FOOTBALL YEARBOOK 2014-2015

Compiled by
John Anderson

headline

Front cover photographs: (left and background)
Vincent Kompany (Manchester City) – *Action Images/Jason Cairnduff*;
(centre) Eden Hazard (Chelsea) – *Darren Walsh/Chelsea FC/Press Association Images*;
(right) Tim Howard (Everton) – *Laurence Griffiths/Getty Images Sport*

Spine photograph: Philipp Lahm of Germany lifts the World Cup trophy,
FIFA World Cup 2014 – *Amin Mohammad Jamali/Getty Images Sport*

Back cover photographs: (above) Ricardo van Rhijn (Ajax) and James Forrest (Celtic),
UEFA Champions League Group H – *VI Images/Press Association Images*;
(below) Mario Götze of Germany celebrates his goal at the FIFA World Cup Final, 2014
Ian MacNicol/Getty Images Sport

Cataloguing in Publication Data is available from the British Library

ISBN 978 1 4722 1252 8 (Hardback)
ISBN 978 1 4722 1251 1 (Trade paperback)

Typeset by Wearset Ltd, Boldon, Tyne and Wear

Printed and bound in the UK by
CPI Mackays, Chatham ME5 8TD

Headline's policy is to use papers that are natural, renewable and recyclable products an
made from wood grown in sustainable forests. The logging and manufacturing processe
are expected to conform to the environmental regulations of the country of origin.

HEADLINE PUBLISHING GROUP
An Hachette UK Company
338 Euston Road
London NW1 3BH

www.headline.co.uk
www.hachette.co.uk

CONTENTS

WELCOME

Welcome to the 2014–15 edition of the *Sky Sports Football Yearbook*.

Last season was a fantastic year for football and for Sky Sports. There were twists and turns at both ends of the Premier League table with some terrific stories including Sunderland's great escape and Manchester City's composure under pressure. In April alone, Sky Sports viewers enjoyed 16 Premier League matches featuring top-of-the-table teams, and after a thrilling climax to the title race, we reported that audiences for live Premier League football were significantly up on last year.

This season there's even more live football on Sky Sports. Not only are we showing extensive coverage of the Barclays Premier League and Football League, but we have also added a new channel, Sky Sports 5. With over 600 matches from the top competitions in Europe, Sky Sports 5 will be the home of European football. The channel will host 129 UEFA Champions League matches, live UEFA EURO 2016 Qualifiers from September and we're also introducing Netherland's top division Eredivisie. This is all part of our unrivalled schedule of over 800 live matches in the domestic, European and international game.

Every year we aim to raise the bar in terms of production and continue to bring fresh ideas to our established programming. The Royal Television Society recognised Gary Neville's highly praised analysis, awarding him 'Best Sports Presenter, Commentator or Pundit' and *Monday Night Football* received a nomination for an IBC Innovation Award for the most innovative use of technology in content creation. Our unrivalled Football League coverage is a huge part of our schedule too. We show 90 matches live from the three leagues and provide fans with the quickest access to every goal from every game on Sky Sports News every Saturday.

Our expert analysis, on-air touchscreen, interactive coverage, multi-match choice and highlights all give the viewer at home a complete football experience with insight and detailed analysis of the game.

Sky Sports and football have built and maintained a partnership stretching over 23 years. Both home and away, we endeavour to give viewers the best seat in the house. This isn't only during our match coverage, as Sky Sports News continues to ensure its viewers are the first to hear all the breaking stories. Our coverage of the bi-annual Transfer Deadline Day on Sky Sports News is always something I look forward to. I know you do too.

I can't wait for another exciting year of live football on Sky Sports. For all the teams involved I wish you good luck, and for all the fans at home, we look forward to bringing you unrivalled coverage of more of the best matches from the UK and across Europe.

Barney Francis
Sky Sports Managing Director

Barney Francis

FOREWORD

Even in a World Cup summer, the build-up and anticipation ahead of the 2014–15 Premier League has filled the back pages. After the drama of last season, which saw Liverpool go so close but ultimately fall short to deserving champions Manchester City, the feeling is that this season could be one of the tightest campaigns to date.

I see at least five teams harbouring realistic ambitions to be crowned champions in May. Manchester City and Liverpool were the stand-out performers last time around and it would be hard to argue against them challenging again this campaign. Over in north London, there is a widespread belief that Aaron Ramsey's extra-time goal that ended Arsenal's nine-year wait for silverware is just the beginning of the club's resurgence to the top of the English game. Chelsea boasted the best head-to-head record against top four clubs in 2013–14 and a rejuvenated Manchester United under Louis van Gaal will also be looking to challenge for the title.

At the other end of the table, Sunderland pulled off a quite remarkable escape, taking 12 points from the last five games of their season, and Tony Pulis transformed a Crystal Palace team who looked destined for their fifth Premier League relegation before he took over in December. It was a great achievement for newly promoted Palace to stay up and this season they're joined by Leicester City, Burnley and QPR. I was very impressed by Leicester City, who won five more games than anyone else in the Sky Bet Championship and passed the 100-points-in-a-season mark for the first time in the club's history.

This will be my second season out of the changing room and in the studio with Sky Sports, and I still get the new-season nerves and adrenaline rush. There is something special about the start of the season as teams and fans set out on a nine-month journey with a sense of optimism and ambition.

Gary, Ed and I can't wait to get back into the *Monday Night Football* studio. As the players are put through their paces at rigorous pre-season training, we have also been busy preparing for the new campaign. I thoroughly enjoy breaking down the key talking points from the weekend and although the technology takes a lot of practice it is a fantastic tool to help analyse the game in more depth.

Coming straight out of a professional football environment, I have been incredibly impressed by the knowledge and dedication of the team here at Sky. It is clear everyone shares my love for the game and is passionate about producing the best coverage possible. I am honoured to be a part of it and will continue to use my experience from the pitch to give viewers detailed analysis and educated views as the season progresses.

If this season is anything like the last then it promises to be a very exciting campaign. We look forward to you joining us on Sky Sports.

Jamie Carragher

Jamie Carragher

INTRODUCTION

The 45th edition of the Yearbook is our twelfth with sponsors Sky Sports and includes every game of the 2014 World Cup in Brazil. Together with the World Cup Finals this new edition gives full coverage of the World Cup 2014 qualifying competition for Europe and South America including full line-ups for each qualifying match. Results and league tables are included for all of the qualifying matches throughout the rest of the world. Other international football at various levels is also well catered for in this edition.

The concise feature entitled Cups and Ups and Downs is again included with dates of those events affecting cup finals, plus promotion and relegation issues. In the age where football club chairmen change managers at will, a new section is included – Managers In and Out, with a diary of managerial changes throughout the year.

At European level, both the Champions League and Europa League have their usual comprehensive details included, with results, goalscorers, attendances, full line-ups and formations from the qualifying rounds onwards and also including all the league tables from the respective group stages.

The 2013–14 campaign gave us a fantastic ending with Manchester City and Liverpool pushing for the Premier League title all the way to the end of the season. City recorded their biggest ever Premier League victory, 7-0 against Norwich City, and surpassed 100 league goals in the season in which they won both the Premier League title and the Capital One Cup. Liverpool also went past a century of league goals and recorded a club record 10-game winning run in the Premier League era. All of these statistics are reproduced in the pages devoted to not only the Premier League, but the three Football League competitions too, as well as all major allied cup competitions.

While transfer fees are invariably those reported at the time and rarely given as official figures, the edition reflects those listed at the time.

In the club-by-club pages that contain the line-ups of all league matches, appearances are split into starting and substitute appearances. In the Players Directory the totals show figures combined.

The Players Directory and its accompanying A to Z index enables the reader to quickly find the club of any specific player.

Throughout the book players sent off are designated with ■, substitutes in the club pages are 12, 13 and 14. Included again in main competitions are the formations for each team.

In addition to competitions already mentioned there is full coverage of Scottish Premier League and Scottish League and cup competitions. There are also sections devoted to Welsh, Irish, Women's football, the Under-21s and various other UEFA youth levels, schools, reserve team, academies, referees and the leading non-league competitions as well as the work of the chaplains at clubs. The chief tournaments outside the UK at club and national level are not forgotten. The International Directory itself features Europe in some depth as well as every FIFA country's international results for the previous year.

Naturally there are international appearances and goals scored by players for England, Scotland, Northern Ireland, Wales and the Republic. For easy reference, those players making appearances and scoring goals in the season covered are picked out in bold type.

The Yearbook would like to extend its appreciation to the publishers Headline for excellent support in the preparation of this edition, particularly Jonathan Taylor for photographic selection throughout the book and to Graham Green for his continued support.

ACKNOWLEDGEMENTS

In addition the Yearbook is also keen to thank the following individuals and organisations for their co-operation.

Special thanks to Jamie Carragher, Barney Francis and Peter Smith from Sky Sports for their pieces, and to Paul McCarthy for the Editorial.

Thanks are also due to Ian Nannestad for the Obituaries, Did You Know and Fact File features in the club section. Many thanks also to John English for his conscientious proof reading and compilation of the International Directory.

The Football Association, The Scottish Professional Football League, The Football League, Rev. Nigel Sands for his contribution to the Chaplain's page and Bob Bannister.

Sincere thanks to George Schley and Simon Dunnington for their excellent work on the database, and to Andy Cordiner, Geoff Turner, Brian Tait, Mick Carruthers, Robin Middlemiss and the staff at Wearset for their much appreciated efforts in the production of the book throughout the year.

Finally, the Yearbook would like to extend particularly warm thanks to Wearset's John Anderson for ensuring that the publication emerges in the very best possible shape. John's passion for, and dedication to, the Yearbook are remarkable.

EDITORIAL

If it was down to sheer passion, Liverpool would have been crowned Barclays Premier League champions around Easter.

If it was down to pure sentiment, then Liverpool's 24-year drought would have been ended by a tidal wave of goodwill.

And those thousands of fans who flocked to the corner of Anfield Road to pay homage to their passing heroes would have something tangible to celebrate, rather than mere fleeting visions of what might have been.

Instead, Brendan Rodgers and his team were the victims of fine margins. A slip by Steven Gerrard, surrender at Selhurst and Anfield's dreams were crushed.

Perhaps the question even the most fanatical Kopite will be asking themselves is, have we blown the best chance we ever had of reclaiming our long-lost place at the pinnacle of English football?

The beauty of Liverpool's game was made all the more exquisite for their fans by the fact Manchester United were suffering a decline of such horrific proportions.

As Liverpool soared, so United plummeted until a crash landing was inevitable and David Moyes was forced out of Old Trafford with barely a tear shed.

For Liverpool, however, that could have been the worst possible result. Out goes a man with not a trophy to his name, replaced by a serial winner in the shape of Louis van Gaal, armed with a serious reputation and even more serious cheque book.

And if United will be stronger, what of their rivals from the blue half of town? Financial Fair Play may have to be taken into consideration but there is an already ominous depth to the Manchester City squad which will surely stand the champions in fantastic stead.

The calmness with which they chipped away at Liverpool's lead was testament to Manuel Pellegrini's sang froid and ability to harness team spirit without the need for a siege mentality or training ground bust-ups.

Instead, City produced displays of ruthless beauty, of power and strength of will, all without the goal-scoring prowess of Sergio Aguero for long periods of the season. Not that it mattered when Yaya Toure chipped in with 24 goals from midfield.

So both Manchester clubs will either build on an already formidable foundation or strengthen with a new manager at the helm. What then of Chelsea?

It's difficult to believe Jose Mourinho will go a third season without a trophy, especially as Roman Abramovich is certain to indulge him and bring in striking reinforcements and more quality in midfield.

Even in transition Chelsea were a force to be reckoned with. Give Mourinho the extra tools he demands and suddenly Stamford Bridge's title expectations are all the more realistic.

Does that spell outright disaster for Liverpool? Not exactly, given the spending power John W. Henry has promised Rodgers, but fighting on the home front and the Champions League will take its toll.

The dreamers who stand on The Kop will claim it's just a small step to glory, that the addition of two top-class defenders and more attack from midfield is all that's needed to take them back to their rightful perch.

The realists, though, will know the new season provides an even tougher challenge for Rodgers. Last year, Champions League qualification was the goal. Perhaps those ambitions might have to be similarly tailored this time around.

Paul McCarthy, Football Writers' Association

SKY SPORTS TEAM OF THE SEASON

GARY NEVILLE AND JAMIE CARRAGHER'S

PREMIER LEAGUE TEAM OF THE SEASON 2013–14

David Marshall
(Cardiff C)

Seamus Coleman	Gary Cahill	John Terry	Luke Shaw
(Everton)	*(Chelsea)*	*(Chelsea)*	*(Southampton)*

Raheem Sterling	Steven Gerrard	Yaya Toure	Eden Hazard
(Liverpool)	*(Liverpool)*	*(Manchester C)*	*(Chelsea)*

Daniel Sturridge   Luis Suarez
(Liverpool)   *(Liverpool)*

EUROPEAN GOLDEN SHOE

The European Golden Shoe award is presented to the leading goalscorer in European League football. However, the determination of the winner comes from a points system which depends on the status of the country involved. The goals total is multiplied by a factor of either two, one and a half, or just by one.

The top 30 places were as follows:

	Scorer	Team	Country	Goals	Factor	Points
1 =	C. Ronaldo	Real Madrid	Spain	31	2.0	62.0
1 =	L. Suarez	Liverpool	England	31	2.0	62.0
3	L. Messi	Barcelona	Spain	28	2.0	56.0
4	D. Costa	Atletico Madrid	Spain	27	2.0	54.0
5	J. Soriano	Salzburg	Austria	31	1.5	46.5
6	C. Immobile	Torino	Italy	22	2.0	44.0
7	D. Sturridge	Liverpool	England	22	2.0	44.0
8	A. Finnbogason	Heerenveen	Netherlands	29	1.5	43.5
9	R. Lewandowski	Borussia Dortmund	Germany	20	2.0	40.0
10	Y. Toure	Manchester C	England	20	2.0	40.0
11	J. Martinez	Porto	Portugal	20	2.0	40.0
12	L. Toni	Verona	Italy	20	2.0	40.0
13	Z. Ibrahimovic	Paris Saint-Germain	France	26	1.5	39.0
14	Alan	Salzburg	Austria	26	1.5	39.0
15	A. Sanchez	Barcelona	Spain	19	2.0	38.0
16	C. Tevez	Juventus	Italy	19	2.0	38.0
17	M. Mandzukic	Bayern Munich	Germany	18	2.0	36.0
18	G. Pelle	Feyenoord	Netherlands	23	1.5	34.5
19	A. Di Natale	Udinese	Italy	17	2.0	34.0
20	K. Benzema	Real Madrid	Spain	17	2.0	34.0
21	W. Rooney	Manchester U	England	17	2.0	34.0
22	R. Palacio	Inter Milan	Italy	17	2.0	34.0
23	G. Higuain	Napoli	Italy	17	2.0	34.0
24	S. Aguero	Manchester C	England	17	2.0	34.0
25	J. Drmic	Nuremberg	Germany	17	2.0	34.0
26	D. Cop	Dinamo Zagreb	Croatia	22	1.5	33.0
27	M. Robak	Pogon Szczecin	Poland	22	1.5	33.0
28	H. Harbaoui	Lokeren	Belgium	22	1.5	33.0
29	F. Llorente	Juventus	Italy	16	2.0	32.0
30	A. Aduriz	Athletic Bilbao	Spain	16	2.0	32.0

FOOTBALL AWARDS 2013–14

FOOTBALLER OF THE YEAR

The Football Writers' Association Sir Stanley Matthews Trophy for the Footballer of the Year was awarded to Luis Suarez of Liverpool and Uruguay. Steven Gerrard (Liverpool and England) was runner-up and Yaya Toure (Manchester C and Ivory Coast) came third.

Past Winners
1947–48 Stanley Matthews (Blackpool), 1948–49 Johnny Carey (Manchester U), 1949–50 Joe Mercer (Arsenal), 1950–51 Harry Johnston (Blackpool), 1951–52 Billy Wright (Wolverhampton W), 1952–53 Nat Lofthouse (Bolton W), 1953–54 Tom Finney (Preston NE), 1954–55 Don Revie (Manchester C), 1955–56 Bert Trautmann (Manchester C), 1956–57 Tom Finney (Preston NE), 1957–58 Danny Blanchflower (Tottenham H), 1958–59 Syd Owen (Luton T), 1959–60 Bill Slater (Wolverhampton W), 1960–61 Danny Blanchflower (Tottenham H), 1961–62 Jimmy Adamson (Burnley), 1962–63 Stanley Matthews (Stoke C), 1963–64 Bobby Moore (West Ham U), 1964–65 Bobby Collins (Leeds U), 1965–66 Bobby Charlton (Manchester U), 1966–67 Jackie Charlton (Leeds U), 1967–68 George Best (Manchester U), 1968–69 Dave Mackay (Derby Co) shared with Tony Book (Manchester C), 1969–70 Billy Bremner (Leeds U), 1970–71 Frank McLintock (Arsenal), 1971–72 Gordon Banks (Stoke C), 1972–73 Pat Jennings (Tottenham H), 1973–74 Ian Callaghan (Liverpool), 1974–75 Alan Mullery (Fulham), 1975–76 Kevin Keegan (Liverpool), 1976–77 Emlyn Hughes (Liverpool), 1977–78 Kenny Burns (Nottingham F), 1978–79 Kenny Dalglish (Liverpool), 1979–80 Terry McDermott (Liverpool), 1980–81 Frans Thijssen (Ipswich T), 1981–82 Steve Perryman (Tottenham H), 1982–83 Kenny Dalglish (Liverpool), 1983–84 Ian Rush (Liverpool), 1984–85 Neville Southall (Everton), 1985–86 Gary Lineker (Everton), 1986–87 Clive Allen (Tottenham H), 1987–88 John Barnes (Liverpool), 1988–89 Steve Nicol (Liverpool), 1989–90 John Barnes (Liverpool), 1990–91 Gordon Strachan (Leeds U), 1991–92 Gary Lineker (Tottenham H), 1992–93 Chris Waddle (Sheffield W), 1993–94 Alan Shearer (Blackburn R), 1994–95 Jurgen Klinsmann (Tottenham H), 1995–96 Eric Cantona (Manchester U), 1996–97 Gianfranco Zola (Chelsea), 1997–98 Dennis Bergkamp (Arsenal), 1998–99 David Ginola (Tottenham H), 1999–2000 Roy Keane (Manchester U), 2000–01 Teddy Sheringham (Manchester U), 2001–02 Robert Pires (Arsenal), 2002–03 Thierry Henry (Arsenal), 2003–04 Thierry Henry (Arsenal), 2004–05 Frank Lampard (Chelsea), 2005–06 Thierry Henry (Arsenal), 2006–07 Cristiano Ronaldo (Manchester U), 2007–08 Cristiano Ronaldo (Manchester U), 2008–09 Ryan Giggs (Manchester U), 2009–10 Wayne Rooney (Manchester U), 2010–11 Scott Parker (West Ham U), 2011–12 Robin van Persie (Arsenal), 2012–13 Gareth Bale (Tottenham H), 2013–14 Luis Suarez (Liverpool).

THE PFA AWARDS 2014

Player of the Year: Luis Suarez, Liverpool and Uruguay
Young Player of the Year: Eden Hazard, Chelsea and Belgium
Women's Player of the Year: Lucy Bronze, Liverpool and England
Women's Young Player of the Year: Martha Harris, Liverpool and England

SCOTTISH AWARDS 2013–14

SCOTTISH PFA PLAYER OF THE YEAR AWARDS 2014

Player of the Year: Kris Commons, Celtic
Young Player of the Year: Andrew Robertson, Dundee U and Scotland
Manager of the Year: Derek McInnes, Aberdeen
Championship Player of the Year: Kane Hemmings, Cowdenbeath
League One Player of the Year: Lee Wallace, Rangers
League Two Player of the Year: Rory McAllister, Peterhead
Goal of the Season: Jonny Hayes, Aberdeen
Special Merit Award: Frank McKeown, Stranraer

SCOTTISH FOOTBALL WRITERS' ASSOCIATION 2014

Player of the Year: Kris Commons, Celtic
Young Player of the Year: Stevie May, St Johnstone
Manager of the Year: Derek McInnes, Aberdeen

OTHER AWARDS

EUROPEAN FOOTBALLER OF THE YEAR 2013

Frank Ribery, Bayern Munich and France

EUROPEAN WOMEN'S PLAYER OF THE YEAR 2013

Nadine Angerer, Brisbane Roar and Germany

FIFA BALLON D'OR PLAYER OF THE YEAR 2013

Cristiano Ronaldo, Real Madrid and Portugal

FIFA BALLON D'OR WOMEN'S PLAYER OF THE YEAR 2013

Nadine Angerer, Brisbane Roar and Germany

FIFA PUSKAS AWARD GOAL OF THE YEAR

Zlatan Ibrahimovic, Paris Saint-Germain and Sweden – Sweden v England, November 2012

PREMIER LEAGUE AWARDS 2013–14

PLAYER OF THE MONTH AWARDS 2013–14

August	Daniel Sturridge (Liverpool)
September	Aaron Ramsey (Arsenal)
October	Sergio Aguero (Manchester C)
November	Tim Krul (Newcastle U)
December	Luis Suarez (Liverpool)
January	Adam Johnson (Sunderland)
February	Daniel Sturridge (Liverpool)
March	Steven Gerrard and Luis Suarez (Liverpool)
April	Connor Wickham (Sunderland)

MANAGER OF THE MONTH AWARDS 2013–14

August	Brendan Rodgers (Liverpool)
September	Arsene Wenger (Arsenal)
October	Mauricio Pochettino (Southampton)
November	Alan Pardew (Newcastle U)
December	Manuel Pellegrini (Manchester C)
January	Manuel Pellegrini (Manchester C)
February	Sam Allardyce (West Ham U)
March	Brendan Rodgers (Liverpool)
April	Tony Pulis (Crystal Palace)

SKYBET LEAGUE AWARDS 2013–14

SKY BET FOOTBALL LEAGUE PLAYER OF THE MONTH AWARDS 2013–14

	Sky Bet Championship	*Sky Bet League 1*	*Sky Bet League 2*
August	James Vaughan (Huddersfield T)	Nahki Wells (Bradford C)	Gary Roberts (Chesterfield)
September	David McGoldrick (Ipswich T)	David Mooney (Leyton Orient)	Antoni Sarcevic (Fleetwood T)
October	Danny Ings (Burnley)	Patrick Bamford (Milton Keynes D)	Luke James (Hartlepool U)
November	Ross McCormack (Leeds U)	Ryan Lowe (Tranmere R)	Zavon Hines (Dagenham & R)
December	Danny Drinkwater (Leicester C)	Sam Saunders (Brentford)	Deon Burton (Scunthorpe U)
January	Adam Le Fondre (Reading)	Nicky Ajose (Peterborough U)	Ryan Clarke (Oxford U)
February	Sam Vokes (Burnley)	Michael Jacobs (Wolverhampton W)	Scott Hogan (Rochdale)
March	Ravel Morrison (QPR)	Callum Wilson (Coventry C)	Jamie Allen (Rochdale)
April	Rudy Gestede (Blackburn R)	Kieran Agard (Rotherham U)	Josh Morris (Fleetwood T)

SKY BET FOOTBALL LEAGUE MANAGER OF THE MONTH AWARDS 2013–14

	Sky Bet Championship	*Sky Bet League 1*	*Sky Bet League 2*
August	Paul Ince (Blackpool)	Russell Slade (Leyton Orient)	Paul Cook (Chesterfield)
September	Sean Dyche (Burnley)	Simon Grayson (Preston NE)	Keith Hill (Rochdale)
October	Sean Dyche (Burnley)	Steven Pressley (Coventry C)	Colin Cooper (Hartlepool U)
November	Oscar Garcia (Brighton & HA)	Uwe Rosler (Brentford)	Phil Brown (Southend U)
December	Steve McClaren (Derby Co)	Mark Warburton (Brentford)	Mark Yates (Cheltenham T)
January	Nigel Pearson (Leicester C)	Russell Slade (Leyton Orient)	Graham Alexander (Fleetwood T)
February	Uwe Rosler (Wigan Ath)	Nigel Clough (Sheffield U)	David Flitcroft (Bury)
March	Nigel Pearson (Leicester C)	Kenny Jackett (Wolverhampton W)	Nigel Worthington (York C)
April	Sean Dyche (Burnley)	Darren Ferguson (Peterborough U)	Andy Awford (Portsmouth)

LEAGUE MANAGERS ASSOCIATION AWARDS 2013–14

LMA MANAGER OF THE YEAR SPONSORED BY BARCLAYS
Brendan Rodgers, Liverpool

LMA SPECIAL MERIT AWARD
Russ Wilcox, Scunthorpe U

LMA SERVICE TO FOOTBALL AWARD
Norman Rimmington, Barnsley

BARCLAYS PREMIER LEAGUE MANAGER OF THE YEAR
Tony Pulis, Crystal Palace

SKY BET FOOTBALL LEAGUE CHAMPIONSHIP MANAGER OF THE YEAR
Nigel Pearson, Leicester C

SKY BET FOOTBALL LEAGUE 1 JOINT MANAGERS OF THE YEAR
Kenny Jackett, Wolverhampton W and Russell Slade, Leyton Orient

SKY BET FOOTBALL LEAGUE 2 MANAGER OF THE YEAR
Russ Wilcox, Scunthorpe U

BUDWEISER FA CUP MANAGER OF THE YEAR
Nigel Clough, Sheffield U

BARCLAYS PREMIER LEAGUE 2013–14

(P) *Promoted into division at end of 2012–13 season.*

			Total				Home					Away						
		P	W	D	L	F	A	W	D	L	F	A	W	D	L	F	A	GD	Pts
1	Manchester C	38	27	5	6	102	37	17	1	1	63	13	10	4	5	39	24	65	86
2	Liverpool	38	26	6	6	101	50	16	1	2	53	18	10	5	4	48	32	51	84
3	Chelsea	38	25	7	6	71	27	15	3	1	43	11	10	4	5	28	16	44	82
4	Arsenal	38	24	7	7	68	41	13	5	1	36	11	11	2	6	32	30	27	79
5	Everton	38	21	9	8	61	39	13	3	3	38	19	8	6	5	23	20	22	72
6	Tottenham H	38	21	6	11	55	51	11	3	5	30	23	10	3	6	25	28	4	69
7	Manchester U	38	19	7	12	64	43	9	3	7	29	21	10	4	5	35	22	21	64
8	Southampton	38	15	11	12	54	46	8	6	5	32	23	7	5	7	22	23	8	56
9	Stoke City	38	13	11	14	45	52	10	6	3	27	17	3	5	11	18	35	−7	50
10	Newcastle U	38	15	4	19	43	59	8	3	8	23	28	7	1	11	20	31	−16	49
11	Crystal Palace (P)	38	13	6	19	33	48	8	3	8	18	23	5	3	11	15	25	−15	45
12	Swansea C	38	11	9	18	54	54	6	5	8	33	26	5	4	10	21	28	0	42
13	West Ham U	38	11	7	20	40	51	7	3	9	25	26	4	4	11	15	25	−11	40
14	Sunderland	38	10	8	20	41	60	5	3	11	21	27	5	5	9	20	33	−19	38
15	Aston Villa	38	10	8	20	39	61	6	3	10	22	29	4	5	10	17	32	−22	38
16	Hull C (P)	38	10	7	21	38	53	7	4	8	20	21	3	3	13	18	32	−15	37
17	WBA	38	7	15	16	43	59	4	9	6	24	27	3	6	10	19	32	−16	36
18	Norwich C	38	8	9	21	28	62	6	6	7	17	18	2	3	14	11	44	−34	33
19	Fulham	38	9	5	24	40	85	5	3	11	24	38	4	2	13	16	47	−45	32
20	Cardiff C (P)	38	7	9	22	32	74	5	5	9	20	35	2	4	13	12	39	−42	30

LEADING GOALSCORERS 2013–14

	League	FA Cup	Capital One Cup	Other	Total
Luis Suarez *(Liverpool)*	31	0	0	0	31
Sergio Aguero *(Manchester C)*	17	4	1	6	28
Edin Dzeko *(Manchester C)*	16	2	6	2	26
Wilfried Bony *(Swansea C)*	16	3	1	5	25
Daniel Sturridge *(Liverpool)*	22	1	2	0	25
Yaya Toure *(Manchester C)*	20	0	3	1	24
Alvaro Negredo *(Manchester C)*	9	3	6	5	23
Olivier Giroud *(Arsenal)*	16	3	0	3	22
Wayne Rooney *(Manchester U)*	17	0	0	2	19
Eden Hazard *(Chelsea)*	14	0	0	4	18
Robin van Persie *(Manchester U)*	12	0	0	6	18
Jay Rodriguez *(Southampton)*	15	1	1	0	17
Romelu Lukaku *(Everton)*	15	1	0	0	16
Aaron Ramsey *(Arsenal)*	10	1	0	5	16
Steven Gerrard *(Liverpool)*	13	1	0	0	14
Rickie Lambert *(Southampton)*	13	1	0	0	14
Loic Remy *(Newcastle U)*	14	0	0	0	14
Emmanuel Adebayor *(Tottenham H)*	11	0	1	2	14
Samuel Eto'o *(Chelsea)*	9	0	0	3	12
Lukas Podolski *(Arsenal)*	8	3	0	1	12

Other matches consist of European games, Club World Cup, European Super Cup, Community Shield. Players listed in order of League goals total.

BARCLAYS PREMIER LEAGUE – RESULTS 2013-14

Home \ Away	Arsenal	Aston Villa	Cardiff C	Chelsea	Crystal Palace	Everton	Fulham	Hull C	Liverpool	Manchester C	Manchester U	Newcastle U	Norwich C	Southampton	Stoke C	Sunderland	Swansea C	Tottenham H	WBA	West Ham U
Arsenal	—	1-3	2-0	0-0	2-0	1-1	2-0	2-0	2-0	1-1	0-0	3-0	4-1	2-0	3-1	4-1	2-2	1-0	1-0	3-1
Aston Villa	1-2	—	2-0	1-0	0-1	0-2	1-2	3-1	0-1	3-2	0-3	1-2	4-1	0-0	1-4	0-0	1-1	0-2	4-3	0-2
Cardiff C	0-3	0-0	—	1-2	0-3	0-0	3-1	0-4	3-6	3-2	2-2	1-2	2-1	0-3	1-1	2-2	1-0	0-1	1-0	0-2
Chelsea	6-0	2-1	4-1	—	2-1	1-0	2-0	2-0	2-1	3-2	3-1	3-0	0-0	3-1	3-0	1-2	1-0	4-0	2-2	0-0
Crystal Palace	0-2	1-0	2-0	1-0	—	0-0	1-4	1-0	3-3	0-2	0-2	3-0	1-1	0-1	1-0	3-1	1-0	0-1	3-1	1-0
Everton	3-0	2-1	2-1	1-0	2-3	—	4-1	2-1	3-3	2-3	2-0	3-2	2-0	2-1	4-0	0-1	3-2	0-0	2-0	1-0
Fulham	1-3	2-0	1-2	1-3	2-2	1-3	—	2-2	2-3	0-2	1-3	1-0	1-0	0-3	1-0	1-4	1-2	1-2	1-1	2-1
Hull C	0-3	0-0	1-1	0-2	0-1	0-2	6-0	—	3-1	0-2	2-3	1-4	1-0	0-1	0-0	1-0	1-0	1-1	2-0	1-0
Liverpool	5-1	2-2	3-1	2-0	3-1	4-0	5-0	2-0	—	3-2	0-0	3-2	5-1	0-1	1-0	2-1	4-3	4-0	4-1	4-1
Manchester C	6-3	4-0	4-2	0-1	1-0	1-0	4-0	2-0	2-1	—	4-1	0-1	7-0	4-1	1-0	2-2	3-0	6-0	3-1	2-0
Manchester U	1-0	4-1	2-0	0-0	2-0	0-1	2-2	3-1	0-3	2-3	—	0-1	4-0	1-1	2-1	0-3	1-2	1-2	0-1	3-1
Newcastle U	0-1	1-0	3-0	2-0	0-1	0-3	1-0	2-3	2-3	0-4	0-1	—	2-1	1-1	5-1	2-0	1-1	0-4	1-2	0-0
Norwich C	0-2	0-1	0-0	1-3	1-0	2-2	2-0	1-0	2-3	0-0	0-1	0-0	—	1-0	1-1	1-1	1-1	2-3	1-0	3-1
Southampton	2-2	2-3	0-1	0-3	2-0	2-0	4-1	1-0	0-3	1-1	1-1	4-0	4-2	—	2-2	1-1	2-0	2-3	1-0	0-0
Stoke C	1-0	0-1	0-0	3-2	2-1	1-1	4-1	1-0	3-5	0-0	2-1	1-0	0-1	1-1	—	2-0	1-1	0-1	1-0	3-1
Sunderland	1-3	0-1	4-0	0-0	0-0	1-0	0-1	1-0	1-3	1-0	2-1	2-1	0-1	2-2	1-0	—	1-3	1-2	1-2	1-2
Swansea C	1-2	4-1	3-0	0-1	1-1	1-2	2-0	1-1	2-2	1-4	2-2	0-1	3-0	0-1	3-3	4-0	—	1-3	1-1	3-1
Tottenham H	1-0	0-2	1-0	1-1	1-0	0-0	1-1	1-0	0-5	1-0	2-2	0-1	0-1	3-2	3-0	5-1	1-0	—	3-3	0-2
WBA	1-1	2-2	3-3	1-1	3-1	1-1	1-1	1-1	1-1	2-3	0-3	1-0	0-2	0-1	1-2	3-0	0-2	3-3	—	3-3
West Ham U	1-3	0-0	2-0	0-3	1-0	2-3	1-1	1-1	1-2	1-3	0-2	1-3	2-0	3-1	0-1	0-0	2-0	3-0	1-0	—

SKY BET CHAMPIONSHIP 2013–14

(P) *Promoted into division at end of 2012–13 season.*   (R) *Relegated into division at end of 2012–13 season.*

				Total					Home					Away						
		P	W	D	L	F	A	W	D	L	F	A	W	D	L	F	A	GD	Pts
1	Leicester C	46	31	9	6	83	43	17	4	2	46	22	14	5	4	37	21	40	102
2	Burnley	46	26	15	5	72	37	15	6	2	37	14	11	9	3	35	23	35	93
3	Derby Co	46	25	10	11	84	52	14	4	5	46	25	11	6	6	38	27	32	85
4	QPR (R)¶	46	23	11	12	60	44	15	6	2	38	18	8	5	10	22	26	16	80
5	Wigan Ath (R)	46	21	10	15	61	48	12	7	4	35	23	9	3	11	26	25	13	73
6	Brighton & HA	46	19	15	12	55	40	10	7	6	31	21	9	8	6	24	19	15	72
7	Reading (R)	46	19	14	13	70	56	8	10	5	38	25	11	4	8	32	31	14	71
8	Blackburn R	46	18	16	12	70	62	11	7	5	34	21	7	9	7	36	41	8	70
9	Ipswich T	46	18	14	14	60	54	12	6	5	35	24	6	8	9	25	30	6	68
10	Bournemouth (P)	46	18	12	16	67	66	11	5	7	40	27	7	7	9	27	39	1	66
11	Nottingham F	46	16	17	13	67	64	10	7	6	38	29	6	10	7	29	35	3	65
12	Middlesbrough	46	16	16	14	62	50	10	9	4	35	20	6	7	10	27	30	12	64
13	Watford	46	15	15	16	74	64	11	5	7	39	25	4	10	9	35	39	10	60
14	Bolton W	46	14	17	15	59	60	6	11	6	29	23	8	6	9	30	37	−1	59
15	Leeds U	46	16	9	21	59	67	9	5	9	35	31	7	4	12	24	36	−8	57
16	Sheffield W	46	13	14	19	63	65	9	4	10	39	33	4	10	9	24	32	−2	53
17	Huddersfield T	46	14	11	21	58	65	8	6	9	34	32	6	5	12	24	33	−7	53
18	Charlton Ath	46	13	12	21	41	61	7	6	10	21	28	6	6	11	20	33	−20	51
19	Millwall	46	11	15	20	46	74	6	9	8	26	33	5	6	12	20	41	−28	48
20	Blackpool	46	11	13	22	38	66	7	6	10	20	27	4	7	12	18	39	−28	46
21	Birmingham C	46	11	11	24	58	74	2	8	13	29	40	9	3	11	29	34	−16	44
22	Doncaster R (P)	46	11	11	24	39	70	9	4	10	27	32	2	7	14	12	38	−31	44
23	Barnsley	46	9	12	25	44	77	5	8	10	22	36	4	4	15	22	41	−33	39
24	Yeovil T (P)	46	8	13	25	44	75	4	6	13	19	32	4	7	12	25	43	−31	37

¶*QPR promoted via play-offs.*

LEADING GOALSCORERS 2013–14

	League	FA Cup	Capital One Cup	Play-Offs	Total
Ross McCormack *(Leeds U)*	28	0	1	0	29
Danny Ings *(Burnley)*	21	1	4	0	26
Jordan Rhodes *(Blackburn R)*	25	0	0	0	25
Troy Deeney *(Watford)*	24	1	0	0	25
Chris Martin *(Derby Co)*	20	3	0	2	25
Lewis Grabban *(Bournemouth)*	22	0	0	0	22
David Nugent *(Leicester C)*	20	1	1	0	22
Sam Vokes *(Burnley)*	20	1	0	0	21
Charlie Austin *(QPR)*	17	0	1	2	20
Jamie Vardy *(Leicester C)*	16	0	0	0	16
Craig Bryson *(Derby Co)*	16	0	0	0	16
Leonardo Ulloa *(Brighton & HA)*	14	2	0	0	16
David McGoldrick *(Ipswich T)*	14	2	0	0	16
Adam Le Fondre *(Reading)*	15	0	0	0	15
Chris O'Grady *(Barnsley)*	15	0	0	0	15
Rudy Gestede *(Blackburn R)*	13	0	0	0	13
Daryl Murphy *(Ipswich T)*	13	0	0	0	13
Pavel Pogrebnyak *(Reading)*	13	0	0	0	13
Matt Smith *(Leeds U)*	12	0	1	0	13
Albert Adomah *(Middlesbrough)*	12	0	0	0	12

SKY BET CHAMPIONSHIP – RESULTS 2013–14

	Barnsley	Birmingham C	Blackburn R	Blackpool	Bolton W	Bournemouth	Brighton & HA	Burnley	Charlton Ath	Derby Co	Doncaster R	Huddersfield T	Ipswich T	Leeds U	Leicester C	Middlesbrough	Millwall	Nottingham F	QPR	Reading	Sheffield W	Watford	Wigan Ath	Yeovil T
Barnsley	—	0-3	2-2	2-0	0-1	0-1	0-0	0-1	2-2	1-2	0-0	2-1	2-2	0-1	0-3	3-2	1-0	1-0	2-3	1-1	1-1	1-5	0-4	1-1
Birmingham C	1-1	—	2-4	1-1	1-2	2-4	0-1	3-3	0-1	3-3	1-1	1-2	1-1	1-3	1-2	2-2	4-0	0-0	0-2	1-2	4-1	0-1	0-1	0-2
Blackburn R	5-2	2-3	—	2-0	4-1	0-1	3-3	1-2	1-1	1-1	1-0	0-0	2-0	1-0	1-1	1-0	3-2	2-2	4-1	0-0	0-0	1-0	4-3	0-0
Blackpool	1-0	1-2	2-0	—	0-0	0-1	0-2	0-1	0-3	1-3	1-1	1-1	0-0	0-1	2-2	3-1	1-0	0-1	0-1	1-0	2-0	2-1	1-0	1-2
Bolton W	1-0	2-2	4-0	1-0	—	2-2	0-0	0-1	1-1	1-3	1-2	0-1	1-0	1-0	0-2	0-1	3-1	3-0	2-1	1-1	1-1	2-0	1-0	1-1
Bournemouth	1-0	0-2	1-3	1-2	0-2	—	0-2	1-1	2-1	2-2	0-1	0-1	2-3	1-1	0-0	2-2	1-0	1-1	3-0	1-0	2-4	1-1	1-1	3-0
Brighton & HA	1-2	1-0	3-0	3-1	3-1	1-1	—	2-0	3-0	0-1	1-3	1-1	1-1	4-1	0-1	0-0	3-1	1-3	2-2	0-1	1-1	1-1	1-0	2-0
Burnley	1-0	3-0	1-1	0-1	1-1	2-0	0-3	—	3-0	1-2	3-1	2-1	1-1	1-0	3-1	0-2	0-1	1-1	3-3	3-1	1-1	0-0	1-2	2-0
Charlton Ath	1-2	0-2	1-3	0-0	1-1	1-1	3-0	3-0	—	0-2	2-0	1-1	0-1	2-1	0-2	0-1	0-1	3-1	1-0	2-1	3-0	3-1	2-0	3-2
Derby Co	2-1	1-1	1-1	5-1	0-0	1-0	0-2	0-3	3-0	—	2-0	3-2	1-0	2-4	2-1	0-1	0-0	5-0	1-0	0-1	1-0	4-2	2-0	2-1
Doncaster R	2-2	1-3	5-1	1-3	1-2	0-1	1-3	0-3	2-1	0-2	—	2-0	0-1	3-1	1-0	2-1	1-0	2-2	2-1	1-3	0-2	1-2	0-1	5-1
Huddersfield T	5-0	1-3	2-0	1-1	0-1	5-1	1-1	2-1	1-1	3-2	2-0	—	0-0	0-3	0-2	0-0	3-0	0-3	2-1	1-3	2-1	1-1	3-0	2-1
Ipswich T	1-1	1-0	2-4	0-0	1-0	2-2	2-0	0-1	0-1	1-1	0-0	2-1	—	1-2	1-2	2-2	1-2	1-1	1-3	0-1	1-1	3-3	1-0	2-0
Leeds U	0-0	4-0	3-1	0-1	1-5	2-1	2-1	1-2	2-1	1-1	2-4	5-1	1-1	—	0-1	3-1	0-2	0-2	0-1	2-0	2-1	2-2	1-3	2-0
Leicester C	2-1	1-3	1-2	2-1	3-1	2-1	2-1	1-1	3-0	2-1	1-2	2-1	3-0	0-1	—	2-1	2-1	0-2	0-1	2-4	1-1	2-2	2-0	1-1
Middlesbrough	3-1	3-1	2-1	3-1	0-1	3-3	1-4	1-1	1-0	1-1	2-0	0-1	2-0	0-0	2-2	—	3-0	2-1	1-0	1-0	1-1	0-3	2-0	4-1
Millwall	1-0	2-3	0-0	1-1	1-1	1-0	0-1	2-2	0-0	1-0	0-0	1-1	1-0	0-0	0-1	2-0	—	2-2	2-0	0-3	3-3	4-2	0-0	0-1
Nottingham F	3-2	1-0	2-2	0-1	3-0	1-1	1-2	1-1	1-0	1-5	2-0	1-0	0-0	2-0	1-1	0-2	1-1	—	1-0	2-3	2-1	2-1	2-1	3-1
QPR	2-0	1-0	4-1	1-1	2-1	3-0	2-2	3-3	1-0	1-0	2-1	2-1	2-1	1-1	0-1	0-1	2-0	2-0	—	1-3	0-2	4-2	1-4	3-0
Reading	1-3	2-0	0-0	5-1	7-1	1-2	0-0	2-2	0-1	2-1	1-0	1-1	1-1	1-0	1-1	1-3	1-1	2-2	1-1	—	0-2	2-1	1-0	1-1
Sheffield W	1-0	4-1	3-3	0-1	1-3	1-2	2-0	1-2	1-0	0-1	4-1	1-2	3-1	6-0	0-3	3-0	2-2	0-1	3-0	5-2	—	2-1	1-2	1-1
Watford	3-0	1-0	3-3	4-0	0-1	6-1	2-0	1-1	2-3	2-3	1-2	1-4	2-0	3-0	1-0	1-0	4-0	0-1	3-3	3-3	1-0	—	0-3	0-3
Wigan Ath	2-0	0-0	2-1	0-2	1-2	3-0	0-1	0-0	1-1	1-3	0-1	3-0	1-0	1-0	2-2	2-2	0-1	2-1	2-1	1-1	3-3	2-1	—	3-3
Yeovil T	1-4	0-1	0-1	1-0	2-2	1-1	0-0	1-2	2-2	0-3	1-0	1-2	0-1	1-2	1-2	1-4	1-1	3-1	3-0	0-1	1-1	3-3	0-1	—

SKY BET LEAGUE 1 2013–14

(P) *Promoted into division at end of 2012–13 season.* (R) *Relegated into division at end of 2012–13 season.*

			Total						Home						Away						
		P	W	D	L	F	A	W	D	L	F	A	W	D	L	F	A	GD	Pts
1	Wolverhampton W (R)	46	31	10	5	89	31	17	4	2	48	15	14	6	3	41	16	58	103
2	Brentford	46	28	10	8	72	43	19	1	3	44	17	9	9	5	28	26	29	94
3	Leyton Orient	46	25	11	10	85	45	13	3	7	43	23	12	8	3	42	22	40	86
4	Rotherham U (P)¶	46	24	14	8	86	58	10	10	3	44	30	14	4	5	42	28	28	86
5	Preston NE	46	23	16	7	72	46	12	9	2	44	26	11	7	5	28	20	26	85
6	Peterborough U (R)	46	23	5	18	72	58	14	3	6	34	21	9	2	12	38	37	14	74
7	Sheffield U	46	18	13	15	48	46	12	7	4	31	18	6	6	11	17	28	2	67
8	Swindon T	46	19	9	18	63	59	14	3	6	40	27	5	6	12	23	32	4	66
9	Port Vale (P)	46	18	7	21	59	73	13	3	7	35	30	5	4	14	24	43	–14	61
10	Milton Keynes D	46	17	9	20	63	65	8	5	10	29	30	9	4	10	34	35	–2	60
11	Bradford C (P)	46	14	17	15	57	54	8	9	6	35	27	6	8	9	22	27	3	59
12	Bristol C (R)	46	13	19	14	70	67	7	10	6	34	28	6	9	8	36	39	3	58
13	Walsall	46	14	16	16	49	49	7	7	9	21	28	7	9	7	28	21	0	58
14	Crawley T	46	14	15	17	48	54	10	7	6	24	23	4	8	11	24	31	–6	57
15	Oldham Ath	46	14	14	18	50	59	7	8	8	23	28	7	6	10	27	31	–9	56
16	Colchester U	46	13	14	19	53	61	8	5	10	29	29	5	9	9	24	32	–8	53
17	Gillingham (P)	46	15	8	23	60	79	10	5	8	35	31	5	3	15	25	48	–19	53
18	Coventry C*	46	16	13	17	74	77	9	8	6	41	39	7	5	11	33	38	–3	51
19	Crewe Alex	46	13	12	21	54	80	7	7	9	26	34	6	5	12	28	46	–26	51
20	Notts Co	46	15	5	26	64	77	12	2	9	40	28	3	3	17	24	49	–13	50
21	Tranmere R	46	12	11	23	52	79	6	8	9	30	39	6	3	14	22	40	–27	47
22	Carlisle U	46	11	12	23	43	76	8	6	9	27	32	3	6	14	16	44	–33	45
23	Shrewsbury T	46	9	15	22	44	65	6	7	10	22	28	3	8	12	22	37	–21	42
24	Stevenage	46	11	9	26	46	72	7	5	11	29	34	4	4	15	17	38	–26	42

Coventry City deducted 10 points for entering administration. ¶Rotherham U promoted via play-offs.

LEADING GOALSCORERS 2013–14

	League	FA Cup	Capital One Cup	J Paint Trophy	Play-Offs	Total
Britt Assombalonga (*Peterborough U*)	23	5	1	3	1	33
Sam Baldock (*Bristol C*)	24	1	1	0	0	26
Kieran Agard (*Rotherham U*)	21	2	0	2	1	26
Joe Garner (*Preston NE*)	18	5	0	0	1	24
Callum Wilson (*Coventry C*)	21	1	0	0	0	22
David Mooney (*Leyton Orient*)	19	1	0	1	0	21
Jay Emmanuel-Thomas (*Bristol C*)	15	4	1	1	0	21
Ryan Lowe (*Tranmere R*)	19	1	0	0	0	20
Clayton Donaldson (*Brentford*)	17	1	0	0	0	18
Kevin Lisbie (*Leyton Orient*)	16	0	2	0	0	18
Leon Clarke (*Coventry C*)	15	3	0	0	0	18
Dean Cox (*Leyton Orient*)	12	2	1	0	2	17
Cody McDonald (*Gillingham*)	17	0	0	0	0	17
Patrick Bamford (*Milton Keynes D*)	14	1	1	1	0	17
Chuks Aneke (*Crewe Alex*)	14	0	1	1	0	16
Craig Westcarr (*Walsall*)	14	2	0	0	0	16
Tom Pope (*Port Vale*)	12	2	0	2	0	16
Francois Zoko (*Stevenage*)	10	4	0	2	0	16
Nahki Wells (*Bradford C*)	14	0	1	0	0	15
Franck Moussa (*Coventry C*)	13	1	1	0	0	15

SKY BET LEAGUE 1 – RESULTS 2013-14

	Bradford C	Brentford	Bristol C	Carlisle U	Colchester U	Coventry C	Crawley T	Crewe Alex	Gillingham	Leyton Orient	Milton Keynes D	Notts Co	Oldham Ath	Peterborough U	Port Vale	Preston NE	Rotherham U	Sheffield U	Shrewsbury T	Stevenage	Swindon T	Tranmere R	Walsall	Wolverhampton W
Bradford C	—	4-0	1-1	4-0	2-2	3-3	2-1	3-3	1-1	1-1	1-0	1-1	2-3	1-0	1-0	0-0	0-1	2-0	2-1	2-3	1-1	0-1	0-2	1-2
Brentford	2-0	—	1-2	0-0	4-1	3-1	1-0	5-0	2-1	0-2	3-1	3-1	1-0	3-2	2-0	1-0	0-1	3-1	1-0	2-0	3-2	2-0	1-0	0-3
Bristol C	2-2	1-2	—	2-1	1-1	1-2	2-0	0-0	2-1	2-2	2-2	2-1	1-1	0-3	5-0	1-1	1-2	0-1	1-1	4-1	0-0	2-2	1-0	1-2
Carlisle U	1-0	0-0	2-4	—	2-4	0-4	1-1	2-0	1-2	1-5	3-0	2-1	0-1	0-3	5-0	0-1	1-2	1-0	1-1	0-0	1-0	2-2	1-1	1-2
Colchester U	0-2	4-1	2-2	1-1	—	2-1	1-1	1-2	3-0	1-2	3-1	0-4	0-1	1-0	1-0	1-2	0-0	0-1	1-0	0-0	1-0	4-1	1-1	0-3
Coventry C	0-0	0-2	5-4	1-2	2-0	—	2-2	2-2	0-3	3-1	1-2	3-0	1-1	4-2	2-2	4-4	0-3	3-2	1-1	1-0	1-2	1-5	2-1	1-1
Crawley T	1-0	0-1	1-0	0-0	0-0	1-0	—	1-2	0-3	2-1	0-2	1-0	1-0	1-0	0-3	2-2	1-2	0-2	1-1	1-0	0-0	2-0	0-0	1-1
Crewe Alex	0-0	1-3	1-0	2-1	0-1	1-2	2-2	—	1-2	1-2	0-2	1-0	1-1	1-0	1-2	2-2	3-3	0-2	0-0	1-1	0-0	2-0	0-3	1-1
Gillingham	0-1	1-1	1-1	1-0	0-1	0-3	1-0	1-3	—	1-2	3-2	2-0	0-1	2-2	3-2	2-1	3-3	3-0	1-1	0-3	2-0	2-1	0-3	0-2
Leyton Orient	0-1	0-1	1-3	4-0	2-1	4-2	2-3	1-0	5-1	—	2-1	5-1	0-1	2-2	3-2	2-1	1-0	0-1	3-0	2-0	2-0	0-1	2-2	1-3
Milton Keynes D	2-3	2-2	2-2	0-1	0-0	1-3	0-1	4-0	2-0	1-3	—	3-1	3-2	0-2	3-0	0-0	3-2	0-1	3-2	4-1	0-0	0-1	1-1	1-3
Notts Co	3-0	0-1	1-1	4-1	2-0	3-0	3-1	1-1	2-1	0-0	2-1	—	3-2	2-4	4-2	0-1	0-1	2-1	2-3	0-1	2-0	2-0	1-5	0-1
Oldham Ath	1-1	0-0	1-1	1-0	0-2	0-0	1-1	4-2	1-1	1-1	1-2	1-1	—	5-4	3-1	1-3	0-2	1-1	1-2	0-1	2-1	0-1	0-1	0-3
Peterborough U	2-1	1-3	1-2	4-1	2-0	4-2	0-2	1-0	2-0	1-3	2-1	4-3	2-1	—	0-0	2-0	0-1	0-0	1-0	0-1	1-0	3-0	0-0	1-0
Port Vale	2-1	1-1	1-0	2-1	3-2	2-2	2-1	1-0	3-1	0-2	2-2	2-1	1-0	3-1	—	0-2	2-0	2-0	3-1	2-0	2-3	3-2	1-0	1-3
Preston NE	2-2	0-3	1-0	6-1	1-1	1-1	1-0	0-2	0-3	1-1	2-2	2-0	3-2	3-1	3-2	—	3-3	0-0	5-2	3-0	2-3	1-1	2-1	0-0
Rotherham U	0-0	3-0	2-1	0-0	2-2	1-3	2-2	4-2	4-1	2-1	0-1	6-0	0-2	3-1	1-0	0-0	—	3-1	2-2	2-1	0-4	1-1	1-1	3-3
Sheffield U	2-2	0-0	3-0	1-0	0-1	2-1	1-1	1-3	4-1	1-1	0-0	2-1	3-4	3-1	2-0	3-3	1-0	—	2-0	3-1	1-0	3-1	2-1	0-2
Shrewsbury T	2-1	1-1	2-3	1-1	1-0	1-1	2-0	1-3	3-1	0-2	2-3	1-0	0-1	2-0	0-0	2-0	0-3	2-0	—	1-0	2-0	0-1	0-1	0-1
Stevenage	1-1	2-1	1-3	1-3	2-0	0-1	2-0	1-1	3-1	0-1	2-3	0-1	3-4	2-4	1-1	1-1	0-3	0-0	1-3	—	2-0	3-1	0-1	0-1
Swindon T	1-0	1-0	3-2	3-1	2-1	3-1	1-1	5-0	2-2	1-3	0-1	3-2	0-1	0-1	5-2	1-0	1-2	0-0	3-1	2-0	—	1-0	1-3	1-4
Tranmere R	1-2	3-4	1-1	0-0	1-2	0-4	1-1	1-1	1-1	0-4	0-3	1-1	0-0	0-5	0-2	1-0	1-2	2-1	3-1	0-0	1-2	—	1-1	1-1
Walsall	0-2	1-1	0-1	2-0	0-1	1-1	1-2	1-1	1-1	1-1	2-0	2-0	2-0	2-0	0-2	0-3	1-1	2-1	1-0	2-1	2-1	3-1	—	0-3
Wolverhampton W	2-0	0-0	3-1	3-0	4-2	1-1	2-1	2-0	4-0	1-1	0-2	2-0	2-0	2-0	3-0	2-0	6-4	2-0	0-0	2-0	3-2	2-0	0-1	—

SKY BET LEAGUE 2 2013–14

(P) *Promoted into division at end of 2012–13 season.*   (R) *Relegated into division at end of 2012–13 season.*

		P	W	D	L	F	A	W	D	L	F	A	W	D	L	F	A	GD	Pts
						Total				*Home*					*Away*				
1	Chesterfield	46	23	15	8	71	40	12	9	2	36	16	11	6	6	35	24	31	84
2	Scunthorpe U (R)	46	20	21	5	68	44	10	11	2	32	19	10	10	3	36	25	24	81
3	Rochdale	46	24	9	13	69	48	15	3	5	42	22	9	6	8	27	26	21	81
4	Fleetwood T¶	46	22	10	14	66	52	11	6	6	41	30	11	4	8	25	22	14	76
5	Southend U	46	19	15	12	56	39	11	7	5	29	16	8	8	7	27	23	17	72
6	Burton Alb	46	19	15	12	47	42	11	6	6	27	22	8	9	6	20	20	5	72
7	York C	46	18	17	11	52	41	10	9	4	23	15	8	8	7	29	26	11	71
8	Oxford U	46	16	14	16	53	50	8	6	9	24	23	8	8	7	29	27	3	62
9	Dagenham & R	46	15	15	16	53	59	8	7	8	25	25	7	8	8	28	34	−6	60
10	Plymouth Arg	46	16	12	18	51	58	8	7	8	23	26	8	5	10	28	32	−7	60
11	Mansfield T (P)	46	15	15	16	49	58	7	6	10	27	32	8	9	6	22	26	−9	60
12	Bury (R)	46	13	20	13	59	51	8	12	3	33	23	5	8	10	26	28	8	59
13	Portsmouth (R)	46	14	17	15	56	66	9	6	8	26	25	5	11	7	30	41	−10	59
14	Newport Co (P)	46	14	16	16	56	59	10	6	7	37	27	4	10	9	19	32	−3	58
15	Accrington S	46	14	15	17	54	56	6	10	7	33	29	8	5	10	21	27	−2	57
16	Exeter C	46	14	13	19	54	57	6	6	11	22	27	8	7	8	32	30	−3	55
17	Cheltenham T	46	13	16	17	53	63	5	9	9	29	35	8	7	8	24	28	−10	55
18	Morecambe	46	13	15	18	52	64	7	10	6	30	26	6	5	12	22	38	−12	54
19	Hartlepool U (R)	46	14	11	21	50	56	10	3	10	30	27	4	8	11	20	29	−6	53
20	AFC Wimbledon*	46	14	14	18	49	57	8	7	8	27	29	6	7	10	22	28	−8	53
21	Northampton T	46	13	14	19	42	57	7	7	9	24	32	6	7	10	18	25	−15	53
22	Wycombe W	46	12	14	20	46	54	6	6	11	20	27	6	8	9	26	27	−8	50
23	Bristol R	46	12	14	20	43	54	10	6	7	28	21	2	8	13	15	33	−11	50
24	Torquay U	46	12	9	25	42	66	4	8	11	18	31	8	1	14	24	35	−24	45

* AFC Wimbledon deducted 3 points for fielding an ineligible player. ¶Fleetwood T promoted via play-offs.

LEADING GOALSCORERS 2013–14

	League	*FA Cup*	*Capital One Cup*	*J Paint Trophy*	*Play-Offs*	*Total*
Sam Winnall *(Scunthorpe U)*	23	0	0	0	0	23
Ruben Reid *(Plymouth Arg)*	17	4	0	0	0	21
Scott Hogan *(Rochdale)*	17	2	0	0	0	19
Luke James *(Hartlepool U)*	13	2	0	1	0	16
Byron Harrison *(Cheltenham T)*	13	0	2	0	0	15
John-Joe O'Toole *(Bristol R)*	13	2	0	0	0	15
Antoni Sarcevic *(Fleetwood T)*	13	0	0	1	1	15
Billy Kee *(Burton Alb)*	12	2	0	0	0	14
Rhys Murphy *(Dagenham & R)*	13	0	0	0	0	13
Barry Corr *(Southend U)*	12	1	0	0	0	13
Chris Zebroski *(Newport Co)*	12	0	0	1	0	13
Eoin Doyle *(Chesterfield)*	11	0	1	1	0	13
Wes Fletcher *(York C)*	10	3	0	0	0	13
David Ball *(Fleetwood T)*	8	1	1	3	0	13
Sam Clucas *(Mansfield T)*	8	5	0	0	0	13
Kevan Hurst *(Southend U)*	11	1	0	0	0	12
Ian Henderson *(Rochdale)*	11	1	0	0	0	12
Gary Roberts *(Chesterfield)*	11	1	0	0	0	12
James Constable *(Oxford U)*	10	1	0	1	0	12
Adam McGurk *(Burton Alb)*	9	1	0	0	2	12

SKY BET LEAGUE 2 – RESULTS 2013-14

	Accrington S	AFC Wimbledon	Bristol R	Burton Alb	Bury	Cheltenham T	Chesterfield	Dagenham & R	Exeter C	Fleetwood T	Hartlepool U	Mansfield T	Morecambe	Newport Co	Northampton T	Oxford U	Plymouth Arg	Portsmouth	Rochdale	Scunthorpe U	Southend U	Torquay U	Wycombe W	York C
Accrington S	—	3-2	2-1	0-1	0-0	0-1	3-1	1-2	2-3	2-0	0-0	1-1	5-1	3-3	0-1	0-0	1-1	2-2	1-2	2-3	1-1	2-1	1-1	1-1
AFC Wimbledon	1-1	—	0-0	3-1	0-1	4-3	1-1	1-1	2-1	2-0	2-1	0-0	0-3	2-2	0-2	0-2	1-1	4-0	0-3	3-2	0-1	0-2	1-0	1-1
Bristol R	0-1	3-0	—	2-0	1-1	1-0	0-0	1-2	2-1	1-3	2-2	1-0	1-0	3-1	1-0	1-1	2-1	2-0	1-2	0-0	0-0	1-2	0-1	3-2
Burton Alb	2-1	1-1	1-0	—	2-2	2-1	0-2	1-1	1-1	2-4	3-0	1-0	0-1	1-0	1-0	0-2	1-0	1-2	1-0	2-2	0-1	1-3	1-0	1-1
Bury	3-0	1-1	2-1	0-0	—	4-1	0-2	1-1	2-0	2-2	1-0	0-0	0-2	0-0	1-1	1-1	4-0	4-4	1-2	2-2	1-1	1-0	1-0	2-1
Cheltenham T	1-2	1-0	0-0	2-2	2-1	—	1-4	2-3	1-0	1-2	2-2	1-2	3-0	0-0	1-1	2-2	1-3	2-2	1-2	0-2	1-2	1-0	1-1	2-2
Chesterfield	1-0	2-0	3-1	0-2	4-0	2-0	—	1-1	1-1	2-1	1-2	0-1	1-0	1-1	0-0	3-0	2-0	0-0	2-2	1-1	2-1	3-1	2-0	2-2
Dagenham & R	0-0	1-0	2-0	2-1	2-1	1-2	0-1	—	1-1	3-0	1-0	0-0	1-1	1-1	0-3	1-0	1-2	1-4	3-1	3-3	1-1	0-1	2-0	2-0
Exeter C	0-1	2-0	2-1	2-1	2-2	1-1	0-1	1-1	—	0-1	0-3	0-0	1-1	0-2	1-1	0-0	3-1	1-1	0-1	2-0	0-2	1-1	0-1	2-1
Fleetwood T	3-1	1-0	4-0	2-3	2-1	0-1	1-1	3-1	1-2	—	2-0	5-4	2-2	4-1	2-0	1-1	0-4	3-1	0-0	0-1	1-1	4-1	1-0	1-2
Hartlepool U	2-1	3-1	1-1	1-1	0-3	0-1	1-2	2-1	0-2	1-0	—	2-4	2-1	3-0	2-0	1-3	1-0	0-0	0-3	0-0	0-1	3-0	1-2	2-0
Mansfield T	2-3	1-0	2-1	0-0	1-4	0-2	0-0	3-0	0-0	0-1	1-4	—	1-2	2-1	3-0	1-3	0-1	2-2	3-0	0-2	2-1	1-3	2-2	0-1
Morecambe	1-2	1-1	1-0	0-1	0-0	0-1	4-3	2-2	2-0	1-0	1-2	0-1	—	4-1	1-1	1-1	2-1	2-2	1-2	2-2	2-1	1-1	1-1	0-0
Newport Co	4-1	1-2	0-1	1-0	0-3	1-1	3-2	1-2	1-1	1-0	2-0	1-2	4-1	—	1-2	3-2	1-2	1-2	2-1	1-1	3-1	2-1	2-0	3-0
Northampton T	1-0	2-2	1-0	1-2	2-1	1-1	1-3	2-1	1-2	0-2	1-0	1-1	2-3	3-1	—	3-1	0-2	1-2	0-3	0-0	2-1	1-0	1-4	0-2
Oxford U	1-2	2-1	0-1	1-0	2-1	1-1	0-1	2-1	0-0	0-2	2-0	3-0	0-0	0-0	1-0	—	2-3	0-0	1-1	0-2	0-2	1-0	2-2	0-1
Plymouth Arg	0-0	1-2	3-2	0-1	1-0	0-0	2-1	1-0	3-2	0-1	1-0	1-1	3-1	0-0	0-0	0-2	—	1-1	1-0	0-2	1-1	2-0	1-0	0-4
Portsmouth	1-0	1-0	2-0	1-1	1-0	2-0	0-2	0-1	3-1	0-1	3-0	3-0	0-0	0-2	3-2	1-4	3-3	—	3-0	1-2	1-2	0-1	0-3	0-1
Rochdale	2-1	1-2	1-1	1-0	2-2	2-0	2-2	1-1	0-4	0-0	1-0	2-0	3-0	3-0	1-1	3-0	3-0	3-0	—	0-4	0-3	1-0	2-2	0-0
Scunthorpe U	0-2	0-0	1-1	0-0	0-0	1-1	1-1	3-0	2-3	2-0	1-0	3-0	2-1	3-0	2-0	1-0	1-0	5-1	3-0	—	2-2	3-1	3-2	2-2
Southend U	1-0	0-1	1-1	1-1	2-1	4-2	3-0	0-1	1-3	0-0	0-0	0-0	2-0	0-1	3-0	3-0	1-1	2-1	1-1	0-1	—	1-0	0-0	1-1
Torquay U	0-1	1-1	1-1	1-1	1-2	1-2	0-2	2-0	1-1	1-1	2-1	1-1	1-3	0-1	1-2	1-3	0-1	0-1	2-1	0-1	1-0	—	1-1	0-3
Wycombe W	0-0	0-3	1-2	1-2	1-2	0-0	1-0	3-1	2-1	1-1	1-0	1-0	1-1	2-0	1-0	0-1	1-0	0-1	0-2	1-1	2-1	0-3	—	1-1
York C	1-1	0-2	0-0	0-0	1-0	0-0	0-2	2-1	2-1	0-2	0-0	1-2	1-0	1-0	1-0	0-1	1-1	4-2	0-0	4-1	0-1	1-0	2-0	—

FOOTBALL LEAGUE PLAY-OFFS 2013–14

■ *Denotes player sent off.*

SKY BET CHAMPIONSHIP SEMI-FINALS FIRST LEG
Thursday, 8 May 2014
Brighton & HA (1) 1 *(Lingard 18)*
Derby Co (2) 2 *(Martin 29 (pen), Kuszczak 45 (og))* 27,118
Brighton & HA: (433) Kuszczak; Calderon, Greer, Upson, Ward; Forster-Caskey, Andrews, Orlandi (March 70); Buckley (LuaLua 46), Ulloa, Lingard (Mackail-Smith 82).
Derby Co: (433) Grant; Wisdom, Keogh, Buxton, Forsyth; Hendrick, Thorne, Bryson (Hughes 90); Ward (Sammon 72), Martin, Russell (Dawkins 66).

Friday, 9 May 2014
Wigan Ath (0) 0
QPR (0) 0 14,560
Wigan Ath: (343) Carson; Boyce, Caldwell, Kiernan; Perch, Gomez, McArthur, Beausejour; McManaman (Waghorn 76), Fortune (Maynard 76), Maloney.
QPR: (4411) Green; Simpson, Onuoha, Dunne, Hill; Traore (Doyle 70), Barton, O'Neil, Hoilett (Yun 88); Morrison (Kranjcar 78); Austin.

SKY BET CHAMPIONSHIP SEMI-FINALS SECOND LEG
Sunday, 11 May 2014
Derby Co (1) 4 *(Hughes 34, Martin 56, Thorne 76, Hendrick 87)*
Brighton & HA (0) 1 *(LuaLua 89)* 31,708
Derby Co: (433) Grant; Wisdom, Keogh, Buxton, Forsyth; Hendrick, Thorne, Hughes (Eustace 85); Russell (Bamford 78), Martin, Ward (Dawkins S 67).
Brighton & HA: (4231) Kuszczak; Calderon, Greer (Chicksen 24), Dunk, Ward; Andrews, Ince; Buckley (LuaLua 57), Orlandi (Mackail-Smith 57), Lingard; Ulloa.
Derby Co won 6-2 on aggregate.

Monday, 12 May 2014
QPR (0) 2 *(Austin 73 (pen), 96)*
Wigan Ath (1) 1 *(Perch 9)* 17,061
QPR: (442) Green; Simpson, Onuoha, Dunne, Hill (Yun 50); Doyle (Zamora 65), Barton, O'Neil (Morrison 69), Hoilett; Austin, Kranjcar.
Wigan Ath: (343) Carson; Boyce, Caldwell (Barnett 74), Kiernan; Perch, Gomez, McArthur (Espinoza 36), Beausejour; McManaman (Waghorn 71), McClean, Maloney.
aet; QPR won 2-1 on aggregate.

SKY BET CHAMPIONSHIP FINAL (at Wembley)
Saturday, 24 May 2014
Derby Co (0) 0
QPR (0) 1 *(Zamora 90)* 87,348
Derby Co: (433) Grant; Wisdom, Keogh, Buxton, Forsyth; Hendrick, Thorne, Hughes (Bryson 68); Russell (Dawkins S 67), Martin, Ward (Bamford 90).
QPR: (442) Green; Simpson, Onuoha, Dunne, Hill (Henry 67); Hoilett, Barton, O'Neil■, Kranjcar (Traore 33); Austin, Doyle (Zamora 57).
Referee: Lee Mason.

SKY BET LEAGUE ONE SEMI-FINALS FIRST LEG
Saturday, 10 May 2014
Peterborough U (1) 1 *(Assombalonga 16)*
Leyton Orient (0) 1 *(Odubajo 72)* 9519
Peterborough U: (4411) Olejnik; Little, Alcock, Baldwin, Ntlhe; Swanson (Isgrove 71), Bostwick, Payne (McCann 82), Rowe; Ajose (Washington 52); Assombalonga.
Leyton Orient: (442) Jones; Cuthbert, Baudry, Clarke, Omozusi; Odubajo, Vincelot, Lundstram (James 70), Cox; Lisbie (Batt 70), Mooney.

Preston NE (0) 1 *(Garner 49)*
Rotherham U (1) 1 *(Revell 21)* 17,221
Preston NE: (442) Rudd; Clarke, Wright, King, Laird; Holmes (Humphrey 77), Browne (Keane 62), Welsh, Gallagher; Garner, Davies C (Davies K 62).
Rotherham U: (433) Collin; Brindley (O'Connor 23), Morgan, Tavernier, Skarz; Arnason, Frecklington (Davis 62), Milsom; Thomas (Vuckic 83), Revell, Pringle.

SKY BET LEAGUE ONE SEMI-FINALS SECOND LEG
Tuesday, 13 May 2014
Leyton Orient (0) 2 *(Cox 60, Dagnall 88)*
Peterborough U (0) 1 *(Washington 90)* 8545
Leyton Orient: (442) Jones; Cuthbert, Baudry, Clarke, Omozusi; Odubajo, Vincelot, James, Cox (Dagnall 73); Lisbie (Batt 69), Mooney.
Peterborough U: (4411) Olejnik; Little, Baldwin, Knight-Percival (McCann 80), Alcock; Swanson (Washington 75), Bostwick, Payne (Isgrove 75), Rowe; Ajose; Assombalonga.
Leyton Orient won 3-2 on aggregate.

Bobby Zamora drives home QPR's last-gasp winner against Derby County in the Championship Play-off final at Wembley. Rangers are returning to the Premier League at the first attempt. (Action Images/Andrew Couldridge Livepic)

Fleetwood Town's Conor McLaughlin (left) and Burton Albion's Chris Hussey battle for the ball during the League Two Play-off final. Fleetwood won 1-0 to clinch their berth in League One, the club's sixth promotion in ten years.
(John Walton/PA Wire/Press Association Images)

Thursday, 15 May 2014
Rotherham U (2) 3 *(Thomas 24, Frecklington 34, Agard 67)*
Preston NE (1) 1 *(Gallagher 16)*   11,576
Rotherham U: (442) Collin; Tavernier, Morgan, Arnason, Skarz; Agard (O'Connor 90), Frecklington (Milsom 90), Smallwood, Pringle; Thomas (Vuckic 87), Revell.
Preston NE: (352) Rudd; Clarke, King, Wright; Wiseman (Humphrey 53), Welsh (Brownhill 68), Gallagher (Beavon 77), Kilkenny, Buchanan; Garner, Davies K.
Rotherham U won 4-2 on aggregate.

SKY BET LEAGUE ONE FINAL (at Wembley)
Sunday, 25 May 2014
Leyton Orient (2) 2 *(Odubajo 34, Cox 39)*
Rotherham U (0) 2 *(Revell 55, 60)*   43,401
Leyton Orient: (442) Jones; Cuthbert, Baudry, Clarke, Omozusi; Odubajo, James, Vincelot, Cox (Batt 74); Lisbie (Dagnall 76), Mooney (Lundstram 106).
Rotherham U: (442) Collin; Tavernier, Morgan, Arnason, Skarz (Milsom 77); Agard, Frecklington, Smallwood, Pringle; Thomas (Brindley 54), Revell (Vuckic 105).
aet; Rotherham U won 4-3 on penalties.
Referee: David Coote.

SKY BET LEAGUE TWO SEMI-FINALS FIRST LEG
Sunday, 11 May 2014
Burton Alb (1) 1 *(McGurk 45)*
Southend U (0) 0   4581
Burton Alb: (442) Lyness; Edwards, Sharps▪, Holness, Hussey; Ismail (Palmer 46), Weir, Bell, McFadzean; McGurk (Knowles 77), Kee (Gray 63).
Southend U: (433) Bentley; White (Eastwood 65), Sokolik, Egan, Coker; Atkinson, Timlin, Leonard; Hurst, Corr (Barnard 73), Murphy (Straker 65).

Monday, 12 May 2014
York C (0) 0
Fleetwood T (0) 1 *(Blair 50)*   5124
York C: (442) Pope; Oyebanjo, Lowe, McCombe, Davies; Brobbel (Bowman 62), Penn, Reed, Hayhurst; Coulson, Andrew.

Fleetwood T: (41212) Maxwell; McLaughlin, Pond, Roberts, Taylor; Schumacher; Blair, Morris; Sarcevic; Hume, Ball (Murdoch 86).

SKY BET LEAGUE TWO SEMI-FINALS SECOND LEG
Friday, 16 May 2014
Fleetwood T (0) 0
York C (0) 0   5194
Fleetwood T: (41212) Maxwell; McLaughlin, Pond, Roberts, Taylor; Schumacher (Goodall 75); Blair, Morris; Sarcevic (Cresswell 83); Ball, Hume (Parkin 64).
York C: (442) Pope; Oyebanjo, Lowe, McCombe, Davies; Coulson, Penn, Reed (Montrose 84), Hayhurst (Allan 90); Bowman (Jarvis 69), Andrew.
Fleetwood T won 1-0 on aggregate.

Saturday, 17 May 2014
Southend U (2) 2 *(Leonard 32, Straker 39)*
Burton Alb (1) 2 *(Holness 21, McGurk 69)*   9696
Southend U: (433) Bentley; White, Sokolik, Egan, Coker; Atkinson (Payne 79), Leonard, Timlin (Clifford 65); Hurst, Corr, Straker (Eastwood 72).
Burton Alb: (442) Lyness; Edwards, Cansdell-Sherriff, Holness, Hussey; Gray (MacDonald 64), Bell, Weir, McFadzean; Knowles (Kee 53), McGurk.
Burton Alb won 3-2 on aggregate.

SKY BET LEAGUE TWO FINAL (at Wembley)
Monday, 26 May 2014
Burton Alb (0) 0
Fleetwood T (0) 1 *(Sarcevic 75)*   14,007
Burton Alb: (442) Lyness; Edwards, Holness (Diamond 65), Cansdell-Sherriff, McFadzean; MacDonald (Ismail 73), Weir, Bell (Palmer 78), Hussey; McGurk, Kee.
Fleetwood T: (41212) Maxwell; McLaughlin, Pond, Roberts, Taylor; Goodall; Blair (Parkin 74), Morris; Sarcevic; Ball, Hume (Murdoch 86).
Referee: Michael Naylor.

REVIEW OF THE SEASON 2013–14

Change was the key word in the build-up to the 2013–14 Premier League season – and it remained so throughout the campaign, as the league lead switched hands 25 times and relegation favourites surged to survival.

Manchester City eventually emerged victorious, after a thrilling duel with Liverpool for the championship, while Sunderland became just the second side in Premier League history to stay up after being bottom at Christmas.

However, at the start of the year all eyes were on Manchester United, where, for the first time ever, a Premier League season began without Sir Alex Ferguson in charge.

The most successful manager in English football history had hand-picked Everton boss David Moyes to succeed him and, in his farewell speech, called on supporters to be patient as the club went through a transition. However, few would have predicted the on-field failings that were to follow from a squad that had eased to the title by 11 points in 2012–13.

A Community Shield cruise past Wigan – Moyes' first and only honour as United boss – and an opening day 4-1 win at Swansea signalled promise but as the club's summer transfer plans unravelled so too did their performances on the pitch.

A 1-0 defeat at fierce rivals Liverpool caused concern, before a 4-1 embarrassment at City and loss at home to West Brom sounded alarm bells.

Back-to-back home league defeats – the club's first in over 10 years – to Moyes' former club Everton and Newcastle followed at the start of December. Then, despite a £37m splash on Juan Mata, a wretched start to the New Year, including a Capital One Cup semi-final exit to relegation-threatened Sunderland, had United fans flying banners over Old Trafford by the end of March calling for Moyes to be axed.

After being thoroughly outclassed 3-0 at home to both local rivals, Liverpool and then City, Moyes' time seemed to be up and a 2-0 defeat at Goodison Park, where he had received a standing ovation at the end of his 11-year tenure the previous spring, was to be the Scot's final game in charge.

Ryan Giggs – who hung up his boots at the end of the campaign as the most decorated player in English football history – took charge for the final four matches of the season, as United finished seventh, recorded their lowest-ever Premier League points total and failed to qualify for European competition for the first time in 25 years.

However, the other half of Manchester will look back on 2013–14 with extremely fond memories.

City also began the campaign with a new man at the helm and Manuel Pellegrini fared far better than his United counterpart, landing a Premier League–League Cup double and becoming the first non-European to manage a team to the English title.

However, that only tells the bare facts of what was a pulsating Premier League title race as City, early pace-setters Arsenal, surprise package Liverpool and Chelsea, with Jose Mourinho back in charge, looked to capitalise on Ferguson's departure.

Arsene Wenger's Gunners, bolstered by £40m new recruit Mesut Ozil and the insatiable form of Aaron Ramsey, took 25 points from the first ten games, including a 2-0 win at home to Liverpool, to move five clear at the top of the standings and, despite losing one of the games of the season 6-3 at Man City, held the league lead into February.

A 5-1 drubbing at Liverpool knocked them off the summit, though, before a 6-0 annihilation at new leaders Chelsea left them seven points behind their London neighbours in fourth, which is where they would ultimately finish for the second year in a row – although an extra-time FA Cup final triumph over Hull ended their nine-year trophy drought.

Arsenal were pushed hard for the final Champions League spot by Roberto Martinez's Everton who won plaudits throughout the campaign, losing just once before Christmas and sweeping aside the Gunners 3-0 at Goodison Park.

On-loan Chelsea striker Romelu Lukaku netted 15 times for Everton but back at the Bridge Mourinho was adamant throughout the campaign his side could not win the league.

Although his prophecy would prove correct, Chelsea completed the double over both Liverpool and Man City – ending the latter's 100% win record at the Etihad in February –

and, after finishing four points adrift, will regret costly defeats to Aston Villa, Crystal Palace and Sunderland – Mourinho's first ever home league defeat in charge of the Blues.

Reaching the semi-finals of the Champions League and putting themselves back in the title race with two to play with a 2-0 win at Anfield demonstrated Chelsea's potential, yet, while they recorded the joint highest number of clean sheets in the Premier League (16), they simply could not keep up with free-scoring pair City and Liverpool.

For the first time in Premier League history two sides registered over 100 goals, with eventual champions City bagging 102 – one shy of the league's record – to Liverpool's 101. Pellegrini's men had racked up a ton in all competitions by January, as Yaya Toure, Sergio Aguero and Edin Dzeko netted over 15 league goals each, another Premier League record.

A 7-0 destruction of Norwich and a 9-0 aggregate Capital One Cup semi-final success over West Ham highlighted City's strike power, while wonder goals from Toure and Samir Nasri in the League Cup final at Wembley helped land the club's first triumph in that competition since 1976.

Indeed, the Ivorian was the standout player from a team of star performers, scoring 20 times from midfield, but there's no question which player shone brightest in this campaign.

Luis Suarez was linked with moves away from Liverpool in the summer but set aside those rumours to net 31 league goals and form a deadly strike partnership with Daniel Sturridge, who finished second in the scoring standings with 21.

Brendan Rodgers' men began the campaign targeting a Champions League spot but finished it devastated to have missed out on a first league win since 1990. A remarkable 11-game winning streak from February to April, which included thrashings of Arsenal, Cardiff and Tottenham, plus a thrilling 3-2 win over title rivals City at Anfield, put them in pole position to land the championship.

However, with Liverpool five points clear at the top with less than a month of the season remaining, Steven Gerrard's untimely slip against Chelsea proved costly, while a 3-3 draw at Crystal Palace – after leading 3-0 with 11 minutes to play – left the Reds going into the final day needing City to falter at home to West Ham.

Pellegrini's side – who had followed their loss at Liverpool with a shock draw at home to Sunderland – won their final five games, though, to record their second Premier League success.

The drama at the other end of the table was equally enthralling as Sunderland completed a 'miracle' escape. Boss Gus Poyet, who had taken over from Paolo Di Canio, all but wrote off his side's survival hopes after a 5-1 April defeat to eventual sixth-placed Tottenham left them seven points adrift of safety with two games in hand.

Wins at Chelsea and Manchester United plus victories over Cardiff and West Brom and a point at City propelled the Black Cats to a 14th-placed finish and five points clear of the drop zone.

Instead it was Cardiff, who controversially swapped boss Malky Mackay for Ole Gunnar Solskjaer mid-season, Fulham, who worked through three managers, and Norwich, who axed Chris Hughton with four to play, who went down.

Crystal Palace had been among the pre-season favourites for the drop – and looked on course for an immediate return to the Championship after losing seven in a row – but Tony Pulis took over from Ian Holloway and produced a Manager of the Year-winning performance to steer the Eagles to mid-table, with the help of a club record-equalling five-game winning streak.

With the World Cup looming, there was plenty to delight England boss Roy Hodgson at Southampton, where Adam Lallana, Luke Shaw, Rickie Lambert and Jay Rodriguez – whose Brazil dream was wrecked by injury – lit up the league with their attacking play, helping Saints to eighth.

But there was frustration at Spurs as Andre Villas-Boas and then Tim Sherwood struggled to get the best out of the new recruits captured with the proceeds of Gareth Bale's £85m sale to Real Madrid. The White Hart Lane outfit may have recorded their second-highest Premier League points tally – and Sherwood may have achieved the highest win ratio of any Spurs boss in the division – but still it was not enough to secure a top four spot.

Meanwhile, Stoke recorded a best-ever Premier League finish in ninth, one place ahead of Newcastle, who collapsed spectacularly after an impressive start, losing eight of their last ten games after boss Alan Pardew was suspended for head-butting Hull player David Meyler.

Meyler's Hull also exceeded expectations, with boss Steve Bruce among the candidates for Manager of the Year after steering his newly promoted side to the Cup Final and 16th in the league, including a win over Liverpool, and one place above West Brom, whose Steve Clarke was one of a record ten manager changes in the season.

Swansea finished a disappointing 12th after cutting ties with their boss, Michael Laudrup, with Garry Monk stepping in, while West Ham were rewarded for standing by Sam Allardyce, who achieved Premier League survival despite losing eight of the club's last eleven games.

In the Football League, Leicester stormed to the Championship title, booking their place in next season's top flight with a club record 102 points.

The Foxes, who registered a 20-game unbeaten run to April and were fired by 20-goal David Nugent, spent much of the season battling with surprise package Burnley for top spot.

The Clarets were among the pre-season favourites for relegation but the combination of Danny Ings (21 goals in 40 appearances) and Sam Vokes (18 in 36) made a mockery of those predictions while Burnley – who used just 25 players all campaign – had the meanest defence in the division, conceding just 37 goals.

It was resurgent Derby who topped the scoring charts. Former England boss Steve McClaren took over from Nigel Clough with the Rams 14th with 11 points from nine matches and led them to a third-placed finish with a club record 85 points and 84 strikes.

His positive impact failed to stretch to Wembley, though, where Derby succumbed to a 90th minute Bobby Zamora winner in the play-off final against 10-man QPR. Harry Redknapp's men had been tipped for the title but, after an 11-game unbeaten start to the campaign, faltered to fourth before edging out Wigan and Derby in the post-season games.

Brighton was the other team to miss out in the play-offs, losing 6-2 on aggregate to Derby, after a thrilling final day winner from Leonardo Ulloa against Nottingham Forest meant the Seagulls pipped Reading to sixth.

There was more last-gasp drama at the Reebok Stadium, where third-from-bottom Birmingham – who had lost their previous seven – battled back from 2-0 down at Bolton to snatch a 93rd minute equaliser through Paul Caddis and condemn Doncaster to relegation instead.

Rovers – last season's League One winners – will join Barnsley and Yeovil in the third tier after spending much of the season embroiled in a dog fight with Millwall, Charlton and Blackpool in the Championship's lower reaches.

Kenny Jackett's Wolves will be optimistic of avoiding a similar fate when they compete in the second tier next season. The Molineux outfit had suffered consecutive relegations in the past two seasons but got back to winning ways in 2013–14, racking up a third-tier points total record with 103 points from their 46 games.

They finished the season nine clear of Brentford, but the West London outfit had been in title contention for much of the campaign, recording 15 wins from 17 games between October and February before Mark Warburton – who had taken over from Uwe Rosler in December – saw his 19-game unbeaten start as Bees manager come to an end with a 3-0 loss at home to Wolves.

Brentford's club record 94 points secured automatic promotion, though, while Leyton Orient, who were the league's early pace setters – and continued to defy their critics throughout the season – were undone in a thrilling play-off final with Rotherham, which the Millers won on penalties.

Tranmere and Carlisle, meanwhile, joined Shrewsbury in being relegated from the division, after a dramatic final 15 minutes on the last day of the season saw Notts County escape the drop.

There was greater heartache for Bristol Rovers, though, who saw their 94-year stay in the Football League brought to an end by the narrowest of margins at the bottom of League Two.

With Torquay already condemned, Wycombe beat the Gulls 3-0 to stay up at Rovers' expense – with a better goal difference of three. Northampton, who had spent much of the season in the mire also saved their status with a 3-1 win at Oxford on the final day.

A week previously Exeter's St James Park had seen both home and away supporters celebrating as Exeter secured their League Two status by ending Scunthorpe's record breaking 28-game unbeaten run under new manager Russ Wilcox. The record streak for a

Rotherham United's Adam Collin saves the deciding penalty from Leyton Orient's Chris Dagnall in the shoot-out which settled the League One Play-off final. The game finished 2-2 after extra time.
(Mike Egerton/PA Wire/Press Association Images)

manager's first spell in charge may have ended in defeat at Exeter – but Fleetwood's failure to beat Southend ensured the Iron gained promotion to League One.

Chesterfield would secure the title, beating Fleetwood 2-1 on the final day as Scunthorpe were held by York. But Fleetwood celebrated in style after securing their sixth promotion in 10 seasons with a play-off final win over Burton Albion, which ensured they would join third-placed Rochdale in also rising to the third tier.

Peter Smith

CUPS AND UPS AND DOWNS DIARY

JANUARY
11   Welsh Premier League Cup Final: Carmathen T 0 Bala T 0.
      (aet; Carmathen T won 3-1 on penalties)

MARCH
2   Capital One Cup Final: Manchester C 3 Sunderland 1.
11   Hyde relegated from Skrill Premier League.
12   Rangers champions of Scottish League 1 and promoted to Scottish Championship.
      The New Saints champions of Welsh Premier League.
16   Scottish Communities League Cup Final: Aberdeen 0 Inverness CT 0.
      (aet; Aberdeen won 4-2 on penalties)
23   FA Trophy Final: Cambridge U 4 Gosport Bor 0.
26   Celtic champions of Scottish Premiership.
30   Johnstone's Paint Trophy Final: Peterborough 3 Chesterfield 1.

APRIL
5   Leicester C promoted from Championship to Premier League.
      Hearts relegated from Scottish Premiership to Scottish Championship.
6   Scottish Ramsdens Cup Final: Raith R 1 Rangers 0 *(aet)*.
8   Tamworth relegated from Skrill Premier League.
12   Wolverhampton W promoted from Football League 1 to Football League Championship.
      Greenock Morton relegated from Scottish Championship to Scottish League 1.
      Peterhead champions of Scottish League 2 and promoted to Scottish League 1.
15   Luton T champions of Skrill Premier League and promoted to Football League 2.
18   Brentford promoted from Football League 1 to Football League Championship.
21   Burnley promoted from Championship to Premier League.
      Wolverhampton W champions of Football League 1.
      Stevenage relegated from Football League 1 to Football League 2.
      Dartford relegated from Skrill Premier League (later re-instated).
22   Leicester C champions of Football League Championship.
25   Yeovil T relegated from Football League Championship to Football League 1.
26   Barnsley relegated from Football League Championship to Football League 1.
      Shrewsbury T relegated from Football League 1 to Football League 2.
      Rochdale and Scunthorpe U promoted from Football League 2 to Football League 1.
      Torquay U relegated from Football League 2 to Skrill Premier League.
      Chester FC relegated from Skrill Premier League (later re-instated).
27   Chesterfield promoted from Football League 2 to Football League 1.

MAY
3   Cardiff C and Fulham relegated from Premier League to Football League Championship.
      Doncaster R relegated from Football League Championship to Football League 1.
      Carlisle U and Tranmere R relegated from Football League 1 to Football League 2.
      Chesterfield champions of Football League 2.
      Bristol R relegated from Football League 2 to Skrill Premier League.
      Dundee champions of Scottish Championship and promoted to Scottish Premier League.
      Arbroath relegated from Scottish League 1 to Scottish League 2.
      Welsh FA Cup Final: The New Saints 3 Abersystwyth Town 2.
10   FA Vase Final: Sholing 1 West Auckland 1.
11   Manchester C champions of Premier League, Liverpool runners-up.
      Norwich C relegated from Premier League to Football League Championship.
14   UEFA Europa League Final: Benfica 0 Sevilla 0.
      (aet; Sevilla won 4-2 on penalties)
      Scottish Championship League Play-off final 1st leg: Cowdenbeath 1 Dunfermline Ath 1.
      Scottish Football League 1 Play-off final 1st leg: Stirling Alb 1 East Fife 2.
17   FA Cup Final: Arsenal 3 Hull C 2 *(aet)*.
      Scottish FA Cup Final: St Johnstone 2 Dundee U 0.
18   Skrill Premier League Play-off final: Cambridge U 2 Gateshead 1.
      (Cambridge U promoted from Skrill Premier League to Football League 2).
      Scottish Championship League Play-off final 2nd leg: Dunfermline 0 Cowdenbeath 3.
      (Cowdenbeath won 4-1 on aggregate and remain in Scottish Championship).
      Scottish Football League 1 Play-off final 2nd leg: East Fife 0 Stirling Alb 2.
      *(Stirling Alb won 3-2 on aggregate and promoted from Scottish League 2 to Scottish League 1 and East Fife relegated
      from Scottish League 1 to Scottish League 2).*
21   Scottish Premier League Play-off final 1st leg: Hamilton A 0 Hibernian 2.
24   UEFA Champions League Final: Real Madrid 4 Atletico Madrid 1 *(aet)*.
      Football League Championship Play-off final: QPR 1 Derby Co 0.
      (QPR promoted to Premier League).
25   Football League 1 Play-off final: Leyton Orient 2 Rotherham U 2.
      (aet; Rotherham U won 4-3 on penalties and promoted from Football League 1 to Football League Championship).
      Scottish Premier League Play-off final 2nd leg: Hibernian 0 Hamilton A 2.
      *(aet; Hamilton A won 4-3 on penalties and promoted from Scottish Championship to Scottish Premier League and
      Hibernian relegated from Scottish Premier League to Scottish Championship).*
26   Football League 2 Play-off final: Fleetwood T 1 Burton Alb 0.
      (Fleetwood T promoted to Football League 1).
27   Women's FA Cup Final: Arsenal 2 Everton 0.

JUNE
10   Hereford U expelled from Skrill Premier League.

JULY
4   Salisbury C expelled from Skrill Premier League.
13   World Cup Final: Germany 1 Netherlands 0 *(aet)*.

THE FA COMMUNITY SHIELD WINNERS 1908–2013

CHARITY SHIELD 1908–2001

1908	Manchester U v QPR	1-1
Replay	Manchester U v QPR	4-0
1909	Newcastle U v Northampton T	2-0
1910	Brighton v Aston Villa	1-0
1911	Manchester U v Swindon T	8-4
1912	Blackburn R v QPR	2-1
1913	Professionals v Amateurs	7-2
1920	WBA v Tottenham H	2-0
1921	Tottenham H v Burnley	2-0
1922	Huddersfield T v Liverpool	1-0
1923	Professionals v Amateurs	2-0
1924	Professionals v Amateurs	3-1
1925	Amateurs v Professionals	6-1
1926	Amateurs v Professionals	6-3
1927	Cardiff C v Corinthians	2-1
1928	Everton v Blackburn R	2-1
1929	Professionals v Amateurs	3-0
1930	Arsenal v Sheffield W	2-1
1931	Arsenal v WBA	1-0
1932	Everton v Newcastle U	5-3
1933	Arsenal v Everton	3-0
1934	Arsenal v Manchester C	4-0
1935	Sheffield W v Arsenal	1-0
1936	Sunderland v Arsenal	2-1
1937	Manchester C v Sunderland	2-0
1938	Arsenal v Preston NE	2-1
1948	Arsenal v Manchester U	4-3
1949	Portsmouth v Wolverhampton W	1-1*
1950	English World Cup XI v FA Canadian Touring Team	4-2
1951	Tottenham H v Newcastle U	2-1
1952	Manchester U v Newcastle U	4-2
1953	Arsenal v Blackpool	3-1
1954	Wolverhampton W v WBA	4-4*
1955	Chelsea v Newcastle U	3-0
1956	Manchester U v Manchester C	1-0
1957	Manchester U v Aston Villa	4-0
1958	Bolton W v Wolverhampton W	4-1
1959	Wolverhampton W v Nottingham F	3-1
1960	Burnley v Wolverhampton W	2-2*
1961	Tottenham H v FA XI	3-2
1962	Tottenham H v Ipswich T	5-1
1963	Everton v Manchester U	4-0
1964	Liverpool v West Ham U	2-2*
1965	Manchester U v Liverpool	2-2*
1966	Liverpool v Everton	1-0
1967	Manchester U v Tottenham H	3-3*
1968	Manchester C v WBA	6-1
1969	Leeds U v Manchester C	2-1
1970	Everton v Chelsea	2-1
1971	Leicester C v Liverpool	1-0
1972	Manchester C v Aston Villa	1-0
1973	Burnley v Manchester C	1-0
1974	Liverpool v Leeds U	1-1
	Liverpool won 6-5 on penalties.	
1975	Derby Co v West Ham U	2-0
1976	Liverpool v Southampton	1-0
1977	Liverpool v Manchester U	0-0*
1978	Nottingham F v Ipswich T	5-0
1979	Liverpool v Arsenal	3-1
1980	Liverpool v West Ham U	1-0
1981	Aston Villa v Tottenham H	2-2*
1982	Liverpool v Tottenham H	1-0
1983	Manchester U v Liverpool	2-0
1984	Everton v Liverpool	1-0
1985	Everton v Manchester U	2-0
1986	Everton v Liverpool	1-1*
1987	Everton v Coventry C	1-0
1988	Liverpool v Wimbledon	2-1
1989	Liverpool v Arsenal	1-0
1990	Liverpool v Manchester U	1-1*
1991	Arsenal v Tottenham H	0-0*
1992	Leeds U v Liverpool	4-3
1993	Manchester U v Arsenal	1-1
	Manchester U won 5-4 on penalties.	
1994	Manchester U v Blackburn R	2-0
1995	Everton v Blackburn R	1-0
1996	Manchester U v Newcastle U	4-0
1997	Manchester U v Chelsea	1-1
	Manchester U won 4-2 on penalties.	
1998	Arsenal v Manchester U	3-0
1999	Arsenal v Manchester U	2-1
2000	Chelsea v Manchester U	2-0
2001	Liverpool v Manchester U	2-1

COMMUNITY SHIELD 2002–13

2002	Arsenal v Liverpool	1-0
2003	Manchester U v Arsenal	1-1
	Manchester U won 4-3 on penalties.	
2004	Arsenal v Manchester U	3-1
2005	Chelsea v Arsenal	2-1
2006	Liverpool v Chelsea	2-1
2007	Manchester U v Chelsea	1-1
	Manchester U won 3-0 on penalties.	
2008	Manchester U v Portsmouth	0-0
	Manchester U won 3-1 on penalties.	
2009	Chelsea v Manchester U	2-2
	Chelsea won 4-1 on penalties.	
2010	Manchester U v Chelsea	3-1
2011	Manchester U v Manchester C	3-2
2012	Manchester C v Chelsea	3-2
2013	Manchester U v Wigan Ath	2-0

* *Each club retained shield for six months.*

THE FA COMMUNITY SHIELD 2013

Manchester U (1) 2, Wigan Ath (0) 0

at Wembley, Sunday 11 August 2013, attendance 80,235

Manchester U: De Gea; Rafael (Smalling 16), Evra, Jones, Vidic, Giggs (Anderson 67), Carrick, Cleverley, Welbeck (Kagawa 83), van Persie (Januzaj 83), Zaha (Valencia 61).
Scorers: van Persie 6, 59.

Wigan Ath: Carson; Crainey, Boyce, Perch, Barnett, McCarthy (Dicko 86), Watson (Espinoza 71), McArthur (McCann 81), Holt (Fortune 61), Maloney (Gomez 71), McClean (McManaman 62).

Referee: Mark Clattenburg.

ACCRINGTON STANLEY

FOUNDATION

Accrington Football Club, founder members of the Football League in 1888, were not connected with Accrington Stanley. In fact both clubs ran concurrently between 1891 when Stanley were formed and 1895 when Accrington FC folded. Actually Stanley Villa was the original name, those responsible for forming the club living in Stanley Street and using the Stanley Arms as their meeting place. They became Accrington Stanley in 1893. In 1894–95 they joined the Accrington & District League, playing at Moorhead Park. Subsequently they played in the North-East Lancashire Combination and the Lancashire Combination before becoming founder members of the Third Division (North) in 1921, two years after moving to Peel Park. In 1962 they resigned from the Football League, were wound up, re-formed in 1963, disbanded in 1966 only to restart as Accrington Stanley (1968), returning to the Lancashire Combination in 1970.

The Crown Ground, Livingstone Road, Accrington, Lancashire BB5 5BX.

Telephone: (0871) 434 1968.

Fax: (01254) 356 951.

Ticket Office: (0871) 434 1968.

Website: www.accringtonstanley.co.uk

Email: info@accringtonstanley.co.uk

Ground Capacity: 5,070.

Record Attendance: 13,181 v Hull C, Division 3 (N), 28 September 1948 (at Peel Park); 4,368 v Colchester U, FA Cup 1st rd, 3 January 2004 (at Fraser Eagle Stadium – Crown Inn).

Pitch Measurements: 101.5m × 65m (111yd × 71yd)

Chairman: Peter Marsden.

Managing Director: Robert Heys.

Manager: James Beattie.

Assistant Manager: Paul Stephenson.

Physio: Paul Morgan.

Colours: Red shirts with white trim, red shorts, red socks with white trim.

Year Formed: 1891, reformed 1968.

Turned Professional: 1919.

Club Nickname: 'The Reds', 'Stanley'.

Previous Names: 1891, Stanley Villa; 1893, Accrington Stanley.

HONOURS

Football League – Division 3 (N): *Runners-up* 1954–55, 1957–58.

Conference: *Champions* 2005–06.

FA Cup: 4th rd 1927, 1937, 1959, 2010.

Football League Cup: never past 2nd rd.

Northern Premier League: *Champions* 2002–03.

Northern League – Division 1: *Champions* 1999–2000.

North-West Counties: *Runners-up* 1986–87.

Cheshire County League – Division 2: *Champions* 1980–81; *Runners-up* 1979–80.

Lancashire Combination: *Champions* 1973–74, 1977–78; *Runners-up* 1971–72, 1975–76.

Lancashire Combination Cup: *Winners* 1971–72, 1972–73, 1973–74, 1976–77.

Grounds: 1891, Moorhead Park; 1897, Bell's Ground; 1919, Peel Park; 1970, Crown Inn.

First Football League Game: 27 August 1921, Division 3 (N), v Rochdale (a) L 3-6 – Tattersall; Newton, Baines, Crawshaw, Popplewell, Burkinshaw, Oxley, Makin, Green (1), Hosker (2), Hartles.

sky SPORTS FACT FILE

In 1938–39 Accrington Stanley reached the final of the Division Three North Cup yet finished bottom of the division and had to apply for re-election. They lost the final 3-0 to Bradford City and were only narrowly re-elected back into the Football League, seeing off a challenge from Shrewsbury Town.

Record League Victory: 8–0 v New Brighton, Division 3 (N), 17 March 1934 – Maidment; Armstrong (pen), Price, Dodds, Crawshaw, McCulloch, Wyper, Lennox (2), Cheetham (4), Leedham (1), Watson.

Record Cup Victory: 7–0 v Spennymoor U, FA Cup 2nd rd, 8 December 1938 – Tootill; Armstrong, Whittaker, Latham, Curran, Lee, Parry (2), Chadwick, Jepson (3), McLoughlin (2), Barclay.

Record Defeat: 1–9 v Lincoln C, Division 3 (N), 3 March 1951.

Most League Points (2 for a win): 61, Division 3 (N), 1954–55.

Most League Points (3 for a win): 73, FL 2, 2010–11.

Most League Goals: 96, Division 3 (N), 1954–55.

Highest League Scorer in Season: George Stewart, 35, Division 3 (N), 1955–56; George Hudson, 35, Division 4, 1960–61.

Most League Goals in Total Aggregate: George Stewart, 136, 1954–58.

Most League Goals in One Match: 5, Billy Harker v Gateshead, Division 3 (N), 16 November 1935; George Stewart v Gateshead, Division 3 (N), 27 November 1954.

Most Capped Player: Romuald Boco, 19 (48), Benin.

Most League Appearances: Jim Armstrong, 260, 1927–34.

Youngest League Player: Ian Gibson, 15 years 358 days, v Norwich C, 23 March 1959.

Record Transfer Fee Received: £50,000 (rising to £250,00) from Blackpool for Brett Ormerod, March 1997.

Record Transfer Fee Paid: £85,000 (rising to £150,000) to Swansea C for Ian Craney, January 2008.

Football League Record: 1921 Original Member of Division 3 (N); 1958–60 Division 3; 1960–62 Division 4; 2006– FL 2.

MANAGERS

William Cronshaw *c.*1894
John Haworth 1897–1910
Johnson Haworth *c.*1916
Sam Pilkingson 1919–24
  (*Tommy Booth p-m 1923–24*)
Ernie Blackburn 1924–32
Amos Wade 1932–35
John Hacking 1935–49
Jimmy Porter 1949–51
Walter Crook 1951–53
Walter Galbraith 1953–58
George Eastham snr 1958–59
Harold Bodle 1959–60
James Harrower 1960–61
Harold Mather 1962–63
Jimmy Hinksman 1963–64
Terry Neville 1964–65
Ian Bryson 1965
Danny Parker 1965–66
Gerry Keenan
Gary Pierce
Dave Thornley
Phil Staley
Eric Whalley
Stan Allen 1995–96
Tony Greenwood 1996–98
Billy Rodaway 1998
Wayne Harrison 1998–99
John Coleman 1999–2012
Paul Cook 2012
Leam Richardson 2012–13
James Beattie May 2013–

LATEST SEQUENCES

Longest Sequence of League Wins: 7, 27.12.1954 – 5.2.1955.

Longest Sequence of League Defeats: 9, 8.3.1930 – 21.4.1930.

Longest Sequence of League Draws: 4, 10.9.1927 – 27.9.1927.

Longest Sequence of Unbeaten League Matches: 14, 15.3.2011 – 6.8.2011.

Longest Sequence Without a League Win: 18, 17.9.1938 – 31.12.1938.

Successive Scoring Runs: 22 from 14.11.1936.

Successive Non-scoring Runs: 5 from 15.3.1930.

TEN YEAR LEAGUE RECORD

		P	W	D	L	F	A	Pts	Pos
2004-05	Conf	42	18	11	13	72	58	65	10
2005-06	Conf	42	28	7	7	76	45	91	1
2006-07	FL 2	46	13	11	22	70	81	50	20
2007-08	FL 2	46	16	3	27	49	83	51	17
2008-09	FL 2	46	13	11	22	42	59	50	16
2009-10	FL 2	46	18	7	21	62	74	61	15
2010-11	FL 2	46	18	19	9	73	55	73	5
2011-12	FL 2	46	14	15	17	54	66	57	14
2012-13	FL 2	46	14	12	20	51	68	54	18
2013-14	FL 2	46	14	15	17	54	56	57	15

DID YOU KNOW ?

Former Accrington Stanley reserve player Paul Grayson switched codes and went on to become a leading rugby union player. He appeared for Stanley's second string as an 18-year-old but after changing sports made over 30 appearances as a fly half for England and was a member of the squad which won the Rugby World Cup in 2003.

ACCRINGTON STANLEY – FOOTBALL LEAGUE TWO 2013–14 LEAGUE RECORD

Match No.	Date	Venue	Opponents	Result		H/T Score	Lg Pos.	Goalscorers	Attendance
1	Aug 3	A	Newport Co	L	1-4	0-2	22	Webber [68]	4631
2	10	H	Portsmouth	D	2-2	0-0	20	Murphy 2 [48, 85]	2531
3	17	A	Bury	L	0-3	0-2	24		3080
4	24	H	Cheltenham T	L	0-1	0-0	24		1224
5	31	A	Burton Alb	L	0-1	0-0	24		1174
6	Sept 7	A	Chesterfield	L	0-1	0-0	24		6588
7	14	A	Hartlepool U	L	1-2	0-2	24	Gray [57]	3388
8	21	H	Rochdale	L	1-2	1-2	24	Odejayi [24]	2180
9	28	A	Plymouth Arg	D	0-0	0-0	24		6180
10	Oct 4	H	Dagenham & R	L	1-2	0-0	24	Gray [90]	1833
11	12	A	AFC Wimbledon	D	1-1	1-0	24	Odejayi [17]	4585
12	19	H	Oxford U	D	0-0	0-0	24		1476
13	22	H	Bristol R	W	2-1	2-1	24	Gray [19], Naismith [29]	1101
14	26	A	Morecambe	W	2-1	1-0	24	Webber (pen) [19], Murphy [90]	2175
15	Nov 2	H	Wycombe W	D	1-1	0-0	23	Murphy [90]	1268
16	16	A	Scunthorpe U	W	2-0	2-0	22	Bowerman [26], Odejayi [36]	3255
17	23	H	Torquay U	W	2-1	1-1	20	Naismith 2 [42, 74]	1279
18	26	H	Fleetwood T	W	2-0	0-0	19	Webber (pen) [75], Odejayi [82]	1699
19	30	A	Northampton T	L	0-1	0-1	19		4092
20	Dec 14	H	Exeter C	L	2-3	1-3	21	Murphy [38], Naismith [50]	1219
21	21	A	Mansfield T	W	3-2	0-1	17	Naismith 2 [48, 90], Gray [90]	2549
22	26	H	York C	D	1-1	1-1	18	Bowerman [45]	2009
23	29	H	Southend U	D	1-1	0-0	18	Phillips (og) [63]	1333
24	Jan 1	A	Fleetwood T	L	1-3	0-1	21	Odejayi [81]	2446
25	11	H	Newport Co	D	3-3	2-1	22	Murphy 2 [23, 88], Naismith [44]	1318
26	18	A	Cheltenham T	W	2-1	2-0	18	Bowerman [15], Joyce [43]	2648
27	28	A	Bristol R	W	1-0	0-0	17	Murphy [90]	6067
28	Feb 8	A	Wycombe W	D	0-0	0-0	18		3073
29	14	H	Scunthorpe U	L	2-3	2-0	19	Molyneux [18], Murphy [37]	1256
30	18	H	Bury	D	0-0	0-0	20		2184
31	22	A	Torquay U	W	1-0	0-0	19	Naismith [80]	2218
32	25	A	Portsmouth	L	0-1	0-0	22		13,387
33	Mar 1	A	Burton Alb	L	1-2	0-1	22	Winnard [69]	2368
34	8	H	Chesterfield	W	3-1	3-0	22	Molyneux 3 [4, 9, 45]	1968
35	11	H	Hartlepool U	D	0-0	0-0	21		1196
36	15	H	Rochdale	L	1-2	0-0	21	Mingoia [72]	2841
37	18	A	Morecambe	W	5-1	2-0	15	Molyneux 2 [5, 90], Naismith (pen) [11], Winnard [59], Aldred [65]	1525
38	22	H	Plymouth Arg	D	1-1	0-1	16	Aldred [81]	1559
39	25	A	Dagenham & R	D	0-0	0-0	18		1383
40	29	H	Exeter C	W	1-0	1-0	14	Odejayi [45]	3354
41	Apr 5	H	Northampton T	L	0-1	0-1	16		1616
42	12	A	York C	D	1-1	0-0	17	McCartan [90]	3855
43	18	H	Mansfield T	D	1-1	0-0	16	Naismith (pen) [90]	2092
44	21	A	Southend U	L	0-1	0-0	18		5915
45	26	A	Oxford U	W	2-1	1-0	17	Odejayi [18], Gray [54]	5022
46	May 3	H	AFC Wimbledon	W	3-2	2-0	15	Odejayi [6], Gray 2 [19, 47]	1888

Final League Position: 15

GOALSCORERS

League (54): Naismith 10 (2 pens), Murphy 9, Odejayi 8, Gray 7, Molyneux 6, Bowerman 3, Webber 3 (2 pens), Aldred 2, Winnard 2, Joyce 1, McCartan 1, Mingoia 1, own goal 1.
The Budweiser FA Cup (0).
Capital One Cup (2): Carver 1, Mingoia 1.
Johnstone's Paint Trophy (0).

Dunbavin I 4	Murphy P 43 + 1	Liddle M 16 + 3	Atkinson R 11 + 4	Hunt N 36 + 1	Aldred T 46	Richardson M 10 + 5	Joyce L 45 + 1	Webber D 14 + 8	Wilson L 13 + 2	Hatfield W 17 + 14	Carver M 1 + 5	Clark L — + 1	McCartan S 6 + 12	Naismith K 29 + 9	Mingoia P 31 + 6	Gray J 21 + 14	Winnard D 37 + 2	Bettinelli M 39	Mahoney C 1 + 3	Miller G 4	Odejayi K 26 + 6	Naylor L 13	Caton J 1 + 1	Bowerman G 10 + 4	Windass J 4 + 6	Dawber A 3	Molyneux L 14 + 3	Buxton A 11	Match No.
1	2	3	4	5	6	7	8[2]	9[3]	10	11[1]	12	13	14																1
1	7	5	4	2	3	8[1]	12	10		9[1]	11[3]			6	13	14													2
1	7	5[1]	4	2[2]	3	14	6	11[8]	10	9[3]			12	8			13												3
1	2	5	4		3	7[3]	6		10	14	13		11[2]	9	8[1]	12													4
	2	5	4		3	8	7			12	14		9[2]	11	6[1]	10[3]		1	13										5
	2	4		5			9	6	11[1]		12		14	7	10[2]		3	1	13		8[4]								6
	2	3		5			8[5]	6			12		13	7		10[3]	4	1	14		9[3]	11							7
	7	2			4		13	8[2]			14		10	6		12	3	1		9	11		5[1]						8
	10	4	2	3			9	6					8[1]			12		1			7	11	5						9
	6	4	2[1]	3			8		9				10[3]		13	14		1			7[2]	11	5	12					10
	8		2	4	3[1]	10	7			14	13				6[3]	12		1			11[1]		5	9[2]					11
	7		2		3	12	8		11[1]			13	14	6	9[2]	10[3]	4	1					5						12
	8		2		4	14	7		11[1]		12	13		6	9	10[2]	3	1					5						13
	8		2		4	14	7		10[1]		12			6	9[3]	11[2]	3	1					5	13					14
	8	14	2		4		7		10[1]	5[3]				6	9	11[2]	3	1			12			13					15
	8		2		3		7		12				9	6	13		4	1			11[2]	5		10[1]					16
	8	5	2		4		7						6	9	12		3	1			10	11[1]							17
			2	5	3		8	7	12		13		6	9[2]			4	1			10	11[1]							18
	7	5	2		3		8		11[1]			13		6	9[2]	12	4	1			10								19
	8		2		3		7		10[2]			13	6	9	11[1]		4	1				5		12					20
	7		2[2]		3		8				12		6	9	11		4	1				5		13	10[1]				21
	8		2		3		7		12				6	9	11[1]	4						5		10	1				22
	8		2		3	9	7						10	6	12	4						5		11[1]	1				23
	9	5	2[1]		4	6	8				14		13	10[3]	7[2]	3					11			12	1				24
	7		2		3		8		10[2]		12	13		6	9		4	1			11	5[1]							25
	8	14	2		3		7		12	5		13		6	9[2]		4	1			10[3]			11[1]					26
	8		2		3		7		13				5	6[1]	9		4	1			10			11[2]			12		27
	8		2		3		7						5	9[1]	6	13	4	1			10			11[2]			12		28
	7		2		3		8		14			13	5	6		12	4	1			10[3]			11[1]			9[2]		29
	7	12	14	2	4		8			10[2]		13	5[4]	6			3	1			11[1]						9[3]		30
	7	5	2		3		8				12			9			4	1			11				10[1]		6		31
	8	5[1]	2		4		7						11	6	12		3	1			10						9		32
	7	5[1]	2		3		8			12			10	6			4	1			11						9		33
	8[4]	14			3		7	6		11[1]	5			10[1]			4	1			13			12			9	2[2]	34
	14				3		7	6		10[1]	5			12		11[2]	4[3]	1			13					8	9	2	35
	7			5	3		8		10				12	6[2]		11[1]	4	1			14					13	9	2[3]	36
	8[2]	12		5[1]	3		7	6[3]				13	10			11	4	1			14						9	2	37
	8		2		3		7	6[2]				13	10[1]	14		11[3]	4	1			12						9	5	38
	8		2		4		7	6					12			10[1]	3	1			11						9	5	39
	8	12	2		4		7	6[2]				13			11		3	1			10[3]					14	9	5[1]	40
	7		2		3		8	6[1]				13	12			10[2]	4	1			11						9	5	41
	7[3]	5	4		3		8	9				13	12	6		10[2]		1			11					14		2[1]	42
	7	5	2		4		8	6[2]			14	13	11[1]			12	3	1			10						9[3]		43
	7	5			4		8	6[2]		14		13	10	9[1]		11[2]	3	1			12							2	44
	12		2		3		7	6				13		9		11[2]	4	1			10					8[1]		5	45
			2	5	4		7	6[2]				12	13	9		10[1]	3	1			11					8			46

The Budweiser FA Cup
First Round   Tranmere R   (h)   0-1

Capital One Cup
First Round   Middlesbrough   (a)   2-1
Second Round   Cardiff C   (h)   0-2

Johnstone's Paint Trophy
First Round   Crewe Alex   (a)   0-1

AFC WIMBLEDON

FOUNDATION

While the history of AFC Wimbledon is straightforward since it was a new club formed in 2002, there were in effect two clubs operating for two years with Wimbledon connections. The other club was MK Dons, of course. In August 2001, the Football League had rejected the existing Wimbledon's application to move to Milton Keynes. In May 2002, they rejected local sites and were given permission to move by an independent commission set up by the Football League. AFC Wimbledon was founded in the summer of 2002 and held its first trials on Wimbledon Common. In subsequent years, there was considerable debate over the rightful home of the trophies obtained by the former Wimbledon football club. In October 2006, an agreement was reached between Milton Keynes Dons FC, its Supporters Association, the Wimbledon Independent Supporters Association and the Football Supporters Federation to transfer such trophies and honours to the London Borough of Merton.

The Cherry Red Records Stadium, Kingsmeadow, Jack Goodchild Way, 422a Kingston Road, Kingston-upon-Thames, Surrey KT1 3PB.

Telephone: (0208) 547 3528.

Fax: (0808) 2800 816.

Website: www.afcwimbledon.co.uk

Email: info@afcwimbledon.co.uk

Ground Capacity: 5,339.

Record Attendance: 4,763 v Plymouth Arg, FL 2, 29 December 2013.

Pitch Measurements: 104m × 66m (113.5yd × 72yd)

President: Dickie Guy.

Chief Executive: Erik Samuelson.

Manager: Neal Ardley.

Assistant Manager: Neil Cox.

First Team Coach: Simon Bassey.

Physio: Stuart Douglas.

Club Nickname: 'The Dons'.

Colours: All blue with yellow trim.

Year Formed: 2002.

Turned Professional: 2002.

MANAGERS

Terry Eames 2002–04
Nicky English *(Caretaker)* 2004
Dave Anderson 2004–07
Terry Brown 2007–12
Neal Ardley October 2012–

sky SPORTS FACT FILE

In only their second season of existence AFC Wimbledon won the Combined Counties League, finishing the 2003–04 campaign with 130 points from their 46 games. They remained undefeated throughout the season, winning 42 of their 46 games and scoring 180 goals.

First Football League Game: 6 August 2011, FL 2 v Bristol R (h) L 2–3 – Brown; Hatton, Gwillim (Bush), Porter (Minshull), Stuart (1), Johnson B, Moore L, Wellard, Jolley (Ademeno (1)), Midson, Yussuff.

Record League Victory: 4–0 v Burton Alb, FL 2, 24 March 2012 – Brown; Hatton, Gwillim, Moncur (1), Mitchel-King, Balkestein, Moore S (1), Knott (Wellard), Jolley, Midson, Moore L (1) (Harrison (1)); 4-0 v Portsmouth, FL 2, 16 November 2012 – Worner; Bennett, Fuller, Frampton (2), Kennedy, Sweeney (Moore L), Moore S (1), Porter, Pell, Smith (1), Mohamed (Francomb).

Record Cup Victory: 4–3 v York City, FA Cup 1st rd replay, 12 November 2012 – Brown; Fenlon (Osano), Mambo, Mitchel-King, Cummings, Jolley, Gregory, Johnson (Harrison (1)), Yussuff (Long), Midson (1), Strutton (2).

Record Defeat: 2–6 v Burton Alb, FL 2, 25 August 2012.

Most League Points (3 for a win): 54, FL 2, 2011–12.

Most League Goals: 62, FL 2, 2011–12.

Highest League Scorer in Season: Jack Midson, 18, 2011–12.

Most League Goals in Total Aggregate: Kevin Cooper, 107, 2002–04.

Most Capped Player: Shane Smeltz, 5 (50), New Zealand.

Most League Appearances: Jack Midson, 126, 2011–14.

Youngest League Player: George Moncur, 18 years 148 days v Port Vale, 14 January 2012.

Record Transfer Fee Received: £120,000 from Coventry C for Chris Hussey, January 2010.

Record Transfer Fee Paid: £25,000 (in excess of) to Stevenage for Byron Harrison, January 2012.

Football League Record: 2011 Promoted from Conference Premier; 2011– FL 2.

LATEST SEQUENCES

Longest Sequence of League Wins: 4, 17.9.2011 – 8.10.2011.

Longest Sequence of League Defeats: 6, 26.11.2011 – 2.1.2012.

Longest Sequence of League Draws: 3, 12.1.2013 – 2.2.2013.

Longest Sequence of Unbeaten League Matches: 5, 1.1.2013 – 2.2.2013.

Longest Sequence Without a League Win: 12, 15.10.2011 – 2.1.2012.

Successive Scoring Runs: 8 from 16.2.2013.

Successive Non-scoring Runs: 3 from 29.3.2013.

HONOURS

Blue Square Conference: *Runners-up* 2010–11; promoted via play-offs.

Blue Square South: *Champions* 2008–09.

FA Cup: never past 2nd rd.

Football League Cup: never past 1st rd.

Isthmian League – Premier Division: *Play-off Winners* 2007–08. **Division 1:** *Champions* 2004–05.

Combined Counties League: *Champions* 2003–04.

Combined Counties League: *Challenge Cup Winners* 2004.

Surrey Senior Cup: *Winners* 2005; *Runners-up* 2006.

Supporters Direct Cup: *Winners* 2003, 2006, 2010; *Runners-up* 2005, 2007.

Phil Ledger Memorial Cup: *Winners* 2011.

TEN YEAR LEAGUE RECORD

		P	W	D	L	F	A	Pts	Pos
2004-05	Isth DI	42	29	10	3	91	33	97	1
2005-06	Isth PR	42	22	11	9	67	36	77	4
2006-07	Isth PR	42	21	15	6	76	37	75	5
2007-08	Isth PR	42	22	9	11	81	47	75	3
2008-09	Conf S	42	26	10	6	86	36	88	1
2009-10	Conf P	44	18	10	16	61	47	64	8
2010-11	Conf P	46	27	9	10	83	47	90	2
2011-12	FL 2	46	15	9	22	62	78	54	16
2012-13	FL 2	46	14	11	21	54	76	53	20
2013-14	FL 2	46	14	14	18	49	57	53*	20

* 3 pts deducted.

DID YOU KNOW ❓

In 2008–09 AFC Wimbledon reached the first round of the FA Cup for the first time in their history. The Dons, then in Conference South, were drawn at home to League Two club Wycombe Wanderers, going out 4-1 in front of a crowd of 4,528.

AFC WIMBLEDON – FOOTBALL LEAGUE TWO 2013–14 LEAGUE RECORD

Match No.	Date	Venue	Opponents	Result	H/T Score	Lg Pos.	Goalscorers	Attendance
1	Aug 3	A	Torquay U	D	1-1	0-0	13	Pell [87]	3441
2	10	H	Wycombe W	W	1-0	1-0	7	Moore, L [37]	4235
3	17	A	Exeter C	L	0-2	0-2	12		3881
4	24	H	Scunthorpe U	W	3-2	0-2	8	Smith [62], Pell [75], Arthur [87]	3865
5	31	H	Fleetwood T	W	2-0	2-0	4	Pell (pen) [42], Smith [45]	3744
6	Sept 7	A	York C	W	2-0	1-0	3	Smith 2 [31, 73]	3530
7	14	A	Chesterfield	L	0-2	0-1	7		6353
8	21	H	Burton Alb	W	3-1	0-1	3	Smith [55], Midson [69], Frampton [74]	4005
9	28	A	Cheltenham T	L	0-1	0-0	7		3032
10	Oct 5	A	Northampton T	L	0-2	0-1	11		4222
11	12	H	Accrington S	D	1-1	0-1	11	Bennett [86]	4585
12	19	A	Morecambe	D	1-1	0-1	11	Smith [52]	2149
13	22	A	Hartlepool U	L	1-3	0-1	15	Pell (pen) [66]	3652
14	26	H	Oxford U	L	0-2	0-1	15		4685
15	Nov 2	A	Rochdale	W	2-1	0-1	15	Moore, S [54], Frampton [84]	2483
16	16	H	Portsmouth	W	4-0	1-0	9	Frampton 2 [34, 74], Moore, S [82], Smith [90]	4605
17	23	A	Bury	D	1-1	0-1	10	Moore, L [66]	2775
18	26	H	Dagenham & R	D	1-1	1-0	10	Smith [28]	3862
19	30	A	Bristol R	L	0-3	0-2	12		5860
20	Dec 14	H	Mansfield T	D	0-0	0-0	12		3900
21	26	H	Southend U	L	0-1	0-0	16		4561
22	29	H	Plymouth Arg	D	1-1	0-0	15	Smith [47]	4763
23	Jan 1	A	Dagenham & R	L	0-1	0-1	15		2012
24	4	A	Wycombe W	W	3-0	0-0	14	Wyke [52], Moore, S [76], Midson (pen) [82]	3513
25	11	H	Torquay U	L	0-2	0-2	15		4339
26	18	A	Scunthorpe U	D	0-0	0-0	14		4326
27	25	H	Exeter C	W	2-1	1-1	11	Midson [74], Moore, L [37]	4410
28	28	H	Hartlepool U	W	2-1	0-1	9	Antwi [74], Hylton [76]	3730
29	Feb 1	A	Oxford U	L	1-2	0-1	10	Wyke [75]	5748
30	8	H	Rochdale	L	0-3	0-0	12		3837
31	15	A	Portsmouth	L	0-1	0-0	14		15,742
32	22	H	Bury	L	0-1	0-0	16		3740
33	25	A	Newport Co	W	2-1	0-0	11	Sheringham [85], Sainte-Luce [88]	2666
34	Mar 1	A	Fleetwood T	D	0-0	0-0	12		2420
35	8	H	York C	L	0-1	0-1	16		4182
36	11	H	Chesterfield	D	1-1	0-0	15	Francomb [50]	3424
37	15	A	Burton Alb	D	1-1	0-1	15	Jones [90]	2592
38	22	H	Cheltenham T	W	4-3	0-1	15	Hylton 2 [69, 71], Nicholson [70], Midson [90]	3670
39	25	A	Northampton T	D	2-2	1-1	13	Francomb [14], Moore, S [90]	3812
40	29	A	Mansfield T	L	0-1	0-1	16		3292
41	Apr 5	H	Bristol R	D	0-0	0-0	17		4322
42	12	A	Southend U	W	1-0	0-0	14	Midson (pen) [58]	7627
43	18	H	Newport Co	D	2-2	0-2	14	Appiah [49], Francomb [69]	4398
44	21	A	Plymouth Arg	W	2-1	1-1	14	Midson [42], Appiah [59]	6618
45	26	H	Morecambe	L	0-3	0-2	14		4017
46	May 3	A	Accrington S	L	2-3	0-2	20	Midson (pen) [73], Appiah [89]	1888

Final League Position: 20

GOALSCORERS

League (49): Smith 9, Midson 7 (3 pens), Frampton 4, Moore, S 4, Pell 4 (2 pens), Appiah 3, Francomb 3, Hylton 3, Moore, L 3, Wyke 2, Antwi 1, Arthur 1, Bennett 1, Jones 1, Nicholson 1, Sainte-Luce 1, Sheringham 1.
The Budweiser FA Cup (1): Smith 1.
Capital One Cup (1): Moore, L 1.
Johnstone's Paint Trophy (3): Fenlon 1, Francomb 1, Sweeney 1.

Worner R 45	Fuller B 45	Kennedy C 21+1	Sweeney P 18+4	Frampton A 31	Bennett A 32	Francomb G 28+5	Pell H 27+6	Moore L 25+8	Smith M 23	Porter G 17+4	Sheringham C 8+7	Arthur C 2+24	Midson J 19+18	Weston R 6+1	Moore S 40	Sainte-Luce K 3+20	Fenlon J 15+4	Strutton C 1+2	Mohamed K 5	Antwi W 14+4	Wyke C 11+6	Morris A 15+2	Jones D 17+1	Hylton D 10+7	Collins M 9	Richards T 9+1	Nicholson J 3+1	Appiah K 6+1	Brown S 1	Match No.
1	2	3	4	5	6	7^1	8	9	10^3	11^2	12	13	14																	1
1	2	5	9	3	4	14	7	8^1	11		6^2	12	13		10^1															2
1	2	5	7	3	4^1	13	8	9	10		6^2	14		11^3	12															3
1	2	5^1		3			7	9	11	6^3	10^2	12	13		4	8	14													4
1	2			3			6^1	7	10	11	9^2		13	12	4	8	14													5
1	2			3	4		6^1	8	11	10	9^2		13	12		7			5											6
1	2			3	4		6^3	8	11^2	10	9^1		13	12		7			5	14										7
1	2	5^1	14	3	4		6^2	8^3	9	11	13		12	10		7														8
1	2	5^1		4	3		6^1	8	9	11	12		13	10^2		7	14													9
1	2	3^3		4^1	5		6^2	7	9	10	11		13	14		8	12													10
1	2	5^1		3			7	9	10	6		12	11^2		4	8	13													11
1	2^1	12	7	3			6	9^2	11	10					4	8	13		5											12
1	2		10	3			8^2	9	11	6					4	7	12		5	13										13
1	2	5	8^3	3				9	14	13	11	6			4	7	12			10^2										14
1	2	5	8	3	4	10^2	9^1		11	7	13				6	12														15
1	2	5	9^1	3	4	13	7	12	11	6					10					8^2										16
1	2	5	7	3	4			9^3	10	8^2	14		12		6						13	11^1								17
1	2	5	10^2	3	4		7	13	11	6			12		9							8^1								18
1	2	5^1	7^1	4	3		9	12	11	10^2			13		6^3	14						8								19
1	2	5	9	3		6		11^1	8	12	7^2	13			4	10														20
1			4	5^2	7	3		6^8	10^1	11		8^1	14	12	9	13	2													21
1	2^1	5	8	4	3	14		9^1	11		10^2		13	7	6					12										22
1	9	5^2		3	2	6^1	12	7	10	13	11^3		14		8					4										23
1	4			3	5			8	9				10		7	12	6^8			2	11^1									24
1	5	9		4	3^1	8^3		7^2					13	11	6	12				2	10	14								25
1	5	9		4^1	3	7^3	6						14	10	8	13				2	11^2	12								26
1	6	9^1		3	14	8		7^2					12	11^3	5	13				4	10		2							27
1	2^3						8				10^2	14	11^1		9	7	6			5	12	4	3	13						28
1	2		3					9				12	14		8	13	6^2				7^1	11	4^1	5	10					29
1	5^2			4	8	6						14	9		7^1	12	13					10	2	3	11^3					30
1				3			7^2		8			14	12		9	13	2^2				6	10	5	4	11^1					31
1	5			3			7^2	12					14		6	13	9^1					11^3	4	2	10	8				32
1	5			2				7			12		11^2		6	14	9^3				3	13		4	10^1	8				33
1	2							12	9	10^2					8	14					3	13	7^1	4	11^2	6	5			34
	1	5	13						7^2			10^1	14	12	6						4	2	3	11	8	9^3				35
1	5	7^3	4	3	8	14					12				6	9^1					13	2		11^2	10					36
1	5^1		3	4	6	8^2						14			9	10					13		2	11^3	7	12				37
1	2	7^1	4		6			13	10			8									11		3	14	9^3	5^2	12			38
1	2		3^1	4	6^3		12					14	10^8		7					13	11^2	8		9	5					39
1	9		3	11								13			7	14					4	10^3	8	2^1		6	5^2	12		40
1	2	9^1		6	8							11^3				12					3	14	7	4	13		5	10^2		41
1	2	3		6	9	12						11^3									14		7	4	13		5	8^1 10^2		42
1	2	4		6^3	14			13	11			7				5^2					8	3	12				9 ^{1} 10			43
1	2	12	4	6^3	9^1			10	7			14									8^2	3	13		6			5	11	44
	2	13	3	6^2	14	12		5	9			8^3										4	10				7^1 11		1	45
1	2	9^3		3^1	6			14	10			7									4		8	12	13		5^2	11		46

The Budweiser FA Cup
First Round   Coventry C   (h)   1-3

Capital One Cup
First Round   Millwall   (a)   1-2

Johnstone's Paint Trophy
First Round   Brentford   (a)   3-5

ARSENAL

FOUNDATION

Formed by workers at the Royal Arsenal, Woolwich in 1886, they began as Dial Square (name of one of the workshops), and included two former Nottingham Forest players, Fred Beardsley and Morris Bates. Beardsley wrote to his old club seeking help and they provided the new club with a full set of red jerseys and a ball. The club became known as the 'Woolwich Reds' although their official title soon after formation was Woolwich Arsenal.

Emirates Stadium, Highbury House, 75 Drayton Park, Islington, London N5 1BU.

Telephone: (020) 7619 5003.

Fax: (020) 7704 4001.

Ticket Office: (020) 7619 5000.

Website: www.arsenal.com

Email: ask@arsenal.com

Ground Capacity: 60,338.

Record Attendance: 73,295 v Sunderland, Div 1, 9 March 1935 (at Highbury); 73,707 v RC Lens, UEFA Champions League, 25 November 1998 (at Wembley); 60,162 v Manchester U, FA Premier League, 3 November 2007 (at Emirates).

Pitch Measurements: 105m × 68m (114yd × 74yd)

Chairman: Sir John 'Chips' Keswick.

Chief Executive: Ivan Gazidis.

Manager: Arsène Wenger.

Assistant Manager: Steve Bould.

Physio: Colin Lewin.

Colours: Red shirts with white sleeves with blue and red trim, white shorts, white socks with blue and red hoops.

Year Formed: 1886.

Turned Professional: 1891.

Previous Names: 1886, Dial Square; 1886, Royal Arsenal; 1891, Woolwich Arsenal; 1914, Arsenal.

Club Nickname: 'The Gunners'.

Grounds: 1886, Plumstead Common; 1887, Sportsman Ground; 1888, Manor Ground; 1890, Invicta Ground; 1893, Manor Ground; 1913, Highbury; 2006, Emirates Stadium.

HONOURS

FA Premier League:
Champions 1997–98, 2001–02, 2003–04. *Runners-up* 1998–99, 1999–2000, 2000–01, 2002–03, 2004–05.
Football League – Division 1:
Champions 1930–31, 1932–33, 1933–34, 1934–35, 1937–38, 1947–48, 1952–53, 1970–71, 1988–89, 1990–91;
Runners-up 1925–26, 1931–32, 1972–73;
Division 2: *Runners-up* 1903–04.
FA Cup: *Winners* 1930, 1936, 1950, 1971, 1979, 1993, 1998, 2002, 2003, 2005; *Runners-up* 1927, 1932, 1952, 1972, 1978, 1980, 2001.
Double performed: 1970–71, 1997–98, 2001–02.
Football League Cup: *Winners* 1987, 1993; *Runners-up* 1968, 1969, 1988, 2007, 2011.
European Competitions
European Cup: 1971–72, 1991–92.
UEFA Champions League: 1998–99, 1999–2000, 2000–01, 2001–02, 2002–03, 2003–04, 2004–05, 2005–06 (*runners-up*), 2006–07, 2007–08 (*q-f*), 2008–09 (*s-f*), 2009–10, 2010–11, 2011–12, 2012–13, 2013–14.
Fairs Cup: 1963–64, 1969–70 (*winners*), 1970–71. **UEFA Cup:** 1978–79, 1981–82, 1982–83, 1996–97, 1997–98, 1999–2000 (*runners-up*).
European Cup-Winners' Cup: 1979–80 (*runners-up*), 1993–94 (*winners*), 1994–95 (*runners-up*). **Super Cup:** 1994 (*runners-up*).

sky SPORTS FACT FILE

When Arsenal played Moscow Dynamo in 1945 the Gunners fielded only five of their own men together with six guest players including England internationals Stanley Matthews and Stan Mortensen. Mortensen scored twice but Arsenal went down 4-3 in front of a 54,000 crowd.

First Football League Game: 2 September 1893, Division 2, v Newcastle U (h) D 2–2 – Williams; Powell, Jeffrey; Devine, Buist, Howat; Gemmell, Henderson, Shaw (1), Elliott (1), Booth.

Record League Victory: 12–0 v Loughborough T, Division 2, 12 March 1900 – Orr; McNichol, Jackson; Moir, Dick (2), Anderson (1); Hunt, Cottrell (2), Main (2), Gaudie (3), Tennant (2).

Record Cup Victory: 11–1 v Darwen, FA Cup 3rd rd, 9 January 1932 – Moss; Parker, Hapgood; Jones, Roberts, John; Hulme (2), Jack (3), Lambert (2), James, Bastin (4).

Record Defeat: 0–8 v Loughborough T, Division 2, 12 December 1896.

Most League Points (2 for a win): 66, Division 1, 1930–31.

Most League Points (3 for a win): 90, FA Premier League, 2003–04.

Most League Goals: 127, Division 1, 1930–31.

Highest League Scorer in Season: Ted Drake, 42, 1934–35.

Most League Goals in Total Aggregate: Thierry Henry, 175, 1999–2007; 2011–12.

Most League Goals in One Match: 7, Ted Drake v Aston Villa, Division 1, 14 December 1935.

Most Capped Player: Thierry Henry, 81 (123), France.

Most League Appearances: David O'Leary, 558, 1975–93.

Youngest League Player: Jack Wilshere, 16 years 256 days v Blackburn R (as substitute), 13 September 2008.

Record Transfer Fee Received: £25,400,000 (rising to £29,800,000) from Barcelona for Cesc Fabregas, August 2011.

Record Transfer Fee Paid: £42,400,000 to Real Madrid for Mesut Ozil, September 2013.

Football League Record: 1893 Elected to Division 2; 1904–13 Division 1; 1913–19 Division 2; 1919–92 Division 1; 1992– FA Premier League.

MANAGERS

Sam Hollis 1894–97
Tom Mitchell 1897–98
George Elcoat 1898–99
Harry Bradshaw 1899–1904
Phil Kelso 1904–08
George Morrell 1908–15
Leslie Knighton 1919–25
Herbert Chapman 1925–34
George Allison 1934–47
Tom Whittaker 1947–56
Jack Crayston 1956–58
George Swindin 1958–62
Billy Wright 1962–66
Bertie Mee 1966–76
Terry Neill 1976–83
Don Howe 1984–86
George Graham 1986–95
Bruce Rioch 1995–96
Arsène Wenger September 1996–

LATEST SEQUENCES

Longest Sequence of League Wins: 14, 10.2.2002 – 18.8.2002.

Longest Sequence of League Defeats: 7, 12.2.1977 – 12.3.1977.

Longest Sequence of League Draws: 6, 4.3.1961 – 1.4.1961.

Longest Sequence of Unbeaten League Matches: 49, 7.5.2003 – 24.10.2004.

Longest Sequence Without a League Win: 23, 28.9.1912 – 1.3.1913.

Successive Scoring Runs: 55 from 19.5.2001.

Successive Non-scoring Runs: 6 from 25.2.1987.

TEN YEAR LEAGUE RECORD

		P	W	D	L	F	A	Pts	Pos
2004-05	PR Lge	38	25	8	5	87	36	83	2
2005-06	PR Lge	38	20	7	11	68	31	67	4
2006-07	PR Lge	38	19	11	8	63	35	68	4
2007-08	PR Lge	38	24	11	3	74	31	83	3
2008-09	PR Lge	38	20	12	6	68	37	72	4
2009-10	PR Lge	38	23	6	9	83	41	75	3
2010-11	PR Lge	38	19	11	8	72	43	68	4
2011-12	PR Lge	38	21	7	10	74	49	70	3
2012-13	PR Lge	38	21	10	7	72	37	73	4
2013-14	PR Lge	38	24	7	7	68	41	79	4

DID YOU KNOW ?

Alf Kirchen marked his first Football League appearance for Arsenal by scoring two goals in a 6-0 win over rivals Tottenham Hotspur in March 1935. Kirchen, who went on to win three England caps while with the Gunners, also represented his country at clay pigeon shooting.

ARSENAL – FA PREMIERSHIP 2013–14 LEAGUE RECORD

Match No.	Date	Venue	Opponents	Result	H/T Score	Lg Pos.	Goalscorers	Attendance
1	Aug 17	H	Aston Villa	L	1-3	1-1	18	Giroud [6]	60,003
2	24	A	Fulham	W	3-1	2-0	8	Giroud [14], Podolski 2 [41, 68]	25,622
3	Sept 1	H	Tottenham H	W	1-0	1-0	4	Giroud [23]	60,071
4	14	A	Sunderland	W	3-1	1-0	1	Giroud [11], Ramsey 2 [67, 76]	39,055
5	22	H	Stoke C	W	3-1	2-1	1	Ramsey [5], Mertesacker [36], Sagna [72]	60,002
6	28	A	Swansea C	W	2-1	0-0	1	Gnabry [58], Ramsey [62]	20,712
7	Oct 6	A	WBA	D	1-1	0-1	1	Wilshere [63]	24,839
8	19	H	Norwich C	W	4-1	1-0	1	Wilshere [18], Ozil 2 [58, 88], Ramsey [83]	60,009
9	26	A	Crystal Palace	W	2-0	0-0	1	Arteta (pen) [47], Giroud [87]	25,050
10	Nov 2	H	Liverpool	W	2-0	1-0	1	Cazorla [19], Ramsey [59]	60,042
11	10	A	Manchester U	L	0-1	0-1	1		75,138
12	23	H	Southampton	W	2-0	1-0	1	Giroud 2 (1 pen) [22, 86 (p)]	60,007
13	30	A	Cardiff C	W	3-0	1-0	1	Ramsey 2 [29, 90], Flamini [86]	27,948
14	Dec 4	H	Hull C	W	2-0	1-0	1	Bendtner [2], Ozil [47]	60,017
15	8	H	Everton	D	1-1	0-0	1	Ozil [80]	60,001
16	14	A	Manchester C	L	3-6	1-2	1	Walcott 2 [31, 63], Mertesacker [90]	47,229
17	23	H	Chelsea	D	0-0	0-0	2		60,039
18	26	A	West Ham U	W	3-1	0-0	1	Walcott 2 [68, 71], Podolski [79]	34,977
19	29	A	Newcastle U	W	1-0	0-0	1	Giroud [65]	52,161
20	Jan 1	H	Cardiff C	W	2-0	0-0	1	Bendtner [88], Walcott [90]	60,004
21	13	A	Aston Villa	W	2-1	2-0	1	Wilshere [34], Giroud [35]	36,097
22	18	H	Fulham	W	2-0	0-0	1	Cazorla 2 [57, 62]	60,000
23	28	A	Southampton	D	2-2	0-1	1	Giroud [48], Cazorla [52]	31,284
24	Feb 2	H	Crystal Palace	W	2-0	0-0	1	Oxlade-Chamberlain 2 [47, 73]	60,005
25	8	A	Liverpool	L	1-5	0-4	2	Arteta (pen) [69]	44,701
26	12	H	Manchester U	D	0-0	0-0	2		60,021
27	22	H	Sunderland	W	4-1	3-0	2	Giroud 2 [5, 31], Rosicky [42], Koscielny [57]	60,012
28	Mar 1	A	Stoke C	L	0-1	0-0	3		26,711
29	16	H	Tottenham H	W	1-0	1-0	3	Rosicky [2]	35,711
30	22	A	Chelsea	L	0-6	0-4	4		41,614
31	25	H	Swansea C	D	2-2	0-1	4	Podolski [73], Giroud [74]	59,937
32	29	H	Manchester C	D	1-1	0-1	4	Flamini [53]	60,060
33	Apr 6	A	Everton	L	0-3	0-2	4		39,504
34	15	H	West Ham U	W	3-1	1-1	4	Podolski 2 [44, 78], Giroud [55]	59,977
35	20	A	Hull C	W	3-0	2-0	4	Ramsey [31], Podolski 2 [45, 54]	24,762
36	28	H	Newcastle U	W	3-0	2-0	4	Koscielny [26], Ozil [42], Giroud [66]	60,023
37	May 4	A	WBA	W	1-0	1-0	4	Giroud [14]	60,021
38	11	A	Norwich C	W	2-0	0-0	4	Ramsey [53], Jenkinson [62]	26,848

Final League Position: 4

GOALSCORERS

League (68): Giroud 16 (1 pen), Ramsey 10, Podolski 8, Ozil 5, Walcott 5, Cazorla 4, Wilshere 3, Arteta 2 (2 pens), Bendtner 2, Flamini 2, Koscielny 2, Mertesacker 2, Oxlade-Chamberlain 2, Rosicky 2, Gnabry 1, Jenkinson 1, Sagna 1.
The Budweiser FA Cup (16): Cazorla 3, Giroud 3, Podolski 3, Arteta 1 (1 pen), Koscielny 1, Mertesacker 1, Oxlade-Chamberlain 1, Ozil 1, Ramsey 1, Rosicky 1.
Capital One Cup (1): Eisfeld 1.
UEFA Champions League (14): Giroud 4 (1 pen), Ramsey 4, Wilshere 2, Gibbs 1, Ozil 1, Podolski 1, Walcott 1.

Szczesny W 37	Sagna B 34 + 1	Mertesacker P 35	Koscielny L 32	Gibbs K 24 + 4	Ramsey A 20 + 3	Wilshere J 19 + 5	Walcott T 9 + 4	Rosicky T 17 + 10	Oxlade-Chamberlain A 6 + 8	Giroud O 36	Jenkinson C 7 + 7	Cazorla S 30 + 1	Podolski L 14 + 6	Monreal N 13 + 10	Sanogo Y — + 8	Flamini M 18 + 9	Ozil M 25 + 1	Vermaelen T 7 + 7	Akpom C — + 1	Gnabry S 5 + 4	Miyaichi R — + 1	Arteta M 27 + 4	Bendtner N 1 + 8	Kallstrom K 1 + 2	Fabianski L 1	Diaby A — + 1	Match No.
1	2³	3	4	5¹	6	7	8	9	10²	11	12	13	14														1
1	3	4		5	7	12	8	6²		11³	2	9	10¹	13	14												2
1 14	3	4	5	7	6³	8²	9¹		11	2	10		13														3
1	3		4	5	7	9	8³			11¹	2		13			6	10²	12	14								4
1	2	3	4	5	7	10³			11			12		6	9²		8¹	13	14								5
1	2	3	4	5	7	10²			11	14		13		6	9³		8¹	12									6
1		3	4	5	8¹	10		12		11²	2					7	9			6	13						7
1	2	3	4	5	12	8		13		11²		10³				7¹	9			6	14						8
1	2	3	4	5	8	13				11		10¹		14		7²	9			12³	6⁴						9
1	2	3	4	5²	6			8¹		11	14	10²		12			9	13			7						10
1	2		3	5	8	12				11		10¹				6²	9	4	14		7³	13					11
1	2	3	4	5	6	8	12	13		11		10³		14			9¹				7²						12
1	2	3	4	5	7	6¹	14			11		10¹		13		12	9²				6						13
1		3	4			6²	13	12	8¹			2	10		5		7	9				14	11¹				14
1		3	4	5		7²	8³	12	13			11		2	10¹		14	9				6					15
1	2	3	4²		6	10	8			11¹				5		7³	9	12		13			14				16
1	2	3		5	7		8	10		11							9	4				6					17
1	2	3		5	6¹		8			11³		10	12			13	9²	4				7	14				18
1	2	3	4	5¹		7	8²	9		11³	13	10				6						12	14				19
1	2	3	4		9		8	13		10			11²	5		7¹		14				6	12³				20
1	2	3	4	12		6		13³	14	11		10		5²		7	9		8¹								21
1	2	3	4		6			13		11		10	12	5		7	9²		8¹								22
1	2	3	4	13				12	6	11³		10¹	14	5		6⁴	9		8²			7					23
1	2	3	4	13		7		14	8	11²		10	12	5¹			9²					7	14				24
1	2	3	4	13		7		14	8	11²		10	12	5¹			9³					6					25
1	2	3	4	5		7				8¹	12	11		10			9					6					26
1	2	3	4³			7		9¹		11	12	8	10	5²		13				14		6					27
1	2	3	4	5		7¹		9¹	13	11		8		10²		14	12					6					28
1	2	3	4	5				8¹	6¹	11		9	10²	13		12		14				7					29
1	2	3	4²	5¹				8	7³	11	13	9	10¹				14				12	6					30
1	2	3		5				9¹	8⁵	11		10	12			14	6				4	7	13				31
1	2	3		5				9	12	11¹		8	10²			13	7				4	6					32
1	2	3		12				9	13	11¹		8	10³	5	14	6²					4	7					33
1	2	3	4	12				9¹		11	13	8	10				5					6	7				34
1	2	3	4	7				13	11¹		8	10³	5	14	12	9²						6					35
1	2	3	4	7²				12		11¹		8	10	5	14	13	9³					6					36
1	2	3	4					13		11		8²	10	5¹		7	9	14				6¹	12				37
	3		4	5	7¹	12		8²		11³	2		10			13	9					6			1	14	38

The Budweiser FA Cup

Third Round	Tottenham H	(h)	2-0
Fourth Round	Coventry C	(h)	4-0
Fifth Round	Liverpool	(h)	2-1
Sixth Round	Everton	(h)	4-1
Semi-Finals	Wigan Ath	(Wembley)	1-1
(aet; won 4-2 on penalties)			
Final	Hull C	(Wembley)	3-2
(aet)			

Capital One Cup

Third Round	WBA	(a)	1-1
(aet; won 4-3 on penalties)			
Fourth Round	Chelsea	(h)	0-2

UEFA Champions League

Play-Off 1st leg	Fenerbahce	(a)	3-0
Play-Off 2nd leg	Fenerbahce	(h)	2-0
Group F	Marseille	(a)	2-1
Group	Napoli	(h)	2-0
Group	Borussia Dortmund	(h)	1-2
Group	Borussia Dortmund	(a)	1-0
Group	Marseille	(h)	2-0
Group	Napoli	(a)	0-2
Round of 16 1st leg	Bayern Munich	(h)	0-2
Round of 16 2nd leg	Bayern Munich	(a)	1-1

ASTON VILLA

FOUNDATION

Cricketing enthusiasts of Villa Cross Wesleyan Chapel, Aston, Birmingham decided to form a football club during the winter of 1874–75. Football clubs were few and far between in the Birmingham area and in their first game against Aston Brook St Mary's rugby team they played one half rugby and the other soccer. In 1876 they were joined by Scottish soccer enthusiast George Ramsay who was immediately appointed captain and went on to lead Aston Villa from obscurity to one of the country's top clubs in a period of less than ten years.

Villa Park, Birmingham B6 6HE.

Telephone: (0121) 327 2299.

Fax: (0121) 322 2107.

Ticket Office/Consumer Sales: (0800) 612 0970.

Website: www.avfc.co.uk

Email: (via website)

Ground Capacity: 42,682.

Record Attendance: 76,588 v Derby Co, FA Cup 6th rd, 2 March 1946.

Pitch Measurements: 105m × 68m (114yd × 74yd)

Chairman: Randolph Lerner.

Manager: Paul Lambert.

Assistant Manager: Roy Keane.

Physio: Alan Smith.

Colours: Claret shirts, sky blue sleeves with claret trim, white shorts with claret trim, sky blue socks with claret hoops.

Year Formed: 1874.

Turned Professional: 1885.

Club Nickname: 'The Villans'.

Grounds: 1874, Wilson Road and Aston Park (also used Aston Lower Grounds for some matches); 1876, Wellington Road, Perry Barr; 1897, Villa Park.

First Football League Game: 8 September 1888, Football League, v Wolverhampton W (a) D 1–1 – Warner; Cox, Coulton; Yates, Harry Devey, Dawson; Albert Brown, Green (1), Allen, Garvey, Hodgetts.

Record League Victory: 12–2 v Accrington S, Division 1, 12 March 1892 – Warner; Evans, Cox; Harry Devey, Jimmy Cowan, Baird; Athersmith (1), Dickson (2), John Devey (4), Lewis Campbell (4), Hodgetts (1).

HONOURS

FA Premier League:
Runners-up 1992–93.

Football League – Division 1:
Champions 1893–94, 1895–96, 1896–97, 1898–99, 1899–1900, 1909–10, 1980–81;
Runners-up 1888–89, 1902–03, 1907–08, 1910–11, 1912–13, 1913–14, 1930–31, 1932–33, 1989–90;
Division 2: *Champions* 1937–38, 1959–60; *Runners-up* 1974–75, 1987–88;
Division 3: *Champions* 1971–72.

FA Cup: *Winners* 1887, 1895, 1897, 1905, 1913, 1920, 1957;
Runners-up 1892, 1924, 2000.

Double Performed: 1896–97.

Football League Cup: *Winners* 1961, 1975, 1977, 1994, 1996;
Runners-up 1963, 1971, 2010.

European Competitions
European Cup: 1981–82 (*winners*), 1982–83. **UEFA Cup:** 1975–76, 1977–78, 1983–84, 1990–91, 1993–94, 1994–95, 1996–97, 1997–98, 1998–99, 2001–02, 2008–09.
Europa League: 2009–10, 2010–11.
World Club Championship: 1982.
Super Cup: 1982 (*winners*). **Intertoto Cup:** 2000, 2001 (*winners*), 2002, 2008 (*winners*).

sky SPORTS FACT FILE

Con Martin began the 1951–52 season as left back in the Aston Villa team but early in the campaign 'keeper Joe Rutherford suffered an injury. Con, who had previously played Gaelic football, was selected to replace him and made 27 appearances in goal before reverting back to an outfield defensive position before the end of the season.

Record Cup Victory: 13–0 v Wednesbury Old Ath, FA Cup 1st rd, 30 October 1886 – Warner; Coulton, Simmonds; Yates, Robertson, Burton (2); Richard Davis (1), Albert Brown (3), Hunter (3), Loach (2), Hodgetts (2).

Record Defeat: 0–8 v Chelsea, FA Premier League, 23 December 2012.

Most League Points (2 for a win): 70, Division 3, 1971–72.

Most League Points (3 for a win): 78, Division 2, 1987–88.

Most League Goals: 128, Division 1, 1930–31.

Highest League Scorer in Season: 'Pongo' Waring, 49, Division 1, 1930–31.

Most League Goals in Total Aggregate: Harry Hampton, 215, 1904–15.

Most League Goals in One Match: 5, Harry Hampton v Sheffield W, Division 1, 5 October 1912; 5, Harold Halse v Derby Co, Division 1, 19 October 1912; 5, Len Capewell v Burnley, Division 1, 29 August 1925; 5, George Brown v Leicester C, Division 1, 2 January 1932; 5, Gerry Hitchens v Charlton Ath, Division 2, 18 November 1959.

Most Capped Player: Steve Staunton 64 (102), Republic of Ireland.

Most League Appearances: Charlie Aitken, 561, 1961–76.

Youngest League Player: Jimmy Brown, 15 years 349 days v Bolton W, 17 September 1969.

Record Transfer Fee Received: £26,000,000 from Manchester C for James Milner, August 2010.

Record Transfer Fee Paid: £18,000,000 (rising to £24,000,000) to Sunderland for Darren Bent, January 2011.

Football League Record: 1888 Founder Member of the League; 1936–38 Division 2; 1938–59 Division 1; 1959–60 Division 2; 1960–67 Division 1; 1967–70 Division 2; 1970–72 Division 3; 1972–75 Division 2; 1975–87 Division 1; 1987–88 Division 2; 1988–92 Division 1; 1992– FA Premier League.

MANAGERS

George Ramsay 1884–1926 *(Secretary-Manager)*
W. J. Smith 1926–34 *(Secretary-Manager)*
Jimmy McMullan 1934–35
Jimmy Hogan 1936–44
Alex Massie 1945–50
George Martin 1950–53
Eric Houghton 1953–58
Joe Mercer 1958–64
Dick Taylor 1964–67
Tommy Cummings 1967–68
Tommy Docherty 1968–70
Vic Crowe 1970–74
Ron Saunders 1974–82
Tony Barton 1982–84
Graham Turner 1984–86
Billy McNeill 1986–87
Graham Taylor 1987–90
Dr Jozef Venglos 1990–91
Ron Atkinson 1991–94
Brian Little 1994–98
John Gregory 1998–2002
Graham Taylor OBE 2002–03
David O'Leary 2003–06
Martin O'Neill 2006–10
Gerard Houllier 2010–11
Alex McLeish 2011–12
Paul Lambert June 2012–

LATEST SEQUENCES

Longest Sequence of League Wins: 9, 15.10.1910 – 10.12.1910.

Longest Sequence of League Defeats: 11, 23.3.1963 – 4.5.1963.

Longest Sequence of League Draws: 6, 12.9.1981 – 10.10.1981.

Longest Sequence of Unbeaten League Matches: 15, 12.3.1949 – 27.8.1949.

Longest Sequence Without a League Win: 13, 24.3.2012 – 15.9.2012.

Successive Scoring Runs: 35 from 10.11.1895.

Successive Non-scoring Runs: 5 from 29.2.1992.

TEN YEAR LEAGUE RECORD

			P	W	D	L	F	A	Pts	Pos
2004-05	PR Lge	38	12	11	15	45	52	47	10
2005-06	PR Lge	38	10	12	16	42	55	42	16
2006-07	PR Lge	38	11	17	10	43	41	50	11
2007-08	PR Lge	38	16	12	10	71	51	60	6
2008-09	PR Lge	38	17	11	10	54	48	62	6
2009-10	PR Lge	38	17	13	8	52	39	64	6
2010-11	PR Lge	38	12	12	14	48	59	48	9
2011-12	PR Lge	38	7	17	14	37	53	38	16
2012-13	PR Lge	38	10	11	17	47	69	41	15
2013-14	PR Lge	38	10	8	20	39	61	38	15

DID YOU KNOW ?

Vic Milne, a centre half who joined Aston Villa in 1923, was a qualified medical doctor. He made over 150 Football League appearances for Villa and while on the playing staff was appointed as assistant to the club doctor. Vic, who played as an amateur for most of his career, was later a GP in Aldridge, Staffs.

ASTON VILLA – FA PREMIERSHIP 2013–14 LEAGUE RECORD

Match No.	Date	Venue	Opponents	Result	H/T Score	Lg Pos.	Goalscorers	Attendance
1	Aug 17	A	Arsenal	W 3-1	1-1	2	Benteke 2 (1 pen) [22, 61 (p)], Luna [85]	60,003
2	21	A	Chelsea	L 1-2	1-1	5	Benteke [45]	41,527
3	24	H	Liverpool	L 0-1	0-1	8		42,098
4	Sept 14	H	Newcastle U	L 1-2	0-1	16	Benteke [67]	37,554
5	21	A	Norwich C	W 1-0	1-0	12	Kozak [30]	26,813
6	28	H	Manchester C	W 3-2	0-1	9	El Ahmadi [51], Bacuna [73], Weimann [75]	34,063
7	Oct 5	A	Hull C	D 0-0	0-0	10		24,396
8	20	H	Tottenham H	L 0-2	0-1	13		35,391
9	26	H	Everton	L 0-2	0-0	13		35,154
10	Nov 2	A	West Ham U	D 0-0	0-0	13		34,977
11	9	H	Cardiff C	W 2-0	0-0	10	Bacuna [76], Kozak [84]	35,809
12	25	A	WBA	D 2-2	0-2	12	El Ahmadi [67], Westwood [76]	24,902
13	30	H	Sunderland	D 0-0	0-0	10		33,036
14	Dec 4	A	Southampton	W 3-2	1-0	10	Agbonlahor [15], Kozak [64], Delph [80]	29,814
15	8	A	Fulham	L 0-2	0-2	10		22,288
16	15	H	Manchester U	L 0-3	0-2	11		42,682
17	21	A	Stoke C	L 1-2	0-0	13	Kozak [66]	26,003
18	26	H	Crystal Palace	L 0-1	0-0	13		37,752
19	28	H	Swansea C	D 1-1	1-1	13	Agbonlahor [7]	37,028
20	Jan 1	A	Sunderland	W 1-0	1-0	11	Agbonlahor [15]	39,757
21	13	H	Arsenal	L 1-2	0-2	11	Benteke [76]	36,097
22	18	A	Liverpool	D 2-2	2-1	10	Weimann [25], Benteke [36]	44,737
23	29	H	WBA	W 4-3	3-3	10	Delph [37], Weimann [12], Bacuna [24], Benteke (pen) [64]	36,083
24	Feb 1	A	Everton	L 1-2	1-0	10	Bacuna [34]	39,469
25	8	H	West Ham U	L 0-2	0-0	12		36,261
26	11	A	Cardiff C	D 0-0	0-0	11		27,597
27	23	A	Newcastle U	L 0-1	0-0	13		50,417
28	Mar 2	H	Norwich C	W 4-1	4-1	11	Benteke 2 [25, 27], Bacuna [37], Bassong (og) [41]	30,303
29	15	H	Chelsea	W 1-0	0-0	10	Delph [82]	40,084
30	23	H	Stoke C	L 1-4	1-3	11	Benteke [5]	30,292
31	29	A	Manchester U	L 1-4	1-2	12	Westwood [13]	75,368
32	Apr 5	H	Fulham	L 1-2	0-0	13	Holt [70]	33,532
33	12	A	Crystal Palace	L 0-1	0-0	14		25,564
34	19	H	Southampton	D 0-0	0-0	15		35,134
35	26	A	Swansea C	L 1-4	1-2	16	Agbonlahor [22]	20,701
36	May 3	H	Hull C	W 3-1	3-1	14	Westwood [1], Weimann 2 [41, 45]	37,182
37	7	A	Manchester C	L 0-4	0-0	15		47,023
38	11	A	Tottenham H	L 0-3	0-3	15		35,826

Final League Position: 15

GOALSCORERS

League (39): Benteke 10 (2 pens), Bacuna 5, Weimann 5, Agbonlahor 4, Kozak 4, Delph 3, Westwood 3, El Ahmadi 2, Holt 1, Luna 1, own goal 1.
The Budweiser FA Cup (1): Helenius 1.
Capital One Cup (3): Benteke 1, Delph 1, Weimann 1.

Guzan B 38	Lowton M 18+5	Vlaar R 32	Baker N 29+1	Luna A 16+1	El Ahmadi K 26+5	Westwood A 35	Delph F 33+1	Weimann A 31+6	Benteke C 24+2	Agbonlahor G 29+1	Clark C 23+4	Bacuna L 28+7	Okore J 2+1	Tonev A 6+11	Helenius N —+3	Kozak L 8+6	Sylla Y 5+6	Bowery J 2+7	Albrighton M 9+10	Herd C 2	Bertrand R 16	Holt G 3+7	Bennett J 3+2	Robinson C —+4	Grealish J —+1	Match No.
1	2	3	4¹	5	6	7	8	9²	10	11	12	13														1
1	2	3		5	6²	7	8	9	10	11	4¹			12	13											2
1	2¹	3		5	12	6²	8	9¹	10	11				7	4	13	14									3
1	2	3		5	6²	7	8	9²	10	11	12		4¹	14	13											4
1		3		5	8	7		9	11²	10¹	4	2				6²	13	12	14							5
1	2	3	9	6		8		10¹		4	5					11	7	12								6
1		3	5	6	7¹	8	9		11²	4	2				12		10	13								7
1		3	4	5	6³	7	8	9	12	11²		2			14	10¹	13									8
1		3	4	5¹		7	8	6	11	9	12	2			10²	13										9
1	5	2	3		8	7		10¹	11		4	9					12	6								10
1	12	3	4		7²	6		11		5	2			9		10¹	8	13								11
1		3	4		8	6	12	14	10	13	5	2		9²		11³	7¹									12
1		3		5	6¹	7	8	11³	10²	9	4	2		12		14		13								13
1	12	3¹	4	6	7²	8	9	14	13	11	5	2				10³										14
1	13		5		6³	7	8	9²	10	11	4	2		12					14	3¹						15
1	2		4	5	6¹	7		12	10³	11	3	14			13	8²		9								16
1	2		4		7	8	10		5	13			9²	11		12	6¹	3								17
1	2		4	5¹	7	8		9²		11	3	12		14		10¹		13	6							18
1	2		4	5	13	7	8	10²		11	3	6³		9¹		12			14							19
1	2	3¹	4	5		7	8	9	10	11		6							12							20
1	5	2	3¹	9	6²	8	7	13	11	10	4	12														21
1		3	14	6²	7	8	9	10	11³	4	2							13			5¹	12				22
1	2³	3	14		7²	8	9	10¹	11	4	6							13			5	12				23
1		3²	4	12		8	9	7¹	11	5	2		14						13		6	10¹				24
1	2³		4		7	8	9²	10	11	3	6							12			5¹	13	14			25
1		3	4		7	8	12	10	11		2							6			5		9¹			26
1		4	3	6	7¹	8	9	10	11		2							12			5¹	13				27
1		3	4	6	7	8	9²	10¹	11		2							12			5	13				28
1		3	4	6	7	8	9	10	11³	13	2							12				5¹				29
1		3	4	6¹	7²	8	9³	10	11		2							12			13	5	14			30
1	13	3		6	7	9	11	10¹	4	2	12								8²		5					31
1	2	3	4	7		11		6	12				13	9¹		8	10	5²								32
1	5	2	3	6¹	7	8	13	11		4	12							9²	10							33
1		3	4	6¹	7	8	11²		10		2							9			5	12	13			34
1	12	3	4	6¹	7	8	11³		10		2²							9			5	14	13			35
1	2	3	4	13	7	8	10²		11³	5	14							12	6¹		9					36
1	2	3	4		7	8	9	10		5²	12							11³			6¹			13	14	37
1	2	3	4		12	7	8	10		9	6¹							11²			5			13		38

The Budweiser FA Cup
Third Round   Sheffield U   (h)   1-2

Capital One Cup
Second Round   Rotherham U   (h)   3-0
Third Round   Tottenham H   (h)   0-4

BARNSLEY

FOUNDATION

Many clubs owe their inception to the Church and Barnsley are among them, for they were formed in 1887 by the Rev. T. T. Preedy, curate of Barnsley St Peter's, and went under that name until it was dropped in 1897 a year before being admitted to the Second Division of the Football League.

Oakwell Stadium, Grove Street, Barnsley,
South Yorkshire S71 1ET.

Telephone: (01226) 211 211.

Fax: (01226) 211 444.

Ticket Office: (0871) 22 66 777.

Website: www.barnsleyfc.co.uk

Email: thereds@barnsleyfc.co.uk

Ground Capacity: 23,287.

Record Attendance: 40,255 v Stoke C, FA Cup 5th rd, 15 February 1936.

Pitch Measurements: 100.5m × 67m (110yd × 73yd)

Chairman: Maurice Watkins.

Chief Executive: Ben Mansford.

Manager: Danny Wilson.

Assistant Manager: Chris Hutchings.

Head Physio: Craig Sedgwick.

Colours: Red shirts, white shorts, red socks.

Year Formed: 1887.

Turned Professional: 1888.

Previous Name: 1887, Barnsley St Peter's; 1897, Barnsley.

Club Nickname: 'The Tykes', 'The Reds', 'The Colliers'.

Ground: 1887, Oakwell.

HONOURS

Football League – Division 1:
Runners-up 1996–97;
Division 3 (N): *Champions* 1933–34, 1938–39, 1954–55; *Runners-up* 1953–54;
Division 3: *Runners-up* 1980–81;
Division 4: *Runners-up* 1967–68.
FA Cup: *Winners* 1912;
Runners-up 1910.
Football League Cup: Best season: 5th rd, 1982.

First Football League Game: 1 September 1898, Division 2, v Lincoln C (a) L 0–1 – Fawcett; McArtney, Nixon; King, Burleigh, Porteous; Davis, Lees, Murray, McCullough, McGee.

Record League Victory: 9–0 v Loughborough T, Division 2, 28 January 1899 – Greaves; McArtney, Nixon, Porteous, Burleigh, Howard; Davis (4), Hepworth (1), Lees (1), McCullough (1), Jones (2). 9–0 v Accrington S, Division 3 (N), 3 February 1934 – Ellis; Cookson, Shotton; Harper, Henderson, Whitworth; Spence (2), Smith (1), Blight (4), Andrews (1), Ashton (1).

Record Cup Victory: 6–0 v Blackpool, FA Cup 1st rd replay, 20 January 1910 – Mearns; Downs, Ness; Glendinning, Boyle (1), Utley; Bartrop, Gadsby (1), Lillycrop (2), Tufnell (2), Forman. 6–0 v Peterborough U, League Cup 1st rd 2nd leg, 15 September 1981 – Horn; Joyce, Chambers, Glavin (2), Banks, McCarthy, Evans, Parker (2), Aylott (1), McHale, Barrowclough (1).

Record Defeat: 0–9 v Notts Co, Division 2, 19 November 1927.

Most League Points (2 for a win): 67, Division 3 (N), 1938–39.

sky SPORTS FACT FILE

Defender Barry Murphy appeared in a club record of 182 consecutive League and Cup games for Barnsley between March 1967 and October 1970. Murphy went on to set a second record, completing 509 League starts for the Reds plus a further five appearances as a substitute before retiring in the summer of 1978.

Most League Points (3 for a win): 82, Division 1, 1999–2000.

Most League Goals: 118, Division 3 (N), 1933–34.

Highest League Scorer in Season: Cecil McCormack, 33, Division 2, 1950–51.

Most League Goals in Total Aggregate: Ernest Hine, 123, 1921–26 and 1934–38.

Most League Goals in One Match: 5, Frank Eaton v South Shields, Division 3 (N), 9 April 1927; 5, Peter Cunningham v Darlington, Division 3 (N), 4 February 1933; 5, Beau Asquith v Darlington, Division 3 (N), 12 November 1938; 5, Cecil McCormack v Luton T, Division 2, 9 September 1950.

Most Capped Player: Gerry Taggart, 35 (51), Northern Ireland.

Most League Appearances: Barry Murphy, 514, 1962–78.

Youngest League Player: Reuben Noble-Lazarus, 15 years 45 days v Ipswich T, 30 September 2008.

Record Transfer Fee Received: £4,500,000 from Blackburn R for Ashley Ward, December 1998.

Record Transfer Fee Paid: £1,500,000 to Partizan Belgrade for Georgi Hristov, July 1997.

Football League Record: 1898 Elected to Division 2; 1932–34 Division 3 (N); 1934–38 Division 2; 1938–39 Division 3 (N); 1946–53 Division 2; 1953–55 Division 3 (N); 1955–59 Division 2; 1959–65 Division 3; 1965–68 Division 4; 1968–72 Division 3; 1972–79 Division 4; 1979–81 Division 3; 1981–92 Division 2; 1992–97 Division 1; 1997–98 FA Premier League; 1998–2002 Division 1; 2002–04 Division 2; 2004–06 FL 1; 2006–14 FL C; 2014 – FL 1.

LATEST SEQUENCES

Longest Sequence of League Wins: 10, 5.3.1955 – 23.4.1955.

Longest Sequence of League Defeats: 9, 14.3.1953 – 25.4.1953.

Longest Sequence of League Draws: 7, 28.3.1911 – 22.4.1911.

Longest Sequence of Unbeaten League Matches: 21, 1.1.1934 – 5.5.1934.

Longest Sequence Without a League Win: 26, 13.12.1952 – 26.8.1953.

Successive Scoring Runs: 44 from 2.10.1926.

Successive Non-scoring Runs: 6 from 27.11.1971.

MANAGERS

Arthur Fairclough 1898–1901
  (*Secretary-Manager*)
John McCartney 1901–04
  (*Secretary-Manager*)
Arthur Fairclough 1904–12
John Hastie 1912–14
Percy Lewis 1914–19
Peter Sant 1919–26
John Commins 1926–29
Arthur Fairclough 1929–30
Brough Fletcher 1930–37
Angus Seed 1937–53
Tim Ward 1953–60
Johnny Steele 1960–71
  (*continued as General Manager*)
John McSeveney 1971–72
Johnny Steele (*General Manager*)
  1972–73
Jim Iley 1973–78
Allan Clarke 1978–80
Norman Hunter 1980–84
Bobby Collins 1984–85
Allan Clarke 1985–89
Mel Machin 1989–93
Viv Anderson 1993–94
Danny Wilson 1994–98
John Hendrie 1998–99
Dave Bassett 1999–2000
Nigel Spackman 2001
Steve Parkin 2001–02
Glyn Hodges 2002–03
Gudjon Thordarson 2003–04
Paul Hart 2004–05
Andy Ritchie 2005–06
Simon Davey 2007–10
  (*caretaker from November 2006*)
Mark Robins 2009–11
Keith Hill 2011–12
David Flitcroft 2013
Danny Wilson December 2013–

TEN YEAR LEAGUE RECORD

		P	W	D	L	F	A	Pts	Pos
2004-05	FL 1	46	14	19	13	69	64	61	13
2005-06	FL 1	46	18	18	10	62	44	72	5
2006-07	FL C	46	15	5	26	53	85	50	20
2007-08	FL C	46	14	13	19	52	65	55	18
2008-09	FL C	46	13	13	20	45	58	52	20
2009-10	FL C	46	14	12	20	53	69	54	18
2010-11	FL C	46	14	14	18	55	66	56	17
2011-12	FL C	46	13	9	24	49	74	48	21
2012-13	FL C	46	14	13	19	56	70	55	21
2013-14	FL C	46	9	12	25	44	77	39	23

DID YOU KNOW ?

In 1921–22 Barnsley missed out on promotion to the old Division One by the narrowest of margins. The Reds finished level with second-placed Stoke on 52 points but their goal average was 0.076 inferior to the Potteries club despite Barnsley scoring the most goals in the division during the season.

BARNSLEY – FL CHAMPIONSHIP 2013–14 LEAGUE RECORD

Match No.	Date	Venue	Opponents	Result	H/T Score	Lg Pos.	Goalscorers	Attendance
1	Aug 3	H	Wigan Ath	L	0-4	0-1	24		13,096
2	10	A	Blackpool	L	0-1	0-0	24		14,268
3	17	H	Charlton Ath	D	2-2	1-0	23	O'Grady 2 [16, 55]	9554
4	24	A	Blackburn R	L	2-5	1-4	24	Dagnall [13], Cywka [72]	13,058
5	31	H	Huddersfield T	W	2-1	2-0	20	O'Grady [8], Pedersen [32]	13,593
6	Sept 14	A	Nottingham F	L	2-3	1-2	22	O'Grady (pen) [20], Cywka [69]	21,181
7	17	A	Bournemouth	L	0-1	0-0	23		7574
8	21	H	Watford	L	1-5	1-3	23	Scotland [13]	9850
9	28	A	Leicester C	L	1-2	0-0	24	Scotland [73]	21,591
10	Oct 1	H	Reading	D	1-1	0-0	24	O'Grady [79]	9084
11	5	A	QPR	L	0-2	0-0	24		16,202
12	19	H	Middlesbrough	W	3-2	3-0	22	McCourt [26], O'Grady 2 (1 pen) [41, 43 (p)]	11,438
13	26	H	Sheffield W	D	1-1	1-0	23	Pedersen [16]	13,268
14	Nov 1	A	Ipswich T	D	1-1	0-1	22	O'Brien [70]	18,361
15	9	H	Doncaster R	D	0-0	0-0	23		11,843
16	23	A	Millwall	L	0-1	0-0	23		9057
17	30	A	Birmingham C	L	0-3	0-3	24		10,077
18	Dec 3	H	Brighton & HA	W	2-1	1-0	24	McCourt [35], Mellis [50]	25,759
19	7	A	Burnley	L	0-1	0-0	24		11,462
20	14	H	Yeovil T	D	1-1	1-1	24	Tudgay (pen) [34]	13,361
21	21	A	Leeds U	D	0-0	0-0	24		31,031
22	26	H	Bolton W	L	0-1	0-0	24		12,484
23	29	H	Derby Co	L	1-2	0-1	24	Cywka [62]	16,338
24	Jan 1	A	Birmingham C	D	1-1	0-1	24	Mellis [61]	14,422
25	18	H	Blackpool	W	2-0	1-0	24	O'Grady 2 (1 pen) [45 (p), 48]	9866
26	28	A	Blackburn R	D	2-2	1-2	23	Proschwitz [29], O'Grady (pen) [69]	9703
27	Feb 1	A	Sheffield W	L	0-1	0-0	23		25,139
28	8	H	Ipswich T	D	2-2	1-0	23	O'Grady [12], Cywka [74]	9929
29	15	A	Doncaster R	D	2-2	1-1	23	Proschwitz 2 [27, 89]	10,216
30	18	A	Wigan Ath	L	0-2	0-2	23		14,121
31	22	H	Millwall	W	1-0	1-0	23	O'Brien [4]	9653
32	Mar 1	A	Huddersfield T	L	0-5	0-2	24		14,236
33	8	H	Nottingham F	W	1-0	0-0	23	Jennings [51]	12,157
34	11	H	Leicester C	L	0-3	0-1	24		12,539
35	15	A	Watford	L	0-3	0-2	24		14,531
36	22	H	Bournemouth	L	0-1	0-0	24		9392
37	25	A	Reading	W	3-1	1-1	23	Dawson [16], Noble-Lazarus [53], Jennings [57]	16,645
38	29	A	Yeovil T	W	4-1	0-0	22	O'Grady 2 [53, 75], Lawrence [64], Jennings [78]	6579
39	Apr 5	H	Brighton & HA	D	0-0	0-0	22		10,195
40	8	H	Burnley	L	0-1	0-1	23		12,904
41	12	A	Bolton W	L	0-1	0-1	24		15,845
42	15	A	Charlton Ath	W	2-1	1-0	23	Mvoto [32], Kennedy [63]	16,320
43	19	H	Leeds U	L	0-1	0-1	23		15,190
44	21	A	Derby Co	L	1-2	0-2	23	Proschwitz [80]	26,046
45	26	A	Middlesbrough	L	1-3	0-0	23	Mvoto [53]	14,867
46	May 3	H	QPR	L	2-3	0-2	23	O'Grady 2 [54, 90]	10,298

Final League Position: 23

GOALSCORERS

League (44): O'Grady 15 (4 pens), Cywka 4, Proschwitz 4, Jennings 3, McCourt 2, Mellis 2, Mvoto 2, O'Brien 2, Pedersen 2, Scotland 2, Dagnall 1, Dawson 1, Kennedy 1, Lawrence 1, Noble-Lazarus 1, Tudgay 1 (1 pen).
The Budweiser FA Cup (1): O'Brien 1.
Capital One Cup: (1). Dawson 1.

Steele L 31	Wiseman S 23	Kennedy T 44	Dawson S 29+8	Mvoto J 25+3	Cranie M 34+1	Mellis J 24+6	Perkins D 22+1	Dagnall C 5+3	O'Grady C 39+1	Golbourne S 4	Jennings D 24+3	Scotland J 4+16	O'Brien J 19+10	Digby P 2+3	Cywka T 15+15	Noble-Lazarus R 2+10	Etuhu K 16+4	Pedersen M 12+6	Pollitt M 2	Ramage P 24	McCourt P 15+8	Butland J 13	Fox D 7	Rose D 1+2	Hassell B 2+2	Tudgay M 5	Nyatanga L 10+2	Shea B 5+3	McLaughlin R 9	Lawrence L 10+4	Proschwitz N 8+6	Hunt J 9+2	Frimpong E 6+3	Woods M 6+2	Bree J —+1	Match No.
1	2	3^2	4	5	6	7^2	8	9^1	10	11	12^3	13	14																							1
1	2		7	3		13	8	11^3	10	4		12	5	6^2	9^1	14																				2
1	4	2	6	3		7^3	8^2	10^1	11			14	5	13				12																		3
1	4	2	6	3^4		7^2	12	11^3	10^1	9			5				14	8	13																	4
	2	4	6	3			12	7	13	10			9				5^2	8	11^1	1																5
	2	5	7	4^1	12		9	14	11			10^1			6^3		13	8		1	3															6
1	2	5^1	7		4		9	8^1	11		12	13			6^2	14	10			3																7
1	2	5^1	6^2		4	9^3	8		10			11	12			13	7			3	14															8
	2	5		4	3		8	11^3		6^1	13		12	10^2				9	1		7	14														9
	2	5	14		4	9^2	8		10			11^3		13				12		3	6	1	7^1													10
	2	5		3		9^2	8		11			10^1			14			12		4^1	6	1	7	13												11
	2	5		4	3	6^2	8		11			14	12	13				10^3			9^1	1	7													12
	2	5		3	4	9^2	8		11	12	14						13	10^1			6^3	1	7													13
	2	5		3	4	9^1	8		10			13	12				14	11^2			6^1	1	7													14
	2	5	12	3	4		7		11			13	6^3	14				10^1			9	1	8^2													15
	2	5	14	4	3	10^2	7	13				12	6				8^3	11^1			9	1														16
	2	5	8	4	3	12	7^2					14	6^3	13				10			9	1					11^1									17
	2	5	12		4	10^1	7					14	13	8			9^2				3	6^3	1				11									18
	2	5		3	6	7						12	13	8^3				9^2 14			4	10^1	1				11									19
	2	5		14	3	8	7^1					13	12	9				10^2			4	6^3	1				11									20
	2		12		3	9	8					14	7^2		10^1	13					4		1			6^3	11^1	5								21
1	2	5	8		4		9^2		11			10^3	6	13				14			3	12		7^1												22
1	2	5	7		4	9			11			14	6^1		12			8^3 13			3	10^2														23
1		5	9	4	2	10	7		11				6	12							3							8		8^1						24
1		5	7		4	8^1			11^2	6		10	14		12						3							9^1	2	13						25
1		5	6^1		4				11	8^2		9	12	13							3							2^3	7	14	10					26
1		5	12		4	7^4			10^3	9^2		13	14								3							6		11	2^1	8^4				27
1		5	6		4				11	8		9	12								3							7^2	14	10^3	2^1		13			28
1		5			4				11	6		12	8^2							3	13								10	2	7	9^1				29
1		5			4				11^2	9		6								3	14							13	12	2^1	10	7	8^3			30
1		5	12		4	8^2			11	9		6								3								13		10^1	2	7				31
1		5	14		4	7			11	9^3										3	13							12	6	10^1	2	8^2				32
1		5	6		4	9			11	10		8^2								3							13		2	12	7^1				33
1		5	7	12	4^3	6			11	9										3^1	10^2						14			13	2		8			34
1		5	7	3		8			12	10			13							4							6^2	11	2	9^1					35
1		5	7	14		13			11	9		12				10		3^1			4	6					2^2			8^3					36
1		4	6	3					11	9		7	12	8	10^1						2						5^2		13						37
1		5	7	3					11	9		6	12^2	2	10^2						4						8^1			14	13				38
1		5	7	3					11	9		10^2	2^4								4	6^1	8	12	13											39
1		5	8	3		6^2			11	9		10^1	12		13						4	2								7^1						40
1		5	7	3					11	10		8^2	2		12						4	6	9^1	13											41
1		5	7	3	4	13			11	9		10	2^1									6	8		12^2											42
1		5	8^2	3	4				11	9		10	2^1		12							6	7	13												43
1		2	7	4	5	12			11	9		10^3	13		6^1								3	8^1	14											44
1		5	8	4	3				11	9	13			2	10^1				14					6^3	7^2	12										45
1		5	8^1	4^2	2				10	9		7	6^3 12		3				11	14															13	46

The Budweiser FA Cup
Third Round   Coventry C   (h)   1-2

Capital One Cup
First Round   Scunthorpe U   (h)   0-0
(aet; won 5-4 on penalties)
Second Round   Southampton   (h)   1-5

BIRMINGHAM CITY

FOUNDATION

In 1875, cricketing enthusiasts who were largely members of Trinity Church, Bordesley, determined to continue their sporting relationships throughout the year by forming a football club which they called Small Heath Alliance. For their earliest games played on waste land in Arthur Street, the team included three Edden brothers and two James brothers.

St Andrew's Stadium, Birmingham B9 4RL.

Telephone: (0844) 557 1875.

Fax: (0844) 557 1975.

Ticket Office: (0844) 557 1875 (then option 2).

Website: www.bcfc.com

Email: reception@bcfc.com

Ground Capacity: 29,409.

Record Attendance: 66,844 v Everton, FA Cup 5th rd, 11 February 1939.

Pitch Measurements: 100m × 67.7m (109.5yd × 74yd)

Vice-chairman: Peter Pannu.

Manager: Lee Clark.

First Team Coach: Steve Watson.

Head of Sports Science: Tom Little.

Colours: Blue shirts with white front panel, white shorts, blue socks.

Year Formed: 1875.

Turned Professional: 1885.

HONOURS

Football League – FL C:
Runners-up 2006–07, 2008–09;
Division 2: *Champions* 1892–93, 1920–21, 1947–48, 1954–55, 1994–95;
Runners-up 1893–94, 1900–01, 1902–03, 1971–72, 1984–85;
Division 3: *Runners-up* 1991–92.

FA Cup: *Runners-up* 1931, 1956.

Football League Cup: *Winners* 1963, 2011; *Runners-up* 2001.

Leyland DAF Cup: *Winners* 1991.

Auto Windscreens Shield:
Winners 1995.

European Competitions
European Fairs Cup: 1955–58, 1958–60 (*runners-up*), 1960–61 (*runners-up*), 1961–62.
Europa League: 2011–12.

Previous Names: 1875, Small Heath Alliance; 1888, dropped 'Alliance'; 1905, Birmingham; 1945, Birmingham City.

Club Nickname: 'Blues'.

Grounds: 1875, waste ground near Arthur St; 1877, Muntz St, Small Heath; 1906, St Andrew's.

First Football League Game: 3 September 1892, Division 2, v Burslem Port Vale (h) W 5–1 – Charsley; Bayley, Speller; Ollis, Jenkyns, Devey; Hallam (1), Edwards (1), Short (1), Wheldon (2), Hands.

Record League Victory: 12–0 v Walsall T Swifts, Division 2, 17 December 1892 – Charsley; Bayley, Jones; Ollis, Jenkyns, Devey; Hallam (2), Walton (3), Mobley (3), Wheldon (2), Hands (2). 12–0 v Doncaster R, Division 2, 11 April 1903 – Dorrington; Goldie, Wassell; Beer, Dougherty (1), Howard; Athersmith, Leonard (4), McRoberts (1), Wilcox (4), Field (1), (1 og).

Record Cup Victory: 9–2 v Burton W, FA Cup 1st rd, 31 October 1885 – Hedges; Jones, Evetts (1); Fred James, Felton, Arthur James (1); Davenport (2), Stanley (4), Simms, Figures, Morris (1).

Record Defeat: 1–9 v Sheffield W, Division 1, 13 December 1930. 1–9 v Blackburn R, Division 1, 5 January 1895.

sky SPORTS FACT FILE

The first captain of Small Heath Alliance, as the club was then known, was Billy Edmonds. At the time he was living in Cattell Road, adjacent to the current Blues ground. A clerk, he went on to become a chartered accountant and later moved to Nottingham where he died in 1938.

Most League Points (2 for a win): 59, Division 2, 1947–48.

Most League Points (3 for a win): 89, Division 2, 1994–95.

Most League Goals: 103, Division 2, 1893–94 (only 28 games).

Highest League Scorer in Season: Joe Bradford, 29, Division 1, 1927–28.

Most League Goals in Total Aggregate: Joe Bradford, 249, 1920–35.

Most League Goals in One Match: 5, Walter Abbott v Darwen, Division 2, 26 November, 1898; 5, John McMillan v Blackpool, Division 2, 2 March 1901; 5, James Windridge v Glossop, Division 2, 23 January 1915.

Most Capped Player: Maik Taylor, 58 (including 8 on loan at Fulham) (88), Northern Ireland.

Most League Appearances: Frank Womack, 491, 1908–28.

Youngest League Player: Trevor Francis, 16 years 7 months v Cardiff C, 5 September 1970.

Record Transfer Fee Received: £6,700,000 (rising to £8,000,000) from Liverpool for Jermaine Pennant, July 2006.

Record Transfer Fee Paid: £6,000,000 to Valencia for Nikola Zigic, May 2010.

Football League Record: 1892 Elected to Division 2; 1894–96 Division 1; 1896–1901 Division 2; 1901–02 Division 1; 1902–03 Division 2; 1903–08 Division 1; 1908–21 Division 2; 1921–39 Division 1; 1946–48 Division 2; 1948–50 Division 1; 1950–55 Division 2; 1955–65 Division 1; 1965–72 Division 2; 1972–79 Division 1; 1979–80 Division 2; 1980–84 Division 1; 1984–85 Division 2; 1985–86 Division 1; 1986–89 Division 2; 1989–92 Division 3; 1992–94 Division 1; 1994–95 Division 2; 1995–2002 Division 1; 2002–06 FA Premier League; 2006–07 FL C; 2007–08 FA Premier League; 2008–09 FL C; 2009–11 FA Premier League; 2011– FL C.

LATEST SEQUENCES

Longest Sequence of League Wins: 13, 17.12.1892 – 16.9.1893.

Longest Sequence of League Defeats: 8, 28.9.1985 – 23.11.1985.

Longest Sequence of League Draws: 8, 18.9.1990 – 23.10.1990.

Longest Sequence of Unbeaten League Matches: 20, 3.9.1994 – 2.1.1995.

Longest Sequence Without a League Win: 17, 28.9.1985 – 18.1.1986.

Successive Scoring Runs: 24 from 24.9.1892.

Successive Non-scoring Runs: 6 from 11.2.1989.

MANAGERS

Alfred Jones 1892–1908
  (*Secretary-Manager*)
Alec Watson 1908–10
Bob McRoberts 1910–15
Frank Richards 1915–23
Billy Beer 1923–27
William Harvey 1927–28
Leslie Knighton 1928–33
George Liddell 1933–39
William Camkin and Ted Goodier
  were in charge during 1939–45
Harry Storer 1945–48
Bob Brocklebank 1949–54
Arthur Turner 1954–58
Pat Beasley 1959–60
Gil Merrick 1960–64
Joe Mallett 1964–65
Stan Cullis 1965–70
Fred Goodwin 1970–75
Willie Bell 1975–77
Sir Alf Ramsey 1977–78
Jim Smith 1978–82
Ron Saunders 1982–86
John Bond 1986–87
Garry Pendrey 1987–89
Dave Mackay 1989–91
Lou Macari 1991
Terry Cooper 1991–93
Barry Fry 1993–96
Trevor Francis 1996–2001
Steve Bruce 2001–07
Alex McLeish 2007–11
Chris Hughton 2011–12
Lee Clark June 2012–

TEN YEAR LEAGUE RECORD

		P	W	D	L	F	A	Pts	Pos
2004-05	PR Lge	38	11	12	15	40	46	45	12
2005-06	PR Lge	38	8	10	20	28	50	34	18
2006-07	FL C	46	26	8	12	67	42	86	2
2007-08	PR Lge	38	8	11	19	46	62	35	19
2008-09	FL C	46	23	14	9	54	37	83	2
2009-10	PR Lge	38	13	11	14	38	47	50	9
2010-11	PR Lge	38	8	15	15	37	58	39	18
2011-12	FL C	46	20	16	10	78	51	76	4
2012-13	FL C	46	15	16	15	63	69	61	12
2013-14	FL C	46	11	11	24	58	74	44	21

DID YOU KNOW ?

Birmingham failed to apply for exemption from the qualifying rounds of the FA Cup for 1921–22 by the deadline date of 20 March. Rather than face having to play through the qualifying rounds the club chose not to enter the competition that season.

BIRMINGHAM CITY – FL CHAMPIONSHIP 2013–14 LEAGUE RECORD

Match No.	Date	Venue	Opponents	Result	H/T Score	Lg Pos.	Goalscorers	Attendance
1	Aug 3	H	Watford	L	0-1	0-1	20		18,830
2	10	A	Yeovil T	W	1-0	0-0	13	Seaborne (og) [48]	8717
3	17	H	Brighton & HA	L	0-1	0-0	17		14,885
4	24	A	Leicester C	L	2-3	1-0	18	Green [12], Burke [90]	21,229
5	31	H	Ipswich T	D	1-1	0-1	19	Burke [76]	14,328
6	Sept 14	H	QPR	L	0-1	0-0	20		16,953
7	17	A	Burnley	L	0-3	0-1	21		9641
8	21	H	Sheffield W	W	4-1	3-0	18	Lingard 4 [20, 29, 33, 51]	14,379
9	28	A	Reading	L	0-2	0-1	19		18,252
10	Oct 1	A	Millwall	W	4-0	2-0	17	Murphy 2 [19, 34], Adeyemi [68], Lingard [89]	13,133
11	5	H	Bolton W	L	1-2	0-1	19	Novak [69]	13,627
12	20	A	Leeds U	L	0-4	0-3	20		21,301
13	26	A	Derby Co	D	1-1	0-1	19	Novak [66]	27,141
14	Nov 2	H	Charlton Ath	L	0-1	0-0	22		14,070
15	9	A	Huddersfield T	W	3-1	1-1	18	Zigic [11], Bartley 2 [66, 81]	14,161
16	23	H	Blackpool	D	1-1	1-1	20	Lingard [27]	14,480
17	30	A	Barnsley	W	3-0	3-0	19	Caddis 2 (1 pen) [13, 22 (p)], Zigic [37]	10,077
18	Dec 3	H	Doncaster R	D	1-1	1-0	17	Novak [29]	12,663
19	7	A	Middlesbrough	D	2-2	0-1	19	Caddis (pen) [59], Bartley [90]	13,454
20	14	A	Bournemouth	W	2-0	2-0	14	Shinnie [3], Zigic [34]	9256
21	21	H	Nottingham F	D	0-0	0-0	16		23,497
22	26	A	Wigan Ath	D	0-0	0-0	18		14,996
23	29	H	Blackburn R	W	3-2	3-0	17	Novak 2 [12, 18], Burke [36]	14,344
24	Jan 1	H	Barnsley	D	1-1	1-0	17	Zigic [10]	14,422
25	11	A	Brighton & HA	L	0-1	0-0	17		26,796
26	18	H	Yeovil T	L	0-2	0-2	17		13,605
27	28	H	Leicester C	L	1-2	0-1	17	Lovenkrands [90]	14,763
28	Feb 1	H	Derby Co	D	3-3	0-0	18	Howard [48], Burke [78], Macheda [90]	15,224
29	8	A	Charlton Ath	W	2-0	1-0	18	Macheda 2 [22, 79]	15,878
30	11	A	Watford	L	0-1	0-1	18		13,904
31	15	H	Huddersfield T	L	1-2	0-1	18	Lee [90]	14,112
32	22	A	Blackpool	W	2-1	0-1	16	Novak 2 [63, 82]	14,628
33	Mar 1	A	Ipswich T	L	0-1	0-1	17		15,596
34	8	H	QPR	L	0-2	0-1	18		14,500
35	12	A	Burnley	D	3-3	0-1	19	Macheda 2 [64, 90], Huws [69]	16,695
36	15	A	Sheffield W	L	1-4	0-2	19	Novak [80]	20,637
37	22	H	Reading	L	1-2	1-1	20	Caddis (pen) [43]	13,409
38	25	A	Millwall	W	3-2	2-1	19	Ibe [18], Shinnie [35], Zigic [52]	9268
39	29	H	Bournemouth	L	2-4	0-3	20	Macheda 2 [57, 73]	13,875
40	Apr 5	A	Doncaster R	W	3-1	0-1	18	Macheda 2 [57, 76], Novak [71]	9206
41	8	A	Middlesbrough	L	1-3	1-2	18	Huws [37]	13,399
42	19	A	Nottingham F	L	0-1	0-1	18		21,300
43	21	H	Blackburn R	L	2-4	0-4	21	Zigic [63], Gray [84]	17,291
44	26	A	Leeds U	L	1-3	0-0	22	Macheda [83]	19,861
45	29	H	Wigan Ath	L	0-1	0-1	22		20,427
46	May 3	A	Bolton W	D	2-2	0-0	21	Zigic [78], Caddis [90]	19,558

Final League Position: 21

GOALSCORERS

League (58): Macheda 10, Novak 9, Zigic 7, Lingard 6, Caddis 5 (3 pens), Burke 4, Bartley 3, Huws 2, Murphy 2, Shinnie 2, Adeyemi 1, Gray 1, Green 1, Howard 1, Ibe 1, Lee 1, Lovenkrands 1, own goal 1.
The Budweiser FA Cup (4): Burke 2, Novak 1, Robinson 1.
Capital One Cup (13): Adeyemi 2, Allan 2, Bartley 2, Lovenkrands 2, Burn 1, Green 1, Lee 1, Novak 1, Shinnie 1.

Randolph D 46	Eardley N 5	Ferguson S 9+9	Robinson P 40	Burn D 23+1	Bartley K 14+3	Adeyemi T 32+3	Shinnie A 18+8	Green M 7+3	Novak L 33+5	Ibe J 4+7	Elliott W 10+5	Allan S 2+3	Burke C 37+7	Mullins H 7+1	Reilly C 21+4	Arthur K —+1	Spector J 22	Lovenkrands P 3+12	Caddis P 35+3	Ambrose D 1	Hancox M 11+3	Brown R 3+3	Murphy D 6	Lingard J 13	Zigic N 21+12	Gray D 1+6	Lee O 14+2	Dudka D 1+1	McLean A 2+5	Howard B 4+1	Packwood W 12	Bell A 1	Rusnak A 3	Thorpe T 6	Blackett T 6+2	Huws E 17	Martin A 6+2	Macheda F 10+8	Match No.
1	2	3³	4	5	6	7	8	9²	10	11	12	13																											1
1	5	9	4	3		8	6	11¹	10	7				2	12																								2
1	5	9²	4	3		6	10¹	13	11	7	8³	12		2		14																							3
1	5	9³	4	3	13	8	12	11²	10	7		14	2¹				6																						4
1	2³	13	5	4	3	7	9¹	14	10	7		12	6					8	11²																				5
1		12	4	3	2	7¹	11²		10	8			9					6	13	5																			6
1		5²		4	3	6		14	10³	7			9					8		2	11¹	12	13																7
1		12	4	3	2	7			10²			6	9					5	13					8	11¹														8
1		14	4	3			7¹		10²		13		9	5				2	6					8	11	12													9
1		4	3	13	6	10	11³						8	7				2						5¹	9²	12	14												10
1		3	4		6	9¹	11¹	12					8	7				2	14					5²	10	13													11
1		4	3¹	2		12			10²	6			9					5						8	11	13		7											12
1	10³	4	3	14	9¹		13	6	8²	7			2					5						11	12													13
1	13	5	4	3	6		9²		10	7			12	2					11	8¹																			14
1		4	13	3⁴	6	12	9		8³	7			14	2		5			10²	11¹																			15
1		4	3	6		9	8²		7³				2	5		10	11¹	14			12	13																	16
1	10¹	4	3	6		8	12			7			2	5		9	11²				13																		17
1		3	4	6	14	8	13		12	7²			2	5		9¹	11				10³																		18
1		3	4	14		6			12				8					2	5²		9	10		13	7¹	11³													19
1	5	4	3	7	10				6¹	13			2					8²	11		9	12																	20
1	5	4	3	7	10¹			6					2					8²	11	12	9	13																	21
1	5	4	3	6	12		10						8²	14				2		9⁴	11¹	7³	13																22
1	13	5	4	3	6²	9¹		10					8²	12		14	2				11	7																	23
1		5	4	3³		9²			10	13			8	12	7¹		14	2			11	6																	24
1	13	4							10	9²			8	3	7¹			2		5	12			11	6														25
1	12	4			14				10	13			8	3				2		5	6¹			11³	7		9²												26
1			3	8					10				6					12	2			9		7¹					4	5	11								27
1		7¹				11²			14				10	2								9		3			8		4³	5	6	12	13						28
1		5				7¹			11				6					12	2					9			4		7¹	3			8	3	10¹				29
1		5				9²			13				8					14	2	12							13	12	3			6	4	10				30
1		5				7³			11¹				6					14	2		9²			13	12		3					8	4	10				31
1		4				7¹			10	13			8²					2	14	5				12	6		3						9	11³				32
1		5							10¹	12		13						2	8³					11	6		14	4					7	3	9²			33
1	8³		4			6			13	11¹			9					2	5					10²			3					14	7	12				34
1		4				7	11²		10				9					2						13	6¹		3					5	8	12				35
1		4³				9	10		11				8					2	12						6²		3					5¹	7	13	14			36
1		4				10²			9³	13			8	5		6		2						14			3					12	7¹	11				37
1	12	3				7				6¹			8	10		9		2						11								5	4					38
1		4				9¹			13	10			8	7				2	14	6				11²								5	3³	12				39
1		4			13	14			10¹	9⁴			8	5		6		6	2					12							3		7³	11				40
1		4			14	9²			10¹	13			8	5		2²		7						12							3		6	11				41
1	10²	4								12			8	7		2	14	6	5³					11¹							3		9	13				42
1													6	5				11¹	7		13			12	14							3	4²	8	10			43
1		9							10³			13	8	7¹				4	2	5				11	14							3²		6	12			44
1						6¹	14		10²	13	9³	8	3				4	2	5					12										7	11			45
1		4				6			10	13			8²	3	5²		2	9	12					11										7¹	14			46

The Budweiser FA Cup

Third Round	Bristol R	(h)	3-0
Fourth Round	Swansea C	(h)	1-2

Capital One Cup

First Round	Plymouth Arg	(h)	3-2
(aet)			
Second Round	Yeovil T	(a)	3-3
(aet; won 3-2 on penalties)			
Third Round	Swansea C	(h)	3-1
Fourth Round	Stoke C	(h)	4-4
(aet; lost 2-4 on penalties)			

BLACKBURN ROVERS

FOUNDATION

It was in 1875 that some public school old boys called a meeting at which the Blackburn Rovers club was formed and the colours blue and white adopted. The leading light was John Lewis, later to become a founder of the Lancashire FA, a famous referee who was in charge of two FA Cup finals, and a vice-president of both the FA and the Football League.

Ewood Park, Blackburn, Lancashire BB2 4JF.

Telephone: (0871) 702 1875.

Fax: (01254) 671 042.

Ticket Office: (0871) 222 1444.

Website: www.rovers.co.uk

Email: (via website)

Ground Capacity: 31,154.

Record Attendance: 62,522 v Bolton W, FA Cup 6th rd, 2 March 1929.

Pitch Measurements: 105m × 65.84m (115yd × 72yd)

Managing Director: Derek Shaw.

Directors: Robert Coar, Gandhi Babu.

Manager: Gary Bowyer.

Assistant Manager: Terry McPhillips.

Physio: Neil Fitzhenry.

Colours: Blue and white halved shirts, white shorts with blue trim, blue socks.

Year Formed: 1875.

Turned Professional: 1880.

Club Nickname: 'Rovers'.

HONOURS

FA Premier League:
Champions 1994–95;
Runners-up 1993–94.

Football League: Division 1:
Champions 1911–12, 1913–14;
Runners-up 2000–01;
Division 2: *Champions* 1938–39;
Runners-up 1957–58;
Division 3: *Champions* 1974–75;
Runners-up 1979–80.
FA Cup: *Winners* 1884, 1885, 1886, 1890, 1891, 1928; *Runners-up* 1882, 1960.

Football League Cup: *Winners* 2002.

Full Members' Cup: *Winners* 1987.

European Competitions
European Cup: 1995–96.
UEFA Cup: 1994–95, 1998–99, 2002–03, 2003–04, 2006–07, 2007–08.
Intertoto Cup: 2007.

Grounds: 1875, all matches played away; 1876, Oozehead Ground; 1877, Pleasington Cricket Ground; 1878, Alexandra Meadows; 1881, Leamington Road; 1890, Ewood Park.

First Football League Game: 15 September 1888, Football League, v Accrington (h) D 5–5 – Arthur; Beverley, James Southworth; Douglas, Almond, Forrest; Beresford (1), Walton, John Southworth (1), Fecitt (1), Townley (2).

Record League Victory: 9–0 v Middlesbrough, Division 2, 6 November 1954 – Elvy; Suart, Eckersley; Clayton, Kelly, Bell; Mooney (3), Crossan (2), Briggs, Quigley (3), Langton (1).

Record Cup Victory: 11–0 v Rossendale, FA Cup 1st rd, 13 October 1884 – Arthur; Hopwood, McIntyre; Forrest, Blenkhorn, Lofthouse; Sowerbutts (2), Jimmy Brown (1), Fecitt (4), Barton (3), Birtwistle (1).

sky SPORTS FACT FILE

Ewood Park has twice hosted internationals. England beat Scotland 2-1 in 1891 but in the second game the national team lost by the same score to Wales in 1924. The Blackburn Rovers stadium has also hosted six FA Cup semi-finals, the last of which was in 1947 when Liverpool and Burnley fought out a goalless draw.

Record Defeat: 0–8 v Arsenal, Division 1, 25 February 1933.

Most League Points (2 for a win): 60, Division 3, 1974–75.

Most League Points (3 for a win): 91, Division 1, 2000–01.

Most League Goals: 114, Division 2, 1954–55.

Highest League Scorer in Season: Ted Harper, 43, Division 1, 1925–26.

Most League Goals in Total Aggregate: Simon Garner, 168, 1978–92.

Most League Goals in One Match: 7, Tommy Briggs v Bristol R, Division 2, 5 February 1955.

Most Capped Player: Morten Gamst Pedersen, 70 (80), Norway.

Most League Appearances: Derek Fazackerley, 596, 1970–86.

Youngest League Player: Harry Dennison, 16 years 155 days v Bristol C, 8 April 1911.

Record Transfer Fee Received: £18,000,000 from Manchester C for Roque Santa Cruz, June 2009.

Record Transfer Fee Paid: £8,000,000 to Huddersfield T for Jordan Rhodes, August 2012; £8,000,000 to Manchester U for Andy Cole, December 2001.

Football League Record: 1888 Founder Member of the League; 1936–39 Division 2; 1946–48 Division 1; 1948–58 Division 2; 1958–66 Division 1; 1966–71 Division 2; 1971–75 Division 3; 1975–79 Division 2; 1979–80 Division 3; 1980–92 Division 2; 1992–99 FA Premier League; 1999–2001 Division 1; 2001–12 FA Premier League; 2012– FL C.

LATEST SEQUENCES

Longest Sequence of League Wins: 8, 1.3.1980 – 7.4.1980.

Longest Sequence of League Defeats: 7, 12.3.1966 – 16.4.1966.

Longest Sequence of League Draws: 5, 11.10.1975 – 1.11.1975.

Longest Sequence of Unbeaten League Matches: 23, 30.9.1987 – 27.3.1988.

Longest Sequence Without a League Win: 16, 11.11.1978 – 24.3.1979.

Successive Scoring Runs: 32 from 24.4.1954.

Successive Non-scoring Runs: 4 from 25.11.2009.

MANAGERS

Thomas Mitchell 1884–96
(Secretary-Manager)
J. Walmsley 1896–1903
((Secretary-Manager)
R. B. Middleton 1903–25
Jack Carr 1922–26
(Team Manager under Middleton to 1925)
Bob Crompton 1926–31
(Hon. Team Manager)
Arthur Barritt 1931–36
(had been Secretary from 1927)
Reg Taylor 1936–38
Bob Crompton 1938–41
Eddie Hapgood 1944–47
Will Scott 1947
Jack Bruton 1947–49
Jackie Bestall 1949–53
Johnny Carey 1953–58
Dally Duncan 1958–60
Jack Marshall 1960–67
Eddie Quigley 1967–70
Johnny Carey 1970–71
Ken Furphy 1971–73
Gordon Lee 1974–75
Jim Smith 1975–78
Jim Iley 1978
John Pickering 1978–79
Howard Kendall 1979–81
Bobby Saxton 1981–86
Don Mackay 1987–91
Kenny Dalglish 1991–95
Ray Harford 1995–96
Roy Hodgson 1997–98
Brian Kidd 1998–99
Graeme Souness 2000–04
Mark Hughes 2004–08
Paul Ince 2008
Sam Allardyce 2008–10
Steve Kean 2010–12
Henning Berg 2012
Michael Appleton 2013
Gary Bowyer March 2013–

TEN YEAR LEAGUE RECORD

		P	W	D	L	F	A	Pts	Pos
2004-05	PR Lge	38	9	15	14	32	43	42	15
2005-06	PR Lge	38	19	6	13	51	42	63	6
2006-07	PR Lge	38	15	7	16	52	54	52	10
2007-08	PR Lge	38	15	13	10	50	48	58	7
2008-09	PR Lge	38	10	11	17	40	60	41	15
2009-10	PR Lge	38	13	11	14	41	55	50	10
2010-11	PR Lge	38	11	10	17	46	59	43	15
2011-12	PR Lge	38	8	7	23	48	78	31	19
2012-13	FL C	46	14	16	16	55	62	58	17
2013-14	FL C	46	18	16	12	70	62	70	8

DID YOU KNOW ?

In May 1934 Blackburn Rovers went on a tour of Sweden and Denmark at the end of a season which saw the club finish eighth in the old First Division. Rovers comfortably won the first four games against combined teams and the tour culminated with a 3-2 victory over a Danish National XI in Copenhagen.

BLACKBURN ROVERS – FL CHAMPIONSHIP 2013–14 LEAGUE RECORD

Match No.	Date	Venue	Opponents	Result	H/T Score	Lg Pos.	Goalscorers	Attendance
1	Aug 4	A	Derby Co	D	1-1	0-1	11	Best [89]	21,188
2	10	H	Nottingham F	L	0-1	0-0	17		14,496
3	16	A	Doncaster R	L	0-2	0-1	19		8707
4	24	H	Barnsley	W	5-2	4-1	14	Cairney [17], Rhodes 2 [30, 39], King [42], Kane [58]	13,058
5	31	H	Bolton W	W	4-1	2-1	11	Dunn [27], Rhodes 2 [28, 83], Evans [70]	15,828
6	Sept 14	A	Burnley	D	1-1	0-0	10	Rhodes [85]	15,699
7	17	A	Leicester C	L	1-2	0-2	13	Rhodes (pen) [70]	19,153
8	21	H	Huddersfield T	D	0-0	0-0	14		14,582
9	28	A	Bournemouth	W	3-1	3-0	11	Rhodes 2 (1 pen) [10, 41 (p)], Best [24]	9441
10	Oct 1	H	Watford	W	1-0	0-0	8	Rhodes [65]	12,981
11	6	A	Wigan Ath	L	1-2	1-0	9	Spurr [8]	16,996
12	19	A	Charlton Ath	L	0-1	0-1	10		13,915
13	26	A	Blackpool	D	2-2	1-2	12	Rhodes (pen) [21], Davies (og) [90]	15,901
14	Nov 2	H	Middlesbrough	W	1-0	0-0	9	Lowe [76]	16,645
15	9	A	Brighton & HA	L	0-3	0-1	13		27,912
16	23	H	Reading	D	0-0	0-0	14		12,903
17	30	H	Leeds U	W	1-0	1-0	13	Spurr [45]	20,267
18	Dec 3	A	Ipswich T	L	1-3	1-1	13	Rhodes [30]	14,953
19	7	A	QPR	D	0-0	0-0	13		15,987
20	14	H	Millwall	W	3-2	1-1	11	Rhodes [22], Marshall [48], Dunn [85]	12,642
21	21	A	Yeovil T	W	1-0	0-0	11	Rhodes [59]	7179
22	26	H	Sheffield W	D	0-0	0-0	11		18,539
23	29	H	Birmingham C	L	2-3	0-3	12	Rhodes 2 [66, 72]	14,344
24	Jan 1	A	Leeds U	W	2-1	2-0	10	Rhodes [13], Gestede [36]	30,145
25	11	A	Doncaster R	W	1-0	1-0	8	Gestede [45]	13,954
26	18	A	Nottingham F	L	1-4	1-2	8	Marshall [37]	22,456
27	25	H	Derby Co	D	1-1	0-0	9	Gestede [47]	13,796
28	28	A	Barnsley	D	2-2	2-1	9	Cairney [36], Gestede [44]	9703
29	Feb 1	H	Blackpool	W	2-0	1-0	8	Dunn [20], Hanley, G [83]	15,045
30	8	A	Middlesbrough	D	0-0	0-0	9		14,965
31	22	A	Reading	W	1-0	1-0	9	Conway [36]	18,858
32	Mar 1	A	Bolton W	L	0-4	0-2	10		17,541
33	9	H	Burnley	L	1-2	1-0	10	Rhodes [24]	21,589
34	12	H	Bournemouth	L	0-1	0-0	10		13,081
35	15	A	Huddersfield T	W	4-2	1-1	10	Rhodes 3 [4, 55, 81], Conway [65]	13,311
36	22	H	Leicester C	D	1-1	1-1	10	Kilgallon [43]	16,528
37	25	A	Watford	D	3-3	1-1	11	Dunn [27], Conway [64], Gestede [90]	13,921
38	29	A	Millwall	D	2-2	0-0	12	Keane [65], King [90]	8840
39	Apr 1	H	Brighton & HA	D	3-3	2-1	11	Rhodes 2 (1 pen) [25, 86 (p)], Cairney [42]	12,332
40	5	H	Ipswich T	W	2-0	0-0	10	Rhodes [64], Gestede [80]	13,281
41	8	H	QPR	W	2-0	1-0	11	Gestede [9], Spurr [49]	12,915
42	12	A	Sheffield W	D	3-3	3-1	10	Rhodes [15], Conway [36], Keane [43]	22,792
43	18	H	Yeovil T	D	0-0	0-0	10		14,353
44	21	A	Birmingham C	W	4-2	4-0	10	Gestede 3 [10, 20, 45], Kane [24]	17,291
45	26	A	Charlton Ath	W	3-1	1-0	8	Gestede [26], Keane [51], Cairney [64]	15,718
46	May 3	H	Wigan Ath	W	4-3	3-1	8	Cairney [13], Gestede 2 [19, 35], Rhodes [84]	16,996

Final League Position: 8

GOALSCORERS

League (70): Rhodes 25 (4 pens), Gestede 13, Cairney 5, Conway 4, Dunn 4, Keane 3, Spurr 3, Best 2, Kane 2, King 2, Marshall 2, Evans 1, Hanley, G 1, Kilgallon 1, Lowe 1, own goal 1.
The Budweiser FA Cup (1): Dann 1.
Capital One Cup (3): Cairney 1, Judge 1, Taylor 1.

Kean J 18	Kane T 23+4	Spurr T 43	Lowe J 38+1	Dann S 25	Hanley G 38	Judge A 7+4	Marrow A 2+1	Rhodes J 45+1	Rochina R 2+3	King J 20+12	Best L 5+3	Taylor C 14+20	Cairney T 36+1	Dunn D 14+9	Evans C 17+4	Morris J —+4	Nunes F —+1	Marshall B 13+5	Williamson L 22+10	Olsson Marcus 4+4	Kilgallon M 23+2	Campbell D 2+5	Etuhu D —+3	Gestede R 21+6	Eastwood S 7	Henley A 13+1	Robinson P 21	Conway C 16+2	Varney L 3+9	Keane M 13	Feeney L 1+5	Match No.
1	2	3	4	5	6	7	8³	9	10¹	11²	12	13	14																			1
1	2	5	7	3	4	8	9	10		12	11	6¹																				2
1	2	5	9	4	3	6		10				13	14	8¹	11³	7²	12															3
1	2	5	7¹	4	3	10		11		6²		12	9	8¹		13	14															4
1	2	5	7	4	3			11		6²		13	10	8¹	12	14		9³														5
1	2	5	6³	3	4	12		11		10		13	9	8¹				7²	14⁸													6
1	2	5	8	3	4			11		9		13	10	7¹				6²		12												7
1	2	5	7	3	4	12		11		9		13	6³	10¹	8²				14													8
1	2	5	8¹	4	3		14	11		6		10²	9		7³				13	12												9
1	2	5	7	3¹	4			10		9²	11³	6	8					12	13	14												10
1	2	5	7		3⁸			10		9	11¹	13	6³	8²				14	12	4												11
1	2	5	7	3	13					9¹	11²	8						6³	12		4	14										12
1	2	5	7	3	10¹					11	9	13	6						8²		4	12⁸										13
1	2	5¹	7	3	10³					11	9	13	6				12	14	8		4²											14
1	2	5³	7	3	6¹					10	11	9	13				14		8²		4	12										15
1	2	5	8	4	3					11	13	9¹	12	6	10²				7													16
1	2	5	8	3	4					11¹	9	6	7	10²				12			13											17
1	2	5	7	3	4¹					11		9²		8				13	6	12	10³	14										18
		5	8	3	4					11¹	12³	10	9²	14				6	7		13						1	2				19
		5	7	3	4					11²	9¹	10	8	12				6			13						1	2				20
		5	7	3	4					11¹	12	6²	8	10³				9			13			14			1	2				21
		5	7	3	4					11	14	12	10³	8¹				6			13			9²			1	2				22
		5	7	3	4					13	11	10²	14	6				9¹	8³		12						1	2				23
		5		3	4					10		12		6	8			2	7					11¹				9	1			24
		5	7	3	4					10²		13	8¹	12	6	9					14			11²			2	1				25
		5	7	3	4					13		12	10²	8	14			6	9³					11¹			1	2				26
13		5	7		3					11		8	6					9¹	12		4			10³		14	2	1				27
		5	7		3					10		13		12	6	8²		9¹			11						2	1				28
		2	5	6	3					10		13³		7²	8	9¹			14		4			11			1		12			29
2³		5	8	3						10		9	6	7¹					4					11²	12		1		13	14		30
		5	7	3						10		12	6¹					8			4			11²			2	1	9	13		31
14		5		3						10		7²						8³	9	4¹				11			2	1	6	12		32
		5	7		3					11		14		8³	6¹			13									2	1	9	10²	4 12	33
		2	5	7	3²					11		12	8					14						10³			1	6	9¹	4 13		34
12		5	2³							10		14	7²	6				8	4					11¹			1	9	13	3		35
13		5								10	14	12		8				7³	4					11	2¹		1	9	3		6²	36
2		5								11				8¹	6			7	4					10			1	9	12	3		37
		5					4⁸			10²	13	12	7¹	8				6	3						1			9	11	2		38
		5			3					11	13	12	6	10³	7¹			8²	4					14	1		9		2			39
		5			3					11	6	13	8²					7³	4	14	10¹				1		9	12	2			40
		5	7		3					11²	6	12						8³	4	14	10¹				1		9	13	2			41
		5	7		4					10¹	6							8	3		11				1		9	12	2			42
		5³	8		3					11	14	6	13	12				7²	4		10				1		9¹	2				43
2		8			3					11	9³	14	7					5	4		10²				1		6¹	12		13		44
					3					11³	6²	14	7	8				13	5	4				10	1		9¹	2	12			45
		12			3					11	9¹	8	7²					5	4		10				1		6	2	13			46

The Budweiser FA Cup

Third Round	Manchester C	(h)	1-1
Replay	Manchester C	(a)	0-5

Capital One Cup

First Round	Carlisle U	(a)	3-3
(aet; lost 3-4 on penalties)			

BLACKPOOL

FOUNDATION

Old boys of St John's School, who had formed themselves into a football club, decided to establish a club bearing the name of their town and Blackpool FC came into being at a meeting at the Stanley Arms Hotel in the summer of 1887. In their first season playing at Raikes Hall Gardens, the club won both the Lancashire Junior Cup and the Fylde Cup.

Bloomfield Road, Seasiders Way, Blackpool, Lancashire FY1 6JJ.

Telephone: (0871) 6221 953.

Fax: (01253) 405 011.

Ticket Office: (0844) 847 1953.

Website: www.blackpoolfc.co.uk

Email: secretary@blackpoolfc.co.uk

Ground Capacity: 16,007.

Record Attendance: 38,098 v Wolverhampton W, Division 1, 17 September 1955.

Pitch Measurements: 100m × 64m (109.5yd × 70yd)

Chairman: Karl Oyston.

Manager: José Riga.

First Team Coach: John Murphy.

Physio: Phil Horner.

Colours: Tangerine shirts, white shorts, tangerine socks.

Year Formed: 1887.

Turned Professional: 1887.

HONOURS

Football League – Division 1:
Runners-up 1955–56;
Division 2: *Champions* 1929–30;
Runners-up 1936–37, 1969–70;
Division 4: *Runners-up* 1984–85.
FA Cup: *Winners* 1953;
Runners-up 1948, 1951.
Football League Cup: Semi-final 1962.
Anglo-Italian Cup: *Winners* 1971;
Runners-up 1972.
LDV Vans Trophy: *Winners* 2002, 2004.

Previous Name: 'South Shore' combined with Blackpool in 1899, twelve years after the latter had been formed on the breaking up of the old 'Blackpool St John's' club.

Club Nickname: 'The Seasiders'.

Grounds: 1887, Raikes Hall Gardens; 1897, Athletic Grounds; 1899, Raikes Hall Gardens; 1899, Bloomfield Road.

First Football League Game: 5 September 1896, Division 2, v Lincoln C (a) L 1–3 – Douglas; Parr, Bowman; Stuart, Stirzaker, Norris; Clarkin, Donnelly, Robert Parkinson, Mount (1), Jack Parkinson.

Record League Victory: 7–0 v Reading, Division 2, 10 November 1928 – Mercer; Gibson, Hamilton, Watson, Wilson, Grant, Ritchie, Oxberry (2), Hampson (5), Tufnell, Neal. 7–0 v Preston NE (away), Division 1, 1 May 1948 – Robinson; Shimwell, Crosland; Buchan, Hayward, Kelly; Hobson, Munro (1), McIntosh (5), McCall, Rickett (1). 7–0 v Sunderland, Division 1, 5 October 1957 – Farm; Armfield, Garrett, Kelly J, Gratrix, Kelly H, Matthews, Taylor (2), Charnley (2), Durie (2), Perry (1).

Record Cup Victory: 7–1 v Charlton Ath, League Cup 2nd rd, 25 September 1963 – Harvey; Armfield, Martin; Crawford, Gratrix, Cranston; Lea, Ball (1), Charnley (4), Durie (1), Oates (1).

sky SPORTS FACT FILE

George McKnight scored a hat-trick in less than four minutes during Blackpool's First Division clash with Fulham in September 1950. McKnight, who only got his chance at centre forward due to injuries, also had a first-half goal disallowed. Despite his achievement he only made two further first team appearances that season – both at right half.

Record Defeat: 1–10 v Small Heath, Division 2, 2 March 1901 and v Huddersfield T, Division 1, 13 December 1930.

Most League Points (2 for a win): 58, Division 2, 1929–30 and Division 2, 1967–68.

Most League Points (3 for a win): 86, Division 4, 1984–85.

Most League Goals: 98, Division 2, 1929–30.

Highest League Scorer in Season: Jimmy Hampson, 45, Division 2, 1929–30.

Most League Goals in Total Aggregate: Jimmy Hampson, 248, 1927–38.

Most League Goals in One Match: 5, Jimmy Hampson v Reading, Division 2, 10 November 1928; 5, Jimmy McIntosh v Preston NE, Division 1, 1 May 1948.

Most Capped Player: Jimmy Armfield, 43, England.

Most League Appearances: Jimmy Armfield, 568, 1952–71.

Youngest League Player: Matty Kay, 16 years 32 days v Scunthorpe U, 13 November 2005.

Record Transfer Fee Received: £6,750,000 from Liverpool for Charlie Adam, July 2011.

Record Transfer Fee Paid: £1,250,000 to Leicester C for D.J. Campbell, August 2010.

Football League Record: 1896 Elected to Division 2; 1899 Failed re-election; 1900 Re-elected; 1900–30 Division 2; 1930–33 Division 1; 1933–37 Division 2; 1937–67 Division 1; 1967–70 Division 2; 1970–71 Division 1; 1971–78 Division 2; 1978–81 Division 3; 1981–85 Division 4; 1985–90 Division 3; 1990–92 Division 4; 1992–2000 Division 2; 2000–01 Division 3; 2001–04 Division 2; 2004–07 FL 1; 2007–10 FL C; 2010–11 FA Premier League; 2011– FL C.

LATEST SEQUENCES

Longest Sequence of League Wins: 9, 21.11.1936 – 1.1.1937.

Longest Sequence of League Defeats: 8, 26.11.1898 – 7.1.1899.

Longest Sequence of League Draws: 5, 4.12.1976 – 1.1.1977.

Longest Sequence of Unbeaten League Matches: 17, 6.4.1968 – 21.9.1968.

Longest Sequence Without a League Win: 19, 19.12.1970 – 24.4.1971.

Successive Scoring Runs: 33 from 23.2.1929.

Successive Non-scoring Runs: 5 from 25.11.1989.

MANAGERS

Tom Barcroft 1903–33
 (*Secretary-Manager*)
John Cox 1909–11
Bill Norman 1919–23
Maj. Frank Buckley 1923–27
Sid Beaumont 1927–28
Harry Evans 1928–33
 (*Hon. Team Manager*)
Alex 'Sandy' Macfarlane 1933–35
Joe Smith 1935–58
Ronnie Suart 1958–67
Stan Mortensen 1967–69
Les Shannon 1969–70
Bob Stokoe 1970–72
Harry Potts 1972–76
Allan Brown 1976–78
Bob Stokoe 1978–79
Stan Ternent 1979–80
Alan Ball 1980–81
Allan Brown 1981–82
Sam Ellis 1982–89
Jimmy Mullen 1989–90
Graham Carr 1990
Bill Ayre 1990–94
Sam Allardyce 1994–96
Gary Megson 1996–97
Nigel Worthington 1997–99
Steve McMahon 2000–04
Colin Hendry 2004–05
Simon Grayson 2005–08
Ian Holloway 2009–12
Michael Appleton 2012–13
Paul Ince 2013–14
José Riga June 2014–

TEN YEAR LEAGUE RECORD

		P	W	D	L	F	A	Pts	Pos
2004-05	FL 1	46	15	12	19	54	59	57	16
2005-06	FL 1	46	12	17	17	56	64	53	19
2006-07	FL 1	46	24	11	11	76	49	83	3
2007-08	FL C	46	12	18	16	59	64	54	19
2008-09	FL C	46	13	17	16	47	58	56	16
2009-10	FL C	46	19	13	14	74	58	70	6
2010-11	PR Lge	38	10	9	19	55	78	39	19
2011-12	FL C	46	20	15	11	79	59	75	5
2012-13	FL C	46	14	17	15	62	63	59	15
2013-14	FL C	46	11	13	22	38	66	46	20

DID YOU KNOW ?

Jimmy Armfield is the only Blackpool player to captain England. The full back skippered the national team on 15 occasions and in total won 43 caps for his country. He still holds Blackpool's record appearance total, playing 568 Football League games for the club between 1952 and 1971.

BLACKPOOL – FL CHAMPIONSHIP 2013–14 LEAGUE RECORD

Match No.	Date		Venue	Opponents		Result	H/T Score	Lg Pos.	Goalscorers	Attendance
1	Aug	3	A	Doncaster R	W	3-1	1-0	2	Davies [16], MacKenzie [87], Ince [90]	9002
2		10	H	Barnsley	W	1-0	0-0	2	Wiseman (og) [90]	14,268
3		17	A	Middlesbrough	D	1-1	0-0	3	Basham [83]	13,993
4		24	H	Reading	W	1-0	0-0	1	Barkhuizen [75]	12,928
5		31	H	Watford	W	1-0	0-0	1	Ince [81]	13,345
6	Sept	14	A	Bournemouth	W	2-1	1-1	1	Fuller [7], Bishop [48]	9446
7		17	A	Millwall	L	1-3	1-1	3	Ince [16]	8415
8		21	H	Leicester C	D	2-2	1-0	4	Basham [19], Ince (pen) [90]	15,317
9		27	A	Huddersfield T	D	1-1	1-0	2	Fuller [27]	12,337
10	Oct	1	H	Bolton W	D	0-0	0-0	6		13,819
11		5	A	Charlton Ath	D	0-0	0-0	6		15,847
12		19	H	Wigan Ath	W	1-0	1-0	5	Ince (pen) [24]	15,721
13		26	H	Blackburn R	D	2-2	2-1	4	Ince (pen) [13], Gosling [39]	15,901
14	Nov	2	A	Nottingham F	W	1-0	0-0	4	Dobbie [90]	21,581
15		9	H	Ipswich T	L	2-3	1-0	4	Dobbie [23], Davies [90]	13,525
16		23	A	Birmingham C	D	1-1	1-1	4	Fuller [36]	14,480
17		30	H	Sheffield W	W	2-0	1-0	4	Fuller [6], Gosling [73]	14,452
18	Dec	3	A	Yeovil T	L	0-1	0-1	5		5530
19		7	A	Derby Co	L	1-5	1-0	7	Osbourne [3]	24,063
20		14	H	QPR	L	0-2	0-0	9		13,822
21		21	A	Burnley	L	1-2	1-1	10	Cathcart [24]	14,489
22		26	H	Leeds U	D	1-1	0-1	10	Ince [65]	15,552
23		29	H	Brighton & HA	L	0-1	0-1	10		12,280
24	Jan	1	A	Sheffield W	L	0-2	0-0	12		19,447
25		11	H	Middlesbrough	L	0-2	0-0	14		14,421
26		18	A	Barnsley	L	0-2	0-1	14		9866
27		25	H	Doncaster R	D	1-1	0-0	14	Halliday [78]	13,468
28		28	A	Reading	L	1-5	0-2	15	Davies [65]	16,636
29	Feb	1	A	Blackburn R	L	0-2	0-1	15		15,045
30		8	H	Nottingham F	D	1-1	0-1	16	Keogh [86]	15,105
31		15	A	Ipswich T	D	0-0	0-0	16		16,010
32		22	H	Birmingham C	L	1-2	1-0	18	Keogh [22]	14,628
33	Mar	1	A	Watford	L	0-4	0-3	19		14,586
34		8	H	Bournemouth	L	0-1	0-0	19		13,043
35		11	H	Millwall	W	1-0	1-0	18	Fuller [14]	12,412
36		15	A	Leicester C	L	1-3	1-0	18	Goodwillie [41]	27,669
37		22	H	Huddersfield T	W	1-0	1-0	18	Fuller [4]	14,624
38		25	A	Bolton W	L	0-1	0-1	18		14,903
39		29	A	QPR	D	1-1	1-0	19	Goodwillie [11]	16,638
40	Apr	5	H	Yeovil T	L	1-2	0-1	20	Grandin [78]	13,310
41		8	H	Derby Co	L	1-3	1-3	20	Goodwillie [1]	13,435
42		12	A	Leeds U	L	0-2	0-1	20		23,416
43		18	H	Burnley	L	0-1	0-0	21		16,098
44		21	A	Brighton & HA	D	1-1	0-0	22	Dobbie [50]	27,616
45		26	H	Wigan Ath	W	2-0	0-0	18	Keogh [60], Dobbie [70]	19,137
46	May	3	H	Charlton Ath	L	0-3	0-0	20		15,518

Final League Position: 20

GOALSCORERS

League (38): Ince 7 (3 pens), Fuller 6, Dobbie 4, Davies 3, Goodwillie 3, Keogh 3, Basham 2, Gosling 2, Barkhuizen 1, Bishop 1, Cathcart 1, Grandin 1, Halliday 1, MacKenzie 1, Osbourne 1, own goal 1.
The Budweiser FA Cup (1): Barkhuizen 1.
Capital One Cup (0).

Gilks M 46	Broadfoot K 33	Harris R 2 + 2	Ferguson B 18 + 1	MacKenzie G 35	Cathcart C 29 + 1	Martinez A 18 + 8	Osbourne I 23 + 1	Grant R 5 + 1	Davies S 13 + 15	Ince T 22 + 1	Basham C 37 + 3	Robinson J 33 + 1	Chopra M 5 + 13	Eccleston N 2 + 2	Bishop N 29 + 6	Barkhuizen T 2 + 12	Delfouneso N 3 + 8	Fuller R 22 + 5	Caton J — + 2	Orr B 3 + 1	Tyson N — + 10	Dobbie S 23 + 4	Gosling D 13 + 1	Blackett T 5	Zeegelaar M — + 2	McMahon T 18	Perkins D 20	Halliday A 12 + 6	Goodwillie D 8 + 5	Haroun F 5 + 4	Keogh A 9 + 5	Grandin E 3 + 4	Foley K 4 + 1	Earnshaw R — + 1	Vellios A 2	McGahey H 4	Almond L — + 1	Match No.
1	2	3^3	4	5	6	7	8		9^2	10^1	11	12	13	14																								1
1	2		7	3	4		8		9^1	10^2	6	5	11	12^2	13	14																						2
1	2		7	4	3	9^2	6		10^1		8	5	13		11		12																					3
1	3	14	7	4^3		6		11^2			2	5	12		8	13	9	10^1																				4
1	3		7		6	8				12	4	5			2	9^2	11^1	10^1	13																			5
1	4	9	3		7^2	6				10	2^1	$5■$			8		13	11^3		12	14																	6
1	4	5	7	3	8^3	9^2				6	2				10		12	11^1		13	14																	7
1	4	9	3		13	8^2			12	10	6	5					11^1		2	14	7^3																	8
1	2		4	3	$7■$		8			10	5	14		6^2		12	11^1		13	9^3																		9
1	2		4	3		9	10^1		6	7	5	13		12			11^2		8																			10
1	2		4	3		7^3	13		8	6	5			10	14		11^2		9^1	12																		11
1	2		3	4	12	13	8		7	5				10			11^1		9^2	6																		12
1	4		3		7		12		6	2	$5■$			10	13		11^1		8^2	9																		13
1	4		3	7^2		13	6			14	10				11^1	2^3	12	8	9	5																		14
1	3		4	7^3		10^1	12	6			14	5			11^2	2	13	8	9																			15
1	3		4		9	13	10		2	12	6	5			11^1			8^2	7	5																		16
1	3		4	12	7	13	6^2		2	10				11^1			8^2	9	5	14																		17
1	3^3	12	$4■$	9^3		13	6		2	5	14	10^1			$11■$			8^2	7																			18
1	6^2	$13■$	7			10	11	4	5	$2■$				12				9^1	8	3																		19
1	3	7		4	6^1	14	11^3	9	2	5	12			13	10^2			8																				20
1	4	9	3			11^1	6	2	5	12	10						8^2	7	13																			21
1	$2■$	7	4	3		13	6	9	5	11^2	10		12				8^1																					22
1	7	4	3		13	6	2	5	11^3	10^1	14	12					8^2	9																				23
1	7	3	4	9^3		14	6		5	12	2	13	11^1				8	10^2																				24
1	9	4	3	8^1		13	6	7	5		12	2	10^2		11^1	14																						25
1	3	14	7		4	8^2	9^3		11	6	10	5	12	2^1							13																	26
1	3		4		7		10^3		6	5	11^2	9^1						14								2	8	12	13									27
1	3		4	12	6²		11		7	5	10^3	8^1						14								2	9	13										28
1	2		3	4		6	11		7^2									14	12								5	8^1	9^2		10	13						29
1	3		4		7^2		10^1			5								6								2	8	14	13	9^3	11^1	12						30
1	4		3		8		11^1			5^2					13			9								2	7	12	14	6	10^3							31
1	3		4		6^2		11^1			$5■$					13			8^3								2	9	14		7	10	12						32
1	3		4		8				12				13		11			9^3								7	5	14	6^1		10	12		2				33
1	3		4	14	7	12	6^1								11			9								8	5	13	10^2		2^3							34
1	2		3	4		12	7							6^1				10^2								5	8	9	11	13								35
1	4		3	2	13					8	5		7^3					12						14		6	9	10^1	11^2									36
1	4^1		3	6			7			5	13				10^4			12								2	8	11		14	9^2	12						37
1			4	3			8			5					14			11^3								2	6	10		13	9^2	7^1	12					38
1			4	3	14		8^3	5						12	13											2	7	9^1	11			6		10^2				39
1			3	4						6^2	9			5^3	14											2	7	8	11		12	13		10^1				40
1			4	3	6^3					13	5			12	14			7^1								2	8	11		10	9^2							41
1		7	3	4						6^1	5			9												2	8	10^2	11	12	13							42
1	8		4	7^3			6	5^2						10				14								2	9	12	11							3	13	43
1			3	13	7^2					6^1				9				10								2	8	5	14	12	11^3					4		44
1			3	14	7					6				10^3	12		13									2	9	5		11^1						4		45
1			4	6						7^1				8^2	13		12									2	9	5		11^3	14					3		46

The Budweiser FA Cup
Third Round   Bolton W   (a)   1-2

Capital One Cup
First Round   Preston NE   (a)   0-1

BOLTON WANDERERS

FOUNDATION

In 1874 boys of Christ Church Sunday School, Blackburn Street, led by their master Thomas Ogden, established a football club which went under the name of the school and whose president was vicar of Christ Church. Membership was 6d (two and a half pence). When their president began to lay down too many rules about the use of church premises, the club broke away and formed Bolton Wanderers in 1877, holding their earliest meetings at the Gladstone Hotel.

The Reebok Stadium, Burnden Way, Lostock, Bolton BL6 6JW.

Telephone: (0844) 871 2932. *Fax:* (01204) 673 773.

Ticket Office: (0844) 871 2932.

Website: www.bwfc.co.uk

Email: reception@bwfc.co.uk

Ground Capacity: 28,063.

Record Attendance: 69,912 v Manchester C, FA Cup 5th rd, 18 February 1933 (at Burnden Park); 28,353 v Leicester C, FA Premier League, 23 December 2003 (at The Reebok Stadium).

Pitch Measurements: 105m × 68m (115yd × 74.5yd)

Chairman: Phil A. Gartside.

Chief Operating Officer: Bradley Cooper.

Manager: Dougie Freedman.

Assistant Manager: Lennie Lawrence.

Head of Sports Science: Mark Leather.

Colours: White shirts with blue body trim, blue shorts, blue socks with white hoops.

Year Formed: 1874.

Turned Professional: 1880.

Previous Name: 1874, Christ Church FC; 1877, Bolton Wanderers.

Club Nickname: 'The Trotters'.

Grounds: Park Recreation Ground and Cockle's Field before moving to Pike's Lane ground 1881; 1895, Burnden Park; 1997, Reebok Stadium.

First Football League Game: 8 September 1888, Football League, v Derby Co (h) L 3–6 – Harrison; Robinson, Mitchell; Roberts, Weir, Bullough, Davenport (2), Milne, Coupar, Barbour, Brogan (1).

Record League Victory: 8–0 v Barnsley, Division 2, 6 October 1934 – Jones; Smith, Finney; Goslin, Atkinson, George Taylor; George T. Taylor (2), Eastham, Milsom (1), Westwood (4), Cook, (1 og).

Record Cup Victory: 13–0 v Sheffield U, FA Cup 2nd rd, 1 February 1890 – Parkinson; Robinson (1), Jones; Bullough, Davenport, Roberts; Rushton, Brogan (3), Cassidy (5), McNee, Weir (4).

HONOURS

Football League – Division 1:
Champions 1996–97;
Division 2: *Champions* 1908–09, 1977–78; *Runners-up* 1899–1900, 1904–05, 1910–11, 1934–35, 1992–93;
Division 3: *Champions* 1972–73.

FA Cup: *Winners* 1923, 1926, 1929, 1958; *Runners-up* 1894, 1904, 1953.

Football League Cup:
Runners-up 1995, 2004.

Freight Rover Trophy:
Runners-up 1986.

Sherpa Van Trophy: *Winners* 1989.

European Competitions
UEFA Cup: 2005–06, 2007–08.

sky SPORTS FACT FILE

Bolton Wanderers' Reebok Stadium hosted the semi-final of the 2000 Rugby League World Cup. An attendance of 16,032 saw New Zealand reach the final by defeating England 49-6. The Reebok has also staged three Rugby League World Club Challenge games.

Record Defeat: 1–9 v Preston NE, FA Cup 2nd rd, 10 December 1887.

Most League Points (2 for a win): 61, Division 3, 1972–73.

Most League Points (3 for a win): 98, Division 1, 1996–97.

Most League Goals: 100, Division 1, 1996–97.

Highest League Scorer in Season: Joe Smith, 38, Division 1, 1920–21.

Most League Goals in Total Aggregate: Nat Lofthouse, 255, 1946–61.

Most League Goals in One Match: 5, Tony Caldwell v Walsall, Division 3, 10 September 1983.

Most Capped Player: Ricardo Gardner, 72 (112), Jamaica.

Most League Appearances: Eddie Hopkinson, 519, 1956–70.

Youngest League Player: Ray Parry, 15 years 267 days v Wolverhampton W, 13 October 1951.

Record Transfer Fee Received: £15,000,000 from Chelsea for Nicolas Anelka, January 2008.

Record Transfer Fee Paid: £8,200,000 to Toulouse for Johan Elmander, July 2008.

Football League Record: 1888 Founder Member of the League; 1899–1900 Division 2; 1900–03 Division 1; 1903–05 Division 2; 1905–08 Division 1; 1908–09 Division 2; 1909–10 Division 1; 1910–11 Division 2; 1911–33 Division 1; 1933–35 Division 2; 1935–64 Division 1; 1964–71 Division 2; 1971–73 Division 3; 1973–78 Division 2; 1978–80 Division 1; 1980–83 Division 2; 1983–87 Division 3; 1987–88 Division 4; 1988–92 Division 3; 1992–93 Division 2; 1993–95 Division 1; 1995–96 FA Premier League; 1996–97 Division 1; 1997–98 FA Premier League; 1998–2001 Division 1; 2001–12 FA Premier League; 2012– FL C.

LATEST SEQUENCES

Longest Sequence of League Wins: 11, 5.11.1904 – 2.1.1905.

Longest Sequence of League Defeats: 11, 7.4.1902 – 18.10.1902.

Longest Sequence of League Draws: 6, 25.1.1913 – 8.3.1913.

Longest Sequence of Unbeaten League Matches: 23, 13.10.1990 – 9.3.1991.

Longest Sequence Without a League Win: 26, 7.4.1902 – 10.1.1903.

Successive Scoring Runs: 24 from 22.11.1996.

Successive Non-scoring Runs: 5 from 30.1.2010.

MANAGERS

Tom Rawthorne 1874–85
   (*Secretary*)
J. J. Bentley 1885–86
   (*Secretary*)
W. G. Struthers 1886–87
   (*Secretary*)
Fitzroy Norris 1887
   (*Secretary*)
J. J. Bentley 1887–95
   (*Secretary*)
Harry Downs 1895–96
   (*Secretary*)
Frank Brettell 1896–98
   (*Secretary*)
John Somerville 1898–1910
Will Settle 1910–15
Tom Mather 1915–19
Charles Foweraker 1919–44
Walter Rowley 1944–50
Bill Ridding 1951–68
Nat Lofthouse 1968–70
Jimmy McIlroy 1970
Jimmy Meadows 1971
Nat Lofthouse 1971
   (*then Admin. Manager to 1972*)
Jimmy Armfield 1971–74
Ian Greaves 1974–80
Stan Anderson 1980–81
George Mulhall 1981–82
John McGovern 1982–85
Charlie Wright 1985
Phil Neal 1985–92
Bruce Rioch 1992–95
Roy McFarland 1995–96
Colin Todd 1996–99
McFarland and Todd joint
   managers 1995–96
Sam Allardyce 1999–2007
Sammy Lee 2007
Gary Megson 2007–09
Owen Coyle 2010–12
Dougie Freedman October 2012–

TEN YEAR LEAGUE RECORD

		P	W	D	L	F	A	Pts	Pos
2004-05	PR Lge	38	16	10	12	49	44	58	6
2005-06	PR Lge	38	15	11	12	49	41	56	8
2006-07	PR Lge	38	16	8	14	47	52	56	7
2007-08	PR Lge	38	9	10	19	36	54	37	16
2008-09	PR Lge	38	11	8	19	41	53	41	13
2009-10	PR Lge	38	10	9	19	42	67	39	14
2010-11	PR Lge	38	12	10	16	52	56	46	14
2011-12	PR Lge	38	10	6	22	46	77	36	18
2012-13	FL C	46	18	14	14	69	61	68	7
2013-14	FL C	46	14	17	15	59	60	59	14

DID YOU KNOW ?

Bolton Wanderers captain Harry Goslin lost his life serving with the Royal Artillery in December 1943. Goslin, a wing-half who was a wartime England international, made 306 Football League appearances for Wanderers after joining the club in 1930.

BOLTON WANDERERS – FL CHAMPIONSHIP 2013–14 LEAGUE RECORD

Match No.	Date	Venue	Opponents	Result	H/T Score	Lg Pos.	Goalscorers	Attendance
1	Aug 3	A	Burnley	D	1-1	1-1	11	Pratley [37]	12,919
2	10	H	Reading	D	1-1	1-0	16	Pratley [14]	15,551
3	17	A	Nottingham F	L	0-3	0-1	19		22,306
4	24	H	QPR	L	0-1	0-0	21		14,999
5	31	A	Blackburn R	L	1-4	1-2	24	Baptiste [45]	15,828
6	Sept 14	H	Leeds U	L	0-1	0-1	23		19,622
7	17	H	Derby Co	D	2-2	2-2	24	Baptiste [5], Eagles [41]	14,260
8	21	A	Brighton & HA	L	1-3	1-0	24	Lopez (og) [29]	26,319
9	28	H	Yeovil T	D	1-1	0-0	23	Baptiste [90]	14,716
10	Oct 1	A	Blackpool	D	0-0	0-0	23		13,819
11	5	A	Birmingham C	W	2-1	1-0	20	Beckford [12], Danns [64]	13,627
12	19	H	Sheffield W	D	1-1	1-1	21	Beckford [16]	17,177
13	26	H	Ipswich T	D	1-1	0-0	21	Medo [65]	15,222
14	Nov 2	A	Bournemouth	W	2-0	1-0	17	Ngog [37], Beckford [90]	10,015
15	9	H	Millwall	W	3-1	2-1	17	Hall [5], Beckford [43], Moritz [89]	14,830
16	23	A	Watford	W	1-0	1-0	15	Beckford [27]	15,247
17	30	A	Middlesbrough	L	0-1	0-0	16		23,679
18	Dec 3	H	Huddersfield T	L	0-1	0-0	18		15,452
19	7	H	Doncaster R	W	3-0	2-0	15	Mason [33], Moritz [39], Danns [90]	15,471
20	15	A	Wigan Ath	L	2-3	0-2	16	Danns [49], Moritz (pen) [64]	19,226
21	21	H	Charlton Ath	D	1-1	1-1	18	McNaughton [45]	14,923
22	26	A	Barnsley	W	1-0	0-0	17	Danns [64]	12,484
23	29	A	Leicester C	L	3-5	3-3	18	Moritz 2 [15, 39], Beckford [20]	26,614
24	Jan 1	H	Middlesbrough	D	2-2	1-2	18	Baptiste [29], Ngog [90]	17,410
25	11	H	Nottingham F	D	1-1	0-0	18	Mills [75]	17,046
26	18	A	Reading	L	0-1	0-4	18	Ngog [88]	18,629
27	28	A	QPR	L	1-2	0-1	18	Spearing [85]	15,097
28	Feb 1	A	Ipswich T	L	0-1	0-0	20		15,429
29	8	H	Bournemouth	D	2-2	2-1	19	Lee [21], Jutkiewicz [32]	14,336
30	11	H	Burnley	L	0-0	0-0	19		16,439
31	15	A	Millwall	D	1-1	1-0	19	Jutkiewicz [15]	10,007
32	22	H	Watford	W	2-0	2-0	19	Jutkiewicz [35], Mason [45]	15,179
33	Mar 1	A	Blackburn R	W	4-0	2-0	18	Medo [23], Mason [45], Spearing [47], Moritz [90]	17,541
34	8	A	Leeds U	W	5-1	1-0	17	Mason [45], Jutkiewicz [52], Knight [56], Davies, M [72], Moritz [89]	28,904
35	11	A	Derby Co	D	0-0	0-0	16		23,435
36	15	H	Brighton & HA	L	0-2	0-1	17		15,336
37	22	A	Yeovil T	D	2-2	0-2	17	Jutkiewicz [53], Knight [83]	6344
38	25	H	Blackpool	W	1-0	1-0	17	Wheater [16]	14,903
39	29	A	Wigan Ath	D	1-1	1-0	17	Jutkiewicz [31]	18,853
40	Apr 5	A	Huddersfield T	W	1-0	0-0	15	Mason [90]	15,120
41	8	A	Doncaster R	W	2-1	2-1	14	Danns [7], Mason [15]	7508
42	12	H	Barnsley	W	1-0	1-0	14	Beckford [44]	15,845
43	18	A	Charlton Ath	D	0-0	0-0	14		15,773
44	22	H	Leicester C	L	0-1	0-0	14		16,569
45	26	A	Sheffield W	W	3-1	3-1	14	Danns [8], Lee [19], Trotter [29]	23,070
46	May 3	H	Birmingham C	D	2-2	0-0	14	Lee [57], Jutkiewicz [76]	19,558

Final League Position: 14

GOALSCORERS

League (59): Beckford 7, Jutkiewicz 7, Moritz 7 (1 pen), Danns 6, Mason 6, Baptiste 4, Lee 3, Ngog 3, Knight 2, Medo 2, Pratley 2, Spearing 2, Davies, M 1, Eagles 1, Hall 1, McNaughton 1, Mills 1, Trotter 1, Wheater 1, own goal 1.
The Budweiser FA Cup (2): Beckford 1, N'Gog 1.
Capital One Cup (4): Odelusi 2, Beckford 1, Hall 1.

Bogdan A 29	Baptiste A 37+2	Tierney M 8	Andrews K 1	Knight Z 24+2	Wheater D 21+2	Eagles C 13+3	Medo M 30+5	Beckford J 20+13	Pratley D 19+1	Lee C 32+13	Ngog D 10+7	Davies C 2+6	Spearing J 45	Moritz A 7+16	Odelusi S —+5	Hall R 11+11	Ream T 42	Mears T 1	Mills M 31+1	Feeney L 3+1	McNaughton K 13	Danns N 26+7	Lonergan A 17	Mason J 12+4	Davies M 14+4	White H 1+1	Jutkiewicz L 16+4	Trotter L 10+6	Hutton A 9	Kellett A —+3	Lester C —+1	Threlkeld O 2	Youngs T —+1	Match No.
1	2	3	4	5	6	7^2	8	9^1	10	11	12	13																						1
1	2	5		3	4		8	11^3	6	9^1	10^2	13	7	12		14																		2
1	2	5		3	4	6	13	10^8	9		11^2		7	12		8^1																		3
1	2	5		3	4			6	11^2	9	10^1	12	8	13		14	7^3																	4
1	5			3	4	12	7^3	11	6^2	9	10^1	14	8	13			2																	5
1	3	6^1		4^2		7^1	14	12	9	10	11		8			13	5		2															6
1	2	5		3	8		11		10	12		6				9^1	7		4															7
1	2	5		4^1	9		13	8	11^2	10^3	6		14	12		7			3															8
1	2	5^1	14		8	6	12	10^2	11^3	7		9	4			3	13																	9
1	2				8	11	9	12		7			4			3	10^1	5	6															10
1	5			12		7	11^2	9^1	13		14	6				4		3	10	2	8^3													11
1	5					10^2	7	11		12	14	9				13	4		3	6^1	2	8^2												12
	5					12	7	11		6^7	10^1	8	13			4		3	2	9	1													13
	5		13				8	11		6^1	10^2	7	12			4		3	2	9	1													14
	5		13				6	11^1		10^1	14	7	12			8^2	4	3	2	9	1													15
	5					10	11^1	8^3	6	13		7	12	14		3	4	2	9^2	1														16
	5						7^3	11	8^2	6^1	14	9	12			4		3	2	10	1	13												17
	4						7^1	11		12	13	9	8^2			6^3	5	3	2	10	1	14												18
	5					10^2	13	9^3	6			7	8^1	14		4	3	2	12	1	11													19
	5						12	7^2	10^3		6	9	14			4	3	2	8^1	1	11	13												20
	5					8	13	10^3		6	9	14				4	3	2	7^1	1	11^2	12												21
	5			3		8^2	13	7^3	12		6					4	14	2	10^1	1	11	9												22
	2			3			7^2	11	12	10		6	9^2			8^1	5	4			1	14	13											23
	2			3		10		13	7^2	8^3	14	6	12				5	4			1	11^1	9											24
	2			4				11^1		9	10	7	12			5		3	6	1		8												25
	2			4		12		9^1	10	11	6	13				5	3	8		1	7^2													26
	2			4		7	8	13	11^1	6			5^3	3		10^2	1		9	12	14													27
	2			3		12	7^1	9^2	14	6			5	4		10^3	1		8	11	13													28
1	2			4		9^2	12		10	6	13		5	3		14				7^3	11	8^1												29
1	2				4	8	7^1		10	6	12^9		5	3		14				13	11	9^2												30
1	2			13	4	10^1	7		9^2	14	6		5	3		12				8³	11													31
1	2			4		6	9^2	13	7				5	3		12				10^1	8^3	11	14											32
1	2	3		4		7		12	6	13			5			9^1				11	8^2	10^3	14											33
1	2	3		4		7	13		6^1	14			5			9				11^3	8^2	10	12											34
1	5	3	14		7	13		6	9^1				4			8				10^3	11^2	12	2											35
1	5	3^3		7		8^1	6	13	12				4	14		10				11	9^2	2												36
1	5^1	3	14		7	12	6	13					4			9				11^2	8^1	10^3	2											37
1		3	4	7	13	12	6	14					5			9				11^2	8^3	10^1	2											38
1	13	3	4	7	14	6			9	12	10^1		5							11^3	8^2	2												39
1		3	4	7	13	10	6						5			8	12			11^2	9^1	2												40
1		3	4	7	13	8^1	6						5			9	11^2			10	12	2												41
1	5^2	14			11	8	7	9^1	10^1			4	3			12				13	6	2												42
1	12		4		11	8^1	6	13				5	3			7				10	9	2^2												43
1		4	3		12	10^2	9		7^3	6		5			2^1	11	8						13	14										44
1		4			11^3	8^2	6	10^1		5	3	9			12	7				13	2						14					2		45
1	13	4			11^{12}	8^1	7	10^3	5	3	9	1			12	6							14				2							46

AFC BOURNEMOUTH

FOUNDATION

There was a Bournemouth FC as early as 1875, but the present club arose out of the remnants of the Boscombe St John's club (formed 1890). The meeting at which Boscombe FC came into being was held at a house in Gladstone Road in 1899. They began by playing in the Boscombe and District Junior League.

Goldsands Stadium, Dean Court, Kings Park, Bournemouth, Dorset BH7 7AF.

Telephone: (0844) 576 1910.

Fax: (01202) 726 373.

Ticket Office: (0844) 576 1910.

Website: www.afcb.co.uk

Email: enquiries@afcb.co.uk

Ground Capacity: 12,081.

Record Attendance: 28,799 v Manchester U, FA Cup 6th rd, 2 March 1957.

Pitch Measurements: 105m × 67.5m (115yd × 74yd)

Chairman: Jeff Mostyn.

Chief Executive: Neill Blake.

Manager: Eddie Howe.

Assistant Manager: Jason Tindall.

Physio: Steve Hard.

Colours: Red and black striped shirts, black shorts with red side panels, red socks with black hoops.

Year Formed: 1899.

Turned Professional: 1910.

Previous Names: 1890, Boscombe St John's; 1899, Boscombe FC; 1923, Bournemouth & Boscombe Ath FC; 1972, AFC Bournemouth.

Club Nickname: 'Cherries'.

Grounds: 1899, Castlemain Road, Pokesdown; 1910, Dean Court.

First Football League Game: 25 August 1923, Division 3 (S), v Swindon T (a) L 1–3 – Heron; Wingham, Lamb; Butt, Charles Smith, Voisey; Miller, Lister (1), Davey, Simpson, Robinson.

Record League Victory: 7–0 v Swindon T, Division 3 (S), 22 September 1956 – Godwin; Cunningham, Keetley; Clayton, Crosland, Rushworth; Siddall (1), Norris (2), Arnott (1), Newsham (2), Cutler (1). 10–0 win v Northampton T at start of 1939–40 expunged from the records on outbreak of war.

Record Cup Victory: 11–0 v Margate, FA Cup 1st rd, 20 November 1971 – Davies; Machin (1), Kitchener, Benson, Jones, Powell, Cave (1), Boyer, MacDougall (9 incl. 1p), Miller, Scott (De Garis).

Record Defeat: 0–9 v Lincoln C, Division 3, 18 December 1982.

HONOURS

Football League:
Division 3: *Champions* 1986–87;
FL 1: *Runners-up* 2012–13;
Division 3 (S): *Runners-up* 1947–48;
Division 4: *Runners-up* 1970–71.
FL 2: *Runners-up* 2009–10.
FA Cup: Best season: 6th rd, 1957.
Football League Cup: Best season: 4th rd, 1962, 1964.
Associate Members' Cup: *Winners* 1984.
Auto Windscreens Shield: *Runners-up* 1998.

sky SPORTS FACT FILE

James Hayter of Bournemouth scored the fastest hat-trick in Football League history. He came on as a substitute after 84 minutes of the home game with Doncaster Rovers on 24 February 2004 and netted three times in less than 140 seconds. The Cherries won the game 6-0.

Most League Points (2 for a win): 62, Division 3, 1971–72.

Most League Points (3 for a win): 97, Division 3, 1986–87.

Most League Goals: 88, Division 3 (S), 1956–57.

Highest League Scorer in Season: Ted MacDougall, 42, 1970–71.

Most League Goals in Total Aggregate: Ron Eyre, 202, 1924–33.

Most League Goals in One Match: 4, Jack Russell v Clapton Orient, Division 3 (S), 7 January 1933; 4, Jack Russell v Bristol C, Division 3 (S), 28 January 1933; 4, Harry Mardon v Southend U, Division 3 (S), 1 January 1938; 4, Jack McDonald v Torquay U, Division 3 (S), 8 November 1947; 4, Ted MacDougall v Colchester U, 18 September 1970; 4, Brian Clark v Rotherham U, 10 October 1972; 4, Luther Blissett v Hull C, 29 November 1988; 4, James Hayter v Bury, Division 2, 21 October 2000.

Most Capped Player: Gerry Peyton, 7 (33), Republic of Ireland.

Most League Appearances: Steve Fletcher, 628, 1992–2007; 2008–13.

Youngest League Player: Jimmy White, 15 years 321 days v Brentford, 30 April 1958.

Record Transfer Fee Received: £1,000,000 from Burnley for Danny Ings, August 2011.

Record Transfer Fee Paid: £2,500,000 to Malmo for Tokelo Rantie, August 2013.

Football League Record: 1923 Elected to Division 3 (S) and remained a Third Division club for record number of years until 1970; 1970–71 Division 4; 1971–75 Division 3; 1975–82 Division 4; 1982–87 Division 3; 1987–90 Division 2; 1990–92 Division 3; 1992–2002 Division 2; 2002–03 Division 3; 2003–04 Division 2; 2004–08 FL 1; 2008–10 FL 2; 2010–13 FL 1; 2013– FL C.

MANAGERS

Vincent Kitcher 1914–23 (*Secretary-Manager*)
Harry Kinghorn 1923–25
Leslie Knighton 1925–28
Frank Richards 1928–30
Billy Birrell 1930–35
Bob Crompton 1935–36
Charlie Bell 1936–39
Harry Kinghorn 1939–47
Harry Lowe 1947–50
Jack Bruton 1950–56
Fred Cox 1956–58
Don Welsh 1958–61
Bill McGarry 1961–63
Reg Flewin 1963–65
Fred Cox 1965–70
John Bond 1970–73
Trevor Hartley 1974–75
John Benson 1975–78
Alec Stock 1979–80
David Webb 1980–82
Don Megson 1983
Harry Redknapp 1983–92
Tony Pulis 1992–94
Mel Machin 1994–2000
Sean O'Driscoll 2000–06
Kevin Bond 2006–08
Jimmy Quinn 2008
Eddie Howe 2008–11
Lee Bradbury 2011–12
Paul Groves 2012
Eddie Howe October 2012–

LATEST SEQUENCES

Longest Sequence of League Wins: 8, 12.3.2013 – 20.4.2013.

Longest Sequence of League Defeats: 7, 13.8.1994 – 13.9.1994.

Longest Sequence of League Draws: 5, 25.4.2000 – 12.8.2000.

Longest Sequence of Unbeaten League Matches: 18, 6.3.1982 – 28.8.1982.

Longest Sequence Without a League Win: 14, 6.3.1974 – 27.4.1974.

Successive Scoring Runs: 31 from 28.10.2000.

Successive Non-scoring Runs: 6 from 1.2.1975.

TEN YEAR LEAGUE RECORD

		P	W	D	L	F	A	Pts	Pos
2004-05	FL 1	46	20	10	16	77	64	70	8
2005-06	FL 1	46	12	19	15	49	53	55	17
2006-07	FL 1	46	13	13	20	50	64	52	19
2007-08	FL 1	46	17	7	22	62	72	48*	21
2008-09	FL 2	46	17	12	17	59	51	46†	21
2009-10	FL 2	46	25	8	13	61	44	83	2
2010-11	FL 1	46	19	14	13	75	54	71	6
2011-12	FL 1	46	15	13	18	48	52	58	11
2012-13	FL 1	46	24	11	11	76	53	83	2
2013-14	FL C	46	18	12	16	67	66	66	10

10 pts deducted; †17 pts deducted.

DID YOU KNOW ?

When Bournemouth were elected to the Football League in 1923 they were not given exemption from the qualifying rounds of the FA Cup. As a result they were drawn to play Portsea Gas Co in a preliminary round tie, but decided to withdraw from the competition.

AFC BOURNEMOUTH – FL CHAMPIONSHIP 2013–14 LEAGUE RECORD

Match No.	Date	Venue	Opponents	Result	H/T Score	Lg Pos.	Goalscorers	Attendance
1	Aug 3	H	Charlton Ath	W 2-1	1-0	3	Grabban 2 [26, 66]	10,108
2	10	A	Watford	L 1-6	1-1	15	Grabban [30]	16,295
3	17	H	Wigan Ath	W 1-0	1-0	7	Grabban [43]	9097
4	24	A	Huddersfield T	L 1-5	0-3	11	Pugh [68]	12,025
5	31	A	Doncaster R	W 1-0	1-0	6	Pitman [31]	6769
6	Sept 14	H	Blackpool	L 1-2	1-1	9	Grabban [12]	9446
7	17	H	Barnsley	W 1-0	0-0	7	Pugh [78]	7574
8	21	A	Middlesbrough	D 3-3	2-2	8	Pitman 2 (2 pens) [4, 12], Woodgate (og) [83]	13,617
9	28	H	Blackburn R	L 1-3	0-3	10	Fraser [74]	9441
10	Oct 1	A	Leeds U	L 1-2	0-0	13	Grabban [73]	21,749
11	5	H	Millwall	W 5-2	1-2	8	Fraser [43], Cook [50], Arter [55], Grabban (pen) [59], Pitman (pen) [90]	9624
12	19	A	Nottingham F	D 1-1	0-1	9	Pugh [90]	28,070
13	26	A	Leicester C	L 1-2	1-1	11	Pugh [38]	23,357
14	Nov 2	H	Bolton W	L 0-2	0-1	15		10,015
15	9	A	Burnley	D 1-1	0-0	14	Rantie [50]	12,221
16	23	H	Derby Co	L 0-1	0-0	16		10,720
17	30	H	Brighton & HA	D 1-1	1-0	17	Ritchie [29]	9870
18	Dec 3	A	QPR	L 0-3	0-1	19		16,331
19	7	A	Reading	W 2-1	2-0	16	Grabban [37], Ritchie [41]	20,944
20	14	A	Birmingham C	L 0-2	0-2	17		9256
21	21	A	Sheffield W	W 2-1	2-0	15	Ritchie [10], Grabban [27]	21,057
22	26	H	Yeovil T	W 3-0	0-0	15	Ritchie 2 [50, 57], O'Kane [65]	10,717
23	29	H	Ipswich T	D 1-1	0-0	16	Pitman [74]	11,096
24	Jan 1	A	Brighton & HA	D 1-1	1-0	16	Grabban (pen) [14]	28,282
25	11	A	Wigan Ath	L 0-3	0-1	16		12,709
26	18	H	Watford	D 1-1	0-1	16	Grabban (pen) [62]	10,353
27	28	H	Huddersfield T	W 2-1	0-0	14	Grabban (pen) [55], Rantie [72]	7258
28	Feb 1	H	Leicester C	L 0-1	0-0	14		10,719
29	8	A	Bolton W	D 2-2	1-2	15	Grabban [34], Francis [66]	14,336
30	15	H	Burnley	D 1-1	0-0	15	Rantie [51]	10,422
31	22	A	Derby Co	L 0-1	0-0	17		27,306
32	Mar 1	H	Doncaster R	W 5-0	2-0	16	Kermorgant 3 [26, 44, 73], Arter 2 [50, 82]	8983
33	8	A	Blackpool	W 1-0	0-0	15	Grabban (pen) [48]	13,043
34	12	A	Blackburn R	W 1-0	0-0	12	Grabban [67]	13,081
35	15	H	Middlesbrough	D 0-0	0-0	12		9710
36	18	A	Charlton Ath	L 0-1	0-0	12		13,537
37	22	A	Barnsley	W 1-0	0-0	11	Cook [90]	9392
38	25	H	Leeds U	W 4-1	3-0	10	Kermorgant 2 [2, 51], Grabban 2 [18, 28]	10,109
39	29	A	Birmingham C	W 4-2	3-0	10	Ritchie [13], Grabban 2 (1 pen) [20, 28 (p)], Harte [52]	13,875
40	Apr 5	H	QPR	W 2-1	1-0	10	Elphick [45], Grabban [60]	11,307
41	8	H	Reading	W 3-1	3-0	9	Ritchie 2 [7, 19], Kermorgant [45]	11,182
42	12	A	Yeovil T	D 1-1	0-1	9	Fraser [59]	6931
43	18	H	Sheffield W	L 2-4	1-2	9	Pugh [31], Kermorgant [57]	10,864
44	21	A	Ipswich T	D 2-2	1-1	11	Cook [44], Ritchie [80]	20,356
45	26	H	Nottingham F	W 4-1	1-0	9	Kermorgant 2 [43, 90], Grabban 2 (1 pen) [47, 70 (p)]	11,021
46	May 3	A	Millwall	L 0-1	0-1	10		15,779

Final League Position: 10

GOALSCORERS

League (67): Grabban 22 (7 pens), Kermorgant 9, Ritchie 9, Pitman 5 (3 pens), Pugh 5, Arter 3, Cook 3, Fraser 3, Rantie 3, Elphick 1, Francis 1, Harte 1, O'Kane 1, own goal 1.
The Budweiser FA Cup (4): Pitman 2 (1 pen), Elphick 1, Fraser 1.
Capital One Cup (1): O'Kane 1.

Allsop R 11 + 1	Francis S 45 + 1	Daniels C 22 + 1	Arter H 31	Cook S 38	Ward E 22 + 1	Coulibaly M 2 + 5	MacDonald S 11 + 12	Thomas W 1 + 9	Grabban L 43 + 1	Pugh M 32 + 10	Fraser R 23 + 14	Surman A 30 + 5	Pitman B 12 + 22	Harte I 22 + 2	O'Kane E 32 + 5	Elphick T 34 + 4	Hughes R 1 + 4	Rantie T 14 + 15	Collison J 4	Flahavan D — + 1	Henderson S 2	Camp L 33	Ritchie M 28 + 2	McQuoid J 1	Kermorgant Y 11 + 5	Smith A 1 + 4	Match No.
1	2	3	4	5	6		7^3	8	9^1	10^2	11	12	13	14													1
1	2	5^1	7	3	4		8^3		10	9^1	11	6	13	12	14												2
1	2		7	3	4			8	12	10	9^1	6^2		11	5			13									3
1	2			8	4			7	10	13	6	9^1	11^2	5	12^3	3	14										4
1	2	5		8	3	4	12	7	13	11^3	9^1	6^2	10				14										5
1	2	5		3	4			8	12	11	9^1	6		10		7											6
1	2	5^1		4	3			7^3	10	9	6^2			11	8	12	14	13									7
1	2			3	5			13	12	10	6			7	8	4	9^1	11^2									8
1	2			5	3		14	7^1	10	9^2	13	6^3		8	4	12^1		11									9
1	2		4	3					10	9^3	6^2	13	14	5	8		11^1	7	12								10
	2	8^1	4	3					10	9^3	6	12	14	5	13		11^2	7		1							11
12	2	13	7	3	4				10	6		9^3	14	5^2			11	8			1^1						12
1	2	5^2		8	4	3		14	11^1	9	6^3	12			13		11^2	7									13
	2	5		8	4		7^1	12	10	9	6^3	14	13			3		11^2				1					14
	2	5	7		4	3	14	12	6	9^3		11			8^2	13		10^1				1					15
	2	5		4			7	14	10	9^1	12		6^2		8	3		11^3				1	13				16
	2	5		4				12		13	9^1	11			7	3		10^2				1	6^2				17
	2	5		8	4			7^3	12	9	14	10		11^1		3		13				1	6^2				18
	2	5		8	4			14	11^2	9	12	10	13		7^1	3						1	6^3				19
	2	5^1	9		4				11	8^2	12	10^3	14		7	3		13				1	6				20
	2	5		6	4		13		10^3	12	11^1	8^2	14		7	3						1	9				21
	2	5	7^2		3		12		11^1	14	6^3	10			8	4		13				1	9				22
	2	5		4					11	13	10^1	8	12		7	3						1	6	9^2			23
	2	5	7		4				11^1	9	12	10	13		8	3						1	6^2				24
	2	5	7^2		4				11	12	9^1	10	14		8	3		13				1	6^3				25
	2	5		8	4				11	9^2	10		13		7	3		12				1	6				26
	2	5^1		8	4		14		11	9	10^1		12		7	3		13				1	6^2				27
	2		7		4				6		9^2	10^3	14	5	8	3		11^1				1	12		13		28
	2		7	4					14	11^3	9^1	10^2		5	8	3		12				1	6		13		29
	2		7	4					12	10^3	9		14	5	8^1	3		11^2				1	6		13		30
	2		7	4					14	10	9^1	13	8	5		3		11^2				1	6^3		12		31
	2		7	4			14		10^1	13	9^3	8		5		3		12				1	6		11^2		32
	2			4					11	12	9^1	8	10	5	7	3						1	6				33
	2	9^3		4			13	14	11	12	10^1	8		5	6	3						1	7^2				34
	2			8	4		10^3		11	13	12	9^1		5	6	3		14				1	7^2				35
	2			4					11^3	10	7^1	9		5	6^2	3		13				1			12	14	36
	2			4					11		9	8		5	7	3						1	6		10		37
	2	7		4					11	9		8^3	14	5	12	3		13				1	6		10^2		38
	2	7^2	4	14					10	9^1	12	13		5	8	3						1	6		11^1		39
	2	8^1		4					10	9^1	13	7	14	5	12	3						1	6^1		11^2		40
	2			4			14		10^3	9^1	12	8	13	5	7	3						1	6^2		11		41
	2			4					10^1	9^2	8	13	5^1	7	3		14					1	6		11	12	42
	2			4					10	9^1	12	8	14	5^3	7	3						1	6^2		11	13	43
	2	5^1		4	3				11	9^2		8			7			12				1	6		10	13	44
	2			4			14		10^2	9^1	12	8			5	7	3	13				1	6^3		11		45
12	5			4			13			9^3	7	14			8^2	3		10				1	6		11	2^1	46

The Budweiser FA Cup
Third Round   Burton   (h)   4-1
Fourth Round   Liverpool   (h)   0-2

Capital One Cup
First Round   Portsmouth   (h)   1-0
Second Round   Watford   (a)   0-2

BRADFORD CITY

FOUNDATION

Bradford was a rugby stronghold around the turn of the 20th century but after Manningham RFC held an archery contest to help them out of financial difficulties in 1903, they were persuaded to give up the handling code and turn to soccer. So they formed Bradford City and continued at Valley Parade. Recognising this as an opportunity to spread the dribbling code in this part of Yorkshire, the Football League immediately accepted the new club's first application for membership of the Second Division.

Coral Windows Stadium, Valley Parade, Bradford, West Yorkshire BD8 7DY.

Telephone: (0871) 978 1911.

Fax: (01274) 773 356.

Ticket Office: (0871) 978 8000.

Website: www.bradfordcityfc.co.uk

Email: bradfordcityfc@compuserve.com

Ground Capacity: 25,136.

Record Attendance: 39,146 v Burnley, FA Cup 4th rd, 11 March 1911.

Pitch Measurements: 103.5m × 64m (113yd × 70yd)

Joint Chairmen: Julian Rhodes and Mark Lawn.

Director of Operations: David Baldwin.

Manager: Phil Parkinson.

Assistant Manager: Steve Parkin.

Head Physio: Matt Barrass.

Colours: Claret and amber striped shirts, amber shorts, amber socks.

Year Formed: 1903.

Turned Professional: 1903.

Club Nickname: 'The Bantams'.

Ground: 1903, Valley Parade.

HONOURS

Football League –
Division 1: *Runners-up* 1998–99;
Division 2: *Champions* 1907–08;
Division 3: *Champions* 1984–85;
Division 3 (N): *Champions* 1928–29;
Division 4: *Runners-up* 1981–82.
FA Cup: *Winners* 1911.
Football League Cup: *Runners-up* 2012–13.
European Competitions:
Intertoto Cup: 2000.

First Football League Game: 1 September 1903, Division 2, v Grimsby T (a) L 0–2 – Seymour; Wilson, Halliday; Robinson, Millar, Farnall; Guy, Beckram, Forrest, McMillan, Graham.

Record League Victory: 11–1 v Rotherham U, Division 3 (N), 25 August 1928 – Sherlaw; Russell, Watson; Burkinshaw (1), Summers, Bauld; Harvey (2), Edmunds (3), White (3), Cairns, Scriven (2).

Record Cup Victory: 11–3 v Walker Celtic, FA Cup 1st rd (replay), 1 December 1937 – Parker; Rookes, McDermott; Murphy, Mackie, Moore; Bagley (1), Whittingham (1), Deakin (4 incl. 1p), Cooke (1), Bartholomew (4).

sky SPORTS FACT FILE

Peter O'Rourke was the most successful manager in Bradford City's history after being appointed at the age of 29. O'Rourke was in charge when the club won the Second Division in 1908 and the FA Cup in 1911. He departed in 1921 but returned in 1928, leading the team to the Division Three North title in his first season back.

Record Defeat: 1–9 v Colchester U, Division 4, 30 December 1961.

Most League Points (2 for a win): 63, Division 3 (N), 1928–29.

Most League Points (3 for a win): 94, Division 3, 1984–85.

Most League Goals: 128, Division 3 (N), 1928–29.

Highest League Scorer in Season: David Layne, 34, Division 4, 1961–62.

Most League Goals in Total Aggregate: Bobby Campbell, 121, 1981–84, 1984–86.

Most League Goals in One Match: 7, Albert Whitehurst v Tranmere R, Division 3 (N), 6 March 1929.

Most Capped Player: Jamie Lawrence, 19 (24), Jamaica.

Most League Appearances: Cec Podd, 502, 1970–84.

Youngest League Player: Robert Cullingford, 16 years 141 days v Mansfield T, 22 April 1970.

Record Transfer Fee Received: £2,000,000 from Newcastle U for Des Hamilton, March 1997; £2,000,000 from Newcastle U for Andrew O'Brien, March 2001.

Record Transfer Fee Paid: £2,500,000 to Leeds U for David Hopkin, July 2000.

Football League Record: 1903 Elected to Division 2; 1908–22 Division 1; 1922–27 Division 2; 1927–29 Division 3 (N); 1929–37 Division 2; 1937–61 Division 3; 1961–69 Division 4; 1969–72 Division 3; 1972–77 Division 4; 1977–78 Division 3; 1978–82 Division 4; 1982–85 Division 3; 1985–90 Division 2; 1990–92 Division 3; 1992–96 Division 2; 1996–99 Division 1; 1999–2001 FA Premier League; 2001–04 Division 1; 2004–07 FL 1; 2007–13 FL 2; 2013– FL 1.

LATEST SEQUENCES

Longest Sequence of League Wins: 10, 26.11.1983 – 3.2.1984.

Longest Sequence of League Defeats: 8, 21.1.1933 – 11.3.1933.

Longest Sequence of League Draws: 6, 30.1.1976 – 13.3.1976.

Longest Sequence of Unbeaten League Matches: 21, 11.1.1969 – 2.5.1969.

Longest Sequence Without a League Win: 16, 28.8.1948 – 20.11.1948.

Successive Scoring Runs: 30 from 26.12.1961.

Successive Non-scoring Runs: 7 from 18.4.1925.

MANAGERS

Robert Campbell 1903–05
Peter O'Rourke 1905–21
David Menzies 1921–26
Colin Veitch 1926–28
Peter O'Rourke 1928–30
Jack Peart 1930–35
Dick Ray 1935–37
Fred Westgarth 1938–43
Bob Sharp 1943–46
Jack Barker 1946–47
John Milburn 1947–48
David Steele 1948–52
Albert Harris 1952
Ivor Powell 1952–55
Peter Jackson 1955–61
Bob Brocklebank 1961–64
Bill Harris 1965–66
Willie Watson 1966–69
Grenville Hair 1967–68
Jimmy Wheeler 1968–71
Bryan Edwards 1971–75
Bobby Kennedy 1975–78
John Napier 1978
George Mulhall 1978–81
Roy McFarland 1981–82
Trevor Cherry 1982–87
Terry Dolan 1987–89
Terry Yorath 1989–90
John Docherty 1990–91
Frank Stapleton 1991–94
Lennie Lawrence 1994–95
Chris Kamara 1995–98
Paul Jewell 1998–2000
Chris Hutchings 2000
Jim Jefferies 2000–01
Nicky Law 2001–03
Bryan Robson 2003–04
Colin Todd 2004–07
Stuart McCall 2007–10
Peter Taylor 2010–11
Peter Jackson 2011
Phil Parkinson August 2011–

TEN YEAR LEAGUE RECORD

		P	W	D	L	F	A	Pts	Pos
2004-05	FL 1	46	17	14	15	64	62	65	11
2005-06	FL 1	46	14	19	13	51	49	61	11
2006-07	FL 1	46	11	14	21	47	65	47	22
2007-08	FL 2	46	17	11	18	63	61	62	10
2008-09	FL 2	46	18	13	15	66	55	67	9
2009-10	FL 2	46	16	14	16	59	62	62	14
2010-11	FL 2	46	15	7	24	43	68	52	18
2011-12	FL 2	46	12	14	20	54	59	50	18
2012-13	FL 2	46	18	15	13	63	52	69	7
2013-14	FL 1	46	14	17	15	57	54	59	11

DID YOU KNOW ?

Len Shackleton appeared as a guest for Bradford City in their derby clash at Huddersfield Town on the afternoon of Christmas Day 1940 having played in the morning for the Bantams' city rivals Bradford Park Avenue at Leeds United. He finished on the winning side for City as they triumphed 4-3 but Avenue went down 2-1.

BRADFORD CITY – FOOTBALL LEAGUE ONE 2013–14 LEAGUE RECORD

Match No.	Date	Venue	Opponents	Result	H/T Score	Lg Pos.	Goalscorers	Attendance
1	Aug 3	A	Bristol C	D	2-2	1-1	10	Wells [33], McArdle [79]	13,862
2	10	H	Carlisle U	W	4-0	3-0	5	Yeates [20], Wells [25], Hanson [29], Jones [67]	13,641
3	17	A	Port Vale	L	1-2	0-1	9	Wells [60]	6552
4	24	H	Sheffield U	W	2-0	1-0	6	Wells 2 [45, 87]	18,041
5	31	A	Stevenage	D	1-1	0-1	7	Reid [48]	3242
6	Sept 7	H	Brentford	W	4-0	1-0	5	Hanson 2 [41, 69], Wells [60], Thompson [64]	13,621
7	14	H	Colchester U	D	2-2	1-2	7	Wells 2 [15, 53]	13,570
8	21	A	Gillingham	W	1-0	1-0	6	Jones [9]	4965
9	28	A	Shrewsbury T	W	2-1	0-1	5	Reid [60], Hanson [90]	14,128
10	Oct 5	A	Walsall	W	2-0	1-0	4	Reid [45], Hanson [47]	5364
11	13	H	Tranmere R	L	0-1	0-0	4		14,674
12	19	A	Crawley T	L	0-1	0-0	5		3836
13	22	A	Preston NE	D	2-2	1-1	5	Hanson [5], McArdle [73]	11,485
14	26	H	Wolverhampton W	L	1-2	1-2	6	De Vita [14]	18,044
15	Nov 2	A	Crewe Alex	D	0-0	0-0	6		5428
16	17	H	Coventry C	D	3-3	2-3	7	Wells 3 (1 pen) [17, 28, 90 (p)]	14,322
17	23	H	Milton Keynes D	W	3-2	2-1	6	Wells [21], Reid [43], Kennedy [85]	8970
18	26	H	Notts Co	D	1-1	0-1	6	Yeates [69]	12,808
19	Dec 1	A	Oldham Ath	D	1-1	1-1	8	Wells [21]	7180
20	14	H	Leyton Orient	D	1-1	0-1	7	Wells [90]	14,292
21	21	A	Peterborough U	L	1-2	0-2	9	Gray [76]	6597
22	26	H	Rotherham U	L	0-1	0-1	11		18,218
23	29	H	Swindon T	D	1-1	1-0	10	McArdle [16]	13,461
24	Jan 1	A	Notts Co	L	0-3	0-1	12		4919
25	11	A	Bristol C	D	1-1	1-1	12	Hanson [1]	13,050
26	18	A	Sheffield U	D	2-2	0-2	13	Jones [56], Hanson [63]	18,794
27	28	H	Preston NE	D	0-0	0-0	12		13,686
28	Feb 1	A	Wolverhampton W	L	0-2	0-1	13		19,498
29	8	H	Crewe Alex	D	3-3	0-1	13	Hanson [58], Jones 2 [50, 84]	13,343
30	11	A	Carlisle U	L	0-1	0-1	13		3267
31	18	H	Port Vale	W	1-0	0-0	11	McHugh [90]	12,106
32	22	H	Milton Keynes D	W	1-0	0-0	11	Hanson [72]	13,501
33	Mar 1	H	Stevenage	L	2-3	2-1	11	Reach [11], Hanson [42]	13,033
34	8	A	Brentford	L	0-2	0-0	13		8063
35	11	A	Colchester U	W	2-0	1-0	11	Hanson [16], Bennett [56]	2605
36	15	H	Gillingham	D	1-1	1-0	12	McLean [10]	13,089
37	22	A	Shrewsbury T	L	1-2	0-0	13	Davies [79]	5181
38	25	H	Walsall	L	0-2	1-0	15		12,165
39	29	A	Leyton Orient	W	1-0	1-0	12	McLean [27]	5165
40	Apr 1	A	Coventry C	D	0-0	0-0	12		1673
41	5	H	Oldham Ath	L	2-3	1-2	12	Reach [36], Jones [90]	14,920
42	11	A	Rotherham U	D	0-0	0-0	12		9228
43	18	H	Peterborough U	W	1-0	1-0	13	Reach [26]	13,820
44	21	A	Swindon T	L	0-1	0-0	14		8377
45	26	H	Crawley T	W	2-1	0-0	13	McLean [49], Thompson [85]	13,247
46	May 3	A	Tranmere R	W	2-1	0-1	11	Stead [81], McLean [87]	9598

Final League Position: 11

GOALSCORERS

League (57): Wells 14 (1 pen), Hanson 12, Jones 6, McLean 4, Reid 4, McArdle 3, Reach 3, Thompson 2, Yeates 2, Bennett 1, Davies 1, De Vita 1, Gray 1, Kennedy 1, McHugh 1, Stead 1.
The Budweiser FA Cup (0).
Capital One Cup (1): Wells 1.
Johnstone's Paint Trophy (0).

McLaughlin J 46	Darby S 46	Meredith J 24+2	Jones G 43+2	McArdle R 41	Davies A 28	Thompson G 29+15	Ravenhill R 4+4	Wells N 18+1	Hanson J 34+1	Yeates M 10+19	Reid K 21+5	De Vita R 6+14	Doyle N 33+5	Connell A —+13	Oliver L 3+1	Taylor M 1+1	Kennedy J 5+3	Folan C —+6	Bates M 20+2	McBurnie O 2+6	Gray A 2+6	McHugh C 11+3	Clarkson L —+1	McLean A 18+2	Bennett K 14+4	Reach A 18	Atkinson C 1+3	Graham J —+1	Dolan M 9+2	Drury A 11+1	Stead J 8	Match No.
1	2	3	4	5	6	7^2	8	9	10	11^1	12	13																				1
1	2	5	8	4	3	6^1			11^1	10	9^3	13	12		7	14																2
1	2^3	4	7	5	3	9^1		11	10		6^2	12	13	8	14																	3
1	2	5	8	4	3	6^1	14	11	10		9^3	12	13	7^2																		4
1	2	5	7	4	3	6^1	13	10	11	14	9^3	12	8^2																			5
1	2	5	7		3	6		10^3	11	13	9^1		8	12	4^2	14																6
1	2	5	8	4	3	6^2	14	11	10	13	9^2	12	7^1																			7
1	2	5	7	4	3	6		11^2	10	12	9^1		8	13																		8
1	2	5	8		3	6^2		10^3	11	12	9	13	7	14	4^1																	9
1	2	5	8	3	4	7		11^2	10^3	6^1	14	9					12	13														10
1	2	5	8			6^3		11	10	9	14	4	13	3^1			7^2	12														11
1	2	5	8	3		6^3		11	10^2	9	13	7	14					12	4^1													12
1	2	5	7	4		11^1		10		9	6^2	8					12	13	3													13
1	2	5	8	3		11^3		12	10	13	9	6^2	7					14	4^1													14
1	2	5	7	4		12		11^3	10	13	9^1	6^2	8					14	3													15
1	2	5	8	3		6^2		10	11	12	9^1	14	7	13					4^3													16
1	2	5	7	4		6^1		11	10	13	9^2		12				8		3													17
1	2	5	8	4		6^1		11^2	10	13	9		12	14			7^3		3													18
1	2	5	7	4		6^2		11^1	10	12	9		8						3	13												19
1	2	5	7	3		6^3		11	10	12	9	14	8^2	13					4^1													20
1	5	9	8	2		10^2		11		7	13		6	14		3^1			4^3	12												21
1	2	5	8			6^2		10		12	9		7	13	14				4	11^1		3^3										22
1	2	5	7	3		6^3	8^2	11^1	10	12	9		13							14		4										23
1	2	5	8	4		11^2	7		10	13	9						6^1		3^3	12			14									24
1	2	7	4			6	8^3		10	13	9^1		14				12		3	11^1	5											25
1	2	8	3			6			11	12	9^2		13				7^1		4		14	5		10^3								26
1	2	7	4	3			13		10				8^2						5	12				11^1	6^8	9						27
1	5	7	4			9^1							8^8						3	13	10^1	2		11^3	6	12	14					28
1	2	8	4	12		10													3				5	11	6^1	9		7				29
1	2	7	5	4		6^1		11^2			12						3		14					10	13	9		8^3				30
1	2	7	4	3	12			10					8						13	5				11^1	6^2	9						31
1	2	7	4	3	12			10					8							5				11^2	6^3	9^1	13	14				32
1	2	7	4	3^2	6^1			10	13				8						12	14	5			11^1		9						33
1	2	7	3		14								8						4		12	5^1		11^3	6	9	10^2			13		34
1	2		3	4	12			10					7								13			11	6^1	9		8	5^2			35
1	2	12	4	3	13			10					8											11^2	6	9		7^1	5			36
1	2	12	4	3	13			10					8^1											11^2	6	9		7	5			37
1	2	7^1	4	3	12			13					8									10³		11^1	6^2	9		14	5			38
1	2	8	3	4	13								14										12	11^1	6	9		7	5^2	10^3		39
1	2	8	3	4	13																		5	10	6^2	9	12	7^1		11		40
1	2	7	3	4	12			14															13	11^1	6^3	9		8	5	10^2		41
1	2	7	3	4	13						12	8												11^1	6^2	9		9^1	5	11		42
1	2	7	4	3				10			6^1	8												12	13	9			5	11^{12}		43
1	2	12	7	4	3	14					6^1	8^3												13	9^2	11			5	10		44
1	2	8	4^1	3	13			9			6^3	7										12		10^2	14			5	11		45
1	2	12	8	3	4	6^2		9			14	7^1												10	13				5^3	11		46

The Budweiser FA Cup
First Round   Rotherham U   (a)   0-3

Capital One Cup
First Round   Huddersfield T   (a)   1-2

Johnstone's Paint Trophy
First Round   Hartlepool U   (a)   0-5

BRENTFORD

FOUNDATION

Formed as a small amateur concern in 1889 they were very
successful in local circles. They won the championship of the West
London Alliance in 1893 and a year later the West Middlesex
Junior Cup before carrying off the Senior Cup in 1895. After
winning both the London Senior Amateur Cup and the Middlesex
Senior Cup in 1898 they were admitted to the Second Division of
the Southern League.

*Griffin Park, Braemar Road, Brentford, Middlesex
TW8 0NT.*

Telephone: (0845) 3456 442.

Fax: (020) 8380 9937.

Ticket Office: (0845) 3456 442 (option 4).

Website: www.brentfordfc.co.uk

Email: enquiries@brentfordfc.co.uk

Ground Capacity: 12,763.

Record Attendance: 38,678 v Leicester C, FA Cup 6th rd,
26 February 1949.

Pitch Measurements: 101.5m × 68.5m (111yd × 75yd)

Chairman: Cliff Crown.

Chief Executive: Mark Devlin.

Manager: Mark Warburton.

Assistant Manager: David Weir.

Physio: Daryl Martin.

Colours: Red and white striped shirts, black shorts, black
socks with white hoops.

Year Formed: 1889.

Turned Professional: 1899.

Club Nickname: 'The Bees'.

HONOURS

Football League – Division 1: Best
season: 5th, 1935–36;
Division 2: *Champions* 1934–35,
1994–95; **Division 3:** *Champions*
1991–92, 1998–99;
Division 3 (S): *Champions* 1932–33,
Runners-up 1929–30, 1957–58;
Division 4: *Champions* 1962–63;
FL 1: *Runners-up* 2013–14.
FL 2: *Champions* 2008–09.
FA Cup: Best season: 6th rd, 1938,
1946, 1949, 1989.
Football League Cup: Best season:
4th rd, 1983, 2011.
Freight Rover Trophy:
Runners-up 1985.
LDV Vans Trophy: *Runners-up* 2001.
Johnstone's Paint Trophy:
Runners-up 2011.

Grounds: 1889, Clifden Road; 1891, Benns Fields, Little Ealing; 1895, Shotters Field; 1898, Cross
Road, S. Ealing; 1900, Boston Park; 1904, Griffin Park.

First Football League Game: 28 August 1920, Division 3, v Exeter C (a) L 0–3 – Young; Hodson,
Rosier, Jimmy Elliott, Levitt, Amos, Smith, Thompson, Spreadbury, Morley, Henery.

Record League Victory: 9–0 v Wrexham, Division 3, 15 October 1963 – Cakebread; Coote, Jones;
Slater, Scott, Higginson; Summers (1), Brooks (2), McAdams (2), Ward (2), Hales (1), (1 og).

Record Cup Victory: 7–0 v Windsor & Eton (away), FA Cup 1st rd, 20 November 1982 – Roche;
Rowe, Harris (Booker), McNichol (1), Whitehead, Hurlock (2), Kamara, Joseph (1), Mahoney (3),
Bowles, Roberts. *N.B.* 8–0 v Uxbridge: Frail, Jock Watson, Caie, Bellingham, Parsonage (1), Jay,
Atherton, Leigh (1), Bell (2), Buchanan (2), Underwood (2), FA Cup, 3rd Qual rd, 31 October 1903.

sky SPORTS FACT FILE

In 1918–19 Brentford, then members of the Southern League, beat off
the challenge of a number of top clubs to finish as champions of the
London Combination which had been formed to provide a regional
competition for teams in the capital. The Bees netted 94 goals from 36
games and finished the campaign four points clear of runners-up Arsenal.

Record Defeat: 0–7 v Swansea T, Division 3 (S), 8 November 1924; v Walsall, Division 3 (S), 19 January 1957; v Peterborough U, 24 November 2007.

Most League Points (2 for a win): 62, Division 3 (S), 1932–33 and Division 4, 1962–63.

Most League Points (3 for a win): 94, FL 1, 2013–14.

Most League Goals: 98, Division 4, 1962–63.

Highest League Scorer in Season: Jack Holliday, 38, Division 3 (S), 1932–33.

Most League Goals in Total Aggregate: Jim Towers, 153, 1954–61.

Most League Goals in One Match: 5, Jack Holliday v Luton T, Division 3 (S), 28 January 1933; 5, Billy Scott v Barnsley, Division 2, 15 December 1934; 5, Peter McKennan v Bury, Division 2, 18 February 1949.

Most Capped Player: John Buttigieg, 22 (98), Malta.

Most League Appearances: Ken Coote, 514, 1949–64.

Youngest League Player: Danis Salman, 15 years 248 days v Watford, 15 November 1975.

Record Transfer Fee Received: £2,500,000 from Wimbledon for Hermann Hreidarsson, October 1999.

Record Transfer Fee Paid: £750,000 to Crystal Palace for Hermann Hreidarsson, September 1998.

Football League Record: 1920 Original Member of Division 3; 1921–33 Division 3 (S); 1933–35 Division 2; 1935–47 Division 1; 1947–54 Division 2; 1954–62 Division 3 (S); 1962–63 Division 4; 1963–66 Division 3; 1966–72 Division 4; 1972–73 Division 3; 1973–78 Division 4; 1978–92 Division 3; 1992–93 Division 1; 1993–98 Division 2; 1998–99 Division 3; 1999–2004 Division 2; 2004–07 FL 1; 2007–09 FL 2; 2009–14 FL 1; 2014– FL C.

LATEST SEQUENCES

Longest Sequence of League Wins: 9, 30.4.1932 – 24.9.1932.

Longest Sequence of League Defeats: 9, 20.10.1928 – 25.12.1928.

Longest Sequence of League Draws: 5, 16.3.1957 – 6.4.1957.

Longest Sequence of Unbeaten League Matches: 26, 20.2.1999 – 16.10.1999.

Longest Sequence Without a League Win: 18, 9.9.2006 – 26.12.2006.

Successive Scoring Runs: 26 from 4.3.1963.

Successive Non-scoring Runs: 7 from 7.3.2000.

MANAGERS

Will Lewis 1900–03 (*Secretary-Manager*)
Dick Molyneux 1902–06
W. G. Brown 1906–08
Fred Halliday 1908–12, 1915–21, 1924–26 (*only Secretary to 1922*)
Ephraim Rhodes 1912–15
Archie Mitchell 1921–24
Harry Curtis 1926–49
Jackie Gibbons 1949–52
Jimmy Bain 1952–53
Tommy Lawton 1953
Bill Dodgin Snr 1953–57
Malcolm Macdonald 1957–65
Tommy Cavanagh 1965–66
Billy Gray 1966–67
Jimmy Sirrel 1967–69
Frank Blunstone 1969–73
Mike Everitt 1973–75
John Docherty 1975–76
Bill Dodgin Jnr 1976–80
Fred Callaghan 1980–84
Frank McLintock 1984–87
Steve Perryman 1987–90
Phil Holder 1990–93
David Webb 1993–97
Eddie May 1997
Micky Adams 1997–98
Ron Noades 1998–2000
Ray Lewington 2000–01
Steve Coppell 2001–02
Wally Downes 2002–04
Martin Allen 2004–06
Leroy Rosenior 2006
Scott Fitzgerald 2006–07
Terry Butcher 2007
Andy Scott 2007–11
Nicky Forster 2011
Uwe Rosler 2011–13
Mark Warburton December 2013–

TEN YEAR LEAGUE RECORD

		P	W	D	L	F	A	Pts	Pos
2004-05	FL 1	46	22	9	15	57	60	75	4
2005-06	FL 1	46	20	16	10	72	52	76	3
2006-07	FL 1	46	8	13	25	40	79	37	24
2007-08	FL 2	46	17	8	21	52	70	59	14
2008-09	FL 2	46	23	16	7	65	36	85	1
2009-10	FL 1	46	14	20	12	55	52	62	9
2010-11	FL 1	46	17	10	19	55	62	61	11
2011-12	FL 1	46	18	13	15	63	52	67	9
2012-13	FL 1	46	21	16	9	62	47	79	3
2013-14	FL 1	46	28	10	8	72	43	94	2

DID YOU KNOW ?

Former England centre-forward Tommy Lawton lasted just nine months as player-manager of Brentford after taking charge of the then Second Division club in January 1953. Lawton began with a victory over Hull City but by September had stepped down to concentrate on playing and within a fortnight left the club to join Arsenal.

BRENTFORD – FOOTBALL LEAGUE ONE 2013–14 LEAGUE RECORD

Match No.	Date	Venue	Opponents	Result	H/T Score	Lg Pos.	Goalscorers	Attendance
1	Aug 3	A	Port Vale	D	1-1	1-1	12	Logan [27]	7579
2	10	H	Sheffield U	W	3-1	1-0	7	Forshaw [35], Grigg 2 [63, 76]	7316
3	17	A	Gillingham	D	1-1	0-1	6	El Alagui [90]	6225
4	24	H	Walsall	W	1-0	1-0	4	Donaldson [42]	5781
5	31	H	Carlisle U	D	0-0	0-0	4		6035
6	Sept 7	A	Bradford C	L	0-4	0-1	8		13,621
7	14	A	Tranmere R	W	4-3	2-1	8	Taylor [3], Donaldson 2 [14, 71], Forshaw (pen) [90]	4454
8	23	H	Leyton Orient	L	0-2	0-0	10		6439
9	29	A	Coventry C	W	2-0	1-0	10	Donaldson [22], Taylor [68]	2650
10	Oct 5	H	Rotherham U	L	0-1	0-1	10		6614
11	12	A	Stevenage	L	1-2	1-2	11	Donaldson [13]	3225
12	19	H	Colchester U	W	3-1	1-0	11	Trotta [76], Saville [80], Harris [87]	5705
13	22	A	Bristol C	W	2-1	0-0	7	Saunders [79], Donaldson [86]	10,639
14	26	H	Shrewsbury T	W	1-0	1-0	5	Trotta [16]	9783
15	Nov 2	A	Crawley T	W	1-0	1-0	5	Forshaw (pen) [5]	4177
16	16	H	Crewe Alex	W	5-0	1-0	4	Trotta [43], Forshaw [46], Saville [58], Donaldson 2 [63, 73]	6616
17	23	A	Wolverhampton W	D	0-0	0-0	4		19,061
18	26	H	Peterborough U	W	3-2	1-0	4	Zakuani (og) [36], Grigg [81], Donaldson [87]	6014
19	30	A	Notts Co	W	1-0	1-0	4	Grigg [44]	5132
20	Dec 14	H	Oldham Ath	W	1-0	0-0	3	Douglas [90]	6594
21	21	A	Preston NE	W	3-0	2-0	3	Forshaw (pen) [23], Trotta [26], Saunders [73]	10,332
22	26	A	Swindon T	W	3-2	1-1	3	Saunders [27], Donaldson [55], Trotta [71]	8333
23	29	H	Milton Keynes D	W	3-1	1-0	1	Donaldson [2], Trotta [52], Saunders [58]	8010
24	Jan 1	A	Peterborough U	W	3-1	2-1	1	Forshaw (pen) [16], Saunders [36], Donaldson [90]	6343
25	11	H	Port Vale	W	2-0	1-0	1	Trotta [30], Grigg [88]	8327
26	18	A	Walsall	D	1-1	1-1	2	Donaldson [30]	5295
27	24	H	Gillingham	W	2-1	1-0	1	Douglas [22], Trotta (pen) [70]	7713
28	28	H	Bristol C	W	3-1	3-1	1	Flint (og) [9], Judge [26], Trotta [42]	6517
29	Feb 1	A	Shrewsbury T	D	1-1	0-0	1	Trotta [68]	4927
30	15	A	Crewe Alex	W	3-1	1-0	1	Judge 2 [9, 52], Forshaw [61]	4812
31	22	H	Wolverhampton W	L	0-3	0-1	3		11,309
32	Mar 1	A	Carlisle U	D	0-0	0-0	3		3984
33	8	H	Bradford C	W	2-0	0-0	3	Donaldson [61], Saville [76]	8063
34	11	H	Tranmere R	W	2-0	0-0	3	Tarkowski [62], Donaldson [74]	5646
35	15	H	Leyton Orient	W	1-0	1-0	2	Trotta [45]	8335
36	22	H	Coventry C	W	3-1	2-1	2	Donaldson [17], Trotta [20], McCormack [48]	8572
37	25	A	Rotherham U	L	0-3	0-2	2		8365
38	29	A	Oldham Ath	D	0-0	0-0	2		4087
39	Apr 1	A	Sheffield U	D	0-0	0-0	2		15,730
40	5	H	Notts Co	W	3-1	2-0	2	Forshaw (pen) [32], Judge 2 [43, 52]	8188
41	8	H	Crawley T	W	1-0	0-0	2	Douglas [58]	7718
42	12	A	Swindon T	L	0-1	0-1	2		9342
43	18	H	Preston NE	W	1-0	1-0	2	Judge (pen) [30]	10,774
44	21	A	Milton Keynes D	D	2-2	1-0	2	Tarkowski [45], Donaldson [59]	10,549
45	26	A	Colchester U	L	1-4	1-3	2	Dallas [45]	6400
46	May 3	H	Stevenage	W	2-0	0-0	2	Dallas [77], Judge [90]	11,393

Final League Position: 2

GOALSCORERS

League (72): Donaldson 17, Trotta 12 (1 pen), Forshaw 8 (5 pens), Judge 7 (1 pen), Grigg 5, Saunders 5, Douglas 3, Saville 3, Dallas 2, Tarkowski 2, Taylor 2, El Alagui 1, Harris 1, Logan 1, McCormack 1, own goals 2.
The Budweiser FA Cup (7): McCormack 1 (1 pen), Donaldson 1, El Alagui 1, Harris 1, Reeves 1, Trotta 1, own goal 1.
Capital One Cup (3): El Alagui 2, Fillo 1.
Johnstone's Paint Trophy (6): El Alagui 2, Nugent 2, Norris 1, Venta 1.

Button D 42	Logan S 14 + 4	Bidwell J 38	McCormack A 43	O'Connor K 6 + 3	Dean H 30 + 2	Saville G 33 + 7	Forshaw A 36 + 3	Donaldson C 46	Grigg W 16 + 18	McAleny C 3 + 1	Fillo M 4 + 3	Reeves J 6 + 14	Craig T 43 + 1	El Alagui F 1 + 11	Diagouraga T 10 + 9	Venta R — + 1	Barron S 2	Saunders S 6 + 11	Trotta M 28 + 9	Bonham J — + 1	Dallas S 6 + 12	Lee R 4	Taylor M 5	Teixeira J — + 2	Douglas J 35	Norris L — + 1	Harris K 9 + 1	Judge A 22	Akpom C — + 4	Yennaris N 5 + 3	Tarkowski J 13	Adams C — + 3	Clarke J — + 1	Match No.
1	2	3	4	5	6	7	8^2	9	10	11^1	12	13																						1
1	2	5	8^3		4	7	6	10	11^1	9^2	12	13	3	14																				2
1	2	5^1	7		3	9	6	10	11^3	13			4	14	8^2	12																		3
1	2		8		4	7	6	10			11^2	9^1	14		3	12^2		5	13															4
1	2		9		4	8^1	7	11	12			13	3^1	10^2	14		5	6^1																5
1^4	5		2		4	7^1	8	11				9	6	3					10^2	12	13													6
	2		8^1		3	9^2	7	11	10^9		12		5		6				13				1	4	14									7
	2		6^2		3		9	10	11^3		7^1		5		8				13		14		1	4	12									8
	2		7^1		3		6	11	8^2		10^3	14	5	13	9		12						1	4										9
1	2		7^1		4	14	6	11	12				5	13	8^3			9	10^2					3										10
1	2^2	5	9		3	14	6	10				12		8				11^1				4^3		7	13									11
1		5	2		4	8	6^1	9	10^2				3	14				12	11^3					7		13								12
1		5	2		4	8	6	11	10^1				3					13	12				1	7		9^2								13
1		5	2		4	8	6^1	11	14				3		13			12	10^3					7		9^2								14
1		5	2		3	6^1	8	9	14				4		12			13	10^2					7		11^3								15
1		5	2		3	7	6^3	10	12			14	4	13				11^1						8		9^2								16
1		5	2		4	8^1	6	9	12				3	14				13	10^1					7		11^3								17
1		5	2		4	8^1	7	9	12				3	13				14	10^3					6		11^1								18
1	13	5	2^3		4	12	6	9	10				3		8^2			14						7		11^1								19
1		5	2		4	7^3	9	8	11^1				3	14				12	13					6		10^2								20
1		5	2		4	8	6	9	13			14	3					12	10^3					7		11^2								21
1		5	2		4		7	9	11^2			13	3	14				8^3	10^1	12				6										22
1	13	5	10^3		3	2	9^2	11					4	14				6	7^1	12				8										23
1	14	5	7		4		2	10				8^2	3		12			6^1	11	13				9^3										24
1	2	5	3	7		8		10	13				12	4				6^2	9							11^1								25
1	12	5	2	3		9		8	10^3				4					11^2	14				6			7^1	13							26
1	2	5	8	3		9		10					4					11^1					7			6	12							27
1	2	5	8^1	3		6		10	13				12	4				11^3					7			9^2	14							28
1		5	7		4	8	12	10	14				3					11^3					6			9^2	13	2^1						29
1		5	2		4	6	7^1	10	12			13	3					11^2	14				6			9^3								30
1		2	5		4	9^1	8	10	12				3					11					7			6								31
1		5				8	6	9	12				4					10^1					7			11			2	3				32
1		5	2		6	7^2	10^3	11^1				12	3					13	14				8			9				4				33
1		5	2		6^2	12	10	11^1				8	4					13					7			9^3				3	14			34
1		5	2	12		9	6	11					4					10^1					7			8				3^4				35
1		5	2		4	7^1	13	10				8^1	3					9	14				6			11^2	12							36
1		5	2		4		7^1	9	13			8	3					10^3					6			11^2	12		14					37
1		5	6		3		8	9	10^2					13				12	14				7			11^3		2^1	4					38
1		5	2			12	8	7					3	10^2				11	13				6			9^1			4					39
1		5	2	12	13	6^3	10	14					3	8					9				7			11			4^2					40
1		5	2		8^1	6^3	10					12	3	14				13	9				7			11^2			4					41
1	5^1	2			12	6^4	10	14					3	8^3				11^2	13				7			9			4					42
1	5	2			7^3		11	13					4	14				9^2	10^1				8			6			3					43
1	5		12		13	7	11	9					4	14					10				8^3			6^2		2	3^1					44
1		2^1	14		9		6						4					10^2	8				7			11		5^3	3	12	13		45
1	5	2	12		7^2		11^3						10	3^1				13	6				9			8		14	4				46

The Budweiser FA Cup

First Round	Staines T	(h)	5-0
Second Round	Carlisle U	(a)	2-3

Capital One Cup

First Round	Dagenham & R	(h)	3-2
Second Round	Derby Co	(a)	0-5

Johnstone's Paint Trophy

First Round	AFC Wimbledon	(h)	5-3
Second Round	Peterborough U	(a)	1-2

BRIGHTON & HOVE ALBION

FOUNDATION

A professional club Brighton United was formed in November 1897 at the Imperial Hotel, Queen's Road, but folded in March 1900 after less than two seasons in the Southern League at the County Ground. An amateur team Brighton & Hove Rangers was then formed by some prominent United supporters and after one season at Withdean, decided to turn semi-professional and play at the County Ground. Rangers were accepted into the Southern League but folded in June 1901. John Jackson, the former United manager, organised a meeting at the Seven Stars public house, Ship Street on 24 June 1901 at which a new third club Brighton & Hove United was formed. They took over Rangers' place in the Southern League and pitch at County Ground. The name was changed to Brighton & Hove Albion before a match was played because of objections by Hove FC.

American Express Community Stadium, Village Way, Falmer, Brighton BN1 9BL.
Telephone: (0844) 324 6282.
Fax: (01273) 878 238.
Ticket Office: (0844) 327 1901.
Website: www.seagulls.co.uk
Email: supporterservices@bhafc.co.uk
Ground Capacity: 30,303.
Record Attendance: 36,747 v Fulham, Division 2, 27 December 1958 (at Goldstone Ground);
8,691 v Leeds U, FL 1, 20 October 2007 (at Withdean);
30,003 v Wolverhampton W, 4 May 2013 (at Amex).
Pitch Measurements: 105m × 68m (115yd × 74.5yd)
Chairman: Tony Bloom.
Chief Executive: Paul Barber.
Manager: Sammi Hyypia.
First Team Coach: Nathan Jones.
Physio: Adam Brett.
Colours: Blue and white striped shirts with white sleeves and yellow trim, blue shorts, white socks with thin yellow stripes.
Year Formed: 1901.
Turned Professional: 1901.
Club Nickname: 'The Seagulls'.
Grounds: 1901, County Ground; 1902, Goldstone Ground; 1997, groundshare at Gillingham FC; 1999, Withdean Stadium; 2011, American Express Community Stadium.
First Football League Game: 28 August 1920, Division 3, v Southend U (a) L 0–2 – Hayes; Woodhouse, Little; Hall, Comber, Bentley; Longstaff, Ritchie, Doran, Rodgerson, March.
Record League Victory: 9–1 v Newport Co, Division 3 (S), 18 April 1951 – Ball; Tennant (1p), Mansell (1p); Willard, McCoy, Wilson; Reed, McNichol (4), Garbutt, Bennett (2), Keene (1). 9–1 v Southend U, Division 3, 27 November 1965 – Powney; Magill, Baxter; Leck, Gall, Turner; Gould (1), Collins (1), Livesey (2), Smith (3), Goodchild (2).

HONOURS

Football League – Division 1: Best season: 13th, 1981–82;
Division 2: *Champions* 2001–02;
Runners-up 1978–79;
FL 1: *Champions* 2010–11.
Division 3 (S): *Champions* 1957–58;
Runners-up 1953–54, 1955–56;
Division 3: *Champions* 2000–01;
Runners-up 1971–72, 1976–77, 1987–88;
Division 4: *Champions* 1964–65.
FA Cup: *Runners-up* 1983.
Football League Cup: Best season: 5th rd, 1979.
Charity Shield: *Winners* 1910.

sky SPORTS FACT FILE

For the first five years of the FA Charity Shield the fixture was played between the champions of the Football League and the champions of the Southern League. Brighton & Hove Albion, by defeating Aston Villa 1-0 in September 1910, were the only Southern League team to be successful.

Record Cup Victory: 10–1 v Wisbech, FA Cup 1st rd, 13 November 1965 – Powney; Magill, Baxter; Collins (1), Gall, Turner; Gould, Smith (2), Livesey (3), Cassidy (2), Goodchild (1), (1 og).

Record Defeat: 0–9 v Middlesbrough, Division 2, 23 August 1958.

Most League Points (2 for a win): 65, Division 3 (S), 1955–56 and Division 3, 1971–72.

Most League Points (3 for a win): 95, FL 1, 2010–11.

Most League Goals: 112, Division 3 (S), 1955–56.

Highest League Scorer in Season: Peter Ward, 32, Division 3, 1976–77.

Most League Goals in Total Aggregate: Tommy Cook, 114, 1922–29.

Most League Goals in One Match: 5, Jack Doran v Northampton T, Division 3 (S), 5 November 1921; 5, Adrian Thorne v Watford, Division 3 (S), 30 April 1958.

Most Capped Player: Steve Penney, 17, Northern Ireland.

Most League Appearances: 'Tug' Wilson, 509, 1922–36.

Youngest League Player: Ian Chapman, 16 years 259 days v Birmingham C, 14 February 1987.

Record Transfer Fee Received: £8,000,000 from Leicester C for Leonardo Ulloa, July 2014.

Record Transfer Fee Paid: £2,500,000 to Peterborough U for Craig Mackail-Smith, July 2011.

Football League Record: 1920 Original Member of Division 3; 1921–58 Division 3 (S); 1958–62 Division 2; 1962–63 Division 3; 1963–65 Division 4; 1965–72 Division 3; 1972–73 Division 2; 1973–77 Division 3; 1977–79 Division 2; 1979–83 Division 1; 1983–87 Division 2; 1987–88 Division 3; 1988–96 Division 2; 1996–2001 Division 3; 2001–02 Division 2; 2002–03 Division 1; 2003–04 Division 2; 2004–06 FL C; 2006–11 FL 1; 2011– FL C.

LATEST SEQUENCES

Longest Sequence of League Wins: 9, 2.10.1926 – 20.11.1926.

Longest Sequence of League Defeats: 12, 17.8.2002 – 26.10.2002.

Longest Sequence of League Draws: 6, 16.2.1980 – 15.3.1980.

Longest Sequence of Unbeaten League Matches: 16, 8.10.1930 – 28.1.1931.

Longest Sequence Without a League Win: 15, 21.10.1972 – 27.1.1973.

Successive Scoring Runs: 31 from 4.2.1956.

Successive Non-scoring Runs: 6 from 23.9.1970.

MANAGERS

John Jackson 1901–05
Frank Scott-Walford 1905–08
John Robson 1908–14
Charles Webb 1919–47
Tommy Cook 1947
Don Welsh 1947–51
Billy Lane 1951–61
George Curtis 1961–63
Archie Macaulay 1963–68
Fred Goodwin 1968–70
Pat Saward 1970–73
Brian Clough 1973–74
Peter Taylor 1974–76
Alan Mullery 1976–81
Mike Bailey 1981–82
Jimmy Melia 1982–83
Chris Cattlin 1983–86
Alan Mullery 1986–87
Barry Lloyd 1987–93
Liam Brady 1993–95
Jimmy Case 1995–96
Steve Gritt 1996–98
Brian Horton 1998–99
Jeff Wood 1999
Micky Adams 1999–2001
Peter Taylor 2001–02
Martin Hinshelwood 2002
Steve Coppell 2002–03
Mark McGhee 2003–06
Dean Wilkins 2006–08
Micky Adams 2008–09
Russell Slade 2009
Gus Poyet 2009–13
Óscar García 2013–14
Sammi Hyypia June 2014–

TEN YEAR LEAGUE RECORD

		P	W	D	L	F	A	Pts	Pos
2004-05	FL C	46	13	12	21	40	65	51	20
2005-06	FL C	46	7	17	22	39	71	38	24
2006-07	FL 1	46	14	11	21	49	58	53	18
2007-08	FL 1	46	19	12	15	58	50	69	7
2008-09	FL 1	46	13	13	20	55	70	52	16
2009-10	FL 1	46	15	14	17	56	60	59	13
2010-11	FL 1	46	28	11	7	85	40	95	1
2011-12	FL C	46	17	15	14	52	52	66	10
2012-13	FL C	46	19	18	9	69	43	75	4
2013-14	FL C	46	19	15	12	55	40	72	6

DID YOU KNOW

A total of 13 of the 17 professional players for Brighton & Hove Albion enlisted in the Footballers' Battalion during the First World War. Three of these – Jasper Batey, Charles Dexter and Bob Whiting – lost their lives in the conflict.

BRIGHTON & HOVE ALBION – FL CHAMPIONSHIP 2013–14 LEAGUE RECORD

Match No.	Date	Venue	Opponents	Result		H/T Score	Lg Pos.	Goalscorers	Attendance
1	Aug 3	A	Leeds U	L	1-2	1-1	15	Ulloa [13]	33,432
2	10	H	Derby Co	L	1-2	1-1	19	Ulloa [17]	26,238
3	17	A	Birmingham C	W	1-0	0-0	16	Crofts [73]	14,885
4	24	H	Burnley	W	2-0	1-0	10	Crofts [28], Ulloa [72]	26,007
5	31	H	Millwall	D	1-1	0-0	13	Ulloa [89]	26,804
6	Sept 15	A	Reading	D	0-0	0-0	14		18,306
7	18	A	QPR	D	0-0	0-0	13		17,246
8	21	H	Bolton W	W	3-1	0-1	10	Spearing (og) [53], Calderon [55], Buckley [57]	26,319
9	28	A	Ipswich T	L	0-2	0-2	12		16,474
10	Oct 1	H	Sheffield W	D	1-1	0-1	12	Andrews [89]	25,725
11	5	H	Nottingham F	L	1-3	1-0	14	Crofts [31]	27,755
12	19	A	Yeovil T	D	0-0	0-0	14		6873
13	28	H	Watford	D	1-1	0-1	16	Crofts [54]	27,657
14	Nov 2	A	Doncaster R	W	3-1	1-0	12	Forster-Caskey [8], Lita [85], Lopez [90]	7396
15	9	H	Blackburn R	W	3-0	1-0	10	Barnes 2 (1 pen) [35 (p), 77], Forster-Caskey [56]	27,912
16	23	A	Wigan Ath	W	1-0	0-0	9	Crofts [72]	14,057
17	30	A	Bournemouth	D	1-1	0-1	9	Barnes [55]	9870
18	Dec 3	H	Barnsley	L	1-2	0-1	11	Upson [63]	25,759
19	7	H	Leicester C	W	3-1	2-0	10	Barnes 2 (1 pen) [9, 77 (p)], Conway [28]	27,497
20	14	A	Middlesbrough	W	1-0	0-0	8	Upson [86]	13,635
21	21	H	Huddersfield T	D	0-0	0-0	8		27,155
22	26	A	Charlton Ath	L	2-3	1-1	9	Ulloa 2 [22, 90]	17,404
23	29	A	Blackpool	W	1-0	1-0	8	Calderon [38]	12,280
24	Jan 1	H	Bournemouth	D	1-1	0-1	7	Ward [89]	28,282
25	11	H	Birmingham C	W	1-0	0-0	6	Lopez [58]	26,796
26	18	A	Derby Co	L	0-1	0-0	7		25,392
27	28	A	Burnley	D	0-0	0-0	8		11,054
28	Feb 2	A	Watford	L	0-2	0-1	9		16,096
29	8	H	Doncaster R	W	1-0	0-0	8	Ulloa [75]	27,009
30	11	H	Leeds U	W	1-0	0-0	7	Ulloa [64]	27,700
31	22	H	Wigan Ath	L	1-2	0-1	8	Ulloa [78]	27,490
32	Mar 1	A	Millwall	W	1-0	1-0	8	Lopez (pen) [39]	12,149
33	8	H	Reading	D	1-1	1-0	8	Gunter (og) [16]	27,532
34	11	A	QPR	W	2-0	0-0	7	Ulloa [77], Ward [86]	28,019
35	15	A	Bolton W	W	2-0	1-0	8	Buckley 2 [13, 65]	15,336
36	22	H	Ipswich T	L	0-2	0-0	8		29,093
37	25	A	Sheffield W	L	0-1	0-0	9		18,192
38	29	H	Middlesbrough	L	0-2	0-0	9		27,486
39	Apr 1	A	Blackburn R	D	3-3	1-2	9	David Rodriguez [17], Greer [79], Stephens [88]	12,332
40	5	A	Barnsley	D	0-0	0-0	8		10,195
41	8	A	Leicester C	W	4-1	2-0	7	Ward [17], Lingard [24], Ulloa 2 [64, 60]	29,722
42	12	H	Charlton Ath	W	3-0	2-0	6	Lingard [11], Ulloa [43], Forster-Caskey [90]	28,770
43	18	A	Huddersfield T	D	1-1	0-1	6	Saltor [83]	13,460
44	21	H	Blackpool	D	1-1	0-0	6	Stephens [46]	27,610
45	25	H	Yeovil T	W	2-0	0-0	6	LuaLua [78], Lingard [90]	26,901
46	May 3	A	Nottingham F	W	2-1	0-1	6	Ward [53], Ulloa [90]	22,209

Final League Position: 6

GOALSCORERS

League (55): Ulloa 14, Barnes 5 (2 pens), Crofts 5, Ward 4, Buckley 3, Forster-Caskey 3, Lingard 3, Lopez 3 (1 pen), Calderon 2, Stephens 2, Upson 2, Andrews 1, Conway 1, David Rodriguez 1, Greer 1, Lita 1, LuaLua 1, Saltor 1, own goals 2.
The Budweiser FA Cup (6): Ulloa 2, Crofts 1, Ince 1, March 1, Obika 1.
Capital One Cup (1): Barnes 1.
Championship Play-Offs (2): Lingard 1, LuaLua 1.

Kuszczak T 41	Saltor B 31+2	Calderon I 18+5	Crofts A 23	Upson M 43	Greer G 40	Bridcutt L 8+3	Lopez D 26+8	Ulloa J 31+2	Orlandi A 9+5	Barnes A 17+5	Agustien K 5+6	Buckley W 20+10	LuaLua K 11+21	Maksimenko V 1	Ince R 26+2	Andrews K 28+3	March S 7+16	Ward S 44	Forster-Caskey J 19+9	Conway C 11+2	Barker G —+1	Lita L —+5	El-Abd A 5+4	Brezovan P 4	Chicksen A —+1	Obika J —+5	Stephens D 12+2	David Rodriguez S 6+4	Lingard J 15	Dunk L 4+2	Mackail-Smith C —+5	Ankergren C 1	Match No.
1	2	3	4	5	6	7	8^3	9	10^2	11^1	12	13	14																				1
1	2		4	3		8	10		9^1	7	11^2	13	5		6^3	12	14																2
1		2	8	4	3		9^2	11		13	6^3	10^1		14	7			5	12														3
1		2	7	3	4		6^1	10		8^3	11^2	12		9				6^1	14	5													4
1		2	7	3	4	11^2	10	12		8^3	9	13		6^1	14			5															5
1		2	6	4	3	9^1	10^4		12		13	11^2		7			5	8															6
1	13	2	6	4	3	9^2		10		12			14	7		5^3	8^1	11															7
1	13	2	6	4	3	8^3		10^1		9^2	11		7		14	5		12															8
1	6^1	2	8	4	3		10^3		9	12		7	13	5	14	11^2																	9
1	6	2^1	9	4	3	8^3	10^2	14	13	12	11		7		5																		10
1		2^2	6	4	3	12		10^1		9	11		7		5	8^3	13	14															11
1	2		6	4	3	12		10^1		9		8^2	7		5	14	11^3																12
1	2	13	6	4	3		10		9		8	5^1	7	11^2		12																	13
1	2^3	12	6	4	3	13		10		9^1		7		5	8^2	11	14																14
1	2		6	4	3	12	9^2		10^1		7		5	8^3	11	13	14																15
1	2		8	4	3	12	9^2		10		7^1		5	6	11	13																	16
1		2	8	4	3	12	9^3	13	10		7^2	14	5	6^1	11																		17
1	2		6	4	3	7	9^1		10^3	13	12		5	8^2	11	14																	18
	2	9		3^2	6	8^1		11			13	7		5		10		12	1														19
	2	13	6		4	8	9^1	14		10^3		12	7		5^4	11		3	1														20
	2		4		7	9	13	10	8^1	11^2	12	6		5				3	1														21
	2^1	12	8	4		6	11^2	10	13	14	9		7^3	5				3	1														22
1		2	8	4		7	14	10^3	11		9^2	13	6		5^1			3	12														23
1		8^3	4		6	9^2	10	14	13	12		11^1	7		5			3															24
1	2	6^2	4	3		9^3	10^3	13		11	8	7		5		14		12															25
1	2		4	3		8^2	11	10^1	14		7	6	12	5	9^3		13																26
1	2		4	3		9^2	10	12		11^1		6	7	13	5	8																	27
1	2		4	3		9^2	10	11^3		12		7	14	5	8^1											6	13						28
1	2		4	3		13	10	8^2		12		7	11^3	5										14	6	9^1							29
1	2		4	3			10^3	8		13	12	7		9^1	5									14	6	11^2							30
1	2		4	3		8^3	11	9		12	13	6		5^2										14	7	10^1							31
1	2		4	3		11^2	10	8^1		12		7	14	5	13									6		9^3							32
1	2		4	3^4		9^2	10			13		6	7	14	5	8^1										11^3	12						33
1	2		4				10			9^1	12	6	7	5	8^2									13	11	3							34
1	2			3			10			9^1		7	12	5	8									6	13	11^1	4						35
1	2		4	3			10			9^1	12	8	7	13	5	6^3										10^2	11	14					36
1	2		4	3			10			9^1	12	6	7	13	5	8^3										11							37
1	2		4	3		8^1	10			9^3	13	6^2	7	14	5	12										11							38
1	2		4	3			10			14		6^2	7	13	5	8^3								12	11^1	9							39
1		2	4	3		13	10			12		7	6	5										8	11^2	9^1	13						40
1		2	4	3		13	10			11^1		7	9^2	5	12									6		8^3	14						41
	2	13	4	3			10			11^3		7	6^1	5	12									8	14	9^2			1				42
1	2			3		13	10			11^2		7	6	5										8		9^1	4	12					43
1	2		4	3		14	10			12	11^2	7	6^1	5										8		9^3	13						44
1	2		4	3			10	8^1		9^3	13	7	12	5	14									6^3		11	4						45
1	2		4	3			10	8^2		9^3	12	7	13	5	6											11^1		14					46

The Budweiser FA Cup

Third Round	Reading	(h)	1-0
Fourth Round	Port Vale	(a)	3-1
Fifth Round	Hull C	(h)	1-1
Replay	Hull C	(a)	1-2

Capital One Cup

First Round	Newport Co	(h)	1-3
(aet)			

Championship Play-Offs

Semi-Finals 1st leg	Derby Co	(h)	1-2
Semi-Finals 2nd leg	Derby Co	(a)	1-4

BRISTOL CITY

FOUNDATION

The name Bristol City came into being in 1897 when the Bristol South End club, formed three years earlier, decided to adopt professionalism and apply for admission to the Southern League after competing in the Western League. The historic meeting was held at the Albert Hall, Bedminster. Bristol City employed Sam Hollis from Woolwich Arsenal as manager and gave him £40 to buy players. In 1900 they merged with Bedminster, another leading Bristol club.

Ashton Gate Stadium, Bristol BS3 2EJ.

Telephone: (0117) 963 0600.

Fax: (0117) 9630 700.

Ticket Office: (0117) 963 0600.

Website: www.bcfc.co.uk

Email: enquiries@bcfc.co.uk

Ground Capacity: 21,654.

Record Attendance: 43,335 v Preston NE, FA Cup 5th rd, 16 February 1935.

Pitch Measurements: 105m × 68.5m (115yd × 75yd)

Chairman: Keith Dawe.

Chief Executive: Doug Harman.

Manager: Steve Cotterill.

Assistant Manager: John Pemberton.

Physio: Steve Allen.

Colours: Red shirts with white trim, whie shorts with red trim, red socks.

Year Formed: 1894.

Turned Professional: 1897.

Previous Name: 1894, Bristol South End; 1897, Bristol City.

Club Nickname: 'Robins'.

Grounds: 1894, St John's Lane; 1904, Ashton Gate.

First Football League Game: 7 September 1901, Division 2, v Blackpool (a) W 2–0 – Moles; Tuft, Davies; Jones, McLean, Chambers; Bradbury, Connor, Boucher, O'Brien (2), Flynn.

Record League Victory: 9–0 v Aldershot, Division 3 (S), 28 December 1946 – Eddols; Morgan, Fox; Peacock, Roberts, Jones (1); Chilcott, Thomas, Clark (4 incl. 1p), Cyril Williams (1), Hargreaves (3).

Record Cup Victory: 11–0 v Chichester C, FA Cup 1st rd, 5 November 1960 – Cook; Collinson, Thresher; Connor, Alan Williams, Etheridge; Tait (1), Bobby Williams (1), Atyeo (5), Adrian Williams (3), Derrick, (1 og).

HONOURS

Football League –
Division 1: *Runners-up* 1906–07;
Division 2: *Champions* 1905–06;
Runners-up 1975–76, 1997–98;
FL 1: *Runners-up* 2006–07;
Division 3 (S): *Champions* 1922–23,
1926–27, 1954–55;
Runners-up 1937–38;
Division 3: *Runners-up* 1964–65,
1989–90.

FA Cup: *Runners-up* 1909.

Football League Cup: Semi-final
1971, 1989.

Welsh Cup: *Winners* 1934.

Anglo-Scottish Cup: *Winners* 1978.

Freight Rover Trophy: *Winners* 1986;
Runners-up 1987.

Auto Windscreens Shield:
Runners-up 2000.

LDV Vans Trophy: *Winners* 2003.

sky SPORTS FACT FILE

Bristol City won the Welsh Cup in 1934 when they defeated Tranmere Rovers in an all English final. City's only Welsh opponents in the competition were Cardiff City who they beat in a sixth round replay. They then knocked out New Brighton and Port Vale before winning the final by defeating Rovers 3-0 in a replay played on an English ground at Chester with an English referee officiating.

Record Defeat: 0–9 v Coventry C, Division 3 (S), 28 April 1934.

Most League Points (2 for a win): 70, Division 3 (S), 1954–55.

Most League Points (3 for a win): 91, Division 3, 1989–90.

Most League Goals: 104, Division 3 (S), 1926–27.

Highest League Scorer in Season: Don Clark, 36, Division 3 (S), 1946–47.

Most League Goals in Total Aggregate: John Atyeo, 314, 1951–66.

Most League Goals in One Match: 6, Tommy 'Tot' Walsh v Gillingham, Division 3 (S), 15 January 1927.

Most Capped Player: Billy Wedlock, 26, England.

Most League Appearances: John Atyeo, 597, 1951–66.

Youngest League Player: Marvin Brown, 16 years 105 days v Bristol R, 17 October 1999.

Record Transfer Fee Received: £3,500,000 from Wolverhampton W for Ade Akinbiyi, September 1999.

Record Transfer Fee Paid: £2,250,000 to Crewe Alex for Nicky Maynard, August 2008.

Football League Record: 1901 Elected to Division 2; 1906–11 Division 1; 1911–22 Division 2; 1922–23 Division 3 (S); 1923–24 Division 2; 1924–27 Division 3 (S); 1927–32 Division 2; 1932–55 Division 3 (S); 1955–60 Division 2; 1960–65 Division 3; 1965–76 Division 2; 1976–80 Division 1; 1980–81 Division 2; 1981–82 Division 3; 1982–84 Division 4; 1984–90 Division 3; 1990–92 Division 2; 1992–95 Division 1; 1995–98 Division 2; 1998–99 Division 1; 1999–2004 Division 2; 2004–07 FL 1; 2007–13 FL C; 2013– FL 1.

LATEST SEQUENCES

Longest Sequence of League Wins: 14, 9.9.1905 – 2.12.1905.

Longest Sequence of League Defeats: 7, 6.10.2012 – 11.11.2012.

Longest Sequence of League Draws: 4, 6.11.1999 – 27.11.1999.

Longest Sequence of Unbeaten League Matches: 24, 9.9.1905 – 10.2.1906.

Longest Sequence Without a League Win: 21, 16.3.2013 – 22.10.2013.

Successive Scoring Runs: 25 from 26.12.1905.

Successive Non-scoring Runs: 6 from 20.12.1980.

MANAGERS

Sam Hollis 1897–99
Bob Campbell 1899–1901
Sam Hollis 1901–05
Harry Thickett 1905–10
Frank Bacon 1910–11
Sam Hollis 1911–13
George Hedley 1913–17
Jack Hamilton 1917–19
Joe Palmer 1919–21
Alex Raisbeck 1921–29
Joe Bradshaw 1929–32
Bob Hewison 1932–49
   (*under suspension 1938–39*)
Bob Wright 1949–50
Pat Beasley 1950–58
Peter Doherty 1958–60
Fred Ford 1960–67
Alan Dicks 1967–80
Bobby Houghton 1980–82
Roy Hodgson 1982
Terry Cooper 1982–88
   (*Director from 1983*)
Joe Jordan 1988–90
Jimmy Lumsden 1990–92
Denis Smith 1992–93
Russell Osman 1993–94
Joe Jordan 1994–97
John Ward 1997–98
Benny Lennartsson 1998–99
Tony Pulis 1999–2000
Tony Fawthrop 2000
Danny Wilson 2000–04
Brian Tinnion 2004–05
Gary Johnson 2005–10
Steve Coppell 2010
Keith Millen 2010–11
Derek McInnes 2011–13
Sean O'Driscoll 2013
Steve Cotterill December 2013–

TEN YEAR LEAGUE RECORD

		P	W	D	L	F	A	Pts	Pos
2004-05	FL 1	46	18	16	12	74	57	70	7
2005-06	FL 1	46	18	11	17	66	62	65	9
2006-07	FL 1	46	25	10	11	63	39	85	2
2007-08	FL C	46	20	14	12	54	53	74	4
2008-09	FL C	46	15	16	15	54	54	61	10
2009-10	FL C	46	15	18	13	56	65	63	10
2010-11	FL C	46	17	9	20	62	65	60	15
2011-12	FL C	46	12	13	21	44	68	49	20
2012-13	FL C	46	11	8	27	59	84	41	24
2013-14	FL 1	46	13	19	14	70	67	58	12

DID YOU KNOW ?

When Bristol City won the Division Three South championship in 1926–27 they finished the season with a club record 104 goals. Centre forward Tom Walsh was leading scorer with 32 including the winner at Southend in April in the game which clinched the title and promotion to Division Two.

BRISTOL CITY – FOOTBALL LEAGUE ONE 2013–14 LEAGUE RECORD

Match No.	Date	Venue	Opponents	Result	H/T Score	Lg Pos.	Goalscorers	Attendance
1	Aug 3	H	Bradford C	D 2-2	1-1	10	Wagstaff [13], Emmanuel-Thomas [58]	13,862
2	11	A	Coventry C	L 4-5	0-3	15	Baldock 2 [55, 74], Emmanuel-Thomas [62], Elliott, M [85]	2204
3	17	H	Wolverhampton W	L 1-2	0-1	18	Emmanuel-Thomas [53]	14,393
4	24	A	Milton Keynes D	D 2-2	1-0	19	Baldock 2 [36, 66]	7874
5	31	A	Gillingham	D 1-1	1-1	20	Elliott, M [45]	5616
6	Sept 14	H	Peterborough U	L 0-3	0-1	21		11,134
7	17	H	Shrewsbury T	D 1-1	0-1	21	Emmanuel-Thomas [85]	10,143
8	21	A	Swindon T	L 2-3	2-2	21	Flint [9], Emmanuel-Thomas [36]	11,598
9	28	H	Colchester U	D 1-1	0-1	19	Baldock [74]	10,739
10	Oct 5	A	Port Vale	D 1-1	0-0	20	Wagstaff [55]	6275
11	19	A	Crewe Alex	L 0-1	0-0	24		4781
12	22	H	Brentford	L 1-2	0-0	24	Harewood [90]	10,639
13	26	A	Carlisle U	W 4-2	0-1	23	Emmanuel-Thomas 3 [51, 52, 84], Wagstaff [72]	4672
14	Nov 2	H	Oldham Ath	D 1-1	1-0	23	Emmanuel-Thomas [36]	11,352
15	5	H	Crawley T	W 2-0	0-0	20	Emmanuel-Thomas [80], Bryan [87]	10,085
16	16	A	Tranmere R	D 1-1	1-1	19	Baldock [14]	4932
17	23	H	Sheffield U	L 0-1	0-0	22		13,220
18	26	H	Leyton Orient	D 2-2	0-1	22	Baldock [58], Cuthbert (og) [73]	10,659
19	30	A	Preston NE	L 0-1	0-1	23		8803
20	Dec 14	H	Rotherham U	L 1-2	0-2	24	Reid [82]	11,201
21	21	A	Notts Co	D 1-1	0-0	24	Baldock (pen) [41]	6523
22	26	H	Walsall	W 1-0	1-0	21	Baldock (pen) [16]	12,031
23	29	H	Stevenage	W 4-1	2-0	21	Cunningham [7], Baldock [12], Emmanuel-Thomas 2 [69, 72]	12,038
24	Jan 11	A	Bradford C	D 1-1	1-1	23	Wagstaff [11]	13,050
25	18	H	Milton Keynes D	D 2-2	0-2	22	Baldock 2 [57, 76]	11,533
26	25	A	Wolverhampton W	L 1-3	1-2	23	Baldock (pen) [24]	18,501
27	28	A	Brentford	L 1-3	1-3	23	Osborne [12]	6517
28	Feb 1	H	Carlisle U	W 2-1	0-1	20	Elliott, M 2 [68, 70]	11,029
29	4	A	Coventry C	L 1-2	0-2	20	Burns [82]	11,272
30	8	A	Oldham Ath	D 1-1	1-1	22	Flint [10]	3822
31	11	A	Leyton Orient	W 3-1	2-1	17	Baldock [3], Barnett [12], Flint [76]	3928
32	15	H	Tranmere R	D 2-2	1-1	17	Baldock [13], Williams [78]	11,340
33	22	A	Sheffield U	L 0-3	0-1	21		19,271
34	Mar 1	H	Gillingham	W 2-1	1-0	20	Baldock [27], Gillett [83]	11,422
35	8	A	Shrewsbury T	W 3-2	1-1	17	Emmanuel-Thomas [18], Mkandawire (og) [55], Bryan [63]	6069
36	11	A	Peterborough U	W 2-1	2-1	15	Baldock 2 [10, 16]	4352
37	15	H	Swindon T	D 0-0	0-0	15		14,884
38	22	A	Colchester U	D 2-2	1-0	15	Paterson [8], Wagstaff [49]	3805
39	25	H	Port Vale	W 5-0	4-0	13	Emmanuel-Thomas 2 [16, 45], Nosworthy [41], Baldock 2 [45, 74]	10,940
40	29	A	Rotherham U	L 1-2	0-1	15	Elliott, W [48]	8607
41	Apr 5	H	Preston NE	D 1-1	0-0	15	Elliott, W [75]	12,537
42	12	A	Walsall	W 1-0	1-0	13	Baldock (pen) [45]	5110
43	18	H	Notts Co	W 2-1	1-1	14	Baldock 2 [13, 86]	13,427
44	21	A	Stevenage	W 3-1	1-0	12	Elliott, W [42], Baldock [66], Pearson [75]	2901
45	26	H	Crewe Alex	D 0-0	0-0	12		14,477
46	May 3	A	Crawley T	D 1-1	0-1	12	Gillett [62]	4405

Final League Position: 12

GOALSCORERS

League (70): Baldock 24 (4 pens), Emmanuel-Thomas 15, Wagstaff 5, Elliott, M 4, Elliott, W 3, Flint 3, Bryan 2, Gillett 2, Barnett 1, Burns 1, Cunningham 1, Harewood 1, Nosworthy 1, Osborne 1, Paterson 1, Pearson 1, Reid 1, Williams 1, own goals 2.
The Budweiser FA Cup (6): Emmanuel-Thomas 4, Baldock 1, Elliott, M 1.
Capital One Cup (4): Baldock 1, Emmanuel-Thomas 1, Wagstaff 1, Wynter 1.
Johnstone's Paint Trophy (3): Bryan 1, Emmanuel-Thomas 1, Moloney 1.

Fielding F 16	Moloney B 27 + 5	Cunningham G 32 + 5	Wynter J 2 + 1	Flint A 32 + 2	Fontaine L 2 + 1	Wagstaff S 35 + 2	Kilkenny N 3	Baldock S 44 + 1	Emmanuel-Thomas J 42 + 4	Bryan J 11 + 10	Pack M 34 + 9	Taylor R 2 + 5	Elliott M 16 + 8	Williams D 40 + 3	Harewood M —+ 12	Reid B 19 + 5	Shorey N 11 + 3	O'Connor J 3	McLaughlin S —+ 5	Parish E 19	Dunk L 2	Gillett S 21 + 2	Osborne K 25 + 2	Burns W + 19	Carey Louis 1 + 1	Barnett T 7 + 10	El-Abd A 13 + 1	Elliott W 17 + 2	Moore S 11	Pearson S 2 + 4	Nosworthy N 10	Paterson M 6 + 2	Kelly L —+ 2	Match No.
1	2	3	4	5	6	7	8	9	10¹	11²	12	13																						1
1	2	5		3	4	9²	8¹	10	11		6	12²		7	13	14																		2
1	2	5¹	9	3		6	7³	11	8		12	10²		13		4	14																	3
1	2	5	12	4		6		10	11³	9²	14			8	3	13	7¹																	4
1	2	5		3		6		10	11		9			8	4		7¹	12																5
1	2¹	5		3		6		10	11	9	7				12	8²			4	13														6
1		14		3		6		10	11	9³	7			8²	4	12	13		5¹	2														7
1	5	13		3		6		10	11	12	8			7	2²	14			9³	4¹														8
	2			3		6²		10	11	9¹	8			14	4	12	7³	5	13	1														9
	2			3		9		10	11³	6¹	7			12	4	14	8²	5	13	1														10
	2			4		6		11²	10¹	9	7	12		3		8	5	13	1															11
	2					9²		10	11	12	7			8	3	13	6¹	5		1	4													12
	2		12			9			10¹	13	6	11		8	4	14	7³	5		1	3²													13
	2			3		6		14	11	12	8		10³	7²	4		9¹	5		1		13												14
	2¹		12			8		10	9³	11	7			13	3	14		5		1		6²	4											15
	2	5		3				10	11		7	13	12		8²	9				1		6¹	4											16
	2²	5²		3		6		11	10		7			8	12	14		9¹	13	1			4											17
	2	6		3		7		10	11	12	8			13	5¹					1		9²	4											18
	6²	9¹		3		8		10	11	12	5	13		4						1		7	2⁸											19
	2³	5²		3		6		11	10	9¹				8	4			13	12	1		7		14										20
	12	9		3		6		10	11¹		5			13	4			8⁸		1		7²	14	2										21
		6		3		9		10	11¹	14	7			2		8²	12³			1		5	4	13										22
	12	5		3		9¹		10³	11			7	2	6						1		8²	4	13	14									23
		9		3	13	5		11	10²		7			8	4¹		6³			1			2	14		12								24
		9		3		5		10	11		7				12		8³			1		2²	14			13	4							25
		9		3				10	11	14				6	4		7²			1		8³	5¹	12		13	2							26
	12	9		3				10	14		6²			8	5		7³			1		7	4³			11	2	13						27
		6		3		9		10	11		5			12	2²		7³			1		8		13		14	4	8¹	1					28
		9		3		5		10	11	7¹	12			6¹	4					1		8		14		13	2²		1					29
	2			3				10	13		6			7¹	5		8			1			9²			11	4	12	1					30
		6		4				10	11		7			5								12	2			9	3	8	1					31
		10²		4				8	9	14	6			2³	13							5	12			11	3	7	1					32
		9²		4				6	10³		7¹			5	12							2	14			11	3	8	1	13				33
1	2	3						9	10	13				5	11²							7	14	12			4	6²	8¹					34
1	2	14		3³				10	9	11²	12			5								7	13			4	6	8¹						35
1	5	9		6²				10	11³	12	14			4								8	2	13		3⁸	7							36
1	9²	6		7¹				10	11		13			2								8	4	12			5²			3	14			37
1	2	13		8				10	11					5¹								6	3	14			7²	12	4	9¹				38
1		5				9²		10	7		6¹			2								3	14	12			8		4	11³	13			39
1		9²		5				11	7³	12				2								6	3	14	13	8		4	10¹					40
1		12		5				11	9¹		7			8								3	13	14	4²	6		2	10³					41
	12	9		5³				11	8¹		7			4								3		13	6	1	14	2	10²					42
	12	5¹		6				10	8³		9			2								3	13	14	7	1	4	11²						43
	3²	5		14				10	13		8			2								6	9		11³	7¹	1	12	4					44
		9		5²				10	11¹		6			3	14							7³	2	12		8	1		4	13				45
	2²	9¹		12				10	14		7			5								6²	4		11	8	1		3		13			46

Capital One Cup

First Round	Gillingham	(a)	2-0
Second Round	Crystal Palace	(h)	2-1
Third Round	Southampton	(a)	0-2

Johnstone's Paint Trophy

First Round	Bristol R	(h)	2-1
Second Round	Wycombe W	(a)	1-2

The Budweiser FA Cup

First Round	Dagenham & R	(h)	3-0
Second Round	Tamworth	(a)	2-1
Third Round	Watford	(h)	1-1
Replay	Watford	(a)	0-2

BRISTOL ROVERS

FOUNDATION

Bristol Rovers were formed at a meeting in Stapleton Road, Eastville, in 1883. However, they first went under the name of the Black Arabs (wearing black shirts). Changing their name to Eastville Rovers in their second season in 1888–89, they won the Gloucestershire Senior Cup. Original members of the Bristol & District League in 1892, this eventually became the Western League and Eastville Rovers adopted professionalism in 1897.

The Memorial Stadium, Filton Avenue, Horfield, Bristol BS7 0BF.
Telephone: (0117) 909 6648.
Fax: (0117) 907 4312.
Ticket Office: (0117) 909 8848.
Website: www.bristolrovers.co.uk
Email: rodwesson@bristolrovers.co.uk;
dave@bristolrovers.co.uk
Ground Capacity: 11,626.
Record Attendance: 38,472 v Preston NE, FA Cup 4th rd, 30 January 1960 (at Eastville); 9,464 v Liverpool, FA Cup 4th rd, 8 February 1992 (at Twerton Park); 12,011 v WBA, FA Cup 6th rd, 9 March 2008 (at Memorial Stadium).
Pitch Measurements: 100.5m × 67m (110yd × 73yd)
Chairman: Nick Higgs.
Manager: Darrell Clarke.
Assistant Manager: Marcus Stewart.
Physio: Phil Kite.
Colours: Blue and white quarters, white shorts with blue trim, blue socks with white trim.
Year Formed: 1883.
Turned Professional: 1897.
Previous Names: 1883, Black Arabs; 1884, Eastville Rovers; 1897, Bristol Eastville Rovers; 1898, Bristol Rovers. *Club Nicknames:* 'The Pirates', 'The Gas'.
Grounds: 1883, Purdown; Three Acres, Ashley Hill; Rudgeway, Fishponds; 1897, Eastville; 1986, Twerton Park; 1996, The Memorial Stadium.
First Football League Game: 28 August 1920, Division 3, v Millwall (a) L 0–2 – Stansfield; Bethune, Panes; Boxley, Kenny, Steele; Chance, Bird, Sims, Bell, Palmer.
Record League Victory: 7–0 v Brighton & HA, Division 3 (S), 29 November 1952 – Hoyle; Bamford, Fox; Pitt, Warren, Sampson; McIlvenny, Roost (2), Lambden (1), Bradford (1), Petherbridge (2), (1 og). 7–0 v Swansea T, Division 2, 2 October 1954 – Radford; Bamford, Watkins; Pitt, Muir, Anderson; Petherbridge, Bradford (2), Meyer, Roost (1), Hooper (2), (2 og). 7–0 v Shrewsbury T, Division 3, 21 March 1964 – Hall; Hillard, Gwyn Jones; Oldfield, Stone (1), Mabbutt; Jarman (2), Brown (1), Biggs (1p), Hamilton, Bobby Jones (2).
Record Cup Victory: 6–0 v Merthyr Tydfil, FA Cup 1st rd, 14 November 1987 – Martyn; Alexander (Dryden), Tanner, Hibbitt, Twentyman, Vaughan Jones, Holloway, Meacham (1), White (2), Penrice (3) (Reece), Purnell.

HONOURS

Football League – Division 2: Best season: 4th, 1994–95; **Division 3 (S):** *Champions* 1952–53;
Division 3: *Champions* 1989–90; *Runners-up* 1973–74.

FA Cup: Best season: 6th rd, 1951, 1958, 2008.

Football League Cup: Best season: 5th rd, 1971, 1972.

Leyland DAF: *Runners-up* 1990.

Johnstone's Paint Trophy: *Runners-up* 2007.

sky SPORTS FACT FILE

Bristol Rovers' first experience of floodlit football came during a mini tour of the Netherlands in November 1930. After defeating the Dutch national team 3-2 in Amsterdam they faced The Swallows for a midweek evening fixture played under electric lights in The Hague. Rovers were not put off by the new experience and finished the game as 4-1 winners.

Record Defeat: 0–12 v Luton T, Division 3 (S), 13 April 1936.
Most League Points (2 for a win): 64, Division 3 (S), 1952–53.
Most League Points (3 for a win): 93, Division 3, 1989–90.
Most League Goals: 92, Division 3 (S), 1952–53.
Highest League Scorer in Season: Geoff Bradford, 33, Division 3 (S), 1952–53.
Most League Goals in Total Aggregate: Geoff Bradford, 242, 1949–64.
Most League Goals in One Match: 4, Sidney Leigh v Exeter C, Division 3 (S), 2 May 1921; 4, Jonah Wilcox v Bournemouth, Division 3 (S), 12 December 1925; 4, Bill Culley v QPR, Division 3 (S), 5 March 1927; 4, Frank Curran v Swindon T, Division 3 (S), 25 March 1939; 4, Vic Lambden v Aldershot, Division 3 (S), 29 March 1947; 4, George Petherbridge v Torquay U, Division 3 (S), 1 December 1951; 4, Vic Lambden v Colchester U, Division 3 (S), 14 May 1952; 4, Geoff Bradford v Rotherham U, Division 2, 14 March 1959; 4, Robin Stubbs v Gillingham, Division 2, 10 October 1970; 4, Alan Warboys v Brighton & HA, Division 3, 1 December 1973; 4, Jamie Cureton v Reading, Division 2, 16 January 1999.
Most Capped Player: Vitalijs Astafjevs, 31 (167), Latvia.
Most League Appearances: Stuart Taylor, 546, 1966–80.
Youngest League Player: Ronnie Dix, 15 years 173 days v Charlton Ath, 25 February 1928.
Record Transfer Fee Received: £2,100,000 from Fulham for Barry Hayles, November 1998; £2,100,000 from WBA for Jason Roberts, July 2000.
Record Transfer Fee Paid: £375,000 to QPR for Andy Tillson, November 1992.
Football League Record: 1920 Original Member of Division 3; 1921–53 Division 3 (S); 1953–62 Division 2; 1962–74 Division 3; 1974–81 Division 2; 1981–90 Division 3; 1990–92 Division 2. 1992–93 Division 1; 1993–2001 Division 2; 2001–04 Division 3; 2004–07 FL 2; 2007–11 FL 1; 2011–14 FL 2; 2014– Conference Premier.

LATEST SEQUENCES

Longest Sequence of League Wins: 12, 18.10.1952 – 17.1.1953.
Longest Sequence of League Defeats: 8, 26.10.2002 – 21.12.2002.
Longest Sequence of League Draws: 5, 1.11.1975 – 22.11.1975.
Longest Sequence of Unbeaten League Matches: 32, 7.4.1973 – 27.1.1974.
Longest Sequence Without a League Win: 20, 5.4.1980 – 1.11.1980.
Successive Scoring Runs: 26 from 26.3.1927.
Successive Non-scoring Runs: 6 from 14.10.1922.

MANAGERS

Alfred Homer 1899–1920
  (*continued as Secretary to 1928*)
Ben Hall 1920–21
Andy Wilson 1921–26
Joe Palmer 1926–29
Dave McLean 1929–30
Albert Prince-Cox 1930–36
Percy Smith 1936–37
Brough Fletcher 1938–49
Bert Tann 1950–68 (*continued as General Manager to 1972*)
Fred Ford 1968–69
Bill Dodgin Snr 1969–72
Don Megson 1972–77
Bobby Campbell 1978–79
Harold Jarman 1979–80
Terry Cooper 1980–81
Bobby Gould 1981–83
David Williams 1983–85
Bobby Gould 1985–87
Gerry Francis 1987–91
Martin Dobson 1991
Dennis Rofe 1992
Malcolm Allison 1992–93
John Ward 1993–96
Ian Holloway 1996–2001
Garry Thompson 2001
Gerry Francis 2001
Garry Thompson 2001–02
Ray Graydon 2002–04
Ian Atkins 2004–05
Paul Trollope 2005–10
Dave Penney 2011
Paul Buckle 2011
Mark McGhee 2012
John Ward 2012–13
Darrell Clarke March 2014–

TEN YEAR LEAGUE RECORD

		P	W	D	L	F	A	Pts	Pos
2004-05	FL 2	46	13	21	12	60	57	60	12
2005-06	FL 2	46	17	9	20	59	67	60	12
2006-07	FL 2	46	20	12	14	49	42	72	6
2007-08	FL 1	46	12	17	17	45	53	53	16
2008-09	FL 1	46	17	12	17	79	61	63	11
2009-10	FL 1	46	19	5	22	59	70	62	11
2010-11	FL 1	46	11	12	23	48	82	45	22
2011-12	FL 2	46	15	12	19	60	70	57	13
2012-13	FL 2	46	16	12	18	60	69	60	14
2013-14	FL 2	46	12	14	20	43	54	50	23

DID YOU KNOW ?

Bristol Rovers' longest serving post-war manager Bert Tann was originally only given the job in January 1950 on a temporary basis until a new boss was appointed. Two months later Tann, who was previously a coach at the club, got the post on a permanent basis and remained in charge until 1968 when he became general manager.

BRISTOL ROVERS – FOOTBALL LEAGUE TWO 2013–14 LEAGUE RECORD

Match No.	Date	Venue	Opponents	Result	H/T Score	Lg Pos.	Goalscorers	Atten- dance
1	Aug 3	A	Exeter C	L 1-2	0-0	15	Richards [68]	5196
2	10	H	Scunthorpe U	D 0-0	0-0	16		6259
3	17	A	Newport Co	L 0-1	0-1	20		5387
4	24	H	York C	W 3-2	2-1	17	Clarkson 2 [3, 33], O'Toole [67]	5569
5	31	H	Northampton T	W 1-0	1-0	11	Lockyer [2]	5695
6	Sept 7	A	Plymouth Arg	L 0-1	0-0	16		8631
7	14	A	Dagenham & R	L 0-2	0-1	18		1423
8	21	H	Hartlepool U	D 2-2	1-2	19	Harrold [35], O'Toole [90]	5579
9	27	A	Southend U	D 1-1	0-0	17	Harrold [51]	5489
10	Oct 5	H	Fleetwood T	L 1-3	0-0	20	O'Toole [66]	5303
11	12	A	Mansfield T	D 1-1	0-1	20	Santos [84]	3275
12	19	H	Wycombe W	L 0-1	0-0	20		5783
13	22	A	Accrington S	L 1-2	1-2	21	Henshall [5]	1101
14	26	H	Chesterfield	D 0-0	0-0	21		5667
15	Nov 2	A	Oxford U	W 1-0	0-0	20	O'Toole (pen) [71]	6374
16	16	H	Bury	D 1-1	1-1	20	O'Toole (pen) [4]	5534
17	23	A	Burton Alb	L 0-1	0-0	22		2302
18	26	A	Cheltenham T	D 0-0	0-0	22		3556
19	30	H	AFC Wimbledon	W 3-0	2-0	22	Clarkson [19], Parkes [31], Harrold (pen) [89]	5860
20	Dec 14	A	Morecambe	L 1-2	1-0	22	O'Toole [30]	1514
21	21	H	Portsmouth	W 2-0	1-0	18	Clarke [40], Clarkson [77]	7537
22	26	A	Torquay U	D 1-1	1-1	19	Harrold [27]	3461
23	29	A	Rochdale	L 0-2	0-0	21		2576
24	Jan 11	H	Exeter C	W 2-1	1-1	21	O'Toole 2 (1 pen) [21 (p), 90]	6674
25	18	A	York C	D 0-0	0-0	22		3514
26	25	H	Newport Co	W 3-1	1-0	18	Mohamed [45], Richards [48], O'Toole [90]	7288
27	28	A	Accrington S	L 0-1	0-0	20		6067
28	Feb 1	A	Chesterfield	L 1-3	1-2	21	Brown [36]	6048
29	8	H	Oxford U	D 1-1	0-1	21	O'Toole [84]	6493
30	11	H	Cheltenham T	W 1-0	0-0	18	O'Toole [34]	5808
31	21	H	Burton Alb	W 2-0	0-0	16	Clarkson [70], O'Toole [79]	5957
32	25	A	Scunthorpe U	D 1-1	0-1	19	Gillespie [89]	3318
33	Mar 1	A	Northampton T	D 0-0	0-0	17		5058
34	8	H	Plymouth Arg	W 2-1	1-0	14	Beardsley [7], Mohamed [78]	7799
35	11	A	Dagenham & R	L 1-2	1-1	16	O'Toole [7]	5761
36	15	A	Hartlepool U	L 0-4	0-2	18		3480
37	21	H	Southend U	D 0-0	0-0	17		6028
38	25	A	Fleetwood T	L 1-3	0-2	20	Harrison [79]	2023
39	29	H	Morecambe	W 1-0	0-0	20	Mohamed [90]	5647
40	Apr 1	A	Bury	L 1-2	1-1	20	Clarke [45]	2314
41	5	A	AFC Wimbledon	D 0-0	0-0	21		4322
42	12	H	Torquay U	L 1-2	0-0	21	Woodards [90]	6612
43	19	A	Portsmouth	L 2-3	2-2	22	Harrold 2 [22, 41]	17,998
44	21	H	Rochdale	L 1-2	1-0	22	Mohamed [17]	8158
45	26	A	Wycombe W	W 2-1	1-1	21	Brown [11], Clarkson [76]	6752
46	May 3	H	Mansfield T	L 0-1	0-1	23		10,594

Final League Position: 23

GOALSCORERS

League (43): O'Toole 13 (3 pens), Clarkson 6, Harrold 6 (1 pen), Mohamed 4, Brown 2, Clarke 2, Richards 2, Beardsley 1, Gillespie 1, Harrison 1, Henshall 1, Lockyer 1, Parkes 1, Santos 1, Woodards 1.
The Budweiser FA Cup (8): Beardsley 2, O'Toole 2, Richards 2, Harrold 1, Norburn 1.
Capital One Cup (1): Richards 1.
Johnstone's Paint Trophy (1): McChrystal 1.

Mildenhall S 46	Smith M 43	Brown L 41	O'Toole J 41	Parkes T 44	McChrystal M 35	Richards E 18+4	Norburn O 16	Harding M 5+6	Clarkson D 28+6	Harrison E 9+16	Santos A 7+16	Hunter S —+3	Lockyer T 38+3	Brunt R 9+2	Gill M —+1	Harrold M 22+8	Bond A 5	Clucas S 11+6	Clarke O 29+3	Keary P —+1	Packwood W 8	Henshall A 1+1	Beardsley C 16+8	Woodards D 6+3	Mohamed K 20+1	Gow A 4	Gillespie S 3+10	Broghammer F 1+3	Lucas J —+1	Match No.
1	2	3	4	5	6	7	8		9[1]	10[3]	11[2]	12	13	14																1
1	2	5	9	3[1]	4	11	7	13		8[2]	10[3]	12	14	6																2
1	2	4	10[2]	3	5	11	7			6[1]	8	12		9	13															3
1	2	5	8	3	4			9[1]	13	10[2]			6			7	11	12												4
1	2	5	8	3	4	13	7			10[2]	9			6			11[1]		12											5
1	2	5	8	3	4		7			11[1]	9[2]	12	14	6[3]	10				13											6
1	2	5	8	4	3	11[2]	6[3]		13	9[1]	12	14				10	7													7
1	2	5	8	3	4	9[2]			10[1]	13	12		7			11	6													8
1	2	5	7	3	4		6[2]			12			8	10[1]		11	9	13												9
1	2	5	10	3	4		8[1]			13			7	11[2]		12	6	9												10
1	5	2[1]	8	4		13	6[2]		10		14		3	11					9[3]		7	12								11
1	2		8	4		13	10[6]	9[2]	14				5	11[1]					7[3]	6		3	12							12
1	2		8	3		13			10	12			5	11					6	7[1]		4	9[2]							13
1	2		9	4		10				6			5	11					8	7		3								14
1	2		8	4		11			13	6[2]			5	12					9	7		3	10[1]							15
1	2	5	8	4		9			13	6[2]	12			11					7[1]			3	10							16
1	2	5	8[8]	4		9			11[1]				6					12	7			3	10[8]							17
1	2	5		3			8[1]	10	9	6	12		7						11			4								18
1	2	5		4			8[2]	6[1]	9	10	13		7						11			12	3							19
1	2	5	8	3		9	6[2]			11[1]	12		4						10			7	13							20
1	2	5	8	3	4	10	9		6										11			7								21
1	2	5	6	3	4	11[2]	8		9[1]	13	12								10			7								22
1	2	5	7	3	4	12	6[2]		11[3]	14	9[1]								10			8	13							23
1	2	5	9	3	4	8[3]			13	10[2]			6[1]						11			7	12	14						24
1	2	5	11	4	3	9		6[2]					7						10[1]			8	12	13						25
1	2	5	8	3	4	11[1]		12		14			7						9			10[3]	13	6[2]						26
1	2	5	8	3	4	10[1]			12				6			11[2]			7			13		9						27
1	2	5	7	3	4			13	12				9			11[2]			8			6	10[1]							28
1	2	5	8	4									6						7			10			9[1]	11	12			29
1	2	5	8	4				13	11[1]				3					7				10		9	6[2]	12				30
1	2	5	7	3	4			11[1]					8					13				10		6[2]	9	12				31
1	2	5	7	3	4			11[2]					8					13				10		6	9[1]	12				32
1	2	5	9	3	4			8[2]		13			6						7			11[1]		10		12				33
1	2	5	8	3	4			6[1]					7			12		13	9			11[2]		7						34
1	2	5	10	3	4			6[2]		14			7			12			8[1]			11		9[3]		13				35
1	2	7	10	4	9			5[1]		13						6		8[2]	14			12	3[1]	11						36
1	2	5	7[3]	3	4			14		13			6			12			8			11		9[1]		10[2]				37
1	2	5		3	4			9[1]	12				8			11			7			14	6[3]	13		10[2]				38
1	2	5			4					10	12	6	7						8			11[1]	3	9						39
1	5	9	6	3[2]	4								13	8		11		12	7[3]				2[1]	10		14				40
1	5	9	7	3	4						12		2[1]	10		8[2]	6							11	13					41
1	2	5[6]	8		4			14	13	6[1]			12			7						10	3	9	11[2]					42
1	6[2]	5		4[3]	3			10					8			11		12	7			2[1]	9		14	13				43
1		5	7	3[4]	4			12	10[1]				2			11		8	6[2]				9					13	14	44
1		5	7[3]	3	4			10					2			11[2]		8	14			13		6		12	9[1]			45
1		7	4	3				8	13				2			11		6[2]	5			10[1]		9		12				46

The Budweiser FA Cup

First Round	York C	(h)	3-3
Replay	York C	(a)	3-2
Second Round	Crawley T	(h)	0-0
Replay	Crawley T	(a)	2-1
Third Round	Birmingham C	(a)	0-3

Capital One Cup

First Round	Watford	(h)	1-3

Johnstone's Paint Trophy

First Round	Bristol C	(a)	1-2

BURNLEY

FOUNDATION

On 18 May 1882 Burnley (Association) Football Club was still known as Burnley Rovers as members of that rugby club had decided on that date to play Association Football in the future. It was only a matter of days later that the members met again and decided to drop Rovers from the club's name.

Turf Moor, Harry Potts Way, Burnley, Lancashire BB10 4BX.

Telephone: (0871) 221 1882.

Fax: (01282) 700 014.

Ticket Office: (0871) 221 1914.

Website: www.burnleyfootballclub.com

Email: info@burnleyfc.com

Ground Capacity: 21,940.

Record Attendance: 54,775 v Huddersfield T, FA Cup 3rd rd, 23 February 1924.

Pitch Measurements: 103.5m × 65m (113yd × 71yd)

Chairmen: Mike Garlick and John Banaszkiewicz.

Chief Executive: Lee Hoos.

Manager: Sean Dyche.

Assistant Manager: Ian Woan.

Head Physio: Ally Beattie.

Colours: Claret shirts with blue sleeves, white shorts with blue trim, claret socks with blue hoops.

Year Formed: 1882.

Turned Professional: 1883.

Previous Name: 1882, Burnley Rovers; 1882, Burnley.

Club Nickname: 'The Clarets'.

Grounds: 1882, Calder Vale; 1883, Turf Moor.

First Football League Game: 8 September 1888, Football League, v Preston NE (a) L 2–5 – Smith; Lang, Bury, Abrahams, Friel, Keenan, Brady, Tait, Poland (1), Gallocher (1), Yates.

Record League Victory: 9–0 v Darwen, Division 1, 9 January 1892 – Hillman; Walker, McFettridge, Lang, Matthews, Keenan, Nicol (3), Bowes, Espie (1), McLardie (3), Hill (2).

Record Cup Victory: 9–0 v Crystal Palace, FA Cup 2nd rd (replay), 10 February 1909 – Dawson; Barron, McLean; Cretney (2), Leake, Moffat; Morley, Ogden, Smith (3), Abbott (2), Smethams (1). 9–0 v New Brighton, FA Cup 4th rd, 26 January 1957 – Blacklaw; Angus, Winton; Seith, Adamson, Miller; Newlands (1), McIlroy (3), Lawson (3), Cheesebrough (1), Pilkington (1). 9–0 v Penrith, FA Cup 1st rd, 17 November 1984 – Hansbury; Miller, Hampton, Phelan, Overson (Kennedy), Hird (3 incl. 1p), Grewcock (1), Powell (2), Taylor (3), Biggins, Hutchison.

Record Defeat: 0–11 v Darwen, FA Cup 1st rd, 17 October 1885.

HONOURS

Football League – Division 1: *Champions* 1920–21, 1959–60; *Runners-up* 1919–20, 1961–62; **Division 2:** *Champions* 1897–98, 1972–73; *Runners-up* 1912–13, 1946–47, 1999–2000; **Division 3:** *Champions* 1981–82; **Division 4:** *Champions* 1991–92. Record 30 consecutive Division 1 games without defeat 1920–21.

FL C: *Runners-up* 2013–14.

FA Cup: *Winners* 1914; *Runners-up* 1947, 1962.

Football League Cup: Semi-final 1961, 1969, 1983, 2009.

Anglo–Scottish Cup: *Winners* 1979.

Sherpa Van Trophy: *Runners-up* 1988.

European Competitions European Cup: 1960–61. **European Fairs Cup:** 1966–67.

sky SPORTS FACT FILE

Three Burnley players were killed during the First World War – Bill Pickering, John Brown and Alf Lorimer. Pre-war captain Tommy Boyle was severely wounded as was Dick Tranter; while Percy Goodison, Sam Gunton and Tom Bamford were also wounded. Charlie Bates, the club's reserve team trainer spent almost four years as a prisoner of war.

Most League Points (2 for a win): 62, Division 2, 1972–73.

Most League Points (3 for a win): 93, FL C, 2013–14.

Most League Goals: 102, Division 1, 1960–61.

Highest League Scorer in Season: George Beel, 35, Division 1, 1927–28.

Most League Goals in Total Aggregate: George Beel, 179, 1923–32.

Most League Goals in One Match: 6, Louis Page v Birmingham C, Division 1, 10 April 1926.

Most Capped Player: Jimmy McIlroy, 51 (55), Northern Ireland.

Most League Appearances: Jerry Dawson, 522, 1907–28.

Youngest League Player: Tommy Lawton, 16 years 174 days v Doncaster R, 28 March 1936.

Record Transfer Fee Received: £7,000,000 from Southampton for Jay Rodriguez, June 2012.

Record Transfer Fee Paid: £3,000,000 to Hibernian for Steven Fletcher, June 2009.

Football League Record: 1888 Original Member of the Football League; 1897–98 Division 2; 1898–1900 Division 1; 1900–13 Division 2; 1913–30 Division 1; 1930–47 Division 2; 1947–71 Division 1; 1971–73 Division 2; 1973–76 Division 1; 1976–80 Division 2; 1980–82 Division 3; 1982–83 Division 2; 1983–85 Division 3; 1985–92 Division 4; 1992–94 Division 2; 1994–95 Division 1; 1995–2000 Division 2; 2000–04 Division 1; 2004–09 FL C; 2009–10 FA Premier League; 2010–14 FL C; 2014– FA Premier League.

LATEST SEQUENCES

Longest Sequence of League Wins: 10, 16.11.1912 – 18.1.1913.

Longest Sequence of League Defeats: 8, 2.1.1995 – 25.2.1995.

Longest Sequence of League Draws: 6, 21.2.1931 – 28.3.1931.

Longest Sequence of Unbeaten League Matches: 30, 6.9.1920 – 25.3.1921.

Longest Sequence Without a League Win: 24, 16.4.1979 – 17.11.1979.

Successive Scoring Runs: 27 from 13.2.1926.

Successive Non-scoring Runs: 6 from 23.12.2006.

MANAGERS

Harry Bradshaw 1894–99
  (*Secretary-Manager from 1897*)
Club Directors 1899–1900
J. Ernest Mangnall 1900–03
  (*Secretary-Manager*)
Spen Whittaker 1903–10
  (*Secretary-Manager*)
John Haworth 1910–24
  (*Secretary-Manager*)
Albert Pickles 1925–31
  (*Secretary-Manager*)
Tom Bromilow 1932–35
Selection Committee 1935–45
Cliff Britton 1945–48
Frank Hill 1948–54
Alan Brown 1954–57
Billy Dougall 1957–58
Harry Potts 1958–70
  (*General Manager to 1972*)
Jimmy Adamson 1970–76
Joe Brown 1976–77
Harry Potts 1977–79
Brian Miller 1979–83
John Bond 1983–84
John Benson 1984–85
Martin Buchan 1985
Tommy Cavanagh 1985–86
Brian Miller 1986–89
Frank Casper 1989–91
Jimmy Mullen 1991–96
Adrian Heath 1996–97
Chris Waddle 1997–98
Stan Ternent 1998–2004
Steve Cotterill 2004–07
Owen Coyle 2007–10
Brian Laws 2010
Eddie Howe 2011–12
Sean Dyche October 2012–

TEN YEAR LEAGUE RECORD

		P	W	D	L	F	A	Pts	Pos
2004-05	FL C	46	15	15	16	38	39	60	13
2005-06	FL C	46	14	12	20	46	54	54	17
2006-07	FL C	46	15	12	19	52	49	57	15
2007-08	FL C	46	16	14	16	60	67	62	13
2008-09	FL C	46	21	13	12	72	60	76	5
2009-10	PR Lge	38	8	6	24	42	82	30	18
2010-11	FL C	46	18	14	14	65	61	68	8
2011-12	FL C	46	17	11	18	61	58	62	13
2012-13	FL C	46	16	13	17	62	60	61	11
2013-14	FL C	46	26	15	5	72	37	93	2

DID YOU KNOW ?

Burnley lost the first three games of the 1920–21 season and finished off with a run of six games without a win. In between they set a new record of 28 games without defeat, enabling them to finish the campaign as Football League champions with a five-point margin over their closest rivals.

BURNLEY – FL CHAMPIONSHIP 2013–14 LEAGUE RECORD

Match No.	Date	Venue	Opponents	Result	H/T Score	Lg Pos.	Goalscorers	Attendance
1	Aug 3	H	Bolton W	D 1-1	1-1	11	Ings [26]	12,919
2	10	A	Sheffield W	W 2-1	2-0	4	Ings [33], Vokes [38]	22,282
3	17	H	Yeovil T	W 2-0	0-0	3	Treacy [74], Vokes [79]	10,085
4	24	A	Brighton & HA	L 0-2	0-1	9		26,007
5	31	H	Derby Co	W 3-0	2-0	3	Ings [14], Vokes [32], Shackell [74]	23,514
6	Sept 14	H	Blackburn R	D 1-1	0-0	5	Stanislas [76]	15,699
7	17	H	Birmingham C	W 3-0	1-0	4	Ings 2 [3, 54], Arfield [46]	9641
8	21	A	Leeds U	W 2-1	2-0	2	Arfield [17], Vokes [42]	26,465
9	28	H	Charlton Ath	W 3-0	1-0	2	Ings [38], Vokes 2 [67, 86]	10,645
10	Oct 1	A	Doncaster R	W 2-0	1-0	1	Vokes (pen) [45], Jones, R (og) [87]	7836
11	5	H	Reading	W 2-1	1-0	1	Ings [21], Vokes [80]	11,256
12	19	A	Ipswich T	W 1-0	0-0	1	Arfield [80]	16,062
13	26	H	QPR	W 2-0	0-0	1	Ings 2 (1 pen) [65, 88 (p)]	16,074
14	Nov 2	A	Millwall	D 2-2	1-2	1	Vokes [39], Lowry (og) [55]	10,168
15	9	H	Bournemouth	D 1-1	0-0	1	Ings [84]	12,221
16	23	A	Nottingham F	D 1-1	1-1	1	Vokes (pen) [28]	22,877
17	30	A	Huddersfield T	L 1-2	0-0	2	Ings [84]	17,390
18	Dec 3	H	Watford	D 0-0	0-0	3		10,910
19	7	H	Barnsley	W 1-0	0-0	1	Kightly [65]	11,462
20	14	A	Leicester C	D 1-1	0-1	2	Ings [47]	23,143
21	21	H	Blackpool	W 2-1	1-1	1	Ings [7], Arfield [47]	14,489
22	26	A	Middlesbrough	L 0-1	0-1	2		20,689
23	29	A	Wigan Ath	D 0-0	0-0	3		17,712
24	Jan 1	H	Huddersfield T	W 3-2	2-1	2	Ings 2 [6, 41], Trippier [79]	14,105
25	11	A	Yeovil T	W 2-1	1-0	2	Ings [19], Vokes [62]	6293
26	18	H	Sheffield W	D 1-1	1-1	3	Vokes [43]	13,735
27	28	H	Brighton & HA	D 0-0	0-0	3		11,054
28	Feb 1	A	QPR	D 3-3	1-2	3	Ings [25], Vokes 2 [54, 62]	16,393
29	8	H	Millwall	W 3-1	2-1	2	Ings 2 [29, 62], Marney [45]	11,502
30	11	A	Bolton W	W 1-0	0-0	2	Vokes [58]	16,439
31	15	A	Bournemouth	D 1-1	0-0	2	Treacy [67]	10,422
32	22	H	Nottingham F	W 3-1	3-0	2	Arfield [12], Vokes 2 [25, 35]	14,928
33	Mar 1	H	Derby Co	W 2-0	1-0	2	Jones [29], Marney [68]	17,285
34	9	A	Blackburn R	W 2-1	0-1	2	Shackell [73], Ings [79]	21,589
35	12	A	Birmingham C	D 3-3	1-0	2	Marney [30], Duff [67], Vokes [86]	16,695
36	15	H	Leeds U	W 2-1	1-1	2	Pearce (og) [38], Arfield [67]	18,109
37	22	A	Charlton Ath	W 3-0	1-0	2	Barnes [38], Vokes (pen) [55], Kightly [90]	16,113
38	25	H	Doncaster R	W 2-0	0-0	2	Vokes (pen) [47], Stanislas [75]	12,325
39	29	H	Leicester C	L 0-2	0-1	2		16,794
40	Apr 5	A	Watford	D 1-1	0-1	2	Arfield [96]	16,182
41	8	A	Barnsley	W 1-0	1-0	2	Barnes [7]	12,904
42	12	H	Middlesbrough	L 0-1	0-0	2		16,661
43	18	H	Blackpool	W 1-0	0-0	2	Kightly [49]	16,098
44	21	H	Wigan Ath	W 2-0	2-0	2	Barnes [22], Kightly [42]	19,125
45	26	H	Ipswich T	W 1-0	0-0	2	Kightly [54]	14,574
46	May 3	A	Reading	D 2-2	2-1	2	Arfield [20], Ings [28]	23,335

Final League Position: 2

GOALSCORERS

League (72): Ings 21 (1 pen), Vokes 20 (4 pens), Arfield 8, Kightly 5, Barnes 3, Marney 3, Shackell 2, Stanislas 2, Treacy 2, Duff 1, Jones 1, Trippier 1, own goals 3.
The Budweiser FA Cup (3): Ings 1, Long 1, Vokes 1.
Capital One Cup (8): Ings 4, Arfield 1, Jones 1, Stanislas 1, Trippier 1.

Heaton T 46	Trippier K 41	Lafferty D 8+2	Marney D 38	Long K 5+2	Shackell J 46	Wallace R 5+9	Jones D 46	Ings D 40	Vokes S 39	Stanislas J 7+20	Arfield S 42+3	Edgar D 5+12	Treacy K 9+18	Noble R —+1	Cisak A —+1	Duff M 41	Mee B 38	Kightly M 32+4	Stock B 2+7	Hewitt S —+1	Barnes A 11+10	Baird C 5+2	Match No.
1	2	3	4	5	6	7	8	9[2]	10	11[1]	12	13											1
1	2	5	7	4	3	6[1]	8	11	10	9[1]	12	13											2
1	2	5	7	4	3	6[2]	8	11[3]	10	9[1]	12		13	14									3
1[1]	2	5	8	3	4		9[2]	10[3]	11	13	7	14	6[1]		12								4
1	2	7	4				8[2]	11	10	12	9	13	6[1]			3	5						5
1	2	7	4				8	11	10	12	9					3	5	6[1]					6
1	2	12	6		4		7	9[1]	11	13	10		14			3	5[3]	8[2]					7
1	2	6	4				7[2]	9	11	10	12					3	5	8[1]	13				8
1	2	6	4				7[1]	9	11	12	10[3]	14	13			3	5	8[2]					9
1	2		4				7	10[2]	11	9	8	12				3	5	6[1]	13				10
1	2	6	4				7	9	11	10						3	5	8					11
1	2	7[2]	4				8	11	10		9	13	12			3	5	6[1]					12
1	2	6[1]	4				7	9	11		12		8[2]			3	5	10	13				13
1	2		4				8	10	11		9		7			3	5	6[1]	12				14
1	2	7	4				6	9	11	13	10[2]		12			3	5	8[1]					15
1	2		4				8	10	11		6	7	12			3	5	9[1]					16
1	2		4				7	11	10	12	6[1]	8[2]	14			3[4]	5	9[3]	13				17
1	2	3	4				8		10	11[1]	6		9[2]				5	12	7		13		18
1	2		4				7	9	11	13	8		12			3	5	10[1]	6[2]				19
1	2	7	4				6	9	11		8		12			3	5	10[1]					20
1	2	7	4				6	9	11	10			12			3	5	8[1]					21
1	2	5	7	4			6	9	11	12	8[1]		13			3		10[2]					22
1	2	5	6	13	4		7	9	11	10	8[1]					3[2]		12					23
1	2	12	7[2]		4		6	9	11	13	10		8[3]			3	5[1]	14					24
1	2	5	7	4			6	9	11	12	10		8[2]			3					13		25
1	2	5	7		3		8	10	11		9		6[1]			4					12		26
1	2	6	4				7	9	11	10						3	5	8[1]			12		27
1	2	7	4				8	10	11	12	9					3	5	6[1]					28
1	2	6	4	14			7	9	11[2]	13	10[3]					3	5	8			12		29
1	2	6	4				7	9	11	10						3	5	8[1]			12		30
1	2	7	4	12			6	9	11[1]		8[2]		13			3	5	10[3]			14		31
1	2	6	4				7	9	11[1]	10	12					3	5	8[2]			13		32
1	2	8	4	12			7	11[3]	10	14	6[2]					3	5	9[1]			13		33
1	2	8	4	12			7	11	10[2]		6					3	5	9[1]			13		34
1	2	7	4			6[1]	8	10[3]	11	12	9[3]		14			3	5				13		35
1	2	6	4			8[1]	7		11	12	10		13			3	5				9[2]		36
1		8	13		4		7		11	9[2]	6					3[1]	5	12			10	2	37
1		6	4				7		11	8[1]	10		13			3	5	8[4]			9[2]	2	38
1			4	13			6		11[2]	10[1]	7		12	14		3	5	8[4]			9	2	39
			4	12			8[1]		9		6		10[2]			3	5	7	13		11	2	40
1		8	4				7		11[1]		9		12			3	5	6			10	2	41
1	2	8	4				13	7	10		12		9[2]			3	5	6[1]			11		42
1	2	7[2]	4				8		11[1]	12	6		14			3	5	9[3]			10	13	43
1	2[1]	8	4				7		10		9					3	5	6			11	12	44
1	2	8	4				13	7	11[2]	12	9[1]		14			3	5	6[1]			10	13	45
1	2	7	4	12			8		11	13	9[1]					3	5	6[2]			10		46

The Budweiser FA Cup
Third Round   Southampton   (a)   3-4

Capital One Cup
First Round   York C   (a)   4-0
Second Round   Preston NE   (h)   2-0
Third Round   Nottingham F   (h)   2-1
Fourth Round   West Ham U   (h)   0-2

BURTON ALBION

FOUNDATION

Once upon a time there were three Football League clubs bearing the name Burton. Then there was none. In reality it had been two. Originally Burton Swifts and Burton Wanderers competed in it until 1901 when they amalgamated to form Burton United. This club disbanded in 1910. There was no senior club representing the town until 1924 when Burton Town, formerly known as Burton All Saints, played in the Birmingham & District League, subsequently joining the Midland League in 1935–36. When the Second World War broke out the club fielded a team in a truncated version of the Birmingham & District League taking over from the club's reserves. But it was not revived in peacetime. So it was not until a further decade that a club bearing the name of Burton reappeared. Founded in 1950 Burton Albion made progress from the Birmingham & District League, too, then into the Southern League and because of its geographical situation later had spells in the Northern Premier League. In April 2009 Burton Albion restored the name of the town to the Football League competition as champions of the Blue Square Premier League.

Pirelli Stadium, Princess Way, Burton-on-Trent, Staffordshire DE13 0AR.

Telephone: (01283) 565 938.

Fax: (01283) 523 199.

Ticket Office: (01283) 565 938.

Website: www.burtonalbionfc.co.uk

Email: bafc@burtonalbionfc.co.uk

Ground Capactiy: 6,912.

Record Attendance: 5,806 v Weymouth, Southern League Cup final 2nd leg 1964 (at Eton Park); 6,192 v Oxford U, Blue Square Premier, 17 April 2009 (at Pirelli Stadium).

Pitch Measurements: 100m × 68.5m (109.5yd × 75yd)

Chairman: Ben Robinson.

Manager: Gary Rowett.

Assistant Manager: Kevin Summerfield.

Physio: James Rowland.

Colours: Yellow shirts with black trim, black shorts, black socks with yellow trim.

Year Formed: 1950.

Turned Professional: 1950.

HONOURS

Conference: *Champions* 2008–09.
FA Cup: Best season: 4th rd, 2011.
Football League Cup: Best season: 3rd rd, 2013.
FA Trophy: *Runners-up* 1986–87.
Southern League – Premier Division: *Runners-up* 1999–2000, 2000–01; **Division 1 (N):** *Runners-up* 1971–72, 1973–74. **Shared Cup:** 2000.
Southern League Cup: *Winners* 1964, 1997, 2000; *Runners-up* 1989.
Northern Premier League: *Champions* 2001–02.
Northern Premier League Shield: 1983. **Challenge Cup:** *Winners* 1983; *Runners-up* 1987.
President's Cup: *Runners-up* 1983, 1986.
Birmingham Senior Cup: *Winners* 1954, 1997; *Runners-up* 1970, 1971, 1987.
Staffordshire Senior Cup: *Winners* 1956; *Runners-up* 1977.
Midland Floodlit Cup: *Winners* 1976; *Runners-up* 1973.

sky SPORTS FACT FILE

Norman Smith was the first player to sign for Burton Albion following their formation at a public meeting in July 1950. Smith, an inside forward with Football League experience at Accrington Stanley and Oldham Athletic, was a locally born player who lived in the Staffordshire town.

Club Nickname: 'The Brewers'.

Grounds: 1950, Eton Park; 2005, Pirelli Stadium.

First Football League Game: 8 August 2009, FL 2, v Shrewsbury T (a) L 1–3 – Redmond; Edworthy, Boertien, Austin, Branston, McGrath, Maghoma, Penn, Phillips (Stride), Walker, Shroot (Pearson) (1).

Record League Victory: 6-1 v Aldershot T, FL 2, 12 December 2009 – Krysiak; James, Boertien, Stride, Webster, McGrath, Jackson, Penn, Kabba (2), Pearson (3) (Harrad) (1), Gilroy (Maghoma).

Record Cup Victory: 12–1 v Coalville T, Birmingham Senior Cup, 6 September 1954.

Record Defeat: 0–10 v Barnet, Southern League, 7 February 1970.

Most League Points (3 for a win): 76, FL 2, 2012–13.

Most League Goals: 71, FL 2, 2009–10; 2012–13.

Highest League Scorer in Season: Shaun Harrad, 21, 2009–10.

Most League Goals in Total Aggregate: Billy Kee, 37, 2011–14.

Most League Goals in One Match: 3, Greg Pearson v Aldershot T, FL 2, 12 December 2009; 3, Shaun Harrad v Rotherham U, FL 2, 11 September 2010.

Most Capped Player: Jacques Maghoma, 2, DR Congo.

Most League Appearances: Jacques Maghoma, 155, 2009–13.

Youngest League Player: Tom Parkes, 18 years 8 days v Torquay U, 23 January 2010.

Record Transfer Fee Received: £200,000 from Derby Co for Adam Legzdins, June 2011.

Record Transfer Fee Paid: £25,000 to Kidderminster H for Russell Penn, July 2009.

Football League Record: 2009 Promoted from Blue Square Premier; 2009– FL 2.

MANAGERS

Reg Weston
Sammy Crooks 1957
Eddie Shimwell 1958
Bill Townsend 1959–62
Peter Taylor 1962–65
Richie Norman
Reg Gutteridge
Harold Bodle 1974–76
Ian Storey-Moore 1978–81
Neil Warnock 1981–86
Brian Fidler 1986–88
Vic Halom 1988
Bobby Hope 1988
Chris Wright 1988–89
Ken Blair 1989–90
Steve Powell 1990–91
Brian Fidler 1991–92
Brian Kenning 1992–94
John Barton 1994–98
Nigel Clough 1998–2009
Roy McFarland 2009
Paul Peschisolido 2009–12
Gary Rowett March 2012–

LATEST SEQUENCES

Longest Sequence of League Wins: 4, 9.2.2013 – 26.2.2013.

Longest Sequence of League Defeats: 8, 25.2.2012 – 24.3.2012.

Longest Sequence of League Draws: 6, 25.4.2011 – 16.8.2011.

Longest Sequence of Unbeaten League Matches: 10, 23.11.13 – 18.1.14.

Longest Sequence Without a League Win: 16, 31.12.2011 – 24.3.2012.

Successive Scoring Runs: 18 from 16.4.2011 – 8.10.2011.

Successive Non-scoring Runs: 5 from 25.2.2012 – 10.3.2012.

TEN YEAR LEAGUE RECORD

		P	W	D	L	F	A	Pts	Pos
2004-05	Conf	42	13	11	18	50	66	50	16
2005-06	Conf	42	16	12	14	50	52	60	9
2006-07	Conf	46	22	9	15	52	47	75	6
2007-08	BSP	46	23	12	11	79	56	81	5
2008-09	BSP	46	27	7	12	81	52	88	1
2009-10	FL 2	46	17	11	18	71	71	62	13
2010-11	FL 2	46	12	15	19	56	70	51	19
2011-12	FL 2	46	14	12	20	54	81	54	17
2012-13	FL 2	46	22	10	14	71	65	76	4
2013-14	FL 2	46	19	15	12	47	42	72	6

DID YOU KNOW ?

Burton Albion's first-ever league championship came in 2001–02 when they won the Northern Premier League by a margin of 15 points. The Brewers finished the season with a 23-match unbeaten run and attracted an average home gate of more than 1,400 over the campaign.

BURTON ALBION – FOOTBALL LEAGUE TWO 2013–14 LEAGUE RECORD

Match No.	Date	Venue	Opponents	Result	H/T Score	Lg Pos.	Goalscorers	Attendance
1	Aug 3	A	Cheltenham T	D	2-2	1-2	11	Kee (pen) [45], Delap [56]	3189
2	10	H	Rochdale	W	1-0	1-0	6	Lancashire (og) [44]	2679
3	17	A	Fleetwood T	W	3-2	3-0	5	Howe [12], McGurk [25], Hussey [34]	2611
4	24	H	Bury	D	2-2	0-2	5	Symes [83], McGurk [90]	2480
5	31	A	Accrington S	W	1-0	0-0	3	Reed [90]	1174
6	Sept 7	H	Oxford U	L	0-2	0-0	6		3416
7	14	H	Portsmouth	L	1-2	0-1	10	Diamond [90]	3577
8	21	A	AFC Wimbledon	L	1-3	1-0	12	McGurk [26]	4005
9	28	H	Scunthorpe U	D	2-2	1-0	13	Kee [37], Weir [62]	2556
10	Oct 5	A	Wycombe W	W	2-1	1-0	12	Kee 2 (1 pen) [27, 52 (p)]	3518
11	12	H	Southend U	L	0-1	0-0	14		2555
12	19	A	Chesterfield	W	2-0	2-0	12	McGurk 2 [10, 14]	6901
13	22	H	Torquay U	W	2-0	0-0	8	Phillips [70], McGurk [80]	2005
14	26	A	Exeter C	W	1-0	0-0	6	Edwards [88]	3658
15	Nov 2	H	Morecambe	L	0-1	0-1	7		2702
16	16	A	Dagenham & R	L	0-2	0-1	11		1626
17	23	H	Bristol R	W	1-0	0-0	7	Weir [59]	2302
18	26	H	Mansfield T	W	1-0	0-0	7	Kee [78]	2759
19	30	A	Plymouth Arg	W	1-0	1-0	6	McGurk [12]	6294
20	Dec 14	A	York C	D	1-1	0-0	6	Kee [72]	2344
21	21	A	Hartlepool U	D	1-1	1-0	5	Edwards [18]	3595
22	26	H	Northampton T	W	1-0	0-0	4	Sharps [85]	3312
23	29	H	Newport Co	W	1-0	0-0	3	Kee [79]	2692
24	Jan 1	A	Mansfield T	D	0-0	0-0	2		3266
25	11	H	Cheltenham T	W	2-1	0-0	2	Knowles 2 [72, 85]	2510
26	18	A	Bury	D	0-0	0-0	3		2910
27	25	H	Fleetwood T	L	2-4	0-1	5	Roberts (og) [50], Marrow (og) [62]	2396
28	Feb 1	H	Exeter C	D	1-1	0-0	7	McGurk [58]	2227
29	8	A	Morecambe	W	1-0	0-0	5	Ismail [72]	1478
30	15	H	Dagenham & R	D	1-1	0-1	6	Kee [69]	2934
31	18	A	Rochdale	D	1-1	1-0	6	Ismail [35]	2092
32	21	A	Bristol R	L	0-2	0-0	6		5957
33	25	A	Torquay U	D	1-1	1-1	5	McCrory [33]	1583
34	Mar 1	H	Accrington S	W	2-1	1-0	4	Kee 2 (1 pen) [34, 80 (p)]	2368
35	8	A	Oxford U	W	2-1	2-0	4	Knowles [10], Ismail [26]	5413
36	11	A	Portsmouth	D	0-0	0-0	4		12,780
37	15	H	AFC Wimbledon	D	1-1	1-0	5	Kee (pen) [22]	2592
38	22	H	Scunthorpe U	L	0-1	0-0	5		4029
39	25	H	Wycombe W	W	1-0	0-0	5	McGurk [54]	1784
40	29	A	York C	D	0-0	0-0	5		3988
41	Apr 5	H	Plymouth Arg	W	1-0	1-0	5	McFadzean [27]	2962
42	12	A	Northampton T	L	0-1	0-1	5		4604
43	19	H	Hartlepool U	W	3-0	1-0	5	Kee [26], Phillips [58], Bell [86]	2558
44	21	A	Newport Co	D	1-1	1-1	5	Symes (pen) [36]	2630
45	27	H	Chesterfield	L	0-2	0-0	5		4855
46	May 3	A	Southend U	L	0-1	0-1	6		6218

Final League Position: 6

GOALSCORERS

League (47): Kee 12 (4 pens), McGurk 9, Ismail 3, Knowles 3, Edwards 2, Phillips 2, Symes 2 (1 pen), Weir 2, Bell 1, Delap 1, Diamond 1, Howe 1, Hussey 1, McCrory 1, McFadzean 1, Reed 1, Sharps 1, own goals 3.
The Budweiser FA Cup (5): Kee 2, McGurk 1, Palmer 1, Phillips 1.
Capital One Cup (4): Hussey 2, Dyer 1, Symes 1.
Johnstone's Paint Trophy (0).
League Two Play-Offs (3): McGurk 2, Holness 1.

Pickford J 12	Edwards P 39+2	McCrory D 40	Weir R 40+1	Sharps I 39	Holness M 14+3	Reed A 3+2	Delap R 6	MacDonald A 16+19	Kee B 29+8	Hussey C 22+5	Palmer M 31+9	Knowles D 11+17	Dyer J —+4	McGurk A 31+3	Bell L 26+8	Howe R 7+8	Symes M 7+6	Lyness D 20+1	Phillips J 27+6	Diamond Z 6+4	Cansdell-Sherriff S 32	Ismail Z 10+5	Alexander G 7+4	Lainton R 14	Gray D 7+5	Harness M 1+2	McFadzean C 7	Hemmings A 2+3	Match No.
1	2	3	4	5	6	7	8	9^2	10^1	11	12	13	14																1
1		5	7	3	4		2	12	10^2	9				6	8	11^1	13												2
13	5	8	3	4	12	2		6^1		9		14		11^2	7	10^2		1											3
	5	7^1	4	3	2		6^2		9	12	14			10	8	11^3	13	1											4
	5		3	4	8	2		9^1		13	14			6	7	11	10^2	1	12^3										5
12	5		3^4	4	7	2		9	14					6	8^2	11^2	10^1	1	13										6
1	2	5		4				12			13	7		9	8	10^1	11		6	3									7
1	2	4	7	5^6				9^1			11	13	8	6	12	10^1			3										8
1	2	5	7					6^2	11^3	9		14		13	8	12	10^1		3	4									9
1	2	9	8	3				6^1	11^2	5	12	13		10	7					4									10
1	2	5	8	3				6^2	10^4	9^1	12			11	7				13	4									11
1	2	8	7^2	3					10	9	14	11^3	5^1						6	12	4								12
1	2	5	7	4				12	11	9^1	8			10					6	3									13
1	2	5	8	3				12	11^1	6	7			10					9	4									14
1	2	5	8	3				12	10^2	9^3	7	14		11			13		6^1	4^6									15
1	2	5	9	3				6^2	14	10^3	8			11	7^1		12		13	4									16
	2	5	7	3				12	9^2	8	10^1			11^3	13	14		1	6^6	4									17
	2	5	7	3				14	13	9^3	6^1	10^2		11	8	12		1		4									18
	2	5	7	3				9	6^3	10^1				11^2	8	12		1	13	14	4								19
	2	5	8	4				6^2	10	9^1	12			7	11			1	13	3									20
	2	5^1	8	3		14			11^2	9	7			10^3				1	6	12	4								21
	2	8^3	4					12	10^2	9^1	7			11	14	13		1	6	3									22
	2	8^1	3					6^2	11	13	7			10^1		13		1	9	4									23
	2	5	8	4				6^2	11	12	7			10^1		13		1	9	14	3^3								24
	2	6	3^3	7				4^1	9		10	13		11^3	14		1	8	5		12								25
	2	5	8	4				10^2	12	7	13			11^2	14		1	9	3		6^1								26
	2	5	8	4				11			6	10		7^1			1	9	3		12								27
	2	5	8	3				10^1	14	7	13			11^2			1	9^3		4	6	12							28
	2	5	7	3				6^1	14	12	8			11			9^2		4	13	10^3	1							29
	2	5	8	3				13	12	7	14			10^1			9^3		4	6	11^2	1							30
	2	5^1	7	4				14	13	9				8			10		3	6^3	11^2	1	12						31
	2		8^1	3	12			13	11^3	5	6	14		10	12		9^2		3	7		1							32
	2	9	6	3				14	13		8	12		10^1					4	7^3	11^2	1	5						33
	2	5	8	3				12	11		7	10^2		13	14		9^1		4	6		1							34
	2	5	7	3^3	13			10			8	11^1		12			9^3		4	6		1	14						35
	2	5	7	3				12	10^3			11^2		13	8		9^1		4	6		1	14						36
	2	5	7	3				13	11		12	10^1		8			9^3		4	6^2		1	14						37
	2	5	9	4^3				6^2	11		8	12		7^1			10		3			1	14	13					38
	2	5	8	3^2	13			12	10		7			11^3					4	14	1	6		9^1					39
	2	5		3				14	11^1		7			10^3	8				4	12	1	6		9^2	13				40
		5	14	3				12	10^1		8			7		13	9		4	11^2	1	2		6^3				41
	5		8	4				11			7			10			13	9^3	3	14	11	1	2		6^2	12			42
	2		8^1	3	12			6	10^3		13			7		14	1	9	4^1	11			5						43
		3	4		12			14			8	10^2		7			11^3	1	9					2	13	5	6^1		44
	2	7^1	3	4				9	10^2		6	14		8^3			1			13	11				5	12			45
	3	9		4				14		5	7	13		10^3			11^2	1		12				2	6^1		8		46

The Budweiser FA Cup

First Round	Hereford U		(h)	2-0
Second Round	Fleetwood T		(a)	1-1
Replay	Fleetwood T		(h)	1-0
Third Round	Bournemouth		(a)	1-4

Johnstone's Paint Trophy

First Round	Notts Co		(a)	0-1

Capital One Cup

First Round	Sheffield U		(a)	2-1
Second Round	Fulham		(h)	2-2
(aet; lost 4-5 on penalties)				

League Two Play-Offs

Semi-Finals 1st leg	Southend U		(h)	1-0
Semi-Finals 2nd leg	Southend U		(a)	2-2
Final	Fleetwood T	(Wembley)		0-1

BURY

FOUNDATION

A meeting at the Waggon & Horses Hotel, attended largely by members of Bury Wesleyans and Bury Unitarians football clubs, decided to form a new Bury club. This was officially formed at a subsequent gathering at the Old White Horse Hotel, Fleet Street, Bury on 24 April 1885.

Gigg Lane, Bury, Lancashire BL9 9HR.

Telephone: (0871) 222 1885.

Fax: (0161) 764 5521.

Ticket Office: (08445) 790009.

Website: www.buryfc.co.uk

Email: info@buryfc.co.uk

Ground Capacity: 11,313.

Record Attendance: 35,000 v Bolton W, FA Cup 3rd rd, 9 January 1960.

Pitch Measurements: 102.5m × 64m (112yd × 70yd)

Chairman: Stewart Day.

Chief Executive: Glenn Thomas.

Manager: David Flitcroft.

Assistant Manager: Chris Brass.

Physio: Tom Walsh.

Colours: White shirts with blue trim, blue shorts, blue socks with white hoops.

Year Formed: 1885.

Turned Professional: 1885.

Club Nickname: 'The Shakers'.

Ground: 1885, Gigg Lane.

HONOURS

Football League – Division 1: Best season: 4th, 1925–26; **Division 2:** *Champions* 1894–95, 1996–97; *Runners-up* 1923–24; **Division 3:** *Champions* 1960–61; *Runners-up* 1967–68; **FL 2:** *Runners-up* 2010–11. **FA Cup:** *Winners* 1900, 1903. **Football League Cup:** Semi-final 1963.

First Football League Game: 1 September 1894, Division 2, v Manchester C (h) W 4–2 – Lowe; Gillespie, Davies; White, Clegg, Ross; Wylie, Barbour (2), Millar (1), Ostler (1), Plant.

Record League Victory: 8–0 v Tranmere R, Division 3, 10 January 1970 – Forrest; Tinney, Saile; Anderson, Turner, McDermott; Hince (1), Arrowsmith (1), Jones (4), Kerr (1), Grundy, (1 og).

Record Cup Victory: 12–1 v Stockton, FA Cup 1st rd (replay), 2 February 1897 – Montgomery; Darroch, Barbour; Hendry (1), Clegg, Ross (1); Wylie (3), Pangbourn, Millar (4), Henderson (2), Plant, (1 og).

Record Defeat: 0–10 v Blackburn R, FA Cup pr rd, 1 October 1887. 0–10 v West Ham U, Milk Cup 2nd rd 2nd leg, 25 October 1983.

Most League Points (2 for a win): 68, Division 3, 1960–61.

Most League Points (3 for a win): 84, Division 4, 1984–85 and Division 2, 1996–97.

sky SPORTS FACT FILE

Australian goalkeeper Ken Grieves made his debut for Bury in October 1947 and went on to make over 50 first team appearances for the club but was better known as a cricketer who played 452 times for Lancashire CCC. Grieves set a county record of 555 catches during his time with the Red Rose team.

Most League Goals: 108, Division 3, 1960–61.

Highest League Scorer in Season: Craig Madden, 35, Division 4, 1981–82.

Most League Goals in Total Aggregate: Craig Madden, 129, 1978–86.

Most League Goals in One Match: 5, Eddie Quigley v Millwall, Division 2, 15 February 1947; 5, Ray Pointer v Rotherham U, Division 2, 2 October 1965.

Most Capped Player: Bill Gorman, 11 (13), Republic of Ireland and (4), Northern Ireland.

Most League Appearances: Norman Bullock, 506, 1920–35.

Youngest League Player: Brian Williams, 16 years 133 days v Stockport Co, 18 March 1972.

Record Transfer Fee Received: £1,100,000 from Ipswich T for David Johnson, November 1997.

Record Transfer Fee Paid: £200,000 to Ipswich T for Chris Swailes, November 1997; £200,000 to Swindon T for Darren Bullock, February 1999.

Football League Record: 1894 Elected to Division 2; 1895–1912 Division 1; 1912–24 Division 2; 1924–29 Division 1; 1929–57 Division 2; 1957–61 Division 3; 1961–67 Division 2; 1967–68 Division 3; 1968–69 Division 2; 1969–71 Division 3; 1971–74 Division 4; 1974–80 Division 3; 1980–85 Division 4; 1985–96 Division 3; 1996–97 Division 2; 1997–99 Division 1; 1999–2002 Division 2; 2002–04 Division 3; 2004–11 FL 2; 2011–13 FL 1; 2013– FL 2.

LATEST SEQUENCES

Longest Sequence of League Wins: 9, 26.9.1960 – 19.11.1960.

Longest Sequence of League Defeats: 8, 18.8.2001 – 25.9.2001.

Longest Sequence of League Draws: 6, 6.3.1999 – 3.4.1999.

Longest Sequence of Unbeaten League Matches: 18, 4.2.1961 – 29.4.1961.

Longest Sequence Without a League Win: 19, 1.4.1911 – 2.12.1911.

Successive Scoring Runs: 24 from 1.9.1894.

Successive Non-scoring Runs: 6 from 11.1.1969.

MANAGERS

T. Hargreaves 1887
  (*Secretary-Manager*)
H. S. Hamer 1887–1907
  (*Secretary-Manager*)
Archie Montgomery 1907–15
William Cameron 1919–23
James Hunter Thompson 1923–27
Percy Smith 1927–30
Arthur Paine 1930–34
Norman Bullock 1934–38
Charlie Dean 1938–44
Jim Porter 1944–45
Norman Bullock 1945–49
John McNeil 1950–53
Dave Russell 1953–61
Bob Stokoe 1961–65
Bert Head 1965–66
Les Shannon 1966–69
Jack Marshall 1969
Colin McDonald 1970
Les Hart 1970
Tommy McAnearney 1970–72
Alan Brown 1972–73
Bobby Smith 1973–77
Bob Stokoe 1977–78
David Hatton 1978–79
Dave Connor 1979–80
Jim Iley 1980–84
Martin Dobson 1984–89
Sam Ellis 1989–90
Mike Walsh 1990–95
Stan Ternent 1995–98
Neil Warnock 1998–99
Andy Preece 1999–2003
Graham Barrow 2003–05
Chris Casper 2005–08
Alan Knill 2008–11
Richie Barker 2011–12
Kevin Blackwell 2012–13
David Flitcroft December 2013–

TEN YEAR LEAGUE RECORD

		P	W	D	L	F	A	Pts	Pos
2004-05	FL 2	46	14	16	16	54	54	58	17
2005-06	FL 2	46	12	17	17	45	57	52*	19
2006-07	FL 2	46	13	11	22	46	61	50	21
2007-08	FL 2	46	16	11	19	58	61	59	13
2008-09	FL 2	46	21	15	10	63	43	78	4
2009-10	FL 2	46	19	12	15	54	59	69	9
2010-11	FL 2	46	23	12	11	82	50	81	2
2011-12	FL 1	46	15	11	20	60	79	56	14
2012-13	FL 1	46	9	14	23	45	73	41	22
2013-14	FL 2	46	13	20	13	59	51	59	12

*1 pt deducted.

DID YOU KNOW ?

Bury stalwart Teddy Bullen made 188 Football League appearances for the Shakers after joining the club in 1906. He served his country as a gunner in the Royal Field Artillery and continued to appear for Bury in wartime football. Bullen was killed in action on 11 August 1917 at Vaux, close to Arras.

BURY – FOOTBALL LEAGUE TWO 2013–14 LEAGUE RECORD

Match No.	Date	Venue	Opponents	Result	H/T Score	Lg Pos.	Goalscorers	Attendance
1	Aug 3	H	Chesterfield	L	0-2	0-0	20		4337
2	10	A	Oxford U	L	1-2	0-1	22	Soares [70]	5774
3	17	H	Accrington S	W	3-0	2-0	15	Forrester [28], Sinnott [38], Jackson [87]	3080
4	24	A	Burton Alb	D	2-2	2-0	16	Forrester [16], Edjenguele [41]	2480
5	31	H	Cheltenham T	W	4-1	3-1	10	Procter [12], Mayor [9], Cameron [17], Reindorf [76]	2910
6	Sept 7	A	Rochdale	L	0-1	0-1	14		5616
7	14	A	Fleetwood T	L	1-2	1-0	17	Soares [28]	3520
8	21	H	Southend U	D	1-1	0-1	18	Forrester [90]	2895
9	28	A	Dagenham & R	L	1-2	0-1	20	Forrester (pen) [89]	1604
10	Oct 5	H	Newport Co	D	0-0	0-0	18		3093
11	12	H	Morecambe	L	0-2	0-0	21		3082
12	19	A	Portsmouth	L	0-1	0-1	22		15,434
13	22	H	Mansfield T	D	0-0	0-0	20		2518
14	26	A	Wycombe W	W	2-1	0-1	19	Soares [69], Edjenguele [88]	3350
15	Nov 2	H	Torquay U	L	1-3	1-2	22	Cameron [24]	2997
16	16	H	Bristol R	D	1-1	1-1	21	Hylton [36]	5534
17	23	H	AFC Wimbledon	D	1-1	1-0	21	Hylton [35]	2775
18	26	H	Hartlepool U	W	1-0	0-0	20	Nardiello [48]	1998
19	30	A	Exeter C	D	2-2	1-1	20	Nardiello [15], Cameron [47]	3426
20	Dec 14	H	Northampton T	D	1-1	1-1	19	Nardiello (pen) [23]	2835
21	21	A	Plymouth Arg	L	1-2	0-1	23	Sedgwick [49]	6206
22	26	A	Scunthorpe U	D	2-2	0-1	23	Sedgwick [75], Nardiello [90]	3277
23	29	H	York C	W	2-1	2-0	20	Forrester [1], Cameron [19]	3706
24	Jan 1	A	Hartlepool U	W	3-0	2-0	16	Mayor [5], Nardiello [12], Hinds [75]	3529
25	11	A	Chesterfield	L	0-4	0-1	19		6053
26	18	H	Burton Alb	D	0-0	0-0	19		2910
27	Feb 1	H	Wycombe W	W	1-0	1-0	20	Forrester [34]	2818
28	4	A	Oxford U	D	1-1	0-0	17	Jones [56]	2303
29	18	A	Accrington S	D	0-0	0-0	21		2184
30	22	A	AFC Wimbledon	W	1-0	0-0	20	Mayor [90]	3740
31	25	A	Mansfield T	W	4-1	1-0	15	Mayor [25], Nardiello 2 [56, 64], Carroll [71]	2628
32	Mar 1	A	Cheltenham T	L	1-2	1-1	16	Platt [16]	2737
33	7	H	Rochdale	D	0-0	0-0	15		6295
34	11	H	Fleetwood T	D	2-2	0-1	19	Nardiello 2 (1 pen) [47, 61 (p)]	2467
35	15	A	Southend U	D	0-0	0-0	17		5680
36	18	A	Torquay U	L	1-2	0-1	18	Platt [66]	1738
37	22	H	Dagenham & R	D	1-1	0-0	19	Hussey [60]	2705
38	25	A	Newport Co	D	0-0	0-0	19		2160
39	29	A	Northampton T	W	3-0	2-0	16	Hope [18], Mayor [35], Rose [90]	4631
40	Apr 1	H	Bristol R	W	2-1	1-1	12	Hope [3], Soares [80]	2314
41	5	H	Exeter C	W	2-0	0-0	11	Hussey [65], Soares [90]	2718
42	12	A	Scunthorpe U	D	2-2	0-0	11	Soares [69], Rose [90]	4162
43	18	H	Plymouth Arg	W	4-0	1-0	10	Tutte [8], Nardiello 2 (1 pen) [50 (p), 53], Rose [88]	3401
44	21	A	York C	L	0-1	0-1	10		5225
45	26	H	Portsmouth	D	4-4	2-0	10	Hope 3 [10, 34, 87], Procter [49]	4759
46	May 3	A	Morecambe	D	0-0	0-0	12		2944

Final League Position: 12

GOALSCORERS

League (59): Nardiello 11 (3 pens), Forrester 6 (1 pen), Soares 6, Hope 5, Mayor 5, Cameron 4, Rose 3, Edjenguele 2, Hussey 2, Hylton 2, Platt 2, Procter 2, Sedgwick 2, Carroll 1, Hinds 1, Jackson 1, Jones 1, Reindorf 1, Sinnott 1, Tutte 1.
The Budweiser FA Cup (1): Harrad 1.
Capital One Cup (6): Harrad 1 (1 pen), Begley 1, Edjenguele 1, Forrester 1, Hinds 1, Reindorf 1.
Johnstone's Paint Trophy (1): Sedgwick 1.

Lainton R 4	Beeley S 20	Roberts G 11	Procter A 23+9	Hinds R 8+2	Cameron N 25+2	Jones C 33+4	Holden E 2	Plant C 8+9	Harrad S 10+8	Grimes A 6+9	Soares T 24+6	Forrester A 18+10	Jackson M 2+6	Carroll J 5+1	Mayor D 30+9	Young L —+4	Rooney J 1+2	Sinnott J 5+4	Hussey C 10+1	Lockwood A 1	Edjenguele W 18+1	Miller T 25+3	Carson T 5	Charles-Cook R 1+1	Reindorf J 1+3	Obadeyi T —+7	Sedgwick C 32+5	Jensen B 36	Mustoe J 6	Hope H 8	Navas M 1+1	Hylton D 7	Rose D —+6	Walker R —+3	Burgess S 1	Howell D 8	Nardiello D 25+2	Harrison S —+1	Poscha M —+1	Burke J 2	Veseli F 18	McNulty J 21	Mills P 21	Dudley A —+2	Tutte A 19	Akpro Akpro J 5+5	Match No.
1	2	3	4	5	6	7		8^3	9^1	10^1	11	12	13	14																																		1
1	2	5	6	3	4^4	11	7	8^1		10^3	12	14			9^2	13																															2
1	2	4	8	3		9		13	10^2	6^1	5^3	14	12		7	11																															3
1	2	5	7		3	6		12	13		11^1	14			9^3			8^2			4	10																									4
	2	5	8	3	6				10^2	11^1	9^3	13									4	7	1				12	14																			5
	2	5	6	3	10			14	11^3	9^1	8^2										4	7	1				12	13																			6
		5	7	4^3	2	6		12	10^1	11	14	13			8^1						3	9	1																								7
	2	5	7	4	6			10^2		9^1	11		12		14						3	8^3	1				13																				8
	2	5	8	3	6			10			11^2	13			9^1	12					4	7^1	1		11^1		14																				9
	2		8	3				12	10		11^2		14		13	7					4	9^3					12	1	5	6^1																	10
	2		8	3	6^1				10		11	14			13		7^2				4	9^3					12	1	5																		11
	2		7	3				10^2			9	13	12								4	8^1					6	1	5					11													12
	2		7	3				10			6	13	12								4	8^1					9^2	1	5					11													13
	2		7	3				10			8	12	9								4						6	1	5					11^1													14
	2		8	3	14			10^2	13	7	11^1		9								4						6^1	1	5							12											15
	2		7	3^1	4			13	11^3	8			9								12						6^1	1						14		5	10										16
	2		7	3	6			12		8											4						9^1	1						11		5	10										17
	2	13		3^2	6			12		8											4	7					9	1						11		5	10^1										18
	2		7	3	6				8		12										4							1						11		5	10										19
	2		8	3	6			10^2	13	7^1											4						9^1	1						11		5	10										20
2^1			6^3	3	9			14			13	10									4	7					8	1						12		5	11^2										21
	2^3	8	12	3				10^2	14		13		9								4^1	7					6	1								5	11										22
	2^4	8	4	3				14	12		10^3		9^1									7					6	1						11		5		13									23
	8	4	3		12			13							11^2	9^3						7					6	1							14		10^1					2	5				24
	8^2	4	3^1					14	12		11^3				9							7				13	6	1									10					2	5				25
		13						6							7							7				12	5	1									11				2	3	4	14			26
		13									5	12			9^2	10^3						6				14	8	1									12				2	4	3		7	11^1	27
								5			13	9^1	14		10^3							6					7	1									12				3	4	2		8	11^2	28
								5			13				11			8^2				6				14	12	1									9				2^3	4	3		7	10^1	29
								7			12				10^1		2	6				8					13	1									11^2				4	5	3		9^2	13	30
								7			11^1				12		2	6				13					6	1									10^3				4	5	3	14	8		31
											5^1				9^2	13		8	10	14		6^3						12						11							2	6	3		7^2		32
											9	14	13		4	11^1	12					8^3					5										10				2	6	3		7^2		33
											11^2	12	13^3		9^1	7		11	14			8^4				12	5	1									10				2	4	3		6	14	34
											5	11		8^1	14	9^3		12							1		6										10^2				2	4	3		7	13	35
		12									5	7^2			11^3	14		9									6	1									10				2	4	3		7	13	36
		12									6	11^2			8			4									7	1									10				2	5	3		9^1	13	37
		12									6	14			9^1			5									7	1		10^2		13					11^2				2	4	3		8		38
		14									5^1				7			9									6	1		10^3		12		11								2	4	3		8^2		40
											5^2		14		7			9		13							6	1		11^1		12		10								2	4	3		8^3		41
		14									2	13	9^2		6			5^2									8	1	11					12				10^1					3	4		7		42
											5	14	6		9			4		13							7^1	1	11^1					12				10^2					3	2		8		43
			14								2	13	9		6			5									8^1	1	11					12				10^8					3	4^3		7^1		44
		12		14		2		10^1			6				9			5								13	7^1	1	11														3	4		8^3		45
				4		2		10							6												8	1	11^2							13	7^1		12			5	3		9		46

The Budweiser FA Cup

First Round — Cambridge U — (h) — 0-0
Replay — Cambridge U — (a) — 1-2

Capital One Cup

First Round — Crewe Alex — (h) — 3-2
Second Round — Norwich C — (a) — 3-6

Johnstone's Paint Trophy

First Round — Port Vale — (a) — 1-2

CAMBRIDGE UNITED

FOUNDATION

The football revival in Cambridge began soon after World War II when the Abbey United club (formed 1912) decided to turn professional in 1949. In 1951 they changed their name to Cambridge United. They were competing in the United Counties League before graduating to the Eastern Counties League in 1951 and the Southern League in 1958.

The R Costings Abbey Stadium, Newmarket Road, Cambridge CB5 8LN.

Telephone: (01223) 566 500.

Fax: (01223) 729 220.

Ticket Office: (01223) 566 500.

Website: www.cambridgeunited.com

Email: info@cambridge-united.co.uk

Ground Capacity: 8,696.

Record Attendance: 14,000 v Chelsea, Friendly, 1 May 1970.

Pitch Measurements: 100.5m × 67.5m (110yd × 74yd).

Chairman: Dave Doggett.

Vice-chairman: Eddie Clarke.

Head Coach: Richard Money.

Assistant Coach: Alan Neilson.

Physio: Greg Reid.

Colours: Amber shirts with black trim, black shorts, amber stockings.

Year Formed: 1912.

Turned Professional: 1949.

Ltd Co.: 1948.

Previous Name: 1919, Abbey United; 1951, Cambridge United.

Club Nickname: The 'U's'.

First Football League Game: 15 August 1970, Division 4, v Lincoln C (h) D 1–1 – Roberts; Thompson, Meldrum (1), Slack, Eades, Hardy, Leggett, Cassidy, Lindsey, McKinven, Harris.

Record League Victory: 6–0 v Darlington, Division 4, 18 September 1971 – Roberts; Thompson, Akers, Guild, Eades, Foote, Collins (1p), Horrey, Hollett, Greenhalgh (4), Phillips, (1 og). 6–0 v Hartlepool U, Division 4, 11 February 1989 – Vaughan; Beck, Kimble, Turner, Chapple (1), Daish, Clayton, Holmes, Taylor (3 incl. 1p), Bull (1), Leadbitter (1).

Record Cup Victory: 5–1 v Bristol C, FA Cup 5th rd second replay, 27 February 1990 – Vaughan; Fensome, Kimble, Bailie (O'Shea), Chapple, Daish, Cheetham (Robinson), Leadbitter (1), Dublin (2), Taylor (1), Philpott (1).

HONOURS

Football League – Division 2: Best season: 5th, 1991–92; **Division 3: Champions** 1990–91; *Runners-up* 1977–78, 1998–99; **Division 4: Champions** 1976–77; *Promoted from Division 4* 1989–90 (play-offs).

Skrill Conference: *Promoted to FL 2* 2013–14 (play-offs).

FA Cup: Best season: 6th rd, 1990 (shared record for Fourth Division club), 1991.

Football League Cup: Best season: 5th rd, 1993.

LDV Vans Trophy: *Runners-up* 2002.

sky SPORTS FACT FILE

Abbey United, as the U's were then known, enjoyed considerable success during the 1920s, winning the Cambridgeshire Senior Cup three times (once shared), the Cambridgeshire League twice (1925–26 and 1928–29) and the Creake Charity Shield four times (once shared). They won all three trophies in 1928–29 as well as the Bury & District Cup and the Chatteris Nursing Cup.

Record Defeat: 0–7 v Sunderland, League Cup 2nd rd, 1 October 2002.

Most League Points (2 for a win): 65, Division 4, 1976–77.

Most League Points (3 for a win): 86, Division 3, 1990–91.

Most League Goals: 87, Division 4, 1976–77.

Highest League Scorer in Season: David Crown, 24, Division 4, 1985–86.

Most League Goals in Total Aggregate: John Taylor, 86, 1988–92; 1996–2001.

Most League Goals in One Match: 5, Steve Butler v Exeter C, Division 2, 4 April 1994.

Most Capped Player: Tom Finney, 7 (15), Northern Ireland.

Most League Appearances: Steve Spriggs, 416, 1975–87.

Youngest League Player: Andy Sinton, 16 years 228 days v Wolverhampton W, 2 November 1982.

Record Transfer Fee Received: £1,000,000 from Manchester U for Dion Dublin, August 1992; £1,000,000 from Leicester C for Trevor Benjamin, July 2000.

Record Transfer Fee Paid: £192,000 to Luton T for Steve Claridge, November 1992.

Football League Record: 1970 Elected to Division 4; 1973–74 Division 3; 1974–77 Division 4; 1977–78 Division 3; 1978–84 Division 2; 1984–85 Division 3; 1985–90 Division 4; 1990–91 Division 3; 1991–92 Division 2; 1992–93 Division 1; 1993–95 Division 2; 1995–99 Division 3; 1999–2002 Division 2; 2002–04 Division 3; 2004–05 FL2; 2005–14 Conference; 2014– FL 2.

MANAGERS

Bill Whittaker 1949–55
Gerald Williams 1955
Bert Johnson 1955–59
Bill Craig 1959–60
Alan Moore 1960–63
Roy Kirk 1964–66
Bill Leivers 1967–74
Ron Atkinson 1974–78
John Docherty 1978–83
John Ryan 1984–85
Ken Shellito 1985
Chris Turner 1985–90
John Beck 1990–92
Ian Atkins 1992–93
Gary Johnson 1993–95
Tommy Taylor 1995–96
Roy McFarland 1996–2001
John Beck 2001
John Taylor 2002–04
Claude Le Roy 2004
Herve Renard 2004
Steve Thompson 2004–05
Rob Newman 2005–06
Jimmy Quinn 2006–08
Gary Brabin 2008–09
Martin Ling 2009–11
Jez George 2011–12
Richard Money October 2012–

LATEST SEQUENCES

Longest Sequence of League Wins: 7, 19.2.1977 – 1.4.1977.

Longest Sequence of League Defeats: 7, 8.4.1985 – 30.4.1985.

Longest Sequence of League Draws: 6, 6.9.1986 – 30.9.1986.

Longest Sequence of Unbeaten League Matches: 14, 9.9.1972 – 10.11.1972.

Longest Sequence Without a League Win: 31, 8.10.1983 – 23.4.1984.

Successive Scoring Runs: 26 from 9.4.2002.

Successive Non-scoring Runs: 5 from 29.9.1973.

TEN YEAR LEAGUE RECORD

		P	W	D	L	F	A	Pts	Pos
2004-05	FL 2	46	8	16	22	39	62	30*	24
2005-06	Conf	42	15	10	17	51	57	55	12
2006-07	Conf	46	15	10	21	57	66	55	17
2007-08	Conf P	46	25	11	10	68	41	86	2
2008-09	Conf P	46	24	14	8	65	39	86	2
2009-10	Conf P	44	15	14	15	65	53	59	10
2010-11	Conf P	46	11	17	18	53	61	50	17
2011-12	Conf P	46	19	14	13	57	41	71	9
2012-13	Conf P	46	15	14	17	68	69	59	14
2013-14	Conf P	46	23	13	10	72	35	82	2

*10 pts deducted.

DID YOU KNOW ?

Abbey United twice reached the first round proper of the FA Amateur Cup. In 1945–46 they lost 5-3 at home to Hitchin Town, while in 1947–48 they went down 1-0 at home to local rivals Cambridge Town in front of an estimated crowd of 5,000, a new ground record.

CARDIFF CITY

FOUNDATION

Credit for the establishment of a first class professional football club in such a rugby stronghold as Cardiff is due to members of the Riverside club formed in 1899 out of a cricket club of that name. Cardiff became a city in 1905 and in 1908 the South Wales and Monmouthshire FA granted Riverside permission to call themselves Cardiff City. The club turned professional under that name in 1910.

Cardiff City Stadium, Leckwith Road, Cardiff CF11 8AZ.

Telephone: (0845) 365 1115. *Fax:* (0845) 365 1116.

Ticket Office: (0845) 345 1400.

Website: www.cardiffcityfc.co.uk

Email: club@cardiffcityfc.co.uk

Ground Capacity: 28,050.

Record Attendance: 57,893 v Arsenal, Division 1, 22 April 1953 (at Ninian Park); 28,018 v Liverpool, FA Premier League, 22 March 2014 (at Cardiff City Stadium).

Ground Record Attendance: 62,634, Wales v England, 17 October 1959 (at Ninian Park).

Pitch Measurements: 105m × 68m (114yd × 75yd)

Chairman/Chief Executive: Simon Lim.

Manager: Ole Gunnar Solskjaer.

Assistant Manager: Mark Dempsey.

Physio: Sean Connelly.

Colours: Red shirts, black shorts, red socks.

Year Formed: 1899.

Turned Professional: 1910.

Previous Names: 1899, Riverside; 1902, Riverside Albion; 1908, Cardiff City.

Club Nickname: 'The Bluebirds'.

Grounds: Riverside, Sophia Gardens, Old Park and Fir Gardens; 1910, Ninian Park; 2009, Cardiff City Stadium.

HONOURS

Football League Division 1:
Runners-up 1923–24;
Division 2: *Runners-up* 1920–21, 1951–52, 1959–60;
FL C: *Champions* 2012–13;
Division 3 (S): *Champions* 1946–47;
Division 3: *Champions* 1992–93.
Runners-up 1975–76, 1982–83, 2000–01;
Division 4: *Runners-up* 1987–88.
FA Cup: *Winners* 1927 (only occasion the Cup has been won by a club outside England); *Runners-up* 1925, 2008.

Football League Cup: *Runners-up* 2012.

Welsh Cup: *Winners* 22 times (joint record).

Charity Shield: Winners 1927.

European Competitions
European Cup-Winners' Cup:
1964–65, 1965–66, 1967–68 (*s-f*), 1968–69, 1969–70, 1970–71, 1971–72, 1973–74, 1974–75, 1976–77, 1977–78, 1988–89, 1992–93, 1993–94.

First Football League Game: 28 August 1920, Division 2, v Stockport Co (a) W 5–2 – Kneeshaw; Brittan, Leyton; Keenor (1), Smith, Hardy; Grimshaw (1), Gill (2), Cashmore, West, Evans (1).

Record League Victory: 9–2 v Thames, Division 3 (S), 6 February 1932 – Farquharson; Eric Morris, Roberts; Galbraith, Harris, Ronan; Emmerson (1), Keating (1), Jones (1), McCambridge (1), Robbins (5).

Record Cup Victory: 8–0 v Enfield, FA Cup 1st rd, 28 November 1931 – Farquharson; Smith, Roberts; Harris (1), Galbraith, Ronan; Emmerson (2), Keating (3); O'Neill (2), Robbins, McCambridge.

sky SPORTS FACT FILE

The Wales rugby international Wilf Wooller signed amateur forms for Cardiff City in July 1939 as a centre forward only for his football career to be curtailed by the outbreak of war. Wilf, who won 18 caps for Wales at rugby union, also excelled at cricket and later captained Glamorgan for 14 seasons. He also represented Wales at squash.

Record Defeat: 2–11 v Sheffield U, Division 1, 1 January 1926.

Most League Points (2 for a win): 66, Division 3 (S), 1946–47.

Most League Points (3 for a win): 87, FL C, 2012–13.

Most League Goals: 95, Division 3, 2000–01.

Highest League Scorer in Season: Robert Earnshaw, 31, Division 2, 2002–03.

Most League Goals in Total Aggregate: Len Davies, 128, 1920–31.

Most League Goals in One Match: 5, Hugh Ferguson v Burnley, Division 1, 1 September 1928; 5, Walter Robbins v Thames, Division 3 (S), 6 February 1932; 5, William Henderson v Northampton T, Division 3 (S), 22 April 1933.

Most Capped Player: Alf Sherwood, 39 (41), Wales.

Most League Appearances: Phil Dwyer, 471, 1972–85.

Youngest League Player: Bob Adams, 15 years 355 days v Southend U, 18 February 1933.

Record Transfer Fee Received: £5,000,000 from Sunderland for Michael Chopra, August 2006; £5,000,000 from Arsenal for Aaron Ramsey, June 2008; £5,000,000 from Birmingham C for Roger Johnson, June 2009.

Record Transfer Fee Paid: £11,000,000 to Sevilla for Gary Medel, August 2013.

Football League Record: 1920 Elected to Division 2; 1921–29 Division 1; 1929–31 Division 2; 1931–47 Division 3 (S); 1947–52 Division 2; 1952–57 Division 1; 1957–60 Division 2; 1960–62 Division 1; 1962–75 Division 2; 1975–76 Division 3; 1976–82 Division 2; 1982–83 Division 3; 1983–85 Division 2; 1985–86 Division 3; 1986–88 Division 4; 1988–90 Division 3; 1990–92 Division 4; 1992–93 Division 3; 1993–95 Division 2; 1995–99 Division 3; 1999–2000 Division 2; 2000–01 Division 3; 2001–03 Division 2; 2003–04 Division 1; 2004–13 FL C; 2013–14 FA Premier League; 2014– FL C.

LATEST SEQUENCES

Longest Sequence of League Wins: 9, 26.10.1946 – 28.12.1946.

Longest Sequence of League Defeats: 7, 4.11.1933 – 25.12.1933.

Longest Sequence of League Draws: 6, 29.11.1980 – 17.1.1981.

Longest Sequence of Unbeaten League Matches: 21, 21.9.1946 – 1.3.1947.

Longest Sequence Without a League Win: 15, 21.11.1936 – 6.3.1937.

Successive Scoring Runs: 24 from 25.8.2012.

Successive Non-scoring Runs: 8 from 20.12.1952.

MANAGERS

Davy McDougall 1910–11
Fred Stewart 1911–33
Bartley Wilson 1933–34
B. Watts-Jones 1934–37
Bill Jennings 1937–39
Cyril Spiers 1939–46
Billy McCandless 1946–48
Cyril Spiers 1948–54
Trevor Morris 1954–58
Bill Jones 1958–62
George Swindin 1962–64
Jimmy Scoular 1964–73
Frank O'Farrell 1973–74
Jimmy Andrews 1974–78
Richie Morgan 1978–81
Graham Williams 1981–82
Len Ashurst 1982–84
Jimmy Goodfellow 1984
Alan Durban 1984–86
Frank Burrows 1986–89
Len Ashurst 1989–91
Eddie May 1991–94
Terry Yorath 1994–95
Eddie May 1995
Kenny Hibbitt (*Chief Coach*) 1995
Phil Neal 1996
Russell Osman 1996–97
Kenny Hibbitt 1997–98
Frank Burrows 1998–2000
Billy Ayre 2000
Bobby Gould 2000
Alan Cork 2000–02
Lennie Lawrence 2002–05
Dave Jones 2005–11
Malky Mackay 2011–13
Ole Gunnar Solskjaer January 2014–

TEN YEAR LEAGUE RECORD

		P	W	D	L	F	A	Pts	Pos
2004-05	FL C	46	13	15	18	48	51	54	16
2005-06	FL C	46	16	12	18	58	59	60	11
2006-07	FL C	46	17	13	16	57	53	64	13
2007-08	FL C	46	16	16	14	59	55	64	12
2008-09	FL C	46	19	17	10	65	53	74	7
2009-10	FL C	46	22	10	14	73	54	76	4
2010-11	FL C	46	23	11	12	76	54	80	4
2011-12	FL C	46	19	18	9	66	53	75	6
2012-13	FL C	46	25	12	9	72	45	87	1
2013-14	PR Lge	38	7	9	22	32	74	30	20

DID YOU KNOW ?

Cardiff City played a friendly against the reigning Football League champions Aston Villa in September 1910 in the first game to be played on their Ninian Park ground. Villa took a two-goal lead in the first half but Cardiff got the score back to 2-1 by the final whistle in front of an attendance of 7,000.

CARDIFF CITY – FA PREMIERSHIP 2013–14 LEAGUE RECORD

Match No.	Date	Venue	Opponents	Result	H/T Score	Lg Pos.	Goalscorers	Attendance
1	Aug 17	A	West Ham U	L	0-2	0-1	19		34,977
2	25	H	Manchester C	W	3-2	0-0	11	Gunnarsson [60], Campbell 2 [79, 87]	27,068
3	31	H	Everton	D	0-0	0-0	10		27,344
4	Sept 14	A	Hull C	D	1-1	0-1	10	Whittingham [59]	21,949
5	22	H	Tottenham H	L	0-1	0-0	16		27,815
6	28	A	Fulham	W	2-1	1-1	11	Caulker [12], Mutch [90]	23,020
7	Oct 5	H	Newcastle U	L	1-2	0-2	13	Odemwingie [58]	27,538
8	19	A	Chelsea	L	1-4	1-1	16	Mutch [10]	41,475
9	26	A	Norwich C	D	0-0	0-0	15		26,846
10	Nov 3	H	Swansea C	W	1-0	0-0	12	Caulker [62]	27,463
11	9	A	Aston Villa	L	0-2	0-0	13		35,809
12	24	H	Manchester U	D	2-2	1-2	15	Campbell [33], Kim [90]	28,016
13	30	H	Arsenal	L	0-3	0-1	17		27,948
14	Dec 4	A	Stoke C	D	0-0	0-0	15		25,014
15	7	A	Crystal Palace	L	0-2	0-1	16		23,705
16	14	H	WBA	W	1-0	0-0	14	Whittingham [65]	26,632
17	21	A	Liverpool	L	1-3	0-3	15	Mutch [58]	44,621
18	26	H	Southampton	L	0-3	0-3	16		27,929
19	28	H	Sunderland	D	2-2	1-0	16	Mutch [6], Campbell [58]	27,247
20	Jan 1	A	Arsenal	L	0-2	0-0	17		60,004
21	11	H	West Ham U	L	0-2	0-0	18		27,750
22	18	A	Manchester C	L	2-4	1-2	20	Noone [29], Campbell [90]	47,213
23	28	A	Manchester U	L	0-2	0-1	20		75,301
24	Feb 1	H	Norwich C	W	2-1	0-1	19	Bellamy [49], Jones [50]	26,748
25	8	A	Swansea C	L	0-3	0-0	19		20,402
26	11	H	Aston Villa	D	0-0	0-0	19		27,597
27	22	H	Hull C	L	0-4	0-2	19		26,167
28	Mar 2	A	Tottenham H	L	0-1	0-1	19		35,512
29	8	H	Fulham	W	3-1	1-0	18	Caulker 2 [45, 67], Riether (og) [71]	26,796
30	15	A	Everton	L	1-2	0-0	19	Cala [68]	38,018
31	22	H	Liverpool	L	3-6	2-2	19	Mutch 2 [9, 88], Campbell [25]	28,018
32	29	A	WBA	D	3-3	1-2	18	Mutch [30], Caulker [73], Daehli [90]	25,661
33	Apr 5	H	Crystal Palace	L	0-3	0-1	19		27,687
34	12	A	Southampton	W	1-0	0-0	19	Cala [65]	30,526
35	19	H	Stoke C	D	1-1	0-1	18	Whittingham (pen) [51]	27,686
36	27	A	Sunderland	L	0-4	0-2	20		42,397
37	May 3	A	Newcastle U	L	0-3	0-1	20		50,239
38	11	H	Chelsea	L	1-2	1-0	20	Azpilicueta (og) [15]	27,716

Final League Position: 20

GOALSCORERS

League (32): Mutch 7, Campbell 6, Caulker 5, Whittingham 3 (1 pen), Cala 2, Bellamy 1, Daehli 1, Gunnarsson 1, Jones 1, Kim 1, Noone 1, Odemwingie 1, own goals 2.
The Budweiser FA Cup (4): Campbell 3, Noone 1.
Capital One Cup (4): Gestede 1, Maynard 1, Noone 1, Odemwingie 1.

Marshall D 37	Connolly M 3	Caulker S 38	Turner B 30 + 1	John D 16 + 4	Medel G 34	Gunnarsson A 17 + 6	Bellamy C 13 + 9	Kim B 21 + 7	Whittingham P 30 + 2	Campbell F 32 + 5	Gestede R — + 3	Maynard N — + 8	Mutch J 26 + 9	Taylor A 18	Cowie D 10 + 8	Cornelius A — + 8	Lewis J 1	Theophile-Catherine K 26 + 2	Odemwingie P 11 + 4	Noone C 13 + 4	McNaughton K 3 + 2	Hudson M 2	Eikrem M 1 + 5	Daehli M 5 + 8	Da Silva F 13	Jones K 6 + 5	Zaha W 5 + 7	Cala J 7	Berget J — + 1	Healey R — + 1	James T — + 1	Match No.
1	2	3	4	5	6	7	8^2	9^3	10	11^1	12	13	14																			1
1	2	3	4		6	7	8^3	9^1	10	11^1	12	13	14		5																	2
1	2	3	4		6^2	7	8^1	9^3	10	11	12	13	14		5																	3
		3	4	5	6^1	7	8^2	9	10	11^3	12	13	14				1	2														4
1		3	4	5	6	7	8^1	9	10	11^2	12	13						2														5
1		3	4	5	6	7	8	9^1	10^3	11^2	12	13	14					2														6
1		3	4	5	6^2	7	8^1	9	10	11^3	12	13	14					2														7
1		3	4	5	6	7^1	8^3	9	10	11^2	12	13	14					2														8
1		3	4	5	6^3	7^2	8^1	9	10	11^3	12	13	14					2														9
1		3	4	5	6^2	7	8^3	9	10	11^1	12	13	14					2														10
1		3	4	5	6	7	8^3	9	10^1	11^2	12	13	14					2														11
1		3	4	5	6	7	8^3	9	10^1	11^2	12	13	14					2														12
1		3	4	5^1	6	7	8^3	9	10	11^2	12	13	14					2														13
1		3	4	5	6	7	8	9	10	11^1	12							2														14
1		3	4	5	6^2	7	8	9	10^3	11^1	12	13	14					2														15
1		3	4	5	6^3	7^2	8	9	10	11^1	12	13	14					2														16
1		3	4	5	6	7^3	8	9^1	10	11^2	12	13	14					2														17
1		3	4	5^2	6	7	8^1	9	10	11^3	12	13	14					2														18
1		3	4	5	6^1	7	8^2	9	10	11^1	12	13	14					2														19
1		3	4	5	6	7^3	8^2	9	10	11^1	12	13	14					2														20
1		3	4^1	5	6^2	7	8	9	10^3	11	12	13	14					2														21
1		3	4^1	5^1	6	7	8^2	9	10^3	11	12	13	14					2														22
1		3	4^1	5	6^3	7	8^2	9	10	11	12	13	14					2														23
1		3	4	5	6	7	8	9^3	10^1	11	12	13	14					2^2														24
1		3	4	5	6	7	8	9	10^2	11^1	12	13	14					2^3														25
1		3	4	5	6	7	8^2	9^1	10	11	12	13						2														26
1		3	4	5^1	6	7	8	9^3	10^2	11	12	13	14					2														27
1		3	4	5	6	7^3	8	9	10	11^1	12	13	14					2^2														28
1		3	4^3	5	6^2	7	8	9	10^1	11	12	13	14					2														29
1		3	4	5	6	7^2	8	9	10^3	11	12	13	14					2^1														30
1		3	4	5	6^2	7	8	9^3	10	11^1	12	13	14					2														31
1		3	4	5	6	7	8^2	9^3	10	11	12	13	14					2^1														32
1		3	4	5	6^3	7	8	9^1	10^2	11	12	13	14					2														33
1		3	4	5^3	6^1	7	8	9	10^2	11	12	13	14					2														34
1		3	4	5^2	6	7^1	8	9	10^2	11	12	13	14					2														35
1		3	4	5^2	6	7^1	8	9	10	11^3	12	13	14					2														36
1		3	4	5	6^2	7	8	9^3	10	11^2	12	13	14					2^1														37
1		3	4	5	6^2	7	8	9	10^3	11^1	12	13	14					2												13	14	38

The Budweiser FA Cup

Third Round	Newcastle U	(a)	2-1
Fourth Round	Bolton W	(a)	1-0
Fifth Round	Wigan Ath	(h)	1-2

Capital One Cup

Second Round	Accrington S	(a)	2-0
Third Round	West Ham U	(a)	2-3

CARLISLE UNITED

Brunton Park, Warwick Road, Carlisle, Cumbria CA1 1LL.

Telephone: (01228) 526 237.

Fax: (01228) 554 141.

Ticket Office: (0844) 371 1921.

Website: www.carlisleunited.co.uk

Email: enquiries@carlisleunited.co.uk

Ground Capacity: 16,683.

Record Attendance: 27,500 v Birmingham C, FA Cup 3rd rd, 5 January 1957 and v Middlesbrough, FA Cup 5th rd, 7 February 1970.

Pitch Measurements: 102.5m × 67.5m (112yd × 74yd)

Chairman: Andrew Jenkins.

Manager: Graham Kavanagh.

Assistant Manager: Davie Irons.

Physio: Neil Dalton.

Colours: Blue shirts with white and red trim, white shorts with blue trim, white socks with blue trim.

Year Formed: 1904.

Turned Professional: 1921.

Previous Name: 1904, Shaddongate United; 1904, Carlisle United.

Club Nicknames: 'The Cumbrians', 'The Blues'.

Grounds: 1904, Milholme Bank; 1905, Devonshire Park; 1909, Brunton Park.

First Football League Game: 25 August 1928, Division 3 (N), v Accrington S (a) W 3–2 – Prout; Coulthard, Cook; Harrison, Ross, Pigg; Agar (1), Hutchison, McConnell (1), Ward (1), Watson.

Record League Victory: 8–0 v Hartlepool U, Division 3 (N), 1 September 1928 – Prout; Smiles, Cook; Robinson (1) Ross, Pigg; Agar (1), Hutchison (1), McConnell (4), Ward (1), Watson. 8–0 v Scunthorpe U, Division 3 (N), 25 December 1952 – MacLaren; Hill, Scott; Stokoe, Twentyman, Waters; Harrison (1), Whitehouse (5), Ashman (2), Duffett, Bond.

Record Cup Victory: 6–0 v Shepshed Dynamo, FA Cup 1st rd, 16 November 1996 – Caig; Hopper, Archdeacon (pen), Walling, Robinson, Pounewatchy, Peacock (1), Conway (1) (Jansen), Smart (McAlindon (1)), Hayward, Aspinall (Thorpe), (2 og). 6–0 v Tipton T, FA Cup 1st rd, 6 November

HONOURS

Football League – Division 1: 22nd, 1974–75;

Division 3: *Champions* 1964–65, 1994–95; *Runners-up* 1981–82;

Division 4: *Runners-up* 1963–64;

FL 2: *Champions* 2005–06.

FA Cup: 6th rd 1975.

Football League Cup: Semi-final 1970.

Auto Windscreens Shield: *Winners* 1997; *Runners-up* 1995.

LDV Vans Trophy: *Runners-up* 2003, 2006.

Johnstone's Paint Trophy: *Winners* 2011; *Runners-up* 2010.

2010 – Collin; Simek, Murphy, Chester, Cruise, Robson (McKenna), Berrett, Taiwo (Hurst), Marshall, Zoko (Curran) (2), Madine (4).

Record Defeat: 1–11 v Hull C, Division 3 (N), 14 January 1939.

Most League Points (2 for a win): 62, Division 3 (N), 1950–51.

Most League Points (3 for a win): 91, Division 3, 1994–95.

Most League Goals: 113, Division 4, 1963–64.

Highest League Scorer in Season: Jimmy McConnell, 42, Division 3 (N), 1928–29.

Most League Goals in Total Aggregate: Jimmy McConnell, 126, 1928–32.

Most League Goals in One Match: 5, Hugh Mills v Halifax T, Division 3 (N), 11 September 1937; 5, Jim Whitehouse v Scunthorpe U, Division 3 (N), 25 December 1952.

Most Capped Player: Eric Welsh, 4, Northern Ireland.

Most League Appearances: Allan Ross, 466, 1963–79.

Youngest League Player: John Slaven, 16 years 162 days v Scunthorpe U, 16 March 2002.

Record Transfer Fee Received: £1,000,000 from Crystal Palace for Matt Jansen, February 1998.

Record Transfer Fee Paid: £140,000 to Blackburn R for Joe Garner, August 2007.

Football League Record: 1928 Elected to Division 3 (N); 1958–62 Division 4; 1962–63 Division 3; 1963–64 Division 4; 1964–65 Division 3; 1965–74 Division 2; 1974–75 Division 1; 1975–77 Division 2; 1977–82 Division 3; 1982–86 Division 2; 1986–87 Division 3; 1987–92 Division 4; 1992–95 Division 3; 1995–96 Division 2; 1996–97 Division 3; 1997–98 Division 2; 1998–2004 Division 3; 2004–05 Conference; 2005–06 FL 2; 2006–14 FL 1; 2014– FL 2.

LATEST SEQUENCES

Longest Sequence of League Wins: 7, 18.2.2006 – 8.4.2006.

Longest Sequence of League Defeats: 12, 27.9.2003 – 13.12.2003.

Longest Sequence of League Draws: 6, 11.2.1978 – 11.3.1978.

Longest Sequence of Unbeaten League Matches: 19, 1.10.1994 – 11.2.1995.

Longest Sequence Without a League Win: 14, 16.9.2003 – 13.12.2003.

Successive Scoring Runs: 26 from 23.8.1947.

Successive Non-scoring Runs: 5 from 16.8.2003.

MANAGERS

Harry Kirkbride 1904–05
 (*Secretary-Manager*)
McCumiskey 1905–06
 (*Secretary-Manager*)
Jack Houston 1906–08
 (*Secretary-Manager*)
Bert Stansfield 1908–10
Jack Houston 1910–12
Davie Graham 1912–13
George Bristow 1913–30
Billy Hampson 1930–33
Bill Clarke 1933–35
Robert Kelly 1935–36
Fred Westgarth 1936–38
David Taylor 1938–40
Howard Harkness 1940–45
Bill Clark 1945–46
 (*Secretary-Manager*)
Ivor Broadis 1946–49
Bill Shankly 1949–51
Fred Emery 1951–58
Andy Beattie 1958–60
Ivor Powell 1960–63
Alan Ashman 1963–67
Tim Ward 1967–68
Bob Stokoe 1968–70
Ian MacFarlane 1970–72
Alan Ashman 1972–75
Dick Young 1975–76
Bobby Moncur 1976–80
Martin Harvey 1980
Bob Stokoe 1980–85
Bryan 'Pop' Robson 1985
Bob Stokoe 1985–86
Harry Gregg 1986–87
Cliff Middlemass 1987–91
Aidan McCaffery 1991–92
David McCreery 1992–93
Mick Wadsworth (*Director of Coaching*) 1993–96
Mervyn Day 1996–97
David Wilkes and John Halpin (*Directors of Coaching*), and Michael Knighton 1997–99
Nigel Pearson 1998–99
Keith Mincher 1999
Martin Wilkinson 1999–2000
Ian Atkins 2000–01
Roddy Collins 2001–02; 2002–03
Paul Simpson 2003–06
Neil McDonald 2006–07
John Ward 2007–08
Greg Abbott 2008–13
Graham Kavanagh September 2013–

TEN YEAR LEAGUE RECORD

		P	W	D	L	F	A	Pts	Pos
2004-05	Conf	42	20	13	9	74	37	73	3
2005-06	FL 2	46	25	11	10	84	42	86	1
2006-07	FL 1	46	19	11	16	54	55	68	8
2007-08	FL 1	46	23	11	12	64	46	80	4
2008-09	FL 1	46	12	14	20	56	69	50	20
2009-10	FL 1	46	15	13	18	63	66	58	14
2010-11	FL 1	46	16	11	19	60	62	59	12
2011-12	FL 1	46	18	15	13	65	66	69	8
2012-13	FL 1	46	14	13	19	56	77	55	17
2013-14	FL 1	46	11	12	23	43	76	45	22

DID YOU KNOW ?

In 1974–75 Carlisle United, then members of the old First Division, reached the quarter-finals of the FA Cup for the only time in their history. They defeated Preston North End, West Bromwich Albion and Mansfield Town, before losing by a single goal to Fulham.

CARLISLE UNITED – FOOTBALL LEAGUE ONE 2013–14 LEAGUE RECORD

Match No.	Date	Venue	Opponents	Result	H/T Score	Lg Pos.	Goalscorers	Attendance
1	Aug 3	H	Leyton Orient	L	1-5	1-2	23	Amoo (pen) [43]	4951
2	10	A	Bradford C	L	0-4	0-3	23		13,641
3	17	H	Coventry C	L	0-4	0-3	23		4072
4	23	A	Colchester U	D	1-1	1-0	22	Robson [4]	3573
5	31	A	Brentford	D	0-0	0-0	22		6035
6	Sept 7	H	Port Vale	L	0-1	0-0	22		3866
7	14	H	Sheffield U	W	1-0	0-0	19	Robson [54]	4863
8	21	A	Stevenage	W	3-1	1-0	15	Miller [27], Robson [77], Amoo [85]	2526
9	28	H	Notts Co	W	2-1	1-1	14	Robson [41], Amoo [54]	4315
10	Oct 5	A	Shrewsbury T	D	2-2	0-1	13	Amoo [87], O'Hanlon [90]	5215
11	19	A	Oldham Ath	L	0-1	0-1	15		4478
12	22	A	Milton Keynes D	W	1-0	1-0	13	Guy [35]	6675
13	26	H	Bristol C	L	2-4	1-0	15	O'Hanlon [24], Noble [80]	4672
14	Nov 2	A	Gillingham	L	0-1	0-0	18		5697
15	5	H	Wolverhampton W	D	2-2	1-2	16	Buaben [30], Noble (pen) [54]	5369
16	16	H	Crawley T	D	1-1	0-0	16	Noble (pen) [47]	3675
17	23	A	Rotherham U	D	0-0	0-0	18		7520
18	26	H	Crewe Alex	W	2-1	2-0	17	O'Hanlon [45], Robson [45]	2969
19	30	A	Swindon T	L	1-3	0-1	18	O'Hanlon [69]	7671
20	Dec 14	H	Tranmere R	W	4-1	1-0	13	Lawrence 2 [1, 67], Amoo [52], Berrett [76]	3793
21	21	A	Walsall	L	0-2	0-1	16		4062
22	26	H	Preston NE	L	0-1	0-1	16		7934
23	29	H	Peterborough U	W	2-1	0-0	15	Amoo 2 [72, 73]	3904
24	Jan 1	A	Crewe Alex	L	1-2	0-0	15	Lawrence [78]	4458
25	11	A	Leyton Orient	L	0-4	0-1	17		5279
26	18	H	Colchester U	L	2-4	1-2	18	Okuonghae (og) [19], Ehmer [90]	3688
27	28	H	Milton Keynes D	W	3-0	2-0	17	Miller [38], Potts [43], Amoo [59]	3007
28	Feb 1	A	Bristol C	L	1-2	1-0	18	Potts [36]	11,029
29	8	H	Gillingham	L	1-2	0-1	20	Legge (og) [90]	3584
30	11	H	Bradford C	W	1-0	1-0	16	Miller [14]	3267
31	18	H	Coventry C	W	2-1	0-1	14	Noble [55], Byrne [70]	1603
32	22	H	Rotherham U	L	1-2	1-1	15	Miller [45]	4293
33	Mar 1	A	Brentford	D	0-0	0-0	17		3984
34	8	A	Port Vale	L	1-2	1-0	19	Meppen-Walter [39]	5009
35	12	A	Sheffield U	L	0-1	0-1	19		15,437
36	15	H	Stevenage	D	0-0	0-0	20		3672
37	22	A	Notts Co	L	1-4	0-2	21	Berrett [57]	4014
38	25	H	Shrewsbury T	D	0-0	0-0	21		3963
39	29	A	Tranmere R	D	0-0	0-0	21		5215
40	Apr 5	H	Swindon T	W	1-0	1-0	20	Madine [38]	4055
41	12	A	Preston NE	L	1-6	1-2	21	Madine [41]	11,428
42	18	H	Walsall	D	1-1	1-0	21	Noble [13]	4389
43	21	A	Peterborough U	L	1-4	0-1	22	Miller [63]	5921
44	26	H	Oldham Ath	L	0-1	0-0	22		5313
45	29	A	Crawley T	D	0-0	0-0	22		3271
46	May 3	A	Wolverhampton W	L	0-3	0-2	22		29,829

Final League Position: 22

GOALSCORERS

League (43): Amoo 8 (1 pen), Miller 5, Noble 5 (2 pens), Robson 5, O'Hanlon 4, Lawrence 3, Berrett 2, Madine 2, Potts 2, Buaben 1, Byrne 1, Ehmer 1, Guy 1, Meppen-Walter 1, own goals 2.
The Budweiser FA Cup (6): Miller 3 (1 pen), Beck 1, Berrett 1, Robson 1.
Capital One Cup (5): Amoo 3, Berrett 1, Guy 1.
Johnstone's Paint Trophy (0).

Gillespie M 15	Pickford J 18	James R 1	Ekangamene C 4	Noble L 31+3	Potts B 32+5	Byrne S 4+13	Livesey D 8+1	Edwards M 1	Amoo D 39+4	Berrett J 38+2	Miller L 28+6	Redmond D 12+3	Guy L 13+10	Gillies J 3+3	Symington D 14+17	Beck M 5+5	Novo N 2+4	Thirlwell P 27	Brough P 1+2	Feely K 1+1	Lynch J —+1	Pearson J 3	Black P 3+1	O'Hanlon S 33	Campbell A —+1	Butterfield D 1	Brown R 9+3	Robson M 29+3	Archibald-Henville T 4	McSweeney L 8	Townsend C 10+2	Eccleston N —+2	Chimbonda P 25+1	Buaben P 10+2	Chandler C 15+2	Ehmer M 12	Madine G 5	Amos B 9	Morris J 1+5	Lawrence T 8+1	Meppen-Walter C 16+4	Roddan C —+1	Fleming G 4	Drennan M 3+3	Dempsey K —+4	Dawson L 1	Match No.
1	2	3	4	5	6	7	8	9	10^1	11	12	13																																			1
1	2	7^1	4	6	8	11	9^3	10	3	5^2	12	13	14																																		2
1	2	7	6	8	10^2	9^1	13	11	4	5	3	12																																			3
1	8	9^1	3	10^2	7	11	12	13	14	4	5	2	6^3																																		4
1	2	6^1	3	9	8	10^2	13	12	14	7	5^2	11	4																																		5
1	7	14	3^1	6	10^2	11	13	12	9	8^1	4	2	5																																		6
1	14	7^1	6	10	11^3	8^2	13	9	3	5	4	2	12																																		7
1	6	5	7^1	11^2	13	12	4	8	3	9	10	2																																			8
1	13	6^2	3	9	8	12	10^1	7	4	11	2	5																																			9
1	14	6^3	3^1	9	8	12	10^2	7	4	11	2	5	13																																		10
1	6^1	9	8	14	13	10^2	7	3	11	2^3	5	12	4																																		11
1	9^3	8	12	6	14	11^1	13	7	3	10	2^2	5	4																																		12
1	2^3	6	9	8^2	12	10^1	13	7	3	11	5	4	14																																		13
1	8^1	3^3	9	13	10^4	14	12	7	4	11	2	6	5^2																																		14
1	6	11	10^1	12	7	3	8	5	2	9	4																																				15
1	7	6	13	10^2	12	9	3	5	11	2	8^1	4	1																																		16
1	6	12	8	10	9^1	7	3	11	5^1	2	4	1																																				17
1	7^1	10	11	13	6	9^2	3	8	2	12	5	4	1																																		18
1	10	12	6	11	9^3	7^1	3	8^2	2	5	4	1	13	14																																	19
14	6	7	11	9^1	3	5	8	2^2	1	12	10^3	4	13																																		20
13	6	8	11^1	14	9	3	5	7^2	2	1	12^3	10	4^1																																		21
2	14	9	7	10	13	6^3	3	8^2	12	4	1	5^1	11																																		22
2	7	6	8	13	11^1	3	12	9^3	4	1	14	10	5^2																																		23
1	7	9	6	10^1	13	3^3	5	2	8^2	4	1	14	11	12																																	24
7	9^1	8	12	10^1	3	5	13	2	6^3	4	11	14	1																																		25
8^1	9	7	10	5	2	3	6	11	4	1	12																																				26
6	7	9^1	8	10^1	14	3	5	2	11^2	4	1	12	13																																		27
10	6^2	9^1	13	11	8	12	14	4	2	5	3	1	7^1																																		28
1	7	6^1	9	8	10	12	4	5	2	3	11^2																																				29
1	6	12	11^1	8	10	9^1	7	3	5	2	4	13																																				30
1	6	8	7^1	12	13	9	11^2	3	5	2	14	4	10^1																																		31
1	7	8	6^1	12	11	10	9^2	13	3	5	2	4																																				32
1	7	6	11^2	9	10	8^1	2	12	13	4	5	3																																				33
1	8	7	12	10	9^2	11	13	6^1	2	3	5	4																																				34
1	6	8^3	11^1	9	7	10	12	13	14	2	4	3	5^2																																		35
1	7	11	9	6	10	6^1	13	2	4	3^2	5	12																																				36
1	7	11	6	8	10	13	9^1	12	2^2	3	4	5																																				37
1	6	12	8	10	11^2	7^1	5	14	3	2	13	9	4^1	13																																	38
1	8	12	6	11^2	7^1	5	14	3	2	13	9	10	4^3																																		39
1	6	11	7^4	8^1	9	3	4	12	2	5	10	13																																				40
1	6^3	13	10	14	7^2	5	8	3	4	12	2^1	9	11																																		41
1	6	7	13	10^2	8	5	3	12	2	9	11	4^1																																				42
1	6	14	12	7	10	13	5	11^1	2^2	3	9	8^1	4																																		43
1	7^1	8	13	9	6	14	2	11^2	3	4	12^3	5	10																																		44
1	6	7^3	12	10	8	11^1	5	3	4	2^2	9	14	13																																		45
1	7	8^2	13	9^3	6	10	11^1	2	3	4	5	12	14																																		46

The Budweiser FA Cup

First Round	Boreham Wood	(a)	0-0
Replay	Boreham Wood	(h)	2-1
Second Round	Brentford	(h)	3-2
Third Round	Sunderland	(a)	1-3

Capital One Cup

First Round	Blackburn R	(h)	3-3
(aet; won 4-3 on penalties)			
Second Round	Leicester C	(h)	2-5

Johnstone's Paint Trophy

Second Round	Morecambe	(a)	0-0
(aet; won 4-3 on penalties)			
Northern Quarter-Finals	Fleetwood T	(a)	0-2

CHARLTON ATHLETIC

The Valley, Floyd Road, Charlton, London SE7 8BL.

Telephone: (020) 8333 4000.

Fax: (020) 8333 4001.

Ticket Office: (0871) 226 1905.

Website: www.cafc.co.uk

Email: info@cafc.co.uk

Ground Capacity: 27,111.

Record Attendance: 75,031 v Aston Villa, FA Cup 5th rd, 12 February 1938 (at The Valley).

Pitch Measurements: 101.5m × 65.8m (111yd × 72yd)

Non-Executive Chairman: Richard Murray.

Head Coach: Bob Peeters.

Assistant Head Coach: Damian Matthew.

Head Physio: Erol Umut.

Colours: Red shirts with white trim, white shorts, red socks.

Year Formed: 1905.

Turned Professional: 1920.

Club Nickname: 'The Addicks'.

HONOURS

Football League – FL 1 *Champions* 2011–12; **Division 1:** *Champions* 1999–2000; *Runners-up* 1936–37; **Division 2:** *Runners-up* 1935–36, 1985–86; **Division 3 (S):** *Champions* 1928–29, 1934–35.

FA Cup: *Winners* 1947; *Runners-up* 1946.

Football League Cup: Quarter-final 2007.

Full Members' Cup: *Runners-up* 1987.

Grounds: 1906, Siemen's Meadow; 1907, Woolwich Common; 1909, Pound Park; 1913, Horn Lane; 1920, The Valley; 1923, Catford (The Mount); 1924, The Valley; 1985, Selhurst Park; 1991, Upton Park; 1992, The Valley.

First Football League Game: 27 August 1921, Division 3 (S), v Exeter C (h) W 1–0 – Hughes; Johnny Mitchell, Goodman; Dowling (1), Hampson, Dunn; Castle, Bailey, Halse, Green, Wilson.

Record League Victory: 8–1 v Middlesbrough, Division 1, 12 September 1953 – Bartram; Campbell, Ellis; Fenton, Ufton, Hammond; Hurst (2), O'Linn (2), Leary (1), Firmani (3), Kiernan.

Record Cup Victory: 7–0 v Burton A, FA Cup 3rd rd, 7 January 1956 – Bartram; Campbell, Townsend; Hewie, Ufton, Hammond; Hurst (1), Gauld (1), Leary (3), White, Kiernan (2).

Record Defeat: 1–11 v Aston Villa, Division 2, 14 November 1959.

Most League Points (2 for a win): 61, Division 3 (S), 1934–35.

Most League Points (3 for a win): 101, FL 1, 2011–12.

Most League Goals: 107, Division 2, 1957–58.

Highest League Scorer in Season: Ralph Allen, 32, Division 3 (S), 1934–35.

Most League Goals in Total Aggregate: Stuart Leary, 153, 1953–62.

Most League Goals in One Match: 5, Wilson Lennox v Exeter C, Division 3 (S), 2 February 1929; 5, Eddie Firmani v Aston Villa, Division 1, 5 February 1955; 5, John Summers v Huddersfield T, Division 2, 21 December 1957; 5, John Summers v Portsmouth, Division 2, 1 October 1960.

Most Capped Player: Jonatan Johansson, 42 (106), Finland.

Most League Appearances: Sam Bartram, 579, 1934–56.

Youngest League Player: Jonjo Shelvey, 16 years 59 days v Burnley, 26 April 2008.

Record Transfer Fee Received: £16,500,000 from Tottenham H for Darren Bent, May 2007

Record Transfer Fee Paid: £4,750,000 to Wimbledon for Jason Euell, January 2001.

Football League Record: 1921 Elected to Division 3 (S); 1929–33 Division 2; 1933–35 Division 3 (S); 1935–36 Division 2; 1936–57 Division 1; 1957–72 Division 2; 1972–75 Division 3; 1975–80 Division 2; 1980–81 Division 3; 1981–86 Division 2; 1986–90 Division 1; 1990–92 Division 2; 1992–98 Division 1; 1998–99 FA Premier League; 1999–2000 Division 1; 2000–07 FA Premier League; 2007–09 FL C; 2009–12 FL 1; 2012– FL C.

MANAGERS

Walter Rayner 1920–25
Alex Macfarlane 1925–27
Albert Lindon 1928
Alex Macfarlane 1928–32
Albert Lindon 1932–33
Jimmy Seed 1933–56
Jimmy Trotter 1956–61
Frank Hill 1961–65
Bob Stokoe 1965–67
Eddie Firmani 1967–70
Theo Foley 1970–74
Andy Nelson 1974–79
Mike Bailey 1979–81
Alan Mullery 1981–82
Ken Craggs 1982
Lennie Lawrence 1982–91
Steve Gritt/Alan Curbishley 1991–95
Alan Curbishley 1995–2006
Iain Dowie 2006
Les Reed 2006
Alan Pardew 2006–08
Phil Parkinson 2008–10
Chris Powell 2011–14
José Riga 2014
Bob Peeters May 2014–

LATEST SEQUENCES

Longest Sequence of League Wins: 12, 26.12.1999 – 7.3.2000.

Longest Sequence of League Defeats: 10, 11.4.1990 – 15.9.1990.

Longest Sequence of League Draws: 6, 13.12.1992 – 16.1.1993.

Longest Sequence of Unbeaten League Matches: 15, 4.10.1980 – 20.12.1980.

Longest Sequence Without a League Win: 18, 18.10.2008 – 17.1.2009.

Successive Scoring Runs: 25 from 26.12.1935.

Successive Non-scoring Runs: 5 from 6.9.1922.

TEN YEAR LEAGUE RECORD

		P	W	D	L	F	A	Pts	Pos
2004-05	PR Lge	38	12	10	16	42	58	46	11
2005-06	PR Lge	38	13	8	17	41	55	47	13
2006-07	PR Lge	38	8	10	20	34	60	34	19
2007-08	FL C	46	17	13	16	63	58	64	11
2008-09	FL C	46	8	15	23	52	74	39	24
2009-10	FL 1	46	23	15	8	71	48	84	4
2010-11	FL 1	46	15	14	17	62	66	59	13
2011-12	FL 1	46	30	11	5	82	36	101	1
2012-13	FL C	46	17	14	15	65	59	65	9
2013-14	FL C	46	13	12	21	41	61	51	18

DID YOU KNOW ?

Charlton Athletic signed at least 16 players of South African origin during the 1950s. Their line-up in the home game with Preston North End on 18 April 1953 included five of them: John Hewie, Ken Chamberlain, Syd O'Linn, Stuart Leary and Eddie Firmani. The Addicks won the match 2-1.

CHARLTON ATHLETIC – FL CHAMPIONSHIP 2013–14 LEAGUE RECORD

Match No.	Date	Venue	Opponents	Result	H/T Score	Lg Pos.	Goalscorers	Attendance
1	Aug 3	A	Bournemouth	L	1-2	0-1	15	Kermorgant [49]	10,108
2	10	H	Middlesbrough	L	0-1	0-0	21		14,882
3	17	A	Barnsley	D	2-2	0-1	20	Cousins [64], Church [72]	9554
4	31	H	Leicester C	W	2-1	1-0	17	Morrison [27], Kermorgant [59]	15,542
5	Sept 14	A	Watford	D	1-1	0-0	17	Kermorgant (pen) [47]	16,431
6	17	A	Huddersfield T	L	1-2	0-1	17	Stewart [79]	12,248
7	21	H	Millwall	L	0-1	0-1	20		15,917
8	28	A	Burnley	L	0-3	0-1	20		10,645
9	Oct 1	H	Nottingham F	D	1-1	0-1	20	Sordell [50]	15,567
10	5	H	Blackpool	D	0-0	0-0	21		15,847
11	19	A	Blackburn R	W	1-0	1-0	20	Church [7]	13,915
12	27	H	Wigan Ath	D	0-0	0-0	19		23,600
13	Nov 2	A	Birmingham C	W	1-0	0-0	17	Stephens [57]	14,070
14	9	H	Leeds U	L	2-4	1-1	19	Stewart [45], Jackson [70]	17,601
15	23	A	QPR	L	0-1	0-1	21		17,397
16	26	A	Doncaster R	W	2-0	1-0	17	Stephens [39], Church [60]	14,140
17	30	H	Ipswich T	L	0-1	0-1	20		16,645
18	Dec 3	A	Reading	L	0-1	0-1	21		18,149
19	7	A	Yeovil T	D	2-2	2-0	21	Stewart [37], Jackson [45]	6053
20	14	H	Derby Co	L	0-2	0-1	21		16,871
21	21	A	Bolton W	D	1-1	1-1	21	Kermorgant [11]	14,923
22	26	H	Brighton & HA	W	3-2	1-1	19	Wilson 2 [32, 58], Kermorgant [75]	17,404
23	29	H	Sheffield W	D	1-1	0-0	19	Stephens [47]	16,377
24	Jan 1	A	Ipswich T	D	1-1	0-1	19	Jackson [90]	18,731
25	18	H	Middlesbrough	L	0-1	0-1	21		14,548
26	28	A	Doncaster R	L	0-3	0-2	22		7289
27	Feb 1	A	Wigan Ath	L	1-2	1-0	22	Sordell [3]	14,341
28	8	H	Birmingham C	L	0-2	0-1	22		15,878
29	22	H	QPR	W	1-0	0-0	22	Jackson [90]	17,333
30	Mar 1	A	Leicester C	L	0-3	0-1	22		24,742
31	12	H	Huddersfield T	D	0-0	0-0	24		12,974
32	15	A	Millwall	D	0-0	0-0	22		16,102
33	18	H	Bournemouth	W	1-0	0-0	21	Dervite [90]	13,537
34	22	H	Burnley	L	0-3	0-1	21		16,113
35	25	A	Nottingham F	W	1-0	0-0	21	Cousins [81]	17,951
36	29	A	Derby Co	L	0-3	0-2	21		24,429
37	Apr 1	A	Leeds U	W	1-0	0-0	21	Ghoochannejhad [54]	17,343
38	5	H	Reading	L	0-1	0-0	21		15,800
39	8	H	Yeovil T	W	3-2	1-1	21	Ajdarevic [10], Dervite [48], Sordell [51]	15,430
40	12	A	Brighton & HA	L	0-3	0-2	21		28,770
41	15	H	Barnsley	L	1-2	0-1	21	Ajdarevic [90]	16,320
42	18	H	Bolton W	D	0-0	0-0	20		15,773
43	21	A	Sheffield W	W	3-2	2-2	18	Sordell 3 [10, 43, 63]	20,557
44	26	H	Blackburn R	L	1-3	0-1	19	Sordell [54]	15,718
45	29	H	Watford	W	3-1	1-0	20	Harriott 2 [22, 77], Jackson [69]	15,815
46	May 3	A	Blackpool	W	3-0	0-0	18	Harriott 3 [61, 82, 90]	15,515

Final League Position: 18

GOALSCORERS

League (41): Sordell 7, Harriott 5, Jackson 5, Kermorgant 5 (1 pen), Church 3, Stephens 3, Stewart 3, Ajdarevic 2, Cousins 2, Dervite 2, Wilson 2, Ghoochannejhad 1, Morrison 1.
The Budweiser FA Cup (8): Kermorgant 3, Church 2, Green 1, Harriott 1, Morrison 1.
Capital One Cup (6): Church 2, Pigott 1 (1 pen), Green 1, Sordell 1, Stephens 1.

Hamer B 32	Solly C 10 + 2	Wiggins R 38	Hughes A 1 + 6	Morrison M 45	Dervite D 33 + 7	Pritchard B 12 + 5	Gower M 6 + 1	Kermorgant Y 17 + 4	Sordell M 20 + 11	Harriott C 17 + 11	Church S 28 + 10	Stephens D 24 + 2	Green D 5 + 8	Jackson J 34 + 4	Wilson L 39 + 3	Cousins J 37 + 5	Cort L 1 + 2	Evina C 4 + 4	Pigott J 2 + 9	Wood R 18 + 3	Stewart C 15 + 3	Cook J 1 + 2	Ainwick B 10	Thuram-Ulien Y 4	Ajdarevic A 13 + 6	Lennon H 1 + 1	Nego L 1	Poyet D 20	Ghoochannejhad R 10 + 5	Parzyszek P — + 1	Tudgay M — + 2	Obika J 3 + 9	Fox M 5 + 1	Petrucci D — + 5	Match No.
1	2	3	4²	5	6	7*	8³	9	10¹	11	12	13	14																						1
1	2	5		4	3		7	11	10¹	9	13	12		6³	8²	14																			2
1	2	5		3	4³	8	11		9¹	10	7²			6	12	13	14																		3
1		9		2	3	8	13	11		10²	6¹			7³	5	12	4		14																4
1		5		3	4	7		11¹		10²	9			2	6	13			12	8															5
1		9		2	3	7		11²	13	10	6			8³	5				14	4¹	12														6
1		9		2	3	7²		13	14	10	6			8	5				11¹	4³	12														7
1		5		3	4	8¹	7²	14	13	12	11			2	6						10³														8
1		5	12	3	14		6²		9	11	10³	8		2	7			13	4																9
1		5		3		12	6¹		9³	11	10²	8		2	7			14	4	13															10
1		5		3		6		12	9³		10²	8	14	2	7		13		4	11¹															11
1		5		3	13	6		9³	12		10	8	14	2	7²				4¹	11															12
1		5		3	4	9				10	8			6¹	2	7					11	12													13
1		5		3	4	14		12	13	8²	11	8		10	2¹	7					9³														14
1		5		3	4	6³		12	14	13	11¹	9		8	2	7					10²														15
		5	13	3	4			11	12		10³	8	14	9¹	2	7					6²		1												16
		5		3	4			10	14	11²	8	13	9¹	2³	7			12			6		1												17
		5		3	4			10	14	11¹	8³	13	12	2	7		6²				9		1												18
13		5	12	3	4			11		10¹	8		9⁴	2	7²						14	6³	1												19
		5		3	4	8²		11	14	12	13	9	6³	2¹	7						10		1												20
2		5		3	13			11		9¹	7			8	6		12				4	10²	1												21
2		5		3	12	14		11		10³	7			6¹	8		13				4	9²	1												22
				3	12			10		11	8	13	9¹	2	7		5				4	6²	1												23
2		5		3				11	10¹	13	7		14	6³	8						4	9²	12	1											24
	5*			3				11		10	13	9	12	8²	7³						4	6¹		1	14										25
		3	4					10		13	11³	8¹		9	6*	7	5²		12					1	14	2									26
	5²	3	14	13				10³				8			7						4			1	9¹	12	2	6	11						27
		3						10³		13		12	8¹	2	7		5		4					1	9			6¹	11	14					28
	5			3	4			14	11³		6¹	9	2	6¹					4					1	13			8	10²		12				29
1		5	14	3³	12			10	11		9	2	6¹					4							8²			7			13				30
1		5		3	4	12		11³	7²	13		8	2	14											9			6	10¹						31
1		5		3	4	6²		11¹	9	14		8	2	12											10³			7	13						32
1		5		3	4			13	10¹	11	7¹	9	2	8											6						12			33
1		5		3	4			14		11¹	7²	9	2	8											12			6³	13		10				34
1		5		3	4²			11³				10	2	8					12						9¹			6	7		13	14			35
1		5		3				11²	12			9¹	2	8			13	4							10¹			6	7³		10		14		36
1		5		3	4			13				9	2	8¹			11²								10¹			6	7³		12		14		37
1		5		3	4			10	11		7³	2	8¹												9²			6	12		14		13		38
1		5		2	4			11¹	13		9		8	14		3									10³			6	7²		12				39
1	13	5		3	4			11	12	14		9¹	2	8											10²			6	7¹						40
1	2¹			5				3				9	13	8				4							14			6³	12		10				41
1		14		3	4				11³		13	8	2												10¹			6	7²		12	5		42
1	2			3	4			10¹	9²	11³		8	13	6											12			7			14	5		43
1	2			3	4			11	7¹	13		9¹		8											10²			6	12			5	14	44
1	2²	14		3	4			11³	10¹			9	7	8			13								9²			6			12	5		45
1				3	4			11³	10			8	2	7¹			14								9²			6			13	5	12	46

The Budweiser FA Cup

Third Round	Oxford U	(h)	2-2
Replay	Oxford U	(a)	3-0
Fourth Round	Huddersfield T	(a)	1-0
Fifth Round	Sheffield W	(a)	2-1
Sixth Round	Sheffield U	(a)	0-2

Capital One Cup

First Round	Oxford U	(h)	4-0
Second Round	Huddersfield T	(a)	2-3

CHELSEA

FOUNDATION

Chelsea may never have existed but for the fact that Fulham rejected an offer to rent the Stamford Bridge ground from Mr H. A. Mears who had owned it since 1904. Fortunately he was determined to develop it as a football stadium rather than sell it to the Great Western Railway and got together with Frederick Parker, who persuaded Mears of the financial advantages of developing a major sporting venue. Chelsea FC was formed in 1905 and applications made to join both the Southern League and Football League. The latter competition was decided upon because of its comparatively meagre representation in the south of England.

Stamford Bridge, Fulham Road, London SW6 1HS.
Telephone: (0871) 984 1955. *Fax:* (020) 7381 4831.
Ticket Office: (0871) 984 1905.
Website: www.chelseafc.com
Email: enquiries@chelseafc.com
Ground Capacity: 41,798.
Record Attendance: 82,905 v Arsenal, Division 1, 12 October 1935.
Pitch Measurements: 103m × 67.5m (112yd × 74yd)
Chairman: Bruce Buck. *Chief Executive:* Ron Gourlay.
Manager: Jose Mourinho.
Technical Director: Michael Emenalo.
Assistant First Team Coaches: Rui Faria, Steve Holland, Silvino Louro, Jose Morais.
Medical Director: Paco Biosca.
Colours: Reflex blue shirt with white trim, reflex blue shorts with white trim, white socks with reflex blue trim.
Year Formed: 1905. *Turned Professional:* 1905.
Club Nickname: 'The Blues'.
Ground: 1905, Stamford Bridge.
First Football League Game: 2 September 1905, Division 2, v Stockport Co (a) L 0–1 – Foulke; Mackie, McEwan; Key, Harris, Miller; Moran, Jack Robertson, Copeland, Windridge, Kirwan.
Record League Victory: 8–0 v Wigan Ath, FA Premier League, 9 May 2010 – Cech; Ivanovic (Belletti), Ashley Cole (1), Ballack (Matic), Terry, Alex, Kalou (1) (Joe Cole), Lampard (pen), Anelka (2), Drogba (3, 1 pen), Malouda; 8–0 v Aston Villa, FA Premier League, 23 December 2012 – Cech; Azpilicueta, Ivanovic (1), Cahill, Cole, Luiz (1), Lampard (1) (Ramirez (2)), Moses, Mata (Piazon), Hazard (1), Torres (1) (Oscar (1)).

HONOURS

FA Premier League:
Champions 2004–05, 2005–06, 2009–10.
Runners-up 2003–04, 2006–07, 2007–08, 2010–11.
Football League – Division 1:
Champions 1954–55; **Division 2:**
Champions 1983–84, 1988–89;
Runners-up 1906–07, 1911–12, 1929–30, 1962–63, 1976–77.
FA Cup: *Winners* 1970, 1997, 2000, 2007, 2009, 2010, 2012. *Runners-up* 1915, 1967, 1994, 2002.
Football League Cup: *Winners* 1965, 1998, 2005, 2007; *Runners-up* 1972, 2008.
Full Members' Cup: *Winners* 1986.
Zenith Data Systems Cup: *Winners* 1990.
European Competitions
Champions League: 1999–2000, 2003–04 (*s-f*), 2004–05 (*s-f*), 2005–06, 2006–07 (*s-f*), 2007–08 (*runners-up*), 2008–09 (*s-f*), 2009–10, 2010–11, 2011–12 (*winners*), 2012–13, 2013–14 (*s-f*). **European Fairs Cup:** 1958–60, 1965–66, 1968–69.
European Cup-Winners' Cup: 1970–71 (*winners*), 1971–72, 1994–95, 1997–98 (*winners*), 1998–99 (*s-f*). **UEFA Cup:** 2000–01, 2001–02, *2002–03*, 2012. **Super Cup:** 1998–99 (*winners*), **Europa League:** 2012–13 (*winners*). **Club World Cup:** 2012 (*runners-up*).

sky SPORTS FACT FILE

When Ted Drake took over as manager of Chelsea in 1952 he set out to modernise the club and one of his first moves was to change the club nickname from the Pensioners to the Blues. The Chelsea Pensioner which had adorned the club crest since their formation in 1905 was replaced by a blue lion.

Record Cup Victory: 13–0 v Jeunesse Hautcharage, ECWC, 1st rd 2nd leg, 29 September 1971 – Bonetti; Boyle, Harris (1), Hollins (1p), Webb (1), Hinton, Cooke, Baldwin (3), Osgood (5), Hudson (1), Houseman (1).

Record Defeat: 1–8 v Wolverhampton W, Division 1, 26 September 1953.

Most League Points (2 for a win): 57, Division 2, 1906–07.

Most League Points (3 for a win): 99, Division 2, 1988–89.

Most League Goals: 103, FA Premier League, 2009–10.

Highest League Scorer in Season: Jimmy Greaves, 41, 1960–61.

Most League Goals in Total Aggregate: Bobby Tambling, 164, 1958–70.

Most League Goals in One Match: 5, George Hilsdon v Glossop, Division 2, 1 September 1906; 5, Jimmy Greaves v Wolverhampton W, Division 1, 30 August 1958; 5, Jimmy Greaves v Preston NE, Division 1, 19 December 1959; 5, Jimmy Greaves v WBA, Division 1, 3 December 1960; 5, Bobby Tambling v Aston Villa, Division 1, 17 September 1966; 5, Gordon Durie v Walsall, Division 2, 4 February 1989.

Most Capped Player: Frank Lampard, 104 (106), England.

Most League Appearances: Ron Harris, 655, 1962–80.

Youngest League Player: Ian Hamilton, 16 years 138 days v Tottenham H, 18 March 1967.

Record Transfer Fee Received: £50,000,000 from Paris St Germain for David Luiz, July 2014.

Record Transfer Fee Paid: £50,000,000 to Liverpool for Fernando Torres, January 2011.

Football League Record: 1905 Elected to Division 2; 1907–10 Division 1; 1910–12 Division 2; 1912–24 Division 1; 1924–30 Division 2; 1930–62 Division 1; 1962–63 Division 2; 1963–75 Division 1; 1975–77 Division 2; 1977–79 Division 1; 1979–84 Division 2; 1984–88 Division 1; 1988–89 Division 2; 1989–92 Division 1; 1992– FA Premier League.

MANAGERS

John Tait Robertson 1905–07
David Calderhead 1907–33
Leslie Knighton 1933–39
Billy Birrell 1939–52
Ted Drake 1952–61
Tommy Docherty 1961–67
Dave Sexton 1967–74
Ron Suart 1974–75
Eddie McCreadie 1975–77
Ken Shellito 1977–78
Danny Blanchflower 1978–79
Geoff Hurst 1979–81
John Neal 1981–85 (*Director to 1986*)
John Hollins 1985–88
Bobby Campbell 1988–91
Ian Porterfield 1991–93
David Webb 1993
Glenn Hoddle 1993–96
Ruud Gullit 1996–98
Gianluca Vialli 1998–2000
Claudio Ranieri 2000–04
Jose Mourinho 2004–07
Avram Grant 2007–08
Luiz Felipe Scolari 2008–09
Guus Hiddink 2009
Carlo Ancelotti 2009–11
Andre Villas-Boas 2011–12
Roberto Di Matteo 2012
Rafael Benitez 2012–13
Jose Mourinho June 2013–

LATEST SEQUENCES

Longest Sequence of League Wins: 11, 25.4.2009 – 20.9.2009.

Longest Sequence of League Defeats: 7, 1.11.1952 – 20.12.1952.

Longest Sequence of League Draws: 6, 20.8.1969 – 13.9.1969.

Longest Sequence of Unbeaten League Matches: 40, 23.10.2004 – 29.10.2005.

Longest Sequence Without a League Win: 21, 3.11.1987 – 2.4.1988.

Successive Scoring Runs: 27 from 29.10.1988.

Successive Non-scoring Runs: 9 from 14.3.1981.

TEN YEAR LEAGUE RECORD

		P	W	D	L	F	A	Pts	Pos
2004-05	PR Lge	38	29	8	1	72	15	95	1
2005-06	PR Lge	38	29	4	5	72	22	91	1
2006-07	PR Lge	38	24	11	3	64	24	83	2
2007-08	PR Lge	38	25	10	3	65	26	85	2
2008-09	PR Lge	38	25	8	5	68	24	83	3
2009-10	PR Lge	38	27	5	6	103	32	86	1
2010-11	PR Lge	38	21	8	9	69	33	71	2
2011-12	PR Lge	38	18	10	10	65	46	64	6
2012-13	PR Lge	38	22	9	7	75	39	75	3
2013-14	PR Lge	38	25	7	6	71	27	82	3

DID YOU KNOW ?

In February 1908 Chelsea's Stamford Bridge ground staged the first Rugby League match to be held in London. England went down 18-6 to New Zealand in the second of a three-match test series. The game was watched by a crowd of 10,000.

CHELSEA – FA PREMIERSHIP 2013–14 LEAGUE RECORD

Match No.	Date	Venue	Opponents	Result	H/T Score	Lg Pos.	Goalscorers	Attendance
1	Aug 18	H	Hull C	W	2-0	2-0	3	Oscar [13], Lampard [25]	41,374
2	21	H	Aston Villa	W	2-1	1-1	1	Luna (og) [6], Ivanovic [73]	41,527
3	26	A	Manchester U	D	0-0	0-0	1		75,032
4	Sept 14	A	Everton	L	0-1	0-1	6		36,034
5	21	H	Fulham	W	2-0	0-0	1	Oscar [52], Mikel [84]	41,608
6	28	A	Tottenham H	D	1-1	0-1	3	Terry [65]	35,857
7	Oct 6	A	Norwich C	W	3-1	1-0	3	Oscar [4], Hazard [85], Willian [86]	26,840
8	19	H	Cardiff C	W	4-1	1-1	2	Hazard 2 [33, 82], Eto'o [66], Oscar [78]	41,475
9	27	H	Manchester C	W	2-1	1-0	2	Schurrle [33], Torres [90]	41,495
10	Nov 2	A	Newcastle U	L	0-2	0-0	2		51,674
11	9	H	WBA	D	2-2	1-0	4	Eto'o [45], Hazard (pen) [90]	41,623
12	23	A	West Ham U	W	3-0	2-0	3	Lampard 2 (1 pen) [21 (p), 82], Oscar [34]	34,977
13	Dec 1	H	Southampton	W	3-1	0-1	2	Cahill [55], Terry [62], Ba [90]	41,568
14	4	A	Sunderland	W	4-3	2-1	2	Lampard [17], Hazard 2 [36, 62], Bardsley (og) [84]	40,652
15	7	A	Stoke C	L	2-3	1-1	3	Schurrle 2 [9, 53]	25,154
16	14	H	Crystal Palace	W	2-1	2-1	2	Torres [16], Ramires [35]	41,608
17	23	A	Arsenal	D	0-0	0-0	4		60,039
18	26	H	Swansea C	W	1-0	1-0	3	Hazard [29]	41,111
19	29	H	Liverpool	W	2-1	2-1	3	Hazard [17], Eto'o [34]	41,614
20	Jan 1	A	Southampton	W	3-0	0-0	3	Torres [60], Willian [71], Oscar [82]	31,271
21	11	A	Hull C	W	2-0	0-0	1	Hazard [56], Torres [87]	24,924
22	19	H	Manchester U	W	3-1	2-0	3	Eto'o 3 [17, 45, 49]	41,615
23	29	H	West Ham U	D	0-0	0-0	3		41,376
24	Feb 3	A	Manchester C	W	1-0	1-0	3	Ivanovic [32]	47,364
25	8	H	Newcastle U	W	3-0	2-0	1	Hazard 3 (1 pen) [27, 34, 63 (p)]	41,387
26	11	A	WBA	D	1-1	1-0	1	Ivanovic [45]	24,327
27	22	H	Everton	W	1-0	0-0	1	Lampard [90]	41,580
28	Mar 1	A	Fulham	W	3-1	0-0	1	Schurrle 3 [52, 65, 68]	24,577
29	8	H	Tottenham H	W	4-0	0-0	1	Eto'o [56], Hazard (pen) [60], Ba 2 [88, 89]	41,598
30	15	A	Aston Villa	L	0-1	0-0	1		40,084
31	22	A	Arsenal	W	6-0	4-0	1	Eto'o [5], Schurrle [7], Hazard (pen) [17], Oscar 2 [42, 66], Salah [71]	41,614
32	29	A	Crystal Palace	L	0-1	0-0	1		25,166
33	Apr 5	H	Stoke C	W	3-0	1-0	1	Salah [32], Lampard [61], Willian [72]	41,168
34	13	A	Swansea C	W	1-0	0-0	2	Ba [68]	20,761
35	19	H	Sunderland	L	1-2	1-1	2	Eto'o [12]	41,210
36	27	A	Liverpool	W	2-0	1-0	2	Ba [45], Willian [90]	44,726
37	May 4	H	Norwich C	D	0-0	0-0	3		41,602
38	11	A	Cardiff C	W	2-1	0-1	3	Schurrle [72], Torres [75]	27,716

Final League Position: 3

GOALSCORERS

League (71): Hazard 14 (4 pens), Eto'o 9, Oscar 8, Schurrle 8, Lampard 6 (1 pen), Ba 5, Torres 5, Willian 4, Ivanovic 3, Salah 2, Terry 2, Cahill 1, Mikel 1, Ramires 1, own goals 2.
The Budweiser FA Cup (3): Oscar 2, Mikel 1.
Capital One Cup (5): Azpilicueta 1, Lampard 1, Mata 1, Ramires 1, Torres 1.
UEFA Super Cup (2): Hazard 1, Torres 1.
UEFA Champions League (19): Torres 4, Ba 3, Eto'o 3, Hazard 2 (1 pen), Ramires 2, Cahill 1, Lampard 1, Oscar 1, Schurrle 1, own goal 1.

Cech P 34	Ivanovic B 36	Cahill G 29 + 1	Terry J 34	Cole A 15 + 2	Lampard F 20 + 6	Ramires 29 + 1	De Bruyne K 2 + 1	Oscar E 24 + 9	Hazard E 32 + 3	Torres F 16 + 12	Schurrle A 15 + 15	Lukaku R — + 2	van Ginkel M — + 2	Mata J 11 + 2	Ba D 5 + 14	Mikel J 11 + 13	Azpilicueta C 26 + 3	Luiz D 15 + 4	Eto'o S 16 + 5	Willian D 18 + 7	Bertrand R 1	Essien M 2 + 3	Matic N 15 + 2	Salah M 6 + 4	Schwarzer M 4	Kalas T 2	Ake N — + 1	Swift J — + 1	Match No
1	2	3	4	5	6	7	8^2	9^8	10	11^1	12	13	14																1
1	2	3	4	5		7		9^1	10		13	12	14	8^1	11^2														2
1	2	3	4	5	7	6	8^3	9	10^2	12	11^1					13	14												3
1	2		4	5^2	12	6		13	10	14	8^2			9^1		7		3	11										4
1	2	3	4	5	13	6	14	9	10^3	12	8^2					7			11^1										5
1	2		4	5	6	8		9^3	10^1	11^1	13			12			7^2	14	3										6
1	2		4	5^2	7	6		9	13		10			8^1	11^1			3	12	14									7
1	2		4		7	6		12	10	13				8^2			14	3	11^3	9	5^1								8
1	2	3	4	5^1	6			9	8^1	11^1	10^2					13			14	12									9
1	2		4	5	7^1	6		9	10	11^2	14			8^3				3	13	12									10
1	2	3	4		7^2	6		9^2	10					14	12	13	5^1		11	8									11
1	2	3	4		8	6		9^2	11^3		13					12	7	5	10^1			14							12
1	2	3	4		12	7		9^1	10	11^3				8	13	14	5					6^2							13
1	2	3	4		7	6			10	11^3	14			8^1	12	13	5			9^2									14
1	2	3	4		13	6			10	11^3	8^2			9	12	7^1	5		14										15
1	2		4			6		12	10	11^1	13			9^2	14		5	3		8^3		7							16
1	2	3	4		8	6		13	11^2	10^3	12					7	5	14		9^1									17
1	2		4	5	12	6		9^2	10^3		13			8^1			3	11	14										18
1	2^1	3	4	12	7^2			9	8	14						13	5	6	11^3	10									19
	3	4	5		6			13	9^2	11	10^3			8^1		7	2			12			14						20
1	3	4	5		7^1			9^2	10	11	13					12	2	6		8^3		14							21
1	2	3	4			6		9^1	10	13						12	5	7	11^3	8^2		14							22
1	2	3	4		12	6		9^1	10					14		7^1	5^2		11	8			13						23
1	2	3	4			8		12	10^3					13	14	5	7	11^2	9^1			6							24
1	2	3			7			9	10^3		14			12			5	4	11^1	8^2			6	13					25
1	2	3				6^2		9^1	10	12						13	5	4	11^1	8			7	14					26
1	2	3	4		6	12		9^1	10	13	14						5		11^1	8^2			7						27
1	2	3	4		6			9^2	10	11	8^3			13	12		5	14					7						28
1	2	3	4	8^3	6			12	9		11^2			14			5		10^1	13			7						29
1	2	3	4		6^1			9^2	10	11^1	13			12			5		8^1				7						30
1	2	3	4					9^2	10	12	8					14	5	6^1	11^1				7	13					31
1	2	3	4		8^3			12	11	10	9^2			14			5		6^1				7	13					32
1	2	3	4	14	6^1				12	11	10^2						5	13		9^3			7	8					33
1	2	3	4			6^2		12			10^2			11^1	14		5	13	9				7	8					34
	2	3	4			6		9^1		14	13			12			5		11^2	10			7	8^1	1				35
	3	13		5	8					14	11^3			10^1	7	2			12			6	9^2	1	4				36
	2	3	4	5	6^1				13	14	10			11				12		9			7^3	8^2	1				37
	3			5				9	10^2	11	12					6^1	2						7	8^1	1	4	13	14	38

The Budweiser FA Cup

Third Round	Derby Co	(a)	2-0
Fourth Round	Stoke C	(h)	1-0
Fifth Round	Manchester C	(a)	0-2

Capital One Cup

Third Round	Swindon T	(a)	2-0
Fourth Round	Arsenal	(a)	2-0
Quarter-Finals	Sunderland	(a)	1-2

(aet)

UEFA Super Cup

	Bayern Munich	(Prague)	2-2

(aet; lost 5-4 on penalties)

UEFA Champions League

Group E	FC Basel	(h)	1-2
Group E	Steaua Bucharest	(a)	4-0
Group E	Schalke 04	(a)	3-0
Group E	Schalke 04	(h)	3-0
Group E	FC Basel	(a)	0-1
Group E	Steaua Bucharest	(h)	1-0
Round of 16 1st leg	Galatasaray	(a)	1-1
Round of 16 2nd leg	Galatasaray	(h)	2-0
Quarter-Finals 1st leg	Paris Saint-Germain	(a)	3-1
Quarter-Finals 2nd leg	Paris Saint-Germain	(h)	2-0
Semi-Finals 1st leg	Atletico Madrid	(a)	0-0
Semi-Finals 2nd leg	Atletico Madrid	(h)	1-3

CHELTENHAM TOWN

FOUNDATION

Although a scratch team representing Cheltenham played a match against Gloucester in 1884, the earliest recorded match for Cheltenham Town FC was a friendly against Dean Close School on 12 March 1892. The School won 4–3 and the match was played at Prestbury (half a mile from Whaddon Road). Cheltenham Town played Wednesday afternoon friendlies at a local cricket ground until entering the Mid Gloucester League. In those days the club played in deep red coloured shirts and were nicknamed 'the Rubies'. The club moved to Whaddon Lane for season 1901–02 and changed to red and white colours two years later.

The Abbey Business Stadium, Whaddon Road, Cheltenham, Gloucestershire GL52 5NA.

Telephone: (01242) 573 558.

Fax: (01242) 224 675.

Ticket Office: (01242) 588 117.

Website: www.ctfc.com

Email: info@ctfc.com

Ground Capacity: 7,133.

Record Attendance: 10,389 v Blackpool, FA Cup 3rd rd, 13 January 1934 (at Cheltenham Athletic Ground); 8,326 v Reading, FA Cup 1st rd, 17 November 1956 (at Whaddon Road).

Pitch Measurements: 102.5m × 66m (112yd × 72yd)

Chairman: Paul Baker.

Vice-chairman: Colin Farmer.

Manager: Mark Yates.

First Team Coach: Shaun North.

Physio: Ian Weston.

Colours: Red and white striped shirts, red shorts, red socks.

Year Formed: 1892.

Turned Professional: 1932.

Club Nickname: 'The Robins'.

Grounds: Pre-1932, Agg-Gardner's Recreation Ground; Whaddon Lane; Carter's Lane; 1932, Whaddon Road.

First Football League Game: 7 August 1999, Division 3, v Rochdale (h) L 0–2 – Book; Griffin, Victory, Banks, Freeman, Brough (Howarth), Howells, Bloomer (Devaney), Grayson, Watkins (McAuley), Yates.

HONOURS

Football League: Best season: Division 3 2001–02 (4th).

FA Cup: Best season: 5th rd, 2002.

Football League Cup: never past 2nd rd.

Football Conference: *Champions* 1998–99; *Runners-up* 1997–98.

Trophy: *Winners* 1997–98.

Southern League: *Champions* 1984–85; **Southern League Cup:** *Winners* 1957–58, *runners-up* 1968–69, 1984–85; **Southern League Merit Cup:** *Winners* 1984–85; **Southern League Championship Shield:** *Winners* 1985.

Gloucestershire Senior Cup: *Winners* 1998–99; **Gloucestershire Northern Senior Professional Cup:** *Winners* 30 times; **Midland Floodlit Cup:** *Winners* **1985–86, 1986–87, 1987–88;** **Mid Gloucester League:** *Champions* 1896–97; **Gloucester and District League:** *Champions* 1902–03, 1905–06; **Cheltenham League:** *Champions* 1910–11, 1913–14; **North Gloucestershire League:** *Champions* 1913–14; **Gloucestershire Northern Senior League:** *Champions* 1928–29, **1932–33;** **Gloucestershire Northern Senior Amateur Cup:** *Winners* 1929–30, 1930–31, 1932–33, 1933–34, 1934–35; **Leamington Hospital Cup:** *Winners* 1934–35.

sky SPORTS FACT FILE

Former Scottish international Patsy Gallacher attracted a gate of 3,000 to Whaddon Road when he made his debut for Cheltenham Town in a Southern League fixture against Yeovil Town in October 1948. Gallacher, who played for Sunderland and Stoke City before the war, made just eight appearances before departing.

Record League Victory: 5–0 v Mansfield T, FL 2, 6 May 2006 – Higgs; Gallinagh, Bell, McCann (1) (Connolly), Caines, Duff, Wilson, Bird (1p), Gillespie (1) (Spencer), Guinan (Odejayi (1)), Vincent (1).

Record Cup Victory: 12–0 v Chippenham R, FA Cup 3rd qual. rd, 2 November 1935 – Bowles; Whitehouse, Williams; Lang, Devonport (1), Partridge (2); Perkins, Hackett, Jones (4), Black (4), Griffiths (1).

Record Defeat: 1–8 v Crewe Alex, FL 2, 2 April 2011. *N.B.* 1–10 v Merthyr T, Southern League, 8 March 1952.

Most League Points (2 for a win): 60, Southern League Division 1, 1963–64.

Most League Points (3 for a win): 78, Division 3, 2001–02.

Most League Goals: 66, Division 3, 2001–02; 66, FL 2, 2011–12.

Highest League Scorer in Season: Julian Alsop, 20, Division 3, 2001–02.

Most League Goals in Total Aggregate: Julian Alsop, 39, 2000–03; 2009–10.

Most League Goals in One Match: 3, Martin Devaney v Plymouth Arg, Division 3, 23 September 2000; 3, Neil Grayson v Cardiff C, Division 3, 1 April 2001; 3, Damien Spencer v Hull C, Division 3, 23 August 2003; 3, Damien Spencer v Milton Keynes D, FL 1, 31 January 2009; 3, Michael Pook v Burton Alb, FL 2, 13 March 2010.

Most Capped Player: Grant McCann, 7 (39), Northern Ireland.

Most League Appearances: David Bird, 288, 2001–11.

Youngest League Player: Kyle Haynes, 17 years, 2 months, 26 days v Oldham Ath, FL 1, 24 March 2009.

Record Transfer Fee Received: £400,000 from Colchester U for Steve Gillespie, July 2008.

Record Transfer Fee Paid: £60,000 to Aldershot T for Jermaine McGlashan, January 2012.

Football League Record: 1999 Promoted to Division 3; 2002 Division 2; 2003–04 Division 3; 2004–06 FL 2; 2006–09 FL 1; 2009– FL 2.

MANAGERS

George Blackburn 1932–34
George Carr 1934–37
Jimmy Brain 1937–48
Cyril Dean 1948–50
George Summerbee 1950–52
William Raeside 1952–53
Arch Anderson 1953–58
Ron Lewin 1958–60
Peter Donnelly 1960–61
Tommy Cavanagh 1961
Arch Anderson 1961–65
Harold Fletcher 1965–66
Bob Etheridge 1966–73
Willie Penman 1973–74
Dennis Allen 1974–79
Terry Paine 1979
Alan Grundy 1979–82
Alan Wood 1982–83
John Murphy 1983–88
Jim Barron 1988–90
John Murphy 1990
Dave Lewis 1990–91
Ally Robertson 1991–92
Lindsay Parsons 1992–95
Chris Robinson 1995–97
Steve Cotterill 1997–2002
Graham Allner 2002–03
Bobby Gould 2003
John Ward 2003–07
Keith Downing 2007–08
Martin Allen 2008–09
Mark Yates December 2009–

LATEST SEQUENCES

Longest Sequence of League Wins: 5, 29.10.2011 – 10.12.2011.
Longest Sequence of League Defeats: 7, 27.1.2009 – 28.2.2009.
Longest Sequence of League Draws: 5, 5.4.2003 – 21.4.2003.
Longest Sequence of Unbeaten League Matches: 16, 1.12.2001 – 12.3.2002.
Longest Sequence Without a League Win: 14, 20.12.2008 – 7.3.2009.
Successive Scoring Runs: 17 from 16.2.2008.
Successive Non-scoring Runs: 5 from 10.3.2012 – 30.3.2012.

TEN YEAR LEAGUE RECORD

		P	W	D	L	F	A	Pts	Pos
2004-05	FL 2	46	16	12	18	51	54	60	14
2005-06	FL 2	46	19	15	12	65	53	72	5
2006-07	FL 1	46	15	9	22	49	61	54	17
2007-08	FL 1	46	13	12	21	42	64	51	19
2008-09	FL 1	46	9	12	25	51	91	39	23
2009-10	FL 2	46	10	18	18	54	71	48	22
2010-11	FL 2	46	13	13	20	56	77	52	17
2011-12	FL 2	46	23	8	15	66	50	77	6
2012-13	FL 2	46	20	15	11	58	51	75	5
2013-14	FL 2	46	13	16	17	53	63	55	17

DID YOU KNOW ?

Cheltenham Town's first-ever Football League Cup game saw them go down 2-0 to Norwich City at Carrow Road in the opening leg. They levelled things up in the second leg taking the tie into extra time only to go out after conceding in the 100th minute.

CHELTENHAM TOWN – FOOTBALL LEAGUE TWO 2013–14 LEAGUE RECORD

Match No.	Date	Venue	Opponents	Result	H/T Score	Lg Pos.	Goalscorers	Attendance
1	Aug 3	H	Burton Alb	D 2-2	2-1	11	Cureton [18], Harrison [32]	3189
2	10	A	Chesterfield	L 0-2	0-1	18		5367
3	17	H	Plymouth Arg	L 1-3	0-3	21	Richards [72]	3450
4	24	A	Accrington S	W 1-0	0-0	21	Taylor [71]	1224
5	31	A	Bury	L 1-4	1-3	21	Procter (og) [4]	2910
6	Sept 7	H	Portsmouth	D 2-2	1-2	20	McGlashan 2 [36, 90]	4776
7	14	H	Oxford U	D 2-2	1-1	20	Harrison [8], Gornell [51]	3906
8	21	A	Torquay U	L 2-4	1-2	21	Harrison [13], Gornell [65]	2407
9	28	H	AFC Wimbledon	W 1-0	0-0	19	Cureton [90]	3032
10	Oct 5	A	Scunthorpe U	L 0-2	0-1	22		3191
11	12	A	Dagenham & R	W 2-1	1-1	17	Cureton [31], Lowe [59]	1727
12	19	H	Rochdale	L 1-2	0-0	17	Brown, T [63]	2887
13	22	H	Morecambe	W 3-0	1-0	17	Richards [45], Gornell [62], Harrison [82]	2050
14	26	A	Northampton T	D 1-1	1-1	17	Harrison [10]	4033
15	Nov 2	H	York C	D 2-2	2-1	18	Harrison [12], Richards [45]	2706
16	16	A	Wycombe W	W 2-1	0-0	17	Cureton [56], Knott (og) [67]	3207
17	23	H	Newport Co	D 0-0	0-0	17		3501
18	26	H	Bristol R	D 0-0	0-0	16		3556
19	30	A	Southend U	D 1-1	0-1	14	Richards (pen) [90]	5677
20	Dec 7	A	Morecambe	W 1-0	0-0	13	Brown, T [80]	1290
21	14	H	Hartlepool U	D 2-2	2-0	13	McGlashan [4], Roofe [38]	2491
22	21	A	Fleetwood T	W 2-0	1-0	13	Brown, T [1], McGlashan [90]	2300
23	26	H	Exeter C	W 1-0	1-0	10	Cureton [13]	3562
24	29	H	Mansfield T	L 1-2	0-2	10	Jombati [86]	2928
25	Jan 11	A	Burton Alb	L 1-2	0-0	12	Harrison [62]	2510
26	18	H	Accrington S	L 1-2	0-2	12	Cureton [72]	2648
27	25	A	Plymouth Arg	D 1-1	0-0	13	Harrison [53]	6735
28	Feb 1	H	Northampton T	D 1-1	1-0	14	Cureton [2]	2707
29	8	A	York C	D 0-0	0-0	15		3148
30	11	A	Bristol R	L 0-1	0-1	15		5808
31	22	A	Newport Co	W 1-0	1-0	15	Vincent [23]	3130
32	25	H	Chesterfield	L 1-4	0-4	17	Harrison [57]	2317
33	Mar 1	H	Bury	W 2-1	1-1	13	Vincent [18], Harrison [82]	2737
34	8	A	Portsmouth	D 0-0	0-0	12		17,254
35	11	A	Oxford U	D 1-1	0-0	14	Cureton [84]	4606
36	15	H	Torquay U	W 1-0	0-0	11	Richards [75]	3105
37	18	H	Wycombe W	D 1-1	0-0	11	Harrison [68]	2267
38	22	A	AFC Wimbledon	L 3-4	1-3	13	Brown, T [5], McGlashan [49], Taylor [74]	3670
39	25	H	Scunthorpe U	L 0-2	0-1	14		2080
40	29	A	Hartlepool U	W 1-0	0-0	11	McGlashan [74]	3328
41	Apr 5	H	Southend U	L 1-2	1-0	13	Harrison [45]	2949
42	12	A	Exeter C	D 1-1	1-1	15	Harrison [27]	3353
43	18	H	Fleetwood T	L 1-2	1-0	15	Cureton [32]	2890
44	21	A	Mansfield T	W 2-0	0-0	16	Cureton 2 [57, 79]	3586
45	26	A	Rochdale	L 0-2	0-2	16		4372
46	May 3	H	Dagenham & R	L 2-3	2-2	17	Elliott [18], Richards [24]	3002

Final League Position: 17

GOALSCORERS

League (53): Harrison 13, Cureton 11, McGlashan 6, Richards 6 (1 pen), Brown, T 4, Gornell 3, Taylor 2, Vincent 2, Elliott 1, Jombati 1, Lowe 1, Roofe 1, own goals 2.
The Budweiser FA Cup (0).
Capital One Cup (5): Richards 2 (2 pens), Harrison 2, Gornell 1.
Johnstone's Paint Trophy (3): Gillespie 2, Taylor 1.

Brown S 45	Jombati S 38 + 5	Braham-Barrett C 29	Penn R 13 + 6	Brown T 39	Elliott S 32	McGlashan J 38 + 5	Richards M 46	Gornell T 21 + 13	Cureton J 23 + 12	Deering S 29 + 6	Harrison B 35 + 11	Kotwica Z 1 + 17	Vincent A 7 + 11	Gillespie S 3 + 1	Dale B — + 1	Lowe K 12 + 1	Taylor J 25 + 8	Inniss R 2	Noble D 25 + 4	Williams H 3 + 2	Roofe K 7 + 2	Goldson C 3 + 1	Ihiekwe M 13	Lucas L 2	Brundle M 7	Daniels B 2	Hanks J 1 + 1	Roberts C 1	Match No.
1	2	3	4	5	6	7^2	8	9^2	10^1	11	12	13	14																1
1	2	5	8	3	4	9	7	11^1		6^2	10	13	12																2
1	2	5	7	3	4	6	8			9^1	10^3	12	13	11^{12}	14														3
1		5	8	3	4	13	10^2			6	12			11^1		2	7												4
1	12	5^1	6			3^2	10	8	11^3		7	13			14	2	9		4										5
1	5	12			4	6	7	11			9^1	14	13		10^5	2		3^1	8										6
1	5	7			4	6	9	10			11					2	12		8^1	3									7
1	5	6			4	9	7^1	10^1	14		11		12			2	13		8^3	3									8
1	13	9	4			6^2	5	10	12	11						2	8		7^1	3									9
1	14	9	4			6	5	11^2	12		10	13				2^2	8		7^1	3									10
1	2	5	9	3		6	8	12	10^1	11						4	7												11
1	2	5	8	3		9	6	10		11						4	7												12
1	2	3				7^2	5	11	10^1	9	12	14				4	8^2		6	13									13
1	2	7	3				5	11	12	9	10					4	8		6^1										14
1	2	6^2	3				5	12	11^1	9	10	13				4	8		7										15
1	2	5	12	3	4	9	13	10^1	7^2	11						14	8		6^3										16
1	2	5	14	3	4	13	9^1	12	10		8^3	11^2					7		6										17
1	2	5		3	4	12	8	10^2	11	9^1		13	14				7		6^1										18
1	2	5	12	3	4	6	8	13		11	9^2						7				10^1								19
1	2	5		3	4	11	7	12			10						8		6^2		9^1	13							20
1	2	5	12	3	4	9	8^2	13		11							7		6		10^1								21
1	2	5		3		9	8	10^1	12	11							7		6			4							22
1	2	5	12	3		10	8	14	9^2	11^3							7^1		6		13	4							23
1	2	5^2		3		10	8	12	9	14	11^1						7		6^3		13	4							24
1	11	10		5		7	6	8	13		12	3^1	4^2			14			2		9^3								25
1	2	5		3	4	6^3	8	11^2	10		12	13	14						7^1		9								26
1	2	5		3		12	8	10^1		6	11								7		9	4							27
1	2	5		3		13	8	12	10	11^2	7										9		4		6^1				28
1	9	2	3	5	6	13	10^1	12	11^3		14								8				4		7^2				29
1	12	5	3^1	4		9	8	10	11^2	6	13	14							7^3				2						30
1	12	5			4	6	7	11		9	10						8^1						2		3				31
1	5			4	8	6	9	12	7^3	11^2	13	10^1				14							3		2				32
1	5			3	4	9	8	7^3	10^1	6	12	13	11^2			14							2						33
1	5			3	4	8	7	9	6	11	12	10^1							13				2						34
1	5			3	4	8	7	9	12	6^3	11^2	14	10^1						13				2						35
1	5			3	4	6	7	10^1	11^3	8^2	12	9				14			13							2			36
1	5			3	4	8	7	9^1	12	11	6	10^2							13							2			37
1	5			3	4	11	8	9	10	12							7		6^1				2						38
1	5			3	4	11	8	14	12	10^3	7	13					9^2		6^1				2						39
1	7	2		5	6	13	3	4^2			12						8^1						9		10	11			40
1	5			3		10	8	13		11	7	14					12^3		6^1				4		2	9^2			41
1	2	5		3	4	6	8	10^2	12	11		13							7		9^1								42
1	2	5		3	4	7	8^1	10	12	11		13							6		9^2								43
1	2	5	4	3		7^2	8	12	10^1	9	11	13							6										44
1	2	5		3	4	7	8	10^2	9^1	11	13								6^3		14						12		45
	2	5		4		8	7	12		11	10^3	14					13		9^2				3			6^1		1	46

The Budweiser FA Cup
First Round   Tamworth   (a)   0-1

Capital One Cup
First Round   Crawley T   (h)   4-3
(aet)
Second Round   West Ham U   (a)   1-2

Johnstone's Paint Trophy
First Round   Plymouth Arg   (h)   3-3
(aet; lost 4-5 on penalties)

CHESTERFIELD

FOUNDATION

Chesterfield are fourth only to Stoke, Notts County and Nottingham Forest in age for they can trace their existence as far back as 1866, although it is fair to say that they were somewhat casual in the first few years of their history, playing only a few friendlies a year. However, their rules of 1871 are still in existence, showing an annual membership of 2s (10p), but it was not until 1891 that they won a trophy (the Barnes Cup) and followed this a year later by winning the Sheffield Cup, Barnes Cup and the Derbyshire Junior Cup.

The Proact Stadium, 1866 Sheffield Road, Whittington Moor, Chesterfield, Derbyshire S41 8NZ.

Telephone: (01246) 209 765.

Fax: (01246) 556 799.

Ticket Office: (01246) 488 232.

Website: www.chesterfield-fc.co.uk

Email: reception@chesterfield-fc.co.uk

Ground Capacity: 10,300.

Record Attendance: 30,968 v Newcastle U, Division 2, 7 April 1939 (at Saltergate); 10,089 v Rotherham U, FL 2, 18 March 2011 (at b2net Stadium (now called the Proact Stadium)).

Pitch Measurements: 103m × 67m (112.5yd × 73.5yd)

Chairman: Dave Allen.

Chief Executive: Chris Turner.

Manager: Paul Cook.

Assistant Manager: Leam Richardson.

Sports Therapist: Jamie Hewitt.

Colours: Blue shirts with white trim, white shorts with blue trim, blue socks with white trim.

Year Formed: 1866.

Turned Professional: 1891.

Previous Name: 1867, Chesterfield Town; 1919, Chesterfield.

Club Nicknames: 'The Blues', 'The Spireites'.

Grounds: 1867, Drill Field; 1871, Recreation Ground, Saltergate; 2010, b2net Stadium (renamed The Proact Stadium).

First Football League Game: 2 September 1899, Division 2, v Sheffield W (a) L 1–5 – Hancock; Pilgrim, Fletcher; Ballantyne, Bell, Downie; Morley, Thacker, Gooing, Munday (1), Geary.

Record League Victory: 10–0 v Glossop NE, Division 2, 17 January 1903 – Clutterbuck; Thorpe, Lerper; Haig, Banner, Thacker; Tomlinson (2), Newton (1), Milward (3), Munday (2), Steel (2).

Record Cup Victory: 6–1 v Hartlepool U (h), FA Cup 1st rd, 3 November 2012 – O'Donnell; Talbot, Forbes (1), Cooper (Westcarr (1)), Smith, Whitaker, Clay (1), Togwell, Randall (1) (Broadhead), Darika, Boden (1) (Lester (1)).

HONOURS

Football League – Division 2: Best season: 4th, 1946–47;
Division 3 (N): *Champions* 1930–31, 1935–36; *Runners-up* 1933–34;
FL 2: *Champions* 2010–11, 2013–14;
Division 4: *Champions* 1969–70, 1984–85.
FA Cup: Semi-final 1997.
Football League Cup: Best season: 4th rd, 1965, 2007.
Johnstone's Paint Trophy: *Winners* 2012; *Runners-up* 2014.
Anglo-Scottish Cup: *Winners* 1981.

sky SPORTS FACT FILE

Former England goalkeeper Ted Davison led Chesterfield to the Division Three North title and promotion to Division Two in 1930–31 in his third full season as manager of the Spireites. Davison later went on to manage Sheffield United for 20 years before returning to Saltergate for a second spell in charge in 1952.

Record Defeat: 0–10 v Gillingham, Division 3, 5 September 1987.

Most League Points (2 for a win): 64, Division 4, 1969–70.

Most League Points (3 for a win): 91, Division 4, 1984–85.

Most League Goals: 102, Division 3 (N), 1930–31.

Highest League Scorer in Season: Jimmy Cookson, 44, Division 3 (N), 1925–26.

Most League Goals in Total Aggregate: Ernie Moss, 161, 1969–76, 1979–81 and 1984–86.

Most League Goals in One Match: 4, Jimmy Cookson v Accrington S, Division 3 (N), 16 January 1926; 4, Jimmy Cookson v Ashington, Division 3 (N), 1 May 1926; 4, Jimmy Cookson v Wigan Borough, Division 3 (N), 4 September 1926; 4, Tommy Lyon v Southampton, Division 2, 3 December 1938.

Most Capped Player: Walter McMillen, 4 (7), Northern Ireland; Mark Williams, 4 (36), Northern Ireland.

Most League Appearances: Dave Blakey, 613, 1948–67.

Youngest League Player: Dennis Thompson, 16 years 160 days v Notts Co, 26 December 1950.

Record Transfer Fee Received: £750,000 from Southampton for Kevin Davies, May 1997.

Record Transfer Fee Paid: £250,000 to Watford for Jason Lee, August 1998.

Football League Record: 1899 Elected to Division 2; 1909 failed re-election; 1921–31 Division 3 (N); 1931–33 Division 2; 1933–36 Division 3 (N); 1936–51 Division 2; 1951–58 Division 3 (N); 1958–61 Division 3; 1961–70 Division 4; 1970–83 Division 3; 1983–85 Division 4; 1985–89 Division 3; 1989–92 Division 4; 1992–95 Division 3; 1995–2000 Division 2; 2000–01 Division 3; 2001–04 Division 2; 2004–07 FL 1; 2007–11 FL 2; 2011–12 FL 1; 2012–14 FL 2; 2014– FL 1.

LATEST SEQUENCES

Longest Sequence of League Wins: 10, 6.9.1933 – 4.11.1933.

Longest Sequence of League Defeats: 9, 22.10.1960 – 27.12.1960.

Longest Sequence of League Draws: 8, 26.11.2005 – 2.1.2006.

Longest Sequence of Unbeaten League Matches: 21, 26.12.1994 – 29.4.1995.

Longest Sequence Without a League Win: 18, 11.9.1999 – 3.1.2000.

Successive Scoring Runs: 46 from 25.12.1929.

Successive Non-scoring Runs: 7 from 23.9.1977.

MANAGERS

E. Russell Timmeus 1891–95
(*Secretary-Manager*)
Gilbert Gillies 1895–1901
E. F. Hind 1901–02
Jack Hoskin 1902–06
W. Furness 1906–07
George Swift 1907–10
G. H. Jones 1911–13
R. L. Weston 1913–17
T. Callaghan 1919
J. J. Caffrey 1920–22
Harry Hadley 1922
Harry Parkes 1922–27
Alec Campbell 1927
Ted Davison 1927–32
Bill Harvey 1932–38
Norman Bullock 1938–45
Bob Brocklebank 1945–48
Bobby Marshall 1948–52
Ted Davison 1952–58
Duggie Livingstone 1958–62
Tony McShane 1962–67
Jimmy McGuigan 1967–73
Joe Shaw 1973–76
Arthur Cox 1976–80
Frank Barlow 1980–83
John Duncan 1983–87
Kevin Randall 1987–88
Paul Hart 1988–91
Chris McMenemy 1991–93
John Duncan 1993–2000
Nicky Law 2000–01
Dave Rushbury 2002–03
Roy McFarland 2003–07
Lee Richardson 2007–09
John Sheridan 2009–12
Paul Cook October 2012–

TEN YEAR LEAGUE RECORD

		P	W	D	L	F	A	Pts	Pos
2004-05	FL 1	46	14	15	17	55	62	57	17
2005-06	FL 1	46	14	14	18	63	73	56	16
2006-07	FL 1	46	12	11	23	45	53	47	21
2007-08	FL 2	46	19	12	15	76	56	69	8
2008-09	FL 2	46	16	15	15	62	57	63	10
2009-10	FL 2	46	21	7	18	61	62	70	8
2010-11	FL 2	46	24	14	8	85	51	86	1
2011-12	FL 1	46	10	12	24	56	81	42	22
2012-13	FL 2	46	18	13	15	60	45	67	8
2013-14	FL 2	46	23	15	8	71	40	84	1

DID YOU KNOW ?

The attendance of 61,879 to watch Chesterfield play at Tottenham Hotspur on Boxing Day 1949 is the highest gate the Spireites have played in front of. Spurs went on to win the Division Two title that season with Chesterfield finishing in a respectable mid-table position.

CHESTERFIELD – FOOTBALL LEAGUE TWO 2013–14 LEAGUE RECORD

Match No.	Date	Venue	Opponents	Result	H/T Score	Lg Pos.	Goalscorers	Attendance
1	Aug 3	A	Bury	W 2-0	0-0	5	O'Shea [50], Richards [66]	4337
2	10	H	Cheltenham T	W 2-0	1-0	3	Roberts [23], Doyle [90]	5367
3	17	A	Rochdale	D 2-2	1-1	3	Richards [19], Roberts [65]	2899
4	24	H	Southend U	W 2-1	0-0	2	Roberts [59], Gnanduillet [90]	5579
5	31	A	Portsmouth	W 2-0	0-0	1	Gnanduillet [87], Darikwa [90]	15,999
6	Sept 7	H	Accrington S	W 1-0	0-0	1	Darikwa [47]	6588
7	14	A	AFC Wimbledon	W 2-0	1-0	1	Roberts [30], Hird [53]	6353
8	21	A	Oxford U	W 1-0	1-0	1	Humphreys [30]	7187
9	28	H	Mansfield T	L 0-1	0-1	1		10,015
10	Oct 5	A	Morecambe	L 3-4	3-0	1	Doyle 2 [5, 23], McSheffrey [11]	2204
11	12	A	Fleetwood T	D 1-1	0-0	1	Cooper [55]	4521
12	19	H	Burton Alb	L 0-2	0-2	1		6901
13	22	H	York C	D 2-2	1-1	2	Gnanduillet (pen) [64], O'Shea [76]	5907
14	26	A	Bristol R	D 0-0	0-0	4		5667
15	Nov 2	H	Scunthorpe U	D 1-1	1-0	3	Richards [8]	6346
16	16	A	Torquay U	W 2-0	2-0	2	Banks [16], O'Shea [19]	2361
17	23	H	Wycombe W	W 2-0	2-0	2	Banks [32], Gnanduillet [45]	5798
18	26	H	Northampton T	D 0-0	0-0	2		5321
19	Dec 1	A	Newport Co	L 2-3	0-1	2	Ryan [62], Richards [90]	3378
20	14	H	Plymouth Arg	W 2-0	2-0	2	Brown [9], Richards (pen) [42]	5486
21	20	A	Exeter C	W 2-0	0-0	1	Banks [48], Richards [70]	3449
22	26	H	Hartlepool U	D 1-1	1-0	1	Darikwa [31]	7680
23	29	H	Dagenham & R	D 1-1	0-0	1	Richards (pen) [49]	5906
24	Jan 11	H	Bury	W 4-0	1-0	3	Roberts [16], O'Shea [65], Soares (og) [82], Gardner [86]	6053
25	18	A	Southend U	L 0-3	0-1	5		6256
26	21	A	Rochdale	D 2-2	1-0	4	Roberts [40], Richards [70]	5078
27	25	A	Northampton T	W 3-1	1-1	2	Gardner [25], Roberts [53], Gnanduillet [87]	5082
28	28	A	York C	W 2-0	2-0	1	Doyle [2], Roberts [39]	3322
29	Feb 1	H	Bristol R	W 3-1	2-1	1	Morsy [5], Banks [44], Doyle [47]	6048
30	8	A	Scunthorpe U	D 1-1	1-1	1	Doyle (pen) [45]	6131
31	15	H	Torquay U	W 3-1	0-0	1	Doyle [56], O'Shea 2 [80, 90]	5912
32	22	A	Wycombe W	L 0-1	0-1	1		3356
33	25	A	Cheltenham T	W 4-1	4-0	1	Gardner [22], Doyle [23], Banks [26], Cooper [29]	2317
34	Mar 3	H	Portsmouth	D 0-0	0-0	1		5807
35	8	A	Accrington S	L 1-3	0-3	1	Evatt [85]	1968
36	11	A	AFC Wimbledon	D 1-1	0-0	1	Banks [55]	3424
37	15	H	Oxford U	W 3-0	2-0	1	Banks [8], Roberts 2 (1 pen) [16 (p), 90]	6246
38	18	A	Plymouth Arg	L 1-2	0-1	2	Humphreys [57]	6012
39	22	A	Mansfield T	D 0-0	0-0	3		5931
40	25	H	Morecambe	W 1-0	1-0	3	O'Shea [19]	4891
41	Apr 5	H	Newport Co	D 1-1	0-0	3	Ryan [49]	5659
42	12	A	Hartlepool U	W 2-1	1-1	3	Cooper [30], Doyle [49]	3778
43	18	H	Exeter C	D 1-1	0-1	2	Doyle (pen) [78]	7331
44	21	A	Dagenham & R	W 1-0	1-0	2	Doyle [28]	1801
45	27	A	Burton Alb	W 2-0	0-0	1	O'Shea 2 [52, 79]	4855
46	May 3	H	Fleetwood T	W 2-1	0-1	1	Hird [51], Roberts [55]	9037

Final League Position: 1

GOALSCORERS

League (71): Doyle 11 (2 pens), Roberts 11 (1 pen), O'Shea 9, Richards 8 (2 pens), Banks 7, Gnanduillet 5 (1 pen), Cooper 3, Darikwa 3, Gardner 3, Hird 2, Humphreys 2, Ryan 2, Brown 1, Evatt 1, McSheffrey 1, Morsy 1, own goal 1.
The Budweiser FA Cup (3): Darikwa 1, Roberts 1, Ryan 1.
Capital One Cup (1): Doyle 1.
Johnstone's Paint Trophy (9): Banks 2, Darikwa 1, Doyle 1, Evatt 1, Gnanduillet 1, McSheffrey 1, Morsy 1, Ryan 1.

Lee T 46	Talbot D 24+1	Humphreys R 38+4	Togwell S 5+5	Hird S 27+8	Edwards R 4+1	Roberts G 36+4	Morsy S 34	Richards M 21+17	O'Shea J 27+13	Ryan J 39	Doyle E 26+17	Darikwa T 32+9	Smith N 12+1	Cooper L 38+3	Gnanduillet A 10+24	McSheffrey G 2+7	Devitt J 3+4	Evatt I 35	Porter C 2+1	Banks D 23+2	McFadzean C 2+2	Brown M 2+1	Gardner D 11+5	Kearns D 6+4	Bennett M 1+4	Match No.
1	2	3	4[1]	5	6	7	8	9[2]	10[3]	11	12	13														1
1	2	10	14	3	4	8	6	11[2]	9[3]	7	13	12	5[1]													2
1	2	8		4	3[2]	10[2]	7	11	9	6	12	14	5[1]	13												3
1	2	10[1]		4		8	6	11[2]	9[3]	7	13	12	5	4	13											4
1	2	8		3		11	6	10[1]	7[3]	9	12	14	5[2]	4	13											5
1	2[3]	5	14	4		9	7	11[2]	10[1]	6	13	8		3	12											6
1	2	5		3		9	7	11	10[3]	6	12	8[2]		4	14	13										7
1	2	5		3		9	6		10[3]	7	11[2]	8[1]		4	13	12	14									8
1	2[3]	5		3		9[4]	7		10[2]	8	11	6[1]		4	12	13	14									9
1		5		2	12		6		9[1]	7	11	8[2]		4		10[3]	13	3	14							10
1	6[2]	5[1]	14	2			8		13	7	11	9		4			12		3	10[3]						11
1	2[1]	5		3		9[3]	7	14	12	6	10	8		4	13					11[2]						12
1		5		2[2]		9	7	14	13	6	12			4	11[3]	10[1]	8	3								13
1		5	14			9	7[1]	13		10	8[4]	2		4	11			6[2]	3[3]		12					14
1	2	5	12			10		11	9[3]	6		13		3[1]	14			8[2]	4		7					15
1	2	5		8		9		12	7[2]	6	14	13		4	11[1]			3		10[3]						16
1	2	5		7		10			8[1]	6	14	12		4	11[3]			3		9[2]	13					17
1	2	5		7		9		12	6[3]	8	13			4	10[1]		14	3		11[2]						18
1	8			2		10[3]		12	9[2]	5	13			3[4]	11	14		4		6[1]	7					19
1	2	5	8	7				10[3]	13		9	6[3]			11[1]	14		3			12	4[▪]				20
1	2	5	7	4				10[2]	14		11[3]	6			12			3		8	9[1]	13				21
1	2	5	8[3]	4				10	12		9[2]	6		14	11[1]	13		3		7						22
1	2	5	8	4[▪]				10	14		9	6[1]	13	12	11[3]			3		7[2]						23
1	2	12				10[3]	7	11	8	6			5[1]	4	13					9[2]		3	14			24
1	2					10	6	11[3]	8[1]	7	14		5	4				3		9[2]			13			25
1	2[1]		12			10	7	11[4]	8	6		13	5	4	14			3[2]		9[3]						26
1		5	14			10	6		13	7	11[3]	2		4	12			3		9[1]			8[2]			27
1		5	14			10[3]	9	13	12	7	11	2		3				4		8[2]			6[1]			28
1		5				10	7	12	14	6	11[2]	2		4	13			3		9[1]			8[3]			29
1	12	5				11	7	13		6	10[2]	2		4	14			3		9[2]			8[1]			30
1		5	14			12	6		8	7	11[3]	2		4	13			3		9[1]			10[2]			31
1		5	3[3]			10	7	13	9[1]	6	11[2]	6		2	12			4					14			32
1		5	14	13		8	7			10[3]	11	2		4	12			3		9[1]			6[2]			33
1		5				10	6	12	13	7	11[3]	2		4	14			3		9			8[2]			34
1		5				10	7	12	14	6[3]	13	2		4	11[2]			3		9			8[1]			35
1		5				10	6	13	8[2]	7	11[3]	2		4	14			3		9				12		36
1		5				10	9	11	6[2]	7	12	2		4				3		8[2]			14	13		37
1		5				10[3]	7	11	8[1]	6	14	2		3				4		9[2]			12	13		38
1		5	6			10	7	11[3]			13	2		4	14			3		9[1]			8[2]	12		39
1		5				13	6	12	8[3]	7	11[2]	2		4				3		14			10	9[1]		40
1		5	12			10	7	13	8[3]	6	11[2]	2		4				3					9[1]	14		41
1	13		8			12	7	11[3]			10	2	5	4	14			3					6[1]	9[2]		42
1	12		2			10	6[▪]	11[3]			8	5	9[1]	4	13			3					7[2]	14		43
1		7				12		11[3]	13	8	10	2	5	4	14			3					6[1]	9[2]		44
1	13		6			10		14	8	7	11[3]	2	5	3[2]				4					12	9[1]		45
1	2[1]	7	14	4		8[3]		13	10	9	6[2]	11	5					3					12			46

The Budweiser FA Cup

First Round	Daventry T	(h)	2-0
Second Round	Southend U	(h)	1-3

Capital One Cup

First Round	Leeds U	(a)	1-2

Johnstone's Paint Trophy

Second Round	Mansfield T	(a)	1-0
Northern Quarter-Finals	Rochdale	(h)	3-0
Northern Semi-Finals	Oldham Ath	(a)	1-1
(aet; won 6-5 on penalties)			
Northern Final 1st leg	Fleetwood T	(a)	3-1
Northern Final 2nd leg	Fleetwood T	(h)	0-1
Final	Peterborough U	(Wembley)	1-3

COLCHESTER UNITED

FOUNDATION

Colchester United was formed in 1937 when a number of enthusiasts of the much older Colchester Town club decided to establish a professional concern as a limited liability company. The new club continued at Layer Road which had been the amateur club's home since 1909.

Weston Homes Community Stadium, United Way, Colchester, Essex CO4 5UP.

Telephone: (01206) 755 100.

Fax: (01206) 715 327.

Ticket Office: (0845) 437 9089.

Website: www.cu-fc.com

Email: media@colchesterunited.net

Ground Capacity: 10,105.

Record Attendance: 19,072 v Reading, FA Cup 1st rd, 27 November 1948 (at Layer Road); 10,064 v Norwich C, FL 1, 16 January 2010 (at Community Stadium).

Pitch Measurements: 100.5m × 65m (110yd × 71yd)

Executive Chairman: Robbie Cowling.

Vice-chairman: Richard Cowling.

Manager: Joe Dunne.

Assistant Manager: Mark Kinsella.

Physio: Tony Flynn.

Colours: Royal blue and white striped shirts, royal blue shorts, white socks with blue trim.

Year Formed: 1937.

Turned Professional: 1937.

Club Nickname: 'The U's'.

Grounds: 1937, Layer Road; 2008, Weston Homes Community Stadium.

First Football League Game: 19 August 1950, Division 3 (S), v Gillingham (a) D 0–0 – Wright; Kettle, Allen; Bearryman, Stewart, Elder; Jones, Curry, Turner, McKim, Church.

Record League Victory: 9–1 v Bradford C, Division 4, 30 December 1961 – Ames; Millar, Fowler; Harris, Abrey, Ron Hunt; Foster, Bobby Hunt (4), King (4), Hill (1), Wright.

Record Cup Victory: 9-1 v Leamington, FA Cup 1st rd, 5 November 2005 – Davison; Stockley (Garcia), Duguid, Brown (1), Chilvers, Watson (1), Halford (1), Izzet (Danns) (2), Iwelumo (1) (Williams), Cureton (2), Yeates (1).

HONOURS

Football League – FL 1: *Runners-up* 2005–06; **Division 4:** *Runners-up* 1961–62. **FA Cup:** Best season: 6th rd, 1971. **Football League Cup:** Best season: 5th rd, 1975. **Auto Windscreens Shield:** *Runners-up* 1997. **GM Vauxhall Conference:** *Winners* 1991–92. **FA Trophy:** *Winners* 1992.

sky SPORTS FACT FILE

In 1947–48 Colchester United became the first non-league team in over 30 years to reach the last 16 of the FA Cup. The U's, then members of the Southern League, knocked out three Football League teams in Wrexham, Huddersfield Town and Bradford Park Avenue before losing 5-0 at Blackpool in the fifth round.

Record Defeat: 0–8 v Leyton Orient, Division 4, 15 October 1988.

Most League Points (2 for a win): 60, Division 4, 1973–74.

Most League Points (3 for a win): 81, Division 4, 1982–83.

Most League Goals: 104, Division 4, 1961–62.

Highest League Scorer in Season: Bobby Hunt, 38, Division 4, 1961–62.

Most League Goals in Total Aggregate: Martyn King, 130, 1956–64.

Most League Goals in One Match: 4, Bobby Hunt v Bradford C, Division 4, 30 December 1961; 4, Martyn King v Bradford C, Division 4, 30 December 1961; 4, Bobby Hunt v Doncaster R, Division 4, 30 April 1962.

Most Capped Player: Bela Balogh, 2 (9), Hungary.

Most League Appearances: Micky Cook, 613, 1969–84.

Youngest League Player: Lindsay Smith, 16 years 218 days v Grimsby T, 24 April 1971.

Record Transfer Fee Received: £2,500,000 from Reading for Greg Halford, January 2007.

Record Transfer Fee Paid: £400,000 to Cheltenham T for Steve Gillespie, July 2008.

Football League Record: 1950 Elected to Division 3 (S); 1958–61 Division 3; 1961–62 Division 4; 1962–65 Division 3; 1965–66 Division 4; 1966–68 Division 3; 1968–74 Division 4; 1974–76 Division 3, 1976–77 Division 4; 1977–81 Division 3; 1981–90 Division 4; 1990–92 Conference; 1992–98 Division 3; 1998–2004 Division 2; 2004–06 FL 1; 2006–08 FL C; 2008– FL 1.

MANAGERS

Ted Fenton 1946–48
Jimmy Allen 1948–53
Jack Butler 1953–55
Benny Fenton 1955–63
Neil Franklin 1963–68
Dick Graham 1968–72
Jim Smith 1972–75
Bobby Roberts 1975–82
Allan Hunter 1982–83
Cyril Lea 1983–86
Mike Walker 1986–87
Roger Brown 1987–88
Jock Wallace 1989
Mick Mills 1990
Ian Atkins 1990–91
Roy McDonough 1991–94
George Burley 1994
Steve Wignall 1995–99
Mick Wadsworth 1999
Steve Whitton 1999–2003
Phil Parkinson 2003–06
Geraint Williams 2006–08
Paul Lambert 2008–09
Aidy Boothroyd 2009–10
John Ward 2010–12
Joe Dunne September 2012–

LATEST SEQUENCES

Longest Sequence of League Wins: 7, 31.12.2005 – 7.2.2006.

Longest Sequence of League Defeats: 9, 20.11.2012 – 12.1.2013.

Longest Sequence of League Draws: 6, 21.3.1977 – 11.4.1977.

Longest Sequence of Unbeaten League Matches: 20, 22.12.1956 – 19.4.1957.

Longest Sequence Without a League Win: 20, 2.3.1968 – 31.8.1968.

Successive Scoring Runs: 24 from 15.9.1962.

Successive Non-scoring Runs: 5 from 11.2.2006.

TEN YEAR LEAGUE RECORD

		P	W	D	L	F	A	Pts	Pos
2004-05	FL 1	46	14	17	15	60	50	59	15
2005-06	FL 1	46	22	13	11	58	40	79	2
2006-07	FL C	46	20	9	17	70	56	69	10
2007-08	FL C	46	7	17	22	62	86	38	24
2008-09	FL 1	46	18	9	19	58	58	63	12
2009-10	FL 1	46	20	12	14	64	52	72	8
2010-11	FL 1	46	16	14	16	57	63	62	10
2011-12	FL 1	46	13	20	13	61	66	59	10
2012-13	FL 1	46	14	9	23	47	68	51	20
2013-14	FL 1	46	13	14	19	53	61	53	16

DID YOU KNOW ?

Colchester United's total of 94 points beat the previous Conference record when they won the title and promotion back to the Football League in 1991–92. They finished ahead of Wycombe Wanderers on goal difference and went on to complete the double by defeating Witton Albion in the FA Trophy final.

COLCHESTER UNITED – FOOTBALL LEAGUE ONE 2013–14 LEAGUE RECORD

Match No.	Date	Venue	Opponents	Result		H/T Score	Lg Pos.	Goalscorers	Attendance
1	Aug 3	A	Gillingham	W	1-0	0-0	6	Bond [89]	6792
2	10	H	Port Vale	W	1-0	0-0	4	Massey [74]	3201
3	17	A	Sheffield U	D	1-1	1-1	5	Sears [25]	17,167
4	23	H	Carlisle U	D	1-1	0-1	4	Sears [71]	3573
5	31	H	Leyton Orient	L	1-2	1-1	8	Ibehre [35]	5056
6	Sept 8	A	Coventry C	L	0-2	0-1	10		1789
7	14	A	Bradford C	D	2-2	2-1	11	Monakana [28], Ibehre [32]	13,570
8	21	H	Crawley T	D	1-1	1-1	12	Sears [6]	3031
9	28	A	Bristol C	D	1-1	1-0	13	Taylor [30]	10,739
10	Oct 5	H	Wolverhampton W	L	0-3	0-1	14		7295
11	12	H	Walsall	D	1-1	1-0	14	Sears [7]	2945
12	19	A	Brentford	L	1-3	0-0	14	Okuonghae [49]	5705
13	22	A	Shrewsbury T	D	1-1	1-1	16	Bean [44]	4364
14	26	H	Peterborough U	W	1-0	0-0	14	Bonne [70]	4149
15	Nov 2	A	Rotherham U	D	2-2	1-2	14	Bean [7], Lee [90]	7096
16	16	H	Swindon T	L	1-2	0-0	15	Okuonghae [78]	3334
17	23	A	Preston NE	D	1-1	0-1	16	Garbutt [76]	8492
18	26	H	Milton Keynes D	W	3-1	2-0	15	Eastmond [20], Ibehre [44], Bonne [78]	2597
19	30	A	Tranmere R	L	1-2	0-1	16	Morrison [90]	4148
20	Dec 14	H	Notts Co	L	0-4	0-2	18		2961
21	21	A	Oldham Ath	W	2-0	2-0	15	Plummer (og) [8], Ibehre [32]	4036
22	26	H	Stevenage	W	4-0	3-0	13	Turgott [10], Ibehre [14], Eastmond 2 [26, 77]	3919
23	29	H	Crewe Alex	L	1-2	1-0	14	Garbutt [29]	3430
24	Jan 1	A	Milton Keynes D	D	0-0	0-0	14		7879
25	11	H	Gillingham	W	3-0	0-0	13	Watt [50], Morrison [87], Sears [90]	3819
26	18	A	Carlisle U	W	4-2	2-1	12	Watt 2 [16, 45], Bean [68], Ehmer (og) [75]	3688
27	Feb 11	A	Port Vale	L	0-2	0-1	14		3734
28	14	A	Swindon T	D	0-0	0-0	14		6683
29	22	H	Preston NE	L	1-2	0-1	16	Ibehre [55]	3416
30	25	H	Sheffield U	L	0-1	0-0	17		3088
31	Mar 1	A	Leyton Orient	L	1-2	0-1	19	Bean [79]	6323
32	4	H	Rotherham U	D	0-0	0-0	18		2655
33	8	H	Coventry C	W	2-1	2-1	15	Sears [5], Massey [26]	4426
34	11	H	Bradford C	L	0-2	0-1	17		2605
35	15	A	Crawley T	L	0-1	0-1	17		3182
36	18	A	Shrewsbury T	W	1-0	0-0	17	Ibehre [56]	2508
37	22	H	Bristol C	D	2-2	0-1	16	Massey [73], Sears [79]	3805
38	25	A	Wolverhampton W	L	2-4	0-3	16	Gilbey [58], Wright, David [72]	17,041
39	29	A	Notts Co	L	0-2	0-2	18		5230
40	Apr 2	A	Peterborough U	L	0-2	0-1	18		4434
41	5	H	Tranmere R	L	1-2	1-1	18	Sears [45]	3443
42	12	A	Stevenage	W	3-2	1-1	18	Sears 2 [45, 73], Ibehre [50]	3108
43	18	H	Oldham Ath	L	0-1	0-1	18		4252
44	21	A	Crewe Alex	D	0-0	0-0	18		4603
45	26	H	Brentford	W	4-1	3-1	18	Bean [29], Wynter [32], Sears 2 (1 pen) [41 (p), 65]	6400
46	May 3	A	Walsall	W	1-0	0-0	16	Eastmond [54]	4271

Final League Position: 16

GOALSCORERS

League (53): Sears 12 (1 pen), Ibehre 8, Bean 5, Eastmond 4, Massey 3, Watt 3, Bonne 2, Garbutt 2, Morrison 2, Okuonghae 2, Bond 1, Gilbey 1, Lee 1, Monakana 1, Taylor 1, Turgott 1, Wright, David 1, Wynter 1, own goals 2.
The Budweiser FA Cup (2): Bonne 1, Garbutt 1.
Capital One Cup (1): Ibehre 1.
Johnstone's Paint Trophy (1): Wilson 1.

Walker S 46	Wilson B 38	Dickson R 28 + 4	Wright David 33 + 2	Okuonghae M 44	Eastmond C 32 + 7	Bean M 31 + 4	Eastman T 36	Ibehre J 32 + 5	Massey G 22 + 8	Sears F 25 + 7	Gilbey A 26 + 10	Wright Drey 2 + 9	Bond A — + 8	Watt S 19 + 3	Morrison C 17 + 16	Olufemi T 5 + 8	Spence M — + 1	Garbutt L 19	Monakana J 6 + 3	Pappoe D — + 2	Taylor M 5	Ladapo F — + 2	Hubble C — + 1	Szmidics S — + 7	Lee E 4	Bonne M 2 + 12	Bolger C 4	Vose D 19 + 8	Tozer B 1	Turgott B 3 + 1	Sesay A 2 + 1	Sanderson J — + 1	Wynter A 5 + 1	Kent F — + 1	Duguid K — + 1	Match No.
1	2	3	4	5	6^2	7^3	8	9	10	11^1	12	13	14																							1
1	2	5	6	3	7^1	13	4	11	10	9^2	12			8																						2
1	2	5	6	3	7		4	11^3	8	9^1	12	13		10^2	14																					3
1	2		7^1	3	6		4	11	8	10	12	13		9^2		5																				4
1		5	6^1	3	7		4	11	8^3	9^2	13	12		10	14	2																				5
1	4	5^1	6^2		7	8^3	3	10		9	11	14		13	2	12																				6
1	2		7	3	6		4	10	12	13	8^2	9^1						5	11^3	$14^\blacklozenge$																7
1	2		7	3	6		11	10^2	9^3	13							5	8^1	4	12	14															8
1	2		7	3	6^2	12	11	8^3	9	14							5	10^1	4		13															9
1	2		6^2	3	7	12	11^3	10	9								5	8^1	4	14	13															10
1	2		4	7^3	8		11	9^2	10^1	6							5	12	14	3	13															11
1	2		3	6	8		11	12	10^1	7^3	13			9^2			5	14	4																	12
1	2	3^3	4	12			9	6^2	7					10			5	13						11¹	14											13
1	2	14	3	7	8			6						10^3			5	9^2				13	11^1	12	4											14
1	2		3	8^3	7^2		12	13		9			13	11			5	6^1				14	10	12	4											15
1	2	5		3	6^1	7		12	13	10				9									11^2	8	4											16
1	2	5^3		3		6		12	8^1	11^2	7			9	13		10									4	14									17
1	2	10	6	3	7^3		4	11^2				8			13			5				14				12		9^1								18
1	2	10	6^1	3	8		4	11				9^3		13	14			5								12		7^2								19
1	9^1		3	7^2	10		4	11			8		14		10^3	13		5								6				2^3	12					20
1	2	12	9	3	7^2	10	4	11^1				14			13			5								8		6^3								21
1	2^3		7	3	6	9	4	11^2						12	13	14		5								8		10^1								22
1	2		7^3	4	8	6	3	11^1				14			13	12		5								12		9^2		10						23
1	2	11	7	3^2	8^3	6	4	10							13			5								12										24
1	2		8	3	7	6	4			14					9^1	10^2	12	5								13		11^3								25
1	6	14	2^1	3	7	8	4	13				12			11^3	10^2		5								9										26
1	2	5	7^3	4	9	8	3	12	14	13				10	11^1													6^2								27
1	2	5	7	3	8^1	9	4		14	12	13			10^4	11^3													6^2								28
1	2	5	8	3	6^2	7	4	10	11¹	12				13														9								29
1	2	2^2	5	6	3	13	8	4	11					9														7		12						30
1	2	5	6^1	3	7^2	12	4	10	11	8					9^3											13							14			31
1	2	5	6	4		7	3		8^1	9^3				10^2	11	14										12		13								32
1	2	5	6	3	12	7	4		8^3	9^1				10	11^2											13		14								33
1	2	5	6^1	3	12	7^3	4		8	9	14			10	11^2											13										34
1	2	5	7	3	8^3	6	4	10^1	12	9^2				11	14													13								35
1	2	5	13	4	12	6^1	3	11^3	10		7			9												14		8^2								36
1		5	3		6	3		4	11	10	12	7		8^2		14										13		9^1			2^3					37
		5	6	3	9^2		4	11^3	8^1	12	7			13				14								10				2					38
1	2	5	7	3	14	9^1	4	11	12	10	8^3			13														6^2								39
1		5	6^3	3	8		4	13	12	11	7	14		10^2	2													9^1								40
1		5	6^1	3			4	11	7	10	8	14		12		2^3												9^2					13			41
1		2^1	3		6	7	10	8^3	11^2	4				9	14	12										13							5			42
1	2		3		7	4	11	8	9	6^2	13			10^1	14											12							5^1			43
1	2	13	3^3		8	4	10	6	11^2	7	12			9^1	14																		5			44
1	2^2	5	12		13	7	4	11	10	9^1	6^3			8												14							3			45
1		5	3^1	6	7^3	4		9		8	12			11		10^2															2		13	14		46

The Budweiser FA Cup
First Round   Sheffield U   (h) 2-3

Capital One Cup
First Round   Peterborough U   (h) 1-5

Johnstone's Paint Trophy
First Round   Dagenham & R   (a) 1-4

COVENTRY CITY

FOUNDATION

Workers at Singers' cycle factory formed a club in 1883. The first success of Singers' FC was to win the Birmingham Junior Cup in 1891 and this led in 1894 to their election to the Birmingham & District League. Four years later they changed their name to Coventry City and joined the Southern League in 1908 at which time they were playing in blue and white quarters.

Playing at Sixfields Stadium, Upton Way, Northampton NN5 5QA (groundshare with Northampton T). Coventry City Football Club, Citibase, 101 Lockhurst Lane, Coventry CV6 5QE.

Telephone: (02476) 992 326 or (02476) 992 327.

Fax: (0247) 623 4099.

Ticket Office: ticketoffice@ccfc.co.uk

Website: www.ccfc.co.uk

Email: info@ccfc.co.uk

Ground Capacity: 7,500.

Record Attendance: 51,455 v Wolverhampton W, Division 2, 29 April 1967 (at Highfield Road); 31,407 v Chelsea, FA Cup 6th rd, 7 March 2009 (at Ricoh Arena).

Pitch Measurements: 106m × 66m (116yd × 72yd)

Managing Director: Tim Fisher.

Manager: Steven Pressley.

Assistant Manager: Neil MacFarlane.

Physio: David Hart.

Colours: Sky blue shirts with grey horizontal stripes, sky blue shorts, sky blue socks.

Year Formed: 1883.

Turned Professional: 1893.

Previous Name: 1883, Singers' FC; 1898, Coventry City.

Club Nickname: 'Sky Blues'.

Grounds: 1883, Binley Road; 1887, Stoke Road; 1899, Highfield Road; 2005, Ricoh Arena; 2013, Sixfields Stadium (groundshare with Northampton T).

First Football League Game: 30 August 1919, Division 2, v Tottenham H (h) L 0–5 – Lindon; Roberts, Chaplin, Allan, Hawley, Clarke, Sheldon, Mercer, Sambrooke, Lowes, Gibson.

Record League Victory: 9–0 v Bristol C, Division 3 (S), 28 April 1934 – Pearson; Brown, Bisby; Perry, Davidson, Frith; White (2), Lauderdale, Bourton (5), Jones (2), Lake.

Record Cup Victory: 8–0 v Rushden & D, League Cup 2nd rd, 2 October 2002 – Debec; Caldwell, Quinn, Betts (1p), Konjic (Shaw), Davenport, Pipe, Safri (Stanford), Mills (2) (Bothroyd (2)), McSheffery (3), Partridge.

HONOURS

Football League – Division 1: Best season: 6th, 1969–70;
Division 2: *Champions* 1966–67;
Division 3: *Champions* 1963–64;
Division 3 (S): *Champions* 1935–36; *Runners-up* 1933–34;
Division 4: *Runners-up* 1958–59.

FA Cup: *Winners* 1987.

Football League Cup: Semi-final 1981, 1990.

European Competitions
European Fairs Cup: 1970–71.

sky SPORTS FACT FILE

Centre forward Clarrie Bourton proved an instant success after signing for Coventry City in 1931. Bourton scored seven hat-tricks in his first season with the Sky Blues finishing the 1931–32 campaign as the Football League's leading marksman with 49 goals from his 40 appearances in Division Three South.

Record Defeat: 2–10 v Norwich C, Division 3 (S), 15 March 1930.

Most League Points (2 for a win): 60, Division 4, 1958–59 and Division 3, 1963–64.

Most League Points (3 for a win): 66, Division 1, 2001–02.

Most League Goals: 108, Division 3 (S), 1931–32.

Highest League Scorer in Season: Clarrie Bourton, 49, Division 3 (S), 1931–32.

Most League Goals in Total Aggregate: Clarrie Bourton, 171, 1931–37.

Most League Goals in One Match: 5, Clarrie Bourton v Bournemouth, Division 3 (S), 17 October 1931; 5, Arthur Bacon v Gillingham, Division 3 (S), 30 December 1933.

Most Capped Player: Magnus Hedman, 44 (58), Sweden.

Most League Appearances: Steve Ogrizovic, 507, 1984–2000.

Youngest League Player: Ben Mackey, 16 years 167 days v Ipswich T, 12 April 2003.

Record Transfer Fee Received: £13,000,000 from Internazionale for Robbie Keane, July 2000.

Record Transfer Fee Paid: £6,500,000 to Norwich C for Craig Bellamy, August 2000.

Football League Record: 1919 Elected to Division 2; 1925–26 Division 3 (N); 1926–36 Division 3 (S); 1936–52 Division 2; 1952–58 Division 3 (S); 1958–59 Division 4; 1959–64 Division 3; 1964–67 Division 2; 1967–92 Division 1; 1992–2001 FA Premier League; 2001–04 Division 1; 2004–12 FL C; 2012– FL 1.

LATEST SEQUENCES

Longest Sequence of League Wins: 6, 25.4.1964 – 5.9.1964.

Longest Sequence of League Defeats: 9, 30.8.1919 – 11.10.1919.

Longest Sequence of League Draws: 6, 1.11.2003 – 29.11.2003.

Longest Sequence of Unbeaten League Matches: 25, 26.11.1966 – 13.5.1967.

Longest Sequence Without a League Win: 19, 30.8.1919 – 20.12.1919.

Successive Scoring Runs: 25 from 10.9.1966.

Successive Non-scoring Runs: 11 from 11.10.1919.

MANAGERS

H. R. Buckle 1909–10
Robert Wallace 1910–13
  (*Secretary-Manager*)
Frank Scott-Walford 1913–15
William Clayton 1917–19
H. Pollitt 1919–20
Albert Evans 1920–24
Jimmy Kerr 1924–28
James McIntyre 1928–31
Harry Storer 1931–45
Dick Bayliss 1945–47
Billy Frith 1947–48
Harry Storer 1948–53
Jack Fairbrother 1953–54
Charlie Elliott 1954–55
Jesse Carver 1955–56
George Raynor 1956
Harry Warren 1956–57
Billy Frith 1957–61
Jimmy Hill 1961–67
Noel Cantwell 1967–72
Bob Dennison 1972
Joe Mercer 1972–75
Gordon Milne 1972–81
Dave Sexton 1981–83
Bobby Gould 1983–84
Don Mackay 1985–86
George Curtis 1986–87
  (*became Managing Director*)
John Sillett 1987–90
Terry Butcher 1990–92
Don Howe 1992
Bobby Gould 1992–93
  (*Bobby Gould and Don Howe joint managers June 1992*)
Phil Neal 1993–95
Ron Atkinson 1995–96
  (*became Director of Football*)
Gordon Strachan 1996–2001
Roland Nilsson 2001–02
Gary McAllister 2002–04
Eric Black 2004
Peter Reid 2004–05
Micky Adams 2005–07
Iain Dowie 2007–08
Chris Coleman 2008–10
Aidy Boothroyd 2010–11
Andy Thorn 2011–12
Mark Robins 2012–13
Steven Pressley March 2013–

TEN YEAR LEAGUE RECORD

		P	W	D	L	F	A	Pts	Pos
2004-05	FL C	46	13	13	20	61	73	52	19
2005-06	FL C	46	16	15	15	62	65	63	8
2006-07	FL C	46	16	8	22	47	62	56	17
2007-08	FL C	46	14	11	21	52	64	53	21
2008-09	FL C	46	13	15	18	47	58	54	17
2009-10	FL C	46	13	15	18	47	64	54	19
2010-11	FL C	46	14	13	19	54	58	55	18
2011-12	FL C	46	9	13	24	41	65	40	23
2012-13	FL 1	46	18	11	17	66	59	55*	15
2013-14	FL 1	46	16	13	17	74	77	51*	18

* 10 pts deducted.

DID YOU KNOW ?

In 1981 Coventry City installed an extra 8,000 seats at their Highfield Road ground and became the first Football League team to play in an all-seated stadium. The new capacity of the ground was 20,600, resulting in the club's home games becoming all-ticket.

COVENTRY CITY – FOOTBALL LEAGUE ONE 2013–14 LEAGUE RECORD

Match No.	Date	Venue	Opponents	Result		H/T Score	Lg Pos.	Goalscorers	Attendance
1	Aug 3	A	Crawley T	L	2-3	0-2	24	Wilson 61, Moussa 82	3454
2	11	H	Bristol C	W	5-4	3-0	24	Clarke, L (pen) 27, Wilson 2 43, 75, Daniels 2 45, 87	2204
3	17	A	Carlisle U	W	4-0	3-0	24	Clarke, L 2 4, 65, Moussa 6, Daniels 31	4072
4	25	H	Preston NE	D	4-4	1-1	24	Clarke, L 25, Wilson 2 70, 83, Manset 90	2068
5	31	A	Shrewsbury T	D	1-1	1-0	24	Wilson 4	6541
6	Sept 8	H	Colchester U	W	2-0	1-0	23	Wilson 2 38, 59	1789
7	15	H	Gillingham	W	2-1	1-1	20	Clarke, L 2, Moussa 83	2046
8	21	A	Port Vale	L	2-3	2-1	20	Wilson 35, Moussa 43	9218
9	29	H	Brentford	L	0-2	0-1	22		2650
10	Oct 5	A	Stevenage	W	1-0	1-0	18	Clarke, L 33	3325
11	13	H	Sheffield U	W	3-2	2-0	16	Clarke, L 2 6, 49, Wilson 32	2078
12	19	A	Wolverhampton W	D	1-1	0-0	17	Phillips 86	22,939
13	22	H	Leyton Orient	W	3-1	1-0	14	Baker 10, Moussa 67, Clarke, L 77	2386
14	26	A	Walsall	W	1-0	0-0	13	Moussa 54	6519
15	Nov 2	H	Notts Co	W	3-0	0-0	11	Clarke, L 2 47, 58, Wilson 64	2693
16	17	A	Bradford C	D	3-3	3-2	12	Webster 2, Clarke, L 7, Wilson 42	14,322
17	23	H	Tranmere R	L	1-5	0-3	12	Baker (pen) 76	1815
18	26	H	Rotherham U	L	0-3	0-0	13		1961
19	30	A	Milton Keynes D	W	3-1	0-1	11	Dagnall 66, Maguire 2 86, 90	14,988
20	Dec 14	H	Crewe Alex	D	2-2	1-1	11	Moussa 36, Wilson (pen) 56	1618
21	21	A	Swindon T	L	1-2	0-0	13	Clarke, L 61	9291
22	26	H	Peterborough U	W	4-2	1-2	12	Clarke, L 2 45, 48, Moussa 80, Wilson 90	4905
23	29	H	Oldham Ath	D	1-1	0-1	12	Baker 73	3347
24	Jan 1	A	Rotherham U	W	3-1	0-1	10	Baker 2 (1 pen) 71 (p), 90, Moussa 85	9154
25	12	H	Crawley T	D	2-2	1-0	11	Sadler (og) 41, Webster 82	2128
26	18	A	Preston NE	D	1-1	0-0	11	Moussa 90	10,671
27	28	A	Leyton Orient	L	0-2	0-0	11		5077
28	Feb 4	A	Bristol C	W	2-1	2-0	10	Moussa 7, Webster 25	11,272
29	8	A	Notts Co	L	0-3	0-2	12		8149
30	18	A	Carlisle U	L	1-2	1-0	13	Moussa 32	1603
31	22	A	Tranmere R	L	1-3	0-1	13	Petrasso 79	5279
32	Mar 2	H	Shrewsbury T	D	0-0	0-0	13		1966
33	5	H	Walsall	W	2-1	1-0	12	Wilson 22, Delfouneso 84	1637
34	8	A	Colchester U	L	1-2	1-2	12	Wilson 45	4426
35	11	A	Gillingham	L	2-4	0-1	14	Wilson (pen) 50, Baker (pen) 83	5447
36	16	H	Port Vale	D	2-2	0-1	15	Clarke, J 81, Wilson 90	1627
37	22	A	Brentford	L	1-3	1-2	17	Wilson 6	8572
38	26	H	Stevenage	W	1-0	0-0	16	Seaborne 67	1697
39	29	A	Crewe Alex	W	2-1	1-0	13	Wilson 2 27, 81	5042
40	Apr 1	H	Bradford C	D	0-0	0-0	13		1673
41	5	H	Milton Keynes D	L	1-2	0-1	13	Baker 57	2781
42	12	A	Peterborough U	L	0-1	0-1	14		6617
43	18	H	Swindon T	L	1-2	1-1	17	Fleck 43	3091
44	21	A	Oldham Ath	D	0-0	0-0	17		4633
45	26	H	Wolverhampton W	D	1-1	0-0	17	Delfouneso 86	4252
46	May 3	A	Sheffield U	L	1-2	1-0	18	Delfouneso 39	20,723

Final League Position: 18

GOALSCORERS

League (74): Wilson 21 (2 pens), Clarke, L 15 (1 pen), Moussa 12, Baker 7 (3 pens), Daniels 3, Delfouneso 3, Webster 3, Maguire 2, Clarke, J 1, Dagnall 1, Fleck 1, Manset 1, Petrasso 1, Phillips 1, Seaborne 1, own goal 1.
The Budweiser FA Cup (8): Clarke, L 3, Baker 2, Moussa 1, Wilson 1, own goal 1.
Capital One Cup (2): Baker 1, Moussa 1.
Johnstone's Paint Trophy (0).

Murphy J 46	Christie C 33 +1	Adams B 34 +2	Baker C 31 +6	Willis J 21 +7	Clarke J 39 +2	Fleck J 41 +2	Thomas C 40 +3	Clarke L 22 +1	Wilson C 37	Moussa F 36 +3	Phillips A 3 +8	Webster A 40 +1	Daniels B 10 +8	Manset M — +9	Barton A 5 +9	Haynes R 1 +1	Garner L — +3	Loza J — +1	Seaborne D 18 +3	Dagnall C 4 +2	Maguire C 1 +2	Slager D — +3	Thomas G 1	Delfouneso N 8 +6	Marshall M 6 +8	McGeouch D — +8	Petrasso M 7	Akpom C 5 +1	Robinson A 5 +1	Eccleston N 4 +4	Prutton D 8	Match No.
1	2	3	4	5¹	6	7	8	9	10	11	12																					1
1	2	5	12	3	8	6	10	11¹	7²			4	9	13																		2
1	2	5	13	4	7	8³	11	10²	6			3	9¹	12	14																	3
1	2	5		3	8	7	11	10	9			4	6¹	12																		4
1	2		6¹	4	8	7	10	11	9			3	12		5																	5
1	2	5	6²	14	4	8	7	10	11³	9¹		3	12	13																		6
1	2	5	6²	13	4	8	7	10	11	9¹		3	12																			7
1	2	5	6		3	7	8¹	10	11	9		4	12																			8
1	2	5			3	6	8	10	11	7		4	12	9¹																		9
1	2²	4		12	10	6	5	11	9	7		3		8¹	13																	10
1		5	6¹	2¹	4	8	7	11	10	9²13	3	12	14																			11
1		5	6	2²	4	8	7	11	10	9¹13	3	12																				12
1		5	6²	2	4	8	7	10	11³	9¹	3	14	12	13																		13
1		5	6²		4	8	7	11	10	9¹	2	3	13	12																		14
1		5	6³		4	8	7¹	10	11²	9	2	3	13	14	12																	15
1	2	5	6		3	8	7	10	11	9¹12	4																					16
1	2²	5	6		4	8	10	11	9	13	3	12											7¹									17
1	12	5	6		3	8	7	11	9	2	4	10¹																				18
1	2	5	6³		3	8	7	10	9²13	14									4	11¹	12											19
1	2	5	13		3	8	7	12	10	9¹									4	11²	6											20
1	2	5¹	6		4	8	7	10		9									3	11	12											21
1	2	5	6¹	14		8	7	10	11³	9²13	3								4	12												22
1	2	5	6			8¹	7	10	11	12	3	13							4	9²												23
1	2	5	6	3		7¹	10	11²	9³13	4	8	14							12													24
1	5	9¹	6	3	4	10	7		11²	2	8³	13	14									12										25
1	2	5	7²		9¹	6	3	10		11	4	12							8		13											26
1	2	5	6		12	9	7		10¹	3	8²	14							4			13	11³									27
1	2	5	7³		14	12	6		11²	3	9²	8							4					10	13							28
1	2	5	6			13	7		10	3	9²	8¹							4						11		12					29
1	2		6¹		5	8¹	7		11	3	13								4								12	9	10			30
	2¹		6²	13	5	7	8		11	3	9³								4								12	14	10			31
1		13	2	5	8	7		11	9²	3									4								12		6	10¹		32
1	13		2	5	8	7		11¹	3		14								4						12	9²		6	10¹			33
1	9²		2	5	8	7¹		11	12	4³									3					13	9	14	6	10				34
1	12	13	2	5	8	7		11	9¹	3									4⁴					10²	14		6³					35
1	2	5	6	3	4	8	7¹		11	13														12	14			9²	10³			36
1	2	5¹	7	3	4	6	8		11	9²									13					10³	12			14				37
1		5		2	6	8	13		11	9²	3								4					10¹					7	12		38
1		5¹	12	6	3		8³		10	9²	4								2						14			11	13	7		39
1	2	5	6	3			12		10	4														13	9¹	14		8³	11²	7		40
1		8	5	3	6		11		2	4														12	9¹	13		14	10³	7²		41
1	2	12	5	4	7		11		3															13	9	14		6³	10¹	8²		42
1	2	6¹	5	4	9	7	11		3															10³	13			12	8		43
1	2	9¹	5	4	8	13	11		3										14						12			6³	10²	7	44
1	2		5	8	9	4	10		3										12					11¹	6					7	45
1	2	12	4	5	8	6¹	11		3															10	9			13		7²	46

The Budweiser FA Cup

First Round	AFC Wimbledon	(a)	3-1
Second Round	Hartlepool U	(a)	1-1
Replay	Hartlepool U	(h)	2-1
Third Round	Barnsley	(a)	2-1
Fourth Round	Arsenal	(a)	0-4

Capital One Cup

First Round	Leyton Orient	(a)	2-3

Johnstone's Paint Trophy

Second Round	Leyton Orient	(a)	0-0

(aet; lost 2-4 on penalties)

CRAWLEY TOWN

FOUNDATION

Formed in 1896, Crawley Town initially entered the West Sussex League before switching to the mid-Sussex League in 1901, winning the Second Division in its second season. The club remained at such level until 1951 when it became members of the Sussex County League and five years later moved to the Metropolitan League while remaining as an amateur club. It was not until 1962 that the club turned semi-professional and a year later, joined the Southern League. Many honours came the club's way, but the most successful run was achieved in 2010–11 when they reached the fifth round of the FA Cup and played before a crowd of 74,778 spectators at Old Trafford against Manchester United. Crawley Town spent 48 years at the Town Mead ground before a new site was occupied at Broadfield in 1997, ideally suited to access from the neighbouring motorway. History was also made on 9 April when the team won promotion to the Football League after beating Tamworth 3-0 to stretch their unbeaten League record to 26 games. They finished the season with a Conference record points total of 105 and at the same time, established another milestone for the longest unbeaten run, having extended it to 30 matches by the end of the season.

Checkatrade.com Stadium, Winfield Way, Crawley, West Sussex RH11 9RX.

Telephone: (01293) 410 000.

Fax: (01293) 410 002.

Ticket Office: (01293) 410 005.

Website: www.crawleytownfc.com

Email: feedback@crawleytownfc.com

Ground Capacity: 5,973.

Record Attendance: 5,608 v Wolverhampton W, FL 1, 18 March 2014.

Pitch Measurements: 103.5m × 66m (113yd × 72yd)

Chairman: Dave Pottinger.

Chief Executive: Michael Dunford.

Manager: John Gregory.

First-Team Coach: Paul Groves.

Head of Medical: Niall Clarke.

Club Nickname: 'The Red Devils'.

Colours: Red shirts with white trim, red shorts with white trim, red socks with white trim.

Year Formed: 1896.

Turned Professional: 1962.

MANAGERS

Managers have included:
Tom Jarvie
John Hollins
Colin Pates
Francis Vines
Simon Wormull
David Woozley
Steve Evans 2007–12
Sean O'Driscoll 2012
Richie Barker 2012–13
John Gregory December 2013–

sky SPORTS FACT FILE

In 2003–04 Crawley Town gained promotion to the Conference after winning the Southern League championship for the first time in their history. They ended the season 12 points ahead of their nearest rivals and completed the double by defeating Moor Green 4-1 over two legs to win the League Cup.

Grounds: Town Mead to 1997; Broadfield Stadium 1997.

First Football League Game: 6 August 2011, FL 2 v Port Vale (a) D 2-2 – Shearer; Hunt, Howell, Bulman, McFadzean (1), Dempster (Thomas), Simpson, Torres, Tubbs (Neilson), Barnett (1) (Wassmer), Smith.

Record League Victory: 5-2 v AFC Wimbledon, FL 2, 22 October 2011.

Record League Defeat: 6-0 v Morecambe, FL 2, 10 September 2011.

Most League Points (3 for a win): 84, FL 2, 2011–12.

Most League Goals: 76, FL 2, 2011–12.

Highest League Scorer in Season: Tyrone Barnett, 14, 2011–12.

Most League Appearances: Dannie Bulman, 135, 2011–14.

Most League Goals in Total Aggregate: Billy Clarke, 20, 2011–14; Matt Tubbs, 20, 2011–12, 2013–14.

Youngest League Player: Hiram Boateng, 18 years 55 days v Stevenage, 4 March 2014.

Record Transfer Fee Received: £1,100,000 from Peterborough U for Tyrone Barnett, July 2012.

Record Transfer Fee Paid: £100,000 to Peterborough U for Sergio Raul Torres, July 2010.

Football League Record: 2011 Promoted from Conference Premier; 2011–12 FL 2; 2012– FL 1.

LATEST SEQUENCES

Longest Sequence of League Wins: 7, 17.9.2011 – 25.10.2011.

Longest Sequence of League Defeats: 6, 22.3.2014 – 8.4.2014.

Longest Sequence of League Draws: 4, 5.3.2013 – 16.3.2013.

Longest Sequence of Unbeaten League Matches: 13, 17.9.2011 – 17.12.2011.

Longest Sequence Without a League Win: 9, 22.10.2013 – 29.12.2013.

Successive Scoring Runs: 16 from 17.9.2011 – 2.1.2012.

Successive Non-scoring Runs: 4 from 22.10.2013.

HONOURS

Football League – FL 2: Best season: 3rd (promoted) 2011–12.

FA Cup: Best season: 5th rd 2011, 2012.

Football League Cup: Best season: 3rd rd 2013.

Blue Square Premier: *Champions* 2010–11.

Southern League: *Champions* 2003–04.

Southern League Cup: *Winners* 2003, 2004.

Southern League Championship Trophy: *Winners* 2004, 2005.

Southern League Merit Cup: *Winners* 1971.

Sussex Professional Cup: *Winners* 1970.

Sussex Senior Cup: *Winners* 1990, 1991, 2003, 2005.

Sussex Intermediate Cup: *Winners* 1928.

Sussex Floodlit Cup: *Winners* 1991, 1992, 1993, 1999.

Southern Counties Floodlit League: *Champions* 1985–86.

Mid-Sussex Senior League: *Champions* 1902–03.

Montgomery Cup: *Winners* 1926.

Gilbert Rice Floodlit Cup: *Winners* 1980, 1984.

Roy Hayden Trophy: *Winners* 1991, 1992.

William Hill Senior Cup: *Winners* 1993.

Metropolitan League Challenge Cup: *Winners* 1959.

Highest Placed Amateur Award: 1961–62.

FA Ronnie Radford Award: 2011.

TEN YEAR LEAGUE RECORD

		P	W	D	L	F	A	Pts	Pos
2004-05	Conf	42	16	9	17	50	50	57	12
2005-06	Conf	42	12	11	19	48	55	44	17
2006-07	Conf	46	17	12	17	52	52	53	18
2007-08	Conf P	46	19	9	18	73	67	60	15
2008-09	Conf P	46	19	14	13	77	55	70	9
2009-10	Conf P	44	19	9	16	50	57	66	7
2010-11	Conf P	46	31	12	3	93	50	105	1
2011-12	FL 2	46	23	15	8	76	54	84	3
2012-13	FL 1	46	18	14	14	59	58	68	10
2013-14	FL 1	46	14	15	17	48	54	57	14

DID YOU KNOW ?

In August 1997 Crawley Town played their first Southern League match at their new Broadfield Stadium, defeating Gloucester City 3-1 in a game watched by an attendance of 1,178. The ground was officially opened two months later by the then Minister of Sport Tony Banks MP.

CRAWLEY TOWN – FOOTBALL LEAGUE ONE 2013–14 LEAGUE RECORD

Match No.	Date	Venue	Opponents		Result	H/T Score	Lg Pos.	Goalscorers	Attendance
1	Aug 3	H	Coventry C	W	3-2	2-0	4	Proctor [13], Walsh [21], Jones, M [84]	3454
2	10	A	Tranmere R	D	3-3	1-2	8	Walsh 2 [10, 81], Clarke [55]	4763
3	17	H	Rotherham U	L	1-2	1-1	10	Sadler [15]	3110
4	23	A	Wolverhampton W	L	1-2	0-1	12	Clarke [90]	17,406
5	31	A	Peterborough U	W	2-0	1-0	11	Alexander 2 [22, 65]	6761
6	Sept 7	H	Gillingham	W	3-2	0-0	6	McFadzean [55], Clarke 2 [66, 81]	3984
7	14	H	Shrewsbury T	D	1-1	0-0	9	Drury [64]	3202
8	21	A	Colchester U	D	1-1	1-1	9	Sinclair [32]	3031
9	28	H	Oldham Ath	W	1-0	1-0	8	Walsh [7]	3142
10	Oct 4	A	Sheffield U	D	1-1	1-0	8	Proctor [10]	15,401
11	19	H	Bradford C	W	1-0	0-0	8	Sinclair [54]	3836
12	22	H	Port Vale	L	0-3	0-2	11		2748
13	26	A	Stevenage	L	0-2	0-1	12		2804
14	Nov 2	H	Brentford	L	0-1	0-1	13		4177
15	5	A	Bristol C	L	0-2	0-0	13		10,085
16	16	A	Carlisle U	D	1-1	0-0	13	Clarke [88]	3675
17	23	H	Walsall	D	0-0	0-0	13		3296
18	26	H	Swindon T	D	0-0	0-0	12		2868
19	30	A	Crewe Alex	L	0-1	0-0	14		4001
20	Dec 14	H	Preston NE	D	2-2	0-2	14	Walsh [66], Alexander [90]	2407
21	21	A	Leyton Orient	W	3-2	2-1	12	Alexander [36], Drury [45], Adams [76]	4855
22	26	A	Milton Keynes D	L	0-2	0-1	14		3249
23	29	H	Notts Co	W	1-0	0-0	13	Connolly, M [54]	3096
24	Jan 12	A	Coventry C	D	2-2	0-1	14	Proctor [83], Drury [87]	2128
25	25	A	Rotherham U	D	2-2	1-1	15	Tubbs [24], Simpson [65]	7579
26	Feb 22	A	Walsall	W	2-1	1-0	19	Tubbs 2 (1 pen) [4 (p), 51]	3904
27	25	A	Swindon T	D	1-1	0-0	18	Tubbs [80]	7062
28	Mar 1	H	Peterborough U	W	1-0	0-0	13	Tubbs (pen) [86]	3663
29	4	H	Stevenage	D	1-1	0-1	13	Tubbs [90]	2936
30	8	A	Gillingham	L	0-1	0-0	16		5961
31	11	A	Shrewsbury T	D	1-1	1-0	16	Simpson [24]	4039
32	15	H	Colchester U	W	1-0	1-0	14	Jones, M [41]	3182
33	18	H	Wolverhampton W	W	2-1	2-1	12	Clarke [27], Tubbs [32]	5680
34	22	A	Oldham Ath	L	0-1	0-1	12		3389
35	25	H	Sheffield U	L	0-2	0-1	14		3622
36	29	A	Preston NE	L	0-1	0-1	16		8979
37	Apr 1	A	Port Vale	L	1-2	1-0	16	Clarke (pen) [35]	3755
38	5	H	Crewe Alex	L	1-2	0-1	17	Proctor [69]	3024
39	8	A	Brentford	L	0-1	0-0	17		7718
40	12	A	Milton Keynes D	W	2-0	2-0	15	Drury [7], Jones, M [45]	8877
41	15	H	Tranmere R	W	2-0	1-0	12	Tubbs [37], Edwards [86]	3443
42	18	H	Leyton Orient	W	2-1	1-1	12	Edwards [26], Drury [70]	4387
43	21	A	Notts Co	L	0-1	0-1	13		7111
44	26	A	Bradford C	L	1-2	0-0	14	Proctor [65]	13,247
45	29	H	Carlisle U	D	0-0	0-0	14		3271
46	May 3	H	Bristol C	D	1-1	1-0	14	Proctor [26]	4405

Final League Position: 14

GOALSCORERS

League (48): Tubbs 8 (2 pens), Clarke 7 (1 pen), Proctor 6, Drury 5, Walsh 5, Alexander 4, Jones, M 3, Edwards 2, Simpson 2, Sinclair 2, Adams 1, Connolly, M 1, McFadzean 1, Sadler 1.
The Budweiser FA Cup (3): Proctor 1, Sinclair 1, own goal 1.
Capital One Cup (3): Adams 2, Alexander 1.
Johnstone's Paint Trophy (2): Jones, M 1, Sinclair 1.

Jones P 46	Hurst J 11 + 7	Sadler M 46	Adams N 24	Walsh J 39	McFadzean K 41 + 1	Jones M 40 + 2	Bulman D 34 + 5	Alexander G 9 + 12	Proctor J 21 + 23	Simpson J 37 + 1	Drury A 36 + 5	Torres S 6 + 16	Connolly M 32 + 4	Clarke B 28 + 1	Rooney L — + 4	Sinclair E 9 + 6	Essam C — + 2	Bennett K 4	Tubbs M 18	Dicker G 9 + 2	KaiKai S 2 + 3	Connolly P 5 + 2	Boateng H 1	Fallon R 3 + 5	Monakana J — + 4	Edwards G 5 + 1	Match No.
1	2	3	4	5	6	7^2	8	9	10^1	11	12	13															1
1	2	5	6^1	4	13	8	14	12	10^3	7	9			3	11^2												2
1	2^1	5	6		4	9		12	11^2	7	8^3	14		2	9^3												3
1		5	6	4^1	3	8	7^2	11	14	2	9^3			12	10	13											4
1	13	5	6^1	4	3	8^4	7	11^3	12	2	9		14	10^2													5
1	2	5	9^2	4		8	11^4	12	7	6^1	13	3	10^3	14													6
1	2^1	5	6	4	13	8		11^2	7	9	3	10	12														7
1	14	5	9	3	4	7	6	12	2	8^3	13		11^2	10													8
1	13	5	8	4	3	7	6	12	2	9^1	14		10^2	11^3													9
1	13	5	7^2	4	3	8	6	12	11^3	2	9^1	14	10														10
1		5	9^3	4	3	7	8	12	10^1	2	6	13		11^2	14												11
1		5	9	4^3	3	8	7^2	13	11	2	6		14	10^1	12												12
1	14	2	9	7	3	10^2	8^1	4^3	13	6	5		12	11													13
1	14	5	9	3	4	7	8^3	13	11^1	2	6^2		12	10													14
1	2	5^2	7	4	3	6		13	8	9	12		14	11^3	10^1												15
1	2	3		5		7^2	8	13	14	9^3	6		4	12	11^1	10											16
1	2	5	9		4	7	8	12	11^1		6		3	10	13												17
1	2	5	9		4		8	12	11^2	7	6^1		3	10	13												18
1	14	2	9	5	4	12	8		10	7^1	13		3^2	6	11^3												19
1	2^2	6	7	5	4		8	10	13		12		3	9	11^1												20
1		5	6	4	3	9	7	11		8			2	10													21
1	2	5	6^1	3		9	7^2	11	12		8	13	4	10^4													22
1		5	6^1	3	4	7		12	10	13	8	9	2	11^2													23
1		5	6	3	4	9		10^2	13	8^1	7	12	2					11									24
1		5	6	4	3	9		12		7^2	8		2	10				11^1	13								25
1		5	6	4	3	9		12		7^2	8		2	10^4				11^2	6^1								26
1		5		4	3	9	13		10^2	6	7^1		2					11^2	8	12							27
1		5		4	3	6	8		12	9	13		2					10^3	7^1	11^2	14						28
1		5			4	9	12		13	6^2	7		3	11				10			2	8^1					29
1		5		4	3	6^2	8		10^1	7				9				11		13	2	12					30
1		5		4	3	9	7		12	6		13	2	10				8^1		13	2	11^2					31
1		5		4	3	6	7		12	9	8^2	13	2	10				11^1									32
1		2		4	5	8	7		12	9	10		3	6				11^1									33
1		5		4	3	9		13	10	7		2^2	6^1					11		8^3	12	14					34
1	2		8	4	11	9		12		7		6^2	3	5				10^1				13					35
1		5		4		11	9^1		10	6	8	7	3	2							2				12		36
1		5		4		9	8^4		12	6	7	13	3	10^1							2	11^2					37
1		5		4	3	6^2		13	7		8	2	11^3	10^2				11	8	9	14	2					38
1		5		3	4	9	7^1		12	6		13		10^2				11	8	6	2						39
1		5		4	3	9	7		11^1	8	10^3	13	12						6		2^1	14					40
1		5		4	3	6	8		11	9^1	7^1	12	2					10^2	14						13		41
1		5		4	3	9	8		12	6^1	7	13	2					11^2							10		42
1		5		4	3	6	12		10		7^2	2						11	8^1					13	9		43
1		5		4	3	9^2	8		13	10		12	2					11	7^1						6		44
1		5		4	3		8		11		7	6	2					10							9		45
1	2			3	6^2	7		10^1	5	8		4						11			13	12	9				46

The Budweiser FA Cup

First Round	Hednesford T	(a)	2-1
Second Round	Bristol R	(a)	0-0
Replay	Bristol R	(h)	1-2

Capital One Cup

First Round	Cheltenham T	(a)	3-4
(aet)			

Johnstone's Paint Trophy

Second Round	Newport Co	(h)	2-3

CREWE ALEXANDRA

FOUNDATION

The first match played at Crewe was on 1 December 1877 against Basford, the leading North Staffordshire team of that time. During the club's history they have also played in a number of other leagues including the Football Alliance, Football Combination, Lancashire League, Manchester League, Central League and Lancashire Combination. Two former players, Aaron Scragg in 1899 and Jackie Pearson in 1911, had the distinction of refereeing FA Cup finals. Pearson was also capped for England against Ireland in 1892.

The Alexandra Stadium, Gresty Road, Crewe, Cheshire CW2 6EB.

Telephone: (01270) 213 014.

Fax: (01270) 216 320.

Ticket Office: (01270) 252 610.

Website: www.crewealex.net

Email: info@crewealex.net

Ground Capacity: 10,109.

Record Attendance: 20,000 v Tottenham H, FA Cup 4th rd, 30 January 1960.

Pitch Measurements: 100.5m × 67m (110yd × 73.1yd)

Chairman: John Bowler.

Vice-chairman: David Rowlinson.   *Director of Football:* Dario Gradi MBE.

Manager: Steve Davis.

Assistant Manager: Neil Baker.

Physio: Rob Sharp.

Colours: Red shirts with white trim, white shorts with red trim, red socks with white trim.

Year Formed: 1877. *Turned Professional:* 1893.

Club Nickname: 'The Railwaymen'.

Ground: 1898, Gresty Road.

First Football League Game: 3 September 1892, Division 2, v Burton Swifts (a) L 1–7 – Hickton; Moore, Cope; Linnell, Johnson, Osborne; Bennett, Pearson (1), Bailey, Barnett, Roberts.

Record League Victory: 8–0 v Rotherham U, Division 3 (N), 1 October 1932 – Foster; Pringle, Dawson; Ward, Keenor (1), Turner (1); Gillespie, Swindells (1), McConnell (2), Deacon (2), Weale (1).

Record Cup Victory: 8–0 v Hartlepool U, Auto Windscreens Shield 1st rd, 17 October 1995 – Gayle; Collins (1), Booty, Westwood (Unsworth), Macauley (1), Whalley (1), Garvey (1), Murphy (1), Savage (1) (Rivers (1p)), Lennon, Edwards, (1 og). 8–0 v Doncaster R, LDV Vans Trophy 3rd rd, 10 November 2002 – Bankole; Wright, Walker, Foster, Tierney; Lunt (1), Brammer, Sorvel, Vaughan (1) (Bell); Ashton (3) (Miles), Jack (2) (Jones (1)).

HONOURS

Football League – Division 2: *Runners-up* 2002–03.
FA Cup: Semi-final 1888.
Football League Cup: never past 3rd round.
Welsh Cup: *Winners* 1936, 1937.
Johnstone's Paint Trophy: *Winners* 2013.

sky **SPORTS** FACT FILE

Former Crewe Alexandra players Bert Swindells and Peter Ellson are commemorated by streets named after them in the Cheshire town. Herbert Swindells Close and Peter Ellson Close can be found within five minutes' walk of Crewe's Gresty Road ground and are near to Dario Gradi Drive named after the club's long-serving manager and coach.

Record Defeat: 2–13 v Tottenham H, FA Cup 4th rd replay, 3 February 1960.

Most League Points (2 for a win): 59, Division 4, 1962–63.

Most League Points (3 for a win): 86, Division 2, 2002–03.

Most League Goals: 95, Division 3 (N), 1931–32.

Highest League Scorer in Season: Terry Harkin, 35, Division 4, 1964–65.

Most League Goals in Total Aggregate: Bert Swindells, 126, 1928–37.

Most League Goals in One Match: 5, Tony Naylor v Colchester U, Division 3, 24 April 1993.

Most Capped Player: Clayton Ince, 38 (79), Trinidad & Tobago.

Most League Appearances: Tommy Lowry, 436, 1966–78.

Youngest League Player: Steve Walters, 16 years 119 days v Peterborough U, 6 May 1988.

Record Transfer Fee Received: £3,000,000 (rising to £6,000,000) from Manchester U for Nick Powell, June 2012.

Record Transfer Fee Paid: £650,000 to Torquay U for Rodney Jack, June 1998.

Football League Record: 1892 Original Member of Division 2; 1896 Failed re-election; 1921 Re-entered Division (N); 1958–63 Division 4; 1963–64 Division 3; 1964–68 Division 4; 1968–69 Division 3; 1969–89 Division 4; 1989–91 Division 3; 1991–92 Division 4; 1992–94 Division 3; 1994–97 Division 2; 1997–2002 Division 1; 2002–03 Division 2; 2003–04 Division 1; 2004–06 FL C; 2006–09 FL 1; 2009–12 FL 2; 2012– FL 1.

LATEST SEQUENCES

Longest Sequence of League Wins: 7, 30.4.1994 – 3.9.1994.

Longest Sequence of League Defeats: 10, 16.4.1979 – 22.8.1979.

Longest Sequence of League Draws: 5, 18.9.2010 – 9.10.2010.

Longest Sequence of Unbeaten League Matches: 17, 25.3.1995 – 16.9.1995.

Longest Sequence Without a League Win: 30, 22.9.1956 – 6.4.1957.

Successive Scoring Runs: 26 from 7.4.1934.

Successive Non-scoring Runs: 9 from 6.11.1974.

MANAGERS

W. C. McNeill 1892–94
  (Secretary-Manager)
J. G. Hall 1895–96
  (Secretary-Manager)
R. Roberts *(1st team Secretary-Manager)* 1897
J. B. Blomerley 1898–1911
  (Secretary-Manager, continued as Hon. Secretary to 1925)
Tom Bailey *(Secretary only)* 1925–38
George Lillycrop *(Trainer)* 1938–44
Frank Hill 1944–48
Arthur Turner 1948–51
Harry Catterick 1951–53
Ralph Ward 1953–55
Maurice Lindley 1956–57
Willie Cook 1957–58
Harry Ware 1958–60
Jimmy McGuigan 1960–64
Ernie Tagg 1964–71
  (continued as Secretary to 1972)
Dennis Viollet 1971
Jimmy Melia 1972–74
Ernie Tagg 1974
Harry Gregg 1975–78
Warwick Rimmer 1978–79
Tony Waddington 1979–81
Arfon Griffiths 1981–82
Peter Morris 1982–83
Dario Gradi 1983–2007
Steve Holland 2007–08
Gudjon Thordarson 2008–09
Dario Gradi 2009–11
Steve Davis October 2011–

TEN YEAR LEAGUE RECORD

		P	W	D	L	F	A	Pts	Pos
2004-05	FL C	46	12	14	20	66	86	50	21
2005-06	FL C	46	9	15	22	57	86	42	22
2006-07	FL 1	46	17	9	20	66	72	60	13
2007-08	FL 1	46	12	14	20	47	65	50	20
2008-09	FL 1	46	12	10	24	59	82	46	22
2009-10	FL 2	46	15	10	21	68	73	55	18
2010-11	FL 2	46	18	11	17	87	65	65	10
2011-12	FL 2	46	20	12	14	67	59	72	7
2012-13	FL 1	46	18	10	18	54	62	64	13
2013-14	FL 1	46	13	12	21	54	80	51	19

DID YOU KNOW

Crewe Alexandra fielded an amateur team in their early years as a Football League club and in 1894–95 became the only club to take part in the FA Amateur Cup in the same season as competing in the Football League. They defeated Sheffield and Shrewsbury Town before going down 1-0 to Old Carthusians in the quarter-finals.

CREWE ALEXANDRA – FOOTBALL LEAGUE ONE 2013–14 LEAGUE RECORD

Match No.	Date		Venue	Opponents		Result	H/T Score	Lg Pos.	Goalscorers	Attendance
1	Aug	3	H	Rotherham U	D	3-3	2-1	8	Grant [3], Clayton [9], Davis (pen) [48]	5926
2		10	A	Milton Keynes D	L	0-1	0-1	16		6911
3		17	H	Tranmere R	W	2-1	1-0	11	Colclough 2 [42, 85]	4720
4		24	A	Leyton Orient	L	0-2	0-2	13		4455
5		31	A	Swindon T	L	0-5	0-2	19		7419
6	Sept	7	H	Peterborough U	D	2-2	2-1	17	Oliver [15], Leitch-Smith [21]	4509
7		14	H	Walsall	L	0-3	0-0	18		4260
8		21	A	Oldham Ath	D	1-1	1-0	17	Turton [13]	4273
9		28	H	Gillingham	L	0-3	0-1	18		4254
10	Oct	5	A	Notts Co	L	0-4	0-2	21		6249
11		12	A	Preston NE	W	2-0	1-0	17	Moore [27], Inman [64]	9268
12		19	H	Bristol C	W	1-0	0-0	16	Moore (pen) [90]	4781
13		22	H	Stevenage	L	0-3	0-3	18		3682
14		26	A	Sheffield U	L	1-3	0-2	22	Clayton [77]	18,784
15	Nov	2	H	Bradford C	D	0-0	0-0	21		5428
16		16	A	Brentford	L	0-5	0-1	22		6616
17		23	H	Port Vale	L	1-2	1-1	23	Evans [35]	6820
18		26	A	Carlisle U	L	1-2	0-2	23	Davis [90]	2969
19		30	H	Crawley T	W	1-0	0-0	22	Aneke [81]	4001
20	Dec	14	A	Coventry C	D	2-2	1-1	23	Hitchcock [14], Aneke [66]	1618
21		21	H	Shrewsbury T	D	1-1	1-0	23	Hitchcock [21]	4801
22		26	A	Wolverhampton W	L	0-2	0-1	24		22,693
23		29	A	Colchester U	W	2-1	0-1	22	Aneke [73], Hitchcock [76]	3430
24	Jan	1	H	Carlisle U	W	2-1	0-0	21	Aneke [53], Na Bangna [64]	4458
25		11	H	Rotherham U	L	2-4	1-1	22	Inman [12], Mellor [61]	7737
26		18	H	Leyton Orient	L	1-2	0-0	23	Aneke [53]	4830
27		21	H	Milton Keynes D	W	2-0	1-0	19	Aneke [35], Leitch-Smith [69]	3613
28		25	A	Tranmere R	L	0-1	0-1	20		5045
29	Feb	1	H	Sheffield U	W	3-0	2-0	19	Aneke 2 [37, 45], Moore [90]	5437
30		8	A	Bradford C	D	3-3	1-0	18	Ikpeazu 2 [12, 54], Pogba [78]	13,343
31		15	H	Brentford	L	1-3	0-1	20	Aneke (pen) [70]	4812
32		22	A	Port Vale	W	3-1	1-0	20	Pogba [15], Aneke (pen) [48], Inman [73]	7812
33		25	A	Stevenage	L	0-1	0-1	20		1970
34	Mar	1	H	Swindon T	D	1-1	0-0	21	Oliver [77]	4433
35		8	A	Peterborough U	L	2-4	1-2	22	Aneke 2 [13, 58]	5109
36		11	A	Walsall	D	1-1	0-0	22	Aneke [51]	3777
37		15	H	Oldham Ath	D	1-1	0-0	22	Davis [90]	5258
38		22	A	Gillingham	W	3-1	1-1	19	Aneke 2 [5, 53], Pogba [83]	5767
39		25	H	Notts Co	L	1-3	0-1	19	Ellis [90]	3895
40		29	H	Coventry C	L	1-2	0-1	22	Clarke, J (og) [62]	5042
41	Apr	5	A	Crawley T	W	2-1	1-0	21	Ikpeazu [18], Inman [80]	3024
42		12	A	Wolverhampton W	L	0-2	0-1	22		6424
43		18	H	Shrewsbury T	W	3-1	1-0	20	Pogba [38], Ikpeazu [51], Grant [89]	6947
44		21	H	Colchester U	D	0-0	0-0	20		4603
45		26	A	Bristol C	D	0-0	0-0	20		14,477
46	May	3	H	Preston NE	W	2-1	1-0	19	Dugdale [10], Pogba [60]	7458

Final League Position: 19

GOALSCORERS

League (54): Aneke 15 (2 pens), Pogba 5, Ikpeazu 4, Inman 4, Davis 3 (1 pen), Hitchcock 3, Moore 3 (1 pen), Clayton 2, Colclough 2, Grant 2, Leitch-Smith 2, Oliver 2, Dugdale 1, Ellis 1, Evans 1, Mellor 1, Na Bangna 1, Turton 1, own goal 1.
The Budweiser FA Cup (1): Grant 1.
Capital One Cup (2): Davis 1 (1 pen), Aneke 1.
Johnstone's Paint Trophy (1): Aneke 1.

Martin A 7	Tootle M 43	Mellor K 23 + 5	Ray G 5 + 4	Colclough R 5 + 3	Davis H 32	Osman A 26 + 5	Clayton M 9 + 4	Leitch-Smith A 13 + 7	Grant A 34 + 4	Moore B 30 + 10	Aneke C 34 + 6	Turton O 8 + 4	Oliver V 10 + 15	West M — + 2	Inman B 28 + 8	Molyneux L 4 + 3	Ellis M 36 + 1	Robertson G 2 + 1	Phillips S 9	Guthrie J 23	Nolan L 8 + 5	Audel T 1 + 1	Dugdale A 21	Evans G 22 + 1	Etheridge N 4	Waters B 1 + 8	Na Bangna B 6	Hitchcock T 6	Garratt B 26	Pogba M 17 + 5	Ikpeazu U 10 + 5	Park C 3 + 1	Match No.
1	2	3	4	5	6	7	8^3	9^1	10	11^1	12	13	14																				1
1	2	5	3	6	4	8	7^2	11^1	9^3	10	12	13	14																				2
1	2	5	3	6	4	7	12	8	9	11^1			10																				3
1	5	2^1	4	10	3	6^3	8		7				9	14	11^2	12	13																4
1	5	2^1		6	3	7	11	12	9	10^3			8^2	13		4	14																5
	2^1	12			3	7		11	14	13	8		10^2		6	9^3	4	5	1														6
	2			4	8^1	14	10	12	13	7			11^1		6	9^2	3	5	1														7
	2	14		12	4	8	10	11^2		6			7^3		9	13	4		1	5^1	13												8
		12			3^3	7	11^2	10^1		6			8	14	9	13	4		1	5		2											9
	2			12		7	8^3		9^2	10	13	6	11^1		14	3		1	5			2		4									10
	5	2				7			9^1	6	11^2	8	13		10	3		1		12			4										11
	2	5	13			8	12		6	10	11^1	9			7^2	3		1		9			4										12
	5	2				7				12	10	6	11		13		8^1	3		1		9^2	4										13
	5	2	3				9	13		10	6	12	7^2	11		8^1			1				4										14
1		2				3	13	6^2		7	9	10			11^1	12				5			4	8									15
1		5				4	14	11		7	9	6^1		12	10^3					2	13		3	8^2									16
	5	2		12	4	7		9^3		11	13		10^2			3							14	6^1	8	1							17
	7	5			2	8		11^1		9			10	13		4^2							3	6	1	12							18
	2	3			4	6			7	12			11^6										5	8	1			9	10^1				19
	2	3			4	6			7	10			12										5	8				9	11^1	1			20
	5	2				3	7	14		9^3	10		13		12								4^2	8			11	6^1	1			21
	5	2			4	7		14	12	9^3	10		13			3								8^1			11	6^2	1			22
	5	2	14			3	6			12	13	7			10^2		4							9^1			8	11^3	1			23
	2	5				4	7			8	13	10^2		12	6		3				14						9^3	11^1	1			24
	5	2				3	7		11^1	8	6	10			9		4												1	12			25
	2	7				8	6^2		10^1	3	11^3	4			5		9						14						1	13	12		26
	5	2				3	12		11^1	7^2	6	10			9		4							8					1	13			27
	5	2				3			10^1	8	6	6^2	11		9		4							7					1	12	13		28
	5					4			9^2	7	12	10			6		3							8					1	11^1	13		29
	2					4	13			7	12	10			9		3							8^2					1	6	11^1		30
	2					4	6^2			7	12	11			9^1		3							8			13		1	10			31
	2					4				8	6	10			9		3							7					1	11			32
	2					3			7^2	9^1	10		13		6		4			5	8					1	12		1	11			33
	2					4			8	6^3	10		14		9^2		3			5	7					13			1	11^1		12	34
	2					3			7	12	10		14				4			5				8^3		9^1			1	11	13	6^2	35
	2	14				3			7	12	10		13		9^2		4			5				8					1	11^3		6^1	36
	2	14				3			8		10		12		9		4^1			5				7					1	11^2	13	6^3	37
	2	13					12			7^6		11			9		4			5		3	8^1						1	6	10^2		38
	2						7		12			11			9^2		3			5		4	8		13				1	6	10^1		39
	2									8	12	10			9^2		4			5		3	7		13				1	6	11		40
	2	14					3			7	10	8^3		12	13		3			5	9	4							1	11^1	6^2		41
	2									7	6	10^6			9^2		3			5	12	4	8^1	14					1	13	11^3		42
	2									7	9		12	13	10^2		3			5	8	4							1	6	11^1		43
	2									13	7	6			14		9^3	4		5	8	3			12				1	11^2	10^1		44
	5									7	9		6				12			2	8	4							1	10^1	11		45
	2									13	7	10	12	8			4			5	6	3							1	9^1	11^2		46

The Budweiser FA Cup

First Round	Wycombe W	(a)	1-1
Replay	Wycombe W	(h)	0-2

Capital One Cup

First Round	Bury	(a)	2-3

Johnstone's Paint Trophy

First Round	Accrington S	(h)	1-0
Second Round	Fleetwood T	(a)	0-4

CRYSTAL PALACE

FOUNDATION

There was a Crystal Palace club as early as 1861 but the present organisation was born in 1905 after the formation of a club by the company that controlled the Crystal Palace (building) had been rejected by the FA, who did not like the idea of the Cup Final hosts running their own club. A separate company had to be formed and they had their home on the old Cup Final ground until 1915.

Selhurst Park Stadium, Whitehorse Lane, London SE25 6PU.

Telephone: (020) 8768 6000.

Fax: (020) 8771 5311.

Ticket Office: (0871) 200 0071.

Website: www.cpfc.co.uk

Email: info@cpfc.co.uk

Ground Capacity: 26,225.

Record Attendance: 51,482 v Burnley, Division 2, 11 May 1979 (at Selhurst Park).

Pitch Measurements: 100m × 66m (110yd × 72yd)

Co-Chairmen: Steve Parish and Martin Long.

Chief Executive: Phil Alexander.

Manager: Tony Pulis.

Assistant Manager: Keith Millen.

Physio: Alex Manos.

Colours: Red and blue halved shirts, blue shorts, blue socks.

Year Formed: 1905.

Turned Professional: 1905.

Club Nickname: 'The Eagles'.

Grounds: 1905, Crystal Palace; 1915, Herne Hill; 1918, The Nest; 1924, Selhurst Park.

First Football League Game: 28 August 1920, Division 3, v Merthyr T (a) L 1–2 – Alderson; Little, Rhodes; McCracken, Jones, Feebury; Bateman, Conner, Smith, Milligan (1), Whibley.

Record League Victory: 9–0 v Barrow, Division 4, 10 October 1959 – Rouse; Long, Noakes; Truett, Evans, McNichol; Gavin (1), Summersby (4 incl. 1p), Sexton, Byrne (2), Colfar (2).

Record Cup Victory: 8–0 v Southend U, Rumbelows League Cup 2nd rd (1st leg), 25 September 1990 – Martyn; Humphrey (Thompson (1)), Shaw, Pardew, Young, Thorn, McGoldrick, Thomas, Bright (3), Wright (3), Barber (Hodges (1)).

Record Defeat: 0–9 v Burnley, FA Cup 2nd rd replay, 10 February 1909; 0–9 v Liverpool, Division 1, 12 September 1990.

HONOURS

Football League –
Division 1: *Champions* 1993–94;
Division 2: *Champions* 1978–79;
Runners-up 1968–69;
Division 3: *Runners-up* 1963–64;
Division 3 (S): *Champions* 1920–21;
Runners-up 1928–29, 1930–31, 1938–39;
Division 4: *Runners-up* 1960–61.
FA Cup: *Runners-up* 1990.
Football League Cup: Semi-final 1993, 1995, 2001.
Zenith Data Systems Cup: *Winners* 1991.
European Competition
Intertoto Cup: 1998.

sky SPORTS FACT FILE

In December 1972 Crystal Palace, then bottom of the First Division, achieved what was to be their biggest win of the season when they defeated Manchester United 5-0 at Selhurst Park. The result temporarily lifted Palace out of the relegation positions but at the end of the season the Eagles went back down to Division Two.

Most League Points (2 for a win): 64, Division 4, 1960–61.

Most League Points (3 for a win): 90, Division 1, 1993–94.

Most League Goals: 110, Division 4, 1960–61.

Highest League Scorer in Season: Peter Simpson, 46, Division 3 (S), 1930–31.

Most League Goals in Total Aggregate: Peter Simpson, 153, 1930–36.

Most League Goals in One Match: 6, Peter Simpson v Exeter C, Division 3 (S), 4 October 1930.

Most Capped Player: Aleksandrs Kolinko, 23 (88), Latvia.

Most League Appearances: Jim Cannon, 571, 1973–88.

Youngest League Player: John Bostock, 15 years 287 days v Watford, 29 October 2007.

Record Transfer Fee Received: £15,000,000 from Manchester U for Wilfried Zaha, January 2013.

Record Transfer Fee Paid: £4,500,000 to Peterborough U for Dwight Gayle, July 2013.

Football League Record: 1920 Original Members of Division 3; 1921–25 Division 2; 1925–58 Division 3 (S); 1958–61 Division 4; 1961–64 Division 3; 1964–69 Division 2; 1969–73 Division 1; 1973–74 Division 2; 1974–77 Division 3; 1977–79 Division 2; 1979–81 Division 1; 1981–89 Division 2; 1989–92 Division 1; 1992–93 FA Premier League; 1993–94 Division 1; 1994–95 FA Premier League; 1995–97 Division 1; 1997–98 FA Premier League; 1998–2004 Division 1; 2004–05 FA Premier League; 2005–13 FL C; 2013– FA Premier League.

LATEST SEQUENCES

Longest Sequence of League Wins: 8, 9.2.1921 – 26.3.1921.

Longest Sequence of League Defeats: 8, 10.1.1998 – 14.3.1998.

Longest Sequence of League Draws: 5, 21.9.2002 – 19.10.2002.

Longest Sequence of Unbeaten League Matches: 18, 22.2.1969 – 13.8.1969.

Longest Sequence Without a League Win: 20, 3.3.1962 – 8.9.1962.

Successive Scoring Runs: 24 from 27.4.1929.

Successive Non-scoring Runs: 9 from 19.11.1994.

MANAGERS

John T. Robson 1905–07
Edmund Goodman 1907–25
 (Secretary 1905–33)
Alex Maley 1925–27
Fred Mavin 1927–30
Jack Tresadern 1930–35
Tom Bromilow 1935–36
R. S. Moyes 1936
Tom Bromilow 1936–39
George Irwin 1939–47
Jack Butler 1947–49
Ronnie Rooke 1949–50
Charlie Slade and Fred Dawes
 (Joint Managers) 1950–51
Laurie Scott 1951–54
Cyril Spiers 1954–58
George Smith 1958–60
Arthur Rowe 1960–62
Dick Graham 1962–66
Bert Head 1966–72 (*continued as General Manager to 1973*)
Malcolm Allison 1973–76
Terry Venables 1976–80
Ernie Walley 1980
Malcolm Allison 1980–81
Dario Gradi 1981
Steve Kember 1981–82
Alan Mullery 1982–84
Steve Coppell 1984–93
Alan Smith 1993–95
Steve Coppell (*Technical Director*) 1995–96
Dave Bassett 1996–97
Steve Coppell 1997–98
Attilio Lombardo 1998
Terry Venables (*Head Coach*) 1998–99
Steve Coppell 1999–2000
Alan Smith 2000–01
Steve Bruce 2001
Trevor Francis 2001–03
Steve Kember 2003
Iain Dowie 2003–06
Peter Taylor 2006–07
Neil Warnock 2007–10
Paul Hart 2010
George Burley 2010–11
Dougie Freedman 2011–12
Ian Holloway 2012–13
Tony Pulis November 2013–

TEN YEAR LEAGUE RECORD

		P	W	D	L	F	A	Pts	Pos
2004-05	PR Lge	38	7	12	19	41	62	33	18
2005-06	FL C	46	21	12	13	67	48	75	6
2006-07	FL C	46	18	11	17	59	51	65	12
2007-08	FL C	46	18	17	11	58	42	71	5
2008-09	FL C	46	15	12	19	52	55	57	15
2009-10	FL C	46	14	17	15	50	53	49*	21
2010-11	FL C	46	12	12	22	44	69	48	20
2011-12	FL C	46	13	17	16	46	51	56	17
2012-13	FL C	46	19	15	12	73	62	72	5
2013-14	PR Lge	38	13	6	19	33	48	45	11

* 10 pts deducted.

DID YOU KNOW ?

Belgian winger Marcel Gaillard was the first foreign-born player to appear for Crystal Palace after signing from non-league Tonbridge in 1948. Gaillard scored on his debut against Watford and went on to make a total of 21 Football League appearances for the Eagles before returning to Tonbridge.

CRYSTAL PALACE – FA PREMIERSHIP 2013–14 LEAGUE RECORD

Match No.	Date	Venue	Opponents	Result		H/T Score	Lg Pos.	Goalscorers	Attendance
1	Aug 18	H	Tottenham H	L	0-1	0-0	13		23,285
2	24	A	Stoke C	L	1-2	1-0	18	Chamakh [31]	25,270
3	31	H	Sunderland	W	3-1	1-0	12	Gabbidon [9], Gayle (pen) [79], O'Keefe [90]	22,671
4	Sept 14	A	Manchester U	L	0-2	0-1	17		75,170
5	22	H	Swansea C	L	0-2	0-1	19		22,466
6	28	A	Southampton	L	0-2	0-0	19		30,699
7	Oct 5	A	Liverpool	L	1-3	0-3	19	Gayle [76]	44,721
8	21	H	Fulham	L	1-4	1-2	19	Mariappa [7]	24,881
9	26	H	Arsenal	L	0-2	0-0	19		25,050
10	Nov 2	A	WBA	L	0-2	0-1	20		26,397
11	9	H	Everton	D	0-0	0-0	20		25,231
12	23	A	Hull C	W	1-0	0-0	19	Bannan [81]	23,043
13	30	A	Norwich C	L	0-1	0-1	20		26,851
14	Dec 3	H	West Ham U	W	1-0	1-0	19	Chamakh [42]	23,891
15	7	H	Cardiff C	W	2-0	1-0	18	Jerome [6], Chamakh [57]	23,705
16	14	A	Chelsea	L	1-2	1-2	18	Chamakh [29]	41,608
17	21	H	Newcastle U	L	0-3	0-2	18		24,936
18	26	A	Aston Villa	W	1-0	0-0	17	Gayle [90]	37,752
19	28	A	Manchester C	L	0-1	0-0	17		47,107
20	Jan 1	H	Norwich C	D	1-1	1-1	18	Puncheon (pen) [44]	25,189
21	11	A	Tottenham H	L	0-2	0-0	20		36,102
22	18	H	Stoke C	W	1-0	0-0	16	Puncheon [51]	24,440
23	28	H	Hull C	W	1-0	1-0	14	Puncheon [16]	22,519
24	Feb 2	A	Arsenal	L	0-2	0-0	17		60,005
25	8	H	WBA	W	3-1	2-0	14	Ince [15], Ledley [27], Chamakh (pen) [69]	24,501
26	22	H	Manchester U	L	0-2	0-0	15		24,571
27	Mar 2	A	Swansea C	D	1-1	0-1	16	Murray (pen) [82]	20,240
28	8	H	Southampton	L	0-1	0-1	16		25,073
29	15	A	Sunderland	D	0-0	0-0	17		43,636
30	22	A	Newcastle U	L	0-1	0-0	17		51,588
31	29	H	Chelsea	W	1-0	0-0	16	Terry (og) [52]	25,166
32	Apr 5	A	Cardiff C	W	3-0	1-0	14	Puncheon 2 [31, 88], Ledley [71]	27,687
33	12	H	Aston Villa	W	1-0	0-0	12	Puncheon [76]	25,564
34	16	A	Everton	W	3-2	1-0	11	Puncheon [23], Dann [49], Jerome [73]	39,333
35	19	A	West Ham U	W	1-0	0-0	11	Jedinak (pen) [59]	34,977
36	27	H	Manchester C	L	0-2	0-2	11		24,769
37	May 5	H	Liverpool	D	3-3	0-1	11	Delaney [79], Gayle 2 [81, 88]	25,261
38	11	A	Fulham	D	2-2	1-0	11	Gayle 2 [28, 83]	24,447

Final League Position: 11

GOALSCORERS

League (33): Gayle 7 (1 pen), Puncheon 7 (1 pen), Chamakh 5 (1 pen), Jerome 2, Ledley 2, Bannan 1, Dann 1, Delaney 1, Gabbidon 1, Ince 1, Jedinak 1 (1 pen), Mariappa 1, Murray 1 (1 pen), O'Keefe 1, own goal 1.
The Budweiser FA Cup (3): Chamakh 1, Gayle 1, Wilbraham 1.
Capital One Cup (1): Garvan 1.

Speroni J 37	Ward J 36	Gabbidon D 22+1	Delaney D 37	Moxey D 18+2	Jedinak M 38	Dikgacoi K 25+1	Dobbie S 1	Garvan O 1+1	Wilbraham A 1+3	Gayle D 8+15	Phillips K —+4	Williams Jon —+9	Chamakh M 27+5	Puncheon J 29+5	Campana J 4+2	O'Keefe S 2+10	Mariappa A 23+1	Guedioura A 4+4	Jerome C 20+8	Kebe J 2+4	Bannan B 13+2	Thomas J 3+6	Bolasie Y 23+6	Parr J 7+8	McCarthy P —+1	Dann S 14	Ledley J 14	Ince T 5+3	Murray G 3+11	Hennessey W 1	Match No.
1	2	3	4	5	6	7	8^9	9^1	10^2	11	12	13	14																		1
1	2	3	4	5	8	7			13		10	14	12	11^1	6^3	9^2															2
1	2	3	4	5	7	8			13		10^2		12	11^3	6	9^1	14														3
1		3	4	5	7	6				11^1			10^2	9	8^3		2	12	13	14											4
1		3	4^1	5	7				13				10	9	12		2	6	11^3		8^2	14									5
1	2		4	5	7	6			9^3	14			10				3		12		11^1		8^2	13							6
1	2		4	5	7				12				11^1	8	13		6	3	10^3		9^2		14								7
1	2		4	5	7					10^1	14		13	9^3	8^2		6	3			12	11									8
1	2	3	4	5	9	7				14			11				8^2		13				6^3	10^1	12						9
1	2	3	4	5	9	7^2				14			11	12			8^3				6^1		10	13							10
1	2	3	4	5	7	6^1							10^1	14	12						13		8	11^2	9						11
1	2	3	4	5	7	6^2				11^1			10^3	14					13		12		8	9							12
1	2	3	4	5	7	6				14		12	10^3	9^2							11	13	8^1								13
1	2	3	4	5	7	8						14	10^1	6^2	13						11	12	9^3								14
1	2	3	4	5^2	8	7							10	6	13	12					11		9^1								15
1	5	3	4		7	8^1				14			10^2	9			2		12		11		6^3	13							16
1	7	3	4	5^3	8					14			10	9			2		11^1				6^2	12	13						17
1	6	3	4	14	7					13		12	10^2				2		11^1				9^3	8	5						18
1	7	3	4		9					14			13	12	6		2		11^2				8^1	10^3	5						19
1	5	3	4		8	7^1				13			14	11	6		2		10^3				9^2		5						20
1	7	3	4		8					12			13	11	6^1		2	14	10^2				9^3	5							21
1	7	3	4	13	8				14				11^1	6			2	12	10^2				9^3	5							22
1	7	3^1	4	5	8					14			10^2	9			2	13	11				6^3	12							23
1	2	3	4		8	7				13			10^2	6							11^1	12	9	5							24
1	2		4		8	7							11^2	6^2								14	9^1	13		3	5	10	12		25
1	2		4		7					14			10^3	9					12				13	5		3	8	6^2	11^1		26
1	2		4		6	8							11^3						12				14	10	5^1	3	9	7^2	13		27
1	2		4	5	6	8^3								7^1					12				14	10^2		3	9	13	11		28
1	5		4		8	7								14			2	13	12				6^3			3	9	10^2	11^1		29
1	5		4		8	7								6^1			2	14	11^2	12			9^3			3	10		13		30
1	5		4		8	7								6^1			2	12	11^2				9^3	14		3	10		13		31
1	5		4		8	7				12				6			2		11^1				9^2	13		3	10^3		14		32
1	5		4		8	7^3				12				6			2		11^1				9^2	14		3	10		13		33
1	5		4		8								10^1	6			2^3	13	11^2				9	12		3	7		14		34
1	5	13	4		8	7								6^1			2		11^2				9^3	14		3	10		12		35
1	5		4		7					12			10^3	6			2		11^2				9^1			3	8	14	13		36
1	5		4		8	7^2				12			11^1	6^3			2						9			3	10	14	13		37
	5		4		7^2	12				11			10^1	13			2						9			3	8	6^2	14	1	38

The Budweiser FA Cup

Third Round	WBA	(a)	2-0	
Fourth Round	Wigan Ath	(a)	1-2	

Capital One Cup

Second Round	Bristol C	(a)	1-2

DAGENHAM & REDBRIDGE

FOUNDATION

The roots of Dagenham & Redbridge lie firmly in the Essex side of the Greater London area. Though formed only in 1992 their complex origins date back to the 19th century involving Ilford (founded 1881) and Leytonstone (1886) who merged in 1979 to form Leytonstone-Ilford. They and Walthamstow Avenue (1900) joined together in 1988 to become Redbridge Forest who in turn merged with Dagenham FC (1949) in 1992. Victoria Road has existed as a football ground since 1917. Initially used by Sterling Works, in the summer of 1955 Briggs Sports vacated the premises and Dagenham FC moved in and the pitch was enclosed.

The London Borough of Barking and Dagenham Stadium, Victoria Road, Dagenham, Essex RM10 7XL.

Telephone: (020) 8592 1549.

Fax: (020) 8593 7227.

Ticket Office: (020) 8592 1549 (extension 21).

Website: www.daggers.co.uk

Email: info@daggers.co.uk

Ground Capacity: 6,070.

Record Attendance: 4,791 v Shrewsbury T, FL 2, 2 May 2009.

Pitch Measurements: 100.5m × 64m (110yd × 70yd)

Chairman: David Bennett.

Managing Director: Stephen Thompson MBE.

Manager: Wayne Burnett.

First Team Coach: Darren Currie.

Physio: John Gowens.

Colours: Red shirts with blue trim, blue shorts with red trim, blue socks.

Year Formed: 1992.

Turned Professional: 1992.

Club Nickname: 'The Daggers'.

Ground: 1992, Victoria Road.

First Football League Game: 11 August 2007, FL 2 v Stockport Co (a) L 0–1 – Roberts; Foster, Griffiths, Rainford, Uddin, Boardman, Saunders (Strevens), Southam, Benson (Moore), Nurse, Sloma (Huke).

Record League Victory: 6–0 v Chester C, FL 2, 9 August 2008 – Roberts; Okuonghae, Griffiths, Arber, Uddin, Taiwo, Saunders (2), Green (1) (Southam), Benson (1) (Nurse), Strevens (1p) (Nwokeji (1)), Gain.

MANAGERS

John Still 1992–94
Dave Cusack 1994–95
Graham Carr 1995–96
Ted Hardy 1996–99
Garry Hill 1999–2004
John Still 2004–13
Wayne Burnett February 2013–

sky SPORTS FACT FILE

During the 2010–11 campaign Dagenham & Redbridge fielded two players named Danny Green. Danny J. Green was a winger who made 3 appearances as a substitute, while Danny R. Green was a regular in the team, finishing the season as the club's leading scorer in league and cup matches.

Record Cup Victory: 6–1 v Stowmarket T, FA Cup 2nd qual rd, 28 September 1992; 6–1 v Wealdstone (a), FA Cup 3rd qual rd, 12 October 1992.

Record Defeat: 0–9 v Hereford U, Conference, 27 February 2004.

Most League Points (3 for a win): 72, FL 2, 2009–10.

Most League Goals: 77, FL 2, 2008–09.

Highest League Scorer in Season: Paul Benson, 28, Conference, 2006–07.

Most League Goals in Total Aggregate: 40, Paul Benson, 2007–11.

Most League Goals in One Match: 4, Paul Benson v Shrewsbury T, FL 2, 18 August 2009.

Most Capped Player: Jon Nurse, 6, Barbados.

Most League Appearances: Scott Doe, 204, 2009–14.

Youngest League Player: Dominic Green, 18 years 93 days v Brentford, 2 October 2007.

Record Transfer Fee Received: £700,000 from Peterborough U for Dwight Gayle, January 2013.

Record Transfer Fee Paid: £20,000 to Plymouth Arg for Damien McCrory, February 2010.

Football League Record: 2006–07 Promoted from Conference; 2007–10 FL 2; 2010–11 FL 1; 2011– FL 2.

LATEST SEQUENCES

Longest Sequence of League Wins: 5, 12.2.2008 – 1.3.2008.

Longest Sequence of League Defeats: 9, 8.10.2011 – 10.12.2011.

Longest Sequence of League Draws: 3, 21.9.2010 – 28.9.2010.

Longest Sequence of Unbeaten League Matches: 8, 1.3.2014 – 5.4.2014.

Longest Sequence Without a League Win: 10, 8.10.2011 – 17.12.2011.

Successive Scoring Runs: 16 from 12.4.2008.

Successive Non-scoring Runs: 3 from 13.4.2013.

HONOURS

Football League – FL 2: Best season: 7th (promoted via play-offs) 2009–10.

FA Cup: Best season: 3rd rd, 2008, 2012.

Football League Cup: Best season: never beyond 1st rd.

Conference: *Champions* 2006–07. *Runners-up* 2001–02.

Isthmian League (Premier): *Champions* 1999–2000.

Essex Senior Cup: *Winners* 1997–98, 2000–01; *Runners-up* 2001–02.

AS DAGENHAM FC

FA Trophy: *Winners* 1979–80; *Runners-up* 1976–77.

Amateur Cup: *Runners-up* 1969–70, 1970–71.

AS ILFORD

FA Amateur Cup: *Winners* 1929, 1930. **Isthmian League:** *Champions* 1906–07, 1920–21, 1921–22.

AS LEYTONSTONE

FA Amateur Cup: *Winners* 1947, 1948, 1968.
Isthmian League: *Champions* 1918–19, 1937–38, 1938–39, 1946–47, 1947–48, 1949–50, 1950–51, 1951–52, 1965–66.

AS LEYTONSTONE/ILFORD

Isthmian League: *Champions* 1981–82, 1988–89.

AS WALTHAMSTOW AVENUE

FA Amateur Cup: *Winners* 1952, 1961. **Isthmian League:** *Champions* 1945–46, 1948–49, 1952–53, 1954–55.
Athenian League: *Champions* 1929–30, 1932–33, 1933–34, 1937–38, 1938–39.

AS REDBRIDGE FOREST

Isthmian League: *Winners* 1990–91.

TEN YEAR LEAGUE RECORD

		P	W	D	L	F	A	Pts	Pos
2004-05	Conf	42	19	8	15	68	60	65	11
2005-06	Conf	42	16	19	16	63	59	58	10
2006-07	Conf	46	28	11	7	93	48	95	1
2007-08	FL 2	46	13	10	23	49	70	49	20
2008-09	FL 2	46	19	11	16	77	53	68	8
2009-10	FL 2	46	20	12	14	69	58	72	7
2010-11	FL 1	46	12	11	23	52	70	47	21
2011-12	FL 2	46	14	8	24	50	72	50	19
2012-13	FL 2	46	13	12	21	55	62	51	22
2013-14	FL 2	46	15	15	16	53	59	60	9

DID YOU KNOW ?

Dagenham & Redbridge won automatic promotion to the Football League in 2006–07 when they won the Conference title. The Daggers led the table throughout the second half of the campaign and finished 14 points above their nearest rivals, despite winning just two of their last five games.

DAGENHAM & REDBRIDGE – FOOTBALL LEAGUE TWO 2013–14 LEAGUE RECORD

Match No.	Date	Venue	Opponents	Result	H/T Score	Lg Pos.	Goalscorers	Attendance
1	Aug 3	A	Fleetwood T	L 1-3	1-2	19	Murphy [26]	2511
2	10	H	York C	W 2-0	1-0	12	Murphy [36], Woodall [79]	1487
3	17	A	Scunthorpe U	D 1-1	0-0	11	Howell [90]	3694
4	24	H	Newport Co	D 1-1	0-1	12	Ogogo [59]	1564
5	31	A	Mansfield T	L 0-3	0-1	19		3015
6	Sept 7	H	Exeter C	D 1-1	1-0	18	Scott [20]	2003
7	14	H	Bristol R	W 2-0	1-0	14	Ogogo [10], Howell [72]	1423
8	21	A	Morecambe	D 2-2	1-0	13	Ogogo [21], Murphy [90]	1790
9	28	H	Bury	W 2-1	1-0	12	Obafemi [44], Murphy [52]	1604
10	Oct 4	A	Accrington S	W 2-1	0-0	8	Hines [56], Murphy [61]	1833
11	12	H	Cheltenham T	L 1-2	1-1	13	Ogogo [40]	1727
12	19	A	Northampton T	D 2-2	2-1	14	Hines [40], Murphy [42]	4046
13	22	A	Southend U	W 1-0	1-0	13	Murphy [31]	4523
14	26	H	Rochdale	W 3-1	1-0	8	Murphy [9], Elito 2 [52, 90]	1742
15	Nov 2	A	Hartlepool U	L 1-2	0-1	11	Hines [56]	3450
16	16	H	Burton Alb	W 2-0	1-0	7	Hines (pen) [8], Howell [54]	1626
17	23	A	Plymouth Arg	L 1-2	1-1	9	Hines [45]	6184
18	26	A	AFC Wimbledon	D 1-1	0-1	9	Murphy [58]	3862
19	30	H	Wycombe W	W 2-0	1-0	8	Obafemi [24], Murphy (pen) [47]	1618
20	Dec 14	A	Oxford U	L 1-2	1-1	10	Murphy [45]	4901
21	21	H	Torquay U	L 0-1	0-0	10		1675
22	26	A	Portsmouth	L 0-1	0-1	11		15,192
23	29	A	Chesterfield	D 1-1	0-0	12	Ogogo [58]	5906
24	Jan 1	H	AFC Wimbledon	W 1-0	1-0	10	Ogogo [10]	2012
25	4	A	York C	L 1-3	0-0	10	Murphy [80]	3207
26	11	H	Fleetwood T	L 0-1	0-0	10		1679
27	25	H	Scunthorpe U	D 3-3	0-1	10	Ogogo [67], Dickson [77], Norris [89]	2037
28	28	H	Southend U	D 1-1	0-0	11	Norris [68]	2624
29	Feb 1	A	Rochdale	W 1-0	0-0	9	Murphy [63]	2273
30	8	H	Hartlepool U	L 0-2	0-0	9		3357
31	15	A	Burton Alb	D 1-1	1-0	9	D'Ath [45]	2934
32	22	H	Plymouth Arg	L 1-2	1-2	12	Hines [23]	2027
33	Mar 1	H	Mansfield T	D 0-0	0-0	14		1377
34	8	A	Exeter C	D 2-2	0-1	15	Norris [62], Elito (pen) [72]	3057
35	11	A	Bristol R	W 2-1	1-1	12	Azeez 2 [23, 58]	5761
36	15	H	Morecambe	D 1-1	0-0	13	Elito (pen) [52]	1718
37	19	A	Newport Co	W 2-1	2-1	11	Elito 2 [10, 43]	2360
38	22	A	Bury	D 1-1	0-0	10	Norris [67]	2705
39	25	H	Accrington S	D 0-0	0-0	10		1383
40	29	H	Oxford U	W 1-0	0-0	10	Howell [89]	1893
41	Apr 5	A	Wycombe W	L 0-2	0-0	10		3103
42	12	H	Portsmouth	L 1-4	1-2	12	Ogogo [34]	3115
43	18	A	Torquay U	W 1-0	0-0	11	Elito (pen) [67]	2425
44	21	H	Chesterfield	L 0-1	0-1	11		1801
45	26	H	Northampton T	L 0-3	0-3	12		2668
46	May 3	A	Cheltenham T	W 3-2	2-2	9	Jombati (og) [21], Doe [44], Azeez [68]	3002

Final League Position: 9

GOALSCORERS

League (53): Murphy 13 (1 pen), Ogogo 8, Elito 7 (3 pens), Hines 6 (1 pen), Howell 4, Norris 4, Azeez 3, Obafemi 2, D'Ath 1, Dickson 1, Doe 1, Scott 1, Woodall 1, own goal 1.
The Budweiser FA Cup (0).
Capital One Cup (2): Scott 1, own goal 1.
Johnstone's Paint Trophy (9): Hines 2, Saah 2, Dennis 1, Dickson 1, Elito 1, Obafemi 1, Ogogo 1.

Lewington C 42	Hoyte G 42	Ilesanmi F 23+6	Ogogo A 44	Saah B 41+2	Doe S 36+1	Howell L 36+4	Bingham B 23+7	Scott J 6+5	Elito M 36+9	Murphy R 32	Reed J —+2	Ohafemi A 9+13	Woodall B 4+4	Dennis L —+2	Hines Z 26+1	Wilkinson L 18+4	Connors J 23	Shields S 2+10	Dickson C 3+22	Seabright J 4	Saunders M 2+2	Edgar A —+7	D'Ath L 17+4	Samuel D 1	Norris L 16+3	Azeez A 10+5	Chambers A 4+2	Turgott B 3+2	Gayle J 13+1	Nouble J —+1	Match No.
1	2	3	4	5	6	7	8	9[2]	10[1]	11[3]	12	13	14																		1
1	2	5	8	3	4	6[1]	12	9[2]	7	10[3]	14	11	13																		2
1	2	5	7	3	4	8	14	11[1]	6[3]	10[2]	13				9		12														3
1	2	5	7	4	3	8	12	11[2]	6[1]	10[3]		14			9		13														4
1		5	8	4	3	7	6[1]	12	9			13	10[2]		11	2															5
1	2		9	4	3	7	8	11[2]	13	10[1]		12			6		5														6
1	2		7	4	3	6	8		12	10		9[1]			11[2]		5		13												7
1	2		7	4	3	6	8[2]		13	10		9[2]	12		11		5														8
1	2		7	4	3	6	8		12	10		9[1]	13		11[2]		5														9
1	2	12	6	4		7	8		13	10[3]		11[2]			9	3	5[1]				14										10
		7	3	2	6	8[2]	14		13	10[3]		9[1]			11	4	5		12	1											11
1		5	6	4	2	7	12	8[2]	9			13			11	3	10[1]														12
1		6	4	2	7	8		9[2]	10[3]			14			11	3[1]	5		13		12										13
1	2	13	6	4	3	7	8[1]		9	10[3]		12			11		5[2]				14										14
1	2		6	4	3	8[1]	7		9[2]	10		13			11		5				12										15
1	2	5	8	3		7	6		9	10[1]		11[2]			4		12						13								16
1	2	5	7[1]	4	8	6			12	9		10			11		3[2]						13								17
1	2	5		3		7	8[1]	14	6	10[3]		11[2]			9	4					12		13								18
1	2	5	6	4	3	7	14		8[2]	10[3]		11[1]			9					12	13										19
1	2	5	6	4		7		11[1]		10		9				3							12		8						20
1	2	5	7	3	4	8	6[2]			10					11		12		13				9[1]								21
1	2	5	7[3]	3	4	8	6[1]			10					11				9[2]		14		12								22
1	2	13	7	4	3	8	12			10		9				5[2]	11[1]						6								23
1	2	13	8	4	3	7			11	10[3]		9[1]			12	5[2]					14		6								24
1	2	5	6	4	3	8		11[2]		10		9				7[1]							12								25
1	2[3]		6	4	3	7[2]			12	10		13			9	14	5						8		11[1]						26
1	2		6	3		7[1]	8[3]			10[2]					11	4	5		14	13			9		12						27
1	2		8	13	3		9[1]			10					6	4	5		12				7[2]		11						28
1	2		7		4		13		6	10[2]					11[1]	3	5		12				8		9						29
1	2		7		6					10[1]					9	3	5[3]		14	12			8		11[2]	13					30
1	2	12[3]	6	14	4		8		9[1]	10[2]						3	5[*]						7		13	11					31
1	2		8	4	5		7[3]		12	10[2]		9				3			14				6[1]		13	11					32
1	2	5	7	4	3		13	8		10[3]		14					12						6[2]		9	11[1]					33
1	2	5	7	4	3	8[1]		11				13					14				6				10[3]	9[2]	12				34
1	2	5	8	4	13	6	7[1]		9							3[2]	14								10[2]	11	12				35
1	2	5	7	4	3	8	12	11[3]				13					14								10[2]	9	6[1]				36
1	9	2	5	4	3	12	6		7														8		11[1]	10					37
1	2	12	6	4	3	8	14		10										5[1]				7[2]		11	13	9[3]				38
1	2	5	6	3	4		13		7[2]						11				12		14				10	9[1]	8[3]				39
1	2	7	4	3	6		11									5	13								10[2]	12	8		9[1]		40
1	2	7	3	4[*]		8				10[2]		9					5[3]		14				6[1]		11	13		12			41
1	2	6		4		7[3]	8					14				3	5		9[*]				10		12	11[1]	13				42
1	2	5	6	3		8		7		10[2]		14					13								9[3]	11[1]		12	4		43
	2	5		3			14		7[2]						11		12		13				1		6[3]	8	10		9	4	44
	2	5[2]	7	3	4	6		11				9[1]				8	12			1			13		10[3]	14					45
	2		7	3	6					10[3]					12	5	14			1			8		11	9[2]	4[1]	13			46

The Budweiser FA Cup
First Round — Bristol C — (a) — 0-3

Capital One Cup
First Round — Brentford — (a) — 2-3

Johnstone's Paint Trophy
First Round — Colchester U — (h) — 4-1
Second Round — Southend U — (a) — 5-2
Southern Quarter-Finals — Peterborough U — (a) — 0-1

DERBY COUNTY

FOUNDATION

Derby County was formed by members of the Derbyshire County Cricket Club in 1884, when football was booming in the area and the cricketers thought that a football club would help boost finances for the summer game. To begin with, they sported the cricket club's colours of amber, chocolate and pale blue, and went into the game at the top immediately entering the FA Cup.

The iPro Stadium, Pride Park, Derby DE24 8XL.

Telephone: (0871) 472 1884.

Fax: (01332) 667 519.

Ticket Office: (0871) 472 1884 (option 1).

Website: www.dcfc.co.uk

Email: derby.county@dcfc.co.uk

Ground Capacity: 33,010.

Record Attendance: 41,826 v Tottenham H, Division 1, 20 September 1969 (at Baseball Ground); 33,378 v Liverpool, FA Premier League, 18 March 2000 (Stadium Record Attendance at Pride Park).

Stadium Record Attendance: 33,597, England v Mexico, 25 May 2001 (at Pride Park).

Pitch Measurements: 100.5m × 66m (110yd × 72yd)

Chairman: Andy Appleby.

Chief Executive: Sam Rush.

Head Coach: Steve McClaren.

First Team Coach: Paul Simpson.

Physio: Neil Sullivan.

HONOURS

Football League – Division 1:
Champions 1971–72, 1974–75;
Runners-up 1895–96, 1929–30,
1935–36, 1995–96;
Division 2: *Champions* 1911–12,
1914–15, 1968–69, 1986–87;
Runners-up 1925–26;
Division 3 (N): *Champions* 1956–57;
Runners-up 1955–56.
FA Cup: *Winners* 1946;
Runners-up 1898, 1899, 1903.
Football League Cup: Semi-final
1968, 2009.
Texaco Cup: *Winners* 1972.
European Competitions
European Cup: 1972–73, 1975–76.
UEFA Cup: 1974–75, 1976–77.
Anglo-Italian Cup: *Runners-up* 1993.

Colours: White shirts with black trim, black shorts with white trim, white socks with black trim.

Year Formed: 1884.

Turned Professional: 1884.

Club Nickname: 'The Rams'.

Grounds: 1884, Racecourse Ground; 1895, Baseball Ground; 1997, Pride Park (renamed The iPro Stadium 2013).

First Football League Game: 8 September 1888, Football League, v Bolton W (a) W 6–3 – Marshall; Latham, Ferguson, Williamson; Monks, Walter Roulstone; Bakewell (2), Cooper (2), Higgins, Harry Plackett, Lol Plackett (2).

Record League Victory: 9–0 v Wolverhampton W, Division 1, 10 January 1891 – Bunyan; Archie Goodall, Roberts; Walker, Chalmers, Walter Roulstone (1); Bakewell, McLachlan, Johnny Goodall (1), Holmes (2), McMillan (5). 9–0 v Sheffield W, Division 1, 21 January 1899 – Fryer; Methven, Staley; Cox, Archie Goodall, May; Oakden (1), Bloomer (6), Boag, McDonald (1), Allen, (1 og).

sky SPORTS FACT FILE

Fred Barker was on the fringes of the Derby County first team at the start of 1904–05. After scoring two goals from four matches he was selected for the team to play Stoke on 26 November but withdrew due to illness. The day before the match he was taken violently ill with meningitis and died at the age of 21.

Record Cup Victory: 12–0 v Finn Harps, UEFA Cup 1st rd 1st leg, 15 September 1976 – Moseley; Thomas, Nish, Rioch (1), McFarland, Todd (King), Macken, Gemmill, Hector (5), George (3), James (3).

Record Defeat: 2–11 v Everton, FA Cup 1st rd, 1889–90.

Most League Points (2 for a win): 63, Division 2, 1968–69 and Division 3 (N), 1955–56 and 1956–57.

Most League Points (3 for a win): 85, FL C, 2013–14.

Most League Goals: 111, Division 3 (N), 1956–57.

Highest League Scorer in Season: Jack Bowers, 37, Division 1, 1930–31; Ray Straw, 37 Division 3 (N), 1956–57.

Most League Goals in Total Aggregate: Steve Bloomer, 292, 1892–1906 and 1910–14.

Most League Goals in One Match: 6, Steve Bloomer v Sheffield W, Division 1, 2 January 1899.

Most Capped Player: Deon Burton, 42 (59), Jamaica.

Most League Appearances: Kevin Hector, 486, 1966–78 and 1980–82.

Youngest League Player: Mason Bennett, 15 years 99 days v Middlesbrough 22 October 2011.

Record Transfer Fee Received: £7,000,000 from Leeds U for Seth Johnson, October 2001.

Record Transfer Fee Paid: £3,500,000 to Norwich C for Robert Earnshaw, June 2007.

Football League Record: 1888 Founder Member of the Football League; 1907–12 Division 2; 1912–14 Division 1; 1914–15 Division 2; 1915–21 Division 1; 1921–26 Division 2; 1926–53 Division 1; 1953–55 Division 2; 1955–57 Division 3 (N); 1957–69 Division 2; 1969–80 Division 1; 1980–84 Division 2; 1984–86 Division 3; 1986–87 Division 2; 1987–91 Division 1; 1991–92 Division 2; 1992–96 Division 1; 1996–2002 FA Premier League; 2002–04 Division 1; 2004–07 FL C; 2007–08 FA Premier League; 2008– FL C.

MANAGERS

W. D. Clark 1896–1900
Harry Newbould 1900–06
Jimmy Methven 1906–22
Cecil Potter 1922–25
George Jobey 1925–41
Ted Magner 1944–46
Stuart McMillan 1946–53
Jack Barker 1953–55
Harry Storer 1955–62
Tim Ward 1962–67
Brian Clough 1967–73
Dave Mackay 1973–76
Colin Murphy 1977
Tommy Docherty 1977–79
Colin Addison 1979–82
Johnny Newman 1982
Peter Taylor 1982–84
Roy McFarland 1984
Arthur Cox 1984–93
Roy McFarland 1993–95
Jim Smith 1995–2001
Colin Todd 2001–02
John Gregory 2002–03
George Burley 2003–05
Phil Brown 2005–06
Billy Davies 2006–07
Paul Jewell 2007–08
Nigel Clough 2009–13
Steve McClaren September 2013–

LATEST SEQUENCES

Longest Sequence of League Wins: 9, 15.3.1969 – 19.4.1969.

Longest Sequence of League Defeats: 8, 12.12.1987 – 10.2.1988.

Longest Sequence of League Draws: 6, 26.3.1927 – 18.4.1927.

Longest Sequence of Unbeaten League Matches: 22, 8.3.1969 – 20.9.1969.

Longest Sequence Without a League Win: 36, 22.9.2007 – 30.8.2008.

Successive Scoring Runs: 29 from 3.12.1960.

Successive Non-scoring Runs: 8 from 30.10.1920.

TEN YEAR LEAGUE RECORD

		P	W	D	L	F	A	Pts	Pos
2004-05	FL C	46	22	10	14	71	60	76	4
2005-06	FL C	46	10	20	16	53	67	50	20
2006-07	FL C	46	25	9	12	62	46	84	3
2007-08	PR Lge	38	1	8	29	20	89	11	20
2008-09	FL C	46	14	12	20	55	67	54	18
2009-10	FL C	46	15	11	20	53	63	56	14
2010-11	FL C	46	13	10	23	58	71	49	19
2011-12	FL C	46	18	10	18	50	58	64	12
2012-13	FL C	46	16	13	17	65	62	61	10
2013-14	FL C	46	25	10	11	84	52	85	3

DID YOU KNOW ?

Derby County's record goalscorer Steve Bloomer was coaching the Berlin Britannia club when the First World War broke out in August 1914. Shortly afterwards he was interned in the Ruhleben Camp near Berlin. It was not until the end of November 1918 that he was eventually repatriated to England.

DERBY COUNTY – FL CHAMPIONSHIP 2013–14 LEAGUE RECORD

Match No.	Date	Venue	Opponents	Result	H/T Score	Lg Pos.	Goalscorers	Attendance
1	Aug 4	H	Blackburn R	D	1-1	1-0	11	Russell (pen) [43]	21,188
2	10	A	Brighton & HA	W	2-1	1-1	4	Martin 2 [27, 47]	26,238
3	17	H	Leicester C	L	0-1	0-1	10		23,437
4	24	A	Yeovil T	W	3-0	2-0	8	Russell [42], Bryson [45], Martin [58]	7047
5	31	A	Burnley	L	0-3	0-2	14		23,514
6	Sept 14	A	Millwall	W	5-1	2-0	7	Buxton [9], Bryson 3 [45, 57, 81], Bennett [87]	9523
7	17	A	Bolton W	D	2-2	2-2	8	Russell 2 [7, 18]	14,260
8	21	H	Reading	L	1-3	0-0	11	Hughes [80]	21,465
9	28	A	Nottingham F	L	0-1	0-1	14		28,276
10	Oct 1	H	Ipswich T	D	4-4	1-4	14	Whitbread [12], Bryson 2 [47, 88], Ward [61]	21,037
11	5	H	Leeds U	W	3-1	2-1	10	Martin [20], Russell [23], Hughes [78]	26,204
12	19	A	Watford	W	3-2	2-1	8	Ward 2 [8, 45], Sammon [88]	16,180
13	26	H	Birmingham C	D	1-1	1-0	8	Ward [39]	27,141
14	Nov 2	A	QPR	L	1-2	1-1	11	Dawkins, S [23]	18,171
15	9	H	Sheffield W	W	3-0	1-0	9	Buxton [45], Hughes [49], Martin [58]	26,421
16	23	A	Bournemouth	W	1-0	0-0	7	Ward [61]	10,720
17	Dec 1	A	Wigan Ath	W	3-1	3-0	5	Bryson [3], Dawkins, S [15], Martin (pen) [29]	15,097
18	4	H	Middlesbrough	W	2-1	1-0	4	Martin [45], Sammon [90]	24,631
19	7	H	Blackpool	W	5-1	0-1	4	Martin 3 (2 pens) [47 (p), 53, 69 (p)], Bryson [57], Keogh [90]	24,063
20	14	A	Charlton Ath	W	2-0	1-0	4	Ward [32], Bryson [87]	16,871
21	21	A	Doncaster R	W	3-1	1-0	4	Ward [13], Dawkins, S [50], Bryson [78]	26,314
22	26	A	Huddersfield T	D	1-1	1-0	4	Bryson [30]	18,159
23	29	A	Barnsley	W	2-1	1-0	2	Martin 2 [8, 49]	16,338
24	Jan 1	H	Wigan Ath	L	0-1	0-0	4		26,740
25	10	A	Leicester C	L	1-4	0-1	4	De Laet (og) [59]	23,140
26	18	A	Brighton & HA	W	1-0	0-0	4	Bamford [76]	25,392
27	25	A	Blackburn R	D	1-1	0-0	4	Bamford [84]	13,796
28	28	H	Yeovil T	W	3-2	0-2	4	Bamford [50], Bryson [87], Martin [90]	23,615
29	Feb 1	A	Birmingham C	D	3-3	0-0	4	Bamford [49], Martin [59], Forsyth [73]	15,224
30	10	H	QPR	W	1-0	1-0	4	Eustace [20]	23,495
31	18	A	Sheffield W	W	1-0	0-0	3	Bamford [78]	21,039
32	22	H	Bournemouth	W	1-0	0-0	3	Martin [85]	27,306
33	Mar 1	A	Burnley	L	0-2	0-1	3		17,285
34	8	H	Millwall	L	0-1	0-0	3		22,853
35	11	H	Bolton W	D	0-0	0-0	3		23,435
36	15	A	Reading	D	0-0	0-0	3		19,514
37	22	H	Nottingham F	W	5-0	3-0	3	Bryson 3 (1 pen) [6, 32, 69 (p)], Hendrick [37], Russell [54]	33,004
38	25	H	Ipswich T	L	1-2	1-0	4	Bamford [1]	17,399
39	29	H	Charlton Ath	W	3-0	2-0	4	Russell [18], Bamford [38], Martin [84]	24,429
40	Apr 5	A	Middlesbrough	L	0-1	0-0	4		15,234
41	8	A	Blackpool	W	3-1	3-1	4	Martin [3], Bamford [14], Bryson [20]	13,435
42	12	H	Huddersfield T	W	3-1	1-1	3	Russell [28], Smithies (og) [50], Martin (pen) [57]	25,809
43	18	A	Doncaster R	W	2-0	1-0	3	Thorne [45], Martin [79]	11,405
44	21	H	Barnsley	W	2-1	2-0	3	Hendrick [34], Russell [42]	26,046
45	26	H	Watford	W	4-2	1-1	3	Hendrick 2 [28, 81], Forsyth [60], Martin [86]	25,922
46	May 3	A	Leeds U	D	1-1	1-0	3	Dawkins, S [6]	29,724

Final League Position: 3

GOALSCORERS

League (84): Martin 20 (4 pens), Bryson 16 (1 pen), Russell 9 (1 pen), Bamford 8, Ward 7, Dawkins, S 4, Hendrick 4, Hughes 3, Buxton 2, Forsyth 2, Sammon 2, Bennett 1, Eustace 1, Keogh 1, Thorne 1, Whitbread 1, own goals 2.
The Budweiser FA Cup (0).
Capital One Cup (7): Martin 3, Sammon 2, Hughes 1, Jacobs 1.
Championship Play-Offs (6): Martin 2, Hendrick 1, Hughes 1, Thorne 1, own goal 1.

Grant L 46	Freeman K 5+1	Forsyth C 46	Bryson C 43+2	Keogh R 41	Buxton J 43+2	Hendrick J 18+12	Hughes W 37+4	Russell J 23+16	Martin C 44	Ward J 31+7	Coutts P 3+5	Eustace J 28+7	Sammon C 3+34	Smith A 7+1	Davies B 1+3	Bennett M 1+12	Jacobs M —+3	Whitbread Z 4	Dawkins S 20+6	Wisdom A 34	Cisse K 1+2	Keane M 4+3	Bamford P 14+7	Thorne G 9	Naylor L —+4	Bailey J —+1	Match No.
1	2	3	4	5	6	7	8^2	9^1	10^1	11	12	13	14														1
1	2	5	9	3	4	8	7^1	6^2	11	12	10	13															2
1	2	5	7	3	4	6	8	10^2	11	12		9^1	13														3
1	2	5	7	4	3	8^2	6	9^1	10	11^3	13	12	14														4
1	2^2	5	7	3	4		8	11^1	10	9		6^3	14	12	13												5
1	13	5	7	3	4		8	9	10^2	11^1	12	6			14					2^3							6
1		5	7	4	3		8^1	9^2	10	11^3	12	6	14		13					2							7
1		5	7	3	4		8	10^3	11	9	12	6^2	13							2							8
1		5	8	3^4	4		6	10^2	11	9^1		7	12							2							9
1		5	7		3		8	14	10	9^1		13	11^2	2	6^3	12		4									10
1		5	6^3	3	14		8	9	10^1	11^2		7	13	2		12		4									11
1		5	6	3	12		8		10	11^3		7	14	2	9^1		4^2	13									12
1		5	8	4	3		6^1		10^2	11		7	12			13	14	9^3	2								13
1		5	6	3	4		8		10	11		7	12			13		9^1	2^1								14
1		5	6	3	4		8		10^2	11^3			13	14	12		9^1	2	7								15
1		5	6	3	4		8	13	10^3	11^1		7	14		12		9^2	2									16
1		5	6	3	4	13	8^1	11^2	10			7^3				12	9	2	14								17
1		5	6^3	3	4	12	8	13	10	11		7^1					9^2	2									18
1		5	6	3	4^3	14	8	12	10	9^1		7^2				11	2	13									19
1		5	8	3	4	6		12	10^3	9^2		7	13			11^1	2	14									20
1		5	6	3^3	4	13	8	14	10	9^1		7^2				11	2	12									21
1		5	7		4		8^3	12	10^1	9		6	14			11^2	2	13	3								22
1		5	6^1		4		8	9	10^2	12		7	13			14	11^3	2	3								23
1		5	6^1		4	12	8	11	10	9^2		7^3	14			13	2	3									24
1		5	8		4	7	6		10^2	9^3			14		12	11^1	2	3	13								25
1		5	8	3	4	12	6^3		10	9		7	14			11^2	2^1	13									26
1		5	6	3	4	8^1	12		10	9^3		7^2	14			11	2	13									27
1		5	6	3	4		8	14	10	12		7^2	13			11^1	2	9^3									28
1		5	6	3	4	8^1	13	10^2	11		7	14					2	9^3										29
1		5	6	3	4	13	8^1	12	10	11^2		7	14				2	9^3									30
1		5	6^3	3	4	13	8	12	10	11^1		7^2	14				2	9									31
1		5		3	4	6	8	11	10			7^2	12			13	2	9^1									32
1	5	14	3	4	7	9	8^1	11 ●		6²	12			10^3	2	13											33
1	5	6	3	4	7^1	8	13		12		10^3		14	11^2	2	9											34
1		5	6	3	4	8		14	10	9^1		7^2	13			11^3	2	12									35
1		5	6	3	4	12	8^3	14	10	9^1		7				11^2	2	13									36
1		5	8^3	3	4	6	14	12	10^1	11^2			13				2		9	7							37
1		5	6	3	4	8		11	10			12					2		9^1	7^2	13						38
1		5	6	3	4	8	11^3	10			12	13					2		9^1	7^2	14						39
1		5	6	3	4	8	13	11^1	10			12					2		9^3	7^2	14						40
1		5	6	3	4		8^2	11	10		13	12					2		9^3	7^1	14						41
1		5^2	6	3	4	13	8	11	10	12							2		9^3	7^1	14						42
1		5	6	3	4	14	8^1	11^2	10	12						13	2		9^3	7							43
1		5	8	3	4	6		9	10^2	11^3	12	14					13	2		7^3							44
1		5	6	3	4	8	14	9^2	10^3	11^1						12	2		13	7							45
1		5	14	3		6^2	8	13		7	10		12		4	11^3	2		9^1								46

The Budweiser FA Cup
Third Round   Chelsea   (h)   0-2

Capital One Cup
First Round   Oldham Ath   (a)   1-0
Second Round   Brentford   (h)   5-0
Third Round   Leicester C   (a)   1-2

Championship Play-Offs
Semi-Finals 1st leg   Brighton & HA   (a)   2-1
Semi-Finals 2nd leg   Brighton & HA   (h)   4-1
Final   QPR   (Wembley)   0-1

DONCASTER ROVERS

FOUNDATION

In 1879, Mr Albert Jenkins assembled a team to play a match against the Yorkshire Institution for the Deaf. The players remained together as Doncaster Rovers, joining the Midland Alliance in 1889 and the Midland Counties League in 1891.

Keepmoat Stadium, Stadium Way, Lakeside, Doncaster, South Yorkshire DN4 5JW.

Telephone: (01302) 764 664.

Fax: (01302) 363 525.

Ticket Office: (01302) 762 576.

Website: www.doncasterroversfc.co.uk

Email: info@doncasterroversfc.co.uk

Ground Capacity: 15,231.

Record Attendance: 37,149 v Hull C, Division 3 (N), 2 October 1948 (at Belle Vue); 15,001 v Leeds U, FL 1, 1 April 2008 (at Keepmoat Stadium).

Pitch Measurements: 100m × 66m (109.5yd × 72yd)

Joint Chairmen: John Ryan and Louis Tomlinson.

Chief Executive: Gavin Baldwin.

Manager: Paul Dickov.

Assistant Manager: Brian Horton.

Fitness Coach: Ben Rome.

Colours: Red and white hooped shirts, black shorts with red trim, red socks with red trim.

Year Formed: 1879.

Turned Professional: 1885.

Club Nickname: 'Rovers', 'Donny'.

Grounds: 1880–1916, Intake Ground; 1920, Benetthorpe Ground; 1922, Low Pasture, Belle Vue; 2007, Keepmoat Stadium.

HONOURS

Football League Division 3: *Champions* 2003–04; **Division 3 (N):** *Champions* – 1934–35, 1946–47, 1949–50; *Runners-up* 1937–38, 1938–39; **FL 1:** *Champions* 2012–13; **Division 4:** *Champions* 1965–66, 1968–69; *Runners-up* 1983–84.

FA Cup: Best season: 5th rd, 1952, 1954, 1955, 1956.

Football League Cup: Best season: 5th rd, 1976, 2006.

Johnstone's Paint Trophy: *Winners* 2007.

Football Conference: *Champions* 2002–03

Sheffield County Cup: *Winners* 1891, 1912, 1936, 1938, 1956, 1968, 1976, 1986.

Midland Counties League: *Champions* 1897, 1899.

Conference Trophy: *Winners* 1999, 2000.

Sheffield & Hallamshire Senior Cup: *Winners* 2001, 2002.

First Football League Game: 7 September 1901, Division 2, v Burslem Port Vale (h) D 3–3 – Eggett; Simpson, Layton; Longden, Jones, Wright, Langham, Murphy, Price, Goodson (2), Bailey (1).

Record League Victory: 10–0 v Darlington, Division 4, 25 January 1964 – Potter; Raine, Meadows, Windross (1), White, Ripley (2), Robinson, Book (2), Hale (4), Jeffrey, Broadbent (1).

Record Cup Victory: 7–0 v Blyth Spartans, FA Cup 1st rd, 27 November 1937 – Imrie; Shaw, Rodgers, McFarlane, Bycroft, Cyril Smith, Burton (1), Killourhy (4), Morgan (2), Malam, Dutton.

Record Defeat: 0–12 v Small Heath, Division 2, 11 April 1903.

sky SPORTS FACT FILE

Five Keetley brothers played in the Football League in the 1920s, and four of them turned out for Doncaster Rovers. Joe, Harold and Tom played in 1925–26 and although Joe moved on at the end of the season, Rovers signed Frank and all three featured in 1926–27. A fifth brother Charlie played for Leeds United, Bradford City and Reading.

Most League Points (2 for a win): 72, Division 3 (N), 1946–47.

Most League Points (3 for a win): 92, Division 3, 2003–04.

Most League Goals: 123, Division 3 (N), 1946–47.

Highest League Scorer in Season: Clarrie Jordan, 42, Division 3 (N), 1946–47.

Most League Goals in Total Aggregate: Tom Keetley, 180, 1923–29.

Most League Goals in One Match: 6, Tom Keetley v Ashington, Division 3 (N), 16 February 1929.

Most Capped Player: Len Graham, 14, Northern Ireland.

Most League Appearances: Fred Emery, 417, 1925–36.

Youngest League Player: Alick Jeffrey, 15 years 229 days v Fulham, 15 September 1954.

Record Transfer Fee Received: £2,000,000 from Reading for Matthew Mills, July 2009.

Record Transfer Fee Paid: £1,150,000 to Sheffield U for Billy Sharp, August 2010.

Football League Record: 1901 Elected to Division 2; 1903 Failed re-election; 1904 Re-elected; 1905 Failed re-election; 1923 Re-elected to Division 3 (N); 1935–37 Division 2; 1937–47 Division 3 (N); 1947–48 Division 2; 1948–50 Division 3 (N); 1950–58 Division 2; 1958–59 Division 3; 1959–66 Division 4; 1966–67 Division 3; 1967–69 Division 4; 1969–71 Division 3; 1971–81 Division 4; 1981–83 Division 3; 1983–84 Division 4; 1984–88 Division 3; 1988–92 Division 4; 1992–98 Division 3; 1998–2003 Conference; 2003–04 Division 3; 2004–08 FL 1; 2008–12 FL C; 2012–13 FL 1; 2013–14 FL C; 2014– FL 1.

LATEST SEQUENCES

Longest Sequence of League Wins: 10, 22.1.1947 – 4.4.1947.

Longest Sequence of League Defeats: 9, 14.1.1905 – 1.4.1905.

Longest Sequence of League Draws: 4, 29.10.1932 – 19.11.1932.

Longest Sequence of Unbeaten League Matches: 20, 26.12.1968 – 12.4.1969.

Longest Sequence Without a League Win: 20, 9.8.1997 – 29.11.1997.

Successive Scoring Runs: 27 from 10.11.1934.

Successive Non-scoring Runs: 7 from 27.9.1947.

MANAGERS

Arthur Porter 1920–21
Harry Tufnell 1921–22
Arthur Porter 1922–23
Dick Ray 1923–27
David Menzies 1928–36
Fred Emery 1936–40
Bill Marsden 1944–46
Jackie Bestall 1946–49
Peter Doherty 1949–58
Jack Hodgson and Sid Bycroft
    (*Joint Managers*) 1958
Jack Crayston 1958–59
    (*continued as Secretary-Manager to 1961*)
Jackie Bestall (*TM*) 1959–60
Norman Curtis 1960–61
Danny Malloy 1961–62
Oscar Hold 1962–64
Bill Leivers 1964–66
Keith Kettleborough 1966–67
George Raynor 1967–68
Lawrie McMenemy 1968–71
Maurice Setters 1971–74
Stan Anderson 1975–78
Billy Bremner 1978–85
Dave Cusack 1985–87
Dave Mackay 1987–89
Billy Bremner 1989–91
Steve Beaglehole 1991–93
Ian Atkins 1994
Sammy Chung 1994–96
Kerry Dixon (*Player-Manager*)
    1996–97
Dave Cowling 1997
Mark Weaver 1997–98
Ian Snodin 1998–99
Steve Wignall 1999–2001
Dave Penney 2002–06
Sean O'Driscoll 2006–11
Dean Saunders 2011–13
Brian Flynn 2013
Paul Dickov May 2013–

TEN YEAR LEAGUE RECORD

		P	W	D	L	F	A	Pts	Pos
2004-05	FL 1	46	16	18	12	65	60	66	10
2005-06	FL 1	46	20	9	17	55	51	69	8
2006-07	FL 1	46	16	15	15	52	47	63	11
2007-08	FL 1	46	23	11	12	65	41	80	3
2008-09	FL C	46	17	7	22	42	53	58	14
2009-10	FL C	46	15	15	16	59	58	60	12
2010-11	FL C	46	11	15	20	55	81	48	21
2011-12	FL C	46	8	12	26	43	80	36	24
2012-13	FL 1	46	25	9	12	62	44	84	1
2013-14	FL C	46	11	11	24	39	70	44	22

DID YOU KNOW

When Doncaster Rovers reached the FA Youth Cup final in 1987–88 the first leg game against Arsenal at Belle Vue attracted a crowd of 6,451. The two clubs also met at first-team level in the Football League Cup that season, when the gate was lower – 5,469 attending the Belle Vue leg of the tie.

DONCASTER ROVERS – FL CHAMPIONSHIP 2013–14 LEAGUE RECORD

Match No.	Date	Venue	Opponents	Result	H/T Score	Lg Pos.	Goalscorers	Attendance
1	Aug 3	H	Blackpool	L	1-3	0-1	23	Jones, R [60]	9002
2	16	H	Blackburn R	W	2-0	1-0	12	Robinson [37], Husband [59]	8707
3	20	A	Wigan Ath	D	2-2	2-0	11	Robinson [25], Brown [42]	14,304
4	31	H	Bournemouth	L	0-1	0-1	17		6769
5	Sept 14	A	Huddersfield T	D	0-0	0-0	18		13,102
6	17	A	Watford	L	1-2	1-1	18	Brown [16]	13,998
7	21	H	Nottingham F	D	2-2	1-1	19	Macheda 2 [34, 52]	12,253
8	28	A	Sheffield W	W	1-0	0-0	17	Macheda [71]	21,871
9	Oct 1	H	Burnley	L	0-2	0-1	18		7836
10	5	H	Leicester C	W	1-0	1-0	16	Schmeichel (og) [17]	10,003
11	19	A	Reading	L	1-4	1-2	17	Robinson [31]	17,697
12	25	A	Middlesbrough	L	0-4	0-2	17		21,882
13	Nov 2	H	Brighton & HA	L	1-3	0-1	20	Brown [75]	7396
14	9	A	Barnsley	D	0-0	0-0	21		11,843
15	22	H	Yeovil T	W	2-1	1-1	18	Furman [11], Duffy [82]	6620
16	26	A	Charlton Ath	L	0-2	0-0	20		14,140
17	30	H	QPR	W	2-1	0-1	18	Robinson [48], Quinn [89]	8854
18	Dec 3	A	Birmingham C	D	1-1	0-1	15	Cotterill [78]	12,663
19	7	A	Bolton W	L	0-3	0-2	20		15,471
20	14	H	Leeds U	L	0-3	0-1	20		12,192
21	21	A	Derby Co	L	1-3	0-1	20	Buxton (og) [64]	26,314
22	26	H	Ipswich T	L	0-3	0-2	21		7753
23	29	H	Millwall	D	0-0	0-0	21		6454
24	Jan 1	A	QPR	L	1-2	1-0	22	Robinson [43]	15,807
25	11	A	Blackburn R	L	0-1	0-1	22		13,954
26	18	H	Wigan Ath	W	3-0	1-0	22	Brown 2 (1 pen) [7, 69 (p)], Coppinger [52]	8331
27	25	A	Blackpool	D	1-1	0-0	20	Sharp [85]	13,468
28	28	H	Charlton Ath	W	3-0	2-0	19	Meite [26], Brown (pen) [36], Duffy [67]	7289
29	Feb 1	H	Middlesbrough	D	0-0	0-0	19		11,440
30	8	A	Brighton & HA	L	0-1	0-0	20		27,009
31	15	H	Barnsley	D	2-2	1-1	20	Coppinger 2 [45, 55]	10,216
32	22	A	Yeovil T	L	0-1	0-0	20		4934
33	Mar 1	A	Bournemouth	L	0-5	0-2	20		8983
34	8	H	Huddersfield T	W	2-0	1-0	20	Sharp [28], Cotterill [55]	9305
35	11	H	Watford	W	2-1	1-0	20	Brown [24], Sharp [90]	6581
36	15	A	Nottingham F	D	0-0	0-0	20		27,402
37	22	H	Sheffield W	W	1-0	1-0	19	Brown [32]	12,609
38	25	A	Burnley	L	0-2	0-0	20		12,325
39	29	A	Leeds U	W	2-1	2-0	18	Cotterill [23], Sharp [45]	23,476
40	Apr 5	H	Birmingham C	L	1-3	1-0	19	Quinn [36]	9206
41	8	H	Bolton W	L	1-2	1-2	19	Cotterill [18]	7508
42	12	A	Ipswich T	L	1-2	0-0	19	Brown (pen) [83]	19,496
43	18	H	Derby Co	L	0-2	0-1	19		11,405
44	21	A	Millwall	D	0-0	0-0	19		12,026
45	26	H	Reading	L	1-3	1-0	21	Coppinger [25]	10,212
46	May 3	A	Leicester C	L	0-1	0-0	22		31,424

Final League Position: 22

GOALSCORERS

League (39): Brown 9 (3 pens), Robinson 5, Coppinger 4, Cotterill 4, Sharp 4, Macheda 3, Duffy 2, Quinn 2, Furman 1, Husband 1, Jones, R 1, Meite 1, own goals 2.
The Budweiser FA Cup (2): Forrester 1, Wakefield 1.
Capital One Cup (2): Khumalo 1, Paynter 1.

Turnbull R 28	Quinn P 31+4	Husband J 28	Wellens R 36+1	Jones R 12	Khumalo B 30	Duffy M 28+8	Furman D 25+7	Brown C 38+2	Coppinger J 34+7	Cotterill D 25+15	Bennett K —+3	Paynter B 1+8	Syers D —+2	Wabara R 13	Keegan P 34	Robinson T 19+12	Forrester H 3+4	Macheda F 12+3	Yun S 2+1	McCullough L 13+1	De Val Fernandez M 2+3	Paterson A 1+4	Stevens E 11+2	Woods M 3+1	Wakefield L 3+1	Meite A 21	Tamas G 13+1	Sharp B 15+1	Johnstone S 18	Bowery J 3	Neill L 4	McCombe J —+2	Match No.
1	2	3	4¹	5	6	7²	8	9	10³	11	12	13	14																				1
1		5	7	4	3	12		11	6	9²			13	2	8	10¹																	2
1	13	5	7³	3	4		12	10	6¹	9			14	2²	8	11																	3
1		5	8	3	4	13		10	6	9²		12		2¹	7	11³	14																4
1		5	8	4	3			10	6	9				2	7	11																	5
1		5	7¹	3	4		13	10	6	9²				2	8	11		12															6
1	12	5	9	4	3			6	11	13		14		2²	7	8³		10¹															7
1	2	5	7	3	4	14	8²	10	12	13					6	9¹	11³																8
1	2	5	7	4	3	12		11	6	9¹					8²	13		10															9
1	2			3	4	8		6	11	12				5	7	9		10¹															10
1	2		8	4	3	10	9³	11¹	6²		14	13		5	7	12																	11
1	2²		4	3	9	8¹	10	6	13					5	7	11		12															12
1		6		3	9			11	8¹	10	12			2	7					4			5										13
1	2		7		3	9¹		6	10	13	12			5	8	11²				4													14
1	2		7		3	9	8¹		12	6¹	13			5	10³	11²	14			4													15
1	2		8		3	9		6	11¹					5	12			10		4	7²	13											16
1	2		7		3	9	8	6							10	11				4			5										17
1	2		8¹		3	9¹	7	6²	13		14				10	11				4			5	12									18
1	2		7		3	6¹	8	12	13	9³		14			10	11²				4			5										19
1	2		7		3	12		6²	10	13					11			9¹		4			5	8									20
1	2³		7		3	6	8	11²							10	13	12			4			5	9¹	14								21
1	2		8			6	7				13	14			11¹	9³		10²	5	4	12		3										22
1	3		9			8	7			10					12		13			4	11¹	5	6²	2									23
1	3		8			9	7	12		6					10¹	13		11²		4			5	2									24
1	10²			3	13	11	8	14							9³				2¹	6	12		5			4							25
1		5	6¹		3	8	12	11	10	13					7³	9²						14				4	2						26
1		5	7		3	6¹		10	9	12					8											4	2	11					27
1	12	5	8		3	9		10¹	6	13					7							14				4	2²	11³					28
1		5	8		3	9¹	12	10	6	13					7²											4	2	11	1				29
	12	5	8		4	6²		10	9	13					7²											3	2¹	11¹	1				30
		5			3	9	7	11	6	12					8											4	2		1	10¹	11		31
	2	5	8		3	9¹		10	6	12					7											4			1		11		32
	5		7		3			8¹	10	9	13				6	12										4	2	11¹	1		11²		33
	2	5	8			6		10		9					7	12										4	3	11¹	1				34
	2	4	8		5			10	7	9					6								12			3¹		11	1				35
	3	5	8		9			11	2	6					7											4		10	1				36
	4	5	8		6			10	2	9					7											3		11	1				37
	3	5	8		9			6¹	13	11	2				7¹	12										4		10	1				38
	2	5	7²		12			11	9	6					8	13										4		10¹	1			3	39
	4	5			9			6¹	7	10	2				8	12												11	1			3	40
	2	5	8²		12			10	6	9					7											4	13	11	1			3¹	41
	3	5³	12			7¹		11	6	9					8	14							13			4²	2	10	1				42
	3	13				8²		10¹	6	9					7	12						14	5			4	2	11¹	1				43
	3					7		10	6	9					8	11¹							5			4¹	2		1			12	44
	3	12				7¹		10	6	9					8	13							5			4	2³	11²	1			14	45
	5	6²				9³		11	7	10					8	13							12			4	2	14	1			3¹	46

The Budweiser FA Cup
Third Round   Stevenage   (h)   2-3

Capital One Cup
First Round   Rochdale   (h)   1-0
Second Round   Leeds U   (h)   1-3

EVERTON

FOUNDATION

St Domingo Church Sunday School formed a football club in 1878 which played at Stanley Park. Enthusiasm was so great that in November 1879 they decided to expand membership and changed the name to Everton, playing in black shirts with a scarlet sash and nicknamed the 'Black Watch'. After wearing several other colours, royal blue was adopted in 1901.

Goodison Park, Goodison Road, Liverpool L4 4EL.

Telephone: (0871) 663 1878.

Fax: (0151) 286 9112.

Ticket Office: (0871) 663 1878.

Website: www.evertonfc.com

Email: everton@evertonfc.com

Ground Capacity: 39,571.

Record Attendance: 78,299 v Liverpool, Division 1, 18 September 1948.

Pitch Measurements: 100.48m × 68m (109yd × 74yd)

Chairman: Bill Kenwright CBE.

Chief Executive: Robert Elstone.

Manager: Roberto Martinez.

Assistant Manager: Graeme Jones.

Physio: Matt Connery.

Colours: Blue shirts with white trim, white shorts with blue trim, white socks with blue trim.

Year Formed: 1878.

Turned Professional: 1885.

Previous Name: 1878, St Domingo FC; 1879, Everton.

Club Nickname: 'The Toffees'.

Grounds: 1878, Stanley Park; 1882, Priory Road; 1884, Anfield Road; 1892, Goodison Park.

First Football League Game: 8 September 1888, Football League, v Accrington (h) W 2–1 – Smalley; Dick, Ross; Holt, Jones, Dobson; Fleming (2), Waugh, Lewis, Edgar Chadwick, Farmer.

HONOURS

Football League – Division 1:
Champions 1890–91, 1914–15, 1927–28, 1931–32, 1938–39, 1962–63, 1969–70, 1984–85, 1986–87;
Runners-up 1889–90, 1894–95, 1901–02, 1904–05, 1908–09, 1911–12, 1985–86;
Division 2: *Champions* 1930–31;
Runners-up 1953–54.

FA Cup: *Winners* 1906, 1933, 1966, 1984, 1995; *Runners-up* 1893, 1897, 1907, 1968, 1985, 1986, 1989, 2009.

Football League Cup:
Runners-up 1977, 1984.

League Super Cup: *Runners-up* 1986.

Simod Cup: *Runners-up* 1989.

Zenith Data Systems Cup:
Runners-up 1991.

European Competitions
European Cup: 1963–64, 1970–71.
European Cup-Winners' Cup:
1966–67, 1984–85 (*winners*), 1995–96.
European Fairs Cup: 1962–63, 1964–65, 1965–66.
Champions League: 2005–06.
UEFA Cup: 1975–76, 1978–79, 1979–80, 2005–06, 2007–08, 2008–09.
Europa League: 2009–10.

Record League Victory: 9–1 v Manchester C, Division 1, 3 September 1906 – Scott; Balmer, Crelley; Booth, Taylor (1), Abbott (1); Sharp, Bolton (1), Young (4), Settle (2), George Wilson. 9–1 v Plymouth Arg, Division 2, 27 December 1930 – Coggins; Williams, Cresswell; McPherson, Griffiths, Thomson; Critchley, Dunn, Dean (4), Johnson (1), Stein (4).

sky SPORTS FACT FILE

Everton went on a tour of Germany in May 1932 as reigning Football League champions. They won games in Hanover and Dresden but drew three other matches and lost in Nuremberg. Seven years later, when they again won the First Division, they accepted a further invitation to visit Germany only to pull out because of the political situation.

Record Cup Victory: 11–2 v Derby Co, FA Cup 1st rd, 18 January 1890 – Smalley; Hannah, Doyle (1); Kirkwood, Holt (1), Parry; Latta, Brady (3), Geary (3), Edgar Chadwick, Millward (3).

Record Defeat: 4–10 v Tottenham H, Division 1, 11 October 1958.

Most League Points (2 for a win): 66, Division 1, 1969–70.

Most League Points (3 for a win): 90, Division 1, 1984–85.

Most League Goals: 121, Division 2, 1930–31.

Highest League Scorer in Season: William Ralph 'Dixie' Dean, 60, Division 1, 1927–28 (All-time League record).

Most League Goals in Total Aggregate: William Ralph 'Dixie' Dean, 349, 1925–37.

Most League Goals in One Match: 6, Jack Southworth v WBA, Division 1, 30 December 1893.

Most Capped Player: Neville Southall, 92, Wales.

Most League Appearances: Neville Southall, 578, 1981–98.

Youngest League Player: Jose Baxter, 16 years 191 days v Blackburn R, 16 August 2008.

Record Transfer Fee Received: £25,000,000 (rising to £29,000,000) from Manchester U for Wayne Rooney, August 2004.

Record Transfer Fee Paid: £15,000,000 to Standard Liege for Marouane Fellaini, September 2008.

Football League Record: 1888 Founder Member of the Football League; 1930–31 Division 2; 1931–51 Division 1; 1951–54 Division 2; 1954–92 Division 1; 1992– FA Premier League.

MANAGERS

W. E. Barclay 1888–89
(Secretary-Manager)
Dick Molyneux 1889–1901
(Secretary-Manager)
William C. Cuff 1901–18
(Secretary-Manager)
W. J. Sawyer 1918–19
(Secretary-Manager)
Thomas H. McIntosh 1919–35
(Secretary-Manager)
Theo Kelly 1936–48
Cliff Britton 1948–56
Ian Buchan 1956–58
Johnny Carey 1958–61
Harry Catterick 1961–73
Billy Bingham 1973–77
Gordon Lee 1977–81
Howard Kendall 1981–87
Colin Harvey 1987–90
Howard Kendall 1990–93
Mike Walker 1994
Joe Royle 1994–97
Howard Kendall 1997–98
Walter Smith 1998–2002
David Moyes 2002–13
Roberto Martinez July 2013–

LATEST SEQUENCES

Longest Sequence of League Wins: 12, 24.3.1894 – 13.10.1894.

Longest Sequence of League Defeats: 6, 27.8.2005– 15.10.2005.

Longest Sequence of League Draws: 5, 4.5.1977 – 16.5.1977.

Longest Sequence of Unbeaten League Matches: 20, 29.4.1978 – 16.12.1978.

Longest Sequence Without a League Win: 14, 6.3.1937 – 4.9.1937.

Successive Scoring Runs: 40 from 15.3.1930.

Successive Non-scoring Runs: 6 from 27.8.2005.

TEN YEAR LEAGUE RECORD

			P	W	D	L	F	A	Pts	Pos
2004-05	PR Lge	38	18	7	13	45	46	61	4
2005-06	PR Lge	38	14	8	16	34	49	50	11
2006-07	PR Lge	38	15	13	10	52	36	58	6
2007-08	PR Lge	38	19	8	11	55	33	65	5
2008-09	PR Lge	38	17	12	9	55	37	63	5
2009-10	PR Lge	38	16	13	9	60	49	61	8
2010-11	PR Lge	38	13	15	10	51	45	54	7
2011-12	PR Lge	38	15	11	12	50	40	56	7
2012-13	PR Lge	38	16	15	7	55	40	63	6
2013-14	PR Lge	38	21	9	8	61	39	72	5

DID YOU KNOW ?

Harold Hardman was one of the last amateur players to collect an FA Cup winners' medal when he was included in the Everton team which defeated Newcastle United in the 1906 final. Hardman made over 130 appearances for the Toffees and won four full England caps.

EVERTON – FA PREMIERSHIP 2013–14 LEAGUE RECORD

Match No.	Date	Venue	Opponents	Result		H/T Score	Lg Pos.	Goalscorers	Attendance
1	Aug 17	A	Norwich C	D	2-2	0-0	7	Barkley [61], Coleman [65]	26,824
2	24	H	WBA	D	0-0	0-0	13		36,410
3	31	A	Cardiff C	D	0-0	0-0	15		27,344
4	Sept 14	H	Chelsea	W	1-0	1-0	9	Naismith [45]	36,034
5	21	A	West Ham U	W	3-2	0-1	5	Baines 2 [62, 83], Lukaku [85]	34,952
6	30	H	Newcastle U	W	3-2	3-0	4	Lukaku 2 [5, 37], Barkley [25]	33,495
7	Oct 5	A	Manchester C	L	1-3	1-2	5	Lukaku [16]	47,267
8	19	H	Hull C	W	2-1	1-1	6	Barry [8], Pienaar [57]	38,828
9	26	A	Aston Villa	W	2-0	0-0	4	Lukaku [68], Osman [81]	35,154
10	Nov 3	H	Tottenham H	D	0-0	0-0	7		38,378
11	9	A	Crystal Palace	D	0-0	0-0	5		25,231
12	23	H	Liverpool	D	3-3	1-2	5	Mirallas [8], Lukaku 2 [72, 82]	39,576
13	30	H	Stoke C	W	4-0	1-0	4	Deulofeu [45], Coleman [49], Oviedo [58], Lukaku [79]	35,513
14	Dec 4	A	Manchester U	W	1-0	0-0	5	Oviedo [86]	75,210
15	8	A	Arsenal	D	1-1	0-0	5	Deulofeu [84]	60,001
16	14	H	Fulham	W	4-1	1-0	4	Osman [18], Coleman [73], Barry [84], Mirallas [90]	33,796
17	22	A	Swansea C	W	2-1	0-0	4	Coleman [66], Barkley [84]	20,695
18	26	H	Sunderland	L	0-1	0-1	5		39,193
19	29	H	Southampton	W	2-1	1-0	4	Coleman [9], Lukaku [74]	39,092
20	Jan 1	A	Stoke C	D	1-1	0-0	5	Baines (pen) [90]	25,832
21	11	H	Norwich C	W	2-0	1-0	4	Barry [23], Mirallas [59]	36,827
22	20	A	WBA	D	1-1	1-0	6	Mirallas [41]	24,184
23	28	A	Liverpool	L	0-4	0-3	6		44,450
24	Feb 1	H	Aston Villa	W	2-1	0-1	5	Naismith [74], Mirallas [85]	39,469
25	9	A	Tottenham H	L	0-1	0-1	6		35,944
26	22	A	Chelsea	L	0-1	0-0	7		41,580
27	Mar 1	H	West Ham U	W	1-0	0-0	6	Lukaku [81]	38,286
28	15	H	Cardiff C	W	2-1	0-0	6	Deulofeu [59], Coleman [90]	38,018
29	22	A	Swansea C	W	3-2	1-1	5	Baines (pen) [20], Lukaku [53], Barkley [58]	36,260
30	25	H	Newcastle U	W	3-0	1-0	5	Barkley [22], Lukaku [52], Osman [87]	47,622
31	30	A	Fulham	W	3-1	0-0	5	Stockdale (og) [50], Mirallas [79], Naismith [87]	25,454
32	Apr 6	H	Arsenal	W	3-0	2-0	5	Naismith [14], Lukaku [34], Arteta (og) [61]	39,504
33	12	A	Sunderland	W	1-0	0-0	4	Brown (og) [75]	38,445
34	16	H	Crystal Palace	L	2-3	0-1	5	Naismith [61], Mirallas [86]	39,333
35	20	H	Manchester U	W	2-0	2-0	5	Baines (pen) [28], Mirallas [43]	39,436
36	26	A	Southampton	L	0-2	0-2	5		31,313
37	May 3	H	Manchester C	L	2-3	1-2	5	Barkley [11], Lukaku [65]	39,454
38	11	A	Hull C	W	2-0	1-0	5	McCarthy [9], Lukaku [46]	24,848

Final League Position: 5

GOALSCORERS

League (61): Lukaku 15, Mirallas 8, Barkley 6, Coleman 6, Baines 5 (3 pens), Naismith 5, Barry 3, Deulofeu 3, Osman 3, Oviedo 2, McCarthy 1, Pienaar 1, own goals 3.
The Budweiser FA Cup (12): Naismith 3, Jelavic 2, Baines 1 (1 pen), Barkley 1, Coleman 1, Gueye 1, Heitinga 1, Lukaku 1, Traore 1.
Capital One Cup (3): Deulofeu 1, Fellaini 1, Naismith 1.

Howard T 37	Coleman S 36	Jagielka P 26	Distin S 33	Baines L 32	Mirallas K 28 + 4	Barkley R 25 + 9	Osman L 27 + 11	Pienaar S 19 + 4	Fellaini M 3	Jelavic N 5 + 4	Naismith S 13 + 18	Kone A — + 5	Anichebe V — + 1	Deulofeu G 9 + 16	Barry G 32	McCarthy J 31 + 3	Stones J 15 + 6	Lukaku R 29 + 2	Oviedo B 8 + 1	Gibson D — + 1	Robles J 1 + 1	Alcaraz A 5 + 1	Heitinga J — + 1	McGeady A 4 + 12	Hibbert T — + 1	Garbutt L — + 1	Traore L — + 1	Match No.
1	2	3	4	5	6^2	7^1	8	9	10	11^1	12	13	14															1
1	2	3	4	5	8^2	9	6	10	7	11^1	13	12																2
1	2	3	4	5	8^2	9	6	10	7	11^1		12			13													3
1	2	3	4	5	8^2	9	6			11^3	10^1				14	7	12	13										4
1	2	3	4	5	10	9	6^2			11^1	8^3				7	13	12	14										5
1	2	3	4	5	8^1	9^1	10^2				13			12	7	6		14	11									6
1	2	3	4	5	8^2	9	7^3		10		14	13				6		11^1	12									7
1	2	3	4	5	8	9^1	10^2			12	14	13			7	6		11^1										8
1	2	3	4	5	8^1	9^1	12	10^2				13	14		7	6		11										9
1	2	3	4	5	8^3	12	9^1	10			14	13			7	6		11^2										10
1	2	3	4	5	8^1	12	9^2	10			13				7	6		11										11
1	2	3	4	5^2	8^1	9	14	10^3			12				7	6	13	11										12
1	2	3	4		14	9	10^2				13				8	7	6^3	12	11^3			5						13
1	2	3	4		8^1	9^1	13	10^2			14			12	6	7		11				5						14
1	2	3	4		8^3	9^1	12	10^1			14	13			7	6		11				5						15
1	2	3	4		12	9	6	10^1			8^2				7	13		11				5						16
1	2	3	4		8^1	9	13	10^2			12				7	6		11				5						17
1	2	3	4		8^3	13	9^1	10^2			14				7	6		11				5	12					18
	2		4	5	13	9	7^2	12			8				6		11	10^1	3		1							19
1	2			5	8	9	12	10^2			13			14	7	6^1	3	11^3	4									20
1	2		4	5	8	9^2		10^1			13				7	6	3	11	12									21
1	2		4	5	9	10^2	14								7	6	12	11	8^1	13								22
1		3		5	8	9^3	13	10^1			12				7	6	2	11^2	4			14						23
1		3	4	5	11	9^2		10			12	13			7	6	2^1	8^3				14						24
1	2	3	4	5	8	12	9^1	10^2		11^3	13				7	6								14				25
1	2	3	4	5	8^3	12	9^2	10^1		11	13				7	6								14				26
1	2		4	5	14	9^2		10			11^3				7	6	3	8^1	12					13				27
1	2		4	5	9^2		14	10^1			12				7	6	3	8^3	11					13				28
1	2		4	5	8	9^3	13	12							7	6	3	11^1	10^3					14				29
1	2		4	5	9^1	10	12				8				7	6	3	11										30
1	2		4	5	13	9^1		10^2			12				7	6	3	8^1	11					14				31
1	2		4	5	10	12	9^1	8^2			14				7	6	3	11^3		13								32
1	2		4	5	12	10^2	9	8^1							7	6	3	11						13				33
1	2		4	5	9	6	14	12			8^1				7^3	13	3	11						10^2				34
1	2	4^3		5	8^2	10^1	13	9							7	6	3	11		12				14				35
1	2			5^1	9^3	12	8	10^2							7	6	3	11				4	13	14				36
1	5	3^2	8	11	7^1	10	12								6		2	9	4					13				37
1	2	3	4	5	9^2		13	10			12				8	7	6^3	11^1						14				38

The Budweiser FA Cup

Third Round	QPR	(h)	4-0
Fourth Round	Stevenage	(a)	4-0
Fifth Round	Swansea C	(h)	3-1
Sixth Round	Arsenal	(a)	1-4

Capital One Cup

Second Round	Stevenage	(h)	2-1
	(aet)		
Third Round	Fulham	(a)	1-2

EXETER CITY

FOUNDATION

Exeter City was formed in 1904 by the amalgamation of St Sidwell's United and Exeter United. The club first played in the East Devon League and then the Plymouth & District League. After an exhibition match between West Bromwich Albion and Woolwich Arsenal, which was held to test interest as Exeter was then a rugby stronghold, it was decided to form Exeter City. At a meeting at the Red Lion Hotel in 1908, the club turned professional.

St James Park, Stadium Way, Exeter, Devon EX4 6PX.

Telephone: (01392) 411 243.

Fax: (01392) 413 959.

Ticket Office: (01392) 411 243.

Website: www.exetercityfc.co.uk

Email: reception@exetercityfc.co.uk

Training Ground: (01395) 232 784.

Ground Capacity: 8,830.

Record Attendance: 20,984 v Sunderland, FA Cup 6th rd (replay), 4 March 1931.

Pitch Measurements: 104m × 64m (113.5yd × 70yd)

Chairman: Edward Chorlton OBE.

Chief Executive: Guy Wolfenden.

Manager: Paul Tisdale.

Physio: Andrew Proctor.

Colours: Red and white striped shirts with red sleeves, black shorts, white socks with black trim.

Year Formed: 1904.

Turned Professional: 1908.

Club Nickname: 'The Grecians'.

Ground: 1904, St James Park.

First Football League Game: 28 August 1920, Division 3, v Brentford (h) W 3–0 – Pym; Coleburne, Feebury (1p); Crawshaw, Carrick, Mitton; Appleton, Makin, Wright (1), Vowles (1), Dockray.

Record League Victory: 8–1 v Coventry C, Division 3 (S), 4 December 1926 – Bailey; Pollard, Charlton; Pullen, Pool, Garrett; Purcell (2), McDevitt, Blackmore (2), Dent (2), Compton (2). 8–1 v Aldershot, Division 3 (S), 4 May 1935 – Chesters; Gray, Miller; Risdon, Webb, Angus; Jack Scott (1), Wrightson (1), Poulter (3), McArthur (1), Dryden (1), (1 og).

Record Cup Victory: 14–0 v Weymouth, FA Cup 1st qual rd, 3 October 1908 – Fletcher; Craig, Bulcock; Ambler, Chadwick, Wake; Parnell (1), Watson (1), McGuigan (4), Bell (6), Copestake (2).

HONOURS

Football League – Division 3:
Best season: 8th, 1979–80;
Division 3 (S): *Runners-up* 1932–33;
Division 4: *Champions* 1989–90;
Runners-up 1976–77;
FL 2: *Runners-up* 2008–09.

FA Cup: Best season: 6th rd replay, 1931, 6th rd 1981.

Football League Cup: never beyond 4th rd.

Division 3 (S) Cup: *Winners* 1934.

sky SPORTS FACT FILE

Exeter City toured South America in 1914. On 21 July they played against a combined representative team made up of players from Rio de Janeiro and Sao Paulo. City lost the match 2-0 but this is considered to have been the first time an all-Brazil selection had played together and thus marks the beginnings of the country's national side.

Record Defeat: 0–9 v Notts Co, Division 3 (S), 16 October 1948. 0–9 v Northampton T, Division 3 (S), 12 April 1958.

Most League Points (2 for a win): 62, Division 4, 1976–77.

Most League Points (3 for a win): 89, Division 4, 1989–90.

Most League Goals: 88, Division 3 (S), 1932–33.

Highest League Scorer in Season: Fred Whitlow, 33, Division 3 (S), 1932–33.

Most League Goals in Total Aggregate: Tony Kellow, 129, 1976–78, 1980–83, 1985–88.

Most League Goals in One Match: 4, Harold 'Jazzo' Kirk v Portsmouth, Division 3 (S), 3 March 1923; 4, Fred Dent v Bristol R, Division 3 (S), 5 November 1927; 4, Fred Whitlow v Watford, Division 3 (S), 29 October 1932.

Most Capped Player: Dermot Curtis, 1 (17), Eire.

Most League Appearances: Arnold Mitchell, 495, 1952–66.

Youngest League Player: Cliff Bastin, 16 years 31 days v Coventry C, 14 April 1928.

Record Transfer Fee Received: £500,000 from Manchester C for Martin Phillips, November 1995.

Record Transfer Fee Paid: £65,000 to Blackpool for Tony Kellow, March 1980.

Football League Record: 1920 Elected to Division 3; 1921–58 Division 3 (S); 1958–64 Division 4; 1964–66 Division 3; 1966–77 Division 4; 1977–84 Division 3; 1984–90 Division 4; 1990–92 Division 3; 1992–94 Division 2; 1994–2003 Division 3; 2003–08 Conference; 2008–09 FL 2; 2009–12 FL 1; 2012– FL 2.

LATEST SEQUENCES

Longest Sequence of League Wins: 7, 23.4.1977 – 20.8.1977.

Longest Sequence of League Defeats: 7, 14.1.1984 – 25.2.1984.

Longest Sequence of League Draws: 6, 13.9.1986 – 4.10.1986.

Longest Sequence of Unbeaten League Matches: 13, 23.8.1986 – 25.10.1986.

Longest Sequence Without a League Win: 18, 21.2.1995 – 19.8.1995.

Successive Scoring Runs: 22 from 15.9.1958.

Successive Non-scoring Runs: 6 from 17.1.1986.

MANAGERS

Arthur Chadwick 1910–22
Fred Mavin 1923–27
Dave Wilson 1928–29
Billy McDevitt 1929–35
Jack English 1935–39
George Roughton 1945–52
Norman Kirkman 1952–53
Norman Dodgin 1953–57
Bill Thompson 1957–58
Frank Broome 1958–60
Glen Wilson 1960–62
Cyril Spiers 1962–63
Jack Edwards 1963–65
Ellis Stuttard 1965–66
Jock Basford 1966–67
Frank Broome 1967–69
Johnny Newman 1969–76
Bobby Saxton 1977–79
Brian Godfrey 1979–83
Gerry Francis 1983–84
Jim Iley 1984–85
Colin Appleton 1985–87
Terry Cooper 1988–91
Alan Ball 1991–94
Terry Cooper 1994–95
Peter Fox 1995–2000
Noel Blake 2000–01
John Cornforth 2001–02
Neil McNab 2002–03
Gary Peters 2003
Eamonn Dolan 2003–04
Alex Inglethorpe 2004–06
Paul Tisdale June 2006–

TEN YEAR LEAGUE RECORD

		P	W	D	L	F	A	Pts	Pos
2004-05	Conf	42	20	11	11	71	50	71	6
2005-06	Conf	42	18	9	15	65	48	63	7
2006-07	Conf	46	22	12	12	67	48	78	5
2007-08	Conf P	46	22	17	7	83	58	83	4
2008-09	FL 2	46	22	13	11	65	50	79	2
2009-10	FL 1	46	11	18	17	48	60	51	18
2010-11	FL 1	46	20	10	16	66	73	70	8
2011-12	FL 1	46	10	12	24	46	75	42	23
2012-13	FL 2	46	18	10	18	63	62	64	10
2013-14	FL 2	46	14	13	19	54	57	55	16

DID YOU KNOW ?

Exeter was the subject of an air raid on the night of 4 May 1942 which left over 150 dead. Amongst the victims were Exeter City club chairman Lieut-Col Hunter and Albert Potter, who had made 89 appearances as a left half for the club in the 1920s and was on duty as an ARP warden during the raid.

EXETER CITY – FOOTBALL LEAGUE TWO 2013–14 LEAGUE RECORD

Match No.	Date	Venue	Opponents	Result	H/T Score	Lg Pos.	Goalscorers	Attendance
1	Aug 3	H	Bristol R	W	2-1	0-0	7	Coles [60], Parkin [80]	5196
2	10	A	Mansfield T	D	0-0	0-0	7		3284
3	17	H	AFC Wimbledon	W	2-0	2-0	4	O'Flynn 2 [11, 36]	3881
4	24	A	Morecambe	L	0-2	0-0	7		1539
5	31	H	York C	W	2-1	1-1	5	Gow 2 [23, 72]	3448
6	Sept 7	A	Dagenham & R	D	1-1	0-1	5	Parkin [80]	2003
7	14	A	Northampton T	W	2-1	1-1	4	Bennett [35], O'Flynn [90]	4036
8	21	H	Newport Co	L	0-2	0-1	9		4614
9	28	A	Fleetwood T	W	2-1	0-0	6	Bennett 2 [76, 79]	2557
10	Oct 5	H	Plymouth Arg	W	3-1	0-0	3	Davies [56], Gow [83], Bennett [90]	5700
11	12	H	Hartlepool U	L	0-3	0-1	6		3615
12	19	A	Scunthorpe U	W	4-0	1-0	3	Sercombe 2 [34, 50], Davies [49], Parkin [90]	3250
13	22	A	Oxford U	D	0-0	0-0	3		5083
14	26	H	Burton Alb	L	0-1	0-0	5		3658
15	Nov 2	A	Portsmouth	L	2-3	0-1	6	Coles [75], O'Flynn [84]	16,168
16	16	H	Southend U	L	0-2	0-2	10		3547
17	23	A	Rochdale	L	1-3	0-1	13	Gow [46]	2428
18	26	A	Wycombe W	D	1-1	0-1	12	Gow [81]	2357
19	30	H	Bury	D	2-2	1-1	11	Wheeler [41], Nichols [77]	3426
20	Dec 14	A	Accrington S	W	3-2	3-1	11	Nichols 2 [6, 11], Gow [24]	1219
21	20	H	Chesterfield	L	0-2	0-0	11		3449
22	26	A	Cheltenham T	L	0-1	0-1	12		3562
23	29	A	Torquay U	W	3-1	1-0	11	Nichols [38], Wheeler [60], Gow [85]	4231
24	Jan 4	H	Mansfield T	L	0-1	0-1	13		3303
25	11	A	Bristol R	L	1-2	1-1	13	Brown (og) [20]	6674
26	25	A	AFC Wimbledon	L	1-2	1-1	16	Midson (og) [4]	4410
27	28	H	Oxford U	D	0-0	0-0	15		2798
28	Feb 1	A	Burton Alb	D	1-1	0-0	16	Sharps (og) [56]	2227
29	8	H	Portsmouth	D	1-1	0-1	16	Sercombe [90]	5221
30	15	A	Southend U	W	3-2	1-2	13	Keohane [10], Sercombe [82], Richards [87]	5899
31	18	A	Morecambe	D	1-1	1-0	12	Nichols [2]	2620
32	22	H	Rochdale	L	0-1	0-1	14		3169
33	25	H	Wycombe W	L	0-1	0-1	16		2540
34	Mar 1	A	York C	L	1-2	1-2	18	Bennett [29]	3212
35	8	H	Dagenham & R	D	2-2	1-0	21	Nichols [34], Richards [90]	3057
36	11	H	Northampton T	L	0-1	0-0	22		2785
37	16	A	Newport Co	D	1-1	0-0	21	Worley (og) [51]	3159
38	22	H	Fleetwood T	W	3-0	1-0	17	Parkin (og) [25], Richards 2 [62, 65]	2978
39	25	A	Plymouth Arg	W	2-1	0-1	16	Sercombe [69], Richards [83]	13,442
40	29	H	Accrington S	L	0-1	0-1	19		3354
41	Apr 5	A	Bury	L	0-2	0-0	20		2718
42	12	H	Cheltenham T	D	1-1	1-1	20	Moore-Taylor [12]	3353
43	18	A	Chesterfield	D	1-1	1-0	20	Grimes [18]	7331
44	21	H	Torquay U	L	1-2	1-0	20	Bennett [17]	5221
45	26	H	Scunthorpe U	W	2-0	1-0	20	Woodman [48], Keohane [49]	4187
46	May 3	A	Hartlepool U	W	2-0	2-0	16	Keohane [25], Wheeler [44]	4710

Final League Position: 16

GOALSCORERS

League (54): Gow 7, Bennett 6, Nichols 6, Richards 5, Sercombe 5, O'Flynn 4, Keohane 3, Parkin 3, Wheeler 3, Coles 2, Davies 2, Grimes 1, Moore-Taylor 1, Woodman 1, own goals 5.
The Budweiser FA Cup (0).
Capital One Cup (0).
Johnstone's Paint Trophy (0).

Krysiak A 37	Woodman C 41	Bennett S 44+1	Moore-Taylor J 25+4	Coles D 37	Baldwin P 24+1	Wheeler D 20+15	Sercombe L 42+2	Perkin S 17+9	O'Flynn J 18+15	Davies A 27+5	Gow A 18+7	Dawson A 4+1	Doherty T 8+2	Reid J 1+5	Grimes M 23+12	Oakley M 22+2	Keohane J 12+8	Butterfield D 26+3	Gill M 19+5	Nichols T 19+9	Jay M 1+1	Gosling J —+3	Richards E 11+6	Pyn C 9	Tillson J 1	Watkins 0 —+1	Match No.
1	2	3	4	5	6	7	8	9	10^1	11	12																1
1	5	7^2	2^1	4	3	6	8	10	11^3	9		12	13	14													2
1	5		4	3	6^2	12^3	10	11^1	9	14		2	13		7	8											3
1	5	3		4		6^2		10^1	11		9	12		2	7^2	14		8	13								4
1	5	13	2^2		3	4	6^3	14	11	10^1	9	12			7	8											5
1	5	2		4	3	12	6	11		9	10				7^1	8											6
1	5	3		4	2	13	6	10	12	11	9^1				8	7^2											7
1	5	3	13	4	2	6^1	7		11		9^2	10^3		14	8	12											8
1	5	2	14	3^1	4	13	6		9	11				7^1	10^2		8		12								9
1	5	11		3	4	6^1	8		9	10				7^2	13	12^3	14	2									10
1	5	11	12	4	3	6^2	7	14	9	10^3				8			13	2^1									11
1	5	3		4	2		8	14	11	9^1	10^3			7^2	13		6^1		12								12
1	5	4		3	2	13	8	14	11^3	6	10			7^2			9^1		12								13
1	5	2		4	3	12	8	11^1	10^2	6	9			7^3	13			14									14
1	5	2	4^1	3		6	10	12	9	11^3				7^2	8				13	14							15
1	5	2		3	4	6	10	12	9^1					7		14	8^3	13	11^2								16
1	5	2		3	4^3	12	8	10^1	11	6	7^2				13	14	9										17
1	5	3		4		6^2	7	12	11^1	13	10				9	2	8										18
1	5	4		3^2		6^1	10	12	11^1	13	8				9	2	7	14									19
1	5	3	4		12	6	14		9	10^2				8^1	13	2	7	11^3									20
1	5	3	4^3	13	6^2	7	10^1		9	12				14	2	8	11										21
1		3^2	5		4	6	7	12		10				9^1	2	8	11		13								22
1		3	5		4	6	8	11^2	13	9^3				12		14	2	7^1	10								23
1		4	5^3		3	6^1	8	10^2	13	11				9	12	2		7		14							24
1		3	6	5^1	4	7^2	8	13	14	12	10			9	2	7	11										25
1		3	5	4		8^3		14	12	10^2	13			6^1	9	2	7	11									26
1	5	8		4	3^2	6			9	13				12	10	2	7^1	11									27
1	5	7		4	3	6		11	9					8	10	2											28
1	5	7^1	12	4	3^2	14	6		9					8	10^3	2	11		13								29
	5	3		4		13	8		11^3	10				7	6^2	9^1	2	14	12					1			30
	5	3		4		12	6		11^3	10				7	6^2	9^1	2	13	11^3				10	1			31
	5	4		3		14	6		11^3	9^2				8	7	10^1	2	13	12					1			32
	5	3	4			6^2	9	11^1	12					7	14	2	8	13	10^3					1			33
1	5	2	4			6	10	9^2					13	12	8	11^3	7^1	13	14								34
1	5	4	2	3		9^2	6	10					13	7	8			11	12								35
1	5	4	2	3		6^2	9	11^1					13	8	7			10	12								36
1	5	9	3	4		6		12						7		2	8	11^1	10								37
1	5	3	6	4		14	9	12	13						8^1	2	7	11^1	10^2								38
1	5	7	4	3		8		13						12	9	2	6^1	11^2	10								39
1	5	6	4	3		8	13	14						12	9^2	2	7^1	11^3	10								40
1	5	8	4	3^1		14	6	13				2^3		12	10		7^1	11^2	9								41
	5	10	4		3	12	9	6						8	7	2	11		6	1							42
	5	3	8	4		6		10^1						9	7	2	12	11	1								43
	5	8	4		3	13	6	12^3						14	7	2	9^2	11^1	10	1							44
	5	8	4	3		6		11^1						13	7	10	2	12	9^2	1							45
	5	10	3			6	9^1						2^3	7	11		8^2	12	14				1	4	13		46

The Budweiser FA Cup
First Round — Peterborough U — (a) 0-2

Capital One Cup
First Round — QPR — (h) 0-2

Johnstone's Paint Trophy
First Round — Wycombe W — (h) 0-2

FLEETWOOD TOWN

FOUNDATION

Originally formed in 1908 as Fleetwood FC, it was liquidated in 1976. Re-formed as Fleetwood Town in 1977, it folded again in 1996. Once again, it was re-formed a year later as Fleetwood Wanderers, but a sponsorship deal saw the club's name immediately changed to Fleetwood Freeport through the local retail outlet centre. This sponsorship ended in 2002, but since then local energy businessman Andy Pilley took charge and the club has risen through the non-league pyramid until finally achieving Football League status in 2012 as Fleetwood Town.

Highbury Stadium, Park Avenue, Fleetwood, Lancashire FY7 6TX.

Telephone: (01253) 775 080.

Ticket Office: (01253) 775 080

Website: www.fleetwoodtownfc.com

Email: info@fleetwoodtownfc.com

Ground Capacity: 5,311.

Record attendance: (Before 1997) 6,150 v Rochdale, FA Cup 1st rd, 13 November 1965; (Since 1997) 5,092 v Blackpool, FA Cup 3rd rd, 7 January 2012.

Pitch Measurements: 102m × 65m (111.5yd × 71yd)

Chairman: Andy Pilley.

Chief Executive: Steve Curwood.

Secretary: Steve Edwards.

Manager: Graham Alexander.

Assistant Manager: Chris Lucketti.

Physio: Luke Bussey.

Colours: Red shirts with white chest and sleeves, white shorts, red socks.

Year Formed: 1908 (re-formed 1997).

Club Nicknames: 'The Trawlermen', 'The Cod Army'.

Grounds: 1908, North Euston Hotel; 1934, Memorial Park (now Highbury Stadium).

First Football League Game: 18 August 2012, FL 2, v Torquay U (h) D 0–0 – Davies; Beeley, Mawene, McNulty, Howell, Nicolson, Johnson, McGuire, Ball, Parkin, Mangan.

Record League Victory: 13–0 v Oldham T, North West Counties Div 2, 5 December 1998.

MANAGER

Micky Mellon 2008–12
Graham Alexander December 2012–

sky SPORTS FACT FILE

Fleetwood Town enjoyed a meteoric rise to Football League status, gaining promotion just four seasons after progressing to the Conference North in 2007–08. In 2008–09 they won promotion to the Conference Premier and after missing out at the play-off stage in 2010–11 won automatic promotion as champions the following season.

Record Defeat: 0–7 v Billingham T, FA Cup 1st qual rd, 15 September 2001.

Most League Points (3 for a win): 76, FL 2, 2013–14

Most League Goals: 66, FL 2, 2013–14.

Most League Goals in Total Aggregate: Jon Parkin, 17, 2012–14.

Most League Goals in One Match: 3, Steven Schumacher v Newport Co, FL 2, 2 November 2013.

Most League Appearances: Scott Davies, 73, 2012–14.

Youngest League Player: Jamie Allen, 17 years 227 days v Northampton T, 5 January 2013.

Record Transfer Fee Received: £1,000,000 from Leicester C for Jamie Vardy, May 2012.

Record Transfer Fee Paid: £300,000 to Kidderminster H for Jamille Matt, January 2013.

Football League Record: 2012 Promoted from Conference Premier; 2012–14 FL 2; 2014–FL 1.

LATEST SEQUENCES

Longest Sequence of League Wins: 4, 1.1.2014 – 27.1.2014.

Longest Sequence of League Defeats: 4, 6.4.2013 – 27.4.2013.

Longest Sequence of League Draws: 3, 27.10.2012 – 10.11.2012.

Longest Sequence of Unbeaten League Matches: 7, 25.3.2014 – 26.4.2014.

Longest Sequence Without a League Win: 6, 30.3.2013 – 27.4.2013.

Successive Scoring Runs: 7 from 5.4.2014 to 12.5.2014.

Successive Non-scoring Runs: 4 from 22.2.2014.

HONOURS

1908 Foundation

Lancashire Combination: Champions 1923–24. *Runners-Up:* 1933–34, 1934–35.

Northern Premier League Challenge Cup: *Winners:* 1971.

Lancashire Combination Cup: *Winners:* 1926, 1932, 1933, 1934. *Runners-up:* 1953, 1967.

1976 Foundation

Northern Premier League First Division: *Champions:* 1987–88.

North West Counties Football League First Division: *Champions:* 1983–84.

Northern Premier League Presiden's Cup: *Winners:* 1990.

FA Vase: *Runners-cup:* 1984–85.

Northern Premier League Challenge Cup: *Runners-up:* 1989.

1997 Foundation

FL 2: 4th (promoted via play-offs), 2013–14.

FA Cup: 3rd rd 2011–12.

Conference: *Champions:* 2011–12.

Conference North: *Runners-up and Play-off winners:* 2009–10.

Northern Premier League Premier Division: *Champions:* 2007–08.

Northern Premier League First Division: *Runners-up* (promoted): 2005–06.

North West Counties Football League Premier Division: *Champions:* 2004–05.

North West Counties Football League First Divison: *Champions:* 1998–99.

Peter Swales Memorial Shield: *Winners:* 2008.

Northern Premier League Challenge Cup: *Winners:* 2007.

North West Counties Football League First Division Trophy: *Winners:* 1999.

Lancashire League West Division Reserve League: *Winners:* 2008–09.

TEN YEAR LEAGUE RECORD

		P	W	D	L	F	A	Pts	Pos
2004-05	NWC 1	42	31	6	5	107	42	99	1
2005-06	Uni 1	42	22	10	10	72	48	76	2
2006-07	Uni Pr	42	19	10	13	71	60	67	8
2007-08	Uni Pr	40	28	7	5	81	39	91	1
2008-09	Conf N	42	17	11	14	70	66	62	8
2009-10	Conf N	42	26	7	7	86	44	85	2
2010-11	Conf P	46	22	12	12	68	42	78	5
2011-12	Conf P	46	31	10	5	102	48	103	1
2012-13	FL 2	46	15	15	16	55	57	60	13
2013-14	FL 2	46	22	10	14	66	52	76	4

DID YOU KNOW ?

Fleetwood Town received a record transfer fee for a non-league club when Leicester City paid a reported £1 million for striker Jamie Vardy in the summer of 2012. Vardy had led the scoring for the Cod Army in 2011–12 with 31 Conference goals from 34 starts and 2 appearances from the bench.

FLEETWOOD TOWN – FOOTBALL LEAGUE TWO 2013–14 LEAGUE RECORD

Match No.	Date	Venue	Opponents	Result		H/T Score	Lg Pos.	Goalscorers	Attendance
1	Aug 3	H	Dagenham & R	W	3-1	2-1	4	Roberts [6], Hughes, J [10], Cresswell [57]	2511
2	10	A	Plymouth Arg	W	2-0	2-0	2	Ball 2 [10, 12]	7280
3	17	H	Burton Alb	L	2-3	0-3	6	Hughes, J [65], Matt [72]	2611
4	24	A	Hartlepool U	W	1-0	1-0	3	Hughes, J [16]	3297
5	31	A	AFC Wimbledon	L	0-2	0-2	6		3744
6	Sept 7	H	Torquay U	W	4-1	2-0	4	Sarcevic 2 [10, 37], Matt [62], Blair [90]	2426
7	14	H	Bury	W	2-1	0-1	3	Sarcevic [52], Evans [64]	3520
8	21	A	Portsmouth	W	1-0	0-0	2	Bradley (og) [67]	15,809
9	28	H	Exeter C	L	1-2	0-0	4	Blair [71]	2557
10	Oct 5	A	Bristol R	W	3-1	0-0	2	Matt 2 [64, 87], Parkin [90]	5303
11	12	H	Chesterfield	D	1-1	0-0	2	Parkin [89]	4521
12	18	A	Southend U	L	0-2	0-1	2		4996
13	22	H	Scunthorpe U	L	0-1	0-0	5		2492
14	26	A	York C	W	2-0	1-0	3	Evans [24], Matt [66]	3523
15	Nov 2	H	Newport Co	W	4-1	1-0	1	Schumacher 3 (2 pens) [4 (p), 48, 59 (p)], Ball [78]	2354
16	16	A	Northampton T	L	0-1	0-0	4		4076
17	23	H	Mansfield T	W	5-4	2-2	4	Evans 2 [1, 66], Sarcevic 3 (2 pens) [35 (p), 64, 90 (p)]	2831
18	26	A	Accrington S	L	0-2	0-0	5		1699
19	30	H	Oxford U	D	1-1	1-0	7	Schumacher [12]	2739
20	Dec 14	A	Rochdale	W	2-1	1-1	3	Sarcevic (pen) [23], Roberts [83]	2698
21	21	H	Cheltenham T	L	0-2	0-1	4		2300
22	26	A	Morecambe	L	0-1	0-1	8		3008
23	Jan 1	H	Accrington S	W	3-1	1-0	7	Parkin [6], Ball [58], Carr [90]	2446
24	11	A	Dagenham & R	W	1-0	0-0	6	Ball [74]	1679
25	18	H	Hartlepool U	W	2-0	0-0	6	Parkin [67], Marrow [69]	3009
26	25	H	Burton Alb	W	4-2	1-0	3	Ball [19], Pond [51], Parkin [78], Brown [90]	2396
27	27	A	Scunthorpe U	D	0-0	0-0	3		3005
28	Feb 1	H	York C	L	1-2	0-1	4	Mandron [72]	2513
29	11	A	Wycombe W	D	1-1	0-0	6	Parkin [76]	2185
30	15	H	Northampton T	W	2-0	1-0	5	Evans 2 [22, 79]	2521
31	22	A	Mansfield T	L	0-1	0-1	5		2759
32	25	H	Plymouth Arg	L	0-4	0-1	6		2131
33	Mar 1	H	AFC Wimbledon	D	0-0	0-0	6		2420
34	4	A	Newport Co	D	0-0	0-0	6		3728
35	8	A	Torquay U	W	1-0	0-0	5	Matt [74]	2245
36	11	A	Bury	D	2-2	1-0	5	Sarcevic [41], Matt [56]	2467
37	15	H	Portsmouth	W	3-1	2-0	4	Parkin [16], Sarcevic (pen) [26], Matt [56]	3509
38	22	A	Exeter C	L	0-3	0-1	4		2978
39	25	H	Bristol R	W	3-1	2-0	4	Sarcevic [21], Roberts [40], Ball [51]	2023
40	29	H	Rochdale	D	0-0	0-0	4		4261
41	Apr 5	A	Oxford U	W	2-0	1-0	4	Ball [34], Sarcevic [52]	5679
42	12	H	Morecambe	D	2-2	1-1	4	Sarcevic [10], Hume [85]	3114
43	18	A	Cheltenham T	W	2-1	0-1	4	Sarcevic (pen) [55], Morris [65]	2890
44	21	H	Wycombe W	W	1-0	0-0	4	Morris [59]	2711
45	26	H	Southend U	D	1-1	1-1	4	Schumacher [37]	3323
46	May 3	A	Chesterfield	L	1-2	1-0	4	Blair [13]	9037

Final League Position: 4

GOALSCORERS

League (66): Sarcevic 13 (5 pens), Ball 8, Matt 8, Parkin 7, Evans 6, Schumacher 5 (2 pens), Blair 3, Hughes, J 3, Roberts 3, Morris 2, Brown 1, Carr 1, Cresswell 1, Hume 1, Mandron 1, Marrow 1, Pond 1, own goal 1.
The Budweiser FA Cup (3): Ball 1, Hughes, J 1, Parkin 1.
Capital One Cup (2): Ball 1, Evans 1.
Johnstone's Paint Trophy (12): Ball 3, Matt 2, Parkin 2, Blair 1, Hughes, J 1, McLaughlin 1, Pond 1, Sarcevic 1.
League Two Play-Offs (2): Blair 1, Sarcevic 1.

Davies S 28	Hogan L 14+2	Jordan S 10	Schumacher S 31+1	Roberts M 33	Cresswell R 18+2	Brown J 11+10	Hughes J 25	Ball D 24+6	Sarcevic A 39+3	Crowther R 5+2	Murdoch S 25+13	Evans G 22+12	Matt J 14+11	Howell D 6+2	McLaughlin C 32+3	Pond N 40+1	Parkin J 14+17	Blair M 13+11	Taylor C 31+1	Dieseruuwe E —+4	Tyson N 4	Carr D 1+3	Goodall A 18+1	Mandron M 4+7	Marrow A 6+1	Maxwell C 18	Hughes M 1+4	Allen J —+1	Morris J 11+3	Grant R 1	Hume 17+1	Match No.
1	2	3	4^1	5	6	7^2	8	9^3	10	11	12	13	14																			1
1	2	5	7^2	4	3	6^1	8	11	10	9^3	13			12	14																	2
1	2	5	7^1	3	4^3	9	8	10	6	11^2		12	13		14																	3
1	2	5		3		6^1	8	11^2	10	12	7	9^3	13	14		4																4
1	2	5	14	3		6^2	8	9				7^3	11^1	10		4	12	13														5
1		6		4	9	7	13	8^2		12	11^3	10^1	5	2	3		14															6
1	13		9^1	4	10	7	14	8		12	6	11^3	5	2^2	3																	7
1	13		8^3	3	6	7	12	10		14	9^2	11^1	5	2	4																	8
1		9		3	6	7	11^3	8			10^2	13	4	14	12																	9
1	2	8^2		3	12	9		7		6	13	11^3	5		4	14	10^1															10
1	2			4	10	7	12	8^3	6^2	9^1		11	5		3	13	14															11
1	2		3	7^1	9	11	8	10^2	6^3		13		4	12	14	5																12
1	2^3		3	13	7	14	8	9^2	6		12		4	11	10^1	5																13
1	2^1	7^2	4	13	6	8^3	9	10	11		12	3			14	5																14
1	2^1	7	4	6	11^3	8	9	10	12	5			3	13																		15
1		7	4	14	9	11^1	10	8^2	6^3		2	3	12	13	5																	16
1		9	4	6	8	7	10^2		2	3	14	13	5	12	11^1																	17
1		7^3	4	10	9	6^1	8		2^2	3	14	13	5	12	11																	18
1		6	3	13	10	9	7	8^2		2	4		5	12	11^1																	19
1		8	3	12	7	10	14	6^3		2	4		9^2	5	11^1	13																20
1		4	3	8	10		7^1	9		2		12	6	5	11																	21
1		3	4	8	11	10	14	7^3	6^1	2		12	9^2	5	13																	22
1		8^1	2	12	6	11^2	7^3	13			5	3	10	9		14	4															23
1		7^2	2	6	11	8	13			5	3	10^1	9			4	12															24
1		6^2	3	8^1	11	7	14			5	2	10^3	9			4	13	12														25
1		6^1	2	13	10^2	12	7			5	3	11^3	9			4	14	8														26
1		9^2	3	12	11	13	7			2	4	14	5			6	10^2	8^1														27
1		6^2	2	13	11	7	8^1			5	4	10	9			3	12															28
		6^2	3			14	8^1	12	13		2	4	10		5		7^1	11^3	9	1												29
		6^1	3	14		9	12	8	10^2		2	4	11^3		5		13	7	1													30
	2	5	4^2		6		9^3				3	10	13			7^1	11	8	1	12	14											31
	7^1	4^3		8	12	10	11			2	3	13	5			9^2	1	6		14												32
	3		6	8		14	2	4	10^3	5		7	9^2	1	13	12	11^1															33
	8	4	11	6	7	10	5	3	9		2	1																				34
	8	3	7	9^3	10^1	11	2	4	12	5		6^2		1	14	13																35
	8	3	9	12	10	2	4	11^2	5^1	6	13	1	7																				36
	7^1	4	9^3	6	11	2	3	10^2	14	5	12	13	1	8																		37
	7	4^2	14	8	9^1	11	2	3	10^3	13	5	1	6	12																		38
	4	10^1	7	12	14	13	2	3	6^3	5	8	1	9	11^2																		39
	4	11^1	8^1	13	14	2	3	12	6^2	5	7	1	9	10																			40
	3	10^2	9	12	2	4	13	7	6	5	8^1	1	11	11^1																		41
	3^2	10	7	12	2	4	13	6	5	8^1	1	9	11																				42
	5	4	13	11^1	9^2	14	2	3	12	7	6	1	8	10^1																		43
	5	3	10^2	8^3	14	13	12	2	4	6	7^1	1	9	11^1																		44
2	5	8^2	4	10	7	13	3	12	6^1	1	9	11																				45
2	4	7	3	9	6	11	8	5	1	12	10^1																					46

The Budweiser FA Cup

First Round	Gloucester C		(a)	2-0
Second Round	Burton		(h)	1-1
Replay	Burton		(a)	0-1

League Two Play-Offs

Semi-Finals 1st leg	York C		(a)	1-0
Semi-Finals 2nd leg	York C		(h)	0-0
Final	Burton Alb	(Wembley)		1-0

Capital One Cup

First Round	Notts Co		(a)	2-3

Johnstone's Paint Trophy

First Round	Tranmere R		(a)	2-1
Second Round	Crewe Alex		(h)	4-0
Northern Quarter-Finals	Carlisle U		(h)	2-0
Northern Semi-Finals	Rotherham U		(h)	2-1
Northern Final 1st leg	Chesterfield		(h)	1-3
Northern Final 2nd leg	Chesterfield		(a)	1-0

FULHAM

Craven Cottage, Stevenage Road, London SW6 6HH.

Telephone: (0843) 208 1222.

Fax: (0870) 442 0236 (Motspur Park).

Ticket Line: (0843) 208 1234.

Website: www.fulhamfc.co.uk

Email: enquiries@fulhamfc.com

Ground Capacity: 25,700.

Record Attendance: 49,335 v Millwall, Division 2, 8 October 1938.

Pitch Measurements: 100m × 65m (109yd × 71yd)

Chairman: Shadid Khan.

Chief Executive: Alistair Mackintosh.

Manager: Felix Magath.

First Team Coaches: Tomas Oral, Peter Grant.

Director of Sports Medicine and Exercise Science: Mark Taylor.

Colours: White shirts with black trim, black shorts with red trim, white socks with red trim.

Year Formed: 1879.

Turned Professional: 1898.

Reformed: 1987.

Previous Name: 1879, Fulham St Andrew's; 1888, Fulham.

Club Nickname: 'The Cottagers'.

Grounds: 1879, Star Road, Fulham; c.1883, Eel Brook Common, 1884, Lillie Road; 1885, Putney Lower Common; 1886, Ranelagh House, Fulham; 1888, Barn Elms, Castelnau; 1889, Purser's Cross (Roskell's Field), Parsons Green Lane; 1891, Eel Brook Common; 1891, Half Moon, Putney; 1895, Captain James Field, West Brompton; 1896, Craven Cottage.

First Football League Game: 3 September 1907, Division 2, v Hull C (h) L 0–1 – Skene; Ross, Lindsay; Collins, Morrison, Goldie; Dalrymple, Freeman, Bevan, Hubbard, Threlfall.

Record League Victory: 10–1 v Ipswich T, Division 1, 26 December 1963 – Macedo; Cohen, Langley; Mullery (1), Keetch, Robson (1); Key, Cook (1), Leggat (4), Haynes, Howfield (3).

Record Cup Victory: 7–0 v Swansea C, FA Cup 1st rd, 11 November 1995 – Lange; Jupp (1), Herrera, Barkus (Brooker (1)), Moore, Angus, Thomas (1), Morgan, Brazil (Hamill), Conroy (3) (Bolt), Cusack (1).

Record Defeat: 0–10 v Liverpool, League Cup 2nd rd 1st leg, 23 September 1986.

HONOURS

Football League –
Division 1: *Champions* 2000–01;
Division 2: *Champions* 1948–49,
1998–99; *Runners-up* 1958–59;
Division 3 (S): *Champions* 1931–32;
Division 3: *Runners-up* 1970–71,
1996–97.
FA Cup: *Runners-up* 1975.
Football League Cup: Best season:
5th rd, 1968, 1971, 2000, 2005.
European Competitions
UEFA Cup: 2002–03.
Intertoto Cup: 2002 (*winners*).
Europa League: 2009–10 (*runners-up*),
2011–12.

sky SPORTS FACT FILE

Andy Ducat, a centre half who played for Fulham in the early 1920s, was capped by England at both football and cricket. He made six appearances for the national football team and earned his only cricket cap against Australia in 1921. Andy went on to manage the Cottagers between 1924 and 1926.

Most League Points (2 for a win): 60, Division 2, 1958–59 and Division 3, 1970–71.

Most League Points (3 for a win): 101, Division 2, 1998–99. 101, Division 1, 2000–01.

Most League Goals: 111, Division 3 (S), 1931–32.

Highest League Scorer in Season: Frank Newton, 43, Division 3 (S), 1931–32.

Most League Goals in Total Aggregate: Gordon Davies, 159, 1978–84, 1986–91.

Most League Goals in One Match: 5, Fred Harrison v Stockport Co, Division 2, 5 September 1908; 5, Bedford Jezzard v Hull C, Division 2, 8 October 1955; 5, Jimmy Hill v Doncaster R, Division 2, 15 March 1958; 5, Steve Earle v Halifax T, Division 3, 16 September 1969.

Most Capped Player: Johnny Haynes, 56, England.

Most League Appearances: Johnny Haynes, 594, 1952–70.

Youngest League Player: Matthew Briggs, 16 years 65 days v Middlesbrough, 13 May 2007.

Record Transfer Fee Received: £15,000,000 from Tottenham H for Moussa Dembele, August 2012.

Record Transfer Fee Paid: £12,400,00 to Olympiacos for Konstantinos Mitroglou, January 2014.

Football League Record: 1907 Elected to Division 2; 1928–32 Division 3 (S); 1932–49 Division 2; 1949–52 Division 1; 1952–59 Division 2; 1959–68 Division 1; 1968–69 Division 2; 1969–71 Division 3; 1971–80 Division 2; 1980–82 Division 3; 1982–86 Division 2; 1986–92 Division 3; 1992–94 Division 2; 1994–97 Division 3; 1997–99 Division 2; 1999–2001 Division 1; 2001–14 FA Premier League; 2014– FL C.

LATEST SEQUENCES

Longest Sequence of League Wins: 12, 7.5.2000 – 18.10.2000.

Longest Sequence of League Defeats: 11, 2.12.1961 – 24.2.1962.

Longest Sequence of League Draws: 6, 23.12.2006 – 20.1.2007.

Longest Sequence of Unbeaten League Matches: 15, 26.1.1999 – 13.4.1999.

Longest Sequence Without a League Win: 15, 25.2.1950 – 23.8.1950.

Successive Scoring Runs: 26 from 28.3.1931.

Successive Non-scoring Runs: 6 from 21.8.1971.

MANAGERS

Harry Bradshaw 1904–09
Phil Kelso 1909–24
Andy Ducat 1924–26
Joe Bradshaw 1926–29
Ned Liddell 1929–31
Jim McIntyre 1931–34
Jimmy Hogan 1934–35
Jack Peart 1935–48
Frank Osborne 1948–64
 (was Secretary-Manager or General Manager for most of this period and Team Manager 1953–56)
Bill Dodgin Snr 1949–53
Duggie Livingstone 1956–58
Bedford Jezzard 1958–64
 (General Manager for last two months)
Vic Buckingham 1965–68
Bobby Robson 1968
Bill Dodgin Jnr 1968–72
Alec Stock 1972–76
Bobby Campbell 1976–80
Malcolm Macdonald 1980–84
Ray Harford 1984–96
Ray Lewington 1986–90
Alan Dicks 1990–91
Don Mackay 1991–94
Ian Branfoot 1994–96
 (continued as General Manager)
Micky Adams 1996–97
Ray Wilkins 1997–98
Kevin Keegan 1998–99
 (Chief Operating Officer)
Paul Bracewell 1999–2000
Jean Tigana 2000–03
Chris Coleman 2003–07
Lawrie Sanchez 2007
Roy Hodgson 2007–10
Mark Hughes 2010–11
Martin Jol 2011–13
Rene Muelensteen 2013–14
Felix Magath February 2014–

TEN YEAR LEAGUE RECORD

		P	W	D	L	F	A	Pts	Pos
2004-05	PR Lge	38	12	8	18	52	60	44	13
2005-06	PR Lge	38	14	6	18	48	58	48	12
2006-07	PR Lge	38	8	15	15	38	60	39	16
2007-08	PR Lge	38	8	12	18	38	60	36	17
2008-09	PR Lge	38	14	11	13	39	34	53	7
2009-10	PR Lge	38	12	10	16	39	46	46	12
2010-11	PR Lge	38	11	16	11	49	43	49	8
2011-12	PR Lge	38	14	10	14	48	51	52	9
2012-13	PR Lge	38	11	10	17	50	60	43	12
2013-14	PR Lge	38	9	5	24	40	85	32	19

DID YOU KNOW

In October 1908 Fulham played the Denmark team just four days after their opponents had lost to Great Britain in the final of the Olympic Games. Denmark included 10 players who had appeared in the final but the Cottagers triumphed 6-3 in front of an attendance of 3,000.

FULHAM – FA PREMIERSHIP 2013–14 LEAGUE RECORD

Match No.	Date	Venue	Opponents	Result		H/T Score	Lg Pos.	Goalscorers	Attendance
1	Aug 17	A	Sunderland	W	1-0	0-0	4	Kasami [52]	43,905
2	24	H	Arsenal	L	1-3	0-2	11	Bent [77]	25,622
3	31	A	Newcastle U	L	0-1	0-0	16		46,402
4	Sept 14	H	WBA	D	1-1	1-0	13	Sidwell [22]	25,560
5	21	A	Chelsea	L	0-2	0-0	18		41,608
6	28	H	Cardiff C	L	1-2	1-1	18	Ruiz [45]	23,020
7	Oct 5	H	Stoke C	W	1-0	0-0	17	Bent [83]	24,634
8	21	A	Crystal Palace	W	4-1	2-1	13	Kasami [19], Sidwell [45], Berbatov [50], Senderos [55]	24,881
9	26	A	Southampton	L	0-2	0-2	13		28,631
10	Nov 2	H	Manchester U	L	1-3	0-3	15	Kacaniklic [65]	25,700
11	9	A	Liverpool	L	0-4	0-3	17		44,768
12	23	H	Swansea C	L	1-2	0-0	18	Parker [64]	25,258
13	30	A	West Ham U	L	0-3	0-0	18		34,946
14	Dec 4	H	Tottenham H	L	1-2	0-0	18	Dejagah [56]	24,128
15	8	H	Aston Villa	W	2-0	2-0	18	Sidwell [21], Berbatov (pen) [30]	22,288
16	14	A	Everton	L	1-4	0-1	19	Berbatov (pen) [67]	33,796
17	21	H	Manchester C	L	2-4	0-2	19	Kompany (og) [68], Richardson [50]	25,509
18	26	A	Norwich C	W	2-1	1-1	18	Kasami [33], Parker [87]	26,811
19	28	A	Hull C	L	0-6	0-0	18		23,925
20	Jan 1	H	West Ham U	W	2-1	1-1	16	Sidwell [32], Berbatov [66]	25,335
21	11	H	Sunderland	L	1-4	0-2	16	Sidwell [52]	25,564
22	18	A	Arsenal	L	0-2	0-0	17		60,000
23	28	A	Swansea C	L	0-2	0-0	17		20,004
24	Feb 1	H	Southampton	L	0-3	0-0	20		25,700
25	9	A	Manchester U	D	2-2	1-0	20	Sidwell [19], Bent [90]	74,966
26	12	H	Liverpool	L	2-3	1-1	20	Toure (og) [8], Richardson [63]	25,375
27	22	A	WBA	D	1-1	1-0	20	Dejagah [28]	25,782
28	Mar 1	H	Chelsea	L	1-3	0-0	20	Heitinga [74]	24,577
29	8	A	Cardiff C	L	1-3	0-1	20	Holtby [59]	26,796
30	15	A	Newcastle U	W	1-0	0-0	20	Dejagah [68]	25,664
31	22	A	Manchester C	L	0-5	0-1	20		47,262
32	30	H	Everton	L	1-3	0-0	20	Dejagah [71]	25,454
33	Apr 5	A	Aston Villa	W	2-1	0-0	18	Richardson [61], Rodallega [86]	33,532
34	12	H	Norwich C	W	1-0	1-0	18	Rodallega [40]	25,028
35	19	A	Tottenham H	L	1-3	1-1	19	Sidwell [37]	35,841
36	26	H	Hull C	D	2-2	0-0	18	Dejagah [55], Amorebieta [58]	25,700
37	May 3	A	Stoke C	L	1-4	0-1	19	Richardson [80]	27,429
38	11	H	Crystal Palace	D	2-2	0-1	19	Woodrow [61], David [90]	24,447

Final League Position: 19

GOALSCORERS

League (40): Sidwell 7, Dejagah 5, Berbatov 4 (2 pens), Richardson 4, Bent 3, Kasami 3, Parker 2, Rodallega 2, Amorebieta 1, David 1, Heitinga 1, Holtby 1, Kacaniklic 1, Ruiz 1, Senderos 1, Woodrow 1, own goals 2.
The Budweiser FA Cup (5): Bent 2, Dejagah 1, Rodallega 1, Sidwell 1.
Capital One Cup (7): Rodallega 3, Bent 1, Berbatov 1, Karagounis 1, Taarabt 1.

Stekelenburg M 19	Riether S 30+1	Hughes A 11+2	Hangeland B 23	Richardson K 28+3	Duff D 9+6	Boateng D 2+1	Sidwell S 36+2	Taarabt A 7+5	Kasami P 20+9	Berbatov D 18	Briggs M —+2	Karagounis G 6+8	Stockdale D 19+2	Riise J 17+3	Parker S 27+2	Bent D 11+13	Kacaniklic A 15+8	Ruiz B 8+4	Rodallega H 6+7	Senderos P 12	Amorebieta F 20+3	Na Bangna B —+1	Dejagah A 13+9	Zverotic E 5+1	Dembele M 1+1	Dempsey C 4+1	Burn D 6+3	Tankovic M 1+2	Kvist Jorgensen W 7+1	Holtby L 11+2	Heitinga J 14	Tunnicliffe R 2+1	Cole L —+1	Mitroglou K 1+2	Woodrow C 5+1	Roberts P —+2	David C —+1	Diarra M 4	Match No.
1^3	2	3	4	5^2	6	7^1	8	9	10	11	12	13	14																										1
	2	3	4		6^1		8^2	9^3	10	11		14		1	5	7	12	13																					2
	2^2	3	4			7^1	13		10	12				1	5	8	11^3	9	6	14																			3
	2		4	5^3	14		8		10	11^2		1			7			9	6^1	13	3	12																4
	2	3	5	6^3		8	12	10^1		1		7	11	9^2		14		4	13																			5
	2		3	5			8	14	6	10		12^1	1		7^3	11^2		9^1	13		4																	6
	2		4^3	12	9	13	7		6	11^2		8^1	1			14		10			3	5																7
1	2		4^3	5	13		7		9	10^1				8	11^2			6	14	3	12																	8
1	2^1	12		5			7		9	10				8	11^2	14	6^3	13	3	4																		9
1	2			5			8	13	9	11				7^3	14	12	10^2		3	4	6^1																	10
1		13		5			7			10		11^3		14		8			9^2	12	3	4	6	2^1														11
1		3		5		7^1	12	14	8	9						6^3	11	13	10^2			4		2														12
1		3		5^3	9^2		7^1	10	6			13				8	11		12			4		2	14													13
1	2	4			13		12		10	11		7^3		5	8^1		9^2	14		3			6															14
1	2	4			13		6		12	10		8^2		5	7		11^1			3			9															15
1	2	4			14		6		12	10		8^2		5	7	13	11^1			3			9^3															16
1	2	4		11			8	10	13			7^1		5	6	14				3^3	12		9^2															17
	2	3		5	8^3		7	11^1	9					1	14	6			10^2		12		4	13														18
		3		14			7		9			6^3		1	5		13	12	8^2	11		4	10^1	2														19
	2			10^2	8^1		7	9^3	14	11				1	5	6	13	12			3	4																20
	2				8^3		7	9^1	12	11				1	5	6	14			3	4		13			10^2												21
1	2	3	5				7		13	11				6	12	10^1							8^2				9	4										22
1	2	3	5	13			7			11^1				6	12	10							8^3				9^2	4	14									23
1	2	3	5	11^1			8		13					6^2	10												12	4	14	7^3	9								24
1	2			9			8					5	13	12													4	11^1	7^2	10	3	6^3	14						25
1^3	2			9^1			8			13	5		11	12													4		7	10	3	6							26
1	2	4	10^3		7							12	6					11^1		5^2	8			14					9	3			13					27
1	2	4^2	5		8		9^3		14			7^1	11								6			10	12		13	3					13					28
1	2	4	5		7				13			9^1	14	12							6^3							8	3			10	11^2					29
13		3	5		7		10^2			1				9							12^3		14		8	6^2	2					11						30
7		3	11^1		8		14			1		5		9^2						$4^\bullet$						6	12	2					10^3	13				31
2		4	9^3		8		6			1		5								13		11^2				7^1	10	3					12	14				32
7		3	5		8		10^2			1	14			13			4			12						6	2^3						11^1		9			33
2		4	9		7		6^1			1	13			11			5			12						14	10^3	3							8^2			34
		3			9				12	1		5^2	7^2	6			11			4		10	13				8	2^1										35
5		3	12		8^2				1			9^3	6	14			11			4		13					10^1	2							7			36
		4	10		9		14			1		5	8	11						12						2^3		7^2	3		13			6^1			37
		4	9^2		8				1			7	6^1	11			5			13^2	2^3							3	14			10	12					38

The Budweiser FA Cup

Third Round	Norwich C	(a)	1-1
Replay	Norwich C	(h)	3-0
Fourth Round	Sheffield U	(a)	1-1
Replay	Sheffield U	(h)	0-1
(aet)			

Capital One Cup

Second Round	Burton	(a)	2-2
(aet, won 5-4 on penalties)			
Third Round	Everton	(h)	2-1
Fourth Round	Leicester C	(a)	3-4

GILLINGHAM

FOUNDATION

The success of the pioneering Royal Engineers of Chatham excited the interest of the residents of the Medway Towns and led to the formation of many clubs including Excelsior. After winning the Kent Junior Cup and the Chatham District League in 1893, Excelsior decided to go for bigger things and it was at a meeting in the Napier Arms, Brompton, in 1893 that New Brompton FC came into being, buying and developing the ground which is now Priestfield Stadium. They changed their name to Gillingham in 1913, when they also changed their strip from black and white stripes to predominantly blue.

MEMS Priestfield Stadium, Redfern Avenue, Gillingham, Kent ME7 4DD.

Telephone: (01634) 300 000.

Fax: (01634) 850 986.

Ticket Office: (01634) 300 000 (option 1).

Website: www.gillinghamfootballclub.com

Email: info@priestfield.com

Ground Capacity: 11,440.

Record Attendance: 23,002 v QPR, FA Cup 3rd rd, 10 January 1948.

Pitch Measurements: 100.5m × 64m (110yd × 70yd)

Chairman: Paul D. P. Scally.

Vice-chairman: Michael Anderson.

Manager: Peter Taylor.

Assistant Manager: Andy Hessenthaler.

Physio: Gary Hemens.

Colours: Blue shirts with thin white stripes, blue shorts, white socks with blue trim.

Year Formed: 1893.

Turned Professional: 1894.

Previous Name: 1893, New Brompton; 1913, Gillingham.

Club Nickname: 'The Gills'.

Ground: 1893, Priestfield Stadium.

First Football League Game: 28 August 1920, Division 3, v Southampton (h) D 1–1 – Branfield; Robertson, Sissons; Battiste, Baxter, Wigmore; Holt, Hall, Gilbey (1), Roe, Gore.

Record League Victory: 10–0 v Chesterfield, Division 3, 5 September 1987 – Kite; Haylock, Pearce, Shipley (2) (Lillis), West, Greenall (1), Pritchard (2), Shearer (2), Lovell, Elsey (2), David Smith (1).

Record Cup Victory: 10–1 v Gorleston, FA Cup 1st rd, 16 November 1957 – Brodie; Parry, Hannaway; Riggs, Boswell, Laing; Payne, Fletcher (2), Saunders (5), Morgan (1), Clark (2).

HONOURS

Football League –
Division 1: 11th, 2002–03;
Division 3: *Runners-up* 1995–96;
Division 4: *Champions* 1963–64;
Runners-up 1973–74;
FL 2: *Champions* 2012–13.
FA Cup: Best season: 6th rd, 2000.
Football League Cup: Best season: 4th rd, 1964, 1997.

sky SPORTS FACT FILE

In 1919–20 the Gills finished bottom of the Southern League First Division but escaped relegation and instead joined the entire division in forming the Third Division of the Football League for 1920–21. The Gills fared no better in the new competition, again finishing bottom of the table with just 28 points.

Record Defeat: 2–9 v Nottingham F, Division 3 (S), 18 November 1950.

Most League Points (2 for a win): 62, Division 4, 1973–74.

Most League Points (3 for a win): 85, Division 2, 1999–2000.

Most League Goals: 90, Division 4, 1973–74.

Highest League Scorer in Season: Ernie Morgan, 31, Division 3 (S), 1954–55; Brian Yeo, 31, Division 4, 1973–74.

Most League Goals in Total Aggregate: Brian Yeo, 135, 1963–75.

Most League Goals in One Match: 6, Fred Cheesmur v Merthyr T, Division 3 (S), 26 April 1930.

Most Capped Player: Andrew Crofts, 12 (27), Wales.

Most League Appearances: John Simpson, 571, 1957–72.

Youngest League Player: Luke Freeman, 15 years 247 days v Hartlepool U, 24 November 2007.

Record Transfer Fee Received: £1,500,000 from Manchester C for Robert Taylor, November 1999.

Record Transfer Fee Paid: £600,000 to Reading for Carl Asaba, August 1998.

Football League Record: 1920 Original Member of Division 3; 1921 Division 3 (S); 1938 Failed re-election; Southern League 1938–44; Kent League 1944–46; Southern League 1946–50; 1950 Re-elected to Division 3 (S); 1958–64 Division 4; 1964–71 Division 3; 1971–74 Division 4; 1974–89 Division 3; 1989–92 Division 4; 1992–96; Division 3; 1996–2000 Division 2; 2000–04 Division 1; 2004–05 FL C; 2005–08 FL 1; 2008–09 FL 2; 2009–10 FL 1; 2010–13 FL 2; 2013– FL 1.

LATEST SEQUENCES

Longest Sequence of League Wins: 7, 18.12.1954 – 29.1.1955.

Longest Sequence of League Defeats: 10, 20.9.1988 – 5.11.1988.

Longest Sequence of League Draws: 5, 28.8.1993 – 18.9.1993.

Longest Sequence of Unbeaten League Matches: 20, 13.10.1973 – 10.2.1974.

Longest Sequence Without a League Win: 15, 1.4.1972 – 2.9.1972.

Successive Scoring Runs: 20 from 31.10.1959.

Successive Non-scoring Runs: 6 from 11.2.1961.

MANAGERS

W. Ironside Groombridge 1896–1906 *(Secretary-Manager)* *(previously Financial Secretary)*
Steve Smith 1906–08
W. I. Groombridge 1908–19 *(Secretary-Manager)*
George Collins 1919–20
John McMillan 1920–23
Harry Curtis 1923–26
Albert Hoskins 1926–29
Dick Hendrie 1929–31
Fred Mavin 1932–37
Alan Ure 1937–38
Bill Harvey 1938–39
Archie Clark 1939–58
Harry Barratt 1958–62
Freddie Cox 1962–65
Basil Hayward 1966–71
Andy Nelson 1971–74
Len Ashurst 1974–75
Gerry Summers 1975–81
Keith Peacock 1981–87
Paul Taylor 1988
Keith Burkinshaw 1988–89
Damien Richardson 1989–92
Glenn Roeder 1992–93
Mike Flanagan 1993–95
Neil Smillie 1995
Tony Pulis 1995–99
Peter Taylor 1999–2000
Andy Hessenthaler 2000–04
Stan Ternent 2004–05
Neale Cooper 2005
Ronnie Jepson 2005–07
Mark Stimson 2007–10
Andy Hessenthaler 2010–12
Martin Allen 2012–13
Peter Taylor November 2013–

TEN YEAR LEAGUE RECORD

		P	W	D	L	F	A	Pts	Pos
2004-05	FL C	46	12	14	20	45	66	50	22
2005-06	FL 1	46	16	12	18	50	64	60	14
2006-07	FL 1	46	17	8	21	56	77	59	16
2007-08	FL 1	46	11	13	22	44	73	46	22
2008-09	FL 2	46	21	12	13	58	55	75	5
2009-10	FL 1	46	12	14	20	48	64	50	21
2010-11	FL 2	46	17	17	12	67	57	68	8
2011-12	FL 2	46	20	10	16	79	62	70	8
2012-13	FL 2	46	23	14	9	66	39	83	1
2013-14	FL 1	46	15	8	23	60	79	53	17

DID YOU KNOW ?

Gillingham were one of the last Football League clubs to install floodlights. The Gills switched on the lights at their Priestfield Stadium in September 1963 when an attendance of 14,979 turned up to see them defeat Bury 3-0 in a Football League Cup second round tie. The lighting system cost £14,000.

GILLINGHAM – FOOTBALL LEAGUE ONE 2013–14 LEAGUE RECORD

Match No.	Date	Venue	Opponents	Result		H/T Score	Lg Pos.	Goalscorers	Attendance
1	Aug 3	H	Colchester U	L	0-1	0-0	20		6792
2	10	A	Wolverhampton W	L	0-4	0-3	22		19,102
3	17	H	Brentford	D	1-1	1-0	21	Akinfenwa [40]	6225
4	24	A	Swindon T	D	2-2	1-1	20	Kedwell [18], McDonald [85]	7520
5	31	H	Bristol C	D	1-1	1-1	21	Akinfenwa [22]	5616
6	Sept 7	A	Crawley T	L	2-3	0-0	21	Kedwell (pen) [47], Legge [69]	3984
7	15	A	Coventry C	L	1-2	1-1	23	McDonald [10]	2046
8	21	H	Bradford C	L	0-1	0-1	24		4965
9	28	H	Crewe Alex	W	3-0	1-0	17	McDonald [39], Martin [50], Barrett [70]	4254
10	Oct 5	H	Milton Keynes D	W	3-2	2-2	16	Kedwell 2 (2 pens) [11, 13], Hollands [59]	5410
11	12	A	Shrewsbury T	L	0-2	0-1	16		5129
12	19	H	Preston NE	L	1-2	0-0	19	Kedwell [76]	7054
13	22	H	Notts Co	W	2-1	2-0	17	Whelpdale [24], Kedwell [29]	5161
14	26	A	Port Vale	L	1-2	1-0	19	Kedwell [13]	5690
15	Nov 2	H	Carlisle U	W	1-0	0-0	17	Kedwell (pen) [63]	5697
16	16	A	Sheffield U	W	2-1	1-1	14	Kedwell [7], McDonald [47]	16,560
17	23	H	Oldham Ath	L	0-1	0-0	16		6025
18	26	H	Stevenage	W	3-2	0-1	17	Kedwell (pen) [47], Daniels [52], Mousinho [76]	4951
19	30	A	Rotherham U	L	1-4	0-3	17	McDonald [66]	7152
20	Dec 7	A	Notts Co	L	1-3	0-1	17	Dack [47]	3607
21	14	H	Peterborough U	D	2-2	0-1	17	Martin [51], McDonald [70]	6949
22	20	A	Tranmere R	W	2-1	1-0	13	Akinfenwa 2 [45, 69]	6251
23	26	H	Leyton Orient	L	1-2	1-0	15	Akinfenwa [4]	8613
24	29	H	Walsall	D	2-2	0-0	16	McDonald 2 [46, 90]	5394
25	Jan 3	H	Wolverhampton W	W	1-0	0-0	14	McDonald [90]	7758
26	11	A	Colchester U	L	0-3	0-0	15		3819
27	18	H	Swindon T	W	2-0	1-0	14	Legge [18], Harriman [83]	6134
28	24	A	Brentford	L	1-2	0-1	14	McDonald [73]	7713
29	Feb 1	H	Port Vale	W	3-2	1-0	11	Akinfenwa 2 [42, 61], McDonald [64]	6356
30	4	A	Stevenage	L	1-3	0-2	12	McDonald [56]	2399
31	8	A	Carlisle U	W	2-1	1-0	11	Pigott [44], McDonald [88]	3584
32	19	H	Sheffield U	L	0-1	0-1	12		5766
33	22	A	Oldham Ath	L	0-1	0-1	12		3714
34	Mar 1	A	Bristol C	L	1-2	0-1	15	Lee [65]	11,422
35	8	H	Crawley T	W	1-0	0-0	14	Lee [88]	5961
36	11	H	Coventry C	W	4-2	1-0	13	Akinfenwa 2 (2 pens) [25, 75], Weston [56], Hessenthaler [90]	5447
37	15	A	Bradford C	D	1-1	0-1	13	McDonald [56]	13,089
38	22	A	Crewe Alex	L	1-3	1-1	14	Linganzi [30]	5767
39	25	A	Milton Keynes D	W	1-0	0-0	12	Fagan [50]	6760
40	Apr 5	H	Rotherham U	L	3-4	1-1	14	Akinfenwa [30], Weston [57], Dack [84]	6027
41	8	A	Peterborough U	L	0-2	0-1	14		6543
42	12	A	Leyton Orient	L	1-5	0-4	16	Fagan [82]	5128
43	18	H	Tranmere R	W	2-0	0-0	15	Dack [78], McDonald [90]	7343
44	21	A	Walsall	D	1-1	0-0	15	McDonald [84]	3890
45	26	A	Preston NE	L	1-3	1-1	16	McDonald [45]	11,591
46	May 3	H	Shrewsbury T	D	1-1	0-0	17	Barrett [72]	7634

Final League Position: 17

GOALSCORERS

League (60): McDonald 17, Akinfenwa 10 (2 pens), Kedwell 10 (5 pens), Dack 3, Barrett 2, Fagan 2, Lee 2, Legge 2, Martin 2, Weston 2, Daniels 1, Harriman 1, Hessenthaler 1, Hollands 1, Linganzi 1, Mousinho 1, Pigott 1, Whelpdale 1.
The Budweiser FA Cup (1): Dack 1.
Capital One Cup (0).
Johnstone's Paint Trophy (1): Dack 1.

Nelson S 46	Fish M 1+1	Martin J 46	Linganzi A 16+4	Legge L 36+1	Barrett A 45	Whelpdale C 21+3	Gregory S 35+4	McDonald C 35+9	Kedwell D 23+4	Lee C 22+9	Butcher S —+1	Weston M 23+16	Akinfenwa A 17+17	Harriman M 33+1	Dack B 15+13	German A —+9	Allen C 2+3	Hollands D 16+1	McKain D —+1	Muggleton S —+1	Davies C 4+3	Hewitt E 20	Fagan C 12+6	Mousinho J 4	Daniels D 3	Hessenthaler J 18+1	Smith C 6+4	Marriott J —+1	Pigott J 4+3	Inniss R 3	Birchall A —+2	Millbank A —+1	Match No.
1	2^1	3	4	5	6	7	8	9^2	10	11^2	12	13	14																				1
1		5	8	3	4	13	7^2	10^1	11^3	6		9		2	12	14																	2
1		5		3	4	8	7	12	11	9		6^2	10^1	2		13																	3
1		5		4	3	7^2	8	13	11	6		9^3	10^1	2	12	14	13																4
1		5		3	4	6	7	12	11	8^2		9^1	10^3	2		14	13																5
1		5	13	3^2	4	9	7		10	2^4		12	11^3		6			8^1	14														6
1		5	7	3	4		12	11^3	10			9	13	2^2			6	8^1	14														7
1		5	7	3	4	13		11	12	9^2		6^1	10^3	2		14		8															8
1		5			4	6^2	7	11^2	10	9		12		2	14		13	8^1			3												9
1		5			4	6	8	11^2	10	9		12		2				7			3												10
1		5		3	9^3	8^1	11	10^2	2			12	14			13	6	7			4												11
1		5		3	4	7	6	11^3	10	9^2		12	14	2		13		8^1															12
1		5	12	3	4	6	8^1		10	9		11		2				7															13
1		5	8^1	4	3	6		13	10^2	9^3		11		2	14	12		7															14
1		5	8^3	3^4	4	6	14	13	10	9^2		11^1		2	12			7															15
1		5		3	4	10	7^2	13	11^3			14		12				8					2	6^1	9								16
1		5		3	4^3	9^2		11	10			13		2	14			7^1					6	12	8								17
1		5			4			12	10			11		2				8					6	9^1	7	3							18
1		5		3	6^2		11	10^2	9			12	13	2				7								8^1	4	14					19
1		5			4		13	11	7			10	12	2	6			8^1							3	9^2							20
1		5		3	4	9^2	12	11	10			13		2	6			8^1	14						7^1								21
1		5		4	3		8	11		13		9^2	10^1	2	6	12									7								22
1		5		3	4		8	11^2	14	9		10^3		2	6^1	13								12	7								23
1		5		3	4	6^2	7	10	11	14		12	2								13		9^3		8^1								24
1		5		3	4		7	10	9	8^2		13	2	12									11^1		6								25
1		5		3	4		7	10	11			14	12	2	9^3								6^2		8^1	13							26
1		5		3	4		8	11		9^1		10^2	6	12									2	13	7								27
1		5	7^1	3	4		8	10		9^2		13	6	12									2	11^3			14						28
1		5	8^1	3	4		7	11		10^2		6	9	2									13		12								29
1	2		4			6	11		10^1	12		7			3	5^4	13					9^2	8										30
1		5	9	4	3		6	11			13	2	7									12		8^2	10^1								31
1		5	8^2	12	4	13	7	11		14		10	2	6									9^3			3^1							32
1		5		3	4	9^2	7	14		12		13											2	10	8^1	6	11^1						33
1		5	7^3	4	3		6	11		12		13	10		8^2								2		9^1	14							34
1		5		3	4		8	10^2	13			9	12										2	6^1	7		11^3		14				35
1		5	12	3	4		8	11		6^1		9	10^3									14	2	13	7^2								36
1		5	8	4	3			10		13		9	12										2	6	7^2		11^1						37
1		5	8^2	3	4		7^1	11		13		9	10	6^3	12								2				14						38
1		5	7	3	4		8	10		9			6										2	11									39
1		5	13		4		8^2	11	12			9	10^3	2	7	14							6							3			40
1		5	9^3		3		7	11	12			8	13	2	10^1								6			14		4^2					41
1		5	7		3		14	10	4			11^2		2^3									6	9	8^1	13			12				42
1		5		3	4		8	11	13	2^2		9	10^1		12								6		7								43
1		5		3	4	10^3	8	11		14		13	12		9^2								2	6^1	7								44
1		5		3	4	10^2	9	11		8^3		12	13		14								2		7^1	6							45
1	12	5		3^1	4	9	8	11^2	13			10^1	2	6									7									14	46

HARTLEPOOL UNITED

FOUNDATION

The inspiration for the launching of Hartlepool United was the West Hartlepool club which won the FA Amateur Cup in 1904–05. They had been in existence since 1881 and their cup success led in 1908 to the formation of the new professional concern which first joined the North-Eastern League. In those days they were Hartlepools United and won the Durham Senior Cup in their first two seasons.

Victoria Park, Clarence Road, Hartlepool TS24 8BZ.

Telephone: (01429) 272 584.

Fax: (01429) 863 007.

Ticket Office: (01429) 272 584 (option 2).

Website: www.hartlepoolunited.co.uk

Email: enquires@hartlepoolunited.co.uk

Ground Capacity: 7,856.

Record Attendance: 17,426 v Manchester U, FA Cup 3rd rd, 5 January 1957.

Pitch Measurements: 100m × 67m (109.5yd × 73.5yd)

Chairman: Ken Hodcroft.

Chief Executive: Russ Green.

Manager: Colin Cooper.

Assistant Manager: Stephen Pears.

Physio: Ian Gallagher.

Colours: Blue and white striped shirts, blue shorts, white socks with blue trim.

Year Formed: 1908.

Turned Professional: 1908.

Previous Names: 1908, Hartlepools United; 1968, Hartlepool; 1977, Hartlepool United.

Club Nickname: 'The Pool', 'Monkey Hangers'.

Ground: 1908, Victoria Park.

First Football League Game: 27 August 1921, Division 3 (N), v Wrexham (a) W 2–0 – Gill; Thomas, Crilly; Dougherty, Hopkins, Short; Kessler, Mulholland (1), Lister (1), Robertson, Donald.

Record League Victory: 10–1 v Barrow, Division 4, 4 April 1959 – Oakley; Cameron, Waugh; Johnson, Moore, Anderson; Scott (1), Langland (1), Smith (3), Clark (2), Luke (2), (1 og).

Record Cup Victory: 6–0 v North Shields, FA Cup 1st rd, 30 November 1946 – Heywood; Brown, Gregory; Spelman, Lambert, Jones; Price, Scott (2), Sloan (4), Moses, McMahon, 6–0 v Gainsborough Trinity (a), FA Cup 1st rd, 10 November 2007 – Budtz; McCunnie, Humphreys, Liddle (1) (Antwi), Nelson, Clark, Moore (1), Sweeney, Barker (2) (Monkhouse), Mackay (Porter 1), Brown (1).

Record Defeat: 1–10 v Wrexham, Division 4, 3 March 1962.

HONOURS

Football League –
FL 2: *Runners-up* 2006–07;
Division 3: *Runners-up* 2002–03;
Division 3 (N): *Runners-up* 1956–57.

FA Cup: Best season: 4th rd, 1955, 1978, 1989, 1993, 2005, 2009.

Football League Cup: Best season: 4th rd, 1975.

sky SPORTS FACT FILE

Hartlepools United as they were then known, signed their first African-born player back in March 1924. Inside forward Tewfik Abdallah joined Pools from Bridgend Town and scored on his debut against Wrexham. He went on to make 11 appearances for the club before leaving at the end of the season.

Most League Points (2 for a win): 60, Division 4, 1967–68.

Most League Points (3 for a win): 88, FL 2, 2006–07.

Most League Goals: 90, Division 3 (N), 1956–57.

Highest League Scorer in Season: William Robinson, 28, Division 3 (N), 1927–28; Joe Allon, 28, Division 4, 1990–91.

Most League Goals in Total Aggregate: Ken Johnson, 98, 1949–64.

Most League Goals in One Match: 5, Harry Simmons v Wigan Borough, Division 3 (N), 1 January 1931; 5, Bobby Folland v Oldham Ath, Division 3 (N), 15 April 1961.

Most Capped Player: Ambrose Fogarty, 1 (11), Republic of Ireland.

Most League Appearances: Richie Humphreys, 481, 2001–13.

Youngest League Player: David Foley, 16 years 105 days v Port Vale, 25 August 2003.

Record Transfer Fee Received: £750,000 from Ipswich T for Tommy Miller, July 2001.

Record Transfer Fee Paid: £80,000 to Mansfield T for Darrell Clarke, July 2001.

Football League Record: 1921 Original Member of Division 3 (N); 1958–68 Division 4; 1968–69 Division 3; 1969–91 Division 4; 1991–92 Division 3; 1992–94 Division 2; 1994–2003 Division 3; 2003–04 Division 2; 2004–06 FL 1; 2006–07 FL 2; 2007–13 FL 1; 2013– FL 2.

LATEST SEQUENCES

Longest Sequence of League Wins: 9, 18.11.2006 – 1.1.2007.

Longest Sequence of League Defeats: 8, 27.1.1993 – 27.2.1993.

Longest Sequence of League Draws: 6, 30.4.2011 – 20.8.2011.

Longest Sequence of Unbeaten League Matches: 23, 18.11.2006 – 30.3.2007.

Longest Sequence Without a League Win: 20, 8.9.2012 – 26.12.2012.

Successive Scoring Runs: 27 from 18.11.2006.

Successive Non-scoring Runs: 11 from 9.1.1993.

MANAGERS

Alfred Priest 1908–12
Percy Humphreys 1912–13
Jack Manners 1913–20
Cecil Potter 1920–22
David Gordon 1922–24
Jack Manners 1924–27
Bill Norman 1927–31
Jack Carr 1932–35
　(had been Player-Coach from 1931)
Jimmy Hamilton 1935–43
Fred Westgarth 1943–57
Ray Middleton 1957–59
Bill Robinson 1959–62
Allenby Chilton 1962–63
Bob Gurney 1963–64
Alvan Williams 1964–65
Geoff Twentyman 1965
Brian Clough 1965–67
Angus McLean 1967–70
John Simpson 1970–71
Len Ashurst 1971–74
Ken Hale 1974–76
Billy Horner 1976–83
Johnny Duncan 1983
Mike Docherty 1983
Billy Horner 1984–86
John Bird 1986–88
Bobby Moncur 1988–89
Cyril Knowles 1989–91
Alan Murray 1991–93
Viv Busby 1993
John MacPhail 1993–94
David McCreery 1994–95
Keith Houchen 1995–96
Mick Tait 1996–99
Chris Turner 1999–2002
Mike Newell 2002–03
Neale Cooper 2003–05
Martin Scott 2005–06
Danny Wilson 2006–08
Chris Turner 2008–10
Mick Wadsworth 2010–11
Neale Cooper 2011–12
John Hughes 2012–13
Colin Cooper May 2013–

TEN YEAR LEAGUE RECORD

		P	W	D	L	F	A	Pts	Pos
2004-05	FL 1	46	21	8	17	76	66	71	6
2005-06	FL 1	46	11	17	18	44	59	50	21
2006-07	FL 2	46	26	10	10	65	40	88	2
2007-08	FL 1	46	15	9	22	63	66	54	15
2008-09	FL 1	46	13	11	22	66	79	50	19
2009-10	FL 1	46	14	11	21	59	67	50*	20
2010-11	FL 1	46	15	12	19	47	65	57	16
2011-12	FL 1	46	14	14	18	50	55	56	13
2012-13	FL 1	46	9	14	23	39	67	41	23
2013-14	FL 2	46	14	11	21	50	56	53	19

*3 pts deducted.

DID YOU KNOW ?

Hartlepools United played their first-ever game on 2 September 1908 when they defeated Newcastle United reserves 6-0. Three days later they played their first competitive fixture, winning 2-0 away to Hebburn Argyle in a North Eastern League fixture.

HARTLEPOOL UNITED – FOOTBALL LEAGUE TWO 2013–14 LEAGUE RECORD

Match No.	Date	Venue	Opponents	Result	H/T Score	Lg Pos.	Goalscorers	Attendance
1	Aug 3	A	Rochdale	L	0-3	0-1	24		3177
2	10	H	Southend U	L	0-1	0-1	24		3479
3	17	A	York C	D	0-0	0-0	23		4768
4	24	H	Fleetwood T	L	0-1	0-1	23		3297
5	31	A	Torquay U	D	0-0	0-0	23		2646
6	Sept 7	H	Wycombe W	L	1-2	0-0	23	Poole 90	3640
7	14	H	Accrington S	W	2-1	2-0	21	Franks 30, Monkhouse 42	3388
8	21	A	Bristol R	D	2-2	2-1	20	James 2 36, 45	5579
9	28	A	Oxford U	L	1-3	0-1	22	James 48	3799
10	Oct 5	A	Mansfield T	W	4-1	2-0	19	Monkhouse 8, Compton 2 44, 50, Poole 79	3457
11	12	A	Exeter C	W	3-0	1-0	16	Baldwin 21, James 50, Compton 62	3615
12	19	H	Plymouth Arg	W	1-0	0-0	16	James 55	3929
13	22	H	AFC Wimbledon	W	3-1	1-0	14	Walton (pen) 32, James 72, Dolan 83	3652
14	26	A	Scunthorpe U	L	0-1	0-0	14		3613
15	Nov 2	H	Dagenham & R	W	2-1	1-0	13	Poole 12, Monkhouse 79	3450
16	15	A	Newport Co	L	0-2	0-1	13		3094
17	23	H	Northampton T	W	2-0	1-0	12	James 23, Walton (pen) 49	3617
18	26	A	Bury	L	0-1	0-0	13		1998
19	30	H	Portsmouth	D	0-0	0-0	13		4126
20	Dec 14	A	Cheltenham T	D	2-2	0-2	14	Franks 2 54, 71	2491
21	21	H	Burton Alb	D	1-1	0-1	14	Walker 69	3595
22	26	A	Chesterfield	D	1-1	0-1	14	Dolan (pen) 48	7680
23	29	A	Morecambe	W	2-1	1-0	13	Baldwin 18, Franks 90	2081
24	Jan 1	H	Bury	L	0-3	0-2	14		3529
25	11	H	Rochdale	L	0-3	0-0	16		3685
26	18	A	Fleetwood T	L	0-2	0-0	16		3009
27	25	H	York C	W	2-0	0-0	14	James 82, Barmby 89	4673
28	28	A	AFC Wimbledon	L	1-2	1-0	14	James 44	3730
29	Feb 1	H	Scunthorpe U	D	0-0	0-0	15		3727
30	8	A	Dagenham & R	W	2-0	0-0	11	Williams 69, Monkhouse 89	3357
31	15	H	Newport Co	W	3-0	1-0	8	James 41, Sandell (og) 55, Williams 90	3470
32	18	A	Southend U	D	1-1	0-1	9	Walker 59	4361
33	22	A	Northampton T	L	0-2	0-1	9		4083
34	Mar 1	H	Torquay U	W	3-0	1-0	9	Barmby 31, James 54, Harewood 64	3437
35	8	A	Wycombe W	L	1-2	1-0	10	Barmby 42	3073
36	11	A	Accrington S	D	0-0	0-0	10		1196
37	15	H	Bristol R	W	4-0	2-0	10	Harewood 2, Walker 16, Walton (pen) 56, Franks 90	3480
38	21	A	Oxford U	L	0-1	0-0	10		4954
39	25	H	Mansfield T	L	2-4	1-1	11	Harewood 28, James 53	2976
40	29	H	Cheltenham T	L	0-1	0-0	13		3328
41	Apr 5	A	Portsmouth	L	0-1	0-1	15		15,273
42	12	H	Chesterfield	L	1-2	1-1	18	James 24	3778
43	19	A	Burton Alb	L	0-3	0-1	19		2558
44	21	H	Morecambe	W	2-1	0-1	17	Compton 67, Barmby 81	4864
45	26	A	Plymouth Arg	D	1-1	0-1	18	Barmby 67	6617
46	May 3	H	Exeter C	L	0-2	0-2	19		4710

Final League Position: 19

GOALSCORERS

League (50): James 13, Barmby 5, Franks 5, Compton 4, Monkhouse 4, Harewood 3, Poole 3, Walker 3, Walton 3 (3 pens), Baldwin 2, Dolan 2 (1 pen), Williams 2, own goal 1.
The Budweiser FA Cup (5): Baldwin 2, James 2, Monkhouse 1.
Capital One Cup (1): Austin 1.
Johnstone's Paint Trophy (7): Compton 1 (1 pen), Burgess 1, Franks 1, James 1, Monkhouse 1, Poole 1, Rodney 1.

Flinders S 43	Austin N 29	Hartley P 1	Walker B 31 + 5	Collins S 20 + 4	Burgess C 41	Baldwin J 28	Sweeney A 3 + 16	Monkhouse A 34 + 2	Franks J 22 + 17	Compton J 25 + 9	James L 38 + 4	Howard S 3 + 5	Poole J 21 + 12	Holden D 23 + 3	Walton S 37 + 2	Rodney N 1 + 11	Duckworth M 30	Dolan M 20	Richards J 11 + 8	Harewood M 16 + 3	Williams L 7	Barmby J 12 + 5	Hawkins L — + 5	Jones D — + 1	Rutherford G — + 1	Rafferty A 3	Harrison S 5 + 1	Oliver C 2 + 1	Smith C — + 1	Match No.
1	2	3	4¹	5	6	7	8³	9²	10	11	12	13	14																	1
1	2		6	4	3		9¹	7³	10	11²		13			8	5		12	14											2
1	2		7	4	3	6		9	12	11²	10¹				5	8		13												3
1	5		6	4	3		12	9²	14	11	10¹	7³	13		2	8														4
1	5		6	4	3		13	11	9²	12	10¹				8			2	7											5
1	5		7¹	4	3		10	6²	9³	11	14	13			12			2	8											6
1	5		12	4	3		11³	6	9	10¹	13				7	14		2	8²											7
1	5		12	4	3		10²	6¹	9	11		13			8			2	7											8
1	5²			4	3	14	11	6¹	9	10	13¹	12			7³			2	8											9
1	5			4	3	8		10¹	12	9²	11		6		7			2		13										10
1	5			4	3	14	9	12	6²	10¹	11³				7			2	8	13										11
1	5		13	4	3		9	14	6⁴	11³	10¹				7			2²	8	12										12
1	5			4	3	13	11	6¹		10	9²				7			2	8	12										13
1	3	12		5	4	14	9	6		11²		10¹			8³	13		2	7											14
1	5			4	3	12	9	6²		11³		10¹	13	7				2	8	14										15
1	2	14		4	3	13	6	12	9²	11¹	10			8³	5	7														16
1	5	13		4	3	12	9			6	10³	11¹		7	14			2	8²											17
1	5	13		3	4			9³	6¹	11		10		7	14			2	8²	12										18
1	5			4	3	13	9	12	6¹	11		10²		7				2	8											19
1	6			3	4	9²	11	10	12			13	8¹	5				2	7											20
1	5	13		4	3		9	12	6	11		10¹		7²				2	8											21
1	5	7		4	3		9⁴	10²	6¹	11		12		13	2	8														22
1	2	7		3	4			9		11		10	12	6¹	5	8														23
1	5²	7		4	3	12	9³	6		11		10¹	13		14	2	8													24
1	5	7		4	3			10¹		8	12							2												25
1	5	7	12	4	3³	14	9	13	6²	11¹				8					2⁴	10										26
1	2	7		4	3		8²	12		10				5	6				11¹	9	13									27
1	2	7		4	3		8			10				5	6				11¹	9	12									28
1	2¹	3	4	6		12		9⁴	14	10				5	7				13	8	11³									29
1	7	3	4		8		12		11					5	6			2	10¹	9										30
1	8	3	4		7	13		11²						5	6			2	10¹	9	12									31
1	6	3	4		8¹		12		11					5	7			2	10	9										32
1	7	4	3			13	14	11						5	6	2¹		12	10⁹	9	8²									33
1	6¹	3	4		13	9	14	11						5	7			2	10³	8⁶	12									34
1	7	3	4		13	9	12	10						5	8³	14		2	11¹	6²										35
1	6	3	4		13	10	8¹	11³		12				5	7			2	14	9²										36
1	7³	3	4		8¹	13	12	11						5	6			2	10²	9	14									37
1	8	3	4		12	13	7	11		14				5	6⁸			2	10	9²										38
1	6	4	3		13			8¹	9	12				5³			7	2	11²	10	14									39
1	7²	3	4			10³	8	11		12				5	6			2		9¹	13	14								40
	7	4	3³			13	9¹	11	10					5	8			2	6¹	12					1	14				41
	7³	3				13	8¹	11	12	5	6			2			10	9¹						1	4	14				42
	7	3				10	8²	14	11¹	9³	5	6			2			12	13					1	4					43
1	7	3				8²	11	12		9¹	5	6⁴			2			10	13						4					44
1	8	3				9¹	6²	12		13	5				2	14	11	10³							4	7				45
1	8	3				11²	6			9	2				5			10		12					4	7¹	13			46

The Budweiser FA Cup

First Round	Notts Co	(h)	3-2
Second Round	Coventry C	(h)	1-1
Replay	Coventry C	(a)	1-2

Capital One Cup

First Round	Nottingham F	(a)	1-3

Johnstone's Paint Trophy

First Round	Bradford C	(h)	5-0
Second Round	Sheffield U	(a)	1-0
Northern Quarter-Finals	Rotherham U	(h)	1-2

HUDDERSFIELD TOWN

FOUNDATION

A meeting, attended largely by members of the Huddersfield & District FA, was held at the Imperial Hotel in 1906 to discuss the feasibility of establishing a football club in this rugby stronghold. However, it was not until a man with both the enthusiasm and the money to back the scheme came on the scene that real progress was made. This benefactor was Mr Hilton Crowther and it was at a meeting at the Albert Hotel in 1908 that the club formally came into existence with an investment of £2,000 and joined the North-Eastern League.

John Smith's Stadium, Stadium Way, Leeds Road, Huddersfield, West Yorkshire HD1 6PX.

Telephone: (01484) 484 112.

Fax: (01484) 484 101.

Ticket Office: (01484) 484 123.

Website: www.htafc.com

Email: info@htafc.com

Ground Capacity: 24,554.

Record Attendance: 67,037 v Arsenal, FA Cup 6th rd, 27 February 1932 (at Leeds Road); 23,678 v Liverpool, FA Cup 3rd rd, 12 December 1999 (at Alfred McAlpine Stadium).

Pitch Measurements: 105m × 67.5m (115yd × 74yd)

Chairman: Dean Hoyle.

Chief Executive: Nigel Clibbens.

Manager: Mark Robins.

Assistant Manager: Steve Thompson.

Physio: James Haycock.

Colours: Blue and white striped shirts, white shorts with blue trim, black socks with white trim.

Year Formed: 1908.

Turned Professional: 1908.

Club Nickname: 'The Terriers'.

Grounds: 1908, Leeds Road; 1994, The Alfred McAlpine Stadium (renamed the Galpharm Stadium 2004, John Smith's Stadium in 2012).

First Football League Game: 3 September 1910, Division 2, v Bradford PA (a) W 1–0 – Mutch; Taylor, Morris; Beaton, Hall, Bartlett; Blackburn, Wood, Hamilton (1), McCubbin, Jee.

Record League Victory: 10–1 v Blackpool, Division 1, 13 December 1930 – Turner; Goodall, Spencer; Redfern, Wilson, Campbell; Bob Kelly (1), McLean (4), Robson (3), Davies (1), Smailes (1).

Record Cup Victory: 7–0 v Lincoln U, FA Cup 1st rd, 16 November 1991 – Clarke; Trevitt, Charlton, Donovan (2), Mitchell, Doherty, O'Regan (1), Stapleton (1) (Wright), Roberts (2), Onuora (1), Barnett (Ireland). *N.B.* 11–0 v Heckmondwike (a), FA Cup pr rd, 18 September 1909 – Doggart; Roberts, Ewing; Hooton, Stevenson, Randall; Kenworthy (2), McCreadie (1), Foster (4), Stacey (4), Jee.

HONOURS

Football League – Division 1: *Champions* 1923–24, 1924–25, 1925–26; *Runners-up* 1926–27, 1927–28, 1933–34; **Division 2:** *Champions* 1969–70; *Runners-up* 1919–20, 1952–53; **Division 4:** *Champions* 1979–80.

FA Cup: *Winners* 1922; *Runners-up* 1920, 1928, 1930, 1938.

Football League Cup: Semi-final 1968.

Autoglass Trophy: *Runners-up* 1994.

sky SPORTS FACT FILE

Towards the end of 1919 the Huddersfield Town chairman Hilton Crowther announced plans to move the Terriers to Elland Road and become a Leeds-based club. The proposal provoked outrage in the town and sufficient money was raised to buy out Crowther's interest in the club, so stopping the move.

Record Defeat: 1–10 v Manchester C, Division 2, 7 November 1987.

Most League Points (2 for a win): 66, Division 4, 1979–80.

Most League Points (3 for a win): 87, FL 1, 2010–11.

Most League Goals: 101, Division 4, 1979–80.

Highest League Scorer in Season: Sam Taylor, 35, Division 2, 1919–20; George Brown, 35, Division 1, 1925–26; Jordan Rhodes, 35, 2011–12.

Most League Goals in Total Aggregate: George Brown, 142, 1921–29; Jimmy Glazzard, 142, 1946–56.

Most League Goals in One Match: 5, Dave Mangnall v Derby Co, Division 1, 21 November 1931; 5, Alf Lythgoe v Blackburn R, Division 1, 13 April 1935.

Most Capped Player: Jimmy Nicholson, 31 (41), Northern Ireland.

Most League Appearances: Billy Smith, 520, 1914–34.

Youngest League Player: Denis Law, 16 years 303 days v Notts Co, 24 December 1956.

Record Transfer Fee Received: £8,000,000 from Blackburn R for Jordan Rhodes, August 2012.

Record Transfer Fee Paid: £1,500,000 to Bradford C for Nahki Wells, January 2014.

Football League Record: 1910 Elected to Division 2; 1920–52 Division 1; 1952–53 Division 2; 1953–56 Division 1; 1956–70 Division 2; 1970–72 Division 1; 1972–73 Division 2; 1973–75 Division 3; 1975–80 Division 4; 1980–83 Division 3; 1983–88 Division 2; 1988–92 Division 3; 1992–95 Division 2; 1995–2001 Division 1; 2001–03 Division 2; 2003–04 Division 3; 2004–12 FL 1; 2012– FL C.

LATEST SEQUENCES

Longest Sequence of League Wins: 11, 5.4.1920 – 4.9.1920.

Longest Sequence of League Defeats: 7, 8.10.1955 – 19.11.1955.

Longest Sequence of League Draws: 6, 3.3.1987 – 3.4.1987.

Longest Sequence of Unbeaten League Matches: 43, 1.1.2011 – 19.11.2011.

Longest Sequence Without a League Win: 22, 4.12.1971 – 29.4.1972.

Successive Scoring Runs: 27 from 12.3.2005.

Successive Non-scoring Runs: 7 from 14.10.2000.

MANAGERS

Fred Walker 1908–10
Richard Pudan 1910–12
Arthur Fairclough 1912–19
Ambrose Langley 1919–21
Herbert Chapman 1921–25
Cecil Potter 1925–26
Jack Chaplin 1926–29
Clem Stephenson 1929–42
Ted Magner 1942–43
David Steele 1943–47
George Stephenson 1947–52
Andy Beattie 1952–56
Bill Shankly 1956–59
Eddie Boot 1960–64
Tom Johnston 1964–68
Ian Greaves 1968–74
Bobby Collins 1974
Tom Johnston 1975–78
  (had been General Manager since 1975)
Mike Buxton 1978–86
Steve Smith 1986–87
Malcolm Macdonald 1987–88
Eoin Hand 1988–92
Ian Ross 1992–93
Neil Warnock 1993–95
Brian Horton 1995–97
Peter Jackson 1997–99
Steve Bruce 1999–2000
Lou Macari 2000–02
Mick Wadsworth 2002–03
Peter Jackson 2003–07
Andy Ritchie 2007–08
Stan Ternent 2008
Lee Clark 2008–12
Simon Grayson 2012–13
Mark Robins February 2013–

TEN YEAR LEAGUE RECORD

		P	W	D	L	F	A	Pts	Pos
2004-05	FL 1	46	20	10	16	74	65	70	9
2005-06	FL 1	46	19	16	11	72	59	73	4
2006-07	FL 1	46	14	17	15	60	69	59	15
2007-08	FL 1	46	20	6	20	50	62	66	10
2008-09	FL 1	46	18	14	14	62	65	68	9
2009-10	FL 1	46	23	11	12	82	56	80	6
2010-11	FL 1	46	25	12	9	77	48	87	3
2011-12	FL 1	46	21	18	7	79	47	81	4
2012-13	FL C	46	15	13	18	53	73	58	19
2013-14	FL C	46	14	11	21	58	65	53	17

DID YOU KNOW ?

Full back Sam Wadsworth returned home from World War One suffering from shell shock and without a club after Blackburn Rovers released him. He went on to achieve success with Huddersfield Town, making close on 300 first-team appearances and winning nine England caps, four as skipper.

HUDDERSFIELD TOWN – FL CHAMPIONSHIP 2013–14 LEAGUE RECORD

Match No.	Date	Venue	Opponents	Result	H/T Score	Lg Pos.	Goalscorers	Attendance
1	Aug 3	A	Nottingham F	L	0-1	0-0	20		25,535
2	10	H	QPR	D	1-1	1-1	17	Vaughan [35]	13,896
3	17	A	Millwall	W	1-0	0-0	12	Vaughan [57]	9503
4	24	H	Bournemouth	W	5-1	3-0	7	Hammill [14], Vaughan 3 (1 pen) [37, 42, 58 (p)], Clayton [78]	12,025
5	31	A	Barnsley	L	1-2	0-2	12	Vaughan [61]	13,593
6	Sept 14	H	Doncaster R	D	0-0	0-0	11		13,102
7	17	H	Charlton Ath	W	2-1	1-0	9	Vaughan [45], Lynch [65]	12,248
8	21	A	Blackburn R	D	0-0	0-0	9		14,582
9	27	H	Blackpool	D	1-1	0-1	8	Vaughan [62]	12,337
10	Oct 1	A	Middlesbrough	D	1-1	0-0	9	Vaughan [59]	12,793
11	5	H	Watford	L	1-2	1-2	12	Ward [17]	14,311
12	19	A	Leicester C	L	1-2	0-2	13	Konchesky (og) [67]	22,297
13	26	H	Leeds U	W	3-2	1-1	9	Ward [10], Lees (og) [62], Stead [77]	18,309
14	Nov 2	A	Wigan Ath	L	1-2	1-1	14	Norwood [45]	16,112
15	9	H	Birmingham C	L	1-3	1-1	15	Gerrard [31]	14,161
16	23	A	Sheffield W	W	2-1	1-0	14	Paterson [11], Clayton [68]	19,338
17	30	H	Burnley	W	2-1	0-0	12	Norwood [50], Vaughan (pen) [55]	17,390
18	Dec 3	A	Bolton W	W	1-0	0-0	10	Norwood [71]	15,452
19	7	A	Ipswich T	L	1-2	1-0	11	Ward [35]	15,386
20	14	H	Reading	L	0-1	0-1	12		13,572
21	21	A	Brighton & HA	D	0-0	0-0	13		27,155
22	26	H	Derby Co	D	1-1	0-1	14	Paterson [86]	18,159
23	29	H	Yeovil T	W	5-1	3-1	11	Clayton [23], Paterson [40], Lynch [43], Ward 2 [65, 68]	12,946
24	Jan 1	A	Burnley	L	2-3	1-2	13	Paterson 2 [20, 89]	14,105
25	11	H	Millwall	W	1-0	0-0	12	Wells [90]	12,651
26	18	A	QPR	L	1-2	0-0	13	Wells [68]	17,185
27	28	A	Bournemouth	L	1-2	0-0	13	Woods [59]	7258
28	Feb 1	A	Leeds U	L	1-5	1-1	13	Ward [25]	31,103
29	8	H	Wigan Ath	W	1-0	0-0	13	Clayton [85]	15,576
30	11	A	Nottingham F	L	0-3	0-0	14		13,249
31	15	A	Birmingham C	W	2-1	1-0	13	Norwood [10], Clayton [60]	14,112
32	22	H	Sheffield W	L	0-2	0-1	14		16,499
33	Mar 1	H	Barnsley	W	5-0	2-0	13	Southern [29], Ward [32], Hammill [48], Clayton (pen) [58], Scannell [86]	14,236
34	8	A	Doncaster R	L	0-2	0-0	14		9305
35	12	A	Charlton Ath	D	0-0	0-0	14		12,974
36	15	H	Blackburn R	L	2-4	1-1	15	Hammill [25], Wells [71]	13,311
37	22	A	Blackpool	L	0-1	0-1	16		14,624
38	25	H	Middlesbrough	D	2-2	2-1	16	Hammill [3], Wells [34]	11,999
39	29	A	Reading	D	1-1	1-1	16	Wells [4]	17,649
40	Apr 5	H	Bolton W	L	0-1	0-0	17		15,120
41	8	H	Ipswich T	L	0-2	0-2	17		11,857
42	12	A	Derby Co	L	1-3	1-1	17	Wells [14]	25,809
43	18	H	Brighton & HA	L	1-0	1-0	17	Norwood [6]	13,460
44	21	A	Yeovil T	W	2-1	0-0	17	Wells [69], Clayton [90]	5903
45	26	H	Leicester C	L	0-2	0-1	17		16,481
46	May 3	A	Watford	W	4-1	0-0	17	Lolley [46], Ward 3 [55, 65, 87]	15,370

Final League Position: 17

GOALSCORERS

League (58): Vaughan 10 (2 pens), Ward 10, Clayton 7 (1 pen), Wells 7, Norwood 5, Paterson 5, Hammill 4, Lynch 2, Gerrard 1, Lolley 1, Scannell 1, Southern 1, Stead 1, Woods 1, own goals 2.
The Budweiser FA Cup (3): Norwood 1, Paterson 1, own goal 1.
Capital One Cup (5): Vaughan 2, Hammill 1, Hogg 1, Lynch 1.

Smithies A 46	Hunt J 1+1	Dixon P 37	Hogg J 34	Clarke P 24+2	Lynch J 27+2	Clayton A 41+1	Gobern O 12+11	Vaughan J 20+3	Paterson M 13+9	Scannell S 8+30	Ward D 27+11	Hammill A 42+2	Lopez C —+2	Gerrard A 39+1	Norwood O 37+3	Carroll J 4	Woods C 11+8	Stead J 6+6	Richards A 7+2	Holmes D 2+14	Southern K 8+2	Carr D —+2	Smith T 23+1	Wallace M 15+2	Wells N 21+1	Lolley J 1+5	Bunn H —+3	Billing P —+1	Match No.
1	2	3	4	5	6	7	8[2]	9	10[3]	11[1]	12	13	14																1
1	12			2	4	6	8[1]	10	11	14	13	5[2]		3	7	9[3]													2
1		8	3	5	7	14	11	10[2]	12			2[3]		4	9[1]	6	13												3
1		8	3	2	6		10[3]	11[2]	14			5		4[1]	7	9	12	13											4
1		8[1]		2	4	7	10	13	11[3]	12		5		3	6			9[2]	14										5
1		8		2	4	7	10	11[3]	13	14		5[1]		3	6[2]		12	9											6
1	9	8[3]		2	4	7	12	10				6[2]		5[1]	3		14	11	13										7
1	9[1]	8		2	4[3]	6	12	10	13			7		3	14		11[2]	5											8
1		8[1]		2	4	7	14	10	12			5		3	6[2]		11[3]	9	13										9
1		8		2	4	7	6	10[2]	11[1]	12		9[4]		3	13		14	5											10
1		7	3	5[2]	9[1]	11	13	14	10	8				4	6		12						2[1]						11
1	8[2]	7		2	4	14	6[3]	10[4]	13	11		9[1]		3	5		12												12
1		5	7	3	4	14	12	10	8[3]	13		11		2[1]	9[2]	6													13
1		5	7[2]	3	4	12	13	10	8[3]			9		11	2		6[1]	14											14
1		5		3[3]	12	14	9	10	8			4		6[1]	11[3]	2	7	13											15
1	9	6		4	7[1]	13	11	10[2]				5		3	8		12						2						16
1	9	8		4	7	11		10[1]				5		3	6		13						2						17
1	9	5		7		13	11	12	10[1]	8				3	9		6[2]						2						18
1	9	5		6[2]	4	7	11	12	10[1]	8				3	9		13						2						19
1	9			4●	8	6[2]	10[3]	14	11		5[1]	13		3	7		12						2						20
1	9			8[3]	6	11	10[2]		12		5[1]			3	7		13						2	4					21
1	9	6[2]		12	8	11	14	10			5[3]			3[1]	7		13						2	4					22
1	9	6		4	8	11[1]	12	10[2]	5			7[3]					13		14				2	3					23
1	9	6[3]		4[2]	8	10	14	11			5[1]	12			7		13						2	3					24
1	9	6[2]			8	10[1]	14	11[3]	5					3	7		12						2	4	13				25
1	9	6			8	14	12	13	11[3]		5[1]			3	7[2]								2	4	10				26
1	9			6	8[2]	13	11							3	7[1]		5[3]	14					2	4	10	12			27
1	9[1]			6	8[2]	14	12	11						3	7		5						2	4	10[3]	13			28
1	9	6		4	8	10		12	5					3	7								2		11[1]				29
1	9	8		4	6	11[3]	14	13	12		5			3	7[1]								2		10[2]				30
1	9	8	12	4[2]	6	14	11		5					3	7[3]		13						2		10[1]				31
1	9	8	3	6		14	13	11	5[2]					4	7[3]								2		10[1]	12			32
1		5		7		14	12	9[3]	6[2]					3	10		8						2	4	11[1]	13			33
1		5		7		12	13	9[3]	6[2]					3	10[1]		8						2	4	11	14			34
1		5	8	3		10	13	6[2]	9	12				2	7									4	11[1]				35
1	9	8	3	6		12	13	10[3]	5[2]						7[1]								2	4	11		14		36
1	9	8[2]		2	7	10	14	5						3	13		12				6[3]			4[1]	11				37
1	9			2	6	8[2]	12	11	5					3	7		13							4	10[1]				38
1	9		3	6	8		13	11[1]	5					4[2]	7								2	12	10[1]				39
1	9		3	8	6[1]		11	5						4	7		12						2		10				40
1		5		4	7	8	12	9[1]	6[3]					3	10[2]		13						2		11	14			41
1		8	2●	4●	6		14	11	5[2]					3	7[2]	9							12		10[1]	13			42
1		5	7		9	12	6[1]		10[2]					3	8								2	4	11		13		43
1		5	9	7		12	10[2]	6						3	8[1]				13				2	4	11				44
1		5	7[3]	3		9	6		10[2]		4	12			8[1]								2		11		13	14	45
1		5	9	14	4	7	13	12	10			3[1]			8								2		11[2]	6[3]			46

The Budweiser FA Cup

Third Round	Grimsby T	(a)	3-2
Fourth Round	Charlton Ath	(h)	0-1

Capital One Cup

First Round	Bradford C	(h)	2-1
Second Round	Charlton Ath	(h)	3-2
Third Round	Hull C	(a)	0-1

HULL CITY

FOUNDATION

The enthusiasts who formed Hull City in 1904 were brave men indeed. More than that, they were audacious for they immediately put the club on the map in this Rugby League fortress by obtaining a three-year agreement with the Hull Rugby League club to rent their ground! They had obtained quite a number of conversions to the dribbling code, before the Rugby League forbade the use of any of their club grounds by Association Football clubs. By that time, Hull City were well away, having entered the FA Cup in their initial season and the Football League, Second Division after only a year.

The KC Stadium, West Park, Hull, East Yorkshire HU3 6HU.

Telephone: (01482) 504 600.

Fax: (01482) 304 882.

Ticket Office: (01482) 505 600.

Website: www.hullcitytigers.com

Email: info@hulltigers.com

Ground Capacity: 25,400.

Record Attendance: 55,019 v Manchester U, FA Cup 6th rd, 26 February 1949 (at Boothferry Park); 25,512 v Sunderland, FL C, 28 October 2007 (at KC Stadium).

Pitch Measurements: 100.3m × 68m (110yd × 74yd)

Chairman: Dr Assem Allam.

Vice-chairman: Ehab Allam.

Manager: Steve Bruce.

Assistant Manager: Steve Agnew.

Physio: Stuart Leake.

Colours: Amber shirts with black stripes, black shorts, amber socks with black hoops.

Year Formed: 1904.

Turned Professional: 1905.

Club Nickname: 'The Tigers'.

Grounds: 1904, Boulevard Ground (Hull RFC); 1905, Anlaby Road (Hull CC); 1944, Boulevard Ground; 1946, Boothferry Park; 2002, Kingston Communications Stadium.

First Football League Game: 2 September 1905, Division 2, v Barnsley (h) W 4–1 – Spendiff; Langley, Jones; Martin, Robinson, Gordon (2); Rushton, Spence (1); Wilson (1), Howe, Raisbeck.

Record League Victory: 11–1 v Carlisle U, Division 3 (N), 14 January 1939 – Ellis; Woodhead, Dowen; Robinson (1), Blyth, Hardy; Hubbard (2), Richardson (2), Dickinson (2), Davies (2), Cunliffe (2).

Record Cup Victory: 8–2 v Stalybridge Celtic (a), FA Cup 1st rd, 26 November 1932 – Maddison; Goldsmith, Woodhead; Gardner, Hill (1), Denby; Forward (1), Duncan, McNaughton (1), Wainscoat (4), Sargeant (1).

HONOURS

FA Premier League: Best season 17th, 2008–09.

Football League – FL C: *Runners-up* 2012–13;

FL 1: *Runners-up* 2004–05;

Division 3 (N): *Champions* 1932–33, 1948–49;

Division 3: *Champions* 1965–66; *Runners-up* 1958–59, 2003–04;

Division 4: *Runners-up* 1982–83.

FA Cup: Semi-final 1930.

Football League Cup: Best season: 4th, 1974, 1976, 1978.

Associate Members' Cup: *Runners-up* 1984.

sky SPORTS FACT FILE

Ernie Shepherd, a left winger who joined Hull City in March 1949, scored within a minute of his debut and went on to help the Tigers to the Division Three North title. Earlier in the season Shepherd had spells with Fulham and West Bromwich Albion who both also won promotion as the top two teams in the Second Division.

Record Defeat: 0–8 v Wolverhampton W, Division 2, 4 November 1911.

Most League Points (2 for a win): 69, Division 3, 1965–66.

Most League Points (3 for a win): 90, Division 4, 1982–83.

Most League Goals: 109, Division 3, 1965–66.

Highest League Scorer in Season: Bill McNaughton, 39, Division 3 (N), 1932–33.

Most League Goals in Total Aggregate: Chris Chilton, 193, 1960–71.

Most League Goals in One Match: 5, Ken McDonald v Bristol C, Division 2, 17 November 1928; 5, Simon 'Slim' Raleigh v Halifax T, Division 3 (N), 26 December 1930.

Most Capped Player: Theo Whitmore, 28 (105), Jamaica.

Most League Appearances: Andy Davidson, 520, 1952–67.

Youngest League Player: Matthew Edeson, 16 years 63 days v Fulham, 10 October 1992.

Record Transfer Fee Received: £4,000,000 from Sunderland for Michael Turner, August 2009.

Record Transfer Fee Paid: £8,000,000 to Tottenham H for Jake Livermore, June 2014.

Football League Record: 1905 Elected to Division 2; 1930–33 Division 3 (N); 1933–36 Division 2; 1936–49 Division 3 (N); 1949–56 Division 2; 1956–58 Division 3 (N); 1958–59 Division 3; 1959–60 Division 2; 1960–66 Division 3; 1966–78 Division 2; 1978–81 Division 3; 1981–83 Division 4; 1983–85 Division 3; 1985–91 Division 2; 1991–92 Division 3; 1992–96 Division 2; 1996–2004 Division 3; 2004–05 FL 1; 2005–08 FL C; 2008–10 FA Premier League; 2010–13 FL C; 2013– FA Premier League.

LATEST SEQUENCES

Longest Sequence of League Wins: 10, 23.2.1966 – 20.4.1966.

Longest Sequence of League Defeats: 8, 7.4.1934 – 8.9.1934.

Longest Sequence of League Draws: 5, 14.2.2012 – 10.3.2012.

Longest Sequence of Unbeaten League Matches: 19, 13.3.2001 – 22.9.2001.

Longest Sequence Without a League Win: 27, 27.3.1989 – 4.11.1989.

Successive Scoring Runs: 26 from 10.4.1990.

Successive Non-scoring Runs: 6 from 13.11.1920.

MANAGERS

James Ramster 1904–05
  (Secretary-Manager)
Ambrose Langley 1905–13
Harry Chapman 1913–14
Fred Stringer 1914–16
David Menzies 1916–21
Percy Lewis 1921–23
Bill McCracken 1923–31
Haydn Green 1931–34
John Hill 1934–36
David Menzies 1936
Ernest Blackburn 1936–46
Major Frank Buckley 1946–48
Raich Carter 1948–51
Bob Jackson 1952–55
Bob Brocklebank 1955–61
Cliff Britton 1961–70
  (continued as General Manager to 1971)
Terry Neill 1970–74
John Kaye 1974–77
Bobby Collins 1977–78
Ken Houghton 1978–79
Mike Smith 1979–82
Bobby Brown 1982
Colin Appleton 1982–84
Brian Horton 1984–88
Eddie Gray 1988–89
Colin Appleton 1989
Stan Ternent 1989–91
Terry Dolan 1991–97
Mark Hateley 1997–98
Warren Joyce 1998–2000
Brian Little 2000–02
Jan Molby 2002
Peter Taylor 2002–06
Phil Parkinson 2006
Phil Brown *(after caretaker role December 2006)* 2007–10
Ian Dowie *(consultant)* 2010
Nigel Pearson 2010–11
Nick Barmby 2011–12
Steve Bruce June 2012–

TEN YEAR LEAGUE RECORD

		P	W	D	L	F	A	Pts	Pos
2004-05	FL 1	46	26	8	12	80	53	86	2
2005-06	FL C	46	12	16	18	49	55	52	18
2006-07	FL C	46	13	10	23	51	67	49	21
2007-08	FL C	46	21	12	13	65	47	75	3
2008-09	PR Lge	38	8	11	19	39	64	35	17
2009-10	PR Lge	38	6	12	20	34	75	30	19
2010-11	FL C	46	16	17	13	52	51	65	11
2011-12	FL C	46	19	11	16	47	44	68	8
2012-13	FL C	46	24	7	15	61	52	79	2
2013-14	PR Lge	38	10	7	21	38	53	37	16

DID YOU KNOW ?

Hull City's first FA Cup tie saw them drawn at home to Stockton in the preliminary round of the 1904–05 competition. City had to concede home advantage because their ground at The Boulevard was required by their landlords Hull FC for a Rugby League match. The tie at Stockton ended 3-3 and City lost the replay 4-1.

HULL CITY – FA PREMIERSHIP 2013–14 LEAGUE RECORD

Match No.	Date	Venue	Opponents	Result		H/T Score	Lg Pos.	Goalscorers	Attendance
1	Aug 18	A	Chelsea	L	0-2	0-2	18		41,374
2	24	H	Norwich C	W	1-0	1-0	12	Brady (pen) [22]	23,682
3	31	A	Manchester C	L	0-2	0-0	17		46,903
4	Sept 14	H	Cardiff C	D	1-1	1-0	15	Davies [40]	21,949
5	21	A	Newcastle U	W	3-2	1-2	10	Brady [26], Elmohamady [48], Aluko [76]	51,523
6	28	H	West Ham U	W	1-0	1-0	7	Brady (pen) [12]	24,291
7	Oct 5	H	Aston Villa	D	0-0	0-0	8		24,396
8	19	A	Everton	L	1-2	1-1	9	Sagbo [30]	38,828
9	27	A	Tottenham H	L	0-1	0-0	10		36,080
10	Nov 2	H	Sunderland	W	1-0	1-0	10	Cuellar (og) [25]	24,677
11	9	A	Southampton	L	1-4	0-3	12	Sagbo [55]	30,022
12	23	H	Crystal Palace	L	0-1	0-0	13		23,043
13	Dec 1	H	Liverpool	W	3-1	1-1	10	Livermore [20], Meyler [72], Skrtel (og) [87]	24,940
14	4	A	Arsenal	L	0-2	0-1	12		60,017
15	9	A	Swansea C	D	1-1	1-0	12	Graham [9]	19,303
16	14	H	Stoke C	D	0-0	0-0	12		23,324
17	21	A	WBA	D	1-1	1-0	12	Livermore [28]	24,753
18	26	H	Manchester U	L	2-3	2-2	12	Chester [4], Meyler [13]	24,826
19	28	H	Fulham	W	6-0	0-0	10	Elmohamady [49], Koren 2 [60, 84], Boyd [63], Huddlestone [67], Fryatt [74]	23,925
20	Jan 1	A	Liverpool	L	0-2	0-1	10		44,627
21	11	H	Chelsea	L	0-2	0-0	10		24,924
22	18	A	Norwich C	L	0-1	0-0	11		26,655
23	28	A	Crystal Palace	L	0-1	0-1	13		22,519
24	Feb 1	H	Tottenham H	D	1-1	1-0	13	Long [12]	24,932
25	8	A	Sunderland	W	2-0	1-0	11	Long [16], Jelavic [62]	42,810
26	11	H	Southampton	L	0-1	0-0	13		23,670
27	22	A	Cardiff C	W	4-0	2-0	11	Huddlestone [18], Jelavic 2 [38, 57], Livermore [67]	26,167
28	Mar 1	H	Newcastle U	L	1-4	0-2	11	Davies [46]	24,903
29	15	H	Manchester C	L	0-2	0-1	13		24,895
30	22	H	WBA	W	2-0	2-0	12	Rosenior [31], Long [38]	23,486
31	26	A	West Ham U	L	1-2	0-1	13	Huddlestone [48]	31,033
32	29	A	Stoke C	L	0-1	0-0	14		27,029
33	Apr 5	H	Swansea C	W	1-0	1-0	12	Boyd [39]	22,744
34	20	A	Arsenal	L	0-3	0-2	14		24,762
35	26	A	Fulham	D	2-2	0-0	13	Jelavic [75], Long [87]	25,700
36	May 3	A	Aston Villa	L	1-3	1-3	15	Bowery (og) [28]	37,182
37	6	A	Manchester U	L	1-3	0-1	15	Fryatt [63]	75,341
38	11	H	Everton	L	0-2	0-1	16		24,848

Final League Position: 16

GOALSCORERS

League (38): Jelavic 4, Long 4, Brady 3 (2 pens), Huddlestone 3, Livermore 3, Boyd 2, Davies 2, Elmohamady 2, Fryatt 2, Koren 2, Meyler 2, Sagbo 2, Aluko 1, Chester 1, Graham 1, Rosenior 1, own goals 3.
The Budweiser FA Cup (17): Fryatt 4, Davies 3, Meyler 2, Sagbo 2, Chester 1, Huddlestone 1, Koren 1, McLean 1, Proschwitz 1, Quinn 1.
Capital One Cup (4): Brady 1, McShane 1, Proschwitz 1, own goal 1.

McGregor A 26	Elmohamady A 38	Chester C 37	Davies C 37	Figueroa M 31 + 1	Koren R 10 + 12	Meyler D 27 + 3	Brady R 11 + 5	Aluko S 10 + 7	Graham D 12 + 6	Sagbo Y 16 + 12	Livermore J 34 + 2	Huddlestone T 35 + 1	Boyd G 9 + 20	Rosenior L 22 + 7	Quinn S 4 + 11	Faye A 3	Harper S 11 + 2	Bruce A 19 + 1	McShane P 9 + 1	McLean A — + 1	Proschwitz N — + 2	Gedo M — + 2	Fryatt M — + 10	Jelavic N 16	Long S 15	Jakupovic E 1	Match No.
1	2	3	4	5	6	7[2]	8	9[3]	10[1]	11	12	13	14														1
1	2	3	4	5	8[2]		11[1]	9[2]	12	10[4]	6	7	13	14													2
1	2	3	4	5	6[1]		9	10[2]	11		7	8	13		12												3
1	2	3	4	5	6		9[1]	10	11		8	7			12												4
1	2	3	4			13	9[2]	10	11[3]	14	8	7	12	5	6[1]												5
1	6		4	5		13		9[3]	10[2]	11[1]	12		8		7	14		2	3								6
1	6[3]	3	5				14	10[2]	11	9[1]	13	8	7		12			2	4								7
1	6	3	5				9	10[2]	11[1]	12	8	7	13		14	2[2]		4									8
	7	3	6		9	13			11[1]		8	10[1]	12		14	2[2]	1	4	5								9
	6	3	5		12	7[2]	14		11	9	8	10[1]			13	2[3]	1	4									10
	2[3]	3	5		12	7[2]		13	11	8	9	10[1]	6		14		1	4									11
1	2	3	5		6[1]			10[3]	12	11	8	7	9		13		4[2]				14						12
1	5	2	4		10[2]	8	9[1]	14	11[3]		6	7	13		12			3									13
1	5	2	4		7		9[3]	11[2]	10[1]	6	8	13			12			3				14					14
1	5	2	4		9		12	8	11[1]	10	6	7						3									15
1	5	2	4		9		8[2]	12	11[3]	10	6	7	14		13			3[1]									16
1	5	2	4		9		8	11[1]	10[2]	6	7	12						3						13			17
1[2]	5	2	4		9[3]		12	8[1]	11	10	6	7	14				13[3]	3									18
1	6[2]	3	4	5			8	13	11[1]	7[3]	9	10				2			14				12				19
1	5	2	4		9		10[1]	6[2]	14	11[2]	8	7			13			3					12				20
1	5	2[1]	4		9		12	6[1]	11	8	7	10[2]			14			3					13				21
1	5	2[2]	4		12		8[1]	10[3]	6	7[1]	13	9						3					14	11			22
1[1]	5	2		8[2]	6					7	9		13		12			3[1]	4				14	10[3]	11		23
	6[2]	4	5		13	7	9[3]	14		8	12					2	1	3						10[1]	11		24
	6	4	5		12		9	14		13	8	7				2[2]	1	3						11[1]	10[3]		25
	6	3	5				9[1]	14		13	7	8	12			2[2]	1		4					10	11		26
1	2	3	13	5			9			6	7	8[3]	12					4[1]	14					10	11[2]		27
1	2	14	3[1]	5[2]				12	8	13	9	7[3]	6						4					10	11		28
1	6	3	4	5[2]			9[3]	12			8	7	13			2[1]			14					11	10		29
1	2	3	4		12		9	6[3]	14		8	7	5		13									11[1]	10[2]		30
1	5	2	4		9[3]					8	6	7	13	12	14			3[1]						11[2]	10		31
1	5	2	4		6		12	13			7	8[3]	9		14			3[2]						11[1]	10		32
	6	3	4	5[1]	13		9	12	14		8	7				2	1							11[2]	10[3]		33
	2	3	4	5	14		9[1]			6	8	7	13		12		1							10[2]	11[3]		34
	5	2	4				8[3]	12	14	6	7	9[2]	13				1	3[1]						11	10		35
	5	2[3]	3	4			8[3]	14		6	7	9	13		12		1							11	10		36
	5[1]	3	4	10	6	13		14			7	9[3]	8		12	2								11[2]		1	37
1	5		4		9			14	10[1]	6	7	8	13		12	2[2]		3							11[3]		38

The Budweiser FA Cup

Third Round	Middlesbrough	(a)	2-0
Fourth Round	Southend U	(a)	2-0
		(aet)	
Fifth Round	Brighton & HA	(a)	1-1
Replay	Brighton & HA	(h)	2-1
Sixth Round	Sunderland	(h)	3-0
Semi-Finals	Sheffield U	(Wembley)	5-3
Final	Arsenal	(Wembley)	2-3
(aet)			

Capital One Cup

Second Round	Leyton Orient	(a)	1-0
	(aet)		
Third Round	Huddersfield T	(h)	1-0
Fourth Round	Tottenham H	(a)	2-2
(aet; lost 7-8 on penalties)			

IPSWICH TOWN

FOUNDATION

Considering that Ipswich Town only reached the Football League in 1938, many people outside of East Anglia may be surprised to learn that this club was formed at a meeting held in the Town Hall as far back as 1878 when Mr T. C. Cobbold, MP, was voted president. Originally it was the Ipswich Association FC to distinguish it from the older Ipswich Football Club which played rugby. These two amalgamated in 1888 and the handling game was dropped in 1893.

Portman Road, Ipswich, Suffolk IP1 2DA.

Telephone: (01473) 400 500.

Fax: (01473) 400 040.

Ticket Office: (0844) 8011 555.

Website: www.itfc.co.uk

Email: customerservices@itfc.co.uk

Ground Capacity: 30,311.

Record Attendance: 38,010 v Leeds U, FA Cup 6th rd, 8 March 1975.

Pitch Measurements: 102m × 66m (111.5yd × 72yd)

Managing Directors: Ian Milne, Jonathan Symonds.

Manager: Mick McCarthy.

Assistant Manager: Terry Connor.

Physios: Matt Byard, Alex Chapman.

Colours: Blue shirts with white trim, white shorts with blue trim, blue socks with white tops.

Year Formed: 1878.

Turned Professional: 1936.

HONOURS

Football League – Division 1:
Champions 1961–62;
Runners-up 1980–81, 1981–82;
Division 2: *Champions* 1960–61, 1967–68, 1991–92;
Division 3 (S): *Champions* 1953–54, 1956–57.
FA Cup: *Winners* 1978.
Football League Cup: Semi-final 1982, 1985, 2001, 2011.
Texaco Cup: *Winners* 1973.
European Competitions
European Cup: 1962–63.
European Cup-Winners' Cup: 1978–79.
UEFA Cup: 1973–74, 1974–75, 1975–76, 1977–78, 1979–80, 1980–81 (*winners*), 1981–82, 1982–83, 2001–02, 2002–03.

Previous Name: 1878, Ipswich Association FC; 1888, Ipswich Town.

Club Nicknames: 'The Blues', 'Town', 'The Tractor Boys'.

Grounds: 1878, Broom Hill and Brook's Hall; 1884, Portman Road.

First Football League Game: 27 August 1938, Division 3 (S), v Southend U (h) W 4–2 – Burns; Dale, Parry; Perrett, Fillingham, McLuckie; Williams, Davies (1), Jones (2), Alsop (1), Little.

Record League Victory: 7–0 v Portsmouth, Division 2, 7 November 1964 – Thorburn; Smith, McNeil; Baxter, Bolton, Thompson; Broadfoot (1), Hegan (2), Baker (1), Leadbetter, Brogan (3). 7–0 v Southampton, Division 1, 2 February 1974 – Sivell; Burley, Mills (1), Morris, Hunter, Beattie (1), Hamilton (2), Viljoen, Johnson, Whymark (2), Lambert (1) (Woods). 7–0 v WBA, Division 1, 6 November 1976 – Sivell; Burley, Mills, Talbot, Hunter, Beattie (1), Osborne, Wark (1), Mariner (1) (Bertschin), Whymark (4), Woods.

sky SPORTS FACT FILE

Ipswich Town are the only current club in the Premier and Football Leagues to have played in an AFA Senior Cup final. On 31 March 1928 they went down 4-2 to Bank of England in the final tie played at Dulwich Hamlet's Champion Hill ground. Goalscorers were Jackie Green and Clem Burch.

Record Cup Victory: 10–0 v Floriana, European Cup prel. rd, 25 September 1962 – Bailey; Malcolm, Compton; Baxter, Laurel, Elsworthy (1); Stephenson, Moran (2), Crawford (5), Phillips (2), Blackwood.

Record Defeat: 1–10 v Fulham, Division 1, 26 December 1963.

Most League Points (2 for a win): 64, Division 3 (S), 1953–54 and 1955–56.

Most League Points (3 for a win): 87, Division 1, 1999–2000.

Most League Goals: 106, Division 3 (S), 1955–56.

Highest League Scorer in Season: Ted Phillips, 41, Division 3 (S), 1956–57.

Most League Goals in Total Aggregate: Ray Crawford, 204, 1958–63 and 1966–69.

Most League Goals in One Match: 5, Alan Brazil v Southampton, Division 1, 16 February 1981.

Most Capped Player: Allan Hunter, 47 (53), Northern Ireland.

Most League Appearances: Mick Mills, 591, 1966–82.

Youngest League Player: Jason Dozzell, 16 years 56 days v Coventry C, 4 February 1984.

Record Transfer Fee Received: £8,000,000 from Sunderland for Connor Wickham, June 2011.

Record Transfer Fee Paid: £5,000,000 to Sampdoria for Matteo Sereni, August 2001.

Football League Record: 1938 Elected to Division 3 (S); 1954–55 Division 2; 1955–57 Division 3 (S); 1957–61 Division 2; 1961–64 Division 1; 1964–68 Division 2; 1968–86 Division 1; 1986–92 Division 2; 1992–95 FA Premier League; 1995–2000 Division 1; 2000–02 FA Premier League; 2002–04 Division 1; 2004– FL C.

MANAGERS

Mick O'Brien 1936–37
Scott Duncan 1937–55
(continued as Secretary)
Alf Ramsey 1955–63
Jackie Milburn 1963–64
Bill McGarry 1964–68
Bobby Robson 1969–82
Bobby Ferguson 1982–87
Johnny Duncan 1987–90
John Lyall 1990–94
George Burley 1994–2002
Joe Royle 2002–06
Jim Magilton 2006–09
Roy Keane 2009–11
Paul Jewell 2011–12
Mick McCarthy November 2012–

LATEST SEQUENCES

Longest Sequence of League Wins: 8, 23.9.1953 – 31.10.1953.

Longest Sequence of League Defeats: 10, 4.9.1954 – 16.10.1954.

Longest Sequence of League Draws: 7, 10.11.1990 – 21.12.1990.

Longest Sequence of Unbeaten League Matches: 23, 8.12.1979 – 26.4.1980.

Longest Sequence Without a League Win: 21, 28.8.1963 – 14.12.1963.

Successive Scoring Runs: 31 from 7.3.2004.

Successive Non-scoring Runs: 7 from 28.2.1995.

TEN YEAR LEAGUE RECORD

		P	W	D	L	F	A	Pts	Pos
2004-05	FL C	46	24	13	9	85	56	85	3
2005-06	FL C	46	14	14	18	53	66	56	15
2006-07	FL C	46	18	8	20	64	59	62	14
2007-08	FL C	46	18	15	13	65	56	69	8
2008-09	FL C	46	17	15	14	62	53	66	9
2009-10	FL C	46	12	20	14	50	61	56	15
2010-11	FL C	46	18	8	20	62	68	62	13
2011-12	FL C	46	17	10	19	69	77	61	15
2012-13	FL C	46	16	12	18	48	61	60	14
2013-14	FL C	46	18	14	14	60	54	68	9

DID YOU KNOW ?

Ipswich Town did not join the professional ranks until 1936 when they became members of the Southern League. Their first-ever game under their new status took place on 29 August 1936 when they beat Tunbridge Wells Rangers 4-1 in front of a then record Portman Road attendance of 14,211.

IPSWICH TOWN – FL CHAMPIONSHIP 2013–14 LEAGUE RECORD

Match No.	Date	Venue	Opponents	Result	H/T Score	Lg Pos.	Goalscorers	Attendance
1	Aug 3	A	Reading	L	1-2	1-1	15	Tabb [16]	20,456
2	10	H	Millwall	W	3-0	0-0	9	Lowry (og) [63], Smith [70], Anderson [83]	17,183
3	17	A	QPR	L	0-1	0-0	14		17,075
4	24	H	Leeds U	L	1-2	1-1	17	McGoldrick [12]	18,322
5	31	A	Birmingham C	D	1-1	1-0	16	Berra [30]	14,328
6	Sept 14	H	Middlesbrough	W	3-1	1-1	14	McGoldrick 2 [34, 90], Chambers [57]	15,276
7	17	H	Yeovil T	W	2-1	0-1	11	Murphy [52], Cresswell [60]	15,340
8	22	A	Wigan Ath	L	0-2	0-1	14		13,747
9	28	H	Brighton & HA	W	2-0	2-0	9	McGoldrick 2 [20, 24]	16,474
10	Oct 1	A	Derby Co	D	4-4	4-1	10	Berra [7], Murphy 2 [9, 34], Cresswell [14]	21,037
11	5	A	Sheffield W	D	1-1	1-1	11	Anderson [12]	19,599
12	19	H	Burnley	L	0-1	0-0	11		16,062
13	26	A	Bolton W	D	1-1	0-0	13	McGoldrick [73]	15,222
14	Nov 1	H	Barnsley	D	1-1	1-0	10	Murphy [41]	18,361
15	9	A	Blackpool	W	3-2	0-1	11	Nouble [65], Taylor [84], Murphy [90]	13,525
16	23	H	Leicester C	L	1-2	1-0	12	McGoldrick [2]	18,227
17	30	A	Charlton Ath	W	1-0	1-0	11	Smith [5]	16,645
18	Dec 3	H	Blackburn R	W	3-1	1-1	8	Hyam [4], Edwards [48], Nouble [86]	14,953
19	7	H	Huddersfield T	W	2-1	0-1	9	McGoldrick [50], Murphy [89]	15,386
20	14	A	Nottingham F	D	0-0	0-0	10		20,966
21	21	H	Watford	D	1-1	0-0	9	McGoldrick (pen) [73]	16,385
22	26	A	Doncaster R	W	3-0	2-0	7	McGoldrick 2 [24, 51], Chambers [30]	7753
23	29	A	Bournemouth	D	1-1	0-0	6	Murphy [59]	11,096
24	Jan 1	H	Charlton Ath	D	1-1	1-0	6	Wood (og) [24]	18,731
25	11	H	QPR	L	1-3	0-0	9	Smith [90]	18,369
26	18	A	Millwall	L	0-1	0-1	10		12,125
27	25	H	Reading	W	2-0	0-0	7	Murphy [62], Anderson [90]	15,323
28	28	A	Leeds U	D	1-1	0-0	7	McGoldrick [57]	20,461
29	Feb 1	H	Bolton W	W	1-0	0-0	7	McGoldrick (pen) [55]	15,429
30	8	A	Barnsley	D	2-2	0-1	7	Berra [81], McGoldrick [84]	9929
31	15	H	Blackpool	D	0-0	0-0	8		16,010
32	22	A	Leicester C	L	0-3	0-2	10		28,078
33	Mar 1	H	Birmingham C	W	1-0	1-0	9	Murphy [38]	15,596
34	8	A	Middlesbrough	L	0-2	0-2	9		13,965
35	11	A	Yeovil T	W	1-0	1-0	9	Berra [40]	5920
36	15	H	Wigan Ath	L	1-3	1-2	9	Smith [19]	16,047
37	22	A	Brighton & HA	W	2-0	0-0	9	Smith [60], Murphy [79]	29,093
38	25	H	Derby Co	W	2-1	0-1	8	Williams [68], Berra [90]	17,399
39	29	H	Nottingham F	D	1-1	0-1	8	Murphy [78]	17,955
40	Apr 5	A	Blackburn R	L	0-2	0-0	9		13,281
41	8	A	Huddersfield T	W	2-0	2-0	8	Anderson [6], Murphy [33]	11,857
42	12	H	Doncaster R	W	2-1	0-0	7	Murphy [47], Chambers [86]	19,496
43	19	A	Watford	L	1-3	0-1	8	Wordsworth [50]	16,615
44	21	H	Bournemouth	D	2-2	1-1	8	Anderson [36], Green [56]	20,356
45	26	A	Burnley	L	0-1	0-0	10		14,574
46	May 3	H	Sheffield W	W	2-1	1-0	9	Smith [36], Green [67]	20,862

Final League Position: 9

GOALSCORERS

League (60): McGoldrick 14 (2 pens), Murphy 13, Smith 6, Anderson 5, Berra 5, Chambers 3, Cresswell 2, Green 2, Nouble 2, Edwards 1, Hyam 1, Tabb 1, Taylor 1, Williams 1, Wordsworth 1, own goals 2.
The Budweiser FA Cup (3): McGoldrick 2, Nouble 1.
Capital One Cup (0).

Loach S 5+1	Hewitt E 4	Mings T 4+12	Skuse C 43	Chambers L 46	Smith T 45	Edwards C 9+6	Hyam L 33+2	McGoldrick D 30+1	Murphy D 42+3	Tabb J 14+13	Taylor P 4+14	Nouble F 16+22	Anderson P 22+9	Cresswell A 42	Tunnicliffe R 23+4	Berra C 41+1	Gerken D 41	Wordsworth A 6+4	Hunt S 15+8	Graham J —+2	Richardson F 3+4	Green P 6+8	Ebanks-Blake S 1+8	Williams J 11+2	Marriot J —+1	Match No.
1	2	3	4	5	6	7^3	8	9^2	10^1	11	12	13	14													1
1	2		7	3	4	6^1	8	10	11	9^2			12	5^3	13	14										2
1	2		7^2	3	4	6	9	10	11^1		8	13^3	14		5	12										3
1	2		7	3	4	6^3	8	11	10^2	9^1			14	12	5	13										4
			7	2	3	12	8	10	13	14		11^3	6^2	5	9^1	4	1									5
			7	2	4	13	8	11	12	14		10^2	6^1	5	9^3	3	1									6
			7	2	4	6	8	11	10	12				5	9^1	3	1									7
			7	2	4		8^1	11	10^2		12	13	6^1	5	9	3	1	14								8
			7	2	4	13	8	11^2	10^3		12		6^1	5	9	3	1	14								9
			7	2	4	12	8	11^2	10	13		14	6^1	5	9^3	3	1									10
	14		7	2	4		8	11^2	10^3		12	13	6^1	5	9	3	1									11
12			7	2	4		8	11	10^1	14			6^2	5	9	3	1^3									12
			7	2	4	14	8^1	11	10^3	13			6^2	5	9	3	1									13
			8	2	4	7		10^3	11	12	14	13	6^2	5	9^1	3	1									14
	5		2	3		6	7^3	11	10		9^1	13	12		8	4^2	1		14							15
	5^1		7	2	4			11	10		9^2	13	12	6^3	8	3	1		14							16
			7	2	4	13		11	10^3		9^2	12	6^1	5	8	3	1	14								17
12		7^2	2	4	6		8	11^3	13			10		5	14	3	1		9^1							18
	14	6^1	2	4		7	9^3	10	12		11^2			5	8	3	1				13					19
12			7	2	4	6	9	10	11					5	8	3	1									20
		6	2	4		7	10	11	9					5	8	3	1									21
			7	2	4	6	9^2	10^1		13		11^3	14	5	8	3	1					12				22
13			7	2	4	6	9^2	10		12		11^1		5	8	3	1									23
			7	2	4	13	12	10^3	9^2	11^3		14	6	5	8	3	1									24
	14	6	2^3	4		8^1	11		10	12		7^2		5	9	3	1	13								25
			7	2	4	6^2	8^1	10	11	12^3		13	14	5	9	3	1									26
	14		7	2	4	6^1		11^2	10	13		12		5	8	3	1		9^3							27
			7	2	4			11	10	9		12	6^1	5	8	3	1									28
			7^1	2	4		9	10	8	11				5		3	1	12^2	6		13					29
			7	2	4		9	10	8^1			11^2	12			3	1		6		13					30
1			7	2	4	8^2	10	11	12	13				5		3			9^1			6^2	14			31
			7	2	4		10	8^1	14	11^2		12		5		3			9^3			6	13			32
	14		7	2	4		10	6^2	9^1	11^3		12		5		3	1		13			8				33
			7	2	4	12		10	8^2	11^1		9^2		5		3	1					6	13	14		34
13			7	2	4	8	10						6^3	5		3			9^1			14	11^2	12		35
			7^1	2	4	9		11		13			6^3	5		3	1		10			12	14	8^2		36
	14		2	4		9		11	12				6^3	5		3	1	7	10^2			13		8^1		37
		2^3	4		7		11			12			6^1	5		3	1	9	10^2		14		13	8		38
			7	2	4	9		11		13			6^1	5		3	1		10^2		14	12		8^3		39
			7	2	4	8^3	10			9				5		3	1	6^2	13			14	12	11^1		40
12			7	2	4	8		11					6	5^2		3	1	13	9^1		14			10^3		41
	5		7	2	4	9		11				12	6^1			3	1		10^3		14		13	8^2		42
	8		2	4		7^1		11		13		9		5		3	1	6^3	14			12		10^2		43
	14	9	3	4			11			13			6^2	5			1	7^1	10	2		12		8^3		44
	8		2	4			11		12	13				5		3	1		9^1		7^2	6		10		45
			2	4^1			11		12	9^2				5		3	1	8	13			6	7	10^3	14	46

The Budweiser FA Cup
Third Round   Preston NE   (h)   1-1
Replay   Preston NE   (a)   2-3

Capital One Cup
First Round   Stevenage   (a)   0-2

LEEDS UNITED

FOUNDATION

Immediately the Leeds City club (founded in 1904) was wound up by the FA in October 1919, following allegations of illegal payments to players, a meeting was called by a Leeds solicitor, Mr Alf Masser, at which Leeds United was formed. They joined the Midland League, playing their first game in that competition in November 1919. It was in this same month that the new club had discussions with the directors of a virtually bankrupt Huddersfield Town who wanted to move to Leeds in an amalgamation. But Huddersfield survived even that crisis.

Elland Road, Leeds, West Yorkshire LS11 0ES.

Telephone: (0871) 334 1919.

Fax: (0113) 367 6050.

Ticket Office: (0871) 334 1992.

Website: www.leedsunited.com

Email: reception@leedsunited.com

Ground Capacity: 37,890.

Record Attendance: 57,892 v Sunderland, FA Cup 5th rd (replay), 15 March 1967.

Pitch Measurements: 105m × 67.5m (115yd × 74yd)

Chairman: Salah Nooruddin.

Chief Executive: David Halgh.

Manager: Dave Hockaday.

Assistant Manager: Nigel Gibbs.

Physio: Harvey Sharman.

Colours: White shirts with blue and yellow trim, white shorts with blue and yellow trim, white socks with blue and yellow trim.

Year Formed: 1919, as Leeds United after disbandment (by FA order) of Leeds City (formed in 1904).

Turned Professional: 1920.

Club Nickname: 'The Whites'.

Ground: 1919, Elland Road.

HONOURS

Football League – Division 1:
Champions 1968–69, 1973–74, 1991–92; *Runners-up* 1964–65, 1965–66, 1969–70, 1970–71, 1971–72;
Division 2: *Champions* 1923–24, 1963–64, 1989–90;
Runners-up 1927–28, 1931–32, 1955–56; **FL 1:** *Runners-up* 2009–10.

FA Cup: *Winners* 1972;
Runners-up 1965, 1970, 1973.

Football League Cup: *Winners* 1968; *Runners-up* 1996.

European Competitions
European Cup: 1969–70, 1974–75 (*runners-up*).
Champions League: 1992–93, 2000–01 (*s-f*).
European Cup-Winners' Cup: 1972–73 (*runners-up*).
European Fairs Cup: 1965–66, 1966–67 (*runners-up*), 1967–68 (*winners*), 1968–69, 1970–71 (*winners*).
UEFA Cup: 1971–72, 1973–74, 1979–80, 1995–96, 1998–99, 1999–2000 (*s-f*), 2001–02, 2002–03.

First Football League Game: 28 August 1920, Division 2, v Port Vale (a) L 0–2 – Down; Duffield, Tillotson; Musgrove, Baker, Walton; Mason, Goldthorpe, Thompson, Lyon, Best.

Record League Victory: 8–0 v Leicester C, Division 1, 7 April 1934 – Moore; George Milburn, Jack Milburn; Edwards, Hart, Copping; Mahon (2), Firth (2), Duggan (2), Furness (2), Cochrane.

sky SPORTS FACT FILE

Leeds United's first-ever game was a friendly against Yorkshire Amateurs at Elland Road on 15 November 1919, resulting in a 5-2 win. The club's first goal was scored by Thomas Heslop. The first competitive game was a Midland League fixture against Barnsley Reserves the following Saturday which produced a 0-0 draw.

Record Cup Victory: 10–0 v Lyn (Oslo), European Cup 1st rd 1st leg, 17 September 1969 – Sprake; Reaney, Cooper, Bremner (2), Charlton, Hunter, Madeley, Clarke (2), Jones (3), Giles (2) (Bates), O'Grady (1).

Record Defeat: 1–8 v Stoke C, Division 1, 27 August 1934.

Most League Points (2 for a win): 67, Division 1, 1968–69.

Most League Points (3 for a win): 86, FL 1, 2009–10.

Most League Goals: 98, Division 2, 1927–28.

Highest League Scorer in Season: John Charles, 42, Division 2, 1953–54.

Most League Goals in Total Aggregate: Peter Lorimer, 168, 1965–79 and 1983–86.

Most League Goals in One Match: 5, Gordon Hodgson v Leicester C, Division 1, 1 October 1938.

Most Capped Player: Lucas Radebe, 58 (70), South Africa.

Most League Appearances: Jack Charlton, 629, 1953–73.

Youngest League Player: Peter Lorimer, 15 years 289 days v Southampton, 29 September 1962.

Record Transfer Fee Received: £30,800,000 from Manchester U for Rio Ferdinand, July 2002.

Record Transfer Fee Paid: £18,000,000 to West Ham U for Rio Ferdinand, November 2000.

Football League Record: 1920 Elected to Division 2; 1924–27 Division 1; 1927–28 Division 2; 1928–31 Division 1; 1931–32 Division 2; 1932–47 Division 1; 1947–56 Division 2; 1956–60 Division 1; 1960–64 Division 2; 1964–82 Division 1; 1982–90 Division 2; 1990–92 Division 1; 1992–2004 FA Premier League; 2004–07 FL C; 2007–10 FL 1; 2010– FL C.

MANAGERS

Dick Ray 1919–20
Arthur Fairclough 1920–27
Dick Ray 1927–35
Bill Hampson 1935–47
Willis Edwards 1947–48
Major Frank Buckley 1948–53
Raich Carter 1953–58
Bill Lambton 1958–59
Jack Taylor 1959–61
Don Revie OBE 1961–74
Brian Clough 1974
Jimmy Armfield 1974–78
Jock Stein CBE 1978
Jimmy Adamson 1978–80
Allan Clarke 1980–82
Eddie Gray MBE 1982–85
Billy Bremner 1985–88
Howard Wilkinson 1988–96
George Graham 1996–98
David O'Leary 1998–2002
Terry Venables 2002–03
Peter Reid 2003
Eddie Gray *(Caretaker)* 2003–04
Kevin Blackwell 2004–06
Dennis Wise 2006–08
Gary McAllister 2008
Simon Grayson 2008–12
Neil Warnock 2012–13
Brian McDermott 2013–14
Dave Hockaday June 2014–

LATEST SEQUENCES

Longest Sequence of League Wins: 9, 18.4.2009 – 5.9.2009.

Longest Sequence of League Defeats: 6, 28.12.2003 – 7.2.2004.

Longest Sequence of League Draws: 5, 19.4.1997 – 9.8.1997.

Longest Sequence of Unbeaten League Matches: 34, 26.10.1968 – 26.8.1969.

Longest Sequence Without a League Win: 17, 1.2.1947 – 26.5.1947.

Successive Scoring Runs: 30 from 27.8.1927.

Successive Non-scoring Runs: 6 from 30.1.1982.

TEN YEAR LEAGUE RECORD

		P	W	D	L	F	A	Pts	Pos
2004-05	FL C	46	14	18	14	49	52	60	14
2005-06	FL C	46	21	15	10	57	38	78	5
2006-07	FL C	46	13	7	26	46	72	36*	24
2007-08	FL 1	46	27	10	9	72	38	76†	5
2008-09	FL 1	46	26	6	14	77	49	84	4
2009-10	FL 1	46	25	11	10	77	44	86	2
2010-11	FL C	46	19	15	12	81	70	72	7
2011-12	FL C	46	17	10	19	65	68	61	14
2012-13	FL C	46	17	10	19	57	66	61	13
2013-14	FL C	46	16	9	21	59	67	57	15

10 pts deducted; †15 pts deducted.

DID YOU KNOW ?

Between 3 March and 14 April 1928 Leeds United played nine games without conceding a goal. The run pushed them into the Division Two promotion places and even though they lost their last game of the season 5-1 at Stoke they had done enough to go up in second place.

LEEDS UNITED – FL CHAMPIONSHIP 2013–14 LEAGUE RECORD

Match No.	Date		Venue	Opponents	Result		H/T Score	Lg Pos.	Goalscorers	Attendance
1	Aug	3	H	Brighton & HA	W	2-1	1-1	3	McCormack [19], Murphy [90]	33,432
2		11	A	Leicester C	D	0-0	0-0	8		22,725
3		17	H	Sheffield W	D	1-1	0-1	9	McCormack [58]	23,766
4		24	A	Ipswich T	W	2-1	1-1	5	Varney [28], McCormack [49]	18,322
5		31	H	QPR	L	0-1	0-0	10		23,341
6	Sept	14	A	Bolton W	W	1-0	1-0	6	Varney [6]	19,622
7		18	A	Reading	L	0-1	0-0	11		21,167
8		21	H	Burnley	L	1-2	0-2	12	Smith [79]	26,465
9		28	A	Millwall	L	0-2	0-0	15		13,063
10	Oct	1	H	Bournemouth	W	2-1	0-0	11	McCormack [52], Poleon [80]	21,749
11		5	A	Derby Co	L	1-3	1-2	13	Pearce [45]	26,204
12		20	A	Birmingham C	W	4-0	3-0	9	McCormack [18], Austin [33], Smith 2 [45, 74]	21,301
13		26	A	Huddersfield T	L	2-3	1-1	10	Smith [2], Blackstock [73]	18,309
14	Nov	2	H	Yeovil T	W	2-0	0-0	8	McCormack 2 [48, 67]	25,351
15		9	A	Charlton Ath	W	4-2	1-1	8	McCormack 4 (1 pen) [17, 48 (p), 73, 90]	17,601
16		23	H	Middlesbrough	W	2-1	1-0	6	McCormack [35], Pearce [57]	30,367
17		30	A	Blackburn R	L	0-1	0-1	7		20,267
18	Dec	4	H	Wigan Ath	W	2-0	1-0	7	McCormack 2 [15, 77]	25,888
19		7	H	Watford	D	3-3	0-2	8	Pugh [50], Smith [56], McCormack [78]	23,445
20		14	A	Doncaster R	W	3-0	1-0	6	Smith [19], McCormack [76], Austin [87]	12,192
21		21	A	Barnsley	D	0-0	0-0	5		31,031
22		26	A	Blackpool	D	1-1	1-0	6	Peltier [25]	15,552
23		29	A	Nottingham F	L	1-2	0-1	7	McCormack [83]	26,854
24	Jan	1	H	Blackburn R	L	1-2	0-2	8	Smith [53]	30,145
25		11	A	Sheffield W	L	0-6	0-2	11		22,124
26		18	H	Leicester C	L	0-1	0-0	12		22,678
27		28	H	Ipswich T	D	1-1	0-0	12	McCormack (pen) [62]	20,461
28	Feb	1	H	Huddersfield T	W	5-1	1-1	11	McCormack 3 [45, 62, 73], Kebe [50], Mowatt [82]	31,103
29		8	A	Yeovil T	W	2-1	0-1	10	McCormack [46], Warnock [62]	7984
30		11	A	Brighton & HA	L	0-1	0-0	11		27,700
31		22	A	Middlesbrough	D	0-0	0-0	11		20,424
32	Mar	1	A	QPR	D	1-1	1-1	12	McCormack [14]	16,448
33		8	H	Bolton W	L	1-5	0-1	12	Smith [90]	28,904
34		11	H	Reading	L	2-4	0-1	13	Smith [63], Austin [64]	19,915
35		15	A	Burnley	L	1-2	1-1	14	McCormack [27]	18,109
36		22	H	Millwall	W	2-1	2-0	13	Smith [19], McCormack [41]	23,211
37		25	A	Bournemouth	L	1-4	0-3	14	McCormack [69]	10,109
38		29	H	Doncaster R	L	1-2	0-2	15	McCormack [62]	23,476
39	Apr	1	H	Charlton Ath	L	0-1	0-0	15		17,343
40		5	A	Wigan Ath	L	0-1	0-1	16		16,443
41		8	A	Watford	L	0-3	0-2	16		16,212
42		12	H	Blackpool	W	2-0	1-0	16	Murphy 2 [21, 73]	23,416
43		19	A	Barnsley	W	1-0	1-0	16	McCormack [16]	15,190
44		21	H	Nottingham F	L	0-2	0-2	16		20,517
45		26	A	Birmingham C	W	3-1	0-0	15	Smith [58], Pugh [60], Caddis (og) [78]	19,861
46	May	3	H	Derby Co	D	1-1	0-1	15	Smith [50]	29,724

Final League Position: 15

GOALSCORERS

League (59): McCormack 28 (2 pens), Smith 12, Austin 3, Murphy 3, Pearce 2, Pugh 2, Varney 2, Blackstock 1, Kebe 1, Mowatt 1, Peltier 1, Poleon 1, Warnock 1, own goal 1.
The Budweiser FA Cup (0).
Capital One Cup (5): McCormack 1 (1 pen), Brown 1, Poleon 1, Smith 1, Wootton 1.

Kenny P 30	Peltier L 23+2	Warnock S 27	Green P 7+2	Lees T 40+1	Pearce J 45	Murphy L 37	Tonge M 16+7	Varney L 11	Hunt N 13+6	McCormack R 46	Poleon D 2+17	Drury A —+1	Smith M 20+19	Austin R 40	Diouf E 2+4	Wootton S 19+1	Byram S 17+8	White A 2+7	Mowatt A 24+5	Brown M 12+6	Blackstock D 2+2	Zaliukas M 13+2	Pugh D 19+1	Ariyibi G —+2	Stewart C 9+2	Kebe J 9	Butland J 16	Wickham C 5	Match No.
1	2	3[3]	4	5	6	7	8	9[2]	10[1]	11	12	13	14																1
1	2	5	6[2]	3	4	8	14	10[3]	11[1]	9	12		13	7															2
1	2	5	6[1]	3	4	8	12	11[2]	9	10[9]			13	7	14														3
1	2	5	6	3	4	8	13	11[2]	10[1]	9	12			7															4
1	2	5	6[2]		4	8		10[3]	11[1]	9	13		12	7	14	3													5
1	2[1]	5		12	4	8	7	10	11	9				6		3													6
1	5[4]	2		4	8	7	10[2]	11[1]	9	12			13	6		3													7
1		12		4	6[2]	8	11[1]		10	13			14	7	9	3	2[3]	5											8
1	2	5[1]	14	4	8	7[2]	10[3]	11					13	6		3	12		9										9
1	2	5	8	3	4		7		10[1]	11	12			6					9										10
1	2	5	6[1]	3	4		7[3]	11[2]	10	13	12		8	14					9										11
1	9		2	4	6				11	10	7[1]					3	5	8	12										12
1	6		3	4	8[1]				10	11	9			5	2	7			12										13
1	5	9[1]		2	4	8			10	11[2]	6			3		7		13	12										14
1	2			3	5	7			10	13	8		4[1]				9	11[2]	12	6									15
1	2			3	5	7[7]			10	13	8			12		9	14	11[1]	4	6[3]									16
1	2[2]			3	5	7[1]	11[3]		10	14	13	9			12	8			4	6									17
1	2			3	5	7			11	10	9					8			4	6									18
1	3				5	7			11	10	8		2			9			4	6									19
1	2			3	5	7			11[2]	13	10	8				9[1]	12		4	6									20
1	2[2]			3	5	7[1]	13		11	14	10	8			12	9[1]			4	6									21
1	5			2	4		6		10	11	7					8			3	9									22
1	2[1]			3	5	7			11[2]	14	10	8			13		9[3]		4	6	12								23
1			3[3]	5	7[1]				11	13	10	8		2		9[2]	14		4	6	12								24
1	5			2[1]	4				10		12[8]	7			13	6			3	8		9	11[2]						25
1	12	5		3	4		10[2]	11					8	13				7					9	6[1]					26
1	14	5		3	4			11	13		7	10[1]		2[3]			12	8[2]					9	6					27
1		5		3	4	6	12		10		7[2]			2		8[1]	13						11	9					28
1		5		3	4	6			10	12	7			2		8[1]						11	9					29
1		5		3	4	7		13	11	12	8			2		9[2]			10[1]				6					30
	2	5			4	7		10[1]	11	12	8	3										9	6	1				31
	2	5		3	4	7[3]			11		8		14		12	13						9[1]	6[2]	1	10			32
	2[3]	5		3		7			10	14	8	4	12	13								9[2]	6[1]	1	11			33
			2	4	8				11	12	6			5	7		3[1]	9					1	10				34
			3	4	6			11	12	10	7			2		8[1]						5		1	9			35
			3	4	7	12	13	11	10	8	14	2[1]	6[3]									5		1	9[2]			36
			3	4	7[1]			9[2]	11	10	8			2	12	6						5	13	1				37
			3	4	7[1]	13		11		10	8[2]			2	12	6						5	9	1				38
	5		3	4		7		12	11	13	10[2]			2[1]	6	9	8							1				39
	5		3	4		8		9[1]	11	12	10			2	6			7						1				40
	5		3	4		7		11[3]	10[5]	6	13			2	14	9[1]	7					12		1				41
	6		3	5	9	7		12	11	10[1]				2	13	8		4[2]						1				42
	6		3	5	7	9		12	11	10[1]				2	13	8		4[2]						1				43
	5[2]		3	4	7	8[1]		10[3]	11	12	9			2		14	6		13					1				44
			3	4	7[2]	8		13	11	10[3]	5			2	14	12	6		9[1]					1				45
			3	5	9[1]	7			11	10	2			4	12		8		6					1				46

The Budweiser FA Cup
Third Round   Rochdale   (a)   0-2

Capital One Cup
First Round   Chesterfield   (h)   2-1
Second Round   Doncaster R   (a)   3-1
Third Round   Newcastle U   (a)   0-2

LEICESTER CITY

FOUNDATION

In 1884 a number of young footballers, who were mostly old boys of Wyggeston School, held a meeting at a house on the Roman Fosse Way and formed Leicester Fosse FC. They collected 9d (less than 4p) towards the cost of a ball, plus the same amount for membership. Their first professional, Harry Webb from Stafford Rangers, was signed in 1888 for 2s 6d (12p) per week, plus travelling expenses.

King Power Stadium, Filbert Way, Leicester LE2 7FL.

Telephone: (0844) 815 5000.

Fax: (0116) 247 0585.

Ticket Office: (0844) 815 5000.

Website: www.lcfc.co.uk

Email: sales@lcfc.co.uk

Ground Capacity: 32,312.

Record Attendance: 47,298 v Tottenham H, FA Cup 5th rd, 18 February 1928 (at Filbert Street); 32,148 v Manchester U, FA Premier League, 26 December 2003 (at Walkers Stadium).

Pitch Measurements: 110m × 74m (120.5yd × 81yd)

Chairman: Khun Vichai Srivaddhanaprabha.

Chief Executive: Susan Whelan.

Manager: Nigel Pearson.

Assistant Managers: Craig Shakespeare, Steve Walsh.

Physio: Dave Rennie.

Colours: Blue shirts with yellow trim, white shorts with blue and yellow trim, blue socks with white trim.

Year Formed: 1884.

Turned Professional: 1888.

Previous Name: 1884, Leicester Fosse; 1919, Leicester City.

Club Nickname: 'The Foxes'.

Grounds: 1884, Victoria Park; 1887, Belgrave Road; 1888, Victoria Park; 1891, Filbert Street; 2002, Walkers Stadium (now known as King Power Stadium from 2011).

First Football League Game: 1 September 1894, Division 2, v Grimsby T (a) L 3–4 – Thraves; Smith, Bailey; Seymour, Brown, Henrys; Hill, Hughes, McArthur (1), Skea (2), Priestman.

Record League Victory: 10–0 v Portsmouth, Division 1, 20 October 1928 – McLaren; Black, Brown; Findlay, Carr, Watson; Adcock, Hine (3), Chandler (6), Lochhead, Barry (1).

Record Cup Victory: 8–1 v Coventry C (a), League Cup 5th rd, 1 December 1964 – Banks; Sjoberg, Norman (2); Roberts, King, McDerment; Hodgson (2), Cross, Goodfellow, Gibson (1), Stringfellow (2), (1 og).

HONOURS

Football League – Division 1:
Runners-up 1928–29, 2002–03;
Division 2: *Champions* 1924–25,
1936–37, 1953–54, 1956–57, 1970–71,
1979–80; *Runners-up* 1907–08;
FL C: *Champions* 2013–14.
FL 1: *Champions* 2008–09.

FA Cup: *Runners-up* 1949, 1961,
1963, 1969.

Football League Cup: *Winners* 1964,
1997, 2000; *Runners-up* 1965, 1999.

European Competitions
European Cup-Winners' Cup: 1961–62.
UEFA Cup: 1997–98, 2000–01.

sky SPORTS FACT FILE

Charlie Saer, a goalkeeper for Leicester Fosse, was elected as secretary of the Association Footballers' Union, forerunner of the PFA, in October 1898. He also worked as a schoolteacher and two months later he was forced to resign from the position. He remained as a teacher in Fleetwood for many years and a local primary school is named after him.

Record Defeat: 0–12 (as Leicester Fosse) v Nottingham F, Division 1, 21 April 1909.

Most League Points (2 for a win): 61, Division 2, 1956–57.

Most League Points (3 for a win): 102, FL C, 2013–14.

Most League Goals: 109, Division 2, 1956–57.

Highest League Scorer in Season: Arthur Rowley, 44, Division 2, 1956–57.

Most League Goals in Total Aggregate: Arthur Chandler, 259, 1923–35.

Most League Goals in One Match: 6, John Duncan v Port Vale, Division 2, 25 December 1924; 6, Arthur Chandler v Portsmouth, Division 1, 20 October 1928.

Most Capped Player: John O'Neill, 39, Northern Ireland.

Most League Appearances: Adam Black, 528, 1920–35.

Youngest League Player: Dave Buchanan, 16 years 192 days v Oldham Ath, 1 January 1979.

Record Transfer Fee Received: £11,000,000 from Liverpool for Emile Heskey, March 2000.

Record Transfer Fee Paid: £8,000,000 to Brighton & HA for Leonardo Ulloa, July 2014.

Football League Record: 1894 Elected to Division 2; 1908–09 Division 1; 1909–25 Division 2; 1925–35 Division 1; 1935–37 Division 2; 1937–39 Division 1; 1946–54 Division 2; 1954–55 Division 1; 1955–57 Division 2; 1957–69 Division 1; 1969–71 Division 2; 1971–78 Division 1; 1978–80 Division 2; 1980–81 Division 1; 1981–83 Division 2; 1983–87 Division 1; 1987–92 Division 2; 1992–94 Division 1; 1994–95 FA Premier League; 1995–96 Division 1; 1996–2002 FA Premier League; 2002–03 Division 1; 2003–04 FA Premier League; 2004–08 FL C; 2008–09 FL 1; 2009–14 FL C; 2014– FA Premier League.

LATEST SEQUENCES

Longest Sequence of League Wins: 9, 21.12.2013 – 1.2.2014.

Longest Sequence of League Defeats: 8, 17.3.2001 – 28.4.2001.

Longest Sequence of League Draws: 6, 2.10.2004 – 2.11.2004.

Longest Sequence of Unbeaten League Matches: 23, 1.11.2008 – 7.3.2009.

Longest Sequence Without a League Win: 18, 12.4.1975 – 1.11.1975.

Successive Scoring Runs: 31 from 23.11.2013 – onwards.

Successive Non-scoring Runs: 7 from 21.11.1987.

MANAGERS

Frank Gardner 1884–92
Ernest Marson 1892–94
J. Lee 1894–95
Henry Jackson 1895–97
William Clark 1897–98
George Johnson 1898–1912
Jack Bartlett 1912–14
Louis Ford 1914–15
Harry Linney 1915–19
Peter Hodge 1919–26
Willie Orr 1926–32
Peter Hodge 1932–34
Arthur Lochhead 1934–36
Frank Womack 1936–39
Tom Bromilow 1939–45
Tom Mather 1945–46
John Duncan 1946–49
Norman Bullock 1949–55
David Halliday 1955–58
Matt Gillies 1958–68
Frank O'Farrell 1968–71
Jimmy Bloomfield 1971–77
Frank McLintock 1977–78
Jock Wallace 1978–82
Gordon Milne 1982–86
Bryan Hamilton 1986–87
David Pleat 1987–91
Gordon Lee 1991
Brian Little 1991–94
Mark McGhee 1994–95
Martin O'Neill 1995–2000
Peter Taylor 2000–01
Dave Bassett 2001–02
Micky Adams 2002–04
Craig Levein 2004–06
Robert Kelly 2006–07
Martin Allen 2007
Gary Megson 2007
Ian Holloway 2007–08
Nigel Pearson 2008–10
Paulo Sousa 2010
Sven-Göran Eriksson 2010–11
Nigel Pearson November 2011–

TEN YEAR LEAGUE RECORD

		P	W	D	L	F	A	Pts	Pos
2004-05	FL C	46	12	21	13	49	46	57	15
2005-06	FL C	46	13	15	18	51	59	54	16
2006-07	FL C	46	13	14	19	49	64	53	19
2007-08	FL C	46	12	16	18	42	45	52	22
2008-09	FL 1	46	27	15	4	84	39	96	1
2009-10	FL C	46	21	13	12	61	45	76	5
2010-11	FL C	46	19	10	17	76	71	67	10
2011-12	FL C	46	18	12	16	66	55	66	9
2012-13	FL C	46	19	11	16	71	48	68	6
2013-14	FL C	46	31	9	6	83	43	102	1

DID YOU KNOW ?

Full back Harry Thorpe joined Leicester Fosse from Fulham in August 1907. He was a regular in the line-up until March 1908 when a bout of influenza put him out of action. He never recovered and after returning home to Derbyshire he passed away the following September.

LEICESTER CITY – FL CHAMPIONSHIP 2013–14 LEAGUE RECORD

Match No.	Date	Venue	Opponents	Result	H/T Score	Lg Pos.	Goalscorers	Attendance
1	Aug 3	A	Middlesbrough	W 2-1	0-1	3	Drinkwater [60], Vardy [67]	17,223
2	11	H	Leeds U	D 0-0	0-0	8		22,725
3	17	A	Derby Co	W 1-0	1-0	6	Grant (og) [37]	23,437
4	24	H	Birmingham C	W 3-2	0-1	2	Vardy [77], King [82], Nugent (pen) [90]	21,229
5	31	A	Charlton Ath	L 1-2	0-1	5	Drinkwater [62]	15,542
6	Sept 14	H	Wigan Ath	W 2-0	1-0	4	Moore [15], Nugent (pen) [81]	21,810
7	17	H	Blackburn R	W 2-1	2-0	3	Dyer [16], Nugent (pen) [45]	19,153
8	21	A	Blackpool	D 2-2	0-1	3	Konchesky (pen) [72], King [74]	15,317
9	28	H	Barnsley	W 2-1	0-0	3	Nugent 2 (1 pen) [50, 62 (p)]	21,591
10	Oct 1	A	Yeovil T	W 2-1	0-0	3	Dyer [54], Nugent (pen) [63]	6476
11	5	A	Doncaster R	L 0-1	0-1	3		10,003
12	19	H	Huddersfield T	W 2-1	2-0	3	Vardy [11], Gerrard (og) [38]	22,297
13	26	H	Bournemouth	W 2-1	1-1	2	Nugent [18], Vardy [64]	23,357
14	Nov 2	A	Watford	W 3-0	1-0	2	Wood [10], Knockaert [53], Dyer [86]	16,011
15	9	H	Nottingham F	L 0-2	0-2	2		30,416
16	23	A	Ipswich T	W 2-1	0-1	2	Nugent 2 [51, 57]	18,227
17	30	H	Millwall	W 3-0	1-0	1	Dyer [12], Vardy 2 [52, 55]	21,633
18	Dec 3	A	Sheffield W	L 1-2	1-2	1	Knockaert [3]	20,016
19	7	A	Brighton & HA	L 1-3	0-2	3	King [64]	27,497
20	14	H	Burnley	D 1-1	1-0	3	Nugent (pen) [14]	23,143
21	21	A	QPR	W 1-0	1-0	3	Vardy [41]	17,713
22	26	H	Reading	W 1-0	1-0	1	Nugent (pen) [21]	26,722
23	29	H	Bolton W	W 5-3	3-3	1	Drinkwater [5], Knockaert [37], Mills (og) [41], Dyer [75], Taylor-Fletcher [89]	26,614
24	Jan 1	A	Millwall	W 3-1	1-0	1	Knockaert [6], Nugent [48], Schlupp [90]	10,014
25	10	A	Derby Co	W 4-1	1-0	1	De Laet [25], Nugent 2 (1 pen) [48, 60 (p)], Vardy [64]	23,140
26	18	A	Leeds U	W 1-0	0-0	1	Nugent [87]	22,678
27	25	H	Middlesbrough	W 2-0	0-0	1	Vardy [52], De Laet [73]	26,047
28	28	A	Birmingham C	W 2-1	1-0	1	Dyer [24], Vardy [83]	14,763
29	Feb 1	A	Bournemouth	W 1-0	0-0	1	Phillips [81]	10,719
30	8	H	Watford	D 2-2	1-2	1	James [43], Drinkwater [90]	23,635
31	19	A	Nottingham F	D 2-2	1-2	1	Vardy [29], Mahrez [82]	24,808
32	22	H	Ipswich T	W 3-0	2-0	1	Vardy [19], Nugent [31], Wood [88]	28,078
33	Mar 1	H	Charlton Ath	W 3-0	1-0	1	Vardy [7], Drinkwater [48], Nugent [64]	24,742
34	11	A	Barnsley	W 3-0	1-0	1	Vardy 2 [21, 62], Drinkwater [58]	12,539
35	15	H	Blackpool	W 3-1	0-1	1	Mahrez [60], Morgan [82], Phillips [87]	27,669
36	22	A	Blackburn R	D 1-1	1-1	1	Vardy [20]	16,528
37	25	H	Yeovil T	D 1-1	0-1	1	Wood [90]	26,240
38	29	A	Burnley	W 2-0	1-0	1	Nugent [35], Wood [78]	16,794
39	Apr 1	A	Wigan Ath	D 2-2	1-1	1	King [41], Hammond [87]	15,025
40	4	H	Sheffield W	W 2-1	1-1	1	Mahrez [10], Knockaert [61]	26,103
41	8	H	Brighton & HA	L 1-4	0-2	1	Taylor-Fletcher [89]	29,722
42	14	A	Reading	D 1-1	1-1	1	Drinkwater [33]	20,072
43	19	H	QPR	W 1-0	0-0	1	Nugent [68]	27,386
44	22	A	Bolton W	W 1-0	0-0	1	Dyer [62]	16,569
45	26	A	Huddersfield T	W 2-0	1-0	1	Taylor-Fletcher [31], Morgan [75]	16,481
46	May 3	H	Doncaster R	W 1-0	0-0	1	Nugent (pen) [75]	31,424

Final League Position: 1

GOALSCORERS

League (83): Nugent 20 (9 pens), Vardy 16, Drinkwater 7, Knockaert 5, King 4, Wood 4, Mahrez 3, Taylor-Fletcher 3, De Laet 2, Morgan 2, Phillips 2, Hammond 1, James 1, Konchesky 1 (1 pen), Moore 1, Schlupp 1, own goals 3.

The Budweiser FA Cup (1): Nugent 1.

Capital One Cup (14): Wood 4 (1 pen), Dyer 3, Knockaert 2, Nugent 1 (1 pen), Drinkwater 1, Miquel 1, Morgan 1, St Ledger 1.

Schmeichel K 46	De Laet R 35 + 1	Konchesky P 31	St. Ledger S 1	Morgan W 45	Whitbread Z 3	James M 28 + 7	Drinkwater D 43 + 2	Vardy J 36 + 1	Wood C 7 + 19	King A 24 + 6	Moore L 26 + 4	Nugent D 44 + 2	Dyer L 31 + 9	Knockaert A 36 + 6	Schlupp J 15 + 11	Waghorn M — + 2	Miquel I 6 + 1	Hammond D 7 + 22	Taylor-Fletcher G 2 + 19	Wasilewski M 26 + 5	Phillips K 2 + 10	Mahrez R 12 + 7	Match No.
1	2	3	4	5	6^1	7	8	9	10^2	11	12	13											1
1	2^2	6		4	5	7^3	8	11^1	14	9	3	10	12	13									2
1	2		3			6^3	7	10^1	11^2	8	4	9	12	13	5	14							3
1	2			4	5	3^2	6	9^1	8	11	10	12	13	7									4
1	2^3		3	8^4	6	11	13	7	5	10	14	12	9^2		4								5
1	2	5	4			7	11^2	13	8	3	10	9^1	6^3	14			12						6
1	2	5	4			7	11	13	8	3	10	9^2	6^1				12						7
1	2	5		3	14	7	11		8	4	10^1	9^3	6^3	12				13					8
1	2	5		3	13	7	11		8^1	4	10^2	9	6^3				12	14					9
1	2	5		3	12	7^1	11		8	4	10^1	9	6^3	13			14						10
1	2^1	5		3		8	11		7	4	10	9^2	6	13					12				11
1		5		3	12	7	11		8^1	4	10	9^2	6^1	14			13		2				12
1		5	4			7	11^1	12	8^2	2	10^9	9	6	13			14		3		6		13
1			4		12	7		10^2	8	2	11^3	9	6^1	5			13	14	3				14
1		5	4			7	12		8	2	10	9^1	6^3	11^2			13	14	3				15
1		5	4		12	6	11^1	14	8^2	2^1	9			11^2			13	7	3		2		16
1		5		3		8	7^1	10	12			11^2	9^3	6			4	14	13	2			17
1		5		3		8	7	10	13			11^1	9^2	6^3	14		4	12		2			18
1		5		3		7	8	13	9			11^3	10^2	12			4	6^1	14	2			19
1	2^3	5		3		8	7^2	11^2			4	10^1	9	6	14				12	13			20
1	2^2	5		3		7	8	11^1			4	10^2	9	6	13				12	14			21
1	2	5		3		8	7	11^2			4	10^1	9^3	6		12		13	14				22
1	2	5		3		8	7	11^1	14		4	10^1	9	6^2				13	12				23
1	12			3			14				8	4^{1}	11^1	9^2	6	13	5	7	10^3	2			24
1	2	5^1		3		7	8	10^3	13		4	11^2	9	6	12				14				25
1	2^3	5		3		8	7	11^2	14		4	10	9^1	6					12	13			26
1	2	5		3		8	7	11^2			4^1	10	9^3	6					12	13	14		27
1	2	5		4		8	7	10^1			11	9^2	6^3					13	3	14	12		28
1	2	5		4		8^2	7	11^3	13		10^1	9	6					14	3	13	9		29
1	2	5		4		7	8	10^2	14		11	9^1	6						3^2	12	13		30
1	2	5^{1}		4		7	8	11			12	10^1	9^3	6^2					3	14	13		31
1	2			4		8	7	11^2	13			10^1	9^1	6	5				3	14	12		32
1	2			4		8^1	7^3	11^2	12	13		10		9	5			14	3		6		33
1	2			4		8	7	11^1	12			10^3		6^2	5			14	13	3		9	34
1	2			4		8	7	11^1				10^2		6^3	5			14	12	3	13	9	35
1	2^3			4		8^2	7	11		14	13	10		6^1	5			12		3		9	36
1	2			4		8	7	11^1	14			10^2	12	6	5				3^3	13	9		37
1	2			4		7	8	11^3	12			10^2		6	5			14	13	3		9^1	38
1	2	5		4				11^3	8	3	10^2	9	6^1					7	13		14	12	39
1	2			4		7	8	11^1			10	14	9^3	5				13	12	3		6^2	40
1		5		4		8		13	7	2	10	12	6^1					14	3	11^3	9^2		41
1	2			4		8	11^3	12	13		10^2	9		5				7^1	14	3		6	42
1	2			4		12	6		8	14	10	13	9^2	5^1				7^3		3		11	43
1	2	5		4		7	6		12	9^3		11	13	10^2				14		3		8^1	44
1		5		4		7^1	14		11^3	9	2	13	10			3	6	8^2				12	45
1	2	5		4			7			8^2		10	9^1	12				14	13	3	11^3	6	46

The Budweiser FA Cup

Third Round	Stoke C	(a)	1-2

Capital One Cup

First Round	Wycombe W	(a)	2-1
Second Round	Carlisle U	(a)	5-2
Third Round	Derby Co	(h)	2-1
Fourth Round	Fulham	(h)	4-3
Quarter-Finals	Manchester C	(h)	1-3

LEYTON ORIENT

FOUNDATION

There is some doubt about the foundation of Leyton Orient, and, indeed, some confusion with clubs like Leyton and Clapton over their early history. As regards the foundation, the most favoured version is that Leyton Orient was formed originally by members of Homerton Theological College who established Glyn Cricket Club in 1881 and then carried on through the following winter playing football. Eventually many employees of the Orient Shipping Line became involved and so the name Orient was chosen in 1888.

Matchroom Stadium, Brisbane Road, Leyton, London E10 5NF.

Telephone: (0871) 310 1881.

Fax: (0871) 310 1882.

Ticket Office: (0871) 310 1883.

Website: www.leytonorient.com

Email: info@leytonorient.net

Ground Capacity: 9,311.

Record Attendance: 34,345 v West Ham U, FA Cup 4th rd, 25 January 1964.

Pitch Measurements: 100.5m × 65m (110yd × 71yd)

Chairman: Barry Hearn.

Chief Executive: Matthew Porter.

Manager: Russell Slade.

Assistant Manager: Kevin Nugent.

Physio: Mike Preston.

Colours: Red shirts, red shorts, red socks.

Year Formed: 1881.

Turned Professional: 1903.

Previous Names: 1881, Glyn Cricket and Football Club; 1886, Eagle Football Club; 1888, Orient Football Club; 1898, Clapton Orient; 1946, Leyton Orient; 1966, Orient; 1987, Leyton Orient.

Club Nickname: 'The O's'.

Grounds: 1884, Glyn Road; 1896, Whittles Athletic Ground; 1900, Millfields Road; 1930, Lea Bridge Road; 1937, Brisbane Road.

First Football League Game: 2 September 1905, Division 2, v Leicester Fosse (a) L 1–2 – Butler; Holmes, Codling; Lamberton, Boden, Boyle; Kingaby (1), Wootten, Leigh, Evenson, Bourne.

Record League Victory: 8–0 v Crystal Palace, Division 3 (S), 12 November 1955 – Welton; Lee, Earl; Blizzard, Aldous, McKnight; White (1), Facey (3), Burgess (2), Heckman, Hartburn (2). 8–0 v Rochdale, Division 4, 20 October 1987 – Wells; Howard, Dickenson (1), Smalley (1), Day, Hull, Hales (2), Castle (Sussex), Shinners (2), Godfrey (Harvey), Comfort (2). 8–0 v Colchester U, Division 4, 15 October 1988 – Wells; Howard, Dickenson, Hales (1p), Day (1), Sitton (1), Baker (1), Ward, Hull (3), Juryeff, Comfort (1). 8–0 v Doncaster R, Division 3, 28 December 1997 – Hyde; Channing, Naylor, Smith (1p), Hicks, Clark, Ling, Roger Joseph, Griffiths (3) (Harris), Richards (2) (Baker (1)), Inglethorpe (1) (Simpson).

HONOURS

Football League – Division 1: 22nd, 1962–63;

Division 2: *Runners-up* 1961–62;

Division 3: *Champions* 1969–70;

Division 3 (S): *Champions* 1955–56; *Runners-up* 1954–55.

FA Cup: Semi-final 1978.

Football League Cup: Best season: 5th rd, 1963.

sky SPORTS FACT FILE

Clapton Orient staged two 'home' Division Three South matches at Wembley in 1930 after changes were ordered to the pitch at their ground of Lea Bridge Speedway Stadium. The O's beat Brentford 3-0 and Southend United 3-1. They also used Arsenal's Highbury ground for an FA Cup tie before returning to their regular stadium just before Christmas.

Record Cup Victory: 9–2 v Chester, League Cup 3rd rd, 15 October 1962 – Robertson; Charlton, Taylor; Gibbs, Bishop, Lea; Deeley (1), Waites (3), Dunmore (2), Graham (3), Wedge.

Record Defeat: 0–8 v Aston Villa, FA Cup 4th rd, 30 January 1929.

Most League Points (2 for a win): 66, Division 3 (S), 1955–56.

Most League Points (3 for a win): 86, FL 1, 2013–14.

Most League Goals: 106, Division 3 (S), 1955–56.

Highest League Scorer in Season: Tom Johnston, 35, Division 2, 1957–58.

Most League Goals in Total Aggregate: Tom Johnston, 121, 1956–58, 1959–61.

Most League Goals in One Match: 4, Wally Leigh v Bradford C, Division 2, 13 April 1906; 4, Albert Pape v Oldham Ath, Division 2, 1 September 1924; 4, Peter Kitchen v Millwall, Division 3, 21 April 1984.

Most Capped Players: Tunji Banjo, 7 (7), Nigeria; John Chiedozie, 7 (9), Nigeria; Tony Grealish, 7 (45), Republic of Ireland.

Most League Appearances: Peter Allen, 432, 1965–78.

Youngest League Player: Paul Went, 15 years 327 days v Preston NE, 4 September 1965.

Record Transfer Fee Received: £1,000,000 from Fulham for Gabriel Zakuani, July 2006.

Record Transfer Fee Paid: £175,000 to Wigan Ath for Paul Beesley, October 1989.

Football League Record: 1905 Elected to Division 2; 1929–56 Division 3 (S); 1956–62 Division 2; 1962–63 Division 1; 1963–66 Division 2; 1966–70 Division 3; 1970–82 Division 2; 1982–85 Division 3; 1985–89 Division 4; 1989–92 Division 3; 1992–95 Division 2; 1995–2004 Division 3; 2004–06 FL 2; 2006– FL 1.

LATEST SEQUENCES

Longest Sequence of League Wins: 10, 21.1.1956 – 30.3.1956.

Longest Sequence of League Defeats: 9, 1.4.1995 – 6.5.1995.

Longest Sequence of League Draws: 6, 30.11.1974 – 28.12.1974.

Longest Sequence of Unbeaten League Matches: 15, 13.4.2013 – 19.10.2013.

Longest Sequence Without a League Win: 23, 6.10.1962 – 13.4.1963.

Successive Scoring Runs: 22 from 12.3.1927.

Successive Non-scoring Runs: 8 from 19.11.1994.

MANAGERS

Sam Omerod 1905–06
Ike Ivenson 1906
Billy Holmes 1907–22
Peter Proudfoot 1922–29
Arthur Grimsdell 1929–30
Peter Proudfoot 1930–31
Jimmy Seed 1931–33
David Pratt 1933–34
Peter Proudfoot 1935–39
Tom Halsey 1939
Bill Wright 1939–45
Willie Hall 1945
Bill Wright 1945–46
Charlie Hewitt 1946–48
Neil McBain 1948–49
Alec Stock 1949–59
Les Gore 1959–61
Johnny Carey 1961–63
Benny Fenton 1963–64
Dave Sexton 1965
Dick Graham 1966–68
Jimmy Bloomfield 1968–71
George Petchey 1971–77
Jimmy Bloomfield 1977–81
Paul Went 1981
Ken Knighton 1981–83
Frank Clark 1983–91
  (Managing Director)
Peter Eustace 1991–94
Chris Turner/John Sitton 1994–95
Pat Holland 1995–96
Tommy Taylor 1996–2001
Paul Brush 2001–03
Martin Ling 2003–09
Geraint Williams 2009–10
Russell Slade April 2010–

TEN YEAR LEAGUE RECORD

		P	W	D	L	F	A	Pts	Pos
2004-05	FL 2	46	16	15	15	65	67	63	11
2005-06	FL 2	46	22	15	9	67	51	81	3
2006-07	FL 1	46	12	15	19	61	77	51	20
2007-08	FL 1	46	16	12	18	49	63	60	14
2008-09	FL 1	46	15	11	20	45	57	56	14
2009-10	FL 1	46	13	12	21	53	63	51	17
2010-11	FL 1	46	19	13	14	71	62	70	7
2011-12	FL 1	46	13	11	22	48	75	50	20
2012-13	FL 1	46	21	8	17	55	48	71	7
2013-14	FL 1	46	25	11	10	85	45	86	3

DID YOU KNOW

In 1977–78 Orient, then in the Second Division, reached the last four of the FA Cup for the only time in their history after knocking out Norwich City, Blackburn Rovers, Chelsea and Middlesbrough. They were finally defeated by Arsenal, going down 3-0 in a semi-final clash at Stamford Bridge.

LEYTON ORIENT – FOOTBALL LEAGUE ONE 2013–14 LEAGUE RECORD

Match No.	Date	Venue	Opponents	Result	H/T Score	Lg Pos.	Goalscorers	Attendance
1	Aug 3	A	Carlisle U	W 5-1	2-1	1	Lisbie [22], Cuthbert [37], Mooney [70], Cox 2 [81, 90]	4951
2	10	H	Shrewsbury T	W 3-0	0-0	1	Mooney 2 [57, 63], Odubajo [90]	4414
3	17	A	Stevenage	W 1-0	1-0	1	Lisbie [29]	3262
4	24	H	Crewe Alex	W 2-0	2-0	1	Odubajo [7], Mooney (pen) [37]	4455
5	31	A	Colchester U	W 2-1	1-1	1	Mooney [13], Lisbie [63]	5056
6	Sept 14	H	Port Vale	W 3-2	2-1	1	Mooney 2 [24, 45], Lisbie [88]	4888
7	17	H	Notts Co	W 5-1	2-0	1	Lisbie 2 [28, 45], Cox [56], Batt [80], Stockley [84]	4092
8	23	A	Brentford	W 2-0	0-0	1	Mooney (pen) [65], Batt [85]	6439
9	28	A	Walsall	D 1-1	1-0	1	Mooney [38]	5429
10	Oct 5	A	Oldham Ath	D 1-1	0-1	1	Batt [66]	4062
11	12	H	Milton Keynes D	W 2-1	1-1	1	Odubajo [42], Lisbie [67]	6359
12	19	A	Tranmere R	W 4-0	1-0	1	Lisbie 2 [22, 61], Cox [78], Batt [85]	4313
13	22	A	Coventry C	L 1-3	0-1	1	Lasimant [90]	2386
14	26	H	Rotherham U	W 1-0	1-0	1	Lisbie [29]	5609
15	Nov 2	A	Peterborough U	W 3-1	1-1	1	Mooney 2 [39, 58], Cox [49]	10,026
16	16	H	Preston NE	L 0-1	0-1	2		7123
17	23	A	Swindon T	W 3-1	2-1	2	Mooney [24], Odubajo 2 [40, 46]	8634
18	26	A	Bristol C	D 2-2	1-0	2	Mooney [23], Cox [70]	10,659
19	30	H	Sheffield U	D 1-1	0-0	1	Cox [82]	6586
20	Dec 14	A	Bradford C	D 1-1	1-0	1	James [45]	14,292
21	21	H	Crawley T	L 2-3	1-2	1	Odubajo [14], Bartley [86]	4855
22	26	H	Gillingham	W 2-1	0-1	1	Bartley [70], Lasimant [90]	8613
23	29	A	Wolverhampton W	D 1-1	0-1	2	Baudry [60]	28,598
24	Jan 7	A	Shrewsbury T	W 2-0	1-0	2	Odubajo [28], Cuthbert [87]	4194
25	11	H	Carlisle U	W 4-0	1-0	2	Cuthbert [43], Ness [47], Lisbie [66], Coulthirst [90]	5279
26	18	A	Crewe Alex	W 2-1	0-0	2	Dagnall 2 [60, 67]	4830
27	28	H	Coventry C	W 2-0	0-0	2	Cox [57], Mooney [81]	5077
28	Feb 1	A	Rotherham U	L 1-2	0-1	3	Odubajo [76]	8604
29	8	H	Peterborough U	L 1-2	0-0	3	Mooney [70]	6717
30	11	H	Bristol C	L 1-3	1-2	3	Lisbie [44]	3928
31	15	A	Preston NE	D 1-1	1-0	3	Baudry [44]	13,440
32	18	H	Stevenage	W 2-0	2-0	2	Odubajo [14], Dagnall [23]	4171
33	22	H	Swindon T	W 2-0	1-0	1	James 2 (2 pens) [42, 52]	5091
34	Mar 1	H	Colchester U	W 2-1	1-0	2	Mooney [21], Odubajo [83]	6323
35	8	A	Notts Co	D 0-0	0-0	2		4680
36	11	A	Port Vale	W 2-0	1-0	2	Cox [41], Clarke [58]	4235
37	15	H	Brentford	L 0-1	0-1	3		8335
38	22	A	Walsall	D 1-1	0-1	3	Clarke [78]	5779
39	25	H	Oldham Ath	D 1-1	1-0	3	Cuthbert [45]	3645
40	29	H	Bradford C	L 0-1	0-1	3		5165
41	Apr 5	A	Sheffield U	D 1-1	1-0	4	Cox [41]	16,809
42	12	H	Gillingham	W 5-1	4-0	3	Mooney 2 [5, 35], Cox [9], Lisbie [35], Dagnall [78]	5128
43	18	A	Crawley T	L 1-2	1-1	3	Dagnall [40]	4387
44	21	H	Wolverhampton W	L 1-3	0-2	5	Cox [48]	8161
45	26	H	Tranmere R	W 2-0	1-0	4	Lisbie [44], Dagnall [77]	4923
46	May 3	A	Milton Keynes D	W 3-1	2-0	3	Lisbie 2 [17, 45], Mooney [56]	9965

Final League Position: 3

GOALSCORERS

League (85): Mooney 19 (2 pens), Lisbie 16, Cox 12, Odubajo 10, Dagnall 6, Batt 4, Cuthbert 4, James 3 (2 pens), Bartley 2, Baudry 2, Clarke 2, Lasimant 2, Coulthirst 1, Ness 1, Stockley 1.
The Budweiser FA Cup (6): Batt 2, Cox 2, James 1, Mooney 1.
Capital One Cup (3): Lisbie 2, Cox 1.
Johnstone's Paint Trophy (5): Batt 3 (1 pen), James 1 (1 pen), Mooney 1.
League One Play-Offs (5): Cox 2, Odubajo 2, Dagnall 1.

Jones J 28	Cuthbert S 44	Sawyer G 16 + 6	James L 38 + 4	Clarke N 46	Baudry M 38 + 1	Odubajo M 46	Vincelot R 38 + 1	Mooney D 34 + 4	Lishie K 35 + 4	Batt S 7 + 28	Omozusi E 38 + 1	Cox D 44 + 1	Gorman J — + 2	Bartley M 9 + 16	Lasimant Y 1 + 10	Stockley J — + 8	Simpson R 5 + 9	Wright J — + 2	Larkins J 2	Jakupovic E 13	Loza J 1 + 2	Ness J 3 + 10	Coulthirst S — + 1	Dagnall C 11 + 9	Alnwick B 1	Jalal S 2	Lundstram J 6 + 1	Match No.
1	2	3	4	5^1	6	7	8	9	10^2	11^3	12	13	14															1
1	2	8^1	4	3	6	7	11	10^2	12	5	9^3			13	14													2
1	7	12	8^3	4	3^1	11	5	9	10^2	14	2	6		13														3
1	2	7^1	4	3	6	8	11^2	10		5	9	12	13	14														4
1	2	7^2	4	3	6	8	10	11^1	12	5	9			13														5
1	2^2	7^3	4	3	6	8	11	10^1	12	5	9			13			14											6
1	2	8	4	3	6^1	7	11^3	10^2	12	5	9				14	13												7
1	2	7	4	3	6	8	11^2	10^1	12	5	9			13														8
1	5^2	7	3	4	9	8^1	10	11^1	12	2	6			13														9
1	2	7	4	3	6		11	10	12	5	9^2	8^1		13														10
1	2	8	4	3	6	7	11	10^1	12	5	9																	11
1	2	8	4	3	6^1	7	11^2	10^3	12	5	9			13	14													12
1	2	14	8	4	3	6	7	10^2	11^3	5^1	9			13	12													13
1		4	5	8^2	3	6	7	11^1	10^2	12	2	9		13	14													14
1		4	5	7	3	6^2	8	11	10	12	2	9^1		13														15
1	3	5^1	7^3	4	13	6	11^2	10	12	2	9	8			14													16
1	2		4	3	6	7	11^3	10^1	12	5	9	8^2			14	13												17
1	2	7^2	4	3	6	8	11	10^3	12	5	9			13	14													18
1	2^2	8^1	4	3	6	7^3	10	11		5	9	14		13	12													19
1	2	8	4	3	6	7		12	10^1	5	9	13			11^2													20
1	2	5	7^1	3	4	6	8	11	10			13	9^2	12														21
	2^3	13		4	3	6	8	11	10^2	5	9	7	14	12					1									22
	12	2	3	4	6	7^2		10		5	9	8	13	11^1					1									23
	2	7	4	3	6^2		11	5	9	8^3		12	13							1	10^1	14						24
	2	7	3	4	6			10^1		5	9	8^2	11^3							1	13	12	14					25
	4		8	2	5	7	13		11	3		9		10^1						1		6^2		12				26
	2^3	14	7	3	4	9	8	13	10^2	5	6^1									1		12		11				27
	2	8^2	3	4	6	7	12		5	9	13			11^3			14					10^1	1					28
	2	12	8	4	3	6	7	10^3	13	5^1	9			14								11^2				1		29
	2	5		4	3	6	7	12	10^1		9	8^3	14								13	11^2				1		30
	2	5	8	4	3	6^2	7	10	11^1	13	9									1		12						31
	2	5	8^1	4	3	6	7	10		12	9									1		13		11^2				32
	2		8	4	3	6	7	10^1	13	12	5	9								1				11^2				33
	3	5	8^3	4		6	7	11^2	10^1	12	2	9		13						1		14						34
	3	5	8	4		6	7		10	12	2	9								1		11^1						35
	4	5	7	3		9	8^2	10^3	13	2	6	12		14						1		11^1						36
	3	5^2	8^1	4		6	7	11	10^3	12	2	9	14							1		13						37
	2	7^2	4	3	6	8	11		12	5	9			13						1				10^1				38
	2	7	4	3	6		11^3	10^1	5	9	8^2		14							1		12		13				39
1	2	5	12	4	3	6	11^2	10^3	13		9											7		14			8^1	40
1	2	8^1	4	3	6	12	11	13	5		10^2	9												7				41
1	2		4	3	6	7^2	11	10^3	14	5	9											13		12			8	42
1	2	8^1	3	4	6	7^3	11	13	5	9												14		10^2			12	43
1	2	5	13	4	3	6	7^3	10^1	12		9		14											11^2			8	44
1	3	5	12	4		2	7	11	10^2	6^1	9											14		13			8^3	45
1		5	13	4	3	2	7	11^3	10^2	14	6	9												12			8^1	46

The Budweiser FA Cup

First Round	Southport	(h)	5-2
Second Round	Walsall	(h)	1-0
Third Round	Yeovil T	(a)	0-4

Capital One Cup

First Round	Coventry C	(h)	3-2
Second Round	Hull C	(h)	0-1

(aet)

Johnstone's Paint Trophy

First Round	Gillingham	(a)	3-1
Second Round	Coventry C	(h)	0-0

(aet; won 4-2 on penalties)

Southern Quarter-Finals	Stevenage	(a)	2-3

League One Play-Offs

Semi-Finals 1st leg	Peterborough U	(a)	1-1
Semi-Finals 2nd leg	Peterborough U	(h)	2-1
Final	Rotherham U	(Wembley)	2-2

(aet; lost 4-3 on penalties)

LIVERPOOL

FOUNDATION

But for a dispute between Everton FC and their landlord at Anfield in 1892, there may never have been a Liverpool club. This dispute persuaded the majority of Evertonians to quit Anfield for Goodison Park, leaving the landlord, Mr John Houlding, to form a new club. He originally tried to retain the name 'Everton' but when this failed, he founded Liverpool Association FC on 15 March 1892.

Anfield Stadium, Anfield Road, Anfield, Liverpool L4 0TH.

Telephone: (0151) 263 2361.

Fax: (0151) 260 8813.

Ticket Office: (0843) 170 5555.

Website: www.liverpoolfc.com

Email: (via website)

Ground Capacity: 45,276.

Record Attendance: 61,905 v Wolverhampton W, FA Cup 4th rd, 2 February 1952.

Pitch Measurements: 101m × 68m (110yd × 74yd)

Chairman: Tom Werner.

Managing Director: Ian Ayre.

Manager: Brendan Rodgers.

Assistant Manager: Colin Pascoe.

Physio: Chris Morgan.

Colours: Red shirts, red shorts, red socks.

Year Formed: 1892.

Turned Professional: 1892.

Club Nicknames: 'The Reds', 'Pool'.

Ground: 1892, Anfield.

First Football League Game: 2 September 1893, Division 2, v Middlesbrough Ironopolis (a) W 2–0 – McOwen; Hannah, McLean; Henderson, McQue (1), McBride; Gordon, McVean (1), Matt McQueen, Stott, Hugh McQueen.

HONOURS

FA Premier League: *Runners-up* 2001–02, 2008–09, 2013–14.
Football League – Division 1:
Champions 1900–01, 1905–06, 1921–22, 1922–23, 1946–47, 1963–64, 1965–66, 1972–73, 1975–76, 1976–77, 1978–79, 1979–80, 1981–82, 1982–83, 1983–84, 1985–86, 1987–88, 1989–90; *Runners-up* 1898–99, 1909–10, 1968–69, 1973–74, 1974–75, 1977–78, 1984–85, 1986–87, 1988–89, 1990–91;
Division 2: *Champions* 1893–94, 1895–96, 1904–05, 1961–62.
FA Cup: *Winners* 1965, 1974, 1986, 1989, 1992, 2001, 2006; *Runners-up* 1914, 1950, 1971, 1977, 1988, 1996, 2012.
Football League Cup: *Winners* 1981, 1982, 1983, 1984, 1995, 2001, 2003, 2012; *Runners-up* 1978, 1987, 2005.
League Super Cup: *Winners* 1986.
European Competitions: European Cup: 1964–65, 1966–67, 1973–74, 1976–77 (*winners*), 1977–78 (*winners*), 1978–79, 1979–80, 1980–81 (*winners*), 1981–82, 1982–83, 1983–84 (*winners*), 1984–85 (*runners-up*). **Champions League:** 2001–02, 2002–03, 2004–05 (*winners*), 2005–06, 2006–07 (*runners-up*), 2007–08 (*s-f*), 2008–09 (*q-f*), 2009–10. **European Cup-Winners' Cup:** 1965–66 (*runners-up*), 1971–72, 1974–75, 1992–93, 1996–97 (*s-f*). **European Fairs Cup:** 1967–68, 1968–69, 1969–70, 1970–71. **UEFA Cup:** 1972–73 (*winners*), 1975–76 (*winners*), 1991–92, 1995–96, 1997–98, 1998–99, 2000–01 (*winners*), 2002–03, 2003–04.
Europa League: 2009–10, 2010–11, 2012–13. **Super Cup:** 1977 (*winners*), 1978, 1984, 2001 (*winners*), 2005 (*winners*). **World Club Championship:** 1981, 1984. **FIFA Club World Cup:** 2005.

Record League Victory: 10–1 v Rotherham T, Division 2, 18 February 1896 – Storer; Goldie, Wilkie; McCartney, McQue, Holmes; McVean (3), Ross (2), Allan (4), Becton (1), Bradshaw.

sky SPORTS FACT FILE

Liverpool won their first derby clash with Everton 1-0 when the teams met at Bootle in the final of the Liverpool Senior Cup in April 1893. The winning goal was scored by former Everton player Tom Wyllie but the Toffees immediately lodged an objection which meant the cup was not presented until after Liverpool's game the following day against Preston.

Record Cup Victory: 11–0 v Stromsgodset Drammen, ECWC 1st rd 1st leg, 17 September 1974 – Clemence; Smith (1), Lindsay (1p), Thompson (2), Cormack (1), Hughes (1), Boersma (2), Hall, Heighway (1), Kennedy (1), Callaghan (1).

Record Defeat: 1–9 v Birmingham C, Division 2, 11 December 1954.

Most League Points (2 for a win): 68, Division 1, 1978–79.

Most League Points (3 for a win): 90, Division 1, 1987–88.

Most League Goals: 106, Division 2, 1895–96.

Highest League Scorer in Season: Roger Hunt, 41, Division 2, 1961–62.

Most League Goals in Total Aggregate: Roger Hunt, 245, 1959–69.

Most League Goals in One Match: 5, Andy McGuigan v Stoke C, Division 1, 4 January 1902; 5, John Evans v Bristol R, Division 2, 15 September 1954; 5, Ian Rush v Luton T, Division 1, 29 October 1983.

Most Capped Player: Steven Gerrard, 114, England.

Most League Appearances: Ian Callaghan, 640, 1960–78.

Youngest League Player: Jack Robinson, 16 years 250 days v Hull C, 9 May 2010.

Record Transfer Fee Received: £75,000,000 from Barcelona for Luis Suarez, July 2014.

Record Transfer Fee Paid: £35,000,000 to Newcastle U for Andy Carroll, January 2011.

Football League Record: 1893 Elected to Division 2; 1894–95 Division 1; 1895–96 Division 2; 1896–1904 Division 1; 1904–05 Division 2; 1905–54 Division 1; 1954–62 Division 2; 1962–92 Division 1; 1992– FA Premier League.

MANAGERS

W. E. Barclay 1892–96
Tom Watson 1896–1915
David Ashworth 1920–23
Matt McQueen 1923–28
George Patterson 1928–36
(continued as Secretary)
George Kay 1936–51
Don Welsh 1951–56
Phil Taylor 1956–59
Bill Shankly 1959–74
Bob Paisley 1974–83
Joe Fagan 1983–85
Kenny Dalglish 1985–91
Graeme Souness 1991–94
Roy Evans 1994–98
(then Joint Manager)
Gerard Houllier 1998–2004
Rafael Benitez 2004–10
Roy Hodgson 2010–11
Kenny Dalglish 2011–12
Brendan Rodgers June 2012–

LATEST SEQUENCES

Longest Sequence of League Wins: 12, 21.4.1990 – 6.10.1990.

Longest Sequence of League Defeats: 9, 29.4.1899 – 14.10.1899.

Longest Sequence of League Draws: 6, 19.2.1975 – 19.3.1975.

Longest Sequence of Unbeaten League Matches: 31, 4.5.1987 – 16.3.1988.

Longest Sequence Without a League Win: 14, 12.12.1953 – 20.3.1954.

Successive Scoring Runs: 29 from 27.4.1957.

Successive Non-scoring Runs: 5 from 21.4.2000.

TEN YEAR LEAGUE RECORD

		P	W	D	L	F	A	Pts	Pos
2004-05	PR Lge	38	17	7	14	52	41	58	5
2005-06	PR Lge	38	25	7	6	57	25	82	3
2006-07	PR Lge	38	20	8	10	57	27	68	3
2007-08	PR Lge	38	21	13	4	67	28	76	4
2008-09	PR Lge	38	25	11	2	77	27	86	2
2009-10	PR Lge	38	18	9	11	61	35	63	7
2010-11	PR Lge	38	17	7	14	59	44	58	6
2011-12	PR Lge	38	14	10	14	47	40	52	8
2012-13	PR Lge	38	16	13	9	71	43	61	7
2013-14	PR Lge	38	26	6	6	101	50	84	2

DID YOU KNOW ?

Full back Ephraim Longworth made 342 Football League appearances for Liverpool during an 18-year career with the Reds between 1910 and 1928 but failed to score a single goal. Ephraim won five England caps while with the Reds, making his international debut at the age of 32.

LIVERPOOL – FA PREMIERSHIP 2013–14 LEAGUE RECORD

Match No.	Date	Venue	Opponents	Result		H/T Score	Lg Pos.	Goalscorers	Attendance
1	Aug 17	H	Stoke C	W	1-0	1-0	4	Sturridge [37]	44,822
2	24	A	Aston Villa	W	1-0	1-0	2	Sturridge [21]	42,098
3	Sept 1	H	Manchester U	W	1-0	1-0	1	Sturridge [4]	44,411
4	16	A	Swansea C	D	2-2	2-1	1	Sturridge [4], Moses [36]	20,752
5	21	H	Southampton	L	0-1	0-0	2		44,755
6	29	A	Sunderland	W	3-1	2-0	2	Sturridge [28], Suarez 2 [36, 89]	41,415
7	Oct 5	H	Crystal Palace	W	3-1	3-0	2	Suarez [13], Sturridge [17], Gerrard (pen) [38]	44,721
8	19	A	Newcastle U	D	2-2	1-1	3	Gerrard (pen) [42], Sturridge [72]	51,703
9	26	H	WBA	W	4-1	2-0	2	Suarez 3 [12, 17, 55], Sturridge [77]	44,747
10	Nov 2	A	Arsenal	L	0-2	0-1	3		60,042
11	9	H	Fulham	W	4-0	3-0	2	Amorebieta [23], Skrtel [26], Suarez 2 [36, 54]	44,768
12	23	A	Everton	D	3-3	2-1	2	Coutinho [5], Suarez [19], Sturridge [89]	39,576
13	Dec 1	A	Hull C	L	1-3	1-1	4	Gerrard [27]	24,940
14	4	H	Norwich C	W	5-1	3-0	4	Suarez 4 [15, 29, 35, 74], Sterling [88]	44,541
15	7	H	West Ham U	W	4-1	1-0	2	Demel (og) [42], Sakho [47], Suarez 2 [81, 84]	44,781
16	15	A	Tottenham H	W	5-0	2-0	2	Suarez 2 [18, 84], Henderson [40], Flanagan [79], Sterling [89]	36,069
17	21	H	Cardiff C	W	3-1	3-0	1	Suarez 2 [25, 45], Sterling [42]	44,621
18	26	A	Manchester C	L	1-2	1-2	4	Coutinho [24]	47,351
19	29	A	Chelsea	L	1-2	1-2	5	Skrtel [3]	41,614
20	Jan 1	A	Hull C	W	2-0	1-0	4	Agger [36], Suarez [50]	44,627
21	12	A	Stoke C	W	5-3	2-2	4	Shawcross (og) [5], Suarez 2 [32, 71], Gerrard (pen) [51], Sturridge [87]	27,160
22	18	A	Aston Villa	D	2-2	1-2	4	Sturridge [45], Gerrard (pen) [53]	44,737
23	28	H	Everton	W	4-0	3-0	4	Gerrard [21], Sturridge 2 [33, 35], Suarez [50]	44,450
24	Feb 2	A	WBA	D	1-1	0-1	4	Sturridge [24]	26,132
25	8	H	Arsenal	W	5-1	4-0	4	Skrtel 2 [1, 10], Sterling 2 [16, 52], Sturridge [20]	44,701
26	12	H	Fulham	W	3-2	1-1	4	Sturridge [41], Coutinho [72], Gerrard (pen) [90]	25,375
27	23	H	Swansea C	W	4-3	3-2	4	Sturridge 2 [3, 36], Henderson 2 [20, 74]	44,731
28	Mar 1	A	Southampton	W	3-0	1-0	2	Suarez [16], Sterling [58], Gerrard (pen) [90]	31,659
29	16	A	Manchester U	W	3-0	1-0	2	Gerrard 2 (2 pens) [34, 46], Suarez [84]	75,225
30	22	A	Cardiff C	W	6-3	2-2	2	Suarez 3 [16, 60, 90], Skrtel 2 [41, 54], Sturridge [75]	28,018
31	26	H	Sunderland	W	2-1	1-0	2	Gerrard [39], Sturridge [48]	44,524
32	30	H	Tottenham H	W	4-0	2-0	1	Kaboul (og) [2], Suarez [25], Coutinho [55], Henderson [75]	44,762
33	Apr 6	A	West Ham U	W	2-1	1-1	1	Gerrard 2 (2 pens) [44, 71]	34,977
34	13	H	Manchester C	W	3-2	2-0	1	Sterling [6], Skrtel [26], Coutinho [78]	44,601
35	20	A	Norwich C	W	3-2	2-0	1	Sterling 2 [4, 62], Suarez [11]	26,857
36	27	H	Chelsea	L	0-2	0-1	1		44,726
37	May 5	A	Crystal Palace	D	3-3	1-0	1	Allen [18], Delaney (og) [53], Suarez [55]	25,261
38	11	H	Newcastle U	W	2-1	0-1	2	Agger [63], Sturridge [65]	44,724

Final League Position: 2

GOALSCORERS

League (101): Suarez 31, Sturridge 21, Gerrard 13 (10 pens), Sterling 9, Skrtel 7, Coutinho 5, Henderson 4, Agger 2, Allen 1, Flanagan 1, Moses 1, Sakho 1, own goals 5.
The Budweiser FA Cup (5): Gerrard 1 (1 pen), Aspas 1, Moses 1, Sturridge 1, own goal 1.
Capital One Cup (4): Sturridge 2, Henderson 1, Sterling 1.

Mignolet S 38	Johnson G 29	Toure K 15+5	Agger D 16+4	Jose Enrique 6+2	Gerrard S 33+1	Lucas 20+7	Henderson J 35	Aspas I 5+9	Coutinho P 28+5	Sturridge D 26+3	Sterling R 24+9	Cissokho A 12+3	Allen J 15+9	Skrtel M 36	Wisdom A 1+1	Alberto L —+9	Sakho M 17+1	Moses V 6+13	Suarez L 33	Kelly M —+5	Flanagan J 23	Smith B —+1	Ibe J —+1	Teixeira J —+1	Match No.
1	2	3	4	5	6	7	8	9¹	10	11	12														1
1	2	3	4	5	6	7	8	9²	10¹	11			12	13											2
1	2³		4	5	6	7	8	9²	10¹	11	12			3	13	14									3
1	13			5	6	7	8	12	9²	11	14			3			2³	4	10¹						4
1	2		4²	13	6	7	8	9³		11	12			3¹			14	5	10						5
1	2			8	6	7	5		10	12				3		4		9¹	11						6
1	2	13	8	6		7	14		10³	5				3		12	4¹	9²	11						7
1	5¹	2		7		6		10	13	8				3		12	4²	9	11						8
1	5¹	2			6³	7	8		10		9	13		3		14	4		11²	12					9
1	2				6	7	8	12	10		9²			3		4	13	11	5¹						10
1	2		4	12	7²	8	6		9	10¹		5³	13	3			14	11							11
1	2		4		6	7²	9		11	13		8¹		3		12	10		5						12
1	2	3		7	6	9		12		8²		4	13			10¹	11		5						13
1	2		4		6		8¹	13	9	10		7		3		12		11²	5						14
1	2		6¹	12	8		9		10²		7		3	4	13	11	14	5³							15
1	2			7¹	8	11²		9		6		3	12	4	13	10		5							16
1	2	13		7	8	11¹		9		6		3		4		10	12	5²							17
1	2			7¹	8	13	11²		9	5	6	3		4	12	10									18
1	2²	14	5		7	8	13	11		9		6¹	3		4³	10		12							19
1	2²	12	4	13	6	7	8¹	9		10³	5	3		14	11										20
1	2	4		7	8	6		11¹	12	9	5	3		10											21
1	2	4		7	12²	8		9¹	10	6	5	13	3		11										22
1		4		7		8		6²	11¹	9	5	3	14		12	10	13	2³							23
1		4		7		8		6²	11	9	5	13	3		10	12	2¹								24
1		4		7¹		6	14	8	10³	11	5	12	3		9²	2	13								25
1		4	13	7		8		6²	10	9¹	5	3	11	2	12										26
1	5	13	4²	7		6		8	9³	11¹	12	3	14	10	2										27
1	5		4	6		7	13	9¹	10²	12	8	3	11	2											28
1	2	4	6³	13	7	14	12	11²	9¹	8	3	10	5												29
1	2	4	6		7	9³	10²	12	13	8	3	14	11	5¹											30
1	2	4	6		7	9	10¹	12	8	3	11	5													31
1	2	4	7¹	13	6	8³	10	9²	12	3	14	11	5												32
1	2	13	7	12	8	6²	10¹	9	3	4	11	5													33
1	2	7	14	8*	6³	10¹	9²	12	3	4	13	11	5												34
1	2	13	7	6	10¹	9	8²	3	4	12	11	5													35
1	2	7	6²	13	11	12	9	8	3	4	10	5¹													36
1	2	6	7	12	11¹	9	8	3	4	13	10	5													37
1	2	4	6	14	7	13	10³	9	12	8¹	3	11	5²												38

The Budweiser FA Cup

Third Round	Oldham Ath	(h)	2-0
Fourth Round	AFC Bournemouth	(a)	2-0
Fifth Round	Arsenal	(a)	1-2

Capital One Cup

Second Round	Notts Co	(h)	4-2
(aet)			
Third Round	Manchester U	(a)	0-1

LUTON TOWN

FOUNDATION

Formed by an amalgamation of two leading local clubs, Wanderers and Excelsior a works team, at a meeting in Luton Town Hall in April 1885. The Wanderers had three months earlier changed their name to Luton Town Wanderers and did not take too kindly to the formation of another Town club but were talked around at this meeting. Wanderers had already appeared in the FA Cup and the new club entered in its inaugural season.

Kenilworth Road Stadium, 1 Maple Road, Luton, Beds LU4 8AW.

Telephone: (01582) 411 622.

Fax: (01582) 405 070.

Ticket Office: (01582) 416 976.

Website: www.lutontown.co.uk

Email: info@lutontown.co.uk

Ground Capacity: 10,226.

Record Attendance: 30,069 v Blackpool, FA Cup 6th rd replay, 4 March 1959.

Pitch Measurements: 110yd × 72yd.

Chairman: Nick Owen.

Managing Director: Gary Sweet.

Manager: John Still.

Assistant Manager: Terry Harris.

Physio: Simon Parsell.

Colours: Orange shirts, navy blue shorts, white socks with orange trim.

Year Formed: 1885.

Turned Professional: 1890.

Ltd Co.: 1897.

Club Nickname: 'The Hatters'.

Grounds: 1885, Excelsior, Dallow Lane; 1897, Dunstable Road; 1905, Kenilworth Road.

First Football League Game: 4 September 1897, Division 2, v Leicester Fosse (a) D 1–1 – Williams; McCartney, McEwen; Davies, Stewart, Docherty; Gallacher, Coupar, Birch, McInnes, Ekins (1).

Record League Victory: 12–0 v Bristol R, Division 3 (S), 13 April 1936 – Dolman; Mackey, Smith; Finlayson, Nelson, Godfrey; Rich, Martin (1), Payne (10), Roberts (1), Stephenson.

Record Cup Victory: 9–0 v Clapton, FA Cup 1st rd (replay after abandoned game), 30 November 1927 – Abbott; Kingham, Graham; Black, Rennie, Fraser; Pointon, Yardley (4), Reid (2), Woods (1), Dennis (2).

HONOURS

Football League – Division 1: Best season: 7th, 1986–87;
Division 2: *Champions* 1981–82; *Runners-up* 1954–55, 1973–74;
Division 3: *Runners-up* 1969–70, 2001–02; **Division 4:** *Champions* 1967–68; **Division 3 (S):** *Champions* 1936–37; *Runners-up* 1935–36.
FL C: *Champions* 2004–05.

Skrill Premier: *Champions* 2013–14.

FA Cup: *Runners-up* 1959.

Football League Cup: *Winners* 1988; *Runners-up* 1989.

Simod Cup: *Runners-up* 1988.

Johnstone's Paint Trophy: *Winners* 2009.

sky SPORTS FACT FILE

Arthur Wileman, who was the regular inside right for Luton Town during the 1914–15 season, enlisted in the Middlesex Regiment during World War One. He went on to win the Military Medal, but was killed in action on 28 April 1918, by which time he had transferred to the Royal Sussex Regiment.

Record Defeat: 0–9 v Small Heath, Division 2, 12 November 1898.

Most League Points (2 for a win): 66, Division 4, 1967–68.

Most League Points (3 for a win): 98, FL 1 2004–05.

Most League Goals: 103, Division 3 (S), 1936–37.

Highest League Scorer in Season: Joe Payne, 55, Division 3 (S), 1936–37.

Most League Goals in Total Aggregate: Gordon Turner, 243, 1949–64.

Most League Goals in One Match: 10, Joe Payne v Bristol R, Division 3 (S), 13 April 1936.

Most Capped Player: Mal Donaghy, 58 (91), Northern Ireland.

Most League Appearances: Bob Morton, 495, 1948–64.

Youngest League Player: Mike O'Hara, 16 years 32 days v Stoke C, 1 October 1960.

Record Transfer Fee Received: £3,000,000 from WBA for Curtis Davies, August 2005; £3,000,000 from Birmingham C for Rowan Vine, January 2007.

Record Transfer Fee Paid: £850,000 to Odense for Lars Elstrup, August 1989.

Football League Record: 1897 Elected to Division 2; 1900 Failed re-election; 1920 Division 3; 1921–37 Division 3 (S); 1937–55 Division 2; 1955–60 Division 1; 1960–63 Division 2; 1963–65 Division 3; 1965–68 Division 4; 1968–70 Division 3; 1970–74 Division 2; 1974–75 Division 1; 1975–82 Division 2; 1982–96 Division 1; 1996–2001 Division 2; 2001–02 Division 3; 2002–04 Division 2; 2004–05 FL 1; 2005–07 FL C; 2007–08 FL 1; 2008–09 FL 2; 2009–14 Conference Premier; 2014– FL 2.

LATEST SEQUENCES

Longest Sequence of League Wins: 12, 19.2.2002 – 6.4.2002.

Longest Sequence of League Defeats: 8, 11.11.1899 – 6.1.1900.

Longest Sequence of League Draws: 5, 28.8.1971 – 18.9.1971.

Longest Sequence of Unbeaten League Matches: 19, 8.4.1969 – 7.10.1969.

Longest Sequence Without a League Win: 16, 9.9.1964 – 6.11.1964.

Successive Scoring Runs: 25 from 24.10.1931.

Successive Non-scoring Runs: 5 from 10.4.1973.

MANAGERS

Charlie Green 1901–28 (Secretary-Manager)
George Thomson 1925
John McCartney 1927–29
George Kay 1929–31
Harold Wightman 1931–35
Ted Liddell 1936–38
Neil McBain 1938–39
George Martin 1939–47
Dally Duncan 1947–58
Syd Owen 1959–60
Sam Bartram 1960–62
Bill Harvey 1962–64
George Martin 1965–66
Allan Brown 1966–68
Alec Stock 1968–72
Harry Haslam 1972–78
David Pleat 1978–86
John Moore 1986–87
Ray Harford 1987–89
Jim Ryan 1990–91
David Pleat 1991–95
Terry Westley 1995
Lennie Lawrence 1995–2000
Ricky Hill 2000
Lil Fuccillo 2000
Joe Kinnear 2001–03
Mike Newell 2003–07
Kevin Blackwell 2007–08
Mick Harford 2008–09
Richard Money 2009–11
Gary Brabin 2011–12
Paul Buckle 2012–13
John Still February 2013–

TEN YEAR LEAGUE RECORD

		P	W	D	L	F	A	Pts	Pos
2004-05	FL 1	46	29	11	6	87	48	98	1
2005-06	FL C	46	17	10	19	66	67	61	10
2006-07	FL C	46	10	10	26	53	81	40	23
2007-08	FL 1	46	11	10	25	43	63	33*	24
2008-09	FL 2	46	13	17	16	58	65	26†	24
2009-10	Conf P	44	26	10	8	84	40	88	2
2010-11	Conf P	46	23	15	8	85	37	84	3
2011-12	Conf P	46	22	15	9	78	42	81	5
2012-13	Conf P	46	18	13	15	70	62	67	7
2013-14	Conf P	46	30	11	5	102	35	101	1

10 pts deducted; †30 points deducted.

DID YOU KNOW ?

Luton Town won their first nine home games of the 1968–69 season and won 20 of their 23 games at Kenilworth Road that season. Despite this the Hatters missed out on promotion from the old Division Three by three points, with Swindon Town and Watford going up that season.

MANCHESTER CITY

FOUNDATION

Manchester City was formed as a limited company in 1894 after their predecessors Ardwick had been forced into bankruptcy. However, many historians like to trace the club's lineage as far back as 1880 when St Mark's Church, West Gorton added a football section to their cricket club. They amalgamated with Belle Vue for one season before splitting again under the name Gorton Association FC in 1884–85. In 1887 Gorton AFC turned professional and moved ground to Hyde Road under the new name Ardwick AFC.

Etihad Stadium, Etihad Campus, Manchester M11 3FF.
Telephone: (0161) 444 1894.
Fax: (0161) 438 7999.
Ticket Office: (0161) 444 1894.
Website: www.mcfc.co.uk
Email: mcfc@mcfc.co.uk
Ground Capacity: 47,405.
Record Attendance: 84,569 v Stoke C, FA Cup 6th rd, 3 March 1934 (at Maine Road; British record for any game outside London or Glasgow); 47,370 v Tottenham H, FA Premier League, 5 May 2010 (at City of Manchester Stadium).
Pitch Measurements: 105m × 68m (114yd × 74yd)
Chairman: Khaldoon Al Mubarak.
Chief Executive: Ferran Soriano.
Manager: Manuel Pellegrini
Assistant Managers: Ruben Cousillas Fuse, Brian Kidd.
Fitness Coach: Jose Cabello.
Colours: Sky blue shirts, white shorts, white socks with sky blue trim.
Year Formed: 1887 as Ardwick FC; 1894 as Manchester City.
Turned Professional: 1887 as Ardwick FC.
Previous Names: 1880, St Mark's Church, West Gorton; 1884, Gorton; 1887, Ardwick; 1894, Manchester City.
Club Nicknames: 'The Blues', 'The Citizens'.

HONOURS

FA Premier League: *Champions* 2011–12, 2013–14; *Runners-up* 2012–13.
Football League – Division 1: *Champions* 1936–37, 1967–68, 2001–02; *Runners-up* 1903–04, 1920–21, 1976–77, 1999–2000; **Division 2:** *Champions* 1898–99, 1902–03, 1909–10, 1927–28, 1946–47, 1965–66; *Runners-up* 1895–96, 1950–51, 1988–89.
FA Cup: *Winners* 1904, 1934, 1956, 1969, 2011; *Runners-up* 1926, 1933, 1955, 1981, 2013.
Football League Cup: *Winners* 1970, 1976, 2014; *Runners-up* 1974.
Full Members Cup: *Runners-up* 1986.
European Competitions
Champions League: 2011–12, 2012–13, 2013–14. **European Cup:** 1968–69. **European Cup-Winners' Cup:** 1969–70 (*winners*), 1970–71. **UEFA Cup:** 1972–73, 1976–77, 1977–78, 1978–79, 2003–04, 2008–09. **Europa League:** 2010–11, 2011–12.

Grounds: 1880, Clowes Street; 1881, Kirkmanshulme Cricket Ground; 1882, Queens Road; 1884, Pink Bank Lane; 1887, Hyde Road (1894–1923 as City); 1923, Maine Road; 2003, City of Manchester Stadium (now know as Etihad Stadium from 2011).
First Football League Game: 3 September 1892, Division 2, v Bootle (h) W 7–0 – Douglas; McVickers; Robson; Middleton, Russell, Hopkins; Davies (3), Morris (2), Angus (1), Weir (1), Milarvie.
Record League Victory: 10–1 v Huddersfield T, Division 2, 7 November 1987 – Nixon; Gidman, Hinchcliffe, Clements, Lake, Redmond, White (3), Stewart (3), Adcock (3), McNab (1), Simpson.
Record Cup Victory: 10–1 v Swindon T, FA Cup 4th rd, 29 January 1930 – Barber; Felton, McCloy; Barrass, Cowan, Heinemann; Toseland, Marshall (5), Tait (3), Johnson (1), Brook (1).

sky SPORTS FACT FILE

Ardwick defeated Liverpool Stanley 12-0 in their first ever FA Cup tie back in October 1890 but then scratched in the next round, giving opponents Halliwell a walk over. On the day of the Halliwell game Ardwick instead played a friendly against Higher Walton, winning 3-2.

Record Defeat: 1–9 v Everton, Division 1, 3 September 1906.

Most League Points (2 for a win): 62, Division 2, 1946–47.

Most League Points (3 for a win): 99, Division 1, 2001–02.

Most League Goals: 108, Division 2, 1926–27, 108, Division 1, 2001–02.

Highest League Scorer in Season: Tommy Johnson, 38, Division 1, 1928–29.

Most League Goals in Total Aggregate: Tommy Johnson, 158, 1919–30.

Most League Goals in One Match: 5, Fred Williams v Darwen, Division 2, 18 February 1899; 5, Tom Browell v Burnley, Division 2, 24 October 1925; 5, Tom Johnson v Everton, Division 1, 15 September 1928; 5, George Smith v Newport Co, Division 2, 14 June 1947.

Most Capped Player: Colin Bell, 48, England.

Most League Appearances: Alan Oakes, 565, 1959–76.

Youngest League Player: Glyn Pardoe, 15 years 314 days v Birmingham C, 11 April 1962.

Record Transfer Fee Received: £21,000,000 from Chelsea for Shaun Wright-Phillips, July 2005.

Record Transfer Fee Paid: £38,000,000 to Atletico Madrid for Sergio Aguero, July 2011.

Football League Record: 1892 Ardwick elected founder member of Division 2; 1894 Newly-formed Manchester C elected to Division 2; Division 1 1899–1902, 1903–09, 1910–26, 1928–38, 1947–50, 1951–63, 1966–83, 1985–87, 1989–92; Division 2 1902–03, 1909–10, 1926–28, 1938–47, 1950–51, 1963–66, 1983–85, 1987–89; 1992–96 FA Premier League; 1996–98 Division 1; 1998–99 Division 2; 1999–2000 Division 1; 2000–01 FA Premier League; 2001–02 Division 1; 2002– FA Premier League.

LATEST SEQUENCES

Longest Sequence of League Wins: 9, 8.4.1912 – 28.9.1912.

Longest Sequence of League Defeats: 8, 23.8.1995 – 14.10.1995.

Longest Sequence of League Draws: 7, 5.10.2009 – 28.11.2009.

Longest Sequence of Unbeaten League Matches: 22, 16.11.1946 – 19.4.1947.

Longest Sequence Without a League Win: 17, 26.12.1979 – 7.4.1980.

Successive Scoring Runs: 44 from 3.10.1936.

Successive Non-scoring Runs: 6 from 30.1.1971.

MANAGERS

Joshua Parlby 1893–95
(Secretary-Manager)
Sam Omerod 1895–1902
Tom Maley 1902–06
Harry Newbould 1906–12
Ernest Magnall 1912–24
David Ashworth 1924–25
Peter Hodge 1926–32
Wilf Wild 1932–46
(continued as Secretary to 1950)
Sam Cowan 1946–47
John 'Jock' Thomson 1947–50
Leslie McDowall 1950–63
George Poyser 1963–65
Joe Mercer 1965–71
(continued as General Manager to 1972)
Malcolm Allison 1972–73
Johnny Hart 1973
Ron Saunders 1973–74
Tony Book 1974–79
Malcolm Allison 1979–80
John Bond 1980–83
John Benson 1983
Billy McNeill 1983–86
Jimmy Frizzell 1986–87
(continued as General Manager)
Mel Machin 1987–89
Howard Kendall 1989–90
Peter Reid 1990–93
Brian Horton 1993–95
Alan Ball 1995–96
Steve Coppell 1996
Frank Clark 1996–98
Joe Royle 1998–2001
Kevin Keegan 2001–05
Stuart Pearce 2005–07
Sven-Göran Eriksson 2007–08
Mark Hughes 2008–09
Roberto Mancini 2009–13
Manuel Pellegrini June 2013–

TEN YEAR LEAGUE RECORD

		P	W	D	L	F	A	Pts	Pos
2004-05	PR Lge	38	13	13	12	47	39	52	8
2005-06	PR Lge	38	13	4	21	43	48	43	15
2006-07	PR Lge	38	11	9	18	29	44	42	14
2007-08	PR Lge	38	15	10	13	45	53	55	9
2008-09	PR Lge	38	15	5	18	58	50	50	10
2009-10	PR Lge	38	18	13	7	73	45	67	5
2010-11	PR Lge	38	21	8	9	60	33	71	3
2011-12	PR Lge	38	28	5	5	93	29	89	1
2012-13	PR Lge	38	23	9	6	66	34	78	2
2013-14	PR Lge	38	27	5	6	102	37	86	1

DID YOU KNOW ?

Sam Cowan played in three FA Cup finals during an 11-year career with Manchester City before being transferred to Bradford City in 1935. He returned to Maine Road in November 1946 as manager and led City to the Second Division title.

MANCHESTER CITY – FA PREMIERSHIP 2013–14 LEAGUE RECORD

Match No.	Date	Venue	Opponents	Result	H/T Score	Lg Pos.	Goalscorers	Attendance
1	Aug 19	H	Newcastle U	W 4-0	2-0	1	Silva [6], Aguero [22], Toure [50], Nasri [75]	46,842
2	25	A	Cardiff C	L 2-3	0-0	6	Dzeko [52], Negredo [90]	27,068
3	31	H	Hull C	W 2-0	0-0	2	Negredo [65], Toure [90]	46,903
4	Sept 14	A	Stoke C	D 0-0	0-0	4		25,052
5	22	H	Manchester U	W 4-1	2-0	3	Aguero 2 [16, 47], Toure [45], Nasri [50]	47,156
6	28	A	Aston Villa	L 2-3	1-0	4	Toure [45], Dzeko [56]	34,063
7	Oct 5	H	Everton	W 3-1	2-1	3	Negredo [17], Aguero [45], Howard (og) [69]	47,267
8	19	A	West Ham U	W 3-1	1-0	4	Aguero 2 [16, 51], Silva [80]	34,507
9	27	A	Chelsea	L 1-2	0-1	6	Aguero [49]	41,495
10	Nov 2	H	Norwich C	W 7-0	4-0	4	Johnson (og) [16], Silva [20], Martin (og) [25], Negredo [36], Toure [60], Aguero [71], Dzeko [86]	47,066
11	10	A	Sunderland	L 0-1	0-1	8		40,137
12	24	H	Tottenham H	W 6-0	3-0	4	Jesus Navas 2 [1, 90], Sandro (og) [34], Aguero 2 [41, 50], Negredo [55]	47,228
13	Dec 1	H	Swansea C	W 3-0	1-0	3	Negredo [8], Nasri 2 [58, 77]	46,559
14	4	A	WBA	W 3-2	2-0	3	Aguero [9], Toure 2 (1 pen) [24, 74 (p)]	22,943
15	7	A	Southampton	D 1-1	1-1	4	Aguero [10]	31,229
16	14	H	Arsenal	W 6-3	2-1	3	Aguero [14], Negredo [39], Fernandinho 2 [50, 88], Silva [66], Toure (pen) [90]	47,229
17	21	A	Fulham	W 4-2	2-0	1	Toure [23], Kompany [43], Jesus Navas [78], Milner [83]	25,509
18	26	H	Liverpool	W 2-1	2-1	1	Kompany [31], Negredo [45]	47,351
19	28	H	Crystal Palace	W 1-0	0-0	1	Dzeko [66]	47,107
20	Jan 1	A	Swansea C	W 3-2	1-1	2	Fernandinho [14], Toure [58], Kolarov [66]	20,498
21	12	A	Newcastle U	W 2-0	1-0	1	Dzeko [8], Negredo [90]	49,423
22	18	H	Cardiff C	W 4-2	2-1	2	Dzeko [14], Jesus Navas [33], Toure [76], Aguero [79]	47,213
23	29	A	Tottenham H	W 5-1	1-0	1	Aguero [15], Toure (pen) [51], Dzeko [53], Jovetic [78], Kompany [89]	36,071
24	Feb 3	H	Chelsea	L 0-1	0-1	2		47,364
25	8	A	Norwich C	D 0-0	0-0	3		26,832
26	22	H	Stoke C	W 1-0	0-0	3	Toure [70]	47,038
27	Mar 15	A	Hull C	W 2-0	1-0	2	Silva [14], Dzeko [90]	24,895
28	22	H	Fulham	W 5-0	1-0	3	Toure 3 (2 pens) [26 (p), 54 (p), 65], Fernandinho [84], Demichelis [88]	47,262
29	25	A	Manchester U	W 3-0	1-0	2	Dzeko 2 [1, 56], Toure [90]	75,203
30	29	A	Arsenal	D 1-1	1-0	3	Silva [18]	60,060
31	Apr 5	H	Southampton	W 4-1	3-1	3	Toure (pen) [3], Nasri [45], Dzeko [45], Jovetic [81]	47,009
32	13	A	Liverpool	L 2-3	0-2	3	Silva [57], Johnson (og) [62]	44,601
33	16	H	Sunderland	D 2-2	1-1	3	Fernandinho [2], Nasri [88]	47,046
34	21	H	WBA	W 3-1	3-1	3	Zabaleta [3], Aguero [10], Demichelis [36]	46,564
35	27	A	Crystal Palace	W 2-0	2-0	3	Dzeko [4], Toure [43]	24,769
36	May 3	A	Everton	W 3-2	2-1	1	Aguero [22], Dzeko 2 [43, 48]	39,454
37	7	H	Aston Villa	W 4-0	0-0	1	Dzeko 2 [64, 72], Jovetic [89], Toure [90]	47,023
38	11	H	West Ham U	W 2-0	1-0	1	Nasri [39], Kompany [49]	47,300

Final League Position: 1

GOALSCORERS

League (102): Toure 20 (6 pens), Aguero 17, Dzeko 16, Negredo 9, Nasri 7, Silva 7, Fernandinho 5, Jesus Navas 4, Kompany 4, Jovetic 3, Demichelis 2, Kolarov 1, Milner 1, Zabaleta 1, own goals 5.
The Budweiser FA Cup (13): Aguero 4, Negredo 3, Dzeko 2, Nasri 2, Jovetic 1, Kolarov 1.
Capital One Cup (22): Dzeko 6, Negredo 6, Toure 3, Jovetic 2, Navas 2, Aguero 1, Kolarov 1, Nasri 1.
UEFA Champions League (19): Aguero 6 (1 pen), Negredo 5, Dzeko 2, Kolarov 1 (1 pen), Kompany 1, Milner 1, Nasri 1, Silva 1, Toure 1.

Hart J 31	Zabaleta P 34 + 1	Kompany V 28	Lescott J 8 + 2	Clichy G 18 + 2	Jesus Navas G 18 + 12	Toure Y 35	Fernandinho L 29 + 4	Silva D 26 + 1	Aguero S 20 + 3	Dzeko E 23 + 8	Nasri S 29 + 5	Javi Garcia F 14 + 15	Negredo A 21 + 11	Milner J 12 + 19	Nastasic M 11 + 2	Kolarov A 21 + 9	Rodwell J 1 + 4	Jovetic S 2 + 11	Richards M 2	Demichelis M 27	Pantilimon C 7	Boyata D 1	Match No.
1	2	3¹	4	5	6	7	8	9²	10³	11	12	13	14										1
1	2		4	5	6³	7²	8	9	10	11¹	12	3	13	14									2
1	2	3			8	7	6	10²	9³	11¹	13		12	14	4	5							3
1	2				13	6		12		10¹	3	11	8	4	5	7	9²						4
1	2	3		6¹	7	8		10²	13	9	14	11³	12	4	5								5
1	2	3		12	8	7		10¹	9²		11	6	4	5	13								6
1	2	3¹	4	13	6	7	10	9³		14	11	8	12	5²									7
1			5		7	8	9	11²		6¹	3	10³	13	4	12		14	2					8
1	2		5	12	9	7	10	11³		8²	6¹	14		4	13				3				9
	2		5	14	8	7	9	10	12	6³		11²	13	4					3	1			10
	13	4	12	8		10	14	9	7²	11¹	6		5		2³	3	1						11
	2	12	5	6	8	7		10²		9¹	13	11	14	4³		5			3	1			12
	2		4	5	6¹	7	8	10²	14	9		11³	12	13					3	1			13
	2	3		6	8¹	7		11²	10	9³	13		12		5	14			4	1			14
	2	3		12	8²	7		11	14	9	13	10³	6¹		5				4	1			15
	2	3		5	12	8	7	9²	10³		6¹	14	11	13					4	1			16
	1	3		2	12	8	7	9¹		10¹	6²	14	11	13		5			4				17
1	2	3	4		8	6	7	9²		13	10³	14	11¹	12		5			4				18
1		3		5	8		7¹	9		11	13	6	12	10²	4	14						2³	19
1	2	3		6¹	7	8		10	9²	12	11³	13	5	14				4					20
1	2	3		12	6³	7	9		11¹	8²	13	10	14		5			4					21
1	2	3	14	6³	7		9¹	12	11		8	10²	13		5			4					22
1	2	3		5	6	8¹	7	9²	11³	10			13	14		12		4					23
1	2	3		6	8		9	10		11¹			4	5		12	7		4				24
1	2	3		5	6	8		9	12		11²-	7	13			10¹		4					25
1	2	3		13	6	7¹	9		11	8	14	10²		5		12³		4					26
1	2	3⁴	12	5	13	9¹	7	10²		11	8³	6		14				4					27
1	2		4		12	7¹	6	10²		9³			8	5	13	14	3						28
1	2	3		5	8¹	6	7	9		11³	10²	12	14	13				4					29
1	2	3		5	8¹	6	7	9		11²	10²	13	14	12				4					30
1	2	3			8	6	7²	9¹		11³	10	12	13		5		14		4				31
1	2	3		5	8¹	6³	7	9	14	11²	10	12		13				4					32
1	2	3				7³		10¹	13	9	8	11²	6		5	14	12		4				33
1	2	3	5			6	9¹	11²	10¹	8	7		13			14		12	4				34
1	2	3			8³	12		11¹	10²	9	7	14	6		5		13		4				35
1	2	3	5		8²	12	14	11¹	10	9³	7		6	13					4				36
1	2	3			7	13	9¹		11²	10	6	14	8³		5		12		4				37
1	2	3			7³	12	6¹	10	11²	9	8	14	13		5				4				38

The Budweiser FA Cup

Third Round	Blackburn R	(a)	1-1
Replay	Blackburn R	(h)	5-0
Fourth Round	Watford	(h)	4-2
Fifth Round	Chelsea	(h)	2-0
Sixth Round	Wigan Ath	(h)	1-2

Capital One Cup

Third Round	Wigan Ath	(h)	5-0
Fourth Round	Newcastle U	(a)	2-0
(aet)			
Quarter-Finals	Leicester C	(a)	3-1
Semi-Finals 1st leg	West Ham U	(h)	6-0
Semi-Finals 2nd leg	West Ham U	(a)	3-0
Final	Sunderland	(Wembley)	3-1

UEFA Champions League

Group D	Viktoria Plzen	(a)	3-0
Group D	Bayern Munich	(h)	1-3
Group D	CSKA Moscow	(a)	2-1
Group D	CSKA Moscow	(h)	5-2
Group D	Viktoria Plzen	(h)	4-2
Group D	Bayern Munich	(a)	3-2
Round of 16 1st leg	Barcelona	(h)	0-2
Round of 16 2nd leg	Barcelona	(a)	1-2

MANCHESTER UNITED

FOUNDATION

Manchester United was formed as comparatively recently as 1902 after their predecessors, Newton Heath, went bankrupt. However, it is usual to give the date of the club's foundation as 1878 when the dining room committee of the carriage and waggon works of the Lancashire and Yorkshire Railway Company formed Newton Heath L and YR Cricket and Football Club. They won the Manchester Cup in 1886 and as Newton Heath FC were admitted to the Second Division in 1892.

Old Trafford, Sir Matt Busby Way, Manchester M16 0RA.

Telephone: (0161) 868 8000.

Fax: (0161) 868 8804.

Ticket Office: (0161) 868 8000 (option 1).

Website: www.manutd.com

Email: enquiries@manutd.co.uk

Ground Capacity: 75,731.

Record Attendance: 76,098 v Blackburn R, FA Premier League, 31 March 2007.

Ground Record Attendance: 76,962 Wolverhampton W v Grimsby T, FA Cup semi-final, 25 March 1939.

Pitch Measurements: 105m × 68m (114yd × 74yd)

Co-Chairmen: Joel and Avram Glazer.

Chief Executive: Ed Woodward.

Manager: Louis van Gaal.

Assistant Manager: Ryan Giggs.

Physio: Rob Swire.

Colours: Red shirts, white shorts, black socks.

Year Formed: 1878 as Newton Heath LYR; 1902, Manchester United.

Turned Professional: 1885.

Previous Name: 1880, Newton Heath; 1902, Manchester United.

Club Nickname: 'Red Devils'.

Grounds: 1880, North Road, Monsall Road; 1893, Bank Street; 1910, Old Trafford (played at Maine Road 1941–49).

HONOURS

FA Premier League: *Champions* 1992–93, 1993–94, 1995–96, 1996–97, 1998–99, 1999–2000, 2000–01, 2002–03, 2006–07, 2007–08, 2008–09, 2010–11, 2012–13; *Runners-up* 1994–95, 1997–98, 2005–06, 2009–10, 2011–12.

Football League – Division 1: *Champions* 1907–08, 1910–11, 1951–52, 1955–56, 1956–57, 1964–65, 1966–67; *Runners-up* 1946–47, 1947–48, 1948–49, 1950–51, 1958–59, 1963–64, 1967–68, 1979–80, 1987–88, 1991–92. **Division 2:** *Champions* 1935–36, 1974–75; *Runners-up* 1896–97, 1905–06, 1924–25, 1937–38. **FA Cup:** *Winners* 1909, 1948, 1963, 1977, 1983, 1985, 1990, 1994, 1996, 1999, 2004; *Runners-up* 1957, 1958, 1976, 1979, 1995, 2005, 2007.

Football League Cup: *Winners* 1992, 2006, 2009, 2010; *Runners-up* 1983, 1991, 1994, 2003.

European Competitions
European Cup: 1956–57 (*s-f*), 1957–58 (*s-f*), 1965–66 (*s-f*), 1967–68 (*winners*), 1968–69 (*s-f*). **Champions League:** 1993–94, 1994–95, 1996–97 (*s-f*), 1997–98, 1998–99 (*winners*), 1999–2000, 2000–01, 2001–02 (*s-f*), 2002–03, 2003–04, 2004–05, 2005–06, 2006–07 (*s-f*), 2007–08 (*winners*), 2008–09 (*runners-up*), 2009–10, 2010–11 (*runners-up*), 2011–12, 2012–13, 2013–14. **European Cup-Winners' Cup:** 1963–64, 1977–78, 1983–84, 1990–91 (*winners*). 1991–92. **Inter Cities Fairs Cup:** 1964–65. **UEFA Cup:** 1976–77, 1980–81, 1982–83, 1984–85, 1992–93, 1995–96. **Europa League:** 2011–12. **Super Cup:** 1991 (*winners*), 1999, 2008. **World Club Championship:** 1968, 1999 (*winners*). **FIFA Club World Cup:** 2008 (*winners*).
NB: In 1958–59 FA refused permission to compete in European Cup.

First Football League Game: 3 September 1892, Division 1, v Blackburn R (a) L 3–4 – Warner; Clements, Brown; Perrins, Stewart, Erentz; Farman (1), Coupar (1), Donaldson (1), Carson, Mathieson.

Record League Victory (as Newton Heath): 10–1 v Wolverhampton W, Division 1, 15 October 1892 – Warner; Mitchell, Clements; Perrins, Stewart (3), Erentz; Farman (1), Hood (1), Donaldson (3), Carson (1), Hendry (1).

Record League Victory (as Manchester U): 9–0 v Ipswich T, FA Premier League, 4 March 1995 – Schmeichel; Keane (1) (Sharpe), Irwin, Bruce (Butt), Kanchelskis, Pallister, Cole (5), Ince (1), McClair, Hughes (2), Giggs.

Record Cup Victory: 10–0 v RSC Anderlecht, European Cup prel. rd 2nd leg, 26 September 1956 – Wood; Foulkes, Byrne; Colman, Jones, Edwards; Berry (1), Whelan (2), Taylor (3), Viollet (4), Pegg.

Record Defeat: 0–7 v Blackburn R, Division 1, 10 April 1926; 0–7 v Aston Villa, Division 1, 27 December 1930; 0–7 v Wolverhampton W, Division 2, 26 December 1931.

Most League Points (2 for a win): 64, Division 1, 1956–57.

Most League Points (3 for a win): 92, FA Premier League, 1993–94.

Most League Goals: 103, Division 1, 1956–57 and 1958–59.

Highest League Scorer in Season: Dennis Viollet, 32, 1959–60.

Most League Goals in Total Aggregate: Bobby Charlton, 199, 1956–73.

Most Capped Player: Bobby Charlton, 106, England.

Most League Appearances: Ryan Giggs, 672, 1991–2014.

Youngest League Player: Jeff Whitefoot, 16 years 105 days v Portsmouth, 15 April 1950.

Record Transfer Fee Received: £80,000,000 from Real Madrid for Cristiano Ronaldo, July 2009.

Record Transfer Fee Paid: £37,100,000 to Chelsea for Juan Mata, January 2014.

Football League Record: 1892 Newton Heath elected to Division 1; 1894–1906 Division 2; 1906–22 Division 1; 1922–25 Division 2; 1925–31 Division 1; 1931–36 Division 2; 1936–37 Division 1; 1937–38 Division 2; 1938–74 Division 1; 1974–75 Division 2; 1975–92 Division 1; 1992– FA Premier League.

MANAGERS

J. Ernest Mangnall 1903–12
John Bentley 1912–14
John Robson 1914–21
  (Secretary-Manager from 1916)
John Chapman 1921–26
Clarence Hilditch 1926–27
Herbert Bamlett 1927–31
Walter Crickmer 1931–32
Scott Duncan 1932–37
Walter Crickmer 1937–45
  (Secretary-Manager)
Matt Busby 1945–69
  (continued as General Manager then Director)
Wilf McGuinness 1969–70
Sir Matt Busby 1970–71
Frank O'Farrell 1971–72
Tommy Docherty 1972–77
Dave Sexton 1977–81
Ron Atkinson 1981–86
Sir Alex Ferguson 1986–2013
David Moyes 2013–14
Louis van Gaal May 2014–

LATEST SEQUENCES

Longest Sequence of League Wins: 14, 15.10.1904 – 3.1.1905.

Longest Sequence of League Defeats: 14, 26.4.1930 – 25.10.1930.

Longest Sequence of League Draws: 6, 30.10.1988 – 27.11.1988.

Longest Sequence of Unbeaten League Matches: 29, 11.4.2010 – 1.2.2011.

Longest Sequence Without a League Win: 16, 19.4.1930 – 25.10.1930.

Successive Scoring Runs: 36 from 3.12.2007.

Successive Non-scoring Runs: 5 from 7.2.1981.

TEN YEAR LEAGUE RECORD

		P	W	D	L	F	A	Pts	Pos
2004-05	PR Lge	38	22	11	5	58	26	77	3
2005-06	PR Lge	38	25	8	5	72	34	83	2
2006-07	PR Lge	38	28	5	5	83	27	89	1
2007-08	PR Lge	38	27	6	5	80	22	87	1
2008-09	PR Lge	38	28	6	4	68	24	90	1
2009-10	PR Lge	38	27	4	7	86	28	85	2
2010-11	PR Lge	38	23	11	4	78	37	80	1
2011-12	PR Lge	38	28	5	5	89	33	89	2
2012-13	PR Lge	38	28	5	5	86	43	89	1
2013-14	PR Lge	38	19	7	12	64	43	64	7

DID YOU KNOW ?

Ernest Payne, who made two appearances for Manchester United as understudy to Billy Meredith in 1908–09, was also a well-known cyclist. He was a member of the Great Britain squad that won the team pursuit gold medal at the 1908 Olympic Games.

MANCHESTER UNITED – FA PREMIERSHIP 2013–14 LEAGUE RECORD

Match No.	Date	Venue	Opponents	Result	H/T Score	Lg Pos.	Goalscorers	Attendance
1	Aug 17	A	Swansea C	W 4-1	2-0	1	van Persie 2 [34, 72], Welbeck 2 [36, 90]	20,733
2	26	H	Chelsea	D 0-0	0-0	4		75,032
3	Sept 1	A	Liverpool	L 0-1	0-1	7		44,411
4	14	H	Crystal Palace	W 2-0	1-0	5	van Persie (pen) [45], Rooney [81]	75,170
5	22	A	Manchester C	L 1-4	0-2	8	Rooney [87]	47,156
6	28	H	WBA	L 1-2	0-0	12	Rooney [57]	75,042
7	Oct 5	A	Sunderland	W 2-1	0-1	9	Januzaj 2 [55, 61]	45,426
8	19	A	Southampton	D 1-1	1-0	8	van Persie [26]	75,220
9	26	H	Stoke C	W 3-2	1-2	8	van Persie [43], Rooney [78], Hernandez [80]	75,274
10	Nov 2	A	Fulham	W 3-1	3-0	8	Valencia [9], van Persie [20], Rooney [22]	25,700
11	10	H	Arsenal	W 1-0	1-0	5	van Persie [27]	75,138
12	24	A	Cardiff C	D 2-2	2-1	6	Rooney [15], Evra [45]	28,016
13	Dec 1	A	Tottenham H	D 2-2	1-1	8	Rooney 2 (1 pen) [32, 57 (p)]	35,884
14	4	H	Everton	L 0-1	0-0	9		75,210
15	7	H	Newcastle U	L 0-1	0-0	9		75,233
16	15	A	Aston Villa	W 3-0	2-0	8	Welbeck 2 [15, 18], Cleverley [52]	42,682
17	21	H	West Ham U	W 3-1	2-0	7	Welbeck [26], Januzaj [36], Young [72]	75,350
18	26	A	Hull C	W 3-2	2-2	7	Chester (og) [66], Smalling [19], Rooney [26]	24,826
19	28	A	Norwich C	W 1-0	0-0	6	Welbeck [57]	26,851
20	Jan 1	H	Tottenham H	L 1-2	0-1	7	Welbeck [67]	75,265
21	11	A	Swansea C	W 2-0	0-0	7	Valencia [47], Welbeck [59]	75,035
22	19	A	Chelsea	L 1-3	0-2	7	Hernandez [78]	41,615
23	28	H	Cardiff C	W 2-0	1-0	7	van Persie [6], Young [59]	75,301
24	Feb 1	A	Stoke C	L 1-2	0-1	7	van Persie [47]	26,547
25	9	H	Fulham	D 2-2	0-1	7	van Persie [78], Carrick [80]	74,966
26	12	A	Arsenal	D 0-0	0-0	7		60,021
27	22	A	Crystal Palace	W 2-0	0-0	6	Van Persie (pen) [62], Rooney [68]	24,571
28	Mar 8	A	WBA	W 3-0	1-0	6	Jones [34], Rooney [65], Welbeck [82]	26,184
29	16	H	Liverpool	L 0-3	0-1	7		75,225
30	22	A	West Ham U	W 2-0	2-0	7	Rooney 2 [8, 33]	34,237
31	25	H	Manchester C	L 0-3	0-1	7		75,203
32	29	H	Aston Villa	W 4-1	2-1	7	Rooney 2 (1 pen) [20, 45 (p)], Mata [57], Hernandez [90]	75,368
33	Apr 5	A	Newcastle U	W 4-0	1-0	6	Mata 2 [39, 50], Hernandez [64], Januzaj [90]	52,081
34	20	A	Everton	L 0-2	0-2	7		39,436
35	26	H	Norwich C	W 4-0	1-0	7	Rooney 2 (1 pen) [41 (p), 48], Mata 2 [63, 73]	75,208
36	May 3	H	Sunderland	L 0-1	0-1	7		75,347
37	6	H	Hull C	W 3-1	1-0	7	Wilson 2 [31, 61], van Persie [86]	75,341
38	11	A	Southampton	D 1-1	0-1	7	Mata [54]	31,372

Final League Position: 7

GOALSCORERS

League (64): Rooney 17 (3 pens), van Persie 12 (2 pens), Welbeck 9, Mata 6, Hernandez 4, Januzaj 4, Valencia 2, Wilson 2, Young 2, Carrick 1, Cleverley 1, Evra 1, Jones 1, Smalling 1, own goal 1.
The Budweiser FA Cup (1): Hernandez 1.
Capital One Cup (10): Hernandez 4 (1 pen), Evans 1, Evra 1, Fabio 1, Jones 1, Vidic 1, Young 1.
Community Shield (2): van Persie 2.
UEFA Champions League (17): van Persie 4, Rooney 2, Valencia 2, Evans 1, Evra 1, Jones 1, Nani 1, Smalling 1, Vidic 1, Welbeck 1, own goals 2.

De Gea D 37	Jones P 26	Ferdinand R 12+2	Vidic N 23+2	Evra P 33	Cleverley T 18+4	Carrick M 26+3	Valencia A 20+9	Welbeck D 15+10	Giggs R 6+6	Van Persie R 18+3	Rooney W 27+2	Anderson 2+2	Young A 13+7	Nani 7+4	Hernandez J 6+18	Da Silva F 1	Fellaini M 12+4	Januzaj A 15+12	Smalling C 21+4	Evans J 17	Buttner A 5+3	Kagawa S 14+4	Da Silva R 18+1	Zaha W –+2	Fletcher D 9+3	Mata J 14+1	Lindegaard A 1	Lawrence T 1	Wilson J 1	Match No.
1	2	3	4	5	6	7	8	9	10^2	11^1	12	13																		1
1	2	3	4	5	6	7	8^2	10^1	13	11	9		12																	2
1	2^3	3	4	5	7	6	12	9	8^2	11			10^1	13	14															3
1		3	4	5			6	8			11^3	9	7^2	10^1	14	2	12	13												4
1		3	4	5	12	6	8	11			9		10^1			7		2											5
1	2	3			6					13	9	7^1		8	11^3		14	12		4	5	10^2								6
1	3		4	5	7	6	12	13		11	9		8^1				10^2	14					2^1							7
1	3		5		6		13	12	11	9^1			8^1				7^2	10	14	4			2							8
1	3		5	7^2	6	14			11				8^1	13			12	2^3	4		10									9
1	6		4	5	7^3		8		11	9			12	10	14		3^1				13	2^2								10
1	6		4^3	5	12	7	8	13	11^2	9			14				2	3			10^1									11
1		3		5	7		8	12	13	9			11^2				6	10^1	2	4										12
1	6		4	5	7		8^3	10^2		11		14	13	12				2	3			9^1								13
1			4	5		8	10^1	7		11			12	14			6	13	3			9^2	2^3							14
1	7		4	5	8^3		14			10		13	9^1	11			6		3			2^2	12							15
1	3			5	7		6	11	8^1	10^3	12		9^2				4				2	14	13							16
1	6		5^2	7		8	11^1		9	13			12				10^2	3	4	14		2								17
1			5	7	14	8^1	11		9				10^1	13			12	3	4			2^3		6^2						18
1		3	5	7	6		12	9^2		8			11^1				13	2	4			10^2			14					19
1		3	5	7^1	6^2	8	11		9				14	12			10	2^2	4			13								20
1			4	5^1		7	8	11^2		13			9	3			12	10	2			6								21
1	6		3^1	5^2		7	8	11					10^1	13			9	12	4			2								22
1	7			5	13		6		8^1	11^3	12		9				14	3	4			2			10^3					23
1	3^2		5	6	7		13		11^1	9	10		14				2	4^3			12				8					24
1			4	5		7	13		11	9	10^1		14				12	3			2^2		6^3	8						25
1	12	4	5	7	6	8^1		11	9	14							13	3			2^3				10^2					26
1	3	4	5		6	12		13	11^1	9							7^3	10^2	2				14	8						27
1	4	14	5		7		12		11^2	9			6	10^1	3			13	2^3				8							28
1	3	14	4^1	5	12	7		13	11	9			6^2	10^1				2					8^1							29
1	4			3		13			11^2	8	12		7				5	10	2			6	9^1							30
1	4	3		5	6^2	7	13	11^1		10			14	8^3			12	2				9								31
1	4	3			12				11^2	8	14		6	13			5	10^1	2^3			7	9							32
	4		5^3			2				8^2	14	11	7^1	12			13	10				6	9	1						33
1	3				6	12	14		11				8^3	13			2	4^2	5	10^1		7	9							34
1	2	3	4	5	8^1	7	6	11^3		10		13	14					9^2								12				35
1	2	3	4	5		7		14	13	8^1	10^2	11		12								6	9^1							36
1	4^1	12		6	2		14	13		9	8	3		5	7										10^2	11^3				37
1		3	4	5		12	14	10		11^2			13				8	2				7^3			6	9^1				38

The Budweiser FA Cup

Third Round	Swansea C	(h)	1-2

Capital One Cup

Third Round	Liverpool	(h)	1-0
Fourth Round	Norwich C	(h)	4-0
Quarter-Finals	Stoke C	(a)	2-0
Semi-Finals 1st leg	Sunderland	(a)	1-2
Semi-Finals 2nd leg	Sunderland	(h)	2-1

(aet; lost 1-2 on penalties)

Community Shield

	Wigan Ath	(Wembley)	2-0

UEFA Champions League

Group A	Bayer Leverkusen	(h)	4-2
Group A	Shakhtar Donetsk	(a)	1-1
Group A	Real Sociedad	(h)	1-0
Group A	Real Sociedad	(a)	0-0
Group A	Bayer Leverkusen	(a)	5-0
Group A	Shakhtar Donetsk	(h)	1-0
Round of 16 1st leg	Olympiacos	(a)	0-2
Round of 16 2nd leg	Olympiacos	(h)	3-0
Quarter-Finals 1st leg	Bayern Munich	(h)	1-1
Quarter-Finals 2nd leg	Bayern Munich	(a)	1-3

MANSFIELD TOWN

FOUNDATION

The club was formed as Mansfield Wesleyans in 1897, and changed their name to Mansfield Wesley in 1906 and Mansfield Town in 1910. This was after the Mansfield Wesleyan Chapel trustees had requested that the club change its name as 'it has no longer had any connection with either the chapel or school'. The new club participated in the Notts and Derby District League, but in the following season 1911–12 joined the Central Alliance.

One Call Stadium, Quarry Lane, Mansfield, Nottinghamshire NG18 5DA.

Telephone: (01623) 482 482.

Fax: (01623) 482 495.

Ticket Office: (01623) 482 482.

Website: www.mansfieldtown.net

Email: info@mansfieldtown.net

Ground Capacity: 8,186.

Record Attendance: 24,467 v Nottingham F, FA Cup 3rd rd, 10 January 1953.

Pitch Measurements: 103.5m × 64m (113yd × 70yd)

Chairman: John Radford.

Chief Executive: Carolyn Radford.

Manager: Paul Cox.

Assistant Manager: Adam Murray.

Physio: Chris Bowman.

Colours: Yellow shirts with blue trim, blue shorts, yellow socks with blue trim.

Year Formed: 1897.

Turned Professional: 1906.

Ltd Co.: 1922.

Previous Name: 1897, Mansfield Wesleyans; 1906, Mansfield Wesley; 1910, Mansfield Town.

Grounds: 1897–99, Westfield Lane; 1899–1901, Ratcliffe Gate; 1901–12, Newgate Lane; 1912–16, Ratcliffe Gate; 1916, Field Mill (renamed One Call Stadium, 2012).

Club Nickname: 'The Stags'.

First Football League Game: 29 August 1931, Division 3 (S), v Swindon T (h) W 3–2 – Wilson; Clifford, England; Wake, Davis, Blackburn; Gilhespy, Readman (1), Johnson, Broom (2), Baxter.

Record League Victory: 9–2 v Rotherham U, Division 3 (N), 27 December 1932 – Wilson; Anthony, England; Davies, S. Robinson, Slack; Prior, Broom, Readman (3), Hoyland (3), Bowater (3).

Record Cup Victory: 8–0 v Scarborough (a), FA Cup 1st rd, 22 November 1952 – Bramley; Chessell, Bradley; Field, Plummer, Lewis; Scott, Fox (3), Marron (2), Sid Watson (1), Adam (2).

Record Defeat: 1–8 v Walsall, Division 3 (N), 19 January 1933.

HONOURS

Football League: Division 2: Best season: 21st, 1977–78; **Division 3: Champions** 1976–77; Promoted to **Division 2** (3rd) 2001–02; **Division 4: Champions** 1974–75; **Division 3 (N): Runners-up** 1950–51.

FA Cup: Best season: 6th rd, 1969.

Football League Cup: Best season: 5th rd, 1976.

Freight Rover Trophy: *Winners* 1987.

Conference: *Winners* 2012–13.

sky SPORTS FACT FILE

Goalkeeper Arthur Jepson made two appearances as an amateur for Mansfield Town in the 1934–35 season. He later played for Port Vale, Stoke and Lincoln but was better known as a fast-medium bowler for Nottinghamshire, for whom he took 1,051 First Class wickets between 1938 and 1959. He also stood as an umpire in four Test Matches.

Most League Points (2 for a win): 68, Division 4, 1974–75.

Most League Points (3 for a win): 81, Division 4, 1985–86.

Most League Goals: 108, Division 4, 1962–63.

Highest League Scorer in Season: Ted Harston, 55, Division 3 (N), 1936–37.

Most League Goals in Total Aggregate: Harry Johnson, 104, 1931–36.

Most League Goals in One Match: 7, Ted Harston v Hartlepools U, Division 3N, 23 January 1937.

Most Capped Player: John McClelland, 6 (53), Northern Ireland.

Most League Appearances: Rod Arnold, 440, 1970–83.

Youngest League Player: Cyril Poole, 15 years 351 days v New Brighton, 27 February 1937.

Record Transfer Fee Received: £175,000 from Sunderland for Liam Lawrence, June 2004.

Record Transfer Fee Paid: £150,000 to Carlisle U for Lee Peacock, October 1997.

Football League Record: 1931 Elected to Division 3 (S); 1932–37 Division 3 (N); 1937–47 Division 3 (S); 1947–58 Division 3 (N); 1958–60 Division 3; 1960–63 Division 4; 1963–72 Division 3; 1972–75 Division 4; 1975–77 Division 3; 1977–78 Division 2; 1978–80 Division 3; 1980–86 Division 4; 1986–91 Division 3; 1991–92 Division 4; 1992–93 Division 2; 1993–2002 Division 3; 2002–03 Division 2; 2003–04 Division 3; 2004–08 FL 2; 2008–13 Conference Premier; 2013– FL 2.

LATEST SEQUENCES

Longest Sequence of League Wins: 7, 13.9.1991 – 26.10.1991.

Longest Sequence of League Defeats: 7, 18.1.1947 – 15.3.1947.

Longest Sequence of League Draws: 5, 18.10.1986 – 22.11.1986.

Longest Sequence of Unbeaten League Matches: 20, 14.2.1976 – 21.8.1976.

Longest Sequence Without a League Win: 14, 25.3.2000 – 2.9.2000.

Successive Scoring Runs: 27 from 1.10.1962.

Successive Non-scoring Runs: 8 from 25.3.2000.

MANAGERS

John Baynes 1922–25
Ted Davison 1926–28
Jack Hickling 1928–33
Henry Martin 1933–35
Charlie Bell 1935
Harold Wightman 1936
Harold Parkes 1936–38
Jack Poole 1938–44
Lloyd Barke 1944–45
Roy Goodall 1945–49
Freddie Steele 1949–51
George Jobey 1952–53
Stan Mercer 1953–55
Charlie Mitten 1956–58
Sam Weaver 1958–60
Raich Carter 1960–63
Tommy Cummings 1963–67
Tommy Eggleston 1967–70
Jock Basford 1970–71
Danny Williams 1971–74
Dave Smith 1974–76
Peter Morris 1976–78
Billy Bingham 1978–79
Mick Jones 1979–81
Stuart Boam 1981–83
Ian Greaves 1983–89
George Foster 1989–93
Andy King 1993–96
Steve Parkin 1996–99
Billy Dearden 1999–2002
Stuart Watkiss 2002
Keith Curle 2002–05
Carlton Palmer 2005
Peter Shirtliff 2005–06
Billy Dearden 2006–08
Paul Holland 2008
Billy McEwan 2008
David Holdsworth 2008–10
Duncan Russell 2010–11
Paul Cox May 2011–

TEN YEAR LEAGUE RECORD

		P	W	D	L	F	A	Pts	Pos
2004-05	FL 2	46	15	15	16	56	56	60	13
2005-06	FL 2	46	13	15	18	59	66	54	16
2006-07	FL 2	46	14	12	20	58	63	54	17
2007-08	FL 2	46	11	9	26	48	68	42	23
2008-09	Conf P	46	19	9	18	57	55	62	12
2009-10	Conf P	44	17	11	16	69	60	62	9
2010-11	Conf P	46	17	10	19	73	75	61	13
2011-12	Conf P	46	25	14	7	87	48	89	3
2012-13	Conf P	46	30	5	11	92	52	95	1
2013-14	FL 2	46	15	15	16	49	58	60	11

DID YOU KNOW ?

Ernest Bell, who played for Mansfield Town in the 1938–39 season, served in the RAMC during the Second World War. In June 1940 he was posted as missing following the evacuation of British troops at Dunkirk. He was captured and held as a prisoner of war by the Germans until repatriated in October 1943.

MANSFIELD TOWN – FOOTBALL LEAGUE TWO 2013–14 LEAGUE RECORD

Match No.	Date		Venue	Opponents	Result	H/T Score	Lg Pos.	Goalscorers	Attendance
1	Aug	3	A	Scunthorpe U	L 0-2	0-2	20		5241
2		10	H	Exeter C	D 0-0	0-0	19		3284
3		17	A	Wycombe W	W 1-0	0-0	13	Palmer 78	3352
4		24	H	Portsmouth	D 2-2	1-2	14	Hutchinson 33, Meikle 72	4574
5		31	H	Dagenham & R	W 3-0	1-0	9	Clucas 35, McGuire 48, Rhead 72	3015
6	Sept	7	A	Newport Co	D 1-1	0-1	10	Clucas 67	3709
7		14	A	York C	W 2-1	1-1	8	Clucas (pen) 21, Palmer 76	3513
8		21	H	Northampton T	W 3-0	2-0	5	Hutchinson 31, Clucas 34, Kouo-Doumbe (og) 65	3469
9		28	A	Chesterfield	W 1-0	1-0	3	Andrew 37	10,015
10	Oct	5	H	Hartlepool U	L 1-4	0-2	5	Clucas (pen) 75	3457
11		12	H	Bristol R	D 1-1	1-0	7	Stevenson 22	3275
12		19	A	Torquay U	D 0-0	0-0	8		2473
13		22	A	Bury	D 0-0	0-0	7		2518
14		26	H	Plymouth Arg	L 0-1	0-0	11		3379
15	Nov	1	A	Southend U	L 0-3	0-2	12		4824
16		16	H	Oxford U	L 1-3	1-2	15	Stevenson 46	3831
17		23	A	Fleetwood T	L 4-5	2-2	16	Clements 9, Howell 13, Clucas 77, Dyer 89	2831
18		26	A	Burton Alb	L 0-1	0-0	17		2759
19		30	H	Morecambe	L 1-2	1-0	18	Dyer 17	2753
20	Dec	14	A	AFC Wimbledon	D 0-0	0-0	17		3900
21		21	H	Accrington S	L 2-3	1-0	19	McCombe 2 23, 68	2549
22		26	A	Rochdale	L 0-3	0-2	21		2671
23		29	A	Cheltenham T	W 2-1	2-0	19	Howell 21, Rhead 45	2928
24	Jan	1	H	Burton Alb	D 0-0	0-0	18		3266
25		4	A	Exeter C	W 1-0	1-0	16	Stevenson 46	3303
26		11	H	Scunthorpe U	L 0-2	0-1	17		4115
27		18	A	Portsmouth	D 1-1	0-0	17	Stevenson 51	14,686
28		25	H	Wycombe W	D 2-2	0-1	17	Stevenson 54, Palmer 86	2789
29	Feb	1	A	Plymouth Arg	D 1-1	0-0	19	Rhead 74	6248
30		8	H	Southend U	W 2-1	1-0	17	Clucas 36, Jennings 65	3055
31		15	A	Oxford U	L 0-3	0-1	18		5108
32		22	H	Fleetwood T	W 1-0	1-0	17	Rhead 31	2759
33		25	H	Bury	L 1-4	0-1	20	Clucas 71	2628
34	Mar	1	A	Dagenham & R	D 0-0	0-0	20		1377
35		8	A	Newport Co	W 2-1	1-0	17	Tafazolli 28, Howell 90	2756
36		11	H	York C	L 0-1	0-1	18		2865
37		15	A	Northampton T	D 1-1	1-0	16	Palmer 32	5129
38		22	H	Chesterfield	D 0-0	0-0	18		5931
39		25	A	Hartlepool U	W 4-2	1-1	17	Jennings 2 20, 72, Rhead 80, McGuire 90	2976
40		29	H	AFC Wimbledon	W 1-0	1-0	12	Murray 7	3292
41	Apr	5	A	Morecambe	W 1-0	1-0	12	Daniel 42	1772
42		12	H	Rochdale	W 3-0	0-0	10	Riley 72, Rhead 87, Tafazolli 90	3843
43		18	A	Accrington S	D 1-1	0-0	12	Speight 75	2092
44		21	H	Cheltenham T	L 0-2	0-0	12		3586
45		26	H	Torquay U	L 1-3	0-2	13	Jennings 46	3389
46	May	3	A	Bristol R	W 1-0	1-0	11	Daniel 36	10,594

Final League Position: 11

GOALSCORERS

League (49): Clucas 8 (2 pens), Rhead 6, Stevenson 5, Jennings 4, Palmer 4, Howell 3, Daniel 2, Dyer 2, Hutchinson 2, McCombe 2, McGuire 2, Tafazolli 2, Andrew 1, Clements 1, Meikle 1, Murray 1, Riley 1, Speight 1, own goal 1.
The Budweiser FA Cup (10): Clucas 5, Daniel 1, Dyer 1, Howells 1, Palmer 1, Stevenson 1.
Capital One Cup (0).
Johnstone's Paint Trophy (0).

Marriott A 40	Beevers L 24 + 2	Jennings J 32 + 1	Howell A 30 + 3	Dempster J 35 + 1	McCombe J 5	Dyer R 7 + 5	Murray A 16 + 2	Rhead M 28 + 12	Stevenson L 19 + 2	Clucas S 29 + 9	Meikle L 2 + 26	Palmer D 20 + 18	Briscoe L — + 2	Sutton R 35 + 1	Riley M 31	McGuire J 25 + 2	Andrew C 11 + 4	Clements C 23	Hutchinson B 11 + 5	Tafazolli R 24	Speight J 1 + 7	Daniel C 18 + 10	Murtagh K 2 + 1	Blake J 3	Poku G 1 + 3	Mitchell L 1	Pilkington G 2	Alabi J 1	Westlake D 23	Cain M — + 2	Price L 5	Thomas J — + 1	Marsden L 2	Match No.
1	2	3	4	5	6	7^3	8	9	10^1	11	12	13	14																					1
1	5^2	9	7	3			14	13	12	8				10^1	2	4	6	11^3																2
1	5	9	14	3				13				7^1		12	2	4	8	11^2	6	10^3														3
1	5^3	9		4				13				6^1	14	12	2	3	7	10^2	8	11														4
1	8^1	5		3					12			11	14	10^2	4	2	7	13	6	9^3														5
1	8^1	5		3				10^4			9	13	12		2	4	6		7	11^2														6
1	5	9^3	12							11	13	14			2	4^4	8	10	7^1	6^2														7
1	5	9	7	4							13	12	6^3		2		8	10^2	11^1	3	14													8
1	5	9	7	3							14			10^3	12	4		6	11^2		8^1	2	13											9
1	5	9	6	2							13			11	12	14		4		8	10^2	7^3	3^1											10
1	5		8	3							12	7^2	10	13	14		2	4			11^1				9^1	6								11
1	9	5		3							10^2	6^1	11		14		2^1	4	7	13		12				8								12
1	2	5		3^*							10^1		6		11^1		12	4^2	7	14		9		8	13									13
	5			3							10^1		11^3	14	13		2		6	12		9^3		8	7	1	4							14
1	5^*			3							12		13	14			2		6	10^2		9^1		8^1	7		4	11^*						15
1	2	5^1	7	3							10^2	6	12			4		8^*				11	9	13										16
1	5^1	12	6^3	3					14		7^2	10		11		2	4		8			9			13									17
1	5			3							13	10^2	6	12	11	2^1	4		7			9			8									18
1	5		7	4			11					6	14	10^2		3		8^1		13	9^3			12				2						19
1		9^2	3		11	10	13				6		8^1		4	7		12		5								2						20
	8			3	11^2	6	13	9^1			12				2	4	7	10^3		14								5						21
1	5		8		4	10^1	7					12	11^2		3		9	6		13								2						22
1		9	5			11					13	10^2		2	3	8^1		7		4		12						6						23
1		9	7	12	13	6	11^2				10			4	3^1		8		2			13						5						24
1		8	7	3	12	11	9^1		14	10^3				2			6		4			13						5^2						25
1		9	6	3		10	7^2			11^1	12	2				8		4			13						5						26
1		9	8	3	11^1		10^3	6^2		12		2	14			7		4			13						5						27
1		5	6	3^*	11^1		10	8	12			13		4			9		2							7						28
1	12^3	9^1	8	3	13		11^2	10		14					2		6		4							5						29
1		9	8	3			11	7	10					2			6		4							5						30
1		8^1	7^3	3			11	9	10			14			2^2	13	6		4		12						5						31
1		6	3				10	7^1	11^2			13		2				8^1	12	4		9						5						32
1		6	3				10^1	9	11			12		2				7^2	14	4		8						5	13				33
1		6	3				11^2	9^1	10			13		2		7			12	4		8						5						34
1		6	3		7	11		10	13	12		2^1						9^1	4		8						5						35
1	12	8		2^2			7^3	10		9	11	13			4	6		3									5^1	14				36
1		8^1	7	3	14	6	11^1	9^2		13	10^1		2				4		12									5^*					37
1	5	8	9	2^1		6	10		12	13	11		3	7^2			4																38
1	5	9	8^1	3^2		7	11		12	13	10^1		2	4	6			14															39
1	9		6^2			7	11		12	13	10^1		4	3	8		2	14	5^1														40
1	5^1					6	10	7	13		11^2		2	3	8		4	12									9						41
	9					6	10	12		11^1			2^3		8	4	7^4										5		1	13			42
	9					7	11		12	13	10^1		2	3	6	4	14	8^3									5^2		1				43
	9^1	8^2				6	10		11	12	13		4	3	7		2	14									5^1		1				44
	9	13	3			6	10^*		12		11^2		2	4^2		7		14	8^1											1		5	45
	9	8	3	12					10	13	11^1		2	4	7			6^2											1		5	46

The Budweiser FA Cup
First Round   St Albans C   (a)   8-1
Second Round   Oldham Ath   (a)   1-1
Replay   Oldham Ath   (h)   1-4

Capital One Cup
First Round   Tranmere R   (a)   0-2

Johnstone's Paint Trophy
Second Round   Chesterfield   (h)   0-1

MIDDLESBROUGH

FOUNDATION

A previous belief that Middlesbrough Football Club was founded at a tripe supper at the Corporation Hotel has proved to be erroneous. In fact, members of Middlesbrough Cricket Club were responsible for forming it at a meeting in the gymnasium of the Albert Park Hotel in 1875.

Riverside Stadium, Middlesbrough TS3 6RS.

Telephone: (0844) 499 6789.

Fax: (01642) 757 697.

Ticket Office: (0844) 499 1234.

Website: www.mfc.co.uk

Email: enquiries@mfc.co.uk

Ground Capacity: 34,998.

Record Attendance: 53,536 v Newcastle U, Division 1, 27 December 1949 (at Ayresome Park); 34,814 v Newcastle U, FA Premier League, 5 March 2003 (at Riverside Stadium).

Pitch Measurements: 105m × 68m (115yd × 74.5yd)

Chairman: Steve Gibson.

Chief Executive: Neil Bausor.

Head Coach: Aitor Karanka.

Assistant Head Coach: Craig Hignett.

Head of Medical: Chris Moseley.

Colours: Red shirts with white trim, red shorts with black trim, red socks with white hoops.

Year Formed: 1876; re-formed 1986.

Turned Professional: 1889; became amateur 1892, and professional again, 1899.

Club Nickname: 'Boro'.

Grounds: 1877, Old Archery Ground, Albert Park; 1879, Breckon Hill; 1882, Linthorpe Road Ground; 1903, Ayresome Park; 1995, Riverside Stadium.

First Football League Game: 2 September 1899, Division 2, v Lincoln C (a) L 0–3 – Smith; Shaw, Ramsey; Allport, McNally, McCracken; Wanless, Longstaffe, Gettins, Page, Pugh.

Record League Victory: 9–0 v Brighton & HA, Division 2, 23 August 1958 – Taylor; Bilcliff, Robinson; Harris (2p), Phillips, Walley; Day, McLean, Clough (5), Peacock (2), Holliday.

Record Cup Victory: 7–0 v Hereford U, Coca-Cola Cup 2nd rd, 1st leg, 18 September 1996 – Miller; Fleming (1), Branco (1), Whyte, Vickers, Whelan, Emerson (1), Mustoe, Stamp, Juninho, Ravanelli (4).

HONOURS

Football League – Division 1:
Champions 1994–95;
Runners-up 1997–98;
Division 2: *Champions* 1926–27, 1928–29, 1973–74;
Runners-up 1901–02, 1991–92;
Division 3: *Runners-up* 1966–67, 1986–87.
FA Cup: *Runners-up* 1997.
Football League Cup: *Winners* 2004; *Runners-up* 1997, 1998.
Amateur Cup: *Winners* 1895, 1898.
Anglo-Scottish Cup: *Winners* 1976.
Zenith Data Systems Cup:
Runners-up 1990.
European Competitions
UEFA Cup: 2004–05, 2005–06
(*runners-up*).

sky SPORTS FACT FILE

Middlesbrough's first application to join the Football League was unusual in that it was a joint bid with their local rivals Ironopolis. The two clubs had agreed to merge if they were successful, with the title to be Middlesbrough and Ironopolis United Football & Athletic Club. They were not elected and subsequently went their separate ways.

Record Defeat: 0–9 v Blackburn R, Division 2, 6 November 1954.

Most League Points (2 for a win): 65, Division 2, 1973–74.

Most League Points (3 for a win): 94, Division 3, 1986–87.

Most League Goals: 122, Division 2, 1926–27.

Highest League Scorer in Season: George Camsell, 59, Division 2, 1926–27 (Second Division record).

Most League Goals in Total Aggregate: George Camsell, 325, 1925–39.

Most League Goals in One Match: 5, John Wilkie v Gainsborough T, Division 2, 2 March 1901; 5, Andy Wilson v Nottingham F, Division 1, 6 October 1923; 5, George Camsell v Manchester C, Division 2, 25 December 1926; 5, George Camsell v Aston Villa, Division 1, 9 September 1935; 5, Brian Clough v Brighton & HA, Division 2, 22 August 1958.

Most Capped Player: Wilf Mannion, 26, England.

Most League Appearances: Tim Williamson, 563, 1902–23.

Youngest League Player: Luke Williams, 16 years 200 days v Barnsley, 18 December 2009.

Record Transfer Fee Received: £12,000,000 from Atletico Madrid for Juninho, July 1997; £12,000,000 from Aston Villa for Stewart Downing, July 2009.

Record Transfer Fee Paid: £12,000,000 to Heerenveen for Afonso Alves, January 2008.

Football League Record: 1899 Elected to Division 2; 1902–24 Division 1; 1924–27 Division 2; 1927–28 Division 1; 1928–29 Division 2; 1929–54 Division 1; 1954–66 Division 2; 1966–67 Division 3; 1967–74 Division 2; 1974–82 Division 1; 1982–86 Division 2; 1986–87 Division 3; 1987–88 Division 2; 1988–89 Division 1; 1989–92 Division 2; 1992–93 FA Premier League; 1993–95 Division 1; 1995–97 FA Premier League; 1997–98 Division 1; 1998–2009 FA Premier League; 2009– FL C.

MANAGERS

John Robson 1899–1905
Alex Mackie 1905–06
Andy Aitken 1906–09
J. Gunter 1908–10
  (Secretary-Manager)
Andy Walker 1910–11
Tom McIntosh 1911–19
Jimmy Howie 1920–23
Herbert Bamlett 1923–26
Peter McWilliam 1927–34
Wilf Gillow 1934–44
David Jack 1944–52
Walter Rowley 1952–54
Bob Dennison 1954–63
Raich Carter 1963–66
Stan Anderson 1966–73
Jack Charlton 1973–77
John Neal 1977–81
Bobby Murdoch 1981–82
Malcolm Allison 1982–84
Willie Maddren 1984–86
Bruce Rioch 1986–90
Colin Todd 1990–91
Lennie Lawrence 1991–94
Bryan Robson 1994–2001
Steve McClaren 2001–06
Gareth Southgate 2006–09
Gordon Strachan 2009–10
Tony Mowbray 2010–13
Aitor Karanka November 2013–

LATEST SEQUENCES

Longest Sequence of League Wins: 9, 16.2.1974 – 6.4.1974.

Longest Sequence of League Defeats: 8, 26.12.1995 – 17.2.1996.

Longest Sequence of League Draws: 8, 3.4.1971 – 1.5.1971.

Longest Sequence of Unbeaten League Matches: 24, 8.9.1973 – 19.1.1974.

Longest Sequence Without a League Win: 19, 3.10.1981 – 6.3.1982.

Successive Scoring Runs: 26 from 21.9.1946.

Successive Non-scoring Runs: 7, 25.1.2014 – 1.3.2014.

TEN YEAR LEAGUE RECORD

		P	W	D	L	F	A	Pts	Pos
2004-05	PR Lge	38	14	13	11	53	46	55	7
2005-06	PR Lge	38	12	9	17	48	58	45	14
2006-07	PR Lge	38	12	10	16	44	49	46	12
2007-08	PR Lge	38	10	12	16	43	53	42	13
2008-09	PR Lge	38	7	11	20	28	57	32	19
2009-10	FL C	46	16	14	16	58	50	62	11
2010-11	FL C	46	17	11	18	68	68	62	12
2011-12	FL C	46	18	16	12	52	51	70	7
2012-13	FL C	46	18	5	23	61	70	59	16
2013-14	FL C	46	16	16	14	62	50	64	12

DID YOU KNOW ?

In 2013–14 Middlesbrough established a new club record for failing to score. After Emmanuel Ledesma netted against Charlton on 18 January they had to wait a total of 733 minutes before Danny Graham's goal in the 2-0 win over Ipswich on 8 March.

MIDDLESBROUGH – FL CHAMPIONSHIP 2013–14 LEAGUE RECORD

Match No.	Date	Venue	Opponents	Result	H/T Score	Lg Pos.	Goalscorers	Attendance
1	Aug 3	H	Leicester C	L	1-2	1-0	15	St. Ledger (og) [36]	17,223
2	10	A	Charlton Ath	W	1-0	0-0	12	Jutkiewicz [72]	14,882
3	17	H	Blackpool	D	1-1	0-0	10	Emnes [90]	13,993
4	25	A	Wigan Ath	D	2-2	1-1	14	Friend [45], Leadbitter [75]	14,333
5	31	H	Sheffield W	D	1-1	0-1	15	Carayol [49]	15,964
6	Sept 14	A	Ipswich T	L	1-3	1-1	16	Adomah [12]	15,276
7	17	A	Nottingham F	D	2-2	1-0	16	Kamara [17], Friend [55]	19,509
8	21	H	Bournemouth	D	3-3	2-2	16	Kamara [19], Carayol [32], Leadbitter [74]	13,617
9	28	A	QPR	L	0-2	0-2	18		17,081
10	Oct 1	H	Huddersfield T	D	1-1	0-0	19	Gibson [79]	12,793
11	5	H	Yeovil T	W	4-1	2-1	15	Leadbitter [8], Adomah [24], Butterfield [50], Kamara [74]	13,181
12	19	A	Barnsley	L	2-3	0-3	16	Adomah 2 [82, 84]	11,438
13	25	H	Doncaster R	W	4-0	2-0	12	Adomah 2 [8, 35], Kamara [67], Ayala [83]	21,882
14	Nov 2	A	Blackburn R	L	0-1	0-0	16		16,645
15	9	H	Watford	D	2-2	1-1	16	Adomah [23], Ayala [90]	14,344
16	23	A	Leeds U	L	1-2	0-1	18	Carayol [52]	30,367
17	30	H	Bolton W	W	1-0	0-0	15	Leadbitter (pen) [82]	23,679
18	Dec 4	A	Derby Co	L	1-2	0-1	16	Whitehead [74]	24,631
19	7	A	Birmingham C	D	2-2	1-0	18	Carayol [22], Ayala [80]	13,454
20	14	H	Brighton & HA	L	0-1	0-0	19		13,635
21	21	A	Millwall	W	2-0	0-0	17	Ledesma [49], Adomah [89]	11,078
22	26	H	Burnley	W	1-0	1-0	16	Ledesma [24]	20,689
23	29	H	Reading	W	3-0	2-0	15	Adomah [12], Leadbitter 2 (1 pen) [36, 82 (p)]	16,001
24	Jan 1	A	Bolton W	D	2-2	2-1	15	Carayol [9], Main [20]	17,410
25	11	A	Blackpool	W	2-0	0-0	13	Carayol 2 [84, 90]	14,421
26	18	H	Charlton Ath	W	1-0	1-0	9	Ledesma [16]	14,548
27	25	A	Leicester C	L	0-2	0-0	10		26,047
28	28	H	Wigan Ath	D	0-0	0-0	10		13,258
29	Feb 1	A	Doncaster R	D	0-0	0-0	12		11,440
30	8	H	Blackburn R	D	0-0	0-0	12		14,965
31	15	A	Watford	L	0-1	0-0	14		15,391
32	22	H	Leeds U	D	0-0	0-0	13		20,424
33	Mar 1	A	Sheffield W	L	0-1	0-0	13		20,743
34	8	H	Ipswich T	W	2-0	2-0	13	Graham 2 [29, 45]	13,965
35	11	H	Nottingham F	D	1-1	0-0	12	Carayol [53]	14,134
36	15	A	Bournemouth	D	0-0	0-0	13		9710
37	22	H	QPR	L	1-3	1-1	14	Friend [18]	15,075
38	25	A	Huddersfield T	D	2-2	1-2	15	Adomah 2 [10, 47]	11,999
39	29	A	Brighton & HA	W	2-0	0-0	13	Adomah [65], Graham [86]	27,486
40	Apr 5	H	Derby Co	W	1-0	0-0	13	Chalobah [69]	15,234
41	8	H	Birmingham C	W	3-1	2-1	13	Graham [29], Butterfield [31], Tomlin [89]	13,399
42	12	A	Burnley	W	1-0	0-0	12	Butterfield [61]	16,661
43	19	A	Millwall	L	1-2	0-2	13	Ledesma [80]	15,342
44	22	A	Reading	L	0-2	0-2	13		17,228
45	26	H	Barnsley	W	3-1	0-0	12	Tomlin 2 [54, 90], Graham [90]	14,867
46	May 3	A	Yeovil T	W	4-1	3-1	12	Graham [31], Ledesma 2 [40, 47], Tomlin [43]	6477

Final League Position: 12

GOALSCORERS

League (62): Adomah 12, Carayol 8, Graham 6, Leadbitter 6 (2 pens), Ledesma 6, Kamara 4, Tomlin 4, Ayala 3, Butterfield 3, Friend 3, Chalobah 1, Emnes 1, Gibson 1, Jutkiewicz 1, Main 1, Whitehead 1, own goal 1.
The Budweiser FA Cup (0).
Capital One Cup (1): Jutkiewicz 1.

Steele J 16	Parnaby S 1+2	Friend G 39+2	Whitehead D 34+3	Williams R 22	Woodgate J 24+1	Carayol M 24+8	Leadbitter G 37+2	Jutkiewicz L 12+10	Emnes M 14+8	Varga J 29+5	Haroun F —+1	Williams L 4+5	Richardson F 11	Adomah A 38+4	Leutwiler J 1+2	Smallwood R 9+4	Halliday A —+4	Hoyte J 1+2	Butterfield J 20+11	Kamara K 16+9	Ledesma E 16+11	Gibson B 26+5	Hines S 3+1	Ayala D 17+2	Main C 7+16	Given S 16	Chalobah N 15+4	Omeruo K 14	Graham D 17+1	Tomlin L 9+5	Mejias T 1	Konstantopoulos D 12	Reach A 1+1	Morris B —+1	Match No.
1	2^2	3	4	5	6	7^1	8	9	10	11	12	13																							1
1^2		5	7	4	3	10^1	9^3	11	14	6			2	8	12	13																			2
		5	9	4	3	10	7	11	12	8^1			2	6	1																				3
1	12	5	6	4	3	10^1	8	11	13	9				2^2	7^3		14																		4
1		5	8	3	4	10^2	7	11	12	9^1				6			13	2																	5
1		5	8^2	3	4	6^1	7	11	12				2	10					9	13															6
1		5	8	4	3	13	7	14	10^1				2	11^2					6		9^1	12													7
1		5	6^1	4^1	3	10^2	8	13				14		2	7^3				9	11		12													8
1	13	5	9			3^2	7	12		8^3				2	10		14			6^1	11		4													9
1		5	6	3		10^3	9	12					2^1	7			13	14	8^2	11		4													10
1		5	8	3		12	7^1					10^3	14	2^2	9			13	6	11		4													11
1		5	8^1			14	7	11^3	13				2	9		12			6^3	10		4	3												12
			2	3	10^3	7		9	14				8^1	6					12	11^3		5		4	13										13
		5		2	3	13	9	12	10^2	7^1			8^3	6					14	11		4													14
1		14		2		9^2	7	10^3					6			8	13		12	11		5	3^1	4											15
1		5			3	9^2	7	14	10^3				2	6	12	8^1				11		4	13												16
		5	14	2	3	10^3	7		13					6		9^2			8^1	11		12	1												17
		5^1	9	2	3	12			13					6^1		8			7^2	10		4		14	11	1									18
			8	2	3	9^1	7	12	10^3					6					13	11^2	14	5		4		1									19
		5	9	2^2	3^2	10	7	11^1				14		6					8			12		4	13	1									20
		5	6			10^1		14	9^2	2				8	7				13		12	4		3	11^3	1									21
		5	7		3		12	10^3	11^2	2				6	8				9	14		4	13		1										22
		5	7			13	8	11^1	10^2	2				9					14		6^3	4		3	12	1									23
		5		2		10^2	7	12	14					6^1	9				8^3		13	4		3	11	1									24
		5	9	4		12	7	11^1	8^3	2				10					14		6^2			3	13	1									25
		5	7	4		9^2	8	12	11^3	2				13					14	6				3	10^1	1									26
		5	6	4		10	7	11^1		2				8					12	9^2		3			1	13									27
		5	8	4^1		9^2	7	11^3		2				13					14	6	12	3		10	1									28
		5	12			10	7			2				8^2	14	6	4		3^2	11^1	1	9	2	13											29
		5	9		3	10^1	7			2				12		13	6^2	4	14	1	8		11^1												30
		5	9		3^1	12	7			2^2				10		14	6^2	4	13	1	8		11												31
		5			3		7			2				13		8^3	9^1	14	10^1	1	6	4	11	12											32
		5	8^1	3^3						2				9^2		6^1	11	13	12	14		7	4	10		1									33
		5		9^1	7					2				12		13	12	6	3	14	8	4	11^2	10^1		1									34
		5	13	9^1	7					2				12		14	6^1	4	8	3	11	10^3				1									35
		5	8	9^1	7^3					2				6		13	3	14	12	4	11	10^2				1									36
		5	8							2				6		10^2	9^1	13	4	7	3	11	12				1								37
		5	9							2	14			10		8		6^2	4	13	7^3	3	11^1	12				1							38
		5	8		7					2	6			9^1		12	14	4	13	3^3	11	10^2					1								39
		5			7					2	6^3			9^1		13	12	4	14	8	3	11	10^2				1								40
		5^1	12		7					2	10^2			8		9^1	13	4	6	3	11	14					1								41
	6		2	8		12	13	5		7^2	9			4	14		3		10^3	11^1							1								42
	14	8^1	3	6^2		12	9			7^3	5			13					2	4	11	10					1								43
	5	7		12						2	11			6					9^1	4		8^2	3	10	13		1								44
		7	3^1							2				6		8^3			5	14	12		13	4^2	11	10				1	9				45
1		7^2								2				6^1		12			9	5	3	4		8^3			10	11				13	14		46

The Budweiser FA Cup
Third Round   Hull C   (h)   0-2

Capital One Cup
First Round   Accrington S   (h)   1-2

MILLWALL

The Den, Zampa Road, London SE16 3LN.

Telephone: (020) 7232 1222. *Fax:* (020) 7231 3663.

Ticket Office: (0844) 826 2004.

Website: www.millwallfc.co.uk

Email: questions@millwallplc.com

Ground Capacity: 19,734.

Record Attendance: 48,672 v Derby Co, FA Cup 5th rd, 20 February 1937 (at The Den, Cold Blow Lane); 20,093 v Arsenal, FA Cup 3rd rd, 10 January 1994 (at The Den, Bermondsey).

Pitch Measurements: 100.5m × 67.5m (110yd × 74yd)

Chairman: John G. Berylson.

Chief Executive: Andy Ambler.

Manager: Ian Holloway.

Coaches: Marc Bircham, Des Bulpin.

Physio: Bobby Bacic.

Colours: Blue shirts with thin white stripes, white shorts with blue trim, blue socks with white trim.

Year Formed: 1885.

Turned Professional: 1893.

Previous Names: 1885, Millwall Rovers; 1889, Millwall Athletic; 1899, Millwall; 1985, Millwall Football & Athletic Company.

Club Nickname: 'The Lions'.

Grounds: 1885, Glengall Road, Millwall; 1886, Back of 'Lord Nelson'; 1890, East Ferry Road; 1901, North Greenwich; 1910, The Den, Cold Blow Lane; 1993, The Den, Bermondsey.

First Football League Game: 28 August 1920, Division 3, v Bristol R (h) W 2–0 – Lansdale; Fort, Hodge; Voisey (1), Riddell, McAlpine; Waterall, Travers, Broad (1), Sutherland, Dempsey.

Record League Victory: 9–1 v Torquay U, Division 3 (S), 29 August 1927 – Lansdale, Tilling, Hill, Amos, Bryant (3), Graham, Chance, Hawkins (3), Landells (1), Phillips (2), Black. 9–1 v Coventry C, Division 3 (S), 19 November 1927 – Lansdale, Fort, Hill, Amos, Collins (1), Graham, Chance, Landells (4), Cock (2), Phillips (2), Black.

Record Cup Victory: 7–0 v Gateshead, FA Cup 2nd rd, 12 December 1936 – Yuill; Ted Smith, Inns; Brolly, Hancock, Forsyth; Thomas (1), Mangnall (1), Ken Burditt (2), McCartney (2), Thorogood (1).

Record Defeat: 1–9 v Aston Villa, FA Cup 4th rd, 28 January 1946.

Most League Points (2 for a win): 65, Division 3 (S), 1927–28 and Division 3, 1965–66.

Most League Points (3 for a win): 93, Division 2, 2000–01.

Most League Goals: 127, Division 3 (S), 1927–28.

Highest League Scorer in Season: Richard Parker, 37, Division 3 (S), 1926–27.

Most League Goals in Total Aggregate: Neil Harris, 124, 1995–2004; 2006–11.

Most League Goals in One Match: 5, Richard Parker v Norwich C, Division 3 (S), 28 August 1926.

Most Capped Player: Eamonn Dunphy, 22 (23), Republic of Ireland.

Most League Appearances: Barry Kitchener, 523, 1967–82.

Youngest League Player: Moses Ashikodi, 15 years 240 days v Brighton & HA, 22 February 2003.

Record Transfer Fee Received: £2,800,000 from Norwich C for Steve Morison, June 2011.

Record Transfer Fee Paid: £800,000 to Derby Co for Paul Goddard, December 1989.

Football League Record: 1920 Original Members of Division 3; 1921 Division 3 (S); 1928–34 Division 2; 1934–38 Division 3 (S); 1938–48 Division 2; 1948–58 Division 3 (S); 1958–62 Division 4; 1962–64 Division 3; 1964–65 Division 4; 1965–66 Division 3; 1966–75 Division 3; 1975–76 Division 3; 1976–79 Division 2; 1979–85 Division 3; 1985–88 Division 2; 1988–90 Division 1; 1990–92 Division 2; 1992–96 Division 1; 1996–2001 Division 2; 2001–04 Division 1; 2004–06 FL C; 2006–10 FL 1; 2010– FL C.

LATEST SEQUENCES

Longest Sequence of League Wins: 10, 10.3.1928 – 25.4.1928.

Longest Sequence of League Defeats: 11, 10.4.1929 – 16.9.1929.

Longest Sequence of League Draws: 5, 22.12.1973 – 12.1.1974.

Longest Sequence of Unbeaten League Matches: 19, 22.8.1959 – 31.10.1959.

Longest Sequence Without a League Win: 20, 26.12.1989 – 5.5.1990.

Successive Scoring Runs: 22 from 27.11.1954.

Successive Non-scoring Runs: 6 from 27.4.2013.

MANAGERS

F. B. Kidd 1894–99
(Hon. Treasurer/Manager)
E. R. Stopher 1899–1900
(Hon. Treasurer/Manager)
George Saunders 1900–11
(Hon. Treasurer/Manager)
Herbert Lipsham 1911–19
Robert Hunter 1919–33
Bill McCracken 1933–36
Charlie Hewitt 1936–40
Bill Voisey 1940–44
Jack Cock 1944–48
Charlie Hewitt 1948–56
Ron Gray 1956–57
Jimmy Seed 1958–59
Reg Smith 1959–61
Ron Gray 1961–63
Billy Gray 1963–66
Benny Fenton 1966–74
Gordon Jago 1974–77
George Petchey 1978–80
Peter Anderson 1980–82
George Graham 1982–86
John Docherty 1986–90
Bob Pearson 1990
Bruce Rioch 1990–92
Mick McCarthy 1992–96
Jimmy Nicholl 1996–97
John Docherty 1997
Billy Bonds 1997–98
Keith Stevens 1998–2000
(then Joint Manager)
(plus **Alan McLeary** 1999–2000)
Mark McGhee 2000–03
Dennis Wise 2003–05
Steve Claridge 2005
Colin Lee 2005
David Tuttle 2005–06
Nigel Spackman 2006
Willie Donachie 2006–07
Kenny Jackett 2007–13
Steve Lomas 2013
Ian Holloway January 2014–

TEN YEAR LEAGUE RECORD

		P	W	D	L	F	A	Pts	Pos
2004-05	FL C	46	18	12	16	51	45	66	10
2005-06	FL C	46	8	17	21	35	61	40	23
2006-07	FL 1	46	19	9	18	59	62	66	10
2007-08	FL 1	46	14	10	22	45	60	52	17
2008-09	FL 1	46	25	7	14	63	53	82	5
2009-10	FL 1	46	24	13	9	76	44	85	3
2010-11	FL C	46	18	13	15	62	48	67	9
2011-12	FL C	46	15	12	19	55	57	57	16
2012-13	FL C	46	15	11	20	51	62	56	20
2013-14	FL C	46	11	15	20	46	74	48	19

DID YOU KNOW ?

Millwall reached the final of the wartime League South Cup in 1944–45 when they played Chelsea at Wembley Stadium. King George VI and Princess Elizabeth (Queen Elizabeth II) were amongst the 90,000 crowd but the Lions lost 2–0.

MILLWALL – FL CHAMPIONSHIP 2013–14 LEAGUE RECORD

Match No.	Date		Venue	Opponents	Result		H/T Score	Lg Pos.	Goalscorers	Attendance
1	Aug	3	H	Yeovil T	L	0-1	0-0	20		12,404
2		10	A	Ipswich T	L	0-3	0-0	23		17,183
3		17	H	Huddersfield T	L	0-1	0-0	24		9503
4		24	A	Sheffield W	D	2-2	1-2	23	Zayatte (og) [5], Keogh (pen) [87]	20,009
5		31	A	Brighton & HA	D	1-1	0-0	23	Woolford [51]	26,804
6	Sept	14	H	Derby Co	L	1-5	0-2	24	Waghorn [75]	9523
7		17	A	Blackpool	W	3-1	1-1	19	Trotter (pen) [45], Bailey [73], Morison [74]	8415
8		21	A	Charlton Ath	W	1-0	1-0	17	McDonald [38]	15,917
9		28	A	Leeds U	W	2-0	0-0	16	Woolford [65], Malone [76]	13,063
10	Oct	1	A	Birmingham C	L	0-4	0-2	16		13,133
11		5	A	Bournemouth	L	2-5	2-1	18	Waghorn [6], Trotter [10]	9624
12		19	A	QPR	D	2-2	0-1	18	McDonald [51], Easter [90]	13,727
13		26	A	Reading	D	1-1	0-1	17	Trotter (pen) [90]	18,245
14	Nov	2	H	Burnley	D	2-2	2-1	18	McDonald [23], Shittu [38]	10,168
15		9	A	Bolton W	L	1-3	1-2	20	Easter [28]	14,830
16		23	H	Barnsley	W	1-0	0-0	17	Wiseman (og) [77]	9057
17		30	A	Leicester C	L	0-3	0-1	21		21,633
18	Dec	3	H	Nottingham F	D	2-2	1-1	20	Morison [8], Woolford [56]	9029
19		7	H	Wigan Ath	W	2-1	1-0	17	Morison [3], Easter [83]	9519
20		14	A	Blackburn R	L	2-3	1-1	18	Waghorn [42], Morison [89]	12,642
21		21	H	Middlesbrough	L	0-2	0-0	19		11,078
22		26	A	Watford	L	0-4	0-2	20		15,471
23		29	A	Doncaster R	D	0-0	0-0	20		6454
24	Jan	1	H	Leicester C	L	1-3	0-1	21	Chaplow [68]	10,014
25		11	A	Huddersfield T	L	0-1	0-0	21		12,651
26		18	H	Ipswich T	W	1-0	1-0	20	Fredericks [40]	12,125
27		28	H	Sheffield W	D	1-1	0-0	21	Campbell [80]	10,624
28	Feb	1	H	Reading	L	0-3	0-1	21		11,174
29		8	A	Burnley	L	1-3	1-2	21	Woolford [27]	11,502
30		11	A	Yeovil T	D	1-1	0-0	21	Morison [75]	4463
31		15	H	Bolton W	D	1-1	0-1	21	Woolford [82]	10,007
32		22	A	Barnsley	L	0-1	0-1	21		9653
33	Mar	1	H	Brighton & HA	L	0-1	0-1	21		12,149
34		8	A	Derby Co	W	1-0	0-0	21	Morison [61]	22,853
35		11	A	Blackpool	L	0-1	0-1	21		12,412
36		15	H	Charlton Ath	D	0-0	0-0	21		16,102
37		22	A	Leeds U	L	1-2	0-2	22	Campbell [72]	23,211
38		25	A	Birmingham C	L	2-3	1-2	24	Morison [30], Jackson (pen) [88]	9268
39		29	H	Blackburn R	D	2-2	0-0	23	Williams (pen) [57], Jackson (pen) [88]	8840
40	Apr	5	A	Nottingham F	W	2-1	2-0	23	Malone [19], Martin [39]	20,077
41		8	A	Wigan Ath	W	1-0	1-0	22	Edwards [22]	14,124
42		12	A	Watford	D	2-2	0-1	22	Morison [64], Woolford [90]	10,851
43		19	A	Middlesbrough	W	2-1	2-0	20	Maierhofer 2 [16, 30]	15,342
44		21	H	Doncaster R	D	0-0	0-0	20		12,026
45		26	A	QPR	D	1-1	0-0	20	Malone [90]	15,725
46	May	3	H	Bournemouth	W	1-0	1-0	19	Woolford [29]	15,779

Final League Position: 19

GOALSCORERS

League (46): Morison 8, Woolford 7, Easter 3, Malone 3, McDonald 3, Trotter 3 (2 pens), Waghorn 3, Campbell 2, Jackson 2 (2 pens), Maierhofer 2, Bailey 1, Chaplow 1, Edwards 1, Fredericks 1, Keogh 1 (1 pen), Martin 1, Shittu 1, Williams 1 (1 pen), own goals 2.
The Budweiser FA Cup (1): Woolford 1.
Capital One Cup (3): Feeney 1, Keogh 1, Woolford 1.

Forde D 40	Dunne A 28+1	Lowry S 21+1	Wright J 2+1	Shittu D 22	Beevers M 27+1	Henry J 4+1	Abdou N 21+3	Keogh A 6+9	Morison S 25+16	Chaplow R 12+7	Bailey N 26+2	McDonald S 21+11	Feeney L 5+12	Maierhofer S 7+4	Bywater S 6+1	Smith J 3+3	Edwards C 8	Derry S 7	Easter J 6+14	Martin L 16+10	Robinson P 20+5	N'Guessan D —+1	Woolford M 38+2	Trotter L 16+3	Connolly P 3+1	Waghorn M 13+1	Malone S 32+1	Osborne K 1	Hoyte J 4+1	Moussi G 3	Fredericks R 11+3	Campbell D 6+3	Williams S 15+2	Marquis J 1+1	Upson E 10	Jackson S 3+11	Bessone F 1+1	Garvan O 13	Onyedinma F 3+1	Match No.
1	2	3	4^3	5	6	7	8	9^2	10	11^1	12	13	14																											1
		5		3	4	6			11^3	10^1	9^2	8	14	13		1	2	7	12																					2
	2	5		3	4	6^3			14	10	9^2	7	13			1			8	11^1	12																			3
	2	5		4^3	3				11		6	8	10	13	1			7^1	9^2	12	14																			4
1	2^4	5		3	4	8^3	12	9^2	7	11^1	6	14											10	13																5
1	6^4			3	4	12		9^2			8^3	6	10					7^1					11	14	2	13														6
1	2				4		8		12	13	6	10^3								14	3		11^2	7^1		9	5													7
1	2				4		7		12	14	10	11^1								13	3		9	8^2		6^2	5													8
1	2				4			6	13		8									10^2	12		3	9	7	11^1	5													9
1	2				4			6			10^2	13	8^3							14	12	3	11	7		9^1	5													10
1	2^4						6		13		12							8^1		10	3		11	7^1	14	9^3	5	4												11
1		3					7	12	13		8	11^2						14		4			10^3	9^1	2	6	5													12
1		4					10^8		14		7^1	11	13	12				3					8^3	9	2^2	6	5													13
1	12	4						14		8	10	13		2	6^1			3		9	7		11^3	5^2																14
1	5	4					7^2	13		6	12			10^1	14	3			11^3	8		9				2														15
1					4		13	9^6	6	11^1	12			14	3			10		8^2	5		2	7																16
1					4		6	14	12	9^2				11^3	8			13	3	10^1		5		2	7															17
1	2				4		8	12	10		14	13		6^2	3			9^1	7	11^1	5																			18
1	2				4		8	12	10		6^2			13	3			9	7	11^1	5																			19
1	2^3				4		7^1	13	10		6^2			12	3			9	8	11	5	14																		20
1	2				4		7^1	13	10		11^2	6		12	3			9	8		5																			21
1	5	3^4	4				7		10	13				14				9^1	12	11	8^2			2	6^3															22
1	2	3	4				8		11	6^1	7	10^2		13	12			9			5																			23
1	2	3	4				7^2		10	6	8	11		13				14	12	9^3		5^1																		24
1	2	5	4				6^2	13	11	8	7	10^3		3				9^1		12	14																			25
1^2			4	13	3		14	8	11		6^3	9		12				10		7^1		5		2																26
	4^4	3					8^2	11		7^3		14	1					10^1		9	6	5		2	12	13														27
	7^2	3	4^1				10				6^3	1		13	12			9		5		2	11	8	14															28
1	13	3					11	6^2		9	12			14		7		5		2	8^1	4		10^3																29
1	4	3					11		13		10^1	8^3		9		5		2	14	7	6^2	12																		30
1		4	3				11		9^1	12		10		5^2		2	8	6	7^3	13	14																			31
1		4^3	3				12		13	14		10^1		6		2	8	7	11^2	9																				32
1	2	4	3^2				11	14		10^1	12		13		5		8^3	7	6	9																				33
1		4					11^1	14			8^3	3		10		2		7	6	12	5^2	9	13																	34
1	2^3	4					11			13		12		3		10		14	5	6^1	8^2	7	9																	35
1	2	5		4			9			12				3		8		14	11^1	6^3	8	7	10^2																	36
1	2^1	4^3		12		6	10		11		14			3		8		5	9^2	13	7																			37
1		4		3	8		11			10		14		6^2		13	2	5^1	12	7^3	9^3																			38
1	3			4			12	9^2	13		11^1	2^3		6	14	10	5	7	8																					39
1	3			4			14	7			11^2	2^3		6		10	5	12	13	9^1	8																			40
1	3			4			12	6			11^1	2	14	8^2		10	5	7	13	9^1																				41
1	3			4	13		12	6	14		11^2	2	8			10	5	7^3	9^3																					42
1	3			4			12	7	10^2		11^1	2	14	6		9^3	5	8	13																					43
1	3			4			12	6	14		11^1	2	8	8^2		10	5	7	13	9^3																				44
1	3			4^3			8	6			11^2	2		12		10	5^1	14	7	13	9																			45
1	3			4^3			8	6			11^2	2		12		10	5^1	14	7	13	9																			46

The Budweiser FA Cup

Third Round	Southend U	(a)	1-4

Capital One Cup

First Round	AFC Wimbledon	(h)	2-1
Second Round (aet)	Nottingham F	(a)	1-2

MILTON KEYNES DONS

FOUNDATION

In July 2004 Wimbledon became MK Dons and relocated to Milton Keynes. In 2007 it recognised itself as a new club with no connection to the old Wimbledon FC. In August of that year the replica trophies and other Wimbledon FC memorabilia were returned to the London Borough of Merton.

Stadiummk, Stadium Way West, Milton Keynes, Buckinghamshire MK1 1ST.

Telephone: (01908) 622 922.

Fax: (01908) 622 933.

Ticket Office: (01908) 622 900.

Website: www.mkdons.com

Email: info@mkdons.com

Ground Capacity: 22,233.

Record Attendance: 8,306 v Tottenham H, League Cup 3rd rd, 25 October 2006 (at National Hockey Stadium); 20,516 v Wolverhampton W, FL 1, 29 March 2014 (at Stadiummk).

Ground Record Attendance: 20,222, England U21 v Bulgaria U21, 16 November 2007.

Pitch Measurements: 105m × 66m (115yd × 72yd)

Chairman: Pete Winkelman.

Manager: Karl Robinson.

Head of Coaching: Richie Barker.

Head of Sports Medicine: Simon Crampton.

Colours: White shirts with red and black trim, white shorts with red trim, white socks.

Year Formed: 2004.

Turned Professional: 2004.

Club Nickname: 'The Dons'.

Grounds: 2003, The National Hockey Stadium; 2007, Stadiummk.

First Football League Game: 7 August 2004, FL 1, v Barnsley (h) D 1–1 – Rachubka; Palmer, Lewington, Harding, Williams, Oyedele, Kamara, Smith, Smart (Herve), McLeod (1) (Hornuss), Small.

Record League Victory: 6–2 v Oldham Ath, FL 1, 14 March 2009 – Gueret; Cummings, O'Hanlon, Llera, Lewington, Leven, Chadwick (Johnson), Navarro (1) (Belson), Baldock (2) (Gerba (1)), Wilbraham (1), Puncheon (1); 6–2 v Chesterfield, FL 1, 28 August 2011 – Martin; Smith A, Lewington, Chicksen, MacKenzie, Williams (Chadwick) (1), Ibhehre, Gleeson, Baldock (3) (O'Shea (1 pen)), Bowditch (1), Balanta (Powell).

HONOURS

Football League – FL 2: *Champions* 2007–08.

Johnstone's Paint Trophy: *Winners* 2008.

FA Cup: Best season: 5th rd, 2013.

Football League Cup: Best season: 3rd rd, 2007, 2011, 2012.

sky SPORTS FACT FILE

MK Dons have reached the play-offs four times during their short history but on each occasion have lost at the semi-final stage. The Dons' only promotion came in 2007–08 when they finished as champions of League Two, ending the season five points clear of their nearest rivals Peterborough United.

Record Cup Victory: 6–0 v Nantwich T, FA Cup 1st rd, 12 November 2011 – Martin; Chicksen, Baldock G, Doumbe (1), Flanagan, Williams S, Powell (1) (O'Shea (1), Chadwick (Galloway), Bowditch (2), MacDonald (Williams G (1)), Balanta.

Record Defeat: 0–5 v Hartlepool U, FL 1, 31 January 2005; 0–5 v Huddersfield T, FL 1, 18 February 2006; 0–5 v Tottenham H, Carling Cup 3rd rd, 24 October 2006; 0–5 v Rochdale, FL 2, 27 January 2007; 0–5 v Carlisle U, FL 1, 13 February 2010.

Most League Points (3 for a win): 97, FL 2, 2007–08.

Most League Goals: 84, FL 1, 2011–12.

Highest League Scorer in Season: Izale McLeod, 21, 2006–07.

Most League Goals in Total Aggregate: Izale McLeod, 62, 2004–07; 2012–14.

Most Capped Player: Ali Gerba (31), Canada.

Most League Goals in One Match: 3, Clive Platt v Barnet, FL 2, 20 January 2007; 3, Mark Wright v Bury, FL 2, 2 February 2008; 3, Aaron Wilbraham v Cheltenham T, FL 1, 31 January 2009; 3, Sam Baldock v Colchester U, FL 1, 12 March 2011; 3, Sam Baldock v Chesterfield, FL 1, 20 August 2012; 3, Dean Bowditch v Bury, FL 1, 22 September 2012; 3, Dele Alli v Notts Co, FL 1, 11 March 2014.

Most League Appearances: Dean Lewington, 428, 2004–14.

Youngest League Player: Brendon Galloway, 16 years 42 days v Rochdale, 28 April 2012.

Record Transfer Fee Received: £1,000,000 from West Ham U for Sam Baldock, August 2011.

Record Transfer Fee Paid: £100,000 to Plymouth Arg for Scott Taylor, January 2006.

Football League Record: 2004–06 FL 1; 2006–08 FL 2; 2008– FL 1.

MANAGERS

Stuart Murdock 2002–04
Danny Wilson 2004–06
Martin Allen 2006–07
Paul Ince 2007–08
Roberto Di Matteo 2008–09
Paul Ince 2009–10
Karl Robinson May 2010–

LATEST SEQUENCES

Longest Sequence of League Wins: 8, 7.9.2007 – 20.10.2007.
Longest Sequence of League Defeats: 4, 14.11.2009 – 1.12.2009.
Longest Sequence of League Draws: 4, 12.2.2013 – 2.3.2013.
Longest Sequence of Unbeaten League Matches: 18, 29.1.2008 – 3.5.2008.
Longest Sequence Without a League Win: 11, 13.3.2010 – 2.5.2010.
Successive Scoring Runs: 18 from 7.4.2007.
Successive Non-scoring Runs: 4, 17.12.2005.

TEN YEAR LEAGUE RECORD

		P	W	D	L	F	A	Pts	Pos
2004-05	FL 1	46	12	15	19	54	68	51	20
2005-06	FL 1	46	12	14	20	45	66	50	22
2006-07	FL 2	46	25	9	12	76	58	84	4
2007-08	FL 2	46	29	10	7	82	37	97	1
2008-09	FL 1	46	26	9	11	83	47	87	3
2009-10	FL 1	46	17	9	20	60	68	60	12
2010-11	FL 1	46	23	8	15	67	60	77	5
2011-12	FL 1	46	22	14	10	84	47	80	5
2012-13	FL 1	46	19	13	14	62	45	70	8
2013-14	FL 1	46	17	9	20	63	65	60	10

DID YOU KNOW ?

Dean Lewington made his 500th appearance for the Dons against Rotherham United in the 2-2 draw at the New York Stadium in April 2014. Dean played in the club's first ever Football League game against Barnsley in August 2004 and has remained with the Dons ever since.

MILTON KEYNES DONS – FOOTBALL LEAGUE ONE 2013–14 LEAGUE RECORD

Match No.	Date	Venue	Opponents	Result	H/T Score	Lg Pos.	Goalscorers	Attendance
1	Aug 3	A	Shrewsbury T	D 0-0	0-0	14		5144
2	10	H	Crewe Alex	W 1-0	1-0	9	Bamford [20]	6911
3	17	A	Preston NE	D 2-2	1-2	8	Banton [31], Williams (pen) [63]	9944
4	24	H	Bristol C	D 2-2	0-1	10	Bamford [52], Carruthers [69]	7874
5	31	A	Sheffield U	W 1-0	0-0	6	Kay [87]	15,080
6	Sept 7	H	Swindon T	D 1-1	0-1	7	Bamford [55]	7738
7	14	H	Notts Co	W 3-1	2-0	6	Chadwick [5], Williams [37], Bamford [90]	7142
8	21	H	Peterborough U	L 1-2	0-2	8	McLeod [74]	8149
9	28	A	Stevenage	W 4-1	3-1	6	Bamford 2 [12, 22], Alli [23], Williams (pen) [62]	7770
10	Oct 5	A	Gillingham	L 2-3	2-2	7	Bamford 2 [26, 30]	5410
11	12	A	Leyton Orient	L 1-2	1-1	8	Bamford [30]	6359
12	19	H	Rotherham U	W 3-2	1-0	7	Williams (pen) [45], Reeves [66], Bamford [88]	11,564
13	22	A	Carlisle U	L 0-1	0-1	10		6675
14	26	A	Tranmere R	L 2-3	1-1	11	Powell [39], Banton [49]	4100
15	Nov 2	H	Walsall	W 1-0	0-0	8	Williams [65]	7711
16	23	A	Bradford C	L 2-3	1-2	11	Bamford [36], Williams (pen) [72]	8970
17	26	A	Colchester U	L 1-3	0-2	11	Spence, J [56]	2597
18	30	H	Coventry C	L 1-3	1-0	12	Williams (pen) [45]	14,988
19	Dec 14	A	Wolverhampton W	W 2-0	1-0	12	Bamford [31], Reeves [50]	17,142
20	21	H	Port Vale	W 3-0	3-0	11	Gleeson [4], Reeves [13], Bamford [32]	7882
21	26	A	Crawley T	W 2-0	1-0	10	Gleeson [22], Bamford [59]	3249
22	29	A	Brentford	L 1-3	0-1	11	Hodson [73]	8010
23	Jan 1	H	Colchester U	D 0-0	0-0	11		7879
24	11	H	Shrewsbury T	W 3-2	2-1	10	Alli [4], Long [21], Bowditch [75]	7408
25	18	A	Bristol C	D 2-2	2-0	10	Williams [17], Reeves [36]	11,533
26	21	A	Crewe Alex	L 0-2	0-1	10		3613
27	28	A	Carlisle U	L 0-3	0-2	10		3007
28	Feb 1	H	Tranmere R	L 0-1	0-0	10		7460
29	8	A	Walsall	W 3-0	2-0	9	McLeod 2 [30, 70], Reeves (pen) [44]	4116
30	15	H	Oldham Ath	W 2-1	0-1	10	Carruthers [49], Reeves [90]	7385
31	18	H	Preston NE	D 0-0	0-0	9		7279
32	22	A	Bradford C	L 0-1	0-0	9		13,501
33	25	A	Oldham Ath	W 2-1	2-0	9	Baldock [4], McLeod [41]	2792
34	Mar 1	H	Sheffield U	L 0-1	0-1	9		9192
35	8	A	Swindon T	W 2-1	0-1	7	Kay [68], Baldock [90]	7424
36	11	A	Notts Co	W 3-1	1-0	7	Alli 3 [3, 55, 90]	3331
37	15	H	Peterborough U	L 0-2	0-0	7		9590
38	22	A	Stevenage	W 3-2	0-2	7	Spence, J [81], Reeves [84], Lewington [90]	3027
39	25	H	Gillingham	L 0-1	0-0	7		6760
40	29	H	Wolverhampton W	L 0-1	0-0	9		20,516
41	Apr 5	A	Coventry C	W 2-1	1-0	7	Alli [39], McLeod [66]	2781
42	12	A	Crawley T	L 0-2	0-2	8		8877
43	18	A	Port Vale	L 0-1	0-0	10		5074
44	21	H	Brentford	D 2-2	0-1	10	Gleeson (pen) [80], McLeod [90]	10,549
45	26	A	Rotherham U	D 2-2	1-0	9	Kennedy [9], McLeod [72]	9405
46	May 3	H	Leyton Orient	L 1-3	0-2	10	Hall [79]	9965

Final League Position: 10

GOALSCORERS

League (63): Bamford 14, Williams 8 (5 pens), McLeod 7, Reeves 7 (1 pen), Alli 6, Gleeson 3 (1 pen), Baldock 2, Banton 2, Carruthers 2, Kay 2, Spence, J 2, Bowditch 1, Chadwick 1, Hall 1, Hodson 1, Kennedy 1, Lewington 1, Long 1, Powell 1.
The Budweiser FA Cup (9): Reeves 3, McLeod 2, Williams 1 (1 pen), Bamford 1, Chadwick 1, Galloway 1.
Capital One Cup (4): Bamford 1, Banton 1, McLeod 1, Reeves 1.
Johnstone's Paint Trophy (3): Williams 1 (1 pen), Alli 1, Bamford 1.

Martin D 40	Hodson L 23	Lewington D 43	Gleeson S 35	Williams S 25	Kay A 28 + 2	Alli B 24 + 9	Potter D 29	Smith A 14 + 10	Chadwick L 14 + 8	Banton J 10 + 1	Bamford P 22 + 1	McLeod 18 + 18	Baldock G 20 + 18	Reeves B 26 + 2	Otsemobor J 9	Carruthers S 19 + 4	Green D 5	Powell D 22 + 10	Flanagan T 6 + 1	McLoughlin 16 + 2	Spence J 29	Jennings D 6	Galloway B 3 + 5	Long C 4	Bowditch D 3 + 9	Hall R 4 + 7	Odelusi S 6 + 4	Cole L 2 + 1	Rasulo G 1 + 6	Loveridge J 2 + 5	Kennedy M 7	Randall M 1 + 3	Burns C — + 1	Match No.
1	2	3	4	5	6	7	8	9¹	10³	11¹	12	13	14																					1
1	2		7	3	4	10	8		12	9²	11¹	13	6	5																				2
1	2		7	5	3	8¹	9		12	10²	11	14	6³		4	13																		3
1	2³		7	5	4	13	8		10¹	9²	11	14	6		3	12																		4
1	2	5	6	4	3	13	7		12	8²	9	11²	14			10¹																		5
1		5	6	4	3	12	7		9¹	10²	11	13	14		2		8³																	6
1		5	7	4	3	12	8		9²		11	13	14		2		10³	6¹																7
1		3	5	4	11		6	14	7²		8	13	12		2		9³	10¹																8
1	2	5	8	4	3	11³	7¹		9²		10	13		14			6	12																9
1	2³	5	8	4		7	12	10¹		11	13					9²	6	14	3³															10
		5	8	4		7	14	10³		11	13	12				2²	9¹	6	3	1														11
1³		5	8	3		7			9	10	13	14	11²			2¹	6	4	12															12
	2³	5				7	12	10⁴		11	13	14	8		3	9¹	6	4	1															13
		5		4		6		9¹	10	11	12	7²	2	13	8			1	3															14
1²	2	5		4		7	13	9¹	10	11	12			8³			6	14	3															15
	2	5	7		4	10	8			11	9¹	12			6		1	3																16
	2	5	8		4		9⁴		13	10	14	6²		11¹	12		1	3																17
	2	5	7		4	12	9	13		11		8¹	14		6³		1	3	10²															18
1	2	5	7		4	8	13		10	12	11¹	6²						3		9²	14													19
1	2	5	8²		4	13	7		11	12	10	6³						3		9¹	14													20
1	2	5	10	4⁴	12	7		11¹		13	9	6						3		8³														21
1	2	5			4		12	6	7²		11	13		8				3		10¹														22
1	2³	5	7		4		12	6		11	13	9		8²	14			3		10¹														23
1		5	7	4	3	10¹	8		14		2	9		6²		12										11¹²	13							24
1	2	5	6	4	3		7	13		14		2	9¹		10³										11	12								25
	5	7	3	4	11³	6		14		2	9		8²	13											10¹	12								26
1	2	5	6		3	9²	7		12	8		10³	13	4											11¹	14								27
1	2	5	7		3	12	8		13		9		6	11²		4									10¹									28
1	2	5	6			7	14		11³	13	9		10¹	8²		4										12								29
	2¹	5	8		3	14		6²		10	13	7		11		9¹										12								30
	2¹	5	7		3	9		13		11	12	8		10²		6																		31
1		5	7		4	6		8¹		9	11²	2		10		3									12	13								32
1		5	8		4	9		14	10¹	11²	2	7		6²		3									12		13							33
1		5		3	8		13	7²		11	2	9		10¹		3									13		10²	6¹						34
1		5		4	9		7			11	2	8		12		3									13		10²	6¹						35
1		5	6	4	7		9			11	2			8		3									12		10¹							36
1		5	7	4	9		8²	12		11	2					3									13	6¹	10³		14					37
1	2		3	6		10			11²	7	5			4³		9	14								3	8¹			12					38
1		5	7	3	4	11³	6		14		2	9		8²		13									3	12	6¹	10³		14				39
1		5		4	7		8			2				9		3		14		10³	12⁴					13	11¹	6²						40
1		5		4	6		7			13	8			9		3				10¹							12³	11¹²	2	14				41
1		5					8		11¹	2				6		3		4³							12	14	13	10²	7					42
1		5	8		6		3²			11	2			9		4		12						14	10¹		13	7²						43
1		5	8				3²			10	2			9³		4		6		12					11¹	13	7	14						44
1		3	6			7			9²	11	2²						12	4		5⁸		10¹				14		8	13					45
1²		5	7	4	9		8¹			11				13	3	2				10					14		6³	12						46

The Budweiser FA Cup

First Round	Halifax T	(h)	4-1
Second Round	Dover Ath	(h)	1-0
Third Round	Wigan Ath	(a)	3-3
Replay	Wigan Ath	(h)	1-3
(aet)			

Capital One Cup

First Round	Northampton T	(a)	2-1
Second Round	Sunderland	(a)	2-4

Johnstone's Paint Trophy

First Round	Northampton T	(h)	2-0
Second Round	Stevenage	(a)	1-2

MORECAMBE

FOUNDATION

Several attempts to start a senior football club in a rugby stronghold finally succeeded on 7 May 1920 at the West View Hotel, Morecambe and a team competed in the Lancashire Combination for 1920–21. The club shared with a local cricket club at Woodhill Lane for the first season and a crowd of 3,000 watched the first game. The club moved to Roseberry Park, the name of which was changed to Christie Park after J.B. Christie who as President had purchased the ground.

Globe Arena, Christie Way, Westgate, Morecambe, Lancashire LA4 4TB.

Telephone: (01524) 411 797.

Fax: (01524) 832 230.

Ticket Office: (01524) 411 797.

Website: www.morecambefc.com

Email: office@morecambefc.com

Ground Capacity: 6,400.

Record Attendance: 9,383 v Weymouth, FA Cup 3rd rd, 6 January 1962 (at Christie Park). 5,375 v Newcastle U, League Cup, 28 August 2013 (at Globe Arena).

Pitch Measurements: 100.5m × 67.5m (110yd × 74yd)

Chairman: Peter McGuigan.

Manager: Jim Bentley.

Assistant Manager: Ken McKenna.

Physio: Simon Farnworth.

Colours: Red panelled shirts with white trim, white shorts with red trim, red socks with white trim.

Year Formed: 1920.

Turned Professional: 1920.

Club Nickname: 'The Shrimps'.

HONOURS

Football League FL 2: Best season: 4th, 2009–10.
FA Cup: Best season: 3rd rd, 1962, 2001, 2003.
Football League Cup: Best season: 3rd rd, 2008.
Northern Premier League: *Runners-up* – 1994–95.
Presidents Cup: *Winners* 1991–92.
FA Trophy: *Winners* 1973–74.
Lancs Senior Cup: *Winners* 1967–68.
Lancs Combination –
Champions 1924–25, 1961–62, 1962–63, 1967–68.
Runners-up 1925–26.
Lancs Combination Cup:
Winners 1926–27, 1945–46, 1964–65, 1966–67, 1967–68.
Runners-up 1923–24, 1924–25, 1962–63.
Lancs Junior Cup: *Winners* 1927, 1928, 1962, 1963, 1969, 1986, 1987, 1994, 1996, 1999, 2004.

Grounds: 1920, Woodhill Lane; 1921, Christie Park; 2010, Globe Arena.

First Football League game: 11 August 2007, FL 2, v Barnet (h) D 0–0 – Lewis; Yates, Adams, Artell, Bentley, Stanley, Baker (Burns), Sorvel, Twiss (Newby), Curtis, Hunter (Thompson).

sky SPORTS FACT FILE

Morecambe made their first visit to Wembley Stadium in April 1974 when they defeated Dartford 2-1 in the FA Trophy final in front of a 19,000 crowd, with around 9,000 fans travelling down from the North West. The Shrimps' goalscorers were Malcolm Richmond and Jimmy Sutton.

Record League Victory: 6–0 v Crawley T, FL 2, 10 September 2011 – Roche; Reid, Wilson (pen), McCready, Haining (Parrish), Fenton (1), Drummond, McDonald, Price (Jevons), Carlton (3) (Alessandra), Ellison (1).

Record Cup Victory: 6–2 v Nelson (a), Lancashire Trophy, 27 January 2004.

Record Defeat: 2–7 v Port Vale, FL 2, 30 April 2011.

Most League Points (3 for a win): 73, FL 2, 2009–10.

Most League Goals: 73, FL 2, 2009–10.

Highest League Scorer in Season: Phil Jevons, 18, 2009–10.

Most League Goals in Total Aggregate: Kevin Ellison, 36, 2011–14.

Most League Goals in One Match: 3, Jon Newby v Rotherham U, FL 2, 29 March 2008.

Most League Appearances: Stuart Drummond, 263, 2007–14.

Youngest League Player: Aaron McGowan, 16 years 263 days, 20 April 2013.

Record Transfer Fee Received: £225,000 from Stockport C for Carl Baker, July 2008.

Record Transfer Fee Paid: £50,000 to Southport for Carl Baker, July 2007.

Football League Record: 2006–07 Promoted from Conference; 2007– FL 2.

MANAGERS

Jimmy Milne 1947–48
Albert Dainty 1955–56
Ken Horton 1956–61
Joe Dunn 1961–64
Geoff Twentyman 1964–65
Ken Waterhouse 1965–69
Ronnie Clayton 1969–70
Gerry Irving/Ronnie Mitchell 1970
Ken Waterhouse 1970–72
Dave Roberts 1972–75
Alan Spavin 1975–76
Johnny Johnson 1976–77
Tommy Ferber 1977–78
Mick Hogarth 1978–79
Don Curbage 1979–81
Jim Thompson 1981
Les Rigby 1981–84
Sean Gallagher 1984–85
Joe Wojciechowicz 1985–88
Eric Whalley 1988
Billy Wright 1988–89
Lawrie Milligan 1989
Bryan Griffiths 1989–93
Leighton James 1994
Jim Harvey 1994–2006
Sammy McIlroy 2006–11
Jim Bentley May 2011–

LATEST SEQUENCES

Longest Sequence of League Wins: 7, 31.10.2009 – 12.12.2009.

Longest Sequence of League Defeats: 4, 23.2.2008 – 12.3.2008.

Longest Sequence of League Draws: 4, 13.9.2008 – 4.10.2008.

Longest Sequence of Unbeaten League Matches: 12, 31.1.2009 – 21.3.2009.

Longest Sequence Without a League Win: 10, 29.12.2013 – 1.3.2014.

Successive Scoring Runs: 17 from 13.8.2011.

Successive Non-scoring Runs: 3 from 25.3.2014.

TEN YEAR LEAGUE RECORD

		P	W	D	L	F	A	Pts	Pos
2004-05	Conf	42	19	14	9	69	50	71	7
2005-06	Conf	42	22	8	12	68	41	74	5
2006-07	Conf	46	23	12	11	64	46	81	3
2007-08	FL 2	46	16	12	18	59	63	60	11
2008-09	FL 2	46	15	18	13	53	56	63	11
2009-10	FL 2	46	20	13	13	73	64	73	4
2010-11	FL 2	46	13	12	21	54	73	51	20
2011-12	FL 2	46	14	14	18	63	57	56	15
2012-13	FL 2	46	15	13	18	55	61	58	16
2013-14	FL 2	46	13	15	18	52	64	54	18

DID YOU KNOW ?

Morecambe reached the FA Cup third round for the first time in their history in 1961–62. They defeated Clitheroe, Penrith, Burscough, Wigan Athletic, South Shields and Chester before going out to another non-league club, Weymouth. Ian Whitehead scored 8 of the Shrimps' 19 goals.

MORECAMBE – FOOTBALL LEAGUE TWO 2013–14 LEAGUE RECORD

Match No.	Date	Venue	Opponents	Result		H/T Score	Lg Pos.	Goalscorers	Attendance
1	Aug 3	A	Wycombe W	L	0-1	0-1	16		3284
2	10	H	Torquay U	D	1-1	1-0	16	Williams [25]	1555
3	17	A	Portsmouth	L	0-3	0-3	22		14,590
4	24	H	Exeter C	W	2-0	0-0	19	Ellison 2 [47, 81]	1539
5	31	H	Plymouth Arg	W	2-1	1-1	13	Ellison [29], Amond [84]	1800
6	Sept 7	A	Southend U	W	3-1	1-1	7	Fleming 2 [35, 45], Sampson [56]	6080
7	14	A	Newport Co	W	3-2	1-2	6	Naylor 2 (2 ogs) [12, 57], Amond (pen) [71]	3165
8	21	H	Dagenham & R	D	2-2	0-1	8	Amond [53], Hughes [78]	1790
9	28	A	Northampton T	D	0-0	0-0	9		3841
10	Oct 5	H	Chesterfield	W	4-3	0-3	6	Ellison [47], Hughes [62], Sampson [71], Amond [86]	2204
11	12	A	Bury	W	2-0	0-0	4	Williams [62], Diagne [90]	3082
12	19	H	AFC Wimbledon	D	1-1	1-0	6	Ellison [8]	2149
13	22	A	Cheltenham T	L	0-3	0-1	6		2050
14	26	H	Accrington S	L	1-2	0-1	10	Sampson [50]	2175
15	Nov 2	A	Burton Alb	W	1-0	1-0	5	Williams [34]	2702
16	16	H	Rochdale	L	1-2	0-0	8	Amond [89]	2563
17	23	A	Oxford U	L	0-3	0-3	11		4871
18	26	H	York C	D	0-0	0-0	11		1381
19	30	A	Mansfield T	W	2-1	0-1	9	Redshaw [51], Ellison [85]	2753
20	Dec 7	H	Cheltenham T	L	0-1	0-0	10		1290
21	14	H	Bristol R	W	2-1	0-1	9	Amond [57], Redshaw [87]	1514
22	21	A	Scunthorpe U	L	0-2	0-2	9		3510
23	26	H	Fleetwood T	W	1-0	1-0	9	Amond [19]	3008
24	29	H	Hartlepool U	L	1-2	0-1	9	Sampson [87]	2081
25	Jan 1	A	York C	L	0-1	0-1	9		3276
26	4	A	Torquay U	D	1-1	0-1	9	Threlfall [84]	2004
27	11	A	Wycombe W	D	1-1	0-1	9	Ellison [78]	1575
28	25	H	Portsmouth	D	2-2	1-2	9	Hughes [21], Redshaw [76]	2550
29	Feb 8	H	Burton Alb	L	0-1	0-0	13		1478
30	15	A	Rochdale	L	1-2	1-1	15	Redshaw [32]	2344
31	18	A	Exeter C	D	1-1	0-1	13	Amond [54]	2620
32	22	H	Oxford U	D	1-1	0-1	13	Threlfall [90]	1614
33	Mar 1	A	Plymouth Arg	L	0-5	0-2	15		6827
34	8	H	Southend U	W	2-1	1-1	13	Ellison [29], Redshaw [70]	1608
35	11	H	Newport Co	W	4-1	0-1	11	Devitt (pen) [57], Ellison [61], Redshaw 2 [72, 83]	1300
36	15	A	Dagenham & R	D	1-1	0-0	12	Hughes [89]	1718
37	18	A	Accrington S	L	1-5	0-2	12	Amond [84]	1525
38	22	H	Northampton T	D	1-1	0-1	14	Amond [75]	1761
39	25	A	Chesterfield	L	0-1	0-1	15		4891
40	29	A	Bristol R	L	0-1	0-0	17		5647
41	Apr 5	H	Mansfield T	L	0-1	0-1	18		1772
42	12	A	Fleetwood T	D	2-2	1-1	19	Hughes [21], Pond (og) [73]	3114
43	18	H	Scunthorpe U	D	1-1	0-1	18	Sampson [90]	2952
44	21	A	Hartlepool U	L	1-2	1-0	19	Ellison [25]	4864
45	26	A	AFC Wimbledon	W	3-0	2-0	19	Redshaw [43], Devitt [44], Amond (pen) [90]	4017
46	May 3	H	Bury	D	0-0	0-0	18		2944

Final League Position: 18

GOALSCORERS

League (52): Amond 11 (2 pens), Ellison 10, Redshaw 8, Hughes 5, Sampson 5, Williams 3, Devitt 2 (1 pen), Fleming 2, Threlfall 2, Diagne 1, own goals 3.
The Budweiser FA Cup (0).
Capital One Cup (1): Williams 1.
Johnstone's Paint Trophy (0).

Roche B 45	Wright A 30 + 5	McCready C 20 + 2	Fleming A 33 + 2	Hughes M 43 + 1	Diagne T 15 + 12	Williams R 21 + 4	Drummond S 31 + 4	Amond P 33 + 12	Sampson J 31 + 11	Ellison K 38 + 4	Mwasile J 2 + 17	Parrish A 38 + 1	Kenyon A 33 + 6	McGee J 3 + 8	Arestidou A 1	Threlfall R 31 + 3	Marshall M 6 + 9	Doyle C 1 + 2	Redshaw J 14 + 15	McGowan A — + 2	Devitt J 14	Beeley S 11 + 1	Edwards R 8 + 1	Mustoe J 4 + 1	Match No.
1	2	3	4	5	6[2]	7	8	9	10	11[1]	12	13													1
1	2		6	4	5	8	7[1]	9	10	11[2]	3	12	13												2
	5[1]		6	3	4	8	7	11[1]	10[2]		13	2	12		1	9									3
1		3	6	4	5	8[3]	13	14	10[2]	11	12	2	7				9[1]								4
1	12	3[1]	6	4		14	7	10	13	11[2]		2	8				9[2]								5
1	2		8	4	5[1]	14	6	9[2]	10[3]	11	13	3	7			12[4]									6
1	2		4	5	6[1]		7	9	10[2]	11	13	3	8				12								7
1	2		4	5	6		7	9	10[3]	11	13	3[1]	8				12								8
1	2		4	5	6		7	9	10[1]	11	12	3	8												9
1	2	12	4	5[2]	6[1]		7	9[3]	10	11		3	8	14		13									10
1	2		6	3	14	8[3]	7	9	10[1]	11[3]	13	4	12			5									11
1	2		6	3	13	8[2]	7	9[1]	10[1]	11	14	4	12			5									12
1	2		8	3[4]	12	9[1]	6[1]	10	11[2]		13	4	7	14		5									13
1	2		6	4			7	9[1]	10	11		3	8			5	12								14
1	2		6	4			7	8[2]	9[1]	10[1]	11	3	13			5	12		14						15
1	2	3		8[3]	4	5	7[1]	12	10	11	13	6		14			9[2]								16
1	2	14	8	4	5	6	7	9	10[1]	11[2]		3[3]					12		13						17
1			3	4		8[2]	7	9[3]	12	10	14	2	6			5			11[1]			13			18
1			3	13	4	8[2]	7	10[3]	14	11		2	6			5	9[1]		12						19
1	2			9	4			6[2]	10	11[1]		12	3	7		5	13		8						20
1	6			4		8	3	7	9[1]	10		2				5	12		11						21
1	7			4[1]		8[3]	3	6	11[2]	10	12	13	2			5	14		9						22
1			3	8	4	12	7	9[1]	10[2]	14		2	6			5	13		11[3]						23
1			4	6	3	14	7	9	12	10	13	2	8[2]			5[2]			11						24
1	2[2]		6	4		8	7	13	10[2]	11			9[1]			5	3		12		14				25
1	4		7	3	12		13	10	9[2]			2	8	6[1]		5			11						26
1	3		7	4	12	14	8	11[2]	9[3]		13	2	6			5[1]			10						27
1	2		4	6	3[1]		7	10[3]	14	11			8			5		12	13	9[2]					28
1	8		4	12	11[2]		7	14	13	10		3				5[1]			9	6[3]	2				29
1	7[2]		8	3	14	6[3]		12	13	11[1]		4				5			10	9	2				30
1	8		4[1]	7	3		6[2]	12	11	10[3]	14	2				5			13	9[4]					31
1	12		8	4	13		7	9[1]	11	10		3	6[2]	14		5							2[3]		32
1	6		7	4	13		9	10[2]	12			3	8[3]			5	14		11				2[1]		33
1	14	3	6	4			7	9[1]	10[2]	11[3]			8			5			13	9[3]			2[1]		34
1	12		8	4			7	14	10[2]	11		3	6			5			13	9[3]			2[1]		35
1	12	3		4			7[1]	14	10	11		2	6	8[2]		5			13	9[3]					36
1	2	4		3			8	14	12	11[3]		7	6[1]			5	13		10	9[2]					37
1	2		7	3			14	9[3]	10[1]	11[2]			6			5	13		12			8	4		38
1	2			3			6	9	11[2]	13	10		8			5	7[1]		12				4		39
1	2		3[1]	8	12		9	10[2]	11	14			7			5[3]			13			6	4		40
1	8[4]			4			13	10[1]	9			2[2]	7			5[3]			11		6	12	3	14	41
1	7			3				11[2]	10			2	8				12		13		6[1]	5	4	9	42
1	7[3]			3			13	11[1]	14	10		2[2]	8				12				6	5	4	9	43
1	7			3			12[3]	14	10[2]	11		2	6						13		9	5[1]	4	8	44
1	13		8	4	12		14	9				2	7						11[3]		10[2]	6	3	5[1]	45
1			6	4			8[2]	9[1]	13	11		3	7[3]			5			10	12			2	14	46

The Budweiser FA Cup
First Round   Southend U   (h)   0-3

Capital One Cup
First Round   Wolverhampton W   (h)   1-0
Second Round   Newcastle U   (h)   0-2

Johnstone's Paint Trophy
Second Round   Carlisle U   (h)   0-0
(aet; lost 3-4 on penalties)

NEWCASTLE UNITED

FOUNDATION

In October 1882 a club called Stanley, which had been formed in 1881, changed its name to Newcastle East End to avoid confusion with two other local clubs, Stanley Nops and Stanley Albion. Shortly afterwards another club, Rosewood, merged with them. Newcastle West End had been formed in August 1882 and they played on a pitch which was part of the Town Moor. They moved to Brandling Park in 1885 and St James' Park 1886 (home of Newcastle Rangers). West End went out of existence after a bad run and the remaining committee men invited East End to move to St James' Park. They accepted and, at a meeting in Bath Lane Hall in 1892, changed their name to Newcastle United.

St James' Park, Newcastle-upon-Tyne NE1 4ST.

Telephone: (0844) 372 1892

Fax: (0191) 201 8600.

Ticket Office: (0844) 372 1892 (option 1).

Website: www.nufc.co.uk

Email: admin@nufc.co.uk

Ground Capacity: 52,405.

Record Attendance: 68,386 v Chelsea, Division 1, 3 September 1930.

Pitch Measurements: 105m × 68m (114yd × 74yd)

Managing Director: Lee Charnley.

Manager: Alan Pardew.

Assistant Manager: John Carver.

Physio: Derek Wright.

Colours: Black and white striped shirts, black shorts, black socks.

Year Formed: 1881.

Turned Professional: 1889.

Previous Names: 1881, Stanley; 1882, Newcastle East End; 1892, Newcastle United.

Club Nickname: 'The Magpies', 'The Toon'.

Grounds: 1881, South Byker; 1886, Chillingham Road, Heaton; 1892, St James' Park.

First Football League Game: 2 September 1893, Division 2, v Royal Arsenal (a) D 2–2 – Ramsay; Jeffery, Miller; Crielly, Graham, McKane; Bowman, Crate (1), Thompson, Sorley (1), Wallace. Graham not Crate scored according to some reports.

Record League Victory: 13–0 v Newport Co, Division 2, 5 October 1946 – Garbutt; Cowell, Graham; Harvey, Brennan, Wright; Milburn (2), Bentley (1), Wayman (4), Shackleton (6), Pearson.

HONOURS

FA Premier League:
Runners-up 1995–96, 1996–97.

Football League – Division 1:
Champions 1904–05, 1906–07, 1908–09, 1926–27, 1992–93;
Division 2: *Champions* 1964–65;
Runners-up 1897–98, 1947–48;
FL C: *Champions* 2009–10.

FA Cup: *Winners* 1910, 1924, 1932, 1951, 1952, 1955; *Runners-up* 1905, 1906, 1908, 1911, 1974, 1998, 1999.

Football League Cup:
Runners-up 1976.

Texaco Cup: *Winners* 1974, 1975.

European Competitions
Champions League: 1997–98, 2002–03, 2003–04. **European Fairs Cup:** 1968–69 (*winners*), 1969–70, 1970–71.
UEFA Cup: 1977–78, 1994–95, 1996–97, 1999–2000, 2003–04 (*s-f*), 2004–05, 2006–07.
European Cup Winners' Cup: 1998–99.
Europa League: 2012–13.
Anglo-Italian Cup: 1972–73 (*winners*).
Intertoto Cup: 2001 (*runners-up*), 2005, 2006 (*winners*).

sky SPORTS FACT FILE

The list of guest players who turned out for Newcastle United during World War Two includes Tom Finney of Preston North End who played six times in the 1942–43 season. Finney, who was stationed nearby at Catterick at the time, scored a hat-trick for United against Gateshead on 14 November 1942 as the Magpies went on to win 7-4.

Record Cup Victory: 9–0 v Southport (at Hillsborough), FA Cup 4th rd, 1 February 1932 – McInroy; Nelson, Fairhurst; McKenzie, Davidson, Weaver (1); Boyd (1), Jimmy Richardson (3), Cape (2), McMenemy (1), Lang (1).

Record Defeat: 0–9 v Burton Wanderers, Division 2, 15 April 1895.

Most League Points (2 for a win): 57, Division 2, 1964–65.

Most League Points (3 for a win): 102, FL C, 2009–10.

Most League Goals: 98, Division 1, 1951–52.

Highest League Scorer in Season: Hughie Gallacher, 36, Division 1, 1926–27.

Most League Goals in Total Aggregate: Jackie Milburn, 177, 1946–57.

Most League Goals in One Match: 6, Len Shackleton v Newport Co, Division 2, 5 October 1946.

Most Capped Player: Shay Given, 82 (125), Republic of Ireland.

Most League Appearances: Jim Lawrence, 432, 1904–22.

Youngest League Player: Steve Watson, 16 years 223 days v Wolverhampton W, 10 November 1990.

Record Transfer Fee Received: £35,000,000 from Liverpool for Andy Carroll, January 2011.

Record Transfer Fee Paid: £16,000,000 to Real Madrid for Michael Owen, September 2005.

Football League Record: 1893 Elected to Division 2; 1898–1934 Division 1; 1934–48 Division 2; 1948–61 Division 1; 1961–65 Division 2; 1965–78 Division 1; 1978–84 Division 2; 1984–89 Division 1; 1989–92 Division 2; 1992–93 Division 1; 1993–2009 FA Premier League; 2009–10 FL C; 2010– FA Premier League.

LATEST SEQUENCES

Longest Sequence of League Wins: 13, 25.4.1992 – 18.10.1992.

Longest Sequence of League Defeats: 10, 23.8.1977 – 15.10.1977.

Longest Sequence of League Draws: 4, 15.11.2008 – 6.12.2008.

Longest Sequence of Unbeaten League Matches: 17, 13.2.2010 – 2.5.2010.

Longest Sequence Without a League Win: 21, 14.1.1978 – 23.8.1978.

Successive Scoring Runs: 25 from 15.4.1939.

Successive Non-scoring Runs: 6 from 29.10.1988.

MANAGERS

Frank Watt 1895–32
(Secretary-Manager)
Andy Cunningham 1930–35
Tom Mather 1935–39
Stan Seymour 1939–47
(Hon. Manager)
George Martin 1947–50
Stan Seymour 1950–54
(Hon. Manager)
Duggie Livingstone 1954–56
Stan Seymour 1956–58
(Hon. Manager)
Charlie Mitten 1958–61
Norman Smith 1961–62
Joe Harvey 1962–75
Gordon Lee 1975–77
Richard Dinnis 1977
Bill McGarry 1977–80
Arthur Cox 1980–84
Jack Charlton 1984
Willie McFaul 1985–88
Jim Smith 1988–91
Ossie Ardiles 1991–92
Kevin Keegan 1992–97
Kenny Dalglish 1997–98
Ruud Gullit 1998–99
Sir Bobby Robson 1999–2004
Graeme Souness 2004–06
Glenn Roeder 2006–07
Sam Allardyce 2007–08
Kevin Keegan 2008
Joe Kinnear 2008–09
Alan Shearer 2009
Chris Hughton 2009–10
Alan Pardew December 2010–

TEN YEAR LEAGUE RECORD

		P	W	D	L	F	A	Pts	Pos
2004-05	PR Lge	38	10	14	14	47	57	44	14
2005-06	PR Lge	38	17	7	14	47	42	58	7
2006-07	PR Lge	38	11	10	17	38	47	43	13
2007-08	PR Lge	38	11	10	17	45	65	43	12
2008-09	PR Lge	38	7	13	18	40	59	34	18
2009-10	FL C	46	30	12	4	90	35	102	1
2010-11	PR Lge	38	11	13	14	56	57	46	12
2011-12	PR Lge	38	19	8	11	56	51	65	5
2012-13	PR Lge	38	11	8	19	45	68	41	16
2013-14	PR Lge	38	15	4	19	43	59	49	10

DID YOU KNOW ?

Newcastle United have always been a well-supported club and in the first 10 seasons of post-war football they were amongst the top five in the country. In 1947–48 the Magpies set a new Football League record with an average attendance of 56,283, a figure which was not beaten until 1967–68.

NEWCASTLE UNITED – FA PREMIERSHIP 2013–14 LEAGUE RECORD

Match No.	Date	Venue	Opponents	Result		H/T Score	Lg Pos.	Goalscorers	Attendance
1	Aug 19	A	Manchester C	L	0-4	0-2	20		46,842
2	24	H	West Ham U	D	0-0	0-0	17		49,622
3	31	H	Fulham	W	1-0	0-0	11	Ben Arfa [86]	46,402
4	Sept 14	A	Aston Villa	W	2-1	1-0	8	Ben Arfa [18], Gouffran [73]	37,554
5	21	H	Hull C	L	2-3	2-1	11	Remy 2 [10, 44]	51,523
6	30	A	Everton	L	2-3	0-3	16	Cabaye [51], Remy [89]	33,495
7	Oct 5	A	Cardiff C	W	2-1	2-0	11	Remy 2 [30, 38]	27,538
8	19	H	Liverpool	D	2-2	1-1	10	Cabaye [23], Dummett [56]	51,703
9	27	A	Sunderland	L	1-2	0-1	11	Debuchy [57]	46,313
10	Nov 2	H	Chelsea	W	2-0	0-0	9	Gouffran [68], Remy [89]	51,674
11	10	A	Tottenham H	W	1-0	1-0	9	Remy [13]	36,042
12	23	H	Norwich C	W	2-1	2-0	8	Remy [2], Gouffran [38]	51,328
13	30	H	WBA	W	2-1	1-0	5	Gouffran [38], Sissoko [57]	49,298
14	Dec 4	A	Swansea C	L	0-3	0-1	7		20,457
15	7	A	Manchester U	W	1-0	0-0	7	Cabaye [61]	75,233
16	14	H	Southampton	D	1-1	1-0	6	Gouffran [27]	49,164
17	21	A	Crystal Palace	W	3-0	2-0	6	Cabaye [25], Gabbidon (og) [39], Ben Arfa (pen) [86]	24,936
18	26	H	Stoke C	W	5-1	1-1	6	Remy 2 [44, 56], Gouffran [48], Cabaye [66], Cisse (pen) [80]	51,665
19	29	H	Arsenal	L	0-1	0-0	8		52,161
20	Jan 1	A	WBA	L	0-1	0-0	8		26,430
21	12	H	Manchester C	L	0-2	0-1	8		49,423
22	18	A	West Ham U	W	3-1	2-1	8	Cabaye 2 [16, 90], Remy [33]	33,343
23	28	A	Norwich C	D	0-0	0-0	8		26,762
24	Feb 1	H	Sunderland	L	0-3	0-2	8		52,280
25	8	A	Chelsea	L	0-3	0-2	8		41,387
26	12	H	Tottenham H	L	0-4	0-1	9		48,264
27	23	H	Aston Villa	W	1-0	0-0	8	Remy [90]	50,417
28	Mar 1	A	Hull C	W	4-1	2-0	8	Sissoko 2 [10, 55], Remy [42], Anita [90]	24,903
29	15	A	Fulham	L	0-1	0-0	9		25,664
30	22	H	Crystal Palace	W	1-0	0-0	8	Cisse [90]	51,588
31	25	H	Everton	L	0-3	0-1	8		47,622
32	29	A	Southampton	L	0-4	0-1	9		31,360
33	Apr 5	H	Manchester U	L	0-4	0-1	9		52,081
34	12	H	Stoke C	L	0-1	0-1	9		27,400
35	19	H	Swansea C	L	1-2	1-1	9	Ameobi, Shola [23]	51,057
36	28	A	Arsenal	L	0-3	0-2	9		60,023
37	May 3	H	Cardiff C	W	3-0	1-0	9	Ameobi, Shola [18], Remy [87], Taylor, S [90]	50,239
38	11	A	Liverpool	L	1-2	1-0	10	Skrtel (og) [20]	44,724

Final League Position: 10

GOALSCORERS

League (43): Remy 14, Cabaye 7, Gouffran 6, Ben Arfa 3 (1 pen), Sissoko 3, Ameobi, Shola 2, Cisse 2 (1 pen), Anita 1, Debuchy 1, Dummett 1, Taylor, S 1, own goals 2.
The Budweiser FA Cup (1): Cisse 1.
Capital One Cup (4): Cisse 1, Gouffran 1, Ameobi, Sammy 1, Ameobi, Shola 1.

Krul T 36	Debuchy M 28+1	Taylor S 9+1	Coloccini F 27	Yanga-Mbiwa M 17+6	Sissoko M 35	Tiote C 31+2	Gutierrez J 1+1	Ben Arfa H 13+14	Cisse P 15+9	Gouffran Y 31+4	Anita V 28+6	Dummett P 11+7	Ameobi Sam 4+6	Santon D 26+1	Marveaux S 2+7	Ameobi Shola 14+12	Cabaye Y 17+2	Remy L 24+2	Williamson M 32+1	Obertan G —+3	Haidara M 3+8	De Jong L 8+4	Gosling D 4+4	Armstrong A —+4	Elliot R 2	Match No.
1	2	3^4	4	5	6	7	8^3	9^2	10	11^1	12	13	14													1
1	2		4	3	7		6	11^2	13	8		12	5			9^1	10									2
1	2		4	3	7		6	11	12	8^3		5	9^2	10^1	13	14										3
1	2		4	3	6	13		8	11	12	7^3		14	5			9^1	10^2								4
1	2^3		4	3	8	14		9	10^2	12	7			5	13		6^1	11								5
1	2		4	3^2	9	6		10^1	14	8	7^1			5			13	11	12							6
1	2		4		9	6	12	13	11	8				5			7^1	10^2	3							7
1	2		4^4	9^1	7			11^3		8	14	12	13	5			6^2	10	3							8
1	2			6^1	7			10	12	9^3	4		14	5		13	8	11^2	3							9
1	2		4	6	8^1			13		9^2	12			5		11^3	7	10	3	14						10
1	2		4	6	8			13		9^1	12			5		11^3	7	10^2	3	14						11
1		4	2	6	7		14	13	9	9^1	12			5		10^2	8^2	11	3							12
1	2		4	6^2	7			13	9	12				5		10	8	11^1	3							13
1	2		4	14	6	7		9						5^3		10^2	8	11	3^1	13	12					14
1	2^1		4	14	9	7		12		11^2	8			5		13	6^3	10	3							15
1	2		4		6	8		13	12	9^3	7			5^2		10^1		11	3	14						16
1	2		4		8	7		13		10	6			5		12	9^1	11^2	3							17
1	2		4		7			8	14	10^1	6^2			5		12	9^1	11	3	13						18
1	2		4		8^2	7		12		10^3	6^1			5		13	9	11	3	14						19
1	2^1		4^2	13	9	7		12		8^3				5		11^1	6	10	3	14						20
1		4		2^2	8	7		13	12	10^1	6^3			5		9	11	3	14							21
1		4		2	8	6		14		10	7^3	13		5^1		12	9	11^2	3							22
1	2	4			9	7		8^2		6				10^1	5		12	11^4	3	13						23
1	2	4			8	7		9		6^3	13	10^2	5^1	14	11			3			12					24
1	2^1	4		12	9			8^2		6^3	5	10	7	14				3			11	13				25
1	2	4			7			13	11	8	6	12	10^3	5^1	14					9^1	3				★	26
1	2		4		6	7^1		11^2	9	8	5							10	3		12	13				27
1	2			4	6	7			9	8	5							11	3		10^1	12				28
1		4	2	6	7			11^3	9	8^2	5					13	12		3		10^1		14			29
1		4	2	6^3	7			12	11	9^1	8	5				14	13		3		10^2					30
1		4	2^3	6	8			12	11	9^2	7	5				13	14		3		10^1					31
	4		2^1	9^3	7			8^1	11	10^1	6	14	12						3	5	13			1		32
	4				6			12	11	10^1	8		2			13			3	5	9^2	7		1		33
1		2^3	4	12		8		13		10^1	7	5	9			11					6^2	14				34
1	12		4		7			8^1	10	2	5			11	13	3				9^3	6^2	14				35
1	2^3		4	13	8	6		10^2	7	5				12		11			3		9^1	14				36
1	2	14	4		6	7			9^1	8^3	5^2			11		10	3		12	13						37
1	2	3^1	5		7	9^2			10^3	8	14^4	13		11^1					4		6	12				38

The Budweiser FA Cup
Third Round   Cardiff C   (h)   1-2

Capital One Cup
Second Round   Morecambe   (a)   2-0
Third Round   Leeds U   (h)   2-0
Fourth Round   Manchester C   (h)   0-2
(aet)

NEWPORT COUNTY

FOUNDATION

In 1912 Newport County were formed following a meeting at The Tredegar Arms Hotel. A professional football club had existed in the town called Newport FC, but they ceased to exist in 1907. The first season as Newport County was in the second division of the Southern League. They started life playing at Somerton Park where they remained through their League years. They were elected to the Football League for the beginning of the 1920–21 season as founder members of Division 3. At the end of the 1987–88 season, they were relegated from the Football League and replaced by Lincoln City. On February 27 1989, Newport County went out of business and from the ashes Newport AFC was born. Starting down the pyramid in the Hellenic League, they eventally gained promotion to the Conference in 2011 and were promoted to the Football League after a play-off with Wrexham in 2013.

Rodney Parade, Newport, South Wales NP19 0UU.

Telephone: (01633) 670 690.

Ticket Office: (01633) 674 990.

Website: www.newport-county.co.uk

Email: office@newport-county.co.uk

Ground Capacity: 7,850.

Record Attendance: 24,268 v Cardiff C, Division 3 (S), 16 October 1937 (Somerton Park); 4,660 v Swansea C, FA Cup 1st rd, 11 November 2006 (Newport Stadium); 6,615 v Grimsby T, Conference National Play-off Semi-final, 28 April 2013 (Rodney Parade).

Pitch Measurements: 100m × 64m (109.5yd × 70yd)

Chairman: Les Scadding.

Chief Executive: Dave Boddy.

Manager: Justin Edinburgh.

Assistant Manager: Jimmy Dack.

Physio: Adam Roche.

Colours: Amber shirts with black trim, amber shorts with black trim, amber socks with black hoops.

Year Formed: 1912.

Turned Professional: 1912.

Club Nicknames: 'The Exiles', 'The Ironsides', 'The Port', 'The County'.

Grounds: 1912–89, 1990–92, Somerton Park, 1992–94, Meadow Park Stadium; 1994, Newport Stadium, 2012, Rodney Parade.

First Football League Game: 28 August 1920, Division 3, v Reading (h) L 0–1.

HONOURS

Football League – Division 3 (S): *Champions* 1938–39.

FA Cup: Best season: 5th rd, 1949.

Football League Cup: Never past 3rd rd.

Welsh Cup: *Winners* 1980; *Runners-up* 1963, 1987.

FA Trophy: *Runners-up* 2012.

European Competitions
European Cup Winners' Cup: 1980–81 (*quarter-finals*).

sky SPORTS FACT FILE

In July 2013 Newport County drew 2-2 with Carl Zeiss Jena as part of the German club's 110th anniversary celebrations. Newport were invited in recognition of the fact that the former Newport County club had featured in a memorable European Cup Winners' Cup quarter-final tie with Carl Zeiss Jena back in 1981 when the teams had also drawn 2-2 in Germany.

Record League Victory: 10-0 v Merthyr T, Division 3(S), 10 April 1930 – Martin (5), Gittins (2), Thomas (1), Bagley (1), Lawson (1).

Record Cup Victory: 7-0 v Working, FA Cup 1st rd, 24 November 1928 – Young (3), Pugh (2) Gittins (1), Reid (1).

Record Defeat: 0–13 v Newcastle U, Division 2, 5 October 1946.

Most League Points (2 for a win): 61, Division 4, 1979–80.

Most League Points (3 for a win): 78, Division 3, 1982–83.

Most League Goals: 85, Division 4, 1964–65.

Highest League Scorer in Season: Tudor Martin, 34, Division 3 (S), 1929–30.

Most League Goals in Total Aggregate: Reg Parker, 99, 1948–54.

Most League Goals in One Match: 5, Tudor Martin v Merthyr T, Dvision 3 (S), 10 April 1930.

Most Capped Player: Nigel Vaughan, 3 (10), Wales.

Most League Appearances: Len Weare, 526, 1955–70.

Youngest League Player: Jamie Stephens, 19 years 344 days v Accrington S, 3 August 2013.

Record Transfer Fee Received: £500,000 from Peterborough U for Conor Washington, January 2014.

Record Transfer Fee Paid: £80,000 to Swansea C for Alan Waddle, January 1981.

Football League Record: 1920 Original member of Division 3; 1921–31 Divsion 3 (S) – dropped out of Football League; 1932 Re-elected to Division 3 (S); 1932–39 Division 3 (S); 1946–47 Division 2; 1947–58 Division 3 (S); 1958–62 Division 3; 1962–80 Division 4; 1980–87 Division 3; 1987–88 Division 4 (relegated from Football League); 2011 Promoted to Conference; 2011–13 Conference Premier; 2013– FL 2.

LATEST SEQUENCES

Longest Sequence of League Wins: 3, 1.12.2013 – 26.12.2013.

Longest Sequence of League Defeats: 2, 8.3.2014 – 11.3.2014.

Longest Sequence of League Draws: 3, 24.8.2013 – 7.9.2013.

Longest Sequence of Unbeaten League Matches: 6, 15.11.2013 – 26.12.2013.

Longest Sequence Without a League Win: 8, 22.2.2014 – 19.3.2013.

Successive Scoring Runs: 2 from 31.1.2014.

Successive Non-scoring Runs: 9 from 3.8.2013.

MANAGERS

Davy McDougle 1912–13
  (Player-Manager)
Sam Hollis 1913–17
Harry Parkes 1919–22
Jimmy Hindmarsh 1922–35
Louis Page 1935–36
Tom Bromilow 1936–37
Billy McCandless 1937–45
Tom Bromilow 1945–50
Fred Stansfield 1950–53
Billy Lucas 1953–61
Bobby Evans 1961–62
Billy Lucas 1962–67
Leslie Graham 1967–69
Bobby Ferguson 1969–70
  (Player-Manager)
Billy Lucas 1970–74
Brian Harris 1974–75
Dave Elliott 1975–76
  (Player-Manager)
Jimmy Scoular 1976–77
Colin Addison 1977–78
Len Ashurst 1978–82
Colin Addison 1982–85
Bobby Smith 1985–86
John Relish 1986
Jimmy Mullen 1986–87
John Lewis 1987
Brian Eastick 1987–88
David Williams 1988
Eddie May 1988
John Mahoney 1988–89
John Relish 1989–93
Graham Rogers 1993–96
Chris Price 1997
Tim Harris 1997–2002
Peter Nicholas 2002–04
John Cornforth 2004–05
Peter Beadle 2005–08
Dean Holdsworth 2008–11
Anthony Hudson 2011
Justin Edinburgh October 2011–

TEN YEAR LEAGUE RECORD

		P	W	D	L	F	A	Pts	Pos
2004-05	Conf S	42	13	11	18	56	61	50	18
2005-06	Conf S	42	12	8	22	50	67	44	18
2006-07	Conf S	42	21	7	14	83	57	70	6
2007-08	Conf S	42	18	12	12	64	49	66	9
2008-09	Conf S	42	16	11	15	50	51	59	10
2009-10	Conf S	42	32	7	3	93	26	103	1
2010-11	Conf P	46	18	15	13	78	60	69	9
2011-12	Conf P	46	11	14	21	53	65	47	19
2012–13	Conf P	46	25	10	11	85	60	85	3
2013-14	FL 2	46	14	16	16	56	59	58	14

DID YOU KNOW ?

Newport County reached the now-defunct FA Wales Premier Cup final on three occasions. They lost out to Wrexham (2003) and The New Saints (2007) but won the last-ever final by defeating Llanelli 1-0 in March 2008 with a goal from Craig Hughes.

NEWPORT COUNTY – FOOTBALL LEAGUE TWO 2013–14 LEAGUE RECORD

Match No.	Date	Venue	Opponents	Result	H/T Score	Lg Pos.	Goalscorers	Attendance
1	Aug 3	H	Accrington S	W 4-1	2-0	1	Worley [24], Zebroski 2 [43, 66], Jolley [55]	4631
2	10	A	Northampton T	L 1-3	0-2	10	Washington [89]	4319
3	17	H	Bristol R	W 1-0	1-0	7	Sandell (pen) [42]	5387
4	24	A	Dagenham & R	D 1-1	1-0	6	Zebroski [25]	1564
5	31	A	Scunthorpe U	D 1-1	0-1	8	Hughes [62]	3157
6	Sept 7	H	Mansfield T	D 1-1	1-0	9	Zebroski [30]	3709
7	14	H	Morecambe	L 2-3	2-1	12	Jones [3], Willmott [24]	3165
8	21	A	Exeter C	W 2-0	1-0	11	Washington [23], Worley [70]	4614
9	28	H	Torquay U	W 2-1	2-0	8	Yakubu [28], Crow [36]	3557
10	Oct 5	A	Bury	D 0-0	0-0	9		3093
11	12	A	Rochdale	L 0-3	0-2	12		2530
12	19	H	York C	W 3-0	2-0	10	Zebroski [23], Minshull [45], Crow [89]	3475
13	22	A	Plymouth Arg	D 0-0	0-0	9		5689
14	26	H	Southend U	W 3-1	2-1	7	Washington [23], Hughes [45], Yakubu [53]	3652
15	Nov 2	A	Fleetwood T	L 1-4	0-1	10	Zebroski (pen) [71]	2354
16	15	H	Hartlepool U	W 2-0	1-0	4	Worley [7], Washington [64]	3094
17	23	A	Cheltenham T	D 0-0	0-0	6		3501
18	26	A	Oxford U	D 0-0	0-0	8		5042
19	Dec 1	H	Chesterfield	W 3-2	1-0	8	Crow [6], Chapman (pen) [75], Sandell [87]	3378
20	14	A	Portsmouth	W 2-0	0-0	4	Flynn 2 [65, 68]	15,295
21	26	A	Wycombe W	W 1-0	1-0	5	Flynn [31]	3513
22	29	A	Burton Alb	L 0-1	0-0	7		2692
23	Jan 4	H	Northampton T	L 1-2	1-1	8	Worley [45]	3864
24	11	A	Accrington S	D 3-3	1-2	8	Willmott [11], Burge [71], Minshull [90]	1318
25	25	A	Bristol R	L 1-3	0-1	8	Howe [57]	7288
26	31	A	Southend U	D 0-0	0-0	8		5993
27	Feb 15	A	Hartlepool U	L 0-3	0-1	10		3470
28	18	H	Oxford U	W 3-2	1-1	8	Howe [45], Burge [71], Zebroski [83]	3757
29	22	H	Cheltenham T	L 0-1	0-1	8		3130
30	25	H	AFC Wimbledon	L 1-2	0-0	9	Worner (og) [65]	2666
31	Mar 1	H	Scunthorpe U	D 2-2	1-0	11	Minshull [25], Zebroski [90]	2782
32	4	H	Fleetwood T	D 0-0	0-0	10		3728
33	8	A	Mansfield T	L 1-2	0-1	11	Howe [50]	2756
34	11	A	Morecambe	L 1-4	1-0	13	Naylor [13]	1300
35	16	H	Exeter C	D 1-1	0-0	14	Minshull [52]	3159
36	19	H	Dagenham & R	L 1-2	1-2	14	Willmott [45]	2360
37	22	A	Torquay U	W 1-0	1-0	12	Zebroski [8]	2874
38	25	H	Bury	D 0-0	0-0	12		2160
39	29	H	Portsmouth	L 1-2	0-2	15	Yakubu [74]	4261
40	Apr 5	A	Chesterfield	D 1-1	0-0	14	Porter [83]	5659
41	8	H	Plymouth Arg	L 1-2	1-2	14	Zebroski [27]	3381
42	12	A	Wycombe W	W 2-0	0-0	13	Jolley [68], Zebroski [73]	2838
43	18	A	AFC Wimbledon	D 2-2	1-0	13	Zebroski [15], Flynn (pen) [47]	4398
44	21	H	Burton Alb	D 1-1	1-1	15	Sandell [5]	2630
45	26	A	York C	L 0-1	0-0	15		4531
46	May 3	H	Rochdale	W 2-1	1-1	14	O'Connor [41], Feely [88]	4662

Final League Position: 14

GOALSCORERS

League (56): Zebroski 12 (1 pen), Flynn 4 (1 pen), Minshull 4, Washington 4, Worley 4, Crow 3, Howe 3, Sandell 3 (1 pen), Willmott 3, Yakubu 3, Burge 2, Hughes 2, Jolley 2, Chapman 1 (1 pen), Feely 1, Jones 1, Naylor 1, O'Connor 1, Porter 1, own goal 1.
The Budweiser FA Cup (4): Willmott 3, Naylor 1.
Capital One Cup (3): Crow 2, Washington 1.
Johnstone's Paint Trophy (6): Washington 2, Chapman 1 (1 pen), Oshilaja 1, Zebroski 1, own goal 1.

Stephens J 2	Pipe D 22 + 3	Sandell A 21 + 2	Worley H 26	Anthony B 7	Yakubu I 22 + 3	Porter M 15 + 7	Chapman A 35 + 4	Jolley C 20 + 12	Zebroski C 32 + 3	Minshull L 34 + 6	Willmott R 40 + 6	Crow D 13 + 14	Washington C 16 + 8	Hughes A 23 + 3	Pidgeley L 25	Naylor T 24 + 9	Flynn M 18 + 14	Jackson R 26 + 3	Burge R 12 + 5	Jones B 6 + 1	James T 5 + 1	Oshilaja A 8	Barker G — + 2	Howe R 12 + 3	Jeffers S 4 + 10	Parish E 7	McLoughlin I 12	Amadi-Holloway A — + 4	Blake D 8	Feely K 10	O'Connor A 1 + 3	Match No.
1	2	3	4	5	6	7¹	8	9²	10³	11	12	13	14																			1
1	6	9	2		3	8¹	5³	11	10²	7	13	12	14	4																		2
	2	8	9			5	11¹	10²	6	7³	13	12	3	1	4	14																3
	2	6	3			9	11¹	10³	7	8²	14	12	5	1	4	13																4
	2	5				9³	10¹	11²	8	7	13	12	6	1	4	14	3															5
	2	9				6³	11¹	10	7¹	8²		12	3	1	5	13	4	14														6
	5	2	13			6	14	11¹		8	12	10	3	1	4²	7				9³												7
	2	3	4			7		11³		9²	14	10	5	1	13	5				6¹	12											8
	2	4	3			8		12		9³	10¹	11	5	1	13	7²	14			6												9
	5	4	3			6		12	8	14	11³	10	7	1	13	9²				2¹												10
	2	4	3			7		9	6³	11	10	12	5¹	1	14	8¹	13															11
		4¹				6²		10³	8	12	14	11		1	7	13	5			9	2											12
			3			7¹		11²	8	5	13	10		1	6	12	9			2	4											13
13			4			6		10²	7	8	14	11	12³	1	5		9			2	3¹											14
12			3			7	14	10	8¹	9³	13	11³		1	6²		5			2		4										15
		5		3		8	9¹			7	10	11		1	4	12	2²	13			6											16
		2		3		7¹	11²		12	8	9	10		1	6		5			4	13											17
			3	2		6	11		8²	9	10¹	7		1	13		5			4	12											18
	13	3				8	10²		12	6	9¹	11	5	1	7³	14	2			4												19
2	9	4				8	11²	14	7	12	10¹		1	13	6³	5				3												20
2	9	4				7	11³		8²	12	10¹		1	13	6	5	14			3												21
2	5	4¹	12			8	11		9³		10		1	13	7²	6	14			3												22
2	8	4	3³			9	10²		12	6	11	13		1	5	7¹		14														23
5	4		3			12		6	11		9¹			1	2		8	7			10											24
6	5¹	3				13		9	8²	11		12	1	4		2	7			10												25
5	2	3				12	6¹	13		8	9			1	4	14		7³			10	11²										26
2³	6	10				12	3	13	14	4¹	5				9		8				11	7²	1									27
4	10		3	2	12	5²		7¹	6	8							9				11	13	1									28
	9		4	3	12	7²		10	5¹	8	13		2				6				11³	14	1									29
	6	3	4	2	7³	8	11²	10¹	14	5							9				13	12	1									30
	5		3	4	7³	13	12	10	8	9					2	6²					11¹	14	1									31
	4			2²	6¹		11	7	9		13			3	12	5	8				10		1									32
		3			6¹	14	11³	8	7		4			2	12	5	9				10²	13	1									33
12		3			6	9³	11	7	8²		4		2⁴	14	5						10¹					1	13					34
2		5		4¹	6		13	11	7	9	10²		3		14		8³						1	12								35
2⁴			4¹		9³	14	13	11	8	6	10²		5		3	12	7						1									36
			13	8²	11	7	9³	10¹		5	2	6			14							1	12	3	4							37
			13	6	10	7²	8	11¹		5	3	9										1	12	4	2							38
	14		12		6⁴	10	7	8	11²		5	2³	9								13		1		4⁴	3¹						39
			3	8		12	10²	11³	9		5	14	4	7							13	6¹	1		2							40
			6		12	11	7²	8		2		9³	5	14							13	10¹	1		3	4						41
		2			7		9	11	6	12		4	8	5							10¹		1	3	4							42
	5				9	13	8³	6	10	14		7²	2								11¹		1	4	3	12						43
	4				7	13	6²	10	9¹	5	1		8¹	2							14			3	11	12						44
	4¹				7	8³	9²	10	6	11		5		14	2						13		1		3	12						45
					8	6	12	11³	13	7		5		9²	3⁴						14		1		4	2	10¹					46

The Budweiser FA Cup

First Round	Braintree T	(a)	1-1
Replay	Braintree T	(h)	1-0
Second Round	Kidderminster H	(a)	2-4

Capital One Cup

First Round	Brighton & HA	(a)	3-1
(aet)			
Second Round	WBA	(a)	0-3

Johnstone's Paint Trophy

Second Round	Crawley T	(a)	3-2
Southern Quarter-Finals	Portsmouth	(h)	3-0
Southern Semi-Finals	Peterborough U	(h)	0-3

NORTHAMPTON TOWN

FOUNDATION

Formed in 1897 by schoolteachers connected with the Northampton & District Elementary Schools' Association, they survived a financial crisis at the end of their first year when they were £675 in the red and became members of the Midland League – a fast move indeed for a new club. They achieved Southern League membership in 1901.

Sixfields Stadium, Upton Way, Northampton NN5 5QA.

Telephone: (01604) 683 700.

Fax: (01604) 751 613.

Ticket Office: (01604) 683 777.

Website: www.ntfc.co.uk

Email: gareth.willsher@ntfc.tv

Ground Capacity: 7,500.

Record Attendance: 24,523 v Fulham, Division 1, 23 April 1966 (at County Ground); 7,557 v Manchester C, Division 2, 26 September 1998 (at Sixfields Stadium).

Pitch Measurements: 106m × 66m (116yd × 72yd)

Chairman: David Cardoza.

Manager: Chris Wilder.

Assistant Manager: Alan Knill.

Physio: Stuart Barker.

Colours: Red shirts with white trim, white shorts, white socks.

Year Formed: 1897.

Turned Professional: 1901.

Grounds: 1897, County Ground; 1994, Sixfields Stadium.

Club Nickname: 'The Cobblers'.

First Football League Game: 28 August 1920, Division 3, v Grimsby T (a) L 0–2 – Thorpe; Sproston, Hewison; Jobey, Tomkins, Pease; Whitworth, Lockett, Thomas, Freeman, MacKechnie.

Record League Victory: 10–0 v Walsall, Division 3 (S), 5 November 1927 – Hammond; Watson, Jeffs; Allen, Brett, Odell; Daley, Smith (3), Loasby (3), Hoten (1), Wells (3).

Record Cup Victory: 10–0 v Sutton T, FA Cup prel rd, 7 December 1907 – Cooch; Drennan, Lloyd Davies, Tirrell (1), McCartney, Hickleton, Badenock (3), Platt (3), Lowe (1), Chapman (2), McDiarmid.

Record Defeat: 0–11 v Southampton, Southern League, 28 December 1901.

HONOURS

Football League – Division 1: 21st, 1965–66;
Division 2: *Runners-up* 1964–65;
Division 3: *Champions* 1962–63;
Division 3 (S): *Runners-up* 1927–28, 1949–50;
Division 4: *Champions* 1986–87;
Runners-up 1975–76;
FL 2: *Runners-up* 2005–06.

FA Cup: Best season: 5th rd, 1934, 1950, 1970.

Football League Cup: Best season: 5th rd, 1965, 1967.

sky SPORTS FACT FILE

Walter Tull, who made over 100 first-team appearances for Northampton Town, was also a hero of World War One. He served in the Footballers' Battalion and became the first black combat soldier to gain an officer's commission. Appointed to the rank of second lieutenant, he was killed in action in March 1918.

Most League Points (2 for a win): 68, Division 4, 1975–76.

Most League Points (3 for a win): 99, Division 4, 1986–87.

Most League Goals: 109, Division 3, 1962–63 and Division 3 (S), 1952–53.

Highest League Scorer in Season: Cliff Holton, 36, Division 3, 1961–62.

Most League Goals in Total Aggregate: Jack English, 135, 1947–60.

Most League Goals in One Match: 5, Ralph Hoten v Crystal Palace, Division 3 (S), 27 October 1928.

Most Capped Player: Edwin Lloyd Davies, 12 (16), Wales.

Most League Appearances: Tommy Fowler, 521, 1946–61.

Youngest League Player: Adrian Mann, 16 years 297 days v Bury, 5 May 1984.

Record Transfer Fee Received: £470,000 from Blackburn R for Mark Bunn, September 2008.

Record Transfer Fee Paid: £165,000 to Oldham Ath for Josh Low, July 2003.

Football League Record: 1920 Original Member of Division 3; 1921 Division 3 (S); 1958–61 Division 4; 1961–63 Division 3; 1963–65 Division 2; 1965–66 Division 1; 1966–67 Division 2; 1967–69 Division 4; 1969–76 Division 4; 1976–77 Division 3; 1977–87 Division 4; 1987–90 Division 3; 1990–92 Division 4; 1992–97 Division 3; 1997–99 Division 2; 1999–2000 Division 3; 2000–03 Division 2; 2003–04 Division 3; 2004–06 FL 2; 2006–09 FL 1; 2009– FL 2.

LATEST SEQUENCES

Longest Sequence of League Wins: 8, 27.8.1960 – 19.9.1960.

Longest Sequence of League Defeats: 8, 26.10.1935 – 21.12.1935.

Longest Sequence of League Draws: 6, 5.2.2011 – 26.2.2011.

Longest Sequence of Unbeaten League Matches: 21, 27.9.1986 – 6.2.1987.

Longest Sequence Without a League Win: 18, 5.2.2011 – 25.4.2011.

Successive Scoring Runs: 27 from 23.8.1986.

Successive Non-scoring Runs: 7 from 7.4.1939.

MANAGERS

Arthur Jones 1897–1907
(Secretary-Manager)
Herbert Chapman 1907–12
Walter Bull 1912–13
Fred Lessons 1913–19
Bob Hewison 1920–25
Jack Tresadern 1925–30
Jack English 1931–35
Syd Puddefoot 1935–37
Warney Cresswell 1937–39
Tom Smith 1939–49
Bob Dennison 1949–54
Dave Smith 1954–59
David Bowen 1959–67
Tony Marchi 1967–68
Ron Flowers 1968–69
Dave Bowen 1969–72
(continued as General Manager and Secretary 1972–85 when joined the board)
Billy Baxter 1972–73
Bill Dodgin Jnr 1973–76
Pat Crerand 1976–77
By committee 1977
Bill Dodgin Jnr 1977
John Petts 1977–78
Mike Keen 1978–79
Clive Walker 1979–80
Bill Dodgin Jnr 1980–82
Clive Walker 1982–84
Tony Barton 1984–85
Graham Carr 1985–90
Theo Foley 1990–92
Phil Chard 1992–93
John Barnwell 1993–94
Ian Atkins 1995–99
Kevin Wilson 1999–2001
Kevan Broadhurst 2001–03
Terry Fenwick 2003
Martin Wilkinson 2003
Colin Calderwood 2003–06
John Gorman 2006
Stuart Gray 2007–09
Ian Sampson 2009–11
Gary Johnson 2011
Aidy Boothroyd 2011–13
Chris Wilder January 2014–

TEN YEAR LEAGUE RECORD

		P	W	D	L	F	A	Pts	Pos
2004-05	FL 2	46	20	12	14	62	51	72	7
2005-06	FL 2	46	22	17	7	63	37	83	2
2006-07	FL 1	46	15	14	17	48	51	59	14
2007-08	FL 1	46	17	15	14	60	55	66	9
2008-09	FL 1	46	12	13	21	61	65	49	21
2009-10	FL 2	46	18	13	15	62	53	67	11
2010-11	FL 2	46	11	19	16	63	71	52	16
2011-12	FL 2	46	12	12	22	56	79	48	20
2012-13	FL 2	46	21	10	15	64	55	73	6
2013-14	FL 2	46	13	14	19	42	57	53	21

DID YOU KNOW ?

Northampton Town established a club record 14 consecutive home victories between April and December 1927. The run included their best-ever victory, 10-0 over Walsall when three players registered hat-tricks, an 8-0 FA Cup win against Leyton and an amazing 6-5 defeat of Luton Town.

NORTHAMPTON TOWN – FOOTBALL LEAGUE TWO 2013–14 LEAGUE RECORD

Match No.	Date	Venue	Opponents	Result		H/T Score	Lg Pos.	Goalscorers	Attendance
1	Aug 3	A	York C	L	0-1	0-0	16		4388
2	10	H	Newport Co	W	3-1	2-0	11	Blyth [25], O'Donovan [27], Deegan [84]	4319
3	17	A	Southend U	L	0-2	0-1	16		5510
4	24	H	Torquay U	L	1-2	1-0	22	Blyth [30]	4088
5	31	A	Bristol R	L	0-1	0-1	22		5695
6	Sept 7	H	Scunthorpe U	D	1-1	0-0	21	Platt [78]	4132
7	14	H	Exeter C	L	1-2	1-1	22	Blyth [7]	4036
8	21	A	Mansfield T	L	0-3	0-2	23		3469
9	28	H	Morecambe	D	0-0	0-0	23		3841
10	Oct 5	A	AFC Wimbledon	W	2-0	1-0	23	Collins [20], Dallas [73]	4222
11	12	A	Oxford U	L	0-2	0-2	23		6177
12	19	H	Dagenham & R	D	2-2	1-2	23	Norris [28], Morris [62]	4046
13	22	A	Rochdale	L	2-3	2-1	23	Norris [2], Dallas [39]	2362
14	26	H	Cheltenham T	D	1-1	1-1	23	Norris [44]	4033
15	Nov 2	A	Plymouth Arg	L	0-1	0-0	24		6547
16	16	H	Fleetwood T	W	1-0	0-0	24	Norris [90]	4076
17	23	A	Hartlepool U	L	0-2	0-1	24		3617
18	26	A	Chesterfield	D	0-0	0-0	24		5321
19	30	H	Accrington S	W	1-0	1-0	23	Dallas [29]	4092
20	Dec 14	A	Bury	D	1-1	1-1	23	Howell (og) [29]	2835
21	21	H	Wycombe W	L	1-4	0-2	24	McLeod [51]	4353
22	26	A	Burton Alb	L	0-1	0-0	24		3312
23	29	A	Portsmouth	D	0-0	0-0	24		15,426
24	Jan 4	A	Newport Co	W	2-1	1-1	24	Hope [29], Carter [47]	3864
25	11	H	York C	L	0-2	0-0	24		4448
26	25	H	Chesterfield	L	1-3	1-1	24	Carter (pen) [15]	5082
27	Feb 1	A	Cheltenham T	D	1-1	0-1	24	Blair [76]	2707
28	8	H	Plymouth Arg	L	0-2	0-2	24		4845
29	11	A	Torquay U	W	2-1	2-1	24	Sinclair 2 [10, 16]	2051
30	15	A	Fleetwood T	L	0-2	0-1	24		2521
31	22	H	Hartlepool U	W	2-0	1-0	24	Kouo-Doumbe [45], Dickenson [47]	4083
32	25	H	Southend U	W	2-1	1-1	23	Kouo-Doumbe [7], Hackett [57]	3846
33	Mar 1	H	Bristol R	D	0-0	0-0	23		5058
34	8	A	Scunthorpe U	D	1-1	0-0	23	Diamond [65]	3968
35	11	A	Exeter C	W	1-0	0-0	23	Morris [56]	2785
36	15	H	Mansfield T	D	1-1	0-1	23	Carter (pen) [64]	5129
37	18	H	Rochdale	L	0-3	0-1	23		3695
38	22	A	Morecambe	D	1-1	1-0	23	Wright (og) [45]	1761
39	25	H	AFC Wimbledon	D	2-2	1-1	23	Carter 2 (1 pen) [29 (p), 79]	3812
40	29	H	Bury	L	0-3	0-2	23		4631
41	Apr 5	A	Accrington S	W	1-0	1-0	23	Hackett [4]	1616
42	12	H	Burton Alb	W	1-0	0-0	23	Marquis [43]	4604
43	18	A	Wycombe W	D	1-1	1-1	23	Ingram (og) [12]	7004
44	21	H	Portsmouth	L	0-1	0-1	23		6829
45	26	A	Dagenham & R	W	3-0	3-0	22	Toney 2 [8, 40], Morris [12]	2668
46	May 3	H	Oxford U	W	3-1	2-1	21	Marquis [29], Toney [33], Kouo-Doumbe [51]	7529

Final League Position: 21

GOALSCORERS

League (42): Carter 5 (3 pens), Norris 4, Blyth 3, Dallas 3, Kouo-Doumbe 3, Morris 3, Toney 3, Hackett 2, Marquis 2, Sinclair 2, Blair 1, Collins 1, Deegan 1, Diamond 1, Dickenson 1, Hope 1, McLeod 1, O'Donovan 1, Platt 1, own goals 3.
The Budweiser FA Cup (2): Emerton 1, Norris 1.
Capital One Cup (1): O'Donovan 1.
Johnstone's Paint Trophy (0).

Duke M 46	Amankwaah K 21	Widdowson J 24 + 1	Tozer B 21 + 8	Collins L 21 + 1	Heath M 5	Emerton D 11 + 5	Carter D 37	O'Donovan R 10 + 5	Morris I 23 + 10	Deegan G 22 + 5	Hooper J — + 3	Blyth J 8 + 3	Toney I 13 + 10	Demontagnac I 2 + 8	Hackett C 35 + 2	Platt C 7 + 4	Harriott M 2 + 3	Kouo-Doumbe M 30 + 2	Reid P 16	Dallas S 10 + 2	Norris L 8 + 2	Ferdinand K 4	Ravenhill R 25	McLeod 14	Moyo D — + 6	German A 5 + 2	Lopez C — + 3	Hope H 3	McGinty S 2	Horwood E 7 + 1	Blair M 3	Hurst J 1	Langmead K — + 3	Connell A 11 + 5	Sinclair E 15 + 5	McSweeney L 16 + 2	Dickenson B 8 + 5	Robertson G 14 + 1	Marquis J 12 + 2	Diamond Z 14	Match No.
1	2	3	4	5	6	7¹	8*	9	10	11	12																														1
1	4	5	2	3		6²	7	11	9	8			10¹	12	13																										2
1	2	5¹	3	4		9²	7	10		8		11³	14	13	6*	12																									3
1	2	5	3	4		6	7	10	9¹	8		11²			13	12																									4
1	2²	3	4	5		8	10*	7				12	13	6¹	9	11																									5
1	2²	5	13	4	3	9¹	8	11		7		12			6	10																									6
1	2²	5	13	4	3	14	8¹	9³		7		11			6	10	12																								7
1	2	12		5	3¹		7	13	9			10			6	11	8²	4																							8
1	2		12	5		13	7²	11	9	8					10¹	6		4	3																						9
1	2	6		3		8	11²	10	9						13		7¹	5	4	12																					10
1	2		7	5¹		14	8	11²	10³	9	13				12			3	4	6																					11
1	2			5		6		8	7¹						13	12	9	3	4	11	10²																				12
1	2¹	5		12		9		6	8						13	7		4	3	10	11²																				13
1		5	12	2			7		9	8¹					13	6		4	3	10	11²																				14
1		5		2			8		6							7		4	3	10	11	9																			15
1		5	2			9²		14				11		13	6¹			4	3	12	10³	7	8																		16
1		5	2			9		12				10					13	4	3	6¹	11¹	7	8																		17
1	2	5	14			6³						13		11¹	9	12		4	3	10²		7	8																		18
1	2	5				9						14	7³	12	10¹			4	3	6	13		8	11²																	19
1	2	5						12	7						6	11		4	3	9			8	10ᵇ																	20
1	2	5						13	8¹						12	6	10²	4	3³	9	14		7	11																	21
1	2	5	7	3			14	8	12						6			9		4³			11²		10¹	13															22
1	2	5	6	4		7²			8						13	10		9		3			11¹				12														23
1	2		3	4		6¹	8		9				14		7		13	5											12	10³	11²										24
1	2ᵇ		3	4		12	7		8						9¹			14											13	11	10³	5	6								25
1		5	7	3				9²	13	12		8³	14					9												10	11	4	6	2¹							26
1		5	2²	3			8		9									4					7						11				6	10¹	12	13					27
1		5		3¹			8								6			4					7						12					11	10	2	9				28
1		5	14				7								9			3					8						13					10²	6¹	2	11³	4	12		29
1		5	4				8			7					6			4					9²						10¹					13	12	2			11		30
1		5¹					8						14		6			4					7											12	10²	2	9	13	11³	3	31
1							8		13						6			4					7											10	11¹	2	9²	5	12	3	32
1							7		9	6					13			4					8*											11²	12	2		5	10¹	3	33
1							7		12	8					6			3												14				13	10³	2	9¹	5	11²	4	34
1							8		12						6²			4					7						13					11	10	2	9¹	5		3	35
1							8		9				14		6			4					7						13					11²	10	2	12	5³		3¹	36
1	2						7		9	12					6¹			4					8											11	10		5			3	37
1							8		14						6			4					7						12		13			10¹	11	2	9²	5³		3	38
1	14						8		9	12					6¹			4					7²						5					10	2³	13			11	3	39
1	13						7		9						6²			3					8						5					12	11¹	2			10	4	40
1	3								7						5¹			6					14						8		12			9²	10¹	2	13	4	11		41
1	3								8						12			7											6		14			11¹	9²	2	13	5	10	4³	42
1	2						7		12					13	9			3					6³						8		14			10²	5¹		4	11			43
1	3						9		8					11²	2³			4					7						6		14			12	13		5	10¹	4		44
1	2						8		7					10³	5		12	6											9					13		14	4¹	11²	3		45

The Budweiser FA Cup
First Round   Bishop's Stortford   (a)   2-1
Second Round   Grimsby T   (a)   0-2

Capital One Cup
First Round   Milton Keynes D   (h)   1-2

Johnstone's Paint Trophy
First Round   Milton Keynes D   (a)   0-2

NORWICH CITY

FOUNDATION

Formed in 1902, largely through the initiative of two local schoolmasters who called a meeting at the Criterion Cafe, they were shocked by an FA Commission which in 1904 declared the club professional and ejected them from the FA Amateur Cup. However, this only served to strengthen their determination. New officials were appointed and a professional club established at a meeting in the Agricultural Hall in March 1905.

Carrow Road, Norwich, Norfolk NR1 1JE.

Telephone: (01603) 760 760.

Fax: (01603) 613 886.

Ticket Office: (0844) 444 1902.

Website: www.canaries.co.uk

Email: reception@ncfc-canaries.co.uk

Ground Capacity: 27,244.

Record Attendance: 25,037 v Sheffield W, FA Cup 5th rd, 16 February 1935 (at The Nest); 43,984 v Leicester C, FA Cup 6th rd, 30 March 1963 (at Carrow Road).

Pitch Measurements: 105m × 68m (114yd × 74yd)

Chairman: Alan Bowkett.

Joint Majority Shareholders: Delia Smith and Michael Wynn-Jones.

Chief Executive: David McNally.

Manager: Neil Adams.

First Team Coach: Gary Holt.

Physio: Neal Reynolds.

HONOURS

FA Premier League: Best season: 3rd 1992–93.

Football League – Division 1: *Champions* 2003–04;

FL C: *Runners-up* 2010–11;

Division 2: *Champions* 1971–72, 1985–86;

FL 1: *Champions* 2009–10;

Division 3 (S): *Champions* 1933–34; *Runners-up* 1950–51;

Division 3: *Runners-up* 1959–60.

FA Cup: Semi-finals 1959, 1989, 1992.

Football League Cup: *Winners* 1962, 1985; *Runners-up* 1973, 1975.

European Competitions UEFA Cup: 1993–94.

Colours: Yellow shirts with green trim, green shorts with yellow trim, yellow socks with green trim.

Year Formed: 1902.

Turned Professional: 1905.

Club Nickname: 'The Canaries'.

Grounds: 1902, Newmarket Road; 1908, The Nest, Rosary Road; 1935, Carrow Road.

First Football League Game: 28 August 1920, Division 3, v Plymouth Arg (a) D 1–1 – Skermer; Gray, Gadsden; Wilkinson, Addy, Martin; Laxton, Kidger, Parker, Whitham (1), Dobson.

Record League Victory: 10–2 v Coventry C, Division 3 (S), 15 March 1930 – Jarvie; Hannah, Graham; Brown, O'Brien, Lochhead (1); Porter (1), Anderson, Hunt (5), Scott (2), Slicer (1).

Record Cup Victory: 8–0 v Sutton U, FA Cup 4th rd, 28 January 1989 – Gunn; Culverhouse, Bowen, Butterworth, Linighan, Townsend (Crook), Gordon, Fleck (3), Allen (4), Phelan, Putney (1).

Record Defeat: 2–10 v Swindon T, Southern League, 5 September 1908.

sky SPORTS FACT FILE

When Norwich City defeated Sunderland to win the Football League Cup in March 1985 they were expected to take part in the UEFA Cup the following season. However, later that year a ban on English clubs taking part in Europe was introduced and the Canaries had to wait until the 1993–94 season to compete in the competition.

Most League Points (2 for a win): 64, Division 3 (S), 1950–51.

Most League Points (3 for a win): 95, FL 1, 2009–10.

Most League Goals: 99, Division 3 (S), 1952–53.

Highest League Scorer in Season: Ralph Hunt, 31, Division 3 (S), 1955–56.

Most League Goals in Total Aggregate: Johnny Gavin, 122, 1945–54, 1955–58.

Most League Goals in One Match: 5, Tommy Hunt v Coventry C, Division 3 (S), 15 March 1930; 5, Roy Hollis v Walsall, Division 3 (S), 29 December 1951.

Most Capped Player: Mark Bowen, 35 (41), Wales.

Most League Appearances: Ron Ashman, 592, 1947–64.

Youngest League Player: Ryan Jarvis, 16 years 282 days v Walsall, 19 April 2003.

Record Transfer Fee Received: £7,250,000 from West Ham U for Dean Ashton, January 2006.

Record Transfer Fee Paid: £8,500,000 to Sporting Lisbon for Ricky van Wolfswinkel, July 2013.

Football League Record: 1920 Original Member of Division 3; 1921 Division 3 (S): 1934–39 Division 2; 1946–58 Division 3 (S); 1958–60 Division 3; 1960–72 Division 2; 1972–74 Division 1; 1974–75 Division 2; 1975–81 Division 1; 1981–82 Division 2; 1982–85 Division 1; 1985–86 Division 2; 1986–92 Division 1; 1992–95 FA Premier League; 1995–2004 Division 1; 2004–05 FA Premier League; 2005–09 FL C; 2009–10 FL 1; 2010–11 FL C; 2011–14 FA Premier League; 2014– FL C.

LATEST SEQUENCES

Longest Sequence of League Wins: 10, 23.11.1985 – 25.1.1986.

Longest Sequence of League Defeats: 7, 1.4.1995 – 6.5.1995.

Longest Sequence of League Draws: 7, 15.1.1994 – 26.2.1994.

Longest Sequence of Unbeaten League Matches: 20, 31.8.1950 – 30.12.1950.

Longest Sequence Without a League Win: 25, 22.9.1956 – 23.2.1957.

Successive Scoring Runs: 25 from 14.9.2009.

Successive Non-scoring Runs: 5 from 18.9.2007.

MANAGERS

John Bowman 1905–07
James McEwen 1907–08
Arthur Turner 1909–10
Bert Stansfield 1910–15
Major Frank Buckley 1919–20
Charles O'Hagan 1920–21
Albert Gosnell 1921–26
Bert Stansfield 1926
Cecil Potter 1926–29
James Kerr 1929–33
Tom Parker 1933–37
Bob Young 1937–39
Jimmy Jewell 1939
Bob Young 1939–45
Duggie Lochhead 1945–46
Cyril Spiers 1946–47
Duggie Lochhead 1947–50
Norman Low 1950–55
Tom Parker 1955–57
Archie Macaulay 1957–61
Willie Reid 1961–62
George Swindin 1962
Ron Ashman 1962–66
Lol Morgan 1966–69
Ron Saunders 1969–73
John Bond 1973–80
Ken Brown 1980–87
Dave Stringer 1987–92
Mike Walker 1992–94
John Deehan 1994–95
Martin O'Neill 1995
Gary Megson 1995–96
Mike Walker 1996–98
Bruce Rioch 1998–2000
Bryan Hamilton 2000
Nigel Worthington 2000–06
Peter Grant 2006–07
Glenn Roeder 2007–09
Bryan Gunn 2009
Paul Lambert 2009–12
Chris Hughton 2012–14
Neil Adams April 2014–

TEN YEAR LEAGUE RECORD

		P	W	D	L	F	A	Pts	Pos
2004-05	PR Lge	38	7	12	19	42	77	33	19
2005-06	FL C	46	18	8	20	56	65	62	9
2006-07	FL C	46	16	9	21	56	71	57	16
2007-08	FL C	46	15	10	21	49	59	55	17
2008-09	FL C	46	12	10	24	57	70	46	22
2009-10	FL 1	46	29	8	9	89	47	95	1
2010-11	FL C	46	23	15	8	83	58	84	2
2011-12	PR Lge	38	12	11	15	52	66	47	12
2012-13	PR Lge	38	10	14	14	41	58	44	11
2013-14	PR Lge	38	8	9	21	28	62	33	18

DID YOU KNOW ?

Norwich City finished bottom of Division Three South in 1956–57 and had to apply for re-election to the Football League. Just two years later they reached the semi-finals of the FA Cup, defeating Manchester United and Tottenham Hotspur before going out to Luton Town in a replay.

NORWICH CITY – FA PREMIERSHIP 2013–14 LEAGUE RECORD

Match No.	Date	Venue	Opponents		Result	H/T Score	Lg Pos.	Goalscorers	Attendance
1	Aug 17	H	Everton	D	2-2	0-0	7	Whittaker [51], van Wolfswinkel [71]	26,824
2	24	A	Hull C	L	0-1	0-1	14		23,682
3	31	H	Southampton	W	1-0	0-0	8	Redmond [68]	26,819
4	Sept 14	A	Tottenham H	L	0-2	0-1	13		35,952
5	21	H	Aston Villa	L	0-1	0-1	17		26,813
6	29	A	Stoke C	W	1-0	1-0	14	Howson [34]	26,184
7	Oct 6	H	Chelsea	L	1-3	0-1	17	Pilkington [68]	26,840
8	19	A	Arsenal	L	1-4	0-1	18	Howson [70]	60,009
9	26	H	Cardiff C	D	0-0	0-0	18		26,846
10	Nov 2	A	Manchester C	L	0-7	0-4	18		47,066
11	9	H	West Ham U	W	3-1	0-1	15	Hooper (pen) [54], Snodgrass [72], Fer [90]	26,824
12	23	A	Newcastle U	L	1-2	0-2	16	Fer [80]	51,328
13	30	H	Crystal Palace	W	1-0	1-0	14	Hooper [30]	26,851
14	Dec 4	A	Liverpool	L	1-5	0-3	16	Johnson [83]	44,541
15	7	A	WBA	W	2-0	1-0	14	Hooper [13], Fer [89]	23,675
16	15	H	Swansea C	D	1-1	1-1	14	Hooper [45]	26,876
17	21	A	Sunderland	D	0-0	0-0	14		37,778
18	26	H	Fulham	L	1-2	1-1	14	Hooper [13]	26,811
19	28	H	Manchester U	L	0-1	0-0	14		26,851
20	Jan 1	A	Crystal Palace	D	1-1	1-1	15	Johnson [39]	25,189
21	11	A	Everton	L	0-2	0-1	15		36,827
22	18	H	Hull C	W	1-0	0-0	12	Bennett, R [87]	26,655
23	28	H	Newcastle U	D	0-0	0-0	12		26,762
24	Feb 1	A	Cardiff C	L	1-2	1-0	15	Snodgrass [5]	26,748
25	8	H	Manchester C	D	0-0	0-0	16		26,832
26	11	A	West Ham U	L	0-2	0-0	16		31,153
27	23	H	Tottenham H	W	1-0	0-0	14	Snodgrass [47]	26,834
28	Mar 2	A	Aston Villa	L	1-4	1-4	15	Hoolahan [3]	30,303
29	8	H	Stoke C	D	1-1	0-0	15	Johnson [56]	26,646
30	15	A	Southampton	L	2-4	0-1	15	Elmander [85], Snodgrass [86]	29,828
31	22	H	Sunderland	W	2-0	2-0	13	Snodgrass [20], Tettey [32]	26,654
32	29	A	Swansea C	L	0-3	0-2	15		20,371
33	Apr 5	H	WBA	L	0-1	0-1	17		26,859
34	12	A	Fulham	L	0-1	0-1	17		25,028
35	20	H	Liverpool	L	2-3	0-2	17	Hooper [54], Snodgrass [77]	26,857
36	26	A	Manchester U	L	0-4	0-1	17		75,208
37	May 4	A	Chelsea	D	0-0	0-0	18		41,602
38	11	H	Arsenal	L	0-2	0-0	18		26,848

Final League Position: 18

GOALSCORERS

League (28): Hooper 6 (1 pen), Snodgrass 6, Fer 3, Johnson 3, Howson 2, Bennett, R 1, Elmander 1, Hoolahan 1, Pilkington 1, Redmond 1, Tettey 1, van Wolfswinkel 1, Whittaker 1.
The Budweiser FA Cup (1): Snodgrass 1.
Capital One Cup (9): Elmander 2, Hooper 2, Fer 1, Murphy, Josh 1, Olsson 1, Pilkington 1, Whittaker 1.

Ruddy J 38	Whittaker S 16+4	Martin R 29+2	Turner M 22	Garrido J 6	Bennett E 1+1	Howson J 23+4	Johnson B 28+4	Redmond N 23+11	Hoolahan W 10+6	van Wolfswinkel R 16+9	Tettey A 17+4	Olsson M 33+1	Fer L 28+1	Snodgrass R 29+1	Elmander J 16+13	Bassong S 27	Pilkington A 10+5	Bennett R 14+2	Hooper G 22+10	Murphy Josh —+9	Becchio L —+5	Gutierrez J 2+2	Yobo J 8	Loza J —+1	Match No.
1	2	3	4	5	6	7	8	9³	10¹	11	12	13													1
1	2	4	3	5		6	9³	10²	14	11	7¹		8	12	13										2
1	2		3	5		12	8	9		11			7	6	10¹	4¹									3
1	2		3	5		12	8²	9³		11	14		7	6	10¹	4¹	13								4
1	2		3	5			8	9³		11			7	6	10²	4¹	13	12	14						5
1	13	2	3				8			11¹	6	5	9	7	12			10²	4						6
1		2	3				8		13	11¹	6	5	9	7²		4	10		12						7
1		2	3				8		12	13	6²	5	9	7		4	10¹		11						8
1		2	3				8³		13	14	6	5	9	7	12	4	10¹		11²						9
1	7²	2	3				8	6				5	9		12	4	10	11¹	13						10
1		2	3				7	13	12			5	8	6	10		9²	4	11¹						11
1		2	3				8	6²	7¹	13		5	9		12		10³	4	11	14					12
1	14	2					7	12	9	6²		5	8		11¹	4	3	10³	13						13
1	14	2					8	9	10	7²		5	6¹		11³	4	3	13	12						14
1	2³	14	3				7	8	6			5	9		10²	4		11¹	12	13					15
1	2		3				7	8	6²			5	9		11¹	4		10	13	12					16
1	2		3				8	9		12		5	7	6	11¹	4		10							17
1	2		3				8	9	13	12		5	7	6²	10¹	4		11							18
1	2						8	9	10³	12		5	7	6	14	4	3	11²	13						19
1	2	14	3²				8	9	10³			5	7⁴	6	13	4	12	11¹							20
1	2				9²		8	12		10¹		5	7	6			3	11	13						21
1	2						8			10²		5	7	6		4	12	3	11	13	9¹				22
1	2						8⁴	13		10¹	14	5	7	6	12		9³	3	11²						23
1	2						8¹	13		12	7	5	14	6	10²	4	3	11			9¹				24
1	13	2					9	6		12	7	5	8			4	10¹		11²	3					25
1	2					7		10³	14	6¹		5	9	8	12	4		13	11²	3					26
1	2						8	9²	13	11¹	7	5	10	6		4		12		3					27
1	2					14	8	9³	10		7¹	5		6²	13	4	12		11	3					28
1	2					12	8	9	10³	11¹	7²	5		6	13	4		14		3					29
1	2						8	9²	14	12	6	5	7	13	10¹	4	11³			3					30
1	2						8	13	14	9³	11¹	5	7	6	10²	4	12			3					31
1	2						7¹	13		9²	11³	8	5	6	10	4	3	14	12						32
1	2						7		12	9³		8	5¹	6	11²	4	10	13	14	3					33
1	2	3	4				8³	6	11	13	10¹	5	7²	9					12	14					34
1	2	3	4				8	6	11		12	5	7²	9			10¹	13							35
1	2	3	4				9	7	10³	11²	14	5	6¹	8	12			13							36
1	5	2	4				9	7	12			6	10		8	11¹	3								37
1	2		4				14	10	7	9¹		8³	5		6	11²	3	12						13	38

The Budweiser FA Cup

Third Round	Fulham	(h)	1-1
Replay	Fulham	(a)	0-3

Capital One Cup

Second Round	Bury	(h)	6-3
Third Round	Watford	(a)	3-2
(aet)			
Fourth Round	Manchester U	(a)	0-4

NOTTINGHAM FOREST

FOUNDATION

One of the oldest football clubs in the world, Nottingham Forest was formed at a meeting in the Clinton Arms in 1865. Known originally as the Forest Football Club, the game which first drew the founders together was 'shinney', a form of hockey. When they determined to change to football in 1865, one of their first moves was to buy a set of red caps to wear on the field.

The City Ground, Nottingham NG2 5FJ.
Telephone: (0115) 982 4444.
Fax: (0115) 982 4455.
Ticket Office: (0871) 226 1980.
Website: www.nottinghamforest.co.uk
Email: info@nottinghamforest.co.uk
Ground Capacity: 30,445.
Record Attendance: 49,946 v Manchester U, Division 1, 28 October 1967.
Pitch Measurements: 102.5m × 67.5m (112yd × 74yd)
Chairman: Fawaz Mubarak Al-Hasawi.
Manager: Stuart Pearce.
Assistant Manager: Steve Wigley.
Physio: Andrew Balderston.
Colours: Red shirt with white trim, white shorts with red trim, red socks with white trim.
Year Formed: 1865.
Turned Professional: 1889.
Previous Name: Forest Football Club.
Club Nickname: 'The Reds'.
Grounds: 1865, Forest Racecourse; 1879, The Meadows; 1880, Trent Bridge Cricket Ground; 1882, Parkside, Lenton; 1885, Gregory, Lenton; 1890, Town Ground; 1898, City Ground.

HONOURS

Football League – Division 1:
Champions 1977–78, 1997–98;
Runners-up 1966–67, 1978–79, 1993–94; **FL 1:** *Runners-up* 2007–08;
Division 2: *Champions* 1906–07, 1921–22; *Runners-up* 1956–57;
Division 3 (S): *Champions* 1950–51.
FA Cup: *Winners* 1898, 1959; *Runners-up* 1991.
Football League Cup: *Winners* 1978, 1979, 1989, 1990; *Runners-up* 1980, 1992.
Anglo-Scottish Cup: *Winners* 1977.
Simod Cup: *Winners* 1989.
Zenith Data Systems Cup: *Winners*: 1992.
European Competitions
European Cup: 1978–79 (*winners*), 1979–80 (*winners*), 1980–81.
European Fairs Cup: 1961–62, 1967–68. **UEFA Cup:** 1983–84, 1984–85, 1995–96. **Super Cup:** 1979 (*winners*), 1980.
World Club Championship: 1980.

First Football League Game: 3 September 1892, Division 1, v Everton (a) D 2–2 – Brown; Earp, Scott; Hamilton, Albert Smith, McCracken; McCallum, 'Tich' Smith, Higgins (2), Pike, McInnes.
Record League Victory: 12–0 v Leicester Fosse, Division 1, 12 April 1909 – Iremonger; Dudley, Maltby; Hughes (1), Needham, Armstrong; Hooper (3), Marrison, West (3), Morris (2), Spouncer (3 incl. 1p).
Record Cup Victory: 14–0 v Clapton (away), FA Cup 1st rd, 17 January 1891 – Brown; Earp, Scott; Albert Smith, Russell, Jeacock; McCallum (2), 'Tich' Smith (1), Higgins (5), Lindley (4), Shaw (2).
Record Defeat: 1–9 v Blackburn R, Division 2, 10 April 1937.
Most League Points (2 for a win): 70, Division 3 (S), 1950–51.
Most League Points (3 for a win): 94, Division 1, 1997–98.

sky SPORTS FACT FILE

Centre half Joe Mercer of Nottingham Forest enlisted in the Footballers' Battalion during the First World War. He was twice wounded and in April 1917 was taken as a prisoner of war by the Germans. He eventually returned to his football career but was never the same player again due to the effects of poison gas which damaged his lungs.

Most League Goals: 110, Division 3 (S), 1950–51.

Highest League Scorer in Season: Wally Ardron, 36, Division 3 (S), 1950–51.

Most League Goals in Total Aggregate: Grenville Morris, 199, 1898–1913.

Most League Goals in One Match: 4, Enoch West v Sunderland, Division 1, 9 November 1907; 4, Tommy Gibson v Burnley, Division 2, 25 January 1913; 4, Tom Peacock v Port Vale, Division 2, 23 December 1933; 4, Tom Peacock v Barnsley, Division 2, 9 November 1935; 4, Tom Peacock v Port Vale, Division 2, 23 November 1935; 4, Tom Peacock v Doncaster R, Division 2, 26 December 1935; 4, Tommy Capel v Gillingham, Division 3 (S), 18 November 1950; 4, Wally Ardron v Hull C, Division 2, 26 December 1952; 4, Tommy Wilson v Barnsley, Division 2, 9 February 1957; 4, Peter Withe v Ipswich T, Division 1, 4 October 1977; 4, Marlon Harewood v Stoke C, Division 1, 22 February 2003.

Most Capped Player: Stuart Pearce, 76 (78), England.

Most League Appearances: Bob McKinlay, 614, 1951–70.

Youngest League Player: Craig Westcarr, 16 years 257 days v Burnley, 13 October 2001.

Record Transfer Fee Received: £8,500,000 from Liverpool for Stan Collymore, June 1995.

Record Transfer Fee Paid: £4,500,000 to Celtic for Pierre van Hooijdonk, March 1997.

Football League Record: 1892 Elected to Division 1; 1906–07 Division 2; 1907–11 Division 1; 1911–22 Division 2; 1922–25 Division 1; 1925–49 Division 1; 1949–51 Division 3 (S); 1951–57 Division 2; 1957–72 Division 1; 1972–77 Division 2; 1977–92 Division 1; 1992–93 FA Premier League; 1993–94 Division 1; 1994–97 FA Premier League; 1997–98 Division 1; 1998–99 FA Premier League; 1999–2004 Division 1; 2004–05 FL C; 2005–08 FL 1; 2008– FL C.

MANAGERS

Harry Radford 1889–97
(Secretary-Manager)
Harry Haslam 1897–1909
(Secretary-Manager)
Fred Earp 1909–12
Bob Masters 1912–25
John Baynes 1925–29
Stan Hardy 1930–31
Noel Watson 1931–36
Harold Wightman 1936–39
Billy Walker 1939–60
Andy Beattie 1960–63
Johnny Carey 1963–68
Matt Gillies 1969–72
Dave Mackay 1972
Allan Brown 1973–75
Brian Clough 1975–93
Frank Clark 1993–96
Stuart Pearce 1996–97
Dave Bassett 1997–99
(previously General Manager)
Ron Atkinson 1999
David Platt 1999–2001
Paul Hart 2001–04
Joe Kinnear 2004
Gary Megson 2005–06
Colin Calderwood 2006–08
Billy Davies 2009–11
Steve McClaren 2011
Steve Cotterill 2011–12
Sean O'Driscoll 2012
Alex McLeish 2012–13
Billy Davies 2013–14
Stuart Pearce July 2014–

LATEST SEQUENCES

Longest Sequence of League Wins: 7, 9.5.1979 – 1.9.1979.

Longest Sequence of League Defeats: 14, 21.3.1913 – 27.9.1913.

Longest Sequence of League Draws: 7, 29.4.1978 – 2.9.1978.

Longest Sequence of Unbeaten League Matches: 42, 26.11.1977 – 25.11.1978.

Longest Sequence Without a League Win: 19, 8.9.1998 – 16.1.1999.

Successive Scoring Runs: 22 from 28.3.1931.

Successive Non-scoring Runs: 7 from 26.11.2011.

TEN YEAR LEAGUE RECORD

		P	W	D	L	F	A	Pts	Pos
2004-05	FL C	46	9	17	20	42	66	44	23
2005-06	FL 1	46	19	12	15	67	52	69	7
2006-07	FL 1	46	23	13	10	65	41	82	4
2007-08	FL 1	46	22	16	8	64	32	82	2
2008-09	FL C	46	13	14	19	50	65	53	19
2009-10	FL C	46	22	13	11	65	40	79	3
2010-11	FL C	46	20	15	11	69	50	75	6
2011-12	FL C	46	14	8	24	48	63	50	19
2012-13	FL C	46	17	16	13	63	59	67	8
2013-14	FL C	46	16	17	13	67	64	65	11

DID YOU KNOW ?

Tinsley Lindley who played for Nottingham Forest in the 1880s was one of the best centre forwards of his era. He played in 25 FA Cup ties for Forest between 1883 and 1891 and won 13 caps for England. He became a well known barrister operating on the Midlands Circuit and also served as a deputy judge.

NOTTINGHAM FOREST – FL CHAMPIONSHIP 2013–14 LEAGUE RECORD

Match No.	Date	Venue	Opponents	Result		H/T Score	Lg Pos.	Goalscorers	Attendance
1	Aug 3	H	Huddersfield T	W	1-0	0-0	8	Lansbury [53]	25,535
2	10	A	Blackburn R	W	1-0	0-0	3	Henderson [90]	14,496
3	17	H	Bolton W	W	3-0	1-0	1	Mackie [2], Reid [50], Lansbury [65]	22,306
4	25	A	Watford	D	1-1	1-0	1	Reid [6]	16,242
5	31	A	Wigan Ath	L	1-2	1-2	4	Reid [8]	16,270
6	Sept 14	H	Barnsley	W	3-2	2-1	3	Cox [18], Etuhu (og) [45], Henderson [84]	21,181
7	17	H	Middlesbrough	D	2-2	0-1	5	Derbyshire [69], Henderson [79]	19,509
8	21	A	Doncaster R	D	2-2	1-1	6	Cohen [39], Reid [81]	12,253
9	28	H	Derby Co	W	1-0	1-0	5	Hobbs [41]	28,276
10	Oct 1	A	Charlton Ath	D	1-1	1-0	4	Reid [3]	15,567
11	5	A	Brighton & HA	W	3-1	0-1	4	Lansbury 2 (1 pen) [46, 62 (p)], Henderson [60]	27,755
12	19	H	Bournemouth	D	1-1	1-0	4	Lansbury [39]	28,070
13	26	H	Yeovil T	L	1-3	1-3	6	Chalobah [42]	7612
14	Nov 2	H	Blackpool	L	0-1	0-0	6		21,581
15	9	A	Leicester C	W	2-0	2-0	5	Cox [31], Mackie [43]	30,416
16	23	H	Burnley	D	1-1	1-1	5	Cox [42]	22,877
17	29	H	Reading	L	2-3	1-2	6	Cox [40], Henderson [60]	21,199
18	Dec 3	A	Millwall	D	2-2	1-1	7	Reid [37], Chalobah [66]	9029
19	7	A	Sheffield W	W	1-0	0-0	5	Cox [48]	23,414
20	14	H	Ipswich T	D	0-0	0-0	7		20,966
21	21	A	Birmingham C	D	0-0	0-0	7		23,497
22	26	H	QPR	W	2-0	1-0	5	Halford [29], Reid [80]	22,721
23	29	H	Leeds U	W	2-1	1-0	5	Halford [23], Derbyshire [84]	26,854
24	Jan 1	A	Reading	D	1-1	1-0	5	Halford [36]	19,873
25	11	A	Bolton W	D	1-1	0-0	5	Paterson [47]	17,046
26	18	A	Blackburn R	W	4-1	2-1	5	Lansbury 2 (2 pens) [15, 34], Paterson [72], Reid [90]	22,456
27	30	H	Watford	W	4-2	0-1	5	Cox 2 [58, 90], Henderson [73], Mackie [82]	18,510
28	Feb 2	H	Yeovil T	W	3-1	2-1	5	Webster (og) [16], Cox [38], Djebbour [90]	21,393
29	8	A	Blackpool	D	1-1	1-0	5	Lascelles [45]	15,105
30	11	A	Huddersfield T	W	3-0	0-0	5	Paterson 2 [63, 82], Henderson [89]	13,249
31	19	H	Leicester C	D	2-2	2-1	5	Paterson [39], Reid (pen) [43]	24,808
32	22	A	Burnley	L	1-3	0-3	5	Abdoun [80]	14,928
33	Mar 1	H	Wigan Ath	L	1-4	0-1	5	Paterson [54]	23,114
34	8	A	Barnsley	L	0-1	0-0	5		12,157
35	11	A	Middlesbrough	D	1-1	0-0	5	Henderson [80]	14,134
36	15	H	Doncaster R	D	0-0	0-0	6		27,402
37	22	A	Derby Co	L	0-5	0-3	7		33,004
38	25	H	Charlton Ath	L	0-1	0-0	7		17,951
39	29	A	Ipswich T	D	1-1	1-0	7	Collins [4]	17,955
40	Apr 5	H	Millwall	L	1-2	0-2	7	Paterson [53]	20,077
41	8	H	Sheffield W	D	3-3	1-2	10	Mackie [44], Tudgay [77], Paterson [87]	20,185
42	12	A	QPR	L	2-5	1-2	11	Lascelles [37], Derbyshire [75]	17,220
43	19	H	Birmingham C	W	1-0	1-0	9	Derbyshire [2]	21,300
44	21	A	Leeds U	W	2-0	2-0	7	Derbyshire 2 [2, 16]	20,517
45	26	A	Bournemouth	L	1-4	0-1	11	Halford [56]	11,021
46	May 3	H	Brighton & HA	L	1-2	1-0	11	Derbyshire [22]	22,209

Final League Position: 11

GOALSCORERS

League (67): Reid 9 (1 pen), Cox 8, Henderson 8, Paterson 8, Derbyshire 7, Lansbury 7 (3 pens), Halford 4, Mackie 4, Chalobah 2, Lascelles 2, Abdoun 1, Cohen 1, Collins 1, Djebbour 1, Hobbs 1, Tudgay 1, own goals 2.
The Budweiser FA Cup (8): Paterson 4, Abdoun 1 (1 pen), Henderson 1, Mackie 1, Reid 1.
Capital One Cup (6): Derbyshire 3, Halford 1, Lascelles 1, Majewski 1.

Darlow K 43	Lichaj E 21 + 3	Cohen C 16	Lansbury H 28 + 1	Hobbs J 27	Collins D 21 + 2	Mackie J 38 + 7	Guedioura A 5	Cox S 25 + 9	Derbyshire M 8 + 21	Reid A 29 + 3	Paterson J 22 + 10	Henderson D 9 + 25	Miller I — + 4	Wilson K 7 + 2	Majewski R 23 + 1	Halford G 28 + 8	Abdoun D 15 + 7	Harding D 13 + 6	Moussi G 9 + 2	Chalobah N 7 + 5	Blackstock D 1	Jara G 28 + 4	Lascelles J 29	Vaughan D 9	Greening J 7 + 6	Fox D 14	Djebbour R 3 + 4	Gomis K 1	Peltier L 7	Osborn B 6 + 2	Tudgay M 1 + 1	De Vries D 3	McLaughlin S 3	Evtimov D — + 1	Rees J — + 1	Match No.
1	2	3	4	5	6	7^3	8	9^1	10^2	11	12	13	14																							1
1	2	5	9	3		12	7		13	10^2	6^1	11			4	8^3	14																			2
1	2	5	8^2	4	11^1	7		12	9	13				3	10	6^1	14																			3
1	2	5	7	3	11^1	6		12	8	13	14				4	9^3	10^2																			4
1	2	5	9	4	11	7^1		10	13	14				3	6^3	8^2	12																			5
1	2	5	9	3	11			6^2	10	12	13				4	8^1		14	7^3																	6
1	2	5	7	3	11			10^1	13	9	14				4^3	8^2	12		6																	7
1	2	5	9	3	10^1	14		8	13	11	12				4	7^2			6^3																	8
1	2	5	7	3	4	10	8	11^1	9^2	14	13	12				6^1																				9
1	2	5	6	3	4	9	12	11^3	8	14	13								7^2	10^1																10
1	2	5	7	3	4	13		6^1	10	11^3	8^2	14			12				9																	11
1		5	6	3	4^1	13	8^1	14	7	11	12				9^2	10						2														12
1	2	5		3	13	11^3		9	14	10	8^2	12			7^1	6						4														13
1	2	5	6	3	10^2	13		14	11^1	12	9^4				7	4			8^3																	14
1	14	5	6	3	10	11^3	8	9^1	13	12					2	4^2	7																			15
1	2^3	5	7	3	6	11		10^1	14	8^2	13	12			9	4																				16
1	2		7	4	6	11		14	13	10^2					12	8^1			5	9			3													17
1	2	8	4		6^2	11		12	10						3	13	5		9^1			2	3													18
1	12		7	3	10	11		13	8						2	9^2	5		14			6^3	4													19
1			6	4	8^2	11		13	9						12	10^3	5		7^1			2	3		14											20
1	12		8	4	7	11		9	14						2	10^3	5^1		13			3	6^2													21
1	5		7	4	8^2			14	9	13					11	10^2	12					3	6^1													22
1	5		7	4	9^1			14	12	8					6^3	10	11^2		13			2	3													23
1	5		7	4	6^2			13	12	9	10				11^2				8^1			2	3			14										24
1		9	4^3	13		12		7	8	14					11	10^2	5	6				2^1	3													25
1		8		4	6^3	11^1		12	9	10	14				3		5		13			2		7^2												26
1	2			4	14			12	9	10^3	13				11	6^2	5	7				8	3													27
1		8		4	6^1	11		9	10^2	13					12	7						2	3			14	5^3									28
1				4	6^3			10^2	14	9	13				12	8		7				2	3				5		11^1							29
1				4	14	11^3		9	6	13					8	7^1	12					2	3				5		10^2							30
1				4	6	11^2		9^1	10	12					8	13		7				2	3			14	5^3									31
1				4	9	13		8	14						10	6^2		7^3				2	3			12	5		11^1							32
1	2^2			12	6	11		10							8	4	14					7^1	3		9^2		5		13							33
1				8^1	11^1	13		9	12						7	10	14					2^2	3		6		5		4							34
1				4	8	11^1		13	12						9^3	14						2	3		7^3	12	5									35
1				4	12	11^3		14	10^1	8	13				9	2^2						6	3		7	5										36
1				4	6	11^3		14	10^1	12	8	13			9^2	2						3			7	5										37
1				4	6	10^2		14	12	11^2					2	9^1		7				3	8		5	13										38
1				4	6			12	10						8^1	3		7				9	5		2	11										39
1	13			4	11			6	14	12					8^2	3^1	5					2			9^1	7	10									40
1	7^2			$4^•$	6			11	9	10^1	13				5							2^3	3		8	14	12									41
1	9^1			8		10^3		11	14						4	2						7^2	3	12	5		6	13								42
1				4	8^2	14		11^3	9	13					2							3	7^1	12	5		6	10								43
			4	9		10		11^3							2	5		14				3	7^1	12		8						1^2	6		13	44
			4	10		13		11							2	5		12				3^1	8^2		7	9						1	6^3			45
			4	2		12		11						9^3		5						6^2	14		3	8	10^1					1	7		13	46

The Budweiser FA Cup

Third Round	West Ham U	(h)	5-0
Fourth Round	Preston NE	(h)	0-0
Replay	Preston NE	(a)	2-0
Fifth Round	Sheffield U	(a)	1-3

Capital One Cup

First Round	Hartlepool U	(h)	3-1
Second Round	Millwall	(h)	2-1
(aet)			
Third Round	Burnley	(a)	1-2

NOTTS COUNTY

FOUNDATION

According to the official history of Notts County 'the true date of Notts' foundation has to be the meeting at the George Hotel on 7 December 1864'. However, there is documented evidence of continuous play from 1862, when club members played organised matches amongst themselves in The Park in Nottingham. They are the world's oldest professional football club.

Meadow Lane Stadium, Meadow Lane, Nottingham NG2 3HJ.

Telephone: (0115) 952 9000.

Fax: (0115) 955 3994.

Ticket Office: (0115) 955 7204.

Website: www.nottscountyfc.co.uk

Email: office@nottscountyfc.co.uk

Ground Capacity: 20,280.

Record Attendance: 47,310 v York C, FA Cup 6th rd, 12 March 1955.

Pitch Measurements: 103.5m × 64m (113yd × 70yd)

Executive Chairman: Ray Trew.

Chief Executive: James Rodwell.

Manager: Shaun Derry.

Assistant Manager: Greg Abbott.

Physio: Rebecca Knight.

Colours: Black and white striped shirts, black shorts with white trim, white socks with black trim.

HONOURS

Football League – Division 1:
Best season: 3rd, 1890–91, 1900–01;
Division 2: *Champions* 1896–97, 1913–14, 1922–23;
Runners-up 1894–95, 1980–81;
Division 3 (S): *Champions* 1930–31, 1949–50; *Runners-up* 1936–37;
Division 3: *Champions* 1997–98;
Runners-up 1972–73;
Division 4: *Champions* 1970–71;
Runners-up 1959–60;
FL 2: *Champions* 2009–10.

FA Cup: *Winners* 1894;
Runners-up 1891.

Football League Cup: Best season: 5th rd, 1964, 1973, 1976.

Anglo-Italian Cup: *Winners* 1995;
Runners-up 1994.

Year Formed: 1862* (*see Foundation*). *Turned Professional:* 1885.

Club Nickname: 'The Magpies'.

Grounds: 1862, The Park; 1864, The Meadows; 1877, Beeston Cricket Ground; 1880, Castle Ground; 1883, Trent Bridge; 1910, Meadow Lane.

First Football League Game: 15 September 1888, Football League, v Everton (a) L 1–2 – Holland; Guttridge, McLean; Brown, Warburton, Shelton; Hodder, Harker, Jardine, Albert Moore (1), Wardle.

Record League Victory: 11–1 v Newport Co, Division 3 (S), 15 January 1949 – Smith; Southwell, Purvis; Gannon, Baxter, Adamson; Houghton (1), Sewell (4), Lawton (4), Pimbley, Johnston (2).

Record Cup Victory: 15–0 v Rotherham T (at Trent Bridge), FA Cup 1st rd, 24 October 1885 – Sherwin; Snook, Henry Thomas Moore; Dobson (1), Emmett (1), Chapman; Gunn (1), Albert Moore (2), Jackson (3), Daft (2), Cursham (4), (1 og).

Record Defeat: 1–9 v Blackburn R, Division 1, 16 November 1889. 1–9 v Aston Villa, Division 1, 29 September 1888. 1–9 v Portsmouth, Division 2, 9 April 1927.

Most League Points (2 for a win): 69, Division 4, 1970–71.

sky SPORTS FACT FILE

In September 2011 Notts County provided the opposition for Juventus in the inaugural match at the Serie A club's new ground. The invitation was in recognition of the Italian club adopting County's black and white striped shirts as their first choice kit back in 1903. The game, in front of a 41,000 crowd, ended in a 1-1 draw.

Most League Points (3 for a win): 99, Division 3, 1997–98.

Most League Goals: 107, Division 4, 1959–60.

Highest League Scorer in Season: Tom Keetley, 39, Division 3 (S), 1930–31.

Most League Goals in Total Aggregate: Les Bradd, 125, 1967–78.

Most League Goals in One Match: 5, Robert Jardine v Burnley, Division 1, 27 October 1888; 5, Daniel Bruce v Port Vale, Division 2, 26 February 1895; 5, Bertie Mills v Barnsley, Division 2, 19 November 1927.

Most Capped Player: Kevin Wilson, 15 (42), Northern Ireland.

Most League Appearances: Albert Iremonger, 564, 1904–26.

Youngest League Player: Tony Bircumshaw, 16 years 54 days v Brentford, 3 April 1961.

Record Transfer Fee Received: £2,500,000 from Derby Co for Craig Short, September 1992.

Record Transfer Fee Paid: £800,000 to Manchester C for Kasper Schmeichel, July 2009.

Football League Record: 1888 Founder Member of the Football League; 1893–97 Division 2; 1897–1913 Division 1; 1913–14 Division 2; 1914–20 Division 1; 1920–23 Division 2; 1923–26 Division 1; 1926–30 Division 2; 1930–31 Division 3 (S); 1931–35 Division 2; 1935–50 Division 3 (S); 1950–58 Division 2; 1958–59 Division 3; 1959–60 Division 4; 1960–64 Division 3; 1964–71 Division 4; 1971–73 Division 3; 1973–81 Division 2; 1981–84 Division 1; 1984–85 Division 2; 1985–90 Division 3; 1990–91 Division 2; 1991–95 Division 1; 1995–97 Division 2; 1997–98 Division 3; 1998–2004 Division 2; 2004–10 FL 2; 2010– FL 1.

LATEST SEQUENCES

Longest Sequence of League Wins: 10, 3.12.1997 – 31.1.1998.

Longest Sequence of League Defeats: 9, 15.3.2011 – 16.4.2011.

Longest Sequence of League Draws: 6, 16.8.2008 – 20.9.2008.

Longest Sequence of Unbeaten League Matches: 19, 26.4.1930 – 6.12.1930.

Longest Sequence Without a League Win: 20, 3.12.1996 – 31.3.1997.

Successive Scoring Runs: 35 from 10.10.1959.

Successive Non-scoring Runs: 5 from 15.3.2011.

MANAGERS

Edwin Browne 1883–93
Tom Featherstone 1893
Tom Harris 1893–1913
Albert Fisher 1913–27
Horace Henshall 1927–34
Charlie Jones 1934
David Pratt 1935
Percy Smith 1935–36
Jimmy McMullan 1936–37
Harry Parkes 1938–39
Tony Towers 1939–42
Frank Womack 1942–43
Major Frank Buckley 1944–46
Arthur Stollery 1946–49
Eric Houghton 1949–53
George Poyser 1953–57
Tommy Lawton 1957–58
Frank Hill 1958–61
Tim Coleman 1961–63
Eddie Lowe 1963–65
Tim Coleman 1965–66
Jack Burkitt 1966–67
Andy Beattie *(General Manager)* 1967
Billy Gray 1967–68
Jack Wheeler *(Caretaker Manager)* 1968–69
Jimmy Sirrel 1969–75
Ron Fenton 1975–77
Jimmy Sirrel 1978–82 *(continued as General Manager to 1984)*
Howard Wilkinson 1982–83
Larry Lloyd 1983–84
Richie Barker 1984–85
Jimmy Sirrel 1985–87
John Barnwell 1987–88
Neil Warnock 1989–93
Mick Walker 1993–94
Russell Slade 1994–95
Howard Kendall 1995
Colin Murphy 1995–96 *(General Manager)*
Steve Thompson 1995–96
Sam Allardyce 1997–99
Gary Brazil 1999–2000
Jocky Scott 2000–01
Gary Brazil 2001–02
Billy Dearden 2002–04
Gary Mills 2004
Ian Richardson 2004–05
Gudjon Thordarson 2005–06
Steve Thompson 2006–07
Ian McParland 2007–09
Hans Backe 2009
Sven-Göran Eriksson 2009–10 *(Director of Football)*
Steve Cotterill 2010
Craig Short 2010
Paul Ince 2010–11
Martin Allen 2011–12
Keith Curle 2012–13
Chris Kiwomya 2013
Shaun Derry November 2013–

TEN YEAR LEAGUE RECORD

		P	W	D	L	F	A	Pts	Pos
2004-05	FL 2	46	13	13	20	46	62	52	19
2005-06	FL 2	46	12	16	18	48	63	52	21
2006-07	FL 2	46	16	14	16	55	53	62	13
2007-08	FL 2	46	10	18	18	37	53	48	21
2008-09	FL 2	46	11	14	21	49	69	47	19
2009-10	FL 2	46	27	12	7	96	31	93	1
2010-11	FL 1	46	14	8	24	46	60	50	19
2011-12	FL 1	46	21	10	15	75	63	73	7
2012-13	FL 1	46	16	17	13	61	49	65	12
2013-14	FL 1	46	15	5	26	64	77	50	20

DID YOU KNOW

Notts County centre half Arthur Clamp lost his life just three days after he was sent to fight at the front line in 1918. Arthur, who made almost 300 first team appearances for the Magpies, suffered severe wounds and although he was brought back to the United Kingdom he passed away in a Stoke-on-Trent hospital.

NOTTS COUNTY – FOOTBALL LEAGUE ONE 2013–14 LEAGUE RECORD

Match No.	Date	Venue	Opponents	Result	H/T Score	Lg Pos.	Goalscorers	Attendance
1	Aug 2	A	Sheffield U	L	1-2	0-1	23	Showunmi [59]	17,944
2	10	H	Peterborough U	L	2-4	1-1	21	Leacock [26], Arquin (pen) [90]	6582
3	17	A	Walsall	D	1-1	0-0	20	Arquin [74]	4295
4	24	H	Stevenage	L	0-1	0-0	21		3925
5	31	H	Rotherham U	L	0-1	0-1	23		5428
6	Sept 14	A	Milton Keynes D	L	1-3	0-2	24	McGregor [76]	7142
7	17	A	Leyton Orient	L	1-5	0-2	24	Haynes [71]	4092
8	21	H	Tranmere R	W	2-0	1-0	23	Labadie [7], Haber [79]	3938
9	28	A	Carlisle U	L	1-2	1-1	23	McGregor [27]	4315
10	Oct 5	H	Crewe Alex	W	4-0	2-0	19	McGregor 2 [33, 41], Haynes [66], Haber [83]	6249
11	18	A	Swindon T	L	0-2	0-2	22		8188
12	22	H	Gillingham	L	1-2	0-2	23	McGregor [79]	5161
13	26	H	Preston NE	L	0-1	0-0	24		4956
14	29	H	Oldham Ath	W	3-2	1-1	23	Haynes [20], Arquin [60], McGregor [68]	3385
15	Nov 2	A	Coventry C	L	0-3	0-0	24		2693
16	16	H	Wolverhampton W	L	0-1	0-0	24		7520
17	23	A	Shrewsbury T	L	0-1	0-0	24		5008
18	26	A	Bradford C	D	1-1	1-0	24	Liddle [43]	12,808
19	30	H	Brentford	L	0-1	0-1	24		5132
20	Dec 7	H	Gillingham	W	3-1	1-0	24	McGregor 2 [40, 53], Grealish [87]	3607
21	14	A	Colchester U	W	4-0	2-0	22	Grealish [30], Fox [43], McGregor [86], Liddle [89]	2961
22	21	H	Bristol C	D	1-1	0-1	22	Sheehan (pen) [89]	6523
23	26	A	Port Vale	L	1-2	1-1	23	Murray [43]	7028
24	29	A	Crawley T	L	0-1	0-0	24		3096
25	Jan 1	H	Bradford C	W	3-0	1-0	23	Campbell-Ryce [32], McGregor [88], Grealish [90]	4919
26	11	H	Sheffield U	W	2-1	1-1	21	Showunmi [26], Fotheringham [68]	8564
27	18	A	Stevenage	W	1-0	1-0	16	Ball [42]	2877
28	21	H	Peterborough U	L	3-4	2-1	16	Showunmi [4], Murray [7], Grealish [76]	4511
29	25	A	Walsall	L	1-5	0-3	18	McGregor [61]	5701
30	Feb 1	A	Preston NE	L	0-2	0-0	22		9483
31	8	H	Coventry C	W	3-0	2-0	19	Mullins [13], Spencer [33], Sheehan (pen) [87]	8149
32	15	A	Wolverhampton W	L	0-2	0-1	21		18,019
33	22	H	Shrewsbury T	L	2-3	2-1	23	Grealish [8], Sheehan (pen) [13]	5424
34	Mar 1	A	Rotherham U	L	0-6	0-4	24		8383
35	8	H	Leyton Orient	D	0-0	0-0	24		4680
36	11	H	Milton Keynes D	L	1-3	0-1	24	Sheehan (pen) [70]	3331
37	15	A	Tranmere R	L	2-3	1-2	24	Murray [14], Sheehan [61]	4292
38	22	H	Carlisle U	W	4-1	2-0	24	Hollis 2 [33, 47], Murray [40], Liddle [70]	4014
39	25	A	Crewe Alex	W	3-1	1-0	23	Liddle [10], Murray 2 [79, 87]	3895
40	29	H	Colchester U	W	2-0	2-0	19	Murray [5], Hollis [45]	5230
41	Apr 5	A	Brentford	L	1-3	0-2	23	Spencer [84]	8188
42	12	H	Port Vale	W	4-2	2-2	20	Spencer 2 [27, 34], Campbell-Ryce 2 [48, 85]	5613
43	18	A	Bristol C	L	1-2	1-1	22	Hollis [29]	13,427
44	21	H	Crawley T	W	1-0	1-0	21	Spencer [34]	7111
45	26	H	Swindon T	W	2-0	1-0	19	Sheehan [9], McGregor [90]	6714
46	May 3	A	Oldham Ath	D	1-1	0-0	20	Sheehan (pen) [75]	7698

Final League Position: 20

GOALSCORERS

League (64): McGregor 12, Murray 7, Sheehan 7 (5 pens), Grealish 5, Spencer 5, Hollis 4, Liddle 4, Arquin 3 (1 pen), Campbell-Ryce 3, Haynes 3, Showunmi 3, Haber 2, Ball 1, Fotheringham 1, Fox 1, Labadie 1, Leacock 1, Mullins 1.
The Budweiser FA Cup (2): Murray 1, own goal 1.
Capital One Cup (5): Arquin 1, Coombes 1, Haynes 1, McGregor 1, Showunmi 1.
Johnstone's Paint Trophy (2): McGregor 1, Murray 1.

Bialkowski B 44	Dumbuya M 23+1	Sheehan A 42	Boucaud A 26+3	Leacock D 25+1	Liddle G 32	Lahadie J 15	Fotheringham M 23+5	Haynes D 15+6	Campbell-Ryce J 36	Arquin Y 4+8	Showunmi E 9+5	Tempest G 8+6	Zoko F —+1	McGregor C 32+5	Thompson C 8+3	Smith M 20+4	Coombes A 3+3	Bell D 4+6	Balmy J —+1	Nangle J —+1	Stevens E 2	Murray R 15+9	Haber M 5+6	Grealish J 32+5	Spiess F 1	Holt J 2	Haworth A —+2	Tyson N 4+6	Freeman K 16	Fox M 6+1	Hollis H 9+1	Ball C 2+4	Appiah K 1+6	Vela J 7	Pilkington K 1	Roberts G 6	Mullins H 15+1	Spencer J 13	Dixon K —+1	Waite T —+1	Match No.
1	2	3	4	5	6^1	7^1	8	9^3	10	11^2	12	13	14																												1
1	2	4		3		7	8	10	6^2	12	11^1	5		9	13																										2
1	2	5		4		7	8	11^2	6^3	14	10^1			9		3	12	13																							3
1	2			3		7	8	11				5		9		4	10^2	6^1	12	13																					4
1	2		13	4	3	7^3	10^1		6^2	11				9		12	8					5	14																		5
1	2	5	14	4	9	7^2		10^1	13					8		3		6^1				11	12																		6
1		4	6	3	2		9^2	14		12				7	13	10						8^3	11^1	5																	7
1	2	5	7^1	4	3	6	8	10^3		14				11^2								13	9																		8
1	2	5	7	4^3	3	6	8^2	10^1	13	11				14								12	9																		9
1	2	5^3	7	4	3	8	6	10^2			12			11		14						13	9^1																		10
1	2	5	8	4^3	3	6^1	7	10						9		12	11^2	14				13																			11
1	2	5	8		3	6^2	13	11^3	10^1			7		9		4	12					14																			12
	2	4	8		3	7^2	10							9	6	5^3						11^1	12	14	13	1															13
1		4		3		7	6	11^3	13					8	2^2	10								9^1					5	14											14
1		4^3	14	2	3		6^2	7	10^4			12		8	11									9^1					5												15
1		5		3		7	8	6^1	12					9^2		4	14					10^2		13					2												16
1		5	7	4			8^2	11						9	14	12						6^1	13	10^3					2												17
1		8	4			7	12	11^1	6^2			5				3						13	10^4	9					2												18
1		5	7	4	9		11		6^2					10	3^1									8					2			12	13								19
1		4	7		3		11^1	8						10										9					2			5	12								20
1		3	6^2	4	7	13		9						8^1								12		10					2			5	11								21
1		4	7	3	6^1	12		8^3		14				10								13		9					2			5	11^2								22
1	2^3	4	8	3		7	13	9^1	12			10	14									11^2		6					5												23
1	2	5^2	6	3		7^3	13	11^2	10													12		9^1					4												24
1	2		7	4		6		8	11					10		3								9					5												25
1		5	7	4		6	12	8							3							9^1		10					2												26
1		2	8	4		7		9	11						3							5		6^1					10			12									27
1		5	8	3		7	12	9^2	10^1						4							11^1		6					2			13									28
1		5	7	4^2		6	8^1	11^3	14					10								9							2			13	12								29
		5	3			7^2		9	11^1					10		4						6		8					2			12	1	2	13						30
1		4	7			8		10^1						3										9					2			12		5		6^1	11				31
1		3	8^1			14		9						10^2		4								13					2			12		5^1		7^1	11^3				32
1		4	7^3			8		14						10^1		3								13					2			12		5		6^1	11^2				33
1		3	8^2					7^1	6					10^3		4								13					2			11		5		9	6		12	14	34
1	2	5		4	6		8							9	3									10					11								7				35
1	2	5		4^3	6^1	14	8							9^2	3							13		10					11	12							7				36
1	2^1	4		7			6					5		13								9		12					11^2	3						8	10				37
1	2^1	5		7			6							13								11	9						12	4		8				3	10				38
1		5		7			6							13	2							11	9^1						12	3		8				4	10^2				39
1	2	5		6			7							9								11^2	13						12	4		7				3	11				40
1	2^1	5	12	7			6							11^2	13							9	4^1						9	4^1		8				3	10				41
1		4		6			8					2		9^1	10							12							7	5	3	11				4	10				42
1		5		7			6							12	2							11	8						3	9^1						4	10				43
1	12	5		7			6							8^1	2							11^2	9						13	4						3	10				44
1	2	5		7			6							11^1								9^2							13	4						3	10				45
1	2^1	5	3				6							12	7							11	9						4			8					10				46

The Budweiser FA Cup
First Round — Hartlepool U — (a) — 2-3

Capital One Cup
First Round — Fleetwood T — (h) — 3-2
Second Round — Liverpool — (a) — 2-4
(aet)

Johnstone's Paint Trophy
First Round — Burton Alb — (h) — 1-0
Second Round — Wolverhampton W — (a) — 0-0
(aet; won 3-1 on penalties)
Northern Quarter-Finals — Oldham Ath — (a) — 1-5

OLDHAM ATHLETIC

FOUNDATION

It was in 1895 that John Garland, the landlord of the Featherstall and Junction Hotel, decided to form a football club. As Pine Villa they played in the Oldham Junior League. In 1899 the local professional club, Oldham County, went out of existence and one of the liquidators persuaded Pine Villa to take over their ground at Sheepfoot Lane and change their name to Oldham Athletic.

Boundary Park, Furtherwood Road, Oldham, Lancs OL1 2PA.

Telephone: (0161) 624 4972.

Fax: (0161) 627 5915.

Ticket Office: (0161) 785 5150.

Website: www.oldhamathletic.co.uk

Email: enquiries@oldhamathletic.co.uk

Ground Capacity: 10,904.

Record Attendance: 46,471 v Sheffield W, FA Cup 4th rd, 25 January 1930.

Pitch Measurements: 100m × 68.5m (109.5yd × 75yd)

Chairman: Simon Corney.

Chief Executive: Neil Joy.

Manager: Lee Johnson.

Assistant Manager: Tommy Wright.

Head of Sports Medicine: Jon Guy.

Colours: Blue shirts, white shorts with blue trim, blue socks with white trim.

Year Formed: 1895.

Turned Professional: 1899.

Previous Name: 1895, Pine Villa; 1899, Oldham Athletic.

Club Nickname: 'The Latics'.

Grounds: 1895, Sheepfoot Lane; 1900, Hudson Field; 1906, Sheepfoot Lane; 1907, Boundary Park.

First Football League Game: 9 September 1907, Division 2, v Stoke (a) W 3–1 – Hewitson; Hodson, Hamilton; Fay, Walders, Wilson; Ward, Billy Dodds (1), Newton (1), Hancock, Swarbrick (1).

Record League Victory: 11–0 v Southport, Division 4, 26 December 1962 – Bollands; Branagan, Marshall; McCall, Williams, Scott; Ledger (1), Johnstone, Lister (6), Colquhoun (1), Whitaker (3).

Record Cup Victory: 10–1 v Lytham, FA Cup 1st rd, 28 November 1925 – Gray; Wynne, Grundy; Adlam, Heaton, Naylor (1), Douglas, Pynegar (2), Ormston (2), Barnes (3), Watson (2).

HONOURS

Football League – Division 1:
Runners-up 1914–15;
Division 2: *Champions* 1990–91;
Runners-up 1909–10;
Division 3 (N): *Champions* 1952–53;
Division 2: *Champions* 1973–74;
Division 4: *Runners-up* 1962–63.

FA Cup: Semi-final 1913, 1990, 1994.

Football League Cup:
Runners-up 1990.

sky SPORTS FACT FILE

Oldham Athletic first applied for Football League membership in 1906 and came within 1 vote of removing Clapton Orient. They were also unsuccessful 12 months later, but Burslem Port Vale then resigned shortly after the League's Annual Meeting and Oldham were selected to replace them by the Football League Management Committee.

Record Defeat: 4–13 v Tranmere R, Division 3 (N), 26 December 1935.

Most League Points (2 for a win): 62, Division 3, 1973–74.

Most League Points (3 for a win): 88, Division 2, 1990–91.

Most League Goals: 95, Division 4, 1962–63.

Highest League Scorer in Season: Tom Davis, 33, Division 3 (N), 1936–37.

Most League Goals in Total Aggregate: Roger Palmer, 141, 1980–94.

Most League Goals in One Match: 7, Eric Gemmell v Chester, Division 3 (N), 19 January 1952.

Most Capped Player: Gunnar Halle, 24 (64), Norway.

Most League Appearances: Ian Wood, 525, 1966–80.

Youngest League Player: Wayne Harrison, 16 years 347 days v Notts Co, 27 October 1984.

Record Transfer Fee Received: £1,700,000 from Aston Villa for Earl Barrett, February 1992.

Record Transfer Fee Paid: £750,000 to Aston Villa for Ian Olney, June 1992.

Football League Record: 1907 Elected to Division 2; 1910–23 Division 1; 1923–35 Division 2; 1935–53 Division 3 (N); 1953–54 Division 2; 1954–58 Division 3 (N); 1958–63 Division 4; 1963–69 Division 3; 1969–71 Division 4; 1971–74 Division 3; 1974–91 Division 2; 1991–92 Division 1; 1992–94 FA Premier League; 1994–97 Division 1; 1997–2004 Division 2; 2004– FL 1.

LATEST SEQUENCES

Longest Sequence of League Wins: 10, 12.1.1974 – 12.3.1974.

Longest Sequence of League Defeats: 8, 15.12.1934 – 2.2.1935.

Longest Sequence of League Draws: 5, 26.12.1982 – 15.1.1983.

Longest Sequence of Unbeaten League Matches: 20, 1.5.1990 – 10.11.1990.

Longest Sequence Without a League Win: 17, 4.9.1920 – 18.12.1920.

Successive Scoring Runs: 25 from 25.8.1962.

Successive Non-scoring Runs: 6 from 12.2.2011.

MANAGERS

David Ashworth 1906–14
Herbert Bamlett 1914–21
Charlie Roberts 1921–22
David Ashworth 1923–24
Bob Mellor 1924–27
Andy Wilson 1927–32
Bob Mellor 1932–33
Jimmy McMullan 1933–34
Bob Mellor 1934–45
(continued as Secretary to 1953)
Frank Womack 1945–47
Billy Wootton 1947–50
George Hardwick 1950–56
Ted Goodier 1956–58
Norman Dodgin 1958–60
Danny McLennan 1960
Jack Rowley 1960–63
Les McDowall 1963–65
Gordon Hurst 1965–66
Jimmy McIlroy 1966–68
Jack Rowley 1968–69
Jimmy Frizzell 1970–82
Joe Royle 1982–94
Graeme Sharp 1994–97
Neil Warnock 1997–98
Andy Ritchie 1998–2001
Mick Wadsworth 2001–02
Iain Dowie 2002–03
Brian Talbot 2004–05
Ronnie Moore 2005–06
John Sheridan 2006–09
Joe Royle 2009
Dave Penney 2009–10
Paul Dickov 2010–13
Lee Johnson March 2013–

TEN YEAR LEAGUE RECORD

		P	W	D	L	F	A	Pts	Pos
2004-05	FL 1	46	14	10	22	60	73	52	19
2005-06	FL 1	46	18	11	17	58	60	65	10
2006-07	FL 1	46	21	12	13	69	47	75	6
2007-08	FL 1	46	18	13	15	58	46	67	8
2008-09	FL 1	46	16	17	13	66	65	65	10
2009-10	FL 1	46	13	13	20	39	57	52	16
2010-11	FL 1	46	13	17	16	53	60	56	17
2011-12	FL 1	46	14	12	20	50	66	54	16
2012-13	FL 1	46	14	9	23	46	59	51	19
2013-14	FL 1	46	14	14	18	50	59	56	15

DID YOU KNOW ?

After changing their name from Pine Villa, Oldham Athletic played their first competitive game under their new name on 9 September 1899. They defeated Nook Rovers from Hurst by 4-2 in a Manchester & District Alliance fixture.

OLDHAM ATHLETIC – FOOTBALL LEAGUE ONE 2013–14 LEAGUE RECORD

Match No.	Date		Venue	Opponents	Result		H/T Score	Lg Pos.	Goalscorers	Attendance
1	Aug	3	A	Stevenage	W	4-3	0-1	3	Tarkowski [51], Baxter 2 (1 pen) [67, 87 (p)], Montano [70]	3009
2		10	H	Walsall	L	0-1	0-1	10		4538
3		17	A	Peterborough U	L	1-2	0-1	16	MacDonald [90]	6184
4		24	H	Port Vale	W	3-1	1-1	8	Rooney 2 [15, 57], Dayton [77]	4788
5		31	H	Tranmere R	L	0-1	0-0	13		4792
6	Sept	9	A	Preston NE	L	1-2	0-2	14	Tarkowski [83]	10,292
7		14	A	Rotherham U	L	2-3	1-1	15	Montano [44], Lanzoni [53]	8306
8		21	H	Crewe Alex	D	1-1	0-1	16	MacDonald [54]	4273
9		28	A	Crawley T	L	0-1	0-1	16		3142
10	Oct	5	H	Leyton Orient	D	1-1	1-0	17	MacDonald [36]	4062
11		19	H	Carlisle U	W	1-0	1-0	18	Rooney (pen) [26]	4478
12		22	A	Wolverhampton W	L	0-2	0-0	19		15,959
13		26	H	Swindon T	W	2-1	1-0	16	Winchester [32], Philliskirk [77]	3837
14		29	A	Notts Co	L	2-3	1-1	16	Rooney [45], Clarke-Harris [70]	3385
15	Nov	2	A	Bristol C	D	1-1	0-1	16	Dayton [77]	11,352
16		23	A	Gillingham	W	1-0	0-0	15	Petrasso [57]	6025
17		26	H	Shrewsbury T	W	2-1	1-1	14	MacDonald [44], Philliskirk [76]	4563
18	Dec	1	H	Bradford C	D	1-1	1-1	14	Clarke-Harris [23]	7180
19		14	A	Brentford	L	0-1	0-0	16		6594
20		21	H	Colchester U	L	0-2	0-2	18		4036
21		26	A	Sheffield U	D	1-1	1-0	18	Clarke-Harris [6]	19,551
22		29	A	Coventry C	D	1-1	1-0	18	Clarke-Harris [45]	3347
23	Jan	1	H	Shrewsbury T	L	1-2	1-1	19	Grounds [35]	3669
24		11	H	Stevenage	W	1-0	1-0	16	Wesolowski [13]	3460
25		14	A	Walsall	L	0-1	0-0	16		3522
26		18	A	Port Vale	L	0-1	0-0	17		6002
27		25	H	Peterborough U	W	5-4	0-3	16	Harkins 2 (1 pen) [48, 89 (p)], Worrall [54], Wesolowski [68], Kusunga [90]	3571
28		28	H	Wolverhampton W	L	0-3	0-0	16		4343
29	Feb	1	A	Swindon T	W	1-0	0-0	15	Grounds [73]	7391
30		8	H	Bristol C	D	1-1	1-1	15	Philliskirk [5]	3822
31		15	A	Milton Keynes D	L	1-2	1-0	15	Lockwood [37]	7385
32		22	H	Gillingham	W	1-0	1-0	14	Harkins [33]	3714
33		25	H	Milton Keynes D	L	1-2	0-2	15	MacDonald [57]	2792
34	Mar	1	A	Tranmere R	D	2-2	1-1	14	Wesolowski [12], Ridehalgh (og) [59]	5061
35		8	H	Preston NE	L	1-3	0-1	18	Harkins [75]	6698
36		11	H	Rotherham U	L	0-2	0-0	18		3745
37		15	A	Crewe Alex	D	1-1	0-0	18	Harkins [52]	5258
38		22	H	Crawley T	W	1-0	1-0	18	Philliskirk [18]	3389
39		25	A	Leyton Orient	D	1-1	0-1	17	Smith [90]	3645
40		29	H	Brentford	D	0-0	0-0	17		4087
41	Apr	5	A	Bradford C	W	3-2	2-1	16	Wesolowski [22], Clarke-Harris 2 [45, 58]	14,920
42		18	A	Colchester U	W	1-0	1-0	16	Brown [45]	4252
43		21	H	Coventry C	D	0-0	0-0	16		4633
44		26	A	Carlisle U	W	1-0	0-0	15	Dayton [70]	5313
45		29	H	Sheffield U	D	1-1	1-0	15	Wilson [17]	3949
46	May	3	H	Notts Co	D	1-1	0-0	15	Lockwood [68]	7698

Final League Position: 15

GOALSCORERS

League (50): Clarke-Harris 6, Harkins 5 (1 pen), MacDonald 5, Philliskirk 4, Rooney 4 (1 pen), Wesolowski 4, Dayton 3, Baxter 2 (1 pen), Grounds 2, Lockwood 2, Montano 2, Tarkowski 2, Brown 1, Kusunga 1, Lanzoni 1, Petrasso 1, Smith 1, Wilson 1, Winchester 1, Worrall 1, own goal 1.
The Budweiser FA Cup (8): Rooney 2 (1 pen), Philliskirk 2, Clarke-Harris 1, Kusunga 1, Lanzoni 1, Smith 1.
Capital One Cup (0).
Johnstone's Paint Trophy (12): Philliskirk 6 (2 pens), Clarke-Harris 1, Dayton 1, Rooney 1, Schmeltz 1, Tarkowski 1, Wesolowski 1.

Oxley M 36	Mellor D 16 + 4	Brown C 24 + 3	Baxter J 3 + 1	Tarkowski J 26	Grounds J 45	Montano C 6 + 4	Smith K 42	Rooney A 16 + 8	MacDonald C 15 + 15	Dayton J 24 + 10	Clarke-Harris J 23 + 17	Schmeltz S 5 + 12	Byrne C — + 3	Rodgers A 2 + 5	Mills J 11	Wesolowski J 37 + 2	Millar K 2 + 9	Lanzoni M 10	Rusnak A — + 2	Philliskirk D 33 + 5	Kusunga G 18	Winchester C 7 + 5	Petrasso M 9 + 2	Plummer E 3	Pritchard J — + 1	Harkins G 22 + 1	Worrall D 17 + 1	Lockwood A 18 + 1	Wilson J 16	Stead J 4 + 1	Kissock J 2 + 2	Dunfield T 1 + 1	Turner R 1 + 1	Rachubka P 10	Byrom J 2 + 2	Gafaiti A — + 1	Match No.
1	2[3]	3	4	5	6	7	8	9	10	11[1]	12	13	14																								1
1	4[1]	2	8	3	5	9[2]	7	10	11	6[3]		13	12	14																							2
1		2	10[2]	3	4	9[3]	8	10		6		13			5	8	12																				3
1		2[1]	13	3	4	9	8	10		6[3]	11[2]	14	12		5	7																					4
1			3	4	14	8	10	6[3]	11[2]	9				12	5	7[1]	2	13																			5
1			3	4	12	8	11[3]	13	9	14	6[2]				5	7[1]	2			10																	6
1	7[▪]			4	9[2]	8	10[3]			13	6			5	12		2	14	11[1]	3																	7
1		3	4		7	10[3]	11[2]	9[1]	12	6				5	8	14	2	13																			8
1		3	4		7	13	11	9[3]	10[3]	12		6[1]	5	8			2	14																			9
1			4	5	13	8	12	10	6[3]					9	7				11[1]	3	2																10
1		3	4		8	10[3]	11[2]	9	13					5	7	12				6	2																11
1	14		4	3	8	7	13		6[2]	12				5[2]	9					11	2	10[1]															12
1			4	5		8	11		9	12	13			7	10[2]					6	3	2															13
1	5		4		7	10		9[2]	12	14	13			8	11[2]					6	3	2[1]															14
1	5		3	4	12	7	11[2]		9[1]	10	13			8[2]						6	2																15
1		3	4		2	13	14	9	10[3]	12				5	7					11[1]	8[▪]		6[2]														16
1	5	4	3		7		11	9[1]	12	14		8[2]		13			2			10			6[1]														17
1	13		3	4	8	12		6[1]	11	9[3]				7		2				10			14	5[2]													18
1	10[2]		3	4	7	13	11[1]	14		6				9		2	12[3]	8	5																		19
1	9	13	3	4	8	11[1]				12	2			10			7[1]	6	5[2]	14																	20
1	9	2		7	5	8	10		11					12	4			3	6[1]																		21
1	12	2		9	5	7	6		11					13	4[1]			3	8[2]	10																	22
1	8	2		4	5	7	10[3]		9[1]	11	13	14		12				3[1]	6																		23
1	5		3	4	7	13	14	12	11[3]			6		9	2			8[1]					10[2]													24
1	5	4	3		7	14	11[1]	10	12			6		9[3]	2			8[2]					13													25
1	2		3	5	8		9[1]	7[2]	13			6		11[12]	4		12				10	14														26
1	13		4	5	2		11	9[2]	12	7				10[1]	3					8	6															27
1	2		4	5	8		10[3]	6[2]	11	7				13	3[1]	14			9			12														28
1	2			5	8				10[2]	7				11					9	6[1]	4	3	12	13												29
1	12	2		5	7	14				13				3[1]	10				9	6[3]	4	8	11[12]													30
1	13			5	14		6[1]	12	7	11				2[▪]					9[2]	8	3	4	10[3]													31
1	2[2]			5	14	13			7	10[3]	8[1]			9					6	4	3	11	12													32
1	2			5	10	12	13		7	6[3]	14			9					3	4	11[1]	8[2]														33
1	5	2	3		8	11[1]	12		7	10				9					6	4																34
1	5	2		4	7	11[2]	12[▪]		8	10[1]				9	6[3]	3						13	14													35
1	8			5	2	10[1]			7	14	12	13		9		3	4		6[2]	11[3]																	36
	2			5		12		11[1]		7				10		9	6	4	3				1	8													37
	2			5	8	13	12	11[3]		7				10[2]		9	6[1]	4	3				1	14													38
	2			5	7	13	12	10[2]		8[1]	14			11		9	6[3]	4	3				1														39
	2			5	6	13	12	11[2]		8				9		10	7[1]	4	3				1														40
	2			5	6		12	11		7				9		10	8[1]	4	3				1														41
	2			5	8			11		7				10		9	6	3	4				1														42
	2			5	8	13	12	11		7				10[1]		9[2]	6	4	3				1														43
	2			5	7	14	12	11[12]		8				10[1]		9	6[3]	4	3				1	13													44
	5			2	12	6	11[3]	13	14	10[3]				8		13		4	3			7[1]	1	9													45
	2			5	6	14	12	11[3]		8				9[2]		10	7[1]	4[▪]	3				1	13													46

The Budweiser FA Cup

First Round	Wolverhampton W	(h)	1-1
Replay	Wolverhampton W	(a)	2-1
Second Round	Mansfield T	(h)	1-1
Replay	Mansfield T	(a)	4-1
Third Round	Liverpool	(a)	0-2

Capital One Cup

First Round	Derby Co	(h)	0-1

Johnstone's Paint Trophy

First Round	Shrewsbury T	(a)	4-1
Second Round	Preston NE	(a)	2-0
Northern Quarter-Finals	Notts Co	(h)	5-1
Northern Semi-Finals	Chesterfield	(h)	1-1
(aet; lost 5-6 on penalties)			

OXFORD UNITED

FOUNDATION

There had been an Oxford United club around the time of World War I but only in the Oxfordshire Thursday League and there is no connection with the modern club which began as Headington in 1893, adding 'United' a year later. Playing first on Quarry Fields and subsequently Wootten's Fields, they owe much to a Dr Hitchings for their early development.

The Kassam Stadium, Grenoble Road, Oxford OX4 4XP.

Telephone: (01865) 337 500.

Fax: (01865) 337 501.

Ticket Office: (01865) 337 533.

Website: www.oufc.co.uk

Email: admin@oufc.co.uk

Ground Capacity: 12,205.

Record Attendance: 22,730 v Preston NE, FA Cup 6th rd, 29 February 1964 (at Manor Ground); 12,243 v Leyton Orient, FL 2, 6 May 2006 (at The Kassam Stadium).

Pitch Measurements: 105m × 65m (115yd × 71yd)

Executive Chairman: Ian Lenagan.

Head Coach: Michael Appleton.

Assistant Head Coach: Mickey Lewis.

Physio: Andy Lord.

Colours: Yellow shirts, blue shorts, blue socks.

Year Formed: 1893.

Turned Professional: 1949.

Previous Names: 1893, Headington; 1894, Headington United; 1960, Oxford United.

Club Nickname: 'The U's'.

Grounds: 1893, Headington Quarry; 1894, Wootten's Fields; 1898, Sandy Lane Ground; 1902, Britannia Field; 1909, Sandy Lane; 1910, Quarry Recreation Ground; 1914, Sandy Lane; 1922, The Paddock Manor Road; 1925, Manor Ground; 2001, The Kassam Stadium.

First Football League Game: 18 August 1962, Division 4, v Barrow (a) L 2–3 – Medlock; Beavon, Quartermain; Ron Atkinson, Kyle, Jones; Knight, Graham Atkinson (1), Houghton (1), Cornwell, Colfar.

Record League Victory: 7–0 v Barrow, Division 4, 19 December 1964 – Fearnley; Beavon, Quartermain; Ron Atkinson (1), Kyle, Jones; Morris, Booth (3), Willey (1), Graham Atkinson (1), Harrington (1).

Record Cup Victory: 9–1 v Dorchester T, FA Cup 1st rd, 11 November 1995 – Whitehead; Wood (2), Mike Ford (1), Smith, Elliott, Gilchrist, Rush (1), Massey (Murphy), Moody (3), Bobby Ford (1), Angel (Beauchamp (1)).

HONOURS

Football League – Division 1:
Best season: 12th, 1997–98;
Division 2: *Champions* 1984–85;
Runners-up 1995–96;
Division 3: *Champions* 1967–68, 1983–84.

FA Cup: Best season: 6th rd, 1964 (shared record for 4th Division club).

Football League Cup: *Winners* 1986.

sky SPORTS FACT FILE

Dave Sloan was the first Oxford United player to win full international honours. Signed from Scunthorpe United in February 1968 he appeared for Northern Ireland against Israel in September of the same year. He added a second cap against Spain in November 1970.

Record Defeat: 0–7 v Sunderland, Division 1, 19 September 1998.

Most League Points (2 for a win): 61, Division 4, 1964–65.

Most League Points (3 for a win): 95, Division 3, 1983–84.

Most League Goals: 91, Division 3, 1983–84.

Highest League Scorer in Season: John Aldridge, 30, Division 2, 1984–85.

Most League Goals in Total Aggregate: Graham Atkinson, 77, 1962–73.

Most League Goals in One Match: 4, Tony Jones v Newport Co, Division 4, 22 September 1962; 4, Arthur Longbottom v Darlington, Division 4, 26 October 1963; 4, Richard Hill v Walsall, Division 2, 26 December 1988; 4, John Durnin v Luton T, 14 November 1992; 4, Tom Craddock v Accrington S, FL 2, 20 October 2011.

Most Capped Player: Jim Magilton, 18 (52), Northern Ireland.

Most League Appearances: John Shuker, 478, 1962–77.

Youngest League Player: Jason Seacole, 16 years 149 days v Mansfield T, 7 September 1976.

Record Transfer Fee Received: £1,600,000 from Leicester C for Matt Elliott, January 1997.

Record Transfer Fee Paid: £475,000 to Aberdeen for Dean Windass, August 1998.

Football League Record: 1962 Elected to Division 4; 1965–68 Division 3; 1968–76 Division 2; 1976–84 Division 3; 1984–85 Division 2; 1985–88 Division 1; 1988–92 Division 2; 1992–94 Division 1; 1994–96 Division 2; 1996–99 Division 1; 1999–2001 Division 2; 2001–04 Division 3; 2004–06 FL 2; 2006–10 Conference; 2010– FL 2.

MANAGERS

Harry Thompson 1949–58
(Player-Manager) 1949-51
Arthur Turner 1959–69
(continued as General Manager to 1972)
Ron Saunders 1969
Gerry Summers 1969–75
Mick Brown 1975–79
Bill Asprey 1979–80
Ian Greaves 1980–82
Jim Smith 1982–85
Maurice Evans 1985–88
Mark Lawrenson 1988
Brian Horton 1988–93
Denis Smith 1993–97
Malcolm Crosby 1997–98
Malcolm Shotton 1998–99
Micky Lewis 1999–2000
Denis Smith 2000
David Kemp 2000–01
Mark Wright 2001
Ian Atkins 2001–04
Graham Rix 2004
Ramon Diaz 2004–05
Brian Talbot 2005–06
Darren Patterson 2006
Jim Smith 2006–07
Darren Patterson 2007–08
Chris Wilder 2008–14
Gary Waddock March 2014–

LATEST SEQUENCES

Longest Sequence of League Wins: 6, 13.4.2013 – 17.8.2013.

Longest Sequence of League Defeats: 7, 4.5.1991 – 7.9.1991.

Longest Sequence of League Draws: 5, 7.10.1978 – 28.10.1978.

Longest Sequence of Unbeaten League Matches: 20, 17.3.1984 – 29.9.1984.

Longest Sequence Without a League Win: 27, 14.11.1987 – 27.8.1988.

Successive Scoring Runs: 17 from 10.9.1983.

Successive Non-scoring Runs: 6 from 26.3.1988.

TEN YEAR LEAGUE RECORD

		P	W	D	L	F	A	Pts	Pos
2004-05	FL 2	46	16	11	19	50	63	59	15
2005-06	FL 2	46	11	16	19	43	57	49	23
2006-07	Conf	46	22	15	9	66	33	81	2
2007-08	Conf P	46	20	11	15	56	48	71	9
2008-09	Conf P	46	24	10	12	72	51	77*	7
2009-10	Conf P	44	25	11	8	64	31	86	3
2010-11	FL 2	46	17	12	17	58	60	63	12
2011-12	FL 2	46	17	17	12	59	48	68	9
2012-13	FL 2	46	19	8	19	60	61	65	9
2013-14	FL 2	46	16	14	16	53	50	62	8

*5 pts deducted.

DID YOU KNOW ?

Oxford United were elected to the Football League in 1962, their 10th attempt to gain a place. They first applied in 1952 as Headington United and their first five applications received a grand total of two votes, both gained in 1955.

OXFORD UNITED – FOOTBALL LEAGUE TWO 2013–14 LEAGUE RECORD

Match No.	Date	Venue	Opponents	Result	H/T Score	Lg Pos.	Goalscorers	Atten- dance
1	Aug 3	A	Portsmouth	W 4-1	2-1	1	Smalley 2 [34, 72], Potter 2 [38, 64]	18,181
2	10	H	Bury	W 2-1	1-0	1	Rose [34], Mullins [82]	5774
3	17	A	Torquay U	W 3-1	0-0	1	Smalley [49], Constable [63], Hall [77]	3176
4	24	H	Wycombe W	D 2-2	0-1	1	Rose [51], Mullins [90]	7100
5	31	H	Rochdale	D 1-1	1-0	2	Constable [24]	5260
6	Sept 7	A	Burton Alb	W 2-0	0-0	2	Potter [49], Rose [85]	3416
7	14	A	Cheltenham T	D 2-2	1-1	2	Kitson [34], Mullins [57]	3906
8	21	H	Chesterfield	L 0-1	0-1	4		7187
9	28	A	Hartlepool U	W 3-1	1-0	2	Williams [5], Smalley [67], Hall (pen) [90]	3799
10	Oct 5	H	Southend U	L 0-2	0-2	4		5578
11	12	H	Northampton T	W 2-0	2-0	3	Constable [44], Rose (pen) [45]	6177
12	19	A	Accrington S	D 0-0	0-0	4		1476
13	22	A	Exeter C	D 0-0	0-0	4		5083
14	26	A	AFC Wimbledon	W 2-0	1-0	1	Constable [6], Smalley (pen) [82]	4685
15	Nov 2	H	Bristol R	L 0-1	0-0	2		6374
16	16	A	Mansfield T	W 3-1	2-1	1	Rigg [12], Constable [45], Williams [66]	3831
17	23	H	Morecambe	W 3-0	3-0	1	Constable [16], Rigg [25], Williams [31]	4871
18	26	H	Newport Co	D 0-0	0-0	1		5042
19	30	A	Fleetwood T	D 1-1	0-1	1	Kitson [89]	2739
20	Dec 14	H	Dagenham & R	W 2-1	1-1	1	Constable [8], Kitson [90]	4901
21	21	A	York C	D 0-0	0-0	2		3526
22	26	H	Plymouth Arg	L 2-3	0-0	2	Hall [66], Trotman (og) [88]	10,049
23	29	H	Scunthorpe U	L 0-2	0-1	5		6009
24	Jan 11	H	Portsmouth	D 0-0	0-0	7		8443
25	18	A	Wycombe W	W 1-0	0-0	7	Wroe [87]	5751
26	25	H	Torquay U	W 1-0	1-0	6	Smalley [6]	4744
27	28	A	Exeter C	D 0-0	0-0	5		2798
28	Feb 1	H	AFC Wimbledon	W 2-1	1-0	3	Newey [39], Connolly [56]	5748
29	4	A	Bury	D 1-1	0-0	3	Ruffels [58]	2303
30	8	A	Bristol R	D 1-1	1-0	3	Constable [10]	6493
31	15	H	Mansfield T	W 3-0	1-0	3	Connolly [27], Wroe [53], Smalley [69]	5108
32	18	A	Newport Co	L 2-3	1-1	3	Constable [14], Potter [88]	3757
33	22	A	Morecambe	D 1-1	1-0	4	Connolly [13]	1614
34	Mar 1	A	Rochdale	L 0-3	0-1	5		3429
35	8	H	Burton Alb	L 1-2	0-2	6	Williams [52]	5413
36	11	H	Cheltenham T	D 1-1	0-0	6	Williams [78]	4606
37	15	A	Chesterfield	L 0-3	0-2	6		6246
38	21	H	Hartlepool U	W 1-0	0-0	6	Connolly [78]	4954
39	24	A	Southend U	L 0-3	0-2	6		6078
40	29	A	Dagenham & R	L 0-1	0-0	7		1893
41	Apr 5	H	Fleetwood T	L 0-2	0-1	8		5679
42	12	A	Plymouth Arg	W 2-0	1-0	7	Kitson [33], Constable [63]	8161
43	18	H	York C	L 0-1	0-0	8		7118
44	21	A	Scunthorpe U	L 0-1	0-1	8		5241
45	26	H	Accrington S	L 1-2	0-1	8	Williams [67]	5022
46	May 3	A	Northampton T	L 1-3	1-2	8	Williams [7]	7529

Final League Position: 8

GOALSCORERS

League (53): Constable 10, Smalley 7 (1 pen), Williams 7, Connolly 4, Kitson 4, Potter 4, Rose 4 (1 pen), Hall 3 (1 pen), Mullins 3, Rigg 2, Wroe 2, Newey 1, Ruffels 1, own goal 1.
The Budweiser FA Cup (7): Smalley 2 (1 pen), Constable 1, Davies 1, Mullins 1, Rose 1, Williams 1.
Capital One Cup (0).
Johnstone's Paint Trophy (1): Constable 1.

Clarke R 46	Hunt D 46	Newey T 40	Rose D 38 + 2	Wright J 31	Mullins J 35	Potter A 16 + 8	Whing A 17 + 1	Kitson D 27 + 5	Smalley D 23 + 9	Rigg S 20 + 8	Constable J 32 + 12	Hall A 15 + 4	Davies S 7 + 15	Ruffels J 21 + 8	Williams R 27 + 9	Marsh T — +5	Raynes M 25 + 2	O'Dowda C 4 + 6	Wroe N 16 + 2	Bevans M 9 + 1	Connolly D 8 + 8	Long S 3	Match No.
1	2	3	4	5	6	7	8	9²	10¹	11²	12	13	14										1
1	2	5	8	4	6	9	3	10¹	7³	11²	12	13	14										2
1	2	5	8	4	3	10²	7	11	9¹	13	12	6³	14										3
1	2	5	8	4	3	10	7	12	11	9²	6¹	13											4
1	2	5	8	4	3	6	7	10¹	11	9	12												5
1	2	5	8	4	3	6³	7	11²	12	10¹	9	13	14										6
1	2	5	8	3	10²	7	11	12	9	6¹	13						4						7
1	2	5	8³	4	10	7¹	11	6	12	9¹	13	14					3²						8
1	2	5	8	4	10	11³	9¹	12	7	14	13	6¹					3						9
1	2	5	7	3	6	11	10¹	9²	12	8¹	13						4	14					10
1	2	5	8	4	7	6	9	10¹	11	12							3						11
1	2	5	8	7	4	3¹	6	10	11	9	12												12
1	2	5	8	4	7	11■	9	10²	12	6¹	13						3						13
1	5	2	8	3	7	13	9¹	11	10¹	12	14	6²					4						14
1	2²	7	5	4	12²	8	11	13	9	10	14	6¹					3						15
1	2	5	8	4	7¹	10	11²	9³	13	12	14	6					3						16
1	2	5	8	3	10²	9¹	11	7	13	6²	14						4	12					17
1	2	5	7	4	10	11	8	9¹	6								3	12					18
1	2	5	6	4	10	11	8	7	9								3						19
1	2	5	8	4	3	10	13	12	11³	7	9¹	6²					14						20
1	2	5	8	4	3	10	13	12	11	7	9¹	6²											21
1	2	5	7	4	3	10	12	9¹	11	8	6												22
1	2	5	8²	4	3	10	9¹	11	7	14	13³	6						12					23
1	2	5	8	3	7	10¹	11	12	9								4		6				24
1	2	5	8	3	7	12	9³	10	13	14	11²						4¹		6				25
1	2	5	8	4²	3	11	12	10	9¹	6							13		7				26
1	2	5	7	4	9	11²	10	13	8								3¹		6		12		27
1	2	5	8	4	13	10	6¹	11²	9										7		3	12	28
1	3	5	7	4	12	9	10¹	8	11²								6		2		13		29
1	3	5	6	4	10	9	11¹	8											7		2	12	30
1	3	5	8	4	13	9	6	10²	12										7		2	11¹	31
1	6	4	8¹	3	12	9²	11	10	5	13									7		2³	14	32
1	5		7		4	9¹	12	11	2	13	6								8		10²	3	33
1	2	8	5	4	6	12	10	13	9¹								3		7		11²		34
1	2²	5	8	4	3	13	10¹	9³	14	11	6								7		12		35
1	2	5		4	7	12	10¹	9	8	6							3				11		36
1	2	5■	7	4	9	10³	11¹	13	12	8²	6						3■				14		37
1	5		4	12	7	13	9	11²	8	6¹							2				10	3	38
1	5	7²	4		6		11	9¹	10³	13	8	12					2			14		3	39
1	5		4	7	11¹	12	13	6	8	9³							3		14		2	10²	40
1	2	5		4	7¹	13	11²	14	9	8	6						3		12		10³		41
1	2	5		4	12	13	11²	10³	14	8	6						3		9¹		7		42
1	2	5	3		12		11	10		7	6¹		4	9²	8				13				43
1	2	5	14	4		6	11		12		8¹	13		3	9²	7			10¹				44
1	2³	5	14	4		9¹		10		11		13	8	6	3	12	7²						45
1	4	5	8	3		10¹		11²			6	7	9■	13		12		2					46

The Budweiser FA Cup

First Round	Gateshead	(h)	2-2
Replay	Gateshead	(a)	1-0
Second Round	Wrexham	(a)	2-1
Third Round	Charlton Ath	(a)	2-2
Replay	Charlton Ath	(h)	0-3

Capital One Cup

First Round	Charlton Ath	(a)	0-4

Johnstone's Paint Trophy

Second Round	Portsmouth	(h)	1-2

PETERBOROUGH UNITED

FOUNDATION

The old Peterborough & Fletton club, founded in 1923, was suspended by the FA during season 1932–33 and disbanded. Local enthusiasts determined to carry on and in 1934 a new professional club, Peterborough United, was formed and entered the Midland League the following year. Peterborough's first success came in 1939–40, but from 1955–56 to 1959–60 they won five successive titles. During the 1958–59 season they were undefeated in the Midland League. They reached the third round of the FA Cup, won the Northamptonshire Senior Cup, the Maunsell Cup and were runners-up in the East Anglian Cup.

London Road Stadium, London Road, Peterborough PE2 8AL.

Telephone: (01733) 563 947. *Fax:* (01733) 344 140.

Ticket Office: (0844) 847 1934.

Website: www.theposh.com

Email: info@theposh.com

Ground Capacity: 14,989 (11,494 for 2013–14 due to redevelopment).

Record Attendance: 30,096 v Swansea T, FA Cup 5th rd, 20 February 1965.

Pitch Measurements: 102.5m × 64m (112yd × 70yd)

Chairman: Darragh MacAnthony.

Chief Executive: Bob Symns.

Manager: Darren Ferguson.

Assistant Manager: Kevin Russell.

Head of Sports Science and Sports Medicine: Chris Burton.

Colours: Blue shirts with white trim, blue shorts, white socks.

Year Formed: 1934.

Turned Professional: 1934.

Club Nickname: 'The Posh'.

Ground: 1934, London Road Stadium.

First Football League Game: 20 August 1960, Division 4, v Wrexham (h) W 3–0 – Walls; Stafford, Walker; Rayner, Rigby, Norris; Hails, Emery (1), Bly (1), Smith, McNamee (1).

Record League Victory: 9–1 v Barnet (a) Division 3, 5 September 1998 – Griemink; Hooper (1), Drury (Farell), Gill, Bodley, Edwards, Davies, Payne, Grazioli (5), Quinn (2) (Rowe), Houghton (Etherington) (1).

Record Cup Victory: 9–1 v Rushden T, FA Cup 1st qual rd, 6 October 1945 – Hilliard; Bryan, Parrott, Warner, Hobbs, Woods, Polhill (1), Fairchild, Laxton (6), Tasker (1), Rodgers (1); 9–1 v Kingstonian, FA Cup 1st rd, 25 November 1992. Match ordered to be replayed by FA. Peterborough won replay

HONOURS

Football League – Division 1:
Best season: 10th, 1992–93;
Division 2: 1991–92 (play-offs);
FL 1: *Runners-up* 2008–09;
FL 2: *Runners-up* 2007–08;
Division 4: *Champions* 1960–61, 1973–74.

FA Cup: Best season: 6th rd, 1965.

Football League Cup: Semi-final 1966.

Johnstone's Paint Trophy: *Winners* 2014.

sky SPORTS FACT FILE

After being elected to the Football League in 1960, Peterborough United did not meet with defeat to a non-league side in the FA Cup until December 1970 when they went down 2-1 to Wigan Athletic (then of the Northern Premier League) in a second round tie. The winning goal was a dramatic last-minute penalty in front of a crowd of 17,300.

1–0.

Record Defeat: 1–8 v Northampton T, FA Cup 2nd rd (2nd replay), 18 December 1946.

Most League Points (2 for a win): 66, Division 4, 1960–61.

Most League Points (3 for a win): 92, FL 2, 2007–08.

Most League Goals: 134, Division 4, 1960–61.

Highest League Scorer in Season: Terry Bly, 52, Division 4, 1960–61.

Most League Goals in Total Aggregate: Jim Hall, 122, 1967–75.

Most League Goals in One Match: 5, Guiliano Grazioli v Barnet, Division 3, 5 September 1998.

Most Capped Player: Craig Morgan, 19 (23), Wales.

Most League Appearances: Tommy Robson, 482, 1968–81.

Youngest League Player: Matthew Etherington, 15 years 262 days v Brentford, 3 May 1997.

Record Transfer Fee Received: £4,500,000 from Crystal Palace for Dwight Gayle, July 2013.

Record Transfer Fee Paid: £1,250,000 to Watford fro Britt Assombalonga, July 2013.

Football League Record: 1960 Elected to Division 4; 1961–68 Division 3, when they were demoted for financial irregularities; 1968–74 Division 4; 1974–79 Division 3; 1979–91 Division 4; 1991–92 Division 3; 1992–94 Division 1; 1994–97 Division 2; 1997–2000 Division 3; 2000–04 Division 2; 2004–05 FL 1; 2005–08 FL 2; 2008–09 FL 1; 2009–10 FL C; 2010–11 FL 1; 2011–13 FL C; 2013– FL 1.

LATEST SEQUENCES

Longest Sequence of League Wins: 9, 1.2.1992 – 14.3.1992.

Longest Sequence of League Defeats: 8, 16.12.2006 – 27.1.2007.

Longest Sequence of League Draws: 8, 18.12.1971 – 12.2.1972.

Longest Sequence of Unbeaten League Matches: 17, 15.1.2008 – 5.4.2008.

Longest Sequence Without a League Win: 17, 23.9.1978 – 30.12.1978.

Successive Scoring Runs: 33 from 20.9.1960.

Successive Non-scoring Runs: 6 from 13.8.2002.

MANAGERS

Jock Porter 1934–36
Fred Taylor 1936–37
Vic Poulter 1937–38
Sam Haden 1938–48
Jack Blood 1948–50
Bob Gurney 1950–52
Jack Fairbrother 1952–54
George Swindin 1954–58
Jimmy Hagan 1958–62
Jack Fairbrother 1962–64
Gordon Clark 1964–67
Norman Rigby 1967–69
Jim Iley 1969–72
Noel Cantwell 1972–77
John Barnwell 1977–78
Billy Hails 1978–79
Peter Morris 1979–82
Martin Wilkinson 1982–83
John Wile 1983–86
Noel Cantwell 1986–88 *(continued as General Manager)*
Mick Jones 1988–89
Mark Lawrenson 1989–90
Dave Booth 1990–91
Chris Turner 1991–92
Lil Fuccillo 1992–93
Chris Turner 1993–94
John Still 1994–95
Mick Halsall 1995–96
Barry Fry 1996–2005
Mark Wright 2005–06
Steve Bleasdale 2006
Keith Alexander 2006–07
Darren Ferguson 2007–09
Mark Cooper 2009–10
Jim Gannon 2010
Gary Johnson 2010–11
Darren Ferguson January 2011–

TEN YEAR LEAGUE RECORD

		P	W	D	L	F	A	Pts	Pos
2004-05	FL 1	46	9	12	25	49	73	39	23
2005-06	FL 2	46	17	11	18	57	49	62	9
2006-07	FL 2	46	18	11	17	70	61	65	10
2007-08	FL 2	46	28	8	10	84	43	92	2
2008-09	FL 1	46	26	11	9	78	54	89	2
2009-10	FL C	46	8	10	28	46	80	34	24
2010-11	FL 1	46	23	10	13	106	75	79	4
2011-12	FL C	46	13	11	22	67	77	50	18
2012-13	FL C	46	15	9	22	66	75	54	22
2013-14	FL 1	46	23	5	18	72	58	74	6

DID YOU KNOW

Tony Philliskirk scored 5 goals for Peterborough United in their 9-1 FA Cup replay win over Kingstonian in November 1992 only for the match to be declared void and expunged from the records due to missile throwing from the crowd. The replayed tie took place behind closed doors with Posh winning again, but this time only 1-0.

PETERBOROUGH UNITED – FOOTBALL LEAGUE ONE 2013–14 LEAGUE RECORD

Match No.	Date	Venue	Opponents	Result	H/T Score	Lg Pos.	Goalscorers	Attendance
1	Aug 3	H	Swindon T	W	1-0	1-0	6	Assombalonga 9	7178
2	10	A	Notts Co	W	4-2	1-1	2	Rowe 30, Barnett 54, McCann (pen) 58, Assombalonga 71	6582
3	17	H	Oldham Ath	W	2-1	1-0	2	Assombalonga 34, Tomlin (pen) 84	6184
4	24	A	Tranmere R	W	5-0	3-0	2	Rowe 14, Barnett 34, McCann (pen) 38, Assombalonga 59, Little 68	4592
5	31	H	Crawley T	L	0-2	0-1	3		6761
6	Sept 7	A	Crewe Alex	D	2-2	1-2	3	Barnett 45, Bostwick 90	4509
7	14	A	Bristol C	W	3-0	1-0	2	Barnett 24, Assombalonga 2 51, 88	11,134
8	21	H	Milton Keynes D	W	2-1	2-0	2	Tomlin (pen) 12, Assombalonga 34	8149
9	28	A	Rotherham U	W	1-0	0-0	2	McCann (pen) 51	9717
10	Oct 5	H	Preston NE	W	2-0	2-0	2	Barnett 9, McCann 29	7020
11	12	A	Port Vale	W	1-0	0-0	2	Barnett 86	6311
12	19	H	Shrewsbury T	W	1-0	0-0	2	Mendez-Laing 64	6956
13	22	H	Sheffield U	D	0-0	0-0	2		6435
14	26	A	Colchester U	L	0-1	0-0	3		4149
15	Nov 2	H	Leyton Orient	L	1-3	1-1	3	Rowe 26	10,026
16	18	A	Walsall	L	0-2	0-1	3		4597
17	23	H	Stevenage	L	0-1	0-1	3		5707
18	26	A	Brentford	L	2-3	0-1	5	Payne 59, Assombalonga 60	6014
19	30	H	Wolverhampton W	W	1-0	0-0	5	Bostwick 79	8170
20	Dec 14	A	Gillingham	D	2-2	1-0	5	Assombalonga 2 12, 90	6949
21	21	H	Bradford C	W	2-1	2-0	4	Ntlhe 18, Assombalonga 24	6597
22	26	H	Coventry C	L	2-4	2-1	5	Jeffers 21, Tomlin 45	4905
23	29	A	Carlisle U	L	1-2	0-0	5	Tomlin 61	3904
24	Jan 1	H	Brentford	L	1-3	1-2	5	Payne 33	6343
25	11	A	Swindon T	L	1-2	0-1	6	Knight-Percival 78	7794
26	18	A	Tranmere R	W	3-0	1-0	6	Assombalonga 2 (1 pen) 5 (pl), 87, Ajose 75	5297
27	21	H	Notts Co	W	4-3	1-2	5	Ajose 3 30, 74, 85, Assombalonga 54	4511
28	25	A	Oldham Ath	L	4-5	3-0	7	Assombalonga 5, Rowe 25, Tomlin 45, Ajose 63	3571
29	Feb 8	H	Leyton Orient	W	2-1	0-0	6	Assombalonga 88, Rowe 90	6717
30	14	H	Walsall	D	0-0	0-0	6		4263
31	22	H	Stevenage	W	1-0	0-0	6	Ajose 76	4262
32	Mar 1	A	Crawley T	L	0-1	0-0	6		3663
33	4	A	Sheffield U	L	0-2	0-0	6		16,051
34	8	H	Crewe Alex	W	4-2	2-1	6	Assombalonga (pen) 15, Ajose 41, Swanson 60, Washington 88	5109
35	11	A	Bristol C	L	1-2	1-2	6	Bostwick 44	4352
36	15	A	Milton Keynes D	W	2-0	0-0	6	Assombalonga 2 (1 pen) 58, 60 (pl)	9590
37	22	H	Rotherham U	L	0-1	0-1	6		6625
38	25	A	Preston NE	L	1-3	1-1	6	Swanson 18	8206
39	Apr 2	H	Colchester U	W	2-0	1-0	6	Rowe 26, Assombalonga 65	4434
40	5	A	Wolverhampton W	L	0-2	0-0	6		23,204
41	8	H	Gillingham	W	2-0	1-0	6	Assombalonga 42, Rowe 58	6543
42	12	H	Coventry C	W	1-0	1-0	6	Ntlhe 6	6617
43	18	H	Bradford C	L	0-1	0-1	6		13,820
44	21	H	Carlisle U	W	4-1	1-0	6	Washington 14, Assombalonga 2 (2 pens) 55, 73, Bostwick 90	5921
45	26	A	Shrewsbury T	W	4-2	3-2	6	Washington 2 13, 21, Isgrove 28, McQuoid 90	5619
46	May 3	H	Port Vale	D	0-0	0-0	6		6621

Final League Position: 6

GOALSCORERS

League (72): Assombalonga 23 (5 pens), Ajose 7, Rowe 7, Barnett 6, Tomlin 5 (2 pens), Bostwick 4, McCann 4 (3 pens), Washington 4, Ntlhe 2, Payne 2, Swanson 2, Isgrove 1, Jeffers 1, Knight-Percival 1, Little 1, McQuoid 1, Mendez-Laing 1.
The Budweiser FA Cup (9): Assombalonga 5 (1 pen), Jeffers 2, Mendez-Laing 1, Rowe 1.
Capital One Cup (11): Tomlin 5 (2 pens), Assombalonga 1, Barnett 1, Payne 1, Rowe 1, Swanson 1, Zakuani 1.
Johnstone's Paint Trophy (12): Assombalonga 3 (1 pen), McCann 2 (1 pen), Brisley 1, McQuoid 1, Mendez-Laing 1, Ntlhe 1, Vassell 1, own goals 2.
League One Play-Offs (2): Assombalonga 1, Washington 1.

Olejnik R 42	Alcock C 24+4	Bostwick M 40+2	McCann G 26+9	Zakuani G 14+1	Nthe K 22+5	Kearns D 5+6	Tomlin L 19	Barnett T 16+5	Assombalonga B 41+2	Rowe T 33+1	Payne J 29+3	Swanson D 25+10	Gordon J —+1	Little M 34+4	Mendez-Laing N 3+13	Knight-Percival N 12+3	Taylor P 6	Newell J 6+5	Jeffers S 3+5	Brisley S 20+2	Ephraim H 6+2	Vassell K 3+3	Anderson J 9+4	Ferdinand K —+2	Ajose N 19+3	Day J 4	Washington C 12+5	Nugent B 11	McQuoid J 8+6	Baldwin J 10+1	Isgrove L 3+5	Santos R 1	Conlon T —+1	Match No.
1	2	3	4^1	5	6	7	8^2	9	10	11	12	13																						1
1	2	4	6	3	5	7^2		9	10	11^1	8		12	13																				2
1	2^2	4	6^1	3	5	7^3		9	10	11	8	12	14	13																				3
1	2	3	6	4	5^3	7^1		9^2	11	10	8			13	14																			4
1	2	3	6	4	5^1	7^3		9^2	11	10	8			12	13 14																			5
1	5	3	10			7	11	6			8	9^1		2	12	4																		6
1	5	3	13			12	9^2	11	10	8	6	7^1		2		4																		7
1	2	5	12		13		7	10^1	6	8	3	4^2		11^8			9^8																	8
1	2	4	8	3			12		10	11	5	6	7^1				9^2	13																9
1	2	4	6	3	13	12		11	10	5	7^1	8				9^2																		10
1	2^1	4	6	3		14		10	11	5	8	7^2		12	13	9^3																		11
1	3	9		4	12		11	10^1	5	7	6		2^1	13		8^3	14																	12
1	2	4	8^1	3	5		11	13	9	6	7^2			12	10																			13
1		4	6^1	3^1	5		9^8	12	11	7	8	13		2^4		10			14															14
1		3	8	4	5^2			11	10^3	9	7	6^1		2	12			13 14																15
1	4	2	7^3	14	9^1	12		13	10^2		8			5	11					3^4	6													16
1	3^3	9		4	12			6	13		5	7		2^1	10				14		11	8^2												17
1		4		3	5			10^2	6	11		7	12	2^1	13						9		8^1											18
1		3			5			9	10^2		6			2^1	14	12				4	8	11	7^3	13										19
1		4	7		5			8	14	10				2	12			9^2	11^1	3	13		6^3											20
1		3	7		5			8		10		13	14	2				9^1	11^2	4	12		6^3											21
1		3	7		5^1			9	14	10				2		13			11^2	4	8		6^3	12										22
1		3	12		5			8		11		7^3	6^1	2				9^2	14	4	10^8		13											23
1		4	13		5			10				7	6^1	2^8				9	12	3		14	8	11^3										24
1		4	12					9^8		11	8^1	6		2		5				3			7	10										25
1		3^3	13		12				9^3	10	9	7	6	2		4				5		4	8^1	11	1									26
	12		7^1		5^2	14	9^3		10		6	8		2		4				3			13	11	1									27
	4	3					10^8	11	8	7^1	6		2^1		5					3			9	1										28
1	3	7						11	9	6^1	8		5		4					2			10	12										29
1	2	7						10	9	8^2	6^1				5					3			11	12	4	13								30
1		7	8					10^3	9		6^1			2		5^2				3		14	11	12	4	13								31
1		8	7					11	9		6^3			2		5^1				3			10	12	4^2	14	13							32
1	5^1	12	8					13	7		6			2					14	4			10	11^3		9^2	3							33
1		7	8					10	5		6			2						3			9	11	4									34
1		7	8^1					11	5					2		13			12	3^2			6	10	4	9								35
1	5	7						11	8					2									10	9^1	4	6	3	12						36
1	2	4	12					10	9^2	13				5									8	6	7^3	11^1	3	14						37
1	2	8						10		7	6			4		9							11^2	13	5	12	3^1							38
1		3	8					11	5	7	9^2			2					4	14			13	10^9		6^1	12							39
1		4	7					11	5	8^1	6^2			2	14				3				13	10		9^3	12							40
1	12			5^1				11	9	7	6			2									8	10	4		3							41
1	14	13	5					10	8	6	7^1			2					9				11^2	4^3	12	3							42
13	12		5					10	9	8				2			7^2		4^8				6^3	1	11^1			3	14					43
1	2	7	9	5				10	12			13								14			11^3	4	6^1	3	8^2							44
1	4	14	5					11	8	7				2^1	12								6^1	10^3	13	3	9^2							45
1	3		5							13				8^3	5	12				11^1	6						9	4	10^2	2	14			46

The Budweiser FA Cup

First Round	Exeter C	(h)	2-0
Second Round	Tranmere R	(h)	5-0
Third Round	Kidderminster H	(a)	0-0
Replay	Kidderminster H	(h)	2-3

Capital One Cup

First Round	Colchester U	(a)	5-1
Second Round	Reading	(h)	6-0
Third Round	Sunderland	(a)	0-2

Johnstone's Paint Trophy

Second Round	Brentford	(h)	2-1
Southern Quarter-Finals	Dagenham & R	(h)	1-0
Southern Semi-Finals	Newport Co	(a)	3-0
Southern Final 1st leg	Swindon T	(h)	2-2
Southern Final 2nd leg	Swindon T	(a)	1-1

(Peterborough won 4-3 on penalties)

Final	Chesterfield	(Wembley)	3-1

League One Play-Offs

Semi-Finals 1st leg	Leyton Orient	(h)	1-1
Semi-Finals 2nd leg	Leyton Orient	(a)	1-2

PLYMOUTH ARGYLE

FOUNDATION

The club was formed in September 1886 as the Argyle Athletic Club by former public and private school pupils who wanted to continue playing the game. The meeting was held in a room above the Borough Arms (a coffee house), Bedford Street, Plymouth. It was common then to choose a local street/terrace as a club name and Argyle or Argyll was a fashionable name throughout the land due to Queen Victoria's great interest in Scotland.

Home Park, Plymouth, Devon PL2 3DQ.

Telephone: (01752) 562 561.

Fax: (01752) 606 167.

Ticket Office: (0845) 872 3335.

Website: www.pafc.co.uk

Email: argyle@pafc.co.uk

Ground Capacity: 16,388.

Record Attendance: 43,596 v Aston Villa, Division 2, 10 October 1936.

Pitch Measurements: 105m × 68.5m (115yd × 75yd)

Chairman: James Brent.

Chief Executive: Martyn Starnes.

Manager: John Sheridan.

First Team Coach: Sean McCarthy.

Physio: Paul Atkinson.

Colours: Dark green shirts with white trim, white shorts with green trim, white socks with green trim.

Year Formed: 1886.

Turned Professional: 1903.

Previous Name: 1886, Argyle Athletic Club; 1903, Plymouth Argyle.

Club Nickname: 'The Pilgrims'.

Ground: 1886, Home Park.

First Football League Game: 28 August 1920, Division 3, v Norwich C (h) D 1–1 – Craig; Russell, Atterbury; Logan, Dickinson, Forbes; Kirkpatrick, Jack, Bowler, Heeps (1), Dixon.

Record League Victory: 8–1 v Millwall, Division 2, 16 January 1932 – Harper; Roberts, Titmuss; Mackay, Pullan, Reed; Grozier, Bowden (2), Vidler (3), Leslie (1), Black (1), (1 og). 8–1 v Hartlepool U (a), Division 2, 7 May 1994 – Nicholls; Patterson (Naylor), Hill, Burrows, Comyn, McCall (1), Barlow, Castle (1), Landon (3), Marshall (1), Dalton (2).

Record Cup Victory: 6–0 v Corby T, FA Cup 3rd rd, 22 January 1966 – Leiper; Book, Baird; Williams, Nelson, Newman; Jones (1), Jackson (1), Bickle (3), Piper (1), Jennings.

HONOURS

Football League – Division 2: *Champions* 2003–04;
Division 3 (S): *Champions* 1929–30, 1951–52; *Runners-up* 1921–22, 1922–23, 1923–24, 1924–25, 1925–26, 1926–27 (record of six consecutive years);
Division 3: *Champions* 1958–59, 2001–02; *Runners-up* 1974–75, 1985–86.
FA Cup: Semi-final 1984.
Football League Cup: Semi-final 1965, 1974.

sky SPORTS FACT FILE

Plymouth Argyle toured South America in the summer of 1924. The team stayed for five weeks during which they played nine matches in Argentina and Uruguay, winning three, drawing three and losing three. The party left Southampton on 30 May and did not return until 11 August, less than three weeks before the start of the 1924–25 season.

Record Defeat: 0–9 v Stoke C, Division 2, 17 December 1960.

Most League Points (2 for a win): 68, Division 3 (S), 1929–30.

Most League Points (3 for a win): 102, Division 3, 2001–02.

Most League Goals: 107, Division 3 (S), 1925–26 and 1951–52.

Highest League Scorer in Season: Jack Cock, 32, Division 3 (S), 1926–27.

Most League Goals in Total Aggregate: Sammy Black, 180, 1924–38.

Most League Goals in One Match: 5, Wilf Carter v Charlton Ath, Division 2, 27 December 1960.

Most Capped Player: Moses Russell, 20 (23), Wales.

Most League Appearances: Kevin Hodges, 530, 1978–92.

Youngest League Player: Lee Phillips, 16 years 43 days v Gillingham, 29 October 1996.

Record Transfer Fee Received: £2,000,000 from Hull C for Peter Halmosi, July 2008.

Record Transfer Fee Paid: £500,000 to Cardiff C for Steve MacLean, January 2008.

Football League Record: 1920 Original Member of Division 3; 1921–30 Division 3 (S); 1930–50 Division 2; 1950–52 Division 3 (S); 1952–56 Division 2; 1956–58 Division 3 (S); 1958–59 Division 3; 1959–68 Division 2; 1968–75 Division 3; 1975–77 Division 2; 1977–86 Division 3; 1986–95 Division 2; 1995–96 Division 3; 1996–98 Division 2; 1998–2002 Division 3; 2002–04 Division 2; 2004–10 FL C; 2010–11 FL 1; 2011– FL 2.

LATEST SEQUENCES

Longest Sequence of League Wins: 9, 8.3.1986 – 12.4.1986.

Longest Sequence of League Defeats: 9, 12.10.1963 – 7.12.1963.

Longest Sequence of League Draws: 5, 26.2.2000 – 14.3.2000.

Longest Sequence of Unbeaten League Matches: 22, 20.4.1929 – 21.12.1929.

Longest Sequence Without a League Win: 13, 13.4.2009 – 27.9.2009.

Successive Scoring Runs: 39 from 15.4.1939.

Successive Non-scoring Runs: 5 from 21.11.2009.

MANAGERS

Frank Brettell 1903–05
Bob Jack 1905–06
Bill Fullerton 1906–07
Bob Jack 1910–38
Jack Tresadern 1938–47
Jimmy Rae 1948–55
Jack Rowley 1955–60
Neil Dougall 1961
Ellis Stuttard 1961–63
Andy Beattie 1963–64
Malcolm Allison 1964–65
Derek Ufton 1965–68
Billy Bingham 1968–70
Ellis Stuttard 1970–72
Tony Waiters 1972–77
Mike Kelly 1977–78
Malcolm Allison 1978–79
Bobby Saxton 1979–81
Bobby Moncur 1981–83
Johnny Hore 1983–84
Dave Smith 1984–88
Ken Brown 1988–90
David Kemp 1990–92
Peter Shilton 1992–95
Steve McCall 1995
Neil Warnock 1995–97
Mick Jones 1997–98
Kevin Hodges 1998–2000
Paul Sturrock 2000–04
Bobby Williamson 2004–05
Tony Pulis 2005–06
Ian Holloway 2006–07
Paul Sturrock 2007–09
Paul Mariner 2009–10
Peter Reid 2010–11
Carl Fletcher 2011–13
John Sheridan January 2013–

TEN YEAR LEAGUE RECORD

		P	W	D	L	F	A	Pts	Pos
2004-05	FL C	46	14	11	21	52	64	53	17
2005-06	FL C	46	13	17	16	39	46	56	14
2006-07	FL C	46	17	16	13	63	62	67	11
2007-08	FL C	46	17	13	16	60	50	64	10
2008-09	FL C	46	13	12	21	44	57	51	21
2009-10	FL C	46	11	8	27	43	68	41	23
2010-11	FL 1	46	15	7	24	51	74	42*	23
2011-12	FL 2	46	10	16	20	47	64	46	21
2012-13	FL 2	46	13	13	20	46	55	52	21
2013-14	FL 2	46	16	12	18	51	58	60	10

* 10 pts deducted.

DID YOU KNOW ?

Left half Billy Baker made over 200 first-team appearances for Plymouth Argyle between 1909 and 1915. He then enlisted in the 17th Middlesex Regiment (The Footballers' Battalion) and received the Distinguished Conduct Medal. He was killed in action on 22 October 1916.

PLYMOUTH ARGYLE – FOOTBALL LEAGUE TWO 2013–14 LEAGUE RECORD

Match No.	Date	Venue	Opponents	Result	H/T Score	Lg Pos.	Goalscorers	Atten- dance
1	Aug 3	A	Southend U	L 0-1	0-1	16		7055
2	10	H	Fleetwood T	L 0-2	0-2	23		7280
3	17	A	Cheltenham T	W 3-1	3-0	16	Morgan [18], Hourihane [27], Boco [38]	3450
4	24	H	Rochdale	W 1-0	1-0	9	Reid (pen) [25]	6978
5	31	A	Morecambe	L 1-2	1-1	15	Reid (pen) [27]	1800
6	Sept 7	H	Bristol R	W 1-0	0-0	12	Reid [82]	8631
7	14	H	Wycombe W	L 0-3	0-0	16		6702
8	21	A	Scunthorpe U	L 0-1	0-0	17		3298
9	28	H	Accrington S	D 0-0	0-0	15		6180
10	Oct 5	A	Exeter C	L 1-3	0-0	17	Young [69]	5700
11	12	H	Portsmouth	D 1-1	1-1	19	Hourihane [21]	8742
12	19	A	Hartlepool U	L 0-1	0-0	19		3929
13	22	H	Newport Co	D 0-0	0-0	19		5689
14	26	A	Mansfield T	W 1-0	0-0	18	Trotman [90]	3379
15	Nov 2	H	Northampton T	W 1-0	0-0	17	Alessandra [90]	6547
16	16	A	York C	D 1-1	0-0	18	Obadeyi [65]	3803
17	23	H	Dagenham & R	W 2-1	1-1	14	Reid [44], Young [77]	6184
18	26	A	Torquay U	D 1-1	1-1	14	Reid (pen) [9]	3866
19	30	H	Burton Alb	L 0-1	0-1	15		6294
20	Dec 14	A	Chesterfield	L 0-2	0-2	16		5486
21	21	H	Bury	W 2-1	1-0	16	Lavery [11], Reid [78]	6206
22	26	A	Oxford U	W 3-2	0-0	13	Lavery [46], Reid 2 (1 pen) [81 (p), 87]	10,049
23	29	A	AFC Wimbledon	D 1-1	0-0	14	Reid [88]	4763
24	Jan 1	H	Torquay U	W 2-0	0-0	12	Lavery [60], Alessandra [85]	10,126
25	11	A	Southend U	D 1-1	0-0	11	Blizzard [65]	7088
26	18	A	Rochdale	L 0-3	0-1	11		2839
27	25	H	Cheltenham T	D 1-1	0-0	12	Young [84]	6735
28	Feb 1	H	Mansfield T	D 1-1	0-0	12	Alessandra [90]	6248
29	8	A	Northampton T	W 2-0	2-0	10	Reid [5], Alessandra [39]	4845
30	15	H	York C	L 0-4	0-2	12		6502
31	22	A	Dagenham & R	W 2-1	2-1	10	Reid [5], Alessandra [33]	2027
32	25	A	Fleetwood T	W 4-0	1-0	8	Reid [22], Young [47], Blanchard [70], Hourihane [85]	2131
33	Mar 1	H	Morecambe	W 5-0	2-0	8	Berry [5], Alessandra 2 [40, 90], Nelson [77], Gurrieri [87]	6827
34	8	A	Bristol R	L 1-2	1-1	8	Trotman [45]	7799
35	11	A	Wycombe W	W 1-0	0-0	8	Hourihane [48]	3042
36	15	H	Scunthorpe U	L 0-2	0-0	9		8198
37	18	H	Chesterfield	W 2-1	1-0	7	Reid 2 [28, 58]	6012
38	22	A	Accrington S	D 1-1	0-0	8	Reid [32]	1559
39	25	H	Exeter C	L 1-2	1-0	9	Reid (pen) [45]	13,442
40	Apr 5	A	Burton Alb	L 0-1	0-1	9		2962
41	8	A	Newport Co	W 2-1	2-1	9	Harvey [21], Hourihane [30]	3381
42	12	H	Oxford U	L 0-2	0-1	9		8161
43	18	A	Bury	L 0-4	0-1	9		3401
44	21	H	AFC Wimbledon	L 1-2	1-1	9	Hourihane [7]	6618
45	26	H	Hartlepool U	D 1-1	1-0	9	Banton [30]	6617
46	May 3	A	Portsmouth	D 3-3	2-2	10	Reid [35], Hourihane 2 [41, 89]	18,026

Final League Position: 10

GOALSCORERS

League (51): Reid 17 (5 pens), Hourihane 8, Alessandra 7, Young 4, Lavery 3, Trotman 2, Banton 1, Berry 1, Blanchard 1, Blizzard 1, Boco 1, Gurrieri 1, Harvey 1, Morgan 1, Nelson 1, Obadeyi 1.
The Budweiser FA Cup (12): Reid 4 (1 pen), Alessandra 2, Gurrieri 2, Hourihane 1, Nelson 1, Purrington 1, own goal 1.
Capital One Cup (2): Alessandra 2.
Johnstone's Paint Trophy (4): Alessandra 1, Bencherif 1, Blackman 1, Boco 1.

McCormick L 27	Berry D 27 + 5	Blackman A 3 + 3	Hourihane C 45	Wotton P 12 + 3	Nelson C 43 + 1	Alessandra L 39 + 3	Blizzard D 21 + 5	Morgan M 11 + 10	Reid R 44 + 2	Boco R 22 + 5	Richards J — + 1	Harvey T 3 + 18	Young L 20 + 14	Cole J 19 + 1	Trotman N 41	Gurrieri A 19 + 13	Branston G 11 + 1	Blanchard M 34 + 2	Reckord J 11 + 1	Bencherif H 5 + 2	Hayes P 4 + 2	Obadeyi T 5 + 9	Lavery C 4 + 4	Purrington B 11 + 1	Thomas N 2 + 8	Banton J 11 + 2	Parsons M 10	Showunmi E 2 + 5	Match No.
1	2	3	4	5^1	6	7	8^3	9	10^2	11	12	13	14																1
	2	5	8		4	6	7^1	11	10^2	9^3		13	12	1	3	14													2
1		5	8		2	6^2	7^3	11	10^1	9		12	13		3	14	4												3
1	2	13	8		5	6	7^3	11	10^1	9^2			14		4	12	3												4
1	2^1		8		5	6	7	11	10^2	9^3		14			4	13	3	12											5
1	2		8		6			11	10	9			12					3	4	5	7^1								6
1	2	12	8			6^3		11	10	9		14			3	13		4		5	7^2								7
1	2		8	13	6			10^1	11	9		12			3			4		5	7^2								8
1		3	8		2	6^3		9	11^2	10		13	12			14		4		5	7^1								9
1		3	7		2	6^3		10	12	9		14	13					4		5		8^2	11^1						10
1	5		8		4	12			10	7^2		13	6		3			2	9	11^1									11
1	5^3	13	10		4	12			6^1	9		7			3	14		2	11^2		8								12
1		5	7		2	9			10	6^1		12	8^2		3	13		4		14	11^2								13
1	5		7		6	10^3			11	8^1		13			3	12	4	2	9^2		14								14
1	5		8		7	10			11^3	6^2		14	12		3	4^1	2	9	13										15
1	5		8		11				10	7^2			12		4	14	3^3	2	9^1			13							16
1	5		8		4	11^2	13		10^1				6		3	9		2					7	12					17
1	5^1		8		4	10	12		11	14		7^1			3	6^2		2					9^1	13					18
1			8		4	11			10	13		7			3	6		2	5^2				9^1	12					19
1	5^2		6		4	11	7^3		10	8^1		14			3	9		2	13					12					20
1	5				4	6	8		10^1	12		7			3	9		2				13		11^2					21
1			7		4	9	8		10^2			6			3	13		2					12	11^1	5				22
1	12		8		4	9^3	7		10						3	6^1		2					14	11^2	5	13			23
1			8		4	6	7		10^2			12			3	9		2					13	11^1	5				24
1			8		4	10	7		11						3	6		2					5	12	9^1				25
1			7		4	9^2	8		10^3	13			12		3	6^4		2					5	14	11^1				26
1			8		4	11	7^2		10	6^1	13	12			3			2					5^3	14	9				27
1^1			8		4	9	7^2		10			13	6	12	3			2					5^3	14	11				28
			7		4	9	8		10	6		12		1	3			2					5		11^1				29
	12		8		4	9	7		11	10^1				1	3			2					5	13	6^2				30
	2		9	8	4	10			13	11^2		7		1		12		3					14		6^1			5^3	31
	5		8	4	11^2			13	10^1	12		7		1	3			2					14				9		32
	5		8^3	6^1	4	11			13	10^2		12	7	1	3	14		2									9		33
	2		8	7	5	10^1			14	11^3		12	9^2	1	4			3					13				6		34
	2		7	13	9	10^1	8		11			6^2		1	4			3					12				5		35
	5		9		4	11	8^2	12	10^1			7		1	3	13		2^3					14				6		36
			8	7	4	11^1			13	10^2		6		1	3			5					12				9		37
			8		4		7	12	10	5^2				1	3	6		2					11^1		13		9		38
	12		8	7^2	4				13	10		6		1	3	5		2					11^1		14		9^2		39
	5^2		12	4					14	13	11			1	3^1	7		2					9					10	40
	14		6	5	4				13	9^1	10	11^2		1	3	8		2					7^3				12	41
	14		6	8^1	4	11	12		10			7^2		1	3	5		2					9^3				13	42
	2		7		4	10^1	8		11			12		1	3^2	6^1		5					13	9			14	43
			7	3^1	4	11		2	14	10		6		1				5^2	12						9^3	8	13	44
	5		8		4	12			13	9^3		14	7	1	3	6		2						11^1			10^2	45
	5		6	14	4	10			11			7^2	8	1	3^3			2					12	9^1		13		46

The Budweiser FA Cup

First Round	Lincoln C	(a)	0-0
Replay	Lincoln C	(h)	5-0
Second Round	Welling U	(h)	3-1
Third Round	Port Vale	(a)	2-2
Replay	Port Vale	(h)	2-3

Capital One Cup

First Round	Birmingham C	(a)	2-3
(aet)			

Johnstone's Paint Trophy

First Round	Cheltenham T	(a)	3-3
(aet; won 5-4 on penalties)			
Second Round	Swindon T	(a)	1-2

PORT VALE

FOUNDATION

Port Vale Football Club was formed in 1876 and took its name from the venue of the inaugural meeting at 'Port Vale House' situated in a suburb of Stoke-on-Trent. Upon moving to Burslem in 1884 the club changed its name to 'Burslem Port Vale' and after several seasons in the Midland League became founder members of the Football League Division Two in 1892. The prefix 'Burslem' was dropped from the name as a new ground several miles away was acquired.

Vale Park, Hamil Road, Burslem, Stoke-on-Trent, Staffordshire ST6 1AW.

Telephone: (0871) 221 1876.

Fax: (01782) 834 981.

Ticket Office: (0871) 222 1950.

Website: www.port-vale.co.uk

Email: enquiries@port-vale.co.uk

Ground Capacity: 19,148.

Record Attendance: 22,993 v Stoke C, Division 2, 6 March 1920 (at Recreation Ground); 49,768 v Aston Villa, FA Cup 5th rd, 20 February 1960 (at Vale Park).

Pitch Measurements: 104m × 69.5m (114yd × 76yd)

Chairman: Norman Smurthwaite.

Manager: Micky Adams.

Assistant Manager: Rob Page.

Physio: Andrew Foster.

Colours: White shirts with black trim, black shorts with white trim, white socks with black trim.

Year Formed: 1876.

Turned Professional: 1885.

Previous Names: 1876, Port Vale; 1884, Burslem Port Vale; 1909, Port Vale.

Club Nickname: 'Valiants'.

Grounds: 1876, Limekin Lane, Longport; 1881, Westport; 1884, Moorland Road, Burslem; 1886, Athletic Ground, Cobridge; 1913, Recreation Ground, Hanley; 1950, Vale Park.

First Football League Game: 3 September 1892, Division 2, v Small Heath (a) L 1–5 – Frail; Clutton, Elson; Farrington, McCrindle, Delves; Walker, Scarratt, Bliss (1), Jones. (Only 10 men).

Record League Victory: 9–1 v Chesterfield, Division 2, 24 September 1932 – Leckie; Shenton, Poyser; Sherlock, Round, Jones; McGrath, Mills, Littlewood (6), Kirkham (2), Morton (1).

Record Cup Victory: 7–1 v Irthlingborough, FA Cup 1st rd, 12 January 1907 – Matthews; Dunn, Hamilton; Eardley, Baddeley, Holyhead; Carter, Dodds (2), Beats, Mountford (2), Coxon (3).

Record Defeat: 0–10 v Sheffield U, Division 2, 10 December 1892. 0–10 v Notts Co, Division 2, 26 February 1895.

HONOURS

Football League – Division 2:
Runners-up 1993–94;
Division 3 (N): *Champions* 1929–30, 1953–54; *Runners-up* 1952–53;
Division 4: *Champions* 1958–59.

FA Cup: Semi-final 1954, when in Division 3.

Football League Cup: Best season: 4th rd, 2007.

Autoglass Trophy: *Winners* 1993.

Anglo-Italian Cup: *Runners-up* 1996.

LDV Vans Trophy: *Winners* 2001.

sky SPORTS FACT FILE

Jack Shelton joined Port Vale in 1911 and went on to make over 200 appearances, captaining the team. During the First World War he worked in a local colliery before being conscripted into the North Staffordshire Regiment in 1917. His death was reported in the press on 2 October 1918. He left a widow and two children.

Most League Points (2 for a win): 69, Division 3 (N), 1953–54.

Most League Points (3 for a win): 89, Division 2, 1992–93.

Most League Goals: 110, Division 4, 1958–59.

Highest League Scorer in Season: Wilf Kirkham 38, Division 2, 1926–27.

Most League Goals in Total Aggregate: Wilf Kirkham, 154, 1923–29, 1931–33.

Most League Goals in One Match: 6, Stewart Littlewood v Chesterfield, Division 2, 24 September 1922.

Most Capped Player: Chris Birchall, 22 (39), Trinidad & Tobago.

Most League Appearances: Roy Sproson, 761, 1950–72.

Youngest League Player: Malcolm McKenzie, 15 years 347 days v Newport Co, 12 April 1966.

Record Transfer Fee Received: £2,000,000 from Wimbledon for Gareth Ainsworth, October 1998.

Record Transfer Fee Paid: £500,000 to Lincoln C for Gareth Ainsworth, September 1997.

Football League Record: 1892 Original Member of Division 2. Failed re-election in 1896; Re-elected 1898; Resigned 1907; Returned in Oct, 1919, when they took over the fixtures of Leeds City; 1929–30 Division 3 (N); 1930–36 Division 2; 1936–38 Division 3 (N); 1938–52 Division 3 (S); 1952–54 Division 3 (N); 1954–57 Division 2; 1957–58 Division 3 (S); 1958–59 Division 4; 1959–65 Division 3; 1965–70 Division 4; 1970–78 Division 3; 1978–83 Division 4; 1983–84 Division 3; 1984–86 Division 4; 1986–89 Division 3; 1989–94 Division 2; 1994–2000 Division 1; 2000–04 Division 2; 2004–08 FL 1; 2008–13 FL 2; 2013– FL 1.

LATEST SEQUENCES

Longest Sequence of League Wins: 8, 8.4.1893 – 30.9.1893.

Longest Sequence of League Defeats: 9, 9.3.1957 – 20.4.1957.

Longest Sequence of League Draws: 6, 26.4.1981 – 12.9.1981.

Longest Sequence of Unbeaten League Matches: 19, 5.5.1969 – 8.11.1969.

Longest Sequence Without a League Win: 17, 7.12.1991 – 21.3.1992.

Successive Scoring Runs: 22 from 12.9.1992.

Successive Non-scoring Runs: 4 from 7.4.2009.

MANAGERS

Sam Gleaves 1896–1905
(Secretary-Manager)
Tom Clare 1905–11
A. S. Walker 1911–12
H. Myatt 1912–14
Tom Holford 1919–24
(continued as Trainer)
Joe Schofield 1924–30
Tom Morgan 1930–32
Tom Holford 1932–35
Warney Cresswell 1936–37
Tom Morgan 1937–38
Billy Frith 1945–46
Gordon Hodgson 1946–51
Ivor Powell 1951
Freddie Steele 1951–57
Norman Low 1957–62
Freddie Steele 1962–65
Jackie Mudie 1965–67
Sir Stanley Matthews
(General Manager) 1965–68
Gordon Lee 1968–74
Roy Sproson 1974–77
Colin Harper 1977
Bobby Smith 1977–78
Dennis Butler 1978–79
Alan Bloor 1979
John McGrath 1980–83
John Rudge 1983–99
Brian Horton 1999–2004
Martin Foyle 2004–07
Lee Sinnott 2007–08
Dean Glover 2008–09
Micky Adams 2009–10
Jim Gannon 2011
Micky Adams May 2011–

TEN YEAR LEAGUE RECORD

		P	W	D	L	F	A	Pts	Pos
2004-05	FL 1	46	17	5	24	49	59	56	18
2005-06	FL 1	46	16	12	18	49	54	60	13
2006-07	FL 1	46	18	6	22	64	65	60	12
2007-08	FL 1	46	9	11	26	47	81	38	23
2008-09	FL 2	46	13	9	24	44	66	48	18
2009-10	FL 2	46	17	17	12	61	50	68	10
2010-11	FL 2	46	17	14	15	54	49	65	11
2011-12	FL 2	46	20	9	17	68	60	59*	12
2012-13	FL 2	46	21	15	10	87	52	78	3
2013-14	FL 1	46	18	7	21	59	73	61	9

*10 pts deducted.

DID YOU KNOW ?

Port Vale appeared in the final of the Debenhams Cup in May 1977 as one of the two lower division clubs to progress furthest in the FA Cup that season. They played Chester over two legs, losing out 4-3 on aggregate. The competition was short lived, lasting just two seasons before disappearing from football's calendar.

PORT VALE – FOOTBALL LEAGUE ONE 2013–14 LEAGUE RECORD

Match No.	Date	Venue	Opponents	Result	H/T Score	Lg Pos.	Goalscorers	Attendance
1	Aug 3	H	Brentford	D 1-1	1-1	12	Loft [31]	7579
2	10	A	Colchester U	L 0-1	0-0	17		3201
3	17	H	Bradford C	W 2-1	1-0	12	Hughes [43], Loft [66]	6552
4	24	A	Oldham Ath	L 1-3	1-1	14	Myrie-Williams [31]	4788
5	31	H	Wolverhampton W	L 1-3	0-0	16	Pope [90]	12,601
6	Sept 7	A	Carlisle U	W 1-0	0-0	13	Pope [90]	3866
7	14	A	Leyton Orient	L 2-3	1-2	14	Dodds [21], Myrie-Williams [54]	4888
8	21	H	Coventry C	W 3-2	1-2	13	Pope [40], Loft [60], Birchall [83]	9218
9	28	A	Tranmere R	W 1-0	0-0	10	Lines [56]	5334
10	Oct 5	H	Bristol C	D 1-1	0-0	12	Hughes [90]	6275
11	12	A	Peterborough U	L 0-1	0-0	12		6311
12	19	A	Sheffield U	L 1-2	1-1	12	Yates [45]	18,545
13	22	A	Crawley T	W 3-0	2-0	12	Dodds [10], Loft [27], Williamson [57]	2748
14	26	H	Gillingham	W 2-1	0-1	9	Robertson [47], Pope [63]	5690
15	Nov 2	A	Swindon T	L 1-2	0-1	12	Pope [73], Hughes [80]	7637
16	16	H	Shrewsbury T	W 3-1	2-0	9	Robertson [23], Myrie-Williams [30], Hugill [90]	6547
17	23	A	Crewe Alex	W 2-1	1-1	9	Taylor [43], Myrie-Williams [83]	6820
18	26	H	Preston NE	L 0-2	0-1	10		5889
19	30	A	Walsall	W 2-0	1-0	8	Pope [20], Tomlin [66]	4909
20	Dec 14	H	Stevenage	D 2-2	1-2	10	Myrie-Williams (pen) [32], Pope [89]	4967
21	21	A	Milton Keynes D	L 0-3	0-3	10		7882
22	26	H	Notts Co	W 2-1	1-1	9	Myrie-Williams (pen) [24], Tomlin (pen) [79]	7028
23	29	H	Rotherham U	W 2-0	1-0	7	Dodds [8], Tomlin [68]	6738
24	Jan 1	A	Preston NE	L 2-3	0-1	8	Tomlin [69], Hugill [84]	10,653
25	11	A	Brentford	L 0-2	0-1	9		8327
26	18	H	Oldham Ath	W 1-0	0-0	8	Grimmer [53]	6002
27	Feb 1	A	Gillingham	L 2-3	0-1	9	Robertson [81], Hugill [87]	6356
28	8	H	Swindon T	L 2-3	2-0	10	Loft [20], Pope [42]	5306
29	11	H	Colchester U	W 2-0	1-0	9	Loft 2 [15, 53]	3734
30	15	A	Shrewsbury T	D 0-0	0-0	9		5992
31	18	A	Bradford C	L 0-1	0-0	10		12,106
32	22	H	Crewe Alex	L 1-3	0-1	10	Pope [76]	7812
33	Mar 1	A	Wolverhampton W	L 0-3	0-0	10		21,929
34	8	H	Carlisle U	W 2-1	0-1	10	Williamson [56], Pope [61]	5009
35	11	H	Leyton Orient	L 0-2	0-1	10		4235
36	16	A	Coventry C	D 2-2	1-0	11	Loft [1], Williamson [74]	1627
37	22	H	Tranmere R	W 3-2	1-0	10	Pope [3], Knott [47], Williamson [56]	5449
38	25	A	Bristol C	L 0-5	0-4	11		10,940
39	29	A	Stevenage	D 1-1	0-0	11	Pope [48]	2912
40	Apr 1	H	Crawley T	W 2-1	0-1	10	Knott [50], Loft [84]	3755
41	5	H	Walsall	W 1-0	0-0	9	Myrie-Williams (pen) [52]	5569
42	12	A	Notts Co	L 2-4	2-2	9	Thompson (og) [13], Tomlin [25]	5613
43	18	H	Milton Keynes D	W 1-0	0-0	8	Hugill [48]	5074
44	21	A	Rotherham U	L 0-1	0-0	9		7743
45	25	H	Sheffield U	L 1-2	0-0	9	Dodds [51]	6394
46	May 3	A	Peterborough U	D 0-0	0-0	9		6621

Final League Position: 9

GOALSCORERS

League (59): Pope 12, Loft 9, Myrie-Williams 7 (3 pens), Tomlin 5 (1 pen), Dodds 4, Hugill 4, Williamson 4, Hughes 3, Robertson 3, Knott 2, Birchall 1, Grimmer 1, Lines 1, Taylor 1, Yates 1, own goal 1.
The Budweiser FA Cup (13): Myrie-Williams 3, Pope 2, Robertson 2, Williamson 2, Birchall 1, Hugill 1, Taylor 1, Tomlin 1.
Capital One Cup (1): Robertson 1.
Johnstone's Paint Trophy (2): Pope 2.

Neal C 31	Yates A 33 + 1	Jones D 17 + 3	Lines C 33 + 1	Robertson C 36 + 1	Dickinson C 40	Myrie-Williams J 26 + 12	Griffith A 34 + 4	Tomlin G 17 + 7	Pope T 41 + 2	Loft D 37	Hughes L 6 + 7	Mohamed K 3 + 3	Dodds L 16 + 13	Duffy R 26 + 2	Chilvers L 14	Williamson B 18 + 20	Shuker C 1 + 9	Birchall C 14 + 13	Hugill J 7 + 13	Taylor R 1 + 5	Johnstone S 15 + 1	Grinmer J 13	Davis J 11	Cuvelier F 1	Knott B 13 + 5	Lloyd R 2 + 1	Match No.
1	2	3	4	5	6	7^1	8	9^1	10	11^2	12	13	14														1
1		6^2	9	3	5	13	8	10^1	11^3	7	12			2	4	14											2
1	2	5	7	4	3	6^2	13		11	8		10^1	9	12													3
1	2	5	8	3	4	6^2			10	7	11^3	9^1	13			12	14										4
1	2	5^2	7	3	4	9^1	8		10	6	11^3			14	12	13											5
1		3	5	14	7	12	10	8				13	11^1	2	4	9^2		6^1									6
1		3	5	6	7		11	8				9	10^1	2	4	12											7
1	2		7	3	5	9^2	8		11	6		10^1			4	13		12									8
1	2		8	3	5	12	7		10	9		13			4	11^2		6^1									9
1	2		7	3	5	12	8^1		10	9		13	14		4	11^2		6^2									10
1	2	5	9	3	6^1	7^2	11		11	8		10^3	14		4	12		13									11
1	2	5^2	8	4		6^2	7^1		11	9		10^3	13		12	3		14									12
1	2		8	3	5	6			12	9		7			4	11^2		13	10^1								13
1	2		7	3	5	8			12	9		6			4	10			11^1								14
1	2	14	7^2	3	5^1	13	8^3		10	9	12	6			4	11											15
1	2		7^3	3	5	6^1	8		10	9			14		4	11^2		12	13								16
1	2		8	3		6^2	7	13	10	9^3					4	12		14	11^1	5							17
1	2		7	4	5^3	6	8^1	13	10				14	9	3	11^2		12									18
	2		9	3	5	6	7	8^1	11		12				4		10				1						19
	2	13	7	3	5	9	8^1	11^3	10				14		4			6^2	12		1						20
		8^2	7	4	5	9^2	12	11	10					2	3	14		13	6^3		1						21
	2		3	5	6^2	8		9^2	10	7	11^2	14			4	13		12			1						22
	2	6		5		7^3	11^2	10	8			9^1	3	4	14	13		12			1						23
	2		4	13		11	10^3	7	8	5		3	12	9^1				6^2	14		1						24
1	2	6				12	4	10^3	11^1	7	8					13		9^3	14				3	5			25
1		3	5	6^3	8		11^2	9								10	12	14	13			2	4		7^1		26
1		5	7	3		8^2	10		11^1	9						13	12	6^3				2	4		14		27
1			8	3	5	6	12		10^1	11^3	9					14		13				2	4		7^2		28
1	2	9	7		5		8^2		10^1	6	14					12		11^3				3	4		13		29
1	2	9	6		5	13	7^1	12	11^3	8						14		10^2				3	4				30
1	2	9	7		5		8		10	6						11^1		12				3	4				31
1	2	9	7		5	12	8	13	11	6								10^2				3^3	4^1		14		32
1		5	7	3	4	12			11	10				8^1	6^3	13	14					2			9^2		33
1		3	5	9	7				10	8					4	11^1	12	6^2				2			13		34
1	2	12	3	5		9^3	7^2		10	8					4	11		6^1	14						13		35
1	2	8			5	6	12		10	9					4	11^1						3			7		36
1^1	2				5	6^3	7		10	9					4	11^2	13	14	12			3			8		37
	2^1	14	12	5^4	6	7^3	13		10	9					4	11					1	3^2			8		38
	2	8	3			13		9^3	11	7	14				5			6^2	12		1	4			10^1		39
	5	7	4^1	6^2					10^1	11		9	2			13	12	14			1	3			8^1		40
	5	3	4	9^1			11^2		10	8			14	2		12		6	13		1				7^3		41
12			3	5	9	7^2			10	11			14	2		13		6^1			1	4^3			8		42
	2		4	5		8	14	11^2	9	3						10^3		13	12		1				7^1	6	43
	2		3	5		13			11			7	4^3			12	14	6^1	10		1				8^2	9	44
	2	8	3	5	6	7^3			10^2						4	11^1	14	12			1				9	13	45
	2	7	3	5	6^3	11^2			9^1						4	10	14	13	12		1				8		46

The Budweiser FA Cup

First Round	Shortwood U	(a)	3-0
Second Round	Salisbury C	(h)	4-1
Third Round	Plymouth Arg	(h)	2-2
Replay	Plymouth Arg	(a)	3-2
Fourth Round	Brighton & HA	(h)	1-3

Capital One Cup

First Round	Walsall	(h)	1-2

Johnstone's Paint Trophy

First Round	Bury	(h)	2-1
Second Round	Rochdale	(h)	0-1

PORTSMOUTH

FOUNDATION

At a meeting held in his High Street, Portsmouth offices in 1898, solicitor Alderman J. E. Pink and five other business and professional men agreed to buy some ground close to Goldsmith Avenue for £4,950 which they developed into Fratton Park in record breaking time. A team of professionals was signed up by manager Frank Brettell and entry to the Southern League obtained for the new club's September 1899 kick-off.

Fratton Park, Frogmore Road, Portsmouth, Hampshire PO4 8RA.

Telephone: (02392) 731 204.

Fax: (02392) 734 129.

Ticket Office: (02392) 778 559.

Website: www.portsmouthfc.co.uk

Email: info@pompeyfc.co.uk

Ground Capacity: 21,178.

Record Attendance: 51,385 v Derby Co, FA Cup 6th rd, 26 February 1949.

Pitch Measurements: 100m × 66m (109.5yd × 72yd)

Chairman: Iain McInnes.

Chief Executive: Mark Catlin.

Manager: Andy Awford.

Coaches: Alan McLoughlin, Paul Hardyman.

Colours: Blue shirts with white trim, white shorts, red socks.

Year Formed: 1898.

Turned Professional: 1898.

Club Nickname: 'Pompey'.

Ground: 1898, Fratton Park.

First Football League Game: 28 August 1920, Division 3, v Swansea T (h) W 3–0 – Robson; Probert, Potts; Abbott, Harwood, Turner; Thompson, Stringfellow (1), Reid (1), James (1), Beedie.

Record League Victory: 9–1 v Notts Co, Division 2, 9 April 1927 – McPhail; Clifford, Ted Smith; Reg Davies (1), Foxall, Moffat; Forward (1), Mackie (2), Haines (3), Watson, Cook (2).

Record Cup Victory: 7–0 v Stockport Co, FA Cup 3rd rd, 8 January 1949 – Butler; Rookes, Ferrier; Scoular, Flewin, Dickinson; Harris (3), Barlow, Clarke (2), Phillips (2), Froggatt.

Record Defeat: 0–10 v Leicester C, Division 1, 20 October 1928.

Most League Points (2 for a win): 65, Division 3, 1961–62.

HONOURS

Football League – Division 1: *Champions* 1948–49, 1949–50, 2002–03;
Division 2: *Runners-up* 1926–27, 1986–87;
Division 3 (S): *Champions* 1923–24;
Division 3: *Champions* 1961–62, 1982–83.
FA Cup: *Winners* 1939, 2008; *Runners-up* 1929, 1934, 2010.
Football League Cup: Best season: 5th rd, 1961, 1986, 1994, 2010.
European Competitions
UEFA Cup: 2008–09.

sky SPORTS FACT FILE

Bob Blyth signed for Portsmouth in 1899 and went on to become player-manager and eventually chairman of the club. His brother William and son Bob also played for Pompey. Bob's sister Barbara married into the Shankly family; all five of her sons became professional footballers including John, who also played for Pompey, and the legendary Bill Shankly.

Most League Points (3 for a win): 98, Division 1, 2002–03.

Most League Goals: 97, Division 1, 2002–03.

Highest League Scorer in Season: Guy Whittingham, 42, Division 1, 1992–93.

Most League Goals in Total Aggregate: Peter Harris, 194, 1946–60.

Most League Goals in One Match: 5, Alf Strange v Gillingham, Division 3, 27 January 1923; 5, Peter Harris v Aston Villa, Division 1, 3 September 1958.

Most Capped Player: Jimmy Dickinson, 48, England.

Most League Appearances: Jimmy Dickinson, 764, 1946–65.

Youngest League Player: Clive Green, 16 years 259 days v Wrexham, 21 August 1976.

Record Transfer Fee Received: £20,000,000 from Real Madrid for Lassana Diarra, January 2009.

Record Transfer Fee Paid: £9,000,000 (rising to £11,000,000) to Liverpool for Peter Crouch, July 2008.

Football League Record: 1920 Original Member of Division 3; 1921 Division 3 (S); 1924–27 Division 2; 1927–59 Division 1; 1959–61 Division 2; 1961–62 Division 3; 1962–76 Division 2; 1976–78 Division 3; 1978–80 Division 4; 1980–83 Division 3; 1983–87 Division 2; 1987–88 Division 1; 1988–92 Division 2; 1992–2003 Division 1; 2003–10 FA Premier League; 2010–12 FL C; 2012–13 FL 1; 2013– FL 2.

LATEST SEQUENCES

Longest Sequence of League Wins: 7, 17.8.2002 – 17.9.2002.

Longest Sequence of League Defeats: 9, 26.12.2012 – 9.2.2013.

Longest Sequence of League Draws: 5, 16.12.2000 – 13.1.2001.

Longest Sequence of Unbeaten League Matches: 15, 18.4.1924 – 18.10.1924.

Longest Sequence Without a League Win: 25, 29.11.1958 – 22.8.1959.

Successive Scoring Runs: 23 from 30.8.1930.

Successive Non-scoring Runs: 6 from 27.12.1993.

MANAGERS

Frank Brettell 1898–1901
Bob Blyth 1901–04
Richard Bonney 1905–08
Bob Brown 1911–20
John McCartney 1920–27
Jack Tinn 1927–47
Bob Jackson 1947–52
Eddie Lever 1952–58
Freddie Cox 1958–61
George Smith 1961–70
Ron Tindall 1970–73
    (General Manager to 1974)
John Mortimore 1973–74
Ian St John 1974–77
Jimmy Dickinson 1977–79
Frank Burrows 1979–82
Bobby Campbell 1982–84
Alan Ball 1984–89
John Gregory 1989–90
Frank Burrows 1990–91
Jim Smith 1991–95
Terry Fenwick 1995–98
Alan Ball 1998–99
Tony Pulis 2000
Steve Claridge 2000–01
Graham Rix 2001–02
Harry Redknapp 2002–04
Velimir Zajec 2004–05
Alain Perrin 2005
Harry Redknapp 2005–08
Tony Adams 2008–09
Paul Hart 2009
Avram Grant 2009–10
Steve Cotterill 2010–11
Michael Appleton 2011–12
Guy Whittingham 2012–13
Richie Barker 2013–14
Andy Awford May 2014–

TEN YEAR LEAGUE RECORD

		P	W	D	L	F	A	Pts	Pos
2004-05	PR Lge	38	10	9	19	43	59	39	16
2005-06	PR Lge	38	10	8	20	37	62	38	17
2006-07	PR Lge	38	14	12	12	45	42	54	9
2007-08	PR Lge	38	16	9	13	48	40	57	8
2008-09	PR Lge	38	10	11	17	38	57	41	14
2009-10	PR Lge	38	7	7	24	34	66	19*	20
2010-11	FL C	46	15	13	18	53	60	58	16
2011-12	FL C	46	13	11	22	50	59	40†	22
2012-13	FL 1	46	10	12	24	51	69	32‡	24
2013-14	FL 2	46	14	17	15	56	66	59	13

9 pts deducted; † 10 pts deducted; ‡ 10 pts deducted.

DID YOU KNOW ?

When Portsmouth beat Burnley 4-2 on 22 November 1958, they were in 13th position in the First Division table. However, in the remaining 24 fixtures they did not win a single game and finished the season in bottom place with just 21 points, 9 adrift of 21st placed Aston Villa who were also relegated.

PORTSMOUTH – FOOTBALL LEAGUE TWO 2013–14 LEAGUE RECORD

Match No.	Date	Venue	Opponents	Result	H/T Score	Lg Pos.	Goalscorers	Attendance
1	Aug 3	H	Oxford U	L	1-4	1-2	22	Agyemang [25]	18,181
2	10	A	Accrington S	D	2-2	0-0	20	Connolly 2 (1 pen) [57, 79 (p)]	2531
3	17	H	Morecambe	W	3-0	3-0	10	Wallace [20], Connolly [26], Agyemang [39]	14,590
4	24	A	Mansfield T	D	2-2	2-1	11	Barcham [39], Connolly [44]	4574
5	31	H	Chesterfield	L	0-2	0-0	18		15,999
6	Sept 7	A	Cheltenham T	D	2-2	2-1	17	Agyemang [5], Ertl [44]	4776
7	14	A	Burton Alb	W	2-1	1-0	13	Holmes [34], Ferry [52]	3577
8	21	H	Fleetwood T	L	0-1	0-0	15		15,809
9	28	A	York C	L	2-4	0-1	17	Wallace [53], Marquis [88]	4848
10	Oct 5	H	Rochdale	W	3-0	1-0	15	Wallace [24], N'Gala 2 [52, 66]	15,155
11	12	A	Plymouth Arg	D	1-1	1-1	15	Wallace [39]	8742
12	19	H	Bury	W	1-0	1-0	15	N'Gala [4]	15,434
13	26	A	Torquay U	D	1-1	0-1	16	Bird [81]	3843
14	Nov 2	H	Exeter C	W	3-2	1-0	16	Holmes [45], Bird 2 [49, 71]	16,168
15	16	A	AFC Wimbledon	L	0-4	0-1	16		4605
16	23	H	Scunthorpe U	L	1-2	1-1	18	Craddock [36]	14,550
17	26	H	Southend U	L	1-2	1-0	18	Barcham [2]	13,427
18	30	A	Hartlepool U	D	0-0	0-0	17		4126
19	Dec 4	H	Wycombe W	D	2-2	0-1	17	Barcham [73], Agyemang [84]	14,942
20	14	H	Newport Co	L	0-2	0-0	18		15,295
21	21	A	Bristol R	L	0-2	0-1	20		7537
22	26	H	Dagenham & R	W	1-0	1-0	17	Padovani [45]	15,192
23	29	A	Northampton T	D	0-0	0-0	17		15,426
24	Jan 1	A	Southend U	L	1-2	1-1	19	Bradley [30]	7736
25	11	A	Oxford U	D	0-0	0-0	20		8443
26	18	H	Mansfield T	D	1-1	0-0	21	Taylor [78]	14,686
27	25	A	Morecambe	D	2-2	2-1	21	Jervis 2 [10, 43]	2550
28	28	A	Wycombe W	W	1-0	0-0	18	Taylor (pen) [50]	3733
29	Feb 1	H	Torquay U	L	0-1	0-1	18		15,474
30	8	A	Exeter C	D	1-1	1-0	19	Jervis [9]	5221
31	15	H	AFC Wimbledon	W	1-0	0-0	17	Taylor [52]	15,742
32	22	A	Scunthorpe U	L	1-5	0-3	21	Drennan [86]	4165
33	25	H	Accrington S	W	1-0	0-0	18	Jervis [48]	13,387
34	Mar 3	A	Chesterfield	D	0-0	0-0	15		5807
35	8	H	Cheltenham T	D	0-0	0-0	19		17,254
36	11	H	Burton Alb	D	0-0	0-0	17		12,780
37	15	A	Fleetwood T	L	1-3	0-2	19	Wallace [64]	3509
38	22	H	York C	L	0-1	0-1	22		14,814
39	25	A	Rochdale	L	0-3	0-1	22		2746
40	29	A	Newport Co	W	2-1	2-0	21	Taylor (pen) [22], Wallace [40]	4261
41	Apr 5	H	Hartlepool U	W	1-0	1-0	19	Webster [2]	15,273
42	12	A	Dagenham & R	W	4-1	2-1	16	Hollands [4], Drennan 2 [21, 57], Wallace [87]	3115
43	19	A	Bristol R	W	3-2	2-2	14	Webster [12], Taylor [41], Fogden [70]	17,998
44	21	A	Northampton T	W	1-0	1-0	13	East [6]	6829
45	26	A	Bury	D	4-4	0-2	11	Hollands [53], Taylor [82], Bradley [88], Fogden [90]	4759
46	May 3	H	Plymouth Arg	D	3-3	2-2	13	Hollands 3 [32, 38, 47]	18,026

Final League Position: 13

GOALSCORERS

League (56): Wallace 7, Taylor 6 (2 pens), Hollands 5, Agyemang 4, Connolly 4 (1 pen), Jervis 4, Barcham 3, Bird 3, Drennan 3, N'Gala 3, Bradley 2, Fogden 2, Holmes 2, Webster 2, Craddock 1, East 1, Ertl 1, Ferry 1, Marquis 1, Padovani 1.
The Budweiser FA Cup (1): Connolly 1.
Capital One Cup (0).
Johnstone's Paint Trophy (2): Agyemang 1, Moutaouakil 1.

Sullivan J 6	Moutaouakil Y 11+2	Butler D 1	Ertl J 20+9	Devera J 33	Bradley S 29+4	Wallace J 38+6	Ferry S 19+1	Agyemang P 24+17	Connolly D 11+7	Barcham A 18+8	Holmes R 31+9	Padovani R 11+7	Craddock T 2+6	Webster A 3+1	Smith P 4	East D 12+3	Bird R 5+13	Painter M 17	N'Gala B 24+3	Cooper S 7+2	Marquis J 4+1	Carson T 36	Racon T 12+4	Mahon G —+1	Potts D 5	Whatmough J 11+1	Maloney J —+1	Harris A —+1	Alfei D 15	Shorey N 21	Taylor R 15+3	Fogden W 16+3	Jervis J 12+3	Chorley B 12	Diagouraga T 8	Drennan M 5+5	McCabe R 2+2	Hollands D 6+1	Match No.
1	2	3¹	4⁴	5	6	7²	8	9³	10	11	12	13	14																										1
	2			3	4		6	8	11¹	10	9		7		1	5	12																						2
	2²			3	4		6	7¹	11³	10	9	13		8¹	1	12			14	5²	4																	3
13			12	2	3	6	7	10³	11	9			8¹		1				14	5²	4																	4
1	2		7	3	4	13	8	11¹	10⁴	9	6²		14			5³	12																					5
1	2		7	3	4	6	8	11³		9¹	10²	14				5	13				12																	6
1	2⁴		7	3¹	4	6	8	11³		9	10²		14			5			12	13																		7
1			7¹		4	13	8	11³	10	9²	6	12	14			5	3	2																				8
1			8		3	6	7¹	11²	10	9	14	12				2		5³	4		13																	9
			7	2	4	9		11²		13	6	12				5	3		10	1	8¹																	10
2			7	5	4	6		10		9						3			11	1	8																	11
2			8	5	4	6		10²		13	9		1			12	3		11¹		7²	14																12
2			7¹	4		9	8³	11		12	6					13		3	5	10²	1	14																13
2			13	5	4	9¹	8²	10³	14	12	6					11		3			1	7																14
			8²	5	4	6	7	10¹	11	9			14			2	12²	3			1	13																15
			8¹	2⁴	4	9	7		12	6	11³	10				13	14	3			1		5															16
			7	2¹	4	9		10	6	13		11¹				12			8		1		5¹	3	14													17
			7	2	4	6²		13		9¹	10					12	11		8		1		5	3														18
			7³	3	4	6²		14	13	9	10					2¹	11		12	8	1		5															19
2				3	4	13	14	10²	11	6	9¹					12			8³	1	7	5																20
14			7		4	6	8	11	12	9¹	13					10²	5	3	2³	1																		21
			12	3	4	6	9¹	11³		10	8					2	14	5²		1	7		13															22
			8³	3	4	7		11¹	14	10	9					2²	12	5	13	1	6																	23
				2	4	6		13	10²	9¹	14					11	5	3		1	7		8		12³													24
			14	3	4	9	6	11¹		13						12	5			1	8²							2	7	10³								25
				3	4	9²	6¹	11	13							5				1	12							2	7	10	8³	14						26
				4	3	6¹		13		12		8				5				1								2	7	10	9	11²						27
			14	3		13		6³	12	7						5				1								2	9	10	8¹	11²	4					28
				3		6		12	14	9	7²					5³				1								2	8	10	13	11¹	4					29
				3¹	12			14		13	9²					5				1	8							2	7	10	6	11³	4					30
				3	6³			12		14	9²					5				1	7							2	8	10	13	11	4					31
				4	10			14		9¹	13					5				1	7²							2		6	11³	3	8	12				32
					12			14		6¹	7					3				1	13							2	5		9	10³	4	8	11²			33
	2				9			12		6	7					4				1								5		10	11¹	3	8					34
	2				6			13		9						3				1								5	12	7	11¹	4	8	10²				35
	2			12	14			10		9	6					3				1								5	11²	8³	13	4¹	7					36
	4				12			13		9						3				1		8						2	5²	14	6¹	11		7	10³			37
				9				13		12						3				1	6							2	5²	10	11³	4⁴	7	14	8¹			38
	4¹				9		11	10								3				1	7							2	5	12	8		6					39
7³			13	10	14			6		2						1				5²								3	4	11¹	8	12					9	40
13				8	6¹			10³		2						3				1								4	5	11	9²		14	12	7			41
13				9	7¹	14		6³		2						5				1								3	4	10		11²	12	8				42
13				8		14		10		2						3				1								4	5	11³	12		9¹	7²	6			43
			6	3	4	9		11²		14			7³			1				5	2		8	10¹		13		5	2		8	10¹	13		12			44
6¹			14	9		13		10²		12	2³					4				1								5	11	8		3		7				45
12					8²			10		2	6¹					4				1								5	11	9		3		13	7			46

The Budweiser FA Cup
First Round Stevenage (a) 1-2

Capital One Cup
First Round AFC Bournemouth (a) 0-1

Johnstone's Paint Trophy
First Round Torquay U (a) 0-0
(aet; won 5-3 on penalties)
Second Round Oxford U (a) 2-1
Southern Quarter-Finals Newport Co (a) 0-3

PRESTON NORTH END

FOUNDATION

North End Cricket and Rugby Club, which was formed in 1863, indulged in most sports before taking up soccer in about 1879. In 1881 they decided to stick to football to the exclusion of other sports and even a 16–0 drubbing by Blackburn Rovers in an invitation game at Deepdale, a few weeks after taking this decision, did not deter them for they immediately became affiliated to the Lancashire FA.

Deepdale Stadium, Sir Tom Finney Way, Deepdale, Preston, Lancashire PR1 6RU.

Telephone: (0844) 856 1964.

Fax: (01772) 693 366.

Ticket Office: (0844) 856 1966.

Website: www.pne.co.uk

Email: enquiries@pne.co.uk

Ground Capacity: 23,404.

Record Attendance: 42,684 v Arsenal, Division 1, 23 April 1938.

Pitch Measurements: 100.5m × 67.5m (110yd × 74yd)

Directors: Kevin Abbott, Anthony Hughes, Paul Newsham, David Robinson, David Taylor.

Manager: Simon Grayson.

Assistant Manager: Glynn Snodin.

Head Physio: Matthew Jackson.

Colours: White shirts, blue shorts, white socks.

Year Formed: 1880.

Turned Professional: 1885.

Club Nicknames: 'The Lilywhites', 'North End'.

Ground: 1881, Deepdale.

HONOURS

Football League – Division 1:
Champions 1888–89 (first champions) 1889–90; *Runners-up* 1890–91, 1891–92, 1892–93, 1905–06, 1952–53, 1957–58;

Division 2: *Champions* 1903–04, 1912–13, 1950–51, 1999–2000; *Runners-up* 1914–15, 1933–34;

Division 3: *Champions* 1970–71, 1995–96;

Division 4: *Runners-up* 1986–87.

FA Cup: *Winners* 1889, 1938; *Runners-up* 1888, 1922, 1937, 1954, 1964.

Football League Cup: Best season: 4th rd, 2003.

Double Performed: 1888–89.

Football League Cup: Best season: 4th rd, 1963, 1966, 1972, 1981.

First Football League Game: 8 September 1888, Football League, v Burnley (h) W 5–2 – Trainer; Howarth, Holmes; Robertson, William Graham, Johnny Graham; Gordon (1), Jimmy Ross (2), Goodall, Dewhurst (2), Drummond.

Record League Victory: 10–0 v Stoke, Division 1, 14 September 1889 – Trainer; Howarth, Holmes; Kelso, Russell (1), Johnny Graham; Gordon, Jimmy Ross (2), Nick Ross (3), Thomson (2), Drummond (2).

Record Cup Victory: 26–0 v Hyde, FA Cup 1st rd, 15 October 1887 – Addision; Howarth, Nick Ross; Russell (1), Thomson (5), Johnny Graham (1); Gordon (5), Jimmy Ross (8), John Goodall (1), Dewhurst (3), Drummond (2).

Record Defeat: 0–7 v Blackpool, Division 1, 1 May 1948.

Most League Points (2 for a win): 61, Division 3, 1970–71.

Most League Points (3 for a win): 95, Division 2, 1999–2000.

Most League Goals: 100, Division 2, 1927–28 and Division 1, 1957–58.

sky SPORTS FACT FILE

Preston North End won the first-ever televised FA Cup final in April 1938 when they defeated Huddersfield Town with a penalty from George Mutch scored in the last minute of extra time. Television was in its infancy at the time and the match was only accessible to a few thousand households in London and the South East.

Highest League Scorer in Season: Ted Harper, 37, Division 2, 1932–33.

Most League Goals in Total Aggregate: Tom Finney, 187, 1946–60.

Most League Goals in One Match: 4, Jimmy Ross v Stoke, Division 1, 6 October 1888; 4, Nick Ross v Derby Co, Division 1, 11 January 1890; 4, George Drummond v Notts Co, Division 1, 12 December 1891; 4, Frank Becton v Notts Co, Division 1, 31 March 1893; 4, George Harrison v Grimsby T, Division 2, 3 November 1928; 4, Alex Reid v Port Vale, Division 2, 23 February 1929; 4, James McClelland v Reading, Division 2, 6 September 1930; 4, Dick Rowley v Notts Co, Division 2, 16 April 1932; 4, Ted Harper v Burnley, Division 2, 29 August 1932; 4, Ted Harper v Lincoln C, Division 2, 11 March 1933; 4, Charlie Wayman v QPR, Division 2, 25 December 1950; 4, Alex Bruce v Colchester U, Division 3, 28 February 1978.

Most Capped Player: Tom Finney, 76, England.

Most League Appearances: Alan Kelly, 447, 1961–75.

Youngest League Player: Steve Doyle, 16 years 166 days v Tranmere R, 15 November 1974.

Record Transfer Fee Received: £6,000,000 from Portsmouth for David Nugent, August 2007.

Record Transfer Fee Paid: £1,500,000 to Manchester U for David Healy, December 2000.

Football League Record: 1888 Founder Member of League; 1901–04 Division 2; 1904–12 Division 1; 1912–13 Division 2; 1913–14 Division 1; 1914–15 Division 2; 1919–25 Division 1; 1925–34 Division 2; 1934–49 Division 1; 1949–51 Division 2; 1951–61 Division 1; 1961–70 Division 2; 1970–71 Division 3; 1971–74 Division 2; 1974–78 Division 3; 1978–81 Division 2; 1981–85 Division 3; 1985–87 Division 4; 1987–92 Division 3; 1992–93 Division 2; 1993–96 Division 3; 1996–2000 Division 2; 2000–04 Division 1; 2004–11 FL C; 2011– FL 1.

LATEST SEQUENCES

Longest Sequence of League Wins: 14, 25.12.1950 – 27.3.1951.

Longest Sequence of League Defeats: 8, 22.9.1984 – 27.10.1984.

Longest Sequence of League Draws: 6, 24.2.1979 – 20.3.1979.

Longest Sequence of Unbeaten League Matches: 23, 8.9.1888 – 14.9.1889.

Longest Sequence Without a League Win: 15, 14.4.1923 – 20.10.1923.

Successive Scoring Runs: 30 from 15.11.1952.

Successive Non-scoring Runs: 6 from 19.11.1960.

MANAGERS

Charlie Parker 1906–15
Vincent Hayes 1919–23
Jim Lawrence 1923–25
Frank Richards 1925–27
Alex Gibson 1927–31
Lincoln Hayes 1931–32
Run by committee 1932–36
Tommy Muirhead 1936–37
Run by committee 1937–49
Will Scott 1949–53
Scot Symon 1953–54
Frank Hill 1954–56
Cliff Britton 1956–61
Jimmy Milne 1961–68
Bobby Seith 1968–70
Alan Ball Snr 1970–73
Bobby Charlton 1973–75
Harry Catterick 1975–77
Nobby Stiles 1977–81
Tommy Docherty 1981
Gordon Lee 1981–83
Alan Kelly 1983–85
Tommy Booth 1985–86
Brian Kidd 1986
John McGrath 1986–90
Les Chapman 1990–92
Sam Allardyce 1992 (*Caretaker*)
John Beck 1992–94
Gary Peters 1994–98
David Moyes 1998–2002
Kelham O'Hanlon 2002
  (*Caretaker*)
Craig Brown 2002–04
Billy Davies 2004–06
Paul Simpson 2006–07
Alan Irvine 2007–09
Darren Ferguson 2010
Phil Brown 2011
Graham Westley 2012–13
Simon Grayson February 2013–

TEN YEAR LEAGUE RECORD

		P	W	D	L	F	A	Pts	Pos
2004-05	FL C	46	21	12	13	67	58	75	5
2005-06	FL C	46	20	20	6	59	30	80	4
2006-07	FL C	46	22	8	16	64	53	74	7
2007-08	FL C	46	15	11	20	50	56	56	15
2008-09	FL C	46	21	11	14	66	54	74	6
2009-10	FL C	46	13	15	18	58	73	54	17
2010-11	FL C	46	10	12	24	54	79	42	22
2011-12	FL 1	46	13	15	18	54	68	54	15
2012-13	FL 1	46	14	17	15	54	49	59	14
2013-14	FL 1	46	23	16	7	72	46	85	5

DID YOU KNOW ?

In the summer of 1986 Preston North End replaced the turf at Deepdale with an artificial surface or 'plastic pitch'. The surface remained in place for eight years. The final game on 'plastic' was a memorable occasion. Trailing 2-0 from the Division Three play-off semi-final first leg, North End ran out 4-1 winners.

PRESTON NORTH END – FOOTBALL LEAGUE ONE 2013–14 LEAGUE RECORD

Match No.	Date	Venue	Opponents	Result	H/T Score	Lg Pos.	Goalscorers	Attendance
1	Aug 3	H	Wolverhampton W	D	0-0	0-0	14		16,583
2	10	A	Rotherham U	D	0-0	0-0	14		8454
3	17	H	Milton Keynes D	D	2-2	2-1	15	Kay (og) [10], Garner [35]	9944
4	25	A	Coventry C	D	4-4	1-1	12	Clarke [10], Wright [65], Byrom [87], Humphrey [90]	2068
5	31	A	Walsall	W	3-0	1-0	9	Byrom [30], Humphrey [58], Holmes [61]	4205
6	Sept 9	H	Oldham Ath	W	2-1	2-0	6	Beavon [13], Davies, K (pen) [38]	10,292
7	14	H	Stevenage	W	3-0	1-0	5	Huntington [45], Laird [59], Davies, K [84]	8855
8	21	A	Sheffield U	W	1-0	0-0	4	Beavon [68]	16,319
9	28	H	Swindon T	W	2-1	1-0	4	Hume [11], McEveley (og) [48]	9296
10	Oct 5	H	Peterborough U	L	0-2	0-2	5		7020
11	12	H	Crewe Alex	L	0-2	0-1	5		9268
12	19	A	Gillingham	W	2-1	0-0	4	Keane [47], Brownhill [53]	7054
13	22	H	Bradford C	D	2-2	1-1	4	Clarke [32], Wright [68]	11,485
14	26	A	Notts Co	W	1-0	0-0	4	Hume [74]	4956
15	Nov 2	H	Tranmere R	D	1-1	0-0	4	Garner [90]	9496
16	16	A	Leyton Orient	W	1-0	1-0	5	Garner [33]	7123
17	23	H	Colchester U	D	1-1	1-0	4	Garner [45]	8492
18	26	A	Port Vale	W	2-0	1-0	3	Garner 2 (1 pen) [30, 71 (p)]	5889
19	30	H	Bristol C	W	1-0	1-0	3	King [33]	8803
20	Dec 14	A	Crawley T	D	2-2	2-0	4	Huntington [9], Brownhill [16]	2407
21	21	H	Brentford	L	0-3	0-2	5		10,332
22	26	A	Carlisle U	W	1-0	1-0	4	Brownhill [42]	7934
23	29	A	Shrewsbury T	W	1-0	0-0	4	Woods (og) [80]	6379
24	Jan 1	H	Port Vale	W	3-2	1-0	4	Garner 2 [43, 62], Gallagher [50]	10,653
25	11	A	Wolverhampton W	L	0-2	0-1	4		20,434
26	18	H	Coventry C	D	1-1	0-0	4	Davies, K [54]	10,671
27	28	A	Bradford C	D	0-0	0-0	4		13,686
28	Feb 1	H	Notts Co	W	2-0	0-0	4	Davies, C [65], Garner (pen) [71]	9483
29	8	A	Tranmere R	W	2-1	1-1	4	Garner 2 [18, 52]	5895
30	15	H	Leyton Orient	D	1-1	0-1	4	Garner (pen) [64]	13,440
31	18	A	Milton Keynes D	D	0-0	0-0	4		7279
32	22	A	Colchester U	W	2-1	1-0	4	Clarke [28], Wilson (og) [82]	3416
33	25	H	Rotherham U	D	3-3	1-2	4	Davies, C [37], Gallagher [60], Garner [65]	9524
34	Mar 1	H	Walsall	W	2-1	2-1	4	Downing (og) [3], Wright [29]	10,034
35	8	A	Oldham Ath	W	3-1	1-0	4	Keane [6], Garner 2 [71, 88]	6698
36	11	A	Stevenage	D	1-1	1-0	4	Clarke [17]	2448
37	17	H	Sheffield U	D	0-0	0-0	4		8892
38	22	A	Swindon T	L	0-1	0-0	5		7570
39	25	H	Peterborough U	W	3-1	1-1	5	Kilkenny [45], Garner 2 [80, 90]	8206
40	29	H	Crawley T	W	1-0	1-0	5	Garner [13]	8979
41	Apr 5	A	Bristol C	D	1-1	0-0	5	King [69]	12,537
42	12	H	Carlisle U	W	6-1	2-1	5	Beavon [10], Browne [20], Holmes [48], Davies, C 3 [57, 79, 83]	11,428
43	18	A	Brentford	L	0-1	0-1	5		10,774
44	21	H	Shrewsbury T	W	5-2	2-1	5	Holmes [34], Wright [40], Gallagher 3 (1 pen) [58, 62 (pl), 81]	9636
45	26	H	Gillingham	W	3-1	1-1	3	Welsh [8], Gallagher [57], Kilkenny [63]	11,591
46	May 3	A	Crewe Alex	L	1-2	0-1	5	Welsh [90]	7458

Final League Position: 5

GOALSCORERS

League (72): Garner 18 (3 pens), Gallagher 6 (1 pen), Davies, C 5, Clarke 4, Wright 4, Beavon 3, Brownhill 3, Davies, K 3 (1 pen), Holmes 3, Byrom 2, Hume 2, Humphrey 2, Huntington 2, Keane 2, Kilkenny 2, King 2, Welsh 2, Browne 1, Laird 1, own goals 5.
The Budweiser FA Cup (11): Garner 5, Gallagher 3, Davies, K 2, Clarke 1.
Capital One Cup (1): Clarke 1.
Johnstone's Paint Trophy (0).
League One Play-Offs (2): Gallagher 1, Garner 1.

Rudd D 46	Keane K 31 + 7	Buchanan D 16 + 3	Clarke T 42	Huntington P 19 + 4	Wright B 43	Humphrey C 30 + 12	Welsh J 30 + 6	Davies K 26 + 12	Wroe N 1 + 4	Holmes L 17 + 15	Hayhurst W 2 + 4	Hume 18 + 8	Laird S 31 + 3	Garner J 27 + 8	Monakana J — + 2	Beavon S 19 + 8	Mousinho J — + 2	Byron J 7 + 4	Brownhill J 11 + 13	Gallagher P 26 + 2	King J 21 + 3	Kilkenny N 24 + 3	Wiseman S 13 + 2	Davies C 12 + 3	Browne A 4 + 4	Match No.
1	2	3	4	5	6	7²	8	9	10¹	11	12	13														1
1	7	5	2	3	4	6¹	8	11		10²	9³		12	13	14											2
1	8	5	2	3	4	7²	9¹	10	12	6			11³	13	14											3
1	8	5	2	3	4	12	7¹	11		9	6³		10²			13	14									4
1	6	13	2	3	4	5		10	14	9¹		8²		12		11³			7							5
1	6	9	2	3	4		12	11		7	13	5²	14			10³			8¹							6
1	7		2	3	4	6²	12	10		13		9¹	8			11	14		5¹							7
1	6		2	3	4	5		10		12		9²	8	13		11¹			7							8
1	6³		2	3	4	5²	13	10	14	12		9¹	8			11			7							9
1	6		2	3	4	5	12	11	13			9²	8	14		10¹			7³							10
1	6³		2	3	4	5¹	14	10		12		11	8			9			7²	13						11
1	6	13	2	3	4	5³	7	11		14		8		10²		12	9¹									12
1	6	14	2	3	4	5³	7	10		12		13	8			11¹			9²							13
1	6		3	2	4	5	8	10³				13	9	12		11²		14	7¹							14
1	7		2	3	4	6	5	11²		12		9³	8	13		14				10¹						15
1	8		2	13	4	5²	6	11					9	10						7¹	3	12				16
1	14	2²		4	12	8¹	11		6³				5	10				13	9	3	7					17
1	12	2	14	4	5¹	7	10²			13			13	5		10³		12	8²	3	6⁴					18
1	7	2	14	4	6¹		11					13	5			10³		12	8²	9⁴	3					19
1	7	5	4	3	2²	9	10		14	12	13	6				11¹			8³							20
1	6²	3	2	4	5³	7	10		12		14	9	11						8¹		13					21
1	14	5	2	3	4	9¹	6			12			13			11			7	11²	10	8³				22
1		9	2	3	4	5³	7	10¹		12		14		11					8³	13		6				23
1		5	2		4	12	6	13		10²			9¹	14	11				8²	3	7					24
1		5	2		4		7¹	12		6¹		11²		10					14	9	3	8	13			25
1	12	5	3		4	13	8¹	10⁴		6⁴				11						9²	14	7	2			26
1	13		3		4	12	8						9	11					7¹	10	2	6⁴	5²			27
1	14	5	3		4	13	7			6³		12		11					9²		8	2	10¹			28
1	6				4	13	7	12					5	10						11¹	3	8	2	9²		29
1	6²	3			4		7	14		12			5	10		14			13	8³		9	2	11¹		30
1	6³	3			4	12	8	11²					5	10		14			13		9	7	2¹			31
1	7	2		3	5		13						8	10²	14				12	9	4	6¹		11³		32
1	7		3		4	6							5	11					12	9²	13	8	2¹	10		33
1	7		3		4	6²							5	10¹	13				12	9	14	8³	2	11		34
1	8		3			6			14				5	10²	13				12	9	4	7³	2	11¹		35
1	2		3			6¹	7	10²					5	8					12	9²	11		13	14		36
1		5	3		4	6¹			14	12				11		13			8³	9		7	2	10²		37
1		5	3		4	6	12	14					10¹	13					8	9		7²	2	11³		38
1	12	5			4	6⁴	8						10	11					9	3	7²	2¹			14	39
1	2	5	4			13	7			6			10	11³					9¹	3	8²		14	12		40
1	8	3		4	5	6¹	14			9²			11						12		2	7	10³	13		41
1	2	3¹	14				13	6		5			11³						12	9	4	8²	10	7		42
1	2		3		4	6³		14		12			5	10					13	7	9²		11¹	8		43
1		2¹		4	12	7	11³			6²			5	13		10		14	9	3				8		44
1	2			4	12	8				6²			5	11³		10				9	3	13		14	7¹	45
1				2	13	7	14			6¹			5	11		10²				9	3	8³	4		12	46

The Budweiser FA Cup

First Round	Barnet	(h)	6-0
Second Round	Wycombe W	(a)	1-0
Third Round	Ipswich T	(a)	1-1
Replay	Ipswich T	(h)	3-2
Fourth Round	Nottingham F	(a)	0-0
Replay	Nottingham F	(h)	0-2

Johnstone's Paint Trophy

Second Round	Oldham Ath	(h)	0-2

Capital One Cup

First Round	Blackpool	(h)	1-0
Second Round	Burnley	(a)	0-2

League One Play-Offs

Semi-Finals 1st leg	Rotherham U	(h)	1-1
Semi-Finals 2nd leg	Rotherham U	(a)	1-3

QUEENS PARK RANGERS

FOUNDATION

There is an element of doubt about the date of the foundation of this club, but it is believed that in either 1885 or 1886 it was formed through the amalgamation of Christchurch Rangers and St Jude's Institute FC. The leading light was George Wodehouse, whose family maintained a connection with the club until comparatively recent times. Most of the players came from the Queen's Park district so this name was adopted after a year as St Jude's Institute.

Loftus Road Stadium, South Africa Road, Shepherds Bush, London W12 7PJ.

Telephone: (020) 8743 0262.

Fax: (020) 8749 0994.

Ticket Office: (0844) 447 7007.

Website: www.qpr.co.uk

Email: feedback@qpr.co.uk

Ground Capacity: 18,489.

Record Attendance: 41,097 v Leeds U, FA Cup 3rd rd, 9 January 1932 (at White City); 35,353 v Leeds U, Division 1, 27 April 1974 (at Loftus Road).

Pitch Measurements: 100.5m × 66m (110yd × 72.01yd)

Chairman: Tony Fernandes.

Chief Executive: Phil Beard.

Manager: Harry Redknapp.

Assistant Manager: Kevin Bond.

Physio: Nigel Cox.

Colours: Blue and white hooped shirts, white shorts with blue trim, white socks with blue trim.

Year Formed: 1885* (*see Foundation*).

Turned Professional: 1898.

Previous Name: 1885, St Jude's; 1887, Queens Park Rangers. *Club Nicknames:* 'Rangers', 'The Hoops', 'R's'.

Grounds: 1885* (*see Foundation*), Welford's Fields; 1888–99, London Scottish Ground, Brondesbury, Home Farm, Kensal Rise Green, Gun Club Wormwood Scrubs, Kilburn Cricket Ground; 1899, Kensal Rise Athletic Ground; 1901, Latimer Road, Notting Hill; 1904, Agricultural Society, Park Royal; 1907, Park Royal Ground; 1917, Loftus Road; 1931, White City; 1933, Loftus Road; 1962, White City; 1963, Loftus Road.

First Football League Game: 28 August 1920, Division 3, v Watford (h) L 1–2 – Price; Blackman, Wingrove; McGovern, Grant, O'Brien; Faulkner, Birch (1), Smith, Gregory, Middlemiss.

Record League Victory: 9–2 v Tranmere R, Division 3, 3 December 1960 – Drinkwater; Woods, Ingham; Keen, Rutter, Angell; Lazarus (2), Bedford (2), Evans (2), Andrews (1), Clark (2).

Record Cup Victory: 8–1 v Bristol R (a), FA Cup 1st rd, 27 November 1937 – Gilfillan; Smith, Jefferson; Lowe, James, March; Cape, Mallett, Cheetham (3), Fitzgerald (3) Bott (2). 8–1 v Crewe Alex, Milk Cup 1st rd, 3 October 1983 – Hucker; Neill, Dawes, Waddock (1), McDonald (1), Fenwick, Micklewhite (1), Stewart (1), Allen (1), Stainrod (3), Gregory.

HONOURS

Football League – Division 1:
Runners-up 1975–76;
FL C: *Champions* 2010–11;
Division 2: *Champions* 1982–83;
Runners-up 1967–68, 1972–73, 2003–04;
Division 3 (S): *Champions* 1947–48;
Runners-up 1946–47;
Division 3: *Champions* 1966–67.
FA Cup: *Runners-up* 1982.
Football League Cup: *Winners* 1967;
Runners-up 1986.
European Competitions
UEFA Cup: 1976–77, 1984–85.

sky SPORTS FACT FILE

Queens Park Rangers' ground at Shepherds Bush was closed for 14 days from 19 February 1930 due to crowd misconduct. As a result the R's had to play their home game with Coventry City at Highbury. Rangers won 3-1 and the gate of 17,903 was the club's second-best of the season.

Record Defeat: 1–8 v Mansfield T, Division 3, 15 March 1965.
1–8 v Manchester U, Division 1, 19 March 1969.

Most League Points (2 for a win): 67, Division 3, 1966–67.

Most League Points (3 for a win): 88, FL C, 2010–11.

Most League Goals: 111, Division 3, 1961–62.

Highest League Scorer in Season: George Goddard, 37,
Division 3 (S), 1929–30.

Most League Goals in Total Aggregate: George Goddard,
172, 1926–34.

Most League Goals in One Match: 4, George Goddard v
Merthyr T, Division 3 (S), 9 March 1929; 4, George Goddard
v Swindon T, Division 3 (S), 12 April 1930; 4, George
Goddard v Exeter C, Division 3 (S), 20 December 1930; 4,
George Goddard v Watford, Division 3 (S), 19 September
1931; 4, Tom Cheetham v Aldershot, Division 3 (S),
14 September 1935; 4, Tom Cheetham v Aldershot, Division
3 (S), 12 November 1938.

Most Capped Player: Alan McDonald, 52, Northern Ireland.

Most League Appearances: Tony Ingham, 519, 1950–63.

Youngest League Player: Frank Sibley, 16 years 97 days v
Bristol C, 10 March 1964.

Record Transfer Fee Received: £12,000,000 from Anzhi
Makhachkala for Chris Samba, July 2013.

Record Transfer Fee Paid: £12,500,000 to Anzhi Makhachkala
for Chris Samba, January 2013.

Football League Record: 1920 Original Members of Division
3; 1921–48 Division 3 (S); 1948–52 Division 2; 1952–58
Division 3 (S); 1958–67 Division 3; 1967–68 Division 2;
1968–69 Division 1; 1969–73 Division 2; 1973–79 Division 1;
1979–83 Division 2; 1983–92 Division 1; 1992–96 FA Premier
League; 1996–2001 Division 1; 2001–04 Division 2; 2004–11
FL C; 2011–13 FA Premier League; 2013–14 FL C; 2014– FA
Premier League.

LATEST SEQUENCES

Longest Sequence of League Wins: 8, 7.11.1931 – 28.12.1931.

Longest Sequence of League Defeats: 9, 25.2.1969 – 5.4.1969.

Longest Sequence of League Draws: 6, 29.1.2000 – 5.3.2000.

Longest Sequence of Unbeaten League Matches: 20, 11.3.1972
– 23.9.1972.

Longest Sequence Without a League Win: 20, 7.12.1968 –
7.4.1969.

Successive Scoring Runs: 33 from 9.12.1961.

Successive Non-scoring Runs: 6 from 18.3.1939.

MANAGERS

James Cowan 1906–13
Jimmy Howie 1913–20
Ned Liddell 1920–24
Will Wood 1924–25
    (had been Secretary since 1903)
Bob Hewison 1925–31
John Bowman 1931
Archie Mitchell 1931–33
Mick O'Brien 1933–35
Billy Birrell 1935–39
Ted Vizard 1939–44
Dave Mangnall 1944–52
Jack Taylor 1952–59
Alec Stock 1959–65
    (General Manager to 1968)
Bill Dodgin Jnr 1968
Tommy Docherty 1968
Les Allen 1968–71
Gordon Jago 1971–74
Dave Sexton 1974–77
Frank Sibley 1977–78
Steve Burtenshaw 1978–79
Tommy Docherty 1979–80
Terry Venables 1980–84
Gordon Jago 1984
Alan Mullery 1984
Frank Sibley 1984–85
Jim Smith 1985–88
Trevor Francis 1988–89
Don Howe 1989–91
Gerry Francis 1991–94
Ray Wilkins 1994–96
Stewart Houston 1996–97
Ray Harford 1997–98
Gerry Francis 1998–2001
Ian Holloway 2001–06
Gary Waddock 2006
John Gregory 2006–07
Luigi Di Canio 2007–08
Iain Dowie 2008
Paulo Sousa 2008–09
Jim Magilton 2009
Paul Hart 2009–10
Neil Warnock 2010–12
Mark Hughes 2012
Harry Redknapp November 2012–

TEN YEAR LEAGUE RECORD

		P	W	D	L	F	A	Pts	Pos
2004-05	FL C	46	17	11	18	54	58	62	11
2005-06	FL C	46	12	14	20	50	65	50	21
2006-07	FL C	46	14	11	21	54	68	53	18
2007-08	FL C	46	14	16	16	60	66	58	14
2008-09	FL C	46	15	16	15	42	44	61	11
2009-10	FL C	46	14	15	17	58	65	57	13
2010-11	FL C	46	24	16	6	71	32	88	1
2011-12	PR Lge	38	10	7	21	43	66	37	17
2012-13	PR Lge	38	4	13	21	30	60	25	20
2013-14	FL C	46	23	11	12	60	44	80	4

DID YOU KNOW ?

After winning the Southern
League in 1907–08 Queens Park
Rangers travelled to Belgium to
play their first games in Europe in
May 1908. Their results included
a 5-2 win over Racing Club
Brussels and a 1-1 draw with a
local select team.

QUEENS PARK RANGERS – FL CHAMPIONSHIP 2013–14 LEAGUE RECORD

Match No.	Date	Venue	Opponents	Result	H/T Score	Lg Pos.	Goalscorers	Attendance
1	Aug 3	H	Sheffield W	W 2-1	2-1	3	Onuoha [40], Johnson [43]	17,626
2	10	A	Huddersfield T	D 1-1	1-1	4	Hoilett [38]	13,896
3	17	H	Ipswich T	W 1-0	0-0	5	Hitchcock [90]	17,075
4	24	A	Bolton W	W 1-0	0-0	3	Johnson [54]	14,999
5	31	A	Leeds U	W 1-0	0-0	2	Hill [75]	23,341
6	Sept 14	H	Birmingham C	W 1-0	0-0	2	Austin [49]	16,953
7	18	H	Brighton & HA	D 0-0	0-0	1		17,246
8	21	A	Yeovil T	W 1-0	0-0	1	Austin (pen) [75]	9108
9	28	H	Middlesbrough	W 2-0	2-0	1	Barton [4], Austin (pen) [35]	17,081
10	Oct 5	H	Barnsley	W 2-0	0-0	2	Austin 2 (1 pen) [66, 87 (p)]	16,202
11	19	A	Millwall	D 2-2	1-0	2	Kranjcar [26], Austin [69]	13,727
12	26	A	Burnley	L 0-2	0-0	3		16,074
13	30	A	Wigan Ath	D 0-0	0-0	3		13,143
14	Nov 2	H	Derby Co	W 2-1	1-1	3	Jenas [11], Eustace (og) [63]	18,171
15	9	A	Reading	D 1-1	0-0	3	Barton [78]	21,497
16	23	H	Charlton Ath	W 1-0	1-0	3	Austin [40]	17,397
17	30	A	Doncaster R	L 1-2	1-0	3	Austin [43]	8854
18	Dec 3	H	Bournemouth	W 3-0	1-0	2	Austin [27], Hoilett [54], Phillips [77]	16,331
19	7	H	Blackburn R	D 0-0	0-0	2		15,987
20	14	A	Blackpool	W 2-0	0-0	1	Phillips [61], Austin [73]	13,822
21	21	H	Leicester C	L 0-1	0-1	2		17,713
22	26	A	Nottingham F	L 0-2	0-1	3		22,721
23	29	A	Watford	D 0-0	0-0	4		16,625
24	Jan 1	H	Doncaster R	W 2-1	0-1	3	Phillips [55], Austin [90]	15,807
25	11	A	Ipswich T	W 3-1	0-0	3	Kranjcar [52], O'Neil [66], Traore [74]	18,369
26	18	H	Huddersfield T	W 2-1	0-0	2	Austin 2 [55, 79]	17,185
27	28	H	Bolton W	W 2-1	1-0	2	Austin [41], Henry [50]	15,097
28	Feb 1	H	Burnley	D 3-3	2-1	2	Doyle [7], Dunne [34], Maiga [79]	16,393
29	10	A	Derby Co	L 0-1	0-1	3		23,495
30	16	H	Reading	L 1-3	1-1	3	Doyle [20]	16,522
31	22	A	Charlton Ath	L 0-1	0-0	4		17,333
32	Mar 1	H	Leeds U	D 1-1	1-1	4	Jenas [44]	16,448
33	8	A	Birmingham C	W 2-0	1-0	4	Morrison 2 [14, 73]	14,500
34	11	A	Brighton & HA	L 0-2	0-0	4		28,019
35	15	A	Yeovil T	W 3-0	1-0	4	Morrison 2 [25, 90], Zamora [70]	16,667
36	18	A	Sheffield W	L 0-3	0-1	4		18,029
37	22	A	Middlesbrough	W 3-1	1-1	4	Benayoun [45], Morrison [90], Zamora [90]	15,075
38	25	H	Wigan Ath	W 1-0	1-0	3	Benayoun [16]	14,649
39	29	H	Blackpool	D 1-1	0-1	3	Hoilett [78]	16,638
40	Apr 5	A	Bournemouth	L 1-2	0-1	3	Traore [46]	11,307
41	8	A	Blackburn R	L 0-2	0-1	4		12,915
42	12	H	Nottingham F	W 5-2	2-1	4	Benayoun [2], Hoilett [43], Onuoha [84], Morrison [90], Zamora [90]	17,220
43	19	A	Leicester C	L 0-1	0-0	4		27,386
44	21	H	Watford	W 2-1	0-0	4	Barton [76], Austin [90]	16,951
45	26	H	Millwall	D 1-1	0-0	4	Austin (pen) [78]	15,725
46	May 3	A	Barnsley	W 3-2	2-0	4	Austin [42], Mvoto (og) [43], Yun [68]	10,298

Final League Position: 4

GOALSCORERS

League (60): Austin 17 (4 pens), Morrison 6, Hoilett 4, Barton 3, Benayoun 3, Phillips 3, Zamora 3, Doyle 2, Jenas 2, Johnson 2, Kranjcar 2, Onuoha 2, Traore 2, Dunne 1, Henry 1, Hill 1, Hitchcock 1, Maiga 1, O'Neil 1, Yun 1, own goals 2.
The Budweiser FA Cup (0).
Capital One Cup (2): Austin 1, Simpson 1.
Championship Play-Offs (3): Austin 2, Zamora 1.

Green R 45	Simpson D 32+1	Traore A 13+9	Henry K 17+10	Hill C 40	Onuoha N 24+2	Barton J 33+1	Faurlin A 5+2	Zamora B 7+10	Johnson A 10+7	Hoilett J 23+12	Austin C 28+3	Wright-Phillips S 4+7	Jenas J 15+11	Yun S 4+3	Granero E 1	Dunne R 41	O'Neil G 23+6	Hitchcock T —+1	Carroll T 23+3	Phillips M 13+8	Assou-Ekotto B 30+1	Kranjcar N 21+8	Ehmer M —+1	Chevanton J —+2	Benayoun Y 10+6	Doyle K 8+1	Maiga M 2+6	Hughes A 11	Keane W 6+4	Morrison R 14+1	Murphy B 1+1	Young L 1	Donaldson C 1	Petrasso M —+1	Match No.
1	2	3	4	5	6	7³	8	9¹	10	11²	12	13	14																						1
1	2		8²	4	3	7			11	9	10	12	13	5	6¹																				2
1	2		8²	5	4	7			10³		9¹	11	6	13		3	12	14																	3
1	2	13	8	5	3	7			12	11²	10¹	6³	14			4	9																		4
1	2		8¹	5	3	7	13		11³	12	10	9	14			4	6²																		5
1	2			5	4	8			11¹	9¹	10	13	14			3	6		7²	12															6
1	2	14	7¹	5	3²	6				11	8	13				3	4		9			10³	12												7
1	2	11³		4		14			10	12	7					3	6¹		8	9²	5	13													8
1	2	13	4²		7	8¹			14	11						3	6		10		5	9³	12												9
1	2	13	4		6	9²			12	11						3	8¹		7		5	10³	14												10
1	2	6	4		7	12³			9²	10		14				3	8		13	5	11¹														11
1	2	7³	4		6				10	11	12					3	8¹		14	5	9²	13													12
1	2		4		7				13	10²	11	6				3	8		12	5	9¹														13
1	2	13	12	4		6	7¹			8²	11		9			3			10	5															14
1	2		4	13	6				14	10	11		9²			3¹	7³		8	5	12														15
1	2	12	4		6				14		11	13	9¹			3	7		8²	5	10²														16
1	2		4		7				12	13	11	6				3	9²		8	5	10¹														17
1	2	14	4		7				10¹	9¹	11	12				3	6²	8	13	5															18
1	2	14	4		7				11	9²	10					3	13	8	6²	5¹	12														19
1	2	14	4¹	12	7					11		9³				3	8²	6	10	5	13														20
1	2		4		6⁴				12	11						3	7¹	9²	8	5	10			13											21
1	2	6²	4					11¹	13	12		9				3		7	8³	5	10	14													22
1	2	14		3	7				12	11¹						4	13	8³	9	5	10			6²											23
1	2	14		4	7				13	10³	11					3	6		12	5	9¹			8²											24
1	2	13	12	4		7³				11						3	8	6	14	5	9²			10¹											25
1	2	13	6	4					11²	9						3	8¹	7	12	5	10														26
1		5	8	4					12	10		11¹	13			3		7	6	2	9²														27
1		9¹	14	4	2	8			10²	12						3		6³	5	7					11	13									28
1			4		7				11³	12			14			3	6¹	8²	5	9					10	13	2								29
1		9	4		7			12		6						3			5²	8		13	11			2	10¹								30
1		8	4	2				9²		6						3	7¹					14	11³	13		5	12	10							31
1		10	6	5	3				8²			7³				4			13			14	11		2	12	9²								32
1		10		4	2	6			8¹			7				3			12							11³	13	9²							33
1		10		4	2	6			8			7				3			5¹						12		11	9							34
1¹		10³		4	2	7		13	8		6					3							12				5	11²	9	14					35
		7³	5	3	6			11	10¹				13			4⁴	8²	14			12				2		9	1							36
1			4	3	7			13	12				5			14	8		9²			6¹			2	11³	10								37
1		13	5	3	6²			11					14			4	12	7		10¹			8⁴			2		9³							38
1	12		6	5	3¹			11²	13							4			7	10					14	2³	8	9							39
1	2	9¹		4				14		6	12		8²			3			7	5					13	11³		10							40
1	2		6					10	13				14			4			7¹	5²			8		12		11³	9		3					41
1	2	12		3				13	10¹	11²		6¹				4			7	5	14		8					9							42
1	2	7		4				13			12		5			6						10⁴	9¹		8³		11²	3	14						43
1	2¹	10	14	5	3	6			13			12	11³			4			7						8²			9							44
1	2		5	3	6			13			12	11¹				4			7						10³		8²	14		9					45
1		10³	7		4					11²				5			6							12			8¹	9		3	13			2	46

The Budweiser FA Cup

Third Round	Everton	(a)	0-4

Capital One Cup

First Round	Exeter C	(a)	2-0
Second Round	Swindon T	(h)	0-2

Championship Play-Offs

Semi-Finals 1st leg	Wigan Ath	(a)	0-0
Semi-Finals 2nd leg	Wigan Ath	(h)	2-1
Final	Derby Co	(Wembley)	1-0

READING

FOUNDATION

Reading was formed as far back as 1871 at a public meeting held at the Bridge Street Rooms. They first entered the FA Cup as early as 1877 when they amalgamated with the Reading Hornets. The club was further strengthened in 1889 when Earley FC joined them. They were the first winners of the Berks & Bucks Cup in 1878–79.

Madejski Stadium, Junction 11, M4, Reading, Berkshire RG2 0FL.

Telephone: (0118) 968 1100.

Fax: (0118) 968 1101.

Ticket Office: (0844) 249 1871.

Website: www.readingfc.co.uk

Email: customerservice@readingfc.co.uk

Ground Capacity: 24,197.

Record Attendance: 33,042 v Brentford, FA Cup 5th rd, 19 February 1927 (at Elm Park); 24,122 v Aston Villa, FA Premier League, 10 February 2007 (at Madejski Stadium).

Pitch Measurements: 105m × 68m (115yd × 74.5yd)

Chairman: Sir John Madejski

Chief Executive: Nigel Howe.

Manager: Nigel Adkins.

Assistant Manager: Andy Crosby.

Head of Sports Science: Nick Harvey.

HONOURS

FA Premier League: Best season: 8th 2006–07.

Football League – FL C:
Champions 2005–06, 2011–12;
Division 1: *Runners-up* 1994–95;
Division 2: *Champions* 1993–94;
Runners-up 2001–02;
Division 3: *Champions* 1985–86;
Division 3 (S): *Champions* 1925–26;
Runners-up 1931–32, 1934–35, 1948–49, 1951–52;
Division 4: *Champions* 1978–79.

FA Cup: Semi-final 1927.

Football League Cup: Best season: 5th rd, 1996, 1998.

Simod Cup: *Winners* 1988.

Colours: Blue and white hooped shirts, blue shorts with red and white trim, white socks with blue trim.

Year Formed: 1871.

Turned Professional: 1895.

Club Nickname: 'The Royals'.

Grounds: 1871, Reading Recreation; Reading Cricket Ground; 1882, Coley Park; 1889, Caversham Cricket Ground; 1896, Elm Park; 1998, Madejski Stadium.

First Football League Game: 28 August 1920, Division 3, v Newport Co (a) W 1–0 – Crawford; Smith, Horler; Christie, Mavin, Getgood; Spence, Weston, Yarnell, Bailey (1), Andrews.

Record League Victory: 10–2 v Crystal Palace, Division 3 (S), 4 September 1946 – Groves; Glidden, Gulliver; McKenna, Ratcliffe, Young; Chitty, Maurice Edelston (3), McPhee (4), Barney (1), Deverell (2).

Record Cup Victory: 6–0 v Leyton, FA Cup 2nd rd, 12 December 1925 – Duckworth; Eggo, McConnell; Wilson, Messer, Evans; Smith (2), Braithwaite (1), Davey (1), Tinsley, Robson (2).

Record Defeat: 0–18 v Preston NE, FA Cup 1st rd, 1893–94.

sky SPORTS FACT FILE

Harry Baker played his first and only game for Reading against Bristol St George's in a friendly match on 28 January 1899. Tragically he suffered a compound fracture of the right ankle during the match. The injury became infected and he died of tetanus on 5 February. He was just 24 years old.

Most League Points (2 for a win): 65, Division 4, 1978–79.

Most League Points (3 for a win): 106, Championship, 2005–06 (Football League Record).

Most League Goals: 112, Division 3 (S), 1951–52.

Highest League Scorer in Season: Ronnie Blackman, 39, Division 3 (S), 1951–52.

Most League Goals in Total Aggregate: Ronnie Blackman, 158, 1947–54.

Most League Goals in One Match: 6, Arthur Bacon v Stoke C, Division 2, 3 April 1931.

Most Capped Player: Kevin Doyle, 26 (59), Republic of Ireland.

Most League Appearances: Martin Hicks, 500, 1978–91.

Youngest League Player: Peter Castle, 16 years 49 days v Watford, 30 April 2003.

Record Transfer Fee Received: £7,000,000 from TSG 1899 Hoffenheim for Gylfi Sigurdsson, August 2010.

Record Transfer Fee Paid: £2,500,000 to Nantes for Emerse Fae, August 2007.

Football League Record: 1920 Original Member of Division 3; 1921–26 Division 3 (S); 1926–31 Division 2; 1931–58 Division 3 (S); 1958–71 Division 3; 1971–76 Division 4; 1976–77 Division 3; 1977–79 Division 4; 1979–83 Division 3; 1983–84 Division 4; 1984–86 Division 3; 1986–88 Division 2; 1988–92 Division 3; 1992–94 Division 2; 1994–98 Division 1; 1998–2002 Division 2; 2002–04 Division 1; 2004–06 FL C; 2006–08 FA Premier League; 2008–12 FL C; 2012–13 FA Premier League; 2013– FL C.

LATEST SEQUENCES

Longest Sequence of League Wins: 13, 17.8.1985 – 19.10.1985.

Longest Sequence of League Defeats: 8, 29.12.2007 – 24.2.2008.

Longest Sequence of League Draws: 6, 23.3.2002 – 20.4.2002.

Longest Sequence of Unbeaten League Matches: 33, 9.8.2005 – 14.2.2006.

Longest Sequence Without a League Win: 14, 30.4.1927 – 29.10.1927.

Successive Scoring Runs: 32 from 1.10.1932.

Successive Non-scoring Runs: 6 from 29.3.2008.

MANAGERS

Thomas Sefton 1897–1901
(Secretary-Manager)
James Sharp 1901–02
Harry Matthews 1902–20
Harry Marshall 1920–22
Arthur Chadwick 1923–25
H. S. Bray 1925–26
(Secretary only since 1922 and 1926–35)
Andrew Wylie 1926–31
Joe Smith 1931–35
Billy Butler 1935–39
John Cochrane 1939
Joe Edelston 1939–47
Ted Drake 1947–52
Jack Smith 1952–55
Harry Johnston 1955–63
Roy Bentley 1963–69
Jack Mansell 1969–71
Charlie Hurley 1972–77
Maurice Evans 1977–84
Ian Branfoot 1984–89
Ian Porterfield 1989–91
Mark McGhee 1991–94
Jimmy Quinn/Mick Gooding 1994–97
Terry Bullivant 1997–98
Tommy Burns 1998–99
Alan Pardew 1999–2003
Steve Coppell 2003–09
Brendan Rodgers 2009
Brian McDermott 2009–13
Nigel Adkins March 2013–

TEN YEAR LEAGUE RECORD

		P	W	D	L	F	A	Pts	Pos
2004-05	FL C	46	19	13	14	51	44	70	7
2005-06	FL C	46	31	13	2	99	32	106	1
2006-07	PR Lge	38	16	7	15	52	47	55	8
2007-08	PR Lge	38	10	6	22	41	66	36	18
2008-09	FL C	46	21	14	11	72	40	77	4
2009-10	FL C	46	17	12	17	68	63	63	9
2010-11	FL C	46	20	17	9	77	51	77	5
2011-12	FL C	46	27	8	11	69	41	89	1
2012-13	PR Lge	38	6	10	22	43	73	28	19
2013-14	FL C	46	19	14	13	70	56	71	7

DID YOU KNOW

Reading centre forward Allen Foster enlisted with the Footballers' Battalion during the First World War. After suffering severe wounds in the arm, leg and abdomen he was evacuated from the front line, but died of his wounds on 8 August 1916.

READING – FL CHAMPIONSHIP 2013–14 LEAGUE RECORD

Match No.	Date	Venue	Opponents	Result	H/T Score	Lg Pos.	Goalscorers	Atten-dance
1	Aug 3	H	Ipswich T	W 2-1	1-1	3	Le Fondre [45], Guthrie [75]	20,456
2	10	A	Bolton W	D 1-1	0-1	4	Blackman (pen) [51]	15,551
3	17	H	Watford	D 3-3	2-0	8	Le Fondre [8], Karacan 2 [42, 70]	20,875
4	24	A	Blackpool	L 0-1	0-0	12		12,928
5	31	A	Yeovil T	W 1-0	0-0	9	Le Fondre (pen) [77]	7306
6	Sept 15	H	Brighton & HA	D 0-0	0-0	9		18,306
7	18	H	Leeds U	W 1-0	0-0	7	Le Fondre [90]	21,167
8	21	A	Derby Co	W 3-1	0-0	7	Pogrebnyak 2 [47, 62], Blackman [90]	21,465
9	28	H	Birmingham C	W 2-0	1-0	6	Guthrie 2 [32, 75]	18,252
10	Oct 1	A	Barnsley	D 1-1	0-0	5	Robson-Kanu [51]	9084
11	5	A	Burnley	L 1-2	0-1	7	Shackell (og) [82]	11,256
12	19	H	Doncaster R	W 4-1	2-1	6	Guthrie [11], Le Fondre [39], McCleary [80], Pogrebnyak [90]	17,697
13	26	A	Millwall	D 1-1	1-0	5	Morrison [9]	18,245
14	Nov 2	A	Sheffield W	L 2-5	1-3	5	Pogrebnyak [35], Le Fondre (pen) [90]	20,368
15	9	H	QPR	D 1-1	0-0	6	McCleary [62]	21,497
16	23	A	Blackburn R	D 0-0	0-0	8		12,903
17	29	H	Nottingham F	W 3-2	2-1	4	Pogrebnyak [8], Gorkss [13], Obita [74]	21,199
18	Dec 3	H	Charlton Ath	W 1-0	1-0	4	Sharp [13]	18,149
19	7	H	Bournemouth	L 1-2	0-2	6	Le Fondre [90]	20,944
20	14	A	Huddersfield T	W 1-0	1-0	5	Sharp [32]	13,572
21	21	H	Wigan Ath	L 1-2	0-2	6	Pogrebnyak [68]	18,336
22	26	A	Leicester C	L 0-1	0-1	8		26,722
23	29	A	Middlesbrough	L 0-3	0-2	9		16,001
24	Jan 1	H	Nottingham F	D 1-1	0-0	9	Kelly [90]	19,873
25	11	A	Watford	W 1-0	1-0	7	Gorkss [5]	15,725
26	18	H	Bolton W	W 7-1	4-0	6	Le Fondre 3 [12, 28, 33], Pogrebnyak (pen) [41], Gorkss [60], Akpan [74], Blackman [78]	18,629
27	25	A	Ipswich T	L 0-2	0-0	6		15,323
28	28	A	Blackpool	W 5-1	2-0	6	Le Fondre 3 [7, 17, 67], Pogrebnyak [52], Robson-Kanu [82]	16,636
29	Feb 1	A	Millwall	W 3-0	1-0	6	Pogrebnyak [39], Pearce [72], Williams, D [76]	11,174
30	8	H	Sheffield W	L 0-2	0-1	6		19,772
31	16	H	QPR	W 3-1	1-1	6	Williams, D [10], Pearce [56], McCleary [58]	16,522
32	22	H	Blackburn R	L 0-1	0-1	6		18,858
33	Mar 1	H	Yeovil T	D 1-1	0-1	7	Lundstram (og) [68]	18,697
34	8	A	Brighton & HA	D 1-1	0-1	6	Drenthe [64]	27,532
35	11	A	Leeds U	W 4-2	1-0	6	McCleary [25], Drenthe [46], Blackman [48], Robson-Kanu [54]	19,915
36	15	H	Derby Co	D 0-0	0-0	7		19,514
37	22	A	Birmingham C	W 2-1	1-1	6	McAnuff 2 [39, 82]	13,409
38	25	H	Barnsley	L 1-3	1-1	6	Pogrebnyak (pen) [20]	16,645
39	29	H	Huddersfield T	D 1-1	1-1	6	Pogrebnyak (pen) [7]	17,649
40	Apr 5	A	Charlton Ath	W 1-0	0-0	6	Williams, D [73]	15,800
41	8	A	Bournemouth	L 1-3	0-3	6	Robson-Kanu [75]	11,182
42	14	H	Leicester C	D 1-1	1-1	6	Pearce [16]	20,072
43	18	A	Wigan Ath	L 0-3	0-2	7		14,609
44	22	H	Middlesbrough	W 2-0	2-0	6	Le Fondre [9], Friend (og) [14]	17,228
45	26	A	Doncaster R	W 3-1	0-1	5	Le Fondre (pen) [63], Pogrebnyak 2 [86, 90]	10,212
46	May 3	H	Burnley	D 2-2	1-2	7	Trippier (og) [16], McCleary [58]	23,335

Final League Position: 7

GOALSCORERS

League (70): Le Fondre 15 (3 pens), Pogrebnyak 13 (3 pens), McCleary 5, Blackman 4 (1 pen), Guthrie 4, Robson-Kanu 4, Gorkss 3, Pearce 3, Williams, D 3, Drenthe 2, Karacan 2, McAnuff 2, Sharp 2, Akpan 1, Kelly 1, Morrison 1, Obita 1, own goals 4.
The Budweiser FA Cup (0).
Capital One Cup (0).

McCarthy A 44	Gunter C 44	Bridge W 11 + 1	Guthrie D 29 + 3	Pearce A 45	Morrison S 21	McCleary G 35 + 7	Karacan J 7	Le Fondre A 25 + 13	Drenthe R 17 + 6	Robson-Kanu H 19 + 17	Williams D 24 + 6	McAnuff J 28 + 7	Pogrebnyak P 34 + 5	Blackman N 9 + 21	Cummings S 8 + 3	Akpan H 17 + 12	Kelly S 10 + 5	Baird C 9	Obita J 32 + 2	Sharp B 6 + 4	Taylor J — + 8	Federici A 2	Gorkss K 24 + 1	Hector M 4 + 5	Leigertwood M 2 + 2	Match No.
1	2	3	4	5	6	7	8	9³	10³	11¹	12	13	14													1
1	2	5	7¹	4	3	6²	9	12	8	13	14	10		11²												2
1	2	5	7	4	3	14	8³	11	9¹	13	12	6²	10													3
1	2	5	8²	4	3	6²	7	12	9	11¹	13		14	10												4
1	2		8	3	4	6¹	7	10	9²	13	12			11¹	5	14										5
1	2	13	6	4	3		7³	11	9¹	12	8		10⁸	14			5²									6
1		5	6	4	3	14	7²	13	11	9³	8		10³		12		2									7
1	2		6	4	3	11²		9		10	14	13	12	5	7¹	8³										8
1	2	5	8	4	3	9³		11²		6¹		10			12	14	7	13								9
1	2	8²	4	3	9¹		10³		6	12	11			13	5	7		14								10
1	2	5	7	4	3			14		9¹		11¹	10	13			6²	8	12							11
	2	5	8¹	3	4	6		11²		12	13	10		14			7	9³		1						12
	2	5³	6	4	3	9		11¹		12	13	10			14	7	8²		1							13
1	2		8¹	4	3	6²		12		11		10	13		5	7	9									14
1	2	8²		3	6³			10¹		13	11		12	5	7	9	14			4						15
1	2	7	3		8¹		11²		13		9	14		12	5	6²	10			4						16
1	2⁸	7	3	10			6¹	8	12	11³	14		5			9²	13			4						17
1		7	4	6¹			13	8²	9	10	14	2	12	5			11³		3							18
1	2	7	4	9³		14	13	11²	6		12		5			8	10		3¹							19
1	2	3		12		9³		7	6	10	13	5	14			8²	11¹		4							20
1	2	7	3²	13		14	6³	8	9	10		5¹			12	11			4							21
1	2	8	3		13	10²	7	9¹	11	6	5				12				4							22
1	2	8	3	6¹			7	9	11	12	5	13			10²				4⁸							23
1	2	8	3	6²	12	13	7	10	9	4¹	5				11³	14										24
1	2		4	5²	11		6	9	10	12	13	8³		7¹		14			3							25
1	2	3	6¹	11³		7	9	10	12	8				5	13			4²	14							26
1	2	3	6¹	11		7	9	10	12	8				5				4								27
1	2	3	6	11¹	12	8	9²	10	13	7				5				4³	14							28
1	2	3	6	11²	13	7	9	10¹	14	8³				5	12			4								29
1	2	12	4⁸	6	11	14	7¹	9²	10	13		8³		5				3								30
1	2	3	6²	10¹	13	7	9	11³		8	14			5				4⁸	12							31
1	2	12	3	6¹	11	14	13	7	9	10²	8³			5				4								32
1	2	12	3	6	11	13	9¹	7		10	14	8³		5				4²								33
1	2	7	3	12	11	9³	10		13	6¹	8²			5	14			4								34
1	2	9	3	6³		8²	11¹	10		12	14	7		5				4	13							35
1	2	8	3	6	12	10¹	11²	9		13	7			5				4								36
1	2	7	3	12	11¹	10³	6²	9	13	14	8			5				4								37
1	2	3	6	12	10²	13	8	11	9¹	7				5				4								38
1	2	3	4	6³	13	12	10⁸	7¹	8	11	14	9											5			39
1	2	8	3	12	11²	6¹	13	7	9	10				5				4								40
1	2	5³	3	11²	6¹	7		8	10	14		13		9				4					12			41
1	2	5	3	4	9²		14	13	6¹	11	10			8²							7	12⁸				42
1	2	3	4	9¹	14		12	6³	11²	10	13		8	5					7							43
1	2	8²	4	3	6	10	11¹	7	9	12		13		5												44
1	2	4	3	6¹	11³	9	10		8²		5	12							14	13	7					45
1	2	4	3	6	11¹	13	9	10		8²	5	12									7					46

The Budweiser FA Cup
Third Round   Brighton & HA   (a)   0-1

Capital One Cup
Second Round   Peterborough U   (a)   0-6

ROCHDALE

FOUNDATION

Considering the love of rugby in their area, it is not surprising that Rochdale had difficulty in establishing an Association Football club. The earlier Rochdale Town club formed in 1900 went out of existence in 1907 when the present club was immediately established and joined the Manchester League, before graduating to the Lancashire Combination in 1908.

Spotland Stadium, Willbutts Lane, Rochdale, Lancs OL11 5DS.

Telephone: (0844) 826 1907.

Fax: (01706) 648 466.

Ticket Office: (0844) 826 1907 (option 8).

Website: www.rochdaleafc.co.uk

Email: admin@rochdaleafc.co.uk

Ground Capacity: 10,037.

Record Attendance: 24,231 v Notts Co, FA Cup 2nd rd, 10 December 1949.

Pitch Measurements: 104m × 69.5m (114yd × 76yd)

Chairman: Chris Dunphy.

Chief Executive: Colin Garlick.

Manager: Keith Hill.

Assistant Manager: Chris Beech.

Physio: Andy Thorpe.

Colours: Black and blue striped shirts with black sleeves, white shorts with blue trim, blue socks with black trim.

Year Formed: 1907.

Turned Professional: 1907.

Club Nickname: 'The Dale'.

Ground: 1907, St Clements Playing Fields (original name Spotland).

First Football League Game: 27 August 1921, Division 3 (N), v Accrington Stanley (h) W 6–3 – Crabtree; Nuttall, Sheehan; Hill, Farrer, Yarwood; Hoad, Sandiford, Dennison (2), Owens (3), Carney (1).

Record League Victory: 8–1 v Chesterfield, Division 3 (N), 18 December 1926 – Hill; Brown, Ward; Hillhouse, Parkes, Braidwood; Hughes, Bertram, Whitehurst (5), Schofield (2), Martin (1).

Record Cup Victory: 8–2 v Crook T, FA Cup 1st rd, 26 November 1927 – Moody; Hopkins, Ward; Braidwood, Parkes, Barker; Tompkinson, Clennell (3) Whitehurst (4), Hall, Martin (1).

Record Defeat: 1–9 v Tranmere R, Division 3 (N), 25 December 1931.

HONOURS

Football League – FL 1: Best season: 9th 2010–11; **FL 2:** Best season: 3rd 2009–10 (promoted to FL 1); **Division 3 (N):** *Runners-up* 1923–24, 1926–27.

FA Cup: Best season: 5th rd, 1990, 2003.

Football League Cup: *Runners-up* 1962.

sky SPORTS FACT FILE

Rochdale won 18 straight home games between December 1926 and October 1927. The run included consecutive victories over Chesterfield (8-1) and Lincoln City (7-3) with centre forward Bert Whitehurst netting 8 of the 15 goals. Whitehurst netted 117 League goals for Dale, a club record which was later surpassed by Reg Jenkins.

Most League Points (2 for a win): 62, Division 3 (N), 1923–24.

Most League Points (3 for a win): 82, FL 2, 2009–10.

Most League Goals: 105, Division 3 (N), 1926–27.

Highest League Scorer in Season: Albert Whitehurst, 44, Division 3 (N), 1926–27.

Most League Goals in Total Aggregate: Reg Jenkins, 119, 1964–73.

Most League Goals in One Match: 6, Tommy Tippett v Hartlepools U, Division 3 (N), 21 April 1930.

Most Capped Player: Leo Bertos, 6 (56), New Zealand.

Most League Appearances: Gary Jones, 470, 1998–2001; 2003–12.

Youngest League Player: Zac Hughes, 16 years 105 days v Exeter C, 19 September 1987.

Record Transfer Fee Received: £600,000 from WBA for Craig Dawson, August 2010.

Record Transfer Fee Paid: £150,000 to Stoke C for Paul Connor, March 2001.

Football League Record: 1921 Elected to Division 3 (N); 1958–59 Division 3; 1959–69 Division 4; 1969–74 Division 3; 1974–92 Division 4; 1992–2004 Division 3; 2004–10 FL 2; 2010–12 FL 1; 2012–14 FL 2; 2014– FL 1.

LATEST SEQUENCES

Longest Sequence of League Wins: 8, 29.9.1969 – 3.11.1969.

Longest Sequence of League Defeats: 17, 14.11.1931 – 12.3.1932.

Longest Sequence of League Draws: 6, 17.8.1968 – 14.9.1968.

Longest Sequence of Unbeaten League Matches: 20, 15.9.1923 – 19.1.1924.

Longest Sequence Without a League Win: 28, 14.11.1931 – 29.8.1932.

Successive Scoring Runs: 29 from 10.10.2008.

Successive Non-scoring Runs: 9 from 14.3.1980.

MANAGERS

Billy Bradshaw 1920
Run by committee 1920–22
Tom Wilson 1922–23
Jack Peart 1923–30
Will Cameron 1930–31
Herbert Hopkinson 1932–34
Billy Smith 1934–35
Ernest Nixon 1935–37
Sam Jennings 1937–38
Ted Goodier 1938–52
Jack Warner 1952–53
Harry Catterick 1953–58
Jack Marshall 1958–60
Tony Collins 1960–68
Bob Stokoe 1967–68
Len Richley 1968–70
Dick Conner 1970–73
Walter Joyce 1973–76
Brian Green 1976–77
Mike Ferguson 1977–78
Doug Collins 1979
Bob Stokoe 1979–80
Peter Madden 1980–83
Jimmy Greenhoff 1983–84
Vic Halom 1984–86
Eddie Gray 1986–88
Danny Bergara 1988–89
Terry Dolan 1989–91
Dave Sutton 1991–94
Mick Docherty 1994–96
Graham Barrow 1996–99
Steve Parkin 1999–2001
John Hollins 2001–02
Paul Simpson 2002–03
Alan Buckley 2003
Steve Parkin 2003–06
Keith Hill 2007–11
   (caretaker from December 2006)
Steve Eyre 2011
John Coleman 2012–13
Keith Hill January 2013–

TEN YEAR LEAGUE RECORD

		P	W	D	L	F	A	Pts	Pos
2004-05	FL 2	46	16	18	12	54	48	66	9
2005-06	FL 2	46	14	14	18	66	69	56	14
2006-07	FL 2	46	18	12	16	70	50	66	9
2007-08	FL 2	46	23	11	12	77	54	80	5
2008-09	FL 2	46	19	13	14	70	59	70	6
2009-10	FL 2	46	25	7	14	82	48	82	3
2010-11	FL 1	46	18	14	14	63	55	68	9
2011-12	FL 1	46	8	14	24	47	81	38	24
2012-13	FL 2	46	16	13	17	68	70	61	12
2013-14	FL 2	46	24	9	13	69	48	81	3

DID YOU KNOW ?

Rochdale won their first-ever Football League promotion in 1968–69. The team struggled to win in the first half of the season and drew 10 of their first 13 games; included in this was a run of five consecutive 1-1 draws with Steve Melledew scoring the Dale goal on each occasion.

ROCHDALE – FOOTBALL LEAGUE TWO 2013–14 LEAGUE RECORD

Match No.	Date	Venue	Opponents	Result	H/T Score	Lg Pos.	Goalscorers	Attendance
1	Aug 3	H	Hartlepool U	W	3-0	1-0	3	Hogan [14], Donnelly (pen) [50], Henderson [57]	3177
2	10	A	Burton Alb	L	0-1	0-1	9		2679
3	17	H	Chesterfield	D	2-2	1-1	9	Tutte (pen) [29], Hogan [51]	2899
4	24	A	Plymouth Arg	L	0-1	0-1	15		6978
5	31	A	Oxford U	D	1-1	0-1	17	Lund [51]	5260
6	Sept 7	H	Bury	W	1-0	1-0	13	Hogan [36]	5616
7	14	H	Torquay U	W	1-0	0-0	9	Henderson [77]	2138
8	21	A	Accrington S	W	2-1	2-1	7	Lund [7], Hogan [13]	2180
9	28	H	Wycombe W	W	3-2	3-1	5	Hogan [5], Bunney [10], Rose [15]	2303
10	Oct 5	H	Portsmouth	L	0-3	0-1	8		15,155
11	12	H	Newport Co	W	3-0	2-0	5	Vincenti [5], Cummins [38], Hery [72]	2530
12	19	A	Cheltenham T	W	2-1	0-0	3	Henderson 2 [82, 90]	2887
13	22	H	Northampton T	W	3-2	1-2	1	Henderson [26], Rose [88], Donnelly [90]	2362
14	26	A	Dagenham & R	L	1-3	0-1	2	Dicker [64]	1742
15	Nov 2	H	AFC Wimbledon	L	1-2	1-0	4	Allen [35]	2483
16	16	A	Morecambe	W	2-1	0-0	3	Hughes (og) [64], Hogan [66]	2563
17	23	H	Exeter C	W	3-1	1-0	3	Rose [39], Cummins [65], Tutte [87]	2428
18	26	H	Scunthorpe U	L	0-4	0-1	4		2174
19	30	A	York C	D	0-0	0-0	5		3471
20	Dec 14	H	Fleetwood T	L	1-2	1-1	8	Hogan [40]	2698
21	20	A	Southend U	D	1-1	1-1	8	Allen [14]	5104
22	26	H	Mansfield T	W	3-0	2-0	7	Hogan 2 [6, 50], Lund [13]	2671
23	29	H	Bristol R	W	2-0	0-0	4	Hogan [58], Cummins [62]	2576
24	Jan 1	A	Scunthorpe U	L	0-3	0-0	5		4017
25	11	A	Hartlepool U	W	3-0	0-0	4	Donnelly [50], Cavanagh [63], Cummins [90]	3685
26	18	H	Plymouth Arg	W	3-0	1-0	2	Allen [5], Henderson [76], Rose [89]	2839
27	21	A	Chesterfield	D	2-2	0-1	2	Henderson (pen) [90], Vincenti [90]	5078
28	Feb 1	H	Dagenham & R	L	0-1	0-0	6		2273
29	8	A	AFC Wimbledon	W	3-0	0-0	4	Hogan 3 [66, 79, 82]	3837
30	15	H	Morecambe	W	2-1	1-1	4	Hogan [35], Henderson [73]	2344
31	18	H	Burton Alb	D	1-1	0-1	4	Donnelly [67]	2092
32	22	A	Exeter C	W	1-0	1-0	3	Allen [45]	3169
33	Mar 1	H	Oxford U	W	3-0	1-0	3	Hogan 3 [45, 50, 62]	3429
34	7	A	Bury	D	0-0	0-0	2		6295
35	11	A	Torquay U	L	1-2	1-1	3	Allen [39]	1627
36	15	H	Accrington S	W	2-1	0-0	3	Lund 2 [77, 90]	2841
37	18	A	Northampton T	W	3-0	1-0	1	Henderson [6], Lund [54], Bunney [65]	3695
38	22	A	Wycombe W	W	2-0	0-0	1	Allen [52], Vincenti [75]	3594
39	25	H	Portsmouth	W	3-0	1-0	1	Lund [16], Henderson [59], Vincenti [63]	2746
40	29	A	Fleetwood T	D	0-0	0-0	1		4261
41	Apr 5	H	York C	D	0-0	0-0	1		3830
42	12	A	Mansfield T	L	0-3	0-0	2		3843
43	18	H	Southend U	L	0-3	0-2	3		3884
44	21	A	Bristol R	W	2-1	0-1	3	Bunney [46], Lund [63]	8158
45	26	H	Cheltenham T	W	2-0	2-0	1	Vincenti [11], Henderson [16]	4372
46	May 3	A	Newport Co	L	1-2	1-1	3	Donnelly [28]	4662

Final League Position: 3

GOALSCORERS

League (69): Hogan 17, Henderson 11 (1 pen), Lund 8, Allen 6, Donnelly 5 (1 pen), Vincenti 5, Cummins 4, Rose 4, Bunney 3, Tutte 2 (1 pen), Cavanagh 1, Dicker 1, Hery 1, own goal 1.
The Budweiser FA Cup (7): Hogan 2, Vincenti 2, Henderson 1, Lund 1, Rose 1.
Capital One Cup (0).
Johnstone's Paint Trophy (1): Rafferty 1.

Lillis J 45	Rafferty J 31	Rose M 42	Lund M 40	Eastham A 15	Lancashire O 38	Hogan S 29 + 4	Cavanagh P 17 + 3	Donnelly G 16 + 16	Vincenti P 31 + 11	Henderson J 45	Done M 25 + 13	Tutte A 7 + 4	Bunney J 7 + 14	O'Connell J 38	Bennett R 18 + 4	Vidal J 2	Hery B 4 + 8	Barry-Murphy B 3	Cummins G 15 + 12	Dicker G 10 + 2	Allen J 22 + 3	Molyneux L — + 3	Thomson R 1	Kennedy J 4 + 3	Gray R — + 3	Porter G 1 + 1	McGinty S — + 1	Lynch C — + 1	Match No.
1	2	3	4	5	6	7	8	9	10	11^1	12																		1
1	2	5	7	4	3	11	8^4	10	6^3	9^2	13	12	14																2
1	2^2	5	8		3	10^1		11	6	9	12	7		4	13														3
1		5	8		3	11		6	10	9^1	7^2	12		4	2		13												4
1		5	8^1		3	10^2		11	6	9	13			4	2		12	7											5
1		5	7		3	11		10	6^1	9				4	2				8	12									6
1		5	7		3	11		10		9	13			4	12	2^1	14	6^1	8^2										7
1		5	7		3	11^2		10^5	6^1	9	13			4	2				12	8									8
1		5	7		4	11		12	9	6^2				10^1	3	2			13	8									9
1		5^2	8		3	11		13	9	6				10^1	4	2		14	12	7^3									10
1	2	5	9^3		3			13	7	10	14			4					12	11^2	6	8^1							11
1	2	5	8		3			14	7^3	10			13	4					12	11^2	6	9^1							12
1	2	5	8^1		3			13	7	10			12	4				9^3	12	6	14								13
1	2^2	5	9		3			11^1	7^3	10	13	14		4					12	6	8								14
1	2	5	8		3	12			13	7	10^2			4					11^3	6	9^1								15
1	2	5	9	6	3	10^5			12	11		6		4					10^1										16
1	2	5	9	6	3	10^5					8	12	7	4					11										17
1		8	7^3	2	3^1	11			10	13	5^1			4^4	6		12		9^2			14							18
1	2	5	8	4		11			6	9^2	7^1			3					10	12		13							19
1		5		3		11	14		8^2	10	9^1	7^3	13	4	2					6		12							20
1	2	6	8	3^1	4	10^4	12		13	7^2	14			5					11		9								21
1	2	5	7		3	9^1	6		8	10				12	4				11				1						22
1	2	5	7		3	9	6		8	10				4					11										23
1	2	5^4	8		3	11^2	7^3	12	9^1	6	13			4					10		14								24
1		10	7^1		3	6^2	4	12^5	2	11	8	14	9	5					13										25
1		9			3	13	8^1	10^2	6	11	5			4	2				12	7									26
1	2		8^3		3^1	9		14	13	6	5			10	4	12			11^2	7									27
1		9	8	3		12		11^1	6^2	10	5			14	4	2^3			13			7							28
1	2	10	9	8	3	11^3		14	12	6^2	5			13	4					7^1		8							29
1	2	9	8	3		11			12	10	5				4					7^2		6^1	13						30
1	2	8	9	3		11			12	7^2	10	5			4					7^2		6^1	13						31
1	2	10	8^3		3	11^1	6	13	12	7		5			4					9^2		14							32
1	2	9			3	11^1	6	12	7	10		5			4					8									33
1	2	9		4		10^1	7	12	6	11^4	5				3					8^2							13		34
1	2	9^3		3^5		6	11	10		5	13	4						14		8^1				12	7^2				35
1	2	10	9	3		6	12	14	7^2	5	13	4						11^1		8^3									36
1	2	8^3	3			6	12	10	7	5	11^1	4								9									37
1	2	5	3^5	4		7	12	6	11	9	10^1				13					8									38
1	2	8	6	4		10^1	9^2	11	5	13		3								12	7								39
1	2	6^2	8	3		13	11^1	7	10	5	12				4					9^3		14							40
1	2	9	4	12		6		7^2	10	5	11^1	3								13	8								41
1	2	9^2	4	11		6^3	14	7^1	10	5	13	3								8	12								42
1	2	9^3	8	4		11^1	6^2	12	13	7	5	10			3					14									43
1		5	7	4		11^4	6^1	9		12	3	2		10	13					8^3							14		44
1		5	7	3		11^1	6	9		12	4	2	8							10									45
1		2^3	7	4		10^2	6	11	14	13	3	5		8^1						9								12	46

The Budweiser FA Cup

First Round	Torquay U	(a)	2-0
Second Round	Rotherham U	(a)	2-1
Third Round	Leeds U	(h)	2-0
Fourth Round	Sheffield W	(h)	1-2

Capital One Cup

First Round	Doncaster R	(a)	0-1

Johnstone's Paint Trophy

Second Round	Port Vale	(a)	1-0
Northern Quarter-Finals	Chesterfield	(a)	0-3

ROTHERHAM UNITED

FOUNDATION

Rotherham were formed in 1870 before becoming Town in the late 1880s. Thornhill United were founded in 1877 and changed their name to Rotherham County in 1905. The Town amalgamated with Rotherham County to form Rotherham United in 1925.

New York Stadium, New York Way, Rotherham, South Yorkshire S60 1AH

Telephone: (0844) 4140 733.

Fax: (0844) 4140 744.

Ticket Office: (0844) 4140 754.

Website: www.themillers.co.uk

Email: office@rotherhamunited.net

Ground Capacity: 12,009.

Record Attendance: 25,170 v Sheffield U, Division 2, 13 December 1952 (at Millmoor); 7,082 v Aldershot T, FL 2 Play-offs semi-final 2nd leg, 19 May 2010 (at Don Valley); 11,758 v Sheffield U, FL 1, 7 September 2013 (at New York Stadium).

Pitch Measurements: 102m × 66m (111.5yd × 72yd)

Chairman: Tony Stewart.

Manager: Steve Evans.

Assistant Manager: Paul Raynor.

Head of Medical: Denis Circuit.

Colours: Red shirts with white trim, white shorts, red socks with white trim.

Year Formed: 1870. *Turned Professional:* 1905. *Club Nickname:* 'The Millers'.

Previous Names: 1877, Thornhill United; 1905, Rotherham County; 1925, amalgamated with Rotherham Town under Rotherham United.

Grounds: 1870, Red House Ground; 1907, Millmoor; 2008, Don Valley Stadium; 2012, New York Stadium.

First Football League Game: 2 September 1893, Division 2, Rotherham T v Lincoln C (a) D 1–1 – McKay; Thickett, Watson; Barr, Brown, Broadhead; Longden, Cutts, Leatherbarrow, McCormick, Pickering, (1 og). 30 August 1919, Division 2, Rotherham Co v Nottingham F (h) W 2–0 – Branston; Alton, Baines; Bailey, Coe, Stanton; Lee (1), Cawley (1), Glennon, Lees, Lamb.

Record League Victory: 8–0 v Oldham Ath, Division 3 (N), 26 May 1947 – Warnes; Selkirk, Ibbotson; Edwards, Horace Williams, Danny Williams; Wilson (2), Shaw (1), Ardron (3), Guest (1), Hainsworth (1).

Record Cup Victory: 6–0 v Spennymoor U, FA Cup 2nd rd, 17 December 1977 – McAlister; Forrest, Breckin, Womble, Stancliffe, Green, Finney, Phillips (3), Gwyther (2) (Smith), Goodfellow, Crawford (1). 6–0 v Wolverhampton W, FA Cup 1st rd, 16 November 1985 – O'Hanlon; Forrest, Dungworth, Gooding (1), Smith (1), Pickering, Birch (2), Emerson, Tynan (1), Simmons (1), Pugh. 6–0 v Kings Lynn, FA Cup 2nd rd, 6 December 1997 – Mimms; Clark, Hurst (Goodwin), Garner (1) (Hudson) (1), Warner (Bass), Richardson (1), Berry (1), Thompson, Druce (1), Glover (1), Roscoe.

Record Defeat: 1–11 v Bradford C, Division 3 (N), 25 August 1928.

HONOURS

Football League – Division 2:
Runners-up 2000–01;
Division 3: *Champions* 1980–81;
Runners-up 1999–2000;
Division 3 (N): *Champions* 1950–51;
Runners-up 1946–47, 1947–48, 1948–49;
Division 4: *Champions* 1988–89;
Runners-up 1991–92.

FL 2: *Runners-up* 2012–13.

FA Cup: Best season: 5th rd, 1953, 1968.

Football League Cup:
Runners-up 1961.

Auto Windscreens Shield:
Winners 1996.

sky SPORTS FACT FILE

Tommy Docherty was appointed as manager of Rotherham United in November 1967 and within a week he had broken the club transfer record, signing Johnny Quinn from neighbours Sheffield Wednesday for a reported £27,500 fee. Quinn went on to play over 100 games for the Millers before leaving in the summer of 1972.

Most League Points (2 for a win): 71, Division 3 (N), 1950–51.

Most League Points (3 for a win): 91, Division 2, 2000–01.

Most League Goals: 114, Division 3 (N), 1946–47.

Highest League Scorer in Season: Wally Ardron, 38, Division 3 (N), 1946–47.

Most League Goals in Total Aggregate: Gladstone Guest, 130, 1946–56.

Most League Goals in One Match: 4, Roland Bastow v York C, Division 3 (N), 9 November 1935; 4, Roland Bastow v Rochdale, Division 3 (N), 7 March 1936; 4, Wally Ardron v Crewe Alex, Division 3 (N), 5 October 1946; 4, Wally Ardron v Carlisle U, Division 3 (N), 13 September 1947; 4, Wally Ardron v Hartlepools U, Division 3 (N), 13 October 1948; 4, Ian Wilson v Liverpool, Division 2, 2 May 1955; 4, Carl Gilbert v Swansea C, Division 3, 28 September 1971; 4, Carl Airey v Chester, Division 3, 31 August 1987; 4, Shaun Goater v Hartlepool U, Division 3, 9 April 1994; 4, Lee Glover v Hull C, Division 3, 28 December 1997; 4, Darren Byfield v Millwall, Division 1, 10 August 2002; 4, Adam Le Fondre v Cheltenham T, FL 2, 21 August 2010.

Most Capped Player: Shaun Goater, 14 (36), Bermuda.

Most League Appearances: Danny Williams, 459, 1946–62.

Youngest League Player: Kevin Eley, 16 years 72 days v Scunthorpe U, 15 May 1984.

Record Transfer Fee Received: £850,000 from Cardiff C for Alan Lee, August 2003.

Record Transfer Fee Paid: Undisclosed (in excess of £160,000) to Aston Villa for Jordan Bowery, June 2014.

Football League Record: 1893 Rotherham Town elected to Division 2; 1896 Failed re-election; 1919 Rotherham County elected to Division 2; 1923–51 Division 3 (N); 1951–68 Division 2; 1968–73 Division 3; 1973–75 Division 4; 1975–81 Division 3; 1981–83 Division 2; 1983–88 Division 3; 1988–89 Division 4; 1989–91 Division 3; 1991–92 Division 4; 1992–97 Division 2; 1997–2000 Division 3; 2000–01 Division 2; 2001–04 Division 1; 2004–05 FL C; 2005–07 FL 1; 2007–13 FL 2; 2013–14 FL 1; 2014– FL C.

MANAGERS

Billy Heald 1925–29 *(Secretary only for several years)*
Stanley Davies 1929–30
Billy Heald 1930–33
Reg Freeman 1934–52
Andy Smailes 1952–58
Tom Johnston 1958–62
Danny Williams 1962–65
Jack Mansell 1965–67
Tommy Docherty 1967–68
Jimmy McAnearney 1968–73
Jimmy McGuigan 1973–79
Ian Porterfield 1979–81
Emlyn Hughes 1981–83
George Kerr 1983–85
Norman Hunter 1985–87
Dave Cusack 1987–88
Billy McEwan 1988–91
Phil Henson 1991–94
Archie Gemmill/John McGovern 1994–96
Danny Bergara 1996–97
Ronnie Moore 1997–2005
Mick Harford 2005
Alan Knill 2005–07
Mark Robins 2007–09
Ronnie Moore 2009–11
Andy Scott 2011–12
Steve Evans April 2012–

LATEST SEQUENCES

Longest Sequence of League Wins: 9, 2.2.1982 – 6.3.1982.

Longest Sequence of League Defeats: 8, 7.4.1956 – 18.8.1956.

Longest Sequence of League Draws: 6, 13.10.1969 – 22.11.1969.

Longest Sequence of Unbeaten League Matches: 18, 13.10.1969 – 7.2.1970.

Longest Sequence Without a League Win: 21, 9.5.2004 – 20.11.2004.

Successive Scoring Runs: 30 from 3.4.1954.

Successive Non-scoring Runs: 6 from 21.8.2004.

TEN YEAR LEAGUE RECORD

		P	W	D	L	F	A	Pts	Pos
2004-05	FL C	46	5	14	27	35	69	29	24
2005-06	FL 1	46	12	16	18	52	62	52	20
2006-07	FL 1	46	13	9	24	58	75	38	23
2007-08	FL 2	46	21	11	14	62	58	64*	9
2008-09	FL 2	46	21	12	13	60	46	58†	14
2009-10	FL 2	46	21	10	15	55	52	73	5
2010-11	FL 2	46	17	15	14	75	60	66	9
2011-12	FL 2	46	18	13	15	67	63	67	10
2012-13	FL 2	46	24	7	15	74	59	79	2
2013-14	FL 1	46	24	14	8	86	58	86	4

*10 pts deducted; †7 pts deducted.

DID YOU KNOW ❓

Rotherham United came closest to reaching the top flight in the 1954–55 season. They hammered Liverpool 6-1 in their final match leaving them in second place in the Division Two table. Two days later Birmingham City completed their programme with a 5-1 win over Doncaster and pushed the Millers down into third place on goal average.

ROTHERHAM UNITED – FOOTBALL LEAGUE ONE 2013–14 LEAGUE RECORD

Match No.	Date	Venue	Opponents	Result	H/T Score	Lg Pos.	Goalscorers	Attendance
1	Aug 3	A	Crewe Alex	D	3-3	1-2	8	Frecklington 2 [10, 90], Pringle [86]	5926
2	10	H	Preston NE	D	0-0	0-0	13		8454
3	17	A	Crawley T	W	2-1	1-1	7	Agard [36], Worrall [78]	3110
4	24	H	Shrewsbury T	D	2-2	0-1	9	Revell [57], Nardiello [69]	7234
5	31	A	Notts Co	W	1-0	1-0	5	Agard [37]	5428
6	Sept 7	H	Sheffield U	W	3-1	0-1	4	Agard [51], Nardiello (pen) [72], Milsom [75]	11,758
7	14	H	Oldham Ath	W	3-2	1-1	4	Nardiello 2 (1 pen) [21 (pl, 90)], Frecklington [63]	8306
8	21	A	Walsall	D	1-1	1-1	5	Nardiello [21]	5002
9	28	H	Peterborough U	L	0-1	0-0	7		9717
10	Oct 5	A	Brentford	W	1-0	1-0	6	Bradley [14]	6614
11	12	H	Swindon T	L	0-4	0-2	6		8103
12	19	A	Milton Keynes D	L	2-3	0-1	10	Frecklington [73], Flanagan (og) [75]	11,564
13	22	H	Tranmere R	D	1-1	0-0	9	Agard [60]	7511
14	26	A	Leyton Orient	L	0-1	0-1	10		5609
15	Nov 2	H	Colchester U	D	2-2	2-1	10	Tubbs [9], Agard [22]	7096
16	16	A	Stevenage	W	3-0	1-0	7	Pringle [14], Davis [61], O'Connor [66]	2814
17	23	H	Carlisle U	D	0-0	0-0	10		7520
18	26	A	Coventry C	W	3-0	0-0	7	Dicko [58], Revell [70], Agard (pen) [73]	1961
19	30	H	Gillingham	W	4-1	3-0	6	Dicko [9], Agard [23], Pringle [35], Tavernier [76]	7152
20	Dec 14	A	Bristol C	W	2-1	2-0	6	Dicko [3], Pringle [27]	11,201
21	21	H	Wolverhampton W	D	3-3	2-1	6	Dicko 2 [11, 54], Agard [37]	11,092
22	26	A	Bradford C	W	1-0	1-0	6	Vuckic [21]	18,218
23	29	A	Port Vale	L	0-2	0-1	6		6738
24	Jan 1	H	Coventry C	L	1-3	1-0	6	Skarz [35]	9154
25	11	H	Crewe Alex	W	4-2	1-1	5	Agard [29], Frecklington 2 (1 pen) [68 (pl, 90)], Revell [74]	7737
26	18	A	Shrewsbury T	W	3-0	3-0	5	Hitchcock [10], Pringle [18], Tavernier [21]	5116
27	25	H	Crawley T	D	2-2	1-1	5	Agard 2 (1 pen) [34 (pl, 90)]	7579
28	28	A	Tranmere R	W	2-1	1-0	5	Revell 2 [39, 65]	3777
29	Feb 1	H	Leyton Orient	W	2-1	1-0	5	Thomas [10], Revell [90]	8604
30	15	H	Stevenage	W	2-1	1-0	5	Thomas [41], Frecklington [88]	7393
31	22	A	Carlisle U	W	2-1	1-1	5	Thomas [24], Agard [90]	4293
32	25	A	Preston NE	D	3-3	2-1	5	Frecklington 2 [7, 89], Clarke (og) [11]	9524
33	Mar 1	H	Notts Co	W	6-0	4-0	5	Tavernier [12], Vuckic 2 [16, 60], Revell [26], Agard (pen) [29], Hitchcock [83]	8383
34	4	A	Colchester U	D	0-0	0-0	5		2655
35	11	A	Oldham Ath	W	2-0	1-0	5	Bradley [27], Frecklington [64]	3745
36	15	H	Walsall	D	1-1	0-1	5	Adams [89]	8212
37	22	A	Peterborough U	W	1-0	1-0	4	Agard (pen) [45]	6625
38	25	H	Brentford	W	3-0	2-0	4	Agard 2 (1 pen) [14 (pl, 45)], Vuckic [90]	8365
39	29	H	Bristol C	W	2-1	1-0	4	Tavernier 2 [2, 60]	8607
40	Apr 5	A	Gillingham	W	4-3	1-1	3	Agard [2], Hitchcock 3 [69, 86, 90]	6027
41	8	A	Sheffield U	L	0-1	0-0	3		21,529
42	11	H	Bradford C	D	0-0	0-0	3		9228
43	18	A	Wolverhampton W	L	4-6	1-3	3	Agard 3 [14, 61, 88], Skarz [84]	30,110
44	21	H	Port Vale	W	1-0	0-0	3	Agard [79]	7743
45	26	H	Milton Keynes D	D	2-2	0-1	5	O'Connor [79], Revell [90]	9405
46	May 3	A	Swindon T	W	2-1	2-0	4	Thomas 2 [1, 23]	8618

Final League Position: 4

GOALSCORERS

League (86): Agard 21 (5 pens), Frecklington 10 (1 pen), Revell 8, Dicko 5, Hitchcock 5, Nardiello 5 (2 pens), Pringle 5, Tavernier 5, Thomas 5, Vuckic 4, Bradley 2, O'Connor 2, Skarz 2, Adams 1, Davis 1, Milsom 1, Tubbs 1, Worrall 1, own goals 2.
The Budweiser FA Cup (4): Agard 2, Frecklington 1, Revell 1.
Capital One Cup (2): Frecklington 1, Pringle 1.
Johnstone's Paint Trophy (6): Agard 2 (1 pen), Dicko 1, Eaves 1, Revell 1, own goal 1.
League One Play-Offs (6): Revell 3, Agard 1, Frecklington 1, Thomas 1.

Shearer S 12	Brindley R 11 + 5	Skarz J 39 + 2	Frecklington L 39	Arnason K 40	Davis C 14 + 2	Worrall D 1 + 2	Pringle B 44 + 1	Revell A 42 + 3	Morgan C 35	O'Connor M 15 + 14	Agard K 43 + 3	Tubbs M 7 + 10	Bradley M 20 + 2	Milsom R 18 + 9	Tidser M 2 + 8	Nardiello D 5 + 4	Mills P 4 + 6	Eaves T 1 + 7	Hylton D — + 1	Collin A 34	Dicko N 4 + 1	Tavernier J 27	Vuckic H 9 + 13	Addison M 4 + 2	Hitchcock T 4 + 7	Thomas W 8 + 5	Turgott B — + 1	Smallwood R 17 + 1	Adams N 7 + 8	Match No.
1	2	3	4	5	6^2	7^1	8	9	10	11	12	13																		1
1		5	7	4		12		9	10	3	8	6	11^1	2																2
1		5	4	3		12	6	10	9	8^3	11^2	2^1	7	13	14															3
1		5	7	4				9	10	3	8	6^2	11^1	2	13	12^4														4
1	12	5	9	4^2				10^3	11	3	6	8		2^1	7	14	13													5
1	2	5	10		3		8	11	4^1		9			6		12	7													6
1	2	5	7	4	3^3			9	10			6^1	13		8	14	11^2	12												7
1	2^2	5	7	3				9	11^3	4		6^1	14	12	8		10		13											8
1		5^1	7	4				9	10	3		6^2	12	2	8		11			13										9
1		5	7	3				9	10^1	4		6	11^1	2	8^2	13	14	12												10
1		5	7					9	10	3		6	12	2	8^1	13	11^2	4												11
1	2	5	9	4			8^2	11^1	3	10^4	6		7		13	12														12
1	2	5						9	12	3		6	13	7	8		10^1	4	11^2	1										13
1		5^1	7	3			8	11^2	4	6^3	10	14	2	9	12	13				1										14
	14	5	8	4				9^1	10			7^5	6	11^2	2	13	3	12		1										15
	2	5	7^2	3^3				9	11	4	8^1	6	10	12	13	14				1										16
	2	5	7	4				9	10^1	3	8	6	11^2		12					1		13								17
	2	5	7^3	3	14			9	11^2	4		6	13		8		12			1		10^1								18
	12	5^1	8	3				9	11^2	4		6	14				7^3			1		10	2	13						19
		7	8	4				9	10^2	3		6	5				12			1		11^1	2	13						20
		7	3	5^1				9	12	4	13	6	2							1		11	8	10^2						21
	13	6	7	4^2				10	11^1	3	8	2	12		14					1		5	9^3							22
	13	5	8	3^4				9	11^1	4	7^3	6	14		12					1		2	10^2							23
		5	7	3					10	4^4	12	6	2	8^1	13					1		9	11^2							24
	14	7	4					9	10	13	6	2^2	8^1							1		5	11^3	3	12					25
		5	7					9^2	10^1		6	4	8							1		2	13	11^1	12	14				26
		5		4				9	10^3	14	6		8							1		2	13	3	11^1	12		7^2		27
		7^3	4	3				9	11	13	6	2	8^2							1		5	14		10^1	12		7		28
	13	8	4	3^2				9	10	6	2									1		5	12	11^1	7	14				29
		8	3	4^3				9	10^1	6	2									1		5	12	13	11^2	7	14			30
		5	7	3	4			9	10	13	6^1									1		2		11^2	8	12				31
		5^1	7	4	3			9	11	13	6									1		2	14	10^2	8^3	12				32
		5	7^1	3				9^3	10	4	12	6								1		2	11^2	14	8	13				33
		5	7^3					9	10	4	13	6	14	2^1						1		2	11^1	3	8^2	12				34
		5	7^2	3				9^3	10	4	12	11		2^1						1		6	14	8	13					35
	2^3	5	7	3				9	10	4	13	6								1		12			11^1	8^2	14			36
		5	7	8			6	11		4	10									1		3	12		9	2^1				37
		5	7	3				9^1	10	4	6^2	12								1		2	13	8	11					38
		5	7	3	14			9^3	10^1	4	11	13								1		2	12	8	6^2					39
		5	7^3	3				9	10	4	14	11	13							1		2	12	8^2	6^1					40
		5		4				9^1	11	3	12	6	8^2							1		2	14	10^3	13	7				41
		5		3				9	11	4	7	10								1		2	12	8	6^1					42
		5		4				13	11^1	3	7^2	6								1		2	10^3	14	12	8	9			43
		5		4				9	14	3	7^3	13	12							1		2	10^2	11	8^4	6^1				44
		5	7^1	3			6	10	4	8	11	9^2								1		2	14	13				12^3		45
	2	5	7	3	4			9		13	12	8^3								1		6	14	11^1	10^2					46

The Budweiser FA Cup

First Round	Bradford C	(h)	3-0
Second Round	Rochdale	(h)	1-2

League One Play-Offs

Semi-Finals 1st leg	Preston NE	(a)	1-1
Semi-Finals 2nd leg	Preston NE	(h)	3-1
Final	Leyton Orient	(Wembley)	2-2

(aet; won 4-3 on penalties)

Capital One Cup

First Round	Sheffield W	(h)	2-1
Second Round	Aston Villa	(a)	0-3

Johnstone's Paint Trophy

Second Round	York C	(a)	3-0
Northern Quarter-Finals	Hartlepool U	(a)	2-1
Northern Semi-Finals	Fleetwood T	(a)	1-2

SCUNTHORPE UNITED

FOUNDATION

The year of foundation for Scunthorpe United has often been quoted as 1910, but the club can trace its history back to 1899 when Brumby Hall FC, who played on the Old Showground, consolidated their position by amalgamating with some other clubs and changing their name to Scunthorpe United. The year 1910 was when that club amalgamated with North Lindsey United as Scunthorpe and Lindsey United. The link is Mr W. T. Lockwood whose chairmanship covers both years.

Glanford Park, Jack Brownsword Way, Scunthorpe, North Lincolnshire DN15 8TD.

Telephone: (0871) 221 1899.

Fax: (01724) 857 986.

Ticket Office: (0871) 221 1899 (option 1).

Website: www.scunthorpe-united.co.uk

Email: admin@scunthorpe-united.co.uk

Ground Capacity: 9,144.

Record Attendance: 23,935 v Portsmouth, FA Cup 4th rd, 30 January 1954 (at Old Showground); 9,077 v Manchester U, League Cup 3rd rd, 22 September 2010 (at Glanford Park).

Pitch Measurements: 102.5m × 66m (112yd × 72yd)

Chairman: Peter Swann.

Vice-chairman: Rex Garton.

Manager: Russ Wilcox.

Assistant Manager: John Schofield.

Physio: Darren Mouatt.

Colours: Claret and light blue striped shirts, claret shorts, light blue socks.

Year Formed: 1899.

Turned Professional: 1912.

Previous Names: Amalgamated first with Brumby Hall then North Lindsey United to become Scunthorpe and Lindsey United, 1910; 1958, Scunthorpe United.

Club Nickname: 'The Iron'.

Grounds: 1899, Old Showground; 1988, Glanford Park.

First Football League Game: 19 August 1950, Division 3 (N), v Shrewsbury T (h) D 0–0 – Thompson; Barker, Brownsword; Allen, Taylor, McCormick; Mosby, Payne, Gorin, Rees, Boyes.

Record League Victory: 8–1 v Luton T, Division 3, 24 April 1965 – Sidebottom; Horstead, Hemstead; Smith, Neale, Lindsey; Bramley (1), Scott, Thomas (5), Mahy (1), Wilson (1). 8–1 v Torquay U (a), Division 3, 28 October 1995 – Samways; Housham, Wilson, Ford (1), Knill (1), Hope (Nicholson), Thornber, Bullimore (Walsh), McFarlane (4) (Young), Eyre (2), Paterson.

HONOURS

Football League – FL 1: *Champions* 2006–07;
FL 2: *Runners-up* 2004–05, 2013–14;
Division 3 (N): *Champions* 1957–58.

FA Cup: Best season: 5th rd, 1958, 1970.

Football League Cup: Best season: 4th rd, 2010.

Johnstone's Paint Trophy: *Runners-up* 2008–09.

sky SPORTS FACT FILE

Scunthorpe United were originally nicknamed The Nuts after a local vicar said they were a tough nut to crack; this was after the team won five trophies in 1911–12: the North Lindsey League, Frodingham Charity Cup, Grimsby Charity Cup, Ironstone Cup and Scunthorpe Nursing Cup.

Record Cup Victory: 9–0 v Boston U, FA Cup 1st rd, 21 November 1953 – Malan; Hubbard, Brownsword; Sharpe, White, Bushby; Mosby (1), Haigh (3), Whitfield (2), Gregory (1), Mervyn Jones (2).

Record Defeat: 0–8 v Carlisle U, Division 3 (N), 25 December 1952.

Most League Points (2 for a win): 66, Division 3 (N), 1956–57, 1957–58.

Most League Points (3 for a win): 91, FL 1, 2006–07.

Most League Goals: 88, Division 3 (N), 1957–58.

Highest League Scorer in Season: Barrie Thomas, 31, Division 2, 1961–62.

Most League Goals in Total Aggregate: Steve Cammack, 110, 1979–81, 1981–86.

Most League Goals in One Match: 5, Barrie Thomas v Luton T, Division 3, 24 April 1965.

Most Capped Player: Grant McCann, 11 (39), Northern Ireland.

Most League Appearances: Jack Brownsword, 595, 1950–65.

Youngest League Player: Hakeeb Adelakun, 16 years 201 days Tranmere R, 29 December 2012.

Record Transfer Fee Received: £2,500,000 from Celtic for Gary Hooper, August 2010.

Record Transfer Fee Paid: £700,000 to Hibernian for Rob Jones, July 2009.

Football League Record: 1950 Elected to Division 3 (N); 1958–64 Division 2; 1964–68 Division 3; 1968–72 Division 4; 1972–73 Division 3; 1973–83 Division 4; 1983–84 Division 3; 1984–92 Division 4; 1992–99 Division 3; 1999–2000 Division 2; 2000–04 Division 3; 2004–05 FL 2; 2005–07 FL 1; 2007–08 FL C; 2008–09 FL 1; 2009–11 FL C; 2011–13 FL 1; 2013–14 FL 2; 2014– FL 1.

MANAGERS

Harry Allcock 1915–53
(Secretary-Manager)
Tom Crilly 1936–37
Bernard Harper 1946–48
Leslie Jones 1950–51
Bill Corkhill 1952–56
Ron Suart 1956–58
Tony McShane 1959
Bill Lambton 1959
Frank Soo 1959–60
Dick Duckworth 1960–64
Fred Goodwin 1964–66
Ron Ashman 1967–73
Ron Bradley 1973–74
Dick Rooks 1974–76
Ron Ashman 1976–81
John Duncan 1981–83
Allan Clarke 1983–84
Frank Barlow 1984–87
Mick Buxton 1987–91
Bill Green 1991–93
Richard Money 1993–94
David Moore 1994–96
Mick Buxton 1996–97
Brian Laws 1997–2004; 2004–06
Nigel Adkins 2006–10
Ian Baraclough 2010–11
Alan Knill 2011–12
Brian Laws 2012–13
Russ Wilcox December 2013–

LATEST SEQUENCES

Longest Sequence of League Wins: 7, 27.1.2007 – 3.3.2007.
Longest Sequence of League Defeats: 8, 29.11.1997 – 20.1.1998.
Longest Sequence of League Draws: 6, 2.1.1984 – 25.2.1984.
Longest Sequence of Unbeaten League Matches: 28, 23.11.2013 – 21.4.2014.
Longest Sequence Without a League Win: 14, 22.3.1975 – 6.9.1975.
Successive Scoring Runs: 24 from 13.1.2007.
Successive Non-scoring Runs: 7 from 19.4.1975.

TEN YEAR LEAGUE RECORD

		P	W	D	L	F	A	Pts	Pos
2004-05	FL 2	46	22	14	10	69	42	80	2
2005-06	FL 1	46	15	15	16	68	73	60	12
2006-07	FL 1	46	26	13	7	73	35	91	1
2007-08	FL C	46	11	13	22	46	69	46	23
2008-09	FL 1	46	22	10	14	82	63	76	6
2009-10	FL C	46	14	10	22	62	84	52	20
2010-11	FL C	46	12	6	28	43	87	42	24
2011-12	FL 1	46	10	22	14	55	59	52	18
2012-13	FL 1	46	13	9	24	49	73	48	21
2013-14	FL 2	46	20	21	5	68	44	81	2

DID YOU KNOW ?

Scunthorpe United were formed as Scunthorpe & Lindsey United in 1910 and adopted their claret and blue strip based on the colours of Aston Villa. They have maintained these colours for most of their history apart from the period between 1959 and 1982.

SCUNTHORPE UNITED – FOOTBALL LEAGUE TWO 2013–14 LEAGUE RECORD

Match No.	Date	Venue	Opponents	Result		H/T Score	Lg Pos.	Goalscorers	Attendance
1	Aug 3	H	Mansfield T	W	2-0	2-0	5	Sparrow [30], Winnall [41]	5241
2	10	A	Bristol R	D	0-0	0-0	5		6259
3	17	H	Dagenham & R	D	1-1	0-0	8	Mirfin [88]	3694
4	24	A	AFC Wimbledon	L	2-3	2-0	10	Winnall [16], Iwelumo [31]	3865
5	31	H	Newport Co	D	1-1	1-0	14	Winnall [2]	3157
6	Sept 7	A	Northampton T	D	1-1	0-0	15	Canavan [67]	4132
7	13	A	Southend U	W	1-0	0-0	7	Iwelumo [64]	4976
8	21	A	Plymouth Arg	W	1-0	0-0	10	Esajas [62]	3298
9	28	A	Burton Alb	D	2-2	0-1	11	Burton [48], Canavan [52]	2556
10	Oct 5	H	Cheltenham T	W	2-0	1-0	7	Esajas [6], Winnall [90]	3191
11	19	H	Exeter C	L	0-4	0-1	13		3250
12	22	H	Fleetwood T	W	1-0	0-0	12	Winnall [59]	2492
13	26	H	Hartlepool U	W	1-0	0-0	9	Winnall [76]	3613
14	29	A	York C	L	1-4	0-4	9	Winnall [47]	3636
15	Nov 2	A	Chesterfield	D	1-1	0-1	8	Waterfall [88]	6346
16	16	H	Accrington S	L	0-2	0-2	12		3255
17	23	A	Portsmouth	W	2-1	1-1	8	Syers 2 [40, 70]	14,550
18	26	A	Rochdale	W	4-0	1-0	6	Canavan [40], Winnall (pen) [75], Spencer [86], Syers [90]	2174
19	30	H	Torquay U	W	3-1	2-0	4	Winnall [6], O'Connor (og) [30], Adelakun [61]	3358
20	Dec 14	A	Wycombe W	D	1-1	0-0	5	Burton [49]	2888
21	21	H	Morecambe	W	2-0	2-0	3	Burton 2 [17, 33]	3510
22	26	A	Bury	D	2-2	1-0	3	Winnall 2 [39, 68]	3277
23	29	A	Oxford U	W	2-0	1-0	2	Burton [11], Syers [72]	6009
24	Jan 1	H	Rochdale	W	3-0	0-0	1	Syers [58], Winnall 2 [82, 84]	4017
25	11	A	Mansfield T	W	2-0	1-0	1	Hayes 2 [9, 74]	4115
26	18	H	AFC Wimbledon	D	0-0	0-0	1		4326
27	25	A	Dagenham & R	D	3-3	1-0	1	Winnall [18], Burton [56], Hayes [61]	2037
28	27	H	Fleetwood T	D	0-0	0-0	1		3005
29	Feb 1	A	Hartlepool U	D	0-0	0-0	2		3727
30	8	H	Chesterfield	D	1-1	1-1	2	Winnall [15]	6131
31	14	A	Accrington S	W	3-2	0-2	2	Winnall [50], Adelakun [59], Mirfin [90]	1256
32	22	H	Portsmouth	W	5-1	3-0	2	Syers 3 [6, 43, 55], Winnall [36], Madden [48]	4165
33	25	H	Bristol R	D	1-1	1-0	2	Winnall [22]	3318
34	Mar 1	A	Newport Co	D	2-2	0-1	2	Madden [61], Syers [83]	2782
35	8	H	Northampton T	D	1-1	0-0	2	Canavan [52]	3968
36	11	H	Southend U	D	2-2	2-0	2	Sparrow [3], Winnall [39]	3018
37	15	A	Plymouth Arg	W	2-0	0-0	2	Syers [79], Cole (og) [90]	8198
38	22	H	Burton Alb	W	1-0	0-0	2	Madden [60]	4029
39	25	A	Cheltenham T	W	2-0	1-0	2	Winnall 2 [45, 59]	2080
40	29	H	Wycombe W	D	0-0	0-0	2		3867
41	Apr 5	A	Torquay U	W	1-0	1-0	2	Winnall (pen) [31]	2234
42	12	H	Bury	D	2-2	0-0	1	Madden [62], Hayes [77]	4162
43	18	A	Morecambe	D	1-1	1-0	1	Winnall [22]	2952
44	21	H	Oxford U	W	1-0	1-0	1	Sparrow [15]	5241
45	26	A	Exeter C	L	0-2	0-1	2		4187
46	May 3	H	York C	D	2-2	2-1	2	Madden [19], Hawkridge [38]	7482

Final League Position: 2

GOALSCORERS

League (68): Winnall 23 (2 pens), Syers 10, Burton 6, Madden 5, Canavan 4, Hayes 4, Sparrow 3, Adelakun 2, Esajas 2, Iwelumo 2, Mirfin 2, Hawkridge 1, Spencer 1, Waterfall 1, own goals 2.
The Budweiser FA Cup (1): Hawkridge 1.
Capital One Cup (0).
Johnstone's Paint Trophy (0).

Slocombe S 46	Nolan E 37 + 2	Mirfin D 45	Canavan A 45	Dawson A 18	Hawkridge T 37 + 8	Sparrow M 20 + 6	Collins M 9 + 8	Winnall S 43 + 2	Burton D 19 + 10	Welsh A 2 + 2	Godden M — + 4	Iwelumo C 4 + 8	Clark J — + 1	Ribeiro C 19 + 2	McAllister S 37 + 2	Wootton J — + 1	Spencer J 5 + 8	Esajas E 8 + 5	Byrne C 7 + 3	Waterfall L 2 + 7	Syers D 37	Adelakun H 8 + 20	Noble-Lazarus R 2 + 2	Williams M 25 + 1	Boyce A — + 2	Hayes P 5 + 11	Madden P 17 + 4	McSheffrey G 9 + 4	Alabi J — + 1	Match No.
1	2*	3	4	5	6	7	8	9[1]	10[2]	11[3]	12	13	14																	1
1	5	3	4		7[3]	8	6	10[2]	11[1]	14	13	12		2	9															2
1	2	3	4	5	6	7	8	11[3]	10[2]	12				9[1]	14															3
1	2	3	4	5	6	7	8[1]	10[3]	9[2]	11					12		13	14												4
1	8	3	4	5	9[2]	6		11	10[1]					2	7		12	13												5
1	8	3	4	5	12	6		10[3]	14		11			2[1]	7		13	9[2]												6
1	2	3	4	5	6[3]	8		11[1]	12			10		7	9[2]		13	14												7
1	2	3	4[1]	5	6	7		11	13			10[2]		8			14	9[3]	12											8
1	2[1]	3	4	5	9	8		11	10[3]			14		7			13	6[2]	12											9
1		3	4	5	12	6		13	10[1]			14		8	11[3]		9[2]	2		7										10
1		3	4	5	12	6[1]		13	10					7[3]	11		9[2]	2		8	14									11
1		3	4	5	9[2]	6[2]		11	12					13	8		10[1]		2	14	7									12
1		3	4	5	7[3]			11	10[2]			13		12	8		9[1]		2	14	6									13
1	2	3[1]	9	14	6[3]			11	10					5	8		12	4		7[2]	13									14
1		3	5	9				10				13		8			11[2]	6[1]	2	4	7	12								15
1			4	5	12			7	11	10[3]		14			9[2]	2	3	6[1]			13									16
1	13	3	4	5	6[3]			9	10[2]					2	8					14	7	12	11[1]							17
1	12	4	3	5[1]	6			11	10[2]					2	8	13					7	9[3]	14							18
1	5	3	4		6			13	10	11[3]				2	7[2]	14					8	12	9[1]							19
1	5	3	4		6			11	10[2]					2	7	13					8	9[3]		12						20
1	5	3	4		6[1]			10[2]	11	13				2	7[3]						8	12		9	14					21
1	5	4	3		7[1]			11*	10[3]	14				2	8[2]						6	12		9	13					22
1	5	3	4		6			12	10					2	8						7	11[1]		9						23
1	5	3	4		6[2]			12	10	11				2[3]	7				14		8[1]	13		9						24
1	5	4	3		6			12	10[3]					2	7						8[1]	13		9[2]		11	14			25
1	5	3	4		6			14	11[2]	13				2	7[3]						8			9		10[1]	12			26
1	5	4	3		6[3]			13	10	11[1]				2	7						8[2]			9		12		14		27
1	2	3	4		9				10[2]						8						7	12		5		11	13	6[1]		28
1	2	3	4		6[1]				13	10					7[2]						8	14		5		11[3]		9		29
1	5	3	4		6[1]			13		10				2	7[2]						8[2]			9			11	12		30
1	5	3	4		6[1]				10					2[2]	7						8	12		9			11	13		31
1	2	3	4		14	12		10[1]							7						8[2]	6[3]		5		13	11	9		32
1	2	3	4		13			10[1]							7						8	6[2]		5		12	11	9		33
1	6	3	4		9[1]	13		11[3]						2	7[2]					14	8	12		5			10			34
1	2	3	4	5[1]	13			11							7	14					8	6[2]	9[1]			12	10			35
1	2	3	4		6[1]	7		11[2]							8						12		5		10	9	13		36
1	2	3	4		6			10							7[3]					14	8	13		5		12	11[1]	9[2]		37
1	2	3	4		6[2]			11[1]							7						8	12		5		13	10	9		38
1	2	3	4		6	14		11[1]							7[3]						8	13		5		12	10	9[2]		39
1	2	3	4		6[3]	13		10							7[2]						8	14		5[1]		12	11	9		40
1	2	3	4		13	6		8[1]	11[3]	14					9						12			5		7[2]	10			41
1	2	3	4		9	7[1]	12	11[2]	14						8						6[2]			5		13	10			42
1	2	4	3		9	8[2]		10[3]	14						13					7	6[1]			5		12	11			43
1	2	3	4		6			9	8	11					7									5			10			44
1	2	3	4		9[3]	6		8[2]	10[1]	12					7							13		5		14	11			45
1	5	3	4		9[3]	6		7[2]	10[1]	12				2	13						8						11	14		46

The Budweiser FA Cup

First Round	Grimsby T	(a)	0-0
Replay	Grimsby T	(h)	1-2

Capital One Cup

First Round	Barnsley	(a)	0-0

(aet; lost 4-5 on penalties)

Johnstone's Paint Trophy

First Round	Sheffield U	(h)	0-0

(aet; lost 3-5 on penalties)

SHEFFIELD UNITED

FOUNDATION

In March 1889, Yorkshire County Cricket Club formed Sheffield United six days after an FA Cup semi-final between Preston North End and West Bromwich Albion had finally convinced Charles Stokes, a member of the cricket club, that the formation of a professional football club would prove successful at Bramall Lane. The United's first secretary, Mr J. B. Wostinholm, was also secretary of the cricket club.

Bramall Lane Ground, Cherry Street, Bramall Lane, Sheffield, South Yorkshire S2 4SU.

Telephone: (0871) 995 1899.

Fax: (0871) 663 2430.

Ticket Office: (0871) 995 1889.

Website: www.sufc.co.uk

Email: info@sufc.co.uk

Ground Capacity: 32,609.

Record Attendance: 68,287 v Leeds U, FA Cup 5th rd, 15 February 1936.

Pitch Measurements: 100.5m × 67m (110yd × 73yd)

Co-Chairmen: Kevin McCabe, HRH Prince Abdullah bin Mosaad bin Abdulaziz Al Saud.

Manager: Nigel Clough.

Assistant Manager: Gary Crosby.

Physio: Ritson Lloyd.

HONOURS

Football League
Division 1: *Champions* 1897–98;
Runners-up 1896–97, 1899–1900;
Division 2: *Champions* 1952–53;
Runners-up 1892–93, 1938–39,
1960–61, 1970–71, 1989–90;
FL C: *Runners-up* 2005–06;
Division 3: *Runners-up* 1988–89;
Division 4: *Champions* 1981–82.
FA Cup: *Winners* 1899, 1902, 1915,
1925; *Runners-up* 1901, 1936.
Football League Cup: semi-final 2003.

Colours: Red and white striped shirts, black shorts with red and white trim, white socks with red trim.

Year Formed: 1889.   *Turned Professional:* 1889.   *Club Nickname:* 'The Blades'.

Ground: 1889, Bramall Lane.

First Football League Game: 3 September 1892, Division 2, v Lincoln C (h) W 4–2 – Lilley; Witham, Cain; Howell, Hendry, Needham (1); Wallace, Dobson, Hammond (3), Davies, Drummond.

Record League Victory: 10–0 v Burslem Port Vale (a), Division 2, 10 December 1892 – Howlett; Witham, Lilley; Howell, Hendry, Needham; Drummond (1), Wallace (1), Hammond (4), Davies (2), Watson (2). 10-0 v Burnley, Division 1 (h), 19 January 1929.

Record Cup Victory: 6–1 v Scarborough (a), FA Cup 1st qualifying rd, 5 October 1889 – Howlett; Stringer, Gilmartin, Mack, Hobson, Hudson, Galbraith (2), Robertson (1), Fraser (2), Duncan, Mosforth (1). 6–1 v Loughborough, FA Cup 4th qualifying rd, 6 December 1890. 6–1 v Lincoln C, League Cup, 22 August 2000 – Tracey; Uhlenbeek, Weber, Woodhouse (Ford), Murphy, Sandford, Devlin (pen), Ribeiro (Santos), Bent (3), Kelly (1) (Thompson), Jagielka, og (1).

Record Defeat: 0–13 v Bolton W, FA Cup 2nd rd, 1 February 1890.

Most League Points (2 for a win): 60, Division 2, 1952–53.

sky SPORTS FACT FILE

Winger Jimmy Revill made 68 League and Cup appearances for Sheffield United between 1910 and 1915. He later served as a lance corporal in the Royal Engineers and saw plenty of action in France before being severely wounded, losing an arm and a leg leading to his death in April 1917.

Most League Points (3 for a win): 96, Division 4, 1981–82.

Most League Goals: 102, Division 1, 1925–26.

Highest League Scorer in Season: Jimmy Dunne, 41, Division 1, 1930–31.

Most League Goals in Total Aggregate: Harry Johnson, 205, 1919–30.

Most League Goals in One Match: 5, Harry Hammond v Bootle, Division 2, 26 November 1892; 5, Harry Johnson v West Ham U, Division 1, 26 December 1927.

Most Capped Player: Billy Gillespie, 25, Northern Ireland.

Most League Appearances: Joe Shaw, 629, 1948–66.

Youngest League Player: Louis Reed, 16 years 257 days v Rotherham U, 8 April 2014.

Record Transfer Fee Received: £4,000,000 from Everton for Phil Jagielka, July 2007; £4,000,000 from Tottenham H for Kyle Naughton, July 2009; £4,000,000 from Tottenham H for Kyle Walker, July 2009.

Record Transfer Fee Paid: £4,000,000 to Everton for James Beattie, August 2007.

Football League Record: 1892 Elected to Division 2; 1893–1934 Division 1; 1934–39 Division 2; 1946–49 Division 1; 1949–53 Division 2; 1953–56 Division 1; 1956–61 Division 2; 1961–68 Division 1; 1968–71 Division 2; 1971–76 Division 1; 1976–79 Division 2; 1979–81 Division 3; 1981–82 Division 4; 1982–84 Division 3; 1984–88 Division 2; 1988–89 Division 3; 1989–90 Division 2; 1990–92 Division 1; 1992–94 FA Premier League; 1994–2004 Division 1; 2004–06 FL C; 2006–07 FA Premier League; 2007–11 FL C; 2011– FL 1.

LATEST SEQUENCES

Longest Sequence of League Wins: 8, 20.8.2005 – 27.9.2005.

Longest Sequence of League Defeats: 7, 19.8.1975 – 20.9.1975.

Longest Sequence of League Draws: 6, 6.5.2001 – 8.9.2001.

Longest Sequence of Unbeaten League Matches: 22, 2.9.1899 – 13.1.1900.

Longest Sequence Without a League Win: 19, 27.9.1975 – 7.2.1976.

Successive Scoring Runs: 34 from 30.3.1956.

Successive Non-scoring Runs: 6 from 4.12.1993.

MANAGERS

J. B. Wostinholm 1889–99 *(Secretary-Manager)*
John Nicholson 1899–1932
Ted Davison 1932–52
Reg Freeman 1952–55
Joe Mercer 1955–58
Johnny Harris 1959–68 *(continued as General Manager to 1970)*
Arthur Rowley 1968–69
Johnny Harris *(General Manager resumed Team Manager duties)* 1969–73
Ken Furphy 1973–75
Jimmy Sirrel 1975–77
Harry Haslam 1978–81
Martin Peters 1981
Ian Porterfield 1981–86
Billy McEwan 1986–88
Dave Bassett 1988–95
Howard Kendall 1995–97
Nigel Spackman 1997–98
Steve Bruce 1998–99
Adrian Heath 1999
Neil Warnock 1999–2007
Bryan Robson 2007–08
Kevin Blackwell 2008–10
Gary Speed 2010
Micky Adams 2010–11
Danny Wilson 2011–13
David Weir 2013
Nigel Clough October 2013–

TEN YEAR LEAGUE RECORD

		P	W	D	L	F	A	Pts	Pos
2004-05	FL C	46	18	13	15	57	56	67	8
2005-06	FL C	46	26	12	8	76	46	90	2
2006-07	PR Lge	38	10	8	20	32	55	38	18
2007-08	FL C	46	17	15	14	56	51	66	9
2008-09	FL C	46	22	14	10	64	39	80	3
2009-10	FL C	46	17	14	15	62	55	65	8
2010-11	FL C	46	11	9	26	44	79	42	23
2011-12	FL 1	46	27	9	10	92	51	90	3
2012-13	FL 1	46	19	18	9	56	42	75	5
2013-14	FL 1	46	18	13	15	48	46	67	7

DID YOU KNOW ?

Sheffield United reached the final of the Watney Cup in 1971–72 by defeating Notts County and Peterborough United. The final tie was played at Eastville against Bristol Rovers and after the teams had drawn 0-0, Rovers ran out winners on penalties (7-6).

SHEFFIELD UNITED – FOOTBALL LEAGUE ONE 2013–14 LEAGUE RECORD

Match No.	Date		Venue	Opponents		Result	H/T Score	Lg Pos.	Goalscorers	Atten- dance
1	Aug	2	H	Notts Co	W	2-1	1-0	1	McDonald [30], Maguire [67]	17,944
2		10	A	Brentford	L	1-3	0-1	12	Collins [57]	7316
3		17	H	Colchester U	D	1-1	1-1	13	Maguire [45]	17,167
4		24	A	Bradford C	L	0-2	0-1	16		18,041
5		31	H	Milton Keynes D	L	0-1	0-0	17		15,080
6	Sept	7	A	Rotherham U	L	1-3	1-0	19	Baxter [37]	11,758
7		14	A	Carlisle U	L	0-1	0-0	20		4863
8		21	H	Preston NE	L	0-1	0-0	22		16,319
9		28	A	Wolverhampton W	L	0-2	0-0	24		20,417
10	Oct	4	H	Crawley T	D	1-1	0-1	21	King [63]	15,401
11		13	A	Coventry C	L	2-3	0-2	24	Taylor 2 [62, 80]	2078
12		19	A	Port Vale	W	2-1	1-1	20	Collins [12], Doyle [75]	18,545
13		22	A	Peterborough U	D	0-0	0-0	21		6435
14		26	H	Crewe Alex	W	3-1	2-0	20	Maguire 2 [18, 29], Flynn [55]	18,784
15	Nov	2	A	Shrewsbury T	L	0-2	0-1	22		6226
16		16	H	Gillingham	L	1-2	1-1	23	Porter [19]	16,560
17		23	A	Bristol C	W	1-0	0-0	21	Flint (og) [78]	13,220
18		26	H	Walsall	D	1-1	1-0	21	Porter (pen) [45]	14,796
19		30	A	Leyton Orient	D	1-1	0-0	20	Coady [67]	6586
20	Dec	14	H	Swindon T	W	1-0	0-0	19	Baxter [67]	15,430
21		21	A	Stevenage	D	0-0	0-0	19		3003
22		26	H	Oldham Ath	D	1-1	0-1	20	Baxter [54]	19,551
23		29	H	Tranmere R	W	3-1	1-0	17	Murphy [9], Baxter [56], Flynn [67]	17,460
24	Jan	1	A	Walsall	L	1-2	1-0	18	Porter [17]	5015
25		11	A	Notts Co	L	1-2	1-1	19	Coady [2]	8564
26		18	H	Bradford C	D	2-2	2-0	19	Murphy [8], Maguire [40]	18,794
27	Feb	1	A	Crewe Alex	L	0-3	0-2	23		5437
28		8	H	Shrewsbury T	W	2-0	2-0	21	Flynn [11], Scougall [17]	15,987
29		19	A	Gillingham	W	1-0	1-0	18	Coady [41]	5766
30		22	H	Bristol C	W	3-0	1-0	17	Brayford [43], Flynn [58], Baxter (pen) [70]	19,271
31		25	A	Colchester U	W	1-0	0-0	12	Porter (pen) [87]	3088
32	Mar	1	A	Milton Keynes D	W	1-0	1-0	12	Scougall [23]	9192
33		4	H	Peterborough U	W	2-0	0-0	10	Davies [47], Porter [88]	16,051
34		12	H	Carlisle U	W	1-0	1-0	10	Baxter [28]	15,437
35		17	A	Preston NE	D	0-0	0-0	10		8892
36		22	H	Wolverhampton W	L	0-2	0-1	11		21,659
37		25	A	Crawley T	W	2-0	1-0	10	Coady 2 [19, 63]	3622
38		29	A	Swindon T	L	1-2	0-1	10	Doyle [59]	8441
39	Apr	1	H	Brentford	D	0-0	0-0	11		15,730
40		5	H	Leyton Orient	D	1-1	0-1	11	Murphy [63]	16,809
41		8	H	Rotherham U	W	1-0	0-0	11	Davies (pen) [90]	21,529
42		18	H	Stevenage	W	1-0	1-0	9	Mousinho (og) [10]	17,629
43		21	A	Tranmere R	D	0-0	0-0	8		5950
44		25	A	Port Vale	W	2-1	0-0	8	Murphy [83], Porter [90]	6394
45		29	A	Oldham Ath	D	1-1	0-1	8	Porter [84]	3949
46	May	3	H	Coventry C	W	2-1	0-1	7	Flynn [62], Davies [73]	20,723

Final League Position: 7

GOALSCORERS

League (48): Porter 7 (2 pens), Baxter 6 (1 pen), Coady 5, Flynn 5, Maguire 5, Murphy 4, Davies 3 (1 pen), Collins 2, Doyle 2, Scougall 2, Taylor 2, Brayford 1, King 1, McDonald 1, own goals 2.
The Budweiser FA Cup (17): Porter 4 (2 pens), Murphy 3, Baxter 2, Flynn 2, Brayford 1, Coady 1, Maguire 1, Miller 1, Scougall 1, own goal 1.
Capital One Cup (1): Doyle 1.
Johnstone's Paint Trophy (0).

Long G 27	Westlake D 4+3	Williams M 2	Doyle M 42+1	Maguire H 41	Collins N 44	Brandy F 10+4	McGinn S 23+7	Porter C 16+16	McDonald K 1	Murphy J 25+9	McFadzean C 3+4	Taylor L 9+11	Coady C 32+7	McMahon T 23	Reed L —+1	McGinty S 2	Johns J —+1	Flynn R 28+4	Ironside J 1+3	Hill M 24+8	Baxter J 29+6	Howard M 19	Cuvelier F 5+2	Bunn H —+2	Hall R 3+1	King M 7+1	Lappin S 7+2	Miller S 5+8	White A 8	Paynter B 6+7	Brayford J 15	Scougall S 13+2	Harris R 9+2	Davies B 8+10	Kennedy T 3+2	Freeman K 10+2	Khan O —+2	Dimaio C 2+1	Match No.
1	2	3	4^1	5	6	7	8	9^2	10	11^3	12	13	14																										1
1	2	5	7	4	3	10	9^1	12		6^2	13	11	8																										2
1			8	3	4	6				9	10^1	11	7	2	5	12																							3
1			7	3	4	8^1		14		6	10^2	11	9	2	5^3			12	13																				4
1			7	3	4	13^4		8^2		14		9^1	6	2				10^2	12	5	11																		5
			9	3	4			11^1				13	7	2				6^2		5	10	1	8	12															6
1	6^3		7	3	4	10^2				13	12		2					11^1	5	9		8	14																7
1	13		8^2	3	4	6^1	14			12			2					5	10	7		9^3	11																8
1			6	3	4	7^1				12			2					13	5	9		8	10^2	11															9
1			8	3	4	6^2			14				13	12	2					10		7^2	9^1	11	5														10
1	2		8	3	4	9	13						12	7				6^3		5	10^1				14	11^2													11
1	13		8	3	4	6^1	7						10	14	2			9^3		5					11^2	12													12
1	14		8	3	4	10^2	7			13			11^3	9	2			6^1							12	5													13
1			8	3	4		7						11^2	13	2			6		5			14		10^3	9^1	12												14
1			7	3	4^1	12^4	14						10		2			6^2		5					11^3	8	13	9											15
1			8	3	4			13	10				14		2			6^1		5^2	12				7^3	11	9												16
1			7	4	3			8	10				11^3	6	2					13	12				9^1		5												17
1			8		3			7	11^1			13	14	6	2					4	12				9^1	10^2	5												18
1			7	3	4			8	10^1			14	13	6	2					5	11^3					12		9^2											19
1			7	3	4	12			11^1				9^2		8	2		6		13	10					14	5^3												20
1			6	3	4			8	10			12			9					5	11					7	2^1												21
1			8	3	4			6	11			12^3	13		2			14		5	7					10^1	9^2												22
1			8	3	4			7^1	11			9		12	2			6^3		5	10^2	14				13													23
			9	4	3	14		7^1	11			13		6	2			10^2		5	8^3					12													24
1			7	3	4			8^2	11			13		9	2			6^3		5^1	10					14	12												25
1			8	3	4			7^1	12			9		14	2			6		5	10^3					13	11^2												26
1				3	4			13	14			9^2		7				6^1		5	10							11^3	2	8	12								27
			3	4				8^1	13			9		7^2				6		10		1					12		2	11	5								28
			7	2	3			8	10^3			12		6				5^2		4	14	1				11^1			9	13								29
			8	3	4				9^1					7				6^2		12	11	1				14		2	10	5^3	13							30
			8	3	4			13	10^1					7				12		14	11^2	1						2	9	5	6^3							31
			7		3			13	9^1					8				6		4	11	1						2^3	10^3	5	12	14						32
			8	3	4			6^3	14		9^2			7				12		5		1				11	10^1	13		2	3							33
			8	3	4			12	13			9		7				6^1			11^1	1							10^2	5	2		14						34
			7	3	4				14			10		6				8		12^3	11^1	1						9	5^1	13		2						35
			8	3	4				13			9		7				6^1			11^1	1						14	2	10		12		5^2				36
			7	3	4			6	11^1			10^2		8							1							12	2			9^1		5	13	14		37
			6		4			13	12			10		7				8			11^1	1						14	3	9^1			2	5^2				38
			8	3	4			10^2	12			9		7				6^3			13	1						11^1	3			2	14	5				39
			8	3	4			10^2	11^1			9		7				6			1									2	12	14	13	5^3				40
1				3				7						14	13					5	10^3							11				9^1	6	4	2	12	8^2	41
			8	3	4				9					7				6		12	11^1	1						13	2	10^2	5^3	14						42
		13	3^3	4				6^2	10^1		11			7						5	12	1						2		9		14		8				43
			8	3	4^1				13			10		7^2				6		12	11^3	1						2	9	14		5						44
			8	3	4				12			10		7^3				6^2			11^1	1						2	9		13	4	5					45
			8	3	4				12			9		7				6		14	11^3	1						2	10^2		13		5^1					46

The Budweiser FA Cup

First Round	Colchester U	(a)	3-2
Second Round	Cambridge U	(a)	2-0
Third Round	Aston Villa	(a)	2-1
Fourth Round	Fulham	(h)	1-1
Replay	Fulham	(a)	1-0
(aet)			
Fifth Round	Nottingham F	(h)	3-1
Sixth Round	Charlton Ath	(h)	2-0
Semi-Finals	Hull C	(Wembley)	3-5

Capital One Cup

First Round	Burton Alb	(h)	1-2

Johnstone's Paint Trophy

First Round	Scunthorpe U	(a)	0-0
(aet; won 5-3 on penalties)			
Second Round	Hartlepool U	(h)	0-1

SHEFFIELD WEDNESDAY

FOUNDATION

Sheffield being one of the principal centres of early Association Football, this club was formed as long ago as 1867 by the Sheffield Wednesday Cricket Club (formed 1825) and their colours from the start were blue and white. The inaugural meeting was held at the Adelphi Hotel and the original committee included Charles Stokes who was subsequently a founder member of Sheffield United.

Hillsborough Stadium, Sheffield, South Yorkshire S6 1SW.

Telephone: (0871) 995 1867.

Fax: (0114) 221 2122.

Ticket Office: (0871) 900 1867.

Website: www.swfc.co.uk

Email: enquiries@swfc.co.uk

Ground Capacity: 39,702.

Record Attendance: 72,841 v Manchester C, FA Cup 5th rd, 17 February 1934.

Pitch Measurements: 106m × 64m (116yd × 70yd)

Chairman: Milan Mandaric.

Vice-chairman: Paul Aldridge.

Manager: Stuart Gray.

Assistant Manager: John Deehan.

Head Physio: Paul Smith.

HONOURS

Football League – Division 1:
Champions 1902–03, 1903–04, 1928–29, 1929–30;
Runners-up 1960–61;
Division 2: *Champions* 1899–1900, 1925–26, 1951–52, 1955–56, 1958–59;
Runners-up 1949–50, 1983–84.
FL 1: *Runners-up* 2011–12.
FA Cup: *Winners* 1896, 1907, 1935;
Runners-up 1890, 1966, 1993.
Football League Cup: *Winners* 1991;
Runners-up 1993.

European Competitions
European Fairs Cup: 1961–62, 1963–64. **UEFA Cup:** 1992–93.
Intertoto Cup: 1995.

Colours: Blue and white striped shirts, blue shorts with white trim, blue socks with white trim.

Year Formed: 1867 (fifth oldest League club).

Turned Professional: 1887.

Previous Name: The Wednesday until 1929.

Club Nickname: 'The Owls'.

Grounds: 1867, Highfield; 1869, Myrtle Road; 1877, Sheaf House; 1887, Olive Grove; 1899, Owlerton (since 1912 known as Hillsborough). Some games were played at Endcliffe in the 1880s. Until 1895 Bramall Lane was used for some games.

First Football League Game: 3 September 1892, Division 1, v Notts Co (a) W 1–0 – Allan; Tom Brandon (1), Mumford; Hall, Betts, Harry Brandon; Spiksley, Brady, Davis, Bob Brown, Dunlop.

Record League Victory: 9–1 v Birmingham, Division 1, 13 December 1930 – Brown; Walker, Blenkinsop; Strange, Leach, Wilson; Hooper (3), Seed (2), Ball (2), Burgess (1), Rimmer (1).

Record Cup Victory: 12–0 v Halliwell, FA Cup 1st rd, 17 January 1891 – Smith; Thompson, Brayshaw; Harry Brandon (1), Betts, Cawley (2); Winterbottom, Mumford (2), Bob Brandon (1), Woolhouse (5), Ingram (1).

sky SPORTS FACT FILE

Sheffield Wednesday played 17 games in Division Two from January 1975 until the end of the season without winning once. They scored just 2 goals in that period and between 25 February and 19 April, a run of 8 matches, they did not find the net a single time. They finished bottom of the table.

Record Defeat: 0–10 v Aston Villa, Division 1, 5 October 1912.

Most League Points (2 for a win): 62, Division 2, 1958–59.

Most League Points (3 for a win): 93, FL 1, 2011–12.

Most League Goals: 106, Division 2, 1958–59.

Highest League Scorer in Season: Derek Dooley, 46, Division 2, 1951–52.

Most League Goals in Total Aggregate: Andrew Wilson, 199, 1900–20.

Most League Goals in One Match: 6, Doug Hunt v Norwich C, Division 2, 19 November 1938.

Most Capped Player: Nigel Worthington, 50 (66), Northern Ireland.

Most League Appearances: Andrew Wilson, 501, 1900–20.

Youngest League Player: Peter Fox, 15 years 269 days v Orient, 31 March 1973.

Record Transfer Fee Received: £3,000,000 from WBA for Chris Brunt, August 2007.

Record Transfer Fee Paid: £4,500,000 to Celtic for Paolo Di Canio, August 1997.

Football League Record: 1892 Elected to Division 1; 1899–1900 Division 2; 1900–20 Division 1; 1920–26 Division 2; 1926–37 Division 1; 1937–50 Division 2; 1950–51 Division 1; 1951–52 Division 2; 1952–55 Division 1; 1955–56 Division 2; 1956–58 Division 1; 1958–59 Division 2; 1959–70 Division 1; 1970–75 Division 2; 1975–80 Division 3; 1980–84 Division 2; 1984–90 Division 1; 1990–91 Division 2; 1991–92 Division 1; 1992–2000 FA Premier League; 2000–03 Division 1; 2003–04 Division 2; 2004–05 FL 1; 2005–10 FL C; 2010–12 FL 1; 2012– FL C.

LATEST SEQUENCES

Longest Sequence of League Wins: 9, 23.4.1904 – 15.10.1904.

Longest Sequence of League Defeats: 8, 9.9.2000 – 17.10.2000.

Longest Sequence of League Draws: 7, 15.3.2008 – 14.4.2008.

Longest Sequence of Unbeaten League Matches: 19, 10.12.1960 – 8.4.1961.

Longest Sequence Without a League Win: 20, 11.1.1975 – 30.8.1975.

Successive Scoring Runs: 40 from 14.11.1959.

Successive Non-scoring Runs: 8 from 8.3.1975.

MANAGERS

Arthur Dickinson 1891–1920
(Secretary-Manager)
Robert Brown 1920–33
Billy Walker 1933–37
Jimmy McMullan 1937–42
Eric Taylor 1942–58
(continued as General Manager to 1974)
Harry Catterick 1958–61
Vic Buckingham 1961–64
Alan Brown 1964–68
Jack Marshall 1968–69
Danny Williams 1969–71
Derek Dooley 1971–73
Steve Burtenshaw 1974–75
Len Ashurst 1975–77
Jackie Charlton 1977–83
Howard Wilkinson 1983–88
Peter Eustace 1988–89
Ron Atkinson 1989–91
Trevor Francis 1991–95
David Pleat 1995–97
Ron Atkinson 1997–98
Danny Wilson 1998–2000
Peter Shreeves *(Acting)* 2000
Paul Jewell 2000–01
Peter Shreeves 2001
Terry Yorath 2001–02
Chris Turner 2002–04
Paul Sturrock 2004–06
Brian Laws 2006–09
Alan Irvine 2010–11
Gary Megson 2011–12
Dave Jones 2012–13
Stuart Gray January 2014–

TEN YEAR LEAGUE RECORD

		P	W	D	L	F	A	Pts	Pos
2004-05	FL 1	46	19	15	12	77	59	72	5
2005-06	FL C	46	13	13	20	39	52	52	19
2006-07	FL C	46	20	11	15	70	66	71	9
2007-08	FL C	46	14	13	19	54	55	55	16
2008-09	FL C	46	16	13	17	51	58	61	12
2009-10	FL C	46	11	14	21	49	69	47	22
2010-11	FL 1	46	16	10	20	67	67	58	15
2011-12	FL 1	46	28	9	9	81	48	93	2
2012-13	FL C	46	16	10	20	53	61	58	18
2013-14	FL C	46	13	14	19	63	65	53	16

DID YOU KNOW ?

Vivien Simpson, who played for Sheffield Wednesday as an amateur between 1903 and 1907, served as a captain in the York & Lancaster Regiment during World War One. He was awarded the Military Cross, but was killed by a sniper's bullet on 13 April 1918.

SHEFFIELD WEDNESDAY – FL CHAMPIONSHIP 2013–14 LEAGUE RECORD

Match No.	Date	Venue	Opponents	Result	H/T Score	Lg Pos.	Goalscorers	Atten-dance
1	Aug 3	A	QPR	L 1-2	1-2	15	Nuhiu [19]	17,626
2	10	H	Burnley	L 1-2	0-2	19	Prutton [71]	22,282
3	17	A	Leeds U	D 1-1	1-0	20	Zayatte [36]	23,766
4	24	H	Millwall	D 2-2	2-1	20	Johnson, Reda [7], Helan [21]	20,009
5	31	A	Middlesbrough	D 1-1	1-0	21	Antonio [35]	15,964
6	Sept 14	H	Yeovil T	D 1-1	1-0	19	Nuhiu [25]	22,328
7	21	A	Birmingham C	L 1-4	0-3	21	Zayatte [66]	14,379
8	28	H	Doncaster R	L 0-1	0-0	22		21,871
9	Oct 1	A	Brighton & HA	D 1-1	1-0	21	Fryatt [42]	25,725
10	5	H	Ipswich T	D 1-1	1-1	22	Antonio [14]	19,599
11	19	A	Bolton W	D 1-1	1-1	23	Baptiste (og) [26]	17,177
12	26	A	Barnsley	D 1-1	0-1	24	Fryatt [59]	13,268
13	Nov 2	H	Reading	W 5-2	3-1	21	Fryatt 2 [18, 62], Antonio [25], Morrison (og) [42], Wickham [57]	20,368
14	9	A	Derby Co	L 0-3	0-1	22		26,421
15	23	H	Huddersfield T	L 1-2	0-1	22	Wickham [90]	19,338
16	30	A	Blackpool	L 0-2	0-1	23		14,452
17	Dec 3	H	Leicester C	W 2-1	2-1	23	Wickham 2 [9, 25]	20,016
18	7	H	Nottingham F	L 0-1	0-0	23		23,414
19	14	A	Watford	W 1-0	1-0	22	Wickham [24]	15,476
20	21	H	Bournemouth	L 1-2	0-2	22	Maghoma [82]	21,057
21	26	A	Blackburn R	D 0-0	0-0	22		18,539
22	29	A	Charlton Ath	D 1-1	0-0	22	Wickham [58]	16,377
23	Jan 1	H	Blackpool	W 2-0	0-0	20	Wickham [50], Maguire [60]	19,447
24	11	H	Leeds U	W 6-0	2-0	19	Johnson, Reda [20], Nuhiu [45], Wickham [50], Maguire [67], Lavery 2 [80, 90]	22,124
25	18	A	Burnley	D 1-1	1-1	19	Maguire [45]	13,735
26	28	A	Millwall	D 1-1	0-0	20	Coke [69]	10,624
27	Feb 1	H	Barnsley	W 1-0	0-0	17	Maguire [90]	25,139
28	8	A	Reading	W 2-0	1-0	17	Maguire (pen) [10], Afobe [58]	19,772
29	11	H	Wigan Ath	L 0-3	0-2	17		25,279
30	18	H	Derby Co	L 0-1	0-0	17		21,039
31	22	A	Huddersfield T	W 2-0	1-0	15	Helan [40], Maghoma [72]	16,499
32	Mar 1	H	Middlesbrough	W 1-0	0-0	15	Nuhiu (pen) [87]	20,743
33	8	A	Yeovil T	L 0-2	0-1	16		6251
34	12	A	Wigan Ath	L 0-1	0-0	17		15,039
35	15	H	Birmingham C	W 4-1	2-0	16	Lavery 2 [16, 68], Best [21], Packwood (og) [58]	20,637
36	18	H	QPR	W 3-0	1-0	14	Maguire (pen) [35], Best [51], Buxton [71]	18,029
37	22	A	Doncaster R	L 0-1	0-1	15		12,609
38	25	H	Brighton & HA	W 1-0	0-0	13	Best [90]	18,192
39	29	H	Watford	L 1-2	0-2	14	Afobe [54]	22,057
40	Apr 4	A	Leicester C	L 1-2	1-1	14	Antonio [37]	26,103
41	8	A	Nottingham F	D 3-3	2-1	15	Maguire (pen) [15], Buxton [45], Mattock [57]	20,185
42	12	H	Blackburn R	D 3-3	1-3	15	Buxton [30], Nuhiu 2 [72, 90]	22,792
43	18	A	Bournemouth	W 4-2	2-1	15	Nuhiu [16], Hutchinson [34], Best [86], Maguire [90]	10,864
44	21	H	Charlton Ath	L 2-3	2-2	15	Nuhiu [3], Maguire [8]	20,557
45	26	H	Bolton W	L 1-3	1-3	16	Mattock [38]	23,070
46	May 3	A	Ipswich T	L 1-2	0-1	16	Lee [55]	20,862

Final League Position: 16

GOALSCORERS

League (63): Maguire 9 (3 pens), Nuhiu 8 (1 pen), Wickham 8, Antonio 4, Best 4, Fryatt 4, Lavery 4, Buxton 3, Afobe 2, Helan 2, Johnson, Reda 2, Maghoma 2, Mattock 2, Zayatte 2, Coke 1, Hutchinson 1, Lee 1, Prutton 1, own goals 3.
The Budweiser FA Cup (8): Best 1, Johnson J 1, Johnson, Reda 1, Llera 1, Maghoma 1, Maguire 1, Mattock 1, Onyewu 1.
Capital One Cup (1): McCabe 1.

Kirkland C 35	Mattock J 20 + 3	Palmer L 33 + 6	Prutton D 7 + 2	Zayatte K 11	Gardner A 5	Johnson J 5 + 22	Coke G 20 + 8	Antonio M 24 + 3	Helan J 33 + 10	Maghoma J 18 + 7	McCabe R 2 + 5	Madine G — + 1	Floro R 1	Corry P — + 1	Semedo J 17 + 5	Maguire C 23 + 4	Lavery C 9 + 12	Buxton L 20	Johnson Reda 17 + 2	Spence J 4	Llera M 18 + 4	Johnson Roger 17	McPhail S 13	Fryatt M 7 + 2	Olofinjana S 6 + 1	Wickham C 11	Martinez D 11	Lee K 26	Loovens G 21 + 1	Savic A — + 1	Onyewu O 18	Afobe B 4 + 8	Oshilaja A 2	Gardner G 3	Best L 12 + 3	Hutchinson S 8 + 2	Stobbs J — + 1	Match No.
1	2³	3	4	5	6	7	8¹	9	10	11²	12	13	14																									1
1	2	8	4	3					10	9	11	6¹			5²	7	12	13																				2
1	2	8	4	3		7	11	9	10²	13			6¹		5	12																						3
1	6	7	4	3			8¹		10	9	11²							12	13	14	2³	5																4
1	6	9	4	3³	8²	7¹	11	10	14			13							5	2	12																	5
1	6¹	7¹		3			12	8	10	9²	11	14						13	5	2	4																	6
1	6²	7	4				13		10	9	12	11¹			5	2	3	8																				7
1							10¹	7	6	9	11	13			5	2²	3	4	8	12																		8
1	13						12	8²	6	9			14		7	2	5	4	3	10¹	11³																	9
1	14						13	8²	6	9	11				12	2	5¹	3	4	7	10³																	10
1	13	3					12	9²	6	10			7■		2	5	4	8	11¹																			11
1	4						11¹	13	6	9	12		14		2	5	3	7	10²	8³																		12
1	3						13	12	6³	9	14				2	5	4	7¹	10²	8	11																	13
1	14	4					12	13	6	9²					2	5	3	7³	11	8¹	10																	14
	7³						12	13	6¹	5	14				8	2	4	3	9²	10	11							1										15
	5¹	14					12	8²	10	6			7		2³	4	3	13	9	11								1										16
	5	6					13	7¹	11³	9			12		14	3	8	10										1	2		4²							17
	5²	2					14	12	11	9			7		13	3	8¹	10										1	6¹	4								18
	2						10	8²	13	9					5	3	7¹	12	11									1	6	4								19
	14	2					10¹	8	12	11³	9		7²		5	4	3											1	6		13							20
1	14	2					12		9	11¹	10²	13	8		5	3	7³												6		4							21
1	2							9²	12	13			7		10	5	3	8¹			11								6		4							22
1	2						12	13	11³	9			7		8¹	5	3				10								6		4							23
1	2						13		14	11³	9²		7		6¹	12	5	3			10								8		4							24
1	5	2					13	12	9³	14			7		6	11¹					10								8		4							25
1	2						13■	8	11				7		6	12		5	10¹		9								4²		3							26
1	5	2					13■		14	11²	8		8		6	12		4			7								3¹		10³							27
1	4	2					12	5	14	10	8²		9		6³	13		3			7										11¹							28
1	5	2					12	13	11	9³			7¹		6	14		3			8										10²	4						29
1	5	2					7	6	12				10			3					8³	4							14			9¹	11²		13			30
1	5	2						9²	10	11³	8		12			4					14								3¹		6	13			7			31
1	5¹	2					13	7	12	14	9³		6²		10	4		3			11								8									32
	2						13	8³	5	12	10		6²			1		3			4	14							7¹	11		9■						33
	8	12					6	5	14	10¹			13		9	2		1			4	3							7³	11²								34
	14							5	11				6³	9¹	2	13		1			7	4²	3	12				10	8								35
	7	14					12		5	10			9¹	6²	2	1	8	4	3		13			11³														36
1	7²	14						5	10²				9	6¹	2	8	4	3			13			11								12						37
1	5	7					12		10²				6	2	9	4	3	13			11			8¹														38
1	5	7					14	9²	12				6³	13	2	8	4	3			11¹			10														39
1	5	7					13	10	14				9	8³	2	12	6	4¹	3²		11																	40
1	4	7					8	10	5²	13			6	12	2	3		9			11																	41
1	5²	8¹					10	13	11				6	12	2	4		7	3		14			9³														42
1	5	12					13	8	10²	11³			6	2¹	4	7		3			14			9■														43
1	13	2²					12	7	9¹	5	10		6	14	4	8		3			11³																	44
1	5²						8³	10	9	11	2¹	13			6	7	4	3			14			12														45
	5³						8²	10	13	11¹	14				6	9	1	2			4	3		12											7			46

The Budweiser FA Cup

Third Round	Macclesfield T	(a)	1-1	
Replay	Macclesfield T	(h)	4-1	
Fourth Round	Rochdale	(a)	2-1	
Fifth Round	Charlton Ath	(h)	1-2	

Capital One Cup

First Round	Rotherham U	(a)	1-2

SHREWSBURY TOWN

FOUNDATION

Shrewsbury School having provided a number of the early England and Wales international players it is not surprising that there was a Town club as early as 1876 which won the Birmingham Senior Cup in 1879. However, the present Shrewsbury Town club was formed in 1886 and won the Welsh FA Cup as early as 1891.

Greenhous Meadow, Oteley Road, Shrewsbury, Shropshire SY2 6ST.

Telephone: (01743) 289 177.

Fax: (01743) 246 942.

Ticket Office: (01743) 273 943.

Website: www.shrewsburytown.com

Email: info@shrewsburytown.co.uk

Ground Capacity: 9,875.

Record Attendance: 18,917 v Walsall, Division 3, 26 April 1961 (at Gay Meadow); 9,510 v Wolverhampton W, FL 1, 21 September 2013 (at ProStar Stadium).

Pitch Measurements: 105m × 68.5m (115yd × 75yd)

Chairman: Roland Wycherley.

Manager: Micky Mellon.

Assistant Manager: Mike Jackson.

Physio: Chris Skitt.

HONOURS

Football League – Division 2: Best season: 8th, 1983–84, 1984–85; **Division 3:** *Champions* 1978–79, 1993–94; **Division 4:** *Runners-up* 1974–75. **FL 2:** *Runners-up* 2011–12. **FA Cup:** Best season: 6th rd, 1979, 1982. **Football League Cup:** Semi-final 1961. **Welsh Cup:** *Winners* 1891, 1938, 1977, 1979, 1984, 1985; *Runners-up* 1931, 1948, 1980. **Auto Windscreens Shield:** *Runners-up* 1996.

Colours: Blue and yellow striped shirts with blue sleeves, blue shorts, blue socks with yellow trim.

Year Formed: 1886.

Turned Professional: 1896.

Club Nicknames: 'Town', 'Blues', 'Salop'. The name 'Salop' is a colloquialism for the county of Shropshire. Since Shrewsbury is the only club in Shropshire, cries of 'Come on Salop' are frequently used!

Grounds: 1886, Old Racecourse Ground; 1889, Ambler's Field; 1893, Sutton Lane; 1895, Barracks Ground; 1910, Gay Meadow; 2007, New Meadow (re-named Greenhous Meadow 2010).

First Football League Game: 19 August 1950, Division 3 (N), v Scunthorpe U (a) D 0–0 – Egglestone; Fisher, Lewis; Wheatley, Depear, Robinson; Griffin, Hope, Jackson, Brown, Barker.

Record League Victory: 7–0 v Swindon T, Division 3 (S), 6 May 1955 – McBride; Bannister, Skeech; Wallace, Maloney, Candlin; Price, O'Donnell (1), Weigh (4), Russell, McCue (2); 7-0 v Gillingham, FL 2, 13 September 2008 – Daniels; Herd, Tierney, Davies (2), Jackson (1) (Langmead), Coughlan (1), Cansdell-Sherriff (1), Thornton, Hibbert (1) (Hindmarch), Holt (pen), McIntyre (Ashton).

Record Cup Victory: 11–2 v Marine, FA Cup 1st rd, 11 November 1995 – Edwards; Seabury (Dempsey (1)), Withe (1), Evans (1), Whiston (2), Scott (1), Woods, Stevens (1), Spink (3) (Anthrobus), Walton, Berkley, (1 og).

sky SPORTS FACT FILE

Although Shrewsbury Town first entered the FA Cup in 1887–88, they had to wait until December 1952 before they recorded a victory over a Football League side in the competition. After drawing twice with Queens Park Rangers in their first round tie, the Shrews secured a 4-1 win in the second replay at Villa Park.

Record Defeat: 1–8 v Norwich C, Division 3 (S), 13 September 1952; 1–8 v Coventry C, Division 3, 22 October 1963.

Most League Points (2 for a win): 62, Division 4, 1974–75.

Most League Points (3 for a win): 88, FL 2, 2011–12.

Most League Goals: 101, Division 4, 1958–59.

Highest League Scorer in Season: Arthur Rowley, 38, Division 4, 1958–59.

Most League Goals in Total Aggregate: Arthur Rowley, 152, 1958–65 (thus completing his League record of 434 goals).

Most League Goals in One Match: 5, Alf Wood v Blackburn R, Division 3, 2 October 1971.

Most Capped Player: Jimmy McLaughlin, 5 (12), Northern Ireland; Bernard McNally, 5, Northern Ireland.

Most League Appearances: Mickey Brown, 418, 1986–91; 1992–94; 1996–2001.

Youngest League Player: Graham French, 16 years 177 days v Reading, 30 September 1961.

Record Transfer Fee Received: £600,000 from Manchester C for Joe Hart, May 2006.

Record Transfer Fee Paid: £170,000 to Nottingham F for Grant Holt, June 2008.

Football League Record: 1950 Elected to Division 3 (N); 1951–58 Division 3 (S); 1958–59 Division 4; 1959–74 Division 3; 1974–75 Division 4; 1975–79 Division 3; 1979–89 Division 2; 1989–94 Division 3; 1994–97 Division 2; 1997–2003 Division 3; 2003–04 Conference; 2004–12 FL 2; 2012–14 FL 1; 2014– FL 2.

LATEST SEQUENCES

Longest Sequence of League Wins: 7, 28.10.1995 – 16.12.1995.

Longest Sequence of League Defeats: 11, 9.4.2003 – 14.8.2004.

Longest Sequence of League Draws: 6, 30.10.1963 – 14.12.1963.

Longest Sequence of Unbeaten League Matches: 16, 30.10.1993 – 26.2.1994.

Longest Sequence Without a League Win: 18, 8.3.2003 – 14.8.2004.

Successive Scoring Runs: 28 from 7.9.1960.

Successive Non-scoring Runs: 6 from 1.1.1991.

MANAGERS

W. Adams 1905–12
  (Secretary-Manager)
A. Weston 1912–34
  (Secretary-Manager)
Jack Roscamp 1934–35
Sam Ramsey 1935–36
Ted Bousted 1936–40
Leslie Knighton 1945–49
Harry Chapman 1949–50
Sammy Crooks 1950–54
Walter Rowley 1955–57
Harry Potts 1957–58
Johnny Spuhler 1958
Arthur Rowley 1958–68
Harry Gregg 1968–72
Maurice Evans 1972–73
Alan Durban 1974–78
Richie Barker 1978
Graham Turner 1978–84
Chic Bates 1984–87
Ian McNeill 1987–90
Asa Hartford 1990–91
John Bond 1991–93
Fred Davies 1994–97
  (previously Caretaker-Manager 1993–94)
Jake King 1997–99
Kevin Ratcliffe 1999–2003
Jimmy Quinn 2003–04
Gary Peters 2004–08
Paul Simpson 2008–10
Graham Turner 2010–14
Mike Jackson 2014
Micky Mellon May 2014–

TEN YEAR LEAGUE RECORD

		P	W	D	L	F	A	Pts	Pos
2004-05	FL 2	46	11	16	19	48	53	49	21
2005-06	FL 2	46	16	13	17	55	55	61	10
2006-07	FL 2	46	18	17	11	68	46	71	7
2007-08	FL 2	46	12	14	20	56	65	50	18
2008-09	FL 2	46	17	18	11	61	44	69	7
2009-10	FL 2	46	17	12	17	55	54	63	12
2010-11	FL 2	46	22	13	11	72	49	79	4
2011-12	FL 2	46	26	10	10	66	41	88	2
2012-13	FL 1	46	13	16	17	54	60	55	16
2013-14	FL 1	46	9	15	22	44	65	42	23

DID YOU KNOW ?

Shrewsbury Town lost 3-1 to Wolverhampton Wanderers reserves in a Birmingham League game on 2 November 1901 but the game had to be replayed after the referee admitted to ending the match 13 minutes early. Town fared even worse in the second match, losing 4-1.

SHREWSBURY TOWN – FOOTBALL LEAGUE ONE 2013–14 LEAGUE RECORD

Match No.	Date	Venue	Opponents	Result		H/T Score	Lg Pos.	Goalscorers	Attendance
1	Aug 3	H	Milton Keynes D	D	0-0	0-0	14		5144
2	10	A	Leyton Orient	L	0-3	0-0	19		4414
3	17	H	Swindon T	W	2-0	1-0	14	Reach [9], Bradshaw [85]	4943
4	24	A	Rotherham U	D	2-2	1-0	11	Taylor [21], Bradshaw [63]	7234
5	31	H	Coventry C	D	1-1	0-1	14	Bradshaw [48]	6541
6	Sept 14	A	Crawley T	D	1-1	0-0	13	Wildig [47]	3202
7	17	A	Bristol C	D	1-1	1-0	13	Taylor [28]	10,143
8	21	H	Wolverhampton W	L	0-1	0-0	14		9510
9	28	A	Bradford C	L	1-2	1-0	15	Bradshaw [2]	14,128
10	Oct 5	H	Carlisle U	D	2-2	1-0	15	Bradshaw [40], Parry [90]	5215
11	12	H	Gillingham	W	2-0	1-0	13	Jacobson [17], McAlinden [81]	5129
12	19	A	Peterborough U	L	0-1	0-0	13		6956
13	22	H	Colchester U	D	1-1	1-1	15	Lopez [4]	4364
14	26	A	Brentford	L	0-1	0-1	18		9783
15	Nov 2	H	Sheffield U	W	2-0	1-0	15	Jacobson [39], McAlinden [80]	6226
16	16	A	Port Vale	L	1-3	0-2	17	McAlinden [59]	6547
17	23	H	Notts Co	W	1-0	0-0	14	Reach [73]	5008
18	26	H	Oldham Ath	L	1-2	1-1	18	Ugwu [16]	4563
19	30	A	Stevenage	W	3-1	2-1	13	Reach [35], Eaves [38], Jacobson [51]	2675
20	Dec 14	H	Walsall	L	0-1	0-0	15		6015
21	21	A	Crewe Alex	D	1-1	0-1	17	Taylor [56]	4801
22	26	H	Tranmere R	L	0-1	0-1	17		6056
23	29	H	Preston NE	L	0-1	0-0	19		6379
24	Jan 1	A	Oldham Ath	W	2-1	1-1	16	Taylor [23], Wildig [62]	3669
25	7	H	Leyton Orient	L	0-2	0-1	17		4194
26	11	A	Milton Keynes D	L	2-3	1-2	18	Woods [7], Jacobson [86]	7408
27	18	H	Rotherham U	L	0-3	0-3	19		5116
28	25	A	Swindon T	L	1-3	1-1	22	Parry [45]	7448
29	Feb 1	H	Brentford	D	1-1	0-0	21	Eaves [90]	4927
30	8	A	Sheffield U	L	0-2	0-2	23		15,987
31	15	H	Port Vale	D	0-0	0-0	23		5992
32	22	A	Notts Co	W	3-2	1-2	22	Taylor 2 [32, 67], McAllister [70]	5424
33	Mar 2	A	Coventry C	D	0-0	0-0	22		1966
34	8	H	Bristol C	L	2-3	1-1	23	Mkandawire [41], Parry [60]	6069
35	11	A	Crawley T	D	1-1	0-1	23	Parry [56]	4039
36	15	A	Wolverhampton W	D	0-0	0-0	23		24,012
37	18	A	Colchester U	L	0-1	0-0	23		2508
38	22	H	Bradford C	W	2-1	0-0	22	Taylor [80], Miller [90]	5181
39	25	A	Carlisle U	D	0-0	0-0	22		3963
40	29	A	Walsall	L	0-1	0-1	23		4222
41	Apr 5	H	Stevenage	W	1-0	0-0	22	Taylor [57]	5178
42	12	A	Tranmere R	L	1-2	0-1	23	Parry [73]	5698
43	18	H	Crewe Alex	L	1-3	0-1	23	Bradshaw [90]	6947
44	21	A	Preston NE	L	2-5	1-2	23	Miller [43], Summerfield [78]	9636
45	26	H	Peterborough U	L	2-4	2-3	24	Taylor [6], Bradshaw [45]	5619
46	May 3	A	Gillingham	D	1-1	0-0	23	Miller [86]	7634

Final League Position: 23

GOALSCORERS

League (44): Taylor 9, Bradshaw 7, Parry 5, Jacobson 4, McAlinden 3, Miller 3, Reach 3, Eaves 2, Wildig 2, Lopez 1, McAllister 1, Mkandawire 1, Summerfield 1, Ugwu 1, Woods 1.
The Budweiser FA Cup (0).
Capital One Cup (1): Wildig 1.
Johnstone's Paint Trophy (1): Burke 1.

Weale C 35	Tavernier J 1	Jacobson J 40 + 1	Wildig A 27 + 3	Mkandawire T 38 + 1	Jones D 14 + 1	Taylor J 36 + 5	Summerfield L 24 + 4	Marsden J 1 + 2	Bradshaw T 17 + 11	Parry P 31 + 8	McAllister D 16 + 10	Goldson C 30 + 6	McQuade A — + 1	Burke G 1 + 2	Reach A 17 + 5	Asante A 1	Woods R 37 + 4	Main C 4 + 1	Winfield D 15 + 2	Lopez C 4 + 1	McAlinden L 5 + 4	Wroe N 7 + 3	Ugwu C 7	Eaves T 20 + 5	Gayle C 2 + 1	Grandison J 6 + 8	Hall A 14 + 3	Schmeltz S 2 + 2	Fyvie F 4	Ataic B 3 + 10	Mendez-Laing N 3 + 3	Mills J 12 + 1	Anyon J 11	Storey M 4 + 2	Foley S 6 + 3	Iorfa D 6 + 1	Miller S 5 + 3	Match No.
1	2	3	4	5	6[1]	7	8	9[3]	10	11[2]	12	13	14																									1
1		5	8	4	3	6	7[1]		10	9	12	2		11																								2
1		5	8	3	4	6	7		12	10[1]		2					9	11[2]	13																			3
1		5	7	3	6	9			11	8[1]	12	4			10		2																					4
1		5	8	4	3	10	7		11	6[1]							2	9[1]		12																		5
1		5	7		3	9	8		11[1]	10[2]	14	4		12	13		2	6[3]																				6
1		5	7		3	9	8		10[1]	6[2]	13	4			12		2	11																				7
1		5	7	4	6		8		11[1]		13	3		12	9[2]		2	10	4																			8
1		5	8	13	3		7		10[2]		12	2			9		6	11[1]	4																			9
1		5	8	4	3	6	7		10	11					9		2																					10
1		5	8	3		6			10	9[1]	7[2]	12			14		2		4	11[3]	13																	11
1		5	3	10		9			11	2[1]	8[3]	14			13		7		4	6[2]	12																	12
1		5	8	4		6	7[2]		14	13		12			9		2		3	10[1]	11[1]																	13
1		5	8	4		6	14		10[1]	9[3]		13			2		3		12	11[2]	7																	14
1		5[1]	8	4		6	14		10[2]			12			9		2		3	11[3]	13	7																15
1		2[1]	9[1]	3			8		13			5			6		12		4		11	7	10															16
1		5	8[1]	4	3		7			6[2]		13			9		2				11	12	10															17
1		5[2]		4	3		7		13	6	12	2			9						11[1]	8	10															18
1		2		5	4		3			7	12				10		8		14		13			6[3]	9[1]	11[2]												19
1		5		4	3	12	7[3]		14	6[1]					9		8							13	10	11[2]	2											20
1		5		4	3	6	7		12						9		2	4						8	10[1]	11												21
1		5		4			6	7	13	14					9[3]		2[2]		3					8	10[1]	11	12											22
1		5	13	4		6	7	14	10[1]	12	8[2]				9[3]		2		3					11														23
1		5	8[1]	4	13	9[2]	7			6					11		2		3				12	10														24
1		5	9	4		8			12	10	7				2[3]		3						6[2]	11		13	14											25
1		5	9[1]	4		10			13		8	2			7			4						11		12	6											26
1		5		4		6			12	13	14	8	2		7		3							11[3]			10[2]	9[1]										27
1		5		3		10				7	8	4			2									11[3]		12	9	14	6[1]	13								28
1		5		4		6	13			9	7[2]	3			2									10				8		11[3]	12	14						29
1		2[2]		4		10				9	7	3			5									11[3]			14		12	8[1]	13	6						30
		4		13					9	12	6				2										14		3	7		8[2]	10[1]	5	1	11[3]				31
		3		6					9[1]	7	4				2									11		13	8				10[2]	5	1	12				32
		14		3	6				9[1]	7	4				2									10[3]			8			13	11[2]	5	1	12				33
		5[2]		4	6				9[1]	7	3				2									14			8			13	12	5	1	11[3]	10			34
		4	8[2]	6	14				11[3]	12	3				7									13		9				14	13	5	1	10[3]	11[1]			35
		5		3	14				13	7[3]	4				9									12		2	10					8	1	11[1]	6[2]			36
		5[2]		4	13				6	9	7[2]				11[3]		2							8			14					5	1	10	14			37
		13		4	6				9	7[2]	4				11[3]		2							8			14					5	1	10[1]	12			38
		12		3	9				6[1]		4				7		10							2			8			13		5	1	14	11[3]			39
		9	7[2]	3					13	14	4				6[1]									12				8		11[2]		5	1		10	2	11[3]	40
1		5	7[3]	4	6[1]				9		3				12									14		10				8	11[2]	13			2			41
1		5	7	3	6		8		9		4				10									13		11[1]	14			2[3]		12						42
1		5	8	3	6	7[1]	14	9			4				13									11[3]		12				2		10[2]						43
1		4	8[2]	6			14		11[3]	12	3				7									13		9				5		2[1]				10		44
1		5	8	6			7[2]		10	9[1]	4				2		3							12		13	14			11[3]								45
		5	8[3]						9	7	10	12			3		6[2]							14		4				11[1]			1			2	13	46

The Budweiser FA Cup
First Round   Walsall   (a)   0-3

Capital One Cup
First Round   Bolton W   (h)   1-3

Johnstone's Paint Trophy
First Round   Oldham Ath   (h)   1-4

SOUTHAMPTON

FOUNDATION

The club was formed by members of the St Mary's Church of England Young Men's Association at a meeting of the Y.M.A. in November 1885 and it was named as such. For the sake of brevity this was usually shortened to St Mary's Y.M.A. The rector Canon Albert Basil Orme Wilberforce was elected president. The name was changed to plain St Mary's during 1887–88 and did not become Southampton St Mary's until 1894, the inaugural season in the Southern League.

St Mary's Stadium, Britannia Road, Southampton, Hampshire SO14 5FP.

Telephone: (0845) 688 9448.

Fax: (02380) 727 727.

Ticket Office: (0845) 688 9288.

Website: www.saintsfc.co.uk

Email: sfc@saintsfc.co.uk

Ground Capacity: 32,589.

Record Attendance: 31,044 v Manchester U, Division 1, 8 October 1969 (at The Dell); 32,151 v Arsenal, FA Premier League, 29 December 2003 (at St Mary's).

Pitch Measurements: 105m × 68m (114yd × 74yd)

Executive Chairman: Katharina Liebherr.

Manager: Ronald Koeman.

Assistant Manager: Erwin Koeman.

Physio: Matt Radcliffe.

Colours: Red shirt with white trim, red shorts with white trim, red socks with white hoops.

Year Formed: 1885.

Turned Professional: 1894.

Previous Names: 1885, St Mary's Young Men's Association; 1887–88, St Mary's; 1894–95 Southampton St Mary's; 1897, Southampton.

Club Nickname: 'Saints'.

HONOURS

Football League – FL C: *Runners-up* 2011–12; **Division 1:** *Runners-up* 1983–84; **Division 2:** *Runners-up* 1965–66, 1977–78; **Division 3:** *Champions* 1959–60: *Runners-up* 1920–21; **Division 3 (S):** *Champions* 1921–22.

FA Cup: *Winners* 1976; *Runners-up* 1900, 1902, 2003.

Football League Cup: *Runners-up* 1979.

Zenith Data Systems Cup: *Runners-up* 1992.

Johnstone's Paint Trophy: *Winners* 2009–10.

European Competitions
European Fairs Cup: 1969–70.
UEFA Cup: 1971–72, 1981–82, 1982–83, 1984–85, 2003–04.
European Cup-Winners' Cup: 1976–77.

Grounds: 1885, 'The Common' (from 1887 also used the County Cricket Ground and Antelope Cricket Ground); 1889, Antelope Cricket Ground; 1896 The County Cricket Ground; 1898, The Dell; 2001, St Mary's.

First Football League Game: 28 August 1920, Division 3, v Gillingham (a) D 1–1 – Allen; Parker, Titmuss; Shelley, Campbell, Turner; Barratt, Dominy (1), Rawlings, Moore, Foxall.

Record League Victory: 9–3 v Wolverhampton W, Division 2, 18 September 1965 – Godfrey; Jones, Williams; Walker, Knapp, Huxford; Paine (2), O'Brien (1), Melia, Chivers (4), Sydenham (2).

Record Cup Victory: 7–1 v Ipswich T, FA Cup 3rd rd, 7 January 1961 – Reynolds; Davies, Traynor, Conner, Page, Huxford, Paine (1), O'Brien (3 incl. 1p), Reeves, Mulgrew (2), Penk (1).

sky SPORTS FACT FILE

Edward Bell appeared in Southampton's Southern League team in 1906–07 and 1907–08. He later enlisted in the Footballers' Battalion in World War One where he was appointed to the rank of Captain. Bell was awarded the Military Cross in October 1916 with a bar added in February 1918. He was killed in action on 24 March 1918.

Record Defeat: 0–8 v Tottenham H, Division 2, 28 March 1936; 0–8 v Everton, Division 1, 20 November 1971.

Most League Points (2 for a win): 61, Division 3 (S), 1921–22 and Division 3, 1959–60.

Most League Points (3 for a win): 92, FL 1, 2010–11.

Most League Goals: 112, Division 3 (S), 1957–58.

Highest League Scorer in Season: Derek Reeves, 39, Division 3, 1959–60.

Most League Goals in Total Aggregate: Mike Channon, 185, 1966–77, 1979–82.

Most League Goals in One Match: 5, Charlie Wayman v Leicester C, Division 2, 23 October 1948.

Most Capped Player: Peter Shilton, 49 (125), England.

Most League Appearances: Terry Paine, 713, 1956–74.

Youngest League Player: Theo Walcott, 16 years 143 days v Wolverhampton W, 6 August 2005.

Record Transfer Fee Received: £27,000,000 (rising to £32,000,000) from Manchester U for Luke Shaw, July 2014.

Record Transfer Fee Paid: £12,800,000 (rising to £18,000,000) to AS Roma for Pablo Daniel Osvaldo, August 2013.

Football League Record: 1920 Original Member of Division 3; 1921–22 Division 3 (S); 1922–53 Division 2; 1953–58 Division 3 (S); 1958–60 Division 3; 1960–66 Division 2; 1966–74 Division 1; 1974–78 Division 2; 1978–92 Division 1; 1992–2005 FA Premier League; 2005–09 FL C; 2009–11 FL 1; 2011–12 FL C; 2012– FA Premier League.

LATEST SEQUENCES

Longest Sequence of League Wins: 10, 16.4.2011 – 20.8.2011.

Longest Sequence of League Defeats: 5, 16.8.1998 – 12.9.1998.

Longest Sequence of League Draws: 8, 29.8.2005 – 15.10.2005.

Longest Sequence of Unbeaten League Matches: 19, 5.9.1921 – 31.12.1921.

Longest Sequence Without a League Win: 20, 30.8.1969 – 27.12.1969.

Successive Scoring Runs: 28 from 10.2.2008.

Successive Non-scoring Runs: 5 from 2.4.2001.

MANAGERS

Cecil Knight 1894–95
  (Secretary-Manager)
Charles Robson 1895–97
Er Arnfield 1897–1911
  (Secretary-Manager)
  (continued as Secretary)
George Swift 1911–12
Er Arnfield 1912–19
Jimmy McIntyre 1919–24
Arthur Chadwick 1925–31
George Kay 1931–36
George Gross 1936–37
Tom Parker 1937–43
J. R. Sarjantson stepped down
  from the board to act as
  Secretary-Manager 1943–47 with
  the next two listed being Team
  Managers during this period
Arthur Dominy 1943–46
Bill Dodgin Snr 1946–49
Sid Cann 1949–51
George Roughton 1952–55
Ted Bates 1955–73
Lawrie McMenemy 1973–85
Chris Nicholl 1985–91
Ian Branfoot 1991–94
Alan Ball 1994–95
Dave Merrington 1995–96
Graeme Souness 1996–97
Dave Jones 1997–2000
Glenn Hoddle 2000–01
Stuart Gray 2001
Gordon Strachan 2001–04
Paul Sturrock 2004
Steve Wigley 2004
Harry Redknapp 2004–05
George Burley 2005–08
Nigel Pearson 2008
Jan Poortvliet 2008–09
Mark Wotte 2009
Alan Pardew 2009–10
Nigel Adkins 2010–13
Mauricio Pochettino 2013–14
Ronald Koeman June 2014–

TEN YEAR LEAGUE RECORD

		P	W	D	L	F	A	Pts	Pos
2004-05	PR Lge	38	6	14	18	45	66	32	20
2005-06	FL C	46	13	19	14	49	50	58	12
2006-07	FL C	46	21	12	13	77	53	75	6
2007-08	FL C	46	13	15	18	56	72	54	20
2008-09	FL C	46	10	15	21	46	69	45	23
2009-10	FL 1	46	23	14	9	85	47	73*	7
2010-11	FL 1	46	28	8	10	86	38	92	2
2011-12	FL C	46	26	10	10	85	46	88	2
2012-13	PR Lge	38	9	14	15	49	60	41	14
2013-14	PR Lge	38	15	11	12	54	46	56	8

*10 pts deducted.

DID YOU KNOW ?

Southampton were the first club to be relegated from the top flight of English football following the introduction of 'three up, three down' for the 1973–74 season. In fact Saints were fourth from bottom after completing their last but one fixture, but were relegated as Birmingham City overtook their points total from a game in hand.

SOUTHAMPTON – FA PREMIERSHIP 2013–14 LEAGUE RECORD

Match No.	Date	Venue	Opponents	Result	H/T Score	Lg Pos.	Goalscorers	Attendance
1	Aug 17	A	WBA	W	1-0	0-0	4	Lambert (pen) [90]	25,927
2	24	H	Sunderland	D	1-1	0-1	4	Fonte [88]	29,596
3	31	A	Norwich C	L	0-1	0-0	9		26,819
4	Sept 15	H	West Ham U	D	0-0	0-0	11		28,794
5	21	A	Liverpool	W	1-0	0-0	6	Lovren [53]	44,755
6	28	H	Crystal Palace	W	2-0	0-0	4	Osvaldo [47], Lambert [49]	30,699
7	Oct 6	H	Swansea C	W	2-0	1-0	4	Lallana [19], Rodriguez [83]	28,570
8	19	A	Manchester U	D	1-1	0-1	5	Lallana [89]	75,220
9	26	H	Fulham	W	2-0	2-0	3	Lambert [20], Rodriguez [42]	28,631
10	Nov 2	A	Stoke C	D	1-1	1-1	5	Rodriguez [42]	26,053
11	9	H	Hull C	W	4-1	3-0	3	Schneiderlin [16], Lambert (pen) [30], Lallana [37], Davis, S [88]	30,022
12	23	A	Arsenal	L	0-2	0-1	4		60,007
13	Dec 1	A	Chelsea	L	1-3	1-0	7	Rodriguez [1]	41,568
14	4	H	Aston Villa	L	2-3	0-0	8	Rodriguez [48], Osvaldo [69]	29,814
15	7	H	Manchester C	D	1-1	1-1	8	Osvaldo [42]	31,229
16	14	A	Newcastle U	D	1-1	0-1	8	Rodriguez [65]	49,164
17	22	H	Tottenham H	L	2-3	1-1	9	Lallana [13], Lambert [59]	31,455
18	26	A	Cardiff C	W	3-0	3-0	9	Rodriguez 2 [14, 20], Lambert [27]	27,929
19	29	A	Everton	L	1-2	0-1	9	Ramirez [71]	39,092
20	Jan 1	H	Chelsea	L	0-3	0-0	9		31,271
21	11	H	WBA	W	1-0	0-0	9	Lallana [66]	28,610
22	18	A	Sunderland	D	2-2	2-1	9	Rodriguez [4], Lovren [31]	38,115
23	28	A	Arsenal	D	2-2	1-0	9	Fonte [21], Lallana [54]	31,284
24	Feb 1	A	Fulham	W	3-0	0-0	9	Lallana [64], Lambert [70], Rodriguez [75]	25,700
25	8	H	Stoke C	D	2-2	2-2	9	Lambert [6], Davis, S [41]	27,987
26	11	H	Hull C	W	1-0	0-0	8	Fonte [69]	23,670
27	22	A	West Ham U	L	1-3	1-2	8	Yoshida [8]	33,148
28	Mar 1	H	Liverpool	L	0-3	0-1	9		31,659
29	8	A	Crystal Palace	W	1-0	1-0	9	Rodriguez [37]	25,073
30	15	H	Norwich C	W	4-2	1-0	8	Schneiderlin [5], Lambert [57], Rodriguez [72], Gallagher [90]	29,828
31	23	A	Tottenham H	L	2-3	2-1	9	Rodriguez [19], Lallana [28]	35,460
32	29	H	Newcastle U	W	4-0	1-0	8	Rodriguez 2 [45, 89], Lambert [49], Lallana [70]	31,360
33	Apr 5	A	Manchester C	L	1-4	1-3	8	Lambert (pen) [37]	47,009
34	12	H	Cardiff C	L	0-1	0-0	8		30,526
35	19	A	Aston Villa	D	0-0	0-0	8		35,134
36	26	H	Everton	W	2-0	2-0	8	Alcaraz (og) [1], Coleman (og) [31]	31,313
37	May 3	A	Swansea C	W	1-0	0-0	8	Lambert [90]	20,682
38	11	H	Manchester U	D	1-1	1-0	8	Lambert [28]	31,372

Final League Position: 8

GOALSCORERS
League (54): Rodriguez 15, Lambert 13 (3 pens), Lallana 9, Fonte 3, Osvaldo 3, Davis, S 2, Lovren 2, Schneiderlin 2, Gallagher 1, Ramirez 1, Yoshida 1, own goals 2.
The Budweiser FA Cup (6): Guly 1 (1 pen), Clyne 1, Gallagher 1, Lallana 1, Lambert 1, Rodriguez 1.
Capital One Cup (8): Davis, S 2 (1 pen), Ramirez 2, Hooiveld 1, Mayuka 1, Rodriguez 1, Yoshida 1.

Boruc A 29	Chambers C 18 + 4	Fonte J 35 + 1	Lovren D 31	Shaw L 35	Ward-Prowse J 16 + 18	Wanyama V 19 + 4	Schneiderlin M 31 + 2	Rodriguez J 30 + 3	Lambert R 31 + 6	Lallana A 37 + 1	Ramirez G 3 + 15	Davis S 28 + 6	Cork J 21 + 7	Osvaldo P 9 + 4	Clyne N 20 + 5	Fox D 3	Do Prado G — + 9	Hooiveld J 3	Gazzaniga P 7 + 1	Yoshida M 7 + 1	Reed H — + 4	Gallagher S 3 + 15	Davis K 2	Match No.
1	2	3	4	5	6¹	7	8	9²	10	11²	12	13	14											1
1	2	3	4	5¹	8	7	6²	10	11	9³	14			12	13									2
1	2	3	4		8	6	7²	14	11	10³	12	13		9¹		5								3
1	13	3	4	5	12	8	7	6	11	9²				10	2									4
1		3	4	5	13	6	7	10²	11¹	8³	12	14		9	2									5
1		3	4	5	12	6	7	13	11³	8²	14	10¹		9	2									6
1		3	4	5	12	6	7	13	11¹	8		10²		9²	2									7
1		3	4	5	13	7²	6	10¹	12	8	9³	11		14	2									8
1		3	4	5	8¹	7	6	9	11	10		13			2				12					9
1		3	4	5	8	6	7	9	11	10	12				2									10
1		3	4	5	8	6³	7	10	11²	9¹	12	14		13	2									11
1		3		5²	8	6	7	10	11	9¹	12	13			2		4							12
1²		3	4	5	8	6	7²	10	14	9	13	11			2				12					13
	14		4	5	7¹	6²		10	11	9	8	13		12	2²				1	3				14
	2	3	4	5	7			10	12	8¹	13	9²		6			11³		1			14		15
	2	3		5	7²		13	10³	11	12		8		6	9¹			4	1			14		16
	2	3		12				8	11	10	9	13		6	7³	5¹		4	1			14		17
	2	3		5	12			7	8²	11²	10¹	13		9	6				1		4	14		18
	2¹	3	4	5	6²			8	11	10	12	9	7³			14						13	1	19
	2	3	4	5²	14			7	11	13	8	10		9⁶	6²				12				1	20
1		3	4	5	13		7	10³	11	9¹	12	8		6²	2							14		21
1	2	3	4¹	5	13		8	11	10	9	12³	6	7								14			22
1	2	3		5	12		7	8		10		9¹	6				13				4	11²		23
1	2²	3		5		6¹	7	10³	11	8		9	12		13						4	14		24
1	12	3		5			7	10	11	8		9	6	2¹							4			25
1	2	3		5	13	14	7	10	11³	8¹		9²	6				12				4			26
1	2	3		5	14		7	8	11¹	10	12	9²	6³								4	13		27
1	2	3	4	5		14	8	9	10¹	11	12	6²	7²									13		28
1		3	4	5	14	12	7	10	11¹	9		8³	6²	2								13		29
		3	4	5	6		7	10¹	12	11³	9²	8			2		13					14		30
1	12	3	4	5	7			10³	11²	9	13	8	6	2¹								14		31
1	2	3	4	5	7		12	10	11³	9²	13	8	6									14		32
	2	3	4	5	12	14	7	10³	11	8		9²	6¹							1		13		33
	2¹	3	4	5			7		11	10	9³	8	6²	13		14	1					12		34
1		3	4	5	8³	6¹	7		11	9²		10	13	2							14	12		35
1		3	4	5	12	7		9	10²	8⁶		6		2			14					13	11³	36
1		3	4	5	13	7	9		12	8²		10	6¹	2							14		11³	37
1	14	3	4	5¹	13	8	7		10	11²		9	6³	2									12	38

The Budweiser FA Cup

Third Round	Burnley	(h)	4-3
Fourth Round	Yeovil T	(h)	2-0
Fifth Round	Sunderland	(a)	0-1

Capital One Cup

Second Round	Barnsley	(a)	5-1
Third Round	Bristol C	(h)	2-0
Fourth Round	Sunderland	(a)	1-2

SOUTHEND UNITED

FOUNDATION

The leading club in Southend around the turn of the 20th century was Southend Athletic, but they were an amateur concern. Southend United was a more ambitious professional club when they were founded in 1906, employing Bob Jack as secretary-manager and immediately joining the Second Division of the Southern League.

Roots Hall Stadium, Victoria Avenue, Southend-on-Sea, Essex SS2 6NQ.

Telephone: (01702) 304 050.

Fax: (01702) 304 124.

Ticket Office: (08444) 770 077.

Website: www.southendunited.co.uk

Email: info@southend-united.co.uk

Ground Capacity: 12,149.

Record Attendance: 22,862 v Tottenham H, FA Cup 3rd rd replay, 11 January 1936 (at Southend Stadium); 31,090 v Liverpool, FA Cup 3rd rd, 10 January 1979 (at Roots Hall).

Pitch Measurements: 100.5m × 67.5m (110yd × 74yd)

Chairman: Ronald Martin.

Chief Executive: Steve Kavanagh.

Manager: Phil Brown.

Assistant Manager: Dave Penney.

Physio: Ben Clarkson.

Colours: Navy blue shirts with white trim, navy blue shorts, white socks.

Year Formed: 1906.

Turned Professional: 1906.

Club Nicknames: 'The Blues', 'The Shrimpers'.

Grounds: 1906, Roots Hall, Prittlewell; 1920, Kursaal; 1934, Southend Stadium; 1955, Roots Hall Football Ground.

First Football League Game: 28 August 1920, Division 3, v Brighton & HA (a) W 2–0 – Capper; Reid, Newton; Wileman, Henderson, Martin; Nicholls, Nuttall, Fairclough (2), Myers, Dorsett.

Record League Victory: 9–2 v Newport Co, Division 3 (S), 5 September 1936 – McKenzie; Nelson, Everest (1); Deacon, Turner, Carr; Bolan, Lane (1), Goddard (4), Dickinson (2), Oswald (1).

Record Cup Victory: 10–1 v Golders Green, FA Cup 1st rd, 24 November 1934 – Moore; Morfitt, Kelly; Mackay, Joe Wilson, Carr (1); Lane (1), Johnson (5), Cheesmuir (2), Deacon (1), Oswald. 10–1 v Brentwood, FA Cup 2nd rd, 7 December 1968 – Roberts; Bentley, Birks; McMillan (1) Beesley, Kurila; Clayton, Chisnall, Moore (4), Best (5), Hamilton. 10–1 v Aldershot, Leyland DAF Cup Prel rd, 6 November 1990 – Sansome; Austin, Powell, Cornwell, Prior (1), Tilson (3), Cawley, Butler, Ansah (1), Benjamin (1), Angell (4).

HONOURS

Football League – Division 1: Best season: 13th, 1994–95;
FL 1: *Champions* 2005–06;
Division 3: *Runners-up* 1990–91;
Division 4: *Champions* 1980–81; *Runners-up* 1971–72, 1977–78.

FA Cup: Best season: old 3rd rd, 1921; 5th rd, 1926, 1952, 1976, 1993.

Football League Cup: Quarter-final 2007.

LDV Vans Trophy: *Runners-up* 2004, 2005.

Johnstone's Paint Trophy: *Runners-up* 2013.

Record Defeat: 1–9 v Brighton & HA, Division 3, 27 November 1965.

Most League Points (2 for a win): 67, Division 4, 1980–81.

Most League Points (3 for a win): 85, Division 3, 1990–91.

Most League Goals: 92, Division 3 (S), 1950–51.

Highest League Scorer in Season: Jim Shankly, 31, 1928–29; Sammy McCrory, 1957–58, both in Division 3 (S).

Most League Goals in Total Aggregate: Roy Hollis, 122, 1953–60.

Most League Goals in One Match: 5, Jim Shankly v Merthyr T, Division 3 (S), 1 March 1930.

Most Capped Player: George Mackenzie, 9, Eire.

Most League Appearances: Sandy Anderson, 452, 1950–63.

Youngest League Player: Phil O'Connor, 16 years 76 days v Lincoln C, 26 December 1969.

Record Transfer Fee Received: £2,000,000 (rising to £2,750,000) from Nottingham F for Stan Collymore, June 1993.

Record Transfer Fee Paid: £80,000 to Crystal Palace for Stan Collymore, November 1992.

Football League Record: 1920 Original Member of Division 3; 1921–58 Division 3 (S); 1958–66 Division 3; 1966–72 Division 4; 1972–76 Division 3; 1976–78 Division 4; 1978–80 Division 3; 1980–81 Division 4; 1981–84 Division 3; 1984–87 Division 3; 1987–89 Division 3; 1989–90 Division 4; 1990–91 Division 3; 1991–92 Division 2; 1992–97 Division 1; 1997–98 Division 2; 1998–2004 Division 3; 2004–05 FL 2; 2005–06 FL 1; 2006–07 FL C; 2007–10 FL 1; 2010– FL 2.

LATEST SEQUENCES

Longest Sequence of League Wins: 8, 29.8.2005 – 9.10.2005.

Longest Sequence of League Defeats: 6, 14.4.2007 – 18.8.2007.

Longest Sequence of League Draws: 6, 30.1.1982 – 19.2.1982.

Longest Sequence of Unbeaten League Matches: 16, 20.2.1932 – 29.8.1932.

Longest Sequence Without a League Win: 17, 26.8.2006 – 2.12.2006.

Successive Scoring Runs: 24 from 23.3.1929.

Successive Non-scoring Runs: 6 from 6.6.1979.

MANAGERS

Bob Jack 1906–10
George Molyneux 1910–11
O. M. Howard 1911–12
Joe Bradshaw 1912–19
Ned Liddell 1919–20
Tom Mather 1920–21
Ted Birnie 1921–34
David Jack 1934–40
Harry Warren 1946–56
Eddie Perry 1956–60
Frank Broome 1960
Ted Fenton 1961–65
Alvan Williams 1965–67
Ernie Shepherd 1967–69
Geoff Hudson 1969–70
Arthur Rowley 1970–76
Dave Smith 1976–83
Peter Morris 1983–84
Bobby Moore 1984–86
Dave Webb 1986–87
Dick Bate 1987
Paul Clark 1987–88
Dave Webb *(General Manager)* 1988–92
Colin Murphy 1992–93
Barry Fry 1993
Peter Taylor 1993–95
Steve Thompson 1995
Ronnie Whelan 1995–97
Alvin Martin 1997–99
Alan Little 1999–2000
David Webb 2000–01
Rob Newman 2001–03
Steve Wignall 2003
Steve Tilson 2003–10
Paul Sturrock 2010–13
Phil Brown March 2013–

TEN YEAR LEAGUE RECORD

		P	W	D	L	F	A	Pts	Pos
2004-05	FL 2	46	22	12	12	65	46	78	4
2005-06	FL 1	46	23	13	10	72	43	82	1
2006-07	FL C	46	10	12	24	47	80	42	22
2007-08	FL 1	46	22	10	14	70	55	76	6
2008-09	FL 1	46	21	8	17	58	61	71	8
2009-10	FL 1	46	10	13	23	51	72	43	23
2010-11	FL 2	46	16	13	17	62	56	61	13
2011-12	FL 2	46	25	8	13	77	48	83	4
2012-13	FL 2	46	16	13	17	61	55	61	11
2013-14	FL 2	46	19	15	12	56	39	72	5

DID YOU KNOW

Spencer Bassett featured at right half for Southend United in the 1914–15 season. Described as 'a fine specimen of manhood' he served as a bombardier in the Royal Garrison Artillery and died from wounds on 11 April 1917 during the early stages of the Battle of Arras.

SOUTHEND UNITED – FOOTBALL LEAGUE TWO 2013–14 LEAGUE RECORD

Match No.	Date	Venue	Opponents	Result	H/T Score	Lg Pos.	Goalscorers	Attendance
1	Aug 3	H	Plymouth Arg	W 1-0	1-0	8	Corr [15]	7055
2	10	A	Hartlepool U	W 1-0	1-0	4	Eastwood [5]	3479
3	17	H	Northampton T	W 2-0	1-0	2	Straker [38], Eastwood [62]	5510
4	24	A	Chesterfield	L 1-2	0-0	4	Eastwood [68]	5579
5	31	A	Wycombe W	L 1-2	1-2	7	Eastwood [14]	3533
6	Sept 7	H	Morecambe	L 1-3	1-1	11	Hurst [30]	6080
7	13	H	Scunthorpe U	L 0-1	0-0	13		4976
8	21	A	Bury	D 1-1	1-0	14	Coker [23]	2895
9	27	H	Bristol R	D 1-1	0-0	12	Hurst [67]	5489
10	Oct 5	A	Oxford U	W 2-0	2-0	14	Clifford [14], Prosser [30]	5578
11	12	A	Burton Alb	W 1-0	0-0	10	Eastwood [90]	2555
12	18	H	Fleetwood T	W 2-0	1-0	6	Corr 2 (1 pen) [21, 81 (p)]	4996
13	22	H	Dagenham & R	L 0-1	0-1	11		4523
14	26	A	Newport Co	L 1-3	1-2	13	Coker [41]	3652
15	Nov 1	H	Mansfield T	W 3-0	2-0	8	Straker [25], McGuire (og) [44], Hurst [90]	4824
16	16	A	Exeter C	W 2-0	2-0	5	Woodrow [12], Hurst [29]	3547
17	23	H	York C	W 2-1	1-0	5	Hurst [6], Prosser [90]	9018
18	26	A	Portsmouth	W 2-1	0-1	3	Atkinson [76], Corr [82]	13,427
19	30	H	Cheltenham T	D 1-1	1-0	3	Hurst [41]	5677
20	Dec 14	A	Torquay U	L 0-1	0-0	7		2144
21	20	H	Rochdale	D 1-1	1-1	5	Hurst [45]	5104
22	26	A	AFC Wimbledon	W 1-0	0-0	6	Woodrow [76]	4561
23	29	A	Accrington S	D 1-1	0-0	6	Prosser [78]	1333
24	Jan 1	H	Portsmouth	W 2-1	1-1	4	Leonard 2 [45, 90]	7736
25	11	H	Plymouth Arg	D 1-1	0-0	5	Hurst [68]	7088
26	18	H	Chesterfield	W 3-0	1-0	4	Hurst [28], Leonard [59], Corr [61]	6256
27	28	A	Dagenham & R	D 1-1	0-0	6	Hurst [53]	2624
28	31	H	Newport Co	D 0-0	0-0	4		5993
29	Feb 8	A	Mansfield T	L 1-2	0-1	7	Leonard [90]	3055
30	15	H	Exeter C	L 2-3	2-1	7	Phillips 2 [12, 22]	5899
31	18	H	Hartlepool U	D 1-1	1-0	7	Corr [43]	4361
32	22	A	York C	D 0-0	0-0	7		3628
33	25	A	Northampton T	L 1-2	1-1	7	Timlin [17]	3846
34	Mar 1	H	Wycombe W	D 1-1	0-0	7	Corr [63]	5502
35	8	A	Morecambe	L 1-2	1-1	7	Leonard [9]	1608
36	11	A	Scunthorpe U	D 2-2	0-2	7	Egan [62], White [69]	3018
37	15	H	Bury	D 0-0	0-0	7		5680
38	21	A	Bristol R	D 0-0	0-0	8		6028
39	24	H	Oxford U	W 3-0	2-0	7	Atkinson [9], Barnard (pen) [17], Loza [86]	6078
40	29	H	Torquay U	W 1-0	0-0	6	Eastwood [72]	6556
41	Apr 5	A	Cheltenham T	W 2-1	0-1	6	Corr [64], Hurst [67]	2949
42	12	H	AFC Wimbledon	L 0-1	0-0	6		7627
43	18	A	Rochdale	W 3-0	2-0	6	Corr [12], Murphy [44], Timlin [46]	3884
44	21	H	Accrington S	W 1-0	0-0	6	Corr [64]	5915
45	26	A	Fleetwood T	D 1-1	1-1	7	Corr [40]	3323
46	May 3	H	Burton Alb	W 1-0	1-0	5	Corr [22]	6218

Final League Position: 5

GOALSCORERS

League (56): Corr 12 (1 pen), Hurst 11, Eastwood 6, Leonard 5, Prosser 3, Atkinson 2, Coker 2, Phillips 2, Straker 2, Timlin 2, Woodrow 2, Barnard 1 (1 pen), Clifford 1, Egan 1, Loza 1, Murphy 1, White 1, own goal 1.
The Budweiser FA Cup (10): Straker 3, Leonard 2, Atkinson 1, Corr 1, Hurst 1, Laird 1, Timlin 1.
Capital One Cup (0).
Johnstone's Paint Trophy (2): Woodrow 2.
League Two Play-Offs (2): Leonard 1, Straker 1.

Bentley D 46	White J 41	Coker B 45	Laird M 9 + 10	Phillips M 23 + 4	Prosser L 23 + 2	Leonard R 42 + 1	Atkinson W 43 + 2	Corr B 35 + 8	Eastwood F 11 + 20	Straker A 27 + 12	Reid C — + 6	Clifford C 13 + 10	Cowan D — + 2	Thompson A 13 + 3	Payne J — + 11	Hurst K 39 + 3	Timlin M 32 + 4	Woodrow C 10 + 9	Kiernan R 11 + 1	Auger R 1	O'Neill L 1	Barnard L 9 + 4	Gomis B — + 2	Williams J — + 2	Bolger C 1	Egan J 13	Sokolik J 10	Loza J 4 + 3	Murphy J 4 + 3	Match No.
1	2	3	4	5	6	7	8	9²	10¹	11	12	13																		1
1	2	5	8²	3	4	7	6	10¹	11¹	9			12	13																2
1	2	5	8¹		4	7	6	11	10²	9	13	12		3	14															3
1	2	5			4	7	6	11²	10³	9		8¹	13	3		12	14													4
1	2	5			4	7	6³	11	10	9	12	8²		3	14	13														5
1	2	5		3	4	7	13	12	10	9³			14	6	8²	11¹														6
1		5³		3	4	7	9	12	10	13	14		2		6	8¹	11²													7
1	2	5⁴		3	4	7	8	11	10¹	9				6²	13	12														8
1	5		3¹	4	7	8	10	11²	9			2	12	6		13														9
1	2	5			4	7	9	11		13	12	8		3		6			10¹											10
1	2	5		3		7¹	6	10	12	14		8²		13	9		11	4³												11
1	2	5		3		6²	7	10	13	12		8		9¹		11	4													12
1	2	5		3⁴		7	6	10³	12	13		8²		14	9¹		11	4												13
1		2		3	8	5	11		14	7¹		13	6²	12	10³	4	9													14
1	3	5	13		4¹	2	6	10		11²	7¹			9	8			12												15
1	2	5	13	14	4	7	9	12		8²				6²	10	11¹	3													16
1	2	5	7		4		6	10		11¹				9⁴	8	12	3													17
1	2	5	13	14	8		6	10		11	7²		4¹			9²	12⁴	3												18
1	2	5	7¹		4		6	10		11	12		13	9²	8		3													19
1	2	5	6¹		3	12		10	13	9²		8²		14	11	7		4												20
1	2	5		12		4¹	7²	6	10	14	11³			9	8	13	3													21
1	2	5	14	4		9¹	7	11²	13	10³				6	8	12	3													22
1	2	5		3	4	9	8	13	12	10¹		14		6	7³	11²														23
1	2	5		3	4	7	6³	12	13	11¹		14		9	8	10²														24
1		5	14	3	4	2	6	10³	13	11²		7¹		9	8	12														25
1		5		3	4	7	6	10	14	11²		12		9	8³	13		2¹												26
1		5		3	4	7	6	10		11³		14	2	9	8²	13														27
1	2	5		4		7	9	11¹	13	12		14	3	6	8²				10³											28
1	2²	5	14	4		8	6	10	12	13⁴	3	9³	7¹			11														29
1	2	5		4		7	9	10³	13		3	6	8³			11¹	12	14												30
1	2	5		4		7	6	10	12	11¹	3	9	8																	31
1	2	5	13	14		9	7	11		10²		4	12	6	8¹			3³												32
1	3	5	7²	4		2	6	10	12	9²		13	8			11¹	14													33
1	2	5		3		7	6¹	10		11²		12	9	8		13														34
1	2	5	14	3		8³	7²	10		11		12	9	6¹		13		4												35
1	2	5	6	4		8	9¹	10²	13	12		7³		11	14		3													36
1	2	5	6		7	13	12⁴	10¹	11³		8²		9		14			4	3											37
1	2	5		8	6²		11¹	13		9	7		10		4	3	12													38
1	2	5	12		7	9		13		6	8¹		10²		4	3	11													39
1	2	5	14		7	9		13		6	8¹		10²		4	3	11³	12												40
1	2	5		7	6²	12		14		9³	8		10¹		4	3	11	13												41
1	2	5²		7	9¹	12	14		6	8		10²		4	3	11	13													42
1	2	5		14	6	8	11²		12		7³	9		4	3	13	10¹													43
1	2	5		14	7	6	10³		13		11	8¹		4	3	12	9²													44
1	2	5		9	7	11²	13	12		10	8		3	4			6¹													45
1	2	5		7	6	10³	14	13		9	8²		12		4	3	11¹													46

The Budweiser FA Cup

First Round	Morecambe	(a)	3-0
Second Round	Chesterfield	(a)	3-1
Third Round	Millwall	(h)	4-1
Fourth Round	Hull C	(h)	0-2

Capital One Cup

First Round	Yeovil T	(h)	0-1

Johnstone's Paint Trophy

Second Round	Dagenham & R	(h)	2-5

League Two Play-Offs

Semi-Finals 1st leg	Burton Alb	(a)	0-1
Semi-Finals 2nd leg	Burton Alb	(h)	2-2

STEVENAGE

FOUNDATION

There have been several clubs associated with the town of Stevenage. Stevenage Town was formed in 1884. They absorbed Stevenage Rangers in 1955 and later played at Broadhall Way. The club went into liquidation in 1968 and Stevenage Athletic was formed, but they, too, followed a similar path in 1976. Then Stevenage Borough was founded. The Broadhall Way pitch was dug up and remained unused for three years. Thus the new club started its life in the modest surrounds of the King George V playing fields with a roped-off ground in the Chiltern League. A change of competition followed to the Wallspan Southern Combination and by 1980 the club returned to the council-owned Broadhall Way when "Borough" was added to the name. Entry into the United Counties League was so successful the league and cup were won in the first season. On to the Isthmian League Division Two and the climb up the pyramid continued. In 1995–96 Stevenage Borough won the Conference but was denied a place in the Football League as the ground did not measure up to the competition's standards. Subsequent improvements changed this and the 7,100 capacity venue became one of the best appointed grounds in non-league football. After winning elevation to the Football League the club dropped Borough from its title.

Lamex Stadium, Broadhall Way, Stevenage, Hertfordshire SG2 8RH.

Telephone: (01438) 223223.

Fax: (01438) 743666.

Ticket Office: (0871) 855 1696.

Website: stevenagefc.com

Email: info@stevenagefc.com

Ground Capacity: 6,920.

Record Attendance: 6,913 v Everton, FA Cup 4th rd, 25 January 2014.

Pitch Measurements: 103m × 64.5m (112.5yd × 70.5yd)

Chairman: Phil Wallace.

Chief Executive: Barry Webber.

Manager: Graham Westley.

Assistant Manager: Dino Maamria.

Physio: Paul Dando.

Colours: White shirts with red trim, red shorts, red socks with white trim.

HONOURS

Football League – FL 2: Best season: 6th 2010–11 promoted to FL 1.
FA Cup: Best season: 5th rd, 2012.
Football League Cup: Best season: 2nd rd, 2012.
Blue Square Premier League: *Champions* 2009–10.
Conference: *Champions* 1995–96.
FA Trophy: *Winners* 2007, 2009; *Runners-up* 2002, 2010.
Herts Senior Cup: *Winners* 2009.
Isthmian League Premier Division: *Champions* 1993–94.
Isthmian League Division 1: *Champions:* 1991–92.
Isthmian League Division 2 (N): *Champions:* 1985–86, 1990–91.
United Counties League Division 1: *Champions* 1980–81.
United Counties League Cup: *Winners* 1981.

sky SPORTS FACT FILE

Stevenage won the Football Conference title in 1995–96 but were still denied promotion to the Football League as they had not met the relevant financial and ground requirements the previous December. The club took legal action on the grounds of unreasonable restraint of trade. Although they lost the case no club has since been denied promotion on these grounds.

Nickname: 'The Boro'.

Previous Name: Stevenage Borough.

Grounds: 1976, King George V playing fields; 1980, Broadhall Way.

First Football League Game: 7 August 2010, FL 2, v Macclesfield T (h) D 2–2 – Day; Henry, Laird, Bostwick, Roberts, Foster, Wilson (Sinclair), Byrom, Griffin (1), Winn (Odubade), Vincenti (1) (Beardsley).

Year Formed: 1976.

Turned Professional: 1976.

Record League Victory: 6–0 v Yeovil T, FL 2, 14 April 2012 – Day; Lascelles (1), Laird, Roberts (1), Ashton (1), Shroot (Mousinho), Wilson (Myrie-Williams), Long, Agyemang (1), Reid (Slew), Freeman (2).

Record Victory: 11–1 v British Timken Ath 1980–81.

Record Defeat: 0–7 v Southwick 1987–88.

Most League Points (3 for a win): 73, FL 1, 2011–12.

Most League Goals: 69, FL 1, 2011–12.

Highest League Scorer in Season: Francois Zoko, 14, 2013–14.

Most Goals in Total Aggregate: Luke Freeman, 15, 2011–14.

Most League Goals in One Match: 3, Chris Holroyd v Hereford U, FL 2, 28 September 2010; 3, Dani Lopez v Sheffield U, FL 1, 16 March 2013.

Most Capped Player: Marcus Haber, 5 (including 3 on loan at Notts Co) (10), Canada.

Most League Appearances: Chris Day, 151, 2010–14.

Youngest League Player: Ryan Johnson, 17 years 213 days v Brentford, 3 May 2014.

Record Transfer Fee Received: £260,000 from Peterborough U for George Boyd, January 2007.

Record Transfer Fee Paid: £75,000 (rising to £150,000) to Exeter C for James Dunne, May 2012.

Football League Record: 2011 Promoted from Conference Premier; 2010–11 FL 2; 2011–14 FL 1; 2014– FL 2.

MANAGERS
Derek Montgomery 1976–83
Frank Cornwell 1983–87
John Bailey 1987–88
Brian Wilcox 1988–90
Paul Fairclough 1990–98
Richard Hill 1998–2000
Steve Wignall 2000
Paul Fairclough 2000–02
Wayne Turner 2002–03
Graham Westley 2003–06
Mark Stimson 2006–07
Peter Taylor 2007–08
Graham Westley 2008–12
Gary Smith 2012–13
Graham Westley March 2013–

LATEST SEQUENCES

Longest Sequence of League Wins: 6, 12.3.2011 – 2.4.2011.

Longest Sequence of League Defeats: 6, 13.4.2013 – 17.8.2013.

Longest Sequence of League Draws: 5, 17.3.2012 – 31.3.2012.

Longest Sequence of Unbeaten League Matches: 17, 9.4.2012 – 6.10.2012.

Longest Sequence Without a League Win: 10, 11.3.2014 – 21.4.2014.

Successive Scoring Runs: 17 from 9.4.2012.

Successive Non-scoring Runs: 4 from 6.4.2013.

TEN YEAR LEAGUE RECORD

		P	W	D	L	F	A	Pts	Pos
2004-05	Conf	42	22	6	14	65	52	72	5
2005-06	Conf	42	19	12	11	62	47	69	6
2006-07	Conf	46	20	10	16	76	66	70	8
2007-08	Conf P	46	24	7	15	82	55	79	6
2008-09	Conf P	46	23	12	11	73	54	81	5
2009-10	Conf P	44	30	9	5	79	24	99	1
2010-11	FL 2	46	18	15	13	62	45	69	6
2011-12	FL 1	46	18	19	9	69	44	73	6
2012-13	FL 1	46	15	9	22	47	64	54	18
2013-14	FL 1	46	11	9	26	46	72	42	24

DID YOU KNOW ?

Stevenage, then known as Stevenage Borough, played their first-ever FA Cup tie on 3 September 1983. They defeated Milton Keynes City 2-0 in a preliminary round tie in front of an attendance of 303. Borough subsequently went out to Moor Green in a first qualifying round replay.

STEVENAGE – FOOTBALL LEAGUE ONE 2013–14 LEAGUE RECORD

Match No.	Date	Venue	Opponents	Result	H/T Score	Lg Pos.	Goalscorers	Attendance
1	Aug 3	H	Oldham Ath	L	3-4	1-0	18	Charles [45], Tansey [77], Morais [84]	3009
2	10	A	Swindon T	L	0-1	0-1	20		7133
3	17	H	Leyton Orient	L	0-1	0-1	22		3262
4	24	A	Notts Co	W	1-0	0-0	18	Dunne [90]	3925
5	31	H	Bradford C	D	1-1	1-0	15	Tansey (pen) [23]	3242
6	Sept 7	A	Tranmere R	D	0-0	0-0	16		4156
7	14	A	Preston NE	L	0-3	0-1	16		8855
8	21	H	Carlisle U	L	1-3	0-1	18	Tansey (pen) [59]	2526
9	28	A	Milton Keynes D	L	1-4	1-3	20	Potter (og) [42]	7770
10	Oct 5	H	Coventry C	L	0-1	0-1	23		3325
11	12	H	Brentford	W	2-1	2-1	19	Zoko 2 [15, 26]	3225
12	19	A	Walsall	L	1-2	0-1	21	Zoko [72]	3720
13	22	H	Crewe Alex	W	3-0	3-0	20	Morais 2 [11, 20], Freeman [13]	3682
14	26	H	Crawley T	W	2-0	1-0	17	Hartley [8], Doughty [90]	2804
15	Nov 2	A	Wolverhampton W	L	0-2	0-1	19		17,700
16	16	H	Rotherham U	L	0-3	0-1	20		2814
17	23	A	Peterborough U	W	1-0	1-0	20	Akins [20]	5707
18	26	A	Gillingham	L	2-3	1-0	19	Heslop [37], Zoko [59]	4951
19	30	H	Shrewsbury T	L	1-3	1-2	21	Zoko [24]	2675
20	Dec 14	A	Port Vale	D	2-2	2-1	21	Burrow 2 [37, 40]	4967
21	21	H	Sheffield U	D	0-0	0-0	21		3003
22	26	A	Colchester U	L	0-4	0-3	22		3919
23	29	A	Bristol C	L	1-4	0-2	23	Zoko [74]	12,038
24	Jan 11	A	Oldham Ath	L	0-1	0-1	24		3460
25	14	H	Swindon T	W	2-0	1-0	24	Akins [39], Morais (pen) [56]	2167
26	18	H	Notts Co	L	0-1	0-1	24		2877
27	Feb 4	H	Gillingham	W	3-1	2-0	24	Zoko (pen) [22], Charles 2 [30, 59]	2399
28	15	A	Rotherham U	L	1-2	0-1	24	Zoko [86]	7393
29	18	A	Leyton Orient	L	0-2	0-2	24		4171
30	22	H	Peterborough U	L	0-1	0-0	24		4262
31	25	H	Crewe Alex	W	1-0	1-0	24	Zoko [5]	1970
32	Mar 1	A	Bradford C	W	3-2	1-2	23	Zoko [23], Freeman 2 [65, 87]	13,033
33	4	A	Crawley T	D	1-1	1-0	23	Dembele [21]	2936
34	8	H	Tranmere R	W	3-1	1-0	21	Smith, J [21], Charles [71], Mousinho [74]	2577
35	11	A	Preston NE	D	1-1	0-1	20	Smith, J [90]	2448
36	15	A	Carlisle U	D	0-0	0-0	21		3672
37	22	H	Milton Keynes D	L	2-3	2-0	23	Parrett [18], Akins (pen) [35]	3027
38	26	A	Coventry C	L	0-1	0-0	24		1697
39	29	H	Port Vale	D	1-1	0-0	24	Hartley [61]	2912
40	Apr 1	H	Wolverhampton W	D	0-0	0-0	23		4660
41	5	A	Shrewsbury T	L	0-1	0-0	24		5178
42	12	H	Colchester U	L	2-3	1-1	24	Doughty [11], Freeman [89]	3108
43	18	A	Sheffield U	L	0-1	0-1	24		17,629
44	21	H	Bristol C	L	1-3	0-1	24	Freeman [85]	2901
45	26	H	Walsall	W	3-2	1-0	23	Smith, J [35], N'Guessan [53], Freeman [82]	2973
46	May 3	A	Brentford	L	0-2	0-0	24		11,393

Final League Position: 24

GOALSCORERS

League (46): Zoko 10 (1 pen), Freeman 6, Charles 4, Morais 4 (1 pen), Akins 3 (1 pen), Smith, J 3, Tansey 3 (2 pens), Burrow 2, Doughty 2, Hartley 2, Dembele 1, Dunne 1, Heslop 1, Mousinho 1, N'Guessan 1, Parrett 1, own goal 1.
The Budweiser FA Cup (9): Zoko 4, Morais 1 (1 pen), Akins 1, Charles 1, Freeman 1, Hartley 1.
Capital One Cup (3): Morais 1 (1 pen), Burrow 1, Freeman 1.
Johnstone's Paint Trophy (6): Morais 2 (1 pen), Zoko 2, Akins 1, Andrade 1.

Day C 44	Wedgbury S 6 + 8	Hills L 3 + 1	Heslop S 23 + 4	Ashton J 40	Jones L 21 + 5	Akins L 25 + 6	Tansey G 14 + 5	Charles D 17 + 5	Tounkara O 6 + 9	Freeman L 45	Morais F 18 + 9	Haber M 1 + 2	Shroot R 6 + 4	Arnold S 2 + 1	Corry P — + 1	Burrow J 9 + 11	Dunne J 6 + 7	Lopez D 1 + 3	Smith J 40 + 2	Doughty M 28 + 8	Hartley P 29 + 2	Deacon R 12 + 11	Gray D 9 + 2	Cowan D — + 1	Zoko F 33	Andrade B 3 + 10	Parrett D 8 + 4	Chorley B 4	Mousinho J 15 + 1	Reid C 1 + 3	Obeng C 15	Dembele B 13	Banvo A — + 1	N'Guessan J 2 + 3	Flanagan T 1 + 1	Henderson C 3	Gordan R 1 + 2	Okenabirhie F 1 + 2	Match No.
1	2	3[1]	4	5	6[2]	7[3]	8	9	10	11	12	13	14																										1
	2	5	8[1]	3			7	4	10	9	6[2]			14	1	11[3]	12	13																					2
1			3			13	4	11[2]	6				14	8			7	10[3]	2[1]	5	9	12																	3
1		12	3			14	11	13	9[1]		10					7			2[2]	8[3]	4	6	5																4
1			3			8[3]	12	9			11					10[2]	7	13	14	5[1]	4	6	2																5
1	14	7	3			6[2]	12	10			11					13			9[3]	8[1]	4	5	2																6
1	12	9[1]	4	14		13	11	10			6								7[3]	8	3[2]	5	2																7
1	13		3			7[3]	10	6			12			9[2]	11				14	8	4	5[1]	2																8
1	2	5[3]	3			9	13	10			14			6					8[1]	7[2]	4	11	12																9
1			3		14	7[1]		10[2]	9	12	11[3]			8	13	2	6	4	5																				10
1	7		3	4	9[1]		13				6[3]					10[2]	12		8		5		2			11	14												11
1			3	4	10[4]	12			9	6						14			7	8[3]	5[2]	2[1]				11	13												12
1	14	7[2]	4	3		2[3]			11	6[1]						12			8	9	5					10		13											13
1		6	2	3		8[2]			7[3]	4[1]						12	14		9	10	11					5	13												14
1		2	3	4		10[3]	12	9	6[2]							7			8[1]	4						11	13	14											15
1[2]		7		3	11	9[3]		14	5	6[1]		13							2	8	4					10	12												16
1	13		7	2	3	9				6	4[2]								5[3]	10[1]	11		12		8														17
1		8	3	4	10				6	9[2]			13						7	5[1]	14	2[3]			11	12													18
1		7[2]	4	3	11			14	5	6[1]			13						2	8	12				10	9[3]													19
1			3[3]	12		7			9				11[1]	13					8	2[4]		5	14		10	6[2]		4											20
1		8	4	12		9			5	6[1]			10[3]	13					2						11	14	7[2]	3											21
1		6[3]	4	2	12	14		8	9										5	7[1]	13				10	11[2]		3											22
1	6[1]	14	4	3	12	8[3]		11								10			7[2]	13		5	2		9														23
1	7[1]		4	2[2]		13			9	6	11[3]					12			5						10	14	8	3[4]											24
1		7	4	3	9	13		6[2]	11[1]							12			2	8	5	14			10[3]														25
1		7[1]	3	4	11	12	14	9	6[2]										2	8	5				10[3]	13													26
1		7	3	5		10	6												8	13	9	14			11[1]	12	4[2]		2[3]										27
1		6	2[1]	5		11[2]	8	9[3]			14					7			4	12		10		13	3														28
1			4	3	8	13	10	9[2]								2			14	5	12[3]				11		7		6[1]										29
1		6[3]	2	3	5[2]		10		9						13				7		4	12			11[1]		8			14									30
1	14		4		13		11		9	12									7	10[1]	5[2]				6		8[3]					2	3						31
1	13		4		9		11		6										7	8[2]	5[1]	12[3]			10					14		2	3						32
1	12		3	14		8	11[3]		9										6	5[1]		10			13		7[2]		4	2									33
1			3		6		10		9				13						2		12	5			11[2]		4			8	7[1]								34
1			3		9		10		7										6	12		5[1]			11		8[2]			13	2	4							35
1	12		3[3]		6		5		8[1]	14			13						9	10[2]					11				7		2	4							36
1			3		10[1]		5		7	14			13						6	12					11		8[3]		9[2]		2	4							37
1		3[2]	11[1]	12			6	13				1	10[3]			7	8								9				4	14	5	2							38
1	14	4		10		5		6	9[2]										8		12				11				7[1]		2	3[3]	13						39
1	8[2]	3		10[1]		5		6	12										7						11				9	10[2]	2	3	13						40
1	7[3]	4		6		5[1]		9	14										8	12					11				7	2	3		13						41
1	14			10[3]		5	12[4]						13						6	9[2]					11				7	2	3		4	8[1]					42
1		7	3[3]	12	11[2]			6											8		5				10				4	2		13		9[1]	14				43
1	2[1]	7[2]	3	12			11								10				9	4	5				8						14					6[3]	13		44
1			3				9												7	14	5	13			6		2[4]	4		11[1]		8	12	10[2]					45
1			3	12			10							4					7	8	5	9[2]			6		2		11[1]		13								46

The Budweiser FA Cup

First Round	Portsmouth	(h)	2-1
Second Round	Stourbridge	(h)	4-0
Third Round	Doncaster R	(a)	3-2
Fourth Round	Everton	(h)	0-4

Capital One Cup

First Round	Ipswich T	(h)	2-0
Second Round	Everton	(a)	1-2
(aet)			

Johnstone's Paint Trophy

Second Round	Milton Keynes D	(h)	2-1
Southern Quarter-Finals	Leyton Orient	(h)	3-2
Southern Semi-Finals	Swindon T	(a)	1-1
(aet; lost 1-3 on penalties)			

STOKE CITY

FOUNDATION

The date of the formation of this club has long been in doubt. The year 1863 was claimed, but more recent research by local club historian Wade Martin has uncovered nothing earlier than 1868, when a couple of Old Carthusians, who were apprentices at the local works of the old North Staffordshire Railway Company, met with some others from that works, to form Stoke Ramblers. It should also be noted that the old Stoke club went bankrupt in 1908 when a new club was formed.

Britannia Stadium, Stanley Matthews Way, Stoke-on-Trent, Staffordshire ST4 4EG.

Telephone: (01782) 367 598.

Fax: (01782) 592 220.

Ticket Office: (01782) 367 599.

Website: www.stokecityfc.com

Email: info@stokecityfc.com

Ground Capacity: 27,740.

Record Attendance: 51,380 v Arsenal, Division 1, 29 March 1937 (at Victoria Ground); 28,218 v Everton, Division 2, 5 January 2002 (at Britannia Stadium).

Pitch Measurements: 100m × 66m (109yd × 72yd)

Chairman: Peter Coates.

Chief Executive: Tony Scholes.

Manager: Mark Hughes.

Assistant Manager: Mark Bowen.

Physio: Dave Watson.

HONOURS

Football League – Division 1:
Best season: 4th, 1935–36, 1946–47;
FL C: *Runners-up* 2007–08;
Division 2: *Champions* 1932–33, 1962–63, 1992–93;
Runners-up 1921–22;
Division 3 (N): *Champions* 1926–27.

FA Cup: *Runners-up* 2011.

Football League Cup: *Winners* 1972;
Runners-up 1964.

Autoglass Trophy: *Winners:* 1992.

Auto Windscreens Shield:
Winners: 2000.

European Competitions
UEFA Cup: 1972–73, 1974–75.
Europa League: 2011–12.

Colours: Red and white striped shirts with red sleeves and red trim, white shorts with red trim, red socks with white hoops.

Year Formed: 1863* (*see Foundation*).

Turned Professional: 1885.

Previous Names: 1868, Stoke Ramblers; 1870, Stoke; 1925, Stoke City.

Club Nickname: 'The Potters'.

Grounds: 1875, Sweeting's Field; 1878, Victoria Ground (previously known as the Athletic Club Ground); 1997, Britannia Stadium.

First Football League Game: 8 September 1888, Football League, v WBA (h) L 0–2 – Rowley; Clare, Underwood; Ramsey, Shutt, Smith; Sayer, McSkimming, Staton, Edge, Tunnicliffe.

Record League Victory: 10–3 v WBA, Division 1, 4 February 1937 – Doug Westland; Brigham, Harbot; Tutin, Turner (1p), Kirton; Matthews, Antonio (2), Freddie Steele (5), Jimmy Westland, Johnson (2).

Record Cup Victory: 7–1 v Burnley, FA Cup 2nd rd (replay), 20 February 1896 – Clawley; Clare, Eccles; Turner, Grewe, Robertson; Willie Maxwell, Dickson, Alan Maxwell (3), Hyslop (4), Schofield.

Record Defeat: 0–10 v Preston NE, Division 1, 14 September 1889.

Most League Points (2 for a win): 63, Division 3 (N), 1926–27.

Most League Points (3 for a win): 93, Division 2, 1992–93.

Most League Goals: 92, Division 3 (N), 1926–27.

Highest League Scorer in Season: Freddie Steele, 33, Division 1, 1936–37.

Most League Goals in Total Aggregate: Freddie Steele, 142, 1934–49.

Most League Goals in One Match: 7, Neville Coleman v Lincoln C, Division 2, 23 February 1957.

Most Capped Player: Glenn Whelan, 58, Republic of Ireland.

Most League Appearances: Eric Skeels, 506, 1958–76.

Youngest League Player: Peter Bullock, 16 years 163 days v Swansea C, 19 April 1958.

Record Transfer Fee Received: £4,500,000 from VfL Wolfsburg for Tuncay Sanli, January 2011.

Record Transfer Fee Paid: £10,000,000 (rising to £12,000,000) to Tottenham H for Peter Crouch, August 2011.

Football League Record: 1888 Founder Member of Football League; 1890 Not re-elected; 1891 Re-elected; relegated in 1907, and after one year in Division 2, resigned for financial reasons; 1919 re-elected to Division 2; 1922–23 Division 1; 1923–26 Division 2; 1926–27 Division 3 (N); 1927–33 Division 2; 1933–53 Division 1; 1953–63 Division 2; 1963–77 Division 1; 1977–79 Division 2; 1979–85 Division 1; 1985–90 Division 2; 1990–92 Division 3; 1992–93 Division 2; 1993–98 Division 1; 1998–2002 Division 2; 2002–04 Division 1; 2004–08 FL C; 2008– FA Premier League.

LATEST SEQUENCES

Longest Sequence of League Wins: 8, 30.3.1895 – 21.9.1895.

Longest Sequence of League Defeats: 11, 6.4.1985 – 17.8.1985.

Longest Sequence of League Draws: 5, 13.5.2012 – 15.9.2012.

Longest Sequence of Unbeaten League Matches: 25, 5.9.1992 – 20.2.1993.

Longest Sequence Without a League Win: 17, 22.4.1989 – 14.10.1989.

Successive Scoring Runs: 21 from 24.12.1921.

Successive Non-scoring Runs: 8 from 29.12.1984.

MANAGERS

Tom Slaney 1874–83
 (Secretary-Manager)
Walter Cox 1883–84
 (Secretary-Manager)
Harry Lockett 1884–90
Joseph Bradshaw 1890–92
Arthur Reeves 1892–95
William Rowley 1895–97
H. D. Austerberry 1897–1908
A. J. Barker 1908–14
Peter Hodge 1914–15
Joe Schofield 1915–19
Arthur Shallcross 1919–23
John 'Jock' Rutherford 1923
Tom Mather 1923–35
Bob McGrory 1935–52
Frank Taylor 1952–60
Tony Waddington 1960–77
George Eastham 1977–78
Alan A'Court 1978
Alan Durban 1978–81
Richie Barker 1981–83
Bill Asprey 1984–85
Mick Mills 1985–89
Alan Ball 1989–91
Lou Macari 1991–93
Joe Jordan 1993–94
Lou Macari 1994–97
Chic Bates 1997–98
Chris Kamara 1998
Brian Little 1998–99
Gary Megson 1999
Gudjon Thordarson 1999–2002
Steve Cotterill 2002
Tony Pulis 2002–05
Johan Boskamp 2005–06
Tony Pulis 2006–13
Mark Hughes May 2013–

TEN YEAR LEAGUE RECORD

		P	W	D	L	F	A	Pts	Pos
2004-05	FL C	46	17	10	19	36	38	61	12
2005-06	FL C	46	17	7	22	54	63	58	13
2006-07	FL C	46	19	16	11	62	41	73	8
2007-08	FL C	46	21	16	9	69	55	79	2
2008-09	PR Lge	38	12	9	17	38	55	45	12
2009-10	PR Lge	38	11	14	13	34	48	47	11
2010-11	PR Lge	38	13	7	18	46	48	46	13
2011-12	PR Lge	38	11	12	15	36	53	45	14
2012-13	PR Lge	38	9	15	14	34	45	42	13
2013-14	PR Lge	38	13	11	14	45	52	50	9

DID YOU KNOW

Centre forward Tommy Sale scored 56 goals from just 36 appearances for Stoke City in the 1941–42 season. He netted 11 hat-tricks including four in consecutive games against New Brighton, Tranmere Rovers (home and away) and Stockport County.

STOKE CITY – FA PREMIERSHIP 2013–14 LEAGUE RECORD

Match No.	Date	Venue	Opponents	Result	H/T Score	Lg Pos.	Goalscorers	Attendance
1	Aug 17	A	Liverpool	L	0-1	0-1	15		44,822
2	24	H	Crystal Palace	W	2-1	0-1	10	Adam [58], Shawcross [62]	25,270
3	31	A	West Ham U	W	1-0	0-0	5	Pennant [82]	34,946
4	Sept 14	H	Manchester C	D	0-0	0-0	7		25,052
5	22	A	Arsenal	L	1-3	1-2	10	Cameron [26]	60,002
6	29	H	Norwich C	L	0-1	0-1	14		26,184
7	Oct 5	A	Fulham	L	0-1	0-0	16		24,634
8	19	H	WBA	D	0-0	0-0	15		25,904
9	26	A	Manchester U	L	2-3	2-1	17	Crouch [4], Arnautovic [45]	75,274
10	Nov 2	H	Southampton	D	1-1	1-1	16	Begovic [1]	26,053
11	10	A	Swansea C	D	3-3	2-0	17	Walters [8], Ireland [25], Adam (pen) [90]	19,242
12	23	H	Sunderland	W	2-0	1-0	14	Adam [30], Nzonzi [81]	26,007
13	30	A	Everton	L	0-4	0-1	16		35,513
14	Dec 4	H	Cardiff C	D	0-0	0-0	14		25,014
15	7	H	Chelsea	W	3-2	1-1	12	Crouch [42], Ireland [50], Assaidi [90]	25,154
16	14	A	Hull C	D	0-0	0-0	13		23,324
17	21	H	Aston Villa	W	2-1	0-0	10	Adam [50], Crouch [70]	26,003
18	26	A	Newcastle U	L	1-5	1-1	10	Assaidi [29]	51,665
19	29	A	Tottenham H	L	0-3	0-1	12		36,072
20	Jan 1	H	Everton	D	1-1	0-0	12	Assaidi [49]	25,832
21	12	H	Liverpool	L	3-5	2-2	12	Crouch [39], Adam [45], Walters [85]	27,160
22	18	A	Crystal Palace	L	0-1	0-0	13		24,440
23	29	A	Sunderland	L	0-1	0-1	16		34,745
24	Feb 1	H	Manchester U	W	2-1	1-0	11	Carrick (og) [38], Adam [52]	26,547
25	8	A	Southampton	D	2-2	2-2	13	Odemwingie [38], Crouch [44]	27,987
26	12	H	Swansea C	D	1-1	1-0	14	Crouch [17]	24,822
27	22	A	Manchester C	L	0-1	0-0	14		47,038
28	Mar 1	H	Arsenal	W	1-0	0-0	12	Walters (pen) [76]	26,711
29	8	A	Norwich C	D	1-1	0-0	12	Walters (pen) [73]	26,646
30	15	H	West Ham U	W	3-1	1-1	11	Crouch [32], Arnautovic [69], Odemwingie [79]	27,015
31	23	A	Aston Villa	W	4-1	3-1	10	Odemwingie [22], Crouch [26], Nzonzi [42], Cameron [90]	30,292
32	29	H	Hull C	W	1-0	0-0	10	Odemwingie [62]	27,029
33	Apr 5	A	Chelsea	L	0-3	0-1	10		41,168
34	12	H	Newcastle U	W	1-0	1-0	10	Pieters [42]	27,400
35	19	A	Cardiff C	D	1-1	1-0	10	Arnautovic (pen) [45]	27,686
36	26	H	Tottenham H	L	0-1	0-1	10		26,021
37	May 3	H	Fulham	W	4-1	1-0	10	Odemwingie [39], Arnautovic [54], Assaidi [73], Walters [82]	27,429
38	11	A	WBA	W	2-1	1-0	9	McAuley (og) [22], Adam [87]	26,613

Final League Position: 9

GOALSCORERS

League (45): Crouch 8, Adam 7 (1 pen), Odemwingie 5, Walters 5 (2 pens), Arnautovic 4 (1 pen), Assaidi 4, Cameron 2, Ireland 2, Nzonzi 2, Begovic 1, Pennant 1, Pieters 1, Shawcross 1, own goals 2.
The Budweiser FA Cup (2): Adam 1, Jones 1.
Capital One Cup (9): Jones 4, Crouch 2, Arnautovic 1, Assaidi 1, Ireland 1.

Begovic A 32	Cameron G 37	Shawcross R 37	Huth R 12	Pieters E 34 + 2	Wilson M 30 + 3	Walters J 27 + 5	Whelan G 28 + 4	Nzonzi S 34 + 2	Etherington M 5 + 6	Crouch P 30 + 4	Adam C 20 + 11	Pennant J — + 8	Jones K 4 + 3	Jerome C — + 1	Arnautovic M 27 + 3	Ireland S 14 + 11	Palacios W 5 + 11	Assaidi O 12 + 7	Wilkinson A 2 + 3	Muniesa M 7 + 6	Shea B — + 1	Sorensen T 4	Butland J 2 + 1	Guidetti J — + 6	Odemwingie P 15	Match No.
1	2	3	4	5	6	7	8¹	9	10²	11³	12	13	14													1
1	2	3	4	5	6	7	13	8	10³	11¹	9²	12		14												2
1	2	3	4	5	9	6	13	7	10²		8¹	12	11													3
1	2	3	4	5	9	6		7	10²	14	8⁹		11¹		12	13										4
1	2	3	4	5²	9	6		7		8⁹	11¹				10	12	13									5
1	2	3	4	5	7	8¹		6		14	9²	13	11³		10	12										6
1	2	3	4	5	7¹	8²	12	6	10³	14					11	9		13								7
1		3	4	5	13	8²		6				7¹		12	11³	9	14	10	2							8
1	2	3	4	5	12	8	13	7		11		14			10³	9²	6¹									9
1	2	3	4	5		8	6²	7		11					10	9¹	12	13								10
1	2	3	4	5	13	8		6		12	11	14			10¹	9²	7³									11
1	2	3	4¹	5		8		7		6	11	9²			10		13	12								12
1	2	3		5		8²		7		6	11	9¹	13				10		4	12						13
1	2	3		5¹	4		6²	8		11		9			7	13	10	12								14
1	2	3			4	8³	7¹	6		11		9²			10	12	14	13		5						15
1	2	3	12		4		6¹	7		11		14			8³	9	13	10		5²						16
1	2	3		5	4	8		6¹		7	11	12	13		9²			10¹								17
	2	3		5	4²	8		7⁸		6¹	11³	9					13	10²	12	14	1					18
		4	3	5		6		8		11	12	13				10³	7¹	9	2²	14	1					19
	2	3		5	4	8¹	7	6		11		9³	13			14	10						1²	12		20
	2	3		5	4	8		6		7¹	11	9			10	12						1				21
	2	3		5	4	8¹	6³	7		11		9			13	12	10²					1		14		22
1	2	3		5	4	12		7		6⁸	11³	9			13		10⁹							14	8²	23
1	2	3		5	4	9¹	7³			11	6				10²	12	14	13							8	24
1	2	3		5			9	6	12		11	7¹					10²		4				13		8	25
1	2	3		5	4	9²	7³	13		11	6				10¹		12							14	8	26
1	2	3		5	4	9¹	6³		14	11	7				10²	13	12								8	27
1	2	3		5	4	8	7	6	13	11	9¹				10²	12									8	28
1	2	3		5	4	9⁸	7	6	13	11					10¹	14								12²	8²	29
1	2	3		5	4		6	7		11					10	9				12					8	30
1	2	3		5	4		6	9		11					10		7			12					8	31
1	2	3		5	4		6¹	7		11³	13				10²	9	12							14	8	32
1	2³	3		5	4	14	7	8		11³	13				10		9¹		12						6	33
1	2	3		5	4	13	6	7		11	12				10	9²								8¹		34
1	2	3		5²	4	14	7	6		11					10¹	8³	13	12							9	35
1	2	3⁸	12		4		6	7		11¹					10	9²	13	5							8	36
1	2			5	3	14	6	7	13		12				8	9¹	10³	4						11²		37
	2	3			4	11³	7	6	14	12	13				10²	9		5			1				8¹	38

The Budweiser FA Cup

Third Round	Leicester C	(h)	2-1
Fourth Round	Chelsea	(a)	0-1

Capital One Cup

Second Round	Walsall	(h)	3-1
Third Round	Tranmere R	(a)	2-0
Fourth Round	Birmingham C	(a)	4-4

(aet; won 4-2 on penalties)

Quarter-Finals	Manchester U	(h)	0-2

SUNDERLAND

FOUNDATION

A Scottish schoolmaster named James Allan, working at Hendon Board School, took the initiative in the foundation of Sunderland in 1879 when they were formed as The Sunderland and District Teachers' Association FC at a meeting in the Adults School, Norfolk Street. Due to financial difficulties, they quickly allowed members from outside the teaching profession and so became Sunderland AFC in October 1880.

Stadium of Light, Sunderland, Tyne and Wear SR5 1SU.

Telephone: (0871) 911 1200.

Fax: (0191) 551 5123.

Ticket Office: (0871) 911 1973.

Website: www.safc.com

Email: enquiries@safc.com

Ground Capacity: 48,707.

Record Attendance: 75,118 v Derby Co, FA Cup 6th rd replay, 8 March 1933 (at Roker Park); 48,353 v Liverpool, FA Premier League, 13 April 2002 (at Stadium of Light) (FA Premier League figure 46,062).

Pitch Measurements: 105m × 68m (114yd × 74yd)

Chairman: Ellis Short.

Chief Executive: Margaret Byrne.

Head Coach: Gus Poyet.

Assistant Head Coach: Mauricio Taricco.

Physio: Peter Brand.

Colours: Red and white striped shirts, black shorts, black socks.

Year Formed: 1879.

Turned Professional: 1886.

Previous Names: 1879, Sunderland and District Teachers AFC; 1880, Sunderland.

Club Nickname: 'The Black Cats'.

Grounds: 1879, Blue House Field, Hendon; 1882, Groves Field, Ashbrooke; 1883, Horatio Street; 1884, Abbs Field, Fulwell; 1886, Newcastle Road; 1898, Roker Park; 1997, Stadium of Light.

First Football League Game: 13 September 1890, Football League, v Burnley (h) L 2–3 – Kirtley; Porteous, Oliver; Wilson, Auld, Gibson; Spence (1), Miller, Campbell (1), Scott, Davy Hannah.

Record League Victory: 9–1 v Newcastle U (a), Division 1, 5 December 1908 – Roose; Forster, Melton; Daykin, Thomson, Low; Mordue (1), Hogg (3), Brown, Holley (3), Bridgett (2).

Record Cup Victory: 11–1 v Fairfield, FA Cup 1st rd, 2 February 1895 – Doig; McNeill, Johnston; Dunlop, McCreadie (1), Wilson; Gillespie (1), Millar (5), Campbell, Jimmy Hannah (3), Scott (1).

HONOURS

Football League: Division 1: *Champions* 1891–92, 1892–93, 1894–95, 1901–02, 1912–13, 1935–36, 1995–96, 1998–99; *Runners-up* 1893–94, 1897–98, 1900–01, 1922–23, 1934–35; **Division 2:** *Champions* 1975–76; *Runners-up* 1963–64, 1979–80. **FL C:** *Champions* 2004–05, 2006–07; **Division 3:** *Champions* 1987–88.

FA Cup: *Winners* 1937, 1973; *Runners-up* 1913, 1992.

Football League Cup: *Runners-up* 1985, 2014.

European Competitions European Cup-Winners' Cup: 1973–74.

sky SPORTS FACT FILE

Goalkeeper Jimmy Thorpe was an ever-present in the Sunderland line-up in 1935–36 until tragedy struck in February. Thorpe was injured in the home game with Chelsea on 1 February and died in hospital four days later. An inquest found his death to be due to diabetes, accelerated by the rough treatment he had received in the match.

Record Defeat: 0–8 v Sheff Wed, Division 1, 26 December 1911; 0–8 v West Ham U, Division 1, 19 October 1968; 0–8 v Watford, Division 1, 25 September 1982.

Most League Points (2 for a win): 61, Division 2, 1963–64.

Most League Points (3 for a win): 105, Division 1, 1998–99.

Most League Goals: 109, Division 1, 1935–36.

Highest League Scorer in Season: Dave Halliday, 43, Division 1, 1928–29.

Most League Goals in Total Aggregate: Charlie Buchan, 209, 1911–25.

Most League Goals in One Match: 5, Charlie Buchan v Liverpool, Division 1, 7 December 1919; 5, Bobby Gurney v Bolton W, Division 1, 7 December 1935; 5, Dominic Sharkey v Norwich C, Division 2, 20 February 1962.

Most Capped Player: Charlie Hurley, 38 (40), Republic of Ireland.

Most League Appearances: Jim Montgomery, 537, 1962–77.

Youngest League Player: Derek Forster, 15 years 184 days v Leicester C, 22 August 1964.

Record Transfer Fee Received: £19,000,000 (rising to £24,000,000) from Aston Villa for Darren Bent, January 2011.

Record Transfer Fee Paid: £14,000,000 to Wolverhampton W for Steven Fletcher, August 2012.

Football League Record: 1890 Elected to Division 1; 1958–64 Division 2; 1964–70 Division 1; 1970–76 Division 2; 1976–77 Division 1; 1977–80 Division 2; 1980–85 Division 1; 1985–87 Division 2; 1987–88 Division 3; 1988–90 Division 2; 1990–91 Division 1; 1991–92 Division 2; 1992–96 Division 1; 1996–97 FA Premier League; 1997–99 Division 1; 1999–2003 FA Premier League; 2003–04 Division 1; 2004–05 FL C; 2005–06 FA Premier League; 2006–07 FL C; 2007– FA Premier League.

MANAGERS

Tom Watson 1888–96
Bob Campbell 1896–99
Alex Mackie 1899–1905
Bob Kyle 1905–28
Johnny Cochrane 1928–39
Bill Murray 1939–57
Alan Brown 1957–64
George Hardwick 1964–65
Ian McColl 1965–68
Alan Brown 1968–72
Bob Stokoe 1972–76
Jimmy Adamson 1976–78
Ken Knighton 1979–81
Alan Durban 1981–84
Len Ashurst 1984–85
Lawrie McMenemy 1985–87
Denis Smith 1987–91
Malcolm Crosby 1991–93
Terry Butcher 1993
Mick Buxton 1993–95
Peter Reid 1995–2002
Howard Wilkinson 2002–03
Mick McCarthy 2003–06
Niall Quinn 2006
Roy Keane 2006–08
Ricky Sbragia 2008–09
Steve Bruce 2009–11
Martin O'Neill 2011–13
Paolo Di Canio 2013
Gus Poyet October 2013–

LATEST SEQUENCES

Longest Sequence of League Wins: 13, 14.11.1891 – 2.4.1892.

Longest Sequence of League Defeats: 17, 18.1.2003 – 16.8.2003.

Longest Sequence of League Draws: 6, 26.3.1949 – 19.4.1949.

Longest Sequence of Unbeaten League Matches: 19, 3.5.1998 – 14.11.1998.

Longest Sequence Without a League Win: 22, 21.12.2002 – 16.8.2003.

Successive Scoring Runs: 29 from 8.11.1997.

Successive Non-scoring Runs: 10 from 27.11.1976.

TEN YEAR LEAGUE RECORD

		P	W	D	L	F	A	Pts	Pos
2004-05	FL C	46	29	7	10	76	41	94	1
2005-06	PR Lge	38	3	6	29	26	69	15	20
2006-07	FL C	46	27	7	12	76	47	88	1
2007-08	PR Lge	38	11	6	21	36	59	39	15
2008-09	PR Lge	38	9	9	20	34	54	36	16
2009-10	PR Lge	38	11	11	16	48	56	44	13
2010-11	PR Lge	38	12	11	15	45	56	47	10
2011-12	PR Lge	38	11	12	15	45	46	45	13
2012-13	PR Lge	38	9	12	17	41	54	39	17
2013-14	PR Lge	38	10	8	20	41	60	38	14

DID YOU KNOW ?

In the summer of 1967 Sunderland travelled to Canada where they played as Vancouver Royals in the United Soccer Association. The Black Cats lost their first game 6-1 and went on to finish second from bottom of the Western Division with just 3 wins from 12 games.

SUNDERLAND – FA PREMIERSHIP 2013–14 LEAGUE RECORD

Match No.	Date	Venue	Opponents	Result	H/T Score	Lg Pos.	Goalscorers	Attendance
1	Aug 17	H	Fulham	L	0-1	0-0	15		43,905
2	24	A	Southampton	D	1-1	1-0	15	Giaccherini [3]	29,596
3	31	A	Crystal Palace	L	1-3	0-1	19	Fletcher [64]	22,671
4	Sept 14	H	Arsenal	L	1-3	0-1	20	Gardner (pen) [48]	39,055
5	21	A	WBA	L	0-3	0-1	20		24,595
6	29	H	Liverpool	L	1-3	0-2	20	Giaccherini [52]	41,415
7	Oct 5	H	Manchester U	L	1-2	1-0	20	Gardner [5]	45,426
8	19	A	Swansea C	L	0-4	0-0	20		20,245
9	27	H	Newcastle U	W	2-1	1-0	19	Fletcher [5], Borini [84]	46,313
10	Nov 2	A	Hull C	L	0-1	0-1	19		24,677
11	10	H	Manchester C	W	1-0	1-0	19	Bardsley [21]	40,137
12	23	A	Stoke C	L	0-2	0-1	20		26,007
13	30	A	Aston Villa	D	0-0	0-0	19		33,036
14	Dec 4	H	Chelsea	L	3-4	1-2	20	Altidore [14], O'Shea [50], Bardsley [86]	40,652
15	7	H	Tottenham H	L	1-2	1-1	20	Johnson [37]	37,963
16	14	A	West Ham U	D	0-0	0-0	20		31,843
17	21	H	Norwich C	D	0-0	0-0	20		37,778
18	26	A	Everton	W	1-0	1-0	20	Ki (pen) [25]	39,193
19	28	A	Cardiff C	D	2-2	0-1	20	Fletcher [83], Colback [90]	27,247
20	Jan 1	H	Aston Villa	L	0-1	0-1	20		39,757
21	11	A	Fulham	W	4-1	2-0	19	Johnson 3 (1 pen) [29, 69, 85 (p)], Ki [41]	25,564
22	18	H	Southampton	D	2-2	1-2	19	Borini [32], Johnson [71]	38,115
23	29	H	Stoke C	W	1-0	1-0	19	Johnson [17]	34,745
24	Feb 1	A	Newcastle U	W	3-0	2-0	14	Borini (pen) [19], Johnson [23], Colback [80]	52,280
25	8	H	Hull C	L	0-2	0-1	17		42,810
26	22	A	Arsenal	L	1-4	0-3	18	Giaccherini [81]	60,012
27	Mar 15	H	Crystal Palace	D	0-0	0-0	18		43,636
28	22	A	Norwich C	L	0-2	0-2	18		26,654
29	26	A	Liverpool	L	1-2	0-1	18	Ki [76]	44,524
30	31	H	West Ham U	L	1-2	0-1	19	Johnson [65]	37,396
31	Apr 7	A	Tottenham H	L	1-5	1-1	20	Cattermole [17]	34,410
32	12	A	Everton	L	0-1	0-0	20		38,445
33	16	A	Manchester C	D	2-2	0-1	20	Wickham 2 [73, 83]	47,046
34	19	A	Chelsea	W	2-1	1-1	20	Wickham [18], Borini (pen) [82]	41,210
35	27	H	Cardiff C	W	4-0	2-0	17	Wickham 2 [26, 86], Borini (pen) [45], Giaccherini [76]	42,397
36	May 3	A	Manchester U	W	1-0	1-0	17	Larsson [30]	75,347
37	7	H	WBA	W	2-0	2-0	14	Colback [13], Borini [31]	45,181
38	11	H	Swansea C	L	1-3	0-2	14	Borini [50]	45,580

Final League Position: 14

GOALSCORERS

League (41): Johnson 8 (1 pen), Borini 7 (3 pens), Wickham 5, Giaccherini 4, Colback 3, Fletcher 3, Ki 3 (1 pen), Bardsley 2, Gardner 2 (1 pen), Altidore 1, Cattermole 1, Larsson 1, O'Shea 1.
The Budweiser FA Cup (5): Ba 1, Gardner 1, Johnson 1, Mavrias 1, own goal 1.
Capital One Cup (14): Borini 3 (1 pen), Bardsley 2, Wickham 2, Altidore 1, Giaccherini 1, Johnson 1, Ki 1, Larsson 1, Roberge 1, own goal 1.

Westwood K 10	Celustka O 14+7	O'Shea J 33	Roberge V 7+2	Colback J 28+5	Johnson A 28+8	Cabral A 1	Larsson S 24+7	Giaccherini E 16+8	Sessegnon S 2	Altidore J 19+12	Ji D 2+3	Wickham C 10+5	Diakite M 7	Gardner C 7+11	Vaughan D 2+1	Fletcher S 13+7	Mavrias C 1+3	Ki S 25+2	Borini F 25+7	Cattermole L 21+3	Cuellar C 4	Bardsley P 26	Dossena A 6+1	Mannone V 28+1	Brown W 24+1	Alonso M 16	Bridcutt L 9+3	Vergini S 10+1	Scocco I —+6	Ba E —+1	Match No.
1	2[1]	3	4	5	6	7	8	9	10[2]	11	12	13																			1
1	2	4		5[2]	9		8	6[1]	10[3]	11	12	14	3	7		13															2
1	2	4*		5	6		7	9[2]		10[1]	11		3	8		12		13													3
1	2			4	5	6			10			14	3	12	8[2]	11		9[3]	7	13											4
1	2	4		5	6			9[3]		13			3	7[1]		10	12	8	11[2]	14											5
1	12	3		5	9			6[1]		11		10		2				13	8			7[2]	4								6
1	2	3	4	5	11[2]		12	9		10	13	14		6[1]				8[1]	7												7
1	2	3	4	12	9[2]		6	10[1]		14				8		11[3]			13	7		5									8
1	14	4		8	9[2]		6			11				10				13	12	7[3]	3	2[1]	5								9
11		4		8	14		6			11[3]				10				9[2]	7[3]	3	2	5[1]	12	13							10
	2	3		9	10[3]		8	7[1]		13				12				11[1]	6	14		5		1	4						11
	2[2]	3	12	9	7		8	10[1]		14				11[1]				6	13			5		1	4*						12
14		3		12	13		8	7						9[2]		11		6	10[1]			2	5[3]	1	4						13
		3		9[3]	13		12	7[1]		11				8[2]		14		6	10			2	5	1	4						14
	2[1]	3		8[3]	9[2]		6	14		10				11				7	13	12		5		1	4						15
	2	3			12		9	8		11[3]				13				7	10[2]	6		5[1]	14	1	4						16
	2	3	14		12		6[1]	9[1]		10[2]				13				8	11	7		5		1	4*						17
	2		4	9[1]			7	12		13		3		11[2]				8	10	6		5		1							18
		4	14	8[3]	7		11			3	13			12				9	10[2]	6[1]		2	5	1							19
	2	4[1]	8	14			11	9[2]		3				10				6	12	7[3]		5		1							20
14		3		8	9[3]		13			12				10[1]		6		11[2]	7			2		1	4	5					21
	3			13	7		8[3]			11[1]				12		14		9	10	6[2]		2		1	4	5					22
12	3			7	9[3]		6			10[1]				14		13		8	11			2[2]		1	4	5					23
	3			9	7[1]		12			11				13				8	10[2]			2		1	4	5	6				24
	3			8	9			10		14				13				6[2]	11[3]			2		1	4*	5	7[1]	12			25
	4			9	7[1]		13	12		11[2]				8[3]		10				2		1			5	6	3	14			26
	3			9[3]			6[2]			12				13		10[1]		8	11			2		1	4	5	7	14			27
	3			9[2]	7[2]		12			11				8[1]		10		13				2		1	4	5*	6	14			28
	3			14	13		9[2]			10		11[3]		12		7				5	8[1]	1		4		6	2				29
	3[1]			12				11				13						9[2]	10	7[1]		5		1	4	8	6	2	14		30
				11								13						8	10	6[2]	3[1]	5		1	4	9	7	2	12		31
	3			9	8		12			11						7		10	6			2		1	4	5					32
	3			9	7		8[2]	12						11				10[1]	6			1		4	5		2	13			33
14	3			9	7[1]		8[3]	12		13				11[2]				10	6			1		4	5		2				34
	3			8[3]	9[1]		6[2]	12				10		13				11	7			1		4	5	14	2				35
	3			9	7[1]		8[3]	12		13				11[2]				10	6			1		4	5	14	2				36
	3			8	9[1]		6	14		13				10[3]				11	7[3]			1		4	5	12	2				37
12	3[1]			9	7		8[2]			14				11				10				5[1]		1	4		6	2		13	38

The Budweiser FA Cup

Third Round	Carlisle U	(h)	3-1
Fourth Round	Kidderminster H	(h)	1-0
Fifth Round	Southampton	(h)	1-0
Sixth Round	Hull C	(a)	0-3

Capital One Cup

Second Round	Milton Keynes D	(h)	4-2
Third Round	Peterborough U	(h)	2-0
Fourth Round	Southampton	(h)	2-1
Quarter-Finals	Chelsea	(h)	2-1
(aet)			
Semi-Finals 1st leg	Manchester U	(h)	2-1
Semi-Finals 2nd leg	Manchester U	(a)	1-2
(aet: won 2-1 on penalties)			
Final	Manchester C	(Wembley)	1-3

SWANSEA CITY

FOUNDATION

The earliest Association Football in Wales was played in the northern part of the country and no international took place in the south until 1894, when a local paper still thought it necessary to publish an outline of the rules and an illustration of the pitch markings. There had been an earlier Swansea club, but this has no connection with Swansea Town (now City) formed at a public meeting in June 1912.

Liberty Stadium, Morfa, Landore, Swansea SA1 2FA.
Telephone: (01792) 616 600.
Fax: (01792) 616 606.
Ticket Office: (0844) 815 6665.
Website: www.swanseacity.net
Email: info@swanseacityfc.co.uk
Ground Capacity: 20,745.
Record Attendance: 32,796 v Arsenal, FA Cup 4th rd, 17 February 1968 (at Vetch Field); 20,733 v Manchester U, FA Premier League, 17 August 2013 (at Liberty Stadium).
Pitch Measurements: 105m × 68m (114yd × 74yd)
Chairman: Huw Jenkins.
Vice-chairman: Leigh Dineen.
Manager: Garry Monk.
Assistant Manager: Josep Clotet.
Head Physio: Kate Rees.
Colours: White shirts with black trim, white shorts with black trim, white socks with black trim.
Year Formed: 1912.
Turned Professional: 1912.
Previous Name: 1912, Swansea Town; 1970, Swansea City.
Club Nicknames: 'The Swans', 'The Jacks'.
Grounds: 1912, Vetch Field; 2005, Liberty Stadium.

HONOURS

Football League – Division 1:
Best season: 6th, 1981–82;
FL 1: *Champions* 2007–08;
Division 3(S): *Champions* 1924–25, 1948–49; **Division 3:**
Champions 1999–2000.

FA Cup: Semi-finals 1926, 1964.

Football League Cup: *Winners* 2013.

Welsh Cup: *Winners* 11 times;
Runners-up 8 times.

Autoglass Trophy: *Winners* 1994, 2006.

Football League Trophy:
Winners 2006.

European Competitions
Europa League: 2013–14.
European Cup-Winners' Cup:
1961–62, 1966–67, 1981–82, 1982–83, 1983–84, 1989–90, 1991–92.

First Football League Game: 28 August 1920, Division 3, v Portsmouth (a) L 0–3 – Crumley; Robson, Evans; Smith, Holdsworth, Williams; Hole, Ivor Jones, Edmundson, Rigsby, Spottiswood.
Record League Victory: 8–0 v Hartlepool U, Division 4, 1 April 1978 – Barber; Evans, Bartley, Lally (1) (Morris), May, Bruton, Kevin Moore, Robbie James (3 incl. 1p), Curtis (3), Toshack (1), Chappell.
Record Cup Victory: 12–0 v Sliema W (Malta), ECWC 1st rd 1st leg, 15 September 1982 – Davies; Marustik, Hadziabdic (1), Irwin (1), Kennedy, Rajkovic (1), Loveridge (2) (Leighton James), Robbie James, Charles (2), Stevenson (1), Latchford (1) (Walsh (3)).
Record Defeat: 0–8 v Liverpool, FA Cup 3rd rd, 9 January 1990; 0–8 v Monaco, ECWC, 1st rd 2nd leg, 1 October 1991.

sky SPORTS FACT FILE

Swansea City striker Walter Boyd created an unwanted record when he became the first player to enter the field of play and receive a red card before the ball entered play. Boyd came on as a substitute for the Swans against Darlington on 12 March 2000, but was immediately dismissed after becoming involved in an off-the-ball incident.

Most League Points (2 for a win): 62, Division 3 (S), 1948–49.

Most League Points (3 for a win): 92, FL 1, 2007–08.

Most League Goals: 90, Division 2, 1956–57.

Highest League Scorer in Season: Cyril Pearce, 35, Division 2, 1931–32.

Most League Goals in Total Aggregate: Ivor Allchurch, 166, 1949–58, 1965–68.

Most League Goals in One Match: 5, Jack Fowler v Charlton Ath, Division 3S, 27 December 1924.

Most Capped Player: Ivor Allchurch, 42 (68), Wales.

Most League Appearances: Wilfred Milne, 585, 1919–37.

Youngest League Player: Nigel Dalling, 15 years 289 days v Southport, 6 December 1974.

Record Transfer Fee Received: £15,000,000 from Liverpool for Joe Allen, August 2012.

Record Transfer Fee Paid: £12,000,000 to Vitesse Arnhem for Wilfried Bony, July 2013.

Football League Record: 1920 Original Member of Division 3; 1921–25 Division 3 (S); 1925–47 Division 2; 1947–49 Division 3 (S); 1949–65 Division 2; 1965–67 Division 3; 1967–70 Division 4; 1970–73 Division 3; 1973–78 Division 4; 1978–79 Division 3; 1979–81 Division 2; 1981–83 Division 1; 1983–84 Division 2; 1984–86 Division 3; 1986–88 Division 4; 1988–92 Division 3; 1992–96 Division 2; 1996–2000 Division 3; 2000–01 Division 2; 2001–04 Division 3; 2004–05 FL 2; 2005–08 FL 1; 2008–11 FL C; 2011– FA Premier League.

LATEST SEQUENCES

Longest Sequence of League Wins: 9, 27.11.1999 – 22.01.2000.

Longest Sequence of League Defeats: 9, 26.1.1991 – 19.3.1991.

Longest Sequence of League Draws: 8, 25.11.2008 – 28.12.2008.

Longest Sequence of Unbeaten League Matches: 19, 19.10.1970 – 9.3.1971.

Longest Sequence Without a League Win: 15, 25.3.1989 – 2.9.1989.

Successive Scoring Runs: 27 from 28.8.1947.

Successive Non-scoring Runs: 6 from 6.2.1996.

MANAGERS

Walter Whittaker 1912–14
William Bartlett 1914–15
Joe Bradshaw 1919–26
Jimmy Thomson 1927–31
Neil Harris 1934–39
Haydn Green 1939–47
Bill McCandless 1947–55
Ron Burgess 1955–58
Trevor Morris 1958–65
Glyn Davies 1965–66
Billy Lucas 1967–69
Roy Bentley 1969–72
Harry Gregg 1972–75
Harry Griffiths 1975–77
John Toshack 1978–83
(resigned October re-appointed in December) 1983–84
Colin Appleton 1984
John Bond 1984–85
Tommy Hutchison 1985–86
Terry Yorath 1986–89
Ian Evans 1989–90
Terry Yorath 1990–91
Frank Burrows 1991–95
Bobby Smith 1995
Kevin Cullis 1996
Jan Molby 1996–97
Micky Adams 1997
Alan Cork 1997–98
John Hollins 1998–2001
Colin Addison 2001–02
Nick Cusack 2002
Brian Flynn 2002–04
Kenny Jackett 2004–07
Roberto Martinez 2007–09
Paulo Sousa 2009–10
Brendan Rodgers 2010–12
Michael Laudrup 2012–14
Garry Monk February 2014–

TEN YEAR LEAGUE RECORD

		P	W	D	L	F	A	Pts	Pos
2004-05	FL 2	46	24	8	14	62	43	80	3
2005-06	FL 1	46	18	17	11	78	55	71	6
2006-07	FL 1	46	20	12	14	69	53	72	7
2007-08	FL 1	46	27	11	8	82	42	92	1
2008-09	FL C	46	16	20	10	63	50	68	8
2009-10	FL C	46	17	18	11	40	37	69	7
2010-11	FL C	46	24	8	14	69	42	80	3
2011-12	PR Lge	38	12	11	15	44	51	47	11
2012-13	PR Lge	38	11	13	14	47	51	46	9
2013-14	PR Lge	38	11	9	18	54	54	42	12

DID YOU KNOW ?

Swansea Town fans of the 1920s sang their own version of the popular song 'Chick, chick, chick, chicken, lay a little egg for me' in praise of Jack Fowler, the first player to score 100 League goals for the club. 'Fow, Fow, Fow, Fowler' was a popular refrain during his stay at the Vetch Field between 1924 and 1929.

SWANSEA CITY – FA PREMIERSHIP 2013–14 LEAGUE RECORD

Match No.	Date	Venue	Opponents	Result	H/T Score	Lg Pos.	Goalscorers	Attendance
1	Aug 17	H	Manchester U	L	1-4	0-2	20	Bony [82]	20,733
2	25	A	Tottenham H	L	0-1	0-0	20		36,005
3	Sept 1	A	WBA	W	2-0	1-0	16	Davies [22], Hernandez [83]	23,395
4	16	H	Liverpool	D	2-2	1-2	13	Shelvey [2], Michu [64]	20,752
5	22	A	Crystal Palace	W	2-0	1-0	9	Michu [2], Dyer [48]	22,466
6	28	H	Arsenal	L	1-2	0-0	13	Davies [81]	20,712
7	Oct 6	A	Southampton	L	0-2	0-1	15		28,570
8	19	H	Sunderland	W	4-0	0-0	11	Bardsley (og) [57], de Guzman [58], Bony (pen) [64], Fletcher (og) [80]	20,245
9	27	H	West Ham U	D	0-0	0-0	9		20,455
10	Nov 3	A	Cardiff C	L	0-1	0-0	13		27,463
11	10	H	Stoke C	D	3-3	0-2	13	Bony 2 [56, 86], Dyer [74]	19,242
12	23	A	Fulham	W	2-1	0-0	10	Hughes (og) [56], Shelvey [80]	25,258
13	Dec 1	A	Manchester C	L	0-3	0-1	13		46,559
14	4	H	Newcastle U	W	3-0	1-0	11	Dyer [45], Debuchy (og) [66], Shelvey [81]	20,457
15	9	H	Hull C	D	1-1	0-1	10	Chico [60]	19,303
16	15	A	Norwich C	D	1-1	1-1	10	Dyer [12]	26,876
17	22	H	Everton	L	1-2	0-0	11	Oviedo (og) [70]	20,695
18	26	A	Chelsea	L	0-1	0-1	11		41,111
19	28	A	Aston Villa	D	1-1	1-1	11	Lamah [36]	37,028
20	Jan 1	H	Manchester C	L	2-3	1-1	13	Bony 2 [45, 90]	20,498
21	11	A	Manchester U	L	0-2	0-0	13		75,035
22	19	H	Tottenham H	L	1-3	0-1	15	Bony [78]	20,769
23	28	H	Fulham	W	2-0	0-0	10	Shelvey [61], Berbatov (og) [75]	20,004
24	Feb 1	A	West Ham U	L	0-2	0-2	12		31,848
25	8	H	Cardiff C	W	3-0	0-0	10	Routledge [47], Dyer [79], Bony [85]	20,402
26	12	A	Stoke C	D	1-1	0-1	10	Chico [52]	24,822
27	23	A	Liverpool	L	3-4	2-3	12	Shelvey [23], Skrtel (og) [27], Bony (pen) [47]	44,731
28	Mar 2	H	Crystal Palace	D	1-1	1-0	14	de Guzman [25]	20,240
29	15	H	WBA	L	1-2	1-0	14	Lamah [2]	20,703
30	22	A	Everton	L	2-3	1-1	15	Bony [33], Williams [90]	36,260
31	25	A	Arsenal	D	2-2	1-0	15	Bony [11], Flamini (og) [90]	59,937
32	29	H	Norwich C	W	3-0	2-0	13	de Guzman 2 [30, 38], Routledge [75]	20,371
33	Apr 5	A	Hull C	L	0-1	0-1	15		22,744
34	13	H	Chelsea	L	0-1	0-0	15		20,761
35	19	A	Newcastle U	W	2-1	1-1	13	Bony 2 (1 pen) [45, 90 (p)]	51,057
36	26	H	Aston Villa	W	4-1	2-1	12	Bony 2 (1 pen) [10, 90 (p)], Shelvey [26], Hernandez [73]	20,701
37	May 3	H	Southampton	L	0-1	0-0	13		20,682
38	11	A	Sunderland	W	3-1	2-0	12	Dyer [7], Emnes [14], Bony [54]	45,580

Final League Position: 12

GOALSCORERS

League (54): Bony 16 (4 pens), Dyer 6, Shelvey 6, de Guzman 4, Chico 2, Davies 2, Hernandez 2, Lamah 2, Michu 2, Routledge 2, Emnes 1, Williams 1, own goals 8.
The Budweiser FA Cup (5): Bony 3, De Guzman 1, Routledge 1.
Capital One Cup (1): Bony 1.
UEFA Europa League (17): Bony 5, Michu 4, Routledge 3, De Guzman 2, Pozuelo 2, Lamah 1.

Vorm M 26	Rangel A 29 + 1	Chico 30 + 1	Williams A 34	Davies B 32 + 2	Canas J 19 + 4	Britton L 23 + 2	Dyer N 19 + 8	Shelvey J 29 + 3	Routledge W 32 + 3	Michu M 15 + 2	Bony W 27 + 7	Hernandez P 17 + 10	Ki S — + 1	de Guzman J 26 + 8	Pozuelo A 7 + 15	Vazquez A 5 + 7	Tiendalli D 9 + 1	Amat J 13 + 4	Taylor N 6 + 4	Tremmel G 12	Lamah R 4 + 5	Ngog D — 3	Emnes M 2 + 5	Lita L — + 2	Bartley K 1 + 1	Fulton J 1 + 1	Match No.
1	2	3	4	5	6²	7¹	8	9	10³	11	12	13	14														1
1	2	3	4	5		7		9²	10¹	11	13	8		6	12												2
1	2	3	4	5	7		6	10¹	9	11²	8			12	13												3
1	2	3	4	5		6	8¹	7	10	9	11²			12	13												4
1	2	3	4	5	6¹	14	8²	7	10	9				12	13	11³											5
1		3		5	6		8	7¹	10²	11	12			9	13		2	4									6
1	2	3		5	6		8	7	10¹	9	11			12				4									7
1	2	3		5¹			7	8	10¹	9	11³			6	14	13		4	12								8
1	2	3	4				7	8	10¹	9	13	12		6		11²		5									9
1¹	2	3	4				6³	8	10¹	11²	12			9	13	14		5									10
	2	3	4	5	14		7	12	13	8		11		6³	9²					1	10¹						11
1	2	3	4	5	7		8²	12			11			6	9³	14	13				10¹						12
		3	4	5	7		13	9	12			10²		6	8¹	11	2			1							13
1		3	4	5	6		12	9	14			10²		7	8¹	11³	2				13						14
	3	4	5	7			8	9	13	11		10²		6¹	12		2			1							15
1	2		4	5	9		6²	7		11³	13	10¹		8	12			3			14						16
	3	4	5	7			9	10¹		11³	8			6²	14	13	2			1	12						17
	2		4		7¹	6		9	10²		14	12		13	8³	11		3	5	1							18
12	3	4	5	7			9			11³	8			6	13	14	2¹			1	10²						19
	2	3	4	5	7			9¹	10		11	8²		6	13					1	12						20
	2	12	4	5	7¹	6		9²	10		11				8	13		3		1							21
	2	3	4	5		7		9¹	10		11			8		6				1	12						22
	2	3	4	5		6	12	9¹	10		11	8²		7¹	14		13		1								23
	3	4	5			8¹	9³	10		11	13		6	12		2	7²		1		14						24
1	2	3	4	5	13	7	8³		10		11	12	6¹				14					9²					25
1	2	3	4	5	7	6⁴	8¹		10		11	9³	12			14					13						26
1	2	3	4		12	7	8¹	9²	10		11	13	6³				5				14						27
1	2	3⁴	4³	5	12	7	8		10		11¹	9²	6			14						13					28
1	2		4	5	6¹	7²		8	12	11	13		9			3				10³	14						29
1	2	3	4	5	6²	7	8³	12	10	14	11¹	9	13														30
1	2	3	4	13		7	12	8¹	9	10¹	11	14	6			5²											31
1	2	3	4	5		6	13	7	10	9²	11¹	11²	12	8³	14												32
1	2	3	4	5		6¹	12	7	10	9³	11	13	8²											14			33
1	2	3⁴	4	5		6³	8¹	7	10		11	9²	14			12				13							34
1	2		4	5		7		6	10¹	11	9²	8			3							12	13				35
1	2¹		4	5	6			7	10²	11	8	9³			3	12					14			13			36
1			4	5		6	12	7	10	11	9³	8¹		2²	3	14					13						37
				14		13	8	6	10	11		12		2¹	3	5	1				9²			4		7³	38

The Budweiser FA Cup

Third Round	Manchester U	(a)	2-1
Fourth Round	Birmingham C	(a)	2-1
Fifth Round	Everton	(a)	1-3

Capital One Cup

Third Round	Birmingham C	(a)	1-3

UEFA Europa League

Third Qualifying 1st leg	Malmo	(h)	4-0
Third Qualifying 2nd leg	Malmo	(a)	0-0
Play-Off 1st leg	Petrolul	(h)	5-1
Play-Off 2nd leg	Petrolul	(a)	1-2
Group A	Valencia	(a)	3-0
Group A	St Gallen	(h)	1-0
Group A	Kuban Krasnodar	(h)	1-1
Group A	Kuban Krasnodar	(a)	1-1
Group A	Valencia	(h)	0-1
Group A	St Gallen	(a)	0-1
Round of 32 1st leg	Napoli	(h)	0-0
Round of 32 2nd leg	Napoli	(a)	1-3

SWINDON TOWN

FOUNDATION

It is generally accepted that Swindon Town came into being in 1881, although there is no firm evidence that the club's founder, Rev. William Pitt, captain of the Spartans (an offshoot of a cricket club), changed his club's name to Swindon Town before 1883, when the Spartans amalgamated with St Mark's Young Men's Friendly Society.

The County Ground, County Road, Swindon, Wiltshire SN1 2ED.

Telephone: (0871) 876 1879.

Fax: (0844) 880 1112.

Ticket Office: (0871) 876 1993.

Website: www.swindontownfc.co.uk

Email: boxoffice@swindontownfc.co.uk

Ground Capacity: 14,983.

Record Attendance: 32,000 v Arsenal, FA Cup 3rd rd, 15 January 1972.

Pitch Measurements: 100.5m × 67m (110yd × 73.5yd)

Chairman: Lee Power.

General Manager: Steve Anderson.

Manager: Mark Cooper.

First Team Coach: Luke Williams.

Physio: Paul Godfrey.

Colours: Red shirts with white trim, white shorts with red trim, red socks with white trim.

Year Formed: 1881* (*see Foundation*).

Turned Professional: 1894.

Club Nickname: 'The Robins'.

Grounds: 1881, The Croft; 1896, County Ground.

First Football League Game: 28 August 1920, Division 3, v Luton T (h) W 9–1 – Nash; Kay, Macconachie; Langford, Hawley, Wareing; Jefferson (1), Fleming (4), Rogers, Batty (2), Davies (1), (1 og).

Record League Victory: 9–1 v Luton T, Division 3 (S), 28 August 1920 – Nash; Kay, Macconachie; Langford, Hawley, Wareing; Jefferson (1), Fleming (4), Rogers, Batty (2), Davies (1), (1 og).

Record Cup Victory: 10–1 v Farnham U Breweries (away), FA Cup 1st rd (replay), 28 November 1925 – Nash; Dickenson, Weston, Archer, Bew, Adey; Denyer (2), Wall (1), Richardson (4), Johnson (3), Davies.

HONOURS

Football League: FL 2: *Champions* 2011–12; **Division 2:** *Champions* 1995–96; **Division 3:** *Runners-up* 1962–63, 1968–69; **Division 4:** *Champions* 1985–86.

FA Cup: Semi-finals 1910, 1912.

Football League Cup: *Winners* 1969.

Johnstone's Paint Trophy: *Runners-up* 2012.

Anglo-Italian Cup: *Winners* 1970.

sky SPORTS FACT FILE

Two Swindon Town players from 1914–15 lost their lives during World War One. Left back Bombardier Albert Milton of the 64th Brigade, Royal Field Artillery was killed on 11 October 1917, while centre forward Second Lieutenant Freddy Wheatcroft of the 13th Battalion, East Surrey Regiment died on 26 November 1917.

Record Defeat: 1–10 v Manchester C, FA Cup 4th rd (replay), 25 January 1930.

Most League Points (2 for a win): 64, Division 3, 1968–69.

Most League Points (3 for a win): 102, Division 4, 1985–86.

Most League Goals: 100, Division 3 (S), 1926–27.

Highest League Scorer in Season: Harry Morris, 47, Division 3 (S), 1926–27.

Most League Goals in Total Aggregate: Harry Morris, 216, 1926–33.

Most League Goals in One Match: 5, Harry Morris v QPR, Division 3 (S), 18 December 1926; 5, Harry Morris v Norwich C, Division 3 (S), 26 April 1930; 5, Keith East v Mansfield T, Division 3, 20 November 1965.

Most Capped Player: Rod Thomas, 30 (50), Wales.

Most League Appearances: John Trollope, 770, 1960–80.

Youngest League Player: Paul Rideout, 16 years 107 days v Hull C, 29 November 1980.

Record Transfer Fee Received: £1,500,000 (rising to £1,900,000) from WBA for Simon Cox, July 2009.

Record Transfer Fee Paid: £800,000 to West Ham U for Joey Beauchamp, August 1994.

Football League Record: 1920 Original Member of Division 3; 1921–58 Division 3 (S); 1958–63 Division 3; 1963–65 Division 2; 1965–69 Division 3; 1969–74 Division 2; 1974–82 Division 3; 1982–86 Division 4; 1986–87 Division 3; 1987–92 Division 2; 1992–93 Division 1; 1993–94 FA Premier League; 1994–95 Division 1; 1995–96 Division 2; 1996–2000 Division 1; 2000–04 Division 2; 2004–06 FL 1; 2006–07 FL 2; 2007–11 FL 1; 2011–12 FL 2; 2012– FL 1.

MANAGERS

Sam Allen 1902–33
Ted Vizard 1933–39
Neil Harris 1939–41
Louis Page 1945–53
Maurice Lindley 1953–55
Bert Head 1956–65
Danny Williams 1965–69
Fred Ford 1969–71
Dave Mackay 1971–72
Les Allen 1972–74
Danny Williams 1974–78
Bobby Smith 1978–80
John Trollope 1980–83
Ken Beamish 1983–84
Lou Macari 1984–89
Ossie Ardiles 1989–91
Glenn Hoddle 1991–93
John Gorman 1993–94
Steve McMahon 1994–98
Jimmy Quinn 1998–2000
Colin Todd 2000
Andy King 2000–01
Roy Evans 2001
Andy King 2001–05
Iffy Onuora 2005–06
Dennis Wise 2006
Paul Sturrock 2006–07
Maurice Malpas 2008
Danny Wilson 2008–11
Paul Hart 2011
Paolo Di Canio 2011–13
Kevin MacDonald 2013
Mark Cooper August 2013–

LATEST SEQUENCES

Longest Sequence of League Wins: 10, 31.12.2011 – 28.2.2012

Longest Sequence of League Defeats: 8, 29.8.2005 – 8.10.2005.

Longest Sequence of League Draws: 6, 22.11.1991 – 28.12.1991.

Longest Sequence of Unbeaten League Matches: 22, 12.1.1986 – 23.8.86.

Longest Sequence Without a League Win: 19, 30.10.1999 – 4.3.2000.

Successive Scoring Runs: 31 from 17.4.1926.

Successive Non-scoring Runs: 5 from 5.4.1997.

TEN YEAR LEAGUE RECORD

		P	W	D	L	F	A	Pts	Pos
2004-05	FL 1	46	17	12	17	66	68	63	12
2005-06	FL 1	46	11	15	20	46	65	48	23
2006-07	FL 2	46	25	10	11	58	38	85	3
2007-08	FL 1	46	16	13	17	63	56	61	13
2008-09	FL 1	46	12	17	17	68	71	53	15
2009-10	FL 1	46	22	16	8	73	57	82	5
2010-11	FL 1	46	9	14	23	50	72	41	24
2011-12	FL 2	46	29	6	11	75	32	93	1
2012-13	FL 1	46	20	14	12	72	39	74	6
2013-14	FL 1	46	19	9	18	63	59	66	8

DID YOU KNOW ?

Twins Alf and Bull Stephens joined Swindon Town from Leeds United in the summer of 1946 and regularly appeared in the same line-up for the Robins. The two both scored in consecutive wins over Norwich City and Brighton & Hove Albion in September 1946.

SWINDON TOWN – FOOTBALL LEAGUE ONE 2013–14 LEAGUE RECORD

Match No.	Date	Venue	Opponents	Result	H/T Score	Lg Pos.	Goalscorers	Atten-dance
1	Aug 3	A	Peterborough U	L	0-1	0-1	20		7178
2	10	H	Stevenage	W	1-0	1-0	11	Luongo [26]	7133
3	17	A	Shrewsbury T	L	0-2	0-1	17		4943
4	24	H	Gillingham	D	2-2	1-1	15	Byrne [12], Thompson, N [68]	7520
5	31	H	Crewe Alex	W	5-0	2-0	10	Ranger [34], Luongo [43], Mason 3 (1 pen) [46, 55 lpl, 70]	7419
6	Sept 7	A	Milton Keynes D	D	1-1	1-0	9	Pritchard [17]	7738
7	14	A	Wolverhampton W	L	2-3	0-2	12	N'Guessan [82], Mason [90]	19,388
8	21	H	Bristol C	W	3-2	2-2	11	Ajose 2 [19, 43], Ranger [87]	11,598
9	28	A	Preston NE	L	1-2	0-1	12	N'Guessan [86]	9296
10	Oct 5	H	Tranmere R	W	1-0	1-0	11	N'Guessan (pen) [29]	7889
11	12	A	Rotherham U	W	4-0	2-0	7	Pritchard [33], Luongo [45], Ajose [65], N'Guessan [90]	8103
12	18	A	Notts Co	W	2-0	2-0	5	Ranger [11], N'Guessan (pen) [28]	8188
13	22	H	Walsall	L	1-3	0-1	8	Ranger [83]	8188
14	26	A	Oldham Ath	L	1-2	0-1	8	Tarkowski (og) [56]	3837
15	Nov 2	H	Port Vale	W	5-2	1-0	7	N'Guessan [24], Ranger [50], Luongo 2 [57, 90], Byrne [82]	7637
16	16	A	Colchester U	W	2-1	1-0	6	Ajose [28], N'Guessan [47]	3334
17	23	H	Leyton Orient	L	1-3	1-2	7	Ajose [23]	8634
18	26	A	Crawley T	D	0-0	0-0	8		2868
19	30	H	Carlisle U	W	3-1	1-0	7	Luongo [36], Pritchard [72], N'Guessan [90]	7671
20	Dec 14	A	Sheffield U	L	0-1	0-0	8		15,430
21	21	H	Coventry C	W	2-1	0-0	7	Kasim [77], Storey [86]	9291
22	26	A	Brentford	L	2-3	1-1	7	Mason [10], Ajose [53]	8333
23	29	A	Bradford C	D	1-1	0-1	8	Pritchard [63]	13,461
24	Jan 11	H	Peterborough U	W	2-1	1-0	8	Ranger [28], Kasim [70]	7794
25	14	A	Stevenage	L	0-2	0-1	8		2167
26	18	A	Gillingham	L	0-2	0-1	9		6134
27	25	H	Shrewsbury T	W	3-1	1-1	8	Smith, M 2 [30, 90], Ranger [89]	7448
28	28	A	Walsall	D	1-1	0-1	8	Smith, M [71]	4059
29	Feb 1	H	Oldham Ath	L	0-1	0-0	8		7391
30	8	A	Port Vale	W	3-2	0-2	8	Ranger [51], Pritchard [65], Byrne [69]	5306
31	14	A	Colchester U	D	0-0	0-0	8		6683
32	22	A	Leyton Orient	L	0-2	0-1	8		5091
33	25	H	Crawley T	D	1-1	0-0	8	Byrne [49]	7062
34	Mar 1	A	Crewe Alex	D	1-1	0-0	7	Harley [48]	4433
35	8	H	Milton Keynes D	L	1-2	1-0	8	Smith, M [19]	7424
36	11	H	Wolverhampton W	L	1-4	0-3	9	Smith, M [74]	9670
37	15	A	Bristol C	D	0-0	0-0	9		14,884
38	22	H	Preston NE	W	1-0	0-0	8	Smith, M (pen) [56]	7570
39	25	A	Tranmere R	W	2-1	1-1	8	Smith, A [12], Storey [68]	3717
40	29	H	Sheffield U	W	2-1	1-0	7	Storey [18], Thompson, L [90]	8441
41	Apr 5	A	Carlisle U	L	0-1	0-1	8		4055
42	12	H	Brentford	W	1-0	1-0	7	Thompson, L [45]	9342
43	18	A	Coventry C	W	2-1	1-1	7	Pritchard [8], Smith, M [90]	3091
44	21	H	Bradford C	W	1-0	0-0	7	Cox [64]	8377
45	26	A	Notts Co	L	0-2	0-1	7		6714
46	May 3	H	Rotherham U	L	1-2	0-2	8	Smith, M (pen) [60]	8618

Final League Position: 8

GOALSCORERS

League (63): N'Guessan 8 (2 pens), Ranger 8, Smith, M 8 (2 pens), Ajose 6, Luongo 6, Pritchard 6, Mason 5 (1 pen), Byrne 4, Storey 3, Kasim 2, Thompson, L 2, Cox 1, Harley 1, Smith, A 1, Thompson, N 1, own goal 1.
The Budweiser FA Cup (0).
Capital One Cup (3): Pritchard 1, Ranger 1, Williams 1.
Johnstone's Paint Trophy (8): Ajose 4, Barthram 1, Pritchard 1, Ranger 1, own goal 1.

Foderingham W 41	Thompson N 41	Hall G 26+1	Luongo M 44	Ward D 36	Smith A 5+3	Reis T 2+4	Harley R 16+5	Williams A 3	Mason R 13+5	Pritchard A 33+3	Kasim Y 34+3	Storey M 7+11	Byrne N 30+6	Thompson L 17+11	Ranger N 19+4	McCveley J 31+1	Ajose N 12+4	N'Guessan D 14+10	El-Gabbas M —+6	Barthram J 3+8	Gladwin B 6+7	Branco R 13+2	Barker G 2+6	Smith M 20	Reckord J 3+2	Archibald-Henville T 13+1	Murphy J 2+4	Belford T 5	Stephens J 10	Cox L 4+1	Waldon C 1+2	Randall W —+1	Jones M —+1	Match No.
1	2	3	4	5	6	7²	8¹	9	10	11	12	13																						1
1	2	3	7	4	12	6²	10¹	11		9	8		5	13																				2
1	2	3	6	4	13		8	10²		11	7¹	9³	5	12	14																			3
1	2	4	7	3			9		12	10	8		6¹		11	5																		4
1	2	5	6²	7			13		9	8	11³		4¹	14	10	3	12																	5
1	2	3	6²	4			14		9	10³	7		8⁸	11¹	5	12	13																	6
1	2	3	8	4					9	10	6	13		11²	5	7¹	12																	7
1	2	3	7	4						9			8	11	5	6	10¹	12																8
1	2¹	3	8	4					10³	6			7²	9		5	12	11	14	13														9
1	2	3	7	4					9	8			6²		10	5	13	11¹	12															10
1	2	3	6	4					7	8			11	13	10²	5	9¹	12																11
1	2¹	3	7	4					14	9²	8		6		11	5		10³	13	12														12
1	2³	3	7	4					12	10	9		6²		11	5	8¹	13		14														13
1	2	3	6	4					7	11¹	8		9		10			12		5														14
1	5¹	3	7	3					6²	8			9	13	10	4		11¹	14	12														15
1		4	8	3			6			12	7		5	9¹		2	11	10																16
1	2	3	7	4			6			9²	8¹			13		5¹	11	10	12															17
1	2	3	7	4			6²		13	12	8		5²	9			11	10¹																18
1	2	3	7	4			9²		12	8	10			6¹	13	5	11³	14																19
1	2²	3	6	4					13	7	10		8⁹	12	9¹		5	11	14															20
1		3	7	4					6²	8¹	11	13	14	2		10	5³	9		12														21
1	2¹	3	8	4					7	10	9	12	5		11²		6³			14	13													22
1	2	4¹	8	3						11	6²	12	9	7		5¹	10			14	13													23
1	2	3	8	4					7³	10¹	9	14	13	12	11			6²			5													24
1	2³	3	8	4					7	9²	6	14	13		11			10¹			5	12												25
1	2¹	3³	8	4					7³	10	9		13		11	6		14			5	12												26
1	2		7	3			12		9²	6	8		10³		14	5¹						4		11	13									27
1	2		7	3			14			6¹	8³	13		9	11²			12			4		10	5										28
1	2		7¹	3²					9				6	8	13			14		4	10³	11	5	12⁴										29
1	2		6	3			13			9¹			5	7	10		8²							11			4	12						30
1	2		8	3			13			9			5	7	10¹		6²							11			4	12						31
		7	3			13	6			8			2								11¹		12	10	5	4	9²	1						32
	2		3			13	9			8			10	7		4		6		5²				11¹				12	1					33
	2		7	3			8²			6			5	11				12					13	10			4	9¹	1					34
	2¹		7	3			9			10	8³		5	6		13		14						11²			4	12	1					35
		9	3			7				10	8²		2¹	13		5		6³		14			4	12	11				1					36
1	2		7	14			10²			6⁸	12			9		5³				13			8¹	11			4			3				37
1	2	9		8						6	10			5							7¹	12		11			4			3				38
1	6	5		9²						7	11³			4							8¹	3		10	13					2	12	14		39
1	5¹		9							7	10	13	12	4							8²			11	2					3	6	14		40
1	5²	8³	9						12	7	10	13	14	4										11	2					3	6¹			41
1	2	14	8						10³		13	7	9	6						12	5²			11¹	3		4							42
	5	7								11		12	9	8						6¹	4			10	3		2							43
1	5	6								8	11			9						12	2			10	4			3	7¹					44
1	5⁸	6								11		13	4²¹²	8						14	9³			10	3⁴		2	7¹						45
1		9										6	7	5²					2	8³	3	12	11		4					10¹	13	14		46

The Budweiser FA Cup

First Round	Macclesfield T	(a)	0-4

Capital One Cup

First Round	Torquay U	(h)	1-0
Second Round	QPR	(a)	2-0
Third Round	Chelsea	(h)	0-2

Johnstone's Paint Trophy

Second Round	Plymouth Arg	(h)	2-1
Southern Quarter-Finals	Wycombe W	(h)	2-1
Southern Semi-Finals	Stevenage	(h)	1-1
(aet; won 3-1 on penalties)			
Southern Final 1st leg	Peterborough U	(a)	2-2
Southern Final 2nd leg	Peterborough U	(h)	1-1
(Peterborough won 4-3 on penalties)			

TORQUAY UNITED

FOUNDATION

The idea of establishing a Torquay club was agreed by old boys of Torquay College and Torbay College, while sitting in Princess Gardens listening to the band. A proper meeting was subsequently held at Tor Abbey Hotel at which officers were elected. This was on 1 May 1899 and the club's first competition was the Eastern League (later known as the East Devon League). As an amateur club it played at Teignmouth Road, Torquay Recreation Ground and Cricket Field Road before settling down for four years at Torquay Cricket Ground where the rugby club now plays. They became Torquay United in 1921 after merging with Babbacombe FC.

Plainmoor, Torquay, Devon TQ1 3PS.

Telephone: (01803) 328 666 (option 0).

Fax: (01803) 323 976.

Ticket Office: (01803) 328 666 (option 0).

Website: www.torquayunited.com

Email: reception@torquayunited.com

Ground Capacity: 6,200.

Record Attendance: 21,908 v Huddersfield T, FA Cup 4th rd, 29 January 1955.

Pitch Measurements: 100.5m × 66m (110yd × 72yd)

Chairwoman: Thea Bristow.

Chief Executive: Andrew Candy.

Manager: Chris Hargreaves.

Assistant Manager: Lee Hodges.

Physio: Damian Davey.

Colours: Yellow and white striped shirts with blue trim, white shorts, white socks.

Year Formed: 1899.

Turned Professional: 1921.

Previous Name: 1910, Torquay Town; 1921, Torquay United.

Club Nickname: 'The Gulls'.

Grounds: 1899, Teignmouth Road; 1900, Torquay Recreation Ground; 1904, Cricket Field Road; 1906, Torquay Cricket Ground; 1910, Plainmoor Ground.

First Football League Game: 27 August 1927, Division 3 (S), v Exeter C (h) D 1–1 – Millsom; Cook, Smith; Wellock, Wragg, Connor, Mackey, Turner (1), Jones, McGovern, Thomson.

Record League Victory: 9–0 v Swindon T, Division 3 (S), 8 March 1952 – George Webber; Topping, Ralph Calland; Brown, Eric Webber, Towers; Shaw (1), Marchant (1), Tommy Northcott (2), Collins (3), Edds (2).

HONOURS

Football League – Division 3 (S): *Runners-up* 1956–57.

FA Cup: Best season: 4th rd, 1949, 1955, 1971, 1983, 1990, 2009, 2011.

Football League Cup: never past 3rd rd.

Sherpa Van Trophy: *Runners-up* 1989.

sky SPORTS FACT FILE

When Torquay United were elected to the Football League in 1927 they signed up almost a completely new team to compete in Division Three South. Amongst the recruits was Jimmy Jones, a full international for Wales who in 1926–27 had been leading scorer for Aberdare Athletic, the club United had replaced.

Record Cup Victory: 7–1 v Northampton T, FA Cup 1st rd, 14 November 1959 – Gill; Penford, Downs; Bettany, George Northcott, Rawson; Baxter, Cox, Tommy Northcott (1), Bond (3), Pym (3).

Record Defeat: 2–10 v Fulham, Division 3 (S), 7 September 1931; 2–10 v Luton T, Division 3 (S), 2 September 1933.

Most League Points (2 for a win): 60, Division 4, 1959–60.

Most League Points (3 for a win): 81, Division 3, 2003–04.

Most League Goals: 89, Division 3 (S), 1956–57.

Highest League Scorer in Season: Sammy Collins, 40, Division 3 (S), 1955–56.

Most League Goals in Total Aggregate: Sammy Collins, 204, 1948–58.

Most League Goals in One Match: 5, Robin Stubbs v Newport Co, Division 4, 19 October 1963.

Most Capped Player: Tony Bedeau, 4, Grenada.

Most League Appearances: Dennis Lewis, 443, 1947–59.

Youngest League Player: David Byng, 16 years 36 days v Walsall, 14 August 1993.

Record Transfer Fee Received: £650,000 from Crewe Alex for Rodney Jack, June 1998.

Record Transfer Fee Paid: £75,000 to Peterborough U for Leon Constantine, December 2004.

Football League Record: 1927 Elected to Division 3 (S); 1958–60 Division 4; 1960–62 Division 3; 1962–66 Division 4; 1966–72 Division 3; 1972–91 Division 4; 1991–2004 Division 3; 2004–05 FL 1; 2005–07 FL 2; 2007–09 Blue Square Pr; 2009–14 FL 2; 2014– Conference Premier.

LATEST SEQUENCES

Longest Sequence of League Wins: 8, 24.1.1998 – 3.3.1998.

Longest Sequence of League Defeats: 8, 30.9.1995 – 18.11.1995.

Longest Sequence of League Draws: 8, 25.10.1969 – 13.12.1969.

Longest Sequence of Unbeaten League Matches: 15, 5.5.1990 – 3.11.1990.

Longest Sequence Without a League Win: 19, 23.9.2006 – 20.1.2007.

Successive Scoring Runs: 19 from 3.10.1953.

Successive Non-scoring Runs: 7 from 3.9.2006.

MANAGERS

Percy Mackrill 1927–29
A. H. Hoskins 1929
  (Secretary-Manager)
Frank Womack 1929–32
Frank Brown 1932–38
Alf Steward 1938–40
Billy Butler 1945–46
Jack Butler 1946–47
John McNeil 1947–50
Bob John 1950
Alex Massie 1950–51
Eric Webber 1951–65
Frank O'Farrell 1965–68
Alan Brown 1969–71
Jack Edwards 1971–73
Malcolm Musgrove 1973–76
Frank O'Farrell 1976–77
Mike Green 1977–81
Frank O'Farrell 1981–82
  (continued as General Manager to 1983)
Bruce Rioch 1982–84
Dave Webb 1984–85
John Sims 1985
Stuart Morgan 1985–87
Cyril Knowles 1987–89
Dave Smith 1989–91
John Impey 1991
Ivan Golac 1992
Paul Compton 1992–93
Don O'Riordan 1993–95
Eddie May 1995–96
Kevin Hodges *(Head Coach)* 1996–98
Wes Saunders 1998–2001
Roy McFarland 2001–02
Leroy Rosenior 2002–06
Ian Atkins 2006
John Cornforth 2006
Lubos Kubik 2006–07
Keith Curle 2007
Leroy Rosenior 2007
Paul Buckle 2007–11
Martin Ling 2011–13
Alan Knill 2013–14
Chris Hargreaves January 2014–

TEN YEAR LEAGUE RECORD

		P	W	D	L	F	A	Pts	Pos
2004-05	FL 1	46	12	15	19	55	79	51	21
2005-06	FL 2	46	13	13	20	53	66	52	20
2006-07	FL 2	46	7	14	25	36	63	35	24
2007-08	BSP	46	26	8	12	83	57	86	3
2008-09	BSP	46	23	14	9	72	47	83	4
2009-10	FL 2	46	14	15	17	64	55	57	17
2010-11	FL 2	46	17	18	11	74	53	68*	7
2011-12	FL 2	46	23	12	11	63	50	81	5
2012-13	FL 2	46	13	14	19	55	62	53	19
2013-14	FL 2	46	12	9	25	42	66	45	24

*1 pt deducted.

DID YOU KNOW ?

In their early days as a Football League club Torquay United played in black and white and were known as the Magpies. The switch to blue and yellow was made in the 1954–55 season, the colours apparently representing the town's status as a seaside resort with blue skies and yellow sands.

TORQUAY UNITED – FOOTBALL LEAGUE TWO 2013–14 LEAGUE RECORD

Match No.	Date	Venue	Opponents	Result	H/T Score	Lg Pos.	Goalscorers	Attendance
1	Aug 3	H	AFC Wimbledon	D 1-1	0-0	13	Downes [90]	3441
2	10	A	Morecambe	D 1-1	0-1	15	Hawley [55]	1555
3	17	H	Oxford U	L 1-3	0-0	19	Chapell [70]	3176
4	24	A	Northampton T	W 2-1	0-1	13	Chapell 2 [72, 78]	4088
5	31	H	Hartlepool U	D 0-0	0-0	15		2646
6	Sept 7	A	Fleetwood T	L 1-4	0-2	19	Benyon [89]	2426
7	14	A	Rochdale	L 0-1	0-0	19		2138
8	21	H	Cheltenham T	W 4-2	2-1	16	Ball 2 [2, 45], Hawley [49], Chapell [89]	2407
9	28	A	Newport Co	L 1-2	0-2	18	Azeez [58]	3557
10	Oct 5	H	York C	L 0-3	0-0	21		2559
11	12	A	Wycombe W	L 2-3	2-1	22	Azeez [27], Pearce [37]	3466
12	19	H	Mansfield T	D 0-0	0-0	21		2473
13	22	A	Burton Alb	L 0-2	0-0	22		2005
14	26	H	Portsmouth	D 1-1	1-0	22	Chapell [1]	3843
15	Nov 2	A	Bury	W 3-1	2-1	21	Downes [18], McCallum 2 [29, 57]	2997
16	16	H	Chesterfield	L 0-2	0-2	23		2361
17	23	A	Accrington S	L 1-2	1-1	23	McCallum [14]	1279
18	26	H	Plymouth Arg	D 1-1	1-1	23	Benyon [6]	3866
19	30	A	Scunthorpe U	L 1-3	0-2	24	Marquis [78]	3358
20	Dec 14	H	Southend U	W 1-0	0-0	24	Marquis [50]	2144
21	21	A	Dagenham & R	W 1-0	0-0	22	Downes [50]	1675
22	26	H	Bristol R	D 1-1	1-1	22	Marquis (pen) [6]	3461
23	29	H	Exeter C	L 1-3	0-1	23	Hawley [74]	4231
24	Jan 1	A	Plymouth Arg	L 0-2	0-0	23		10,126
25	4	H	Morecambe	D 1-1	1-0	23	Downes [17]	2004
26	11	A	AFC Wimbledon	W 2-0	2-0	23	Pearce [29], Stockley [43]	4339
27	25	A	Oxford U	L 0-1	0-1	23		4744
28	Feb 1	A	Portsmouth	W 1-0	1-0	23	Bodin [27]	15,474
29	11	H	Northampton T	L 1-2	1-2	23	Pearce [45]	2051
30	15	A	Chesterfield	L 1-3	0-0	23	Goodwin [50]	5912
31	22	H	Accrington S	L 0-1	0-0	23		2218
32	25	H	Burton Alb	D 1-1	1-1	24	Benyon [40]	1583
33	Mar 1	A	Hartlepool U	L 0-3	0-1	24		3437
34	8	H	Fleetwood T	L 0-1	0-0	24		2245
35	11	H	Rochdale	W 2-1	1-1	24	Pearce [17], Labadie [82]	1627
36	15	A	Cheltenham T	L 0-1	0-0	24		3105
37	18	H	Bury	W 2-1	1-0	24	Mansell [8], Yeoman [90]	1738
38	22	H	Newport Co	L 0-1	0-1	24		2874
39	25	A	York C	L 0-1	0-1	24		3416
40	29	A	Southend U	L 0-1	0-0	24		6556
41	Apr 5	H	Scunthorpe U	L 0-1	0-1	24		2234
42	12	A	Bristol R	W 2-1	0-0	24	Coulthirst [62], Mansell [75]	6612
43	18	H	Dagenham & R	L 0-1	0-0	24		2425
44	21	A	Exeter C	W 2-1	0-1	24	Cameron [52], Yeoman [56]	5221
45	26	A	Mansfield T	W 3-1	2-0	24	Dempster (og) [13], Yeoman [32], Coulthirst [78]	3389
46	May 3	H	Wycombe W	L 0-3	0-2	24		3149

Final League Position: 24

GOALSCORERS

League (42): Chapell 5, Downes 4, Pearce 4, Benyon 3, Hawley 3, Marquis 3 (1 pen), McCallum 3, Yeoman 3, Azeez 2, Ball 2, Coulthirst 2, Mansell 2, Bodin 1, Cameron 1, Goodwin 1, Labadie 1, Stockley 1, own goal 1.
The Budweiser FA Cup (0).
Capital One Cup (0).
Johnstone's Paint Trophy (0).

Rice M 32	Tonge D 36	Nicholson K 28 + 1	Mansell L 41 + 2	Downes K 30 + 2	Pearce K 35	Cameron C 15 + 9	Harding B 16 + 1	Benyon E 23 + 14	Ball C 9	Bodin B 23 + 4	Hawley K 22 + 5	Chapell J 23 + 13	Thompson N 1 + 2	Lathrope D 19 + 4	Sullivan D — + 4	Cruise T 18 + 3	Azeez A 6 + 3	O'Connor A 30 + 1	McCourt J 10 + 1	Craig N 6 + 7	McCallum P 4 + 1	Mozika D 9 + 3	Marquis J 5	Stockley J 7 + 12	Poke M 14	Labadie J 10	Goodwin S 11 + 1	O'Brien A — + 3	Wilkinson C 2 + 1	Stevens D 2 + 4	Showunmi E 7	Yeoman A 2 + 7	Coulthirst S 5 + 1	Cargill B 5	Match No.
1	2³	3	4	5	6	7²	8	9¹	10	11	12	13	14																						1
1	2⁴	5	7	3	4	12	8	11		9³	10²	6¹	13	14																					2
1		5	7	3	4	6¹	8²	11		9¹	10	13		12			2																		3
1	2	5	7	4	3	9¹	8	13		11	12	10²		6³	14																				4
1	2	5	7	3	4	12	8¹	14		11	9¹	10³		6			13																		5
1	2	5	7	3	4	9¹	8	12		10	11²	6					13																		6
1	2	5²	7	4	3			8		11	9	10	6¹			12	13																		7
1	2		7	3	4			8		12	11	9	10¹	6				5																	8
1	2³	5	7		4			8		14	10²	11	13	9¹		6	3	12																	9
1	2	5	7					14		8¹	13			9³	10		12	13	4	11²	3														10
1	2	5	7³			3	14			11¹		9	8			4	10		12	13															11
1	2	5	7		3⁴			14				9²	11³	6¹		13	10	4	8	12															12
1	2	5	6					14				9¹	11³	13			4	8	3	7	10²	12													13
1	2	5	7			3	13					11	6²				9	4	8		10¹	12													14
1	2	5	7	4				11¹				12	9²				6	3	8³	13	10	14													15
1			2	3	4	14		12				11²	6³			13	5				7	9	10¹	8											16
1	2		6	3				10¹				9					5	12	4		7	11	8												17
1	2		8	3				10¹				13	6				5	12²	4		9		7	11											18
1	2		8	4				11¹					9				5	3	6		7	10	12												19
	2		7	3				12		10		6¹					5	4	9		8	11		1											20
	2		8	3				10				6¹					5	4	7	12	9	11		1											21
	2		7	3				10				6¹					5	4	8²	13	9	11	12	1											22
	2		7	3		6²		12		8	11	13					5	4	9¹		10		1												23
	2		7	3				12		6	11	8²					5	4	10		9¹		13	1											24
		5	8	4	3			9		11¹	10			7				2						12	1	6									25
		5	6	4	3			11		12	10			7				2					9¹	1	8										26
		5	6	3	4			11²		14	9¹	12		7³				2					10	1	8	13									27
1	2	5	12		4			9		11²				7		13		3					10¹	1	8	6¹	14								28
		5	6		3			11²		9¹	13	12		7				2					10	1	8	4³	14								29
	2		7	13	3	14						8³		9¹		5	4						11²	1	10	6		12							30
	2	12	7³	3						11²	6			5¹		4							1	8	10	13	9	14							31
		5		4	3		7	10		13		14		8			2						12	1		9³		11¹	6²						32
		5		4	3	12	8	11³			13		9				2						14	1	6				7¹	10²					33
1	2	5	8²	3	4	12		9²		11¹	14		7				13			6						10									34
1	2	5		3	4	9	10						7				12			8	6					11¹									35
1	2	5	13	3	4	9					12		7				10			8²	6					11¹									36
1	2	5	6	3	4	9¹		11³					7				13			8			12		10²	14									37
1	2³	5¹	7	4	3			10	9				8				14	13							6⁴		11¹	12							38
1		5	7	3	4		8	11¹	9			6					2								13		10²	12							39
1		5	8	4	3	6²	7		9	11³	13						2								10¹		14	12							40
1	2		6		3	11²		13		10	9¹		7		5		4								12⁴		14	8³							41
1	2		7	13	3	9¹	8	10²									4									11		12			6	5			42
1	2²		7		3	9¹	8	10	6¹		14						4											12		13	11	5			43
1	2		6	3	11	13	10					12	7				4	8¹											9²	5					44
1	2		8	4	9	11¹					12		7				3								13				10	6²	5				45
1	2		7		3	9		11¹				6²	8				4⁴	13							12				10		5				46

The Budweiser FA Cup
First Round   Rochdale   (h)   0-2

Capital One Cup
First Round   Swindon T   (a)   0-1

Johnstone's Paint Trophy
First Round   Portsmouth   (h)   0-0
(aet; lost 3-5 on penalties)

TOTTENHAM HOTSPUR

FOUNDATION

The Hotspur Football Club was formed from an older cricket club in 1882. Most of the founders were old boys of St John's Presbyterian School and Tottenham Grammar School. The Casey brothers were well to the fore as the family provided the club's first goalposts (painted blue and white) and their first ball. They soon adopted the local YMCA as their meeting place, but after a couple of moves settled at the Red House, which is still their headquarters, although now known simply as 748 High Road.

White Hart Lane, Bill Nicholson Way, 748 High Road, Tottenham, London N17 0AP.

Telephone: (0844) 499 5000.

Fax: (020) 3544 8563.

Ticket Office: (0844) 844 0102 (option 1).

Website: www.tottenhamhotspur.com

Email: email@tottenhamhotspur.com

Ground Capacity: 36,284.

Record Attendance: 75,038 v Sunderland, FA Cup 6th rd, 5 March 1938.

Pitch Measurements: 100m × 67m (109yd × 73yd)

Chairman: Daniel Levy.

Head Coach: Mauricio Pochettino.

Assistant Head Coach: Jesus Perez.

Head Physio: Geoff Scott.

Colours: White shirts, navy blue shorts, navy blue socks with white trim.

Year Formed: 1882. *Turned Professional:* 1895.

Previous Name: 1882, Hotspur Football Club; 1884, Tottenham Hotspur.

Club Nickname: 'Spurs'.

Grounds: 1882, Tottenham Marshes; 1888, Northumberland Park; 1899, White Hart Lane.

HONOURS

Football League – Division 1: *Champions* 1950–51, 1960–61; *Runners-up* 1921–22, 1951–52, 1956–57, 1962–63; **Division 2:** *Champions* 1919–20, 1949–50; *Runners-up* 1908–09, 1932–33.

FA Cup: *Winners* 1901 (as non-League club), 1921, 1961, 1962, 1967, 1981, 1982, 1991; *Runners-up* 1987.

Football League Cup: *Winners* 1971, 1973, 1999, 2008; *Runners-up* 1982, 2002, 2009.

European Competitions European Cup: 1961–62. **Champions League:** 2010–11. **European Cup-Winners' Cup:** 1962–63 (*winners*), 1963–64, 1967–68, 1981–82, 1982–83, 1991–92. **UEFA Cup:** 1971–72 (*winners*), 1972–73, 1973–74 (*runners-up*), 1983–84 (*winners*), 1984–85, 1999–2000, 2006–07, 2007–08, 2008–09. **Europa League:** 2011–12, 2012–13, 2013–14. **Intertoto Cup:** 1995.

First Football League Game: 1 September 1908, Division 2, v Wolverhampton W (h) W 3–0 – Hewitson; Coquet, Burton; Morris (1), Danny Steel, Darnell; Walton, Woodward (2), Macfarlane, Bobby Steel, Middlemiss.

Record League Victory: 9–0 v Bristol R, Division 2, 22 October 1977 – Daines; Naylor, Holmes, Hoddle (1), McAllister, Perryman, Pratt, McNab, Moores (3), Lee (4), Taylor (1).

Record Cup Victory: 13–2 v Crewe Alex, FA Cup 4th rd (replay), 3 February 1960 – Brown; Hills, Henry; Blanchflower, Norman, Mackay; White, Harmer (1), Smith (4), Allen (5), Jones (3 incl. 1p).

sky SPORTS FACT FILE

Tottenham Hotspur entered the very first FA Amateur Cup competition in 1893–94. After receiving a bye in the first qualifying round, they defeated Vampires 3-1 and were drawn at home to Clapham Rovers in the third qualifying round. However, the club was suspended by the London FA following allegations of professionalism and their opponents received a walkover.

Record Defeat: 0–8 v Cologne, UEFA Intertoto Cup, 22 July 1995.

Most League Points (2 for a win): 70, Division 2, 1919–20.

Most League Points (3 for a win): 77, Division 1, 1984–85.

Most League Goals: 115, Division 1, 1960–61.

Highest League Scorer in Season: Jimmy Greaves, 37, Division 1, 1962–63.

Most League Goals in Total Aggregate: Jimmy Greaves, 220, 1961–70.

Most League Goals in One Match: 5, Ted Harper v Reading, Division 2, 30 August 1930; 5, Alf Stokes v Birmingham C, Division 1, 18 September 1957; 5, Bobby Smith v Aston Villa, Division 1, 29 March 1958; 5, Jermain Defoe v Wigan Ath, FA Premier League, 22 November 2009.

Most Capped Player: Pat Jennings, 74 (119), Northern Ireland.

Most League Appearances: Steve Perryman, 655, 1969–86.

Youngest League Player: Ally Dick, 16 years 301 days v Manchester C, 20 February 1982.

Record Transfer Fee Received: £85,300,000 from Real Madrid for Gareth Bale, September 2013.

Record Transfer Fee Paid: £30,000,000 to AS Roma for Erik Lamela, August 2013.

Football League Record: 1908 Elected to Division 2; 1909–15 Division 1; 1919–20 Division 2; 1920–28 Division 1; 1928–33 Division 2; 1933–35 Division 1; 1935–50 Division 2; 1950–77 Division 1; 1977–78 Division 2; 1978–92 Division 1; 1992– FA Premier League.

LATEST SEQUENCES

Longest Sequence of League Wins: 13, 23.4.1960 – 1.10.1960.

Longest Sequence of League Defeats: 7, 1.1.1994 – 27.2.1994.

Longest Sequence of League Draws: 6, 9.1.1999 – 27.2.1999.

Longest Sequence of Unbeaten League Matches: 22, 31.8.1949 – 31.12.1949.

Longest Sequence Without a League Win: 16, 29.12.1934 – 13.4.1935.

Successive Scoring Runs: 32 from 24.2.1962.

Successive Non-scoring Runs: 6 from 28.12.1985.

MANAGERS

Frank Brettell 1898–99
John Cameron 1899–1906
Fred Kirkham 1907–08
Peter McWilliam 1912–27
Billy Minter 1927–29
Percy Smith 1930–35
Jack Tresadern 1935–38
Peter McWilliam 1938–42
Arthur Turner 1942–46
Joe Hulme 1946–49
Arthur Rowe 1949–55
Jimmy Anderson 1955–58
Bill Nicholson 1958–74
Terry Neill 1974–76
Keith Burkinshaw 1976–84
Peter Shreeves 1984–86
David Pleat 1986–87
Terry Venables 1987–91
Peter Shreeves 1991–92
Doug Livermore 1992–93
Ossie Ardiles 1993–94
Gerry Francis 1994–97
Christian Gross *(Head Coach)* 1997–98
George Graham 1998–2001
Glenn Hoddle 2001–03
David Pleat *(Caretaker)* 2003–04
Jacques Santini 2004
Martin Jol 2004–07
Juande Ramos 2007–08
Harry Redknapp 2008–12
Andre Villas-Boas 2012–13
Tim Sherwood 2013–14
Mauricio Pochettino May 2014–

TEN YEAR LEAGUE RECORD

		P	W	D	L	F	A	Pts	Pos
2004-05	PR Lge	38	14	10	14	47	41	52	9
2005-06	PR Lge	38	18	11	9	53	38	65	5
2006-07	PR Lge	38	17	9	12	57	54	60	5
2007-08	PR Lge	38	11	13	14	66	61	46	11
2008-09	PR Lge	38	14	9	15	45	45	51	8
2009-10	PR Lge	38	21	7	10	67	41	70	4
2010-11	PR Lge	38	16	14	8	55	46	62	5
2011-12	PR Lge	38	20	9	9	66	41	69	4
2012-13	PR Lge	38	21	9	8	66	46	72	5
2013-14	PR Lge	38	21	6	11	55	51	69	6

DID YOU KNOW

John Cameron was one of the founder members of the Association Footballers' Union in December 1897 and he was the organisation's first secretary and treasurer. In May 1898 he was transferred to Tottenham Hotspur and went on to become a successful manager of the club, winning both the FA Cup and the Southern League.

TOTTENHAM HOTSPUR – FA PREMIERSHIP 2013–14 LEAGUE RECORD

Match No.	Date	Venue	Opponents	Result	H/T Score	Lg Pos.	Goalscorers	Attendance
1	Aug 18	A	Crystal Palace	W 1-0	0-0	5	Soldado (pen) [50]	23,285
2	25	H	Swansea C	W 1-0	0-0	2	Soldado (pen) [58]	36,005
3	Sept 1	A	Arsenal	L 0-1	0-1	6		60,071
4	14	H	Norwich C	W 2-0	1-0	2	Sigurdsson 2 [28, 49]	35,952
5	22	A	Cardiff C	W 1-0	0-0	2	Paulinho [90]	27,815
6	28	H	Chelsea	D 1-1	1-0	2	Sigurdsson [19]	35,857
7	Oct 6	H	West Ham U	L 0-3	0-0	6		35,977
8	20	A	Aston Villa	W 2-0	1-0	5	Townsend [31], Soldado [69]	35,391
9	27	H	Hull C	W 1-0	0-0	4	Soldado (pen) [80]	36,080
10	Nov 3	A	Everton	D 0-0	0-0	4		38,378
11	10	H	Newcastle U	L 0-1	0-1	7		36,042
12	24	A	Manchester C	L 0-6	0-3	9		47,228
13	Dec 1	H	Manchester U	D 2-2	1-1	9	Walker [18], Sandro [54]	35,884
14	4	A	Fulham	W 2-1	0-0	6	Chiriches [73], Holtby [82]	24,128
15	7	A	Sunderland	W 2-1	1-1	6	Paulinho [43], O'Shea (og) [50]	37,963
16	15	H	Liverpool	L 0-5	0-2	7		36,069
17	22	A	Southampton	W 3-2	1-1	7	Adebayor 2 [25, 64], Hooiveld (og) [54]	31,455
18	26	H	WBA	D 1-1	1-1	8	Eriksen [36]	35,545
19	29	H	Stoke C	W 3-0	1-0	7	Soldado (pen) [37], Dembele [65], Lennon [69]	36,072
20	Jan 1	A	Manchester U	W 2-1	1-0	6	Adebayor [34], Eriksen [66]	75,265
21	11	H	Crystal Palace	W 2-0	0-0	5	Eriksen [50], Defoe [72]	36,102
22	19	A	Swansea C	W 3-1	1-0	5	Adebayor 2 [35, 71], Chico (og) [53]	20,769
23	29	H	Manchester C	L 1-5	0-1	6	Capoue [59]	36,071
24	Feb 1	H	Hull C	D 1-1	0-1	6	Paulinho [61]	24,932
25	9	H	Everton	W 1-0	0-0	5	Adebayor [65]	35,944
26	12	A	Newcastle U	W 4-0	1-0	5	Adebayor 2 [19, 82], Paulinho [53], Chadli [88]	48,264
27	23	A	Norwich C	L 0-1	0-0	5		26,834
28	Mar 2	H	Cardiff C	W 1-0	1-0	5	Soldado [28]	35,512
29	8	A	Chelsea	L 0-4	0-0	5		41,598
30	16	H	Arsenal	L 0-1	0-1	5		35,711
31	23	H	Southampton	W 3-2	1-2	5	Eriksen 2 [31, 46], Sigurdsson [90]	35,460
32	30	A	Liverpool	L 0-4	0-2	6		44,762
33	Apr 7	H	Sunderland	W 5-1	1-1	6	Adebayor 2 [28, 86], Kane [59], Eriksen [78], Sigurdsson [90]	34,410
34	12	A	WBA	D 3-3	1-3	6	Olsson (og) [34], Kane [70], Eriksen [90]	25,398
35	19	H	Fulham	W 3-1	1-1	6	Paulinho [35], Kane [48], Kaboul [62]	35,841
36	26	A	Stoke C	W 1-0	1-0	6	Rose [33]	26,021
37	May 3	A	West Ham U	L 0-2	0-2	6		34,977
38	11	H	Aston Villa	W 3-0	3-0	6	Paulinho [14], Baker (og) [35], Adebayor (pen) [38]	35,826

Final League Position: 6

GOALSCORERS

League (55): Adebayor 11 (1 pen), Eriksen 7, Paulinho 6, Soldado 6 (4 pens), Sigurdsson 5, Kane 3, Capoue 1, Chadli 1, Chiriches 1, Defoe 1, Dembele 1, Holtby 1, Kaboul 1, Lennon 1, Rose 1, Sandro 1, Townsend 1, Walker 1, own goals 5.
The Budweiser FA Cup (0).
Capital One Cup (7): Defoe 2, Adebayor 1, Chadli 1, Kane 1, Paulinho 1, Sigurdsson 1.
UEFA Europa League (29): Defoe 7 (1 pen), Soldado 5, Chadli 3, Eriksen 3, Adebayor 2, Holtby 2, Dembele 1, Lamela 1, Paulinho 1, Rose 1, Townsend 1, Vertonghen 1, own goal 1.

Lloris H 37	Walker K 26	Dawson M 31 + 1	Vertonghen J 23	Rose D 22	Dembele M 22 + 6	Paulinho J 28 + 2	Lennon A 26 + 1	Sigurdsson G 14 + 11	Chadli N 15 + 9	Soldado R 22 + 6	Capoue E 8 + 4	Defoe J 3 + 11	Kaboul Y 11 + 2	Townsend A 12 + 13	Sandro 10 + 7	Lamela E 3 + 6	Eriksen C 23 + 2	Holtby L 6 + 7	Naughton K 19 + 3	Kane H 6 + 4	Chiriches V 16 + 1	Friedel B 1	Adebayor E 20 + 1	Fryers Z 3 + 4	Bentaleb N 11 + 4	Veljkovic M — + 2	Pritchard A — + 1	Match No.
1	2	3	4	5¹	6²	7	8	9	10	11³	12	13	14															1
1	2	3	4	5	9¹	6	12	10	11²	7		13		8³	14													2
1	2	3	4	5	9²	7		10	11	6¹		12		8¹	14	13												3
1	2	3	4	5	6³	7		10²	11	8		13	14				9¹	12										4
1	2	3	4		6	7		10²	11	8¹		12	14				9³		5	13								5
1	2	3	4		6	7		10	11³	8¹		12	14				9²		5	13								6
1	2	3	4		6	7		10¹	11	8	12	13	14				9³		5²									7
1	2	3		5	6	7		10³	11²	8		12	14		13		9¹							4				8
1	2	3		5	6	7³		10²	11	8		12	14		13		9¹							4				9
1	2	3		5	7	6¹		10²	11	8		12	14		13		9³							4				10
	2	3		5	7³	6		10²	11	8	12	13	14				9					1		4¹				11
1	2	3		5	7³	8		11¹	14		4	6	10				9²		12					13				12
1	2	3		5	7	9	8¹	14	10³	11¹	13	12	6										4					13
1	2	3		5		9	10		13			7²	11	14	6¹	8³		12			4							14
1	2		4		7²	6	8	14	10³		3	11		13	12		9¹	5										15
1	2		4		7³	9⁴	8		10	11	3		14	6¹			12	5²					13					16
1	2	3		5	8³			9	13	11¹		14			6²	7			4	10			12					17
1	2	3		5				9	6²	10		13	8	7¹					4	11			12					18
1		3			8	7²	6¹	14	11	12		13	9			2			4	10³	5							19
1	2	3		5	8		6		13	11²	7³		9				14		4	10¹			12					20
	2¹	3		5	8		6		14	11³		13	9²				12		4	10			7					21
1	2	3		5	7			8¹	12	10²			9		13				4	11	6							22
1	2	3		5⁴	7²			8	10¹				9³	14	13				4	11	6							23
1	2	3	4	5			8	6		11			9				12			10¹	7							24
1	2	3	4	5	8¹	9¹				13	14		12			11²				10	6							25
1	2		4		7²	8	10¹		13	14	6	3	12			5			11³		9							26
	3	4	5¹	7	8³	10		12	13	6¹			14			2				11	9							27
1		3	4		7	8²	6		12	11¹			9³	13		2	14			10	5							28
1	8	3¹	5			12	9	10³				4⁴	6			2				11	13		7					29
1		4	5		12			13	8²	14		3	6	7³		10¹			2	11			9					30
1		4	5	7²				8¹	12	9	11		3	13		10			2		6							31
1	12	4²	5	14				8³	7	9	11		3	13		10			2		6¹							32
1			5		6²	7³	12	9¹				4	13		8		2	11	3	10							14	33
1			5²		7	6	13	8³				4	14		9		2	11	3¹	10	12							34
1			5	12	7	6		8¹	13			3	14		9³		2	11²		10	4							35
1	3		5¹		8	6¹	13	7²				4	14		9		2	10		11	12							36
1	3		5		7³	6	8²		14			4⁴		13	9		2	11	12	10								37
1	3		5		8¹		6³					7²			9		2	11	4	10					13	12	14	38

The Budweiser FA Cup

Third Round	Arsenal	(a)	0-2

Capital One Cup

Third Round	Aston Villa	(a)	4-0
Fourth Round	Hull C	(h)	2-2
(aet; won 8-7 on penalties)			
Quarter-Finals	West Ham U	(h)	1-2

UEFA Europa League

Play-Off 1st leg	Dinamo Tbilisi	(a)	5-0
Play-Off 2nd leg	Dinamo Tbilisi	(h)	3-0
Group K	Tromso	(h)	3-0
Group K	Anzhi Makhachkala	(a)	2-0
Group K	Serif Tiraspol	(a)	2-0
Group K	Serif Tiraspol	(h)	2-1
Group K	Tromso	(a)	2-0
Group K	Anzhi Makhachkala	(h)	4-1
Round of 32 1st leg	Dnipro Dnipropetrovsk	(a)	0-1
Round of 32 2nd leg	Dnipro Dnipropetrovsk	(h)	3-1
Round of 16 1st leg	Benfica	(h)	1-3
Round of 16 2nd leg	Benfica	(a)	2-2

TRANMERE ROVERS

FOUNDATION

Formed in 1884 as Belmont they adopted their present title the following year and eventually joined their first league, the West Lancashire League, in 1889–90, the same year as their first success in the Wirral Challenge Cup. The club almost folded in 1899–1900 when all the players left en bloc to join a rival club, but they survived the crisis and went from strength to strength, winning the 'Combination' title in 1907–08 and the Lancashire Combination in 1913–14. They joined the Football League in 1921 from the Central League.

Prenton Park, Prenton Road West, Birkenhead, Merseyside CH42 9PY.

Telephone: (0871) 221 2001.

Fax: (0151) 609 0606.

Ticket Office: (0871) 221 2001.

Website: www.tranmererovers.co.uk

Email: info@tranmererovers.co.uk

Ground Capacity: 16,151.

Record Attendance: 24,424 v Stoke C, FA Cup 4th rd, 5 February 1972.

Pitch Measurements: 100.5m × 64m (110yd × 70yd)

Chairman: Peter Johnson.

Chief Executive: Mick Horton.

Manager: Robert Edwards.

Assistant Manager: John McMahon.

Physio: Gregg Blundell.

Colours: White shirts with blue sleeves, white shorts with blue trim, white socks with blue trim.

Year Formed: 1884.

Turned Professional: 1912.

Previous Name: 1884, Belmont AFC; 1885, Tranmere Rovers.

Club Nickname: 'Rovers'.

Grounds: 1884, Steeles Field; 1887, Ravenshaws Field/Old Prenton Park; 1912, Prenton Park.

First Football League Game: 27 August 1921, Division 3 (N), v Crewe Alex (h) W 4–1 – Bradshaw; Grainger, Stuart (1); Campbell, Milnes (1), Heslop; Moreton, Groves (1), Hyam, Ford (1), Hughes.

Record League Victory: 13–4 v Oldham Ath, Division 3 (N), 26 December 1935 – Gray; Platt, Fairhurst; McLaren, Newton, Spencer; Eden, MacDonald (1), Bell (9), Woodward (2), Urmson (1).

Record Cup Victory: 13–0 v Oswestry U, FA Cup 2nd prel rd, 10 October 1914 – Ashcroft; Stevenson, Bullough, Hancock, Taylor, Holden (1), Moreton (1), Cunningham (2), Smith (5), Leck (3), Gould (1).

HONOURS

Football League Division 1: Best season: 4th, 1992–93;
Division 3 (N): *Champions* 1937–38;
Division 4: *Runners-up* 1988–89.

FA Cup: Best season: 6th rd, 2000, 2001, 2004.

Football League Cup: *Runners-up* 2000.

Welsh Cup: *Winners* 1935; *Runners-up* 1934.

Leyland DAF Cup: *Winners* 1990; *Runners-up* 1991.

sky SPORTS FACT FILE

Tranmere Rovers applied for membership of the Central League in June 1915, but were unsuccessful, receiving just four votes. In October 1919 they joined the competition as a replacement for the expelled Leeds City club. Their first game took place on 25 October 1919 resulting in a 1-1 draw away Bolton Wanderers Reserves at Burnden Park.

Record Defeat: 1–9 v Tottenham H, FA Cup 3rd rd (replay), 14 January 1953.

Most League Points (2 for a win): 60, Division 4, 1964–65.

Most League Points (3 for a win): 80, Division 4, 1988–89; Division 3, 1989–90; Division 2, 2002–03.

Most League Goals: 111, Division 3 (N), 1930–31.

Highest League Scorer in Season: Bunny Bell, 35, Division 3 (N), 1933–34.

Most League Goals in Total Aggregate: Ian Muir, 142, 1985–95.

Most League Goals in One Match: 9, Bunny Bell v Oldham Ath, Division 3 (N), 26 December 1935.

Most Capped Player: John Aldridge, 30 (69), Republic of Ireland.

Most League Appearances: Harold Bell, 595, 1946–64 (incl. League record 401 consecutive appearances).

Youngest League Player: Iain Hume, 16 years 167 days v Swindon T, 15 April 2000.

Record Transfer Fee Received: £2,250,000 from WBA for Jason Koumas, August 2002.

Record Transfer Fee Paid: £450,000 to Aston Villa for Shaun Teale, August 1995.

Football League Record: 1921 Original Member of Division 3 (N): 1938–39 Division 2; 1946–58 Division 3 (N); 1958–61 Division 3; 1961–67 Division 4; 1967–75 Division 3; 1975–76 Division 4; 1976–79 Division 3; 1979–89 Division 4; 1989–91 Division 3; 1991–92 Division 2; 1992–2001 Division 1; 2001–04 Division 2; 2004–14 FL 1; 2014– FL 2.

MANAGERS

Bert Cooke 1912–35
Jackie Carr 1935–36
Jim Knowles 1936–39
Bill Ridding 1939–45
Ernie Blackburn 1946–55
Noel Kelly 1955–57
Peter Farrell 1957–60
Walter Galbraith 1961
Dave Russell 1961–69
Jackie Wright 1969–72
Ron Yeats 1972–75
John King 1975–80
Bryan Hamilton 1980–85
Frank Worthington 1985–87
Ronnie Moore 1987
John King 1987–96
John Aldridge 1996–2001
Dave Watson 2001–02
Ray Mathias 2002–03
Brian Little 2003–06
Ronnie Moore 2006–09
John Barnes 2009
Les Parry 2009–12
Ronnie Moore 2012–14
Robert Edwards May 2014–

LATEST SEQUENCES

Longest Sequence of League Wins: 9, 9.2.1990 – 19.3.1990.

Longest Sequence of League Defeats: 8, 29.10.1938 – 17.12.1938.

Longest Sequence of League Draws: 5, 26.12.1997 – 31.1.1998.

Longest Sequence of Unbeaten League Matches: 18, 16.3.1970 – 4.9.1970.

Longest Sequence Without a League Win: 16, 8.11.1969 – 14.3.1970.

Successive Scoring Runs: 32 from 24.2.1934.

Successive Non-scoring Runs: 7 from 20.12.1997.

TEN YEAR LEAGUE RECORD

		P	W	D	L	F	A	Pts	Pos
2004-05	FL 1	46	22	13	11	73	55	79	3
2005-06	FL 1	46	13	15	18	50	52	54	18
2006-07	FL 1	46	18	13	15	58	53	67	9
2007-08	FL 1	46	18	11	17	52	47	65	11
2008-09	FL 1	46	21	11	14	62	49	74	7
2009-10	FL 1	46	14	9	23	45	72	51	19
2010-11	FL 1	46	15	11	20	53	60	56	17
2011-12	FL 1	46	14	14	18	49	53	56	12
2012-13	FL 1	46	19	10	17	58	48	67	11
2013-14	FL 1	46	12	11	23	52	79	47	21

DID YOU KNOW ?

Tranmere Rovers were one of 16 clubs to take part in the Football league Centenary tournament at Wembley Stadium in April 1988. Matches lasted for 40 minutes only for the first two rounds, then 60 minutes for the semi-finals, and Rovers defeated Wimbledon and Newcastle United before going out on penalties to eventual winners Nottingham Forest in the last four.

TRANMERE ROVERS – FOOTBALL LEAGUE ONE 2013–14 LEAGUE RECORD

Match No.	Date	Venue	Opponents	Result	H/T Score	Lg Pos.	Goalscorers	Attendance
1	Aug 3	A	Walsall	L	1-3	1-2	22	Robinson [40]	4788
2	10	H	Crawley T	D	3-3	2-1	18	Thompson 2 [16, 44], Lowe [90]	4763
3	17	A	Crewe Alex	L	1-2	0-1	19	Akpa Akpro [87]	4720
4	24	H	Peterborough U	L	0-5	0-3	22		4592
5	31	A	Oldham Ath	W	1-0	0-0	18	Lowe (pen) [90]	4792
6	Sept 7	H	Stevenage	D	0-0	0-0	18		4156
7	14	H	Brentford	L	3-4	1-2	17	Atkinson [44], Dugdale [55], Stockton [90]	4454
8	21	A	Notts Co	L	0-2	0-1	19		3938
9	28	H	Port Vale	L	0-1	0-0	21		5334
10	Oct 5	A	Swindon T	L	0-1	0-1	24		7889
11	13	A	Bradford C	W	1-0	0-0	21	Lowe [69]	14,674
12	19	H	Leyton Orient	L	0-4	0-1	22		4313
13	22	A	Rotherham U	D	1-1	0-0	22	Lowe (pen) [84]	7511
14	26	H	Milton Keynes D	W	3-2	1-1	21	Lowe 2 (1 pen) [7, 66 (p)], Rowe [84]	4100
15	Nov 2	A	Preston NE	D	1-1	0-0	20	Atkinson [55]	9496
16	16	H	Bristol C	D	1-1	1-1	21	Ridehalgh [41]	4932
17	23	A	Coventry C	W	5-1	3-0	19	Lowe 3 [4, 44, 54], Kirby [37], Wallace [89]	1815
18	26	A	Wolverhampton W	L	0-2	0-2	20		14,989
19	30	H	Colchester U	W	2-1	1-0	19	Lowe 2 (1 pen) [32, 56 (p)]	4148
20	Dec 14	A	Carlisle U	L	1-4	0-1	20	Lowe [81]	3793
21	20	H	Gillingham	L	1-2	0-1	20	Lowe [77]	6251
22	26	A	Shrewsbury T	W	1-0	1-0	19	Robinson [45]	6056
23	29	A	Sheffield U	L	1-3	0-1	20	Taylor [85]	17,460
24	Jan 1	H	Wolverhampton W	D	1-1	1-0	20	Lowe [34]	6158
25	11	H	Walsall	D	1-1	0-1	20	Stockton [78]	4871
26	18	A	Peterborough U	L	0-3	0-1	21		5297
27	25	H	Crewe Alex	W	1-0	1-0	17	Pennington [28]	5045
28	28	H	Rotherham U	L	1-2	0-1	18	Robinson [90]	3777
29	Feb 1	A	Milton Keynes D	W	1-0	0-0	17	Lowe [90]	7460
30	8	H	Preston NE	L	1-2	1-1	17	Taylor [45]	5895
31	15	A	Bristol C	D	2-2	1-1	18	Cassidy [19], Koumas [80]	11,340
32	22	H	Coventry C	W	3-1	1-0	18	Lowe (pen) [12], Wallace [48], Kirby [64]	5279
33	Mar 1	H	Oldham Ath	D	2-2	1-1	18	Grounds (og) [31], Lowe [76]	5061
34	8	A	Stevenage	L	1-3	0-1	20	Obeng (og) [88]	2577
35	11	A	Brentford	L	0-2	0-0	21		5646
36	15	H	Notts Co	W	3-2	2-1	19	Koumas [25], Lowe [28], Jennings [84]	4292
37	22	A	Port Vale	L	2-3	0-1	20	Taylor [58], Koumas [60]	5449
38	25	H	Swindon T	L	1-2	1-1	20	Power [15]	3717
39	29	H	Carlisle U	D	0-0	0-0	20		5215
40	Apr 5	A	Colchester U	W	2-1	1-1	19	Akpa Akpro [36], Lowe [63]	3443
41	12	H	Shrewsbury T	W	2-1	1-0	19	Power [19], Brown [85]	5698
42	15	A	Crawley T	L	0-2	0-1	19		3443
43	18	A	Gillingham	L	0-2	0-0	19		7343
44	21	H	Sheffield U	D	0-0	0-0	19		5950
45	26	A	Leyton Orient	L	0-2	0-1	21		4923
46	May 3	H	Bradford C	L	1-2	1-0	21	Pennington [7]	9598

Final League Position: 21

GOALSCORERS

League (52): Lowe 19 (5 pens), Koumas 3, Robinson 3, Taylor 3, Akpa Akpro 2, Atkinson 2, Kirby 2, Pennington 2, Power 2, Stockton 2, Thompson 2, Wallace 2, Brown 1, Cassidy 1, Dugdale 1, Jennings 1, Ridehalgh 1, Rowe 1, own goals 2.
The Budweiser FA Cup (1): Lowe 1.
Capital One Cup (3): Atkinson 1, Robinson 1, Stockton 1.
Johnstone's Paint Trophy (1): Horwood 1.

Fon Williams O 43	Holmes D 25 + 3	Horwood E 12 + 6	Atkinson C 22	Taylor A 41 + 1	Foster S 4	Robinson A 9 + 10	Power M 27 + 6	Lowe R 44 + 1	Sodje A 3 + 6	Akpa Akpro J 21 + 4	Koumas J 24 + 7	Bell-Baggie A 4 + 8	Thompson J 6	Jones A 1 + 1	Rowe J 7 + 12	Goodison I 15 + 3	Stockton C 2 + 19	Mooney J 3	Dugdale A 4	Hateley T 8	Ridehalgh L 36	McNulty J 12	Kirby J 19 + 12	Jennings S 23 + 2	Wallace J 16 + 2	Otsemobor J 2	Peterson K 6	Pennington M 17	Arthurworrey S 15 + 2	Kennedy M 8	Cassidy J 19	Brown J 8 + 1	Ariyibi G — + 2	Match No.
1	3		4²	5	6	7	8	9	10	11¹	12	13																						1
1	2	5	7	3	4	9	8²	10		11¹	12	13		6																				2
1	2⁴	5	7	3	4	9¹	8²	10		11	13		6¹	12	14																			3
1		5	7	3	4¹	9	8	10²		11	12	6²		2⁴		13	14																	4
1	2	5	7	3			6	12	13	11²	8¹			9	4	10																		5
	2	5	6	12			7	10	13	11			9²	8	4²		1	3																6
1	2	5	8			13	6	10¹		9		14	11³	7²	4	12	3																	7
1		5	8				9	10		11		12	6²	7¹	3	13		4	2															8
1		8	3			13	10	14	9				6³	7¹	12	11²		4	2	5⁴														9
1	2	8	3			9	6	11²		14			13	4	12			7¹	10³	5														10
1	2	12	8	3		9	11³		13			4	14		7	10	5	6²																11
1	2		8	3		7	11	13		12			4¹			9²	10¹	5	6															12
1	2		7¹	3		6	11			12			14	13		9¹	5	4	10	8³														13
1	2¹	14	6	3		8	10			9²		13				7²	5	4	11	12														14
1	2		7	3		10	11		12	8				9¹	5	4	6																	15
	2		8	3		6	10	12	7	9¹				1		5	4	11																16
1	2	13	7	3⁴			8²	11	14	9	10³				5	4	6		12															17
1	2	8				7²	11	13	9	10¹	14		4			5	3	6³		12														18
1	12	13	8				11		10			14	3¹			5	4	6	7²	2³	9													19
1		9¹	3				11		10	8		12				5	4		7	2	6													20
1	2	12		3	14		10		11²	7			13			5	4⁴	9¹		8		6³												21
1	2	5	9²	3		10³	14	11		7			4				12	13	8¹	6														22
1	2³	5	9²	4		10¹	12	11		13	7			3			14	8		6														23
1			3			10¹	13	11		8²				5		12	7	9⁴		6	2	4												24
1			3			10²		11		14	9¹		8		13	5	12	6			2	4	7²											25
1	12		3				13	10		8²			6³		14	5¹	11	7			2	4	9											26
1	5		3				12	10		8							9¹	7			2	4	6	11²										27
1	5		3			12		10		13							9³	7²	8		2	4	6¹	11										28
1			4					10		6						5	12	7	8		2	3	9¹	11										29
1			3	13				11		12						5	6²	8	7		2	4	9¹	10										30
1			3				8			6						5	12	9	7		2	4	10¹	11										31
1			4	14			10²			8					13	5	12	7	6		2	3	9³	11¹										32
1	2		3			10²		6		7¹		13				5	12	8	9			4		11										33
1	2		3	12		10		8								9¹			7	6		4		5	11									34
1	2		3	12		10		8					13			9			7	6		4		5²	11¹									35
1	2		3	13	12	11¹				7²						5	6	8	9³			4		10										36
1			4			8	11			9				12	13	5	6	7			3¹		10	2²										37
1	2²		3	13	6	11							14	4		5	9	7¹	8³			10		12										38
1			3			7	10	9						4		5	6¹	8³		2		11		12										39
1	12		3			7	11¹	9	6²					14		5	13	8		2	4³	10												40
1			3			6	10	9	8²				4¹			5		7		2	13	11	12											41
1			3			7		11					13	4	12	5	6¹	8		2		10	9²											42
1	12		3			7	10¹	6	8²				4²	13		5				2	14	11	9											43
1	2		3			8	10	9¹					13	14		5²	12	7		4		11³	6											44
1	2		3			7	11	9¹					12			5	13	8		4		10²	6											45
			4			6²	10		11	8			12	3		1	5¹	13	7		2		9⁴											46

The Budweiser FA Cup

First Round	Accrington S	(a)	1-0
Second Round	Peterborough U	(a)	0-5

Johnstone's Paint Trophy

First Round	Fleetwood T	(h)	1-2

Capital One Cup

First Round	Mansfield T	(h)	2-0
Second Round	Bolton W	(h)	1-1
(aet; won 4-2 on penalties)			
Third Round	Stoke C	(h)	0-2

WALSALL

FOUNDATION

Two of the leading clubs around Walsall in the 1880s were Walsall Swifts (formed 1877) and Walsall Town (formed 1879). The Swifts were winners of the Birmingham Senior Cup in 1881, while the Town reached the 4th round (5th round modern equivalent) of the FA Cup in 1883. These clubs amalgamated as Walsall Town Swifts in 1888, becoming simply Walsall in 1895.

Banks's Stadium, Bescot Crescent, Walsall WS1 4SA.
Telephone: (01922) 622 791. *Fax:* (01922) 613 202.
Ticket Office: (01922) 651 414/416.
Website: www.saddlers.co.uk
Email: info@walsallfc.co.uk
Ground Capacity: 10,989.
Record Attendance: 25,453 v Newcastle U, Division 2, 29 August 1961 (at Fellows Park); 11,049 v Rotherham U, Division 1, 9 May 2004 (at Bescot Stadium).
Pitch Measurements: 100.5m × 67m (110yd × 73yd)
Chairman: Jeff Bonser.
Chief Executive: Stefan Gamble.
Manager: Dean Smith.
First Team Coach: Richard O'Kelly.
Physio: Jon Whitney.
Colours: Red shirts with thin white stripes, white shorts with red trim, white socks with red trim.
Year Formed: 1888.
Turned Professional: 1888.
Previous Names: Walsall Swifts (founded 1877) and Walsall Town (founded 1879) amalgamated in 1888 as Walsall Town Swifts; 1895, Walsall.
Club Nickname: 'The Saddlers'.
Grounds: 1888, Fellows Park; 1990, Bescot Stadium.
First Football League Game: 3 September 1892, Division 2, v Darwen (h) L 1–2 – Hawkins; Withington, Pinches; Robinson, Whitrick, Forsyth; Marshall, Holmes, Turner, Gray (1), Pangbourn.
Record League Victory: 10–0 v Darwen, Division 2, 4 March 1899 – Tennent; Ted Peers (1), Davies; Hickinbotham, Jenkyns, Taggart; Dean (3), Vail (2), Aston (4), Martin, Griffin.
Record Cup Victory: 7–0 v Macclesfield T (a), FA Cup 2nd rd, 6 December 1997 – Walker; Evans, Marsh, Viveash (1), Ryder, Peron, Boli (2 incl. 1p) (Ricketts), Porter (2), Keates, Watson (Platt), Hodge (2 incl. 1p).
Record Defeat: 0–12 v Small Heath, 17 December 1892; 0–12 v Darwen, 26 December 1896, both Division 2.
Most League Points (2 for a win): 65, Division 4, 1959–60.
Most League Points (3 for a win): 89, FL 2, 2006–07.
Most League Goals: 102, Division 4, 1959–60.
Highest League Scorer in Season: Gilbert Alsop, 40, Division 3 (N), 1933–34 and 1934–35.

HONOURS

Football League –
Division 2: *Runners-up*, 1998–99;
FL 2: *Champions* 2006–07;
Division 3: *Runners-up* 1960–61, 1994–95;
Division 4: *Champions* 1959–60; *Runners-up* 1979–80.
FA Cup: Best season: 5th rd, 1939, 1975, 1978, 1987, 2002, 2003 and last 16 1889.
Football League Cup: Semi-final 1984.

sky SPORTS FACT FILE

In 1986 it was announced that Walsall would leave their historic home at Fellows Park and ground share with Birmingham City. The proposals were met with outrage by the club's fans who campaigned against the switch and the Save Walsall Action Group was successful in stopping the move.

Most League Goals in Total Aggregate: Tony Richards, 184, 1954–63; Colin Taylor, 184, 1958–63, 1964–68, 1969–73.

Most League Goals in One Match: 5, Gilbert Alsop v Carlisle U, Division 3 (N), 2 February 1935; 5, Bill Evans v Mansfield T, Division 3 (N), 5 October 1935; 5, Johnny Devlin v Torquay U, Division 3 (S), 1 September 1949.

Most Capped Player: Mick Kearns, 15 (18), Republic of Ireland.

Most League Appearances: Colin Harrison, 467, 1964–82.

Youngest League Player: Geoff Morris, 16 years 218 days v Scunthorpe U, 14 September 1965.

Record Transfer Fee Received: £1,000,000 from Coventry C for Scott Dann, January 2008.

Record Transfer Fee Paid: £175,000 to Birmingham C for Alan Buckley, June 1979.

Football League Record: 1892 Elected to Division 2; 1895 Failed re-election; 1896–1901 Division 2; 1901 Failed re-election; 1921 Original Member of Division 3 (N); 1927–31 Division 3 (S); 1931–36 Division 3 (N); 1936–58 Division 3 (S); 1958–60 Division 4; 1960–61 Division 3; 1961–63 Division 2; 1963–79 Division 3; 1979–80 Division 4; 1980–88 Division 3; 1988–89 Division 2; 1989–90 Division 3; 1990–92 Division 4; 1992–95 Division 3; 1995–99 Division 2; 1999–2000 Division 1; 2000–01 Division 2; 2001–04 Division 1; 2004–06 FL 1; 2006–07 FL 2; 2007– FL 1.

LATEST SEQUENCES

Longest Sequence of League Wins: 7, 9.4.2005 – 9.8.2005.

Longest Sequence of League Defeats: 15, 29.10.1988 – 4.2.1989.

Longest Sequence of League Draws: 5, 7.5.1988 – 17.9.1988.

Longest Sequence of Unbeaten League Matches: 21, 6.11.1979 – 22.3.1980.

Longest Sequence Without a League Win: 18, 15.10.1988 – 4.2.1989.

Successive Scoring Runs: 27 from 6.11.1979.

Successive Non-scoring Runs: 5 from 10.4.2004.

MANAGERS

H. Smallwood 1888–91 *(Secretary-Manager)*
A. G. Burton 1891–93
J. H. Robinson 1893–95
C. H. Ailso 1895–96 *(Secretary-Manager)*
A. E. Parsloe 1896–97 *(Secretary-Manager)*
L. Ford 1897–98 *(Secretary-Manager)*
G. Hughes 1898–99 *(Secretary-Manager)*
L. Ford 1899–1901 *(Secretary-Manager)*
J. E. Shutt 1908–13 *(Secretary-Manager)*
Haydn Price 1914–20
Joe Burchell 1920–26
David Ashworth 1926–27
Jack Torrance 1927–28
James Kerr 1928–29
Sid Scholey 1929–30
Peter O'Rourke 1930–32
Bill Slade 1932–34
Andy Wilson 1934–37
Tommy Lowes 1937–44
Harry Hibbs 1944–51
Tony McPhee 1951
Brough Fletcher 1952–53
Major Frank Buckley 1953–55
John Love 1955–57
Billy Moore 1957–64
Alf Wood 1964
Reg Shaw 1964–68
Dick Graham 1968
Ron Lewin 1968–69
Billy Moore 1969–72
John Smith 1972–73
Ronnie Allen 1973
Doug Fraser 1973–77
Dave Mackay 1977–78
Alan Ashman 1978
Frank Sibley 1979
Alan Buckley 1979–86
Neil Martin *(Joint Manager with Buckley)* 1981–82
Tommy Coakley 1986–88
John Barnwell 1989–90
Kenny Hibbitt 1990–94
Chris Nicholl 1994–97
Jan Sorensen 1997–98
Ray Graydon 1998–2002
Colin Lee 2002–04
Paul Merson 2004–06
Kevin Broadhurst 2006
Richard Money 2006–08
Jimmy Mullen 2008–09
Chris Hutchings 2009–10
Dean Smith January 2011–

TEN YEAR LEAGUE RECORD

		P	W	D	L	F	A	Pts	Pos
2004-05	FL 1	46	16	12	18	65	69	60	14
2005-06	FL 1	46	11	14	21	47	70	47	24
2006-07	FL 2	46	25	14	7	66	34	89	1
2007-08	FL 1	46	16	16	14	52	46	64	12
2008-09	FL 1	46	17	10	19	61	66	61	13
2009-10	FL 1	46	16	14	16	60	63	62	10
2010-11	FL 1	46	12	12	22	56	75	48	20
2011-12	FL 1	46	10	20	16	51	57	50	19
2012-13	FL 1	46	17	17	12	65	58	68	9
2013-14	FL 1	46	14	16	16	49	49	58	13

DID YOU KNOW ?

Walsall followed up their tremendous FA Cup victory over Arsenal in January 1933 with an 8-1 win over Mansfield Town five days later. The game was played on a midweek afternoon and although school children were given a half holiday and free admission, the attendance was just 3,068.

WALSALL – FOOTBALL LEAGUE ONE 2013–14 LEAGUE RECORD

Match No.	Date	Venue	Opponents	Result	H/T Score	Lg Pos.	Goalscorers	Attendance
1	Aug 3	H	Tranmere R	W 3-1	2-1	2	Westcarr 2 [4, 71], Lalkovic [25]	4788
2	10	A	Oldham Ath	W 1-0	1-0	3	Baxendale [25]	4538
3	17	H	Notts Co	D 1-1	0-0	4	Sawyers [50]	4295
4	24	A	Brentford	L 0-1	0-1	7		5781
5	31	H	Preston NE	L 0-3	0-1	12		4205
6	Sept 14	A	Crewe Alex	W 3-0	0-0	10	Westcarr 2 (1 pen) [66, 69 (p)], Baxendale [84]	4260
7	17	A	Wolverhampton W	W 1-0	0-0	7	Butler [69]	22,240
8	21	H	Rotherham U	D 1-1	1-1	7	Mantom [33]	5002
9	28	A	Leyton Orient	D 1-1	0-1	9	Westcarr [71]	5429
10	Oct 5	H	Bradford C	L 0-2	0-1	9		5364
11	12	A	Colchester U	D 1-1	0-1	10	Taylor [90]	2945
12	19	H	Stevenage	W 2-1	1-0	9	Sawyers [11], Westcarr [55]	3720
13	22	A	Swindon T	W 3-1	1-0	6	Hemmings 2 [18, 78], Mantom [48]	8188
14	26	H	Coventry C	L 0-1	0-0	7		6519
15	Nov 2	A	Milton Keynes D	L 0-1	0-0	9		7711
16	18	H	Peterborough U	W 2-0	1-0	7	Lalkovic [26], Sawyers [69]	4597
17	23	A	Crawley T	D 0-0	0-0	8		3296
18	26	A	Sheffield U	D 1-1	0-1	9	Westcarr [47]	14,796
19	30	H	Port Vale	L 0-2	0-1	10		4909
20	Dec 14	A	Shrewsbury T	W 1-0	0-0	9	Lalkovic [54]	6015
21	21	H	Carlisle U	W 2-0	1-0	8	Sawyers [15], Lalkovic [66]	4062
22	26	A	Bristol C	L 0-1	0-1	8		12,031
23	29	A	Gillingham	D 2-2	0-0	9	Sawyers [62], Gray [90]	5394
24	Jan 1	H	Sheffield U	W 2-1	0-1	7	Westcarr (pen) [52], Chambers, J [62]	5015
25	11	A	Tranmere R	D 1-1	1-0	7	Lalkovic [19]	4871
26	14	H	Oldham Ath	W 1-0	0-0	6	Mantom [65]	3522
27	18	H	Brentford	D 1-1	1-1	7	Westcarr [45]	5295
28	25	A	Notts Co	W 5-1	3-0	6	Brandy 3 [24, 33, 45], Butler [49], Westcarr [53]	5701
29	28	H	Swindon T	D 1-1	1-0	6	Sawyers [37]	4059
30	Feb 8	H	Milton Keynes D	L 0-3	0-2	7		4116
31	14	A	Peterborough U	D 0-0	0-0	7		4263
32	22	H	Crawley T	L 1-2	0-1	7	Mantom [64]	3904
33	Mar 1	A	Preston NE	L 1-2	1-2	8	Mantom [5]	10,034
34	5	A	Coventry C	L 1-2	0-1	8	Benning [54]	1637
35	8	H	Wolverhampton W	L 0-3	0-1	9		10,139
36	11	H	Crewe Alex	D 1-1	0-0	8	Ellis (og) [90]	3777
37	15	A	Rotherham U	D 1-1	1-0	8	Lalkovic [19]	8212
38	22	H	Leyton Orient	D 1-1	1-0	9	Downing [14]	5779
39	25	A	Bradford C	W 2-0	0-0	9	Westcarr 2 [68, 78]	12,165
40	29	H	Shrewsbury T	W 1-0	1-0	8	Westcarr [5]	4222
41	Apr 5	A	Port Vale	L 0-1	0-0	10		5569
42	12	H	Bristol C	L 0-1	0-1	10		5110
43	18	A	Carlisle U	D 1-1	1-1	11	Ngoo [82]	4389
44	21	H	Gillingham	D 1-1	0-0	11	Brandy [55]	3890
45	26	H	Stevenage	L 2-3	0-1	11	Benning [46], Westcarr [50]	2973
46	May 3	H	Colchester U	L 0-1	0-0	13		4271

Final League Position: 13

GOALSCORERS

League (49): Westcarr 14 (2 pens), Lalkovic 6, Sawyers 6, Mantom 5, Brandy 4, Baxendale 2, Benning 2, Butler 2, Hemmings 2, Chambers, J 1, Downing 1, Gray 1, Ngoo 1, Taylor 1, own goal 1.
The Budweiser FA Cup (3): Westcarr 2, Sawyers 1.
Capital One Cup (3): Hemmings 2, Baxendale 1.
Johnstone's Paint Trophy (2): Hemmings 1, Hewitt 1.

O'Donnell R 46	Chambers J 40	Benning M 14 + 2	Mantom S 43	Butler A 45	Downing P 43 + 1	Baxendale J 25 + 15	Chambers A 45	Westcar C 40 + 3	Lalkovic M 30 + 8	Hemmings A 14 + 13	Featherstone N 15 + 10	Sawyers R 29 + 15	Hewitt T 8 + 19	McQuilkin J 2 + 7	Taylor A 32 + 1	Purkiss B 10 + 4	Gray J — + 12	Brandy F 20	Ngoo M 4 + 10	Bakayoko A — + 6	Morris K 1 + 1	Match No.
1	2	3	4	5	6	7[1]	8[2]	9[3]	10	11	12	13	14									1
1	2	5	8	3	4	6	7	10[1]	11[2]	9[3]	13	12	14									2
1	2	5	8	4	3	6[1]	7	10		9[2]	13	11	12									3
1	2	5	7	3	4	6[1]	8[3]	10[1]	11	9[2]	13	12		14								4
1	2	5[3]	7	3	4	6	8	10[1]	11	9[2]	13	12			14							5
1	2		7	4	3		12	6[2]	10	14	9[1]	8	13	11[3]	5							6
1	2		8	4	3		12	6	10[1]	13	9[3]	7	14	11[2]	5							7
1	2		8	4	3		9[4]	6	13	12	14	7	11	10[3]	5							8
1	2[2]	14	7	4[4]	3	13	9	6	8[1]	10[3]	11				5	12						9
1	2		8	3	4	12	9	10	7[3]	13	6[2]	14	11[1]		5							10
1	5		8	3	4	11[1]	7	10		9[3]	6[2]	13	14		2	12						11
1	2		7	3	4	6[2]	8	11	13	9[1]	10[3]	12			5	14						12
1	2		8	3	4	6[3]	9	11[1]	13	10[2]	7	14			5	12						13
1	2		6	4	3	9[1]	8	11[2]	10[3]	7	14	13			5	12						14
1	2		8	4	3	9[3]	6	10	13	11[2]	7[1]	12	14		5							15
1	2		8	4	3	9[1]	7	11[3]	6[2]	12	10	14			5	13						16
1	2		8	4	3	6[3]	7	11	9[2]	12	10[1]	14			5	13						17
1	2		8	3	4	6[2]	7	11	10[1]	12	9[3]	13	14		5							18
1	2		6	4	3	10[3]	7	11	8[3]	12	9[1]	14			5	13						19
1			7	3	4	6	8	10	9[1]	12	11				5	2						20
1			7	3	4	6	9[2]	11[2]	10[1]	13	8	12			5	2	14					21
1			7	3	4	11[1]		10[2]	9[3]	12	8	6	13		5	2	14					22
1			8	3	4	6[2]	7	11		9[1]	10	13			5	2	12					23
1	2		8	4	3	6[2]	7	12	9[1]	14	10	11[3]			5	13						24
1	2		7	3	4	13	8	11[3]	6[1]	9[2]	10	14			5	12						25
1	2		7	3	4		8	11[2]	9	12	10	13			5			6[1]				26
1	2[3]	12	7	4	3	14	8	11	9	10[2]					5[1]	13		6				27
1	2[2]	5	8	4	3	14	7[1]	11	9	12	6	13						10[3]				28
1	2[1]	5	8	4	3		7	11	9	13	6[2]	14				12		10[3]				29
1		5	6	4[3]	3		7	11[1]	10	13	9[3]	14			2			8[1]	12			30
1	4	5	8	3		13	7	10	9[2]	14	12				2			6[3]	11[1]			31
1		5	7	4	3	13	8	10	9[1]	14	12				2			6[2]	11[3]			32
1	2	5	7[3]	3	4	12	6	11	10[2]	9[1]	13							8[3]	14			33
1	2	5		4	3	13	7	11[2]	10[3]	6	9	14						8[1]	12			34
1	2		4	12		7	13	9[3]	8	10	11[1]	5	3					6[2]	14			35
1	3		4			7	10	12	6[2]	9[1]	11[3]	14			5	2		8	13			36
1	3		7	4	12		6	11[2]	10[1]	9					5	2[7]		8	13			37
1	2		8	3	4	12	7	11	9[1]	10					5			6				38
1	2		7	3	4	12	8	11	9[2]	10	13				5			6[1]				39
1	2		7	3	4	9[2]	8	10[4]	11[1]	12					5			6	13			40
1	2		8	3	4	9[1]	7	12	10	14					5			6[2]	11[3]	13		41
1	2		6	4	3	10[3]	7[2]	14		9	13				5	11		8[1]	12			42
1	2		8	3	4	9[3]	7	10		6[1]					5			11[2]	12	14	13	43
1	2	5	7	4	3		6	10		8	9[1]							11[2]	12	13		44
1	4	2	7	3	5		12	8[1]	9	11[3]	6							10[2]	14	13		45
1	2		7	4	3	6[1]	8	10		13	12	11[3]			5					14	9[2]	46

The Budweiser FA Cup

First Round	Shrewsbury T	(h)	3-0
Second Round	Leyton Orient	(a)	0-1

Capital One Cup

First Round	Port Vale	(a)	2-1
Second Round	Stoke C	(a)	1-3

Johnstone's Paint Trophy

First Round	Wolverhampton W	(a)	2-2
(aet; lost 2-4 on penalties)			

WATFORD

FOUNDATION

The club was formed as Watford Rovers in 1881. The name was changed to West Herts in 1893 and then the name Watford was adopted after rival club Watford St Mary's was absorbed in 1898.

Vicarage Road Stadium, Vicarage Road, Watford, Hertfordshire WD18 0ER.

Telephone: (01923) 496 000.

Fax: (01923) 496 001.

Ticket Office: (01923) 496 001.

Website: www.watfordfc.com

Email: yourvoice@watfordfc.com

Ground Capacity: 17,477.

Record Attendance: 34,099 v Manchester U, FA Cup 4th rd (replay), 3 February 1969.

Pitch Measurements: 103m × 66.1m (112.5yd × 72.5yd)

Chairman: Raffaele Riva.

Chief Executive: Scott Duxbury.

Head Coach: Beppe Sannino.

HONOURS

Football League – Division 1:
Runners-up 1982–83;
Division 2: *Champions* 1997–98;
Runners-up 1981–82;
Division 3: *Champions* 1968–69;
Runners-up 1978–79;
Division 4: *Champions* 1977–78.
FA Cup: *Runners-up* 1984, semi-finals 1970, 1984, 1987, 2003, 2007.
Football League Cup: Semi-final 1979, 2005.
European Competitions
UEFA Cup: 1983–84.

Assistant Coaches: Francesco Troise, Giovanni Cusatis, Paulo De Toffal, Alberto Sebastiani.

Head of Medicine: Marco Cesarini.

Colours: Yellow shirts with black trim, black shorts with yellow trim, yellow socks with black trim.

Year Formed: 1881.

Turned Professional: 1897.

Previous Names: 1881, Watford Rovers; 1893, West Herts; 1898, Watford.

Club Nickname: 'The Hornets'.

Grounds: 1883, Vicarage Meadow, Rose and Crown Meadow; 1889, Colney Butts; 1890, Cassio Road; 1922, Vicarage Road.

First Football League Game: 28 August 1920, Division 3, v QPR (a) W 2–1 – Williams; Horseman, Fred Gregory; Bacon, Toone, Wilkinson; Bassett, Ronald (1), Hoddinott, White (1), Waterall.

Record League Victory: 8–0 v Sunderland, Division 1, 25 September 1982 – Sherwood; Rice, Rostron, Taylor, Terry, Bolton, Callaghan (2), Blissett (4), Jenkins (2), Jackett, Barnes.

Record Cup Victory: 10–1 v Lowestoft T, FA Cup 1st rd, 27 November 1926 – Yates; Prior, Fletcher (1); Frank Smith, Bert Smith, Strain; Stephenson, Warner (3), Edmonds (3), Swan (1), Daniels (1), (1 og).

Record Defeat: 0–10 v Wolverhampton W, FA Cup 1st rd (replay), 24 January 1912.

sky SPORTS FACT FILE

Frank Jackett made 14 appearances for Watford between 1949 and 1953, featuring as a wing half or inside forward. His son Kenny went on to become one of the Hornets' all-time greats, making over 400 appearances as a player. They are the only father and son combination to play for the club in the Football League.

Most League Points (2 for a win): 71, Division 4, 1977–78.

Most League Points (3 for a win): 88, Division 2, 1997–98.

Most League Goals: 92, Division 4, 1959–60.

Highest League Scorer in Season: Cliff Holton, 42, Division 4, 1959–60.

Most League Goals in Total Aggregate: Luther Blissett, 148, 1976–83, 1984–88, 1991–92.

Most League Goals in One Match: 5, Eddie Mummery v Newport Co, Division 3 (S), 5 January 1924.

Most Capped Players: John Barnes, 31 (79), England; Kenny Jackett, 31, Wales.

Most League Appearances: Luther Blissett, 415, 1976–83, 1984–88, 1991–92.

Youngest League Player: Keith Mercer, 16 years 125 days v Tranmere R, 16 February 1973.

Record Transfer Fee Received: £9,600,000 from Aston Villa for Ashley Young, January 2007.

Record Transfer Fee Paid: £3,250,000 to WBA for Nathan Ellington, August 2007.

Football League Record: 1920 Original Member of Division 3; 1921–58 Division 3 (S); 1958–60 Division 4; 1960–69 Division 3; 1969–72 Division 2; 1972–75 Division 3; 1975–78 Division 4; 1978–79 Division 3; 1979–82 Division 2; 1982–88 Division 1; 1988–92 Division 2; 1992–96 Division 1; 1996–98 Division 2; 1998–99 Division 1; 1999–2000 FA Premier League; 2000–04 Division 1; 2004–06 FL C; 2006–07 FA Premier League; 2007– FL C.

LATEST SEQUENCES

Longest Sequence of League Wins: 7, 28.8.2000 – 14.10.2000.

Longest Sequence of League Defeats: 9, 26.12.1972 – 27.2.1973.

Longest Sequence of League Draws: 7, 16.2.2008 – 22.3.2008.

Longest Sequence of Unbeaten League Matches: 22, 1.10.1996 – 1.3.1997.

Longest Sequence Without a League Win: 19, 27.11.1971 – 8.4.1972.

Successive Scoring Runs: 22 from 20.8.1985.

Successive Non-scoring Runs: 7 from 18.12.1971.

MANAGERS

John Goodall 1903–10
Harry Kent 1910–26
Fred Pagnam 1926–29
Neil McBain 1929–37
Bill Findlay 1938–47
Jack Bray 1947–48
Eddie Hapgood 1948–50
Ron Gray 1950–51
Haydn Green 1951–52
Len Goulden 1952–55
    (General Manager to 1956)
Johnny Paton 1955–56
Neil McBain 1956–59
Ron Burgess 1959–63
Bill McGarry 1963–64
Ken Furphy 1964–71
George Kirby 1971–73
Mike Keen 1973–77
Graham Taylor 1977–87
Dave Bassett 1987–88
Steve Harrison 1988–90
Colin Lee 1990
Steve Perryman 1990–93
Glenn Roeder 1993–96
Kenny Jackett 1996–97
Graham Taylor 1997–2001
Gianluca Vialli 2001–02
Ray Lewington 2002–05
Adrian Boothroyd 2005–08
Brendan Rodgers 2008–09
Malky Mackay 2009–11
Sean Dyche 2011–12
Gianfranco Zola 2012–13
Beppe Sannino December 2013–

TEN YEAR LEAGUE RECORD

		P	W	D	L	F	A	Pts	Pos
2004-05	FL C	46	12	16	18	52	59	52	18
2005-06	FL C	46	22	15	9	77	53	81	3
2006-07	PR Lge	38	5	13	20	29	59	28	20
2007-08	FL C	46	18	16	12	62	56	70	6
2008-09	FL C	46	16	10	20	68	72	58	13
2009-10	FL C	46	14	12	20	61	68	54	16
2010-11	FL C	46	16	13	17	77	71	61	14
2011-12	FL C	46	16	16	14	56	64	64	11
2012-13	FL C	46	23	8	15	85	58	77	3
2013-14	FL C	46	15	15	16	74	64	60	13

DID YOU KNOW

Winger Jimmy Carr made 18 Southern League appearances for Watford in 1913–14 before moving on to West Ham United. In later life he became a prominent bowls player and represented England at the Empire Games in Vancouver in 1954.

WATFORD – FL CHAMPIONSHIP 2013–14 LEAGUE RECORD

Match No.	Date	Venue	Opponents	Result		H/T Score	Lg Pos.	Goalscorers	Attendance
1	Aug 3	A	Birmingham C	W	1-0	1-0	8	Deeney [11]	18,830
2	10	H	Bournemouth	W	6-1	1-1	1	Angella 2 [13, 53], Deeney 3 (1 pen) [56, 88, 90 (p)], McGugan [66]	16,295
3	17	A	Reading	D	3-3	0-2	2	Faraoni [66], Deeney (pen) [76], Fabbrini [90]	20,875
4	25	H	Nottingham F	D	1-1	0-1	5	McGugan [54]	16,242
5	31	A	Blackpool	L	0-1	0-0	7		13,345
6	Sept14	H	Charlton Ath	D	1-1	0-0	8	Pudil [71]	16,431
7	17	H	Doncaster R	W	2-1	1-1	6	McGugan 2 (1 pen) [13, 87 (p)]	13,998
8	21	A	Barnsley	W	5-1	3-1	5	Deeney [7], Faraoni [17], Forestieri [43], Murray [69], Anya [79]	9850
9	28	H	Wigan Ath	W	1-0	0-0	4	Battocchio [82]	14,999
10	Oct 1	A	Blackburn R	L	0-1	0-0	7		12,981
11	5	A	Huddersfield T	W	2-1	2-1	5	Forestieri [18], Pudil [43]	14,311
12	19	H	Derby Co	L	2-3	1-2	7	Forestieri [12], McGugan [68]	16,180
13	28	H	Brighton & HA	D	1-1	1-0	7	Murray [4]	27,657
14	Nov 2	H	Leicester C	L	0-3	0-1	7		16,011
15	9	A	Middlesbrough	D	2-2	1-1	7	Deeney [32], Forestieri [73]	14,344
16	23	H	Bolton W	L	0-1	0-1	10		15,247
17	30	H	Yeovil T	L	0-3	0-1	10		15,263
18	Dec 3	A	Burnley	D	0-0	0-0	12		10,910
19	7	A	Leeds U	D	3-3	2-0	12	Deeney 2 [12, 86], Battocchio [45]	23,445
20	14	H	Sheffield W	L	0-1	0-1	13		15,476
21	21	A	Ipswich T	D	1-1	0-0	14	Deeney [81]	16,385
22	26	A	Millwall	W	4-0	2-0	12	Deeney (pen) [10], Forestieri [26], Anya [48], McGugan (pen) [60]	15,471
23	29	H	QPR	D	0-0	0-0	13		16,625
24	Jan 11	H	Reading	L	0-1	0-1	15		15,725
25	18	A	Bournemouth	D	1-1	1-0	15	Angella [45]	10,353
26	30	A	Nottingham F	L	2-4	1-0	16	Angella 2 [33, 47]	18,510
27	Feb 2	H	Brighton & HA	W	2-0	1-0	13	Anya [13], Forestieri [60]	16,096
28	8	A	Leicester C	D	2-2	2-1	14	Forestieri [9], Murray [41]	23,635
29	11	H	Birmingham C	W	1-0	1-0	13	Deeney [33]	13,904
30	15	H	Middlesbrough	W	1-0	0-0	12	Deeney (pen) [50]	15,391
31	18	A	Yeovil T	D	0-0	0-0	11		6042
32	22	A	Bolton W	L	0-2	0-2	12		15,179
33	Mar 1	A	Blackpool	W	4-0	3-0	11	Ranegie 2 [15, 39], Deeney 2 [35, 74]	14,586
34	11	A	Doncaster R	L	1-2	0-1	11	Anya [68]	6581
35	15	H	Barnsley	W	3-0	2-0	11	Battocchio [5], Deeney [16], Merkel [74]	14,531
36	22	A	Wigan Ath	L	1-2	1-1	12	McGugan [36]	14,556
37	25	A	Blackburn R	D	3-3	1-1	12	Cassetti [4], Deeney (pen) [71], Battocchio [88]	13,921
38	29	A	Sheffield W	W	4-1	2-0	11	Angella [5], McGugan [23], Deeney 2 [49, 50]	22,057
39	Apr 5	H	Burnley	D	1-1	1-0	12	Deeney [9]	16,182
40	8	H	Leeds U	W	3-0	2-0	12	Abdi [9], Anya [32], Deeney [67]	16,212
41	12	A	Millwall	D	2-2	1-0	13	McGugan [17], Abdi [86]	10,851
42	19	H	Ipswich T	W	3-1	1-0	12	Riera [21], Angella [63], McGugan [65]	16,615
43	21	A	QPR	L	1-2	0-0	12	Ranegie [51]	16,951
44	26	A	Derby Co	L	2-4	1-1	13	Deeney [5], Ranegie [70]	25,922
45	29	A	Charlton Ath	L	1-3	0-1	13	Deeney [60]	15,815
46	May 3	H	Huddersfield T	L	1-4	0-0	13	Deeney (pen) [90]	15,370

Final League Position: 13

GOALSCORERS

League (74): Deeney 24 (6 pens), McGugan 10 (2 pens), Angella 7, Forestieri 7, Anya 5, Battocchio 4, Ranegie 4, Murray 3, Abdi 2, Faraoni 2, Pudil 2, Cassetti 1, Fabbrini 1, Merkel 1, Riera 1.
The Budweiser FA Cup (5): Deeney 1, Faraoni 1, Forestieri 1, McGugan 1, Murray 1.
Capital One Cup (7): Murray 2, Acuna 1, Angella 1, Battocchio 1, Faraoni 1, own goal 1.

Almunia M 37	Faraoni M 26 + 12	Anya I 29 + 6	Cassetti M 32 + 3	Angella G 39 + 1	Doyley L 23 + 1	McGugan L 31 + 3	Iriney S 12 + 3	Deeney T 44	Forestieri F 19 + 9	Abdi A 9 + 4	Battocchio C 21 + 14	Fabbrini D 8 + 13	Pudil D 29 + 8	Ekstrand J 31 + 2	Brown R — +1	Acuna J 3 + 6	Murray S 22 + 12	Belkalem E 5 + 3	Smith C 1	McEachran J 5 + 2	Nosworthy N 5	Thorne G 8	Bond J 9 + 1	Mensah B — +1	Bellerin H 6 + 2	Hall F 3 + 2	Merkel A 7 + 4	Tozser D 20	Diakite S 1 + 5	Park C 1 + 1	Hoban T 5 + 2	Ranegie M 8 + 2	Neill L — +1	O'Nien L — +1	Riera A 6 + 2	Jakubiak A 1	Doherty J — +1	Match No.
1	2	3^1	4	5	6	7^2	8	9	10^3	11	12	13	14																									1
1	8^2	5	4	2	3	6^2	9	10	11^1	7	14	13	12																									2
1	5	9		2	4	8	7^1	10	11^2	6		13		3^2	12	14																						3
1	14	5	4	3	2	8^1	7^2	10	13	6		11	9^3				12																					4
1	5	9	2	3		7	6^2	10	12	8^1		11^3		4			13	14																				5
1	6^3	12	2	3			5	9	10	11^2			8^1	7			13	14	4																			6
1	5		3	2		8	14	11	12	6^3		9	4				10^2	13		7^1																		7
1	9^3	5	4	3	2^1	7^2	8	11	10	13			14				6	12																				8
1	13	5		3	2	7	8^3	11	10		12	14	9^1	4			6^2																					9
1	5	9	4	3		7	8^2	11	14	6^1	12				10^1		2			13																		10
1	5	13		3	2	7	12	11	10^1			14	9^2	4			6			8^3																		11
1			5	2		8	6^2	11			10^1	9	4	13			12	3		7																		12
1	5			3	2	7		11	10			12	9	4^1			6			8																		13
1	14	5	13	3	2^1	7		10	11			12	9^2	4			6^3			8																		14
1	5		4	3	2^2	7^3	8^1	11	10	14			9				6	12		13																		15
1^1	5	2						10		7	13	9	4	11^2			8			3^3	6	12	14															16
	14	2				7		10	11			13	9^1	4			12	8^3		3^2	6	1		5														17
	2	4^2				7		11			8	12	13	5			10^1			3	9	1	6															18
	2^1	10	13					9^2	11			8^2		5	4		12			3	7	1	6	14														19
	2^3	10	5				14	11	13			8^1	12				7			3	9	1	6	4^2														20
1	13	5	3	2	7			11	14		12	10^1	9^3	4			6^2			8																		21
1	9^1	5	3	2	7^2	12	11	10				13		4			8			6^1			14															22
1		5	3	2	7			11				13	10^2	4			12	8^1		6		9																23
1	14		3	2^2	7			10	12			13	11	9	4		8^3						5^1	6^8														24
1	5	14	3^8		7^1	6^2	10		12	8	11^3	9	4				13						2															25
1	5	11^2	13	4	2			10	9^1	12^3	6	14	8	3		7									6^3	8	13	14										26
1	9	5	2					10	11^1			7^1			4		12			3					13	14	7											27
1	5^3	9	3	2				10	11^1			8^2	12	4			6										14	8^3	6									28
1	5		2	3	12			10	11			7^1	9	4^2			13								14		8^3	6										29
	5^2	13	2	3	4^1			10	11^3			14	9				7						1				8^8	6^8		12								30
1	13	5	3	2				10				7	9^2	4			12									8^1	6			11								31
1	2	6	4^2	3				11				14	12	5			8									7^3	9		10^1	13								32
1	12	5	4	3^2	2			10				7	9^3				6^1	13									14	8		11								33
	13	5	3	4	2			10	12			7^2	9										1				8^1	6		11^8								34
1	5	10	3	4	2^2	8^1		11				7	9^3													12	6			13	14							35
1	5	10	3	4		8^1		11				7	9	12			2^2									6	13											36
	10	5	3			13		11			12	9	4			7^1										8^3	6	14	2^2									37
1	14	5^1		3	2	8^2		10	13	7		9^1	4				6												11				12					38
1	13	5	2			8^2		10	12	7		9	4				6												11^3				14					39
1	5	10	2	3		12		11	6^3			13	4			8^1										14	7						9^2					40
1	5	11^2		3		7^3		10	12	6		13	4			14											8		2				9^1					41
1	5		4			7^3		10	6^1	12		13	3			14											8		2	11			9^2					42
		3	4		7^1			10	6	12		9	2										8				11						5					43
	14	13	3^8		2	7^7		10			6	9	4^1										1				8		12	11^3			5					44
	5^1	11		13	2^3			10	7			6^2	4										1				8	14	3	9^8			5					45
	13	5	3	4				10	7^2			6^3	9										1				8	12	2				11^1	14				46

The Budweiser FA Cup

Third Round	Bristol C	(a)	1-1
Replay	Bristol C	(h)	2-0
Fourth Round	Manchester C	(a)	2-4

Capital One Cup

First Round	Bristol R	(a)	3-1
Second Round	AFC Bournemouth	(h)	2-0
Third Round	Norwich C	(h)	2-3
(aet)			

WEST BROMWICH ALBION

FOUNDATION

There is a well known story that when employees of Salter's Spring Works in West Bromwich decided to form a football club, they had to send someone to the nearby Association Football stronghold of Wednesbury to purchase a football. A weekly subscription of 2d (less than 1p) was imposed and the name of the new club was West Bromwich Strollers.

The Hawthorns, West Bromwich, West Midlands B71 4LF.

Telephone: (0871) 271 1100.

Fax: (0871) 271 9851.

Ticket Office: (0121) 227 2227.

Website: www.wba.co.uk

Email: enquiries@wbafc.co.uk

Ground Capacity: 26,445.

Record Attendance: 64,815 v Arsenal, FA Cup 6th rd, 6 March 1937.

Pitch Measurements: 105m × 68m (114yd × 74yd)

Chairman: Jeremy Peace.

Chief Executive: Mark Jenkins.

Head Coach: Alan Irvine.

Assistant Head Coaches: Keith Downing, Rob Kelly.

Physio: Richie Rawlins.

Colours: Navy blue and white striped shirts, navy blue shorts with white trim, navy blue socks with white hoops.

Year Formed: 1878.

Turned Professional: 1885.

Previous Name: 1878, West Bromwich Strollers; 1881, West Bromwich Albion.

Club Nicknames: 'The Throstles', 'The Baggies', 'Albion'.

Grounds: 1878, Coopers Hill; 1879, Dartmouth Park; 1881, Bunns Field, Walsall Street; 1882, Four Acres (Dartmouth Cricket Club); 1885, Stoney Lane; 1900, The Hawthorns.

First Football League Game: 8 September 1888, Football League, v Stoke (a) W 2–0 – Roberts; Jack Horton, Green; Ezra Horton, Perry, Bayliss; Bassett, Woodhall (1), Hendry, Pearson, Wilson (1).

Record League Victory: 12–0 v Darwen, Division 1, 4 April 1892 – Reader; Jack Horton, McCulloch; Reynolds (2), Perry, Groves; Bassett (3), McLeod, Nicholls (1), Pearson (4), Geddes (1), (1 og).

Record Cup Victory: 10–1 v Chatham (away), FA Cup 3rd rd, 2 March 1889 – Roberts; Jack Horton, Green; Timmins (1), Charles Perry, Ezra Horton; Bassett (2), Walter Perry (1), Bayliss (2), Pearson, Wilson (3), (1 og).

HONOURS

Football League – Division 1: *Champions* 1919–20; *Runners-up* 1924–25, 1953–54, 2001–02, 2003–04. **FL C:** *Champions* 2007–08; *Runners-up* 2009–10. **Division 2:** *Champions* 1901–02, 1910–11; *Runners-up* 1930–31, 1948–49.

FA Cup: *Winners* 1888, 1892, 1931, 1954, 1968; *Runners-up* 1886, 1887, 1895, 1912, 1935.

Football League Cup: *Winners* 1966; *Runners-up* 1967, 1970.

European Competitions European Cup-Winners' Cup: 1968–69. **European Fairs Cup:** 1966–67. **UEFA Cup:** 1978–79, 1979–80, 1981–82.

sky SPORTS FACT FILE

West Bromwich Albion were the first team from England to tour China. In the summer of 1978 they played four games in mainland China and one in Hong Kong. The Baggies won all five games including a 2-0 victory over the China national team in Beijing in front of an attendance of 89,400.

Record Defeat: 3–10 v Stoke C, Division 1, 4 February 1937.

Most League Points (2 for a win): 60, Division 1, 1919–20.

Most League Points (3 for a win): 91, FL C, 2009–10.

Most League Goals: 105, Division 2, 1929–30.

Highest League Scorer in Season: William 'Ginger' Richardson, 39, Division 1, 1935–36.

Most League Goals in Total Aggregate: Tony Brown, 218, 1963–79.

Most League Goals in One Match: 6, Jimmy Cookson v Blackpool, Division 2, 17 September 1927.

Most Capped Player: Stuart Williams, 33 (43), Wales.

Most League Appearances: Tony Brown, 574, 1963–80.

Youngest League Player: Charlie Wilson, 16 years 73 days v Oldham Ath, 1 October 1921.

Record Transfer Fee Received: £8,000,000 from Aston Villa for Curtis Davies, July 2008.

Record Transfer Fee Paid: £10,000,000 to Dynamo Kiev for Brown Ideye, July 2014.

Football League Record: 1888 Founder Member of Football League; 1901–02 Division 2; 1902–04 Division 1; 1904–11 Division 2; 1911–27 Division 1; 1927–31 Division 2; 1931–38 Division 1; 1938–49 Division 2; 1949–73 Division 1; 1973–76 Division 2; 1976–86 Division 1; 1986–91 Division 2; 1991–92 Division 3; 1992–93 Division 2; 1993–2002 Division 1; 2002–03 FA Premier League; 2003–04 Division 1; 2004–06 FA Premier League; 2006–08 FL C; 2008–09 FA Premier League; 2009–10 FL C; 2010– FA Premier League.

LATEST SEQUENCES

Longest Sequence of League Wins: 11, 5.4.1930 – 8.9.1930.

Longest Sequence of League Defeats: 11, 28.10.1995 – 26.12.1995.

Longest Sequence of League Draws: 5, 30.8.1999 – 3.10.1999.

Longest Sequence of Unbeaten League Matches: 17, 7.9.1957 – 7.12.1957.

Longest Sequence Without a League Win: 15, 16.10.2004 – 16.1.2005.

Successive Scoring Runs: 36 from 26.4.1958.

Successive Non-scoring Runs: 4 from 1.3.2003.

MANAGERS

Louis Ford 1890–92
(Secretary-Manager)
Henry Jackson 1892–94
(Secretary-Manager)
Edward Stephenson 1894–95
(Secretary-Manager)
Clement Keys 1895–96
(Secretary-Manager)
Frank Heaven 1896–1902
(Secretary-Manager)
Fred Everiss 1902–48
Jack Smith 1948–52
Jesse Carver 1952
Vic Buckingham 1953–59
Gordon Clark 1959–61
Archie Macaulay 1961–63
Jimmy Hagan 1963–67
Alan Ashman 1967–71
Don Howe 1971–75
Johnny Giles 1975–77
Ronnie Allen 1977
Ron Atkinson 1978–81
Ronnie Allen 1981–82
Ron Wylie 1982–84
Johnny Giles 1984–85
Nobby Stiles 1985–86
Ron Saunders 1986–87
Ron Atkinson 1987–88
Brian Talbot 1988–91
Bobby Gould 1991–92
Ossie Ardiles 1992–93
Keith Burkinshaw 1993–94
Alan Buckley 1994–97
Ray Harford 1997
Denis Smith 1997–1999
Brian Little 1999–2000
Gary Megson 2000–04
Bryan Robson 2004–06
Tony Mowbray 2006–09
Roberto Di Matteo 2009–11
Roy Hodgson 2011–12
Steve Clarke 2012–13
Pepe Mel 2014
Alan Irvine June 2014–

TEN YEAR LEAGUE RECORD

		P	W	D	L	F	A	Pts	Pos
2004-05	PR Lge	38	6	16	16	36	61	34	17
2005-06	PR Lge	38	7	9	22	31	58	30	19
2006-07	FL C	46	22	10	14	81	55	76	4
2007-08	FL C	46	23	12	11	88	55	81	1
2008-09	PR Lge	38	8	8	22	36	67	32	20
2009-10	FL C	46	26	13	7	89	48	91	2
2010-11	PR Lge	38	12	11	15	56	71	47	11
2011-12	PR Lge	38	13	8	17	45	52	47	10
2012-13	PR Lge	38	14	7	17	53	57	49	8
2013-14	PR Lge	38	7	15	16	43	59	36	17

DID YOU KNOW

West Bromwich Albion scored five goals or more in three consecutive visits to Birmingham City's St Andrew's ground in the 1950s. They won 5-3 in December 1957, 6-0 in September 1958 and 7-1 in April 1960. Surprisingly all three home games with the Blues in these seasons were drawn.

WEST BROMWICH ALBION – FA PREMIERSHIP 2013–14 LEAGUE RECORD

Match No.	Date	Venue	Opponents	Result	H/T Score	Lg Pos.	Goalscorers	Attendance
1	Aug 17	H	Southampton	L 0-1	0-0	15		25,927
2	24	A	Everton	D 0-0	0-0	16		36,410
3	Sept 1	H	Swansea C	L 0-2	0-1	20		23,395
4	14	A	Fulham	D 1-1	0-1	19	McAuley [90]	25,560
5	21	H	Sunderland	W 3-0	1-0	13	Sessegnon [20], Ridgewell [76], Amalfitano [90]	24,595
6	28	A	Manchester U	W 2-1	0-0	10	Amalfitano [54], Berahino [67]	75,042
7	Oct 6	H	Arsenal	D 1-1	1-0	12	Yacob [42]	24,839
8	19	A	Stoke C	D 0-0	0-0	13		25,904
9	26	A	Liverpool	L 1-4	0-2	12	Morrison (pen) [66]	44,747
10	Nov 2	H	Crystal Palace	W 2-0	1-0	11	Berahino [44], McAuley [83]	26,397
11	9	A	Chelsea	D 2-2	0-1	9	Long [60], Sessegnon [68]	41,623
12	25	H	Aston Villa	D 2-2	2-0	11	Long 2 [3, 11]	24,902
13	30	A	Newcastle U	L 1-2	0-1	12	Brunt [53]	49,298
14	Dec 4	H	Manchester C	L 2-3	0-2	13	Pantilimon (og) [85], Anichebe [90]	22,943
15	7	H	Norwich C	L 0-2	0-1	15		23,675
16	14	A	Cardiff C	L 0-1	0-0	16		26,632
17	21	H	Hull C	D 1-1	0-1	16	Vydra [86]	24,753
18	26	A	Tottenham H	D 1-1	1-1	15	Olsson [38]	35,545
19	28	A	West Ham U	D 3-3	2-1	16	Anelka 2 [40, 45], Berahino [69]	34,946
20	Jan 1	H	Newcastle U	W 1-0	0-0	14	Berahino (pen) [87]	26,430
21	11	A	Southampton	L 0-1	0-1	14		28,610
22	20	H	Everton	D 1-1	0-1	13	Lugano [75]	24,184
23	29	A	Aston Villa	L 3-4	3-3	15	Brunt [4], Delph (og) [9], Mulumbu [43]	36,083
24	Feb 2	H	Liverpool	D 1-1	0-1	16	Anichebe [67]	26,132
25	8	A	Crystal Palace	L 1-3	0-2	18	Thievy [46]	24,501
26	11	H	Chelsea	D 1-1	0-1	17	Anichebe [87]	24,327
27	22	H	Fulham	D 1-1	0-1	16	Vydra [86]	25,782
28	Mar 8	H	Manchester U	L 0-3	0-1	17		26,184
29	15	A	Swansea C	W 2-1	0-1	16	Sessegnon [52], Mulumbu [85]	20,703
30	22	A	Hull C	L 0-2	0-2	16		23,486
31	29	H	Cardiff C	D 3-3	2-1	17	Amalfitano [2], Dorrans [9], Thievy [90]	25,661
32	Apr 5	A	Norwich C	W 1-0	1-0	16	Amalfitano [16]	26,859
33	12	H	Tottenham H	D 3-3	3-1	16	Vydra [1], Brunt [4], Sessegnon [31]	25,398
34	21	A	Manchester C	L 1-3	1-3	16	Dorrans [16]	46,564
35	26	H	West Ham U	W 1-0	1-0	15	Berahino [11]	26,541
36	May 4	A	Arsenal	L 0-1	0-1	16		60,021
37	7	A	Sunderland	L 0-2	0-2	17		45,181
38	11	H	Stoke C	L 1-2	0-1	17	Sessegnon [56]	26,613

Final League Position: 17

GOALSCORERS

League (43): Berahino 5 (1 pen), Sessegnon 5, Amalfitano 4, Anichebe 3, Brunt 3, Long 3, Vydra 3, Anelka 2, Dorrans 2, McAuley 2, Mulumbu 2, Thievy 2, Lugano 1, Morrison 1 (1 pen), Olsson 1, Ridgewell 1, Yacob 1, own goals 2.
The Budweiser FA Cup (0).
Capital One Cup (4): Berahino 4 (1 pen).

Foster B 24	Jones B 21	McAuley G 32	Olsson J 32	Ridgewell L 33	Morrison J 23+9	Mulumbu Y 33+4	Yacob C 22+5	Dorrans G 12+2	Anelka N 11+1	Long S 11+4	Vydra M 7+16	Rosenberg M 1+3	Daniels L —+1	Brunt C 25+3	Myhill B 14	Sinclair S 4+4	Berahino S 11+21	Amalfitano M 26+2	Anichebe V 11+13	Sessegnon S 23+3	Lugano D 7+2	Reid S 16	Popov G 1+1	Gera Z 5+9	Dawson C 10+2	Thievy K 3+3	O'Neil L —+3	Match No.
1	2	3	4	5	6	7	8	9	10^1	11^2	12	13																1
1^3	2	3	4	5	6	7	8	9		10^2	12	11^1	13	14														2
	2	3	4	5	6^3	8	7^1	12	10	11				13	1		9^2	14										3
	2	3	4	5	12	7	8^9		10					9	1		13	14	6^2	11^1								4
	2	3	4	5		7	6	13		11^2					1		10^3	14	8	12	9^1							5
	2	3	4	5			7	6					14		1		10^2	12	8	11^2	13							6
	2	3	4	5	13	7	6			11^2	12			14	1		10	8^1	9^2									7
	2	3	4	5	12	7	6	13		14					1		10^1	8^2	11^2	9								8
	2	3	4	5	12	6	7^2			11^1	14			13	1		8^1	10	9									9
	2^2	3	4	5	6^3	7	13			11	14			10	1		12	8	9^1									10
		3	4	5	13	6	7			11^3				10	1		8^2	12	9^1					2	14			11
		3	4		12	6	7			11				10	1		8	13	9^1					2	5^2			12
	2	3	4	5	6	7				11				10^1	1		12	8^3	13	9^2					14			13
		3	4	5	6^3		7			11^1	14			9	1		10	8^2	13					2	12			14
	2	3		5^2		7	6				12		14	10	1		13	8^1	11^3	9	4							15
	2	3	4	5		6	7^1			11^3	14			10	1		13	8^2	9									16
1	2	3	4	5^1	9	7				11	13			6			10^3	12		8^2					14			17
1			4	5	9	12	6			11^1							14	10^2		13	3	7		8^2	2			18
1	5	2	3	9	6^1	7	13		11					8			10^2	12		14	4^3							19
1	2^9	3	4	5		6	7		11^1					10			12	8	9^2					14				20
1	3^2	4	5		8	7				10^2	11	14		9			12	6^1					2	13				21
1		4	5	7	13	8				11^2				10^3			9	14		12	3	2		6^1				22
1		4	5	6	8	7				11^3				14			9	13	12	10^2	3	2^1						23
1	2	3	4^2	5		6	7	14						11^1			10	8^3	13	12			9					24
1	2	3		5^2	9	7	6^1							10			12	14	11				8^2	4	13			25
1		3		5	6	12	7^3							14			8	11	9^1	13		2		4	10^2			26
1	2^2	3	4	5	7	8								14			9	10^2	6	12				13		11^1		27
1		3	4	5	12	7	6^3										14	8	11	13		2^1		9				28
1		3	4	6	9	8					7^1						11^3	10^2			2	12		5	13	14		29
1		3^1		5	7	6				8				14		13	11^2	9			2			4	10^3			30
1			5		7	8					9^2			11^2			12	6^1	10		2			14	4	13		31
1		3	4	5	7	8					9^1			11^2			12	6	10		2			13^3		14		32
1		3	4^2	5		7	12	8			11^3			9			13	6	10^1		2			14				33
1	2		4	5	14	6^2		10			11^{12}			7			13	8	12	9^1				3				34
1	5		4		12	6	14	7						10			11^3	8	13	9^2		2^1		3				35
1		4		8	7^2		9							13			11	6^1	12	10	3				2			36
1	3			7	12	6^1	10							14			5	8^2	11	9	4	2^3			13			37
1		3	4		9	6^1		7						14			5	11	8^2	12	10				2^3	13		38

The Budweiser FA Cup
Third Round   Crystal Palace   (h)   0-2

Capital One Cup
Second Round   Newport Co   (h)   3-0
Third Round   Arsenal   (h)   1-1
(aet; lost 3-4 on penalties)

WEST HAM UNITED

The Boleyn Ground, Upton Park, Green Street, London E13 9AZ.

Telephone: (0871) 222 2700.

Fax: (020) 8548 2758.

Ticket Office: (0871) 529 1966.

Website: www.whufc.com

Email: customerservices@westhamunited.co.uk

Ground Capacity: 35,016.

Record Attendance: 42,322 v Tottenham H, Division 1, 17 October 1970.

Pitch Measurements: 100.58m × 66.84m (109yd × 73yd)

Joint Chairmen: David Sullivan and David Gold.

Vice-chairman: Karren Brady.

Manager: Sam Allardyce.

Assistant Manager: Neil McDonald.

Head of Sports Medicine: Dominic Rogan.

Colours: Claret shirts with sky blue trim, white shorts with claret and sky blue trim, white socks with claret and sky blue trim.

Year Formed: 1895.

Turned Professional: 1900.

Previous Name: 1895, Thames Iron Works FC; 1900, West Ham United.

Club Nicknames: 'The Hammers', 'The Irons'.

Grounds: 1895, Memorial Recreation Ground, Canning Town; 1904, Boleyn Ground.

First Football League Game: 30 August 1919, Division 2, v Lincoln C (h) D 1–1 – Hufton; Cope, Lee; Lane, Fenwick, McCrae; David Smith, Moyes (1), Puddefoot, Morris, Bradshaw.

Record League Victory: 8–0 v Rotherham U, Division 2, 8 March 1958 – Gregory; Bond, Wright; Malcolm, Brown, Lansdowne; Grice, Smith (2), Keeble (2), Dick (4), Musgrove. 8–0 v Sunderland, Division 1, 19 October 1968 – Ferguson; Bonds, Charles; Peters, Stephenson, Moore (1); Redknapp, Boyce, Brooking (1), Hurst (6), Sissons.

HONOURS

Football League – Division 1:
Runners-up 1992–93
Division 2: *Champions* 1957–58, 1980–81; *Runners-up* 1922–23, 1990–91.
FA Cup: *Winners* 1964, 1975, 1980; *Runners-up* 1923, 2006.
Football League Cup:
Runners-up 1966, 1981.
European Competitions
European Cup-Winners' Cup:
1964–65 (*winners*), 1965–66, 1975–76 (*runners-up*), 1980–81.
UEFA Cup: 1999–2000; 2006–07.
Intertoto Cup: 1999 (*winners*).

sky SPORTS FACT FILE

West Ham United's Hammer of the Year is one of the oldest player-of-the-year awards in English football. The first winner was Andy Malcolm back in 1957–58. Trevor Brooking has won the most awards – five (1971–72, 1975–76, 1976–77, 1977–78 and 1983–84), while Bobby Moore, Billy Bonds and Julian Dicks won the award four times.

Record Cup Victory: 10–0 v Bury, League Cup 2nd rd (2nd leg), 25 October 1983 – Parkes; Stewart (1), Walford, Bonds (Orr), Martin (1), Devonshire (2), Allen, Cottee (4), Swindlehurst, Brooking (2), Pike.

Record Defeat: 2–8 v Blackburn R, Division 1, 26 December 1963.

Most League Points (2 for a win): 66, Division 2, 1980–81.

Most League Points (3 for a win): 88, Division 1, 1992–93.

Most League Goals: 101, Division 2, 1957–58.

Highest League Scorer in Season: Vic Watson, 42, Division 1, 1929–30.

Most League Goals in Total Aggregate: Vic Watson, 298, 1920–35.

Most League Goals in One Match: 6, Vic Watson v Leeds U, Division 1, 9 February 1929; 6, Geoff Hurst v Sunderland, Division 1, 19 October 1968.

Most Capped Player: Bobby Moore, 108, England.

Most League Appearances: Billy Bonds, 663, 1967–88.

Youngest League Player: Billy Williams, 16 years 221 days v Blackpool, 6 May 1922.

Record Transfer Fee Received: £18,000,000 from Leeds U for Rio Ferdinand, November 2000.

Record Transfer Fee Paid: £15,000,000 to Liverpool for Andy Carroll, July 2013.

Football League Record: 1919 Elected to Division 2; 1923–32 Division 1; 1932–58 Division 2; 1958–78 Division 1; 1978–81 Division 2; 1981–89 Division 1; 1989–91 Division 2; 1991–93 Division 1; 1993–2003 FA Premier League; 2003–04 Division 1; 2004–05 FL C; 2005–11 FA Premier League; 2011–12 FL C; 2012– FA Premier League.

MANAGERS

Syd King 1902–32
Charlie Paynter 1932–50
Ted Fenton 1950–61
Ron Greenwood 1961–74
  (continued as General Manager to 1977)
John Lyall 1974–89
Lou Macari 1989–90
Billy Bonds 1990–94
Harry Redknapp 1994–2001
Glenn Roeder 2001–03
Alan Pardew 2003–06
Alan Curbishley 2006–08
Gianfranco Zola 2008–10
Avram Grant 2010–11
Sam Allardyce June 2011–

LATEST SEQUENCES

Longest Sequence of League Wins: 9, 19.10.1985 – 14.12.1985.

Longest Sequence of League Defeats: 9, 28.3.1932 – 29.8.1932.

Longest Sequence of League Draws: 5, 7.3.2012 – 24.3.2012.

Longest Sequence of Unbeaten League Matches: 27, 27.12.80 – 10.10.81.

Longest Sequence Without a League Win: 17, 31.1.1976 – 21.8.1976.

Successive Scoring Runs: 27 from 5.10.1957.

Successive Non-scoring Runs: 5 from 17.9.2006.

TEN YEAR LEAGUE RECORD

		P	W	D	L	F	A	Pts	Pos
2004-05	FL C	46	21	10	15	66	56	73	6
2005-06	PR Lge	38	16	7	15	52	55	55	9
2006-07	PR Lge	38	12	5	21	35	59	41	15
2007-08	PR Lge	38	13	10	15	42	50	49	10
2008-09	PR Lge	38	14	9	15	42	45	51	9
2009-10	PR Lge	38	8	11	19	47	66	35	17
2010-11	PR Lge	38	7	12	19	43	70	33	20
2011-12	FL C	46	24	14	8	81	48	86	3
2012-13	PR Lge	38	12	10	16	45	53	46	10
2013-14	PR Lge	38	11	7	20	40	51	40	13

DID YOU KNOW ?

Syd Puddefoot led the scoring charts for West Ham United for their first three seasons in the Football League. In February 1922 he was transferred to Falkirk, where he had previously played as a guest in the 1918–19 season. The transfer was announced as a new world record fee of £5,000.

WEST HAM UNITED – FA PREMIERSHIP 2013–14 LEAGUE RECORD

Match No.	Date	Venue	Opponents	Result	H/T Score	Lg Pos.	Goalscorers	Attendance
1	Aug 17	H	Cardiff C	W 2-0	1-0	3	Cole, J [13], Nolan [76]	34,977
2	24	A	Newcastle U	D 0-0	0-0	3		49,622
3	31	H	Stoke C	L 0-1	0-0	7		34,946
4	Sept 15	A	Southampton	D 0-0	0-0	10		28,794
5	21	H	Everton	L 2-3	1-0	13	Morrison [31], Noble (pen) [76]	34,952
6	28	A	Hull C	L 0-1	0-1	16		24,291
7	Oct 6	A	Tottenham H	W 3-0	0-0	13	Reid [66], Vaz Te [72], Morrison [79]	35,977
8	19	H	Manchester C	L 1-3	0-1	14	Vaz Te [58]	34,507
9	27	A	Swansea C	D 0-0	0-0	15		20,455
10	Nov 2	H	Aston Villa	D 0-0	0-0	14		34,977
11	9	A	Norwich C	L 1-3	1-0	16	Morrison [32]	26,824
12	23	H	Chelsea	L 0-3	0-2	17		34,977
13	30	H	Fulham	W 3-0	0-0	15	Diame [47], Cole, C [82], Cole, J [88]	34,946
14	Dec 3	A	Crystal Palace	L 0-1	0-1	25		23,891
15	7	A	Liverpool	L 1-4	0-1	17	Skrtel (og) [66]	44,781
16	14	H	Sunderland	D 0-0	0-0	17		31,843
17	21	A	Manchester U	L 1-3	0-2	17	Cole, C [81]	75,350
18	26	H	Arsenal	L 1-3	0-0	19	Cole, C [46]	34,977
19	28	H	WBA	D 3-3	1-2	19	Cole, J [4], Maiga [65], Nolan [67]	34,946
20	Jan 1	A	Fulham	L 1-2	1-1	19	Diame [7]	25,335
21	11	A	Cardiff C	W 2-0	1-0	17	Cole, C [42], Noble [90]	27,750
22	18	H	Newcastle U	L 1-3	1-2	18	Cole, C [45]	33,343
23	29	A	Chelsea	D 0-0	0-0	18		41,376
24	Feb 1	H	Swansea C	W 2-0	2-0	18	Nolan 2 [26, 45]	31,848
25	8	A	Aston Villa	W 2-0	0-0	15	Nolan 2 [46, 48]	36,261
26	11	A	Norwich C	W 2-0	0-0	10	Collins [84], Diame [90]	31,153
27	22	H	Southampton	W 3-1	2-1	10	Jarvis [20], Cole, C [23], Nolan [71]	33,148
28	Mar 1	A	Everton	L 0-1	0-0	10		38,286
29	15	A	Stoke C	L 1-3	1-1	12	Carroll [5]	27,015
30	22	H	Manchester U	L 0-2	0-2	14		34,237
31	26	H	Hull C	W 2-1	1-0	11	Noble (pen) [26], Chester (og) [54]	31,033
32	31	A	Sunderland	W 2-1	1-0	11	Carroll [9], Diame [50]	37,396
33	Apr 6	H	Liverpool	L 1-2	1-1	11	Demel [45]	34,977
34	15	A	Arsenal	L 1-3	1-1	11	Jarvis [40]	59,977
35	19	H	Crystal Palace	L 0-1	0-0	12		34,977
36	26	A	WBA	L 0-1	0-1	14		26,541
37	May 3	H	Tottenham H	W 2-0	2-0	12	Kane (og) [27], Downing [44]	34,977
38	11	A	Manchester C	L 0-2	0-1	13		47,300

Final League Position: 13

GOALSCORERS

League (40): Nolan 7, Cole, C 6, Diame 4, Cole, J 3, Morrison 3, Noble 3 (2 pens), Carroll 2, Jarvis 2, Vaz Te 2, Collins 1, Demel 1, Downing 1, Maiga 1, Reid 1, own goals 3.
The Budweiser FA Cup (0).
Capital One Cup (9): Jarvis 2, Morrison 2, Vaz Te 2, Collison 1 (1 pen), Taylor 1 (1 pen), Maiga 1.

Jaaskelainen J 18	Demel G 30 + 2	Collins J 22 + 2	Reid W 18 + 4	O'Brien J 13 + 4	Noble M 38	Diame M 29 + 6	Cole J 6 + 14	Nolan K 33	Jarvis M 23 + 9	Maiga M 11 + 3	Downing S 29 + 3	Diarra A 1 + 2	Vaz Te R 3 + 5	Morrison R 12 + 4	Collison J 6 + 4	Lee E — + 1	Rat R 11 + 4	Taylor M 16 + 4	Petric M — + 3	Tomkins J 31	Cole C 9 + 17	McCartney G 20 + 2	Adrian 20	Johnson R 2 + 2	Carroll A 12 + 3	Nocerino A 2 + 8	Borriello M — + 2	Armero P 3 + 2	Match No.
1	2	3	4	5	6	7[1]	8[2]	9	10[1]	11	12	13	14																1
1	2	3	4	5	7	6[2]	12	8	11	10	9[1]			13															2
1	2	3	4	5	6[1]	7[7]		9	10	11	8[3]	12	13	14															3
1	2[1]	3	4	5	7	8		9	10	11[3]		13		6[2]	12	14													4
1		3	4	2	7	8		9[2]	10[1]	11[3]		13		6			5	14	12										5
1			4	2	7	6[1]		9	10[2]	11[3]	14		13	8			5	12	3										6
1	2	12	4	14	6[1]	8[3]	13	9	10	11[2]			7				5			3									7
1	2[3]		4	12	6	11		7[2]	13		8		9[1]	10			5		14	3									8
1	2		4		7	11[2]	14	6	12		8		9[1]	10[3]			5			3	13								9
1	2		4		7	14	12	10	9[2]		8		11	6[3]			5[1]			3	13								10
1	2	3			7[3]	12	10[2]	11	14		8		9	6[1]			5			4	13								11
1	2	3		5	7	12		8[2]	11[1]	14	13	10		9	6[3]					4									12
1	2	3			7	6	12	9[2]	10[3]	11[1]	8			13						4	14	5							13
1		3		2	6	10	12	7[2]		13	8			9			5[1]			4	11[3]	14							14
1	2	3	13	6	7	12		9[4]	10[3]	11	8[1]							14		4[2]		5							15
1	2[3]	3	13	7	9	8[1]		10[2]	11		6	12								4	14	5							16
	2	3[3]		6	8			10[2]	11					9	12		14	7[1]		4	13	5	1						17
		4			7	9[2]	14	10[1]			8				12		6[3]	5	2		11		1		3	13			18
1	12			2	6	7	8[2]	9	10	13							14	5		3[1]	11[3]	4							19
1	2			3	7[1]	6[2]		9[4]			11[2]	13	4		8		12	10			14	5							20
	2[3]			6				10			8	14			9[2]		5	7		4[1]	11[1]	12	1	3	13				21
		4			7	9[2]	14	10[1]			8				12		6[3]	5	2		11		1	3	13				22
	2	3		5	6	8[3]		9[2]	12		10							7		4	13		1		11[1]	14			23
	2	3	13		6			9[1]	8[3]		10							7[4]		4	12	5	1		11	14			24
	2	3	14		6			9[2]	8[1]		10							7		4	11[3]	5	1		13	12			25
	2	3			6	13		9	8[3]		10							7[2]		4	11[1]	5	1		14	12			26
	2	3	13		6	12		9[2]	8[1]		10							7		4	11	5	1						27
	2[3]	3	14		7	13		10	6[2]		9							8		4	11[1]	5	1		12				28
	2	3			6	8	12	9			10[1]							4		13	5	1	11[3]	7[2]		14			29
	2	3			7	8[2]		9[3]	12		10						6[1]	4		13	5	1	11		14				30
	2	3[2]			7	10[1]	13	9			8						6	4			5	1	12	11					31
	2		4		6	10[3]		9[2]			8						7	3			5[1]	1	13	11	14		12		32
	2		4		6	8[3]		9[1]	13		10						7[2]	3	14		1		11	12		5			33
	2		4		6	8	13		11[2]		9[3]		12					3	14		1		10[1]	7		5			34
		4			7	8	13	6[3]	11[2]		9[1]							3	12	2	1		10	14		5			35
	2	12		4	7	6	13	9	10[3]		8[1]							3	14		5	1	11						36
	2		4		6	10		9[2]	13		8						7	3			5	1	12	11[1]					37
		4	2		6	10[1]	14	9[3]	12		8						7	3			5	1	11[2]						38

The Budweiser FA Cup

Third Round	Nottingham F	(a)	0-5

Capital One Cup

Second Round	Cheltenham T	(h)	2-1
Third Round	Cardiff C	(h)	3-2
Fourth Round	Burnley	(a)	2-0
Quarter-Finals	Tottenham H	(a)	2-1
Semi-Finals 1st leg	Manchester C	(a)	0-6
Semi-Finals 2nd leg	Manchester C	(h)	0-3

WIGAN ATHLETIC

FOUNDATION

Following the demise of Wigan Borough and their resignation from the Football League in 1931, a public meeting was called in Wigan at the Queen's Hall in May 1932 at which a new club, Wigan Athletic, was founded in the hope of carrying on in the Football League. With this in mind, they bought Springfield Park for £2,250, but failed to gain admission to the Football League until 46 years later.

The DW Stadium, Loire Drive, Wigan, Lancashire WN5 0UZ.

Telephone: (01942) 774 000.

Fax: (01942) 770 477.

Ticket Office: (0871) 663 3552.

Website: www.wiganlatics.co.uk

Email: feedback@wiganathletic.com

Ground Capacity: 25,133.

Record Attendance: 27,526 v Hereford U, 12 December 1953 (at Springfield Park); 25,133 v Manchester U, FA Premier League, 11 May 2008 (at DW Stadium).

Pitch Measurements: 103.4m × 68m (113yd × 74.5yd)

Chairman: David Whelan.

Chief Executive: Jonathan Jackson.

Manager: Uwe Rosler.

First Team Coach: Graham Barrow.

Physio: Andy Mitchell.

Colours: Blue and white striped shirts with blue sleeves, blue shorts, blue socks with white trim.

Year Formed: 1932.

Turned Professional: 1932.

Club Nickname: 'The Latics'.

Grounds: 1932, Springfield Park; 1999, JJB Stadium (renamed the DW Stadium in 2009).

First Football League Game: 19 August 1978, Division 4, v Hereford U (a) D 0–0 – Brown; Hinnigan, Gore, Gillibrand, Ward, Davids, Corrigan, Purdie, Houghton, Wilkie, Wright.

Record League Victory: 7–1 v Scarborough, Division 3, 11 March 1997 – Lee Butler; John Butler, Sharp (Morgan), Greenall, McGibbon (Biggins (1)), Martinez (1), Diaz (2), Jones (Lancashire (1)), Lowe (2), Rogers, Kilford.

Record Cup Victory: 6–0 v Carlisle U (a), FA Cup 1st rd, 24 November 1934 – Caunce; Robinson, Talbot; Paterson, Watson, Tufnell; Armes (2), Robson (1), Roberts (2), Felton, Scott (1).

Record Defeat: 1–9 v Tottenham H, FA Premier League, 22 November 2009.

HONOURS

Football League – FL C:
Runners-up 2004–05;
Division 2: *Champions* 2002–03;
Division 3: *Champions* 1996–97.

FA Cup: *Winners* 2013.

Football League Cup:
Runners-up 2006.

Freight Rover Trophy: *Winners* 1985.

Auto Windscreens Shield:
Winners 1999.

European Competitions
Europa League: 2013–14.

sky SPORTS FACT FILE

Wigan Athletic played their first competitive game on 27 August 1932. The match was a Cheshire County League fixture against Port Vale Reserves. Over 5,000 turned out at Springfield Park, but the Latics went down to a 2-0 defeat, both goals coming in the second half.

Most League Points (2 for a win): 55, Division 4, 1978–79 and 1979–80.

Most League Points (3 for a win): 100, Division 2, 2002–03.

Most League Goals: 84, Division 3, 1996–97.

Highest League Scorer in Season: Graeme Jones, 31, Division 3, 1996–97.

Most League Goals in Total Aggregate: Andy Liddell, 70, 1998–2004.

Most League Goals in One Match: Not more than three goals by one player.

Most Capped Players: Kevin Kilbane, 22 (110), Republic of Ireland; Henri Camara, 22 (99), Senegal.

Most League Appearances: Kevin Langley, 317, 1981–86, 1990–94.

Youngest League Player: Steve Nugent, 16 years 132 days v Leyton Orient, 16 September 1989.

Record Transfer Fee Received: £15,250,000 from Manchester U for Antonio Valencia, June 2009.

Record Transfer Fee Paid: £6,500,000 to Estudiantes for Mauro Boselli, August 2010.

Football League Record: 1978 Elected to Division 4; 1982–92 Division 3; 1992–93 Division 2; 1993–97 Division 3; 1997–2003 Division 2; 2003–04 Division 1; 2004–05 FL C; 2005–13 FA Premier League; 2013– FL C.

LATEST SEQUENCES

Longest Sequence of League Wins: 11, 2.11.2002 – 18.1.2003.

Longest Sequence of League Defeats: 8, 10.9.2011 – 6.11.2011.

Longest Sequence of League Draws: 6, 11.12.2001 – 5.1.2002.

Longest Sequence of Unbeaten League Matches: 25, 8.5.1999 – 3.1.2000.

Longest Sequence Without a League Win: 14, 9.5.1989 – 17.10.1989.

Successive Scoring Runs: 24 from 27.4.1996.

Successive Non-scoring Runs: 4 from 17.2.2001.

MANAGERS

Charlie Spencer 1932–37
Jimmy Milne 1946–47
Bob Pryde 1949–52
Ted Goodier 1952–54
Walter Crook 1954–55
Ron Suart 1955–56
Billy Cooke 1956
Sam Barkas 1957
Trevor Hitchen 1957–58
Malcolm Barrass 1958–59
Jimmy Shirley 1959
Pat Murphy 1959–60
Allenby Chilton 1960
Johnny Ball 1961–63
Allan Brown 1963–66
Alf Craig 1966–67
Harry Leyland 1967–68
Alan Saunders 1968
Ian McNeill 1968–70
Gordon Milne 1970–72
Les Rigby 1972–74
Brian Tiler 1974–76
Ian McNeill 1976–81
Larry Lloyd 1981–83
Harry McNally 1983–85
Bryan Hamilton 1985–86
Ray Mathias 1986–89
Bryan Hamilton 1989–93
Dave Philpotts 1993
Kenny Swain 1993–94
Graham Barrow 1994–95
John Deehan 1995–98
Ray Mathias 1998–99
John Benson 1999–2000
Bruce Rioch 2000–01
Steve Bruce 2001
Paul Jewell 2001–07
Chris Hutchings 2007
Steve Bruce 2007–09
Roberto Martinez 2009–13
Owen Coyle 2013
Uwe Rosler December 2013–

TEN YEAR LEAGUE RECORD

		P	W	D	L	F	A	Pts	Pos
2004-05	FL C	46	25	12	9	79	35	87	2
2005-06	PR Lge	38	15	6	17	45	52	51	10
2006-07	PR Lge	38	10	8	20	37	59	38	17
2007-08	PR Lge	38	10	10	18	34	51	40	14
2008-09	PR Lge	38	12	9	17	34	45	45	11
2009-10	PR Lge	38	9	9	20	37	79	36	16
2010-11	PR Lge	38	9	15	14	40	61	42	16
2011-12	PR Lge	38	11	10	17	42	62	43	15
2012-13	PR Lge	38	9	9	20	47	73	36	18
2013-14	FL C	46	21	10	15	61	48	73	5

DID YOU KNOW ?

In August 1950 Wigan Athletic signed 23-year-old Jack Casey from Oldham Rugby League club. Casey, who played soccer as a centre forward and rugby as a three-quarter back, had also previously played for Wigan RL club.

WIGAN ATHLETIC – FL CHAMPIONSHIP 2013–14 LEAGUE RECORD

Match No.	Date	Venue	Opponents	Result	H/T Score	Lg Pos.	Goalscorers	Attendance
1	Aug 3	A	Barnsley	W 4-0	1-0	1	Watson [37], Holt [55], Barnett [80], Maloney [88]	13,096
2	17	A	Bournemouth	L 0-1	0-1	13		9097
3	20	H	Doncaster R	D 2-2	0-2	10	Maloney [57], Barnett [89]	14,304
4	25	H	Middlesbrough	D 2-2	1-1	12	Holt (pen) [17], Gomez [85]	14,333
5	31	H	Nottingham F	W 2-1	2-1	8	Maloney (pen) [14], Gomez [35]	16,270
6	Sept 14	A	Leicester C	L 0-2	0-1	12		21,810
7	22	H	Ipswich T	W 2-0	1-0	11	Shotton [12], Powell [90]	13,747
8	28	A	Watford	L 0-1	0-0	13		14,999
9	Oct 6	H	Blackburn R	W 2-1	0-1	12	Spurr (og) [69], Boyce [90]	16,996
10	19	A	Blackpool	L 0-1	0-1	12		15,721
11	27	A	Charlton Ath	D 0-0	0-0	14		23,600
12	30	H	QPR	D 0-0	0-0	13		13,143
13	Nov 2	H	Huddersfield T	W 2-1	1-1	10	Barnett [21], Powell [49]	16,112
14	10	A	Yeovil T	W 1-0	0-0	10	Fortune [78]	6149
15	23	H	Brighton & HA	L 0-1	0-0	11		14,057
16	Dec 1	H	Derby Co	L 1-3	0-3	14	Powell [50]	15,097
17	4	A	Leeds U	L 0-2	0-1	14		25,888
18	7	A	Millwall	L 1-2	0-1	14	McArthur [84]	9519
19	15	H	Bolton W	W 3-2	2-0	14	Watson (pen) [11], Powell [24], McManaman [68]	19,226
20	21	A	Reading	W 2-1	2-0	12	McCann [10], Powell [12]	18,336
21	26	H	Birmingham C	D 0-0	0-0	13		14,996
22	29	H	Burnley	D 0-0	0-0	14		17,712
23	Jan 1	A	Derby Co	W 1-0	0-0	11	Beausejour [69]	26,740
24	11	H	Bournemouth	W 3-0	1-0	10	Fortune [5], Ward (og) [57], Gomez [90]	12,709
25	18	A	Doncaster R	L 0-3	0-1	11		8331
26	28	A	Middlesbrough	D 0-0	0-0	11		13,258
27	Feb 1	H	Charlton Ath	W 2-1	0-1	10	Fortune [88], Gomez [90]	14,341
28	8	A	Huddersfield T	L 0-1	0-0	11		15,576
29	11	A	Sheffield W	W 3-0	2-0	9	Maynard 2 [31, 38], Fortune [90]	25,279
30	18	H	Barnsley	W 2-0	2-0	7	Maynard [35], Waghorn [44]	14,121
31	22	A	Brighton & HA	W 2-1	1-0	7	McArthur [21], McCann [50]	27,490
32	Mar 1	A	Nottingham F	W 4-1	1-0	6	Waghorn [36], Boyce [66], McArthur [71], Gomez [90]	23,114
33	12	H	Sheffield W	W 1-0	0-0	7	Gomez (pen) [88]	15,039
34	15	A	Ipswich T	W 3-1	2-1	5	McClean 2 [22, 77], Barnett [42]	16,047
35	18	H	Yeovil T	D 3-3	0-0	5	Powell [56], McArthur [86], Webster (og) [88]	12,970
36	22	H	Watford	W 2-1	1-1	5	Beausejour [40], Waghorn [57]	14,556
37	25	A	QPR	L 0-1	0-1	5		14,649
38	29	A	Bolton W	D 1-1	0-1	5	Powell [88]	18,853
39	Apr 1	H	Leicester C	D 2-2	1-1	5	Ramis [37], Kiernan [62]	15,025
40	5	H	Leeds U	W 1-0	1-0	5	Waghorn [33]	16,443
41	8	H	Millwall	L 0-1	0-1	5		14,124
42	18	H	Reading	W 3-0	2-0	5	Gomez [30], Waghorn [42], McManaman [51]	14,609
43	21	A	Burnley	L 0-2	0-2	5		19,125
44	26	H	Blackpool	L 0-2	0-0	6		19,137
45	29	A	Birmingham C	W 1-0	1-0	5	McManaman [3]	20,427
46	May 3	A	Blackburn R	L 3-4	1-3	5	Ramis [17], McClean [59], Maynard [87]	16,996

Final League Position: 5

GOALSCORERS

League (61): Gomez 7 (1 pen), Powell 7, Waghorn 5, Barnett 4, Fortune 4, Maynard 4, McArthur 4, Maloney 3 (1 pen), McClean 3, McManaman 3, Beausejour 2, Boyce 2, Holt 2 (1 pen), McCann 2, Ramis 2, Watson 2 (1 pen), Kiernan 1, Shotton 1, own goals 3.
The Budweiser FA Cup (13): Gomez 3 (2 pens), Powell 2, Watson 2, Espinoza 1, Fortune 1, McCann 1, McClean 1, McManaman 1, Perch 1.
Capital One Cup (0). Community Shield (0). Championship Play-Offs (1): Perch 1.
UEFA Europa League (6): Powell 3, Gomez 1 (1 pen), Barnett 1, Watson 1.

Carson S 16	Boyce E 39+3	Crainey S 14+6	Watson B 25	Barnett J 39+2	Perch J 38+2	Beausejour J 30+3	McCarthy J 5	Holt G 9+7	Maloney S 9+1	McArthur J 37+4	McManaman C 17+13	McClean J 23+14	McCann C 22+5	Fortune M 16+20	Gomez J 22+9	Espinoza R 7+11	Rogne T 10+2	Powell N 23+8	Shotton R 7+2	Nicholls L 6	Albrighton M 2+2	Ramis I 15	Keane W 2+2	Al Habsi A 24	Kiernan R 7+5	Browning T 1+1	Maynard N 11+5	McEachran J 5+3	Waghorn M 15	Tunnicliffe R 3+2	Collison J 5+4	Caldwell G 2	Holgersson M —+1	Match No.
1	2	3	4	5	6	7^3	8	9^1	10	11^2	12	13	14																					1
1	2	5	9	3	4	10^2	8	11^1	6	7^3	12^4	14	13																					2
1	2	5	7^2	4	3	13	6	10	9				8^3	12	11^1	14																		3
1	2	5		3	4	9	7	11^3			8^2		6^1	10	14	12	13																	4
1	2		6^1	4		5	9		10	12		13	11^3	14	8	7^2	3																	5
1	2		7	4	9	5		6^3		12		11	14	8^2	10^1	3	13																	6
1	13		8	3	4^1	6^3		9		7^2	14		10		12	5	11	2																7
1	13		7	4	5			8	12		11^2	9	6		3^1	10	2																	8
1	13		7	4	5	9		12		8^1		14		6	10		3^3	11^1	2^2															9
1	2		8	4	5	14		13		7	6^3		12	9^4	10^1		3	11^2																10
	2	9^1	4	5		11^3		7	12	6	14	10^2		13	3	8			1															11
	2		4	5		11^2		7	8^3	6	12	13	10^1		9	3	1	14																12
	2	6	4	5		13			10^1	7	11^3	14	8^2		9	3	1	12																13
	2	6	4	5		12		14	10^1	7	11^3		13		9	3	1	8^2																14
	2	6	4	5		12		10^3	7	11^1	13	14			9	3	1	8^2																15
	2	5	6^1	4		13		7	10^3		14	8	12		11		1		1		9^2													16
1	2	6	4	5	10^1	13		7	14	8		12			11^3			3	9^2															17
1	2^2	5^1	7	4		11		9	12	8		6		14		10^1	13	3																18
1	2	12	6^2	4	14	5^1		11^3		8	10	7		13		9		3																19
		14	6	3	2	9^3			7	5^1	8		11	13		4	10^3				12	1												20
			3	6	9			11		7	5	8^1		10^3	13		2^2		12		4	14	1											21
	5	9		3	4			6		8^2	11^3	12	7^1	13		10					2		1	14										22
	2	12		4	5	9		8	13	7	11^1			6^3		10					3^2		1	14										23
	3		9^2	4	2^1	5		6^3	7	11		13	14		10							1			12									24
	3		7^1	4		5		6	12	8	13		11^2	14		10						1			2	9^3								25
	2	9	6^3	3	4	5		12		8	11^3	13		7		10^2						1				14								26
	3		7	4	2	5		6^2	8	9^3	12	10	14			10						1				11^1	13							27
	3	5	6	4	2	10		9^3	12	13	11			7^2								1				14		8^1						28
	3	13	9	4	2	5		8^3		7	12	6^1									1	14				11		10^2						29
	3		6^2	4	2	5		7		9	13	10		14								1				11^1	12^1	8						30
	2		4	12	5			9		6		10^2	13	14					3			1				11	7^3	8^1						31
	3	12		4	2	5^1		7		6	13	11	8									1				10^2		9^3	14					32
	3			4	2	5		6^1	12	14	11^2	7			13							1				10		9^1	8					33
	2	14		4^1	5			7		10	11^2	6		12				3			1	13				9^1	8							34
	3			2^3	5			7	9	13		8	12	11		4		1								10^2	6^1	14						35
	3			2	5			6		10	11^3	8	14	13		4		1	7^2							9^1	12							36
	9^3			5	12			6			11	13	2^1	10		3		1	4	14	8^2					7								37
	3			4	2	5		9^3	12		11	10^2	8		14			1					6	7^1	13									38
	2	9		5				6		13	12	8^2		11^1		3		1	4	10^3	14				7									39
	3	6		2				7	9^1	14	13	8		11^3		4		1	5				10^2	12										40
1	2		3	5		9^1	13		12	10^1		14			4			11^2	7^3	8	6													41
	3		4	2	5	11^1	7	9		12		8	6^2	13					1					10^2	14									42
	3	5^1	4	2	10			7	12	11		8^2	9^1				1	13	14				6											43
	3		4	2	5		11^1	6	9	13	14	7	8^3	12			1						10^2										44
1	3	14	2	6		10^2	8	7^3	12	9							5	13	11^1			4												45
1		5	12			13			11		6				3^3			4	10^1	7	9^2		8	2^1	14									46

The Budweiser FA Cup

Third Round	Milton Keynes D	(h)	3-3
Replay	Milton Keynes D	(a)	3-1
(aet)			
Fourth Round	Crystal Palace	(h)	2-1
Fifth Round	Cardiff C	(a)	2-1
Sixth Round	Manchester C	(a)	2-1
Semi-Finals	Arsenal	(Wembley)	1-1
(aet; lost 2-4 on penalties)			

Capital One Cup

Third Round	Manchester C	(a)	0-5

Community Shield Manchester U (Wembley) 0-2

UEFA Europa League

Group D	Zulte Waregem	(a)	0-0	(h)	1-2
Group D	Maribor Teatanic	(h)	3-1	(a)	1-2
Group D	Rubin Kazan	(h)	1-1	(a)	0-1

Championship Play-Offs

Semi-Finals 1st leg	QPR	(h)	0-0
Semi-Finals 2nd leg	QPR	(a)	1-2

WOLVERHAMPTON WANDERERS

FOUNDATION

Enthusiasts of the game at St Luke's School, Blakenhall formed a club in 1877. In the same neighbourhood a cricket club called Blakenhall Wanderers had a football section. Several St Luke's footballers played cricket for them and shortly before the start of the 1879–80 season the two amalgamated and Wolverhampton Wanderers FC was brought into being.

Molineux Stadium, Waterloo Road, Wolverhampton WV1 4QR.

Telephone: (0871) 222 2220.

Fax: (01902) 687 006.

Ticket Office: (0871) 222 1877.

Website: wolves.co.uk

Email: info@wolves.co.uk

Ground Capacity: 30,852.

Record Attendance: 61,315 v Liverpool, FA Cup 5th rd, 11 February 1939.

Pitch Measurements: 103.5m × 68m (113yd × 74.5yd)

Chairman: Steve Morgan OBE.

Chief Executive: Jez Moxey.

Head Coach: Kenny Jackett.

Assistant Head Coach: Joe Gallen.

Physio: Carl Howarth.

Colours: Gold shirts with black trim, black shorts with gold trim, gold socks with black trim.

Year Formed: 1877* (*see Foundation*).

Turned Professional: 1888.

Previous Names: 1879, St Luke's combined with Wanderers Cricket Club to become Wolverhampton Wanderers (1923) Ltd. New limited companies followed in 1982 and 1986 (current).

Club Nickname: 'Wolves'.

HONOURS

Football League – Division 1: *Champions* 1953–54, 1957–58, 1958–59; *Runners-up* 1937–38, 1938–39, 1949–50, 1954–55, 1959–60; **Division 2:** *Champions* 1931–32, 1976–77; *Runners-up* 1966–67, 1982–83; **FL C:** *Champions* 2008–09; **Division 3 (N):** *Champions* 1923–24; **Division 3:** *Champions* 1988–89; **Division 4:** *Champions* 1987–88; **FL 1:** *Champions* 2013–14.

FA Cup: *Winners* 1893, 1908, 1949, 1960; *Runners-up* 1889, 1896, 1921, 1939.

Football League Cup: *Winners* 1974, 1980.

Texaco Cup: *Winners* 1971.

Sherpa Van Trophy: *Winners* 1988.

European Competitions
European Cup: 1958–59, 1959–60.
European Cup-Winners' Cup: 1960–61. **UEFA Cup:** 1971–72 (*runners-up*), 1973–74, 1974–75, 1980–81.

Grounds: 1877, Windmill Field; 1879, John Harper's Field; 1881, Dudley Road; 1889, Molineux.

First Football League Game: 8 September 1888, Football League, v Aston Villa (h) D 1–1 – Baynton; Baugh, Mason; Fletcher, Allen, Lowder; Hunter, Cooper, Anderson, White, Cannon, (1 og).

Record League Victory: 10–1 v Leicester C, Division 1, 15 April 1938 – Sidlow; Morris, Dowen; Galley, Cullis, Gardiner; Maguire (1), Horace Wright, Westcott (4), Jones (1), Dorsett (4).

Record Cup Victory: 14–0 v Crosswell's Brewery, FA Cup 2nd rd, 13 November 1886 – Ike Griffiths; Baugh, Mason; Pearson, Allen (1), Lowder; Hunter, Knight (2), Brodie (4), Bernie Griffiths (2), Wood. Plus one goal 'scrambled through'.

sky SPORTS FACT FILE

In December 1954 Wolverhampton Wanderers defeated Honved 3-2 at Molineux after trailing 2-0. Although a friendly match the game attracted an attendance of nearly 55,000 and is regarded as one of the club's greatest post-war victories. The result restored confidence in English football after two heavy defeats by the Hungary national team the previous season.

Record Defeat: 1–10 v Newton Heath, Division 1, 15 October 1892.

Most League Points (2 for a win): 64, Division 1, 1957–58.

Most League Points (3 for a win): 103, FL 1, 2013–14.

Most League Goals: 115, Division 2, 1931–32.

Highest League Scorer in Season: Dennis Westcott, 38, Division 1, 1946–47.

Most League Goals in Total Aggregate: Steve Bull, 250, 1986–99.

Most League Goals in One Match: 5, Joe Butcher v Accrington, Division 1, 19 November 1892; 5, Tom Phillipson v Barnsley, Division 2, 26 April 1926; 5, Tom Phillipson v Bradford C, Division 2, 25 December 1926; 5, Billy Hartill v Notts Co, Division 2, 12 October 1929; 5, Billy Hartill v Aston Villa, Division 1, 3 September 1934.

Most Capped Player: Billy Wright, 105, England (70 consecutive).

Most League Appearances: Derek Parkin, 501, 1967–82.

Youngest League Player: Jimmy Mullen, 16 years 43 days v Leeds U, 18 February 1939.

Record Transfer Fee Received: £14,000,000 from Sunderland for Steven Fletcher, August 2012.

Record Transfer Fee Paid: £6,500,000 to Reading for Kevin Doyle, June 2009; £6,500,000 to Burnley for Steven Fletcher, June 2010.

Football League Record: 1888 Founder Member of Football League: 1906–23 Division 2; 1923–24 Division 3 (N); 1924–32 Division 2; 1932–65 Division 1; 1965–67 Division 2; 1967–76 Division 1; 1976–77 Division 2; 1977–82 Division 1; 1982–83 Division 2; 1983–84 Division 1; 1984–85 Division 2; 1985–86 Division 3; 1986–88 Division 4; 1988–89 Division 3; 1989–92 Division 2; 1992–2003 Division 1; 2003–04 FA Premier League; 2004–09 FL C; 2009–12 FA Premier League; 2012–13 FL C; 2013–14 FL 1; 2014– FL C.

MANAGERS

George Worrall 1877–85
  (Secretary-Manager)
John Addenbrooke 1885–1922
George Jobey 1922–24
Albert Hoskins 1924–26
  (had been Secretary since 1922)
Fred Scotchbrook 1926–27
Major Frank Buckley 1927–44
Ted Vizard 1944–48
Stan Cullis 1948–64
Andy Beattie 1964–65
Ronnie Allen 1966–68
Bill McGarry 1968–76
Sammy Chung 1976–78
John Barnwell 1978–81
Ian Greaves 1982
Graham Hawkins 1982–84
Tommy Docherty 1984–85
Bill McGarry 1985
Sammy Chapman 1985–86
Brian Little 1986
Graham Turner 1986–94
Graham Taylor 1994–95
Mark McGhee 1995–98
Colin Lee 1998–2000
Dave Jones 2001–04
Glenn Hoddle 2004–06
Mick McCarthy 2006–12
Stale Solbakken 2012–13
Dean Saunders 2013
Kenny Jackett May 2013–

LATEST SEQUENCES

Longest Sequence of League Wins: 9, 11.1.2014 – 11.3.2014.

Longest Sequence of League Defeats: 8, 5.12.1981 – 13.2.1982.

Longest Sequence of League Draws: 6, 22.4.1995 – 20.8.1995.

Longest Sequence of Unbeaten League Matches: 21, 15.1.2005 – 13.8.2005.

Longest Sequence Without a League Win: 19, 1.12.1984 – 6.4.1985.

Successive Scoring Runs: 41 from 20.12.1958.

Successive Non-scoring Runs: 7 from 2.2.1985.

TEN YEAR LEAGUE RECORD

		P	W	D	L	F	A	Pts	Pos
2004-05	FL C	46	15	21	10	72	59	66	9
2005-06	FL C	46	16	19	11	50	42	67	7
2006-07	FL C	46	22	10	14	59	56	76	5
2007-08	FL C	46	18	16	12	53	48	70	7
2008-09	FL C	46	27	9	10	80	52	90	1
2009-10	PR Lge	38	9	11	18	32	56	38	15
2010-11	PR Lge	38	11	7	20	46	66	40	17
2011-12	PR Lge	38	5	10	23	40	82	25	20
2012-13	FL C	46	14	9	23	55	69	51	23
2013-14	FL 1	46	31	10	5	89	31	103	1

DID YOU KNOW ?

In 1957–58 Wolverhampton Wanderers won four league titles: the first team won the Football League championship, while the reserves won the Central League, the 'A' team won the Birmingham League and the 'B' team the Worcestershire Combination. For good measure the U18s also won the FA Youth Cup.

WOLVERHAMPTON WANDERERS –
FOOTBALL LEAGUE ONE 2013–14 LEAGUE RECORD

Match No.	Date	Venue	Opponents	Result	H/T Score	Lg Pos.	Goalscorers	Attendance
1	Aug 3	A	Preston NE	D 0-0	0-0	14		16,583
2	10	H	Gillingham	W 4-0	3-0	6	Griffiths 2 (1 pen) [5, 68 (p)], Evans [26], Sako [31]	19,102
3	17	A	Bristol C	W 2-1	1-0	3	Sako [22], Doherty [85]	14,393
4	23	H	Crawley T	W 2-1	1-0	1	Sigurdarson [7], Griffiths (pen) [90]	17,406
5	31	A	Port Vale	W 3-1	0-0	2	Griffiths [56], Sigurdarson [75], McDonald [83]	12,601
6	Sept 14	H	Swindon T	W 3-2	2-0	3	Golbourne [3], Doyle [43], Foley [90]	19,388
7	17	H	Walsall	L 0-1	0-0	3		22,240
8	21	A	Shrewsbury T	W 1-0	0-0	3	Sako (pen) [84]	9510
9	28	H	Sheffield U	W 2-0	0-0	3	Griffiths [66], Sako [90]	20,417
10	Oct 5	A	Colchester U	W 3-0	1-0	3	Griffiths 2 (1 pen) [20 (p), 48], Doyle [55]	7295
11	19	H	Coventry C	D 1-1	0-0	3	Griffiths [68]	22,939
12	22	H	Oldham Ath	W 2-0	0-0	3	Henry [50], Griffiths [66]	15,959
13	26	A	Bradford C	W 2-1	2-1	2	Henry [28], Stearman [32]	18,044
14	Nov 2	A	Stevenage	W 2-0	1-0	2	Doyle [7], Henry [81]	17,700
15	5	A	Carlisle U	D 2-2	2-1	2	Sako [8], Griffiths [42]	5369
16	16	A	Notts Co	W 1-0	0-0	3	Ebanks-Landell [76]	7520
17	23	H	Brentford	D 0-0	0-0	2		19,061
18	26	H	Tranmere R	W 2-0	2-0	1	Griffiths [17], Edwards [42]	14,989
19	30	A	Peterborough U	L 0-1	0-0	2		8170
20	Dec 14	H	Milton Keynes D	L 0-2	0-1	2		17,142
21	21	A	Rotherham U	D 3-3	1-2	2	Batth [10], Sako (pen) [59], Henry [64]	11,092
22	26	H	Crewe Alex	W 2-0	1-0	2	Jacobs [3], Griffiths [90]	22,693
23	29	H	Leyton Orient	D 1-1	1-0	3	Ebanks-Landell [5]	28,598
24	Jan 1	A	Tranmere R	D 1-1	0-1	2	Edwards [55]	6158
25	3	A	Gillingham	L 0-1	0-0	2		7758
26	11	H	Preston NE	W 2-0	1-0	3	Edwards [28], Evans [55]	20,434
27	25	H	Bristol C	W 3-1	2-1	3	Dicko [10], Williams (og) [43], Sako [76]	18,501
28	28	A	Oldham Ath	W 3-0	0-0	3	McDonald [50], Jacobs [89], Henry [90]	4343
29	Feb 1	A	Bradford C	W 2-0	1-0	2	McDonald [45], Dicko [57]	19,498
30	15	H	Notts Co	W 2-0	1-0	2	Jacobs 2 [17, 54]	18,019
31	22	A	Brentford	W 3-0	1-0	2	Henry [45], Jacobs 2 [72, 85]	11,309
32	Mar 1	H	Port Vale	W 3-0	0-0	1	Sako [52], Dicko 2 [73, 75]	21,929
33	8	A	Walsall	W 3-0	1-0	1	Dicko 2 [31, 48], Sako [67]	10,139
34	11	A	Swindon T	W 4-1	3-0	1	Sako 2 [9, 34], Dicko [19], Clarke [90]	9670
35	15	H	Shrewsbury T	D 0-0	0-0	1		24,012
36	18	A	Crawley T	L 1-2	1-2	1	Henry [25]	5680
37	22	A	Sheffield U	W 2-0	1-0	1	Henry [13], Edwards [53]	21,659
38	25	H	Colchester U	W 4-2	3-0	1	Jacobs [2], Edwards [27], Henry [44], Dicko [90]	17,041
39	29	A	Milton Keynes D	W 1-0	0-0	1	McAlinden [81]	20,516
40	Apr 1	A	Stevenage	D 0-0	0-0	1		4660
41	5	H	Peterborough U	W 2-0	0-0	1	Batth [48], Edwards [69]	23,204
42	12	A	Crewe Alex	W 2-0	1-0	1	McDonald [45], Edwards [66]	6424
43	18	H	Rotherham U	W 6-4	3-1	1	Dicko 3 [21, 34, 80], Edwards [36], Ricketts [90], McDonald [90]	30,110
44	21	A	Leyton Orient	W 3-1	2-0	1	Stearman [17], Sako [32], Henry [90]	8161
45	26	A	Coventry C	D 1-1	0-0	1	Edwards [84]	4252
46	May 3	H	Carlisle U	W 3-0	2-0	1	Ricketts [5], Jacobs [24], Dicko [57]	29,829

Final League Position: 1

GOALSCORERS

League (89): Dicko 12, Griffiths 12 (3 pens), Sako 12 (2 pens), Henry 10, Edwards 9, Jacobs 8, McDonald 5, Doyle 3, Batth 2, Ebanks-Landell 2, Evans 2, Ricketts 2, Sigurdarson 2, Stearman 2, Clarke 1, Doherty 1, Foley 1, Golbourne 1, McAlinden 1, own goal 1.
The Budweiser FA Cup (2): Golbourne 1, Griffiths 1.
Capital One Cup (0).
Johnstone's Paint Trophy (2): McAlinden 1, Sako 1.

Ikeme C 41	Doherty M 15+3	Ricketts S 42+2	Davis D 12+6	Stearman R 39+1	Batth D 46	Sigurdarson B 7+11	Evans L 19+7	Griffiths L 18+8	Edwards D 22+8	Sako B 36+4	Elokobi G 1+5	Cassidy J 4+10	Foley K —+5	Ismail Z 5+4	Doyle K 16+7	Price J 20+6	McDonald K 39+2	Golbourne S 39+1	Forde A —+3	Henry J 26+6	Ebanks-Landell E 4+3	O'Hara J —+2	Jacobs M 28+2	McAlinden L 2+5	McCarey A 5	Dicko N 16+3	Clarke L 4+9	Match No.
1	2	3	4	5²	6	7	8	9	10¹	11	12³	13	14															1
1	2¹	5	7	3	4	12	8	11		9				14	6²	10³	13											2
1	5	2	7	3	4	13	8	11³		9		12			6²	10¹	14											3
1	2	5	7	4	3	8³	9¹	12		10	14				6²	11	13											4
1	2	5	8	3	4	13	12	11							6²	10¹	7	9²	14									5
1	2	4	7¹		3	13	6	11²		9³				14	12	10	8	5										6
1	2	4	7		3	10	6²	12		9		13			11		8¹	5										7
1	2	3	7		4	10²	11	13	9	12	14				6³		8	5										8
1	2	4		3		10¹		11²	6³	9		13			12	8	7	5	14									9
1	2	5	13	4	3	12			10¹	11²						7	8	9	14	6³								10
1	2	4	12	3		13		11²	9	10						8¹	7	5		6								11
1	2³	4	12	3		8²		11³	13	9			14			10	7	5		6								12
1	4	7	2²	3		14	8³	11¹	10						12	9		5		6	13							13
1	2	7	4	3		10¹	8	12		9²					11			5		6	13							14
1	2	7		3	4	14	8²	11¹		9		13				10³		5		6	12							15
1		7³	3	4	14	12	8	10	13	11²	9							5		6¹		2						16
1	2	5		3	4	14		11¹	7	9		13			12	10¹	8						6²					17
	2		4	3				11¹	7	9³		12			14	10	13	8	5				6²					18
	2		3	4	12			11¹	7	9		13			14	10²	8	5					6¹					19
1		2	4	3				10²	7	9³		14			11		8³	5			13	12						20
1		2	13	3	4	10¹		12	7	9					11	8²		5		6¹		14						21
1		2		4	3			13	8¹				11³		14	9	7	5²		6	12		10					22
1		5		4	3			13	12	8		11³			14	9¹	7			6²	2		10					23
1		5	14	2¹	4			10	8³	6		11¹			13	7	12			3²			9					24
	2			3				12	8	11	4	13			10²	7	5		6¹			9		1			25
	2	12		3	4	9²	11¹	7³		14					10	5		6			8	13	1					26
	2			3	4¹		10			12		13			8	7	5		6²			9		1	11		27
	2			3	4		9¹			10²	12					8	7	5		13			8		1	11		28
	2		4	3			9¹									8	7	5	12				6		1	11	10	29
1	2		3	4		12				8¹						9	7	5		6			10			11		30
1	2	14		3	4					12	8					9	7³	5		6¹			10	13		11²		31
1	12	2		4¹	3		14			13		9²				7	8	5		6			10²			11		32
1		2		4	3					13		9¹				8	7	5		6			10			11²	12	33
1		2		4	3					12		9²				8	7	5		6	14		10			11³	13	34
1	12			3	4					8						7	9	5		6¹	2²		10			11	13	35
1		2		4	3	14				13		9¹				8³	7	5		6			10²			11	12	36
1	2³	13		3	4	7¹				10	14				12	8	5		6			9²			11		37
1	2		3	4		7³				9¹	14				12	6	5	8		10			13	11²				38
1	2		4	3					8						9²	7	5	10		6	13		11¹	12				39
1	5		3	4		13	2									7	9	8¹		6	11²		12	10				40
1	2		4	3		14			9³	10¹					8	7	5		6			12	11¹	13				41
1	2		3	4		7				9	8²				6	5		12			10		11¹	13				42
1	14	2		4	3	6¹			9²	10³					13	7	5	12		8			11					43
1		2		3	4	14			9	10²					7	6	5	13		8¹			11²	12				44
1	2	14		3	4	7			9	13					6	5²	8			10²	11¹		12					45
1		2		4	3	6			9¹	10²	14				7	5	12			8			11³	13				46

The Budweiser FA Cup

First Round	Oldham Ath	(a)	1-1
Replay	Oldham Ath	(h)	1-2

Capital One Cup

First Round	Morecambe	(a)	0-1

Johnstone's Paint Trophy

First Round	Walsall	(h)	2-2
(aet; won 4-2 on penalties)			
Second Round	Notts Co	(h)	0-0
(aet; lost 1-3 on penalties)			

WYCOMBE WANDERERS

FOUNDATION

In 1887 a group of young furniture trade workers called a meeting at the Steam Engine public house with the aim of forming a football club and entering junior football. It is thought that they were named after the famous FA Cup winners, The Wanderers, who had visited the town in 1877 for a tie with the original High Wycombe club. It is also possible that they played informally before their formation, although there is no proof of this.

Adams Park, Hillbottom Road, High Wycombe, Buckinghamshire HP12 4HJ.

Telephone: (01494) 472 100. *Fax:* (01494) 441 589.

Ticket Office: (01494) 441 118.

Website: www.wwfc.com

Email: wwfc@wwfc.com

Ground Capacity: 10,000.

Record Attendance: 15,850 v St Albans C, FA Amateur Cup 4th rd, 25 February 1950 (at Loakes Park); 9,921 v Fulham, FA Cup 3rd rd, 9 January 2002 (at Adams Park).

Pitch Measurements: 105m × 68.5m (115yd × 75yd)

Chairman: Don Woodward.

Manager: Gareth Ainsworth.

Assistant Manager: Richard Dobson.

Physio: Theo Farley.

Colours: Light blue and dark blue quartered shirts, dark blue shorts with light blue trim, dark blue socks.

Year Formed: 1887.

Turned Professional: 1974.

Club Nicknames: 'The Chairboys' (after High Wycombe's tradition of furniture making), 'The Blues'.

Grounds: 1887, The Rye; 1893, Spring Meadow; 1895, Loakes Park; 1899, Daws Hill Park; 1901, Loakes Park; 1990, Adams Park.

First Football League Game: 14 August 1993, Division 3 v Carlisle U (a) D 2–2: Hyde; Cousins, Horton (Langford), Kerr, Crossley, Ryan, Carroll, Stapleton, Thompson, Scott, Guppy (1) (Hutchinson), (1 og).

Record League Victory: 5–0 v Burnley, Division 2, 15 April 1997 – Parkin; Cousins, Bell, Kavanagh, McCarthy, Forsyth, Carroll (2p) (Simpson), Scott (Farrell), Stallard (1), McGavin (1) (Read (1)), Brown. 5–0 v Northampton T, Division 2, 4 January 2003 – Talia; Senda, Ryan, Thomson, McCarthy, Johnson, Bulman, Simpson (1), Faulconbridge (Harris), Dixon (1) (Roberts 3), Brown (Currie).

Record Cup Victory: 5–0 v Hitchin T (a), FA Cup 2nd rd, 3 December 1994 – Hyde; Cousins, Brown, Crossley, Evans, Ryan (1), Carroll, Bell (1), Thompson, Garner (3) (Hemmings), Stapleton (Langford).

HONOURS

Football League – Division 2: Best season: 6th, 1994–95; **FL 2:** Best season: 3rd, 2008–09 (promoted to FL 1), 2010–11 (promoted to FL 1).

FA Amateur Cup: *Winners* 1931.

FA Trophy: *Winners* 1991, 1993.

GM Vauxhall Conference: *Winners* 1992–93.

FA Cup: semi-final 2001.

Football League Cup: semi-final 2007.

sky SPORTS FACT FILE

Wycombe Wanderers were an amateur club up until 1974 when the status was abolished. They reached the final of the FA Amateur Cup on two occasions. In 1930–31 they defeated Hayes 1-0 at Highbury and in 1956–57 they lost out 3-1 to Bishop Auckland in front of a 90,000 crowd at Wembley Stadium.

Record Defeat: 0–7 v Shrewsbury T, Johnstone's Paint Trophy, 7 October 2008.

Most League Points (3 for a win): 80, FL 2, 2010-11.

Most League Goals: 72, FL 2, 2005–06.

Highest League Goalscorer in Season: Scott McGleish, 25, 2007–08.

Most League Goals in Total Aggregate: Nathan Tyson, 42, 2004–06.

Most League Goals in One Match: 3, Miquel Desouza v Bradford C, Division 2, 2 September 1995; 3, John Williams v Stockport Co, Division 2, 24 February 1996; 3, Mark Stallard v Walsall, Division 2, 21 October 1997; 3, Sean Devine v Reading, Division 2, 2 October 1999; 3, Sean Divine v Bury, Division 2, 26 February 2000; 3, Stuart Roberts v Northampton T, Division 2, 4 January 2003; 3, Nathan Tyson v Lincoln C, FL 2, 5 March 2005; 3, Nathan Tyson v Kidderminster H, FL 2, 2 April 2005; 3, Nathan Tyson v Stockport Co, FL 2, 10 September 2005; 3, Kevin Betsy v Mansfield T, FL 2, 24 September 2005; 3, Scott McGleish v Mansfield T, FL 2, 8 January 2008; 3, Stuart Roberts v Northampton T, Division 2, 4 January 2003.

Most Capped Player: Mark Rogers, 7, Canada; Marvin McCoy, 7, Antigua and Barbuda.

Most League Appearances: Steve Brown, 371, 1994–2004.

Youngest League Player: Jordon Ibe, 15 years 311 days v Hartlepool U, 15 October 2011.

Record Transfer Fee Received: £675,000 from Nottingham F for Nathan Tyson, January 2006.

Record Transfer Fee Paid: £200,000 to Barnet for Sean Devine, 15 April 1999.

Football League Record: 1993 Promoted to Division 3 from Conference; 1993–94 Division 3; 1994–2004 Division 2; 2004–09 FL 2; 2009–10 FL 1; 2010–11 FL 2; 2011–12 FL 1; 2012– FL 2.

MANAGERS

First coach appointed 1951. *Prior to Brian Lee's appointment in 1969 the team was selected by a Match Committee which met every Monday evening.*

James McCormack 1951–52
Sid Cann 1952–61
Graham Adams 1961–62
Don Welsh 1962–64
Barry Darvill 1964–68
Brian Lee 1969–76
Ted Powell 1976–77
John Reardon 1977–78
Andy Williams 1978–80
Mike Keen 1980–84
Paul Bence 1984–86
Alan Gane 1986–87
Peter Suddaby 1987–88
Jim Kelman 1988–90
Martin O'Neill 1990–95
Alan Smith 1995–96
John Gregory 1996–98
Neil Smillie 1998–99
Lawrie Sanchez 1999–2003
Tony Adams 2003–04
John Gorman 2004–06
Paul Lambert 2006–08
Peter Taylor 2008–09
Gary Waddock 2009–12
Gareth Ainsworth November 2012–

LATEST SEQUENCES

Longest Sequence of League Wins: 6, 19.8.2006 – 16.9.2006.

Longest Sequence of League Defeats: 6, 18.3.2006 – 17.4.2006.

Longest Sequence of League Draws: 5, 24.1.2004 – 21.2.2004.

Longest Sequence of Unbeaten League Matches: 21, 6.8.2005 – 10.12.2005.

Longest Sequence Without a League Win: 13, 16.8.2003 – 18.10.2003 and 10.1.2004 – 20.3.2004.

Successive Scoring Runs: 15 from 28.12.2004.

Successive Non-scoring Runs: 5 from 15.10.1996.

TEN YEAR LEAGUE RECORD

		P	W	D	L	F	A	Pts	Pos
2004-05	FL 2	46	17	14	15	58	52	65	10
2005-06	FL 2	46	18	17	11	72	56	71	6
2006-07	FL 2	46	16	14	16	52	47	62	12
2007-08	FL 2	46	22	12	12	56	42	78	7
2008-09	FL 2	46	20	18	8	54	33	78	3
2009-10	FL 1	46	10	15	21	56	76	45	22
2010-11	FL 2	46	22	14	10	69	50	80	3
2011-12	FL 1	46	11	10	25	65	88	43	21
2012-13	FL 2	46	17	9	20	50	60	60	15
2013-14	FL 2	46	12	14	20	46	54	50	22

DID YOU KNOW ?

Wycombe Wanderers were one of the top amateur clubs of the early 1970s. The club had the distinction of providing four members of the England amateur team that played against both Denmark and Italy in May 1972: Derek Gamblin, John Delaney, Ted Powell and Larry Pritchard.

WYCOMBE WANDERERS – FOOTBALL LEAGUE TWO 2013–14 LEAGUE RECORD

Match No.	Date	Venue	Opponents	Result	H/T Score	Lg Pos.	Goalscorers	Attendance
1	Aug 3	H	Morecambe	W 1-0	1-0	8	Cowan-Hall [7]	3284
2	10	A	AFC Wimbledon	L 0-1	0-1	13		4235
3	17	H	Mansfield T	L 0-1	0-0	18		3352
4	24	A	Oxford U	D 2-2	1-0	18	Morgan 2 (1 pen) [44, 59 (p)]	7100
5	31	H	Southend U	W 2-1	2-1	11	Morgan [7], Craig [32]	3533
6	Sept 7	H	Hartlepool U	W 2-1	0-0	8	Kretzschmar 2 [51, 69]	3640
7	14	A	Plymouth Arg	W 3-0	0-0	5	Wood [70], Morgan [74], Knott [90]	6702
8	21	H	York C	D 1-1	0-0	6	Morgan [70]	4015
9	28	A	Rochdale	L 2-3	1-3	10	McClure [42], Kuffour [58]	2303
10	Oct 5	H	Burton Alb	L 1-2	0-1	13	McClure [90]	3518
11	12	H	Torquay U	W 3-2	1-2	9	Kuffour [28], Cowan-Hall 2 [53, 77]	3466
12	19	A	Bristol R	W 1-0	0-0	7	Kretzschmar [82]	5783
13	26	H	Bury	L 1-2	1-0	12	Stewart [16]	3350
14	Nov 2	A	Accrington S	D 1-1	0-0	12	Stewart [72]	1268
15	16	H	Cheltenham T	L 1-2	0-0	13	McClure [66]	3207
16	23	A	Chesterfield	L 0-2	0-2	15		5798
17	26	H	Exeter C	D 1-1	1-0	15	Craig [10]	2357
18	30	A	Dagenham & R	L 0-2	0-1	16		1618
19	Dec 4	A	Portsmouth	D 2-2	1-0	14	McClure [23], Stewart [90]	14,942
20	14	H	Scunthorpe U	D 1-1	0-0	15	Johnson [90]	2888
21	21	A	Northampton T	W 4-1	2-0	13	Kuffour [1], Hause [14], Lewis [80], Morgan [85]	4353
22	26	H	Newport Co	L 0-1	0-1	15		3513
23	Jan 4	A	AFC Wimbledon	L 0-3	0-0	19		3513
24	11	A	Morecambe	D 1-1	1-0	18	Cowan-Hall [41]	1575
25	18	H	Oxford U	L 0-1	0-0	19		5751
26	25	A	Mansfield T	D 2-2	1-0	19	Lewis [9], Scowen [48]	2789
27	28	H	Portsmouth	L 0-1	0-0	21		3733
28	Feb 1	A	Bury	L 0-1	0-1	22		2818
29	8	H	Accrington S	D 0-0	0-0	22		3073
30	11	H	Fleetwood T	D 1-1	1-0	22	Lewis [45]	2185
31	22	H	Chesterfield	W 1-0	1-0	22	Kretzschmar (pen) [35]	3356
32	25	A	Exeter C	W 1-0	1-0	21	Kretzschmar [23]	2540
33	Mar 1	A	Southend U	D 1-1	0-0	21	Bentley (og) [70]	5502
34	8	H	Hartlepool U	W 2-1	0-1	18	Morgan [52], McClure [70]	3073
35	11	H	Plymouth Arg	L 0-1	0-0	20		3042
36	15	A	York C	L 0-2	0-2	20		3455
37	18	A	Cheltenham T	D 1-1	0-0	19	Morgan (pen) [79]	2267
38	22	H	Rochdale	L 0-2	0-0	21		3594
39	25	A	Burton Alb	L 0-1	0-0	21		1784
40	29	A	Scunthorpe U	D 0-0	0-0	22		3867
41	Apr 5	H	Dagenham & R	W 2-0	0-0	22	Craig (pen) [47], Kretzschmar [58]	3103
42	12	A	Newport Co	L 0-2	0-0	22		2838
43	18	H	Northampton T	D 1-1	1-1	21	Pierre [18]	7004
44	21	A	Fleetwood T	L 0-1	0-0	21		2711
45	26	H	Bristol R	L 1-2	1-1	23	McClure [20]	6752
46	May 3	A	Torquay U	W 3-0	2-0	22	Wood [6], Craig (pen) [42], McClure [62]	3149

Final League Position: 22

GOALSCORERS

League (46): Morgan 8 (2 pens), McClure 7, Kretzschmar 6 (1 pen), Cowan-Hall 4, Craig 4 (2 pens), Kuffour 3, Lewis 3, Stewart 3, Wood 2, Hause 1, Johnson 1, Knott 1, Pierre 1, Scowen 1, own goal 1.
The Budweiser FA Cup (3): Craig 1 (1 pen), Cowan-Hall 1, Doherty 1.
Capital One Cup (1): Kuffour 1.
Johnstone's Paint Trophy (5): McClure 2, Bloomfield 1, Knott 1, Stewart 1.

Ingram M 46	McCoy M 32+1	Dunne C 9	Scowen J 36+1	Stewart A 26+7	Johnson L 30	Cowan-Hall P 20+5	Lewis S 36	Pittman J 2+8	Morgan D 19+10	Wood S 42+1	Arnold N 30+1	Kretzschmar M 21+14	Spring M 2+3	Kuffour J 11+13	Craig S 17+10	Doherty G 19+1	McClure B 24+12	Knott M 24+12	Hause K 13+1	Bloomfield M 25+7	Morias J —+9	Mustoe J 3	Styche R 8+6	Jeffrey A 1+10	Kewley-Graham J 1	Togwell S 3+1	Pierre A 8	Rowe D 7	Match No.
1	2	3	4	5	6	7^2	8	9	10^1	11	12	13																	1
1	2	5	7	3	4	6	8^1	11^2	10^3	9^1				12	13	14													2
1	2	5	8	3		9^2		12	13	6^3	14	7	11		4	10^1		7^3											3
1	2	5^4	9	3			12	11^2	10	6		14	13	8^1	4		7^3												4
1	2	8^1	4			10	9	6^2	12				11^3	5	14	7	3	13											5
1	5		14	3		8		6	9^1	12		13	11^3	4	10^2	7	2												6
1	2		3	8		10^2	9		6^3		13	11^1	4	12	7	5	14												7
1	2		4	7		11^2	9		6		12		3	10^1	8^3	5	14	13											8
1	2		14	3		7	13		9		6^2	11		4	10	8^3	5^1	12											9
1	2	5^4	12			6^2	8		9		14		10^5	4	11	7^2	3		13										10
1		9	4		6^3	8	12		5	2	13	14	11^1			7	3	10^2											11
1		5	7	4	8^4	6	14		2	13		11^1		12	9	3	10^2												12
1		5	6	3	9^1	7		12		2	14	11^2		13	10^1	4	8^4												13
1	2	5	8	3	6^1	7	14	11^3	9		12		13		10²	10^2	4												14
1	2	7	3	4	6^3	8	10^1	5	11^2		14	12	9			13													15
1	2	7	3		6^2	8	12	5		13		10	4	11^1	9^1		14												16
1	2	6^1	3	14	8	10^2	5		12		11^3	4	13	9		7													17
1	2	5	8	3^4	4	6	7	12		9^2		11^1	13	10^3		14													18
1	2		12	3^1	9	7		10^3	5		14	6	13		4	11	6^2												19
1	7^1	3	4	6^2	8	12	9	2		13	10^1		11^3		5	14													20
1	2		3			8	11	5	6	9^1		10^2		13	12	4	7												21
1	2		3		14	8	10^1	5	6	9^2		11^3		12	13	4	7												22
1	2^3	8	3^4	4	10	7		5	6			11^3	13		12	9^2		14											23
1		8		3	6	7		5	2			12^1	11^1	4	10		9												24
1	2	8^2		3		7		5	6	13		12^1	11^1	4	10^1		9^3	14											25
1	5	8		4		7			6	9				3	10^2	13				14	2	11^1	12						26
1	2	7		3		8			9^1	6^2				4	10		13			5	11	12							27
1	2	7	12	4^1	13	8		9	6					3	10^3					5^2	11	14							28
1		7	3	6^2	8	10	5	2				12	4	13			9			11^1									29
1		7	14	3	10^2	8	11^1	5	2	6^3				4	13		9			12									30
1		7	12	3	13	6		5	2	9				4^1	11^3		8			14	10^2								31
1	2	8	3	4	10^2			5	6	9				7						11^1	13								32
1	2	8	3	4	13			12	5	6^1	9		14^1	11^2		10^3		7											33
1	2	6	3	4	11^1			10^2	5	7	9			13		12		8											34
1	2		3	4				10^2	5	6^3	9		13	12		11^1		7			14		8						35
1	2		3	4				10^1	5	6	9^2		11^2	12				7			13	14		8^4					36
1	2	6	3	4				12	5	7	8		13^1	10^2		11^1		9^1											37
1	2	6	4	3		7^2	14	10	5		9^1							8			11^3	12		13					38
1	2	8	3				13	10^2	5	9^3			12					7			11^1	14				6	4		39
1		9				8			5	2	7			11				10								6	4	3	40
1	12	7				8	13		5	2	6		11^2			10^3		9^1			14					3	4		41
1	2	6				7		12	8	5^3	9^1		13^1	10^2		11					14					3	4		42
1		7	13	3	6^1	8	12	5		14^1			10^3			11		9									4^2	2	43
1		7	4			9		12	5	6^3	10^1					11		8^2	13		11^1	14				3	2		44
1		7	3			8			5	9^1			10^2			11		6	13		12					4	2		45
1		7	3	4		8			9				10^1			11		6	12							5	2		46

The Budweiser FA Cup

First Round	Crewe Alex	(h)	1-1
Replay	Crewe Alex	(a)	2-0
Second Round	Preston NE	(h)	0-1

Capital One Cup

First Round	Leicester C	(h)	1-2

Johnstone's Paint Trophy

First Round	Exeter C	(a)	2-0
Second Round	Bristol C	(h)	2-1
Southern Quarter-Finals	Swindon T	(a)	1-2

YEOVIL TOWN

FOUNDATION

One of the prime movers of Yeovil football was Ernest J. Sercombe. His association with the club began in 1895 as a playing member of Yeovil Casuals, of which team he became vice-captain and in his last season 1899–1900, he was chosen to play for Somerset against Devon. Upon the reorganisation of the club, he became secretary of the old Yeovil Town FC and with the amalgamation with Petters United in 1914, he continued to serve until his resignation in 1930.

Huish Park, Lufton Way, Yeovil, Somerset BA22 8YF.

Telephone: (01935) 423 662.

Fax: (01935) 847 886.

Ticket Office: (01935) 847 888.

Website: www.ytfc.net

Email: info@ytfc.net

Ground Capacity: 9,565.

Record Attendance: 16,318 v Sunderland, FA Cup 4th rd, 29 January 1949 (at Huish); 9,527 v Leeds U, FL 1, 25 April 2008 (at Huish Park).

Pitch Measurements: 108m × 67m (118yd × 73.5yd)

Chairman: John R. Fry.

Manager: Gary Johnson.

Assistant Manager: Terry Skiverton.

Physios: Simon Baker, Mike Micciche.

Colours: Green and white hooped shirts, white shorts with green trim, green and white hooped socks.

Year Formed: 1895.

Turned Professional: 1921.

Previous Names: 1895, Yeovil Casuals; 1907, Yeovil Town; 1915, Yeovil & Petters United; 1946, Yeovil Town.

Club Nickname: 'The Glovers'.

HONOURS

Football League – FL 2: *Winners* 2004–05.

Conference: *Champions* 2002–03.

FA Cup: 5th rd 1949.

League Cup: never past 2nd rd.

Southern League: *Champions* 1954–55, 1963–64, 1970–71; *Runners-up:* 1923–24, 1931–32, 1934–35, 1969–70, 1972–73.

Southern League Cup: *Winners* 1948–49, 1954–55, 1960–61, 1965–66; *Runners-up:* 1946–47, 1955–56.

Isthmian League: *Winners* 1987–88; *Runners-up:* 1985–86, 1986–87, 1996–97.

AC Delco Cup: *Winners* 1987–88.

Bob Lord Trophy: *Winners* 1989–90.

FA Trophy: *Winners* 2002.

London Combination: *Runners-up* 1930–31, 1932–33.

Grounds: 1895, Pen Mill Ground; 1921, Huish; 1990, Huish Park.

First Football League Game: 9 August 2003, Division 3 v Rochdale (a) W 3-1: Weale; Williams (Lindegaard), Crittenden, Lockwood, O'Brien, Pluck (Rodrigues), Gosling (El Kholti), Way, Jackson, Gall (2), Johnson (1).

Record League Victory: 6–1 v Oxford U, FL 2, 18 September 2004 – Weale; Rose, O'Brien, Way, Skiverton, Fontaine, Caceres (Tarachulski), Johnson, Jevons (3), Stoicers (2) (Mirza), Terry (Gall 1).

Record Cup Victory: 12–1 v Westbury United, FA Cup 1st qual rd, 1923–24.

sky SPORTS FACT FILE

Yeovil & Petters United reached the FA Cup third round for the first time in 1934–35. Drawn at home to Liverpool they took the lead on 5 minutes through McNeill and were level at half time only to collapse in the second half with the final score being 6-2 to the Merseysiders.

Record Defeat: 0–8 v Manchester United, FA Cup 5th rd, 12 February 1949.

Most League Points (3 for a win): 83, FL 2, 2004–05.

Most League Goals: 90, FL 2, 2004–05.

Highest League Goalscorer in Season: Phil Jevons, 27, 2004–05.

Most League Goals in Total Aggregate: Phil Jevons, 42, 2004–06.

Most League Goals in One Match: 3, Phil Jevons v Oxford U, FL 2, 18 September 2004; 3, Phil Jevons v Chester C, FL 2, 30 October 2004; 3, Phil Jevons v Bristol R, FL 2, 12 February 2005; 3, Arron Davies v Chesterfield, FL 1, 4 March 2006.

Most Capped Players: Andrejs Stolcers, 1 (81), Latvia; Arron Davies, 1, Wales.

Most League Appearances: Terry Skiverton, 195, 2003–09.

Youngest League Player: Steven Caulker, 17 years 222 days v Tranmere R, 8 August 2009.

Record Transfer Fee Received: £1,000,000 from Nottingham F for Arron Davies and Chris Cohen, July 2007.

Record Transfer Fee Paid: £250,000 to Quilmes for Pablo Bastianini, August 2005.

Football League Record: 2003 Promoted to Division 3 from Conference; 2003–04 Division 3; 2004–05 FL 2; 2005–13 FL 1; 2013–14 FL C; 2014– FL 1.

LATEST SEQUENCES

Longest Sequence of League Wins: 8, 29.12.2012 – 16.2.2013.

Longest Sequence of League Defeats: 6, 8.9.2012 – 2.10.2012.

Longest Sequence of League Draws: 3, 18.3.2014 – 25.3.2014.

Longest Sequence of Unbeaten League Matches: 9, 29.12.2012 – 23.2.2013.

Longest Sequence Without a League Win: 11, 10.8.2013 – 19.10.2013.

Successive Scoring Runs: 22 from 30.10.2004.

Successive Non-scoring Runs: 4 from 10.8.2013.

MANAGERS

Jack Gregory 1922–28
Tommy Lawes 1928–29
Dave Pratt 1929–33
Louis Page 1933–35
Dave Halliday 1935–38
Billy Kingdon 1938–46
Alec Stock 1946–49
George Patterson 1949–51
Harry Lowe 1951–53
Ike Clarke 1953–57
Norman Dodgin 1957
Jimmy Baldwin 1957–60
Basil Hayward 1960–64
Glyn Davies 1964–65
Joe McDonald 1965–67
Ron Saunders 1967–69
Mike Hughes 1969–72
Cecil Irwin 1972–75
Stan Harland 1975–81
Barry Lloyd 1978–81
Malcolm Allison 1981
Jimmy Giles 1981–83
Trevor Finnigan/Mike Hughes 1983
Steve Coles 1983–84
Ian McFarlane 1984
Gerry Gow 1984–87
Brian Hall 1987–90
Clive Whitehead 1990–91
Steve Rutter 1991–93
Brian Hall 1994–95
Graham Roberts 1995–98
Colin Lippiatt 1998–99
Steve Thompson 1999–2000
Dave Webb 2000
Gary Johnson 2001–05
Steve Thompson 2005–06
Russell Slade 2006–09
Terry Skiverton 2009–12
Gary Johnson January 2012–

TEN YEAR LEAGUE RECORD

		P	W	D	L	F	A	Pts	Pos
2004-05	FL 2	46	25	8	13	90	65	83	1
2005-06	FL 1	46	15	11	20	54	62	56	15
2006-07	FL 1	46	23	10	13	55	39	79	5
2007-08	FL 1	46	14	10	22	38	59	52	18
2008-09	FL 1	46	12	15	19	41	66	51	17
2009-10	FL 1	46	13	14	19	55	59	53	15
2010-11	FL 1	46	16	11	19	56	66	59	14
2011-12	FL 1	46	14	12	20	59	80	54	17
2012-13	FL 1	46	23	8	15	71	56	77	4
2013-14	FL C	46	8	13	25	44	75	37	24

DID YOU KNOW ?

Yeovil Town applied to join the Football League every year between 1947 and 1960 without success, never receiving more than two votes. They did not gain a single vote between 1954 and 1960.

YEOVIL TOWN – FL CHAMPIONSHIP 2013–14 LEAGUE RECORD

Match No.	Date	Venue	Opponents	Result	H/T Score	Lg Pos.	Goalscorers	Attendance
1	Aug 3	A	Millwall	W 1-0	0-0	8	Upson [89]	12,404
2	10	H	Birmingham C	L 0-1	0-0	13		8717
3	17	A	Burnley	L 0-2	0-0	18		10,085
4	24	H	Derby Co	L 0-3	0-2	19		7047
5	31	H	Reading	L 0-1	0-0	22		7306
6	Sept 14	A	Sheffield W	D 1-1	0-1	21	Ralls [64]	22,328
7	17	A	Ipswich T	L 1-2	1-0	22	Grant [43]	15,340
8	21	H	QPR	L 0-1	0-0	22		9108
9	28	A	Bolton W	D 1-1	0-0	21	Upson [79]	14,716
10	Oct 1	H	Leicester C	L 1-2	0-0	22	Hayter (pen) [84]	6476
11	5	A	Middlesbrough	L 1-4	1-2	23	Davis [4]	13,181
12	19	H	Brighton & HA	D 0-0	0-0	24		6873
13	26	H	Nottingham F	W 3-1	3-1	22	Upson 2 [8, 40], Webster [43]	7612
14	Nov 2	A	Leeds U	L 0-2	0-0	24		25,351
15	10	H	Wigan Ath	L 0-1	0-0	24		6149
16	22	A	Doncaster R	L 1-2	1-1	24	Webster [43]	6620
17	30	A	Watford	W 3-0	1-0	22	Webster [45], Miller [53], Edwards [90]	15,263
18	Dec 3	H	Blackpool	W 1-0	1-0	22	Lundstram [21]	5530
19	7	H	Charlton Ath	D 2-2	0-2	22	Morrison (og) [72], Miller (pen) [76]	6053
20	14	A	Barnsley	D 1-1	1-1	23	Grant [10]	13,361
21	21	H	Blackburn R	L 0-1	0-0	23		7179
22	26	A	Bournemouth	L 0-3	0-0	23		10,717
23	29	A	Huddersfield T	L 1-5	1-3	23	Miller [14]	12,946
24	Jan 11	A	Burnley	L 1-2	1-0	23	Moore [80]	6293
25	18	A	Birmingham C	W 2-0	2-0	23	Hayter 2 [12, 19]	13,605
26	28	A	Derby Co	L 2-3	2-0	24	Lundstram [25], Miller [34]	23,615
27	Feb 2	A	Nottingham F	L 1-3	1-2	24	Moore [25]	21,393
28	8	H	Leeds U	L 1-2	1-0	24	Miller [32]	7984
29	11	H	Millwall	D 1-1	0-0	24	Ralls [64]	4463
30	18	H	Watford	D 0-0	0-0	24		6042
31	22	H	Doncaster R	W 1-0	0-0	24	Hayter (pen) [59]	4934
32	Mar 1	A	Reading	D 1-1	1-0	23	Duffy [20]	18,697
33	8	H	Sheffield W	W 2-0	1-0	22	Miller 2 [41, 51]	6251
34	11	H	Ipswich T	L 0-1	0-1	22		5920
35	15	A	QPR	L 0-3	0-1	23		16,667
36	18	A	Wigan Ath	D 3-3	0-0	23	Miller 2 [62, 85], Ayling [90]	12,970
37	22	D	Bolton W	D 2-2	2-0	23	Miller [33], Dawson [42]	6344
38	25	A	Leicester C	D 1-1	1-0	22	Ralls [22]	26,240
39	29	H	Barnsley	L 1-4	0-0	24	Ayling [70]	6579
40	Apr 5	A	Blackpool	W 2-1	1-0	24	Hayter (pen) [16], Lawrence [74]	13,310
41	8	H	Charlton Ath	L 2-3	1-1	24	Grant [12], Moore [74]	15,430
42	12	H	Bournemouth	D 1-1	1-0	23	Moore [26]	6931
43	18	A	Blackburn R	D 0-0	0-0	24		14,353
44	21	H	Huddersfield T	L 1-2	0-0	24	Lawrence [73]	5903
45	25	A	Brighton & HA	L 0-2	0-0	24		26,901
46	May 3	H	Middlesbrough	L 1-4	1-3	24	Hayter [38]	6477

Final League Position: 24

GOALSCORERS

League (44): Miller 10 (1 pen), Hayter 6 (3 pens), Moore 4, Upson 4, Grant 3, Ralls 3, Webster 3, Ayling 2, Lawrence 2, Lundstram 2, Davis 1, Dawson 1, Duffy 1, Edwards 1, own goal 1.
The Budweiser FA Cup (4): Hayter 2, Grant 1, Moore 1.
Capital One Cup (4): Ayling 1, Dawson 1, Upson 1, Webster 1.

Stech M 26	Ayling L 41+1	Tate A 4	Edwards J 46	Webster B 40+1	Seaborne D 10	Dawson K 17+18	Upson E 21+3	Madden P 7+2	Hayter J 24+13	Foley S 4+3	Ngoo M 1+5	Hoskins S 6+13	Davis L 18+9	Stewart G —+1	Johnstone S 1	Ralls J 33+4	Hennessey W 12	Williams A 7+2	Grant J 27+7	McAllister J 35+3	Fontaine L 4+1	Moore K 10+10	Duffy S 37	Fyvie F 2	Dunn C 7+1	Lundstram J 13+1	Miller I 19	Morgan A 3+9	Bakayogo Z 1	Lanzoni M 2+4	Lawrence T 17+2	Holmes D 5	Palazuelos R 6+3	Nana Ofori-Twumasi S —+3	Match No.
1	2	3	4	5	6	7	8	9^3	10^1	11^2	12	13	14																						1
1^2	2	5	7	3	4	6	8	11	10	9^1	14	13			12																				2
	2	5^2	8	3	4	6^1	7	11	10^3			13	12	9		1	14																		3
	2	4^2	7	3	5	6	9	13				11^3	10						8^1	1	12	14													4
	2		7	3	4	13	8		10^1			14	12						9^2	1	11	6^3	5												5
	2		7	3^4	4	13	8		10^1										9^3	1	11	6^2	5	12	14										6
	2	9^5		3		7			11^2			14	13						10	1	8	6^1	5	4	12										7
	2		7	3	12	9			13			14	10						8	1	11^2	6^1	5	4^3											8
	2		7	3	12	8	10						5						9	1	11	6^1	4												9
2^2		8	12	3^3		7	10	14					5						9	1	11	6	4		13										10
	2	4	14	7		10^2	12	9					8			1	11		6	5^1		13	3												11
12	2	3		6	7	11^1			10			9³				1	14	13	5		4	8^2													12
	2	4		6	7							10	9			8	1		11	5		3													13
	2	3	6^3	7	13		14		10^2	9^1		8	1			11			5		12	4													14
	2	7	4	6^2	10		9^1		13	12		8	1			11			5			3													15
	2	6	3	12	7	14	10^2	13				9				11	5^1		4	8^3	1														16
	2	6	3	14	8	13	12	5				9^1				4			1	7	10^3	11^2													17
	2	6	3	8			12	5				13				9^2			4	1	7	10	11^1												18
	2	6	3	13	8		12	5^2								9	14		4	1	7^2	11	10^1												19
	2	6	3	12	8^3	13		9								11	5		4	1	7^2	10^1	14												20
1	2	6	3^3	12	14	13		9^2	8							10	5		4	7^1	11														21
1		2^2	6	8	12	14	13	9								10	5^1	3	4	7^2	11														22
1^3	3	8	2	7^1	10		14	9								12			6	5^2	4				13	11									23
1	2	7	3	6^3	13	10^1		5								9			11			8^2	14												24
1	2	8	3	14	10^1			9								6	12^3		11	4		7					5^2	13							25
1	2	8	3	12	13			9								6^2	5		11	4		7	10^1												26
1	2	7	3			11^2										9^1			6	5	10	4	8					13	12						27
1	2	8	3	6^2	14											9	5^1		11	4		7^3	10	12		13									28
1	2	7	4	13			12									9^2	5		10^1	3		8	11	14		6^3									29
1	2	7	3		11^2											8	5		12	4		6^1	10	13		9									30
1	2	7	3^4	13		10										8	5		12	4		11^1	9			6^2									31
1	2	7	3	10^3												8^4	5^1		11^4	4		12				9	6^3	13	14						32
1	2	7	3	13		10^1						12				5			4			11^3	14			9	6^3	8							33
1	2	7	3	11^1				13								5			12	4		10^2	14			9	6^3	8							34
1	2	7	3	12												11^2			5^1	4		10	13		8	9	6^3		14						35
1	9	7	3	12												10			6^2	5	13	4				11	2^1	8							36
1	2	7	3	6^2		12						8				13	5		11	4		10				9									37
1	2	7	3	6		12						13				8	5		11	4		10^2				9^1									38
1	2	7	3	6^1		12						13				8	5		11^1	4		10	14			9^2									39
	2	7	3	13		10			9^1							8	6^2	5		4	1					11		12							40
	2	7	3			10			9							8^2	6^1	5	12	4	1					11		13							41
1	2	8	3	11^1				12				9				5			10	4		6				7									42
1	2	6	3	11^1				13				9^2	8			12	5			4		10				7									43
1	2	8	3	6^3		11	14					9^2				13	5			4		12				10							7^1		44
1	2	6	3	14		11^2	10									12	8		5	4		13				9^3							7^1		45
1	2	7	3	6^1		11	9^2	10^3				12	8			13	5		4															14	46

The Budweiser FA Cup

Third Round	Leyton Orient	(h)	4-0
Fourth Round	Southampton	(a)	0-2

Capital One Cup

First Round	Southend U	(a)	1-0
Second Round	Birmingham C	(h)	3-3

(aet; lost 2-3 on penalties)

YORK CITY

Bootham Crescent, York YO30 7AQ.

Telephone: (01904) 624 447.

Fax: (01904) 631 457.

Ticket Office: (01904) 624 447 (ext 1).

Website: www.yorkcityfootballclub.co.uk

Email: enquiries@yorkcityfootballclub.co.uk

Ground Capacity: 8,105.

Record Attendance: 28,123 v Huddersfield T, FA Cup 6th rd, 5 March 1938.

Pitch Measurements: 104m × 64m (113.5yd × 70yd)

Chairman: Jason McGill.

Manager: Nigel Worthington.

Assistant Manager: Steve Torpey.

Physio: Jeff Miller.

Colours: Red shirts with white sleeves, blue shorts, white socks with blue trim.

Year Formed: 1922.

Turned Professional: 1922.

Ltd Co.: 1922.

Club Nickname: 'Minstermen'.

Previous Grounds: 1922, Fulfordgate; 1932, Bootham Crescent.

First Football League Game: 31 August 1929, Division 3 (N), v Wigan Borough (a) W 2–0 – Farmery; Archibald, Johnson; Beck, Davis, Thompson; Evans, Gardner, Cowie (1), Smailes, Stockill (1).

Record League Victory: 9–1 v Southport, Division 3 (N), 2 February 1957 – Forgan; Phillips, Howe; Brown (1), Cairney, Mollatt; Hill, Bottom (4 incl. 1p), Wilkinson (2), Wragg (1), Fenton (1).

Record Cup Victory: 6–0 v South Shields (a), FA Cup 1st rd, 16 November 1968 – Widdowson; Baker (1p), Richardson; Carr, Jackson, Burrows; Taylor, Ross (3), MacDougall (2), Hodgson, Boyer.

Record Defeat: 0–12 v Chester, Division 3 (N), 1 February 1936.

Most League Points (2 for a win): 62, Division 4, 1964–65.

HONOURS

Football League – Division 3: *Promoted* 1973–74 (3rd); **Division 4:** *Champions* 1983–84. 1992–93 *(play-offs).*

FA Cup: *Semi-finals* 1955, *when in Division 3.*

Football League Cup: Best season: 5th rd, 1962.

FA Trophy: *Winners* 2012; *Runners-up* 2009.

sky SPORTS FACT FILE

York City's record goalscorer Norman Wilkinson was a part-time footballer who also worked as a boot and shoe repairer throughout his playing career. He netted twice for the Minstermen on his debut against Wrexham and was one of the heroes of the team that reached the FA Cup semi-final in 1954–55.

Most League Points (3 for a win): 101, Division 4, 1983–84.

Most League Goals: 96, Division 4, 1983–84.

Highest League Scorer in Season: Bill Fenton, 31, Division 3 (N), 1951–52; Arthur Bottom, 31, Division 3 (N), 1954–55 and 1955–56.

Most League Goals in Total Aggregate: Norman Wilkinson, 125, 1954–66.

Most League Goals in One Match: 5, Alf Patrick v Rotherham U, Division 3N, 20 November 1948.

Most Capped Player: Peter Scott, 7 (10), Northern Ireland.

Most League Appearances: Barry Jackson, 481, 1958–70.

Youngest League Player: Reg Stockill, 15 years 281 days v Wigan Borough, 31 August 1929.

Record Transfer Fee Received: £950,000 from Sheffield W for Richard Cresswell, March 1999.

Record Transfer Fee Paid: £140,000 to Burnley for Adrian Randall, December 1995.

Football League Record: 1929 Elected to Division 3 (N); 1958–59 Division 4; 1959–60 Division 3; 1960–65 Division 4; 1965–66 Division 3; 1966–71 Division 4; 1971–74 Division 3; 1974–76 Division 2; 1976–77 Division 3; 1977–84 Division 4; 1984–88 Division 3; 1988–92 Division 4; 1992–93 Division 3; 1993–99 Division 2; 1999–04 Division 3; 2004–07 Conference; 2007–12 Conference Premier; 2012– FL 2.

MANAGERS

Bill Sherrington 1924–60
(was Secretary for most of this time but virtually Secretary-Manager for a long pre-war spell)
John Collier 1929–36
Tom Mitchell 1936–50
Dick Duckworth 1950–52
Charlie Spencer 1952–53
Jimmy McCormick 1953–54
Sam Bartram 1956–60
Tom Lockie 1960–67
Joe Shaw 1967–68
Tom Johnston 1968–75
Wilf McGuinness 1975–77
Charlie Wright 1977–80
Barry Lyons 1980–81
Denis Smith 1982–87
Bobby Saxton 1987–88
John Bird 1988–91
John Ward 1991–93
Alan Little 1993–99
Neil Thompson 1999–2000
Terry Dolan 2000–03
Chris Brass 2003–04
Billy McEwan 2005–07
Colin Walker 2007–08
Martin Foyle 2008–10
Gary Mills 2010–13
Nigel Worthington March 2013–

LATEST SEQUENCES

Longest Sequence of League Wins: 7, 31.10.1964 – 26.12.1964.

Longest Sequence of League Defeats: 8, 14.11.1966 – 31.12.1966.

Longest Sequence of League Draws: 6, 26.12.1992 – 22.1.1993.

Longest Sequence of Unbeaten League Matches: 21, 10.9.1973 – 12.1.1974.

Longest Sequence Without a League Win: 21, 17.1.2004 – 18.8.2012.

Successive Scoring Runs: 24 from 3.3.1984.

Successive Non-scoring Runs: 7 from 28.8.1972.

TEN YEAR LEAGUE RECORD

		P	W	D	L	F	A	Pts	Pos
2004-05	Conf	42	11	10	21	39	66	43	17
2005-06	Conf	42	17	12	13	63	48	63	8
2006-07	Conf	46	23	11	12	65	45	80	4
2007-08	Conf P	46	17	11	18	71	74	62	14
2008-09	Conf P	46	11	19	16	47	51	52	17
2009-10	Conf P	44	22	12	10	62	35	78	5
2010-11	Conf P	46	19	14	13	55	50	71	8
2011-12	Conf P	46	23	14	9	81	45	83	4
2012-13	FL 2	46	12	19	15	50	60	55	17
2013-14	FL 2	46	18	17	11	52	41	71	7

DID YOU KNOW ?

York City applied for membership of the Football League before they had even played a competitive match. The club was formed early in 1922 but received just one vote at that year's AGM and were not elected. They made two more unsuccessful applications before replacing Ashington in 1929.

YORK CITY – FOOTBALL LEAGUE TWO 2013–14 LEAGUE RECORD

Match No.	Date	Venue	Opponents	Result	H/T Score	Lg Pos.	Goalscorers	Attendance
1	Aug 3	H	Northampton T	W 1-0	0-0	8	Jarvis [90]	4388
2	10	A	Dagenham & R	L 0-2	0-1	14		1487
3	17	A	Hartlepool U	D 0-0	0-0	13		4768
4	24	A	Bristol R	L 2-3	1-2	19	Jarvis 2 (1 pen) [41, 64 (p)]	5569
5	31	A	Exeter C	L 1-2	1-1	20	Jarvis [19]	3448
6	Sept 7	H	AFC Wimbledon	L 0-2	0-1	22		3530
7	14	H	Mansfield T	L 1-2	1-1	23	Brobbel [2]	3513
8	21	A	Wycombe W	D 1-1	0-0	22	McGurk [64]	4015
9	28	H	Portsmouth	W 4-2	1-0	21	Fletcher 2 [4, 66], Montrose [58], Jarvis [64]	4848
10	Oct 5	A	Torquay U	W 3-0	0-0	16	Fletcher [53], Carson [67], Jarvis [73]	2559
11	19	A	Newport Co	L 0-3	0-2	18		3475
12	22	A	Chesterfield	D 2-2	1-0	18	O'Neill [35], Jarvis [61]	5907
13	26	H	Fleetwood T	L 0-2	0-1	20		3523
14	29	H	Scunthorpe U	W 4-1	4-0	18	Carson [3], Fletcher [12], Brobbel 2 [21, 40]	3636
15	Nov 2	A	Cheltenham T	D 2-2	1-2	19	Bowman 2 [20, 54]	2706
16	16	H	Plymouth Arg	D 1-1	0-0	19	Bowman [54]	3803
17	23	A	Southend U	L 1-2	0-1	19	Bowman [56]	9018
18	26	A	Morecambe	D 0-0	0-0	21		1381
19	30	H	Rochdale	D 0-0	0-0	21		3471
20	Dec 14	A	Burton Alb	D 1-1	0-0	20	Cansdell-Sherriff (og) [64]	2344
21	21	H	Oxford U	D 0-0	0-0	21		3526
22	26	A	Accrington S	D 1-1	1-1	20	Fletcher (pen) [35]	2009
23	29	A	Bury	L 1-2	0-2	22	Coulson [73]	3706
24	Jan 1	H	Morecambe	W 1-0	1-0	20	Jarvis [30]	3276
25	4	A	Dagenham & R	W 3-1	0-0	17	Bowman [52], Fletcher 2 [65, 71]	3207
26	11	A	Northampton T	W 2-0	0-0	14	Bowman [68], Fletcher (pen) [70]	4448
27	18	H	Bristol R	D 0-0	0-0	13		3514
28	25	A	Hartlepool U	L 0-2	0-0	15		4673
29	28	H	Chesterfield	L 0-2	0-2	16		3322
30	Feb 1	A	Fleetwood T	W 2-1	1-0	13	McLaughlin (og) [45], Fletcher [90]	2513
31	8	H	Cheltenham T	D 0-0	0-0	14		3148
32	15	A	Plymouth Arg	W 4-0	2-0	11	Fletcher (pen) [12], McCombe 2 [45, 89], Carson [90]	6502
33	22	H	Southend U	D 0-0	0-0	11		3628
34	Mar 1	H	Exeter C	W 2-1	2-1	10	McCombe [17], Coulson [27]	3212
35	8	A	AFC Wimbledon	W 1-0	1-0	9	Coulson [41]	4182
36	11	A	Mansfield T	W 1-0	1-0	9	Bowman (pen) [32]	2865
37	15	H	Wycombe W	W 2-0	2-0	8	Bowman (pen) [7], Carson [45]	3455
38	22	A	Portsmouth	W 1-0	1-0	7	Coulson [6]	14,814
39	25	H	Torquay U	W 1-0	1-0	7	Hayhurst [11]	3416
40	29	H	Burton Alb	D 0-0	0-0	8		3988
41	Apr 5	A	Rochdale	D 0-0	0-0	7		3830
42	12	H	Accrington S	D 1-1	0-0	8	Coulson (pen) [61]	3855
43	18	A	Oxford U	W 1-0	0-0	7	Coulson (pen) [48]	7118
44	21	H	Bury	W 1-0	1-0	7	Lowe [5]	5225
45	26	H	Newport Co	W 1-0	0-0	6	Coulson [77]	4531
46	May 3	A	Scunthorpe U	D 2-2	1-2	7	Brobbel [45], Andrew [71]	7482

Final League Position: 7

GOALSCORERS

League (52): Fletcher 10 (3 pens), Bowman 8 (2 pens), Jarvis 8 (1 pen), Coulson 7 (2 pens), Brobbel 4, Carson 4, McCombe 3, Andrew 1, Hayhurst 1, Lowe 1, McGurk 1, Montrose 1, O'Neill 1, own goals 2.
The Budweiser FA Cup (5): Fletcher 3 (1 pen), Carson 1, Jarvis 1.
Capital One Cup (0).
Johnstone's Paint Trophy (0).
League Two Play-Offs (0).

Ingham M 19	Oyebanjo L 41	Davies B 44	Puri S 3+5	McGurk D 21+2	Smith C 8+1	Clay C 6+2	Platt T 11+9	Jarvis R 21+14	Cresswell R 3+3	Chambers A 8+7	Bowman R 22+15	Coulson M 22+11	Montrose L 26+7	Fletcher W 24+8	Allan T 4+1	Parslow D 13	Taft G 2+1	Brobbel R 16+3	Chamberlain T —+2	Fyfield J 1+1	Whitehouse E 15	Carson J 29+2	O'Neill L 15	Pope N 22	Lowe K 30	McCarey A 5	Penn R 21	Reed A 17+2	McCombe J 18+1	Hayhurst W 14+4	Dickinson C —+2	Andrew C 5+3	Match No.
1	2	3	4¹	5	6	7	8	9	10	11	12																						1
1	2	5		4	3	12	8	10	11³	9¹	14	6	7¹	13																			2
1	2	5		4	6	8	10¹	11²	9¹	14	12		13	3	7																		3
1	2	5	14	3	6	7	10			9¹	12¹	13		11¹	4	8³																	4
1	2	5		3	7	8	10		11¹		9¹	6²			4	12	13	14															5
1	2	5	9		3	6¹	8	10		11²		12	7		4		13																6
1	2	5	6¹	3			11	13⁸				7	10²		4	14	9¹		8	12													7
1	2	5	14	3			11			13	12		7	10¹		4		9²		8	6¹												8
1	2	5	13	3			12	11			14		7¹	10³		4			8	6													9
1		5		4		8	14	11		12	13			10²		3		9¹		7	6	2³											10
1			3				11³	14		6¹	13		7	10²		4		12	5	9	8	2											11
1	2	5		3			12	11²				6	13		4		10¹		8	7	9												12
1	2²	5		3¹			11³			14		7	13	12	4		10		9	6	8												13
1		5		12			14	13	10	7	11³		4¹	3	9		8	6²	2														14
1		5	12	3		7	13	14		11³			10²		4		9¹		8	6	2												15
1	6	5		3	13		9¹	12	11		7	10		4			8		2²														16
	2	5	12				11⁸		7	10		4¹				8	9	6	1	3													17
	2	5	4			11¹		12			7	10		8	9	6	1	3															18
	6¹	5	3		8	11	10¹		13	7		12		9	2	4	1																19
	6	5	3			10		12	7	11		8	9	2¹	4	1																	20
		5	4		8	11²	13		12	7	10		9⁴		6	2	3	1															21
	6¹	5	4			11²		13	12	8	10		7	9	2	3	1																22
	6	5	3		13	14		11³	12	8¹	10		7	9²	2	4	1																23
1	6²	5	3		8	10¹		12	9	7	11		13	2	4																		24
1	2	5	12	3		8		13	10	9²	7	11		6¹		4																	25
1	2	5		3		13	12²		11	9	7	10¹		6		4	8																26
	2	5		4			13		11²	9	8	10		6		1	3	7¹	12														27
	2	5		4			12²		11¹	9	8	10		6		1	3	7	13														28
	2¹	6	4³		14				11²	13	10		7		1	5	8	9	3	12													29
	2	5						11	12		10		6¹		1	3	8	7	4	9¹													30
	2	5						11	9		10		6¹		1	3	7	8	4	12													31
	2	5						10³	12	13	11¹		6		1	3	7²	8	4	9	14												32
	2	5						11¹	10²			6		1	3	7	8	4	9	13													33
	2	5			14		12		10²	11	13		6		1	3	8	7³	4	9¹													34
	2	5			14			11	10	13	12		6³		1	3	7	8²	4	9¹													35
	2	5				14		10¹	11²	13	12		6		1	3	7	8³	4	9													36
	2	5				13		11¹	10¹	14	12		6		1	3	7	8³	4	9													37
	2	5				13		11	10		12⁴		6¹		1	3	8	7	4	9													38
	2	5			13	6¹		10	11			1	3	7	8	4	9²	12															39
	2	5			13		11¹	10		6		1	3	7	8	4	9²	12															40
	2				13		11³	10	14	5	9		1	3	7	8³	4	6¹	12														41
	2	5				12	10		6		1	3	7	8	4	9¹	11																42
	2	5	12			14	10	13	9		1	3	8	7⁴	4	6¹	11³																43
	2	5				13	10²	8		6		1	3	7	12	4	9¹	11															44
	2	5				12	11	8²		6¹		1	3	7	9	4	13	10															45
	2	5			13		10	7¹		6²		1	3	8	9	4	12	11															46

The Budweiser FA Cup
First Round — Bristol R — (a) — 3-3
Replay — Bristol R — (h) — 2-3

Capital One Cup
First Round — Burnley — (h) — 0-4

Johnstone's Paint Trophy
Second Round — Rotherham U — (h) — 0-3

League Two Play-Offs
Semi-Finals 1st leg — Fleetwood T — (h) — 0-1
Semi-Finals 2nd leg — Fleetwood T — (a) — 0-0

ENGLISH LEAGUE PLAYERS DIRECTORY

Players listed represent those with their clubs during the 2013–14 season.

Players are listed alphabetically on pages 538–543.

The number alongside each player corresponds to the team number heading. (Abbott, Brad 5 = team 5 (Barnsley)). Club names in italic indicate loans.

ACCRINGTON S (1)

ALDRED, Tom (D)   71   2
H: 6 2   W: 13 02   b.Bolton 11-9-90
Internationals: Scotland U19.

2008–09	Carlisle U	0	0	
2009–10	Carlisle U	5	0	5 0
2010–11	Watford	0	0	
2010–11	*Stockport Co*	7	0	7 0
2011–12	Watford	0	0	
2011–12	Colchester U	0	0	
2011–12	*Torquay U*	0	0	
2012–13	Colchester U	0	0	
2012–13	Accrington S	13	0	
2013–14	Accrington S	46	2	59 2

ATKINSON, Rob (D)   147   5
H: 6 1   W: 12 03   b.Beverley 29-4-87
Internationals: England C.

2003–04	Barnsley	1	0	
2004–05	Barnsley	1	0	
2005–06	Barnsley	0	0	
2006–07	Barnsley	6	0	
2007–08	Barnsley	0	0	8 0
2007–08	*Rochdale*	2	0	2 0
2007–08	*Grimsby T*	24	1	
2008–09	Grimsby T	31	2	
2009–10	Grimsby T	37	2	92 5
2012–13	Fleetwood T	18	0	18 0
2012–13	*Accrington S*	12	0	
2013–14	Accrington S	15	0	27 0

BEATTIE, James (F)   443 131
H: 6 1   W: 13 06   b.Lancaster 27-2-78
Internationals: England R, Full caps.

1994–95	Blackburn R	0	0	
1995–96	Blackburn R	0	0	
1996–97	Blackburn R	1	0	
1997–98	Blackburn R	3	0	4 0
1998–99	Southampton	35	5	
1999–2000	Southampton	18	0	
2000–01	Southampton	37	11	
2001–02	Southampton	28	12	
2002–03	Southampton	38	23	
2003–04	Southampton	37	14	
2004–05	Southampton	11	3	204 68
2004–05	Everton	11	1	
2005–06	Everton	32	10	
2006–07	Everton	33	2	76 13
2007–08	Sheffield U	39	22	
2008–09	Sheffield U	23	12	
2008–09	Stoke C	16	7	
2009–10	Stoke C	22	3	38 10
2010–11	*Rangers*	7	0	7 0
2010–11	*Blackpool*	9	0	9 0
2011–12	Sheffield U	18	0	
2012–13	Sheffield U	0	0	80 34
2012–13	Accrington S	25	6	
2013–14	Accrington S	0	0	25 6

BOWERMAN, George (F)   64 12
H: 5 10   W: 10 07   b.Sedgley 6-11-91

2010–11	Walsall	0	0	
2011–12	Walsall	22	3	
2012–13	Walsall	28	6	
2013–14	Walsall	0	0	50 9
2013–14	Accrington S	14	3	14 3

CARVER, Marcus (F)   19   0
H: 5 11   W: 11-11   b.Blackburn 22-10-93

2011–12	Accrington S	2	0	
2012–13	Accrington S	11	0	
2013–14	Accrington S	6	0	19 0

CLARK, Luke (D)   9   0
H: 5 10   W: 11 05   b.Preston 24-5-94

2011–12	Preston NE	2	0	2 0
2012–13	Accrington S	6	0	
2013–14	Accrington S	1	0	7 0

DAWBER, Andrew (G)   5   0
b. 20-11-94

2012–13	Accrington S	2	0	
2013–14	Accrington S	3	0	5 0

DUNBAVIN, Ian (G)   247
H: 6 1   W: 12 10   b.Knowsley 27-5-80

1998–99	Liverpool	0	0	
1999–2000	Liverpool	0	0	
1999–2000	Shrewsbury T	7	0	
2000–01	Shrewsbury T	22	0	
2001–02	Shrewsbury T	34	0	
2002–03	Shrewsbury T	33	0	
2003–04	Shrewsbury T	0	0	96 0

From Halifax T.

2006–07	Accrington S	23	0	
2007–08	Accrington S	23	0	
2008–09	Accrington S	4	0	
2009–10	Accrington S	27	0	
2010–11	Accrington S	25	0	
2011–12	Accrington S	25	0	
2012–13	Accrington S	20	0	
2013–14	Accrington S	4	0	151 0
2013–14	*Chesterfield*	0	0	

GRAY, James (F)   51   9
H: 5 11   b.Stockton on Tees 17-10-92
Internationals: Northern Ireland U16, U17, U19, U21.

2012–13	Accrington S	16	2	
2013–14	Accrington S	35	7	51 9

HATFIELD, Will (M)   80   5
H: 5 8   W: 10 00   b.Liversedge 10-10-91

2009–10	Leeds U	0	0	
2010–11	Leeds U	0	0	
2011–12	Leeds U	0	0	
2011–12	*Accrington S*	17	3	
2012–13	Accrington S	32	2	
2013–14	Accrington S	31	0	80 5

HUNT, Nicky (D)   241   2
H: 6 1   W: 13 07   b.Westhoughton 3-9-83
Internationals: England U21.

2000–01	Bolton W	1	0	
2001–02	Bolton W	0	0	
2002–03	Bolton W	0	0	
2003–04	Bolton W	31	1	
2004–05	Bolton W	29	0	
2005–06	Bolton W	20	0	
2006–07	Bolton W	33	0	
2007–08	Bolton W	14	0	
2008–09	Bolton W	0	0	
2008–09	*Birmingham C*	11	0	11 0
2009–10	Bolton W	0	0	128 1
2009–10	*Derby Co*	21	0	21 0
2010–11	Bristol C	7	0	
2011–12	Bristol C	0	0	7 0
2011–12	Preston NE	17	1	17 1
2012–13	Rotherham U	9	0	9 0
2012–13	Accrington S	11	0	
2013–14	Accrington S	37	0	48 0

JOYCE, Luke (M)   227   7
H: 5 11   W: 12 03   b.Bolton 9-7-87

2005–06	Wigan Ath	0	0	
2005–06	Carlisle U	0	0	
2006–07	Carlisle U	16	1	
2007–08	Carlisle U	3	1	
2008–09	Carlisle U	7	0	26 2
2009–10	Accrington S	41	1	
2010–11	Accrington S	27	1	
2011–12	Accrington S	43	2	
2012–13	Accrington S	44	0	
2013–14	Accrington S	46	1	201 5

LIDDLE, Michael (D)   86   0
H: 5 6   W: 11 00   b.Hounslow 25-12-89
Internationals: Republic of Ireland U21.

2007–08	Sunderland	0	0	
2008–09	Sunderland	0	0	
2008–09	*Carlisle U*	22	0	22 0
2009–10	Sunderland	0	0	
2010–11	Sunderland	0	0	
2010–11	*Leyton Orient*	1	0	1 0
2011–12	Sunderland	0	0	
2011–12	*Accrington S*	12	0	
2012–13	Accrington S	32	0	
2013–14	Accrington S	19	0	63 0

McCARTAN, Shay (M)   19   1
H: 5 10   W: 11 09   b.Newry 18-5-94

2011–12	Burnley	1	0	
2012–13	Burnley	0	0	1 0
2013–14	Accrington S	18	1	18 1

MILLER, George (M)   36   3
H: 5 9   W: 12 02   b.Eccleston 25-11-91

2009–10	Preston NE	0	0	
2010–11	Preston NE	1	0	
2011–12	Preston NE	6	0	7 0
2012–13	Accrington S	25	3	
2013–14	Accrington S	4	0	29 3

MINGOIA, Piero (M)   49   2
H: 5 6   W: 10 12   b.Enfield 20-10-91

2010–11	Watford	5	0	
2011–12	Watford	0	0	
2011–12	*Brentford*	0	0	
2012–13	Watford	0	0	
2012–13	*Accrington S*	7	1	
2013–14	Watford	0	0	5 0
2013–14	Accrington S	37	1	44 2

MURPHY, Peter (D)   155 18
H: 6 0   W: 11 10   b.Liverpool 13-2-90

2007–08	Accrington S	2	0	
2008–09	Accrington S	3	0	
2009–10	Accrington S	10	0	
2010–11	Accrington S	13	0	
2011–12	Accrington S	38	4	
2012–13	Accrington S	45	5	
2013–14	Accrington S	44	9	155 18

NAISMITH, Kal (F)   38 10
H: 5 7   W: 13 02   b.Glasgow 18-2-92
Internationals: Scotland U16, U19.

2013–14	Accrington S	38	10	38 10

WEBBER, Danny (F)   250 49
H: 5 10   W: 11 04   b.Manchester 28-12-81
Internationals: England U20.

1998–99	Manchester U	0	0	
1999–2000	Manchester U	0	0	
2000–01	Manchester U	0	0	
2001–02	Manchester U	0	0	
2001–02	*Port Vale*	4	0	4 0
2001–02	*Watford*	5	2	
2002–03	Manchester U	0	0	
2002–03	*Watford*	2	0	
2003–04	Watford	27	5	
2004–05	Watford	28	12	72 21
2004–05	*Sheffield U*	7	3	
2005–06	Sheffield U	35	10	
2006–07	Sheffield U	22	3	
2007–08	Sheffield U	14	3	
2008–09	Sheffield U	36	4	
2009–10	Sheffield U	0	0	114 23
2009–10	Portsmouth	17	1	
2010–11	Portsmouth	8	0	
2011–12	Portsmouth	0	0	25 1
2011–12	Leeds U	13	1	13 1
2013–14	Accrington S	22	3	22 3

WILSON, Laurence (D)   278 16
H: 5 10   W: 10 09   b.Huyton 10-10-86
Internationals: England U18, U19.

2004–05	Everton	0	0	
2005–06	Everton	0	0	
2005–06	*Mansfield T*	15	1	15 1
2006–07	Chester C	41	1	
2007–08	Chester C	40	2	
2008–09	Chester C	34	1	115 4

2009–10	Morecambe	41	3	
2010–11	Morecambe	38	3	
2011–12	Morecambe	30	5	109 11
2012–13	Rotherham U	5	0	5 0
2012–13	Accrington S	19	0	
2013–14	Accrington S	15	0	34 0

WINDASS, Josh (M)   10 0
b.Hull 9-1-93
| 2013–14 | Accrington S | 10 | 0 | 10 0 |

WINNARD, Dean (D)   198 5
H: 5 9 W: 10 04 b.Wigan 20-8-89
2006–07	Blackburn R	0	0	
2007–08	Blackburn R	0	0	
2008–09	Blackburn R	0	0	
2009–10	Accrington S	44	0	
2010–11	Accrington S	45	1	
2011–12	Accrington S	30	1	
2012–13	Accrington S	40	1	
2013–14	Accrington S	39	2	198 5

Scholars
Atkinson, Connor Michael; Barker, Dalian Aaron; Clarke, Joseph Paul; Downey, Dieter; Goulding, Liam John; Greaves, Luke Andrew James; Hazeldine, Max Cameron; Hennigan, Daniel Stephen; Hudson, Nathan Paul; Jenkins, James Edward; Quansah, Keenan Elliott; Steenson, Kealan Joseph; Walsh, Callum Joseph; Wolland, Kieran Fred.

AFC WIMBLEDON (2)

ANTWI, Will (D)   87 2
H: 6 1 W: 13 07 b.London 19-10-82
Internationals: Ghana Full caps.
2002–03	Crystal Palace	4	0	
2003–04	Crystal Palace	0	0	4 0

From Aldershot T
2005–06	Wycombe W	5	0	
2006–07	Wycombe W	25	0	
2007–08	Wycombe W	6	0	
2008–09	Wycombe W	6	0	42 1

From Dagenham & R, Luton T, Grimsby T
2012–13	AFC Wimbledon	23	0	
2013–14	AFC Wimbledon	18	1	41 1

ARTHUR, Chris (M)   33 1
H: 5 10 W: 12 02 b.Enfield 25-1-90
2011–12	Northampton T	7	0	7 0
2013–14	AFC Wimbledon	26	1	26 1

BAYES, Ashley (G)   307 0
H: 6 1 W: 13 04 b.Lincoln 19-4-72
Internationals: England U18.
1989–90	Brentford	1	0	
1990–91	Brentford	1	0	
1991–92	Brentford	1	0	
1992–93	Brentford	2	0	4 0
1993–94	Torquay U	32	0	
1994–95	Torquay U	37	0	
1995–96	Torquay U	28	0	97 0
1996–97	Exeter C	41	0	
1997–98	Exeter C	45	0	
1998–99	Exeter C	41	0	127 0
2000–01	Leyton Orient	39	0	
2001–02	Leyton Orient	13	0	52 0
2002–03	Bohemians	27	0	27 0

From Woking, Hornchurch, Grays Ath, Crawley T, Stevenage, Basingstoke
2013–14	AFC Wimbledon	0	0	

BEERE, Tom (F)   0 0
b. 27-1-95
2012–13	AFC Wimbledon	0	0	
2013–14	AFC Wimbledon	0	0	

BENNETT, Alan (D)   212 7
H: 6 2 W: 12 08 b.Cork 4-10-81
Internationals: Republic of Ireland U21, B, Full caps.
2006–07	Reading	0	0	
2007–08	Reading	0	0	
2007–08	*Southampton*	10	0	10 0
2007–08	*Brentford*	11	1	
2008–09	Reading	0	0	
2008–09	*Brentford*	44	1	
2009–10	Brentford	13	0	68 2
2009–10	*Wycombe W*	6	1	
2010–11	Wycombe W	17	0	23 1

2011–12	Cheltenham T	44	2	
2012–13	Cheltenham T	17	0	61 2
2012–13	AFC Wimbledon	18	1	
2013–14	AFC Wimbledon	32	1	50 2

BROWN, Sebastian (G)   61 0
H: 6 2 W: 13 07 b.Carshalton 24-11-89
Internationals: England C.
2008–09	Brentford	0	0	
2009–10	Brentford	0	0	
2011–12	AFC Wimbledon	44	0	
2012–13	AFC Wimbledon	16	0	
2013–14	AFC Wimbledon	1	0	61 0

FAYERS, Charlie (M)   0 0
b.Hastings 6-2-95
2013–14	AFC Wimbledon	0	0	

FENLON, Jim (D)   36 1
b. 3-3-94
2012–13	AFC Wimbledon	17	1	
2013–14	AFC Wimbledon	19	0	36 1

FRAMPTON, Andrew (D)   363 12
H: 5 11 W: 10 10 b.Wimbledon 3-9-79
1998–99	Crystal Palace	6	0	
1999–2000	Crystal Palace	9	0	
2000–01	Crystal Palace	10	0	
2001–02	Crystal Palace	2	0	
2002–03	Crystal Palace	1	0	28 0
2002–03	Brentford	15	0	
2003–04	Brentford	16	0	
2004–05	Brentford	35	0	
2005–06	Brentford	36	3	
2006–07	Brentford	32	1	134 4
2007–08	Millwall	30	1	
2008–09	Millwall	37	1	
2009–10	Millwall	21	2	
2010–11	Millwall	0	0	88 4
2010–11	*Leyton Orient*	1	0	1 0
2010–11	*Swindon T*	23	0	23 0
2011–12	Gillingham	28	0	
2012–13	Gillingham	30	0	
2013–14	Gillingham	0	0	58 0
2013–14	AFC Wimbledon	31	4	31 4

FRANCOMB, George (D)   77 3
H: 5 11 W: 11 07 b.Hackney 8-9-91
2009–10	Norwich C	2	0	
2010–11	Norwich C	0	0	
2010–11	*Barnet*	13	0	13 0
2011–12	Norwich C	0	0	
2011–12	*Hibernian*	14	0	14 0
2012–13	Norwich C	0	0	2 0
2012–13	*AFC Wimbledon*	15	0	
2013–14	AFC Wimbledon	33	3	48 3

FULLER, Barry (D)   233 7
H: 5 10 W: 11 10 b.Ashford 25-9-84
Internationals: England C.
2004–05	Charlton Ath	0	0	
2005–06	Charlton Ath	0	0	
2005–06	*Barnet*	15	1	

From Stevenage B.
2007–08	Gillingham	10	0	
2008–09	Gillingham	37	0	
2009–10	Gillingham	36	0	
2010–11	Gillingham	42	0	
2011–12	Gillingham	9	0	
2012–13	Gillingham	0	0	134 0
2012–13	Barnet	39	0	54 1
2013–14	AFC Wimbledon	45	0	45 0

JACQUART, Chace (M)   0 0
b. 16-7-95
2013–14	AFC Wimbledon	0	0	

JONES, Darren (D)   213 7
H: 6 0 W: 14 12 b.Newport 28-8-83
Internationals: Wales Schools, Youth.
2000–01	Bristol C	0	0	
2001–02	Bristol C	2	0	
2002–03	Bristol C	0	0	
2003–04	Bristol C	0	0	2 0
2003–04	*Cheltenham T*	14	1	14 1

From Forest Green R.
2009–10	Hereford U	41	3	41 3
2010–11	Aldershot T	43	1	
2011–12	Aldershot T	42	0	85 1
2012–13	Shrewsbury T	38	1	
2013–14	Shrewsbury T	15	0	53 1
2013–14	AFC Wimbledon	18	1	18 1

KENNEDY, Callum (D)   80 1
H: 6 1 W: 12 10 b.Chertsey 9-11-89
2007–08	Swindon T	0	0	
2008–09	Swindon T	4	0	
2009–10	Swindon T	8	0	
2010–11	Swindon T	3	0	
2010–11	*Gillingham*	3	0	3 0
2010–11	*Rotherham U*	5	0	5 0
2011–12	Swindon T	18	1	33 1
2012–13	Scunthorpe U	17	0	17 0
2013–14	AFC Wimbledon	22	0	22 0

MIDSON, Jack (F)   156 46
H: 5 8 W: 11 07 b.Stevenage 21-7-83
2010–11	Oxford U	21	6	21 6
2010–11	*Southend U*	4	2	4 2
2010–11	*Barnet*	5	0	5 0
2011–12	AFC Wimbledon	46	18	
2012–13	AFC Wimbledon	43	13	
2013–14	AFC Wimbledon	37	7	126 38

MOORE, Luke (F)   105 16
H: 5 11 W: 11 07 b.Gravesend 27-4-88
Internationals: England C.
2011–12	AFC Wimbledon	37	9	
2012–13	AFC Wimbledon	35	4	
2013–14	AFC Wimbledon	33	3	105 16

Transferred to Chivas February 2014.

MOORE, Sammy (M)   130 14
H: 5 8 W: 9 00 b.Dover 7-9-87
2006–07	Ipswich T	1	0	
2007–08	Ipswich T	0	0	
2007–08	*Brentford*	20	2	20 2
2008–09	Ipswich T	0	0	1 0
2011–12	AFC Wimbledon	41	6	
2012–13	AFC Wimbledon	28	2	
2013–14	AFC Wimbledon	40	4	109 12

MORRIS, Aaron (D)   116 2
H: 6 1 W: 12 05 b.Cardiff 30-12-89
Internationals: Wales Youth, U21.
2008–09	Cardiff C	1	0	
2009–10	Cardiff C	1	0	1 0
2010–11	Aldershot T	22	0	
2011–12	Aldershot T	39	2	
2012–13	Aldershot T	37	0	98 2
2013–14	AFC Wimbledon	17	0	17 0

NICHOLSON, Jake (M)   6 1
H: 6 0 W: 11 07 b.Harrow 19-7-92
Internationals: England U19.
2010–11	Tottenham H	0	0	
2010–11	*MyPa*	2	0	2 0
2011–12	Tottenham H	0	0	
2012–13	Tottenham H	0	0	
2013–14	AFC Wimbledon	4	1	4 1

NIGHTINGALE, Will (M)   0 0
2013–14	AFC Wimbledon	0	0	

OAKLEY, George (F)   0 0
2013–14	AFC Wimbledon	0	0	

PELL, Harry (M)   97 9
H: 6 4 W: 13 05 b.Tilbury 21-10-91
2010–11	Bristol R	10	0	10 0
2010–11	Hereford U	7	0	
2011–12	Hereford U	30	3	37 3
2012–13	AFC Wimbledon	17	2	
2013–14	AFC Wimbledon	33	4	50 6

SAINTE-LUCE, Kevin (M)   37 3
H: 5 10 W: 11 11 b.Paris 28-4-93
2012–13	Cardiff C	0	0	
2012–13	AFC Wimbledon	14	2	
2013–14	AFC Wimbledon	23	1	37 3

SHERINGHAM, Charlie (F)   21 2
H: 6 1 W: 11 06 · b.Chingford 17-4-88
2006–07	Crystal Palace	0	0	
2007–08	Crystal Palace	0	0	

From Welling U, Bishop's Stortford, Histon, Dartford.
2011–12	Bournemouth	6	1	
2012–13	Bournemouth	0	0	6 1
2013–14	AFC Wimbledon	15	1	15 1

STRUTTON, Charlie (F)   17 0
b.Brent 17-4-89
2011–12	AFC Wimbledon	0	0	
2012–13	AFC Wimbledon	14	0	
2013–14	AFC Wimbledon	3	0	17 0

SWEENEY, Peter (M) 276 16
H: 6 0 W: 12 11 b.Glasgow 25-9-84
Internationals: Scotland U21, B.

2001–02	Millwall	1	0		
2002–03	Millwall	5	1		
2003–04	Millwall	29	2		
2004–05	Millwall	24	2	59	5
2005–06	Stoke C	17	1		
2006–07	Stoke C	13	1		
2006–07	Yeovil T	8	0	8	0
2007–08	Stoke C	5	0	35	2
2007–08	Walsall	7	0	7	0
2007–08	Leeds U	9	0		
2008–09	Leeds U	0	0	9	0
2008–09	Grimsby T	8	0		
2009–10	Grimsby T	40	4	48	4
2010–11	Bury	25	0		
2011–12	Bury	41	4		
2012–13	Bury	16	1	82	5
2012–13	AFC Wimbledon	6	0		
2013–14	AFC Wimbledon	22	0	28	0

WESTON, Rhys (D) 321 3
H: 6 1 W: 12 11 b.Kingston 27-10-80
Internationals: Wales U21, Full caps.

1999–2000	Arsenal	1	0		
2000–01	Arsenal	0	0	1	0
2000–01	Cardiff C	28	0		
2001–02	Cardiff C	37	0		
2002–03	Cardiff C	38	2		
2003–04	Cardiff C	24	0		
2004–05	Cardiff C	25	0		
2005–06	Cardiff C	30	0	182	2
2006	Viking FK	1	0	1	0
2006–07	Port Vale	15	0	15	0
2007–08	Walsall	44	0		
2008–09	Walsall	31	1		
2009–10	Walsall	27	0	102	1
2012	KR Reykjavik	13	0	13	0
2013–14	AFC Wimbledon	7	0	7	0

WORNER, Ross (G) 76 0
H: 6 1 W: 12 05 b.Hindhead 3-10-89

2010–11	Charlton Ath	8	0	8	0
2011–12	Aldershot T	22	0		
2012–13	Aldershot T	1	0	23	0
2013–14	AFC Wimbledon	45	0	45	0

Scholars
Agyei, Daniel Ebenezer Kwasi; Basker,
Harlan Jay; Bishop, Billy; Frost, Billy James;
Gallagher, Daniel Lee; Haines, Oliver
George; Harrison, Ben Nicholas; Kaja, Egli;
Obaye-Daley, Oluseyi; Overton, Callum
Peter William; Pearse, Daniel; Roles, Taylor
Lewis; Sweeney, Ryan Joseph; Tarbie,
Kieron; Vlietinck, Christopher David;
Wilson, Callum Anthony.

ARSENAL (3)

AFOBE, Benik (F) 68 9
H: 5 10 W: 11 00 b.Leyton 12-2-93
Internationals: England U16, U17, U19, U21.

2009–10	Arsenal	0	0		
2010–11	Arsenal	0	0		
2010–11	Huddersfield T	28	5	28	5
2011–12	Arsenal	0	0		
2011–12	Reading	3	0	3	0
2012–13	Arsenal	0	0		
2012–13	Bolton W	20	2	20	2
2012–13	Millwall	5	0	5	0
2013–14	Arsenal	0	0		
2013–14	Sheffield W	12	2	12	2

AKPOM, Chuba (F) 11 0
b.London 9-10-95

2012–13	Arsenal	0	0		
2013–14	Arsenal	1	0	1	0
2013–14	Brentford	4	0	4	0
2013–14	Coventry C	6	0	6	0

ANEKE, Chuks (M) 83 22
H: 6 3 W: 13 01 b.Newham 3-7-93
Internationals: England Youth.

2010–11	Arsenal	0	0		
2011–12	Arsenal	0	0		
2011–12	Stevenage	6	0	6	0
2011–12	Preston NE	7	1	7	1
2012–13	Arsenal	.	0	0	

2012–13	Crewe Alex	30	6		
2013–14	Arsenal	0	0		
2013–14	Crewe Alex	40	15	70	21

ARTETA, Mikel (M) 405 59
H: 5 9 W: 10 08 b.San Sebastian 26-3-82
Internationals: Spain U16, U17, U18, U21.

1999–2000	Barcelona B	26	1		
2000–01	Barcelona B	16	2	42	3
2000–01	Paris St Germain	6	1		
2001–02	Paris St Germain	25	1	31	2
2002–03	Rangers	27	4		
2003–04	Rangers	23	8	50	12
2004–05	Real Sociedad	14	1	14	1
2004–05	Everton	12	1		
2005–06	Everton	29	1		
2006–07	Everton	35	9		
2007–08	Everton	28	1		
2008–09	Everton	26	5		
2009–10	Everton	13	6		
2010–11	Everton	29	3		
2011–12	Everton	2	1	174	27
2011–12	Arsenal	29	6		
2012–13	Arsenal	34	6		
2013–14	Arsenal	31	2	94	14

BELLERIN, Hector (D) 8 0
H: 5 10 W: 11 09 b.Barcelona 19-3-95
Internationals: Spain U16, U17, U19.

2012–13	Arsenal	0	0		
2013–14	Arsenal	0	0		
2013–14	Watford	8	0	8	0

BENDTNER, Nicklas (F) 187 43
H: 6 2 W: 13 00 b.Copenhagen 16-1-88
Internationals: Denmark U16, U17, U19, U21,
Full caps.

2005–06	Arsenal	0	0		
2006–07	Arsenal	0	0		
2006–07	Birmingham C	42	11	42	11
2007–08	Arsenal	27	5		
2008–09	Arsenal	31	9		
2009–10	Arsenal	23	6		
2010–11	Arsenal	17	2		
2011–12	Arsenal	1	0		
2011–12	Sunderland	28	8	28	8
2012–13	Arsenal	0	0		
2012–13	Juventus	9	0	9	0
2013–14	Arsenal	9	2	108	24

BOATENG, Daniel (D) 7 0
H: 6 0 W: 12 04 b.Enfield 2-9-92

2010–11	Arsenal	0	0		
2011–12	Arsenal	0	0		
2011–12	Swindon T	2	0	2	0
2012–13	Arsenal	0	0		
2012–13	Oxford U	2	0	2	0
2013–14	Arsenal	0	0		
2013–14	Hibernian	3	0	3	0

CAMPBELL, Joel (F) 93 13
H: 5 10 W: 12 00 b.Costa Rica 26-6-92
Internationals: Costa Rica U17, U20, Full
caps.

2009–10	Saprissa	1	0		
2010–11	Saprissa	2	0	3	0
2010–11	Puntarenas	5	0	5	0
2011–12	Arsenal	0	0		
2011–12	Lorient	25	3	25	3
2012–13	Arsenal	0	0		
2012–13	Real Betis	28	2	28	2
2013–14	Arsenal	0	0		
2013–14	Olympiacos	32	8	32	8

CAZORLA, Santi (M) 321 55
H: 5 5 W: 10 07 b.Lugo De Llanera
13-12-84
Internationals: Spain U21, Full caps.

2003–04	Villarreal	2	0		
2004–05	Villarreal	28	2		
2005–06	Villarreal	23	0		
2006–07	Recreativo Huelva	34	5	34	5
2007–08	Villarreal	36	5		
2008–09	Villarreal	30	8		
2009–10	Villarreal	24	5		
2010–11	Villarreal	37	5	180	25
2011–12	Malaga	38	9		
2012–13	Malaga	0	0	38	9
2012–13	Arsenal	38	12		
2013–14	Arsenal	31	4	69	16

COQUELIN, Francis (M) 61 1
H: 5 10 W: 11 08 b.Laval 13-5-91
Internationals: France U17, U18, U19, U20,
U21.

2008–09	Arsenal	0	0		
2009–10	Arsenal	0	0		
2010–11	Arsenal	0	0		
2010–11	Lorient	24	1	24	1
2011–12	Arsenal	10	0		
2012–13	Arsenal	11	0		
2013–14	Arsenal	0	0	21	0
2013–14	SC Freiburg	16	0	16	0

DIABY, Abou (M) 134 15
H: 6 2 W: 12 04 b.Paris 11-5-86
Internationals: France U19, U21, Full caps.

2004–05	Auxerre	5	0		
2005–06	Auxerre	5	1	10	1
2005–06	Arsenal	12	1		
2006–07	Arsenal	12	1		
2007–08	Arsenal	15	1		
2008–09	Arsenal	24	3		
2009–10	Arsenal	29	6		
2010–11	Arsenal	16	2		
2011–12	Arsenal	4	0		
2012–13	Arsenal	11	0		
2013–14	Arsenal	1	0	124	14

DJOUROU, Johan (D) 136 1
H: 6 2 W: 12 05 b.Ivory Coast 18-1-87
Internationals: Switzerland U16, U17, U19,
U20, U21, Full caps.

2004–05	Arsenal	0	0		
2005–06	Arsenal	7	0		
2006–07	Arsenal	21	0		
2007–08	Arsenal	2	0		
2007–08	Birmingham C	13	0	13	0
2008–09	Arsenal	15	0		
2009–10	Arsenal	1	0		
2010–11	Arsenal	22	1		
2011–12	Arsenal	18	0		
2012–13	Arsenal	0	0		
2012–13	Hannover 96	14	0	14	0
2013–14	Arsenal	0	0	86	1
2013–14	Hamburg	23	0	23	0

EISFELD, Thomas (M) 0 0
H: 5 10 W: 10 03 b.Finsterwalde 18-1-93

2011–12	Arsenal	0	0
2012–13	Arsenal	0	0
2013–14	Arsenal	0	0

FABIANSKI, Lukasz (G) 85 0
H: 6 3 W: 13 01 b.Costrzyn nad Odra
18-4-85
Internationals: Poland U21, Full caps.

2005–06	Legia	30	0		
2006–07	Legia	23	0	53	0
2007–08	Arsenal	3	0		
2008–09	Arsenal	6	0		
2009–10	Arsenal	4	0		
2010–11	Arsenal	14	0		
2011–12	Arsenal	0	0		
2012–13	Arsenal	4	0		
2013–14	Arsenal	1	0	32	0

FLAMINI, Mathieu (M) 235 16
H: 5 10 W: 10 07 b.Marseille 7-3-84
Internationals: France U21, Full caps.

2003–04	Marseille	14	0	14	0
2004–05	Arsenal	21	1		
2005–06	Arsenal	31	0		
2006–07	Arsenal	20	3		
2007–08	Arsenal	30	3		
2008–09	AC Milan	28	0		
2009–10	AC Milan	23	0		
2010–11	AC Milan	22	2		
2011–12	AC Milan	2	1		
2012–13	AC Milan	17	4	92	7
2013–14	Arsenal	27	2	129	9

GALINDO, Samuel (M) 0 0
b.Santa Cruz 18-4-89

2012–13	Arsenal	0	0

GIBBS, Kieran (D) 96 1
H: 5 10 W: 10 02 b.Lambeth 26-9-89
Internationals: England U19, U20, U21, Full
caps

2007–08	Arsenal	0	0		
2007–08	Norwich C	7	0	7	0
2008–09	Arsenal	8	0		
2009–10	Arsenal	3	0		

Season	Club	Apps	Gls	Tot	Tot
2010–11	Arsenal	7	0		
2011–12	Arsenal	16	1		
2012–13	Arsenal	27	0		
2013–14	Arsenal	28	0	89	1

GIROUD, Olivier (F)   222 91
H: 6 3 W: 13 11 b.Chambery 30-9-86
Internationals: France Full caps.

Season	Club	Apps	Gls	Tot	Tot
2005–06	Grenoble	3	0		
2006–07	Grenoble	15	2	18	2
2008–09	Tours	23	8		
2009–10	Tours	38	21	61	29
2010–11	Montpellier	37	12		
2011–12	Montpellier	36	21	73	33
2012–13	Arsenal	34	11		
2013–14	Arsenal	36	16	70	27

GNABRY, Serge (M)   10 1
H: 5 9 W: 11 06 b.Stuttgart 14-7-95
Internationals: Germany U16, U17, U18, U19.

Season	Club	Apps	Gls	Tot	Tot
2012–13	Arsenal	1	0		
2013–14	Arsenal	9	1	10	1

HAYDEN, Isaac (D)   0 0
b.Chelmsford 22-3-95
Internationals: England U16, U17, U18, U19.

Season	Club	Apps	Gls
2011–12	Arsenal	0	0
2012–13	Arsenal	0	0
2013–14	Arsenal	0	0

ILIEV, Dejan (G)   0 0
H: 6 5 b.Strumica 25-2-95
Internationals: Macedonia Youth, U21.

Season	Club	Apps	Gls
2012–13	Arsenal	0	0
2013–14	Arsenal	0	0

IWOBI, Alex (M)   0 0
H: 5 11 W: 11 11 b. 3-5-96
Internationals: England U16.

Season	Club	Apps	Gls
2012–13	Arsenal	0	0
2013–14	Arsenal	0	0

JEBB, Jack (M)   0 0
b. 11-9-95
Internationals: England U16, U17.

Season	Club	Apps	Gls
2012–13	Arsenal	0	0
2013–14	Arsenal	0	0

JENKINSON, Carl (D)   45 1
H: 6 1 W: 12 02 b.Harlow 8-2-92
Internationals: Finland U19, U21. England U17, U21, Full caps.

Season	Club	Apps	Gls	Tot	Tot
2010–11	Charlton Ath	8	0	8	0
2010–11	Arsenal	0	0		
2011–12	Arsenal	9	0		
2012–13	Arsenal	14	0		
2013–14	Arsenal	14	1	37	1

KALLSTROM, Kim (M)   430 80
H: 6 0 W: 13 00 b.Sandviken 24-8-82

Season	Club	Apps	Gls	Tot	Tot
1999	BK Hacken	21	4		
2000	BK Hacken	18	2		
2001	BK Hacken	29	8	68	14
2002	Djurgarden	22	12		
2003	Djurgarden	26	14	48	26
2003–04	Rennes	18	7		
2004–05	Rennes	31	5		
2005–06	Rennes	34	8	83	20
2006–07	Lyon	33	3		
2007–08	Lyon	37	5		
2008–09	Lyon	32	2		
2009–10	Lyon	32	4		
2010–11	Lyon	33	3		
2011–12	Lyon	32	0	199	17
2012–13	Spartak Moscow	19	2		
2013–14	Spartak Moscow	10	1	29	3

On loan from Spartak Moscow

Season	Club	Apps	Gls	Tot	Tot
2013–14	Arsenal	3	0	3	0

KOSCIELNY, Laurent (D)   263 17
H: 6 1 W: 11 11 b.Tulle 10-9-85
Internationals: France Full caps.

Season	Club	Apps	Gls	Tot	Tot
2004–05	Guingamp	11	0		
2005–06	Guingamp	9	0		
2006–07	Guingamp	21	0	41	0
2007–08	Tours	33	1		
2008–09	Tours	34	5	67	6
2009–10	Lorient	35	3	35	3
2010–11	Arsenal	30	2		
2011–12	Arsenal	33	2		
2012–13	Arsenal	25	2		
2013–14	Arsenal	32	2	120	8

LIPMAN, Austin (M)   0 0
Internationals: England U17.

Season	Club	Apps	Gls
2012–13	Arsenal	0	0
2013–14	Arsenal	0	0

MACEY, Matt (G)   0 0
H: 6 6 b.Bristol 9-9-94

Season	Club	Apps	Gls
2011–12	Bristol R	0	0
2012–13	Bristol R	0	0
2013–14	Arsenal	0	0

MARTINEZ, Damian (G)   12 0
H: 6 3 W: 13 05 b.Mar del Plata 2-9-92
Internationals: Argentina U17, U20.

Season	Club	Apps	Gls	Tot	Tot
2010–11	Arsenal	0	0		
2011–12	Arsenal	0	0		
2011–12	Oxford U	1	0	1	0
2012–13	Arsenal	0	0		
2013–14	Arsenal	0	0		
2013–14	Sheffield W	11	0	11	0

MERTESACKER, Per (D)   310 24
H: 6 6 W: 14 -02 b.Hannover 29-9-84
Internationals: Germany U20, U21, Full caps.

Season	Club	Apps	Gls	Tot	Tot
2003–04	Hannover	13	0		
2004–05	Hannover	31	2		
2005–06	Hannover	30	5	74	7
2006–07	Werder Bremen	25	2		
2007–08	Werder Bremen	32	1		
2008–09	Werder Bremen	23	2		
2009–10	Werder Bremen	33	5		
2010–11	Werder Bremen	29	2		
2011–12	Werder Bremen	4	0	146	12
2011–12	Arsenal	21	0		
2012–13	Arsenal	34	3		
2013–14	Arsenal	35	2	90	5

MIQUEL, Ignasi (D)   12 0
H: 6 4 W: 13 05 b.Barcelona 28-9-92
Internationals: Spain U16, U19, U21.

Season	Club	Apps	Gls	Tot	Tot
2009–10	Arsenal	0	0		
2010–11	Arsenal	0	0		
2011–12	Arsenal	4	0		
2012–13	Arsenal	1	0		
2013–14	Arsenal	0	0	5	0
2013–14	Leicester C	7	0	7	0

MIYAICHI, Ryo (F)   17 0
H: 6 0 W: 11 02 b.Okazaki 14-12-92
Internationals: Japan U15, U16, U17, U19, Full caps.

Season	Club	Apps	Gls	Tot	Tot
2010–11	Arsenal	0	0		
2011–12	Arsenal	0	0		
2011–12	Bolton W	12	0	12	0
2012–13	Arsenal	0	0		
2012–13	Wigan Ath	4	0	4	0
2013–14	Arsenal	1	0	1	0

MONREAL, Nacho (D)   206 4
H: 5 10 W: 11 04 b.Pamplona 26-2-86
Internationals: Spain U19, U21, Full caps.

Season	Club	Apps	Gls	Tot	Tot
2006–07	Osasuna	11	0		
2007–08	Osasuna	27	0		
2008–09	Osasuna	28	0		
2009–10	Osasuna	31	1		
2010–11	Osasuna	31	1	128	2
2011–12	Malaga	31	0		
2012–13	Malaga	14	1	45	1
2012–13	Arsenal	10	1		
2013–14	Arsenal	23	0	33	1

OLSSON, Kristoffer (M)   0 0
b.Vrinnevi 30-6-95
Internationals: Sweden U17, U19, U21.

Season	Club	Apps	Gls
2012–13	Arsenal	0	0
2013–14	Arsenal	0	0

ORMONDE-OTTEWILL, Brandon (D)   0 0
b. 21-12-95
Internationals: England U16, U19.

Season	Club	Apps	Gls
2012–13	Arsenal	0	0
2013–14	Arsenal	0	0

OXLADE-CHAMBERLAIN, Alex (M)   91 14
H: 5 11 W: 11 00 b.Portsmouth 15-8-93
Internationals: England U18, U19, U21, Full caps.

Season	Club	Apps	Gls	Tot	Tot
2009–10	Southampton	2	0		
2010–11	Southampton	34	9	36	9
2011–12	Arsenal	16	2		
2012–13	Arsenal	25	1		
2013–14	Arsenal	14	2	55	5

OZIL, Mesut (M)   231 37
H: 5 11 W: 11 06 b.Gelsenkirchen 15-10-88
Internationals: Germany U19, U21, Full caps.

Season	Club	Apps	Gls	Tot	Tot
2005–06	Schalke 04	0	0		
2006–07	Schalke 04	19	0		
2007–08	Schalke 04	11	0	30	0
2007–08	Werder Bremen	12	1		
2008–09	Werder Bremen	27	3		
2009–10	Werder Bremen	31	9		
2010–11	Werder Bremen	0	0	70	13
2010–11	Real Madrid	36	6		
2011–12	Real Madrid	35	4		
2012–13	Real Madrid	32	9		
2013–14	Real Madrid	2	0	105	19
2013–14	Arsenal	26	5	26	5

PARK, Chu-Young (F)   185 51
H: 6 0 W: 11 11 b.Daegu 10-7-85
Internationals: South Korea Youth, U23, Full caps.

Season	Club	Apps	Gls	Tot	Tot
2005	Seoul	19	12		
2006	Seoul	26	7		
2007	Seoul	11	2		
2008	Seoul	13	2	69	23
2008–09	Monaco	31	5		
2009–10	Monaco	27	8		
2010–11	Monaco	33	12	91	25
2011–12	Arsenal	1	0		
2012–13	Arsenal	0	0		
2012–13	Celta Vigo	22	3	22	3
2013–14	Arsenal	0	0	1	0
2013–14	Watford	2	0	2	0

PODOLSKI, Lukas (F)   275 110
H: 6 0 W: 13 00 b.Gleiwitz, Poland 4-6-85
Internationals: Germany U17, U18, U19, U21, Full caps.

Season	Club	Apps	Gls	Tot	Tot
2003–04	Cologne	19	10		
2004–05	Cologne	12	21		
2005–06	Cologne	32	12		
2006–07	Bayern Munich	22	4		
2007–08	Bayern Munich	25	5		
2008–09	Bayern Munich	24	6	71	15
2009–10	Cologne	27	2		
2010–11	Cologne	32	13		
2011–12	Cologne	29	18	151	76
2012–13	Arsenal	33	11		
2013–14	Arsenal	20	8	53	19

RAMSEY, Aaron (M)   154 19
H: 5 9 W: 10 07 b.Caerphilly 26-12-90
Internationals: Wales U17, U21, Full caps. Great Britain.

Season	Club	Apps	Gls	Tot	Tot
2006–07	Cardiff C	1	0		
2007–08	Cardiff C	15	1		
2008–09	Arsenal	9	0		
2009–10	Arsenal	18	3		
2010–11	Arsenal	7	1		
2010–11	Nottingham F	5	0	5	0
2010–11	Cardiff C	6	1	22	2
2011–12	Arsenal	34	2		
2012–13	Arsenal	35	0		
2013–14	Arsenal	23	10	127	17

ROSICKY, Tomas (M)   345 44
H: 5 10 W: 10 10 b.Prague 4-10-80
Internationals: Czech Republic U15, U16, U17, U21, Full caps.

Season	Club	Apps	Gls	Tot	Tot
1998–99	Sparta Prague	3	0		
1999–2000	Sparta Prague	24	5		
2000–01	Sparta Prague	14	3	41	8
2000–01	Borussia Dortmund	15	0		
2001–02	Borussia Dortmund	30	5		
2002–03	Borussia Dortmund	30	3		
2003–04	Borussia Dortmund	19	2		
2004–05	Borussia Dortmund	27	4		
2005–06	Borussia Dortmund	28	5	149	19
2006–07	Arsenal	26	3		
2007–08	Arsenal	18	6		
2008–09	Arsenal	0	0		
2009–10	Arsenal	25	3		
2010–11	Arsenal	21	0		
2011–12	Arsenal	28	1		
2012–13	Arsenal	10	2		
2013–14	Arsenal	27	2	155	17

SAGNA, Bakari (D)   300 4
H: 5 10 W: 11 05 b.Sens 14-2-83
Internationals: France U21, Full caps.

Season	Club	Apps	Gls
2003–04	Auxerre	0	0
2004–05	Auxerre	26	0
2005–06	Auxerre	23	0

2006–07	Auxerre	38	0	87 0
2007–08	Arsenal	29	1	
2008–09	Arsenal	35	0	
2009–10	Arsenal	35	0	
2010–11	Arsenal	33	1	
2011–12	Arsenal	21	1	
2012–13	Arsenal	25	0	
2013–14	Arsenal	35	1	213 4

SANOGO, Yaya (F)   **28 10**
H: 6 3   W: 11 08   b.Massy 27-1-93
Internationals: France U16, U17, U19, U20, U21.

2009–10	Auxerre	0	0	
2010–11	Auxerre	0	0	
2011–12	Auxerre	7	1	
2012–13	Auxerre	13	9	20 10
2013–14	Arsenal	8	0	8 0

SILVA, Wellington (M)   **53 5**
H: 5 6   W: 10 00   b.Rio de Janeiro 6-1-93
Internationals: Brazil Youth.

2010–11	Arsenal	0	0	
2010–11	*Levante*	2	0	2 0
2011–12	Arsenal	0	0	
2011–12	*Alcoyano*	16	3	16 3
2012–13	Arsenal	0	0	
2013–14	Arsenal	0	0	
2013–14	*Murcia*	35	2	35 2

SZCZESNY, Wojciech (G)   **143 0**
H: 5 10   W: 11 11   b.Warsaw 18-4-90
Internationals: Poland U20, U21, Full caps.

2007–08	Arsenal	0	0	
2008–09	Arsenal	0	0	
2009–10	Arsenal	0	0	
2009–10	*Brentford*	28	0	28 0
2010–11	Arsenal	15	0	
2011–12	Arsenal	38	0	
2012–13	Arsenal	25	0	
2013–14	Arsenal	37	0	115 0

VERMAELEN, Thomas (D)   **222 22**
H: 6 0   W: 11 11   b.Antwerp 14-11-85
Internationals: Belgium U18, U19, U21, U23, Full caps.

2003–04	Ajax	1	0	
2004–05	*RKC Waalwijk*	13	2	13 2
2005–06	Ajax	24	3	
2006–07	Ajax	23	0	
2007–08	Ajax	20	0	
2008–09	Ajax	31	4	99 7
2009–10	Arsenal	33	7	
2010–11	Arsenal	5	0	
2011–12	Arsenal	29	6	
2012–13	Arsenal	29	0	
2013–14	Arsenal	14	0	110 13

WALCOTT, Theo (F)   **215 49**
H: 5 9   W: 11 01   b.Stanmore 16-3-89
Internationals: England U16, U17, U19, U21, Full caps.

2005–06	Southampton	21	4	21 4
2005–06	Arsenal	0	0	
2006–07	Arsenal	16	0	
2007–08	Arsenal	25	4	
2008–09	Arsenal	22	2	
2009–10	Arsenal	23	3	
2010–11	Arsenal	28	9	
2011–12	Arsenal	35	8	
2012–13	Arsenal	32	14	
2013–14	Arsenal	13	5	194 45

WILSHERE, Jack (M)   **100 5**
H: 5 7   W: 11 03   b.Stevenage 1-1-92
Internationals: England U16, U17, U19, U21, Full caps.

2008–09	Arsenal	1	0	
2009–10	Arsenal	1	0	
2009–10	*Bolton W*	14	1	14 1
2010–11	Arsenal	35	1	
2011–12	Arsenal	0	0	
2012–13	Arsenal	25	0	
2013–14	Arsenal	24	3	86 4

ZELALEM, Gedion (M)   **0 0**
H: 5 10   b.Berlin 26-1-97

2013–14	Arsenal	0	0	

Scholars
Crowley, Daniel; Kamara, Glen; Maitland-Niles, Ainsley; Moore, Tafari Lalibela; O'Connor, Stefan Ramone Sewell; Smith, Renny Piers; Vickers, Josh; Wright, Elliot.

ASTON VILLA (4)

AGBONLAHOR, Gabriel (F)   **283 66**
H: 5 11   W: 12 05   b.Birmingham 13-10-86
Internationals: England U21, Full caps.

2005–06	Aston Villa	9	1	
2005–06	*Watford*	2	0	2 0
2005–06	*Sheffield W*	8	0	8 0
2006–07	Aston Villa	38	9	
2007–08	Aston Villa	37	11	
2008–09	Aston Villa	36	11	
2009–10	Aston Villa	36	13	
2010–11	Aston Villa	26	3	
2011–12	Aston Villa	33	5	
2012–13	Aston Villa	28	9	
2013–14	Aston Villa	30	4	273 66

ALBRIGHTON, Marc (M)   **90 7**
H: 6 2   W: 12 06   b.Tamworth 18-11-89
Internationals: England U20, U21.

2008–09	Aston Villa	0	0	
2009–10	Aston Villa	3	0	
2010–11	Aston Villa	29	5	
2011–12	Aston Villa	26	2	
2012–13	Aston Villa	9	0	
2013–14	Aston Villa	19	0	86 7
2013–14	*Wigan Ath*	4	0	4 0

BACUNA, Leandro (M)   **88 12**
H: 6 2   W: 12 00   b.Groningen 21-8-91
Internationals: Netherlands U19, U21.

2009–10	FC Groningen	20	2	
2012–13	FC Groningen	33	5	53 7
2013–14	Aston Villa	35	5	35 5

BAKER, Nathan (D)   **92 0**
H: 6 2   W: 11 11   b.Worcester 23-4-91
Internationals: England U19, U20, U21.

2008–09	Aston Villa	0	0	
2009–10	Aston Villa	0	0	
2009–10	*Lincoln C*	18	0	18 0
2010–11	Aston Villa	4	0	
2011–12	Aston Villa	8	0	
2011–12	*Millwall*	6	0	6 0
2012–13	Aston Villa	26	0	
2013–14	Aston Villa	30	0	68 0

BENNETT, Joe (D)   **115 1**
H: 5 10   W: 10 04   b.Rochdale 28-3-90
Internationals: England U19, U20, U21.

2008–09	Middlesbrough	1	0	
2009–10	Middlesbrough	12	0	
2010–11	Middlesbrough	31	0	
2011–12	Middlesbrough	41	1	
2012–13	Middlesbrough	0	0	85 1
2012–13	Aston Villa	25	0	
2013–14	Aston Villa	5	0	30 0

BENT, Darren (F)   **386 154**
H: 5 11   W: 12 07   b.Wandsworth 6-2-84
Internationals: England U15, U16, U17, U19, U21, Full caps.

2001–02	Ipswich T	5	1	
2002–03	Ipswich T	35	12	
2003–04	Ipswich T	37	16	
2004–05	Ipswich T	45	20	122 49
2005–06	Charlton Ath	36	18	
2006–07	Charlton Ath	32	13	68 31
2007–08	Tottenham H	27	6	
2008–09	Tottenham H	33	12	
2009–10	Tottenham H	0	0	60 18
2009–10	Sunderland	38	24	
2010–11	Sunderland	20	8	58 32
2010–11	Aston Villa	16	9	
2011–12	Aston Villa	22	9	
2012–13	Aston Villa	16	3	
2013–14	Aston Villa	0	0	54 21
2013–14	*Fulham*	24	3	24 3

BENTEKE, Christian (F)   **164 65**
H: 6 3   W: 13 00   b.Kinshasa 3-12-90
Internationals: Belgium U17, U18, U19, U21, Full caps.

2007–08	Genk	7	0	
2008–09	Genk	3	0	
2008–09	Standard Liege	9	3	
2009–10	KV Kortrijk	24	9	24 9
2010–11	Standard Liege	5	0	
2010–11	KV Mechelen	15	5	15 5
2011–12	Standard Liege	4	0	18 3
2011–12	Genk	32	16	

2012–13	Genk	5	3	47 19
2012–13	Aston Villa	34	19	
2013–14	Aston Villa	26	10	60 29

BOWERY, Jordan (F)   **105 10**
H: 6 1   W: 12 00   b.Nottingham 2-7-91

2008–09	Chesterfield	3	0	
2009–10	Chesterfield	10	0	
2010–11	Chesterfield	27	1	
2011–12	Chesterfield	40	8	
2012–13	Chesterfield	3	1	83 10
2012–13	Aston Villa	10	0	
2013–14	Aston Villa	9	0	19 0
2013–14	*Doncaster R*	3	0	3 0

BURKE, Graham (F)   **3 0**
H: 5 11   W: 11 11   b.Dublin 21-9-93
Internationals: Republic of Ireland U19, U21.

2010–11	Aston Villa	0	0	
2011–12	Aston Villa	0	0	
2012–13	Aston Villa	0	0	
2013–14	Aston Villa	0	0	
2013–14	*Shrewsbury T*	3	0	3 0

CARRUTHERS, Samir (F)   **26 2**
H: 5 8   W: 11 00   b.Islington 4-4-93
Internationals: Republic of Ireland U19, U21.

2011–12	Aston Villa	3	0	
2012–13	Aston Villa	0	0	
2013–14	Aston Villa	0	0	3 0
2013–14	*Milton Keynes D*	23	2	23 2

CLARK, Ciaran (D)   **91 5**
H: 6 2   W: 12 00   b.Harrow 26-9-89
Internationals: England U17, U18, U19, U20. Republic of Ireland Full caps.

2008–09	Aston Villa	0	0	
2009–10	Aston Villa	1	0	
2010–11	Aston Villa	19	3	
2011–12	Aston Villa	15	1	
2012–13	Aston Villa	29	1	
2013–14	Aston Villa	27	0	91 5

DELFOUNESO, Nathan (F)   **111 12**
H: 6 1   W: 12 04   b.Birmingham 2-2-91
Internationals: England U16, U17, U19, U21.

2007–08	Aston Villa	0	0	
2008–09	Aston Villa	4	0	
2009–10	Aston Villa	9	1	
2010–11	Aston Villa	11	1	
2010–11	*Burnley*	11	1	11 1
2011–12	Aston Villa	6	0	
2011–12	*Leicester C*	4	0	4 0
2012–13	*Blackpool*	40	6	
2013–14	Aston Villa	0	0	31 2
2013–14	*Blackpool*	11	0	51 6
2013–14	*Coventry C*	14	3	14 3

DELPH, Fabian (D)   **133 9**
H: 5 8   W: 11 00   b.Bradford 21-11-89
Internationals: England U19, U21.

2006–07	Leeds U	1	0	
2007–08	Leeds U	1	0	
2008–09	Leeds U	42	6	
2009–10	Aston Villa	8	0	
2010–11	Aston Villa	11	0	
2011–12	*Leeds U*	5	0	49 6
2012–13	Aston Villa	24	0	
2013–14	Aston Villa	34	3	84 3

DONACIEN, Janoi (D)   **0 0**
b.St Lucia

2011–12	Aston Villa	0	0	
2012–13	Aston Villa	0	0	
2013–14	Aston Villa	0	0	

DRENNAN, Michael (F)   **16 3**
b.Kilkenny 2-2-94
Internationals: Republic of Ireland U16, U17, U19, U21.

2010–11	Aston Villa	0	0	
2011–12	Aston Villa	0	0	
2012–13	Aston Villa	0	0	
2013–14	Aston Villa	0	0	
2013–14	*Carlisle U*	6	0	6 0
2013–14	*Portsmouth*	10	3	10 3

EL AHMADI, Karim (M)   **234 10**
H: 6 1   W: 12 03   b.Enschede 27-1-85
Internationals: Morocco Full caps.

2003–04	FC Twente	7	0	
2004–05	FC Twente	19	1	

Season	Club	Apps	Gls	Total Apps	Total Gls
2005–06	FC Twente	8	0		
2006–07	FC Twente	22	2		
2007–08	FC Twente	33	0	89	3
2008–09	Feyenoord	22	2		
2009–10	Feyenoord	26	0		
2010–11	Feyenoord	15	0		
2011–12	Feyenoord	31	2	94	4
2012–13	Aston Villa	20	1		
2013–14	Aston Villa	31	2	51	3

GARDNER, Gary (M) 23 1
H: 6 2 W: 12 13 b.Solihull 29-6-92
Internationals: England U17, U19, U20, U21.

Season	Club	Apps	Gls	Total Apps	Total Gls
2009–10	Aston Villa	0	0		
2010–11	Aston Villa	0	0		
2011–12	Aston Villa	14	0		
2011–12	*Coventry C*	4	1	4	1
2012–13	Aston Villa	2	0		
2013–14	Aston Villa	0	0	16	0
2013–14	*Sheffield W*	3	0	3	0

GIVEN, Shay (G) 478 0
H: 6 0 W: 13 03 b.Lifford 20-4-76
Internationals: Republic of Ireland U21, Full caps.

Season	Club	Apps	Gls	Total Apps	Total Gls
1994–95	*Blackburn R*	0	0		
1994–95	*Swindon T*	0	0		
1995–96	*Blackburn R*	0	0		
1995–96	*Swindon T*	5	0	5	0
1995–96	*Sunderland*	17	0	17	0
1996–97	*Blackburn R*	2	0	2	0
1997–98	Newcastle U	24	0		
1998–99	Newcastle U	31	0		
1999–2000	Newcastle U	14	0		
2000–01	Newcastle U	34	0		
2001–02	Newcastle U	38	0		
2002–03	Newcastle U	38	0		
2003–04	Newcastle U	38	0		
2004–05	Newcastle U	36	0		
2005–06	Newcastle U	38	0		
2006–07	Newcastle U	22	0		
2007–08	Newcastle U	19	0		
2008–09	Newcastle U	22	0	354	0
2008–09	Manchester C	15	0		
2009–10	Manchester C	35	0		
2010–11	Manchester C	0	0	50	0
2011–12	Aston Villa	32	0		
2012–13	Aston Villa	2	0		
2013–14	Aston Villa	0	0	34	0
2013–14	*Middlesbrough*	16	0	16	0

GRAHAM, Jordan (M) 3 0
b.Coventry 5-3-95

Season	Club	Apps	Gls	Total Apps	Total Gls
2011–12	Aston Villa	0	0		
2012–13	Aston Villa	0	0		
2013–14	Aston Villa	0	0		
2013–14	*Ipswich T*	2	0	2	0
2013–14	*Bradford C*	1	0	1	0

GREALISH, Jack (M) 38 5
b.Birmingham 10-9-95
Internationals: Republic of Ireland U17, U18, U21.

Season	Club	Apps	Gls	Total Apps	Total Gls
2012–13	Aston Villa	0	0		
2013–14	Aston Villa	1	0	1	0
2013–14	*Notts Co*	37	5	37	5

GUZAN, Brad (G) 177 0
H: 6 4 W: 14 11 b.Chicago 9-9-84
Internationals: USA U23, Full caps.

Season	Club	Apps	Gls	Total Apps	Total Gls
2005	Chivas USA	24	0		
2006	Chivas USA	13	0		
2007	Chivas USA	27	0		
2008	Chivas USA	15	0	79	0
2008–09	Aston Villa	1	0		
2009–10	Aston Villa	0	0		
2010–11	Aston Villa	0	0		
2010–11	*Hull C*	16	0	16	0
2011–12	Aston Villa	7	0		
2012–13	Aston Villa	36	0		
2013–14	Aston Villa	38	0	82	0

HELENIUS, Nicklas (F) 98 35
H: 6 5 W: 13 00 b.Svenstrup 8-5-91
Internationals: Denmark U20, U21, Full caps.

Season	Club	Apps	Gls	Total Apps	Total Gls
2009–10	Aalborg	1	0		
2010–11	Aalborg	29	5		
2011–12	Aalborg	32	14		
2012–13	Aalborg	33	16	95	35
2013–14	Aston Villa	3	0	3	0

HERD, Chris (M) 71 7
H: 5 9 W: 11 04 b.Perth 4-4-89
Internationals: Australia U20.

Season	Club	Apps	Gls	Total Apps	Total Gls
2007–08	Aston Villa	0	0		
2007–08	*Port Vale*	11	2	11	2
2007–08	*Wycombe W*	4	0	4	0
2008–09	Aston Villa	0	0		
2009–10	Aston Villa	0	0		
2009–10	*Lincoln C*	20	4	20	4
2010–11	Aston Villa	6	0		
2011–12	Aston Villa	19	1		
2012–13	Aston Villa	9	0		
2013–14	Aston Villa	2	0	36	1

HUTTON, Alan (D) 208 3
H: 6 1 W: 11 05 b.Glasgow 30-11-84
Internationals: Scotland U21, Full caps.

Season	Club	Apps	Gls	Total Apps	Total Gls
2004–05	Rangers	10	0		
2005–06	Rangers	19	0		
2006–07	Rangers	33	1		
2007–08	Rangers	20	0	82	1
2007–08	Tottenham H	14	0		
2008–09	Tottenham H	8	0		
2009–10	Tottenham H	8	0		
2009–10	*Sunderland*	11	0	11	0
2010–11	Tottenham H	21	2		
2011–12	Tottenham H	0	0	51	2
2011–12	Aston Villa	31	0		
2012–13	*Nottingham F*	7	0	7	0
2012–13	*Mallorca*	17	0	17	0
2013–14	Aston Villa	0	0	31	0
2013–14	*Bolton W*	9	0	9	0

JOHNSON, Daniel (M) 5 0
H: 5 8 W: 10 07 b.Kingston, Jam 8-10-92

Season	Club	Apps	Gls	Total Apps	Total Gls
2010–11	Aston Villa	0	0		
2011–12	Aston Villa	0	0		
2012–13	Aston Villa	0	0		
2012–13	*Yeovil T*	5	0	5	0
2013–14	Aston Villa	0	0		

KOZAK, Libor (F) 96 18
H: 6 4 W: 12 11 b.Brumov-Bylnice 30-5-89
Internationals: Czech Republic U19, U21, Full caps.

Season	Club	Apps	Gls	Total Apps	Total Gls
2008–09	Lazio	3	0		
2009–10	Brescia	25	4	25	4
2010–11	Lazio	19	6		
2011–12	Lazio	16	4		
2012–13	Lazio	19	0	57	10
2013–14	Aston Villa	14	4	14	4

LOWTON, Matt (M) 143 12
H: 5 11 W: 12 04 b.Chesterfield 9-6-89

Season	Club	Apps	Gls	Total Apps	Total Gls
2008–09	Sheffield U	0	0		
2009–10	Sheffield U	2	0		
2009–10	*Ferencvaros*	5	0	5	0
2010–11	Sheffield U	32	4		
2011–12	Sheffield U	44	6	78	10
2012–13	Aston Villa	37	2		
2013–14	Aston Villa	23	0	60	2

LUNA, Antonio (D) 62 2
H: 5 10 W: 10 09 b.Son Servera 17-3-91

Season	Club	Apps	Gls	Total Apps	Total Gls
2009–10	Sevilla	1	0		
2010–11	Sevilla	2	0		
2010–11	*Almeria*	13	0	13	0
2011–12	Sevilla	14	1		
2012–13	Sevilla	4	0	21	1
2012–13	*Mallorca*	11	0	11	0
2013–14	Aston Villa	17	1	17	1

N'ZOGBIA, Charles (M) 251 28
H: 5 9 W: 11 00 b.Le Havre 28-5-86
Internationals: France U21, Full caps.

Season	Club	Apps	Gls	Total Apps	Total Gls
2004–05	Newcastle U	14	0		
2005–06	Newcastle U	32	5		
2006–07	Newcastle U	22	0		
2007–08	Newcastle U	31	3		
2008–09	Newcastle U	18	1	117	9
2008–09	Wigan Ath	13	1		
2009–10	Wigan Ath	36	5		
2010–11	Wigan Ath	34	9	83	15
2011–12	Aston Villa	30	2		
2012–13	Aston Villa	21	2		
2013–14	Aston Villa	0	0	51	4

OKORE, Jores (D) 68 5
H: 6 0 W: 12 07 b.Abidjan 11-8-92
Internationals: Denmark U21, Full caps.

Season	Club	Apps	Gls	Total Apps	Total Gls
2010–11	Nordsjaelland	11	0		
2011–12	Nordsjaelland	25	1		
2012–13	Nordsjaelland	29	4	65	5
2013–14	Aston Villa	3	0	3	0

ROBINSON, Callum (F) 4 0
b.Birmingham 2-2-95
Internationals: England U16, U17, U19.

Season	Club	Apps	Gls	Total Apps	Total Gls
2013–14	Aston Villa	4	0	4	0

SIEGRIST, Benjamin (G) 0 0
H: 6 4 W: 13 05 b.Basle 31-1-92
Internationals: Switzerland Youth.

Season	Club	Apps	Gls	Total Apps	Total Gls
2008–09	Aston Villa	0	0		
2009–10	Aston Villa	0	0		
2010–11	Aston Villa	0	0		
2011–12	Aston Villa	0	0		
2012–13	Aston Villa	0	0		
2013–14	Aston Villa	0	0		
2013–14	*Burton Alb*	0	0		

STEER, Jed (G) 12 0
H: 6 2 W: 14 00 b.Norwich 23-9-92
Internationals: England U16, U17, U19.

Season	Club	Apps	Gls	Total Apps	Total Gls
2009–10	Norwich C	0	0		
2010–11	Norwich C	0	0		
2011–12	Norwich C	0	0		
2011–12	*Yeovil T*	12	0	12	0
2012–13	*Cambridge U*	0	0		
2012–13	Norwich C	0	0		
2013–14	Aston Villa	0	0		

STEVENS, Enda (D) 99 0
H: 6 0 W: 12 04 b.Dublin 9-7-90
Internationals: Republic of Ireland U21.

Season	Club	Apps	Gls	Total Apps	Total Gls
2008	UCD	2	0	2	0
2009	St Patrick's Ath	30	0	30	0
2010	Shamrock R	18	0		
2011	Shamrock R	27	0	45	0
2011–12	Aston Villa	0	0		
2012–13	Aston Villa	7	0		
2013–14	Aston Villa	0	0	7	0
2013–14	*Notts Co*	2	0	2	0
2013–14	*Doncaster R*	13	0	13	0

SYLLA, Yacouba (M) 86 0
H: 6 0 W: 12 07 b.Etampes 29-11-90
Internationals: France U21. Mali Full caps.

Season	Club	Apps	Gls	Total Apps	Total Gls
2010–11	Clermont Foot	20	0		
2011–12	Clermont Foot	23	0		
2012–13	Clermont Foot	21	0	64	0
2012–13	Aston Villa	11	0		
2013–14	Aston Villa	11	0	22	0

TONEV, Aleksandar (M) 135 12
H: 5 10 W: 10 11 b.elin pelin 3-2-90
Internationals: Bulgaria U19, U21, Full caps.

Season	Club	Apps	Gls	Total Apps	Total Gls
2008–09	CSKA Sofia	19	2		
2009–10	CSKA Sofia	0	0		
2009–10	*Sliven 2000*	22	1	22	1
2010–11	CSKA Sofia	23	2	42	4
2011–12	Lech Poznan	28	3		
2012–13	Lech Poznan	26	4	54	7
2013–14	Aston Villa	17	0	17	0

VLAAR, Ron (D) 201 10
H: 5 11 W: 12 05 b.Hensbraek 16-2-85
Internationals: Netherlands U19, U21, Full caps.

Season	Club	Apps	Gls	Total Apps	Total Gls
2004–05	AZ	3	0		
2005–06	AZ	7	0	10	0
2005–06	Feyenoord	16	0		
2006–07	Feyenoord	20	1		
2007–08	Feyenoord	4	1		
2008–09	Feyenoord	32	4		
2009–10	Feyenoord	26	2		
2010–11	Feyenoord	34	0		
2011–12	Feyenoord	0	0	132	8
2012–13	Aston Villa	27	2		
2013–14	Aston Villa	32	0	59	2

WEIMANN, Andreas (F) 103 18
H: 5 9 W: 11 09 b.Vienna 5-8-91
Internationals: Austria U17, U19, U20, U21, Full caps.

Season	Club	Apps	Gls	Total Apps	Total Gls
2008–09	Aston Villa	0	0		
2009–10	Aston Villa	0	0		
2010–11	Aston Villa	1	0		
2010–11	*Watford*	18	4		
2011–12	*Watford*	14	2		
2011–12	*Watford*	3	0	21	4
2012–13	Aston Villa	30	7		
2013–14	Aston Villa	37	5	82	14

WESTWOOD, Ashley (M) — 193 17
H: 5 10 W: 11 00 b.Nantwich 1-4-90

Season	Club	Apps	Gls	Tot A	Tot G
2008-09	Crewe Alex	2	0		
2009-10	Crewe Alex	36	6		
2010-11	Crewe Alex	46	5		
2011-12	Crewe Alex	41	3		
2012-13	Crewe Alex	3	0	128	14
2012-13	Aston Villa	30	0		
2013-14	Aston Villa	35	3	65	3

Scholars

Abdo, Khalid; Bannister, Charlie Brendan Alec; Cowans, Henry Gordon Mander; Forth, Dylan Carl; Hale, Rory Danny; Lewis, Harry James; Lyons-Foster, Kodi; McKirdy, Harry; O'Brien, Daniel William; Strain, Ryan; Strain, Thomas James; Toner, Kevin Stephen; Wildin, Courtney James.

BARNSLEY (5)

ABBOTT, Brad (M) — 0 0
b. 24-12-94

Season	Club	Apps	Gls	Tot A	Tot G
2013-14	Barnsley	0	0		

BREE, James (D) — 1 0

Season	Club	Apps	Gls	Tot A	Tot G
2013-14	Barnsley	1	0	1	0

CLARK, Jordan (F) — 9 0
H: 6 0 W: 11 07 b.Barnsley 22-9-93

Season	Club	Apps	Gls	Tot A	Tot G
2010-11	Barnsley	4	0		
2011-12	Barnsley	2	0		
2012-13	Barnsley	0	0		
2012-13	*Chesterfield*	2	0	2	0
2013-14	Barnsley	0	0	6	0
2013-14	*Scunthorpe U*	1	0	1	0

CRANIE, Martin (D) — 243
H: 6 1 W: 12 09 b.Yeovil 23-9-86
Internationals: England U17, U18, U19, U20, U21.

Season	Club	Apps	Gls	Tot A	Tot G
2003-04	Southampton	1	0		
2004-05	Southampton	3	0		
2004-05	*Bournemouth*	3	0	3	0
2005-06	Southampton	11	0		
2006-07	Southampton	1	0	16	0
2006-07	*Yeovil T*	12	0	12	0
2007-08	Portsmouth	2	0		
2007-08	*QPR*	6	0	6	0
2008-09	Portsmouth	0	0		
2008-09	*Charlton Ath*	19	0	19	0
2009-10	Portsmouth	0	0	2	0
2009-10	Coventry C	40	1		
2010-11	Coventry C	36	0		
2011-12	Coventry C	38	0	114	1
2012-13	Barnsley	36	0		
2013-14	Barnsley	35	0	71	0

CYWKA, Thomasz (M) — 111 14
H: 5 10 W: 11 09 b.Gliwice 27-6-88
Internationals: Poland U18, U19, U20, U21.

Season	Club	Apps	Gls	Tot A	Tot G
2006-07	Wigan Ath	0	0		
2006-07	*Oldham Ath*	4	0	4	0
2007-08	Wigan Ath	0	0		
2008-09	Wigan Ath	0	0		
2009-10	Wigan Ath	0	0		
2009-10	*Derby Co*	5	0		
2010-11	Derby Co	31	4		
2011-12	Derby Co	8	1	44	5
2011-12	*Reading*	4	0	4	0
2012-13	Barnsley	29	5		
2013-14	Barnsley	30	4	59	9

DAWSON, Stephen (M) — 346 18
H: 5 9 W: 11 09 b.Dublin 4-12-85
Internationals: Republic of Ireland U21.

Season	Club	Apps	Gls	Tot A	Tot G
2003-04	Leicester C	0	0		
2004-05	Leicester C	0	0		
2005-06	Mansfield T	40	1		
2006-07	Mansfield T	34	1		
2007-08	Mansfield T	43	2	117	4
2008-09	Bury	43	2		
2009-10	Bury	45	4	88	6
2010-11	Leyton Orient	40	2		
2011-12	Leyton Orient	20	1	60	3
2011-12	Barnsley	12	0		
2012-13	Barnsley	32	4		
2013-14	Barnsley	37	1	81	5

DIBBLE, Christian (G) — 0 0
H: 6 4 W: 13 11 b.Wilmslow 11-5-94

Season	Club	Apps	Gls	Tot A	Tot G
2012-13	Bury	0	0		
2013-14	Barnsley	0	0		

DIGBY, Paul (M) — 9 0
H: 5 9 W: 10 00 b.Sheffield 2-2-95
Internationals: England U19.

Season	Club	Apps	Gls	Tot A	Tot G
2011-12	Barnsley	4	0		
2012-13	Barnsley	0	0		
2013-14	Barnsley	5	0	9	0

ETUHU, Kelvin (F) — 93 4
H: 5 11 W: 11 02 b.Kano 30-5-88

Season	Club	Apps	Gls	Tot A	Tot G
2005-06	Manchester C	0	0		
2006-07	Manchester C	0	0		
2006-07	*Rochdale*	4	2	4	2
2007-08	Manchester C	6	1		
2007-08	*Leicester C*	4	0	4	0
2008-09	Manchester C	4	0		
2009-10	Manchester C	0	0		
2009-10	*Cardiff C*	16	0	16	0
2010-11	Manchester C	0	0	10	1
2011-12	Kavala	0	0		
2011-12	Portsmouth	13	1		
2012-13	Portsmouth	0	0	13	1
2012-13	Barnsley	26	0		
2013-14	Barnsley	20	0	46	0

FRIMPONG, Emmanuel (M) — 32 0
H: 5 11 W: 10 07 b.Ghana 10-1-92
Internationals: England U16, U17. Ghana Full caps.

Season	Club	Apps	Gls	Tot A	Tot G
2008-09	Arsenal	0	0		
2009-10	Arsenal	0	0		
2010-11	Arsenal	0	0		
2011-12	Arsenal	0	0		
2011-12	*Wolverhampton W*	5	0	5	0
2012-13	Arsenal	0	0		
2012-13	*Charlton Ath*	6	0	6	0
2012-13	*Fulham*	6	0	6	0
2013-14	Arsenal	0	0	6	0
2013-14	Barnsley	9	0	9	0

HASSELL, Bobby (D) — 427 10
H: 5 10 W: 12 00 b.Derby 4-6-80

Season	Club	Apps	Gls	Tot A	Tot G
1997-98	Mansfield T	9	0		
1998-99	Mansfield T	3	0		
1999-2000	Mansfield T	11	1		
2000-01	Mansfield T	40	1		
2001-02	Mansfield T	43	1		
2002-03	Mansfield T	20	0		
2003-04	Mansfield T	34	0	160	3
2004-05	Barnsley	39	0		
2005-06	Barnsley	28	2		
2006-07	Barnsley	39	2		
2007-08	Barnsley	20	0		
2008-09	Barnsley	40	0		
2009-10	Barnsley	24	1		
2010-11	Barnsley	37	1		
2011-12	Barnsley	19	0		
2012-13	Barnsley	17	1		
2013-14	Barnsley	4	0	267	7

JENNINGS, Dale (F) — 62 9
H: 5 7 W: 11 00 b.Liverpool 21-12-92

Season	Club	Apps	Gls	Tot A	Tot G
2010-11	Tranmere R	29	6	29	6
2013-14	Barnsley	27	3	27	3
2013-14	*Milton Keynes D*	6	0	6	0

JONES, Andrai (D) — 26 0
H: 5 11 W: 10 10 b.Liverpool 1-1-92

Season	Club	Apps	Gls	Tot A	Tot G
2010-11	Bury	1	0		
2011-12	Bury	11	0		
2012-13	Bury	10	0	22	0
2012-13	Barnsley	2	0		
2013-14	Barnsley	0	0	2	0
2013-14	*Tranmere R*	2	0	2	0

KENNEDY, Tom (D) — 379 15
H: 5 10 W: 11 01 b.Bury 24-6-85

Season	Club	Apps	Gls	Tot A	Tot G
2002-03	Bury	0	0		
2003-04	Bury	27	0		
2004-05	Bury	46	1		
2005-06	Bury	33	4		
2006-07	Bury	37	0	143	5
2007-08	Rochdale	43	2		
2008-09	Rochdale	45	4		
2009-10	Rochdale	44	3		
2010-11	Leicester C	1	0		
2010-11	*Rochdale*	6	0	138	9
2010-11	Peterborough U	14	0		
2011-12	Leicester C	0	0		
2011-12	Peterborough U	10	0	24	0
2012-13	Leicester C	0	0	6	0
2012-13	Bury	24	0		
2013-14	Barnsley	44	1	68	1

LAWRENCE, Liam (M) — 427 79
H: 5 11 W: 12 06 b.Retford 14-12-81
Internationals: Republic of Ireland Full caps.

Season	Club	Apps	Gls	Tot A	Tot G
1999-2000	Mansfield T	2	0		
2000-01	Mansfield T	18	4		
2001-02	Mansfield T	32	2		
2002-03	Mansfield T	43	10		
2003-04	Mansfield T	41	18	136	34
2004-05	Sunderland	32	7		
2005-06	Sunderland	29	3		
2006-07	Sunderland	12	0	73	10
2006-07	Stoke C	27	5		
2007-08	Stoke C	41	14		
2008-09	Stoke C	20	3		
2009-10	Stoke C	25	1		
2010-11	Stoke C	0	0	113	23
2010-11	Portsmouth	31	7		
2011-12	Portsmouth	23	0	54	7
2011-12	*Cardiff C*	13	1	13	1
2012-13	PAOK Salonika	22	3		
2013-14	PAOK Salonika	2	0	24	3
2013-14	Barnsley	14	1	14	1

McCOURT, Paddy (M) — 247 32
H: 5 10 W: 10 13 b.Londonderry 16-12-83
Internationals: Northern Ireland U21, B, Full caps.

Season	Club	Apps	Gls	Tot A	Tot G
2001-02	Rochdale	23	4		
2002-03	Rochdale	26	3		
2003-04	Rochdale	24	2		
2004-05	Rochdale	6	0	79	9
2005	Shamrock R	17	7	17	7
2005	Derry C	15	1		
2006	Derry C	22	2		
2007	Derry C	17	2		
2008	Derry C	8	0	62	5
2008-09	Celtic	4	0		
2009-10	Celtic	9	2		
2010-11	Celtic	25	7		
2011-12	Celtic	13	0		
2012-13	Celtic	15	0	66	9
2013-14	Barnsley	23	2	23	2

McHALE, Dominic (M) — 0 0
b. 1-1-95

Season	Club	Apps	Gls	Tot A	Tot G
2013-14	Barnsley	0	0		

MELLIS, Jacob (M) — 93 10
H: 5 11 W: 10 11 b.Nottingham 8-1-91
Internationals: England U16, U17, U19.

Season	Club	Apps	Gls	Tot A	Tot G
2009-10	Chelsea	0	0		
2009-10	*Southampton*	12	0	12	0
2010-11	Chelsea	0	0		
2010-11	*Barnsley*	15	2		
2012-13	Barnsley	36	6		
2013-14	Barnsley	30	2	81	10

MVOTO, Jean Yves (D) — 28 2
H: 6 4 W: 14 07 b.Paris 6-9-88

Season	Club	Apps	Gls	Tot A	Tot G
2009-10	Southend U	0	0		
2010-11	Oldham Ath	0	0		
2012-13	Oldham Ath	0	0		
2013-14	Barnsley	28	2	28	2

NOBLE-LAZARUS, Reuben (F) — 49 3
H: 5 11 W: 13 07 b.Huddersfield 16-8-93

Season	Club	Apps	Gls	Tot A	Tot G
2008-09	Barnsley	2	0		
2009-10	Barnsley	2	0		
2010-11	Barnsley	7	1		
2011-12	Barnsley	8	0		
2012-13	Barnsley	14	1		
2013-14	Barnsley	12	1	45	3
2013-14	*Scunthorpe U*	4	0	4	0

NYATANGA, Lewin (D) — 245 10
H: 6 2 W: 12 08 b.Burton 18-8-88
Internationals: Wales U17, U21, Full caps.

Season	Club	Apps	Gls	Tot A	Tot G
2005-06	Derby Co	24	1		
2006-07	Derby Co	7	1		
2006-07	*Sunderland*	11	0	11	0
2006-07	*Barnsley*	10	1		
2007-08	Derby Co	9	0		
2007-08	*Barnsley*	41	1		
2008-09	Derby Co	30	1	63	4
2009-10	Bristol C	37	1		
2010-11	Bristol C	20	1		
2010-11	*Peterborough U*	29	0	3	0
2011-12	Bristol C	0	0		

2012–13	Bristol C	19	2	105	4
2013–14	Barnsley	12	0	63	2

O'BRIEN, Jim (F) 211 12
H: 6 0 W: 11 11 b.Alexandria 28-9-87
Internationals: Republic of Ireland U19, U21.

2006–07	Celtic	0	0		
2006–07	*Dunfermline Ath*	13	1	13	1
2007–08	Celtic	1	0	1	0
2007–08	*Dundee U*	10	0	10	0
2008–09	Motherwell	29	1		
2009–10	Motherwell	35	3	64	4
2010–11	Barnsley	33	1		
2011–12	Barnsley	31	2		
2012–13	Barnsley	30	2		
2013–14	Barnsley	29	2	123	7

O'GRADY, Chris (F) 344 80
H: 6 3 W: 12 04 b.Nottingham 25-1-86
Internationals: England Youth.

2002–03	Leicester C	1	0		
2003–04	Leicester C	0	0		
2004–05	Leicester C	0	0		
2004–05	*Notts Co*	9	0	9	0
2005–06	Leicester C	13	1		
2005–06	*Rushden & D*	22	4	22	4
2006–07	Leicester C	10	0	24	1
2006–07	Rotherham U	13	4		
2007–08	Rotherham U	38	9	51	13
2008–09	Oldham Ath	13	0		
2008–09	*Bury*	6	0	6	0
2008–09	*Bradford C*	2	0	2	0
2008–09	*Stockport Co*	18	2	18	2
2009–10	Oldham Ath	0	0	13	0
2009–10	Rochdale	43	22		
2010–11	Rochdale	46	9		
2011–12	Rochdale	1	0	90	31
2011–12	Sheffield W	32	5		
2012–13	Sheffield W	21	4	53	9
2012–13	*Barnsley*	16	5		
2013–14	Barnsley	40	15	56	20

OATES, Rhys (F) 0 0
b.Pontefract 4-12-94

2012–13	Barnsley	0	0
2013–14	Barnsley	0	0

PEDERSEN, Marcus (F) 132 43
H: 5 11 b.Hamar 8-6-90

2007	Ham-Kam	4	0		
2008	Ham-Kam	4	1	8	1
2009	Stromsgodset	24	10		
2010	Stromsgodset	16	8	40	18
2010–11	Vitesse	16	5		
2011–12	Vitesse	9	0		
2012	Valerenga	15	8	15	8
2012–13	Odense BK	24	8	24	8
2013–14	Vitesse	2	1	27	6

On loan from Vitesse

2013–14	Barnsley	18	2	18	2

ROSE, Danny (F) 22 4
H: 5 8 W: 9 00 b.Barnsley 10-12-93

2010–11	Barnsley	1	0		
2011–12	Barnsley	4	0		
2012–13	Barnsley	8	1		
2013–14	Barnsley	3	0	16	1
2013–14	*Bury*	6	3	6	3

SCOTLAND, Jason (F) 363 113
H: 5 8 W: 11 10 b.Morvant 18-2-79
Internationals: Trinidad and Tobago Full caps.

2003–04	Dundee U	21	4		
2004–05	Dundee U	39	3	50	7
2005–06	St Johnstone	31	15		
2006–07	St Johnstone	35	18	66	33
2007–08	Swansea C	45	24		
2008–09	Swansea C	45	21		
2009–10	Swansea C	0	0	90	45
2009–10	Wigan Ath	32	1		
2010–11	Wigan Ath	0	0	32	1
2010–11	Ipswich T	39	10		
2011–12	Ipswich T	36	8		
2012–13	Ipswich T	12	1	87	19
2012–13	Barnsley	18	6		
2013–14	Barnsley	20	2	38	8

Transferred to Hamilton A February 2014

STEELE, Luke (G) 250 0
H: 6 2 W: 12 00 b.Peterborough 24-9-84
Internationals: England U18, U19, U20.

2001–02	Peterborough U	2	0	2	0

2001–02	Manchester U	0	0		
2002–03	Manchester U	0	0		
2003–04	Manchester U	0	0		
2004–05	Manchester U	0	0		
2004–05	*Coventry C*	32	0		
2005–06	Manchester U	0	0		
2006–07	WBA	0	0		
2006–07	*Coventry C*	5	0	37	0
2007–08	WBA	2	0	2	0
2007–08	*Barnsley*	14	0		
2008–09	Barnsley	10	0		
2009–10	Barnsley	39	0		
2010–11	Barnsley	46	0		
2011–12	Barnsley	36	0		
2012–13	Barnsley	33	0		
2013–14	Barnsley	31	0	209	0

WOODS, Martin (M) 180 11
H: 5 11 W: 11 13 b.Airdrie 1-1-86
Internationals: Scotland U17, U19, U20.

2002–03	Leeds U	0	0		
2003–04	Leeds U	0	0		
2004–05	Leeds U	1	0	1	0
2004–05	*Hartlepool U*	6	0	6	0
2005–06	Sunderland	7	0	7	0
2006–07	Rotherham U	36	4	36	4
2007–08	Doncaster R	15	0		
2007–08	*Yeovil T*	3	0	3	0
2008–09	Doncaster R	41	2		
2009–10	Doncaster R	24	4		
2010–11	Doncaster R	15	1		
2011–12	Doncaster R	4	0		
2012–13	Doncaster R	16	0		
2013–14	Doncaster R	4	0	119	7
2013–14	*Barnsley*	8	0	8	0

Scholars
Alexander-Salmon, Omari Keither Jayden; Biggins, Harrison; Chadderton, Elliot; Cooke, Joshua James Alan; Cowgill, Jack Nicholas; Freeman, Dean Thomas; Gooda, Bailey Roy; Goodwin, Sean; Hancock, Charlie; Holgate, Mason Anthony; MacKey, Conor Laurence; Maris, George Thomas; McKnight, Darren James; Moore, Jamie Stephen; Ndlovu, Talent; Pilkington, Callum Jon; Rogerson, Edward James; Rusling, Danny William; Smith, George Thomas; Templeton, Matthew; Yiadom, Nana Emeka Boakye.

BIRMINGHAM C (6)

ADAMS, Charlee (M) 0 0
H: 5 11 W: 12 01 b.Redbridge 16-2-95

2013–14	Birmingham C	0	0

ADEYEMI, Tom (M) 146 10
H: 6 1 W: 12 04 b.Milton Keynes 24-10-91

2008–09	Norwich C	0	0		
2009–10	Norwich C	11	0		
2010–11	Norwich C	0	0		
2010–11	*Bradford C*	34	5	34	5
2011–12	Norwich C	0	0		
2011–12	*Oldham Ath*	36	2	36	2
2012–13	Norwich C	0	0	11	0
2012–13	*Brentford*	30	2	30	2
2013–14	Birmingham C	35	1	35	1

AMBROSE, Darren (M) 316 61
H: 6 0 W: 11 00 b.Harlow 29-2-84
Internationals: England U21.

2001–02	Ipswich T	1	0		
2002–03	Ipswich T	29	8		
2002–03	Newcastle U	1	0		
2003–04	Newcastle U	24	2		
2004–05	Newcastle U	12	3	37	5
2005–06	Charlton Ath	28	3		
2006–07	Charlton Ath	26	3		
2007–08	Charlton Ath	37	7		
2008–09	Charlton Ath	21	0	112	13
2008–09	*Ipswich T*	9	0	39	8
2009–10	Crystal Palace	46	15		
2010–11	Crystal Palace	28	7		
2011–12	Crystal Palace	36	7	110	29
2012–13	Birmingham C	6	0		
2013–14	Birmingham C	1	0	7	0
2013–14	*Apollon Smyrni*	11	6	11	6

ARTHUR, Koby (M) 3 0
H: 5 6 W: 10 09 b.Kumasi 3-1-96

2012–13	Birmingham C	2	0		
2013–14	Birmingham C	1	0	3	0

ASANTE, Akwasi (F) 12 2
H: 5 7 W: 10 00 b.Amsterdam 22-9-92

2010–11	Birmingham C	0	0		
2011–12	Birmingham C	0	0		
2011–12	*Northampton T*	4	1	4	1
2012–13	Birmingham C	0	0		
2012–13	*Shrewsbury T*	7	1		
2013–14	Birmingham C	0	0		
2013–14	*Shrewsbury T*	1	0	8	1

BELL, Amari (D) 1 0
H: 5 11 W: 12 00 b. 5-5-94

2012–13	Birmingham C	0	0		
2013–14	Birmingham C	1	0	1	0

BROWN, Reece (M) 6 0
b. 3-3-96
Internationals: England U16, U17, U18.

2013–14	Birmingham C	6	0	6	0

BURKE, Chris (M) 328 50
H: 5 9 W: 10 10 b.Glasgow 2-12-83
Internationals: Scotland U21, B, Full caps.

2001–02	Rangers	2	1		
2002–03	Rangers	20	3		
2003–04	Rangers	12	0		
2004–05	Rangers	27	3		
2005–06	Rangers	22	2		
2006–07	Rangers	11	2		
2007–08	Rangers	1	0	95	11
2008–09	Cardiff C	14	1		
2009–10	Cardiff C	44	9		
2010–11	Cardiff C	44	5	102	15
2011–12	Birmingham C	46	12		
2012–13	Birmingham C	41	8		
2013–14	Birmingham C	44	4	131	24

CADDIS, Paul (D) 170 10
H: 5 7 W: 10 07 b.Irvine 19-4-88
Internationals: Scotland U19, U21.

2007–08	Celtic	2	0		
2008–09	Celtic	5	0		
2008–09	*Dundee U*	11	0	11	0
2009–10	Celtic	10	0	17	0
2010–11	Swindon T	38	1		
2011–12	Swindon T	39	4		
2012–13	Swindon T	0	0		
2012–13	*Birmingham C*	27	0		
2013–14	Swindon T	0	0	77	5
2013–14	Birmingham C	38	5	65	5

DOYLE, Colin (G) 47 0
H: 6 5 W: 14 05 b.Cork 12-8-85
Internationals: Republic of Ireland U21, B, Full caps.

2004–05	Birmingham C	0	0		
2004–05	*Chester C*	0	0		
2004–05	*Nottingham F*	3	0	3	0
2005–06	Birmingham C	0	0		
2005–06	*Millwall*	14	0	14	0
2006–07	Birmingham C	19	0		
2007–08	Birmingham C	3	0		
2008–09	Birmingham C	2	0		
2009–10	Birmingham C	0	0		
2010–11	Birmingham C	1	0		
2011–12	Birmingham C	5	0		
2012–13	Birmingham C	0	0		
2013–14	Birmingham C	0	0	30	0

DUDKA, Dariusz (M) 263 11
H: 6 0 W: 12 07 b.Kostrzyn nad odra 9-12-83
Internationals: Poland Full caps.

1999–2000	Amica Wronki	2	0		
2000–01	Amica Wronki	17	0		
2001–02	Amica Wronki	23	0		
2002–03	Amica Wronki	4	0		
2003–04	Amica Wronki	23	0		
2004–05	Amica Wronki	1	0	70	0
2005–06	Wisła Krakow	29	1		
2006–07	Wisła Krakow	28	3		
2007–08	Wisła Krakow	20	1	77	5
2008–09	Auxerre	28	1		
2009–10	Auxerre	19	0		
2010–11	Auxerre	30	3		
2011–12	Auxerre	34	2	111	6
2012–13	Levante	3	0	3	0

EARDLEY, Neal (M) 222 12
H: 5 11 W: 11 10 b.Llandudno 6-11-88
Internationals: Wales U17, U19, U21, Full caps.

Season	Club				
2005–06	Oldham Ath	1	0		
2006–07	Oldham Ath	36	2		
2007–08	Oldham Ath	42	6		
2008–09	Oldham Ath	34	2		
2009–10	Oldham Ath	0	0	113	10
2009–10	Blackpool	24	0		
2010–11	Blackpool	31	1		
2011–12	Blackpool	26	1		
2012–13	Blackpool	23	0	104	2
2013–14	Birmingham C	5	0	5	0

ELLIOTT, Wade (M) 579 61
H: 5 10 W: 10 03 b.Eastleigh 14-12-78

Season	Club				
1999–2000	Bournemouth	12	3		
2000–01	Bournemouth	36	9		
2001–02	Bournemouth	46	8		
2002–03	Bournemouth	44	4		
2003–04	Bournemouth	39	3		
2004–05	Bournemouth	43	4	220	31
2005–06	Burnley	36	3		
2006–07	Burnley	42	4		
2007–08	Burnley	46	2		
2008–09	Burnley	42	4		
2009–10	Burnley	38	4		
2010–11	Burnley	44	2		
2011–12	Burnley	4	0	252	19
2011–12	Birmingham C	29	2		
2012–13	Birmingham C	44	6		
2013–14	Birmingham C	15	0	88	8
2013–14	Bristol C	19	3	19	3

FRY, James (D) 0 0
H: 5 11 W: 12 03 b.Solihull 3-2-95

Season	Club		
2012–13	Birmingham C	0	0
2013–14	Birmingham C	0	0

GRAY, Demarai (M) 7 1
H: 5 10 W: 10 04 b.Birmingham 28-6-96
Internationals: England U18.

Season	Club				
2013–14	Birmingham C	7	1	7	1

GREEN, Matt (F) 56 1
H: 6 0 W: 12 09 b.Bath 1-8-87

Season	Club				
2006–07	Cardiff C	6	0		
2007–08	Cardiff C	0	0	6	0
2007–08	Darlington	4	0	4	0
From Torquay U					
2010–11	Oxford U	17	0	17	0
2010–11	Cheltenham T	19	0	19	0
From Mansfield T					
2013–14	Birmingham C	10	1	10	1

HANCOX, Mitch (D) 33 0
H: 5 10 W: 11 03 b.Solihull 9-11-93

Season	Club				
2011–12	Birmingham C	0	0		
2012–13	Birmingham C	19	0		
2013–14	Birmingham C	14	0	33	0

HOWARD, Brian (M) 326 41
H: 5 8 W: 11 00 b.Winchester 23-1-83
Internationals: England U16, U17, U19, U20.

Season	Club				
1999–2000	Southampton	0	0		
2000–01	Southampton	0	0		
2001–02	Southampton	0	0		
2002–03	Southampton	0	0		
2003–04	Swindon T	35	4		
2004–05	Swindon T	35	5	70	9
2005–06	Barnsley	31	5		
2006–07	Barnsley	42	8		
2007–08	Barnsley	41	13		
2008–09	Barnsley	7	1	121	27
2008–09	Sheffield U	26	2		
2009–10	Sheffield U	4	0	30	2
2009–10	Reading	34	2		
2010–11	Reading	24	0		
2011–12	Reading	1	0	59	2
2011–12	Millwall	12	0	12	0
2012–13	Portsmouth	23	0	23	0
2012–13	Bristol C	6	0		
2013–14	Bristol C	0	0		
2013–14	Birmingham C	5	1	5	1

LEE, Oliver (M) 56 4
H: 5 11 W: 12 07 b.Hornchurch 11-7-91

Season	Club				
2009–10	West Ham U	0	0		
2010–11	West Ham U	0	0		
2010–11	Dagenham & R	5	0		
2011–12	West Ham U	0	0		
2011–12	Dagenham & R	16	3	21	3
2011–12	Gillingham	8	0	8	0
2012–13	Barnet	11	0	11	0
2012–13	Birmingham C	0	0		
2013–14	Birmingham C	16	1	16	1

LOVENKRANDS, Peter (F) 320 77
H: 5 11 W: 11 02 b.Copenhagen 29-1-80
Internationals: Denmark U19, U21, Full caps.

Season	Club				
1998–99	AB Copenhagen	8	1		
1999–2000	AB Copenhagen	14	5	32	7
2000–01	Rangers	8	0		
2001–02	Rangers	18	2		
2002–03	Rangers	28	9		
2003–04	Rangers	25	8		
2004–05	Rangers	17	3		
2005–06	Rangers	33	14	129	36
2006–07	Schalke	24	6		
2007–08	Schalke	20	0	44	6
2008–09	Schalke B	3	2	3	2
2008–09	Newcastle U	12	3		
2009–10	Newcastle U	29	13		
2010–11	Newcastle U	25	6		
2011–12	Newcastle U	9	0	75	22
2012–13	Birmingham C	22	3		
2013–14	Birmingham C	15	1	37	4

MARTIN, Aaron (D) 44 1
H: 6 3 W: 11 13 b.Newport (IW) 29-9-89

Season	Club				
2009–10	Southampton	2	0		
2010–11	Southampton	8	0		
2011–12	Southampton	10	1		
2012–13	Southampton	0	0		
2012–13	Crystal Palace	4	0	4	0
2012–13	Coventry C	12	0	12	0
2013–14	Southampton	0	0	20	1
2013–14	Birmingham C	8	0	8	0

MULLINS, Hayden (D) 575 28
H: 5 11 W: 11 12 b.Reading 27-3-79
Internationals: England U21.

Season	Club				
1996–97	Crystal Palace	0	0		
1997–98	Crystal Palace	0	0		
1998–99	Crystal Palace	40	5		
1999–2000	Crystal Palace	45	10		
2000–01	Crystal Palace	41	1		
2001–02	Crystal Palace	43	0		
2002–03	Crystal Palace	43	2		
2003–04	Crystal Palace	10	0	222	18
2003–04	West Ham U	27	0		
2004–05	West Ham U	37	1		
2005–06	West Ham U	35	0		
2006–07	West Ham U	30	2		
2007–08	West Ham U	34	0		
2008–09	West Ham U	17	1	180	4
2008–09	Portsmouth	17	0		
2009–10	Portsmouth	18	0		
2010–11	Portsmouth	34	1	114	3
2011–12	Reading	7	0	7	0
2012–13	Birmingham C	28	2		
2013–14	Birmingham C	8	0	36	2
2013–14	Notts Co	16	1	16	1

MURPHY, David (D) 236 13
H: 6 1 W: 12 03 b.Hartlepool 1-3-84
Internationals: England U16.

Season	Club				
2001–02	Middlesbrough	5	0		
2002–03	Middlesbrough	8	0		
2003–04	Middlesbrough	0	0	13	0
2003–04	Barnsley	10	2	10	2
2004–05	Hibernian	27	1		
2005–06	Hibernian	30	1		
2006–07	Hibernian	33	0		
2007–08	Hibernian	17	2	107	4
2007–08	Birmingham C	14	1		
2008–09	Birmingham C	30	0		
2009–10	Birmingham C	0	0		
2010–11	Birmingham C	10	0		
2011–12	Birmingham C	33	4		
2012–13	Birmingham C	13	0		
2013–14	Birmingham C	6	2	106	7

NOVAK, Lee (F) 182 43
H: 6 0 W: 12 04 b.Newcastle 28-9-88

Season	Club				
2008–09	Huddersfield T	0	0		
2009–10	Huddersfield T	37	12		
2010–11	Huddersfield T	31	5		
2011–12	Huddersfield T	41	13		
2012–13	Huddersfield T	35	4	144	34
2013–14	Birmingham C	38	9	38	9

PACKWOOD, Will (M) 25 0
H: 6 3 W: 12 08 b.Concord 21-5-93
Internationals: USA U17, U18, U20.

Season	Club				
2011–12	Birmingham C	0	0		
2012–13	Birmingham C	5	0		
2013–14	Birmingham C	12	0	17	0
2013–14	Bristol R	8	0	8	0

RANDOLPH, Darren (G) 201 0
H: 6 1 W: 12 02 b.Dublin 12-5-87
Internationals: Republic of Ireland U21, B, Full caps.

Season	Club				
2004–05	Charlton Ath	0	0		
2005–06	Charlton Ath	0	0		
2006–07	Charlton Ath	1	0		
2006–07	Gillingham	3	0	3	0
2007–08	Charlton Ath	1	0		
2007–08	Bury	14	0	14	0
2008–09	Charlton Ath	1	0		
2008–09	Hereford U	13	0	13	0
2009–10	Charlton Ath	11	0	14	0
2010–11	Motherwell	37	0		
2011–12	Motherwell	38	0		
2012–13	Motherwell	36	0	111	0
2013–14	Birmingham C	46	0	46	0

REILLY, Callum (M) 43 1
H: 6 1 W: 12 03 b.Warrington 3-10-93
Internationals: Republic of Ireland U21.

Season	Club				
2012–13	Birmingham C	18	1		
2013–14	Birmingham C	25	0	43	1

ROBINSON, Paul (D) 595 12
H: 5 9 W: 11 12 b.Watford 14-12-78
Internationals: England U21.

Season	Club				
1996–97	Watford	12	0		
1997–98	Watford	22	2		
1998–99	Watford	29	0		
1999–2000	Watford	32	0		
2000–01	Watford	39	0		
2001–02	Watford	38	3		
2002–03	Watford	37	3		
2003–04	Watford	10	0	219	8
2003–04	WBA	31	0		
2004–05	WBA	30	1		
2005–06	WBA	33	0		
2006–07	WBA	42	2		
2007–08	WBA	43	1		
2008–09	WBA	35	0		
2009–10	WBA	0	0	214	4
2009–10	Bolton W	25	0		
2010–11	Bolton W	35	0		
2011–12	Bolton W	17	0	77	0
2011–12	Leeds U	10	0	10	0
2012–13	Birmingham C	35	0		
2013–14	Birmingham C	40	0	75	0

SHINNIE, Andrew (M) 85 21
H: 5 11 W: 10 13 b.Aberdeen 17-7-89
Internationals: Scotland U19, U21, Full caps.

Season	Club				
2005–06	Rangers	2	0		
2006–07	Rangers	2	0		
2007–08	Rangers	0	0		
2008–09	Rangers	0	0		
2009–10	Rangers	0	0		
2010–11	Rangers	0	0	2	0
2011–12	Inverness CT	19	7		
2012–13	Inverness CT	38	12	57	19
2013–14	Birmingham C	26	2	26	2

SPECTOR, Jonathan (D) 206 1
H: 6 0 W: 12 08 b.Chicago 1-3-86
Internationals: USA U17, U20, Full caps.

Season	Club				
2003–04	Manchester U	0	0		
2004–05	Manchester U	3	0		
2005–06	Manchester U	0	0	3	0
2005–06	Charlton Ath	20	0	20	0
2006–07	West Ham U	25	0		
2007–08	West Ham U	26	0		
2008–09	West Ham U	9	0		
2009–10	West Ham U	27	0		
2010–11	West Ham U	14	1	101	1
2011–12	Birmingham C	31	0		
2012–13	Birmingham C	29	0		
2013–14	Birmingham C	22	0	82	0

TOWNSEND, Nick (G) 0 0
H: 5 11 W: 13 11 b.Solihull 1-11-94

Season	Club		
2012–13	Birmingham C	0	0
2013–14	Birmingham C	0	0

TRUSLOVE, Liam (M) 0 0
H: 5 11 W: 10 11 b.5-9-95
| 2013–14 | Birmingham C | 0 | 0 | | |

ZIGIC, Nikola (F) 404 208
H: 6 8 W: 14 02 b.Backa Topola 25-9-80
Internationals: Serbia Full caps.
1998–99	Backa Topola	14	8		
1999–2000	Backa Topola	28	28		
2000–01	Backa Topola	30	30		
2001–02	Backa Topola	4	2	76	68
2001–02	Mornar Bar	23	15	23	15
2002–03	Kolubara	8	3	8	3
2002–03	Spartak Subotica	11	14	11	14
2003–04	Red Star Belgrade	28	19		
2004–05	Red Star Belgrade	25	15		
2005–06	Red Star Belgrade	23	11		
2006–07	Red Star Belgrade	3	2	79	47
2006–07	Santander	32	11		
2007–08	Valencia	15	1		
2008–09	Santander	19	13	51	24
2009–10	Valencia	13	4	28	5
2010–11	Birmingham C	25	5		
2011–12	Birmingham C	35	11		
2012–13	Birmingham C	35	9		
2013–14	Birmingham C	33	7	128	32

Scholars
Bernard, Dominic Archie; Cooper, Charlie Terrence; Cotton, Perry Kevin; Dacres-Cogley, Joshua Jacob; Deadfield, Samuel Jack; Denton, Peter Richard; Dunbar, Kieron Paul; Harding, Wesley Nathan Hylton; Kalenda, Jean; Kelly, Nathaniel; Lang, Thomas Antoni Robert; McDonald, Wesley Nurettin; McFarlane, Raewkon Kyle; McGee, George David; Moseley, Bobby James; O'Neill, George Connor; Preston, Callum; Solomon-Otabor, Viv Efosa; Trueman, Connal Joe; Weaver, Jacob William Robert; Webb, Reece.

BLACKBURN R (7)

BEST, Leon (F) 226 54
H: 6 1 W: 13 03 b.Nottingham 19-9-86
Internationals: Republic of Ireland U21, Full caps.
2004–05	Southampton	3	0		
2004–05	QPR	5	0	5	0
2005–06	Southampton	3	0		
2005–06	Sheffield W	13	2		
2006–07	Southampton	9	4	15	4
2006–07	Bournemouth	15	3	15	3
2006–07	Yeovil T	15	10	15	10
2007–08	Coventry C	34	8		
2008–09	Coventry C	31	2		
2009–10	Coventry C	27	9	92	19
2009–10	Newcastle U	13	0		
2010–11	Newcastle U	11	6		
2011–12	Newcastle U	18	4	42	10
2012–13	Blackburn R	6	0		
2013–14	Blackburn R	8	2	14	2
2013–14	Sheffield W	15	4	28	6

CAIRNEY, Tom (M) 107 7
H: 6 0 W: 11 05 b.Nottingham 20-1-91
Internationals: Scotland U19, U21.
2009–10	Hull C	11	1		
2010–11	Hull C	22	1		
2011–12	Hull C	27	0		
2012–13	Hull C	10	0		
2013–14	Hull C	0	0	70	2
2013–14	Blackburn R	37	5	37	5

CAMPBELL, Dudley (F) 232 69
H: 5 10 W: 11 00 b.Hammersmith 12-11-81
Internationals: England C.
2005–06	Brentford	23	9	23	9
2005–06	Birmingham C	11	0		
2006–07	Birmingham C	32	9	43	9
2007–08	Leicester C	28	4		
2008–09	Leicester C	7	0		
2008–09	Blackpool	20	9		
2009–10	Leicester C	3	0		
2009–10	Derby Co	8	3	8	3
2009–10	Blackpool	15	8		
2010–11	Leicester C	3	1	41	5
2010–11	Blackpool	31	13	66	30
2011–12	QPR	11	1		
2012–13	QPR	0	0	11	1
2012–13	Ipswich T	17	10	17	10
2012–13	Blackburn R	7	0		
2013–14	Blackburn R	7	0	14	0
2013–14	Millwall	9	2	9	2

CONWAY, Craig (M) 286 30
H: 5 7 W: 10 07 b.Irvine 2-5-85
Internationals: Scotland Full caps.
2002–03	Ayr U	1	0		
2003–04	Ayr U	6	0		
2004–05	Ayr U	23	3		
2005–06	Ayr U	31	4	61	7
2006–07	Dundee U	30	0		
2007–08	Dundee U	15	1		
2008–09	Dundee U	36	5		
2009–10	Dundee U	33	4		
2010–11	Dundee U	22	3	136	13
2011–12	Cardiff C	31	3		
2012–13	Cardiff C	27	2		
2013–14	Cardiff C	0	0	58	5
2013–14	Brighton & HA	13	1	13	1
2013–14	Blackburn R	18	4	18	4

DALY, Kellen (D) 0 0
b. 17-1-95
| 2012–13 | Blackburn R | 0 | 0 | | |
| 2013–14 | Blackburn R | 0 | 0 | | |

DUNN, David (M) 365 57
H: 5 9 W: 12 03 b.Gt Harwood 27-12-79
Internationals: England U18, U21, Full caps.
1997–98	Blackburn R	0	0		
1998–99	Blackburn R	15	1		
1999–2000	Blackburn R	22	2		
2000–01	Blackburn R	42	12		
2001–02	Blackburn R	29	7		
2002–03	Blackburn R	28	8		
2003–04	Birmingham C	28	2		
2004–05	Birmingham C	11	2		
2005–06	Birmingham C	15	2		
2006–07	Birmingham C	11	1	58	7
2006–07	Blackburn R	11	0		
2007–08	Blackburn R	31	1		
2008–09	Blackburn R	15	1		
2009–10	Blackburn R	23	9		
2010–11	Blackburn R	27	2		
2011–12	Blackburn R	26	2		
2012–13	Blackburn R	15	1		
2013–14	Blackburn R	23	4	307	50

EASTWOOD, Simon (G) 57 0
H: 6 2 W: 10 13 b.Huddersfield 26-6-89
Internationals: England U18, U19.
2005–06	Huddersfield T	0	0		
2006–07	Huddersfield T	0	0		
2007–08	Huddersfield T	0	0		
2008–09	Huddersfield T	1	0		
2009–10	Huddersfield T	0	0	1	0
2009–10	Bradford C	22	0	22	0
2012–13	Portsmouth	27	0	27	0
2013–14	Blackburn R	7	0	7	0

EDWARDS, Ryan (D) 49 0
b.Liverpool 7-10-93
2011–12	Blackburn R	0	0		
2012–13	Rochdale	26	0	26	0
2012–13	Blackburn R	0	0		
2012–13	Fleetwood T	9	0	9	0
2013–14	Blackburn R	0	0		
2013–14	Chesterfield	5	0	5	0
2013–14	Tranmere R	9	0		
2013–14	Morecambe	9	0	9	0

ETUHU, Dickson (M) 342 28
H: 6 2 W: 13 04 b.Kano 8-6-82
Internationals: Nigeria Full caps.
1999–2000	Manchester C	0	0		
2000–01	Manchester C	0	0		
2001–02	Manchester C	12	0	12	0
2001–02	Preston NE	16	3		
2002–03	Preston NE	39	6		
2003–04	Preston NE	31	3		
2004–05	Preston NE	35	3		
2005–06	Preston NE	13	2	134	17
2005–06	Norwich C	19	0		
2006–07	Norwich C	43	6	62	6
2007–08	Sunderland	20	1		
2008–09	Sunderland	0	0	20	1
2008–09	Fulham	21	1		
2009–10	Fulham	20	0		
2010–11	Fulham	28	2		
2011–12	Fulham	22	0		
2012–13	Fulham	0	0	91	3
2012–13	Blackburn R	20	1		
2013–14	Blackburn R	3	0	23	1

EVANS, Corry (M) 115 7
H: 5 8 W: 10 12 b.Belfast 30-7-90
Internationals: Northern Ireland U16, U17, U19, U21, B, Full caps.
2007–08	Manchester U	0	0		
2008–09	Manchester U	0	0		
2009–10	Manchester U	0	0		
2010–11	Manchester U	0	0		
2010–11	Carlisle U	1	0	1	0
2010–11	Hull C	18	3		
2011–12	Hull C	43	2		
2012–13	Hull C	32	1		
2013–14	Hull C	0	0	93	6
2013–14	Blackburn R	21	1	21	1

FORRESTER, Anton (F) 28 6
H: 6 0 W: 12 00 b.Liverpool 11-2-94
2010–11	Everton	0	0		
2011–12	Everton	0	0		
2012–13	Blackburn R	0	0		
2013–14	Blackburn R	0	0		
2013–14	Bury	28	6	28	6

GESTEDE, Rudy (F) 123 28
H: 6 4 W: 13 07 b.Nancy 10-10-88
Internationals: France U19. Benin Full caps.
2008–09	Metz	5	0		
2009–10	Cannes	22	4	22	4
2010–11	Metz	11	3	16	3
2010–11	Metz B	3	1	3	1
2011–12	Cardiff C	25	2		
2012–13	Cardiff C	27	5		
2013–14	Cardiff C	3	0	55	7
2013–14	Blackburn R	27	13	27	13

GOODWILLIE, David (F) 200 45
H: 5 9 W: 11 02 b.Stirling 28-3-89
Internationals: Scotland U16, U17, U19, U21, Full caps.
2005–06	Dundee U	10	1		
2006–07	Dundee U	17	0		
2007–08	Dundee U	2	0		
2007–08	Raith R	23	9	23	9
2008–09	Dundee U	16	3		
2009–10	Dundee U	33	8		
2010–11	Dundee U	37	16		
2011–12	Dundee U	1	0		
2011–12	Blackburn R	20	2		
2012–13	Blackburn R	8	0		
2012–13	Crystal Palace	1	0	1	0
2013–14	Blackburn R	0	0	28	2
2013–14	Dundee U	19	3	135	31
2013–14	Blackpool	13	3	13	3

HANLEY, Grant (D) 108 4
H: 6 2 W: 12 00 b.Dumfries 20-11-91
Internationals: Scotland U19, U21, Full caps.
2008–09	Blackburn R	0	0		
2009–10	Blackburn R	1	0		
2010–11	Blackburn R	7	0		
2011–12	Blackburn R	23	1		
2012–13	Blackburn R	39	2		
2013–14	Blackburn R	38	1	108	4

HENLEY, Adam (D) 36 0
H: 5 10 W: 12 02 b.Knoxville 14-6-94
Internationals: Wales U19, U21.
2011–12	Blackburn R	7	0		
2012–13	Blackburn R	15	0		
2013–14	Blackburn R	14	0	36	0

JORGE, Paulo (M) 1 0
H: 5 10 W: 11 01 b.Braga 18-1-93
Internationals: Portugal U17, U19.
| 2012–13 | Blackburn R | 1 | 0 | | |
| 2013–14 | Blackburn R | 0 | 0 | 1 | 0 |

KEAN, Jake (G) 70 0
H: 6 4 W: 11 13 b.Derby 4-2-91
Internationals: England U20.
2010–11	Blackburn R	0	0		
2010–11	Hartlepool U	19	0	19	0
2011–12	Blackburn R	0	0		
2011–12	Rochdale	14	0	14	0
2012–13	Blackburn R	18	0		
2013–14	Blackburn R	18	0	37	0

KILGALLON, Matthew (D) 252 8
H: 6 1 W: 12 10 b.York 8-1-84
Internationals: England U20, U21.

Season	Club				
2000–01	Leeds U	0	0		
2001–02	Leeds U	0	0		
2002–03	Leeds U	2	0		
2003–04	Leeds U	8	2		
2003–04	West Ham U	3	0	3	0
2004–05	Leeds U	26	0		
2005–06	Leeds U	25	1		
2006–07	Leeds U	19	0	80	3
2006–07	Sheffield U	6	0		
2007–08	Sheffield U	40	2		
2008–09	Sheffield U	40	1		
2009–10	Sheffield U	21	1	107	4
2009–10	Sunderland	7	0		
2010–11	Sunderland	0	0		
2010–11	Middlesbrough	2	0	2	0
2010–11	Doncaster R	12	0	12	0
2011–12	Sunderland	10	0		
2012–13	Sunderland	6	0	23	0
2013–14	Blackburn R	25	1	25	1

KING, Josh (F) 76 5
H: 5 11 W: 11 09 b.Oslo 15-1-92
Internationals: Norway U15, U16, U18, U19, U21, Full caps.

Season	Club				
2008–09	Manchester U	0	0		
2009–10	Manchester U	0	0		
2010–11	Manchester U	0	0		
2010–11	Preston NE	8	0	8	0
2011–12	Manchester U	0	0		
2011–12	Moenchengladbach	2	0	2	0
2011–12	Hull C	18	1	18	1
2012–13	Manchester U	0	0		
2012–13	Blackburn R	16	2		
2013–14	Blackburn R	32	2	48	4

LENIHAN, Darragh (M) 0 0
b.Dublin 16-3-94
Internationals: Republic of Ireland U17.

Season	Club				
2011–12	Blackburn R	0	0		
2012–13	Blackburn R	0	0		
2013–14	Blackburn R	0	0		

LOWE, Jason (M) 115 3
H: 6 0 W: 12 08 b.Wigan 2-9-91
Internationals: England U20, U21.

Season	Club				
2009–10	Blackburn R	0	0		
2010–11	Blackburn R	1	0		
2010–11	Oldham Ath	7	2	7	2
2011–12	Blackburn R	32	0		
2012–13	Blackburn R	36	0		
2013–14	Blackburn R	39	1	108	1

MAHONEY, Connor (M) 4 0
Internationals: England U17.

Season	Club				
2013–14	Accrington S	4	0	4	0
2013–14	Blackburn R	0	0		

MARROW, Alex (M) 92 2
H: 6 1 W: 13 00 b.Tyldesley 21-1-90

Season	Club				
2007–08	Blackburn R	0	0		
2008–09	Blackburn R	0	0		
2009–10	Blackburn R	0	0		
2009–10	Oldham Ath	32	1	32	1
2010–11	Blackburn R	0	0		
2010–11	Crystal Palace	21	0		
2011–12	Crystal Palace	1	0		
2011–12	Preston NE	4	0	4	0
2012–13	Crystal Palace	4	0	26	0
2012–13	Fleetwood T	20	0		
2013–14	Blackburn R	3	0	3	0
2013–14	Fleetwood T	7	1	27	1

MARSHALL, Ben (F) 170 24
H: 5 11 W: 11 13 b.Salford 29-3-91
Internationals: England U21.

Season	Club				
2009–10	Stoke C	0	0		
2009–10	Northampton T	15	2	15	2
2009–10	Cheltenham T	6	2	6	2
2009–10	Carlisle U	20	3		
2010–11	Stoke C	0	0		
2010–11	Carlisle U	33	3	53	6
2011–12	Stoke C	0	0		
2011–12	Sheffield W	22	5	22	5
2011–12	Leicester C	16	3		
2012–13	Leicester C	40	4		
2013–14	Leicester C	0	0	56	7
2013–14	Blackburn R	18	2	18	2

MORRIS, Josh (M) 50 2
H: 5 9 W: 10 00 b.Preston 30-9-91
Internationals: England U20.

Season	Club				
2010–11	Blackburn R	4	0		
2011–12	Blackburn R	2	0		
2011–12	Yeovil T	5	0	5	0
2012–13	Blackburn R	10	0		
2012–13	Rotherham U	5	0	5	0
2013–14	Blackburn R	4	0	20	0
2013–14	Carlisle U	6	0	6	0
2013–14	Fleetwood T	14	2	14	2

NUNES, Fabio (M) 7 0
H: 5 9 W: 11 10 b.portimao 24-7-92
Internationals: Portugal U18, U19, U20.

Season	Club				
2012–13	Blackburn R	6	0		
2013–14	Blackburn R	1	0	7	0

Transferred to Latino January 2014.

O'CONNELL, Jack (D) 59 0
b.Liverpool 29-3-94
Internationals: England U18, U19.

Season	Club				
2012–13	Blackburn R	0	0		
2012–13	Rotherham U	3	0	3	0
2012–13	York C	18	0	18	0
2013–14	Blackburn R	0	0		
2013–14	Rochdale	38	0	38	0

O'CONNOR, Anthony (D) 77 0
H: 6 2 W: 12 06 b.Cork 25-10-92
Internationals: Republic of Ireland U17, U19, U21.

Season	Club				
2010–11	Blackburn R	0	0		
2011–12	Blackburn R	0	0		
2012–13	Blackburn R	0	0		
2012–13	Burton Alb	46	0	46	0
2013–14	Blackburn R	0	0		
2013–14	Torquay U	31	0	31	0

O'SULLIVAN, John (M) 1 0
b.Birmingham 18-9-93
Internationals: Republic of Ireland U19, U21.

Season	Club				
2011–12	Blackburn R	0	0		
2012–13	Blackburn R	1	0		
2013–14	Blackburn R	0	0	1	0

OLSSON, Marcus (M) 143 13
H: 5 11 W: 10 10 b.Gavle 17-5-88
Internationals: Sweden U21, Full caps.

Season	Club				
2008	Halmstad	21	2		
2009	Halmstad	20	4		
2010	Halmstad	30	4		
2011	Halmstad	29	2	100	12
2011–12	Blackburn R	12	0		
2012–13	Blackburn R	23	1		
2013–14	Blackburn R	8	0	43	1

ORR, Bradley (D) 320 13
H: 6 0 W: 11 11 b.Liverpool 1-11-82

Season	Club				
2001–02	Newcastle U	0	0		
2002–03	Newcastle U	0	0		
2003–04	Newcastle U	0	0		
2003–04	Burnley	4	0	4	0
2004–05	Bristol C	37	0		
2005–06	Bristol C	38	1		
2006–07	Bristol C	35	4		
2007–08	Bristol C	42	4		
2008–09	Bristol C	38	1		
2009–10	Bristol C	39	2	229	12
2010–11	QPR	33	1		
2011–12	QPR	6	0	39	1
2011–12	Blackburn R	12	0		
2012–13	Blackburn R	19	0		
2012–13	Ipswich T	13	0	13	0
2013–14	Blackburn R	0	0	31	0
2013–14	Blackpool	4	0	4	0

RAYA, David (G) 0 0
b.Barcelona 15-9-95

Season	Club				
2013–14	Blackburn R	0	0		

RHODES, Jordan (F) 242 134
H: 6 1 W: 11 03 b.Oldham 5-2-90
Internationals: Scotland U21, Full caps.

Season	Club				
2007–08	Ipswich T	8	1		
2008–09	Ipswich T	2	0	10	1
2008–09	Rochdale	5	2	5	2
2008–09	Brentford	14	7	14	7
2009–10	Huddersfield T	45	19		
2010–11	Huddersfield T	37	16		
2011–12	Huddersfield T	40	35		
2012–13	Huddersfield T	2	2	124	72
2012–13	Blackburn R	43	27		
2013–14	Blackburn R	46	25	89	52

RITTENBERG, Dean (F) 0 0
b. 13-5-96
Internationals: England U18.

Season	Club				
2013–14	Blackburn R	0	0		

ROBINSON, Paul (G) 414 1
H: 6 1 W: 14 07 b.Beverley 15-10-79
Internationals: England U21, Full caps.

Season	Club				
1996–97	Leeds U	0	0		
1997–98	Leeds U	0	0		
1998–99	Leeds U	5	0		
1999–2000	Leeds U	0	0		
2000–01	Leeds U	16	0		
2001–02	Leeds U	0	0		
2002–03	Leeds U	38	0		
2003–04	Leeds U	36	0	95	0
2003–04	Tottenham H	0	0		
2004–05	Tottenham H	36	0		
2005–06	Tottenham H	38	0		
2006–07	Tottenham H	38	1		
2007–08	Tottenham H	25	0	137	1
2008–09	Blackburn R	35	0		
2009–10	Blackburn R	35	0		
2010–11	Blackburn R	36	0		
2011–12	Blackburn R	34	0		
2012–13	Blackburn R	21	0		
2013–14	Blackburn R	21	0	182	0

ROCHINA, Ruben (F) 91 13
H: 5 11 W: 11 00 b.Sagunto 23-3-91
Internationals: Spain U17, U18, U19.

Season	Club				
2008–09	Barcelona B	10	2		
2009–10	Barcelona B	3	0	13	2
2010–11	Blackburn R	4	0		
2011–12	Blackburn R	18	2		
2012–13	Blackburn R	19	5		
2012–13	Real Zaragoza	15	1	15	1
2013–14	Blackburn R	5	0	46	7
2013–14	Rayo Vallecano	17	3	17	3

SLEW, Jordan (F) 51 4
H: 6 3 W: 12 11 b.Sheffield 7-9-92
Internationals: England U19.

Season	Club				
2010–11	Sheffield U	7	2		
2011–12	Sheffield U	4	1	11	3
2011–12	Blackburn R	1	0		
2011–12	Stevenage	9	0	9	0
2012–13	Blackburn R	0	0		
2012–13	Oldham Ath	3	0	3	0
2012–13	Rotherham U	7	0	7	0
2013–14	Blackburn R	0	0	1	0
2013–14	Ross Co	20	1	20	1

SONGO'O, Yann (D) 35 4
H: 6 0 W: 12 00 b.Yaounde 17-11-91
Internationals: France U16. Cameroon U20.

Season	Club				
2011–12	Sabadell	6	0	6	0
2013	Sporting Kansas C	0	0		
2013	Orlando	12	1	12	1
2013–14	Blackburn R	0	0		
2013–14	Ross Co	17	3	17	3

SPURR, Tommy (D) 300 9
H: 6 1 W: 11 05 b.Leeds 13-9-87

Season	Club				
2005–06	Sheffield W	0	0		
2006–07	Sheffield W	36	0		
2007–08	Sheffield W	41	2		
2008–09	Sheffield W	41	2		
2009–10	Sheffield W	46	1		
2010–11	Sheffield W	26	0	192	5
2011–12	Doncaster R	19	0		
2012–13	Doncaster R	46	1		
2013–14	Doncaster R	0	0	65	1
2013–14	Blackburn R	43	3	43	3

TAYLOR, Chris (M) 310 36
H: 5 11 W: 11 00 b.Oldham 20-12-86

Season	Club				
2005–06	Oldham Ath	14	0		
2006–07	Oldham Ath	44	4		
2007–08	Oldham Ath	42	5		
2008–09	Oldham Ath	42	10		
2009–10	Oldham Ath	32	1		
2010–11	Oldham Ath	42	11		
2011–12	Oldham Ath	38	2	254	33
2012–13	Millwall	22	3	22	3
2013–14	Blackburn R	34	0	34	0

WILLIAMSON, Lee (M) 452 36
H: 5 10 W: 10 04 b.Derby 7-6-82

Season	Club				
1999–2000	Mansfield T	4	0		
2000–01	Mansfield T	15	0		

2001–02	Mansfield T	46	˙3		
2002–03	Mansfield T	40	0		
2003–04	Mansfield T	35	0		
2004–05	Mansfield T	4	0	144	3
2004–05	Northampton T	37	0	37	0
2005–06	Rotherham U	37	4		
2006–07	Rotherham U	19	5	56	9
2006–07	Watford	5	0		
2007–08	Watford	32	2		
2008–09	Watford	34	2	71	4
2008–09	*Preston NE*	5	1	5	1
2009–10	Sheffield U	20	3		
2010–11	Sheffield U	16	3		
2011–12	Sheffield U	40	13		
2012–13	Sheffield U	0	0	76	19
2012–13	Portsmouth	22	0	22	0
2012–13	Blackburn R	9	0		
2013–14	Blackburn R	32	0	41	0

Scholars

Anderson, Jordan Jacob; Bauress, Bradley Stephen; Brown, Thomas Hayden; Butterwick, William Peter; Cham, Modou; Doyle, Jack Marc; Edgar, Mark David Arthur; Edo Martin, Adrian; Green, Devarn Rohan; Harris, Callum Lee; Joel, Samuel Robert Edward; Langford, Liam James; Lavelle, Samuel Mark; Paul, Thomas; Pierce, George Ramon; Scott, Cameron Henry; Tanner, Hyuga; Torres Martinez, Yeray; Vicars, Ian Paul; Wall, Luke Sky; Wassi, Brice; Williams, Callum James.

BLACKPOOL (8)

ALMOND, Louis (F) 5 0
H: 5 11 W: 12 00 b.Blackburn 5-1-92

2009–10	Blackpool	0	0		
2009–10	*Cheltenham T*	4	0	4	0
2010–11	Blackpool	0	0		
2011–12	Blackpool	0	0		
2012–13	Blackpool	0	0		
2013–14	Blackpool	1	0	1	0

BANVO, Anderson (F) 1 0
H: 6 1 b.Paris 4-2-94
Internationals: Ivory Coast Youth.

2012–13	Blackpool	0	0		
2013–14	Blackpool	0	0		
2013–14	*Stevenage*	1	0	1	0

BARKHUIZEN, Tom (F) 65 13
H: 5 9 W: 11 00 b.Blackpool 4-7-93

2011–12	Blackpool	0	0		
2011–12	*Hereford U*	38	11	38	11
2012–13	Blackpool	0	0		
2012–13	*Fleetwood T*	13	1	13	1
2013–14	Blackpool	14	1	14	1

BASHAM, Chris (M) 117 6
H: 5 11 W: 12 08 b.Hebburn 20-7-88

2007–08	Bolton W	0	0		
2007–08	*Rochdale*	13	0	13	0
2008–09	Bolton W	11	1		
2009–10	Bolton W	8	0	19	1
2010–11	Blackpool	2	0		
2011–12	Blackpool	17	2		
2012–13	Blackpool	26	1		
2013–14	Blackpool	40	2	85	5

BISHOP, Neil (M) 286 15
H: 6 1 W: 12 10 b.Stockton 7-8-81
Internationals: England C.

2007–08	Barnet	39	2		
2008–09	Barnet	44	1	83	3
2009–10	Notts Co	43	1		
2010–11	Notts Co	43	1		
2011–12	Notts Co	41	2		
2012–13	Notts Co	41	7	168	11
2013–14	Blackpool	35	1	35	1

BROADFOOT, Kirk (D) 297 16
H: 6 3 W: 13 13 b.Irvine 8-8-84

2002–03	St Mirren	23	1		
2003–04	St Mirren	31	3		
2004–05	St Mirren	36	4		
2005–06	St Mirren	27	2		
2006–07	St Mirren	37	3	154	13
2007–08	Rangers	15	1		
2008–09	Rangers	27	0		
2009–10	Rangers	12	0		
2010–11	Rangers	8	0		
2011–12	Rangers	16	0	78	1
2012–13	Blackpool	32	2		
2013–14	Blackpool	33	0	65	2

CAPRICE, Jake (M) 14 0
H: 5 10 W: 11 07 b.Lambeth 11-11-92

2011–12	Crystal Palace	0	0		
2012–13	Blackpool	0	0		
2012–13	*Dagenham & R*	8	0	8	0
2013–14	Blackpool	0	0		
2013–14	*St Mirren*	6	0	6	0

CATHCART, Craig (D) 168 6
H: 6 2 W: 11 06 b.Belfast 6-2-89
Internationals: Northern Ireland U16, U17, U20, U21, Full caps.

2005–06	Manchester U	0	0		
2006–07	Manchester U	0	0		
2007–08	Manchester U	0	0		
2007–08	*Antwerp*	13	2	13	2
2008–09	Manchester U	0	0		
2008–09	*Plymouth Arg*	31	1	31	1
2009–10	Manchester U	0	0		
2009–10	*Watford*	12	0	12	0
2010–11	Blackpool	30	1		
2011–12	Blackpool	27	0		
2012–13	Blackpool	25	1		
2013–14	Blackpool	30	1	112	3

CATON, James (M) 4 0
b.Bolton 4-1-94

2012–13	Blackpool	0	0		
2013–14	Blackpool	2	0	2	0
2013–14	*Accrington S*	2	0	2	0

CHOPRA, Michael (F) 347 105
H: 5 9 W: 10 10 b.Newcastle 23-12-83
Internationals: England U16, U17, U19, U20, U21.

2000–01	Newcastle U	0	0		
2001–02	Newcastle U	0	0		
2002–03	Newcastle U	1	0		
2002–03	*Watford*	5	5	5	5
2003–04	Newcastle U	6	0		
2003–04	*Nottingham F*	5	0	5	0
2004–05	Newcastle U	1	0		
2004–05	*Barnsley*	39	17	39	17
2005–06	Newcastle U	13	1	21	1
2006–07	Cardiff C	42	22		
2007–08	Sunderland	33	6		
2008–09	Sunderland	6	2	39	8
2008–09	*Cardiff C*	27	9		
2009–10	Cardiff C	41	16		
2010–11	Cardiff C	32	9	142	56
2011–12	Ipswich T	45	14		
2012–13	Ipswich T	33	4	78	18
2013–14	Blackpool	18	0	18	0

DAVIES, Steve (F) 208 41
H: 6 0 W: 12 00 b.Liverpool 29-12-87

2005–06	Tranmere R	22	2		
2006–07	Tranmere R	28	1		
2007–08	Tranmere R	19	2	60	5
2008–09	Derby Co	19	3		
2009–10	Derby Co	18	1		
2010–11	Derby Co	20	5		
2011–12	Derby Co	26	11		
2012–13	Derby Co	0	0	83	20
2012–13	*Bristol C*	37	13	37	13
2013–14	Blackpool	28	3	28	3

DUNNE, Charles (F) 50 0
H: 5 9 W: 11 09 b.Lambeth 13-2-93

2011–12	Wycombe W	3	0		
2012–13	Wycombe W	38	0		
2013–14	Blackpool	0	0		
2013–14	*Wycombe W*	9	0	50	0

EARNSHAW, Robert (F) 409 165
H: 5 6 W: 9 09 b.Mulfulira 6-4-81
Internationals: Wales U21, Full caps.

1997–98	Cardiff C	5	0		
1998–99	Cardiff C	5	1		
1998–99	*Middlesbrough*	0	0		
1999–2000	Cardiff C	6	1		
1999–2000	*Morton*	3	2	3	2
2000–01	Cardiff C	36	19		
2001–02	Cardiff C	30	11		
2002–03	Cardiff C	46	31		
2003–04	Cardiff C	46	21		
2004–05	Cardiff C	4	1		
2004–05	WBA	31	11		
2005–06	WBA	12	1	43	12
2005–06	Norwich C	15	8		
2006–07	Norwich C	30	19	45	27
2007–08	Derby Co	22	1	22	1
2008–09	Nottingham F	32	12		
2009–10	Nottingham F	32	15		
2010–11	Nottingham F	34	8	98	35
2011–12	Cardiff C	19	3		
2012–13	Cardiff C	0	0	197	88
2012–13	*Toronto FC*	2	0		
2013–14	Blackpool	1	0	1	0

ECCLESTON, Nathan (F) 60 6
H: 5 10 W: 12 00 b.Manchester 30-12-90
Internationals: England U17.

2007–08	Liverpool	0	0		
2008–09	Liverpool	0	0		
2009–10	Liverpool	0	0		
2009–10	*Huddersfield T*	11	1	11	1
2010–11	Liverpool	1	0		
2010–11	*Charlton Ath*	21	3	21	3
2011–12	Liverpool	0	0		
2011–12	*Rochdale*	5	1	5	1
2012–13	Liverpool	0	0	2	0
2012–13	Blackpool	6	1		
2012–13	*Tranmere R*	1	0	1	0
2013–14	Blackpool	4	0	10	1
2013–14	*Carlisle U*	2	0	2	0
2013–14	*Coventry C*	8	0	8	0

FERGUSON, Barry (M) 484 48
H: 5 7 W: 9 10 b.Hamilton 2-2-78
Internationals: Scotland U21, Full caps.

1994–95	Rangers	0	0		
1995–96	Rangers	0	0		
1996–97	Rangers	1	0		
1997–98	Rangers	7	0		
1998–99	Rangers	23	1		
1999–2000	Rangers	31	4		
2000–01	Rangers	30	2		
2001–02	Rangers	22	1		
2002–03	Rangers	36	16		
2003–04	Rangers	3	0		
2003–04	Blackburn R	15	1		
2004–05	Blackburn R	21	2	36	3
2004–05	Rangers	13	2		
2005–06	Rangers	32	5		
2006–07	Rangers	32	4		
2007–08	Rangers	38	7		
2008–09	Rangers	22	2	290	44
2009–10	Birmingham C	37	0		
2010–11	Birmingham C	35	0	72	0
2011–12	Blackpool	42	1		
2012–13	Blackpool	19	0		
2012–13	*Fleetwood T*	6	0	6	0
2013–14	Blackpool	19	0	80	1

FULLER, Ricardo (F) 398 101
H: 6 3 W: 12 10 b.Kingston, Jamaica 31-10-79
Internationals: Jamaica Full caps.

2000–01	Crystal Palace	8	0	8	0
2001–02	Hearts	27	8	27	8

From Tivoli Gardens.

2002–03	Preston NE	18	9		
2003–04	Preston NE	38	17		
2004–05	Preston NE	2	1	58	27
2004–05	Portsmouth	31	1	31	1
2005–06	Southampton	30	9		
2005–06	*Ipswich T*	3	2	3	2
2006–07	Southampton	1	0	31	9
2006–07	Stoke C	30	10		
2007–08	Stoke C	42	15		
2008–09	Stoke C	34	11		
2009–10	Stoke C	35	3		
2010–11	Stoke C	28	4		
2011–12	Stoke C	13	0	182	43
2012–13	Charlton Ath	31	5		
2013–14	Charlton Ath	31	3	31	5
2013–14	Blackpool	27	6	27	6

GILKS, Matthew (G) 362 0
H: 6 3 W: 13 12 b.Rochdale 4-6-82
Internationals: Scotland Full caps.

2000–01	Rochdale	3	0		
2001–02	Rochdale	19	0		
2002–03	Rochdale	20	0		
2003–04	Rochdale	12	0		
2004–05	Rochdale	30	0		
2005–06	Rochdale	46	0		
2006–07	Rochdale	46	0	176	0

2007–08	Norwich C	0	0		
2008–09	Blackpool	5	0		
2008–09	*Shrewsbury T*	4	0	**4**	**0**
2009–10	Blackpool	26	0		
2010–11	Blackpool	18	0		
2011–12	Blackpool	42	0		
2012–13	Blackpool	45	0		
2013–14	Blackpool	46	0	**182**	**0**

GRANDIN, Elliot (F)   **148 19**
H: 5 10   W: 10 07   b.Caen 17-10-87
Internationals: France U21.

2004–05	Caen	0	0		
2005–06	Caen	19	3		
2006–07	Caen	23	2		
2007–08	Caen	12	1	**55**	**6**
2007–08	Marseille	8	0		
2008–09	Marseille	8	2	**16**	**2**
2008–09	*Grenoble*	8	0	**8**	**0**
2009–10	CSKA Sofia	10	4		
2010–11	CSKA Sofia	1	0	**11**	**4**
2010–11	Blackpool	23	1		
2011–12	Blackpool	7	2		
2011–12	*Nice*	9	0	**9**	**0**
2012–13	Blackpool	12	3		
2013–14	Crystal Palace	0	0		
2013–14	Blackpool	7	1	**49**	**7**

GRANT, Robert (M)   **181 42**
H: 5 11   W: 12 00   b.Liverpool 1-7-90

2006–07	Accrington S	1	0		
2007–08	Accrington S	7	0		
2008–09	Accrington S	15	1		
2009–10	Accrington S	42	14		
2010–11	Scunthorpe U	27	0		
2010–11	*Rochdale*	6	2		
2011–12	Scunthorpe U	29	7		
2011–12	*Accrington S*	8	3	**73**	**18**
2012–13	Scunthorpe U	3	0	**59**	**7**
2012–13	Rochdale	36	15	**42**	**17**
2013–14	Blackpool	6	0	**6**	**0**
2013–14	*Fleetwood T*	1	0	**1**	**0**

HAROUN, Faris (M)   **260 45**
H: 6 2   W: 13 00   b.Brussels 22-9-85
Internationals: Belgium U18, U19, U21, Full caps.

2003–04	Genk	12	3		
2004–05	Genk	23	4		
2005–06	Genk	20	0		
2006–07	Genk	21	5		
2007–08	Genk	28	4	**104**	**16**
2008–09	Beerschot	31	8		
2009–10	Beerschot	31	10		
2010–11	Beerschot	29	5	**91**	**23**
2011–12	Middlesbrough	32	2		
2012–13	Middlesbrough	23	4		
2013–14	Middlesbrough	1	0	**56**	**6**
2013–14	Blackpool	9	0	**9**	**0**

INCE, Tom (M)   **75 26**
H: 5 10   W: 10 06   b.Stockport 30-1-92
Internationals: England U17, U19, U21.

2011–12	Blackpool	0	0		
2012–13	Blackpool	44	18		
2013–14	Blackpool	23	7	**67**	**25**
2013–14	*Crystal Palace*	8	1	**8**	**1**

KETTINGS, Chris (G)   **2 0**
H: 6 2   W: 12 04   b.Bolton 25-10-92
Internationals: Scotland Youth, U21.

2011–12	Blackpool	0	0		
2011–12	*Birmingham C*	0	0		
2011–12	*Morecambe*	2	0	**2**	**0**
2012–13	Blackpool	0	0		
2013–14	Blackpool	0	0		
2013–14	*York C*	0	0		

MACKENZIE, Gary (D)   **210 8**
H: 6 3   W: 13 01   b.Lanark 15-10-85

2003–04	Rangers	2	0		
2004–05	Rangers	0	0		
2005–06	Rangers	0	0	**2**	**0**
2006–07	Dundee	21	0		
2007–08	Dundee	33	1		
2008–09	Dundee	19	0		
2009–10	Dundee	25	1	**98**	**2**
2010–11	Milton Keynes D	26	2		
2011–12	Milton Keynes D	26	1		
2012–13	Milton Keynes D	11	0	**63**	**3**
2012–13	*Blackpool*	12	2		
2013–14	Blackpool	35	1	**47**	**3**

MARTINEZ, Angel (M)   **202 10**
H: 5 9   W: 11 13   b.Girona 31-1-86
Internationals: Spain U19, U21.

2006–07	Espanyol B	27	5	**27**	**5**
2006–07	Espanyol	7	0		
2007–08	Espanyol	28	2		
2008–09	Espanyol	15	0	**50**	**2**
2009–10	Rayo Vallecano	27	2	**27**	**2**
2010–11	Girona	36	0	**36**	**0**
2011–12	Blackpool	15	1		
2012–13	Blackpool	21	0		
2013–14	Blackpool	26	0	**62**	**1**

McGAHEY, Harrison (D)   **4 0**

2013–14	Blackpool	4	0	**4**	**0**

McMAHON, Tony (D)   **215 6**
H: 5 10   W: 11 04   b.Bishop Auckland 24-3-86

2003–04	Middlesbrough	0	0		
2004–05	Middlesbrough	13	0		
2005–06	Middlesbrough	3	0		
2006–07	Middlesbrough	0	0		
2007–08	Middlesbrough	1	0		
2007–08	*Blackpool*	2	0		
2008–09	Middlesbrough	13	0		
2008–09	*Sheffield W*	15	1	**15**	**1**
2009–10	Middlesbrough	21	0		
2010–11	Middlesbrough	34	2		
2011–12	Middlesbrough	34	1	**119**	**3**
2012–13	Sheffield U	38	2		
2013–14	Sheffield U	23	0	**61**	**2**
2013–14	Blackpool	18	0	**20**	**0**

OSBOURNE, Isaiah (M)   **128 3**
H: 6 2   W: 12 06   b.Birmingham 5-11-87
Internationals: England U16.

2005–06	Aston Villa	0	0		
2006–07	Aston Villa	11	0		
2007–08	Aston Villa	8	0		
2008–09	Aston Villa	0	0		
2008–09	*Nottingham F*	8	0	**8**	**0**
2009–10	Aston Villa	0	0		
2009–10	*Middlesbrough*	9	0	**9**	**0**
2010–11	Aston Villa	0	0	**19**	**0**
2010–11	*Sheffield W*	10	0	**10**	**0**
2011–12	Hibernian	30	1	**30**	**1**
2012–13	Blackpool	28	1		
2013–14	Blackpool	24	1	**52**	**2**

PERKINS, David (D)   **283 14**
H: 5 6   W: 11 06   b.Heysham 21-6-82
Internationals: England C.

2006–07	Rochdale	18	0		
2007–08	Rochdale	40	4	**58**	**4**
2008–09	Colchester U	38	5		
2009–10	Colchester U	5	1		
2009–10	*Chesterfield*	13	1	**13**	**1**
2009–10	*Stockport Co*	22	0	**22**	**0**
2010–11	Colchester U	36	1	**79**	**7**
2011–12	Barnsley	33	1		
2012–13	Barnsley	35	1		
2013–14	Barnsley	23	0	**91**	**2**
2013–14	Blackpool	20	0	**20**	**0**

TYSON, Nathan (F)   **381 84**
H: 5 10   W: 10 02   b.Reading 4-5-82
Internationals: England U20.

1999–2000	Reading	1	0		
2000–01	Reading	0	0		
2001–02	Reading	1	0		
2001–02	*Swansea C*	11	1	**11**	**1**
2001–02	*Cheltenham T*	8	1	**8**	**1**
2002–03	Reading	23	1		
2003–04	Reading	8	0	**33**	**1**
2003–04	Wycombe W	21	9		
2004–05	Wycombe W	42	22		
2005–06	Wycombe W	15	11	**78**	**42**
2005–06	Nottingham F	21	9		
2006–07	Nottingham F	24	7		
2007–08	Nottingham F	34	9		
2008–09	Nottingham F	35	5		
2009–10	Nottingham F	33	2		
2010–11	Nottingham F	30	2	**184**	**35**
2011–12	Derby Co	23	0		
2012–13	Derby Co	16	4		
2012–13	*Millwall*	4	0	**4**	**0**
2013–14	Derby Co	0	0	**39**	**4**
2013–14	Blackpool	10	0	**10**	**0**
2013–14	*Fleetwood T*	4	0	**4**	**0**
2013–14	*Notts Co*	10	0	**10**	**0**

ZEEGELAAR, Marvin (F)   **56 0**
H: 6 1   W: 13 02   b.Amsterdam 12-8-90

2008–09	Ajax	0	0		
2009–10	Ajax	2	0		
2010–11	Ajax	2	0	**4**	**0**
2010–11	*Excelsior*	16	0	**16**	**0**
2012–13	Elazigspor	19	0		
2013–14	Elazigspor	15	0	**34**	**0**
On loan from Elazigspor					
2013–14	Blackpool	2	0	**2**	**0**

Scholars
Cameron, Henry Anthony; Charles, Dion; Clayton, Mitchell James; Higham, Luke; Hunt, Connor Charles; Lomax, George John Paul; McGahey, Harrison; Milton, Daniel Brian; Moulden, Joseph Luke; Ready, Conor David; Richardson, Rowan Francis; Rowley, Ashley James; Shaw, Kieran John; Staunton-Turner, Sam Christopher; Telford, Dominic; Waddington, Mark Thomas.

BOLTON W (9)

ANDREWS, Keith (M)   **361 42**
H: 6 0   W: 12 04   b.Dublin 13-9-80
Internationals: Republic of Ireland U17, Full caps.

1997–98	Wolverhampton W	0	0		
1998–99	Wolverhampton W	0	0		
1999–2000	Wolverhampton W	2	0		
2000–01	Wolverhampton W	22	0		
2000–01	*Oxford U*	4	1	**4**	**1**
2001–02	Wolverhampton W	11	0		
2002–03	Wolverhampton W	9	0		
2003–04	Wolverhampton W	1	0		
2003–04	*Stoke C*	16	0	**16**	**0**
2003–04	*Walsall*	10	2	**10**	**2**
2004–05	Wolverhampton W	20	0	**65**	**0**
2005–06	Hull C	26	0		
2006–07	Hull C	3	0	**29**	**0**
2006–07	Milton Keynes D	34	6		
2007–08	Milton Keynes D	41	12		
2008–09	Milton Keynes D	1	0	**76**	**18**
2008–09	Blackburn R	33	4		
2009–10	Blackburn R	32	1		
2010–11	Blackburn R	5	0		
2011–12	Blackburn R	0	0	**70**	**5**
2011–12	*Ipswich T*	20	9	**20**	**9**
2011–12	WBA	14	2	**14**	**2**
2012–13	Bolton W	25	4		
2013–14	Bolton W	1	0	**26**	**4**
2013–14	*Brighton & HA*	31	1	**31**	**1**

BAPTISTE, Alex (D)   **383 17**
H: 6 0   W: 11 11   b.Sutton-in-Ashfield 31-1-86

2002–03	Mansfield T	4	0		
2003–04	Mansfield T	17	0		
2004–05	Mansfield T	41	1		
2005–06	Mansfield T	41	1		
2006–07	Mansfield T	46	3		
2007–08	Mansfield T	25	0	**174**	**5**
2008–09	Blackpool	21	1		
2009–10	Blackpool	42	3		
2010–11	Blackpool	21	2		
2011–12	Blackpool	43	1		
2012–13	Blackpool	43	1	**170**	**8**
2013–14	Bolton W	39	4	**39**	**4**

BASTOS, Yannick (M)   **33 5**
b. 30-5-93
Internationals: Luxembourg Full caps.

2012–13	FC Differdange	20	2		
2013–14	FC Differdange	13	3	**33**	**5**
2013–14	Bolton W	0	0		

BECKFORD, Jermaine (F)   **279 112**
H: 6 2   W: 13 02   b.Ealing 9-12-83
Internationals: Jamaica Full caps.

2005–06	Leeds U	5	0		
2006–07	Leeds U	5	0		
2006–07	*Carlisle U*	4	1	**4**	**1**
2006–07	*Scunthorpe U*	18	8	**18**	**8**
2007–08	Leeds U	40	20		
2008–09	Leeds U	34	26		
2009–10	Leeds U	42	25	**126**	**71**
2010–11	Everton	32	8		
2011–12	Everton	2	0	**34**	**8**
2011–12	Leicester C	39	9		

2012–13	Leicester C	4	0	43	9
2012–13	*Huddersfield T*	21	8	21	8
2013–14	Bolton W	33	7	33	7

BOGDAN, Adam (G)   95   0
H: 6 4   W: 14 02   b.Budapest 27-9-87
Internationals: Hungary U21, Full caps.

2007–08	Bolton W	0	0		
2008–09	Bolton W	0	0		
2009–10	Bolton W	0	0		
2009–10	*Crewe Alex*	1	0	1	0
2010–11	Bolton W	4	0		
2011–12	Bolton W	20	0		
2012–13	Bolton W	41	0		
2013–14	Bolton W	29	0	94	0

BOLGER, Cian (D)   53   2
H: 6 4   W: 12 05   b.Co. Kildare 12-3-92
Internationals: Republic of Ireland U21.

2009–10	Leicester C	0	0		
2010–11	Leicester C	0	0		
2010–11	*Bristol R*	6	0		
2011–12	Leicester C	0	0		
2011–12	*Bristol R*	39	2		
2012–13	Leicester C	0	0		
2012–13	*Bristol R*	3	0	48	2
2012–13	Bolton W	0	0		
2013–14	Bolton W	0	0		
2013–14	*Colchester U*	4	0	4	0
2013–14	*Southend U*	1	0	1	0

CLOUGH, Zach (F)   0   0
b.Manchester 8-3-95

2013–14	Bolton W	0	0

DANNS, Neil (M)   320   58
H: 5 10   W: 10 12   b.Liverpool 23-11-82

2000–01	Blackburn R	0	0		
2001–02	Blackburn R	0	0		
2002–03	Blackburn R	2	0		
2003–04	Blackpool	12	2	12	2
2003–04	Blackburn R	1	0		
2003–04	*Hartlepool U*	9	1	9	1
2004–05	Colchester U	32	11		
2005–06	Colchester U	41	8	73	19
2006–07	Birmingham C	29	3		
2007–08	Birmingham C	2	0	31	3
2007–08	Crystal Palace	4	0		
2008–09	Crystal Palace	20	2		
2009–10	Crystal Palace	42	8		
2010–11	Crystal Palace	37	8	103	18
2011–12	Leicester C	29	5		
2012–13	Leicester C	1	0		
2012–13	*Bristol C*	9	2	9	2
2012–13	*Huddersfield T*	17	2	17	2
2013–14	Leicester C	0	0	30	5
2013–14	Bolton W	33	6	33	6

DAVIES, Craig (F)   315   82
H: 6 2   W: 13 05   b.Burton-on-Trent 9-1-86
Internationals: Wales U19, U17, U21, Full caps.

2004–05	Oxford U	28	6		
2005–06	Oxford U	20	2	48	8
2005–06	Verona	0	0		
2006–07	Wolverhampton W	23	0	23	0
2007–08	Oldham Ath	32	10		
2008–09	Oldham Ath	12	0	44	10
2008–09	*Stockport Co*	9	5	9	5
2008–09	Brighton & HA	16	1		
2009–10	Brighton & HA	5	0	21	1
2009–10	*Yeovil T*	4	0	4	0
2009–10	*Port Vale*	24	7	24	7
2010–11	Chesterfield	41	23	41	23
2011–12	Barnsley	40	11		
2012–13	Barnsley	20	8	60	19
2012–13	Bolton W	18	4		
2013–14	Bolton W	8	0	26	4
2013–14	*Preston NE*	15	5	15	5

DAVIES, Mark (M)   162   14
H: 5 11   W: 11 08   b.Willenhall 18-2-88
Internationals: England U16, U17, U19.

2004–05	Wolverhampton W	0	0		
2005–06	Wolverhampton W	20	1		
2006–07	Wolverhampton W	7	0		
2007–08	Wolverhampton W	0	0	27	1
2008–09	Wolverhampton W	0	0		
2008–09	*Leicester C*	7	1	7	1
2008–09	Bolton W	10	0		
2009–10	Bolton W	17	0		
2010–11	Bolton W	24	1		
2011–12	Bolton W	35	4		
2012–13	Bolton W	24	6		
2013–14	Bolton W	18	1	128	12

EAGLES, Chris (M)   289   47
H: 5 10   W: 11 07   b.Hemel Hempstead 19-11-85
Internationals: England Youth.

2003–04	Manchester U	0	0		
2004–05	Manchester U	0	0		
2004–05	*Watford*	13	1		
2005–06	Manchester U	0	0		
2005–06	*Sheffield W*	25	3	25	3
2005–06	*Watford*	17	3	30	4
2006–07	Manchester U	2	1		
2006–07	*NEC Nijmegen*	15	1	15	1
2007–08	Manchester U	4	0	6	1
2008–09	Burnley	43	8		
2009–10	Burnley	34	2		
2010–11	Burnley	43	11	120	21
2011–12	Bolton W	34	4		
2012–13	Bolton W	43	12		
2013–14	Bolton W	16	1	93	17

EAVES, Tom (M)   77   15
H: 6 3   W: 13 07   b.Liverpool 14-1-92

2009–10	Oldham Ath	15	0		
2010–11	Bolton W	0	0		
2010–11	*Oldham Ath*	0	0	15	0
2011–12	Bolton W	0	0		
2012–13	Bolton W	3	0		
2012–13	*Bristol R*	16	7	16	7
2013–14	Bolton W	0	0	3	0
2013–14	*Rotherham U*	8	0	8	0
2013–14	*Shrewsbury T*	25	2	35	8

HALL, Robert (F)   55   6
H: 6 2   W: 10 05   b.Aylesbury 20-10-93
Internationals: England U16, U17, U18, U19.

2010–11	West Ham U	0	0		
2011–12	West Ham U	3	0		
2011–12	*Oxford U*	13	5	13	5
2011–12	*Milton Keynes D*	2	0	2	0
2012–13	West Ham U	1	0	4	0
2012–13	*Birmingham C*	13	0	13	0
2012–13	*Bolton W*	1	0		
2013–14	Bolton W	22	1	23	1

ILIEV, Georg (M)   0   0
Internationals: Bulgaria U17, U19, U21.

2013–14	Bolton W	0	0

KAMARA, Mohammed (M)   0   0

2012–13	Bolton W	0	0
2013–14	Bolton W	0	0

KELLETT, Andy (D)   3   0
H: 5 8   b. 10-11-93

2012–13	Bolton W	0	0		
2013–14	Bolton W	3	0	3	0

KNIGHT, Aaron (M)   0   0

2012–13	Bolton W	0	0
2013–14	Bolton W	0	0

KNIGHT, Zat (D)   366   9
H: 6 6   W: 15 02   b.Solihull 2-5-80
Internationals: England U21, Full caps.

1998–99	Fulham	0	0		
1999–2000	Fulham	0	0		
1999–2000	*Peterborough U*	8	0	8	0
2000–01	Fulham	0	0		
2001–02	Fulham	10	0		
2002–03	Fulham	17	0		
2003–04	Fulham	31	0		
2004–05	Fulham	35	1		
2005–06	Fulham	30	0		
2006–07	Fulham	23	2		
2007–08	Fulham	0	0	150	3
2007–08	Aston Villa	27	1		
2008–09	Aston Villa	13	1		
2009–10	Aston Villa	0	0	40	2
2009–10	Bolton W	35	1		
2010–11	Bolton W	34	1		
2011–12	Bolton W	25	0		
2012–13	Bolton W	43	0		
2013–14	Bolton W	31	2	168	4

LEE, Chung Yong (M)   204   24
H: 5 11   W: 10 09   b.Seoul 2-7-88
Internationals: South Korea U19, U20, Full caps.

2006	FC Seoul	2	0		
2007	FC Seoul	15	3		
2008	FC Seoul	20	5		
2009	FC Seoul	14	2	51	10
2009–10	Bolton W	34	4		
2010–11	Bolton W	31	3		
2011–12	Bolton W	2	0		
2012–13	Bolton W	41	4		
2013–14	Bolton W	45	3	153	14

LESTER, Chris (M)   1   0
b.Salford 27-10-94
Internationals: Northern Ireland U21.

2012–13	Bolton W	0	0		
2013–14	Bolton W	1	0	1	0

LONERGAN, Andrew (G)   270   1
H: 6 4   W: 13 02   b.Preston 19-10-83
Internationals: Republic of Ireland U16. England U20.

2000–01	Preston NE	1	0		
2001–02	Preston NE	0	0		
2002–03	Preston NE	0	0		
2002–03	*Darlington*	2	0	2	0
2003–04	Preston NE	8	0		
2004–05	Preston NE	23	1		
2005–06	Preston NE	0	0		
2005–06	*Wycombe W*	2	0	2	0
2006–07	Preston NE	13	0		
2006–07	*Swindon T*	1	0	1	0
2007–08	Preston NE	43	0		
2008–09	Preston NE	46	0		
2009–10	Preston NE	45	0		
2010–11	Preston NE	29	0	208	1
2011–12	Leeds U	35	0	35	0
2012–13	Bolton W	5	0		
2013–14	Bolton W	17	0	22	0

MEARS, Tyrone (D)   231   7
H: 5 11   W: 11 10   b.Stockport 18-2-83
Internationals: Jamaica Full caps.

2000–01	Manchester C	0	0		
2001–02	Manchester C	1	0	1	0
2002–03	Preston NE	22	1		
2003–04	Preston NE	12	1		
2004–05	Preston NE	4	0		
2005–06	Preston NE	32	2	70	4
2006–07	West Ham U	5	0	5	0
2006–07	Derby Co	13	1		
2007–08	Derby Co	25	1		
2008–09	Derby Co	3	0	41	2
2008–09	Marseille	4	0	4	0
2009–10	Burnley	38	0		
2010–11	Burnley	44	1		
2011–12	Burnley	0	0	82	1
2011–12	Bolton W	1	0		
2012–13	Bolton W	26	0		
2013–14	Bolton W	1	0	28	0

MEDO, Mohamed (M)   60   16
H: 5 9   W: 10 12   b.Serabu 27-12-81
Internationals: Sierra Leone U17, Full caps.

2007–08	HJK Helsinki	4	4		
2008–09	HJK Helsinki	4	4		
2009–10	HJK Helsinki	3	3		
2010–11	HJK Helsinki	2	2	13	13
2012–13	Partizan Belgrade	0	0		
2012–13	Bolton W	12	1		
2013–14	Bolton W	35	2	47	3

MILLS, Matthew (D)   242   13
H: 6 3   W: 12 12   b.Swindon 14-7-86
Internationals: England U18, U19.

2004–05	Southampton	0	0		
2004–05	*Coventry C*	4	0	4	0
2004–05	*Bournemouth*	12	3	12	3
2005–06	Southampton	4	0		
2005–06	Manchester C	1	0		
2006–07	Manchester C	1	0		
2006–07	*Colchester U*	9	0	9	0
2007–08	Manchester C	0	0		
2007–08	*Doncaster R*	34	3		
2008–09	Doncaster R	41	0		
2009–10	Doncaster R	0	0	75	3
2009–10	Reading	23	2		
2010–11	Reading	38	2	61	4
2011–12	Leicester C	25	1	25	1
2012–13	Bolton W	18	1		
2013–14	Bolton W	32	1	50	2

MORITZ, Andre (M)   144   31
H: 6 2   W: 13 00   b.Florianopolis 6-8-86

2007–08	Kasimpasa	20	4		
2009–10	Kasimpasa	21	9	41	13

2010–11	Kayserispor	21	2	**21**	**2**
2011–12	Mersin Idmanyurdu	32	4	**32**	**4**
2012–13	Crystal Palace	27	5	**27**	**5**
2013–14	Bolton W	23	7	**23**	**7**

ODELUSI, Sanmi (F)   **16**   **0**
b.London 11-6-93

2012–13	Bolton W	1	0		
2013–14	Bolton W	5	0	**6**	**0**
2013–14	*Milton Keynes D*	10	0	**10**	**0**

PRATLEY, Darren (M)   **300**   **36**
H: 6 1   W: 10 12   b.Barking 22-4-85

2001–02	Fulham	0	0		
2002–03	Fulham	0	0		
2003–04	Fulham	1	0		
2004–05	Fulham	0	0		
2004–05	*Brentford*	14	1		
2005–06	Fulham	0	0	**1**	**0**
2005–06	*Brentford*	32	4	**46**	**5**
2006–07	Swansea C	28	1		
2007–08	Swansea C	42	5		
2008–09	Swansea C	37	4		
2009–10	Swansea C	36	7		
2010–11	Swansea C	34	9	**177**	**26**
2011–12	Bolton W	25	1		
2012–13	Bolton W	31	2		
2013–14	Bolton W	20	2	**76**	**5**

REAM, Tim (D)   **229**   **7**
H: 6 1   W: 11 05   b.St Louis 5-10-87
Internationals: USA Full caps.

2006	St Louis Billikens	19	0		
2007	St Louis Billikens	19	0		
2008	St Louis Billikens	22	0		
2008	Chicago Fire	12	0		
2009	Chicago Fire	7	0	**19**	**0**
2009	St Louis Billikens	22	6	**82**	**6**
2010	New York RB	30	1		
2011	New York RB	28	0	**58**	**1**
2011–12	Bolton W	13	0		
2012–13	Bolton W	15	0		
2013–14	Bolton W	42	0	**70**	**0**

RILEY, Joe (D)   **3**   **0**
H: 6 0   W: 11 02   b.Salford 13-10-91

2011–12	Bolton W	3	0		
2012–13	Bolton W	0	0		
2013–14	Bolton W	0	0	**3**	**0**

SORDELL, Marvin (F)   **139**   **33**
H: 5 9   W: 12 06   b.Pinner 17-2-91
Internationals: England U20, U21. Great Britain.

2009–10	Watford	6	1		
2009–10	*Tranmere R*	8	1	**8**	**1**
2010–11	Watford	43	12		
2011–12	Watford	26	8	**75**	**21**
2011–12	Bolton W	3	0		
2012–13	Bolton W	22	4		
2013–14	Bolton W	0	0	**25**	**4**
2013–14	*Charlton Ath*	31	7	**31**	**7**

SPEARING, Jay (M)   **119**   **5**
H: 5 6   W: 11 01   b.Wallasey 25-11-88

2006–07	Liverpool	0	0		
2007–08	Liverpool	0	0		
2008–09	Liverpool	0	0		
2009–10	Liverpool	3	0		
2009–10	*Leicester C*	7	1	**7**	**1**
2010–11	Liverpool	11	0		
2011–12	Liverpool	16	0		
2012–13	Liverpool	0	0		
2012–13	*Bolton W*	37	2		
2013–14	Liverpool	0	0	**30**	**0**
2013–14	Bolton W	45	2	**82**	**4**

THRELKELD, Oscar (D)   **2**   **0**
b.Bolton 15-12-94

2013–14	Bolton W	2	0	**2**	**0**

TIERNEY, Marc (D)   **238**   **2**
H: 5 11   W: 11 04   b.Prestwich 23-8-85

2003–04	Oldham Ath	2	0		
2004–05	Oldham Ath	11	0		
2005–06	Oldham Ath	19	0		
2006–07	Oldham Ath	5	0	**37**	**0**
2006–07	Shrewsbury T	18	0		
2007–08	Shrewsbury T	43	1		
2008–09	Shrewsbury T	18	0	**79**	**1**
2008–09	Colchester U	26	1		
2009–10	Colchester U	41	0		
2010–11	Colchester U	13	0	**80**	**1**
2010–11	Norwich C	16	0		
2011–12	Norwich C	17	0		
2012–13	Norwich C	1	0	**34**	**0**
2013–14	Bolton W	8	0	**8**	**0**

VELA, Joshua (M)   **14**   **0**
H: 5 11   W: 11 07   b.Salford 14-12-93

2010–11	Bolton W	0	0		
2011–12	Bolton W	3	0		
2012–13	Bolton W	4	0		
2013–14	Bolton W	0	0	**7**	**0**
2013–14	*Notts Co*	7	0	**7**	**0**

WHEATER, David (D)   **221**   **15**
H: 6 5   W: 12 12   b.Redcar 14-2-87
Internationals: England U16, U17, U18, U19, U21.

2004–05	Middlesbrough	0	0		
2005–06	Middlesbrough	6	0		
2005–06	*Doncaster R*	7	1	**7**	**1**
2006–07	Middlesbrough	2	1		
2006–07	*Wolverhampton W*	1	0	**1**	**0**
2006–07	*Darlington*	15	2	**15**	**2**
2007–08	Middlesbrough	34	3		
2008–09	Middlesbrough	32	1		
2009–10	Middlesbrough	42	1		
2010–11	Middlesbrough	24	3	**140**	**9**
2010–11	Bolton W	7	0		
2011–12	Bolton W	24	2		
2012–13	Bolton W	4	0		
2013–14	Bolton W	23	1	**58**	**3**

WHITE, Hayden (D)   **2**   **0**
b. 15-4-95

2013–14	Bolton W	2	0	**2**	**0**

WILKINSON, Conor (F)   **3**   **0**
Internationals: Republic of Ireland U19.

2012–13	Millwall	0	0		
2013–14	Bolton W	0	0		
2013–14	*Torquay U*	3	0	**3**	**0**

WOODLAND, Luke (M)   **0**   **0**
b. 21-7-97
Internationals: England U17.

2013–14	Bolton W	0	0		

YOUNGS, Tom (F)   **1**   **0**
b.London 6-9-94

2013–14	Bolton W	1	0	**1**	**0**

Scholars
Bailey, Sam Lewis; Ball, James Cameron; Campbell, Harry Joseph Gordon; Cvetko, Christopher Brian; Garratt, Tyler John; Gibson, Liam Robert; Hamer, Saul Michael; Hendrie, Jordan Lee; Hinchcliffe, Jamie Sidebottom; Holding, Robert Samuel; Kennedy, Carl Harvey; Maher, Niall Callum James Peter; Matthews, Glenn William; Newby, Elliot Christian; Nolan, Kieran Nathan; Thomas, Jamie Carl; Torres, Guillermo Garcia; Walker, Thomas James.

AFC BOURNEMOUTH (10)

ADDISON, Miles (D)   **116**   **4**
H: 6 2   W: 13 03   b.Newham 7-1-89
Internationals: England U21.

2005–06	Derby Co	2	0		
2006–07	Derby Co	1	0		
2007–08	Derby Co	1	0		
2008–09	Derby Co	28	1		
2009–10	Derby Co	13	2		
2010–11	Derby Co	21	0		
2011–12	Derby Co	0	0		
2011–12	*Barnsley*	11	0	**11**	**0**
2011–12	*Bournemouth*	14	1		
2012–13	Derby Co	0	0	**65**	**3**
2012–13	Bournemouth	20	0		
2013–14	Bournemouth	0	0	**34**	**1**
2013–14	*Rotherham U*	6	0	**6**	**0**

ALLSOP, Ryan (G)   **42**   **0**
H: 6 2   W: 12 06   b.Birmingham 17-6-92
Internationals: England U17.

2012–13	*Leyton Orient*	20	0	**20**	**0**
2012–13	Bournemouth	10	0		
2013–14	Bournemouth	12	0	**22**	**0**

ARTER, Harry (M)   **125**   **17**
H: 5 9   W: 11 07   b.Sidcup 28-12-89
Internationals: Republic of Ireland U19.

2007–08	Charlton Ath	0	0		
2008–09	Charlton Ath	0	0		
From Woking.					
2010–11	Bournemouth	18	0		
2010–11	*Carlisle U*	5	1	**5**	**1**
2011–12	Bournemouth	34	5		
2012–13	Bournemouth	37	8		
2013–14	Bournemouth	31	3	**120**	**16**

BASSELE, Aristide (M)   **0**   **0**
b.London 15-6-94

2012–13	Bournemouth	0	0		
2013–14	Bournemouth	0	0		

CAMP, Lee (G)   **379**   **0**
H: 5 11   W: 11 11   b.Derby 22-8-84
Internationals: England U21. Northern Ireland Full caps.

2002–03	Derby Co	1	0		
2003–04	Derby Co	0	0		
2003–04	*QPR*	12	0		
2004–05	Derby Co	45	0		
2005–06	Derby Co	40	0		
2006–07	Derby Co	3	0	**89**	**0**
2006–07	*Norwich C*	3	0		
2006–07	*QPR*	11	0		
2007–08	QPR	46	0		
2008–09	QPR	4	0	**73**	**0**
2008–09	*Nottingham F*	15	0		
2009–10	Nottingham F	45	0		
2010–11	Nottingham F	46	0		
2011–12	Nottingham F	46	0		
2012–13	Nottingham F	26	0	**178**	**0**
2012–13	*Norwich C*	3	0	**6**	**0**
2013–14	WBA	0	0		
2013–14	Bournemouth	33	0	**33**	**0**

CARGILL, Baily (D)   **5**   **0**
b. 13-10-95

2012–13	Bournemouth	0	0		
2013–14	Bournemouth	0	0		
2013–14	*Torquay U*	5	0	**5**	**0**

CARMICHAEL, Josh (M)   **4**   **0**
H: 6 0   W: 12 06   b.Poole 27-9-94
Internationals: Scotland U16.

2011–12	Bournemouth	1	0		
2012–13	Bournemouth	3	0		
2013–14	Bournemouth	0	0	**4**	**0**

COOK, Steve (D)   **100**   **4**
H: 6 1   W: 12 13   b.Hastings 19-4-91

2008–09	Brighton & HA	2	0		
2009–10	Brighton & HA	0	0		
2010–11	Brighton & HA	0	0		
2011–12	Brighton & HA	1	0	**3**	**0**
2011–12	Bournemouth	26	0		
2012–13	Bournemouth	33	1		
2013–14	Bournemouth	38	3	**97**	**4**

CORNICK, Harry (F)   **0**   **0**
b. 6-3-95

2013–14	Bournemouth	0	0		

COULIBALY, Mohamed (M)   **17**   **0**
b.Bakel 7-8-88

2011–12	Grasshoppers	5	0		
2012–13	Grasshoppers	5	0	**10**	**0**
2013–14	Bournemouth	7	0	**7**	**0**

DANIELS, Charlie (M)   **233**   **11**
H: 6 1   W: 12 12   b.Harlow 7-9-86

2005–06	Tottenham H	0	0		
2006–07	Tottenham H	0	0		
2006–07	*Chesterfield*	2	0	**2**	**0**
2007–08	Tottenham H	0	0		
2007–08	*Leyton Orient*	31	2		
2008–09	Tottenham H	0	0		
2008–09	*Gillingham*	5	1	**5**	**1**
2008–09	*Leyton Orient*	21	2		
2009–10	Leyton Orient	41	0		
2010–11	Leyton Orient	42	0		
2011–12	Leyton Orient	13	0	**148**	**4**
2011–12	Bournemouth	21	2		
2012–13	Bournemouth	34	4		
2013–14	Bournemouth	23	0	**78**	**6**

ELPHICK, Tommy (M)   **225**   **10**
H: 5 11   W: 11 07   b.Brighton 7-9-87

2005–06	Brighton & HA	1	0		
2006–07	Brighton & HA	3	0		
2007–08	Brighton & HA	39	2		
2008–09	Brighton & HA	39	1		
2009–10	Brighton & HA	44	3		
2010–11	Brighton & HA	27	1		

2011–12	Brighton & HA	0	0		
2012–13	Brighton & HA	0	0	153	7
2012–13	Bournemouth	34	2		
2013–14	Bournemouth	38	1	72	3

FLAHAVAN, Darryl (G) 356 0
H: 5 11 W: 12 05 b.Southampton 9-9-77
From Woking.

2000–01	Southend U	29	0		
2001–02	Southend U	41	0		
2002–03	Southend U	41	0		
2003–04	Southend U	37	0		
2004–05	Southend U	28	0		
2005–06	Southend U	43	0		
2006–07	Southend U	46	0		
2007–08	Southend U	26	0	291	0
2008–09	Crystal Palace	1	0		
2008–09	Leeds U	0	0		
2009–10	Crystal Palace	1	0		
2009–10	Oldham Ath	18	0	18	0
2010–11	Crystal Palace	0	0	2	0
2011–12	Bournemouth	44	0		
2012–13	Bournemouth	0	0		
2013–14	Bournemouth	1	0	45	0

FRANCIS, Simon (D) 397 8
H: 6 0 W: 12 06 b.Nottingham 16-2-85
Internationals: England U20.

2002–03	Bradford C	25	1		
2003–04	Bradford C	30	0	55	1
2003–04	Sheffield U	5	0		
2004–05	Sheffield U	6	0		
2005–06	Sheffield U	1	0	12	0
2005–06	Grimsby T	5	0	5	0
2005–06	Tranmere R	17	1	17	1
2006–07	Southend U	40	1		
2007–08	Southend U	27	2		
2008–09	Southend U	45	0		
2009–10	Southend U	45	1	157	4
2010–11	Charlton Ath	34	0		
2011–12	Charlton Ath	0	0	34	0
2011–12	Bournemouth	29	0		
2012–13	Bournemouth	42	1		
2013–14	Bournemouth	46	1	117	2

FRASER, Ryan (M) 63 3
H: 5 4 W: 10 13 b.Aberdeen 24-2-94
Internationals: Scotland U18, U21.

2010–11	Aberdeen	2	0		
2011–12	Aberdeen	2	0		
2012–13	Aberdeen	16	0	21	0
2012–13	Bournemouth	5	0		
2013–14	Bournemouth	37	3	42	3

GILKES, Harrison (M) 0 0

| 2012–13 | Bournemouth | 0 | 0 |
| 2013–14 | Bournemouth | 0 | 0 |

GOODSHIP, Brandon (F) 0 0
b. 1-1-86

| 2013–14 | Bournemouth | 0 | 0 |

GRABBAN, Lewis (F) 239 70
H: 6 0 W: 11 03 b.Croydon 12-1-88

2005–06	Crystal Palace	0	0		
2006–07	Crystal Palace	8	1		
2006–07	Oldham Ath	9	0	9	0
2007–08	Crystal Palace	2	0	10	1
2007–08	Motherwell	6	0	6	0
2007–08	Millwall	13	3		
2008–09	Millwall	31	6		
2009–10	Millwall	11	0		
2009–10	Brentford	7	2		
2010–11	Millwall	1	0	56	9
2010–11	Brentford	22	5	29	7
2011–12	Rotherham U	43	18	43	18
2012–13	Bournemouth	42	13		
2013–14	Bournemouth	44	22	86	35

HARTE, Ian (D) 419 64
H: 5 11 W: 12 06 b.Drogheda 31-8-77
Internationals: Republic of Ireland Full caps.

1995–96	Leeds U	4	0		
1996–97	Leeds U	14	2		
1997–98	Leeds U	12	0		
1998–99	Leeds U	35	4		
1999–2000	Leeds U	33	6		
2000–01	Leeds U	29	7		
2001–02	Leeds U	36	5		
2002–03	Leeds U	27	3		
2003–04	Leeds U	23	1	213	28
2004–05	Levante	24	1		
2005–06	Levante	0	0		
2006–07	Levante	6	0	30	1
2007–08	Sunderland	8	0	8	0
2008–09	Blackpool	4	0	4	0
2008–09	Carlisle U	3	1		
2009–10	Carlisle U	45	16		
2010–11	Carlisle U	4	2	52	19
2010–11	Reading	40	11		
2011–12	Reading	32	4		
2012–13	Reading	16	0	88	15
2013–14	Bournemouth	24	1	24	1

HUGHES, Richard (M) 300 16
H: 6 0 W: 12 13 b.Glasgow 25-6-79
Internationals: Scotland Full caps.

1998–99	Bournemouth	44	2		
1999–2000	Bournemouth	21	2		
2000–01	Bournemouth	44	8		
2001–02	Bournemouth	22	2		
2002–03	Portsmouth	6	0		
2002–03	Grimsby T	12	1	12	1
2003–04	Portsmouth	11	0		
2004–05	Portsmouth	16	0		
2005–06	Portsmouth	26	0		
2006–07	Portsmouth	18	0		
2007–08	Portsmouth	13	0		
2008–09	Portsmouth	20	0		
2009–10	Portsmouth	10	0		
2010–11	Portsmouth	11	0	131	0
2012–13	Bournemouth	21	1		
2013–14	Bournemouth	5	0	157	15

JALAL, Shwan (G) 170 0
H: 6 2 W: 14 02 b.Baghdad 14-8-83
Internationals: England C.

2001–02	Tottenham H	0	0		
2002–03	Tottenham H	0	0		
2003–04	Tottenham H	0	0		
From Woking.					
2006–07	Sheffield W	0	0		
2006–07	Peterborough U	1	0		
2007–08	Peterborough U	7	0		
2007–08	Morecambe	12	0	12	0
2008–09	Peterborough U	0	0	8	0
2008–09	Bournemouth	41	0		
2009–10	Bournemouth	44	0		
2010–11	Bournemouth	43	0		
2011–12	Bournemouth	3	0		
2012–13	Bournemouth	17	0		
2013–14	Bournemouth	0	0	148	0
2013–14	Oxford U	0	0		
2013–14	Leyton Orient	2	0	2	0

KERMORGANT, Yann (F) 305 85
H: 6 0 W: 13 03 b.Vannes 8-11-81
Internationals: Brittany Full caps.

2004–05	Chatellerault	29	14	29	14
2005–06	Grenoble	26	6		
2006–07	Grenoble	32	10	58	16
2007–08	Reims	33	4		
2008–09	Reims	34	9	67	13
2009–10	Leicester C	20	1		
2010–11	Leicester C	0	0	20	1
2010–11	Arles-Avignon	26	3	26	3
2011–12	Charlton Ath	36	12		
2012–13	Charlton Ath	32	12		
2013–14	Charlton Ath	21	5	89	29
2013–14	Bournemouth	16	9	16	9

MACDONALD, Shaun (M) 161 10
H: 6 1 W: 11 04 b.Swansea 17-6-88
Internationals: Wales U19, U21, Full caps.

2005–06	Swansea C	7	0		
2006–07	Swansea C	8	0		
2007–08	Swansea C	1	0		
2008–09	Swansea C	5	0		
2008–09	Yeovil T	4	2		
2009–10	Swansea C	3	0		
2009–10	Yeovil T	31	3		
2010–11	Swansea C	0	0		
2010–11	Yeovil T	26	4	61	9
2011–12	Swansea C	0	0	24	0
2011–12	Bournemouth	25	1		
2012–13	Bournemouth	28	0		
2013–14	Bournemouth	23	0	76	1

MATTHEWS, Sam (M) 0 0
b. 1-3-97

| 2013–14 | Bournemouth | 0 | 0 |

McCARTHY, Jake (D) 0 0
b. 2-4-96

| 2013–14 | Bournemouth | 0 | 0 |

McQUOID, Josh (F) 151 16
H: 5 9 W: 10 10 b.Southampton 15-12-89
Internationals: Northern Ireland U19, U21, B, Full caps.

2006–07	Bournemouth	2	0		
2007–08	Bournemouth	5	0		
2008–09	Bournemouth	16	0		
2009–10	Bournemouth	29	1		
2010–11	Bournemouth	17	9		
2010–11	Millwall	11	1		
2011–12	Millwall	5	0	16	1
2011–12	Burnley	17	1	17	1
2012–13	Bournemouth	34	3		
2013–14	Bournemouth	0	0	104	13
2013–14	Peterborough U	14	1	14	1

MULEBA, Jonathan (D) 0 0

| 2013–14 | Bournemouth | 0 | 0 |

O'HANLON, Josh (F) 22 7
b. 25-9-95

| 2013 | Longford T | 22 | 7 | 22 | 7 |
| 2013–14 | Bournemouth | 0 | 0 | | |

O'KANE, Eunan (M) 193 18
H: 5 8 W: 13 04 b.Derry 10-7-90
Internationals: Northern Ireland U16, U17, U19, U20, U21. Republic of Ireland U21.

2007–08	Everton	0	0		
2008–09	Everton	0	0		
2009–10	Coleraine	13	4	13	4
2009–10	Torquay U	16	1		
2010–11	Torquay U	45	6		
2011–12	Torquay U	45	5		
2012–13	Torquay U	0	0	106	12
2012–13	Bournemouth	37	1		
2013–14	Bournemouth	37	1	74	2

PARTINGTON, Joe (M) 52 2
H: 5 11 W: 11 13 b.Portsmouth 1-4-90
Internationals: Wales U17, U19, U21.

2007–08	Bournemouth	6	1		
2008–09	Bournemouth	11	1		
2009–10	Bournemouth	11	0		
2010–11	Bournemouth	5	0		
2011–12	Bournemouth	5	0		
2012–13	Bournemouth	14	0		
2013–14	Bournemouth	0	0	52	2

PITMAN, Brett (F) 311 102
H: 6 0 W: 11 00 b.Jersey 31-1-88

2005–06	Bournemouth	19	1		
2006–07	Bournemouth	29	5		
2007–08	Bournemouth	39	6		
2008–09	Bournemouth	39	17		
2009–10	Bournemouth	46	26		
2010–11	Bournemouth	2	3		
2010–11	Bristol C	39	13		
2011–12	Bristol C	35	7		
2012–13	Bristol C	3	0	77	20
2012–13	Bournemouth	26	19		
2013–14	Bournemouth	34	5	234	82

PUGH, Marc (M) 303 53
H: 5 11 W: 11 04 b.Bacup 2-4-87

2005–06	Burnley	0	0		
2005–06	Bury	6	1		
2006–07	Bury	35	3	41	4
2007–08	Shrewsbury T	37	4		
2008–09	Shrewsbury T	7	0	44	4
2008–09	Luton T	4	0	4	0
2008–09	Hereford U	9	1		
2009–10	Hereford U	40	13	49	14
2010–11	Bournemouth	41	12		
2011–12	Bournemouth	42	8		
2012–13	Bournemouth	40	6		
2013–14	Bournemouth	42	5	165	31

RANTIE, Tokelo (F) 81 20
b.Parys 8-9-90
Internationals: South Africa Full caps.

2011–12	Orlando Pirates	20	7	20	7
2012	Malmo FF	11	3		
2013	Malmo FF	21	7	32	10
2013–14	Bournemouth	29	3	29	3

RITCHIE, Matt (M) 214 52
H: 5 8 W: 11 00 b.Gosport 10-9-89

2008–09	Portsmouth	0	0		
2008–09	Dagenham & R	37	11	37	11
2009–10	Portsmouth	2	0		
2009–10	Notts Co	16	3	16	3
2009–10	Swindon T	4	0		

2010–11	Portsmouth	5	0	7	0
2010–11	Swindon T	36	7		
2011–12	Swindon T	40	10		
2012–13	Swindon T	27	9	107	26
2012–13	Bournemouth	17	3		
2013–14	Bournemouth	30	9	47	12

SMITH, Adam (D)   116   4
H: 5 8   W: 10 07   b.Leytonstone 29-4-91
Internationals: England U16, U17, U19, U20, U21.

2007–08	Tottenham H	0	0		
2008–09	Tottenham H	0	0		
2009–10	Tottenham H	0	0		
2009–10	Wycombe W	3	0	3	0
2009–10	Torquay U	16	0	16	0
2010–11	Tottenham H	0	0		
2010–11	Bournemouth	38	1		
2011–12	Tottenham H	1	0		
2011–12	Milton Keynes D	17	2	17	2
2011–12	Leeds U	3	0	3	0
2012–13	Tottenham H	0	0		
2012–13	Millwall	25	1	25	1
2013–14	Tottenham H	0	0	1	0
2013–14	Derby Co	8	0	8	0
2013–14	Bournemouth	5	0	43	1

STOCKLEY, Jayden (F)   52   5
H: 6 2   W: 12 07   b.Poole 10-10-93

2009–10	Bournemouth	2	0		
2010–11	Bournemouth	4	0		
2011–12	Bournemouth	10	0		
2011–12	Accrington S	9	3	9	3
2012–13	Bournemouth	0	0		
2013–14	Bournemouth	0	0	16	0
2013–14	Leyton Orient	8	1	8	1
2013–14	Torquay U	19	1	19	1

TUBBS, Matt (F)   105   29
H: 5 9   W: 11 00   b.Salisbury 15-7-84
Internationals: England C.
On loan from Salisbury C.

2008–09	Bournemouth	8	1		
2009–10	Bournemouth	0	0		
2011–12	Crawley T	24	12		
2011–12	Bournemouth	7	1		
2012–13	Bournemouth	31	- 6		
2013–14	Bournemouth	0	0	46	8
2013–14	Rotherham U	17	1	17	1
2013–14	Crawley T	18	8	42	20

WAKEFIELD, Josh (M)   3   0
H: 5 11   W: 11 05   b.Frimley 6-11-93

2011–12	Bournemouth	2	0		
2012–13	Bournemouth	1	0		
2012–13	Dagenham & R	0	0		
2013–14	Bournemouth	0	0	3	0

WARD, Elliot (D)   266   20
H: 6 2   W: 13 00   b.Harrow 19-1-85

2001–02	West Ham U	0	0		
2002–03	West Ham U	0	0		
2003–04	West Ham U	0	0		
2004–05	West Ham U	11	0		
2004–05	Bristol R	3	0	3	0
2005–06	West Ham U	4	0	15	0
2005–06	Plymouth Arg	16	1	16	1
2006–07	Coventry C	39	3		
2007–08	Coventry C	37	6		
2008–09	Coventry C	33	5		
2009–10	Coventry C	8	0	117	14
2009–10	Doncaster R	6	1	6	1
2009–10	Preston NE	4	0	4	0
2010–11	Norwich C	39	1		
2011–12	Norwich C	12	0		
2012–13	Norwich C	0	0	51	1
2012–13	Nottingham F	31	3	31	3
2013–14	Bournemouth	23	0	23	0

WHITFIELD, Ben (M)   0   0

2013–14	Bournemouth	0	0		

ZUBAR, Stephane (D)   120   3
H: 6 1   W: 12 11   b.Guadeloupe 9-10-86
Internationals: Guadeloupe Full caps.

2006–07	Caen	0	0		
2006–07	Pau	10	0	10	0
2007–08	Caen	0	0		
2007–08	FC Brussels	11	0	11	0
2008–09	Vaslui	10	0		
2009–10	Vaslui	26	1	36	1
2010–11	Plymouth Arg	29	2		
2011–12	Plymouth Arg	4	0	33	2

2011–12	Bournemouth	22	0		
2012–13	Bournemouth	2	0		
2012–13	Bury	6	0	6	0
2013–14	Bournemouth	0	0	24	0

Scholars
Banaghan, Macually James; Blackman, Daryl Henry Antony; Buckley, Callum Ralph; Butcher, Matthew David; Hansford, Curtis Jake; Harris, Anthony; Holmes, Jordan Thomas; Holmes, Luke Harold; Kaye, Joshua Joseph; Kirkwood, Samuel Jack; Lee, Jordan Michael; Quigley, Joseph Richard; Randall, Declan Samuel; Roberts, Kieran Matthew; Simpson, Jack Benjamin; Walsh, Mason Anthony; West, Jamie David.

BRADFORD C (11)

BATES, Matthew (D)   148   6
H: 5 10   W: 12 03   b.Stockton 10-12-86
Internationals: England U18, U19.

2003–04	Middlesbrough	0	0		
2004–05 -	Middlesbrough	2	0		
2004–05	Darlington	4	0	4	0
2005–06	Middlesbrough	16	0		
2006–07	Middlesbrough	1	0		
2006–07	Ipswich T	2	0	2	0
2007–08	Middlesbrough	0	0		
2007–08	Norwich C	3	0	3	0
2008–09	Middlesbrough	17	1		
2009–10	Middlesbrough	0	0		
2010–11	Middlesbrough	31	3		
2011–12	Middlesbrough	37	2	104	6
2012–13	Bristol C	13	0		
2013–14	Bristol C	0	0	13	0
2013–14	Bradford C	22	0	22	0

CLARKSON, Lewis (F)   1   0
H: 5 8   W: 11 12   b.Beverley 8-11-93

2013–14	Bradford C	1	0	1	0

DARBY, Stephen (D)   152   0
H: 5 9   W: 10 00   b.Liverpool 6-10-88
Internationals: England U19.

2006–07	Liverpool	0	0		
2007–08	Liverpool	0	0		
2008–09	Liverpool	0	0		
2009–10	Liverpool	1	0		
2009–10	Swindon T	12	0	12	0
2010–11	Liverpool	0	0		
2010–11	Notts Co	23	0	23	0
2011–12	Liverpool	0	0	1	0
2011–12	Rochdale	35	0	35	0
2012–13	Bradford C	35	0		
2013–14	Bradford C	46	0	81	0

DAVIES, Andrew (D)   215   10
H: 6 3   W: 14 08   b.Stockton 17-12-84
Internationals: England U21.

2002–03	Middlesbrough	0	0		
2003–04	Middlesbrough	10	0		
2004–05	Middlesbrough	3	0		
2004–05	QPR	9	0	9	0
2005–06	Middlesbrough	12	0		
2005–06	Derby Co	23	3	23	3
2006–07	Middlesbrough	23	0		
2007–08	Middlesbrough	4	0		
2007–08	Southampton	23	0		
2008–09	Southampton	0	0	23	0
2008–09	Stoke C	2	0		
2008–09	Preston NE	5	0	5	0
2009–10	Stoke C	0	0		
2009–10	Sheffield U	8	0	8	0
2010–11	Stoke C	0	0		
2010–11	Walsall	3	0	3	0
2010–11	Middlesbrough	6	0	59	0
2011–12	Stoke C	0	0	2	0
2011–12	Crystal Palace	1	0	1	0
2011–12	Bradford C	26	2		
2012–13	Bradford C	28	4		
2013–14	Bradford C	28	1	82	7

DE VITA, Raffaele (F)   161   35
H: 6 0   W: 11 09   b.Rome 23-9-87

2005–06	Blackburn R	0	0		
2006–07	Blackburn R	0	0		
2007–08	Blackburn R	0	0		
2008–09	Livingston	7	1		
2009–10	Livingston	29	9		

2010–11	Livingston	31	12	67	22
2011–12	Swindon T	38	4		
2012–13	Swindon T	36	8	74	12
2013–14	Bradford C	20	1	20	1

DOYLE, Nathan (M)   232   4
H: 5 11   W: 12 06   b.Derby 12-1-87
Internationals: England U16, U17, U18, U19.

2003–04	Derby Co	2	0		
2004–05	Derby Co	3	0		
2005–06	Derby Co	4	0		
2005–06	Notts Co	12	0	12	0
2006–07	Derby Co	0	0	9	0
2006–07	Bradford C	28	0		
2006–07	Hull C	1	0		
2007–08	Hull C	1	0		
2008–09	Hull C	3	0		
2009–10	Hull C	0	0	5	0
2009–10	Barnsley	34	0		
2010–11	Barnsley	43	2		
2011–12	Barnsley	21	0	98	2
2011–12	Preston NE	5	0	5	0
2012–13	Bradford C	37	2		
2013–14	Bradford C	38	0	103	2

FOLAN, Caleb (F)   212   34
H: 6 2   W: 14 07   b.Leeds 26-10-82
Internationals: Republic of Ireland Full caps.

1999–2000	Leeds U	0	0		
2000–01	Leeds U	0	0		
2001–02	Leeds U	0	0		
2001–02	Rushden & D	6	0	6	0
2001–02	Hull C	1	0		
2002–03	Leeds U	0	0		
2002–03	Chesterfield	13	1		
2003–04	Chesterfield	7	0		
2004–05	Chesterfield	32	6		
2005–06	Chesterfield	27	0		
2006–07	Chesterfield	23	8	102	15
2006–07	Wigan Ath	13	2		
2007–08	Wigan Ath	2	0	15	2
2007–08	Hull C	29	8		
2008–09	Hull C	15	1		
2009–10	Hull C	8	2		
2009–10	Middlesbrough	1	0	1	0
2010–11	Hull C	3	0	56	11
2010–11	Colorado Rapids	26	4	26	6
2011–12	Birmingham C	0	0		
2013–14	Bradford C	6	0	6	0

Transferred to FC Edmonton March 2014

GRAY, Andy (F)   490   108
H: 6 1   W: 13 00   b.Harrogate 15-11-77
Internationals: Scotland Youth, B, Full caps.

1995–96	Leeds U	15	0		
1996–97	Leeds U	7	0		
1997–98	Leeds U	0	0		
1997–98	Bury	6	1	6	1
1998–99	Leeds U	0	0		
1998–99	Nottingham F	8	0		
1998–99	Preston NE	5	0	5	0
1998–99	Oldham Ath	4	0	4	0
1999–2000	Nottingham F	22	0		
2000–01	Nottingham F	18	0		
2001–02	Nottingham F	16	1	64	1
2002–03	Bradford C	44	15		
2003–04	Bradford C	33	5		
2003–04	Sheffield U	14	9		
2004–05	Sheffield U	43	15		
2005–06	Sheffield U	1	1	58	25
2005–06	Sunderland	21	1	21	1
2005–06	Burnley	9	3		
2006–07	Burnley	35	14		
2007–08	Burnley	25	11	69	28
2007–08	Charlton Ath	16	2		
2008–09	Charlton Ath	27	7		
2009–10	Charlton Ath	2	0	45	9
2009–10	Barnsley	30	6		
2010–11	Barnsley	34	7		
2011–12	Barnsley	32	8	96	21
2012–13	Leeds U	8	1	30	1
2013–14	Bradford C	7	0		
2013–14	Bradford C	8	1	92	21

HANSON, James (F)   187   53
H: 6 4   W: 12 04   b.Bradford 9-11-87

2009–10	Bradford C	34	12		
2010–11	Bradford C	36	6		
2011–12	Bradford C	39	13		
2012–13	Bradford C	43	10		
2013–14	Bradford C	35	12	187	53

JONES, Gary (M) — 618 84
H: 5 11 W: 12 05 b.Birkenhead 3-6-77

Season	Club	A	G	A	G
1997–98	Swansea C	8	0	8	0
1997–98	Rochdale	17	2		
1998–99	Rochdale	20	0		
1999–2000	Rochdale	39	7		
2000–01	Rochdale	44	8		
2001–02	Rochdale	20	5		
2001–02	Barnsley	25	1		
2002–03	Barnsley	31	1		
2003–04	Barnsley	0	0	56	2
2003–04	Rochdale	26	4		
2004–05	Rochdale	39	8		
2005–06	Rochdale	42	4		
2006–07	Rochdale	27	3		
2007–08	Rochdale	43	7		
2008–09	Rochdale	28	0		
2009–10	Rochdale	34	4		
2010–11	Rochdale	46	17		
2011–12	Rochdale	45	5	470	74
2012–13	Bradford C	39	2		
2013–14	Bradford C	45	6	84	8

KENNEDY, Jason (M) — 298 23
H: 6 1 W: 13 02 b.Stockton 11-9-86

Season	Club	A	G	A	G
2004–05	Middlesbrough	1	0		
2005–06	Middlesbrough	3	0		
2006–07	Middlesbrough	0	0		
2006–07	*Boston U*	13	1	13	1
2006–07	*Bury*	12	0	12	0
2007–08	Middlesbrough	0	0	4	0
2007–08	*Livingston*	18	2	18	2
2007–08	*Darlington*	13	2		
2008–09	Darlington	46	5	59	7
2009–10	Rochdale	42	0		
2010–11	Rochdale	45	4		
2011–12	Rochdale	44	4		
2012–13	Rochdale	46	4		
2013–14	Bradford C	8	1	8	1
2013–14	*Rochdale*	7	0	184	12

McARDLE, Rory (D) — 283 13
H: 6 1 W: 11 04 b.Doncaster 1-5-87
Internationals: Northern Ireland U21, Full caps.

Season	Club	A	G	A	G
2005–06	Sheffield W	0	0		
2005–06	*Rochdale*	19	1		
2006–07	Sheffield W	1	0	1	0
2006–07	Rochdale	25	0		
2007–08	Rochdale	43	3		
2008–09	Rochdale	41	2		
2009–10	Rochdale	20	0	148	6
2010–11	Aberdeen	28	2		
2011–12	Aberdeen	25	0	53	2
2012–13	Bradford C	40	2		
2013–14	Bradford C	41	3	81	5

McBURNIE, Oliver (F) — 8 0
H: 6 2 W: 10 04 b.Bradford 6-4-96

Season	Club	A	G	A	G
2013–14	Bradford C	8	0	8	0

McHUGH, Carl (D) — 30 2
b.Co. Donegal 5-2-93
Internationals: Republic of Ireland U17, U19, U21.

Season	Club	A	G	A	G
2011–12	Reading	0	0		
2012–13	Bradford C	16	1		
2013–14	Bradford C	14	1	30	2

McLAUGHLIN, Jon (G) — 125 0
H: 6 2 W: 13 00 b.Edinburgh 9-9-87

Season	Club	A	G	A	G
2008–09	Bradford C	1	0		
2009–10	Bradford C	7	0		
2010–11	Bradford C	25	0		
2011–12	Bradford C	23	0		
2012–13	Bradford C	23	0		
2013–14	Bradford C	46	0	125	0

McLEAN, Aaron (F) — 308 87
H: 5 9 W: 10 10 b.Hammersmith 25-5-83
Internationals: England C.

Season	Club	A	G	A	G
1999–2000	Leyton Orient	3	0		
2000–01	Leyton Orient	2	1		
2001–02	Leyton Orient	27	1		
2002–03	Leyton Orient	8	0	40	2

From Aldershot T, Grays Ath

Season	Club	A	G	A	G
2006–07	Peterborough U	16	7		
2007–08	Peterborough U	45	29		
2008–09	Peterborough U	42	18		
2009–10	Peterborough U	35	7		
2010–11	Peterborough U	19	10	157	71
2010–11	Hull C	23	3		
2011–12	Hull C	39	5		
2012–13	Hull C	14	1		
2012–13	*Ipswich T*	7	1	7	1
2013–14	Hull C	1	0	77	9
2013–14	*Birmingham C*	7	0	7	0
2013–14	Bradford C	20	4	20	4

MEREDITH, James (D) — 62 1
H: 6 1 W: 11 06 b.Albury, Australia 4-4-88

Season	Club	A	G	A	G
2006–07	Derby Co	0	0		
2006–07	*Chesterfield*	1	0	1	0
2007–08	*Shrewsbury T*	3	0	3	0

From York C

Season	Club	A	G	A	G
2012–13	Bradford C	32	1		
2013–14	Bradford C	26	0	58	1

OLIVER, Luke (D) — 145 4
H: 6 6 W: 14 05 b.Acton 1-5-84

Season	Club	A	G	A	G
2002–03	Wycombe W	2	0		
2003–04	Wycombe W	2	0		

From Woking

Season	Club	A	G	A	G
2005–06	*Yeovil T*	3	0	3	0

From Stevenage B.

Season	Club	A	G	A	G
2008–09	Wycombe W	8	0		
2009–10	Wycombe W	23	0	35	0
2009–10	*Bradford C*	7	2		
2010–11	Bradford C	42	1		
2011–12	Bradford C	39	1		
2012–13	Bradford C	15	0		
2013–14	Bradford C	4	0	107	4

REID, Kyel (M) — 198 18
H: 5 10 W: 12 05 b.Deptford 26-11-87
Internationals: England U17, U18, U19.

Season	Club	A	G	A	G
2004–05	West Ham U	0	0		
2005–06	West Ham U	2	0		
2006–07	West Ham U	0	0		
2006–07	*Barnsley*	26	2	26	2
2007–08	West Ham U	1	0		
2007–08	*Crystal Palace*	2	0	2	0
2008–09	West Ham U	0	0	3	0
2008–09	*Blackpool*	7	0	7	0
2008–09	*Wolverhampton W*	8	1	8	1
2009–10	*Sheffield U*	7	0	7	0
2009–10	Charlton Ath	17	4		
2010–11	Charlton Ath	32	1	49	5
2011–12	Bradford C	37	4		
2012–13	Bradford C	33	2		
2013–14	Bradford C	26	4	96	10

TAYLOR, Matthew (D) — 165 10
H: 6 0 W: 12 04 b.Chorley 30-1-82

Season	Club	A	G	A	G
2008–09	Exeter C	31	2		
2009–10	Exeter C	46	5		
2010–11	Exeter C	28	2	105	9
2011–12	Charlton Ath	41	0		
2012–13	Charlton Ath	12	0	53	0
2013–14	Bradford C	2	0	2	0
2013–14	*Colchester U*	5	1	5	1

THOMPSON, Gary (M) — 236 35
H: 6 0 W: 14 02 b.Kendal 24-11-80

Season	Club	A	G	A	G
2007–08	Morecambe	40	7	40	7
2007–08	Scunthorpe U	24	3		
2009–10	Scunthorpe U	36	9		
2010–11	Scunthorpe U	12	1		
2011–12	Scunthorpe U	39	7	111	20
2012–13	Bradford C	41	6		
2013–14	Bradford C	44	2	85	8

YEATES, Mark (F) — 311 43
H: 5 8 W: 13 03 b.Dublin 11-1-85
Internationals: Republic of Ireland U21, B.

Season	Club	A	G	A	G
2002–03	Tottenham H	0	0		
2003–04	Tottenham H	1	0		
2003–04	*Brighton & HA*	9	0	9	0
2004–05	Tottenham H	2	0		
2004–05	*Swindon T*	4	0	4	0
2005–06	Tottenham H	0	0		
2005–06	Colchester U	44	5		
2006–07	Tottenham H	0	0	3	0
2006–07	*Hull C*	5	0	5	0
2006–07	*Leicester C*	9	1	9	1
2007–08	Colchester U	29	8		
2008–09	Colchester U	43	12	116	25
2009–10	Middlesbrough	19	1	19	1
2009–10	Sheffield U	20	2		
2010–11	Sheffield U	35	5	55	7
2011–12	Watford	33	3		
2012–13	Watford	29	4	62	7
2013–14	Bradford C	29	2	29	2

Scholars
Barker, Elliott Austin; Bentley, Jack; Brennan, Joseph James; Chippendale, Callum Ross; Curtis, Nathan Robert; Heaton, Niall Michael; Hepworth, Calum; Jenkinson, Rhys Brandon; King, James Taylor; Mottley-Henry, Dylan; Pollard, James Harry; Stockdill, Jack Peter; Wright, Samuel Lee.

BRENTFORD (12)

ADAMS, Charlie (M) — 4 0
H: 5 6 W: 9 10 b.London 16-5-94

Season	Club	A	G	A	G
2012–13	Brentford	1	0		
2013–14	Brentford	3	0	4	0

BARRON, Scott (D) — 139 2
H: 5 9 W: 9 08 b.Preston 2-9-85

Season	Club	A	G	A	G
2003–04	Ipswich T	0	0		
2004–05	Ipswich T	0	0		
2005–06	Ipswich T	15	0		
2006–07	Ipswich T	0	0	15	0
2006–07	*Wrexham*	3	0	3	0
2007–08	Millwall	12	0		
2008–09	Millwall	14	0		
2009–10	Millwall	23	0		
2010–11	Millwall	38	2		
2011–12	Millwall	20	0		
2012–13	Millwall	0	0	107	2
2012–13	Brentford	12	0		
2013–14	Brentford	2	0	14	0

BIDWELL, Jake (D) — 102 0
H: 6 0 W: 11 00 b.Southport 21-3-93
Internationals: England U16, U17, U18, U19.

Season	Club	A	G	A	G
2009–10	Everton	0	0		
2010–11	Everton	0	0		
2011–12	Everton	0	0		
2011–12	*Brentford*	24	0		
2012–13	Everton	0	0		
2012–13	*Brentford*	40	0		
2013–14	Brentford	38	0	102	0

BONHAM, Jack (G) — 2 0
H: 6 4 W: 14 13 b.Stevenage 14-9-93
Internationals: Republic of Ireland U17.

Season	Club	A	G	A	G
2010–11	Watford	0	0		
2011–12	Watford	0	0		
2012–13	Watford	1	0	1	0
2013–14	Brentford	1	0	1	0

BUTTON, David (G) — 137 0
H: 6 3 W: 13 00 b.Stevenage 27-2-89
Internationals: England U16, U17, U19, U20.

Season	Club	A	G	A	G
2005–06	Tottenham H	0	0		
2006–07	Tottenham H	0	0		
2007–08	*Rochdale*	0	0		
2007–08	Tottenham H	0	0		
2008–09	*Bournemouth*	4	0	4	0
2008–09	*Luton T*	0	0		
2008–09	*Dagenham & R*	3	0	3	0
2009–10	Tottenham H	0	0		
2009–10	*Crewe Alex*	10	0	10	0
2009–10	*Shrewsbury T*	26	0	26	0
2010–11	Tottenham H	0	0		
2010–11	*Plymouth Arg*	30	0	30	0
2011–12	Tottenham H	0	0		
2011–12	*Leyton Orient*	1	0	1	0
2011–12	*Doncaster R*	7	0	7	0
2011–12	*Barnsley*	9	0	9	0
2012–13	Tottenham H	0	0		
2012–13	*Charlton Ath*	5	0	5	0
2013–14	Brentford	42	0	42	0

CALVET, Raphael (D) — 1 0
H: 6 0 W: 10 13 b.Paris 7-2-94

Season	Club	A	G	A	G
2012–13	Auxerre	1	0	1	0
2013–14	Brentford	0	0		

CLARKE, Josh (M) — 1 0
b. 5-7-95

Season	Club	A	G	A	G
2012–13	Brentford	0	0		
2013–14	Brentford	1	0	1	0

CRAIG, Tony (D) — 324 7
H: 6 0 W: 10 03 b.Greenwich 20-4-85

Season	Club	A	G	A	G
2002–03	Millwall	2	1		
2003–04	Millwall	9	0		
2004–05	Millwall	10	0		
2004–05	*Wycombe W*	14	0	14	0

Season	Club				
2005–06	Millwall	28	0		
2006–07	Millwall	30	1		
2007–08	Crystal Palace	13	0	13	0
2007–08	*Millwall*	5	1		
2008–09	Millwall	44	2		
2009–10	Millwall	30	2		
2010–11	Millwall	24	0		
2011–12	Millwall	23	0	205	7
2011–12	*Leyton Orient*	4	0	4	0
2012–13	Brentford	44	0		
2013–14	Brentford	44	0	88	0

DALLAS, Stuart (M)   58   29
H: 6 0   W: 12 09   b.Cookstown 19-4-91
Internationals: Northern Ireland U21, U23, Full caps.

Season	Club				
2010–11	Crusaders	13	16		
2011–12	Crusaders	8	8	21	24
2012–13	Brentford	7	0		
2013–14	Brentford	18	2	25	2
2013–14	*Northampton T*	12	3	12	3

DEAN, Harlee (M)   103   4
H: 6 0   W: 12   b.Basingstoke 26-7-91

Season	Club				
2008–09	Dagenham & R	0	0		
2009–10	Dagenham & R	1	0	1	0
2010–11	Southampton	0	0		
2011–12	Southampton	0	0		
2011–12	*Brentford*	26	1		
2012–13	Brentford	44	3		
2013–14	Brentford	32	0	102	4

DIAGOURAGA, Toumani (M)   274   10
H: 6 2   W: 11 05   b.Paris 10-6-87

Season	Club				
2004–05	Watford	0	0		
2005–06	Watford	1	0		
2005–06	*Swindon T*	8	0	8	0
2006–07	Watford	0	0		
2006–07	*Rotherham U*	7	0	7	0
2007–08	Watford	0	0	1	0
2007–08	*Hereford U*	41	2		
2008–09	Hereford U	45	2	86	4
2009–10	Peterborough U	19	0	19	0
2009–10	*Brentford*	20	0		
2010–11	Brentford	32	1		
2011–12	Brentford	35	4		
2012–13	Brentford	39	1		
2013–14	Brentford	19	0	145	6
2013–14	*Portsmouth*	8	0	8	0

DONALDSON, Clayton (F)   272   98
H: 6 1   W: 11 07   b.Bradford 7-2-84

Season	Club				
2002–03	Hull C	2	0		
2003–04	Hull C	0	0		
2004–05	Hull C	0	0	2	0
From York C					
2007–08	Hibernian	17	5	17	5
2008–09	Crewe Alex	37	6		
2009–10	Crewe Alex	37	13		
2010–11	Crewe Alex	43	28	117	47
2011–12	Brentford	46	11		
2012–13	Brentford	44	18		
2013–14	Brentford	46	17	136	46

DOUGLAS, Jonathan (M)   398   25
H: 5 11   W: 11 11   b.Monaghan 22-11-81
Internationals: Republic of Ireland Full caps.

Season	Club				
1999–2000	Blackburn R	0	0		
2000–01	Blackburn R	0	0		
2001–02	Blackburn R	0	0		
2002–03	Blackburn R	1	0		
2002–03	*Chesterfield*	7	1	7	1
2003–04	*Blackpool*	16	3	16	3
2003–04	Blackburn R	14	1		
2004–05	Blackburn R	1	0		
2004–05	*Gillingham*	10	0	10	0
2005–06	Blackburn R	0	0		
2005–06	*Leeds U*	40	5		
2006–07	Blackburn R	0	0	16	1
2006–07	Leeds U	35	1		
2007–08	Leeds U	24	3		
2008–09	Leeds U	43	1	142	10
2009–10	Swindon T	43	0		
2010–11	Swindon T	39	1	82	1
2011–12	Brentford	46	2		
2012–13	Brentford	44	4		
2013–14	Brentford	35	3	125	9

EL ALAGUI, Farid (F)   69   25
H: 6 1   W: 13 00   b.Marmande 28-8-85

Season	Club				
2011–12	Falkirk	33	18	33	18
2012–13	Brentford	11	3		
2013–14	Brentford	12	1	23	4
2013–14	*Dundee U*	13	3	13	3

FILLO, Martin (M)   230   42
H: 5 10   W: 11 04   b.Plana 7-2-86

Season	Club				
2003–04	Plzen	8	2		
2004–05	Plzen	25	5		
2005–06	Plzen	29	6		
2006–07	Plzen	28	7		
2007–08	Plzen	14	5		
2008	Viking FK	25	6		
2009	Viking FK	25	3		
2010	Viking FK	15	5	65	14
2010–11	Plzen	10	0		
2011–12	Plzen	9	0		
2011–12	*Mlada Boleslav*	13	2		
2012–13	Plzen	14	1		
2012–13	*Mlada Boleslav*	8	0	21	2
2013–14	Plzen	0	0	137	26
On loan from Plzen					
2013–14	*Brentford*	7	0	7	0

FORSHAW, Adam (M)   90   11
H: 6 1   W: 11 02   b.Liverpool 8-10-91

Season	Club				
2009–10	Everton	0	0		
2010–11	Everton	1	0		
2011–12	Everton	0	0	1	0
2011–12	*Brentford*	7	0		
2012–13	Brentford	43	3		
2013–14	Brentford	39	8	89	11

GRIGG, Will (M)   133   32
H: 5 11   W: 11 00   b.Solihull 3-7-91
Internationals: Northern Ireland U19, U21, Full caps.

Season	Club				
2008–09	Walsall	1	0		
2009–10	Walsall	0	0		
2010–11	Walsall	28	4		
2011–12	Walsall	29	4		
2012–13	Walsall	41	19	99	27
2013–14	Brentford	34	5	34	5

HUTTON, Louis (M)   0   0
H: 5 9   b.Bradford 9-9-94
Internationals: England U16, U17.

Season	Club				
2013–14	Manchester C	0	0		
2013–14	Brentford	0	0		

JUDGE, Alan (F)   188   30
H: 5 6   W: 11 03   b.Dublin 11-11-88
Internationals: Republic of Ireland U18, U19, U21, U23.

Season	Club				
2006–07	Blackburn R	0	0		
2007–08	Blackburn R	0	0		
2008–09	Blackburn R	0	0		
2008–09	*Plymouth Arg*	17	2		
2009–10	Blackburn R	0	0		
2009–10	*Plymouth Arg*	37	5	54	7
2010–11	Blackburn R	0	0		
2010–11	Notts Co	19	1		
2011–12	Notts Co	43	7		
2012–13	Notts Co	39	8	101	16
2013–14	Blackburn R	11	0	11	0
2013–14	Brentford	22	7	22	7

LEE, Richard (G)   158   0
H: 6 0   W: 12 06   b.Oxford 5-10-82
Internationals: England U20.

Season	Club				
2000–01	Watford	0	0		
2001–02	Watford	0	0		
2002–03	Watford	4	0		
2003–04	Watford	0	0		
2004–05	Watford	33	0		
2005–06	Watford	0	0		
2005–06	*Blackburn R*	0	0		
2006–07	Watford	10	0		
2007–08	Watford	35	0		
2008–09	Watford	10	0		
2009–10	Watford	0	0	92	0
2010–11	Brentford	22	0		
2011–12	Brentford	37	0		
2012–13	Brentford	3	0		
2013–14	Brentford	4	0	66	0

LOGAN, Shaleum (D)   153   7
H: 6 1   W: 12 07   b.Wythenshawe 29-1-88

Season	Club				
2006–07	Manchester C	0	0		
2007–08	Manchester C	0	0		
2007–08	*Grimsby T*	5	2	5	2
2007–08	*Scunthorpe U*	4	0	4	0
2007–08	*Stockport Co*	7	0	7	0
2008–09	Manchester C	1	0		
2009–10	Manchester C	0	0		
2009–10	*Tranmere R*	33	0	33	0
2010–11	Manchester C	0	0	1	0
2011–12	Brentford	27	3		
2012–13	Brentford	45	0		
2013–14	Brentford	18	1	90	4
2013–14	*Aberdeen*	13	1	13	1

MAWSON, Alfie (D)   0   0
b. 19-1-94

Season	Club				
2012–13	Brentford	0	0		
2013–14	Brentford	0	0		

McCORMACK, Alan (M)   338   24
H: 5 8   W: 11 00   b.Dublin 10-1-84

Season	Club				
2002–03	Preston NE	0	0		
2003–04	Preston NE	5	0		
2003–04	*Leyton Orient*	10	0	10	0
2004–05	Preston NE	3	0		
2004–05	*Southend U*	7	2		
2005–06	Preston NE	0	0		
2005–06	*Motherwell*	24	2	24	2
2006–07	Preston NE	3	0	11	0
2006–07	Southend U	22	3		
2007–08	Southend U	42	8		
2008–09	Southend U	34	2		
2009–10	Southend U	41	3	146	18
2010–11	Charlton Ath	24	1	24	1
2011–12	Swindon T	40	2		
2012–13	Swindon T	40	0	80	2
2013–14	Brentford	43	1	43	1

MILLER-RODNEY, Tyrell (M)   0   0
H: 5 9   W: 10 04   b.Stonebridge 23-4-94

Season	Club				
2013–14	Brentford	0	0		

MORRIS, Kieran (M)   0   0
H: 6 0   W: 12 03   b.Stourbridge 26-6-95

Season	Club				
2013–14	Brentford	0	0		

NORRIS, Luke (F)   31   8
H: 6 1   W: 13 05   b.Stevenage 3-6-93

Season	Club				
2011–12	Brentford	1	0		
2012–13	Brentford	0	0		
2013–14	Brentford	1	0	2	0
2013–14	*Northampton T*	10	4	10	4
2013–14	*Dagenham & R*	19	4	19	4

O'BRIEN, Liam (G)   21   0
H: 6 1   W: 12 06   b.Ruislip 30-11-91
Internationals: England U19.

Season	Club				
2008–09	Portsmouth	0	0		
2009–10	Portsmouth	0	0		
2010–11	Barnet	8	0		
2011–12	Barnet	10	0		
2012–13	Barnet	3	0	21	0
2013–14	Brentford	0	0		

O'CONNOR, Kevin (F)   420   32
H: 5 11   W: 12 00   b.Blackburn 24-2-82
Internationals: Republic of Ireland U21.

Season	Club				
1999–2000	Brentford	6	0		
2000–01	Brentford	11	1		
2001–02	Brentford	25	0		
2002–03	Brentford	45	5		
2003–04	Brentford	43	1		
2004–05	Brentford	37	2		
2005–06	Brentford	30	7		
2006–07	Brentford	39	6		
2007–08	Brentford	37	3		
2008–09	Brentford	28	0		
2009–10	Brentford	43	4		
2010–11	Brentford	41	2		
2011–12	Brentford	14	1		
2012–13	Brentford	12	0		
2013–14	Brentford	9	0	420	32

OYELEKE, Emmanuel (M)   3   0
H: 5 9   W: 11 11   b.Wandsworth 24-12-92

Season	Club				
2011–12	Brentford	1	0		
2012–13	Brentford	0	0		
2012–13	*Northampton T*	2	0	2	0
2013–14	Brentford	0	0	1	0

PIERRE, Aaron (D)   8   1
H: 6 1   W: 13 12   b.Southall 17-2-93

Season	Club				
2011–12	Brentford	0	0		
2012–13	Brentford	0	0		
2013–14	Brentford	0	0		
2013–14	*Wycombe W*	8	1	8	1

REEVES, Jake (M)   40   0
H: 5 8   W: 11 11   b.Lewisham 30-6-93

Season	Club				
2010–11	Brentford	1	0		
2011–12	Brentford	8	0		
2012–13	Brentford	6	0		

2012–13	AFC Wimbledon	5	0	5	0
2013–14	Brentford	20	0	35	0

SAUNDERS, Sam (M) 194 35
H: 5 6 W: 11 04 b.Erith 29-8-83

2007–08	Dagenham & R	22	0		
2008–09	Dagenham & R	40	14	62	14
2009–10	Brentford	26	1		
2010–11	Brentford	21	2		
2011–12	Brentford	37	10		
2012–13	Brentford	31	3		
2013–14	Brentford	17	5	132	21

TARKOWSKI, James (D) 85 7
H: 6 1 W: 12 10 b.Manchester 19-11-92

2010–11	Oldham Ath	9	0		
2011–12	Oldham Ath	16	1		
2012–13	Oldham Ath	21	2		
2013–14	Oldham Ath	26	2	72	5
2013–14	Brentford	13	2	13	2

VENTA, Rodriguez (D) 284 2
H: 5 11 W: 11 06 b.Oviedo 13-12-75

2001–02	Tenerife	29	1	29	1
2002–03	Villarreal	16	0		
2003–04	Villarreal	23	0		
2004–05	Villarreal	32	0		
2005–06	Villarreal	25	0		
2006–07	Villarreal	20	0		
2007–08	Villarreal	25	1		
2008–09	Villarreal	22	0		
2009–10	Villarreal	18	0		
2010–11	Levante	33	0		
2011–12	Levante	26	0	59	0
2012–13	Villarreal	14	0	195	1
2013–14	Brentford	1	0	1	0

YENNARIS, Nico (D) 11 0
H: 5 7 W: 10 03 b.Leytonstone 23-5-93
Internationals: England U17, U18, U19.

2010–11	Arsenal	0	0		
2011–12	Arsenal	1	0		
2011–12	Notts Co	2	0	2	0
2012–13	Arsenal	0	0		
2013–14	Arsenal	0	0	1	0
2013–14	Bournemouth	0	0		
2013–14	Brentford	8	0	8	0

Scholars
Bryan, Richard Edward; Ferry, James Patrick; Field, Thomas; Jatta, Seika; Khanye, Makhosini Ryan; Laucys, Audrius; Lavender, Lewis Henry; Milenge, Gradi; Moore, Montell; Onowvigun, Michael; Pilbeam, George; Rowe, Fabian Troy; Senior, Courtney Fitzroy; Stockwell, Joshua James; Stone, Lionel Junior Richard; Taylor, Joseph Stuart; Webster, Daniel James; Westbrooke, Zain Sam.

BRIGHTON & HA (13)

AGUSTIEN, Kemy (M) 206 8
H: 5 10 W: 11 05 b.Tilburg 20-8-86
Internationals: Netherlands U19, U20, U21.

2004–05	Willem II	21	1		
2005–06	Willem II	34	2	55	3
2006–07	Roda JC	31	2	31	2
2007–08	AZ	25	2	25	2
2008–09	Birmingham C	18	0	18	0
2009–10	RKC Waalwijk	19	1	19	1
2010–11	Swansea C	8	0		
2010–11	Crystal Palace	8	0	8	0
2011–12	Swansea C	13	0		
2012–13	Swansea C	18	0	39	0
2013–14	Brighton & HA	11	0	11	0

ANKERGREN, Casper (G) 273 0
H: 6 3 W: 14 07 b.Koge 9-11-79
Internationals: Denmark U17, U21.

2001–02	Brondby	1	0		
2002–03	Brondby	16	0		
2003–04	Brondby	1	0		
2004–05	Brondby	32	0		
2005–06	Brondby	18	0		
2006–07	Brondby	18	0	86	0
2006–07	Leeds U	14	0		
2007–08	Leeds U	43	0		
2008–09	Leeds U	33	0		
2009–10	Leeds U	29	0	119	0
2010–11	Brighton & HA	45	0		
2011–12	Brighton & HA	19	0		
2012–13	Brighton & HA	3	0		
2013–14	Brighton & HA	1	0	68	0

ASMUNDSSON, Emil (M) 6 1
b. 8-1-95
Internationals: Iceland U17, U19.

2012	Fylkir	6	1	6	1
2012–13	Brighton & HA	0	0		
2013–14	Brighton & HA	0	0		

BARRY, Bradley (D) 0 0

2013–14	Brighton & HA	0	0		

BREZOVAN, Peter (G) 140 0
H: 6 6 W: 14 13 b.Bratislava 9-12-79
Internationals: Slovakia U21.

2002–03	Brno	10	0		
2003–04	Brno	2	0		
2004–05	Inter Bratislava	8	0	8	0
2005–06	Brno	7	0	19	0
2006–07	Swindon T	14	0		
2007–08	Swindon T	31	0		
2008–09	Swindon T	21	0	66	0
2009–10	Brighton & HA	20	0		
2010–11	Brighton & HA	2	0		
2011–12	Brighton & HA	20	0		
2012–13	Brighton & HA	1	0		
2013–14	Brighton & HA	4	0	47	0

BUCKLEY, Will (F) 193 37
H: 6 0 W: 13 00 b.Oldham 12-8-88

2007–08	Rochdale	7	0		
2008–09	Rochdale	37	10		
2009–10	Rochdale	15	3	59	13
2009–10	Watford	6	1		
2010–11	Watford	33	4	39	5
2011–12	Brighton & HA	29	8		
2012–13	Brighton & HA	36	8		
2013–14	Brighton & HA	30	3	95	19

CALDERON, Inigo (D) 351 22
H: 5 10 W: 12 02 b.Vitoria 4-1-82

2002–03	Alaves B	35	1		
2003–04	Alaves B	33	0	68	1
2004–05	Alicante	25	0		
2005–06	Alicante	31	4		
2006–07	Alicante	28	1	84	5
2007–08	Alaves	20	0		
2008–09	Alaves	33	2	53	2
2009–10	Brighton & HA	19	1		
2010–11	Brighton & HA	44	7		
2011–12	Brighton & HA	32	4		
2012–13	Brighton & HA	28	0		
2013–14	Brighton & HA	23	2	146	14

CHICKSEN, Adam (D) 77 2
H: 5 8 W: 11 09 b.Milton Keynes 27-9-91

2008–09	Milton Keynes D	1	0		
2009–10	Milton Keynes D	6	0		
2010–11	Milton Keynes D	14	0		
2011–12	Milton Keynes D	20	0		
2011–12	Leyton Orient	3	0	3	0
2012–13	Milton Keynes D	32	2		
2013–14	Milton Keynes D	0	0	73	2
2013–14	Brighton & HA	1	0	1	0

CROFTS, Andrew (D) 342 35
H: 5 10 W: 12 09 b.Chatham 29-5-84
Internationals: Wales U19, U21, Full caps.

2000–01	Gillingham	1	0		
2001–02	Gillingham	0	0		
2002–03	Gillingham	0	0		
2003–04	Gillingham	8	0		
2004–05	Gillingham	27	2		
2005–06	Gillingham	45	2		
2006–07	Gillingham	43	8		
2007–08	Gillingham	41	5		
2008–09	Gillingham	9	0	174	17
2008–09	Peterborough U	9	0	9	0
2009–10	Brighton & HA	44	5		
2010–11	Norwich C	44	8		
2011–12	Norwich C	24	0		
2012–13	Norwich C	0	0	68	8
2012–13	Brighton & HA	24	0		
2013–14	Brighton & HA	23	5	91	10

DALLISON, Tom (M) 0 0
H: 5 10 W: 14 01 b. 2-2-96

2012–13	Arsenal	0	0		
2013–14	Brighton & HA	0	0		

DICKENSON, Brennan (F) 31 4
H: 6 0 W: 12 07 b.Ferndown 26-2-93

2012–13	Brighton & HA	0	0		
2012–13	Chesterfield	11	1	11	1
2012–13	AFC Wimbledon	7	2	7	2
2013–14	Brighton & HA	0	0		
2013–14	Northampton T	13	1	13	1

DUNK, Lewis (D) 53 0
H: 6 3 W: 12 02 b.Brighton 1-12-91

2009–10	Brighton & HA	1	0		
2010–11	Brighton & HA	5	0		
2011–12	Brighton & HA	31	0		
2012–13	Brighton & HA	8	0		
2013–14	Brighton & HA	6	0	51	0
2013–14	Bristol C	2	0	2	0

FORSTER-CASKEY, Jake (M) 52 7
H: 5 10 W: 10 00 b.Southend 25-4-94
Internationals: England U16, U17, U18, U21.

2009–10	Brighton & HA	1	0		
2010–11	Brighton & HA	4	1		
2011–12	Brighton & HA	3	0		
2012–13	Oxford U	16	3	16	3
2013–14	Brighton & HA	28	3	36	4

GOODWIN, Shamir (M) 12 1

2011–12	Brighton & HA	0	0		
2013–14	Brighton & HA	0	0		
2013–14	Torquay U	12	1	12	1

GREER, Gordon (D) 369 10
H: 6 2 W: 12 05 b.Glasgow 14-12-80
Internationals: Scotland B, Full caps.

2000–01	Clyde	30	0	30	0
2000–01	Blackburn R	0	0		
2001–02	Blackburn R	0	0		
2002–03	Blackburn R	0	0		
2002–03	Stockport Co	5	1	5	1
2003–04	Kilmarnock	25	0		
2004–05	Kilmarnock	22	1		
2005–06	Kilmarnock	27	2		
2006–07	Kilmarnock	33	0	107	3
2007–08	Doncaster R	11	1		
2008–09	Doncaster R	1	0	12	1
2008–09	Swindon T	19	1		
2009–10	Swindon T	44	1	63	2
2010–11	Brighton & HA	32	0		
2011–12	Brighton & HA	42	1		
2012–13	Brighton & HA	38	1		
2013–14	Brighton & HA	40	1	152	3

HUNT, Robert (M) 0 0

2013–14	Brighton & HA	0	0		

INCE, Rohan (D) 30 0
H: 6 3 W: 12 08 b.Whitechapel 8-11-92

2010–11	Chelsea	0	0		
2011–12	Chelsea	0	0		
2012–13	Chelsea	0	0		
2012–13	Yeovil T	2	0	2	0
2013–14	Brighton & HA	28	0	28	0

KUSZCZAK, Tomasz (G) 160 0
H: 6 3 W: 13 03 b.Krosno Odrzansia 20-3-82
Internationals: Poland U16, U18, U21, Full caps.

2001–02	Hertha Berlin	0	0		
2002–03	Hertha Berlin	0	0		
2003–04	Hertha Berlin	0	0		
2004–05	WBA	3	0		
2005–06	WBA	28	0		
2006–07	WBA	0	0	31	0
2006–07	Manchester U	6	0		
2007–08	Manchester U	9	0		
2008–09	Manchester U	4	0		
2009–10	Manchester U	8	0		
2010–11	Manchester U	5	0		
2011–12	Manchester U	0	0	32	0
2011–12	Watford	13	0	13	0
2012–13	Brighton & HA	43	0		
2013–14	Brighton & HA	41	0	84	0

LOPEZ, David (M) 258 34
H: 5 11 W: 11 06 b.Logrono 10-9-82

2004–05	Osasuna	12	1		
2005–06	Osasuna	34	6		
2006–07	Osasuna	31	4	77	11
2007–08	Athletic Bilbao	30	1		
2008–09	Athletic Bilbao	29	3		
2009–10	Athletic Bilbao	17	0		

2010–11	Athletic Bilbao	28	6	
2011–12	Athletic Bilbao	12	1	116 11
2012–13	Brighton & HA	31	9	
2013–14	Brighton & HA	34	3	65 12

LUALUA, Kazenga (F)   115 11
H: 5 11 W: 12 00 b.Kinshasa 10-12-90

2007–08	Newcastle U	2	0	
2008–09	Newcastle U	3	0	
2008–09	*Doncaster R*	4	0	4 0
2009–10	Newcastle U	1	0	
2009–10	*Brighton & HA*	11	0	
2010–11	Newcastle U	2	0	
2010–11	*Brighton & HA*	11	4	
2011–12	Newcastle U	0	0	8 0
2011–12	Brighton & HA	27	1	
2012–13	Brighton & HA	22	5	
2013–14	Brighton & HA	32	1	103 11

MACKAIL-SMITH, Craig (F)   264 100
H: 6 3 W: 12 04 b.Watford 25-2-84
Internationals: England C. Scotland Full caps.

2006–07	Peterborough U	15	8	
2007–08	Peterborough U	36	12	
2008–09	Peterborough U	46	23	
2009–10	Peterborough U	43	10	
2010–11	Peterborough U	45	27	185 80
2011–12	Brighton & HA	45	9	
2012–13	Brighton & HA	29	11	
2013–14	Brighton & HA	5	0	79 20

MAKSIMENKO, Vitalijs (D)   87 3
H: 6 1 W: 11 11 b.Riga 8-12-90
Internationals: Latvia U17, U19, U21, Full caps.

2010	Skonto FC	24	0	
2011	Skonto FC	19	0	
2012	Skonto FC	32	2	75 2
2012–13	Brighton & HA	0	0	
2012–13	*Yeovil T*	3	0	3 0
2013–14	Brighton & HA	1	0	1 0
2013–14	*Kilmarnock*	8	1	8 1

MARCH, Solly (M)   23 0
b.Lewes 26-7-94
Internationals: England U21.

2012–13	Brighton & HA	0	0	
2013–14	Brighton & HA	23	0	23 0

MONAKANA, Jeffrey (M)   53 5
b.Enfield 5-11-93

2012–13	Preston NE	38	4	
2013–14	Preston NE	2	0	40 4
2013–14	*Colchester U*	9	1	9 1
2013–14	Brighton & HA			
2013–14	*Crawley T*	4	0	4 0

ORLANDI, Andrea (M)   189 14
H: 6 0 W: 12 01 b.Barcelona 3-8-84

2005–06	Alaves	0	0	
2005–06	*Barcelona*	1	0	1 0
2005–06	*Barcelona B*	32	4	
2006–07	*Barcelona B*	35	1	67 5
2007–08	Swansea C	8	0	
2008–09	Swansea C	11	1	
2009–10	Swansea C	30	1	
2010–11	Swansea C	20	0	
2011–12	Swansea C	3	1	
2012–13	Swansea C	0	0	72 3
2012–13	Brighton & HA	35	6	
2013–14	Brighton & HA	14	0	49 6

REA, Glen (D)   0 0
b. 3-9-94

2013–14	Brighton & HA	0	0	

RODRIGUEZ, David (F)   194 59
H: 5 8 W: 11 04 b.Talavera de la Reina 14-2-86
Internationals: Spain U16, U17, U18, U19.

2007–08	Salamanca	36	13	36 13
2008–09	Almeria	0	0	
2008–09	*Celta Vigo*	34	7	
2009–10	Almeria	9	1	9 1
2010–11	Celta Vigo	37	17	
2011–12	Celta Vigo	26	9	
2012–13	Celta Vigo	0	0	
2012–13	*Sporting Gijon*	37	11	37 11
2013–14	Celta Vigo	5	0	102 33
2013–14	Brighton & HA	10	1	10 1

SALTOR, Bruno (D)   265 3
H: 5 10 W: 11 10 b.Masnou (Barca) 1-10-80

2001–02	Espanyol	1	0	1 0
2001–02	*Gimnastic*	12	0	12 0
2004–05	Lleida	1	1	
2005–06	Lleida	38	0	39 1
2006–07	Almeria	23	0	
2007–08	Almeria	34	0	
2008–09	Almeria	34	0	91 0
2009–10	Valencia	26	0	
2010–11	Valencia	19	0	
2011–12	Valencia	14	0	59 0
2012–13	Brighton & HA	30	1	
2013–14	Brighton & HA	33	1	63 2

SMITH, Josh (G)   0 0

2013–14	Brighton & HA	0	0	

STEPHENS, Dale (M)   179 25
H: 5 7 W: 11 04 b.Bolton 12-6-89

2006–07	Bury	3	0	
2007–08	Bury	6	1	9 1
2008–09	Oldham Ath	0	0	
2009–10	Oldham Ath	26	2	
2009–10	*Rochdale*	6	1	6 1
2010–11	Oldham Ath	34	9	60 11
2010–11	*Southampton*	6	0	6 0
2011–12	Charlton Ath	30	5	
2012–13	Charlton Ath	28	2	
2013–14	Charlton Ath	26	3	84 10
2013–14	Brighton & HA	14	2	14 2

ULLOA, Jose (F)   227 98
H: 6 1 W: 11 10 b.General Roca 26-7-86

2004–05	San Lorenzo	0	0	
2005–06	San Lorenzo	22	3	
2006–07	San Lorenzo	6	0	25 3
2007–08	Arsenal Sarandi	6	1	6 1
2007–08	Olimpo	8	1	8 1
2008–09	Castellon	33	17	
2009–10	Castellon	32	14	
2010–11	Castellon	1	0	66 31
2010–11	Almeria	34	7	
2011–12	Almeria	28	29	
2012–13	Almeria	10	3	72 39
2012–13	Brighton & HA	17	9	
2013–14	Brighton & HA	33	14	50 23

UPSON, Matthew (D)   377 14
H: 6 1 W: 11 04 b.Eye 18-4-79
Internationals: England U21, Full caps.

1995–96	Luton T	0	0	
1996–97	Luton T	1	0	1 0
1996–97	Arsenal	0	0	
1997–98	Arsenal	5	0	
1998–99	Arsenal	5	0	
1999–2000	Arsenal	8	0	
2000–01	Arsenal	2	0	
2000–01	*Nottingham F*	1	0	1 0
2000–01	*Crystal Palace*	7	0	7 0
2001–02	Arsenal	14	0	
2002–03	Arsenal	0	0	34 0
2002–03	*Reading*	14	0	14 0
2002–03	Birmingham	14	0	
2003–04	Birmingham	30	0	
2004–05	Birmingham	36	2	
2005–06	Birmingham	24	1	
2006–07	Birmingham	9	2	113 5
2006–07	West Ham U	14	1	
2007–08	West Ham U	29	1	
2008–09	West Ham U	37	0	
2009–10	West Ham U	33	3	
2010–11	West Ham U	30	0	131 4
2011–12	Stoke C	14	1	
2012–13	Stoke C	1	1	15 2
2012–13	*Brighton & HA*	18	1	
2013–14	Brighton & HA	43	2	61 3

WALTON, Christian (G)   0 0
b. 9-11-95
Internationals: England U19.

2011–12	Plymouth Arg	0	0	
2012–13	Plymouth Arg	0	0	
2013–14	Brighton & HA	0	0	

Scholars
Barclay, Benjamin Philip; Barnett, Dylan Mark; Benham, Matthew Richard; Collar, William Guy; Colquhoun, Luke Ray; Courtney, Josh; Davis, Jason Mytton; Deen, Robin; Harris, Charles Haddon; Horncastle, Jamie Edward; Hutchinson, Desmond John; Lall, Dylan; Larusson, Ragnar Mar; Muitt, James Andrew; Pring, Connor Mark; Rowe-Hurst, Jack Michael; Tighe, Connor Jay; Wiltshire, Cameron Anthony; Wray, Oliver.

BRISTOL C (14)

AJALA, Toby (M)   14 0
H: 5 9 W: 11 11 b. 27-7-91

2012–13	AFC Wimbledon	12	0	12 0
2012–13	Bristol C	2	0	
2013–14	Bristol C	0	0	2 0
2013–14	*Cheltenham T*	0	0	

BALDOCK, Sam (F)   202 72
H: 5 7 W: 10 07 b.Buckingham 15-3-89
Internationals: England U20.

2005–06	Milton Keynes D	0	0	
2006–07	Milton Keynes D	1	0	
2007–08	Milton Keynes D	5	0	
2008–09	Milton Keynes D	40	12	
2009–10	Milton Keynes D	20	5	
2010–11	Milton Keynes D	30	12	
2011–12	Milton Keynes D	4	4	100 33
2011–12	West Ham U	23	5	
2012–13	West Ham U	0	0	23 5
2012–13	Bristol C	34	10	
2013–14	Bristol C	45	24	79 34

BATTEN, Jack (M)   0 0

2012–13	Bristol C	0	0	
2013–14	Bristol C	0	0	

BRUNDLE, Mitch (D)   7 0
H: 5 10 W: 12 04 b.London 4-12-94

2012–13	Yeovil T	0	0	
2013–14	Bristol C	0	0	
2013–14	*Cheltenham T*	7	0	7 0

BRYAN, Joe (D)   45 3
H: 5 7 W: 11 05 b.Bristol 17-9-93

2011–12	Bristol C	1	0	
2012–13	Bristol C	13	0	
2012–13	*Plymouth Arg*	10	1	10 1
2013–14	Bristol C	21	2	35 2

BURNS, Wes (F)   26 1
b.Cardiff 28-12-95

2012–13	Bristol C	6	0	
2013–14	Bristol C	20	1	26 1

CAREY, Louis (D)   582 12
H: 5 10 W: 11 00 b.Bristol 20-1-77
Internationals: Scotland U21.

1995–96	Bristol C	23	0	
1996–97	Bristol C	42	0	
1997–98	Bristol C	38	0	
1998–99	Bristol C	41	0	
1999–2000	Bristol C	22	0	
2000–01	Bristol C	46	3	
2001–02	Bristol C	35	0	
2002–03	Bristol C	24	1	
2003–04	Bristol C	41	1	
2004–05	*Coventry C*	23	0	23 0
2004–05	Bristol C	14	0	
2005–06	Bristol C	38	3	
2006–07	Bristol C	38	2	
2007–08	Bristol C	33	0	
2008–09	Bristol C	28	0	
2009–10	Bristol C	37	2	
2010–11	Bristol C	21	0	
2011–12	Bristol C	20	0	
2012–13	Bristol C	16	0	
2013–14	Bristol C	2	0	559 12

CUNNINGHAM, Greg (D)   109 2
H: 6 0 W: 11 00 b.Galway 31-1-91
Internationals: Republic of Ireland U17, U21, Full caps.

2008–09	Manchester C	0	0	
2009–10	Manchester C	2	0	
2010–11	Manchester C	0	0	
2010–11	*Leicester C*	13	0	13 0
2011–12	Manchester C	0	0	
2011–12	*Nottingham F*	27	0	27 0
2012–13	Manchester C	0	0	2 0
2012–13	Bristol C	30	1	
2013–14	Bristol C	37	1	67 2

EL-ABD, Adam (D) 314 5
H: 5 10 W: 13 05 b.Brighton 11-9-84
Internationals: Egypt Full caps.

2003–04	Brighton & HA	11	0	
2004–05	Brighton & HA	16	0	
2005–06	Brighton & HA	29	0	
2006–07	Brighton & HA	42	1	
2007–08	Brighton & HA	35	1	
2008–09	Brighton & HA	31	0	
2009–10	Brighton & HA	35	1	
2010–11	Brighton & HA	37	1	
2011–12	Brighton & HA	23	0	
2012–13	Brighton & HA	32	1	
2013–14	Brighton & HA	9	0	300 5
2013–14	Bristol C	14	0	14 0

ELLIOTT, Marvin (M) 386 28
H: 6 0 W: 12 02 b.Wandsworth 15-9-84
Internationals: Jamaica Full caps.

2001–02	Millwall	0	0	
2002–03	Millwall	1	0	
2003–04	Millwall	21	0	
2004–05	Millwall	41	1	
2005–06	Millwall	39	2	
2006–07	Millwall	42	0	144 3
2007–08	Bristol C	45	5	
2008–09	Bristol C	28	3	
2009–10	Bristol C	39	1	
2010–11	Bristol C	46	8	
2011–12	Bristol C	28	2	
2012–13	Bristol C	32	2	
2013–14	Bristol C	24	4	242 25

EMMANUEL-THOMAS, Jay (M) 157 31
H: 5 9 W: 11 05 b.Forest Gate 27-12-90
Internationals: England U17, U19.

2008–09	Arsenal	0	0	
2009–10	Arsenal	0	0	
2009–10	*Blackpool*	11	1	11 1
2009–10	*Doncaster R*	14	5	14 5
2010–11	Arsenal	1	0	1 0
2010–11	*Cardiff C*	14	2	14 2
2011–12	Ipswich T	42	6	
2012–13	Ipswich T	29	2	71 8
2013–14	Bristol C	46	15	46 15

FIELDING, Frank (G) 181 0
H: 5 11 W: 12 00 b.Blackburn 4-4-88
Internationals: England U19, U21.

2006–07	Blackburn R	0	0	
2007–08	Blackburn R	0	0	
2007–08	*Wycombe W*	36	0	36 0
2008–09	Blackburn R	0	0	
2008–09	*Northampton T*	12	0	12 0
2008–09	*Rochdale*	23	0	
2009–10	Blackburn R	0	0	
2009–10	*Rochdale*	18	0	41 0
2010–11	Blackburn R	0	0	
2010–11	Derby Co	16	0	
2011–12	Derby Co	44	0	
2012–13	Derby Co	16	0	76 0
2013–14	Bristol C	16	0	16 0

FLINT, Aiden (D) 98 7
H: 6 2 W: 12 00 b.Pinxton 11-7-89
Internationals: England C.

2010–11	Swindon T	3	0	
2011–12	Swindon T	32	2	
2012–13	Swindon T	29	2	64 4
2013–14	Bristol C	34	3	34 3

FONTAINE, Liam (D) 293 6
H: 5 11 W: 11 09 b.Beckenham 7-1-86
Internationals: England U16, U17, U20.

2003–04	Fulham	0	0	
2004–05	Fulham	1	0	
2004–05	*Yeovil T*	15	0	
2005–06	Fulham	0	0	1 0
2005–06	*Yeovil T*	10	0	
2005–06	*Bristol C*	15	0	
2006–07	Bristol C	30	0	
2007–08	Bristol C	38	1	
2008–09	Bristol C	42	2	
2009–10	Bristol C	36	2	
2010–11	Bristol C	31	0	
2011–12	Bristol C	26	0	
2012–13	Bristol C	41	1	
2013–14	Bristol C	3	0	262 6
2013–14	*Yeovil T*	5	0	30 0

HALL, Lewis (M) 0 0
2012–13	Bristol C	0	0	
2013–14	Bristol C	0	0	

KELLY, Liam (M) 121 15
H: 6 2 W: 13 11 b.Milton Keynes 10-2-90
Internationals: Scotland U18, U21, Full caps.

2009–10	Kilmarnock	15	1	
2010–11	Kilmarnock	32	7	
2011–12	Kilmarnock	34	1	
2012–13	Kilmarnock	19	6	100 15
2012–13	Bristol C	19	0	
2013–14	Bristol C	2	0	21 0

LEMONHEIGH-EVANS, Connor (F) 0 0
b. 24-1-97
Internationals: Wales U17.

2013–14	Bristol C	0	0	

MAFUTA, Gus (M) 0 0
H: 5 10 W: 11 01 b.Clevedon 28-8-94

2013–14	Bristol C	0	0	

MOLONEY, Brendan (M) 121 2
H: 6 1 W: 11 12 b.Killarney 18-1-89
Internationals: Republic of Ireland U21.

2005–06	Nottingham F	0	0	
2006–07	Nottingham F	1	0	
2007–08	Nottingham F	2	0	
2007–08	*Chesterfield*	9	1	9 1
2008–09	Nottingham F	12	0	
2009–10	Nottingham F	0	0	
2009–10	*Notts Co*	18	1	18 1
2009–10	*Scunthorpe U*	3	0	3 0
2010–11	Nottingham F	6	0	
2011–12	Nottingham F	8	0	
2012–13	Nottingham F	13	0	42 0
2012–13	Bristol C	17	0	
2013–14	Bristol C	32	0	49 0

MONELLE, Liam (F) 0 0
H: 5 10 W: 11 04

2013–14	Bristol C	0	0	

MORRELL, Joe (M) 0 0
H: 5 3 W: 11 04 b.Ipswich 3-1-97
Internationals: Wales U17.

2013–14	Bristol C	0	0	

OSBORNE, Karleigh (D) 202 8
H: 6 2 W: 12 04 b.Southall 19-3-88

2004–05	Brentford	1	0	
2005–06	Brentford	1	0	
2006–07	Brentford	21	0	
2007–08	Brentford	29	1	
2008–09	Brentford	23	4	
2009–10	Brentford	19	0	
2010–11	Brentford	42	1	
2011–12	Brentford	25	0	161 6
2012–13	Millwall	13	1	
2013–14	Millwall	1	0	14 1
2013–14	Bristol C	27	1	27 1

PACK, Marlon (M) 193 15
H: 6 2 W: 11 09 b.Portsmouth 25-3-91

2008–09	Portsmouth	0	0	
2009–10	Portsmouth	0	0	
2009–10	*Wycombe W*	8	0	8 0
2009–10	*Dagenham & R*	17	1	17 1
2010–11	Portsmouth	0	0	1 0
2010–11	*Cheltenham T*	38	2	
2011–12	*Cheltenham T*	43	5	
2012–13	*Cheltenham T*	43	7	
2013–14	*Cheltenham T*	0	0	124 14
2013–14	Bristol C	43	0	43 0

PARISH, Elliot (G) 37 0
H: 6 2 W: 13 00 b.Towcester 20-5-90
Internationals: England U20.

2008–09	Aston Villa	0	0	
2009–10	Aston Villa	0	0	
2010–11	Aston Villa	0	0	
2010–11	*Lincoln C*	9	0	9 0
2011–12	Aston Villa	0	0	
2011–12	*Cardiff C*	0	0	
2012–13	*Wycombe W*	2	0	2 0
2012–13	*Cardiff C*	0	0	
2013–14	Bristol C	19	0	19 0
2013–14	*Newport Co*	7	0	7 0

PEARSON, Stephen (M) 322 28
H: 6 0 W: 11 01 b.Lanark 2-10-82
Internationals: Scotland U21, B, Full caps.

2000–01	Motherwell	6	0	

2001–02	Motherwell	27	2	
2002–03	Motherwell	29	6	
2003–04	Motherwell	18	4	80 12
2003–04	Celtic	17	3	
2004–05	Celtic	8	0	
2005–06	Celtic	18	2	
2006–07	Celtic	13	1	56 6
2006–07	Derby Co	9	0	
2007–08	Derby Co	24	0	
2007–08	*Stoke C*	4	0	4 0
2008–09	Derby Co	12	1	
2009–10	Derby Co	37	1	
2010–11	Derby Co	30	1	
2011–12	Derby Co	0	0	112 3
2011–12	Bristol C	28	3	
2012–13	Bristol C	36	3	
2013–14	Bristol C	6	1	70 7

REID, Bobby (M) 37 2
H: 5 7 W: 10 10 b.Bristol 1-3-93

2010–11	Bristol C	1	0	
2011–12	Bristol C	0	0	
2011–12	*Cheltenham T*	1	0	1 0
2012–13	Bristol C	4	1	
2012–13	*Oldham Ath*	7	0	7 0
2013–14	Bristol C	24	1	29 2

RICHARDS, Dave (G) 0 0
2013–14	Cardiff C	0	0	
2013–14	Bristol C	0	0	

WAGSTAFF, Scott (M) 166 22
H: 5 10 W: 10 03 b.Maidstone 31-3-90

2007–08	Charlton Ath	2	0	
2008–09	Charlton Ath	2	0	
2008–09	*Bournemouth*	5	0	5 0
2009–10	Charlton Ath	30	4	
2010–11	Charlton Ath	40	8	
2011–12	Charlton Ath	34	4	
2012–13	Charlton Ath	9	1	117 17
2012–13	*Leyton Orient*	7	0	7 0
2013–14	Bristol C	37	5	37 5

WILLIAMS, Derrick (D) 44 1
H: 5 11 W: 11 11 b.Waterford 17-1-93
Internationals: Republic of Ireland U19, U21.

2009–10	Aston Villa	0	0	
2010–11	Aston Villa	0	0	
2011–12	Aston Villa	0	0	
2012–13	Aston Villa	1	0	1 0
2013–14	Bristol C	43	1	43 1

WYNTER, Jordan (M) 3 0
2012–13	Arsenal	0	0	
2013–14	Bristol C	3	0	3 0

Scholars
Bishop, Marley Lyndon; Cable, Conor James;
Fry, Thomas Owain; Horgan, Jamie
Alexander; Last, Benjamin Frederick; Long,
Matthew Terence; Mattis, Matthew David;
Mitchell, Pierce Jonty; Nelson, Elliott Joshua;
Paice, Harry; Pollard, Tyson John; Vyner,
Zachary George Onyego; Withey, Ben
Stephen; Wollacott, Joseph Luke.

BRISTOL R (15)

BROGHAMMER, Fabian (D) 40 3
H: 5 10 W: 11 00
Internationals: Germany Youth.

2012–13	Bristol R	36	3	
2013–14	Bristol R	4	0	40 3

BROWN, Lee (D) 123 12
H: 6 0 W: 12 06 b.Bromley 10-8-90

2008–09	QPR	0	0	
2009–10	QPR	1	0	
2010–11	QPR	0	0	1 0
2011–12	Bristol R	42	7	
2012–13	Bristol R	39	3	
2013–14	Bristol R	41	2	122 12

BRUNT, Ryan (F) 62 9
H: 6 1 W: 11 11 b.Birmingham 26-5-93

2011–12	Stoke C	0	0	
2011–12	*Tranmere R*	15	1	15 1
2012–13	Stoke C	0	0	
2012–13	*Leyton Orient*	18	3	18 3
2012–13	Bristol R	18	5	
2013–14	Bristol R	11	0	29 5

CLARKE, Ollie (M)   38 2
H: 5 11 W: 11 11 b.Bristol 29-6-92

Season	Club				
2009–10	Bristol R	0	0		
2010–11	Bristol R	1	0		
2011–12	Bristol R	0	0		
2012–13	Bristol R	5	0		
2013–14	Bristol R	32	2	38	2

CLARKSON, David (F)   349 73
H: 5 10 W: 10 03 b.Airdrie 10-9-85
Internationals: Scotland U21, B, Full caps.

2002–03	Motherwell	19	3		
2003–04	Motherwell	38	12		
2004–05	Motherwell	35	3		
2005–06	Motherwell	32	4		
2006–07	Motherwell	29	2		
2007–08	Motherwell	35	12		
2008–09	Motherwell	33	13	221	49
2009–10	Bristol C	26	4		
2010–11	Bristol C	34	7		
2011–12	Bristol C	4	0	64	11
2011–12	*Brentford*	4	1	4	1
2012–13	Bristol R	26	6		
2013–14	Bristol R	34	6	60	12

CLUCAS, Seanan (M)   39 0
H: 5 10 W: 12 00 b.Dungannon 8-11-92
Internationals: Northern Ireland U17, U19, U21.

2011–12	Preston NE	1	0	1	0
2011–12	*Burton Alb*	2	0	2	0
2012–13	Bristol R	19	0		
2013–14	Bristol R	17	0	36	0

GILLESPIE, Steven (F)   235 60
H: 5 9 W: 11 02 b.Liverpool 4-6-84

2004–05	Bristol C	8	0		
2004–05	*Cheltenham T*	12	5		
2005–06	Bristol C	4	1	12	1
2005–06	Cheltenham T	14	5		
2006–07	Cheltenham T	23	5		
2007–08	Cheltenham T	37	14		
2008–09	Colchester U	17	4		
2009–10	Colchester U	30	1		
2010–11	Colchester U	18	9		
2011–12	Colchester U	33	11	98	25
2012–13	Fleetwood T	22	4		
2013–14	Fleetwood T	0	0	22	4
2013–14	*Cheltenham T*	4	0	90	29
2013–14	Bristol R	13	1	13	1

HARDING, Mitch (F)   17 0
b.Weston-Super-Mare 27-1-94

2011–12	Bristol R	1	0		
2012–13	Bristol R	5	0		
2013–14	Bristol R	11	0	17	0

HARRISON, Ellis (F)   39 4
H: 5 11 W: 12 06 b.Newport 1-2-94
Internationals: Wales U21.

2010–11	Bristol R	1	0		
2011–12	Bristol R	0	0		
2012–13	Bristol R	13	3		
2013–14	Bristol R	25	1	39	4

HARROLD, Matt (F)   327 65
H: 6 1 W: 11 10 b.Leyton 25-7-84

2003–04	Brentford	13	2		
2004–05	Brentford	19	0	32	2
2004–05	*Grimsby T*	6	2	6	2
2005–06	Yeovil T	42	9		
2006–07	Yeovil T	5	0	47	9
2006–07	Southend U	36	3		
2007–08	Southend U	16	0		
2008–09	Southend U	0	0	52	3
2008–09	Wycombe W	37	9		
2009–10	Wycombe W	36	8	73	17
2010–11	Shrewsbury T	41	8	41	8
2011–12	Bristol R	40	16		
2012–13	Bristol R	6	2		
2013–14	Bristol R	30	6	76	24

HUNTER, Shaquille (M)   3 0
H: 5 10 W: 11 03 b.Bristol 29-8-95

2012–13	Bristol R	0	0		
2013–14	Bristol R	3	0	3	0

KEARY, Pat (D)   1 0
b. 22-11-92

2013–14	Bristol R	1	0	1	0

LOCKYER, Tom (D)   45 1
b.Bristol 30-12-94

2012–13	Bristol R	4	0		
2013–14	Bristol R	41	1	45	1

LUCAS, Jamie (F)   1 0

2013–14	Bristol R	1	0	1	0

McCHRYSTAL, Mark (D)   174 3
H: 6 1 W: 13 07 b.Derry 26-6-84
Internationals: Northern Ireland U18, U21.

2001–02	Wolverhampton W	0	0		
2003	Derry C	5	0		
2003	*Institute*	6	0	6	0
2004	Derry C	9	1		
2005	Derry C	9	0		
2006–07	Partick Thistle	15	1	15	1
2007	Derry C	3	0		
2008	Derry C	11	0		
2009	Derry C	13	0	50	1
2009–10	Lisburn Distillery	3	0	3	0
2010–11	Tranmere R	23	0		
2011–12	Tranmere R	18	1		
2012–13	Tranmere R	0	0	41	1
2012–13	*Scunthorpe U*	3	0	3	0
2012–13	Bristol R	21	0		
2013–14	Bristol R	35	0	56	0

MILDENHALL, Steve (G)   401 1
H: 6 4 W: 14 01 b.Swindon 13-5-78

1996–97	Swindon T	1	0		
1997–98	Swindon T	4	0		
1998–99	Swindon T	0	0		
1999–2000	Swindon T	5	0		
2000–01	Swindon T	23	0	33	0
2001–02	Notts Co	26	0		
2002–03	Notts Co	21	0		
2003–04	Notts Co	28	0		
2004–05	Notts Co	1	0	76	0
2004–05	Oldham Ath	6	0	6	0
2005–06	Grimsby T	46	1	46	1
2006–07	Yeovil T	46	0		
2007–08	Yeovil T	29	0	75	0
2008–09	Southend U	34	0		
2009–10	Southend U	44	0		
2010–11	Southend U	0	0	78	0
2010–11	Millwall	0	0		
2011–12	Millwall	10	0		
2012–13	Millwall	0	0	10	0
2012–13	*Scunthorpe U*	9	0	9	0
2012–13	Bristol R	22	0		
2013–14	Bristol R	46	0	68	0

NORBURN, Oliver (M)   56 3
b.Leicester 26-10-92

2011–12	Leicester C	0	0		
2011–12	*Bristol R*	5	0		
2012–13	Bristol R	35	3		
2013–14	Bristol R	16	0	56	3

O'TOOLE, John (M)   197 29
H: 6 2 W: 13 07 b.Harrow 30-9-88
Internationals: Republic of Ireland U21.

2007–08	Watford	35	3		
2008–09	Watford	22	7		
2008–09	*Sheffield U*	9	1	9	1
2009–10	Watford	0	0	57	10
2009–10	Colchester U	31	2		
2010–11	Colchester U	11	0		
2011–12	Colchester U	15	0		
2012–13	Colchester U	15	0	72	2
2012–13	*Bristol R*	18	3		
2013–14	Bristol R	41	13	59	16

PARKES, Tom (D)   130 3
H: 6 3 W: 12 05 b.Sutton-in-Ashfield 15-1-92
Internationals: England U17.

2008–09	Leicester C	0	0		
2009–10	Leicester C	0	0		
2009–10	*Burton Alb*	22	1		
2010–11	Leicester C	0	0		
2010–11	*Yeovil T*	1	0	1	0
2010–11	*Burton Alb*	5	0		
2011–12	Leicester C	0	0		
2011–12	*Burton Alb*	4	0	31	1
2011–12	*Bristol R*	14	0		
2012–13	Leicester C	0	0		
2012–13	Bristol R	40	1		
2013–14	Bristol R	44	1	98	2

RICHARDS, Eliot (M)   129 21
H: 5 9 W: 11 09 b.New Tredegar 1-9-91
Internationals: Wales U19, U21.

2009–10	Bristol R	5	0		
2010–11	Bristol R	13	1		
2011–12	Bristol R	32	7		
2012–13	Bristol R	40	6		
2013–14	Bristol R	22	2	112	16
2013–14	*Exeter C*	17	5	17	5

SANTOS, Alefe (M)   24 1
b. 28-1-95

2012–13	Bristol R	1	0		
2013	Ponte Preta	0	0		
2013–14	Bristol R	23	1	24	1

SMITH, Michael (D)   276 17
H: 5 11 W: 11 02 b.Ballyclare 4-9-88
Internationals: Northern Ireland U23.

2005–06	Ballyclare Com	1	0		
2006–07	Ballyclare Com	25	2		
2007–08	Ballyclare Com	39	1		
2008–09	Ballyclare Com	27	7	92	10
2008–09	Ballymena U	12	1		
2009–10	Ballymena U	37	2		
2010–11	Ballymena U	34	3	83	6
2011–12	Bristol R	20	0		
2012–13	Bristol R	38	1		
2013–14	Bristol R	43	0	101	1

WOODARDS, Danny (D)   220 5
H: 5 11 W: 11 01 b.Forest Gate 7-10-83
Internationals: England C.

2003–04	Chelsea	0	0		
2004–05	Chelsea	0	0		
2005–06	Chelsea	0	0		
From Exeter C.					
2006–07	Crewe Alex	11	0		
2007–08	Crewe Alex	36	0		
2008–09	Crewe Alex	37	0	84	0
2009–10	Milton Keynes D	29	0		
2010–11	Milton Keynes D	37	1	66	1
2011–12	Bristol R	39	1		
2012–13	Bristol R	22	2		
2013–14	Bristol R	9	1	70	4

Scholars
Anderson, Treyvond Theophilus; Broom, Ryan James; Bryan, Aaron Victor; Davis-Wilson, Laurent; Douglas, Chad Castrus; Ezewele, Louis Osezenoria; Gonzalez-Barra, Carlos; Greenslade, Daniel; Malpas, Jay Robert Alexander; Palmer, Mitchell; Preston, Kieran; Thomas, Dominic William; Trueman, Harrison William; Ward-Baptiste, Aaron James; Wilson, Donovan Junior.

BURNLEY (16)

ANDERSON, Thomas (M)   0 0

2012–13	Burnley	0	0		
2013–14	Burnley	0	0		

ARFIELD, Scott (M)   249 28
H: 5 10 W: 10 01 b.Livingston 1-11-88
Internationals: Scotland U19, U21, B.

2007–08	Falkirk	35	3		
2008–09	Falkirk	37	7		
2009–10	Falkirk	36	3	108	13
2010–11	Huddersfield T	40	4		
2011–12	Huddersfield T	35	2		
2012–13	Huddersfield T	21	1	96	7
2013–14	Burnley	45	8	45	8

BAIRD, Chris (D)   229 7
H: 5 10 W: 11 11 b.Ballymoney 25-2-82
Internationals: Northern Ireland U18, U21, Full caps.

2000–01	Southampton	0	0		
2001–02	Southampton	0	0		
2002–03	Southampton	3	0		
2003–04	Southampton	4	0		
2003–04	*Walsall*	10	0	10	0
2003–04	*Watford*	8	0	8	0
2004–05	Southampton	0	0		
2005–06	Southampton	17	0		
2006–07	Southampton	44	3	68	3
2007–08	Fulham	18	0		
2008–09	Fulham	10	0		
2009–10	Fulham	32	0		
2010–11	Fulham	29	2		

2011–12	Fulham	19	0		
2012–13	Fulham	19	2	127	4
2013–14	Reading	9	0	9	0
2013–14	Burnley	7	0	7	0

BARNES, Ashley (F)   198 51
H: 6 0 W: 12 00 b.Bath 30-10-89
Internationals: Austria U20.

2006–07	Plymouth Arg	0	0		
2007–08	Plymouth Arg	0	0		
2008–09	Plymouth Arg	15	1		
2009–10	Plymouth Arg	7	1	22	2
2009–10	Torquay U	6	0	6	0
2009–10	Brighton & HA	8	4		
2010–11	Brighton & HA	42	18		
2011–12	Brighton & HA	43	11		
2012–13	Brighton & HA	34	8		
2013–14	Brighton & HA	22	5	149	46
2013–14	Burnley	21	3	21	3

BARTLEY, Marvyn (M)   203 8
H: 6 1 W: 12 04 b.Reading 4-7-86

2007–08	Bournemouth	20	1		
2008–09	Bournemouth	33	1		
2009–10	Bournemouth	34	0		
2010–11	Bournemouth	26	1	113	3
2010–11	Burnley	5	0		
2011–12	Burnley	39	3		
2012–13	Burnley	21	0		
2013–14	Burnley	0	0	65	3
2013–14	Leyton Orient	25	2	25	2

CISAK, Aleksander (G)   71 0
H: 6 3 W: 14 11 b.Krakow 19-5-89
Internationals: Australia U20.

2006–07	Leicester C	0	0		
2007–08	Leicester C	0	0		
2008–09	Leicester C	0	0		
2009–10	Leicester C	0	0		
2010–11	Accrington S	21	0	21	0
2011–12	Oldham Ath	38	0		
2012–13	Oldham Ath	10	0	48	0
2012–13	Portsmouth	1	0	1	0
2013–14	Burnley	1	0	1	0

DUFF, Michael (D)   498 19
H: 6 1 W: 11 08 b.Belfast 11-1-78
Internationals: Northern Ireland B, Full caps.

1999–2000	Cheltenham T	31	2		
2000–01	Cheltenham T	39	5		
2001–02	Cheltenham T	45	3		
2002–03	Cheltenham T	44	2		
2003–04	Cheltenham T	42	0	201	12
2004–05	Burnley	42	0		
2005–06	Burnley	41	0		
2006–07	Burnley	44	2		
2007–08	Burnley	8	1		
2008–09	Burnley	27	1		
2009–10	Burnley	11	0		
2010–11	Burnley	28	1		
2011–12	Burnley	31	0		
2012–13	Burnley	24	1		
2013–14	Burnley	41	1	297	7

DUMMIGAN, Cameron (D)   0 0
Internationals: Northern Ireland U17, U19.

2013–14	Burnley	0	0		

EDGAR, David (D)   123 7
H: 6 2 W: 12 13 b.Ontario 19-5-87
Internationals: Canada U17, U20, Full caps.

2005–06	Newcastle U	0	0		
2006–07	Newcastle U	3	1		
2007–08	Newcastle U	5	0		
2008–09	Newcastle U	11	1		
2009–10	Newcastle U	0	0	19	2
2009–10	Burnley	4	0		
2009–10	Swansea C	5	1	5	1
2010–11	Burnley	7	0		
2011–12	Burnley	44	2		
2012–13	Burnley	27	2		
2013–14	Burnley	17	0	99	4

FROST, Jamie (F)   0 0
b. 6-10-96

2013–14	Burnley	0	0		

GALLAGHER, Luke (M)   0 0
b. 29-7-94
Internationals: Republic of Ireland U17, U19.

2013–14	Burnley	0	0		

GILCHRIST, Jason (F)   0 0
b. 17-12-94

2013–14	Burnley	0	0		

HEATON, Tom (G)   181 0
H: 6 1 W: 13 12 b.Chester 15-4-86
Internationals: England 16, U17, U18, U19, U21.

2003–04	Manchester U	0	0		
2004–05	Manchester U	0	0		
2005–06	Manchester U	0	0		
2005–06	Swindon T	14	0	14	0
2006–07	Manchester U	0	0		
2007–08	Manchester U	0	0		
2008–09	Manchester U	0	0		
2008–09	Cardiff C	21	0		
2009–10	Manchester U	0	0		
2009–10	Rochdale	12	0	12	0
2009–10	Wycombe W	16	0	16	0
2010–11	Cardiff C	27	0		
2011–12	Cardiff C	2	0	50	0
2012–13	Bristol C	43	0	43	0
2013–14	Burnley	46	0	46	0

HEWITT, Steven (M)   2 0
H: 5 7 W: 11 00 b.Manchester 5-12-93

2011–12	Burnley	1	0		
2012–13	Burnley	1	0		
2013–14	Burnley	1	0	2	0

HOWIESON, Cameron (M)   2 0
H: 5 9 W: 11 00 b.Dunedin 22-12-94
Internationals: New Zealand U17, U20, U23, Full caps.

2011–12	Burnley	2	0		
2012–13	Doncaster R	0	0		
2012–13	Burnley	0	0		
2013–14	Burnley	0	0	2	0

INGS, Danny (F)   114 34
H: 5 10 W: 11 07 b.Winchester 16-3-92
Internationals: England U21.

2009–10	Bournemouth	0	0		
2010–11	Bournemouth	26	7		
2011–12	Bournemouth	1	0	27	7
2011–12	Burnley	15	3		
2012–13	Burnley	32	3		
2013–14	Burnley	40	21	87	27

JONES, David (M)   236 25
H: 5 11 W: 10 10 b.Southport 4-11-84
Internationals: England U21.

2003–04	Manchester U	0	0		
2004–05	Manchester U	0	0		
2005–06	Manchester U	0	0		
2005–06	Preston NE	24	3	24	3
2005–06	NEC Nijmegen	17	6	17	6
2006–07	Manchester U	0	0		
2006–07	Derby Co	28	6		
2007–08	Derby Co	14	1	42	7
2008–09	Wolverhampton W	34	4		
2009–10	Wolverhampton W	20	1		
2010–11	Wolverhampton W	12	1	66	6
2011–12	Wigan Ath	16	0		
2012–13	Wigan Ath	13	0	29	0
2012–13	Blackburn R	12	2	12	2
2013–14	Burnley	46	1	46	1

LAFFERTY, Danny (D)   99 8
H: 6 0 W: 12 08 b.Derry 1-4-89
Internationals: Northern Ireland U17, U19, U21, B, Full caps.

2009–10	Celtic	0	0		
2009–10	Ayr U	14	1	14	1
2010	Derry C	12	0		
2011	Derry C	34	7	46	7
2011–12	Burnley	5	0		
2012–13	Burnley	24	0		
2013–14	Burnley	10	0	39	0

LONG, Kevin (D)   97 4
H: 6 3 W: 13 01 b.Cork 18-8-90

2009	Cork C	16	0	16	0
2009–10	Burnley	0	0		
2010–11	Burnley	0	0		
2010–11	Accrington S	15	0		
2011–12	Burnley	0	0		
2011–12	Accrington S	24	4	39	4
2011–12	Rochdale	16	0	16	0
2012–13	Burnley	14	0		
2012–13	Portsmouth	5	0	5	0
2013–14	Burnley	7	0	21	0

MARNEY, Dean (M)   309 19
H: 5 10 W: 11 09 b.Barking 31-1-84
Internationals: England U21.

2002–03	Tottenham H	0	0		
2002–03	Swindon T	9	0	9	0
2003–04	Tottenham H	3	0		
2003–04	QPR	2	0	2	0
2004–05	Tottenham H	5	2		
2004–05	Gillingham	3	0	3	0
2005–06	Tottenham H	0	0	8	2
2005–06	Norwich C	13	0	13	0
2006–07	Hull C	37	2		
2007–08	Hull C	41	6		
2008–09	Hull C	31	0		
2009–10	Hull C	16	1	125	9
2009–10	Burnley	0	0		
2010–11	Burnley	36	3		
2011–12	Burnley	37	0		
2012–13	Burnley	38	2		
2013–14	Burnley	38	3	149	8

MEE, Ben (D)   103 1
H: 5 11 W: 11 09 b.Sale 21-9-89
Internationals: England U19, U20, U21.

2007–08	Manchester C	0	0		
2008–09	Manchester C	0	0		
2009–10	Manchester C	0	0		
2010–11	Manchester C	0	0		
2010–11	Leicester C	15	0	15	0
2011–12	Manchester C	0	0		
2011–12	Burnley	31	0		
2012–13	Burnley	19	1		
2013–14	Burnley	38	0	88	1

MILLS, Joseph (D)   107 2
H: 5 9 W: 11 00 b.Swindon 30-10-89
Internationals: England U17, U18.

2006–07	Southampton	0	0		
2007–08	Southampton	0	0		
2008–09	Southampton	8	0		
2008–09	Scunthorpe U	14	0	14	0
2009–10	Southampton	16	0		
2010–11	Southampton	2	0		
2010–11	Doncaster R	18	2	18	2
2011–12	Southampton	0	0	26	0
2011–12	Reading	15	0		
2012–13	Reading	0	0	15	0
2012–13	Burnley	10	0		
2013–14	Burnley	0	0	10	0
2013–14	Oldham Ath	11	0	11	0
2013–14	Shrewsbury T	13	0	13	0

NOBLE, Ryan (F)   28 3
H: 6 0 W: 11 00 b.Sunderland 6-11-91
Internationals: England U17, U19.

2009–10	Sunderland	0	0		
2009–10	Watford	0	0		
2010–11	Sunderland	3	0		
2010–11	Derby Co	1	0		
2011–12	Sunderland	2	0		
2011–12	Derby Co	2	0	3	0
2011–12	Hartlepool U	9	2		
2012–13	Sunderland	0	0	5	0
2012–13	Hartlepool U	10	1	19	3
2013–14	Burnley	1	0	1	0

O'NEILL, Luke (D)   22 1
H: 6 0 W: 11 04 b.Slough 20-8-91
Internationals: England U17.

2009–10	Leicester C	1	0	1	0
2009–10	Tranmere R	4	0	4	0

From Kettering T (loan), Mansfield T

2012–13	Burnley	1	0		
2013–14	Burnley	0	0	1	0
2013–14	York C	15	1	15	1
2013–14	Southend U	1	0	1	0

SHACKELL, Jason (D)   346 12
H: 6 4 W: 13 06 b.Stevenage 27-9-83

2002–03	Norwich C	2	0		
2003–04	Norwich C	6	0		
2004–05	Norwich C	11	0		
2005–06	Norwich C	17	0		
2006–07	Norwich C	43	3		
2007–08	Norwich C	39	0		
2008–09	Norwich C	15	0	133	3
2008–09	Wolverhampton W	12	0		
2009–10	Wolverhampton W	0	0	12	0
2009–10	Doncaster R	21	1	21	1
2010–11	Barnsley	44	3		
2011–12	Barnsley	0	0	44	3
2011–12	Derby Co	46	1	46	1

Season	Club	Apps	Gls		
2012–13	Burnley	44	2		
2013–14	Burnley	46	2	90	4

STANISLAS, Junior (M) 141 14
H: 6 0　W: 12 00　b.Kidbrooke 26-11-89
Internationals: England U20, U21.

Season	Club	Apps	Gls		
2007–08	West Ham U	0	0		
2008–09	West Ham U	9	2		
2008–09	*Southend U*	6	1	6	1
2009–10	West Ham U	26	3		
2010–11	West Ham U	6	1		
2011–12	West Ham U	1	0	42	6
2011–12	Burnley	31	0		
2012–13	Burnley	35	5		
2013–14	Burnley	27	2	93	7

STOCK, Brian (M) 377 34
H: 5 11　W: 11 02　b.Winchester 24-12-81
Internationals: Wales U21, Full caps.

Season	Club	Apps	Gls		
1999–2000	Bournemouth	5	0		
2000–01	Bournemouth	1	0		
2001–02	Bournemouth	26	2		
2002–03	Bournemouth	27	2		
2003–04	Bournemouth	19	3		
2004–05	Bournemouth	41	6		
2005–06	Bournemouth	26	3	145	16
2005–06	Preston NE	6	1		
2006–07	Preston NE	2	0	8	1
2006–07	Doncaster R	36	3		
2007–08	Doncaster R	40	5		
2008–09	Doncaster R	36	6		
2009–10	Doncaster R	15	0		
2010–11	Doncaster R	37	2		
2011–12	Doncaster R	26	1		
2012–13	Doncaster R	0	0	190	17
2012–13	Burnley	25	0		
2013–14	Burnley	9	0		

TREACY, Keith (M) 160 16
H: 6 0　W: 13 02　b.Dublin 13-9-88
Internationals: Republic of Ireland U21, Full caps.

Season	Club	Apps	Gls		
2005–06	Blackburn R	0	0		
2006–07	Blackburn R	0	0		
2006–07	*Stockport Co*	4	0	4	0
2007–08	Blackburn R	0	0		
2008–09	Blackburn R	12	0		
2009–10	Blackburn R	0	0	12	0
2009–10	*Sheffield U*	16	1	16	1
2009–10	Preston NE	17	2		
2010–11	Preston NE	38	7	55	9
2011–12	Burnley	24	2		
2011–12	*Sheffield W*	7	1	7	1
2012–13	Burnley	15	1		
2013–14	Burnley	27	2	66	5

TRIPPIER, Keiran (D) 174 6
H: 5 10　W: 11 00　b.Bury 19-9-90
Internationals: England U18, U19, U20, U21.

Season	Club	Apps	Gls		
2007–08	Manchester C	0	0		
2008–09	Manchester C	0	0		
2009–10	Manchester C	0	0		
2009–10	*Barnsley*	3	0		
2010–11	Manchester C	0	0		
2010–11	*Barnsley*	39	2	42	2
2011–12	Manchester C	0	0		
2011–12	Burnley	46	3		
2012–13	Burnley	45	0		
2013–14	Burnley	41	1	132	4

VOKES, Sam (F) 228 54
H: 6 1　W: 13 10　b.Lymington 21-10-89
Internationals: Wales U21, Full caps.

Season	Club	Apps	Gls		
2006–07	Bournemouth	13	4		
2007–08	Bournemouth	41	12	54	16
2008–09	Wolverhampton W	36	6		
2009–10	Wolverhampton W	5	0		
2009–10	*Leeds U*	8	1	8	1
2010–11	Wolverhampton W	2	0		
2010–11	*Bristol C*	1	0	1	0
2010–11	*Sheffield U*	6	1	6	1
2010–11	*Norwich C*	4	1	4	1
2011–12	Wolverhampton W	4	0		
2011–12	*Burnley*	9	2		
2011–12	*Brighton & HA*	14	3	14	3
2012–13	Wolverhampton W	0	0	47	6
2012–13	Burnley	46	4		
2013–14	Burnley	39	20	94	26

WALLACE, Ross (M) 304 32
H: 5 6　W: 9 12　b.Dundee 23-5-85
Internationals: Scotland U18, U19, U21, B, Full caps.

Season	Club	Apps	Gls		
2001–02	Celtic	0	0		
2002–03	Celtic	0	0		
2003–04	Celtic	8	1		
2004–05	Celtic	16	0		
2005–06	Celtic	11	0		
2006–07	Celtic	2	0	37	1
2006–07	Sunderland	32	6		
2007–08	Sunderland	21	2		
2008–09	Sunderland	0	0	53	8
2008–09	Preston NE	39	5		
2009–10	Preston NE	41	7	80	12
2010–11	Burnley	40	3		
2011–12	Burnley	44	5		
2012–13	Burnley	36	3		
2013–14	Burnley	14	0	134	11

Scholars
Azam, Muhammed Waqas; Bianga, Andreas Ntuntumuna; Daly, Luke Thomas; Galvin, Evan; Hill, Christian Stephen; Holt, Charlie George; Jackson, Bradley Allen; Jakovleks, Callum David; Lowe, Nathan Patrick; Ly, Kevin Lap Chi; Massanka, Ntumba; Mitchell, Conor; Nuttall, Lewis Lee; Richardson, Callum John; Whitmore, Alexander James; Wilson, Brandon James.

BURTON ALB (17)

ALEXANDER, Gary (F) 560 156
H: 6 0　W: 13 04　b.Lambeth 15-8-79

Season	Club	Apps	Gls		
1998–99	West Ham U	0	0		
1999–2000	West Ham U	0	0		
1999–2000	*Exeter C*	37	16	37	16
2000–01	Swindon T	37	7	37	7
2001–02	Hull C	43	17		
2002–03	Hull C	25	6	68	23
2002–03	Leyton Orient	17	2		
2003–04	Leyton Orient	44	15		
2004–05	Leyton Orient	28	9		
2005–06	Leyton Orient	44	14		
2006–07	Leyton Orient	44	12	179	52
2007–08	Millwall	36	7		
2008–09	Millwall	35	11		
2009–10	Millwall	15	1	86	19
2010–11	Brentford	38	9		
2011–12	Brentford	24	12	62	21
2011–12	*Crawley T*	14	7		
2012–13	Crawley T	27	4		
2012–13	*AFC Wimbledon*	18	3	18	3
2013–14	Crawley T	21	4	62	15
2013–14	Burton Alb	11	0	11	0

BELL, Lee (M) 312 13
H: 5 11　W: 12 04　b.Alsager 26-1-83

Season	Club	Apps	Gls		
2000–01	Crewe Alex	0	0		
2001–02	Crewe Alex	0	0		
2002–03	Crewe Alex	17	1		
2003–04	Crewe Alex	3	0		
2004–05	Crewe Alex	17	0		
2005–06	Crewe Alex	17	2		
2006–07	Crewe Alex	9	0		
2007–08	Mansfield T	23	1	23	1
2008–09	Macclesfield T	41	1		
2009–10	Macclesfield T	42	2	83	3
2010–11	Crewe Alex	45	1		
2011–12	Crewe Alex	30	0		
2012–13	Crewe Alex	0	0	129	4
2012–13	Burton Alb	43	4		
2013–14	Burton Alb	34	1	77	5

DELAP, Rory (M) 504 33
H: 6 3　W: 13 00　b.Sutton Coldfield 6-7-76
Internationals: Republic of Ireland U21, B, Full caps.

Season	Club	Apps	Gls		
1992–93	Carlisle U	1	0		
1993–94	Carlisle U	1	0		
1994–95	Carlisle U	3	0		
1995–96	Carlisle U	19	3		
1996–97	Carlisle U	32	4		
1997–98	Carlisle U	9	0	65	7
1997–98	Derby Co	13	0		
1998–99	Derby Co	23	0		
1999–2000	Derby Co	34	8		
2000–01	Derby Co	33	3	103	11
2001–02	Southampton	28	2		
2002–03	Southampton	24	0		
2003–04	Southampton	27	1		
2004–05	Southampton	37	2		
2005–06	Southampton	16	0	132	5
2005–06	Sunderland	6	1		
2006–07	Sunderland	6	0	12	1
2006–07	Stoke C	2	0		
2007–08	Stoke C	44	2		
2008–09	Stoke C	34	2		
2009–10	Stoke C	36	0		
2010–11	Stoke C	37	2		
2011–12	Stoke C	26	2		
2012–13	Stoke C	1	0	180	8
2012–13	*Barnsley*	6	0	6	0
2013–14	Burton Alb	6	1	6	1

DIAMOND, Zander (D) 288 24
H: 6 2　W: 11 07　b.Alexandria 3-12-85
Internationals: Scotland U21.

Season	Club	Apps	Gls		
2003–04	Aberdeen	19	2		
2004–05	Aberdeen	29	3		
2005–06	Aberdeen	33	0		
2006–07	Aberdeen	21	0		
2007–08	Aberdeen	26	3		
2008–09	Aberdeen	28	4		
2009–10	Aberdeen	16	3		
2010–11	Aberdeen	32	1	204	16
2011–12	Oldham Ath	23	2	23	2
2012–13	Burton Alb	37	4		
2013–14	Burton Alb	10	1	47	5
2013–14	*Northampton T*	14	1	14	1

DYER, Jack (M) 54 1
H: 5 9　W: 11 00　b.Sutton Coldfield 11-12-91

Season	Club	Apps	Gls		
2010–11	Burton Alb	5	0		
2011–12	Burton Alb	17	1		
2012–13	Burton Alb	28	0		
2013–14	Burton Alb	4	0	54	1

EDWARDS, Phil (D) 310 25
H: 5 8　W: 11 03　b.Bootle 8-11-85

Season	Club	Apps	Gls		
2005–06	Wigan Ath	0	0		
2006–07	Accrington S	33	1		
2007–08	Accrington S	31	1		
2008–09	Accrington S	46	0		
2009–10	Accrington S	46	8		
2010–11	Accrington S	44	13	200	23
2011–12	Stevenage	22	0	22	0
2011–12	*Rochdale*	3	0		
2012–13	Rochdale	44	0	47	0
2013–14	Burton Alb	41	2	41	2

GRAY, David (F) 137 0
H: 5 11　W: 11 02　b.Edinburgh 4-5-88
Internationals: Scotland U19, U21.

Season	Club	Apps	Gls		
2005–06	Manchester U	0	0		
2006–07	Manchester U	0	0		
2007–08	Manchester U	0	0		
2007–08	*Crewe Alex*	1	0	1	0
2008–09	Manchester U	0	0		
2008–09	*Plymouth Arg*	14	0		
2009–10	Manchester U	0	0		
2009–10	*Plymouth Arg*	12	0	26	0
2010–11	Preston NE	22	0		
2011–12	Preston NE	23	0	45	0
2012–13	Stevenage	42	0		
2013–14	Stevenage	11	0	53	0
2013–14	Burton Alb	12	0	12	0

HARNESS, Marcus (M) 3 0

Season	Club	Apps	Gls		
2013–14	Burton Alb	3	0	3	0

HOLNESS, Marcus (D) 147 5
H: 6 0　W: 12 02　b.Swinton 8-12-88

Season	Club	Apps	Gls		
2007–08	Oldham Ath	0	0		
2007–08	Rochdale	19	0		
2008–09	Rochdale	8	0		
2009–10	Rochdale	11	0		
2010–11	Rochdale	46	1		
2011–12	Rochdale	24	3	108	4
2012–13	Burton Alb	22	1		
2013–14	Burton Alb	17	0	39	1

HUSSEY, Chris (D) 115 3
H: 5 10　W: 10 03　b.Hammersmith 2-1-89

Season	Club	Apps	Gls		
2009–10	Coventry C	8	0		
2010–11	Coventry C	11	0		
2010–11	*Crewe Alex*	0	0		
2011–12	Coventry C	29	0		
2012–13	Coventry C	10	0	58	0
2012–13	AFC Wimbledon	19	0		

Season	Club				
2013–14	AFC Wimbledon	0	0	19	0
2013–14	Burton Alb	27	1	27	1
2013–14	Bury	11	2	11	2

KEE, Billy (F) 178 55
H: 5 9 W: 11 04 b.Loughborough 1-12-90
Internationals: Northern Ireland U19, U21.

2009–10	Leicester C	0	0		
2009–10	*Accrington S*	37	9	37	9
2010–11	*Torquay U*	40	9		
2011–12	*Torquay U*	4	0	44	9
2011–12	Burton Alb	20	12		
2012–13	Burton Alb	40	13		
2013–14	Burton Alb	37	12	97	37

KNOWLES, Dominic (F) 28 3
H: 5 9 W: 11 05 b.Accrington 13-2-92

2010–11	Burnley	0	0		
2011–12	Burnley	0	0		
2013–14	Burton Alb	28	3	28	3

LYNESS, Dean (G) 36 0
H: 6 3 W: 11 12 b.Birmingham 20-7-91
Internationals: England U17.

| 2012–13 | Burton Alb | 15 | 0 | | |
| 2013–14 | Burton Alb | 21 | 0 | 36 | 0 |

MACDONALD, Alex (F) 116 8
H: 5 7 W: 11 04 b.Warrington 14-4-90
Internationals: Scotland U19, U21.

2007–08	Burnley	2	0		
2008–09	Burnley	3	0		
2009–10	Burnley	0	0		
2009–10	*Falkirk*	11	1	11	1
2010–11	Burnley	0	0		
2010–11	*Inverness CT*	10	1	10	1
2011–12	Burnley	5	0		
2011–12	*Plymouth Arg*	18	4		
2012–13	Burnley	1	0	11	0
2012–13	*Plymouth Arg*	16	1	34	5
2012–13	*Burton Alb*	15	1		
2013–14	Burton Alb	35	0	50	1

McCRORY, Damien (M) 185 3
H: 6 2 W: 12 10 b.Limerick 22-2-90
Internationals: Republic of Ireland U18, U19.

2008–09	Plymouth Arg	0	0		
2008–09	*Port Vale*	12	0		
2009–10	Plymouth Arg	0	0		
2009–10	*Port Vale*	5	0	17	0
2009–10	*Grimsby T*	10	0	10	0
2009–10	Dagenham & R	20	0		
2010–11	Dagenham & R	23	0		
2011–12	Dagenham & R	33	1	76	1
2012–13	Burton Alb	42	1		
2013–14	Burton Alb	40	1	82	2

McGURK, Adam (F) 113 19
H: 5 9 W: 12 13 b.Larne 24-1-89
Internationals: Northern Ireland U21.

2005–06	Aston Villa	0	0		
2006–07	Aston Villa	0	0		
2007–08	Aston Villa	0	0		
2008–09	Aston Villa	0	0		
2009–10	Aston Villa	0	0		

From Hednesford T.

2010–11	Tranmere R	21	3		
2011–12	Tranmere R	31	4		
2012–13	Tranmere R	27	3	79	10
2013–14	Burton Alb	34	9	34	9

PALMER, Chris (D) 216 14
H: 5 7 W: 11 00 b.Derby 16-10-83

2003–04	Derby Co	0	0		
2004–05	Notts Co	25	4		
2005–06	Notts Co	29	1	54	5
2006–07	Wycombe W	32	0		
2007–08	Wycombe W	1	0	33	0
2007–08	*Darlington*	4	0	4	0
2008–09	Walsall	44	1	44	1
2009–10	Gillingham	20	1		
2010–11	Gillingham	18	4	38	5
2011–12	Burton Alb	34	3		
2012–13	Burton Alb	9	0		
2013–14	Burton Alb	0	0	43	3

PALMER, Matthew (M) 42 0
H: 5 10 W: 12 06 b.Derby 1-8-93

| 2012–13 | Burton Alb | 2 | 0 | | |
| 2013–14 | Burton Alb | 40 | 0 | 42 | 0 |

PHILLIPS, Jimmy (M) 120 3
H: 5 7 W: 10 00 b.Stoke 20-9-89

2008–09	Stoke C	0	0		
2009–10	Burton Alb	24	1		
2010–11	Burton Alb	23	0		
2011–12	Burton Alb	33	0		
2012–13	Burton Alb	7	0		
2013–14	Burton Alb	33	2	120	3

SHARPS, Ian (D) 494 18
H: 6 3 W: 14 07 b.Warrington 23-10-80

1998–99	Tranmere R	1	0		
1999–2000	Tranmere R	0	0		
2000–01	Tranmere R	0	0		
2001–02	Tranmere R	29	0		
2002–03	Tranmere R	30	3		
2003–04	Tranmere R	27	1		
2004–05	Tranmere R	44	1		
2005–06	Tranmere R	39	1	170	6
2006–07	Rotherham U	38	2		
2007–08	Rotherham U	33	2		
2008–09	Rotherham U	45	4		
2009–10	Rotherham U	44	2		
2010–11	Shrewsbury T	43	1		
2011–12	Shrewsbury T	43	1	86	2
2011–12	Rotherham U	23	1	183	9
2012–13	Burton Alb	16	0		
2013–14	Burton Alb	39	1	55	1

SLADE, Liam (D) 0 0

| 2013–14 | Burton Alb | 0 | 0 | | |

SYMES, Michael (F) 242 55
H: 6 3 W: 12 04 b.Gt Yarmouth 31-10-83

2001–02	Everton	0	0		
2002–03	Everton	0	0		
2003–04	Everton	0	0		
2003–04	*Crewe Alex*	4	1	4	1
2004–05	Bradford C	12	2		
2004–05	*Darlington*	0	0		
2005–06	Bradford C	3	1		
2005–06	*Stockport Co*	1	0	1	0
2006–07	Bradford C	0	0	15	3
2006–07	Shrewsbury T	33	9		
2007–08	Shrewsbury T	21	3		
2007–08	*Macclesfield T*	14	1	14	1
2008–09	Shrewsbury T	8	2	62	14
2008–09	Bournemouth	5	0		
2008–09	*Accrington S*	7	1		
2009–10	Accrington S	41	13	48	14
2010–11	Bournemouth	22	8		
2011–12	Bournemouth	15	3	42	11
2011–12	Rochdale	15	4	15	4
2012–13	Leyton Orient	13	1	13	1
2013–14	*Burton Alb*	13	2	28	6

WEIR, Robbie (M) 140 10
H: 5 9 W: 11 07 b.Belfast 9-12-88
Internationals: Northern Ireland U18, U19, U21, B.

2007–08	Sunderland	0	0		
2008–09	Sunderland	0	0		
2009–10	Sunderland	0	0		
2010–11	Sunderland	0	0		
2010–11	*Tranmere R*	18	0		
2011–12	Tranmere R	39	3	57	3
2012–13	Burton Alb	42	5		
2013–14	Burton Alb	41	2	83	7

Scholars
Allen, Shay Courtney; Austin, Samuel Joseph; Coggins, Brad Michael William; Currie, Isaac Konata; Doyle-Charles, Joseph; Horton, Alex Thomas; Markall, Ben; Murfin, Matthew Adam; O'Brien, Jack Christopher; Richards, Christopher Crushi; Shelton, Mark John; Stanley-Browne, Leandro Jamaal; Thorpe, Ashley Nicholas; Ware, Charlie Peter; Yates, Shae Steven.

Non Contract
Poole, Kevin.

BURY (18)

BURGESS, Scott (M) 1 0

| 2013–14 | Bury | 1 | 0 | 1 | 0 |

CAMERON, Nathan (D) 78 4
H: 6 2 W: 12 04 b.Birmingham 21-11-91
Internationals: England U20.

2009–10	Coventry C	0	0		
2010–11	Coventry C	25	0		
2011–12	Coventry C	14	0		
2012–13	Coventry C	9	0	48	0
2012–13	*Northampton T*	3	0	3	0
2013–14	Bury	27	4	27	4

CARSON, Trevor (G) 132 0
H: 6 0 W: 14 11 b.Downpatrick 5-3-88
Internationals: Northern Ireland U21, B.

2004–05	Sunderland	0	0		
2005–06	Sunderland	0	0		
2006–07	Sunderland	0	0		
2007–08	Sunderland	0	0		
2008–09	Sunderland	0	0		
2008–09	*Chesterfield*	18	0	18	0
2009–10	Sunderland	0	0		
2010–11	Sunderland	0	0		
2010–11	*Lincoln C*	16	0	16	0
2010–11	*Brentford*	1	0	1	0
2011–12	Sunderland	0	0		
2011–12	*Hull C*	0	0		
2011–12	Bury	17	0		
2012–13	Bury	39	0		
2013–14	Bury	5	0	61	0
2013–14	*Portsmouth*	36	0	36	0

CHARLES-COOK, Reice (G) 2 0
b.London 8-4-94

| 2013–14 | Bury | 2 | 0 | 2 | 0 |

DUDLEY, Anthony (F) 2 0

| 2013–14 | Bury | 2 | 0 | 2 | 0 |

EDJENGUELE, William (D) 108 6
H: 6 2 W: 13 00 b.Paris 7-5-87

2008–09	Neuchatel Xamax	23	0		
2009–10	Neuchatel Xamax	15	1	38	1
2011–12	Panetolikos	18	2	18	2
2012–13	Coventry C	33	1		
2013–14	Coventry C	0	0	33	1
2013–14	Bury	19	2	19	2

GRIMES, Ashley (M) 141 35
H: 6 0 W: 11 02 b.Swinton 9-12-86

2006–07	Manchester C	0	0		
2006–07	*Swindon T*	4	0	4	0
2007–08	Manchester C	0	0		
2008–09	Millwall	17	2		
2009–10	Millwall	4	0		
2010–11	Millwall	0	0	21	2
2010–11	*Lincoln C*	15	15	27	15
2011–12	Rochdale	36	8		
2012–13	Rochdale	38	10	74	18
2013–14	Bury	15	0	15	0

HARRAD, Shaun (F) 192 51
H: 5 10 W: 12 04 b.Nottingham 11-12-84
Internationals: England C. Scotland Full caps.

2002–03	Notts Co	5	0		
2003–04	Notts Co	8	0		
2004–05	Notts Co	16	1	29	1
2009–10	Burton Alb	42	21		
2010–11	Burton Alb	20	10	62	31
2010–11	*Northampton T*	18	6		
2011–12	Northampton T	0	0	18	6
2011–12	Bury	26	2		
2011–12	*Rotherham U*	8	3	8	3
2012–13	Bury	0	0		
2012–13	*Cheltenham T*	31	8	31	8
2013–14	Bury	18	0	44	2

HINDS, Richard (D) 305 14
H: 6 2 W: 12 02 b.Sheffield 22-8-80

1998–99	Tranmere R	2	0		
1999–2000	Tranmere R	6	0		
2000–01	Tranmere R	29	0		
2001–02	Tranmere R	10	0		
2002–03	Tranmere R	8	0	55	0
2003–04	Hull C	39	1		
2004–05	Hull C	6	0	45	1
2004–05	Scunthorpe U	7	0		
2005–06	Scunthorpe U	42	6		
2006–07	Scunthorpe U	44	2	93	8
2007–08	Sheffield W	38	2		
2008–09	Sheffield W	0	0		
2009–10	Sheffield W	11	0		
2010–11	Sheffield W	4	0		
2011–12	Sheffield W	0	0	67	2

From Lincoln C

2011–12	Yeovil T	16	1		
2012–13	Yeovil T	19	1	35	2
2013–14	Bury	10	1	10	1

HOLDEN, Euan (D) — 3 0
H: 6 1 W: 12 11 b.Aberdeen 2-2-88

Season	Club				
2012–13	Bury	1	0		
2013–14	Bury	2	0	3	0

JACKSON, Marlon (F) — 55 3
H: 5 11 W: 11 12 b.Bristol 6-12-90

Season	Club				
2009–10	Bristol C	0	0		
2009–10	*Hereford U*	5	0	5	0
2009–10	*Aldershot T*	22	1		
2010–11	Bristol C	4	0		
2010–11	*Aldershot T*	9	0	31	1
2011–12	Bristol C	0	0	4	0
2011–12	*Northampton T*	6	1	6	1
2011–12	*Cheltenham T*	1	0	1	0
2013–14	Bury	8	1	8	1

JENSEN, Brian (G) — 354 0
H: 6 1 W: 12 04 b.Copenhagen 8-6-75

Season	Club				
1997–98	AZ	0	0		
1998–99	AZ	1	0	1	0
1999–2000	WBA	12	0		
2000–01	WBA	33	0		
2001–02	WBA	1	0		
2002–03	WBA	0	0	46	0
2003–04	Burnley	46	0		
2004–05	Burnley	27	0		
2005–06	Burnley	39	0		
2006–07	Burnley	31	0		
2007–08	Burnley	19	0		
2008–09	Burnley	45	0		
2009–10	Burnley	38	0		
2010–11	Burnley	21	0		
2011–12	Burnley	4	0		
2012–13	Burnley	1	0	271	0
2013–14	Bury	36	0	36	0

JONES, Craig (M) — 171 28
H: 5 7 W: 10 13 b.Chester 20-3-87

Season	Club				
2004–05	Airbus UK	2	2		
2005–06	Airbus UK	7	6	9	8
2007–08	Rhyl	27	8		
2008–09	Rhyl	14	2	41	10
2008–09	Connah's Quay	12	0	12	0
2009–10	New Saints FC	26	7	26	7
2010–11	Port Talbot	14	1		
2011–12	Port Talbot	7	0	21	1
2012–13	Bury	25	1		
2013–14	Bury	37	1	62	2

LAINTON, Robert (G) — 18 0
H: 6 2 W: 12 06 b.Ashton-under-Lyne 12-10-89

Season	Club				
2009–10	Bolton W	0	0		
2010–11	Bolton W	0	0		
2011–12	Bolton W	0	0		
2012–13	Bolton W	0	0		
2013–14	Bury	4	0	4	0
2013–14	*Burton Alb*	14	0	14	0

MAYOR, Danny (M) — 119 7
H: 6 0 W: 11 12 b.Leyland 18-10-90

Season	Club				
2008–09	Preston NE	0	0		
2008–09	*Tranmere R*	3	0	3	0
2009–10	Preston NE	7	0		
2010–11	Preston NE	21	0		
2011–12	Preston NE	36	2		
2012–13	Preston NE	0	0	64	2
2012–13	Sheffield W	8	0		
2012–13	*Southend U*	5	0	5	0
2013–14	Sheffield W	0	0		
2013–14	Bury	39	5	39	5

McNULTY, Jim (D) — 182 5
H: 6 1 W: 12 00 b.Runcorn 13-2-85
Internationals: Scotland U17, U19.

Season	Club				
2006–07	Macclesfield T	15	0		
2007–08	Macclesfield T	19	1	34	1
2007–08	Stockport Co	11	0		
2008–09	Stockport Co	26	1	37	1
2008–09	Brighton & HA	5	1		
2009–10	Brighton & HA	8	0		
2009–10	*Scunthorpe U*	3	0		
2010–11	Brighton & HA	0	0	13	1
2010–11	*Scunthorpe U*	6	0	9	0
2011–12	Barnsley	44	2		
2012–13	Barnsley	12	0		
2013–14	Barnsley	0	0	56	2
2013–14	*Tranmere R*	12	0	12	0
2013–14	Bury	21	0	21	0

MILLER, Tommy (M) — 505 90
H: 6 0 W: 11 07 b.Shotton 8-1-79

Season	Club				
1997–98	Hartlepool U	13	1		
1998–99	Hartlepool U	34	4		
1999–2000	Hartlepool U	44	14		
2000–01	Hartlepool U	46	16		
2001–02	Hartlepool U	0	0	137	35
2001–02	Ipswich T	8	0		
2002–03	Ipswich T	30	6		
2003–04	Ipswich T	34	11		
2004–05	Ipswich T	45	13		
2005–06	Sunderland	29	3		
2006–07	Sunderland	4	0	33	3
2006–07	*Preston NE*	7	0	7	0
2007–08	Ipswich T	37	5		
2008–09	Ipswich T	32	5	186	40
2009–10	Sheffield W	20	1		
2010–11	Sheffield W	34	9	54	10
2011–12	Huddersfield T	26	1	26	1
2012–13	Swindon T	34	1		
2013–14	Swindon T	0	0	34	1
2013–14	Bury	28	0	28	0

MILLS, Pablo (D) — 276 6
H: 5 9 W: 11 04 b.Birmingham 27-5-84
Internationals: England U16, U18, U19.

Season	Club				
2002–03	Derby Co	16	0		
2003–04	Derby Co	19	0		
2004–05	Derby Co	22	0		
2005–06	Derby Co	0	0	58	0
2005–06	*Milton Keynes D*	16	1	16	1
2005–06	Walsall	14	0	14	0
2006–07	Rotherham U	31	1		
2007–08	Rotherham U	33	1		
2008–09	Rotherham U	35	1		
2009–10	Rotherham U	37	0		
2011–12	Crawley T	21	2	21	2
2013–14	Rotherham U	10	0	146	3
2013–14	Bury	21	0		

NARDIELLO, Daniel (F) — 296 91
H: 5 11 W: 11 04 b.Coventry 22-10-82
Internationals: Wales Full caps.

Season	Club				
1999–2000	Manchester U	0	0		
2000–01	Manchester U	0	0		
2001–02	Manchester U	0	0		
2002–03	Manchester U	0	0		
2003–04	Manchester U	0	0		
2003–04	*Swansea C*	4	0	4	0
2003–04	*Barnsley*	16	7		
2004–05	Manchester U	0	0		
2004–05	Barnsley	28	7		
2005–06	Barnsley	34	5		
2006–07	Barnsley	30	9		
2007–08	QPR	8	0	8	0
2007–08	Barnsley	11	2	119	30
2008–09	Blackpool	2	0		
2008–09	*Hartlepool U*	12	3	12	3
2009–10	Blackpool	5	0	7	0
2009–10	*Bury*	6	4		
2009–10	*Oldham Ath*	2	0	2	0
2010–11	Exeter C	30	10		
2011–12	Exeter C	36	9	66	19
2012–13	Rotherham U	36	19		
2013–14	Rotherham U	9	5	45	24
2013–14	Bury	27	11	33	15

NAVAS, Marco (M) — 4 0
H: 5 9 b.Los Palacios 21-9-82

Season	Club				
2012–13	Recreativo Huelva	2	0	2	0
2013–14	Bury	2	0	2	0

OBADEYI, Temitope (F) — 78 5
H: 5 10 W: 11 09 b.Birmingham 29-10-89
Internationals: England U19, U20.

Season	Club				
2006–07	Bolton W	0	0		
2007–08	Bolton W	0	0		
2008–09	Bolton W	3	0		
2008–09	Bolton W	0	0		
2009–10	*Swindon T*	12	2	12	2
2009–10	*Rochdale*	11	1		
2010–11	Bolton W	0	0		
2010–11	*Shrewsbury T*	9	0	9	0
2011–12	Bolton W	0	0	3	0
2011–12	*Chesterfield*	5	0	5	0
2011–12	*Rochdale*	6	1	17	2
2012–13	Rio Ave	11	0	11	0
2013–14	Bury	7	0	7	0
2013–14	*Plymouth Arg*	14	1	14	1

PLATT, Clive (F) — 615 110
H: 6 4 W: 12 07 b.Wolverhampton 27-10-77

Season	Club				
1995–96	Walsall	4	2		
1996–97	Walsall	1	0		
1997–98	Walsall	20	1		
1998–99	Walsall	7	1		
1999–2000	Rochdale	0	0	32	4
1999–2000	Rochdale	41	9		
2000–01	Rochdale	43	8		
2001–02	Rochdale	43	7		
2002–03	Rochdale	42	6	169	30
2003–04	Notts Co	19	3	19	3
2003–04	Peterborough U	18	2		
2004–05	Peterborough U	19	4	37	6
2004–05	Milton Keynes D	20	3		
2005–06	Milton Keynes D	40	6		
2006–07	Milton Keynes D	42	18	102	27
2007–08	Colchester U	41	8		
2008–09	Colchester U	43	10		
2009–10	Colchester U	41	7	125	25
2010–11	Coventry C	34	3		
2011–12	Coventry C	33	4	67	7
2012–13	Northampton T	36	5		
2013–14	Northampton T	11	1	47	6
2013–14	Bury	17	2	17	2

POSCHA, Marcus (D) — 1 0

Season	Club				
2013–14	Bury	1	0	1	0

PROCTER, Andy (M) — 301 31
H: 6 0 W: 12 04 b.Blackburn 13-3-83
Internationals: England C.

Season	Club				
2006–07	Accrington S	43	3		
2007–08	Accrington S	43	10		
2008–09	Accrington S	37	3		
2009–10	Accrington S	44	5		
2010–11	Accrington S	43	6		
2011–12	Accrington S	25	2	235	29
2011–12	Preston NE	19	0		
2012–13	Preston NE	15	0	34	0
2013–14	Bury	32	2	32	2

REINDORF, Jessy (F) — 4 1
H: 6 5 b.10-7-91
Internationals: Rwanda Full caps.

Season	Club				
2013–14	Bury	4	1	4	1

ROONEY, John (M) — 49 3
H: 5 10 W: 11 08 b.Liverpool 17-12-90

Season	Club				
2007–08	Macclesfield T	2	0		
2008–09	Macclesfield T	14	2		
2009–10	Macclesfield T	25	1	41	3
2010–11	New York RB	2	0		
2011–12	New York RB	3	0	5	0
2012–13	Barnsley	0	0		
2013–14	Bury	3	0	3	0

SEDGWICK, Chris (M) — 556 36
H: 5 11 W: 11 10 b.Sheffield 28-4-80

Season	Club				
1997–98	Rotherham U	4	0		
1998–99	Rotherham U	33	4		
1999–2000	Rotherham U	38	5		
2000–01	Rotherham U	21	2		
2001–02	Rotherham U	44	1		
2002–03	Rotherham U	43	1		
2003–04	Rotherham U	40	2		
2004–05	Rotherham U	20	2	243	17
2004–05	Preston NE	24	3		
2005–06	Preston NE	46	4		
2006–07	Preston NE	43	1		
2007–08	Preston NE	42	2		
2008–09	Preston NE	40	1		
2009–10	Preston NE	34	1	229	12
2010–11	Sheffield W	33	4		
2011–12	Sheffield W	10	1	43	5
2012–13	Scunthorpe U	4	0	4	0
2013–14	Bury	37	2	37	2

SOARES, Tom (M) — 255 24
H: 6 0 W: 11 04 b.Reading 10-7-86
Internationals: England U20, U21.

Season	Club				
2003–04	Crystal Palace	3	0		
2004–05	Crystal Palace	22	0		
2005–06	Crystal Palace	44	1		
2006–07	Crystal Palace	37	3		
2007–08	Crystal Palace	39	6		
2008–09	Crystal Palace	4	1	149	11
2008–09	Stoke C	9	0		
2008–09	*Charlton Ath*	11	1	11	1
2009–10	Stoke C	0	0		
2009–10	*Sheffield W*	25	2	25	2

2010–11	Stoke C	0	0		
2011–12	Stoke C	0	0	7	0
2011–12	*Hibernian*	10	2	10	2
2012–13	Bury	23	2		
2013–14	Bury	30	6	53	8

TUTTE, Andrew (M) — 131 13
H: 5 9 W: 10 10 b.Huyton 21-9-90
Internationals: England U19, U20.

2007–08	Manchester C	0	0		
2008–09	Manchester C	0	0		
2009–10	Manchester C	0	0		
2010–11	Manchester C	0	0		
2010–11	*Rochdale*	7	0		
2010–11	*Shrewsbury T*	2	0	2	0
2010–11	*Yeovil T*	15	2	15	2
2011–12	Rochdale	40	1		
2012–13	Rochdale	37	7		
2013–14	Rochdale	11	2	95	10
2013–14	Bury	19	1	19	1

WALKER, Regan (F) — 3 0
b. 4-6-96

| 2013–14 | Bury | 3 | 0 | 3 | 0 |

YOUNG, Lewis (M) — 75 0
H: 5 10 W: 11 02 b.Stevenage 27-9-89

2008–09	Watford	1	0		
2009–10	Watford	0	0		
2009–10	*Hereford U*	6	0	6	0
2010–11	*Burton Alb*	19	0	19	0
2011–12	*Northampton T*	30	0	30	0
2012–13	Yeovil T	15	0		
2013–14	Yeovil T	0	0	15	0
2013–14	Bury	4	0	4	0

Scholars
Bickett, Liam Matthew; Brown, Joseph Andrew; Burgess, Scott Andrew; Cliffe, Jake Oliver; Cook, Matthew John Barton; Dickinson, Samuel Jack; Dudley, Anthony Ryan; Nasseri, Navid; Poscha, Marcus Anthony; Potter, Benjamin Oliver; Shaw, Brayden Lewis; Willis, Connor Nathan; Wordingham, Henry Robert.

CARDIFF C (19)

AMONDARAIN, Maximiliano (D) — 0 0
H: 6 1 W: 12 05 b.Salto 22-1-93
Internationals: Uruguay U20.

| 2013–14 | Cardiff C | 0 | 0 | | |

BELLAMY, Craig (F) — 458 134
H: 5 9 W: 10 12 b.Cardiff 13-7-79
Internationals: Wales Schools, U18, U21, Full caps. Great Britain.

1996–97	Norwich C	3	0		
1997–98	Norwich C	36	13		
1998–99	Norwich C	40	17		
1999–2000	Norwich C	4	2		
2000–01	Norwich C	0	0	84	32
2000–01	Coventry C	34	6	34	6
2001–02	Newcastle U	27	9		
2002–03	Newcastle U	29	7		
2003–04	Newcastle U	16	4		
2004–05	Newcastle U	21	7	93	27
2004–05	*Celtic*	12	7	12	7
2005–06	Blackburn R	27	13	27	13
2006–07	Liverpool	27	7		
2007–08	West Ham U	8	2		
2008–09	West Ham U	16	5	24	7
2008–09	Manchester C	8	3		
2009–10	Manchester C	32	10		
2010–11	Manchester C	0	0		
2010–11	*Cardiff C*	35	11		
2011–12	Manchester C	0	0	40	13
2011–12	Liverpool	27	6		
2012–13	Liverpool	0	0	54	13
2012–13	Cardiff C	33	4		
2013–14	Cardiff C	22	1	90	16

BERGET, Jo Inge (F) — 125 28
H: 6 0 W: 12 03 b.Gjlovile 11-9-90
Internationals: Norway U21, U23, Full caps.

2007	Lyn	3	0		
2008	Lyn	2	0		
2008–09	Udinese	0	0		
2009	*Lyn*	26	3	31	3
2009–10	Udinese	0	0		
2010	*Stromsgodset*	18	6		
2010–11	Udinese	0	0		
2011	*Stromsgodset*	13	2	31	8
2011	Molde	9	2		
2012	Molde	28	8		
2013	Molde	25	7	62	17
2013–14	Cardiff C	1	0	1	0

BRAYFORD, John (D) — 205 7
H: 5 8 W: 11 02 b.Stoke 29-12-87
Internationals: England C.

2008–09	Crewe Alex	36	2		
2009–10	Crewe Alex	45	0	81	2
2010–11	Derby Co	46	1		
2011–12	Derby Co	23	0		
2012–13	Derby Co	40	1	109	2
2013–14	Cardiff C	0	0		
2013–14	*Sheffield U*	15	1	15	1

CALA, Juan (D) — 77 11
H: 6 1 W: 12 03 b.Lebrija 26-11-89
Internationals: Spain U19.

2008–09	Sevilla	0	0		
2009–10	Sevilla	5	3		
2010–11	Sevilla	0	0		
2010–11	*Cartagena*	25	3	25	3
2011–12	Sevilla	8	1		
2011–12	*AEK Athens*	13	1	13	1
2012–13	Sevilla	10	0		
2013–14	Sevilla	9	1	32	5
2013–14	Cardiff C	7	2	7	2

CAMPBELL, Frazier (F) — 153 35
H: 5 11 W: 12 04 b.Huddersfield 13-9-87
Internationals: England U16, U17, U18, U21, Full caps.

2005–06	Manchester U	0	0		
2006–07	Manchester U	0	0		
2007–08	Manchester U	1	0		
2007–08	*Hull C*	34	15	34	15
2008–09	Manchester U	1	0		
2008–09	*Tottenham H*	10	1	10	1
2009–10	Manchester U	0	0	2	0
2009–10	Sunderland	31	4		
2010–11	Sunderland	3	0		
2011–12	Sunderland	12	1		
2012–13	Sunderland	12	1	58	6
2012–13	Cardiff C	12	7		
2013–14	Cardiff C	37	6	49	13

CAULKER, Steven (D) — 155 9
H: 6 3 W: 12 00 b.Feltham 29-12-91
Internationals: England U19 U21, Full caps. Great Britain.

2009–10	Tottenham H	0	0		
2009–10	*Yeovil T*	44	0	44	0
2010–11	Tottenham H	0	0		
2010–11	*Bristol C*	29	2	29	2
2011–12	Tottenham H	0	0		
2011–12	*Swansea C*	26	0	26	0
2012–13	Tottenham H	18	2	18	2
2013–14	Cardiff C	38	5	38	5

CONNOLLY, Matthew (D) — 182 10
H: 6 1 W: 11 03 b.Barnet 24-9-87
Internationals: England Youth.

2005–06	Arsenal	0	0		
2006–07	Arsenal	0	0		
2007–08	*Bournemouth*	5	1	5	1
2007–08	Arsenal	0	0		
2007–08	*Colchester U*	16	2	16	2
2007–08	QPR	20	0		
2008–09	QPR	35	0		
2009–10	QPR	19	2		
2010–11	QPR	36	0		
2011–12	QPR	6	0		
2011–12	*Reading*	6	0	6	0
2012–13	QPR	0	0	116	2
2012–13	Cardiff C	36	5		
2013–14	Cardiff C	3	0	39	5

CORNELIUS, Andreas (F) — 42 18
H: 6 3 W: 13 13 b.Copenhagen 16-3-93

2011–12	FC Copenhagen	2	0		
2012–13	FC Copenhagen	32	18	34	18
2013–14	Cardiff C	8	0	8	0

Transferred to FC Copenhagen January 2014

COWIE, Don (M) — 399 44
H: 5 5 W: 8 05 b.Inverness 15-2-83
Internationals: Scotland Full caps.

2000–01	Ross Co	0	0		
2001–02	Ross Co	18	0		
2002–03	Ross Co	30	1		
2003–04	Ross Co	23	0		
2004–05	Ross Co	34	5		
2005–06	Ross Co	32	4		
2006–07	Ross Co	28	7	166	17
2007–08	Inverness CT	37	9		
2008–09	Inverness CT	22	3	59	12
2008–09	Watford	10	3		
2009–10	Watford	41	2		
2010–11	Watford	37	4	88	9
2011–12	Cardiff C	43	4		
2012–13	Cardiff C	25	2		
2013–14	Cardiff C	18	0	86	6

DA SILVA, Fabio (M) — 56 1
H: 5 8 W: 10 03 b.Rio de Janeiro 9-7-90
Internationals: Brazil U17, Full caps.

2008–09	Manchester U	0	0		
2009–10	Manchester U	5	0		
2010–11	Manchester U	11	1		
2011–12	Manchester U	5	0		
2012–13	Manchester U	0	0		
2012–13	*QPR*	21	0	21	0
2013–14	Manchester U	1	0	22	1
2013–14	Cardiff C	13	0	13	0

DAEHLI, Mats (M) — 13 1
b.Oslo 2-3-95
Internationals: Norway U15, U16, U19, U21, Full caps.

2011–12	Manchester U	0	0		
2012–13	Manchester U	0	0		
2013–14	Cardiff C	13	1	13	1

EIKREM, Magnus Wolff (M) — 87 8
H: 5 8 W: 10 11 b.Molde 8-8-90
Internationals: Norway U17, U19, U21, Full caps.

2009–10	Manchester U	0	0		
2010–11	Manchester U	0	0		
2011	Molde	28	4		
2012	Molde	27	0		
2013	Molde	13	2	68	6
2013–14	*Heerenveen*	13	2	13	2
2013–14	Cardiff C	6	0	6	0

GUNNARSSON, Aron (M) — 233 20
H: 5 9 W: 11 00 b.Akureyri 22-9-89
Internationals: Iceland U17, U19, U21, Full caps.

2007–08	AZ	1	0	1	0
2008–09	Coventry C	40	1		
2009–10	Coventry C	40	1		
2010–11	Coventry C	42	4	122	6
2011–12	Cardiff C	42	5		
2012–13	Cardiff C	45	8		
2013–14	Cardiff C	23	1	110	14

HARRIS, Kedeem (M) — 29 1
H: 5 9 W: 10 08 b.Westminster 8-6-93

2009–10	Wycombe W	2	0		
2010–11	Wycombe W	0	0		
2011–12	Wycombe W	17	0	19	0
2011–12	Cardiff C	0	0		
2012–13	Cardiff C	0	0		
2013–14	Cardiff C	0	0		
2013–14	*Brentford*	10	1	10	1

HEALEY, Rhys (M) — 1 0

| 2012–13 | Cardiff C | 0 | 0 | | |
| 2013–14 | Cardiff C | 1 | 0 | 1 | 0 |

HILL, Gethyn (F) — 0 0
H: 6 0 W: 11 10 b.Pontypool 18-1-95
Internationals: Wales U17, U19.

| 2012–13 | Cardiff C | 0 | 0 | | |
| 2013–14 | Cardiff C | 0 | 0 | | |

HUDSON, Mark (D) — 319 21
H: 6 1 W: 12 01 b.Guildford 30-3-82

1998–99	Fulham	0	0		
1999–2000	Fulham	0	0		
2000–01	Fulham	0	0		
2001–02	Fulham	0	0		
2002–03	Fulham	0	0		
2003–04	Fulham	0	0		
2003–04	*Oldham Ath*	15	0	15	0
2003–04	*Crystal Palace*	14	0		
2004–05	Crystal Palace	7	1		
2005–06	Crystal Palace	15	0		
2006–07	Crystal Palace	39	4		
2007–08	Crystal Palace	45	2	120	7
2008–09	Charlton Ath	43	3	43	3
2009–10	Cardiff C	27	2		
2010–11	Cardiff C	40	0		

2011–12	Cardiff C	39	5		
2012–13	Cardiff C	33	4		
2013–14	Cardiff C	2	0	141	11

JAMES, Tom (D) 1 0
2013–14	Cardiff C	1	0	1	0

JOHN, Declan (M) 26 0
H: 5 10 W: 11 10 b.Merthyr Tydfil 30-6-95
Internationals: Wales U17, U19, Full caps.
2010–11	Llanelli	1	0	1	0
2011–12	Afan Lido	5	0	5	0
2012–13	Cardiff C	0	0		
2013–14	Cardiff C	20	0	20	0

JONES, Kenwyne (F) 284 69
H: 6 2 W: 13 06 b.Trinidad & Tobago 5-10-84
Internationals: Trinidad & Tobago Youth, U23, Full caps.
2004–05	Southampton	2	0		
2004–05	Sheffield W	7	7	7	7
2004–05	Stoke C	13	3		
2005–06	Southampton	34	4		
2006–07	Southampton	34	14		
2007–08	Southampton	1	1	71	19
2007–08	Sunderland	33	7		
2008–09	Sunderland	29	10		
2009–10	Sunderland	32	9	94	26
2010–11	Stoke C	34	9		
2011–12	Stoke C	21	1		
2012–13	Stoke C	26	3		
2013–14	Stoke C	7	0	101	16
2013–14	Cardiff C	11	1	11	1

KIM, Bo-Kyung (M) 124 26
H: 5 10 W: 11 06 b.Oita 6-10-89
Internationals: South Korea U20, U23, Full caps.
2010	Oita Trinita	27	8	27	8
2011	Cerezo Osaka	26	8		
2012	Cerezo Osaka	15	7	41	15
2012–13	Cardiff C	28	2		
2013–14	Cardiff C	28	1	56	3

KISS, Filip (M) 100 17
H: 6 1 W: 11 11 b.Dunajska 13-10-90
Internationals: Slovakia U19, U21, Full caps.
2009–10	Petrzalka	25	4	25	4
2010–11	Slovan Bratislava	29	6		
2011–12	Slovan Bratislava	1	0	30	6
2011–12	*Cardiff C*	26	1		
2012–13	*Cardiff C*	2	0		
2013–14	Cardiff C	0	0	28	1
2013–14	*Ross Co*	17	6	17	6

LAPPIN, Simon (M) 286 13
H: 5 11 W: 9 06 b.Glasgow 25-1-83
Internationals: Scotland U21.
2001–02	St Mirren	1	0		
2002–03	St Mirren	34	0		
2003–04	St Mirren	24	4		
2004–05	St Mirren	34	1		
2005–06	St Mirren	35	3		
2006–07	St Mirren	24	1	152	9
2006–07	Norwich C	14	1		
2007–08	*Motherwell*	14	2	14	2
2007–08	Norwich C	15	1		
2008–09	Norwich C	5	0		
2009–10	Norwich C	44	0		
2010–11	Norwich C	27	0		
2011–12	Norwich C	4	0		
2012–13	Norwich C	0	0	109	2
2012–13	Cardiff C	2	0		
2013–14	Cardiff C	0	0	2	0
2013–14	*Sheffield U*	9	0	9	0

LEWIS, Joe (G) 192 0
H: 6 5 W: 12 10 b.Bungay 6-10-87
Internationals: England U16, U17, U19, U21.
2004–05	Norwich C	0	0		
2005–06	Norwich C	0	0		
2006–07	Norwich C	0	0		
2006–07	*Stockport Co*	5	0	5	0
2007–08	Norwich C	0	0		
2007–08	*Morecambe*	19	0	19	0
2007–08	Peterborough U	22	0		
2008–09	Peterborough U	46	0		
2009–10	Peterborough U	43	0		
2010–11	Peterborough U	45	0		
2011–12	Peterborough U	11	0	167	0
2012–13	Cardiff C	0	0		
2013–14	Cardiff C	1	0	1	0

MARSHALL, David (G) 311 0
H: 6 3 W: 13 04 b.Glasgow 5-3-85
Internationals: Scotland Youth, U21, B, Full caps.
2003–04	Celtic	11	0		
2004–05	Celtic	18	0		
2005–06	Celtic	4	0		
2006–07	Celtic	2	0	35	0
2006–07	Norwich C	2	0		
2007–08	Norwich C	46	0		
2008–09	Norwich C	46	0	94	0
2008–09	Cardiff C	0	0		
2009–10	Cardiff C	43	0		
2010–11	Cardiff C	11	0		
2011–12	Cardiff C	45	0		
2012–13	Cardiff C	46	0		
2013–14	Cardiff C	37	0	182	0

MASON, Joe (F) 136 31
H: 5 9 W: 11 11 b.Plymouth 13-5-91
Internationals: Republic of Ireland Youth, U21.
2009–10	Plymouth Arg	19	3		
2010–11	Plymouth Arg	34	7	53	10
2011–12	Cardiff C	39	9		
2012–13	Cardiff C	28	6		
2013–14	Cardiff C	0	0	67	15
2013–14	*Bolton W*	16	6	16	6

MAYNARD, Nicky (F) 226 83
H: 5 11 W: 11 00 b.Winsford 11-12-86
2005–06	Crewe Alex	1	1		
2006–07	Crewe Alex	31	16		
2007–08	Crewe Alex	27	14	59	31
2008–09	Bristol C	43	11		
2009–10	Bristol C	42	20		
2010–11	Bristol C	13	6		
2011–12	Bristol C	27	8	125	45
2011–12	West Ham U	14	2		
2012–13	West Ham U	0	0	14	2
2012–13	Cardiff C	4	1		
2013–14	Cardiff C	8	0	12	1
2013–14	*Wigan Ath*	16	4	16	4

McNAUGHTON, Kevin (D) 443 5
H: 5 10 W: 10 06 b.Dundee 28-8-82
Internationals: Scotland B, Full caps.
1999–2000	Aberdeen	1	0		
2000–01	Aberdeen	33	0		
2001–02	Aberdeen	34	0		
2002–03	Aberdeen	22	1		
2003–04	Aberdeen	17	0		
2004–05	Aberdeen	35	2		
2005–06	Aberdeen	34	0	175	3
2006–07	Cardiff C	42	0		
2007–08	Cardiff C	35	1		
2008–09	Cardiff C	39	0		
2009–10	Cardiff C	21	0		
2010–11	Cardiff C	44	0		
2011–12	Cardiff C	42	0		
2012–13	Cardiff C	27	0		
2013–14	Cardiff C	5	0	255	1
2013–14	*Bolton W*	13	1	13	1

MEDEL, Gary (M) 199 20
H: 5 8 W: 11 08 b.Santiago 3-8-87
Internationals: Chile U20, U23, Full caps.
2008	Univ Catolica	28	4		
2009	Univ Catolica	13	1	41	5
2009–10	Boca Juniors	29	7		
2010–11	Boca Juniors	17	0	46	7
2010–11	Sevilla	15	0		
2011–12	Sevilla	31	2		
2012–13	Sevilla	32	6	78	8
2013–14	Cardiff C	34	0	34	0

MOORE, Simon (G) 75 0
H: 6 3 W: 12 02 b.Sandown 19-5-90
Internationals: Isle of Wight Full caps.
2009–10	Brentford	1	0		
2010–11	Brentford	10	0		
2011–12	Brentford	10	0		
2012–13	Brentford	43	0	64	0
2013–14	Cardiff C	0	0		
2013–14	*Bristol C*	11	0	11	0

MUTCH, Jordon (M) 124 16
H: 5 9 W: 10 03 b.Derby 2-12-91
Internationals: England U17, U19, U20, U21.
2007–08	Birmingham C	0	0		
2008–09	Birmingham C	0	0		
2009–10	Birmingham C	0	0		
2009–10	*Hereford U*	3	0	3	0
2009–10	*Doncaster R*	17	2	17	2
2010–11	Birmingham C	3	0		
2010–11	*Watford*	23	5	23	5
2011–12	Birmingham C	21	2	24	2
2012–13	Cardiff C	22	0		
2013–14	Cardiff C	35	7	57	7

NOONE, Craig (M) 170 19
H: 6 3 W: 12 07 b.Kirkby 17-11-87
2008–09	Plymouth Arg	21	1		
2009–10	Plymouth Arg	17	1		
2009–10	*Exeter C*	7	2	7	2
2010–11	Plymouth Arg	17	3	55	5
2010–11	Brighton & HA	23	2		
2011–12	Brighton & HA	33	2		
2012–13	Brighton & HA	3	0	59	4
2012–13	Cardiff C	32	7		
2013–14	Cardiff C	17	1	49	8

NUGENT, Ben (D) 23 1
H: 6 1 W: 13 00 b.Street 28-11-93
2012–13	Cardiff C	12	1		
2013–14	Cardiff C	0	0	12	1
2013–14	*Brentford*	0	0		
2013–14	*Peterborough U*	11	0	11	0

O'SULLIVAN, Tommy (M) 0 0
H: 5 9 W: 11 06 b.Mountain Ash 18-1-95
Internationals: Wales U17, U19, U21.
2012–13	Cardiff C	0	0		
2013–14	Cardiff C	0	0		

OSHILAJA, Adedeji (D) 10 0
H: 5 11 W: 11 06 b.Bermondsey 16-7-93
2012–13	Cardiff C	0	0		
2013–14	Cardiff C	0	0		
2013–14	*Newport Co*	8	0	8	0
2013–14	*Sheffield W*	2	0	2	0

RALLS, Joe (M) 51 4
H: 5 10 W: 11 00 b.Farnborough 13-10-93
Internationals: England U19.
2011–12	Cardiff C	10	1		
2012–13	Cardiff C	4	0		
2013–14	Cardiff C	0	0	14	1
2013–14	*Yeovil T*	37	3	37	3

TAYLOR, Andrew (D) 271 5
H: 5 10 W: 11 04 b.Hartlepool 1-8-86
Internationals: England U16, U17, U18, U19. U20, U21.
2003–04	Middlesbrough	0	0		
2004–05	Middlesbrough	0	0		
2005–06	Middlesbrough	13	0		
2005–06	*Bradford C*	24	0	24	0
2006–07	Middlesbrough	34	0		
2007–08	Middlesbrough	19	0		
2008–09	Middlesbrough	26	0		
2009–10	Middlesbrough	12	0		
2010–11	Middlesbrough	21	3	125	3
2010–11	*Watford*	19	1	19	1
2011–12	Cardiff C	42	1		
2012–13	Cardiff C	43	0		
2013–14	Cardiff C	18	0	103	1

THEOPHILE-CATHERINE, Kevin (D) 125 3
H: 5 11 W: 12 00 b.Saint Brieuc 28-10-89
Internationals: France U20, U21.
2008–09	Rennes	0	0		
2009–10	Rennes	3	0		
2010–11	Rennes	26	2		
2011–12	Rennes	36	0		
2012–13	Rennes	29	1		
2013–14	Rennes	3	0	97	3
2013–14	Cardiff C	28	0	28	0

TURNER, Ben (D) 180 7
H: 6 4 W: 14 04 b.Birmingham 21-1-88
Internationals: England U19.
2005–06	Coventry C	1	0		
2006–07	Coventry C	1	0		
2006–07	*Peterborough U*	8	0	8	0
2006–07	*Oldham Ath*	1	0	1	0
2007–08	Coventry C	19	0		
2008–09	Coventry C	24	0		
2009–10	Coventry C	13	0		
2010–11	Coventry C	14	4	72	4
2011–12	Cardiff C	37	2		
2012–13	Cardiff C	31	1		
2013–14	Cardiff C	31	0	99	3

VELIKONJA, Etien (F) 162 54
H: 5 10 W: 11 04 b.Sempeter Pri Gorici 26-12-88
Internationals: Slovenia U19, U21, Full caps.

2006–07	Gorica	7	1		
2007–08	Gorica	31	5		
2008–09	Gorica	32	17		
2009–10	Gorica	16	5		
2010–11	Gorica	18	4	104	32
2010–11	Maribor	16	6		
2011–12	Maribor	30	15		
2012–13	Maribor	2	0	48	21
2012–13	Cardiff C	3	0		
2013–14	Cardiff C	0	0	3	0
2013–14	*Rio Ave*	7	1	7	1

WHARTON, Theo (M) 0 0
b.Cwmbran 15-11-94
Internationals: Wales U17, U19.

2011–12	Cardiff C	0	0
2012–13	Cardiff C	0	0
2013–14	Cardiff C	0	0

WHITTINGHAM, Peter (M) 371 67
H: 5 10 W: 9 13 b.Nuneaton 8-9-84
Internationals: England U20, U21.

2002–03	Aston Villa	4	0		
2003–04	Aston Villa	32	0		
2004–05	Aston Villa	13	1		
2004–05	*Burnley*	7	0	7	0
2005–06	Aston Villa	4	0		
2005–06	*Derby Co*	11	0	11	0
2006–07	Aston Villa	3	0	56	1
2006–07	Cardiff C	19	4		
2007–08	Cardiff C	41	5		
2008–09	Cardiff C	33	3		
2009–10	Cardiff C	41	20		
2010–11	Cardiff C	45	11		
2011–12	Cardiff C	46	12		
2012–13	Cardiff C	40	8		
2013–14	Cardiff C	32	3	297	66

WILSON, Ben (G) 0 0
b.Stanley 9-8-92

2010–11	Sunderland	0	0
2011–12	Sunderland	0	0
2013–14	Accrington S	0	0
2013–14	Cardiff C	0	0

Scholars
Baker, Ashley Thomas; Bellamy, Ellis; Bowen, Jaye Ricky; Burridge, Thomas Sean; Lavery, Gary Francis; Noor, Abdifatah Mohamed; Patten, Robbie; Pearson, Thomas James; Phipps, Elijah; Rees, Dylan Patrick James; Roche, Tyler Paul; Southam, Macauley Anthony; Taylor, William Margam Raymond; Tutonda, David; Tevale, Jamie Lawrence; Watkins, Benjamin Lewis; Watkins, Curtis James; Watkins, Jake Kristian; Wickham, Bradley; Williams, Bradley Jason.

CARLISLE U (20)

AMOO, David (F) 108 14
H: 5 10 W: 12 03 b.Southwark 23-4-91

2007–08	Liverpool	0	0		
2008–09	Liverpool	0	0		
2009–10	Liverpool	0	0		
2010–11	Liverpool	0	0		
2010–11	*Milton Keynes D*	3	0	3	0
2010–11	*Hull C*	7	1	7	1
2011–12	Liverpool	0	0		
2011–12	*Bury*	27	4	27	4
2012–13	Preston NE	17	0	17	0
2012–13	Tranmere R	11	1		
2013–14	Tranmere R	0	0	11	1
2013–14	Carlisle U	43	8	43	8

BECK, Mark (F) 39 4
H: 6 5 W: 12 08 b.Sunderland 2-2-94
Internationals: Scotland U19, U21.

2011–12	Carlisle U	2	0		
2012–13	Carlisle U	27	4		
2013–14	Carlisle U	10	0	39	4

BERRETT, James (M) 205 25
H: 5 10 W: 10 13 b.Halifax 13-1-89
Internationals: Republic of Ireland U18, U19, U21.

2006–07	Huddersfield T	2	0		
2007–08	Huddersfield T	15	1		
2008–09	Huddersfield T	9	1		
2009–10	Huddersfield T	9	0	35	2
2010–11	Carlisle U	46	10		
2011–12	Carlisle U	42	9		
2012–13	Carlisle U	42	2		
2013–14	Carlisle U	40	2	170	23

BROUGH, Patrick (M) 3 0
H: 5 8 b.Carlisle 20-2-96

2013–14	Carlisle U	3	0	3	0

BUABEN, Prince (M) 153 9
H: 6 0 W: 11 09 b.Akosombo 23-4-88
Internationals: Ghana Full caps.

2007–08	Dundee U	24	3		
2008–09	Dundee U	22	1		
2009–10	Dundee U	34	2		
2010–11	Dundee U	19	1	99	7
2011–12	Watford	30	1		
2012–13	Watford	1	0	31	1
2013–14	Carlisle U	12	1	12	1
2013–14	*Partick Thistle*	11	0	11	0

CHANTLER, Chris (M) 54 0
H: 5 8 W: 11 00 b.Cheadle Hulme 16-12-90

2009–10	Manchester C	0	0		
2010–11	Manchester C	0	0		
2011–12	Manchester C	0	0		
2011–12	Carlisle U	12	0		
2012–13	Carlisle U	25	0		
2013–14	Carlisle U	17	0	54	0

CHIMBONDA, Pascal (D) 346 15
H: 5 10 W: 11 05 b.Les Abymes 21-2-79
Internationals: Guadeloupe Full caps. France Full caps.

1999–2000	Le Havre	2	0		
2000–01	Le Havre	32	1		
2001–02	Le Havre	27	2		
2002–03	Le Havre	24	2	85	5
2003–04	Bastia	31	1		
2004–05	Bastia	36	3	67	4
2005–06	Wigan Ath	37	2		
2006–07	Wigan Ath	1	0	38	2
2006–07	Tottenham H	33	1		
2007–08	Tottenham H	32	2		
2008–09	Sunderland	13	0	13	0
2008–09	Tottenham H	3	0	68	3
2009–10	Blackburn R	24	1		
2010–11	Blackburn R	6	0	30	1
2010–11	QPR	3	0	3	0
2011–12	Doncaster R	16	0		
2012–13	Doncaster R	0	0		
2013–14	Doncaster R	0	0	16	0
2013–14	Carlisle U	26	0	26	0

DEMPSEY, Kyle (M) 4 0

2013–14	Carlisle U	4	0	4	0

EDWARDS, Mike (D) 509 27
H: 6 0 W: 12 10 b.Hessle 25-4-80

1997–98	Hull C	21	0		
1998–99	Hull C	30	0		
1999–2000	Hull C	40	1		
2000–01	Hull C	42	4		
2001–02	Hull C	39	1		
2002–03	Hull C	6	0	178	6
2002–03	Colchester U	5	0	5	0
2003–04	Grimsby T	33	1	33	1
2004–05	Notts Co	9	0		
2005–06	Notts Co	46	7		
2006–07	Notts Co	45	3		
2007–08	Notts Co	19	1		
2008–09	Notts Co	43	2		
2009–10	Notts Co	40	5		
2010–11	Notts Co	37	1		
2011–12	Notts Co	30	1	269	20
2012–13	Carlisle U	23	0		
2013–14	Carlisle U	1	0	24	0

FLEMING, Greg (G) 109 0
H: 5 11 W: 12 09 b.Dunfermline 27-9-86
Internationals: Scotland U21.

2006–07	Gretna	2	0		
2007–08	Gretna	28	0	30	0
2008–09	Oldham Ath	18	0		
2009–10	Oldham Ath	0	0		
2009–10	*Dunfermline Ath*	26	0	26	0
2010–11	Oldham Ath	0	0	18	0
2010–11	*Galway U*	21	0	21	0
2011–12	Chesterfield	10	0	10	0
2013–14	Carlisle U	4	0	4	0

GILLESPIE, Mark (G) 51 0
H: 6 3 W: 13 07 b.Newcastle 27-3-92

2009–10	Carlisle U	1	0		
2010–11	Carlisle U	0	0		
2011–12	Carlisle U	0	0		
2012–13	Carlisle U	35	0		
2013–14	Carlisle U	15	0	51	0

GILLIES, Josh (M) 6 0
b. 12-6-96
Internationals: England C.

2013–14	Carlisle U	6	0	6	0

GUY, Lewis (F) 229 25
H: 5 10 W: 10 07 b.Penrith 27-8-85
Internationals: England U20.

2002–03	Newcastle U	0	0		
2003–04	Newcastle U	0	0		
2004–05	Newcastle U	0	0		
2004–05	Doncaster R	9	3		
2005–06	Doncaster R	31	3		
2006–07	Doncaster R	36	4		
2007–08	Doncaster R	29	6		
2008–09	Doncaster R	29	2		
2008–09	*Hartlepool U*	4	0	4	0
2009–10	Doncaster R	13	0	147	18
2009–10	*Oldham Ath*	12	3	12	3
2010–11	Milton Keynes D	34	2		
2011–12	Milton Keynes D	1	0	35	2
2011–12	*Oxford U*	8	1	8	1
2013–14	Carlisle U	23	1	23	1

LIVESEY, Danny (D) 290 17
H: 6 3 W: 13 01 b.Salford 31-12-84

2002–03	Bolton W	2	0		
2003–04	Bolton W	0	0		
2003–04	*Notts Co*	11	0	11	0
2003–04	*Rochdale*	13	0	13	0
2004–05	Bolton W	0	0	2	0
2004–05	*Blackpool*	1	0	1	0
2005–06	Carlisle U	36	4		
2006–07	Carlisle U	31	1		
2007–08	Carlisle U	45	6		
2008–09	Carlisle U	27	0		
2009–10	Carlisle U	38	2		
2010–11	Carlisle U	10	0		
2011–12	Carlisle U	28	1		
2012–13	Carlisle U	39	3		
2013–14	Carlisle U	9	0	263	17

LYNCH, Jack (M) 1 0
b. 22-6-95

2013–14	Carlisle U	1	0	1	0

MEPPEN-WALTER, Courtney (D) 20 1
H: 6 0 W: 12 00 b.Bury 24-8-95
Internationals: England U17, U18.

2012–13	Manchester C	0	0		
2013–14	Carlisle U	20	1	20	1

MILLER, Lee (F) 410 112
H: 6 0 W: 11 07 b.Lanark 18-5-83
Internationals: Scotland B, Full caps.

2000–01	Falkirk	0	0		
2001–02	Falkirk	27	11		
2002–03	Falkirk	34	17	61	28
2003–04	Bristol C	42	8		
2004–05	Bristol C	7	0	49	8
2004–05	Hearts	18	8	18	8
2005–06	Dundee U	34	8		
2006–07	Dundee U	3	0	37	8
2006–07	Aberdeen	32	4		
2007–08	Aberdeen	36	12		
2008–09	Aberdeen	34	10		
2009–10	Aberdeen	18	3	120	29
2009–10	Middlesbrough	10	0		
2009–10	Middlesbrough	1	0		
2010–11	*Notts Co*	6	2	6	2
2010–11	*Scunthorpe U*	18	1	18	1
2011–12	Middlesbrough	0	0	11	0
2011–12	Carlisle U	33	14		
2012–13	Carlisle U	23	9		
2013–14	Carlisle U	34	5	90	28

NOBLE, Liam (M) 130 20
H: 5 9 W: 10 05 b.Newcastle 8-5-91

2009–10	Sunderland	0	0
2010–11	Sunderland	0	0

2010–11	Carlisle U	21	3		
2011–12	Sunderland	0	0		
2011–12	Carlisle U	40	6		
2012–13	Carlisle U	35	6		
2013–14	Carlisle U	34	5	130	20

NOVO, Nacho (F)   341 87
H: 5 9   W: 10 13   b.Ferrol 26-3-79

2002–03	Dundee	36	7		
2003–04	Dundee	35	20	71	27
2004–05	Rangers	35	19		
2005–06	Rangers	24	2		
2006–07	Rangers	28	5		
2007–08	Rangers	28	10		
2008–09	Rangers	29	5		
2009–10	Rangers	35	6	179	47
2010–11	Sporting Gijon	30	4		
2011–12	Sporting Gijon	11	3	41	7
2011–12	Legia Warsaw	11	0	11	0
2012–13	Huesca	33	6	33	6
2013–14	Carlisle U	6	0	6	0

O'HANLON, Sean (D)   337 30
H: 6 1   W: 12 04   b.Liverpool 2-1-83
Internationals: England U20.

2003–04	Swindon T	21	1		
2004–05	Swindon T	40	3		
2005–06	Swindon T	40	4	101	8
2006–07	Milton Keynes D	38	4		
2007–08	Milton Keynes D	43	4		
2008–09	Milton Keynes D	40	3		
2009–10	Milton Keynes D	6	0		
2010–11	Milton Keynes D	34	4	161	15
2011–12	Hibernian	22	2		
2012–13	Hibernian	1	0	23	2
2012–13	Carlisle U	19	1		
2013–14	Carlisle U	33	4	52	5

POTTS, Brad (M)   64 2
H: 6 2   W: 12 09   b.Carlisle 3-7-94
Internationals: England U19.

2012–13	Carlisle U	27	0		
2013–14	Carlisle U	37	2	64	2

ROBSON, Matty (D)   311 29
H: 5 10   W: 11 02   b.Spennymoor 23-1-85

2002–03	Hartlepool U	0	0		
2003–04	Hartlepool U	23	1		
2004–05	Hartlepool U	27	2		
2005–06	Hartlepool U	19	1		
2006–07	Hartlepool U	20	2		
2007–08	Hartlepool U	17	1		
2008–09	Hartlepool U	29	2	135	9
2009–10	Carlisle U	39	4		
2010–11	Carlisle U	42	2		
2011–12	Carlisle U	36	7		
2012–13	Carlisle U	36	2		
2013–14	Carlisle U	32	5	176	20

SYMINGTON, David (M)   62 3
H: 5 8   W: 12 03   b.Carlisle 28-1-94

2012–13	Carlisle U	31	3		
2013–14	Carlisle U	31	0	62	3

THIRLWELL, Paul (M)   353 8
H: 5 11   W: 12 08   b.Washington 13-2-79
Internationals: England U21.

1996–97	Sunderland	0	0		
1997–98	Sunderland	0	0		
1998–99	Sunderland	2	0		
1999–2000	Sunderland	8	0		
1999–2000	Swindon T	12	0	12	0
2000–01	Sunderland	5	0		
2001–02	Sunderland	14	0		
2002–03	Sunderland	19	0		
2003–04	Sunderland	29	0	77	0
2004–05	Sheffield U	30	1	30	1
2005–06	Derby Co	21	0		
2006–07	Derby Co	0	0	21	0
2006–07	Carlisle U	30	0		
2007–08	Carlisle U	13	0		
2008–09	Carlisle U	34	4		
2009–10	Carlisle U	28	1		
2010–11	Carlisle U	23	1		
2011–12	Carlisle U	26	1		
2012–13	Carlisle U	32	0		
2013–14	Carlisle U	27	0	213	7

Scholars
Blackburn, Jason James; Brass, Lewis Alan Shaun; Brough, Patrick John; Chisholm, Cameron Albert; Eccles, Daniel John; Elliott, Jack;

Hammell, Connor Rhys; Marshall, Jordan Aaron; Moyes, Harvey Kenneth; Thomson, Connor Keegan; Wallace, Frankie; White, Thomas Alan.

CHARLTON ATH (21)

AJAYI, Semi (D)   0 0
H: 6 4   W: 13 00   b.Croydon 9-11-93
Internationals: Nigeria U21.

2012–13	Charlton Ath	0	0
2013–14	Charlton Ath	0	0

AJDAREVIC, Astrit (M)   102 15
H: 6 1   W: 11 08   b.Kosovo 17-4-90
Internationals: Sweden U17, U19, U21.

2006–07	Falkenberg	4	1	4	1
2006–07	Liverpool	0	0		
2007–08	Liverpool	0	0		
2008–09	Liverpool	0	0		
2008–09	Leicester C	5	0		
2009–10	Leicester C	0	0	5	0
2009–10	Hereford U	1	0	1	0
2010	Orebro	13	5	13	5
2011	IFK Norrkoping	28	4		
2012	IFK Norrkoping	12	2	40	6
2012–13	Standard Liege	20	1		
2013–14	Standard Liege	0	0	20	1
On loan from Standard Liege					
2013–14	Charlton Ath	19	2	19	2

AZEEZ, Adebayo (F)   29 5
H: 6 0   W: 12 07   b.Orpington 8-1-94
Internationals: England U19.

2012–13	Charlton Ath	0	0		
2012–13	Wycombe W	4	0	4	0
2012–13	Leyton Orient	1	0	1	0
2013–14	Charlton Ath	0	0		
2013–14	Torquay U	9	2	9	2
2013–14	Dagenham & R	15	3	15	3

CHURCH, Simon (F)   189 32
H: 6 0   W: 13 04   b.Amersham 10-12-88
Internationals: Wales U21, Full caps.

2007–08	Reading	0	0		
2007–08	Crewe Alex	12	1	12	1
2007–08	Yeovil T	6	0	6	0
2008–09	Reading	0	0		
2008–09	Wycombe W	9	0	9	0
2008–09	Leyton Orient	13	5	13	5
2009–10	Reading	36	10		
2010–11	Reading	37	5		
2011–12	Reading	31	7		
2012–13	Reading	0	0	104	22
2012–13	Huddersfield T	7	1	7	1
2013–14	Charlton Ath	38	3	38	3

COOK, Jordan (F)   41 5
H: 5 10   W: 10 10   b.Hetton-le-Hole 20-3-90

2007–08	Sunderland	0	0		
2008–09	Sunderland	0	0		
2009–10	Sunderland	0	0		
2009–10	Darlington	5	0	5	0
2010–11	Sunderland	3	0		
2010–11	Walsall	8	1	8	1
2011–12	Sunderland	0	0	3	0
2011–12	Carlisle U	14	4	14	4
2012–13	Charlton Ath	7	0		
2012–13	Yeovil T	1	0	1	0
2013–14	Charlton Ath	3	0	10	0

CORT, Leon (D)   396 38
H: 6 3   W: 13 01   b.Bermondsey 11-9-79
Internationals: Guyana Full caps.

1997–98	Millwall	0	0		
1998–99	Millwall	0	0		
1999–2000	Millwall	0	0		
2000–01	Millwall	0	0		
2001–02	Southend U	45	4		
2002–03	Southend U	46	6		
2003–04	Southend U	46	1	137	11
2004–05	Hull C	44	6		
2005–06	Hull C	42	4	86	10
2006–07	Crystal Palace	37	7		
2007–08	Crystal Palace	12	0	49	7
2007–08	Stoke C	33	8		
2008–09	Stoke C	11	0		
2009–10	Stoke C	0	0	44	8
2009–10	Burnley	15	0		
2010–11	Burnley	4	0		
2010–11	Preston NE	13	0	13	0

2011–12	Burnley	0	0	19	0
2011–12	Charlton Ath	15	0		
2012–13	Charlton Ath	30	2		
2013–14	Charlton Ath	3	0	48	2

COUSINS, Jordan (D)   42 2
H: 5 10   W: 11 05   b.Greenwich 6-3-94
Internationals: England U16, U17, U18, U21.

2011–12	Charlton Ath	0	0		
2012–13	Charlton Ath	0	0		
2013–14	Charlton Ath	42	2	42	2

DERVITE, Dorian (D)   99 5
H: 6 3   W: 13 06   b.Lille 25-7-88
Internationals: France U16, U17, U18, U19, U21.

2008–09	Southend U	18	0	18	0
2010–11	Villarreal B	9	0		
2011–12	Villarreal B	2	0	11	0
2012–13	Villarreal	0	0		
2012–13	Charlton Ath	30	3		
2013–14	Charlton Ath	40	2	70	5

EVINA, Cedric (D)   50 2
H: 5 11   W: 12 08   b.Cameroon 16-11-91

2009–10	Arsenal	0	0		
2010–11	Arsenal	0	0		
2010–11	Oldham Ath	27	2	27	2
2011–12	Charlton Ath	3	0		
2012–13	Charlton Ath	12	0		
2013–14	Charlton Ath	8	0	23	0

FEELY, Kevin (D)   40 2
H: 5 10   W: 11 07   b.Dublin 30-8-92

2011	Bohemians	5	0		
2012	Bohemians	23	1	28	1
2012–13	Charlton Ath	0	0		
2013–14	Charlton Ath	0	0		
2013–14	Carlisle U	2	0	2	0
2013–14	AFC Wimbledon	0	0		
2013–14	Newport Co	10	1	10	1

FOX, Morgan (D)   13 1
H: 6 1   W: 12 03   b.Chelmsford 21-9-93
Internationals: Wales U21.

2012–13	Charlton Ath	0	0		
2013–14	Charlton Ath	6	0	6	0
2013–14	Notts Co	7	1	7	1

GHOOCHANNEJHAD, Reza (F)   130 48
H: 5 11   W: 11 12   b.Mashdad 20-9-87
Internationals: Netherlands U16, U17, U18, U19. Iran Full caps

2005–06	Heerenveen	1	0		
2006–07	Heerenveen	0	0		
2006–07	Go Ahead Eagles	13	4		
2007–08	Heerenveen	0	0		
2008–09	Heerenveen	1	0	2	0
2008–09	Emmen	11	1	11	1
2009–10	Go Ahead Eagles	10	6	23	10
2009–10	Cambuur	13	2		
2010–11	Cambuur	24	13	37	15
2011–12	St. Truidense	22	11		
2012–13	St. Truidense	10	6	32	17
2012–13	Standard Liege	9	3		
2013–14	Standard Liege	1	1	10	4
2013–14	Charlton Ath	15	1	15	1

GOWER, Mark (M)   367 40
H: 5 11   W: 11 12   b.Edmonton 5-10-78

1996–97	Tottenham H	0	0		
1997–98	Tottenham H	0	0		
1998–99	Tottenham H	0	0		
1998–99	Motherwell	9	1	9	1
1999–2000	Tottenham H	0	0		
2000–01	Tottenham H	0	0		
2000–01	Barnet	14	1		
2001–02	Barnet	0	0		
2002–03	Barnet	0	0	14	1
2003–04	Southend U	40	6		
2004–05	Southend U	38	6		
2005–06	Southend U	40	6		
2006–07	Southend U	43	8		
2007–08	Southend U	42	9	203	35
2008–09	Swansea C	36	0		
2009–10	Swansea C	31	1		
2010–11	Swansea C	40	2		
2011–12	Swansea C	20	0		
2012–13	Swansea C	1	0	128	3
2012–13	Charlton Ath	6	0		
2013–14	Charlton Ath	7	0	13	0

GREEN, Danny (M)   154   28
H: 5 11   W: 12 00   b.Harlow 9-7-88
2006–07	Northampton T	0	0		
2007–08	Nottingham F	0	0		

From Bishop's Stortford.
2009–10	Dagenham & R	46	13		
2010–11	Dagenham & R	41	11	87	24
2011–12	Charlton Ath	32	3		
2012–13	Charlton Ath	17	1		
2013–14	Charlton Ath	13	0	62	4
2013–14	*Milton Keynes D*	5	0	5	0

HAMER, Ben (G)   207   0
H: 5 11   W: 12 04   b.Chard 20-11-87
2006–07	Reading	0	0		
2007–08	Reading	0	0		
2007–08	*Brentford*	20	0		
2008–09	Reading	0	0		
2008–09	*Brentford*	45	0		
2009–10	Reading	0	0		
2010–11	Reading	0	0		
2010–11	*Brentford*	10	0	75	0
2010–11	*Exeter C*	18	0	18	0
2011–12	Charlton Ath	41	0		
2012–13	Charlton Ath	41	0		
2013–14	Charlton Ath	32	0	114	0

HARRIOTT, Callum (M)   45   7
H: 5 5   W: 10 05   b.Norbury 4-3-94
Internationals: England U19.
2010–11	Charlton Ath	3	0		
2011–12	Charlton Ath	0	0		
2012–13	Charlton Ath	14	2		
2013–14	Charlton Ath	28	5	45	7

HOLLANDS, Danny (M)   294   40
H: 6 0   W: 11 11   b.Ashford (Middlesex)
6-11-85
2003–04	Chelsea	0	0		
2004–05	Chelsea	0	0		
2005–06	Chelsea	0	0		
2005–06	*Torquay U*	10	1	10	1
2006–07	Bournemouth	33	1		
2007–08	Bournemouth	37	4		
2008–09	Bournemouth	42	6		
2009–10	Bournemouth	39	6		
2010–11	Bournemouth	42	7	193	24
2011–12	Charlton Ath	43	7		
2012–13	Charlton Ath	14	0		
2012–13	*Swindon T*	10	2	10	2
2013–14	Charlton Ath	0	0	57	7
2013–14	*Gillingham*	17	1	17	1
2013–14	*Portsmouth*	7	5	7	5

HOLMES-DENNIS, Tareiq (M)   0   0
2012–13	Charlton Ath	0	0
2013–14	Charlton Ath	0	0

HUGHES, Andy (M)   544   39
H: 5 11   W: 12 01   b.Stockport 2-1-78
1995–96	Oldham Ath	15	1		
1996–97	Oldham Ath	8	0		
1997–98	Oldham Ath	10	0	33	1
1997–98	Notts Co	15	2		
1998–99	Notts Co	30	3		
1999–2000	Notts Co	35	7		
2000–01	Notts Co	30	5	110	17
2001–02	Reading	39	6		
2002–03	Reading	43	9		
2003–04	Reading	43	3		
2004–05	Reading	41	0	166	18
2005–06	Norwich C	36	2		
2006–07	Norwich C	36	0	72	2
2007–08	Leeds U	40	1		
2008–09	Leeds U	27	0		
2009–10	Leeds U	39	0		
2010–11	Leeds U	10	0	116	1
2010–11	Scunthorpe U	19	0	19	0
2011–12	Charlton Ath	15	0		
2012–13	Charlton Ath	6	0		
2013–14	Charlton Ath	7	0	28	0

JACKSON, Johnnie (M)   349   61
H: 6 1   W: 12 00   b.Camden 15-8-82
Internationals: England U17, U18, U20.
1999–2000	Tottenham H	0	0		
2000–01	Tottenham H	0	0		
2001–02	Tottenham H	0	0		
2002–03	Tottenham H	0	0		
2002–03	*Swindon T*	13	1	13	1
2002–03	*Colchester U*	8	0		
2003–04	Tottenham H	11	1		

JORDAN, Bradley (M)   0   0
H: 5 8   W: 10 09   b.Ashford 21-1-94
2012–13	Charlton Ath	0	0
2013–14	Charlton Ath	0	0
2013–14	*Notts Co*	0	0

LENNON, Harry (M)   2   0
2012–13	Charlton Ath	0	0
2013–14	Charlton Ath	2	0	2	0

MORRISON, Michael (D)   223   11
H: 6 0   W: 12 00   b.Bury St Edmunds 3-3-88
Internationals: England C.
2008–09	Leicester C	35	3		
2009–10	Leicester C	31	2		
2010–11	Leicester C	11	0	77	5
2010–11	*Sheffield W*	12	0	12	0
2011–12	Charlton Ath	45	4		
2012–13	Charlton Ath	44	1		
2013–14	Charlton Ath	45	1	134	6

MUNNS, Jack (M)   0   0
b.Dagenham 18-11-93
2012–13	*Aldershot T*	0	0
2013–14	Charlton Ath	0	0

NEGO, Loic (D)   20   1
H: 5 10   W: 10 00   b.Paris 15-1-91
Internationals: France U16, U17, U18, U19,
U20.
2008–09	Nantes	0	0		
2009–10	Nantes	1	0		
2010–11	Nantes	12	0	13	0
2011–12	Roma	0	0		
2012–13	Roma	0	0		
2012–13	*Standard Liege*	2	0	2	0
2013–14	Roma	0	0		
2013–14	*Ujpest*	4	1	4	1
2013–14	Charlton Ath	1	0	1	0

OSBORNE, Harry (D)   0   0
H: 6 0   W: 12 03   b.Greenwich 3-3-94
2011–12	Charlton Ath	0	0
2012–13	Charlton Ath	0	0
2013–14	Charlton Ath	0	0

PARZYSZEK, Piotr (F)   47   25
H: 6 2   W: 11 08   b.Torun 8-6-93
Internationals: Poland U18, U20, U21.
2012–13	De Graafschap	26	10		
2013–14	De Graafschap	20	15	46	25
2013–14	Charlton Ath	1	0	1	0

PHILLIPS, Dillon (M)   0   0
2012–13	Charlton Ath	0	0
2013–14	Charlton Ath	0	0

PIGOTT, Joe (F)   18   1
H: 6 0   W: 9 05   b.London 24-11-93
2012–13	Charlton Ath	0	0		
2013–14	Charlton Ath	11	0	11	0
2013–14	*Gillingham*	7	1	7	1

POPE, Nick (G)   23   0
H: 6 3   W: 11 13   b.Cambridge 19-4-92
2011–12	Charlton Ath	0	0		
2012–13	Charlton Ath	1	0		
2013–14	Charlton Ath	0	0	1	0
2013–14	*York C*	22	0	22	0

POYET, Diego (M)   20   0
b. 8-4-95
Internationals: England U17.
2011–12	Charlton Ath	0	0		
2012–13	Charlton Ath	0	0		
2013–14	Charlton Ath	20	0	20	0

PRITCHARD, Bradley (M)   79   3
H: 6 1   W: 14 02   b.Zimbabwe 19-12-85
2011–12	Charlton Ath	20	0

2012–13	Charlton Ath	42	3		
2013–14	Charlton Ath	17	0	79	3

SHO-SILVA, Oluwatobi (M)   0   0
2012–13	Charlton Ath	0	0
2013–14	Charlton Ath	0	0

SOLLY, Chris (D)   125   2
H: 5 8   W: 10 07   b.Rochester 20-1-91
Internationals: England U16, U17.
2008–09	Charlton Ath	1	0		
2009–10	Charlton Ath	9	0		
2010–11	Charlton Ath	14	1		
2011–12	Charlton Ath	44	0		
2012–13	Charlton Ath	45	1		
2013–14	Charlton Ath	12	0	125	2

THURAM-ULIEN, Yohann (G)   90   0
H: 6 2   W: 13 04   b.Courcouronnes 31-10-88
Internationals: France U20, U21.
2008–09	Monaco	3	0		
2009–10	Monaco	1	0		
2010–11	Monaco	0	0		
2010–11	*Tours*	20	0	20	0
2011–12	Monaco	0	0	4	0
2011–12	Troyes	21	0		
2012–13	Troyes	38	0	59	0
2013–14	Standard Liege	3	0	3	0

On loan from Standard Liege
2013–14	Charlton Ath	4	0	4	0

WIGGINS, Rhoys (D)   171   3
H: 5 8   W: 11 05   b.Uxbridge 4-11-87
Internationals: Wales U17, U19, U21.
2006–07	Crystal Palace	0	0		
2007–08	Crystal Palace	0	0		
2008–09	Crystal Palace	1	0	1	0
2008–09	Bournemouth	13	0		
2009–10	Norwich C	0	0		
2009–10	Bournemouth	19	0		
2010–11	Bournemouth	35	2	67	2
2011–12	Charlton Ath	45	1		
2012–13	Charlton Ath	20	0		
2013–14	Charlton Ath	38	0	103	1

WILSON, Lawrie (D)   160   14
H: 5 11   W: 11 06   b.London 11-9-87
2006–07	Colchester U	0	0		
2010–11	Stevenage	42	5		
2011–12	Stevenage	46	5	88	10
2012–13	Charlton Ath	30	2		
2013–14	Charlton Ath	42	2	72	4

WOOD, Richard (D)   309   15
H: 6 3   W: 12 13   b.Ossett 5-7-85
2002–03	Sheffield W	3	1		
2003–04	Sheffield W	12	0		
2004–05	Sheffield W	34	1		
2005–06	Sheffield W	30	1		
2006–07	Sheffield W	12	0		
2007–08	Sheffield W	27	2		
2008–09	Sheffield W	42	0		
2009–10	Sheffield W	11	2	171	7
2009–10	Coventry C	24	3		
2010–11	Coventry C	40	1		
2011–12	Coventry C	17	1		
2012–13	Coventry C	36	3	117	8
2013–14	Charlton Ath	21	0	21	0

Scholars

Afolabi, Emmanuel Mayowa; Barnes, Aaron
Christopher; Bokciu, Sevdar; Brown, Ellis
Ryan; Charles-Cook, Regan Evans; Doherty,
Harry Daniel; Edwards, Archie David;
Gomez, Joseph David; Hanlan, Brandon
Alex Graham; Kelly, Alexander Lawrence;
Kennedy, Mikhail Caolan Patrick; Leon,
Connor Stephen Williams; Martin, Brian
Micheal; Neavin, Darien Aaron; O'Hanlon,
Cathal; Pyke, Levander; Shehaj, Lamce;
Thomas, Terell Mondasia; Umerah, Joshua
Chukwudinma.

CHELSEA (22)

AKE, Nathan (M)   4   0
H: 5 11   W: 11 01   b.Den Haag 18-2-95
Internationals: Netherlands U15, U16, U17,
U19, U21.
2012–13	Chelsea	3	0		
2013–14	Chelsea	1	0	4	0

ATSU, Christian (F)   70 12
H: 5 8   W: 10 09   b.Ada Foah 10-1-92
Internationals: Ghana Full caps.

Season	Club				
2010–11	Porto	0	0		
2011–12	Porto	0	0		
2011–12	*Rio Ave*	27	6	**27**	**6**
2012–13	Porto	17	1	**17**	**1**
2013–14	Chelsea	0	0		
2013–14	*Vitesse*	26	5	**26**	**5**

AZPILICUETA, Cesar (D)   202 1
H: 5 10   W: 10 13   b.Pamplona 28-8-89
Internationals: Spain U16, U17, U19, U20, U21, U23, Full caps.

Season	Club				
2006–07	Osasuna	1	0		
2007–08	Osasuna	29	0		
2008–09	Osasuna	36	0		
2009–10	Osasuna	33	0	**99**	**0**
2010–11	Marseille	15	0		
2011–12	Marseille	30	1		
2012–13	Marseille	2	0	**47**	**1**
2012–13	Chelsea	27	0		
2013–14	Chelsea	29	0	**56**	**0**

BA, Demba (F)   234 110
H: 6 2   W: 12 13   b.Sevres 25-5-85
Internationals: Senegal Full caps.

Season	Club				
2005–06	Rouen	26	22	**26**	**22**
2006–07	Mouscron	10	8		
2007–08	Mouscron	2	0	**12**	**8**
2007–08	Hoffenheim	30	12		
2008–09	Hoffenheim	33	14		
2009–10	Hoffenheim	17	5		
2010–11	Hoffenheim	17	6	**97**	**37**
2010–11	West Ham U	12	7	**12**	**7**
2011–12	Newcastle U	34	16		
2012–13	Newcastle U	20	13	**54**	**29**
2012–13	Chelsea	14	2		
2013–14	Chelsea	19	5	**33**	**7**

BAKER, Lewis (M)   0 0
Internationals: England U17, U18.

Season	Club				
2012–13	Chelsea	0	0		
2013–14	Chelsea	0	0		

BAMFORD, Patrick (F)   60 26
H: 6 1   W: 11 02   b.Newark 5-9-93
Internationals: Republic of Ireland U18. England U18, U19, U21.

Season	Club				
2010–11	Nottingham F	0	0		
2011–12	Nottingham F	2	0	**2**	**0**
2011–12	Chelsea	0	0		
2012–13	Chelsea	0	0		
2012–13	*Milton Keynes D*	14	4		
2013–14	Chelsea	0	0		
2013–14	*Milton Keynes D*	23	14	**37**	**18**
2013–14	*Derby Co*	21	8	**21**	**8**

BERTRAND, Ryan (D)   189 4
H: 5 10   W: 11 00   b.Southwark 5-8-89
Internationals: England U16, U17, U18, U19, U20, U21, Full caps. Great Britain.

Season	Club				
2006–07	Chelsea	0	0		
2006–07	*Bournemouth*	5	0	**5**	**0**
2007–08	Chelsea	0	0		
2007–08	*Oldham Ath*	21	0	**21**	**0**
2007–08	*Norwich C*	18	0		
2008–09	Chelsea	0	0		
2008–09	*Norwich C*	38	0	**56**	**0**
2009–10	Chelsea	0	0		
2009–10	*Reading*	44	1	**44**	**1**
2010–11	Chelsea	1	0		
2010–11	*Nottingham F*	19	0	**19**	**0**
2011–12	Chelsea	7	0		
2012–13	Chelsea	19	0		
2013–14	Chelsea	1	0	**28**	**0**
2013–14	*Aston Villa*	16	0	**16**	**0**

BLACKMAN, Jamal (G)   0 0
b.Croydon 27-10-93
Internationals: England U16, U17, U18, U19.

Season	Club				
2011–12	Chelsea	0	0		
2012–13	Chelsea	0	0		
2013–14	Chelsea	0	0		

BROWN, Isaiah (M)   1 0
H: 6 0   W: 10 13   b.Peterborough 7-1-97
Internationals: England U16, U17.

Season	Club				
2012–13	WBA	1	0	**1**	**0**
2013–14	Chelsea	0	0		

CAHILL, Gary (D)   267 21
H: 6 2   W: 12 06   b.Dronfield 19-12-85
Internationals: England U20, U21, Full caps.

Season	Club				
2003–04	Aston Villa	0	0		
2004–05	Aston Villa	0	0		
2004–05	*Burnley*	27	1	**27**	**1**
2005–06	Aston Villa	7	1		
2006–07	Aston Villa	20	0		
2007–08	Aston Villa	1	0	**28**	**1**
2007–08	*Sheffield U*	16	2	**16**	**2**
2007–08	Bolton W	13	0		
2008–09	Bolton W	33	3		
2009–10	Bolton W	29	5		
2010–11	Bolton W	36	3		
2011–12	Bolton W	19	2	**130**	**13**
2011–12	Chelsea	10	1		
2012–13	Chelsea	26	2		
2013–14	Chelsea	30	1	**66**	**4**

CECH, Petr (G)   454 0
H: 6 5   W: 14 07   b.Plzen 20-5-82
Internationals: Czech Republic U15, U16, U17, U18, U20, U21, Full caps.

Season	Club				
1998–99	Viktoria Plzen	0	0		
1999–2000	Chmel	1	0		
2000–01	Chmel	26	0	**27**	**0**
2001–02	Sparta Prague	26	0	**26**	**0**
2002–03	Rennes	37	0		
2003–04	Rennes	38	0	**75**	**0**
2004–05	Chelsea	35	0		
2005–06	Chelsea	34	0		
2006–07	Chelsea	20	0		
2007–08	Chelsea	26	0		
2008–09	Chelsea	35	0		
2009–10	Chelsea	34	0		
2010–11	Chelsea	38	0		
2011–12	Chelsea	34	0		
2012–13	Chelsea	36	0		
2013–14	Chelsea	34	0	**326**	**0**

CHALOBAH, Nathaniel (D)   69 8
H: 6 1   W: 11 11   b.Sierra Leone 12-12-94
Internationals: England U16, U17, U19, U21.

Season	Club				
2010–11	Chelsea	0	0		
2011–12	Chelsea	0	0		
2012–13	Chelsea	0	0		
2012–13	*Watford*	38	5	**38**	**5**
2013–14	Chelsea	0	0		
2013–14	*Nottingham F*	12	2	**12**	**2**
2013–14	*Middlesbrough*	19	1	**19**	**1**

CHRISTENSEN, Andreas (D)   0 0
H: 6 2   b.Allerod 10-4-96
Internationals: Denmark U16, U17, U19, U21.

Season	Club				
2012–13	Chelsea	0	0		
2013–14	Chelsea	0	0		

CLIFFORD, Billy (M)   18 1
H: 5 7   W: 10 03   b.Slough 18-10-92

Season	Club				
2010–11	Chelsea	0	0		
2011–12	Chelsea	0	0		
2012–13	Chelsea	0	0		
2012–13	*Colchester U*	18	1	**18**	**1**
2013–14	Chelsea	0	0		
2013–14	*Yeovil T*	0	0		

COLE, Ashley (D)   399 16
H: 5 8   W: 10 05   b.Stepney 20-12-80
Internationals: England U20, U21, B, Full caps.

Season	Club				
1998–99	Arsenal	0	0		
1999–2000	Arsenal	1	0		
1999–2000	*Crystal Palace*	14	1	**14**	**1**
2000–01	Arsenal	17	3		
2001–02	Arsenal	29	2		
2002–03	Arsenal	31	1		
2003–04	Arsenal	32	0		
2004–05	Arsenal	35	2		
2005–06	Arsenal	11	0		
2006–07	Arsenal	0	0	**156**	**8**
2006–07	Chelsea	23	0		
2007–08	Chelsea	27	1		
2008–09	Chelsea	34	1		
2009–10	Chelsea	27	4		
2010–11	Chelsea	38	0		
2011–12	Chelsea	32	0		
2012–13	Chelsea	31	1		
2013–14	Chelsea	17	0	**229**	**7**

COURTOIS, Thibaut (G)   152 0
H: 6 6   W: 14 02   b.Bree 11-5-92
Internationals: Belgium U18, Full caps.

Season	Club				
2008–09	Genk	1	0		
2009–10	Genk	0	0		
2010–11	Genk	40	0	**41**	**0**
2011–12	Chelsea	0	0		
2011–12	*Atletico Madrid*	37	0		
2012–13	Chelsea	0	0		
2012–13	*Atletico Madrid*	37	0		
2013–14	Chelsea	0	0		
2013–14	*Atletico Madrid*	37	0	**111**	**0**

CUEVAS, Cristian (M)   13 1
b. 2-4-95
Internationals: Chile U20.

Season	Club				
2013–14	Chelsea	0	0		
2013–14	*Vitesse*	0	0		
2013–14	*Eindhoven*	13	1	**13**	**1**

DAVEY, Alex (M)   0 0
Internationals: Scotland U19.

Season	Club				
2012–13	Chelsea	0	0		
2013–14	Chelsea	0	0		

DAVILA PLASCENCIA, Ulises Alejandro (F)   85 10
H: 5 8   W: 13 04   b. 13-4-91
Internationals: Mexico U20, U23.

Season	Club				
2008–09	Guadalajara	0	0		
2009–10	Guadalajara	7	0		
2010–11	Guadalajara	8	0	**15**	**0**
2011–12	Chelsea	0	0		
2011–12	*Vitesse*	2	0	**2**	**0**
2012–13	Chelsea	0	0		
2012–13	*Sabadell*	35	4	**35**	**4**
2013–14	Chelsea	0	0		
2013–14	*Cordoba*	33	6	**33**	**6**

DE BRUYNE, Kevin (M)   115 24
H: 5 11   W: 12 00   b.Ghent 28-6-91
Internationals: Belgium U18, U19, U21, Full caps.

Season	Club				
2008–09	Genk	2	0		
2009–10	Genk	30	3		
2010–11	Genk	32	5		
2011–12	Genk	15	6	**79**	**14**
2011–12	Chelsea	0	0		
2012–13	Chelsea	0	0		
2012–13	*Werder Bremen*	33	10	**33**	**10**
2013–14	Chelsea	3	0	**3**	**0**

Transferred to Wolfsburg January 2014

DELAC, Matej (G)   70 0
b.Bosnia 20-8-92
Internationals: Croatia U15, U16, U17, U19, U20, U21.

Season	Club				
2009–10	Inter Zapresic	38	0		
2010–11	Chelsea	0	0		
2011–12	Chelsea	0	0		
2011–12	*Dynamo Ceske*	1	0	**1**	**0**
2012–13	Chelsea	0	0		
2012–13	*Inter Zapresic*	14	0	**52**	**0**
2013–14	Chelsea	0	0		
2013–14	*Vojvodina*	10	0	**10**	**0**
2013–14	*FK Sarajevo*	7	0	**7**	**0**

ESSIEN, Michael (M)   326 37
H: 5 10   W: 13 06   b.Accra 3-12-82
Internationals: Ghana Full caps.

Season	Club				
2000–01	Bastia	13	1		
2001–02	Bastia	24	4		
2002–03	Bastia	29	6	**66**	**11**
2003–04	Lyon	34	3		
2004–05	Lyon	37	4	**71**	**7**
2005–06	Chelsea	31	2		
2006–07	Chelsea	33	2		
2007–08	Chelsea	27	6		
2008–09	Chelsea	11	1		
2009–10	Chelsea	14	3		
2010–11	Chelsea	33	3		
2011–12	Chelsea	14	0		
2012–13	*Real Madrid*	21	2	**21**	**2**
2013–14	Chelsea	5	0	**168**	**17**

Transferred to AC Milan January 2014

ETO'O, Samuel (F)   402 221
H: 5 11   W: 11 10   b.Nkon 10-3-81
Internationals: Cameroon U23, Full caps.

Season	Club				
2000–01	Mallorca	28	11		
2001–02	Mallorca	30	6		
2002–03	Mallorca	30	14		

2003–04	Mallorca	32	17	120	48
2004–05	Barcelona	37	24		
2005–06	Barcelona	34	26		
2006–07	Barcelona	19	11		
2007–08	Barcelona	18	16		
2008–09	Barcelona	36	30	144	107
2009–10	Inter Milan	30	11		
2010–11	Inter Milan	34	21	64	32
2011–12	Anzhi Makhachkala	22	13		
2012–13	Anzhi Makhachkala	25	10		
2013–14	Anzhi Makhachkala	6	2	53	25
2013–14	Chelsea	21	9	21	9

FERUZ, Islam (F)   0 0
b.Somalia 10-9-95
Internationals: Scotland U16, U17, U19, U20, U21.

2011–12	Chelsea	0	0
2013–14	Chelsea	0	0

HAZARD, Eden (M)   215 59
H: 5 7 W: 8 11 b.La Louviere 7-1-91
Internationals: Belgium U15, U16, U17, U19, Full caps.

2007–08	Lille	3	0		
2008–09	Lille	30	4		
2009–10	Lille	37	5		
2010–11	Lille	38	7		
2011–12	Lille	38	20	146	36
2012–13	Chelsea	34	9		
2013–14	Chelsea	35	14	69	23

HAZARD, Thorgan (M)   87 19
H: 5 8 W: 10 11 b.La Louviere 29-3-93
Internationals: Belgium U15, U16, U17, U18, U19, Full caps.

2011–12	Lens	14	0	14	0
2012–13	Chelsea	0	0		
2012–13	Zulte-Waregem	34	5		
2013–14	Chelsea	0	0		
2013–14	Zulte-Waregem	39	14	73	19

HUTCHINSON, Sam (M)   25 2
H: 6 0 W: 11 07 b.Windsor 3-8-89
Internationals: England U18, U19.

2006–07	Chelsea	1	0		
2007–08	Chelsea	0	0		
2008–09	Chelsea	0	0		
2009–10	Chelsea	2	0		
2010–11	Chelsea	0	0		
2011–12	Chelsea	2	0		
2012–13	Chelsea	0	0		
2012–13	Nottingham F	9	1	9	1
2013–14	Chelsea	0	0	5	0
2013–14	Vitesse	1	0	1	0
2013–14	Sheffield W	10	1	10	1

IVANOVIC, Branislav (M)   305 28
H: 6 0 W: 12 04 b.Sremska Mitreovica 22-2-84
Internationals: Serbia U21, Full caps.

2002–03	Sremska	19	2	19	2
2003–04	OFK Belgrade	13	0		
2004–05	OFK Belgrade	27	2		
2005–06	OFK Belgrade	15	3	55	5
2006	Loko Moscow	28	2		
2007	Loko Moscow	26	3	54	5
2007–08	Chelsea	0	0		
2008–09	Chelsea	16	0		
2009–10	Chelsea	28	1		
2010–11	Chelsea	34	4		
2011–12	Chelsea	29	3		
2012–13	Chelsea	34	5		
2013–14	Chelsea	36	3	177	16

KAKUTA, Gael (F)   67 7
H: 5 8 W: 10 03 b.Lille 21-6-91
Internationals: France U16, U17, U18, U19, U20, U21.

2008–09	Chelsea	0	0		
2009–10	Chelsea	1	0		
2010–11	Chelsea	5	0		
2010–11	Fulham	7	1	7	1
2011–12	Chelsea	0	0		
2011–12	Bolton W	4	0	4	0
2011–12	Dijon	14	4	14	4
2012–13	Chelsea	0	0		
2012–13	Vitesse	22	1		
2013–14	Chelsea	0	0	6	0
2013–14	Vitesse	13	1	35	2
2013–14	Lazio	1	0	1	0

KALAS, Tomas (D)   41 1
H: 6 0 W: 12 00 b.Olomouc 15-5-93
Internationals: Czech Republic U17, U18, U19, U21, Full caps.

2009–10	Sigma Olomouc	1	0		
2010–11	Chelsea	0	0		
2010–11	Sigma Olomouc	4	0	5	0
2011–12	Chelsea	0	0		
2012–13	Chelsea	0	0		
2012–13	Vitesse	34	1	34	1
2013–14	Chelsea	2	0	2	0

KANE, Todd (D)   44 2
H: 5 11 W: 11 00 b.Huntingdon 17-9-93
Internationals: England U19.

2011–12	Chelsea	0	0		
2012–13	Chelsea	0	0		
2012–13	Preston NE	3	0	3	0
2012–13	Blackburn R	14	0		
2013–14	Chelsea	0	0		
2013–14	Blackburn R	27	2	41	2

LALKOVIC, Milan (F)   54 6
b.Kosice 9-12-92
Internationals: Slovakia U17, U19, U21.

2010–11	Chelsea	0	0		
2011–12	Chelsea	0	0		
2011–12	Doncaster R	6	0	6	0
2011–12	Den Haag	2	0	2	0
2012–13	Chelsea	0	0		
2012–13	Vitoria Guimaraes	8	0	8	0
2013–14	Chelsea	0	0		
2013–14	Walsall	38	6	38	6

LAMPARD, Frank (M)   586 172
H: 6 0 W: 14 02 b.Romford 20-6-78
Internationals: England U21, B, Full caps.

1994–95	West Ham U	0	0		
1995–96	West Ham U	2	0		
1995–96	Swansea C	9	1	9	1
1996–97	West Ham U	13	0		
1997–98	West Ham U	31	5		
1998–99	West Ham U	38	5		
1999–2000	West Ham U	34	7		
2000–01	West Ham U	30	7	148	24
2001–02	Chelsea	37	5		
2002–03	Chelsea	38	6		
2003–04	Chelsea	38	10		
2004–05	Chelsea	38	13		
2005–06	Chelsea	35	16		
2006–07	Chelsea	37	11		
2007–08	Chelsea	24	10		
2008–09	Chelsea	37	12		
2009–10	Chelsea	36	22		
2010–11	Chelsea	24	10		
2011–12	Chelsea	30	11		
2012–13	Chelsea	29	15		
2013–14	Chelsea	26	6	429	147

LOFTUS-CHEEK, Ruben (M)   0 0
b. 23-1-96
Internationals: England U17, U19.

2012–13	Chelsea	0	0
2013–14	Chelsea	0	0

LUIZ, David (D)   189 11
H: 6 2 W: 13 03 b.Sao Paulo 22-4-87
Internationals: Brazil U20, Full caps.

2005	Vitoria	1	0		
2006	Vitoria	26	1	26	1
2006–07	Benfica	10	0		
2007–08	Benfica	8	0		
2008–09	Benfica	19	2		
2009–10	Benfica	29	2		
2010–11	Benfica	16	0	82	4
2010–11	Chelsea	12	2		
2011–12	Chelsea	20	2		
2012–13	Chelsea	30	2		
2013–14	Chelsea	19	0	81	6

LUKAKU, Romelu (F)   149 65
H: 6 3 W: 13 00 b.Antwerp 13-5-93
Internationals: Belgium U15, U18, U21, Full caps.

2008–09	Anderlecht	1	0		
2009–10	Anderlecht	33	15		
2010–11	Anderlecht	37	16		
2011–12	Anderlecht	2	2	73	33
2011–12	Chelsea	8	0		
2012–13	Chelsea	0	0		
2012–13	WBA	35	17	35	17

2013–14	Chelsea	2	0	10	0
2013–14	Everton	31	15	31	15

MARIN, Marko (M)   172 17
H: 5 7 W: 9 12 b.Gradiska 13-3-89
Internationals: Germany U16, U17, U18, U21, Full caps.

2006–07	Moenchengladbach	3	0		
2007–08	Moenchengladbach	25	4		
2008–09	Moenchengladbach	33	4	61	8
2009–10	Werder Bremen	32	4		
2010–11	Werder Bremen	34	3		
2011–12	Werder Bremen	21	1	87	8
2012–13	Chelsea	6	1		
2013–14	Chelsea	0	0	6	1
2013–14	Sevilla	18	0	18	0

MATIC, Nemanja (M)   185 12
H: 6 4 W: 13 02 b.Sabac 1-8-88
Internationals: Serbia U21, Full caps.

2005–06	Jedinstvo	7	0		
2006–07	Jedinstvo	9	0	16	0
2006–07	Kosice	13	1		
2007–08	Kosice	25	1		
2008–09	Kosice	29	2	67	4
2009–10	Chelsea	2	0		
2010–11	Chelsea	0	0		
2010–11	Vitesse	27	2	27	2
2011–12	Benfica	16	1		
2012–13	Benfica	26	3		
2013–14	Benfica	14	2	56	6
2013–14	Chelsea	17	0	19	0

McEACHRAN, Josh (D)   68 0
H: 5 10 W: 10 03 b.Oxford 1-3-93
Internationals: England U16, U17, U19, U21.

2010–11	Chelsea	9	0		
2011–12	Chelsea	2	0		
2011–12	Swansea C	4	0	4	0
2012–13	Chelsea	0	0		
2012–13	Middlesbrough	38	0	38	0
2013–14	Chelsea	0	0	11	0
2013–14	Watford	7	0	7	0
2013–14	Wigan Ath	8	0	8	0

MIKEL, John Obi (M)   212 2
H: 6 0 W: 13 05 b.Plateau State 22-4-87
Internationals: Nigeria Youth, Full caps.

2005	Lyn	6	1	6	1
2006–07	Chelsea	22	0		
2007–08	Chelsea	29	0		
2008–09	Chelsea	34	0		
2009–10	Chelsea	25	0		
2010–11	Chelsea	28	0		
2011–12	Chelsea	22	0		
2012–13	Chelsea	22	0		
2013–14	Chelsea	24	1	206	1

MOSES, Victor (M)   174 21
H: 5 10 W: 11 07 b.Lagos 12-12-90
Internationals: England U16, U17, U19, U21. Nigeria Full caps.

2007–08	Crystal Palace	13	3		
2008–09	Crystal Palace	27	2		
2009–10	Crystal Palace	18	6	58	11
2009–10	Wigan Ath	14	1		
2010–11	Wigan Ath	21	1		
2011–12	Wigan Ath	38	6		
2012–13	Wigan Ath	1	0	74	8
2012–13	Chelsea	23	1		
2013–14	Chelsea	0	0	23	1
2013–14	Liverpool	19	1	19	1

OMERUO, Kenneth (D)   41 0
H: 6 1 W: 12 00 b.Nigeria 17-10-93
Internationals: Nigeria U17, U20, Full caps.

2011–12	Chelsea	0	0		
2012–13	Chelsea	0	0		
2012–13	ADO Den Haag	27	0	27	0
2013–14	Chelsea	0	0		
2013–14	Middlesbrough	14	0	14	0

OSCAR, Emboaba (M)   105 22
H: 5 11 W: 10 04 b.Americana 9-9-91
Internationals: Brazil U20, U23, Full caps.

2008–09	Sao Paulo	1	0		
2009–10	Sao Paulo	3	0	4	0
2010–11	Internacional	7	2		
2011–12	Internacional	27	8	34	10
2012–13	Chelsea	34	4		
2013–14	Chelsea	33	8	67	12

PAPPOE, Daniel (D) 2 0
b.Accra 30-12-93
Internationals: Ghana U20.

2011–12	Chelsea	0	0	
2012–13	Chelsea	0	0	
2013–14	Chelsea	0	0	
2013–14	Colchester U	2	0	2 0

PERICA, Stipe (F) 45 14
H: 6 3 b.Zadar 7-7-95
Internationals: Croatia U19, U20, U21.

2012–13	Zadar	20	8	20 8
2013–14	Chelsea	0	0	
2013–14	NAC Breda	25	6	25 6

PIAZON, Lucas (M) 41 11
H: 6 0 W: 11 11 b.Curitiba 20-1-94
Internationals: Brazil U15, U17.

2011–12	Chelsea	0	0	
2012–13	Chelsea	1	0	
2012–13	*Malaga*	11	0	11 0
2013–14	Chelsea	0	0	
2013–14	*Vitesse*	29	11	29 11

RAMIRES (M) 225 30
H: 5 11 W: 10 03 b.Rio de Janeiro 24-3-87
Internationals: Brazil U23, Full caps.

2006	Joinville	14	3	14 3
2007	Cruzeiro	32	3	
2008	Cruzeiro	25	6	
2009	Cruzeiro	4	1	61 10
2009–10	Benfica	26	4	26 4
2010–11	Chelsea	29	2	
2011–12	Chelsea	30	5	
2012–13	Chelsea	35	5	
2013–14	Chelsea	30	1	124 13

ROMEU, Oriol (M) 85 1
H: 6 0 W: 12 06 b.Ulldecona 24-9-91
Internationals: Spain U17, U19, U20, U21, U23.

2008–09	Barcelona B	5	0	
2009–10	Barcelona B	26	0	
2010–11	Barcelona B	18	1	49 1
2010–11	Barcelona	1	0	1 0
2011–12	Chelsea	16	0	
2012–13	Chelsea	6	0	
2013–14	Chelsea	0	0	22 0
2013–14	*Valencia*	13	0	13 0

SALAH, Mohamed (M) 93 22
H: 5 9 W: 11 04 b.Basion 15-6-92
Internationals: Egypt U20, U23, Full caps

2010–11	Al-Mokawloon	21	4	
2011–12	Al-Mokawloon	15	7	36 11
2012–13	Basle	29	5	
2013–14	Basle	18	4	47 9
2013–14	Chelsea	10	2	10 2

SAVILLE, George (M) 43 3
H: 5 9 W: 11 07 b.Camberley 1-6-93

2010–11	Chelsea	0	0	
2011–12	Chelsea	0	0	
2012–13	Chelsea	0	0	
2012–13	*Millwall*	3	0	3 0
2013–14	Chelsea	0	0	
2013–14	*Brentford*	40	3	40 3

SCHURRLE, Andre (F) 161 46
H: 6 0 W: 11 06 b.Ludwigshafen 6-11-90
Internationals: Germany U19, U20, U21, Full caps.

2009–10	Mainz	33	5	
2010–11	Mainz	33	15	66 20
2011–12	Bayer Leverkusen	31	7	
2012–13	Bayer Leverkusen	34	11	65 18
2013–14	Chelsea	30	8	30 8

SCHWARZER, Mark (G) 620 0
H: 6 4 W: 14 07 b.Sydney 6-10-72
Internationals: Australia U17, U20, U23, Full caps.

1990–91	Marconi Stallions	1	0	
1991–92	Marconi Stallions	9	0	
1992–93	Marconi Stallions	25	0	
1993–94	Marconi Stallions	25	0	58 0
1994–95	Dynamo Dresden	2	0	2 0
1995–96	Kaiserslautern	4	0	
1996–97	Kaiserslautern	0	0	4 0
1996–97	Bradford C	13	0	13 0
1996–97	Middlesbrough	7	0	
1997–98	Middlesbrough	35	0	
1998–99	Middlesbrough	34	0	
1999–2000	Middlesbrough	37	0	
2000–01	Middlesbrough	31	0	
2001–02	Middlesbrough	21	0	
2002–03	Middlesbrough	38	0	
2003–04	Middlesbrough	36	0	
2004–05	Middlesbrough	31	0	
2005–06	Middlesbrough	27	0	
2006–07	Middlesbrough	36	0	
2007–08	Middlesbrough	34	0	367 0
2008–09	Fulham	38	0	
2009–10	Fulham	37	0	
2010–11	Fulham	31	0	
2011–12	Fulham	30	0	
2012–13	Fulham	36	0	172 0
2013–14	Chelsea	4	0	4 0

SWIFT, John (M) 1 0
b.Portsmouth 23-6-95
Internationals: England U16, U17, U18, U19.

2013–14	Chelsea	1	0	1 0

TERRY, John (D) 427 34
H: 6 1 W: 14 02 b.Barking 7-12-80
Internationals: England U21, Full caps.

1997–98	Chelsea	0	0	
1998–99	Chelsea	2	0	
1999–2000	Chelsea	4	0	
1999–2000	Nottingham F	6	0	6 0
2000–01	Chelsea	22	1	
2001–02	Chelsea	33	1	
2002–03	Chelsea	20	3	
2003–04	Chelsea	33	2	
2004–05	Chelsea	36	3	
2005–06	Chelsea	36	4	
2006–07	Chelsea	28	1	
2007–08	Chelsea	23	1	
2008–09	Chelsea	35	1	
2009–10	Chelsea	37	2	
2010–11	Chelsea	33	3	
2011–12	Chelsea	31	6	
2012–13	Chelsea	14	4	
2013–14	Chelsea	34	2	421 34

TORRES, Fernando (F) 386 160
H: 5 9 W: 12 03 b.Madrid 20-3-84
Internationals: Spain U15, U16, U17, U18, U19, U21, Full caps.

2002–03	Atletico Madrid	29	13	
2003–04	Atletico Madrid	35	19	
2004–05	Atletico Madrid	38	16	
2005–06	Atletico Madrid	36	13	
2006–07	Atletico Madrid	36	14	174 75
2007–08	Liverpool	33	24	
2008–09	Liverpool	24	14	
2009–10	Liverpool	22	18	
2010–11	Liverpool	23	9	102 65
2010–11	Chelsea	14	1	
2011–12	Chelsea	32	6	
2012–13	Chelsea	36	8	
2013–14	Chelsea	28	5	110 20

TRAORE, Bertrand (M) 13 3
H: 5 10 b.Bob-Dioulasso 6-9-95
Internationals: Burkina Faso U17, Full caps

2013–14	Chelsea	0	0	
2013–14	*Vitesse*	13	3	13 3

VAN AANHOLT, Patrick (D) 111 6
H: 5 9 W: 10 08 b.Den Bosch 3-7-88
Internationals: Netherlands U16, U17, U18, U19, U20, U21, Full caps.

2007–08	Chelsea	0	0	
2008–09	Chelsea	0	0	
2009–10	Chelsea	2	0	
2009–10	Coventry C	20	0	20 0
2009–10	Newcastle U	7	0	7 0
2010–11	Chelsea	0	0	
2010–11	Leicester C	12	1	12 1
2011–12	Chelsea	0	0	
2011–12	Wigan Ath	3	0	3 0
2011–12	Vitesse	9	0	
2012–13	Chelsea	0	0	
2012–13	Vitesse	31	1	
2013–14	Chelsea	0	0	2 0
2013–14	*Vitesse*	27	4	67 5

VAN GINKEL, Marco (M) 98 18
H: 6 1 W: 12 11 b.Amersfoort 1-12-92
Internationals: Netherlands U15, U19, U21, Full caps

2009–10	Vitesse	3	0	
2010–11	Vitesse	26	5	
2011–12	Vitesse	34	5	
2012–13	Vitesse	33	8	96 18
2013–14	Chelsea	2	0	2 0

WALLACE, Oliveira (D) 24 1
H: 5 9 W: 10 09 b.Rio de Jainero 1-5-94
Internationals: Brazil U17, U20.

2011	Fluminense	3	0	
2012	Fluminense	18	1	21 1
2013–14	Chelsea	0	0	
2013–14	*Inter Milan*	3	0	3 0

WILLIAN, da Silva (M) 161 25
H: 5 9 W: 11 10 b.Ribeirao 9-8-88
Internationals: Brazil U20, Full caps.

2006	Corinthians	5	0	
2007	Corinthians	0	0	5 0
2008–09	Shakhtar Donetsk	29	5	
2009–10	Shakhtar Donetsk	22	5	
2010–11	Shakhtar Donetsk	28	3	
2011–12	Shakhtar Donetsk	27	5	
2012–13	Shakhtar Donetsk	14	2	120 20
2012–13	Anzhi Makhachkala	7	1	
2013–14	Anzhi Makhachkala	4	0	11 1
2013–14	Chelsea	25	4	25 4

ZOUMA, Kurt (D) 61 3
H: 6 2 W: 13 04 b.Lyon 27-10-94
Internationals: France U16, U17, U19, U20, U21.

2011–12	St Etienne	20	1	
2012–13	St Etienne	18	2	
2013–14	Chelsea	0	0	
2013–14	*St Etienne*	23	0	61 3

Scholars
Boga, Jeremie; Brady, George; Collins, Bradley Ray; Palmer, Kasey Remel.

CHELTENHAM T (23)

BRAHAM-BARRETT, Craig (D) 29 0
H: 5 9 b.England 1-9-88

2013–14	Cheltenham T	29	0	29 0

BROWN, Scott P (G) 252 0
H: 6 2 W: 13 01 b.Wolverhampton 26-4-85
From Welshpool T

2003–04	Bristol C	0	0	
2004–05	Cheltenham T	0	0	
2005–06	Cheltenham T	1	0	
2006–07	Cheltenham T	11	0	
2007–08	Cheltenham T	0	0	
2008–09	Cheltenham T	35	0	
2009–10	Cheltenham T	46	0	
2010–11	Cheltenham T	46	0	
2011–12	Cheltenham T	22	0	
2012–13	Cheltenham T	46	0	
2013–14	Cheltenham T	45	0	252 0

BROWN, Troy (D) 109 10
H: 6 1 W: 12 01 b.Croydon 17-9-90
Internationals: Wales U17, U19, U21.

2009–10	Ipswich T	1	0	
2010–11	Ipswich T	12	0	13 0
2011–12	Rotherham U	6	1	6 1
2011–12	Aldershot T	17	2	
2012–13	Aldershot T	34	3	51 5
2013–14	Cheltenham T	39	4	39 4

CURETON, Jamie (F) 672 237
H: 5 8 W: 10 07 b.Bristol 28-8-75
Internationals: England Youth.

1992–93	Norwich C	0	0	
1993–94	Norwich C	0	0	
1994–95	Norwich C	17	4	
1995–96	Norwich C	12	2	
1995–96	*Bournemouth*	5	0	5 0
1996–97	Norwich C	12	0	
1996–97	Bristol R	38	11	
1997–98	Bristol R	43	13	
1998–99	Bristol R	46	25	
1999–2000	Bristol R	46	22	
2000–01	Bristol R	1	1	174 72
2000–01	Reading	43	26	
2001–02	Reading	38	15	
2002–03	Reading	27	9	108 50
From Busan Icons				
2003–04	QPR	13	2	
2004–05	QPR	30	4	43 6
2005–06	Swindon T	30	7	30 7
2005–06	*Colchester U*	8	4	

2006–07	Colchester U	44	23	52	27
2007–08	Norwich C	41	12		
2008–09	Norwich C	22	2		
2008–09	*Barnsley*	8	2	8	2
2009–10	Norwich C	6	2	98	22
2009–10	*Shrewsbury T*	12	0	12	0
2010–11	Exeter C	41	17		
2011–12	Leyton Orient	19	1	19	1
2011–12	*Exeter C*	7	1		
2012–13	Exeter C	40	21	88	39
2013–14	Cheltenham T	35	11	35	11

DALE, Bobbie (F)   1   0
2013–14	Cheltenham T	1	0	1	0

DEERING, Sam (M)   133   5
H: 5 5   W: 10 00   b.Stepney 26-2-91
Internationals: England C.
2010–11	Oxford U	6	0	6	0
2010–11	Barnet	16	2		
2011–12	Barnet	44	3	60	5
2012–13	Cheltenham T	32	0		
2013–14	Cheltenham T	35	0	67	0

ELLIOTT, Steve (D)   476   25
H: 6 1   W: 14 00   b.Derby 29-10-78
Internationals: England U21.
1996–97	Derby Co	0	0		
1997–98	Derby Co	3	0		
1998–99	Derby Co	11	0		
1999–2000	Derby Co	20	0		
2000–01	Derby Co	6	0		
2001–02	Derby Co	6	0		
2002–03	Derby Co	23	1		
2003–04	Derby Co	4	0	73	1
2003–04	*Blackpool*	28	0	28	0
2004–05	Bristol R	41	2		
2005–06	Bristol R	45	2		
2006–07	Bristol R	39	5		
2007–08	Bristol R	33	3		
2008–09	Bristol R	39	3		
2009–10	Bristol R	21	1	218	16
2010–11	Cheltenham T	41	1		
2011–12	Cheltenham T	38	2		
2012–13	Cheltenham T	46	4		
2013–14	Cheltenham T	32	1	157	8

GORNELL, Terry (F)   197   37
H: 5 11   W: 12 04   b.Liverpool 16-12-89
2008–09	Tranmere R	10	1		
2008–09	*Accrington S*	11	4		
2009–10	Tranmere R	27	2		
2010–11	Tranmere R	3	0	40	3
2010–11	Accrington S	40	13	51	17
2011–12	Shrewsbury T	41	9		
2012–13	Shrewsbury T	12	0	53	9
2012–13	*Rochdale*	19	5	19	5
2013–14	Cheltenham T	34	3	34	3

HANKS, Joe (M)   3   0
b.Gloucester 2-3-95
2012–13	Cheltenham T	1	0		
2013–14	Cheltenham T	2	0	3	0

HARRISON, Byron (F)   141   34
H: 6 3   W: 13 02   b.Wandsworth 15-6-87
2010–11	Stevenage	20	8		
2011–12	Stevenage	18	2	38	10
2011–12	AFC Wimbledon	19	2		
2012–13	AFC Wimbledon	21	8	40	10
2012–13	Cheltenham T	17	1		
2013–14	Cheltenham T	46	13	63	14

JOMBATI, Sido (D)   116   4
H: 6 0   W: 11 11   b.Lisbon 20-8-87
2011–12	Cheltenham T	36	2		
2012–13	Cheltenham T	37	1		
2013–14	Cheltenham T	43	1	116	4

KOTWICA, Zack (M)   18   0
b. 18-1-95
2013–14	Cheltenham T	18	0	18	0

McGLASHAN, Jermaine (M)   165   17
H: 5 7   W: 10 00   b.Croydon 14-4-88
2010–11	Aldershot T	38	1		
2011–12	Aldershot T	23	4	61	5
2011–12	Cheltenham T	16	2		
2012–13	Cheltenham T	45	4		
2013–14	Cheltenham T	43	6	104	12

RICHARDS, Matt (D)   417   39
H: 5 8   W: 11 00   b.Harlow 26-12-84
Internationals: England U16, U17, U18, U21.
2001–02	Ipswich T	0	0		
2002–03	Ipswich T	13	0		
2003–04	Ipswich T	44	1		
2004–05	Ipswich T	24	1		
2005–06	Ipswich T	38	4		
2006–07	Ipswich T	28	2		
2007–08	Ipswich T	0	0		
2007–08	*Brighton & HA*	28	0		
2008–09	Brighton & HA	23	1	51	1
2008–09	*Wycombe W*	0	0		
2008–09	*Notts Co*	1	0	1	0
2008–09	Ipswich T	1	0	148	8
2009–10	Walsall	40	4		
2010–11	Walsall	46	8	86	12
2011–12	Shrewsbury T	42	5		
2012–13	Shrewsbury T	43	7	85	12
2013–14	Cheltenham T	46	6	46	6

ROBERTS, Connor (G)   1   0
b.Wrexham 8-12-92
Internationals: Wales U19, U21.
2009–10	Everton	0	0		
2010–11	Everton	0	0		
2011–12	Everton	0	0		
2012–13	Colwyn Bay	0	0		
2013–14	Cheltenham T	0	0		
2013–14	Cheltenham T	1	0	1	0

TAYLOR, Jason (M)   294   19
H: 6 1   W: 11 03   b.Ashton-under-Lyne 28-1-87
2005–06	Oldham Ath	0	0		
2005–06	*Stockport Co*	9	0		
2006–07	Stockport Co	45	1		
2007–08	Stockport Co	42	4		
2008–09	Stockport Co	8	1	104	6
2008–09	Rotherham U	15	1		
2009–10	Rotherham U	2	0		
2009–10	*Rochdale*	23	1	23	1
2010–11	Rotherham U	42	5		
2011–12	Rotherham U	39	2		
2012–13	Rotherham U	20	2	118	10
2012–13	Cheltenham T	16	0		
2013–14	Cheltenham T	33	2	49	2

VINCENT, Ashley (M)   233   27
H: 5 10   W: 11 08   b.Oldbury 26-5-85
2004–05	Cheltenham T	26	1		
2005–06	Cheltenham T	13	2		
2006–07	Cheltenham T	5	0		
2007–08	Cheltenham T	37	2		
2008–09	Cheltenham T	29	3		
2008–09	*Colchester U*	6	1		
2009–10	Colchester U	19	3		
2010–11	Colchester U	37	5		
2011–12	Colchester U	9	1	71	10
2012–13	Port Vale	34	7	34	7
2013–14	Cheltenham T	18	2	128	10

WILLIAMS, Harry (M)   5   0
2013–14	Cheltenham T	5	0	5	0

Scholars
Bowen, James Malcolm Robert; Craddock, Callum David; Dale, Robson Louis; Daly, Reece John; Goodwin, Jamie Liam; Hamilton, Spencer Jon; Keightley, Elliott Nigel; Kirkpatrick-Jones, Zachary Daniel; Lawrence, Jamal Courtney; Marshall, Callum; McFarlane, Callum Robert; Powell, Adam Thomas; Reynolds, Danny James; Reynolds, Harry; Rivers, Harvey Charles; Sheppard, Liam Paul; Whitehead, Kieran John; Williams, Harry John Robert.

CHESTERFIELD (24)

BANKS, Oliver (D)   26   8
H: 6 3   W: 11 11   b.Rotherham 21-9-92
2010–11	Rotherham U	1	1		
2011–12	Rotherham U	0	0	1	1
2013–14	Chesterfield	25	7	25	7

BROADHEAD, Jack (D)   0   0
b. 2-10-94
2012–13	Chesterfield	0	0		
2013–14	Chesterfield	0	0		

BROWN, Matt (D)   3   1
2013–14	Chesterfield	3	1	3	1

CHAPMAN, Aaron (G)   0   0
b. 29-5-90
2013–14	Chesterfield	0	0		

COOPER, Liam (D)   91   6
H: 6 2   W: 13 07   b.Hull 30-8-91
Internationals: Scotland U17, U19.
2008–09	Hull C	0	0		
2009–10	Hull C	2	0		
2009–10	Hull C	2	0		
2010–11	*Carlisle U*	6	1	6	1
2011–12	Hull C	7	0		
2011–12	*Huddersfield T*	4	0	4	0
2012–13	Hull C	0	0	11	0
2012–13	Chesterfield	29	2		
2013–14	Chesterfield	41	3	70	5

DARIKWA, Tendayi (M)   79   8
H: 6 2   W: 12 02   b.Nottingham 13-12-91
2010–11	Chesterfield	0	0		
2011–12	Chesterfield	2	0		
2012–13	Chesterfield	36	5		
2013–14	Chesterfield	41	3	79	8

DEVITT, Jamie (F)   91   13
H: 5 10   W: 10 05   b.Dublin 6-7-90
Internationals: Republic of Ireland U21.
2007–08	Hull C	0	0		
2008–09	Hull C	0	0		
2009–10	Hull C	0	0		
2009–10	*Darlington*	6	1	6	1
2009–10	*Shrewsbury T*	9	2	9	2
2009–10	*Grimsby T*	15	5	15	5
2010–11	Hull C	16	0		
2011–12	Hull C	0	0		
2011–12	*Bradford C*	7	1	7	1
2011–12	*Accrington S*	16	2	16	2
2012–13	Hull C	0	0	16	0
2012–13	*Rotherham U*	1	0	1	0
2013–14	Chesterfield	7	0	7	0
2013–14	*Morecambe*	14	2	14	2

DOYLE, Eoin (F)   176   51
H: 6 0   b. 12-3-88
2009	Sligo	15	3		
2010	Sligo	35	6		
2011	Sligo	34	20	84	29
2011–12	Hibernian	13	1		
2012–13	Hibernian	36	10	49	11
2013–14	Chesterfield	43	11	43	11

EVATT, Ian (D)   421   19
H: 6 3   W: 13 12   b.Coventry 19-11-81
1998–99	Derby Co	0	0		
1999–2000	Derby Co	0	0		
2000–01	Derby Co	1	0		
2001–02	*Northampton T*	11	0	11	0
2001–02	Derby Co	3	0		
2002–03	Derby Co	30	0	34	0
2003–04	Chesterfield	43	5		
2004–05	Chesterfield	41	4		
2005–06	QPR	27	0		
2006–07	QPR	0	0	27	0
2006–07	Blackpool	44	0		
2007–08	Blackpool	29	0		
2008–09	Blackpool	33	1		
2009–10	Blackpool	36	4		
2010–11	Blackpool	38	1		
2011–12	Blackpool	39	3		
2012–13	Blackpool	11	0	230	9
2013–14	Chesterfield	35	1	119	10

GARDNER, Dan (M)   18   3
H: 6 1   W: 12 05   b.Manchester 5-4-90
2009–10	Crewe Alex	2	0	2	0

From Droylsden, FC Halifax T
2013–14	Chesterfield	16	3	16	3

GNANDUILLET, Armand (F)   47   8
H: 6 4   W: 13 12   b.Angers 13-2-92
Internationals: Ivory Coast U20.
2012–13	Chesterfield	13	3		
2013–14	Chesterfield	34	5	47	8

HIRD, Samuel (D)   238   5
H: 5 7   W: 10 12   b.Askern 7-9-87
2005–06	Leeds U	0	0		
2006–07	Leeds U	0	0		
2006–07	*Doncaster R*	5	0		
2007–08	Doncaster R	4	0		
2007–08	*Grimsby T*	17	0	17	0
2008–09	Doncaster R	37	1		
2009–10	Doncaster R	36	0		

2010–11	Doncaster R	32	0	
2011–12	Doncaster R	31	0	145 1
2012–13	Chesterfield	41	2	
2013–14	Chesterfield	35	2	76 4

HUMPHREYS, Richie (M) 619 47
H: 5 11 W: 12 07 b.Sheffield 30-11-77
Internationals: England U20, U21.

1995–96	Sheffield W	5	0	
1996–97	Sheffield W	29	3	
1997–98	Sheffield W	7	0	
1998–99	Sheffield W	19	1	
1999–2000	Sheffield W	0	0	
1999–2000	*Scunthorpe U*	6	2	6 2
1999–2000	*Cardiff C*	9	2	9 2
2000–01	Sheffield W	7	0	67 4
2000–01	Cambridge U	7	3	7 3
2001–02	Hartlepool U	46	5	
2002–03	Hartlepool U	46	11	
2003–04	Hartlepool U	46	3	
2004–05	Hartlepool U	46	3	
2005–06	Hartlepool U	46	2	
2006–07	Hartlepool U	38	3	
2006–07	*Port Vale*	7	0	7 0
2007–08	Hartlepool U	45	3	
2008–09	Hartlepool U	45	0	
2009–10	Hartlepool U	38	0	
2010–11	Hartlepool U	25	2	
2011–12	Hartlepool U	29	1	
2012–13	Hartlepool U	31	1	481 34
2013–14	Chesterfield	42	2	42 2

LEE, Tommy (G) 303 0
H: 6 2 W: 12 00 b.Keighley 3-1-86

2005–06	Manchester U	0	0	
2005–06	Macclesfield T	11	0	
2006–07	Macclesfield T	34	0	
2007–08	Macclesfield T	18	0	63 0
2007–08	*Rochdale*	11	0	11 0
2008–09	Chesterfield	28	0	
2009–10	Chesterfield	42	0	
2010–11	Chesterfield	46	0	
2011–12	Chesterfield	35	0	
2012–13	Chesterfield	32	0	
2013–14	Chesterfield	46	0	229 0

MORSY, Sam (M) 105 5
H: 5 9 W: 12 06 b.Wolverhampton 10-9-91

2009–10	Port Vale	1	0	
2010–11	Port Vale	16	1	
2011–12	Port Vale	26	1	
2012–13	Port Vale	28	2	71 4
2013–14	Chesterfield	34	1	34 1

O'SHEA, Jay (M) 193 38
H: 5 9 W: 12 00 b.Dun Laoghaire 10-8-88
Internationals: Republic of Ireland U19, U21, U23.

2007	Bray Wanderers	27	4	27 4
2008	Galway U	29	8	
2009	Galway U	19	3	48 11
2009–10	Birmingham C	1	0	
2009–10	*Middlesbrough*	2	0	2 0
2010–11	Birmingham C	0	0	1 0
2010–11	*Stevenage*	5	0	5 0
2010–11	*Port Vale*	5	1	5 1
2011–12	Milton Keynes D	28	5	
2012–13	Milton Keynes D	11	3	39 6
2012–13	*Chesterfield*	26	7	
2013–14	Chesterfield	40	9	66 16

ROBERTS, Gary (F) 313 57
H: 5 10 W: 11 09 b.Chester 18-3-84
Internationals: England C.

2006–07	Accrington S	14	8	14 8
2006–07	Ipswich T	33	2	
2007–08	Ipswich T	21	1	54 3
2007–08	*Crewe Alex*	4	0	4 0
2008–09	Huddersfield T	43	9	
2009–10	Huddersfield T	43	7	
2010–11	Huddersfield T	37	9	
2011–12	Huddersfield T	39	6	162 31
2012–13	Swindon T	39	4	39 4
2013–14	Chesterfield	40	11	40 11

RYAN, James (M) 241 28
H: 5 8 W: 11 08 b.Maghull 6-9-88
Internationals: Republic of Ireland U21.
Northern Ireland Full caps.

2006–07	Liverpool	0	0	
2007–08	Liverpool	0	0	
2007–08	*Shrewsbury T*	4	0	4 0
2008–09	Accrington S	44	10	
2009–10	Accrington S	39	3	
2010–11	Accrington S	46	9	129 22
2011–12	Scunthorpe U	24	2	
2012–13	Scunthorpe U	45	2	69 4
2013–14	Chesterfield	39	2	39 2

SMITH, Nathan (D) 181 1
H: 5 11 W: 12 00 b.Enfield 11-1-87
Internationals: Jamaica Full caps.

2007–08	Yeovil T	7	0	
2008–09	Yeovil T	33	1	
2009–10	Yeovil T	34	0	
2010–11	Yeovil T	40	0	114 1
2011–12	Chesterfield	25	0	
2012–13	Chesterfield	29	0	
2013–14	Chesterfield	13	0	67 0

TALBOT, Drew (F) 282 23
H: 5 11 W: 11 00 b.Barnsley 19-7-86

2003–04	Sheffield W	0	0	
2004–05	Sheffield W	21	4	
2005–06	Sheffield W	0	0	
2006–07	Sheffield W	8	0	29 4
2006–07	*Scunthorpe U*	3	1	3 1
2006–07	Luton T	15	3	
2007–08	Luton T	27	0	
2008–09	Luton T	7	0	49 3
2008–09	*Chesterfield*	17	2	
2009–10	Chesterfield	30	6	
2010–11	Chesterfield	44	3	
2011–12	Chesterfield	43	2	
2012–13	Chesterfield	42	2	
2013–14	Chesterfield	25	0	201 15

TOGWELL, Sam (M) 321 12
H: 5 11 W: 12 04 b.Beaconsfield 14-10-84

2002–03	Crystal Palace	1	0	
2003–04	Crystal Palace	0	0	
2004–05	Crystal Palace	0	0	
2004–05	*Oxford U*	4	0	4 0
2004–05	*Northampton T*	8	0	8 0
2005–06	Crystal Palace	0	0	1 0
2005–06	*Port Vale*	27	2	27 2
2006–07	Barnsley	44	1	
2007–08	Barnsley	22	1	66 2
2008–09	Scunthorpe U	40	2	
2009–10	Scunthorpe U	41	2	
2010–11	Scunthorpe U	36	0	
2011–12	Scunthorpe U	39	1	156 5
2012–13	Chesterfield	45	3	
2013–14	Chesterfield	10	0	55 3
2013–14	*Wycombe W*	4	0	4 0

Scholars
Bayne, Joseph John; Beesley, Jake Elliott; Brock, Oliver; Colton, Thomas Edward; Coy, Mason Taylor; Dakwa, Edward Junior Munashe; Edridge, Regan William John; Hewitt, Alex James Joel; Johnson, Fabian Jacob; Maguire, Laurence Henry; Mason, Cameron Francis; Massey, Joseph Paul; Mathers, Joseph Jordan; McNicholas, Jamie; Partridge, Benjamin Jon; Sugden, Lewis Jack; Walshaw, Jordan Thomas.

COLCHESTER U (25)

BEAN, Marcus (M) 329 24
H: 5 11 W: 11 06 b.Hammersmith 2-11-84
Internationals: Jamaica Full caps.

2002–03	QPR	7	0	
2003–04	QPR	31	1	
2004–05	QPR	20	1	
2004–05	Swansea C	8	0	
2005–06	QPR	9	0	67 2
2005–06	Swansea C	9	1	17 1
2005–06	Blackpool	17	1	
2006–07	Blackpool	6	0	
2007–08	Blackpool	0	0	23 1
2007–08	*Rotherham U*	12	1	12 1
2008–09	Brentford	44	9	
2009–10	Brentford	31	0	
2010–11	Brentford	37	3	
2011–12	Brentford	32	2	144 14
2012–13	Colchester U	31	0	
2013–14	Colchester U	35	5	66 5

BOND, Andy (M) 127 11
H: 5 10 W: 11 07 b.Wigan 16-3-86
Internationals: England C.

2010–11	Colchester U	43	7	
2011–12	Colchester U	40	3	
2012–13	Colchester U	27	0	
2012–13	Crewe Alex	4	0	4 0
2013–14	Colchester U	8	1	118 11
2013–14	*Bristol R*	5	0	5 0

BONNE, Macauley (F) 14 2
b. 26-10-95

2013–14	Colchester U	14	2	14 2

BRANSGROVE, James (G) 0 0
b. 12-5-95

2013–14	Colchester U	0	0	

COUSINS, Mark (G) 58 0
H: 6 2 W: 12 02 b.Chelmsford 9-1-87

2005–06	Colchester U	0	0	
2006–07	Colchester U	0	0	
2007–08	Colchester U	2	0	
2008–09	Colchester U	9	0	
2009–10	Colchester U	0	0	
2010–11	Colchester U	14	0	
2011–12	Colchester U	10	0	
2012–13	Colchester U	23	0	
2013–14	Colchester U	0	0	58 0

CURTIS, Jack (M) 0 0

2013–14	Colchester U	0	0	

DICKSON, Ryan (M) 185 7
H: 5 10 W: 11 05 b.Saltash 14-12-86

2004–05	Plymouth Arg	3	0	
2005–06	Plymouth Arg	0	0	
2006–07	Plymouth Arg	2	0	
2006–07	*Torquay U*	9	1	9 1
2007–08	Plymouth Arg	0	0	5 0
2007–08	Brentford	31	0	
2008–09	Brentford	39	1	
2009–10	Brentford	27	2	97 3
2010–11	Southampton	23	1	
2011–12	Southampton	0	0	
2011–12	*Yeovil T*	5	1	5 1
2011–12	*Leyton Orient*	9	0	9 0
2012–13	Southampton	0	0	23 1
2012–13	*Bradford C*	5	1	5 1
2013–14	Colchester U	32	0	32 0

DUGUID, Karl (M) 523 47
H: 5 11 W: 11 06 b.Letchworth 21-3-78

1995–96	Colchester U	16	1	
1996–97	Colchester U	20	3	
1997–98	Colchester U	21	3	
1998–99	Colchester U	33	4	
1999–2000	Colchester U	41	12	
2000–01	Colchester U	41	5	
2001–02	Colchester U	41	4	
2002–03	Colchester U	27	3	
2003–04	Colchester U	30	2	
2004–05	Colchester U	0	0	
2005–06	Colchester U	35	0	
2006–07	Colchester U	43	5	
2007–08	Colchester U	37	0	
2008–09	Plymouth Arg	39	1	
2009–10	Plymouth Arg	42	1	
2010–11	Plymouth Arg	26	0	107 2
2011–12	Colchester U	25	3	
2012–13	Colchester U	5	0	
2013–14	Colchester U	1	0	416 45

EASTMAN, Tom (D) 106 5
H: 6 3 W: 13 12 b.Clacton 21-10-91

2009–10	Ipswich T	1	0	
2010–11	Ipswich T	9	0	10 0
2011–12	Colchester U	25	3	
2011–12	*Crawley T*	6	0	6 0
2012–13	Colchester U	29	2	
2013–14	Colchester U	36	0	90 5

EASTMOND, Craig (D) 75 6
H: 6 0 W: 11 11 b.Wandsworth 9-12-90

2009–10	Arsenal	4	0	
2010–11	Arsenal	0	0	
2010–11	*Millwall*	6	0	6 0
2011–12	Arsenal	0	0	
2011–12	*Wycombe W*	14	0	14 0
2012–13	Arsenal	0	0	4 0
2012–13	*Colchester U*	12	2	
2013–14	Colchester U	39	4	51 6

GILBEY, Alex (M)   39   1
H: 6 0   W: 11 07   b.Dagenham 9-12-94

2011–12	Colchester U	0	0		
2012–13	Colchester U	3	0		
2013–14	Colchester U	36	1	39	1

HUBBLE, Connor (M)   1   0
b. 29-11-94

2013–14	Colchester U	1	0	1	0

IBEHRE, Jabo (F)   433   79
H: 6 2   W: 13 13   b.Islington 28-1-83

1999–2000	Leyton Orient	3	0		
2000–01	Leyton Orient	5	2		
2001–02	Leyton Orient	28	4		
2002–03	Leyton Orient	25	5		
2003–04	Leyton Orient	35	4		
2004–05	Leyton Orient	19	2		
2005–06	Leyton Orient	33	8		
2006–07	Leyton Orient	30	4		
2007–08	Leyton Orient	31	7	209	36
2008–09	Walsall	39	10	39	10
2009–10	Milton Keynes D	10	1		
2009–10	Southend U	4	0	4	0
2009–10	Stockport Co	20	5	20	5
2010–11	Milton Keynes D	42	3		
2011–12	Milton Keynes D	39	8		
2012–13	Milton Keynes D	3	0	94	12
2012–13	Colchester U	30	8		
2013–14	Colchester U	37	8	67	16

KENT, Frankie (D)   1   0

2013–14	Colchester U	1	0	1	0

LADAPO, Freddie (F)   6   0
H: 6 0   W: 12 06   b.Romford 1-2-93

2011–12	Colchester U	0	0		
2012–13	Colchester U	4	0		
2013–14	Colchester U	2	0	6	0

LAPSLIE, Tom (M)   0   0
b. 5-5-95

2013–14	Colchester U	0	0		

MASSEY, Gavin (F)   101   12
H: 5 11   W: 11 06   b.Watford 14-10-92

2009–10	Watford	1	0		
2010–11	Watford	3	0		
2011–12	Watford	3	0		
2011–12	Yeovil T	16	3	16	3
2011–12	Colchester U	8	0		
2012–13	Watford	0	0	7	0
2012–13	Colchester U	40	6		
2013–14	Colchester U	30	3	78	9

MORRISON, Clinton (F)   592   152
H: 6 0   W: 12 00   b.Tooting 14-5-79
Internationals: Republic of Ireland U21, Full caps.

1996–97	Crystal Palace	0	0		
1997–98	Crystal Palace	1	1		
1998–99	Crystal Palace	37	12		
1999–2000	Crystal Palace	29	13		
2000–01	Crystal Palace	45	14		
2001–02	Crystal Palace	45	22		
2002–03	Birmingham C	28	6		
2003–04	Birmingham C	32	4		
2004–05	Birmingham C	26	4		
2005–06	Birmingham C	1	0	87	14
2005–06	Crystal Palace	40	13		
2006–07	Crystal Palace	41	12		
2007–08	Crystal Palace	43	16	281	103
2008–09	Coventry C	45	10		
2009–10	Coventry C	46	11	91	21
2010–11	Sheffield W	35	6		
2011–12	Sheffield W	19	1	54	7
2011–12	Milton Keynes D	6	3	6	3
2011–12	Brentford	8	0	8	0
2012–13	Colchester U	32	2		
2013–14	Colchester U	33	2	65	4

NWACHUKU, Nnamdi (F)   0   0
b. 27-11-84

2013–14	Colchester U	0	0		

O'DONOGHUE, Michael (D)   0   0
b. 18-1-96

2013–14	Colchester U	0	0		

OKUONGHAE, Magnus (D)   264   10
H: 6 3   W: 13 04   b.Nigeria 16-2-86

2003–04	Rushden & D	1	0		
2004–05	Rushden & D	0	0		
2005–06	Rushden & D	21	1		
2006–07	Rushden & D	0	0	22	1
2007–08	Dagenham & R	10	0		
2008–09	Dagenham & R	45	2	55	2
2009–10	Colchester U	44	0		
2010–11	Colchester U	14	2		
2011–12	Colchester U	42	0		
2012–13	Colchester U	43	3		
2013–14	Colchester U	44	2	187	7

OLUFEMI, Tosin (M)   14   0
H: 5 8   W: 10 13   b.Hackney 13-5-94

2012–13	Colchester U	1	0		
2013–14	Colchester U	13	0	14	0

ROAST, Billy (D)   0   0
b. 6-6-95

2013–14	Colchester U	0	0		

ROSE, Michael (D)   302   21
H: 5 11   W: 12 04   b.Salford 28-7-82
Internationals: England C.

1999–2000	Manchester U	0	0		
2000–01	Manchester U	0	0		
2001–02	Manchester U	0	0		

From Hereford U

2004–05	Yeovil T	40	1		
2005–06	Yeovil T	1	0	41	1
2005–06	Cheltenham T	3	0	3	0
2005–06	Scunthorpe U	15	0	15	0
2006–07	Stockport Co	25	3		
2007–08	Stockport Co	28	3		
2008–09	Stockport Co	27	0		
2009–10	Stockport Co	24	2	104	8
2009–10	Norwich C	12	1	12	1
2010–11	Swindon T	35	3	35	3
2010–11	Colchester U	0	0		
2011–12	Colchester U	14	0		
2012–13	Colchester U	22	2		
2012–13	Rochdale	14	2		
2013–14	Colchester U	0	0	36	2
2013–14	Rochdale	42	4	56	6

SANDERSON, Jordan (M)   2   0
H: 6 0   W: 11 02   b.Chingford 7-8-93

2010–11	Colchester U	1	0		
2011–12	Colchester U	0	0		
2012–13	Colchester U	0	0		
2013–14	Colchester U	1	0	2	0

SEARS, Freddie (F)   161   23
H: 5 8   W: 10 01   b.Hornchurch 27-11-89
Internationals: England U19, U20, U21.

2007–08	West Ham U	7	1		
2008–09	West Ham U	17	0		
2009–10	West Ham U	1	0		
2009–10	Crystal Palace	18	0	18	0
2009–10	Coventry C	10	0	10	0
2010–11	West Ham U	11	1		
2010–11	Scunthorpe U	9	0	9	0
2011–12	West Ham U	10	0	46	2
2011–12	Colchester U	11	2		
2012–13	Colchester U	37	7		
2013–14	Colchester U	32	12	78	21

SEMBIE-FERRIS, Dion (F)   0   0

2013–14	Colchester U	0	0		

SPENCE, Mason (D)   1   0
b.Milton Keynes 20-11-94
Internationals: Wales U19.

2012–13	Milton Keynes D	0	0		
2013–14	Colchester U	1	0	1	0

SZMIDICS, Sammie (M)   7   0

2013–14	Colchester U	7	0	7	0

THOMPSON, Josh (D)   83   6
H: 6 4   W: 12 00   b.Bolton 25-2-91
Internationals: England U19.

2008–09	Stockport Co	9	0	9	0
2009–10	Celtic	18	3	18	3
2010–11	Rochdale	12	1	12	1
2011–12	Chesterfield	20	1	20	1
2012–13	Portsmouth	2	0	2	0
2012–13	Colchester U	22	1		
2013–14	Colchester U	0	0	22	1

VOSE, Dominic (M)   29   0
b.Lambeth 23-11-93

2010–11	West Ham U	0	0		
2011–12	West Ham U	0	0		
2012–13	Barnet	0	0	2	0
2013–14	Colchester U	27	0	27	0

WALKER, Sam (G)   124   0
H: 6 5   W: 14 00   b.Gravesend 2-10-91

2009–10	Chelsea	0	0		
2010–11	Chelsea	0	0		
2010–11	Barnet	7	0	7	0
2011–12	Chelsea	0	0		
2011–12	Northampton T	21	0	21	0
2011–12	Yeovil T	20	0	20	0
2012–13	Chelsea	0	0		
2012–13	Bristol R	11	0	11	0
2012–13	Colchester U	19	0		
2013–14	Colchester U	46	0	65	0

WATT, Sanchez (M)   78   8
H: 5 11   W: 12 00   b.Hackney 14-2-91
Internationals: England U16, U17, U19.

2008–09	Arsenal	0	0		
2009–10	Arsenal	0	0		
2009–10	Southend U	4	0	4	0
2009–10	Leeds U	6	0		
2010–11	Arsenal	0	0		
2010–11	Leeds U	22	1	28	1
2011–12	Arsenal	0	0		
2011–12	Sheffield W	4	0	4	0
2011–12	Crawley T	14	2	14	2
2012–13	Arsenal	0	0		
2012–13	Colchester U	6	2		
2013–14	Colchester U	22	3	28	5

WILSON, Brian (D)   342   16
H: 5 10   W: 11 00   b.Manchester 9-5-83

2001–02	Stoke C	1	0		
2002–03	Stoke C	3	0		
2003–04	Stoke C	2	0	6	0
2003–04	Cheltenham T	14	0		
2004–05	Cheltenham T	43	3		
2005–06	Cheltenham T	43	9		
2006–07	Cheltenham T	25	2	125	14
2006–07	Bristol C	19	0		
2007–08	Bristol C	18	1		
2008–09	Bristol C	20	0		
2009–10	Bristol C	3	0	60	1
2010–11	Colchester U	26	1		
2011–12	Colchester U	46	0		
2012–13	Colchester U	41	0		
2013–14	Colchester U	38	0	151	1

WRIGHT, David (D)   486   9
H: 5 11   W: 11 01   b.Warrington 1-5-80
Internationals: England Youth.

1997–98	Crewe Alex	3	0		
1998–99	Crewe Alex	20	1		
1999–2000	Crewe Alex	45	0		
2000–01	Crewe Alex	42	0		
2001–02	Crewe Alex	30	0		
2002–03	Crewe Alex	31	1		
2003–04	Crewe Alex	40	1	211	3
2004–05	Wigan Ath	31	0		
2005–06	Wigan Ath	2	0		
2005–06	Norwich C	5	0	5	0
2006–07	Wigan Ath	12	0	45	0
2006–07	Ipswich T	19	1		
2007–08	Ipswich T	41	2		
2008–09	Ipswich T	34	1		
2009–10	Ipswich T	26	1	120	5
2010–11	Crystal Palace	28	0		
2011–12	Crystal Palace	22	0		
2012–13	Crystal Palace	1	0	51	0
2012–13	Gillingham	7	0	7	0
2012–13	Colchester U	12	0		
2013–14	Colchester U	35	1	47	1

WRIGHT, Drey (M)   32   3
H: 5 9   W: 10 11   b.Greenwich 30-4-94

2012–13	Colchester U	21	3		
2013–14	Colchester U	11	0	32	3

Scholars
Andrews, Marley Patrick; Atkin, Joel;
Brampton, Tyler Victor; Carroll, Ronnie
James Alfred; Clarke, Conor Patrick;
Gardiner, Terence Michael; Harrison,
Callum John; Monk, Thomas Edward;
O'Shea, Patrick James; Rogers, Callum Ron.

COVENTRY C (26)

ADAMS, Blair (D) 81 0
H: 5 11 W: 11 05 b.South Shields 8-9-91
Internationals: England U20.

Season	Club				
2010–11	Sunderland	0	0		
2011–12	Sunderland	0	0		
2011–12	Brentford	7	0	7	0
2011–12	Northampton T	22	0	22	0
2012–13	Sunderland	0	0		
2012–13	Coventry C	16	0		
2013–14	Coventry C	36	0	52	0

BAKER, Carl (M) 244 43
H: 6 2 W: 12 06 b.Prescot 26-12-82
Internationals: England C.

2007–08	Morecambe	42	10	42	10
2008–09	Stockport Co	22	3		
2009–10	Stockport Co	20	9	42	12
2009–10	Coventry C	22	0		
2010–11	Coventry C	32	1		
2011–12	Coventry C	26	1		
2012–13	Coventry C	43	12		
2013–14	Coventry C	37	7	160	21

BARTON, Adam (M) 86 4
H: 5 11 W: 12 01 b.Clitheroe 7-1-91
Internationals: Republic of Ireland U21.
Northern Ireland Full caps.

2008–09	Preston NE	0	0		
2009–10	Preston NE	1	0		
2010–11	Preston NE	33	1		
2011–12	Preston NE	16	0		
2012–13	Preston NE	0	0	50	1
2012–13	Coventry C	22	3		
2013–14	Coventry C	14	0	36	3
2013–14	Fleetwood T	0	0		

BURGE, Lee (G) 0 0
H: 5 11 W: 11 00 b.Hereford 9-1-93

2011–12	Coventry C	0	0		
2012–13	Coventry C	0	0		
2013–14	Coventry C	0	0		

CHRISTIE, Cyrus (D) 102 2
H: 6 2 W: 12 03 b.Coventry 30-9-92

2011–12	Coventry C	37	0		
2012–13	Coventry C	31	2		
2013–14	Coventry C	34	0	102	2

CLARKE, Jordan (D) 113 3
H: 6 0 W: 11 02 b.Coventry 19-11-91
Internationals: England U19, U20.

2009–10	Coventry C	12	0		
2010–11	Coventry C	21	1		
2011–12	Coventry C	19	1		
2012–13	Coventry C	20	0		
2013–14	Coventry C	41	1	113	3

DANIELS, Billy (F) 24 3
H: 6 0 W: 11 07 b.Bristol 3-7-94

2012–13	Coventry C	4	0		
2013–14	Coventry C	18	3	22	3
2013–14	Cheltenham T	2	0	2	0

FLECK, John (M) 126 6
H: 5 9 W: 11 05 b.Glasgow 24-8-91
Internationals: Scotland U17, U19, U21.

2007–08	Rangers	1	0		
2008–09	Rangers	8	1		
2009–10	Rangers	15	1		
2010–11	Rangers	13	0		
2011–12	Rangers	4	0	41	2
2011–12	Blackpool	7	0	7	0
2012–13	Coventry C	35	3		
2013–14	Coventry C	43	1	78	4

GARNER, Louis (M) 3 0
H: 5 10 W: 11 07 b.Manchester 31-10-94

2012–13	Coventry C	0	0		
2013–14	Coventry C	3	0	3	0

HAYNES, Ryan (D) 3 0
H: 5 7 W: 10 10 b.Northampton 27-9-95

2012–13	Coventry C	1	0		
2013–14	Coventry C	2	0	3	0

MANSET, Mathieu (F) 108 18
H: 6 1 W: 13 08 b.Metz 5-8-89

2009–10	Hereford U	29	3		
2010–11	Hereford U	21	7	50	10
2010–11	Reading	13	2		
2011–12	Reading	15	3	28	5
2011–12	Shanghai S	9	1	9	1
2012–13	FC Sion	5	1	5	1
2012–13	Carlisle U	7	0		
2013–14	Carlisle U	0	0	7	0
2013–14	Coventry C	9	1	9	1

Transferred to Royal Antwerp January 2014.

MARSHALL, Mark (M) 112 7
H: 5 7 W: 10 07 b.Jamaica 9-5-86

2008–09	Swindon T	12	0		
2009–10	Swindon T	7	0	19	0
2009–10	Hereford U	8	0	8	0
2010–11	Barnet	46	6		
2011–12	Barnet	25	1	71	7
2013–14	Coventry C	14	0	14	0

McGEOUCH, Dylan (M) 27 2
H: 5 10 W: 10 11 b.Glasgow 15-1-93
Internationals: Scotland U16, U17, U19, U21.

2011–12	Celtic	6	1		
2012–13	Celtic	12	1		
2013–14	Celtic	1	0	19	2

On loan from Celtic

2013–14	Coventry C	8	0	8	0

MOUSSA, Franck (M) 208 32
H: 5 8 W: 10 08 b.Brussels 24-7-89

2005–06	Southend U	1	0		
2006–07	Southend U	4	0		
2007–08	Southend U	16	0		
2008–09	Southend U	26	2		
2008–09	Wycombe W	9	0	9	0
2009–10	Southend U	43	5	90	7
2010–11	Leicester C	8	1		
2010–11	Doncaster R	14	2	14	2
2011–12	Leicester C	0	0	8	1
2011–12	Chesterfield	10	4	10	4
2012–13	Nottingham F	0	0		
2012–13	Coventry C	38	6		
2013–14	Coventry C	39	12	77	18

MURPHY, Joe (G) 445 0
H: 6 2 W: 13 06 b.Dublin 21-8-81
Internationals: Republic of Ireland Youth, U21, Full caps.

1999–2000	Tranmere R	21	0		
2000–01	Tranmere R	20	0		
2001–02	Tranmere R	22	0	63	0
2002–03	WBA	2	0		
2003–04	WBA	3	0		
2004–05	WBA	0	0	5	0
2004–05	Walsall	25	0		
2005–06	Sunderland	0	0		
2005–06	Walsall	14	0	39	0
2006–07	Scunthorpe U	45	0		
2007–08	Scunthorpe U	45	0		
2008–09	Scunthorpe U	42	0		
2009–10	Scunthorpe U	40	0		
2010–11	Scunthorpe U	29	0	201	0
2011–12	Coventry C	46	0		
2012–13	Coventry C	45	0		
2013–14	Coventry C	46	0	137	0

PHILLIPS, Aaron (D) 11 1
b. 20-11-93

2012–13	Coventry C	0	0		
2013–14	Coventry C	11	1	11	1

SEABORNE, Danny (D) 147 2
H: 6 0 W: 11 10 b.Barnstaple 5-3-87

2008–09	Exeter C	33	1		
2009–10	Exeter C	19	0	52	1
2009–10	Southampton	16	0		
2010–11	Southampton	24	0		
2011–12	Southampton	4	0		
2012–13	Southampton	0	0	44	0
2012–13	Charlton Ath	7	0	7	0
2012–13	Bournemouth	13	0	13	0
2013–14	Yeovil T	10	0	10	0
2013–14	Coventry C	21	1	21	1

SLAGER, Denzel (F) 17 1
H: 6 0 W: 12 00 b.Utrecht 2-5-93
Internationals: Curacao U20.

2012–13	RKC	5	0		
2013–14	RKC	9	1	14	1
2013–14	Coventry C	3	0	3	0

THOMAS, Conor (M) 81 1
H: 6 1 W: 11 05 b.Coventry 29-10-93
Internationals: England U17, U18.

2010–11	Liverpool	0	0		
2010–11	Coventry C	0	0		
2011–12	Coventry C	27	1		
2012–13	Coventry C	11	0		
2013–14	Coventry C	43	0	81	1

THOMAS, George (M) 1 0
Internationals: Wales U17.

2013–14	Coventry C	1	0	1	0

URQUHART, Stuart (D) 0 0
b.Glasgow 26-3-95
Internationals: Scotland U17.

2013–14	Coventry C	0	0		

WEBSTER, Andy (D) 299 17
H: 6 0 W: 9 13 b.Dundee 23-4-82
Internationals: Scotland U21, B, Full caps.

2000–01	Hearts	4	0		
2001–02	Hearts	26	1		
2002–03	Hearts	21	1		
2003–04	Hearts	32	2		
2004–05	Hearts	35	1		
2005–06	Hearts	30	1		
2006–07	Wigan Ath	4	0		
2007–08	Wigan Ath	0	0	4	0
2007–08	Rangers	1	0		
2008–09	Rangers	0	0		
2008–09	Bristol C	5	0	5	0
2009–10	Rangers	0	0		
2009–10	Dundee U	26	3	26	3
2010–11	Rangers	1	0	2	0
2010–11	Hearts	9	0		
2011–12	Hearts	31	4		
2012–13	Hearts	33	1	221	11
2013–14	Coventry C	41	3	41	3

WILLIS, Jordan (D) 32 0
H: 5 11 W: 11 00 b.Coventry 24-8-94
Internationals: England U18, U19.

2011–12	Coventry C	3	0		
2012–13	Coventry C	1	0		
2013–14	Coventry C	28	0	32	0

WILSON, Callum (M) 49 22
H: 5 11 W: 10 06 b.Coventry 27-2-92

2009–10	Coventry C	0	0		
2010–11	Coventry C	1	0		
2011–12	Coventry C	0	0		
2012–13	Coventry C	11	1		
2013–14	Coventry C	37	21	49	22

Scholars
Baker-Richardson, Courtney Romello; Bako, Elisha Thomas; Barnett, Kyle James; Bromley, Luke William; Finch, Jack Jonathon; Forrester, Jordan Kyle John; Gott, Alex George; Harries, Cian William Thomas; Kelly-Evans, Devon Jerome; Kelly-Evans, Dion Jermaine; Lawton, Ivor James John; Maddison, James Daniel; Quinn, Ryan John; Richards, Jake James; Smith, Jordan Nathaniel; Smith, Ryan Anthony; Stevenson, Ben Edward; Thomas, George Stanley.

CRAWLEY T (27)

BULMAN, Dannie (M) 323 18
H: 5 9 W: 11 12 b.Ashford 24-1-79

1998–99	Wycombe W	11	1		
1999–2000	Wycombe W	29	1		
2000–01	Wycombe W	36	4		
2001–02	Wycombe W	46	5		
2002–03	Wycombe W	42	3		
2003–04	Wycombe W	38	0	202	14

From Stevenage, Crawley T

2010–11	Oxford U	5	0	5	0
2011–12	Crawley T	41	3		
2012–13	Crawley T	36	1		
2013–14	Crawley T	39	0	116	4

CLARKE, Billy (F) 210 43
H: 5 7 W: 10 01 b.Cork 13-12-87
Internationals: Republic of Ireland U17, U19, U21.

2004–05	Ipswich T	0	0		
2005–06	Ipswich T	2	0		
2005–06	Colchester U	6	0	6	0
2006–07	Ipswich T	27	3		
2007–08	Ipswich T	20	0		
2007–08	Falkirk	8	1	8	1
2008–09	Ipswich T	0	0	49	3
2008–09	Darlington	20	8	20	8
2008–09	Northampton T	5	3	5	3

2008–09	Brentford	8	6	8	6
2009–10	Blackpool	18	1		
2010–11	Blackpool	0	0		
2011–12	Blackpool	9	0	27	1
2011–12	*Sheffield U*	5	1	5	1
2011–12	Crawley T	17	3		
2012–13	Crawley T	36	10		
2013–14	Crawley T	29	7	82	20

CONNOLLY, Mark (D)   77 3
H: 6 1   W: 12 01   b.Monaghan 16-12-91
Internationals: Republic of Ireland U21.

2009–10	Bolton W	0	0		
2009–10	*St Johnstone*	1	0	1	0
2010–11	Bolton W	0	0		
2011–12	Bolton W	0	0		
2011–12	*Macclesfield T*	7	0	7	0
2012–13	Crawley T	33	2		
2013–14	Crawley T	36	1	69	3

CONNOLLY, Paul (D)   318 2
H: 6 0   W: 11 09   b.Liverpool 29-9-83

2000–01	Plymouth Arg	1	0		
2001–02	Plymouth Arg	0	0		
2002–03	Plymouth Arg	2	0		
2003–04	Plymouth Arg	29	0		
2004–05	Plymouth Arg	19	0		
2005–06	Plymouth Arg	31	0		
2006–07	Plymouth Arg	38	0		
2007–08	Plymouth Arg	42	1	162	1
2008–09	Derby Co	40	1		
2009–10	Derby Co	21	0	61	1
2009–10	*Sheffield U*	7	0	7	0
2010–11	Leeds U	30	0		
2011–12	Leeds U	28	0		
2012–13	Leeds U	0	0	58	0
2012–13	*Portsmouth*	4	0	4	0
2012–13	*Preston NE*	15	0	15	0
2013–14	Millwall	4	0	4	0
2013–14	Crawley T	7	0	7	0

DICKER, Gary (M)   284 12
H: 6 0   W: 12 00   b.Dublin 31-7-86
Internationals: Republic of Ireland U19, U21.

2004	UCD	9	1		
2005	UCD	31	2		
2006	UCD	28	2	68	5
2006–07	Birmingham C	0	0		
2007–08	Stockport Co	30	0		
2008–09	Stockport Co	25	0	55	0
2008–09	*Brighton & HA*	9	1		
2009–10	Brighton & HA	42	2		
2010–11	Brighton & HA	46	3		
2011–12	Brighton & HA	18	0		
2012–13	Brighton & HA	23	0		
2013–14	Brighton & HA	0	0	138	6
2013–14	*Rochdale*	12	1	12	1
2013–14	Crawley T	11	0	11	0

DRURY, Andy (M)   139 16
H: 5 11   W: 12 06   b.Sittingbourne 28-11-83

2010–11	Luton T	23	6	23	6
2010–11	Ipswich T	12	0		
2011–12	*Crawley T*	13	3		
2012–13	Ipswich T	29	0	62	2
2013–14	Crawley T	41	5	54	8

ESSAM, Connor (D)   29 1
H: 6 0   W: 12 00   b.Sheerness 9-7-92

2010–11	Gillingham	0	0		
2011–12	Gillingham	18	0		
2012–13	Gillingham	0	0	18	0
2012–13	Crawley T	9	1		
2013–14	Crawley T	2	0	11	1

FALLON, Rory (F)   398 72
H: 6 2   W: 11 09   b.Gisborne 20-3-82
Internationals: England Youth. New Zealand Full caps.

1998–99	Barnsley	0	0		
1999–2000	Barnsley	0	0		
2000–01	Barnsley	1	0		
2001–02	Barnsley	9	0		
2001–02	*Shrewsbury T*	11	0	11	0
2002–03	Barnsley	26	7		
2003–04	Barnsley	16	4	52	11
2003–04	Swindon T	19	6		
2004–05	Swindon T	31	3		
2004–05	*Yeovil T*	6	1		
2005–06	Swindon T	25	12	75	21
2005–06	Swansea C	17	4		
2006–07	Swansea C	24	8	41	12

2006–07	Plymouth Arg	15	1		
2007–08	Plymouth Arg	29	7		
2008–09	Plymouth Arg	44	5		
2009–10	Plymouth Arg	33	5		
2010–11	Plymouth Arg	28	4	149	22
2010–11	*Ipswich T*	6	1	6	1
2011–12	*Yeovil T*	5	0	11	1
2011–12	Aberdeen	22	2		
2012–13	Aberdeen	15	1	37	3
2013–14	St Johnstone	8	1	8	1
2013–14	Crawley T	8	0	8	0

HURST, James (D)   53 2
H: 5 8   W: 11 11   b.Sutton Coldfield 31-1-92
Internationals: England U16, U17, U19, U20.

2008–09	Portsmouth	0	0		
2009–10	Portsmouth	0	0		
2010–11	Portsmouth	0	0		
2010–11	WBA	1	0		
2011–12	WBA	0	0		
2011–12	*Blackpool*	2	0	2	0
2011–12	*Shrewsbury T*	7	0		
2011–12	*Chesterfield*	10	0	10	0
2012–13	WBA	0	0	1	0
2012–13	*Birmingham C*	3	0	3	0
2012–13	*Shrewsbury T*	4	0	11	0
2013	Valur Reykjavik	7	2	7	2
2013–14	Crawley T	18	0	18	0
2013–14	*Northampton T*	1	0	1	0

Transferred to Valur Reykjavik May 2014

JONES, Mike (M)   268 26
H: 5 11   W: 12 04   b.Birkenhead 15-8-87

2005–06	Tranmere R	1	0		
2006–07	Tranmere R	0	0		
2006–07	*Shrewsbury T*	13	1	13	1
2007–08	Tranmere R	9	1	10	1
2008–09	Bury	46	4		
2009–10	Bury	41	5		
2010–11	Bury	42	8		
2011–12	Bury	24	3	153	20
2011–12	Sheffield W	10	0		
2012–13	Sheffield W	0	0	10	0
2012–13	Crawley T	40	1		
2013–14	Crawley T	42	3	82	4

JONES, Paul (G)   218 0
H: 6 3   W: 13 00   b.Maidstone 28-6-86

2008–09	Exeter C	46	0		
2009–10	Exeter C	26	0		
2010–11	Exeter C	18	0	90	0
2010–11	*Peterborough U*	1	0		
2011–12	Peterborough U	35	0	36	0
2012–13	Crawley T	46	0		
2013–14	Crawley T	46	0	92	0

McFADZEAN, Kyle (D)   96 6
H: 6 1   W: 13 04   b.Sheffield 20-2-87
Internationals: England C.

2004–05	Sheffield U	0	0		
2005–06	Sheffield U	0	0		
2006–07	Sheffield U	0	0		

From Alfreton T

2011–12	Crawley T	37	2		
2012–13	Crawley T	17	3		
2013–14	Crawley T	42	1	96	6

PROCTOR, Jamie (F)   108 17
H: 6 2   W: 12 03   b.Preston 25-3-92

2009–10	Preston NE	1	0		
2010–11	Preston NE	5	1		
2010–11	*Stockport Co*	0	0	7	0
2011–12	Preston NE	31	3		
2012–13	Preston NE	0	0	37	4
2012–13	Swansea C	0	0		
2012–13	*Shrewsbury T*	2	0	2	0
2012–13	Crawley T	18	7		
2013–14	Crawley T	44	6	62	13

SADLER, Matthew (D)   292 3
H: 5 11   W: 11 08   b.Birmingham 26-2-85
Internationals: England U17, U18, U19.

2001–02	Birmingham C	0	0		
2002–03	Birmingham C	2	0		
2003–04	Birmingham C	0	0		
2003–04	*Northampton T*	7	0	7	0
2004–05	Birmingham C	8	0		
2005–06	Birmingham C	8	0		
2006–07	Birmingham C	36	0		
2007–08	Birmingham C	5	0	51	0
2007–08	Watford	15	0		
2008–09	Watford	15	0		
2009–10	Watford	0	0		

2009–10	*Stockport Co*	20	0	20	0
2010–11	Watford	0	0	30	0
2010–11	Shrewsbury T	46	0	46	0
2011–12	Walsall	46	1	46	1
2012–13	Crawley T	46	1		
2013–14	Crawley T	46	1	92	2

SIMPSON, Josh (M)   152 11
H: 5 10   W: 12 02   b.Cambridge 6-3-87
Internationals: England C.

2009–10	Peterborough U	21	2		
2010–11	Peterborough U	0	0	21	2
2010–11	Southend U	17	1	17	1
2011–12	Crawley T	40	2		
2012–13	Crawley T	36	4		
2013–14	Crawley T	38	2	114	8

SINCLAIR, Emile (F)   204 32
H: 6 0   W: 11 04   b.Leeds 29-12-87

2007–08	Nottingham F	12	1		
2007–08	*Brentford*	4	0	4	0
2008–09	Nottingham F	3	0	15	1
2008–09	*Macclesfield T*	17	1		
2009–10	Macclesfield T	42	7		
2010–11	Macclesfield T	31	5		
2011–12	Macclesfield T	5	1	95	14
2011–12	Peterborough U	35	10		
2012–13	Peterborough U	12	3		
2012–13	*Barnsley*	4	0	4	0
2012–13	*Doncaster R*	4	0	4	0
2013–14	Peterborough U	0	0	47	13
2013–14	*Crawley T*	15	2	15	2
2013–14	*Northampton T*	20	2	20	2

TORRES, Sergio (M)   201 11
H: 6 2   W: 12 04   b.Mar del Plata 8-11-83

2005–06	Wycombe W	24	1		
2006–07	Wycombe W	20	0		
2007–08	Wycombe W	42	5	86	6
2008–09	Peterborough U	15	1		
2009–10	Peterborough U	9	0		
2009–10	*Lincoln C*	8	1	8	1
2010–11	Peterborough U	0	0	24	1
2011–12	Crawley T	38	3		
2012–13	Crawley T	23	0		
2013–14	Crawley T	0	0	83	3

WALSH, Joe (D)   69 7
H: 5 11   W: 11 00   b.Cardiff 15-5-92
Internationals: Wales U17, U18, U21.

2010–11	Swansea C	0	0		
2011–12	Swansea C	0	0		
2012–13	Crawley T	30	2		
2013–14	Crawley T	39	5	69	7

WILLIAMS, Tony (G)   263 0
H: 6 2   W: 13 09   b.Maesteg 20-9-77
Internationals: Wales U21.

1996–97	Blackburn R	0	0		
1997–98	Blackburn R	0	0		
1997–98	*QPR*	0	0		
1998–99	Blackburn R	0	0		
1998–99	*Macclesfield T*	4	0		
1998–99	*Huddersfield T*	0	0		
1998–99	*Bristol R*	9	0	9	0
1999–2000	Blackburn R	0	0		
1999–2000	*Gillingham*	2	0	2	0
1999–2000	*Macclesfield T*	11	0	15	0
2000–01	Hartlepool U	41	0		
2001–02	Hartlepool U	43	0		
2002–03	Hartlepool U	46	0		
2003–04	Hartlepool U	1	0	131	0
2003–04	*Swansea C*	0	0		
2003–04	*Stockport Co*	15	0	15	0
2004–05	Grimsby T	46	0	46	0
2005–06	Carlisle U	11	0		
2005–06	*Bury*	3	0		
2006–07	Carlisle U	0	0	11	0
2006–07	Wrexham	9	0		
2007–08	Wrexham	22	0		
2008–09	Wrexham	0	0		
2009–10	Wrexham	0	0	31	0

From Neath.

2011–12	Bury	0	0		
2012–13	Bury	0	0	3	0
2013–14	Crawley T	0	0		

Scholars
Eden, Jack William; Fowodu, Temitope; Haigh, Christopher David; Isaacs, Bradley James; Jackson, Edward Tom Charles; Kouadio, William; Laing, Alex Neil; Low,

Sonnie Frank; Melford-Rowe, Emmanuel
Joshua; Melville, Scott Andrew; Read,
Alexander Nicholas; Richefond, Ryan James;
Robinson, Malachi Tramaine Jahvan; Smith,
Vincent Cudal Nelson; Thomas, Cecil Jee;
Woon, William Ernest Henry.

CREWE ALEX (28)

AUDEL, Thierry (D)   11   1
b. 15-1-87
Internationals: France U19.

2007–08	Triestina	2	0	
2008–09	Triestina	0	0	
2009–10	Triestina	7	1	9 1
From Macclesfield T				
2013–14	Crewe Alex	2	0	2 0

CLAYTON, Max (F)   74   9
H: 5 9   W: 11 00   b.Crewe 9-8-94
Internationals: England U16, U17, U18, U19.

2010–11	Crewe Alex	2	0
2011–12	Crewe Alex	24	3
2012–13	Crewe Alex	35	4
2013–14	Crewe Alex	13	2	74 9

COLCLOUGH, Ryan (F)   26   3
H: 6 3   W: 13 01   b.Budapest 27-12-94

2012–13	Crewe Alex	18	1
2013–14	Crewe Alex	8	2	26 3

DAVIS, Harry (D)   117   9
H: 6 2   W: 12 04   b.Burnley 24-9-91

2009–10	Crewe Alex	1	0
2010–11	Crewe Alex	1	0
2011–12	Crewe Alex	41	5
2012–13	Crewe Alex	42	1
2013–14	Crewe Alex	32	3	117 9

DUGDALE, Adam (D)   108   6
H: 6 3   W: 12 07   b.Liverpool 12-9-87

2006–07	Crewe Alex	0	0
2006–07	*Accrington S*	2	0	2 0

From Southport, Droylsden, Montagnee,
Barrow, AFC Telford U.

2010–11	Crewe Alex	20	1
2011–12	Crewe Alex	43	3
2012–13	Crewe Alex	18	0
2013–14	Crewe Alex	21	1	102 5
2013–14	*Tranmere R*	4	1	4 1

ELLIS, Mark (D)   170   14
H: 6 2   W: 12 04   b.Kingsbridge 30-9-88

2007–08	Bolton W	0	0
2009–10	Torquay U	27	3
2010–11	Torquay U	27	2
2011–12	Torquay U	35	3	89 8
2012–13	Crewe Alex	44	5
2013–14	Crewe Alex	37	1	81 6

GARRATT, Ben (G)   27   0
H: 6 1   W: 10 06   b.Market Drayton 25-4-94
Internationals: England U17, U18, U19.

2011–12	Crewe Alex	0	0
2012–13	Crewe Alex	1	0
2013–14	Crewe Alex	26	0	27 0

GRANT, Anthony (M)   285   12
H: 5 10   W: 11 01   b.Lambeth 4-6-87
Internationals: England U16, U17, U19.

2004–05	Chelsea	1	0
2005–06	Chelsea	0	0
2005–06	*Oldham Ath*	2	0	2 0
2006–07	Chelsea	0	0
2006–07	*Wycombe W*	40	0	40 0
2007–08	Chelsea	0	0	1 0
2007–08	*Luton T*	4	0	4 0
2007–08	*Southend U*	10	0
2008–09	Southend U	35	1
2009–10	Southend U	38	0
2010–11	Southend U	43	8
2011–12	Southend U	33	1	159 10
2012–13	Stevenage	41	0	41 0
2013–14	Crewe Alex	38	2	38 2

GUTHRIE, Jon (D)   25   0
H: 5 10   W: 11 00   b.Devizes 1-2-93

2011–12	Crewe Alex	0	0
2012–13	Crewe Alex	2	0
2013–14	Crewe Alex	23	0	25 0

INMAN, Bradden (M)   57   9
H: 5 9   W: 11 03   b.Adelaide 10-12-91
Internationals: Scotland U19, U21.

2009–10	Newcastle U	0	0
2010–11	Newcastle U	0	0
2011–12	Newcastle U	0	0
2012–13	Newcastle U	0	0
2012–13	*Crewe Alex*	21	5
2013–14	Newcastle U	0	0
2013–14	Crewe Alex	36	4	57 9

JOHNSTON, John (F)   0   0

2013–14	Crewe Alex	0	0

LEITCH-SMITH, AJ (F)   121   24
H: 5 11   W: 12 04   b.Crewe 6-3-90

2008–09	Crewe Alex	5	0
2009	*IBV*	18	5	18 5
2009–10	Crewe Alex	1	0
2010–11	Crewe Alex	16	5
2011–12	Crewe Alex	38	8
2012–13	Crewe Alex	28	4
2013–14	Crewe Alex	20	2	103 19

MARTIN, Alan (G)   55   0
H: 6 0   W: 11 11   b.Glasgow 1-1-89
Internationals: Scotland U19, U21.

2007–08	Leeds U	0	0
2008–09	Leeds U	0	0
2009–10	Leeds U	0	0
2009–10	*Accrington S*	7	0	7 0
2010–11	Leeds U	0	0
2010–11	*Ayr U*	15	0	15 0
2011–12	Crewe Alex	0	0
2012–13	Crewe Alex	26	0
2013–14	Crewe Alex	7	0	33 0

MELLOR, Kelvin (D)   76   2
H: 5 10   W: 11 09   b.Copenhagen 25-1-91

2007–08	Crewe Alex	0	0
2008–09	Crewe Alex	0	0
2009–10	Crewe Alex	0	0
2010–11	Crewe Alex	1	0
2011–12	Crewe Alex	12	1
2012–13	Crewe Alex	35	0
2013–14	Crewe Alex	28	1	76 2

MOLYNEUX, Lee (D)   79   14
H: 6 1   W: 12 09   b.Liverpool 24-2-89
Internationals: England U16, U17, U18.

2005–06	Everton	0	0
2006–07	Everton	0	0
2007–08	Everton	0	0
2008–09	Southampton	4	0
2009–10	Southampton	0	0	4 0
2010–11	Plymouth Arg	9	0	9 0
2012–13	Accrington S	39	8
2013–14	Crewe Alex	7	0	7 0
2013–14	*Rochdale*	3	0	3 0
2013–14	*Accrington S*	17	6	56 14

MOORE, Byron (M)   262   30
H: 6 0   W: 10 06   b.Stoke 24-8-88

2006–07	Crewe Alex	0	0
2007–08	Crewe Alex	33	3
2008–09	Crewe Alex	36	3
2009–10	Crewe Alex	32	3
2010–11	Crewe Alex	38	6
2011–12	Crewe Alex	42	8
2012–13	Crewe Alex	41	4
2013–14	Crewe Alex	40	3	262 30

NOLAN, Liam (D)   13   0
H: 5 9   W: 10 12   b.Liverpool 20-9-94
Internationals: Northern Ireland U21.

2012–13	Crewe Alex	0	0
2013–14	Crewe Alex	13	0	13 0

OLIVER, Vadaine (F)   25   2
b.Sheffield 21-10-91

2010–11	Sheffield W	0	0
2011–12	Sheffield W	0	0
2013–14	Crewe Alex	25	2	25 2

OSMAN, Abdul (M)   191   8
H: 6 0   W: 11 00   b.Accra 27-2-87

2007–08	Gretna	18	1	18 1
2008–09	Northampton T	36	2
2009–10	Northampton T	30	2
2010–11	Northampton T	38	3
2011–12	Northampton T	0	0	104 7
2012–13	Crewe Alex	38	0
2013–14	Crewe Alex	31	0	69 0

PHILLIPS, Steve (G)   510   0
H: 6 1   W: 11 10   b.Bath 6-5-78

1996–97	Bristol C	0	0	
1997–98	Bristol C	0	0	
1998–99	Bristol C	15	0	
1999–2000	Bristol C	21	0	
2000–01	Bristol C	42	0	
2001–02	Bristol C	22	0	
2002–03	Bristol C	46	0	
2003–04	Bristol C	46	0	
2004–05	Bristol C	46	0	
2005–06	Bristol C	19	0	257 0
2006–07	Bristol R	44	0	
2007–08	Bristol R	46	0	
2008–09	Bristol R	46	0	
2009–10	Bristol R	0	0	136 0
2009–10	*Shrewsbury T*	11	0	11 0
2009–10	*Crewe Alex*	28	0	
2010–11	Crewe Alex	3	0	
2011–12	Crewe Alex	46	0	
2012–13	Crewe Alex	20	0	
2013–14	Crewe Alex	9	0	106 0

POGBA, Mathias (F)   56   17
H: 6 3   W: 12 13   b.Conakry 19-8-90
Internationals: Guinea

2010–11	Wrexham	0	0
2012–13	Crewe Alex	34	12
2013–14	Crewe Alex	22	5	56 17

RAY, George (D)   13   0
H: 5 10   W: 11 03   b.Warrington 13-10-93
Internationals: Wales U21.

2011–12	Crewe Alex	0	0
2012–13	Crewe Alex	4	0
2013–14	Crewe Alex	9	0	13 0

TOOTLE, Matt (D)   184   2
H: 5 9   W: 11 00   b.Widnes 11-10-90

2009–10	Crewe Alex	28	1
2010–11	Crewe Alex	39	0
2011–12	Crewe Alex	37	0
2012–13	Crewe Alex	37	1
2013–14	Crewe Alex	43	0	184 2

TURTON, Oliver (D)   35   1
H: 5 11   W: 11 11   b.Manchester 6-12-92

2010–11	Crewe Alex	1	0
2011–12	Crewe Alex	2	0
2012–13	Crewe Alex	20	0
2013–14	Crewe Alex	12	1	35 1

WATERS, Billy (M)   9   0
H: 5 9   W: 11 07   b.Epsom 15-10-94

2012–13	Crewe Alex	0	0
2013–14	Crewe Alex	9	0	9 0

WEST, Michael (M)   10   0
H: 5 9   W: 12 06   b.Maidstone 9-2-91

2012–13	Crewe Alex	8	0
2013–14	Crewe Alex	2	0	10 0

Scholars

Allcock, Ryan; Baillie, James; Brown, Andre
Dave; Howell, Joseph Edward James;
Johnson, Louis Darryl; Johnson, Robbie
James Michael; Jones, James Charles; Kearns,
Joseph Glen; Matthews, Liam Elliott; Moran,
Jonathan Lewis Daniel; Mullarkey, Tobias;
Murdoch, Fraser; Ng, Perry; O'Neill, Liam
Kieron; Pino, Michael Roberto; Prichard-
Ellis, Callum; Saunders, Callum; Smith,
Dominic; Speed, Christopher David.

CRYSTAL PALACE (29)

ALLASSANI, Reise (M)   0   0
b.Wandsworth 3-1-96

2013–14	Crystal Palace	0	0

APPIAH, Kwesi (F)   27   3
H: 5 11   W: 12 08   b.Thamesmead 12-8-90

2008–09	Peterborough U	0	0

From Brackley T, Thurrock, Margate.

2011–12	Crystal Palace	4	0
2012–13	Crystal Palace	2	0
2012–13	*Aldershot T*	2	0	2 0
2012–13	*Yeovil T*	5	0	5 0
2013–14	Crystal Palace	0	0	6 0
2013–14	*Notts Co*	7	0	7 0
2013–14	*AFC Wimbledon*	7	3	7 3

BANNAN, Barry (D) 116 4
H: 5 10 W: 10 08 b.Glasgow 1-12-89
Internationals: Scotland U21, Full caps.

Season	Club				
2008–09	Aston Villa	0	0		
2008–09	Derby Co	10	1	**10**	**1**
2009–10	Aston Villa	0	0		
2009–10	Blackpool	20	1	**20**	**1**
2010–11	Aston Villa	12	0		
2010–11	Leeds U	7	0	**7**	**0**
2011–12	Aston Villa	28	1		
2012–13	Aston Villa	24	0		
2013–14	Aston Villa	0	0	**64**	**1**
2013–14	Crystal Palace	15	1	**15**	**1**

BLAKE, Darcy (M) 115 4
H: 5 10 W: 12 05 b.New Tredegar 13-12-88
Internationals: Wales Youth, U17, U19, U21, Full caps.

Season	Club				
2005–06	Cardiff C	1	0		
2006–07	Cardiff C	10	0		
2007–08	Cardiff C	8	0		
2008–09	Cardiff C	7	0		
2009–10	Cardiff C	0	0		
2009–10	Plymouth Arg	7	0	**7**	**0**
2010–11	Cardiff C	26	0		
2011–12	Cardiff C	20	0		
2012–13	Cardiff C	0	0	**90**	**0**
2012–13	Crystal Palace	10	0		
2013–14	Crystal Palace	0	0	**10**	**0**
2013–14	Newport Co	8	0	**8**	**0**

BOATENG, Hiram (M) 1 0
b. 8-1-96

Season	Club				
2012–13	Crystal Palace	0	0		
2013–14	Crystal Palace	0	0		
2013–14	Crawley T	1	0	**1**	**0**

BOLASIE, Yannick (M) 188 17
H: 6 2 W: 13 02 b.DR Congo 24-5-89
Internationals: DR Congo Full caps.

Season	Club				
2008–09	Plymouth Arg	0	0		
2008–09	Barnet	20	3		
2009–10	Plymouth Arg	16	1		
2009–10	Barnet	22	2	**42**	**5**
2010–11	Plymouth Arg	35	7	**51**	**8**
2011–12	Bristol C	23	1		
2012–13	Bristol C	0	0	**23**	**1**
2012–13	Crystal Palace	43	3		
2013–14	Crystal Palace	29	0	**72**	**3**

CAMPANA, Jose (M) 36 1
H: 5 9 W: 8 8 b.Seville 31-5-93
Internationals: Spain U16, U17, U18, U19, U20, U21.

Season	Club				
2011–12	Sevilla	15	0		
2012–13	Sevilla	5	0	**20**	**0**
2013–14	Crystal Palace	6	0	**6**	**0**
2013–14	Nuremberg	10	1	**10**	**1**

CHAMAKH, Marouane (F) 305 69
H: 6 1 W: 11 00 b.Tonnens 10-1-84
Internationals: France U19. Morocco Full caps.

Season	Club				
2002–03	Bordeaux	10	1		
2003–04	Bordeaux	25	6		
2004–05	Bordeaux	33	10		
2005–06	Bordeaux	29	7		
2006–07	Bordeaux	29	5		
2007–08	Bordeaux	32	4		
2008–09	Bordeaux	34	13		
2009–10	Bordeaux	38	10	**230**	**56**
2010–11	Arsenal	29	7		
2011–12	Arsenal	11	1		
2012–13	Arsenal	0	0		
2012–13	West Ham U	3	0	**3**	**0**
2013–14	Arsenal	0	0	**40**	**8**
2013–14	Crystal Palace	32	5	**32**	**5**

DANN, Scott (D) 268 18
H: 6 2 W: 12 00 b.Liverpool 14-2-87
Internationals: England U21.

Season	Club				
2004–05	Walsall	1	0		
2005–06	Walsall	0	0		
2006–07	Walsall	30	4		
2007–08	Walsall	28	3	**59**	**7**
2007–08	Coventry C	16	0		
2008–09	Coventry C	31	3	**47**	**3**
2009–10	Birmingham C	30	0		
2010–11	Birmingham C	20	2		
2011–12	Birmingham C	0	0	**50**	**2**
2011–12	Blackburn R	27	1		
2012–13	Blackburn R	46	4		
2013–14	Blackburn R	25	0	**98**	**5**
2013–14	Crystal Palace	14	1	**14**	**1**

DE SILVA, Kyle (F) 10 0
H: 5 10 W: 11 05 b.Croydon 29-11-93

Season	Club				
2010–11	Crystal Palace	0	0		
2011–12	Crystal Palace	6	0		
2012–13	Crystal Palace	1	0		
2012–13	Barnet	3	0	**3**	**0**
2013–14	Crystal Palace	0	0	**7**	**0**

DELANEY, Damien (D) 482 14
H: 6 3 W: 14 00 b.Cork 20-7-81
Internationals: Republic of Ireland Full caps.

Season	Club				
2000–01	Leicester C	5	0		
2001–02	Leicester C	3	0		
2001–02	Stockport Co	12	1	**12**	**1**
2001–02	Huddersfield T	2	0	**2**	**0**
2002–03	Leicester C	0	0	**8**	**0**
2002–03	Mansfield T	7	0	**7**	**0**
2002–03	Hull C	30	1		
2003–04	Hull C	46	2		
2004–05	Hull C	43	1		
2005–06	Hull C	46	0		
2006–07	Hull C	37	1		
2007–08	Hull C	22	0	**224**	**5**
2007–08	QPR	17	1		
2008–09	QPR	37	1		
2009–10	QPR	0	0	**54**	**2**
2009–10	Ipswich T	36	0		
2010–11	Ipswich T	32	2		
2011–12	Ipswich T	29	0		
2012–13	Ipswich T	1	0	**98**	**2**
2012–13	Crystal Palace	40	3		
2013–14	Crystal Palace	37	1	**77**	**4**

DIKGACOI, Kagisho (M) 208 15
H: 5 11 W: 12 10 b.Brandfort 24-11-84
Internationals: South Africa Full caps.

Season	Club				
2004–05	Bloemfontein YT	10	0	**10**	**0**
2005–06	Lamontville GA	9	0		
2006–07	Lamontville GA	25	0		
2007–08	Lamontville GA	23	4		
2008–09	Lamontville GA	23	4	**80**	**8**
2009–10	Fulham	12	0		
2010–11	Fulham	1	0	**13**	**0**
2010–11	Crystal Palace	13	1		
2011–12	Crystal Palace	27	2		
2012–13	Crystal Palace	39	4		
2013–14	Crystal Palace	26	0	**105**	**7**

DOBBIE, Stephen (F) 302 94
H: 5 10 W: 11 00 b.Glasgow 5-12-82

Season	Club				
2002–03	Rangers	0	0		
2002–03	Northern Spirit	3	3	**3**	**3**
2003–04	Hibernian	28	2		
2004–05	Hibernian	7	0	**35**	**2**
2004–05	St Johnstone	8	2		
2005–06	St Johnstone	20	1	**28**	**3**
2006–07	Dumbarton	17	10	**17**	**10**
2006–07	Queen of the South	15	10		
2007–08	Queen of the South	36	16		
2008–09	Queen of the South	32	23	**83**	**49**
2009–10	Swansea C	6	0		
2009–10	Blackpool	16	4		
2010–11	Swansea C	41	9		
2011–12	Swansea C	8	0		
2011–12	Blackpool	7	5		
2012–13	Swansea C	0	0	**55**	**9**
2012–13	Brighton & HA	15	2	**15**	**2**
2012–13	Crystal Palace	15	3		
2013–14	Crystal Palace	1	0	**16**	**3**
2013–14	Blackpool	27	4	**50**	**13**

GABBIDON, Daniel (D) 363 12
H: 6 0 W: 13 05 b.Cwmbran 8-8-79
Internationals: Wales Youth, U21, Full caps.

Season	Club				
1998–99	WBA	2	0		
1999–2000	WBA	18	0		
2000–01	WBA	0	0	**20**	**0**
2000–01	Cardiff C	43	3		
2001–02	Cardiff C	44	3		
2002–03	Cardiff C	24	0		
2003–04	Cardiff C	41	3		
2004–05	Cardiff C	45	1	**197**	**10**
2005–06	West Ham U	32	0		
2006–07	West Ham U	14	0		
2007–08	West Ham U	10	0		
2008–09	West Ham U	18	0		
2009–10	West Ham U	10	0		
2010–11	West Ham U	26	0	**96**	**0**
2011–12	QPR	17	0	**17**	**0**
2012–13	Crystal Palace	10	1		
2013–14	Crystal Palace	23	1	**33**	**2**

GARVAN, Owen (M) 254 23
H: 6 0 W: 10 07 b.Dublin 29-1-88
Internationals: Republic of Ireland U21.

Season	Club				
2005–06	Ipswich T	32	3		
2006–07	Ipswich T	27	1		
2007–08	Ipswich T	43	2		
2008–09	Ipswich T	37	7		
2009–10	Ipswich T	25	0	**164**	**13**
2010–11	Crystal Palace	26	3		
2011–12	Crystal Palace	22	3		
2012–13	Crystal Palace	27	4		
2013–14	Crystal Palace	2	0	**77**	**10**
2013–14	Millwall	13	0	**13**	**0**

GAYLE, Dwight (F) 70 27
H: 5 10 W: 11 07 b.Walthamstow 20-10-89

Season	Club				
2011–12	Dagenham & R	0	0		
2012–13	Dagenham & R	18	7	**18**	**7**
2012–13	Peterborough U	29	13	**29**	**13**
2013–14	Crystal Palace	23	7	**23**	**7**

GUEDIOURA, Adlene (M) 196 17
H: 6 1 W: 12 08 b.La Roche-sur-Yon 12-11-85
Internationals: Algeria Full caps.

Season	Club				
2004–05	Sedan	0	0		
2005–06	Noisy-Le-Sec	15	1	**15**	**1**
2006–07	L'Entente	21	3	**21**	**3**
2007–08	Creteil	24	6	**24**	**6**
2008–09	Kortrijk	10	0	**10**	**0**
2008–09	Charleroi	12	0		
2009–10	Charleroi	13	1	**25**	**1**
2009–10	Wolverhampton W	14	1		
2010–11	Wolverhampton W	10	1		
2011–12	Wolverhampton W	10	0	**34**	**2**
2011–12	Nottingham F	19	1		
2012–13	Nottingham F	35	3		
2013–14	Nottingham F	5	0	**59**	**4**
2013–14	Crystal Palace	8	0	**8**	**0**

HENNESSEY, Wayne (G) 180 0
H: 6 0 W: 11 06 b.Anglesey 24-1-87
Internationals: Wales U17, U19, U21, Full caps.

Season	Club				
2004–05	Wolverhampton W	0	0		
2005–06	Wolverhampton W	0	0		
2006–07	Wolverhampton W	0	0		
2006–07	Bristol C	0	0		
2006–07	Stockport Co	15	0	**15**	**0**
2007–08	Wolverhampton W	46	0		
2008–09	Wolverhampton W	35	0		
2009–10	Wolverhampton W	13	0		
2010–11	Wolverhampton W	24	0		
2011–12	Wolverhampton W	34	0		
2012–13	Wolverhampton W	0	0		
2013–14	Wolverhampton W	0	0	**152**	**0**
2013–14	Yeovil T	12	0	**12**	**0**
2013–14	Crystal Palace	1	0	**1**	**0**

HUNT, Jack (D) 135 2
H: 5 9 W: 11 02 b.Rothwell 6-12-90

Season	Club				
2009–10	Huddersfield T	0	0		
2010–11	Huddersfield T	19	1		
2010–11	Chesterfield	20	0	**20**	**0**
2011–12	Huddersfield T	43	1		
2012–13	Huddersfield T	40	0		
2013–14	Huddersfield T	2	0	**104**	**2**
2013–14	Crystal Palace	0	0		
2013–14	Barnsley	11	0	**11**	**0**

INNISS, Ryan (D) 5 0
H: 6 5 W: 13 02 b.Kent 5-6-95
Internationals: England U16, U17.

Season	Club				
2012–13	Crystal Palace	0	0		
2013–14	Crystal Palace	0	0		
2013–14	Cheltenham T	2	0	**2**	**0**
2013–14	Gillingham	3	0	**3**	**0**

JEDINAK, Mile (M) 303 34
H: 6 2 W: 13 12 b.Sydney 3-8-84
Internationals: Australia U20, Full caps.

Season	Club				
2000–01	Sydney U	3	0		
2001–02	Sydney U	7	1		
2002–03	Sydney U	18	2		
2003–04	Varteks	0	0		
2004–05	Sydney U	24	3		
2005–06	Sydney U	30	6	**82**	**12**
2006–07	Central Coast M	8	0		
2007–08	Central Coast M	22	2		
2008–09	Central Coast M	15	6	**45**	**8**

2008–09	Genclerbirligi	15	1		
2009–10	Genclerbirligi	2	0		
2009–10	Antalya	28	5	28	5
2010–11	Genclerbirligi	21	3	38	4
2011–12	Crystal Palace	31	1		
2012–13	Crystal Palace	41	3		
2013–14	Crystal Palace	38	1	110	5

KAIKAI, Sullay (F)   **5 0**

2013–14	Crystal Palace	0	0		
2013–14	Crawley T	5	0	5	0

KEBE, Jimmy (M)   **224 37**
H: 6 2   W: 11 07   b.Paris 19-1-84
Internationals: Mali U23, Full caps.

2005–06	Lens	0	0		
2006–07	*Chateauroux*	18	2	18	2
2007–08	Lens	0	0		
2007–08	*Boulogne*	16	5	16	5
2007–08	Reading	5	0		
2008–09	Reading	41	2		
2009–10	Reading	42	10		
2010–11	Reading	36	9		
2011–12	Reading	33	3		
2012–13	Reading	18	5		
2013–14	Reading	0	0	175	29
2013–14	Crystal Palace	6	0	6	0
2013–14	*Leeds U*	9	1	9	1

LEDLEY, Joe (M)   **346 47**
H: 6 0   W: 11 06   b.Cardiff 23-1-87
Internationals: Wales U17, U19, U21, Full caps.

2004–05	Cardiff C	28	3		
2005–06	Cardiff C	42	3		
2006–07	Cardiff C	46	2		
2007–08	Cardiff C	41	10		
2008–09	Cardiff C	40	4		
2009–10	Cardiff C	29	3	226	25
2010–11	Celtic	29	2		
2011–12	Celtic	32	7		
2012–13	Celtic	25	7		
2013–14	Celtic	20	4	106	20
2013–14	Crystal Palace	14	2	14	2

MARIAPPA, Adrian (D)   **269 6**
H: 5 10   W: 11 12   b.Harrow 3-10-86
Internationals: Jamaica Full caps.

2005–06	Watford	3	0		
2006–07	Watford	19	0		
2007–08	Watford	25	0		
2008–09	Watford	39	1		
2009–10	Watford	46	1		
2010–11	Watford	45	1		
2011–12	Watford	39	1	216	4
2012–13	Reading	29	1		
2013–14	Reading	0	0	29	1
2013–14	Crystal Palace	24	1	24	1

McCARTHY, Patrick (D)   **253 11**
H: 6 2   W: 13 07   b.Dublin 31-5-83
Internationals: Republic of Ireland U17, U21, B.

2000–01	Manchester C	0	0		
2001–02	Manchester C	0	0		
2002–03	Manchester C	0	0		
2002–03	*Boston U*	12	0	12	0
2002–03	*Notts Co*	6	0	6	0
2003–04	Manchester C	0	0		
2004–05	Manchester C	0	0		
2004–05	Leicester C	12	0		
2005–06	Leicester C	38	2		
2006–07	Leicester C	22	1	72	3
2007–08	Charlton Ath	29	2	29	2
2008–09	Crystal Palace	27	3		
2009–10	Crystal Palace	20	0		
2010–11	Crystal Palace	43	1		
2011–12	Crystal Palace	43	2		
2012–13	Crystal Palace	0	0		
2013–14	Crystal Palace	0	0	134	6

MOXEY, Dean (D)   **186 7**
H: 6 2   W: 11 00   b.Exeter 14-1-86
Internationals: England C.

2008–09	Exeter C	43	4	43	4
2009–10	Derby Co	30	0		
2010–11	Derby Co	22	2	52	2
2010–11	Crystal Palace	17	1		
2011–12	Crystal Palace	24	0		
2012–13	Crystal Palace	30	0		
2013–14	Crystal Palace	20	0	91	1

MURRAY, Glenn (F)   **304 122**
H: 6 1   W: 12 12   b.Maryport 25-9-83

2005–06	Carlisle U	26	3		
2006–07	Carlisle U	1	0	27	3
2006–07	*Stockport Co*	11	3	11	3
2006–07	Rochdale	31	16		
2007–08	Rochdale	23	9	54	25
2007–08	Brighton & HA	21	9		
2008–09	Brighton & HA	23	11		
2009–10	Brighton & HA	32	12		
2010–11	Brighton & HA	42	22	118	54
2011–12	Crystal Palace	38	6		
2012–13	Crystal Palace	42	30		
2013–14	Crystal Palace	14	1	94	37

O'KEEFFE, Stuart (M)   **44 1**
H: 5 8   W: 10 00   b.Eye 4-3-91

2008–09	Southend U	3	0		
2009–10	Southend U	7	0		
2010–11	Southend U	0	0	10	0
2011–12	Crystal Palace	13	0		
2012–13	Crystal Palace	5	0		
2013–14	Crystal Palace	12	1	34	1

PARR, Jonathan (M)   **213 10**
H: 6 0   W: 11 11   b.Oslo 21-10-88
Internationals: Norway U17, U19, U21, Full caps.

2006	Lyn	11	0	11	0
2007	Aalesund	19	1		
2008	Aalesund	24	4		
2009	Aalesund	27	2		
2010	Aalesund	25	0		
2011	Aalesund	15	1	110	8
2011–12	Crystal Palace	39	2		
2012–13	Crystal Palace	38	0		
2013–14	Crystal Palace	15	0	92	2

PRICE, Lewis (G)   **107 0**
H: 6 3   W: 13 05   b.Bournemouth 19-7-84
Internationals: Wales U19, U21, Full caps.

2002–03	Ipswich T	0	0		
2003–04	Ipswich T	1	0		
2004–05	Ipswich T	8	0		
2004–05	*Cambridge U*	6	0	6	0
2005–06	Ipswich T	25	0		
2006–07	Ipswich T	34	0	68	0
2007–08	Derby Co	6	0		
2008–09	Derby Co	0	0		
2008–09	*Milton Keynes D*	2	0	2	0
2008–09	*Luton T*	1	0	1	0
2009–10	Derby Co	0	0	6	0
2009–10	*Brentford*	13	0	13	0
2010–11	Crystal Palace	1	0		
2011–12	Crystal Palace	5	0		
2012–13	Crystal Palace	0	0		
2013–14	Crystal Palace	0	0	6	0
2013–14	*Mansfield T*	5	0	5	0

PUNCHEON, Jason (M)   **297 51**
H: 5 9   W: 12 05   b.Croydon 26-6-86

2003–04	Wimbledon	8	0	8	0
2004–05	Milton Keynes D	25	1		
2005–06	Milton Keynes D	1	0		
2006–07	Barnet	37	5		
2007–08	Barnet	41	10	78	15
2008–09	Plymouth Arg	6	0		
2008–09	*Milton Keynes D*	27	4		
2009–10	Plymouth Arg	0	0		
2009–10	*Milton Keynes D*	24	7	77	12
2009–10	Southampton	19	3		
2010–11	Southampton	15	0		
2010–11	*Millwall*	7	5	7	5
2010–11	*Blackpool*	11	3	11	3
2011–12	Southampton	8	0		
2011–12	*QPR*	2	0	2	0
2012–13	Southampton	32	6		
2013–14	Southampton	0	0	74	9
2013–14	Crystal Palace	34	7	34	7

RAMAGE, Peter (D)   **214 6**
H: 6 3   W: 11 02   b.Whitley Bay 22-11-83

2003–04	Newcastle U	0	0		
2004–05	Newcastle U	4	0		
2005–06	Newcastle U	23	0		
2006–07	Newcastle U	21	0		
2007–08	Newcastle U	3	0	51	0
2008–09	QPR	31	0		
2009–10	QPR	33	2		
2010–11	QPR	4	0		
2011–12	QPR	0	0	68	2
2011–12	Crystal Palace	17	0		
2011–12	*Birmingham C*	14	0	14	0
2012–13	Crystal Palace	40	4		
2013–14	Crystal Palace	0	0	57	4
2013–14	*Barnsley*	24	0	24	0

SOW, Osman (F)   **28 5**
H: 6 4   b.Stockholm 22-4-90

2011–12	FC Dacia	13	1		
2012–13	FC Dacia	8	2	21	3
2013	Syrianska FC	7	2	7	2
2013–14	Crystal Palace	0	0		

SPERONI, Julian (G)   **415 0**
H: 6 0   W: 11 00   b.Buenos Aires 18-5-79
Internationals: Argentina U20, U21.

1999–2000	Platense	2	0		
2000–01	Platense	0	0	2	0
2001–02	Dundee	17	0		
2002–03	Dundee	38	0		
2003–04	Dundee	37	0	92	0
2004–05	Crystal Palace	6	0		
2005–06	Crystal Palace	4	0		
2006–07	Crystal Palace	5	0		
2007–08	Crystal Palace	46	0		
2008–09	Crystal Palace	45	0		
2009–10	Crystal Palace	45	0		
2010–11	Crystal Palace	45	0		
2011–12	Crystal Palace	42	0		
2012–13	Crystal Palace	46	0		
2013–14	Crystal Palace	37	0	321	0

THOMAS, Jerome (M)   **230 22**
H: 5 9   W: 11 09   b.Wembley 23-3-83
Internationals: England U19, U20, U21.

2001–02	Arsenal	0	0		
2001–02	*QPR*	4	1		
2002–03	Arsenal	0	0		
2002–03	*QPR*	6	2	10	3
2003–04	Arsenal	0	0		
2003–04	Charlton Ath	1	0		
2004–05	Charlton Ath	24	3		
2005–06	Charlton Ath	25	1		
2006–07	Charlton Ath	20	3		
2007–08	Charlton Ath	32	0		
2008–09	Charlton Ath	1	0	103	7
2008–09	Portsmouth	3	0		
2009–10	Portsmouth	0	0	3	0
2009–10	WBA	27	7		
2010–11	WBA	33	3		
2011–12	WBA	29	1		
2012–13	WBA	10	0	99	11
2012–13	*Leeds U*	6	1	6	1
2013–14	Crystal Palace	9	0	9	0

WARD, Joel (D)   **171 7**
H: 6 2   W: 11 13   b.Emsworth 29-10-89

2008–09	Portsmouth	1	0		
2008–09	*Bournemouth*	21	1	21	1
2009–10	Portsmouth	3	0		
2010–11	Portsmouth	42	3		
2011–12	Portsmouth	44	3	89	6
2012–13	Crystal Palace	25	0		
2013–14	Crystal Palace	36	0	61	0

WILBRAHAM, Aaron (F)   **424 91**
H: 6 3   W: 12 04   b.Knutsford 21-10-79

1997–98	Stockport Co	7	1		
1998–99	Stockport Co	26	4		
1999–2000	Stockport Co	26	4		
2000–01	Stockport Co	36	12		
2001–02	Stockport Co	21	3		
2002–03	Stockport Co	15	7		
2003–04	Stockport Co	41	8	172	35
2004–05	Hull C	9	2	9	2
2004–05	*Oldham Ath*	4	2	4	2
2005–06	Milton Keynes D	31	4		
2005–06	*Bradford C*	5	1	5	1
2006–07	Milton Keynes D	32	7		
2007–08	Milton Keynes D	35	10		
2008–09	Milton Keynes D	33	8		
2009–10	Milton Keynes D	35	10		
2010–11	Milton Keynes D	10	2	176	49
2010–11	Norwich C	12	1		
2011–12	Norwich C	11	1	23	2
2012–13	Crystal Palace	21	0		
2013–14	Crystal Palace	4	0	25	0

WILLIAMS, Jon (M)   **65 1**
H: 5 6   W: 10 00   b.Tunbridge Wells 9-10-93
Internationals: Wales U17, U19, U21, Full caps.

2010–11	Crystal Palace	0	0		

2011–12	Crystal Palace	14	0		
2012–13	Crystal Palace	29	0		
2013–14	Crystal Palace	9	0	52	0
2013–14	*Ipswich T*	13	1	13	1

WYNTER, Alex (M) 6 1
H: 6 0 W: 13 04 b.Camberwell 15-9-93

2009–10	Crystal Palace	0	0		
2010–11	Crystal Palace	0	0		
2011–12	Crystal Palace	0	0		
2012–13	Crystal Palace	0	0		
2013–14	Crystal Palace	0	0		
2013–14	*Colchester U*	6	1	6	1

Scholars
Berkeley-Agyepong, Jacob Kwame; Black, Sonny Jamaal; Clement-Peter, Shawnikki Tau Kamaius Kwakou; Comins, Bradley Jonathan; Dsane, Eddie-Louis Kweku; Egbo, Mandela; Forte, Spencer Ellis Henderson; Gabsi, Elijah Yousef Septe; George, Matthew; Hoare, William James; Howlett-Mundle Jahmal; List, Elliott Ricardo Wignal; Lumeya, Joel; Martin, Kiye; Mohammed, Hussein Ali; O'Dwyer, Oliver; Spence, Kyle Cameron Walter.

DAGENHAM & R (30)

BINGHAM, Billy (D) 83 4
H: 5 11 W: 11 02 b.Welling 15-7-90

2008–09	Dagenham & R	0	0		
2009–10	Dagenham & R	2	0		
2010–11	Dagenham & R	6	0		
2011–12	Dagenham & R	27	2		
2012–13	Dagenham & R	18	2		
2013–14	Dagenham & R	30	0	83	4

CONNORS, Jack (D) 23 0
b. 24-10-94
Internationals: Republic of Ireland U21.

2013–14	Dagenham & R	23	0	23	0

DENNIS, Louis (F) 8 0
H: 5 10 W: 10 12 b.Hendon 9-10-92

2011–12	Dagenham & R	0	0		
2012–13	Dagenham & R	6	0		
2013–14	Dagenham & R	2	0	8	0

DICKSON, Chris (F) 108 17
H: 5 11 W: 11 08 b.Plumstead 28-12-84
Internationals: Ghana Full caps.

2006–07	Charlton Ath	0	0		
2007–08	Charlton Ath	2	0		
2007–08	*Crewe Alex*	3	0	3	0
2007–08	*Gillingham*	12	7		
2008–09	Charlton Ath	21	0		
2009–10	Charlton Ath	5	0	28	0
2009–10	*Bristol R*	14	4	14	4
2009–10	*Gillingham*	9	1	21	8
2011–12	Nea Salamina	17	4		
2012–13	Nea Salamina	0	0	17	4
2013–14	Dagenham & R	25	1	25	1

DOE, Scott (D) 204 10
H: 6 0 W: 11 06 b.Reading 6-11-88
Internationals: England C.

2009–10	Dagenham & R	42	0		
2010–11	Dagenham & R	38	0		
2011–12	Dagenham & R	41	6		
2012–13	Dagenham & R	46	3		
2013–14	Dagenham & R	37	1	204	10

EDGAR, Anthony (M) 31 2
H: 5 8 W: 11 00 b.Newham 30-9-90

2009–10	West Ham U	0	0		
2009–10	*Bournemouth*	3	0	3	0
2010–11	West Ham U	0	0		
2011–12	*Yeovil T*	10	1	10	1
2012–13	*Barnet*	11	1	11	1
2013–14	Dagenham & R	7	0	7	0

ELITO, Medy (M) 158 23
H: 6 2 W: 13 00 b.Kinshasa 20-3-90
Internationals: England U17, U18, U19.

2007–08	Colchester U	11	1		
2008–09	Colchester U	5	0		
2009–10	Colchester U	3	0		
2009–10	*Cheltenham T*	12	3		
2010–11	Colchester U	0	0	19	1
2010–11	*Dagenham & R*	10	2		
2010–11	*Cheltenham T*	2	0	14	3

2011–12	Dagenham & R	24	4		
2012–13	Dagenham & R	46	6		
2013–14	Dagenham & R	45	7	125	19

GAYLE, Ian (D) 4 0
b.Welling 23-10-92

2011–12	Dagenham & R	0	0		
2012–13	Dagenham & R	0	0		
2013–14	Dagenham & R	4	0	4	0

HINES, Zavon (F) 109 11
H: 5 10 W: 10 07 b.Jamaica 27-12-88
Internationals: England U21.

2007–08	West Ham U	0	0		
2007–08	*Coventry C*	7	1	7	1
2008–09	West Ham U	0	0		
2009–10	West Ham U	13	1		
2010–11	West Ham U	9	0	22	1
2011–12	*Burnley*	13	0	13	0
2011–12	*Bournemouth*	8	1	8	1
2012–13	*Bradford C*	32	2		
2013–14	*Bradford C*	0	0	32	2
2013–14	Dagenham & R	27	6	27	6

HOWELL, Luke (D) 175 15
H: 5 10 W: 10 05 b.Heathfield 5-1-87

2006–07	Gillingham	1	0	1	0
2007–08	Milton Keynes D	8	0		
2008–09	Milton Keynes D	15	1		
2009–10	Milton Keynes D	29	0		
2010–11	Milton Keynes D	1	0	53	1
2010–11	*Lincoln C*	25	1	25	1
2011–12	Dagenham & R	10	0		
2012–13	Dagenham & R	46	9		
2013–14	Dagenham & R	40	4	96	13

HOYTE, Gavin (D) 109 0
H: 5 11 W: 11 00 b.Waltham Forest 6-6-90
Internationals: England U20.

2007–08	Arsenal	0	0		
2008–09	Arsenal	1	0		
2008–09	*Watford*	7	0	7	0
2009–10	Arsenal	0	0		
2009–10	*Brighton & HA*	18	0	18	0
2010–11	Arsenal	0	0		
2010–11	*Lincoln C*	12	0	12	0
2011–12	Arsenal	0	0	1	0
2011–12	*AFC Wimbledon*	3	0	3	0
2012–13	Dagenham & R	26	0		
2013–14	Dagenham & R	42	0	68	0

ILESANMI, Femi (D) 117 1
H: 6 1 W: 11 13 b.Southwark 18-4-91

2011–12	Dagenham & R	25	0		
2011–12	Dagenham & R	17	0		
2012–13	Dagenham & R	46	1		
2013–14	Dagenham & R	29	0	117	1

LEWINGTON, Chris (G) 127 0
H: 6 1 W: 12 00 b.Sidcup 23-8-88

2009–10	Dagenham & R	0	0		
2010–11	Dagenham & R	3	0		
2011–12	Dagenham & R	41	0		
2012–13	Dagenham & R	41	0		
2013–14	Dagenham & R	42	0	127	0

MURPHY, Rhys (F) 68 21
H: 6 1 W: 11 13 b.Shoreham 6-11-90
Internationals: England U16, U17, 19. Republic of Ireland U15, U21.

2007–08	Arsenal	0	0		
2008–09	Arsenal	0	0		
2009–10	Arsenal	0	0		
2009–10	*Brentford*	5	0	5	0
2010–11	Arsenal	0	0		
2011–12	Arsenal	0	0		
2011–12	*Preston NE*	5	0	5	0
2012–13	Arsenal	0	0		
2012–13	*Stormvogels Telstar*	26	8	26	8
2013–14	Dagenham & R	32	13	32	13

NOUBLE, Jon (F) 1 0

2013–14	Dagenham & R	1	0	1	0

OBAFEMI, Affy (F) 31 2
H: 6 2 W: 13 02 b.London 25-11-94

2011–12	Leyton Orient	1	0		
2012–13	Leyton Orient	8	0	9	0
2013–14	Dagenham & R	22	2	22	2

OGOGO, Abu (D) 202 14
H: 5 8 W: 10 02 b.Epsom 3-11-89

2007–08	Arsenal	0	0		
2008–09	Arsenal	0	0		
2008–09	*Barnet*	9	1	9	1

2009–10	Dagenham & R	30	2		
2010–11	Dagenham & R	33	1		
2011–12	Dagenham & R	40	1		
2012–13	Dagenham & R	46	1		
2013–14	Dagenham & R	44	8	193	13

REED, Jake (F) 31 1
H: 5 9 W: 11 07 b.Great Yarmouth 13-5-91

2011–12	Dagenham & R	7	0		
2012–13	Dagenham & R	22	1		
2013–14	Dagenham & R	2	0	31	1

SAAH, Brian (M) 214 3
H: 6 3 W: 12 03 b.Rush Green 16-12-86
Internationals: England C.

2003–04	Leyton Orient	6	0		
2004–05	Leyton Orient	12	0		
2005–06	Leyton Orient	3	0		
2006–07	Leyton Orient	32	0		
2007–08	Leyton Orient	25	1		
2008–09	Leyton Orient	15	0	93	1

From Cambridge U.

2011–12	Torquay U	35	1		
2012–13	Torquay U	43	1	78	2
2013–14	Dagenham & R	43	0	43	0

SAUNDERS, Matthew (M) 59 7
H: 5 11 W: 11 05 b.Chertsey 12-9-89

2008–09	Fulham	0	0		
2009–10	Fulham	0	0		
2009–10	*Lincoln C*	18	3	18	3
2010–11	Fulham	0	0		
2011–12	Fulham	0	0		
2011–12	Dagenham & R	5	1		
2012–13	Dagenham & R	32	3		
2013–14	Dagenham & R	4	0	41	4

SCOTT, Josh (F) 105 15
H: 6 1 W: 12 00 b.Camden 10-5-85

2009–10	Dagenham & R	40	10		
2010–11	Dagenham & R	16	1		
2011–12	Dagenham & R	20	1		
2012–13	Dagenham & R	18	2		
2013–14	Dagenham & R	11	1	105	15

SEABRIGHT, Jordan (G) 8 0
H: 6 2 W: 12 06 b.Poole 1-5-94

2011–12	Bournemouth	0	0		
2012–13	Bournemouth	0	0		
2012–13	Dagenham & R	4	0		
2013–14	Dagenham & R	4	0	8	0

SHIELDS, Sean (F) 13 0
b.Enfield 20-1-92
Internationals: Northern Ireland U21.

2012–13	Dagenham & R	1	0		
2013–14	Dagenham & R	12	0	13	0

WILKINSON, Luke (D) 65 6
H: 6 2 W: 11 09 b.Wells 2-12-92

2009–10	Portsmouth	0	0		
2010–11	Dagenham & R	0	0		
2011–12	Dagenham & R	0	0		
2012–13	Dagenham & R	43	6		
2013–14	Dagenham & R	22	0	65	6

WOODALL, Brian (F) 75 13
H: 5 10 W: 11 09 b.Bielefeld 28-12-87

2011–12	Dagenham & R	39	11		
2012–13	Dagenham & R	28	1		
2013–14	Dagenham & R	8	1	75	13

Scholars
Bolton, Tyler Jon; Clark, Lewis James; Crickmay, Benjamin Michael; Enigbokan-Bloomfield, Mason Ozail; Ferguson, Nathan James Decalvia; Fitchett, James David; Grimme-Yexley, Charles John; Hursit, Lee; Martinsen-Hickman, Tristan Nicholas; Nouble, Joel Jonathan; Olukoga, Ayodeji Sulaimon Olakuseyin Onotayo O; Pykes, Kurtis; Rumens, Daniel; Sidhu, Jordan; Stewart, Montana; Tweddell, Harrison; Walker, Omari.

DERBY CO (31)

ATKINS, Ross (G) 50 0
H: 6 0 W: 13 00 b.Derby 3-11-89
Internationals: England U18, U19.

2008–09	Derby Co	0	0		
2009–10	Derby Co	0	0		
2010–11	Derby Co	1	0		

2011–12 Derby Co 0 0
2011–12 *Burton Alb* 45 0
2012–13 Derby Co 0 0
2012–13 *Burton Alb* 4 0 49 0
2013–14 Derby Co 0 0 1 0
2013–14 *Crawley T* 0 0

BAILEY, James (M) 135 3
H: 6 0 W: 12 05 b.Bollington 18-9-88
2006–07 Crewe Alex 0 0
2007–08 Crewe Alex 1 0
2008–09 Crewe Alex 24 0
2009–10 Crewe Alex 21 0 46 0
2010–11 Derby Co 36 1
2011–12 Derby Co 22 0
2012–13 Derby Co 0 0
2012–13 *Coventry C* 30 2 30 2
2013–14 Derby Co 1 0 59 1

BALL, Callum (F) 59 6
H: 6 1 W: 10 03 b.Leicester 8-10-92
2009–10 Derby Co 1 0
2010–11 Derby Co 5 0
2011–12 Derby Co 23 3
2012–13 *Coventry C* 15 0 15 0
2013–14 Derby Co 0 0 29 3
2013–14 *Torquay U* 9 2 9 2
2013–14 *Notts Co* 6 1 6 1

BARKER, Shaun (D) 355 18
H: 6 2 W: 12 08 b.Nottingham 19-9-82
2002–03 Rotherham U 11 0
2003–04 Rotherham U 36 2
2004–05 Rotherham U 33 2
2005–06 Rotherham U 43 3 123 7
2006–07 Blackpool 45 3
2007–08 Blackpool 46 2
2008–09 Blackpool 43 0 134 5
2009–10 Derby Co 35 5
2010–11 Derby Co 43 1
2011–12 Derby Co 20 0
2012–13 Derby Co 0 0
2013–14 Derby Co 0 0 98 6

BENNETT, Mason (F) 33 1
H: 5 10 W: 10 02 b.Shirebrook 15-7-96
Internationals: England U16, U17, U19.
2011–12 Derby Co 9 0
2012–13 Derby Co 6 0
2013–14 Derby Co 13 1 28 1
2013–14 *Chesterfield* 5 0 5 0

BRYSON, Craig (M) 339 47
H: 5 7 W: 10 00 b.Rutherglen 6-11-86
Internationals: Scotland U21, Full caps.
2003–04 Clyde 0 0
2004–05 Clyde 28 3
2005–06 Clyde 33 2
2006–07 Clyde 34 3 95 8
2007–08 Kilmarnock 19 4
2008–09 Kilmarnock 33 2
2009–10 Kilmarnock 33 4
2010–11 Kilmarnock 33 2 118 12
2011–12 Derby Co 44 6
2012–13 Derby Co 37 5
2013–14 Derby Co 45 16 126 27

BUXTON, Jake (D) 268 13
H: 6 1 W: 13 05 b.Sutton-in-Ashfield 4-3-85
2002–03 Mansfield T 3 0
2003–04 Mansfield T 9 1
2004–05 Mansfield T 30 1
2005–06 Mansfield T 39 0
2006–07 Mansfield T 30 1
2007–08 Mansfield T 40 2
2008–09 Mansfield T 0 0 151 5
From Burton Alb.
2008–09 Derby Co 0 0
2009–10 Derby Co 19 1
2010–11 Derby Co 1 0
2011–12 Derby Co 21 2
2012–13 Derby Co 31 3
2013–14 Derby Co 45 2 117 8

CAPITANI, Matteo (F) 0 0
2013–14 Derby Co 0 0

CISSE, Kalifa (M) 193 9
H: 6 2 W: 12 11 b.Dreux 1-9-84
Internationals: Mali U20, Full caps.
2004–05 Estoril 6 0 6 0
2005–06 Boavista 15 0
2006–07 Boavista 27 0 42 0

2007–08 Reading 22 1
2008–09 Reading 36 5
2009–10 Reading 17 1 75 7
2010–11 Bristol C 29 0
2011–12 Bristol C 32 2 61 2
2013 *N.E Revolution* 6 0 6 0
2013–14 Derby Co 3 0 3 0
Transferred to Bangkok United January 2014.

COUTTS, Paul (M) 182 7
H: 5 9 W: 11 11 b.Aberdeen 22-7-88
Internationals: Scotland U21.
2008–09 Peterborough U 37 0
2009–10 Peterborough U 16 0 53 0
2010–11 Preston NE 13 1
2010–11 Preston NE 23 1
2011–12 Preston NE 41 2 77 4
2012–13 Derby Co 44 3
2013–14 Derby Co 8 0 52 3

DAVIES, Ben (M) 373 69
H: 5 7 W: 12 03 b.Birmingham 27-5-81
2000–01 Kidderminster H 3 0
2001–02 Kidderminster H 9 0 12 0
2004–05 Chester C 44 2
2005–06 Chester C 45 7 89 9
2006–07 Shrewsbury T 43 12
2007–08 Shrewsbury T 27 6
2008–09 Shrewsbury T 42 12 112 30
2009–10 Notts Co 45 15
2010–11 Notts Co 22 5 67 20
2010–11 Derby Co 13 1
2011–12 Derby Co 35 2
2012–13 Derby Co 23 4
2013–14 Derby Co 4 0 75 7
2013–14 *Sheffield U* 18 3 18 3

DAWKINS, Simon (F) 96 18
H: 5 10 W: 11 01 b.Edgware 1-12-87
Internationals: Jamaica Full caps.
2005–06 Tottenham H 0 0
2006–07 Tottenham H 0 0
2007–08 Tottenham H 0 0
2008–09 Tottenham H 0 0
2008–09 *Leyton Orient* 11 0 11 0
2009–10 Tottenham H 0 0
2010–11 Tottenham H 0 0
2011 *San Jose E* 26 6
2011–12 Tottenham H 0 0
2012 *San Jose E* 29 8 55 14
2012–13 Tottenham H 0 0
2012–13 *Aston Villa* 4 0 4 0
2013–14 Tottenham H 0 0
2013–14 Derby Co 26 4 26 4

ETHERIDGE, Ross (G) 0 0
2013–14 Derby Co 0 0

EUSTACE, John (M) 381 31
H: 5 11 W: 11 12 b.Solihull 3-11-79
1996–97 Coventry C 0 0
1997–98 Coventry C 0 0
1998–99 Coventry C 0 0
1998–99 Dundee U 11 1 11 1
1999–2000 Coventry C 16 1
2000–01 Coventry C 32 2
2001–02 Coventry C 6 0
2002–03 Coventry C 32 4 86 7
2002–03 *Middlesbrough* 1 0 1 0
2003–04 Stoke C 26 5
2004–05 Stoke C 7 0
2005–06 Stoke C 0 0
2006–07 Stoke C 15 0
2006–07 *Hereford U* 8 0 8 0
2007–08 Stoke C 26 0 74 5
2007–08 Watford 13 0
2008–09 Watford 17 2
2008–09 *Derby Co* 9 1
2009–10 Watford 42 4
2010–11 Watford 41 6
2011–12 Watford 39 4
2012–13 Watford 5 0 157 16
2013–14 Derby Co 35 1 44 2

FORSYTH, Craig (M) 179 17
H: 6 0 W: 12 00 b.Carnoustie 24-2-89
2006–07 Dundee 1 0
2007–08 Dundee 0 0
2007–08 *Montrose* 9 0 9 0
2008–09 Dundee 1 0
2008–09 *Arbroath* 26 2 26 2
2009–10 Dundee 24 2

2010–11 Dundee 33 8 59 10
2011–12 Watford 20 3
2012–13 Watford 2 0 22 3
2012–13 *Bradford C* 7 0 7 0
2012–13 *Derby Co* 10 0
2013–14 Derby Co 46 2 56 2

FREEMAN, Kieron (D) 72 1
H: 5 10 W: 12 05 b.Nottingham 21-3-92
Internationals: Wales U17, U19, U21.
2010–11 Nottingham F 0 0
2011–12 Nottingham F 0 0
2011–12 *Notts Co* 19 1
2012–13 Derby Co 19 0
2013–14 Derby Co 6 0 25 0
2013–14 *Notts Co* 16 0 35 1
2013–14 *Sheffield U* 12 0 12 0

GRANT, Lee (G) 387 0
H: 6 3 W: 13 01 b.Hemel Hempstead 27-1-83
Internationals: England U16, U17, U18, U19, U21.
2000–01 Derby Co 0 0
2001–02 Derby Co 0 0
2002–03 Derby Co 29 0
2003–04 Derby Co 36 0
2004–05 Derby Co 2 0
2005–06 Derby Co 0 0
2005–06 *Burnley* 1 0
2005–06 *Oldham Ath* 16 0 16 0
2006–07 Derby Co 7 0
2007–08 Sheffield W 44 0
2008–09 Sheffield W 46 0
2009–10 Sheffield W 46 0 136 0
2010–11 Burnley 25 0
2011–12 Burnley 43 0
2012–13 Burnley 46 0 115 0
2013–14 Derby Co 46 0 120 0

HANSON, Jamie (F) 0 0
2012–13 Derby Co 0 0
2013–14 Derby Co 0 0

HENDRICK, Jeff (M) 121 13
H: 6 1 W: 11 11 b.Dublin 31-1-92
Internationals: Republic of Ireland U17, U19, U21, Full caps.
2010–11 Derby Co 4 0
2011–12 Derby Co 42 3
2012–13 Derby Co 45 6
2013–14 Derby Co 30 4 121 13

HUGHES, Will (M) 79 5
H: 6 1 W: 11 08 b.Weybridge 7-4-95
Internationals: England U17, U21.
2011–12 Derby Co 3 0
2012–13 Derby Co 35 2
2013–14 Derby Co 41 3 79 5

KEOGH, Richard (D) 320 14
H: 6 0 W: 11 02 b.Harlow 11-8-86
Internationals: Republic of Ireland U21, Full caps.
2004–05 Stoke C 0 0
2005–06 Bristol C 9 1
2005–06 *Wycombe W* 3 0 3 0
2006–07 Bristol C 31 2
2007–08 Bristol C 0 0 40 3
2007–08 *Huddersfield T* 9 1 9 1
2007–08 *Carlisle U* 7 0
2007–08 *Cheltenham T* 10 0 10 0
2008–09 Carlisle U 32 1
2009–10 Carlisle U 41 3 80 4
2010–11 Coventry C 46 1
2011–12 Coventry C 45 0 91 1
2012–13 Derby Co 46 4
2013–14 Derby Co 41 1 87 5

LELAN, Josh (D) 0 0
b.Derby 21-12-94
2012–13 Derby Co 0 0
2013–14 Derby Co 0 0

MARTIN, Chris (F) 237 66
H: 6 2 W: 12 06 b.Beccles 4-11-88
Internationals: England U19. Scotland Full caps.
2006–07 Norwich C 18 4
2007–08 Norwich C 7 0
2007–08 Norwich C 0 0
2008–09 *Luton T* 40 11 40 11
2009–10 Norwich C 42 17
2010–11 Norwich C 30 4

2011–12	Norwich C	4	0		
2011–12	*Crystal Palace*	26	7	26	7
2012–13	Norwich C	1	0	102	25
2012–13	*Swindon T*	12	1	12	1
2012–13	Derby Co	13	2		
2013–14	Derby Co	44	20	57	22

MORCH, Mats (G)   0   0
b.Mandal

2010–11	Derby Co	0	0		
2011–12	Derby Co	0	0		
2012–13	Derby Co	0	0		
2013–14	Derby Co	0	0		
2013–14	*Burton Alb*	0	0		

NAYLOR, Lee (D)   439   17
H: 5 9   W: 11 03   b.Walsall 19-3-80
Internationals: England U21.

1997–98	Wolverhampton W	16	0		
1998–99	Wolverhampton W	23	1		
1999–2000	Wolverhampton W	30	2		
2000–01	Wolverhampton W	46	1		
2001–02	Wolverhampton W	27	0		
2002–03	Wolverhampton W	32	1		
2003–04	Wolverhampton W	38	0		
2004–05	Wolverhampton W	38	1		
2005–06	Wolverhampton W	40	1		
2006–07	Wolverhampton W	3	0	293	7
2006–07	Celtic	32	0		
2007–08	Celtic	33	1		
2008–09	Celtic	23	1		
2009–10	Celtic	12	1	100	3
2010–11	Cardiff C	27	2		
2011–12	Cardiff C	2	0	29	2
2013–14	Accrington S	13	0	13	0
2013–14	Derby Co	4	0	4	0

NAYLOR, Tom (D)   46   1
H: 5 11   W: 11 05   b.Sutton-in-Ashfield 28-6-91

2011–12	Derby Co	8	0		
2012–13	Derby Co	0	0		
2012–13	*Bradford C*	5	0	5	0
2013–14	Derby Co	0	0	8	0
2013–14	*Newport Co*	33	1	33	1

O'BRIEN, Mark (D)   32   0
H: 5 11   W: 12 02   b.Dublin 20-11-92
Internationals: Republic of Ireland U17, U19, U21.

2008–09	Derby Co	1	0		
2009–10	Derby Co	0	0		
2010–11	Derby Co	2	0		
2011–12	Derby Co	20	0		
2012–13	Derby Co	9	0		
2013–14	Derby Co	0	0	32	0

O'CONNOR, James (D)   295   6
H: 5 10   W: 12 05   b.Birmingham 20-11-84

2003–04	Aston Villa	0	0		
2004–05	Aston Villa	0	0		
2004–05	Port Vale	13	0	13	0
2004–05	Bournemouth	6	0		
2005–06	Bournemouth	39	1	45	1
2006–07	Doncaster R	40	1		
2007–08	Doncaster R	40	0		
2008–09	Doncaster R	32	1		
2009–10	Doncaster R	38	0		
2010–11	Doncaster R	34	2		
2011–12	Doncaster R	28	0	212	4
2012–13	Derby Co	22	1		
2013–14	Derby Co	0	0	22	1
2013–14	*Bristol C*	3	0	3	0

ROOS, Kelle (G)   0   0

| 2013–14 | Derby Co | 0 | 0 | | |

RUSSELL, Johnny (F)   141   40
H: 5 10   W: 12 03   b.Glasgow 8-4-90
Internationals: Scotland U19, U21.

2006–07	Dundee U	1	0		
2007–08	Dundee U	2	0		
2008–09	Dundee U	0	0		
2009–10	Dundee U	0	0		
2010–11	Dundee U	30	9		
2011–12	Dundee U	37	9		
2012–13	Dundee U	32	13	102	31
2013–14	Derby Co	39	9	39	9

SAMMON, Conor (F)   264   44
H: 5 10   W: 11 11   b.Dublin 13-4-87
Internationals: Republic of Ireland U21, U23, Full caps.

2005	UCD	7	0		
2006	UCD	31	7		
2007	UCD	31	6	69	13
2008	Derry C	16	3	16	3
2008–09	Kilmarnock	17	1		
2009–10	Kilmarnock	25	1		
2010–11	Kilmarnock	23	15	65	17
2010–11	Wigan Ath	7	1		
2011–12	Wigan Ath	25	0	32	1
2012–13	Derby Co	45	8		
2013–14	Derby Co	37	2	82	10

SHARPE, Rhys (D)   0   0
b. 17-10-94
Internationals: Republic of Ireland U21.

| 2013–14 | Derby Co | 0 | 0 | | |

THOMAS, Kwame (F)   0   0
b. 28-9-95

2011–12	Derby Co	0	0		
2012–13	Derby Co	0	0		
2013–14	Derby Co	0	0		

WARD, Jamie (M)   277   76
H: 5 5   W: 9 04   b.Birmingham 12-5-86
Internationals: Northern Ireland U18, U21, Full caps.

2003–04	Aston Villa	0	0		
2004–05	Aston Villa	0	0		
2005–06	Aston Villa	0	0		
2005–06	Stockport Co	9	1	9	1
2006–07	Torquay U	25	9	25	9
2006–07	Chesterfield	9	3		
2007–08	Chesterfield	35	12		
2008–09	Chesterfield	23	14	67	29
2008–09	Sheffield U	16	2		
2009–10	Sheffield U	28	7		
2010–11	Sheffield U	19	0	63	9
2010–11	Derby Co	13	5		
2011–12	Derby Co	37	4		
2012–13	Derby Co	25	12		
2013–14	Derby Co	38	7	113	28

Scholars
Adams, Mohammed; Behrens, Eric; Bennett, Thomas Paul; Clennett, Guy James; Dryden, Samuel; Guy, Callum; Lowe, Max Josef; Moulton, Jorna Anthony Junior; Nash, Joshua Samuel James; Rawson, Farrend James; Revan, Kurtis; Rigby, Thomas James; Tuite, Jack Patrick; Vernam, Charles Terence Priestley; Zanzala, Offrande.

DONCASTER R (32)

BENNETT, Kyle (F)   128   10
H: 5 5   W: 9 08   b.Telford 9-9-90
Internationals: England U18.

2007–08	Wolverhampton W	0	0		
2008–09	Wolverhampton W	0	0		
2009–10	Wolverhampton W	0	0		
2010–11	Bury	32	2	32	2
2011–12	Doncaster R	36	4		
2012–13	Doncaster R	35	3		
2013–14	Doncaster R	3	0	74	7
2013–14	*Crawley T*	4	0	4	0
2013–14	*Bradford C*	18	1	18	1

BROWN, Chris (F)   312   58
H: 6 3   W: 13 01   b.Doncaster 11-12-84

2002–03	Sunderland	0	0		
2003–04	Sunderland	0	0		
2003–04	*Doncaster R*	22	10		
2004–05	Sunderland	37	5		
2005–06	Sunderland	13	1		
2005–06	Hull C	13	1	13	1
2006–07	Sunderland	16	3	66	9
2006–07	Norwich C	4	0		
2007–08	Norwich C	14	1	18	1
2007–08	Preston NE	17	5		
2008–09	Preston NE	30	6		
2009–10	Preston NE	43	6		
2010–11	Preston NE	16	1	106	18
2011–12	Doncaster R	11	2		
2012–13	Doncaster R	36	8		
2013–14	Doncaster R	40	9	109	29

COPPINGER, James (F)   434   46
H: 5 7   W: 10 03   b.Middlesbrough 10-1-81
Internationals: England U16.

1997–98	Newcastle U	0	0		
1998–99	Newcastle U	0	0		
1999–2000	Newcastle U	0	0		
1999–2000	*Hartlepool U*	10	3		
2000–01	Newcastle U	1	0		
2001–02	Newcastle U	0	0	1	0
2001–02	*Hartlepool U*	14	2	24	5
2002–03	Exeter C	43	5		
2003–04	Exeter C	0	0	43	5
2004–05	Doncaster R	31	0		
2005–06	Doncaster R	36	5		
2006–07	Doncaster R	39	4		
2007–08	Doncaster R	39	3		
2008–09	Doncaster R	32	5		
2009–10	Doncaster R	39	4		
2010–11	Doncaster R	40	7		
2011–12	Doncaster R	38	2		
2012–13	Doncaster R	25	2		
2012–13	*Nottingham F*	6	0	6	0
2013–14	Doncaster R	41	4	360	36

COTTERILL, David (F)   279   35
H: 5 9   W: 11 02   b.Cardiff 4-12-87
Internationals: Wales U19, U21, Full caps.

2004–05	Bristol C	7	0		
2005–06	Bristol C	45	7		
2006–07	Bristol C	5	1	62	8
2006–07	Wigan Ath	16	1		
2007–08	Wigan Ath	2	0	18	1
2007–08	*Sheffield U*	16	0		
2008–09	Sheffield U	24	4		
2009–10	Sheffield U	14	2	54	6
2009–10	Swansea C	21	3		
2009–10	Swansea C	14	1		
2010–11	*Portsmouth*	15	1	15	1
2011–12	Swansea C	0	0	35	4
2011–12	*Barnsley*	11	1	11	1
2012–13	Doncaster R	44	10		
2013–14	Doncaster R	40	4	84	14

DE VAL FERNANDEZ, Marc (M)   5   0
b. 15-2-90

| 2013–14 | Doncaster R | 5 | 0 | 5 | 0 |

DUFFY, Mark (M)   204   15
H: 5 9   W: 11 05   b.Liverpool 7-10-85

2008–09	Morecambe	9	1		
2009–10	Morecambe	35	4		
2010–11	Morecambe	22	0	66	5
2010–11	Scunthorpe U	22	1		
2011–12	Scunthorpe U	37	2		
2012–13	Scunthorpe U	43	5	102	8
2013–14	Doncaster R	36	2	36	2

FORRESTER, Harry (F)   69   8
H: 5 9   W: 11 03   b.Milton Keynes 2-1-91
Internationals: England U16, U17.

2007–08	Aston Villa	0	0		
2008–09	Aston Villa	0	0		
2009–10	Aston Villa	0	0		
2010–11	Aston Villa	0	0		
2010–11	*Kilmarnock*	7	0	7	0
2011–12	Brentford	19	0		
2012–13	Brentford	36	8	55	8
2013–14	Doncaster R	7	0	7	0

FURMAN, Dean (M)   204   13
H: 6 0   W: 11 08   b.Cape Town 22-6-88
Internationals: South Africa Full caps.

2007–08	Rangers	0	0	1	0
2008–09	*Bradford C*	32	4	32	4
2009–10	Oldham Ath	38	0		
2010–11	Oldham Ath	42	5		
2011–12	Oldham Ath	23	1		
2012–13	Oldham Ath	28	2	131	8
2012–13	Doncaster R	8	0		
2013–14	Doncaster R	32	1	40	1

HUSBAND, James (D)   64   4
H: 5 10   W: 10 00   b.Leeds 3-1-94

2011–12	Doncaster R	3	0		
2012–13	Doncaster R	33	3		
2013–14	Doncaster R	28	1	64	4

JONES, Rob (D)   312   30
H: 6 7   W: 12 02   b.Stockton 30-11-79

2002–03	Stockport Co	0	0		
2003–04	Stockport Co	16	2	16	2
2003–04	*Macclesfield T*	1	0	1	0
2004–05	Grimsby T	20	1		
2005–06	Grimsby T	40	4	60	5
2006–07	Hibernian	34	4		
2007–08	Hibernian	30	0		
2008–09	Hibernian	32	4	96	8
2009–10	Scunthorpe U	28	1		

Season	Club				
2010–11	Scunthorpe U	14	1	**42**	**2**
2010–11	*Sheffield W*	8	1		
2011–12	Sheffield W	33	4	**41**	**5**
2012–13	Doncaster R	44	7		
2013–14	Doncaster R	12	1	**56**	**8**

KEEGAN, Paul (M)   **232 13**
H: 5 11 W: 11 05 b.Dublin 5-7-84
Internationals: Republic of Ireland U16, U21, U23.

Season	Club				
2000–01	Leeds U	0	0		
2001–02	Leeds U	0	0		
2002–03	Leeds U	0	0		
2003–04	Leeds U	0	0		
2003–04	*Scunthorpe U*	2	0	**2**	**0**
2004–05	Leeds U	0	0		
2005	Drogheda	11	0		
2006	Drogheda	25	4		
2007	Drogheda	30	1		
2008	Drogheda	27	1	**93**	**6**
2009	Bohemians	34	2		
2010	Bohemians	32	4	**66**	**6**
2010–11	Doncaster R	10	0		
2011–12	Doncaster R	2	0		
2012–13	Doncaster R	25	1		
2013–14	Doncaster R	34	0	**71**	**1**

McCOMBE, Jamie (D)   **364 26**
H: 6 5 W: 12 05 b.Scunthorpe 1-1-83

Season	Club				
2001–02	Scunthorpe U	17	0		
2002–03	Scunthorpe U	31	1		
2003–04	Scunthorpe U	15	0	**63**	**1**
2003–04	Lincoln C	8	0		
2004–05	Lincoln C	41	3		
2005–06	Lincoln C	38	4	**87**	**7**
2006–07	Bristol C	41	4		
2007–08	Bristol C	34	3		
2008–09	Bristol C	28	1		
2009–10	Bristol C	16	1	**119**	**9**
2010–11	Huddersfield T	34	5		
2011–12	Huddersfield T	20	3		
2011–12	*Preston NE*	6	0	**6**	**0**
2012–13	Huddersfield T	0	0	**54**	**8**
2012–13	Doncaster R	33	1		
2013–14	Doncaster R	2	0	**35**	**1**

McCULLOUGH, Luke (D)   **15 0**
b.Portadown 15-2-94
Internationals: Northern Ireland U16, U17, U19, U20, U21, Full caps.

Season	Club				
2012–13	Manchester U	0	0		
2012–13	*Cheltenham T*	1	0	**1**	**0**
2013–14	Doncaster R	14	0	**14**	**0**

MEITE, Abdoulaye (D)   **296 4**
H: 6 1 W: 12 11 b.Paris 6-10-80
Internationals: Ivory Coast Full caps.

Season	Club				
1998–99	Red Star 93	4	1		
1999–2000	Red Star 93	0	0	**4**	**1**
2000–01	Marseille	1	0		
2001–02	Marseille	10	0		
2002–03	Marseille	28	0		
2003–04	Marseille	30	0		
2004–05	Marseille	34	1		
2005–06	Marseille	13	0	**116**	**1**
2006–07	Bolton W	35	0		
2007–08	Bolton W	21	0	**56**	**0**
2008–09	WBA	18	0		
2009–10	WBA	20	0		
2010–11	WBA	10	0	**48**	**0**
2011–12	Dijon	25	1	**25**	**1**
2013	FC Honka	26	0	**26**	**0**
2013–14	Doncaster R	21	1	**21**	**1**

PAYNTER, Billy (F)   **406 98**
H: 6 1 W: 14 01 b.Liverpool 13-7-84

Season	Club				
2000–01	Port Vale	0	0		
2001–02	Port Vale	7	0		
2002–03	Port Vale	31	5		
2003–04	Port Vale	44	13		
2004–05	Port Vale	45	10		
2005–06	Port Vale	16	2	**144**	**30**
2005–06	Hull C	22	3	**22**	**3**
2006–07	Southend U	9	0		
2006–07	*Bradford C*	15	4	**15**	**4**
2007–08	Southend U	0	0	**9**	**0**
2007–08	Swindon T	36	8		
2008–09	Swindon T	42	11		
2009–10	Swindon T	42	26	**120**	**45**
2010–11	Leeds U	22	1		
2011–12	Leeds U	5	2		
2011–12	*Brighton & HA*	10	0	**10**	**0**
2012–13	Leeds U	0	0	**27**	**3**
2012–13	Doncaster R	37	13		
2013–14	Doncaster R	9	0	**46**	**13**
2013–14	*Sheffield U*	13	0	**13**	**0**

PETERSON, Alex (F)   **5 0**
b. 17-10-94

Season	Club				
2013–14	Doncaster R	5	0	**5**	**0**

QUINN, Paul (D)   **280 6**
H: 6 0 W: 11 04 b.Wishaw 21-7-85
Internationals: Scotland U21.

Season	Club				
2002–03	Motherwell	4	0		
2003–04	Motherwell	26	0		
2004–05	Motherwell	23	0		
2005–06	Motherwell	18	0		
2006–07	Motherwell	26	0		
2007–08	Motherwell	31	2		
2008–09	Motherwell	33	1	**161**	**3**
2009–10	Cardiff C	22	0		
2010–11	Cardiff C	23	1		
2011–12	Cardiff C	1	0	**46**	**1**
2012–13	Doncaster R	38	0		
2013–14	Doncaster R	35	2	**73**	**2**

ROBINSON, Theo (F)   **235 61**
H: 5 9 W: 10 03 b.Birmingham 22-1-89
Internationals: Jamaica Full caps.

Season	Club				
2005–06	Watford	1	0		
2006–07	Watford	1	0		
2007–08	Watford	0	0		
2007–08	Hereford U	43	13	**43**	**13**
2008–09	Watford	3	0	**5**	**0**
2008–09	Southend U	21	7	**21**	**7**
2009–10	Huddersfield T	37	13		
2010–11	Huddersfield T	1	0		
2010–11	Millwall	11	3		
2010–11	Derby Co	13	2		
2011–12	Derby Co	39	10		
2012–13	Derby Co	28	8		
2012–13	*Huddersfield T*	6	0	**44**	**13**
2013–14	Millwall	0	0	**11**	**3**
2013–14	Derby Co	0	0	**80**	**20**
2013–14	Doncaster R	31	5	**31**	**5**

TAMAS, Gabriel (D)   **276 12**
H: 6 2 W: 12 02 b.Brasov 9-11-83
Internationals: Romania U16, U19, U21, Full caps.

Season	Club				
1998–99	Brasov	1	0		
1999–2000	Brasov	0	0	**1**	**0**
2000–01	Tractorul	15	1		
2001–02	Tractorul	19	2	**34**	**3**
2002–03	Din Bucharest	19	4		
2003–04	Galatasaray	6	0	**6**	**0**
2004	Spartak Moscow	14	0		
2004–05	Din Bucharest	13	0		
2005–06	Din Bucharest	14	1		
2006	Spartak Moscow	3	0		
2006–07	Celta Vigo	29	0	**29**	**0**
2007–08	Auxerre	27	0	**27**	**0**
2008–09	Din Bucharest	22	0		
2009–10	Din Bucharest	12	2	**80**	**7**
2009–10	WBA	23	2		
2010–11	WBA	26	0		
2011–12	WBA	8	0		
2012–13	WBA	11	0		
2013–14	WBA	0	0	**68**	**2**
2013–14	Doncaster R	14	0	**14**	**0**

TURNBULL, Ross (G)   **126 0**
H: 6 4 W: 15 00 b.Bishop Auckland 4-1-85
Internationals: England U16, U17, U18, U19.

Season	Club				
2002–03	Middlesbrough	0	0		
2003–04	Middlesbrough	0	0		
2003–04	*Darlington*	1	0	**1**	**0**
2003–04	Barnsley	3	0		
2004–05	Middlesbrough	0	0		
2004–05	*Bradford C*	2	0	**2**	**0**
2004–05	*Barnsley*	23	0	**26**	**0**
2005–06	Middlesbrough	2	0		
2005–06	*Crewe Alex*	29	0	**29**	**0**
2006–07	Middlesbrough	3	0		
2007–08	Middlesbrough	3	0		
2007–08	*Cardiff C*	6	0	**6**	**0**
2008–09	Middlesbrough	22	0		
2009–10	Middlesbrough	0	0	**27**	**0**
2009–10	Chelsea	2	0		
2010–11	Chelsea	2	0		
2011–12	Chelsea	2	0		
2012–13	Chelsea	3	0	**7**	**0**
2013–14	Doncaster R	28	0	**28**	**0**

WAKEFIELD, Liam (D)   **4 0**
H: 6 0 W: 11 00 b.Doncaster 9-4-94

Season	Club				
2012–13	Doncaster R	0	0		
2013–14	Doncaster R	4	0	**4**	**0**

WELLENS, Richard (M)   **532 37**
H: 5 9 W: 11 06 b.Manchester 26-3-80

Season	Club				
1996–97	Manchester U	0	0		
1997–98	Manchester U	0	0		
1998–99	Manchester U	0	0		
1999–2000	Manchester U	0	0		
1999–2000	Blackpool	8	0		
2000–01	Blackpool	36	8		
2001–02	Blackpool	36	1		
2002–03	Blackpool	39	1		
2003–04	Blackpool	41	3		
2004–05	Blackpool	28	3	**188**	**16**
2005–06	Oldham Ath	45	4		
2006–07	Oldham Ath	42	4	**87**	**8**
2007–08	Doncaster R	45	6		
2008–09	Doncaster R	39	3		
2009–10	Leicester C	41	1		
2010–11	Leicester C	45	2		
2011–12	Leicester C	41	1		
2012–13	Leicester C	2	0		
2012–13	*Ipswich T*	7	0	**7**	**0**
2013–14	Leicester C	0	0	**129**	**4**
2013–14	Doncaster R	37	0	**121**	**9**

Scholars
Askins, Benjamin Jack; Brown, Scott Peter; Burnyeat, Ryan Mark; Davies, Matthew Allen; Dawson, Jacob Thomas; Ferguson, Lewis Edward; Gordon, Aron Josiah; Head, Alexander; Lund, Spencer Declan; Lund, Mitchell Perry; Mandeville, Liam; McKay, Jack; McKay, Paul; McLaren, Jack Maurice Peter; Steadman, Jack Alan; Terrell, Callum Burton; Whitehouse, Billy Haywood.

EVERTON (33)

ALCARAZ, Antolin (D)   **255 13**
H: 6 0 W: 12 08 b.Roque Gonzalez 30-7-82
Internationals: Paraguay Full caps.

Season	Club				
2002–03	Beira-Mar	7	0		
2003–04	Beira-Mar	24	1		
2004–05	Beira-Mar	24	1		
2005–06	Beira-Mar	31	0		
2006–07	Beira-Mar	26	3	**112**	**5**
2007–08	Club Brugge	10	1		
2008–09	Club Brugge	29	3		
2009–10	Club Brugge	29	1	**68**	**5**
2010–11	Wigan Ath	34	1		
2011–12	Wigan Ath	25	2		
2012–13	Wigan Ath	10	0	**69**	**3**
2013–14	Everton	6	0	**6**	**0**

BAINES, Leighton (D)   **376 25**
H: 5 8 W: 11 00 b.Liverpool 11-12-84
Internationals: England U21, Full caps.

Season	Club				
2002–03	Wigan Ath	6	0		
2003–04	Wigan Ath	26	0		
2004–05	Wigan Ath	41	1		
2005–06	Wigan Ath	37	0		
2006–07	Wigan Ath	35	3		
2007–08	Wigan Ath	0	0	**145**	**4**
2007–08	Everton	22	0		
2008–09	Everton	31	1		
2009–10	Everton	37	1		
2010–11	Everton	38	5		
2011–12	Everton	33	4		
2012–13	Everton	38	5		
2013–14	Everton	32	5	**231**	**21**

BARKLEY, Ross (M)   **64 10**
H: 6 2 W: 12 00 b.Liverpool 5-12-93
Internationals: England U16, U17, U19, U20, U21, Full caps.

Season	Club				
2010–11	Everton	0	0		
2011–12	Everton	6	0		
2012–13	Everton	7	0		
2012–13	*Sheffield W*	13	4	**13**	**4**
2012–13	*Leeds U*	4	0	**4**	**0**
2013–14	Everton	34	6	**47**	**6**

BROWNING, Tyias (D)   **2 0**
H: 5 11 W: 12 00 b.Liverpool 27-5-94
Internationals: England U17, U19, U21.

Season	Club				
2011–12	Everton	0	0		

2012–13	Everton	0	0	
2013–14	Everton	0	0	
2013–14	Wigan Ath	2	0	**2 0**

COLEMAN, Seamus (D) **126 11**
H: 6 4 W: 10 07 b.Donegal 11-10-88
Internationals: Republic of Ireland U21, U23, Full caps.

2008–09	Everton	0	0	
2009–10	Everton	3	0	
2009–10	*Blackpool*	9	1	**9 1**
2010–11	Everton	34	4	
2011–12	Everton	18	0	
2012–13	Everton	26	0	
2013–14	Everton	36	6	**117 10**

DEULOFEU, Gerard (F) **27 3**
H: 5 10 W: 11 01 b.Riudarenes 13-3-94
Internationals: Spain U16, U17, U19, U20, U21, Full caps.

2010–11	Barcelona	0	0	
2011–12	Barcelona	1	0	
2012–13	Barcelona	1	0	
2013–14	Barcelona	0	0	**2 0**

On loan from Barcelona

2013–14	Everton	25	3	**25 3**

DISTIN, Sylvain (D) **531 11**
H: 6 3 W: 14 06 b.Bagnolet 16-12-77

1998–99	Tours	26	3	**26 3**
1999–2000	Gueugnon	33	1	**33 1**
2000–01	Paris St Germain	28	0	**28 0**
2001–02	Newcastle U	28	0	**28 0**
2002–03	Manchester C	34	0	
2003–04	Manchester C	38	2	
2004–05	Manchester C	38	1	
2005–06	Manchester C	31	0	
2006–07	Manchester C	37	2	**178 0**
2007–08	Portsmouth	36	0	
2008–09	Portsmouth	38	0	
2009–10	Portsmouth	3	0	**77 0**
2009–10	Everton	29	0	
2010–11	Everton	38	2	
2011–12	Everton	27	0	
2012–13	Everton	34	0	
2013–14	Everton	33	0	**161 2**

DUFFUS, Courtney (F) **0 0**
b.Cheltenham 24-10-95

2013–14	Everton	0	0

DUFFY, Shane (D) **61 3**
H: 6 4 W: 12 00 b.Derry 1-1-92
Internationals: Northern Ireland U16, U17, U19, U21, B. Republic of Ireland U19, U21, Full caps.

2008–09	Everton	0	0	
2009–10	Everton	0	0	
2010–11	Everton	0	0	
2010–11	*Burnley*	1	0	**1 0**
2011–12	Everton	4	0	
2011–12	*Scunthorpe U*	18	2	**18 2**
2012–13	Everton	1	0	
2013–14	Everton	0	0	**5 0**
2013–14	*Yeovil T*	37	1	**37 1**

GARBUTT, Luke (D) **54 4**
H: 5 10 W: 11 07 b.Harrogate 21-5-93
Internationals: England U16, U17, U18, U19, U20, U21.

2010–11	Everton	0	0	
2011–12	Everton	0	0	
2011–12	*Cheltenham T*	34	2	**34 2**
2012–13	Everton	0	0	
2013–14	Everton	1	0	**1 0**
2013–14	*Colchester U*	19	2	**19 2**

GIBSON, Darron (M) **87 6**
H: 6 0 W: 12 04 b.Derry 25-10-87
Internationals: Republic of Ireland U21, B, Full caps.

2005–06	Manchester U	0	0	
2006–07	Manchester U	0	0	
2007–08	Manchester U	0	0	
2007–08	*Wolverhampton W*	21	1	**21 1**
2008–09	Manchester U	3	1	
2009–10	Manchester U	15	2	
2010–11	Manchester U	12	0	
2011–12	Manchester U	1	0	**31 3**
2011–12	Everton	11	1	
2012–13	Everton	23	1	
2013–14	Everton	1	0	**35 2**

GRANT, Conor (M) **0 0**
b.Fazakerley 18-4-95

2013–14	Everton	0	0

GREEN, George (M) **0 0**
b.Dewsbury 2-1-96

2013–14	Everton	0	0

GUEYE, Magaye (F) **58 10**
H: 5 10 W: 11 07 b.Paris 6-7-90
Internationals: France U16, U19, U20, U21. Senegal U23.

2008–09	Strasbourg	3	0	
2009–10	Strasbourg	24	9	**27 9**
2010–11	Everton	5	0	
2011–12	Everton	17	1	
2012–13	Everton	2	0	
2012–13	*Brest*	7	0	**7 0**
2013–14	Everton	0	0	**24 1**

HEITINGA, Johnny (D) **308 11**
H: 5 11 W: 11 05 b.Alphen aan den Rijn 15-11-83
Internationals: Netherlands Full caps.

2000–01	Ajax	0	0	
2001–02	Ajax	15	0	
2002–03	Ajax	1	0	
2003–04	Ajax	26	3	
2004–05	Ajax	26	1	
2005–06	Ajax	19	1	
2006–07	Ajax	32	0	
2007–08	Ajax	33	0	**152 5**
2008–09	Atletico Madrid	27	3	**27 3**
2009–10	Everton	31	0	
2010–11	Everton	27	1	
2011–12	Everton	30	1	
2012–13	Everton	26	0	
2013–14	Everton	1	0	**115 2**
2013–14	*Fulham*	14	1	**14 1**

HIBBERT, Tony (D) **260 0**
H: 5 9 W: 11 05 b.Liverpool 20-2-81

1998–99	Everton	0	0	
1999–2000	Everton	0	0	
2000–01	Everton	3	0	
2001–02	Everton	10	0	
2002–03	Everton	24	0	
2003–04	Everton	25	0	
2004–05	Everton	36	0	
2005–06	Everton	29	0	
2006–07	Everton	13	0	
2007–08	Everton	24	0	
2008–09	Everton	17	0	
2009–10	Everton	20	0	
2010–11	Everton	20	0	
2011–12	Everton	32	0	
2012–13	Everton	6	0	
2013–14	Everton	1	0	**260 0**

HOPE, Hallam (F) **11 6**
b.Manchester 17-3-94
Internationals: England U16, U17, U18, U19.

2010–11	Everton	0	0	
2011–12	Everton	0	0	
2013–14	Everton	0	0	
2013–14	*Northampton T*	3	1	**3 1**
2013–14	*Bury*	8	5	**8 5**

HOWARD, Tim (G) **427 1**
H: 6 3 W: 14 12 b.North Brunswick 6-3-79
Internationals: USA U21, U23, Full caps.

1998	NY/NJ MetroStars	1	0	
1999	NY/NJ MetroStars	9	0	
2000	NY/NJ MetroStars	9	0	
2001	NY/NJ MetroStars	26	0	
2002	NY/NJ MetroStars	27	0	
2003	NY/NJ MetroStars	13	0	**85 0**
2003–04	Manchester U	32	0	
2004–05	Manchester U	12	0	
2005–06	Manchester U	1	0	
2006–07	Manchester U	0	0	**45 0**
2006–07	Everton	36	0	
2007–08	Everton	36	0	
2008–09	Everton	38	0	
2009–10	Everton	38	0	
2010–11	Everton	38	1	
2011–12	Everton	38	0	
2012–13	Everton	36	0	
2013–14	Everton	37	0	**297 1**

JAGIELKA, Phil (D) **459 24**
H: 6 0 W: 13 01 b.Manchester 17-8-82
Internationals: England U20, U21, B, Full caps.

1999–2000	Sheffield U	1	0	
2000–01	Sheffield U	15	0	
2001–02	Sheffield U	23	3	
2002–03	Sheffield U	42	0	
2003–04	Sheffield U	43	3	
2004–05	Sheffield U	46	0	
2005–06	Sheffield U	46	8	
2006–07	Sheffield U	38	4	**254 18**
2007–08	Everton	34	1	
2008–09	Everton	34	0	
2009–10	Everton	12	0	
2010–11	Everton	33	1	
2011–12	Everton	30	2	
2012–13	Everton	36	2	
2013–14	Everton	26	0	**205 6**

JUNIOR, Francisco (M) **10 1**
H: 5 4 W: 10 02 b.Bissau 18-1-92
Internationals: Portugal U19, U21.

2012–13	Everton	0	0	
2013–14	Everton	0	0	
2013–14	*Vitesse*	2	0	**2 0**
2013–14	*Stromsgodset*	8	1	**8 1**

KENNEDY, Matthew (M) **29 1**
H: 5 9 W: 10 02 b.Irvine 1-11-94
Internationals: Scotland U16, U17, U18, U19, U21.

2011–12	Kilmarnock	11	0	
2012–13	Kilmarnock	3	0	**14 0**
2012–13	Everton	0	0	
2013–14	Everton	0	0	
2013–14	*Tranmere R*	8	0	**8 0**
2013–14	*Milton Keynes D*	7	1	**7 1**

KONE, Arouna (F) **256 87**
H: 6 0 W: 11 08 b.Anyama 11-11-83
Internationals: Ivory Coast Full caps.

2002–03	Lierse	21	11	**21 11**
2003–04	Roda JC	28	11	
2004–05	Roda JC	32	14	
2005–06	Roda JC	1	1	**61 26**
2005–06	PSV Eindhoven	21	11	
2006–07	PSV Eindhoven	31	10	
2007–08	PSV Eindhoven	1	0	**53 21**
2007–08	Sevilla	21	1	
2008–09	Sevilla	6	0	
2009–10	Sevilla	12	0	
2009–10	*Hannover 96*	8	2	**8 2**
2010–11	Sevilla	1	0	**40 1**
2011–12	Levante	34	15	**34 15**
2012–13	Wigan Ath	34	11	**34 11**
2013–14	Everton	5	0	**5 0**

LONG, Chris (F) **4 1**
b.Huyton 25-2-95
Internationals: England U16, U17, U18, U19, U20.

2013–14	Everton	0	0	
2013–14	*Milton Keynes D*	4	1	**4 1**

LUNDSTRAM, John (M) **35 2**
H: 5 11 W: 11 09 b.Liverpool 18-2-94
Internationals: England U17, U18, U19, U20.

2011–12	Everton	0	0	
2012–13	Everton	0	0	
2012–13	*Doncaster R*	14	0	**14 0**
2013–14	Everton	0	0	
2013–14	*Yeovil T*	14	2	**14 2**
2013–14	*Leyton Orient*	7	0	**7 0**

McALENY, Conor (F) **9 0**
H: 5 10 W: 12 05 b.Liverpool 12-8-92

2009–10	Everton	0	0	
2010–11	Everton	0	0	
2011–12	Everton	2	0	
2011–12	*Scunthorpe U*	3	0	**3 0**
2012–13	Everton	0	0	
2013–14	Everton	0	0	**2 0**
2013–14	*Brentford*	4	0	**4 0**

McCARTHY, James (M) **249 22**
H: 5 11 W: 11 05 b.Glasgow 12-11-90
Internationals: Republic of Ireland U17, U18, U19, U21, Full caps.

2006–07	Hamilton A	23	1	
2007–08	Hamilton A	35	7	
2008–09	Hamilton A	37	6	**95 14**
2009–10	Wigan Ath	20	1	

2010–11	Wigan Ath	24	3		
2011–12	Wigan Ath	33	0		
2012–13	Wigan Ath	38	3		
2013–14	Wigan Ath	5	0	120	7
2013–14	Everton	34	1	34	1

McGEADY, Aiden (M) 273 42
H: 5 10 W: 11 03 b.Glasgow 4-4-86
Internationals: Republic of Ireland Full caps.

2003–04	Celtic	4	1		
2004–05	Celtic	27	4		
2005–06	Celtic	20	4		
2006–07	Celtic	34	5		
2007–08	Celtic	36	7		
2008–09	Celtic	29	3		
2009–10	Celtic	35	7	185	31
2010–11	Spartak Moscow	11	2		
2011–12	Spartak Moscow	31	3		
2012–13	Spartak Moscow	17	5		
2013–14	Spartak Moscow	13	1	72	11
2013–14	Everton	16	0	16	0

McLAUGHLIN, Ben (M) 0 0
b.Dundalk 15-4-95
Internationals: Republic of Ireland U19.

2013–14	Everton	0	0

MIRALLAS, Kevin (F) 236 61
H: 6 0 W: 11 10 b.Leige 5-10-87
Internationals: Belgium U16, U17, U18, U19, U21, Full caps.

2004–05	Lille	1	1		
2005–06	Lille	15	1		
2006–07	Lille	23	2		
2007–08	Lille	35	6	74	10
2008–09	St Etienne	30	3		
2009–10	St Etienne	23	0	53	3
2010–11	Olympiacos	26	14		
2011–12	Olympiacos	24	20		
2012–13	Olympiacos	0	0	50	34
2012–13	Everton	27	6		
2013–14	Everton	32	8	59	14

NAISMITH, Steven (F) 262 66
H: 5 10 W: 11 04 b.Irvine 14-9-86
Internationals: Scotland U21, B, Full caps.

2003–04	Kilmarnock	1	0		
2004–05	Kilmarnock	24	1		
2005–06	Kilmarnock	36	13		
2006–07	Kilmarnock	37	15		
2007–08	Kilmarnock	4	0	102	29
2007–08	Rangers	21	5		
2008–09	Rangers	7	0		
2009–10	Rangers	28	3		
2010–11	Rangers	31	11		
2011–12	Rangers	11	9	98	28
2012–13	Everton	31	4		
2013–14	Everton	31	5	62	9

OSMAN, Leon (F) 351 46
H: 5 8 W: 10 09 b.Billinge 17-5-81
Internationals: England U16, Full caps.

1998–99	Everton	0	0		
1999–2000	Everton	0	0		
2000–01	Everton	0	0		
2001–02	Everton	0	0		
2002–03	Everton	2	0		
2002–03	*Carlisle U*	12	1	12	1
2003–04	Everton	4	1		
2003–04	*Derby Co*	17	3	17	3
2004–05	Everton	29	6		
2005–06	Everton	35	3		
2006–07	Everton	34	3		
2007–08	Everton	28	4		
2008–09	Everton	34	6		
2009–10	Everton	26	2		
2010–11	Everton	26	4		
2011–12	Everton	30	5		
2012–13	Everton	36	5		
2013–14	Everton	38	3	322	42

OVIEDO, Bryan (M) 68 4
H: 5 8 W: 10 09 b.Alajuela 18-2-90
Internationals: Costa Rica U20, Full caps.

2009–10	FC Copenhagen	3	0		
2010–11	FC Copenhagen	5	0		
2010–11	*Nordsjaelland*	14	0	14	0
2011–12	FC Copenhagen	22	2		
2012–13	FC Copenhagen	4	0	30	2
2012–13	Everton	15	0		
2013–14	Everton	9	2	24	2

PENNINGTON, Matthew (D) 17 2
H: 6 1 b.Warrington 6-10-94
Internationals: England U19.

2013–14	Everton	0	0		
2013–14	*Tranmere R*	17	2	17	2

PIENAAR, Steven (M) 305 35
H: 5 10 W: 10 06 b.Westbury 17-3-82
Internationals: South Africa U17, Full caps.

2001–02	Ajax	8	1		
2002–03	Ajax	31	5		
2003–04	Ajax	16	3		
2004–05	Ajax	24	4		
2005–06	Ajax	15	2	94	15
2006–07	Bor Dortmund	25	0	25	0
2007–08	Everton	28	2		
2008–09	Everton	28	2		
2009–10	Everton	30	4		
2010–11	Everton	18	1		
2010–11	Tottenham H	8	0		
2011–12	Tottenham H	2	0		
2011–12	*Everton*	14	4		
2012–13	Tottenham H	0	0	10	0
2012–13	Everton	35	6		
2013–14	Everton	23	1	176	20

ROBLES, Joel (G) 26 0
H: 6 5 W: 13 04 b.Leganes 17-6-90
Internationals: Spain U16, U17, U21, U23.

2009–10	Atletico Madrid	2	0		
2011–12	*Rayo Vallecano*	13	0	13	0
2012–13	Atletico Madrid	0	0	2	0
2012–13	*Wigan Ath*	9	0	9	0
2013–14	Everton	2	0	2	0

SANTOS, Francisco (M) 0 0
b.Guinea-Bissau 18-1-92
Internationals: Portugal U19, U21.

2011–12	Everton	0	0
2012–13	Everton	0	0
2013–14	Everton	0	0

STANEK, Jindrich (G) 0 0
Internationals: Czech Republic U19.

2013–14	Everton	0	0

STONES, John (D) 45 0
H: 6 2 W: 11 00 b.Barnsley 28-5-94
Internationals: England U19, U20, U21, Full caps

2011–12	Barnsley	2	0		
2012–13	Barnsley	22	0	24	0
2012–13	Everton	0	0		
2013–14	Everton	21	0	21	0

TRAORE, Lacina (F) 97 40
H: 6 8 W: 11 10 b.Abidjan 20-8-90
Internationals: Ivory Coast U23, Full caps.

2008–09	CFR Cluj-Napoca	6	1		
2009–10	CFR Cluj-Napoca	25	6		
2010–11	CFR Cluj-Napoca	13	7	44	14
2011–12	Kuban Krasnodar	23	13	23	13
2012–13	Anzhi Makhachkala	24	12		
2013–14	Anzhi Makhachkala	5	1	29	13
2013–14	Monaco	0	0		
On loan from Monaco					
2013–14	Everton	1	0	1	0

VELLIOS, Apostolos (F) 46 7
H: 6 3 W: 12 06 b.Salonika 8-1-92
Internationals: Greece U17, U19, U21.

2008–09	Iraklis	1	0		
2009–10	Iraklis	9	2		
2010–11	Iraklis	12	2	22	4
2010–11	Everton	3	0		
2011–12	Everton	13	3		
2012–13	Everton	6	0		
2013–14	Everton	0	0	22	3
2013–14	*Blackpool*	2	0	2	0

Scholars

Adelson, Jake Joseph Clifford; Birch, Arlen Tom; Charsley, Henry William James; Dyson, Calum William; Edge, Charley Joseph; Graham, Aidan James; Griffiths, Russell John; Hewelt, Mateusz Tomasz; Jones, Gethin Wynne; Kenny, Jon Joe; Langton, Curtis John; Ledson, Ryan Graham; Newell, George Stephen; Robinson, Antonee; Thorniley, Jordan; Williams, Joseph Michael.

EXETER C (34)

BALDWIN, Pat (D) 309 3
H: 6 3 W: 12 07 b.City of London 12-11-82

2002–03	Colchester U	19	0		
2003–04	Colchester U	4	0		
2004–05	Colchester U	38	0		
2005–06	Colchester U	25	0		
2006–07	Colchester U	38	1		
2007–08	Colchester U	26	0		
2008–09	Colchester U	35	0		
2009–10	Colchester U	7	0		
2009–10	*Bristol R*	6	0	6	0
2009–10	Southend U	18	1		
2010–11	Colchester U	11	0		
2011–12	Colchester U	5	0	208	1
2011–12	Southend U	2	0	20	1
2011–12	Exeter C	9	0		
2012–13	Exeter C	41	1		
2013–14	Exeter C	25	0	75	1

BENNETT, Scott (D) 104 15
H: 5 10 W: 12 10 b.Newquay 30-11-90

2008–09	Exeter C	0	0		
2009–10	Exeter C	0	0		
2010–11	Exeter C	1	0		
2011–12	Exeter C	15	3		
2012–13	Exeter C	43	6		
2013–14	Exeter C	45	6	104	15

BUTTERFIELD, Danny (D) 448 9
H: 5 10 W: 11 06 b.Boston 21-11-79

1997–98	Grimsby T	7	0		
1998–99	Grimsby T	12	0		
1999–2000	Grimsby T	29	0		
2000–01	Grimsby T	30	1		
2001–02	Grimsby T	46	2	124	3
2002–03	Crystal Palace	46	1		
2003–04	Crystal Palace	45	4		
2004–05	Crystal Palace	7	0		
2005–06	Crystal Palace	13	0		
2006–07	Crystal Palace	28	0		
2007–08	Crystal Palace	30	0		
2008–09	Crystal Palace	26	1		
2008–09	*Charlton Ath*	12	0	12	0
2009–10	Crystal Palace	37	0	232	6
2010–11	Southampton	34	0		
2011–12	Southampton	10	0		
2012–13	Southampton	0	0		
2012–13	*Bolton W*	6	0	6	0
2013–14	Southampton	0	0	44	0
2013–14	Carlisle U	1	0	1	0
2013–14	Exeter C	29	0	29	0

COLES, Danny (D) 398 16
H: 6 1 W: 11 05 b.Bristol 31-10-81

1999–2000	Bristol C	1	0		
2000–01	Bristol C	2	0		
2001–02	Bristol C	23	0		
2002–03	Bristol C	39	2		
2003–04	Bristol C	45	2		
2004–05	Bristol C	38	1	148	5
2005–06	Hull C	9	0		
2006–07	Hull C	21	0		
2007–08	Hull C	1	0	31	0
2007–08	*Hartlepool U*	3	0	3	0
2007–08	Bristol R	24	1		
2008–09	Bristol R	5	1		
2009–10	Bristol R	36	1		
2010–11	Bristol R	37	0	102	3
2011–12	Exeter C	31	2		
2012–13	Exeter C	46	4		
2013–14	Exeter C	37	2	114	8

DAVIES, Arron (M) 260 33
H: 5 9 W: 11 00 b.Cardiff 22-6-84
Internationals: Wales U19, 21, Full caps.

2002–03	Southampton	0	0		
2003–04	Southampton	0	0		
2003–04	*Barnsley*	4	0	4	0
2004–05	Southampton	0	0		
2004–05	Yeovil T	23	8		
2005–06	Yeovil T	39	8		
2006–07	Yeovil T	39	6		
2007–08	Nottingham F	19	1		
2008–09	Nottingham F	13	0		
2009–10	Nottingham F	0	0	32	1
2009–10	*Brighton & HA*	7	0	7	0
2009–10	Yeovil T	10	0	111	32
2010–11	Peterborough U	22	1	22	1

Season	Club				
2011–12	Northampton T	15	4	15	4
2012–13	Exeter C	37	3		
2013–14	Exeter C	32	2	69	5

DAWSON, Aaron (M) 14 0
H: 5 10 W: 10 10 b.Exmouth 24-3-92

2010–11	Exeter C	0	0		
2011–12	Exeter C	2	0		
2012–13	Exeter C	7	0		
2013–14	Exeter C	5	0	14	0

DOHERTY, Tommy (M) 358 9
H: 5 8 W: 9 12 b.Bristol 17-3-79
Internationals: Northern Ireland B, Full caps.

1997–98	Bristol C	30	2		
1998–99	Bristol C	23	1		
1999–2000	Bristol C	1	0		
2000–01	Bristol C	0	0		
2001–02	Bristol C	34	1		
2002–03	Bristol C	38	0		
2003–04	Bristol C	33	2		
2004–05	Bristol C	29	1	188	7
2005–06	QPR	15	0		
2005–06	Yeovil T	1	0	1	0
2006–07	QPR	0	0	15	0
2006–07	Wycombe W	26	2		
2007–08	Wycombe W	24	0		
2008–09	Wycombe W	34	0		
2009–10	Wycombe W	12	0	96	2
2010–11	Bradford C	18	0	18	0
From Newport Co, Bath C					
2012–13	Exeter C	30	0		
2013–14	Exeter C	10	0	40	0

GILL, Matthew (M) 344 16
H: 5 11 W: 11 10 b.Cambridge 8-11-80

1997–98	Peterborough U	2	0		
1998–99	Peterborough U	26	0		
1999–2000	Peterborough U	20	1		
2000–01	Peterborough U	17	1		
2001–02	Peterborough U	12	2		
2002–03	Peterborough U	41	1		
2003–04	Peterborough U	33	0		
2004–05	Notts Co	43	0		
2005–06	Notts Co	14	0	57	0
2008–09	Exeter C	43	9		
2009–10	Norwich C	8	0		
2010–11	Norwich C	4	0	12	0
2010–11	Peterborough U	4	0	155	5
2010–11	Walsall	8	2	8	2
2011–12	Bristol R	33	0		
2012–13	Bristol R	11	0		
2013–14	Bristol R	1	0	45	0
2013–14	Exeter C	24	0	67	9

GOSLING, Jake (M) 15 1
b.Newquay 11-8-93
Internationals: Gibraltar Full caps

2011–12	Exeter C	0	0		
2012–13	Exeter C	12	1		
2013–14	Exeter C	3	0	15	1

GOW, Alan (M) 312 64
H: 6 0 W: 11 00 b.Clydebank 9-10-82
Internationals: Scotland B.

2000–01	Clydebank	3	0		
2001–02	Clydebank	5	0	8	0
2002–03	Airdrie U	27	5		
2003–04	Airdrie U	32	12		
2004–05	Airdrie U	26	9	85	26
2005–06	Falkirk	34	6		
2006–07	Falkirk	36	7	70	13
2007–08	Rangers	0	0		
2008–09	Blackpool	17	5	17	5
2008–09	Norwich C	13	0	13	0
2009–10	Plymouth Arg	14	2	14	2
2009–10	Hibernian	7	0	7	0
2010–11	Motherwell	15	1	15	1
2010–11	Notts Co	16	1	16	1
2010–11	East Bengal	5	2	5	2
2011–12	Exeter C	7	3		
2012–13	Exeter C	26	4		
2013–14	Exeter C	25	7	58	14
2013–14	Bristol R	4	0	4	0

GRIMES, Matt (M) 35 1
b. 15-7-95

2013–14	Exeter C	35	1	35	1

JAY, Matt (D) 2 0
b. 27-2-96

2013–14	Exeter C	2	0	2	0

KEOHANE, Jimmy (M) 57 6
H: 5 11 W: 11 05 b.Wexford 22-1-91
Internationals: Republic of Ireland U19.

2010–11	Bristol C	0	0		
2011–12	Bristol C	0	0		
2011–12	Exeter C	4	0		
2012–13	Exeter C	33	3		
2013–14	Exeter C	20	3	57	6

KRYSIAK, Artur (G) 172 0
H: 6 1 W: 12 00 b.Lodz 11-8-89
Internationals: Poland U19.

2006–07	Birmingham C	0	0		
2007–08	Gretna	4	0	4	0
2007–08	Birmingham C	0	0		
2008–09	Birmingham C	0	0		
2008–09	Motherwell	1	0	1	0
2008–09	Swansea C	2	0	2	0
2009–10	Birmingham C	0	0		
2009–10	Burton Alb	38	0	38	0
2010–11	Exeter C	10	0		
2011–12	Exeter C	38	0		
2012–13	Exeter C	42	0		
2013–14	Exeter C	37	0	127	0

MOORE-TAYLOR, Jordan (D) 36 1
b. 21-1-94

2012–13	Exeter C	7	0		
2013–14	Exeter C	29	1	36	1

NICHOLS, Tom (F) 39 7
H: 5 10 W: 10 10 b.Wellington 1-9-93

2010–11	Exeter C	1	0		
2011–12	Exeter C	7	1		
2012–13	Exeter C	3	0		
2013–14	Exeter C	28	6	39	7

O'FLYNN, John (F) 351 120
H: 5 11 W: 11 11 b.Cobh 11-7-82
Internationals: Republic of Ireland U21.

2001–02	Peterborough U	0	0		
2002–03	Cork C	27	15		
2003	Cork C	23	15		
2004	Cork C	28	12		
2005	Cork C	21	11		
2006	Cork C	15	6		
2007	Cork C	25	5		
2008	Cork C	19	4	158	68
2008–09	Barnet	34	17		
2009–10	Barnet	36	12	70	29
2010–11	Exeter C	31	6		
2011–12	Exeter C	24	2		
2012–13	Exeter C	35	11		
2013–14	Exeter C	33	4	123	23

OAKLEY, Matthew (M) 521 33
H: 5 10 W: 12 06 b.Peterborough 17-8-77
Internationals: England U21.

1994–95	Southampton	1	0		
1995–96	Southampton	10	0		
1996–97	Southampton	28	3		
1997–98	Southampton	33	1		
1998–99	Southampton	22	2		
1999–2000	Southampton	31	3		
2000–01	Southampton	35	1		
2001–02	Southampton	27	1		
2002–03	Southampton	31	0		
2003–04	Southampton	7	0		
2004–05	Southampton	7	1		
2005–06	Southampton	29	2	261	14
2006–07	Derby Co	37	6		
2007–08	Derby Co	19	3	56	9
2007–08	Leicester C	20	0		
2008–09	Leicester C	45	8		
2009–10	Leicester C	38	0		
2010–11	Leicester C	34	2		
2011–12	Leicester C	0	0	137	10
2011–12	Exeter C	7	0		
2012–13	Exeter C	36	0		
2013–14	Exeter C	24	0	67	0

PARKIN, Sam (F) 371 106
H: 6 2 W: 12 13 b.Roehampton 14-3-81
Internationals: Scotland B.

1998–99	Chelsea	0	0		
1999–2000	Chelsea	0	0		
2000–01	Chelsea	0	0		
2000–01	Millwall	7	4	7	4
2000–01	Wycombe W	8	1	8	1
2000–01	Oldham Ath	7	3	7	3
2001–02	Chelsea	0	0		
2001–02	Northampton T	40	4	40	4
2002–03	Swindon T	43	25		
2003–04	Swindon T	40	19		
2004–05	Swindon T	41	23	124	67
2005–06	Ipswich T	20	5		
2006–07	Ipswich T	2	0	22	5
2006–07	Luton T	8	1		
2007–08	Luton T	19	5		
2008–09	Luton T	23	4	50	10
2008–09	Leyton Orient	13	0	13	0
2009–10	Walsall	24	3	24	3
2010–11	St Johnstone	21	4		
2011–12	St Johnstone	2	0	23	4
2012–13	St Mirren	27	2	27	2
2013–14	Exeter C	26	3	26	3

PYN, Christy (G) 9 0
b. 24-4-95

2012–13	Exeter C	0	0		
2013–14	Exeter C	9	0	9	0

REID, Jamie (F) 10 2
b.Torquay 15-7-94
Internationals: Northern Ireland U21.

2012–13	Exeter C	4	2		
2013–14	Exeter C	6	0	10	2

SERCOMBE, Liam (M) 196 19
H: 5 10 W: 10 10 b.Exeter 25-4-90

2008–09	Exeter C	29	2		
2009–10	Exeter C	28	1		
2010–11	Exeter C	42	3		
2011–12	Exeter C	33	7		
2012–13	Exeter C	20	1		
2013–14	Exeter C	44	5	196	19

TILLSON, Jordan (D) 1 0

2012–13	Exeter C	0	0		
2013–14	Exeter C	1	0	1	0

WATKINS, Ollie (F) 1 0

2013–14	Exeter C	1	0	1	0

WHEELER, David (M) 35 3
b.Brighton 4-10-90
Internationals: England U18.

2013–14	Exeter C	35	3	35	3

WOODMAN, Craig (D) 385 7
H: 5 9 W: 10 11 b.Tiverton 22-12-82

1999–2000	Bristol C	0	0		
2000–01	Bristol C	2	0		
2001–02	Bristol C	6	0		
2002–03	Bristol C	10	0		
2003–04	Bristol C	21	0		
2004–05	Bristol C	3	0		
2004–05	Mansfield T	8	1	8	1
2004–05	Torquay U	22	1		
2005–06	Bristol C	37	1		
2005–06	Torquay U	2	0	24	1
2006–07	Bristol C	11	0	90	1
2007–08	Wycombe W	29	0		
2008–09	Wycombe W	46	1		
2009–10	Wycombe W	44	1	119	2
2010–11	Brentford	41	1		
2011–12	Brentford	18	0	59	1
2012–13	Exeter C	44	0		
2013–14	Exeter C	41	1	85	1

Scholars
Billingsley, Dean Albert Joseph; Byrne, Alex John; Byrne, James Joseph; Charles, Joseph Paul; Gill, Cameron Louis; Harkness, Jamie Scott; Heidari, Hussein; Madden, Charlie Thomas; Mitchison, James Russell Colin; Pope, Jason Warren; Read, Joshua John Peter; Riley-Lowe, Connor; Watkins, Oliver George Arthur.

FLEETWOOD T (35)

ALLEN, Jamie (M) 5 1

2012–13	Fleetwood T	4	1		
2013–14	Fleetwood T	1	0	5	1

BALL, David (F) 137 29
H: 6 0 W: 11 08 b.Whitefield 14-12-89

2007–08	Manchester C	0	0		
2008–09	Manchester C	0	0		
2009–10	Manchester C	0	0		
2010–11	Manchester C	0	0		
2010–11	Swindon T	18	2	18	2
2010–11	Peterborough U	19	5		
2011–12	Peterborough U	22	4		

2011–12 Rochdale 14 3 **14 3**
2012–13 Peterborough U 0 0 **41 9**
2012–13 Fleetwood T 34 7
2013–14 Fleetwood T 30 8 **64 15**

BLAIR, Matty (M)   **71 10**
H: 5 10 W: 11 09 b.Coventry 30-11-87
Internationals: England C.
2012–13 York C 44 6 **44 6**
2013–14 Fleetwood T 24 3 **24 3**
2013–14 *Northampton T* 3 1 **3 1**

BROWN, Junior (D)   **74 13**
H: 5 9 W: 10 09 b.Crewe 7-5-89
2006–07 Crewe Alex 0 0
2007–08 Crewe Alex 1 0 **1 0**
2012–13 Fleetwood T 43 11
2013–14 Fleetwood T 21 1 **64 12**
2013–14 Tranmere R 9 1 **9 1**

CRESSWELL, Ryan (D)   **178 17**
H: 5 9 W: 10 05 b.Rotherham 22-12-87
2006–07 Sheffield U 0 0
2007–08 Sheffield U 0 0
2007–08 Rotherham U 3 0
2007–08 Morecambe 2 0 **2 0**
2007–08 Macclesfield T 19 1 **19 1**
2008–09 Bury 25 1
2009–10 Bury 28 0 **53 1**
2010–11 Rotherham U 22 4
2011–12 Rotherham U 16 4 **41 8**
2012–13 Southend U 43 6 **43 6**
2013–14 Fleetwood T 20 1 **20 1**

CROWTHER, Ryan (M)   **22 2**
H: 5 11 b.Stockport 17-9-88
2012–13 Fleetwood T 15 2
2013–14 Fleetwood T 7 0 **22 2**

DAVIES, Scott (G)   **84 0**
H: 6 0 W: 10 13 b.Blackpool 27-2-87
2007–08 Morecambe 10 0
2008–09 Morecambe 0 0
2009–10 Morecambe 1 0 **11 0**
2012–13 Fleetwood T 45 0
2013–14 Fleetwood T 28 0 **73 0**

EVANS, Gary (F)   **256 49**
H: 6 0 W: 12 08 b.Stockport 26-4-88
2007–08 Macclesfield T 42 7
2008–09 Macclesfield T 40 12 **82 19**
2009–10 Bradford C 43 11
2010–11 Bradford C 36 3 **79 14**
2011–12 Rotherham U 32 7
2012–13 Rotherham U 13 2 **45 9**
2013–14 Fleetwood T 16 1
2013–14 Fleetwood T 34 6 **50 7**

GOODALL, Alan (D)   **260 16**
H: 5 9 W: 11 06 b.Birkenhead 2-12-81
2004–05 Rochdale 34 2
2005–06 Rochdale 40 3
2006–07 Rochdale 46 3
2007–08 Luton T 29 1 **29 1**
2008–09 Chesterfield 28 3
2009–10 Chesterfield 17 0 **45 3**
2010–11 Rochdale 5 0 **125 8**
2010–11 Stockport Co 13 0 **13 0**
2012–13 Fleetwood T 29 4
2013–14 Fleetwood T 19 0 **48 4**

HAUGHTON, Nick (M)   **0 0**
2013–14 Fleetwood T 0 0

HOGAN, Liam (D)   **16 0**
H: 6 0 W: 12 02 b. 8-2-89
2012–13 Fleetwood T 0 0
2013–14 Fleetwood T 16 0 **16 0**

HOWELL, Dean (D)   **112 5**
H: 6 1 W: 12 05 b.Burton-on-Trent 29-11-80
1999–2000 Notts Co 1 0 **1 0**
2000–01 Crewe Alex 1 0 **1 0**
2000–01 *Rochdale* 3 0 **3 0**
From Southport, Morecambe, Halifax T
2005–06 Colchester U 4 0 **4 0**
From Halifax, Weymouth, Grays, Rushden
2008–09 Aldershot T 14 0
2008–09 Bury 3 0
2009–10 Aldershot T 3 1
2010–11 Aldershot T 0 0 **17 1**
2011–12 Crawley T 37 3 **37 3**
2012–13 Fleetwood T 30 1

2013–14 Fleetwood T 8 0 **38 1**
2013–14 *Bury* 8 0 **11 0**

HUGHES, Jeff (D)   **373 61**
H: 6 1 W: 11 00 b.Larne 29-5-85
Internationals: Northern Ireland U21, Full caps.
2003–04 Larne 21 1
2004–05 Larne 29 0 **50 1**
2005–06 Lincoln C 22 2
2006–07 Lincoln C 41 6 **63 8**
2007–08 Crystal Palace 10 0 **10 0**
2007–08 *Peterborough U* 7 1 **7 1**
2008–09 Bristol R 43 6
2009–10 Bristol R 44 12
2010–11 Bristol R 42 10 **129 28**
2011–12 Notts Co 45 13
2012–13 Notts Co 44 7 **89 20**
2013–14 Fleetwood T 25 3 **25 3**

HUGHES, Matty (M)   **5 0**
2013–14 Fleetwood T 5 0 **5 0**

JORDAN, Stephen (D)   **187 0**
H: 6 1 W: 13 00 b.Warrington 6-3-82
1998–99 Manchester C 0 0
1999–2000 Manchester C 0 0
2000–01 Manchester C 0 0
2001–02 Manchester C 0 0
2002–03 Manchester C 1 0
2002–03 *Cambridge U* 11 0 **11 0**
2003–04 Manchester C 2 0
2004–05 Manchester C 19 0
2005–06 Manchester C 18 0
2006–07 Manchester C 13 0 **53 0**
2007–08 Burnley 21 0
2008–09 Burnley 27 0
2009–10 Burnley 25 0
2010–11 Burnley 0 0 **73 0**
2010–11 Sheffield U 15 0 **15 0**
2010–11 *Huddersfield T* 6 0 **6 0**
2011–12 Rochdale 19 0 **19 0**
2013–14 Fleetwood T 10 0 **10 0**

MATT, Jamille (F)   **39 11**
b.Walsall 20-10-89
2012–13 Fleetwood T 14 3
2013–14 Fleetwood T 25 8 **39 11**

MAXWELL, Chris (G)   **18 0**
b.Wrexham 30-7-90
Internationals: Wales U17, U19, U21, U23.
2012–13 Fleetwood T 0 0
2013–14 Fleetwood T 18 0 **18 0**

McLAUGHLIN, Conor (D)   **82 0**
H: 6 0 W: 11 02 b.Belfast 26-7-91
Internationals: Northern Ireland U21, Full caps.
2009–10 Preston NE 0 0
2010–11 Preston NE 7 0
2011–12 Preston NE 17 0 **24 0**
2011–12 *Shrewsbury T* 4 0 **4 0**
2012–13 Fleetwood T 19 0
2013–14 Fleetwood T 35 0 **54 0**

MURDOCH, Stewart (M)   **41 0**
H: 6 0 W: 12 00 b.Aberdeen 9-5-90
2007–08 Falkirk 0 0
2008–09 Falkirk 0 0
2009–10 Falkirk 3 0 **3 0**
2013–14 Fleetwood T 38 0 **38 0**

PARKIN, Jon (F)   **419 112**
H: 6 4 W: 13 07 b.Barnsley 30-12-81
1998–99 Barnsley 2 0
1999–2000 Barnsley 0 0
2000–01 Barnsley 4 0
2001–02 Barnsley 4 0 **10 0**
2001–02 *Hartlepool U* 1 0 **1 0**
2001–02 York C 18 2
2002–03 York C 41 10
2003–04 York C 15 2 **74 14**
2003–04 Macclesfield T 12 1
2004–05 Macclesfield T 42 22
2005–06 Macclesfield T 11 7 **65 30**
2005–06 Hull C 18 5
2006–07 Hull C 29 6 **47 11**
2006–07 *Stoke C* 6 3
2007–08 Stoke C 29 2
2008–09 Stoke C 0 0 **35 5**
2008–09 Preston NE 39 11
2009–10 Preston NE 43 10
2010–11 Preston NE 19 7 **101 28**

2010–11 Cardiff C 11 1
2011–12 Cardiff C 0 0 **11 1**
2011–12 Doncaster R 5 0 **5 0**
2011–12 Huddersfield T 3 0 **3 0**
2011–12 Scunthorpe U 14 6 **14 6**
2012–13 Fleetwood T 22 10
2013–14 Fleetwood T 31 7 **53 17**

POND, Nathan (M)   **53 1**
H: 6 3 W: 11 00 b.Preston 5-1-85
2012–13 Fleetwood T 12 0
2013–14 Fleetwood T 41 1 **53 1**

ROBERTS, Mark (D)   **206 17**
H: 6 1 W: 12 00 b.Northwich 16-10-83
2002–03 Crewe Alex 0 0
2003–04 Crewe Alex 0 0
2004–05 Crewe Alex 6 0
2005–06 Crewe Alex 0 0
2005–06 *Chester C* 1 0 **1 0**
2006–07 Crewe Alex 0 0 **6 0**
2007–08 Accrington S 34 0 **34 0**
From Northwich Vic.
2010–11 Stevenage 42 6
2011–12 Stevenage 46 6
2012–13 Stevenage 44 2 **132 14**
2013–14 Fleetwood T 33 3 **33 3**

SARCEVIC, Antoni (M)   **54 14**
H: 5 10 W: 11 00 b. 13-3-92
Internationals: England C.
2009–10 Crewe Alex 0 0
2010–11 Crewe Alex 6 1
2011–12 Crewe Alex 6 0 **12 1**
2013–14 Fleetwood T 42 13 **42 13**

SCHUMACHER, Steven (M)   **340 48**
H: 5 10 W: 11 00 b.Liverpool 30-4-84
2000–01 Everton 0 0
2001–02 Everton 0 0
2002–03 Everton 0 0
2003–04 Everton 0 0
2003–04 *Carlisle U* 4 0 **4 0**
2004–05 Bradford C 43 6
2005–06 Bradford C 30 1
2006–07 Bradford C 44 6 **117 13**
2007–08 Crewe Alex 26 1
2008–09 Crewe Alex 15 2
2009–10 Crewe Alex 32 4 **73 7**
2010–11 Bury 43 9
2011–12 Bury 32 6
2012–13 Bury 39 8 **114 23**
2013–14 Fleetwood T 32 5 **32 5**

WRIGHT, Richard (M)   **0 0**
2013–14 Fleetwood T 0 0

Scholars
Barrett, Dominic; Bleeker, Liam James Jan; Bromley, Robbie; Cartwright, Max Jonathan; Deacon, Keano; Folksman, Jonathan; Glean, Shane Eric Dalglish; Lazenbury, Jordan; Martin, Oliver; Olapade, Lanre; Rajab, Abdul Rahman; Smith, Conor James; Vaughan-Muscat, Michael; Vile, Daniel Oscar; Wainwright, Aden; Williams, Matthew Thomas; Willoughby, Kurt Henry.

FULHAM (36)

AMOREBIETA, Fernando (D)   **218 4**
H: 6 3 W: 12 00 b.Iurreta 29-3-85
Internationals: Spain U19. Venezuela Full caps.
2004–05 Athletic Bilbao 0 0
2005–06 Athletic Bilbao 15 0
2006–07 Athletic Bilbao 27 0
2007–08 Athletic Bilbao 34 0
2008–09 Athletic Bilbao 29 0
2009–10 Athletic Bilbao 34 0
2010–11 Athletic Bilbao 17 0
2011–12 Athletic Bilbao 28 3
2012–13 Athletic Bilbao 11 0 **195 3**
2013–14 Fulham 21 1 **23 1**

ARTHURWORREY, Stephen (D)   **17 0**
H: 6 4 W: 13 12 b.Hackney 15-10-94
2011–12 Fulham 0 0
2012–13 Fulham 0 0
2013–14 Fulham 0 0
2013–14 *Tranmere R* 17 0 **17 0**

BERBATOV, Dimitar (F) — 445 194

H: 6 2 W: 12 06 b.Blagoevgrad 30-1-81
Internationals: Bulgaria U18, 21, Full caps.

Season	Club	A	G		
1998–99	CSKA Sofia	11	3		
1999–2000	CSKA Sofia	27	14		
2000–01	CSKA Sofia	12	8	50	25
2000–01	Leverkusen	6	0		
2001–02	Leverkusen	24	8		
2002–03	Leverkusen	24	4		
2003–04	Leverkusen	33	16		
2004–05	Leverkusen	33	20		
2005–06	Leverkusen	34	21	154	69
2006–07	Tottenham H	33	12		
2007–08	Tottenham H	36	15		
2008–09	Tottenham H	1	0	70	27
2008–09	Manchester U	31	9		
2009–10	Manchester U	33	12		
2010–11	Manchester U	32	20		
2011–12	Manchester U	12	7	108	48
2012–13	Fulham	33	15		
2013–14	Fulham	18	4	51	19
2013–14	*Monaco*	12	6	12	6

BETTINELLI, Marcus (G) — 39 0

b.Camberwell 24-5-92

Season	Club	A	G		
2010–11	Fulham	0	0		
2011–12	Fulham	0	0		
2012–13	Fulham	0	0		
2013–14	Fulham	0	0		
2013–14	*Accrington S*	39	0	39	0

BOATENG, Derek (M) — 258 20

H: 6 1 W: 12 03 b.Accra 2-5-83
Internationals: Ghana Full caps.

Season	Club	A	G		
2000–01	Panathinaikos	14	1		
2001–02	Panathinaikos	10	1		
2002–03	Panathinaikos	0	0	24	2
2002–03	*OFI Crete*	12	1	12	1
2003–04	AIK	19	2		
2004–05	AIK	16	1		
2005–06	AIK	10	1		
2006–07	AIK	7	1	52	5
2006–07	Beitar	30	4		
2007–08	Beitar	31	4		
2008–09	Beitar	12	0	73	8
2008–09	Cologne	10	0	10	0
2009–10	Getafe	29	0		
2010–11	Getafe	32	2	61	2
2011–12	Dnipro	21	2		
2012–13	Dnipro	2	0	23	2
2013–14	Fulham	3	0	3	0

BRIGGS, Matthew (D) — 30 1

H: 6 1 W: 11 12 b.Wandsworth 6-3-91
Internationals: England U16, U17, U19, U20, U21.

Season	Club	A	G		
2006–07	Fulham	1	0		
2007–08	Fulham	0	0		
2008–09	Fulham	0	0		
2009–10	Fulham	0	0		
2009–10	*Leyton Orient*	1	0	1	0
2010–11	Fulham	3	0		
2011–12	Fulham	2	0		
2011–12	*Peterborough U*	5	0	5	0
2012–13	Fulham	5	0		
2012–13	*Bristol C*	4	0	4	0
2012–13	*Watford*	7	1	7	1
2013–14	Fulham	2	0	13	0

BURN, Dan (D) — 71 2

H: 6 6 W: 13 00 b.Blyth 1-5-92

Season	Club	A	G		
2009–10	Darlington	4	0	4	0
2010–11	Fulham	0	0		
2011–12	Fulham	0	0		
2012–13	Fulham	0	0		
2012–13	*Yeovil T*	34	2	34	2
2013–14	Fulham	9	0	9	0
2013–14	*Birmingham C*	24	0	24	0

CHRISTENSEN, Lasse Vigen (M) — 0 0

H: 5 10 W: 10 04 b.Esbjerg 15-8-94
Internationals: Denmark U16, U17, U18, U19, U21.

Season	Club	A	G
2012–13	Fulham	0	0
2013–14	Fulham	0	0

COLE, Larnell (M) — 4 0

H: 5 4 W: 12 04 b.Manchester 9-3-93
Internationals: England U19, U20.

Season	Club	A	G		
2011–12	Manchester U	0	0		
2012–13	Manchester U	0	0		
2013–14	Manchester U	0	0		
2013–14	Fulham	1	0	1	0
2013–14	*Milton Keynes D*	3	0	3	0

DAVID, Chris (F) — 1 1

H: 5 7 W: 11 01 b.Amsterdam 6-3-93
Internationals: Netherlands U17, U18, U19.

Season	Club	A	G		
2013–14	Fulham	1	1	1	1

DEJAGAH, Ashkan (F) — 197 24

H: 5 11 W: 11 08 b.Tehran 5-7-86
Internationals: Germany U17, U18, U19, U20, U21. Iran Full caps.

Season	Club	A	G		
2004–05	Hertha Berlin	1	0		
2005–06	Hertha Berlin	3	0		
2006–07	Hertha Berlin	22	1	26	1
2007–08	Wolfsburg	31	8		
2008–09	Wolfsburg	27	3		
2009–10	Wolfsburg	22	1		
2010–11	Wolfsburg	21	3		
2011–12	Wolfsburg	26	3		
2012–13	Wolfsburg	1	0	128	18
2012–13	Fulham	21	0		
2013–14	Fulham	22	5	43	5

DELLA-VERDE, Lyle (M) — 0 0

b.Leeds 9-1-95

Season	Club	A	G
2011–12	Fulham	0	0
2012–13	Fulham	0	0
2013–14	Fulham	0	0

DEMBELE, Moussa (F) — 2 0

H: 6 0 W: 11 08 b.Pontoise 12-7-96
Internationals: France U16, U17, U18.

Season	Club	A	G		
2013–14	Fulham	2	0	2	0

DIARRA, Mahamadou (M) — 359 27

H: 6 0 W: 11 13 b.Bamako 18-5-81
Internationals: Mali Full caps.

Season	Club	A	G		
1996	CSK Bamako	0	0		
1997	CSK Bamako	24	6		
1998	CSK Bamako	0	0	24	6
1998–99	OFI Crete	21	2	21	2
1999–2000	Vitesse	16	2		
2000–01	Vitesse	29	4		
2001–02	Vitesse	24	3	69	9
2002–03	Lyon	25	0		
2003–04	Lyon	28	1		
2004–05	Lyon	36	2		
2005–06	Lyon	32	3		
2006–07	Lyon	2	0	123	6
2006–07	Real Madrid	33	3		
2007–08	Real Madrid	30	0		
2008–09	Real Madrid	9	0		
2009–10	Real Madrid	15	0		
2010–11	Real Madrid	3	0	90	3
2010–11	Monaco	9	0	9	0
2011–12	Fulham	11	1		
2012–13	Fulham	8	0		
2013–14	Fulham	4	0	23	1

DONNELLY, Liam (D) — 0 0

b.Dungannon 7-3-96
Internationals: Northern Ireland U16, U17, U21, Full caps

Season	Club	A	G
2013–14	Fulham	0	0

DUFF, Damien (F) — 464 61

H: 5 9 W: 12 06 b.Ballyboden 2-3-79
Internationals: Republic of Ireland U20, B, Full caps.

Season	Club	A	G		
1995–96	Blackburn R	0	0		
1996–97	Blackburn R	1	0		
1997–98	Blackburn R	26	4		
1998–99	Blackburn R	28	1		
1999–2000	Blackburn R	39	5		
2000–01	Blackburn R	32	1		
2001–02	Blackburn R	32	7		
2002–03	Blackburn R	26	9	184	27
2003–04	Chelsea	23	5		
2004–05	Chelsea	30	6		
2005–06	Chelsea	28	3	81	14
2006–07	Newcastle U	22	1		
2007–08	Newcastle U	16	0		
2008–09	Newcastle U	30	3		
2009–10	Newcastle U	1	1	69	5
2009–10	Fulham	32	6		
2010–11	Fulham	24	4		
2011–12	Fulham	28	2		
2012–13	Fulham	31	3		
2013–14	Fulham	15	0	130	15

ETHERIDGE, Neil (G) — 16 0

H: 6 3 W: 14 00 b.Enfield 7-2-90
Internationals: England U16. Philippines Full caps.

Season	Club	A	G		
2008–09	Fulham	0	0		
2009–10	Fulham	0	0		
2010–11	Fulham	0	0		
2011–12	Fulham	0	0		
2012–13	Fulham	0	0		
2012–13	*Bristol R*	12	0	12	0
2013–14	Fulham	0	0		
2013–14	*Crewe Alex*	4	0	4	0

EVANS, Jordan (M) — 0 0

b.Wrexham 23-9-95
Internationals: Wales U19.

Season	Club	A	G
2013–14	Fulham	0	0

GRIMMER, Jack (M) — 17 1

H: 6 0 W: 12 06 b.Aberdeen 25-1-94
Internationals: Scotland U15, U16, U17, U18, U19, U21.

Season	Club	A	G		
2009–10	Aberdeen	2	0		
2010–11	Aberdeen	2	0		
2011–12	Aberdeen	0	0	4	0
2011–12	Fulham	0	0		
2012–13	Fulham	0	0		
2013–14	Fulham	0	0		
2013–14	*Port Vale*	13	1	13	1

HANGELAND, Brede (D) — 394 17

H: 6 4 W: 13 05 b.Houston 20-6-81
Internationals: Norway U21, Full caps.

Season	Club	A	G		
2000	Vidar				
2001	Viking	22	0		
2002	Viking	26	2		
2003	Viking	26	1		
2004	Viking	14	3		
2005	Viking	26	0	114	6
2005–06	FC Copenhagen	13	1		
2006–07	FC Copenhagen	32	0		
2007–08	FC Copenhagen	18	2	63	3
2007–08	Fulham	15	0		
2008–09	Fulham	37	1		
2009–10	Fulham	32	1		
2010–11	Fulham	37	6		
2011–12	Fulham	38	0		
2012–13	Fulham	35	0		
2013–14	Fulham	23	0	217	8

HYNDMAN, Emerson (M) — 0 0

b.Dallas 9-4-96
Internationals: USA Youth.

Season	Club	A	G
2013–14	Fulham	0	0

JORONEN, Jesse (G) — 0 0

b.Rautjarvi 21-3-93
Internationals: Finland U17, U19, U21, Full caps.

Season	Club	A	G
2013–14	Fulham	0	0
2013–14	*FC Lahti*	0	0

KACANIKLIC, Alex (M) — 65 6

H: 5 11 W: 10 05 b.Helsingborg 13-8-91
Internationals: Sweden U17, U19, Full caps.

Season	Club	A	G		
2008–09	Liverpool	0	0		
2009–10	Liverpool	0	0		
2010–11	Fulham	0	0		
2011–12	Fulham	4	0		
2011–12	*Watford*	12	1	12	1
2012–13	Fulham	20	4		
2012–13	*Burnley*	6	0	6	0
2013–14	Fulham	23	1	47	5

KARAGOUNIS, Giorgos (M) — 226 20

H: 5 9 W: 11 08 b.Pyrgos 6-3-77
Internationals: Greece U21, Full caps.

Season	Club	A	G		
2000–01	Panathinaikos	1	1		
2001–02	Panathinaikos	13	3		
2002–03	Panathinaikos	13	3		
2003–04	Inter Milan	9	0		
2004–05	Inter Milan	11	0	20	0
2005–06	Benfica	19	1		
2006–07	Benfica	26	2	45	3
2007–08	Panathinaikos	27	2		
2008–09	Panathinaikos	15	3		
2009–10	Panathinaikos	23	2		
2010–11	Panathinaikos	22	1		
2011–12	Panathinaikos	18	1	122	16
2012–13	Fulham	25	1		
2013–14	Fulham	14	0	39	1

KASAMI, Pajtim (M) 78 6
H: 6 2 W: 11 00 b.Macedonia 2-6-92
Internationals: Switzerland U17, U18, U21, U23, Full caps.

Season	Club				
2009–10	Bellinzona	10	2	10	2
2010–11	Palermo	14	0	14	0
2011–12	Fulham	7	0		
2012–13	Fulham	2	0		
2012–13	Lucerne	16	1	16	1
2013–14	Fulham	29	3	38	3

KAVANAGH, Sean (D) 0 0
b.Dublin 20-1-94
Internationals: Republic of Ireland U17, U19.

Season	Club		
2011–12	Fulham	0	0
2012–13	Fulham	0	0
2013–14	Fulham	0	0

KVIST JORGENSEN, William (M) 255 8
H: 6 0 W: 12 07 b.Odder 24-2-85
Internationals: Denmark U16, U17, U18, U19, U20, U21, Full caps.

Season	Club				
2004–05	Copenhagen	1	0		
2005–06	Copenhagen	20	0		
2006–07	Copenhagen	31	2		
2007–08	Copenhagen	32	0		
2008–09	Copenhagen	29	4		
2009–10	Copenhagen	33	2		
2010–11	Copenhagen	33	0	179	8
2011–12	Stuttgart	33	0		
2012–13	Stuttgart	23	0		
2013–14	Stuttgart	12	0	68	0

On loan from Stuttgart

Season	Club				
2013–14	Fulham	8	0	8	0

MITROGLOU, Konstantinos (F) 140 66
H: 6 2 W: 12 06 b.Kavala 12-3-88
Internationals: Greece U19, U21, Full caps.

Season	Club				
2007–08	Olympiacos	11	4		
2008–09	Olympiacos	7	2		
2009–10	Olympiacos	32	9		
2010–11	Olympiacos	5	1		
2010–11	Panionios	11	8	11	8
2011–12	Olympiacos	0	0		
2011–12	Atromitos	34	17	34	17
2012–13	Olympiacos	25	11		
2013–14	Olympiacos	12	14	92	41
2013–14	Fulham	3	0	3	0

NA BANGNA, Buomesca (M) 7 1
H: 5 9 W: 10 03 b.Guinea-Bissau 6-5-93
Internationals: Portugal U17, U18, U19.

Season	Club				
2011–12	Fulham	0	0		
2012–13	Fulham	0	0		
2013–14	Fulham	1	0	1	0
2013–14	Crewe Alex	6	1	6	1

O'HALLORAN, Dean (M) 0 0
b.Waterford 2-1-96
Internationals: Republic of Ireland U17, U19.

Season	Club		
2013–14	Fulham	0	0

OBERSCHMIDT, Max (G) 0 0
b.Germany 25-1-95
Internationals: Germany U15, U16.

Season	Club		
2011–12	Fulham	0	0
2012–13	Fulham	0	0
2013–14	Fulham	0	0
2013–14	Celtic	0	0

PARKER, Scott (M) 396 27
H: 5 9 W: 11 10 b.Lambeth 13-10-80
Internationals: England U16, U18, U21, Full caps.

Season	Club				
1997–98	Charlton Ath	3	0		
1998–99	Charlton Ath	4	0		
1999–2000	Charlton Ath	15	1		
2000–01	Charlton Ath	20	1		
2000–01	Norwich C	6	1	6	1
2001–02	Charlton Ath	38	1		
2002–03	Charlton Ath	28	4		
2003–04	Charlton Ath	20	2	128	9
2003–04	Chelsea	11	1		
2004–05	Chelsea	4	0	15	1
2005–06	Newcastle U	26	1		
2006–07	Newcastle U	29	3	55	4
2007–08	West Ham U	18	1		
2008–09	West Ham U	28	1		
2009–10	West Ham U	31	2		
2010–11	West Ham U	32	5		
2011–12	West Ham U	4	1	113	10
2011–12	Tottenham H	29	0		
2012–13	Tottenham H	21	0		
2013–14	Tottenham H	0	0	50	0
2013–14	Fulham	29	2	29	2

PASSLEY, Josh (D) 0 0
b. 21-9-93

Season	Club		
2013–14	Fulham	0	0

PLUMAIN, Ange (F) 20 1
b.Paris 2-3-95
Internationals: France U16, U18.

Season	Club				
2012–13	Lens	20	1	20	1
2013–14	Fulham	0	0		

RICHARDS, Tom (D) 10 0

Season	Club				
2013–14	Fulham	0	0		
2013–14	AFC Wimbledon	10	0	10	0

RICHARDSON, Kieran (M) 232 24
H: 5 9 W: 11 13 b.Greenwich 21-10-84
Internationals: England U18, U21, Full caps.

Season	Club				
2002–03	Manchester U	2	0		
2003–04	Manchester U	0	0		
2004–05	Manchester U	2	0		
2004–05	WBA	12	3	12	3
2005–06	Manchester U	22	1		
2006–07	Manchester U	15	1	41	2
2007–08	Sunderland	17	3		
2008–09	Sunderland	32	4		
2009–10	Sunderland	29	1		
2010–11	Sunderland	26	4		
2011–12	Sunderland	29	2		
2012–13	Sunderland	1	0	134	14
2012–13	Fulham	14	1		
2013–14	Fulham	31	4	45	5

RIETHER, Sascha (D) 324 11
H: 5 8 W: 10 13 b.Lahr 23-3-83
Internationals: Germany U20, U21, Full caps.

Season	Club				
2002–03	SC Freiburg	6	0		
2003–04	SC Freiburg	33	3		
2004–05	SC Freiburg	23	1		
2005–06	SC Freiburg	30	0		
2006–07	SC Freiburg	17	0	109	4
2007–08	Wolfsburg	27	1		
2008–09	Wolfsburg	28	2		
2009–10	Wolfsburg	33	1		
2010–11	Wolfsburg	28	2	116	6
2011–12	Cologne	33	0	33	0

On loan from Cologne

Season	Club				
2012–13	Fulham	35	1		
2013–14	Fulham	31	0	66	1

RIISE, John Arne (M) 489 37
H: 6 1 W: 14 00 b.Molde 24-9-80
Internationals: Norway U15, U16, U17, U18, U19, U21, Full caps.

Season	Club				
1997	Aalesund	8	1		
1998	Aalesund	17	4	25	5
1998–99	Monaco	7	0		
1999–2000	Monaco	21	1		
2000–01	Monaco	16	3	44	4
2001–02	Liverpool	38	7		
2002–03	Liverpool	37	6		
2003–04	Liverpool	28	0		
2004–05	Liverpool	37	6		
2005–06	Liverpool	32	1		
2006–07	Liverpool	33	1		
2007–08	Liverpool	29	0	234	21
2008–09	Roma	31	2		
2009–10	Roma	36	5		
2010–11	Roma	32	0	99	7
2011–12	Fulham	36	0		
2012–13	Fulham	31	0		
2013–14	Fulham	20	0	87	0

ROBERTS, Patrick (M) 2 0
b. 5-2-97
Internationals: England U16, U17.

Season	Club				
2013–14	Fulham	2	0	2	0

RODALLEGA, Hugo (F) 311 106
H: 5 11 W: 11 05 b.Valle del Cauca 25-7-85
Internationals: Colombia U20, Full caps.

Season	Club				
2004	Quindio	32	31	32	31
2005	Dep Cali	26	12	26	12
2005–06	Monterrey	14	3		
2006–07	Atlas	17	5	17	5
2006–07	Monterrey	15	1	29	4
2007–08	Necaxa	36	16		
2008–09	Necaxa	17	9	53	25
2008–09	Wigan Ath	15	3		
2009–10	Wigan Ath	38	10		
2010–11	Wigan Ath	36	9		
2011–12	Wigan Ath	23	2	112	24

RUIZ, Bryan (M) 291 95
H: 6 2 W: 12 04 b.Alajuela 18-8-85
Internationals: Costa Rica Full caps.

Season	Club				
2004–05	Alajuelense	31	13		
2005–06	Alajuelense	35	8	66	21
2006–07	Gent	15	3		
2007–08	Gent	31	11		
2008–09	Gent	32	12	78	26
2009–10	Twente	34	24		
2010–11	Twente	27	9		
2011–12	Twente	4	2	65	35
2011–12	Fulham	27	2		
2012–13	Fulham	29	5		
2013–14	Fulham	12	1	68	8
2013–14	PSV Eindhoven	14	5	14	5

SENDEROS, Philippe (D) 163 9
H: 6 1 W: 13 10 b.Geneva 14-2-85
Internationals: Switzerland U20, U21, Full caps.

Season	Club				
2001–02	Servette	3	0		
2002–03	Servette	23	3	26	3
2003–04	Arsenal	0	0		
2004–05	Arsenal	13	0		
2005–06	Arsenal	20	2		
2006–07	Arsenal	14	0		
2007–08	Arsenal	17	2		
2008–09	Arsenal	0	0		
2008–09	AC Milan	14	0	14	0
2009–10	Arsenal	0	0	64	4
2009–10	Everton	2	0	2	0
2010–11	Fulham	3	0		
2011–12	Fulham	21	1		
2012–13	Fulham	21	0		
2013–14	Fulham	12	1	57	2

Transferred to Valencia January 2014

SIDWELL, Steve (M) 362 55
H: 5 10 W: 11 00 b.Wandsworth 14-12-82
Internationals: England U20, U21.

Season	Club				
2001–02	Arsenal	0	0		
2001–02	Brentford	30	4	30	4
2002–03	Arsenal	0	0		
2002–03	Brighton & HA	12	5	12	5
2002–03	Reading	13	2		
2003–04	Reading	43	8		
2004–05	Reading	44	5		
2005–06	Reading	33	10		
2006–07	Reading	35	4	168	29
2007–08	Chelsea	15	0	15	0
2008–09	Aston Villa	16	3		
2009–10	Aston Villa	25	0		
2010–11	Aston Villa	4	0	45	3
2010–11	Fulham	12	2		
2011–12	Fulham	14	1		
2012–13	Fulham	28	4		
2013–14	Fulham	38	7	92	14

STEKELENBURG, Maarten (G) 257 0
H: 6 6 W: 14 05 b.Haarlem 22-9-82
Internationals: Netherlands U21, Full caps.

Season	Club				
2001–02	Ajax	0	0		
2002–03	Ajax	9	0		
2003–04	Ajax	10	0		
2004–05	Ajax	11	0		
2005–06	Ajax	27	0		
2006–07	Ajax	32	0		
2007–08	Ajax	31	0		
2008–09	Ajax	12	0		
2009–10	Ajax	33	0		
2010–11	Ajax	26	0	191	0
2011–12	Roma	29	0		
2012–13	Roma	18	0	47	0
2013–14	Fulham	19	0	19	0

STOCKDALE, David (G) 166 0
H: 6 3 W: 13 04 b.Leeds 20-9-85
Internationals: England C.

Season	Club				
2002–03	York C	1	0		
2003–04	York C	0	0	1	0
2006–07	Darlington	6	0		
2007–08	Darlington	41	0	47	0
2008–09	Fulham	0	0		
2008–09	Rotherham U	8	0	8	0
2008–09	Leicester C	8	0	8	0
2009–10	Fulham	0	0		
2009–10	Plymouth Arg	21	0	21	0
2010–11	Fulham	7	0		
2011–12	Fulham	8	0		

Season	Club				
2011–12	Ipswich T	18	0	18	0
2012–13	Fulham	2	0		
2012–13	Hull C	24	0	24	0
2013–14	Fulham	21	0	39	0

TANKOVIC, Muamer (F) 3 0
H: 5 11 W: 11 06 b.Norrkoping 22-2-95
Internationals: Sweden U17, U19, Full caps.

Season	Club				
2011–12	Fulham	0	0		
2012–13	Fulham	0	0		
2013–14	Fulham	3	0	3	0

TROTTA, Marcello (F) 69 26
H: 6 1 W: 12 12 b.Caserta 29-9-92
Internationals: Italy U16, U18, U19, U20, U21.

Season	Club				
2009–10	Fulham	0	0		
2010–11	Fulham	0	0		
2011–12	Fulham	1	0		
2011–12	Wycombe W	8	8	8	8
2011–12	Watford	1	0	1	0
2012–13	Fulham	0	0		
2012–13	Brentford	22	6		
2013–14	Fulham	0	0	1	0
2013–14	Brentford	37	12	59	18

TUNNICLIFFE, Ryan (M) 64 0
H: 6 0 W: 14 02 b.Bury 30-12-92
Internationals: England U16, U17.

Season	Club				
2009–10	Manchester U	0	0		
2010–11	Manchester U	0	0		
2011–12	Manchester U	0	0		
2011–12	Peterborough U	27	0	27	0
2012–13	Manchester U	0	0		
2012–13	Barnsley	2	0	2	0
2013–14	Manchester U	0	0		
2013–14	Ipswich T	27	0	27	0
2013–14	Fulham	3	0	3	0
2013–14	Wigan Ath	5	0	5	0

WILLIAMS, George (F) 2 0
H: 5 10 W: 12 04 b.Milton Keynes 7-9-95
Internationals: Wales U17, U19, U21, Full caps.

Season	Club				
2011–12	Milton Keynes D	2	0	2	0
2012–13	Fulham	0	0		
2013–14	Fulham	0	0		

WILLIAMS, Ryan (F) 40 7
H: 5 11 W: 12 00 b.Perth 28-10-93
Internationals: Australia U20.

Season	Club				
2011–12	Portsmouth	4	0	4	0
2011–12	Fulham	0	0		
2012–13	Fulham	0	0		
2013–14	Fulham	0	0		
2013–14	Oxford U	36	7	36	7

WOODROW, Cauley (F) 25 3
b.Hemel Hempstead 2-12-94
Internationals: England U17, U21.

Season	Club				
2011–12	Fulham	0	0		
2012–13	Fulham	0	0		
2013–14	Fulham	6	1	6	1
2013–14	Southend U	19	2	19	2

ZVEROTIC, Elsad (D) 149 3
H: 5 10 W: 11 10 b.Berane 31-10-86
Internationals: Switzerland U18. Montenegro U21, Full caps.

Season	Club				
2008–09	Lucerne	27	1		
2009–10	Lucerne	31	0		
2010–11	Lucerne	27	1	85	2
2011–12	Young Boys	23	0		
2012–13	Young Boys	28	1		
2013–14	Young Boys	7	0	58	1
2013–14	Fulham	6	0	6	0

Scholars
Elworthy, Shane; Leacock-Mcleod, Mekhi; Norman, Magnus; Redford, Aaron; Sambou, Solomon; Sheckleford, Ryheem Cole; Smile, Joshua Clifford.

GILLINGHAM (37)

AKINFENWA, Adebayo (F) 385 129
H: 5 11 W: 13 07 b.Nigeria 10-5-82

Season	Club				
2001	Atlanta	19	4		
2002	Atlanta	4	1	23	5
From Barry T					
2003–04	Boston U	3	0	3	0
2003–04	Leyton Orient	1	0	1	0
2003–04	Rushden & D	0	0		
2003–04	Doncaster R	9	4	9	4
2004–05	Torquay U	37	14	37	14
2005–06	Swansea C	34	9		
2006–07	Swansea C	25	5		
2007–08	Swansea C	0	0	59	14
2007–08	Millwall	7	0	7	0
2007–08	Northampton T	15	7		
2008–09	Northampton T	33	13		
2009–10	Northampton T	40	17		
2010–11	Gillingham	44	11		
2011–12	Northampton T	39	18		
2012–13	Northampton T	41	16	168	71
2013–14	Gillingham	34	10	78	21

ALLEN, Charlie (M) 46 2
H: 6 0 W: 11 10 b.Slough 24-3-92

Season	Club				
2011–12	Notts Co	9	0	9	0
2012–13	Gillingham	32	2		
2013–14	Gillingham	5	0	37	2

BARRETT, Adam (D) 556 40
H: 5 10 W: 12 00 b.Dagenham 29-11-79

Season	Club				
1998–99	Plymouth Arg	1	0		
1999–2000	Plymouth Arg	42	3		
2000–01	Plymouth Arg	9	0	52	3
2000–01	Mansfield T	8	1		
2001–02	Mansfield T	29	0	37	1
2002–03	Bristol R	45	1		
2003–04	Bristol R	45	4	90	5
2004–05	Southend U	43	11		
2005–06	Southend U	45	3		
2006–07	Southend U	28	3		
2007–08	Southend U	45	6		
2008–09	Southend U	45	2		
2009–10	Southend U	41	2	247	27
2010–11	Crystal Palace	7	0	7	0
2010–11	Leyton Orient	14	0	14	0
2011–12	Bournemouth	21	1		
2012–13	Bournemouth	0	0	21	1
2012–13	Gillingham	43	1		
2013–14	Gillingham	45	2	88	3

BIRCHALL, Adam (F) 169 25
H: 5 7 W: 10 09 b.Maidstone 2-12-84
Internationals: Wales U21.

Season	Club				
2002–03	Arsenal	0	0		
2003–04	Arsenal	0	0		
2004–05	Arsenal	0	0		
2004–05	Wycombe W	12	4	12	4
2005–06	Mansfield T	31	2		
2006–07	Mansfield T	5	0	36	2
2006–07	Barnet	23	6		
2007–08	Barnet	42	11		
2008–09	Barnet	39	2	104	19
From Dover Ath.					
2011–12	Gillingham	0	0		
2012–13	Gillingham	15	0		
2013–14	Gillingham	2	0	17	0

BRUNT, Thomas (M) 0 0
b.Chatham 5-1-93

Season	Club				
2011–12	Gillingham	0	0		
2012–13	Gillingham	0	0		
2013–14	Gillingham	0	0		

BUTCHER, Stephen (D) 1 0

Season	Club				
2013–14	Gillingham	1	0	1	0

DACK, Bradley (M) 44 4
b.Greenwich 31-12-93

Season	Club				
2012–13	Gillingham	16	1		
2013–14	Gillingham	28	3	44	4

DAVIES, Callum (D) 24 0
H: 6 1 W: 11 11 b.Sittingbourne 8-2-93

Season	Club				
2010–11	Gillingham	1	0		
2011–12	Gillingham	2	0		
2012–13	Gillingham	14	0		
2013–14	Gillingham	7	0	24	0

FAGAN, Craig (F) 309 40
H: 5 11 W: 11 11 b.Birmingham 11-12-82

Season	Club				
2001–02	Birmingham C	0	0		
2002–03	Birmingham C	1	0		
2002–03	Bristol C	6	1	6	1
2003–04	Birmingham C	0	0	1	0
2003–04	Colchester U	37	9		
2004–05	Colchester U	26	8	63	17
2004–05	Hull C	12	4		
2005–06	Hull C	41	5		
2006–07	Hull C	27	6		
2006–07	Derby Co	17	1		
2007–08	Derby Co	2	0	39	1
2007–08	Hull C	8	0		
2008–09	Hull C	22	3		
2009–10	Hull C	25	2		
2010–11	Hull C	5	0	140	20
2011–12	Bradford C	31	7	31	7
2012–13	Bury	11	1		
2013–14	Bury	0	0	11	1
2013–14	Gillingham	18	2	18	2

FISH, Matt (D) 69 3
b.Croydon 5-1-89

Season	Club				
2011–12	Gillingham	23	1		
2012–13	Gillingham	44	2		
2013–14	Gillingham	2	0	69	3

GERMAN, Antonio (F) 56 4
H: 5 10 W: 12 03 b.Wembley 26-12-91

Season	Club				
2008–09	QPR	3	0		
2009–10	QPR	13	2		
2009–10	Aldershot T	3	0	3	0
2010–11	QPR	2	0		
2010–11	Southend U	4	0	4	0
2010–11	Yeovil T	4	0	4	0
2011–12	QPR	0	0	18	2
From Stockport Co, Bromley.					
2011–12	Brentford	2	0		
2012–13	Brentford	2	1	4	1
2012–13	Gillingham	7	1		
2013–14	Gillingham	9	0	16	1
2013–14	Northampton T	7	0	7	0

GREGORY, Steven (D) 103 2
H: 6 1 W: 12 04 b.Haddenham 19-3-87
Internationals: England C.

Season	Club				
2005–06	Wycombe W	1	0		
2006–07	Wycombe W	3	0	4	0
From AFC Wimbledon, Hayes & Yeading U.					
2011–12	Bournemouth	28	2		
2012–13	Bournemouth	0	0	28	2
2012–13	AFC Wimbledon	15	0	15	0
2012–13	Gillingham	17	0		
2013–14	Gillingham	39	0	56	0

HARE, Josh (D) 0 0
b.Cantebury 12-8-94

Season	Club				
2012–13	Gillingham	0	0		
2013–14	Gillingham	0	0		

HESSENTHALER, Jake (M) 19 1
b.Gravesend 20-4-94

Season	Club				
2012–13	Gillingham	0	0		
2013–14	Gillingham	19	1	19	1

KEDWELL, Danny (F) 105 36
H: 5 11 W: 12 13 b.Gillingham 3-8-83

Season	Club				
2011–12	Gillingham	40	12		
2012–13	Gillingham	38	14		
2013–14	Gillingham	27	10	105	36

LEE, Charlie (M) 257 25
H: 5 11 W: 11 07 b.Whitechapel 5-1-87

Season	Club				
2005–06	Tottenham H	0	0		
2006–07	Tottenham H	0	0		
2006–07	Millwall	5	0	5	0
2007–08	Peterborough U	42	6		
2008–09	Peterborough U	44	5		
2009–10	Peterborough U	33	2		
2010–11	Peterborough U	34	1	153	14
2010–11	Gillingham	4	1		
2011–12	Gillingham	33	6		
2012–13	Gillingham	31	2		
2013–14	Gillingham	31	2	99	11

LEGGE, Leon (D) 153 13
H: 6 1 W: 11 02 b.Bexhill 1-7-85

Season	Club				
2009–10	Brentford	29	2		
2010–11	Brentford	30	3		
2011–12	Brentford	28	4		
2012–13	Brentford	7	0	94	9
2012–13	Gillingham	22	2		
2013–14	Gillingham	37	2	59	4

LINGANZI, Amine (M) 39 1
H: 6 1 W: 10 00 b.Algiers 16-11-89
Internationals: DR Congo Full caps.

Season	Club				
2008–09	St Etienne	3	0		
2009–10	St Etienne	0	0	3	0
2009–10	Blackburn R	1	0		
2010–11	Blackburn R	1	0		
2010–11	Preston NE	1	0	1	0
2011–12	Blackburn R	0	0		
2012–13	Blackburn R	0	0	2	0
2012–13	Accrington S	13	0	13	0
2013–14	Gillingham	20	1	20	1

MARTIN, Joe (M) 158 6
H: 6 0　W: 12 13　b.Dagenham 29-11-88
Internationals: England U16, U17.

Season	Club				
2005–06	Tottenham H	0	0		
2006–07	Tottenham H	0	0		
2007–08	Tottenham H	0	0		
2007–08	*Blackpool*	1	0		
2008–09	Blackpool	15	0		
2009–10	Blackpool	6	0	22	0
2010–11	Gillingham	17	1		
2011–12	Gillingham	35	1		
2012–13	Gillingham	38	2		
2013–14	Gillingham	46	2	136	6

McDONALD, Cody (F) 159 57
H: 5 10　W: 11 03　b.Witham 30-5-86

2008–09	Norwich C	7	1		
2009–10	Norwich C	17	3		
2010–11	Norwich C	0	0		
2010–11	*Gillingham*	41	25		
2011–12	Norwich C	0	0	24	4
2011–12	Coventry C	23	4		
2012–13	Coventry C	20	3	43	7
2012–13	*Gillingham*	7	4		
2013–14	Gillingham	44	17	92	46

McKAIN, Devante (F) 2 0
b.26-6-94

2012–13	Gillingham	1	0		
2013–14	Gillingham	1	0	2	0

MILLBANK, Aaron (F) 1 0

2013–14	Gillingham	1	0	1	0

MUGGLETON, Sam (D) 2 0
b.Melton Mowbray 17-11-95

2012–13	Gillingham	1	0		
2013–14	Gillingham	1	0	2	0

NELSON, Stuart (G) 316 0
H: 6 1　W: 12 12　b.Stroud 17-9-81

2003–04	Brentford	9	0		
2004–05	Brentford	43	0		
2005–06	Brentford	45	0		
2006–07	Brentford	19	0	116	0
2007–08	Leyton Orient	30	0	30	0
2008–09	Norwich C	0	0		
2010–11	Notts Co	33	0		
2011–12	Notts Co	46	0	79	0
2012–13	Gillingham	45	0		
2013–14	Gillingham	46	0	91	0

RICHARDSON, Michael (M) 20 0
H: 5 10　W: 12 02　b.Newcastle 17-3-92

2010–11	Newcastle U	0	0		
2011–12	Newcastle U	0	0		
2011–12	*Leyton Orient*	3	0	3	0
2012–13	Newcastle U	0	0		
2012–13	*Gillingham*	2	0		
2013–14	Gillingham	0	0	2	0
2013–14	*Accrington S*	15	0	15	0

WESTON, Myles (M) 257 25
H: 5 11　W: 12 05　b.Lewisham 12-3-88
Internationals: England U16, U17, U18, U19.

2006–07	Charlton Ath	0	0		
2006–07	*Notts Co*	4	0		
2007–08	Notts Co	25	0		
2008–09	Notts Co	44	3	73	3
2009–10	Brentford	40	8		
2010–11	Brentford	42	3		
2011–12	Brentford	26	1		
2012–13	Brentford	0	0	108	12
2012–13	*Gillingham*	37	8		
2013–14	Gillingham	39	2	76	10

WHELPDALE, Chris (M) 233 35
H: 6 0　W: 12 08　b.Harold Wood 27-1-87

2007–08	Peterborough U	35	3		
2008–09	Peterborough U	39	7		
2009–10	Peterborough U	29	1		
2010–11	Peterborough U	22	1	125	12
2010–11	*Gillingham*	4	3		
2011–12	Gillingham	39	12		
2012–13	Gillingham	41	7		
2013–14	Gillingham	24	1	108	23

Scholars
Bent, Daniel David; Blanchard, Aidan James; Butcher, Stephen James; Cundle, Gregory Vincent; Dickenson, Mitchell Jack; Emptage, Callum James; Freiter, Michael Thomas John; Haysman, Kane Cruz; Hendricks, Connor Ian; Ibbertson, Ross Adam; Leonard, Danny Claydon; Millbank, Aaron Craig; Muggleton, Samuel Alexander; Nalder, Luke Justin; Romeo, Mahlon Beresford Baker; Sellens, Jack Aaron; Staunton, Joshua Michael; Webster, Charlie Ronald.

HARTLEPOOL U (38)

AUSTIN, Neil (D) 387 13
H: 5 10　W: 11 09　b.Barnsley 26-4-83
Internationals: England U16, U17.

1999–2000	Barnsley	0	0		
2000–01	Barnsley	0	0		
2001–02	Barnsley	0	0		
2002–03	Barnsley	34	0		
2003–04	Barnsley	37	0		
2004–05	Barnsley	15	0		
2005–06	Barnsley	38	0		
2006–07	Barnsley	24	0	148	0
2007–08	Darlington	29	2		
2008–09	Darlington	33	3	62	5
2009–10	Hartlepool U	39	3		
2010–11	Hartlepool U	24	2		
2011–12	Hartlepool U	46	1		
2012–13	Hartlepool U	39	2		
2013–14	Hartlepool U	29	0	177	8

COLLINS, Sam (D) 518 19
H: 6 2　W: 14 03　b.Pontefract 5-6-77

1994–95	Huddersfield T	0	0		
1995–96	Huddersfield T	0	0		
1996–97	Huddersfield T	4	0		
1997–98	Huddersfield T	10	0		
1998–99	Huddersfield T	23	0	37	0
1999–2000	Bury	19	0		
2000–01	Bury	34	2		
2001–02	Bury	29	0	82	2
2002–03	Port Vale	44	5		
2003–04	Port Vale	43	4		
2004–05	Port Vale	33	2		
2005–06	Port Vale	15	0	135	11
2005–06	Hull C	17	0		
2006–07	Hull C	6	0		
2007–08	Hull C	0	0	23	0
2007–08	*Swindon T*	4	0	4	0
2007–08	Hartlepool U	10	2		
2008–09	Hartlepool U	40	1		
2009–10	Hartlepool U	44	0		
2010–11	Hartlepool U	42	2		
2011–12	Hartlepool U	36	1		
2012–13	Hartlepool U	41	0		
2013–14	Hartlepool U	24	0	237	6

COMPTON, Jack (M) 104 7
H: 5 8　W: 10 07　b.Torquay 2-9-88
From Havant & Waterloovlle,
Weston-Super-Mare.

2010–11	Falkirk	24	3		
2011–12	Falkirk	13	0	37	3
2011–12	*Bradford C*	14	0	14	0
2011–12	*St Johnstone*	0	0		
2012–13	Portsmouth	12	0	12	0
2012–13	*Colchester U*	7	0	7	0
2013–14	Hartlepool U	34	4	34	4

DUCKWORTH, Michael (M) 30 0
2013–14	Hartlepool U	30	0	30	0

FLINDERS, Scott (G) 258 1
H: 6 4　W: 13 00　b.Rotherham 12-6-86
Internationals: England U20.

2004–05	Barnsley	11	0		
2005–06	Barnsley	3	0	14	0
2006–07	Crystal Palace	0	0		
2006–07	*Gillingham*	9	0	9	0
2006–07	*Brighton & HA*	12	0	12	0
2007–08	Crystal Palace	0	0		
2007–08	*Yeovil T*	9	0	9	0
2008–09	Crystal Palace	0	0	8	0
2009–10	Hartlepool U	46	0		
2010–11	Hartlepool U	26	1		
2011–12	Hartlepool U	45	0		
2012–13	Hartlepool U	46	0		
2013–14	Hartlepool U	43	0	206	1

FRANKS, Jonathan (F) 127 15
H: 5 9　W: 11 03　b.Stockton 8-4-90
Internationals: England U16, U17, U18, U19, U20.

2007–08	Middlesbrough	0	0		
2008–09	Middlesbrough	1	0		
2009–10	Middlesbrough	23	3		
2010–11	Middlesbrough	4	0		
2011–12	Middlesbrough	0	0	28	3
2011–12	*Oxford U*	1	0	1	0
2011–12	*Yeovil T*	14	3	14	3
2012–13	Hartlepool U	45	4		
2013–14	Hartlepool U	39	5	84	9

HAREWOOD, Marlon (F) 482 128
H: 6 1　W: 13 07　b.Hampstead 25-8-79

1996–97	Nottingham F	0	0		
1997–98	Nottingham F	1	0		
1998–99	Nottingham F	23	1		
1998–99	*Ipswich T*	6	1	6	1
1999–2000	Nottingham F	34	4		
2000–01	Nottingham F	33	3		
2001–02	Nottingham F	28	11		
2002–03	Nottingham F	44	20		
2003–04	Nottingham F	19	12		
2003–04	West Ham U	28	13		
2004–05	West Ham U	45	17		
2005–06	West Ham U	37	14		
2006–07	West Ham U	32	3	142	47
2007–08	Aston Villa	23	5		
2008–09	Aston Villa	6	0		
2008–09	*Wolverhampton W*	5	0	5	0
2009–10	Aston Villa	0	0	29	5
2009–10	*Newcastle U*	15	5	15	5
2010–11	Blackpool	16	5	16	5
2010–11	*Barnsley*	10	4		
2011	Guangzhou	10	4	10	4
2011–12	Nottingham F	4	0	186	51
2012–13	Barnsley	32	2		
2013–14	Barnsley	0	0	42	6
2013–14	Bristol C	12	1	12	1
2013–14	Hartlepool U	19	3	19	3

HAWKINS, Lewis (M) 7 0
H: 5 10　W: 12 04　b.Middlesbrough 15-6-93

2011–12	Hartlepool U	1	0		
2012–13	Hartlepool U	1	0		
2013–14	Hartlepool U	5	0	7	0

HOLDEN, Darren (D) 47 0
H: 5 11　W: 11 00　b.Krugersdorp 27-8-93

2010–11	Hartlepool U	1	0		
2011–12	Hartlepool U	3	0		
2012–13	Hartlepool U	17	0		
2013–14	Hartlepool U	26	0	47	0

HOWARD, Steve (F) 700 189
H: 6 3　W: 15 00　b.Durham 10-5-76
Internationals: Scotland B.

1995–96	Hartlepool U	39	7		
1996–97	Hartlepool U	32	8		
1997–98	Hartlepool U	43	7		
1998–99	Hartlepool U	28	5		
1998–99	Northampton T	12	0		
1999–2000	Northampton T	41	10		
2000–01	Northampton T	33	8	86	18
2000–01	Luton T	12	3		
2001–02	Luton T	42	24		
2002–03	Luton T	41	22		
2003–04	Luton T	34	14		
2004–05	Luton T	40	18		
2005–06	Luton T	43	14	212	95
2006–07	Derby Co	43	16		
2007–08	Derby Co	20	1	63	17
2007–08	Leicester C	21	6		
2008–09	Leicester C	41	13		
2009–10	Leicester C	36	5		
2010–11	Leicester C	29	4		
2011–12	Leicester C	20	0	147	28
2012–13	Hartlepool U	34	3		
2012–13	*Sheffield W*	8	1	8	1
2013–14	Hartlepool U	8	0	184	30

JAMES, Luke (M) 87 19
H: 6 0　W: 12 08　b.Amble 4-11-94

2011–12	Hartlepool U	19	3		
2012–13	Hartlepool U	26	3		
2013–14	Hartlepool U	42	13	87	19

JONES, Dan (D) 1 0
H: 6 0　W: 12 05　b. 14-12-94

2013–14	Hartlepool U	1	0	1	0

MONKHOUSE, Andy (M) 436 58
H: 6 1　W: 11 06　b.Leeds 23-10-80

1998–99	Rotherham U	5	1		
1999–2000	Rotherham U	0	0		
2000–01	Rotherham U	12	0		

Season	Club				
2001–02	Rotherham U	38	2		
2002–03	Rotherham U	20	0		
2003–04	Rotherham U	27	3		
2004–05	Rotherham U	14	2		
2005–06	Rotherham U	12	1	128	9
2006–07	Swindon T	10	2	10	2
2006–07	Hartlepool U	26	7		
2007–08	Hartlepool U	25	2		
2008–09	Hartlepool U	44	6		
2009–10	Hartlepool U	43	11		
2010–11	Hartlepool U	44	7		
2011–12	Hartlepool U	45	3		
2012–13	Hartlepool U	35	7		
2013–14	Hartlepool U	36	4	298	47

POOLE, James (F)   108 15
H: 5 11 W: 12 05 b.Stockport 20-3-90

2008–09	Manchester C	0	0		
2009–10	Manchester C	0	0		
2009–10	Bury	9	0	9	0
2010–11	Manchester C	0	0		
2010–11	*Hartlepool U*	3	1		
2011–12	*Hartlepool U*	27	7		
2012–13	Hartlepool U	36	4		
2013–14	Hartlepool U	33	3	99	15

RAFFERTY, Andy (G)   5 0
H: 6 6 W: 13 07 b.Sidcup 27-5-88

2010–11	Hartlepool U	1	0		
2011–12	Hartlepool U	1	0		
2012–13	Hartlepool U	0	0		
2013–14	Hartlepool U	3	0	5	0

RICHARDS, Jordan (M)   32 0
H: 5 9 W: 11 05 b.Sunderland 25-4-93

2011–12	Hartlepool U	2	0		
2012–13	Hartlepool U	11	0		
2013–14	Hartlepool U	19	0	32	0

RODNEY, Nialle (F)   23 0
H: 6 1 W: 11 11 b.Nottingham 28-2-91

2008–09	Nottingham F	0	0		
2009–10	Nottingham F	0	0		
2010–11	Nottingham F	3	0	3	0
2010–11	*Burton Alb*	3	0	3	0
2011–12	Bradford C	5	0	5	0
2013–14	Hartlepool U	12	0	12	0

ROWBOTHAM, Josh (M)   2 0
H: 5 11 W: 11 00 b.Stockton 7-1-94

2011–12	Hartlepool U	1	0		
2012–13	Hartlepool U	0	0		
2013–14	Hartlepool U	0	0	2	0

RUTHERFORD, Greg (M)   9 1
H: 5 10 W: 12 06 b.North Shields 17-5-94

2011–12	Hartlepool U	1	0		
2012–13	Hartlepool U	7	1		
2013–14	Hartlepool U	1	0	9	1

SMITH, Connor (M)   1 0
b. 14-10-96

2013–14	Hartlepool U	1	0	1	0

SWEENEY, Anthony (M)   385 52
H: 6 0 W: 11 07 b.Stockton 5-9-83

2001–02	Hartlepool U	2	0		
2002–03	Hartlepool U	4	0		
2003–04	Hartlepool U	11	1		
2004–05	Hartlepool U	44	13		
2005–06	Hartlepool U	35	5		
2006–07	Hartlepool U	35	4		
2007–08	Hartlepool U	36	4		
2008–09	Hartlepool U	44	5		
2009–10	Hartlepool U	42	2		
2010–11	Hartlepool U	40	9		
2011–12	Hartlepool U	39	8		
2012–13	Hartlepool U	34	1		
2013–14	Hartlepool U	19	0	385	52

WALKER, Brad (M)   36 3
b. 25-4-95

2012–13	Hartlepool U	0	0		
2013–14	Hartlepool U	36	3	36	3

WALTON, Simon (M)   240 20
H: 6 1 W: 13 05 b.Sherburn-in-Elmet 13-9-87
Internationals: England U16, U17, U19.

2004–05	Leeds U	30	3		
2005–06	Leeds U	4	0	34	3
2006–07	Charlton Ath	0	0		
2006–07	*Ipswich T*	19	3	19	3
2006–07	*Cardiff C*	6	0	6	0
2007–08	QPR	5	0	5	0
2007–08	Hull C	10	0	10	0
2008–09	Plymouth Arg	13	0		
2008–09	*Blackpool*	1	0	1	0
2009–10	Plymouth Arg	0	0		
2009–10	*Crewe Alex*	31	1	31	1
2010–11	Plymouth Arg	7	1		
2010–11	*Sheffield U*	0	0		
2011–12	Plymouth Arg	41	8	61	9
2012–13	Hartlepool U	34	1		
2013–14	Hartlepool U	39	3	73	4

Scholars
Armstrong, Dylan Michael; Barber, Jonathan Frederick; Bridges, Andrew; Carr, Jonathon Wesley; Foden, Mark Andrew; Green, Kieran Thomas; Harbottle, Rhys Lee; Mitchinson, Thomas Peter; Nearney, Joshua William; Nellis, Keelan Paul; Smith, Connor Charles; Turner, Daniel; Wood, Callum Peter.

HUDDERSFIELD T (39)

ALLINSON, Lloyd (G)   0 0
H: 6 2 W: 13 00 b.Rothwell 7-9-93

2010–11	Huddersfield T	0	0
2011–12	Huddersfield T	0	0
2012–13	Huddersfield T	0	0
2013–14	Huddersfield T	0	0

ATKINSON, Chris (M)   51 8
H: 6 1 W: 11 13 b. 13-2-92

2010–11	Huddersfield T	2	0		
2011–12	Huddersfield T	1	0		
2012–13	Huddersfield T	7	1		
2012–13	*Chesterfield*	15	5	15	5
2013–14	Huddersfield T	0	0	10	1
2013–14	*Tranmere R*	22	2	22	2
2013–14	*Bradford C*	4	0	4	0

BAJAJ, Florent (M)   0 0
b. 13-4-96

2013–14	Huddersfield T	0	0

BILLING, Phillip (M)   1 0
b. 11-6-96

2013–14	Huddersfield T	1	0	1	0

BURKE, James (D)   2 0
H: 5 11 W: 13 03 b.Shepley 16-4-94

2012–13	Huddersfield T	0	0		
2013–14	Huddersfield T	0	0		
2013–14	*Bury*	2	0	2	0

CARR, Daniel (F)   6 1
H: 5 11 W: 11 13 b. 30-11-93

2013–14	Huddersfield T	2	0	2	0
2013–14	*Fleetwood T*	4	1	4	1

CARROLL, Jake (D)   43 2
H: 6 0 W: 12 03 b. 11-1-91
Internationals: Republic of Ireland U18.

2011	St Patricks	7	0		
2012	St Patricks	19	1		
2013	St Patricks	7	0	33	1
2013–14	Huddersfield T	4	0	4	0
2013–14	*Bury*	6	1	6	1

CHARLES, Jake (M)   0 0
b.Leeds 28-2-96
Internationals: Wales U16, U17.

2013–14	Huddersfield T	0	0

CLARKE, Peter (D)   445 34
H: 6 0 W: 12 00 b.Southport 3-1-82
Internationals: England U20, U21.

1998–99	Everton	0	0		
1999–2000	Everton	0	0		
2000–01	Everton	1	0		
2001–02	Everton	7	0		
2002–03	Everton	0	0		
2002–03	*Blackpool*	16	3		
2002–03	*Port Vale*	13	1	13	1
2003–04	Everton	1	0		
2003–04	*Coventry C*	5	0	5	0
2004–05	Everton	0	0	9	0
2004–05	Blackpool	38	5		
2005–06	Blackpool	46	6	100	14
2006–07	Southend U	38	2		
2007–08	Southend U	45	4		
2008–09	Southend U	43	4	126	10
2009–10	Huddersfield T	46	5		
2010–11	Huddersfield T	46	4		
2011–12	Huddersfield T	31	0		
2012–13	Huddersfield T	43	0		
2013–14	Huddersfield T	26	0	192	9

CLAYTON, Adam (M)   173 19
H: 5 9 W: 11 11 b.Manchester 14-1-89
Internationals: England U20.

2007–08	Manchester C	0	0		
2008–09	Manchester C	0	0		
2009–10	Manchester C	0	0		
2009–10	*Carlisle U*	28	1	28	1
2010–11	Leeds U	4	0		
2010–11	*Peterborough U*	7	0	7	0
2010–11	*Milton Keynes D*	6	1	6	1
2011–12	Leeds U	43	6	47	6
2012–13	Huddersfield T	43	4		
2013–14	Huddersfield T	42	7	85	11

CROOKS, Matt (M)   0 0
H: 6 0 W: 11 05 b.Leeds 20-1-94

2011–12	Huddersfield T	0	0
2012–13	Huddersfield T	0	0
2013–14	Huddersfield T	0	0

DIXON, Paul (D)   287 6
H: 5 9 W: 11 01 b.Aberdeen 11-10-86
Internationals: Scotland U21, Full caps.

2005–06	Dundee	29	2		
2006–07	Dundee	33	0		
2007–08	Dundee	30	0	92	2
2008–09	Dundee U	29	1		
2009–10	Dundee U	25	0		
2010–11	Dundee U	30	0		
2011–12	Dundee U	37	3	121	4
2012–13	Huddersfield T	37	0		
2013–14	Huddersfield T	37	0	74	0

GERRARD, Anthony (D)   341 17
H: 6 2 W: 13 07 b.Huyton 6-2-86
Internationals: Republic of Ireland U18.

2004–05	Everton	0	0		
2004–05	*Walsall*	8	0		
2005–06	Walsall	34	0		
2006–07	Walsall	35	1		
2007–08	Walsall	44	3		
2008–09	Walsall	42	3	163	7
2009–10	Cardiff C	39	2		
2010–11	Cardiff C	0	0		
2010–11	*Hull C*	41	5	41	5
2011–12	Cardiff C	20	1		
2012–13	Cardiff C	0	0	59	3
2012–13	Huddersfield T	38	1		
2013–14	Huddersfield T	40	1	78	2

GOBERN, Oscar (M)   82 3
H: 5 11 W: 10 10 b.Birmingham 26-1-91
Internationals: England U19.

2008–09	Southampton	6	0		
2009–10	Southampton	4	0		
2009–10	*Milton Keynes D*	2	0	2	0
2010–11	Southampton	11	1	21	1
2011–12	Huddersfield T	21	2		
2012–13	Huddersfield T	15	0		
2013–14	Huddersfield T	23	0	59	2

HAMMILL, Adam (M)   231 21
H: 5 11 W: 11 07 b.Liverpool 25-1-88
Internationals: England U19, U21.

2005–06	Liverpool	0	0		
2006–07	Liverpool	0	0		
2006–07	*Dunfermline Ath*	13	1	13	1
2007–08	Liverpool	0	0		
2007–08	*Southampton*	25	0	25	0
2008–09	Liverpool	0	0		
2008–09	*Blackpool*	22	1	22	1
2008–09	*Barnsley*	14	1		
2009–10	Liverpool	0	0		
2009–10	Barnsley	39	4		
2010–11	Barnsley	25	8	78	13
2010–11	Wolverhampton W	10	0		
2011–12	Wolverhampton W	9	0		
2011–12	*Middlesbrough*	10	0	10	0
2012–13	Wolverhampton W	4	0	23	0
2012–13	*Huddersfield T*	16	2		
2013–14	Huddersfield T	44	4	60	6

HOGG, Jonathan (M)   141 1
H: 5 7 W: 10 05 b.Middlesbrough 6-12-88

2007–08	Aston Villa	0	0		
2008–09	Aston Villa	0	0		
2009–10	Aston Villa	0	0		
2009–10	*Darlington*	5	1	5	1
2010–11	Aston Villa	5	0		

2010–11	Portsmouth	19	0	19	0
2011–12	Aston Villa	0	0	5	0
2011–12	Watford	40	0		
2012–13	Watford	38	0	78	0
2013–14	Huddersfield T	34	0	34	0

HOLMES, Duane (M) 21 0
b.Wakefield 6-11-94

2012–13	Huddersfield T	0	0		
2013–14	Huddersfield T	16	0	16	0
2013–14	*Yeovil T*	5	0	5	0

LOLLEY, Joe (F) 6 1
b. 25-8-92
Internationals: England C.

2013–14	Huddersfield T	6	1	6	1

LOPEZ, Cristian (F) 10 1
H: 6 0 W: 11 10 b.Elche 24-2-94

2013–14	Huddersfield T	2	0	2	0
2013–14	*Shrewsbury T*	5	1	5	1
2013–14	*Northampton T*	3	0	3	0

LYNCH, Joel (D) 210 8
H: 6 1 W: 12 10 b.Eastbourne 3-10-87
Internationals: England Youth. Wales Full caps.

2005–06	Brighton & HA	16	1		
2006–07	Brighton & HA	39	0		
2007–08	Brighton & HA	22	1		
2008–09	Brighton & HA	2	0	79	2
2008–09	Nottingham F	23	0		
2009–10	Nottingham F	10	0		
2010–11	Nottingham F	12	0		
2011–12	Nottingham F	35	3	80	3
2012–13	Huddersfield T	22	1		
2013–14	Huddersfield T	29	2	51	3

NORWOOD, Oliver (M) 118 11
H: 5 11 W: 11 13 b.Burnley 12-4-91
Internationals: England U16, U17. Northern Ireland U19, U21, B, Full caps.

2009–10	Manchester U	0	0		
2010–11	Manchester U	0	0		
2010–11	*Carlisle U*	6	0	6	0
2011–12	Manchester U	0	0		
2011–12	*Scunthorpe U*	15	1	15	1
2011–12	*Coventry C*	18	2	18	2
2012–13	Huddersfield T	39	3		
2013–14	Huddersfield T	40	5	79	8

PATERSON, Martin (F) 230 55
H: 5 9 W: 10 11 b.Tunstall 13-5-87
Internationals: Northern Ireland U21, Full caps.

2004–05	Stoke C	3	0		
2005–06	Stoke C	3	0		
2006–07	Stoke C	9	1	15	1
2006–07	*Grimsby T*	15	6	15	6
2007–08	Scunthorpe U	40	13	40	13
2008–09	Burnley	43	12		
2009–10	Burnley	23	4		
2010–11	Burnley	11	2		
2011–12	Burnley	14	3		
2012–13	Burnley	39	8	130	29
2013–14	Huddersfield T	22	5	22	5
2013–14	*Bristol C*	8	1	8	1

RIDEHALGH, Liam (D) 121 2
H: 5 11 W: 11 05 b.Halifax 20-4-91

2009–10	Huddersfield T	0	0		
2010–11	Huddersfield T	20	0		
2011–12	Huddersfield T	0	0		
2011–12	*Swindon T*	11	0	11	0
2011–12	*Chesterfield*	20	1		
2012–13	Huddersfield T	0	0		
2012–13	*Chesterfield*	14	0	34	1
2012–13	*Rotherham U*	20	0	20	0
2013–14	Huddersfield T	0	0	20	0
2013–14	*Tranmere R*	36	1	36	1

ROBINSON, Anton (M) 153 11
H: 5 9 W: 10 03 b.Harrow 17-2-86
Internationals: England C.

2004–05	Millwall	0	0		
2005–06	Millwall	0	0		

From Ex C, Eastb B, Fish A, Weymouth.

2008–09	Bournemouth	17	1		
2009–10	Bournemouth	44	4		
2010–11	Bournemouth	45	3	106	10
2011–12	Huddersfield T	25	1		
2012–13	Huddersfield T	2	0		
2012–13	*Gillingham*	14	0	14	0

2013–14	Huddersfield T	0	0	27	1
2013–14	*Coventry C*	6	0	6	0

SCANNELL, Sean (F) 202 15
H: 5 9 W: 11 07 b.Croydon 19-9-90
Internationals: Republic of Ireland U17, U18, U19, U21, B.

2007–08	Crystal Palace	23	2		
2008–09	Crystal Palace	25	2		
2009–10	Crystal Palace	26	2		
2010–11	Crystal Palace	19	2		
2011–12	Crystal Palace	37	4	130	12
2012–13	Huddersfield T	34	2		
2013–14	Huddersfield T	38	1	72	3

SINNOTT, Jordan (M) 10 1
H: 5 11 W: 11 12 b. 14-2-94

2012–13	Huddersfield T	1	0		
2013–14	Huddersfield T	0	0	1	0
2013–14	*Bury*	9	1	9	1

SMITH, Tommy (D) 24 0
b. 14-4-92

2012–13	Huddersfield T	0	0		
2013–14	Huddersfield T	24	0	24	0

SMITHIES, Alex (G) 202 0
H: 6 1 W: 10 01 b.Huddersfield 25-3-90
Internationals: England U16, U17, U18, U19.

2006–07	Huddersfield T	0	0		
2007–08	Huddersfield T	2	0		
2008–09	Huddersfield T	27	0		
2009–10	Huddersfield T	46	0		
2010–11	Huddersfield T	22	0		
2011–12	Huddersfield T	13	0		
2012–13	Huddersfield T	46	0		
2013–14	Huddersfield T	46	0	202	0

SOUTHERN, Keith (M) 369 27
H: 5 10 W: 12 06 b.Gateshead 24-4-81

1998–99	Everton	0	0		
1999–2000	Everton	0	0		
2000–01	Everton	0	0		
2001–02	Everton	0	0		
2002–03	Everton	0	0		
2002–03	Blackpool	38	1		
2003–04	Blackpool	28	2		
2004–05	Blackpool	27	6		
2005–06	Blackpool	42	0		
2006–07	Blackpool	39	5		
2007–08	Blackpool	30	3		
2008–09	Blackpool	35	3		
2009–10	Blackpool	45	2		
2010–11	Blackpool	21	0		
2011–12	Blackpool	25	1	330	25
2012–13	Huddersfield T	29	1		
2013–14	Huddersfield T	10	1	39	2

STEAD, Jon (F) 379 86
H: 6 3 W: 13 03 b.Huddersfield 7-4-83
Internationals: England U21.

2001–02	Huddersfield T	0	0		
2002–03	Huddersfield T	42	6		
2003–04	Huddersfield T	26	16		
2003–04	Blackburn R	13	6		
2004–05	Blackburn R	29	2	42	8
2005–06	Sunderland	30	1		
2006–07	Sunderland	5	1	35	2
2006–07	*Derby Co*	17	3	17	3
2006–07	Sheffield U	14	5		
2007–08	Sheffield U	24	3		
2008–09	Sheffield U	1	0	39	8
2008–09	Ipswich T	39	12		
2009–10	Ipswich T	22	6		
2009–10	*Coventry C*	10	2	10	2
2010–11	Ipswich T	3	1	64	19
2010–11	Bristol C	27	9		
2011–12	Bristol C	24	6		
2012–13	Bristol C	28	5	79	20
2013–14	Huddersfield T	12	1	80	23
2013–14	*Oldham Ath*	5	0	5	0
2013–14	*Bradford C*	8	1	8	1

TRONSTAD, Sondre (M) 9 1
H: 5 8 W: 10 13 b. 26-8-95
Internationals: Norway U16, U17, U18.

2013	IK Start	9	1	9	1
2013–14	Huddersfield T	0	0		

VAUGHAN, James (F) 140 40
H: 5 11 W: 13 00 b.Birmingham 14-7-88
Internationals: England U17, U19, U21.

2004–05	Everton	2	1		
2005–06	Everton	1	0		
2006–07	Everton	14	4		
2007–08	Everton	8	1		
2008–09	Everton	13	0		
2009–10	Everton	8	1		
2009–10	*Derby Co*	2	0	2	0
2010–11	Everton	1	0	47	7
2010–11	*Crystal Palace*	30	9	30	9
2011–12	Norwich C	5	0		
2012–13	Norwich C	0	0	5	0
2012–13	*Huddersfield T*	33	14		
2013–14	Huddersfield T	23	10	56	24

WALLACE, Murray (D) 42 3
H: 6 2 W: 11 07 b.Glasgow 10-1-93
Internationals: Scotland U20, U21.

2011–12	Falkirk	19	2	19	2
2011–12	Huddersfield T	0	0		
2012–13	Huddersfield T	6	1		
2013–14	Huddersfield T	17	0	23	1

WARD, Danny (M) 147 26
H: 5 11 W: 12 05 b.Bradford 11-12-91

2008–09	Bolton W	5	0		
2009–10	Bolton W	2	0		
2009–10	*Swindon T*	28	7	28	7
2010–11	Bolton W	0	0	2	0
2010–11	*Coventry C*	5	0	5	0
2010–11	*Huddersfield T*	7	3		
2011–12	Huddersfield T	39	4		
2012–13	Huddersfield T	28	2		
2013–14	Huddersfield T	38	10	112	19

WELLS, Nahki (F) 116 49
H: 5 7 W: 11 00 b.Bermuda 1-6-90
Internationals: Bermuda Full caps.

2010–11	Carlisle U	3	0	3	0
2011–12	Bradford C	33	10		
2012–13	Bradford C	39	18		
2013–14	Bradford C	19	14	91	42
2013–14	Huddersfield T	22	7	22	7

WILCZYNSKI, Ed (G) 0 0
H: 6 2 W: 12 08 b. 6-11-94

2013–14	Huddersfield T	0	0		

WOODS, Calum (D) 200 11
H: 5 11 W: 11 07 b.Liverpool 5-2-87
Internationals: England Youth.

2006–07	Dunfermline Ath	12	0		
2007–08	Dunfermline Ath	25	0		
2008–09	Dunfermline Ath	30	2		
2009–10	Dunfermline Ath	29	2		
2010–11	Dunfermline Ath	32	3	128	10
2011–12	Huddersfield T	26	0		
2012–13	Huddersfield T	0	0		
2013–14	Huddersfield T	19	1	72	1

WRIGHT, Joe (D) 0 0

2013–14	Huddersfield T	0	0		

Scholars
Atkinson, Benjamin Louis; Boyle, William Sam Douglas Harry; Carroll, Bradley John; Goddard, Kedesh Malachi; Guthrie, Sam Alan; Holmes, Benjamin; Horsfall, Fraser Matthew; Kane, Danny; Pells, Nathaniel William; Rodgers, Sheiden Lee Tosh; Senior, Jack Christopher Senior; Starkey, Michael Jay; Wilkinson, Joseph.

HULL C (40)

AIMSON, William (D) 0 0
b.Christchurch 1-1-94

2013–14	Hull C	0	0		

ALUKO, Sone (M) 164 31
H: 5 8 W: 9 10 b.Birmingham 19-2-89
Internationals: England U16, U17, U18, U19. Nigeria U20, Full caps.

2005–06	Birmingham C	0	0		
2006–07	Birmingham C	0	0		
2007–08	Birmingham C	0	0		
2007–08	*Aberdeen*	20	3		
2008–09	Birmingham C	0	0		
2008–09	*Blackpool*	0	1	1	0
2008–09	*Aberdeen*	32	2		
2009–10	Aberdeen	22	3		
2010–11	Aberdeen	28	2	102	10
2011–12	Rangers	21	12	21	12
2012–13	Hull C	23	8		
2013–14	Hull C	17	1	40	9

BOYD, George (M) 311 71
H: 5 10 W: 11 07 b.Chatham 2-10-85
Internationals: Scotland B, Full caps.

2006–07	Peterborough U	20	6
2007–08	Peterborough U	46	12
2008–09	Peterborough U	46	9
2009–10	Peterborough U	32	9
2009–10	*Nottingham F*	6	1	6	1
2010–11	Peterborough U	43	15
2011–12	Peterborough U	45	7
2012–13	Peterborough U	31	6	263	64
2012–13	Hull C	13	4
2013–14	Hull C	29	2	42	6

BRADY, Robert (F) 87 10
H: 5 9 W: 10 12 b.Belfast 14-1-92
Internationals: Republic of Ireland Youth, U21, Full caps.

2008–09	Manchester U	0	0
2009–10	Manchester U	0	0
2010–11	Manchester U	0	0
2011–12	Manchester U	0	0
2011–12	*Hull C*	39	3
2012–13	Manchester U	0	0
2012–13	Hull C	32	4
2013–14	Hull C	16	3	87	10

BRUCE, Alex (D) 237 3
H: 6 0 W: 11 06 b.Norwich 28-9-84
Internationals: Republic of Ireland B, U21, Full caps. Northern Ireland Full caps.

2002–03	Blackburn R	0	0
2003–04	Blackburn R	0	0
2004–05	Blackburn R	0	0
2004–05	*Oldham Ath*	12	0	12	0
2004–05	Birmingham C	0	0
2004–05	*Sheffield W*	6	0	6	0
2005–06	Birmingham C	6	0	6	0
2005–06	*Tranmere R*	11	0	11	0
2006–07	Ipswich T	41	0
2007–08	Ipswich T	36	0
2008–09	Ipswich T	25	1
2009–10	Ipswich T	13	1
2009–10	*Leicester C*	3	0	3	0
2010–11	Ipswich T	0	0	115	2
2010–11	Leeds U	21	1
2011–12	Leeds U	8	0	29	1
2011–12	*Huddersfield T*	3	0	3	0
2012–13	Hull C	32	0
2013–14	Hull C	20	0	52	0

CHESTER, James (D) 159 7
H: 5 11 W: 11 04 b.Warrington 23-1-89
Internationals: Wales Full caps.

2007–08	Manchester U	0	0
2008–09	Manchester U	0	0
2008–09	*Peterborough U*	5	0	5	0
2009–10	Manchester U	0	0
2009–10	*Plymouth Arg*	3	0	3	0
2010–11	Manchester U	0	0
2010–11	*Carlisle U*	18	2	18	2
2010–11	Hull C	21	1
2011–12	Hull C	44	2
2012–13	Hull C	44	1
2013–14	Hull C	24	1	133	5

CRACKNELL, Joe (G) 0 0
H: 6 0 W: 11 02 b. 5-6-94

2012–13	Hull C	0	0
2013–14	Hull C	0	0

DAVIES, Curtis (D) 308 20
H: 6 2 W: 11 13 b.Waltham Forest 15-3-85
Internationals: England U21.

2003–04	Luton T	6	0
2004–05	Luton T	44	1
2005–06	Luton T	6	1	56	2
2005–06	WBA	33	2
2006–07	WBA	32	0
2007–08	WBA	0	0	65	2
2007–08	*Aston Villa*	12	1
2008–09	Aston Villa	35	1
2009–10	Aston Villa	2	1
2010–11	Aston Villa	0	0	49	3
2010–11	*Leicester C*	12	0	12	0
2010–11	Birmingham C	6	0
2011–12	Birmingham C	42	5
2012–13	Birmingham C	41	6	89	11
2013–14	Hull C	37	2	37	2

ELMOHAMADY, Ahmed (M) 210 20
H: 5 11 W: 12 10 b.El Mahalla El-Kubra 9-9-87
Internationals: Egypt Full caps.

2003–04	Ghazi Al-Mehalla	0	0
2004–05	Ghazi Al-Mehalla	14	4
2005–06	Ghazi Al-Mehalla	3	0	17	4
2006–07	ENPPI	12	2
2007–08	ENPPI	28	6
2008–09	ENPPI	28	6
2009–10	ENPPI	12	1	58	10
2010–11	Sunderland	36	0
2011–12	Sunderland	18	1
2012–13	Sunderland	2	0	56	1
2012–13	*Hull C*	41	3
2013–14	Hull C	38	2	79	5

FAYE, Aboulaye (M) 320 18
H: 6 2 W: 13 10 b.Dakar 26-2-78
Internationals: Senegal Full caps.

2001–02	Jeanne D'Arc	32	4	32	4
2002–03	Lens	15	0
2003–04	Lens	19	0	34	0
2004–05	Istres	28	0	28	0
2005–06	Bolton W	27	1
2006–07	Bolton W	32	2
2007–08	Bolton W	0	0	60	3
2007–08	Newcastle U	22	1	22	1
2008–09	Stoke C	36	3
2009–10	Stoke C	31	2
2010–11	Stoke C	14	1	81	6
2011–12	West Ham U	29	0	29	0
2012–13	Hull C	31	4
2013–14	Hull C	3	0	34	4

FIGUEROA, Maynor (D) 235 6
H: 5 11 W: 12 02 b.Jutiapa 2-5-83
Internationals: Honduras U20, U23, Full caps.

2000–01	Victoria La Ceiba	1	0
2001–02	Victoria La Ceiba	22	2	24	2
2007–08	Wigan Ath	2	0
2008–09	Wigan Ath	38	1
2009–10	Wigan Ath	35	1
2010–11	Wigan Ath	33	1
2011–12	Wigan Ath	38	0
2012–13	Wigan Ath	33	1
2013–14	Wigan Ath	0	0	179	4
2013–14	Hull C	32	0	32	0

FRYATT, Matty (F) 339 110
H: 5 10 W: 11 00 b.Nuneaton 5-3-86
Internationals: England U19.

2002–03	Walsall	0	0
2003–04	Walsall	11	1
2003–04	*Carlisle U*	10	1	10	1
2004–05	Walsall	36	15
2005–06	Walsall	23	11	70	27
2005–06	Leicester C	19	6
2006–07	Leicester C	32	3
2007–08	Leicester C	30	2
2008–09	Leicester C	46	27
2009–10	Leicester C	29	11
2010–11	Leicester C	12	2	168	51
2010–11	Hull C	22	9
2011–12	Hull C	46	16
2012–13	Hull C	4	0
2013–14	Hull C	10	2	82	27
2013–14	*Sheffield W*	9	4	9	4

GEDO, Mohamed (F) 52 17
b.Damanhur 30-10-84
Internationals: Egypt Full caps.

2010–11	Al Ahly Cairo	24	8
2011–12	Al Ahly Cairo	14	4	38	12
2012–13	Hull C	12	5
2013–14	Hull C	2	0	14	5

HARPER, Steve (G) 215 0
H: 6 2 W: 13 10 b.Easington 14-3-75

1993–94	Newcastle U	0	0
1994–95	Newcastle U	0	0
1995–96	Newcastle U	0	0
1995–96	*Bradford C*	1	0	1	0
1996–97	Newcastle U	0	0
1996–97	*Stockport Co*	0	0
1997–98	Newcastle U	0	0
1997–98	*Hartlepool U*	15	0	15	0
1997–98	*Huddersfield T*	24	0	24	0
1998–99	Newcastle U	8	0
1999–2000	Newcastle U	18	0
2000–01	Newcastle U	5	0
2001–02	Newcastle U	0	0

2002–03	Newcastle U	0	0
2003–04	Newcastle U	0	0
2004–05	Newcastle U	2	0
2005–06	Newcastle U	0	0
2006–07	Newcastle U	18	0
2007–08	Newcastle U	21	0
2008–09	Newcastle U	16	0
2009–10	Newcastle U	45	0
2010–11	Newcastle U	18	0
2011–12	Newcastle U	0	0
2011–12	*Brighton & HA*	5	0	5	0
2012–13	Newcastle U	6	0	157	0
2013–14	Hull C	13	0	13	0

HENDERSON, Conor (M) 5 0
H: 6 1 W: 11 13 b.Sidcup 8-9-91
Internationals: England U17. Republic of Ireland U19, U21.

2008–09	Arsenal	0	0
2009–10	Arsenal	0	0
2010–11	Arsenal	0	0
2011–12	Arsenal	0	0
2012–13	Arsenal	0	0
2012–13	*Coventry C*	2	0	2	0
2013–14	Hull C	0	0
2013–14	*Stevenage*	3	0	3	0

HUDDLESTONE, Tom (M) 281 12
H: 6 2 W: 11 02 b.Nottingham 28-12-86
Internationals: England U16, U17, U19, U20, U21, Full caps.

2003–04	Derby Co	43	0
2004–05	Derby Co	45	0	88	0
2005–06	Tottenham H	4	0
2005–06	*Wolverhampton W*	13	1	13	1
2006–07	Tottenham H	21	1
2007–08	Tottenham H	28	3
2008–09	Tottenham H	22	0
2009–10	Tottenham H	33	2
2010–11	Tottenham H	14	2
2011–12	Tottenham H	2	0
2012–13	Tottenham H	20	0
2013–14	Tottenham H	0	0	144	8
2013–14	Hull C	36	3	36	3

JAHRALDO-MARTIN, Calaum (F) 0 0
b.St Johns 27-4-93
Internationals: Antigua and Barbuda U20.

2013–14	Hull C	0	0

JAKUPOVIC, Eldin (G) 132 1
H: 6 3 W: 13 00 b.Kozarac 2-10-84
Internationals: Bosnia & Herzegovina U21, Switzerland U21, Full caps.

2004–05	Grasshoppers	8	0
2005–06	FC Thun	23	0	23	0
2007–08	Grasshoppers	23	1
2008–09	Grasshoppers	32	0	63	1
2010–11	Olympiacos Volou	26	0	26	0
2011–12	Aris Salonika	1	0	1	0
2012–13	Hull C	5	0
2013–14	Hull C	0	0	6	0
2013–14	*Leyton Orient*	13	0	13	0

JELAVIC, Nikica (F) 248 83
H: 6 2 W: 13 12 b.Capljina 27-8-85
Internationals: Croatia U17, U18, Full caps.

2002–03	Hajduk Split	2	0
2003–04	Hajduk Split	2	0
2004–05	Hajduk Split	0	0
2005–06	Hajduk Split	9	0
2006–07	Hajduk Split	22	5	35	5
2007–08	Waregem	23	3	23	3
2008–09	Rapid Vienna	34	7
2009–10	Rapid Vienna	33	17
2010–11	Rapid Vienna	3	1	70	25
2010–11	Rangers	23	16
2011–12	Rangers	22	14	45	30
2011–12	Everton	13	9
2012–13	Everton	37	7
2013–14	Everton	9	0	59	16
2013–14	Hull C	16	4	16	4

KOREN, Robert (M) 485 96
H: 5 10 W: 11 03 b.Ljubljana 20-9-80
Internationals: Slovenia U21, Full caps.

1999–2000	Dravograd	31	2
2000–01	Dravograd	31	9	62	11
2001–02	Publikum	31	5
2002–03	Publikum	31	0
2003–04	Publikum	15	5	78	22
2004	Lillestrom	23	1
2005	Lillestrom	26	8

2006	Lillestrom	26	10	75	19
2006–07	WBA	18	1		
2007–08	WBA	40	9		
2008–09	WBA	35	1		
2009–10	WBA	34	5	127	16
2010–11	Hull C	40	7		
2011–12	Hull C	41	10		
2012–13	Hull C	40	9		
2013–14	Hull C	22	2	143	28

LONG, Shane (F) 271 67
H: 5 10 W: 11 02 b.Co. Tipperary 22-1-87
Internationals: Republic of Ireland B, U21, Full caps.

2005	Cork C	1	0	1	0
2005–06	Reading	11	3		
2006–07	Reading	21	2		
2007–08	Reading	29	3		
2008–09	Reading	37	9		
2009–10	Reading	31	6		
2010–11	Reading	44	21		
2011–12	Reading	1	0	174	44
2011–12	WBA	32	8		
2012–13	WBA	34	8		
2013–14	WBA	15	3	81	19
2013–14	Hull C	15	4	15	4

MARGETTS, Jonathan (F) 0 0
b.Edenthorpe

| 2013–14 | Hull C | 0 | 0 | | |

McGREGOR, Allan (G) 284 0
H: 6 0 W: 11 08 b.Edinburgh 31-1-82
Internationals: Scotland U21, B, Full caps.

1998–99	Rangers	0	0		
1999–2000	Rangers	0	0		
2000–01	Rangers	0	0		
2001–02	Rangers	2	0		
2002–03	Rangers	0	0		
2003–04	Rangers	4	0		
2004–05	Rangers	2	0		
2005–06	Rangers	0	0		
2005–06	Dunfermline Ath	26	0	26	0
2006–07	Rangers	31	0		
2007–08	Rangers	31	0		
2008–09	Rangers	27	0		
2009–10	Rangers	34	0		
2010–11	Rangers	37	0		
2011–12	Rangers	37	0	205	0
2012–13	Besiktas	27	0	27	0
2013–14	Hull C	26	0	26	0

McSHANE, Paul (D) 218 10
H: 6 0 W: 11 05 b.Wicklow 6-1-86
Internationals: Republic of Ireland U21, Full caps.

2002–03	Manchester U	0	0		
2003–04	Manchester U	0	0		
2004–05	Manchester U	0	0		
2004–05	Walsall	4	1	4	1
2005–06	Manchester U	0	0		
2005–06	Brighton & HA	38	3	38	3
2006–07	WBA	32	2	32	2
2007–08	Sunderland	21	0		
2008–09	Sunderland	3	0		
2008–09	Hull C	17	1		
2009–10	Sunderland	0	0	24	0
2009–10	Hull C	27	0		
2010–11	Hull C	19	0		
2010–11	Barnsley	10	1	10	1
2011–12	Hull C	1	0		
2011–12	Crystal Palace	11	0	11	0
2012–13	Hull C	25	2		
2013–14	Hull C	10	0	99	0

MEYLER, David (M) 85 7
H: 6 3 W: 11 09 b.Cork 29-5-89
Internationals: Republic of Ireland U21, Full caps.

2008	Cork C	2	0	2	0
2008–09	Sunderland	0	0		
2009–10	Sunderland	10	0		
2010–11	Sunderland	5	0		
2011–12	Sunderland	7	0		
2012–13	Sunderland	3	0	25	0
2012–13	Hull C	28	5		
2013–14	Hull C	30	2	58	7

OXLEY, Mark (G) 43 0
H: 5 11 W: 11 05 b.Aston 2-6-90
Internationals: England U18, U20.

| 2008–09 | Hull C | 0 | 0 | | |
| 2009–10 | Hull C | 0 | 0 | | |

2009–10	Grimsby T	3	0	3	0
2010–11	Hull C	0	0		
2011–12	Hull C	0	0		
2012–13	Hull C	1	0		
2012–13	Burton Alb	3	0	3	0
2013–14	Hull C	0	0	1	0
2013–14	Oldham Ath	36	0	36	0

PROSCHWITZ, Nick (F) 106 32
H: 6 3 W: 12 11 b.Weibenfels 28-11-86

2010–11	FC Thun	31	8	31	8
2011–12	Paderborn	32	17	32	17
2012–13	Hull C	27	3		
2013–14	Hull C	2	0	29	3
2013–14	Barnsley	14	4	14	4

QUINN, Stephen (M) 294 23
H: 5 6 W: 9 08 b.Dublin 4-4-86
Internationals: Republic of Ireland U21, Full caps.

2005–06	Sheffield U	0	0		
2005–06	Milton Keynes D	15	0	15	0
2005–06	Rotherham U	16	0	16	0
2006–07	Sheffield U	15	2		
2007–08	Sheffield U	19	2		
2008–09	Sheffield U	43	7		
2009–10	Sheffield U	44	4		
2010–11	Sheffield U	37	1		
2011–12	Sheffield U	45	4		
2012–13	Sheffield U	3	0	206	20
2012–13	Hull C	42	3		
2013–14	Hull C	15	0	57	3

ROSENIOR, Liam (D) 335 4
H: 5 10 W: 11 05 b.Wandsworth 9-7-84
Internationals: England U20, U21.

2001–02	Bristol C	1	0		
2002–03	Bristol C	21	2		
2003–04	Bristol C	0	0	22	2
2003–04	Fulham	0	0		
2003–04	Torquay U	10	0	10	0
2004–05	Fulham	17	0		
2005–06	Fulham	24	0		
2006–07	Fulham	38	0		
2007–08	Fulham	0	0	79	0
2007–08	Reading	17	0		
2008–09	Reading	42	0		
2009–10	Reading	5	0		
2009–10	Ipswich T	29	1	29	1
2010–11	Reading	0	0	64	0
2010–11	Hull C	26	0		
2011–12	Hull C	44	0		
2012–13	Hull C	32	0		
2013–14	Hull C	29	1	131	1

SAGBO, Yannick (F) 146 27
H: 6 0 W: 12 03 b.Marseille 12-7-88
Internationals: Ivory Coast U23, Full caps.

2008–09	Monaco	5	0		
2009–10	Monaco	14	0		
2010–11	Monaco	1	0	20	0
2010–11	Evian TG	30	9		
2011–12	Evian TG	33	10		
2012–13	Evian TG	35	6	98	25
2013–14	Hull C	28	2	28	2

STEWART, Cameron (M) 97 4
H: 5 8 W: 11 05 b.Manchester 8-4-91
Internationals: England U17, U19, U20.

2009–10	Manchester U	0	0		
2010–11	Manchester U	0	0		
2010–11	Yeovil T	5	0	5	0
2010–11	Hull C	14	0		
2011–12	Hull C	31	1		
2012–13	Hull C	2	0		
2012–13	Burnley	9	0	9	0
2012–13	Blackburn R	7	0	7	0
2013–14	Hull C	0	0	47	1
2013–14	Charlton Ath	18	3	18	3
2013–14	Leeds U	11	0	11	0

TOWNSEND, Conor (D) 32 1
H: 5 4 W: 9 11 b.Hessle 4-3-93

2011–12	Hull C	0	0		
2012–13	Hull C	0	0		
2012–13	Chesterfield	20	1	20	1
2013–14	Hull C	0	0		
2013–14	Carlisle U	12	0	12	0

Scholars
Annan, William John; Buckle, Jake Alexander; Clackstone, Joshua Philip; Clark, Max Oliver; Dawson, Leon Stanley;

Fallowfield, Ryan Jack Glenn; McCawl, Eoghan Martin; Newman-Morton, Devonte; Penny, Alexander James Robert Kevin; Rodgers, Harvey; Rose, Jacob; Walker, Joseph Michael; Watson, Rory.

IPSWICH T (41)

ANDERSON, Paul (M) 207 24
H: 5 9 W: 10 04 b.Leicester 23-7-88
Internationals: England U19.

2005–06	Hull C	0	0		
2005–06	Liverpool	0	0		
2006–07	Liverpool	0	0		
2007–08	Liverpool	0	0		
2007–08	Swansea C	31	7	31	7
2008–09	Liverpool	0	0		
2008–09	Nottingham F	26	2		
2009–10	Nottingham F	37	4		
2010–11	Nottingham F	36	3		
2011–12	Nottingham F	17	0		
2012–13	Nottingham F	0	0	116	9
2012–13	Bristol C	29	3	29	3
2013–14	Ipswich T	31	5	31	5

BERRA, Christophe (D) 306 9
H: 6 1 W: 12 10 b.Edinburgh 31-1-85
Internationals: Scotland U21, B, Full caps.

2003–04	Hearts	6	0		
2004–05	Hearts	12	0		
2005–06	Hearts	12	1		
2006–07	Hearts	35	1		
2007–08	Hearts	35	2		
2008–09	Hearts	23	0	123	4
2008–09	Wolverhampton W	15	0		
2009–10	Wolverhampton W	32	0		
2010–11	Wolverhampton W	32	0		
2011–12	Wolverhampton W	32	0		
2012–13	Wolverhampton W	30	0	141	0
2013–14	Ipswich T	42	5	42	5

CHAMBERS, Luke (D) 419 24
H: 6 1 W: 11 13 b.Kettering 29-8-85

2002–03	Northampton T	1	0		
2003–04	Northampton T	24	0		
2004–05	Northampton T	27	0		
2005–06	Northampton T	43	0		
2006–07	Northampton T	29	1	124	1
2006–07	Nottingham F	14	0		
2007–08	Nottingham F	42	6		
2008–09	Nottingham F	39	2		
2009–10	Nottingham F	23	3		
2010–11	Nottingham F	44	6		
2011–12	Nottingham F	43	0	205	17
2012–13	Ipswich T	44	3		
2013–14	Ipswich T	46	3	90	6

CRESSWELL, Aaron (D) 202 11
H: 5 7 W: 10 05 b.Liverpool 15-12-89

2008–09	Tranmere R	13	1		
2009–10	Tranmere R	14	0		
2010–11	Tranmere R	43	4	70	5
2011–12	Ipswich T	44	1		
2012–13	Ipswich T	46	3		
2013–14	Ipswich T	42	2	132	6

CROWE, Michael (G) 0 0
b.London 13-11-95
Internationals: Wales U19.

| 2013–14 | Ipswich T | 0 | 0 | | |

DOHERTY, Jack (M) 30 5
b.Clonmel 3-8-94

2012	Waterford U	9	2		
2013	Waterford U	10	1		
2013–14	Ipswich T	0	0		
2014	Waterford U	11	2	30	5

EBANKS-BLAKE, Sylvan (F) 252 82
H: 5 10 W: 13 04 b.Cambridge 29-3-86
Internationals: England U21.

2004–05	Manchester U	0	0		
2005–06	Manchester U	0	0		
2006–07	Plymouth Arg	41	10		
2007–08	Plymouth Arg	25	11	66	21
2007–08	Wolverhampton W	20	12		
2008–09	Wolverhampton W	41	25		
2009–10	Wolverhampton W	23	2		
2010–11	Wolverhampton W	30	7		
2011–12	Wolverhampton W	23	1		
2012–13	Wolverhampton W	40	14	177	61
2013–14	Ipswich T	9	0	9	0

EDWARDS, Carlos (M) — 474 46
H: 5 8 W: 11 02 b.Port of Spain 24-10-78
Internationals: Trinidad & Tobago Full caps.

Season	Club				
2000–01	Wrexham	36	4		
2001–02	Wrexham	26	5		
2002–03	Wrexham	44	8		
2003–04	Wrexham	42	5		
2004–05	Wrexham	18	1	166	23
2005–06	Luton T	42	2		
2006–07	Luton T	26	6	68	8
2006–07	Sunderland	15	5		
2007–08	Sunderland	13	0		
2008–09	Sunderland	22	0		
2008–09	*Wolverhampton W*	6	0	6	0
2009–10	Sunderland	0	0	50	5
2009–10	Ipswich T	28	2		
2010–11	Ipswich T	45	3		
2011–12	Ipswich T	45	0		
2012–13	Ipswich T	43	3		
2013–14	Ipswich T	15	1	176	9
2013–14	*Millwall*	8	1	8	1

GERKEN, Dean (G) — 210 0
H: 6 3 W: 12 08 b.Southend 22-5-85

Season	Club				
2003–04	Colchester U	1	0		
2004–05	Colchester U	13	0		
2005–06	Colchester U	7	0		
2006–07	Colchester U	27	0		
2007–08	Colchester U	40	0		
2008–09	Colchester U	21	0	109	0
2008–09	*Darlington*	7	0	7	0
2009–10	Bristol C	39	0		
2010–11	Bristol C	1	0		
2011–12	Bristol C	10	0		
2012–13	Bristol C	3	0	53	0
2013–14	Ipswich T	41	0	41	0

HEWITT, Elliott (D) — 53 0
H: 5 11 W: 11 10 b.Rhyl 30-5-94
Internationals: Wales U17, U19.

Season	Club				
2010–11	Macclesfield T	1	0		
2011–12	Macclesfield T	21	0	22	0
2012–13	Ipswich T	7	0		
2013–14	Ipswich T	4	0	11	0
2013–14	*Gillingham*	20	0	20	0

HUNT, Steve (M) — 401 55
H: 5 9 W: 10 10 b.Port Laoise 1-8-80
Internationals: Republic of Ireland U21, B, Full caps.

Season	Club				
1999–2000	Crystal Palace	3	0		
2000–01	Crystal Palace	0	0	3	0
2001–02	Brentford	35	4		
2002–03	Brentford	42	7		
2003–04	Brentford	40	11		
2004–05	Brentford	19	3	136	25
2005–06	Reading	38	2		
2006–07	Reading	35	4		
2007–08	Reading	37	5		
2008–09	Reading	46	6		
2009–10	Reading	0	0	156	17
2009–10	*Hull C*	27	6	27	6
2010–11	Wolverhampton W	20	3		
2011–12	Wolverhampton W	24	3		
2012–13	Wolverhampton W	12	1	56	7
2013–14	Ipswich T	23	0	23	0

HYAM, Luke (M) — 83 2
H: 5 10 W: 11 05 b.Ipswich 24-10-91

Season	Club				
2010–11	Ipswich T	10	0		
2011–12	Ipswich T	8	0		
2012–13	Ipswich T	30	1		
2013–14	Ipswich T	35	1	83	2

LAWRENCE, Byron (M) — 1 0
H: 5 7 W: 10 03 b.Cambridge 12-3-96

Season	Club				
2011–12	Ipswich T	1	0		
2012–13	Ipswich T	0	0		
2013–14	Ipswich T	0	0	1	0

LOACH, Scott (G) — 204 0
H: 6 1 W: 13 01 b.Nottingham 27-5-88
Internationals: England U21.

Season	Club				
2006–07	Watford	0	0		
2007–08	Watford	0	0		
2007–08	*Morecambe*	2	0	2	0
2007–08	*Bradford C*	20	0	20	0
2008–09	Watford	31	0		
2009–10	Watford	46	0		
2010–11	Watford	46	0		
2011–12	Watford	31	0	154	0
2012–13	Ipswich T	22	0		
2013–14	Ipswich T	6	0	28	0

MARRIOTT, Jack (F) — 3 0
H: 5 8 W: 11 03 b.Beverley 9-9-94

Season	Club				
2012–13	Ipswich T	1	0		
2013–14	Ipswich T	1	0	2	0
2013–14	*Gillingham*	1	0	1	0

McGOLDRICK, David (F) — 236 63
H: 6 1 W: 11 10 b.Nottingham 29-11-87

Season	Club				
2003–04	Notts Co	4	0		
2004–05	Notts Co	0	0		
2005–06	Southampton	1	0		
2005–06	*Notts Co*	6	0	10	0
2006–07	Southampton	9	0		
2006–07	*Bournemouth*	12	6	12	6
2007–08	Southampton	8	0		
2007–08	*Port Vale*	17	2	17	2
2008–09	Southampton	46	12	64	12
2009–10	Nottingham F	33	3		
2010–11	Nottingham F	21	5		
2011–12	Nottingham F	9	0		
2011–12	*Sheffield W*	4	1	4	1
2012–13	Nottingham F	0	0	63	8
2012–13	*Coventry C*	22	16	22	16
2012–13	Ipswich T	13	4		
2013–14	Ipswich T	31	14	44	18

MINGS, Tyrone (D) — 17 0
H: 6 3 W: 12 00 b.Bath 19-3-93

Season	Club				
2012–13	Ipswich T	1	0		
2013–14	Ipswich T	16	0	17	0

MURPHY, Daryl (F) — 268 47
H: 6 2 W: 13 12 b.Waterford 15-3-83
Internationals: Republic of Ireland U21, Full caps.

Season	Club				
2000–01	Luton T	0	0		
2001–02	Luton T	0	0		
2005–06	Sunderland	18	1		
2005–06	*Sheffield W*	4	0	4	0
2006–07	Sunderland	38	10		
2007–08	Sunderland	28	3		
2008–09	Sunderland	23	0		
2009–10	Sunderland	3	0	110	14
2009–10	*Ipswich T*	18	6		
2010–11	Celtic	18	3		
2011–12	*Ipswich T*	33	4		
2012–13	Celtic	14	0	19	3

On loan from Celtic

Season	Club				
2012–13	Ipswich T	39	7		
2013–14	Ipswich T	45	13	135	30

NOUBLE, Frank (F) — 119 12
H: 6 3 W: 12 08 b.Lewisham 24-9-91
Internationals: England U17, U19.

Season	Club				
2009–10	West Ham U	8	0		
2009–10	*WBA*	3	0	3	0
2009–10	*Swindon T*	8	0	8	0
2010–11	West Ham U	2	0		
2010–11	*Swansea C*	6	1	6	1
2010–11	*Barnsley*	4	0		
2010–11	*Charlton Ath*	9	1	9	1
2011–12	West Ham U	3	1	13	1
2011–12	*Gillingham*	13	5	13	5
2011–12	*Barnsley*	6	0	10	0
2012–13	*Wolverhampton W*	2	0	2	0
2012–13	Ipswich T	17	2		
2013–14	Ipswich T	38	2	55	4

SKUSE, Cole (M) — 322 9
H: 6 1 W: 11 05 b.Bristol 29-3-86

Season	Club				
2004–05	Bristol C	7	0		
2005–06	Bristol C	38	2		
2006–07	Bristol C	42	0		
2007–08	Bristol C	25	0		
2008–09	Bristol C	33	2		
2009–10	Bristol C	43	2		
2010–11	Bristol C	30	1		
2011–12	Bristol C	36	2		
2012–13	Bristol C	25	0	279	9
2013–14	Ipswich T	43	0	43	0

SMITH, Tommy (D) — 161 15
H: 6 2 W: 12 02 b.Macclesfield 31-3-90
Internationals: England U17, U18. New Zealand Full caps.

Season	Club				
2007–08	Ipswich T	0	0		
2008–09	Ipswich T	2	0		
2009–10	Ipswich T	14	0		
2009–10	*Brentford*	8	0	8	0
2010–11	Ipswich T	22	3		
2010–11	*Colchester U*	6	0	6	0
2011–12	Ipswich T	26	3		
2012–13	Ipswich T	38	3		
2013–14	Ipswich T	45	6	147	15

TABB, Jay (M) — 348 33
H: 5 7 W: 10 00 b.Tooting 21-2-84
Internationals: Republic of Ireland U21.

Season	Club				
2000–01	Brentford	2	0		
2001–02	Brentford	3	0		
2002–03	Brentford	5	0		
2003–04	Brentford	36	9		
2004–05	Brentford	40	5		
2005–06	Brentford	42	6	128	20
2006–07	Coventry C	31	3		
2007–08	Coventry C	42	5		
2008–09	Coventry C	22	3	95	11
2008–09	Reading	9	0		
2009–10	Reading	28	0		
2010–11	Reading	21	0		
2011–12	Reading	19	0		
2012–13	Reading	12	0	89	0
2012–13	*Ipswich T*	9	1		
2013–14	Ipswich T	27	1	36	2

TAYLOR, Paul (F) — 88 13
H: 5 11 W: 11 02 b.Liverpool 4-11-87

Season	Club				
2008–09	Chester C	9	0	9	0
2009–10	Montegnee	1	0	1	0
2009–10	Charleoi	3	0	3	0
2010–11	Anderlecht	0	0		
2010–11	Peterborough U	1	0		
2011–12	Peterborough U	44	12		
2012–13	Peterborough U	3	0		
2012–13	*Ipswich T*	3	0		
2013–14	*Ipswich T*	18	1	21	1
2013–14	Peterborough U	6	0	54	12

VESELI, Frederic (D) — 18 0
H: 6 0 W: 12 08 b.Kosovo 20-11-92
Internationals: Switzerland U15, U16, U17, U18, U19, U20, U21.

Season	Club				
2009–10	Manchester C	0	0		
2010–11	Manchester C	0	0		
2011–12	Manchester C	0	0		
2011–12	Manchester U	0	0		
2012–13	Manchester U	0	0		
2013–14	Ipswich T	0	0		
2013–14	*Bury*	18	0	18	0

WORDSWORTH, Anthony (M) — 194 37
H: 6 1 W: 12 00 b.Camden 3-1-89

Season	Club				
2007–08	Colchester U	3	0		
2008–09	Colchester U	30	3		
2009–10	Colchester U	41	11		
2010–11	Colchester U	35	5		
2011–12	Colchester U	44	13		
2012–13	Colchester U	24	3	177	35
2013–14	*Ipswich T*	7	1		
2013–14	Ipswich T	10	1	17	2

Scholars
Berkane, Amir; Bishop, Edward James; Clarke, Matthew Edward Barkell; Ellis, Edward William Colin; Emmanuel, Joshua Oluwadurotimi; Galvin, Cory; Hammond, Kyle James; Marsden, Jacob Anthony; McDermid, Samuel David; McLoughlin, Shane Daniel; Ramadan, Cemal; Robinson, Joe Alan; Smith, Jonathan William Robert; Sowunmi, Omar Kolawole Olufemi; Thompson, Rory Peter Francis; Walton-Owen, Amon Jesse Enos; Willbye, Jack Thomas; Winter, Thomas James.

Non Contract
Lee, Alan Desmond.

LEEDS U (42)

ARIYIBI, Gboly (M) — 4 0

Season	Club				
2013–14	Leeds U	2	0	2	0
2013–14	*Tranmere R*	2	0	2	0

AUSTIN, Rodolph (M) — 161 20
H: 6 0 W: 12 03 b.Clarendon 1-6-85
Internationals: Jamaica Full caps.

Season	Club				
2008–09	SK Brann	19	2		
2009–10	SK Brann	20	2		
2010–11	SK Brann	22	1		
2011–12	SK Brann	29	10	90	15

Season	Club				
2012–13	Leeds U	31	2		
2013–14	Leeds U	40	3	71	5

BROWN, Michael (M) 510 38
H: 5 9 W: 12 04 b.Hartlepool 25-1-77
Internationals: England U21.

Season	Club				
1994–95	Manchester C	0	0		
1995–96	Manchester C	21	0		
1996–97	Manchester C	11	0		
1996–97	*Hartlepool U*	6	1	6	1
1997–98	Manchester C	26	0		
1998–99	Manchester C	31	2		
1999–2000	Manchester C	0	0	89	2
1999–2000	Portsmouth	4	0		
1999–2000	Sheffield U	24	3		
2000–01	Sheffield U	36	1		
2001–02	Sheffield U	36	5		
2002–03	Sheffield U	40	16		
2003–04	Sheffield U	15	2	151	27
2003–04	Tottenham H	17	1		
2004–05	Tottenham H	24	1		
2005–06	Tottenham H	9	0	50	2
2005–06	Fulham	7	0		
2006–07	Fulham	34	0	41	0
2007–08	Wigan Ath	31	0		
2008–09	Wigan Ath	25	0		
2009–10	Wigan Ath	2	0	58	0
2009–10	Portsmouth	24	2		
2010–11	Portsmouth	21	2	49	4
2011–12	Leeds U	24	1		
2012–13	Leeds U	24	1		
2013–14	Leeds U	18	0	66	2

BYRAM, Samuel (M) 69 3
H: 5 11 W: 11 04 b.Thurrock 16-9-93

Season	Club				
2012–13	Leeds U	44	3		
2013–14	Leeds U	25	0	69	3

CAIRNS, Alex (G) 1 0
H: 6 0 W: 11 05 b.Doncaster 4-1-93

Season	Club				
2011–12	Leeds U	1	0		
2012–13	Leeds U	0	0		
2013–14	Leeds U	0	0	1	0

COKER, Afolabi (D) 0 0
b. 3-9-95

Season	Club				
2013–14	Leeds U	0	0		

DAWSON, Chris (M) 1 0
b.Dewsbury 2-9-94
Internationals: Wales U21.

Season	Club				
2012–13	Leeds U	1	0		
2013–14	Leeds U	0	0	1	0

DIOUF, El Hadji (F) 419 59
H: 5 11 W: 11 11 b.Dakar 15-1-81
Internationals: Senegal Full caps.

Season	Club				
1998–99	Sochaux	15	0	15	0
1999–2000	Rennes	28	1	28	1
2000–01	Lens	28	8		
2001–02	Lens	26	10	54	18
2002–03	Liverpool	29	3		
2003–04	Liverpool	26	0		
2004–05	Liverpool	0	0	55	3
2004–05	Bolton W	27	9		
2005–06	Bolton W	20	3		
2006–07	Bolton W	33	5		
2007–08	Bolton W	34	4	114	21
2008–09	Sunderland	14	0	14	0
2008–09	Blackburn R	14	1		
2009–10	Blackburn R	26	3		
2010–11	Blackburn R	20	0		
2010–11	*Rangers*	15	1	15	1
2011–12	Blackburn R	0	0	60	4
2011–12	Doncaster R	22	6		
2012–13	Doncaster R	0	0	22	6
2012–13	Leeds U	36	5		
2013–14	Leeds U	6	0	42	5

DRURY, Adam (D) 499 6
H: 5 10 W: 11 09 b.Cambridge 29-8-78

Season	Club				
1995–96	Peterborough U	1	0		
1996–97	Peterborough U	5	1		
1997–98	Peterborough U	31	0		
1998–99	Peterborough U	40	0		
1999–2000	Peterborough U	42	1		
2000–01	Peterborough U	29	0	148	2
2000–01	Norwich C	6	0		
2001–02	Norwich C	35	0		
2002–03	Norwich C	45	2		
2003–04	Norwich C	42	0		
2004–05	Norwich C	33	1		
2005–06	Norwich C	39	0		
2006–07	Norwich C	39	0		
2007–08	Norwich C	9	0		
2008–09	Norwich C	11	0		
2009–10	Norwich C	35	0		
2010–11	Norwich C	20	1		
2011–12	Norwich C	12	0	326	4
2012–13	Leeds U	12	0		
2013–14	Leeds U	1	0	13	0
2013–14	*Bradford C*	12	0	12	0

GREEN, Paul (M) 378 39
H: 5 9 W: 10 02 b.Pontefract 10-4-83
Internationals: Republic of Ireland Full caps.

Season	Club				
2003–04	Doncaster R	43	8		
2004–05	Doncaster R	42	7		
2005–06	Doncaster R	34	3		
2006–07	Doncaster R	41	2		
2007–08	Doncaster R	38	5	198	25
2008–09	Derby Co	29	3		
2009–10	Derby Co	33	2		
2010–11	Derby Co	36	2		
2011–12	Derby Co	27	1	125	8
2012–13	Leeds U	32	4		
2013–14	Leeds U	9	0	41	4
2013–14	*Ipswich T*	14	2	14	2

GRIMES, Eric (G) 0 0
b. 4-2-94
Internationals: Republic of Ireland U17 U19.

Season	Club				
2013–14	Leeds U	0	0		

HUNT, Noel (F) 308 64
H: 5 8 W: 11 05 b.Waterford 26-12-82
Internationals: Republic of Ireland U21, B, Full caps.

Season	Club				
2002–03	Dunfermline Ath	12	1		
2003–04	Dunfermline Ath	13	2		
2004–05	Dunfermline Ath	23	1		
2005–06	Dunfermline Ath	32	4	80	8
2006–07	Dundee U	28	10		
2007–08	Dundee U	36	13	64	23
2008–09	Reading	37	11		
2009–10	Reading	10	2		
2010–11	Reading	33	10		
2011–12	Reading	41	8		
2012–13	Reading	24	2	145	33
2013–14	Leeds U	19	0	19	0

KENNY, Paddy (G) 564 0
H: 6 1 W: 14 01 b.Halifax 17-5-78
Internationals: Republic of Ireland Full caps.

Season	Club				
1998–99	Bury	0	0		
1999–2000	Bury	46	0		
2000–01	Bury	46	0		
2001–02	Bury	41	0		
2002–03	Bury	0	0	133	0
2002–03	Sheffield U	45	0		
2003–04	Sheffield U	27	0		
2004–05	Sheffield U	40	0		
2005–06	Sheffield U	46	0		
2006–07	Sheffield U	34	0		
2007–08	Sheffield U	40	0		
2008–09	Sheffield U	44	0		
2009–10	Sheffield U	2	0	278	0
2010–11	QPR	44	0		
2011–12	QPR	33	0	77	0
2012–13	Leeds U	46	0		
2013–14	Leeds U	30	0	76	0

KILLOCK, Ross (D) 0 0
b. 12-7-94

Season	Club				
2012–13	Leeds U	0	0		
2013–14	Leeds U	0	0		

LEES, Tom (D) 207 7
H: 6 1 W: 12 04 b.Warwick 28-11-90
Internationals: England U21.

Season	Club				
2008–09	Leeds U	0	0		
2009–10	Leeds U	0	0		
2009–10	*Accrington S*	39	0	39	0
2010–11	Leeds U	0	0		
2010–11	*Bury*	45	4	45	4
2011–12	Leeds U	42	3		
2012–13	Leeds U	40	1		
2013–14	Leeds U	41	0	123	3

McCORMACK, Ross (F) 296 95
H: 5 9 W: 11 00 b.Glasgow 18-8-86
Internationals: Scotland U21, B, Full caps.

Season	Club				
2003–04	Rangers	2	1		
2004–05	Rangers	1	0		
2005–06	Rangers	8	1	11	2
2005–06	Doncaster R	19	4	19	4
2006–07	Motherwell	12	2		
2007–08	Motherwell	36	9	48	11
2008–09	Cardiff C	38	21		
2009–10	Cardiff C	34	4		
2010–11	Cardiff C	2	0	74	25
2010–11	Leeds U	21	2		
2011–12	Leeds U	45	18		
2012–13	Leeds U	32	5		
2013–14	Leeds U	46	28	144	53

MORISON, Steven (F) 215 59
H: 6 2 W: 13 07 b.Enfield 29-8-83
Internationals: England C. Wales Full caps.

Season	Club				
2001–02	Northampton T	1	0		
2002–03	Northampton T	13	1		
2003–04	Northampton T	5	1		
2004–05	Northampton T	4	1	23	3
From Stevenage B.					
2008–09	Millwall	0	0		
2009–10	Millwall	43	20		
2010–11	Millwall	40	15		
2011–12	Norwich C	34	9		
2012–13	Norwich C	19	1	53	10
2012–13	Leeds U	15	3		
2013–14	Leeds U	0	0	15	3
2013–14	*Millwall*	41	8	124	43

MOWATT, Alex (D) 29 1
b. 13-2-95
Internationals: England U19.

Season	Club				
2013–14	Leeds U	29	1	29	1

MURPHY, Luke (M) 198 24
H: 6 1 W: 11 05 b.Alsager 21-10-89

Season	Club				
2008–09	Crewe Alex	9	1		
2009–10	Crewe Alex	32	3		
2010–11	Crewe Alex	39	3		
2011–12	Crewe Alex	42	8		
2012–13	Crewe Alex	39	6	161	21
2013–14	Leeds U	37	3	37	3

NORRIS, David (M) 408 52
H: 5 7 W: 11 06 b.Stamford 22-2-81

Season	Club				
1999–2000	Bolton W	0	0		
2000–01	Bolton W	0	0		
2001–02	Bolton W	0	0		
2001–02	*Hull C*	6	1	6	1
2002–03	Bolton W	0	0		
2002–03	Plymouth Arg	33	6		
2003–04	Plymouth Arg	45	5		
2004–05	Plymouth Arg	35	3		
2005–06	Plymouth Arg	45	2		
2006–07	Plymouth Arg	41	6		
2007–08	Plymouth Arg	27	5	226	27
2007–08	Ipswich T	9	1		
2008–09	Ipswich T	37	3		
2009–10	Ipswich T	24	1		
2010–11	Ipswich T	36	8	106	13
2011–12	Portsmouth	40	8	40	8
2012–13	Leeds U	30	3		
2013–14	Leeds U	0	0	30	3

PARKIN, Luke (F) 0 0
b. 15-8-95

Season	Club				
2013–14	Leeds U	0	0		

PEARCE, Jason (D) 283 11
H: 5 11 W: 12 00 b.Hillingdon 6-12-87

Season	Club				
2006–07	Portsmouth	0	0		
2007–08	Bournemouth	33	1		
2008–09	Bournemouth	44	2		
2009–10	Bournemouth	39	1		
2010–11	Bournemouth	46	3	162	7
2011–12	Portsmouth	43	2	43	2
2011–12	Leeds U	0	0		
2012–13	Leeds U	33	0		
2013–14	Leeds U	45	2	78	2

PELTIER, Lee (D) 269 5
H: 5 10 W: 12 00 b.Liverpool 11-12-86
Internationals: England U18.

Season	Club				
2004–05	Liverpool	0	0		
2005–06	Liverpool	0	0		
2006–07	Liverpool	0	0		
2006–07	*Hull C*	7	0	7	0
2007–08	Liverpool	0	0		
2007–08	Yeovil T	34	0		
2008–09	Yeovil T	35	1	69	1
2009–10	Huddersfield T	42	0		
2010–11	Huddersfield T	38	1	80	1
2011–12	Leicester C	40	2		
2012–13	Leicester C	0	0	40	2
2012–13	Leeds U	41	0		

Season	Club	App	Gls	Tot App	Tot Gls
2013–14	Leeds U	25	1	66	1
2013–14	*Nottingham F*	7	0	7	0

POLEON, Dominic (F) 39 5
H: 6 3 W: 12 13 b.Newham 7-9-93

Season	Club	App	Gls	Tot App	Tot Gls
2012–13	Leeds U	6	2		
2012–13	*Bury*	7	2	7	2
2012–13	*Sheffield U*	7	0	7	0
2013–14	Leeds U	19	1	25	3

PUGH, Danny (M) 249 15
H: 6 0 W: 12 10 b.Cheadle Hulme 19-10-82

Season	Club	App	Gls	Tot App	Tot Gls
2000–01	Manchester U	0	0		
2001–02	Manchester U	0	0		
2002–03	Manchester U	1	0		
2003–04	Manchester U	0	0	1	0
2004–05	Leeds U	38	5		
2005–06	Leeds U	12	0		
2006–07	Preston NE	45	4		
2007–08	Preston NE	7	0		
2007–08	Stoke C	30	0		
2008–09	Stoke C	17	0		
2009–10	Stoke C	7	1		
2010–11	Stoke C	10	0		
2010–11	*Preston NE*	5	0	57	4
2011–12	Stoke C	3	0	67	1
2011–12	Leeds U	34	2		
2012–13	Leeds U	4	0		
2012–13	*Sheffield W*	16	1	16	1
2013–14	Leeds U	20	2	108	9

SMITH, Matt (F) 109 22
H: 6 6 W: 14 00 b.Birmingham 7-6-89

Season	Club	App	Gls	Tot App	Tot Gls
2011–12	Oldham Ath	28	3		
2011–12	*Macclesfield T*	8	1	8	1
2012–13	Oldham Ath	34	6	62	9
2013–14	Leeds U	39	12	39	12

STOKES, Eoghan (F) 0 0
b. 22-11-95
Internationals: Republic of Ireland U17.

Season	Club	App	Gls	Tot App	Tot Gls
2013–14	Leeds U	0	0		

TAYLOR, Charlie (D) 48 0
H: 5 9 W: 11 00 b.York 18-9-93
Internationals: England U19.

Season	Club	App	Gls	Tot App	Tot Gls
2011–12	Leeds U	2	0		
2011–12	*Bradford C*	3	0	3	0
2012–13	Leeds U	0	0		
2012–13	*York C*	4	0	4	0
2012–13	*Inverness CT*	7	0	7	0
2013–14	Leeds U	0	0	2	0
2013–14	*Fleetwood T*	32	0	32	0

TONGE, Michael (M) 372 28
H: 6 0 W: 11 10 b.Manchester 7-4-83
Internationals: England U20, U21.

Season	Club	App	Gls	Tot App	Tot Gls
2000–01	Sheffield U	2	0		
2001–02	Sheffield U	30	3		
2002–03	Sheffield U	44	6		
2003–04	Sheffield U	46	4		
2004–05	Sheffield U	34	2		
2005–06	Sheffield U	30	3		
2006–07	Sheffield U	27	2		
2007–08	Sheffield U	45	1		
2008–09	Sheffield U	4	0	262	21
2008–09	Stoke C	10	0		
2009–10	Stoke C	0	0		
2009–10	*Preston NE*	7	0		
2009–10	*Derby Co*	18	2	18	2
2010–11	Stoke C	2	0		
2010–11	*Preston NE*	5	1	12	1
2011–12	Stoke C	0	0		
2011–12	*Barnsley*	10	0	10	0
2012–13	Stoke C	0	0	12	0
2012–13	Leeds U	35	4		
2013–14	Leeds U	23	0	58	4

VARNEY, Luke (F) 324 66
H: 5 11 W: 11 00 b.Leicester 28-9-82

Season	Club	App	Gls	Tot App	Tot Gls
2002–03	Crewe Alex	0	0		
2003–04	Crewe Alex	8	1		
2004–05	Crewe Alex	26	4		
2005–06	Crewe Alex	27	5		
2006–07	Crewe Alex	34	17	95	27
2007–08	Charlton Ath	39	8		
2008–09	Charlton Ath	18	2	57	10
2008–09	*Sheffield W*	4	2		
2008–09	Derby Co	10	1		
2009–10	Derby Co	0	0		
2009–10	*Sheffield W*	39	9	43	11
2010–11	Derby Co	1	0	12	1
2010–11	Blackpool	30	5	30	5
2011–12	Portsmouth	30	6	30	6
2012–13	Leeds U	34	4		
2013–14	Leeds U	11	2	45	6
2013–14	*Blackburn R*	12	0	12	0

WALTERS, Lewis (F) 0 0
b. 28-3-95

Season	Club	App	Gls	Tot App	Tot Gls
2013–14	Leeds U	0	0		

WARNOCK, Stephen (D) 326 14
H: 5 7 W: 11 09 b.Ormskirk 12-12-81
Internationals: England Full caps.

Season	Club	App	Gls	Tot App	Tot Gls
1998–99	Liverpool	0	0		
1999–2000	Liverpool	0	0		
2000–01	Liverpool	0	0		
2001–02	Liverpool	0	0		
2002–03	Liverpool	0	0		
2002–03	*Bradford C*	12	1	12	1
2003–04	Liverpool	0	0		
2003–04	*Coventry C*	44	3	44	3
2004–05	Liverpool	19	0		
2005–06	Liverpool	20	1		
2006–07	Liverpool	0	0	40	1
2006–07	Blackburn R	13	1		
2007–08	Blackburn R	37	1		
2008–09	Blackburn R	37	3		
2009–10	Blackburn R	1	0	88	5
2009–10	Aston Villa	30	0		
2010–11	Aston Villa	19	0		
2011–12	Aston Villa	35	2		
2012–13	Aston Villa	0	0	84	2
2012–13	*Bolton W*	15	0	15	0
2012–13	Leeds U	16	1		
2013–14	Leeds U	27	1	43	2

WHITE, Aidan (D) 116 5
H: 5 7 W: 10 00 b.Otley 10-10-91
Internationals: England U19. Republic of Ireland U21.

Season	Club	App	Gls	Tot App	Tot Gls
2008–09	Leeds U	5	0		
2009–10	Leeds U	8	0		
2010–11	Leeds U	2	0		
2010–11	*Oldham Ath*	24	4	24	4
2011–12	Leeds U	36	0		
2012–13	Leeds U	24	1		
2013–14	Leeds U	9	0	84	1
2013–14	*Sheffield U*	8	0	8	0

WOOTTON, Scott (D) 53 2
H: 6 2 W: 13 00 b.Birkenhead 12-9-91
Internationals: England U17.

Season	Club	App	Gls	Tot App	Tot Gls
2009–10	Manchester U	0	0		
2010–11	Manchester U	0	0		
2010–11	*Tranmere R*	7	1	7	1
2011–12	Manchester U	0	0		
2011–12	*Peterborough U*	11	0		
2011–12	*Nottingham F*	13	0	13	0
2012–13	Manchester U	0	0		
2012–13	*Peterborough U*	2	1	13	1
2013–14	Manchester U	0	0		
2013–14	Leeds U	20	0	20	0

ZALIUKAS, Marius (D) 236 13
H: 6 3 W: 13 02 b. 10-11-83
Internationals: Lithuania U21, Full caps.

Season	Club	App	Gls	Tot App	Tot Gls
2004–05	FBK Kaunas	21	2		
2006–07	FBK Kaunas	8	0	29	2
2006–07	Hearts	27	2		
2007–08	Hearts	26	1		
2008–09	Hearts	28	2		
2009–10	Hearts	22	2		
2010–11	Hearts	28	1		
2011–12	Hearts	36	1		
2012–13	Hearts	25	2	192	11
2013–14	Leeds U	15	0	15	0

Scholars
Amiri, Ali; Assenso, Isaac Kofi Boateng; Atkinson, Daniel Joseph; Bennett, Liam Christopher; Berry, Lewie Jacob; Booker, Luke Thomas; Coyle, Lewie Jacob; Crouz Chydrick, Piteu Munyaradzi; Denton, Tyler Jake; Dixon, Bradley John; Lyman, Thomas Ian; Mbanje, Munyaradzi; Molloy, Ian Patrick; Mulhern, Euan Francis Peter; Peacock-Farrell, Bailey; Phillips, Kalvin Mark; Purver, Alex William; Roper, Corey Lee Russell; Skelton, Jake Daniel.

LEICESTER C (43)

BAKAYOGO, Zaoumana (D) 144 5
H: 5 9 W: 10 08 b.Paris 11-8-86
Internationals: Ivory Coast U23.

Season	Club	App	Gls	Tot App	Tot Gls
2006–07	Millwall	5	0		
2007–08	Millwall	10	0	15	0

From Alfortville.

Season	Club	App	Gls	Tot App	Tot Gls
2009–10	Tranmere R	29	0		
2010–11	Tranmere R	27	1		
2011–12	Tranmere R	26	0		
2012–13	Tranmere R	46	4	128	5
2013–14	Leicester C	0	0		
2013–14	*Yeovil T*	1	0	1	0

BARRINGTON, Marcel (F) 0 0
b.London 28-8-95

Season	Club	App	Gls	Tot App	Tot Gls
2013–14	Stoke C	0	0		
2013–14	Leicester C	0	0		

BLYTH, Jacob (F) 17 3
b.Nuneaton 14-8-92

Season	Club	App	Gls	Tot App	Tot Gls
2012–13	Leicester C	0	0		
2012–13	*Burton Alb*	2	0	2	0
2012–13	*Notts Co*	4	0	4	0
2013–14	Leicester C	0	0		
2013–14	*Northampton T*	11	3	11	3

CAIN, Michael (M) 2 0
b. 4-12-94

Season	Club	App	Gls	Tot App	Tot Gls
2011–12	Leicester C	0	0		
2012–13	Leicester C	0	0		
2013–14	Leicester C	0	0		
2013–14	*Mansfield T*	2	0	2	0

DAWSON, Adam (M) 0 0
H: 5 9 W: 12 02 b.Bury 5-10-92

Season	Club	App	Gls	Tot App	Tot Gls
2011–12	Wigan Ath	0	0		
2012–13	Wigan Ath	0	0		
2012–13	*Accrington S*	0	0		
2013–14	Leicester C	0	0		

DE LAET, Ritchie (D) 119 4
H: 6 1 W: 12 02 b.Antwerp 28-11-88
Internationals: Belgium U21, Full caps.

Season	Club	App	Gls	Tot App	Tot Gls
2007–08	Stoke C	0	0		
2008–09	Stoke C	0	0		
2008–09	Manchester U	1	0		
2009–10	Manchester U	2	0		
2010–11	Manchester U	0	0		
2010–11	*Sheffield U*	6	0	6	0
2010–11	*Preston NE*	5	0	5	0
2010–11	*Portsmouth*	22	0	22	0
2011–12	Manchester U	0	0	3	0
2011–12	*Norwich C*	6	1	6	1
2012–13	Leicester C	41	1		
2013–14	Leicester C	36	2	77	3

DODOO, Joseph (F) 0 0
Internationals: England U18.

Season	Club	App	Gls	Tot App	Tot Gls
2013–14	Leicester C	0	0		

DRINKWATER, Daniel (M) 177 13
H: 5 10 W: 11 00 b.Manchester 5-3-90
Internationals: England U18, U19.

Season	Club	App	Gls	Tot App	Tot Gls
2008–09	Manchester U	0	0		
2009–10	Manchester U	0	0		
2009–10	*Huddersfield T*	33	2	33	2
2010–11	Manchester U	0	0		
2010–11	*Cardiff C*	9	0	9	0
2010–11	*Watford*	12	0	12	0
2011–12	Manchester U	0	0		
2011–12	*Barnsley*	17	1	17	1
2011–12	Leicester C	19	2		
2012–13	Leicester C	42	1		
2013–14	Leicester C	45	7	106	10

DYER, Lloyd (M) 371 49
H: 5 8 W: 10 03 b.Birmingham 13-9-82

Season	Club	App	Gls	Tot App	Tot Gls
2001–02	WBA	0	0		
2002–03	WBA	0	0		
2003–04	WBA	17	2		
2003–04	*Kidderminster H*	7	1	7	1
2004–05	WBA	4	0		
2004–05	*Coventry C*	6	0	6	0
2005–06	WBA	0	0	21	2
2005–06	*QPR*	15	0	15	0
2005–06	*Millwall*	6	0	6	0
2006–07	Milton Keynes D	41	5		
2007–08	Milton Keynes D	45	11	86	16
2008–09	Leicester C	44	10		
2009–10	Leicester C	33	3		

2010–11	Leicester C	35	3		
2011–12	Leicester C	36	4		
2012–13	Leicester C	42	3		
2013–14	Leicester C	40	7	230	30

ELDER, Callum (D) 0 0
b. 27-1-95
Internationals: Australia U20.

2013–14	Leicester C	0	0		

FUTACS, Marko (F) 112 23
H: 6 5 W: 14 00 b.Budapest 22-2-90
Internationals: Hungary UK18, U20, U21, Full caps.

2008–09	Nancy B	12	3	12	3
2009–10	Werder Bremen II	13	3	13	3
2010–11	Ingolstadt	23	2	23	2
2011–12	Portsmouth	29	5	29	5
2012–13	Leicester C	9	1		
2012–13	*Blackpool*	4	0	4	0
2013–14	Leicester C	0	0	9	1
2013–14	*Diosgyor*	22	9	22	9

GALLAGHER, Paul (F) 316 63
H: 6 1 W: 11 00 b.Glasgow 9-8-84
Internationals: Scotland U21, B, Full caps.

2002–03	Blackburn R	1	0		
2003–04	Blackburn R	26	3		
2004–05	Blackburn R	16	2		
2005–06	Blackburn R	1	0		
2005–06	*Stoke C*	37	11		
2006–07	Blackburn R	16	1		
2007–08	Blackburn R	0	0		
2007–08	*Preston NE*	19	1		
2007–08	*Stoke C*	7	0	44	11
2008–09	Blackburn R	0	0		
2008–09	*Plymouth Arg*	40	13	40	13
2009–10	Blackburn R	1	0	61	6
2009–10	Leicester C	41	7		
2010–11	Leicester C	41	10		
2011–12	Leicester C	28	8		
2012–13	Leicester C	8	0		
2012–13	*Sheffield U*	6	1	6	1
2013–14	Leicester C	0	0	118	25
2013–14	*Preston NE*	28	6	47	7

HOPPER, Tom (F) 22 3
H: 6 1 W: 12 00 b.Boston 14-12-93
Internationals: England Youth.

2011–12	Leicester C	0	0		
2012–13	Leicester C	0	0		
2012–13	*Bury*	22	3	22	3
2013–14	Leicester C	0	0		

JAMES, Matthew (M) 87 6
H: 6 0 W: 11 12 b.Bacup 22-7-91
Internationals: England U16, U17, U19, U20.

2007–08	Manchester U	0	0		
2008–09	Manchester U	0	0		
2009–10	Manchester U	0	0		
2009–10	*Preston NE*	18	2		
2010–11	Manchester U	0	0		
2010–11	*Preston NE*	10	0	28	2
2011–12	Manchester U	0	0		
2012–13	Leicester C	24	3		
2013–14	Leicester C	35	1	59	4

KING, Andy (M) 246 49
H: 6 0 W: 11 10 b.Barnstaple 29-10-88
Internationals: Wales U19, U21, Full caps.

2007–08	Leicester C	11	1		
2008–09	Leicester C	45	9		
2009–10	Leicester C	43	9		
2010–11	Leicester C	45	15		
2011–12	Leicester C	30	4		
2012–13	Leicester C	42	7		
2013–14	Leicester C	30	4	246	49

KNOCKAERT, Anthony (M) 118 23
H: 5 8 W: 10 11 b.Lille 20-11-91
Internationals: France U20, U21.

2011–12	Guingamp	34	10	34	10
2012–13	Leicester C	42	8		
2013–14	Leicester C	42	5	84	13

KONCHESKY, Paul (D) 459 13
H: 5 10 W: 11 07 b.Barking 15-5-81
Internationals: England U18, U20, U21, Full caps.

1997–98	Charlton Ath	3	0		
1998–99	Charlton Ath	2	0		
1999–2000	Charlton Ath	8	0		
2000–01	Charlton Ath	23	0		
2001–02	Charlton Ath	34	1		
2002–03	Charlton Ath	30	3		
2003–04	Charlton Ath	21	0		
2003–04	*Tottenham H*	12	0	12	0
2004–05	Charlton Ath	28	1	149	5
2005–06	West Ham U	37	1		
2006–07	West Ham U	22	0	59	1
2007–08	Fulham	33	0		
2008–09	Fulham	36	1		
2009–10	Fulham	27	1		
2010–11	Fulham	1	0	97	2
2010–11	Liverpool	15	0	15	0
2010–11	*Nottingham F*	15	1	15	1
2011–12	Leicester C	42	2		
2012–13	Leicester C	39	1		
2013–14	Leicester C	31	1	112	4

LOGAN, Conrad (G) 134 0
H: 6 2 W: 14 00 b.Letterkenny 18-4-86
Internationals: Republic of Ireland U16, U17, U18, U19.

2003–04	Leicester C	0	0		
2004–05	Leicester C	0	0		
2005–06	Leicester C	0	0		
2005–06	*Boston U*	13	0	13	0
2006–07	Leicester C	18	0		
2007–08	Leicester C	0	0		
2007–08	*Stockport Co*	34	0		
2008–09	Leicester C	0	0		
2008–09	*Luton T*	22	0	22	0
2008–09	*Stockport Co*	7	0	41	0
2009–10	Leicester C	2	0		
2010–11	Leicester C	3	0		
2010–11	*Bristol R*	16	0	16	0
2011–12	Leicester C	0	0		
2011–12	*Rotherham U*	19	0	19	0
2012–13	Leicester C	0	0		
2013–14	Leicester C	0	0	23	0

MAHREZ, Riyad (M) 77 9
H: 5 10 W: 9 10 b.Sarcelles 21-2-91
Internationals: Algeria Full caps.

2011–12	Le Havre	9	0		
2012–13	Le Havre	32	4		
2013–14	Le Havre	17	2	58	6
2013–14	Leicester C	19	3	19	3

McCOURT, Jak (M) 11 0

2013–14	Leicester C	0	0		
2013–14	*Torquay U*	11	0	11	0

MOORE, Liam (D) 72 1
H: 6 1 W: 13 08 b.Loughborough 31-1-93
Internationals: England U17, U21.

2011–12	Leicester C	2	0		
2011–12	*Bradford C*	17	0	17	0
2012–13	Leicester C	16	0		
2012–13	*Brentford*	7	0	7	0
2013–14	Leicester C	30	1	48	1

MORGAN, Wes (D) 464 16
H: 6 2 W: 14 00 b.Nottingham 21-1-84

2002–03	Nottingham F	0	0		
2002–03	*Kidderminster H*	5	1	5	1
2003–04	Nottingham F	32	2		
2004–05	Nottingham F	43	1		
2005–06	Nottingham F	43	2		
2006–07	Nottingham F	38	0		
2007–08	Nottingham F	42	1		
2008–09	Nottingham F	42	1		
2009–10	Nottingham F	44	3		
2010–11	Nottingham F	46	1		
2011–12	Nottingham F	22	1	352	12
2011–12	Leicester C	17	0		
2012–13	Leicester C	45	1		
2013–14	Leicester C	45	2	107	3

NUGENT, Dave (F) 420 122
H: 5 11 W: 12 13 b.Liverpool 2-5-85
Internationals: England U20, U21, Full caps.

2001–02	Bury	5	0		
2002–03	Bury	31	4		
2003–04	Bury	26	3		
2004–05	Bury	26	11	88	18
2004–05	Preston NE	18	8		
2005–06	Preston NE	32	10		
2006–07	Preston NE	44	15	94	33
2007–08	Portsmouth	16	3		
2008–09	Portsmouth	16	3		
2009–10	Portsmouth	3	0		
2009–10	*Burnley*	30	6	30	6
2010–11	Portsmouth	44	13	78	16
2011–12	Leicester C	42	15		
2012–13	Leicester C	42	14		
2013–14	Leicester C	46	20	130	49

PANAYIOTOU, Harry (F) 1 1
b.Leicester 28-10-94

2011–12	Leicester C	1	1		
2012–13	Leicester C	0	0		
2013–14	Leicester C	0	0	1	1

PEARSON, James (D) 3 0

2013–14	Leicester C	0	0		
2013–14	*Carlisle U*	3	0	3	0

PHILLIPS, Kevin (F) 580 246
H: 5 7 W: 11 00 b.Hitchin 25-7-73
Internationals: England B, Full caps.

1994–95	Watford	16	9		
1995–96	Watford	27	11		
1996–97	Watford	16	4	59	24
1997–98	Sunderland	43	29		
1998–99	Sunderland	26	23		
1999–2000	Sunderland	36	30		
2000–01	Sunderland	34	14		
2001–02	Sunderland	37	11		
2002–03	Sunderland	32	6	208	113
2003–04	Southampton	34	12		
2004–05	Southampton	30	10	64	22
2005–06	Aston Villa	23	4		
2006–07	Aston Villa	0	0	23	4
2006–07	WBA	36	16		
2007–08	WBA	35	22	71	38
2008–09	Birmingham C	36	14		
2009–10	Birmingham C	19	4		
2010–11	Birmingham C	14	1	69	19
2011–12	Blackpool	38	16		
2012–13	Blackpool	18	2	56	18
2012–13	Crystal Palace	14	6		
2013–14	Crystal Palace	4	0	18	6
2013–14	Leicester C	12	2	12	2

SCHLUPP, Jeffrey (M) 75 12
H: 5 8 W: 11 00 b.Hamburg 23-12-92
Internationals: Ghana Full caps.

2010–11	Leicester C	0	0		
2010–11	*Brentford*	9	6	9	6
2011–12	Leicester C	21	2		
2012–13	Leicester C	19	3		
2013–14	Leicester C	26	1	66	6

SCHMEICHEL, Kasper (G) 297 0
H: 6 1 W: 13 00 b.Copenhagen 5-11-86
Internationals: Denmark U19, U20, U21, Full caps.

2003–04	Manchester C	0	0		
2004–05	Manchester C	0	0		
2005–06	Manchester C	0	0		
2005–06	*Darlington*	4	0	4	0
2005–06	*Bury*	15	0		
2006–07	Manchester C	0	0		
2006–07	*Falkirk*	15	0	15	0
2006–07	*Bury*	14	0	29	0
2007–08	Manchester C	7	0		
2007–08	*Cardiff C*	14	0	14	0
2007–08	*Coventry C*	9	0	9	0
2008–09	Manchester C	1	0		
2009–10	Manchester C	0	0	8	0
2009–10	Notts Co	43	0	43	0
2010–11	Leeds U	37	0	37	0
2011–12	Leicester C	46	0		
2012–13	Leicester C	46	0		
2013–14	Leicester C	46	0	138	0

SESAY, Alie (D) 3 0
b. 25-7-93

2013–14	Leicester C	0	0		
2013–14	*Colchester U*	3	0	3	0

SMITH, Adam (D) 0 0
H: 5 11 W: 11 00 b.Sunderland 23-11-92

2010–11	Leicester C	0	0		
2011–12	Leicester C	0	0		
2011–12	*Chesterfield*	0	0		
2011–12	*Bristol R*	0	0		
2012–13	Leicester C	0	0		
2013–14	Leicester C	0	0		
2013–14	*Stevenage*	0	0		

ST. LEDGER, Sean (D) 321 13
H: 6 0 W: 11 09 b.Solihull 28-12-84
Internationals: Republic of Ireland Full caps.

2002–03	Peterborough U	1	0		
2003–04	Peterborough U	2	0		
2004–05	Peterborough U	33	0		
2005–06	Peterborough U	43	1	79	1

2006–07	Preston NE	41	1	
2007–08	Preston NE	37	1	
2008–09	Preston NE	46	5	
2009–10	Preston NE	30	2	
2009–10	Middlesbrough	15	2	15 2
2010–11	Preston NE	31	1	185 10
2011–12	Leicester C	26	0	
2012–13	Leicester C	9	0	
2012–13	Millwall	6	0	6 0
2013–14	Leicester C	1	0	36 0

TAFT, George (D) 3 0
H: 5 9 W: 11 09 b.Leicester 29-7-93
Internationals: England U18, U19.

2010–11	Leicester C	0	0
2011–12	Leicester C	0	0
2012–13	Leicester C	0	0
2013–14	Leicester C	0	0
2013–14	York C	3	0 3 0

TAYLOR-FLETCHER, Gary (F) 424 88
H: 6 0 W: 11 00 b.Widnes 4-6-81

2000–01	Hull C	5	0	5 0
2001–02	Leyton Orient	9	0	
2002–03	Leyton Orient	12	1	21 1
2003–04	Lincoln C	42	16	
2004–05	Lincoln C	38	11	80 27
2005–06	Huddersfield T	43	10	
2006–07	Huddersfield T	39	11	82 21
2007–08	Blackpool	42	6	
2008–09	Blackpool	38	5	
2009–10	Blackpool	32	6	
2010–11	Blackpool	31	6	
2011–12	Blackpool	37	8	
2012–13	Blackpool	35	5	215 36
2013–14	Leicester C	21	3	21 3

VARDY, Jamie (F) 63 20
H: 5 10 W: 11 12 b.Sheffield 11-1-87

2012–13	Leicester C	26	4	
2013–14	Leicester C	37	16	63 20

WASILEWSKI, Marcin (D) 272 32
H: 6 1 W: 13 11 b.Krakow 9-6-80
Internationals: Poland Full caps.

2002–03	Wisla Plock	24	1	
2003–04	Wisla Plock	21	1	
2004–05	Wisla Plock	15	1	60 3
2005–06	Amica Wronki	24	4	24 4
2006–07	Lech Poznan	14	5	14 5
2006–07	Anderlecht	14	2	
2007–08	Anderlecht	26	3	
2008–09	Anderlecht	30	8	
2009–10	Anderlecht	6	1	
2010–11	Anderlecht	17	3	
2011–12	Anderlecht	30	3	
2012–13	Anderlecht	20	0	143 20
2013–14	Leicester C	31	0	31 0

WATSON, Ryan (M) 0 0
H: 6 1 W: 11 07 b.Crewe 7-7-93

2011–12	Wigan Ath	0	0
2012–13	Wigan Ath	0	0
2012–13	Accrington S	0	0
2013–14	Leicester C	0	0

WHITBREAD, Zak (D) 167 6
H: 6 2 W: 12 07 b.Houston 4-3-84
Internationals: USA U20.

2002–03	Liverpool	0	0	
2003–04	Liverpool	0	0	
2004–05	Liverpool	0	0	
2005–06	Liverpool	0	0	
2005–06	Millwall	25	0	
2006–07	Millwall	14	0	
2007–08	Millwall	23	3	
2008–09	Millwall	38	0	
2009–10	Millwall	0	0	100 3
2009–10	Norwich C	4	0	
2010–11	Norwich C	22	1	
2011–12	Norwich C	18	0	44 1
2012–13	Leicester C	16	1	
2013–14	Leicester C	3	0	19 1
2013–14	Derby Co	4	1	4 1

WOOD, Chris (F) 164 45
H: 6 3 W: 12 10 b.Auckland 7-12-91
Internationals: New Zealand U17, U23, Full caps.

2008–09	WBA	2	0	
2009–10	WBA	18	1	
2010–11	WBA	1	0	
2010–11	Barnsley	7	0	7 0
2010–11	Brighton & HA	29	8	29 8
2011–12	WBA	0	0	
2011–12	Birmingham C	23	9	23 9
2011–12	Bristol C	19	3	19 3
2012–13	WBA	0	0	21 1
2012–13	Millwall	19	11	19 11
2012–13	Leicester C	20	9	
2013–14	Leicester C	26	4	46 13

Scholars
Anderson, Conor Rhys; Bailey, Kyle Stuart; Burke, Sean Joseph; Casey, Dylan; Chilwell, Benjamin James; Dombrauskis, Tomas; Dusabe, Chris; Fox, Brandon Levi; Jones, Samuel James Cooper; King, Keenan Rakwarne; King, Macauley; Kipre, Cedric; Miles, Matthew Richard; Moore, Elliott Jordan; Olukanmi, Andre Cameron; Pepe-Ngoma, Herve; Rowe, Daniel Isaiah; Samba, Eddy; Sharpe, Liam James; Smith-Varnam, Max Presley; Stankevicius, Simonas.

LEYTON ORIENT (44)

ALNWICK, Ben (G) 68 0
H: 6 2 W: 13 12 b.Prudhoe 1-1-87
Internationals: England U16, U17, U18, U19, U21.

2003–04	Sunderland	0	0	
2004–05	Sunderland	3	0	
2005–06	Sunderland	5	0	
2006–07	Sunderland	11	0	19 0
2006–07	Tottenham H	0	0	
2007–08	Tottenham H	0	0	
2007–08	Luton T	4	0	4 0
2007–08	Leicester C	8	0	8 0
2008–09	Tottenham H	0	0	
2008–09	Carlisle U	6	0	6 0
2009–10	Tottenham H	1	0	
2009–10	Norwich C	3	0	3 0
2010–11	Tottenham H	0	0	
2010–11	Leeds U	0	0	
2010–11	Doncaster R	0	0	
2011–12	Tottenham H	0	0	
2011–12	Leyton Orient	6	0	
2012–13	Tottenham H	0	0	1 0
2012–13	Barnsley	10	0	
2013–14	Barnsley	0	0	10 0
2013–14	Charlton Ath	0	0	10 0
2013–14	Leyton Orient	1	0	7 0

BATT, Shaun (M) 137 14
H: 6 3 W: 12 08 b.Harlow 22-2-87

2008–09	Peterborough U	30	2	
2009–10	Peterborough U	20	2	50 4
2009–10	Millwall	16	3	
2010–11	Millwall	0	0	
2010–11	Millwall	4	0	
2011–12	Crawley T	5	0	5 0
2012–13	Millwall	16	1	
2012–13	Leyton Orient	11	2	
2013–14	Millwall	0	0	36 4
2013–14	Leyton Orient	35	4	46 6

BAUDRY, Mathieu (D) 110 7
H: 6 2 W: 12 08 b.Le Havre 24-2-88

2007–08	Troyes	2	1	
2008–09	Troyes	17	0	
2009–10	Troyes	7	0	26 1
2010–11	Bournemouth	3	1	
2011–12	Bournemouth	7	0	10 1
2011–12	Dagenham & R	0	0	11 0
2012–13	Leyton Orient	24	3	
2013–14	Leyton Orient	39	2	63 5

CLARKE, Nathan (D) 389 11
H: 6 2 W: 12 00 b.Halifax 30-11-83

2001–02	Huddersfield T	36	1	
2002–03	Huddersfield T	3	0	
2003–04	Huddersfield T	26	1	
2004–05	Huddersfield T	37	0	
2005–06	Huddersfield T	46	0	
2006–07	Huddersfield T	16	0	
2007–08	Huddersfield T	44	2	
2008–09	Huddersfield T	38	3	
2009–10	Huddersfield T	17	1	
2010–11	Huddersfield T	1	0	
2010–11	Colchester U	18	0	18 0
2011–12	Huddersfield T	0	0	264 8
2011–12	Oldham Ath	16	1	16 1
2011–12	Bury	11	0	11 0
2012–13	Leyton Orient	34	0	
2013–14	Leyton Orient	46	2	80 2

COX, Dean (M) 318 50
H: 5 4 W: 9 08 b.Cuckfield 12-8-87

2005–06	Brighton & HA	1	0	
2006–07	Brighton & HA	42	6	
2007–08	Brighton & HA	42	6	
2008–09	Brighton & HA	40	4	
2009–10	Brighton & HA	21	0	146 16
2010–11	Leyton Orient	45	11	
2011–12	Leyton Orient	38	7	
2012–13	Leyton Orient	44	4	
2013–14	Leyton Orient	45	12	172 34

CUTHBERT, Scott (D) 208 11
H: 6 2 W: 14 00 b.Alexandria 15-6-87
Internationals: Scotland U19, U20, U21, B.

2004–05	Celtic	0	0	
2005–06	Celtic	0	0	
2006–07	Celtic	0	0	
2006–07	Livingston	4	1	4 1
2007–08	Celtic	0	0	
2008–09	Celtic	0	0	
2008–09	St Mirren	29	0	29 0
2009–10	Swindon T	39	3	
2010–11	Swindon T	41	2	80 5
2011–12	Leyton Orient	33	1	
2012–13	Leyton Orient	18	0	
2013–14	Leyton Orient	44	4	95 5

DAGNALL, Chris (F) 342 84
H: 5 8 W: 12 03 b.Liverpool 15-4-86

2003–04	Tranmere R	10	1	
2004–05	Tranmere R	23	6	
2005–06	Tranmere R	6	0	39 7
2005–06	Rochdale	21	3	
2006–07	Rochdale	37	17	
2007–08	Rochdale	14	7	
2008–09	Rochdale	40	7	
2009–10	Rochdale	45	20	157 54
2010–11	Scunthorpe U	37	5	
2011–12	Scunthorpe U	23	4	60 9
2011–12	Barnsley	9	0	
2011–12	Bradford C	7	1	7 1
2012–13	Barnsley	36	5	
2013–14	Barnsley	8	1	53 6
2013–14	Coventry C	6	1	6 1
2013–14	Leyton Orient	20	6	20 6

GORMAN, Johnny (M) 5 0
H: 5 9 W: 11 00 b.Sheffield 26-10-92
Internationals: Republic of Ireland U16. Northern Ireland U16, U17, U18, U19, U20, U21, Full caps.

2009–10	Wolverhampton W	0	0	
2010–11	Wolverhampton W	0	0	
2011–12	Wolverhampton W	1	0	
2012–13	Wolverhampton W	0	0	1 0
2012–13	Plymouth Arg	2	0	2 0
2013–14	Leyton Orient	2	0	2 0

GRAINGER, Charlie (G) 0 0
b. 31-7-96
Internationals: England U18.

2012–13	Leyton Orient	0	0
2013–14	Leyton Orient	0	0

JAMES, Lloyd (M) 198 6
H: 5 11 W: 11 01 b.Bristol 16-2-88
Internationals: Wales U17, U19, U21.

2005–06	Southampton	0	0	
2006–07	Southampton	0	0	
2007–08	Southampton	0	0	
2008–09	Southampton	41	0	
2009–10	Southampton	30	2	71 2
2010–11	Colchester U	28	0	
2011–12	Colchester U	23	1	51 1
2011–12	Crawley T	6	0	6 0
2012–13	Colchester U	28	0	
2013–14	Leyton Orient	42	3	70 3

JONES, Jamie (G) 151 0
H: 6 2 W: 14 05 b.Kirkby 18-2-89

2007–08	Everton	0	0	
2008–09	Leyton Orient	20	0	
2009–10	Leyton Orient	36	0	
2010–11	Leyton Orient	35	0	
2011–12	Leyton Orient	6	0	
2012–13	Leyton Orient	26	0	
2013–14	Leyton Orient	28	0	151 0

LAIRD, Marc (M) 166 11
H: 6 1 W: 10 07 b.Edinburgh 23-1-86
2003-04	Manchester C	0	0		
2004-05	Manchester C	0	0		
2005-06	Manchester C	0	0		
2006-07	Manchester C	0	0		
2006-07	Northampton T	6	0	6	0
2007-08	Manchester C	0	0		
2007-08	Port Vale	7	1	7	1
2007-08	Millwall	17	1		
2008-09	Millwall	38	5		
2009-10	Millwall	20	0		
2010-11	Millwall	1	0	76	6
2010-11	Brentford	4	1	4	1
2010-11	Walsall	8	0	8	0
2011-12	Leyton Orient	22	2		
2012-13	Leyton Orient	1	0		
2012-13	Southend U	23	1		
2013-14	Leyton Orient	0	0	23	2
2013-14	Southend U	19	0	42	1

LARKINS, Jake (G) 2 0
H: 5 9 W: 11 00 b.Barking 11-1-94
2010-11	West Ham U	0	0		
2011-12	West Ham U	0	0		
2012-13	West Ham U	0	0		
2013-14	Leyton Orient	2	0	2	0

LASIMANT, Yohann (F) 78 5
H: 5 11 W: 10 13 b.Besancon 4-9-89
Internationals: France U19, U20.
2008-09	Rennes	1	0	1	0
2009-10	Sedan	18	0	18	0
2010-11	Grenoble	33	2	33	2
2011-12	Larissa	9	0	9	0
2012-13	Eger	6	1	6	1
2013-14	Leyton Orient	11	2	11	2

LEE, Harry (M) 1 0
H: 6 0 W: 11 09 b.Hackney 20-3-95
| 2012-13 | Leyton Orient | 1 | 0 | | |
| 2013-14 | Leyton Orient | 0 | 0 | 1 | 0 |

LISBIE, Kevin (F) 427 106
H: 5 10 W: 11 06 b.Hackney 17-10-78
Internationals: England Youth. Jamaica Full caps.
1996-97	Charlton Ath	25	1		
1997-98	Charlton Ath	17	1		
1998-99	Charlton Ath	1	0		
1998-99	Gillingham	7	4	7	4
1999-2000	Charlton Ath	0	0		
1999-2000	Reading	2	0	2	0
2000-01	Charlton Ath	18	0		
2000-01	QPR	2	0	2	0
2001-02	Charlton Ath	22	5		
2002-03	Charlton Ath	32	4		
2003-04	Charlton Ath	9	4		
2004-05	Charlton Ath	17	1		
2005-06	Charlton Ath	6	0		
2005-06	Norwich C	6	1	6	1
2005-06	Derby Co	7	1	7	1
2006-07	Charlton Ath	8	0	155	16
2007-08	Colchester U	42	17		
2008-09	Ipswich T	41	6		
2009-10	Ipswich T	0	0		
2009-10	Colchester U	41	13	83	30
2010-11	Ipswich T	0	0		
2010-11	Millwall	20	4	20	4
2011-12	Ipswich T	0	0	41	6
2011-12	Leyton Orient	37	12		
2012-13	Leyton Orient	28	16		
2013-14	Leyton Orient	39	16	104	44

MOONEY, David (F) 287 89
H: 6 2 W: 12 06 b.Dublin 30-10-84
Internationals: Republic of Ireland U23.
2005	Longford T	13	4		
2005	Shamrock R	14	2	14	2
2006	Longford T	21	3		
2007	Longford T	32	19	66	26
2008	Cork C	22	15	22	15
2008-09	Reading	0	0		
2008-09	Stockport Co	2	0	2	0
2008-09	Norwich C	9	3	9	3
2009-10	Reading	0	0		
2009-10	Charlton Ath	28	5	28	5
2010-11	Reading	0	0		
2010-11	Colchester U	39	9	39	9
2011-12	Leyton Orient	37	5		
2012-13	Leyton Orient	32	5		
2013-14	Leyton Orient	38	19	107	29

ODUBAJO, Moses (M) 93 13
H: 5 9 W: 11 05 b.Greenwich 28-7-93
2011-12	Leyton Orient	3	1		
2012-13	Leyton Orient	44	2		
2013-14	Leyton Orient	46	10	93	13

OMOZUSI, Elliot (D) 133 0
H: 5 11 W: 12 09 b.Hackney 15-12-88
Internationals: England U16, U17, U18, U19.
2005-06	Fulham	0	0		
2006-07	Fulham	0	0		
2007-08	Fulham	8	0		
2008-09	Fulham	0	0		
2008-09	Norwich C	21	0	21	0
2009-10	Fulham	0	0	8	0
2009-10	Charlton Ath	9	0	9	0
2010-11	Leyton Orient	40	0		
2011-12	Leyton Orient	10	0		
2012-13	Leyton Orient	6	0		
2013-14	Leyton Orient	39	0	95	0

SAWYER, Gary (D) 214 6
H: 6 0 W: 11 08 b.Bideford 5-7-85
2004-05	Plymouth Arg	0	0		
2005-06	Plymouth Arg	0	0		
2006-07	Plymouth Arg	22	0		
2007-08	Plymouth Arg	31	1		
2008-09	Plymouth Arg	13	3		
2009-10	Plymouth Arg	29	1	95	5
2009-10	Bristol C	2	0	2	0
2010-11	Bristol R	37	0		
2011-12	Bristol R	24	0	61	0
2012-13	Leyton Orient	34	1		
2013-14	Leyton Orient	22	0	56	1

SIMPSON, Robbie (F) 181 16
H: 6 1 W: 11 11 b.Poole 15-3-85
2007-08	Coventry C	28	1		
2008-09	Coventry C	33	3	61	4
2009-10	Huddersfield T	13	0		
2010-11	Huddersfield T	0	0		
2010-11	Brentford	27	4	27	4
2011-12	Huddersfield T	0	0	13	0
2011-12	Oldham Ath	29	6		
2012-13	Oldham Ath	37	2		
2013-14	Oldham Ath	0	0	66	8
2013-14	Leyton Orient	14	0	14	0

VINCELOT, Romain (M) 199 17
H: 5 9 W: 11 02 b.Poitiers 29-10-85
2004-05	Chamois Niortais	3	0	3	0
2005-06	Chemois Niortais	28	1		
2006-07	Chemois Niortais	9	0		
2007-08	Chemois Niortais	6	0	43	1
2008-09	Gueugnon	20	0	20	0
2009-10	Dagenham & R	9	1		
2010-11	Dagenham & R	46	12	55	13
2011-12	Brighton & HA	15	1		
2012-13	Brighton & HA	0	0	15	1
2012-13	Gillingham	9	1	9	1
2012-13	Leyton Orient	15	1		
2013-14	Leyton Orient	39	0	54	1

Scholars
Adams, Kane James Arthur Peter; Agyemang, Montel Kofi Owusu; Bridle-Card, Benjamin William Daniel; Brown, Nicholas Joseph; Finney, Alex; Humphrey, Jack Peter; Ling, Samuel Jack; Moncur, Freddy Daniel; Nikolaou, Andys Antreas; Okimeji, Lawson; Oladipo, Oluwanishola Kelvin Amusa Opeyemi Farouq; Sandy, Sinclaire; Uzun, Josh.

LIVERPOOL (45)

ADORJAN, Krisztian (F) 19 3
H: 5 9 b.Budapest 19-1-93
Internationals: Hungary U17, U19, U21.
2010-11	Liverpool	0	0		
2011-12	Liverpool	0	0		
2012-13	Liverpool	0	0		
2013-14	Liverpool	0	0		
2013-14	FC Groningen	19	3	19	3

AGGER, Daniel (D) 209 14
H: 6 2 W: 12 06 b.Hvidovre 12-12-84
Internationals: Denmark U20, U21, Full caps.
2004-05	Brondby	26	5		
2005-06	Brondby	8	0	34	5
2005-06	Liverpool	4	0		
2006-07	Liverpool	27	2		
2007-08	Liverpool	5	0		
2008-09	Liverpool	18	1		
2009-10	Liverpool	23	0		
2010-11	Liverpool	16	0		
2011-12	Liverpool	27	1		
2012-13	Liverpool	35	3		
2013-14	Liverpool	20	2	175	9

ALBERTO, Luis (M) 16 0
H: 6 0 b.San Jose Del Valle 28-9-92
Internationals: Spain U18, U19, U21.
2009-10	Sevilla	0	0		
2010-11	Sevilla	2	0		
2011-12	Sevilla	5	0		
2012-13	Sevilla	0	0	7	0
2013-14	Liverpool	9	0	9	0

ALLEN, Joe (M) 178 8
H: 5 6 W: 9 10 b.Carmarthen 14-3-90
Internationals: Wales U17, U19, U21, Full caps. Great Britain.
2006-07	Swansea C	1	0		
2007-08	Swansea C	6	0		
2008-09	Swansea C	23	1		
2009-10	Swansea C	21	0		
2010-11	Swansea C	40	2		
2011-12	Swansea C	36	4		
2012-13	Swansea C	0	0	127	7
2012-13	Liverpool	27	0		
2013-14	Liverpool	24	1	51	1

ASPAS, Iago (F) 148 46
H: 5 9 W: 10 11 b.Moana 1-8-87
2008-09	Celta Vigo	3	2		
2009-10	Celta Vigo	36	4		
2010-11	Celta Vigo	28	4		
2011-12	Celta Vigo	33	24		
2012-13	Celta Vigo	34	12	134	46
2013-14	Liverpool	14	0	14	0

ASSAIDI, Oussama (F) 122 33
H: 5 10 W: 10 13 b.Beni Boughari 15-8-88
Internationals: Holland U20. Morocco Full caps.
2007-08	Almere City FC	3	3	3	3
2008-09	De Graafschap	13	1		
2009-10	De Graafschap	3	5	16	6
2009-10	Heerenveen	21	1		
2010-11	Heerenveen	31	9		
2011-12	Heerenveen	27	10		
2012-13	Heerenveen	1	0	80	20
2012-13	Liverpool	4	0		
2013-14	Liverpool	0	0	4	0
2013-14	Stoke C	19	4	19	4

BORINI, Fabio (F) 82 23
H: 5 10 W: 11 08 b.Bentivoglio 23-3-91
Internationals: Italy U17, U19, U21, Full caps.
2008-09	Chelsea	0	0		
2009-10	Chelsea	4	0		
2010-11	Chelsea	0	0	4	0
2010-11	Swansea C	9	6	9	6
2011-12	Roma	24	9	24	9
2012-13	Liverpool	13	1		
2013-14	Liverpool	0	0	13	1
2013-14	Sunderland	32	7	32	7

BRANNAGAN, Cameron (M) 0 0
b.Manchester 9-5-96
Internationals: England U18.
| 2013-14 | Liverpool | 0 | 0 | | |

CISSOKHO, Aly (D) 182 3
H: 5 11 W: 11 10 b.Blois 15-9-87
Internationals: France Full caps.
2006-07	Gueugnon	1	0		
2007-08	Gueugnon	21	0	22	0
2008-09	Vitoria Setubal	13	0	13	0
2008-09	Porto	15	0	15	0
2009-10	Lyon	30	0		
2010-11	Lyon	29	1		
2011-12	Lyon	31	0		
2012-13	Lyon	2	0	92	1
2012-13	Valencia	25	2		
2013-14	Valencia	0	0	25	2
On loan from Valencia
2013-14	Liverpool	15	0	15	0

COADY, Conor (D) 40 5
H: 6 1 W: 11 05 b.Liverpool 25-2-93
Internationals: England U16, U17, U18, U19, U20.
| 2010-11 | Liverpool | 0 | 0 | | |

Season	Club	Apps	Gls	Tot	TGls
2011–12	Liverpool	0	0		
2012–13	Liverpool	1	0		
2013–14	Liverpool	0	0	1	0
2013–14	*Sheffield U*	39	5	39	5

COATES, Sebastian (D)   **67 5**
H: 6 5 W: 13 12 b.Montevideo 7-10-90
Internationals: Uruguay U20, U23, Full caps.

Season	Club	Apps	Gls	Tot	TGls
2008–09	Nacional	6	1		
2009–10	Nacional	21	2		
2010–11	Nacional	27	1		
2011–12	Nacional	1	0	55	4
2011–12	Liverpool	7	1		
2012–13	Liverpool	5	0		
2013–14	Liverpool	0	0	12	1

COUTINHO, Phillippe (M)   **96 17**
H: 5 7 W: 10 09 b.Rio de Janeiro 12-6-92
Internationals: Brazil U17, U20, Full caps.

Season	Club	Apps	Gls	Tot	TGls
2009–10	Vasco da Gama	7	1	7	1
2010–11	Inter Milan	12	1		
2011–12	Inter Milan	5	1		
2011–12	*Espanyol*	16	5	16	5
2012–13	Inter Milan	10	1	27	3
2012–13	Liverpool	13	3		
2013–14	Liverpool	33	5	46	8

DUNN, Jack (M)   **0 0**
b.Liverpool 19-11-94
Internationals: England U17, U18, U19.

Season	Club	Apps	Gls
2011–12	Liverpool	0	0
2012–13	Liverpool	0	0
2013–14	Liverpool	0	0

FLANAGAN, John (D)   **35 1**
H: 5 11 W: 12 06 b.Liverpool 1-1-93
Internationals: England U19, U20, U21, Full caps.

Season	Club	Apps	Gls	Tot	TGls
2010–11	Liverpool	7	0		
2011–12	Liverpool	5	0		
2012–13	Liverpool	0	0		
2013–14	Liverpool	23	1	35	1

GERRARD, Steven (M)   **475 111**
H: 6 0 W: 12 05 b.Huyton 30-5-80
Internationals: England U21, Full caps.

Season	Club	Apps	Gls	Tot	TGls
1997–98	Liverpool	0	0		
1998–99	Liverpool	12	0		
1999–2000	Liverpool	29	1		
2000–01	Liverpool	33	7		
2001–02	Liverpool	28	3		
2002–03	Liverpool	34	5		
2003–04	Liverpool	34	4		
2004–05	Liverpool	30	7		
2005–06	Liverpool	32	10		
2006–07	Liverpool	36	7		
2007–08	Liverpool	34	11		
2008–09	Liverpool	31	16		
2009–10	Liverpool	33	9		
2010–11	Liverpool	21	4		
2011–12	Liverpool	18	5		
2012–13	Liverpool	36	9		
2013–14	Liverpool	34	13	475	111

HENDERSON, Jordan (M)   **183 16**
H: 6 0 W: 10 07 b.Sunderland 17-6-90
Internationals: England U19, U20, U21, Full caps.

Season	Club	Apps	Gls	Tot	TGls
2008–09	Sunderland	1	0		
2008–09	*Coventry C*	10	1	10	1
2009–10	Sunderland	33	1		
2010–11	Sunderland	37	3	71	4
2011–12	Liverpool	37	2		
2012–13	Liverpool	30	5		
2013–14	Liverpool	35	4	102	11

IBE, Jordan (F)   **20 2**
H: 5 9 W: 11 00 b.Southwark 8-12-95
Internationals: England U18, U19.

Season	Club	Apps	Gls	Tot	TGls
2011–12	Wycombe W	7	1	7	1
2011–12	Liverpool	0	0		
2012–13	Liverpool	1	0		
2013–14	Liverpool	1	0	2	0
2013–14	*Birmingham C*	11	1	11	1

JOHNSON, Glen (D)   **290 14**
H: 6 0 W: 13 04 b.Greenwich 23-8-84
Internationals: England U20, U21, Full caps.

Season	Club	Apps	Gls	Tot	TGls
2001–02	West Ham U	0	0		
2002–03	West Ham U	15	0	15	0
2002–03	*Millwall*	8	0	8	0
2003–04	Chelsea	19	3		
2004–05	Chelsea	17	0		
2005–06	Chelsea	4	0		
2006–07	Chelsea	0	0		
2006–07	*Portsmouth*	26	0		
2007–08	Chelsea	2	0	42	3
2007–08	Portsmouth	29	1		
2008–09	Portsmouth	29	3		
2009–10	Portsmouth	0	0	84	4
2009–10	Liverpool	25	3		
2010–11	Liverpool	28	2		
2011–12	Liverpool	23	1		
2012–13	Liverpool	36	1		
2013–14	Liverpool	29	0	141	7

JONES, Brad (G)   **108 0**
H: 6 3 W: 12 01 b.Armidale 19-3-82
Internationals: Australia U20, U23, Full caps.

Season	Club	Apps	Gls	Tot	TGls
1998–99	Middlesbrough	0	0		
1999–2000	Middlesbrough	0	0		
2000–01	Middlesbrough	0	0		
2001–02	Middlesbrough	0	0		
2002	Shelbourne	2	0	2	0
2002–03	Middlesbrough	0	0		
2002–03	*Stockport Co*	1	0	1	0
2003–04	Middlesbrough	1	0		
2003–04	*Blackpool*	5	0		
2003–04	*Rotherham U*	0	0		
2004–05	Middlesbrough	5	0		
2004–05	*Blackpool*	12	0	17	0
2005–06	Middlesbrough	9	0		
2006–07	Middlesbrough	2	0		
2006–07	*Sheffield W*	15	0	15	0
2007–08	Middlesbrough	1	0		
2008–09	Middlesbrough	16	0		
2009–10	Middlesbrough	24	0	58	0
2010–11	Liverpool	0	0		
2010–11	*Derby Co*	7	0	7	0
2011–12	Liverpool	1	0		
2012–13	Liverpool	7	0		
2013–14	Liverpool	0	0	8	0

JONES, Lloyd (D)   **0 0**
b.Plymouth 7-10-95
Internationals: Wales U17, U18.

Season	Club	Apps	Gls
2012–13	Liverpool	0	0
2013–14	Liverpool	0	0

JOSE ENRIQUE (D)   **247 4**
H: 6 0 W: 12 00 b.Valencia 23-1-86
Internationals: Spain U16, U19, U21.

Season	Club	Apps	Gls	Tot	TGls
2004–05	Levante	19	1	19	1
2005–06	Valencia	0	0		
2005–06	*Celta Vigo*	14	0	14	0
2006–07	*Villarreal*	23	0	23	0
2007–08	Newcastle U	23	0		
2008–09	Newcastle U	26	0		
2009–10	Newcastle U	34	1		
2010–11	Newcastle U	36	0	119	1
2011–12	Liverpool	35	0		
2012–13	Liverpool	29	2		
2013–14	Liverpool	8	0	72	2

KELLY, Martin (D)   **40 1**
H: 6 3 W: 12 02 b.Bolton 27-4-90
Internationals: England U19, U20, U21, Full caps.

Season	Club	Apps	Gls	Tot	TGls
2007–08	Liverpool	0	0		
2008–09	Liverpool	0	0		
2008–09	*Huddersfield T*	7	1	7	1
2009–10	Liverpool	1	0		
2010–11	Liverpool	11	0		
2011–12	Liverpool	12	0		
2012–13	Liverpool	4	0		
2013–14	Liverpool	5	0	33	0

LUCAS (M)   **209 5**
H: 5 10 W: 11 09 b.Dourados 9-1-87
Internationals: Brazil U20, U23, Full caps.

Season	Club	Apps	Gls	Tot	TGls
2005	Gremio	3	0		
2006	Gremio	30	4	33	4
2007–08	Liverpool	18	0		
2008–09	Liverpool	25	1		
2009–10	Liverpool	35	0		
2010–11	Liverpool	33	0		
2011–12	Liverpool	12	0		
2012–13	Liverpool	26	0		
2013–14	Liverpool	27	0	176	1

LUSSEY, Jordan (M)   **0 0**
b.Ormskirk 2-11-94
Internationals: England U16, U17.

Season	Club	Apps	Gls
2011–12	Liverpool	0	0
2012–13	Liverpool	0	0
2013–14	Liverpool	0	0

McLAUGHLIN, Ryan (D)   **9 0**
b.Belfast 30-9-94
Internationals: Northern Ireland U16, U17, U19, U21, Full caps.

Season	Club	Apps	Gls	Tot	TGls
2011–12	Liverpool	0	0		
2013–14	Liverpool	0	0		
2013–14	*Barnsley*	9	0	9	0

MIGNOLET, Simon (G)   **250 1**
H: 6 4 W: 13 10 b.St Truiden 6-3-88
Internationals: Belgium U16, U17, U18, U19, U20, U21, Full caps.

Season	Club	Apps	Gls	Tot	TGls
2006–07	St Truiden	2	0		
2007–08	St Truiden	25	0		
2008–09	St Truiden	35	1		
2009–10	St Truiden	37	0		
2010–11	St Truiden	23	0	122	1
2010–11	Sunderland	23	0		
2011–12	Sunderland	29	0		
2012–13	Sunderland	38	0	90	0
2013–14	Liverpool	38	0	38	0

MUKENDI, Henoc (F)   **7 0**
H: 6 3 W: 12 11 b.Congo DR 20-1-93

Season	Club	Apps	Gls	Tot	TGls
2012–13	Liverpool	0	0		
2012–13	*Northampton T*	7	0	7	0
2013–14	Liverpool	0	0		
2013–14	*Partick Thistle*	0	0		

NGOO, Michael (F)   **35 5**
b.Walthamstow 23-10-92
Internationals: England U19, U20.

Season	Club	Apps	Gls	Tot	TGls
2009–10	Liverpool	0	0		
2010–11	Liverpool	0	0		
2011–12	Liverpool	0	0		
2012–13	Liverpool	0	0		
2012–13	*Hearts*	15	4	15	4
2013–14	Liverpool	0	0		
2013–14	*Yeovil T*	6	0	6	0
2013–14	*Walsall*	14	1	14	1

PELOSI, Marc (D)   **0 0**
b.Bad Sackingen 17-6-94
Internationals: USA U17.

Season	Club	Apps	Gls
2011–12	Liverpool	0	0
2012–13	Liverpool	0	0
2013–14	Liverpool	0	0

PETERSON, Kristoffer (M)   **6 0**
b.Gothenburg 28-11-94
Internationals: Sweden U17, U21.

Season	Club	Apps	Gls	Tot	TGls
2011–12	Liverpool	0	0		
2012–13	Liverpool	0	0		
2013–14	Liverpool	0	0		
2013–14	*Tranmere R*	6	0	6	0

RANDALL, Conor (M)   **0 0**
b.Liverpool 21-10-95

Season	Club	Apps	Gls
2013–14	Liverpool	0	0

REINA, Jose (G)   **484 0**
H: 6 2 W: 14 06 b.Madrid 31-8-82
Internationals: Spain U16, U17, U18, U21, Full caps.

Season	Club	Apps	Gls	Tot	TGls
1999–2000	Barcelona B	30	0	30	0
2000–01	Barcelona	19	0		
2001–02	Barcelona	11	0	30	0
2002–03	Villarreal	33	0		
2003–04	Villarreal	38	0		
2004–05	Villarreal	38	0	109	0
2005–06	Liverpool	33	0		
2006–07	Liverpool	35	0		
2007–08	Liverpool	38	0		
2008–09	Liverpool	38	0		
2009–10	Liverpool	38	0		
2010–11	Liverpool	38	0		
2011–12	Liverpool	34	0		
2012–13	Liverpool	31	0		
2013–14	Liverpool	0	0	285	0
2013–14	*Napoli*	30	0	30	0

ROBINSON, Jack (D)   **48 0**
H: 5 11 W: 10 08 b.Warrington 1-9-93
Internationals: England U16, U17, U18, U19, U21.

Season	Club	Apps	Gls	Tot	TGls
2009–10	Liverpool	1	0		
2010–11	Liverpool	2	0		
2011–12	Liverpool	0	0		
2012–13	Liverpool	0	0		
2012–13	*Wolverhampton W*	11	0	11	0
2013–14	Liverpool	0	0	3	0
2013–14	*Blackpool*	34	0	34	0

RODDAN, Craig (M)   1   0
b.Kirkby 22-4-93

2011–12	Liverpool	0	0	
2012–13	Liverpool	0	0	
2013–14	Liverpool	0	0	
2013–14	Carlisle U	1	0	1 0

ROSSITER, Jordan (M)   0   0
b.Liverpool 24-3-97

2013–14	Liverpool	0	0

SAKHO, Mamadou (D)   169   8
H: 6 2 W: 12 07 b.Paris 13-2-90
Internationals: France U16, U17, U18, U19, U21, Full caps.

2006–07	Paris St Germain	0	0	
2007–08	Paris St Germain	12	0	
2008–09	Paris St Germain	23	1	
2009–10	Paris St Germain	32	0	
2010–11	Paris St Germain	35	4	
2011–12	Paris St Germain	30	0	
2012–13	Paris St Germain	27	2	151 7
2013–14	Liverpool	18	1	18 1

SINCLAIR, Jerome (F)   0   0
b. 20-9-96
Internationals: England U16, U17.

2012–13	Liverpool	0	0
2013–14	Liverpool	0	0

SKRTEL, Martin (D)   296   17
H: 6 3 W: 12 10 b.Handlova 15-12-84
Internationals: Slovakia Full caps.

2002–03	Trencin	1	0	
2003–04	Trencin	34	0	35 0
2004	Zenit	7	0	
2005	Zenit	18	1	
2006	Zenit	26	1	
2007	Zenit	23	1	74 3
2007–08	Liverpool	14	0	
2008–09	Liverpool	21	0	
2009–10	Liverpool	19	1	
2010–11	Liverpool	38	2	
2011–12	Liverpool	34	2	
2012–13	Liverpool	25	2	
2013–14	Liverpool	36	7	187 14

SMITH, Bradley (D)   1   0
b.New South Wales 9-4-94
Internationals: England U17, U19, U21.

2011–12	Liverpool	0	0	
2012–13	Liverpool	0	0	
2013–14	Liverpool	1	0	1 0

SOKOLIK, Jakub (D)   10   0
H: 5 6 b.Ostrava 28-8-93
Internationals: Czech Republic U16, U17.

2010–11	Liverpool	0	0	
2011–12	Liverpool	0	0	
2012–13	Liverpool	0	0	
2013–14	Liverpool	0	0	
2013–14	Southend U	10	0	10 0

STERLING, Raheem (F)   60   11
H: 5 7 W: 10 00 b.Kingston 8-12-94
Internationals: England U16, U17, U18, U19, U21, Full caps.

2011–12	Liverpool	3	0	
2012–13	Liverpool	24	2	
2013–14	Liverpool	33	9	60 11

STURRIDGE, Daniel (F)   139   57
H: 6 2 W: 12 00 b.Birmingham 1-9-89
Internationals: England U16, U17, U18, U19, U20, U21, Full caps. Great Britain.

2006–07	Manchester C	2	0	
2007–08	Manchester C	3	1	
2008–09	Manchester C	16	4	
2009–10	Manchester C	0	0	21 5
2009–10	Chelsea	13	1	
2010–11	Chelsea	13	0	
2010–11	Bolton W	12	8	12 8
2011–12	Chelsea	30	11	
2012–13	Chelsea	7	1	63 13
2012–13	Liverpool	14	10	
2013–14	Liverpool	29	21	43 31

SUAREZ, Luis (F)   276   170
H: 5 11 W: 12 10 b.Salto 24-1-87
Internationals: Uruguay U20, Full caps.

2005–06	Nacional	27	10	27 10
2006–07	Groningen	29	10	29 10
2007–08	Ajax	33	17	
2008–09	Ajax	31	22	
2009–10	Ajax	33	35	
2010–11	Ajax	13	7	110 81
2010–11	Liverpool	13	4	
2011–12	Liverpool	31	11	
2012–13	Liverpool	33	23	
2013–14	Liverpool	33	31	110 69

SUSO (M)   67   10
H: 5 8 W: 10 12 b.Cadiz 19-11-93
Internationals: Spain U17, U18, U19, U20, U21.

2010–11	Cadiz B	20	7	20 7
2010–11	Liverpool	0	0	
2011–12	Liverpool	14	0	
2013–14	Liverpool	0	0	14 0
2013–14	Almeria	33	3	33 3

TEIXEIRA, Joao Carlos (M)   3   0
b.Braga 18-1-93
Internationals: Portugal U16, U17, U18, U19, U20, U21.

2011–12	Liverpool	0	0	
2012–13	Liverpool	0	0	
2013–14	Liverpool	1	0	1 0
2013–14	Brentford	2	0	2 0

TIAGO ILORI, Almeida (D)   21   1
H: 6 3 W: 12 07 b.London 26-2-93
Internationals: Portugal U18, U19, U20, U21.

2011–12	Sporting Lisbon	1	0	
2012–13	Sporting Lisbon	11	1	12 1
2013–14	Liverpool	0	0	
2013–14	Granada	9	0	9 0

TOURE, Kolo (D)   327   11
H: 5 10 W: 13 08 b.Sokoura Bouake 19-3-81
Internationals: Ivory Coast Full caps.

2001–02	Arsenal	0	0	
2002–03	Arsenal	26	2	
2003–04	Arsenal	37	1	
2004–05	Arsenal	35	0	
2005–06	Arsenal	33	0	
2006–07	Arsenal	35	3	
2007–08	Arsenal	30	2	
2008–09	Arsenal	29	1	
2009–10	Arsenal	0	0	225 9
2009–10	Manchester C	31	1	
2010–11	Manchester C	22	1	
2011–12	Manchester C	14	0	
2012–13	Manchester C	15	0	82 2
2013–14	Liverpool	20	0	20 0

WARD, Danny (G)   0   0
H: 5 11 W: 13 12 b.Wrexham 22-6-93
Internationals: Wales U17, U19, U21.

2011–12	Liverpool	0	0
2012–13	Liverpool	0	0
2013–14	Liverpool	0	0

WISDOM, Andre (D)   48   0
H: 6 1 W: 12 04 b.Leeds 9-5-93
Internationals: England U16, U17, U18, U19, U21.

2009–10	Liverpool	0	0	
2010–11	Liverpool	0	0	
2012–13	Liverpool	12	0	
2013–14	Liverpool	2	0	14 0
2013–14	Derby Co	34	0	34 0

YESIL, Samed (F)   1   0
H: 5 10 W: 10 13 b.Dusseldorf 25-5-94
Internationals: Germany U16, U17, U18, U19.

2011–12	Bayer Leverkusen	1	0	1 0
2012–13	Liverpool	0	0	
2013–14	Liverpool	0	0	

Scholars
Alexander, Jack; Brewitt, Tom; Canos, Tenes Sergi; Chirivella, Burgos Pedro; Cleary, Daniel; Crump, Ryan; Firth, Andrew; Hart, Samuel James; Maguire, Joseph; Marsh, William George; Ojo, Oluwaseyi; Roberts, David; Virtue, Thick Matthew Joseph; Waldron, Dahrius Nathaniel; Williams, Michael Jordan; Wilson, Harry.

MANCHESTER C (46)

ADJEI-BOATENG, Bismark (M)   26   7
b.Accra 10-5-94

2011–12	Manchester C	0	0	
2012	*Stromsgodset*	8	0	
2012–13	Manchester C	0	0	
2013	*Stromsgodset*	17	7	
2013–14	Manchester C	0	0	
2014	*Stromsgodset*	1	0	26 7

AGUERO, Sergio (F)   316   149
H: 5 8 W: 11 09 b.Buenos Aires 2-6-88
Internationals: Argentina U17, U20, U23, Full caps.

2002–03	Independiente	1	0	
2003–04	Independiente	5	0	
2004–05	Independiente	12	5	
2005–06	Independiente	36	18	54 23
2006–07	Atletico Madrid	38	6	
2007–08	Atletico Madrid	37	19	
2008–09	Atletico Madrid	37	17	
2009–10	Atletico Madrid	31	12	
2010–11	Atletico Madrid	32	20	175 74
2011–12	Manchester C	34	23	
2012–13	Manchester C	30	12	
2013–14	Manchester C	23	17	87 52

BARRY, Gareth (M)   529   50
H: 5 11 W: 12 06 b.Hastings 23-2-81
Internationals: England B, U21, Full caps.

1997–98	Aston Villa	5	0	
1998–99	Aston Villa	32	2	
1999–2000	Aston Villa	30	1	
2000–01	Aston Villa	30	0	
2001–02	Aston Villa	20	0	
2002–03	Aston Villa	35	3	
2003–04	Aston Villa	36	3	
2004–05	Aston Villa	34	7	
2005–06	Aston Villa	36	3	
2006–07	Aston Villa	35	8	
2007–08	Aston Villa	37	9	
2008–09	Aston Villa	38	5	365 41
2009–10	Manchester C	34	2	
2010–11	Manchester C	33	2	
2011–12	Manchester C	34	1	
2012–13	Manchester C	31	1	
2013–14	Manchester C	0	0	132 6
2013–14	*Everton*	32	3	32 3

BOSSAERTS, Mathias (D)   0   0
H: 6 0 W: 11 12 b.Gooreind 10-7-96
Internationals: Belgium U17.

BOYATA, Dedryck (M)   30   1
H: 6 2 W: 12 00 b.Brussels 8-9-90
Internationals: Belgium U19, 21, Full caps.

2008–09	Manchester C	0	0	
2009–10	Manchester C	3	0	
2010–11	Manchester C	7	0	
2011–12	Manchester C	0	0	
2011–12	*Bolton W*	14	1	14 1
2012–13	Manchester C	0	0	
2012–13	*FC Twente*	5	0	5 0
2013–14	Manchester C	1	0	11 0

BUNN, Harry (F)   27   1
H: 5 9 W: 11 10 b.Oldham 25-11-92

2010–11	Manchester C	0	0	
2011–12	Manchester C	0	0	
2011–12	*Rochdale*	6	0	6 0
2011–12	*Preston NE*	1	1	1 1
2011–12	*Oldham Ath*	11	0	
2012–13	Manchester C	0	0	
2012–13	*Oldham Ath*	0	0	11 0
2012–13	*Crewe Alex*	4	0	4 0
2013–14	Manchester C	0	0	
2013–14	*Sheffield U*	2	0	2 0
2013–14	*Huddersfield T*	3	0	3 0

BYTYQI, Sinan (M)   0   0
H: 6 1 W: 12 11 b.Prizren 15-1-95
Internationals: Austria U17, U18, U19.

2013–14	Manchester C	0	0

CLICHY, Gael (D)   263   1
H: 5 9 W: 10 04 b.Toulouse 26-7-85
Internationals: France U15, U17, U18, U19, 21, B, Full caps.

2003–04	Arsenal	12	0
2004–05	Arsenal	15	0

2005–06	Arsenal	7	0		
2006–07	Arsenal	27	0		
2007–08	Arsenal	38	0		
2008–09	Arsenal	31	1		
2009–10	Arsenal	24	0		
2010–11	Arsenal	33	0	187	1
2011–12	Manchester C	28	0		
2012–13	Manchester C	28	0		
2013–14	Manchester C	20	0	76	0

COLE, Devante (F)   0 0
H: 6 1 W: 11 06 b.Alderley Edge 10-5-95
Internationals: England U17, U18, U19.

2013–14	Manchester C	0	0

DEMICHELIS, Martin (D)   336 24
H: 6 0 W: 12 03 b.Cordoba 20-12-80
Internationals: Argentina Full caps.

2001	River Plate	0	0		
2002	River Plate	17	0		
2003	River Plate	35	1	52	1
2003–04	Bayern Munich	14	2		
2004–05	Bayern Munich	23	0		
2005–06	Bayern Munich	27	1		
2006–07	Bayern Munich	26	3		
2007–08	Bayern Munich	28	1		
2008–09	Bayern Munich	29	4		
2009–10	Bayern Munich	21	1		
2010–11	Bayern Munich	6	1	174	13
2010–11	Malaga	17	1		
2011–12	Malaga	35	3		
2012–13	Malaga	31	4	83	8
2013–14	Atletico Madrid	0	0		
2013–14	Manchester C	27	2	27	2

DENAYER, Jason (D)   0 0
H: 6 0 b.Brussels 28-6-95
Internationals: Belgium U19, U21.

2013–14	Manchester C	0	0

DONYOH, Godsway (F)   13 1
H: 5 11 W: 11 01 b. 14-10-94

2012–13	Manchester C	0	0		
2012–13	Djurgarden	7	0	7	0
2013–14	Manchester C	0	0		
2013–14	Falkenburg	6	1	6	1

DRURY, Adam (M)   12 0
b.Grimsby 21-9-93

2010–11	Manchester C	0	0		
2011–12	Manchester C	0	0		
2012–13	Manchester C	0	0		
2012–13	Burton Alb	12	0	12	0
2013–14	Manchester C	0	0		

DZEKO, Edin (F)   290 135
H: 6 3 W: 12 08 b.Doboj 17-3-86
Internationals: Bosnia & Herzegovina U19, U21, Full caps.

2004–05	Zeljeznicar	13	1	13	1
2005–06	Usti nad Labem	15	6	15	6
2005–06	Teplice	13	3		
2006–07	Teplice	30	13	43	16
2007–08	Wolfsburg	28	8		
2008–09	Wolfsburg	32	26		
2009–10	Wolfsburg	34	22		
2010–11	Wolfsburg	17	10	111	66
2010–11	Manchester C	15	2		
2011–12	Manchester C	30	14		
2012–13	Manchester C	32	14		
2013–14	Manchester C	31	16	108	46

EVANS, George (M)   23 1
H: 6 0 W: 11 12 b.Cheadle 13-1-96
Internationals: England U17, U19.

2012–13	Manchester C	0	0		
2013–14	Manchester C	0	0		
2013–14	Crewe Alex	23	1	23	1

FACEY, Shay (D)   0 0
H: 5 10 W: 10 00 b.Manchester 7-1-95
Internationals: England U16, U17, U19.

2013–14	Manchester C	0	0

FERNANDINHO, Luis (M)   259 39
H: 5 10 W: 10 09 b.Londrina 4-5-85
Internationals: Brazil Full caps.

2003	Paranaense	29	5		
2004	Paranaense	41	9		
2005	Paranaense	2	0	72	14
2005–06	Shakhtar Donetsk	22	1		
2006–07	Shakhtar Donetsk	25	1		
2008–09	Shakhtar Donetsk	21	5		
2009–10	Shakhtar Donetsk	24	4		
2010–11	Shakhtar Donetsk	15	3		
2011–12	Shakhtar Donetsk	24	4		
2012–13	Shakhtar Donetsk	23	2	154	20
2013–14	Manchester C	33	5	33	5

FOFANA, Seko (M)   0 0
H: 6 0 W: 11 08 b.Paris 7-5-95
Internationals: France U16, U17, U18, U19.

2013–14	Manchester C	0	0

GLENDON, George (M)   0 0
H: 5 10 b.Manchester 3-5-95
Internationals: England U16, U17.

2013–14	Manchester C	0	0

GUIDETTI, John (F)   19 4
H: 5 11 W: 11 00 b.Stockholm 15-4-92
Internationals: Sweden U17, U19, U21, Full caps.

2009–10	Manchester C	0	0		
2009–10	Brommapojkana	8	3	8	3
2010–11	Manchester C	0	0		
2010–11	Burnley	5	1	5	1
2011–12	Manchester C	0	0		
2012–13	Manchester C	0	0		
2013–14	Manchester C	0	0		
2013–14	Stoke C	6	0	6	0

GUNN, Angus (G)   0 0
H: 6 0 b.Norwich 22-1-96
Internationals: England U16, U17, U18.

2013–14	Manchester C	0	0

HART, Joe (G)   294 0
H: 6 3 W: 13 03 b.Shrewsbury 19-4-87
Internationals: England U19, U21, Full caps.

2004–05	Shrewsbury T	6	0		
2005–06	Shrewsbury T	46	0	52	0
2006–07	Manchester C	1	0		
2006–07	Tranmere R	6	0	6	0
2006–07	Blackpool	5	0	5	0
2007–08	Manchester C	26	0		
2008–09	Manchester C	23	0		
2009–10	Manchester C	0	0		
2009–10	Birmingham C	36	0	36	0
2010–11	Manchester C	38	0		
2011–12	Manchester C	38	0		
2012–13	Manchester C	38	0		
2013–14	Manchester C	31	0	195	0

HENSHALL, Alex (M)   9 1
b.Swindon 15-2-94
Internationals: England U16, U17.

2010–11	Manchester C	0	0		
2011–12	Manchester C	0	0		
2012–13	Manchester C	0	0		
2012–13	Chesterfield	7	0	7	0
2013–14	Manchester C	0	0		
2013–14	Bristol R	2	1	2	1
2013–14	Ipswich T	0	0		

HIWULA, Jordy (F)   0 0
H: 5 10 W: 11 12 b.Manchester 24-9-94
Internationals: England U18, U19.

2013–14	Manchester C	0	0

HUWS, Emyr (M)   27 2
b.Llanelli 30-9-93
Internationals: Wales U17, U19, U21, Full caps.

2010–11	Manchester C	0	0		
2011–12	Manchester C	0	0		
2012–13	Manchester C	0	0		
2012–13	Northampton T	10	0	10	0
2013–14	Manchester C	0	0		
2013–14	Birmingham C	17	2	17	2

JAVI GARCIA, Francisco (M)   215 16
H: 6 2 W: 13 02 b.Madrid 8-2-87
Internationals: Spain U16, U17, U19, U20, U21, Full caps.

2004–05	Real Madrid	3	0		
2005–06	RM Castilla	28	4		
2006–07	RM Castilla	17	2	45	6
2007–08	Osasuna	25	2	25	2
2008–09	Real Madrid	15	0	18	0
2009–10	Benfica	26	3		
2010–11	Benfica	24	2		
2011–12	Benfica	22	1		
2012–13	Benfica	2	0	74	6
2012–13	Manchester C	24	2		
2013–14	Manchester C	29	0	53	2

JESUS NAVAS, Gonzalez (M)   315 27
H: 5 7 W: 9 05 b.Los Palacios 21-11-85
Internationals: Spain U21, Full caps.

2003–04	Sevilla	5	0		
2004–05	Sevilla	23	2		
2005–06	Sevilla	34	2		
2006–07	Sevilla	29	1		
2007–08	Sevilla	36	4		
2008–09	Sevilla	35	4		
2009–10	Sevilla	34	4		
2010–11	Sevilla	15	1		
2011–12	Sevilla	37	5		
2012–13	Sevilla	37	0	285	23
2013–14	Manchester C	30	4	30	4

JOHANSEN, Eirik (G)   0 0
H: 6 4 W: 14 00 b.Tonsberg 12-7-92
Internationals: Norway U15, U16, U17, U18, U19, U21, U23.

2010–11	Manchester C	0	0
2011–12	Manchester C	0	0
2012–13	Manchester C	0	0
2013–14	Manchester C	0	0

JOVETIC, Stevan (F)   178 50
H: 6 0 W: 12 05 b.Podgorica 2-11-89
Internationals: Montenegro U21, Full caps.

2005–06	Partizan Belgrade	2	0		
2006–07	Partizan Belgrade	22	1		
2007–08	Partizan Belgrade	27	12	51	13
2008–09	Fiorentina	29	2		
2009–10	Fiorentina	27	5		
2010–11	Fiorentina	0	0		
2011–12	Fiorentina	27	14		
2012–13	Fiorentina	31	13	114	34
2013–14	Manchester C	13	3	13	3

KENNEDY, Kieran (D)   0 0
b.Urmston 23-9-93
Internationals: England U19.

2011–12	Manchester C	0	0
2012–13	Manchester C	0	0
2013–14	Manchester C	0	0
2013–14	Leicester C	0	0

KOLAROV, Aleksandar (D)   250 18
H: 6 2 W: 13 05 b.Belgrade 10-11-85
Internationals: Serbia U21, Full caps.

2004–05	Cukaricki	27	2		
2005–06	Cukaricki	17	0	44	2
2005–06	OFK Belgrade	11	1		
2006–07	OFK Belgrade	27	4	38	5
2007–08	Lazio	24	1		
2008–09	Lazio	25	2		
2009–10	Lazio	33	3	82	6
2010–11	Manchester C	24	1		
2011–12	Manchester C	12	2		
2012–13	Manchester C	20	1		
2013–14	Manchester C	30	1	86	5

KOMPANY, Vincent (D)   271 16
H: 6 3 W: 13 05 b.Brussels 10-4-86
Internationals: Belgium U16, U17, Full caps.

2004–05	Anderlecht	29	2		
2005–06	Anderlecht	32	2	61	4
2006–07	Hamburg	6	0		
2007–08	Hamburg	22	1		
2008–09	Hamburg	1	0	29	1
2008–09	Manchester C	34	1		
2009–10	Manchester C	25	2		
2010–11	Manchester C	37	0		
2011–12	Manchester C	31	3		
2012–13	Manchester C	26	1		
2013–14	Manchester C	28	4	181	11

LAWLOR, Ian (G)   0 · 0
b.Dublin 27-10-94
Internationals: Republic of Ireland U17, U19, U21.

2011–12	Manchester C	0	0
2012–13	Manchester C	0	0
2013–14	Manchester C	0	0

LEIGH, Greg (D)   0 0
H: 5 11 b.Manchester 30-9-94
Internationals: England U19.

2013–14	Manchester C	0	0

LESCOTT, Jolean (D)   432 34
H: 6 2 W: 13 00 b.Birmingham 16-8-82
Internationals: England U17, U18, U20, U21, B, Full caps.

1999–2000	Wolverhampton W	0	0

2000–01	Wolverhampton W	37	2		
2001–02	Wolverhampton W	44	5		
2002–03	Wolverhampton W	44	1		
2003–04	Wolverhampton W	0	0		
2004–05	Wolverhampton W	41	4		
2005–06	Wolverhampton W	46	1	212	13
2006–07	Everton	38	2		
2007–08	Everton	38	8		
2008–09	Everton	36	4		
2009–10	Everton	1	0	113	14
2009–10	Manchester C	18	1		
2010–11	Manchester C	22	3		
2011–12	Manchester C	31	2		
2012–13	Manchester C	26	1		
2013–14	Manchester C	10	0	107	7

LOPES, Marcos (F)   0   0
H: 5 8   W: 10 09   b.Belem 28-12-95
Internationals: Portugal U17, U18, U19, U21.

| 2012–13 | Manchester C | 0 | 0 | | |
| 2013–14 | Manchester C | 0 | 0 | | |

MILNER, James (M)   363   33
H: 5 9   W: 11 00   b.Leeds 4-1-86
Internationals: England U16, U17, U19, U20, U21, Full caps.

2002–03	Leeds U	18	2		
2003–04	Leeds U	30	3	48	5
2003–04	Swindon T	6	2	6	2
2004–05	Newcastle U	25	1		
2005–06	Newcastle U	3	0		
2005–06	Aston Villa	27	1		
2006–07	Newcastle U	35	3		
2007–08	Newcastle U	29	2		
2008–09	Newcastle U	2	0	94	6
2008–09	Aston Villa	36	3		
2009–10	Aston Villa	36	7		
2010–11	Aston Villa	1	1	100	12
2010–11	Manchester C	32	0		
2011–12	Manchester C	26	3		
2012–13	Manchester C	26	4		
2013–14	Manchester C	31	1	115	8

NASRI, Samir (M)   299   43
H: 5 9   W: 11 11   b.Marseille 26-6-87
Internationals: France U16, U17, U18, U19, U21, Full caps.

2004–05	Marseille	24	1		
2005–06	Marseille	30	1		
2006–07	Marseille	37	3		
2007–08	Marseille	30	6	121	11
2008–09	Arsenal	29	6		
2009–10	Arsenal	26	2		
2010–11	Arsenal	30	10		
2011–12	Arsenal	1	0	86	18
2011–12	Manchester C	30	5		
2012–13	Manchester C	28	2		
2013–14	Manchester C	34	7	92	14

NASTASIC, Matija (D)   60   2
H: 6 2   W: 12 05   b.Valjevo 28-3-93
Internationals: Serbia Youth, U21, Full caps.

2011–12	Fiorentina	25	2		
2012–13	Fiorentina	1	0	26	2
2012–13	Manchester C	21	0		
2013–14	Manchester C	13	0	34	0

NEGREDO, Alvaro (F)   241   110
H: 6 1   W: 12 11   b.Madrid 20-8-85
Internationals: Spain U21, Full caps.

2007–08	Almeria	36	13		
2008–09	Almeria	34	18	70	31
2009–10	Sevilla	35	11		
2010–11	Sevilla	38	20		
2011–12	Sevilla	30	14		
2012–13	Sevilla	36	25	139	70
2013–14	Sevilla	32	9	32	9

NTCHAM, Jules Olivier (M)   0   0
H: 5 11   W: 12 07   b.Longjumeau 9-2-96
Internationals: France U16, U17, U18.

| 2013–14 | Manchester C | 0 | 0 | | |

NUHU, Razak (D)   45   1
b.Ghana 14-4-91
Internationals: Ghana Full caps.

2010–11	Manchester C	0	0		
2011	Stromsgodset	11	0		
2011–12	Manchester C	0	0		
2012	Stromsgodset	25	1		
2012–13	Manchester C	0	0		
2013	Stromsgodset	4	0	40	1

| 2013–14 | Manchester C | 0 | 0 | | |
| 2013–14 | Apollon Limassol | 5 | 0 | 5 | 0 |

PANTILIMON, Costel (G)   109   0
H: 6 5   W: 15 02   b.Bacau 1-2-87
Internationals: Romania U17, U19, U21, Full caps.

2005–06	Aerostar Bacau	9	0	9	0
2006–07	Poli Timisoara	8	0		
2007–08	Poli Timisoara	5	0	13	0
2008–09	Timisoara	31	0		
2009–10	Timisoara	21	0		
2010–11	Timisoara	28	0	80	0
2011–12	Manchester C	0	0		
2012–13	Manchester C	0	0		
2013–14	Manchester C	7	0	7	0

PLUMMER, Ellis (D)   3   0
b.Denton 2-9-94
Internationals: England U16, U17.

2011–12	Manchester C	0	0		
2012–13	Manchester C	0	0		
2013–14	Manchester C	0	0		
2013–14	Oldham Ath	3	0	3	0

POZO, Jose (M)   0   0
H: 5 7   b.Malaga 15-3-96
Internationals: Spain U16, U17, U18.

| 2013–14 | Manchester C | 0 | 0 | | |

REKIK, Karim (D)   39   1
H: 6 0   W: 12 00   b.Den Haag 2-12-94
Internationals: Netherlands U16, U17, U19, U21, Full caps.

2011–12	Manchester C	0	0		
2011–12	Portsmouth	8	0	8	0
2012–13	Manchester C	1	0		
2012–13	Blackburn R	5	0	5	0
2013–14	Manchester C	0	0	1	0
2013–14	PSV Eindhoven	25	1	25	1

RICHARDS, Micah (D)   179   7
H: 5 11   W: 13 00   b.Birmingham 24-6-88
Internationals: England U16, U19, U21, Full caps. Great Britain.

2005–06	Manchester C	13	0		
2006–07	Manchester C	28	1		
2007–08	Manchester C	25	0		
2008–09	Manchester C	34	1		
2009–10	Manchester C	23	3		
2010–11	Manchester C	18	1		
2011–12	Manchester C	29	1		
2012–13	Manchester C	7	0		
2013–14	Manchester C	2	0	179	7

RODWELL, Jack (D)   101   6
H: 6 2   W: 12 08   b.Southport 11-3-91
Internationals: England U16, U17, U19, U21, Full caps.

2007–08	Everton	2	0		
2008–09	Everton	19	0		
2009–10	Everton	26	2		
2010–11	Everton	24	0		
2011–12	Everton	14	2		
2012–13	Everton	0	0	85	4
2012–13	Manchester C	11	2		
2013–14	Manchester C	5	0	16	2

RUSNAK, Albert (M)   5   0
b.Kosice 7-7-94
Internationals: Slovakia U19, U21.

2011–12	Manchester C	0	0		
2012–13	Manchester C	0	0		
2013–14	Manchester C	0	0		
2013–14	Oldham Ath	2	0	2	0
2013–14	Birmingham C	3	0	3	0

SCAPUZZI, Luca (F)   63   1
H: 6 0   W: 11 11   b.Milan 15-4-91

2009–10	Portogruaro	22	0		
2010–11	Portogruaro	7	0	29	0
2011–12	Manchester C	0	0		
2011–12	Oldham Ath	10	1	10	1
2011–12	Portsmouth	2	0	2	0
2012–13	Manchester C	0	0		
2012–13	Varese	10	0	10	0
2013–14	Manchester C	0	0		
2013–14	Siena	12	0	12	0

SILVA, David (F)   332   51
H: 5 7   W: 10 07   b.Arguineguin 8-1-86
Internationals: Spain U16, U17, U18, U19, U20, U21, Full caps.

| 2003–04 | Mestalla | 14 | 1 | 14 | 1 |

2004–05	Eibar	35	5	35	5
2005–06	Celta Vigo	34	3	34	3
2006–07	Valencia	36	5		
2007–08	Valencia	34	4		
2008–09	Valencia	19	4		
2009–10	Valencia	30	8	119	21
2010–11	Manchester C	35	4		
2011–12	Manchester C	36	6		
2012–13	Manchester C	32	4		
2013–14	Manchester C	27	7	130	21

SINCLAIR, Scott (F)   173   34
H: 5 10   W: 10 00   b.Bath 26-3-89
Internationals: England U17, U18, U19, U20, U21. Great Britain.

2004–05	Bristol R	2	0	2	0
2005–06	Chelsea	0	0		
2006–07	Chelsea	2	0		
2006–07	Plymouth Arg	15	2	15	2
2007–08	Chelsea	1	0		
2007–08	QPR	9	1	9	1
2007–08	Charlton Ath	3	0	3	0
2007–08	Crystal Palace	6	2	6	2
2008–09	Chelsea	2	0		
2008–09	Birmingham C	14	0	14	0
2009–10	Chelsea	0	0	5	0
2009–10	Wigan Ath	18	1	18	1
2010–11	Swansea C	43	19		
2011–12	Swansea C	38	8		
2012–13	Swansea C	1	1	82	28
2012–13	Manchester C	11	0		
2013–14	Manchester C	0	0	11	0
2013–14	WBA	8	0	8	0

SWANN, George (D)   0   0
H: 6 3   b.Plymouth 10-9-91

2012–13	Manchester C	0	0		
2013–14	Manchester C	0	0		
2013–14	Sheffield W	0	0		

TOURE, Yaya (M)   358   59
H: 6 3   W: 14 02   b.Sokoura Bouake 13-5-83
Internationals: Ivory Coast Full caps.

2001–02	Beveren	28	0		
2002–03	Beveren	30	3		
2003–04	Beveren	12	0	70	3
2003–04	Metalurgs Donetsk	11	1		
2004–05	Metalurgs Donetsk	22	2	33	3
2005–06	Olympiacos	20	3	20	3
2006–07	Monaco	27	5	27	5
2007–08	Barcelona	26	1		
2008–09	Barcelona	25	2		
2009–10	Barcelona	23	1	74	4
2010–11	Manchester C	35	8		
2011–12	Manchester C	32	6		
2012–13	Manchester C	32	7		
2013–14	Manchester C	35	20	134	41

WABARA, Reece (D)   46   0
H: 6 0   W: 12 06   b.Birmingham 28-12-91
Internationals: England U20.

2008–09	Manchester C	0	0		
2009–10	Manchester C	0	0		
2010–11	Manchester C	1	0		
2011–12	Manchester C	0	0		
2011–12	Ipswich T	6	0	6	0
2012–13	Manchester C	0	0		
2012–13	Oldham Ath	25	0	25	0
2012–13	Blackpool	1	0	1	0
2013–14	Manchester C	0	0	1	0
2013–14	Doncaster R	13	0	13	0

WRIGHT, Richard (G)   380   0
H: 6 2   W: 14 04   b.Ipswich 5-11-77
Internationals: England U18, U21, Full caps.

1994–95	Ipswich T	3	0		
1995–96	Ipswich T	23	0		
1996–97	Ipswich T	40	0		
1997–98	Ipswich T	46	0		
1998–99	Ipswich T	46	0		
1999–2000	Ipswich T	46	0		
2000–01	Ipswich T	36	0		
2001–02	Arsenal	12	0	12	0
2002–03	Everton	33	0		
2003–04	Everton	4	0		
2004–05	Everton	7	0		
2005–06	Everton	15	0		
2006–07	Everton	1	0	60	0
2007–08	West Ham U	0	0		
2007–08	Southampton	7	0	7	0
2008–09	Ipswich T	46	0		
2009–10	Ipswich T	12	0		

2010–11	Ipswich T	0	0		
2010–11	Sheffield U	2	0	2	0
2011–12	Ipswich T	1	0	299	0
2012–13	Manchester C	0	0		
2013–14	Manchester C	0	0		

ZABALETA, Pablo (D)   314 18
H: 5 8   W: 10 12   b.Buenos Aires 16-1-85
Internationals: Argentina U20, U23, Full caps.

2002–03	San Lorenzo	11	0		
2003–04	San Lorenzo	27	3		
2004–05	San Lorenzo	28	5	66	8
2005–06	Espanyol	27	2		
2006–07	Espanyol	21	0		
2007–08	Espanyol	32	1	80	3
2008–09	Manchester C	29	1		
2009–10	Manchester C	27	0		
2010–11	Manchester C	26	2		
2011–12	Manchester C	21	1		
2012–13	Manchester C	30	2		
2013–14	Manchester C	35	1	168	7

Scholars
Albinson, Charlie; Ambrose, Thierry;
Barbosa, Intima Jorge Fernando; Barker,
Brandon Lee; Boadu-Adjei, Denzeil; Brooks,
David; Bryan, Kean Shay; Celina, Bersant;
Esmoris, Tasende Jose Angel; Hardy, James;
Holland, Thomas; Horsfield, James; Maffeo,
Becerra Pablo; Nuttall, Joseph; O'Brien, Billy
Thomas; Oseni, Nathaniel Adeyomi Andrew;
Samuelsen, Martin; Smith-Brown, Ashley;
Tattum, Sam; Vasi, Emanuel; Wassi, Yvan.

MANCHESTER U (47)

AMOS, Ben (G)   44 0
H: 6 1   W: 13 00   b.Macclesfield 10-4-90
Internationals: England U16, U17, U18, U19,
U20, U21.

2007–08	Manchester U	0	0		
2008–09	Manchester U	0	0		
2009–10	Manchester U	0	0		
2009–10	*Peterborough U*	1	0	1	0
2010–11	Manchester U	0	0		
2010–11	*Oldham Ath*	16	0	16	0
2011–12	Manchester U	1	0		
2012–13	Manchester U	0	0		
2012–13	*Hull C*	17	0	17	0
2013–14	Manchester U	0	0	1	0
2013–14	*Carlisle U*	9	0	9	0

ANDERSON (M)   134 8
H: 5 8   W: 10 07   b.Porto Alegre 13-4-88
Internationals: Brazil U17, U23, Full caps.

2004–05	Gremio	5	1	5	1
2005–06	Porto	3	0		
2006–07	Porto	15	2	18	2
2007–08	Manchester U	24	0		
2008–09	Manchester U	17	0		
2009–10	Manchester U	14	1		
2010–11	Manchester U	18	1		
2011–12	Manchester U	10	2		
2012–13	Manchester U	17	1		
2013–14	Manchester U	4	0	104	5
2013–14	*Fiorentina*	7	0	7	0

BARMBY, Jack (M)   17 5
Internationals: England U16, U18, U19.

2013–14	Manchester U	0	0		
2013–14	*Hartlepool U*	17	5	17	5

BEBE (F)   76 18
H: 6 3   W: 11 11   b.Agualva-cacem 12-7-90
Internationals: Portugal U21.

2009–10	Amadora	26	4	26	4
2010–11	Guimaraes	8	0		
2010–11	Manchester U	2	0		
2011–12	Manchester U	0	0		
2011–12	*Besiktas*	4	0	4	0
2012–13	Manchester U	0	0		
2012–13	*Rio Ave*	17	1	17	1
2013–14	Manchester U	0	0	2	0
2013–14	*Pacos Ferreira*	27	13	27	13

BLACKETT, Tyler (D)   13 0
H: 6 1   W: 11 12   b. 2-4-94
Internationals: England U16, U17, U18, U19.

2012–13	Manchester U	0	0		
2013–14	Manchester U	0	0		

2013–14	*Blackpool*	5	0	5	0
2013–14	*Birmingham C*	8	0	8	0

BUTTNER, Alexander (D)   119 12
H: 5 8   W: 11 10   b.Doetinchem 11-2-89
Internationals: Netherlands U19, U20.

2007–08	Vitesse	1	0		
2008–09	Vitesse	23	3		
2009–10	Vitesse	26	2		
2010–11	Vitesse	24	0		
2011–12	Vitesse	32	5	106	10
2012–13	Manchester U	5	2		
2013–14	Manchester U	8	0	13	2

BYRNE, Sam (F)   17 1
Internationals: Republic of Ireland U15, U16,
U17, U19.

2013–14	Manchester U	0	0		
2013–14	*Carlisle U*	17	1	17	1

CARRICK, Michael (M)   453 26
H: 6 1   W: 11 10   b.Wallsend 28-7-81
Internationals: England U18, U21, B, Full
caps.

1998–99	West Ham U	0	0		
1999–2000	West Ham U	8	1		
1999–2000	*Swindon T*	6	2	6	2
1999–2000	*Birmingham C*	2	0	2	0
2000–01	West Ham U	33	1		
2001–02	West Ham U	30	2		
2002–03	West Ham U	30	1		
2003–04	West Ham U	35	1		
2004–05	West Ham U	0	0	136	6
2004–05	Tottenham H	29	0		
2005–06	Tottenham H	35	2	64	2
2006–07	Manchester U	33	3		
2007–08	Manchester U	31	2		
2008–09	Manchester U	28	4		
2009–10	Manchester U	30	3		
2010–11	Manchester U	28	0		
2011–12	Manchester U	30	2		
2012–13	Manchester U	36	1		
2013–14	Manchester U	29	1	245	16

CLEVERLEY, Tom (M)   127 19
H: 5 9   W: 10 07   b.Basingstoke 12-8-89
Internationals: England U20, U21, Full caps.
Great Britain.

2007–08	Manchester U	0	0		
2008–09	Manchester U	0	0		
2008–09	*Leicester C*	15	2	15	2
2009–10	Manchester U	0	0		
2009–10	*Watford*	33	11	33	11
2010–11	Manchester U	0	0		
2010–11	*Wigan Ath*	25	3	25	3
2011–12	Manchester U	10	0		
2012–13	Manchester U	22	2		
2013–14	Manchester U	22	1	54	3

DA SILVA, Rafael (D)   99 5
H: 5 8   W: 10 03   b.Rio de Janeiro 9-7-90
Internationals: Brazil U17, U23, Full caps.

2008–09	Manchester U	16	1		
2009–10	Manchester U	8	1		
2010–11	Manchester U	16	0		
2011–12	Manchester U	12	0		
2012–13	Manchester U	28	3		
2013–14	Manchester U	19	0	99	5

DE GEA, David (G)   151 0
H: 6 3   W: 12 13   b.Madrid 7-11-90
Internationals: Spain U15, U17, U19, U20,
U21, U23, Full caps.

2009–10	Atletico Madrid	19	0		
2010–11	Atletico Madrid	38	0	57	0
2011–12	Manchester U	29	0		
2012–13	Manchester U	28	0		
2013–14	Manchester U	37	0	94	0

EKANGAMENE, Charni (M)   4 0
b.Antwerp 16-2-94
Internationals: Belgium U15, U19.

2011–12	Manchester U	0	0		
2012–13	Manchester U	0	0		
2013–14	Manchester U	0	0		
2013–14	*Carlisle U*	4	0	4	0

EVANS, Jonny (D)   164 7
H: 6 2   W: 12 02   b.Belfast 3-1-88
Internationals: Northern Ireland U16, U17,
U21, Full caps.

2004–05	Manchester U	0	0		
2005–06	Manchester U	0	0		
2006–07	Manchester U	0	0		

2006–07	*Antwerp*	14	2	14	2
2006–07	*Sunderland*	18	1		
2007–08	Manchester U	0	0		
2007–08	*Sunderland*	15	0	33	1
2008–09	Manchester U	17	0		
2009–10	Manchester U	18	0		
2010–11	Manchester U	13	0		
2011–12	Manchester U	29	1		
2012–13	Manchester U	23	3		
2013–14	Manchester U	17	0	117	4

EVRA, Patrice (D)   459 12
H: 5 8   W: 11 10   b.Dakar 15-5-81
Internationals: France U21, Full caps.

1998–99	Marsala	24	3	24	3
1999–2000	Monza	3	0	3	0
2000–01	Nice	5	0		
2001–02	Nice	34	1	39	1
2002–03	Monaco	36	1		
2003–04	Monaco	33	0		
2004–05	Monaco	36	0		
2005–06	Monaco	15	0	120	1
2005–06	Manchester U	11	0		
2006–07	Manchester U	24	1		
2007–08	Manchester U	33	0		
2008–09	Manchester U	28	0		
2009–10	Manchester U	38	0		
2010–11	Manchester U	35	1		
2011–12	Manchester U	37	0		
2012–13	Manchester U	34	4		
2013–14	Manchester U	33	1	273	7

FELLAINI, Marouane (M)   219 31
H: 6 4   W: 13 05   b.Brussels 22-11-87
Internationals: Belgium U18, U19, U21, Full
caps.

2006–07	Standard Liege	29	0		
2007–08	Standard Liege	30	6		
2008–09	Standard Liege	3	0	62	6
2008–09	Everton	30	8		
2009–10	Everton	23	2		
2010–11	Everton	20	1		
2011–12	Everton	34	3		
2012–13	Everton	31	11		
2013–14	Everton	3	0	141	25
2013–14	Manchester U	16	0	16	0

FERDINAND, Rio (D)   503 11
H: 6 2   W: 13 12   b.Peckham 7-11-78
Internationals: England U18, U21, B, Full
caps.

1995–96	West Ham U	1	0		
1996–97	West Ham U	15	2		
1996–97	*Bournemouth*	10	0	10	0
1997–98	West Ham U	35	0		
1998–99	West Ham U	31	0		
1999–2000	West Ham U	33	0		
2000–01	West Ham U	12	0	127	2
2000–01	Leeds U	23	2		
2001–02	Leeds U	31	0	54	2
2002–03	Manchester U	28	0		
2003–04	Manchester U	20	0		
2004–05	Manchester U	31	0		
2005–06	Manchester U	37	3		
2006–07	Manchester U	33	1		
2007–08	Manchester U	35	2		
2008–09	Manchester U	24	0		
2009–10	Manchester U	13	0		
2010–11	Manchester U	19	0		
2011–12	Manchester U	30	0		
2012–13	Manchester U	28	1		
2013–14	Manchester U	14	0	312	7

FLETCHER, Darren (M)   212 18
H: 6 0   W: 11 09   b.Edinburgh 1-2-84
Internationals: Scotland U20, U21, B, Full
caps.

2000–01	Manchester U	0	0		
2001–02	Manchester U	0	0		
2002–03	Manchester U	0	0		
2003–04	Manchester U	22	0		
2004–05	Manchester U	18	3		
2005–06	Manchester U	27	1		
2006–07	Manchester U	24	3		
2007–08	Manchester U	16	0		
2008–09	Manchester U	26	3		
2009–10	Manchester U	30	4		
2010–11	Manchester U	26	2		
2011–12	Manchester U	8	1		
2012–13	Manchester U	3	1		
2013–14	Manchester U	12	0	212	18

GIGGS, Ryan (F)   672 114
H: 5 11   W: 11 02   b.Cardiff 29-11-73
Internationals: England Schools. Wales U18, U21, Full caps. Great Britain.

1990–91	Manchester U	2	1		
1991–92	Manchester U	38	4		
1992–93	Manchester U	41	9		
1993–94	Manchester U	38	13		
1994–95	Manchester U	29	1		
1995–96	Manchester U	33	11		
1996–97	Manchester U	26	3		
1997–98	Manchester U	29	8		
1998–99	Manchester U	24	3		
1999–2000	Manchester U	30	6		
2000–01	Manchester U	31	5		
2001–02	Manchester U	25	7		
2002–03	Manchester U	36	8		
2003–04	Manchester U	33	7		
2004–05	Manchester U	32	5		
2005–06	Manchester U	27	3		
2006–07	Manchester U	30	4		
2007–08	Manchester U	31	3		
2008–09	Manchester U	28	2		
2009–10	Manchester U	25	5		
2010–11	Manchester U	25	2		
2011–12	Manchester U	25	2		
2012–13	Manchester U	22	2		
2013–14	Manchester U	12	0	672	114

GOLLINI, Pierluigi (G)   0 0
b.Bologna 18-3-95
Internationals: Italy U18, U19.

2013–14	Manchester U	0	0

GRIMSHAW, Liam (D)   0 0
Internationals: England U18.

2013–14	Manchester U	0	0
2013–14	Morecambe	0	0

HENRIQUEZ, Angelo (F)   45 11
H: 5 10   W: 10 11   b.Santiago 13-4-94
Internationals: Chile U15, U17, U20, Full caps.

2012	Universidad de Chile	17	11	17	11
2012–13	Manchester U	0	0		
2012–13	*Wigan Ath*	4	1	4	1
2013–14	Manchester U	0	0		
2013–14	*Real Zaragoza*	24	6	24	6

HERNANDEZ, Javier (F)   208 74
H: 5 8   W: 9 11   b.Guadalajara 1-6-88
Internationals: Mexico U20, Full caps.

2005–06	Tapatio	11	0		
2006–07	Tapatio	12	3		
2006–07	Guadalajara	7	1		
2007–08	Guadalajara	5	0		
2007–08	Tapatio	15	6		
2008–09	Tapatio	7	2	45	11
2008–09	Guadalajara	22	4		
2009–10	Guadalajara	28	21	62	26
2010–11	Manchester U	27	13		
2011–12	Manchester U	28	10		
2012–13	Manchester U	22	10		
2013–14	Manchester U	24	4	101	37

HOLGEBAUM PEREIRA, Andreas (M)   0 0
b.Duffel 1-1-96
Internationals: Belgium U15, U16, U17.

2013–14	Manchester U	0	0

JAMES, Reece (D)   1 0
H: 5 6   b. 7-11-93

2012–13	Manchester U	0	0		
2013–14	Manchester U	0	0		
2013–14	*Carlisle U*	1	0	1	0

JANUZAJ, Adrian (M)   27 4
H: 5 11   W: 11 11   b.Brussels 5-2-95
Internationals: Belgium Full caps.

2011–12	Manchester U	0	0		
2012–13	Manchester U	0	0		
2013–14	Manchester U	27	4	27	4

JOHNSTONE, Samuel (G)   38 0
H: 6 0   W: 12 10   b.Preston 25-3-93
Internationals: England U16, U17, U19, U20.

2009–10	Manchester U	0	0		
2010–11	Manchester U	0	0		
2011–12	Manchester U	0	0		
2011–12	*Scunthorpe U*	12	0	12	0
2012–13	Manchester U	0	0		
2012–13	*Walsall*	7	0	7	0

2013–14	Manchester U	0	0		
2013–14	*Yeovil T*	1	0	1	0
2013–14	*Doncaster R*	18	0	18	0

JONES, Phil (D)   107 2
H: 5 11   W: 11 02   b.Preston 21-2-92
Internationals: England U19, U21, Full caps.

2009–10	Blackburn R	9	0		
2010–11	Blackburn R	26	0	35	0
2011–12	Manchester U	29	1		
2012–13	Manchester U	17	0		
2013–14	Manchester U	26	1	72	2

KAGAWA, Shinji (M)   98 34
H: 5 8   W: 10 00   b.Tarumi-ku 17-3-89
Internationals: Japan 19, U20, U23, Full caps.

2009–10	Cerezo Osaka	11	7	11	7
2010–11	Borussia Dortmund	18	8		
2011–12	Borussia Dortmund	31	13	49	21
2012–13	Manchester U	20	6		
2013–14	Manchester U	18	0	38	6

KEANE, Michael (D)   42 5
H: 5 7   W: 12 13   b.Stockport 11-1-93
Internationals: Republic of Ireland U17. England U19, U21.

2011–12	Manchester U	0	0		
2012–13	Manchester U	0	0		
2012–13	*Leicester C*	22	2	22	2
2013–14	Manchester U	0	0		
2013–14	*Derby Co*	7	0	7	0
2013–14	*Blackburn R*	13	3	13	3

KEANE, Will (F)   15 0
H: 6 2   W: 11 05   b.Stockport 11-1-93
Internationals: England U16, U17, U19, U21.

2009–10	Manchester U	0	0		
2010–11	Manchester U	0	0		
2011–12	Manchester U	1	0		
2012–13	Manchester U	0	0		
2013–14	Manchester U	0	0	1	0
2013–14	*Wigan Ath*	4	0	4	0
2013–14	*QPR*	10	0	10	0

LAWRENCE, Tom (M)   29 5
b. 13-1-94
Internationals: Wales U17, U19, U21.

2012–13	Manchester U	0	0		
2013–14	Manchester U	1	0	1	0
2013–14	*Carlisle U*	9	3	9	3
2013–14	*Yeovil T*	19	2	19	2

LINDEGAARD, Anders (G)   91 0
H: 6 4   W: 12 08   b.Odense 13-4-84
Internationals: Denmark U19, U20, Full caps.

2003–04	Odense	0	0		
2004–05	Odense	0	0		
2005–06	Odense	0	0		
2006–07	Odense	1	0		
2007–08	Odense	1	0		
2008–09	*Kolding*	10	0	10	0
2009	Aalesund	26	0		
2009	Odense	4	0	6	0
2010	Aalesund	30	0	56	0
2010–11	Manchester U	0	0		
2011–12	Manchester U	8	0		
2012–13	Manchester U	10	0		
2013–14	Manchester U	1	0	19	0

LINGARD, Jesse (M)   33 9
H: 5 3   W: 11 11   b.Warrington 15-12-92
Internationals: England U17, U21.

2011–12	Manchester U	0	0		
2012–13	Manchester U	0	0		
2012–13	*Leicester C*	5	0	5	0
2013–14	Manchester U	0	0		
2013–14	*Birmingham C*	13	6	13	6
2013–14	*Brighton & HA*	15	3	15	3

MACHEDA, Federico (F)   83 17
H: 6 0   W: 11 13   b.Rome 22-8-91
Internationals: Italy U16, U17, U19, 21.

2008–09	Manchester U	4	2		
2009–10	Manchester U	5	1		
2010–11	Manchester U	7	1		
2010–11	*Sampdoria*	14	0	14	0
2011–12	Manchester U	3	0		
2011–12	*QPR*	3	0	3	0
2012–13	Manchester U	0	0		
2012–13	*Stuttgart*	14	0	14	0
2013–14	Manchester U	0	0	19	4
2013–14	*Doncaster R*	15	3	15	3
2013–14	*Birmingham C*	18	10	18	10

MATA, Juan (M)   265 67
H: 5 7   W: 11 00   b.Ocon de Villafranca 28-4-88
Internationals: Spain U16, U17, U19, U20, U21, U23, Full caps.

2006–07	Real Madrid B	39	10	39	10
2007–08	Valencia	24	5		
2008–09	Valencia	37	11		
2009–10	Valencia	35	9		
2010–11	Valencia	33	8	129	33
2011–12	Chelsea	34	6		
2012–13	Chelsea	35	12		
2013–14	Chelsea	13	0	82	18
2013–14	Manchester U	15	6	15	6

NANI (M)   204 35
H: 5 9   W: 10 04   b.Cape Verde 17-11-86
Internationals: Portugal U21, Full caps.

2005–06	Sporting Lisbon	29	4		
2006–07	Sporting Lisbon	29	5	58	9
2007–08	Manchester U	26	3		
2008–09	Manchester U	13	1		
2009–10	Manchester U	23	4		
2010–11	Manchester U	33	9		
2011–12	Manchester U	29	8		
2012–13	Manchester U	11	1		
2013–14	Manchester U	11	0	146	26

PETRUCCI, Davide (M)   9 1
H: 6 2   W: 13 10   b.Rome 5-10-91
Internationals: Italy U19.

2008–09	Manchester U	0	0		
2009–10	Manchester U	0	0		
2010–11	Manchester U	0	0		
2011–12	Manchester U	0	0		
2012–13	Manchester U	0	0		
2012–13	*Peterborough U*	4	1	4	1
2013–14	Manchester U	0	0		
2013–14	*Charlton Ath*	5	0	5	0

POWELL, Nick (F)   88 22
H: 6 0   W: 10 05   b.Crewe 23-3-94
Internationals: England U16, U17, U18, U19, U21.

2010–11	Crewe Alex	17	0		
2011–12	Crewe Alex	38	14	55	14
2012–13	Manchester U	2	1		
2013–14	Manchester U	0	0	2	1
2013–14	*Wigan Ath*	31	7	31	7

ROONEY, Wayne (F)   374 173
H: 5 10   W: 12 13   b.Liverpool 24-10-85
Internationals: England U15, U16, U19, Full caps.

2002–03	Everton	33	6		
2003–04	Everton	34	9	67	15
2004–05	Manchester U	29	11		
2005–06	Manchester U	36	16		
2006–07	Manchester U	35	14		
2007–08	Manchester U	27	12		
2008–09	Manchester U	30	12		
2009–10	Manchester U	32	26		
2010–11	Manchester U	28	11		
2011–12	Manchester U	34	27		
2012–13	Manchester U	27	12		
2013–14	Manchester U	29	17	307	158

SMALLING, Chris (D)   88 2
H: 6 4   W: 14 02   b.Greenwich 22-11-89
Internationals: England U18, U20, U21, Full caps.

2008–09	Fulham	1	0		
2009–10	Fulham	12	0	13	0
2010–11	Manchester U	16	0		
2011–12	Manchester U	19	1		
2012–13	Manchester U	15	0		
2013–14	Manchester U	25	1	75	2

THORPE, Tom (D)   6 0
H: 6 0   W: 14 00   b.Manchester 13-1-93
Internationals: England U16, U17, U18, U19, U20, U21.

2010–11	Manchester U	0	0		
2011–12	Manchester U	0	0		
2012–13	Manchester U	0	0		
2013–14	Manchester U	0	0		
2013–14	*Birmingham C*	6	0	6	0

VALENCIA, Antonio (M)   303 31
H: 5 10   W: 12 04   b.Lago Agrio 5-8-85
Internationals: Ecuador U20, 21, U23, Full caps.

2002	El Nacional	1	0		

Season	Club	App	Gls	Tot	TG
2003	El Nacional	26	2		
2004	El Nacional	42	5		
2005	El Nacional	14	4	**83**	**11**
2005–06	Villarreal	2	0	**2**	**0**
2005–06	*Recreativo*	4	0	**4**	**0**
2006–07	Wigan Ath	22	1		
2007–08	Wigan Ath	31	3		
2008–09	Wigan Ath	31	3	**84**	**7**
2009–10	Manchester U	34	5		
2010–11	Manchester U	10	1		
2011–12	Manchester U	27	4		
2012–13	Manchester U	30	1		
2013–14	Manchester U	29	2	**130**	**13**

VAN PERSIE, Robin (F)   **314 148**
H: 6 0   W: 11 00   b.Rotterdam 6-8-83
Internationals: Netherlands U17, U19, U21, Full caps.

Season	Club	App	Gls	Tot	TG
2001–02	Feyenoord	10	0		
2002–03	Feyenoord	23	8		
2003–04	Feyenoord	28	6	**61**	**14**
2004–05	Arsenal	26	5		
2005–06	Arsenal	24	5		
2006–07	Arsenal	22	11		
2007–08	Arsenal	15	7		
2008–09	Arsenal	28	11		
2009–10	Arsenal	16	9		
2010–11	Arsenal	25	18		
2011–12	Arsenal	38	30		
2012–13	Arsenal	0	0	**194**	**96**
2012–13	Manchester U	38	26		
2013–14	Manchester U	21	12	**59**	**38**

VARELA, Guillermo (D)   **0 0**
H: 5 7   W: 10 11   b.Montevideo 24-3-93
Internationals: Uruguay U17, U20.

Season	Club	App	Gls
2013–14	Manchester U	0	0

VERMIJL, Marnick (D)   **28 3**
H: 5 11   W: 11 12   b.Overpelt 13-1-92
Internationals: Belgium U17, U18, U19, U21.

Season	Club	App	Gls	Tot	TG
2010–11	Manchester U	0	0		
2011–12	Manchester U	0	0		
2012–13	Manchester U	0	0		
2013–14	Manchester U	0	0		
2013–14	*NEC*	28	3	**28**	**3**

VIDIC, Nemanja (D)   **345 37**
H: 6 1   W: 13 02   b.Uzice 21-10-81
Internationals: Serbia Full caps.

Season	Club	App	Gls	Tot	TG
2000–01	Subotica	27	6	**27**	**6**
2001–02	Red Star Belgrade	22	2		
2002–03	Red Star Belgrade	26	5		
2003–04	Red Star Belgrade	20	5	**68**	**12**
2004	Spartak Moscow	12	2		
2005	Spartak Moscow	27	2	**39**	**4**
2005–06	Manchester U	11	0		
2006–07	Manchester U	25	3		
2007–08	Manchester U	32	1		
2008–09	Manchester U	34	4		
2009–10	Manchester U	24	1		
2010–11	Manchester U	35	5		
2011–12	Manchester U	6	0		
2012–13	Manchester U	19	1		
2013–14	Manchester U	25	0	**211**	**15**

WELBECK, Danny (F)   **124 28**
H: 6 1   W: 11 07   b.Manchester 26-11-90
Internationals: England U17, U18, U19, U21, Full caps.

Season	Club	App	Gls	Tot	TG
2007–08	Manchester U	0	0		
2008–09	Manchester U	3	1		
2009–10	Manchester U	5	0		
2009–10	*Preston NE*	8	2	**8**	**2**
2010–11	Manchester U	2	0		
2010–11	*Sunderland*	26	6	**26**	**6**
2011–12	Manchester U	30	9		
2012–13	Manchester U	27	1		
2013–14	Manchester U	25	9	**90**	**20**

WILSON, James (F)   **1 2**
b.Biddulph 1-12-95
Internationals: England U16, U19.

Season	Club	App	Gls	Tot	TG
2013–14	Manchester U	1	2	**1**	**2**

YOUNG, Ashley (M)   **319 57**
H: 5 10   W: 10 03   b.Stevenage 9-7-85
Internationals: England U21, Full caps.

Season	Club	App	Gls	Tot	TG
2002–03	Watford	0	0		
2003–04	Watford	5	3		
2004–05	Watford	34	0		
2005–06	Watford	39	13		
2006–07	Watford	20	3	**98**	**19**
2006–07	Aston Villa	13	2		
2007–08	Aston Villa	37	9		
2008–09	Aston Villa	36	7		
2009–10	Aston Villa	37	5		
2010–11	Aston Villa	34	7	**157**	**30**
2011–12	Manchester U	25	6		
2012–13	Manchester U	19	0		
2013–14	Manchester U	20	2	**64**	**8**

ZAHA, Wilfried (F)   **140 13**
H: 5 11   W: 10 05   b.Ivory Coast 10-11-92
Internationals: England U19, U21, Full caps.

Season	Club	App	Gls	Tot	TG
2009–10	Crystal Palace	1	0		
2010–11	Crystal Palace	41	1		
2011–12	Crystal Palace	41	6		
2012–13	Crystal Palace	43	6	**126**	**13**
2012–13	Manchester U	0	0		
2013–14	Manchester U	2	0	**2**	**0**
2013–14	*Cardiff C*	12	0	**12**	**0**

Scholars
Borthwick-Jackson, Cameron Jake; Croskery, Ruairi; Dorrington, George Edward; Evans, Callum Leeroy; Fletcher, Ashley Michael; Goss, Sean Richard; Harrop, Josh; Henderson, Dean Bradley; McConnell, Ryan Peter; McNair, Patrick James Coleman; Mctominay, Scott; Mitchell, Demetri Karim; Redmond, Devonte Vincent; Riley, Joe; Rowley, Louis James; Thompson, Jordan Andrew; Willock, Matthew.

MANSFIELD T (48)

BEEVERS, Lee (D)   **322 12**
H: 6 2   W: 11 07   b.Doncaster 4-12-83
Internationals: Wales U21.

Season	Club	App	Gls	Tot	TG
2000–01	Ipswich T	0	0		
2001–02	Ipswich T	0	0		
2002–03	Ipswich T	0	0		
2002–03	*Boston U*	1	0		
2003–04	Boston U	40	2		
2004–05	Boston U	31	1	**72**	**3**
2004–05	Lincoln C	8	0		
2005–06	Lincoln C	33	1		
2006–07	Lincoln C	44	5		
2007–08	Lincoln C	37	1		
2008–09	Lincoln C	44	2	**166**	**9**
2009–10	Colchester U	4	0		
2010–11	Colchester U	19	0	**23**	**0**
2011–12	Walsall	35	0	**35**	**0**
2013–14	Mansfield T	26	0	**26**	**0**

BLACK, Paul (D)   **74 1**
H: 6 0   W: 12 10   b.Middleton 18-5-90

Season	Club	App	Gls	Tot	TG
2007–08	Oldham Ath	2	0		
2008–09	Oldham Ath	3	0		
2009–10	Oldham Ath	13	1		
2010–11	Oldham Ath	29	0		
2011–12	Oldham Ath	13	0	**60**	**1**
2012–13	Tranmere R	10	0		
2013–14	Tranmere R	0	0	**10**	**0**
2013–14	Mansfield T	0	0		
2013–14	*Carlisle U*	4	0	**4**	**0**

BRISCOE, Louis (F)   **6 0**
H: 5 11   W: 13 06   b.Burton-on-Trent 2-4-88
Internationals: England C.

Season	Club	App	Gls	Tot	TG
2005–06	Port Vale	4	0		
2006–07	Port Vale	0	0		
2007–08	Port Vale	0	0	**4**	**0**
2013–14	Mansfield T	2	0	**2**	**0**

CLEMENTS, Chris (M)   **38 2**
H: 5 9   W: 10 04   b.Birmingham 6-2-90

Season	Club	App	Gls	Tot	TG
2008–09	Crewe Alex	0	0		
2009	*IBV*	15	1	**15**	**1**
2009–10	Crewe Alex	0	0		
2010–11	Crewe Alex	0	0		
2013–14	Mansfield T	23	1	**23**	**1**

CLUCAS, Sam (M)   **55 8**
H: 5 10   W: 11 08   b.Lincoln 25-9-90

Season	Club	App	Gls	Tot	TG
2009–10	Lincoln C	0	0		
2011–12	Hereford U	17	0	**17**	**0**
2013–14	Mansfield T	38	8	**38**	**8**

DANIEL, Colin (M)   **167 16**
H: 5 11   W: 11 06   b.Eastwood 15-2-88

Season	Club	App	Gls	Tot	TG
2006–07	Crewe Alex	0	0		
2007–08	Crewe Alex	1	0		
2008–09	Crewe Alex	13	1	**14**	**1**
2008–09	*Macclesfield T*	8	0		
2009–10	Macclesfield T	38	3		
2010–11	Macclesfield T	43	8		
2011–12	Macclesfield T	36	2	**125**	**13**
2013–14	Mansfield T	28	2	**28**	**2**

DEMPSTER, John (D)   **115 5**
H: 6 1   W: 11 07   b.Kettering 1-4-83
Internationals: Scotland U21.

Season	Club	App	Gls	Tot	TG
2001–02	Rushden & D	2	0		
2002–03	Rushden & D	16	1		
2003–04	Rushden & D	19	0		
2004–05	Rushden & D	15	0		
2005–06	Rushden & D	14	3	**66**	**4**
2005–06	Oxford U	6	0	**6**	**0**
From Kettering T					
2011–12	*Crawley T*	7	1	**7**	**1**
2013–14	Mansfield T	36	0	**36**	**0**

DYER, Ross (F)   **12 2**

Season	Club	App	Gls	Tot	TG
2013–14	Mansfield T	12	2	**12**	**2**

HOWELL, Anthony (M)   **33 3**
b.27-5-86

Season	Club	App	Gls	Tot	TG
2013–14	Mansfield T	33	3	**33**	**3**

HUTCHINSON, Ben (F)   **79 8**
H: 5 11   W: 12 09   b.Nottingham 27-11-87

Season	Club	App	Gls	Tot	TG
2005–06	Middlesbrough	0	0		
2006–07	Middlesbrough	0	0		
2007–08	Middlesbrough	8	1	**8**	**1**
2007–08	Celtic	2	0		
2008–09	Celtic	3	0		
2009–10	Celtic	0	0		
2009–10	*Swindon T*	10	1	**10**	**1**
2010–11	Celtic	0	0	**5**	**0**
2010–11	*Lincoln C*	36	4	**36**	**4**
2011–12	Kilmarnock	4	0	**4**	**0**
2013–14	Mansfield T	16	2	**16**	**2**

JENNINGS, James (D)   **71 4**
H: 5 10   W: 12 00   b.Manchester 2-9-87

Season	Club	App	Gls	Tot	TG
2006–07	Macclesfield T	9	0		
2007–08	Macclesfield T	11	0		
2008–09	Macclesfield T	18	0	**38**	**0**
From Kettering T, Cambridge U					
2013–14	Mansfield T	33	4	**33**	**4**

MARRIOTT, Alan (G)   **391 0**
H: 6 0   W: 12 07   b.Bedford 3-9-78

Season	Club	App	Gls	Tot	TG
1997–98	Tottenham H	0	0		
1998–99	Tottenham H	0	0		
1999–2000	Lincoln C	18	0		
2000–01	Lincoln C	30	0		
2001–02	Lincoln C	43	0		
2002–03	Lincoln C	46	0		
2003–04	Lincoln C	46	0		
2004–05	Lincoln C	45	0		
2005–06	Lincoln C	43	0		
2006–07	Lincoln C	46	0		
2007–08	Lincoln C	34	0	**351**	**0**
2013–14	Mansfield T	40	0	**40**	**0**

MARSDEN, Liam (D)   **2 0**
b. 21-11-94

Season	Club	App	Gls	Tot	TG
2013–14	Mansfield T	2	0	**2**	**0**

McGUIRE, Jamie (M)   **64 3**
H: 5 7   W: 10 13   b.Birkenhead 13-11-83

Season	Club	App	Gls	Tot	TG
2001–02	Tranmere R	0	0		
2002–03	Tranmere R	0	0		
2003–04	Tranmere R	0	0		
From Northwich Vic (loan), Droylsden					
2012–13	Fleetwood T	37	1	**37**	**1**
2013–14	Mansfield T	27	2	**27**	**2**

MEIKLE, Lindon (F)   **28 1**
b. 21-3-88
Internationals: England C.

Season	Club	App	Gls	Tot	TG
2013–14	Mansfield T	28	1	**28**	**1**

MITCHELL, Liam (G)   **1 0**
H: 6 3   W: 14 00   b.Nottingham 18-9-92

Season	Club	App	Gls	Tot	TG
2011–12	Notts Co	0	0		
2012–13	Notts Co	0	0		
2013–14	Mansfield T	1	0	**1**	**0**

MURRAY, Adam (M)   **236 17**
H: 5 9   W: 10 01   b.Birmingham 30-9-81

Season	Club	App	Gls	Tot	TG
1998–99	Derby Co	4	0		
1999–2000	Derby Co	8	0		
2000–01	Derby Co	14	0		
2001–02	Derby Co	6	0		
2001–02	*Mansfield T*	13	7		

2002–03	Derby Co	24	0	56	0
2003–04	Kidderminster H	22	3	22	3

From Burton Alb

2003–04	Notts Co	3	0	3	0
2004–05	Mansfield T	32	5		
2005–06	Carlisle U	37	1	37	1
2006–07	Torquay U	21	0	21	0
2006–07	Macclesfield T	11	0		
2007–08	Macclesfield T	23	0	34	0

From Oxford U, Luton T

2013–14	Mansfield T	18	1	63	13

MURTAGH, Keiran (M) 63 3
H: 6 2 W: 11 12 b.Wapping 29-10-88
Internationals: Republic of Ireland U17. Antigua and Barbuda Full caps.

2008–09	Yeovil T	26	0		
2009–10	Yeovil T	27	3	53	3
2010–11	Wycombe W	7	0	7	0

From Cambridge U, Macclesfield T

2013–14	Mansfield T	3	0	3	0

PALMER, Oliver (F) 38 4

2013–14	Mansfield T	38	4	38	4

PILKINGTON, George (D) 251 11
H: 5 11 W: 12 04 b.Rugeley 7-11-81

2002–03	Everton	0	0		
2002–03	*Exeter C*	7	0	7	0
2003–04	Port Vale	44	1		
2004–05	Port Vale	43	0		
2005–06	Port Vale	46	2		
2006–07	Port Vale	46	6		
2007–08	Port Vale	45	2	224	11
2008–09	Luton T	18	0	18	0
2013–14	Mansfield T	2	0	2	0

POKU, Godfrey (M) 4 0

2013–14	Mansfield T	4	0	4	0

RHEAD, Matt (F) 40 6

2013–14	Mansfield T	40	6	40	6

RILEY, Martin (D) 57 1
H: 6 2 W: 12 10 b.Wolverhampton 5-12-86
Internationals: England C.

2006–07	Wolverhampton W	0	0		
2007–08	Wolverhampton W	0	0		

From Kidderminster H

2010–11	Cheltenham T	26	0	26	0

From Wrexham

2013–14	Mansfield T	31	1	31	1

SPEIGHT, Jake (F) 70 8
H: 5 8 W: 12 09 b.Sheffield 28-9-83

2005–06	Bury	17	2		
2006–07	Bury	13	0	30	2

From Northwich Vic, Droylsden, Mansfield T

2010–11	Bradford C	28	4	28	4
2010–11	*Port Vale*	4	1	4	1

From Wrexham

2013–14	Mansfield T	8	1	8	1

STEVENSON, Lee (M) 21 5
b. 1-6-84

2013–14	Mansfield T	21	5	21	5

SUTTON, Ritchie (D) 47 0
H: 6 0 W: 11 04 b.Stoke-on-Trent 29-4-86

2005–06	Crewe Alex	0	0		

From Stafford R, Northwich Vic, FC Halifax T, Nantwich T

2010–11	Port Vale	11	0	11	0
2013–14	Mansfield T	36	0	36	0

TAFAZOLLI, Ryan (D) 24 2
H: 6 5 W: 12 03 b.Sutton 28-9-91

2010–11	Southampton	0	0		

From Salisbury, Cambridge C, Carshalton Ath

2013–14	Mansfield T	24	2	24	2

THOMAS, Jack (M) 1 0
b. 3-6-96

2013–14	Mansfield T	1	0	1	0

MIDDLESBROUGH (49)

ADOMAH, Albert (F) 285 48
H: 6 1 W: 11 08 b.Lambeth 13-12-87
Internationals: Ghana Full caps.

2007–08	Barnet	22	5		
2008–09	Barnet	45	9		
2009–10	Barnet	45	5	112	19

2010–11	Bristol C	46	5		
2011–12	Bristol C	45	5		
2012–13	Bristol C	40	7		
2013–14	Bristol C	0	0	131	17
2013–14	Middlesbrough	42	12	42	12

ATKINSON, David (D) 0 0
b.Shildon 27-4-93

2010–11	Middlesbrough	0	0		
2011–12	Middlesbrough	0	0		
2012–13	Middlesbrough	0	0		
2013–14	Middlesbrough	0	0		

AYALA, Daniel (M) 72 5
H: 6 3 W: 13 03 b.Sevilla 7-11-90
Internationals: Spain U21.

2007–08	Liverpool	0	0		
2008–09	Liverpool	0	0		
2009–10	Liverpool	5	0		
2010–11	Liverpool	0	0	5	0
2010–11	Hull C	12	1	12	1
2010–11	Derby Co	17	0	17	0
2011–12	Norwich C	7	0		
2012–13	Norwich C	0	0		
2012–13	*Nottingham F*	12	1	12	1
2013–14	Norwich C	0	0	7	0
2013–14	Middlesbrough	19	3	19	3

BENNETT, Andre (D) 0 0
H: 5 8 W: 10 02 b.Houghton-le-Spring 22-10-94

2012–13	Middlesbrough	0	0		
2013–14	Middlesbrough	0	0		

BROBBEL, Ryan (M) 19 4
b.Hartlepool 5-3-93
Internationals: Northern Ireland U17, U19, U21.

2011–12	Middlesbrough	0	0		
2012–13	Middlesbrough	0	0		
2013–14	Middlesbrough	0	0		
2013–14	*York C*	19	4	19	4

BURGESS, Christian (D) 42 0
H: 6 5 W: 13 02 b. 7-10-91

2012–13	Middlesbrough	1	0		
2013–14	Middlesbrough	0	0	1	0
2013–14	*Hartlepool U*	41	0	41	0

BUTTERFIELD, Jacob (D) 138 11
H: 5 10 W: 11 00 b.Bradford 10-6-90
Internationals: England U21.

2007–08	Barnsley	3	0		
2008–09	Barnsley	3	0		
2009–10	Barnsley	20	1		
2010–11	Barnsley	40	2		
2011–12	Barnsley	24	5	90	8
2012–13	Norwich C	0	0		
2012–13	*Bolton W*	8	0	8	0
2012–13	*Crystal Palace*	9	0	9	0
2013–14	Norwich C	0	0		
2013–14	Middlesbrough	31	3	31	3

CARAYOL, Mustapha (F) 133 24
H: 5 10 W: 11 11 b.Gambia 10-6-89

2007–08	Milton Keynes D	0	0		
2009–10	Torquay U	20	6	20	6
2010–11	Lincoln C	33	3	33	3
2011–12	Bristol R	30	4		
2012–13	Bristol R	0	0	30	4
2012–13	Middlesbrough	18	3		
2013–14	Middlesbrough	32	8	50	11

CODDINGTON, Luke (G) 0 0
b.Middlesbrough 6-6-95
Internationals: England U17, U18, U19.

2013–14	Middlesbrough	0	0		

DOLAN, Matthew (M) 39 3
b.Hartlepool 11-2-93

2010–11	Middlesbrough	0	0		
2011–12	Middlesbrough	0	0		
2012–13	Middlesbrough	0	0		
2012–13	*Yeovil T*	8	1	8	1
2013–14	Middlesbrough	0	0		
2013–14	*Hartlepool U*	20	2	20	2
2013–14	*Bradford C*	11	0	11	0

EMNES, Marvin (M) 209 36
H: 5 11 W: 10 06 b.Rotterdam 27-5-88
Internationals: Netherlands U16, U17, U19, U20, U21.

2005–06	Sparta Rotterdam	11	1		
2006–07	Sparta Rotterdam	16	0		

2007–08	Sparta Rotterdam	29	8	56	9
2008–09	Middlesbrough	15	0		
2009–10	Middlesbrough	16	1		
2010–11	Middlesbrough	23	3		
2010–11	*Swansea C*	4	2		
2011–12	Middlesbrough	42	14		
2012–13	Middlesbrough	24	5		
2013–14	Middlesbrough	22	1	142	24
2013–14	*Swansea C*	7	1	11	3

FEWSTER, Bradley (F) 0 0
b. 27-1-96
Internationals: England U16, U17, U18.

2013–14	Middlesbrough	0	0		

FRIEND, George (D) 174 6
H: 6 2 W: 13 01 b.Barnstaple 19-10-87

2008–09	Exeter C	4	0		
2008–09	Wolverhampton W	6	0		
2009–10	Wolverhampton W	1	0	7	0
2009–10	Millwall	6	0	6	0
2009–10	Southend U	6	1	6	1
2009–10	Scunthorpe U	4	0	4	0
2009–10	*Exeter C*	13	1	17	1
2010–11	Doncaster R	32	1		
2011–12	Doncaster R	27	0		
2012–13	Middlesbrough	0	0	59	1
2012–13	Middlesbrough	34	0		
2013–14	Middlesbrough	41	3	75	3

GIBSON, Ben (D) 74 2
H: 6 1 W: 12 04 b.Nunthorpe 15-1-93
Internationals: England U17, U18, U21.

2010–11	Middlesbrough	1	0		
2011–12	Middlesbrough	0	0		
2011–12	*Plymouth Arg*	13	0	13	0
2012–13	Middlesbrough	0	0		
2012–13	*Tranmere R*	28	1	28	1
2013–14	Middlesbrough	31	1	31	1

HALLIDAY, Andrew (M) 105 17
H: 5 8 W: 10 07 b.Glasgow 11-10-91

2008–09	Livingston	1	1		
2009–10	Livingston	32	14	44	15
2010–11	Middlesbrough	12	1		
2011–12	Middlesbrough	1	0		
2011–12	*Walsall*	7	0	7	0
2012–13	Middlesbrough	19	0		
2013–14	Middlesbrough	4	0	36	1
2013–14	*Blackpool*	18	1	18	1

HINES, Seb (D) 70 3
H: 6 1 W: 12 02 b.Wetherby 29-5-88
Internationals: England U16, U17, U19.

2005–06	Middlesbrough	0	0		
2006–07	Middlesbrough	0	0		
2007–08	Middlesbrough	1	0		
2008–09	Middlesbrough	1	0		
2008–09	*Derby Co*	0	0		
2008–09	*Oldham Ath*	4	0	4	0
2009–10	Middlesbrough	2	0		
2010–11	Middlesbrough	14	1		
2011–12	Middlesbrough	23	1		
2012–13	Middlesbrough	21	1		
2013–14	Middlesbrough	4	0	66	3

JACKSON, Adam (D) 0 0
b.Darlington 18-5-94
Internationals: England Youth.

2011–12	Middlesbrough	0	0		
2012–13	Middlesbrough	0	0		
2013–14	Middlesbrough	0	0		

JONES, Jordan (M) 0 0
H: 5 8 W: 9 07 b.Kettering 24-10-94

2012–13	Middlesbrough	0	0		
2013–14	Middlesbrough	0	0		

JUTKIEWICZ, Lucas (F) 234 53
H: 6 1 W: 12 11 b.Southampton 20-3-89

2005–06	Swindon T	5	0		
2006–07	Swindon T	33	5	38	5
2006–07	Everton	0	0		
2007–08	Everton	0	0		
2007–08	*Plymouth Arg*	3	0	3	0
2008–09	Everton	0	0		
2008–09	*Huddersfield T*	7	0	7	0
2009–10	Everton	0	0	1	0
2009–10	*Motherwell*	33	12	33	12
2010–11	Coventry C	42	9		
2011–12	Coventry C	25	9	67	18
2011–12	Middlesbrough	19	2		

Season	Club	Apps	Gls	Tot Apps	Tot Gls
2012–13	Middlesbrough	24	8		
2013–14	Middlesbrough	22	1	65	11
2013–14	Bolton W	20	7	20	7

KAMARA, Kei (F)   **230 57**
H: 6 2 W: 11 10 b.Lawndale 1-9-84
Internationals: Sierra Leone, Full caps.

Season	Club	Apps	Gls	Tot Apps	Tot Gls
2006	Columbus Crew	19	3		
2007	Columbus Crew	17	2	36	5
2008	San Jose E	12	2	12	2
2008	Houston D	12	3		
2009	Houston D	22	5	34	8
2010	Sporting Kansas C	29	10		
2011	Sporting Kansas C	33	9		
2012	Sporting Kansas C	35	11		
2012–13	Norwich C	11	1	11	1
2013	Sporting Kansas C	15	7	112	37
2013–14	Middlesbrough	25	4	25	4

KONSTANTOPOULOS, Dimitrios (G)   **226 0**
H: 6 4 W: 14 02 b.Kalamata 29-11-78
Internationals: Greece U21, Full caps.

Season	Club	Apps	Gls	Tot Apps	Tot Gls
2003–04	Hartlepool U	0	0		
2004–05	Hartlepool U	25	0		
2005–06	Hartlepool U	46	0		
2006–07	Hartlepool U	46	0	117	0
2007–08	Coventry C	21	0		
2008–09	Coventry C	0	0		
2008–09	Swansea C	4	0	4	0
2008–09	Cardiff C	6	0	6	0
2009–10	Coventry C	3	0	24	0
2010–11	Kerkyra	30	0	30	0
2011–12	AEK Athens	9	0		
2012–13	AEK Athens	24	0	33	0
2013–14	Middlesbrough	12	0	12	0

LEADBITTER, Grant (M)   **313 34**
H: 5 9 W: 11 06 b.Chester-le-Street 7-1-86
Internationals: England U16, U17, U19, U20, U21.

Season	Club	Apps	Gls	Tot Apps	Tot Gls
2002–03	Sunderland	0	0		
2003–04	Sunderland	0	0		
2004–05	Sunderland	0	0		
2005–06	Sunderland	12	0		
2005–06	Rotherham U	5	1	5	1
2006–07	Sunderland	44	7		
2007–08	Sunderland	31	2		
2008–09	Sunderland	23	2		
2009–10	Sunderland	1	0	111	11
2009–10	Ipswich T	38	3		
2010–11	Ipswich T	44	5		
2011–12	Ipswich T	34	5		
2012–13	Ipswich T	0	0	116	13
2012–13	Middlesbrough	42	3		
2013–14	Middlesbrough	39	6	81	9

LEDESMA, Emmanuel (M)   **119 16**
H: 5 11 W: 12 02 b.Quilmes 24-5-88

Season	Club	Apps	Gls	Tot Apps	Tot Gls
2007–08	Genoa	1	0	1	0
2008–09	Salernitana	8	1	8	1
2008–09	QPR	17	1	17	1
2009–10	Novara	8	1	8	1
2010–11	Crotone	10	0	10	0
2010–11	Walsall	10	1		
2011–12	Walsall	10	4	20	5
2012–13	Middlesbrough	28	2		
2013–14	Middlesbrough	27	6	55	8

LEUTWILER, Jayson (G)   **3 0**
H: 6 3 W: 12 07 b.Basel 25-4-89
Internationals: Switzerland U16, U17, U18, U19, U20, U21.

Season	Club	Apps	Gls	Tot Apps	Tot Gls
2012–13	Middlesbrough	0	0		
2013–14	Middlesbrough	3	0	3	0

MAIN, Curtis (F)   **98 11**
H: 5 9 W: 12 02 b.South Shields 20-6-92

Season	Club	Apps	Gls	Tot Apps	Tot Gls
2007–08	Darlington	1	0		
2008–09	Darlington	18	2		
2009–10	Darlington	26	3		
2010–11	Darlington	0	0	45	5
2011–12	Middlesbrough	12	2		
2012–13	Middlesbrough	13	3		
2013–14	Middlesbrough	23	1	48	6
2013–14	Shrewsbury T	5	0	5	0

MEJIAS, Tomas (G)   **2 0**
H: 6 5 W: 13 02 b.Madrid 30-1-89
Internationals: Spain U19, U20.

Season	Club	Apps	Gls	Tot Apps	Tot Gls
2010–11	Real Madrid	1	0		
2011–12	Real Madrid	0	0		
2012–13	Real Madrid	0	0		
2013–14	Real Madrid	0	0	1	0
	On loan from Real Madrid				
2013–14	Middlesbrough	1	0	1	0

MORRIS, Bryn (M)   **2 0**
H: 6 0 W: 11 01 b.Hartlepool 25-4-96
Internationals: England U16, U17, U18.

Season	Club	Apps	Gls	Tot Apps	Tot Gls
2012–13	Middlesbrough	1	0		
2013–14	Middlesbrough	1	0	2	0

PARK, Cameron (M)   **11 0**
H: 5 10 W: 11 02 b.Marske 6-7-92
Internationals: Scotland U19, U21.

Season	Club	Apps	Gls	Tot Apps	Tot Gls
2010–11	Middlesbrough	4	0		
2011–12	Middlesbrough	0	0		
2011–12	Barnsley	3	0	3	0
2012–13	Middlesbrough	0	0		
2013–14	Middlesbrough	0	0	4	0
2013–14	Crewe Alex	4	0	4	0

PARNABY, Stuart (D)   **161 2**
H: 5 11 W: 12 00 b.Durham 19-7-82
Internationals: England U20, U21.

Season	Club	Apps	Gls	Tot Apps	Tot Gls
2000–01	Middlesbrough	0	0		
2000–01	Halifax T	6	0	6	0
2001–02	Middlesbrough	0	0		
2002–03	Middlesbrough	21	0		
2003–04	Middlesbrough	13	0		
2004–05	Middlesbrough	19	0		
2005–06	Middlesbrough	20	2		
2006–07	Middlesbrough	18	0		
2007–08	Birmingham C	13	0		
2008–09	Birmingham C	21	0		
2009–10	Birmingham C	8	0		
2010–11	Birmingham C	5	0	47	0
2012–13	Middlesbrough	14	0		
2013–14	Middlesbrough	3	0	108	2

REACH, Adam (M)   **60 9**
H: 6 1 W: 11 07 b.Gateshead 3-2-93
Internationals: England U19, U20.

Season	Club	Apps	Gls	Tot Apps	Tot Gls
2010–11	Middlesbrough	1	1		
2011–12	Middlesbrough	1	0		
2012–13	Middlesbrough	16	2		
2013–14	Middlesbrough	2	0	20	3
2013–14	Shrewsbury T	22	3	22	3
2013–14	Bradford C	18	3	18	3

RICHARDSON, Frazer (D)   **278 5**
H: 5 11 W: 11 12 b.Rotherham 29-10-82
Internationals: England U20.

Season	Club	Apps	Gls	Tot Apps	Tot Gls
1999–2000	Leeds U	0	0		
2000–01	Leeds U	0	0		
2001–02	Leeds U	0	0		
2002–03	Leeds U	0	0		
2002–03	Stoke C	7	0		
2003–04	Leeds U	4	0		
2003–04	Stoke C	6	1	13	1
2004–05	Leeds U	38	1		
2005–06	Leeds U	23	1		
2006–07	Leeds U	22	0		
2007–08	Leeds U	39	1		
2008–09	Leeds U	23	0	149	3
2009–10	Charlton Ath	38	1	38	1
2010–11	Southampton	21	0		
2011–12	Southampton	34	0		
2012–13	Southampton	5	0	60	0
2013–14	Middlesbrough	11	0	11	0
2013–14	Ipswich T	7	0	7	0

RIPLEY, Connor (G)   **3 0**
H: 5 11 W: 11 13 b.Middlesbrough 13-2-93
Internationals: England U19, U20.

Season	Club	Apps	Gls	Tot Apps	Tot Gls
2010–11	Middlesbrough	1	0		
2011–12	Middlesbrough	1	0		
2011–12	Oxford U	1	0	1	0
2012–13	Middlesbrough	0	0		
2013–14	Middlesbrough	0	0	2	0
2013–14	Bradford C	0	0		

SMALLWOOD, Richard (M)   **79 3**
H: 5 11 W: 11 05 b.Redcar 29-12-90
Internationals: England U19.

Season	Club	Apps	Gls	Tot Apps	Tot Gls
2008–09	Middlesbrough	0	0		
2009–10	Middlesbrough	0	0		
2010–11	Middlesbrough	13	1		
2011–12	Middlesbrough	13	0		
2012–13	Middlesbrough	22	2		
2013–14	Middlesbrough	13	0	61	3
2013–14	Rotherham U	18	0	18	0

STEELE, Jason (G)   **144 0**
H: 6 2 W: 12 07 b.Newton Aycliffe 18-8-90
Internationals: England U16, U17, U19, U21. Great Britain.

Season	Club	Apps	Gls	Tot Apps	Tot Gls
2007–08	Middlesbrough	0	0		
2008–09	Middlesbrough	0	0		
2009–10	Middlesbrough	0	0		
2009–10	Northampton T	13	0	13	0
2010–11	Middlesbrough	35	0		
2011–12	Middlesbrough	34	0		
2012–13	Middlesbrough	46	0		
2013–14	Middlesbrough	16	0	131	0

TOMLIN, Lee (F)   **149 36**
H: 5 11 W: 11 09 b.Leicester 12-1-89
Internationals: England C.

Season	Club	Apps	Gls	Tot Apps	Tot Gls
2010–11	Peterborough U	37	8		
2011–12	Peterborough U	37	8		
2012–13	Peterborough U	42	11		
2013–14	Peterborough U	19	5	135	32
2013–14	Middlesbrough	14	4	14	4

VARGA, Jozsef (M)   **140 2**
H: 5 9 W: 11 01 b. 6-6-88
Internationals: Hungary U21, Full caps.

Season	Club	Apps	Gls	Tot Apps	Tot Gls
2008–09	Debrecen	20	0		
2009–10	Debrecen	19	1		
2010–11	Debrecen	21	0		
2011–12	Debrecen	26	1		
2012–13	Debrecen	14	0		
2012–13	Greuther Furth	6	0	6	0
2013–14	Debrecen	0	0	100	2
	On loan from Debrecen				
2013–14	Middlesbrough	34	0	34	0

WHITEHEAD, Dean (M)   **476 26**
H: 5 11 W: 12 06 b.Abingdon 12-1-82

Season	Club	Apps	Gls	Tot Apps	Tot Gls
1999–2000	Oxford U	0	0		
2000–01	Oxford U	20	0		
2001–02	Oxford U	40	1		
2002–03	Oxford U	18	1		
2003–04	Oxford U	44	7	122	9
2004–05	Sunderland	42	5		
2005–06	Sunderland	37	3		
2006–07	Sunderland	45	4		
2007–08	Sunderland	27	1		
2008–09	Sunderland	34	0		
2009–10	Sunderland	0	0	185	13
2009–10	Stoke C	36	0		
2010–11	Stoke C	37	2		
2011–12	Stoke C	33	0		
2012–13	Stoke C	26	1	132	3
2013–14	Middlesbrough	37	1	37	1

WILLIAMS, Luke (F)   **37 4**
H: 6 1 W: 11 08 b.Middlesbrough 11-6-93
Internationals: England U17, U19, U20.

Season	Club	Apps	Gls	Tot Apps	Tot Gls
2009–10	Middlesbrough	4	0		
2010–11	Middlesbrough	6	0		
2011–12	Middlesbrough	0	0		
2012–13	Middlesbrough	11	2		
2013–14	Middlesbrough	9	0	30	2
2013–14	Hartlepool U	7	2	7	2

WILLIAMS, Rhys (M)   **141 5**
H: 6 2 W: 11 05 b.Perth 14-7-88
Internationals: Wales U21. Australia Full caps.

Season	Club	Apps	Gls	Tot Apps	Tot Gls
2006–07	Middlesbrough	0	0		
2007–08	Middlesbrough	0	0		
2008–09	Middlesbrough	0	0		
2008–09	Burnley	17	0	17	0
2009–10	Middlesbrough	32	2		
2010–11	Middlesbrough	12	1		
2011–12	Middlesbrough	35	2		
2012–13	Middlesbrough	23	0		
2013–14	Middlesbrough	22	0	124	5

WOODGATE, Jonathan (D)   **302 7**
H: 6 2 W: 12 06 b.Middlesbrough 22-1-80
Internationals: England U16, U18, U21, Full caps.

Season	Club	Apps	Gls	Tot Apps	Tot Gls
1996–97	Leeds U	0	0		
1997–98	Leeds U	0	0		
1998–99	Leeds U	25	2		
1999–2000	Leeds U	34	1		
2000–01	Leeds U	14	1		
2001–02	Leeds U	13	0		
2002–03	Leeds U	18	0	104	4
2002–03	Newcastle U	10	0		
2003–04	Newcastle U	18	0	28	0
2004–05	Real Madrid	0	0		

2005–06	Real Madrid	9	0	9	0
2006–07	Middlesbrough	30	0		
2007–08	Middlesbrough	16	0		
2007–08	Tottenham H	12	1		
2008–09	Tottenham H	34	1		
2009–10	Tottenham H	3	0		
2010–11	Tottenham H	0	0	49	2
2011–12	Stoke C	17	0	17	0
2012–13	Middlesbrough	24	1		
2013–14	Middlesbrough	25	0	95	1

WYKE, Charlie (F) 42 4
b.Middlesbrough 6-12-92

2011–12	Middlesbrough	0	0		
2012–13	Middlesbrough	0	0		
2012–13	*Hartlepool U*	25	2	25	2
2013–14	Middlesbrough	0	0		
2013–14	*AFC Wimbledon*	17	2	17	2

Scholars
Armstrong, Luke Thomas; Burn, Jonathan David; Coleby, Jonathan James; Cooke, Callum James; Elsdon, Matthew; Fry, Dael Jonathan; Fryer, Joseph Luke; Griffiths, Priestley David; Helm, Jonathan David; Johnson, Callum Charles; Jowers, Jordan; Kitching, Mark Stephen; Maloney, Lewis Terence James; McAloon, Thomas; McCarthy, Scott; McGinley, Nathan; McNab, Ross; Okosieme, Ejiro Onyemachie Denzel; O'Neill, Conor Martin; O'Neill, Stephen Charles; Plews, Nathan Paul; Scoble, Lewis Clive; Tinkler, Robbie; Warnett, James Peter; Weledji, Kieran Wembanesi; Wheatley, Josef James; Wyke, Matthew Gerald.

MILLWALL (50)

ABDOU, Nadjim (M) 353 9
H: 5 10 W: 11 02 b.Martigues 13-7-84
Internationals: Comoros Full caps.

2002–03	Martigues	26	1	26	1
2003–04	Sedan	17	0		
2004–05	Sedan	32	2		
2005–06	Sedan	14	0		
2006–07	Sedan	17	0	80	2
2007–08	Plymouth Arg	31	1	31	1
2008–09	Millwall	36	3		
2009–10	Millwall	34	0		
2010–11	Millwall	40	0		
2011–12	Millwall	39	1		
2013–14	Millwall	24	0	216	5

BAILEY, Nicky (M) 348 51
H: 5 10 W: 12 06 b.Hammersmith 10-6-84
Internationals: England C.

2005–06	Barnet	45	7		
2006–07	Barnet	44	5	89	12
2007–08	Southend U	44	9		
2008–09	Southend U	1	0	45	9
2008–09	Charlton Ath	43	13		
2009–10	Charlton Ath	44	12	87	25
2010–11	Middlesbrough	34	0		
2011–12	Middlesbrough	37	2		
2012–13	Middlesbrough	28	2	99	4
2013–14	Millwall	28	1	28	1

BEEVERS, Mark (D) 217 4
H: 6 4 W: 13 00 b.Barnsley 21-11-89
Internationals: England U19.

2006–07	Sheffield W	2	0		
2007–08	Sheffield W	28	0		
2008–09	Sheffield W	34	0		
2009–10	Sheffield W	35	0		
2010–11	Sheffield W	28	2		
2011–12	Sheffield W	7	0		
2011–12	*Milton Keynes D*	14	1	14	1
2012–13	Sheffield W	6	0	140	2
2012–13	Millwall	35	1		
2013–14	Millwall	28	0	63	1

BESSONE, Fede (D) 73 1
H: 5 11 W: 11 13 b.Cordoba 23-1-84

2007–08	*Gimnastic*	10	0	10	0
2008–09	Swansea C	15	0		
2009–10	Swansea C	21	1		
2010–11	Leeds U	6	0		
2010–11	*Charlton Ath*	13	0	13	0
2011–12	Leeds U	0	0	6	0
2011–12	Swansea C	1	0		
2012–13	Swansea C	0	0	37	1
2012–13	Swindon T	5	0		
2013–14	Swindon T	0	0	5	0
2013–14	Millwall	2	0	2	0

BYWATER, Steve (G) 293 0
H: 6 2 W: 12 10 b.Manchester 7-6-81
Internationals: England U20, U21.

1997–98	Rochdale	7	0		
1998–99	West Ham U	0	0		
1999–2000	West Ham U	4	0		
1999–2000	*Wycombe W*	2	0	2	0
1999–2000	*Hull C*	4	0	4	0
2000–01	West Ham U	1	0		
2001–02	West Ham U	0	0		
2001–02	*Wolverhampton W*	0	0		
2001–02	*Cardiff C*	0	0		
2002–03	West Ham U	0	0		
2003–04	West Ham U	17	0		
2004–05	West Ham U	36	0		
2005–06	West Ham U	1	0		
2005–06	*Coventry C*	14	0	14	0
2006–07	West Ham U	0	0	59	0
2006–07	Derby Co	37	0		
2007–08	Derby Co	18	0		
2007–08	*Ipswich T*	17	0	17	0
2008–09	Derby Co	31	0		
2009–10	Derby Co	42	0		
2010–11	Derby Co	22	0		
2010–11	*Cardiff C*	8	0	8	0
2011–12	Derby Co	0	0	150	0
2011–12	Sheffield W	32	0		
2012–13	Sheffield W	0	0	32	0
2013–14	Millwall	7	0	7	0

CHAPLOW, Richard (M) 272 25
H: 5 9 W: 9 03 b.Accrington 2-2-85
Internationals: England U19, U20, U21.

2002–03	Burnley	7	0		
2003–04	Burnley	39	5		
2004–05	Burnley	21	2	67	7
2004–05	WBA	4	0		
2005–06	WBA	7	0		
2005–06	*Southampton*	11	1		
2006–07	WBA	28	1		
2007–08	WBA	5	0	44	1
2007–08	Preston NE	12	3		
2008–09	Preston NE	25	3		
2009–10	Preston NE	31	2		
2010–11	Preston NE	0	0	68	8
2010–11	Southampton	33	4		
2011–12	Southampton	25	3		
2012–13	Southampton	3	0	72	8
2012–13	*Millwall*	4	0		
2013–14	Millwall	19	1	23	1

DUNNE, Alan (D) 302 15
H: 5 10 W: 10 13 b.Dublin 23-8-82

1999–2000	Millwall	0	0		
2000–01	Millwall	0	0		
2001–02	Millwall	1	0		
2002–03	Millwall	4	0		
2003–04	Millwall	8	0		
2004–05	Millwall	19	3		
2005–06	Millwall	40	0		
2006–07	Millwall	32	6		
2007–08	Millwall	19	3		
2008–09	Millwall	24	0		
2009–10	Millwall	32	2		
2010–11	Millwall	39	0		
2011–12	Millwall	30	0		
2012–13	Millwall	25	1		
2013–14	Millwall	29	0	302	15

EASTER, Jermaine (F) 339 77
H: 5 9 W: 12 02 b.Cardiff 15-1-82
Internationals: Wales Full caps.

2000–01	Wolverhampton W	0	0		
2000–01	Hartlepool U	4	0		
2001–02	Hartlepool U	12	2		
2002–03	Hartlepool U	8	0		
2003–04	Hartlepool U	3	0	27	2
2003–04	*Cambridge U*	15	2		
2004–05	Cambridge U	24	6	39	8
2004–05	Boston U	9	3	9	3
2005–06	Stockport Co	19	8	19	8
2005–06	Wycombe W	5	2		
2006–07	Wycombe W	38	17		
2007–08	Wycombe W	6	2	59	21
2007–08	Plymouth Arg	32	6		
2008–09	Plymouth Arg	4	0	36	6
2008–09	*Millwall*	5	1		
2008–09	Colchester U	5	2	5	2
2009–10	Milton Keynes D	36	14		
2010–11	Milton Keynes D	14	0	50	14
2010–11	*Swansea C*	6	1	6	1
2010–11	Crystal Palace	14	1		
2011–12	Crystal Palace	33	5		
2012–13	Crystal Palace	8	1	55	7
2012–13	*Millwall*	9	1		
2013–14	Millwall	20	3	34	5

FEENEY, Liam (M) 193 17
H: 5 10 W: 12 02 b.Hammersmith 21-1-87

2008–09	Southend U	1	0	1	0
2008–09	Bournemouth	14	3		
2009–10	Bournemouth	44	5		
2010–11	Bournemouth	46	4		
2011–12	Bournemouth	5	0	109	12
2011–12	Millwall	34	4		
2012–13	Millwall	22	1		
2013–14	Millwall	17	0	73	5
2013–14	*Bolton W*	4	0	4	0
2013–14	*Blackburn R*	6	0	6	0

FORDE, David (G) 341 0
H: 6 3 W: 13 06 b.Galway 20-12-79
Internationals: Republic of Ireland Full caps.

2001–02	West Ham U	0	0		
2002–03	West Ham U	0	0		
2003–04	West Ham U	0	0		
2004	Derry C	11	0		
2005	Derry C	33	0		
2006	Derry C	29	0	73	0
2006–07	Cardiff C	7	0		
2007–08	Cardiff C	0	0	7	0
2007–08	*Luton T*	5	0	5	0
2007–08	*Bournemouth*	11	0	11	0
2008–09	Millwall	46	0		
2009–10	Millwall	46	0		
2010–11	Millwall	46	0		
2011–12	Millwall	27	0		
2012–13	Millwall	40	0		
2013–14	Millwall	40	0	245	0

GERRARD, Denzel (G) 0 0

2013–14	Millwall	0	0		

GOODMAN, Jake (D) 0 0
b. 5-8-93

2012–13	Millwall	0	0		
2013–14	Millwall	0	0		

HENRY, James (M) 203 32
H: 6 1 W: 11 11 b.Reading 10-6-89
Internationals: Scotland U16, U19. England U18, U19.

2006–07	Reading	0	0		
2006–07	*Nottingham F*	1	0	1	0
2007–08	Reading	0	0		
2007–08	*Bournemouth*	11	4	11	4
2007–08	*Norwich C*	3	0	3	0
2008–09	Reading	7	0		
2008–09	*Millwall*	16	3		
2009–10	Reading	3	0	10	0
2009–10	*Millwall*	9	5		
2010–11	Millwall	42	5		
2011–12	Millwall	39	0		
2012–13	Millwall	35	5		
2013–14	Millwall	5	0	146	18
2013–14	*Wolverhampton W*	32	10	32	10

HOYTE, Justin (D) 208 4
H: 5 11 W: 11 00 b.Waltham Forest 20-11-84
Internationals: England U16, U19, U20, U21. Trinidad and Tobago Full caps.

2002–03	Arsenal	1	0		
2003–04	Arsenal	1	0		
2004–05	Arsenal	5	0		
2005–06	Arsenal	0	0		
2005–06	*Sunderland*	27	1	27	1
2006–07	Arsenal	22	1		
2007–08	Arsenal	5	0	34	1
2008–09	Middlesbrough	22	0		
2009–10	Middlesbrough	30	1		
2010–11	Middlesbrough	17	0		
2011–12	Middlesbrough	39	0		
2012–13	Middlesbrough	31	1		
2013–14	Middlesbrough	3	0	142	2
2013–14	Millwall	5	0	5	0

JACKSON, Simeon (M) 214 59
H: 5 10 W: 10 12 b.Kingston, Jamaica 28-3-87
Internationals: Canada U20, Full caps.

Season	Club	App	Gls	Tot App	Tot Gls
2004–05	Rushden & D	3	0		
2005–06	Rushden & D	14	5		
2006–07	Rushden & D	0	0		
2007–08	Rushden & D	0	0	17	5
2007–08	Gillingham	18	4		
2008–09	Gillingham	41	17		
2009–10	Gillingham	42	14	101	35
2010–11	Norwich C	38	13		
2011–12	Norwich C	22	3		
2012–13	Norwich C	13	1	73	17
2013–14	E Braunschweig	9	0	9	0
2013–14	Millwall	14	2	14	2

KEOGH, Andy (F) 349 67
H: 6 0 W: 11 00 b.Dublin 16-5-86
Internationals: Republic of Ireland B, U21, Full caps.

Season	Club	App	Gls	Tot App	Tot Gls
2003–04	Leeds U	0	0		
2004–05	Leeds U	0	0		
2004–05	Bury	4	2	4	2
2004–05	Scunthorpe U	25	3		
2005–06	Scunthorpe U	45	11		
2006–07	Scunthorpe U	28	7	98	21
2006–07	Wolverhampton W	17	5		
2007–08	Wolverhampton W	43	8		
2008–09	Wolverhampton W	42	5		
2009–10	Wolverhampton W	13	1		
2010–11	Wolverhampton W	1	0		
2010–11	Cardiff C	16	2	16	2
2010–11	Bristol C	9	1	9	1
2011–12	Wolverhampton W	0	0	116	19
2011–12	Leeds U	22	2	22	2
2011–12	Millwall	18	10		
2012–13	Millwall	37	6		
2013–14	Millwall	15	1	70	17
2013–14	Blackpool	14	3	14	3

LOWRY, Shane (D) 124 2
H: 6 1 W: 13 01 b.Perth 12-6-89
Internationals: Republic of Ireland U17, U21.

Season	Club	App	Gls	Tot App	Tot Gls
2007–08	Aston Villa	0	0		
2008–09	Aston Villa	0	0		
2009–10	Aston Villa	0	0		
2009–10	Plymouth Arg	13	0	13	0
2009–10	Leeds U	11	0	11	0
2010–11	Aston Villa	0	0		
2010–11	Sheffield U	17	0	17	0
2011–12	Aston Villa	0	0		
2011–12	Millwall	22	1		
2012–13	Millwall	39	1		
2013–14	Millwall	22	0	83	2

MAIERHOFER, Stefan (F) 272 110
H: 6 8 W: 14 11 b.Vienna 16-8-82
Internationals: Austria Full caps.

Season	Club	App	Gls	Tot App	Tot Gls
2002–03	First Vienna	0	0		
2003–04	Langenrohr	28	10		
2004–05	Langenrohr	25	16	53	26
2005–06	Bayern Munich II	28	10		
2006–07	Bayern Munich II	14	11	42	21
2006–07	Bayern Munich	2	0		
2006–07	Koblenz	14	3	14	3
2007–08	Furth	10	2	10	2
2007–08	Rapid Vienna	11	7		
2008–09	Rapid Vienna	35	23		
2009–10	Rapid Vienna	3	1	49	31
2009–10	Wolverhampton W	8	1		
2009–10	Bristol C	3	0	3	0
2010–11	Wolverhampton W	0	0		
2010–11	Duisburg	27	8	27	8
2011–12	Wolverhampton W	1	0	9	1
2011–12	Salzburg	29	14		
2012–13	Salzburg	10	1	39	15
2012–13	Cologne	13	1	13	1
2013–14	Millwall	11	2	11	2

MALONE, Scott (D) 126 11
H: 6 2 W: 11 11 b.Rowley Regis 25-3-91
Internationals: England U19.

Season	Club	App	Gls	Tot App	Tot Gls
2008–09	Wolverhampton W	0	0		
2008–09	Ujpest	7	1	7	1
2009–10	Wolverhampton W	0	0		
2009–10	Southend U	17	0	17	0
2010–11	Wolverhampton W	0	0		
2010–11	Burton Alb	22	1	22	1
2011–12	Wolverhampton W	0	0		
2011–12	Bournemouth	32	5	32	5
2012–13	Millwall	15	1		
2013–14	Millwall	33	3	48	4

MARQUIS, John (F) 65 11
H: 6 1 W: 11 03 b.Lewisham 16-5-92

Season	Club	App	Gls	Tot App	Tot Gls
2009–10	Millwall	1	0		
2010–11	Millwall	11	4		
2011–12	Millwall	17	1		
2012–13	Millwall	10	0		
2013–14	Millwall	2	0	41	5
2013–14	Portsmouth	5	1	5	1
2013–14	Torquay U	5	3	5	3
2013–14	Northampton T	14	2	14	2

MARTIN, Lee (M) 198 13
H: 5 10 W: 10 03 b.Taunton 9-2-87
Internationals: England Youth.

Season	Club	App	Gls	Tot App	Tot Gls
2004–05	Manchester U	0	0		
2005–06	Manchester U	0	0		
2006–07	Manchester U	0	0		
2006–07	Rangers	7	0	7	0
2006–07	Stoke C	13	1	13	1
2007–08	Manchester U	0	0		
2007–08	Plymouth Arg	12	2	12	2
2007–08	Sheffield U	6	0	6	0
2008–09	Manchester U	1	0		
2008–09	Nottingham F	13	1	13	1
2009–10	Manchester U	0	0	1	0
2009–10	Ipswich T	16	1		
2010–11	Ipswich T	16	0		
2010–11	Charlton Ath	20	2	20	2
2011–12	Ipswich T	34	5		
2012–13	Ipswich T	34	0		
2013–14	Ipswich T	0	0	100	6
2013–14	Millwall	26	1	26	1

McDONALD, Scott (F) 372 136
H: 5 7 W: 12 07 b.Melbourne 21-8-83
Internationals: Australia U17, U20, U23, Full caps.

Season	Club	App	Gls	Tot App	Tot Gls
1998–99	Eastern Pride	3	0	3	0
1999–2000	Southampton	0	0		
2000–01	Southampton	2	0		
2001–02	Southampton	2	0		
2002–03	Southampton	0	0	2	0
2002–03	Huddersfield T	13	1	13	1
2002–03	Bournemouth	7	1	7	1
2003–04	Wimbledon	2	0	2	0
2003–04	Motherwell	15	2		
2004–05	Motherwell	27	15		
2005–06	Motherwell	35	11		
2006–07	Motherwell	32	15	109	43
2007–08	Celtic	36	25		
2008–09	Celtic	34	16		
2009–10	Celtic	18	10	88	51
2009–10	Middlesbrough	13	4		
2010–11	Middlesbrough	38	12		
2011–12	Middlesbrough	33	9		
2012–13	Middlesbrough	32	12	116	37
2013–14	Millwall	32	3	32	3

O'BRIEN, Aiden (F) 12 0
H: 5 8 W: 10 12 b.Islington 4-10-93
Internationals: Republic of Ireland U17, U19, U21.

Season	Club	App	Gls	Tot App	Tot Gls
2010–11	Millwall	0	0		
2011–12	Millwall	0	0		
2012–13	Millwall	0	0		
2012–13	Crawley T	9	0	9	0
2013–14	Millwall	0	0		
2013–14	Torquay U	3	0	3	0

ONYEDINMA, Fred (M) 4 0
b. 24-11-96

Season	Club	App	Gls	Tot App	Tot Gls
2013–14	Millwall	4	0	4	0

POWELL, Jack (M) 0 0

Season	Club	App	Gls	Tot App	Tot Gls
2013–14	Millwall	0	0		

ROBINSON, Paul (D) 316 16
H: 6 1 W: 11 09 b.Barnet 7-1-82

Season	Club	App	Gls	Tot App	Tot Gls
2000–01	Millwall	0	0		
2001–02	Millwall	0	0		
2002–03	Millwall	14	0		
2003–04	Millwall	9	0		
2004–05	Millwall	0	0		
2004–05	Torquay U	12	0	12	0
2005–06	Millwall	32	0		
2006–07	Millwall	38	3		
2007–08	Millwall	45	3		
2008–09	Millwall	26	2		
2009–10	Millwall	34	4		
2010–11	Millwall	37	3		
2011–12	Millwall	41	1		
2012–13	Millwall	3	0		
2013–14	Millwall	25	0	304	16

SHITTU, Dan (D) 342 28
H: 6 2 W: 16 03 b.Lagos 2-9-80
Internationals: Nigeria Full caps.

Season	Club	App	Gls	Tot App	Tot Gls
1999–2000	Charlton Ath	0	0		
2000–01	Charlton Ath	0	0		
2000–01	Blackpool	17	2	17	2
2001–02	Charlton Ath	0	0		
2001–02	QPR	27	2		
2002–03	QPR	43	7		
2003–04	QPR	20	0		
2004–05	QPR	34	4		
2005–06	QPR	45	4		
2006–07	Watford	30	1		
2007–08	Watford	39	7	69	8
2008–09	Bolton W	10	0		
2009–10	Bolton W	0	0		
2010–11	Bolton W	0	0	10	0
2010–11	Millwall	9	0		
2011–12	QPR	7	0		
2011–12	QPR	0	0	176	17
2012–13	Millwall	39	0		
2013–14	Millwall	22	1	70	1

SIAFA, Josh (D) 0 0
b. 7-10-94

Season	Club	App	Gls	Tot App	Tot Gls
2013–14	Millwall	0	0		

SMITH, Jack (D) 259 12
H: 5 11 W: 11 05 b.Hemel Hempstead 14-10-83

Season	Club	App	Gls	Tot App	Tot Gls
2001–02	Watford	0	0		
2002–03	Watford	1	0		
2003–04	Watford	17	2		
2004–05	Watford	7	0	25	2
2005–06	Swindon T	38	0		
2006–07	Swindon T	41	3		
2007–08	Swindon T	21	1		
2008–09	Swindon T	38	5	138	9
2009–10	Millwall	31	0		
2010–11	Millwall	9	1		
2011–12	Millwall	33	0		
2012–13	Millwall	17	0		
2013–14	Millwall	6	0	96	1

TROTTER, Liam (M) 213 30
H: 6 2 W: 12 02 b.Ipswich 24-8-88

Season	Club	App	Gls	Tot App	Tot Gls
2005–06	Ipswich T	1	0		
2006–07	Ipswich T	0	0		
2006–07	Millwall	2	0		
2007–08	Ipswich T	7	1		
2008–09	Ipswich T	3	1		
2008–09	Grimsby T	15	2	15	2
2008–09	Scunthorpe U	12	1	12	1
2009–10	Ipswich T	12	0	23	2
2009–10	Millwall	20	1		
2010–11	Millwall	35	7		
2011–12	Millwall	35	7		
2012–13	Millwall	36	6		
2013–14	Millwall	19	3	147	24
2013–14	Bolton W	16	1	16	1

UPSON, Edward (M) 148 10
H: 5 10 W: 11 07 b.Bury St Edmunds 21-11-89
Internationals: England U17, U19.

Season	Club	App	Gls	Tot App	Tot Gls
2006–07	Ipswich T	0	0		
2007–08	Ipswich T	0	0		
2008–09	Ipswich T	0	0		
2009–10	Ipswich T	0	0		
2009–10	Barnet	9	1	9	1
2010–11	Yeovil T	23	0		
2011–12	Yeovil T	41	3		
2012–13	Yeovil T	41	2		
2013–14	Yeovil T	24	4	129	9
2013–14	Millwall	10	0	10	0

WILLIAMS, Shaun (M) 208 43
H: 5 9 W: 11 11 b.Dublin 19-10-86
Internationals: Republic of Ireland U21, U23.

Season	Club	App	Gls	Tot App	Tot Gls
2007	Drogheda U	0	0		
2007	Dundalk	19	9	19	9
2008	Drogheda U	4	0		
2008	Finn Harps	14	2	14	2
2009	Drogheda U	1	0	5	0
2009	Sporting Fingal	13	7		
2010	Sporting Fingal	32	5	45	12
2011–12	Milton Keynes D	39	8		
2012–13	Milton Keynes D	44	3		

2013–14	Milton Keynes D	25	8	108	19
2013–14	Millwall	17	1	17	1

WOOLFORD, Martyn (M)   213   27
H: 6 0   W: 11 09   b.Castleford 13-10-85
Internationals: England C.

2008–09	Scunthorpe U	39	4		
2009–10	Scunthorpe U	40	5		
2010–11	Scunthorpe U	24	6	103	15
2010–11	Bristol C	15	0		
2011–12	Bristol C	25	1		
2012–13	Bristol C	15	3	55	4
2012–13	Millwall	15	1		
2013–14	Millwall	40	7	55	8

WRIGHT, Josh (M)   162   2
H: 6 1   W: 11 07   b.Bethnal Green 6-11-89
Internationals: England U17, U18, U19.

2007–08	Charlton Ath	0	0		
2007–08	Barnet	32	1	32	1
2008–09	Charlton Ath	2	0	2	0
2008–09	Brentford	5	0	5	0
2008–09	Gillingham	5	0	5	0
2009–10	Scunthorpe U	35	0		
2010–11	Scunthorpe U	36	0	71	0
2011–12	Millwall	18	1		
2012–13	Millwall	24	0		
2013–14	Millwall	3	0	45	1
2013–14	Leyton Orient	2	0	2	0

Scholars
Adeloye, Oluwatomisin; Beadle, Tommy;
Bryon, Zak Lewis; Danquah, Richie
Kwabena; Farrell, Kyron Cassius Daniel;
Goodman, Max John; Guinchard, Joe;
Nelson, Sidney Raymond Kenneth; Parr,
Christopher John; Pavey, Alfie Martin Kevin;
Peter, Dexter Washington; Philpot, James
Frederick; Rylah, John-Prince Timothy;
Thompson, Ben Rhys; Twardek, Kristopher
David; Webb, Callum Michael; Wood,
Keaton Matthew Tate.

MILTON KEYNES D (51)

ALLI, Bamidele (M)   33   6
H: 6 1   W: 11 12   b.Watford 11-4-96
Internationals: England U17, U18.

2012–13	Milton Keynes D	0	0		
2013–14	Milton Keynes D	33	6	33	6

BALDOCK, George (M)   48   2
H: 5 9   W: 10 07   b.Buckingham 26-1-93

2009–10	Milton Keynes D	1	0		
2010–11	Milton Keynes D	2	0		
2011–12	Milton Keynes D	0	0		
2011–12	Northampton T	5	0	5	0
2012–13	Milton Keynes D	2	0		
2013–14	Milton Keynes D	38	2	43	2

BOWDITCH, Dean (F)   284   61
H: 5 11   W: 11 05   b.Bishops Stortford
15-6-86
Internationals: England U16, U17, U18.

2002–03	Ipswich T	5	0		
2003–04	Ipswich T	16	4		
2004–05	Ipswich T	21	3		
2004–05	Burnley	10	1	10	1
2005–06	Ipswich T	21	0		
2005–06	Wycombe W	11	1	11	1
2006–07	Ipswich T	9	1		
2006–07	Brighton & HA	3	1		
2007–08	Ipswich T	0	0		
2007–08	Northampton T	10	2	10	2
2007–08	Brighton & HA	5	0	8	1
2008–09	Ipswich T	1	0	73	8
2008–09	Brentford	9	2	9	2
2009–10	Yeovil T	30	10		
2010–11	Yeovil T	41	15	71	25
2011–12	Milton Keynes D	41	12		
2012–13	Milton Keynes D	39	8		
2013–14	Milton Keynes D	12	1	92	21

BURNS, Charlie (G)   1   0
2012–13	Milton Keynes D	0	0		
2013–14	Milton Keynes D	1	0	1	0

CHADWICK, Luke (M)   384   33
H: 5 11   W: 11 08   b.Cambridge 18-11-80
Internationals: England U18, U21.

1998–99	Manchester U	0	0		

1999–2000	Manchester U	0	0		
2000–01	Manchester U	16	2		
2001–02	Manchester U	8	0		
2001–02	Manchester U	1	0		
2002–03	Reading	15	1	15	1
2003–04	Manchester U	0	0	25	2
2003–04	Burnley	36	5	36	5
2004–05	West Ham U	32	1		
2005–06	West Ham U	0	0	32	1
2005–06	Stoke C	36	2		
2006–07	Stoke C	15	3	51	5
2006–07	Norwich C	4	1		
2007–08	Norwich C	13	1		
2008–09	Norwich C	0	0	17	2
2008–09	Milton Keynes D	24	6		
2009–10	Milton Keynes D	40	2		
2010–11	Milton Keynes D	44	0		
2011–12	Milton Keynes D	42	2		
2012–13	Milton Keynes D	36	6		
2013–14	Milton Keynes D	22	1	208	17

FLANAGAN, Tom (D)   55   4
H: 6 2   W: 11 05   b.Hammersmith 21-10-91
Internationals: Northern Ireland U21.

2009–10	Milton Keynes D	1	0		
2010–11	Milton Keynes D	2	0		
2011–12	Milton Keynes D	21	3		
2012–13	Milton Keynes D	0	0		
2012–13	Gillingham	13	1	13	1
2012–13	Barnet	9	0	9	0
2013–14	Milton Keynes D	7	0	31	3
2013–14	Stevenage	2	0	2	0

GALLOWAY, Brendon (M)   10   0
H: 6 2   W: 13 10   b.Zimbabwe 17-3-96
Internationals: England U17, U18, U19.

2011–12	Milton Keynes D	1	0		
2012–13	Milton Keynes D	1	0		
2013–14	Milton Keynes D	8	0	10	0

GLEESON, Stephen (M)   222   20
H: 6 2   W: 11 00   b.Dublin 3-8-88
Internationals: Republic of Ireland U21, Full
caps.

2006–07	Wolverhampton W	3	0		
2006–07	Stockport Co	14	2		
2007–08	Wolverhampton W	0	0		
2007–08	Hereford U	4	0	4	0
2007–08	Stockport Co	6	0		
2008–09	Wolverhampton W	0	0	3	0
2008–09	Stockport Co	21	2	41	4
2008–09	Milton Keynes D	5	0		
2009–10	Milton Keynes D	29	0		
2010–11	Milton Keynes D	36	0		
2011–12	Milton Keynes D	39	5		
2012–13	Milton Keynes D	30	6		
2013–14	Milton Keynes D	35	3	174	16

HALL, Ryan (M)   118   22
H: 5 10   W: 10 04   b.Dulwich 4-1-88
Internationals: England C.

2005–06	Crystal Palace	0	0		
2006–07	Crystal Palace	0	0		
2007–08	Crystal Palace	1	0	1	0
2007–08	Dagenham & R	8	2	8	2
From Bromley.					
2010–11	Southend U	41	9		
2011–12	Southend U	43	10		
2012–13	Southend U	2	0	86	19
2012–13	Leeds U	8	0		
2013–14	Leeds U	0	0	8	0
2013–14	Sheffield U	4	0	4	0
2013–14	Milton Keynes D	11	1	11	1

HODSON, Lee (D)   119   2
H: 5 11   W: 11 02   b.Boreham Wood
2-10-91
Internationals: Northern Ireland U19, U21,
Full caps.

2008–09	Watford	1	0		
2009–10	Watford	31	0		
2010–11	Watford	29	1		
2011–12	Watford	20	0		
2012–13	Watford	2	0	83	1
2012–13	Brentford	13	0	13	0
2013–14	Milton Keynes D	23	1	23	1

KAY, Antony (D)   414   41
H: 5 11   W: 11 08   b.Barnsley 21-10-82
Internationals: England Youth.

1999–2000	Barnsley	0	0		
2000–01	Barnsley	7	0		
2001–02	Barnsley	1	0		

2002–03	Barnsley	16	0		
2003–04	Barnsley	43	3		
2004–05	Barnsley	39	6		
2005–06	Barnsley	36	1		
2006–07	Barnsley	32	1	174	11
2007–08	Tranmere R	38	6		
2008–09	Tranmere R	44	11	82	17
2009–10	Huddersfield T	40	6		
2010–11	Huddersfield T	27	3		
2011–12	Huddersfield T	28	1		
2012–13	Huddersfield T	0	0	95	10
2012–13	Milton Keynes D	33	1		
2013–14	Milton Keynes D	30	2	63	3

LEWINGTON, Dean (D)   457   16
H: 5 11   W: 11 07   b.Kingston 18-5-84

2002–03	Wimbledon	1	0		
2003–04	Wimbledon	28	1	29	1
2004–05	Milton Keynes D	43	2		
2005–06	Milton Keynes D	44	1		
2006–07	Milton Keynes D	45	1		
2007–08	Milton Keynes D	45	0		
2008–09	Milton Keynes D	40	2		
2009–10	Milton Keynes D	42	1		
2010–11	Milton Keynes D	42	1		
2011–12	Milton Keynes D	46	3		
2012–13	Milton Keynes D	38	1		
2013–14	Milton Keynes D	43	1	428	15

MARTIN, David E (G)   217   0
H: 6 1   W: 13 04   b.Romford 22-1-86
Internationals: England U16, U17, U18, U19.

2003–04	Wimbledon	2	0	2	0
2004–05	Milton Keynes D	15	0		
2005–06	Milton Keynes D	0	0		
2005–06	Liverpool	0	0		
2006–07	Liverpool	0	0		
2006–07	Accrington S	10	0	10	0
2007–08	Liverpool	0	0		
2008–09	Liverpool	0	0		
2008–09	Leicester C	25	0	25	0
2009–10	Liverpool	0	0		
2009–10	Tranmere R	3	0	3	0
2009–10	Leeds U	0	0		
2009–10	Derby Co	2	0	2	0
2010–11	Milton Keynes D	43	0		
2011–12	Milton Keynes D	46	0		
2012–13	Milton Keynes D	31	0		
2013–14	Milton Keynes D	40	0	175	0

McLEOD, Izale (F)   356   114
H: 6 1   W: 11 02   b.Birmingham 15-10-84
Internationals: England U21.

2002–03	Derby Co	29	3		
2003–04	Derby Co	10	1	39	4
2003–04	Sheffield U	7	0	7	0
2004–05	Milton Keynes D	43	16		
2005–06	Milton Keynes D	39	17		
2006–07	Milton Keynes D	34	21		
2007–08	Charlton Ath	18	1		
2008–09	Charlton Ath	2	0		
2008–09	Millwall	7	2	7	2
2009–10	Charlton Ath	11	2		
2009–10	Peterborough U	4	0	4	0
2010–11	Charlton Ath	0	0	31	3
2010–11	Barnet	29	14		
2011–12	Barnet	44	18	73	32
2012–13	Portsmouth	24	10	24	10
2013–14	Milton Keynes D	36	7	165	62
2013–14	Northampton T	4	1	4	1

McLOUGHLIN, Ian (G)   48   0
H: 6 3   W: 13 08   b.Dublin 9-8-91
Internationals: Republic of Ireland U19, U21.

2008–09	Ipswich T	0	0		
2009–10	Ipswich T	0	0		
2010–11	Ipswich T	0	0		
2010–11	Stockport Co	5	0	5	0
2011–12	Milton Keynes D	1	0		
2012–13	Milton Keynes D	16	0		
2012–13	Walsall	6	0	6	0
2013–14	Milton Keynes D	8	0	25	0
2013–14	Newport Co	12	0	12	0

OTSEMOBOR, John (D)   265   7
H: 5 10   W: 12 07   b.Liverpool 23-3-83
Internationals: England U20.

1999–2000	Liverpool	0	0		
2000–01	Liverpool	0	0		
2001–02	Liverpool	0	0		

2002–03	Liverpool	0	0		
2002–03	*Hull C*	9	3	9	3
2003–04	Liverpool	4	0		
2003–04	*Bolton W*	1	0	1	0
2004–05	Liverpool	0	0	4	0
2004–05	*Crewe Alex*	14	1		
2005–06	Rotherham U	10	0	10	0
2005–06	Crewe Alex	16	0		
2006–07	Crewe Alex	27	0	57	1
2007–08	Norwich C	43	1		
2008–09	Norwich C	37	0		
2009–10	Norwich C	13	1	93	2
2009–10	Southampton	19	0	19	0
2010–11	Sheffield W	15	0		
2011–12	Sheffield W	11	0	26	0
2012–13	Milton Keynes D	35	1		
2013–14	Milton Keynes D	9	0	44	1
2013–14	*Tranmere R*	2	0	2	0

POTTER, Darren (M)   279 14
H: 6 0   W: 10 08   b.Liverpool 21-12-84
Internationals: Republic of Ireland Youth, B, U21, Full caps.

2001–02	Liverpool	0	0		
2002–03	Liverpool	0	0		
2003–04	Liverpool	0	0		
2004–05	Liverpool	2	0		
2005–06	Liverpool	0	0		
2005–06	Southampton	10	0	10	0
2006–07	Liverpool	0	0	2	0
2006–07	Wolverhampton W	38	0		
2007–08	Wolverhampton W	18	0		
2008–09	Wolverhampton W	0	0	56	0
2008–09	*Sheffield W*	17	2		
2009–10	Sheffield W	46	3		
2010–11	Sheffield W	33	3	96	8
2011–12	Milton Keynes D	40	2		
2012–13	Milton Keynes D	46	4		
2013–14	Milton Keynes D	29	0	115	6

POWELL, Daniel (F)   147 25
H: 5 11   W: 13 03   b.Luton 12-3-91

2008–09	Milton Keynes D	7	1		
2009–10	Milton Keynes D	2	1		
2010–11	Milton Keynes D	29	9		
2011–12	Milton Keynes D	43	6		
2012–13	Milton Keynes D	34	7		
2013–14	Milton Keynes D	32	1	147	25

RANDALL, Mark (M)   87 3
H: 6 0   W: 12 12   b.Milton Keynes 28-9-89
Internationals: England U17, U18.

2006–07	Arsenal	0	0		
2007–08	Arsenal	1	0		
2007–08	*Burnley*	10	0	10	0
2008–09	Arsenal	1	0		
2009–10	Arsenal	0	0		
2009–10	*Milton Keynes D*	16	0		
2010–11	Arsenal	0	0	2	0
2010–11	*Rotherham U*	10	1	10	1
2011–12	Chesterfield	16	1		
2012–13	Chesterfield	29	1		
2013–14	Chesterfield	0	0	45	2
2013–14	Milton Keynes D	4	0	20	0

RASULO, Georgio (M)   8 0
b.Banbury 23-1-97
Internationals: England U16, U17.

| 2012–13 | Milton Keynes D | 1 | 0 | | |
| 2013–14 | Milton Keynes D | 7 | 0 | 8 | 0 |

REEVES, Ben (D)   48 8
H: 5 10   W: 10 07   b.Verwood 19-11-91

2008–09	Southampton	0	0		
2009–10	Southampton	0	0		
2010–11	Southampton	0	0		
2011–12	Southampton	0	0		
2011–12	*Dagenham & R*	5	0	5	0
2012–13	Southampton	3	0	5	0
2012–13	*Southend U*	10	1	10	1
2013–14	Milton Keynes D	28	7	28	7

SMITH, Alan (F)   384 47
H: 5 10   W: 12 04   b.Rothwell 28-10-80
Internationals: England U21, B, Full caps.

1997–98	Leeds U	7	2		
1998–99	Leeds U	22	7		
1999–2000	Leeds U	26	4		
2000–01	Leeds U	33	11		
2001–02	Leeds U	23	4		
2002–03	Leeds U	33	3		
2003–04	Leeds U	35	9	172	38
2004–05	Manchester U	31	6		
2005–06	Manchester U	21	1		
2006–07	Manchester U	9	0	61	7
2007–08	Newcastle U	33	0		
2008–09	Newcastle U	6	0		
2009–10	Newcastle U	32	0		
2010–11	Newcastle U	11	0		
2011–12	Newcastle U	2	0	84	0
2011–12	*Milton Keynes D*	16	1		
2012–13	Milton Keynes D	27	1		
2013–14	Milton Keynes D	24	0	67	2

Scholars
Burns, Charlie Peter John; Daffern, Jacob Bempton Lewis; Forrester, Remy Lezlee; Galloway, Brendan Joel Zibusiso; Grant, Benjamin Matthew; Hickford, Harry Samuel; Okito, Gedeon; Osei-Addo, Kelvin Kwame; Rasulo, Giorgio Antonio; Summerfield, William Oliver; Tilney, Benjamin Rowland; Tingey, Luke Steven; Tshimanga, Kabongo; Vaughan, Laurence Murcot; Weston, Aaran Charles; Wiltshire, Kyran Tonell.

MORECAMBE (52)

AMOND, Padraig (F)   242 64
H: 5 11   W: 12 05   b.Carlow 15-4-88
Internationals: Republic of Ireland U21.

2006	Shamrock R	10	1		
2007	Shamrock R	6	1		
2007	*Kildare Co*	13	5	13	5
2008	Shamrock R	26	9		
2009	Shamrock R	20	4	62	15
2010	Sligo R	27	17	27	17
2010–11	Pacos	17	0	17	0
2011–12	Accrington S	42	7		
2012–13	Accrington S	36	9		
2013–14	Accrington S	0	0	78	16
2013–14	Morecambe	45	11	45	11

ARESTIDOU, Andreas (G)   16 0
H: 6 2   W: 13 00   b.Lambeth 6-12-89

2007–08	Blackburn R	0	0		
2008–09	Blackburn R	0	0		
2009–10	Shrewsbury T	2	0	2	0
2010–11	Preston NE	0	0		
2011–12	Preston NE	7	0	7	0
2012–13	Morecambe	6	0		
2013–14	Morecambe	1	0	7	0

BEELEY, Shaun (D)   66 0
H: 5 10   W: 11 05
Internationals: England C.

2012–13	Fleetwood T	34	0	34	0
2013–14	Bury	20	0	20	0
2013–14	Morecambe	12	0	12	0

DIAGNE, Tony (D)   108 6
H: 6 0   W: 11 10   b.Aubergenville 17-9-90

2010–11	Aubervilliers	20	1	20	1
2010–11	Macclesfield T	20	1		
2011–12	Macclesfield T	41	3	61	4
2013–14	Morecambe	27	1	27	1

DOYLE, Chris (D)   7 0

| 2012–13 | Morecambe | 4 | 0 | | |
| 2013–14 | Morecambe | 3 | 0 | 7 | 0 |

DRUMMOND, Stuart (M)   417 53
H: 6 2   W: 13 08   b.Preston 11-12-75

2004–05	Chester C	45	6		
2005–06	Chester C	42	6	87	12
2006–07	Shrewsbury T	9	0		
2007–08	Shrewsbury T	23	3	67	7
2007–08	Morecambe	18	2		
2008–09	Morecambe	44	10		
2009–10	Morecambe	43	9		
2010–11	Morecambe	41	6		
2011–12	Morecambe	38	5		
2012–13	Morecambe	44	2		
2013–14	Morecambe	35	0	263	34

ELLISON, Kevin (M)   417 84
H: 6 0   W: 12 00   b.Liverpool 23-2-79

2000–01	Leicester C	1	0		
2001–02	Leicester C	0	0		
2001–02	Stockport Co	11	0		
2002–03	Stockport Co	23	1		
2003–04	Stockport Co	14	1	48	2
2003–04	*Lincoln C*	11	0	11	0
2004–05	Chester C	24	9		
2004–05	Hull C	16	1		
2005–06	Hull C	23	1	39	2
2006–07	Tranmere R	34	4	34	4
2007–08	Chester C	36	11		
2008–09	Chester C	39	8	99	28
2008–09	Rotherham U	0	0		
2009–10	Rotherham U	39	8		
2010–11	Rotherham U	23	3	62	11
2010–11	*Bradford C*	7	1	7	1
2011–12	Morecambe	34	15		
2012–13	Morecambe	40	11		
2013–14	Morecambe	42	10	116	36

FLEMING, Andy (M)   120 11
H: 6 1   W: 12 00   b.Liverpool 18-2-89
Internationals: England C.

2006–07	Wrexham	2	0		
2007–08	Wrexham	4	0	6	0
2010–11	Morecambe	30	2		
2011–12	Morecambe	17	2		
2012–13	Morecambe	32	5		
2013–14	Morecambe	35	2	114	11

HUGHES, Mark (D)   254 15
H: 6 1   W: 13 03   b.Liverpool 9-12-86

2004–05	Everton	0	0		
2005–06	Everton	0	0		
2005–06	*Stockport Co*	3	1	3	1
2006–07	Everton	1	0	1	0
2006–07	Northampton T	17	2		
2007–08	Northampton T	35	1		
2008–09	Northampton T	41	1	93	4
2009–10	Walsall	26	1	26	1
2010–11	N Queensland F	30	4	30	4
2011–12	Bury	25	0		
2012–13	Bury	27	0	52	0
2012–13	*Accrington S*	5	0	5	0
2013–14	Morecambe	44	5	44	5

KENYON, Alex (M)   39 0
H: 5 11   W: 11 12   b.Preston 17-7-92

| 2013–14 | Morecambe | 39 | 0 | 39 | 0 |

MARSHALL, Marcus (F)   111 5
H: 5 10   W: 11 06   b.Hammersmith 7-10-89

2007–08	Blackburn R	0	0		
2008–09	Blackburn R	0	0		
2009–10	Blackburn R	0	0		
2009–10	*Rotherham U*	22	0		
2010–11	Rotherham U	36	3		
2011–12	Rotherham U	15	1	73	4
2011–12	*Macclesfield T*	14	1	14	1
2012–13	Bury	9	0	9	0
2013–14	Morecambe	15	0	15	0

McCREADY, Chris (D)   323 9
H: 6 1   W: 12 05   b.Ellesmere Port 5-9-81

2000–01	Crewe Alex	0	0		
2001–02	Crewe Alex	1	0		
2002–03	Crewe Alex	8	0		
2003–04	Crewe Alex	22	0		
2004–05	Crewe Alex	20	0		
2005–06	Crewe Alex	25	0		
2006–07	Tranmere R	42	1		
2007–08	Crewe Alex	34	1		
2008–09	Crewe Alex	5	1	115	2
2009–10	Northampton T	14	0	14	0
2009–10	*Tranmere R*	8	0	50	1
2010–11	Morecambe	36	4		
2011–12	Morecambe	46	0		
2012–13	Morecambe	40	2		
2013–14	Morecambe	22	0	144	6

McGEE, Joe (M)   15 0
H: 5 11   W: 10 12   b.Liverpool 6-3-93

2011–12	Morecambe	1	0		
2012–13	Morecambe	3	0		
2013–14	Morecambe	11	0	15	0

McGOWAN, Aaron (D)   3 0

| 2012–13 | Morecambe | 1 | 0 | | |
| 2013–14 | Morecambe | 2 | 0 | 3 | 0 |

MWASIŁE, Joe (M)   24 0
H: 5 8   W: 10 00   b.Zambia 6-7-93

2011–12	Morecambe	0	0		
2012–13	Morecambe	5	0		
2013–14	Morecambe	19	0	24	0

PARRISH, Andy (D)   234 2
H: 6 0   W: 11 00   b.Bolton 22-6-88

2005–06	Bury	8	0		
2006–07	Bury	9	0		
2007–08	Bury	26	1	43	1

2008–09	Morecambe	13	0		
2009–10	Morecambe	35	0		
2010–11	Morecambe	41	0		
2011–12	Morecambe	38	0		
2012–13	Morecambe	25	1		
2013–14	Morecambe	39	0	191	1

REDSHAW, Jack (F)   82 25
H: 5 6   W: 10 00   b.Salford 20-11-90

2009–10	Manchester C	0	0		
2010–11	Rochdale	2	0	2	0

From Salford C, Altrincham

2011–12	Morecambe	11	2		
2012–13	Morecambe	40	15		
2013–14	Morecambe	29	8	80	25

ROCHE, Barry (G)   400 0
H: 6 5   W: 14 08   b.Dublin 6-4-82
Internationals: Republic of Ireland U17.

1999–2000	Nottingham F	0	0		
2000–01	Nottingham F	2	0		
2001–02	Nottingham F	0	0		
2002–03	Nottingham F	1	0		
2003–04	Chesterfield	8	0		
2004–05	Nottingham F	2	0	13	0
2005–06	Chesterfield	41	0		
2006–07	Chesterfield	40	0		
2007–08	Chesterfield	45	0	126	0
2008–09	Morecambe	46	0		
2009–10	Morecambe	42	0		
2010–11	Morecambe	42	0		
2011–12	Morecambe	44	0		
2012–13	Morecambe	42	0		
2013–14	Morecambe	45	0	261	0

SAMPSON, Jack (F)   56 5
H: 6 2   W: 12 04   b.Wigan 14-4-93
Internationals: England U19.

2010–11	Bolton W	0	0		
2011–12	Bolton W	0	0		
2011–12	Southend U	9	0	9	0
2012–13	Bolton W	0	0		
2012–13	Accrington S	5	0		
2013–14	Accrington S	0	0	5	0
2013–14	Morecambe	42	5	42	5

THRELFALL, Robbie (D)   131 5
H: 5 11   W: 11 00   b.Liverpool 25-11-88
Internationals: England U19.

2006–07	Liverpool	0	0		
2007–08	Liverpool	0	0		
2007–08	Hereford U	9	0		
2008–09	Liverpool	0	0		
2008–09	Hereford U	3	0	12	0
2008–09	Stockport Co	2	0	2	0
2009–10	Liverpool	0	0		
2009–10	Northampton T	4	0	4	0
2009–10	Bradford C	17	2		
2010–11	Bradford C	20	0		
2011–12	Bradford C	17	0	54	2
2012–13	Morecambe	25	1		
2013–14	Morecambe	34	2	59	3

WILLIAMS, Ryan (F)   41 5
H: 5 8   W: 10 09   b.Birkenhead 8-4-91

2012–13	Morecambe	16	2		
2013–14	Morecambe	25	3	41	5

WRIGHT, Andrew (M)   162 0
H: 6 1   W: 13 07   b.Formby 15-1-85
From West Virginia Univ, Cape Cod Crusaders.

2007–08	Scunthorpe U	2	0		
2008–09	Scunthorpe U	28	0		
2009–10	Scunthorpe U	19	0		
2010–11	Scunthorpe U	20	0		
2011–12	Scunthorpe U	18	0	87	0
2012–13	Morecambe	40	0		
2013–14	Morecambe	35	0	75	0

Scholars
Bailey, Charlie Ellis; Dunleavy, Daniel Mark; Hilton, Ross Thomas George; Kitchen, William George; Lewis, Kyle Francis; McGowan, Aaron Joseph; Naylor, Alexander Ryan; Newton, Michael Callum; Preston, Jack; Reynolds, Adam Alexander; Roberts, James Peter; Smith, James Michael; Towers, Danny Harry; Woods, Thomas Andrew.

NEWCASTLE U (53)

ABEID, Mehdi (M)   59 10
H: 6 1   W: 12 08   b.Paris 6-8-92
Internationals: France U16, U17, U18. Algeria U23.

2008–09	Lens B	0	0		
2009–10	Lens B	8	0		
2010–11	Lens B	11	3	19	3
2011–12	Newcastle U	0	0		
2012–13	Newcastle U	0	0		
2012–13	*St Johnstone*	12	0	12	0
2013–14	Newcastle U	0	0		
2013–14	*Panathinaikos*	28	7	28	7

ALNWICK, Jak (G)   0 0
H: 6 2   W: 12 13   b.Hexham 17-6-93
Internationals: England U17, U18, U19, U20.

2010–11	Newcastle U	0	0		
2011–12	Newcastle U	0	0		
2012–13	Newcastle U	0	0		
2013–14	Newcastle U	0	0		

AMALFITANO, Romain (M)   80 10
H: 5 9   W: 10 11   b.Nice 27-8-89

2010–11	Reims	31	5		
2011–12	Reims	26	3	57	8
2012–13	Newcastle U	0	0		
2013–14	Newcastle U	0	0		
2013–14	*Dijon*	23	2	23	2

AMEOBI, Sam (F)   38 1
H: 6 3   W: 10 04   b.Newcastle 1-5-92
Internationals: Nigeria U20. England U21.

2010–11	Newcastle U	0	0		
2011–12	Newcastle U	10	0		
2012–13	Newcastle U	8	0		
2012–13	*Middlesbrough*	9	1	9	1
2013–14	Newcastle U	10	0	29	0

AMEOBI, Shola (F)   318 53
H: 6 3   W: 11 13   b.Zaria 12-10-81
Internationals: England U21. Nigeria Full caps.

1998–99	Newcastle U	0	0		
1999–2000	Newcastle U	0	0		
2000–01	Newcastle U	20	2		
2001–02	Newcastle U	15	0		
2002–03	Newcastle U	28	5		
2003–04	Newcastle U	26	7		
2004–05	Newcastle U	31	2		
2005–06	Newcastle U	30	9		
2006 07	Newcastle U	12	3		
2007–08	Newcastle U	6	0		
2007–08	*Stoke C*	6	0	6	0
2008–09	Newcastle U	22	4		
2009–10	Newcastle U	18	10		
2010–11	Newcastle U	28	6		
2011–12	Newcastle U	27	2		
2012–13	Newcastle U	23	1		
2013–14	Newcastle U	26	2	312	53

ANITA, Vurnon (M)   168 6
H: 5 5   W: 10 04   b.Willemstad 4-4-89
Internationals: Netherlands U15, U17, U19, U20, U21, Full caps.

2005–06	Ajax	1	0		
2006–07	Ajax	1	0		
2008–09	Ajax	16	0		
2009–10	Ajax	26	0		
2010–11	Ajax	31	3		
2011–12	Ajax	33	2		
2012–13	Ajax	1	0	109	5
2012–13	Newcastle U	25	0		
2013–14	Newcastle U	34	1	59	1

ARMSTRONG, Adam (F)   4 0
Internationals: England U16, U17.

2013–14	Newcastle U	4	0	4	0

BEN ARFA, Hatem (M)   235 38
H: 5 8   W: 10 08   b.Clamart 7-3-87
Internationals: France U16, U17, U18, U19, U21, Full caps.

2003–04	Lyon B	3	2		
2004–05	Lyon B	10	3		
2004–05	Lyon	9	0		
2005–06	Lyon B	12	0		
2005–06	Lyon	10	1		
2006–07	Lyon B	9	3	32	9
2006–07	Lyon	13	1		
2007–08	Lyon	30	6	64	7

2008–09	Marseille	33	6		
2009–10	Marseille	29	3		
2010–11	Marseille	1	0	63	9
2010–11	Newcastle U	4	1		
2011–12	Newcastle U	26	5		
2012–13	Newcastle U	19	4		
2013–14	Newcastle U	27	3	76	13

BIGIRIMANA, Gael (M)   39 1
H: 5 9   W: 11 09   b.Burundi 22-10-93
Internationals: England U20.

2011–12	Coventry C	26	0	26	0
2012–13	Newcastle U	13	1		
2013–14	Newcastle U	0	0	13	1

CABAYE, Yohan (M)   270 48
H: 5 9   W: 11 05   b.Tourcoing 14-1-86
Internationals: France U16, U18, U19, U20, U21, Full caps.

2004–05	Lille	6	0		
2005–06	Lille	27	1		
2006–07	Lille	22	3		
2007–08	Lille	36	7		
2008–09	Lille	32	5		
2009–10	Lille	32	13		
2010–11	Lille	36	2	191	31
2011–12	Newcastle U	34	4		
2012–13	Newcastle U	26	6		
2013–14	Newcastle U	19	7	79	17

Transferred to Paris St Germain January 2014

CAMPBELL, Adam (F)   15 2
H: 5 7   W: 11 07   b.North Shields 1-1-95
Internationals: England U16, U17, U19.

2011–12	Newcastle U	0	0		
2012–13	Newcastle U	3	0		
2013–14	Newcastle U	0	0	3	0
2013–14	*Carlisle U*	1	0	1	0
2013–14	*St Mirren*	11	2	11	2

CISSE, Papiss (F)   316 136
H: 6 0   W: 11 07   b.Dakar 3-6-85
Internationals: Senegal Full caps.

2003–04	AS Douanes	26	23	26	23
2004–05	Metz B	10	3		
2005–06	Metz B	3	0	13	3
2005–06	Metz	1	0		
2005–06	*Cherbourg*	28	11	28	11
2006–07	Metz	32	12		
2007–08	Metz	9	0		
2007–08	*Chateauroux*	15	4	15	4
2008–09	Metz	37	15		
2009–10	Metz	16	8	95	35
2009 10	Freiburg	16	6		
2010–11	Freiburg	32	22		
2011–12	Freiburg	17	9	65	37
2011–12	Newcastle U	14	13		
2012–13	Newcastle U	36	8		
2013–14	Newcastle U	24	2	74	23

COLOCCINI, Fabricio (D)   408 20
H: 6 0   W: 12 04   b.Cordoba 22-1-82
Internationals: Argentina Full caps.

1998–99	Boca Juniors	1	1		
1999–2000	Boca Juniors	1	0	2	1
1999–2000	AC Milan	0	0		
2000–01	AC Milan	0	0		
2000–01	San Lorenzo	19	3	19	3
2001–02	Alaves	33	6	33	6
2002–03	Atletico Madrid	27	0	27	0
2003–04	Villarreal	31	1	31	1
2004–05	AC Milan	1	0	1	0
2004–05	La Coruna	15	1		
2005–06	La Coruna	26	0		
2006–07	La Coruna	26	0		
2007–08	La Coruna	38	4	105	5
2008–09	Newcastle U	34	0		
2009–10	Newcastle U	37	2		
2010–11	Newcastle U	35	2		
2011–12	Newcastle U	35	0		
2012–13	Newcastle U	22	0		
2013–14	Newcastle U	27	0	190	4

DE JONG, Luuk (F)   139 47
H: 6 2   W: 12 07   b.Aigle 27-8-90
Internationals: Netherlands U19, U21, Full caps.

2008–09	De Graafschap	14	2	14	2
2009–10	FC Twente	12	2		
2010–11	FC Twente	12	2		
2011–12	FC Twente	33	25	77	39
2012–13	Moenchengladbach	23	6		
2013–14	Moenchengladbach	13	0	36	6

On loan from Moenchengladbach

Season	Club	Apps	Gls	Tot A	Tot G
2013–14	Newcastle U	12	0	12	0

DEBUCHY, Mathieu (D)   272 17
H: 5 10 W: 12 02 b.Fretin 28-7-85
Internationals: France U21, Full caps.

Season	Club	Apps	Gls	Tot A	Tot G
2003–04	Lille	6	0		
2004–05	Lille	16	3		
2005–06	Lille	26	4		
2006–07	Lille	22	1		
2007–08	Lille	16	0		
2008–09	Lille	30	0		
2009–10	Lille	31	1		
2010–11	Lille	35	2		
2011–12	Lille	32	5		
2012–13	Lille	15	0	229	16
2012–13	Newcastle U	14	0		
2013–14	Newcastle U	29	1	43	1

DUMMETT, Paul (D)   48 3
H: 5 10 W: 10 02 b.Newcastle 26-9-91
Internationals: Wales U21, Full caps.

Season	Club	Apps	Gls	Tot A	Tot G
2010–11	Newcastle U	0	0		
2011–12	Newcastle U	0	0		
2012–13	Newcastle U	0	0		
2012–13	*St Mirren*	30	2	30	2
2013–14	Newcastle U	18	1	18	1

ELLIOT, Rob (G)   119 0
H: 6 3 W: 14 10 b.Chatham 30-4-86
Internationals: Republic of Ireland U19, Full caps.

Season	Club	Apps	Gls	Tot A	Tot G
2004–05	Charlton Ath	0	0		
2004–05	*Notts Co*	4	0	4	0
2005–06	Charlton Ath	0	0		
2006–07	Charlton Ath	0	0		
2006–07	*Accrington S*	7	0	7	0
2007–08	Charlton Ath	1	0		
2008–09	Charlton Ath	23	0		
2009–10	Charlton Ath	33	0		
2010–11	Charlton Ath	35	0		
2011–12	Charlton Ath	4	0	96	0
2011–12	Newcastle U	0	0		
2012–13	Newcastle U	10	0		
2013–14	Newcastle U	2	0	12	0

FERGUSON, Shane (D)   52 1
H: 5 9 W: 10 01 b.Limavady 12-7-91
Internationals: Northern Ireland U17, U19, U21, B, Full caps.

Season	Club	Apps	Gls	Tot A	Tot G
2008–09	Newcastle U	0	0		
2009–10	Newcastle U	0	0		
2010–11	Newcastle U	7	0		
2011–12	Newcastle U	7	0		
2012–13	Newcastle U	9	0		
2012–13	*Birmingham C*	11	1		
2013–14	Newcastle U	0	0	23	0
2013–14	*Birmingham C*	18	0	29	1

GOOD, Curtis (D)   31 2
H: 6 2 W: 13 05 b.Melbourne 23-3-93
Internationals: Australia U20, U23, Full caps.

Season	Club	Apps	Gls	Tot A	Tot G
2011–12	Melbourne Heart	24	1	24	1
2012–13	Newcastle U	0	0		
2012–13	*Bradford C*	3	0	3	0
2013–14	Newcastle U	0	0		
2013–14	*Dundee U*	4	1	4	1

GOSLING, Dan (M)   82 9
H: 6 0 W: 11 00 b.Brixham 2-2-90
Internationals: England U17, U18, U19, U21.

Season	Club	Apps	Gls	Tot A	Tot G
2006–07	Plymouth Arg	12	2		
2007–08	Plymouth Arg	10	0	22	2
2007–08	Everton	0	0		
2008–09	Everton	11	2		
2009–10	Everton	11	2	22	4
2010–11	Newcastle U	1	0		
2011–12	Newcastle U	12	1		
2012–13	Newcastle U	3	0		
2013–14	Newcastle U	8	0	24	1
2013–14	*Blackpool*	14	2	14	2

GOUFFRAN, Yoan (F)   299 74
H: 5 9 W: 11 11
b.Villeneuve-Saint-Georges 25-5-86
Internationals: France U21.

Season	Club	Apps	Gls	Tot A	Tot G
2004–05	Caen	8	0		
2005–06	Caen	29	8		
2006–07	Caen	37	15		
2007–08	Caen	36	10	110	33
2008–09	Bordeaux	32	3		
2009–10	Bordeaux	32	5		
2010–11	Bordeaux	21	2		
2011–12	Bordeaux	34	14		
2012–13	Bordeaux	20	8	139	32
2012–13	Newcastle U	15	3		
2013–14	Newcastle U	35	6	50	9

GUTIERREZ, Jonas (M)   375 16
H: 6 0 W: 11 07 b.Buenos Aires 5-7-82
Internationals: Argentina Full caps.

Season	Club	Apps	Gls	Tot A	Tot G
2001–02	Velez Sarsfield	17	0		
2002–03	Velez Sarsfield	21	1		
2003–04	Velez Sarsfield	27	0		
2004–05	Velez Sarsfield	33	0	98	1
2005–06	Mallorca	30	2		
2006–07	Mallorca	36	3		
2007–08	Mallorca	30	0	96	5
2008–09	Newcastle U	30	0		
2009–10	Newcastle U	37	4		
2010–11	Newcastle U	37	3		
2011–12	Newcastle U	37	2		
2012–13	Newcastle U	34	1		
2013–14	Newcastle U	2	0	177	10
2013–14	*Norwich C*	4	0	4	0

HAIDARA, Massadio (D)   59 0
H: 5 11 W: 11 10 b.Trappes 2-12-92
Internationals: France U19, U20, U21.

Season	Club	Apps	Gls	Tot A	Tot G
2010–11	AS Nancy	8	0		
2011–12	AS Nancy	19	0		
2012–13	AS Nancy	17	0	44	0
2012–13	Newcastle U	4	0		
2013–14	Newcastle U	11	0	15	0

KEMEN, Olivier (M)   0 0
Internationals: France U16, U17, U18.

Season	Club	Apps	Gls	Tot A	Tot G
2013–14	Newcastle U	0	0		

KRUL, Tim (G)   153 0
H: 6 2 W: 11 08 b.Den Haag 3-4-88
Internationals: Netherlands U15, U16, U17, U19, U20, U21, Full caps.

Season	Club	Apps	Gls	Tot A	Tot G
2005–06	Newcastle U	0	0		
2006–07	Newcastle U	0	0		
2007–08	*Falkirk*	22	0	22	0
2007–08	Newcastle U	0	0		
2008–09	Newcastle U	0	0		
2008–09	*Carlisle U*	9	0	9	0
2009–10	Newcastle U	3	0		
2010–11	Newcastle U	21	0		
2011–12	Newcastle U	38	0		
2012–13	Newcastle U	24	0		
2013–14	Newcastle U	36	0	122	0

MARVEAUX, Sylvain (M)   140 17
H: 5 8 W: 10 05 b.Vannes 15-4-86
Internationals: France U21.

Season	Club	Apps	Gls	Tot A	Tot G
2006–07	Rennes	28	5		
2007–08	Rennes	24	0		
2008–09	Rennes	5	0		
2009–10	Rennes	35	10		
2010–11	Rennes	10	1	102	16
2011–12	Newcastle U	7	0		
2012–13	Newcastle U	22	1		
2013–14	Newcastle U	9	0	38	1

MBABU, Kevin (D)   1 0
H: 6 0 W: 12 03 b.Zurich 19-4-95
Internationals: Switzerland U16, U17, U18, U19.

Season	Club	Apps	Gls	Tot A	Tot G
2012–13	*Servette*	1	0	1	0
2012–13	Newcastle U	0	0		
2013–14	Newcastle U	1	0		

OBERTAN, Gabriel (F)   123 5
H: 6 1 W: 12 06 b.Paris 26-2-89
Internationals: France U16, U17, U18, U19, U21.

Season	Club	Apps	Gls	Tot A	Tot G
2006–07	Bordeaux	17	1		
2007–08	Bordeaux	26	2		
2008–09	Bordeaux	11	0	54	3
2008–09	*Lorient*	15	1	15	1
2009–10	Manchester U	7	0		
2010–11	Manchester U	7	0	14	0
2011–12	Newcastle U	23	1		
2012–13	Newcastle U	14	0		
2013–14	Newcastle U	3	0	40	1

SANTON, Davide (D)   133 1
H: 6 2 W: 13 00 b.Portomaggiore 2-1-91
Internationals: Italy U16, U17, U20, U21, Full caps.

Season	Club	Apps	Gls	Tot A	Tot G
2008–09	Internazionale	16	0		
2009–10	Internazionale	12	0		
2010–11	Internazionale	12	0	40	0
2010–11	*Cesena*	11	0	11	0
2011–12	Newcastle U	24	0		
2012–13	Newcastle U	31	1		
2013–14	Newcastle U	27	0	82	1

SATKA, Lubomir (D)   0 0
Internationals: Slovakia U19, U21, U23.

Season	Club	Apps	Gls	Tot A	Tot G
2013–14	Newcastle U	0	0		

SISSOKO, Moussa (M)   237 26
H: 6 2 W: 13 00 b.Le Blanc Mesnil 16-8-89
Internationals: France U16, U17, U18, U19, U21, Full caps.

Season	Club	Apps	Gls	Tot A	Tot G
2007–08	Toulouse	29	1		
2008–09	Toulouse	35	4		
2009–10	Toulouse	37	7		
2010–11	Toulouse	35	5		
2011–12	Toulouse	35	2		
2012–13	Toulouse	19	1	190	20
2012–13	Newcastle U	12	3		
2013–14	Newcastle U	35	3	47	6

STREETE, Remie (D)   0 0
H: 6 2 W: 12 13 b.Boldon 2-11-94

Season	Club	Apps	Gls	Tot A	Tot G
2011–12	Newcastle U	0	0		
2012–13	Newcastle U	0	0		
2013–14	Newcastle U	0	0		

TAVERNIER, James (D)   59 5
H: 5 9 W: 11 00 b.Bradford 31-10-91

Season	Club	Apps	Gls	Tot A	Tot G
2009–10	Newcastle U	0	0		
2010–11	Newcastle U	0	0		
2011–12	Newcastle U	0	0		
2011–12	*Carlisle U*	16	0	16	0
2011–12	*Sheffield W*	6	0	6	0
2011–12	*Milton Keynes D*	7	0	7	0
2012–13	Newcastle U	2	0		
2013–14	Newcastle U	0	0	2	0
2013–14	*Shrewsbury T*	1	0	1	0
2013–14	*Rotherham U*	27	5	27	5

TAYLOR, Ryan (M)   232 26
H: 5 8 W: 10 04 b.Liverpool 19-8-84
Internationals: England U21.

Season	Club	Apps	Gls	Tot A	Tot G
2001–02	Tranmere R	0	0		
2002–03	Tranmere R	25	1		
2003–04	Tranmere R	30	5		
2004–05	Tranmere R	43	8	98	14
2005–06	Wigan Ath	11	0		
2006–07	Wigan Ath	16	1		
2007–08	Wigan Ath	17	3		
2008–09	Wigan Ath	12	2	56	6
2008–09	Newcastle U	10	0		
2009–10	Newcastle U	31	4		
2010–11	Newcastle U	5	0		
2011–12	Newcastle U	31	2		
2012–13	Newcastle U	1	0		
2013–14	Newcastle U	0	0	78	6

TAYLOR, Steven (D)   201 12
H: 6 2 W: 13 01 b.Greenwich 23-1-86
Internationals: England U16, U17, U20, U21, B.

Season	Club	Apps	Gls	Tot A	Tot G
2002–03	Newcastle U	0	0		
2003–04	Newcastle U	1	0		
2003–04	*Wycombe W*	6	0	6	0
2004–05	Newcastle U	13	0		
2005–06	Newcastle U	12	0		
2006–07	Newcastle U	27	2		
2007–08	Newcastle U	31	1		
2008–09	Newcastle U	27	4		
2009–10	Newcastle U	21	1		
2010–11	Newcastle U	14	3		
2011–12	Newcastle U	14	0		
2012–13	Newcastle U	25	0		
2013–14	Newcastle U	10	1	195	12

TIOTE, Cheik (M)   195 4
H: 5 11 W: 12 06 b.Yamoussoukro 21-6-86
Internationals: Ivory Coast Full caps.

Season	Club	Apps	Gls	Tot A	Tot G
2005–06	Anderlecht	0	0		
2006–07	Anderlecht	2	0	4	0
2007–08	Roda JC	26	2	26	2
2008–09	Twente	28	0		
2009–10	Twente	28	1		
2010–11	Twente	2	0	58	1
2010–11	Newcastle U	26	1		
2011–12	Newcastle U	24	0		
2012–13	Newcastle U	24	0		
2013–14	Newcastle U	33	0	107	1

VUCKIC, Haris (F)   38   5
H: 6 2   W: 12 02   b.Ljubljana 21-8-92
Internationals: Slovenia U17, U19, U21, Full caps.

2007–08	Domzale	1	0	
2008–09	Domzale	4	0	5 0
2009–10	Newcastle U	2	0	
2010–11	Newcastle U	0	0	
2011–12	Newcastle U	4	0	
2011–12	*Cardiff C*	5	1	5 1
2012–13	Newcastle U	0	0	
2013–14	Newcastle U	0	0	6 0
2013–14	*Rotherham U*	22	4	22 4

WILLIAMSON, Mike (D)   297   13
H: 6 4   W: 13 03   b.Stoke 8-11-83

2001–02	Torquay U	3	0	
2001–02	Southampton	0	0	
2002–03	Southampton	0	0	
2003–04	Southampton	0	0	
2003–04	*Torquay U*	11	0	14 0
2003–04	*Doncaster R*	0	0	
2004–05	Southampton	0	0	
2004–05	Wycombe W	37	2	
2005–06	Wycombe W	39	5	
2006–07	Wycombe W	33	1	
2007–08	Wycombe W	12	0	
2008–09	Wycombe W	22	3	143 11
2008–09	Watford	17	1	
2009–10	Watford	4	1	21 2
2009–10	Portsmouth	0	0	
2009–10	Newcastle U	16	0	
2010–11	Newcastle U	29	0	
2011–12	Newcastle U	22	0	
2012–13	Newcastle U	19	0	
2013–14	Newcastle U	33	0	119 0

YANGA-MBIWA, Mapou (D)   222   4
H: 6 0   W: 12 12   b.Bangui 15-5-89
Internationals: France U21, Full caps.

2006–07	Montpellier	1	0	
2007–08	Montpellier	33	1	
2008–09	Montpellier	29	1	
2009–10	Montpellier	36	0	
2010–11	Montpellier	36	1	
2011–12	Montpellier	34	1	
2012–13	Montpellier	16	0	185 4
2012–13	Newcastle U	14	0	
2013–14	Newcastle U	23	0	37 0

Scholars
Atkinson, James Lewis; Barlaser, Daniel Tan; Cameron, Kyle Milne; Cobain, Jamie Anthony; Drennan, Ben; Gibson, Liam Steven; Gillesphey, Macauley; Hall, Andrew; Heardman, Tom; Kerridge, Joseph George; Laidler, Adam; McKinnon, Ryan; Olley, Greg Thomas; Pearson, Brendan Conor; Quinn, Jonathyn Stephen; Roberts, Callum; Smith, Liam Phillip; Sterry, Jamie Michael; Storey, Jordan Jay; Williams, Callum Dylan.

NEWPORT CO (54)

AMADI-HOLLOWAY, Aaron (D)   4   0
H: 6 2   W: 13 00   b.Newark 21-2-93
Internationals: Wales U17, U19.

2012–13	Bristol C	0	0	
2013–14	Bristol C	0	0	
2013–14	Newport Co	4	0	4 0

ANTHONY, Byron (D)   185   8
H: 6 1   W: 11 02   b.Newport 20-9-84
Internationals: Wales U21.

2003–04	Cardiff C	0	0	
2004–05	Cardiff C	0	0	
2005–06	*Cardiff C*	0	0	
2006–07	Bristol R	23	0	
2007–08	Bristol R	20	1	
2008–09	Bristol R	30	2	
2009–10	Bristol R	37	0	
2010–11	Bristol R	37	3	
2011–12	Bristol R	16	1	163 7
2011–12	*Hereford U*	15	1	15 1
2013–14	Newport Co	7	0	7 0

BURGE, Ryan (M)   55   4
H: 5 10   W: 10 03   b.Cheltenham 12-10-88

2005–06	Birmingham C	0	0	
2006–07	Birmingham C	0	0	

2007–08	Birmingham C	0	0	
2008–09	Barnet	2	0	2 0
From Jerez Industrial.				
2010–11	*Doncaster R*	1	0	1 0
2010–11	*Oxford U*	5	0	5 0
2011–12	Port Vale	0	0	
2012–13	Port Vale	30	2	
2013–14	Port Vale	0	0	30 2
2013–14	Newport Co	17	2	17 2

CHAPMAN, Adam (M)   79   3
H: 5 10   W: 11 00   b.Doncaster 29-11-89
Internationals: Northern Ireland U21.

2008–09	Sheffield U	0	0	
2009–10	Sheffield U	0	0	
2010–11	Oxford U	0	0	
2011–12	Oxford U	14	1	
2012–13	Oxford U	26	1	40 2
2013–14	*Mansfield T*	0	0	
2013–14	Newport Co	39	1	39 1

CROW, Danny (F)   131   30
H: 5 9   W: 13 02   b.Great Yarmouth 26-1-86

2004–05	Norwich C	3	0	3 0
2004–05	*Northampton T*	10	2	10 2
2005–06	Peterborough U	38	15	
2006–07	Peterborough U	35	6	
2007–08	Peterborough U	4	2	77 23
2007–08	*Notts Co*	14	2	14 2
From Cambridge U, Luton T				
2013–14	Newport Co	27	3	27 3

FLYNN, Michael (M)   317   42
H: 5 10   W: 13 04   b.Newport 17-10-80

2002–03	Wigan Ath	17	1	
2003–04	Wigan Ath	8	0	
2004–05	Wigan Ath	13	1	38 2
2004–05	*Blackpool*	6	0	
2004–05	Gillingham	16	3	
2005–06	Gillingham	36	6	
2006–07	Gillingham	45	10	97 19
2007–08	Blackpool	28	3	34 3
2008–09	*Darlington*	0	0	
2008–09	Huddersfield T	25	4	25 4
2009–10	Bradford C	42	6	
2010–11	Bradford C	19	0	
2011–12	Bradford C	30	4	91 10
2013–14	Newport Co	32	4	32 4

HOWE, Rene (F)   230   60
H: 6 0   W: 14 03   b.Bedford 22-10-86

2007–08	Peterborough U	15	1	
2007–08	*Rochdale*	20	9	20 9
2008–09	Peterborough U	0	0	
2008–09	*Morecambe*	37	10	37 10
2009–10	Peterborough U	0	0	
2009–10	*Lincoln C*	17	5	17 5
2009–10	*Gillingham*	18	2	18 2
2010–11	Peterborough U	0	0	15 1
2010–11	*Bristol R*	12	1	12 1
2011–12	Torquay U	39	12	
2012–13	Torquay U	42	16	81 28
2013–14	Burton Alb	15	1	15 1
2013–14	Newport Co	15	3	15 3

HUGHES, Andrew (D)   26   2
Internationals: Wales U23.

2013–14	Newport Co	26	2	26 2

JACKSON, Ryan (M)   36   0
H: 5 9   W: 10 03   b.Streatham 31-7-90
Internationals: England C.

2011–12	AFC Wimbledon	7	0	7 0
2012–13	Newport Co	29	0	29 0

JAMES, Tony (D)   111   1
H: 5 10   W: 13 04   b.Abergavenny 9-10-78

2009–10	Burton Alb	42	1	
2010–11	Burton Alb	27	0	
2010–11	*Hereford U*	6	0	6 0
2011–12	Burton Alb	30	0	99 1
2013–14	Newport Co	6	0	6 0

JEFFERS, Shaun (F)   51   2
H: 6 1   W: 11 03   b.Bedford 14-4-92
Internationals: England U19.

2009–10	Coventry C	4	0	
2010–11	Coventry C	0	0	
2010–11	*Cheltenham T*	22	1	22 1
2011–12	Coventry C	3	0	
2012–13	Coventry C	0	0	7 0
2013–14	Peterborough U	8	1	8 1
2013–14	Newport Co	14	0	14 0

JOLLEY, Christian (F)   84   9
H: 6 0   W: 10 00   b.Fleet 12-5-88
Internationals: England C.

2011–12	AFC Wimbledon	37	7	
2012–13	AFC Wimbledon	15	0	52 7
2013–14	Newport Co	32	2	32 2

JONES, Billy (D)   249   10
H: 6 1   W: 11 05   b.Chatham 26-3-83
Internationals: England C.

2000–01	Leyton Orient	1	0	
2001–02	Leyton Orient	16	0	
2002–03	Leyton Orient	24	0	
2003–04	Leyton Orient	31	0	
2004–05	Leyton Orient	0	0	72 0
2004–05	Kidderminster H	12	0	
2005–06	Kidderminster H	0	0	
2006–07	Kidderminster H	0	0	12 0
2007–08	Crewe Alex	22	0	
2008–09	Crewe Alex	38	6	
2009–10	Crewe Alex	11	2	71 8
2010–11	Exeter C	29	0	
2011–12	Exeter C	19	1	48 1
2012–13	Cheltenham T	39	0	
2013–14	Cheltenham T	0	0	39 0
2013–14	Newport Co	7	1	7 1

MINSHULL, Lee (M)   58   4
H: 6 2   W: 14 07   b.Chatham 11-11-85

2011–12	AFC Wimbledon	18	0	18 0
2013–14	Newport Co	40	4	40 4

O'CONNOR, Aaron (F)   7   1
b.Nottingham 9-8-83

2002–03	Scunthorpe U	3	0	3 0
From Ilkeston T, Gresley, Grays Ath, Mansfield T, Rushden & D, Luton T				
2013–14	Newport Co	4	1	4 1

PARKER, Joe (F)   0   0

2013–14	Newport Co	0	0	

PIDGELEY, Lenny (G)   157   0
H: 6 4   W: 14 09   b.Twickenham 7-2-84
Internationals: England U16, U18, U19, U20.

2003–04	Chelsea	0	0	
2003–04	*Watford*	27	0	27 0
2004–05	Chelsea	1	0	
2005–06	Chelsea	1	0	2 0
2005–06	*Millwall*	0	0	
2006–07	Millwall	42	0	
2007–08	Millwall	13	0	
2008–09	Millwall	0	0	55 0
2009–10	Carlisle U	17	0	17 0
From Woking				
2010–11	Bradford C	21	0	21 0
2011–12	Exeter C	10	0	10 0
2013–14	Newport Co	25	0	25 0

PIPE, David (M)   281   8
H: 5 9   W: 12 01   b.Caerphilly 5-11-83
Internationals: Wales U21, Full caps.

2002–03	Coventry C	21	1	
2003–04	Coventry C	0	0	21 1
2003–04	Notts Co	18	0	
2004–05	Notts Co	41	2	
2005–06	Notts Co	43	2	
2006–07	Notts Co	39	0	141 4
2007–08	Bristol R	40	2	
2008–09	Bristol R	39	1	
2009–10	Bristol R	7	0	86 3
2009–10	*Cheltenham T*	8	0	8 0
2013–14	Newport Co	25	0	25 0

PORTER, Max (M)   93   7
H: 5 10   W: 12 04   b.Hornchurch 29-6-87
Internationals: England C.

2007–08	Barnet	30	1	
2008–09	Barnet	26	0	56 1
From Rushden & D.				
2011–12	AFC Wimbledon	15	1	15 1
2013–14	Newport Co	22	1	22 1

SANDELL, Andy (D)   160   20
H: 5 11   W: 11 09   b.Calne 8-9-83

2005–06	Bristol R	0	0	
2006–07	Bristol R	36	3	
2008–09	Bristol R	0	0	36 0
From Salisbury C.				
2008–09	Aldershot T	29	2	
2009–10	Aldershot T	29	5	58 7
2010–11	Wycombe W	32	7	

2011–12	Wycombe W	11	0	**43**	**7**
2013–14	Newport Co	23	3	**23**	**3**

STEPHENS, Jamie (G)   15   0
b.Wotton 24-8-93

2012–13	Liverpool	0	0		
2012–13	*Airbus UK*	13	0	**13**	**0**
2013–14	Newport Co	2	0	**2**	**0**

WILLMOTT, Robbie (M)   46   3
H: 5 9   W: 12 00   b. 16-5-90
Internationals: England C.

2013–14	Newport Co	46	3	**46**	**3**

WORLEY, Harry (D)   132   7
H: 6 3   W: 13 00   b.Warrington 25-11-88

2005–06	Chelsea	0	0		
2006–07	Chelsea	0	0		
2006–07	*Doncaster R*	10	0	**10**	**0**
2007–08	Chelsea	0	0		
2007–08	*Carlisle U*	1	0	**1**	**0**
2007–08	Leicester C	2	0		
2008–09	Leicester C	0	0		
2008–09	*Luton T*	8	0	**8**	**0**
2009–10	Leicester C	0	0	**2**	**0**
2009–10	*Crewe Alex*	23	1	**23**	**1**
2010–11	Oxford U	43	1		
2011–12	Oxford U	10	0		
2012–13	Oxford U	9	1		
2013–14	Oxford U	0	0	**62**	**2**
2013–14	Newport Co	26	4	**26**	**4**

YAKUBU, Ismail (D)   171   12
H: 5 11   W: 11 12   b.Kano 8-4-85
Internationals: England C.

2005–06	Barnet	26	1		
2006–07	Barnet	29	1		
2007–08	Barnet	28	2		
2008–09	Barnet	38	3		
2009–10	Barnet	25	2	**146**	**9**

From AFC Wimbledon, Cambridge U

2013–14	Newport Co	25	3	**25**	**3**

ZEBROSKI, Chris (F)   246   52
H: 6 1   W: 11 08   b.Swindon 29-10-86

2005–06	Plymouth Arg	4	0		
2006–07	Plymouth Arg	0	0	**4**	**0**
2006–07	Millwall	25	3		
2007–08	Millwall	0	0	**25**	**3**
2008–09	Wycombe W	33	7		
2009–10	Wycombe W	15	2	**48**	**9**
2009–10	Torquay U	30	6		
2010–11	Torquay U	44	14	**74**	**20**
2011–12	Bristol R	39	3		
2012–13	Bristol R	0	0		
2012–13	*Cheltenham T*	21	5	**21**	**5**
2013–14	Newport Co	35	12	**35**	**12**

Scholars
Brooks, Ben; Keating, Jake Alexander; Owen-Evans, Thomas; Redman, Ellis Anthony David; Ward, Joseph Adam; Wood, Spencer; Zanotti, Alexander.

NORTHAMPTON T (55)

AMANKWAAH, Kevin (D)   319   7
H: 6 1   W: 12 12   b.Harrow 19-5-82
Internationals: England Youth.

1999–2000	Bristol C	5	0		
2000–01	Bristol C	14	0		
2001–02	Bristol C	24	1		
2002–03	Bristol C	1	0		
2002–03	*Torquay U*	6	0	**6**	**0**
2003–04	Bristol C	5	0		
2003–04	*Cheltenham T*	12	0	**12**	**0**
2004–05	Bristol C	5	0	**54**	**1**
2004–05	Yeovil T	15	0		
2005–06	Yeovil T	38	1	**53**	**1**
2006–07	Swansea C	29	0		
2007–08	Swansea C	0	0	**29**	**0**
2008–09	Swindon T	31	2		
2009–10	Swindon T	36	3		
2010–11	Swindon T	19	0		
2011–12	Swindon T	0	0	**86**	**5**
2011–12	*Burton Alb*	8	0	**8**	**0**
2011–12	*Rochdale*	16	0	**16**	**0**
2012–13	Exeter C	34	0	**34**	**0**
2013–14	Northampton T	21	0	**21**	**0**

CARTER, Darren (M)   283   23
H: 6 2   W: 12 03   b.Solihull 18-12-83
Internationals: England U19, U20.

2001–02	Birmingham C	13	1		
2002–03	Birmingham C	12	0		
2003–04	Birmingham C	5	0		
2004–05	Birmingham C	15	2	**45**	**3**
2004–05	*Sunderland*	10	1	**10**	**1**
2005–06	WBA	20	1		
2006–07	WBA	33	3	**53**	**4**
2007–08	Preston NE	39	4		
2008–09	Preston NE	18	0		
2009–10	Preston NE	23	0		
2010–11	Preston NE	14	0	**94**	**4**
2010–11	*Millwall*	10	0	**10**	**0**
2012–13	Cheltenham T	34	6	**34**	**6**
2013–14	Northampton T	37	5	**37**	**5**

COLLINS, Lee (D)   210   5
H: 6 1   W: 11 10   b.Telford 23-9-83
Internationals: England Youth.

2006–07	Wolverhampton W	0	0		
2007–08	Wolverhampton W	0	0		
2007–08	*Hereford U*	16	0	**16**	**0**
2008–09	Wolverhampton W	0	0		
2008–09	Port Vale	39	1		
2009–10	Port Vale	45	1		
2010–11	Port Vale	42	2		
2011–12	Port Vale	16	0	**142**	**4**
2011–12	Barnsley	7	0		
2012–13	Barnsley	0	0	**7**	**0**
2012–13	*Shrewsbury T*	8	0	**8**	**0**
2012–13	Northampton T	15	0		
2013–14	Northampton T	22	1	**37**	**1**

CONNELL, Alan (F)   305   60
H: 6 0   W: 12 00   b.Enfield 5-2-83

2002–03	Bournemouth	13	6		
2003–04	Bournemouth	7	0		
2004–05	Bournemouth	34	2		
2005–06	Torquay U	22	7	**22**	**7**
2006–07	*Hereford U*	44	9	**44**	**9**
2007–08	Brentford	42	12		
2008–09	Brentford	2	0	**44**	**12**
2008–09	Bournemouth	12	0		
2009–10	Bournemouth	38	5	**104**	**13**

From Grimsby T.

2011–12	Swindon T	32	11	**32**	**11**
2012–13	Bradford C	30	8		
2013–14	Bradford C	13	0	**43**	**8**
2013–14	Northampton T	16	0	**16**	**0**

DEEGAN, Gary (M)   169   18
H: 5 9   W: 11 11   b.Dublin 28-9-87

2005–06	Shelbourne	0	0		
2006	*Kilkenny City*	18	4	**18**	**4**
2007	*Longford Town*	30	3	**30**	**3**
2008	Galway U	17	0	**17**	**0**
2008	Bohemians	12	3	**12**	**3**
2009	Bohemians	23	2	**23**	**2**
2009–10	Coventry C	17	2		
2010–11	Coventry C	1	0		
2011–12	Coventry C	24	3		
2012–13	Coventry C	0	0	**42**	**5**
2012–13	Hibernian	0	0		
2013–14	Northampton T	27	1	**27**	**1**

DEMONTAGNAC, Ishmel (F)   163   15
H: 5 10   W: 11 05   b.Newham 15-6-88
Internationals: England U18, U19.

2005–06	Walsall	24	2		
2006–07	Walsall	19	1		
2007–08	Walsall	30	3		
2008–09	Walsall	10	3		
2009–10	Walsall	0	0	**83**	**9**
2009–10	Blackpool	8	0		
2009–10	*Chesterfield*	10	3	**10**	**3**
2010–11	Blackpool	1	0	**9**	**0**
2010–11	*Stockport Co*	7	2	**7**	**2**
2011–12	Notts Co	17	0	**17**	**0**
2012–13	Northampton T	27	1		
2013–14	Northampton T	10	0	**37**	**1**

DUKE, Matt (G)   155   0
H: 6 5   W: 13 04   b.Sheffield 16-7-77

1999–2000	Sheffield U	0	0		
2000–01	Sheffield U	0	0		
2001–02	Sheffield U	0	0		
2004–05	Hull C	2	0		
2005–06	Hull C	2	0		
2005–06	*Stockport Co*	3	0	**3**	**0**
2005–06	*Wycombe W*	5	0	**5**	**0**

2006–07	Hull C	1	0		
2007–08	Hull C	3	0		
2008–09	Hull C	10	0		
2009–10	Hull C	11	0		
2010–11	Hull C	21	0	**50**	**0**
2011–12	Bradford C	18	0		
2011–12	*Northampton T*	9	0		
2012–13	Bradford C	24	0	**42**	**0**
2013–14	Northampton T	46	0	**55**	**0**

EMERTON, Danny (M)   16   0
H: 5 10   W: 11 02   b.Beverley 27-9-91

2010–11	Hull C	0	0		
2011–12	Hull C	0	0		
2012–13	Hull C	0	0		
2013–14	Hull C	0	0		
2013–14	Northampton T	16	0	**16**	**0**

HACKETT, Chris (M)   338   22
H: 6 0   W: 12 08   b.Oxford 1-3-83

1999–2000	Oxford U	2	0		
2000–01	Oxford U	16	2		
2001–02	Oxford U	15	0		
2002–03	Oxford U	12	0		
2003–04	Oxford U	22	1		
2004–05	Oxford U	37	4		
2005–06	Oxford U	21	2	**125**	**9**
2005–06	*Hearts*	2	0	**2**	**0**
2006–07	Millwall	33	3		
2007–08	Millwall	6	0		
2008–09	Millwall	22	0		
2009–10	Millwall	40	2		
2010–11	Millwall	16	0		
2011–12	Millwall	3	0	**120**	**5**
2011–12	*Exeter C*	5	0	**5**	**0**
2011–12	*Wycombe W*	8	0	**8**	**0**
2012–13	Northampton T	41	6		
2013–14	Northampton T	37	2	**78**	**8**

HARRIOTT, Matty (M)   11   0
H: 6 0   W: 12 10   b.Luton 23-9-92

2010–11	Sheffield U	2	0		
2011–12	Sheffield U	0	0		
2011–12	*Burton Alb*	4	0	**4**	**0**
2012–13	Sheffield U	0	0		
2013–14	Sheffield U	0	0	**2**	**0**
2013–14	Northampton T	5	0	**5**	**0**

HEATH, Matt (D)   254   16
H: 6 4   W: 13 13   b.Leicester 1-11-81

2000–01	Leicester C	5	0		
2001–02	Leicester C	5	0		
2002–03	Leicester C	11	3		
2003–04	Leicester C	13	0		
2003–04	*Stockport Co*	8	0	**8**	**0**
2004–05	Leicester C	22	3	**51**	**6**
2005–06	Coventry C	25	1		
2006–07	Coventry C	7	0	**32**	**1**
2006–07	Leeds U	26	3		
2007–08	Leeds U	26	1	**52**	**4**
2007–08	Colchester U	5	0		
2008–09	Colchester U	14	0		
2008–09	*Brighton & HA*	6	1	**6**	**1**
2009–10	Colchester U	18	0		
2009–10	*Southend U*	4	0	**4**	**0**
2010–11	Colchester U	27	2		
2011–12	Colchester U	26	2		
2012–13	Colchester U	6	0	**96**	**4**
2013–14	Northampton T	5	0	**5**	**0**

HOOPER, JJ (F)   3   0

2013–14	Northampton T	3	0	**3**	**0**

HORNBY, Lewis (M)   25   0
H: 5 10   W: 10 13   b.Kettering 25-4-94

2012–13	Northampton T	25	0		
2013–14	Northampton T	0	0	**25**	**0**

KOUO-DOUMBE, Mathias (D)   332   20
H: 6 1   W: 12 05   b.Paris 28-10-79
Internationals: France U21.

2001–02	Hibernian	0	0		
2002–03	Hibernian	0	0		
2003–04	Hibernian	33	2	**45**	**2**
2004–05	Plymouth Arg	26	2		
2005–06	Plymouth Arg	43	1		
2006–07	Plymouth Arg	29	0		
2007–08	Plymouth Arg	12	0		
2008–09	Plymouth Arg	4	1	**134**	**4**
2009–10	Milton Keynes D	33	1		
2010–11	Milton Keynes D	44	5		
2011–12	Milton Keynes D	20	4		
2012–13	Milton Keynes D	24	1	**121**	**11**
2013–14	Northampton T	32	3	**32**	**3**

LANGMEAD, Kelvin (D)   368 35
H: 6 1   W: 12 00   b.Coventry 23-3-85

2003–04	Preston NE	0	0		
2003–04	Carlisle U	11	1	11	1
2004–05	Preston NE	1	0	1	0
2004–05	*Kidderminster H*	10	1	10	1
2004–05	Shrewsbury T	28	3		
2005–06	Shrewsbury T	42	9		
2006–07	Shrewsbury T	45	3		
2007–08	Shrewsbury T	39	1		
2008–09	Shrewsbury T	33	0		
2009–10	Shrewsbury T	44	3	231	19
2010–11	Peterborough U	32	3		
2011–12	Peterborough U	0	0	32	3
2011–12	Northampton T	41	4		
2012–13	Northampton T	39	7		
2013–14	Northampton T	3	0	83	11

McSWEENEY, Leon (F)   229 13
H: 5 10   W: 10 11   b.Cork 19-2-83

2001–02	Leicester C	0	0		
2002–03	Leicester C	0	0		

From Scarborough, Hucknall T, Hednesford T, Ilkeston T.

2007	Cork C	18	5	18	5
2007–08	Stockport Co	11	1		
2008–09	Stockport Co	36	4	47	5
2009–10	Hartlepool U	31	1		
2010–11	Hartlepool U	46	2	77	3
2011–12	Leyton Orient	29	0		
2012–13	Leyton Orient	32	0	61	0
2013–14	Carlisle U	8	0	8	0
2013–14	Northampton T	18	0	18	0

MORRIS, Ian (D)   219 17
H: 6 0   W: 11 05   b.Dublin 27-2-87
Internationals: Republic of Ireland U19, U21.

2003–04	Leeds U	0	0		
2004–05	Leeds U	0	0		
2005–06	Leeds U	0	0		
2005–06	*Blackpool*	30	3	30	3
2006–07	Leeds U	0	0		
2006–07	Scunthorpe U	28	3		
2007–08	Scunthorpe U	25	3		
2008–09	Scunthorpe U	20	1		
2008–09	*Carlisle U*	6	0	6	0
2009–10	Scunthorpe U	3	0		
2009–10	*Chesterfield*	7	0		
2010–11	Scunthorpe U	0	0	76	7
2010–11	*Chesterfield*	19	1	26	1
2011–12	Torquay U	37	2		
2012–13	Torquay U	11	1	48	3
2013–14	Northampton T	33	3	33	3

MOYO, David (F)   11 0
b.Harare 17-12-94

2012–13	Northampton T	5	0		
2013–14	Northampton T	6	0	11	0

O'DONOVAN, Roy (F)   195 49
H: 5 10   W: 11 07   b.Cork 10-8-85
Internationals: Republic of Ireland U21, B.

2002–03	Coventry C	0	0		
2003–04	Coventry C	0	0		
2004–05	Coventry C	0	0		
2005	Cork C	26	6		
2006	Cork C	29	11		
2007	Cork C	19	14	74	31
2007–08	Sunderland	17	0		
2008–09	Sunderland	0	0		
2008–09	*Dundee U*	11	1	11	1
2008–09	*Blackpool*	12	0	12	0
2009–10	Sunderland	0	0	17	0
2009–10	*Southend U*	4	1	4	1
2009–10	*Hartlepool U*	15	9	15	9
2010–11	Coventry C	2	0		
2011–12	Coventry C	11	0		
2011–12	*Hibernian*	14	1	14	1
2012–13	Coventry C	4	0	17	0
2012–13	Northampton T	16	5		
2013–14	Northampton T	15	1	31	6

Transferred to Brunei DPMM February 2014.

RAVENHILL, Ricky (M)   366 22
H: 5 10   W: 11 02   b.Doncaster 16-1-81

2003–04	Doncaster R	36	3		
2004–05	Doncaster R	35	3		
2005–06	Doncaster R	27	3	98	9
2006–07	Chester C	3	0	3	0
2006–07	Grimsby T	17	2	17	2
2006–07	Darlington	15	1		
2007–08	Darlington	35	3		
2008–09	Darlington	38	2	88	6
2008–09	Notts Co	0	0		
2009–10	Notts Co	40	3		
2010–11	Notts Co	34	0		
2011–12	Notts Co	5	0	79	3
2011–12	Bradford C	26	1		
2012–13	Bradford C	22	1		
2013–14	Bradford C	8	0	56	2
2013–14	Northampton T	25	0	25	0

REID, Paul (D)   333 9
H: 6 2   W: 11 08   b.Carlisle 18-2-82
Internationals: England U19, U20.

1998–99	Carlisle U	0	0		
1999–2000	Carlisle U	19	0		
2000–01	Rangers	0	0		
2001–02	Rangers	0	0		
2001–02	*Preston NE*	1	1	1	1
2002–03	Rangers	0	0		
2002–03	*Northampton T*	19	0		
2003–04	Northampton T	33	2		
2004–05	Barnsley	41	3		
2005–06	Barnsley	33	0		
2006–07	Barnsley	37	0		
2007–08	Barnsley	3	0	114	3
2007–08	*Carlisle U*	1	0	20	0
2008–09	Colchester U	26	1		
2009–10	Colchester U	12	0		
2010–11	Colchester U	18	0	56	1
2010–11	Scunthorpe U	12	0		
2011–12	Scunthorpe U	36	1		
2012–13	Scunthorpe U	26	1		
2013–14	Scunthorpe U	0	0	74	2
2013–14	Northampton T	16	0	68	2

ROBERTSON, Gregor (D)   252 4
H: 6 0   W: 12 04   b.Edinburgh 19-1-84
Internationals: Scotland U21.

2000–01	Nottingham F	0	0		
2001–02	Nottingham F	0	0		
2002–03	Nottingham F	0	0		
2003–04	Nottingham F	16	0		
2004–05	Nottingham F	20	0	36	0
2005–06	Rotherham U	35	1		
2006–07	Rotherham U	18	0	53	1
2007–08	Chesterfield	35	1		
2008–09	Chesterfield	38	2		
2009–10	Chesterfield	10	0		
2010–11	Chesterfield	21	0		
2011–12	Chesterfield	12	0	116	3
2012–13	Crewe Alex	29	0		
2013–14	Crewe Alex	3	0	32	0
2013–14	Northampton T	15	0	15	0

SNEDKER, Dean (G)   0 0
H: 6 0   W: 11 13   b.Northampton 17-11-94
Internationals: England U19.

2011–12	Northampton T	0	0	
2012–13	Northampton T	0	0	
2013–14	Northampton T	0	0	

TONEY, Ivan (F)   13 3
b.Northampton 16-3-96

2012–13	Northampton T	0	0		
2013–14	Northampton T	13	3	13	3

TOZER, Ben (D)   155 6
H: 6 1   W: 12 11   b.Plymouth 1-3-90

2007–08	Swindon T	2	0	2	0
2007–08	Newcastle U	0	0		
2008–09	Newcastle U	0	0		
2009–10	Newcastle U	1	0		
2010–11	Newcastle U	0	0	1	0
2010–11	*Northampton T*	31	3		
2011–12	Northampton T	45	3		
2012–13	Northampton T	46	0		
2013–14	Northampton T	29	0	151	6
2013–14	*Colchester U*	1	0	1	0

WIDDOWSON, Joe (D)   191 1
H: 6 0   W: 12 00   b.Forest Gate 28-3-89

2007–08	West Ham U	0	0		
2008–09	*Rotherham U*	3	0	3	0
2008–09	West Ham U	0	0		
2008–09	*Grimsby T*	20	1		
2009–10	Grimsby T	38	0	58	1
2010–11	Rochdale	34	0		
2011–12	Rochdale	32	0	66	0
2012–13	Northampton T	39	0		
2013–14	Northampton T	25	0	64	0

Scholars
Agbenu, Dodzi; Brown, Brendan Thomas; Clifton, Daniel Paul; Cooke, Ryan Lewis; Fitzgerald, Keran Michael; Harmon, Danny Patrick; Heath, Benjamin Michael; Jackson, Ben Robert; Parker, Richard Jonathan; Powell, Callum James; Reeve, Tyler Lewis; Roberts, Connor Harvey Hugh; Warburton, Samuel Jake.

NORWICH C (56)

BASSONG, Sebastien (D)   224 6
H: 6 2   W: 11 07   b.Paris 9-7-86
Internationals: France U21. Cameroon Full caps.

2005–06	Metz	23	0		
2006–07	Metz	37	1		
2007–08	Metz	19	0	79	1
2008–09	Newcastle U	30	0		
2009–10	Newcastle U	0	0	30	0
2009–10	Tottenham H	28	1		
2010–11	Tottenham H	12	1		
2011–12	Tottenham H	5	0		
2011–12	*Wolverhampton W*	9	0	9	0
2012–13	Tottenham H	0	0	45	2
2012–13	Norwich C	34	3		
2013–14	Norwich C	27	0	61	3

BECCHIO, Luciano (F)   303 107
H: 6 2   W: 13 05   b.Cordoba 28-12-83

2003–04	Mallorca B	0	0		
2004–05	Mallorca B	0	0		
2004–05	Murcia	16	3	16	3
2005–06	Terrassa	24	2	24	2
2006–07	Barcelona Athletic	10	0	10	0
2006–07	Merida	12	5		
2007–08	Merida	38	22	50	27
2008–09	Leeds U	45	15		
2009–10	Leeds U	37	15		
2010–11	Leeds U	41	19		
2011–12	Leeds U	41	11		
2012–13	Leeds U	26	15	190	75
2012–13	Norwich C	8	0		
2013–14	Norwich C	5	0	13	0

BENNETT, Elliott (M)   222 20
H: 5 9   W: 10 11   b.Telford 18-12-88

2006–07	Wolverhampton W	0	0		
2007–08	Wolverhampton W	0	0		
2007–08	*Crewe Alex*	9	1	9	1
2007–08	*Bury*	19	1		
2008–09	Wolverhampton W	0	0		
2008–09	*Bury*	46	3	65	4
2009–10	Wolverhampton W	0	0		
2009–10	Brighton & HA	43	7		
2010–11	Brighton & HA	46	6	89	13
2011–12	Norwich C	33	1		
2012–13	Norwich C	24	1		
2013–14	Norwich C	2	0	59	2

BENNETT, Ryan (M)   230 14
H: 6 2   W: 11 00   b.Thurrock 6-3-90
Internationals: England U18, U21.

2006–07	Grimsby T	5	0		
2007–08	Grimsby T	40	1		
2008–09	Grimsby T	45	5		
2009–10	Grimsby T	13	0	103	6
2009–10	Peterborough U	22	1		
2010–11	Peterborough U	34	4		
2011–12	Peterborough U	32	1	88	6
2011–12	Norwich C	8	0		
2012–13	Norwich C	15	1		
2013–14	Norwich C	16	1	39	2

BUNN, Mark (G)   154 0
H: 6 0   W: 12 02   b.Southgate 16-11-84

2004–05	Northampton T	0	0		
2005–06	Northampton T	0	0		
2006–07	Northampton T	42	0		
2007–08	Northampton T	45	0		
2008–09	Northampton T	3	0	90	0
2008–09	Blackburn R	0	0		
2008–09	*Leicester C*	3	0	3	0
2009–10	Blackburn R	0	0		
2009–10	*Sheffield U*	32	0	32	0
2010–11	Blackburn R	3	0		
2011–12	Blackburn R	3	0		
2012–13	Blackburn R	0	0	6	0

Season	Club				
2012–13	Norwich C	23	0		
2013–14	Norwich C	0	0	23	0

ELMANDER, Johan (F)   441 110
H: 6 2 W: 13 02 b.Alingsas 27-5-81
Internationals: Sweden U16, U18, U21, Full caps.

Season	Club				
1997	Holmalund	5	0		
1998	Holmalund	19	5	24	5
1999	Orgryte	18	2		
2000	Orgryte	21	2	39	4
2000–01	Feyenoord	16	2		
2001–02	Feyenoord	22	1		
2002	*Djurgaarden*	8	5		
2002–03	Feyenoord	1	0	39	3
2003	*Djurgaarden*	11	7	19	12
2003–04	*NAC Breda*	31	7	31	7
2004–05	Brondby	27	9		
2005–06	Brondby	31	13	58	22
2006–07	Toulouse	32	11		
2007–08	Toulouse	32	11	64	22
2008–09	Bolton W	30	5		
2009–10	Bolton W	25	3		
2010–11	Bolton W	37	10	92	18
2011–12	Galatasaray	30	12		
2012–13	Galatasaray	16	4		
2013–14	Galatasaray	0	0	46	16

On loan from Galatasaray

Season	Club				
2013–14	Norwich C	29	1	29	1

FER, Leroy (M)   183 30
H: 6 2 W: 12 05 b.Zortermeer 5-1-90
Internationals: Netherlands U16, U17, U19, U21, Full caps.

Season	Club				
2007–08	Feyenoord	13	1		
2008–09	Feyenoord	31	6		
2009–10	Feyenoord	31	2		
2010–11	Feyenoord	23	3		
2011–12	Feyenoord	4	2	102	14
2011–12	FC Twente	26	8		
2012–13	FC Twente	26	5	52	13
2013–14	Norwich C	29	3	29	3

FOX, David (M)   185 11
H: 5 9 W: 11 08 b.Leek 13-12-83
Internationals: England U16, U18, U19, U20.

Season	Club				
2000–01	Manchester U	0	0		
2001–02	Manchester U	0	0		
2002–03	Manchester U	0	0		
2003–04	Manchester U	0	0		
2004–05	Manchester U	0	0		
2004–05	*Shrewsbury T*	4	1	4	1
2005–06	Manchester U	0	0		
2005–06	Blackpool	7	1		
2006–07	Blackpool	37	4		
2007–08	Blackpool	28	1		
2008–09	Blackpool	22	0	94	6
2009–10	Colchester U	18	3	18	3
2010–11	Norwich C	32	1		
2011–12	Norwich C	28	0		
2012–13	Norwich C	2	0		
2013–14	Norwich C	0	0	62	1
2013–14	*Barnsley*	7	0	7	0

GAFAITI, Adel (D)   1 0
b.London 13-9-94
Internationals: Algeria U20.

Season	Club				
2013–14	Norwich C	0	0		
2013–14	*Oldham Ath*	1	0	1	0

GARRIDO, Javier (D)   196 3
H: 5 10 W: 11 12 b.Irun, Spain 15-3-85
Internationals: Spain U17, U20, U21.

Season	Club				
2004–05	Real Sociedad	28	0		
2005–06	Real Sociedad	33	0		
2006–07	Real Sociedad	25	1	86	1
2007–08	Manchester C	27	0		
2008–09	Manchester C	13	1		
2009–10	Manchester C	9	1	49	2
2010–11	Lazio	10	0		
2011–12	Lazio	11	0		
2012–13	Lazio	0	0	21	0

On loan from Lazio

Season	Club				
2012–13	Norwich C	34	0		
2013–14	Norwich C	6	0	40	0

HALL-JOHNSON, Reece (M)   0 0
b.Aylesbury 9-5-95

Season	Club				
2013–14	Norwich C	0	0		

HOOLAHAN, Wes (M)   398 53
H: 5 6 W: 10 03 b.Dublin 10-8-83
Internationals: Republic of Ireland U21, B, Full caps.

Season	Club				
2001–02	Shelbourne	20	3		
2002–03	Shelbourne	23	0		
2004	Shelbourne	31	2		
2005	Shelbourne	29	4	103	9
2005–06	Livingston	16	0	16	0
2006–07	Blackpool	42	8		
2007–08	Blackpool	45	5	87	13
2008–09	Norwich C	32	2		
2009–10	Norwich C	37	11		
2010–11	Norwich C	41	10		
2011–12	Norwich C	33	4		
2012–13	Norwich C	33	3		
2013–14	Norwich C	16	1	192	31

HOOPER, Gary (F)   262 127
H: 5 9 W: 11 02 b.Loughton 26-1-88

Season	Club				
2006–07	Southend U	19	0		
2006–07	*Leyton Orient*	4	2	4	2
2007–08	Southend U	13	2	32	2
2007–08	*Hereford U*	19	11	19	11
2008–09	Scunthorpe U	45	24		
2009–10	Scunthorpe U	35	19	80	43
2010–11	Celtic	26	20		
2011–12	Celtic	37	24		
2012–13	Celtic	32	19	95	63
2013–14	Norwich C	32	6	32	6

HOWSON, Jonathan (M)   253 28
H: 5 11 W: 12 01 b.Morley 21-5-88
Internationals: England U21.

Season	Club				
2006–07	Leeds U	9	1		
2007–08	Leeds U	26	3		
2008–09	Leeds U	40	4		
2009–10	Leeds U	45	4		
2010–11	Leeds U	46	10		
2011–12	Leeds U	19	1	185	23
2011–12	Norwich C	11	1		
2012–13	Norwich C	30	2		
2013–14	Norwich C	27	2	68	5

JOHNSON, Brad (M)   278 33
H: 6 0 W: 12 10 b.Hackney 28-4-87

Season	Club				
2004–05	Cambridge U	1	0	1	0
2005–06	Northampton T	3	0		
2006–07	Northampton T	27	5		
2007–08	Northampton T	23	2	53	7
2007–08	Leeds U	21	3		
2008–09	Leeds U	15	1		
2008–09	*Brighton & HA*	10	4	10	4
2009–10	Leeds U	36	7		
2010–11	Leeds U	45	5	117	16
2011–12	Norwich C	28	2		
2012–13	Norwich C	37	1		
2013–14	Norwich C	32	3	97	6

LOZA, Jamar (F)   12 1
H: 5 10 W: 11 01 b.Kingston 10-5-94
Internationals: Jamaica Full caps.

Season	Club				
2013–14	Norwich C	1	0	1	0
2013–14	*Coventry C*	1	0	1	0
2013–14	*Leyton Orient*	3	0	3	0
2013–14	*Southend U*	7	1	7	1

MARTIN, Russell (M)   339 16
H: 6 0 W: 11 08 b.Brighton 4-1-86
Internationals: Scotland Full caps.

Season	Club				
2004–05	Wycombe W	7	0		
2005–06	Wycombe W	23	3		
2006–07	Wycombe W	42	2		
2007–08	Wycombe W	44	0	116	5
2008–09	Peterborough U	46	1		
2009–10	Peterborough U	10	0	56	1
2009–10	Norwich C	26	0		
2010–11	Norwich C	46	5		
2011–12	Norwich C	33	2		
2012–13	Norwich C	31	3		
2013–14	Norwich C	31	0	167	10

MURPHY, Jacob (M)   13 1
b.Wembley 24-2-95
Internationals: England U18, U19.

Season	Club				
2013–14	Norwich C	0	0		
2013–14	*Swindon T*	6	0	6	0
2013–14	*Southend U*	7	1	7	1

MURPHY, Josh (F)   9 0
H: 5 8 W: 10 07 b.London 24-2-95
Internationals: England U18, U19.

Season	Club				
2012–13	Norwich C	0	0		
2013–14	Norwich C	9	0	9	0

NASH, Carlo (G)   243 0
H: 6 5 W: 14 01 b.Bolton 13-9-73

Season	Club				
1996–97	Crystal Palace	21	0		
1997–98	Crystal Palace	0	0	21	0
1998–99	Stockport Co	43	0		
1999–2000	Stockport Co	38	0		
2000–01	Stockport Co	8	0	89	0
2000–01	Manchester C	6	0		
2001–02	Manchester C	23	0		
2002–03	Manchester C	9	0	38	0
2003–04	Middlesbrough	1	0		
2004–05	Middlesbrough	2	0	3	0
2004–05	Preston NE	7	0		
2005–06	Preston NE	46	0		
2006–07	Preston NE	29	0	82	0
2007–08	Wigan Ath	0	0		
2007–08	*Stoke C*	10	0		
2008–09	Wigan Ath	0	0		
2008–09	Everton	0	0		
2009–10	Everton	0	0		
2010–11	Stoke C	0	0		
2011–12	Stoke C	0	0		
2012–13	Stoke C	0	0	10	0
2013–14	Norwich C	0	0		

OLSSON, Martin (D)   151 3
H: 5 7 W: 12 12 b.Gavle 17-5-88
Internationals: Sweden U19, U21, Full caps.

Season	Club				
2005–06	Blackburn R	0	0		
2006–07	Blackburn R	0	0		
2007–08	Blackburn R	2	0		
2008–09	Blackburn R	9	0		
2009–10	Blackburn R	21	1		
2010–11	Blackburn R	29	2		
2011–12	Blackburn R	27	0		
2012–13	Blackburn R	29	0	117	3
2013–14	Norwich C	34	0	34	0

PILKINGTON, Anthony (M)   242 49
H: 5 11 W: 12 00 b.Blackburn 3-11-87
Internationals: Republic of Ireland U21, Full caps.

Season	Club				
2006–07	Stockport Co	24	5		
2007–08	Stockport Co	29	6		
2008–09	Stockport Co	24	5	77	16
2008–09	Huddersfield T	16	2		
2009–10	Huddersfield T	43	7		
2010–11	Huddersfield T	31	10	90	19
2011–12	Norwich C	30	8		
2012–13	Norwich C	30	5		
2013–14	Norwich C	15	1	75	14

REDMOND, Nathan (M)   96 8
H: 5 8 W: 11 11 b.Birmingham 6-3-94
Internationals: England U16, U17, U18, U19, U21.

Season	Club				
2011–12	Birmingham C	24	5		
2012–13	Birmingham C	38	2	62	7
2013–14	Norwich C	34	1	34	1

RUDD, Declan (G)   70 0
H: 6 3 W: 12 06 b.Diss 16-1-91
Internationals: England U16, U17, U19, U20, U21.

Season	Club				
2008–09	Norwich C	0	0		
2009–10	Norwich C	7	0		
2010–11	Norwich C	1	0		
2011–12	Norwich C	2	0		
2012–13	Norwich C	0	0		
2012–13	*Preston NE*	14	0		
2013–14	Norwich C	0	0	10	0
2013–14	*Preston NE*	46	0	60	0

RUDDY, John (G)   269 0
H: 6 3 W: 12 07 b.St Ives 24-10-86
Internationals: England Full caps.

Season	Club				
2003–04	Cambridge U	1	0		
2004–05	Cambridge U	38	0	39	0
2005–06	Everton	1	0		
2005–06	*Walsall*	5	0	5	0
2005–06	*Rushden & D*	3	0	3	0
2005–06	*Chester C*	4	0	4	0
2006–07	Everton	0	0		
2006–07	*Stockport Co*	11	0		
2006–07	*Wrexham*	5	0	5	0
2006–07	*Bristol C*	1	0	1	0

2007–08	Everton	0	0		
2007–08	*Stockport Co*	12	0	23	0
2008–09	Everton	0	0		
2008–09	*Crewe Alex*	19	0	19	0
2009–10	Everton	0	0	1	0
2009–10	Motherwell	34	0	34	0
2010–11	Norwich C	45	0		
2011–12	Norwich C	37	0		
2012–13	Norwich C	15	0		
2013–14	Norwich C	38	0	135	0

SNODGRASS, Robert (M)   326   67
H: 6 0   W: 12 02   b.Glasgow 7-9-87
Internationals: Scotland U20, U21, Full caps.

2003–04	Livingston	0	0		
2004–05	Livingston	17	2		
2005–06	Livingston	27	4		
2006–07	Livingston	6	0		
2006–07	*Stirling Alb*	12	5	12	5
2007–08	Livingston	31	9	81	15
2008–09	Leeds U	42	9		
2009–10	Leeds U	44	7		
2010–11	Leeds U	37	6		
2011–12	Leeds U	43	13	166	35
2012–13	Norwich C	37	6		
2013–14	Norwich C	30	6	67	12

SURMAN, Andrew (M)   264   30
H: 5 10   W: 11 06   b.Johannesburg 20-8-86
Internationals: England U21.

2003–04	Southampton	0	0		
2004–05	Southampton	0	0		
2004–05	*Walsall*	14	2	14	2
2005–06	Southampton	12	2		
2005–06	Bournemouth	24	6		
2006–07	Southampton	37	4		
2007–08	Southampton	40	2		
2008–09	Southampton	44	7		
2009–10	Southampton	0	0	133	15
2009–10	Wolverhampton W	7	0	7	0
2010–11	Norwich C	22	3		
2011–12	Norwich C	25	4		
2012–13	Norwich C	4	0		
2013–14	Norwich C	0	0	51	7
2013–14	Bournemouth	35	0	59	6

TETTEY, Alexander (M)   193   15
H: 5 11   W: 10 09   b.Accra 4-4-86
Internationals: Norway U18, U19, U21, Full caps.

2004–05	Rosenborg	0	0		
2005–06	Rosenborg	10	1		
2006–07	Rosenborg	21	1		
2007–08	Rosenborg	25	4		
2008–09	Rosenborg	28	6		
2009–10	Rosenborg	1	0	85	12
2009–10	Rennes	24	0		
2010–11	Rennes	17	1		
2011–12	Rennes	19	1	60	2
2012–13	Norwich C	27	0		
2013–14	Norwich C	21	1	48	1

TURNER, Michael (D)   343   21
H: 6 4   W: 13 05   b.Lewisham 9-11-83

2001–02	Charlton Ath	0	0		
2002–03	Charlton Ath	0	0		
2002–03	*Leyton Orient*	7	1	7	1
2003–04	Charlton Ath	0	0		
2004–05	Charlton Ath	0	0		
2004–05	Brentford	45	1		
2005–06	Brentford	46	2	91	3
2006–07	Hull C	43	3		
2007–08	Hull C	44	5		
2008–09	Hull C	38	4		
2009–10	Hull C	4	0	129	12
2009–10	Sunderland	29	2		
2010–11	Sunderland	15	0		
2011–12	Sunderland	24	0		
2012–13	Sunderland	0	0	68	2
2012–13	Norwich C	26	3		
2013–14	Norwich C	22	0	48	3

VAN WOLFSWINKEL, Ricky (F)   176   63
H: 6 1   W: 10 13   b.Amersfoort 27-1-89
Internationals: Netherlands U19, U21, Full caps.

2007–08	Vitesse	1	0		
2008–09	Vitesse	32	8	33	8
2009–10	FC Utrecht	35	11		
2010–11	FC Utrecht	29	15	64	26
2011–12	Sporting Lisbon	25	14		

2012–13	Sporting Lisbon	29	14	54	28
2013–14	Norwich C	25	1	25	1

WHITTAKER, Steven (D)   324   25
H: 6 1   W: 13 07   b.Edinburgh 16-6-84
Internationals: Scotland U21, Full caps.

2001–02	Hibernian	1	0		
2002–03	Hibernian	6	0		
2003–04	Hibernian	28	1		
2004–05	Hibernian	37	1		
2005–06	Hibernian	34	1		
2006–07	Hibernian	35	1	141	4
2007–08	Rangers	30	4		
2008–09	Rangers	24	2		
2009–10	Rangers	35	7		
2010–11	Rangers	36	4		
2011–12	Rangers	25	2	150	19
2012–13	Norwich C	13	1		
2013–14	Norwich C	20	1	33	2

YOBO, Joseph (D)   389   12
H: 6 1   W: 13 00   b.Kano 6-9-80
Internationals: Nigeria B, Full caps.

1998–99	Standard Liege	0	0		
1999–2000	Standard Liege	18	0		
2000–01	Standard Liege	30	2	48	2
2001–02	Marseille	23	0	23	0
2002–03	Everton	24	0		
2003–04	Everton	28	2		
2004–05	Everton	27	0		
2005–06	Everton	29	1		
2006–07	Everton	38	2		
2007–08	Everton	30	1		
2008–09	Everton	27	1		
2009–10	Everton	17	1		
2010–11	Everton	0	0		
2010–11	*Fenerbahce*	30	1		
2011–12	Everton	0	0		
2011–12	*Fenerbahce*	39	1		
2012–13	Everton	0	0	220	8
2012–13	*Fenerbahce*	20	0		
2013–14	Fenerbahce	1	0	90	2

On loan from Fenerbahce
2013–14	Norwich C	8	0	8	0

Scholars
Awuah, Reiss; Burgess, Ben; Byrne-Hewitt, Lewis Christopher; Cole, Oliver; Eaton-Collins, Jamie; Efete, Michee; Fox, Nathan Ross; Grant, Raymond Michael; Heath, Harrison; Killip, Ben; King, Cameron; Norman, Cameron; Scales, Christian Stephen; Simpson, Jake Mark.

NOTTINGHAM F (57)

ABDOUN, Djamel (M)   192   23
H: 5 9   W: 10 02   b.Montreuil-sous-Bois 14-2-86
Internationals: France U18, U19, U20. Algeria Full caps.

2003–04	Ajaccio	1	0		
2004–05	Ajaccio	2	0		
2005–06	Ajaccio	7	2		
2006–07	Ajaccio	2	0		
2006–07	*Manchester C*	0	0		
2007–08	Ajaccio	0	0	12	2
2007–08	Sedan	32	5	32	5
2008–09	Nantes	22	1		
2009–10	Nantes	27	2		
2010–11	Nantes	1	0	50	3
2010–11	Kavala	26	3	26	3
2011–12	Olympiacos	23	2		
2012–13	Olympiacos	27	7	50	9
2013–14	Nottingham F	22	1	22	1

BLACKSTOCK, Dexter (F)   287   75
H: 6 2   W: 13 00   b.Oxford 20-5-86
Internationals: England U18, U19, U20, U21. Antigua and Barbuda Full caps.

2004–05	Southampton	9	1		
2004–05	*Plymouth Arg*	14	4	14	4
2005–06	Southampton	19	3	28	4
2005–06	*Derby Co*	9	3	9	3
2006–07	QPR	39	13		
2007–08	QPR	35	6		
2008–09	QPR	36	11	110	30
2008–09	*Nottingham F*	6	2		
2009–10	Nottingham F	39	12		
2010–11	Nottingham F	17	5		

2011–12	Nottingham F	22	8		
2012–13	Nottingham F	37	6		
2013–14	Nottingham F	1	0	122	33
2013–14	*Leeds U*	4	1	4	1

BLAKE, Jack (M)   3   0
b.Scotland 22-9-94
Internationals: Scotland U19.

2011–12	Nottingham F	0	0		
2012–13	Nottingham F	0	0		
2013–14	Nottingham F	0	0		
2013–14	*Mansfield T*	3	0	3	0

COHEN, Chris (M)   321   19
H: 5 11   W: 10 11   b.Norwich 5-3-87
Internationals: England Youth.

2003–04	West Ham U	7	0		
2004–05	West Ham U	11	0		
2005–06	West Ham U	0	0	18	0
2005–06	Yeovil T	30	1		
2006–07	Yeovil T	44	6	74	7
2007–08	Nottingham F	41	2		
2008–09	Nottingham F	41	2		
2009–10	Nottingham F	44	3		
2010–11	Nottingham F	42	2		
2011–12	Nottingham F	7	0		
2012–13	Nottingham F	38	2		
2013–14	Nottingham F	16	1	229	12

COLLINS, Danny (D)   301   9
H: 6 2   W: 11 13   b.Buckley 6-8-80
Internationals: England C. Wales Full caps.

2004–05	Chester C	12	1	12	1
2004–05	Sunderland	14	0		
2005–06	Sunderland	23	1		
2006–07	Sunderland	38	0		
2007–08	Sunderland	36	1		
2008–09	Sunderland	35	1		
2009–10	Sunderland	3	0	149	3
2009–10	Stoke C	25	0		
2010–11	Stoke C	25	0		
2011–12	Stoke C	0	0	50	0
2011–12	*Ipswich T*	16	3	16	3
2011–12	*West Ham U*	11	1	11	1
2012–13	Nottingham F	40	0		
2013–14	Nottingham F	23	1	63	1

COX, Simon (F)   242   70
H: 5 10   W: 10 12   b.Reading 28-4-87
Internationals: Republic of Ireland Full caps.

2005–06	Reading	2	0		
2006–07	Reading	0	0		
2006–07	*Brentford*	13	0	13	0
2007–08	*Northampton T*	8	3	8	3
2007–08	Reading	0	0	2	0
2007–08	Swindon T	36	15		
2008–09	Swindon T	45	29	81	44
2009–10	WBA	28	9		
2010–11	WBA	19	1		
2011–12	WBA	18	0		
2012–13	WBA	0	0	65	10
2012–13	Nottingham F	39	5		
2013–14	Nottingham F	34	8	73	13

DARLOW, Karl (G)   73   0
H: 6 1   W: 12 05   b.Northampton 8-10-90

2009–10	Nottingham F	0	0		
2010–11	Nottingham F	1	0		
2011–12	Nottingham F	0	0		
2012–13	Nottingham F	20	0		
2012–13	*Walsall*	9	0	9	0
2013–14	Nottingham F	43	0	64	0

DE VRIES, Dorus (G)   353   0
H: 6 1   W: 12 08   b.Beverwijk 29-12-80

1999–2000	Telstar	1	0		
2000–01	Telstar	27	0		
2001–02	Telstar	27	0		
2002–03	Telstar	26	0	81	0
2003–04	Den Haag	18	0		
2004–05	Den Haag	32	0		
2005–06	Den Haag	0	0	50	0
2006–07	Dunfermline Ath	27	0	27	0
2007–08	Swansea C	46	0		
2008–09	Swansea C	40	0		
2009–10	Swansea C	46	0		
2010–11	Swansea C	46	0	178	0
2011–12	Wolverhampton W	4	0		
2012–13	Wolverhampton W	10	0	14	0
2013–14	Nottingham F	3	0	3	0

DEMETRIOU, James (F) 0 0
b. 14-8-95
Internationals: Cyrpus U21.

| 2013–14 | Nottingham F | 0 | 0 | | |

DERBYSHIRE, Matt (F) 204 43
H: 5 10 W: 11 01 b.Gt Harwood 14-4-86
Internationals: England U21.

2003–04	Blackburn R	0	0		
2004–05	Blackburn R	1	0		
2005–06	Blackburn R	0	0		
2005–06	Plymouth Arg	12	0	12	0
2005–06	Wrexham	16	10	16	10
2006–07	Blackburn R	22	5		
2007–08	Blackburn R	23	3		
2008–09	Blackburn R	17	2	63	10
2008–09	Olympiacos	7	5		
2009–10	Olympiacos	19	6		
2010–11	Olympiacos	0	0	26	11
2010–11	Birmingham C	13	0	13	0
2011–12	Nottingham F	15	1		
2012–13	Nottingham F	0	0		
2012–13	Oldham Ath	18	4	18	4
2012–13	Blackpool	12	0		
2013–14	Blackpool	0	0	12	0
2013–14	Nottingham F	29	7	44	8

DJEBBOUR, Rafik (F) 191 84
H: 6 1 W: 13 00 b.Grenoble 8-3-84
Internationals: Algeria Full caps.

2004–05	La Louviere	19	3	19	3
2005–06	Atromitos	12	5		
2006–07	Atromitos	2	0	14	5
2006–07	Panionios	14	4		
2007–08	Panionios	23	14	37	18
2008–09	AEK Athens	23	7		
2009–10	AEK Athens	14	4		
2010–11	AEK Athens	15	5	48	16
2010–11	Olympiacos	10	7		
2011–12	Olympiacos	21	12		
2012–13	Olympiacos	25	20	56	39
2013–14	Sivasspor	10	2	10	2
2013–14	Nottingham F	7	1	7	1

EVTIMOV, Dimitar (G) 1 0
H: 6 3 W: 13 00 b.Plevan 7-9-93
Internationals: Bulgaria U19, U21.

2012–13	Nottingham F	0	0		
2013–14	Nottingham F	1	0	1	0

FENTON, Kieran (D) 0 0
b. 25-11-94
Internationals: England U19.

| 2013–14 | Nottingham F | 0 | 0 | | |

FOX, Danny (D) 310 15
H: 5 11 W: 12 06 b.Winsford 29-5-86
Internationals: England U21. Scotland Full caps.

2004–05	Everton	0	0		
2004–05	Stranraer	11	1	11	1
2005–06	Walsall	33	0		
2006–07	Walsall	44	3		
2007–08	Walsall	22	3	99	6
2007–08	Coventry C	18	1		
2008–09	Coventry C	39	5		
2009–10	Coventry C	0	0	57	6
2009–10	Celtic	15	0	15	0
2009–10	Burnley	14	1		
2010–11	Burnley	35	0		
2011–12	Burnley	1	0	50	1
2011–12	Southampton	41	0		
2012–13	Southampton	20	1		
2013–14	Southampton	3	0	64	1
2013–14	Nottingham F	14	0	14	0

GILLETT, Simon (M) 202 8
H: 5 6 W: 11 07 b.Oxford 6-11-85

2003–04	Southampton	0	0		
2004–05	Southampton	0	0		
2005–06	Southampton	0	0		
2005–06	Walsall	2	0	2	0
2006–07	Southampton	0	0		
2006–07	Blackpool	31	1	31	1
2007–08	Bournemouth	7	1	7	1
2007–08	Southampton	2	0		
2007–08	Yeovil T	4	0	4	0
2008–09	Southampton	27	0		
2009–10	Southampton	2	0	31	0
2009–10	Doncaster R	11	0		
2010–11	Doncaster R	22	1		
2011–12	Doncaster R	46	3		
2012–13	Doncaster R	0	0	79	4
2012–13	Nottingham F	25	0		
2013–14	Nottingham F	0	0	25	0
2013–14	Bristol C	23	2	23	2

GNAHORE, Wilfried (M) 0 0
b. 30-12-95
Internationals: Ivory Coast U19.

| 2013–14 | Nottingham F | 0 | 0 | | |

GOMIS, Kevin (D) 81 2
H: 6 1 W: 13 04 b.Paris 20-1-89

2009–10	Naval	22	0		
2010–11	Naval	21	2	43	2
2011–12	Nice	15	0		
2012–13	Nice	13	0		
2013–14	Nice	9	0	37	0

On loan from Nice

| 2013–14 | Nottingham F | 1 | 0 | 1 | 0 |

GRANT, Jorge (M) 0 0

| 2013–14 | Nottingham F | 0 | 0 | | |

GREENING, Jonathan (M) 422 15
H: 5 11 W: 11 00 b.Scarborough 2-1-79
Internationals: England U21.

1996–97	York C	5	0		
1997–98	York C	20	2	25	2
1997–98	Manchester U	0	0		
1998–99	Manchester U	3	0		
1999–2000	Manchester U	4	0		
2000–01	Manchester U	7	0	14	0
2001–02	Middlesbrough	36	1		
2002–03	Middlesbrough	38	2		
2003–04	Middlesbrough	25	1	99	4
2004–05	WBA	34	0		
2005–06	WBA	38	2		
2006–07	WBA	42	2		
2007–08	WBA	46	1		
2008–09	WBA	34	2		
2009–10	WBA	2	0	196	7
2009–10	Fulham	23	1		
2010–11	Fulham	10	0	33	1
2011–12	Nottingham F	31	0		
2012–13	Nottingham F	5	0		
2012–13	Barnsley	6	1	6	1
2013–14	Nottingham F	13	0	49	0

HALFORD, Greg (D) 369 43
H: 6 0 W: 12 10 b.Chelmsford 8-12-84
Internationals: England U21.

2002–03	Colchester U	1	0		
2003–04	Colchester U	18	4		
2004–05	Colchester U	44	4		
2005–06	Colchester U	45	7		
2006–07	Colchester U	28	3	136	18
2006–07	Reading	3	0	3	0
2007–08	Sunderland	8	0		
2007–08	Charlton Ath	16	2	16	2
2008–09	Sunderland	0	0		
2008–09	Sheffield U	41	4	41	4
2009–10	Sunderland	0	0	8	0
2009–10	Wolverhampton W	15	0		
2010–11	Wolverhampton W	2	0	17	0
2010–11	Portsmouth	33	5		
2011–12	Portsmouth	42	7	75	12
2012–13	Nottingham F	37	3		
2013–14	Nottingham F	36	4	73	7

HARDING, Dan (D) 326 7
H: 6 0 W: 11 11 b.Gloucester 23-12-83
Internationals: England U21.

2002–03	Brighton & HA	1	0		
2003–04	Brighton & HA	23	0		
2004–05	Brighton & HA	43	1	67	1
2005–06	Leeds U	20	0	20	0
2006–07	Ipswich T	42	0		
2007–08	Ipswich T	30	1		
2008–09	Ipswich T	1	0	73	1
2008–09	Southend U	19	1	19	1
2008–09	Reading	3	0	3	0
2009–10	Southampton	42	3		
2010–11	Southampton	36	0		
2011–12	Southampton	20	1	98	4
2012–13	Nottingham F	27	0		
2013–14	Nottingham F	19	0	46	0

HENDERSON, Darius (F) 396 108
H: 6 3 W: 14 03 b.Sutton 7-9-81

1999–2000	Reading	6	0		
2000–01	Reading	4	0		
2001–02	Reading	38	7		
2002–03	Reading	22	4		
2003–04	Reading	1	0	71	11
2003–04	Brighton & HA	10	2	10	2
2003–04	Gillingham	4	0		
2004–05	Gillingham	32	9	36	9
2004–05	Swindon T	6	5	6	5
2005–06	Watford	30	14		
2006–07	Watford	35	3		
2007–08	Watford	40	12	105	29
2008–09	Sheffield U	32	6		
2009–10	Sheffield U	32	12		
2010–11	Sheffield U	8	2	72	20
2011–12	Millwall	31	15		
2012–13	Millwall	20	7	51	22
2012–13	Nottingham F	11	2		
2013–14	Nottingham F	34	8	45	10

HOBBS, Jack (D) 228 4
H: 6 3 W: 13 05 b.Portsmouth 18-8-88
Internationals: England U19.

2004–05	Lincoln C	1	0	1	0
2005–06	Liverpool	0	0		
2006–07	Liverpool	0	0		
2007–08	Liverpool	0	0		
2007–08	Scunthorpe U	9	1	9	1
2008–09	Liverpool	0	0	2	0
2008–09	Leicester C	44	1		
2009–10	Leicester C	44	0		
2010–11	Leicester C	26	0	114	1
2010–11	Hull C	13	0		
2011–12	Hull C	40	1		
2012–13	Hull C	22	0	75	1
2013–14	Nottingham F	27	1	27	1

JARA, Gonzalo (D) 252 5
H: 5 10 W: 12 02 b.Hualpen 29-8-85
Internationals: Chile Full caps.

2002	Huachipato	0	0		
2003	Huachipato	17	1		
2004	Huachipato	11	0		
2005	Huachipato	23	0		
2006	Huachipato	18	1	69	2
2007	Colo Colo	23	1		
2008	Colo Colo	25	0		
2009	Colo Colo	16	0	64	1
2009–10	WBA	22	1		
2010–11	WBA	29	1		
2011–12	WBA	4	0		
2011–12	Brighton & HA	14	0	14	0
2012–13	WBA	1	0	56	2
2012–13	Nottingham F	17	0		
2013–14	Nottingham F	32	0	49	0

LANSBURY, Henri (M) 162 26
H: 6 0 W: 13 06 b.Enfield 12-10-90
Internationals: England U16, U17, U19, U21.

2007–08	Arsenal	0	0		
2008–09	Arsenal	0	0		
2008–09	Scunthorpe U	16	4	16	4
2009–10	Arsenal	1	0		
2009–10	Watford	37	5	37	5
2010–11	Arsenal	0	0		
2010–11	Norwich C	23	4	23	4
2011–12	Arsenal	2	0		
2011–12	West Ham U	22	1	22	1
2012–13	Arsenal	0	0	3	0
2012–13	Nottingham F	32	5		
2013–14	Nottingham F	29	7	61	12

LASCELLES, Jamaal (D) 39 3
H: 6 2 W: 13 01 b.Derby 11-11-93
Internationals: England U18, U19, U20.

2010–11	Nottingham F	0	0		
2011–12	Nottingham F	1	0		
2011–12	Stevenage	7	1	7	1
2012–13	Nottingham F	2	0		
2013–14	Nottingham F	29	2	32	2

LICHAJ, Eric (D) 87 2
H: 5 11 W: 12 07 b.Chicago 17-11-88
Internationals: USA U17, U20, Full caps.

2007–08	Aston Villa	0	0		
2008–09	Aston Villa	0	0		
2009–10	Aston Villa	0	0		
2009–10	Lincoln C	6	0	6	0
2009–10	Leyton Orient	9	1	9	1
2010–11	Aston Villa	5	0		
2010–11	Leeds U	16	0	16	0
2011–12	Aston Villa	10	1		
2012–13	Aston Villa	17	0	32	1
2013–14	Nottingham F	24	0	24	0

MACKIE, Jamie (F) 244 38
H: 5 8 W: 11 00 b.Dorking 22-9-85
Internationals: Scotland Full caps.

2003–04	Wimbledon	13	0	13	0
2004–05	Milton Keynes D	3	0	3	0
From Exeter C					
2007–08	Plymouth Arg	13	3		
2008–09	Plymouth Arg	43	5		
2009–10	Plymouth Arg	42	8	98	16
2010–11	QPR	25	9		
2011–12	QPR	31	7		
2012–13	QPR	29	2	85	18
2013–14	Nottingham F	45	4	45	4

MAJEWSKI, Radoslaw (M) 215 21
H: 5 7 W: 10 06 b.Pruszkow 15-12-86
Internationals: Poland U21, U23, Full caps.

2006–07	Groclin	14	0		
2007–08	Groclin	28	4	42	4
2008–09	Polonia Warsaw	29	1	29	1
2009–10	Nottingham F	35	3		
2010–11	Nottingham F	26	2		
2011–12	Nottingham F	28	6		
2012–13	Nottingham F	31	5		
2013–14	Nottingham F	24	0	144	16

McLAUGHLIN, Stephen (M) 65 13
H: 5 9 W: 11 12 b.Derry 14-6-90

2011	Derry C	33	3		
2012	Derry C	24	10	57	13
2012–13	Nottingham F	0	0		
2013–14	Nottingham F	3	0	3	0
2013–14	*Bristol C*	5	0	5	0

MILLER, Ishmael (F) 168 33
H: 6 3 W: 14 00 b.Manchester 5-3-87

2005–06	Manchester C	1	0		
2006–07	Manchester C	16	0		
2007–08	Manchester C	0	0	17	0
2007–08	WBA	34	9		
2008–09	WBA	15	3		
2009–10	WBA	15	2		
2010–11	WBA	6	0	70	14
2010–11	*QPR*	12	1	12	1
2011–12	Nottingham F	21	3		
2012–13	Nottingham F	0	0		
2012–13	*Middlesbrough*	25	5	25	5
2013–14	Nottingham F	4	0	25	3
2013–14	*Yeovil T*	19	10	19	10

MOUSSI, Guy (M) 230 5
H: 6 1 W: 12 11 b.Paris 23-1-85

2004–05	Angers	15	1		
2005–06	Angers	9	0		
2006–07	Angers	32	0		
2007–08	Angers	35	1	91	2
2008–09	Nottingham F	15	0		
2009–10	Nottingham F	27	3		
2010–11	Nottingham F	31	0		
2011–12	Nottingham F	34	0		
2012–13	Nottingham F	18	0		
2013–14	Nottingham F	11	0	136	3
2013–14	*Millwall*	3	0	3	0

OSBORN, Ben (D) 8 0
b.Derby 5-8-94
Internationals: England U18, U19.

2011–12	Nottingham F	0	0		
2012–13	Nottingham F	0	0		
2013–14	Nottingham F	8	0	8	0

OTIM, Derrick (F) 0 0
b. 21-3-96

2013–14	Nottingham F	0	0		

PATERSON, Jamie (F) 126 23
H: 5 9 W: 10 07 b.Coventry 20-12-91

2010–11	Walsall	14	0		
2011–12	Walsall	34	3		
2012–13	Walsall	46	12	94	15
2013–14	Nottingham F	32	8	32	8

POLIMOS, Ilias (D) 0 0
b. 1-9-95
Internationals: Greece U18, U19.

2013–14	Nottingham F	0	0		

REES, Josh (M) 1 0
H: 5 9 W: 11 00 b.Hemel Hempstead 4-10-93
Internationals: England U16, U17.

2011–12	Arsenal	0	0		
2013–14	Nottingham F	1	0	1	0

REID, Andy (M) 403 51
H: 5 9 W: 12 08 b.Dublin 29-7-82
Internationals: Republic of Ireland U21, Full caps.

1999–2000	Nottingham F	0	0		
2000–01	Nottingham F	14	2		
2001–02	Nottingham F	29	0		
2002–03	Nottingham F	30	1		
2003–04	Nottingham F	46	13		
2004–05	Nottingham F	25	5		
2004–05	Tottenham H	13	1		
2005–06	Tottenham H	13	0	26	1
2006–07	Charlton Ath	16	2		
2007–08	Charlton Ath	22	5	38	7
2007–08	Sunderland	13	1		
2008–09	Sunderland	32	1		
2009–10	Sunderland	21	2		
2010–11	Sunderland	2	0	68	4
2010–11	*Sheffield U*	9	2	9	2
2010–11	*Blackpool*	5	0	5	0
2011–12	Nottingham F	39	2		
2012–13	Nottingham F	42	5		
2013–14	Nottingham F	32	9	257	37

SCHOENECKER, Edouard (M) 0 0
b. 20-10-95

2013–14	Nottingham F	0	0		

SMITH, Jordan (G) 0 0
Internationals: Costa Rica U17, U20, Full caps.

2013–14	Nottingham F	0	0		

TUDGAY, Marcus (F) 364 83
H: 5 10 W: 12 04 b.Shoreham 3-2-83

2002–03	Derby Co	8	0		
2003–04	Derby Co	29	6		
2004–05	Derby Co	34	9		
2005–06	Derby Co	21	2	92	17
2005–06	Sheffield W	18	5		
2006–07	Sheffield W	40	11		
2007–08	Sheffield W	35	7		
2008–09	Sheffield W	42	14		
2009–10	Sheffield W	43	10		
2010–11	Sheffield W	17	2	195	49
2010–11	Nottingham F	22	7		
2011–12	Nottingham F	34	5		
2012–13	Nottingham F	3	0		
2012–13	*Barnsley*	9	3		
2013–14	Nottingham F	2	1	61	13
2013–14	*Barnsley*	5	1	14	4
2013–14	*Charlton Ath*	2	0	2	0

WHOLEY, Jake (D) 2 0
H: 5 10 W: 12 04 b.Nottingham 1-12-93

2010–11	Notts Co	1	0		
2011–12	Notts Co	0	0		
2012–13	Notts Co	1	0		
2013–14	Notts Co	0	0	2	0
2013–14	Nottingham F	0	0		

WILSON, Kelvin (D) 284 4
H: 6 2 W: 12 01 b.Nottingham 3-9-85

2003–04	Notts Co	3	0		
2004–05	Notts Co	41	2		
2005–06	Notts Co	34	1	78	3
2005–06	*Preston NE*	6	0		
2006–07	Preston NE	21	1	27	1
2007–08	Nottingham F	42	0		
2008–09	Nottingham F	36	0		
2009–10	Nottingham F	35	0		
2010–11	Nottingham F	10	0		
2011–12	Celtic	15	0		
2012–13	Celtic	32	0	47	0
2013–14	Nottingham F	9	0	132	0

Scholars
Arrowsmith, David James; Burke, Oliver Jasen; Dearle, Richard Alexander; Durrant, Ross Eric; Elliott, Daniel John Eniton Squire; Garcia Worthington, Jermaine Ramon; Karo, Antreas; Kelly, Jack Brent; Mulraney, Jake David; Myles, Aaron Jack; Petravicius, Deimantas; Thomas, Luke Washington; Walker, Tyler J Andrew; Walton, Kasheme Emmanuel Alphonsian; Worrall, Joseph Adrian.

NOTTS CO (58)

ARQUIN, Yoann (F) 138 33
H: 6 2 W: 13 04 b.Le Havre 15-4-88
Internationals: Martinique Full caps.

2008–09	Quimper	24	9	24	9
2010–11	Red Star 93	11	2	11	2
2011–12	Hereford U	34	8	34	8
2012–13	Notts Co	41	7		
2013–14	Notts Co	12	3	53	10
2013–14	Ross Co	16	4	16	4

BALMY, Jeremy (M) 1 0

2013–14	Notts Co	1	0	1	0

BELL, David (M) 325 22
H: 5 10 W: 11 05 b.Wellingborough 21-4-84
Internationals: Republic of Ireland Youth, U21, B.

2001–02	Rushden & D	0	0		
2002–03	Rushden & D	30	3		
2003–04	Rushden & D	37	1		
2004–05	Rushden & D	40	3		
2005–06	Rushden & D	14	3	121	10
2005–06	Luton T	9	0		
2006–07	Luton T	34	3		
2007–08	Luton T	32	4	75	7
2007–08	*Leicester C*	6	0	6	0
2008–09	Norwich C	19	0	19	0
2008–09	Coventry C	9	1		
2009–10	Coventry C	28	2		
2010–11	Coventry C	22	2		
2011–12	Coventry C	28	0		
2012–13	Coventry C	7	0	94	5
2013–14	Notts Co	10	0	10	0

BIALKOWSKI, Bartosz (G) 115 0
H: 6 3 W: 12 10 b.Braniewo 6-7-87
Internationals: Poland U20, U21.

2004–05	Gornik Zabrze	7	0	7	0
2005–06	Southampton	5	0		
2006–07	Southampton	8	0		
2007–08	Southampton	1	0		
2008–09	Southampton	0	0		
2009–10	Southampton	7	0		
2009–10	*Barnsley*	2	0	2	0
2010–11	Southampton	0	0		
2011–12	Southampton	1	0	22	0
2012–13	Notts Co	40	0		
2013–14	Notts Co	44	0	84	0

BOUCAUD, Andre (M) 117 3
H: 5 8 W: 11 01 b.Enfield 10-10-84
Internationals: Trinidad & Tobago Full caps.

2002–03	Reading	0	0		
2002–03	*Peterborough U*	6	0		
2003–04	Reading	0	0		
2003–04	*Peterborough U*	8	1		
2004–05	*Peterborough U*	22	1		
2005–06	*Peterborough U*	3	0	39	2
From Kettering T					
2007–08	Wycombe W	10	0	10	0
From Kettering T, York C, Luton T					
2012–13	Notts Co	39	1		
2013–14	Notts Co	29	0	68	1

CAMPBELL-RYCE, Jamal (M) 364 30
H: 5 7 W: 12 03 b.Lambeth 6-4-83
Internationals: Jamaica Full caps.

2002–03	Charlton Ath	1	0		
2002–03	*Leyton Orient*	17	2		
2003–04	Charlton Ath	2	0		
2003–04	*Wimbledon*	4	0	4	0
2004–05	Charlton Ath	3	0	3	0
2004–05	*Chesterfield*	14	0	14	0
2004–05	Rotherham U	24	0		
2005–06	Rotherham U	7	0	31	0
2005–06	*Southend U*	13	0		
2005–06	*Colchester U*	4	0	4	0
2006–07	Southend U	43	2		
2007–08	Southend U	2	0	58	2
2007–08	Barnsley	37	3		
2008–09	Barnsley	40	9		
2009–10	Barnsley	13	0	90	12
2009–10	Bristol C	14	0		
2010–11	Bristol C	31	2		
2011–12	Bristol C	17	0	62	2
2011–12	*Leyton Orient*	8	1	25	3
2012–13	Notts Co	37	8		
2013–14	Notts Co	36	3	73	11

COOMBES, Adam (F) 9 0
H: 6 1 W: 12 07 b.London 19-6-91
Internationals: England U16, U17.

Season	Club				
2010–11	Chelsea	0	0		
2010–11	Yeovil T	3	0	3	0
2011–12	Chelsea	0	0		
2012–13	Chelsea	0	0		
2013–14	Notts Co	6	0	6	0

DIXON, Kyle (M) 1 0
H: 5 9 W: 11 11 b.Nottingham 20-12-94

Season	Club				
2012–13	Notts Co	0	0		
2013–14	Notts Co	1	0	1	0

DUMBUYA, Mustapha (D) 100 0
H: 5 7 W: 11 00 b.Sierra Leone 7-8-87
Internationals: Sierra Leone Full caps.

Season	Club				
2009–10	Doncaster R	3	0		
2010–11	Doncaster R	23	0		
2011–12	Doncaster R	10	0		
2011–12	Crystal Palace	2	0	2	0
2012–13	Doncaster R	0	0	36	0
2012–13	Portsmouth	23	0	23	0
2012–13	Crawley T	15	0	15	0
2013–14	Notts Co	24	0	24	0

FOTHERINGHAM, Mark (M) 212 10
H: 5 11 W: 11 12 b.Dundee 22-10-83
Internationals: Scotland U21

Season	Club				
1999–2000	Celtic	2	0		
2000–01	Celtic	1	0		
2001–02	Celtic	0	0		
2002–03	Celtic	0	0	3	0
2003–04	Dundee	24	4		
2004–05	Dundee	27	0	51	4
2005–06	Freiburg	9	0	9	0
2006–07	Aarau	13	0	13	0
2006–07	Norwich C	14	0		
2007–08	Norwich C	28	2		
2008–09	Norwich C	27	1	69	3
2009–10	Dundee U	3	0	3	0
2009–10	Anorthosis	7	1		
2010–11	Anorthosis	15	1	22	2
From Livingston, Dundee					
2012–13	Ross Co	14	0	14	0
2013–14	Notts Co	28	1	28	1

HAWORTH, Andrew (M) 69 3
H: 5 11 W: 11 10 b.Lancaster 28-11-88

Season	Club				
2007–08	Blackburn R	0	0		
2008–09	Blackburn R	0	0		
2009–10	Blackburn R	0	0		
2009–10	Rochdale	7	0		
2010–11	Bury	40	3		
2011–12	Bury	6	0	46	3
2011–12	Oxford U	4	0	4	0
2011–12	Bradford C	3	0	3	0
2012–13	Falkirk	0	0		
2012–13	Rochdale	7	0	14	0
2013–14	Notts Co	2	0	2	0

HAYNES, Danny (F) 266 46
H: 5 11 W: 12 04 b.Peckham 19-1-88
Internationals: England U19.

Season	Club				
2005–06	Ipswich T	19	3		
2006–07	Ipswich T	31	7		
2006–07	Millwall	5	2	5	2
2007–08	Ipswich T	40	7		
2008–09	Ipswich T	24	0	114	17
2009–10	Bristol C	38	7		
2010–11	Bristol C	13	1	51	8
2010–11	Barnsley	20	6		
2011–12	Barnsley	12	0	32	6
2011–12	Charlton Ath	14	2		
2012–13	Charlton Ath	20	7	34	9
2013–14	Notts Co	21	3	21	3
2013–14	Hibernian	9	1	9	1

HOLLIS, Haydn (D) 17 4
H: 6 4 W: 13 01 b.Selston 14-10-92

Season	Club				
2011–12	Notts Co	1	0		
2012–13	Notts Co	6	0		
2013–14	Notts Co	10	4	17	4

HOLT, Jordan (D) 2 0
Internationals: Wales U19.

Season	Club				
2013–14	Notts Co	2	0	2	0

LABADIE, Joss (M) 151 23
H: 5 7 W: 11 02 b.Croydon 31-8-90

Season	Club				
2008–09	WBA	0	0		
2008–09	Shrewsbury T	1	0		
2009–10	WBA	0	0		
2009–10	Shrewsbury T	13	5	14	5
2009–10	Cheltenham T	11	0	11	0
2009–10	Tranmere R	9	3		
2010–11	Tranmere R	34	2		
2011–12	Tranmere R	27	5	70	10
2012–13	Notts Co	24	2		
2012–13	Torquay U	7	4		
2013–14	Notts Co	15	1	39	3
2013–14	Torquay U	10	1	17	5

LEACOCK, Dean (D) 222 3
H: 6 2 W: 12 04 b.Croydon 10-6-84
Internationals: England U18, U19, U20.

Season	Club				
2002–03	Fulham	0	0		
2003–04	Fulham	4	0		
2004–05	Fulham	0	0		
2004–05	Coventry C	13	0	13	0
2005–06	Fulham	5	0		
2006–07	Fulham	0	0	9	0
2006–07	Derby Co	38	0		
2007–08	Derby Co	26	0		
2008–09	Derby Co	11	0		
2009–10	Derby Co	17	0		
2010–11	Derby Co	25	1		
2011–12	Derby Co	0	0	117	1
2011–12	Leyton Orient	15	0	15	0
2012–13	Notts Co	42	1		
2013–14	Notts Co	26	1	68	2

LIDDLE, Gary (D) 325 22
H: 6 1 W: 12 06 b.Middlesbrough 15-6-86
Internationals: England Youth.

Season	Club				
2003–04	Middlesbrough	0	0		
2004–05	Middlesbrough	0	0		
2005–06	Middlesbrough	0	0		
2006–07	Hartlepool U	42	3		
2007–08	Hartlepool U	41	2		
2008–09	Hartlepool U	43	0		
2009–10	Hartlepool U	40	3		
2010–11	Hartlepool U	42	6		
2011–12	Hartlepool U	39	4	247	18
2012–13	Notts Co	46	0		
2013–14	Notts Co	32	4	78	4

McGREGOR, Callum (M) 37 12
H: 5 11 W: 11 06 b.Irvine 14-6-93
Internationals: Scotland U15, U16, U17, U19, U20, U21.

Season	Club				
2011–12	Celtic	0	0		
2012–13	Celtic	0	0		
2013–14	Celtic	0	0		
On loan from Celtic					
2013–14	Notts Co	37	12	37	12

MURRAY, Ronan (F) 73 12
H: 5 7 W: 11 00 b.Mayo 12-9-91
Internationals: Republic of Ireland U17, U19, U21.

Season	Club				
2010–11	Ipswich T	8	0		
2010–11	Torquay U	7	1	7	1
2011–12	Ipswich T	0	0		
2011–12	Swindon T	20	3	20	3
2012–13	Ipswich T	1	0	9	0
2012–13	Plymouth Arg	13	1		
2013–14	Plymouth Arg	0	0	13	1
2013–14	Notts Co	24	7	24	7

NANGLE, Romello (F) 8 1
b.Nottingham 20-12-94

Season	Club				
2012–13	Notts Co	7	1		
2013–14	Notts Co	1	0	8	1

PILKINGTON, Kevin (G) 362 0
H: 6 1 W: 13 08 b.Hitchin 8-3-74

Season	Club				
1992–93	Manchester U	0	0		
1993–94	Manchester U	0	0		
1994–95	Manchester U	1	0		
1995–96	Manchester U	3	0		
1995–96	Rochdale	6	0	6	0
1996–97	Manchester U	0	0		
1996–97	Rotherham U	17	0	17	0
1997–98	Manchester U	2	0	6	0
1998–99	Port Vale	8	0		
1999–2000	Port Vale	15	0	23	0
2000–01	Mansfield T	2	0		
2001–02	Mansfield T	45	0		
2002–03	Mansfield T	32	0		
2003–04	Mansfield T	46	0		
2004–05	Mansfield T	42	0	167	0
2005–06	Notts Co	45	0		
2006–07	Notts Co	39	0		
2007–08	Notts Co	32	0		
2008–09	Notts Co	25	0		
From Luton T, Mansfield T					
2012–13	Notts Co	1	0		
2013–14	Notts Co	1	0	143	0

ROBERTS, Gareth (D) 550 22
H: 5 8 W: 11 12 b.Wrexham 6-2-78
Internationals: Wales U21, B, Full caps.

Season	Club				
1995–96	Liverpool	0	0		
1996–97	Liverpool	0	0		
1997–98	Liverpool	0	0		
1998–99	Liverpool	0	0		
1998–99	Panionios	15	0	15	0
1999–2000	Tranmere R	37	1		
2000–01	Tranmere R	34	0		
2001–02	Tranmere R	45	2		
2002–03	Tranmere R	37	4		
2003–04	Tranmere R	44	1		
2004–05	Tranmere R	40	3		
2005–06	Tranmere R	44	2	281	13
2006–07	Doncaster R	30	1		
2007–08	Doncaster R	37	3		
2008–09	Doncaster R	32	1		
2009–10	Doncaster R	42	3	141	8
2010–11	Derby Co	26	0		
2011–12	Derby Co	41	1		
2012–13	Derby Co	29	0	96	1
2013–14	Bury	11	0	11	0
2013–14	Notts Co	6	0	6	0

SHEEHAN, Alan (D) 222 15
H: 5 11 W: 11 02 b.Athlone 14-9-86
Internationals: Republic of Ireland U21.

Season	Club				
2004–05	Leicester C	1	0		
2005–06	Leicester C	0	0		
2006–07	Leicester C	0	0		
2006–07	Mansfield T	10	0	10	0
2007–08	Leicester C	20	1	23	1
2007–08	Leeds U	10	1		
2008–09	Leeds U	11	1		
2008–09	Crewe Alex	3	0	3	0
2009–10	Leeds U	0	0		
2009–10	Oldham Ath	8	1	8	1
2009–10	Swindon T	22	1		
2010–11	Leeds U	0	0	21	2
2010–11	Swindon T	21	1	43	2
2011–12	Notts Co	39	2		
2012–13	Notts Co	33	0		
2013–14	Notts Co	42	7	114	9

SHOWUNMI, Enoch (F) 297 47
H: 6 3 W: 14 11 b.Kilburn 21-4-82
Internationals: Nigeria Full caps.

Season	Club				
2003–04	Luton T	26	7		
2004–05	Luton T	35	6		
2005–06	Luton T	41	1	102	14
2006–07	Bristol C	33	10		
2007–08	Bristol C	17	3	50	13
2007–08	Sheffield W	10	0	10	0
2008–09	Leeds U	8	2		
2009–10	Leeds U	7	0	15	2
2010–11	Tranmere R	43	11		
2011–12	Tranmere R	27	3	70	14
2012–13	Notts Co	22	1		
2013–14	Notts Co	14	3	36	4
2013–14	Torquay U	7	0	7	0
2013–14	Plymouth Arg	7	0	7	0

SMITH, Manny (D) 153 7
H: 6 2 W: 12 03 b.Birmingham 8-11-88

Season	Club				
2005–06	Walsall	0	0		
2006–07	Walsall	3	0		
2007–08	Walsall	4	0		
2008–09	Walsall	26	0		
2009–10	Walsall	33	4		
2010–11	Walsall	25	2		
2011–12	Walsall	33	1	124	7
2012–13	Notts Co	5	0		
2013–14	Notts Co	24	0	29	0

SPENCER, James (F) 102 24
H: 6 1 W: 13 00 b.Leeds 13-12-91

Season	Club				
2008–09	Huddersfield T	0	0		
2009–10	Huddersfield T	0	0		
2010–11	Huddersfield T	0	0		
2010–11	Morecambe	32	8	32	8
2011–12	Huddersfield T	0	0		
2011–12	Cheltenham T	41	10	41	10
2012–13	Huddersfield T	1	0		
2012–13	Brentford	2	0	2	0
2013–14	Huddersfield T	0	0	2	0
2013–14	Scunthorpe U	13	1	13	1
2013–14	Notts Co	13	5	13	5

SPIESS, Fabian (G) 8 0
H: 6 2 W: 12 09 b.Germany 30-11-93

2011–12	Notts Co	0	0	
2012–13	Notts Co	7	0	
2013–14	Notts Co	1	0	8 0

TEMPEST, Greg (M) 17 0
H: 6 0 W: 11 04 b.Nottingham 28-12-95
Internationals: Northern Ireland U21.

2012–13	Notts Co	3	0	
2013–14	Notts Co	14	0	17 0

THOMPSON, Curtis (M) 13 0
H: 5 10 W: 12 06 b.Nottingham 2-9-93

2011–12	Notts Co	0	0	
2012–13	Notts Co	2	0	
2013–14	Notts Co	11	0	13 0

WAITE, Tyrell (F) 9 1
H: 5 11 W: 12 08 b.Derby 1-7-94

2011–12	Notts Co	0	0	
2012–13	Notts Co	8	1	
2013–14	Notts Co	1	0	9 1

Scholars
Andrews, Harry Marcus; Bange, Glodi; Bishop, Colby David; Brown, Elliot George; Duncan, Kieran McKenzie; Dwyer, Anthony O'Neil; Fyfe, Reece Terence; Geldenhuys, Kieran; Golding, Jack Callum; Guy, Tyler Richard; Hodge, Elliot Stephen; Kelleher, Gino James T J; Kenlock, Alexander James; McGowan, Brad; Myers, Rhys Anthony; Richards, Jordan Elijah; Sarpong, Nana Owiredu Lartey; Symons, Kyle Sean.

OLDHAM ATH (59)

BROWN, Connor (D) 52 1
H: 5 8 W: 10 12 b.Sheffield 2-10-91

2010–11	Sheffield U	0	0	
2011–12	Sheffield U	0	0	
2012–13	Oldham Ath	25	0	
2013–14	Oldham Ath	27	1	52 1

BYRNE, Cliff (D) 324 10
H: 6 0 W: 12 11 b.Dublin 27-4-82
Internationals: Republic of Ireland U19, U21.

1999-2000	Sunderland	0	0	
2000–01	Sunderland	0	0	
2001–02	Sunderland	0	0	
2002–03	Sunderland	0	0	
2002–03	*Scunthorpe U*	13	0	
2003–04	Scunthorpe U	39	1	
2004–05	Scunthorpe U	29	1	
2005–06	Scunthorpe U	32	1	
2006–07	Scunthorpe U	24	0	
2007–08	Scunthorpe U	25	0	
2008–09	Scunthorpe U	43	2	
2009–10	Scunthorpe U	36	2	
2010–11	Scunthorpe U	21	2	
2011–12	Scunthorpe U	14	0	
2012–13	Oldham Ath	35	1	
2013–14	Scunthorpe U	10	0	286 9
2013–14	Oldham Ath	3	0	38 1

CLARKE-HARRIS, Jonson (F) 55 10
H: 6 0 W: 11 01 b.Leicester 21-7-94

2012–13	Peterborough U	1	0	
2012–13	*Southend U*	3	0	3 0
2012–13	*Bury*	12	4	12 4
2013–14	Oldham Ath	40	6	40 6

DAYTON, James (M) 102 9
H: 5 8 W: 10 00 b.Enfield 12-12-88

2007–08	Crystal Palace	0	0	
2008–09	Crystal Palace	0	0	
2008–09	*Yeovil T*	2	0	2 0

From Bishop's Stortford, Bromley

2010–11	Kilmarnock	10	2	
2011–12	Kilmarnock	29	3	
2012–13	Kilmarnock	27	1	66 6
2013–14	Oldham Ath	34	3	34 3

DUNFIELD, Terry (M) 237 13
H: 5 7 W: 10 03 b.Vancouver 20-2-82
Internationals: Canada U20, U23, Full caps.

1998–99	Manchester C	0	0	
1999-2000	Manchester C	0	0	
2000–01	Manchester C	1	0	
2001–02	Manchester C	0	0	
2002–03	Manchester C	0	0	1 0
2002–03	Bury	29	2	
2003–04	Bury	30	2	
2004–05	Bury	15	1	74 5
2007–08	Macclesfield T	41	1	
2008–09	Macclesfield T	20	1	61 2
2008–09	Shrewsbury T	17	0	
2009–10	Shrewsbury T	30	2	47 2
2011	Vancouver W	12	1	12 1
2011	Toronto FC	6	0	
2012	Toronto FC	30	3	
2013	Toronto FC	4	0	40 3
2013–14	Oldham Ath	2	0	2 0

GROUNDS, Jonathan (D) 165 7
H: 6 1 W: 13 10 b.Thornaby 2-2-88

2007–08	Middlesbrough	5	0	
2008–09	Middlesbrough	2	0	
2008–09	*Norwich C*	16	3	16 3
2009–10	Middlesbrough	20	0	
2010–11	Middlesbrough	6	1	
2011–12	Middlesbrough	0	0	33 1
2011–12	*Chesterfield*	13	0	13 0
2011–12	*Yeovil T*	14	0	14 0
2012–13	Oldham Ath	44	1	
2013–14	Oldham Ath	45	2	89 3

HARKINS, Gary (M) 127 12
H: 6 2 W: 12 09 b.Glasgow 2-1-85

2003–04	Blackburn R	0	0	
2003–04	*Huddersfield T*	3	0	3 0
2004–05	Blackburn R	0	0	
2004–05	*Bury*	5	0	5 0
2005–06	Blackburn R	0	0	
2005–06	*Blackpool*	4	1	4 1
2006–07	Grimsby T	17	0	17 0

From Partick Thistle, Dundee

2011–12	Kilmarnock	30	1	
2012–13	Kilmarnock	16	2	46 3
2012–13	Dundee	14	2	14 2
2013–14	St Mirren	15	1	15 1

On loan from St Mirren

2013–14	Oldham Ath	23	5	23 5

KISSOCK, John Paul (M) 22 0
H: 5 6 W: 10 07 b.Liverpool 2-12-89
Internationals: England U16, U18. England C.

2006–07	Everton	0	0	
2007–08	Everton	0	0	
2007–08	*Gretna*	11	0	11 0
2008–09	Everton	0	0	
2008–09	*Accrington S*	5	0	5 0
2009–10	Hamilton A	2	0	2 0

From Southport, Luton T

2013–14	Macclesfield T	0	0	

On loan from Macclesfield T

2013–14	Oldham Ath	4	0	4 0

KUSUNGA, Generic (D) 50 1
Internationals: Switzerland U21. Angola Full caps.

2010–11	Basle	7	0	
2011–12	Basle	6	0	13 0
2012–13	*Servette*	19	0	19 0
2013–14	Oldham Ath	18	1	18 1

LOCKWOOD, Adam (D) 270 18
H: 6 0 W: 12 07 b.Wakefield 26-10-81

2003–04	Yeovil T	43	4	
2004–05	Yeovil T	10	0	
2005–06	Yeovil T	20	0	73 4
2005–06	*Torquay U*	9	3	9 3
2006–07	Doncaster R	44	2	
2007–08	Doncaster R	39	3	
2008–09	Doncaster R	22	0	
2009–10	Doncaster R	16	2	
2010–11	Doncaster R	16	1	
2011–12	Doncaster R	14	0	151 8
2012–13	Bury	17	1	
2013–14	Bury	1	0	18 1
2013–14	Oldham Ath	19	2	19 2

MACDONALD, Charlie (F) 265 64
H: 5 8 W: 12 10 b.Southwark 13-2-81

1998–99	Charlton Ath	0	0	
1999-2000	Charlton Ath	3	0	
2000–01	Charlton Ath	3	0	
2000–01	*Cheltenham T*	8	2	8 2
2001–02	Charlton Ath	2	1	8 1
2001–02	*Torquay U*	5	0	5 0
2001–02	*Colchester U*	4	1	4 1

From Margate, Stevenage, Crawley T, Gravesend & N

2007–08	Southend U	25	1	25 1
2008–09	Brentford	38	16	
2009–10	Brentford	40	15	
2010–11	Brentford	30	9	
2011–12	Brentford	3	0	111 40
2011–12	Milton Keynes D	5	0	
2012–13	Milton Keynes D	19	2	54 11
2012–13	Leyton Orient	20	3	20 3
2013–14	Oldham Ath	30	5	30 5

MELLOR, David (D) 46 1
H: 5 9 W: 11 09 b.Oldham 10-7-93

2011–12	Oldham Ath	21	1	
2012–13	Oldham Ath	5	0	
2013–14	Oldham Ath	20	0	46 1

MILLAR, Kirk (M) 39 1
H: 5 9 W: 10 07 b.Belfast 7-7-92
Internationals: Northern Ireland U21.

2008–09	Linfield	1	0	1 0
2009–10	Oldham Ath	6	0	
2010–11	Oldham Ath	5	0	
2011–12	Oldham Ath	4	0	
2012–13	Oldham Ath	12	1	
2013–14	Oldham Ath	11	0	38 1

MONTANO, Cristian (F) 78 13
H: 5 11 W: 12 00 b.Cali 11-12-91

2010–11	West Ham U	0	0	
2011–12	West Ham U	0	0	
2011–12	*Notts Co*	15	4	15 4
2011–12	*Swindon T*	4	1	4 1
2011–12	*Dagenham & R*	10	3	10 3
2011–12	*Oxford U*	9	2	9 2
2012–13	Swindon T	30	1	
2013–14	Oldham Ath	10	2	40 3

PHILLISKIRK, Daniel (M) 48 4
H: 5 10 W: 11 05 b.Oldham 10-4-91
Internationals: England U17.

2008–09	Chelsea	0	0	
2009–10	Chelsea	0	0	
2010–11	Chelsea	0	0	
2010–11	*Oxford U*	1	0	
2010–11	*Sheffield U*	3	0	
2011–12	Sheffield U	0	0	
2011–12	*Oxford U*	4	0	5 0
2012–13	Sheffield U	1	0	4 0
2012–13	Coventry C	0	0	
2013–14	Coventry C	0	0	1 0
2013–14	Oldham Ath	38	4	38 4

PRITCHARD, John (F) 1 0

2013–14	Oldham Ath	1	0	1 0

RACHUBKA, Paul (G) 284 0
H: 6 1 W: 13 05 b.San Luis Opispo 21-5-81
Internationals: England U16, U18, U20.

1999-2000	Manchester U	0	0	
2000–01	Manchester U	1	0	
2001–02	Manchester U	0	0	1 0
2001–02	*Oldham Ath*	16	0	
2001–02	Charlton Ath	0	0	
2002–03	Charlton Ath	0	0	
2003–04	Charlton Ath	0	0	
2003–04	*Huddersfield T*	13	0	
2004–05	Charlton Ath	0	0	
2004–05	*Milton Keynes D*	4	0	4 0
2004–05	*Northampton T*	10	0	10 0
2004–05	Huddersfield T	29	0	
2005–06	Huddersfield T	34	0	
2006–07	Huddersfield T	0	0	76 0
2006–07	*Peterborough U*	4	0	4 0
2006–07	*Blackpool*	8	0	
2007–08	Blackpool	46	0	
2008–09	Blackpool	42	0	
2009–10	Blackpool	20	0	
2010–11	Blackpool	2	0	118 0
2011–12	Leeds U	6	0	
2011–12	*Tranmere R*	10	0	10 0
2011–12	*Leyton Orient*	8	0	8 0
2012–13	Leeds U	0	0	6 0
2012–13	*Accrington S*	21	0	21 0
2013–14	Oldham Ath	10	0	26 0

RODGERS, Anton (M) 9 0
H: 5 7 b.Reading 26-1-93
Internationals: Republic of Ireland U21.

2011–12	Brighton & HA	0	0	
2012–13	Exeter C	0	0	2 0
2013–14	Oldham Ath	7	0	7 0

ROONEY, Adam (F) 242 82
H: 5 10 W: 12 03 b.Dublin 21-4-87
Internationals: Republic of Ireland U21.

2005–06	Stoke C	5	4		
2006–07	Stoke C	10	0		
2006–07	*Yeovil T*	3	0	3	0
2007–08	Stoke C	0	0	15	4
2007–08	*Chesterfield*	22	7	22	7
2007–08	*Bury*	16	3	16	3
2008–09	Inverness CT	30	5		
2009–10	Inverness CT	35	24		
2010–11	Inverness CT	37	15	102	44
2011–12	Birmingham C	18	4		
2012–13	Birmingham C	0	0	18	4
2012–13	Swindon T	29	9	29	9
2013–14	Oldham Ath	24	4	24	4
2013–14	Aberdeen	13	7	13	7

SCHMELTZ, Sidney (M) 103 8
H: 5 10 W: 11 04 b.Nieuwegein 8-6-89

2008–09	Willem II	4	0		
2009–10	Willem II	2	0	6	0
2010–11	Almere C	33	4	33	4
2011–12	S Rotterdam	17	2	17	2
2012–13	Veendam	26	2	26	2
2013–14	Oldham Ath	17	0	17	0
2013–14	*Shrewsbury T*	4	0	4	0

SMITH, Korey (M) 148 5
H: 5 9 W: 11 01 b.Hatfield 31-1-91

2008–09	Norwich C	2	0		
2009–10	Norwich C	37	4		
2010–11	Norwich C	28	0		
2011–12	Norwich C	0	0		
2011–12	*Barnsley*	12	0	12	0
2012–13	Norwich C	0	0	67	4
2012–13	*Yeovil T*	17	0	17	0
2012–13	*Oldham Ath*	10	0		
2013–14	Oldham Ath	42	1	52	1

TURNER, Rhys (F) 2 0

| 2013–14 | Oldham Ath | 2 | 0 | 2 | 0 |

WESOLOWSKI, James (M) 212 13
H: 5 8 W: 11 11 b.Sydney 25-8-87
Internationals: Australia U20.

2004–05	Leicester C	0	0		
2005–06	Leicester C	5	0		
2006–07	Leicester C	19	0		
2007–08	Leicester C	22	0		
2008–09	Leicester C	0	0		
2008–09	*Dundee U*	8	0	8	0
2008–09	*Cheltenham T*	4	0	4	0
2009–10	Leicester C	0	0	46	0
2009–10	*Hamilton A*	29	4	29	4
2010–11	Peterborough U	32	2	32	2
2011–12	Oldham Ath	21	3		
2012–13	Oldham Ath	33	0		
2013–14	Oldham Ath	39	4	93	7

WILSON, James (D) 78 1
H: 6 2 W: 11 05 b.Chepstow 26-2-89
Internationals: Wales U19. U21, Full caps.

2005–06	Bristol C	0	0		
2006–07	Bristol C	0	0		
2007–08	Bristol C	0	0		
2008–09	Bristol C	2	0		
2008–09	*Brentford*	14	0		
2009–10	Bristol C	0	0		
2009–10	*Brentford*	13	0	27	0
2010–11	Bristol C	2	0		
2011–12	Bristol C	21	0		
2012–13	Bristol C	6	0		
2013–14	Bristol C	0	0	31	0
2013–14	*Cheltenham T*	4	0	4	0
2013–14	Oldham Ath	16	1	16	1

WINCHESTER, Carl (D) 39 2
H: 5 10 W: 11 08 b.Belfast 12-4-93
Internationals: Northern Ireland U16, U17, U18, U19, U21, Full caps.

2010–11	Oldham Ath	6	1		
2011–12	Oldham Ath	12	0		
2012–13	Oldham Ath	9	0		
2013–14	Oldham Ath	12	1	39	2

Scholars
Bove, Jordon; Brewster, Michael; Byrnes, Daniel Aaron; Clarke, Tomos Allen; Coleman, Joel; Edmundson, Samuel George Alan; Ellison, Ryan Henry; Etches, Callum Christopher; Foulds, Haydn James; Fulwood, Edward-Paul Mugabe; Hardman, Kyle; Kinder, William Michael; Pritchard, John Vincent; Tansinda, Emil Denzel; Truelove, Jack Christopher; Tuohy, Jack Samuel; Tyson, Paul Stephen; Walters, Jordache Dave Akyme.

Non Contract
Jacobs, DeVante Rogea.

OXFORD U (60)

BEVANS, Matt (D) 10 0
b.Oxford 19-9-93

| 2013–14 | Oxford U | 10 | 0 | 10 | 0 |

CLARKE, Ryan (G) 232 0
H: 6 3 W: 13 00 b.Bristol 30-4-82

2001–02	Bristol R	1	0		
2002–03	Bristol R	2	0		
2003–04	Bristol R	2	0		
2004–05	Bristol R	18	0	23	0
2004–05	*Southend U*	1	0	1	0
2004–05	*Kidderminster H*	6	0	6	0

From Salisbury C

2009–10	Oxford U	44	0		
2010–11	Oxford U	46	0		
2011–12	Oxford U	42	0		
2012–13	Oxford U	24	0		
2013–14	Oxford U	46	0	202	0

CONSTABLE, James (F) 204 52
H: 6 2 W: 12 12 b.Malmesbury 4-10-84
Internationals: England C.

| 2005–06 | Walsall | 17 | 3 | | |
| 2006–07 | Walsall | 6 | 0 | 23 | 3 |

From Kidderminster H.

2007–08	*Shrewsbury T*	14	4	14	4
2010–11	Oxford U	44	15		
2011–12	Oxford U	40	11		
2012–13	Oxford U	39	9		
2013–14	Oxford U	44	10	167	45

CROCOMBE, Max (G) 4 0
H: 6 4 b. 12-8-93
Internationals: New Zealand U20.

| 2012–13 | Oxford U | 4 | 0 | | |
| 2013–14 | Oxford U | 0 | 0 | 4 | 0 |

DAVIES, Scott (M) 141 21
H: 5 11 W: 12 00 b.Aylesbury 10-3-88
Internationals: Republic of Ireland U19, U21.

2006–07	Reading	0	0		
2007–08	Reading	0	0		
2008–09	Reading	0	0		
2008–09	*Aldershot T*	41	13		
2009–10	Reading	4	0		
2009–10	*Wycombe W*	15	3		
2009–10	*Yeovil T*	4	0	4	0
2010–11	Reading	0	0	4	0
2010–11	*Wycombe W*	8	1	23	4
2010–11	*Bristol R*	7	0	7	0
2011–12	Crawley T	20	2		
2011–12	*Aldershot T*	8	1	49	14
2012–13	Crawley T	0	0	20	2
2012–13	*Oxford U*	12	1		
2013–14	Oxford U	22	0	34	1

HUNT, David (M) 312 11
H: 5 11 W: 11 09 b.Dulwich 10-9-82

2002–03	Crystal Palace	2	0	2	0
2003–04	Leyton Orient	38	1		
2004–05	Leyton Orient	27	0	65	1
2004–05	Northampton T	4	0		
2005–06	Northampton T	40	3		
2006–07	Northampton T	29	0	73	3
2007–08	Shrewsbury T	2	0		
2008–09	Shrewsbury T	2	0	29	2
2008–09	Brentford	20	2		
2009–10	Brentford	24	3		
2010–11	Brentford	3	0	47	5
2011–12	Crawley T	27	0		
2012–13	Crawley T	23	0	50	0
2013–14	Oxford U	46	0	46	0

KITSON, Dave (F) 420 129
H: 6 3 W: 12 07 b.Hitchin 21-1-80

2000–01	Cambridge U	8	1		
2001–02	Cambridge U	33	9		
2002–03	Cambridge U	44	20		
2003–04	Cambridge U	17	10	102	40
2003–04	Reading	17	5		
2004–05	Reading	37	19		
2005–06	Reading	34	18		
2006–07	Reading	13	2		
2007–08	Reading	34	10		
2008–09	Stoke C	16	0		
2008–09	*Reading*	10	2	145	56
2009–10	Stoke C	18	3		
2009–10	*Middlesbrough*	6	3	6	3
2010–11	Stoke C	0	0	34	3
2010–11	Portsmouth	35	8		
2011–12	Portsmouth	33	4		
2012–13	Portsmouth	0	0	68	12
2012–13	Sheffield U	33	11	33	11
2013–14	Oxford U	32	4	32	4

LONG, Sam (D) 4 0
b.Oxford 16-1-95

| 2012–13 | Oxford U | 1 | 0 | | |
| 2013–14 | Oxford U | 3 | 0 | 4 | 0 |

MARSH, Tyrone (F) 7 0
b. 24-12-93

| 2012–13 | Oxford U | 2 | 0 | | |
| 2013–14 | Oxford U | 5 | 0 | 7 | 0 |

MEADES, Jonathan (M) 26 1
H: 6 1 W: 13 00 b.Cardiff 2-3-92
Internationals: Wales Youth, U17, U21.

2010–11	Cardiff C	0	0		
2011–12	Cardiff C	0	0		
2012–13	Bournemouth	0	0		
2012–13	*AFC Wimbledon*	26	1	26	1
2013–14	Oxford U	0	0		

MULLINS, John (D) 318 22
H: 5 11 W: 12 07 b.Hampstead 6-11-85

2004–05	Reading	0	0		
2004–05	*Kidderminster H*	21	2	21	2
2005–06	Reading	0	0		
2006–07	Mansfield T	43	2		
2007–08	Mansfield T	43	2	86	4
2008–09	Stockport Co	33	3		
2009–10	Stockport Co	36	1	69	4
2010–11	Rotherham U	35	1		
2011–12	Rotherham U	35	2		
2012–13	Rotherham U	29	4	99	7
2013–14	*Oxford U*	8	2		
2013–14	Oxford U	35	3	43	5

NEWEY, Tom (D) 407 8
H: 5 10 W: 10 02 b.Sheffield 31-10-82

2000–01	Leeds U	0	0		
2001–02	Leeds U	0	0		
2002–03	Leeds U	0	0		
2002–03	*Cambridge U*	0	0		
2002–03	*Darlington*	7	1	7	1
2003–04	Leyton Orient	34	2		
2004–05	Leyton Orient	20	1	54	3
2004–05	*Cambridge U*	16	0	22	0
2005–06	Grimsby T	38	1		
2006–07	Grimsby T	43	1		
2007–08	Grimsby T	42	1		
2008–09	Grimsby T	24	0		
2008–09	*Rochdale*	2	0	2	0
2009–10	Grimsby T	0	0	147	3
2009–10	*Bury*	32	0	32	0
2010–11	Rotherham U	38	0		
2011–12	Rotherham U	20	0	58	0
2012–13	Scunthorpe U	45	0	45	0
2013–14	Oxford U	40	1	40	1

O'DOWDA, Callum (M) 10 0
b.Oxford 23-4-95

| 2012–13 | Oxford U | 0 | 0 | | |
| 2013–14 | Oxford U | 10 | 0 | 10 | 0 |

POTTER, Alfie (M) 132 18
H: 5 7 W: 9 06 b.Islington 9-1-89

| 2007–08 | Peterborough U | 2 | 0 | 2 | 0 |

From Kettering T.

| 2010–11 | Oxford U | 38 | 2 | | |

From Kettering T.

2011–12	Oxford U	25	2		
2012–13	Oxford U	43	10		
2013–14	Oxford U	24	4	130	18

RAYNES, Michael (D) 272 6
H: 6 4 W: 12 00 b.Wythenshawe 15-10-87

2004–05	Stockport Co	19	0		
2005–06	Stockport Co	25	1		
2006–07	Stockport Co	9	0		
2007–08	Stockport Co	27	0		
2008–09	Stockport Co	35	3		
2009–10	Stockport Co	25	1	140	4

2009–10	Scunthorpe U	12	0		
2010–11	Scunthorpe U	22	0	34	0
2011–12	Rotherham U	33	0	33	0
2012–13	Oxford U	38	1		
2013–14	Oxford U	27	0	65	1

RIGG, Sean (F)   222 25
H:5 9   W:12 01   b.Bristol 1-10-88

2006–07	Bristol R	18	1		
2007–08	Bristol R	31	1		
2008–09	Bristol R	8	0		
2009–10	Bristol R	0	0	57	2
2009–10	Port Vale	26	3		
2010–11	Port Vale	25	3		
2011–12	Port Vale	42	10	93	16
2012–13	Oxford U	44	5		
2013–14	Oxford U	28	2	72	7

ROSE, Danny (M)   74 6
H:5 7   W:10 04   b.Bristol 21-2-88
Internationals: England C.

2006–07	Manchester U	0	0		
2007–08	Manchester U	0	0		
From Oxford U, Newport Co					
2012–13	Fleetwood T	0	0		
2012–13	*Aldershot T*	34	2	34	2
2013–14	Oxford U	40	4	40	4

RUFFELS, Joshua (M)   30 1
H:5 10   W:11 11   b.Oxford 23-10-93

2011–12	Coventry C	1	0		
2012–13	Coventry C	0	0	1	0
2013–14	Oxford U	29	1	29	1

SHAMA, Josh (M)   0 0

| 2013–14 | Oxford U | 0 | 0 | | |

SMALLEY, Deane (M)   230 35
H:6 0   W:11 10   b.Chadderton 5-9-88

2006–07	Oldham Ath	2	0		
2007–08	Oldham Ath	37	2		
2008–09	Oldham Ath	34	5		
2009–10	Oldham Ath	29	3		
2010–11	Oldham Ath	3	0	105	10
2010–11	*Rochdale*	3	0	3	0
2010–11	Chesterfield	28	12	28	12
2011–12	Oxford U	22	1		
2011–12	*Bradford C*	13	0	13	0
2012–13	Oxford U	27	5		
2013–14	Oxford U	32	7	81	13

WHING, Andrew (D)   325 6
H:6 0   W:12 00   b.Birmingham 20-9-84

2002–03	Coventry C	14	0		
2003–04	Coventry C	28	1		
2004–05	Coventry C	16	1		
2005–06	Coventry C	32	0		
2006–07	Coventry C	16	0	106	2
2006–07	Brighton & HA	12	0		
2007–08	Brighton & HA	42	0		
2008–09	Brighton & HA	40	0		
2009–10	Brighton & HA	9	0		
2009–10	*Chesterfield*	11	0	11	0
2010–11	Brighton & HA	0	0	103	0
2010–11	*Leyton Orient*	24	2	24	2
2011–12	Oxford U	41	0		
2012–13	Oxford U	22	2		
2013–14	Oxford U	18	0	81	2

WRIGHT, Jake (D)   158 0
H:5 10   W:11 07   b.Keighley 11-3-86

2005–06	Bradford C	1	0	1	0
From Halifax T, Crawley T					
2009–10	*Brighton & HA*	6	0	6	0
2010–11	Oxford U	35	0		
2011–12	Oxford U	43	0		
2012–13	Oxford U	42	0		
2013–14	Oxford U	31	0	151	0

Scholars
Ashby, Joshua James; Calvin, Jamie; Cavanagh, Edward Roger; Clarke, James Moses; Conte, Muctaru; Cundy, Robbie David; Ekpiteta, Marvin Akpereogene Paul Edem; George, Adriel Jared; Grant, Freddie Tom; Hackett, Gregory James; Hill, Joshua William Robert; Humphreys, Samuel Aston; Ingram, Conor Patrick; Roberts, James Anthony.

PETERBOROUGH U (61)

AJOSE, Nicholas (F)   125 33
H:5 8   W:11 00   b.Bury 7-10-91
Internationals: England U16, U17.

2009–10	Manchester U	0	0		
2010–11	Manchester U	0	0		
2010–11	*Bury*	28	13		
2011–12	Peterborough U	2	0		
2011–12	*Scunthorpe U*	7	0	7	0
2011–12	*Chesterfield*	12	1	12	1
2012–13	*Crawley T*	19	2	19	2
2012–13	Peterborough U	0	0		
2012–13	*Bury*	19	4	47	17
2013–14	Peterborough U	22	7	24	7
2013–14	*Swindon T*	16	6	16	6

ALCOCK, Craig (D)   203 3
H:5 8   W:11 00   b.Cornwall 8-12-87

2006–07	Yeovil T	1	0		
2007–08	Yeovil T	8	0		
2008–09	Yeovil T	30	1		
2009–10	Yeovil T	42	1		
2010–11	Yeovil T	26	1	107	3
2011–12	Peterborough U	41	0		
2012–13	Peterborough U	27	0		
2013–14	Peterborough U	28	0	96	0

ANDERSON, Jermaine (M)   14 0
b. 16-5-96
Internationals: England U18.

| 2012–13 | Peterborough U | 1 | 0 | | |
| 2013–14 | Peterborough U | 13 | 0 | 14 | 0 |

ASSOMBALONGA, Britt (F)   90 38
H:5 9   W:11 13   b.Kinshasa 6-12-92

2010–11	Watford	0	0		
2011–12	Watford	4	0		
2012–13	Watford	0	0		
2012–13	*Southend U*	43	15	43	15
2013–14	Watford	0	0	4	0
2013–14	Peterborough U	43	23	43	23

BALDWIN, Jack (D)   88 4
H:6 1   W:11 00   b.Barking 30-6-93

2011–12	Hartlepool U	17	0		
2012–13	Hartlepool U	32	2		
2013–14	Hartlepool U	28	2	77	4
2013–14	Peterborough U	11	0	11	0

BARNETT, Tyrone (F)   143 39
H:6 3   W:13 05   b.Stevenage 28-10-85

2010–11	Macclesfield T	45	13	45	13
2011–12	*Crawley T*	26	14	26	14
2011–12	Peterborough U	13	4		
2012–13	Peterborough U	18	1		
2012–13	*Ipswich T*	3	0	3	0
2013–14	Peterborough U	21	6	52	11
2013–14	*Bristol C*	17	1	17	1

BOSTWICK, Michael (D)   165 18
H:6 4   W:14 00   b.Eltham 17-5-88
Internationals: England C.

2006–07	Millwall	0	0		
From Rushden & D, Ebbsfleet U					
2010–11	Stevenage	41	2		
2011–12	Stevenage	43	7	84	9
2012–13	Peterborough U	39	5		
2013–14	Peterborough U	42	4	81	9

BRISLEY, Shaun (M)   185 6
H:6 2   W:12 02   b.Macclesfield 6-5-90

2007–08	Macclesfield T	10	2		
2008–09	Macclesfield T	38	0		
2009–10	Macclesfield T	33	1		
2010–11	Macclesfield T	14	0		
2011–12	Macclesfield T	29	3	124	6
2011–12	Peterborough U	11	0		
2012–13	Peterborough U	28	0		
2013–14	Peterborough U	22	0	61	0

CONLON, Tom (M)   1 0

| 2013–14 | Peterborough U | 1 | 0 | 1 | 0 |

COULSON, Charlie (M)   1 0
b.Kettering 11-1-96

2011–12	Peterborough U	1	0		
2012–13	Peterborough U	0	0		
2013–14	Peterborough U	0	0	1	0

DAY, Joe (G)   4 0
H:6 1   W:12 00   b.Brighton 13-8-90

2011–12	Peterborough U	0	0		
2012–13	Peterborough U	0	0		
2013–14	Peterborough U	4	0	4	0

FERDINAND, Kane (D)   99 11
H:6 1   W:13 07   b.Newham 7-10-92
Internationals: Republic of Ireland U18, U19, U21.

2010–11	Southend U	22	2		
2011–12	Southend U	36	7		
2012–13	Southend U	3	1	61	10
2012–13	Peterborough U	32	1		
2013–14	Peterborough U	2	0	34	1
2013–14	*Northampton T*	4	0	4	0

KEARNS, Daniel (M)   110 9
H:5 10   W:12 00   b.Belfast 26-8-91
Internationals: Northern Ireland U19.
Republic of Ireland U19, U21, U23.

2010	Dundalk	12	0		
2011	Dundalk	37	9	49	9
2011–12	Peterborough U	20	0		
2012–13	Peterborough U	1	0		
2012–13	*York C*	9	0	9	0
2012–13	*Rotherham U*	10	0	10	0
2013–14	Peterborough U	11	0	32	0
2013–14	*Chesterfield*	0	0	10	0

KNIGHT-PERCIVAL, Nathaniel (M)   46 1
H:6 0   W:11 06   b.Cambridge 31-3-87

| 2012–13 | Peterborough U | 31 | 0 | | |
| 2013–14 | Peterborough U | 15 | 1 | 46 | 1 |

LITTLE, Mark (D)   222 3
H:6 1   W:12 10   b.Worcester 20-8-88
Internationals: England U19.

2005–06	Wolverhampton W	0	0		
2006–07	Wolverhampton W	26	0		
2007–08	Wolverhampton W	1	0		
2007–08	*Northampton T*	17	0		
2008–09	Wolverhampton W	0	0		
2008–09	*Northampton T*	9	0	26	0
2009–10	Wolverhampton W	0	0	27	0
2009–10	*Chesterfield*	12	0	12	0
2009–10	*Peterborough U*	9	0		
2010–11	Peterborough U	35	0		
2011–12	Peterborough U	35	1		
2012–13	Peterborough U	40	1		
2013–14	Peterborough U	38	1	157	3

McCANN, Grant (M)   493 85
H:5 10   W:11 00   b.Belfast 14-4-80
Internationals: Northern Ireland U21, Full caps.

1998–99	West Ham U	0	0		
1999–2000	West Ham U	0	0		
2000–01	West Ham U	1	0		
2000–01	*Notts Co*	2	0	2	0
2000–01	*Cheltenham T*	30	3		
2001–02	West Ham U	3	0		
2002–03	West Ham U	0	0	4	0
2002–03	Cheltenham T	27	6		
2003–04	Cheltenham T	43	8		
2004–05	Cheltenham T	39	4		
2005–06	Cheltenham T	39	8		
2006–07	Cheltenham T	15	5	193	34
2006–07	Barnsley	20	2		
2007–08	Barnsley	19	3	41	4
2007–08	Scunthorpe U	14	1		
2008–09	Scunthorpe U	43	9		
2009–10	Scunthorpe U	42	8	99	18
2010–11	Peterborough U	38	9		
2011–12	Peterborough U	41	8		
2012–13	Peterborough U	40	8		
2013–14	Peterborough U	35	4	154	29

MENDEZ-LAING, Nathaniel (M)   92 10
H:5 10   W:11 12   b.Birmingham 15-4-92
Internationals: England U16, U17.

2009–10	Wolverhampton W	0	0		
2010–11	Wolverhampton W	0	0		
2010–11	*Peterborough U*	33	5		
2011–12	Wolverhampton W	0	0		
2011–12	*Sheffield U*	8	1	8	1
2012–13	Peterborough U	21	3		
2012–13	*Portsmouth*	8	0	8	0
2013–14	Peterborough U	16	1	70	9
2013–14	*Shrewsbury T*	6	0	6	0

NEWELL, Joe (M)   57 1
H:5 11   W:11 02   b.Tamworth 15-3-93

| 2010–11 | Peterborough U | 2 | 0 | | |
| 2011–12 | Peterborough U | 14 | 1 | | |

2012–13	Peterborough U	30	0
2013–14	Peterborough U	11 0	**57 1**

NTLHE, Kgosietsile (D) 41 3
H: 5 9 W: 10 05 b.Pretoria 21-2-94
Internationals: South Africa U20, Full caps.

2010–11	Peterborough U	0	0
2011–12	Peterborough U	2	0
2012–13	Peterborough U	12	1
2013–14	Peterborough U	27 2	**41 3**

OLEJNIK, Robert (G) 236 0
H: 6 0 W: 15 06 b.Vienna 26-11-86
Internationals: Austria U21.

2004–05	Aston Villa	0	0
2005–06	Aston Villa	0	0
2006–07	Aston Villa	0	0
2006–07	*Lincoln C*	0	0
2007–08	Falkirk	13	0
2008–09	Falkirk	15	0
2009–10	Falkirk	38	0
2010–11	Falkirk	36 0	**102 0**
2011–12	Torquay U	46 0	**46 0**
2012–13	Peterborough U	46	0
2013–14	Peterborough U	42 0	**88 0**

PAYNE, Jack (M) 147 7
H: 5 9 W: 9 02 b.Gravesend 5-12-91

2008–09	Gillingham	2	0
2009–10	Gillingham	19	0
2010–11	Gillingham	31	1
2011–12	Gillingham	30	2
2012–13	Gillingham	19 2	**101 5**
2012–13	*Peterborough U*	14	0
2013–14	Peterborough U	32 2	**46 2**

RICHENS, Michael (D) 0 0
b.Bedford 28-2-95

2012–13	Peterborough U	0	0
2013–14	Peterborough U	0	0

ROWE, Tommy (M) 247 36
H: 5 11 W: 12 11 b.Manchester 1-5-89

2006–07	Stockport Co	4	0
2007–08	Stockport Co	24	6
2008–09	Stockport Co	44 7	**72 13**
2008–09	Peterborough U	0	0
2009–10	Peterborough U	32	2
2010–11	Peterborough U	35	5
2011–12	Peterborough U	43	4
2012–13	Peterborough U	31	5
2013–14	Peterborough U	34 7	**175 23**

SANTOS, Ricardo (D) 1 0
b.Almada 18-6-95

2012–13	Dagenham & R	0	0
2013–14	Dagenham & R	0	0
2013–14	Peterborough U	1 0	**1 0**

SWANSON, Danny (M) 214 20
H: 5 6 W: 9 03 b.Edinburgh 28-12-86

2005–06	Berwick R	27	1
2006–07	Berwick R	3	0
2007–08	Berwick R	14 3	**44 4**
2007–08	Dundee U	12	2
2008–09	Dundee U	30	0
2009–10	Dundee U	31	5
2010–11	Dundee U	21	2
2011–12	Dundee U	14 3	**108 12**
2012–13	Peterborough U	27	2
2013–14	Peterborough U	35 2	**62 4**

VASSELL, Kyle (F) 6 0
b. 7-2-93

2013–14	Peterborough U	6 0	**6 0**

WASHINGTON, Conor (F) 41 8

2013–14	Newport Co	24 4	**24 4**
2013–14	Peterborough U	17 4	**17 4**

ZAKUANI, Gaby (D) 310 9
H: 6 1 W: 12 13 b.DR Congo 31-5-86
Internationals: DR Congo Full caps.

2002–03	Leyton Orient	1	0
2003–04	Leyton Orient	10	2
2004–05	Leyton Orient	33	0
2005–06	Leyton Orient	43 1	**87 3**
2006–07	Fulham	0	0
2006–07	*Stoke C*	9	0
2007–08	Fulham	0	0
2007–08	*Stoke C*	19 0	**28 0**
2008–09	Fulham	0	0
2008–09	Peterborough U	32	1
2009–10	Peterborough U	29	0
2010–11	Peterborough U	30	2
2011–12	Peterborough U	41	1
2012–13	Peterborough U	33	1
2013–14	Peterborough U	15 0	**180 5**
2013–14	*Kalloni*	15 1	**15 1**

Scholars
Burgess, Joe Oliver William; Carter, Matthew Philip; Carthey, Regan; Duggan, Robert John; Edwards, Jonathan Dvonte; Friend, Jack Peter; Luto, Oliver; Lynch, Alexander Patrick; Marshall, Liam Sanuel Hugh; Moore-Azille, Tarik Armani Carlos; O'Reilly, Luke Patrick; Phillips, Tye Gregory; Stewart, Greig; Ward, James Christopher; Wright, Levi Mark.

PLYMOUTH ARG (62)

ALESSANDRA, Lewis (F) 191 22
H: 5 9 W: 11 07 b.Heywood 8-2-89

2007–08	Oldham Ath	15	2
2008–09	Oldham Ath	32	5
2009–10	Oldham Ath	1	0
2010–11	Oldham Ath	19 1	**67 8**
2011–12	Morecambe	42	4
2012–13	Morecambe	40 3	**82 7**
2013–14	Plymouth Arg	42 7	**42 7**

BANTON, Jason (F) 39 9
H: 5 10 W: 11 05 b.Tottenham 15-12-92
Internationals: England U17.

2009–10	Blackburn R	0	0
2010–11	Blackburn R	0	0
2010–11	Liverpool	0	0
2011–12	Liverpool	0	0
2011–12	*Burton Alb*	1 0	**1 0**
2012–13	Crystal Palace	0	0
2012–13	*Plymouth Arg*	14	6
2013–14	Crystal Palace	0	0
2013–14	*Milton Keynes D*	11 2	**11 2**
2013–14	Plymouth Arg	13 1	**27 7**

BENCHERIF, Hamza (D) 110 19
H: 5 9 W: 12 03 b.Paris 9-2-88
Internationals: Algeria U20.

2006–07	Nottingham F	0	0
2007–08	*Lincoln C*	12 1	**12 1**
2008–09	Nottingham F	0	0
2009–10	Macclesfield T	19	5
2010–11	Macclesfield T	41 11	**60 16**
2011–12	Notts Co	20	2
2012–13	Notts Co	11 0	**31 2**
2013–14	Plymouth Arg	7 0	**7 0**

Transferred to JS Kabylie January 2014.

BERRY, Durrell (D) 95 1
H: 5 11 W: 11 11 b.Derby 27-5-92

2010–11	Aston Villa	0	0
2011–12	Plymouth Arg	35	0
2012–13	Plymouth Arg	28	0
2013–14	Plymouth Arg	32 1	**95 1**

BLACKMAN, Andre (D) 11 0
H: 5 11 W: 11 05 b.Lambeth 10-11-90

2009–10	Bristol C	0	0
2011–12	Celtic	3	0
2012–13	Celtic	0 0	**3 0**
2012–13	*Inverness CT*	2 0	**2 0**
2013–14	Plymouth Arg	6 0	**6 0**

BLANCHARD, Maximo (D) 220 6
H: 5 11 W: 11 13 b.Alencon 27-9-86

2006–07	Laval	4	0
2007–08	Laval	22 0	**26 0**
2008–09	Entente	35 1	**35 1**
2009–10	Moulins	35 1	**35 1**
2010–11	Tranmere R	20 0	**20 0**
2011–12	Plymouth Arg	28	2
2012–13	Plymouth Arg	40	1
2013–14	Plymouth Arg	36 1	**104 4**

BLIZZARD, Dominic (M) 222 12
H: 6 2 W: 12 04 b.High Wycombe 2-9-83

2001–02	Watford	0	0
2002–03	Watford	0	0
2003–04	Watford	2	1
2004–05	Watford	17	1
2005–06	Watford	10	0
2006–07	Watford	0 0	**29 2**
2006–07	*Stockport Co*	7	0
2006–07	*Milton Keynes D*	8 0	**8 0**
2007–08	Stockport Co	27	1
2008–09	Stockport Co	31 3	**65 4**
2009–10	Bristol R	34	1
2010–11	Bristol R	5 0	**39 1**
2010–11	*Port Vale*	1 0	**1 0**
2011–12	Yeovil T	30	3
2012–13	Yeovil T	24 1	**54 4**
2013–14	Plymouth Arg	26 1	**26 1**

BOCO, Romuald (F) 120 14
H: 5 10 W: 10 13 b.Bernay 8-7-85
Internationals: Benin Full caps.

2006–07	Accrington S	32	3
2007–08	Accrington S	11	0
2008–09	Accrington S	0	0
2009–10	Burton Alb	8 0	**8 0**

From Sligo

2012–13	Accrington S	42 10	**85 13**
2013–14	Plymouth Arg	27 1	**27 1**

BRANSTON, Guy (D) 381 22
H: 6 1 W: 15 01 b.Leicester 9-1-79

1997–98	Leicester C	0	0
1997–98	*Colchester U*	12	1
1998–99	Leicester C	0	0
1998–99	*Colchester U*	1 0	**13 1**
1998–99	*Plymouth Arg*	7	1
1999–2000	Leicester C	0	0
1999–2000	*Lincoln C*	4 0	**4 0**
1999–2000	Rotherham U	30	4
2000–01	Rotherham U	41	6
2001–02	Rotherham U	10	1
2002–03	Rotherham U	15	2
2003–04	Rotherham U	8	0
2003–04	*Wycombe W*	9 0	**9 0**
2004–05	Sheffield W	11 0	**11 0**
2004–05	*Peterborough U*	4	1
2004–05	Oldham Ath	7	1
2005–06	Oldham Ath	38 1	**45 2**
2006–07	Peterborough U	24	0
2007–08	Peterborough U	2 0	**44 1**
2007–08	*Rochdale*	4 0	**4 0**
2007–08	*Northampton T*	3 0	**3 0**
2007–08	Notts Co	1 0	**1 0**

From Kettering T

2009–10	Burton Alb	19 0	**19 0**
2009–10	Torquay U	16	0
2010–11	Torquay U	45 0	**61 2**
2011–12	Bradford C	16 1	**16 1**
2011–12	*Rotherham U*	2 0	**106 13**
2012–13	Aldershot T	3 0	**3 0**
2012–13	*Bristol R*	4 1	**4 1**
2012–13	Plymouth Arg	19	0
2013–14	Plymouth Arg	12 0	**38 1**

COLE, Jake (G) 184 0
H: 6 2 W: 13 00 b.Hammersmith 11-9-85

2005–06	QPR	3	0
2006–07	QPR	3	0
2007–08	QPR	0	0
2008–09	QPR	0 0	**6 0**
2008–09	*Barnet*	10	0
2009–10	Barnet	46	0
2010–11	Barnet	31 0	**87 0**
2011–12	Plymouth Arg	37	0
2012–13	Plymouth Arg	34	0
2013–14	Plymouth Arg	20 0	**91 0**

GURRIERI, Andres (M) 115 4
H: 5 6 W: 10 05 b.Winterthur 3-7-89

2007–08	Ternana	0	0
2008–09	Ternana	6	0
2008–09	*Colligiana*	16 2	**16 2**
2009–10	Ternana	0 0	**6 0**
2010–11	Sud America	20 0	**20 0**
2011–12	Burton Alb	13 0	**13 0**
2012–13	Plymouth Arg	28	1
2013–14	Plymouth Arg	32 1	**60 2**

HARVEY, Tyler (F) 31 2
b.Plymouth 29-6-95

2012–13	Plymouth Arg	10	1
2013–14	Plymouth Arg	21 1	**31 2**

HOURIHANE, Conor (M) 125 15
H: 5 11 W: 9 11 b.Cork 2-2-91
Internationals: Republic of Ireland U19, U21.

2008–09	Sunderland	0	0
2009–10	Sunderland	0	0
2010–11	Ipswich T	0	0
2011–12	Plymouth Arg	38	2
2012–13	Plymouth Arg	42	5
2013–14	Plymouth Arg	45 8	**125 15**

LECOINTE, Matt (F)   25   2
H: 5 10   W: 10 07   b.Plymouth 28-10-94
Internationals: England U18.
2011–12	Plymouth Arg	19	2		
2012–13	Plymouth Arg	6	0		
2013–14	Plymouth Arg	0	0	25	2

McCORMICK, Luke (G)   42   0
H: 6 0   W: 13 12   b.Coventry 15-8-83
| 2012–13 | Oxford U | 15 | 0 | 15 | 0 |
| 2013–14 | Plymouth Arg | 27 | 0 | 27 | 0 |

MORGAN, Marvin (F)   206   42
H: 6 4   W: 12 08   b.Manchester 13-4-83
2008–09	Aldershot T	32	6		
2009–10	Aldershot T	40	15		
2010–11	Aldershot T	19	5	91	26
2010–11	Dagenham & R	12	0	12	0
2011–12	Shrewsbury T	42	8		
2012–13	Shrewsbury T	40	7	82	15
2013–14	Plymouth Arg	21	1	21	1

NELSON, Curtis (D)   123   4
H: 6 0   W: 11 07   b.Newcastle-u-Lyme 21-5-93
Internationals: England U18.
2010–11	Plymouth Arg	35	0		
2011–12	Plymouth Arg	17	0		
2012–13	Plymouth Arg	27	3		
2013–14	Plymouth Arg	44	1	123	4

PARSONS, Matthew (D)   28   0
H: 5 10   W: 11 09   b.Catford 23-12-91
2010–11	Crystal Palace	2	0		
2010–11	Barnet	8	0	8	0
2011–12	Crystal Palace	4	0		
2012–13	Crystal Palace	0	0		
2012–13	Wycombe W	4	0	4	0
2013–14	Crystal Palace	0	0	6	0
2013–14	Plymouth Arg	10	0	10	0

PURRINGTON, Ben (D)   12   0
| 2013–14 | Plymouth Arg | 12 | 0 | 12 | 0 |

REID, Reuben (F)   235   55
H: 6 0   W: 12 02   b.Bristol 26-7-88
2005–06	Plymouth Arg	1	0		
2006–07	Plymouth Arg	6	0		
2006–07	Rochdale	2	0	2	0
2006–07	Torquay U	7	2	7	2
2007–08	Plymouth Arg	0	0		
2007–08	Wycombe W	11	1	11	1
2007–08	Brentford	10	1	10	1
2008–09	Rotherham U	41	18	41	18
2009–10	WBA	4	0		
2009–10	Peterborough U	13	0	13	0
2010–11	WBA	0	0	4	0
2010–11	Walsall	18	3	18	3
2010–11	Oldham Ath	19	2		
2011–12	Oldham Ath	20	5	39	7
2012–13	Yeovil T	19	4	19	4
2013–14	Plymouth Arg	46	17	71	19

RICHARDS, Jamie (D)   2   0
b.Newton Abbot 24-6-94
2011–12	Plymouth Arg	0	0		
2012–13	Plymouth Arg	1	0		
2013–14	Plymouth Arg	1	0	2	0

THOMAS, Nathan (F)   10   0
| 2013–14 | Plymouth Arg | 10 | 0 | 10 | 0 |

TROTMAN, Neal (D)   191   8
H: 6 3   W: 13 08   b.Manchester 11-3-87
2006–07	Oldham Ath	1	0		
2007–08	Oldham Ath	17	1		
2007–08	Preston NE	3	0		
2008–09	Preston NE	0	0		
2008–09	Colchester U	6	0	6	0
2009–10	Preston NE	0	0		
2009–10	Southampton	18	2	18	2
2009–10	Huddersfield T	21	2	21	2
2010–11	Preston NE	0	0	3	0
2010–11	Oldham Ath	18	0	36	1
2011–12	Rochdale	12	0	12	0
2011–12	Chesterfield	23	1		
2012–13	Chesterfield	31	0	54	1
2013–14	Plymouth Arg	41	2	41	2

WOTTON, Paul (D)   552   61
H: 5 11   W: 12 00   b.Plymouth 17-8-77
1994–95	Plymouth Arg	7	0		
1995–96	Plymouth Arg	1	0		
1996–97	Plymouth Arg	9	1		
1997–98	Plymouth Arg	34	1		
1998–99	Plymouth Arg	36	1		
1999–2000	Plymouth Arg	23	0		
2000–01	Plymouth Arg	42	4		
2001–02	Plymouth Arg	46	5		
2002–03	Plymouth Arg	43	8		
2003–04	Plymouth Arg	38	9		
2004–05	Plymouth Arg	40	12		
2005–06	Plymouth Arg	45	8		
2006–07	Plymouth Arg	22	4		
2007–08	Plymouth Arg	8	1		
2008–09	Southampton	29	0		
2009–10	Southampton	26	0		
2010–11	Southampton	2	0	57	0
2010–11	Oxford U	4	0	4	0
2010–11	Yeovil T	23	2		
2011–12	Yeovil T	22	2	45	4
2011–12	Plymouth Arg	18	1		
2012–13	Plymouth Arg	19	2		
2013–14	Plymouth Arg	15	0	446	57

YOUNG, Luke (M)   99   8
H: 5 8   W: 11 05   b.Ivybridge 22-2-93
2010–11	Plymouth Arg	5	0		
2011–12	Plymouth Arg	28	2		
2012–13	Plymouth Arg	32	2		
2013–14	Plymouth Arg	34	4	99	8

Scholars
Allen, River Brian Zach; Asumadu-Sakyi, Kieran; Bentley, Aaron Stuart James; Hall, Callum James; Hannah, Andrew James; Hughes, Mason Richard; Hutchinson, Joshua; Lane, Ryan Alan John; Moxham, Thomas Neal; Rooney, Louis John; Sargent, William Michael; Stark, Ethan; Summers, Nathan Rick Alexander; Wheatley, Solomon Patrick.

PORT VALE (63)

BIRCHALL, Chris (M)   249   13
H: 6 2   W: 12 07   b.Liverpool 5-5-84
Internationals: Trinidad & Tobago Full caps.
2001–02	Port Vale	1	0		
2002–03	Port Vale	2	0		
2003–04	Port Vale	10	0		
2004–05	Port Vale	34	6		
2005–06	Port Vale	31	1		
2006–07	Coventry C	28	2		
2007–08	Coventry C	1	0		
2007–08	St Mirren	9	0	9	0
2008–09	Coventry C	0	0	29	2
2008–09	Carlisle U	2	0	2	0
2008–09	Brighton & HA	9	0	9	0
2009	LA Galaxy	11	0		
2010	LA Galaxy	28	0		
2011	LA Galaxy	27	1	66	1
2012	Columbus Crew	18	1	18	1
2012–13	Port Vale	11	1		
2013–14	Port Vale	27	1	116	9

BOOT, Ryan (G)   0   0
b. 9-11-94
| 2012–13 | Port Vale | 0 | 0 | | |
| 2013–14 | Port Vale | 0 | 0 | | |

CHILVERS, Liam (D)   310   8
H: 6 2   W: 12 03   b.Chelmsford 6-11-81
2000–01	Arsenal	0	0		
2000–01	Northampton T	7	0	7	0
2001–02	Arsenal	0	0		
2001–02	Notts Co	9	1		
2002–03	Arsenal	0	0		
2002–03	Colchester U	6	0		
2003–04	Arsenal	0	0		
2003–04	Colchester U	32	0		
2004–05	Colchester U	41	1		
2005–06	Colchester U	34	2	113	3
2006–07	Preston NE	45	2		
2007–08	Preston NE	28	0		
2008–09	Preston NE	1	0		
2009–10	Preston NE	23	0	97	2
2010–11	Notts Co	21	0		
2011–12	Notts Co	17	0	47	1
2011–12	Port Vale	12	0		
2012–13	AFC Telford U	0	0		
2012–13	Port Vale	20	2		
2013–14	Port Vale	14	0	46	2

DAVIS, Joe (D)   27   0
H: 6 0   W: 11 07   b.Burnley 10-11-93
2010–11	Port Vale	1	0		
2011–12	Port Vale	8	0		
2012–13	Port Vale	7	0		
2013–14	Port Vale	11	0	27	0

DICKINSON, Carl (D)   224   3
H: 6 1   W: 12 04   b.Swadlincote 31-3-87
2004–05	Stoke C	1	0		
2005–06	Stoke C	5	0		
2006–07	Stoke C	13	0		
2006–07	Blackpool	7	0	7	0
2007–08	Stoke C	27	0		
2008–09	Stoke C	5	0		
2008–09	Leeds U	7	0	7	0
2009–10	Stoke C	0	0		
2009–10	Barnsley	28	1	28	1
2010–11	Stoke C	0	0	51	0
2010–11	Portsmouth	36	0		
2011–12	Watford	39	2		
2012–13	Watford	4	0	43	2
2012–13	Portsmouth	6	0	42	0
2012–13	Coventry C	6	0	6	0
2013–14	Port Vale	40	0	40	0

DODDS, Louis (M)   268   50
H: 5 10   W: 12 04   b.Sheffield 8-10-86
2005–06	Leicester C	0	0		
2006–07	Leicester C	0	0		
2006–07	Rochdale	12	2	12	2
2007–08	Leicester C	0	0		
2007–08	Lincoln C	41	9	41	9
2008–09	Port Vale	44	7		
2009–10	Port Vale	44	6		
2010–11	Port Vale	33	7		
2011–12	Port Vale	35	8		
2012–13	Port Vale	30	7		
2013–14	Port Vale	29	4	215	39

DUFFY, Richard (D)   286   5
H: 5 9   W: 10 03   b.Swansea 30-8-85
Internationals: Wales U17, U19, U21, Full caps.
2002–03	Swansea C	0	0		
2003–04	Swansea C	18	1		
2003–04	Portsmouth	1	0		
2004–05	Portsmouth	0	0		
2004–05	Burnley	7	1	7	1
2004–05	Coventry C	14	0		
2005–06	Portsmouth	0	0		
2005–06	Coventry C	32	0		
2006–07	Portsmouth	0	0		
2006–07	Coventry C	13	0		
2006–07	Swansea C	11	0	29	1
2007–08	Portsmouth	0	0		
2007–08	Coventry C	2	0	61	0
2008–09	Portsmouth	0	0	1	0
2008–09	Millwall	12	0	12	0
2009–10	Exeter C	42	1		
2010–11	Exeter C	42	2		
2011–12	Exeter C	28	0	112	3
2012–13	Port Vale	36	0		
2013–14	Port Vale	28	0	64	0

GRIFFITH, Anthony (M)   240   2
H: 6 0   W: 12 00   b.Huddersfield 28-10-86
Internationals: Montserrat Full caps.
2005–06	Doncaster R	4	0		
2005–06	Oxford U	0	0		
2006–07	Doncaster R	2	0		
2006–07	Darlington	4	0	4	0
2007–08	Doncaster R	0	0	6	0
2007–08	Port Vale	0	0		
2008–09	Port Vale	38	0		
2009–10	Port Vale	40	0		
2010–11	Port Vale	40	1		
2011–12	Port Vale	43	1		
2012–13	Port Vale	10	0		
2012–13	Leyton Orient	21	0	21	0
2013–14	Port Vale	38	0	209	2

HUGHES, Lee (F)   470   202
H: 5 10   W: 12 00   b.Smethwick 22-5-76
1997–98	WBA	37	14		
1998–99	WBA	42	31		
1999–2000	WBA	36	12		
2000–01	WBA	41	21		
2001–02	Coventry C	38	14		
2002–03	Coventry C	4	1	42	15
2002–03	WBA	23	0		
2003–04	WBA	32	11	211	89

Season	Club	Apps	Gls	Tot A	Tot G
2007–08	Oldham Ath	18	7		
2008–09	Oldham Ath	37	18	55	25
2008–09	*Blackpool*	3	1	3	1
2009–10	Notts Co	39	30		
2010–11	Notts Co	31	13		
2011–12	Notts Co	40	10		
2012–13	Notts Co	18	6	128	59
2012–13	Port Vale	18	10		
2013–14	Port Vale	13	3	31	13

HUGILL, Jordan (F) 20 4
b. 4-6-92

Season	Club	Apps	Gls	Tot A	Tot G
2013–14	Port Vale	20	4	20	4

JOHNSON, Sam (G) 16 0
H: 6 0 W: 12 04 b.Newcastle-under-Lyme 1-12-92

Season	Club	Apps	Gls	Tot A	Tot G
2011–12	Port Vale	0	0		
2012–13	Port Vale	0	0		
2013–14	Port Vale	16	0	16	0

JONES, Daniel (D) 163 5
H: 6 2 W: 13 00 b.Rowley Regis 14-7-86

Season	Club	Apps	Gls	Tot A	Tot G
2005–06	Wolverhampton W	1	0		
2006–07	Wolverhampton W	8	0		
2007–08	Wolverhampton W	1	0		
2007–08	*Northampton T*	33	3	33	3
2008–09	Wolverhampton W	0	0		
2008–09	*Oldham Ath*	23	1	23	1
2009–10	Wolverhampton W	0	0	10	0
2009–10	*Notts Co*	7	0	7	0
2009–10	*Bristol R*	17	0	17	0
2010–11	Sheffield W	25	0		
2011–12	Sheffield W	3	0		
2012–13	Sheffield W	9	0	37	0
2012–13	Port Vale	16	1		
2013–14	Port Vale	20	0	36	1

LINES, Chris (M) 265 24
H: 6 2 W: 12 00 b.Bristol 30-11-88

Season	Club	Apps	Gls	Tot A	Tot G
2005–06	Bristol R	4	0		
2006–07	Bristol R	7	0		
2007–08	Bristol R	27	3		
2008–09	Bristol R	45	4		
2009–10	Bristol R	42	10		
2010–11	Bristol R	42	3		
2011–12	Bristol R	1	0	168	20
2011–12	Sheffield W	41	3		
2012–13	Sheffield W	6	0	47	3
2012–13	*Milton Keynes D*	16	0	16	0
2013–14	Port Vale	34	1	34	1

LLOYD, Ryan (M) 12 0
H: 5 10 W: 10 03 b.Newcastle-u-Lyme 1-2-94

Season	Club	Apps	Gls	Tot A	Tot G
2010–11	Port Vale	1	0		
2011–12	Port Vale	2	0		
2012–13	Port Vale	6	0		
2013–14	Port Vale	3	0	12	0

LOFT, Doug (M) 224 20
H: 6 0 W: 12 01 b.Maidstone 25-12-86

Season	Club	Apps	Gls	Tot A	Tot G
2005–06	Brighton & HA	3	1		
2006–07	Brighton & HA	11	1		
2007–08	Brighton & HA	13	0		
2008–09	Brighton & HA	12	0	39	2
2008–09	*Dagenham & R*	11	0	11	0
2009–10	Port Vale	32	3		
2010–11	Port Vale	29	1		
2011–12	Port Vale	44	4		
2012–13	Port Vale	32	1		
2013–14	Port Vale	37	9	174	18

MOHAMED, Kaid (F) 234 51
H: 5 11 W: 12 06 b.Cardiff 23-7-84

Season	Club	Apps	Gls	Tot A	Tot G
2003–04	Cwmbran T	29	3		
2004–05	Cwmbran T	15	2		
2004–05	Llanelli	3	1		
2005–06	Carmarthen T	14	4		
2005–06	Cwmbran T	11	7	55	12
2006–07	Llanelli	5	0	8	1
2006–07	Carmarthen T	30	15	44	19
2007–08	Swindon T	11	0	11	0

From Forest Green R, Bath C, AFC Wimbledon.

Season	Club	Apps	Gls	Tot A	Tot G
2011–12	Cheltenham T	45	11		
2012–13	Cheltenham T	39	4	84	15
2013–14	Port Vale	6	0	6	0
2013–14	*AFC Wimbledon*	5	0	5	0
2013–14	*Bristol R*	21	4	21	4

MYRIE-WILLIAMS, Jennison (F) 226 26
H: 5 11 W: 12 08 b.Lambeth 17-5-88
Internationals: England U18.

Season	Club	Apps	Gls	Tot A	Tot G
2005–06	Bristol C	1	0		
2006–07	Bristol C	25	2		
2007–08	Bristol C	0	0		
2007–08	Cheltenham T	12	0		
2007–08	*Tranmere R*	25	3	25	3
2008–09	Bristol C	0	0		
2008–09	*Cheltenham T*	5	1	17	1
2008–09	*Carlisle U*	8	0	8	0
2008–09	*Hereford U*	15	2	15	2
2009–10	Bristol C	0	0	26	2
2009–10	Dundee U	24	1	24	1
2010–11	St Johnstone	6	0	6	0
2011–12	Stevenage	17	0	17	0
2011–12	*Port Vale*	6	1		
2012–13	Port Vale	44	9		
2013–14	Port Vale	38	7	88	17

NEAL, Chris (G) 142 0
H: 6 2 W: 12 04 b.St Albans 23-10-85

Season	Club	Apps	Gls	Tot A	Tot G
2004–05	Preston NE	1	0		
2005–06	Preston NE	0	0		
2006–07	Preston NE	0	0		
2007–08	*Shrewsbury T*	0	0		
2007–08	*Morecambe*	0	0		
2007–08	Preston NE	0	0		
2008–09	Preston NE	0	0	1	0
2009–10	Shrewsbury T	7	0		
2010–11	Shrewsbury T	22	0		
2011–12	Shrewsbury T	35	0	64	0
2012–13	Port Vale	46	0		
2013–14	Port Vale	31	0	77	0

POPE, Tom (F) 252 72
H: 6 3 W: 11 03 b.Stoke 27-8-85

Season	Club	Apps	Gls	Tot A	Tot G
2005–06	Crewe Alex	0	0		
2006–07	Crewe Alex	4	0		
2007–08	Crewe Alex	26	7		
2008–09	Crewe Alex	26	10	56	17
2009–10	Rotherham U	35	3		
2010–11	Rotherham U	18	1	53	4
2010–11	*Port Vale*	13	3		
2011–12	Port Vale	41	5		
2012–13	Port Vale	46	31		
2013–14	Port Vale	43	12	143	51

ROBERTSON, Chris (D) 199 10
H: 6 3 W: 11 08 b.Dundee 11-10-85

Season	Club	Apps	Gls	Tot A	Tot G
2005–06	Sheffield U	0	0		
2005–06	*Chester C*	1	0	1	0
2006–07	Sheffield U	0	0		
2006–07	Torquay U	9	1		
2009–10	Torquay U	45	2		
2010–11	Torquay U	43	2		
2011–12	Torquay U	25	1	122	6
2011–12	Preston NE	18	1		
2012–13	Preston NE	21	0	39	1
2013–14	Port Vale	37	3	37	3

SHUKER, Chris (M) 352 37
H: 5 5 W: 9 03 b.Liverpool 9-5-82

Season	Club	Apps	Gls	Tot A	Tot G
1999–2000	Manchester C	0	0		
2000–01	Manchester C	0	0		
2000–01	*Macclesfield T*	9	1	9	1
2001–02	Manchester C	2	0		
2002–03	Manchester C	3	0		
2002–03	*Walsall*	5	0	5	0
2003–04	Manchester C	0	0	5	0
2003–04	*Rochdale*	14	1	14	1
2003–04	*Hartlepool U*	14	1	14	1
2004–05	Barnsley	9	0		
2004–05	Barnsley	45	7		
2005–06	Barnsley	46	10	100	17
2006–07	Tranmere R	46	6		
2007–08	Tranmere R	23	3		
2008–09	Tranmere R	28	3		
2009–10	Tranmere R	26	2	123	14
2010–11	Morecambe	27	2		
2011–12	Morecambe	0	0	27	2
2011–12	Port Vale	16	1		
2012–13	Port Vale	29	0		
2013–14	Port Vale	10	0	55	1

TAYLOR, Rob (D) 160 15
H: 6 0 W: 12 08 b.Shrewsbury 16-1-85

Season	Club	Apps	Gls	Tot A	Tot G
2008–09	Port Vale	20	3		
2009–10	Port Vale	39	8		
2010–11	Port Vale	36	1		
2011–12	Port Vale	31	2		
2012–13	Port Vale	28	0		
2013–14	Port Vale	6	1	160	15

TOMLIN, Gavin (F) 204 44
H: 6 0 W: 12 02 b.Gillingham 13-1-83

Season	Club	Apps	Gls	Tot A	Tot G
2006–07	Brentford	12	0		
2007–08	Brentford	0	0	12	0

From Fisher Ath.

Season	Club	Apps	Gls	Tot A	Tot G
2008–09	Yeovil T	42	7		
2009–10	Yeovil T	35	7	77	14
2010–11	Dagenham & R	19	2		
2010–11	*Torquay U*	12	4	12	4
2011–12	Dagenham & R	17	0	36	2
2011–12	*Gillingham*	10	6	10	6
2012–13	Southend U	33	13		
2013–14	Southend U	0	0	33	13
2013–14	Port Vale	24	5	24	5

WILLIAMSON, Ben (F) 122 23
H: 5 11 W: 11 13 b.Lambeth 25-12-88

Season	Club	Apps	Gls	Tot A	Tot G
2010–11	Jerez Industrial	12	8	12	8
2010–11	Bournemouth	4	0		
2011–12	Bournemouth	0	0	4	0
2011–12	Port Vale	35	3		
2012–13	Port Vale	33	8		
2013–14	Port Vale	38	4	106	15

YATES, Adam (D) 252 3
H: 5 10 W: 10 07 b.Stoke 28-5-83
Internationals: England C.

Season	Club	Apps	Gls	Tot A	Tot G
2000–01	Crewe Alex	0	0		
2001–02	Crewe Alex	0	0		
2002–03	Crewe Alex	0	0		
2003–04	Crewe Alex	0	0		
2004–05	Crewe Alex	0	0		
2005–06	Crewe Alex	0	0		
2006–07	Crewe Alex	0	0		
2007–08	Morecambe	44	0		
2008–09	Morecambe	32	0	76	0
2009–10	Port Vale	32	0		
2010–11	Port Vale	46	0		
2011–12	Port Vale	38	2		
2012–13	Port Vale	26	0		
2013–14	Port Vale	34	1	176	3

Scholars
Beesley, Luke Edward; Bergin, Lewis Thomas; Clarke, Kyle Benito; Davies, Macauley Craid; Haughton, Omar Raheen Samuel; Kapend, Jonathan; Lander, David William; Lewis, Luke Charles; Osborne, Elliot James; Reeves, William David; Smith, Nathan James; Steele, Chekaine Craig; Swaby, Ricardo Nicholas; Wakeham, Daniel James; Warner, Matthew; Wright, Luke James.

PORTSMOUTH (64)

AGYEMANG, Patrick (F) 455 72
H: 6 1 W: 12 00 b.Walthamstow 29-9-80
Internationals: Ghana Full caps.

Season	Club	Apps	Gls	Tot A	Tot G
1998–99	Wimbledon	0	0		
1999–2000	Wimbledon	0	0		
1999–2000	*Brentford*	12	0	12	0
2000–01	Wimbledon	29	4		
2001–02	Wimbledon	33	4		
2002–03	Wimbledon	33	5		
2003–04	Wimbledon	26	7	121	20
2003–04	Gillingham	20	6		
2004–05	Gillingham	13	2	33	8
2004–05	Preston NE	27	4		
2005–06	Preston NE	42	6		
2006–07	Preston NE	31	7		
2007–08	Preston NE	22	4	122	21
2007–08	QPR	17	8		
2008–09	QPR	20	2		
2009–10	QPR	17	3		
2009–10	*Bristol C*	7	0	7	0
2010–11	QPR	19	2		
2011–12	QPR	2	0	75	15
2011–12	*Millwall*	2	0	2	0
2011–12	Stevenage	13	1		
2012–13	Stevenage	14	0	27	1
2012–13	Portsmouth	15	3		
2013–14	Portsmouth	41	4	56	7

BARCHAM, Andy (F) 225 32
H: 5 8 W: 11 10 b.Basildon 16-12-86
Internationals: England U16.

Season	Club				
2005–06	Tottenham H	0	0		
2006–07	Tottenham H	0	0		
2007–08	Tottenham H	0	0		
2007–08	Leyton Orient	25	1	25	1
2008–09	Tottenham H	0	0		
2008–09	Gillingham	33	6		
2009–10	Gillingham	42	7		
2010–11	Gillingham	24	6	99	19
2011–12	Scunthorpe U	41	9		
2012–13	Scunthorpe U	34	0	75	9
2013–14	Portsmouth	26	3	26	3

BIRD, Ryan (F) 18 3

2013–14	Portsmouth	18	3	18	3

BRADLEY, Sonny (D) 91 3
H: 6 0 W: 11 05 b.Hedon 14-6-92

2011–12	Hull C	2	0		
2011–12	Aldershot T	14	0		
2012–13	Hull C	0	0	2	0
2012–13	Aldershot T	42	1	56	1
2013–14	Portsmouth	33	2	33	2

BUTLER, Dan (D) 18 0

2012–13	Portsmouth	17	0		
2013–14	Portsmouth	1	0	18	0

CHORLEY, Ben (D) 385 15
H: 6 3 W: 13 02 b.Sidcup 30-9-82

2001–02	Arsenal	0	0		
2002–03	Arsenal	0	0		
2002–03	Brentford	2	0	2	0
2002–03	Wimbledon	10	0		
2003–04	Wimbledon	35	2	45	2
2004–05	Milton Keynes D	41	2		
2005–06	Milton Keynes D	26	0		
2006–07	Milton Keynes D	13	1	80	3
2006–07	Gillingham	27	1	27	1
2007–08	Tranmere R	31	1		
2008–09	Tranmere R	45	1	76	2
2009–10	Leyton Orient	42	1		
2010–11	Leyton Orient	29	3		
2011–12	Leyton Orient	32	1		
2012–13	Leyton Orient	28	2	131	7
2012–13	Stevenage	8	0		
2013–14	Stevenage	4	0	12	0
2013–14	Portsmouth	12	0	12	0

CONNOLLY, David (F) 436 164
H: 5 9 W: 11 00 b.Willesden 6-6-77
Internationals: Republic of Ireland U21, Full caps.

1994–95	Watford	2	0		
1995–96	Watford	11	8		
1996–97	Watford	13	2	26	10
1997–98	Feyenoord	10	2		
1998–99	Wolverhampton W	32	6	32	6
1999–2000	Excelsior	32	29	32	29
2000–01	Feyenoord	15	5	25	7
2001–02	Wimbledon	35	18		
2002–03	Wimbledon	28	24	63	42
2003–04	West Ham U	39	10	39	10
2004–05	Leicester C	44	13		
2005–06	Leicester C	5	4	49	17
2005–06	Wigan Ath	17	1		
2006–07	Wigan Ath	2	0	19	1
2006–07	Sunderland	36	13		
2007–08	Sunderland	3	0		
2008–09	Sunderland	0	0	39	13
2009–10	Southampton	20	5		
2010–11	Southampton	15	3		
2011–12	Southampton	26	6	61	14
2012–13	Portsmouth	17	7		
2013–14	Portsmouth	18	4	35	11
2013–14	Oxford U	16	4	16	4

CRADDOCK, Tom (F) 170 59
H: 5 11 W: 11 10 b.Durham 14-10-86

2005–06	Middlesbrough	1	0		
2006–07	Middlesbrough	0	0		
2006–07	Wrexham	1	1	1	1
2007–08	Middlesbrough	3	0		
2007–08	Hartlepool U	4	0	4	0
2008–09	Middlesbrough	0	0	4	0
2008–09	Luton T	27	10		
2009–10	Luton T	46	22	73	32
2010–11	Oxford U	39	14		
2011–12	Oxford U	9	1		
2012–13	Oxford U	32	10	80	25
2013–14	Portsmouth	8	1	8	1

DEVERA, Joe (D) 263 4
H: 6 2 W: 12 00 b.Southgate 6-2-87

2005–06	Barnet	0	0		
2006–07	Barnet	26	0		
2007–08	Barnet	41	0		
2008–09	Barnet	34	1		
2009–10	Barnet	33	0		
2010–11	Barnet	43	1	177	2
2011–12	Swindon T	28	2		
2012–13	Swindon T	25	0	53	2
2013–14	Portsmouth	33	0	33	0

EAST, Danny (D) 31 1
H: 5 10 W: 11 03 b.Hessle 26-12-91

2011–12	Hull C	0	0		
2012–13	Hull C	0	0		
2012–13	Northampton T	14	0	14	0
2012–13	Gillingham	2	0	2	0
2013–14	Portsmouth	15	1	15	1

ERTL, Johannes (D) 263 7
H: 6 2 W: 12 08 b.Graz 13-11-82
Internationals: Austria Full caps.

2003–04	Kalzdorf	11	3	11	3
2004–05	Sturm Graz	26	0		
2005–06	Sturm Graz	27	0		
2006–07	Sturm Graz	5	0	58	0
2006–07	FK Austria	24	0		
2007–08	FK Austria	24	2	48	3
2008–09	Crystal Palace	12	0		
2009–10	Crystal Palace	33	0	45	0
2010–11	Sheffield U	28	0		
2011–12	Sheffield U	7	0		
2012–13	Sheffield U	0	0	35	0
2012–13	Portsmouth	37	0		
2013–14	Portsmouth	29	1	66	1

FERRY, Simon (M) 167 9
H: 5 8 W: 11 00 b.Dundee 11-1-88
Internationals: Scotland U19.

2005–06	Celtic	0	0		
2006–07	Celtic	0	0		
2007–08	Celtic	0	0		
2008–09	Celtic	0	0		
2009–10	Celtic	0	0		
2009–10	Swindon T	40	2		
2010–11	Swindon T	21	0		
2011–12	Swindon T	44	1		
2012–13	Swindon T	42	5	147	8
2013–14	Portsmouth	20	1	20	1

FOGDEN, Wes (F) 75 6
H: 5 8 W: 10 04 b.Brighton 12-4-88

2006–07	Brighton & HA	0	0		
2007–08	Brighton & HA	3	0	3	0

From Dorchester T, Havant & Waterlooville.

2011–12	Bournemouth	27	3		
2012–13	Bournemouth	26	1		
2013–14	Bournemouth	0	0	53	4
2013–14	Portsmouth	19	2	19	2

HARRIS, Ashley (M) 32 3
H: 5 8 W: 10 00 b.Waterlooville 9-12-93

2011–12	Portsmouth	5	0		
2012–13	Portsmouth	26	3		
2013–14	Portsmouth	1	0	32	3

HOLMES, Ricky (M) 131 17
H: 6 2 W: 11 11 b.Southend 19-6-87
Internationals: England C.

2010–11	Barnet	25	2		
2011–12	Barnet	41	8		
2012–13	Barnet	25	5	91	15
2013–14	Portsmouth	40	2	40	2

JERVIS, Jake (F) 71 17
H: 6 3 W: 12 13 b.Birmingham 17-9-91

2009–10	Birmingham C	0	0		
2009–10	Hereford U	7	2		
2010–11	Birmingham C	0	0		
2010–11	Notts Co	10	0	10	0
2010–11	Hereford U	4	0	11	2
2011–12	Birmingham C	0	0		
2011–12	Swindon T	12	3	12	3
2011–12	Preston NE	5	2	5	2
2012–13	Birmingham C	2	0	2	0
2012–13	Carlisle	5	3	5	3
2012–13	Tranmere R	4	1	4	1
2012–13	Portsmouth	3	1		
2013–14	Elazigspor	4	1	4	1
2013–14	Portsmouth	15	4	18	5

MAHON, Gavin (M) 452 19
H: 5 11 W: 13 07 b.Birmingham 2-1-77

1995–96	Wolverhampton W	0	0		
1996–97	Hereford U	11	1		
1997–98	Hereford U	0	0		
1998–99	Hereford U	0	0	11	1
1998–99	Brentford	29	4		
1999–2000	Brentford	37	3		
2000–01	Brentford	40	1		
2001–02	Brentford	35	0	141	8
2001–02	Watford	6	0		
2002–03	Watford	17	0		
2003–04	Watford	32	2		
2004–05	Watford	43	0		
2005–06	Watford	38	3		
2006–07	Watford	34	1		
2007–08	Watford	19	0	189	6
2007–08	QPR	16	1		
2008–09	QPR	35	2		
2009–10	QPR	7	1		
2010–11	QPR	0	0	58	4
2010–11	Crystal Palace	0	0		
2011–12	Notts Co	31	0		
2012–13	Notts Co	12	0	43	0
2012–13	Stevenage	9	0	9	0
2013–14	Portsmouth	1	0	1	0

MALONEY, Jack (M) 10 0

2012–13	Portsmouth	9	0		
2013–14	Portsmouth	1	0	10	0

MOUTAOUAKIL, Yassin (D) 95 0
H: 5 11 W: 11 06 b.Nice 18-7-86
Internationals: France U21.

2005–06	Chateauroux	16	0		
2006–07	Chateauroux	13	0	29	0
2007–08	Charlton Ath	10	0		
2008–09	Charlton Ath	11	0	21	0
2009–10	Motherwell	13	0	13	0
2012–13	Portsmouth	19	0		
2013–14	Portsmouth	13	0	32	0

N'GALA, Bondz (D) 129 6
H: 6 0 W: 12 03 b.Forest Gate 13-9-89

2007–08	West Ham U	0	0		
2008–09	West Ham U	0	0		
2008–09	Milton Keynes D	3	0	3	0
2009–10	West Ham U	0	0		
2009–10	Scunthorpe U	2	0	2	0
2009–10	Plymouth Arg	9	0		
2010–11	Plymouth Arg	26	1	35	1
2011–12	Yeovil T	31	2	31	2
2012–13	Stevenage	25	0		
2012–13	Barnet	6	0	6	0
2013–14	Stevenage	0	0	25	0
2013–14	Portsmouth	27	3	27	3

PADOVANI, Romain (M) 18 1
b.Nizza 23-1-89

2013–14	Portsmouth	18	1	18	1

PAINTER, Marcos (D) 182 1
H: 5 11 W: 12 04 b.Solihull 17-8-86
Internationals: Republic of Ireland U21.

2005–06	Birmingham C	4	0		
2006–07	Birmingham C	1	0	5	0
2006–07	Swansea C	23	0		
2007–08	Swansea C	30	0		
2008–09	Swansea C	11	0		
2009–10	Swansea C	4	0	68	0
2009–10	Brighton & HA	19	0		
2010–11	Brighton & HA	46	1		
2011–12	Brighton & HA	20	0		
2012–13	Brighton & HA	5	0		
2012–13	Bournemouth	2	0	2	0
2013–14	Brighton & HA	0	0	90	1
2013–14	Portsmouth	17	0	17	0

RACON, Therry (M) 167 10
H: 5 10 W: 10 02 b.Paris 1-5-84
Internationals: Guadeloupe Full caps.

2004–05	Lorient	28	3	28	3
2005–06	Guingamp	0	0		
2006–07	Guingamp	0	0		
2007–08	Charlton Ath	4	0		
2007–08	Brighton & HA	8	0	8	0
2008–09	Charlton Ath	19	3		
2009–10	Charlton Ath	36	1		
2010–11	Charlton Ath	39	3		
2011–12	Charlton Ath	0	0	98	7
2011–12	Millwall	0	0		
2012–13	Millwall	1	0	1	0

2012–13	Portsmouth	16	0	
2013–14	Portsmouth	16	0	32	0

SHOREY, Nicky (D) 429 12
H: 5 9 W: 10 08 b.Romford 19-2-81
Internationals: England B, Full caps.

1999–2000	Leyton Orient	7	0		
2000–01	Leyton Orient	8	0	15	0
2000–01	Reading	0	0		
2001–02	Reading	32	0		
2002–03	Reading	43	2		
2003–04	Reading	35	2		
2004–05	Reading	44	3		
2005–06	Reading	40	2		
2006–07	Reading	37	1		
2007–08	Reading	36	2		
2008–09	Aston Villa	21	0		
2009–10	Aston Villa	3	0	24	0
2009–10	Nottingham F	9	0	9	0
2009–10	Fulham	9	0	9	0
2010–11	WBA	28	0		
2011–12	WBA	25	0	53	0
2012–13	Reading	17	0	284	12
2013–14	Bristol C	14	0	14	0
2013–14	Portsmouth	21	0	21	0

SMITH, Phil (G) 121 0
H: 6 1 W: 13 11 b.Harrow 14-12-79
Internationals: England C.

1997–98	Millwall	0	0		
1998–99	Millwall	5	0	5	0

From Folkestone, Dover, Margate, Crawley

2006–07	Swindon T	31	0		
2007–08	Swindon T	15	0		
2008–09	Swindon T	25	0		
2009–10	Swindon T	6	0		
2010–11	Swindon T	27	0		
2011–12	Swindon T	8	0	112	0
2012–13	Portsmouth	4	0		
2013–14	Portsmouth	4	0	4	0

SULLIVAN, John (G) 54 0
H: 5 10 W: 11 04 b.Brighton 8-3-88

2005–06	Brighton & HA	0	0		
2006–07	Brighton & HA	0	0		
2007–08	Brighton & HA	0	0		
2008–09	Brighton & HA	13	0	13	0
2009–10	Millwall	0	0		
2010–11	Millwall	0	0		
2010–11	Yeovil T	13	0	13	0
2010–11	Charlton Ath	4	0		
2011–12	Charlton Ath	3	0		
2012–13	Charlton Ath	0	0	7	0
2012–13	Colchester U	4	0	4	0
2012–13	AFC Wimbledon	11	0	11	0
2013–14	Portsmouth	6	0	6	0

TAYLOR, Ryan (F) 196 29
H: 6 2 W: 10 10 b.Rotherham 4-5-88

2005–06	Rotherham U	1	0		
2006–07	Rotherham U	10	0		
2007–08	Rotherham U	35	6		
2008–09	Rotherham U	33	4		
2009–10	Rotherham U	19	0		
2009–10	Exeter C	7	0	7	0
2010–11	Rotherham U	34	11	132	21
2011–12	Bristol C	7	1		
2012–13	Bristol C	25	1		
2013–14	Bristol C	7	0	39	2
2013–14	Portsmouth	18	6	18	6

WALLACE, Jed (M) 66 13
b.Reading 15-12-93
Internationals: England U19.

2011–12	Portsmouth	0	0		
2012–13	Portsmouth	22	6		
2013–14	Portsmouth	44	7	66	13

WEBSTER, Adam (D) 25 2
H: 6 1 W: 11 11 b.West Wittering 4-1-95
Internationals: England U18, U19.

2011–12	Portsmouth	3	0		
2012–13	Portsmouth	18	0		
2013–14	Portsmouth	4	2	25	2

WHATMOUGH, Jack (D) 12 0
b.Gosport 19-8-96
Internationals: England U18.

2012–13	Portsmouth	0	0		
2013–14	Portsmouth	12	0	12	0

Scholars
Chaplin, Conor Mark; Close, Ben Easton; Field, Chad Paul; Gill, Lewis James; Granger, James John Keith; Haunstrup, Brandon Neil; Horsburgh, Lewis David; Kim, Jae Heon; Medway, Harry George; Nilsen, Snorre; Rwakarambwe, Fahad Ali; Tarbuck, Bradley Mark.

PRESTON NE (65)

BEARDSLEY, Chris (F) 159 16
H: 6 0 W: 12 12 b.Derby 28-2-84

2002–03	Mansfield T	5	0		
2003–04	Mansfield T	15	1		
2004–05	Doncaster R	4	0	4	0
2004–05	Kidderminster H	25	5	25	5
2005–06	Mansfield T	3	0		
2006–07	Mansfield T	10	0	33	1

From Rushden & D, York C, Kettering T

2010–11	Stevenage	23	1		
2011–12	Stevenage	31	7	54	8
2012–13	Preston NE	19	1		
2013–14	Preston NE	0	0	19	1
2013–14	Bristol R	24	1	24	1

BEAVON, Stuart (F) 173 37
H: 5 7 W: 10 10 b.Reading 5-5-84

2008–09	Wycombe W	8	0		
2009–10	Wycombe W	25	3		
2010–11	Wycombe W	37	3		
2011–12	Wycombe W	43	21		
2012–13	Wycombe W	2	1	115	28
2012–13	Preston NE	31	6		
2013–14	Preston NE	27	3	58	9

BROWNE, Alan (M) 8 1
Internationals: Republic of Ireland U19.

2013–14	Preston NE	8	1	8	1

BROWNHILL, Josh (M) 24 3
b. 19-12-95

2013–14	Preston NE	24	3	24	3

BUCHANAN, David (M) 307 2
H: 5 7 W: 11 03 b.Rochdale 6-5-86
Internationals: Northern Ireland U19, U21.

2004–05	Bury	3	0		
2005–06	Bury	23	0		
2006–07	Bury	41	0		
2007–08	Bury	35	0		
2008–09	Bury	46	0		
2009–10	Bury	38	0	186	0
2010–11	Hamilton A	28	1	28	1
2011–12	Tranmere R	41	1	41	1
2012–13	Preston NE	33	0		
2013–14	Preston NE	19	0	52	0

BYROM, Joel (M) 77 8
H: 6 0 W: 12 04 b.Accrington 14-9-86
Internationals: England C.

2004–05	Blackburn R	0	0		
2005–06	Blackburn R	0	0		
2006–07	Accrington S	1	0	1	0

From Clitheroe, Southport, Clitheroe, Northwich Vic.

2010–11	Stevenage	7	0		
2011–12	Stevenage	32	4	39	4
2012–13	Preston NE	22	2		
2013–14	Preston NE	11	2	33	4
2013–14	Oldham Ath	4	0	4	0

CANSDELL-SHERRIFF, Shane (D) 386 23
H: 5 11 W: 11 08 b.Sydney 10-11-82
Internationals: Australia U17, U23.

1999–2000	Leeds U	0	0		
2000–01	Leeds U	0	0		
2001–02	Leeds U	0	0		
2002–03	Leeds U	0	0		
2002–03	Rochdale	3	0		
2003–04	Aarhus	29	4		
2004–05	Aarhus	26	2		
2005–06	Aarhus	27	1	82	7
2006–07	Tranmere R	8	0		
2007–08	Tranmere R	44	3	87	6
2008–09	Shrewsbury T	31	2		
2009–10	Shrewsbury T	41	1		
2010–11	Shrewsbury T	41	2		
2011–12	Shrewsbury T	37	4	150	9
2012–13	Preston NE	15	1		
2012–13	Rochdale	17	0	20	0

2013–14	Preston NE	0	0	15	1
2013–14	Burton Alb	32	0	32	0

CLARKE, Tom (D) 154 7
H: 6 0 W: 11 02 b.Sowerby Bridge 21-12-87
Internationals: England U18, U19.

2004–05	Huddersfield T	12	0		
2005–06	Huddersfield T	17	1		
2006–07	Huddersfield T	9	0		
2007–08	Huddersfield T	3	0		
2008–09	Huddersfield T	15	1		
2008–09	Bradford C	6	0	6	0
2009–10	Huddersfield T	21	0		
2010–11	Huddersfield T	5	1		
2011–12	Huddersfield T	14	0		
2011–12	Leyton Orient	10	0	10	0
2012–13	Huddersfield T	0	0	96	3
2013–14	Preston NE	42	4	42	4

CUMMINS, Graham (F) 228 84
H: 6 2 W: 11 11 b.Cork 29-12-87
Internationals: Republic of Ireland U23.

2006	Cobh Ramblers	14	5		
2007	Cobh Ramblers	35	11		
2008	Cobh Ramblers	28	1	77	17
2009	Waterford U	28	17	28	17
2010	Cork C	32	18		
2011	Cork C	30	24	62	42
2011–12	Preston NE	15	2		
2012–13	Preston NE	19	2		
2013–14	Preston NE	0	0	34	4
2013–14	Rochdale	27	4	27	4

DAVIES, Ben (D) 47 0

2012–13	Preston NE	3	0		
2013–14	Preston NE	0	0	3	0
2013–14	York C	44	0	44	0

DAVIES, Kevin (F) 657 121
H: 6 0 W: 12 10 b.Sheffield 26-3-77
Internationals: England U18, U21, Full caps.

1993–94	Chesterfield	24	4		
1994–95	Chesterfield	41	11		
1995–96	Chesterfield	30	4		
1996–97	Chesterfield	34	3	129	22
1996–97	Southampton	0	0		
1997–98	Southampton	25	9		
1998–99	Blackburn R	21	1		
1999–2000	Blackburn R	2	0	23	1
1999–2000	Southampton	23	6		
2000–01	Southampton	27	1		
2001–02	Southampton	23	2		
2002–03	Southampton	9	1	107	19
2002–03	Millwall	9	3	9	3
2003–04	Bolton W	38	9		
2004–05	Bolton W	35	8		
2005–06	Bolton W	37	7		
2006–07	Bolton W	30	8		
2007–08	Bolton W	32	3		
2008–09	Bolton W	38	11		
2009–10	Bolton W	37	9		
2010–11	Bolton W	38	8		
2011–12	Bolton W	31	6		
2012–13	Bolton W	35	6	351	73
2013–14	Preston NE	38	3	38	3

GARNER, Joe (F) 220 60
H: 5 10 W: 11 02 b.Blackburn 12-4-88
Internationals: England U16, U17, U19.

2004–05	Blackburn R	0	0		
2005–06	Blackburn R	0	0		
2006–07	Blackburn R	0	0		
2006–07	Carlisle U	18	5		
2007–08	Carlisle U	31	14		
2008–09	Nottingham F	28	7		
2009–10	Nottingham F	18	2		
2010–11	Nottingham F	0	0		
2010–11	Huddersfield T	16	0	16	0
2010–11	Scunthorpe U	18	6	18	6
2011–12	Nottingham F	2	0	48	9
2011–12	Watford	22	1		
2012–13	Watford	2	0	24	1
2012–13	Carlisle U	16	7	65	26
2012–13	Preston NE	14	0		
2013–14	Preston NE	35	18	49	18

HAYHURST, Will (M) 47 5
H: 5 10 W: 11 02 b.Longridge 24-2-94
Internationals: Republic of Ireland U17, U19, U21.

2011–12	Preston NE	2	0		
2012–13	Preston NE	21	4		

| 2013–14 | Preston NE | 6 | 0 | 29 | 4 |
| 2013–14 | York C | 18 | 1 | 18 | 1 |

HOLMES, Lee (M)   202 17
H: 5 8   W: 10 06   b.Mansfield 2-4-87
Internationals: England U16, U17, U19.

2002–03	Derby Co	2	0		
2003–04	Derby Co	23	2		
2004–05	Derby Co	3	0		
2004–05	Swindon T	15	1		
2005–06	Derby Co	18	0		
2006–07	Derby Co	0	0		
2006–07	*Bradford C*	16	0	16	0
2007–08	Derby Co	0	0	46	2
2007–08	*Walsall*	19	4	19	4
2008–09	Southampton	11	0		
2009–10	Southampton	5	0		
2010–11	Southampton	7	0		
2011–12	Southampton	6	1	29	1
2011–12	*Oxford U*	7	2	7	2
2011–12	*Swindon T*	10	1	25	2
2012–13	Preston NE	28	3		
2013–14	Preston NE	32	3	60	6

HUME, Iain (F)   439 104
H: 5 7   W: 11 02   b.Ontario 31-10-83
Internationals: Canada Youth, U20, Full caps.

1999–2000	Tranmere R	3	0		
2000–01	Tranmere R	10	0		
2001–02	Tranmere R	14	0		
2002–03	Tranmere R	35	6		
2003–04	Tranmere R	40	10		
2004–05	Tranmere R	42	15		
2005–06	Tranmere R	6	1	150	32
2005–06	Leicester C	37	9		
2006–07	Leicester C	45	13		
2007–08	Leicester C	40	11	122	33
2008–09	Barnsley	15	4		
2009–10	Barnsley	35	5		
2010–11	Barnsley	1	0	51	9
2010–11	Preston NE	31	12		
2011–12	Preston NE	28	9		
2012–13	Preston NE	0	0		
2012–13	*Doncaster R*	33	6	33	6
2013–14	Preston NE	16	2	75	23
2013–14	*Fleetwood T*	8	1	8	1

HUMPHREY, Chris (M)   248 12
H: 5 11   W: 11 07   b.Walsall 19-9-87
Internationals: Jamaica Full caps.

2006–07	Shrewsbury T	12	0		
2007–08	Shrewsbury T	25	0		
2008–09	Shrewsbury T	37	2	74	2
2009–10	Motherwell	28	0		
2010–11	Motherwell	36	3		
2011–12	Motherwell	35	2		
2012–13	Motherwell	33	3	132	8
2013–14	Preston NE	42	2	42	2

HUNTINGTON, Paul (D)   195 15
H: 6 3   W: 12 08   b.Carlisle 17-9-87
Internationals: England U18.

2005–06	Newcastle U	0	0		
2006–07	Newcastle U	11	1		
2007–08	Newcastle U	0	0	11	1
2007–08	Leeds U	17	2		
2008–09	Leeds U	4	0		
2009–10	Leeds U	0	0	21	2
2009–10	*Stockport Co*	26	0	26	0
2010–11	Yeovil T	40	5		
2011–12	Yeovil T	37	2	77	7
2012–13	Preston NE	37	3		
2013–14	Preston NE	23	2	60	5

JAMES, Steven (G)   0 0

| 2012–13 | Preston NE | 0 | 0 | | |
| 2013–14 | Preston NE | 0 | 0 | | |

KEANE, Keith (M)   193 7
H: 5 9   W: 11 01   b.Luton 20-11-86
Internationals: Republic of Ireland U19, U21.

2003–04	Luton T	15	1		
2004–05	Luton T	17	0		
2005–06	Luton T	10	1		
2006–07	Luton T	19	1		
2007–08	Luton T	28	1		
2008–09	Luton T	40	0	129	4
2012–13	Preston NE	26	1		
2013–14	Preston NE	38	2	64	3

KILKENNY, Neil (M)   286 16
H: 5 8   W: 10 08   b.Enfield 19-12-85
Internationals: England U18, U20. Australia U23, Full caps.

2003–04	Birmingham C	0	0		
2004–05	Birmingham C	0	0		
2004–05	*Oldham Ath*	27	4		
2005–06	Birmingham C	18	0		
2006–07	Birmingham C	8	0		
2007–08	Birmingham C	0	0	26	0
2007–08	*Oldham Ath*	20	1	47	5
2007–08	Leeds U	16	1		
2008–09	Leeds U	30	4		
2009–10	Leeds U	35	2		
2010–11	Leeds U	37	1	118	8
2011–12	Bristol C	41	1		
2012–13	Bristol C	24	0		
2013–14	Bristol C	3	0	68	1
2013–14	Preston NE	27	2	27	2

KING, Jack (M)   60 6
b.Oxford 20-8-85

| 2012–13 | Preston NE | 36 | 4 | | |
| 2013–14 | Preston NE | 24 | 2 | 60 | 6 |

LAIRD, Scott (D)   143 17
H: 5 11   W: 11 05   b.Taunton 15-5-88
Internationals: Scotland U16. England C.

2006–07	Plymouth Arg	0	0		
2007–08	Plymouth Arg	0	0		
2010–11	Stevenage	44	4		
2011–12	Stevenage	46	8	90	12
2012–13	Preston NE	19	4		
2013–14	Preston NE	34	1	53	5

MOUSINHO, John (M)   240 18
H: 6 1   W: 12 07   b.Hounslow 30-4-86

2005–06	Brentford	7	0		
2006–07	Brentford	34	0		
2007–08	Brentford	23	2	64	2
2008–09	Wycombe W	34	2		
2009–10	Wycombe W	39	1	73	3
2010–11	Stevenage	38	7		
2011–12	Stevenage	19	3		
2012–13	Preston NE	24	1		
2013–14	Preston NE	2	0	26	1
2013–14	*Gillingham*	4	1	4	1
2013–14	*Stevenage*	16	1	73	11

STUCKMANN, Thorsten (G)   331 0
H: 6 6   W: 14 11   b.Gutersloh 3-3-81

2000–01	Pr Munster	25	0		
2001–02	Pr Munster	19	0		
2002–03	Pr Munster	30	0	74	0
2003–04	E Braunschweig	21	0		
2004–05	E Braunschweig	36	0		
2005–06	E Braunschweig	34	0		
2006–07	E Braunschweig	34	0	125	0
2007–08	A Aachen	16	0		
2008–09	A Aachen	34	0		
2009–10	A Aachen	31	0		
2010–11	A Aachen	1	0	82	0
2011–12	Preston NE	28	0		
2012–13	Preston NE	22	0		
2013–14	Preston NE	0	0	50	0

WELSH, John (M)   271 17
H: 5 7   W: 12 02   b.Liverpool 10-1-84
Internationals: England U20, U21.

2000–01	Liverpool	0	0		
2001–02	Liverpool	0	0		
2002–03	Liverpool	0	0		
2003–04	Liverpool	1	0		
2004–05	Liverpool	3	0		
2005–06	Liverpool	0	0	4	0
2005–06	Hull C	32	2		
2006–07	Hull C	18	1		
2007–08	Hull C	0	0		
2007–08	*Chester C*	6	0	6	0
2008–09	Hull C	0	0	50	3
2008–09	*Carlisle U*	4	0	4	0
2008–09	*Bury*	5	0	5	0
2009–10	Tranmere R	45	4		
2010–11	Tranmere R	8	0		
2011–12	Tranmere R	44	3	130	11
2012–13	Preston NE	36	1		
2013–14	Preston NE	36	2	72	3

WISEMAN, Scott (D)   275 3
H: 6 0   W: 11 06   b.Hull 9-10-85
Internationals: England U20. Gibraltar Full caps.

2003–04	Hull C	2	0		
2004–05	Hull C	3	0		
2004–05	*Boston U*	2	0	2	0
2005–06	Hull C	11	0		
2006–07	Hull C	0	0	16	0
2006–07	*Rotherham U*	18	1	18	1
2006–07	Darlington	10	0		
2007–08	Darlington	7	0	17	0
2008–09	Rochdale	32	0		
2009–10	Rochdale	36	1		
2010–11	Rochdale	37	0	105	1
2011–12	Barnsley	43	1		
2012–13	Barnsley	36	0		
2013–14	Barnsley	23	0	102	1
2013–14	Preston NE	15	0	15	0

WRIGHT, Bailey (D)   96 7
H: 5 9   W: 13 05   b.Melbourne 28-7-92
Internationals: Australia U17.

2010–11	Preston NE	2	0		
2011–12	Preston NE	13	1		
2012–13	Preston NE	38	2		
2013–14	Preston NE	43	4	96	7

WROE, Nicky (M)   246 30
H: 5 11   W: 10 02   b.Sheffield 28-9-85
Internationals: England C.

2002–03	Barnsley	1	0		
2003–04	Barnsley	2	1		
2004–05	Barnsley	31	0		
2005–06	Barnsley	12	0		
2006–07	Barnsley	3	0	49	1
2006–07	*Bury*	5	0	5	0

From York C.

2009–10	Torquay U	45	9		
2010–11	Torquay U	20	3	65	12
2010–11	Shrewsbury T	18	3		
2011–12	Shrewsbury T	38	4		
2012–13	Preston NE	38	8		
2013–14	Preston NE	5	0	43	8
2013–14	*Shrewsbury T*	10	0	66	7
2013–14	*Oxford U*	18	2	18	2

Scholars
Dalton, Ross Anthony; Gray, George Robert; Hagon, Harold Jack; Holmes, Sean Lewis; Hornby-Forbes, Tyler Cecil; Livesey, Sam Anthony; Magolis, Lyle Daleroy; Pritchard, Luke Gerard; Quigley, James Alan; Quinn, Thomas Taylor; Roscoe, Bradley Samuel; Ryan, Jack Liam; Sampson, Joshua William; Scott, Jordan Lee; Whittington, Joseph Eric; Wicks, Bradley Dalton; Wilmer-Anderton, Nicholas Jack.

QPR (66)

ANDRADE, Bruno (M)   39 2
H: 5 9   W: 11 09   b.Aveiro 2-10-93

2010–11	QPR	1	0		
2011–12	QPR	1	0		
2011–12	*Aldershot T*	1	0	1	0
2012–13	QPR	0	0		
2012–13	*Wycombe W*	23	2	23	2
2013–14	QPR	0	0	2	0
2013–14	*Stevenage*	13	0	13	0

AUSTIN, Charlie (F)   167 89
H: 6 2   W: 13 03   b.Hungerford 5-7-89

2009–10	Swindon T	33	19		
2010–11	Swindon T	21	12	54	31
2010–11	Burnley	4	0		
2011–12	Burnley	41	16		
2012–13	Burnley	37	25	82	41
2013–14	QPR	31	17	31	17

BARTON, Joey (M)   301 28
H: 5 11   W: 12 05   b.Huyton 2-9-82
Internationals: England U21, Full caps.

2001–02	Manchester C	0	0		
2002–03	Manchester C	7	1		
2003–04	Manchester C	28	1		
2004–05	Manchester C	31	1		
2005–06	Manchester C	31	6		
2006–07	Manchester C	33	6	130	15
2007–08	Newcastle U	23	1		

Season	Club	Apps	Gls	Tot	Gls
2008–09	Newcastle U	9	1		
2009–10	Newcastle U	15	1		
2010–11	Newcastle U	32	4		
2011–12	Newcastle U	2	0	81	7
2011–12	QPR	31	3		
2012–13	QPR	0	0		
2012–13	*Marseille*	25	0	25	0
2013–14	QPR	34	3	65	6

BENAYOUN, Yossi (M) 431 115
H: 5 10 W: 11 00 b.Beer Sheva 6-6-80
Internationals: Israel Full caps.

Season	Club	Apps	Gls	Tot	Gls
1997–98	Hapoel Beer Sheva	25	15	25	15
1998–99	Maccabi Haifa	29	16		
1999–2000	Maccabi Haifa	38	19		
2000–01	Maccabi Haifa	37	13		
2001–02	Maccabi Haifa	26	7	130	55
2002–03	Santander	31	4		
2003–04	Santander	35	7		
2004–05	Santander	0	0	66	11
2005–06	West Ham U	34	5		
2006–07	West Ham U	29	3		
2007–08	Liverpool	30	4		
2008–09	Liverpool	32	8		
2009–10	Liverpool	30	6	92	18
2010–11	Chelsea	7	1		
2011–12	Chelsea	1	0		
2011–12	Arsenal	19	4	19	4
2012–13	Chelsea	6	0	14	1
2012–13	*West Ham U*	6	0	69	8
2013–14	QPR	16	3	16	3

CHEVANTON, Javier (F) 269 127
H: 5 10 W: 11 10 b.Juan Lacaze 12-8-80
Internationals: Uruguay Full caps.

Season	Club	Apps	Gls	Tot	Gls
1997	Danubio	1	0		
1998	Danubio	1	0		
1999	Danubio	9	3		
2000	Danubio	30	32	41	35
2001–02	Lecce	27	12		
2002–03	Lecce	30	16		
2003–04	Lecce	30	19		
2004–05	Monaco	27	11		
2005–06	Monaco	23	10	50	21
2006–07	Sevilla	17	4		
2007–08	Sevilla	8	1		
2008–09	Sevilla	8	3		
2009–10	Sevilla	1	0	34	8
2009–10	*Atalanta*	12	2	12	2
2010–11	Lecce	14	2		
2011–12	*Colon Santa Fe*	15	6	15	6
2012–13	Lecce	14	6	115	55
2013–14	QPR	2	0	2	0

Transferred to Liverpool (Uruguay) January 2014

DERRY, Shaun (M) 575 12
H: 5 10 W: 10 13 b.Nottingham 6-12-77

Season	Club	Apps	Gls	Tot	Gls
1995–96	Notts Co	12	0		
1996–97	Notts Co	39	2		
1997–98	Notts Co	28	2	79	4
1997–98	Sheffield U	12	0		
1998–99	Sheffield U	26	0		
1999–2000	Sheffield U	34	0	72	0
1999–2000	Portsmouth	9	1		
2000–01	Portsmouth	28	0		
2001–02	Portsmouth	12	0	49	1
2002–03	Crystal Palace	39	1		
2003–04	Crystal Palace	37	2		
2004–05	Crystal Palace	7	0		
2004–05	*Nottingham F*	7	0	7	0
2004–05	Leeds U	7	2		
2005–06	Leeds U	41	0		
2006–07	Leeds U	23	1		
2007–08	Leeds U	0	0	71	3
2007–08	Crystal Palace	30	0		
2008–09	Crystal Palace	39	0		
2009–10	Crystal Palace	46	0	198	3
2010–11	QPR	45	0		
2011–12	QPR	29	1		
2012–13	QPR	18	0		
2013–14	QPR	0	0	92	1
2013–14	*Millwall*	7	0	7	0

DIAKITE, Samba (M) 124 1
H: 6 1 W: 11 13 b.Montfermeil 24-1-89
Internationals: Mali Full caps.

Season	Club	Apps	Gls	Tot	Gls
2007–08	Valenciennes B	7	0	7	0
2008–09	Olympique N-le-Sec	28	0	28	0
2009–10	Nancy B	19	0	19	0
2009–10	Nancy	3	0		
2010–11	Nancy	23	0		
2011–12	Nancy	15	0	41	0
2011–12	QPR	9	1		
2012–13	QPR	14	0		
2013–14	QPR	0	0	23	1
2013–14	*Watford*	6	0	6	0

DONALDSON, Coll (D) 1 0
H: 6 2 W: 12 13 b.Edinburgh 9-4-95

Season	Club	Apps	Gls	Tot	Gls
2013–14	QPR	1	0	1	0

DOUGHTY, Michael (M) 62 2
H: 6 1 W: 12 10 b.Westminster 20-11-92
Internationals: Wales U19, U21.

Season	Club	Apps	Gls	Tot	Gls
2010–11	QPR	0	0		
2011–12	QPR	0	0		
2011–12	*Crawley T*	16	0	16	0
2011–12	*Aldershot T*	5	0		
2012–13	QPR	0	0		
2012–13	*Aldershot T*	0	0	5	0
2012–13	*St Johnstone*	5	0	5	0
2013–14	QPR	0	0		
2013–14	*Stevenage*	36	2	36	2

DUNNE, Richard (D) 492 13
H: 6 2 W: 15 10 b.Dublin 21-9-79
Internationals: Republic of Ireland U21, B, Full caps.

Season	Club	Apps	Gls	Tot	Gls
1996–97	Everton	7	0		
1997–98	Everton	3	0		
1998–99	Everton	16	0		
1999–2000	Everton	31	0		
2000–01	Everton	3	0	60	0
2000–01	Manchester C	25	0		
2001–02	Manchester C	43	1		
2002–03	Manchester C	25	0		
2003–04	Manchester C	29	0		
2004–05	Manchester C	35	2		
2005–06	Manchester C	32	3		
2006–07	Manchester C	38	1		
2007–08	Manchester C	36	0		
2008–09	Manchester C	31	1		
2009–10	Manchester C	2	0	296	8
2009–10	Aston Villa	35	3		
2010–11	Aston Villa	32	0		
2011–12	Aston Villa	28	1		
2012–13	Aston Villa	0	0	95	4
2013–14	QPR	41	1	41	1

EHMER, Max (M) 79 2
H: 6 2 W: 11 00 b.Frankfurt 3-2-92

Season	Club	Apps	Gls	Tot	Gls
2009–10	QPR	0	0		
2010–11	QPR	0	0		
2010–11	*Yeovil T*	27	0		
2011–12	QPR	0	0		
2011–12	*Yeovil T*	24	0	51	0
2011–12	*Preston NE*	9	0	9	0
2012–13	QPR	0	0		
2012–13	*Stevenage*	6	1	6	1
2013–14	QPR	1	0	1	0
2013–14	*Carlisle U*	12	1	12	1

EPHRAIM, Hogan (F) 161 10
H: 5 9 W: 10 06 b.Islington 31-3-88
Internationals: England U16, U17, U18, U19.

Season	Club	Apps	Gls	Tot	Gls
2004–05	West Ham U	0	0		
2005–06	West Ham U	0	0		
2006–07	West Ham U	0	0		
2006–07	*Colchester U*	21	1	21	1
2007–08	West Ham U	1	0		
2007–08	QPR	29	3		
2008–09	QPR	27	1		
2009–10	QPR	22	0		
2009–10	*Leeds U*	3	0	3	0
2010–11	QPR	28	3		
2011–12	QPR	2	0		
2011–12	*Charlton Ath*	5	1	5	1
2011–12	*Bristol C*	5	1	5	1
2012–13	QPR	0	0		
2012–13	*Toronto FC*	11	0	11	0
2013–14	QPR	0	0	108	7
2013–14	*Peterborough U*	8	0	8	0

FAURLIN, Alejandro (M) 193 13
H: 6 1 W: 12 06 b.Argentina 9-8-86
Internationals: Argentina U17.

Season	Club	Apps	Gls	Tot	Gls
2004	Rosario Central	1	0		
2005	Rosario Central	0	0		
2006	Rosario Central	0	0	1	0
2007	Atletico Rafaela	40	1	40	1
2008–09	Instituto	27	7	27	7
2009–10	QPR	41	1		
2010–11	QPR	40	3		
2011–12	QPR	20	1		
2012–13	QPR	11	0		
2012–13	*Palermo*	6	0	6	0
2013–14	QPR	7	0	119	5

GIBBONS, Jordan (M) 1 0
H: 5 10 W: 10 12 b. 18-11-93

Season	Club	Apps	Gls	Tot	Gls
2011–12	QPR	0	0		
2012–13	QPR	0	0		
2012–13	*Inverness CT*	1	0	1	0
2013–14	QPR	0	0		

GRANERO, Esteban (M) 182 17
H: 5 11 W: 11 04 b.Madrid 2-7-87
Internationals: Spain U16, U17, U19, U20, U21.

Season	Club	Apps	Gls	Tot	Gls
2005–06	RM Castilla	1	0		
2006–07	RM Castilla	23	4	24	4
2007–08	Getafe	27	3		
2008–09	Getafe	35	5	62	8
2009–10	Real Madrid	31	3		
2010–11	Real Madrid	19	1		
2011–12	Real Madrid	17	0	67	4
2012–13	QPR	24	1		
2013–14	QPR	1	0	25	1
2013–14	*Real Sociedad*	4	0	4	0

GREEN, Rob (G) 503 0
H: 6 3 W: 14 09 b.Chertsey 18-1-80
Internationals: England U16, U18, B, Full caps.

Season	Club	Apps	Gls	Tot	Gls
1997–98	Norwich C	0	0		
1998–99	Norwich C	2	0		
1999–2000	Norwich C	3	0		
2000–01	Norwich C	5	0		
2001–02	Norwich C	41	0		
2002–03	Norwich C	46	0		
2003–04	Norwich C	46	0		
2004–05	Norwich C	38	0		
2005–06	Norwich C	42	0	223	0
2006–07	West Ham U	26	0		
2007–08	West Ham U	38	0		
2008–09	West Ham U	38	0		
2009–10	West Ham U	38	0		
2010–11	West Ham U	37	0		
2011–12	West Ham U	42	0	219	0
2012–13	QPR	16	0		
2013–14	QPR	45	0	61	0

HARAN, James (D) 0 0

Season	Club	Apps	Gls	Tot	Gls
2013–14	QPR	0	0		

HARRIMAN, Michael (D) 56 1
H: 5 6 W: 11 10 b.Chichester 23-10-92
Internationals: Republic of Ireland U18, U19, U21.

Season	Club	Apps	Gls	Tot	Gls
2010–11	QPR	0	0		
2011–12	QPR	1	0		
2012–13	QPR	1	0		
2012–13	*Wycombe W*	20	0	20	0
2013–14	QPR	0	0	2	0
2013–14	*Gillingham*	34	1	34	1

HENRY, Karl (M) 406 9
H: 6 0 W: 12 00 b.Wolverhampton 26-11-82
Internationals: England U20.

Season	Club	Apps	Gls	Tot	Gls
1999–2000	Stoke C	0	0		
2000–01	Stoke C	0	0		
2001–02	Stoke C	24	0		
2002–03	Stoke C	18	1		
2003–04	Stoke C	20	0		
2003–04	*Cheltenham T*	9	1	9	1
2004–05	Stoke C	34	0		
2005–06	Stoke C	24	0	120	1
2006–07	Wolverhampton W	34	3		
2007–08	Wolverhampton W	40	3		
2008–09	Wolverhampton W	43	0		
2009–10	Wolverhampton W	34	0		
2010–11	Wolverhampton W	29	0		
2011–12	Wolverhampton W	31	0		
2012–13	Wolverhampton W	39	0	250	6
2013–14	QPR	27	1	27	1

HILL, Clint (D) 493 28
H: 6 0 W: 11 06 b.Liverpool 19-10-78

Season	Club	Apps	Gls	Tot	Gls
1997–98	Tranmere R	14	0		
1998–99	Tranmere R	33	4		
1999–2000	Tranmere R	29	5		
2000–01	Tranmere R	34	5		
2001–02	Tranmere R	30	2	140	16
2002–03	Oldham Ath	17	1	17	1
2003–04	Stoke C	12	0		

2004–05	Stoke C	32	1		
2005–06	Stoke C	13	0		
2006–07	Stoke C	18	2		
2007–08	Stoke C	5	0	80	3
2007–08	Crystal Palace	28	3		
2008–09	Crystal Palace	43	1		
2009–10	Crystal Palace	43	1	114	5
2010–11	QPR	44	2		
2011–12	QPR	22	0		
2011–12	*Nottingham F*	5	0	5	0
2012–13	QPR	31	0		
2013–14	QPR	40	1	137	3

HITCHCOCK, Tom (F)   43 12
H: 5 11 W: 12 08 b.Hemel Hempstead 1-10-92

2009–10	Blackburn R	0	0		
2010–11	Blackburn R	0	0		
2011–12	Blackburn R	0	0		
2011–12	*Plymouth Arg*	8	0	8	0
2011–12	QPR	0	0		
2012–13	QPR	0	0		
2012–13	*Bristol R*	17	3	17	3
2013–14	QPR	1	1	1	1
2013–14	*Crewe Alex*	6	3	6	3
2013–14	*Rotherham U*	11	5	11	5

HOILETT, Junior (M)   175 24
H: 5 8 W: 11 00 b.Ottawa 5-6-90

2007–08	Blackburn R	0	0		
2007–08	*Paderborn*	12	1	12	1
2008–09	Blackburn R	0	0		
2008–09	*St Pauli*	21	6	21	6
2009–10	Blackburn R	23	0		
2010–11	Blackburn R	24	5		
2011–12	Blackburn R	34	7	81	12
2012–13	QPR	26	1		
2013–14	QPR	35	4	61	5

HUGHES, Aaron (D)   466 5
H: 6 0 W: 11 02 b.Cookstown 8-11-79
Internationals: Northern Ireland Youth, B, Full caps.

1996–97	Newcastle U	0	0		
1997–98	Newcastle U	4	0		
1998–99	Newcastle U	14	0		
1999–2000	Newcastle U	27	2		
2000–01	Newcastle U	35	0		
2001–02	Newcastle U	34	0		
2002–03	Newcastle U	35	1		
2003–04	Newcastle U	34	0		
2004–05	Newcastle U	22	1	205	4
2005–06	Aston Villa	35	0		
2006–07	Aston Villa	19	0	54	0
2007–08	Fulham	30	0		
2008–09	Fulham	38	0		
2009–10	Fulham	34	0		
2010–11	Fulham	38	1		
2011–12	Fulham	19	0		
2012–13	Fulham	24	0		
2013–14	Fulham	13	0	196	1
2013–14	QPR	11	0	11	0

JENAS, Jermaine (M)   341 39
H: 5 11 W: 11 00 b.Nottingham 18-2-83
Internationals: England U16, U17, U18, U19, U21, B, Full caps.

1999–2000	Nottingham F	0	0		
2000–01	Nottingham F	1	0		
2001–02	Nottingham F	28	4		
2001–02	Newcastle U	12	0		
2002–03	Newcastle U	32	6		
2003–04	Newcastle U	31	2		
2004–05	Newcastle U	31	1		
2005–06	Newcastle U	4	0	110	9
2005–06	Tottenham H	30	6		
2006–07	Tottenham H	25	6		
2007–08	Tottenham H	29	4		
2008–09	Tottenham H	32	4		
2009–10	Tottenham H	19	1		
2010–11	Tottenham H	19	0		
2011–12	Tottenham H	0	0		
2011–12	*Aston Villa*	3	0	3	0
2012–13	Tottenham H	1	0	155	21
2012–13	*Nottingham F*	6	1	35	5
2012–13	QPR	12	2		
2013–14	QPR	26	2	38	4

JOHNSON, Andy (F)   390 114
H: 5 7 W: 10 09 b.Bedford 10-2-81
Internationals: England U20, Full caps.

1997–98	Birmingham C	0	0		
1998–99	Birmingham C	4	0		
1999–2000	Birmingham C	22	1		
2000–01	Birmingham C	34	4		
2001–02	Birmingham C	23	3	83	8
2002–03	Crystal Palace	28	11		
2003–04	Crystal Palace	42	27		
2004–05	Crystal Palace	37	21		
2005–06	Crystal Palace	33	15	140	74
2006–07	Everton	32	11		
2007–08	Everton	29	6	61	17
2008–09	Fulham	31	7		
2009–10	Fulham	8	0		
2010–11	Fulham	27	3		
2011–12	Fulham	20	3	86	13
2012–13	QPR	3	0		
2013–14	QPR	17	2	20	2

JULIO CESAR, Soares (G)   252 0
H: 6 1 W: 12 05 b.Rio de Janeiro 3-9-79
Internationals: Brazil Full caps.

2005–06	Inter Milan	29	0		
2006–07	Inter Milan	32	0		
2007–08	Inter Milan	35	0		
2008–09	Inter Milan	36	0		
2009–10	Inter Milan	38	0		
2010–11	Inter Milan	25	0		
2011–12	Inter Milan	33	0	228	0
2012–13	QPR	24	0		
2013–14	QPR	0	0	24	0

KRANJCAR, Niko (M)   309 57
H: 6 1 W: 12 13 b.Zagreb 13-8-84
Internationals: Croatia U17, U19, U21, Full caps.

2001–02	Dynamo Zagreb	24	3		
2002–03	Dynamo Zagreb	21	4		
2003–04	Dynamo Zagreb	24	10		
2004–05	Dynamo Zagreb	16	2	85	19
2004–05	Hajduk Split	13	1		
2005–06	Hajduk Split	32	10		
2006–07	Hajduk Split	5	3	50	14
2006–07	Portsmouth	24	2		
2007–08	Portsmouth	34	4		
2008–09	Portsmouth	21	3		
2009–10	Portsmouth	4	0	83	9
2009–10	Tottenham H	24	6		
2010–11	Tottenham H	13	2		
2011–12	Tottenham H	12	1	49	9
2012–13	Dynamo Kiev	13	4		
2013–14	Dynamo Kiev	0	0	13	4

On loan from Dynamo Kiev

| 2013–14 | QPR | 29 | 2 | 29 | 2 |

LAURENT, Josh (M)   0 0
b. 6-5-95

| 2013–14 | QPR | 0 | 0 | | |

LENNOX, Aaron (G)   0 0
b.Sydney 19-2-93
Internationals: Australia U23.

2011–12	QPR	0	0		
2012–13	QPR	0	0		
2013–14	QPR	0	0		

LUMLEY, Joe (G)   0 0

| 2013–14 | QPR | 0 | 0 | | |

MBIA, Stephane (M)   222 13
H: 6 2 W: 12 11 b.Yaounde 20-5-86
Internationals: Cameroon Full caps.

2005–06	Rennes	22	0		
2006–07	Rennes	31	1		
2007–08	Rennes	25	3		
2008–09	Rennes	27	0	105	4
2009–10	Marseille	27	3		
2010–11	Marseille	26	1		
2011–12	Marseille	15	2		
2012–13	Marseille	1	0	69	6
2012–13	QPR	29	0		
2013–14	QPR	0	0	29	0
2013–14	*Sevilla*	19	3	19	3

MONTHE, Emmanuel (D)   0 0

| 2013–14 | QPR | 0 | 0 | | |

MURPHY, Brian (G)   133 0
H: 6 0 W: 13 00 b.Waterford 7-5-83
Internationals: Republic of Ireland U16, U21.

2000–01	Manchester C	0	0		
2001–02	Manchester C	0	0		
2002–03	Manchester C	0	0		
2002–03	*Oldham Ath*	0	0		
2002–03	*Peterborough U*	1	0	1	0

From Waterford

2003–04	Swansea C	11	0		
2004–05	Swansea C	2	0		
2005–06	Swansea C	0	0		
2006–07	Swansea C	0	0	13	0
2007	Bohemians	29	0		
2008	Bohemians	33	0		
2009	Bohemians	35	0	97	0
2009–10	Ipswich T	16	0		
2010–11	Ipswich T	4	0		
2011–12	Ipswich T	0	0	20	0
2011–12	QPR	0	0		
2012–13	QPR	0	0		
2013–14	QPR	2	0	2	0

O'NEIL, Gary (M)   377 29
H: 5 11 W: 11 00 b.Beckenham 18-5-83
Internationals: England U19, U20, U21.

1999–2000	Portsmouth	1	0		
2000–01	Portsmouth	10	1		
2001–02	Portsmouth	33	1		
2002–03	Portsmouth	31	3		
2003–04	Portsmouth	3	2		
2003–04	*Walsall*	7	0	7	0
2004–05	Portsmouth	24	2		
2004–05	*Cardiff C*	9	1	9	1
2005–06	Portsmouth	36	6		
2006–07	Portsmouth	35	1		
2007–08	Portsmouth	2	0	175	16
2007–08	Middlesbrough	26	0		
2008–09	Middlesbrough	29	4		
2009–10	Middlesbrough	36	4		
2010–11	Middlesbrough	18	0	109	8
2010–11	West Ham U	8	0		
2011–12	West Ham U	16	2		
2012–13	West Ham U	24	1	48	3
2013–14	QPR	29	1	29	1

ONUOHA, Nedum (D)   191 6
H: 6 2 W: 12 04 b.Warri 12-11-86
Internationals: England U20, U21.

2004–05	Manchester C	17	0		
2005–06	Manchester C	10	0		
2006–07	Manchester C	18	0		
2007–08	Manchester C	16	1		
2008–09	Manchester C	23	1		
2009–10	Manchester C	10	1		
2010–11	Manchester C	0	0		
2010–11	*Sunderland*	31	1	31	1
2011–12	Manchester C	1	0	95	3
2011–12	QPR	16	0		
2012–13	QPR	23	0		
2013–14	QPR	26	2	65	2

PARK, Ji-Sung (M)   316 45
H: 5 9 W: 11 06 b.Seoul 25-2-81
Internationals: South Korea U23, Full caps.

2000	Kyoto Purple S	13	1		
2001	Kyoto Purple S	38	3		
2002	Kyoto Purple S	25	7	76	11
2002–03	PSV Eindhoven	28	0		
2003–04	PSV Eindhoven	28	8		
2004–05	PSV Eindhoven	28	7		
2005–06	Manchester U	33	1		
2006–07	Manchester U	14	5		
2007–08	Manchester U	12	1		
2008–09	Manchester U	25	2		
2009–10	Manchester U	17	3		
2010–11	Manchester U	15	5		
2011–12	Manchester U	17	2	133	19
2012–13	QPR	20	0		
2013–14	QPR	0	0	20	0
2013–14	*PSV Eindhoven*	23	2	87	15

PATTIE, Ben (F)   0 0

| 2013–14 | QPR | 0 | 0 | | |

PETRASSO, Michael (M)   19 2
b. 9-7-95
Internationals: Canada U17, U20.

2013–14	QPR	1	0	1	0
2013–14	*Oldham Ath*	11	1	11	1
2013–14	*Coventry C*	7	1	7	1

PHILLIPS, Matthew (M)   199 28
H: 6 0 W: 12 10 b.Aylesbury 13-3-91
Internationals: England U19, U20. Scotland Full caps.

2007–08	Wycombe W	2	0		
2008–09	Wycombe W	37	3		
2009–10	Wycombe W	36	5		
2010–11	Wycombe W	3	0	78	8
2010–11	Blackpool	27	1		
2011–12	Blackpool	33	7		

2011–12	*Sheffield U*	6	5	6	5
2012–13	Blackpool	34	4		
2013–14	Blackpool	0	0	94	12
2013–14	QPR	21	3	21	3

REMY, Loic (F) 204 75
H: 6 0 W: 10 04 b.Lyon 2-1-87
Internationals: France U20, U21, Full caps.

2006–07	Lyon	6	0		
2007–08	Lyon	6	0	12	0
2007–08	Lens	10	3	10	3
2008–09	Nice	32	10		
2009–10	Nice	34	14		
2010–11	Nice	2	1	68	25
2010–11	Marseille	31	15		
2011–12	Marseille	29	11		
2012–13	Marseille	14	1	74	27
2012–13	QPR	14	6		
2013–14	QPR	0	0	14	6
2013–14	Newcastle U	26	14	26	14

SENDLES-WHITE, Jamie (D) 0 0
b.Kingston
Internationals: Northern Ireland U19, U21.

2011–12	QPR	0	0		
2012–13	QPR	0	0		
2013–14	QPR	0	0		
2013–14	*Colchester U*	0	0		

SIMPSON, Danny (D) 193 1
H: 5 9 W: 11 05 b.Eccles 4-1-87

2005–06	Manchester U	0	0		
2006–07	Manchester U	0	0		
2006–07	*Sunderland*	14	0	14	0
2007–08	Manchester U	3	0		
2007–08	*Ipswich T*	8	0	8	0
2008–09	Manchester U	0	0		
2008–09	*Blackburn R*	12	0	12	0
2009–10	Manchester U	0	0	3	0
2009–10	Newcastle U	39	1		
2010–11	Newcastle U	30	0		
2011–12	Newcastle U	35	0		
2012–13	Newcastle U	19	0	123	1
2013–14	QPR	33	0	33	0

SUTHERLAND, Frankie (M) 1 0
H: 5 9 W: 10 00 b.Hillingdon 6-12-93
Internationals: Republic of Ireland U17, U19, U21.

2010–11	QPR	0	0		
2011–12	QPR	0	0		
2012–13	QPR	0	0		
2012–13	*Portsmouth*	1	0	1	0
2013–14	QPR	0	0		
2013–14	*Leyton Orient*	0	0		

TAARABT, Adel (M) 186 38
H: 5 9 W: 10 12 b.Marseille 24-5-89
Internationals: France Youth. Morocco Full caps.

2006–07	Lens	1	0	1	0
2006–07	Tottenham H	2	0		
2007–08	Tottenham H	6	0		
2008–09	Tottenham H	1	0		
2008–09	*QPR*	7	1		
2009–10	Tottenham H	0	0	9	0
2009–10	*QPR*	41	7		
2010–11	QPR	44	19		
2011–12	QPR	27	2		
2012–13	QPR	31	5		
2013–14	QPR	0	0	150	34
2013–14	*Fulham*	12	0	12	0
2013–14	*AC Milan*	14	4	14	4

TRAORE, Armand (D) 113 3
H: 6 1 W: 12 12 b.Paris 8-10-89
Internationals: France U19, U21. Senegal Full caps.

2006–07	Arsenal	0	0		
2007–08	Arsenal	3	0		
2008–09	Arsenal	0	0		
2008–09	*Portsmouth*	19	1	19	1
2009–10	Arsenal	9	0		
2010–11	Arsenal	0	0		
2010–11	*Juventus*	10	0	10	0
2011–12	Arsenal	1	0	13	0
2011–12	QPR	23	0		
2012–13	QPR	26	0		
2013–14	QPR	22	2	71	2

WRIGHT-PHILLIPS, Shaun (M) 362 40
H: 5 5 W: 10 01 b.Lewisham 25-10-81
Internationals: England U21, Full caps.

1998–99	Manchester C	0	0		
1999–2000	Manchester C	4	0		
2000–01	Manchester C	15	0		
2001–02	Manchester C	35	8		
2002–03	Manchester C	31	1		
2003–04	Manchester C	34	7		
2004–05	Manchester C	34	10		
2005–06	Chelsea	27	0		
2006–07	Chelsea	27	2		
2007–08	Chelsea	27	2		
2008–09	Chelsea	1	0	82	4
2008–09	Manchester C	27	5		
2009–10	Manchester C	30	4		
2010–11	Manchester C	7	0		
2011–12	Manchester C	0	0	217	35
2011–12	QPR	32	0		
2012–13	QPR	20	1		
2013–14	QPR	11	0	63	1

YOUNG, Luke (D) 379 7
H: 6 0 W: 12 04 b.Harlow 19-7-79
Internationals: England U18, U21, Full caps.

1997–98	Tottenham H	0	0		
1998–99	Tottenham H	15	0		
1999–2000	Tottenham H	20	0		
2000–01	Tottenham H	23	0	58	0
2001–02	Charlton Ath	34	0		
2002–03	Charlton Ath	32	0		
2003–04	Charlton Ath	24	0		
2004–05	Charlton Ath	36	2		
2005–06	Charlton Ath	32	1		
2006–07	Charlton Ath	29	1	187	4
2007–08	Middlesbrough	35	1	35	1
2008–09	Aston Villa	34	1		
2009–10	Aston Villa	16	0		
2010–11	Aston Villa	23	1		
2011–12	Aston Villa	2	0	75	2
2011–12	QPR	23	2		
2012–13	QPR	0	0		
2013–14	QPR	17	3	24	2

YUN, Suk-Young (D) 10 1
H: 6 0 b.Suwon 13-2-90
Internationals: South Korea U17, U20, U23, Full caps.

2012–13	QPR	0	0		
2013–14	QPR	7	1	7	1
2013–14	*Doncaster R*	3	0	3	0

ZAMORA, Bobby (F) 418 135
H: 6 1 W: 11 11 b.Barking 16-1-81
Internationals: England U21, Full caps.

1999–2000	Bristol R	4	0	4	0
1999–2000	*Brighton & HA*	6	6		
2000–01	Brighton & HA	43	28		
2001–02	Brighton & HA	41	28		
2002–03	Brighton & HA	35	14	125	76
2003–04	Tottenham H	16	0	16	0
2003–04	West Ham U	17	5		
2004–05	West Ham U	34	7		
2005–06	West Ham U	34	6		
2006–07	West Ham U	32	11		
2007–08	West Ham U	13	1	130	30
2008–09	Fulham	35	2		
2009–10	Fulham	27	8		
2010–11	Fulham	14	5		
2011–12	Fulham	15	5	91	20
2011–12	QPR	14	2		
2012–13	QPR	21	4		
2013–14	QPR	17	3	52	9

Scholars
Beckles, Benjamin John; Butler, George Douglas; Corkery, Nathan Ryan; Garnett, Addison Righteous Adam; Grego-Cox, Reece Randall; Herdman, Martin John; Hudnott, Conor John James; Kakay, Osman Jovan; Komodikis, Andreas; Mitford, Tyrell Lee; O'Sullivan, Callum Liam; Page, William Alexander; Shodipo, Olamide Oluwatimilehin Babatunde Oluwaka; Smith, Mark David; Williams, Trey Preston; Young, Ryan Lee.

READING (67)

AKPAN, Hope (M) 87 6
H: 6 0 W: 10 08 b.Liverpool 14-8-91

2007–08	Everton	0	0		
2008–09	Everton	0	0		
2009–10	Everton	0	0		
2010–11	Everton	0	0		
2010–11	*Hull C*	2	0	2	0
2011–12	Crawley T	26	1		
2012–13	Crawley T	21	4	47	5
2012–13	Reading	9	0		
2013–14	Reading	29	1	38	1

ANDERSEN, Mikkel (G) 92 0
H: 6 5 W: 12 08 b.Copenhagen 17-12-88
Internationals: Denmark U19, U20, U21.

2006–07	Reading	0	0		
2007–08	Reading	0	0		
2008–09	Reading	0	0		
2008–09	*Brentford*	1	0	1	0
2008–09	*Brighton & HA*	5	0	5	0
2009–10	Reading	0	0		
2009–10	*Bristol R*	39	0		
2010–11	Reading	0	0		
2010–11	*Bristol R*	19	0	58	0
2011–12	Reading	0	0		
2012–13	Reading	0	0		
2012–13	*Portsmouth*	18	0	18	0
2013–14	Reading	0	0		
2013–14	*Randers FC*	10	0	10	0

ARNOLD, Nick (D) 31 0
H: 5 11 W: 12 12 b.Tadley 3-7-93

2011–12	Reading	0	0		
2012–13	Reading	0	0		
2013–14	Reading	0	0		
2013–14	*Wycombe W*	31	0	31	0

BLACKMAN, Nick (F) 132 30
H: 6 2 W: 11 08 b.Whitefield 11-11-89

2006–07	Macclesfield T	1	0		
2007–08	Macclesfield T	11	1		
2008–09	Macclesfield T	0	0	12	1
2008–09	Blackburn R	0	0		
2008–09	*Blackpool*	5	1	5	1
2009–10	Blackburn R	0	0		
2009–10	*Oldham Ath*	12	1	12	1
2010–11	Blackburn R	0	0		
2010–11	*Motherwell*	18	10	18	10
2010–11	*Aberdeen*	15	2	15	2
2011–12	Blackburn R	1	0		
2012–13	Blackburn R	0	0	1	0
2012–13	*Sheffield U*	28	11	28	11
2012–13	Reading	11	0		
2013–14	Reading	30	4	41	4

BRIDGE, Wayne (D) 365 6
H: 5 10 W: 12 13 b.Southampton 5-8-80
Internationals: England U18, U21, Full caps.

1997–98	Southampton	0	0		
1998–99	Southampton	23	0		
1999–2000	Southampton	19	1		
2000–01	Southampton	38	0		
2001–02	Southampton	38	0		
2002–03	Southampton	34	1	152	2
2003–04	Chelsea	33	1		
2004–05	Chelsea	15	0		
2005–06	Chelsea	0	0		
2005–06	*Fulham*	12	0	12	0
2006–07	Chelsea	22	0		
2007–08	Chelsea	11	0		
2008–09	Chelsea	6	0	87	1
2008–09	Manchester C	16	0		
2009–10	Manchester C	23	0		
2010–11	Manchester C	0	0		
2010–11	*West Ham U*	15	0	15	0
2011–12	Manchester C	0	0		
2011–12	*Sunderland*	8	0	8	0
2012–13	Manchester C	0	0	42	0
2012–13	*Brighton & HA*	37	3	37	3
2013–14	Reading	12	0	12	0

COOPER, Jake (D) 0 0
Internationals: England U18, 19.

2013–14	Reading	0	0	

CUMMINGS, Shaun (D) 107 0
H: 6 0 W: 11 10 b.Hammersmith 25-2-89
Internationals: Jamaica Full caps.

2007–08	Chelsea	0	0	

2008–09	Chelsea	0	0		
2008–09	*Milton Keynes D*	32	0	32	0
2009–10	Chelsea	0	0		
2009–10	*WBA*	3	0	3	0
2009–10	Reading	8	0		
2010–11	Reading	10	0		
2011–12	Reading	34	0		
2012–13	Reading	9	0		
2013–14	Reading	11	0	72	0

D'ATH, Lawson (M)   45 4
H: 5 9   W: 12 02   b.Witney 24-12-92

2010–11	Reading	0	0		
2011–12	Reading	0	0		
2011–12	*Yeovil T*	14	1	14	1
2012–13	Reading	0	0		
2012–13	*Cheltenham T*	2	1	2	1
2012–13	*Exeter C*	8	1	8	1
2013–14	Reading	0	0		
2013–14	*Dagenham & R*	21	1	21	1

DRENTHE, Royston (M)   133 11
H: 5 6   W: 10 07   b.Rotterdam 8-4-87
Internationals: Netherlands U18, U19, U21, B, Full caps.

2005–06	Feyenoord	3	0		
2006–07	Feyenoord	26	0	29	0
2007–08	Real Madrid	18	2		
2008–09	Real Madrid	20	0		
2009–10	Real Madrid	8	0	46	2
2010–11	*Hercules*	14	4	14	4
2011–12	Everton	21	3		
2012–13	Everton	0	0	21	3
2012–13	*Alania Vladikavkaz*	0	0		
2013–14	Reading	23	2	23	2

EDWARDS, Ryan (M)   0 0
H: 5 7   W: 11 07   b.Sydney 17-11-93
Internationals: Australia U20, U23.

2011–12	Reading	0	0
2012–13	Reading	0	0
2012–13	*Rochdale*	0	0
2013–14	Reading	0	0

FEDERICI, Adam (G)   176 1
H: 6 2   W: 14 02   b.Nowra 31-1-85
Internationals: Australia U20, U23, Full caps.

2005–06	Reading	0	0		
2006–07	Reading	2	0		
2007–08	Reading	0	0		
2008–09	Reading	15	1		
2008–09	*Southend U*	10	0	10	0
2009–10	Reading	46	0		
2010–11	Reading	34	0		
2011–12	Reading	46	0		
2012–13	Reading	21	0		
2013–14	Reading	2	0	166	1

FOSU, Tarique (M)   0 0
Internationals: England U18.

2013–14	Reading	0	0

FRIDJONSSON, Sammi (M)   0 0
b. 22-2-96
Internationals: Iceland U17, U19.

2013–14	Reading	0	0

GORKSS, Kaspars (D)   371 24
H: 6 3   W: 13 05   b.Riga 6-11-81
Internationals: Latvia U21, Full caps.

2002	Auda Riga	28	0	28	0
2003	Oster	8	0		
2004	Oster	24	1	32	1
2005	Assyriska	23	0	23	0
2006	Ventspils	28	5	28	5
2006–07	Blackpool	10	0		
2007–08	Blackpool	40	5	50	5
2008–09	QPR	31	0		
2009–10	QPR	41	3		
2010–11	QPR	42	3		
2011–12	QPR	0	0	114	6
2011–12	Reading	42	3		
2012–13	Reading	14	1		
2012–13	*Wolverhampton W*	15	0	15	0
2013–14	Reading	25	3	81	7

GRIFFIN, Shane (D)   0 0
Internationals: Republic of Ireland U19, U21.

2013–14	Reading	0	0

GUNTER, Chris (D)   238 2
H: 5 11   W: 11 02   b.Newport 21-7-89
Internationals: Wales U17, U19, U21, Full caps.

2006–07	Cardiff C	15	0		
2007–08	Cardiff C	13	0	28	0
2007–08	Tottenham H	2	0		
2008–09	Tottenham H	3	0	5	0
2008–09	Nottingham F	8	0		
2009–10	Nottingham F	44	1		
2010–11	Nottingham F	43	0		
2011–12	Nottingham F	46	1	141	2
2012–13	Reading	20	0		
2013–14	Reading	44	0	64	0

GUTHRIE, Danny (M)   183 12
H: 5 9   W: 11 06   b.Shrewsbury 18-4-87
Internationals: England U16.

2004–05	Liverpool	0	0		
2005–06	Liverpool	0	0		
2006–07	Liverpool	3	0		
2006–07	*Southampton*	10	0	10	0
2007–08	Liverpool	0	0	3	0
2007–08	*Bolton W*	25	0	25	0
2008–09	Newcastle U	24	2		
2009–10	Newcastle U	38	4		
2010–11	Newcastle U	14	0		
2011–12	Newcastle U	16	1	92	7
2012–13	Reading	21	1		
2013–14	Reading	32	4	53	5

HECTOR, Michael (D)   101 7
H: 6 4   W: 12 13   b.Newham 19-7-92

2009–10	Reading	0	0		
2010–11	Reading	0	0		
2011	*Dundalk*	11	2	11	2
2011–12	Reading	0	0		
2011–12	*Barnet*	27	2	27	2
2012–13	Reading	0	0		
2012–13	*Shrewsbury T*	8	0	8	0
2012–13	*Aldershot T*	8	1	8	1
2013–14	Reading	9	0	9	0
2013–14	*Aberdeen*	20	1	20	1

HENLY, Jonathan (M)   0 0
H: 6 3   W: 13 00   b.Reading 7-6-94
Internationals: Scotland U19.

2012–13	Reading	0	0
2013–14	Reading	0	0
2013–14	*Oxford U*	0	0

KARACAN, Jem (M)   167 11
H: 5 10   W: 11 13   b.Lewisham 21-2-89
Internationals: Turkey U17, U18, U19, U21.

2007–08	Reading	0	0		
2007–08	*Bournemouth*	13	1	13	1
2007–08	*Millwall*	7	0	7	0
2008–09	Reading	15	1		
2009–10	Reading	27	0		
2010–11	Reading	40	3		
2011–12	Reading	37	3		
2012–13	Reading	21	1		
2013–14	Reading	7	2	147	10

KELLY, Stephen (D)   227 3
H: 6 0   W: 12 04   b.Dublin 6-9-83
Internationals: Republic of Ireland U16, U20, U21, Full caps.

2000–01	Tottenham H	0	0		
2001–02	Tottenham H	0	0		
2002–03	Tottenham H	0	0		
2002–03	*Southend U*	10	0	10	0
2002–03	*QPR*	7	0	7	0
2003–04	Tottenham H	11	0		
2003–04	*Watford*	13	0	13	0
2004–05	Tottenham H	17	2		
2005–06	Tottenham H	9	0	37	2
2006–07	Birmingham C	36	0		
2007–08	Birmingham C	38	0		
2008–09	Birmingham C	5	0		
2008–09	*Stoke C*	6	0	6	0
2009–10	Birmingham C	0	0	79	0
2009–10	Fulham	8	0		
2010–11	Fulham	10	0		
2011–12	Fulham	24	0		
2012–13	Fulham	2	0	44	0
2012–13	Reading	16	0		
2013–14	Reading	15	1	31	1

KEOWN, Niall (D)   0 0

2013–14	Reading	0	0

LE FONDRE, Adam (F)   358 146
H: 5 9   W: 11 04   b.Stockport 2-12-86

2004–05	Stockport Co	20	4		
2005–06	Stockport Co	22	6		
2006–07	Stockport Co	21	7	63	17
2006–07	*Rochdale*	7	4		
2007–08	Rochdale	46	16		
2008–09	Rochdale	44	18		
2009–10	Rochdale	1	0	98	38
2009–10	Rotherham U	44	25		
2010–11	Rotherham U	45	23		
2011–12	Rotherham U	4	4	93	52
2011–12	Reading	32	12		
2012–13	Reading	34	12		
2013–14	Reading	38	15	104	39

LEIGERTWOOD, Mikele (D)   372 22
H: 6 1   W: 11 04   b.Enfield 12-11-82
Internationals: Antigua and Barbuda Full caps.

2001–02	Wimbledon	1	0		
2001–02	*Leyton Orient*	8	0	8	0
2002–03	Wimbledon	28	0		
2003–04	Wimbledon	27	2	56	2
2003–04	Crystal Palace	12	0		
2004–05	Crystal Palace	20	1		
2005–06	Crystal Palace	27	0	59	1
2006–07	Sheffield U	19	0		
2007–08	Sheffield U	2	0	21	0
2007–08	QPR	40	5		
2008–09	QPR	42	2		
2009–10	QPR	40	5		
2010–11	QPR	9	0	131	12
2010–11	*Reading*	22	1		
2011–12	Reading	41	5		
2012–13	Reading	30	1		
2013–14	Reading	4	0	97	7

LINCOLN, Daniel (G)   0 0

2013–14	Reading	0	0

LONG, Sean (D)   0 0
Internationals: Republic of Ireland U17, U19.

2013–14	Reading	0	0

McANUFF, Jobi (M)   498 48
H: 5 11   W: 11 05   b.Edmonton 9-11-81
Internationals: Jamaica Full caps.

2000–01	Wimbledon	0	0		
2001–02	Wimbledon	38	4		
2002–03	Wimbledon	31	4		
2003–04	Wimbledon	27	5	96	13
2003–04	West Ham U	12	1		
2004–05	West Ham U	1	0	13	1
2004–05	Cardiff C	43	2	43	2
2005–06	Crystal Palace	41	8		
2006–07	Crystal Palace	34	5	75	13
2007–08	Watford	39	2		
2008–09	Watford	40	3		
2009–10	Watford	3	0	82	5
2009–10	Reading	36	3		
2010–11	Reading	40	4		
2011–12	Reading	40	5		
2012–13	Reading	38	2		
2013–14	Reading	35	2	189	14

McCARTHY, Alex (G)   137 0
H: 6 4   W: 11 12   b.Guildford 3-12-89
Internationals: England U21.

2008–09	Reading	0	0		
2008–09	*Aldershot T*	4	0	4	0
2009–10	Reading	0	0		
2009–10	*Yeovil T*	44	0	44	0
2010–11	Reading	13	0		
2010–11	*Brentford*	3	0	3	0
2011–12	Reading	0	0		
2011–12	*Leeds U*	6	0	6	0
2011–12	*Ipswich T*	10	0	10	0
2012–13	Reading	13	0		
2013–14	Reading	44	0	70	0

McCLEARY, Garath (M)   184 21
H: 5 10   W: 12 06   b.Oxford 15-5-87
Internationals: Jamaica Full caps.

2007–08	Nottingham F	8	1		
2008–09	Nottingham F	39	1		
2009–10	Nottingham F	24	0		
2010–11	Nottingham F	18	2		
2011–12	Nottingham F	22	9	111	13
2011–12	Reading	0	0		
2012–13	Reading	31	3		
2013–14	Reading	42	5	73	8

MOORE, Stuart (G)   **0 0**

Season	Club				
2013–14	Reading	0	0		

MORRISON, Sean (D)   **114 10**
H: 6 4   W: 14 00   b.Plymouth 8-1-91

Season	Club				
2007–08	Swindon T	2	0		
2008–09	Swindon T	20	1		
2009–10	Swindon T	9	1		
2009–10	*Southend U*	8	0	**8**	**0**
2010–11	Swindon T	19	4	**50**	**6**
2010–11	Reading	0	0		
2010–11	*Huddersfield T*	0	0		
2011–12	Reading	0	0		
2011–12	*Huddersfield T*	19	1	**19**	**1**
2012–13	Reading	16	2		
2013–14	Reading	21	1	**37**	**3**

OBITA, Jordan (M)   **61 5**
H: 5 11   W: 11 08   b.Oxford 8-12-93
Internationals: England U18, U19, U21.

Season	Club				
2010–11	Reading	0	0		
2011–12	Reading	0	0		
2011–12	*Barnet*	5	0	**5**	**0**
2011–12	*Gillingham*	6	3	**6**	**3**
2012–13	Reading	0	0		
2012–13	*Portsmouth*	8	1	**8**	**1**
2012–13	*Oldham Ath*	8	0	**8**	**0**
2013–14	Reading	34	1	**34**	**1**

PEARCE, Alex (D)   **218 17**
H: 6 0   W: 11 10   b.Wallingford 9-11-88
Internationals: Scotland U19, U21, Full caps.

Season	Club				
2006–07	Reading	0	0		
2006–07	*Northampton T*	15	1	**15**	**1**
2007–08	Reading	0	0		
2007–08	*Bournemouth*	11	0	**11**	**0**
2007–08	*Norwich C*	11	0	**11**	**0**
2008–09	Reading	16	1		
2008–09	*Southampton*	9	2	**9**	**2**
2009–10	Reading	25	4		
2010–11	Reading	21	1		
2011–12	Reading	46	5		
2012–13	Reading	19	0		
2013–14	Reading	45	3	**172**	**14**

POGREBNYAK, Pavel (F)   **325 101**
H: 6 2   W: 14 05   b.Moscow 8-11-83
Internationals: Russia Full caps.

Season	Club				
2002	Spartak Moscow	2	0		
2003	Baltika	40	15	**40**	**15**
2004	Spartak Moscow	16	2	**18**	**2**
2004	Khimki				
2005	Shinnik	23	4	**23**	**4**
2006	Tomsk	26	13	**26**	**13**
2007	Zenit	24	11		
2008	Zenit	19	6		
2009	Zenit	15	5	**58**	**22**
2009–10	Stuttgart	28	6		
2010–11	Stuttgart	26	8		
2011–12	Stuttgart	14	1	**68**	**15**
2011–12	Fulham	12	6	**12**	**6**
2012–13	Reading	29	5		
2013–14	Reading	39	13	**68**	**18**

ROBSON-KANU, Hal (F)   **183 29**
H: 5 7   W: 11 08   b.Acton 21-5-89
Internationals: England U19, U20. Wales U21, Full caps.

Season	Club				
2007–08	Reading	0	0		
2007–08	*Southend U*	8	3		
2008–09	Reading	0	0		
2008–09	*Southend U*	14	2	**22**	**5**
2008–09	*Swindon T*	20	4	**20**	**4**
2009–10	Reading	17	0		
2010–11	Reading	27	5		
2011–12	Reading	36	4		
2012–13	Reading	25	7		
2013–14	Reading	36	4	**141**	**20**

SAMUEL, Dominic (F)   **4 0**
H: 6 0   W: 14 00   b.Southwark 1-4-94
Internationals: England U19.

Season	Club				
2011–12	Reading	0	0		
2012–13	Reading	1	0		
2012–13	*Colchester U*	2	0	**2**	**0**
2013–14	Reading	0	0		
2013–14	*Dagenham & R*	1	0	**1**	**0**

SHAUGHNESSY, Conor Glynn (M)   **0 0**

Season	Club				
2013–14	Reading	0	0		

SWEENEY, Pierce (D)   **0 0**
H: 5 10   W: 12 07   b. 11-9-94
Internationals: Republic of Ireland U17, U19, U21.

Season	Club				
2012–13	Reading	0	0		
2013–14	Reading	0	0		

TANNER, Craig (F)   **0 0**
b.Reading 27-10-94

Season	Club				
2011–12	Reading	0	0		
2012–13	Reading	0	0		
2013–14	Reading	0	0		

TAYLOR, Jake (M)   **54 4**
H: 5 10   W: 12 01   b.Ascot 1-12-91
Internationals: Wales U17, U19, U21.

Season	Club				
2010–11	Reading	1	0		
2011–12	Reading	0	0		
2011–12	*Aldershot T*	3	0	**3**	**0**
2011–12	*Exeter C*	30	3	**30**	**3**
2012–13	Reading	0	0		
2012–13	*Cheltenham T*	8	1	**8**	**1**
2012–13	*Crawley T*	4	0	**4**	**0**
2013–14	Reading	8	0	**9**	**0**

TSHIBOLA, Aaron (M)   **0 0**
H: 6 3   W: 11 01   b.Newham 2-1-95
Internationals: England U18.

Season	Club				
2011–12	Reading	0	0		
2012–13	Reading	0	0		
2013–14	Reading	0	0		

UGWU, Chigozie (F)   **28 4**
H: 6 2   W: 12 00   b.Oxford 22-4-93

Season	Club				
2011–12	Reading	0	0		
2012–13	Reading	0	0		
2012–13	*Yeovil T*	15	3	**15**	**3**
2012–13	*Plymouth Arg*	6	0	**6**	**0**
2013–14	Reading	0	0		
2013–14	*Shrewsbury T*	7	1	**7**	**1**

VASTSUK, Bogdan (F)   **0 0**
b. 4-10-95
Internationals: Estonia U16, U17, U19, U21.

Season	Club				
2013–14	Reading	0	0		

WILLIAMS, Daniel (M)   **88 4**
H: 6 0   W: 11 12   b.Karlsruhe 8-3-89
Internationals: USA Full caps.

Season	Club				
2009–10	SC Freiburg	5	0		
2010–11	SC Freiburg	7	0		
2011–12	SC Freiburg	1	0	**13**	**0**
2011–12	Hoffenheim	24	0		
2012–13	Hoffenheim	21	1	**45**	**1**
2013–14	Reading	30	3	**30**	**3**

Scholars
Cardwell, Harry James; Collins, Lewis James; Dickie, Robert; Ethelston, Marc Connor; Husin, Noor; Ismajli, Shpat; Jeffrey, Jack Len David; Jules, Zak Kennedy; Lawal, Hammed; McLennan, George; Ofori, Germaine; Owusu, Nana; Sheppard, Jake Edwin; Taylor-Crossdale, De'juane Ardell Kyle; Urbancic, Tomas Ingi; Ward, Lewis Moore; Waritay, Amadu; Watson, Tennai Rosharne; Williams, Daniel Olamide Cecil.

ROCHDALE (68)

ALLEN, Jamie (M)   **25 6**
H: 5 11   b. 29-1-95

Season	Club				
2012–13	Rochdale	0	0		
2013–14	Rochdale	25	6	**25**	**6**

BARRY-MURPHY, Brian (M)   **457 17**
H: 5 10   W: 13 01   b.Cork 27-7-78
Internationals: Republic of Ireland U21.

Season	Club				
1995–96	Cork C	13	0		
1996–97	Cork C	25	0		
1997–98	Cork C	15	1		
1998–99	Cork C	27	1	**80**	**2**
1999–2000	Preston NE	1	0		
2000–01	Preston NE	14	0		
2001–02	Preston NE	4	0		
2001–02	*Southend U*	8	1	**8**	**1**
2002–03	Preston NE	2	0	**21**	**0**
2002–03	*Hartlepool U*	7	0	**7**	**0**
2002–03	Sheffield W	17	0		
2003–04	Sheffield W	41	0	**58**	**0**
2004–05	Bury	45	6		
2005–06	Bury	40	3		
2006–07	Bury	14	0		
2007–08	Bury	31	1		
2008–09	Bury	42	2		
2009–10	Bury	46	1	**218**	**13**
2010–11	Rochdale	32	0		
2011–12	Rochdale	22	1		
2012–13	Rochdale	8	0		
2013–14	Rochdale	3	0	**65**	**1**

BENNETT, Rhys (D)   **41 0**
b.Manchester 1-9-91

Season	Club				
2011–12	Bolton W	0	0		
2011–12	*Falkirk*	19	0	**19**	**0**
2013–14	Rochdale	22	0	**22**	**0**

BUCKLEY, Kyle (M)   **0 0**
H: 1 11   W: 9 12   b.Droylsden 9-6-89

Season	Club				
2012–13	Rochdale	0	0		
2013–14	Rochdale	0	0		

BUNNEY, Joe (F)   **22 4**
b.Manchester 26-9-93

Season	Club				
2012–13	Rochdale	1	1		
2013–14	Rochdale	21	3	**22**	**4**

CAMPS, Callum (M)   **2 0**
b.Stockport 30-11-95
Internationals: Northern Ireland U18.

Season	Club				
2012–13	Rochdale	2	0		
2013–14	Rochdale	0	0	**2**	**0**

CAVANAGH, Peter (D)   **125 8**
H: 5 11   W: 11 08   b.Liverpool 14-10-81
Internationals: England C.

Season	Club				
2006–07	Accrington S	26	4		
2007–08	Accrington S	19	1		
2008–09	Accrington S	29	1	**74**	**6**
From Fleetwood T					
2012–13	Rochdale	31	1		
2013–14	Rochdale	20	1	**51**	**2**

DONE, Matt (M)   **244 10**
H: 5 10   W: 10 04   b.Oswestry 22-6-88

Season	Club				
2005–06	Wrexham	6	0		
2006–07	Wrexham	34	1		
2007–08	Wrexham	26	0	**66**	**1**
2008–09	Hereford U	36	0		
2009–10	Hereford U	20	0	**56**	**0**
2010–11	Rochdale	33	5		
2011–12	Barnsley	31	4		
2012–13	Barnsley	13	0	**44**	**4**
2012–13	*Hibernian*	7	0	**7**	**0**
2013–14	Rochdale	38	0	**71**	**5**

DONNELLY, George (F)   **147 31**
H: 6 2   W: 13 03   b.Liverpool 28-5-88
Internationals: England C.

Season	Club				
2008–09	Plymouth Arg	2	0		
2009–10	Plymouth Arg	0	0		
2009–10	*Stockport Co*	19	4		
2010–11	Plymouth Arg	0	0	**2**	**0**
2010–11	*Stockport Co*	23	8	**42**	**12**
From Fleetwood T					
2011–12	*Macclesfield T*	28	6	**28**	**6**
2011–12	Rochdale	0	0		
2012–13	Rochdale	43	8		
2013–14	Rochdale	32	5	**75**	**13**

EASTHAM, Ashley (D)   **94 2**
H: 6 3   W: 12 06   b.Preston 22-3-91

Season	Club				
2009–10	Blackpool	1	0		
2009–10	*Cheltenham T*	20	0		
2010–11	Blackpool	0	0		
2010–11	*Cheltenham T*	9	0	**29**	**0**
2010–11	*Carlisle U*	0	0		
2011–12	Blackpool	0	0		
2011–12	*Bury*	25	2		
2012–13	Blackpool	0	0	**1**	**0**
2012–13	*Fleetwood T*	1	0	**1**	**0**
2012–13	*Notts Co*	4	0	**4**	**0**
2012–13	*Bury*	19	0	**44**	**2**
2013–14	Rochdale	15	0	**15**	**0**

GRAY, Reece (F)   **13 2**
H: 5 7   W: 8 08   b.Oldham 1-9-92

Season	Club				
2009–10	Rochdale	2	1		
2010–11	Rochdale	2	1		
2011–12	Rochdale	4	1		
2012–13	Rochdale	2	0		
2013–14	Rochdale	3	0	**13**	**2**

HENDERSON, Ian (F)   **307 46**
H: 5 10   W: 11 06   b.Thetford 25-1-85
Internationals: England U18, U20.

Season	Club				
2002–03	Norwich C	20	1		

Season	Club				
2003–04	Norwich C	19	4		
2004–05	Norwich C	3	0		
2005–06	Norwich C	24	1		
2006–07	Norwich C	2	0	68	6
2006–07	Rotherham U	18	1	18	1
2007–08	Northampton T	23	0		
2008–09	Northampton T	3	0	26	0
2008–09	Luton T	19	1	19	1
2009–10	Colchester U	13	2		
2009–10	*Ankaragucu*	2	0	2	0
2010–11	Colchester U	36	10		
2011–12	Colchester U	46	9		
2012–13	Colchester U	22	3	117	24
2012–13	Rochdale	12	3		
2013–14	Rochdale	45	11	57	14

HERY, Bastien (M) 12 1
b.Brou sur Chantereine 23-3-92

Season	Club				
2012–13	Sheffield W				
2013–14	Rochdale	12	1	12	1

HOGAN, Scott (F) 33 17

Season	Club				
2009–10	Rochdale	0	0		
2013–14	Rochdale	33	17	33	17

LANCASHIRE, Oliver (D) 137 2
H: 6 1 W: 11 10 b.Basingstoke 13-12-88

Season	Club				
2006–07	Southampton	0	0		
2007–08	Southampton	0	0		
2008–09	Southampton	11	0		
2009–10	Southampton	2	0	13	0
2009–10	Grimsby T	25	1	25	1
2010–11	Walsall	29	0		
2011–12	Walsall	20	1	49	1
2012–13	Aldershot T	12	0	12	0
2013–14	Rochdale	38	0	38	0

LILLIS, Josh (G) 162 0
H: 6 0 W: 12 08 b.Derby 24-6-87

Season	Club				
2006–07	Scunthorpe U	1	0		
2007–08	Scunthorpe U	3	0		
2008–09	Scunthorpe U	5	0		
2008–09	*Notts Co*	5	0	5	0
2009–10	Scunthorpe U	8	0		
2009–10	*Grimsby T*	4	0	4	0
2009–10	*Rochdale*	1	0		
2010–11	Scunthorpe U	15	0		
2010–11	*Rochdale*	23	0		
2011–12	Scunthorpe U	6	0	38	0
2012–13	Rochdale	46	0		
2013–14	Rochdale	45	0	115	0

LOGAN, Joel (F) 5 0
b.Manchester 25-1-95

Season	Club				
2012–13	Rochdale	5	0		
2013–14	Rochdale	0	0	5	0

LUND, Matthew (M) 88 13
H: 6 0 W: 11 13 b.Manchester 21-11-90
Internationals: Northern Ireland U21.

Season	Club				
2009–10	Stoke C	0	0		
2010–11	Stoke C	0	0		
2010–11	Hereford U	2	0	2	0
2011–12	Stoke C	0	0		
2011–12	*Oldham Ath*	3	0	3	0
2012–13	Stoke C	0	0		
2012–13	*Bristol R*	3	2		
2012–13	*Bristol R*	18	2	31	4
2012–13	Southend U	12	1	12	1
2013–14	Rochdale	40	8	40	8

LYNCH, Craig (F) 9 1
H: 5 9 W: 10 01 b.Chester-le-Street 25-3-92

Season	Club				
2010–11	Sunderland	2	0		
2011–12	Sunderland	0	0		
2012–13	Sunderland	0	0		
2012–13	*Hartlepool U*	6	1	6	1
2013–14	Rochdale	1	0	1	0

O'CONNOR, Darcy (D) 1 0
b.Oldham

Season	Club				
2012–13	Rochdale	1	0		
2013–14	Rochdale	0	0	1	0

PORTER, George (F) 77 2
H: 5 10 W: 12 06 b.Sidcup 27-6-92

Season	Club				
2010–11	Leyton Orient	1	0		
2011–12	Leyton Orient	34	1	35	1
2012–13	Burnley	0	0		
2012–13	*Colchester U*	19	1	19	1
2013–14	Burnley	0	0		
2013–14	*AFC Wimbledon*	21	0	21	0
2013–14	Rochdale	2	0	2	0

RAFFERTY, Joe (D) 52 0
b. 6-10-93
Internationals: Republic of Ireland U18, U19.

Season	Club				
2012–13	Rochdale	21	0		
2013–14	Rochdale	31	0	52	0

TANSER, Scott (D) 1 0

Season	Club				
2012–13	Rochdale	1	0		
2013–14	Rochdale	0	0	1	0

THOMSON, Robbie (G) 1 0
b.Dundee 7-3-93

Season	Club				
2012–13	Celtic	0	0		
2013–14	Rochdale	1	0	1	0

VIDAL, Javan (D) 25 0
H: 5 10 W: 10 09 b.Manchester 10-5-89
Internationals: England U19, U20.

Season	Club				
2007–08	Manchester C	0	0		
2008–09	Manchester C	0	0		
2008–09	Grimsby T	3	0	3	0
2008–09	*Aberdeen*	13	0	13	0
2009–10	Manchester C	0	0		
2009–10	*Derby Co*	1	0	1	0
2010–11	Manchester C	0	0		
2010–11	*Chesterfield*	6	0	6	0
From Stockport Co					
2013–14	Rochdale	2	0	2	0

VINCENTI, Peter (F) 151 20
H: 6 2 W: 11 13 b.St Peter 7-7-86

Season	Club				
2007–08	Millwall	0	0		
2010–11	Stevenage	5	1	5	1
2010–11	Aldershot T	23	6		
2011–12	Aldershot T	42	6		
2012–13	Aldershot T	39	2	104	14
2013–14	Rochdale	42	5	42	5

Scholars
Antoine-Clarke, Shaquille Maurice; Ashley, Aaron John; Bell, Nyal Aston Nathanial; Cannon, Andrew Francis; Cowan-Thompson, Connor Richard; Hasler-Cregg, William David; Hooper, James; Horan, Jack; Martin, Connor Jay; Reid, Dominic Michael; Samuels, Abayomi Jonathan Akinwale; Sinclair, Omar Jermaine Kareem; Tuanzebe, Dimitri Gobula; Whitehall, Daniel.

ROTHERHAM U (69)

AGARD, Kieran (F) 114 34
H: 5 10 W: 10 10 b.Newham 10-10-89

Season	Club				
2006–07	Everton	0	0		
2007–08	Everton	0	0		
2008–09	Everton	0	0		
2009–10	Everton	1	0		
2010–11	Everton	0	0	1	0
2010–11	*Kilmarnock*	8	1	8	1
2010–11	*Peterborough U*	0	0		
2011–12	*Yeovil T*	29	6	29	6
2012–13	Rotherham U	30	6		
2013–14	Rotherham U	46	21	76	27

AINSWORTH, Lionel (F) 200 29
H: 5 9 W: 9 10 b.Nottingham 1-10-87
Internationals: England U16, U17, U18, U19.

Season	Club				
2005–06	Derby Co	2	0		
2006–07	Derby Co	0	0	2	0
2006–07	Bournemouth	7	0	7	0
2006–07	Wycombe W	7	0	7	0
2007–08	Hereford U	15	4		
2007–08	Watford	8	0		
2008–09	Watford	7	0	15	0
2008–09	*Hereford U*	7	3	22	7
2008–09	Huddersfield T	14	0		
2009–10	Huddersfield T	11	0		
2009–10	*Brentford*	9	0	9	0
2010–11	Shrewsbury T	33	9		
2010–11	*Huddersfield T*	0	0	25	0
2011–12	Shrewsbury T	21	2	54	11
2011–12	*Burton Alb*	7	0	7	0
2012–13	Rotherham U	16	0		
2012–13	*Aldershot T*	7	0	7	0
2013–14	Rotherham U	7	0	7	0
2013–14	Motherwell	29	11	29	11

ARNASON, Kari (M) 313 14
H: 6 3 W: 13 06 b.Reykjavik 13-10-82
Internationals: Iceland Full caps.

Season	Club				
2001	Vikingur	5	2		
2002	Vikingur	5	1		
2003	Vikingur	16	0		
2004	Vikingur	15	0	41	3
2005	Djurgarden	21	0		
2006	Djurgarden	14	0	35	0
2006–07	Aarhus	14	2		
2007–08	Aarhus	25	0		
2008–09	Aarhus	12	1	51	3
2008–09	*Esbjerg*	8	0	8	0
2009–10	Plymouth Arg	32	2		
2010–11	Plymouth Arg	40	1	72	3
2011–12	Aberdeen	33	3	33	3
2012–13	Rotherham U	33	2		
2013–14	Rotherham U	40	0	73	2

BRADLEY, Mark (D) 187 9
H: 6 0 W: 11 05 b.Dudley 14-1-88
Internationals: Wales Youth, U21, Full caps.

Season	Club				
2004–05	Walsall	1	0		
2005–06	Walsall	3	0		
2006–07	Walsall	1	0		
2007–08	Walsall	35	3		
2008–09	Walsall	28	2		
2009–10	Walsall	28	0	96	5
2010–11	Rotherham U	21	0		
2011–12	Rotherham U	21	1		
2012–13	Rotherham U	27	1		
2013–14	Rotherham U	22	2	91	4

BRINDLEY, Richard (D) 28 0
H: 5 10 W: 11 09 b.Coventry 30-11-87

Season	Club				
2012–13	Chesterfield	12	0	12	0
2013–14	Rotherham U	16	0	16	0

COLLIN, Adam (G) 167 0
H: 6 2 W: 12 00 b.Penrith 9-12-84

Season	Club				
2003–04	Newcastle U	0	0		
2003–04	*Oldham Ath*	0	0		
From Workington					
2009–10	Carlisle U	29	0		
2010–11	Carlisle U	46	0		
2011–12	Carlisle U	46	0		
2012–13	Carlisle U	12	0	133	0
2013–14	Rotherham U	34	0	34	0

DAVIS, Claude (D) 270 8
H: 6 3 W: 14 04 b.Kingston, Jamaica 6-3-79
Internationals: Jamaica Full caps.

Season	Club				
2003–04	Preston NE	22	1		
2004–05	Preston NE	32	0		
2005–06	Preston NE	40	3	94	4
2006–07	Sheffield U	21	0	21	0
2007–08	Derby Co	19	0		
2008–09	Derby Co	8	0		
2009–10	Derby Co	0	0	27	0
2009–10	Crystal Palace	21	0		
2010–11	Crystal Palace	24	0		
2011–12	Crystal Palace	0	0	52	0
2011–12	Crawley T	29	3		
2012–13	Crawley T	16	0	45	3
2012–13	*Rotherham U*	15	0		
2013–14	Rotherham U	16	1	31	1

FRECKLINGTON, Lee (M) 287 45
H: 5 8 W: 11 00 b.Lincoln 8-9-85
Internationals: Republic of Ireland B.

Season	Club				
2003–04	Lincoln C	0	0		
2004–05	Lincoln C	3	0		
2005–06	Lincoln C	18	2		
2006–07	Lincoln C	42	8		
2007–08	Lincoln C	34	4		
2008–09	Lincoln C	27	7	124	21
2008–09	Peterborough U	7	0		
2009–10	Peterborough U	35	2		
2010–11	Peterborough U	9	1		
2011–12	Peterborough U	37	5		
2012–13	Peterborough U	5	0	93	8
2012–13	*Rotherham U*	31	6		
2013–14	Rotherham U	39	10	70	16

HYLTON, Danny (F) 179 35
H: 6 0 W: 11 13 b.Camden 25-2-89

Season	Club				
2008–09	Aldershot T	29	5		
2009–10	Aldershot T	21	3		
2010–11	Aldershot T	33	5		
2011–12	Aldershot T	44	13		
2012–13	Aldershot T	27	4	154	30
2013–14	Rotherham U	1	0	1	0
2013–14	*Bury*	7	2	7	2
2013–14	*AFC Wimbledon*	17	3	17	3

MILSOM, Robert (M) — 107 3
H: 5 10 W: 11 04 b.Redhill 2-1-87

Season	Club				
2005–06	Fulham	0	0		
2006–07	Fulham	0	0		
2007–08	Fulham	0	0		
2007–08	Brentford	6	0	6	0
2008–09	Fulham	1	0		
2008–09	Southend U	6	0	6	0
2009–10	Fulham	0	0		
2010	TPS Turku	14	0	14	0
2010–11	Fulham	0	0	1	0
2010–11	Aberdeen	18	1		
2011–12	Aberdeen	22	1		
2012–13	Aberdeen	13	0	53	2
2013–14	Rotherham U	27	1	27	1

MORGAN, Craig (D) — 327 9
H: 6 0 W: 11 04 b.Flint 18-6-85
Internationals: Wales U17, U19, U21, Full caps.

Season	Club				
2001–02	Wrexham	2	0		
2002–03	Wrexham	6	1		
2003–04	Wrexham	18	0		
2004–05	Wrexham	26	0		
2005–06	Milton Keynes D	40	0		
2006–07	Milton Keynes D	3	0	43	0
2006–07	Wrexham	1	0	53	1
2006–07	Peterborough U	23	1		
2007–08	Peterborough U	41	2		
2008–09	Peterborough U	27	0		
2009–10	Peterborough U	34	1	125	4
2010–11	Preston NE	31	2		
2011–12	Preston NE	19	1		
2012–13	Preston NE	0	0	50	3
2012–13	Rotherham U	21	1		
2013–14	Rotherham U	35	0	56	1

NOBLE, David (M) — 291 18
H: 6 0 W: 12 04 b.Hitchin 2-2-82
Internationals: England U20. Scotland U21, B.

Season	Club				
2000–01	Arsenal	0	0		
2001–02	Arsenal	0	0		
2001–02	Watford	15	1	15	1
2002–03	Arsenal	0	0		
2002–03	West Ham U	0	0		
2003–04	West Ham U	3	0	3	0
2003–04	Boston U	14	2		
2004–05	Boston U	32	3		
2005–06	Boston U	11	0	57	5
2005–06	Bristol C	24	1		
2006–07	Bristol C	26	3		
2007–08	Bristol C	26	2		
2008–09	Bristol C	9	1	85	7
2008–09	Yeovil T	2	0	2	0
2009–10	Exeter C	0	0		
2010–11	Exeter C	36	0		
2011–12	Exeter C	42	2	78	2
2012–13	Rotherham U	22	3		
2013–14	Rotherham U	0	0	22	3
2013–14	Cheltenham T	29	0	29	0

O'CONNOR, Michael (M) — 248 23
H: 6 1 W: 11 08 b.Belfast 6-10-87
Internationals: Northern Ireland U21, B, Full caps.

Season	Club				
2005–06	Crewe Alex	2	0		
2006–07	Crewe Alex	29	0		
2007–08	Crewe Alex	23	0		
2008–09	Crewe Alex	23	3	77	3
2008–09	Lincoln C	10	1	10	1
2009–10	Scunthorpe U	32	2		
2010–11	Scunthorpe U	32	8		
2011–12	Scunthorpe U	33	1	97	11
2012–13	Rotherham U	35	6		
2013–14	Rotherham U	29	2	64	8

ODEJAYI, Kayode (F) — 421 65
H: 6 2 W: 12 02 b.Ibadon 21-2-82
Internationals: Nigeria Full caps.

Season	Club				
1999–2000	Bristol C	3	0		
2000–01	Bristol C	3	0		
2001–02	Bristol C	0	0		
2002–03	Bristol C	0	0	6	0
2003–04	Cheltenham T	30	5		
2004–05	Cheltenham T	32	1		
2005–06	Cheltenham T	41	11		
2006–07	Cheltenham T	45	13	148	30
2007–08	Barnsley	39	3		
2008–09	Barnsley	28	1		
2008–09	Scunthorpe U	6	1	6	1
2009–10	Barnsley	5	0	72	4
2009–10	Colchester U	28	9		
2010–11	Colchester U	44	4		
2011–12	Colchester U	43	4	115	17
2012–13	Rotherham U	42	5		
2013–14	Rotherham U	0	0	42	5
2013–14	Accrington S	32	8	32	8

PRINGLE, Ben (M) — 132 16
H: 5 8 W: 11 10 b.Whitley Bay 25-7-88

Season	Club				
2009–10	Derby Co	5	0		
2010–11	Derby Co	15	0	20	0
2010–11	Torquay U	5	0	5	0
2011–12	Rotherham U	21	4		
2012–13	Rotherham U	41	7		
2013–14	Rotherham U	45	5	107	16

REVELL, Alex (F) — 345 67
H: 6 3 W: 13 00 b.Cambridge 7-7-83

Season	Club				
2000–01	Cambridge U	4	0		
2001–02	Cambridge U	24	2		
2002–03	Cambridge U	9	0		
2003–04	Cambridge U	20	3	57	5
From Braintree T.					
2006–07	Brighton & HA	38	7		
2007–08	Brighton & HA	21	6	59	13
2007–08	Southend U	8	0		
2008–09	Southend U	23	4		
2009–10	Southend U	3	0	34	4
2009–10	Swindon T	10	2	10	2
2009–10	Wycombe W	6	6	15	6
2010–11	Leyton Orient	39	13		
2011–12	Leyton Orient	5	0	44	13
2011–12	Rotherham U	40	10		
2012–13	Rotherham U	41	6		
2013–14	Rotherham U	45	8	126	24

ROSE, Mitchell (M) — 5 0
H: 5 9 W: 12 03 b.4-7-94

Season	Club				
2012–13	Rotherham U	5	0		
2013–14	Rotherham U	0	0	5	0

ROWE, Daniel (D) — 7 0
b.Middlesbrough 24-10-95

Season	Club				
2012–13	Rotherham U	0	0		
2013–14	Rotherham U	0	0		
2013–14	Wycombe W	7	0	7	0

SHEARER, Scott (G) — 286 0
H: 6 3 W: 12 00 b.Glasgow 15-2-81
Internationals: Scotland B.

Season	Club				
2000–01	Albion R	3	0		
2001–02	Albion R	10	0		
2002–03	Albion R	36	0	49	0
2003–04	Coventry C	30	0		
2004–05	Coventry C	8	0	38	0
2004–05	Rushden & D	13	0	13	0
2005–06	Bristol R	45	0		
2006–07	Bristol R	2	0	47	0
2006–07	Shrewsbury T	20	0	20	0
2007–08	Wycombe W	5	0		
2008–09	Wycombe W	29	0		
2009–10	Wycombe W	29	0		
2010–11	Wycombe W	0	0	63	0
2011–12	Crawley T	25	0	25	0
2012–13	Rotherham U	19	0		
2013–14	Rotherham U	12	0	31	0

SKARZ, Joe (D) — 274 7
H: 5 10 W: 11 04 b.Huddersfield 13-7-89

Season	Club				
2006–07	Huddersfield T	17	0		
2007–08	Huddersfield T	27	0		
2008–09	Huddersfield T	9	1		
2008–09	Hartlepool U	7	0	7	0
2009–10	Huddersfield T	15	0	68	1
2009–10	Shrewsbury T	20	0	20	0
2010–11	Bury	46	0		
2011–12	Bury	45	1		
2012–13	Bury	39	2	130	4
2012–13	Rotherham U	8	0		
2013–14	Rotherham U	41	2	49	2

THOMAS, Wesley (F) — 166 47
H: 5 10 W: 11 00 b.Barking 23-1-87

Season	Club				
2008–09	Dagenham & R	5	0		
2009–10	Dagenham & R	23	3	28	3
2010–11	Cheltenham T	41	18	41	18
2011–12	Crawley T	6	1	6	1
2011–12	Bournemouth	36	11		
2012–13	Bournemouth	0	0		
2012–13	Portsmouth	6	3	6	3
2012–13	Blackpool	9	3	9	3
2012–13	Birmingham C	11	3	11	3
2013–14	Bournemouth	10	0	52	11
2013–14	Rotherham U	13	5	13	5

THOMPSON, Tony (G) — 0 0
b.Liverpool 4-11-94

Season	Club		
2012–13	Rotherham U	0	0
2013–14	Rotherham U	0	0

TIDSER, Michael (M) — 26 0
H: 6 0 W: 11 13 b.Glasgow 15-1-90
Internationals: Scotland U18, U19.

Season	Club				
2013–14	Rotherham U	10	0	10	0
2013–14	Ross Co	16	0	16	0

WALKER, Nicky (D) — 2 0
b.Rotherham 8-9-94

Season	Club				
2012–13	Rotherham U	2	0		
2013–14	Rotherham U	0	0	2	0

WORRALL, David (M) — 197 13
H: 6 0 W: 11 03 b.Manchester 12-6-90

Season	Club				
2006–07	Bury	1	0		
2007–08	Bury	0	0		
2007–08	WBA	0	0		
2008–09	Accrington S	4	0	4	0
2008–09	Shrewsbury T	9	0	9	0
2009–10	WBA	0	0		
2009–10	Bury	40	4		
2010–11	Bury	40	2		
2011–12	Bury	41	3		
2012–13	Bury	41	2	163	11
2013–14	Rotherham U	3	1	3	1
2013–14	Oldham Ath	18	1	18	1

Scholars
Bell, Connor Harry James; Bevins, Ayrton Niall; Bryan, Charlie; Cadman, James; Fenton, Jake; Gibson, Luke; Hallatt, Max; Johnson, Adam; Johnson, Connor Nicholas; Lucas, Reece; Norfolk, Andrew Brian; Warren, Mason Rhys; Watson, Alistair Clark; Wigley, Harley; Wiles, Alexander Peter; Williamson, Michael; Yates, Jerry Arron.

SCUNTHORPE U (70)

ADELAKUN, Hakeeb (F) — 30 2
b. 11-6-96

Season	Club				
2012–13	Scunthorpe U	2	0		
2013–14	Scunthorpe U	28	2	30	2

BOYCE, Andrew (D) — 2 0
b.Doncaster

Season	Club				
2013–14	Scunthorpe U	2	0	2	0

BURTON, Deon (F) — 587 140
H: 5 10 W: 11 08 b.Ashford 25-10-76
Internationals: Jamaica Full caps.

Season	Club				
1993–94	Portsmouth	2	0		
1994–95	Portsmouth	7	2		
1995–96	Portsmouth	32	7		
1996–97	Portsmouth	21	1		
1996–97	Cardiff C	5	2	5	2
1997–98	Derby Co	29	3		
1998–99	Derby Co	21	9		
1998–99	Barnsley	3	0	3	0
1999–2000	Derby Co	19	4		
2000–01	Derby Co	32	5		
2001–02	Derby Co	17	1		
2001–02	Stoke C	12	2	12	2
2002–03	Derby Co	7	3	125	25
2002–03	Portsmouth	15	4		
2003–04	Portsmouth	1	0	78	14
2003–04	Walsall	3	0	3	0
2003–04	Swindon T	4	1	4	1
2004–05	Brentford	40	10	40	10
2005–06	Rotherham U	24	12	24	12
2005–06	Sheffield W	17	3		
2006–07	Sheffield W	42	12		
2007–08	Sheffield W	40	7		
2008–09	Sheffield W	17	1	116	23
2008–09	Charlton Ath	20	5		
2009–10	Charlton Ath	39	13	59	18
2010–11	Gabala	28	9		
2011–12	Gabala	21	6	49	15
2012–13	Gillingham	40	12	40	12
2013–14	Scunthorpe U	29	6	29	6

CANAVAN, Niall (D) — 115 12
H: 6 3 W: 12 00 b.Guiseley 11-4-91
Internationals: Republic of Ireland U21.

Season	Club		
2009–10	Scunthorpe U	7	1
2010–11	Scunthorpe U	8	0

Season	Club	Apps	Gls	Tot A	Tot G
2010–11	Shrewsbury T	3	0	3	0
2011–12	Scunthorpe U	12	1		
2012–13	Scunthorpe U	40	6		
2013–14	Scunthorpe U	45	4	112	12

COLLINS, Michael (M) 261 21
H: 6 0 W: 11 00 b.Halifax 30-4-86
Internationals: Republic of Ireland U18, U19, U21.

Season	Club	Apps	Gls	Tot A	Tot G
2004–05	Huddersfield T	8	0		
2005–06	Huddersfield T	17	1		
2006–07	Huddersfield T	43	4		
2007–08	Huddersfield T	41	2		
2008–09	Huddersfield T	36	9		
2009–10	Huddersfield T	28	3	173	19
2010–11	Scunthorpe U	32	1		
2011–12	Scunthorpe U	1	0		
2012–13	Scunthorpe U	29	1		
2013–14	Scunthorpe U	17	0	79	2
2013–14	*AFC Wimbledon*	9	0	9	0

DAWSON, Andy (D) 506 16
H: 5 9 W: 11 02 b.Leyburn 20-10-78

Season	Club	Apps	Gls	Tot A	Tot G
1995–96	Nottingham F	0	0		
1996–97	Nottingham F	0	0		
1997–98	Nottingham F	0	0		
1998–99	Nottingham F	0	0		
1998–99	Scunthorpe U	24	0		
1999–2000	Scunthorpe U	43	2		
2000–01	Scunthorpe U	41	4		
2001–02	Scunthorpe U	44	0		
2002–03	Scunthorpe U	43	2		
2003–04	Hull C	33	3		
2004–05	Hull C	34	0		
2005–06	Hull C	18	0		
2006–07	Hull C	38	2		
2007–08	Hull C	29	1		
2008–09	Hull C	25	1		
2009–10	Hull C	35	1		
2010–11	Hull C	45	0		
2011–12	Hull C	32	0		
2012–13	Hull C	4	0	293	8
2013–14	Scunthorpe U	18	0	213	8

ESAJAS, Etienne (F) 120 10
H: 5 7 W: 10 03 b.Amsterdam 4-11-84

Season	Club	Apps	Gls	Tot A	Tot G
2005–06	Vitesse	11	1		
2006–07	Vitesse	21	2	32	3
2007–08	Sheffield W	18	0		
2008–09	Sheffield W	22	3		
2009–10	Sheffield W	20	2	60	5
2010–11	Helmond Sp	9	0	9	0
2011–12	Swindon T	6	0	6	0
2013–14	Scunthorpe U	13	2	13	2

GODDEN, Matthew (F) 18 0
H: 6 1 W: 12 03 b.Canterbury 29-7-91

Season	Club	Apps	Gls	Tot A	Tot G
2009–10	Scunthorpe U	0	0		
2010–11	Scunthorpe U	5	0		
2011–12	Scunthorpe U	1	0		
2012–13	Scunthorpe U	8	0		
2013–14	Scunthorpe U	4	0	18	0

HAWKRIDGE, Terry (M) 45 1

Season	Club	Apps	Gls	Tot A	Tot G
2013–14	Scunthorpe U	45	1	45	1

HAYES, Paul (F) 418 95
H: 6 0 W: 12 12 b.Dagenham 20-9-83

Season	Club	Apps	Gls	Tot A	Tot G
2002–03	Scunthorpe U	18	8		
2003–04	Scunthorpe U	35	2		
2004–05	Scunthorpe U	46	18		
2005–06	Barnsley	45	6		
2006–07	Barnsley	30	5		
2006–07	*Huddersfield T*	4	1	4	1
2007–08	Scunthorpe U	40	8		
2008–09	Scunthorpe U	44	17		
2009–10	Scunthorpe U	45	9		
2010–11	Preston NE	23	2	23	2
2010–11	*Barnsley*	7	0	82	11
2011–12	Charlton Ath	19	3	19	3
2011–12	*Wycombe W*	6	6	6	6
2012–13	Brentford	23	4		
2012–13	*Crawley T*	11	2	11	2
2013–14	Brentford	0	0	23	4
2013–14	*Plymouth Arg*	6	0	6	0
2013–14	Scunthorpe U	16	4	244	66

HOWE, Callum (D)
H: 6 0 W: 11 07 b.Doncaster 9-4-94

Season	Club	Apps	Gls
2012–13	Scunthorpe U	0	0
2013–14	Scunthorpe U	0	0

IWELUMO, Chris (F) 484 106
H: 6 3 W: 15 03 b.Coatbridge 1-8-78
Internationals: Scotland B, Full caps.

Season	Club	Apps	Gls	Tot A	Tot G
1996–97	St Mirren	14	0		
1997–98	St Mirren	12	0	26	0
1998–99	Aarhus Fremad	27	4	27	4
1999–2000	Stoke C	3	0		
2000–01	Stoke C	2	1		
2000–01	York C	12	2	12	2
2000–01	*Cheltenham T*	4	1	4	1
2001–02	Stoke C	38	10		
2002–03	Stoke C	32	5		
2003–04	Stoke C	9	0	84	16
2003–04	Brighton & HA	4	4	10	4
2004–05	Aachen	9	0	9	0
2005–06	Colchester U	46	17		
2006–07	Colchester U	46	18	92	35
2007–08	Charlton Ath	46	10	46	10
2008–09	Wolverhampton W	31	14		
2009–10	Wolverhampton W	15	0	46	14
2009–10	*Bristol C*	7	2	7	2
2010–11	Burnley	45	11	45	11
2011–12	Watford	39	4		
2012–13	Watford	7	0	46	4
2012–13	*Notts Co*	5	0	5	0
2012–13	*Oldham Ath*	7	1	7	1
2013–14	Scunthorpe U	12	2	12	2
2013–14	St Johnstone	6	0	6	0

MADDEN, Patrick (F) 164 49
H: 6 0 W: 11 13 b.Dublin 4-3-90
Internationals: Republic of Ireland U19, U21, U23, Full caps.

Season	Club	Apps	Gls	Tot A	Tot G
2008	Bohemians	18	4		
2009	Bohemians	2	0		
2009	Shelbourne	13	6	13	6
2010	Bohemians	34	10	54	14
2010–11	Carlisle U	13	0		
2011–12	Carlisle U	18	1		
2012–13	Carlisle U	1	1	32	2
2012–13	Yeovil T	35	22		
2013–14	Yeovil T	9	0	44	22
2013–14	Scunthorpe U	21	5	21	5

McALLISTER, Sean (M) 151 5
H: 5 8 W: 10 07 b.Bolton 15-8-87

Season	Club	Apps	Gls	Tot A	Tot G
2005–06	Sheffield W	2	0		
2006–07	Sheffield W	6	1		
2007–08	Sheffield W	8	0		
2007–08	*Mansfield T*	7	0	7	0
2007–08	Bury	0	0		
2008–09	Sheffield W	40	3		
2009–10	Sheffield W	12	0	68	4
2010–11	Shrewsbury T	18	0		
2011–12	Shrewsbury T	17	1	35	1
2012–13	Port Vale	2	0	2	0
2013–14	Scunthorpe U	39	0	39	0

McSHEFFREY, Gary (F) 394 90
H: 5 8 W: 10 06 b.Coventry 13-8-82
Internationals: England U18, U20.

Season	Club	Apps	Gls	Tot A	Tot G
1998–99	Coventry C	1	0		
1999–2000	Coventry C	3	0		
2000–01	Coventry C	0	0		
2001–02	*Stockport Co*	5	1	5	1
2001–02	Coventry C	8	1		
2002–03	Coventry C	29	4		
2003–04	Coventry C	19	11		
2003–04	*Luton T*	18	9		
2004–05	Coventry C	37	12		
2004–05	*Luton T*	5	1	23	10
2005–06	Coventry C	43	15		
2006–07	Coventry C	3	1		
2006–07	Birmingham C	40	13		
2007–08	Birmingham C	32	3		
2008–09	Birmingham C	6	0		
2008–09	*Nottingham F*	4	0	4	0
2009–10	Birmingham C	5	0	83	16
2009–10	*Leeds U*	10	1	10	1
2010–11	Coventry C	33	8		
2011–12	Coventry C	39	8		
2012–13	Coventry C	32	1		
2013–14	Coventry C	0	0	247	61
2013–14	Chesterfield	9	1	9	1
2013–14	Scunthorpe U	13	0	13	0

MIRFIN, David (D) 352 16
H: 6 3 W: 13 00 b.Sheffield 18-4-85

Season	Club	Apps	Gls	Tot A	Tot G
2002–03	Huddersfield T	1	0		
2003–04	Huddersfield T	21	2		
2004–05	Huddersfield T	41	4		
2005–06	Huddersfield T	31	1		
2006–07	Huddersfield T	38	1		
2007–08	Huddersfield T	29	1	161	9
2008–09	Scunthorpe U	33	0		
2009–10	Scunthorpe U	37	1		
2010–11	Scunthorpe U	23	3		
2011–12	Watford	4	0	4	0
2011–12	*Scunthorpe U*	19	1		
2012–13	Scunthorpe U	30	0		
2013–14	Scunthorpe U	45	2	187	7

NOLAN, Eddie (D) 185 2
H: 6 0 W: 13 05 b.Waterford 5-8-88
Internationals: Republic of Ireland U21, B, Full caps.

Season	Club	Apps	Gls	Tot A	Tot G
2005–06	Blackburn R	0	0		
2006–07	Blackburn R	0	0		
2006–07	*Stockport Co*	4	0	4	0
2007–08	Blackburn R	0	0		
2007–08	*Hartlepool U*	11	0	11	0
2008–09	Blackburn R	0	0		
2008–09	Preston NE	21	0		
2009–10	Preston NE	19	0		
2009–10	*Sheffield W*	14	1	14	1
2010–11	Preston NE	0	0	40	0
2010–11	Scunthorpe U	35	0		
2011–12	Scunthorpe U	30	1		
2012–13	Scunthorpe U	12	0		
2013–14	Scunthorpe U	39	0	116	1

RIBEIRO, Christian (D) 87 2
H: 5 11 W: 12 02 b.Neath 14-12-89
Internationals: Wales U17, U19, U21, Full caps.

Season	Club	Apps	Gls	Tot A	Tot G
2006–07	Bristol C	0	0		
2007–08	Bristol C	0	0		
2008–09	Bristol C	0	0		
2009–10	Bristol C	5	0		
2009–10	*Stockport Co*	7	0	7	0
2009–10	*Colchester U*	2	0	2	0
2010–11	Bristol C	9	0		
2011–12	Bristol C	0	0	14	0
2011–12	*Carlisle U*	5	0	5	0
2011–12	*Scunthorpe U*	10	0		
2012–13	Scunthorpe U	28	2		
2013–14	Scunthorpe U	21	0	59	2

SEVERN, James (G) 2 0
H: 6 4 W: 14 11 b.Nottingham 10-10-91
Internationals: England U17, U19, U20.

Season	Club	Apps	Gls	Tot A	Tot G
2010–11	Derby Co	1	0		
2011–12	Derby Co	0	0	1	0
2012–13	Scunthorpe U	1	0		
2013–14	Scunthorpe U	0	0	1	0

SLOCOMBE, Sam (G) 106 0
H: 6 0 W: 11 11 b.Scunthorpe 5-6-88

Season	Club	Apps	Gls	Tot A	Tot G
2008–09	Scunthorpe U	0	0		
2009–10	Scunthorpe U	1	0		
2010–11	Scunthorpe U	2	0		
2011–12	Scunthorpe U	28	0		
2012–13	Scunthorpe U	29	0		
2013–14	Scunthorpe U	46	0	106	0

SPARROW, Matt (M) 426 49
H: 5 11 W: 10 06 b.Wembley 3-10-81

Season	Club	Apps	Gls	Tot A	Tot G
1999–2000	Scunthorpe U	11	0		
2000–01	Scunthorpe U	11	4		
2001–02	Scunthorpe U	24	1		
2002–03	Scunthorpe U	42	9		
2003–04	Scunthorpe U	38	3		
2004–05	Scunthorpe U	44	5		
2005–06	Scunthorpe U	39	5		
2006–07	Scunthorpe U	29	4		
2007–08	Scunthorpe U	32	1		
2008–09	Scunthorpe U	36	4		
2009–10	Scunthorpe U	30	1		
2010–11	Brighton & HA	29	4		
2011–12	Brighton & HA	18	2	47	6
2012–13	Crawley T	17	3	17	3
2013–14	Scunthorpe U	26	3	362	40

SYERS, Dave (M) 126 23
H: 5 11 W: 11 07 b.Leeds 30-11-87

Season	Club	Apps	Gls	Tot A	Tot G
2010–11	Bradford C	37	8		
2011–12	Bradford C	18	2	55	10
2012–13	Doncaster R	32	3		
2013–14	Doncaster R	2	0	34	3
2013–14	Scunthorpe U	37	10	37	10

WATERFALL, Luke (D) 9 1
H: 6 2 W: 13 02 b.Sheffield 30-7-90

Season	Club	Apps	Gls
2008–09	Tranmere R	0	0

From Ilkeston, Gainsborough T

2013–14	Scunthorpe U	9	1	**9 1**

WELSH, Andy (M) **310 14**
H: 5 8 W: 10 03 b.Manchester 24-11-83
Internationals: Scotland U19.

2001–02	Stockport Co	15	0	
2002–03	Stockport Co	13	2	
2002–03	*Macclesfield T*	6	2	**6 2**
2003–04	Stockport Co	34	1	
2004–05	Stockport Co	13	0	**75 3**
2004–05	Sunderland	7	1	
2005–06	Sunderland	14	0	
2005–06	*Leicester C*	10	1	
2006–07	Sunderland	0	0	**21 1**
2006–07	*Leicester C*	7	0	**17 1**
2007	Toronto Lynx	20	1	**20 1**
2007–08	Blackpool	21	0	
2008–09	Blackpool	0	0	**21 0**
2008–09	Yeovil T	37	0	
2009–10	Yeovil T	42	2	
2010–11	Yeovil T	34	4	**113 6**
2011–12	Carlisle U	21	0	
2012–13	Carlisle U	12	0	**33 0**
2013–14	Scunthorpe U	4	0	**4 0**

WILLIAMS, Marcus (D) **242 0**
H: 5 8 W: 10 07 b.Doncaster 8-4-86

2003–04	Scunthorpe U	1	0	
2004–05	Scunthorpe U	4	0	
2005–06	Scunthorpe U	29	0	
2006–07	Scunthorpe U	35	0	
2007–08	Scunthorpe U	34	0	
2008–09	Scunthorpe U	26	0	
2009–10	Scunthorpe U	37	0	
2010–11	Reading	3	0	
2010–11	*Peterborough U*	3	0	**3 0**
2010–11	*Scunthorpe U*	5	0	
2011–12	Reading	0	0	**3 0**
2011–12	Sheffield U	19	0	
2012–13	Sheffield U	18	0	
2013–14	Scunthorpe U	0	0	**39 0**
2013–14	Scunthorpe U	26	0	**197 0**

WINNALL, Sam (F) **78 32**
H: 5 9 W: 11 04 b.Wolverhampton 19-1-91

2009–10	Wolverhampton W	0	0	
2010–11	Wolverhampton W	0	0	
2010–11	*Burton Alb*	19	7	**19 7**
2011–12	Wolverhampton W	0	0	
2011–12	*Hereford U*	8	2	**8 2**
2011–12	*Inverness CT*	2	0	**2 0**
2012–13	Wolverhampton W	0	0	
2012–13	*Shrewsbury T*	4	0	**4 0**
2013–14	Scunthorpe U	45	23	**45 23**

WOOTTON, Jamie (F) **2 0**

2012–13	Scunthorpe U	1	0	
2013–14	Scunthorpe U	1	0	**2 0**

Scholars
Bateson, Curtis Devan; Beresford, Billy Jack; Cowling, Zac Christopher; Hare, Taron Jay; Hawley, Ryan Joseph; Hood, Jacob Sebastian; Mawson, Jack Lewis; Mosanya, Reece Olusola James Adekunle; Oliver-Stothard, Emilio Austin; Purdue, Connor; Smythe, Connor Elliott; Sutton, Jack Levi; Weaver, Patrick Anthony; Wooton, Kyle Leon.

SHEFFIELD U (71)

BAXTER, Jose (F) **99 24**
H: 5 10 W: 11 07 b.Bootle 7-2-92
Internationals: England U16, U17.

2008–09	Everton	3	0	
2009–10	Everton	2	0	
2010–11	Everton	1	0	
2011–12	Everton	0	0	
2011–12	*Tranmere R*	14	3	**14 3**
2012–13	Everton	0	0	**7 0**
2012–13	Crystal Palace	0	0	
2012–13	Oldham Ath	39	13	
2013–14	Oldham Ath	4	2	**43 15**
2013–14	Sheffield U	35	6	**35 6**

BRANDY, Febian (F) **132 19**
H: 5 6 W: 9 13 b.Manchester 4-2-89
Internationals: England U16, U17, U18, U19, U20.

2006–07	Manchester U	0	0	

2007–08	Manchester U	0	0	
2007–08	*Swansea C*	19	3	
2008–09	Manchester U	0	0	
2008–09	*Swansea C*	14	0	**33 3**
2008–09	*Hereford U*	15	4	**15 4**
2009–10	Manchester U	0	0	
2009–10	*Gillingham*	7	1	**7 1**
2010–11	Notts Co	9	0	**9 0**
2012–13	Walsall	34	7	
2013–14	Sheffield U	14	0	**14 0**
2013–14	*Walsall*	20	4	**54 11**

COLLINS, Neill (D) **411 22**
H: 6 3 W: 12 07 b.Irvine 2-9-83
Internationals: Scotland U21, B.

2000–01	Queen's Park	4	0	
2001–02	Queen's Park	28	0	**32 0**
2002–03	Dumbarton	33	2	
2003–04	Dumbarton	30	2	**63 4**
2004–05	Sunderland	11	0	
2005–06	Sunderland	0	0	
2005–06	*Hartlepool U*	22	0	**22 0**
2005–06	*Sheffield C*	2	0	
2006–07	Sunderland	7	1	**18 1**
2006–07	Wolverhampton W	22	2	
2007–08	Wolverhampton W	39	3	
2008–09	Wolverhampton W	23	4	
2009–10	Wolverhampton W	0	0	**84 9**
2009–10	Preston NE	21	1	**21 1**
2009–10	*Leeds U*	9	0	
2010–11	Leeds U	21	0	**30 0**
2010–11	Sheffield U	14	0	
2011–12	Sheffield U	42	2	
2012–13	Sheffield U	39	3	
2013–14	Sheffield U	44	2	**141 7**

COYNE, Danny (G) **441 0**
H: 6 0 W: 13 00 b.Prestatyn 27-8-73
Internationals: Wales U21, B, Full caps.

1991–92	Tranmere R	0	0	
1992–93	Tranmere R	1	0	
1993–94	Tranmere R	5	0	
1994–95	Tranmere R	5	0	
1995–96	Tranmere R	46	0	
1996–97	Tranmere R	21	0	
1997–98	Tranmere R	16	0	
1998–99	Tranmere R	17	0	
1999–2000	Grimsby T	44	0	
2000–01	Grimsby T	46	0	
2001–02	Grimsby T	45	0	
2002–03	Grimsby T	46	0	**181 0**
2003–04	Leicester C	4	0	
2004–05	Burnley	20	0	
2005–06	Burnley	8	0	
2006–07	Burnley	12	0	**40 0**
2007–08	Tranmere R	41	0	
2008–09	Tranmere R	39	0	**191 0**
2009–10	Middlesbrough	23	0	
2010–11	Middlesbrough	1	0	
2011–12	Middlesbrough	1	0	**25 0**
2012–13	Sheffield U	0	0	
2013–14	Sheffield U	0	0	
2013–14	*Shrewsbury T*	0	0	

CUVELIER, Florent (M) **46 6**
H: 6 0 W: 11 05 b.Brussels 12-9-92
Internationals: Belgium U16, U17, U18, U19, U20, U21.

2009–10	Portsmouth	0	0	
2010–11	Stoke C	0	0	
2011–12	Stoke C	0	0	
2011–12	*Walsall*	18	4	
2012–13	Stoke C	0	0	
2012–13	*Walsall*	19	2	**37 6**
2012–13	*Peterborough U*	1	0	**1 0**
2013–14	Stoke C	0	0	
2013–14	*Sheffield U*	7	0	**7 0**
2013–14	*Port Vale*	1	0	**1 0**

DE GIROLAMO, Diago (F) **2 0**
Internationals: Italy U18, U19.

2012–13	Sheffield U	2	0	
2013–14	Sheffield U	0	0	**2 0**

DIMAIO, Connor (D) **3 0**
Internationals: Republic of Ireland U16, U17, U19.

2013–14	Sheffield U	3	0	**3 0**

DOYLE, Micky (M) **452 28**
H: 5 10 W: 11 00 b.Dublin 8-7-81
Internationals: Republic of Ireland U21, Full caps.

2003–04	Coventry C	40	5	
2004–05	Coventry C	44	2	
2005–06	Coventry C	44	0	
2006–07	Coventry C	40	3	
2007–08	Coventry C	42	7	
2008–09	Coventry C	37	2	
2009–10	Coventry C	0	0	
2009–10	*Leeds U*	42	0	**42 0**
2010–11	Coventry C	18	1	**265 20**
2010–11	Sheffield U	16	0	
2011–12	Sheffield U	43	3	
2012–13	Sheffield U	43	3	
2013–14	Sheffield U	43	2	**145 8**

FLYNN, Ryan (M) **163 20**
H: 5 8 W: 10 00 b.Falkirk 4-9-88
Internationals: Scotland U19.

2006–07	Liverpool	0	0	
2007–08	*Hereford U*	0	0	
2007–08	Liverpool	0	0	
2008–09	Liverpool	0	0	
2009–10	Liverpool	0	0	
2009–10	*Falkirk*	36	5	
2010–11	Falkirk	33	5	**69 10**
2011–12	Sheffield U	26	2	
2012–13	Sheffield U	36	3	
2013–14	Sheffield U	32	5	**94 10**

HARRIS, Robert (D) **184 11**
H: 5 8 W: 10 00 b.Glasgow 28-8-87

2004–05	Clyde	1	0	
2005–06	Clyde	20	0	
2006–07	Clyde	24	0	**45 0**
2007–08	Queen of the South	26	2	
2008–09	Queen of the South	21	2	
2009–10	Queen of the South	32	4	
2010–11	Queen of the South	31	2	**110 10**
2011–12	Blackpool	5	0	
2012–13	Blackpool	4	0	
2012–13	*Rotherham U*	5	1	**5 1**
2013–14	Blackpool	4	0	**13 0**
2013–14	Sheffield U	11	0	**11 0**

HILL, Matt (D) **439 8**
H: 5 7 W: 12 06 b.Bristol 26-3-81

1998–99	Bristol C	3	0	
1999–2000	Bristol C	14	0	
2000–01	Bristol C	34	0	
2001–02	Bristol C	40	1	
2002–03	Bristol C	42	3	
2003–04	Bristol C	42	0	
2004–05	Bristol C	23	0	**198 6**
2004–05	Preston NE	14	0	
2005–06	Preston NE	26	0	
2006–07	Preston NE	38	0	
2007–08	Preston NE	26	0	
2008–09	Preston NE	1	0	**105 0**
2008–09	Wolverhampton W	13	0	
2009–10	Wolverhampton W	2	0	
2009–10	*QPR*	16	0	**16 0**
2010–11	Wolverhampton W	0	0	**15 0**
2010–11	Barnsley	23	2	**23 2**
2011–12	Blackpool	4	0	**4 0**
2011–12	*Sheffield U*	12	0	
2012–13	Sheffield U	34	0	
2013–14	Sheffield U	32	0	**78 0**

HOWARD, Mark (G) **96 0**
H: 6 0 W: 11 13 b.Southwark 21-9-86

2005–06	Falkirk	8	0	**8 0**
2006–07	Cardiff C	0	0	
2006–07	Swansea C	0	0	
2007–08	St Mirren	10	0	
2008–09	St Mirren	33	0	
2009–10	St Mirren	2	0	**45 0**
2010–11	Aberdeen	9	0	**9 0**
2011–12	Blackpool	4	0	**4 0**
2011–12	*Sheffield U*	0	0	
2012–13	Sheffield U	11	0	
2013–14	Sheffield U	19	0	**30 0**

IRONSIDE, Joe (F) **16 0**

2012–13	Sheffield U	12	0	
2013–14	Sheffield U	4	0	**16 0**

JOHNS, Jasper (D)   1 0
b. 6-2-95
Internationals: England U16.

2013–14	Sheffield U	1	0	1	0

KENNEDY, Terry (D)   7 0
H: 5 10 W: 12 04 b.Barnsley 14-11-93

2010–11	Sheffield U	1	0		
2011–12	Sheffield U	0	0		
2012–13	Sheffield U	1	0		
2013–14	Sheffield U	5	0	7	0

KHAN, Otis (M)   2 0

2013–14	Sheffield U	2	0	2	0

KING, Marlon (F)   448 150
H: 5 10 W: 12 10 b.Dulwich 26-4-80
Internationals: Jamaica Full caps.

1998–99	Barnet	22	6		
1999–2000	Barnet	31	8	53	14
2000–01	Gillingham	38	15		
2001–02	Gillingham	42	17		
2002–03	Gillingham	10	4		
2003–04	Gillingham	11	4	101	40
2003–04	Nottingham F	24	5		
2004–05	Nottingham F	26	5		
2004–05	Leeds U	9	0	9	0
2005–06	Nottingham F	0	0	50	10
2005–06	Watford	41	21		
2006–07	Watford	13	4		
2007–08	Watford	27	11	81	36
2007–08	Wigan Ath	15	1		
2008–09	Wigan Ath	0	0		
2008–09	Hull C	20	5	20	5
2008–09	Middlesbrough	13	2	13	2
2009–10	Wigan Ath	3	0	18	1
2010–11	Coventry C	28	12	28	12
2011–12	Birmingham C	40	16		
2012–13	Birmingham C	27	13		
2013–14	Birmingham C	0	0	67	29
2013–14	Sheffield U	8	1	8	1

LONG, George (G)   66 0
H: 6 0 W: 12 05 b.Sheffield 5-11-93
Internationals: England U18.

2010–11	Sheffield U	1	0		
2011–12	Sheffield U	2	0		
2012–13	Sheffield U	36	0		
2013–14	Sheffield U	27	0	66	0

MAGUIRE, Harry (D)   134 9
H: 6 2 W: 12 06 b.Mosborough 5-3-93
Internationals: England U21.

2010–11	Sheffield U	5	0		
2011–12	Sheffield U	44	1		
2012–13	Sheffield U	44	3		
2013–14	Sheffield U	41	5	134	9

McFADZEAN, Callum (D)   26 1
b.Sheffield 16-1-94
Internationals: England U16.

2010–11	Sheffield U	0	0		
2011–12	Sheffield U	0	0		
2012–13	Sheffield U	8	0		
2013–14	Sheffield U	7	0	15	0
2013–14	Chesterfield	4	0	4	0
2013–14	Burton Alb	7	1	7	1

McGINN, Stephen (M)   159 11
H: 5 9 W: 10 01 b.Glasgow 2-12-88
Internationals: Scotland U19, U21.

2006–07	St Mirren	4	1		
2007–08	St Mirren	25	2		
2008–09	St Mirren	26	1		
2009–10	St Mirren	18	3	73	7
2009–10	Watford	9	0		
2010–11	Watford	29	2		
2011–12	Watford	0	0		
2012–13	Watford	0	0	38	2
2012–13	Shrewsbury T	18	2	18	2
2013–14	Sheffield U	30	0	30	0

McGINTY, Sean (D)   13 0
H: 6 0 W: 11 09 b.Maidstone 11-8-93
Internationals: Republic of Ireland U17, U19, U21.

2010–11	Manchester U	0	0		
2011–12	Manchester U	0	0		
2011–12	Morecambe	4	0	4	0
2012–13	Manchester U	0	0		
2012–13	Oxford U	0	0		
2012–13	Carlisle U	1	0	1	0
2012–13	Tranmere R	3	0	3	0
2013–14	Sheffield U	2	0	2	0
2013–14	Northampton T	2	0	2	0
2013–14	Rochdale	1	0	1	0

MILLER, Shaun (F)   199 45
H: 5 10 W: 11 08 b.Alsager 25-9-87

2006–07	Crewe Alex	7	3		
2007–08	Crewe Alex	15	1		
2008–09	Crewe Alex	33	4		
2009–10	Crewe Alex	33	7		
2010–11	Crewe Alex	42	18		
2011–12	Crewe Alex	33	5		
2012–13	Crewe Alex	0	0	163	38
2012–13	Sheffield U	15	4		
2013–14	Sheffield U	13	0	28	4
2013–14	Shrewsbury T	8	3	8	3

MURPHY, Jamie (F)   227 40
H: 6 0 W: 12 00 b. 28-8-89
Internationals: Scotland U19, U21.

2006–07	Motherwell	2	0		
2007–08	Motherwell	16	1		
2008–09	Motherwell	30	2		
2009–10	Motherwell	35	6		
2010–11	Motherwell	35	6		
2011–12	Motherwell	36	9		
2012–13	Motherwell	22	10	176	34
2012–13	Sheffield U	17	2		
2013–14	Sheffield U	34	4	51	6

PORTER, Chris (F)   335 95
H: 6 1 W: 12 09 b.Wigan 12-12-83

2002–03	Bury	2	0		
2003–04	Bury	37	9		
2004–05	Bury	32	9	71	18
2005–06	Oldham Ath	31	7		
2006–07	Oldham Ath	35	21	66	28
2007–08	Motherwell	37	14		
2008–09	Motherwell	22	9	59	23
2008–09	Derby Co	5	3		
2009–10	Derby Co	21	4		
2010–11	Derby Co	18	2	44	9
2011–12	Sheffield U	34	5		
2012–13	Sheffield U	21	4		
2012–13	Shrewsbury T	5	1	5	1
2013–14	Sheffield U	32	7	87	16
2013–14	Chesterfield	3	0	3	0

REED, Louis (M)   1 0
b. 25-7-97

2013–14	Sheffield U	1	0	1	0

SCOUGALL, Stefan (M)   15 2
H: 5 7 W: 8 13 b.Edinburgh 7-12-92
Internationals: Scotland U21.

2013–14	Sheffield U	15	2	15	2

TAYLOR, Lyle (F)   77 11
H: 6 2 W: 12 00 b.Greenwich 29-3-90

2007–08	Millwall	0	0		
2008–09	Millwall	0	0		

From Concord R

2010–11	Bournemouth	11	0		
2011–12	Bournemouth	18	0	29	0
2011–12	Hereford U	8	2	8	2
2013–14	Sheffield U	20	2	20	2
2013–14	Partick Thistle	20	7	20	7

WESTLAKE, Darryl (D)   108 1
H: 5 9 W: 11 00 b.Sutton Coldfield 1-3-91

2009–10	Walsall	22	0		
2010–11	Walsall	28	1		
2011–12	Walsall	17	0	67	1
2012–13	Sheffield U	11	0		
2013–14	Sheffield U	7	0	18	0
2013–14	Mansfield T	23	0	23	0

WHITEHOUSE, Elliott (M)   18 0

2012–13	Sheffield U	3	0		
2013–14	Sheffield U	0	0	3	0
2013–14	York C	15	0	15	0

WILLIS, George (G)   0 0
Internationals: England U16, U17, U19.

2012–13	Sheffield U	0	0		
2013–14	Sheffield U	0	0		

Scholars
Banton, Julian Daniel Anthony; Calvert-Lewin, Dominic; Cheeseman, Joe; Cockerline, Daniel; Coustrain, Joel; Dimaio, Connor James; Eastwood, Jake; Evans, Ioan Thomas; Eyre, Jake; Fixter, Robbie Ian; Heh, Kler Low Eh Hmoo; Ismael, Fahad Abdisamad; Kedman, Michael Junior Wells; Khan, Otis Jan Mohammed; McDonagh, Jamie-dean Cantona; Owen, Gareth Thomas; Paling, Jason Dean; Ptak, Elliott; Reed, Louis Samuel; Scarisbrick, Kyle Roy; Whiteman, Benjamin; Wright, Jake David.

SHEFFIELD W (72)

ANTONIO, Michael (M)   158 25
H: 6 0 W: 11 11 b.Wandsworth 28-3-90

2008–09	Reading	0	0		
2008–09	*Cheltenham T*	9	0	9	0
2009–10	Reading	1	0		
2009–10	*Southampton*	28	3	28	3
2010–11	Reading	21	1		
2011–12	Reading	6	0		
2011–12	*Colchester U*	15	4	15	4
2011–12	*Sheffield W*	14	5		
2012–13	Reading	0	0	28	1
2012–13	Sheffield W	37	8		
2013–14	Sheffield W	27	4	78	17

BETRA, Franck (F)   0 0

2013–14	Sheffield W	0	0		

BUXTON, Lewis (D)   317 7
H: 6 1 W: 13 11 b.Newport (IW) 10-12-83

2000–01	Portsmouth	0	0		
2001–02	Portsmouth	29	0		
2002–03	Portsmouth	1	0		
2002–03	*Exeter C*	4	0	4	0
2002–03	*Bournemouth*	17	0		
2003–04	Portsmouth	0	0		
2003–04	*Bournemouth*	26	0	43	0
2004–05	Portsmouth	0	0	30	0
2004–05	Stoke C	16	0		
2005–06	Stoke C	32	1		
2006–07	Stoke C	1	0		
2007–08	Stoke C	4	0		
2008–09	Stoke C	0	0	53	1
2008–09	Sheffield W	32	1		
2009–10	Sheffield W	28	0		
2010–11	Sheffield W	30	1		
2011–12	Sheffield W	37	1		
2012–13	Sheffield W	40	0		
2013–14	Sheffield W	20	3	187	6

COKE, Giles (M)   259 25
H: 6 0 W: 11 11 b.Westminster 3-6-86

2004–05	Mansfield T	9	0		
2005–06	Mansfield T	40	4		
2006–07	Mansfield T	21	1	70	5
2007–08	Northampton T	20	5		
2008–09	Northampton T	32	2	52	7
2009–10	Motherwell	32	2	32	2
2010–11	Sheffield W	27	4		
2011–12	Sheffield W	0	0		
2011–12	*Bury*	30	6	30	6
2012–13	Sheffield W	16	0		
2012–13	*Swindon T*	4	0	4	0
2013–14	Sheffield W	28	1	71	5

CORRY, Paul (M)   94 7
H: 6 2 W: 11 12 b.Dublin 3-2-91
Internationals: Republic of Ireland U21, U23.

2010	UCD	28	4		
2011	UCD	36	2		
2012	UCD	17	1	81	7
2012–13	Sheffield W	6	0		
2012–13	*Tranmere R*	6	0	6	0
2013–14	Sheffield W	1	0	7	0

DAWSON, Cameron (G)   0 0
b. 7-7-95
Internationals: England U18, U19.

2013–14	Sheffield W	0	0		
2013–14	*Plymouth Arg*	0	0		

DIESERUVWE, Emmanuel (F)   4 0
b. 5-1-94

2013–14	Sheffield W	0	0		
2013–14	*Fleetwood T*	4	0	4	0

FLORO, Rafael (D)   1 0
b. 19-1-94
Internationals: Portugal U18, U20.

2013–14	Sheffield W	1	0	1	0

GARDNER, Anthony (D)   285 7
H: 6 3 W: 14 00 b.Stone 19-9-80
Internationals: England U21, Full caps.

1998–99	Port Vale	15	1		
1999–2000	Port Vale	26	3	41	4

Season	Club	A	G	Tot A	Tot G
1999–2000	Tottenham H	0	0		
2000–01	Tottenham H	8	0		
2001–02	Tottenham H	15	0		
2002–03	Tottenham H	12	1		
2003–04	Tottenham H	33	0		
2004–05	Tottenham H	17	0		
2005–06	Tottenham H	17	0		
2006–07	Tottenham H	8	0		
2007–08	*Everton*	0	0		
2007–08	Tottenham H	4	1	114	2
2008–09	Hull C	6	0		
2009–10	Hull C	24	0		
2010–11	Hull C	2	0	32	0
2010–11	*Crystal Palace*	28	1		
2011–12	*Crystal Palace*	28	0	56	1
2012–13	Sheffield W	37	0		
2013–14	Sheffield W	5	0	42	0

HELAN, Jeremy (M) — 76 3
H: 5 11 W: 12 00 b.Paris 9-5-92
Internationals: France U19.

Season	Club	A	G	Tot A	Tot G
2009–10	Manchester C	0	0		
2010–11	Manchester C	0	0		
2011–12	Manchester C	0	0		
2011–12	*Carlisle U*	2	0	2	0
2012–13	Manchester C	0	0		
2012–13	*Shrewsbury T*	3	0	3	0
2012–13	*Sheffield W*	28	1		
2013–14	Sheffield W	43	2	71	3

JAMESON, Arron (G) — 2 0
H: 6 3 W: 13 01 b.Sheffield 7-11-89

Season	Club	A	G	Tot A	Tot G
2008–09	Sheffield W	0	0		
2009–10	Sheffield W	0	0		
2010–11	Sheffield W	2	0		
2011–12	Sheffield W	0	0		
2012–13	Sheffield W	0	0		
2012–13	*York C*	0	0		
2013–14	Sheffield W	0	0	2	0
2013–14	*Bradford C*	0	0		

JOHNSON, Jermaine (M) — 309 38
H: 5 11 W: 11 05 b.Kingston, Jamaica 25-6-80
Internationals: Jamaica Full caps.

Season	Club	A	G	Tot A	Tot G
2001–02	Bolton W	10	0		
2002–03	Bolton W	2	0		
2003–04	Bolton W	0	0	12	0
2003–04	Oldham Ath	20	5		
2004–05	Oldham Ath	19	4		
2005–06	Oldham Ath	0	0	39	9
2006–07	Bradford C	27	4	27	4
2006–07	Sheffield W	7	2		
2007–08	Sheffield W	35	1		
2008–09	Sheffield W	37	3		
2009–10	Sheffield W	34	5		
2010–11	Sheffield W	26	4		
2011–12	Sheffield W	24	4		
2012–13	Sheffield W	41	6		
2013–14	Sheffield W	27	0	231	25

JOHNSON, Reda (D) — 132 20
H: 6 2 W: 13 10 b.Marseille 21-3-88
Internationals: Benin Full caps.

Season	Club	A	G	Tot A	Tot G
2005–06	Gueugnon	0	0		
2006–07	Gueugnon	0	0		
2007–08	Amiens	8	0		
2008–09	Amiens	7	0	15	0
2009–10	Plymouth Arg	25	0		
2010–11	Plymouth Arg	17	2	42	2
2010–11	Sheffield W	16	3		
2011–12	Sheffield W	24	7		
2012–13	Sheffield W	16	6		
2013–14	Sheffield W	19	2	75	18

KIRKLAND, Chris (G) — 275 0
H: 6 5 W: 14 08 b.Barwell 2-5-81
Internationals: England U21, Full caps.

Season	Club	A	G	Tot A	Tot G
1997–98	Coventry C	0	0		
1998–99	Coventry C	0	0		
1999–2000	Coventry C	0	0		
2000–01	Coventry C	23	0		
2001–02	Coventry C	1	0	24	0
2001–02	Liverpool	1	0		
2002–03	Liverpool	8	0		
2003–04	Liverpool	6	0		
2004–05	Liverpool	10	0		
2005–06	Liverpool	0	0		
2005–06	*WBA*	10	0	10	0
2006–07	Liverpool	0	0	25	0
2006–07	Wigan Ath	26	0		
2007–08	Wigan Ath	37	0		
2008–09	Wigan Ath	32	0		
2009–10	Wigan Ath	32	0		
2010–11	Wigan Ath	4	0		
2010–11	*Leicester C*	3	0	3	0
2011–12	Wigan Ath	0	0	131	0
2011–12	*Doncaster R*	1	0	1	0
2012–13	Sheffield W	46	0		
2013–14	Sheffield W	35	0	81	0

LAVERY, Caolan (F) — 32 7
H: 5 11 W: 11 12 b.Red Deer 22-10-92
Internationals: Canada U17. Northern Ireland U19, U21.

Season	Club	A	G	Tot A	Tot G
2012–13	Sheffield W	0	0		
2012–13	*Southend U*	3	0	3	0
2013–14	Sheffield W	21	4	21	4
2013–14	*Plymouth Arg*	8	3	8	3

LEE, Kieran (D) — 174 6
H: 6 1 W: 12 00 b.Stalybridge 22-6-88

Season	Club	A	G	Tot A	Tot G
2006–07	Manchester U	1	0		
2007–08	Manchester U	0	0	1	0
2007–08	*QPR*	7	0	7	0
2008–09	Oldham Ath	7	0		
2009–10	Oldham Ath	24	1		
2010–11	Oldham Ath	43	2		
2011–12	Oldham Ath	43	2	117	5
2012–13	Sheffield W	23	0		
2013–14	Sheffield W	26	1	49	1

LLERA, Miguel (D) — 220 23
H: 6 3 W: 13 12 b.Seville 7-8-79

Season	Club	A	G	Tot A	Tot G
2005–06	Gimnastic	27	3		
2006–07	Gimnastic	12	2	39	5
2007–08	Heracles	13	1	13	1
2008–09	Milton Keynes D	34	2	34	2
2009–10	Charlton Ath	25	4		
2010–11	Charlton Ath	15	1		
2011–12	Charlton Ath	0	0	40	5
2011–12	*Brentford*	11	0	11	0
2011–12	*Sheffield W*	20	4		
2012–13	Sheffield W	41	6		
2013–14	Sheffield W	22	0	83	10

LOOVENS, Glenn (D) — 266 13
H: 5 10 W: 11 08 b.Doetrinchem 22-10-83
Internationals: Netherlands U21, Full caps.

Season	Club	A	G	Tot A	Tot G
2001–02	Feyenoord	8	0		
2002–03	Feyenoord	12	0		
2003–04	Feyenoord	1	0		
2003–04	Excelsior	24	2	24	2
2004–05	Feyenoord	6	0	27	0
2004–05	De Graafschap	11	0	11	0
2005–06	Cardiff C	33	2		
2006–07	Cardiff C	30	1		
2007–08	Cardiff C	36	0		
2008–09	Cardiff C	1	0	100	3
2008–09	Celtic	17	3		
2009–10	Celtic	20	3		
2010–11	Celtic	13	1		
2011–12	Celtic	11	1	61	8
2012–13	Real Zaragoza	21	0	21	0
2013–14	Sheffield W	22	0	22	0

MADINE, Gary (F) — 178 41
H: 6 1 W: 12 00 b.Gateshead 24-8-90

Season	Club	A	G	Tot A	Tot G
2007–08	Carlisle U	11	0		
2008–09	Carlisle U	14	1		
2008–09	*Rochdale*	3	0	3	0
2009–10	Carlisle U	20	4		
2009–10	*Coventry C*	9	0	9	0
2009–10	*Chesterfield*	4	0	4	0
2010–11	Carlisle U	21	8		
2010–11	Sheffield W	22	5		
2011–12	Sheffield W	38	18		
2012–13	Sheffield W	30	3		
2013–14	Sheffield W	1	0	91	26
2013–14	*Carlisle U*	5	2	71	15

MAGHOMA, Jacques (M) — 180 28
H: 5 9 W: 11 06 b.Lubumbashi 23-10-87
Internationals: DR Congo Full caps.

Season	Club	A	G	Tot A	Tot G
2005–06	Tottenham H	0	0		
2006–07	Tottenham H	0	0		
2007–08	Tottenham H	0	0		
2008–09	Tottenham H	0	0		
2009–10	Burton Alb	35	3		
2010–11	Burton Alb	41	4		
2011–12	Burton Alb	36	4		
2012–13	Burton Alb	43	15	155	26
2013–14	Sheffield W	25	2	25	2

MAGUIRE, Chris (F) — 203 36
H: 5 10 W: 10 05 b.Bellshill 16-1-89
Internationals: Scotland U16, U19, U21, Full caps.

Season	Club	A	G	Tot A	Tot G
2005–06	Aberdeen	1	0		
2006–07	Aberdeen	19	1		
2007–08	Aberdeen	28	4		
2008–09	Aberdeen	31	3		
2009–10	Aberdeen	17	1		
2009–10	*Kilmarnock*	14	4	14	4
2010–11	Aberdeen	35	7	131	16
2011–12	Derby Co	7	1	7	1
2011–12	Portsmouth	11	3	11	3
2012–13	Sheffield W	10	1		
2013–14	Sheffield W	27	9	37	10
2013–14	*Coventry C*	3	2	3	2

MATTOCK, Joe (D) — 160 4
H: 5 11 W: 12 05 b.Leicester 15-5-90
Internationals: England U17, U19, U21.

Season	Club	A	G	Tot A	Tot G
2006–07	Leicester C	4	0		
2007–08	Leicester C	31	0		
2008–09	Leicester C	31	1		
2009–10	Leicester C	0	0	66	1
2009–10	WBA	29	0		
2010–11	WBA	0	0		
2010–11	*Sheffield U*	13	0	13	0
2011–12	WBA	0	0	29	0
2011–12	*Portsmouth*	7	0	7	0
2011–12	*Brighton & HA*	15	1	15	1
2012–13	Sheffield W	7	0		
2013–14	Sheffield W	23	2	30	2

McCABE, Rhys (M) — 42 1
H: 5 10 W: 11 08 b.Polbeth 24-7-92
Internationals: Scotland U21.

Season	Club	A	G	Tot A	Tot G
2011–12	Rangers	9	0	9	0
2012–13	Sheffield W	22	1		
2013–14	Sheffield W	7	0	29	1
2013–14	*Portsmouth*	4	0	4	0

McKENZIE, Taylor (D) — 0 0

Season	Club	A	G	Tot A	Tot G
2013–14	Sheffield W	0	0		

McPHAIL, Stephen (M) — 364 10
H: 5 8 W: 11 04 b.Westminster 9-12-79
Internationals: Republic of Ireland U17, U21, B, Full caps.

Season	Club	A	G	Tot A	Tot G
1996–97	Leeds U	0	0		
1997–98	Leeds U	4	0		
1998–99	Leeds U	17	0		
1999–2000	Leeds U	24	2		
2000–01	Leeds U	7	0		
2001–02	Leeds U	1	0		
2001–02	*Millwall*	3	0	3	0
2002–03	Leeds U	13	0		
2003–04	Leeds U	12	1	78	3
2003–04	*Nottingham F*	14	0	14	0
2004–05	Barnsley	36	2		
2005–06	Barnsley	34	2	70	4
2006–07	Cardiff C	43	0		
2007–08	Cardiff C	43	3		
2008–09	Cardiff C	32	0		
2009–10	Cardiff C	21	0		
2010–11	Cardiff C	28	0		
2011–12	Cardiff C	19	0		
2012–13	Cardiff C	0	0	186	3
2013–14	Sheffield W	13	0	13	0

NUHIU, Atdhe (F) — 171 31
Internationals: Austria U19, U20, U21.

Season	Club	A	G	Tot A	Tot G
2008–09	Austria Karnten	16	2		
2009–10	Austria Karnten	3	0	19	2
2009–10	SV Ried	27	6	27	6
2010–11	Rapid Vienna	28	5		
2011–12	Rapid Vienna	31	8	59	13
2012–13	Eskisehirspor	28	2	28	2
2013–14	Sheffield W	38	8	38	8

OLOFINJANA, Seyi (M) — 273 36
H: 6 4 W: 11 10 b.Lagos 30-6-80
Internationals: Nigeria Full caps.

Season	Club	A	G	Tot A	Tot G
2003	Brann	25	9		
2004	Brann	9	2	34	11
2004–05	Wolverhampton W	42	5		
2005–06	Wolverhampton W	13	0		
2006–07	Wolverhampton W	44	8		
2007–08	Wolverhampton W	36	3	135	16
2008–09	Stoke C	18	2		
2008–09	Stoke C	0	0	18	2
2009–10	Hull C	19	1		
2010–11	Hull C				

2010–11	Cardiff C	39	6	39	6
2011–12	Hull C	3	0		
2012–13	Hull C	12	0	34	1
2012–13	Sheffield W	6	0		
2013–14	Sheffield W	7	0	13	0

ONYEWU, Oguchi (D) 224 16
H: 6 5 W: 15 04 b.Washington DC 13-5-82
Internationals: USA U17, U20, Full caps.

2002–03	Metz	3	0		
2003–04	Metz	2	0	5	0
2003–04	La Louviere	24	1	24	1
2004–05	Standard Liege	30	3		
2005–06	Standard Liege	29	2		
2006–07	Standard Liege	15	1		
2006–07	Newcastle U	11	0	11	0
2007–08	Standard Liege	33	2		
2008–09	Standard Liege	32	3	139	11
2009–10	AC Milan	0	0		
2010–11	AC Milan	0	0		
2010–11	FC Twente	8	0	8	0
2011–12	Sporting Lisbon	17	4		
2012–13	Sporting Lisbon	0	0	17	4
2012–13	Malaga	2	0	2	0
2013–14	QPR	0	0		
2013–14	Sheffield W	18	0	18	0

PALMER, Liam (M) 105 1
H: 6 2 W: 12 10 b.Worksop 19-9-91
Internationals: Scotland U19, U21.

2010–11	Sheffield W	9	0		
2011–12	Sheffield W	14	1		
2012–13	Sheffield W	0	0		
2012–13	Tranmere R	43	0		
2013–14	Tranmere R	0	0	43	0
2013–14	Sheffield W	39	0	62	1

PRUTTON, David (M) 439 25
H: 5 10 W: 13 00 b.Hull 12-9-81
Internationals: England U21.

1998–99	Nottingham F	0	0		
1999–2000	Nottingham F	34	2		
2000–01	Nottingham F	42	1		
2001–02	Nottingham F	43	3		
2002–03	Nottingham F	24	1		
2002–03	Southampton	12	0		
2003–04	Southampton	27	1		
2004–05	Southampton	23	1		
2005–06	Southampton	17	0		
2006–07	Southampton	3	1	82	3
2006–07	Nottingham F	12	2	155	9
2007–08	Leeds U	43	4		
2008–09	Leeds U	16	0		
2009–10	Leeds U	6	0	65	4
2009–10	Colchester U	19	3	19	3
2010–11	Swindon T	41	3	41	3
2011–12	Sheffield W	25	2		
2012–13	Sheffield W	22	0		
2012–13	Scunthorpe U	13	0	13	0
2013–14	Sheffield W	9	1	56	3
2013–14	Coventry C	8	0	8	0

SAVIC, Andelko (F) 1 0
b. 11-3-93
Internationals: Switzerland U15, U16, U17, U18, U19, U21.

| 2012–13 | Sampdoria | 0 | 0 | | |
| 2013–14 | Sampdoria | 0 | 0 | | |

On loan from Sampdoria

| 2013–14 | Sheffield W | 1 | 0 | 1 | 0 |

SEMEDO, Jose (D) 284 5
H: 6 0 W: 12 08 b.Setubal 11-1-85
Internationals: Portugal U17, U18, U19, U20, U21, B.

2004–05	Sporting Lisbon	0	0		
2004–05	Casa Pia	34	2	34	2
2005–06	Feirense	18	0	18	0
2006–07	Cagliari	3	0	3	0
2007–08	Charlton Ath	37	0		
2008–09	Charlton Ath	18	0		
2009–10	Charlton Ath	38	1		
2010–11	Charlton Ath	42	1	135	2
2011–12	Sheffield W	46	1		
2012–13	Sheffield W	26	0		
2013–14	Sheffield W	22	0	94	1

STOBBS, Jack (M) 1 0

| 2013–14 | Sheffield W | 1 | 0 | 1 | 0 |

TAYLOR, Martin (D) 312 20
H: 6 4 W: 15 00 b.Ashington 9-11-79
Internationals: England U18, U21.

1997–98	Blackburn R	0	0		
1998–99	Blackburn R	3	0		
1999–2000	Blackburn R	6	0		
1999–2000	Darlington	4	0	4	0
1999–2000	Stockport Co	7	0	7	0
2000–01	Blackburn R	16	3		
2001–02	Blackburn R	19	0		
2002–03	Blackburn R	33	2		
2003–04	Blackburn R	11	0	88	5
2003–04	Birmingham C	12	1		
2004–05	Birmingham C	7	0		
2005–06	Birmingham C	21	0		
2006–07	Birmingham C	31	0		
2007–08	Birmingham C	4	0		
2007–08	Norwich C	8	1	8	1
2008–09	Birmingham C	24	1		
2009–10	Birmingham C	0	0	99	2
2009–10	Watford	19	2		
2010–11	Watford	46	6		
2011–12	Watford	22	1		
2012–13	Watford	3	1	90	10
2012–13	Sheffield W	11	0		
2013–14	Sheffield W	0	0	11	0
2013–14	Brentford	5	2	5	2

WILDSMITH, Joe (G) 0 0

| 2013–14 | Sheffield W | 0 | 0 | | |

ZAYATTE, Kamil (D) 185 9
H: 6 2 W: 13 08 b.Conakry 7-3-85
Internationals: Guinea Full caps.

2005–06	Lens	0	0		
2006–07	Lens	1	0	1	0
2006–07	Young Boys	18	0		
2007–08	Young Boys	23	1		
2008–09	Young Boys	6	1	47	2
2008–09	Hull C	32	1		
2009–10	Hull C	23	2		
2010–11	Hull C	16	0	71	3
2010–11	Konyaspor	13	1	13	1
2011–12	Istanbul Buyuksehir	17	0		
2012–13	Istanbul Buyuksehir	25	1	42	1
2013–14	Sheffield W	11	2	11	2

Scholars
Beatson, Bradley Lewis; Davies, Rhys Calum; Dawes, Charlie; Ellam, Jake James; Foster, Seanan James; Frost, Harry Michael; Fusco, Jonathan Nicholas; Harvey, Adam Dominic; Kanteh, Emmanuel Saah; Law, Glenn Jonathan; Lee, Ryan Simon; Mullan, Sean Francis; Smith, Luke Adam; Taylor, Jack Edward.

SHREWSBURY T (73)

ANYON, Joe (G) 11 0
H: 6 4 W: 14 01 b.Blackpool 29-12-86
Internationals: England U16.

2006–07	Port Vale	0	0		
2010–11	Lincoln C	0	0		
2010–11	Morecambe	0	0		
2012–13	Shrewsbury T	0	0		
2013–14	Shrewsbury T	11	0	11	0

ATAJIC, Bahrudin (F) 17 1
H: 5 11 W: 11 12 b.Vastervik 16-11-93
Internationals: Bosnia & Herzegovina U21.

| 2012–13 | Celtic | 1 | 0 | | |
| 2013–14 | Celtic | 3 | 1 | 4 | 1 |

On loan from Celtic

| 2013–14 | Shrewsbury T | 13 | 0 | 13 | 0 |

BRADSHAW, Tom (F) 89 17
H: 5 5 W: 11 02 b.Shrewsbury 27-7-92
Internationals: Wales U19, U21.

2009–10	Shrewsbury T	9	3		
2010–11	Shrewsbury T	26	6		
2011–12	Shrewsbury T	8	1		
2012–13	Shrewsbury T	21	0		
2013–14	Shrewsbury T	28	7	89	17

GOLDSON, Connor (D) 64 1
H: 6 3 W: 13 05 b.York 18-12-92

2010–11	Shrewsbury T	3	0		
2011–12	Shrewsbury T	4	0		
2012–13	Shrewsbury T	17	1		
2013–14	Shrewsbury T	36	0	60	1
2013–14	Cheltenham T	4	0	4	0

GRANDISON, Jermaine (D) 108 3
H: 6 4 W: 13 03 b.Birmingham 15-12-90

2008–09	Coventry C	2	0		
2009–10	Coventry C	3	0		
2010–11	Coventry C	0	0	5	0
2010–11	Tranmere R	8	0	8	0
2011–12	Shrewsbury T	13	0		
2011–12	Shrewsbury T	38	2		
2012–13	Shrewsbury T	30	1		
2013–14	Shrewsbury T	14	0	95	3

HALL, Asa (M) 244 34
H: 6 2 W: 11 09 b.Sandwell 29-11-86
Internationals: England U19, U20.

2004–05	Birmingham C	0	0		
2005–06	Birmingham C	0	0		
2005–06	Boston U	12	0	12	0
2006–07	Birmingham C	0	0		
2007–08	Birmingham C	0	0		
2007–08	Shrewsbury T	15	3		
2008–09	Luton T	42	10		
2009–10	Luton T	33	5	75	15
2010–11	Oxford U	41	4		
2011–12	Oxford U	34	7		
2012–13	Shrewsbury T	15	2		
2012–13	Aldershot T	16	0	16	0
2013–14	Shrewsbury T	17	0	47	5
2013–14	Oxford U	19	3	94	14

JACOBSON, Joe (D) 232 11
H: 5 11 W: 12 06 b.Cardiff 17-11-86
Internationals: Wales U21.

2005–06	Cardiff C	1	0		
2006–07	Cardiff C	0	0	1	0
2006–07	Accrington S	6	1		
2006–07	Bristol R	11	0		
2007–08	Bristol R	40	1		
2008–09	Bristol R	22	0	73	1
2009–10	Oldham Ath	15	0		
2010–11	Oldham Ath	1	0	16	0
2010–11	Accrington S	26	2	32	3
2011–12	Shrewsbury T	39	1		
2012–13	Shrewsbury T	30	2		
2013–14	Shrewsbury T	41	4	110	7

MARSDEN, John (F) 3 0

| 2013–14 | Shrewsbury T | 3 | 0 | 3 | 0 |

McALLISTER, David (M) 154 30
H: 5 10 W: 11 09 b.Dublin 29-12-88

2008	Drogheda U	0	0		
2008	Shelbourne	16	7		
2009	Shelbourne	30	16	46	23
2010	St Patrick's Ath	32	3	32	3
2010–11	Sheffield U	2	1		
2011–12	Sheffield U	4	0		
2011–12	Shrewsbury T	0	0		
2012–13	Sheffield U	14	1	20	2
2012–13	Shrewsbury T	15	1		
2013–14	Shrewsbury T	26	1	56	2

McQUADE, Alex (D) 1 0
H: 6 1 W: 10 13 b.Manchester 7-11-92

| 2012–13 | Bolton W | 0 | 0 | | |
| 2013–14 | Shrewsbury T | 1 | 0 | 1 | 0 |

MKANDAWIRE, Tamika (D) 258 19
H: 6 1 W: 12 03 b.Malawi 28-5-83
Internationals: England C.

2002–03	WBA	0	0		
2003–04	WBA	0	0		
2006–07	Hereford U	39	2	39	2
2007–08	Leyton Orient	35	3		
2008–09	Leyton Orient	36	5		
2009–10	Leyton Orient	43	7	114	15
2010–11	Millwall	35	1		
2011–12	Millwall	13	0		
2012–13	Millwall	0	0	48	1
2012–13	Southend U	18	0		
2013–14	Southend U	0	0	18	0
2013–14	Shrewsbury T	39	1	39	1

PARRY, Paul (M) 341 41
H: 5 11 W: 12 12 b.Chepstow 19-8-80
Internationals: Wales Full caps.

2003–04	Cardiff C	17	1		
2004–05	Cardiff C	24	4		
2005–06	Cardiff C	27	1		
2006–07	Cardiff C	42	6		
2007–08	Cardiff C	41	10		
2008–09	Cardiff C	40	2	191	24

2009–10	Preston NE	17	2		
2010–11	Preston NE	23	0		
2011–12	Preston NE	40	4	80	6
2012–13	Shrewsbury T	31	6		
2013–14	Shrewsbury T	39	5	70	11

SUMMERFIELD, Luke (M)   206   12
H: 6 0   W: 11 00   b.Ivybridge 6-12-87

2004–05	Plymouth Arg	1	0		
2005–06	Plymouth Arg	0	0		
2006–07	Plymouth Arg	23	1		
2006–07	*Bournemouth*	8	1	8	1
2007–08	Plymouth Arg	7	0		
2008–09	Plymouth Arg	29	2		
2009–10	Plymouth Arg	12	0		
2009–10	*Leyton Orient*	14	0	14	0
2010–11	Plymouth Arg	7	1	79	4
2011–12	Cheltenham T	41	4	41	4
2012–13	Shrewsbury T	36	2		
2013–14	Shrewsbury T	28	1	64	3

TAYLOR, Jon (M)   133   22
H: 5 11   W: 12 04   b.Liverpool 23-12-89

2009–10	Shrewsbury T	2	0		
2010–11	Shrewsbury T	20	6		
2011–12	Shrewsbury T	33	4		
2012–13	Shrewsbury T	37	7		
2013–14	Shrewsbury T	41	9	133	22

WARD, Gavin (G)   0   0
H: 6 3   W: 14 10   b.Sutton Coldfield 30-6-70

1992–93	Cardiff C	0	0
1994–95	Leicester C	0	0
1995–96	Bradford C	0	0
1997–98	Bolton W	0	0
1998–99	*Burnley*	0	0
2000–01	Stoke C	0	0
2002–03	Walsall	0	0
2003–04	Coventry C	0	0
2003–04	Barnsley	0	0
2004–05	Preston NE	0	0
2006–07	Tranmere R	0	0
2007–08	Wrexham	0	0
2012–13	Shrewsbury T	0	0
2013–14	Shrewsbury T	0	0

WEALE, Chris (G)   278   1
H: 6 2   W: 13 03   b.Chard 9-2-82

2003–04	Yeovil T	35	0		
2004–05	Yeovil T	38	0		
2005–06	Yeovil T	25	0		
2006–07	Bristol C	1	0		
2007–08	Hereford U	1	0		
2007–08	Bristol C	3	0		
2008–09	Bristol C	5	0	9	0
2008–09	*Hereford U*	1	0	2	0
2008–09	*Yeovil T*	10	1	108	1
2009–10	Leicester C	45	0		
2010–11	Leicester C	29	0		
2011–12	Leicester C	1	0	75	0
2011–12	*Northampton T*	3	0	3	0
2012–13	Shrewsbury T	46	0		
2013–14	Shrewsbury T	35	0	81	0

WILDIG, Aaron (M)   79   6
H: 5 9   W: 11 02   b.Hereford 15-4-92
Internationals: Wales U16.

2009–10	Cardiff C	11	1		
2010–11	Cardiff C	2	0		
2010–11	*Hamilton A*	3	0	3	0
2011–12	Cardiff C	0	0	13	1
2011–12	*Shrewsbury T*	12	2		
2012–13	Shrewsbury T	21	1		
2013–14	Shrewsbury T	30	2	63	5

WINFIELD, Dave (D)   143   8
H: 6 3   W: 13 08   b.Aldershot 24-3-88

2008–09	Aldershot T	10	0		
2009–10	Aldershot T	25	2	35	2
2010–11	Wycombe W	37	2		
2011–12	Wycombe W	25	2		
2012–13	Wycombe W	29	2		
2013–14	Wycombe W	0	0	91	6
2013–14	Shrewsbury T	17	0	17	0

WOODS, Ryan (M)   43   1
H: 5 8   b. 13-12-93

2012–13	Shrewsbury T	2	0		
2013–14	Shrewsbury T	41	1	43	1

Scholars
Anderson, Kaiman Selern; Ashton, Alexander Neil; Astley, Thomas Ryan; Burton, Benjamin Kenneth; Burton, Callum Alex David; Carpenter, George William; Easthope, David Robert; Fletcher, Alexander John; Flint, Niall Daniel; Ginnelly, Joshua Llyod; Hickman, Ryan Luke; Jones, Matthew Stephen; Molyneux, Sam Lee; Richards, Jack Liam; Rowley, Shaun Keith; Ryan, Scott James; Smith, Dominic James; Watkins, Jeff Trevor.

SOUTHAMPTON (74)

BARNARD, Lee (F)   208   69
H: 5 10   W: 11 00   b.Romford 18-7-84

2002–03	Tottenham H	0	0		
2002–03	*Exeter C*	3	0	3	0
2003–04	Tottenham H	0	0		
2004–05	Tottenham H	0	0		
2004–05	*Leyton Orient*	8	0	8	0
2004–05	*Northampton T*	5	0	5	0
2005–06	Tottenham H	3	0		
2006–07	Tottenham H	0	0		
2007–08	Tottenham H	0	0	3	0
2007–08	*Crewe Alex*	10	3	10	3
2007–08	Southend U	15	9		
2008–09	Southend U	35	11		
2009–10	Southend U	25	15		
2009–10	Southampton	20	9		
2010–11	Southampton	36	14		
2011–12	Southampton	6	0		
2012–13	Southampton	0	0		
2012–13	*Bournemouth*	15	4	15	4
2012–13	*Oldham Ath*	14	3	14	3
2013–14	Southampton	0	0	62	23
2013–14	*Southend U*	13	1	88	36

BORUC, Artur (G)   273   0
H: 6 4   W: 13 08   b.Siedlce 20-2-80
Internationals: Poland Full caps.

2005–06	Celtic	34	0		
2006–07	Celtic	36	0		
2007–08	Celtic	30	0		
2008–09	Celtic	34	0		
2009–10	Celtic	28	0	162	0
2010–11	Fiorentina	26	0		
2011–12	Fiorentina	36	0	62	0
2012–13	Southampton	20	0		
2013–14	Southampton	29	0	49	0

CHAMBERS, Calum (M)   22   0
H: 6 0   W: 10 05   b.Petersfield 20-1-95
Internationals: England U17, U19.

2011–12	Southampton	0	0		
2012–13	Southampton	0	0		
2013–14	Southampton	22	0	22	0

CLYNE, Nathaniel (D)   181   2
H: 5 9   W: 10 07   b.Stockwell 5-4-91
Internationals: England U19, U21.

2008–09	Crystal Palace	26	0		
2009–10	Crystal Palace	22	1		
2010–11	Crystal Palace	46	0		
2011–12	Crystal Palace	28	0	122	1
2012–13	Southampton	34	1		
2013–14	Southampton	25	0	59	1

CORK, Jack (D)   257   6
H: 6 0   W: 10 12   b.Carshalton 25-6-89
Internationals: England U17, U18, U19, U20, U21.

2006–07	Chelsea	0	0		
2006–07	*Bournemouth*	7	0	7	0
2007–08	Chelsea	0	0		
2007–08	*Scunthorpe U*	34	2	34	2
2008–09	Chelsea	0	0		
2008–09	*Southampton*	23	0		
2008–09	*Watford*	19	0	19	0
2009–10	Chelsea	0	0		
2009–10	*Coventry C*	21	0	21	0
2009–10	*Burnley*	1	0		
2010–11	Chelsea	0	0		
2010–11	*Burnley*	40	3	51	4
2011–12	Southampton	46	0		
2012–13	Southampton	28	0		
2013–14	Southampton	28	0	125	0

CROPPER, Cody (G)   0   0
H: 6 3   W: 14 05   b.Atlanta 16-2-93
Internationals: USA U20.

2011–12	Ipswich T	0	0
2012–13	Ipswich T	0	0
2012–13	Southampton	0	0
2013–14	Southampton	0	0

DAVIS, Kelvin (G)   606   0
H: 6 1   W: 11 05   b.Bedford 29-9-76
Internationals: England U21.

1993–94	Luton T	1	0		
1994–95	Luton T	9	0		
1994–95	*Torquay U*	2	0	2	0
1995–96	Luton T	6	0		
1996–97	Luton T	6	0		
1997–98	Luton T	32	0		
1997–98	*Hartlepool U*	2	0	2	0
1998–99	Luton T	44	0	92	0
1999–2000	Wimbledon	0	0		
2000–01	Wimbledon	45	0		
2001–02	Wimbledon	40	0		
2002–03	Wimbledon	46	0	131	0
2003–04	Ipswich T	45	0		
2004–05	Ipswich T	39	0	84	0
2005–06	Sunderland	33	0	33	0
2006–07	Southampton	38	0		
2007–08	Southampton	35	0		
2008–09	Southampton	46	0		
2009–10	Southampton	40	0		
2010–11	Southampton	46	0		
2011–12	Southampton	45	0		
2012–13	Southampton	10	0		
2013–14	Southampton	2	0	262	0

DAVIS, Steven (M)   331   27
H: 5 8   W: 11 04   b.Ballymena 1-1-85
Internationals: Northern Ireland U15, U16, U17, U19, U21, U23, Full caps.

2004–05	Aston Villa	28	1		
2005–06	Aston Villa	35	4		
2006–07	Aston Villa	28	0	91	5
2007–08	Fulham	22	0	22	0
2007–08	*Rangers*	12	0		
2008–09	Rangers	34	6		
2009–10	Rangers	36	3		
2010–11	Rangers	37	4		
2011–12	Rangers	33	5	152	18
2012–13	Southampton	32	2		
2013–14	Southampton	34	2	66	4

DO PRADO, Guilherme (F)   239   49
H: 6 2   W: 12 04   b.Sao Paulo 31-12-81

2002	Portuguese Santista	22	7	22	7
2002–03	Catania	6	0	6	0
2003–04	Perugia	17	0		
2004–05	Perugia	17	4	34	4
2005–06	Fiorentina	0	0		
2006–07	Fiorentina	0	0		
2006–07	Spezia	12	1	12	1
2007–08	Mantoba	14	2	14	2
2008–09	Pro Patria	14	7	14	7
2009–10	Cesena	34	9	34	9
2010–11	Southampton	34	9		
2011–12	Southampton	42	10		
2012–13	Southampton	18	0		
2013–14	Southampton	9	0	103	19

FONTE, Jose (D)   331   22
H: 6 2   W: 12 08   b.Penafiel 22-12-83
Internationals: Portugal U21.

2004–05	Felgueiros	28	1	28	1
2005–06	Setubal	15	0	15	0
2005–06	Benfica	1	0	1	0
2005–06	Pacos	11	1	11	1
2006–07	Amadora	25	1	25	1
2007–08	Crystal Palace	22	1		
2008–09	Crystal Palace	38	4		
2009–10	Crystal Palace	22	1	82	6
2009–10	Southampton	21	0		
2010–11	Southampton	43	7		
2011–12	Southampton	42	1		
2012–13	Southampton	27	2		
2013–14	Southampton	36	3	169	13

GALLAGHER, Sam (F)   18   1
H: 6 4   b.Crediton 15-9-95
Internationals: Scotland U19, England U19.

2013–14	Southampton	18	1	18	1

GAPE, Dominic (M)   0   0
H: 5 11   W: 10 13   b.Southampton 9-9-94

2012–13	Southampton	0	0
2013–14	Southampton	0	0

GAZZANIGA, Paulo (G)   37   0
H: 6 5   W: 14 02   b.Santa Fe 2-1-92

2011–12	Gillingham	20	0	20	0

| 2012–13 | Southampton | 9 | 0 | | |
| 2013–14 | Southampton | 8 | 0 | 17 | 0 |

HAMMOND, Dean (M) 390 39
H: 6 0 W: 11 09 b.Hastings 7-3-83

2002–03	Brighton & HA	4	0		
2003–04	Brighton & HA	0	0		
2003–04	Leyton Orient	8	0	8	0
2004–05	Brighton & HA	30	4		
2005–06	Brighton & HA	41	4		
2006–07	Brighton & HA	37	8		
2007–08	Brighton & HA	24	5		
2007–08	Colchester U	13	0		
2008–09	Colchester U	41	5		
2009–10	Colchester U	2	0	56	5
2009–10	Southampton	40	5		
2010–11	Southampton	41	4		
2011–12	Southampton	43	1		
2012–13	Southampton	0	0		
2012–13	*Brighton & HA*	37	2	173	23
2013–14	Southampton	0	0	124	10
2013–14	*Leicester C*	29	1	29	1

HOOIVELD, Jos (D) 225 14
H: 6 3 W: 11 11 b.Zeijen 22-4-83
Internationals: Netherlands U19.

2002–03	Heerenveen	1	0		
2003–04	Heerenveen	12	0	13	0
2004–05	Zwolle	14	2		
2005–06	Zwolle	30	1	44	3
2006–07	Kapfenberger	14	0	14	0
2007	Inter Turku	26	0		
2008	Inter Turku	26	4	52	4
2009	AIK Stockholm	28	0	28	0
2009–10	Celtic	2	0		
2010–11	Celtic	5	0	7	0
2011–12	Southampton	39	7		
2012–13	Southampton	25	0		
2013–14	Southampton	3	0	67	7

ISGROVE, Lloyd (M) 8 1
H: 5 10 W: 11 05 b.Yeovil 12-1-93
Internationals: Wales U21.

2011–12	Southampton	0	0		
2012–13	Southampton	0	0		
2013–14	Southampton	0	0		
2013–14	*Peterborough U*	8	1	8	1

JOHNS, Christopher (G) 0 0
b. 13-5-95
Internationals: Northern Ireland U15, U16, U17, U19.

| 2013–14 | Southampton | 0 | 0 | | |

LALLANA, Adam (M) 238 48
H: 5 8 W: 11 06 b.St Albans 10-5-88
Internationals: England U18, U19, U21, Full caps.

2005–06	Southampton	0	0		
2006–07	Southampton	1	0		
2007–08	Southampton	5	1		
2007–08	*Bournemouth*	3	0	3	0
2008–09	Southampton	40	1		
2009–10	Southampton	44	15		
2010–11	Southampton	36	8		
2011–12	Southampton	41	11		
2012–13	Southampton	30	3		
2013–14	Southampton	38	9	235	48

LAMBERT, Ricky (F) 544 212
H: 6 2 W: 14 08 b.Liverpool 16-2-82
Internationals: England Full caps.

1999–2000	Blackpool	3	0		
2000–01	Blackpool	0	0	3	0
2000–01	Macclesfield T	9	0		
2001–02	Macclesfield T	35	8	44	8
2001–02	Stockport Co	0	0		
2002–03	Stockport Co	29	2		
2003–04	Stockport Co	40	12		
2004–05	Stockport Co	29	4	98	18
2004–05	Rochdale	15	6		
2005–06	Rochdale	46	22		
2006–07	Rochdale	3	0	64	28
2006–07	Bristol R	36	8		
2007–08	Bristol R	46	14		
2008–09	Bristol R	45	29		
2009–10	Bristol R	1	1	128	52
2009–10	Southampton	45	30		
2010–11	Southampton	45	21		
2011–12	Southampton	42	27		
2012–13	Southampton	38	15		
2013–14	Southampton	37	13	207	106

LOVREN, Dejan (D) 190 6
H: 6 2 W: 13 02 b.Karlovac 5-7-89
Internationals: Croatia U17, U18, U19, U20, U21, Full caps.

2005–06	Dinamo Zagreb	1	0		
2006–07	Dinamo Zagreb	0	0		
2006–07	Inter Zapresic	21	0		
2007–08	Dinamo Zagreb	0	0		
2007–08	Inter Zapresic	29	1	50	1
2008–09	Dinamo Zagreb	22	1		
2009–10	Dinamo Zagreb	14	0	37	1
2009–10	Lyon	8	0		
2010–11	Lyon	28	0		
2011–12	Lyon	18	1		
2012–13	Lyon	18	1	72	2
2013–14	Southampton	31	2	31	2

MAGABI, Bevis (M) 0 0
b. 1-5-95

| 2013–14 | Southampton | 0 | 0 | | |

MAYUKA, Emmanuel (F) 161 39
H: 5 9 W: 11 01 b.Kabwe 21-11-90
Internationals: Zambia Full caps.

2006	Kabwe Warriors	1	0		
2007	Kabwe Warriors	16	4		
2008	Kabwe Warriors	9	3	26	7
2008–09	Maccabi Tel Aviv	12	1		
2009–10	Maccabi Tel Aviv	29	7	41	8
2010–11	Young Boys	27	9		
2011–12	Young Boys	28	9		
2012–13	Young Boys	7	2	62	20
2012–13	Southampton	11	0		
2013–14	Southampton	0	0	11	0
2013–14	*Sochaux*	21	4	21	4

McCARTHY, Jason (D) 0 0
b.Southampton 7-11-95

| 2013–14 | Southampton | 0 | 0 | | |

McQUEEN, Sam (M) 0 0
b.Southampton 6-2-95

2011–12	Southampton	0	0		
2012–13	Southampton	0	0		
2013–14	Southampton	0	0		

OSVALDO, Pablo (F) 236 79
H: 6 0 W: 11 06 b.Buenos Aires 12-1-86
Internationals: Italy U21, Full caps.

2005–06	Huracan	33	11	33	11
2005–06	Atalanta	3	1		
2006–07	Atalanta	0	0	3	1
2006–07	*Lecce*	31	8	31	8
2007–08	Fiorentina	13	5		
2008–09	Fiorentina	8	0	21	5
2008–09	Bologna	12	0		
2009–10	Bologna	13	3	25	3
2009–10	Espanyol	20	7		
2010–11	Espanyol	24	13	44	20
2011–12	Roma	26	11		
2012–13	Roma	29	16	55	27
2013–14	Southampton	13	3	13	3
2013–14	*Juventus*	11	1	11	1

RAMIREZ, Gaston (M) 101 18
H: 6 0 W: 12 00 b.Montevideo 2-12-90
Internationals: Uruguay U20, U23, Full caps.

2010–11	Bologna	24	4		
2011–12	Bologna	33	8	57	12
2012–13	Southampton	26	5		
2013–14	Southampton	18	1	44	6

REED, Harrison (M) 4 0
b. 27-1-95
Internationals: England U19.

2011–12	Southampton	0	0		
2012–13	Southampton	0	0		
2013–14	Southampton	4	0	4	0

RODRIGUEZ, Jay (F) 190 56
H: 6 0 W: 12 00 b.Burnley 29-7-89
Internationals: England U21, Full caps.

2007–08	Burnley	1	0		
2007–08	*Stirling Alb*	11	3	11	3
2008–09	Burnley	25	2		
2009–10	Burnley	0	0		
2009–10	*Barnsley*	6	1	6	1
2010–11	Burnley	42	14		
2011–12	Burnley	37	15	105	31
2012–13	Southampton	35	6		
2013–14	Southampton	33	15	68	21

ROWE, Omar (M) 0 0
b.Southampton 30-10-94

| 2013–14 | Southampton | 0 | 0 | | |

SCHNEIDERLIN, Morgan (M) 210 10
H: 5 11 W: 11 11 b.Obernai 8-11-89
Internationals: France U16, U17, U18, U19, U20, U21, Full caps.

2007–08	Strasbourg	5	0	5	0
2008–09	Southampton	30	0		
2009–10	Southampton	37	1		
2010–11	Southampton	27	0		
2011–12	Southampton	42	2		
2012–13	Southampton	36	5		
2013–14	Southampton	33	2	205	10

SEAGER, Ryan (F) 0 0
b. 5-2-96
Internationals: England U17.

| 2013–14 | Southampton | 0 | 0 | | |

SHARP, Billy (F) 315 135
H: 5 9 W: 11 00 b.Sheffield 5-2-86

2004–05	Sheffield U	2	0		
2004–05	*Rushden & D*	16	9	16	9
2005–06	Sheffield U	0	0		
2005–06	Scunthorpe U	37	23		
2006–07	Scunthorpe U	45	30	82	53
2007–08	Sheffield U	29	4		
2008–09	Sheffield U	22	4		
2009–10	Sheffield U	0	0	53	8
2009–10	*Doncaster R*	33	15		
2010–11	Doncaster R	29	15		
2011–12	Doncaster R	20	10		
2011–12	Southampton	15	9		
2012–13	Southampton	2	0		
2012–13	*Nottingham F*	39	10	39	10
2013–14	Southampton	0	0	17	9
2013–14	*Reading*	10	2	10	2
2013–14	*Doncaster R*	16	4	98	44

SHAW, Luke (D) 60 0
H: 6 1 W: 11 11 b.Kingston 12-7-95
Internationals: England U16, U17, U21, Full caps.

2011–12	Southampton	0	0		
2012–13	Southampton	25	0		
2013–14	Southampton	35	0	60	0

SINCLAIR, Jake (F) 0 0
H: 5 7 W: 11 00 b.Bath 29-11-94

2011–12	Southampton	0	0		
2012–13	Southampton	0	0		
2013–14	Southampton	0	0		

STEPHENS, Jack (D) 15 0
H: 6 1 W: 13 03 b.Torpoint 27-1-94
Internationals: England U18, U19.

2010–11	Plymouth Arg	5	0	5	0
2011–12	Southampton	0	0		
2012–13	Southampton	0	0		
2013–14	Southampton	0	0		
2013–14	*Swindon T*	10	0	10	0

TARGETT, Matt (D) 0 0
b.Edinburgh 18-9-95
Internationals: Scotland U19, England U19.

| 2013–14 | Southampton | 0 | 0 | | |

TURNBULL, Jordan (D) 0 0
b.Swindon 30-10-94
Internationals: England U19.

2011–12	Southampton	0	0		
2012–13	Southampton	0	0		
2013–14	Southampton	0	0		

WANYAMA, Victor (M) 133 12
H: 6 2 W: 11 12 b.Nairobi 25-6-91
Internationals: Kenya Full caps.

2009–10	Beerschot	9	0		
2010–11	Beerschot	30	2	49	2
2011–12	Celtic	29	4		
2012–13	Celtic	32	6	61	10
2013–14	Southampton	23	0	23	0

WARD-PROWSE, James (M) 49 0
H: 5 8 W: 10 06 b.Portsmouth 1-11-94
Internationals: England U17, U19, U20, U21.

2011–12	Southampton	0	0		
2012–13	Southampton	15	0		
2013–14	Southampton	34	0	49	0

YOSHIDA, Maya (D) 94 6
H: 6 2 W: 12 03 b.Nagasaki 24-8-88
Internationals: Japan U23, Full caps.

2010–11	VVV	20	0		
2011–12	VVV	32	5		
2012–13	VVV	0	0	54	5
2012–13	Southampton	32	0		
2013–14	Southampton	8	1	40	1

Scholars
Clinton, Kyle; Deasy, Colm; Demkiv, Daniel Steven; Irvine, Mark Joshua; Little, Armani; Mason, Niall Aadya; Mells, George John; Regis, Christopher; Wood, William Nicholas.

SOUTHEND U (75)

ATKINSON, Will (M) 182 15
H: 5 10 W: 10 07 b.Beverley 14-10-88

2006–07	Hull C	0	0		
2007–08	Hull C	0	0		
2007–08	*Port Vale*	4	0	4	0
2007–08	*Mansfield T*	12	0	12	0
2008–09	Hull C	0	0		
2009–10	Hull C	2	1		
2009–10	*Rochdale*	15	3		
2010–11	Hull C	4	0		
2010–11	*Rotherham U*	3	1	3	1
2010–11	*Rochdale*	21	2	36	5
2011–12	Hull C	0	0	6	1
2011–12	*Plymouth Arg*	22	4	22	4
2011–12	*Bradford C*	12	1		
2012–13	Bradford C	42	1	54	2
2013–14	Southend U	45	2	45	2

AUGER, Ryan (M) 1 0

| 2012–13 | Southend U | 0 | 0 | | |
| 2013–14 | Southend U | 1 | 0 | 1 | 0 |

BENTLEY, Daniel (G) 56 0
H: 6 2 W: 11 05 b.Wickford 13-7-93

2011–12	Southend U	1	0		
2012–13	Southend U	9	0		
2013–14	Southend U	46	0	56	0

CLIFFORD, Conor (M) 49 2
H: 5 8 W: 10 08 b.Dublin 1-10-91
Internationals: Republic of Ireland U17, U19, U21.

2008–09	Chelsea	0	0		
2009–10	Chelsea	0	0		
2010–11	Chelsea	0	0		
2010–11	*Plymouth Arg*	7	0	7	0
2010–11	*Notts Co*	9	0	9	0
2011–12	Chelsea	0	0		
2011–12	*Yeovil T*	7	0	7	0
2012–13	Chelsea	0	0		
2012–13	*Portsmouth*	2	1	2	1
2012–13	*Crawley T*	1	0	1	0
2012–13	*Leicester C*	0	0		
2013–14	Southend U	23	1	23	1

COKER, Ben (D) 86 2
H: 5 11 W: 11 09 b.Hatfield 17-6-89

2010–11	Colchester U	20	0		
2011–12	Colchester U	20	0		
2012–13	Colchester U	1	0	41	0
2013–14	Southend U	45	2	45	2

CORR, Barry (F) 206 49
H: 6 3 W: 12 07 b.Co Wicklow 2-4-85
Internationals: Republic of Ireland Youth.

2001–02	Leeds U	0	0		
2002–03	Leeds U	0	0		
2003–04	Leeds U	0	0		
2004–05	Leeds U	0	0		
2005–06	Sheffield W	16	0		
2006–07	Sheffield W	1	0	17	0
2006–07	*Bristol C*	3	0	3	0
2006–07	*Swindon T*	8	3		
2007–08	Swindon T	17	5		
2008–09	Swindon T	11	2	36	10
2009–10	Exeter C	34	3	34	3
2010–11	Southend U	41	18		
2011–12	Southend U	0	0		
2012–13	Southend U	32	6		
2013–14	Southend U	43	12	116	36

EASTWOOD, Freddy (F) 323 84
H: 5 11 W: 12 04 b.Epsom 29-10-83
Internationals: Wales Full caps.

2004–05	Southend U	33	19		
2005–06	Southend U	40	23		
2006–07	Southend U	42	11		
2007–08	Wolverhampton W	31	3	31	3
2008–09	Coventry C	46	4		
2009–10	Coventry C	36	8		
2010–11	Coventry C	27	5		
2011–12	Coventry C	4	0	113	17
2011–12	*Southend U*	7	2		
2012–13	Southend U	26	3		
2013–14	Southend U	31	6	179	64

GOMIS, Bedsente (M) 2 0
H: 5 10 W: 10 04 b. 14-4-88
From Lens, Puertollano, Almeria

| 2013–14 | Southend U | 2 | 0 | 2 | 0 |

HURST, Kevan (M) 326 34
H: 5 10 W: 11 07 b.Chesterfield 27-8-85

2003–04	*Boston U*	7	1	7	1
2004–05	Sheffield U	1	0		
2004–05	*Stockport Co*	14	1	14	1
2005–06	Sheffield U	0	0		
2005–06	*Chesterfield*	37	4		
2006–07	Sheffield U	0	0	1	0
2006–07	*Chesterfield*	25	3	62	7
2006–07	*Scunthorpe U*	13	0		
2007–08	Scunthorpe U	33	1		
2008–09	Scunthorpe U	20	2	66	3
2009–10	Carlisle U	33	2		
2010–11	Carlisle U	2	0	35	2
2010–11	*Morecambe*	21	2	21	2
2011–12	Walsall	34	2	34	2
2012–13	Southend U	44	5		
2013–14	Southend U	42	11	86	16

LEONARD, Ryan (D) 83 8
H: 6 0 W: 11 01 b.Plympton 24-5-92

2009–10	Plymouth Arg	1	0		
2010–11	Plymouth Arg	0	0	1	0
2011–12	Southend U	17	1		
2012–13	Southend U	22	2		
2013–14	Southend U	43	5	82	8

PAYNE, Jack (M) 11 0
b. 25-10-94

| 2013–14 | Southend U | 11 | 0 | 11 | 0 |

PHILLIPS, Mark (D) 222 14
H: 6 2 W: 11 00 b.Lambeth 27-1-82

1999–2000	Millwall	0	0		
2000–01	Millwall	0	0		
2001–02	Millwall	1	0		
2002–03	Millwall	7	0		
2003–04	Millwall	0	0		
2004–05	Millwall	25	1		
2005–06	Millwall	22	0		
2006–07	Millwall	12	0		
2006–07	*Darlington*	8	0	8	0
2007–08	Millwall	0	0	67	1
2008–09	Brentford	33	1		
2009–10	Brentford	22	0	55	1
2010–11	Southend U	5	0		
2011–12	Southend U	39	7		
2012–13	Southend U	21	3		
2013–14	Southend U	27	2	92	12

PINNOCK, Mitch (M) 2 0
H: 5 10 b. 12-12-94

| 2012–13 | Southend U | 2 | 0 | | |
| 2013–14 | Southend U | 0 | 0 | 2 | 0 |

PROSSER, Luke (D) 121 7
H: 6 2 W: 12 04 b.Waltham Cross 28-5-88

2005–06	Port Vale	0	0		
2006–07	Port Vale	0	0		
2007–08	Port Vale	5	0		
2008–09	Port Vale	26	1		
2009–10	Port Vale	2	1	33	2
2010–11	Southend U	17	1		
2011–12	Southend U	21	1		
2012–13	Southend U	25	0		
2013–14	Southend U	25	3	88	5

SMITH, Ted (G) 0 0
Internationals: England U18.

| 2012–13 | Southend U | 0 | 0 | | |
| 2013–14 | Southend U | 0 | 0 | | |

STRAKER, Anthony (D) 222 8
H: 5 9 W: 11 11 b.Ealing 23-9-88
Internationals: England U18. Grenada Full caps.

2008–09	Aldershot T	32	0		
2009–10	Aldershot T	37	2		
2010–11	Aldershot T	38	2		
2010–11	*Wycombe W*	4	0	4	0
2011–12	Aldershot T	44	2	151	6
2012–13	Southend U	28	0		
2013–14	Southend U	39	2	67	2

THOMPSON, Adam (D) 53 1
H: 6 2 W: 12 10 b.Harlow 28-9-92
Internationals: Northern Ireland U17, U19, U21, Full caps.

2010–11	Watford	10	1		
2011–12	Watford	0	0		
2011–12	*Brentford*	20	0	20	0
2012–13	Watford	4	0		
2012–13	*Wycombe W*	2	0	2	0
2012–13	*Barnet*	1	0	1	0
2013–14	Watford	0	0	14	1
2013–14	Southend U	16	0	16	0

TIMLIN, Michael (M) 231 13
H: 5 8 W: 11 08 b.New Cross 19-3-85
Internationals: Republic of Ireland Youth, U21.

2002–03	Fulham	0	0		
2003–04	Fulham	0	0		
2004–05	Fulham	0	0		
2005–06	Fulham	0	0		
2005–06	*Scunthorpe U*	1	0	1	0
2005–06	*Doncaster R*	3	0	3	0
2006–07	Fulham	0	0		
2006–07	*Swindon T*	24	1		
2007–08	Fulham	0	0		
2007–08	*Swindon T*	10	1		
2008–09	Swindon T	41	2		
2009–10	Swindon T	21	0		
2010–11	Swindon T	22	2		
2010–11	*Southend U*	8	1		
2011–12	Swindon T	1	0	119	6
2011–12	Southend U	39	4		
2012–13	Southend U	25	0		
2013–14	Southend U	36	2	108	7

WHITE, John (D) 273 1
H: 6 0 W: 12 01 b.Maldon 26-7-86

2004–05	Colchester U	20	0		
2005–06	Colchester U	35	0		
2006–07	Colchester U	16	0		
2007–08	Colchester U	21	0		
2008–09	Colchester U	26	0		
2009–10	Colchester U	39	0		
2009–10	*Southend U*	5	0		
2010–11	Colchester U	22	0		
2011–12	Colchester U	26	0		
2012–13	Colchester U	22	0	227	0
2013–14	Southend U	41	1	46	1

WILLIAMS, Jason (F) 2 0

| 2013–14 | Southend U | 2 | 0 | 2 | 0 |

Scholars
Adeyeye, Emmanuel Adekunle; Agyakwa, Marlon; Alawode-Williams, Jordan; Banton, Joshua Jordan Lee-Winston; Barlow, Charlie Harry; Bridge, Jack; Cotton, Nico Lewis; Edwards, Jack; Farrell, Kane Stephen William; Gard, Frederick Jack; Johnson, Ross Anthony; Keating, Macauley Anthony; King, Daniel Charles Lewis; Matsuzaka, Daniel Lewis; Norman, Harry Alan; Scott, Brandon Montel; Snook, Daniel John; Tatham, Aaron Jon; Williams, Jason Norrel.

STEVENAGE (76)

AKINS, Lucas (F) 179 21
H: 5 10 W: 11 07 b.Huddersfield 25-2-89

2006–07	Huddersfield T	2	0		
2007–08	Huddersfield T	3	0	5	0
2008–09	Hamilton A	11	0		
2008–09	*Partick Thistle*	9	1	9	1
2009–10	Hamilton A	0	0	11	0
2010–11	Tranmere R	33	2		
2011–12	Tranmere R	44	5		
2012–13	Tranmere R	0	0	77	7

| 2012–13 | Stevenage | 46 | 10 | | |
| 2013–14 | Stevenage | 31 | 3 | 77 | 13 |

ALLEN, George (D)   0   0

| 2012–13 | Stevenage | 0 | 0 |
| 2013–14 | Stevenage | 0 | 0 |

ARNOLD, Steve (G)   33   0
H: 6 1   W: 13 02   b.Welham Green 22-8-89

| 2012–13 | Stevenage | 30 | 0 | | |
| 2013–14 | Stevenage | 3 | 0 | 33 | 0 |

ASHTON, Jon (D)   237   3
H: 6 2   W: 13 12   b.Nuneaton 4-10-82
Internationals: England C.

2000–01	Leicester C	0	0		
2001–02	Leicester C	7	0		
2002–03	Notts Co	4	0	4	0
2003–04	Leicester C	0	0	7	0
2003–04	Oxford U	34	0		
2004–05	Oxford U	30	0		
2005–06	Oxford U	33	1	97	1

From Rushden & D, Grays Ath.

2010–11	Stevenage	38	1		
2011–12	Stevenage	43	1		
2012–13	Stevenage	8	0		
2013–14	Stevenage	40	0	129	2

BURROW, Jordan (F)   71   7
H: 6 1   W: 11 13   b.Sheffield 12-9-92

2011–12	Morecambe	19	4		
2012–13	Morecambe	32	1		
2013–14	Morecambe	0	0	51	5
2013–14	Stevenage	20	2	20	2

CHARLES, Darius (M)   152   12
H: 6 1   W: 13 05   b.Ealing 10-12-87
Internationals: England C.

2004–05	Brentford	1	0		
2005–06	Brentford	2	0		
2006–07	Brentford	17	1		
2007–08	Brentford	17	0	37	1

From Ebbsfleet U.

2010–11	Stevenage	28	2		
2011–12	Stevenage	28	4		
2012–13	Stevenage	37	1		
2013–14	Stevenage	22	4	115	11

COWAN, Don (F)   51   8
H: 5 10   W: 13 05   b.New York 16-11-89

2009	Shamrock R	5	0		
2010	Shamrock R	3	0	8	0
2010	Longford T	13	0		
2011	Longford T	19	8	32	8
2011–12	Stevenage	8	0		
2012–13	Stevenage	0	0		
2012–13	Braintree T	0	0		
2012–13	Dundee	0	0		
2013–14	Southend U	2	0	2	0
2013–14	Stevenage	1	0	9	0

DAY, Chris (G)   333   0
H: 6 2   W: 13 07   b.Whipps Cross 28-7-75
Internationals: England U18, U21.

1992–93	Tottenham H	0	0		
1993–94	Tottenham H	0	0		
1994–95	Tottenham H	0	0		
1995–96	Tottenham H	0	0		
1996–97	Crystal Palace	24	0	24	0
1997–98	Watford	0	0		
1998–99	Watford	0	0		
1999–2000	Watford	11	0		
2000–01	Watford	0	0	11	0
2000–01	Lincoln C	14	0	14	0
2001–02	QPR	16	0		
2002–03	QPR	12	0		
2003–04	QPR	29	0		
2004–05	QPR	30	0	87	0
2004–05	Preston NE	6	0	6	0
2005–06	Oldham Ath	30	0	30	0
2006–07	Millwall	5	0		
2007–08	Millwall	5	0	10	0
2010–11	Stevenage	46	0		
2011–12	Stevenage	44	0		
2012–13	Stevenage	17	0		
2013–14	Stevenage	44	0	151	0

DEACON, Roarie (M)   24   0
Internationals: England U19.

| 2012–13 | Stevenage | 1 | 0 | | |
| 2013–14 | Stevenage | 23 | 0 | 24 | 0 |

DEMBELE, Bira (D)   55   2
H: 6 2   W: 11 10   b. 22-3-88
Internationals: France U21.

2007–08	Rennes	7	0		
2008–09	Rennes	2	0		
2009–10	Rennes	0	0		
2009–10	Boulogne	23	1	23	1
2010–11	Rennes	0	0	9	0
2011–12	Sedan	1	0		
2011–12	Red Star 93	9	0	9	0
2012–13	Sedan	0	0	1	0
2013–14	Stevenage	13	1	13	1

DUNNE, James (M)   178   11
H: 5 11   W: 10 12   b.Bromley 18-9-89

2007–08	Arsenal	0	0		
2008–09	Arsenal	0	0		
2008–09	Nottingham F	0	0		
2009–10	Exeter C	23	3		
2010–11	Exeter C	42	1		
2011–12	Exeter C	45	2	110	6
2012–13	Stevenage	42	4		
2013–14	Stevenage	13	1	55	5
2013–14	St Johnstone	13	0	13	0

FREEMAN, Luke (F)   124   17
H: 6 0   W: 10 00   b.Dartford 22-3-92
Internationals: England U16, 17.

2007–08	Gillingham	1	0	1	0
2008–09	Arsenal	0	0		
2009–10	Arsenal	0	0		
2010–11	Arsenal	0	0		
2010–11	Yeovil T	13	2	13	2
2011–12	Arsenal	0	0		
2011–12	Stevenage	26	7		
2012–13	Stevenage	39	2		
2013–14	Stevenage	45	6	110	15

GORDAN, Rohdell (M)   3   0

| 2013–14 | Stevenage | 3 | 0 | 3 | 0 |

HABER, Marcus (F)   103   12
H: 6 3   W: 13 04   b.Vancouver 11-1-89
Internationals: Canada U16, U17, U20, U23 U23, Full caps.

2009–10	WBA	0	0		
2009–10	Exeter C	5	0	5	0
2010–11	WBA	0	0		
2010–11	St Johnstone	11	1		
2011–12	St Johnstone	31	2	42	3
2012–13	Stevenage	42	7		
2013–14	Stevenage	3	0	45	7
2013–14	Notts Co	11	2	11	2

HARTLEY, Peter (D)   210   12
H: 6 0   W: 12 06   b.Hartlepool 3-4-88

2006–07	Sunderland	0	0		
2007–08	Sunderland	0	0		
2007–08	Chesterfield	12	0	12	0
2008–09	Sunderland	0	0	1	0
2009–10	Hartlepool U	38	2		
2010–11	Hartlepool U	40	2		
2011–12	Hartlepool U	44	4		
2012–13	Hartlepool U	43	2		
2013–14	Hartlepool U	1	0	166	10
2013–14	Stevenage	31	2	31	2

HESLOP, Simon (M)   127   8
H: 5 11   W: 11 00   b.York 1-5-87

2005–06	Barnsley	0	0		
2006–07	Barnsley	1	0		
2007–08	Barnsley	0	0		
2008–09	Barnsley	0	0		
2008–09	Grimsby T	8	0	8	0
2009–10	Barnsley	0	0	1	0
2010–11	Oxford U	38	3		
2011–12	Oxford U	29	3		
2012–13	Oxford U	24	1		
2013–14	Oxford U	0	0	91	7
2013–14	Stevenage	27	1	27	1

HILLS, Lee (D)   72   1
H: 5 10   W: 11 11   b.Croydon 13-4-90
Internationals: England U18, U19.

2007–08	Crystal Palace	12	1		
2008–09	Crystal Palace	14	0		
2008–09	Colchester U	2	0	2	0
2009–10	Crystal Palace	19	0		
2009–10	Oldham Ath	3	0	3	0
2010–11	Crystal Palace	0	0		
2011–12	Crystal Palace	0	0		
2011–12	Southend U	7	0	7	0
2012–13	Crystal Palace	0	0	45	1

| 2012–13 | Stevenage | 11 | 0 | | |
| 2013–14 | Stevenage | 4 | 0 | 15 | 0 |

JOHNSON, Ryan (D)   1   0
b. 2-10-96

| 2013–14 | Stevenage | 1 | 0 | 1 | 0 |

JONES, Luke (D)   48   0
H: 6 0   W: 13 04   b.Darwen 10-4-87

2005–06	Blackburn R	0	0		
2005–06	Cercle Brugge	8	0	8	0
2006–07	Shrewsbury T	7	0		
2007–08	Shrewsbury T	7	0	14	0

From Kidderminster H, Mansfield T, Forest Green R

| 2013–14 | Stevenage | 26 | 0 | 26 | 0 |

LOPEZ, Daniel (F)   31   12
H: 5 9   W: 9 08

2012–13	Stevenage	10	3		
2012–13	Aldershot T	12	6	12	6
2012–13	Barnet	5	3	5	3
2013–14	Stevenage	4	0	14	3

MORAIS, Filipe (M)   224   23
H: 5 9   W: 11 10   b.Lisbon 21-11-85
Internationals: Portugal U21.

2003–04	Chelsea	0	0		
2004–05	Chelsea	0	0		
2005–06	Chelsea	0	0		
2005–06	Milton Keynes D	13	0	13	0
2006–07	Millwall	12	1	12	1
2006–07	St Johnstone	13	1		
2007–08	Hibernian	28	1		
2008–09	Hibernian	2	0	30	1
2008–09	Inverness CT	12	3	12	3
2009–10	St Johnstone	30	2	43	3
2010–11	Oldham Ath	23	3		
2011–12	Oldham Ath	36	5		
2012–13	Oldham Ath	0	0	59	8
2012–13	Stevenage	28	3		
2013–14	Stevenage	27	4	55	7

N'GUESSAN, Joseph (M)   6   1

| 2012–13 | Stevenage | 1 | 0 | | |
| 2013–14 | Stevenage | 5 | 1 | 6 | 1 |

OKENABIRHIE, Fejiri (F)   3   0

| 2013–14 | Stevenage | 3 | 0 | 3 | 0 |

PARRETT, Dean (M)   46   4
H: 5 10   W: 11 04   b.Hampstead 16-11-91
Internationals: England U16, U17, U19, U20.

2008–09	Tottenham H	0	0		
2009–10	Tottenham H	0	0		
2009–10	Aldershot T	4	0	4	0
2010–11	Tottenham H	0	0		
2010–11	Plymouth Arg	8	1	8	1
2010–11	Charlton Ath	9	1	9	1
2011–12	Tottenham H	0	0		
2011–12	Yeovil T	10	1	10	1
2012–13	Tottenham H	0	0		
2012–13	Swindon T	3	0	3	0
2013–14	Stevenage	12	1	12	1

REID, Craig (F)   112   19
H: 5 10   W: 11 10   b.Coventry 17-12-85

2004–05	Coventry C	0	0		
2005–06	Coventry C	0	0		
2006–07	Cheltenham T	6	0		
2007–08	Cheltenham T	8	0	14	0

From Grays Ath, Newport Co.

2010–11	Stevenage	20	2		
2011–12	Stevenage	29	6		
2012–13	Stevenage	0	0		
2012–13	Aldershot T	39	11	39	11
2013–14	Southend U	6	0	6	0
2013–14	Stevenage	4	0	53	8

SHROOT, Robin (M)
H: 5 9   W: 11 05   b.Hammersmith 26-3-88
Internationals: Northern Ireland U21.

2008–09	Birmingham C	0	0		
2008–09	Walsall	5	0	5	0
2009–10	Birmingham C	0	0		
2009–10	Burton Alb	7	0	7	0
2010–11	Birmingham C	0	0		
2010–11	Cheltenham T	7	1	7	1
2011–12	Stevenage	25	3		
2012–13	Stevenage	26	6		
2013–14	Stevenage	10	0	61	9

Transferred to IL Hodd March 2014

SMITH, Jimmy (M) 253 27
H: 6 0 W: 10 03 b.Newham 7-1-87
Internationals: England U16, U17, U19.

Season	Club				
2004–05	Chelsea	0	0		
2005–06	Chelsea	1	0		
2006–07	Chelsea	0	0		
2006–07	QPR	29	6	29	6
2007–08	Chelsea	0	0		
2007–08	Norwich C	9	0	9	0
2008–09	Chelsea	0	0	1	0
2008–09	Sheffield W	12	0	12	0
2008–09	Leyton Orient	16	0		
2009–10	Leyton Orient	40	2		
2010–11	Leyton Orient	31	7		
2011–12	Leyton Orient	38	6		
2012–13	Leyton Orient	35	3		
2013–14	Leyton Orient	0	0	160	18
2013–14	Stevenage	42	3	42	3

TANSEY, Greg (M) 206 28
H: 6 1 W: 12 03 b.Huyton 21-11-88

Season	Club				
2006–07	Stockport Co	3	0		
2007–08	Stockport Co	13	0		
2008–09	Stockport Co	12	1		
2009–10	Stockport Co	32	2		
2010–11	Stockport Co	38	10	98	13
2011–12	Inverness CT	36	4		
2012–13	Stevenage	37	6		
2013–14	Stevenage	19	3	56	9
2013–14	Inverness CT	16	2	52	6

TOUNKARA, Oumare (F) 76 10
H: 6 1 W: 12 08 b.Paris 25-5-90

Season	Club				
2009–10	Sunderland	0	0		
2010–11	Sunderland	0	0		
2010–11	Oldham Ath	44	7		
2011–12	Sunderland	0	0		
2011–12	Oldham Ath	8	1		
2012–13	Oldham Ath	0	0	52	8
2012–13	Bristol R	9	2		
2013–14	Bristol R	0	0	9	2
2013–14	Stevenage	15	0	15	0

WEDGBURY, Sam (M) 82 3
H: 5 10 W: 12 07 b.West Midlands 26-2-89
Internationals: England C.

Season	Club				
2006–07	Sheffield U	0	0		
2007–08	Sheffield U	0	0		
2008–09	Sheffield U	0	0		
2009–10	Sheffield U	0	0		
2009–10	Ferencvaros	6	1	6	1
2010–11	Macclesfield T	23	1		
2011–12	Macclesfield T	39	1	62	2
2013–14	Stevenage	14	0	14	0

ZOKO, Francois (F) 385 70
H: 6 0 W: 11 05 b.Daloa 13-9-83
Internationals: Ivory Coast U20, U23.

Season	Club				
2001–02	Nancy	24	3		
2002–03	Nancy	28	2		
2003–04	Nancy	19	3	71	8
2004–05	Laval	27	7		
2005–06	Laval	33	2	60	9
2006–07	Mons	23	4		
2007–08	Mons	32	8	55	12
2008–09	Hacettepe	27	1	27	1
2009–10	Ostend	11	4	11	4
2010–11	Carlisle U	44	6		
2011–12	Carlisle U	45	13		
2012–13	Carlisle U	0	0	89	19
2012–13	Notts Co	38	7		
2013–14	Notts Co	1	0	39	7
2013–14	Stevenage	33	10	33	10

Scholars
Carey-Morrell, James Mark; Casey, George James; Cathline, Alex Raymond Kwamena; Gordon, Rohdell Antonio; Gorman, Dale Anthony; Hartley, Jimmy; Johnson, Ryan Anthony; Jones, Jack Lewis; Joseph, Harold Michael Oluwatimilehin Alao Olufe; Kennedy, Ben James; Millard, Ross Alan; Okenabirhie, Fejiri Shaun China; Reading, Tyler Joel; Towner, Ryan Alfie; Udoh, Dominic Daniel.

STOKE C (77)

ADAM, Charlie (M) 275 62
H: 6 1 W: 12 00 b.Dundee 10-12-85
Internationals: Scotland U21, B, Full caps.

Season	Club				
2004–05	Rangers	1	0		
2004–05	Ross Co	10	2	10	2
2005–06	Rangers	1	0		
2005–06	St Mirren	29	5	29	5
2006–07	Rangers	32	11		
2007–08	Rangers	16	2		
2008–09	Rangers	9	0	59	13
2008–09	Blackpool	13	2		
2009–10	Blackpool	43	16		
2010–11	Blackpool	35	12	91	30
2011–12	Liverpool	28	2	28	2
2012–13	Stoke C	27	3		
2013–14	Stoke C	31	7	58	10

ALABI, James (F) 11 1

Season	Club				
2012–13	Stoke C	0	0		
2012–13	Scunthorpe U	9	1		
2013–14	Stoke C	0	0		
2013–14	Mansfield T	1	0	1	0
2013–14	Scunthorpe U	1	0	10	1

ARNAUTOVIC, Marko (F) 149 30
H: 6 4 W: 13 00 b.Floridsdorf 19-4-89
Internationals: Austria U18, U19, U21, Full caps.

Season	Club				
2006–07	FC Twente	2	0		
2007–08	FC Twente	14	0		
2008–09	FC Twente	28	12		
2009–10	FC Twente	0	0	44	12
2009–10	Inter Milan	3	0	3	0
2010–11	Werder Bremen	25	3		
2011–12	Werder Bremen	19	6		
2012–13	Werder Bremen	26	5		
2013–14	Werder Bremen	2	0	72	14
2013–14	Stoke C	30	4	30	4

BACHMANN, Daniel (G) 0 0
b.Vienna 9-7-94
Internationals: Austria U17, U18, U19.

Season	Club		
2011–12	Stoke C	0	0
2012–13	Stoke C	0	0
2013–14	Stoke C	0	0

BEGOVIC, Asmir (G) 169 1
H: 6 5 W: 13 01 b.Trebinje 20-6-87
Internationals: Canada U20. Bosnia & Herzegovina Full caps.

Season	Club				
2006–07	Portsmouth	0	0		
2006–07	Macclesfield T	3	0	3	0
2007–08	Portsmouth	0	0		
2007–08	Bournemouth	8	0	8	0
2007–08	Yeovil T	2	0		
2008–09	Portsmouth	2	0		
2008–09	Yeovil T	14	0	16	0
2009–10	Portsmouth	9	0	11	0
2009–10	Ipswich T	6	0	6	0
2009–10	Stoke C	4	0		
2010–11	Stoke C	28	0		
2011–12	Stoke C	23	0		
2012–13	Stoke C	38	0		
2013–14	Stoke C	32	1	125	1

BUTLAND, Jack (G) 102 0
H: 6 4 W: 12 00 b.Clevedon 10-3-93
Internationals: England U16, U17, U19, U20, U21, Full caps.

Season	Club				
2009–10	Birmingham C	0	0		
2010–11	Birmingham C	0	0		
2011–12	Birmingham C	0	0		
2011–12	Cheltenham T	24	0	24	0
2012–13	Birmingham C	46	0	46	0
2012–13	Stoke C	0	0		
2013–14	Stoke C	3	0	3	0
2013–14	Barnsley	13	0	13	0
2013–14	Leeds U	16	0	16	0

CAMERON, Geoff (D) 196 13
H: 6 3 W: 13 02 b.Attleboro 11-7-85
Internationals: USA Full caps.

Season	Club				
2008	Houston D	24	1		
2009	Houston D	32	2		
2010	Houston D	16	3		
2011	Houston D	37	5		
2012	Houston D	15	0	124	11
2012–13	Stoke C	35	0		
2013–14	Stoke C	37	2	72	2

CROUCH, Peter (F) 454 120
H: 6 7 W: 13 03 b.Macclesfield 30-1-81
Internationals: England U20, U21, B, Full caps.

Season	Club				
1998–99	Tottenham H	0	0		
1999–2000	Tottenham H	0	0		
2000–01	QPR	42	10	42	10
2001–02	Portsmouth	37	18		
2001–02	Aston Villa	7	2		
2002–03	Aston Villa	14	0		
2003–04	Aston Villa	16	4	37	6
2003–04	Norwich C	15	4	15	4
2004–05	Southampton	27	12	27	12
2005–06	Liverpool	32	8		
2006–07	Liverpool	32	9		
2007–08	Liverpool	21	5	85	22
2008–09	Portsmouth	38	11		
2009–10	Portsmouth	0	0	75	29
2009–10	Tottenham H	38	8		
2010–11	Tottenham H	34	4		
2011–12	Tottenham H	1	0	73	12
2011–12	Stoke C	32	10		
2012–13	Stoke C	34	7		
2013–14	Stoke C	34	8	100	25

DAWSON, Lucas (M) 1 0
H: 5 9 W: 11 10 b.Stoke-on-Trent 12-11-93

Season	Club				
2011–12	Stoke C	0	0		
2012–13	Stoke C	0	0		
2013–14	Stoke C	0	0		
2013–14	Carlisle U	1	0	1	0

EDU, Maurice (M) 146 15
H: 6 0 W: 12 00 b.Fontana, California 18-4-86
Internationals: USA U23, Full caps.

Season	Club				
2007	Toronto FC	25	4		
2008	Toronto FC	13	2	38	6
2008–09	Rangers	12	2		
2009–10	Rangers	15	2		
2010–11	Rangers	33	2		
2011–12	Rangers	36	3	96	9
2012–13	Stoke C	1	0		
2012–13	Bursaspor	11	0	11	0
2013–14	Stoke C	1	0	1	0

ETHERINGTON, Matthew (M) 426 37
H: 5 10 W: 10 12 b.Truro 14-8-81
Internationals: England U16, U18, U20, U21.

Season	Club				
1996–97	Peterborough U	1	0		
1997–98	Peterborough U	2	0		
1998–99	Peterborough U	29	3		
1999–2000	Peterborough U	19	3	51	6
1999–2000	Tottenham H	5	0		
2000–01	Tottenham H	6	0		
2001–02	Bradford C	13	1	13	1
2001–02	Tottenham H	11	0		
2002–03	Tottenham H	23	1	45	1
2003–04	West Ham U	35	5		
2004–05	West Ham U	39	4		
2005–06	West Ham U	33	2		
2006–07	West Ham U	27	0		
2007–08	West Ham U	18	3		
2008–09	West Ham U	13	2	165	16
2008–09	Stoke C	14	0		
2009–10	Stoke C	34	5		
2010–11	Stoke C	32	5		
2011–12	Stoke C	30	3		
2012–13	Stoke C	31	0		
2013–14	Stoke C	11	0	152	13

EVE, Dale (G) 0 0
Internationals: Bermuda U17, Full caps.

Season	Club		
2013–14	Stoke C	0	0
2013–14	Fleetwood T	0	0

GRANT, Alex (D) 0 0
b.Perth 23-1-94
Internationals: Australia U17.

Season	Club		
2011–12	Portsmouth	0	0
2013–14	Stoke C	0	0

HUTH, Robert (D) 243 15
H: 6 3 W: 14 07 b.Berlin 18-8-84
Internationals: Germany U21, Full caps.

Season	Club				
2001–02	Chelsea	1	0		
2002–03	Chelsea	2	0		
2003–04	Chelsea	16	0		
2004–05	Chelsea	10	0		
2005–06	Chelsea	13	0	42	0
2006–07	Middlesbrough	12	1		
2007–08	Middlesbrough	13	1		

2008–09	Middlesbrough	24	0		
2009–10	Middlesbrough	4	0	53	2
2009–10	Stoke C	32	3		
2010–11	Stoke C	35	6		
2011–12	Stoke C	34	3		
2012–13	Stoke C	35	1		
2013–14	Stoke C	12	0	148	13

IRELAND, Stephen (F)   212 19
H: 5 8   W: 10 07   b.Cork 22-8-86
Internationals: Republic of Ireland U21, Full caps.

2005–06	Manchester C	24	0		
2006–07	Manchester C	24	1		
2007–08	Manchester C	33	4		
2008–09	Manchester C	35	9		
2009–10	Manchester C	22	2		
2010–11	Manchester C	0	0	138	16
2010–11	Aston Villa	10	0		
2010–11	Newcastle U	2	0	2	0
2011–12	Aston Villa	24	1		
2012–13	Aston Villa	13	0		
2013–14	Aston Villa	0	0	47	1
2013–14	Stoke C	25	2	25	2

JEROME, Cameron (F)   332 70
H: 6 1   W: 13 06   b.Huddersfield 14-8-86
Internationals: England U21.

2004–05	Cardiff C	29	6		
2005–06	Cardiff C	44	18	73	24
2005–06	Birmingham C	0	0		
2006–07	Birmingham C	38	7		
2007–08	Birmingham C	33	7		
2008–09	Birmingham C	43	9		
2009–10	Birmingham C	32	11		
2010–11	Birmingham C	34	3		
2011–12	Birmingham C	1	0	181	37
2011–12	Stoke C	23	4		
2012–13	Stoke C	26	3		
2013–14	Stoke C	1	0	50	7
2013–14	*Crystal Palace*	28	2	28	2

KIGHTLY, Michael (F)   197 34
H: 5 10   W: 10 10   b.Basildon 24-1-86
Internationals: England U21.

2002–03	Southend U	1	0		
2003–04	Southend U	11	0		
2004–05	Southend U	1	0	13	0

From Grays Ath.

2006–07	Wolverhampton W	24	8		
2007–08	Wolverhampton W	21	4		
2008–09	Wolverhampton W	38	8		
2009–10	Wolverhampton W	9	0		
2010–11	Wolverhampton W	4	0		
2011–12	Wolverhampton W	18	3		
2011–12	*Watford*	12	3	12	3
2012–13	Wolverhampton W	0	0	114	23
2012–13	Stoke C	22	3		
2013–14	Stoke C	0	0	22	3
2013–14	*Burnley*	36	5	36	5

LECYGNE, Eddy (M)   0 0
b.Pabu 6-8-96

2013–14	Stoke C	0	0

MUNIESA, Marc (D)   15 0
H: 5 10   W: 11 04   b.Lloret de Mar 27-3-92
Internationals: Spain U16, U17, U19, U21.

2008–09	Barcelona	1	0		
2009–10	Barcelona	0	0		
2010–11	Barcelona	0	0		
2011–12	Barcelona	1	0		
2012–13	Barcelona	0	0	2	0
2013–14	Stoke C	13	0	13	0

NARDIELLO, Jack (F)   0 0
b. 21-10-94
Internationals: Wales U19.

2013–14	Stoke C	0	0

NESS, Jamie (M)   29 2
H: 6 2   W: 10 13   b.Irvine 2-3-91
Internationals: Scotland U17, U19, U21.

2010–11	Rangers	11	0		
2011–12	Rangers	5	1	16	1
2012–13	Stoke C	0	0		
2013–14	Stoke C	0	0		
2013–14	*Leyton Orient*	13	1	13	1

NZONZI, Steven (M)   194 9
H: 6 3   W: 11 11   b.Paris 15-12-88
Internationals: France U21.

2007–08	Amiens	3	0		
2008–09	Amiens	34	1	37	1

2009–10	Blackburn R	33	2		
2010–11	Blackburn R	21	1		
2011–12	Blackburn R	32	2	86	5
2012–13	Stoke C	35	1		
2013–14	Stoke C	36	2	71	3

O'REILLY, Ryan (D)   0 0
b.Crover 7-7-95
Internationals: Republic of Ireland U17.

2013–14	Stoke C	0	0

ODEMWINGIE, Peter (F)   311 89
H: 6 0   W: 11 09   b.Tashkent 15-7-81
Internationals: Nigeria Full caps.

2002–03	La Louviere	14	2		
2003–04	La Louviere	27	5		
2004–05	La Louviere	3	2	44	9
2004–05	Lille	20	4		
2005–06	Lille	26	14		
2006–07	Lille	29	5	75	23
2007	Loko Moscow	14	4		
2008	Loko Moscow	26	10		
2009	Loko Moscow	25	7		
2010	Loko Moscow	10	0	75	21
2010–11	WBA	32	15		
2011–12	WBA	30	10		
2012–13	WBA	25	5	87	30
2013–14	Cardiff C	15	1	15	1
2013–14	Stoke C	15	5	15	5

PALACIOS, Wilson (D)   147 1
H: 5 11   W: 11 11   b.La Ceiba 29-7-84
Internationals: Honduras Full caps.

2007–08	Birmingham C	7	0	7	0
2007–08	Wigan Ath	16	0		
2008–09	Wigan Ath	21	0	37	0
2008–09	Tottenham H	11	0		
2009–10	Tottenham H	33	1		
2010–11	Tottenham H	21	0		
2011–12	Tottenham H	0	0	65	1
2011–12	Stoke C	18	0		
2012–13	Stoke C	4	0		
2013–14	Stoke C	16	0	38	0

PENNANT, Jermaine (M)   292 16
H: 5 9   W: 10 06   b.Nottingham 15-1-83
Internationals: England U21.

1998–99	Notts Co	0	0		
1998–99	Arsenal	0	0		
1999–2000	Arsenal	0	0		
2000–01	Arsenal	0	0		
2001–02	Arsenal	0	0		
2001–02	Watford	9	2		
2002–03	Arsenal	5	3		
2002–03	Watford	12	0	21	2
2003–04	Arsenal	0	0		
2003–04	*Leeds U*	36	2	36	2
2004–05	Arsenal	7	0	12	3
2004–05	Birmingham C	12	0		
2005–06	Birmingham C	38	2	50	2
2006–07	Liverpool	34	1		
2007–08	Liverpool	18	2		
2008–09	Liverpool	3	0	55	3
2008–09	Portsmouth	13	0	13	0
2009–10	Zaragoza	25	0	25	0
2010–11	Stoke C	29	3		
2011–12	Stoke C	27	0		
2012–13	Stoke C	1	0		
2012–13	*Wolverhampton W*	15	0	15	0
2013–14	Stoke C	8	1	65	4

PIETERS, Erik (D)   180 3
H: 6 0   W: 13 00   b.Tiel 7-8-88
Internationals: Netherlands U17, U19, U21, Full caps.

2006–07	FC Utrecht	20	0		
2007–08	FC Utrecht	31	2	51	2
2008–09	PSV Eindhoven	17	0		
2009–10	PSV Eindhoven	27	0		
2010–11	PSV Eindhoven	31	0		
2011–12	PSV Eindhoven	16	0		
2012–13	PSV Eindhoven	2	0	93	0
2013–14	Stoke C	36	1	36	1

SHAWCROSS, Ryan (D)   245 17
H: 6 3   W: 13 13   b.Buckley 4-10-87
Internationals: England U21, Full caps.

2006–07	Manchester U	0	0
2007–08	Manchester U	0	0
2007–08	Stoke C	41	7
2008–09	Stoke C	30	3
2009–10	Stoke C	28	2
2010–11	Stoke C	35	1

2011–12	Stoke C	36	2		
2012–13	Stoke C	37	1		
2013–14	Stoke C	37	1	245	17

SHEA, Brek (M)   114 19
H: 6 3   W: 12 11   b.College Station, Texas 28-2-90
Internationals: USA U17, U20, U23, Full caps.

2008	FC Dallas	2	0		
2009	FC Dallas	19	0		
2010	FC Dallas	29	5		
2011	FC Dallas	32	11		
2012	FC Dallas	21	3	103	19
2012–13	Stoke C	2	0		
2013–14	Stoke C	1	0	3	0
2013–14	*Barnsley*	8	0	8	0

SHOTTON, Ryan (D)   120 7
H: 6 3   W: 13 05   b.Stoke 30-9-88

2006–07	Stoke C	0	0		
2007–08	Stoke C	0	0		
2008–09	Stoke C	0	0		
2008–09	*Tranmere R*	33	5	33	5
2009–10	Stoke C	0	0		
2009–10	*Barnsley*	30	0	30	0
2010–11	Stoke C	2	0		
2011–12	Stoke C	23	1		
2012–13	Stoke C	23	0		
2013–14	Stoke C	0	0	48	1
2013–14	*Wigan Ath*	9	1	9	1

SORENSEN, Thomas (G)   409 0
H: 6 4   W: 13 10   b.Fredericia 12-6-76
Internationals: Denmark U19, U21, B, Full caps.

1998–99	Sunderland	45	0		
1999–2000	Sunderland	37	0		
2000–01	Sunderland	34	0		
2001–02	Sunderland	34	0		
2002–03	Sunderland	21	0	171	0
2003–04	Aston Villa	38	0		
2004–05	Aston Villa	36	0		
2005–06	Aston Villa	36	0		
2006–07	Aston Villa	29	0		
2007–08	Aston Villa	0	0	139	0
2008–09	Stoke C	36	0		
2009–10	Stoke C	33	0		
2010–11	Stoke C	10	0		
2011–12	Stoke C	16	0		
2012–13	Stoke C	0	0		
2013–14	Stoke C	4	0	99	0

THOMAS, Adam (M)   0 0
b.Wiral 4-2-94

2013–14	Stoke C	0	0

WALTERS, Jon (F)   407 77
H: 6 0   W: 12 06   b.Birkenhead 20-9-83
Internationals: Republic of Ireland U21, B, Full caps.

2001–02	Bolton W	0	0		
2002–03	Bolton W	4	0		
2002–03	*Hull C*	11	5		
2003–04	Bolton W	0	0	4	0
2003–04	Crewe Alex	0	0		
2003–04	*Barnsley*	8	0	8	0
2003–04	Hull C	16	1		
2004–05	Hull C	21	1	48	7
2004–05	*Scunthorpe U*	3	0	3	0
2005–06	Wrexham	38	5	38	5
2006–07	Chester C	26	9	26	9
2006–07	Ipswich T	16	4		
2007–08	Ipswich T	40	13		
2008–09	Ipswich T	36	5		
2009–10	Ipswich T	43	8		
2010–11	Ipswich T	1	0	136	30
2010–11	Stoke C	36	6		
2011–12	Stoke C	38	7		
2012–13	Stoke C	38	8		
2013–14	Stoke C	32	5	144	26

WARD, Charlie (M)   0 0
b.Stoke 19-2-96

2013–14	Stoke C	0	0

WARING, George (F)   0 0
b.Chester 2-2-94

2013–14	Stoke C	0	0

WATKINS-CLARK, Mason (D)   0 0
b.Dublin 1-1-95
Internationals: Republic of Ireland U21.

2013–14	Stoke C	0	0

WESTLEY, Samuel (D) 0 0
b. 5-2-94
| 2013–14 | Stoke C | 0 | 0 | | |

WHEELER, Elliot (D) 0 0
H: 5 11 W: 11 10 b.Stoke 19-12-93
| 2013–14 | Stoke C | 0 | 0 | | |

WHELAN, Glenn (M) 351 17
H: 5 11 W: 12 07 b.Dublin 13-1-84
Internationals: Republic of Ireland U16, U21, B, Full caps.
2000–01	Manchester C	0	0		
2001–02	Manchester C	0	0		
2002–03	Manchester C	0	0		
2003–04	Manchester C	0	0		
2003–04	*Bury*	13	0	13	0
2004–05	Sheffield W	36	2		
2005–06	Sheffield W	43	1		
2006–07	Sheffield W	38	7		
2007–08	Sheffield W	25	2	142	12
2007–08	Stoke C	14	1		
2008–09	Stoke C	26	1		
2009–10	Stoke C	33	2		
2010–11	Stoke C	29	0		
2011–12	Stoke C	30	1		
2012–13	Stoke C	32	0		
2013–14	Stoke C	32	0	196	5

WILKINSON, Andy (D) 176 0
H: 5 11 W: 11 00 b.Stone 6-8-84
2001–02	Stoke C	0	0		
2002–03	Stoke C	0	0		
2003–04	Stoke C	3	0		
2004–05	Stoke C	1	0		
2004–05	*Shrewsbury T*	9	0	9	0
2005–06	Stoke C	6	0		
2006–07	Stoke C	4	0		
2006–07	*Blackpool*	7	0	7	0
2007–08	Stoke C	23	0		
2008–09	Stoke C	22	0		
2009–10	Stoke C	25	0		
2010–11	Stoke C	22	0		
2011–12	Stoke C	25	0		
2012–13	Stoke C	24	0		
2013–14	Stoke C	5	0	160	0

WILSON, Marc (M) 182 4
H: 6 2 W: 12 07 b.Lisburn 17-8-87
Internationals: Republic of Ireland U18, U19, U21, Full caps.
2005–06	Portsmouth	0	0		
2005–06	*Yeovil T*	2	0	2	0
2006–07	Portsmouth	0	0		
2006–07	*Bournemouth*	19	3		
2007–08	Portsmouth	0	0		
2007–08	*Bournemouth*	7	0	26	3
2007–08	*Luton T*	4	0	4	0
2008–09	Portsmouth	3	0		
2009–10	Portsmouth	28	0		
2010–11	Portsmouth	4	0	35	0
2010–11	Stoke C	28	1		
2011–12	Stoke C	35	0		
2012–13	Stoke C	19	0		
2013–14	Stoke C	33	0	115	1

Scholars
Banks, Lewis; Coban, Yusuf; Cook, Jake Benjamin; Coulson, Samuel Philip; Douglas, Kelvin Isaac; Edwards, Liam; Gyollai, Daniel; Kurasik, Dominic; Monlouis, Keiran Dion; Pickerill, Lee; Renee-Pringle, Johnville Isaacs Joseph; Ricketts-Hopkinson, Nathan Alton; Roberts, Oliver James; Strong, Curtis; Taylor, Joel; Vassell, Theo Gary Carlstan; Weston-Hayles, Charles-Anthony Noel.

SUNDERLAND (78)

ALONSO, Marcus (D) 91 8
H: 6 2 W: 13 05 b.Madrid 28-12-90
Internationals: Spain U19.
2008–09	RM Castilla	11	0		
2009–10	RM Castilla	28	3	39	3
2009–10	Real Madrid	1	0	1	0
2010–11	Bolton W	4	0		
2011–12	Bolton W	5	1		
2012–13	Bolton W	26	4	35	5
2013–14	Fiorentina	0	0		

On loan from Fiorentina
| 2013–14 | Sunderland | 16 | 0 | 16 | 0 |

ALTIDORE, Jozy (F) 184 57
H: 5 10 W: 12 07 b.Florida 6-11-89
Internationals: USA U17, U20, U23, Full caps.
2006	NY Red Bulls	7	3		
2007	NY Red Bulls	22	9		
2008	NY Red Bulls	8	3	37	15
2008–09	Villarreal	6	1		
2009–10	Villarreal	0	0		
2009–10	*Hull C*	28	1	28	1
2010–11	Villarreal	3	0	9	1
2010–11	*Bursaspor*	12	1	12	1
2011–12	AZ	34	15		
2012–13	AZ	33	23	67	38
2013–14	Sunderland	31	1	31	1

BA, El-Hadji (M) 1 0
H: 6 0 W: 11 08 b.Paris 5-3-93
Internationals: France U18, U19, U20.
| 2013–14 | Sunderland | 1 | 0 | 1 | 0 |

BARDSLEY, Phillip (D) 222 8
H: 5 11 W: 11 13 b.Salford 28-6-85
Internationals: Scotland Full caps.
2003–04	Manchester U	0	0		
2004–05	Manchester U	0	0		
2005–06	Manchester U	8	0		
2005–06	*Burnley*	6	0	6	0
2006–07	Manchester U	0	0		
2006–07	*Rangers*	5	1	5	1
2006–07	*Aston Villa*	13	0	13	0
2007–08	Manchester U	0	0	8	0
2007–08	*Sheffield U*	16	0	16	0
2007–08	Sunderland	11	0		
2008–09	Sunderland	28	0		
2009–10	Sunderland	26	0		
2010–11	Sunderland	34	3		
2011–12	Sunderland	31	1		
2012–13	Sunderland	18	1		
2013–14	Sunderland	26	2	174	7

BRIDCUTT, Liam (M) 174 2
H: 5 9 W: 11 07 b.Reading 8-5-89
Internationals: Scotland Full caps.
2007–08	Chelsea	0	0		
2007–08	*Yeovil T*	9	0	9	0
2008–09	Chelsea	0	0		
2008–09	*Watford*	6	0	6	0
2009–10	Chelsea	0	0		
2009–10	*Stockport Co*	15	0	15	0
2010–11	Chelsea	0	0		
2010–11	Brighton & HA	37	2		
2011–12	Brighton & HA	43	0		
2012–13	Brighton & HA	41	0		
2013–14	Brighton & HA	11	0	132	2
2013–14	Sunderland	12	0	12	0

BROWN, Wes (D) 277 4
H: 6 1 W: 13 08 b.Manchester 13-10-79
Internationals: England U21, Full caps.
1996–97	Manchester U	0	0		
1997–98	Manchester U	2	0		
1998–99	Manchester U	14	0		
1999–2000	Manchester U	0	0		
2000–01	Manchester U	28	0		
2001–02	Manchester U	17	0		
2002–03	Manchester U	22	0		
2003–04	Manchester U	17	0		
2004–05	Manchester U	21	1		
2005–06	Manchester U	19	0		
2006–07	Manchester U	22	0		
2007–08	Manchester U	36	1		
2008–09	Manchester U	8	1		
2009–10	Manchester U	19	0		
2010–11	Manchester U	7	0	232	3
2011–12	Sunderland	20	1		
2012–13	Sunderland	0	0		
2013–14	Sunderland	25	0	45	1

CABRAL, Adilson (M) 107 2
H: 5 10 W: 11 10 b.Praia 22-10-88
Internationals: Switzerland U18, U19, U20, U21. Cape Verde Full caps.
2007–08	Basle	9	0		
2008–09	Basle	0	0		
2009–10	Basle	23	1		
2010–11	Basle	20	0		
2011–12	Basle	20	1		
2012–13	Basle	27	0	99	2

| 2013–14 | Sunderland | 1 | 0 | 1 | 0 |
| 2013–14 | Genoa | 7 | 0 | 7 | 0 |

CATTERMOLE, Lee (M) 204 5
H: 5 10 W: 11 13 b.Stockton 21-3-88
Internationals: England U16, U17, U18, U19, U21.
2005–06	Middlesbrough	14	1		
2006–07	Middlesbrough	31	1		
2007–08	Middlesbrough	24	1	69	3
2008–09	Wigan Ath	33	1		
2009–10	Wigan Ath	0	0	33	1
2009–10	Sunderland	22	0		
2010–11	Sunderland	23	0		
2011–12	Sunderland	23	0		
2012–13	Sunderland	10	0		
2013–14	Sunderland	24	1	102	1

CELUSTKA, Ondrej (D) 142 7
H: 6 1 W: 12 05 b.Zlin 18-6-89
Internationals: Czech Republic U19, U20, U21, Full caps.
2007–08	Tescoma Zlin	2	0		
2008–09	Tescoma Zlin	22	3	24	3
2009–10	Slavia Prague	13	1		
2009–10	*Palermo*	1	0	1	0
2010–11	Slavia Prague	28	2	41	3
2011–12	Trabzonspor	36	1		
2012–13	Trabzonspor	19	0		
2013–14	Trabzonspor	0	0	55	1
On loan from Trabzonspor
2013–14	Sunderland	21	0	21	0

COLBACK, Jack (M) 165 8
H: 5 9 W: 11 05 b.Killingworth 24-10-89
Internationals: England U20.
2007–08	Sunderland	0	0		
2008–09	Sunderland	0	0		
2009–10	Sunderland	1	0		
2009–10	*Ipswich T*	37	4		
2010–11	Sunderland	11	0		
2010–11	*Ipswich T*	13	0	50	4
2011–12	Sunderland	35	1		
2012–13	Sunderland	35	0		
2013–14	Sunderland	33	3	115	4

CUELLAR, Carlos (D) 320 13
H: 6 3 W: 13 03 b.Madrid 23-8-81
2000–01	Calahorra	27	0	27	0
2001–02	Numancia	23	1		
2002–03	Numancia	39	3	62	4
2003–04	Osasuna	5	0		
2004–05	Osasuna	14	0		
2005–06	Osasuna	29	1		
2006–07	Osasuna	23	1	71	2
2007–08	Rangers	36	4	36	4
2008–09	Aston Villa	28	0		
2009–10	Aston Villa	36	2		
2010–11	Aston Villa	12	0		
2011–12	Aston Villa	18	0	94	2
2012–13	Sunderland	26	1		
2013–14	Sunderland	4	0	30	1

DIAKITE, Modibo (D) 79 2
H: 6 3 W: 13 02 b.Paris 2-3-87
2006–07	Lazio	3	0		
2007–08	Lazio	0	0		
2008–09	Lazio	9	1		
2009–10	Lazio	18	0		
2010–11	Lazio	8	0		
2011–12	Lazio	25	1		
2012–13	Lazio	0	0	63	2
2013–14	Sunderland	7	0	7	0
2013–14	Fiorentina	9	0	9	0

DIXON, Joel (G) 0 0
b.Middlesbrough 30-11-92
| 2012–13 | Sunderland | 0 | 0 | | |
| 2013–14 | Sunderland | 0 | 0 | | |

DOSSENA, Andrea (D) 302 9
H: 5 11 W: 11 08 b.Lodi 11-9-81
Internationals: Italy U20, Full caps.
2001–02	Verona	2	0		
2002–03	Verona	21	1		
2003–04	Verona	37	1		
2004–05	Verona	39	1	99	3
2005–06	Treviso	21	0	21	0
2006–07	Udinese	28	0		
2007–08	Udinese	35	2	63	2
2008–09	Liverpool	16	1		
2009–10	Liverpool	2	0	18	1
2009–10	Napoli	10	0		

2010–11	Napoli	33	1		
2011–12	Napoli	33	2		
2012–13	Napoli	7	0	83	3
2012–13	*Palermo*	11	0	11	0
2013–14	Sunderland	7	0	7	0

EGAN, John (D)   19 1
H: 6 1 W: 11 11 b.Cork 20-10-92
Internationals: Republic of Ireland U17, U19, U21.

2009–10	Sunderland	0	0		
2010–11	Sunderland	0	0		
2011–12	Sunderland	0	0		
2011–12	*Crystal Palace*	1	0	1	0
2011–12	*Sheffield U*	1	0	1	0
2012–13	Sunderland	0	0		
2012–13	*Bradford C*	4	0	4	0
2013–14	Sunderland	0	0		
2013–14	*Southend U*	13	1	13	1

FERGUSON, David (D)   0 0
b.Sunderland 7-6-94

| 2012–13 | Sunderland | 0 | 0 | | |
| 2013–14 | Sunderland | 0 | 0 | | |

FLETCHER, Steven (F)   300 87
H: 6 1 W: 12 00 b.Shrewsbury 26-3-87
Internationals: Scotland U20, U21, B, Full caps.

2003–04	Hibernian	5	0		
2004–05	Hibernian	20	5		
2005–06	Hibernian	34	8		
2006–07	Hibernian	31	6		
2007–08	Hibernian	32	13		
2008–09	Hibernian	34	11	156	43
2009–10	Burnley	35	8	35	8
2010–11	Wolverhampton W	29	10		
2011–12	Wolverhampton W	32	12	61	22
2012–13	Sunderland	28	11		
2013–14	Sunderland	20	3	48	14

GARDNER, Craig (M)   182 25
H: 5 10 W: 11 13 b.Solihull 25-11-86
Internationals: England U21.

2004–05	Aston Villa	0	0		
2005–06	Aston Villa	8	0		
2006–07	Aston Villa	13	2		
2007–08	Aston Villa	23	3		
2008–09	Aston Villa	14	0		
2009–10	Aston Villa	1	0	59	5
2009–10	Birmingham C	13	1		
2010–11	Birmingham C	29	8	42	9
2011–12	Sunderland	30	3		
2012–13	Sunderland	33	6		
2013–14	Sunderland	18	2	81	11

GIACCHERINI, Emanuele (M)   161 28
H: 5 3 W: 10 07 b.Forlì 5-5-85
Internationals: Italy Full caps.

2008–09	Cesena	29	5		
2009–10	Cesena	32	8		
2010–11	Cesena	36	7	97	20
2011–12	Juventus	23	1		
2012–13	Juventus	17	3	40	4
2013–14	Sunderland	24	4	24	4

GRAHAM, Danny (F)   339 99
H: 5 11 W: 12 05 b.Gateshead 12-8-85
Internationals: England U20.

2003–04	Middlesbrough	0	0		
2003–04	*Darlington*	9	2	9	2
2004–05	Middlesbrough	11	1		
2005–06	Middlesbrough	3	0		
2005–06	*Derby Co*	14	0	14	0
2005–06	*Leeds U*	3	0	3	0
2006–07	Middlesbrough	1	0		
2006–07	*Blackpool*	4	1	4	1
2006–07	*Carlisle U*	11	7		
2007–08	Carlisle U	45	14		
2008–09	Carlisle U	44	15	100	36
2009–10	Watford	46	14		
2010–11	Watford	45	23	91	37
2011–12	Swansea C	36	12		
2012–13	Swansea C	18	3	54	15
2012–13	Sunderland	13	0		
2013–14	Sunderland	0	0	13	0
2013–14	*Hull C*	18	1	18	1
2013–14	*Middlesbrough*	18	6	33	7

HARRISON, Scott (D)   7 0
b.Middlesbrough 3-9-93

| 2012–13 | Sunderland | 0 | 0 | | |
| 2013–14 | Sunderland | 0 | 0 | | |

| 2013–14 | *Bury* | 1 | 0 | 1 | 0 |
| 2013–14 | *Hartlepool U* | 6 | 0 | 6 | 0 |

JI, Dong-Won (F)   74 17
H: 6 2 W: 12 04 b.Jeju 28-5-91
Internationals: South Korea U20, U23, Full caps.

2010	Chunnam D	22	7		
2011	Chunnam D	11	3	33	10
2011–12	Sunderland	19	2		
2012–13	Sunderland	0	0		
2012–13	*Augsburg*	17	5	17	5
2013–14	Sunderland	5	0	24	2

Transferred to Augsburg January 2014.

JOHNSON, Adam (M)   257 42
H: 5 8 W: 10 00 b.Sunderland 14-7-87
Internationals: England U19, U21, Full caps.

2004–05	Middlesbrough	0	0		
2005–06	Middlesbrough	13	1		
2006–07	Middlesbrough	12	0		
2006–07	*Leeds U*	5	0	5	0
2007–08	Middlesbrough	19	1		
2007–08	*Watford*	12	5	12	5
2008–09	Middlesbrough	26	0		
2009–10	Middlesbrough	26	11	96	13
2009–10	Manchester C	16	1		
2010–11	Manchester C	31	4		
2011–12	Manchester C	26	6		
2012–13	Manchester C	0	0	73	11
2012–13	Sunderland	35	5		
2013–14	Sunderland	36	8	71	13

KNOTT, Billy (M)   56 6
H: 5 8 W: 11 02 b.Canvey Island 28-11-92
Internationals: England U16, U17, U20.

2010–11	Sunderland	0	0		
2011–12	Sunderland	0	0		
2011–12	*AFC Wimbledon*	20	3	20	3
2012–13	Sunderland	1	0		
2013–14	Sunderland	0	0	1	0
2013–14	*Wycombe W*	17	1	17	1
2013–14	*Port Vale*	18	2	18	2

LARSSON, Sebastian (M)   288 28
H: 5 11 W: 11 02 b.Eskilstuna 6-6-85
Internationals: Sweden U16, U17, U19, U21, Full caps.

2002–03	Arsenal	0	0		
2003–04	Arsenal	0	0		
2004–05	Arsenal	0	0		
2005–06	Arsenal	3	0		
2006–07	Arsenal	0	0	3	0
2006–07	Birmingham C	43	4		
2007–08	Birmingham C	35	6		
2008–09	Birmingham C	38	1		
2009–10	Birmingham C	33	4		
2010–11	Birmingham C	35	4	184	19
2011–12	Sunderland	32	7		
2012–13	Sunderland	38	1		
2013–14	Sunderland	31	1	101	9

MANDRON, Mikael (F)   13 1
H: 6 3 W: 12 13 b.Boulogne 11-10-94

2011–12	Sunderland	0	0		
2012–13	Sunderland	2	0		
2013–14	Sunderland	0	0	2	0
2013–14	*Fleetwood T*	11	1	11	1

MANNONE, Vito (G)   77 0
H: 6 0 W: 11 08 b.Milan 2-3-88
Internationals: Italy U21.

2005–06	Arsenal	0	0		
2006–07	Arsenal	0	0		
2006–07	*Barnsley*	2	0	2	0
2007–08	Arsenal	0	0		
2008–09	Arsenal	1	0		
2009–10	Arsenal	5	0		
2010–11	Arsenal	0	0		
2011–12	*Hull C*	10	0		
2011–12	Arsenal	0	0		
2011–12	*Hull C*	21	0	31	0
2012–13	Arsenal	9	0	15	0
2013–14	Sunderland	29	0	29	0

MAVRIAS, Charis (M)   55 3
H: 5 10 W: 11 08 b.Zakynthos 21-2-94
Internationals: Greece U17, U19, U21, Full caps.

2010–11	Panathinaikos	4	0		
2011–12	Panathinaikos	21	1		
2012–13	Panathinaikos	26	2	51	3
2013–14	Sunderland	4	0	4	0

MOBERG KARLSSON, David (M)   34 2
H: 5 10 W: 11 12 b.Mariestad 20-3-94
Internationals: Sweden U17, U19.

2011	IFK Goteborg	2	0		
2012	IFK Goteborg	18	0		
2013	IFK Goteborg	10	2	30	2
2013–14	Sunderland	0	0		
2013–14	*Kilmarnock*	4	0	4	0

N'DIAYE, Alfred (M)   153 7
H: 6 2 W: 13 08 b.Paris 6-3-90
Internationals: France U17, U19, U20, U21. Senegal Full caps.

2008–09	AS Nancy	24	0		
2009–10	AS Nancy	23	0		
2010–11	AS Nancy	13	0	60	0
2011–12	Bursaspor	32	3		
2012–13	Bursaspor	13	1	45	4
2012–13	Sunderland	16	0		
2013–14	Sunderland	0	0	16	0
2013–14	*Eskisehirspor*	16	3	16	3
2013–14	*Real Betis*	16	0	16	0

O'SHEA, John (D)   362 14
H: 6 3 W: 13 07 b.Waterford 30-4-81
Internationals: Republic of Ireland U21, Full caps.

1998–99	Manchester U	0	0		
1999–2000	Manchester U	0	0		
1999–2000	*Bournemouth*	10	1	10	1
2000–01	Manchester U	9	0		
2001–02	Manchester U	9	0		
2002–03	Manchester U	32	0		
2003–04	Manchester U	33	2		
2004–05	Manchester U	23	2		
2005–06	Manchester U	34	1		
2006–07	Manchester U	32	4		
2007–08	Manchester U	28	0		
2008–09	Manchester U	30	0		
2009–10	Manchester U	15	1		
2010–11	Manchester U	20	0	256	10
2011–12	Sunderland	29	0		
2012–13	Sunderland	34	2		
2013–14	Sunderland	33	1	96	3

OLIVER, Connor (D)   3 0

| 2013–14 | Sunderland | 0 | 0 | | |
| 2013–14 | *Hartlepool U* | 3 | 0 | 3 | 0 |

PICKFORD, Jordan (G)   30 0
b.Washington 7-3-94
Internationals: England U16, U17, U18, U19.

2010–11	Sunderland	0	0		
2011–12	Sunderland	0	0		
2012–13	Sunderland	0	0		
2013–14	Sunderland	0	0		
2013–14	*Burton Alb*	12	0	12	0
2013–14	*Carlisle U*	18	0	18	0

ROBERGE, Valentin (D)   111 2
H: 6 1 W: 11 06 b.Montreuil 9-6-87

2008–09	Aris Thessaloniki	20	0		
2009–10	Aris Thessaloniki	5	0	25	0
2010–11	Maritimo	25	1		
2011–12	Maritimo	25	0		
2012–13	Maritimo	27	1	77	2
2013–14	Sunderland	9	0	9	0

SCOCCO, Ignacio (F)   291 96
H: 5 8 W: 11 04 b.Hughes 29-5-85
Internationals: Argentina U20, Full caps.

2003–04	Newell's Old Boys	7	0		
2004–05	Newell's Old Boys	36	3		
2005–06	Newell's Old Boys	35	13		
2006–07	UNAM Pumas	28	10		
2007–08	UNAM Pumas	25	8	53	18
2008–09	AEK Athens	31	7		
2009–10	AEK Athens	29	9		
2010–11	AEK Athens	28	10	88	26
2011–12	Al-Ain	19	9	19	9
2012–13	Newell's Old Boys	32	24	108	40
2013	Internacional	17	3	17	3
2013–14	Sunderland	6	0	6	0

SMITH, Martin (F)   0 0

| 2013–14 | Sunderland | 0 | 0 | | |

VAUGHAN, David (M)   359 26
H: 5 7 W: 11 00 b.Abergele 18-2-83
Internationals: Wales U19, U21, Full caps.

2000–01	Crewe Alex	1	0		
2001–02	Crewe Alex	13	0		
2002–03	Crewe Alex	32	3		

2003–04	Crewe Alex	31	0		
2004–05	Crewe Alex	44	6		
2005–06	Crewe Alex	34	5		
2006–07	Crewe Alex	29	4		
2007–08	Crewe Alex	1	0	185	18
2007–08	Real Sociedad	7	1	7	1
2008–09	Blackpool	33	1		
2009–10	Blackpool	41	1		
2010–11	Blackpool	35	2	109	4
2011–12	Sunderland	22	2		
2012–13	Sunderland	24	1		
2013–14	Sunderland	3	0	49	3
2013–14	*Nottingham F*	9	0	9	0

VERGINI, Santiago (D)   113 6
H: 6 3 W: 13 00 b.Maximo Paz 3-8-88
Internationals: Argentina Full caps.

2008–09	Olimpia	0	0		
2009–10	Olimpia	0	0		
2010–11	Olimpia	0	0	4	0
2010–11	*Verona*	15	1	15	1
2011–12	Newell's Old Boys	32	3		
2012–13	Newell's Old Boys	34	1	66	4
2013–14	Estudiantes	17	1	17	1

On loan from Estudiantes

2013–14	Sunderland	11	0	11	0

WATMORE, Duncan (F)   9 1
b. 8-3-94

2013–14	Sunderland	0	0		
2013–14	*Hibernian*	9	1	9	1

WESTWOOD, Keiren (G)   277 0
H: 6 1 W: 13 10 b.Manchester 23-10-84
Internationals: Republic of Ireland Full caps.

2001–02	Manchester C	0	0		
2002–03	Manchester C	0	0		
2003–04	Manchester C	0	0		
2003–04	*Oldham Ath*	0	0		
2004–05	Manchester C	0	0		
2005–06	Manchester C	0	0		
2005–06	Carlisle U	35	0		
2006–07	Carlisle U	46	0		
2007–08	Carlisle U	46	0	127	0
2008–09	Coventry C	46	0		
2009–10	Coventry C	44	0		
2010–11	Coventry C	41	0	131	0
2011–12	Sunderland	9	0		
2012–13	Sunderland	0	0		
2013–14	Sunderland	10	0	19	0

WICKHAM, Connor (F)   130 28
H: 6 0 W: 14 01 b.Hereford 31-3-93
Internationals: England U16, U17, U19, U21.

2008–09	Ipswich T	2	0		
2009–10	Ipswich T	26	4		
2010–11	Ipswich T	37	9	65	13
2011–12	Sunderland	16	1		
2012–13	Sunderland	12	0		
2012–13	*Sheffield W*	6	1		
2013–14	Sunderland	15	5	43	6
2013–14	*Sheffield W*	11	8	17	9
2013–14	*Leeds U*	5	0	5	0

Scholars
Agnew, Liam John; Beadling, Thomas; Blinco, Jordan William; Burke, Peter; Cartwright, Andrew; Colquhoun, Ross; Ellison, Ryan; Greenwood, Rees; Lawson, Carl; Ledger, Michael; McEvoy, Dylan James; McNamee, Thomas Gerard; Robson, Thomas; Sukar, Jassem Mohamed.

SWANSEA C (79)

ALFEI, Daniel (D)   16 0
H: 5 11 W: 12 02 b.Swansea 23-2-92
Internationals: Wales U17, U19, U21.

2010–11	Swansea C	1	0		
2011–12	Swansea C	0	0		
2012–13	Swansea C	0	0		
2013–14	Swansea C	0	0	1	0
2013–14	*Portsmouth*	15	0	15	0

AMAT, Jordi (D)   85 1
H: 6 0 W: 12 03 b.Barcelona 21-3-92
Internationals: Spain U16, U17, U18, U19, U20, U21.

2009–10	Espanyol	6	0		
2010–11	Espanyol	26	0		
2011–12	Espanyol	9	0		
2012–13	Espanyol	0	0	41	0
2012–13	*Rayo Vallecano*	27	1	27	1
2013–14	Swansea C	17	0	17	0

BARTLEY, Kyle (D)   80 4
H: 5 11 W: 11 00 b.Stockport 22-5-91
Internationals: England U16, U17.

2008–09	Arsenal	0	0		
2009–10	Arsenal	0	0		
2009–10	*Sheffield U*	14	0		
2010–11	Arsenal	0	0		
2010–11	*Sheffield U*	21	0	35	0
2010–11	*Rangers*	5	1		
2011–12	Arsenal	0	0		
2011–12	*Rangers*	19	0	24	1
2012–13	Arsenal	0	0		
2012–13	Swansea C	2	0		
2013–14	Swansea C	2	0	4	0
2013–14	*Birmingham C*	17	3	17	3

BONY, Wilfried (F)   157 84
H: 6 0 W: 13 11 b.Bingerville 10-12-88
Internationals: Ivory Coast Full caps.

2008–09	Sparta Prague	16	3		
2009–10	Sparta Prague	29	9		
2010–11	Sparta Prague	13	10	58	22
2010–11	Vitesse	7	3		
2011–12	Vitesse	28	12		
2012–13	Vitesse	30	31	65	46
2013–14	Vitesse	34	16	34	16

BRAY, Alex (M)   0 0
b.Bath 25-7-95
Internationals: Wales U19.

2013–14	Swansea C	0	0		

BRITTON, Leon (M)   430 11
H: 5 6 W: 10 00 b.Merton 16-9-82
Internationals: England Youth.

1999–2000	West Ham U	0	0		
2000–01	West Ham U	0	0		
2001–02	West Ham U	0	0		
2002–03	West Ham U	0	0		
2002–03	*Swansea C*	25	0		
2003–04	Swansea C	42	3		
2004–05	Swansea C	30	1		
2005–06	Swansea C	38	4		
2006–07	Swansea C	41	2		
2007–08	Swansea C	40	0		
2008–09	Swansea C	43	0		
2009–10	Swansea C	36	0		
2010–11	Sheffield U	24	0	24	0
2010–11	Swansea C	17	1		
2011–12	Swansea C	36	0		
2012–13	Swansea C	33	0		
2013–14	Swansea C	25	0	406	11

CANAS, Jose Alberto (M)   89 0
H: 5 10 W: 10 00 b.Jerez de la Frontera 27-5-87

2008–09	Real Betis	2	0		
2009–10	Real Betis	0	0		
2010–11	Real Betis	15	0		
2011–12	Real Betis	22	0		
2012–13	Real Betis	27	0	66	0
2013–14	Swansea C	23	0	23	0

CHICO (D)   154 3
H: 6 2 W: 11 10 b.Cadiz 6-3-87
Internationals: Spain U21.

2006–07	Cadiz	1	0	1	0
2008–09	Almeria	20	1		
2009–10	Almeria	27	0	47	1
2010–11	Genoa	16	0	16	0
2011–12	*Mallorca*	33	0	33	0
2012–13	Swansea C	26	0		
2013–14	Swansea C	31	2	57	2

CORNELL, David (G)   30 0
H: 5 11 W: 11 07 b.Gorseinon 28-3-91
Internationals: Wales U17, U19, U21.

2009–10	Swansea C	0	0		
2010–11	Swansea C	0	0		
2011–12	Swansea C	0	0		
2011–12	*Hereford U*	25	0	25	0
2012–13	Swansea C	0	0		
2013–14	Swansea C	0	0		
2013–14	*St Mirren*	5	0	5	0

DAVIES, Ben (D)   71 3
H: 5 7 W: 12 00 b.Neath 24-4-93
Internationals: Wales U19, Full caps.

2011–12	Swansea C	0	0		
2012–13	Swansea C	37	1		
2013–14	Swansea C	34	2	71	3

DAVIES, Oliver (G)   0 0
b.Neath 31-12-94

2013–14	Swansea C	0	0		

DE GUZMAN, Jonathan (M)   233 37
H: 5 8 W: 10 02 b.Toronto 13-9-87
Internationals: Netherlands U21, Full caps.

2005–06	Feyenoord	29	4		
2006–07	Feyenoord	32	7		
2007–08	Feyenoord	33	8		
2008–09	Feyenoord	2	0		
2009–10	Feyenoord	13	3	109	22
2010–11	Mallorca	33	5		
2011–12	Mallorca	1	1	34	6
2011–12	Villarreal	19	0		
2012–13	Villarreal	0	0		
2012–13	*Swansea C*	37	5		
2013–14	Villarreal	0	0	19	0

On loan from Villarreal

2013–14	Swansea C	34	4	71	9

DONNELLY, Rory (F)   49 20
H: 6 2 W: 12 10 b.Belfast 18-2-92
Internationals: Northern Ireland U21.

2010–11	Cliftonville	31	7		
2011–12	Cliftonville	18	13	49	20
2011–12	Swansea C	0	0		
2012–13	Swansea C	0	0		
2013–14	Swansea C	0	0		
2013–14	*Coventry C*	0	0		

DYER, Nathan (M)   269 24
H: 5 5 W: 9 00 b.Trowbridge 29-11-87
Internationals: England Youth.

2005–06	Southampton	17	0		
2005–06	*Burnley*	5	2	5	2
2006–07	Southampton	18	0		
2007–08	Southampton	17	1		
2008–09	Southampton	0	0	56	1
2008–09	*Sheffield U*	7	1	7	1
2008–09	Swansea C	17	2		
2009–10	Swansea C	40	2		
2010–11	Swansea C	46	2		
2011–12	Swansea C	34	5		
2012–13	Swansea C	37	3		
2013–14	Swansea C	27	6	201	20

EDWARDS, Gwion (M)   25 2
H: 5 9 W: 12 00 b.Carmarthen 1-3-93
Internationals: Wales U19, U21

2011–12	Swansea C	0	0		
2012–13	Swansea C	0	0		
2012–13	*St Johnstone*	6	0		
2013–14	Swansea C	0	0		
2013–14	*St Johnstone*	13	0	19	0
2013–14	*Crawley T*	6	2	6	2

EVANS, Sam (M)   0 0
b.Swansea 12-5-95
Internationals: Wales U19.

2013–14	Swansea C	0	0		

FULTON, Jay (M)   2 0
H: 5 10 W: 10 08 b.Bolton 4-4-94
Internationals: Scotland U18, U19.

2013–14	Swansea C	2	0	2	0

GOGIC, Alex (M)   0 0
H: 6 1 b.Nicosia 13-4-94
Internationals: Serbia U17. Cyprus U19.

2013–14	Swansea C	0	0		

GORRE, Kenji (M)   0 0
b.Paramaribo 29-9-94

2013–14	Swansea C	0	0		

HANLEY, Raheem (D)   0 0
H: 5 8 W: 11 00 b.Blackburn 24-3-94
Internationals: England U19.

2011–12	Blackburn R	0	0		
2012–13	Blackburn R	0	0		
2013–14	Blackburn R	0	0		
2013–14	Swansea C	0	0		

HEDGES, Ryan (M)   0 0
b.Swansea 7-9-95
Internationals: Wales U19.

2013–14	Swansea C	0	0		

HERNANDEZ, Pablo (M)   210 29
H: 5 8 W: 10 00 b.Castellon 11-4-85
Internationals: Spain Full caps.

2005–06	Valencia	1	0		

2006–07	Cadiz	14	4	14	4
2007–08	Getafe	28	3	28	3
2008–09	Valencia	21	4		
2009–10	Valencia	33	5		
2010–11	Valencia	26	5		
2011–12	Valencia	30	3	111	17
2012–13	Swansea C	30	3		
2013–14	Swansea C	27	2	57	5

JONES, Henry (M) 0 0
H: 6 0 W: 13 02 b.Swansea 18-9-93

| 2012–13 | Swansea C | 0 | 0 | | |
| 2013–14 | Swansea C | 0 | 0 | | |

KI, Sung-Yeung (M) 123 12
H: 6 2 W: 11 10 b.Gwangju 24-1-89
Internationals: South Korea U17, U20, U23, Full caps.

2009–10	Celtic	10	0		
2010–11	Celtic	26	3		
2011–12	Celtic	30	6	66	9
2012–13	Swansea C	29	0		
2013–14	Swansea C	1	0	30	0
2013–14	Sunderland	27	3	27	3

KING, Adam (M) 2 0
H: 5 11 W: 11 10 b.Edinburgh 11-10-95
Internationals: Scotland U18, U19.

2012–13	Hearts	0	0		
2013–14	Hearts	2	0	2	0
2013–14	Swansea C	0	0		

LAMAH, Roland (F) 188 26
H: 5 11 W: 11 01 b.Leige 31-12-87
Internationals: Belgium U19, U20, U21, Full caps.

2006–07	Anderlecht	5	0	5	0
2007–08	Roda JC	32	11	32	11
2008–09	Le Mans	32	3		
2009–10	Le Mans	31	4		
2010–11	Le Mans	25	3		
2011–12	Le Mans	4	0	92	10
2011–12	Osasuna	30	1		
2012–13	Osasuna	15	2		
2012–13	Swansea C	5	0		
2013–14	Osasuna	0	0	45	3

On loan from Osusana

| 2013–14 | Swansea C | 9 | 2 | 14 | 2 |

LITA, Leroy (F) 320 93
H: 5 7 W: 11 12 b.DR Congo 28-12-84
Internationals: England U21.

2002–03	Bristol C	15	2		
2003–04	Bristol C	26	5		
2004–05	Bristol C	44	24	85	31
2005–06	Reading	26	11		
2006–07	Reading	33	7		
2007–08	Reading	14	1		
2007–08	Charlton Ath	8	3	8	3
2008–09	Reading	10	1	83	20
2008–09	Norwich C	16	7	16	7
2009–10	Middlesbrough	40	8		
2010–11	Middlesbrough	38	12	78	20
2011–12	Swansea C	16	2		
2012–13	Swansea C	0	0		
2012–13	Birmingham C	10	3	10	3
2012–13	Sheffield W	17	6	17	6
2013–14	Swansea C	2	0	18	2
2013–14	Brighton & HA	5	1	5	1

LOVERIDGE, James (F) 7 0
H: 6 2 W: 13 04 b.Swansea 16-5-94
Internationals: Wales U17, U19.

2012–13	Swansea C	0	0		
2013–14	Swansea C	0	0		
2013–14	Milton Keynes D	7	0	7	0

LUCAS, Lee (M) 4 0
H: 5 11 W: 11 08 b.Aberdare 10-6-92
Internationals: Wales U17, U19, U21.

2010–11	Swansea C	1	0		
2011–12	Swansea C	0	0		
2011–12	Burton Alb	1	0	1	0
2012–13	Swansea C	0	0		
2013–14	Swansea C	0	0	1	0
2013–14	Cheltenham T	2	0	2	0

MARCH, Kurtis (M) 0 0
H: 5 9 W: 11 03 b.Swansea 30-4-93
Internationals: Wales U19.

2011–12	Swansea C	0	0		
2012–13	Swansea C	0	0		
2013–14	Swansea C	0	0		

MICHU, Miguel (M) 176 50
H: 6 1 W: 12 07 b.Oviedo 21-3-86
Internationals: Spain Full caps.

2007–08	Celta Vigo	12	1		
2008–09	Celta Vigo	18	1		
2009–10	Celta Vigo	27	6		
2010–11	Celta Vigo	30	7	87	15
2011–12	Rayo Vallecano	37	15	37	15
2012–13	Swansea C	35	18		
2013–14	Swansea C	17	2	52	20

NGOG, David (F) 165 24
H: 6 3 W: 12 04 b.Paris 1-4-89
Internationals: France U16, U17, U18, U19, U21.

2006–07	Paris St Germain	4	0		
2007–08	Paris St Germain	14	1	18	1
2008–09	Liverpool	14	2		
2009–10	Liverpool	24	5		
2010–11	Liverpool	25	2		
2011–12	Liverpool	0	0	63	9
2011–12	Bolton W	33	3		
2012–13	Bolton W	31	8		
2013–14	Bolton W	17	3	81	14
2013–14	Swansea C	3	0	3	0

OBENG, Curtis (D) 24 0
H: 5 6 W: 10 05 b.Manchester 14-2-89
Internationals: England U19.

| 2007–08 | Manchester C | 0 | 0 | | |
| 2008–09 | Manchester C | 0 | 0 | | |

From Wrexham

2011–12	Swansea C	0	0		
2012–13	Swansea C	0	0		
2012–13	Fleetwood T	5	0	5	0
2013–14	York C	4	0	4	0
2013–14	Swansea C	0	0		
2013–14	Stevenage	15	0	15	0

POZUELO, Alejandro (M) 51 3
H: 5 7 W: 9 12 b.Seville 20-9-91

2011–12	Real Betis	18	2		
2012–13	Real Betis	11	1	29	3
2013–14	Swansea C	22	0	22	0

RANGEL, Angel (D) 290 10
H: 5 11 W: 11 09 b.Barcelona 28-10-82

2006–07	Terrassa	34	2	34	2
2007–08	Swansea C	43	2		
2008–09	Swansea C	40	1		
2009–10	Swansea C	38	0		
2010–11	Swansea C	38	2		
2011–12	Swansea C	34	0		
2012–13	Swansea C	33	3		
2013–14	Swansea C	30	0	256	8

RICHARDS, Ashley (M) 49 0
H: 6 1 W: 12 04 b.Swansea 12-4-91
Internationals: Wales U17, U19, U21, Full caps.

2009–10	Swansea C	15	0		
2010–11	Swansea C	6	0		
2011–12	Swansea C	8	0		
2012–13	Swansea C	0	0		
2012–13	Crystal Palace	11	0	11	0
2013–14	Swansea C	0	0	29	0
2013–14	Huddersfield T	9	0	9	0

ROUTLEDGE, Wayne (M) 360 31
H: 5 6 W: 11 02 b.Sidcup 7-1-85
Internationals: England U20, U21.

2001–02	Crystal Palace	2	0		
2002–03	Crystal Palace	26	4		
2003–04	Crystal Palace	44	6		
2004–05	Crystal Palace	38	0	110	10
2005–06	Tottenham H	3	0		
2005–06	Portsmouth	13	0	13	0
2006–07	Tottenham H	0	0		
2006–07	Fulham	24	0	24	0
2007–08	Tottenham H	2	0	5	0
2007–08	Aston Villa	1	0		
2008–09	Aston Villa	1	0	2	0
2008–09	Cardiff C	9	2	9	2
2008–09	QPR	19	1		
2009–10	QPR	25	2		
2009–10	Newcastle U	17	3		
2010–11	Newcastle U	17	0	34	3
2010–11	QPR	20	5	64	8
2011–12	Swansea C	28	1		
2012–13	Swansea C	36	5		
2013–14	Swansea C	35	2	99	8

SCOTT, Kris (M) 0 0
b.Brsitol 23-5-95
Internationals: Republic of Ireland U19.

| 2013–14 | Swansea C | 0 | 0 | | |

SHEEHAN, Josh (M) 0 0
b.Pembrey 30-3-95
Internationals: Wales U19.

| 2013–14 | Swansea C | 0 | 0 | | |

SHELVEY, Jonjo (M) 131 21
H: 6 1 W: 11 02 b.Romford 27-2-92
Internationals: England U16, U17, U19, U21, Full caps.

2007–08	Charlton Ath	2	0		
2008–09	Charlton Ath	16	3		
2009–10	Charlton Ath	24	4	42	7
2010–11	Liverpool	15	0		
2011–12	Liverpool	13	1		
2011–12	Blackpool	10	6	10	6
2012–13	Liverpool	19	1	47	2
2013–14	Swansea C	32	6	32	6

SHEPHARD, Liam (D) 0 0
b.Rhondda 22-11-94

| 2013–14 | Swansea C | 0 | 0 | | |

TANCOCK, Scott (D) 0 0
H: 6 1 W: 11 10 b.Swansea 29-12-92
Internationals: Wales U21.

| 2012–13 | Swansea C | 0 | 0 | | |
| 2013–14 | Swansea C | 0 | 0 | | |

TATE, Alan (D) 311 5
H: 6 1 W: 13 05 b.Seaham 2-9-82

2000–01	Manchester U	0	0		
2001–02	Manchester U	0	0		
2002–03	Manchester U	0	0		
2002–03	Swansea C	27	0		
2003–04	Manchester U	0	0		
2003–04	Swansea C	26	1		
2004–05	Swansea C	23	0		
2005–06	Swansea C	43	0		
2006–07	Swansea C	38	1		
2007–08	Swansea C	21	1		
2008–09	Swansea C	29	1		
2009–10	Swansea C	39	1		
2010–11	Swansea C	40	0		
2011–12	Swansea C	5	0		
2012–13	Swansea C	3	0		
2012–13	Leeds U	10	0	10	0
2013–14	Swansea C	0	0	290	5
2013–14	Yeovil T	4	0	4	0
2013–14	Aberdeen	7	0	7	0

TAYLOR, Neil (D) 107 0
H: 5 9 W: 10 02 b.Ruthin 7-2-89
Internationals: Wales U17, U19, U21, Full caps. Great Britain.

2007–08	Wrexham	26	0	26	0
2010–11	Swansea C	29	0		
2011–12	Swansea C	36	0		
2012–13	Swansea C	, 6	0		
2013–14	Swansea C	10	0	81	0

TIENDALLI, Dwight (D) 183 5
H: 5 9 W: 11 08 b.Surinam 21-10-85
Internationals: Netherlands U21, Full caps.

2004–05	FC Utrecht	10	1		
2005–06	FC Utrecht	29	2		
2006–07	FC Utrecht	1	0	40	3
2006–07	Feyenoord	13	0		
2007–08	S Rotterdam	13	0	13	0
2008–09	Feyenoord	22	0	35	0
2009–10	FC Twente	26	1		
2010–11	FC Twente	18	0		
2011–12	FC Twente	27	0	71	1
2012–13	Swansea C	14	1		
2013–14	Swansea C	10	0	24	1

TREMMEL, Gerhard (G) 120 0
H: 6 3 W: 14 00 b.Munich 16-11-78

2006–07	Energie Cottbus	24	0		
2007–08	Energie Cottbus	24	0		
2008–09	Energie Cottbus	34	0		
2009–10	Energie Cottbus	34	0	93	0
2011–12	Swansea C	1	0		
2012–13	Swansea C	14	0		
2013–14	Swansea C	12	0	27	0

VAZQUEZ, Alvaro (F) 101 14
H: 6 0 W: 11 10 b.Barcelona 27-4-91
Internationals: Spain U20, U21, U23.

| 2010–11 | Espanyol | 30 | 4 | | |

2011–12	Espanyol	28	5		
2012–13	Espanyol	2	1	60	10
2012–13	Getafe	29	4		
2013–14	Getafe	0	0	29	4

On loan from Getafe

2013–14	Swansea C	12	0	12	0

VORM, Michel (G) 260 0
H: 6 0 W: 13 03 b.Nieuwegein 20-10-83
Internationals: Netherlands Full caps.

2005–06	Den Bosch	35	0	35	0
2006–07	Utrecht	33	0		
2007–08	Utrecht	11	0		
2008–09	Utrecht	26	0		
2009–10	Utrecht	33	0		
2010–11	Utrecht	33	0	136	0
2011–12	Swansea C	37	0		
2012–13	Swansea C	26	0		
2013–14	Swansea C	26	0	89	0

WILLIAMS, Ashley (D) 411 15
H: 6 0 W: 11 02 b.Wolverhampton 23-8-84
Internationals: Wales Full caps.

2003–04	Stockport Co	10	0		
2004–05	Stockport Co	44	1		
2005–06	Stockport Co	36	1		
2006–07	Stockport Co	46	1		
2007–08	Stockport Co	26	0	162	3
2007–08	Swansea C	3	0		
2008–09	Swansea C	46	2		
2009–10	Swansea C	46	5		
2010–11	Swansea C	46	3		
2011–12	Swansea C	37	1		
2012–13	Swansea C	37	0		
2013–14	Swansea C	34	1	249	12

ZABRET, Gregor (G) 0 0
H: 6 2 W: 12 11 b.Ljubljana 18-8-95
Internationals: Slovenia U16, U17, U19.

2013–14	Swansea C	0	0		

Scholars
Atyeo, Thomas David Benjamin; Copp, Kyle Thomas; Davies, Keston Ellis; Fallon, Stephen; Francis, Corey Benjamin; Gilchrist, Cameron Philip; Jones, Joseph Michael; Jones, Owain Rhys; Latham, Jamie Edward; Owens, Cai Raymond Lewis; Roberts, Connor Richard Jones; Samuel, Alexander Kinloch; Sherman, Jordan; Thomas, Dylan.

SWINDON T (80)

AGOMBAR, Harry (M) 0 0
H: 5 10 b.London 12-7-92

2013–14	Swindon T	0	0		

ARCHIBALD-HENVILLE, Troy (D) 138 3
H: 6 2 W: 13 03 b.Newham 4-11-88

2007–08	Tottenham H	0	0		
2008–09	Tottenham H	0	0		
2008–09	Norwich C	0	0		
2008–09	Exeter C	19	0		
2009–10	Tottenham H	0	0		
2009–10	Exeter C	15	0		
2010–11	Exeter C	36	1		
2011–12	Exeter C	45	2	115	3
2012–13	Swindon T	5	0		
2013–14	Carlisle U	4	0	4	0
2013–14	Swindon T	14	0	19	0

BARKER, George (F) 15 0
H: 5 8 W: 11 02 b.Portsmouth 26-9-91

2010–11	Brighton & HA	0	0		
2011–12	Brighton & HA	0	0		
2012–13	Brighton & HA	3	0		
2012–13	Barnet	1	0	1	0
2013–14	Brighton & HA	1	0	4	0
2013–14	Newport Co	2	2	0	
2013–14	Swindon T	8	0	8	0

BARTHRAM, Jack (D) 11 0
H: 5 8 W: 11 09 b.Newham 13-10-93

2012–13	Tottenham H	0	0		
2013–14	Swindon T	11	0	11	0

BELFORD, Tyrell (G) 5 0
b.Nuneaton 6-5-94
Internationals: England U16, U17.

2011–12	Liverpool	0	0		
2012–13	Liverpool	0	0		
2013–14	Swindon T	5	0	5	0

BRANCO, Raphael Rossi (D) 15 0
b. 25-7-90

2013–14	Swindon T	15	0	15	0

BYRNE, Nathan (D) 75 5
H: 5 10 W: 10 10 b.St Albans 5-6-92

2010–11	Tottenham H	0	0		
2010–11	Brentford	11	0	11	0
2011–12	Tottenham H	0	0		
2011–12	Bournemouth	9	0	9	0
2012–13	Tottenham H	0	0		
2012–13	Crawley T	12	1	12	1
2012–13	Swindon T	7	0		
2013–14	Swindon T	36	4	43	4

COX, Lee (M) 105 7
H: 6 1 W: 12 02 b.Leicester 26-6-90

2007–08	Leicester C	0	0		
2008–09	Leicester C	0	0		
2008–09	Yeovil T	0	0		
2009–10	Inverness CT	35	2		
2010–11	Inverness CT	27	1		
2011–12	Inverness CT	7	0	69	3
2011–12	Swindon T	7	0		
2012–13	Swindon T	0	0		
2012–13	Oxford U	14	0	14	0
2012–13	Plymouth Arg	10	0		
2013–14	Plymouth Arg	0	0	10	0
2013–14	Swindon T	5	1	12	1

EL-GABBAS, Mohamed (F) 122 25
Internationals: Egypt Full caps.

2008–09	Al Masry	24	9	24	9
2009–10	Lierse	7	1		
2010–11	Lierse	28	4		
2011–12	Lierse	30	6		
2012–13	Lierse	27	5	92	16

Transferred to Arles.

2013–14	Swindon T	6	0	6	0

FODERINGHAM, Wesley (G) 120 0
H: 6 1 W: 12 00 b.Hammersmith 14-1-91
Internationals: England U16, U17, U19.

2009–10	Fulham	0	0		
2010–11	Crystal Palace	0	0		
2011–12	Crystal Palace	0	0		
2011–12	Swindon T	33	0		
2012–13	Swindon T	46	0		
2013–14	Swindon T	41	0	120	0

GLADWIN, Ben (D) 13 0

2013–14	Swindon T	13	0	13	0

HARLEY, Ryan (M) 166 27
H: 5 11 W: 11 00 b.Bristol 22-1-85

2004–05	Bristol C	2	0		
2005–06	Bristol C	0	0	2	0
2008–09	Exeter C	31	4		
2009–10	Exeter C	44	10		
2010–11	Exeter C	21	6		
2010–11	Swansea C	0	0		
2010–11	Exeter C	21	4	117	24
2011–12	Swansea C	0	0		
2011–12	Brighton & HA	16	2		
2012–13	Brighton & HA	2	0	18	2
2012–13	Milton Keynes D	8	0	8	0
2013–14	Swindon T	21	1	21	1

JONES, Matthew (D) 1 0

2012–13	Swindon T	0	0		
2013–14	Swindon T	1	0	1	0

KASIM, Yaser (M) 38 2
H: 5 11 W: 11 07 b.Bagdad 10-5-91
Internationals: Iraq U23, Iraq Full caps.

2010–11	Brighton & HA	1	0		
2011–12	Brighton & HA	0	0		
2012–13	Brighton & HA	0	0	1	0
2013–14	Swindon T	37	2	37	2

McEVELEY, James (D) 270 7
H: 6 1 W: 13 03 b.Liverpool 11-2-85
Internationals: England U20, U21. Scotland B, Full caps.

2002–03	Blackburn R	9	0		
2003–04	Blackburn R	0	0		
2003–04	Burnley	4	0	4	0
2004–05	Blackburn R	5	0		
2004–05	Gillingham	10	1	10	1
2005–06	Blackburn R	0	0		
2005–06	Ipswich T	19	1	19	1
2006–07	Blackburn R	4	0	18	0
2006–07	Derby Co	15	0		
2007–08	Derby Co	29	2		

2008–09	Derby Co	15	0		
2008–09	Preston NE	7	0	7	0
2008–09	Charlton Ath	6	0	6	0
2009–10	Derby Co	33	2	92	4
2010–11	Barnsley	17	1		
2011–12	Barnsley	29	0	46	1
2011–12	Swindon T	8	0		
2012–13	Swindon T	28	0		
2013–14	Swindon T	32	0	68	0

N'GUESSAN, Dany (M) 215 38
H: 6 0 W: 12 13 b.Paris 11-8-87

2006–07	Boston U	23	5	23	5
2006–07	Lincoln C	9	0		
2007–08	Lincoln C	37	7		
2008–09	Lincoln C	45	8	91	15
2009–10	Leicester C	27	3		
2010–11	Leicester C	5	0	32	3
2010–11	Scunthorpe U	3	1	3	1
2010–11	Southampton	6	0	6	0
2011–12	Millwall	15	1		
2011–12	Charlton Ath	7	4	7	4
2012–13	Millwall	13	1		
2013–14	Millwall	1	0	29	2
2013–14	Swindon T	24	8	24	8

RANDALL, Will (M) 1 0

2013–14	Swindon T	1	0	1	0

RANGER, Nile (F) 87 12
H: 6 2 W: 13 03 b.Wood Green 11-4-91
Internationals: England U19.

2008–09	Newcastle U	0	0		
2009–10	Newcastle U	25	2		
2010–11	Newcastle U	24	0		
2011–12	Newcastle U	0	0		
2011–12	Barnsley	5	0	5	0
2011–12	Sheffield W	8	2	8	2
2012–13	Newcastle U	2	0	51	2
2013–14	Swindon T	23	8	23	8

REIS, Tijane (F) 6 0
H: 5 11 W: 10 07 b.Canchungo 28-6-91
Internationals: Portugal U21.

2013–14	Swindon T	6	0	6	0

ROONEY, Luke (M) 94 8
H: 5 8 W: 11 07 b.Southwark 28-12-90

2009–10	Gillingham	13	2		
2010–11	Gillingham	23	1		
2011–12	Gillingham	17	3	53	6
2011–12	Swindon T	20	2		
2012–13	Swindon T	11	0		
2012–13	Burton Alb	3	0	3	0
2012–13	Rotherham U	3	0	3	0
2013–14	Swindon T	0	0	31	2
2013–14	Crawley T	4	0	4	0

SMITH, Alex (D) 11 1
H: 5 9 W: 8 09 b.Clapham 31-10-91

2009–10	Fulham	0	0		
2010–11	Fulham	0	0		
2011–12	Fulham	0	0		
2012–13	Fulham	1	0	1	0
2012–13	Leyton Orient	2	0	2	0
2013–14	Swindon T	8	1	8	1

SMITH, Michael (F) 57 21
H: 6 4 W: 11 02 b.Wallsend 17-10-91

2011–12	Charlton Ath	0	0		
2011–12	Accrington S	6	3	6	3
2012–13	Charlton Ath	0	0		
2012–13	Colchester U	8	1	8	1
2013–14	Charlton Ath	0	0		
2013–14	AFC Wimbledon	23	9	23	9
2013–14	Swindon T	20	8	20	8

STOREY, Miles (F) 38 6
H: 5 11 W: 11 00 b.West Bromwich 4-1-94
Internationals: England U19.

2010–11	Swindon T	2	0		
2011–12	Swindon T	4	0		
2012–13	Swindon T	8	1		
2013–14	Swindon T	18	3	32	4
2013–14	Shrewsbury T	6	0	6	0

THOMPSON, Louis (M) 32 2
H: 5 11 W: 11 10 b.Bristol 19-12-94
Internationals: Wales U19.

2012–13	Swindon T	4	0		
2013–14	Swindon T	28	2	32	2

THOMPSON, Nathan (D) 75 1
H: 5 7 W: 11 02 b.Chester 9-11-90

2009–10	Swindon T	0	0		

2010–11	Swindon T	3	0		
2011–12	Swindon T	5	0		
2012–13	Swindon T	26	0		
2013–14	Swindon T	41	1	75	1

WALDON, Connor (F)   4   0

| 2012–13 | Swindon T | 1 | 0 | | |
| 2013–14 | Swindon T | 3 | 0 | 4 | 0 |

WARD, Darren (D)   502   16
H: 6 3   W: 11 04   b.Harrow 13-9-78

1995–96	Watford	1	0		
1996–97	Watford	7	0		
1997–98	Watford	0	0		
1998–99	Watford	1	0		
1999–2000	Watford	9	1		
1999–2000	*QPR*	14	0	14	0
2000–01	Watford	40	1		
2001–02	Watford	1	0		
2001–02	Millwall	14	0		
2002–03	Millwall	39	1		
2003–04	Millwall	46	3		
2004–05	Millwall	43	0		
2005–06	Crystal Palace	43	5		
2006–07	Crystal Palace	20	0	63	5
2007–08	Wolverhampton W	30	0		
2008–09	Wolverhampton W	1	0		
2008–09	Watford	9	1	68	3
2008–09	*Charlton Ath*	16	0	16	0
2009–10	Wolverhampton W	0	0	31	0
2009–10	Millwall	31	1		
2010–11	Millwall	31	1		
2011–12	Millwall	30	0		
2012–13	Millwall	1	0	235	6
2012–13	*Swindon T*	39	2		
2013–14	Swindon T	36	0	75	2

WILLIAMS, Andy (F)   279   51
H: 5 11   W: 11 09   b.Hereford 14-8-86

2006–07	Hereford U	41	8		
2007–08	Bristol R	41	4		
2008–09	Bristol R	4	1		
2008–09	*Hereford U*	26	2	67	10
2009–10	Bristol R	43	3	88	8
2010–11	Yeovil T	37	6		
2011–12	Yeovil T	35	16		
2012–13	Swindon T	40	11		
2013–14	Swindon T	3	0	43	11
2013–14	*Yeovil T*	9	0	81	22

Scholars
Cooke, Joshua Ian Ron; Da-Costa, Claude; Da-Costa, Curtis; English, Joe; Gied Galib, Amir; Holland, Tom; Jones, Mathew Ryan; Kisitu, Salvyn Joshua Kajoba; Marshall, Lee James; Matthews, Luke Benjamin; McCormack, Callum Francis; Moody, Aaron Luke; Randall-Hurren, William; Walsh, Liam Thomas.

TORQUAY U (81)

BENYON, Elliot (F)   162   34
H: 5 9   W: 10 01   b.High Wycombe 29-8-87

2005–06	Bristol C	0	0		
2006–07	Bristol C	0	0		
2009–10	Torquay U	45	11		
2010–11	Torquay U	23	13		
2010–11	Swindon T	12	1		
2011–12	Swindon T	0	0	12	1
2011–12	*Wycombe W*	9	0	9	0
2011–12	Southend U	16	2		
2012–13	Southend U	5	0	21	2
2012–13	*Torquay U*	15	4		
2013–14	Torquay U	37	3	120	31

BODIN, Billy (M)   111   14
H: 5 11   W: 11 00   b.Swindon 24-3-92
Internationals: Wales U17, U19, U21.

2009–10	Swindon T	0	0		
2010–11	Swindon T	5	0		
2011–12	Swindon T	11	3	16	3
2011–12	*Torquay U*	17	5		
2011–12	*Crewe Alex*	8	0	8	0
2012–13	Torquay U	43	5		
2013–14	Torquay U	27	1	87	11

CAMERON, Courtney (D)   39   2
b.Northampton 22-1-93

2011–12	Aston Villa	0	0		
2012–13	*Rotherham U*	15	1	15	1
2013–14	Torquay U	24	1	24	1

CHAPELL, Jordan (M)   46   6
H: 5 10   W: 10 09   b.Sheffield 8-9-91

2011–12	Sheffield U	0	0		
2012–13	Sheffield U	2	0	2	0
2012–13	*Burton Alb*	2	1	2	1
2012–13	*Torquay U*	6	0		
2013–14	Torquay U	36	5	42	5

COOPER, Shaun (D)   268   3
H: 5 10   W: 10 05   b.Newport (IW) 5-10-83

2000–01	Portsmouth	0	0		
2001–02	Portsmouth	7	0		
2002–03	Portsmouth	0	0		
2003–04	Portsmouth	0	0		
2003–04	*Leyton Orient*	9	0	9	0
2004–05	Portsmouth	0	0		
2004–05	*Kidderminster H*	10	0	10	0
2005–06	Bournemouth	0	0		
2005–06	Bournemouth	35	0		
2006–07	Bournemouth	33	0		
2007–08	Bournemouth	38	1		
2008–09	Bournemouth	37	0		
2009–10	Bournemouth	6	0		
2010–11	Bournemouth	36	0		
2011–12	Bournemouth	26	0	211	1
2012–13	Crawley T	8	0	8	0
2012–13	Portsmouth	14	2		
2013–14	Portsmouth	9	0	30	2
2013–14	Torquay U	0	0		

CRAIG, Nathan (M)   43   1
H: 5 11   W: 10 11   b.Bangor 25-10-91
Internationals: Wales U17, U19, U21.

| 2012–13 | Torquay U | 30 | 1 | | |
| 2013–14 | Torquay U | 13 | 0 | 43 | 1 |

CRUISE, Thomas (D)   40   0
H: 5 6   W: 12 07   b.London 9-3-91
Internationals: England U16, U17, U19.

2008–09	Arsenal	0	0		
2009–10	Arsenal	0	0		
2010–11	Arsenal	0	0		
2010–11	*Carlisle U*	3	0	3	0
2012–13	Torquay U	16	0		
2013–14	Torquay U	21	0	37	0

DOWNES, Aaron (D)   252   19
H: 6 2   W: 13 02   b.Mudgee 15-5-85
Internationals: Australia Youth, U20, U21, U23.

2004–05	Chesterfield	9	2		
2005–06	Chesterfield	22	0		
2006–07	Chesterfield	45	3		
2007–08	Chesterfield	40	2		
2008–09	Chesterfield	42	2		
2009–10	Chesterfield	7	1		
2010–11	Chesterfield	0	0		
2011–12	Chesterfield	9	0	174	10
2011–12	*Bristol R*	8	0	8	0
2012–13	Torquay U	38	5		
2013–14	Torquay U	32	4	70	9

HARDING, Ben (M)   226   14
H: 5 10   W: 11 02   b.Carshalton 6-9-84
Internationals: England C.

2001–02	Wimbledon	0	0		
2002–03	Wimbledon	0	0		
2003–04	Wimbledon	15	0	15	0
2004–05	Milton Keynes D	26	4		
2005–06	Milton Keynes D	10	2		
2006–07	Milton Keynes D	0	0	36	6
2008–09	Aldershot T	29	3		
2009–10	Aldershot T	33	1		
2010–11	Aldershot T	35	2	97	6
2011–12	*Wycombe W*	7	0	7	0
2011–12	Northampton T	19	0		
2012–13	Northampton T	35	2	54	2
2013–14	Torquay U	17	0	17	0

HAWLEY, Karl (F)   303   67
H: 5 8   W: 12 02   b.Walsall 6-12-81
Internationals: England C.

2000–01	Walsall	0	0		
2001–02	Walsall	1	0		
2002–03	Walsall	0	0		
2002–03	*Raith R*	17	7		
2003–04	Walsall	0	0	1	0
2003–04	*Raith R*	11	2	28	9
2004–05	Carlisle U	0	0		
2005–06	Carlisle U	46	22		
2006–07	Carlisle U	32	12	78	34
2007–08	Preston NE	25	3		
2008–09	Preston NE	5	0	30	3
2008–09	*Northampton T*	11	2	11	2
2008–09	*Colchester U*	4	0	4	0
2009–10	Notts Co	31	3		
2010–11	Notts Co	24	0		
2011–12	Notts Co	26	2	81	5
2011–12	*Crawley T*	4	0	4	0
2012–13	Scunthorpe U	39	11		
2013–14	Scunthorpe U	0	0	39	11
2013–14	Torquay U	27	3	27	3

HUTCHINGS, Jake (D)   0   0
b.North London 20-12-95

| 2012–13 | Torquay U | 0 | 0 | | |
| 2013–14 | Torquay U | 0 | 0 | | |

LATHROPE, Damon (M)   109   0
H: 5 8   W: 10 02   b.Stevenage 28-10-89

2007–08	Norwich C	0	0		
2008–09	Norwich C	0	0		
2009–10	Norwich C	0	0		
2010–11	Torquay U	18	0		
2011–12	Torquay U	40	0		
2012–13	Torquay U	28	0		
2013–14	Torquay U	23	0	109	0

MANSELL, Lee (D)   350   31
H: 5 10   W: 11 10   b.Gloucester 28-10-82

2000–01	Luton T	18	5		
2001–02	Luton T	11	1		
2002–03	Luton T	1	0		
2003–04	Luton T	16	2		
2004–05	Luton T	1	0	47	8
2005–06	Oxford U	44	1	44	1
2006–07	Torquay U	45	4		
2009–10	Torquay U	39	2		
2010–11	Torquay U	45	0		
2011–12	Torquay U	45	12		
2012–13	Torquay U	42	2		
2013–14	Torquay U	43	2	259	22

MOZIKA, Damien (M)   128   9
H: 6 0   W: 11 13   b.Corbeil-Essonnes 15-4-87

2006–07	Nancy	0	0		
2007–08	*Louhans*	28	0	28	0
2008–09	*Chester C*	22	2	22	2
From Tarbiat Yazd.					
2010–11	Bury	33	2		
2011–12	Bury	4	1	37	3
2011–12	Scunthorpe U	18	2		
2012–13	Scunthorpe U	11	2	29	4
2013–14	Torquay U	12	0	12	0

NICHOLSON, Kevin (D)   291   11
H: 5 8   W: 12 05   b.Derby 2-10-80
Internationals: England C.

1997–98	Sheffield W	0	0		
1998–99	Sheffield W	0	0		
1999–2000	Sheffield W	0	0		
2000–01	Sheffield W	1	0	1	0
From Forest Green R.					
2000–01	*Northampton T*	7	0	7	0
2000–01	Notts Co	11	2		
2001–02	Notts Co	24	1		
2002–03	Notts Co	37	0		
2003–04	Notts Co	23	0	95	3
From Scarborough, Forest Green R.					
2009–10	Torquay U	27	0		
2010–11	Torquay U	44	3		
2011–12	Torquay U	46	4		
2012–13	Torquay U	42	1		
2013–14	Torquay U	29	0	188	8

PEARCE, Krystian (D)   170   11
H: 6 1   W: 13 05   b.Birmingham 5-1-90
Internationals: England U17, U19.

2006–07	Birmingham C	0	0		
2007–08	Birmingham C	0	0		
2007–08	*Port Vale*	12	0	12	0
2007–08	*Notts Co*	8	1		
2008–09	Birmingham C	0	0		
2008–09	*Scunthorpe U*	39	0	39	0
2009–10	Birmingham C	0	0		
2009–10	*Peterborough U*	2	0	2	0
2009–10	*Huddersfield T*	1	0	1	0
2010–11	Notts Co	27	1		
2011–12	Notts Co	27	3		
2012–13	Notts Co	2	1	64	6
2012–13	*Barnet*	17	1	17	1
2013–14	Torquay U	35	4	35	4

POKE, Michael (G) 　98　0
H: 6 1　W: 13 12　b.Staines 21-11-85

Season	Club		
2003–04	Southampton	0	0
2004–05	Southampton	0	0
2005–06	Southampton	0	0
2005–06	*Oldham Ath*	0	0
2005–06	*Northampton T*	0	0
2006–07	Southampton	0	0
2007–08	Southampton	4	0
2008–09	Southampton	0	0
2009–10	Southampton	0	0	4 0
2009–10	Torquay U	29	0
2010–11	Brighton & HA	0	0
2011–12	Brighton & HA	0	0
2011–12	*Bristol R*	8	0	8 0
2012–13	Torquay U	43	0
2013–14	Torquay U	14	0	86 0

RICE, Martin (G) 　37　0
H: 5 11　W: 13 01　b.Exeter 7-3-86

2011–12	Torquay U	0	0
2012–13	Torquay U	5	0
2013–14	Torquay U	32	0	37 0

STEVENS, Danny (M) 　135　15
H: 5 5　W: 9 09　b.Enfield 26-11-86

2004–05	Luton T	0	0
2005–06	Luton T	1	0
2006–07	Luton T	0	0	1 0
2009–10	Torquay U	27	1
2010–11	Torquay U	37	3
2011–12	Torquay U	41	8
2012–13	Torquay U	23	3
2013–14	Torquay U	6	0	134 15

SULLIVAN, Daniel (F) 　4　0
b.Plymouth 1-9-94

2012–13	Torquay U	0	0
2013–14	Torquay U	4	0	4 0

THOMPSON, Niall (M) 　21　0
b.Derby 3-9-93

2012–13	Torquay U	18	0
2013–14	Torquay U	3	0	21 0

TONGE, Dale (D) 　247　1
H: 5 10　W: 10 06　b.Doncaster 7-5-85

2003–04	Barnsley	1	0
2004–05	Barnsley	14	0
2005–06	Barnsley	24	0
2006–07	Barnsley	6	0	45 0
2006–07	*Gillingham*	3	0	3 0
2007–08	Rotherham U	37	0
2008–09	Rotherham U	39	1
2009–10	Rotherham U	21	0
2010–11	Rotherham U	23	0
2011–12	Rotherham U	32	0
2012–13	Rotherham U	11	0	163 1
2013–14	Torquay U	36	0	36 0

YEOMAN, Ashley (F) 　23　5
H: 5 10　W: 12 01　b.Kingsbridge 25-2-92

2010–11	Torquay U	0	0
2011–12	Torquay U	1	0
2012–13	Torquay U	13	2
2013–14	Torquay U	9	3	23 5

Scholars
Alexandrou, Jamie Lenos; Berrow, Monty
Joshua Hepburn; Buckle, Johnny Joseph;
Campbell, Jordan Michael; Chaney, Sam;
Coleman, Christopher John; Deery, Cormac
Paul Andrew; Ives, Levi Paul; Lavercombe,
Daniel; Lynch, Joshua Stephen; Mace, Jack;
McCallion, Kevin Patrick; Mouzouros,
Charalampos; Oduola-Odofin, O'Neil
Olawale Odunayo; Palmer, Freddie James;
Parcell, Mickey Charles; Prynn, Liam David.

TOTTENHAM H (82)

ADEBAYOR, Emmanuel (F) 　353　132
H: 6 4　W: 11 08　b.Lome 26-2-84
Internationals: Togo Full caps.

2001–02	Metz	10	2
2002–03	Metz	34	13	44 15
2003–04	Monaco	31	8
2004–05	Monaco	34	9
2005–06	Monaco	13	1	78 18
2005–06	Arsenal	13	4
2006–07	Arsenal	29	8

2007–08	Arsenal	36	24
2008–09	Arsenal	26	10	104 46
2009–10	Manchester C	26	14
2010–11	Manchester C	8	1
2010–11	*Real Madrid*	14	5	14 5
2011–12	Manchester C	0	0
2011–12	*Tottenham H*	33	17
2012–13	Manchester C	0	0	34 15
2012–13	Tottenham H	25	5
2013–14	Tottenham H	21	11	79 33

ARCHER, Jordan (G) 　27　0
H: 6 1　W: 12 08　b.Walthamstow 12-4-93
Internationals: Scotland U19, U20, U21.

2011–12	Tottenham H	0	0
2012–13	Tottenham H	0	0
2012–13	*Wycombe W*	27	0	27 0
2013–14	Tottenham H	0	0

ASSOU-EKOTTO, Benoit (M) 　252　4
H: 5 10　W: 10 12　b.Arras 24-3-84
Internationals: Cameroon B, Full caps.

2003–04	Lens	3	0
2004–05	Lens	29	0
2005–06	Lens	34	0	66 0
2006–07	Tottenham H	16	0
2007–08	Tottenham H	1	0
2008–09	Tottenham H	29	0
2009–10	Tottenham H	30	1
2010–11	Tottenham H	30	0
2011–12	Tottenham H	34	2
2012–13	Tottenham H	15	1
2013–14	Tottenham H	0	0	155 4
2013–14	*QPR*	31	0	31 0

BALL, Dominic (M) 　0　0
Internationals: Northern Ireland U15, U16,
U17, U19, U21. England U19.

2013–14	Tottenham H	0	0

BENTALEB, Nabil (M) 　15　0
H: 6 2　W: 10 09　b.Lille, France 24-11-94
Internationals: France U18. Algeria Full caps.

2012–13	Tottenham H	0	0
2013–14	Tottenham H	15	0	15 0

CAPOUE, Etienne (M) 　186　14
H: 6 2　W: 11 10　b.Niort 11-7-88
Internationals: France U18, U19, U21, Full caps.

2006–07	Toulouse	0	0
2007–08	Toulouse	5	0
2008–09	Toulouse	32	1
2009–10	Toulouse	33	0
2010–11	Toulouse	37	2
2011–12	Toulouse	33	3
2012–13	Toulouse	34	7	174 13
2013–14	Tottenham H	12	1	12 1

CARROLL, Tommy (M) 　57　1
H: 5 10　W: 10 00　b.Watford 28-5-92
Internationals: England U19, U21.

2010–11	Tottenham H	0	0
2010–11	*Leyton Orient*	12	0	12 0
2011–12	Tottenham H	0	0
2011–12	*Derby Co*	12	1	12 1
2012–13	Tottenham H	7	0
2013–14	Tottenham H	0	0	7 0
2013–14	*QPR*	26	0	26 0

CHADLI, Nacer (M) 　200　54
H: 6 2　W: 12 07　b.Liege 3-6-88
Internationals: Morocco Full caps. Belgium
Full caps.

2007–08	AGOVV	19	2
2008–09	AGOVV	34	9
2009–10	AGOVV	39	17	92 28
2010–11	FC Twente	33	7
2011–12	FC Twente	25	6
2012–13	FC Twente	26	12	84 25
2013–14	Tottenham H	24	1	24 1

CHIRICHES, Vlad (D) 　139　3
H: 6 0　W: 11 10　b.Bacau 14-11-89
Internationals: Romania U21, Full caps.

2008–09	Curtea-de-Arges	26	1
2009–10	Curtea-de-Arges	15	0	41 1
2010–11	Pandurii T-J	24	0
2011–12	Pandurii T-J	15	0	39 0
2011–12	Steaua Bucuresti	14	0
2012–13	Steaua Bucuresti	26	1
2013–14	Steaua Bucuresti	2	0	42 1
2013–14	Tottenham H	17	1	17 1

COULIBALY, Souleymane (F) 　0　0
b.Anguededou 26-12-94
Internationals: Ivory Coast U17.

2013–14	Tottenham H	0	0

COULTHIRST, Shaquile (F) 　7　3
b.Hackney 2-1-94
Internationals: England U19.

2012–13	Tottenham H	0	0
2013–14	Tottenham H	0	0
2013–14	*Leyton Orient*	1	1	1 1
2013–14	*Torquay U*	6	2	6 2

DAWSON, Michael (D) 　319　14
H: 6 2　W: 12 02　b.Leyburn 18-11-83
Internationals: England U21, B, Full caps.

2000–01	Nottingham F	0	0
2001–02	Nottingham F	1	0
2002–03	Nottingham F	38	5
2003–04	Nottingham F	30	1
2004–05	Nottingham F	14	1	83 7
2004–05	Tottenham H	5	0
2005–06	Tottenham H	32	0
2006–07	Tottenham H	37	1
2007–08	Tottenham H	27	1
2008–09	Tottenham H	16	1
2009–10	Tottenham H	29	2
2010–11	Tottenham H	24	1
2011–12	Tottenham H	7	0
2012–13	Tottenham H	27	1
2013–14	Tottenham H	32	0	236 7

DEFOE, Jermain (F) 　429　153
H: 5 7　W: 10 04　b.Beckton 7-10-82
Internationals: England U16, U18, U21, B, Full caps.

1999–2000	West Ham U	0	0
2000–01	West Ham U	1	0
2000–01	*Bournemouth*	29	18	29 18
2001–02	West Ham U	35	10
2002–03	West Ham U	38	8
2003–04	West Ham U	19	11	93 29
2003–04	Tottenham H	15	7
2004–05	Tottenham H	35	13
2005–06	Tottenham H	36	9
2006–07	Tottenham H	34	10
2007–08	Tottenham H	19	4
2007–08	Portsmouth	12	8
2008–09	Portsmouth	19	7	31 15
2008–09	Tottenham H	8	3
2009–10	Tottenham H	34	18
2010–11	Tottenham H	22	4
2011–12	Tottenham H	25	11
2012–13	Tottenham H	34	11
2013–14	Tottenham H	14	1	276 91

Transferred to Toronto January 2014.

DEMBELE, Mousa (M) 　291　41
H: 5 9　W: 10 01　b.Wilrijk 17-7-87
Internationals: Belgium U16, U17, U18, U19, Full caps.

2003–04	Beerschot	1	0
2004–05	Beerschot	19	1	20 1
2005–06	Willem II	33	9	33 9
2006–07	AZ	33	6
2007–08	AZ	33	4
2008–09	AZ	23	10
2009–10	AZ	29	4	118 24
2010–11	Fulham	24	3
2011–12	Fulham	36	2
2012–13	Fulham	2	0	62 5
2012–13	Tottenham H	30	1
2013–14	Tottenham H	28	1	58 2

DEMPSEY, Clint (M) 　295　83
H: 6 1　W: 12 02　b.Nacogdoches 9-3-83
Internationals: USA U21, Full caps.

2004	New England Rev	24	7
2005	New England Rev	30	11
2006	New England Rev	23	8	77 26
2006–07	Fulham	10	1
2007–08	Fulham	36	6
2008–09	Fulham	35	7
2009–10	Fulham	29	7
2010–11	Fulham	37	12
2011–12	Fulham	37	17
2012–13	Fulham	0	0
2012–13	Tottenham H	29	7
2013–14	Tottenham H	0	0	29 7
2013–14	*Fulham*	5	0	189 50

ERIKSEN, Christian (M) — 138 32
H: 5 9 W: 10 02 b.Middelfart 14-2-92
Internationals: Denmark U17, U18, U19, U21, Full caps.

Season	Club				
2009-10	Ajax	15	0		
2010-11	Ajax	28	6		
2011-12	Ajax	33	7		
2012-13	Ajax	33	10		
2013-14	Ajax	4	2	113	25
2013-14	Tottenham H	25	7	25	7

FALQUE, Iago (M) — 89 17
H: 5 8 W: 11 00 b.Vigo 4-4-90
Internationals: Spain Youth, U21.

Season	Club				
2008-09	Barcelona B	1	1	1	1
2008-09	Juventus	0	0		
2009-10	Juventus	0	0		
2009-10	Bari	0	0		
2010-11	Juventus	0	0		
2010-11	Villarreal B	36	11	36	11
2011-12	Tottenham H	0	0		
2011-12	Southampton	1	0	1	0
2012-13	Tottenham H	1	0		
2012-13	Almeria	22	2	22	2
2013-14	Tottenham H	0	1	0	0
2013-14	Rayo Vallecano	28	3	28	3

FREDERICKS, Ryan (M) — 18 1
H: 5 8 W: 11 10 b.Potters Bar 10-10-92
Internationals: England U19.

Season	Club				
2010-11	Tottenham H	0	0		
2011-12	Tottenham H	0	0		
2012-13	Tottenham H	0	0		
2012-13	Brentford	4	0	4	0
2013-14	Tottenham H	0	0		
2013-14	Millwall	14	1	14	1

FRIEDEL, Brad (G) — 515 1
H: 6 3 W: 14 00 b.Lakewood 18-5-71
Internationals: USA Full caps.

Season	Club				
1996	Columbus Crew	9	0		
1997	Columbus Crew	29	0	38	0
1997-98	Liverpool	11	0		
1998-99	Liverpool	12	0		
1999-2000	Liverpool	2	0		
2000-01	Liverpool	0	0	25	0
2000-01	Blackburn R	27	0		
2001-02	Blackburn R	36	0		
2002-03	Blackburn R	37	0		
2003-04	Blackburn R	36	1		
2004-05	Blackburn R	38	0		
2005-06	Blackburn R	38	0		
2006-07	Blackburn R	38	0		
2007-08	Blackburn R	38	0	288	1
2008-09	Aston Villa	38	0		
2009-10	Aston Villa	38	0		
2010-11	Aston Villa	38	0	114	0
2011-12	Tottenham H	38	0		
2012-13	Tottenham H	11	0		
2013-14	Tottenham H	1	0	50	0

FRYERS, Zeki (D) — 16 0
H: 6 0 W: 12 00 b.Manchester 9-9-92
Internationals: England U16, U17, U19.

Season	Club				
2011-12	Manchester U	2	0		
2012-13	Manchester U	0	0	2	0
2012-13	Standard Liege	7	0	7	0
2013-14	Tottenham H	0	0		
2013-14	Tottenham H	7	0	7	0

GOMELT, Tomislav (M) — 0 0
b.Sisak 7-1-95
Internationals: Croatia U19.

Season	Club		
2013-14	Tottenham H	0	0

HALL, Grant (D) — 28 0
H: 5 9 W: 11 02 b.Brighton 29-10-91

Season	Club				
2009-10	Brighton & HA	0	0		
2010-11	Brighton & HA	0	0		
2011-12	Brighton & HA	1	0	1	0
2012-13	Tottenham H	0	0		
2013-14	Tottenham H	0	0		
2013-14	Swindon T	27	0	27	0

HOLTBY, Lewis (M) — 169 26
H: 5 8 W: 10 04 b.Erkelenz 18-9-90
Internationals: Germany U18, U19, U20, U21, Full caps.

Season	Club				
2007-08	Alemania Aachen	2	0		
2008-09	Alemania Aachen	31	7	33	7
2009-10	Schalke 04	9	0		
2009-10	VfL Bochum	14	2	14	2
2010-11	Mainz	30	5	30	5
2011-12	Schalke 04	27	6		
2012-13	Schalke 04	19	4	55	10
2012-13	Tottenham H	11	0		
2013-14	Tottenham H	13	1	24	1
2013-14	Fulham	13	1	13	1

KABOUL, Younes (D) — 190 13
H: 6 2 W: 13 07 b.Annemasse 4-1-86
Internationals: France U21, Full caps.

Season	Club				
2004-05	Auxerre	12	1		
2005-06	Auxerre	9	0		
2006-07	Auxerre	31	2	52	3
2007-08	Tottenham H	21	3		
2008-09	Portsmouth	20	1		
2009-10	Portsmouth	19	3	39	4
2009-10	Tottenham H	10	0		
2010-11	Tottenham H	21	1		
2011-12	Tottenham H	33	1		
2012-13	Tottenham H	1	0		
2013-14	Tottenham H	13	1	99	6

KANE, Harry (F) — 67 17
H: 6 0 W: 10 00 b.Chingford 28-7-93
Internationals: England U17, U19, U20, U21.

Season	Club				
2010-11	Tottenham H	0	0		
2010-11	Leyton Orient	18	5	18	5
2011-12	Tottenham H	0	0		
2011-12	Millwall	22	7	22	7
2012-13	Tottenham H	1	0		
2012-13	Norwich C	3	0	3	0
2012-13	Leicester C	13	2	13	2
2013-14	Tottenham H	10	3	11	3

KHUMALO, Bongani (D) — 194 12
H: 6 2 W: 12 13 b.Swaziland 6-1-87
Internationals: South Africa Full caps.

Season	Club				
2005-06	Pretoria Univ	22	0		
2006-07	Pretoria Univ	24	4	50	4
2007-08	Supersport U	25	4		
2008-09	Supersport U	23	3		
2009-10	Supersport U	26	1		
2010-11	Supersport U	7	0	81	8
2010-11	Tottenham H	0	0		
2010-11	Preston NE	6	0	6	0
2011-12	Tottenham H	0	0		
2011-12	Reading	4	0	4	0
2012-13	Tottenham H	0	0		
2012-13	PAOK Salonika	23	0	23	0
2013-14	Tottenham H	0	0		
2013-14	Doncaster R	30	0	30	0

LAMELA, Erik (F) — 104 23
H: 6 0 W: 10 13 b.Buenos Aires 4-3-92
Internationals: Argentina U20, Full caps.

Season	Club				
2009-10	River Plate	1	0		
2009-10	River Plate	1	0		
2010-11	River Plate	32	4	34	4
2011-12	Roma	29	4		
2012-13	Roma	32	15	61	19
2013-14	Tottenham H	9	0	9	0

LENNON, Aaron (M) — 295 27
H: 5 6 W: 10 03 b.Leeds 16-4-87
Internationals: England U17, U19, U21, B, Full caps.

Season	Club				
2003-04	Leeds U	11	0		
2004-05	Leeds U	27	1	38	1
2005-06	Tottenham H	27	2		
2006-07	Tottenham H	26	3		
2007-08	Tottenham H	29	2		
2008-09	Tottenham H	35	5		
2009-10	Tottenham H	22	3		
2010-11	Tottenham H	34	3		
2011-12	Tottenham H	23	3		
2012-13	Tottenham H	34	4		
2013-14	Tottenham H	27	1	257	26

LIVERMORE, Jake (M) — 119 5
H: 5 9 W: 12 08 b.Enfield 14-11-89
Internationals: England Full caps.

Season	Club				
2006-07	Tottenham H	0	0		
2007-08	Tottenham H	0	0		
2007-08	Milton Keynes D	5	0	5	0
2008-09	Tottenham H	0	0		
2008-09	Crewe Alex	0	0		
2009-10	Tottenham H	1	0		
2009-10	Derby Co	16	1	16	1
2009-10	Peterborough U	9	1	9	1
2010-11	Tottenham H	0	0		
2010-11	Ipswich T	12	0	12	0
2010-11	Leeds U	5	0	5	0
2011-12	Tottenham H	24	0		
2012-13	Tottenham H	11	0		
2013-14	Tottenham H	0	0	36	0
2013-14	Hull C	36	3	36	3

LLORIS, Hugo (G) — 282 0
H: 6 2 W: 12 03 b.Nice 26-12-86
Internationals: France U18, U19, U20, U21, Full caps.

Season	Club				
2005-06	Nice	5	0		
2006-07	Nice	37	0		
2007-08	Nice	30	0	72	0
2008-09	Lyon	35	0		
2009-10	Lyon	36	0		
2010-11	Lyon	37	0		
2011-12	Lyon	36	0		
2012-13	Lyon	2	0	146	0
2012-13	Tottenham H	27	0		
2013-14	Tottenham H	37	0	64	0

LUONGO, Massimo (F) — 60 7
H: 5 8 W: 11 10 b.Sydney 25-9-92
Internationals: Australia U20, Full caps.

Season	Club				
2010-11	Tottenham H	0	0		
2011-12	Tottenham H	0	0		
2012-13	Tottenham H	0	0		
2012-13	Ipswich T	9	0	9	0
2012-13	Swindon T	7	1		
2013-14	Tottenham H	0	0		
2013-14	Swindon T	44	6	51	7

MASON, Ryan (F) — 70 11
H: 5 9 W: 10 00 b.Enfield 13-6-91
Internationals: England U19, U20.

Season	Club				
2007-08	Tottenham H	0	0		
2008-09	Tottenham H	0	0		
2009-10	Tottenham H	0	0		
2009-10	Yeovil T	28	6	28	6
2010-11	Tottenham H	0	0		
2010-11	Doncaster R	15	0		
2011-12	Tottenham H	0	0		
2011-12	Doncaster R	4	0	19	0
2011-12	Millwall	5	0	5	0
2012-13	Tottenham H	0	0		
2012-13	Lorient	0	0		
2013-14	Tottenham H	0	0		
2013-14	Swindon T	18	5	18	5

McEVOY, Kenneth (M) — 0 0
b.Waterford 4-9-94
Internationals: Republic of Ireland U17, U19, U21.

Season	Club		
2013-14	Tottenham H	0	0

NAUGHTON, Kyle (M) — 176 6
H: 5 11 W: 11 07 b.Sheffield 11-11-88
Internationals: England U21.

Season	Club				
2006-07	Sheffield U	0	0		
2007-08	Gretna	18	0	18	0
2007-08	Sheffield U	0	0		
2008-09	Sheffield U	40	1		
2009-10	Sheffield U	0	0	40	1
2009-10	Tottenham H	1	0		
2009-10	Middlesbrough	15	0	15	0
2010-11	Tottenham H	0	0		
2010-11	Leicester C	34	5	34	5
2011-12	Tottenham H	0	0		
2011-12	Norwich C	32	0	32	0
2012-13	Tottenham H	14	0		
2013-14	Tottenham H	22	0	37	0

OBIKA, Jonathan (F) — 122 23
H: 6 0 W: 12 00 b.Enfield 12-9-90
Internationals: England U19, U20.

Season	Club				
2008-09	Tottenham H	0	0		
2008-09	Yeovil T	10	4		
2009-10	Tottenham H	0	0		
2009-10	Yeovil T	22	6		
2009-10	Millwall	12	2	12	2
2010-11	Tottenham H	0	0		
2010-11	Crystal Palace	7	0	7	0
2010-11	Peterborough U	1	1	1	1
2010-11	Swindon T	5	0	5	0
2010-11	Yeovil T	11	3		
2011-12	Tottenham H	0	0		
2011-12	Yeovil T	27	4	70	17
2012-13	Tottenham H	0	0		
2012-13	Charlton Ath	10	3		
2013-14	Tottenham H	0	0		
2013-14	Brighton & HA	5	0	5	0
2013-14	Charlton Ath	12	0	22	3

ODUWA, Nathan (F)   0 0
b.London 5-3-96
Internationals: England U17, U18.

Season	Club	A	G		
2013–14	Tottenham H	0	0		

ONOMAH, Joshua (M)   0 0
Internationals: England U16, U17.

Season	Club	A	G		
2013–14	Tottenham H	0	0		

PAULINHO (M)   199 37
H: 5 11   W: 12 00   b.Sao Paulo 25-7-88
Internationals: Brazil Full caps.

Season	Club	A	G	T A	T G
2006	FK Vilnius	17	2		
2007	FK Vilnius	21	3	38	5
2007–08	LKS Lodz	17	0	17	0
2009	Bragantino	28	6	28	6
2010	Corinthians	27	4		
2011	Corinthians	35	8		
2012	Corinthians	23	7		
2013	Corinthians	1	1	86	20
2013–14	Tottenham H	30	6	30	6

PRITCHARD, Alex (M)   43 6
H: 5 7   W: 9 11   b.Grays 3-5-93
Internationals: England U20.

Season	Club	A	G	T A	T G
2011–12	Tottenham H	0	0		
2012–13	Tottenham H	0	0		
2012–13	Peterborough U	6	0	6	0
2013–14	Tottenham H	1	0	1	0
2013–14	Swindon T	36	6	36	6

ROSE, Danny (M)   89 3
H: 5 8   W: 11 11   b.Doncaster 2-6-90
Internationals: England U17, U19, U21. Great Britain.

Season	Club	A	G	T A	T G
2007–08	Tottenham H	0	0		
2008–09	Tottenham H	0	0		
2008–09	Watford	7	0	7	0
2009–10	Tottenham H	1	1		
2010–11	Tottenham H	4	0		
2010–11	Bristol C	17	0	17	0
2011–12	Tottenham H	11	0		
2012–13	Tottenham H	0	0		
2012–13	Sunderland	27	1	27	1
2013–14	Tottenham H	22	1	38	2

SANDRO (M)   124 7
H: 6 2   W: 11 11   b.Riachinho 15-3-89
Internationals: Brazil U20, U23, Full caps.

Season	Club	A	G	T A	T G
2008	Internacional	7	2		
2009	Internacional	27	1		
2010	Internacional	9	1	43	4
2010–11	Tottenham H	19	1		
2011–12	Tottenham H	23	0		
2012–13	Tottenham H	22	1		
2013–14	Tottenham H	17	1	81	3

SIGURDSSON, Gylfi (M)   172 46
H: 6 1   W: 12 02   b.Reykjavik 9-9-89
Internationals: Iceland U17, U18, U19, U21, Full caps.

Season	Club	A	G	T A	T G
2007–08	Reading	0	0		
2008–09	Reading	0	0		
2008–09	Shrewsbury T	5	1	5	1
2008–09	Crewe Alex	15	3	15	3
2009–10	Reading	38	16		
2010–11	Reading	2		42	18
2010–11	Hoffenheim	28	9		
2011–12	Hoffenheim	6	0	34	9
2011–12	Swansea C	18	7	18	7
2012–13	Tottenham H	0	0		
2013–14	Tottenham H	25	5	58	8

SOLDADO, Roberto (F)   235 107
H: 5 9   W: 11 06   b.Valencia 27-5-85
Internationals: Spain U15, U17, U17, U19, U21, Full caps.

Season	Club	A	G	T A	T G
2005–06	Real Madrid	11	2		
2006–07	Real Madrid	0	0		
2006–07	Osasuna	30	11	30	11
2007–08	Real Madrid	5	0	16	2
2008–09	Getafe	34	13		
2009–10	Getafe	26	16	60	29
2010–11	Valencia	34	18		
2011–12	Valencia	32	17		
2012–13	Valencia	35	24	101	59
2013–14	Tottenham H	28	6	28	6

TOWNSEND, Andros (M)   131 12
H: 6 0   W: 12 00   b.Chingford 16-7-91
Internationals: England U16, U17, U19, U21, Full caps.

Season	Club	A	G	T A	T G
2008–09	Tottenham H	0	0		
2008–09	Yeovil T	10	1	10	1
2009–10	Tottenham H	0	0		
2009–10	Leyton Orient	22	2	22	2
2009–10	Milton Keynes D	9	2	9	2
2010–11	Tottenham H	0	0		
2010–11	Ipswich T	13	1	13	1
2010–11	Watford	3	0	3	0
2010–11	Millwall	11	2	11	2
2011–12	Tottenham H	0	0		
2011–12	Leeds U	6	1	6	1
2011–12	Birmingham C	15	0	15	0
2012–13	Tottenham H	5	0		
2012–13	QPR	12	2	12	2
2013–14	Tottenham H	25	1	30	1

VELJKOVIC, Milos (D)   2 0
b.Basel 26-9-95
Internationals: Serbia U17, U19.

Season	Club	A	G	T A	T G
2012–13	Tottenham H	0	0		
2013–14	Tottenham H	2	0	2	0

VERTONGHEN, Jan (D)   224 30
H: 6 2   W: 12 05   b.Sint-Niklaas 24-4-87
Internationals: Belgium U16, U21, Full caps.

Season	Club	A	G	T A	T G
2006–07	Ajax	3	0		
2006–07	RKC	12	3	12	3
2007–08	Ajax	31	2		
2008–09	Ajax	26	4		
2009–10	Ajax	32	3		
2010–11	Ajax	32	6		
2011–12	Ajax	31	8	155	23
2012–13	Tottenham H	34	4		
2013–14	Tottenham H	23	0	57	4

WALKER, Kyle (D)   174 4
H: 5 10   W: 11 07   b.Sheffield 28-5-90
Internationals: England U19, U21, Full caps.

Season	Club	A	G	T A	T G
2008–09	Sheffield U	2	0		
2008–09	Northampton T	9	0	9	0
2009–10	Tottenham H	2	0		
2009–10	Sheffield U	26	0	28	0
2010–11	Tottenham H	1	0		
2010–11	QPR	20	0	20	0
2010–11	Aston Villa	15	1	15	1
2011–12	Tottenham H	37	2		
2012–13	Tottenham H	36	0		
2013–14	Tottenham H	26	1	102	3

Scholars
Akindayini, Daniel Oluwaseun; Amos, Luke Ayodele; Campbell-Young, Channing Shelby; Georgiou, Anthony Michael; Goddard, Cy; Harrison, Shayon; Lameiras, Ruben; Lesniak, Filip; McEneff, Aaron; McGee, Luke Paul; McQueen, Alexander Luke; Miller, William; Ogilvie, Connor Stuart; Pritchard, Joe Cameron; Ross, Lloyd; Sonupe, Emmanuel Olukolade; Voss, Harry William; Walker-Peters, Kyle; Walkes, Anton; Winks, Harry.

TRANMERE R (83)

AKPA AKPRO, Jean-Louis (F)   237 34
H: 6 0   W: 10 12   b.Toulouse 4-1-85

Season	Club	A	G	T A	T G
2004–05	Toulouse	13	0		
2005–06	Toulouse	14	3	27	3
2006–07	Brest	15	2	15	2
2007–08	FC Brussels	3	0	3	0
2008–09	Grimsby T	20	3		
2009–10	Grimsby T	36	5	56	8
2010–11	Rochdale	32	4		
2011–12	Rochdale	41	7	73	11
2012–13	Tranmere R	28	8		
2013–14	Tranmere R	25	2	53	10
2013–14	Bury	10	0	10	0

BELL-BAGGIE, Abdulai (F)   57 1
H: 5 6   W: 10 00   b.London 28-4-92
Internationals: England U16, U17. Sierra Leone Full caps.

Season	Club	A	G	T A	T G
2009–10	Reading	0	0		
2009–10	Rotherham U	11	0	11	0
2010–11	Reading	0	0		
2010–11	Port Vale	3	0	3	0
From Hayes & Y, Salisbury C					
2012–13	Tranmere R	31	1		
2013–14	Tranmere R	12	0	43	1

BOLAND, Antoine (M)   0 0
b. 30-12-94

Season	Club	A	G		
2012–13	Barnsley	0	0		
2013–14	Barnsley	0	0		
2013–14	Tranmere R	0	0		

FON WILLIAMS, Owain (G)   233 0
H: 6 1   W: 12 09   b.Penygroes 17-3-87
Internationals: Wales U17, U19, U21.

Season	Club	A	G	T A	T G
2005–06	Crewe Alex	0	0		
2006–07	Crewe Alex	0	0		
2007–08	Crewe Alex	0	0		
2008–09	Stockport Co	33	0		
2009–10	Stockport Co	44	0		
2010–11	Stockport Co	5	0	82	0
2010–11	Bury	6	0	6	0
2010–11	Rochdale	22	0	22	0
2011–12	Tranmere R	35	0		
2012–13	Tranmere R	45	0		
2013–14	Tranmere R	43	0	123	0

FOSTER, Stephen (D)   465 25
H: 6 0   W: 11 05   b.Warrington 10-9-80

Season	Club	A	G	T A	T G
1998–99	Crewe Alex	1	0		
1999–2000	Crewe Alex	0	0		
2000–01	Crewe Alex	30	0		
2001–02	Crewe Alex	34	5		
2002–03	Crewe Alex	35	4		
2003–04	Crewe Alex	45	2		
2004–05	Crewe Alex	34	1		
2005–06	Crewe Alex	39	3	218	15
2006–07	Burnley	17	0		
2007–08	Burnley	0	0	17	0
2007–08	Barnsley	41	1		
2008–09	Barnsley	38	3		
2009–10	Barnsley	42	2		
2010–11	Barnsley	33	1		
2011–12	Barnsley	41	1		
2012–13	Barnsley	31	2	226	10
2013–14	Tranmere R	4	0	4	0

GOODISON, Ian (D)   434 12
H: 6 1   W: 13 04   b.St James, Jamaica 21-11-72
Internationals: Jamaica Full caps.

Season	Club	A	G	T A	T G
1999–2000	Hull C	18	0		
2000–01	Hull C	36	1		
2001–02	Hull C	16	0		
2002–03	Hull C	0	0	70	1
From Seba U.					
2003–04	Tranmere R	12	0		
2004–05	Tranmere R	44	1		
2005–06	Tranmere R	38	1		
2006–07	Tranmere R	40	0		
2007–08	Tranmere R	42	0		
2008–09	Tranmere R	33	1		
2009–10	Tranmere R	44	3		
2010–11	Tranmere R	40	4		
2011–12	Tranmere R	43	1		
2012–13	Tranmere R	10	0		
2013–14	Tranmere R	18	0	364	11

HATELEY, Tom (M)   156 9
b. 12-9-89

Season	Club	A	G	T A	T G
2008–09	Reading	0	0		
2009–10	Motherwell	38	2		
2010–11	Motherwell	38	2		
2011–12	Motherwell	38	2		
2012–13	Motherwell	34	3	148	9
2013–14	Tranmere R	8	0	8	0

Transferred to Slask Wroclaw January 2014.

HOLMES, Danny (D)   156 5
H: 6 0   W: 11 13   b.Birkenhead 6-1-89

Season	Club	A	G	T A	T G
2007–08	Tranmere R	0	0		
2008–09	Tranmere R	1	0		
2009–10	The New Saints	32	0		
2010–11	The New Saints	26	3	58	3
2011–12	Tranmere R	26	0		
2012–13	Tranmere R	43	2		
2013–14	Tranmere R	28	0	98	2

HORWOOD, Evan (D)   270 6
H: 6 0   W: 10 06   b.Billingham 10-3-86

Season	Club	A	G	T A	T G
2004–05	Sheffield U	0	0		
2004–05	Stockport Co	10	0	10	0
2005–06	Sheffield U	0	0		
2005–06	Scunthorpe U	0	0		
2005–06	Chester C	1	0	1	0
2006–07	Sheffield U	0	0		
2006–07	Darlington	20	0	20	0
2007–08	Sheffield U	0	0		
2007–08	Gretna	15	1	15	1
2007–08	Carlisle U	19	0		
2008–09	Carlisle U	24	0		
2009–10	Carlisle U	32	0	75	0

2010–11	Hartlepool U	45	2		
2011–12	Hartlepool U	41	1		
2012–13	Hartlepool U	37	2	123	6
2013–14	Tranmere R	18	0	18	0
2013–14	*Northampton T*	8	0	8	0

JENNINGS, Steven (M)   308 10
H: 5 5   W: 12 00   b.Liverpool 28-10-84

2003–04	Tranmere R	4	0		
2004–05	Tranmere R	11	0		
2005–06	Tranmere R	38	1		
2006–07	Tranmere R	2	0		
2006–07	*Hereford U*	11	0	11	0
2007–08	Tranmere R	41	2		
2008–09	Tranmere R	44	3		
2009–10	Motherwell	29	2		
2010–11	Motherwell	30	0		
2011–12	Motherwell	34	0	93	2
2012–13	Coventry C	39	0		
2013–14	Coventry C	0	0	39	0
2013–14	Tranmere R	25	1	165	7

KIRBY, Jake (M)   36 2
H: 5 11   W: 12 04   b.Liverpool 9-5-94

2011–12	Tranmere R	1	0		
2012–13	Tranmere R	4	0		
2013–14	Tranmere R	31	2	36	2

KOUMAS, Jason (M)   402 67
H: 5 10   W: 11 07   b.Wrexham 25-9-79
Internationals: Wales Full caps.

1997–98	Tranmere R	0	0		
1998–99	Tranmere R	23	3		
1999–2000	Tranmere R	23	2		
2000–01	Tranmere R	39	10		
2001–02	Tranmere R	38	8		
2002–03	Tranmere R	4	2		
2002–03	WBA	32	4		
2003–04	WBA	42	10		
2004–05	WBA	10	0		
2005–06	WBA	0	0		
2005–06	*Cardiff C*	44	12		
2006–07	WBA	39	9	123	23
2007–08	Wigan Ath	30	1		
2008–09	Wigan Ath	16	0		
2009–10	Wigan Ath	8	1		
2010–11	Wigan Ath	0	0		
2010–11	*Cardiff C*	23	2	67	4
2011–12	Wigan Ath	0	0		
2012–13	Wigan Ath	0	0	54	2
2013–14	Tranmere R	31	3	158	28

MOONEY, Jason (G)   4 0
H: 6 9   W: 14 00

2011–12	Wycombe W	0	0		
2012–13	Tranmere R	1	0		
2013–14	Tranmere R	3	0	4	0

POWER, Max (M)   64 5
H: 5 11   W: 11 13   b.Bebington 27-7-93

2010–11	Tranmere R	0	0		
2011–12	Tranmere R	4	0		
2012–13	Tranmere R	27	3		
2013–14	Tranmere R	33	2	64	5

ROBINSON, Andy (M)   327 63
H: 5 8   W: 11 04   b.Birkenhead 3-11-79

2002–03	Tranmere R	0	0		
2003–04	Swansea C	37	8		
2004–05	Swansea C	37	8		
2005–06	Swansea C	39	12		
2006–07	Swansea C	39	7		
2007–08	Swansea C	40	8	192	43
2008–09	Leeds U	32	2		
2009–10	Leeds U	6	0		
2009–10	*Tranmere R*	5	1		
2010–11	Leeds U	0	0	38	2
2010–11	Tranmere R	15	0		
2011–12	Tranmere R	25	4		
2012–13	Tranmere R	33	10		
2013–14	Tranmere R	19	3	97	18

ROWE, James (M)   19 1
H: 5 11   W: 10 02   b. 21-10-91

2010–11	Reading	0	0		
2011–12	Reading	0	0		
From Forest Green R					
2013–14	Tranmere R	19	1	19	1

SODJE, Akpo (F)   244 55
H: 6 2   W: 12 07   b.London 31-1-80

2004–05	Huddersfield T	7	0	7	0
2004–05	*Darlington*	7	1		
2005–06	Darlington	36	8	43	9

2006–07	Port Vale	43	14		
2007–08	Port Vale	3	0	46	14
2007–08	Sheffield W	19	7		
2008–09	Sheffield W	11	2		
2009–10	Sheffield W	11	0	41	9
2009–10	Charlton Ath	25	5		
2010–11	Charlton Ath	15	1	40	6
2010–11	Hibernian	15	6		
2011–12	Hibernian	12	0	27	6
2011–12	Tianjin Taida	1	1	1	1
2012–13	Preston NE	14	4	14	4
2012–13	Scunthorpe U	16	6	16	6
2013–14	Tranmere R	9	0	9	0

STOCKTON, Cole (F)   53 5
H: 6 1   W: 11 11   b.Huyton 13-3-94

2011–12	Tranmere R	1	0		
2012–13	Tranmere R	31	3		
2013–14	Tranmere R	21	2	53	5

TAYLOR, Ash (M)   183 8
H: 6 0   W: 12 00   b.Bromborough 2-9-90
Internationals: Wales U19, U21

2008–09	Tranmere R	1	0		
2009–10	Tranmere R	33	1		
2010–11	Tranmere R	26	0		
2011–12	Tranmere R	37	2		
2012–13	Tranmere R	44	2		
2013–14	Tranmere R	42	3	183	8

THOMPSON, Joe (M)   172 18
H: 6 0   W: 9 07   b.Rochdale 5-3-89

2005–06	Rochdale	1	0		
2006–07	Rochdale	13	0		
2007–08	Rochdale	11	1		
2008–09	Rochdale	30	5		
2009–10	Rochdale	36	6		
2010–11	Rochdale	32	2		
2011–12	Rochdale	17	1		
2012–13	Rochdale	19	1		
2013–14	*Rochdale*	7	0	147	15
2013–14	Tranmere R	6	2	25	3

WALLACE, James (M)   72 7
H: 5 11   W: 12 08   b.Fazackerly 19-12-91
Internationals: England U19, U20.

2008–09	Everton	0	0		
2009–10	Everton	0	0		
2010–11	Everton	0	0		
2010–11	*Stockport Co*	14	1	14	1
2010–11	*Bury*	0	0		
2011–12	Everton	0	0		
2011–12	*Shrewsbury T*	3	0	3	0
2011–12	*Stevenage*	0	0		
2011–12	*Tranmere R*	18	2		
2012–13	Tranmere R	19	2		
2013–14	Everton	0	0		
2013–14	Tranmere R	18	2	55	6

Scholars

Davies, Liam; Duggan, Mitchel James; Gumbs, Evan; Jago, Ben; Lamb, Joe; Maher, Benjamin Thomas; Moynes, Lewis John; Newton, Joseph Luke; Phillips, Jake Terence Kenneth Lee; Pilling, Luke Arthur; Ramsbottom, Sam Nicholas; Riley, Leo Paul; Shackleton, Connor Edward; Shaw, Daniel Thomas; Smith, Liam Alexander.

WALSALL (84)

BAKAYOKO, Amadou (F)   6 0

2013–14	Walsall	6	0	6	0

BAXENDALE, James (M)   75 6
H: 5 8   W: 10 03   b.Thorne 16-9-92

2011–12	Doncaster R	2	0		
2011–12	*Hereford U*	1	0	1	0
2012–13	Doncaster R	0	0	2	0
2012–13	Walsall	32	4		
2013–14	Walsall	40	2	72	6

BENNING, Malvind (D)   26 2
H: 5 10   W: 12 00   b.Sandwell 2-11-93

2012–13	Walsall	10	0		
2013–14	Walsall	16	2	26	2

BUTLER, Andy (D)   358 34
H: 6 0   W: 13 00   b.Doncaster 4-11-83

2003–04	Scunthorpe U	35	2		
2004–05	Scunthorpe U	37	10		
2005–06	Scunthorpe U	16	1		

2006–07	Scunthorpe U	11	1		
2006–07	*Grimsby T*	4	0	4	0
2007–08	Scunthorpe U	36	2	135	16
2008–09	Huddersfield T	42	4		
2009–10	Huddersfield T	11	0	53	4
2009–10	*Blackpool*	7	0	7	0
2010–11	Walsall	31	4		
2011–12	Walsall	42	5		
2012–13	Walsall	41	3		
2013–14	Walsall	45	2	159	14

CHAMBERS, Adam (D)   354 12
H: 5 10   W: 11 12   b.Sandwell 20-11-80

1998–99	WBA	0	0		
1999–2000	WBA	11	0		
2000–01	WBA	11	1		
2001–02	WBA	32	0		
2002–03	WBA	13	0		
2003–04	WBA	0	0		
2003–04	*Sheffield W*	11	0	11	0
2004–05	WBA	0	0	56	1
2004–05	Kidderminster H	2	0	2	0
2006–07	Leyton Orient	38	4		
2007–08	Leyton Orient	45	3		
2008–09	Leyton Orient	33	1		
2009–10	Leyton Orient	29	1		
2010–11	Leyton Orient	29	0	174	9
2011–12	Walsall	29	2		
2012–13	Walsall	37	0		
2013–14	Walsall	45	0	111	2

CHAMBERS, James (D)   350 1
H: 5 10   W: 11 11   b.West Bromwich 20-11-80

1998–99	WBA	0	0		
1999–2000	WBA	12	0		
2000–01	WBA	31	0		
2001–02	WBA	5	0		
2002–03	WBA	8	0		
2003–04	WBA	17	0		
2004–05	WBA	0	0	73	0
2005–06	Watford	40	0		
2005–06	Watford	38	0		
2006–07	Watford	12	0	90	0
2006–07	*Cardiff C*	7	0	7	0
2007–08	Leicester C	24	0	24	0
2008–09	Doncaster R	37	0		
2009–10	Doncaster R	43	0		
2010–11	Doncaster R	7	0		
2011–12	Doncaster R	0	0	87	0
2011–12	*Hereford U*	7	0	7	0
2012–13	Walsall	22	0		
2013–14	Walsall	40	1	62	1

DOWNING, Paul (D)   107 2
H: 6 1   W: 12 06   b.Taunton 26-10-91

2009–10	WBA	0	0		
2009–10	*Hereford U*	6	0		
2010–11	WBA	0	0		
2010–11	*Hereford U*	0	0	6	0
2010–11	*Swansea C*	0	0		
2011–12	WBA	0	0		
2011–12	*Barnet*	26	0	26	0
2012–13	Walsall	31	1		
2013–14	Walsall	44	1	75	2

FEATHERSTONE, Nicky (M)   137 1
H: 5 7   W: 11 02   b.Ferriby 22-9-88

2006–07	Hull C	2	0		
2007–08	Hull C	6	0		
2008–09	Hull C	0	0		
2009–10	Hull C	0	0	8	0
2009–10	*Grimsby T*	8	0	8	0
2010–11	Hereford U	27	1		
2011–12	Hereford U	38	0	65	1
2012–13	Walsall	31	0		
2013–14	Walsall	25	0	56	0

FLANAGAN, Reece (M)   0 0
H: 5 7   W: 11 02

2013–14	Walsall	0	0		

GEORGE, Ben (D)   1 0
H: 5 8   W: 10 13   b. 14-11-93

2012–13	Walsall	1	0		
2013–14	Walsall	0	0	1	0

GRAY, Julian (M)   358 40
H: 6 1   W: 10 13   b.Lewisham 21-9-79

1998–99	Arsenal	0	0		
1999–2000	Arsenal	1	0	1	0
2000–01	Crystal Palace	23	1		
2001–02	Crystal Palace	43	2		
2002–03	Crystal Palace	35	5		

Season	Club				
2003–04	Crystal Palace	24	2	**125**	**10**
2003–04	*Cardiff C*	9	0	**9**	**0**
2004–05	Birmingham C	32	2		
2005–06	Birmingham C	21	1		
2006–07	Birmingham C	7	0	**60**	**3**
2007–08	Coventry C	26	3		
2008–09	Coventry C	3	1	**29**	**4**
2008–09	Fulham	1	0	**1**	**0**
2009–10	Barnsley	5	0	**5**	**0**
2009–10	Walsall	18	4		
2010–11	Walsall	43	10		
2011–12	Nea Salamina	24	5		
2012–13	Nea Salamina	31	3	**55**	**8**
2013–14	Walsall	12	1	**73**	**15**

HEATH, Jake (M)   **0 0**
b. 9-3-95

2013–14	Walsall	0	0		

HEMMINGS, Ashley (M)   **95 5**
H: 5 8 W: 11 06 b.Lewisham 3-3-91
Internationals: England U17.

2008–09	Wolverhampton W	2	0		
2008–09	*Cheltenham T*	1	0	**1**	**0**
2009–10	Wolverhampton W	0	0		
2010–11	Wolverhampton W	0	0		
2010–11	*Torquay U*	9	0	**9**	**0**
2011–12	Wolverhampton W	0	0	**2**	**0**
2011–12	*Plymouth Arg*	23	2	**23**	**2**
2012–13	Walsall	28	1		
2013–14	Walsall	27	2	**55**	**3**
2013–14	*Burton Alb*	5	0	**5**	**0**

HEWITT, Troy (F)   **42 2**
H: 6 0 W: 12 05 b.Newham 10-2-90

2010–11	QPR	0	0		
2011–12	QPR	0	0		
2011–12	*Dagenham & R*	6	0	**6**	**0**
2012–13	QPR	0	0		
2012–13	*Bury*	8	2	**8**	**2**
2012–13	*Colchester U*	1	0	**1**	**0**
2013–14	Walsall	27	0	**27**	**0**

KINSELLA, Liam (M)   **0 0**
b. 23-2-96

2013–14	Walsall	0	0		

MANTOM, Sam (M)   **91 10**
H: 5 9 W: 11 00 b.Stourbridge 20-2-92
Internationals: England U17.

2010–11	WBA	0	0		
2010–11	*Tranmere R*	2	0	**2**	**0**
2010–11	*Oldham Ath*	4	0	**4**	**0**
2011–12	WBA	0	0		
2011–12	*Walsall*	13	3		
2012–13	WBA	0	0		
2012–13	Walsall	29	2		
2013–14	Walsall	43	5	**85**	**10**

McQUILKIN, James (M)   **82 5**
H: 5 8 W: 11 08 b.Belfast 9-1-89
Internationals: Northern Ireland U21.

2007–08	Zlin	4	0		
2008–09	Zlin	2	0	**6**	**0**
2009–10	Hereford U	22	2		
2010–11	Hereford U	38	3		
2011–12	Hereford U	7	0	**67**	**5**
2013–14	Walsall	9	0	**9**	**0**

MORRIS, Kieron (M)   **2 0**
H: 5 10 W: 11 01

2012–13	Walsall	0	0		
2013–14	Walsall	2	0	**2**	**0**

O'DONNELL, Richard (G)   **90 0**
H: 6 2 W: 13 05 b.Sheffield 12-9-88

2007–08	Sheffield W	0	0		
2007–08	*Rotherham U*	0	0		
2007–08	*Oldham Ath*	4	0	**4**	**0**
2008–09	Sheffield W	0	0		
2009–10	Sheffield W	0	0		
2010–11	Sheffield W	9	0		
2011–12	Sheffield W	6	0	**15**	**0**
2011–12	*Macclesfield T*	11	0	**11**	**0**
2012–13	Chesterfield	14	0	**14**	**0**
2013–14	Walsall	46	0	**46**	**0**

PRESTON, Matt (D)   **0 0**
b. 16-3-95

2013–14	Walsall	0	0		

PURKISS, Ben (D)   **79 0**
H: 6 2 W: 10 13 b.Sheffield 1-4-84

2001–02	Sheffield U	0	0		
2002–03	Sheffield U	0	0		

From Gainsborough T, York C

2010–11	Oxford U	23	0	**23**	**0**
2011–12	Hereford U	15	0	**15**	**0**
2012–13	Walsall	27	0		
2013–14	Walsall	14	0	**41**	**0**

SAWYERS, Romaine (M)   **56 6**
H: 5 9 W: 11 00 b.Birmingham 2-11-91
Internationals: St Kitts and Nevis U23, Full caps.

2009–10	WBA	0	0		
2010–11	WBA	0	0		
2010–11	*Port Vale*	1	0	**1**	**0**
2011–12	WBA	0	0		
2011–12	*Shrewsbury T*	7	0	**7**	**0**
2012–13	WBA	0	0		
2012–13	Walsall	4	0		
2013–14	Walsall	44	6	**48**	**6**

TAYLOR, Andy (D)   **193 4**
H: 5 11 W: 11 07 b.Blackburn 14-3-86
Internationals: England U16, U17, U18, U19, U20.

2004–05	Blackburn R	0	0		
2005–06	Blackburn R	0	0		
2005–06	*QPR*	3	0	**3**	**0**
2005–06	*Blackpool*	3	0	**3**	**0**
2006–07	Blackburn R	0	0		
2006–07	*Crewe Alex*	4	0	**4**	**0**
2006–07	*Huddersfield T*	8	0	**8**	**0**
2007–08	Blackburn R	0	0		
2007–08	Tranmere R	30	2		
2008–09	Tranmere R	39	1	**69**	**3**
2009–10	Sheffield U	26	0		
2010–11	Sheffield U	9	0		
2011–12	Sheffield U	4	0		
2012–13	Sheffield U	0	0	**39**	**0**
2012–13	Nottingham F	0	0		
2013–14	Walsall	34	0		
2013–14	Walsall	33	1	**67**	**1**

WESTCARR, Craig (F)   **240 52**
H: 5 11 W: 11 04 b.Nottingham 29-1-85
Internationals: England U18.

2001–02	Nottingham F	8	0		
2002–03	Nottingham F	11	1		
2003–04	Nottingham F	3	0		
2004–05	Nottingham F	1	0	**23**	**1**
2004–05	*Lincoln C*	6	1	**6**	**1**
2004–05	*Milton Keynes D*	4	0	**4**	**0**

From Cambridge U, Kettering T

2009–10	Notts Co	42	9		
2010–11	Notts Co	41	12		
2011–12	Notts Co	4	0	**87**	**21**
2011–12	Chesterfield	38	8		
2012–13	Chesterfield	15	2	**53**	**10**
2012–13	*Walsall*	24	5		
2013–14	Walsall	43	14	**67**	**19**

Scholars
Ashmore, Jamie Russell; Christophorou, Aris James; Dallison, Alexander Fredrick; Delaney, Luke; Garner, Jordan Craig; Henry, Rico; Jones, Richard James; Lovett, Rhys Christian; McKenzie, Carlton Nesta Coral; Probert, Lewis Jon; Reid, Romario Rashaun; Reid, Alex Michael; Rowley, Kyle Jake; Rowley, Levi James; Rush, Westleigh Taylor; Shakespeare, Tevin McKoy Jhevon.

WATFORD (85)

ABDI, Almen (M)   **232 45**
H: 5 11 W: 12 11 b.Prizren 21-10-86
Internationals: Switzerland, U21, Full caps.

2003–04	FC Zurich	11	0		
2004–05	FC Zurich	5	0		
2005–06	FC Zurich	12	0		
2006–07	FC Zurich	28	5		
2007–08	FC Zurich	31	7		
2008–09	FC Zurich	32	19		
2009–10	FC Zurich	8	0	**127**	**31**
2009–10	Le Mans	13	0	**13**	**0**
2010–11	Udinese	19	0		
2011–12	Udinese	22	0	**41**	**0**
2012–13	*Watford*	38	12		
2013–14	Watford	13	2	**51**	**14**

ACUNA, Javier (F)   **134 27**
H: 5 9 W: 10 13 b.Encarnacion 23-6-88
Internationals: Paraguay U17, U20.

2006–07	Cadiz	23	2		
2007–08	Cadiz	0	0	**23**	**2**
2007–08	*Salamanca*	21	1	**21**	**1**
2008–09	Real Madrid	0	0		
2009–10	Real Madrid	0	0		
2010–11	Real Madrid	0	0		
2010–11	*Recreativo Huelva*	12	1	**12**	**1**
2011–12	Real Madrid	0	0		
2011–12	Girona	17	4		
2012–13	Real Madrid	0	0		
2012–13	Girona	36	16	**53**	**20**
2013–14	*Watford*	9	0	**9**	**0**
2013–14	Osasuna	16	3	**16**	**3**

ALMUNIA, Manuel (G)   **324 0**
H: 6 3 W: 13 00 b.Pamplona 19-5-77

1996–97	Osasuna B	2	0		
1997–98	Osasuna B	31	0		
1998–99	Osasuna B	13	0	**46**	**0**
1999–2000	*Cartagena*	3	0	**3**	**0**
2000–01	Sabadell	25	0	**25**	**0**
2000–01	Celta Vigo	0	0		
2001–02	Celta Vigo	0	0		
2001–02	Eibar	35	0	**35**	**0**
2002–03	*Recreativo*	2	0	**2**	**0**
2003–04	Albacete	24	0	**24**	**0**
2004–05	Arsenal	10	0		
2005–06	Arsenal	0	0		
2006–07	Arsenal	1	0		
2007–08	Arsenal	29	0		
2008–09	Arsenal	32	0		
2009–10	Arsenal	29	0		
2010–11	Arsenal	8	0		
2011–12	Arsenal	0	0		
2011–12	*West Ham U*	4	0	**4**	**0**
2012–13	Arsenal	0	0	**109**	**0**
2012–13	Watford	39	0		
2013–14	Watford	37	0	**76**	**0**

ANGELLA, Gabriele (D)   **129 12**
H: 6 2 W: 12 05 b.Firenze 28-4-89
Internationals: Italy U21.

2008–09	Empoli	11	0		
2009–10	Empoli	35	0		
2010–11	Empoli	2	0	**48**	**0**
2010–11	Udinese	8	0		
2011–12	Udinese	0	0		
2011–12	Siena	0	0		
2011–12	*Reggina*	19	1	**19**	**1**
2012–13	Udinese	14	4	**22**	**4**
2013–14	Watford	40	7	**40**	**7**

ANYA, Ikechi (M)   **93 11**
H: 5 5 W: 11 04 b.Glasgow 3-1-88
Internationals: Scotland Full caps.

2004–05	Wycombe W	3	0		
2005–06	Wycombe W	2	0		
2006–07	Wycombe W	13	0		
2007–08	Wycombe W	0	0	**18**	**0**
2008–09	Northampton T	14	3	**14**	**3**
2010–11	Celta Vigo	1	0	**1**	**0**

From Cadiz

2012–13	*Watford*	25	3		
2013–14	Watford	35	5	**60**	**8**

BATTOCCHIO, Cristian (M)   **63 6**
H: 5 10 W: 10 13 b.Buenos Aires 10-2-92
Internationals: Italy U20, U21.

2010–11	Udinese	1	0		
2011–12	Udinese	4	0		
2012–13	Udinese	1	0	**6**	**0**
2012–13	*Watford*	22	2		
2013–14	Watford	35	4	**57**	**6**

BELKALEM, Essaid (D)   **73 5**
H: 6 3 W: 13 04 b.Mekla 1-1-89
Internationals: Algeria U20, U23, Full caps.

2009–10	JS Kabylie	19	1		
2010–11	JS Kabylie	12	0		
2011–12	JS Kabylie	12	2		
2012–13	JS Kabylie	22	2	**65**	**5**
2013–14	Granada	0	0		

On loan from Granada

2013–14	Watford	8	0	**8**	**0**

BOND, Jonathan (G) 30 0
H: 6 3 W: 13 03 b.Hemel Hempstead 19-5-93
Internationals: Wales U17, U19. England U21.

2010–11	Watford	0	0		
2011–12	Watford	1	0		
2011–12	Dagenham & R	5	0	5	0
2011–12	Bury	6	0	6	0
2012–13	Watford	8	0		
2013–14	Watford	10	0	19	0

BROWN, Reece (D) 41 0
H: 6 2 W: 13 02 b.Manchester 1-11-91
Internationals: England U19, U20.

2010–11	Manchester U	0	0		
2010–11	Bradford C	3	0	3	0
2011–12	Manchester U	0	0		
2011–12	Doncaster R	3	0	3	0
2011–12	Oldham Ath	15	0	15	0
2012–13	Manchester U	0	0		
2012–13	Coventry C	6	0	6	0
2012–13	Ipswich T	1	0	1	0
2013–14	Watford	1	0	1	0
2013–14	Carlisle U	12	0	12	0

CASSETTI, Marco (D) 425 26
H: 6 1 W: 12 11 b.Milano 29-5-75
Internationals: Italy Full caps.

1995–96	Lumezzane	0	0		
1996–97	Montichiari	1	0		
1997–98	Montichiari	29	6	30	6
1998–99	Lumezzane	19	2		
1999–2000	Lumezzane	31	2	50	4
2000–01	Verona	11	0		
2001–02	Verona	14	0		
2002–03	Verona	11	2	36	2
2003–04	Lecce	30	5		
2004–05	Lecce	34	4		
2005–06	Lecce	29	0	93	9
2006–07	Roma	28	2		
2007–08	Roma	27	0		
2008–09	Roma	20	0		
2009–10	Roma	29	2		
2010–11	Roma	32	0		
2011–12	Roma	7	0	143	4
2012–13	Udinese	0	0		
2012–13	Watford	38	0		
2013–14	Watford	35	1	73	1

DEENEY, Troy (F) 286 84
H: 5 11 W: 12 00 b.Solihull 29-6-88

2006–07	Walsall	1	0		
2007–08	Walsall	35	1		
2008–09	Walsall	45	12		
2009–10	Walsall	42	14	123	27
2010–11	Watford	36	3		
2011–12	Watford	43	11		
2012–13	Watford	40	19		
2013–14	Watford	44	24	163	57

DOHERTY, Josh (M) 1 0
b. 15-3-96
Internationals: Northern Ireland U17, U19.

2013–14	Watford	1	0	1	0

DOYLEY, Lloyd (D) 389 6
H: 5 10 W: 12 13 b.Whitechapel 1-12-82
Internationals: Jamaica Full caps.

2000–01	Watford	0	0		
2001–02	Watford	20	0		
2002–03	Watford	22	0		
2003–04	Watford	9	0		
2004–05	Watford	29	0		
2005–06	Watford	44	0		
2006–07	Watford	21	0		
2007–08	Watford	36	0		
2008–09	Watford	37	0		
2009–10	Watford	44	1		
2010–11	Watford	36	0		
2011–12	Watford	33	0		
2012–13	Watford	34	1		
2013–14	Watford	24	0	389	6

EKSTRAND, Joel (D) 151 2
H: 6 2 W: 12 00 b.Lund 4-2-89
Internationals: Sweden U17, U19, U21, Full caps.

2007–08	Helsingborgs IF	12	0		
2008–09	Helsingborgs IF	24	0		
2009–10	Helsingborgs IF	25	1		
2010–11	Helsingborgs IF	12	0	73	1
2010–11	Udinese	1	0		
2011–12	Udinese	12	0	13	0
2012–13	Watford	32	1		
2013–14	Watford	33	0	65	1

FABBRINI, Diego (F) 114 8
H: 5 11 W: 11 12 b.San Giuliano terme 31-7-90
Internationals: Italy U21, Full caps.

2009–10	Empoli	29	1		
2010–11	Empoli	26	2	55	3
2011–12	Udinese	14	2		
2012–13	Udinese	6	0	20	2
2012–13	Palermo	8	1	8	1
2013–14	Watford	21	1	21	1
2013–14	Siena	10	1	10	1

FARAONI, Marco (M) 62 3
H: 5 10 W: 11 08 b.Bracciano 25-10-91
Internationals: Italy U16, U17, U18, U19, U20, U21.

2007–08	Lazio	0	0		
2008–09	Lazio	0	0		
2009–10	Lazio	0	0		
2010–11	Inter Milan	0	0		
2011–12	Inter Milan	14	1	14	1
2012–13	Udinese	10	0	10	0
2013–14	Watford	38	2	38	2

FORESTIERI, Fernando (F) 152 28
H: 5 8 W: 10 07 b.Rosario 16-1-90
Internationals: Italy U17, U19, U20, U21.

2006–07	Genoa	1	1	1	1
2007–08	Siena	17	1		
2008–09	Siena	2	0	19	1
2008–09	Vicenza	13	5	13	5
2009–10	Malaga	19	1	19	1
2010–11	Empoli	17	3	17	3
2011–12	Bari	27	2	27	2
2012–13	Udinese	0	0		
2012–13	Watford	28	8		
2013–14	Watford	28	7	56	15

HALL, Fitz (D) 273 12
H: 6 3 W: 13 00 b.Leytonstone 20-12-80

2001–02	Oldham Ath	4	1		
2002–03	Oldham Ath	40	4	44	5
2003–04	Southampton	11	0	11	0
2004–05	Crystal Palace	36	2		
2005–06	Crystal Palace	39	1	75	3
2006–07	Wigan Ath	24	0		
2007–08	Wigan Ath	1	0	25	0
2007–08	QPR	14	0		
2008–09	QPR	24	2		
2009–10	QPR	14	0		
2009–10	Newcastle U	7	0	7	0
2010–11	QPR	19	1		
2011–12	QPR	14	0	85	3
2012–13	Watford	21	1		
2013–14	Watford	5	0	26	1

HOBAN, Tommie (D) 27 2
H: 6 2 W: 11 13 b.Walthamstow 24-1-94
Internationals: Republic of Ireland U17, U19.

2010–11	Watford	1	0		
2011–12	Watford	0	0		
2012–13	Watford	19	2		
2013–14	Watford	7	0	27	2

IKPEAZU, Uche (F) 15 4
b.London 28-2-95

2013–14	Watford	0	0		
2013–14	Crewe Alex	15	4	15	4

IRINEY, Santos (M) 232 5
H: 5 10 W: 12 07 b. 23-4-81

2005–06	Celta Vigo	29	0		
2006–07	Celta Vigo	26	2	55	2
2007–08	Almeria	8	0		
2008–09	Almeria	18	0	26	0
2009–10	Real Betis	33	0		
2010–11	Real Betis	36	3		
2011–12	Real Betis	31	0	100	3
2012–13	Granada	25	0	25	0
2013–14	Watford	15	0	15	0
2013–14	Mallorca	11	0	11	0

JAKUBIAK, Alex (F) 1 0
b. 27-8-96

2013–14	Watford	1	0	1	0

McGUGAN, Lewis (M) 236 50
H: 5 9 W: 11 06 b.Long Eaton 25-10-88
Internationals: England U17, U19.

2006–07	Nottingham F	13	2		
2007–08	Nottingham F	33	6		
2008–09	Nottingham F	33	5		
2009–10	Nottingham F	18	3		
2010–11	Nottingham F	40	13		
2011–12	Nottingham F	35	3		
2012–13	Nottingham F	30	8	202	40
2013–14	Watford	34	10	34	10

MENSAH, Bernard (F) 1 0
b.Hounslow 29-12-94

2011–12	Watford	0	0		
2012–13	Watford	0	0		
2013–14	Watford	1	0	1	0

MERKEL, Alexander (M) 42 2
H: 5 10 W: 11 10 b.Stuttgart 22-2-92
Internationals: Germany U15, U16, U17, U18, U19, U20.

2009–10	AC Milan	0	0		
2010–11	AC Milan	6	0		
2011–12	Genoa	13	0		
2011–12	AC Milan	1	0	7	0
2012–13	Genoa	6	1	19	1
2012–13	Udinese	5	0		
2013–14	Udinese	0	0	5	0
On loan from Udinese					
2013–14	Watford	11	1	11	1

MURRAY, Sean (M) 69 11
H: 5 9 W: 10 10 b.Abbots Langley 11-10-93
Internationals: Republic of Ireland U17, U19, U21.

2010–11	Watford	2	0		
2011–12	Watford	18	7		
2012–13	Watford	15	1		
2013–14	Watford	34	3	69	11

NEILL, Lucas (D) 86 4
H: 6 1 W: 12 03 b.Sydney 9-3-78
Internationals: Australia U20, U23, Full caps.

2009–10	Galatasaray	14	1		
2010–11	Galatasaray	25	0	39	1
2011–12	Al-Jazira	19	3	19	3
2012–13	Al-Wasl	11	0	11	0
2012–13	Sydney FC	3	0	3	0
2013	Omiya Ardija	9	0	9	0
2013–14	Watford	1	0	1	0
2013–14	Doncaster R	4	0	4	0

NOSWORTHY, Nyron (D) 405 8
H: 6 0 W: 12 08 b.Brixton 11-10-80
Internationals: Jamaica Full caps.

1998–99	Gillingham	3	0		
1999–2000	Gillingham	29	1		
2000–01	Gillingham	10	0		
2001–02	Gillingham	29	0		
2002–03	Gillingham	39	2		
2003–04	Gillingham	27	2		
2004–05	Gillingham	37	0	174	5
2005–06	Sunderland	30	0		
2006–07	Sunderland	29	0		
2007–08	Sunderland	29	0		
2008–09	Sunderland	16	0		
2009–10	Sunderland	10	0		
2009–10	Sheffield U	19	0		
2010–11	Sunderland	0	0		
2010–11	Sheffield U	32	0	51	0
2011–12	Sunderland	0	0	114	0
2011–12	Watford	19	0		
2012–13	Watford	5	0	56	2
2013–14	Bristol C	10	1	10	1

O'NIEN, Luke (M) 1 0
b. 21-11-94

2013–14	Watford	1	0	1	0

PUDIL, Daniel (D) 211 24
H: 6 1 W: 12 11 b.Prague 27-9-85
Internationals: Czech Republic U19, U21, Full caps.

2003–04	Blsany	2	2	2	2
2005–06	Liberec	3	4		
2006–07	Liberec	3	3	6	7
2007–08	Slavia Prague	16	6	16	6
2008–09	Genk	29	4		
2009–10	Genk	27	1		
2010–11	Genk	32	0		

Season	Club	App	Gls	Tot App	Tot Gls
2011–12	Genk	18	0	**106**	**5**
2011–12	Cesena	7	1	**7**	**1**
2012–13	Watford	37	1		
2013–14	Watford	37	2	**74**	**3**

RANEGIE, Mathias (F) **159 56**
H: 6 5 W: 14 07 b.Gothenburg 14-7-84
Internationals: Sweden Full caps.

Season	Club	App	Gls	Tot App	Tot Gls
2007	IFK Goteborg	5	0		
2008	IFK Goteborg	9	1	**14**	**1**
2008–09	Go Ahead Eagles	5	1	**5**	**1**
2009	BK Hacken	28	6		
2010	BK Hacken	30	12		
2011	BK Hacken	22	18	**80**	**36**
2011	Malmo FF	7	3		
2012	Malmo FF	19	10	**26**	**13**
2012–13	Udinese	20	1		
2013–14	Udinese	4	0	**24**	**1**
2013–14	Watford	10	4	**10**	**4**

RIERA, Albert (M) **319 32**
H: 6 2 W: 12 01 b.Manacor 15-4-82
Internationals: Spain U18, U21, Full caps.

Season	Club	App	Gls	Tot App	Tot Gls
2000–01	Mallorca	3	1		
2001–02	Mallorca	8	1		
2002–03	Mallorca	35	4	**46**	**6**
2003–04	Bordeaux	32	2		
2004–05	Bordeaux	21	2	**53**	**4**
2005–06	Espanyol	8	0		
2005–06	*Manchester C*	15	1	**15**	**1**
2006–07	Espanyol	28	4		
2007–08	Espanyol	35	4	**71**	**8**
2008–09	Liverpool	28	3		
2009–10	Liverpool	12	0	**40**	**3**
2010–11	Olympiacos	26	6	**26**	**6**
2011–12	Galatasaray	30	1		
2012–13	Galatasaray	26	2		
2013–14	Galatasaray	4	0	**60**	**3**
2013–14	Watford	8	1	**8**	**1**

SMITH, Connor (M) **18 0**
H: 5 11 W: 11 06 b.London 18-2-93
Internationals: Republic of Ireland U19, U21.

Season	Club	App	Gls	Tot App	Tot Gls
2012–13	Watford	7	0		
2013–14	Watford	1	0	**8**	**0**
2013–14	Gillingham	10	0	**10**	**0**

TOZSER, Daniel (M) **258 23**
H: 6 1 W: 11 08 b.Szolnok 12-5-85
Internationals: Hungary U21, Full caps.

Season	Club	App	Gls	Tot App	Tot Gls
2002–03	Debrecen	0	0		
2003–04	Debrecen	1	0	**1**	**0**
2004–05	Ferencvaros	24	1		
2005–06	Ferencvaros	30	2	**54**	**3**
2006–07	AEK Athens	23	2		
2007–08	AEK Athens	12	1	**35**	**3**
2008–09	Genk	25	2		
2009–10	Genk	38	5		
2010–11	Genk	39	8		
2011–12	Genk	25	2	**127**	**17**
2012–13	Genoa	21	0		
2013–14	Genoa	0	0	**21**	**0**

On loan from Genoa

Season	Club	App	Gls	Tot App	Tot Gls
2013–14	Watford	20	0	**20**	**0**

Scholars
Ammann, Arie Michael; Barnum-Bobb, Jazzi; Bawling, Alfred Bobson; Byers, George William; Choi, Il Myeong; Cox, Ollie Jaspar Charlie; Cumberbatch, Kurtis Benjamin; Dillon, Christopher; Doherty, Josh; Hall, Matthew Stuart; Hope, Ryan Clifford; Johnson, Jorell James; Kyprianou, Harry Kypros; Lewis, Dennon Elliot; Martin, Mahlando Javion; Otudeko, Joseph Adekunle Ayodeji Ibukun Onwumere; Rosenthal, Tom; Stewart, Carl Leon; Wilks, Daniel John; Young, Alfie Mac.

WBA (86)

ALLAN, Scott (M) **45 3**
H: 5 9 W: 11 00 b.Glasgow 28-11-91
Internationals: Scotland U17, U21.

Season	Club	App	Gls	Tot App	Tot Gls
2010–11	Dundee U	0	0		
2010–11	Forfar Ath	4	1	**4**	**1**
2011–12	Dundee U	8	0	**8**	**0**
2011–12	WBA	0	0		
2011–12	Portsmouth	15	1		
2012–13	*Milton Keynes D*	4	0	**4**	**0**
2012–13	WBA	0	0		
2012–13	Portsmouth	9	1	**24**	**2**
2013–14	WBA	0	0		
2013–14	*Birmingham C*	5	0	**5**	**0**

AMALFITANO, Morgan (M) **324 20**
H: 5 9 W: 10 09 b.Nice 20-3-85
Internationals: France Full caps.

Season	Club	App	Gls	Tot App	Tot Gls
2004–05	Sedan	26	0		
2005–06	Sedan	34	0		
2006–07	Sedan	31	0		
2007–08	Sedan	35	0	**126**	**0**
2008–09	Lorient	35	3		
2009–10	Lorient	37	6		
2010–11	Lorient	38	5	**110**	**14**
2011–12	Marseille	32	1		
2012–13	Marseille	26	1		
2013–14	Marseille	2	0	**60**	**2**

On loan from Marseille

Season	Club	App	Gls	Tot App	Tot Gls
2013–14	WBA	28	4	**28**	**4**

ANELKA, Nicolas (F) **495 155**
H: 6 1 W: 13 03 b.Versailles 14-3-79
Internationals: France U20, U21, Full caps.

Season	Club	App	Gls	Tot App	Tot Gls
1995–96	Paris St Germain	2	0		
1996–97	Paris St Germain	8	1		
1996–97	Arsenal	4	0		
1997–98	Arsenal	26	6		
1998–99	Arsenal	35	17	**65**	**23**
1999–2000	Real Madrid	19	2	**19**	**2**
2000–01	Paris St Germain	27	8		
2001–02	Paris St Germain	12	2	**49**	**11**
2001–02	Liverpool	20	4	**20**	**4**
2002–03	Manchester C	38	14		
2003–04	Manchester C	32	16		
2004–05	Manchester C	19	7	**89**	**37**
2004–05	Fenerbahce	14	4		
2005–06	Fenerbahce	25	10	**39**	**14**
2006–07	Bolton W	35	11		
2007–08	Bolton W	18	10	**53**	**21**
2007–08	Chelsea	14	1		
2008–09	Chelsea	37	19		
2009–10	Chelsea	33	11		
2010–11	Chelsea	32	6		
2011–12	Chelsea	9	1	**125**	**38**
2012	Shanghai S	22	3	**22**	**3**
2012–13	Juventus	2	0	**2**	**0**
2013–14	WBA	12	2	**12**	**2**

ANICHEBE, Victor (F) **155 20**
H: 6 1 W: 13 00 b.Nigeria 23-4-88
Internationals: Nigeria U23, Full caps.

Season	Club	App	Gls	Tot App	Tot Gls
2005–06	Everton	2	1		
2006–07	Everton	19	3		
2007–08	Everton	27	1		
2008–09	Everton	17	1		
2009–10	Everton	11	1		
2010–11	Everton	16	0		
2011–12	Everton	12	4		
2012–13	Everton	26	6		
2013–14	Everton	1	0	**131**	**17**
2013–14	WBA	24	3	**24**	**3**

BERAHINO, Saido (F) **64 17**
H: 5 10 W: 11 13 b.Burundi 4-8-93
Internationals: England U16, U17, U18, U19, U20, U21.

Season	Club	App	Gls	Tot App	Tot Gls
2010–11	WBA	0	0		
2011–12	WBA	0	0		
2011–12	*Northampton T*	14	6	**14**	**6**
2011–12	*Brentford*	8	4	**8**	**4**
2012–13	WBA	0	0		
2012–13	*Peterborough U*	10	2	**10**	**2**
2013–14	WBA	32	5	**32**	**5**

BRUNT, Chris (M) **370 60**
H: 6 1 W: 13 04 b.Belfast 14-12-84
Internationals: Northern Ireland U19, U21, U23, Full caps.

Season	Club	App	Gls	Tot App	Tot Gls
2002–03	Middlesbrough	0	0		
2003–04	Middlesbrough	0	0		
2003–04	Sheffield W	9	2		
2004–05	Sheffield W	42	4		
2005–06	Sheffield W	44	7		
2006–07	Sheffield W	44	11		
2007–08	Sheffield W	1	0	**140**	**24**
2007–08	WBA	34	4		
2008–09	WBA	34	8		
2009–10	WBA	40	13		
2010–11	WBA	34	4		
2011–12	WBA	29	2		
2012–13	WBA	31	2		
2013–14	WBA	28	3	**230**	**36**

DANIELS, Donervorn (D) **16 2**
H: 6 1 W: 14 05 b.Montserrat 24-11-93
Internationals: England U20.

Season	Club	App	Gls	Tot App	Tot Gls
2011–12	WBA	0	0		
2012–13	WBA	0	0		
2012–13	*Tranmere R*	13	1	**13**	**1**
2013–14	WBA	0	0		
2013–14	*Gillingham*	3	1	**3**	**1**

DANIELS, Luke (G) **97 0**
H: 6 1 W: 12 10 b.Bolton 5-1-88
Internationals: England U19.

Season	Club	App	Gls	Tot App	Tot Gls
2006–07	WBA	0	0		
2007–08	*Motherwell*	2	0	**2**	**0**
2007–08	WBA	0	0		
2008–09	WBA	0	0		
2008–09	*Shrewsbury T*	38	0	**38**	**0**
2009–10	WBA	0	0		
2009–10	*Tranmere R*	37	0	**37**	**0**
2010–11	*Charlton Ath*	0	0		
2010–11	*Rochdale*	1	0	**1**	**0**
2010–11	*Bristol R*	9	0	**9**	**0**
2011–12	WBA	0	0		
2011–12	*Southend U*	9	0	**9**	**0**
2012–13	WBA	0	0		
2013–14	WBA	1	0	**1**	**0**

DAWSON, Craig (D) **124 23**
H: 6 0 W: 12 04 b.Rochdale 6-5-90
Internationals: England U21. Great Britain.

Season	Club	App	Gls	Tot App	Tot Gls
2008–09	Rochdale	0	0		
2009–10	Rochdale	42	9		
2010–11	WBA	0	0		
2010–11	*Rochdale*	45	10	**87**	**19**
2011–12	WBA	8	0		
2012–13	WBA	1	0		
2012–13	*Bolton W*	16	4	**16**	**4**
2013–14	WBA	12	0	**21**	**0**

DORRANS, Graham (F) **236 41**
H: 5 9 W: 11 07 b.Glasgow 5-5-87
Internationals: Scotland U20, U21, Full caps.

Season	Club	App	Gls	Tot App	Tot Gls
2006–07	Livingston	8	0		
2006–07	*Partick Thistle*	15	5	**15**	**5**
2006–07	Livingston	34	5		
2007–08	Livingston	34	11	**76**	**16**
2008–09	WBA	8	0		
2009–10	WBA	45	13		
2010–11	WBA	21	1		
2011–12	WBA	31	3		
2012–13	WBA	26	1		
2013–14	WBA	14	2	**145**	**20**

FOSTER, Ben (G) **233 0**
H: 6 2 W: 12 08 b.Leamington Spa 3-4-83
Internationals: England Full caps.

Season	Club	App	Gls	Tot App	Tot Gls
2000–01	Stoke C	0	0		
2001–02	Stoke C	0	0		
2002–03	Stoke C	0	0		
2003–04	Stoke C	0	0		
2004–05	Stoke C	0	0		
2004–05	*Kidderminster H*	2	0	**2**	**0**
2005–06	*Wrexham*	17	0	**17**	**0**
2005–06	Manchester U	0	0		
2006–07	Watford	44	0		
2006–07	*Watford*	29	0	**73**	**0**
2007–08	Manchester U	1	0		
2008–09	Manchester U	0	0		
2009–10	Manchester U	9	0	**12**	**0**
2010–11	Birmingham C	38	0		
2011–12	Birmingham C	0	0	**38**	**0**
2011–12	*WBA*	37	0		
2012–13	WBA	30	0		
2013–14	WBA	24	0	**91**	**0**

GARMSTON, Bradley (D) **13 0**
H: 5 9 W: 10 12 b.Greenwich 18-1-94
Internationals: Republic of Ireland U19.

Season	Club	App	Gls	Tot App	Tot Gls
2012–13	WBA	0	0		
2012–13	*Colchester U*	13	0	**13**	**0**
2013–14	WBA	0	0		

GAYLE, Cameron (D) **21 1**
H: 5 11 W: 11 00 b.Birmingham 22-11-92

Season	Club	App	Gls	Tot App	Tot Gls
2010–11	WBA	0	0		
2011–12	WBA	0	0		
2012–13	WBA	0	0		
2012–13	*Shrewsbury T*	18	1		
2013–14	WBA	0	0		
2013–14	*Shrewsbury T*	3	0	**21**	**1**

GERA, Zoltan (M) **385 66**
H: 6 0 W: 11 11 b.Pecs 22-4-79
Internationals: Hungary U21, Full caps.

Season	Club	App	Gls	Tot App	Tot Gls
1999–2000	Pecsi	15	4	**15**	**4**

2000–01	Ferencvaros	32	7		
2001–02	Ferencvaros	27	8		
2002–03	Ferencvaros	26	6		
2003–04	Ferencvaros	30	11	115	32
2004–05	WBA	38	6		
2005–06	WBA	15	2		
2006–07	WBA	40	5		
2007–08	WBA	43	8		
2008–09	Fulham	32	2		
2009–10	Fulham	27	2		
2010–11	Fulham	27	1	86	5
2011–12	WBA	3	0		
2012–13	WBA	16	4		
2013–14	WBA	14	0	169	25

JONES, Billy (M) 358 22
H: 5 11 W: 13 00 b.Shrewsbury 24-3-87
Internationals: England U16, U17, U19, U20.

2003–04	Crewe Alex	27	1		
2004–05	Crewe Alex	20	0		
2005–06	Crewe Alex	44	6		
2006–07	Crewe Alex	41	1	132	8
2007–08	Preston NE	29	0		
2008–09	Preston NE	44	3		
2009–10	Preston NE	44	4		
2010–11	Preston NE	43	6	160	13
2011–12	WBA	18	0		
2012–13	WBA	27	1		
2013–14	WBA	21	0	66	1

LUGANO, Diego (D) 311 35
H: 6 2 W: 13 01 b.Canelones 2-11-80
Internationals: Uruguay Full caps.

1999	Nacional	2	0		
2000	Nacional	6	0		
2001	Plaza Colonia	12	0		
2002	Plaza Colonia	34	4	46	4
2003	Nacional	5	0	13	0
2003	Sao Paulo	24	1		
2004	Sao Paulo	34	1		
2005	Sao Paulo	27	6		
2006	Sao Paulo	11	0	96	8
2006–07	Fenerbahce	23	4		
2007–08	Fenerbahce	23	0		
2008–09	Fenerbahce	25	7		
2009–10	Fenerbahce	25	3		
2010–11	Fenerbahce	28	8	124	22
2011–12	Paris St Germain	12	0		
2012–13	Paris St Germain	0	0	12	0
2012–13	Malaga	11	0	11	0
2013–14	WBA	9	1	9	1

McAULEY, Gareth (D) 361 27
H: 6 3 W: 13 00 b.Larne 5-12-79
Internationals: Northern Ireland B, Full caps.

2004–05	Lincoln C	37	3		
2005–06	Lincoln C	35	5	72	8
2006–07	Leicester C	30	3		
2007–08	Leicester C	44	2	74	5
2008–09	Ipswich T	35	0		
2009–10	Ipswich T	41	5		
2010–11	Ipswich T	39	2	115	7
2011–12	WBA	32	2		
2012–13	WBA	36	3		
2013–14	WBA	32	2	100	7

MORRISON, James (M) 271 26
H: 5 10 W: 10 06 b.Darlington 25-5-86
Internationals: England U17, U18, U19, U20. Scotland Full caps.

2003–04	Middlesbrough	1	0		
2004–05	Middlesbrough	14	0		
2005–06	Middlesbrough	24	1		
2006–07	Middlesbrough	28	2	67	3
2007–08	WBA	35	4		
2008–09	WBA	30	3		
2009–10	WBA	11	1		
2010–11	WBA	31	4		
2011–12	WBA	30	5		
2012–13	WBA	35	5		
2013–14	WBA	32	1	204	23

MULUMBU, Youssef (M) 216 16
H: 5 9 W: 10 03 b.Kinshasa 25-1-87
Internationals: France U20, U21. DR Congo Full caps.

2006–07	Paris St Germain	12	0		
2007–08	Paris St Germain	1	0		
2007–08	Amiens	23	1	23	1
2008–09	Paris St Germain	0	0	13	0
2008–09	WBA	6	0		
2009–10	WBA	40	3		
2010–11	WBA	34	7		
2011–12	WBA	35	1		
2012–13	WBA	28	2		
2013–14	WBA	37	2	180	15

MYHILL, Boaz (G) 346 0
H: 6 3 W: 14 06 b.California 9-11-82
Internationals: England U20. Wales Full caps.

2000–01	Aston Villa	0	0		
2001–02	Aston Villa	0	0		
2001–02	Stoke C	0	0		
2002–03	Aston Villa	0	0		
2002–03	Bristol C	0	0		
2002–03	Bradford C	2	0	2	0
2003–04	Aston Villa	0	0		
2003–04	Macclesfield T	15	0	15	0
2003–04	Stockport Co	2	0	2	0
2003–04	Hull C	23	0		
2004–05	Hull C	45	0		
2005–06	Hull C	45	0		
2006–07	Hull C	46	0		
2007–08	Hull C	43	0		
2008–09	Hull C	28	0		
2009–10	Hull C	27	0	257	0
2010–11	WBA	6	0		
2011–12	WBA	0	0		
2011–12	Birmingham C	42	0	42	0
2012–13	WBA	8	0		
2013–14	WBA	14	0	28	0

NABI, Adil (F) 0 0
H: 5 9 W: 10 10 b.Birmingham 28-2-94
Internationals: England U16, U17.

2010–11	WBA	0	0		
2011–12	WBA	0	0		
2012–13	WBA	0	0		
2013–14	WBA	0	0		

O'NEIL, Liam (D) 17 0
H: 6 0 W: 12 06 b.Cambridge 31-7-93

2011–12	WBA	0	0		
2011–12	VPS	14	0	14	0
2012–13	WBA	0	0		
2013–14	WBA	3	0	3	0

OLSSON, Jonas (D) 345 16
H: 6 4 W: 12 08 b.Landskrona 10-3-83
Internationals: Sweden U21, Full caps.

2002	Landskrona	0	0		
2003	Landskrona	22	0		
2004	Landskrona	22	1		
2005	Landskrona	12	0	56	1
2005–06	NEC Nijmegen	34	0		
2006–07	NEC Nijmegen	32	2		
2007–08	NEC Nijmegen	27	3	93	5
2008–09	WBA	28	2		
2009–10	WBA	43	4		
2010–11	WBA	24	1		
2011–12	WBA	33	2		
2012–13	WBA	36	0		
2013–14	WBA	32	1	196	10

POPOV, Goran (D) 180 5
H: 6 2 W: 14 08 b.Strumica 2-10-84
Internationals: Macedonia U19, U21, Full caps.

2003–04	AEK Athens	8	0	8	0
2004–05	Wodzislaw Slaski	11	0	11	0
2005–06	Aigaleo	19	0		
2006–07	Aigaleo	25	1	44	1
2007–08	Levadiakos	20	0	20	0
2008–09	Heerenveen	24	1		
2009–10	Heerenveen	27	1	51	2
2010–11	Dynamo Kiev	15	1		
2011–12	Dynamo Kiev	16	1		
2012–13	Dynamo Kiev	1	0		
2012–13	WBA	12	0		
2013–14	Dynamo Kiev	0	0	32	2

On loan from Dynamo Kiev

2013–14	WBA	2	0	14	0

REID, Steven (M) 336 27
H: 6 0 W: 12 07 b.Kingston 10-3-81
Internationals: England U16. Republic of Ireland U21, Full caps.

1997–98	Millwall	1	0		
1998–99	Millwall	25	0		
1999–2000	Millwall	21	0		
2000–01	Millwall	37	7		
2001–02	Millwall	35	5		
2002–03	Millwall	20	6	139	18
2003–04	Blackburn R	16	0		
2004–05	Blackburn R	28	2		
2005–06	Blackburn R	34	4		
2006–07	Blackburn R	3	0		
2007–08	Blackburn R	24	0		
2008–09	Blackburn R	4	0		
2009–10	Blackburn R	4	0	113	6
2009–10	QPR	2	0	2	0
2009–10	WBA	10	1		
2010–11	WBA	23	1		

2011–12	WBA	22	1		
2012–13	WBA	11	0		
2013–14	WBA	16	0	82	3

RIDGEWELL, Liam (D) 312 17
H: 5 10 W: 10 03 b.Bexley 21-7-84
Internationals: England U19, U20, U21.

2001–02	Aston Villa	0	0		
2002–03	Aston Villa	0	0		
2002–03	Bournemouth	5	0	5	0
2003–04	Aston Villa	11	0		
2004–05	Aston Villa	15	0		
2005–06	Aston Villa	32	5		
2006–07	Aston Villa	21	1	79	6
2007–08	Birmingham C	35	1		
2008–09	Birmingham C	36	1		
2009–10	Birmingham C	31	3		
2010–11	Birmingham C	36	4		
2011–12	Birmingham C	14	0	152	9
2011–12	WBA	13	1		
2012–13	WBA	30	0		
2013–14	WBA	33	1	76	2

ROOFE, Kemar (M) 15 1
H: 5 10 W: 11 03 b.Walsall 6-1-93

2011–12	WBA	0	0		
2012–13	WBA	0	0		
2012–13	Northampton T	6	0	6	0
2013–14	WBA	0	0		
2013–14	Cheltenham T	9	1	9	1

ROSENBERG, Markus (F) 249 84
H: 6 0 W: 12 06 b.Linhamm 27-9-82
Internationals: Sweden U21, Full caps.

2001–02	Malmo FF	1	1		
2002–03	Malmo FF	2	2		
2003–04	Malmo FF	1	1		
2003–04	Halmstads BK	3	3		
2004–05	Halmstads BK	10	11	13	14
2004–05	Malmo FF	6	4		
2005–06	Malmo FF	4	3	14	11
2005–06	Ajax	30	11		
2006–07	Ajax	8	0	38	11
2006–07	Werder Bremen	14	8		
2007–08	Werder Bremen	30	14		
2008–09	Werder Bremen	29	7		
2009–10	Werder Bremen	17	1		
2010–11	Racing Santander	33	8	33	8
2011–12	Werder Bremen	33	10	123	40
2012–13	WBA	24	0		
2013–14	WBA	4	0	28	0

SESSEGNON, Stephane (M) 321 46
H: 5 8 W: 11 05 b.Allahe 1-6-84
Internationals: Benin Full caps.

2003–04	Requins	2	0	2	0
2004–05	Creteil	35	5		
2005–06	Creteil	33	5	68	10
2006–07	Le Mans	31	1		
2007–08	Le Mans	30	5	61	6
2008–09	Paris St Germain	34	5		
2009–10	Paris St Germain	29	3		
2010–11	Paris St Germain	14	0	77	8
2010–11	Sunderland	14	3		
2011–12	Sunderland	36	7		
2012–13	Sunderland	35	7		
2013–14	Sunderland	2	0	87	17
2013–14	WBA	26	5	26	5

THIEVY, Koulossa (F) 73 17
H: 5 11 W: 11 08 b.Saint Denis 13-5-92
Internationals: France U20, U21.

2010–11	Espanyol	2	0		
2011–12	Espanyol	19	1		
2012–13	Espanyol	0	0		
2012–13	Las Palmas	35	11	35	11
2013–14	Espanyol	11	3	32	4

On loan from Espanyol

2013–14	WBA	6	2	6	2

THORNE, George (M) 48 2
H: 6 2 W: 13 01 b.Chatham 4-1-93
Internationals: England U16, U17, U18, U19.

2009–10	WBA	1	0		
2010–11	WBA	1	0		
2011–12	WBA	3	0		
2011–12	Portsmouth	14	0	14	0
2012–13	WBA	5	0		
2012–13	Peterborough U	7	1	7	1
2013–14	WBA	0	0	10	0
2013–14	Watford	8	0	8	0
2013–14	Derby Co	9	1	9	1

VYDRA, Matej (F) 80 27
H: 5 10 W: 11 09 b.Chotebor 1-5-92
Internationals: Czech Republic U16, U17, U18, U19, U21, Full caps.

2009-10	Banik Ostrava	13	4	13	4
2010-11	Udinese	2	0		
2011-12	Club Brugge	1	0	1	0
2012-13	Udinese	0	0		
2012-13	*Watford*	41	20	41	20
2013-14	Udinese	0	0	2	0
On loan from Udinese					
2013-14	*WBA*	23	3	23	3

YACOB, Claudio (M) 182 5
H: 5 11 W: 11 06 b.Carcarana 18-7-87
Internationals: Argentina U20, Full caps.

2006-07	Racing Club	12	0		
2007-08	Racing Club	24	0		
2008-09	Racing Club	25	1		
2009-10	Racing Club	26	0		
2010-11	Racing Club	21	2		
2011-12	Racing Club	17	1	125	4
2012-13	WBA	30	0		
2013-14	WBA	27	1	57	1

Scholars
Atkinson, Wesley; Barrow, Daniel; Birch, Aaron; Campbell, Tahvon; Cater, George; Cleet, George Henry; Donnellan, Shaun; Ezewele, Joshua Aizenose; Gannon, Philip; Greenidge, Reiss James; Gregory, Jamie; Hallahan, Jack; Howkins, Kyle; Jones, Alexander; Jones, Callam; Jones, Jon-Pierre; Miller, Ben Nicholas; Moran, Evan; Nabi, Samir; Pace, Ryan; Palmer, Alexander; Ross, Ethan Walker; Smart, Tom; Vaikla, Andreas; Ward, Joseph; Wedderburn, Rees; Wright, Andre.

WEST HAM U (87)

ADRIAN (G) 52 0
H: 6 2 W: 12 00 b.Seville 3-1-87

2008-09	Real Betis	0	0		
2009-10	Real Betis	0	0		
2010-11	Real Betis	0	0		
2011-12	Real Betis	0	0		
2012-13	Real Betis	32	0	32	0
2013-14	West Ham U	20	0	20	0

ARMERO, Pablo (D) 283 12
H: 5 8 W: 11 01 b.Tumaco 2-11-86
Internationals: Columbia Full caps.

2004	America Cali	28	3		
2005	America Cali	25	0		
2006	America Cali	24	1		
2007	America Cali	31	2		
2008	America Cali	36	2	144	8
2009	Palmeiras	29	1		
2010	Palmeiras	7	0	36	1
2010-11	Udinese	31	2		
2011-12	Udinese	28	1		
2012-13	Udinese	10	0	69	3
2012-13	*Napoli*	15	0		
2013-14	Napoli	14	0	29	0
On loan from Napoli					
2013-14	West Ham U	5	0	5	0

BORRIELLO, Marco (F) 291 82
H: 5 11 W: 11 06 b.Napoli 18-6-82
Internationals: Italy U20, U21, Full caps.

2000-01	Triestina	9	1	9	1
2001-02	AC Milan	0	0		
2001-02	*Treviso*	27	10		
2002-03	AC Milan	3	0		
2002-03	*Empoli*	12	1	12	1
2003-04	AC Milan	4	0		
2004-05	AC Milan	0	0		
2004-05	*Reggina*	29	2	29	2
2005-06	AC Milan	0	0		
2005-06	*Sampdoria*	11	2	11	2
2005-06	*Treviso*	20	5	47	15
2006-07	AC Milan	9	1		
2007-08	AC Milan	0	0		
2007-08	*Genoa*	35	19		
2008-09	AC Milan	7	1		
2009-10	AC Milan	29	14		
2010-11	AC Milan	14	0	53	16
2010-11	Roma	34	11		
2011-12	Roma	7	0		
2011-12	*Juventus*	13	2	13	2
2012-13	Roma	0	0		
2012-13	*Genoa*	28	12	63	31
2013-14	Roma	11	1	52	12
On loan from Roma					
2013-14	West Ham U	2	0	2	0

CARROLL, Andy (F) 174 47
H: 6 4 W: 11 00 b.Gateshead 6-1-89
Internationals: England U19, U21, Full caps.

2006-07	Newcastle U	4	0		
2007-08	Newcastle U	4	0		
2007-08	*Preston NE*	11	1	11	1
2008-09	Newcastle U	14	3		
2009-10	Newcastle U	39	17		
2010-11	Newcastle U	19	11	80	31
2010-11	Liverpool	7	2		
2011-12	Liverpool	35	4		
2012-13	Liverpool	2	0	44	6
2012-13	*West Ham U*	24	7		
2013-14	West Ham U	15	2	39	9

CHAMBERS, Leo (D) 0 0
H: 6 1 W: 13 00 b.London 5-8-95
Internationals: England U16, U17, U18, U19.

2012-13	West Ham U	0	0
2013-14	West Ham U	0	0

COLE, Carlton (F) 313 65
H: 6 3 W: 14 02 b.Croydon 12-11-83
Internationals: England U19, U20, U21, Full caps.

2000-01	Chelsea	0	0		
2001-02	Chelsea	3	1		
2002-03	Chelsea	13	3		
2002-03	*Wolverhampton W*	7	1	7	1
2003-04	Chelsea	0	0		
2003-04	*Charlton Ath*	21	4	21	4
2004-05	Chelsea	0	0		
2004-05	*Aston Villa*	27	3	27	3
2005-06	Chelsea	9	0	25	4
2006-07	West Ham U	17	2		
2007-08	West Ham U	31	4		
2008-09	West Ham U	27	10		
2009-10	West Ham U	30	10		
2010-11	West Ham U	35	5		
2011-12	West Ham U	40	14		
2012-13	West Ham U	27	2		
2013-14	West Ham U	26	6	233	53

COLE, Joe (M) 397 49
H: 5 9 W: 11 09 b.Camden 8-11-81
Internationals: England U16, U18, U21, B, Full caps.

1998-99	West Ham U	8	0		
1999-2000	West Ham U	22	1		
2000-01	West Ham U	30	5		
2001-02	West Ham U	30	0		
2002-03	West Ham U	36	4		
2003-04	Chelsea	35	1		
2004-05	Chelsea	28	8		
2005-06	Chelsea	34	7		
2006-07	Chelsea	13	0		
2007-08	Chelsea	33	7		
2008-09	Chelsea	14	2		
2009-10	Chelsea	26	2	183	27
2010-11	Liverpool	20	2		
2011-12	Liverpool	0	0		
2011-12	*Lille*	31	4	31	4
2012-13	Liverpool	6	1	26	3
2012-13	*West Ham U*	11	2		
2013-14	West Ham U	20	3	157	15

COLLINS, James M (D) 264 11
H: 6 2 W: 14 05 b.Newport 23-8-83
Internationals: Wales U19, U20, U21, Full caps.

2000-01	Cardiff C	3	0		
2001-02	Cardiff C	7	1		
2002-03	Cardiff C	2	0		
2003-04	Cardiff C	20	1		
2004-05	Cardiff C	14	2	66	3
2005-06	West Ham U	14	2		
2006-07	West Ham U	16	0		
2007-08	West Ham U	3	0		
2008-09	West Ham U	18	0		
2009-10	West Ham U	30	0		
2009-10	Aston Villa	27	1		
2010-11	Aston Villa	32	3		
2011-12	Aston Villa	32	1	91	5
2012-13	West Ham U	29	0		
2013-14	West Ham U	24	1	107	3

COLLISON, Jack (M) 118 11
H: 6 0 W: 13 10 b.Watford 2-10-88
Internationals: Wales U21, Full caps.

2007-08	West Ham U	0	0
2008-09	West Ham U	20	3
2009-10	West Ham U	22	2
2010-11	West Ham U	3	0
2011-12	West Ham U	31	4
2012-13	West Ham U	17	2

2013-14	West Ham U	10	0	105	11
2013-14	*Bournemouth*	4	0	4	0
2013-14	*Wigan Ath*	9	0	9	0

DEMEL, Guy (D) 275 12
H: 6 2 W: 13 12 b.Paris 13-6-81
Internationals: Ivory Coast Full caps.

1999-2000	Nimes	1	0	1	0
2000-01	Arsenal	0	0		
2001-02	Bor Dortmund II	16	3		
2002-03	Bor Dortmund II	24	6	40	9
2002-03	Bor Dortmund	4	0		
2003-04	Bor Dortmund	13	0		
2004-05	Bor Dortmund	16	0	33	0
2005-06	Hamburg	22	1		
2006-07	Hamburg	8	0		
2007-08	Hamburg	26	0		
2008-09	Hamburg	28	0		
2009-10	Hamburg	26	1		
2010-11	Hamburg	21	0	131	2
2011-12	West Ham U	7	0		
2012-13	West Ham U	31	0		
2013-14	West Ham U	32	1	70	1

DIAME, Mohamed (M) 230 15
H: 6 1 W: 11 02 b.Creteil 14-6-87
Internationals: Senegal U23, Full caps.

2006-07	Lens	0	0		
2007-08	Linares	31	1	31	1
2008-09	Rayo Vallecano	35	2	35	2
2009-10	Wigan Ath	34	1		
2010-11	Wigan Ath	36	1		
2011-12	Wigan Ath	26	3	96	5
2012-13	West Ham U	33	3		
2013-14	West Ham U	35	4	68	7

DIARRA, Alou (M) 323 22
H: 6 3 W: 12 05 b.Villepinte 15-7-81
Internationals: France U20, U21, Full caps.

2002-03	Liverpool	0	0		
2002-03	*Le Havre*	25	0	25	0
2003-04	Liverpool	0	0		
2003-04	*Bastia*	35	4	35	4
2004-05	Liverpool	0	0		
2004-05	*Lens*	34	2		
2005-06	Lens	30	2	64	4
2006-07	Lyon	15	1	15	1
2007-08	Bordeaux	36	4		
2008-09	Bordeaux	35	2		
2009-10	Bordeaux	30	1		
2010-11	Bordeaux	32	4	133	11
2011-12	Marseille	33	2		
2012-13	Marseille	0	0	33	2
2012-13	*West Ham U*	3	0		
2012-13	*Rennes*	12	0	12	0
2013-14	West Ham U	3	0	6	0

DOWNING, Stewart (M) 348 33
H: 5 11 W: 10 04 b.Middlesbrough 22-7-84
Internationals: England U21, B, Full caps.

2001-02	Middlesbrough	3	0		
2002-03	Middlesbrough	2	0		
2003-04	Middlesbrough	20	0		
2003-04	*Sunderland*	7	3	7	3
2004-05	Middlesbrough	35	5		
2005-06	Middlesbrough	12	1		
2006-07	Middlesbrough	34	2		
2007-08	Middlesbrough	38	9		
2008-09	Middlesbrough	37	0	181	17
2009-10	Aston Villa	25	2		
2010-11	Aston Villa	38	7	63	9
2011-12	Liverpool	36	0		
2012-13	Liverpool	29	3		
2013-14	Liverpool	0	0	65	3
2013-14	West Ham U	32	1	32	1

FANIMO, Matthias (M) 0 0
H: 5 8 W: 11 03 b.Lambeth 28-1-94
Internationals: England U16, U17, U18.

2011-12	West Ham U	0	0
2012-13	West Ham U	0	0
2013-14	West Ham U	0	0

GORDON, Jaanai (F) 4 0
H: 5 10 W: 10 02 b.Northampton 7-12-95

2012-13	Peterborough U	3	0		
2013-14	Peterborough U	1	0	4	0
2013-14	West Ham U	0	0		

HENDERSON, Stephen (G) 97 0
H: 6 3 W: 11 00 b.Dublin 2-5-88
Internationals: Republic of Ireland U16, U17, U19, U21.

2005-06	Aston Villa	0	0

2006–07	Aston Villa	0	0		
2007–08	Bristol C	1	0		
2008–09	Bristol C	1	0		
2009–10	Bristol C	3	0		
2009–10	*Aldershot T*	8	0	8	0
2010–11	Bristol C	0	0	5	0
2010–11	*Yeovil T*	33	0	33	0
2011–12	Portsmouth	25	0	25	0
2011–12	*West Ham U*	0	0		
2012–13	West Ham U	0	0		
2012–13	*Ipswich T*	24	0	24	0
2013–14	West Ham U	0	0		
2013–14	*Bournemouth*	2	0	2	0

JAASKELAINEN, Jussi (G) 648 0
H: 6 3 W: 12 10 b.Vaasa 19-4-75
Internationals: Finland U21, Full caps.

1992	MP	6	0		
1993	MP	6	0		
1994	MP	26	0		
1995	MP	26	0	64	0
1996	VPS	27	0		
1997	VPS	27	0	54	0
1997–98	Bolton W	0	0		
1998–99	Bolton W	34	0		
1999–2000	Bolton W	34	0		
2000–01	Bolton W	27	0		
2001–02	Bolton W	34	0		
2002–03	Bolton W	38	0		
2003–04	Bolton W	38	0		
2004–05	Bolton W	36	0		
2005–06	Bolton W	38	0		
2006–07	Bolton W	38	0		
2007–08	Bolton W	28	0		
2008–09	Bolton W	38	0		
2009–10	Bolton W	38	0		
2010–11	Bolton W	35	0		
2011–12	Bolton W	18	0	474	0
2012–13	West Ham U	38	0		
2013–14	West Ham U	18	0	56	0

JARVIS, Matthew (M) 338 35
H: 5 8 W: 11 10 b.Middlesbrough 22-5-86
Internationals: England Full caps.

2003–04	Gillingham	10	0		
2004–05	Gillingham	30	3		
2005–06	Gillingham	35	3		
2006–07	Gillingham	35	6	110	12
2007–08	Wolverhampton W	26	1		
2008–09	Wolverhampton W	28	3		
2009–10	Wolverhampton W	34	3		
2010–11	Wolverhampton W	37	4		
2011–12	Wolverhampton W	37	8		
2012–13	Wolverhampton W	0	0	164	19
2012–13	West Ham U	32	2		
2013–14	West Ham U	32	2	64	4

LEE, Elliot (F) 5 1
H: 5 11 W: 11 05 b.Co. Durham 16-12-94

2011–12	West Ham U	0	0		
2012–13	West Ham U	0	0		
2013–14	West Ham U	1	0	1	0
2013–14	*Colchester U*	4	1	4	1

LLETGET, Sebastian (M) 0 0
H: 5 10 W: 10 11 b.San Francisco 3-9-92
Internationals: USA U17, U20, U23.

2010–11	West Ham U	0	0	
2011–12	West Ham U	0	0	
2012–13	West Ham U	0	0	
2013–14	West Ham U	0	0	

MAGUIRE, Sean (F) 44 14
H: 5 9 W: 11 10 b.Luton 1-5-94
Internationals: Republic of Ireland U19.

2010–11	West Ham U	0	0		
2011	*Waterford U*	8	1		
2011–12	West Ham U	0	0		
2012	*Waterford U*	26	13	34	14
2012–13	West Ham U	0	0		
2013–14	West Ham U	0	0		
2014	*Sligo R*	10	0	10	0

MAIGA, Modibo (F) 186 43
H: 6 1 W: 12 07 b.Bamako 3-9-87
Internationals: Mali Full caps.

2007–08	Le Mans	19	0		
2008–09	Le Mans	37	8		
2009–10	Le Mans	32	7	88	15
2010–11	Sochaux	36	15		
2011–12	Sochaux	23	9	59	24
2012–13	West Ham U	17	2		
2013–14	West Ham U	14	1	31	3
2013–14	*QPR*	8	1	8	1

McCALLUM, Paul (F) 29 10
H: 6 3 W: 12 00 b.Streatham 28-7-93

2010–11	West Ham U	0	0		
2011–12	West Ham U	0	0		
2011–12	*Rochdale*	0	0		
2012–13	West Ham U	0	0		
2012–13	*AFC Wimbledon*	9	4	9	4
2012–13	*Aldershot T*	9	3	9	3
2013–14	West Ham U	0	0		
2013–14	*Torquay U*	5	3	5	3
2013–14	*Hearts*	6	0	6	0

McCARTNEY, George (D) 340 2
H: 5 11 W: 11 02 b.Belfast 29-4-81
Internationals: Northern Ireland U18, U21, Full caps.

1998–99	Sunderland	0	0		
1999–2000	Sunderland	0	0		
2000–01	Sunderland	2	0		
2001–02	Sunderland	18	0		
2002–03	Sunderland	24	0		
2003–04	Sunderland	41	0		
2004–05	Sunderland	36	0		
2005–06	Sunderland	13	0		
2006–07	West Ham U	22	0		
2007–08	West Ham U	38	1		
2008–09	West Ham U	1	0		
2008–09	Sunderland	16	0		
2009–10	Sunderland	25	0		
2010–11	Sunderland	0	0		
2010–11	*Leeds U*	32	0	32	0
2011–12	Sunderland	0	0	175	0
2011–12	*West Ham U*	38	1		
2012–13	West Ham U	12	0		
2013–14	West Ham U	22	0	133	2

MONCUR, George (M) 22 3
H: 5 9 W: 10 00 b.Swindon 18-8-93
Internationals: England U18.

2010–11	West Ham U	0	0		
2011–12	West Ham U	0	0		
2011–12	*AFC Wimbledon*	20	2	20	2
2012–13	West Ham U	0	0		
2013–14	West Ham U	0	0		
2013–14	*Partick Thistle*	2	1	2	1

MORRISON, Ravel (M) 59 12
H: 5 9 W: 11 02 b.Wythenshawe 2-2-93
Internationals: England U16, U17, U18, U21.

2009–10	Manchester U	0	0		
2010–11	Manchester U	0	0		
2011–12	Manchester U	0	0		
2011–12	West Ham U	1	0		
2012–13	West Ham U	0	0		
2012–13	*Birmingham C*	27	3	27	3
2013–14	West Ham U	16	3	17	3
2013–14	*QPR*	15	6	15	6

NOBLE, Mark (M) 270 30
H: 5 11 W: 12 00 b.West Ham 8-5-87
Internationals: England U16, U17, U18, U19, U21.

2004–05	West Ham U	13	0		
2005–06	West Ham U	5	0		
2005–06	*Hull C*	5	0	5	0
2006–07	West Ham U	10	2		
2006–07	*Ipswich T*	13	1	13	1
2007–08	West Ham U	31	3		
2008–09	West Ham U	29	3		
2009–10	West Ham U	27	2		
2010–11	West Ham U	26	4		
2011–12	West Ham U	45	8		
2012–13	West Ham U	28	4		
2013–14	West Ham U	38	3	252	29

NOCERINO, Antonio (M) 336 24
H: 5 9 W: 11 06 b.Napoli 9-4-85
Internationals: Italy U19, U20, U21, U23, Full caps.

2003–04	Juventus	0	0		
2003–04	*Avellino*	34	0	34	0
2004–05	Juventus	0	0		
2004–05	*Genoa*	5	0	5	0
2004–05	*Catanzaro*	21	0	21	0
2005–06	Juventus	0	0		
2005–06	*Crotone*	15	0	15	0
2005–06	*Messina*	11	0	11	0
2006–07	Juventus	0	0		
2006–07	*Piacenza*	37	6	37	6
2007–08	Juventus	30	0	30	0
2008–09	Palermo	32	0		
2009–10	Palermo	33	2		
2010–11	Palermo	37	4	102	6
2011–12	AC Milan	35	10		
2012–13	AC Milan	25	2		
2013–14	AC Milan	11	0	71	12

On loan from AC Milan

2013–14	West Ham U	10	0	10	0

NOLAN, Kevin (M) 491 98
H: 6 0 W: 14 00 b.Liverpool 24-6-82
Internationals: England U20, U21.

1999–2000	Bolton W	4	0		
2000–01	Bolton W	31	1		
2001–02	Bolton W	35	8		
2002–03	Bolton W	33	1		
2003–04	Bolton W	37	9		
2004–05	Bolton W	36	4		
2005–06	Bolton W	36	9		
2006–07	Bolton W	31	3		
2007–08	Bolton W	33	5		
2008–09	Bolton W	20	0	296	40
2008–09	Newcastle	11	0		
2009–10	Newcastle	44	17		
2010–11	Newcastle	30	12	85	29
2011–12	West Ham U	42	12		
2012–13	West Ham U	35	10		
2013–14	West Ham U	33	7	110	29

O'BRIEN, Joey (M) 151 5
H: 5 11 W: 10 13 b.Dublin 17-2-86
Internationals: Republic of Ireland U19, U21, Full caps.

2004–05	Bolton W	1	0		
2004–05	*Sheffield W*	15	2		
2005–06	Bolton W	23	0		
2006–07	Bolton W	0	0		
2007–08	Bolton W	19	0		
2008–09	Bolton W	7	0		
2009–10	Bolton W	0	0		
2010–11	Bolton W	0	0	50	0
2010–11	*Sheffield W*	4	0	19	2
2011–12	West Ham U	32	1		
2012–13	West Ham U	33	2		
2013–14	West Ham U	17	0	82	3

PETRIC, Mladen (F) 259 105
H: 6 1 W: 12 09 b.Dubrave 1-1-81
Internationals: Croatia Full caps.

2002–03	Grasshoppers	5	5		
2003–04	Grasshoppers	28	6	33	11
2004–05	Basle	17	5		
2005–06	Basle	31	15		
2006–07	Basle	24	18	72	38
2007–08	Borussia Dortmund	29	13	29	13
2008–09	Hamburg	25	12		
2009–10	Hamburg	26	8		
2010–11	Hamburg	22	11		
2011–12	Hamburg	26	7	99	38
2012–13	Fulham	23	5	23	5
2013–14	West Ham U	3	0	3	0

Transferred to Panathinaikos January 2014

POTTS, Danny (D) 15 0
H: 5 8 W: 11 00 b.Barking 13-4-94
Internationals: USA U20. England U18, U19, U20.

2011–12	West Ham U	3	0		
2012–13	West Ham U	2	0		
2012–13	*Colchester U*	5	0	5	0
2013–14	West Ham U	0	0	5	0
2013–14	*Portsmouth*	5	0	5	0

RAT, Razvan (D) 190 6
H: 5 11 W: 11 04 b.Slatina 26-5-81
Internationals: Romania U21, Full caps.

2003–04	Shakhtar Donetsk	27	1		
2004–05	Shakhtar Donetsk	20	2		
2005–06	Shakhtar Donetsk	18	0		
2006–07	Shakhtar Donetsk	14	0		
2007–08	Shakhtar Donetsk	20	2		
2008–09	Shakhtar Donetsk	17	0		
2009–10	Shakhtar Donetsk	18	1		
2010–11	Shakhtar Donetsk	17	0		
2011–12	Shakhtar Donetsk	8	0		
2012–13	Shakhtar Donetsk	16	0	175	6
2013–14	West Ham U	15	0	15	0

Transferred to Rayo Vallecano February 2014

REID, Winston (D) 176 7
H: 6 3 W: 13 10 b.North Shore 3-7-88
Internationals: Denmark U19, U20, U21. New Zealand Full caps.

2005–06	Midtjylland	9	0		
2006–07	Midtjylland	11	0		
2007–08	Midtjylland	9	0		
2008–09	Midtjylland	25	2		
2009–10	Midtjylland	29	0	83	2
2010–11	West Ham U	7	0		
2011–12	West Ham U	28	3		

2012–13	West Ham U	36	1		
2013–14	West Ham U	22	1	93	5

SADLIER, Kieran (F)   0   0
b. 14-9-94
Internationals: Republic of Ireland U19, U21.

2013–14	West Ham U	0	0		

SPENCE, Jordan (D)   90   2
H: 6 2 W: 12 07 b.Woodford 24-5-90
Internationals: England U16, U17, U18, U19, U21.

2007–08	West Ham U	0	0		
2008–09	West Ham U	0	0		
2008–09	*Leyton Orient*	20	0	20	0
2009–10	West Ham U	1	0		
2009–10	*Scunthorpe U*	9	0	9	0
2010–11	West Ham U	2	0		
2010–11	*Bristol C*	11	0		
2011–12	West Ham U	0	0		
2011–12	*Bristol C*	10	0	21	0
2012–13	West Ham U	4	0		
2013–14	West Ham U	0	0	7	0
2013–14	*Sheffield W*	4	0	4	0
2013–14	*Milton Keynes D*	29	2	29	2

SPIEGEL, Raphael (G)   0   0
H: 6 5 W: 15 00 b.Zurich 19-12-92
Internationals: Switzerland U17, U19, U21.

2012–13	Grasshoppers	0	0		
2012–13	West Ham U	0	0		
2013–14	West Ham U	0	0		

TAYLOR, Matthew (D)   507   64
H: 5 11 W: 12 03 b.Oxford 27-11-81
Internationals: England U21, B.

1998–99	Luton T	0	0		
1999–2000	Luton T	41	4		
2000–01	Luton T	45	1		
2001–02	Luton T	43	11	129	16
2002–03	Portsmouth	35	7		
2003–04	Portsmouth	30	0		
2004–05	Portsmouth	32	1		
2005–06	Portsmouth	34	6		
2006–07	Portsmouth	35	8		
2007–08	Portsmouth	13	1	179	23
2007–08	Bolton W	16	3		
2008–09	Bolton W	34	10		
2009–10	Bolton W	37	8		
2010–11	Bolton W	36	2	123	23
2011–12	West Ham U	28	1		
2012–13	West Ham U	28	1		
2013–14	West Ham U	20	0	76	2

TOMKINS, James (D)   168   7
H: 6 3 W: 11 10 b.Basildon 29-3-89
Internationals: England U16, U17, U18, U19, U20 Youth, U21.

2005–06	West Ham U	0	0		
2006–07	West Ham U	0	0		
2007–08	West Ham U	6	0		
2008–09	West Ham U	12	1		
2008–09	*Derby Co*	7	0	7	0
2009–10	West Ham U	23	0		
2010–11	West Ham U	19	1		
2011–12	West Ham U	44	4		
2012–13	West Ham U	26	1		
2013–14	West Ham U	31	0	161	7

TURGOTT, Blair (M)   14   1
H: 6 0 W: 10 03 b.Bromley 22-5-94
Internationals: England U16, U17, U18, U19.

2011–12	West Ham U	0	0		
2012–13	*Bradford C*	4	0	4	0
2013–14	West Ham U	0	0		
2013–14	*Colchester U*	4	1	4	1
2013–14	*Rotherham U*	1	0	1	0
2013–14	*Dagenham & R*	5	0	5	0

VAZ TE, Ricardo (F)   133   28
H: 6 2 W: 12 07 b.Lisbon 1-10-86
Internationals: Portugal U17, U19, U20, U21, U23.

2003–04	Bolton W	1	0		
2004–05	Bolton W	7	0		
2005–06	Bolton W	22	3		
2006–07	Bolton W	25	0		
2006–07	*Hull C*	6	0	6	0
2007–08	Bolton W	1	0		
2008–09	Bolton W	2	0		
2009–10	Bolton W	0	0		
2010–11	Bolton W	0	0	58	3
2011–12	*Barnsley*	22	10	22	10
2011–12	West Ham U	15	10		
2012–13	West Ham U	24	3		
2013–14	West Ham U	8	2	47	15

WHITEHEAD, Danny (M)   0   0
H: 5 10 W: 10 11 b.Trafford 23-10-93

2013–14	West Ham U	0	0

Scholars
Amoo, Jeremiah; Bailey, Kieran; Brown, Tim; Burke, Reece; Bywater, Kieran; Cullen, Joshua Jon; Harney, Jamie; Knoyle, Kyle; Makasi, Kusu Moses; Marlow, Ben John; Martins, Marcio Filipe; Mavila, Nathan; Nasha, Amos Lawrence; Page, Lewis Robert; Parfitt-Williams, Djair Terraii Carl; Pike, Alexander George; Tombides, Taylor James.

WIGAN ATH (88)

AL HABSI, Ali (G)   197   0
H: 6 4 W: 12 06 b.Oman 30-12-81
Internationals: Oman Full caps.

2003	Lyn	13	0		
2004	Lyn	24	0		
2005	Lyn	25	0	62	0
2005–06	Bolton W	0	0		
2006–07	Bolton W	0	0		
2007–08	Bolton W	10	0		
2008–09	Bolton W	0	0		
2009–10	Bolton W	0	0		
2010–11	Bolton W	0	0	10	0
2010–11	*Wigan Ath*	34	0		
2011–12	Wigan Ath	38	0		
2012–13	Wigan Ath	29	0		
2013–14	Wigan Ath	24	0	125	0

BARNETT, Leon (D)   223   12
H: 6 0 W: 12 04 b.Stevenage 30-11-85

2003–04	Luton T	0	0		
2004–05	Luton T	0	0		
2005–06	Luton T	20	0		
2006–07	Luton T	39	3	59	3
2007–08	WBA	32	3		
2008–09	WBA	11	0		
2009–10	WBA	2	0		
2009–10	*Coventry C*	20	0	20	0
2010–11	WBA	0	0	45	3
2010–11	*Norwich C*	25	1		
2011–12	*Norwich C*	17	1		
2012–13	*Norwich C*	8	0		
2012–13	*Cardiff C*	8	0	8	0
2013–14	*Norwich C*	0	0	50	2
2013–14	Wigan Ath	41	4	41	4

BEAUSEJOUR, Jean (M)   337   36
H: 5 10 W: 12 08 b.Santiago 1-6-84
Internationals: Chile Full caps.

2002	Univ Catolica	1	0		
2003	Univ Concepcion	30	3	30	3
2004	Univ Catolica	15	3	16	3
2004–05	Servette	11	1	11	1
2005–06	Gremio	55	7	55	7
2006–07	Gent	0	0		
2007–08	Cobreloa	22	0	22	0
2008	O'Higgins	34	13	34	13
2008–09	America	17	0		
2009–10	America	28	3		
2010–11	America	0	0	47	3
2010–11	Birmingham C	17	2		
2011–12	Birmingham C	22	1	39	3
2011–12	Wigan Ath	16	0		
2012–13	Wigan Ath	34	1		
2013–14	Wigan Ath	33	2	83	3

BOYCE, Emmerson (D)   491   23
H: 6 0 W: 12 03 b.Aylesbury 24-9-79
Internationals: Barbados Full caps.

1997–98	Luton T	0	0		
1998–99	Luton T	1	0		
1999–2000	Luton T	30	1		
2000–01	Luton T	42	3		
2001–02	Luton T	37	0		
2002–03	Luton T	42	3		
2003–04	Luton T	42	4	186	8
2004–05	Crystal Palace	27	0		
2005–06	Crystal Palace	42	2	69	2
2006–07	Wigan Ath	34	0		
2007–08	Wigan Ath	25	0		
2008–09	Wigan Ath	27	1		
2009–10	Wigan Ath	24	3		
2010–11	Wigan Ath	22	0		
2011–12	Wigan Ath	26	3		
2012–13	Wigan Ath	36	4		
2013–14	Wigan Ath	42	2	236	13

BUXTON, Adam (D)   11   0
H: 6 1 W: 12 10 b.Liverpool 12-5-92

2010–11	Wigan Ath	0	0		
2011–12	Wigan Ath	0	0		
2012–13	Wigan Ath	0	0		
2013–14	Wigan Ath	0	0		
2013–14	*Burton Alb*	0	0		
2013–14	*Accrington S*	11	0	11	0

CALDWELL, Gary (D)   356   16
H: 5 11 W: 11 10 b.Stirling 12-4-82
Internationals: Scotland U21, Full caps.

1998–99	Newcastle U	0	0		
1999–2000	Newcastle U	0	0		
2000–01	Newcastle U	0	0		
2001–02	Newcastle U	0	0		
2001–02	*Darlington*	4	0	4	0
2001–02	*Hibernian*	11	0		
2002–03	Newcastle U	0	0		
2002–03	*Coventry C*	36	0	36	0
2003–04	Newcastle U	0	0		
2003–04	*Derby Co*	9	0	9	0
2003–04	Hibernian	17	1		
2004–05	Hibernian	37	3		
2005–06	Hibernian	34	1	99	5
2006–07	Celtic	21	0		
2007–08	Celtic	35	1		
2008–09	Celtic	36	3		
2009–10	Celtic	14	1	106	5
2009–10	Wigan Ath	16	2		
2010–11	Wigan Ath	23	0		
2011–12	Wigan Ath	36	3		
2012–13	Wigan Ath	25	1		
2013–14	Wigan Ath	2	0	102	6

CARSON, Scott (G)   276   0
H: 6 0 W: 13 06 b.Whitehaven 3-9-85
Internationals: England U18, U21, B, Full caps.

2002–03	Leeds U	0	0		
2003–04	Leeds U	3	0		
2004–05	Leeds U	0	0	3	0
2004–05	*Liverpool*	4	0		
2005–06	Liverpool	0	0		
2005–06	*Sheffield W*	9	0	9	0
2006–07	Liverpool	0	0		
2006–07	*Charlton Ath*	36	0	36	0
2007–08	Liverpool	0	0	4	0
2007–08	*Aston Villa*	35	0	35	0
2008–09	WBA	35	0		
2009–10	WBA	43	0		
2010–11	WBA	32	0	110	0
2011–12	Bursaspor	34	0		
2011–12	Bursaspor	29	0	63	0
2013–14	Wigan Ath	16	0	16	0

CHOW, Tim (M)   0   0
W: 11 06 b.Wigan 18-1-94

2011–12	Wigan Ath	0	0		
2012–13	Wigan Ath	0	0		
2013–14	Wigan Ath	0	0		

CRAINEY, Stephen (D)   332   4
H: 5 9 W: 9 11 b.Glasgow 22-6-81
Internationals: Scotland B, U21, Full caps.

1999–2000	Celtic	9	0		
2000–01	Celtic	2	0		
2001–02	Celtic	15	0		
2002–03	Celtic	13	0		
2003–04	Celtic	2	0	41	0
2003–04	*Southampton*	5	0	5	0
2004–05	Leeds U	9	0		
2005–06	Leeds U	24	0		
2006–07	Leeds U	19	0	52	0
2007–08	Blackpool	40	1		
2008–09	Blackpool	17	0		
2009–10	Blackpool	41	0		
2010–11	Blackpool	31	0		
2011–12	Blackpool	42	3		
2012–13	Blackpool	43	0	214	4
2013–14	Wigan Ath	20	0	20	0

CVETKOVIC, Alex (M)   0   0
b. 29-11-96

2013–14	Wigan Ath	0	0

ESPINOZA, Roger (M)   144   3
H: 5 10 W: 11 06 b.Puerto Cortes 25-10-86
Internationals: Honduras Full caps.

2008	Sporting Kansas C	24	1		
2009	Sporting Kansas C	10	0		
2010	Sporting Kansas C	25	0		
2011	Sporting Kansas C	27	1		
2012	Sporting Kansas C	28	0	114	2
2012–13	Wigan Ath	12	1		
2013–14	Wigan Ath	18	0	30	1

FORTUNE, Marc-Antoine (F)   415 80
H: 6 0   W: 11 13   b.Cayenne 2-7-81

Season	Club				
2000-01	Angouleme	18	3		
2001-02	Angouleme	36	12	54	15
2002-03	Nancy	19	1		
2002-03	Lille	15	0	15	0
2003-04	Rouen	34	10	34	10
2004-05	Brest	33	10	33	10
2005-06	Utrecht	31	6		
2006-07	Utrecht	22	5	53	11
2006-07	Nancy	15	5		
2007-08	Nancy	37	6		
2008-09	Nancy	19	1	90	13
2009-10	Celtic	30	10		
2010-11	Celtic	2	0	32	10
2010-11	WBA	25	2		
2011-12	WBA	17	2		
2011-12	Doncaster R	5	1	5	1
2012-13	WBA	21	2	63	6
2013-14	Wigan Ath	36	4	36	4

FYVIE, Fraser (M)   65 2
H: 5 8   W: 9 05   b.Aberdeen 27-3-93
Internationals: Scotland U15, U16, U17, U19, U21.

Season	Club				
2009-10	Aberdeen	26	1		
2010-11	Aberdeen	5	0		
2011-12	Aberdeen	27	1	58	2
2012-13	Wigan Ath	1	0		
2013-14	Wigan Ath	0	0	1	0
2013-14	Yeovil T	2	0	2	0
2013-14	Shrewsbury T	4	0	4	0

GARCIA, Juan (D)   133 5
H: 5 11   W: 11 12   b.Tela 8-3-88
Internationals: Honduras Full caps.

Season	Club				
2007-08	Marathon	11	0		
2008-09	Marathon	22	1		
2009-10	Marathon	20	0	53	1
2010-11	Olimpia	30	0		
2011-12	Olimpia	27	2		
2012-13	Olimpia	23	2	80	4
2013-14	Wigan Ath	0	0		

GOMEZ, Jordi (M)   194 29
H: 5 10   W: 11 09   b.Barcelona 24-5-85
Internationals: Spain U17.

Season	Club				
2006-07	Espanyol B	21	0	21	0
2007-08	Espanyol	2	0	2	0
2008-09	Swansea C	44	12	44	12
2009-10	Wigan Ath	23	1		
2010-11	Wigan Ath	13	1		
2011-12	Wigan Ath	28	5		
2012-13	Wigan Ath	32	3		
2013-14	Wigan Ath	31	7	127	17

HOLGERSSON, Markus (D)   173 13
H: 6 3   W: 12 05   b. 12-4-85
Internationals: Sweden Full caps.

Season	Club				
2008	Angelholm	29	5	29	5
2009	Helsingborgs IF	23	1		
2010	Helsingborgs IF	28	2		
2011	Helsingborgs IF	29	2	80	5
2012	NY Red Bulls	31	3		
2013	NY Red Bulls	32	0	63	3
2013-14	Wigan Ath	1	0	1	0

HOLT, Grant (F)   428 150
H: 6 1   W: 14 02   b.Carlisle 12-4-81

Season	Club				
1999-2000	Halifax T	4	0		
2000-01	Halifax T	2	0	6	0

From Sengkang, Barrow

Season	Club				
2002-03	Sheffield W	7	1		
2003-04	Sheffield W	17	2	24	3
2003-04	Rochdale	14	4		
2004-05	Rochdale	40	17		
2005-06	Rochdale	21	14	75	35
2005-06	Nottingham F	19	4		
2006-07	Nottingham F	45	14		
2007-08	Nottingham F	32	3	96	21
2007-08	Blackpool	4	0	4	0
2008-09	Shrewsbury T	43	20	43	20
2009-10	Norwich C	39	24		
2010-11	Norwich C	45	21		
2011-12	Norwich C	36	15		
2012-13	Norwich C	34	8	154	68
2013-14	Wigan Ath	16	2	16	2
2013-14	Aston Villa	10	1	10	1

JENNINGS, Ryan (F)   0 0
2013-14   Wigan Ath   0 0

JOHNSON, Joseph (F)   0 0
2013-14   Wigan Ath   0 0

KIERNAN, Rob (D)   58 1
H: 6 1   W: 11 13   b.Rickmansworth 13-1-91
Internationals: Republic of Ireland U19, U21.

Season	Club				
2008-09	Watford	0	0		
2009-10	Watford	0	0		
2009-10	Kilmarnock	4	0	4	0
2010-11	Watford	0	0		
2010-11	Yeovil T	3	0	3	0
2010-11	Bradford C	8	0	8	0
2010-11	Wycombe W	2	0	2	0
2011-12	Wigan Ath	0	0		
2011-12	Accrington S	3	0	3	0
2012-13	Wigan Ath	0	0		
2012-13	Burton Alb	6	0	6	0
2012-13	Brentford	8	0	8	0
2013-14	Wigan Ath	12	1	12	1
2013-14	Southend U	12	0	12	0

MALONEY, Shaun (M)   248 56
H: 5 7   W: 10 01   b.Miri 24-1-83
Internationals: Scotland U20, U21, B, Full caps.

Season	Club				
1999-2000	Celtic	0	0		
2000-01	Celtic	4	0		
2001-02	Celtic	16	5		
2002-03	Celtic	20	3		
2003-04	Celtic	17	5		
2004-05	Celtic	2	0		
2005-06	Celtic	36	13		
2006-07	Celtic	9	0		
2006-07	Aston Villa	8	1		
2007-08	Aston Villa	22	4	30	5
2008-09	Celtic	21	4		
2009-10	Celtic	10	4		
2010-11	Celtic	21	5		
2011-12	Celtic	3	0	159	39
2011-12	Wigan Ath	13	3		
2012-13	Wigan Ath	36	6		
2013-14	Wigan Ath	10	3	59	12

McARTHUR, James (M)   292 19
H: 5 6   W: 9 13   b.Glasgow 7-10-87
Internationals: Scotland U21, Full caps.

Season	Club				
2004-05	Hamilton A	6	0		
2005-06	Hamilton A	20	1		
2006-07	Hamilton A	36	1		
2007-08	Hamilton A	34	4		
2008-09	Hamilton A	37	2		
2009-10	Hamilton A	35	1	168	9
2010-11	Wigan Ath	18	0		
2011-12	Wigan Ath	31	3		
2012-13	Wigan Ath	34	3		
2013-14	Wigan Ath	41	4	124	10

McCANN, Chris (M)   265 29
H: 6 1   W: 11 11   b.Dublin 21-7-87
Internationals: Republic of Ireland U19.

Season	Club				
2005-06	Burnley	23	2		
2006-07	Burnley	38	5		
2007-08	Burnley	35	5		
2008-09	Burnley	44	6		
2009-10	Burnley	7	0		
2010-11	Burnley	4	1		
2011-12	Burnley	46	4		
2012-13	Burnley	41	4	238	27
2013-14	Wigan Ath	27	2	27	2

McCLEAN, James (M)   169 28
H: 5 11   W: 11 00   b.Derry 22-4-89
Internationals: Northern Ireland U21. Republic of Ireland Full caps.

Season	Club				
2009	Derry C	27	1		
2010	Derry C	30	10		
2011	Derry C	16	7	73	18
2011-12	Sunderland	23	5		
2012-13	Sunderland	36	2		
2013-14	Sunderland	0	0	59	7
2013-14	Wigan Ath	37	3	37	3

McMANAMAN, Callum (F)   70 7
H: 5 9   W: 11 03   b.Huyton 25-4-91
Internationals: England U20.

Season	Club				
2008-09	Wigan Ath	1	0		
2009-10	Wigan Ath	0	0		
2010-11	Wigan Ath	3	0		
2011-12	Wigan Ath	2	0		
2011-12	Blackpool	14	2	14	2
2012-13	Wigan Ath	20	2		
2013-14	Wigan Ath	30	3	56	5

MUSTOE, Jordan (M)   57 1
H: 5 11   W: 11 11   b.Birkenhead 28-1-91

Season	Club				
2009-10	Wigan Ath	0	0		
2010-11	Wigan Ath	0	0		
2011-12	Wigan Ath	0	0		
2011-12	Barnet	18	0	18	0
2012-13	Wigan Ath	0	0		
2012-13	Morecambe	11	0		
2012-13	Carlisle U	14	1	14	1
2013-14	Wigan Ath	0	0		
2013-14	Bury	6	0	6	0
2013-14	Wycombe W	3	0	3	0
2013-14	Morecambe	5	0	16	0

NICHOLLS, Lee (G)   61 0
H: 6 3   W: 13 05   b.Huyton 5-10-92
Internationals: England U19.

Season	Club				
2009-10	Wigan Ath	0	0		
2010-11	Wigan Ath	0	0		
2010-11	Hartlepool U	0	0		
2010-11	Shrewsbury T	0	0		
2010-11	Sheffield W	0	0		
2011-12	Wigan Ath	0	0		
2011-12	Accrington S	9	0	9	0
2012-13	Wigan Ath	0	0		
2012-13	Northampton T	46	0	46	0
2013-14	Wigan Ath	6	0	6	0

PERCH, James (D)   295 13
H: 5 11   W: 11 05   b.Mansfield 29-9-85

Season	Club				
2002-03	Nottingham F	0	0		
2003-04	Nottingham F	0	0		
2004-05	Nottingham F	22	0		
2005-06	Nottingham F	38	3		
2006-07	Nottingham F	46	5		
2007-08	Nottingham F	30	0		
2008-09	Nottingham F	37	3		
2009-10	Nottingham F	17	1	190	12
2010-11	Newcastle U	13	0		
2011-12	Newcastle U	25	0		
2012-13	Newcastle U	27	1	65	1
2013-14	Wigan Ath	40	0	40	0

POLLITT, Mike (G)   505 0
H: 6 4   W: 15 03   b.Farnworth 29-2-72

Season	Club				
1990-91	Manchester U	0	0		
1990-91	Oldham Ath	0	0		
1991-92	Bury	0	0		
1992-93	Lincoln C	27	0		
1993-94	Lincoln C	30	0	57	0
1994-95	Darlington	40	0		
1995-96	Darlington	15	0	55	0
1995-96	Notts Co	8	0		
1996-97	Notts Co	8	0		
1997-98	Notts Co	2	0	10	0
1997-98	Oldham Ath	16	0	16	0
1997-98	Gillingham	6	0	6	0
1997-98	Brentford	5	0	5	0
1997-98	Sunderland	0	0		
1998-99	Rotherham U	46	0		
1999-2000	Rotherham U	46	0		
2000-01	Chesterfield	46	0	46	0
2001-02	Rotherham U	46	0		
2002-03	Rotherham U	41	0		
2003-04	Rotherham U	43	0		
2004-05	Rotherham U	45	0	267	0
2005-06	Wigan Ath	24	0		
2006-07	Wigan Ath	3	0		
2006-07	Ipswich T	1	0	1	0
2006-07	Burnley	4	0	4	0
2007-08	Wigan Ath	1	0		
2008-09	Wigan Ath	3	0		
2009-10	Wigan Ath	4	0		
2010-11	Wigan Ath	1	0		
2011-12	Wigan Ath	0	0		
2012-13	Wigan Ath	0	0		
2013-14	Wigan Ath	0	0	36	0
2013-14	Barnsley	2	0	2	0

POOLE, Declan (M)   0 0
b. 5-9-95
2013-14   Wigan Ath   0 0

RAMIS, Ivan (D)   222 13
H: 6 2   W: 12 11   b.Sa Pobla 25-10-84
Internationals: Spain U19, U21, U23.

Season	Club				
2003-04	Mallorca	9	1		
2004-05	Mallorca	22	0		
2005-06	Valladolid	27	0	27	0
2006-07	Mallorca	7	0		
2007-08	Mallorca	14	3		
2008-09	Mallorca	19	0		
2009-10	Mallorca	26	0		
2010-11	Mallorca	33	3		
2011-12	Mallorca	34	2	164	9
2012-13	Wigan Ath	16	2		
2013-14	Wigan Ath	15	2	31	4

REDMOND, Daniel (D)   33 5
H: 5 11   W: 10 07   b.Liverpool 2-3-91

Season	Club			
2009-10	Wigan Ath	0	0
2010-11	Wigan Ath	0	0

Season	Club				
2011–12	Wigan Ath	0	0		
2011–12	*Hamilton A*	18	5	18	5
2012–13	Wigan Ath	0	0		
2013–14	Wigan Ath	0	0		
2013–14	*Carlisle U*	15	0	15	0

ROGNE, Thomas (D)   75 3
H: 6 4   W: 12 11   b.Baerum 29-6-90
Internationals: Norway U19, U21, Full caps.

Season	Club				
2007	Stabaek	3	0		
2008	Stabaek	0	0		
2009	Stabaek	10	1	13	1
2009–10	Celtic	4	0		
2010–11	Celtic	16	1		
2011–12	Celtic	7	0		
2012–13	Celtic	13	0	50	2
2013–14	Wigan Ath	12	0	12	0

WAGHORN, Martyn (F)   150 30
H: 5 9   W: 13 01   b.South Shields 23-1-90
Internationals: England U19, U21.

Season	Club				
2007–08	Sunderland	3	0		
2008–09	Sunderland	1	0		
2008–09	*Charlton Ath*	7	1	7	1
2009–10	Sunderland	0	0		
2009–10	Leicester C	43	12		
2010–11	Sunderland	2	0	6	0
2010–11	Leicester C	30	4		
2011–12	Leicester C	4	1		
2011–12	*Hull C*	5	1	5	1
2012–13	Leicester C	24	3		
2013–14	Leicester C	2	0	103	20
2013–14	*Millwall*	14	3	14	3
2013–14	*Wigan Ath*	15	5	15	5

WATSON, Ben (M)   294 33
H: 5 10   W: 10 11   b.Camberwell 9-7-85
Internationals: England U21.

Season	Club				
2002–03	Crystal Palace	5	0		
2003–04	Crystal Palace	16	1		
2004–05	Crystal Palace	21	0		
2005–06	Crystal Palace	42	4		
2006–07	Crystal Palace	25	3		
2007–08	Crystal Palace	42	5		
2008–09	Crystal Palace	18	5	169	18
2008–09	Wigan Ath	10	2		
2009–10	Wigan Ath	5	1		
2009–10	*QPR*	16	2	16	2
2009–10	*WBA*	7	1	7	1
2010–11	Wigan Ath	29	3		
2011–12	Wigan Ath	21	3		
2012–13	Wigan Ath	12	1		
2013–14	Wigan Ath	25	2	102	12

WILSON, Michael (D)   0 0
b. 24-1-95

Season	Club		
2013–14	Wigan Ath	0	0

Scholars
Anson, Adam James; Balogun, Oluwamayowa Nathaniel Oluwatoyin; Bannister, Lloyd Andrew; Carey, Omar; Cosgrove, Sam Benjamin; Flores, Jordan Michael; Foukamene, Dieu Le Veut; Gibbons, Ellis; Hamilton, Matthew Lewis; Harrison, Sean Thomas; Keane, Connor Owen; Lambert, Liam James; Leigh, Daniel; Mather, Christian; McNally, Reece Patrick; Purzycki, Adrian Cyprian; Robles, Louis Gabriel; Unsworth, Jordan James.

WOLVERHAMPTON W (89)

BANCESSI, Eusebio (M)   0 0
b. 4-8-95

Season	Club		
2013–14	Wolverhampton W	0	0

BATTH, Danny (D)   130 6
H: 6 3   W: 13 05   b.Brierley Hill 21-9-90

Season	Club				
2009–10	Wolverhampton W	0	0		
2009–10	*Colchester U*	17	1	17	1
2010–11	Wolverhampton W	0	0		
2010–11	*Sheffield U*	1	0	1	0
2010–11	*Sheffield W*	10	0		
2011–12	Wolverhampton W	0	0		
2011–12	*Sheffield W*	44	2	54	2
2012–13	Wolverhampton W	0	0		
2013–14	Wolverhampton W	46	2	58	3

BOUKARI, Razak (M)   209 27
H: 6 0   W: 10 13   b.Lome 25-4-87

Season	Club				
2004–05	Chateauroux	5	5		
2005–06	Chateauroux	35	3	40	8
2006–07	Lens	29	0		
2007–08	Lens	18	0		
2008–09	Lens	26	4		
2009–10	Lens	27	4		
2010–11	Lens	17	4	117	12
2010–11	Rennes	18	4		
2011–12	Rennes	20	3	38	7
2012–13	Wolverhampton W	4	0		
2013–14	Wolverhampton W	0	0	4	0
2013–14	*Sochaux*	10	0	10	0

CASSIDY, Jake (F)   75 17
H: 5 10   W: 11 02   b.Glan Conwy 9-2-93
Internationals: Wales U21.

Season	Club				
2010–11	Wolverhampton W	0	0		
2011–12	Wolverhampton W	0	0		
2011–12	*Tranmere R*	10	5		
2012–13	Wolverhampton W	6	0		
2012–13	*Tranmere R*	26	11		
2013–14	Wolverhampton W	14	0	20	0
2013–14	*Tranmere R*	19	1	55	17

CLARKE, Leon (F)   297 88
H: 6 2   W: 14 02   b.Birmingham 10-2-85

Season	Club				
2003–04	Wolverhampton W	13	0		
2003–04	*Kidderminster H*	4	0	4	0
2004–05	Wolverhampton W	28	7		
2005–06	Wolverhampton W	24	1		
2005–06	*QPR*	1	0		
2005–06	*Plymouth Arg*	5	0	5	0
2006–07	Wolverhampton W	22	5		
2006–07	Sheffield W	10	1		
2006–07	*Oldham Ath*	5	3	5	3
2007–08	Sheffield W	8	3		
2007–08	*Southend U*	16	8	16	8
2008–09	Sheffield W	29	8		
2009–10	Sheffield W	36	6	83	18
2010–11	QPR	13	0	14	0
2010–11	*Preston NE*	6	1	6	1
2011–12	*Swindon T*	2	0	2	0
2011–12	*Chesterfield*	14	9	14	9
2011–12	Charlton Ath	7	0		
2011–12	*Crawley T*	4	1	4	1
2012–13	Charlton Ath	0	0		
2012–13	*Scunthorpe U*	15	11	15	11
2012–13	Coventry C	12	8		
2013–14	Coventry C	23	15	35	23
2013–14	Wolverhampton W	13	1	87	14

DAVIS, David (M)   93 2
H: 5 8   W: 12 03   b.Smethwick 20-2-91

Season	Club				
2009–10	Wolverhampton W	0	0		
2009–10	*Darlington*	5	0	5	0
2010–11	Wolverhampton W	0	0		
2010–11	*Walsall*	7	0	7	0
2010–11	*Shrewsbury T*	19	2	19	2
2011–12	Wolverhampton W	7	0		
2011–12	*Chesterfield*	9	0	9	0
2012–13	Wolverhampton W	28	0		
2013–14	Wolverhampton W	18	0	53	0

DICKO, Nouha (M)   105 39
H: 5 8   W: 11 00   b.Paris 14-5-92
Internationals: Mali Full caps.

Season	Club				
2009–10	Strasbourg B	14	8		
2010–11	Strasbourg B	24	8	42	12
2010–11	Strasbourg	3	0	3	0
2011–12	Wigan Ath	0	0		
2011–12	*Blackpool*	10	4		
2012–13	Wigan Ath	0	0		
2012–13	*Blackpool*	22	5	32	9
2012–13	*Wolverhampton W*	4	1		
2013–14	Wigan Ath	0	0		
2013–14	*Rotherham U*	5	5	5	5
2013–14	Wolverhampton W	19	12	23	13

DOHERTY, Matthew (M)   62 5
H: 6 0   W: 12 08   b.Dublin 17-1-92
Internationals: Republic of Ireland U19, U21.

Season	Club				
2010–11	Wolverhampton W	0	0		
2011–12	Wolverhampton W	1	0		
2011–12	*Hibernian*	13	2	13	2
2012–13	Wolverhampton W	13	1		
2012–13	*Bury*	17	1	17	1
2013–14	Wolverhampton W	18	1	32	2

DOUMBIA, Tongo (M)   117 8
H: 6 3   W: 12 05   b.Vernon 6-8-89
Internationals: Mali U21, Full caps.

Season	Club				
2008–09	Chateauroux	1	0	1	0
2009–10	Rennes	3	0		
2010–11	Rennes	19	0		
2011–12	Rennes	25	2	47	2
2012–13	Wolverhampton W	33	2		
2013–14	Wolverhampton W	0	0	33	2
2013–14	*Valenciennes*	36	4	36	4

DOYLE, Kevin (F)   364 107
H: 5 11   W: 12 06   b.Adamstown 18-9-83
Internationals: Republic of Ireland U21, Full caps.

Season	Club				
2004	Cork C	32	13		
2005	Cork C	11	7	43	20
2005–06	Reading	45	18		
2006–07	Reading	32	13		
2007–08	Reading	36	6		
2008–09	Reading	41	18	154	55
2009–10	Wolverhampton W	34	9		
2010–11	Wolverhampton W	26	5		
2011–12	Wolverhampton W	33	4		
2012–13	Wolverhampton W	42	9		
2013–14	Wolverhampton W	23	3	158	30
2013–14	*QPR*	9	2	9	2

EBANKS-LANDELL, Ethan (M)   31 2
H: 5 6   W: 11 02   b.Oldbury 16-12-92

Season	Club				
2009–10	Wolverhampton W	0	0		
2010–11	Wolverhampton W	0	0		
2011–12	Wolverhampton W	0	0		
2012–13	Wolverhampton W	0	0		
2012–13	*Bury*	24	0	24	0
2013–14	Wolverhampton W	7	2	7	2

EDWARDS, Dave (M)   291 36
H: 5 11   W: 11 04   b.Shrewsbury 3-2-86
Internationals: Wales U21, Full caps.

Season	Club				
2002–03	Shrewsbury T	1	0		
2003–04	Shrewsbury T	0	0		
2004–05	Shrewsbury T	27	5		
2005–06	Shrewsbury T	30	2		
2006–07	Shrewsbury T	45	5	103	12
2007–08	Luton T	19	4	19	4
2007–08	Wolverhampton W	10	1		
2008–09	Wolverhampton W	44	3		
2009–10	Wolverhampton W	20	1		
2010–11	Wolverhampton W	15	1		
2011–12	Wolverhampton W	26	3		
2012–13	Wolverhampton W	24	2		
2013–14	Wolverhampton W	30	9	169	20

ELOKOBI, George (D)   142 4
H: 5 10   W: 13 02   b.Cameroon 31-1-86

Season	Club				
2004–05	Colchester U	0	0		
2004–05	*Chester C*	5	0	5	0
2005–06	Colchester U	12	1		
2006–07	Colchester U	10	0		
2007–08	Colchester U	17	1	39	2
2007–08	Wolverhampton W	15	0		
2008–09	Wolverhampton W	4	0		
2009–10	Wolverhampton W	22	0		
2010–11	Wolverhampton W	27	2		
2011–12	Wolverhampton W	13	0		
2011–12	*Nottingham F*	12	0	12	0
2012–13	Wolverhampton W	2	0		
2012–13	*Bristol C*	1	0	1	0
2013–14	Wolverhampton W	6	0	85	2

ERDEI, Carlo (M)   0 0
Internationals: Romania U18.

Season	Club		
2013–14	Wolverhampton W	0	0

EVANS, Lee (M)   26 2
Internationals: Wales U21.

Season	Club				
2012–13	Wolverhampton W	0	0		
2013–14	Wolverhampton W	26	2	26	2

FLATT, Jonathan (G)   0 0

Season	Club		
2013–14	Wolverhampton W	0	0

FOLEY, Kevin (D)   350 8
H: 5 9   W: 11 11   b.Luton 1-11-84
Internationals: Republic of Ireland U21, B, Full caps.

Season	Club				
2002–03	Luton T	2	0		
2003–04	Luton T	33	1		
2004–05	Luton T	39	2		
2005–06	Luton T	38	0		
2006–07	Luton T	39	0		
2007–08	Luton T	0	0	151	3
2007–08	Wolverhampton W	44	1		
2008–09	Wolverhampton W	45	1		
2009–10	Wolverhampton W	25	0		
2010–11	Wolverhampton W	33	2		
2011–12	Wolverhampton W	16	0		
2012–13	Wolverhampton W	26	0		
2013–14	Wolverhampton W	5	1	194	5
2013–14	*Blackpool*	5	0	5	0

FORDE, Anthony (M) 29 0
H: 5 9 W: 10 10 b.Limerick 16-11-93
Internationals: Republic of Ireland U19, U21.

2011–12	Wolverhampton W	6	0		
2012–13	Wolverhampton W	12	0		
2012–13	Scunthorpe U	8	0	8	0
2013–14	Wolverhampton W	3	0	21	0

GOLBOURNE, Scott (M) 254 6
H: 5 8 W: 11 08 b.Bristol 29-2-88
Internationals: England U17, U19

2004–05	Bristol C	9	0		
2005–06	Bristol C	5	0	14	0
2005–06	Reading	1	0		
2006–07	Reading	0	0		
2006–07	Wycombe W	34	1	34	1
2007–08	Reading	1	0		
2007–08	Bournemouth	5	0	5	0
2008–09	Reading	0	0	2	0
2008–09	Oldham Ath	8	0	8	0
2009–10	Exeter C	34	0		
2010–11	Exeter C	44	2		
2011–12	Exeter C	26	0	104	2
2011–12	Barnsley	12	1		
2012–13	Barnsley	31	1		
2013–14	Barnsley	4	0	47	2
2013–14	Wolverhampton W	40	1	40	1

GRIFFITHS, Leigh (F) 201 94
H: 5 07 W: 10 01 b.Leith 20-8-90
Internationals: Scotland U19, U21, B, Full caps.

2006–07	Livingston	4	1		
2007–08	Livingston	18	5		
2008–09	Livingston	27	17	49	23
2009–10	Dundee	29	13		
2010–11	Dundee	18	8	47	21
2010–11	Wolverhampton W	0	0		
2011–12	Wolverhampton W	0	0		
2011–12	Hibernian	30	8		
2012–13	Wolverhampton W	0	0		
2012–13	Hibernian	36	23	66	31
2013–14	Wolverhampton W	26	12	26	12
2013–14	Celtic	13	7	13	7

HAUSE, Kortney (D) 23 2
b. 16-7-95

2012–13	Wycombe W	9	1		
2013–14	Wycombe W	14	1	23	2
2013–14	Wolverhampton W	0	0		

IHIEKWE, Michael (D) 13 0
H: 6 1 W: 12 02 b.Liverpool 20-11-92

2011–12	Wolverhampton W	0	0		
2012–13	Wolverhampton W	0	0		
2013–14	Wolverhampton W	0	0		
2013–14	Cheltenham T	13	0	13	0

IKEME, Carl (G) 155 0
H: 6 2 W: 13 09 b.Sutton Coldfield 8-6-86

2005–06	Wolverhampton W	0	0		
2005–06	Stockport Co	9	0	9	0
2006–07	Wolverhampton W	1	0		
2007–08	Wolverhampton W	0	0		
2008–09	Wolverhampton W	12	0		
2009–10	Wolverhampton W	0	0		
2009–10	Charlton Ath	4	0	4	0
2009–10	Sheffield U	2	0	2	0
2009–10	QPR	17	0	17	0
2010–11	Wolverhampton W	0	0		
2010–11	Leicester C	5	0	5	0
2011–12	Wolverhampton W	1	0		
2011–12	Middlesbrough	10	0	10	0
2011–12	Doncaster R	15	0	15	0
2012–13	Wolverhampton W	38	0		
2013–14	Wolverhampton W	41	0	93	0

IORFA, Dominic (D) 7 0
b. 24-6-95
Internationals: England U18.

| 2013–14 | Wolverhampton W | 0 | 0 | | |
| 2013–14 | Shrewsbury T | 7 | 0 | 7 | 0 |

ISMAIL, Zeli (M) 31 3
b.Serbia 12-12-93
Internationals: England U16, U17.

2010–11	Wolverhampton W	0	0		
2011–12	Wolverhampton W	0	0		
2012–13	Wolverhampton W	0	0		
2012–13	Milton Keynes D	7	0	7	0
2013–14	Wolverhampton W	9	0	9	0
2013–14	Burton Alb	15	3	15	3

JACOBS, Michael (M) 158 21
H: 5 9 W: 11 08 b.Rothwell 23-3-92

2009–10	Northampton T	0	0		
2010–11	Northampton T	41	5		
2011–12	Northampton T	46	6	87	11
2012–13	Derby Co	38	2		
2013–14	Derby Co	3	0	41	2
2013–14	Wolverhampton W	30	8	30	8

JOHNSON, Roger (D) 442 35
H: 6 3 W: 11 00 b.Ashford (Middlesex) 28-4-83

1999–2000	Wycombe W	1	0		
2000–01	Wycombe W	1	0		
2001–02	Wycombe W	7	1		
2002–03	Wycombe W	33	3		
2003–04	Wycombe W	28	2		
2004–05	Wycombe W	42	6		
2005–06	Wycombe W	45	7	157	19
2006–07	Cardiff C	32	2		
2007–08	Cardiff C	42	5		
2008–09	Cardiff C	45	5	119	12
2009–10	Birmingham C	38	0		
2010–11	Birmingham C	38	2	76	2
2011–12	Wolverhampton W	27	0		
2012–13	Wolverhampton W	42	2		
2013–14	Wolverhampton W	0	0	69	2
2013–14	Sheffield W	17	0	17	0
2013–14	West Ham U	4	0	4	0

KEITA, Ibrahim (F) 0 0
b. 18-1-96
Internationals: France U16.

| 2013–14 | Wolverhampton W | 0 | 0 | | |

KELLERMANN, James (M) 0 0

| 2013–14 | Wolverhampton W | 0 | 0 | | |

MARGREITTER, Georg (D) 97 4
H: 6 1 W: 12 09 b.Schruns 7-11-88
Internationals: Austria U19, U20, U21.

2007–08	LASK Linz	7	0		
2009–10	LASK Linz	19	2	26	2
2010–11	FK Austria	25	1		
2011–12	FK Austria	29	1		
2012–13	FK Austria	3	0	57	2
2012–13	Wolverhampton W	1	0		
2013–14	Wolverhampton W	0	0	1	0
2013–14	FC Copenhagen	13	0	13	0

McALINDEN, Liam (F) 17 4
b.Cannock 26-9-93
Internationals: Northern Ireland U21. Republic of Ireland U21.

2010–11	Wolverhampton W	0	0		
2011–12	Wolverhampton W	0	0		
2012–13	Wolverhampton W	1	0		
2013–14	Wolverhampton W	7	1	8	1
2013–14	Shrewsbury T	9	3	9	3

McCAREY, Aaron (G) 24 0
H: 6 1 W: 11 09 b.Monaghan 14-1-92
Internationals: Republic of Ireland U17, U18, U19, U21.

2009–10	Wolverhampton W	0	0		
2010–11	Wolverhampton W	0	0		
2011–12	Wolverhampton W	0	0		
2012–13	Wolverhampton W	0	0		
2012–13	Walsall	14	0	14	0
2013–14	Wolverhampton W	5	0	5	0
2013–14	York C	5	0	5	0

McDONALD, Kevin (M) 276 27
H: 6 2 W: 13 03 b.Carnoustie 4-11-88
Internationals: Scotland U19, U21.

2005–06	Dundee	26	3		
2006–07	Dundee	31	2		
2007–08	Dundee	34	9	91	14
2008–09	Burnley	25	1		
2009–10	Burnley	26	1		
2010–11	Burnley	0	0	51	2
2010–11	Scunthorpe U	5	1	5	1
2010–11	Notts Co	11	0	11	0
2011–12	Sheffield U	31	3		
2012–13	Sheffield U	45	1		
2013–14	Wolverhampton W	1	1	77	5
2013–14	Wolverhampton W	41	5	41	5

O'HARA, Jamie (M) 148 16
H: 5 11 W: 12 04 b.Dartford 25-9-86
Internationals: England U21.

2004–05	Tottenham H	0	0		
2005–06	Tottenham H	0	0		
2005–06	Chesterfield	19	5	19	5
2006–07	Tottenham H	0	0		
2007–08	Tottenham H	17	1		
2007–08	Millwall	14	2	14	2
2008–09	Tottenham H	15	1		
2009–10	Tottenham H	2	0		
2009–10	Portsmouth	26	2	26	2
2010–11	Tottenham H	0	0	34	2
2010–11	Wolverhampton W	14	3		
2011–12	Wolverhampton W	19	2		
2012–13	Wolverhampton W	20	0		
2013–14	Wolverhampton W	2	0	55	5

PRICE, Jack (M) 26 0
H: 6 3 W: 13 10 b.Shrewsbury 19-12-92

2011–12	Wolverhampton W	0	0		
2012–13	Wolverhampton W	0	0		
2013–14	Wolverhampton W	26	0	26	0

RECKORD, Jamie (D) 50 0
H: 5 10 W: 11 11 b.Wolverhampton 9-3-92
Internationals: England U16, U17.

2010–11	Wolverhampton W	0	0		
2010–11	Northampton T	7	0	7	0
2011–12	Wolverhampton W	0	0		
2011–12	Scunthorpe U	17	0	17	0
2012–13	Wolverhampton W	0	0		
2012–13	Coventry C	9	0	9	0
2013–14	Wolverhampton W	0	0		
2013–14	Plymouth Arg	12	0	12	0
2013–14	Swindon T	5	0	5	0

REID, Bradley (F) 0 0
Internationals: Wales U19.

| 2013–14 | Wolverhampton W | 0 | 0 | | |

RICKETTS, Sam (D) 384 6
H: 6 1 W: 12 01 b.Aylesbury 11-10-81
Internationals: England C. Wales Full caps.

1999–2000	Oxford U	0	0		
2000–01	Oxford U	14	0		
2001–02	Oxford U	29	1		
2002–03	Oxford U	2	0	45	1
From Telford U					
2004–05	Swansea C	42	0		
2005–06	Swansea C	44	1	86	1
2006–07	Hull C	40	1		
2007–08	Hull C	44	0		
2008–09	Hull C	29	0		
2009–10	Hull C	0	0	113	1
2009–10	Bolton W	27	0		
2010–11	Bolton W	17	0		
2011–12	Bolton W	20	1		
2012–13	Bolton W	32	0	96	1
2013–14	Wolverhampton W	44	2	44	2

SAKO, Bakary (M) 247 44
H: 5 11 W: 11 12 b.Ivry Sur Seine 26-4-88
Internationals: France U21. Mali U17, Full caps.

2006–07	Chateauroux	17	0		
2007–08	Chateauroux	12	1		
2008–09	Chateauroux	35	9	64	10
2009–10	St Etienne	30	1		
2010–11	St Etienne	38	7		
2011–12	St Etienne	36	5		
2012–13	St Etienne	0	0	106	13
2012–13	Wolverhampton W	37	9		
2013–14	Wolverhampton W	40	12	77	21

SIGURDARSON, Bjorn (F) 125 24
H: 6 1 W: 12 09 b.Akranes 26-12-91
Internationals: Iceland U17, U19, U21, Full caps.

2008–09	Lillestrom	5	0		
2009–10	Lillestrom	19	4		
2010–11	Lillestrom	22	4		
2011–12	Lillestrom	24	9	70	17
2012–13	Wolverhampton W	37	5		
2013–14	Wolverhampton W	18	2	55	7

STEARMAN, Richard (D) 297 12
H: 6 2 W: 10 08 b.Wolverhampton 19-8-87
Internationals: England U16, U17, U19, U21.

2004–05	Leicester C	8	1		
2005–06	Leicester C	34	3		
2006–07	Leicester C	35	1		
2007–08	Leicester C	39	2	116	7
2008–09	Wolverhampton W	37	1		
2009–10	Wolverhampton W	16	1		
2010–11	Wolverhampton W	31	0		
2011–12	Wolverhampton W	30	0		
2012–13	Wolverhampton W	12	1		
2012–13	Ipswich T	15	0	15	0
2013–14	Wolverhampton W	40	2	166	5

TORRAS, Albert (M) 0 0
b. 13-6-96
2013–14 Wolverhampton W 0 0

WARD, Stephen (D) 338 24
H: 5 11 W: 12 02 b.Dublin 20-8-85
Internationals: Republic of Ireland U20, U21, B, Full caps.
2003 Bohemians 6 0
2004 Bohemians 16 2
2005 Bohemians 29 7
2006 Bohemians 21 2 72 11
2006–07 Wolverhampton W 18 3
2007–08 Wolverhampton W 29 0
2008–09 Wolverhampton W 42 0
2009–10 Wolverhampton W 22 0
2010–11 Wolverhampton W 34 1
2011–12 Wolverhampton W 38 3
2012–13 Wolverhampton W 39 2
2013–14 Wolverhampton W 0 0 222 9
2013–14 *Brighton & HA* 44 4 44 4

Scholars
Breslin, Anthony Patrick; Burgoyne, Harry James; Devers, Jesse James; Dutton, Scott James; Hayden, Aaron Edward-George; Hill, Thomas Adam; Keane, Cieron Macaully; Matinyadze, Tendai Regis; Murray, Daniel Michael; O'Hanlon, Ben Joseph; Priest, Ben Charles; Rainey, Ryan Gavin; Smith, Peter Joseph; Streete, Andre Ramone; Stringer-Moth, Dylan Mark; Upton, Regan David; Weeks, Declan Lee.

WYCOMBE W (90)

BLOOMFIELD, Matt (M) 286 24
H: 5 9 W: 11 00 b.Felixstowe 8-2-84
Internationals: England U19.
2001–02 Ipswich T 0 0
2002–03 Ipswich T 0 0
2003–04 Ipswich T 0 0
2003–04 Wycombe W 12 1
2004–05 Wycombe W 26 2
2005–06 Wycombe W 39 5
2006–07 Wycombe W 41 4
2007–08 Wycombe W 35 4
2008–09 Wycombe W 20 0
2009–10 Wycombe W 14 2
2010–11 Wycombe W 34 3
2011–12 Wycombe W 31 2
2012–13 Wycombe W 2 1
2013–14 Wycombe W 32 0 286 24

COWAN-HALL, Paris (F) 69 7
H: 5 8 W: 11 08 b.Portsmouth 5-10-90
2008–09 Portsmouth 0 0
2009–10 Portsmouth 0 0
2009–10 *Grimsby T* 3 0 3 0
2010–11 Portsmouth 0 0
2010–11 Scunthorpe U 1 0 1 0
2012–13 Plymouth Arg 40 3 40 3
2013–14 Wycombe W 25 4 25 4

CRAIG, Steven (F) 81 11
H: 5 11 W: 12 02 b.Preston 5-2-81
2002–03 Motherwell 13 2
2003–04 Motherwell 24 3 37 5
2004–05 Aberdeen 14 2
2005–06 Aberdeen 3 0 17 2
From Dundee, Livingston, Ross Co, Partick Thistle
2013–14 Wycombe W 27 4 27 4

DOHERTY, Gary (D) 433 30
H: 6 3 W: 13 13 b.Co. Donegal 31-1-80
Internationals: Republic of Ireland U20, U21, Full caps.
1997–98 Luton T 10 0
1998–99 Luton T 20 6
1999–2000 Luton T 40 6 70 12
1999–2000 Tottenham H 5 0
2000–01 Tottenham H 22 3
2001–02 Tottenham H 7 0
2002–03 Tottenham H 15 1
2003–04 Tottenham H 17 0
2004–05 Tottenham H 1 0 64 4
2004–05 Norwich C 20 2
2005–06 Norwich C 42 1
2006–07 Norwich C 34 0
2007–08 Norwich C 34 0
2008–09 Norwich C 34 3
2009–10 Norwich C 38 5 202 11
2010–11 Charlton Ath 38 0
2011–12 Charlton Ath 3 0 41 0
2011–12 *Wycombe W* 13 1
2012–13 Wycombe W 23 2
2013–14 Wycombe W 20 0 56 3

FLETCHER, Tommy (D) 0 0
2013–14 Wycombe W 0 0

HORLOCK, Charlie (G) 0 0
2012–13 Stevenage 0 0
2013–14 Wycombe W 0 0

INGRAM, Matt (G) 54 0
H: 6 3 W: 12 13 b.Croydon 18-12-93
2011–12 Wycombe W 0 0
2012–13 Wycombe W 8 0
2013–14 Wycombe W 46 0 54 0

JEFFREY, Anthony (M) 12 0
2012–13 Arsenal 0 0
2012–13 *Stevenage* 1 0 1 0
2013–14 Wycombe W 11 0 11 0

JOHNSON, Leon (D) 325 9
H: 6 1 W: 13 05 b.Shoreditch 10-5-81
Internationals: Grenada Full caps.
1999–2000 Southend U 0 0
2000–01 Southend U 20 1
2001–02 Southend U 28 2 48 3
2002–03 Gillingham 18 0
2003–04 Gillingham 20 0
2004–05 Gillingham 8 0
2005–06 Gillingham 28 1
2006–07 Gillingham 24 1 98 2
2007–08 Wycombe W 45 0
2008–09 Wycombe W 29 2
2009–10 Wycombe W 5 0
2010–11 Wycombe W 23 1
2011–12 Wycombe W 27 0
2012–13 Wycombe W 20 0
2013–14 Wycombe W 30 1 179 4

KEWLEY-GRAHAM, Jesse (M) 9 0
H: 5 10 W: 11 11 b.Hounslow 15-6-93
2011–12 Wycombe W 1 0
2012–13 Wycombe W 7 0
2013–14 Wycombe W 1 0 9 0

KRETZSCHMAR, Max (M) 35 6
b. 12-10-93
2011–12 Wycombe W 0 0
2012–13 Wycombe W 0 0
2013–14 Wycombe W 35 6 35 6

KUFFOUR, Jo (F) 458 101
H: 5 8 W: 11 11 b.Edmonton 17-11-81
2000–01 Arsenal 0 0
2001–02 Arsenal 0 0
2001–02 *Swindon U* 11 2 11 2
2002–03 Torquay U 30 5
2003–04 Torquay U 41 10
2004–05 Torquay U 34 6
2005–06 Torquay U 43 8 148 29
2006–07 Brentford 39 12 39 12
2007–08 Bournemouth 42 12
2008–09 Bournemouth 2 0 44 12
2008–09 Bristol R 41 11
2009–10 Bristol R 42 14
2010–11 Bristol R 42 6
2011–12 Bristol R 5 1 130 32
2011–12 Gillingham 30 9 30 9
2012–13 Wycombe W 32 2
2013–14 Wycombe W 24 3 56 5

LEWIS, Stuart (M) 211 9
H: 5 10 W: 11 06 b.Welwyn 15-10-87
Internationals: England, C, U16, U17.
2005–06 Tottenham H 0 0
2006–07 Tottenham H 0 0
2006–07 *Barnet* 4 0 4 0
From Stevenage B
2007–08 Gillingham 10 0
2008–09 Gillingham 21 0
2009–10 Gillingham 20 1 51 1
2010–11 *Dagenham & R* 10 0 10 0
2010–11 Wycombe W 25 2
2011–12 Wycombe W 41 1
2012–13 Wycombe W 44 2
2013–14 Wycombe W 36 3 146 8

McCLURE, Matt (F) 83 19
H: 5 10 W: 11 00 b.Slough 17-11-91
Internationals: Northern Ireland U19, U21.
2010–11 Wycombe W 8 0
2011–12 Wycombe W 12 1
2012–13 Wycombe W 27 11
2013–14 Wycombe W 36 7 83 19

McCOY, Marvin (D) 91 0
H: 5 11 W: 11 00 b.Walthamstow 2-10-88
Internationals: Antigua and Barbuda Full caps.
2007–08 Hereford U 0 0
From Leyton, Wealdstone
2010–11 Wycombe W 21 0
2011–12 Wycombe W 28 0
2012–13 Wycombe W 9 0
2013–14 Wycombe W 33 0 91 0

MORGAN, Dean (M) 367 51
H: 5 11 W: 13 00 b.Enfield 3-10-83
Internationals: Montserrat Full caps.
2000–01 Colchester U 4 0
2001–02 Colchester U 30 0
2002–03 Colchester U 37 6
2003–04 Colchester U 0 0 71 6
2003–04 Reading 13 1
2004–05 Reading 18 2 31 3
2005–06 Luton T 36 6
2006–07 Luton T 36 4
2007–08 Luton T 16 1
2007–08 *Southend U* 8 0 8 0
2007–08 *Crewe Alex* 9 1 9 1
2008–09 Luton T 0 0
2008–09 *Leyton Orient* 32 5 32 5
2009–10 Luton T 0 0 88 11
2009–10 *Milton Keynes D* 9 1 9 1
2009–10 *Aldershot T* 9 4 9 4
2010–11 Chesterfield 21 1
2011–12 Chesterfield 17 3 38 4
2011–12 *Oxford U* 10 1 10 1
2012–13 Wycombe W 33 7
2013–14 Wycombe W 29 8 62 15

MORIAS, Junior (F) 28 0
b. 4-7-95
2012–13 Wycombe W 19 0
2013–14 Wycombe W 9 0 28 0

PITTMAN, Jon-Paul (F) 133 21
H: 5 9 W: 11 00 b.Oklahoma City 24-10-86
Internationals: England C.
2005–06 Nottingham F 0 0
2005–06 Hartlepool U 3 0 3 0
2006–07 Bury 9 1 9 1
2006–07 Doncaster R 0 0
From Crawley T.
2008–09 Wycombe W 17 3
2009–10 Wycombe W 41 7
2010–11 Wycombe W 19 4
2011–12 Oxford U 15 3
2011–12 *Crawley T* 4 1 4 1
2012–13 Oxford U 15 2 30 5
2013–14 Wycombe W 10 0 87 14

SCOWEN, Josh (M) 73 2
H: 5 10 W: 11 09 b.Cheshunt 28-3-93
2010–11 Wycombe W 2 0
2011–12 Wycombe W 0 0
2012–13 Wycombe W 34 1
2013–14 Wycombe W 37 1 73 2

SPRING, Matthew (M) 512 53
H: 5 11 W: 12 05 b.Harlow 17-11-79
1997–98 Luton T 12 0
1998–99 Luton T 45 3
1999–2000 Luton T 45 6
2000–01 Luton T 41 4
2001–02 Luton T 42 6
2002–03 Luton T 41 5
2003–04 Luton T 24 1
2004–05 Leeds U 13 1
2005–06 Leeds U 0 0 13 1
2005–06 Watford 39 8
2006–07 Watford 6 0 45 8
2006–07 Luton T 14 1
2007–08 Luton T 44 9
2008–09 Luton T 0 0 308 35
2008–09 *Sheffield U* 11 1 11 1
2008–09 Charlton Ath 13 2
2009–10 Charlton Ath 12 0 25 2
2010–11 Leyton Orient 39 2
2011–12 Leyton Orient 41 4 80 6
2012–13 Wycombe W 25 0
2013–14 Wycombe W 5 0 30 0

STEWART, Anthony (D) 56 4
H: 5 10 W: 12 03 b.Brixton 18-9-92
2011–12 Wycombe W 4 0
2012–13 Wycombe W 19 1
2013–14 Wycombe W 33 3 56 4

STYCHE, Reece (F)   14 0
H: 6 1 W: 12 11 b. 3-5-89
Internationals: England C. Gibraltar Full caps.

2013–14	Wycombe W	14	0	14	0

WOOD, Sam (M)   212 10
H: 6 0 W: 11 05 b.Sidcup 9-8-86

2008–09	Brentford	40	1		
2009–10	Brentford	43	2		
2010–11	Brentford	20	1		
2011–12	Brentford	5	0	108	4
2011–12	Rotherham U	26	1	26	1
2012–13	Wycombe W	35	3		
2013–14	Wycombe W	43	2	78	5

Non Contract
Ainsworth, Gareth; Richardson, Barry

YEOVIL T (91)

AYLING, Luke (D)   166 2
H: 5 11 W: 10 08 b.Lambeth 25-8-91

2009–10	Arsenal	0	0		
2009–10	Yeovil T	4	0		
2010–11	Yeovil T	37	0		
2011–12	Yeovil T	44	0		
2012–13	Yeovil T	39	0		
2013–14	Yeovil T	42	2	166	2

DAVIS, Liam (M)   191 12
H: 5 9 W: 11 07 b.Wandsworth 23-11-86

2005–06	Coventry C	2	0		
2006–07	Coventry C	3	0		
2006–07	Peterborough U	7	0	7	0
2007–08	Coventry C	6	0	11	0
2008–09	Northampton T	29	4		
2009–10	Northampton T	17	2		
2010–11	Northampton T	33	2	79	8
2011–12	Oxford U	44	2		
2012–13	Oxford U	23	1	67	3
2013–14	Yeovil T	27	1	27	1

DAWSON, Kevin (M)   106 7
H: 5 10 W: 12 08 b.Dublin 30-6-90
Internationals: Republic of Ireland U18.

2011	Shelbourne	26	2		
2012	Shelbourne	25	2	51	4
2012–13	Yeovil T	20	2		
2013–14	Yeovil T	35	1	55	3

DUNN, Chris (G)   109 0
H: 6 5 W: 13 11 b.Brentwood 23-10-87

2006–07	Northampton T	0	0		
2007–08	Northampton T	1	0		
2008–09	Northampton T	29	0		
2009–10	Northampton T	29	0		
2010–11	Northampton T	39	0	98	0
2011–12	Coventry C	2	0		
2012–13	Coventry C	1	0		
2013–14	Coventry C	0	0	3	0
2013–14	Yeovil T	8	0	8	0

EDWARDS, Joe (D)   89 4
H: 5 8 W: 11 07 b.Gloucester 31-10-90

2009–10	Bristol C	0	0		
2010–11	Bristol C	2	0		
2011–12	Bristol C	2	0		
2011–12	Yeovil T	4	1		
2012–13	Bristol C	0	0	4	0
2012–13	Yeovil T	35	2		
2013–14	Yeovil T	46	1	85	4

FOLEY, Sam (M)   57 5
H: 6 0 W: 11 08 b.St Albans 17-10-86

2012–13	Yeovil T	41	5		
2013–14	Yeovil T	7	0	48	5
2013–14	Shrewsbury T	9	0	9	0

GRANT, Joel (F)   208 33
H: 6 0 W: 12 01 b.Acton 26-8-87
Internationals: Jamaica U20, Full caps.

2005–06	Watford	7	0		
2006–07	Watford	0	0	7	0
From Aldershot T					
2008–09	Crewe Alex	28	2		
2009–10	Crewe Alex	43	9		
2010–11	Crewe Alex	25	5	96	16
2011–12	Wycombe W	30	4		
2012–13	Wycombe W	41	10	71	14
2013–14	Yeovil T	34	3	34	3

HAYTER, James (F)   601 147
H: 5 9 W: 10 13 b.Sandown 9-4-79

1996–97	Bournemouth	0	0		
1997–98	Bournemouth	5	0		
1998–99	Bournemouth	20	2		
1999–2000	Bournemouth	31	2		
2000–01	Bournemouth	40	11		
2001–02	Bournemouth	44	7		
2002–03	Bournemouth	45	9		
2003–04	Bournemouth	44	14		
2004–05	Bournemouth	39	19		
2005–06	Bournemouth	46	20		
2006–07	Bournemouth	42	10	358	94
2007–08	Doncaster R	34	7		
2008–09	Doncaster R	27	4		
2009–10	Doncaster R	38	9		
2010–11	Doncaster R	32	9		
2011–12	Doncaster R	31	4	162	33
2012–13	Yeovil T	14	4		
2013–14	Yeovil T	37	6	81	20

HOSKINS, Sam (F)   41 3
H: 5 8 W: 10 07 b.Dorchester 4-2-93

2011–12	Southampton	0	0		
2011–12	Preston NE	0	0		
2011–12	Rotherham U	8	2	8	2
2012–13	Southampton	0	0		
2012–13	Stevenage	14	1	14	1
2013–14	Yeovil T	19	0	19	0

LANZONI, Matteo (D)   99 2
H: 6 0 W: 12 05 b.Como 18-7-88
Internationals: Italy U19.

2007–08	Sampdoria	0	0		
2008–09	Sampdoria	0	0		
2008–09	Bari	0	0		
2009–10	Sampdoria	0	0		
2009–10	Mantova	20	1	20	1
2010–11	Portogruaro	18	0	18	0
2011–12	Sampdoria	0	0		
2011–12	Foggia	24	0	24	0
2012–13	Sampdoria	0	0		
2012–13	Carrarese	21	0	21	0
2013–14	Oldham Ath	10	1	10	1
2013–14	Yeovil T	6	0	6	0

McALLISTER, Jamie (D)   510 4
H: 5 10 W: 11 00 b.Glasgow 26-4-78
Internationals: Scotland Full caps.

1995–96	Queen of the South	2	0		
1996–97	Queen of the South	6	0		
1997–98	Queen of the South	15	0		
1998–99	Queen of the South	27	0	50	0
1999–2000	Aberdeen	34	0		
2000–01	Aberdeen	25	0		
2001–02	Aberdeen	29	0		
2002–03	Aberdeen	29	0	117	0
2003–04	Livingston	34	1	34	1
2004–05	Hearts	30	0		
2005–06	Hearts	17	0	47	0
2006–07	Bristol C	31	1		
2007–08	Bristol C	41	0		
2008–09	Bristol C	35	1		
2009–10	Bristol C	33	0		
2010–11	Bristol C	34	1		
2011–12	Bristol C	12	0	186	3
2011–12	Preston NE	4	0	4	0
2012–13	Yeovil T	34	0		
2013–14	Yeovil T	38	0	72	0

MOORE, Kieffer (F)   20 4

2013–14	Yeovil T	20	4	20	4

MORGAN, Adam (F)   13 0
H: 5 10 W: 11 03 b.Liverpool 21-4-94
Internationals: England U17, U19.

2011–12	Liverpool	0	0		
2012–13	Liverpool	0	0		
2012–13	Rotherham U	1	0	1	0
2013–14	Liverpool	0	0		
2013–14	Yeovil T	12	0	12	0

NANA OFORI-TWUMASI, Seth (D) 3 0
H: 5 8 W: 11 09 b.Accra 15-5-90
Internationals: England U16, U17, U18, U20.

2009–10	Dagenham & R	0	0		
2010–11	Peterborough U	0	0		
2010–11	Northampton T	0	0		
2011–12	Northampton T	0	0		
2012–13	Northampton T	0	0		
2013–14	Yeovil T	3	0	3	0

PALAZUELOS, Ruben (M)   204 9
H: 6 3 W: 13 02 b. 11-4-83

2006–07	Aris Thessaloniki	21	0	21	0
2007–08	Hearts	29	1		
2008–09	Hearts	25	2		
2009–10	Hearts	27	0		
2010–11	Hearts	33	0	114	3
2011–12	Alaves	16	3	16	3
2012–13	Botev Plovdiv	14	0	14	0
2013	FC Honka	30	3	30	0
2013–14	Yeovil T	9	0	9	0

STECH, Marek (G)   82 0
H: 6 3 W: 14 00 b.Prague 28-1-90
Internationals: Czech Republic U17 U21, Full caps.

2008–09	West Ham U	0	0		
2008–09	Wycombe W	2	0	2	0
2009–10	West Ham U	0	0		
2009–10	Bournemouth	1	0	1	0
2010–11	West Ham U	0	0		
2010–11	West Ham U	0	0		
2011–12	Yeovil T	5	0		
2011–12	Leyton Orient	2	0	2	0
2012–13	Yeovil T	46	0		
2013–14	Yeovil T	26	0	77	0

STEWART, Gareth (G)   166 0
H: 6 0 W: 12 08 b.Preston 3-2-80

1996–97	Blackburn R	0	0		
1997–98	Blackburn R	0	0		
1998–99	Blackburn R	0	0		
1999–2000	Bournemouth	3	0		
2000–01	Bournemouth	35	0		
2001–02	Bournemouth	45	0		
2002–03	Bournemouth	1	0		
2003–04	Bournemouth	0	0		
2004–05	Bournemouth	42	0		
2005–06	Bournemouth	20	0		
2006–07	Bournemouth	18	0		
2008–09	Bournemouth	0	0	164	0
2011–12	Yeovil T	1	0		
2012–13	Yeovil T	3	0		
2013–14	Yeovil T	1	0	2	0

WEBSTER, Byron (D)   143 12
H: 6 5 W: 12 07 b.Sherburn-in-Elmet 31-3-87

2007–08	Siad Most	23	4		
2008–09	Siad Most	0	0	23	4
2009–10	Doncaster R	5	0		
2010–11	Doncaster R	7	0	12	0
2010–11	Hereford U	2	0	2	0
2010–11	Northampton T	8	0		
2011–12	Northampton T	13	0	21	0
2012–13	Yeovil T	44	5		
2013–14	Yeovil T	41	3	85	8

YORK C (92)

ALLAN, Tom (D)   10 0
b.York 30-10-94

2012–13	York C	5	0		
2013–14	York C	5	0	10	0

ANDREW, Calvin (F)   196 12
H: 6 0 W: 12 11 b.Luton 19-12-86

2004–05	Luton T	8	0		
2005–06	Luton T	1	1		
2005–06	Grimsby T	8	1	8	1
2005–06	Bristol C	3	0	3	0
2006–07	Luton T	7	1		
2007–08	Luton T	39	2	55	4
2008–09	Crystal Palace	7	0		
2008–09	Brighton & HA	9	2	9	2
2009–10	Crystal Palace	27	1		
2010–11	Crystal Palace	13	0		
2010–11	Millwall	0	0	3	0
2010–11	Swindon T	10	1	10	1
2011–12	Crystal Palace	6	0	53	1
2011–12	Leyton Orient	10	0	10	0
2012–13	Port Vale	22	1		
2013–14	Port Vale	0	0	22	1
2013–14	Mansfield T	15	1	15	1
2013–14	York C	8	1	8	1

BOWMAN, Ryan (F)   46 8
H: 6 2 W: 11 12 b.Carlisle 30-11-91

2009–10	Carlisle U	6	0		
2010–11	Carlisle U	3	0	9	0
From Darlington, Hereford U					
2013–14	York C	37	8	37	8

CARSON, Josh (M)   67 9
H: 5 9 W: 11 00 b.Ballymena 3-6-93
Internationals: Northern Ireland U16, U17, U18, U19, U21, Full caps.

2010–11	Ipswich T	9	3		
2011–12	Ipswich T	16	2		
2012–13	Ipswich T	6	0		
2012–13	York C	5	0		

Season	Club	App	Gls	Tot App	Tot Gls
2013–14	Ipswich T	0	0	31	5
2013–14	York C	31	4	36	4

CHAMBERLAIN, Tom (F) 2 0

Season	Club	App	Gls	Tot App	Tot Gls
2013–14	York C	2	0	2	0

CHAMBERS, Ashley (F) 65 10
H: 5 10 W: 11 06 b.Leicester 1-3-90
Internationals: England C, U16, U17, U18, U19.

Season	Club	App	Gls	Tot App	Tot Gls
2005–06	Leicester C	0	0		
2006–07	Leicester C	0	0		
2007–08	Leicester C	5	0		
2008–09	Leicester C	1	0		
2009–10	Leicester C	0	0	6	0
2009–10	Wycombe W	0	0		
2009–10	Grimsby T	0	0		
2012–13	York C	38	10		
2013–14	York C	15	0	53	10
2013–14	Dagenham & R	6	0	6	0

CLAY, Craig (M) 35 1
H: 5 11 W: 11 07 b.Nottingham 5-5-92

Season	Club	App	Gls	Tot App	Tot Gls
2010–11	Chesterfield	3	1		
2011–12	Chesterfield	5	0		
2012–13	Chesterfield	19	0	27	1
2013–14	York C	8	0	8	0

COULSON, Michael (F) 97 16
H: 5 10 W: 10 00 b.Scarborough 4-4-88
Internationals: England C.

Season	Club	App	Gls	Tot App	Tot Gls
2006–07	Barnsley	2	0		
2007–08	Barnsley	12	0		
2008–09	Barnsley	2	0		
2009–10	Barnsley	0	0	16	0
2009–10	Grimsby T	29	5	29	5
2012–13	York C	19	4		
2013–14	York C	33	7	52	11

CRESSWELL, Richard (F) 573 122
H: 6 0 W: 11 08 b.Bridlington 20-9-77
Internationals: England U21.

Season	Club	App	Gls	Tot App	Tot Gls
1995–96	York C	16	1		
1996–97	York C	17	0		
1996–97	*Mansfield T*	5	1	5	1
1997–98	York C	26	4		
1998–99	York C	36	16		
1998–99	Sheffield W	7	1		
1999–2000	Sheffield W	20	1		
2000–01	Sheffield W	4	0	31	2
2000–01	Leicester C	8	0	8	0
2000–01	Preston NE	11	2		
2001–02	Preston NE	40	13		
2002–03	Preston NE	42	16		
2003–04	Preston NE	45	2		
2004–05	Preston NE	46	16		
2005–06	Preston NE	3	0	187	49
2005–06	Leeds U	16	5		
2006–07	Leeds U	22	4	38	9
2007–08	Stoke C	43	11		
2008–09	Stoke C	29	0		
2009–10	Stoke C	2	0	74	11
2009–10	Sheffield U	31	12		
2010–11	Sheffield U	35	5		
2011–12	Sheffield U	42	9		
2012–13	Sheffield U	16	1	124	27
2012–13	*York C*	5	2		
2013–14	York C	6	0	106	23

DICKINSON, Chris (F) 2 0

Season	Club	App	Gls	Tot App	Tot Gls
2013–14	York C	2	0	2	0

FLETCHER, Wes (F) 64 15
H: 5 11 W: 12 06 b.Ormskirk 28-2-91

Season	Club	App	Gls	Tot App	Tot Gls
2009–10	Burnley	0	0		
2009–10	*Grimsby T*	6	1	6	1
2010–11	Burnley	0	0		
2010–11	*Stockport Co*	9	1	9	1
2011–12	Burnley	0	0		
2011–12	*Accrington S*	10	2	10	2
2011–12	*Crewe Alex*	6	1	6	1
2012–13	Burnley	0	0		
2012–13	*Yeovil T*	1	0	1	0
2013–14	York C	32	10	32	10

FYFIELD, Jamal (D) 35 0
b.Leyton 17-3-89

Season	Club	App	Gls	Tot App	Tot Gls
2012–13	York C	33	0		
2013–14	York C	2	0	35	0

INGHAM, Michael (G) 195 0
H: 6 4 W: 13 08 b.Preston 9-7-80
Internationals: Northern Ireland U18, U21, Full caps.

Season	Club	App	Gls	Tot App	Tot Gls
1998–99	Cliftonville	18	0	18	0
1999–2000	Sunderland	0	0		
1999–2000	*Carlisle U*	7	0	7	0
2000–01	Sunderland	0	0		
2001–02	Sunderland	0	0		
2001–02	*Stoke C*	0	0		
2002–03	Sunderland	0	0		
2002–03	*Darlington*	3	0	3	0
2002–03	*York C*	17	0		
2003–04	Sunderland	0	0		
2003–04	*Wrexham*	11	0		
2004–05	Sunderland	2	0	2	0
2004–05	*Doncaster R*	1	0	1	0
2005–06	Wrexham	40	0		
2006–07	Wrexham	31	0	82	0
2012–13	York C	46	0		
2013–14	York C	19	0	82	0

JARVIS, Ryan (F) 268 41
H: 6 1 W: 11 11 b.Fakenham 11-7-86
Internationals: England U16, U17, U19.

Season	Club	App	Gls	Tot App	Tot Gls
2002–03	Norwich C	3	0		
2003–04	Norwich C	12	1		
2004–05	Norwich C	4	1		
2004–05	*Colchester U*	6	0	6	0
2005–06	Norwich C	4	1		
2006–07	Norwich C	5	0		
2006–07	*Leyton Orient*	14	6		
2007–08	Norwich C	1	0	29	3
2007–08	*Kilmarnock*	9	1	9	1
2007–08	*Notts Co*	17	2	17	2
2008–09	Leyton Orient	31	0		
2009–10	Leyton Orient	42	8		
2010–11	Leyton Orient	11	2	98	16
2010–11	*Northampton T*	3	0	3	0
2011–12	Walsall	19	2	19	2
2011–12	Torquay U	14	2		
2012–13	Torquay U	38	7	52	9
2013–14	York C	35	8	35	8

LOWE, Keith (D) 238 13
H: 6 2 W: 13 03 b.Wolverhampton 13-9-85

Season	Club	App	Gls	Tot App	Tot Gls
2004–05	Wolverhampton W	11	0		
2005–06	Wolverhampton W	3	0		
2005–06	*Burnley*	16	0	16	0
2005–06	*QPR*	1	0	1	0
2005–06	*Swansea C*	4	0	4	0
2006–07	Wolverhampton W	0	0		
2006–07	*Brighton & HA*	0	0		
2006–07	*Cheltenham T*	16	1		
2007–08	Wolverhampton W	0	0		
2007–08	*Port Vale*	28	3	28	3
2008–09	Wolverhampton W	0	0	14	0
2009–10	Hereford U	19	1	19	1
2010–11	Cheltenham T	36	1		
2011–12	Cheltenham T	30	1		
2012–13	Cheltenham T	31	4		
2013–14	Cheltenham T	13	1	126	8
2013–14	York C	30	1	30	1

McCOMBE, John (D) 250 19
H: 6 2 W: 13 00 b.Pontefract 7-5-85

Season	Club	App	Gls	Tot App	Tot Gls
2001–02	Huddersfield T	1	0		
2003–04	Huddersfield T	0	0		
2004–05	Huddersfield T	5	0		
2005–06	Huddersfield T	1	0		
2005–06	*Torquay U*	0	0		
2006–07	Huddersfield T	7	0	14	0
2007–08	Hereford U	27	0	27	0
2008–09	Port Vale	31	2		
2009–10	Port Vale	40	3		
2010–11	Port Vale	42	4		
2011–12	Port Vale	40	1		
2012–13	Port Vale	32	1		
2013–14	Port Vale	0	0	185	14
2013–14	*Mansfield T*	5	2	5	2
2013–14	York C	3	1	19	3

McGURK, David (D) 90 7
H: 6 0 W: 11 08 b.Middlesbrough 30-9-82

Season	Club	App	Gls	Tot App	Tot Gls
2001–02	Darlington	12	0		
2002–03	Darlington	4	0		
2003–04	Darlington	27	4		
2004–05	Darlington	10	2		
2005–06	Darlington	3	0	56	6
2012–13	York C	11	0		
2013–14	York C	23	1	34	1

MONTROSE, Lewis (M) 157 10
H: 6 0 W: 12 00 b.Manchester 17-11-88

Season	Club	App	Gls	Tot App	Tot Gls
2006–07	Wigan Ath	0	0		
2007–08	Wigan Ath	0	0		
2008–09	Wigan Ath	0	0		
2008–09	*Cheltenham T*	5	0	5	0
2008–09	*Chesterfield*	12	0	12	0
2009–10	Wycombe W	14	0		
2010–11	Wycombe W	36	4	50	4
2011–12	Gillingham	37	4		
2012–13	Gillingham	15	1	52	5
2012–13	*Oxford U*	5	0	5	0
2013–14	York C	33	1	33	1

MURRAY, Cameron (M) 0 0

Season	Club	App	Gls	Tot App	Tot Gls
2013–14	York C	0	0		

OYEBANJO, Lanre (D) 71 0
H: 6 1 W: 11 04 b.Hackney 24-4-90
Internationals: Republic of Ireland U19, U21.

Season	Club	App	Gls	Tot App	Tot Gls
2012–13	York C	30	0		
2013–14	York C	41	0	71	0

PARSLOW, Daniel (D) 58 1
H: 5 11 W: 12 05 b.Cardiff 11-9-85
Internationals: Wales U17, U19, U21.

Season	Club	App	Gls	Tot App	Tot Gls
2012–13	York C	45	1		
2013–14	York C	13	0	58	1

PENN, Russ (M) 207 9
H: 5 11 W: 12 13 b.Dudley 8-11-85
Internationals: England C.

Season	Club	App	Gls	Tot App	Tot Gls
2009–10	Burton Alb	40	4		
2010–11	Burton Alb	41	3	81	7
2011–12	Cheltenham T	43	1		
2012–13	Cheltenham T	43	1		
2013–14	Cheltenham T	19	0	105	2
2013–14	York C	21	0	21	0

PLATT, Tom (M) 27 0
H: 6 1 W: 12 13 b.Pontefract 1-10-93

Season	Club	App	Gls	Tot App	Tot Gls
2012–13	York C	7	0		
2013–14	York C	20	0	27	0

PURI, Sander (M) 176 44
H: 5 10 W: 10 02 b.Tartu 7-5-88
Internationals: Estonia Full caps.

Season	Club	App	Gls	Tot App	Tot Gls
2004	Tartu	18	12	18	12
2005	Levadia Tallinn	13	2		
2006	Levadia Tallinn	6	1		
2007	Levadia Tallinn	1	0		
2007	*Tulevik Viljandi*	14	4	14	4
2008	Levadia Tallinn	34	11		
2009	Levadia Tallinn	19	10	73	24
2009–10	Larissa	11	1		
2010–11	Larissa	10	0		
2010–11	*Korona Kielce*	8	1	8	1
2011–12	Larissa	0	0	21	1
2011–12	*Papa*	12	0	12	0
2012	KuPS Kuopio	19	2	19	2
2012–13	St Mirren	3	0	3	0
2013–14	York C	8	0	8	0

REED, Adam (M) 66 3
H: 5 5 W: 10 03 b.Hartlepool 8-5-91

Season	Club	App	Gls	Tot App	Tot Gls
2009–10	Sunderland	0	0		
2010–11	Sunderland	0	0		
2010–11	*Brentford*	11	0	11	0
2011–12	Sunderland	0	0		
2011–12	*Bradford C*	4	0	4	0
2011–12	*Leyton Orient*	11	0	11	0
2012–13	Sunderland	0	0		
2012–13	*Portsmouth*	10	0	10	0
2012–13	*York C*	6	2		
2013–14	Sunderland	0	0		
2013–14	*Burton Alb*	5	1	5	1
2013–14	York C	19	0	25	2

SMITH, Chris (D) 133 4
H: 5 10 W: 12 05 b.Derby 30-6-81

Season	Club	App	Gls	Tot App	Tot Gls
1999–2000	Reading	0	0		
2000–01	Reading	0	0		
2001–02	York C	15	0		
2002–03	York C	36	0		
2003–04	York C	28	0		

From Tamworth, Mansfield T

Season	Club	App	Gls	Tot App	Tot Gls
2012–13	York C	45	4		
2013–14	York C	9	0	133	4

Scholars
Andrew, Daniel Paul; Archer, Joshua; Banks, Christopher James; Bowkett, Joshua Vincent; Chamberlain, Thomas Liam; Coates, Harry Ryan; Collis, Aaron Luke; Green, James; Hardey, Liam Thomas; Morley, Adam Alan; Outerbridge, Jordan Isaiah; Rzonca, Callum James; Smith, Oliver Henry Canvin; Tilsley, Niall Joshua; Wilson, George Daniel; Wright, Daniel Mark.

ENGLISH LEAGUE PLAYERS – INDEX

NATIONAL LIST OF REFEREES FOR SEASON 2014–15

REFEREES

First Year Referee

Adcock, JG (James) – Nottinghamshire
Atkinson, M (Martin) – West Yorkshire
Attwell, SB (Stuart) – Warwickshire
Bankes, P (Peter) – Merseyside*
Berry, CJ (Carl) – Surrey
Bond, D (Darren) – Lancashire
Boyeson, C (Carl) – East Yorkshire
Bratt, S (Stephen) – West Midlands
Breakspear, C (Charles) – Surrey
Brown, M (Mark) – East Yorkshire
Bull, M (Michael) – Essex
Clark, R (Richard) – Northumberland
Clattenburg, M (Mark) – County Durham
Collins, LM (Lee) – Surrey
Coote, D (David) – West Yorkshire
Davies, A (Andy) – Hampshire
Deadman, D (Darren) – Cambridgeshire
Dean, ML (Mike) – Wirral
Dowd, P (Phil) – Staffordshire
Drysdale, D (Darren) – Lincolnshire
Duncan, S (Scott) – Northumberland
D'urso, AP (Andy) – Essex
East, R (Roger) – Wiltshire
Eltringham, G (Geoff) – Tyne & Wear
Foy, CJ (Chris) – Merseyside

Friend, KA (Kevin) – Leicestershire
Gibbs, PN (Phil) – West Midlands
Graham F (Fred) – Essex
Haines, A (Andy) – Tyne & Wear
Handley, D (Darren) – Lancashire*
Harrington, T (Tony) – Cleveland
Haywood, M (Mark) – West Yorkshire
Heywood, M (Mark) – Cheshire
Hill, K (Keith) – Hertfordshire
Hooper, SA (Simon) – Wiltshire
Horwood, G (Graham) – Bedfordshire
Ilderton, EL (Eddie) – Tyne & Wear
Johnson, K (Kevin) – Somerset*
Jones, MJ (Michael) – Cheshire
Kavanagh, C (Chris) – Manchester*
Kettle, TM (Trevor) – Leicestershire
Langford, O (Oliver) – West Midlands
Lewis, RL (Rob) – Shropshire
Linington, JJ (James) – Isle of Wight
Madley, AJ (Andy) – West Yorkshire
Madley, RJ (Bobby) – West Yorkshire
Malone, BJ (Brendan) – Wiltshire
Marriner, AM (André) – West Midlands
Martin, S (Stephen) – Staffordshire
Mason, LS (Lee) – Lancashire
Mathieson, SW (Scott) – Cheshire
Miller, NS (Nigel) – County Durham
Miller, P (Pat) – Bedfordshire

Mohareb, D (Dean) – Cheshire
Moss, J (Jon) – West Yorkshire
Naylor, MA (Michael) – South Yorkshire
Oliver, M (Michael) – Northumberland
Pawson, CL (Craig) – South Yorkshire
Probert, LW (Lee) – Wiltshire
Robinson, T (Tim) – West Sussex
Russell, MP (Mick) – Hertfordshire
Salisbury, G (Graham) – Lancashire
Sarginson, CD (Chris) – Staffordshire
Scott, GD (Graham) – Oxfordshire
Sheldrake, D (Darren) – Surrey
Simpson, J (Jeremy) – Lancashire
Stockbridge, S (Seb) – Tyne & Wear
Stroud, KP (Keith) – Hampshire
Sutton, GJ (Gary) – Lincolnshire
Swarbrick, ND (Neil) – Lancashire
Taylor, A (Anthony) – Cheshire
Tierney, P Paul) – Lancashire
Ward, GL (Gavin) – Surrey
Webb, D (David) – County Durham
Webb, HM (Howard) – South Yorkshire
Whitestone, D (Dean) – Northamptonshire
Williamson, IG (Iain) – Berkshire
Woolmer, KA (Andy) – Northamptonshire
Wright, KK (Kevin) – Merseyside

ASSISTANT REFEREES

First Year Assistant

Akers, C (Chris) – South Yorkshire
Amey, JR (Justin) – Dorset
Amphlett, MJ (Marvyn) – Worcestershire
Astley, MA (Mark) – Manchester
Atkin, R (Robert) – Lincolnshire
Atkin, RT (Ryan) – London
Avent, D (David) – Northamptonshire
Aylott, A (Andrew) – Bedfordshire
Backhouse, A (Anthony) – Cumbria
Barnard, N (Nicholas) – Cheshire*
Barratt, W (Wayne) – Worcestershire
Barrow, SJ (Simon) – Staffordshire
Bartlett, R (Richard) – Cheshire
Beck, S (Simon_ – Bedfordshire
Bennett, A (Andrew) – Devon
Bennett, S (Simon) – Staffordshire
Benton, DK (David) – South Yorkshire
Beswick, G (Gary) – County Durham
Betts, L (Lee) – Norfolk
Bingham, M (Michael) – Warwickshire
Blunden, D (Darren) – Kent

Bramall, T (Thomas) – Sheffield*
Bristow, M (Matthew) – Manchester
Bromley, A (Adam) – Devon
Brook, C (Carl) – East Sussex
Brooks, J (John) – Leicestershire
Bryan, D (Dave) – Lincolnshire
Bull, W (William) – Hampshire
Buonassisi, M (Mathew) – Northamptonshire
Burt, S (Stuart) – Northamptonshire
Busby, J (John) – Oxfordshire
Bushell, DD (David) – London
Butler, S (Stuart) – Kent
Byrne, H (Helen) – Liverpool*
Cann, D (Darren) – Norfolk
Cheosiaua, D-R (Dumitru-Ravel) – Worcestershire*
Child, S (Stephen) – Kent
Clark, J (Joseph) – West Midlands
Clayton, A (Alan) – Cheshire
Clayton, S (Simon) – County Durham
Coggins, A (Anthony) – Oxfordshire
Collin, J (Jake) – Merseyside
Cook, D (Daniel) – Hampshire
Cook, P (Paul) – East Yorkshire
Cooper, IJ (Ian) – Kent
Cooper, N (Nicholas) – Suffolk

Copeland, SJ (Steven) – Merseyside
Corlett, M (Matthew) – Liverpool*
Coy, M (Martin) – Durham
Cropp, B (Barry) – Lancashire
Crysell, A (Adam) – Essex
D'aguilar, M (Michael) – Staffordshire
Dale, A (Alan) – Suffolk
Daly, SDJ (Stephen) – Middlesex
Davies, N (Neil) – London
Degnarain, A (Ashvin) – London
Denton, MJ (Michael) – Lancashire
Dermott, P (Philip) – Lancashire
Derrien, M (Mark) – Dorset
Dicicco, M (Matthew) – Cleveland
Donohue, M (Matthew) – Manchester*
Dudley, IA (Ian) – Nottinghamshire
Duncan, M (Mark) – Cheshire
Durie, B (Brian) – Gloucestershire*
Dwyer, M (Mark) – West Yorkshire
Eagland, S (Stuart) – Staffordshire*
Eaton, D (Derek) – Gloucestershire
Edwards, M (Marc) – Durham*
England, D (Darren) – South Yorkshire
Evans, K (Karl) – Lancashire

Farries, J (John) – Oxfordshire
Fearn, AE (Amy) – Leicestershire
Finch, S (Steven) – Southampton
Fissenden, I (Ian) – Kent
Fitch, C (Carl) – Suffolk
Flynn, J (John) – Wiltshire
Foley, MJ (Matt) – London
Ford, D (Declan) – Lincolnshire
Fox, A (Andrew) – Warwickshire
Fyvie, G (Graeme) – Tyne & Wear
Ganfield, R (Ron) – Somerset
Garratt, A (Andy) – West Midlands
Garratt, S (Sarah) – West Midlands
George, M (Mike) – Norfolk
Gibbons, N (Nick) – Lancashire
Gooch, P (Peter) – Lancashire
Gordon, B (Barry) – County Durham
Graham, P (Paul) – Manchester
Gratton, D (Danny) – Staffordshire
Greenhalgh, N (Nick) – Lancashire
Greenwood, AH (Alf) –
   North Yorkshire
Griffiths, M (Mark) –
   South Yorkshire
Grunnill, W (Wayne) –
   East Yorkshire
Hair, NA (Neil) – Cambridgeshire
Halliday, A (Andy) –
   North Yorkshire
Hanley, M (Michael) – Liverpool*
Harris, P (Paul) – Kent
Hart, G (Glen) – County Durham
Hatzidakis, C (Constantine) – Kent
Haycock, KW (Ken) –
   South Yorkshire
Hendley, AR (Andy) –
   West Midlands
Hicks, C (Craig) – Surrey
Hillier, J(Jake) – Hertfordshire
Hilton, G (Gary) – Lancashire
Hobbis, N (Nick) – West Midlands
Hobday, P (Paul) – West Midlands
Hodges, R (Robert) –
   Buckinghamshire
Hodskinson, P (Paul) – Lancashire
Holderness, BC (Barry) – Essex
Holmes, A (Adrian) –
   West Yorkshire
Hopkins, AJ (Adam) – Devon
Hopton, N (Nicholas) – Derbyshire*
Howes, M (Mark) – Birmingham
Howson, A (Akil) – Leicestershire*
Hudson, S (Shaun) – Tyne & Wear
Hull, J (Joe) – Cheshire
Hulme, R (Richard) – Somerset
Hunt, J (Jonathan) – Liverpool
Husband, C (Christopher) –
   Worcestershire*
Hussin, I (Ian) – Merseyside
Huxtable, B (Brett) – Devon
Hyde, RA (Robert) – London
Johnson, RL (Ryan) – Manchester
Jones, M (Matthew) – Staffordshire*
Jones, MT (Mark) – Nottinghamshire
Jones, RJ (Robert) – Merseyside
Joyce, R (Ross) – Cleveland
Kane, G (Graham) – East Sussex
Kaye, E (Elliott) – Essex
Kelly, P (Paul) – Kent
Kendall, R (Richard) – Bedfordshire

Kettlewell, PT (Paul) – Lancashire
Khatib, B (Billy) – County Durham
Kinseley, N (Nick) – Essex
Kirk, T (Thomas) – Cheshire*
Kirkup, P (Peter) –
   Northamptonshire
Knapp, SC (Simon) – Bristol
Knowles, CJ (Chris) –
   Northamptonshire
Laver, AA (Andrew) – Hampshire
Law, GC (Geoff) – Leicestershire
Law, J (John) – Worcestershire
Lawson, KD (Keith) –
   South Humberside
Leach, D (Daniel) – Oxfordshire
Ledger, S (Scott) – South Yorkshire
Lennard, H (Harry) – East Sussex
Liddle, G (Geoff) – County Durham
Linden, W (Wes) – Middlesex
Long, S (Simon) – Cornwall
Lucas, S (Simeon) – Lancashire
Lugg, N (Nigel) – Surrey
Lymer, C (Colin) – Hampshire
Mcdonough, M (Mick) –
   Northumberland
Mcgrath, M (Matt) – East Yorkshire
Mackay, R (Rob) – Bedfordshire
Magill, JP (John) – Essex
Mainwaring, J (James) – Lancashire
Markham, DR (Danny) –
   Tyne & Wear
Marsden, PR (Paul) – Lancashire
Martin, RJ (Richard) –
   Weston-super-Mare
Massey-Ellis, R (Rob) –
   West Midlands
Massey-Ellis, S (Sian) –
   West Midlands
Mather, S (Simon) – Manchester
Matthews, A (Adam) –
   Gloucestershire
Mattocks, KJ (Kevin) – Lancashire
Meeson, DP (Daniel) – Staffordshire
Mellor, G (Gareth) –
   West Yorkshire*
Mellor, JM (Mark) – Hertfordshire
Merchant, R (Rob) – Staffordshire
Meredith, S (Steven) –
   Nottinghamshire
Metcalfe, RL (Lee) – Lancashire
Morris, K (Kevin) – Herefordshire*
Muge, G (Gavin) – Bedfordshire
Mullarkey, M (Mike) – Devon
Mulraine, K (Kevin) – Cumbria
Newbold, AM (Andy) –
   Leicestershire
Nield, T (Tom) – West Yorkshire
Norcott, WG (Wade) – Essex
Nunn, A (Adam) – Wiltshire
O'brien, J (John) – London
O'donnell, CJ (Chris) – Bedfordshire
Oldham, SA (Scott) – Lancashire
Parry, MJ (Matthew) – Liverpool
Pashley, A (Alix) – Derbyshire*
Peart, T (Tony) – North Yorkshire
Perry, M (Marc) – West Midlands
Plane, S (Steven) – Worcestershire
Plowright, DP (David) –
   Nottinghamshire
Pollard, C (Christopher) – Suffolk*

Porter, W (Wayne) – Lincolnshire
Pottage, M (Mark) – Dorset
Powell, CI (Chris) – Dorset
Purkiss, S (Sam) – London
Quin, A (Andrew) – Devon*
Radford, N (Neil) – Worcestershire
Ramsey, T (Thomas) – Essex
Rashid, L (Lisa) – Birmingham*
Rathbone, I (Ian) –
   Northamptonshire
Rees, P (Paul) – Somerset
Richardson, D (David) –
   West Yorkshire
Robathan, DM (Daniel) – Surrey
Roberts, B (Bob) – Lancashire
Rock, DK (David) – Hertfordshire
Ross, SJ (Stephen) – Lincolnshire
Rushton, S (Steven) – Staffordshire
Russell, GR (Geoff) –
   Northamptonshire
Russell, M (Mark) – Somerset
Salisbury, M (Michael) – Lancashire
Saliy, O (Oleksandr) – Middlesex
Sannerude, A (Adrian) – Suffolk
Scholes, M (Mark) –
   Buckinghamshire
Scregg, AJ (Andrew) – Liverpool
Sharp, N (Neil) – Cleveland
Siddall, I (Iain) – Lancashire
Slaughter, A (Ashley) – West Sussex
Smallwood, W (William) – Cheshire
Smart, E (Eddie) – West Midlands
Smith, M (Michael) – Essex
Smith, N (Nigel) – Derbyshire
Smith, R (Rob) – Hertfordshire*
Storrie, D (David) – West Yorkshire
Strain, D (Darren) – Cheshire
Street, DR (Duncan) –
   West Yorkshire
Stretton, GS (Guy) – Leicestershire
Swabey, L (Lee) – Devon
Tankard, A (Anthony) –
   South Yorkshire
Taylor, G (Grant) – Warwickshire
Thompson, PI (Paul) – Derbyshire
Toner, B (Ben) – Lancashire
Tranter, A (Adrian) – Dorset
Treleaven, D (Dean) – West Sussex
Turner, A (Andrew) – Devon
Tyas, J (Jason) – West Yorkshire
Venamore, L (Lee) – Kent
Wade, C (Christopher) – Hampshire*
Wade, S (Stephen) – East Yorkshire*
Webb, MP (Michael) – Surrey
West, R (Richard) – East Riding
Whiteley, J (Jason) – West Yorkshire
Whitton, RP (Rob) – Essex
Wigglesworth, RJ (Richard) –
   South Yorkshire
Wild, R (Richard) – Lancashire*
Wilkes, M (Matthew) –
   West Midlands
Wilson, J (James) – Cheshire
Wilson, M (Marc) – Cambridgeshire
Wood, T (Tim) – Gloucestershire
Wootton, R (Ricky) –
   West Yorkshire
Wright, P (Peter) – Merseyside
Yates, O (Oliver) – Staffordshire
Young, A (Alan) – Cambridgeshire

MANAGERS – IN AND OUT 2013–14

JULY 2013
13   Manager Kevin McDonald leaves Swindon T by mutual consent; Mark Cooper appointed caretaker.
16   Gus Poyet's sacking as manager of Brighton & HA is confirmed after he lost his internal disciplinary appeal for gross misconduct.
23   Gareth Southgate appointed manager of England U21 team.

AUGUST 2013
20   Mark Cooper appointed manager of Swindon T after being in temporary charge.
    Hope Powell sacked as manager of England Women's team after 15 years in charge.

SEPTEMBER 2013
9   Greg Abbott sacked as manager of Carlisle U; assistant manager Graham Kavanagh appointed caretaker. Only Arsene Wenger at Arsenal and Exeter's Paul Tisdale were longer-serving managers than Abbott when he was dismissed.
23   Paolo Di Canio sacked as manager of Sunderland after only 6 months and 12 league games in charge; Kevin Ball appointed caretaker for the second time, he was previously caretaker in 2006 after Mick McCarthy had been sacked. Oscar Garcia appointed caretaker of Brighton & HA.
28   Nigel Clough sacked as manager of Derby Co after 4 years in charge. He was the longest serving manager in the Championship.
30   Former England coach, Steve McClaren appointed manager of Derby Co.
    Graham Kavanagh appointed manager of Carlisle U after being in temporary charge.

OCTOBER 2013
8   Gus Poyet appointed manager of Sunderland.
11   David Weir sacked as manager of Sheffield U after only 13 games in charge; Chris Morgan appointed caretaker for the second time, he was caretaker last season when he took the reins after Danny Wilson left.
13   Martin Allen sacked as manager of Gillingham; John Schofield appointed caretaker.
14   Kevin Blackwell sacked as manager of Bury; Ronnie Jepson appointed caretaker.
    Peter Taylor takes over as caretaker manager of Gillingham.
21   Tony Mowbray sacked as manager of Middlesbrough; Mark Venus appointed caretaker.
23   Crystal Palace manager Ian Holloway leaves by mutual consent; Keith Millen appointed caretaker.
    Nigel Clough appointed manager of Sheffield U.
27   Notts Co manager Chris Kiwomya leaves by mutual consent; Steve Hodge appointed caretaker.

NOVEMBER 2013
5   Martin O'Neill confirmed as manager of Republic of Ireland with Roy Keane as his assistant.
6   Shaun Derry appointed manager of Notts Co.
11   Peter Taylor confirmed as manager of Gillingham after spell as caretaker.
13   Aitor Karanka appointed as manager of Middlesbrough, he had previously worked as assistant to Jose Mourinho at Real Madrid.
20   Brian Laws sacked as manager of Scunthorpe U; Russ Wilcox appointed caretaker.
23   Tony Pulis appointed manager of Crystal Palace.
25   Guy Wittingham sacked as manager of Portsmouth; Andy Awford appointed caretaker.
27   Richie Barker sacked as manager of Crawley T; Martin Hishelwood and Gary Alexander appointed caretakers.
28   Sean O'Driscoll sacked as manager of Bristol C; John Pemberton appointed caretaker.
30   David Flitcroft sacked as manager of Barnsley; Micky Mellon appointed caretaker.

DECEMBER 2013
1   Dave Jones sacked as manager of Sheffield W; Stuart Gray appointed caretaker.
    Martin Jol sacked as manager of Fulham; assistant manager Rene Muelensteen appointed manager.
2   Owen Coyle sacked as manager of Wigan Ath; Graham Barrow appointed caretaker.
3   John Gregory appointed manager of Crawley T after a six-year managerial exile.
    Steve Cotterill appointed manager of Bristol C.
7   Uwe Rosler appointed manager of Wigan Ath after leaving his post as manager of Brentford.
9   Richie Barker appointed manager of Portsmouth.
10   David Flitcroft appointed manager of Bury.
    Mark Warburton appointed manager of Brentford swapping his role from Sporting Director at the club.
14   Steve Clarke sacked as manager of WBA; Keith Downing appointed caretaker.
16   Andre Villas Boas sacked as manager of Tottenham H; Tim Sherwood and Les Ferdinand appointed caretakers.
    Gianfranco Zola resigns as manager of Watford.
18   Giuseppe Sannino appointed manager of Watford.

17   Danny Wilson appointed manager of Barnsley for the second time, 15 years after his first spell in charge.
21   Aidy Boothroyd sacked as manger of Northampton T; Andy King appointed caretaker.
23   Tim Sherwood appointed manager of Tottenham H.
24   Russ Wilcox appointed manager of Scunthorpe U after being in temporary charge.
26   Steve Lomas sacked as manager of Millwall; Neil Harris appointed caretaker.
27   Malky Mackay sacked as manger of Cardiff C; David Kerslake appointed caretaker.

JANUARY 2014
2   Ole Gunnar Solskaer appointed manager of Cardiff C.
    Alan Knill sacked as manager of Torquay U.
6   Ian Holloway appointed manager of Millwall.
    Chris Hargreaves appointed manager of Torquay U.
9   Pepe Mel appointed manager of WBA.
18   Edgar Davids resigns as manager of Skrill Premier Barnet.
21   Paul Ince sacked as manager of Blackpool; Barry Ferguson appointed caretaker.
    Graham Turner resigns as manager of Shrewsbury T; Mike Jackson appointed caretaker.
25   Stuart Gray appointed manager of Sheffield W after being in temporary charge.
26   Chris Wilder resigns as manager of Oxford U; Micky Lewis appointed caretaker.
27   Chris Wilder appointed manager of Northampton T.

FEBRUARY 2014
4   Michael Laudrup sacked as manager of Swansea C; Garry Monk appointed caretaker.
14   Rene Muelensteen sacked as manager of Fulham; Felix Magath, one-time manager of Bayern Munich appointed manager.
17   Ronnie Moore suspended as manager of Tranmere R pending a FA investigation into a potential breach of betting rules; assistant John McMahon appointed caretaker manager.
21   Mike Jackson appointed manager of Shrewsbury T after being in temporary charge.

MARCH 2014
11   Chris Powell sacked as manager of Charlton Ath; former Standard Liege boss Jose Riga appointed manager.
22   Gary Waddock appointed manager of Oxford U.
24   Billy Davies sacked as manager of Nottingham F; Gary Brazil appointed caretaker.
27   Richie Barker sacked as manager of Portsmouth; Andy Awford takes temporary charge for the second time this season.
28   John Ward leaves job as manager of Bristol R to take up a new role as Director of Football with his assistant Darrell Clarke becoming the manager.

APRIL 2014
4   Stuart Pearce appointed manager of Nottingham F with his appointment beginning 1 July. Gary Brazil remains in temporary charge.
6   Chris Hughton sacked as manager of Norwich C; youth team coach Neil Adams appointed manager.
9   Ronnie Moore sacked as manager of Tranmere R after being suspended since February; John McMahon continues as caretaker manager.
22   David Moyes sacked as manager of Manchester U; Ryan Giggs appointed caretaker manager.

MAY 2014
1   Andy Awford appointed manager of Portsmouth after being in temporary charge.
7   Gary Monk appointed manager of Swansea C after being in temporary charge.
12   Pepe Mel leaves as manager of WBA by mutual consent.
    Oscar Garcia resigns as manager of Brighton & HA.
    Mike Jackson sacked as manager of Shrewsbury T; Micky Mellon appointed manager. Jackson stays on as Mellon's assistant manager.
13   Tim Sherwood sacked as manager of Tottenham H.
19   Louis van Gaal appointed manager of Manchester U; Ryan Giggs appointed assistant manager.
23   Jose Riga leaves Charlton Athletic by mutual consent.
27   Mauricio Pochettino leaves Southampton to take up manager's position at Tottenham H.
    Bob Peeters appointed as manager of Charlton Athletic.
    Rob Edwards appointed manager of Tranmere R.
30   Brian McDermott sacked as manager of Leeds U.

JUNE 2014
6   Sami Hyypia appointed manager of Brighton & HA.
11   Jose Riga appointed manager of Blackpool.
14   Alan Irvine appointed manager of WBA.
16   Ronald Koeman appointed manager of Southampton.

JULY 2014
1   Roy Keane appointed assistant manager at Aston Villa.
4   Gary Waddock sacked as manager of Oxford U. Michael Appleton appointed manager.

TRANSFERS 2013–14

JUNE 2013 TRANSFERS	From	To	Fee in £
24 Adeyemi, Tom	Norwich C	Birmingham C	Free
18 Affane, Amin	Chelsea	Energie Cottbus	Free
11 Alessandra, Lewis	Morecambe	Plymouth Arg	Free
14 Amoo, David	Tranmere R	Carlisle U	Free
27 Arshavin, Andrey	Arsenal	Zenit St Petersburg	Free
24 Audel, Thierry	Macclesfield T	Crewe Alex	Undisclosed
25 Barthram, Jack	Tottenham H	Swindon T	Free
24 Batt, Shaun	Millwall	Leyton Orient	Free
17 Bidwell, Jake	Everton	Brentford	Undisclosed
25 Blizzard, Dominic	Yeovil T	Plymouth Arg	Free
12 Bonham, Jack	Watford	Brentford	Free
28 Boselli, Mauro	Wigan Ath	Club Leon	Undisclosed
25 Brandy, Fabien	Walsall	Sheffield U	Free
7 Bridge, Wayne	Manchester C	Reading	Free
13 Bruma, Jeffrey	Chelsea	PSV	Undisclosed
24 Bywater, Stephen	Sheffield W	Millwall	Free
28 Cameron, Nathan	Coventry C	Bury	Free
19 Carroll, Andrew Thomas	Liverpool	West Ham U	£15m
5 Chapman, Adam	Oxford U	Newport Co	Undisclosed
13 Cisak, Alex	Oldham Ath	Burnley	Free
21 Clucas, Sam	Hereford U	Mansfield T	Tribunal
27 Compton, Jack	Colchester U	Hartlepool U	Free
24 Cowan-Hall, Paris Dedan Joseph	Plymouth Arg	Wycombe W	Free
28 Crainey, Stephen	Blackpool	Wigan Ath	Free
17 Cureton, Jamie	Exeter C	Cheltenham T	Free
24 Davies, Curtis Eugene	Birmingham C	Hull C	£2.25m
14 Denilson	Arsenal	Sao Paolo	Free
6 Diagne, Tony	Macclesfield T	Morecambe	Undisclosed
28 Dillon, Kealan	Hull C	St Mirren	Free
17 Drury, Andy	Ipswich T	Crawley T	Free
24 Duke, Matt	Bradford C	Northampton T	Free
20 Eastham, Ashley	Blackpool	Rochdale	Free
29 Edwards, Phil	Rochdale	Burton Alb	Free
27 Elmohamady, Ahmed	Sunderland	Hull C	£2m
26 Fielding, Francis David	Derby Co	Bristol C	Undisclosed
17 Figueroa, Maynor	Wigan Ath	Hull C	Free
13 Fletcher, Wes	Burnley	York C	Free
11 Flint, Aden	Swindon T	Bristol C	£300,000
19 Foster, Stephen	Barnsley	Tranmere R	Free
26 Francomb, George	Norwich C	AFC Wimbledon	Free
28 Gameiro, Corey	Fulham	Sydney FC	Free
27 German, Antonio	Brentford	Gillingham	Undisclosed
3 Gower, Mark	Swansea C	Charlton Ath	Free
26 Grant, Joel	Wycombe W	Yeovil T	Free
21 Grimes, Ashley	Rochdale	Bury	Free
7 Gulacsi, Peter	Liverpool	Red Bull Salzburg	Undisclosed
18 Hammar, Johan	Everton	Malmo	Free
24 Hammill, Adam James	Wolverhampton W	Huddersfield T	Undisclosed
28 Harte, Ian	Reading	Bournemouth	Free
22 Holman, Brett	Aston Villa	Al Nasr	Free
19 Horwood, Evan	Hartlepool U	Tranmere R	Free
26 Hoskins, Sam	Southampton	Yeovil T	Free
4 Humphrey, Chris	Motherwell	Preston NE	Free
13 Hunt, David	Crawley T	Oxford U	Free
20 Hunt, Nicky	Rotherham U	Accrington S	Free
28 Hussey, Chris	AFC Wimbledon	Burton Alb	Free
3 Iwelumo, Chris	Watford	Scunthorpe U	Free
20 Jara, Gonzalo	WBA	Nottingham F	Free
25 Johns, Jasper	Everton	Sheffield U	Free
26 Jones, Joe	Leicester C	Yeovil T	Free
27 Kitson, Dave	Sheffield U	Oxford U	Free
6 Larkins, Jake	West Ham U	Leyton Orient	Free
19 Lichaj, Eric	Aston Villa	Nottingham F	Free
10 Linganzi, Amine	Accrington S	Gillingham	Free
21 Lowe, Ryan	Milton Keynes D	Tranmere R	Free
21 Lund, Matthew	Stoke C	Rochdale	Free
18 MacDonald, Alex	Burnley	Burton Alb	Free
26 Maghoma, Jacques	Burton Alb	Sheffield W	Free
19 Marshall, Marcus	Bury	Morecambe	Free
26 McCann, Chris	Burnley	Wigan Ath	Free
24 McCormack, Alan	Swindon T	Brentford	Free
25 McGinn, Stephen	Watford	Sheffield U	Free
25 McGinty, Sean	Manchester U	Sheffield U	Free
30 McGoldrick, David James	Nottingham F	Ipswich T	Undisclosed

25 Mignolet, Simon	Sunderland	Liverpool	£9m
24 Milsom, Rob	Aberdeen	Rotherham U	Free
21 Mkandawire, Tamika	Millwall	Shrewsbury T	Free
1 Mohamed, Kaid	Cheltenham T	Port Vale	Free
28 Montrose, Lewis	Gillingham	York C	Free
26 Morris, Ian	Torquay U	Northampton T	Free
29 Morsy, Sam	Port Vale	Chesterfield	Undisclosed
14 Murdoch, Stewart	Falkirk	Fleetwood T	Free
7 Murphy, Daryl	Celtic	Ipswich T	Free
19 O'Grady, Christopher	Sheffield W	Barnsley	Undisclosed
10 Oliver, Vadaine	Lincoln C	Crewe Alex	Undisclosed
25 Paterson, Martin	Burnley	Huddersfield T	Free
27 Pittman, Jon-Paul	Oxford U	Wycombe W	Free
14 Puri, Sander	St Mirren	York C	Free
18 Reed, Adam	Sunderland	Burton Alb	Free
27 Roberts, Gareth	Derby Co	Bury	Free
22 Roberts, Gary	Swindon T	Chesterfield	Free
27 Robertson, Chris	Preston NE	Port Vale	Free
13 Rose, Daniel	Fleetwood T	Oxford U	Free
10 Russell, Johnny	Dundee U	Derby Co	£750,000
5 Ryan, Jimmy	Scunthorpe U	Chesterfield	Free
26 Sampson, Jack	Bolton W	Morecambe	Free
14 Shama, Josh	Reading	Oxford U	Free
29 Sharps, Ian	Rotherham U	Burton Alb	Free
21 Sheringham, Charlie	Bournemouth	AFC Wimbledon	Free
27 Simpson, Danny	Newcastle U	QPR	Free
25 Smith, Alex	Fulham	Swindon T	Free
10 Smith, Jimmy	Leyton Orient	Stevenage	Free
20 Smith, Korey	Norwich C	Oldham Ath	Free
10 Smith, Matt	Oldham Ath	Leeds U	Free
24 Stead, Jon	Bristol C	Huddersfield T	Free
26 Steer, Jed	Norwich C	Aston Villa	Compensation
29 Symes, Michael	Leyton Orient	Burton Alb	Free
5 Tabb, Jay	Reading	Ipswich T	Free
26 Tevez, Carlos	Manchester C	Juventus	£12m
27 Tomlin, Gavin	Southend U	Port Vale	Free
18 Ward, Elliott	Norwich C	Bournemouth	Free
28 Watt, Sanchez	Arsenal	Colchester U	Free
24 Welsh, Andy	Carlisle U	Scunthorpe U	Free
24 White, Hayden	Sheffield W	Bolton W	Free
27 White, John	Colchester U	Southend U	Free
24 Williams, Derrick Shaun	Aston Villa	Bristol C	Free
30 Wilson, Danny	Liverpool	Hearts	Free
21 Worley, Harry	Oxford U	Newport Co	Free
24 Wylde, Gregg	Bolton W	Aberdeen	Free
18 Zola, Calvin	Burton Alb	Aberdeen	Free
JULY 2013			
27 Agdestein, Torbjorn	Brighton & HA	Inverness CT	Free
2 Akinfenwa, Adebayo	Northampton T	Gillingham	Free
9 Alcaraz, Antolin	Wigan Ath	Everton	Free
29 Amankwaah, Kevin	Exeter C	Northampton T	Free
8 Anderson, Paul	Bristol C	Ipswich T	Swap
19 Arfield, Scott	Huddersfield T	Burnley	Free
31 Assombalonga, Britt Curtis	Watford	Peterborough U	Undisclosed
16 Atkinson, Rob	Fleetwood T	Accrington S	Free
4 Atkinson, Will	Bradford C	Southend U	Free
19 Bailey, Nicky	Middlesbrough	Millwall	Free
22 Bakayogo, Zoumana	Tranmere R	Leicester C	Free
1 Baptiste, Alex	Blackpool	Bolton W	Free
31 Barnett, Leon Peter	Norwich C	Wigan Ath	Undisclosed
15 Beckford, Jermaine Paul	Leicester C	Bolton W	Undisclosed
31 Belford, Tyrell	Liverpool	Swindon T	Free
19 Bell, David	Coventry C	Notts Co	Free
2 Benyon, Elliot	Southend U	Torquay U	Free
20 Berra, Christophe	Wolverhampton W	Ipswich T	Free
24 Bird, Ryan	Burnham	Portsmouth	Undisclosed
29 Blackman, Andre	Celtic	Plymouth Arg	Free
17 Boco, Romuald	Accrington S	Plymouth Arg	Free
11 Bostock, John	Tottenham H	Royal Antwerp	Free
26 Brayford, John	Derby Co	Cardiff C	£1.5m
22 Brown, Reece	Manchester U	Watford	Free
22 Burton Alb, Deon	Gillingham	Scunthorpe U	Free
30 Button, David Robert	Charlton Ath	Brentford	Undisclosed
9 Byrne, Nathan	Tottenham H	Swindon T	Undisclosed
2 Cameron, Courtney	Aston Villa	Torquay U	Free
4 Campbell, DJ	QPR	Blackburn R	Free
9 Carter, Darren	Cheltenham T	Northampton T	Free
31 Caulker, Steven	Tottenham H	Cardiff C	£8m
9 Chapell, Jordan	Sheffield U	Torquay U	Free

17 Chaplow, Richard	Southampton	Millwall	Free
14 Charles-Cook, Reice	Arsenal	Bury	Free
14 Chicksen, Adam	Milton Keynes D	Brighton & HA	Undisclosed
23 Chippendale, Aidan	Accrington S	Bury	Free
25 Chopra, Michael	Ipswich T	Blackpool	Free
19 Cofie, John	Manchester U	Barnsley	Free
15 Coker, Ben	Colchester U	Southend U	Free
29 Collins, James	Swindon T	Hibernian	£200,000
22 Craig, Steven	Partick Th	Wycombe W	Free
16 Cresswell, Richard	Sheffield U	York C	Free
22 Cresswell, Ryan Anthony	Southend U	Fleetwood T	Undisclosed
11 Cruz, Roque Santa	Manchester C	Malaga	Free
10 Davies, Kevin	Bolton W	Preston NE	Free
25 Davies, Steven Gary	Bristol C	Blackpool	£500,000
30 Davis, Liam	Oxford U	Yeovil T	Free
3 De Vries, Dorus	Wolverhampton W	Nottingham F	Free
25 Deegan, Gary	Hibernian	Northampton T	Free
18 Delap, Rory	Stoke C	Burton Alb	Free
19 Devitt, Jamie	Hull C	Chesterfield	Free
1 Dibble, Christian	Bury	Barnsley	Free
25 Dickinson, Carl	Watford	Port Vale	Undisclosed
26 Dickson, Ryan	Southampton	Colchester U	Free
1 Dilo, Christopher	Blackburn R	St Mirren	Free
1 Dobbie, Stephen	Brighton & HA	Crystal Palace	Undisclosed
8 Done, Matt	Barnsley	Rochdale	Free
14 Duffy, Mark	Scunthorpe U	Doncaster R	Undisclosed
2 Dumbuya, Mustapha	Crawley T	Notts Co	Free
15 Dunne, Richard	Aston Villa	QPR	Free
8 Emmanuel-Thomas, Jay Aston	Ipswich T	Bristol C	Swap
30 Evatt, Ian	Blackpool	Chesterfield	Free
25 Ferry, Simon	Swindon T	Portsmouth	Free
1 Fornasier, Michele	Manchester U	Sampdoria	Free
11 Forren, Vegard	Southampton	Molde FK	Undisclosed
1 Forsyth, Craig	Watford	Derby Co	£150,000
5 Fortune, Marc-Antoine	WBA	Wigan Ath	Free
24 Fotheringham, Mark	Ross Co	Notts Co	Free
11 Fraser, Gary	Hamilton A	Bolton W	Free
1 Gayle, Dwight Devon Boyd	Peterborough U	Crystal Palace	Undisclosed
12 Gerken, Dean	Bristol C	Ipswich T	Free
12 Gornell, Terry	Rochdale	Cheltenham T	Free
12 Grant, Anthony Paul	Stevenage	Crewe Alex	Free
18 Grant, Robert	Rochdale	Blackpool	Undisclosed
2 Green, Devarn	Burton Alb	Blackburn R	Undisclosed
3 Green, Matt	Mansfield T	Birmingham C	Free
16 Griffith, Anthony	Leyton Orient	Port Vale	Free
1 Grigg, Will	Walsall	Brentford	Compensation
25 Guy, Lewis	St Mirren	Carlisle U	Free
1 Hall, Robert	West Ham U	Bolton W	Compensation
14 Harding, Ben	Northampton T	Torquay U	Free
26 Harley, Ryan	Brighton & HA	Swindon T	Free
15 Harper, Steve	Newcastle U	Hull C	Free
1 Haworth, Andy	Rochdale	Notts Co	Free
11 Haynes, Danny	Charlton Ath	Notts Co	Free
1 Helan, Jeremy	Manchester C	Sheffield W	Undisclosed
23 Henry, Karl	Wolverhampton W	QPR	Undisclosed
16 Hewitt, Troy	QPR	Walsall	Free
17 Hinds, Richard	Yeovil T	Bury	Free
19 Hodson, Lee James Stephen	Watford	Milton Keynes D	Free
29 Hogg, Jonathan Lee	Watford	Huddersfield T	Undisclosed
8 Holt, Grant	Norwich C	Wigan Ath	£2m
26 Hooper, Gary	Celtic	Norwich C	£5m
25 Hooper, JJ	Newcastle U	Northampton T	Free
13 Howe, Rene	Torquay U	Burton Alb	Free
9 Hughes, Mark	Bury	Morecambe	Free
15 Humphreys, Ritchie	Hartlepool U	Chesterfield	Free
3 Hunt, Noel	Reading	Leeds U	Free
1 Hurst, James	WBA	Crawley T	Free
1 Ikpeazu, Uche	Reading	Watford	Free
31 Jackson, Marlon	Hereford U	Bury	Free
10 Jackson, Simeon	Norwich C	Eintracht Braunschweig	Free
19 Jovetic, Stevan	Fiorentina	Manchester C	£22m
4 Kennedy, Callum	Scunthorpe U	AFC Wimbledon	Free
2 Kennedy, Jason	Rochdale	Bradford C	Free
1 Kerr, Fraser	Birmingham C	Motherwell	Free
8 Kilgallon, Matt	Sunderland	Blackburn R	Free
8 Kone, Arouna	Wigan Ath	Everton	£6m
8 Lainton, Rob	Bolton W	Bury	Free
6 Lines, Chris	Sheffield W	Port Vale	Free
5 MacDonald, Charlie	Leyton Orient	Oldham Ath	Free

5 MacKenzie, Gary	Milton Keynes D	Blackpool	Undisclosed
25 Mackie, James Charles	QPR	Nottingham F	£1m
18 Maicon	Manchester C	Roma	Undisclosed
18 Malouda, Florent	Chelsea	Trabzonspor	Free
1 Mannone, Vito	Arsenal	Sunderland	Undisclosed
9 Marrow, Alex James	Crystal Palace	Blackburn R	Undisclosed
19 McAllister, Sean	Cowdenbeath	Scunthorpe U	Free
2 McCartan, Shay	Burnley	Accrington S	Free
25 McCullough, Luke	Manchester U	Doncaster R	Free
10 McDonald, Cody	Coventry C	Gillingham	Free
23 McDonald, Scott	Middlesbrough	Millwall	Free
2 McGugan, Lewis	Nottingham F	Watford	Free
15 McManus, Stephen	Middlesbrough	Motherwell	Free
29 McQuilkin, James	Hereford U	Walsall	Free
16 Meade, Jernade	Arsenal	Swansea C	Free
1 Mills, Joseph Nathan	Reading	Burnley	Free
26 Mohsni, Bilel	Southend U	Rangers	Free
1 Molyneux, Lee	Accrington S	Crewe Alex	Free
29 Moore, Simon	Brentford	Cardiff C	Undisclosed
1 Morgan, Marvin	Shrewsbury T	Plymouth Arg	Free
18 Mucha, Jan	Everton	Krylia Sovetov Samara	Free
22 Mullins, John	Rotherham U	Oxford U	Undisclosed
1 Murphy, Luke John	Crewe Alex	Leeds U	£1m
23 M'Voto, Jean-Yves	Oldham Ath	Barnsley	Free
10 Nash, Carlo	Stoke C	Norwich C	Free
4 Newey, Tom	Scunthorpe U	Oxford U	Free
19 Noble, Ryan	Sunderland	Burnley	Free
9 Nyatanga, Lewin	Bristol C	Barnsley	Free
11 Obafemi, Afolabi	Leyton Orient	Dagenham & R	Free
18 O'Donnell, Richard	Chesterfield	Walsall	Free
10 Olsson, Martin Tony Waikwa	Blackburn R	Norwich C	Free
24 O'Toole, John-Joe	Colchester U	Bristol R	Undisclosed
26 Parish, Elliot	Cardiff C	Bristol C	Free
9 Parkin, Sam	St Mirren	Exeter C	Free
1 Paterson, Jamie Charles Stuart	Walsall	Nottingham F	Undisclosed
1 Payne, Jack Stephen	Gillingham	Peterborough U	Undisclosed
30 Pearce, Krystian	Notts Co	Torquay U	Free
3 Perch, James Robert	Newcastle U	Wigan Ath	Undisclosed
20 Phillips, Kevin	Blackpool	Crystal Palace	Free
1 Procter, Andy	Preston NE	Bury	Free
4 Redmond, Nathan Daniel Jerome	Birmingham C	Norwich C	£3.2m
14 Reeves, Ben	Southampton	Milton Keynes D	Free
5 Richards, Matt	Shrewsbury T	Cheltenham T	Free
4 Ricketts, Sam	Bolton W	Wolverhampton W	Free
3 Roberts, Mark	Stevenage	Fleetwood T	Free
26 Roberts, Philip	Arsenal	Falkirk	Free
12 Rodgers, Anton	Brighton & HA	Oldham Ath	Free
1 Rogne, Thomas	Celtic	Wigan Ath	Free
10 Rooney, John	Barnsley	Bury	Free
30 Ruffels, Josh	Coventry C	Oxford U	Free
21 Saah, Brian	Torquay U	Dagenham & R	Free
5 Samba, Christopher	QPR	Anzhi Makhachkala	£12m
20 Santos, Andre	Arsenal	Flamengo	Undisclosed
19 Sawyers, Romaine	WBA	Walsall	Free
9 Schwarzer, Mark	Fulham	Chelsea	Free
19 Seaborne, Dan	Southampton	Yeovil T	Free
3 Shelvey, Jonjo	Liverpool	Swansea C	£5m
15 Sodje, Akpo	Scunthorpe U	Tranmere R	Free
4 Sparrow, Matt	Crawley T	Scunthorpe U	Free
18 Squillaci, Sebastien	Arsenal	Bastia	Free
9 Stephens, Jamie	Liverpool	Newport Co	Free
17 Taylor, Lyle	Falkirk	Sheffield U	Undisclosed
10 Thomas, Jerome	WBA	Crystal Palace	Free
26 Thomson, Robbie	Celtic	Rochdale	Free
3 Tidser, Michael	Greenock Morton	Rotherham U	£50,000
2 Tonge, Dale	Rotherham U	Torquay U	Free
2 Toure, Kolo	Manchester C	Liverpool	Free
18 Tremarco, Carl	Macclesfield T	Inverness CT	Free
10 Upson, Matthew	Stoke C	Brighton & HA	Free
3 Vaughan, James Oliver	Norwich C	Huddersfield T	Undisclosed
19 Veseli, Frederic	Manchester U	Ipswich T	Free
17 Vincent, Ashley	Port Vale	Cheltenham T	Free
30 Vita, Raffaele De	Swindon T	Bradford C	Free
3 Vries, Dorus De	Wolverhampton W	Nottingham F	Free
8 Wagstaff, Scott	Charlton Ath	Bristol C	Free
11 Wanyama, Victor	Celtic	Southampton	£12.5m
15 Weaver, Nicky	Sheffield W	Aberdeen	Free
2 Whitehead, Dean	Stoke C	Middlesbrough	Free
2 Wilkinson, Conor	Millwall	Bolton W	Compensation

24 Windass, Josh	Huddersfield T	Accrington S	Free
29 Winnall, Sam	Wolverhampton W	Scunthorpe U	Free
19 Wood, Richard	Coventry C	Charlton Ath	Free
1 Worrall, David	Bury	Rotherham U	Free
24 Wright-Phillips, Bradley	Charlton Ath	New York Red Bulls	Free
3 Yeates, Mark	Watford	Bradford C	Free

AUGUST 2013

6 Adomah, Albert	Bristol C	Middlesbrough	£1m
1 Agustien, Kemy	Swansea C	Brighton & HA	Free
15 Alexander, Neil	Rangers	Crystal Palace	Free
1 Amond, Padraig	Accrington S	Morecambe	Free
22 Anderson, Myles	Exeter C	AC Monza	Free
1 Austin, Charles	Burnley	QPR	Undisclosed
29 Baxter, Jose	Oldham Ath	Sheffield U	Undisclosed
16 Bennett, Callum	Ipswich T	Notts Co	Free
1 Bennett, Julian	Sheffield W	Southend U	Free
2 Bishop, Neal	Notts Co	Blackpool	Free
23 Butterfield, Danny	Southampton	Carlisle U	Free
15 Capoue, Etienne	Toulouse	Tottenham H	£9m
10 Chamakh, Marouane	Arsenal	Crystal Palace	Free
1 Church, Simon	Reading	Charlton Ath	Free
1 Clifford, Conor	Leicester C	Southend U	Free
5 Cowan, Don	Dundee	Southend U	Free
3 Dempsey, Clint	Tottenham H	Seattle Sounders	£6m
13 Downing, Stewart	Liverpool	West Ham U	£5m
17 Dunn, Chris	Coventry C	Yeovil T	Free
21 Dunne, Charles	Wycombe W	Blackpool	Undisclosed
22 Edjenguele, William	Coventry C	Bury	Free
1 Emerton, Danny	Hull C	Northampton T	Free
2 Evans, Corry John	Hull C	Blackburn R	Undisclosed
15 Fuller, Ricardo	Charlton Ath	Blackpool	Free
8 Gervinho	Arsenal	Roma	£8m
30 Givet, Gael	Blackburn R	Arles-Avignon	Undisclosed
30 Golbourne, Julio Scott	Barnsley	Wolverhampton W	Undisclosed
1 Gorman, Johnny	Wolverhampton W	Leyton Orient	Free
1 Grandin, Elliot	Blackpool	Crystal Palace	Free
30 Hammond, Dean	Southampton	Leicester C	Undisclosed
2 Harewood, Marlon	Barnsley	Bristol C	Free
30 Harriott, Matty	Sheffield U	Northampton T	Free
7 Hartley, Peter	Hartlepool U	Stevenage	Undisclosed
1 Hawley, Karl	Scunthorpe U	Torquay U	Free
1 Heath, Matt	Colchester U	Northampton T	Free
8 Higginbotham, Kallum	Huddersfield T	Partick Th	Free
22 Hines, Zavon	Bradford C	Dagenham & R	Free
16 Holt, Jordan	St Mirren	Notts Co	Free
14 Huddlestone, Thomas Andrew	Tottenham H	Hull C	£5m
22 Inman, Brad	Newcastle U	Crewe Alex	Undisclosed
1 Jones, David	Wigan Ath	Burnley	Free
31 Luongo, Massimo	Tottenham H	Swindon T	£400,000
7 Manset, Mathieu	Carlisle U	Coventry C	Free
8 Marshall, Andy	Aston Villa	Millwall	Free
28 Marshall, Ben	Leicester C	Blackburn R	Undisclosed
7 McClean, James	Sunderland	Wigan Ath	£1.5m
22 McCourt, Paddy	Celtic	Barnsley	Free
14 McDonald, Kevin	Sheffield U	Wolverhampton W	Undisclosed
5 McGurk, Adam	Tranmere R	Burton Alb	Free
19 Miller, Tommy	Swindon T	Bury	Free
1 Mingoia, Piero	Watford	Accrington S	Free
1 Moritz, Andre	Crystal Palace	Bolton W	Free
16 Murray, Ronan	Ipswich T	Notts Co	Free
10 Naismith, Kal	Rangers	Accrington S	Free
2 N'Gala, Bondz	Stevenage	Portsmouth	Free
17 Nicholson, Barry	Fleetwood T	Kilmarnock	Free
15 O'Brien, Liam	Barnet	Brentford	Free
7 O'Neil, Gary	West Ham U	QPR	Free
2 Pack, Marlon	Cheltenham T	Bristol C	£100,000
15 Painter, Marcos	Brighton & HA	Portsmouth	Free
19 Parker, Scott Matthew	Tottenham H	Fulham	Undisclosed
29 Pedersen, Morten Gamst	Blackburn R	Kardemir Karabukspor	Undisclosed
23 Phillips, Matthew	Blackpool	QPR	Undisclosed
16 Philliskirk, Danny	Coventry C	Oldham Ath	Free
2 Richardson, Frazer	Southampton	Middlesbrough	Free
1 Ridder, Steve de	Southampton	Utrecht	Free
15 Robinson, Theo	Derby Co	Doncaster R	Undisclosed
1 Rooney, Adam	Birmingham C	Oldham Ath	Free
14 Santo, Franco Di	Wigan Ath	Werder Bremen	Free
30 Shorey, Nicky	Reading	Bristol C	Free
29 Sinclair, Emile Anthony	Peterborough U	Crawley T	£100,000
8 Spearing, Jay Francis	Liverpool	Bolton W	Undisclosed

1 Spurr, Tommy	Doncaster R	Blackburn R	Free
22 Suarez, Denis	Manchester C	Barcelona	Undisclosed
1 Taylor, Matt	Charlton Ath	Bradford C	Free
5 Trotman, Neal	Chesterfield	Plymouth Arg	Free
18 Tumwa, Aaron	Watford	Blackburn R	Free
1 Turnbull, Ross	Chelsea	Doncaster R	Free
2 Wellens, Richie	Leicester C	Doncaster R	Free
27 Wilson, Ben	Cambridge U	Accrington S	Free
9 Wilson, Kelvin	Celtic	Nottingham F	£2.5m
21 Wootton, Scott	Manchester U	Leeds U	Undisclosed

SEPTEMBER 2013

2 Anichebe, Victor	Everton	WBA	£6m
1 Atsu, Christian	Porto	Chelsea	£3.5m
1 Bale, Gareth	Tottenham H	Real Madrid	£85.3m
2 Bannan, Barry	Aston Villa	Crystal Palace	Undisclosed
2 Bencherif, Hamza	Notts Co	Plymouth Arg	Free
2 Butterfield, Jacob	Norwich C	Middlesbrough	Undisclosed
2 Caddis, Paul	Swindon T	Birmingham C	Undisclosed
2 Camp, Lee	Norwich C	WBA	Free
2 Cuvelier, Florent	Stoke C	Sheffield U	Undisclosed
2 Fellaini Bakkioui, Marouane	Everton	Manchester U	£27.5m
2 Guedioura, Adlene	Nottingham F	Crystal Palace	Undisclosed
2 Hunt, Jack	Huddersfield T	Crystal Palace	Undisclosed
2 Jensen, Brian	Burnley	Bury	Free
1 Kebe, Jimmy Boubou	Reading	Crystal Palace	Undisclosed
2 Mariappa, Adrian Joseph	Reading	Crystal Palace	Undisclosed
2 McCarthy, James	Wigan Ath	Everton	Undisclosed
2 N'Guessan, Dany	Millwall	Swindon T	Free
2 Odemwingie, Peter	WBA	Cardiff C	£2.25m
2 Pacheco, Daniel	Liverpool	AD Alcorcon	Undisclosed
2 Sessegnon, Stephane	Sunderland	WBA	Undisclosed
2 Tyson, Nathan	Derby Co	Blackpool	Free
18 Urquhart, Stuart	Rangers	Coventry C	Undisclosed

OCTOBER 2013

23 Macey, Matt	Bristol R	Arsenal	Compensation

DECEMBER 2013

31 Gordon, Jaanai	Peterborough U	West Ham U	Undisclosed
13 Mahoney, Connor	Accrington S	Blackburn R	Undisclosed

JANUARY 2014

31 Adams, Nicholas	Crawley T	Rotherham U	Undisclosed
31 Alexander, Gary	Crawley T	Burton Alb	Undisclosed
31 Alnwick, Ben	Charlton Ath	Leyton Orient	Undisclosed
15 Arquin, Yoann	Notts Co	Ross Co	Free
24 Ayala, Daniel Sanchez	Norwich C	Middlesbrough	£350,000
31 Baldwin, Jack	Hartlepool U	Peterborough U	£500,000
8 Banton, Jason Steve	Crystal Palace	Plymouth Arg	Free
7 Barker, George	Brighton & HA	Swindon T	Undisclosed
9 Barnes, Ashley Luke	Brighton & HA	Burnley	Undisclosed
31 Bartley, Marvin	Burnley	Leyton Orient	Free
6 Boyce, Andrew Thomas	Lincoln C	Scunthorpe U	Undisclosed
30 Bridcutt, Liam Robert	Brighton & HA	Sunderland	£2.5m
18 Bruyne, Kevin de	Chelsea	Wolfsburg	Undisclosed
1 Burke, James	Huddersfield T	Bury	Free
29 Cabaye, Yohan	Newcastle U	Paris St-Germain	£19m
2 Cairney, Thomas	Hull C	Blackburn R	Undisclosed
5 Camp, Lee	WBA	Bournemouth	Free
21 Chorley, Ben	Stevenage	Portsmouth	Free
30 Clarke, Leon Marvin	Coventry C	Wolverhampton W	£750,000
31 Cole, Larnell James	Manchester U	Fulham	Undisclosed
30 Connell, Alan	Bradford C	Northampton T	Free
31 Conway, Craig	Cardiff C	Blackburn R	Undisclosed
31 Dann, Scott	Blackburn R	Crystal Palace	Undisclosed
3 Dawkins, Simon Jonathan	Tottenham H	Derby Co	Undisclosed
23 Dicker, Gary	Rochdale	Crawley T	Free
13 Dicko, Nouha	Wigan Ath	Wolverhampton W	Undisclosed
2 Dobie, Luke Jeffrey	Bristol City	Wigan Athletic	Undisclosed
30 Donaldson, Coll	Livingston	QPR	Undisclosed
16 Dong-Won, Ji	Sunderland	Augsburg	Undisclosed
16 El-Abd, Adam	Brighton & HA	Bristol C	Undisclosed
27 Essien, Michael	Chelsea	AC Milan	Undisclosed
16 Fogden, Wes	Bournemouth	Portsmouth	Free
10 Fraser, Gary	Bolton W	Partick Thistle	Free
31 Frimpong, Emmanuel Yaw	Arsenal	Barnsley	Undisclosed
31 Fulton, Jay	Falkirk	Swansea C	£200,000
2 Gestede, Rudy	Cardiff C	Blackburn R	Undisclosed
2 Gill, Matt	Bristol R	Exeter C	Undisclosed
1 Gordon, Jaanai Derece	Peterborough United	West Ham United	Undisclosed

31 Gray, David	Stevenage	Burton Alb	Free
31 Griffiths, Leigh	Wolverhampton W	Celtic	Undisclosed
13 Harewood, Marlon	Bristol C	Hartlepool U	Free
31 Haroun, Faris	Middlesbrough	Blackpool	Free
31 Harris, Robert	Blackpool	Sheffield U	Undisclosed
31 Hause, Kortney	Wycombe W	Wolverhampton W	Undisclosed
1 Hayes, Paul	Brentford	Scunthorpe U	Free
31 Heitinga, John Gjsbert Alan	Everton	Fulham	Free
31 Hennessey, Wayne Robert	Wolverhampton W	Crystal Palace	£3m
2 Henry, James	Millwall	Wolverhampton W	Undisclosed
31 Hobbs, Jack	Hull C	Nottingham F	Undisclosed
9 Howe, Rene	Burton Alb	Newport Co	Free
31 Hughes, Aaron William	Fulham	QPR	Undisclosed
10 Ireland, Stephen	Aston Villa	Stoke C	Undisclosed
23 Iwelumo, Chris	Scunthorpe U	St Johnstone	Free
7 Jacobs, Michael Edward	Derby Co	Wolverhampton W	Undisclosed
28 Jeffers, Shaun	Peterborough U	Newport Co	Undisclosed
23 Jeffrey, Anthony	Arsenal	Wycombe W	Free
13 Jelavic, Nikica	Everton	Hull C	Undisclosed
23 Jones, Darren	Shrewsbury T	AFC Wimbledon	Free
28 Jones, Kenwyne	Stoke C	Cardiff C	Swap
24 Junior, Edinho	Blackburn R	Harrisburg C Islanders	Free
31 Kermogant, Yann	Charlton Ath	Bournemouth	Undisclosed
6 Kilkenny, Neil	Bristol C	Preston NE	Free
28 King, Adam	Hearts	Swansea C	£150,000
31 Labadie, Joss	Notts Co	Torquay U	Undisclosed
31 Ledley, Joe	Celtic	Crystal Palace	Undisclosed
17 Long, Shane Patrick	WBA	Hull C	Rising to £7m
5 Lowe, Keith Stephen	Cheltenham T	York C	Undisclosed
9 Madden, Patrick	Yeovil T	Scunthorpe U	Undisclosed
30 Martin, Aaron	Southampton	Birmingham C	Free
25 Mata Garcia, Juan Manuel	Chelsea	Manchester U	£37.1m
11 McIntyre, Robbie	Huddersfield T	Bury	Free
16 Mclean, Aaron	Hull C	Bradford C	Undisclosed
30 McMahon, Anthony	Sheffield U	Blackpool	Undisclosed
17 McNulty, Jim	Barnsley	Bury	Free
14 McSheffrey, Gary	Chesterfield	Scunthorpe U	Free
30 McSweeney, Leon	Carlisle U	Northampton T	Free
3 Mills, Pablo	Rotherham U	Bury	Free
14 Monakana, Jeffrey	Preston NE	Brighton & HA	Undisclosed
1 Morgan, Adam Joseph	Liverpool	Yeovil T	Free
28 Muleba, Jonathan Mukendi	Chelsea	Bournemouth	Undisclosed
29 Nardiello, Daniel	Rotherham U	Bury	Free
27 Ngog, David	Bolton W	Swansea C	Undisclosed
24 Nunes, Fabio	Blackburn R	Latina	Free
28 Odemwingie, Peter	Cardiff C	Stoke C	Swap
11 Onyewu, Oguchi	QPR	Sheffield W	Free
6 Osborne, Karleigh Anthony Jon	Millwall	Bristol C	Undisclosed
16 Parsons, Matthew John	Crystal Palace	Plymouth Arg	Undisclosed
6 Penn, Russell Anthony	Cheltenham T	York C	Undisclosed
17 Perkins, David	Barnsley	Blackpool	Free
24 Platt, Clive	Northampton T	Bury	Free
31 Porter, George	Burnley	Rochdale	Free
31 Puncheon, Jason David Ian	Southampton	Crystal Palace	Undisclosed
30 Ravenhill, Ricky	Bradford C	Northampton T	Free
2 Ribeiro, Bruno	Blackburn R	Clube Atletico Linense	Free
3 Ridehalgh, Liam	Huddersfield T	Tranmere R	Undisclosed
31 Roberts, Gareth	Bury	Notts Co	Free
23 Rooney, Adam	Oldham Ath	Aberdeen	Free
22 Scotland, Jason	Barnsley	Hamilton A	Free
24 Scougall, Stefan	Livingston	Sheffield U	Undisclosed
13 Seaborne, Daniel Anthony Sag	Yeovil T	Coventry C	Free
31 Senderos, Philippe	Fulham	Valencia	Undisclosed
9 Shorey, Nicky	Bristol C	Portsmouth	Free
28 Silva, Fabio da	Manchester U	Cardiff C	Undisclosed
27 Smith, Adam David	Tottenham H	Bournemouth	Undisclosed
23 Smith, Michael John	Charlton Ath	Swindon T	Undisclosed
30 Stephens, Dale	Charlton Ath	Brighton & HA	Undisclosed
10 Syers, David	Doncaster R	Scunthorpe U	Undisclosed
17 Tansey, Greg	Stevenage	Inverness CT	Free
30 Tarkowski, James	Oldham Ath	Brentford	Undisclosed
9 Taylor, Ryan	Bristol C	Portsmouth	Free
14 Thomas, Wesley	Bournemouth	Rotherham U	Undisclosed
8 Thompson, Adam Lee	Watford	Southend U	Undisclosed
31 Tunnicliffe, Ryan	Manchester U	Fulham	Undisclosed
24 Tutte, Andrew	Rochdale	Bury	Free
31 Upson, Edward James	Yeovil T	Millwall	Undisclosed
20 Walker, Samuel Colin	Chelsea	Colchester U	Free
28 Washington, Conor	Newport Co	Peterborough U	Undisclosed

10 Wells, Nahki	Bradford C	Huddersfield T	Undisclosed
10 Williams, Marcus	Sheffield U	Scunthorpe U	Free
27 Williams, Shaun	Milton Keynes D	Millwall	Undisclosed
31 Wilson, James	Bristol C	Oldham Ath	Free
10 Wiseman, Scott	Barnsley	Preston NE	Free
27 Yennaris, Nicholas Harry	Arsenal	Brentford	Undisclosed

FEBRUARY 2014

4 Baxter, Sam	West Ham U	Gillingham	Free
11 Bergqvist, Doug	Exeter C	Ostersunds	Free
1 Cala, Juan	Sevilla	Cardiff C	Free
28 Defoe, Jermain	Tottenham H	Toronto	£6m
17 Fallon, Rory	St Johnstone	Crawley T	Free
6 Gillespie, Steven	Fleetwood T	Bristol R	Free
6 Grandin, Elliot	Crystal Palace	Blackpool	Free
4 Hall, Ryan	Leeds U	Milton Keynes D	Free
18 Lynch, Craig	Sunderland	Rochdale	Free
14 McPhail, Stephen	Sheffield W	Shamrock R	Free
27 Naylor, Lee	Accrington S	Derby Co	Free
19 Nicholson, Jake	Morton	AFC Wimbledon	Free
4 Robertson, Gregor	Crewe Alex	Northampton T	Free
3 Spencer, James	Huddersfield T	Notts Co	Free
14 Tomlin, Lee	Peterborough U	Middlesbrough	Undisclosed

MARCH 2014

| 14 Nosworthy, Nyron | Watford | Bristol C | |
| 5 Vidic, Nemanja | Manchester U | Inter Milan | Free |

To be completed at the end of the season.

| 27 Wynter, Alex | Crystal Palace | Colchester | |

APRIL 2014

| 4 Waghorn, Martyn | Leicester C | Wigan Ath | Free |

MAY 2014

16 Adams, Nicky	Rotherham U	Bury	Undisclosed
28 Andrew, Danny	Macclesfield T	Fleetwood T	Undisclosed
28 Brown, Scott	Cheltenham T	Aberdeen	Undisclosed
28 Cansdell-Sherriff, Shane	Preston NE	Burton Alb	Free
12 Cox, Lee	Swindon U	Plymouth Arg	Free
30 Derbyshire, Matt	Nottingham F	Rotherham U	Free
20 Devitt, Jamie	Chesterfield	Morecambe	Free
7 Diamond, Zander	Burton Alb	Northampton T	Free
16 Dolan, Matthew	Middlesbrough	Bradford C	Free
21 Edwards, Carlos	Ipswich T	Millwall	Free
20 Edwards, Ryan	Blackburn R	Morecambe	Free
30 Ellis, Mark	Crewe Alex	Shrewsbury T	Free
9 Fox, Danny	Southampton	Nottingham F	Free
29 Gill, Matt	Exeter C	Tranmere R	Free
23 Green, Danny	Charlton Ath	Milton Keynes D	Free
28 Hall, Asa	Shrewsbury T	Cheltenham T	Free
22 Hamer, Ben	Charlton Ath	Leicester C	Free
15 Hayes, Paul	Scunthorpe U	Wycombe W	Free
22 Hollands, Danny	Charlton Ath	Portsmouth	Free
27 Jensen, Brian	Bury	Crawley T	Free
23 Jombati, Sido	Cheltenham T	Wycombe W	Free
20 Jones, Darren	AFC Wimbledon	Newport Co	Free
28 Jones, Luke	Stevenage	Mansfield T	Free
23 Knight-Percival, Nat	Peterborough U	Shrewsbury T	Free
28 Le Fondre, Adam	Reading	Cardiff C	Undisclosed
19 Lowe, Ryan	Tranmere R	Bury	Undisclosed
3 Mayor, Danny	Sheffield W	Bury	Undisclosed
21 McKenzie, Taylor	Sheffield W	Notts Co	Free
19 McNulty, Marc	Livingston	Sheffield U	Undisclosed
23 Newton, Conor	Newcastle U	Rotherham U	Free
29 O'Brien, Liam	Brentford	Dagenham & R	Free
16 Pierre, Aaron	Brentford	Wycombe W	Undisclosed
23 Richards, Eliot	Bristol R	Tranmere R	Free
14 Richards, Marc	Chesterfield	Northampton T	Free
22 Rigg, Sean	Oxford U	AFC Wimbledon	Free
20 Smalley, Deane	Oxford U	Plymouth Arg	Free
20 Smith, Alan	Milton Keynes D	Notts Co	Free
19 Smith, Jimmy	Stevenage	Crawley T	Undisclosed
30 Taft, George	Leicester C	Burton Alb	Free
27 Tamas, Gabriel	Doncaster R	Watford	Free
28 Taylor, Ash	Tranmere R	Aberdeen	Undisclosed
20 Vincent, Ashley	Cheltenham T	Shrewsbury T	Free

THE NEW FOREIGN LEGION 2013–14

	From	To	Fee in £
JUNE 2013	*From*	*To*	*Fee in £*
5 Adrian	Real Betis	West Ham U	Free
22 Alberto, Luis	Sevilla	Liverpool	£6.8m
27 Amat, Jordi	Espanyol	Swansea C	£2.5m
23 Aspas, Iago	Celta Vigo	Liverpool	£7m
13 Bacuna, Leandro	FC Groningen	Aston Villa	Undisclosed
6 Canas, Jose	Real Betis	Swansea C	Free
21 Drenthe, Royston	Alania Vladikavkaz	Reading	Undisclosed
24 Fernandez, Marc De Val	Real Madrid	Doncaster R	Free
6 Fernandinho	Shakhtar Donetsk	Manchester C	£30m
18 Helenius, Nicklas	AaB Aalborg	Aston Villa	Rising to £2m
8 Jennings, Dale	Bayern Munich	Barnsley	£250,000
19 Karlsson, David Moberg	IFK Gothenburg	Sunderland	Undisclosed
14 Lovren, Dejan	Lyon	Southampton	£8.5m
20 Luna, Antonio	Sevilla	Aston Villa	Undisclosed
11 Navas, Jesus	Sevilla	Manchester C	£14.9m
13 Okore, Jores	Nordsjaelland	Aston Villa	Undisclosed
28 Pieters, Erik	PSV Eindhoven	Stoke C	£3m
25 Schurrle, Andre	Bayer Leverkusen	Chelsea	£18m
5 Stekelenburg, Maarten	Roma	Fulham	Undisclosed
7 Tonev, Aleksandar	Lech Poznan	Aston Villa	Undisclosed
7 Varela, Guillermo	Atletico Penarol	Manchester U	Undisclosed
25 Williams, Danny	Hoffenheim	Reading	Undisclosed
JULY 2013			
19 Abdi, Almen	Udinese	Watford	Free
25 Abdoun, Djamel	Olympiacos	Nottingham F	£1.55m
19 Acuna, Javier	Udinese	Watford	Free
9 Altidore, Jozy	AZ Alkmaar	Sunderland	Undisclosed
4 Anelka, Nicolas	Juventus	WBA	Free
19 Angella, Gabriele	Udinese	Watford	Free
22 Anya, Ikechi	Granada	Watford	Undisclosed
10 Ba, El Hadji	Le Havre	Sunderland	Free
19 Battocchio, Cristian	Udinese	Watford	Free
11 Bony, Wilfried	Vitesse Arnhem	Swansea C	£12m
1 Cabral	FC Basel	Sunderland	Free
18 Campana, Jose	Sevilla	Crystal Palace	Undisclosed
4 Carson, Scott	Bursaspor	Wigan Ath	Undisclosed
5 Cassetti, Marco	Udinese	Watford	Undisclosed
26 Chadli, Nacer	FC Twente	Tottenham H	£7m
1 Cornelius, Andreas	FC Copenhagen	Cardiff C	£7.5m
11 Coulibaly, Mohamed	Grasshoppers	Bournemouth	Free
23 Cuevas, Cristian	O'Higgins	Chelsea	£3m
1 Diakite, Modibo	Lazio	Sunderland	Free
24 Ekstrand, Joel	Udinese	Watford	Free
19 Fabbrini, Diego	Udinese	Watford	Free
19 Faraoni, Davide	Udinese	Watford	Free
13 Fer, Leroy	FC Twente	Norwich C	Undisclosed
26 Garcia, Juan Carlos	Olimpia	Wigan Ath	Free
16 Giaccherini, Emanuele	Juventus	Sunderland	£6.5m
5 Ginkel, Marco van	Vitesse Arnhem	Chelsea	£8m
2 Gogic, Alex	Olympiacos	Swansea C	Undisclosed
24 Iriney	Granada	Watford	Free
4 Kemen, Olivier	Metz	Newcastle U	Undisclosed
31 Lopez, Cristian	Atletico Baleares	Huddersfield T	Free
2 McGregor, Allan	Besiktas	Hull C	£1.5m
2 Muniesa, Marc	Barcelona	Stoke C	Free
22 Murphy, Rhys	Telstar	Dagenham & R	Free
19 Negredo, Alvaro	Sevilla	Manchester C	£20m
25 Nuhiu, Atdhe	Eskisehirspor	Sheffield W	Free
6 Paulinho	Corinthians	Tottenham H	£17m
25 Plumain, Ange-Freddy	Lens	Fulham	Free
2 Pozuelo, Alejandro	Real Betis	Swansea C	Undisclosed
5 Pudil, Daniel	Granada	Watford	Undisclosed
25 Reindorf, Jessy	Union Royale Namur	Bury	Free
1 Roberge, Valentin	Maritimo	Sunderland	Free
9 Robles, Joel	Atletico Madrid	Everton	Undisclosed
26 Sagbo, Yannick	Evian	Hull C	Undisclosed
1 Sanogo, Yaya	Auxerre	Arsenal	Free
11 Venta, Javi	Villarreal	Brentford	Free
2 Zabret, Gregor	NK Domzale	Swansea C	Undisclosed
AUGUST 2013			
16 Balmy, Jeremy	Le Havre	Notts Co	Free
30 Chiriches, Vlad	Steaua Bucharest	Tottenham H	£8.5m
30 Eriksen, Christian	Ajax	Tottenham H	£11.5m
29 Eto'o, Samuel	Anzhi Makhachkala	Chelsea	Free

29 Flamini, Mathieu	AC Milan	Arsenal	Free
16 Konstantopoulos, Dimitrios	AEK Athens	Middlesbrough	Free
30 Lamela, Erik	Roma	Tottenham H	£25.7m
29 Lanzoni, Matteo	Carrarese	Oldham Ath	Free
2 Lugano, Diego	Paris Saint-Germain	WBA	Free
16 Marange, Florian	Bordeaux	Crystal Palace	Free
22 Mavrias, Charis	Panathinaikos	Sunderland	Undisclosed
10 Medel, Gary	Sevilla	Cardiff C	£11m
16 Navas, Marcos	Recreativo Huelva	Bury	Free
16 Obadeyi, Temitope Ayoluwa	Rio Ave	Bury	Free
18 Osvaldo, Pablo	Roma	Southampton	£15m
2 Perica, Stipe	Zadar	Chelsea	Undisclosed
28 Rantie, Tokelo	Malmo	Bournemouth	Undisclosed
5 Soldado, Roberto	Valencia	Tottenham H	£26m
5 Songo'o, Yann	Sporting Kansas City	Blackburn R	Free
31 Theophile-Catherine, Kevin	Stade Rennais	Cardiff C	£2.1m
7 Weston, Rhys	KR Reykjavik	AFC Wimbledon	Free
28 Willian	Anzhi Makhachkala	Chelsea	£30m
2 Zayatte, Kamil	Istanbul BB	Sheffield W	Free

SEPTEMBER 2013

2 Arnautovic, Marko	Werder Bremen	Stoke C	Undisclosed
2 Calvet, Raphael	Auxerre	Brentford	Undisclosed
1 Demichelis, Martin	Atletico Madrid	Manchester C	£4.2m
2 Dossena, Andrea	Napoli	Sunderland	Undisclosed
2 Ilori, Tiago	Sporting Lisbon	Liverpool	£7m
2 Janko, Saidy	FC Zurich	Manchester U	£700,000
2 Kamara, Kei	Sporting Kansas City	Middlesbrough	Undisclosed
2 Kozak, Libor	Lazio	Aston Villa	£7m
2 Kusunga, Genseric	FC Basel	Oldham Ath	Free
2 Ozil, Mesut	Real Madrid	Arsenal	£42.4m
2 Sakho, Mamadou	Paris Saint-Germain	Liverpool	£18m
2 Zverotic, Elsad	Young Boys	Fulham	Undisclosed

JANUARY 2014

21 Agudelo, Juan	New England Revolution	Stoke C	Free
31 Bastos, Yannick	Differdange 03	Bolton W	Undisclosed
24 Berget, Jo Inge	Molde	Cardiff C	Undisclosed
28 Bouzanis, Dean	Aris	Carlisle U	Free
11 Daehli, Mats Moller	Molde	Cardiff C	Undisclosed
29 Djebbour, Rafik	Olympiacos	Nottingham F	Undisclosed
8 Eikrem, Magnus Wolff	Heerenveen	Cardiff C	Undisclosed
30 Ghoochannejhad, Reza	Standard Liege	Charlton Ath	Undisclosed
14 Howard, Brian	CSKA Sofia	Birmingham C	Free
21 Kebbie, Elliott	Atletico Madrid	Hull C	Free
16 Lawrence, Liam	PAOK Salonika	Barnsley	Free
11 Mahrez, Riyad	Le Havre	Leicester C	Undisclosed
15 Matic, Nemanja	Benfica	Chelsea	£21m
11 McGeady, Aiden	Spartak Moscow	Everton	Undisclosed
31 Mitroglou, Konstantinos	Olympiacos	Fulham	£11m
30 Nego, Loic	Ujpest	Charlton Ath	Undisclosed
31 Parzyszek, Piotr	De Graafschap	Charlton Ath	Undisclosed
3 Ranegie, Mathias	Udinese	Watford	Undisclosed
30 Razak, Abdul	Anzhi Makhachkala	West Ham U	Undisclosed
31 Rodriguez, David	Celta Vigo	Brighton & HA	Free
26 Salah, Mohamed	FC Basel	Chelsea	£11m
30 Scocco, Ignacio	Internacional	Sunderland	Undisclosed
5 Slager, Denzel	RKC Waalwijk	Coventry C	Free
31 Stanek, Jindrich	Sparta Prague	Everton	Undisclosed
1 Traore, Bertrand	Association Jeunes Espoirs	Chelsea	Free
21 Tronstad, Sondre	IK Start	Huddersfield T	Undisclosed
21 Ustari, Oscar	Almeria	Sunderland	Free
31 Zouma, Kurt	Saint-Etienne	Chelsea	£12m

FEBRUARY 2014

22 Dembele, Bira	CS Sedan	Stevenage	Free
5 Holgersson, Markus	New York Red Bulls	Wigan Ath	Free
1 Jackson, Simeon	Eintracht Braunschweig	Millwall	Free

MAY 2014

23 Burgstaller, Guido	Rapid Vienna	Cardiff C	Undisclosed
21 Guerra, Javi	Real Valladolid	Cardiff C	Free
17 Milinkovic, Vanja	Vojvodina	Manchester U	Undisclosed
20 Toko, Nzuzi	Grasshoppers	Brighton & HA	Free
28 Zarate, Mauro	Velez Sarsfield	West Ham U	Undisclosed

ENGLISH LEAGUE HONOURS 1888–2014

*Won or placed on goal average (ratio), goal difference or most goals scored. ‡Not promoted after play-offs. No official competition during 1915–19 and 1939–46, regional leagues operated.

FOOTBALL LEAGUE (1888–89 to 1891–92) – TIER 1

MAXIMUM POINTS: a 44; b 60

1	1888–89a	Preston NE	40	Aston Villa	29	Wolverhampton W	28
1	1889–90a	Preston NE	33	Everton	31	Blackburn R	27
1	1890–91a	Everton	29	Preston NE	27	Notts Co	26
1	1891–92b	Sunderland	42	Preston NE	37	Bolton W	36

DIVISION 1 (1892–93 to 1991–92)

MAXIMUM POINTS: a 44; b 52; c 60; d 68; e 76; f 84; g 126; h 120; k 114.

1	1892–93c	Sunderland	48	Preston NE	37	Everton	36
1	1893–94c	Aston Villa	44	Sunderland	38	Derby Co	36
1	1894–95c	Sunderland	47	Everton	42	Aston Villa	39
1	1895–96c	Aston Villa	45	Derby Co	41	Everton	39
1	1896–97c	Aston Villa	47	Sheffield U*	36	Derby Co	36
1	1897–98c	Sheffield U	42	Sunderland	37	Wolverhampton W*	35
1	1898–99d	Aston Villa	45	Liverpool	43	Burnley	39
1	1899–1900d	Aston Villa	50	Sheffield U	48	Sunderland	41
1	1900–01d	Liverpool	45	Sunderland	43	Notts Co	40
1	1901–02d	Sunderland	44	Everton	41	Newcastle U	37
1	1902–03d	The Wednesday	42	Aston Villa*	41	Sunderland	41
1	1903–04d	The Wednesday	47	Manchester C	44	Everton	43
1	1904–05d	Newcastle U	48	Everton	47	Manchester C	46
1	1905–06e	Liverpool	51	Preston NE	47	The Wednesday	44
1	1906–07e	Newcastle U	51	Bristol C	48	Everton*	45
1	1907–08e	Manchester U	52	Aston Villa*	43	Manchester C	43
1	1908–09e	Newcastle U	53	Everton	46	Sunderland	44
1	1909–10e	Aston Villa	53	Liverpool	48	Blackburn R*	45
1	1910–11e	Manchester U	52	Aston Villa	51	Sunderland*	45
1	1911–12e	Blackburn R	49	Everton	46	Newcastle U	44
1	1912–13e	Sunderland	54	Aston Villa	50	Sheffield W	49
1	1913–14e	Blackburn R	51	Aston Villa	44	Middlesbrough*	43
1	1914–15e	Everton	46	Oldham Ath	45	Blackburn R*	43
1	1919–20f	WBA	60	Burnley	51	Chelsea	49
1	1920–21f	Burnley	59	Manchester C	54	Bolton W	52
1	1921–22f	Liverpool	57	Tottenham H	51	Burnley	49
1	1922–23f	Liverpool	60	Sunderland	54	Huddersfield T	53
1	1923–24f	Huddersfield T*	57	Cardiff C	57	Sunderland	53
1	1924–25f	Huddersfield T	58	WBA	56	Bolton W	55
1	1925–26f	Huddersfield T	57	Arsenal	52	Sunderland	48
1	1926–27f	Newcastle U	56	Huddersfield T	51	Sunderland	49
1	1927–28f	Everton	53	Huddersfield T	51	Leicester C	48
1	1928–29f	Sheffield W	52	Leicester C	51	Aston Villa	50
1	1929–30f	Sheffield W	60	Derby Co	50	Manchester C*	47
1	1930–31f	Arsenal	66	Aston Villa	59	Sheffield W	52
1	1931–32f	Everton	56	Arsenal	54	Sheffield W	50
1	1932–33f	Arsenal	58	Aston Villa	54	Sheffield W	51
1	1933–34f	Arsenal	59	Huddersfield T	56	Tottenham H	49
1	1934–35f	Arsenal	58	Sunderland	54	Sheffield W	49
1	1935–36f	Sunderland	56	Derby Co*	48	Huddersfield T	48
1	1936–37f	Manchester C	57	Charlton Ath	54	Arsenal	52
1	1937–38f	Arsenal	52	Wolverhampton W	51	Preston NE	49
1	1938–39f	Everton	59	Wolverhampton W	55	Charlton Ath	50
1	1946–47f	Liverpool	57	Manchester U*	56	Wolverhampton W	56
1	1947–48f	Arsenal	59	Manchester U*	52	Burnley	52
1	1948–49f	Portsmouth	58	Manchester U*	53	Derby Co	53
1	1949–50f	Portsmouth*	53	Wolverhampton W	53	Sunderland	52
1	1950–51f	Tottenham H	60	Manchester U	56	Blackpool	50
1	1951–52f	Manchester U	57	Tottenham H*	53	Arsenal	53
1	1952–53f	Arsenal*	54	Preston NE	54	Wolverhampton W	51
1	1953–54f	Wolverhampton W	57	WBA	53	Huddersfield T	51
1	1954–55f	Chelsea	52	Wolverhampton W*	48	Portsmouth*	48
1	1955–56f	Manchester U	60	Blackpool*	49	Wolverhampton W	49
1	1956–57f	Manchester U	64	Tottenham H*	56	Preston NE	56
1	1957–58f	Wolverhampton W	64	Preston NE	59	Tottenham H	51
1	1958–59f	Wolverhampton W	61	Manchester U	55	Arsenal*	50
1	1959–60f	Burnley	55	Wolverhampton W	54	Tottenham H	53
1	1960–61f	Tottenham H	66	Sheffield W	58	Wolverhampton W	57
1	1961–62f	Ipswich T	56	Burnley	53	Tottenham H	52
1	1962–63f	Everton	61	Tottenham H	55	Burnley	54
1	1963–64f	Liverpool	57	Manchester U	53	Everton	52
1	1964–65f	Manchester U*	61	Leeds U	61	Chelsea	56
1	1965–66f	Liverpool	61	Leeds U*	55	Burnley	55
1	1966–67f	Manchester U	60	Nottingham F*	56	Tottenham H	56
1	1967–68f	Manchester C	58	Manchester U	56	Liverpool	55
1	1968–69f	Leeds U	67	Liverpool	61	Everton	57
1	1969–70f	Everton	66	Leeds U	57	Chelsea	55
1	1970–71f	Arsenal	65	Leeds U	64	Tottenham H*	52

1	1971–72f	Derby Co	58	Leeds U*	57	Liverpool*	57
1	1972–73f	Liverpool	60	Arsenal	57	Leeds U	53
1	1973–74f	Leeds U	62	Liverpool	57	Derby Co	48
1	1974–75f	Derby Co	53	Liverpool*	51	Ipswich T	51
1	1975–76f	Liverpool	60	QPR	59	Manchester U	56
1	1976–77f	Liverpool	57	Manchester C	56	Ipswich T	52
1	1977–78f	Nottingham F	64	Liverpool	57	Everton	55
1	1978–79f	Liverpool	68	Nottingham F	60	WBA	59
1	1979–80f	Liverpool	60	Manchester U	58	Ipswich T	53
1	1980–81f	Aston Villa	60	Ipswich T	56	Arsenal	53
1	1981–82g	Liverpool	87	Ipswich T	83	Manchester U	78
1	1982–83g	Liverpool	82	Watford	71	Manchester U	70
1	1983–84g	Liverpool	80	Southampton	77	Nottingham F*	74
1	1984–85g	Everton	90	Liverpool*	77	Tottenham H	77
1	1985–86g	Liverpool	88	Everton	86	West Ham U	84
1	1986–87g	Everton	86	Liverpool	77	Tottenham H	71
1	1987–88h	Liverpool	90	Manchester U	81	Nottingham F	73
1	1988–89k	Arsenal*	76	Liverpool	76	Nottingham F	64
1	1989–90k	Liverpool	79	Aston Villa	70	Tottenham H	63
1	1990–91k	Arsenal[1]	83	Liverpool	76	Crystal Palace	69
1	1991–92g	Leeds U	82	Manchester U	78	Sheffield W	75

[1]*Arsenal deducted 2pts due to player misconduct in match on 20/10/1990 v Manchester U at Old Trafford.*

FA PREMIER LEAGUE (1992–93 to 2013–14)

MAXIMUM POINTS: *a* 126; *b* 114.

1	1992–93a	Manchester U	84	Aston Villa	74	Norwich C	72
1	1993–94a	Manchester U	92	Blackburn R	84	Newcastle U	77
1	1994–95a	Blackburn R	89	Manchester U	88	Nottingham F	77
1	1995–96b	Manchester U	82	Newcastle U	78	Liverpool	71
1	1996–97b	Manchester U	75	Newcastle U*	68	Arsenal*	68
1	1997–98b	Arsenal	78	Manchester U	77	Liverpool	65
1	1998–99b	Manchester U	79	Arsenal	78	Chelsea	75
1	1999–2000b	Manchester U	91	Arsenal	73	Leeds U	69
1	2000–01b	Manchester U	80	Arsenal	70	Liverpool	69
1	2001–02b	Arsenal	87	Liverpool	80	Manchester U	77
1	2002–03b	Manchester U	83	Arsenal	78	Newcastle U	69
1	2003–04b	Arsenal	90	Chelsea	79	Manchester U	75
1	2004–05b	Chelsea	95	Arsenal	83	Manchester U	77
1	2005–06b	Chelsea	91	Manchester U	83	Liverpool	82
1	2006–07b	Manchester U	89	Chelsea	83	Liverpool*	68
1	2007–08b	Manchester U	87	Chelsea	85	Arsenal	83
1	2008–09b	Manchester U	90	Liverpool	86	Chelsea	83
1	2009–10b	Chelsea	86	Manchester U	85	Arsenal	75
1	2010–11b	Manchester U	80	Chelsea*	71	Manchester C	71
1	2011–12b	Manchester C*	89	Manchester U	89	Arsenal	70
1	2012–13b	Manchester U	89	Manchester C	78	Chelsea	75
1	2013–14b	Manchester C	86	Liverpool	84	Chelsea	82

DIVISION 2 (1892–93 to 1991–92) – TIER 2

MAXIMUM POINTS: *a* 44; *b* 56; *c* 60; *d* 68; *e* 76; *f* 84; *g* 126; *h* 132; *k* 138.

2	1892–93a	Small Heath	36	Sheffield U	35	Darwen	30
2	1893–94b	Liverpool	50	Small Heath	42	Notts Co	39
2	1894–95c	Bury	48	Notts Co	39	Newton Heath*	38
2	1895–96c	Liverpool*	46	Manchester C	46	Grimsby T*	42
2	1896–97c	Notts Co	42	Newton Heath	39	Grimsby T	38
2	1897–98c	Burnley	48	Newcastle U	45	Manchester C	39
2	1898–99d	Manchester C	52	Glossop NE	46	Leicester Fosse	45
2	1899–1900d	The Wednesday	54	Bolton W	52	Small Heath	46
2	1900–01d	Grimsby T	49	Small Heath	48	Burnley	44
2	1901–02d	WBA	55	Middlesbrough	51	Preston NE*	42
2	1902–03d	Manchester C	54	Small Heath	51	Woolwich A	48
2	1903–04d	Preston NE	50	Woolwich A	49	Manchester U	48
2	1904–05d	Liverpool	58	Bolton W	56	Manchester U	53
2	1905–06e	Bristol C	66	Manchester U	62	Chelsea	53
2	1906–07e	Nottingham F	60	Chelsea	57	Leicester Fosse	48
2	1907–08e	Bradford C	54	Leicester Fosse	52	Oldham Ath	50
2	1908–09e	Bolton W	52	Tottenham H*	51	WBA	51
2	1909–10e	Manchester C	54	Oldham Ath*	53	Hull C*	53
2	1910–11e	WBA	53	Bolton W	51	Chelsea	49
2	1911–12e	Derby Co*	54	Chelsea	54	Burnley	52
2	1912–13e	Preston NE	53	Burnley	50	Birmingham	46
2	1913–14e	Notts Co	53	Bradford PA*	49	Woolwich A	49
2	1914–15e	Derby Co	53	Preston NE	50	Barnsley	47
2	1919–20f	Tottenham H	70	Huddersfield T	64	Birmingham	56
2	1920–21f	Birmingham*	58	Cardiff C	58	Bristol C	51
2	1921–22f	Nottingham F	56	Stoke C*	52	Barnsley	52
2	1922–23f	Notts Co	53	West Ham U*	51	Leicester C	51
2	1923–24f	Leeds U	54	Bury*	51	Derby Co	51
2	1924–25f	Leicester C	59	Manchester U	57	Derby Co	55
2	1925–26f	Sheffield W	60	Derby Co	57	Chelsea	52
2	1926–27f	Middlesbrough	62	Portsmouth*	54	Manchester C	54
2	1927–28f	Manchester C	59	Leeds U	57	Chelsea	54
2	1928–29f	Middlesbrough	55	Grimsby T	53	Bradford PA*	48
2	1929–30f	Blackpool	58	Chelsea	55	Oldham Ath	53

2	1930–31f	Everton	61	WBA	54	Tottenham H	51
2	1931–32f	Wolverhampton W	56	Leeds U	54	Stoke C	52
2	1932–33f	Stoke C	56	Tottenham H	55	Fulham	50
2	1933–34f	Grimsby T	59	Preston NE	52	Bolton W*	51
2	1934–35f	Brentford	61	Bolton W*	56	West Ham U	56
2	1935–36f	Manchester U	56	Charlton Ath	55	Sheffield U*	52
2	1936–37f	Leicester C	56	Blackpool	55	Bury	52
2	1937–38f	Aston Villa	57	Manchester U*	53	Sheffield U	53
2	1938–39f	Blackburn R	55	Sheffield U	54	Sheffield W	53
2	1946–47f	Manchester C	62	Burnley	58	Birmingham C	55
2	1947–48f	Birmingham C	59	Newcastle U	56	Southampton	52
2	1948–49f	Fulham	57	WBA	56	Southampton	55
2	1949–50f	Tottenham H	61	Sheffield W*	52	Sheffield U*	52
2	1950–51f	Preston NE	57	Manchester C	52	Cardiff C	50
2	1951–52f	Sheffield W	53	Cardiff C*	51	Birmingham C	51
2	1952–53f	Sheffield U	60	Huddersfield T	58	Luton T	52
2	1953–54f	Leicester C*	56	Everton	56	Blackburn R	55
2	1954–55f	Birmingham C*	54	Luton T*	54	Rotherham U	54
2	1955–56f	Sheffield W	55	Leeds U	52	Liverpool*	48
2	1956–57f	Leicester C	61	Nottingham F	54	Liverpool	53
2	1957–58f	West Ham U	57	Blackburn R	56	Charlton Ath	55
2	1958–59f	Sheffield W	62	Fulham	60	Sheffield U*	53
2	1959–60f	Aston Villa	59	Cardiff C	58	Liverpool*	50
2	1960–61f	Ipswich T	59	Sheffield U	58	Liverpool	52
2	1961–62f	Liverpool	62	Leyton Orient	54	Sunderland	53
2	1962–63f	Stoke C	53	Chelsea*	52	Sunderland	52
2	1963–64f	Leeds U	63	Sunderland	61	Preston NE	56
2	1964–65f	Newcastle U	57	Northampton T	56	Bolton W	50
2	1965–66f	Manchester C	59	Southampton	54	Coventry C	53
2	1966–67f	Coventry C	59	Wolverhampton W	58	Carlisle U	52
2	1967–68f	Ipswich T	59	QPR*	58	Blackpool	58
2	1968–69f	Derby Co	63	Crystal Palace	56	Charlton Ath	50
2	1969–70f	Huddersfield T	60	Blackpool	53	Leicester C	51
2	1970–71f	Leicester C	59	Sheffield U	56	Cardiff C*	53
2	1971–72f	Norwich C	57	Birmingham C	56	Millwall	55
2	1972–73f	Burnley	62	QPR	61	Aston Villa	50
2	1973–74f	Middlesbrough	65	Luton T	50	Carlisle U	49
2	1974–75f	Manchester U	61	Aston Villa	58	Norwich C	53
2	1975–76f	Sunderland	56	Bristol C*	53	WBA	53
2	1976–77f	Wolverhampton W	57	Chelsea	55	Nottingham F	52
2	1977–78f	Bolton W	58	Southampton	57	Tottenham H*	56
2	1978–79f	Crystal Palace	57	Brighton & HA*	56	Stoke C	56
2	1979–80f	Leicester C	55	Sunderland	54	Birmingham C*	53
2	1980–81f	West Ham U	66	Notts Co	53	Swansea C*	50
2	1981–82g	Luton T	88	Watford	80	Norwich C	71
2	1982–83g	QPR	85	Wolverhampton W	75	Leicester C	70
2	1983–84g	Chelsea*	88	Sheffield W	88	Newcastle U	80
2	1984–85g	Oxford U	84	Birmingham C	82	Manchester C*	74
2	1985–86g	Norwich C	84	Charlton Ath	77	Wimbledon	76
2	1986–87g	Derby Co	84	Portsmouth	78	Oldham Ath‡	75
2	1987–88h	Millwall	82	Aston Villa*	78	Middlesbrough	78
2	1988–89k	Chelsea	99	Manchester C	82	Crystal Palace	81
2	1989–90k	Leeds U*	85	Sheffield U	85	Newcastle U‡	80
2	1990–91k	Oldham Ath	88	West Ham U	87	Sheffield W	82
2	1991–92k	Ipswich T	84	Middlesbrough	80	Derby Co	78

FIRST DIVISION (1992–93 to 2003–04)

MAXIMUM POINTS: 138

2	1992–93	Newcastle U	96	West Ham U*	88	Portsmouth‡	88
2	1993–94	Crystal Palace	90	Nottingham F	83	Millwall‡	74
2	1994–95	Middlesbrough	82	Reading‡	79	Bolton W	77
2	1995–96	Sunderland	83	Derby Co	79	Crystal Palace‡	75
2	1996–97	Bolton W	98	Barnsley	80	Wolverhampton W‡	76
2	1997–98	Nottingham F	94	Middlesbrough	91	Sunderland‡	90
2	1998–99	Sunderland	105	Bradford C	87	Ipswich T‡	86
2	1999–2000	Charlton Ath	91	Manchester C	89	Ipswich T	87
2	2000–01	Fulham	101	Blackburn R	91	Bolton W	87
2	2001–02	Manchester C	99	WBA	89	Wolverhampton W‡	86
2	2002–03	Portsmouth	98	Leicester C	92	Sheffield U‡	80
2	2003–04	Norwich C	94	WBA	86	Sunderland‡	79

FOOTBALL LEAGUE CHAMPIONSHIP (2004–05 to 2013–14)

MAXIMUM POINTS: 138

2	2004–05	Sunderland	94	Wigan Ath	87	Ipswich T‡	85
2	2005–06	Reading	106	Sheffield U	90	Watford	81
2	2006–07	Sunderland	88	Birmingham C	86	Derby Co	84
2	2007–08	WBA	81	Stoke C	79	Hull C	75
2	2008–09	Wolverhampton W	90	Birmingham C	83	Sheffield U‡	80
2	2009–10	Newcastle U	102	WBA	91	Nottingham F‡	79
2	2010–11	QPR	88	Norwich C	84	Swansea C*	80
2	2011–12	Reading	89	Southampton	88	West Ham U	86
2	2012–13	Cardiff C	87	Hull C	79	Watford‡	77
2	2013–14	Leicester C	102	Burnley	93	Derby Co‡	85

DIVISION 3 (1920–1921) – TIER 3

MAXIMUM POINTS: *a* 84.

3	1920–21*a*	Crystal Palace	59	Southampton	54	QPR	53

DIVISION 3—SOUTH (1921–22 to 1957–58)

MAXIMUM POINTS: *a* 84; *b* 92.

3	1921–22*a*	Southampton*	61	Plymouth Arg	61	Portsmouth	53
3	1922–23*a*	Bristol C	59	Plymouth Arg*	53	Swansea T	53
3	1923–24*a*	Portsmouth	59	Plymouth Arg	55	Millwall	54
3	1924–25*a*	Swansea T	57	Plymouth Arg	56	Bristol C	53
3	1925–26*a*	Reading	57	Plymouth Arg	56	Millwall	53
3	1926–27*a*	Bristol C	62	Plymouth Arg	60	Millwall	56
3	1927–28*a*	Millwall	65	Northampton T	55	Plymouth Arg	53
3	1928–29*a*	Charlton Ath*	54	Crystal Palace	54	Northampton T*	52
3	1929–30*a*	Plymouth Arg	68	Brentford	61	QPR	51
3	1930–31*a*	Notts Co	59	Crystal Palace	51	Brentford	50
3	1931–32*a*	Fulham	57	Reading	55	Southend U	53
3	1932–33*a*	Brentford	62	Exeter C	58	Norwich C	57
3	1933–34*a*	Norwich C	61	Coventry C*	54	Reading*	54
3	1934–35*a*	Charlton Ath	61	Reading	53	Coventry C	51
3	1935–36*a*	Coventry C	57	Luton T	56	Reading	54
3	1936–37*a*	Luton T	58	Notts Co	56	Brighton & HA	53
3	1937–38*a*	Millwall	56	Bristol C	55	QPR*	53
3	1938–39*a*	Newport Co	55	Crystal Palace	52	Brighton & HA	49
3	1946–47*a*	Cardiff C	66	QPR	57	Bristol C	51
3	1947–48*a*	QPR	61	Bournemouth	57	Walsall	51
3	1948–49*a*	Swansea T	62	Reading	55	Bournemouth	52
3	1949–50*a*	Notts Co	58	Northampton T*	51	Southend U	51
3	1950–51*b*	Nottingham F	70	Norwich C	64	Reading*	57
3	1951–52*b*	Plymouth Arg	66	Reading*	61	Norwich C	61
3	1952–53*b*	Bristol R	64	Millwall*	62	Northampton T	62
3	1953–54*b*	Ipswich T	64	Brighton & HA	61	Bristol C	56
3	1954–55*b*	Bristol C	70	Leyton Orient	61	Southampton	59
3	1955–56*b*	Leyton Orient	66	Brighton & HA	65	Ipswich T	64
3	1956–57*b*	Ipswich T*	59	Torquay U	59	Colchester U	58
3	1957–58*b*	Brighton & HA	60	Brentford*	58	Plymouth Arg	58

DIVISION 3—NORTH (1921–22 to 1957–58)

MAXIMUM POINTS: *a* 76; *b* 84; *c* 80; *d* 92.

3	1921–22*a*	Stockport Co	56	Darlington*	50	Grimsby T	50
3	1922–23*a*	Nelson	51	Bradford PA	47	Walsall	46
3	1923–24*b*	Wolverhampton W	63	Rochdale	62	Chesterfield	54
3	1924–25*b*	Darlington	58	Nelson*	53	New Brighton	53
3	1925–26*b*	Grimsby T	61	Bradford PA	60	Rochdale	59
3	1926–27*b*	Stoke C	63	Rochdale	58	Bradford PA	55
3	1927–28*b*	Bradford PA	63	Lincoln C	55	Stockport Co	54
3	1928–29*b*	Bradford C	63	Stockport Co	62	Wrexham	52
3	1929–30*b*	Port Vale	67	Stockport Co	63	Darlington*	50
3	1930–31*b*	Chesterfield	58	Lincoln C	57	Wrexham*	54
3	1931–32*c*	Lincoln C*	57	Gateshead	57	Chester	50
3	1932–33*b*	Hull C	59	Wrexham	57	Stockport Co	54
3	1933–34*b*	Barnsley	62	Chesterfield	61	Stockport Co	59
3	1934–35*b*	Doncaster R	57	Halifax T	55	Chester	54
3	1935–36*b*	Chesterfield	60	Chester*	55	Tranmere R	55
3	1936–37*b*	Stockport Co	60	Lincoln C	57	Chester	53
3	1937–38*b*	Tranmere R	56	Doncaster R	54	Hull C	53
3	1938–39*b*	Barnsley	67	Doncaster R	56	Bradford C	52
3	1946–47*b*	Doncaster R	72	Rotherham U	64	Chester	56
3	1947–48*b*	Lincoln C	60	Rotherham U	59	Wrexham	50
3	1948–49*b*	Hull C	65	Rotherham U	62	Doncaster R	50
3	1949–50*b*	Doncaster R	55	Gateshead	53	Rochdale*	51
3	1950–51*d*	Rotherham U	71	Mansfield T	64	Carlisle U	62
3	1951–52*d*	Lincoln C	69	Grimsby T	66	Stockport Co	59
3	1952–53*d*	Oldham Ath	59	Port Vale	58	Wrexham	56
3	1953–54*d*	Port Vale	69	Barnsley	58	Scunthorpe U	57
3	1954–55*d*	Barnsley	65	Accrington S	61	Scunthorpe U*	58
3	1955–56*d*	Grimsby T	68	Derby Co	63	Accrington S	59
3	1956–57*d*	Derby Co	63	Hartlepools U	59	Accrington S*	58
3	1957–58*d*	Scunthorpe U	66	Accrington S	59	Bradford C	57

DIVISION 3 (1958–59 to 1991–92)

MAXIMUM POINTS: 92; 138 FROM 1981–82.

3	1958–59	Plymouth Arg	62	Hull C	61	Brentford*	57
3	1959–60	Southampton	61	Norwich C	59	Shrewsbury T*	52
3	1960–61	Bury	68	Walsall	62	QPR	60
3	1961–62	Portsmouth	65	Grimsby T	62	Bournemouth*	59
3	1962–63	Northampton T	62	Swindon T	58	Port Vale	54
3	1963–64	Coventry C*	60	Crystal Palace	60	Watford	58
3	1964–65	Carlisle U	60	Bristol C*	59	Mansfield T	59
3	1965–66	Hull C	69	Millwall	65	QPR	57
3	1966–67	QPR	67	Middlesbrough	55	Watford	54

3	1967–68	Oxford U	57	Bury	56	Shrewsbury T	55
3	1968–69	Watford*	64	Swindon T	64	Luton T	61
3	1969–70	Orient	62	Luton T	60	Bristol R	56
3	1970–71	Preston NE	61	Fulham	60	Halifax T	56
3	1971–72	Aston Villa	70	Brighton & HA	65	Bournemouth*	62
3	1972–73	Bolton W	61	Notts Co	57	Blackburn R	55
3	1973–74	Oldham Ath	62	Bristol R*	61	York C	61
3	1974–75	Blackburn R	60	Plymouth Arg	59	Charlton Ath	55
3	1975–76	Hereford U	63	Cardiff C	57	Millwall	56
3	1976–77	Mansfield T	64	Brighton & HA	61	Crystal Palace*	59
3	1977–78	Wrexham	61	Cambridge U	58	Preston NE*	56
3	1978–79	Shrewsbury T	61	Watford*	60	Swansea C	60
3	1979–80	Grimsby T	62	Blackburn R	59	Sheffield W	58
3	1980–81	Rotherham U	61	Barnsley*	59	Charlton Ath	59
3	1981–82	Burnley*	80	Carlisle U	80	Fulham	78
3	1982–83	Portsmouth	91	Cardiff C	86	Huddersfield T	82
3	1983–84	Oxford U	95	Wimbledon	87	Sheffield U*	83
3	1984–85	Bradford C	94	Millwall	90	Hull C	87
3	1985–86	Reading	94	Plymouth Arg	87	Derby Co	87
3	1986–87	Bournemouth	97	Middlesbrough	94	Swindon T	87
3	1987–88	Sunderland	93	Brighton & HA	84	Walsall	82
3	1988–89	Wolverhampton W	92	Sheffield U*	84	Port Vale	84
3	1989–90	Bristol R	93	Bristol C	91	Notts Co	87
3	1990–91	Cambridge U	86	Southend U	85	Grimsby T*	83
3	1991–92	Brentford	82	Birmingham C	81	Huddersfield T‡	78

SECOND DIVISION (1992–93 to 2003–04)

MAXIMUM POINTS: 138

3	1992–93	Stoke C	93	Bolton W	90	Port Vale‡	89
3	1993–94	Reading	89	Port Vale	88	Plymouth Arg*‡	85
3	1994–95	Birmingham C	89	Brentford‡	85	Crewe Alex‡	83
3	1995–96	Swindon T	92	Oxford U	83	Blackpool‡	82
3	1996–97	Bury	84	Stockport Co	82	Luton T‡	78
3	1997–98	Watford	88	Bristol C	85	Grimsby T	72
3	1998–99	Fulham	101	Walsall	87	Manchester C	82
3	1999–2000	Preston NE	95	Burnley	88	Gillingham	85
3	2000–01	Millwall	93	Rotherham U	91	Reading‡	86
3	2001–02	Brighton & HA	90	Reading	84	Brentford*‡	83
3	2002–03	Wigan Ath	100	Crewe Alex	86	Bristol C*‡	83
3	2003–04	Plymouth Arg	90	QPR	83	Bristol C‡	82

FOOTBALL LEAGUE 1 (2004–05 to 2013–14)

MAXIMUM POINTS: 138

3	2004–05	Luton T	98	Hull C	86	Tranmere R‡	79
3	2005–06	Southend U	82	Colchester U	79	Brentford‡	76
3	2006–07	Scunthorpe U	91	Bristol C	85	Blackpool	83
3	2007–08	Swansea C	92	Nottingham F	82	Doncaster R*	80
3	2008–09	Leicester C	96	Peterborough U	89	Milton Keynes D‡	87
3	2009–10	Norwich C	95	Leeds U	86	Millwall	85
3	2010–11	Brighton & HA	95	Southampton	92	Huddersfield T‡	87
3	2011–12	Charlton Ath	101	Sheffield W	93	Sheffield U‡	90
3	2012–13	Doncaster R	84	Bournemouth	83	Brentford‡	79
3	2013-14	Wolverhampton W	103	Brentford	94	Leyton Orient‡	86

DIVISION 4 (1958–59 to 1991–92) – TIER 4

MAXIMUM POINTS: 92; 138 FROM 1981–82.

4	1958–59	Port Vale	64	Coventry C*	60	York C	60	Shrewsbury T	58
4	1959–60	Walsall	65	Notts Co*	60	Torquay U	60	Watford	57
4	1960–61	Peterborough U	66	Crystal Palace	64	Northampton T*	60	Bradford PA	60
4	1961–62²	Millwall	56	Colchester U	55	Wrexham	53	Carlisle U	52
4	1962–63	Brentford	62	Oldham Ath*	59	Crewe Alex	59	Mansfield T*	57
4	1963–64	Gillingham*	60	Carlisle U	60	Workington	59	Exeter C	58
4	1964–65	Brighton & HA	63	Millwall*	62	York C	62	Oxford U	61
4	1965–66	Doncaster R*	59	Darlington	59	Torquay U	58	Colchester U*	56
4	1966–67	Stockport Co	64	Southport*	59	Barrow	59	Tranmere R	58
4	1967–68	Luton T	66	Barnsley	61	Hartlepools U	60	Crewe Alex	58
4	1968–69	Doncaster R	59	Halifax T	57	Rochdale*	56	Bradford C	56
4	1969–70	Chesterfield	64	Wrexham	61	Swansea C	60	Port Vale	59
4	1970–71	Notts Co	69	Bournemouth	60	Oldham Ath	59	York C	56
4	1971–72	Grimsby T	63	Southend U	60	Brentford	59	Scunthorpe U	57
4	1972–73	Southport	62	Hereford U	58	Cambridge U	57	Aldershot*	56
4	1973–74	Peterborough U	65	Gillingham	62	Colchester U	60	Bury	59
4	1974–75	Mansfield T	68	Shrewsbury T	62	Rotherham U	59	Chester*	57
4	1975–76	Lincoln C	74	Northampton T	68	Reading	60	Tranmere R	58
4	1976–77	Cambridge U	65	Exeter C	62	Colchester U*	59	Bradford C	59
4	1977–78	Watford	71	Southend U	60	Swansea C*	56	Brentford	56
4	1978–79	Reading	65	Grimsby T*	61	Wimbledon*	61	Barnsley	61
4	1979–80	Huddersfield T	66	Walsall	64	Newport Co	61	Portsmouth*	60
4	1980–81	Southend U	67	Lincoln C	65	Doncaster R	56	Wimbledon	55
4	1981–82	Sheffield U	96	Bradford C*	91	Wigan Ath	91	Bournemouth	88
4	1982–83	Wimbledon	98	Hull C	90	Port Vale	88	Scunthorpe U	83
4	1983–84	York C	101	Doncaster R	85	Reading*	82	Bristol C	82
4	1984–85	Chesterfield	91	Blackpool	86	Darlington	85	Bury	84
4	1985–86	Swindon T	102	Chester C	84	Mansfield T	81	Port Vale	79
4	1986–87	Northampton T	99	Preston NE	90	Southend U	80	Wolverhampton W‡	79

4	1987–88	Wolverhampton W	90	Cardiff C	85	Bolton W	78	Scunthorpe U*‡	77
4	1988–89	Rotherham U	82	Tranmere R	80	Crewe Alex	78	Scunthorpe U*‡	77
4	1989–90	Exeter C	89	Grimsby T	79	Southend U	75	Stockport Co‡	74
4	1990–91	Darlington	83	Stockport Co*	82	Hartlepool U	82	Peterborough U	80
4	1991–92[3]	Burnley	83	Rotherham U*	77	Mansfield T	77	Blackpool	76

[2]*Maximum points:* 88 owing to Accrington Stanley's resignation.
[3]*Maximum points:* 126 owing to Aldershot being expelled (and only 23 teams started the competition).

THIRD DIVISION (1992–93 to 2003–04)

MAXIMUM POINTS: *a* 126; *b* 138.

4	1992–93a	Cardiff C	83	Wrexham	80	Barnet	79	York C	75
4	1993–94a	Shrewsbury T	79	Chester C	74	Crewe Alex	73	Wycombe W	70
4	1994–95a	Carlisle U	91	Walsall	83	Chesterfield	81	Bury‡	80
4	1995–96b	Preston NE	86	Gillingham	83	Bury	79	Plymouth Arg*	78
4	1996–97b	Wigan Ath*	87	Fulham	87	Carlisle U	84	Northampton T	72
4	1997–98b	Notts Co	99	Macclesfield T	82	Lincoln C	72	Colchester U*	74
4	1998–99b	Brentford	85	Cambridge U	81	Cardiff C	80	Scunthorpe U	74
4	1999–2000b	Swansea C	85	Rotherham U	84	Northampton T	82	Darlington‡	79
4	2000–01b	Brighton & HA	92	Cardiff C	82	Chesterfield[4]	80	Hartlepool U‡	77
4	2001–02b	Plymouth Arg	102	Luton T	97	Mansfield T	79	Cheltenham T	78
4	2002–03b	Rushden & D	87	Hartlepool U	85	Wrexham	84	Bournemouth	74
4	2003–04b	Doncaster R	92	Hull C	88	Torquay U*	81	Huddersfield T	81

[4]*Chesterfield deducted 9pts for irregularities.*

FOOTBALL LEAGUE 2 (2004–05 to 2013–14)

MAXIMUM POINTS: 138

4	2004–05	Yeovil T	83	Scunthorpe U*	80	Swansea C	80	Southend U	80
4	2005–06	Carlisle U	86	Northampton T	83	Leyton Orient	81	Grimsby T‡	78
4	2006–07	Walsall	89	Hartlepool U	88	Swindon T	85	Milton Keynes D‡	84
4	2007–08	Milton Keynes D	97	Peterborough U	92	Hereford U	88	Stockport Co	82
4	2008–09	Brentford	85	Exeter C	79	Wycombe W*	78	Bury‡	78
4	2009–10	Notts Co	93	Bournemouth	83	Rochdale	82	Morecambe*‡	73
4	2010–11	Chesterfield	86	Bury	81	Wycombe W	80	Shrewsbury T‡	79
4	2011–12	Swindon T	93	Shrewsbury T	88	Crawley T	84	Southend U‡	83
4	2012–13	Gillingham	83	Rotherham U	79	Port Vale	78	Burton Alb	76
4	2013-14	Chesterfield	84	Scunthorpe U*	81	Rochdale	81	Fleetwood T	76

LEAGUE TITLE WINS

DIVISION 1 (1888–89 to 1991–92) – TIER 1
Liverpool 18, Arsenal 10, Everton 9, Aston Villa 7, Manchester U 7, Sunderland 6, Newcastle U 4, Sheffield W 4 (2 as The Wednesday), Leeds U 3, Wolverhampton W 3, Blackburn R 2, Burnley 2, Derby Co 2, Manchester C 2, Portsmouth 2, Preston NE 2, Tottenham H 2, Chelsea 2, Ipswich T 1, Nottingham F 1, Sheffield U 1, WBA 1.

FA PREMIER LEAGUE (1992–93 to 2013–14) – TIER 1
Manchester U 13, Arsenal 3, Chelsea 3, Manchester C 2, Blackburn R 1.

DIVISION 2 (1892–93 TO 1991–92) – TIER 2
Leicester C 6, Manchester C 6, Sheffield W 5 (1 as The Wednesday), Birmingham C 4 (1 as Small Heath), Derby Co 4, Liverpool 4, Ipswich T 3, Leeds U 3, Middlesbrough 3, Notts Co 3, Preston NE 3, Aston Villa 2, Bolton W 2, Burnley 2, Chelsea 2, Grimsby T 2, Manchester U 2, Norwich C 2, Nottingham F 2, Stoke C 2, Tottenham H 2, WBA 2, West Ham U 2, Wolverhampton W 2, Blackburn R 1, Blackpool 1, Bradford C 1, Brentford 1, Bristol C 1, Bury 1, Coventry C 1, Crystal Palace 1, Everton 1, Fulham 1, Huddersfield T 1, Luton T 1, Millwall 1, Newcastle U 1, Oldham Ath 1, Oxford U 1, QPR 1, Sheffield U 1, Sunderland 1.

FIRST DIVISION (1992–93 to 2003–04) – TIER 2
Sunderland 2, Bolton W 2, Charlton Ath 1, Crystal Palace 1, Fulham 1, Manchester C 1, Middlesbrough 1, Newcastle U 1, Norwich C 1, Nottingham F 1, Portsmouth 1.

FOOTBALL LEAGUE CHAMPIONSHIP (2004–05 to 2013–14) – TIER 2
Reading 2, Sunderland 2, Cardiff C 1, Leicester C 1, Newcastle U 1, QPR 1, WBA 1, Wolverhampton W 1.

DIVISION 3—SOUTH (1920–21 to 1957–58) – TIER 3
Bristol C 3, Charlton Ath 2, Ipswich T 2, Millwall 2, Notts Co 2, Plymouth Arg 2, Swansea T 2, Brentford 2, Brighton & HA 1, Bristol R 1, Cardiff C 1, Coventry C 1, Crystal Palace 1, Fulham 1, Leyton Orient 1, Luton T 1, Newport Co 1, Norwich C 1, Nottingham F 1, Portsmouth 1, QPR 1, Reading 1, Southampton 1.

DIVISION 3—NORTH (1921–22 to 1957–58) – TIER 3
Barnsley 3, Doncaster R 3, Lincoln C 3, Chesterfield 2, Grimsby T 2, Hull C 2, Port Vale 2, Stockport Co 2, Bradford C 1, Bradford PA 1, Darlington 1, Derby Co 1, Nelson 1, Oldham Ath 1, Rotherham U 1, Scunthorpe U 1, Stoke C 1, Tranmere R 1, Wolverhampton W 1.

DIVISION 3 (1958–59 to 1991–92) – TIER 3
Oxford U 2, Portsmouth 2, Aston Villa 1, Blackburn R 1, Bolton W 1, Bournemouth 1, Bradford C 1, Brentford 1, Bristol R 1, Burnley 1, Bury 1, Cambridge U 1, Carlisle U 1, Coventry C 1, Grimsby T 1, Hereford U 1, Hull C 1, Mansfield T 1, Northampton T 1, Oldham Ath 1, Orient 1, Plymouth Arg 1, Preston NE 1, QPR 1, Reading 1, Rotherham U 1, Shrewsbury T 1, Southampton 1, Sunderland 1, Watford 1, Wolverhampton W 1, Wrexham 1.

SECOND DIVISION (1992–93 to 2003–04) – TIER 3
Birmingham C 1, Brighton & HA 1, Bury 1, Fulham 1, Millwall 1, Plymouth Arg 1, Preston NE 1, Reading 1, Stoke C 1, Swindon T 1, Watford 1, Wigan Ath 1.

FOOTBALL LEAGUE 1 (2004–05 to 2013–14) – TIER 3
Brighton & HA 1, Charlton Ath 1, Doncaster R 1, Leicester C 1, Luton T 1, Norwich C 1, Scunthorpe U 1, Southend U 1, Swansea C 1, Wolverhampton W 1.

DIVISION 4 (1958–59 to 1991–92) – TIER 4
Chesterfield 2, Doncaster R 2, Peterborough U 2, Brentford 1, Brighton & HA 1, Burnley 1, Cambridge U 1, Darlington 1, Exeter C 1, Gillingham 1, Grimsby T 1, Huddersfield T 1, Lincoln C 1, Luton T 1, Mansfield T 1, Millwall †, Northampton T 1, Notts Co 1, Port Vale 1, Reading 1, Rotherham U 1, Sheffield U 1, Southend U 1, Southport 1, Stockport Co 1, Swindon T 1, Walsall 1, Watford 1, Wimbledon 1, Wolverhampton W 1, York C 1.

THIRD DIVISION (1992–93 to 2003–04) – TIER 4
Brentford 1, Brighton & HA 1, Cardiff C 1, Carlisle U 1, Doncaster R 1, Notts Co 1, Plymouth Arg 1, Preston NE 1, Rushden & D 1, Shrewsbury T 1, Swansea C 1, Wigan Ath 1.

FOOTBALL LEAGUE 2 (2004–05 to 2013–14) – TIER 4
Chesterfield 2, Brentford 1, Carlisle U 1, Gillingham 1, Milton Keynes D 1, Notts Co 1, Swindon T 1, Walsall 1, Yeovil T 1.

PROMOTED AFTER PLAY-OFFS

1986–87	Charlton Ath to Division 1; Swindon T to Division 2; Aldershot to Division 3
1987–88	Middlesbrough to Division 1; Walsall to Division 2; Swansea C to Division 3
1988–89	Crystal Palace to Division 1; Port Vale to Division 2; Leyton Orient to Division 3
1989–90	Sunderland to Division 1; Notts Co to Division 2; Cambridge U to Division 3
1990–91	Notts Co to Division 1; Tranmere R to Division 2; Torquay U to Division 3
1991–92	Blackburn R to Premier League; Peterborough U to First Division; Blackpool to Second Division
1992–93	Swindon T to Premier League; WBA to First Division; York C to Second Division
1993–94	Leicester C to Premier League; Burnley to First Division; Wycombe W to Second Division
1994–95	Bolton W to Premier League; Huddersfield T to First Division; Wycome Wanderers to Second Division
1995–96	Leicester C to Premier League; Bradford C to First Division; Plymouth Arg to Second Division
1996–97	Crystal Palace to Premier League; Crewe Alex to First Division; Northampton T to Second Division
1997–98	Charlton Ath to Premier League; Grimsby T to First Division; Colchester U to Second Division
1998–99	Watford to Premier League; Manchester C to First Division; Scunthorpe U to Second Division
1999–2000	Ipswich to Premier League; Gillingham to First Division; Peterborough to Second Division
2000–01	Bolton W to Premier league; Walsall to First Division; Blackpool to Second Division
2001–02	Birmingham C to Premier League; Stoke C to First Division; Cheltenham T to Second Division
2002–03	Wolverhampton W to Premier League; Cardiff C to First Division; Bournemouth to Second Division
2003–04	Crystal Palace to Premier League; Brighton & HA to First Division; Huddersfield T to Second Division
2004–05	West Ham U to Premier League; Sheffield W to Championship; Southend U to Football League 1
2005–06	Watford to Premier League; Barnsley to Championship; Cheltenham T to Football League 1
2006–07	Derby Co to Premier League; Blackpool to Championship; Bristol R to Football League 1
2007–08	Hull C to Premier League; Doncaster R to Championship; Stockport Co to Football League 1
2008–09	Burnley to Premier League; Scunthorpe U to Championship; Gillingham to Football League 1
2009–10	Blackpool to Premier League; Millwall to Championship; Dagenham & R to Football League 1
2010–11	Swansea C to Premier League; Peterborough U to Championship; Stevenage to Football League 1
2011–12	West Ham U to Premier League; Huddersfield T to Championship; Crewe Alex to Football League 1
2012–13	Crystal Palace to Premier League; Yeovil T to Championship; Bradford C to Football League 1
2013–14	QPR to Premier League; Rotherham U to Championship; Fleetwood T to Football League 1

RELEGATED CLUBS

1891–92 League extended. Newton Heath, Sheffield W and Nottingham F admitted. *Second Division formed* including Darwen.

1892–93 In Test matches, Sheffield U and Darwen won promotion in place of Notts Co and Accrington S.

1893–94 In Tests, Liverpool and Small Heath won promotion. Newton Heath and Darwen relegated.

1894–95 After Tests, Bury promoted, Liverpool relegated.

1895–96 After Tests, Liverpool promoted, Small Heath relegated.

1896–97 After Tests, Notts Co promoted, Burnley relegated.

1897–98 Test system abolished after success of Stoke C and Burnley. League extended. Blackburn R and Newcastle U elected to First Division. *Automatic promotion and relegation introduced.*

DIVISION 1 TO DIVISION 2 (1898–99 to 1991–92)

1898–99	Bolton W and Sheffield W
1899–1900	Burnley and Glossop
1900–01	Preston NE and WBA
1901–02	Small Heath and Manchester C
1902–03	Grimsby T and Bolton W
1903–04	Liverpool and WBA
1904–05	League extended. Bury and Notts Co, two bottom clubs in First Division, re-elected.
1905–06	Nottingham F and Wolverhampton W
1906–07	Derby Co and Stoke C
1907–08	Bolton W and Birmingham C
1908–09	Manchester C and Leicester Fosse
1909–10	Bolton W and Chelsea
1910–11	Bristol C and Nottingham F
1911–12	Preston NE and Bury
1912–13	Notts Co and Woolwich Arsenal
1913–14	Preston NE and Derby Co
1914–15	Tottenham H and Chelsea*
1919–20	Notts Co and Sheffield W
1920–21	Derby Co and Bradford PA
1921–22	Bradford C and Manchester U
1922–23	Stoke C and Oldham Ath
1923–24	Chelsea and Middlesbrough
1924–25	Preston NE and Nottingham F
1925–26	Manchester C and Notts Co
1926–27	Leeds U and WBA
1927–28	Tottenham H and Middlesbrough
1928–29	Bury and Cardiff C
1929–30	Burnley and Everton
1930–31	Leeds U and Manchester U
1931–32	Grimsby T and West Ham U
1932–33	Bolton W and Blackpool
1933–34	Newcastle U and Sheffield U
1934–35	Leicester C and Tottenham H
1935–36	Aston Villa and Blackburn R
1936–37	Manchester U and Sheffield W
1937–38	Manchester C and WBA
1938–39	Birmingham C and Leicester C
1946–47	Brentford and Leeds U
1947–48	Blackburn R and Grimsby T
1948–49	Preston NE and Sheffield U
1949–50	Manchester C and Birmingham C
1950–51	Sheffield W and Everton
1951–52	Huddersfield T and Fulham

1952–53	Stoke C and Derby Co
1953–54	Middlesbrough and Liverpool
1954–55	Leicester C and Sheffield W
1955–56	Huddersfield T and Sheffield U
1956–57	Charlton Ath and Cardiff C
1957–58	Sheffield W and Sunderland
1958–59	Portsmouth and Aston Villa
1959–60	Luton T and Leeds U
1960–61	Preston NE and Newcastle U
1961–62	Chelsea and Cardiff C
1962–63	Manchester C and Leyton Orient
1963–64	Bolton W and Ipswich T
1964–65	Wolverhampton W and Birmingham C
1965–66	Northampton T and Blackburn R
1966–67	Aston Villa and Blackpool
1967–68	Fulham and Sheffield U
1968–69	Leicester C and QPR
1969–70	Sunderland and Sheffield W
1970–71	Burnley and Blackpool
1971–72	Huddersfield T and Nottingham F
1972–73	Crystal Palace and WBA
1973–74	Southampton, Manchester U, Norwich C
1974–75	Luton T, Chelsea, Carlisle U
1975–76	Wolverhampton W, Burnley, Sheffield U
1976–77	Sunderland, Stoke C, Tottenham H
1977–78	West Ham U, Newcastle U, Leicester C
1978–79	QPR, Birmingham C, Chelsea
1979–80	Bristol C, Derby Co, Bolton W
1980–81	Norwich C, Leicester C, Crystal Palace
1981–82	Leeds U, Wolverhampton W, Middlesbrough
1982–83	Manchester C, Swansea C, Brighton & HA
1983–84	Birmingham C, Notts Co, Wolverhampton W
1984–85	Norwich C, Sunderland, Stoke C
1985–86	Ipswich T, Birmingham C, WBA
1986–87	Leicester C, Manchester C, Aston Villa
1987–88	Chelsea**, Portsmouth, Watford, Oxford U
1988–89	Middlesbrough, West Ham U, Newcastle U
1989–90	Sheffield W, Charlton Ath, Millwall
1990–91	Sunderland and Derby Co
1991–92	Luton T, Notts Co, West Ham U

***Relegated after play-offs.*

**Subsequently re-elected to Division 1 when League was extended after the War.*

FA PREMIER LEAGUE TO DIVISION 1 (1992–93 to 2003–04)

1992–93 Crystal Palace, Middlesbrough, Nottingham F	1998–99 Charlton Ath, Blackburn R, Nottingham F
1993–94 Sheffield U, Oldham Ath, Swindon T	1999–2000 Wimbledon, Sheffield W, Watford
1994–95 Crystal Palace, Norwich C, Leicester C, Ipswich T	2000–01 Manchester C, Coventry C, Bradford C
1995–96 Manchester C, QPR, Bolton W	2001–02 Ipswich T, Derby Co, Leicester C
1996–97 Sunderland, Middlesbrough, Nottingham F	2002–03 West Ham U, WBA, Sunderland
1997–98 Bolton W, Barnsley, Crystal Palace	2003–04 Leicester C, Leeds U, Wolverhampton W

FA PREMIER LEAGUE TO CHAMPIONSHIP (2004–05 to 2013–14)

2004–05 Crystal Palace, Norwich C, Southampton	2009–10 Burnley, Hull C, Portsmouth
2005–06 Birmingham C, WBA, Sunderland	2010–11 Birmingham C, Blackpool, West Ham U
2006–07 Sheffield U, Charlton Ath, Watford	2011–12 Bolton W, Blackburn R, Wolverhampton W
2007–08 Reading, Birmingham C, Derby Co	2012–13 Wigan Ath, Reading, QPR
2008–09 Newcastle U, Middlesbrough, WBA	2013–14 Norwich C, Fulham, Cardiff C

DIVISION 2 TO DIVISION 3 (1920–21 to 1991–92)

1920–21 Stockport Co	1960–61 Lincoln C and Portsmouth
1921–22 Bradford PA and Bristol C	1961–62 Brighton & HA and Bristol R
1922–23 Rotherham Co and Wolverhampton W	1962–63 Walsall and Luton T
1923–24 Nelson and Bristol C	1963–64 Grimsby T and Scunthorpe U
1924–25 Crystal Palace and Coventry C	1964–65 Swindon T and Swansea T
1925–26 Stoke C and Stockport Co	1965–66 Middlesbrough and Leyton Orient
1926–27 Darlington and Bradford C	1966–67 Northampton T and Bury
1927–28 Fulham and South Shields	1967–68 Plymouth Arg and Rotherham U
1928–29 Port Vale and Clapton Orient	1968–69 Fulham and Bury
1929–30 Hull C and Notts Co	1969–70 Preston NE and Aston Villa
1930–31 Reading and Cardiff C	1970–71 Blackburn R and Bolton W
1931–32 Barnsley and Bristol C	1971–72 Charlton Ath and Watford
1932–33 Chesterfield and Charlton Ath	1972–73 Huddersfield T and Brighton & HA
1933–34 Millwall and Lincoln C	1973–74 Crystal Palace, Preston NE, Swindon T
1934–35 Oldham Ath and Notts Co	1974–75 Millwall, Cardiff C, Sheffield W
1935–36 Port Vale and Hull C	1975–76 Oxford U, York C, Portsmouth
1936–37 Doncaster R and Bradford C	1976–77 Carlisle U, Plymouth Arg, Hereford U
1937–38 Barnsley and Stockport Co	1977–78 Blackpool, Mansfield T, Hull C
1938–39 Norwich C and Tranmere R	1978–79 Sheffield U, Millwall, Blackburn R
1946–47 Swansea T and Newport Co	1979–80 Fulham, Burnley, Charlton Ath
1947–48 Doncaster R and Millwall	1980–81 Preston NE, Bristol C, Bristol R
1948–49 Nottingham F and Lincoln C	1981–82 Cardiff C, Wrexham, Orient
1949–50 Plymouth Arg and Bradford PA	1982–83 Rotherham U, Burnley, Bolton W
1950–51 Grimsby T and Chesterfield	1983–84 Derby Co, Swansea C, Cambridge U
1951–52 Coventry C and QPR	1984–85 Notts Co, Cardiff C, Wolverhampton W
1952–53 Southampton and Barnsley	1985–86 Carlisle U, Middlesbrough, Fulham
1953–54 Brentford and Oldham Ath	1986–87 Sunderland**, Grimsby T, Brighton & HA
1954–55 Ipswich T and Derby Co	1987–88 Huddersfield T, Reading, Sheffield U**
1955–56 Plymouth Arg and Hull C	1988–89 Shrewsbury T, Birmingham C, Walsall
1956–57 Port Vale and Bury	1989–90 Bournemouth, Bradford C, Stoke C
1957–58 Doncaster R and Notts Co	1990–91 WBA and Hull C
1958–59 Barnsley and Grimsby T	1991–92 Plymouth Arg, Brighton & HA, Port Vale
1959–60 Bristol C and Hull C	

FIRST DIVISION TO SECOND DIVISION (1992–93 to 2003–04)

1992–93 Brentford, Cambridge U, Bristol R	1998–99 Bury, Oxford U, Bristol C
1993–94 Birmingham C, Oxford U, Peterborough U	1999–2000 Walsall, Port Vale, Swindon T
1994–95 Swindon T, Burnley, Bristol C, Notts Co	2000–01 Huddersfield T, QPR, Tranmere R
1995–96 Millwall, Watford, Luton T	2001–02 Crewe Alex, Barnsley, Stockport Co
1996–97 Grimsby T, Oldham Ath, Southend U	2002–03 Sheffield W, Brighton & HA, Grimsby T
1997–98 Manchester C, Stoke C, Reading	2003–04 Walsall, Bradford C, Wimbledon

FOOTBALL LEAGUE CHAMPIONSHIP TO FOOTBALL LEAGUE 1 (2004–05 to 2013–14)

2004–05 Gillingham, Nottingham F, Rotherham U	2009–10 Sheffield W, Plymouth Arg, Peterborough U
2005–06 Crewe Alex, Millwall, Brighton & HA	2010–11 Preston NE, Sheffield U, Scunthorpe U
2006–07 Southend U, Luton T, Leeds U	2011–12 Portsmouth, Coventry C, Doncaster R
2007–08 Leicester C, Scunthorpe U, Colchester U	2012–13 Peterborough U, Wolverhampton W, Bristol C
2008–09 Norwich C, Southampton, Charlton Ath	2013–14 Doncaster R, Barnsley, Yeovil T

DIVISION 3 TO DIVISION 4 (1958–59 to 1991–92)

1958–59 Stockport Co, Doncaster R, Notts Co, Rochdale	1971–72 Mansfield T, Barnsley, Torquay U, Bradford C
1959–60 York C, Mansfield T, Wrexham, Accrington S	1972–73 Rotherham U, Brentford, Swansea C, Scunthorpe U
1960–61 Tranmere R, Bradford C, Colchester U, Chesterfield	1973–74 Cambridge U, Shrewsbury T, Southport, Rochdale
1961–62 Torquay U, Lincoln C, Brentford, Newport Co	1974–75 Bournemouth, Tranmere R, Watford, Huddersfield T
1962–63 Bradford PA, Brighton & HA, Carlisle U, Halifax T	1975–76 Aldershot, Colchester U, Southend U, Halifax T
1963–64 Millwall, Crewe Alex, Wrexham, Notts Co	1976–77 Reading, Northampton T, Grimsby T, York C
1964–65 Luton T, Port Vale, Colchester U, Barnsley	1977–78 Port Vale, Bradford C, Hereford U, Portsmouth
1965–66 Southend U, Exeter C, Brentford, York C	1978–79 Peterborough U, Walsall, Tranmere R, Lincoln C
1966–67 Swansea T, Darlington, Doncaster R, Workington	1979–80 Bury, Southend U, Mansfield T, Wimbledon
1967–68 Grimsby T, Colchester U, Scunthorpe U, Peterborough U (demoted)	1980–81 Sheffield U, Colchester U, Blackpool, Hull C
1968–69 Northampton T, Hartlepool, Crewe Alex, Oldham Ath	1981–82 Wimbledon, Swindon T, Bristol C, Chester
1969–70 Bournemouth, Southport, Barrow, Stockport Co	1982–83 Reading, Wrexham, Doncaster R, Chesterfield
1970–71 Reading, Bury, Doncaster R, Gillingham	1983–84 Scunthorpe U, Southend U, Port Vale, Exeter C
	1984–85 Burnley, Orient, Preston NE, Cambridge U

1985–86	Lincoln C, Cardiff C, Wolverhampton W, Swansea C
1986–87	Bolton W**, Carlisle U, Darlington, Newport Co
1987–88	Rotherham U**, Grimsby T, York C, Doncaster R
1988–89	Southend U, Chesterfield, Gillingham, Aldershot

1989–90	Cardiff C, Northampton T, Blackpool, Walsall
1990–91	Crewe Alex, Rotherham U, Mansfield T
1991–92	Bury, Shrewsbury T, Torquay U, Darlington

** *Relegated after play-offs.*

SECOND DIVISION TO THIRD DIVISION (1992–93 to 2003–04)

1992–93	Preston NE, Mansfield T, Wigan Ath, Chester C
1993–94	Fulham, Exeter C, Hartlepool U, Barnet
1994–95	Cambridge U, Plymouth Arg, Cardiff C, Chester C, Leyton Orient
1995–96	Carlisle U, Swansea C, Brighton & HA, Hull C
1996–97	Peterborough U, Shrewsbury T, Rotherham U, Notts Co
1997–98	Brentford, Plymouth Arg, Carlisle U, Southend U
1998–99	York C, Northampton T, Lincoln C, Macclesfield T

1999–2000	Cardiff C, Blackpool, Scunthorpe U, Chesterfield
2000–01	Bristol R, Luton T, Swansea C, Oxford U
2001–02	Bournemouth, Bury, Wrexham, Cambridge U
2002–03	Cheltenham T, Huddersfield T, Mansfield T Northampton T
2003–04	Grimsby T, Rushden & D, Notts Co, Wycombe W

FOOTBALL LEAGUE 1 TO FOOTBALL LEAGUE 2 (2004–05 to 2013–14)

2004–05	Torquay U, Wrexham, Peterborough U, Stockport Co
2005–06	Hartlepool U, Milton Keynes D, Swindon T, Walsall
2006–07	Chesterfield, Bradford C, Rotherham U, Brentford
2007–08	Bournemouth, Gillingham, Port Vale, Luton T
2008–09	Northampton T, Crewe Alex, Cheltenham T, Hereford U

2009–10	Gillingham, Wycombe W, Southend U, Stockport Co
2010–11	Dagenham & R, Bristol R, Plymouth Arg, Swindon T
2011–12	Wycombe W, Chesterfield, Exeter C, Rochdale
2012–13	Scunthorpe U, Bury, Hartlepool U, Portsmouth
2013–14	Tranmere R, Carlisle U, Shrewsbury T, Stevenage

LEAGUE STATUS FROM 1986–87

RELEGATED FROM LEAGUE

1986–87 Lincoln C	1987–88 Newport Co
1988–89 Darlington	1989–90 Colchester U
1990–91 —	1991–92 —
1992–93 Halifax T	1993–94 —
1994–95 —	1995–96 —
1996–97 Hereford U	1997–98 Doncaster R
1998–99 Scarborough	1999–2000 Chester C
2000–01 Barnet	2001–02 Halifax T
2002–03 Shrewsbury T, Exeter C	
2003–04 Carlisle U, York C	
2004–05 Kidderminster H, Cambridge U	
2005–06 Oxford U, Rushden & D	
2006–07 Boston U, Torquay U	
2007–08 Mansfield T, Wrexham	
2008–09 Chester C, Luton T	
2009–10 Grimsby T, Darlington	
2010–11 Lincoln C, Stockport Co	
2011–12 Hereford U, Macclesfield T	
2012–13 Barnet, Aldershot T	
2013–14 Bristol R, Torquay U	

PROMOTED TO LEAGUE

1986–87 Scarborough	1987–88 Lincoln C
1988–89 Maidstone U	1989–90 Darlington
1990–91 Barnet	1991–92 Colchester U
1992–93 Wycombe W	1993–94 —
1994–95 —	1995–96 —
1996–97 Macclesfield T	1997–98 Halifax T
1998–99 Cheltenham T	1999–2000 Kidderminster H
2000–01 Rushden & D	2001–02 Boston U
2002–03 Yeovil T, Doncaster R	
2003–04 Chester C, Shrewsbury T	
2004–05 Barnet, Carlisle U	
2005–06 Accrington S, Hereford U	
2006–07 Dagenham & R, Morecambe	
2007–08 Aldershot T, Exeter C	
2008–09 Burton Alb, Torquay U	
2009–10 Stevenage B, Oxford U	
2010–11 Crawley T, AFC Wimbledon	
2011–12 Fleetwood T, York C	
2012–13 Mansfield T, Newport Co	
2013–14 Luton T, Cambridge U	

APPLICATIONS FOR RE-ELECTION

FOURTH DIVISION

Eleven: Hartlepool U.

Seven: Crewe Alex.

Six: Barrow (lost League place to Hereford U 1972), Halifax T, Rochdale, Southport (lost League place to Wigan Ath 1978), York C.

Five: Chester C, Darlington, Lincoln C, Stockport Co, Workington (lost League place to Wimbledon 1977).

Four: Bradford PA (lost League place to Cambridge U 1970), Newport Co, Northampton T.

Three: Doncaster R, Hereford U.

Two: Bradford C, Exeter C, Oldham Ath, Scunthorpe U, Torquay U.

One: Aldershot, Colchester U, Gateshead (lost League place to Peterborough U 1960), Grimsby T, Swansea C, Tranmere R, Wrexham, Blackpool, Cambridge U, Preston NE.

Accrington S resigned and Oxford U were elected 1962.

Port Vale were forced to re-apply following expulsion in 1968.

Aldershot expelled March 1992. Maidstone U resigned August 1992.

THIRD DIVISIONS NORTH & SOUTH

Seven: Walsall.

Six: Exeter C, Halifax T, Newport Co.

Five: Accrington S, Barrow, Gillingham, New Brighton, Southport.

Four: Rochdale, Norwich C.

Three: Crystal Palace, Crewe Alex, Darlington, Hartlepool U, Merthyr T, Swindon T.

Two: Aberdare Ath, Aldershot, Ashington, Bournemouth, Brentford, Chester, Colchester U, Durham C, Millwall, Nelson, QPR, Rotherham U, Southend U, Tranmere R, Watford, Workington.

One: Bradford C, Bradford PA, Brighton & HA, Bristol R, Cardiff C, Carlisle U, Charlton Ath, Gateshead, Grimsby T, Mansfield T, Shrewsbury T, Torquay U, York C.

LEAGUE ATTENDANCES SINCE 1946–47

Season	Matches	Total	Div. 1	Div. 2	Div. 3 (S)	Div. 3 (N)
1946–47	1848	35,604,606	15,005,316	11,071,572	5,664,004	3,863,714
1947–48	1848	40,259,130	16,732,341	12,286,350	6,653,610	4,586,829
1948–49	1848	41,271,414	17,914,667	11,353,237	6,998,429	5,005,081
1949–50	1848	40,517,865	17,278,625	11,694,158	7,104,155	4,440,927
1950–51	2028	39,584,967	16,679,454	10,780,580	7,367,884	4,757,109
1951–52	2028	39,015,866	16,110,322	11,066,189	6,958,927	4,880,428
1952–53	2028	37,149,966	16,050,278	9,686,654	6,704,299	4,708,735
1953–54	2028	36,174,590	16,154,915	9,510,053	6,311,508	4,198,114
1954–55	2028	34,133,103	15,087,221	8,988,794	5,996,017	4,051,071
1955–56	2028	33,150,809	14,108,961	9,080,002	5,692,479	4,269,367
1956–57	2028	32,744,405	13,803,037	8,718,162	5,622,189	4,601,017
1957–58	2028	33,562,208	14,468,652	8,663,712	6,097,183	4,332,661

Season	Matches	Total	Div. 1	Div. 2	Div. 3	Div. 4
1958–59	2028	33,610,985	14,727,691	8,641,997	5,946,600	4,276,697
1959–60	2028	32,538,611	14,391,227	8,399,627	5,739,707	4,008,050
1960–61	2028	28,619,754	12,926,948	7,033,936	4,784,256	3,874,614
1961–62	2015	27,979,902	12,061,194	7,453,089	5,199,106	3,266,513
1962–63	2028	28,885,852	12,490,239	7,792,770	5,341,362	3,261,481
1963–64	2028	28,535,022	12,486,626	7,594,158	5,419,157	3,035,081
1964–65	2028	27,641,168	12,708,752	6,984,104	4,436,245	3,512,067
1965–66	2028	27,206,980	12,480,644	6,914,757	4,779,150	3,032,429
1966–67	2028	28,902,596	14,242,957	7,253,819	4,421,172	2,984,648
1967–68	2028	30,107,298	15,289,410	7,450,410	4,013,087	3,354,391
1968–69	2028	29,382,172	14,584,851	7,382,390	4,339,656	3,075,275
1969–70	2028	29,600,972	14,868,754	7,581,728	4,223,761	2,926,729
1970–71	2028	28,194,146	13,954,337	7,098,265	4,377,213	2,764,331
1971–72	2028	28,700,729	14,484,603	6,769,308	4,697,392	2,749,426
1972–73	2028	25,448,642	13,998,154	5,631,730	3,737,252	2,081,506
1973–74	2027	24,982,203	13,070,991	6,326,108	3,421,624	2,163,480
1974–75	2028	25,577,977	12,613,178	6,955,970	4,086,145	1,992,684
1975–76	2028	24,896,053	13,089,861	5,798,405	3,948,449	2,059,338
1976–77	2028	26,182,800	13,647,585	6,250,597	4,152,218	2,132,400
1977–78	2028	25,392,872	13,255,677	6,474,763	3,332,042	2,330,390
1978–79	2028	24,540,627	12,704,549	6,153,223	3,374,558	2,308,297
1979–80	2028	24,623,975	12,163,002	6,112,025	3,999,328	2,349,620
1980–81	2028	21,907,569	11,392,894	5,175,442	3,637,854	1,701,379
1981–82	2028	20,006,961	10,420,793	4,750,463	2,836,915	1,998,790
1982–83	2028	18,766,158	9,295,613	4,974,937	2,943,568	1,552,040
1983–84	2028	18,358,631	8,711,448	5,359,757	2,729,942	1,557,484
1984–85	2028	17,849,835	9,761,404	4,030,823	2,667,008	1,390,600
1985–86	2028	16,488,577	9,037,854	3,551,968	2,490,481	1,408,274
1986–87	2028	17,379,218	9,144,676	4,168,131	2,350,970	1,715,441
1987–88	2030	17,959,732	8,094,571	5,341,599	2,751,275	1,772,287
1988–89	2036	18,464,192	7,809,993	5,887,805	3,035,327	1,791,067
1989–90	2036	19,445,442	7,883,039	6,867,674	2,803,551	1,891,178
1990–91	2036	19,508,202	8,618,709	6,285,068	2,835,759	1,768,666
1991–92	2064*	20,487,273	9,989,160	5,809,787	2,993,352	1,694,974

Season	Matches	Total	FA Premier	Div. 1	Div. 2	Div. 3
1992–93	2028	20,657,327	9,759,809	5,874,017	3,483,073	1,540,428
1993–94	2028	21,683,381	10,644,551	6,487,104	2,972,702	1,579,024
1994–95	2028	21,856,020	11,213,168	6,044,293	3,037,752	1,560,807
1995–96	2036	21,844,416	10,469,107	6,566,349	2,843,652	1,965,308
1996–97	2036	22,783,163	10,804,762	6,931,539	3,195,223	1,851,639
1997–98	2036	24,692,608	11,092,106	8,330,018	3,503,264	1,767,220
1998–99	2036	25,435,542	11,620,326	7,543,369	4,169,697	2,102,150
1999-2000	2036	25,341,090	11,668,497	7,810,208	3,700,433	2,161,952
2000–01	2036	26,030,167	12,472,094	7,909,512	3,488,166	2,160,395
2001–02	2036	27,756,977	13,043,118	8,352,128	3,963,153	2,398,578
2002–03	2036	28,343,386	13,468,965	8,521,017	3,892,469	2,460,935
2003–04	2036	29,197,510	13,303,136	8,772,780	4,146,495	2,975,099

Season	Matches	Total	FA Premier	Championship	League 1	League 2
2004–05	2036	29,245,870	12,878,791	9,612,761	4,270,674	2,483,644
2005–06	2036	29,089,084	12,871,643	9,719,204	4,183,011	2,315,226
2006–07	2036	29,541,949	13,058,115	10,057,813	4,135,599	2,290,422
2007–08	2036	29,914,212	13,708,875	9,397,036	4,412,023	2,396,278
2008–09	2036	29,881,966	13,527,815	9,877,552	4,171,834	2,304,765
2009–10	2036	30,057,892	12,977,251	9,909,882	5,043,099	2,127,660
2010–11	2036	29,459,105	13,406,990	9,595,236	4,150,547	2,306,332
2011–12	2036	29,454,401	13,148,465	9,784,100	4,091,897	2,429,939
2012–13	2036	29,225,443	13,653,958	9,662,232	3,485,290	2,423,963
2013–14	2036	29,629,309	13,930,810	9,168,922	4,126,701	2,402,876

*Figures include matches played by Aldershot.
Football League official total for their three divisions in 2001–02 was 14,716,162.

ENGLISH LEAGUE ATTENDANCES 2013–14

BARCLAYS PREMIER LEAGUE ATTENDANCES

	Average Gate			Season 2013–14	
	2012–13	*2013–14*	*+/–%*	*Highest*	*Lowest*
Arsenal	60,079	60,013	–0.11	60,071	59,937
Aston Villa	35,060	36,081	+2.91	42,682	30,292
Cardiff C	22,999	27,430	+19.26	28,018	26,167
Chelsea	41,462	41,482	+0.05	41,623	41,111
Crystal Palace	17,280	24,377	+41.07	25,564	22,466
Everton	36,356	37,732	+3.78	39,576	33,495
Fulham	25,394	24,977	–1.64	25,700	22,288
Hull C	17,369	24,117	+38.85	24,940	21,949
Liverpool	44,749	44,671	–0.17	44,822	44,411
Manchester C	46,974	47,080	+0.23	47,364	46,559
Manchester U	75,530	75,207	–0.43	75,368	74,966
Newcastle U	50,517	50,395	–0.24	52,280	46,402
Norwich C	26,672	26,805	+0.50	26,876	26,646
Southampton	30,874	30,212	–2.15	31,659	27,987
Stoke C	26,922	26,137	–2.92	27,429	24,822
Sunderland	40,544	41,090	+1.35	46,313	34,745
Swansea C	20,370	20,407	+0.18	20,769	19,242
Tottenham H	36,030	35,808	–0.61	36,102	34,410
WBA	25,360	25,194	–0.66	26,613	22,943
West Ham U	34,720	33,986	–2.11	34,977	31,033

TOTAL ATTENDANCES: 13,930,810 (380 games)
Average 36,660 (+2.03%)
HIGHEST: 75,368 Manchester U v Aston Villa
LOWEST: 19,242 Swansea C v Stoke C
HIGHEST AVERAGE: 75,207 Manchester U
LOWEST AVERAGE: 20,407 Swansea C

SKY BET FOOTBALL LEAGUE: CHAMPIONSHIP ATTENDANCES

	Average Gate			Season 2013–14	
	2012–13	*2013–14*	*+/–%*	*Highest*	*Lowest*
Barnsley	10,207	11,557	+13.23	16,338	9,084
Birmingham C	16,703	15,458	–7.45	23,497	12,663
Blackburn R	14,997	14,960	–0.25	21,589	12,332
Blackpool	13,917	14,217	+2.16	16,098	12,280
Bolton W	18,094	16,141	–10.79	19,622	14,260
Bournemouth	6,852	9,952	+45.24	11,307	7,258
Brighton & HA	26,236	27,283	+3.99	29,093	25,725
Burnley	12,928	13,722	+6.14	19,125	9,641
Charlton Ath	18,500	16,134	–12.79	23,600	12,974
Derby Co	23,228	24,933	+7.34	33,004	21,037
Doncaster R	7,239	9,041	+24.89	12,609	6,454
Huddersfield T	15,166	14,213	–6.28	18,309	11,857
Ipswich T	17,526	17,111	–2.37	20,862	14,953
Leeds U	21,572	25,088	+16.30	33,432	17,343
Leicester C	22,054	24,995	+13.33	31,424	19,153
Middlesbrough	16,794	15,748	–6.23	23,679	12,793
Millwall	10,559	11,063	+4.77	16,102	8,415
Nottingham F	23,082	22,630	–1.96	28,276	17,951
QPR	17,779	16,656	–6.32	18,171	14,649
Reading	23,862	19,167	–19.68	23,335	16,636
Sheffield W	24,078	21,278	–11.63	25,279	18,029
Watford	13,454	15,512	+15.29	16,625	13,904
Wigan Ath	19,375	15,177	–21.67	19,226	12,709
Yeovil T	4,072	6,616	+62.48	9,108	4,463

TOTAL ATTENDANCES: 9,168,922 (552 games)
Average 16,610 (–5.11%)
HIGHEST: 33,432 Leeds U v Brighton & HA
LOWEST: 4,463 Yeovil T v Millwall
HIGHEST AVERAGE: 27,283 Brighton & HA
LOWEST AVERAGE: 6,616 Yeovil T

Premier League and Football League attendance averages and highest crowd figures for 2013–14 are unofficial.

SKY BET FOOTBALL LEAGUE: DIVISION 1 ATTENDANCES

	Average Gate			Season 2013–14	
	2012–13	2013–14	+/–%	Highest	Lowest
Bradford C	10,322	14,121	+36.80	18,218	12,106
Brentford	6,303	7,716	+22.41	11,393	5,646
Bristol C	13,348	11,929	–10.63	14,884	10,085
Carlisle U	4,302	4,243	–1.36	7,934	2,969
Colchester U	3,530	3,735	+5.81	7,295	2,508
Coventry C	10,864	2,348	–78.38	4,905	1,603
Crawley T	3,408	3,486	+2.29	5,680	2,407
Crewe Alex	4,903	4,932	+0.60	7,458	3,613
Gillingham	6,601	6,219	–5.78	8,613	4,951
Leyton Orient	4,002	5,468	+36.62	8,335	3,645
Milton Keynes D	8,612	9,047	+5.05	20,516	6,675
Notts Co	5,522	5,508	–0.24	8,564	3,331
Oldham Ath	4,129	4,415	+6.94	7,698	2,792
Peterborough U	8,215	6,340	–22.82	10,026	4,263
Port Vale	5,727	6,249	+9.12	12,601	3,734
Preston NE	9,263	10,234	+10.48	16,583	8,206
Rotherham U	7,967	8,450	+6.06	11,758	7,096
Sheffield U	18,612	17,507	–5.94	21,659	14,796
Shrewsbury T	5,736	5,581	–2.71	9,510	4,039
Stevenage	3,170	2,964	–6.51	4,660	1,970
Swindon T	8,528	8,130	–4.67	11,598	6,683
Tranmere R	6,196	5,113	–17.48	9,598	3,717
Walsall	4,234	4,807	+13.53	10,139	3,522
Wolverhampton W	21,789	20,879	–4.18	30,110	14,989

TOTAL ATTENDANCES:	4,126,701 (552 games)
	Average 7,476 (+18.4%)
HIGHEST:	30,110 Wolverhampton W v Rotherham U
LOWEST:	1,603 Coventry C v Carlisle U
HIGHEST AVERAGE:	20,879 Wolverhampton W
LOWEST AVERAGE:	2,348 Coventry C

SKY BET FOOTBALL LEAGUE: DIVISION 2 ATTENDANCES

	Average Gate			Season 2013–14	
	2012–13	2013–14	+/–%	Highest	Lowest
Accrington S	1,675	1,606	–4.15	2,531	1,101
AFC Wimbledon	4,060	4,135	+1.84	4,763	3,424
Bristol R	6,309	6,421	+1.77	10,594	5,303
Burton Alb	2,859	2,720	–4.85	4,855	1,784
Bury	2,749	3,139	+14.18	6,295	1,998
Cheltenham T	3,253	2,989	–8.13	4,776	2,050
Chesterfield	5,431	6,318	+16.33	10,015	4,891
Dagenham & R	1,903	1,920	+0.89	3,357	1,377
Exeter C	4,142	3,701	–10.65	5,700	2,540
Fleetwood T	2,856	2,819	–1.29	4,521	2,023
Hartlepool U	3,613	3,723	+3.04	4,864	2,976
Mansfield T	2,758	3,385	+22.74	5,931	2,549
Morecambe	1,954	1,939	–0.75	3,008	1,290
Newport Co	2,371	3,453	+45.65	5,387	2,160
Northampton T	4,785	4,548	–4.95	7,529	3,695
Oxford U	5,955	5,923	–0.53	10,049	4,606
Plymouth Arg	7,096	7,305	+2.94	13,442	5,689
Portsmouth	12,232	15,461	+26.40	18,181	12,780
Rochdale	2,439	2,900	+18.91	5,616	2,092
Scunthorpe U	3,465	4,013	+15.81	7,482	3,005
Southend U	5,003	5,960	+19.12	9,018	4,361
Torquay U	2,709	2,642	–2.49	4,231	1,583
Wycombe W	3,721	3,681	–1.08	7,004	2,185
York C	3,879	3,773	–2.73	5,225	3,148

TOTAL ATTENDANCES:	2,402,876 (552 games)
	Average 4,353 (–0.86%)
HIGHEST:	18,181 Portsmouth v Oxford U
LOWEST:	1,101 Accrington S v Bristol R
HIGHEST AVERAGE:	15,461 Portsmouth
LOWEST AVERAGE:	1,606 Accrington S

LEAGUE CUP FINALS 1961–2014

Played as a two-leg final until 1966. All subsequent finals played at Wembley except between 2001 and 2007 (inclusive) which were played at Millennium Stadium, Cardiff.

FOOTBALL LEAGUE CUP

1961	Rotherham U v Aston Villa	2-0
	Aston Villa v Rotherham U	3-0*
	Aston Villa won 3-2 on aggregate.	
1962	Rochdale v Norwich C	0-3
	Norwich C v Rochdale	1-0
	Norwich C won 4-0 on aggregate.	
1963	Birmingham C v Aston Villa	3-1
	Aston Villa v Birmingham C	0-0
	Birmingham C won 3-1 on aggregate.	
1964	Stoke C v Leicester C	1-1
	Leicester C v Stoke C	3-2
	Leicester C won 4-3 on aggregate.	
1965	Chelsea v Leicester C	3-2
	Leicester C v Chelsea	0-0
	Chelsea won 3-2 on aggregate.	
1966	West Ham U v WBA	2-1
	WBA v West Ham U	4-1
	WBA won 5-3 on aggregate.	
1967	QPR v WBA	3-2
1968	Leeds U v Arsenal	1-0
1969	Swindon T v Arsenal	3-1*
1970	Manchester C v WBA	2-1*
1971	Tottenham H v Aston Villa	2-0
1972	Stoke C v Chelsea	2-1
1973	Tottenham H v Norwich C	1-0
1974	Wolverhampton W v Manchester C	2-1
1975	Aston Villa v Norwich C	1-0
1976	Manchester C v Newcastle U	2-1
1977	Aston Villa v Everton	0-0
Replay	Aston Villa v Everton	1-1*
	(at Hillsborough)	
Replay	Aston Villa v Everton	3-2*
	(at Old Trafford)	
1978	Nottingham F v Liverpool	0-0*
Replay	Nottingham F v Liverpool	1-0
	(at Old Trafford)	
1979	Nottingham F v Southampton	3-2
1980	Wolverhampton W v Nottingham F	1-0
1981	Liverpool v West Ham U	1-1*
Replay	Liverpool v West Ham U	2-1
	(at Villa Park)	

MILK CUP

1982	Liverpool v Tottenham H	3-1*
1983	Liverpool v Manchester U	2-1*
1984	Liverpool v Everton	0-0*
Replay	Liverpool v Everton	1-0
	(at Maine Road)	
1985	Norwich C v Sunderland	1-0
1986	Oxford U v QPR	3-0

LITTLEWOODS CUP

1987	Arsenal v Liverpool	2-1
1988	Luton T v Arsenal	3-2
1989	Nottingham F v Luton T	3-1
1990	Nottingham F v Oldham Ath	1-0

RUMBELOWS LEAGUE CUP

1991	Sheffield W v Manchester U	1-0
1992	Manchester U v Nottingham F	1-0

COCA-COLA CUP

1993	Arsenal v Sheffield W	2-1
1994	Aston Villa v Manchester U	3-1
1995	Liverpool v Bolton W	2-1
1996	Aston Villa v Leeds U	3-0
1997	Leicester C v Middlesbrough	1-1*
Replay	Leicester C v Middlesbrough	1-0*
	(at Hillsborough)	
1998	Chelsea v Middlesbrough	2-0*

WORTHINGTON CUP

1999	Tottenham H v Leicester C	1-0
2000	Leicester C v Tranmere R	2-1
2001	Liverpool v Birmingham C	1-1*
	Liverpool won 5-4 on penalties.	
2002	Blackburn R v Tottenham H	2-1
2003	Liverpool v Manchester U	2-0

CARLING CUP

2004	Middlesbrough v Bolton W	2-1
2005	Chelsea v Liverpool	3-2*
2006	Manchester U v Wigan Ath	4-0
2007	Chelsea v Arsenal	2-1
2008	Tottenham H v Chelsea	2-1*
2009	Manchester U v Tottenham H	0-0*
	Manchester U won 4-1 on penalties.	
2010	Manchester U v Aston Villa	2-1
2011	Birmingham C v Arsenal	2-1
2012	Liverpool v Cardiff C	2-2*
	Liverpool won 3-2 on penalties.	

CAPITAL ONE CUP

2013	Swansea C v Bradford C	5-0
2014	Manchester C v Sunderland	3-1

After extra time.

LEAGUE CUP WINS

Liverpool 8, Aston Villa 5, Chelsea 4, Manchester U 4, Nottingham F 4, Tottenham H 4, Leicester C 3, Manchester C 3, Arsenal 2, Birmingham C 2, Norwich C 2, Wolverhampton W 2, Blackburn R 1, Leeds U 1, Luton T 1, Middlesbrough 1, Oxford U 1, QPR 1, Sheffield W 1, Stoke C 1, Swansea C 1, Swindon T 1, WBA 1.

APPEARANCES IN FINALS

Liverpool 11, Aston Villa 8, Manchester U 8, Arsenal 7, Tottenham H 7, Chelsea 6, Nottingham F 6, Leicester C 5, Manchester C 4, Norwich C 4, Birmingham C 3, Middlesbrough 3, WBA 3, Bolton W 2, Everton 2, Leeds U 2, Luton T 2, QPR 2, Sheffield W 2, Stoke C 2, Sunderland 2, West Ham U 2, Wolverhampton W 2, Blackburn R 1, Bradford C 1, Cardiff C 1, Newcastle U 1, Oldham Ath 1, Oxford U 1, Rochdale 1, Rotherham U 1, Southampton 1, Swansea C 1, Swindon T 1, Tranmere R 1, Wigan Ath 1.

APPEARANCES IN SEMI-FINALS

Arsenal 14, Aston Villa 14, Liverpool 14, Manchester U 13, Tottenham H 13, Chelsea 11, West Ham U 9, Manchester C 8, Blackburn R 6, Nottingham F 6, Birmingham C 5, Leeds U 5, Leicester C 5, Middlesbrough 5, Norwich C 5, Bolton W 4, Burnley 4, Crystal Palace 4, Everton 4, Ipswich T 4, Sheffield W 4, Sunderland 4, WBA 4, QPR 3, Swindon T 3, Wolverhampton W 3, Bristol C 2, Cardiff C 2, Coventry C 2, Derby Co 2, Luton T 2, Oxford U 2, Plymouth Arg 2, Southampton 2, Stoke C 2, Tranmere R 2, Watford 2, Wimbledon 2, Blackpool 1, Bradford C 1, Bury 1, Carlisle U 1, Chester C 1, Huddersfield T 1, Newcastle U 1, Oldham Ath 1, Peterborough U 1, Rochdale 1, Rotherham U 1, Sheffield U 1, Shrewsbury T 1, Stockport Co 1, Swansea C 1, Walsall 1, Wigan Ath 1, Wycombe W 1.

CAPITAL ONE CUP 2013–14

■ *Denotes player sent off.*

FIRST ROUND

Monday, 5 August 2013

Preston NE (0) 1 *(Clarke 87)*

Blackpool (0) 0 17,470

Preston NE: (442) Rudd; Clarke, Huntington, Wright, Buchanan; Holmes, Keane, Welsh, Hayhurst (Davies K 90); Hume (Humphrey 80), Garner (King 68).
Blackpool: (433) Gilks; Broadfoot, Cathcart, MacKenzie, Robinson; Basham, Ferguson, Martinez (Grant 74); Ince, Davies, Chopra.
Referee: Andrew Madley.

Tuesday, 6 August 2013

Barnsley (0) 0

Scunthorpe U (0) 0 5238

Barnsley: (442) Steele; Kennedy (Cywka 81), Golbourne, Dawson, Mvoto; Cranie (Wiseman 63), Mellis (Scotland 55), Perkins, Dagnall; O'Grady, O'Brien.
Scunthorpe U: (442) Slocombe; Ribeiro, Dawson, McAllister (Godden 79), Mirfin; Canavan, Sparrow, Collins, Winnall (Welsh 71); Burton (Iwelumo 72), Hawkridge.
aet; Barnsley win 5-4 on penalties.
Referee: Paul Tierney.

Birmingham C (0) 3 *(Allan 49, 84, Bartley 92)*

Plymouth Arg (0) 2 *(Alessandra 61, 90)* 10,178

Birmingham C: (433) Doyle; Eardley, Ferguson (Lee 90), Allan, Burn; Bartley, Adeyemi (Elliott 77), Reilly; Novak, Burke, Arthur (Robinson 71).
Plymouth Arg: (442) Cole; Berry, Blackman, Blizzard (Young 106), Trotman; Nelson, Alessandra, Hourihane, Morgan; Reid (Harvey 78), Boco (Vassell 88).
aet.
Referee: Graham Salisbury.

Bournemouth (0) 1 *(O'Kane 54)*

Portsmouth (0) 0 7620

Bournemouth: (4411) Allsop; Francis, Harte, O'Kane, Cook; Elphick, Fraser (MacDonald 88), Hughes, Thomas (Daniels 73); McDermott; Surman (Arter 83).
Portsmouth: (442) Smith; Butler (Ferry 65), N'Gala, East, Devera; Bradley, Padovani, Wallace (Barcham 71), Craddock; Agyemang (Bird 72), Holmes.
Referee: Fred Graham.

Brentford (0) 3 *(El Alagui 62, 90, Fillo 64)*

Dagenham & R (1) 2 *(Nugent 18 (og), Scott 81)* 3586

Brentford: (451) Bonham; Venta, Barron, Reeves, Nugent; O'Connor (Craig 46), Fillo, Oyeleke (El Alagui 54), Hayes, Saunders; Dallas.
Dagenham & R: (433) Lewington; Hoyte, Ilesanmi, Ogogo, Saah; Doe, Elito (Woodall 72), Howell; Murphy, Reed (Obafemi 68), Scott.
Referee: Pat Miller.

Brighton & HA (1) 1 *(Barnes 18)*

Newport Co (0) 3 *(Crow 81, 94, Washington 103)* 8409

Brighton & HA: (433) Ankergren; Ince (Bridcutt 84), Calderon■, Forster-Caskey (Ulloa 96), Greer; El-Abd, Lopez, Agustien; Barnes, Buckley, LuaLua (Maksimenko 73).
Newport Co: (442) Stephens; Jackson, Anthony (Hughes 72), Minshull, Yakubu; Worley, Willmott (Washington 66), Chapman, Jolley; Zebroski (Crow 66), Sandell.
aet.
Referee: Brendan Malone.

Bristol R (1) 1 *(Richards 41)*

Watford (3) 3 *(Murray 19, 35, Angella 30)* 4875

Bristol R: (442) Mildenhall; Smith, Brown, Norburn, Parkes; McChrystal, Lockyer (Harding 74), O'Toole, Richards (Hunter 81); Clarkson (Santos 69), Harrison.
Watford: (352) Bond; Faraoni (Cassetti 54), Pudil, Ekstrand; Angella (Doyley 46), Brown, Battocchio (Abdi 74), Smith, Fabbrini; Acuna, Murray.
Referee: Darren Sheldrake.

Bury (2) 3 *(Beeley 20, Harrad 29 (pen), Hinds 49)*

Crewe Alex (1) 2 *(Aneke 5, Davis 75 (pen))* 2146

Bury: (442) Lainton; Beeley, Roberts, Holden, Hinds; Cameron, Soares, Procter, Grimes (Forrester 71); Harrad (Rooney 77), Jones.
Crewe Alex: (442) Martin; Mellor, Tootle, Osman, Davis; Ray, Colclough, Grant (Turton 67), Aneke (West 89); Leitch-Smith (Oliver 67), Clayton.
Referee: Mark Brown.

Charlton Ath (1) 4 *(Church 18, 57, Green 49, Pigott 90 (pen))*

Oxford U (0) 0 4935

Charlton Ath: (442) Hamer; Wilson, Evina, Stephens (Cousins 88), Cort; Wood, Green, Hollands, Church (Sordell 77); Pigott, Cook (Harriott 82).
Oxford U: (4411) Clarke; Hunt, Newey, Whing, Mullins; Wright, Williams (Rigg 76), Rose, Constable (Smalley 65); Hall (Potter 65); O'Dowda.
Referee: Andy Davies.

Cheltenham T (1) 4 *(Richards 40 (pen), Gornell 70, Harrison 75, 114)*

Crawley T (1) 3 *(Alexander 23, Adams 59, 65)* 1562

Cheltenham T: (442) Brown S; Jombati, Braham-Barrett, Penn, Brown T; Elliott (Lowe 104), McGlashan (Kotwica 109), Richards, Gornell; Harrison, Deering (Vincent 101).
Crawley T: (442) Jones P; Hurst (Rooney 102), Sadler, Bulman (Drury 79), McFadzean; Walsh, Adams, Simpson, Alexander; Proctor (Clarke 71), Jones M.
aet.
Referee: Oliver Langford.

Colchester U (0) 1 *(Ibehre 47)*

Peterborough U (1) 5 *(Zakuani 42, Barnett 59, Rowe 68, Tomlin 71, 80)* 2368

Colchester U: (442) Walker; Wilson, Dickson, Eastmond, Okuonghae; Eastman, Bond (Wright Drey 65), Wright David, Morrison; Ibehre, Gilbey (Watt 65).
Peterborough U: (442) Olejnik; Alcock (Little 84), Ntlhe, Tomlin, Bostwick; Zakuani, Kearns, McCann (Payne 82), Barnett; Assombalonga, Rowe (Swanson 81).
Referee: Trevor Kettle.

Doncaster R (0) 1 *(Khumalo 89)*

Rochdale (0) 0 4368

Doncaster R: (442) Turnbull; Wabara (Quinn 71), Husband, Brown (Paynter 86), Furman; Jones R, Duffy (Syers 63), Khumalo, Coppinger; Wellens, Cotterill.
Rochdale: (442) Lillis; Rafferty, Tutte, Hogan (Donnelly 63), Lund; Eastham, Lancashire, Hery (Henderson 46), O'Connell; Vincenti, Done.
Referee: Gary Sutton.

Exeter C (0) 0

QPR (1) 2 *(Austin 3, Simpson 50)* 5253

Exeter C: (442) Krysiak; Woodman, Moore-Taylor, Doherty (Davies 46), Coles; Baldwin, Sercombe, Bennett, Reid; Gow (O'Flynn 54), Wheeler (Parkin 54).
QPR: (442) Murphy; Yun, Simpson, Faurlin (Derry 63), Hill; Dunne, Barton, Jenas, Austin; Zamora (Johnson 46), Hoilett (Wright-Phillips 74).
Referee: Jeremy Simpson.

Gillingham (0) 0

Bristol C (1) 2 *(Baldock 21, Wynter 66)* 2585

Gillingham: (442) Nelson; Harriman, Martin, Barrett, Legge; Davies (Weston 69), Whelpdale, Gregory, German (McDonald 59); Akinfenwa (Kedwell 59), Dack.
Bristol C: (442) Fielding; Moloney, Cunningham (Williams 86), Wynter, Fontaine; Flint, Pack, Kilkenny (Reid 81), Emmanuel-Thomas (Harewood 75); Baldock, Elliott M.
Referee: Darren Deadman.

Huddersfield T (1) 2 *(Vaughan 42, 54)*
Bradford C (0) 1 *(Wells 90)*   11,630
Huddersfield T: (352) Smithies; Hunt (Hammill 46), Carroll, Clarke; Gerrard (Wallace 84), Lynch, Hogg, Clayton, Paterson; Vaughan (Stead 63), Norwood.
Bradford C: (442) McLaughlin; Darby, McHugh, Ravenhill, Taylor (Meredith 64); Doyle, Reid, Kennedy, Thompson; Connell (Hanson 63), De Vita (Wells 63).
Referee: Mark Haywood.

Leyton Orient (2) 3 *(Lisbie 26, 89, Cox 37)*
Coventry C (1) 2 *(Baker 22, Moussa 59)*   2871
Leyton Orient: (442) Jones; Omozusi, Sawyer, Vincelot, Cuthbert; Baudry, Odubajo, James, Mooney; Lisbie, Cox (Lasimant 85).
Coventry C: (442) Murphy; Christie, Adams, Thomas, Clarke J; Willis, Baker■, Fleck, Wilson; Clarke L, Moussa.
Referee: Dean Whitestone.

Middlesbrough (1) 1 *(Jutkiewicz 9)*
Accrington S (1) 2 *(Carver 40, Mingoia 81)*   6774
Middlesbrough: (442) Leutwiler; Hoyte, Friend, Leadbitter, Gibson; Williams R, Carayol, Varga, Emnes (Williams L 78); Jutkiewicz (Reach 74), Ledesma (Main 74).
Accrington S: (442) Dunbavin; Hunt, Atkinson, Richardson, Liddle; Aldred, Hatfield, Mingoia (Wilson 90), Clark (McCartan 73); Carver (Gray 73), Murphy.
Referee: Scott Duncan.

Millwall (0) 2 *(Keogh 52, Woolford 76)*
AFC Wimbledon (0) 1 *(Moore L 90)*   4443
Millwall: (442) Bywater; Smith, Malone, Abdou, Robinson; Beevers, Henry (Martin 75), Bailey (Wright 71), Keogh (McDonald 78); Easter, Woolford.
AFC Wimbledon: (4411) Worner; Fuller, Kennedy, Moore S, Frampton; Bennett, Francomb (Midson 56), Sweeney (Arthur 56), Sheringham; Porter (Moore L 70); Pell.
Referee: James Linington.

Morecambe (0) 1 *(Williams 84)*
Wolverhampton W (0) 0   2545
Morecambe: (433) Roche; Wright, Diagne, Fleming, Parrish; Hughes, Williams (McGee 89), Drummond; Sampson, Amond, Mwasile (Kenyon 77).
Wolverhampton W: (442) Ikeme; Doherty, Reckord, Foley, Batth; Ebanks-Landell, Ismail (Evans 66), Davis, Griffiths; Cassidy (Doyle 57), Forde (McAlinden 88).
Referee: Geoff Eltringham.

Northampton T (0) 1 *(O'Donovan 77)*
Milton Keynes D (1) 2 *(Reeves 13, Banton 54)*   3486
Northampton T: (442) Duke; Amankwaah (Demontagnac 70), Widdowson, Tozer, Heath; Collins, Emerton (Moyo 85), Deegan, Hooper (Toney 74); O'Donovan, Morris.
Milton Keynes D: (4411) McLoughlin; Hodson, Williams, Reeves, Otsemobor; Flanagan, Bamford (McLeod 69), Gleeson, Baldock; Alli (Chadwick 62); Banton (Galloway 80).
Referee: Christopher Sarginson.

Nottingham F (1) 3 *(Majewski 33, Halford 65, Derbyshire 67)*
Hartlepool U (0) 1 *(Austin 76)*   9081
Nottingham F: (442) De Vries; Jara, Harding, Guedioura, Hobbs; Halford, Paterson, Majewski, Cox (Derbyshire 26); Henderson (Miller 70), Mackie (Reid 61).
Hartlepool U: (433) Flinders (Rafferty 46); Austin, Holden, Walker, Baldwin; Burgess, Walton, Sweeney; Franks, Compton (Howard 61), James (Rodney 84).
Referee: Stephen Martin.

Oldham Ath (0) 0
Derby Co (1) 1 *(Jacobs 20)*   5000
Oldham Ath: (442) Oxley; Brown, Grounds, Smith, Tarkowski; Mellor, Dayton (Schmeltz 66), Baxter, Clarke-Harris (Wesolowski 56); Rooney (Millar 67), Montano.
Derby Co: (4411) Grant; Smith, Forsyth, Hendrick, Keogh; Buxton, Coutts, Eustace, Sammon (Martin 76); Jacobs (Hughes 72); Davies.
Referee: Rob Lewis.

Port Vale (0) 1 *(Robertson 59)*
Walsall (1) 2 *(Hemmings 43, Baxendale 84)*   4013
Port Vale: (442) Neal; Yates, Jones, Lines, Robertson; Dickinson, Myrie-Williams (Hughes 85), Griffith (Mohamed 63), Tomlin (Williamson 85); Pope, Loft.
Walsall: (442) O'Donnell; Chambers J, Benning, Mantom (Featherstone 86), Butler; Downing, Baxendale, Chambers A, Lalkovic (Sawyers 66); Westcarr, Hemmings.
Referee: Andy Haines.

Rotherham U (2) 2 *(Pringle 10, Frecklington 38)*
Sheffield W (1) 1 *(McCabe 23)*   11,433
Rotherham U: (442) Shearer; Bradley, Skarz, O'Connor, Arnason; Morgan, Agard (Noble 90), Frecklington (Tidser 72), Tubbs (Worrall 81); Revell, Pringle.
Sheffield W: (4231) Kirkland; Palmer, Floro (Maguire 70), McCabe, Gardner; Zayatte, Maghoma (Johnson J■ 58); Prutton, Nuhiu (Madine 52), Antonio; Helan.
Referee: Darren Drysdale.

Sheffield U (0) 1 *(Doyle 64)*
Burton Alb (0) 2 *(Hussey 50, 90)*   6191
Sheffield U: (4231) Howard; Westlake, Williams, Doyle, Maguire; Collins, McFadzean; Coady, Porter (Taylor 61), McDonald; Flynn (Brandy 74).
Burton Alb: (4231) Pickford; Edwards, McCrory, Bell, Sharps; Holness, McGurk; Delap (Kee 82), Symes (MacDonald 82), Weir (Palmer 72); Hussey.
Referee: Eddie Ilderton.

Shrewsbury T (1) 1 *(Wildig 29)*
Bolton W (2) 3 *(Hall 26, Odelusi 43, 52)*   3456
Shrewsbury T: (442) Weale; Tavernier, Jacobson, Wildig, Jones (Goldson 86); Mkandawire, Taylor (McAllister 53), Summerfield, Bradshaw; Marsden (McQuade 18), Parry.
Bolton W: (442) Lonergan; Mears, Tierney, Pratley (Baptiste 86), Knight; Ream, Hall (Andrews 81), Medo, Davies C; Ngog (Moritz 61), Odelusi.
Referee: Steve Bratt.

Southend U (0) 0
Yeovil T (1) 1 *(Dawson 36)*   2971
Southend U: (442) Bentley; White, Bennett (Corr 60), Clifford, Phillips; Prosser, Atkinson, Payne (Leonard 58), Reid; Cowan (Coker 71), Straker.
Yeovil T: (442) Stech; Ayling, Davis, Clifford, Webster; Tate, Dawson (Madden 69), Edwards (Upson 63), Hoskins; Ngoo (Moore 82), Grant.
Referee: Lee Collins.

Stevenage (0) 2 *(Morais 51 (pen), Burrow 76)*
Ipswich T (0) 0   3212
Stevenage: (442) Arnold; Wedgbury, Hills, Heslop, Charles; Ashton, Morais (Shroot 72), Tansey, Burrow (Jones 90); Tounkara (Haber 72), Freeman.
Ipswich T: (442) Gerken; Chambers, Hyam, Skuse, Smith; Berra, Veseli, Tabb (Edwards 34), Taylor (McGoldrick 56); Nouble (Murphy 56), Anderson.
Referee: Gavin Ward.

Swindon T (0) 1 *(Williams 83)*
Torquay U (0) 0   5662
Swindon T: (451) Foderingham; Barthram, Byrne, Thompson N, Ward; Hall, Reis (Storey 46), Mason (Luongo 46), Williams, Pritchard (Smith A 87); Kasim.
Torquay U: (442) Rice; Tonge (Thompson 89), Nicholson, Mansell, Downes; Pearce, Chapell, Harding, Ball; Hawley (Benyon 70 (Cameron 81)), Bodin.
Referee: Andy D'Urso.

Tranmere R (2) 2 *(Robinson 2, Atkinson 45)*
Mansfield T (0) 0   3067
Tranmere R: (442) Fon Williams; Holmes, Horwood, Atkinson, Taylor; Foster, Thompson, Rowe (Koumas 64), Sodje (Akpa Akpro 72); Lowe, Robinson.
Mansfield T: (442) Marriott; Beevers, Jennings, Howell, Dempster; McCombe (Sutton 46), Briscoe (Speight 74), Murray, Palmer (Rhead 79); Clucas, Meikle.
Referee: David Webb.

Wycombe W (1) 1 *(Kuffour 21)*
Leicester C (1) 2 *(Nugent 14 (pen), St Ledger 90)*   3158
Wycombe W: (41212) Ingram; McCoy, Dunne, Spring, Stewart; Hause; Scowen, Morgan (Kretzschmar 89); Kuffour (Cowan-Hall 90); Craig (Pittman 75), Lewis.
Leicester C: (352) Schmeichel; Dyer, De Laet, Moore; Morgan, St Ledger, Danns, James (Knockaert 51), Wood; Nugent (Schlupp 61), King.
Referee: Tim Robinson.

York C (0) 0
Burnley (1) 4 *(Jones 12, Stanislas 61, Ings 78, Arfield 82)*
                                                         3922
York C: (442) Ingham; Oyebanjo, Fyfield, Platt (Montrose 67), Smith; McGurk, Puri (Coulson 22), Clay, Jarvis (Fletcher 70); Bowman, Chambers.
Burnley: (442) Heaton; Trippier, Lafferty, Marney, Long; Shackell, Stanislas, Jones (Edgar 70), Ings; Vokes (Stock 80), Wallace (Arfield 62).
Referee: Tony Harrington.

Wednesday, 7 August 2013

Carlisle U (1) 3 *(Amoo 14, 114, Guy 62)*
Blackburn R (0) 3 *(Cairney 52, Taylor 56, Judge 95)* 4372
Carlisle U: (442) Gillespie; Potts, James (Brough 43), Noble, Livesey; Thirlwell, Amoo, Berrett, Guy (Salmon 101); Beck, Gillies (Symington 89).
Blackburn R: (442) Eastwood; Kane, Morris, Marrow (Lowe 48), Songo'o; Givet, Taylor, Cairney▪, Dunn (Rhodes 93); King, Olsson (Judge 91).
aet; Carlisle U won 4-3 on penalties.
Referee: Richard Clark.

Leeds U (2) 2 *(Brown 28, Poleon 32)*
Chesterfield (1) 1 *(Doyle 19)*   17,466
Leeds U: (442) Kenny; Thompson, Drury, Norris (Murphy 59), Lees; Pearce, Green, Brown, Smith; Poleon, White (McCormack 59).
Chesterfield: (4231) Lee; Talbot, Smith, Humphreys (Richards 77), Edwards; Hird, Darikwa (O'Shea 64); Morsy, Doyle (Gnanduillet 67), Ryan; Roberts.
Referee: Carl Boyeson.

Notts Co (2) 3 *(Showunmi 28, Haynes 40, McGregor 73)*
Fleetwood T (1) 2 *(Evans 16, Ball 88)*   2115
Notts Co: (442) Bialkowski; Dumbuya, Sheehan, Labadie, Smith▪; Leacock, McGregor (Boucaud 90), Fotheringham, Haynes; Showunmi (Arquin 89), Tempest.
Fleetwood T: (4411) Davies; Hogan, Jordan, Sarcevic, Roberts; Cresswell, Evans (Brown 42), Murdoch (Matt 74), Ball; Blair (Crowther 68); Hughes J.
Referee: Keith Hill.

SECOND ROUND

Tuesday, 27 August 2013

Barnsley (0) 1 *(Dawson 53)*
Southampton (1) 5 *(Davis S 26, 89 (pen), Rodriguez 49, Mayuka 66, Ramirez 90)*   6574
Barnsley: (352) Pollitt; Wiseman, McNulty, Kennedy (Dagnall 55); O'Brien, Mellis, Dawson, Etuhu (Cywka 66), Golbourne; O'Grady, Pedersen (Scotland 55).
Southampton: (442) Davis K; Clyne, Yoshida, Fonte, Fox; Ramirez, Davis S, Cork, Isgrove (Rowe 72); Rodriguez (Reed 81), Mayuka (Sinclair 90).
Referee: Scott Duncan.

Bristol C (0) 2 *(Emmanuel-Thomas 59, Wagstaff 71)*
Crystal Palace (0) 1 *(Garvan 90)*   6816
Bristol C: (442) Parish; Moloney, Flint, Williams (Fontaine 74), Cunningham; Reid, Elliott M, Wagstaff, Bryan (Pack 64); Emmanuel-Thomas, Baldock (Harewood 72).
Crystal Palace: (442) Alexander; Wynter (De Silva 68), O'Keefe, Ramage, Marange; Garvan, Williams Jonathan, Wilbraham (Appiah 55), Dobbie (Phillips 46); Grandin, Williams Jerome.
Referee: Iain Williamson.

Burnley (2) 2 *(Trippier 6, Ings 34)*
Preston NE (0) 0   10,648
Burnley: (4411) Cisak; Trippier, Duff, Shackell, Mee; Arfield, Edgar, Jones (Stock 81), Treacy (Marney 66); Ings (Stanislas 84); Vokes.

Preston NE: (352) Stuckmann; Clarke, Huntington, Wright; Humphrey, Keane, Holmes (Wroe 73), Byrom, Laird; Beavon (Garner 89), Hume (Davies K 73).
Referee: Paul Tierney.

Burton Alb (0) 2 *(Dyer 85, Symes 101)*
Fulham (1) 2 *(Taarabt 35, Rodallega 117)*   4002
Burton Alb: (4141) Lyness; Edwards, Sharps, Holness, McCrory; Bell (Phillips 61); Dyer, Palmer, Weir (Reed 61), Hussey; Howe (Symes 78).
Fulham: (4411) Stockdale; Riether, Hangeland, Hughes, Riise; Dejagah (Kasami 84), Parker, Karagounis (Rodallega 103), Taarabt (Kacaniklic 46); Ruiz; Bent.
aet; Fulham won 5-4 on penalties.
Referee: Andrew Madley.

Carlisle U (1) 2 *(Amoo 16, Berrett 71)*
Leicester C (1) 5 *(Wood 38, 59 (pen), 63, Dyer 47, Knockaert 51)*   3308
Carlisle U: (451) Gillespie; Butterfield, Livesey, Thirlwell, Black; Amoo (Symington 74), Noble (Guy 56), Berrett, Potts, Robson; Miller (Beck 80).
Leicester C: (442) Logan; Moore, Miquel, Whitbread, Bakayogo (Schlupp 84); Knockaert, Drinkwater, Danns, Dyer; Vardy (Waghorn 62), Wood (Hopper 66).
Referee: Graham Salisbury.

Derby Co (3) 5 *(Martin 19, 77, Sammon 36, 71, Hughes 38)*
Brentford (0) 0   9076
Derby Co: (442) Grant; Smith, Keogh, Buxton, Forsyth; Coutts, Bryson (Davies 73), Eustace, Hughes (Jacobs 75); Martin (Bennett 78), Sammon.
Brentford: (433) Bonham; Venta, O'Connor, Nugent, Barron (Pierre 46); Saunders (Mawson 73), Diagouraga, Reeves; Clarke, El Alagui (Norris 61), Dallas.
Referee: Darren Bond.

Doncaster R (0) 1 *(Paynter 63)*
Leeds U (1) 3 *(Wootton 41, Smith 77, McCormack 80 (pen))*   10,890
Doncaster R: (442) Turnbull; Wabara, Khumalo, Jones R, Husband; Coppinger (Duffy 46), Furman (Forrester 84), Wellens, Cotterill; Brown, Robinson (Paynter 60).
Leeds U: (41212) Kenny; Peltier, Wootton, Pearce, Drury, Austin; Mowatt (Murphy 74), Tonge; McCormack; Smith, Poleon.
Referee: Scott Mathieson.

Huddersfield T (1) 3 *(Lynch 40, Hogg 77, Hammill 82)*
Charlton Ath (1) 2 *(Stephens 32, Sordell 59)*   6250
Huddersfield T: (352) Smithies; Clarke, Gerrard, Lynch; Hammill, Norwood, Clayton (Stead 71), Hogg, Carroll (Hunt 55); Vaughan, Paterson (Scannell 46).
Charlton Ath: (352) Hamer; Morrison, Wood (Cort 79), Dervite; Wilson, Stephens, Pritchard, Jackson (Kermorgant 85), Evina; Sordell, Pigott (Green 85).
Referee: Geoff Eltringham.

Leyton Orient (0) 0
Hull C (0) 1 *(Brady 107)*   3181
Leyton Orient: (442) Jones; Odubajo, Cuthbert, Clarke, Omozusi; Bartley (Gorman 69), Vincelot, James, Cox; Lisbie (Lasimant 66), Mooney.
Hull C: (442) Harper; Rosenior, Bruce, McShane, Dudgeon; Mclean (Brady 106), Meyler, Boyd, Stewart (Townsend 55); Fryatt, Proschwitz (Jahraldo-Martin 67).
aet.
Referee: Gavin Ward.

Liverpool (2) 4 *(Sterling 4, Sturridge 29, 105, Henderson 110)*
Notts Co (0) 2 *(Arquin 62, Coombes 84)*   42,231
Liverpool: (4231) Mignolet; Johnson, Toure, Wisdom, Cissokho (Agger 10); Gerrard, Allen (Henderson 65); Ibe, Alberto (Coutinho 72), Sterling; Sturridge.
Notts Co: (4411) Bialkowski; Dumbuya, Smith, Liddle, Stevens; Campbell-Ryce (Thompson 71), Labadie, Fotheringham (Boucaud 77), Bell (Coombes 82); McGregor; Arquin.
aet.
Referee: Stuart Atwell.

Norwich C (2) 6 *(Olsson 23, Pilkington 31,*
Elmander 52, 75, Fer 84, Whittaker 90)
Bury (0) 3 *(Forrester 72, Edjenguele 79, Reindorf 90)*
16,107
Norwich C: (3421) Bunn; Bennett R (Whittaker 73),
Bassong, Olsson; Snodgrass, Martin, Johnson, Pilkington
(Becchio 76); Fer (Redmond 84), Hoolahan; Elmander.
Bury: (442) Lainton; Beeley, Cameron, Edjenguele,
Roberts; Jones, Procter, Miller, Mayor (Sedgwick 85);
Forrester (Grimes 85), Jackson (Reindorf 77).
Referee: James Adcock.

Peterborough U (3) 6 *(Assombalonga 4,*
Tomlin 19, 54 (pen), 79 (pen), Swanson 28, Payne 90)
Reading (0) 0 4496
Peterborough U: (41212) Olejnik; Little, Bostwick,
Knight-Percival, Alcock; Payne; Swanson, Rowe
(Gordon 80); Tomlin (Mendez-Laing 81); Assombalonga
(Anderson 80), Barnett.
Reading: (442) Federici; Gunter, Mariappa, Gorkss,
Cummings; Robson-Kanu, Williams D, Akpan, Obita; Le
Fondre, Pogrebnyak.
Referee: Keith Hill.

QPR (0) 0
Swindon T (1) 2 *(Ranger 38, Pritchard 90)* 9715
QPR: (442) Murphy; Simpson, Onuoha, Hill, Yun; Jenas,
Diakite (Johnson 56), Faurlin (Hitchcock 89), Wright-
Phillips; Zamora (Shariff 56), Austin.
Swindon T: (4321) Foderingham; Thompson N, Ward,
Hall, Byrne; Luongo, Kasim, Harley (Thompson L 60);
Smith A (Mason 39), Pritchard; Ranger (Storey 65).
Referee: David Phillips.

Sunderland (0) 4 *(Altidore 78, Wickham 87, 89, Johnson 90)*
Milton Keynes D (1) 2 *(Bamford 7, McLeod 55)* 18,992
Sunderland: (442) Mannone; Celustka, O'Shea, Roberge,
Colback; Johnson, Vaughan, Cabral (Larsson 61),
Moberg Karlsson (Mavrias 65); Ji (Wickham 49),
Altidore.
Milton Keynes D: (4231) McLoughlin; Baldock, Kay,
Williams, Reeves; Smith, Alli; Bamford (Otsemobor 67),
Gleeson, Carruthers (Banton 66); McLeod (Chadwick
82).
Referee: David Coote.

Tranmere R (1) 1 *(Stockton 45)*
Bolton W (0) 1 *(Beckford 66)* 3379
Tranmere R: (41212) Fon Williams; Holmes, Taylor,
Goodison, Horwood; Koumas (Kirby 74); Atkinson
(Bell-Baggie 112), Power; Rowe; Akpa Akpro, Stockton.
Bolton W: (4411) Lonergan; Mears, Mills, Knight,
Baptiste; Odelusi (Moritz 64), Medo, Vela (Beckford 60),
Hall (Youngs 96); Pratley; Eaves.
aet; Tranmere R won 4-2 on penalties.
Referee: Stephen Martin.

WBA (3) 3 *(Berahino 7, 26, 38 (pen))*
Newport Co (0) 0 8955
WBA: (442) Daniels; Jones (Gayle 70), Dawson, Lugano,
Popov; Dorrans, Brunt, Yacob (Morrison 65), Sinclair;
Berahino, Vydra (Rosenberg 43).
Newport Co: (532) Pidgeley; Jackson, Hughes, Naylor,
Worley, Sandell; Chapman (James 63), Willmott,
Minshull (Flynn 53); Crow (Zebroski 72), Washington.
Referee: Andy D'Urso.

West Ham U (1) 2 *(Vaz Te 42, Morrison 46)*
Cheltenham T (0) 1 *(Richards 59 (pen))* 23,440
West Ham U: (4231) Adrian; Chambers, McCartney,
Tomkins, Rat; Diarra (Diame 34), Cole J (Downing 46);
Collison, Taylor, Morrison; Vaz Te.
Cheltenham T: (451) Brown; Lowe, Inniss, Elliott,
Braham-Barrett; Deering (Harrison 63), Taylor,
McGlashan, Penn (Vincent 83), Richards; Gornell
(Kotwica 77).
Referee: Graham Scott.

Yeovil T (1) 3 *(Upson 22, Webster 90, Ayling 105)*
Birmingham C (2) 3 *(Bartley 20, Shinnie 44, Novak 106)*
3769
Yeovil T: (442) Hennessey; Ayling, Webster, Seaborne,
McAllister; Grant, Edwards, Upson, Davis (Hoskins 66);
Hayter (Tate 80), Moore (Dawson 80).
Birmingham C: (352) Doyle; Bartley, Burn, Robinson;
Eardley, Adeyemi, Shinnie (Ambrose 87), Spector,
Burke; Novak, Green (Allan 77).
aet; Birmingham C won 3-2 on penalties.
Referee: Darren Sheldrake.

Wednesday, 28 August 2013

Accrington S (0) 0
Cardiff C (0) 2 *(Maynard 61, Gestede 62)* 1617
Accrington S: (4231) Bettinelli; Murphy (McCartan 83),
Aldred, Atkinson, Liddle; Joyce, Richardson; Naismith
(Carver 72), Hatfield, Mingoia (Mahoney 72); Clark.
Cardiff C: (442) Lewis; Brayford, Hudson, McNaughton,
John; Smith (Conway 65), Mutch, Cowie, Noone;
Cornelius (Gestede 45), Maynard (Mason 75).
Referee: David Webb.

Aston Villa (2) 3 *(Weimann 19, Benteke 40, Delph 53)*
Rotherham U (0) 0 22,447
Aston Villa: (433) Steer; Bacuna, Okore, Vlaar, Bennett;
El Ahmadi, Westwood, Delph (Sylla 60); Weimann,
Benteke (Helenius 67), Agbonlahor (Tonev 67).
Rotherham U: (442) Shearer; Bradley, Morgan, Arnason,
Skarz; Agard (Tubbs 84), Frecklington, O'Connor,
Pringle (Brindley 84); Revell, Milsom (Tidser 58).
Referee: Simon Hooper.

Everton (1) 2 *(Deulofeu 45, Fellaini 115)*
Stevenage (1) 1 *(Freeman 36)* 22,730
Everton: (4411) Robles; Hibbert (Coleman 66), Heitinga,
Jagielka (Distin 46), Naismith; Deulofeu, Stones, Osman,
Oviedo; Barkley (Fellaini 96); Kone.
Stevenage: (4411) Day; Smith J (Tansey 53), Ashton,
Hartley, Gray; Deacon, Dunne, Doughty (Heslop 89),
Freeman; Shroot; Charles (Tounkara 27).
aet.
Referee: Keith Stroud.

Morecambe (0) 0
Newcastle U (0) 2 *(Ameobi Shola 84, Ameobi Sammy 90)*
5375
Morecambe: (433) Roche; Wright, Hughes, Parrish,
Diagne; Fleming (Kenyon 77), Drummond (Mwasile 87),
Williams; Amond (Marshall 57), Sampson, Ellison.
Newcastle U: (4231) Elliot; Debuchy, Yanga-Mbiwa,
Good, Dummett; Bigirimana, Gosling; Marveaux
(Sissoko 58), Vuckic (Ameobi Shola 46), Ameobi
Sammy; Gouffran (Ben Arfa 71).
Referee: Mark Haywood.

Nottingham F (0) 2 *(Derbyshire 59, Lascelles 94)*
Millwall (0) 1 *(Feeney 86)* 12,201
Nottingham F: (442) De Vries; Jara, Lascelles, Collins,
Harding; Paterson, Moussi, Gillett, Abdoun (Halford 77);
Cox (Blackstock 60), Derbyshire (Miller 66).
Millwall: (451) Bywater; Smith, Robinson, Beevers,
Malone; Feeney, Bailey (Chaplow 72), Woolford, Abdou,
Martin (Marquis 62); McDonald (Keogh 62).
aet.
Referee: Mark Haywood.

Stoke C (2) 3 *(Jones 22, 31, 84)*
Walsall (0) 1 *(Hemmings 57)* 9796
Stoke C: (451) Sorensen; Wilkinson, Shawcross, Huth,
Muniesa; Pennant, Whelan, Palacios (Wilson 46), Adam
(Nzonzi 75), Shea (Assaidi 46); Jones.
Walsall: (442) O'Donnell; Chambers J, Butler, Downing,
Taylor; Baxendale (McQuilkin 81), Mantom,
Featherstone (Morris 86), Hemmings; Westcarr (Hewitt
81), Sawyers.
Referee: Michael Naylor.

Watford (1) 2 *(Ward 15 (og), Battocchio 66)*
Bournemouth (0) 0   9824
Watford: (532) Bond; Battocchio, Brown (Angella 63),
Belkalem, Ekstrand, Murray; Pudil, Faraoni (Anya 72),
Smith; Acuna (McGugan 84), Forestieri.
Bournemouth: (451) Allsop; Francis, Elphick, Ward,
Harte; Pugh (McDermott 83), Surman, Hughes,
MacDonald (Thomas 63), Fraser (Coulibaly 63); Pitman.
Referee: Darren Deadman.

THIRD ROUND

Tuesday, 24 September 2013
Aston Villa (0) 0
Tottenham H (1) 4 *(Defoe 45, 90, Paulinho 49, Chadli 86)*
                                                        22,975
Aston Villa: (4231) Steer; Lowton, Vlaar, Baker, Bennett;
El Ahmadi (Bowery 46), Sylla; Albrighton, Bacuna,
Tonev (Robinson 82); Kozak (Helenius 46).
Tottenham H: (4231) Friedel; Walker (Dawson 80),
Chiriches, Vertonghen, Fryers; Paulinho (Dembele 64),
Sandro; Lamela, Holtby, Defoe; Kane (Chadli 73).
Referee: Jon Moss.

Burnley (1) 2 *(Ings 45, 68)*
Nottingham F (1) 1 *(Derbyshire 24)*   6405
Burnley: (4231) Heaton; Trippier, Long, Shackell, Mee;
Edgar, Marney (Stock 34); Treacy (Arfield 83), Ings,
Stanislas; Vokes (Kightly 88).
Nottingham F: (442) De Vries; Jara, Collins, Lascelles,
Harding; Paterson, Moussi (Cohen 64), Gillett, Majewski
(Miller 73); Derbyshire, Blackstock (Cox 64).
Referee: Darren Drysdale.

Fulham (0) 2 *(Berbatov 54, Bent 68)*
Everton (1) 1 *(Naismith 12)*   14,627
Fulham: (4411) Stockdale; Zverotic, Senderos,
Hangeland, Riise (Amorebieta 64); Kacaniklic, Parker,
Karagounis, Taarabt (Bent 65); Kasami; Berbatov.
Everton: (4231) Robles; Coleman, Stones, Distin, Oviedo;
Gibson (Jagielka 69), Heitinga (Barry 69); Deulofeu,
McCarthy, Naismith (Mirallas 80); Lukaku.
Referee: Martin Atkinson.

Hull C (0) 1 *(Proschwitz 59)*
Huddersfield T (0) 0   7151
Hull C: (433) Harper; Rosenior, Bruce, Faye, Dudgeon;
Boyd, Meyler, Quinn (Henderson 74); Fryatt (Gedo 68),
Proschwitz, Sagbo.
Huddersfield T: (442) Smithies; Woods, Wallace, Smith,
Carroll; Norwood (Hammill 67), Gobern, Southern, Carr
(Holmes 50); Scannell, Paterson (Lopez 53).
Referee: Simon Hooper.

Leicester C (0) 2 *(Knockaert 78, Drinkwater 81)*
Derby Co (1) 1 *(Martin 42)*   14,043
Leicester C: (433) Schmeichel; Moore, Wasilewski,
Miquel, Bakayogo (Dyer 46); Hammond, James,
Drinkwater; Taylor-Fletcher (Knockaert 63), Hopper
(Nugent 46), Schlupp.
Derby Co: (442) Grant; Freeman, Keogh, Buxton,
Forsyth; Coutts (Davies 28), Bryson, Hughes (Jacobs 90),
Russell; Sammon, Martin.
Referee: Dean Whitestone.

Manchester C (1) 5 *(Dzeko 33, Jovetic 60, 83, Toure 76,
Jesus Navas 86)*
Wigan Ath (0) 0   25,519
Manchester C: (442) Pantilimon; Richards, Boyata,
Lescott, Clichy; Milner, Fernandinho (Toure 46), Javi
Garcia, Lopes (Jesus Navas 71); Jovetic, Dzeko (Negredo
79).
Wigan Ath: (4141) Nicholls; Boyce, Rogne, Barnett
(Shotton 59), Crainey (Redmond 68); Espinoza; Gomez,
Fyvie, McCann, Garcia; Dicko (Powell 80).
Referee: Kevin Friend.

Southampton (1) 2 *(Ramirez 15, Hooiveld 83)*
Bristol C (0) 0   8539
Southampton: (4231) Davis K; Chambers, Yoshida,
Hooiveld, Fox; Davis S (Rowe 87), Cork; Ward-Prowse,
Ramirez, Do Prado (Reed 74); Lee (Rodriguez 74).
Bristol C: (451) Parish; Moloney, Flint, Williams, Shorey;
Wagstaff (Kilkenny 76), Pack, McLaughlin, Reid
(Baldock 84), Bryan (Harewood 70); Emmanuel-Thomas.
Referee: Graham Scott.

Sunderland (1) 2 *(Giaccherini 32, Roberge 74)*
Peterborough U (0) 0   18,126
Sunderland: (451) Westwood; Gardner, O'Shea (Roberge
61), Cuellar, Colback; Johnson, Ki, Larsson, Cattermole,
Giaccherini (Borini 81); Altidore (Wickham 85).
Peterborough U: (442) Olejnik; Ntlhe, Bostwick, Zakuani,
Alcock; Swanson, Payne (Mendez-Laing 76), Rowe
(McCann 64), Tomlin (Newell 11); Assombalonga, Barnett.
Referee: Michael Naylor.

Swindon T (0) 0
Chelsea (2) 2 *(Torres 29, Ramires 35)*   14,924
Swindon T: (4231) Foderingham; Thompson N, Hall,
Ward, McEveley; Luongo, Kasim; Ajose (El-Gabbas 73),
Pritchard, N'Guessan; Ranger (Thompson L 46).
Chelsea: (4231) Schwarzer; Azpilicueta, Cahill, Luiz,
Bertrand; van Ginkel (Ramires 10 (Terry 46)), Essien;
De Bruyne (Ba 78), Mata, Willian; Torres.
Referee: Michael Oliver.

Watford (1) 2 *(Acuna 23, Faraoni 55)*
Norwich C (0) 3 *(Murphy Josh 77, Hooper 90, 115)* 11,178
Watford: (352) Bond; Ekstrand, Belkalem, Cassetti;
Faraoni, Murray, McEachran (Smith 39), Battocchio,
Pudil; Acuna (Deeney 52), Fabbrini (Forestieri 86).
Norwich C: (442) Bunn; Whittaker, Martin, Bennett R,
Garrido (Elmander 46); Redmond, Johnson (Murphy
Josh 67), Tettey, Olsson; Hoolahan (Fer 74), Hooper.
aet.
Referee: Stephen Martin.

West Ham U (2) 3 *(Morrison 1, Jarvis 8, Vaz Te 88)*
Cardiff C (1) 2 *(Noone 45, Odemwingie 76)*   18,611
West Ham U: (433) Adrian; Chambers, Tomkins, Collins,
McCartney (Rat 82); Jarvis, Morrison (Diame 58),
Taylor; Vaz Te, Maiga (Petric 46); Collison.
Cardiff C: (442) Lewis; Connolly, Hudson, Brayford
(McNaughton 46); John; Odemwingie, Mutch, Cowie,
Noone; Mason (Smith 56), Maynard (Gestede 90).
Referee: Roger East.

Wednesday, 25 September 2013
Birmingham C (0) 3 *(Burn 57, Green 61, Adeyemi 81)*
Swansea C (0) 1 *(Bony 90)*   7470
Birmingham C: (343) Doyle; Spector, Burn, Robinson;
Reilly, Caddis, Adeyemi, Hancox; Burke, Green,
Ferguson (Shinnie 83).
Swansea C: (4231) Tremmel; Tiendalli, Amat, Monk,
Taylor; Lamah (Routledge 82), de Guzman (Vazquez
64); Britton, Pozuelo, Shelvey (Canas 73); Bony.
Referee: Keith Stroud.

Manchester U (0) 1 *(Hernandez 46)*
Liverpool (0) 0   65,701
Manchester U: (4231) De Gea; Da Silva R, Smalling,
Evans, Buttner; Jones, Giggs; Nani (Welbeck 90),
Rooney, Kagawa (Januzaj 73); Hernandez (Carrick 74).
Liverpool: (4231) Mignolet; Toure, Skrtel, Sakho;
Henderson, Gerrard, Moses (Sterling 82), Lucas (Kelly
67), Jose Enrique; Sturridge, Suarez.
Referee: Mark Clattenburg.

Newcastle U (1) 2 *(Cisse 31, Gouffran 67)*
Leeds U (0) 0   36,220
Newcastle U: (442) Krul; Debuchy, Williamson,
Coloccini, Dummett; Gouffran, Anita (Gosling 80),
Tiote, Marveaux; Ameobi Sammy, Cisse (Obertan 71).
Leeds U: (41212) Kenny; Byram, Wootton, Pearce,
Warnock; Austin; Mowatt, Tonge (Diouf 63);
McCormack; Smith, Poleon (White 63).
Referee: Mike Jones.

Tranmere R (0) 0

Stoke C (1) 2 *(Ireland 23, Crouch 90)*   5559

Tranmere R: (442) Fon Williams; Hateley, Dugdale, Taylor, Horwood (Holmes 46); Rowe (Bell-Baggie 74), Atkinson, Power, Akpa Akpro; Lowe, Stockton.
Stoke C: (433) Sorensen; Cameron, Huth, Shawcross, Muniesa; Whelan, Palacios, Ireland (Assaidi 61); Pennant (Walters 76), Crouch, Arnautovic (Etherington 77).
Referee: David Coote.

WBA (0) 1 *(Berahino 71)*

Arsenal (0) 1 *(Eisfeld 61)*   18,649

WBA: (4411) Daniels; Reid, Dawson, Lugano, Popov; Berahino (Amalfitano 101), Mulumbu (Morrison 91), Dorrans, Sinclair; Sessegnon; Long (Rosenberg 91).
Arsenal: (4411) Fabianski; Jenkinson, Mertesacker, Vermaelen, Monreal; Gnabry, Hayden (Olsson 84), Arteta (Bellerin 95), Miyaichi; Eisfeld (Akpom 82); Bendtner.
aet; Arsenal won 4-3 on penalties.
Referee: Robert Madley.

FOURTH ROUND

Tuesday, 29 October 2013

Arsenal (0) 0

Chelsea (1) 2 *(Azpilicueta 25, Mata 66)*   59,455

Arsenal: (4231) Fabianski; Jenkinson, Koscielny, Vermaelen, Monreal; Wilshere, Ramsey (Park 81); Miyaichi (Ozil 63), Rosicky, Cazorla; Bendtner (Giroud 67).
Chelsea: (4231) Schwarzer; Azpilicueta, Cahill, Luiz, Bertrand; Essien, Mikel; De Bruyne (Ramires 69), Mata (Kalas 90), Willian; Eto'o (Ba 81).
Referee: Phil Dowd.

Birmingham C (1) 4 *(Adeyemi 28, Lovenkrands 85, 90, Lee 118)*

Stoke C (1) 4 *(Assaidi 10, Crouch 55, Arnautovic 71, Jones 94)*   13,436

Birmingham C: (4231) Doyle; Caddis, Robinson, Burn, Hancox; Adeyemi (Lee 79), Reilly; Elliott■, Novak, Ferguson (Gray 68); Zigic (Lovenkrands 79).
Stoke C: (4411) Sorensen; Muniesa, Shawcross, Huth, Wilson; Pennant (Shea 76), Palacios, Nzonzi, Assaidi; Crouch (Jones 81); Arnautovic (Ireland 71).
aet; Stoke C won 4-2 on penalties.
Referee: Andy D'Urso.

Burnley (0) 0

West Ham U (0) 2 *(Taylor 76 (pen), Collison 90 (pen))*   14,376

Burnley: (4231) Heaton; Trippier, Long, Shackell, Mee; Stock, Edgar (Noble 90); Treacy■, Ings, Stanislas (Kightly 84); Vokes.
West Ham U: (352) Adrian; Ruddock, Potts, Tomkins (Nolan 71); Chambers, Cole J, Diame (Collison 46), Taylor, O'Brien; Maiga, Cole C (Downing 60).
Referee: Robert Madley.

Leicester C (2) 4 *(Morgan 41, Wood 45, Miquel 53, Dyer 89)*

Fulham (1) 3 *(Rodallega 18, 54, Karagounis 87)*   17,932

Leicester C: (442) Schmeichel; Wasilewski, Morgan, Miquel, Konchesky (Dyer 46); Knockaert (Nugent 87), James, Drinkwater, Hammond; Schlupp, Wood (Vardy 87).
Fulham: (4411) Stekelenburg; Zverotic, Senderos, Hughes, Riise; Duff (Ruiz 56), Karagounis, Boateng (Sidwell 80), Kacaniklic; Taarabt; Rodallega (Bent 65).
Referee: Keith Stroud.

Manchester U (1) 4 *(Hernandez 20 (pen), 54, Jones 88, Da Silva F 90)*

Norwich C (0) 0   58,663

Manchester U: (4411) Lindegaard; Da Silva R, Ferdinand, Vidic, Buttner; Zaha (Rooney 78), Jones, Cleverley (Anderson 90), Young; Januzaj (Da Silva F 90); Hernandez.
Norwich C: (442) Bunn; Whittaker, Bassong, Bennett R, Garrido; Snodgrass (Pilkington 65), Fer, Johnson, Redmond (Murphy Josh 76); Hoolahan (Hooper 89), Elmander.
Referee: Kevin Friend.

Wednesday, 30 October 2013

Newcastle U (0) 0

Manchester C (0) 2 *(Negredo 99, Dzeko 105)*   33,846

Newcastle U: (4231) Krul; Debuchy, Williamson, Yanga-Mbiwa, Haidara (Dummett 46 (Ben Arfa 81)); Tiote, Anita; Sissoko, Ameobi Shola (Cabaye 67), Gouffran; Cisse.
Manchester C: (4231) Pantilimon; Richards (Zabaleta 83), Boyata, Lescott, Kolarov; Javi Garcia, Rodwell (Silva 64); Jesus Navas, Jovetic (Negredo 10), Milner; Dzeko.
aet.
Referee: Neil Swarbrick.

Tottenham H (1) 2 *(Sigurdsson 16, Kane 108)*

Hull C (0) 2 *(Friedel 53 (og), McShane 99)*   35,617

Tottenham H: (4231) Friedel; Walker, Kaboul, Vertonghen, Naughton (Chiriches 68); Dembele, Paulinho; Lamela, Eriksen (Chadli 68 (Kane 78)), Sigurdsson; Defoe.
Hull C: (3511) Jakupovic; Davies, Bruce (Proschwitz 34), McShane; Elmohamady, Meyler, Koren (Gedo 81), Quinn, Rosenior; Boyd; Graham (Mclean 46).
aet; Tottenham H won 8-7 on penalties.
Referee: Jon Moss.

Wednesday, 6 November 2013

Sunderland (0) 2 *(Bardsley 59, Larsson 86)*

Southampton (0) 1 *(Yoshida 88)*   15,966

Sunderland: (451) Mannone; Celustka (Larsson 70), Brown, O'Shea, Bardsley; Johnson, Gardner, Ki, Colback, Giaccherini (Fletcher 90); Altidore.
Southampton: (4231) Davis K; Chambers, Yoshida, Hooiveld, Fox; Cork, Reed; Rodriguez, Ramirez (Gallagher 79), Davis S (Lallana 70); Lee (Ward-Prowse 57).
Referee: Lee Mason.

QUARTER-FINALS

Tuesday, 17 December 2013

Leicester C (0) 1 *(Dyer 77)*

Manchester C (2) 3 *(Kolarov 8, Dzeko 41, 53)*   31,319

Leicester C: (442) Schmeichel; Wasilewski, Morgan, Miquel, Konchesky; Knockaert (Vardy 46), Drinkwater, King, Dyer; Taylor-Fletcher (James 46), Nugent (Schlupp 68).
Manchester C: (4231) Hart; Zabaleta (Boyata 12), Kompany, Lescott, Kolarov; Javi Garcia, Rodwell; Jesus Navas (Nasri 70), Milner; Dzeko.
Referee: Roger East.

Sunderland (0) 2 *(Borini 88, Ki 118)*

Chelsea (0) 1 *(Lampard 46)*   20,731

Sunderland: (4141) Mannone; Celustka, O'Shea, Brown, Dossena; Cattermole; Johnson (Borini 74), Larsson, Gardner (Ki 63), Giaccherini (Bardsley 120); Altidore.
Chelsea: (4231) Schwarzer; Azpilicueta (Essien 70), Cahill, Luiz, Cole; Mikel, Lampard; De Bruyne, Willian, Schurrle (Hazard 83); Eto'o (Ba 74).
aet.
Referee: Anthony Taylor.

Wednesday, 18 December 2013

Stoke C (0) 0

Manchester U (0) 2 *(Young 62, Evra 78)*   25,928

Stoke C: (4231) Sorensen; Cameron, Shawcross (Adam 76), Wilson, Pieters; Palacios, Whelan; Walters, Ireland, Assaidi (Arnautovic 62); Crouch.
Manchester U: (433) De Gea; Da Silva, Smalling, Evans, Evra; Cleverley, Jones, Anderson (Hernandez 58); Valencia, Welbeck (Fletcher 82), Young.
Referee: Mark Clattenburg.

Tottenham H (0) 1 *(Adebayor 67)*

West Ham U (0) 2 *(Jarvis 80, Maiga 85)*   34,080

Tottenham H: (442) Lloris; Walker, Capoue, Chiriches, Rose (Fryers 62); Lennon, Dembele, Sigurdsson, Townsend (Chadli 73); Adebayor (Holtby 78), Defoe.
West Ham U: (433) Adrian; O'Brien, Collins, McCartney, Rat; Collison, Diarra (Morrison 79), Taylor; Cole J (Diame 70), Cole C (Maiga 65), Jarvis.
Referee: Neil Swarbrick.

SEMI-FINALS FIRST LEG

Tuesday, 7 January 2014

Sunderland (1) 2 *(Giggs 45 (og), Borini 64 (pen))*

Manchester U (0) 1 *(Vidic 52)*   31,547

Sunderland: (433) Mannone; Bardsley, O'Shea, Brown, Alonso; Larsson, Cattermole, Ki; Giaccherini (Johnson 56), Fletcher (Altidore 72), Borini.
Manchester U: (4231) De Gea; Da Silva R, Vidic, Evans (Smalling 61), Evra; Carrick, Cleverley (Fletcher 74); Valencia (Hernandez 87), Giggs, Januzaj; Welbeck.
Referee: Andre Marriner.

Wednesday, 8 January 2014

Manchester C (3) 6 *(Negredo 12, 26, 49, Toure 40, Dzeko 60, 89)*

West Ham U (0) 0   30,381

Manchester C: (4222) Pantilimon, Zabaleta, Kompany, Lescott, Clichy, Toure (Demichelis 66), Javi Garcia, Nasri, Silva (Lopes 73), Dzeko, Negredo (Kolarov 79).
West Ham U: (433) Adrian; Demel, Johnson, McCartney, O'Brien (Rat 75); Noble (Diarra 57), Diame, Taylor; Downing, Maiga (Cole C 46), Cole J.
Referee: Jon Moss.

SEMI-FINALS SECOND LEG

Tuesday, 21 January 2014

West Ham U (0) 0

Manchester C (2) 3 *(Negredo 3, 59, Aguero 24)*   14,390

West Ham U: (4231) Jaaskelainen; Taylor, Johnson, Tomkins, Rat; Diarra, Morrison; Diame (Collison 89), Nolan, Cole J (Downing 47); Carroll (Cole C 46).
Manchester C: (442) Pantilimon; Boyata, Lescott, Nastasic, Clichy; Jesus Navas (Kolarov 79), Javi Garcia (Rodwell 63), Fernandinho, Lopes; Negredo, Aguero (Jovetic 65).
Referee: Chris Foy.

Wednesday, 22 January 2014

Manchester U (1) 2 *(Evans 37, Hernandez 120)*

Sunderland (0) 1 *(Bardsley 119)*   71,019

Manchester U: (4231) De Gea; Da Silva R, Smalling, Evans, Buttner (Evra 85); Fletcher, Carrick (Jones 95); Januzaj, Welbeck, Kagawa (Valencia 61); Hernandez.
Sunderland: (4141) Mannone; Bardsley, O'Shea, Brown, Alonso; Cattermole (Gardner 82); Johnson, Ki, Colback, Borini (Altidore 86); Fletcher.
aet; Sunderland won 2-1 on penalties.
Referee: Lee Mason.

CAPITAL ONE CUP FINAL 2014

Sunday, 2 March 2014

(at Wembley Stadium, attendance 84,697)

Manchester C (0) 3   Sunderland (1) 1

Manchester C: (442) Pantilimon; Zabaleta, Kompany, Demichelis, Kolarov; Nasri, Toure, Fernandinho, Silva (Javi Garcia 77); Dzeko (Negredo 88), Aguero (Jesus Navas 58).
Scorers: Toure 55, Nasri 56, Jesus Navas 90.

Sunderland: (4141) Mannone; Bardsley, O'Shea, Brown, Alonso; Cattermole (Giaccherini 77); Johnson (Gardner 60), Larsson (Fletcher 60), Ki, Colback; Borini.
Scorer: Borini 10.

Referee: Martin Atkinson.

Despite a desperate challenge from Sunderland's Wes Brown, Jesus Navas scores Manchester City's third goal in a 3-1 victory in the Capital One Cup final. This was City's first League Cup trophy since 1976.
(John Walton/EMPICS Sport)

LEAGUE CUP ATTENDANCES

Season	Attendances	Games	Average
1960–61	1,204,580	112	10,755
1961–62	1,030,534	104	9,909
1962–63	1,029,893	102	10,097
1963–64	945,265	104	9,089
1964–65	962,802	98	9,825
1965–66	1,205,876	106	11,376
1966–67	1,394,553	118	11,818
1967–68	1,671,326	110	15,194
1968–69	2,064,647	118	17,497
1969–70	2,299,819	122	18,851
1970–71	2,035,315	116	17,546
1971–72	2,397,154	123	19,489
1972–73	1,935,474	120	16,129
1973–74	1,722,629	132	13,050
1974–75	1,901,094	127	14,969
1975–76	1,841,735	140	13,155
1976–77	2,236,636	147	15,215
1977–78	2,038,295	148	13,772
1978–79	1,825,643	139	13,134
1979–80	2,322,866	169	13,745
1980–81	2,051,576	161	12,743
1981–82	1,880,682	161	11,681
1982–83	1,679,756	160	10,498
1983–84	1,900,491	168	11,312
1984–85	1,876,429	167	11,236
1985–86	1,579,916	163	9,693
1986–87	1,531,498	157	9,755
1987–88	1,539,253	158	9,742
1988–89	1,552,780	162	9,585
1989–90	1,836,916	168	10,934
1990–91	1,675,496	159	10,538
1991–92	1,622,337	164	9,892
1992–93	1,558,031	161	9,677
1993–94	1,744,120	163	10,700
1994–95	1,530,478	157	9,748
1995–96	1,776,060	162	10,963
1996–97	1,529,321	163	9,382
1997–98	1,484,297	153	9,701
1998–99	1,555,856	153	10,169
1999–2000	1,354,233	153	8,851
2000–01	1,501,304	154	9,749
2001–02	1,076,390	93	11,574
2002–03	1,242,478	92	13,505
2003–04	1,267,729	93	13,631
2004–05	1,313,693	93	14,216
2005–06	1,072,362	93	11,531
2006–07	1,098,403	93	11,811
2007–08	1,332,841	94	14,179
2008–09	1,329,753	93	14,298
2009–10	1,376,405	93	14,800
2010–11	1,197,917	93	12,881
2011–12	1,209,684	93	13,007
2012–13	1,210,031	93	13,011
2013–14	1,362,360	93	14,649

CAPITAL ONE CUP 2013–14

Round	Aggregate	Games	Average
One	197,461	35	5,642
Two	275,819	25	11,033
Three	295,697	16	18,481
Four	249,291	8	31,161
Quarter-finals	112,058	4	28,015
Semi-finals	147,337	4	36,834
Final	84,697	1	84,697
Total	1,362,360	93	14,649

FOOTBALL LEAGUE TROPHY
FINALS 1984–2014

The 1984 final was played at Boothferry Park, Hull. All subsequent finals played at Wembley except between 2001 and 2007 (inclusive) which were played at Millennium Stadium, Cardiff.

ASSOCIATE MEMBERS' CUP
1984	Bournemouth v Hull C	2-1

FREIGHT ROVER TROPHY
1985	Wigan Ath v Brentford	3-1
1986	Bristol C v Bolton W	3-0
1987	Mansfield T v Bristol C	1-1*
	Mansfield T won 5-4 on penalties	

SHERPA VANS TROPHY
1988	Wolverhampton W v Burnley	2-0
1989	Bolton W v Torquay U	4-1

LEYLAND DAF CUP
1990	Tranmere R v Bristol R	2-1
1991	Birmingham C v Tranmere R	3-2

AUTOGLASS TROPHY
1992	Stoke C v Stockport Co	1-0
1993	Port Vale v Stockport Co	2-1
1994	Swansea C v Huddersfield T	1-1*
	Swansea C won 3-1 on penalties	

AUTO WINDSCREENS SHIELD
1995	Birmingham C v Carlisle U	1-0*
1996	Rotherham U v Shrewsbury T	2-1
1997	Carlisle U v Colchester U	0-0*
	Carlisle U won 4-3 on penalties	
1998	Grimsby T v Bournemouth	2-1
1999	Wigan Ath v Millwall	1-0
2000	Stoke C v Bristol C	2-1

LDV VANS TROPHY
2001	Port Vale v Brentford	2-1
2002	Blackpool v Cambridge U	4-1
2003	Bristol C v Carlisle U	2-0
2004	Blackpool v Southend U	2-0
2005	Wrexham v Southend U	2-0*

FOOTBALL LEAGUE TROPHY
2006	Swansea C v Carlisle U	2-1

JOHNSTONE'S PAINT TROPHY
2007	Doncaster R v Bristol R	3-2*
2008	Milton Keynes D v Grimsby T	2-0
2009	Luton T v Scunthorpe U	3-2*
2010	Southampton v Carlisle U	4-1
2011	Carlisle U v Brentford	1-0
2012	Chesterfield v Swindon T	2-0
2013	Crewe Alex v Southend U	2-0
2014	Peterborough U v Chesterfield	3-1

After extra time.

FOOTBALL LEAGUE TROPHY WINS

Birmingham C 2, Blackpool 2, Bristol C 2, Carlisle U 2, Port Vale 2, Stoke C 2, Swansea C 2, Wigan Ath 2, Bolton W 1, Bournemouth 1, Chesterfield 1, Crewe Alex 1, Doncaster R 1, Grimsby T 1, Luton T 1, Mansfield T 1, Milton Keynes D 1, Peterborough U 1, Rotherham U 1, Southampton 1, Tranmere R 1, Wolverhampton W 1, Wrexham 1.

APPEARANCES IN FINALS

Carlisle U 6, Bristol C 4, Brentford 3, Southend U 3, Birmingham C 2, Blackpool 2, Bolton W 2, Bournemouth 2, Bristol R 2, Chesterfield 2, Grimsby T 2, Port Vale 2, Stockport Co 2, Stoke C 2, Swansea C 2, Tranmere R 2, Wigan Ath 2, Burnley 1, Cambridge U 1, Colchester U 1, Crewe Alex 1, Doncaster R 1, Huddersfield T 1, Hull C 1, Luton T 1, Mansfield T 1, Millwall 1, Milton Keynes D 1, Peterborough U 1, Rotherham U 1, Scunthorpe U 1, Shrewsbury T 1, Southampton 1, Swindon T 1, Torquay U 1, Wolverhampton W 1, Wrexham 1.

JOHNSTONE'S PAINT TROPHY 2013–14

■ *Denotes player sent off.*

NORTHERN SECTION FIRST ROUND

Tuesday, 3 September 2013

Crewe Alex (0) 1 *(Aneke 79)*

Accrington S (0) 0   2077

Crewe Alex: (433) Phillips; Tootle, Davis, Ellis, Robertson; Grant (Molyneux 65), Osman, Inman; Clayton (Oliver 73), Aneke, Colclough (Leitch-Smith 58).
Accrington S: (442) Wilson; Clark, Aldred, Atkinson, Liddle; McCartan (Mahoney 61), Joyce (Miller 46), Richardson, Mingoia; Gray, Webber (Hatfield 68).
Referee: Tony Harrington.

Hartlepool U (1) 5 *(James 25, Franks 48, Burgess 56, Compton 59 (pen), Rodney 87)*

Bradford C (0) 0   1740

Hartlepool U: (442) Flinders; Duckworth, Baldwin, Burgess, Austin; Monkhouse, Walker (Walton 69), Dolan, Compton (Poole 76); James (Rodney 69), Franks.
Bradford C: (451) Ripley; Darby, Taylor, McArdle (Connell 52), Meredith (McHugh 46); De Vita, Doyle, Kennedy, Ravenhill, Yeates; Thompson (Reid 75).
Referee: Richard Clark.

Notts Co (1) 1 *(McGregor 40)*

Burton Alb (0) 0   1240

Notts Co: (442) Bialkowski; Liddle, Smith, Leacock, Stevens; McGregor, Labadie (Nangle 41), Fotheringham, Bell; Arquin, Thompson.
Burton Alb: (4141) Lyness; Edwards, Sharps, Holness, McCrory; Palmer (Howe 68); Dyer (Harness 76), Weir, Knowles, Reed; Symes.
Referee: Darren Bond.

Port Vale (0) 2 *(Pope 80, 90)*

Bury (0) 1 *(Sedgwick 71)*   2351

Port Vale: (442) Neal; Duffy, Chilvers, Robertson, Dickinson; Birchall (Myrie-Williams 72), Griffith (Shuker 46), Dodds (Mohamed 72), Loft; Williamson, Pope.
Bury: (442) Jensen; Beeley, Hinds, Edjenguele, Holden; Grimes, Procter, Sinnott, Sedgwick (Navas 78); Harrad, Obadeyi.
Referee: David Coote.

Scunthorpe U (0) 0

Sheffield U (0) 0   2352

Scunthorpe U: (442) Slocombe; Ribeiro, Mirfin, Canavan, Dawson; Esajas (Hawkridge 75), McAllister, Nolan, Sparrow (Welsh 89); Spencer, Winnall (Burton 73).
Sheffield U: (4231) Howard; McMahon (McGinty 73), Collins, Maguire, Westlake; McGinn, Coady; Flynn, McFadzean, Cuvelier (Baxter 67); Ironside (Taylor 62).
Sheffield U win 5-3 on penalties.
Referee: Jeremy Simpson.

Shrewsbury T (1) 1 *(Burke 45)*

Oldham Ath (3) 4 *(Philliskirk 9, 26, Rooney 42, Schmeltz 76)*   1748

Shrewsbury T: (442) Anyon; Woods, Goldson, Mkandawire (Jones 8), Jacobson; Taylor, McAllister (Summerfield 81), Wildig, Reach; Burke (Parry 81), Main.
Oldham Ath: (442) Oxley; Lanzoni, Grounds, Tarkowski, Mills; Schmeltz, Smith, Rodgers (Mellor 71), Rusnak (Clarke-Harris 79); Rooney, Philliskirk (Millar 78).
Referee: Seb Stockbridge.

Tranmere R (1) 1 *(Horwood 37)*

Fleetwood T (0) 2 *(Matt 48, 66)*   1937

Tranmere R: (41212) Fon Williams; Jones, Taylor, Goodison, Horwood; Atkinson; Power, Rowe (Thompson 65); Lowe; Stockton (Kirby 64), Sodje (Akpa Akpro 81).
Fleetwood T: (4411) Davies; McLaughlin, Cresswell, Pond, Howell; Brown, Murdoch, Schumacher, Blair (Hughes J 74); Evans; Matt (Ball 81 (Parkin 89)).
Referee: Carl Boyeson.

Wolverhampton W (1) 2 *(McAlinden 5, Sako 64)*

Walsall (0) 2 *(Hemmings 54, Hewitt 85)*   13,481

Wolverhampton W: (442) McCarey; Doherty, Batth, Elokobi (Stearman 56), Golbourne; Price, Davis, McDonald, Sako; Sigurdarson, McAlinden (Forde 76).
Walsall: (4411) O'Donnell; Chambers J, Butler, Downing, Taylor; Baxendale (Hewitt 76), Chambers A, Featherstone, Hemmings (Mantom 82); Sawyers; Lalkovic (Westcarr 46).
Wolverhampton W won 4-2 on penalties.
Referee: Darren Deadman.

SOUTHERN SECTION FIRST ROUND

Tuesday, 3 September 2013

Brentford (1) 5 *(El Alagui 42, 54, Norris 52, Nugent 64, Venta 69)*

AFC Wimbledon (0) 3 *(Fenlon 56, Francomb 82, Sweeney 90)*   4189

Brentford: (442) Button; Logan (Venta 46), O'Connor, Nugent, Barron (Pierre 46); Dallas, Diagouraga, Saville (Reeves 22), Saunders; El Alagui, Norris.
AFC Wimbledon: (442) Worner; Francomb, Fenlon, Weston (Fuller 46), Kennedy; Sainte-Luce (Porter 29), Moore S, Sweeney, Arthur (Pell 63); Midson, Smith.
Referee: Lee Collins.

Cheltenham T (1) 3 *(Gillespie 6, 63, Taylor 67)*

Plymouth Arg (2) 3 *(Boco 16, Alessandra 17, Bencherif 58)*   1236

Cheltenham T: (442) Brown S; Lowe, Inniss, Taylor, Jombati; Vincent (McGlashan 69), Penn (Noble 46), Deering, Kotwica; Harrison, Gillespie (Gornell 83).
Plymouth Arg: (442) Cole; Nelson■, Branston, Blanchard, Reckord; Boco, Bencherif, Hourihane, Blackman; Reid (Morgan 65), Alessandra.
Plymouth Arg won 5-4 on penalties.
Referee: Mark Heywood.

Dagenham & R (0) 4 *(Elito 53, Saah 64, Ogogo 78, Dennis 85)*

Colchester U (1) 1 *(Wilson 38)*   1050

Dagenham & R: (442) Seabright; Hoyte, Doe, Saah, Connors; Elito (Saunders 76), Bingham, Ogogo, Hines (Shields 86); Obafemi (Dennis 84), Scott.
Colchester U: (433) Walker; Wilson, Okuonghae■, Eastman, Dickson; Gilbey, Eastmond (Wright David 70), Bond; Olufemi, Morrison (Thompson 65), Massey (Ibehre 46).
Referee: Charles Breakspear.

Exeter C (0) 0

Wycombe W (1) 2 *(McClure 30, Stewart 83)*   1654

Exeter C: (442) Krysiak; Moore-Taylor, Bennett, Baldwin, Woodman; Sercombe, Doherty (Jay 69), Gosling, Wheeler (Grimes 46); Gow (Reid 79), Parkin.
Wycombe W: (442) Ingram; McCoy (Fletcher 90), Stewart, Hause, Wood; Arnold (Craig 74), Knott, Lewis, Kretzschmar (Bloomfield 82); McClure, Kuffour.
Referee: Steve Bratt.

Gillingham (0) 1 *(Dack 69)*

Leyton Orient (2) 3 *(Batt 26 (pen), 45, 59)*   1630

Gillingham: (442) Nelson; Harriman, Legge, Barrett, Martin; Whelpdale (Weston 67), Gregory (Allen 46), Hollands, Dack; McDonald, German (Kedwell 74).
Leyton Orient: (442) Jones; Odubajo, Clarke, Baudry, Omozusi; Bartley (Cox 90), Vincelot, James, Gorman (Cuthbert 81); Batt (Mooney 65), Stockley.
Referee: Michael Bull.

Milton Keynes D (0) 2 *(Bamford 53, Alli 58)*

Northampton T (0) 0   4299

Milton Keynes D: (4411) McLoughlin; Otsemobor, Williams (Galloway 84), Kay, Lewington; Green (Baldock 78), Alli (Chadwick 71), Reeves, Banton; Smith; Bamford.
Northampton T: (451) Duke; Amankwaah, Heath, Collins, Tozer; Hackett (Emerton 65), Deegan (Toney 86), Demontagnac■, Carter, Harriott (Hooper 90); Blyth.
Referee: Graham Horwood.

Torquay U (0) 0
Portsmouth (0) 0 1951

Torquay U: (442) Rice; Tonge, Downes, Pearce, Cruise; Chapell (Sullivan 59), Lathrope (Mansell 90), Harding, Cameron (Hawley 90); Benyon, Ball.
Portsmouth: (442) Sullivan; Moutaouakil, Devera, Bradley, East; Wallace, Ertl (Padovani 71), Ferry, Barcham; Bird (Craddock 68), Holmes.
Portsmouth won 5-3 on penalties.
Referee: Keith Hill.

Wednesday, 4 September 2013

Bristol C (1) 2 *(Emmanuel-Thomas 12, Bryan 76)*
Bristol R (0) 1 *(McChrystal 59)* 17,888

Bristol C: (4411) Parish; Moloney, Flint, O'Connor, Shorey; Wagstaff, Pack, Reid (Wynter 90), Bryan (Carey 88); Emmanuel-Thomas; Harewood (Baldock 69).
Bristol R: (442) Mildenhall; Smith, Parkes, McChrystal, Brown; Norburn, Lockyer, O'Toole, Harrison; Clarkson (Santos 81), Harrold (Brunt 80).
Referee: Simon Hooper.

NORTHERN SECTION SECOND ROUND

Tuesday, 8 October 2013

Fleetwood T (2) 4 *(Ball 40, Parkin 44, Pond 47, Blair 90)*
Crewe Alex (0) 0 1928

Fleetwood T: (442) Davies; McLaughlin, Pond, Roberts, Hogan; Crowther (Sarcevic 83), Brown, Murdoch, Evans (Blair 71); Ball, Parkin.
Crewe Alex: (442) Phillips; Mellor, Ellis, Dugdale, Tootle; Grant, Osman, Turton (Inman 68), Moore; Oliver (Leitch-Smith 67), Clayton (Aneke 78).
Referee: Eddie Ilderton.

Mansfield T (0) 0
Chesterfield (0) 1 *(McSheffrey 72)* 4834

Mansfield T: (4411) Marriott; Sutton (Jennings 81), Dempster, Riley, Beevers; Clucas, Murtagh, McGuire (Howell 70), Daniel; Stevenson (Palmer 87); Andrew.
Chesterfield: (4231) Lee; Edwards, Hird, Evatt, Cooper; Ryan, Morsy; Devitt (Darikwa 90), O'Shea, McSheffrey (Banks 90); Porter.
Referee: Michael Naylor.

Morecambe (0) 0
Carlisle U (0) 0 2297

Morecambe: (352) Arestidou; Parrish, Hughes, Diagne (Ellison 64); Wright, McGee (Williams 73), Fleming, Kenyon, Threlfall; Mwasile (Sampson 81), Amond.
Carlisle U: (433) Gillespie; McSweeney, O'Hanlon, Thirlwell, Robson; Noble, Potts (Townsend 81), Berrett; Eccleston (Gillies 84), Amoo, Guy (Symington 73).
Carlisle U won 4-3 on penalties.
Referee: David Webb.

Port Vale (0) 0
Rochdale (1) 1 *(Rafferty 40)* 2612

Port Vale: (442) Neal; Yates, Robertson, Dickinson, Jones; Myrie-Williams, Dodds (Birchall 70), Lines, Loft; Pope, Williamson (Hughes 63).
Rochdale: (442) Lillis; Rafferty, Lancashire, O'Connell, Rose; Dicker, Hery (Hogan 58), Allen, Vincenti; Cummins (Bunney 88), Henderson.
Referee: Scott Mathieson.

Preston NE (0) 0
Oldham Ath (2) 2 *(Philliskirk 2, Wesolowski 9)* 5987

Preston NE: (352) Stuckmann; Laird, Huntington, Mousinho (Clarke 46); Nicholson, Welsh, Wroe (Brownhill 75), Croasdale (Beavon 46), Buchanan; Holmes, Garner.
Oldham Ath: (442) Rachubka; Smith, Tarkowski (Mellor 56), Kusunga (Belezika 74), Grounds; Dayton, Wesolowski, Schmeltz, Mills (Montano 83); Rooney, Philliskirk.
Referee: Oliver Langford.

Sheffield U (0) 0
Hartlepool U (1) 1 *(Poole 37)* 4189

Sheffield U: (442) Howard; Westlake, Maguire, Collins, Lappin; Baxter, Coady, Doyle, Murphy (Hall 56); Taylor (Ironside 57), King.
Hartlepool U: (451) Flinders; Duckworth, Austin, Burgess, Holden; Compton (Franks 79), Walton, Monkhouse (Richards 84), Walker, Poole; James (Rodney 85).
Referee: Mick Russell.

Wolverhampton W (0) 0
Notts Co (0) 0 7166

Wolverhampton W: (442) Ikeme; Foley, Ebanks-Landell, Stearman, Elokobi (Sigurdarson 46); Henry, Price, McDonald, Golbourne; Cassidy (McAlinden 62), Griffiths.
Notts Co: (433) Spiess; Thompson, Leacock, Liddle, Dumbuya; Labadie, Boucaud, Fotheringham; Campbell-Ryce (Haynes 72), Arquin (Haworth 81), Coombes.
Notts Co won 3-1 on penalties.
Referee: Andy D'Urso.

York C (0) 0
Rotherham U (1) 3 *(Smith 17 (og), Agard 63 (pen), Revell 69)* 2372

York C: (442) Ingham; O'Neill, Smith, Parslow, Davies; Platt (Murray 75), Whitehouse, Montrose, Chambers (Bowman 69); Jarvis, Fletcher (Cresswell 69).
Rotherham U: (442) Collin; Brindley, Mills, Morgan (Rowe 87), Skarz; Agard (Bradley 90), Frecklington, Tidser, Pringle (Milsom 90); Revell, Hylton.
Referee: Mark Heywood.

SOUTHERN SECTION SECOND ROUND

Tuesday, 8 October 2013

Crawley T (2) 2 *(Sinclair 13, Jones M 23)*
Newport Co (1) 3 *(Zebroski 43, Chapman 48 (pen), Essam 61 (og))* 1350

Crawley T: (442) Jones P; Hurst■, Connolly M, Essam, Sadler; Adams, Simpson, Jones M (Alexander 68), Torres (Bulman 63); Proctor, Sinclair (Drury 63).
Newport Co: (433) Stephens; Jackson, Yakubu (Chapman 15), James, Hughes; Minshull, Naylor, Flynn (Pipe 84); Willmott (Washington 87), Crow, Zebroski.
Referee: Rob Lewis.

Leyton Orient (0) 0
Coventry C (0) 0 2151

Leyton Orient: (442) Jones; Omozusi, Cuthbert, Clarke, Sawyer; Batt (Mooney 65), Vincelot, James, Odubajo; Lasimant (Cox 74), Stockley (Bartley 84).
Coventry C: (442) Murphy; Willis (Phillips 66), Clarke J, Webster, Adams; Moussa, Thomas, Fleck, Barton (Daniels 74); Clarke L, Wilson.
Leyton Orient won 4-2 on penalties.
Referee: Tim Robinson.

Oxford U (0) 1 *(Constable 90)*
Portsmouth (0) 2 *(Agyemang 66, Marquis 83)* 3697

Oxford U: (4411) Clarke; Hunt, Mullins, Raynes, Newey; Williams (Hall 73), Davies, Ruffels, O'Dowda; Potter (Smalley 42); Constable.
Portsmouth: (451) Carson; Moutaouakil, Bradley, N'Gala, Painter (Cooper 17); Wallace, Ertl, Mahon, Padovani (Agyemang 60), Holmes (Barcham 78); Marquis.
Referee: Iain Williamson.

Peterborough U (1) 2 *(Taylor 18 (og), McCann 70 (pen))*
Brentford (0) 1 *(Nugent 80)* 5261

Peterborough U: (442) Olejnik; Alcock, Zakuani (Brisley 46), Bostwick, Little; Swanson, Kearns (Mendez-Laing 68), Payne (Gordon 73), McCann; Assombalonga, Taylor.
Brentford: (4231) Button; Bidwell, Calvet, Taylor (Nugent 62), Saville; Craig, Douglas; Saunders (El Alagui 71), Diagouraga, Fillo (Clarke 46); Trotta.
Referee: Andy Davies.

Southend U (0) 2 *(Woodrow 51, 53)*

Dagenham & R (1) 5 *(Hines 26, 60, Saah 58, Dickson 64, Obafemi 66)*   3236

Southend U: (433) Smith; White, Phillips, Prosser (Corr 89), Coker; Payne, Clifford, Timlin; Hurst, Reid (Woodrow 46), Straker (Atkinson 65).
Dagenham & R: (433) Seabright; Hoyte■, Wilkinson, Saah, Ilesanmi; Saunders, Ogogo, Elito; Dickson (Woodall 81), Murphy (Obafemi 56), Hines (Bingham 81).
Referee: Gavin Ward.

Stevenage (0) 2 *(Zoko 51, Morais 61 (pen))*

Milton Keynes D (1) 1 *(Williams 25 (pen))*   1456

Stevenage: (442) Day; Smith J, Ashton, Hartley, Jones; Morais (Wedgbury 81), Doughty, Heslop, Akins (Andrade 74); Zoko (Cowan 73), Freeman.
Milton Keynes D: (442) McLoughlin; Lewington, Williams, Powell (Banton 65), Reeves; Gleeson, Potter, Smith (Rasulo 65), Baldock; McLeod (Carruthers 65), Bamford.
Referee: Fred Graham.

Swindon T (1) 2 *(Barthram 19, Ajose 46)*

Plymouth Arg (1) 1 *(Blackman 7)*   4211

Swindon T: (451) Belford; Branco, Hall, Ward, Barthram (N'Guessan 70); Byrne, Pritchard, Thompson L (Cox 65), Luongo, Ajose; El-Gabbas (Ranger 82).
Plymouth Arg: (442) Cole; Nelson, Blanchard, Trotman, Reckord (Berry 58); Boco, Young (Bencherif 69), Hourihane, Blackman; Reid, Hayes (Harvey 58).
Referee: James Linington.

Wycombe W (2) 2 *(Knott 9, Bloomfield 27)*

Bristol C (0) 1 *(Moloney 56)*   1279

Wycombe W: (4411) Ingram; Arnold (McCoy 88), Hause, Stewart, Wood; Bloomfield (Kretzschmar 70), Scowen, Lewis, Cowan-Hall; Knott (Spring 81); Kuffour.
Bristol C: (442) Fielding; Moloney, Dunk, Flint, Cunningham; Wagstaff, Pack, Bryan (Baldock 46), McLaughlin; Harewood (Emmanuel-Thomas 69), Morrell (Reid 46).
Referee: Keith Stroud.

NORTHERN SECTION QUARTER-FINALS

Tuesday, 12 November 2013

Chesterfield (1) 3 *(Banks 45, 79, Gnanduillet 73)*

Rochdale (0) 0   2897

Chesterfield: (442) Lee; Talbot, Cooper, Evatt, Hird; Ryan, Humphreys, Banks (Darikwa 82), Roberts; O'Shea (Doyle 88), Gnanduillet (Richards 81).
Rochdale: (352) Lillis; Eastham, Lancashire, O'Connell; Done, Tutte (Allen 66), Dicker, Vidal (Rose 18), Henderson; Vincenti (Cummins 55), Hogan.
Referee: Christopher Sarginson.

Hartlepool U (1) 1 *(Monkhouse 24)*

Rotherham U (2) 2 *(Eaves 9, Agard 45)*   2911

Hartlepool U: (442) Flinders; Duckworth, Baldwin, Collins, Austin; Franks (Richards 87), Walton, Dolan (Sweeney 80), Monkhouse; Poole (Walker 85), James.
Rotherham U: (442) Collin; Brindley, Morgan, Mills, Skarz (Pringle 60); Milsom, Tidser, Frecklington, Agard; Tubbs (Nardiello 67), Eaves (Revell 68).
Referee: Darren Drysdale.

Oldham Ath (2) 5 *(Tarkowski 30, Philliskirk 45 (pen), 84, Dayton 67, Clarke-Harris 90)*

Notts Co (1) 1 *(Murray 13)*   2646

Oldham Ath: (442) Rachubka; Kusunga (Brown 71), Tarkowski, Grounds, Mills; Dayton, Smith, Rodgers (Bove■ 85), Montano (Schmeltz 76); Clarke-Harris, Philliskirk.
Notts Co: (442) Spiess; Liddle, Smith, Leacock■, Sheehan; Campbell-Ryce, Labadie, Fotheringham (Freeman 46), Grealish (Bell 46); Arquin, Murray (Showunmi 78).
Referee: Andy Haines.

Wednesday, 13 November 2013

Fleetwood T (1) 2 *(Ball 5, Sarcevic 54)*

Carlisle U (0) 0   2446

Fleetwood T: (4231) Davies; McLaughlin, Cresswell, Roberts, Taylor; Schumacher, Murdoch; Evans, Sarcevic (Dieseruvwe 86), Hughes J (Brown 78); Ball (Parkin 85).
Carlisle U: (3421) Fleming; Ehmer, O'Hanlon, Townsend; Symington, Potts, Berrett, Robson (Guy 46); Amoo (Gillies 66), Buaben (Lynch 66); Beck.
Referee: Stuart Attwell.

SOUTHERN SECTION QUARTER-FINALS

Tuesday, 12 November 2013

Newport Co (2) 3 *(Washington 5, 83, Oshilaja 19)*

Portsmouth (0) 0   2849

Newport Co: (442) Stephens; Pipe■, Yakubu, Naylor, Oshilaja; Crow, Willmott, Flynn (Minshull 61), Worley; Washington, Jolley (Jackson 72).
Portsmouth: (442) Carson; N'Gala, Devera, Bradley, East; Holmes, Cooper, Barcham, Padovani; Craddock (Connolly 55), Bird.
Referee: Graham Scott.

Peterborough U (0) 1 *(Assombalonga 57)*

Dagenham & R (0) 0   4830

Peterborough U: (352) Olejnik; Alcock, Brisley, Bostwick; Little, Ephraim (Barnett 81), McCann, Swanson, Nthle; Assombalonga (Jeffers 87), Mendez-Laing (Conlon 87).
Dagenham & R: (433) Lewington; Hoyte, Wilkinson, Saah, Ilesanmi; Ogogo (Howell 86), Bingham, Hines; Elito, Dickson, Obafemi (Scott 71).
Referee: Mark Haywood.

Stevenage (3) 3 *(Zoko 3, Akins 12, Morais 16 (pen))*

Leyton Orient (2) 2 *(Mooney 14, James 45 (pen))*   1532

Stevenage: (442) Day; Smith J, Jones, Hartley, Deacon■; Morais, Heslop, Doughty, Freeman (Wedgbury 64); Akins, Zoko (Burrow 90).
Leyton Orient: (442) Jones; Omozusi, Cuthbert, Sawyer, Stockley (Simpson 79); Cox, James, Bartley, Odubajo; Mooney (Lisbie 70), Batt (Lasimant 74).
Referee: James Adcock.

Swindon T (0) 2 *(Ajose 78, 90)*

Wycombe W (1) 1 *(McClure 45)*   3940

Swindon T: (451) Belford; Byrne, Hall, Ward, McEveley; Ajose, Luongo, Kasim (Harley 46), Thompson L, Pritchard; N'Guessan (El-Gabbas 72).
Wycombe W: (442) Ingram; McCoy, Hause, Doherty, Wood; Lewis, Scowen, Kuffour (Knott 84), Kretzschmar; Craig (Dunne 73), McClure (Morgan 45).
Referee: Carl Berry.

NORTHERN SECTION SEMI-FINALS

Tuesday, 10 December 2013

Fleetwood T (1) 2 *(Hughes J 19, McLaughlin 70)*

Rotherham U (0) 1 *(Dicko 56)*   2224

Fleetwood T: (451) Davies; McLaughlin, Pond, Roberts, Taylor; Blair (Brown 78), Schumacher, Sarcevic, Hughes J, Evans (Cresswell 89); Tyson (Carr 76).
Rotherham U: (433) Collin; Bradley (Brindley 46), Arnason, Morgan, Tavernier; Agard, Frecklington, Pringle; Revell, Vuckic (Davis 79), Dicko.
Referee: Scott Duncan.

Oldham Ath (1) 1 *(Philliskirk 21)*

Chesterfield (1) 1 *(Darikwa 28)*   3534

Oldham Ath: (442) Rachubka; Lanzoni, Tarkowski, Kusunga, Grounds; Petrasso (Rooney 81), Wesolowski (Rodgers 86), Smith, Mellor; Philliskirk, Clarke-Harris.
Chesterfield: (4231) Lee; Talbot, Evatt, Cooper (McSheffrey 90), Humphreys; Hird, Ryan; Darikwa, Banks, Doyle; Richards.
Chesterfield won 6-5 on penalties.
Referee: Kevin Wright.

SOUTHERN SECTION SEMI-FINALS

Tuesday, 10 December 2013

Newport Co (0) 0
Peterborough U (1) 3 *(Ntlhe 13, McCann 90, Mendez-Laing 90)* 1765
Newport Co: (352) Stephens (Pidgeley 60); Pipe, Hughes (Crow 46), Chapman; Washington, Willmott, Naylor (Flynn 46), Sandell, Oshilaja; Worley, Jolley.
Peterborough U: (442) Olejnik; Little (Knight-Percival 37), Ntlhe, McCann, Bostwick; Anderson, Brisley, Swanson (Ferdinand 61), Jeffers (Mendez-Laing 71); Assombalonga, Tomlin.
Referee: Trevor Kettle.

Swindon T (1) 1 *(Ajose 24)*
Stevenage (0) 1 *(Zoko 82)* 3804
Swindon T: (433) Belford; Barthram, Hall, Ward, McEveley; Mason (Kasim 67), Luongo (Gladwin 67), Harley; Ajose, N'Guessan (El-Gabbas 84), Pritchard.
Stevenage: (352) Day; Chorley, Ashton, Hartley (Andrade 72); Smith J, Parrett (Akins 60), Heslop, Doughty (Wedgbury 90); Freeman; Morais, Zoko.
Swindon T won 3-1 on penalties.
Referee: Stephen Martin.

NORTHERN FINAL

Tuesday, 4 February 2014

Fleetwood T (1) 1 *(Ball 45)*
Chesterfield (2) 3 *(Evatt 21, Morsy 24, Ryan 65)* 3508
Fleetwood: (41212) Davies; McLaughlin, Roberts, Pond, Taylor; Goodall; Murdoch (Evans 75), Brown; Sarcevic; Ball (Mandron 68), Parkin.
Chesterfield: (4231) Lee; Darikwa, Evatt, Cooper, Humphreys; Morsy, Ryan (Hird 85); Gardner (Talbot 53), Banks, Roberts; Doyle (Richards 77).
Referee: David Coote.

Tuesday, 18 February 2014

Chesterfield (0) 0
Fleetwood T (0) 1 *(Parkin 90)* 6358
Chesterfield: (4141) Lee; Darikwa, Evatt, Cooper, Humphreys; Hird; O'Shea (Doyle 76), Morsy, Ryan (Gnanduillet 86), Roberts; Richards (Banks 76).
Fleetwood T: (442) Maxwell; McLaughlin, Roberts (Hughes J 74), Pond, Taylor; Sarcevic, Goodall (Mandron 63), Marrow (Brown 63), Evans; Parkin, Matt.
Referee: David Webb.

SOUTHERN FINAL

Wednesday, 5 February 2014

Peterborough U (2) 2 *(Branco 10 (og), Vassell 14)*
Swindon T (2) 2 *(Ranger 31, Brisley 45 (og))* 3312
Peterborough U: (442) Olejnik; Alcock, Brisley (Newell 77), Bostwick, Knight-Percival; Swanson, Payne, McCann (Anderson 46), Rowe; Vassell, Assombalonga (Kearns 41).
Swindon T: (41212) Foderingham; Thompson N, Branco, Ward, McEveley■; Thompson L; Kasim, Luongo; Gladwin (Byrne 89); Ranger, N'Guessan.
Referee: Paul Tierney.

Monday, 17 February 2014

Swindon T (1) 1 *(Pritchard 34)*
Peterborough U (0) 1 *(Assombalonga 75)* 6825
Swindon T: (352) Foderingham; Archibald-Henville, Branco, Ward; Pritchard, Luongo, Kasim, Thompson L, Byrne; Murphy (Reis 85), N'Guessan (Gladwin 81).
Peterborough U: (442) Olejnik; Little, Brisley, Knight-Percival, Alcock; Swanson, Payne (McCann 60), Bostwick, Rowe; Vassell (McQuoid 46), Assombalonga.
Peterborough U won 4-3 on penalties.
Referee: Keith Stroud.

JOHNSTONE'S PAINT TROPHY FINAL 2014

Sunday, 30 March 2014

(at Wembley Stadium, attendance 35,663)

Chesterfield (0) 1 Peterborough U (2) 3

Chesterfield: (4231) Lee; Darikwa, Humphreys, Cooper, Evatt; Ryan, Morsy; O'Shea (Bennett 72), Banks (Hird 12 (Richards 79)), Roberts; Doyle.
Scorer: Doyle 53.

Peterborough U: (4411) Olejnik; Little, Bostwick, Brisley (Alcock 72), Knight-Percival; McQuoid (Isgrove 83), McCann (Payne 67), Rowe, Newell■; Swanson; Assombalonga.
Scorers: McQuoid 7, Brisley 38, Assombalonga 78 (pen)).

Referee: Andy D'Urso.

JOHNSTONE'S PAINT TROPHY
ATTENDANCES 2013–14

Round	Aggregate	Games	Average
One	60,823	16	3,801
Two	54,026	16	3,377
Area Quarter-finals	24,051	8	3,006
Area Semi-finals	11,327	4	2,832
Area finals	20,003	4	5,001
Final	35,663	1	35,663
Total	205,893	49	4,202

FA CUP FINALS 1872–2014

VENUES

1872 and 1874–92	Kennington Oval	1895–1914	Crystal Palace
1873	Lillie Bridge	1915	Old Trafford, Manchester
1893	Fallowfield, Manchester	1920–22	Stamford Bridge
1894	Everton	2001–2006	Millennium Stadium, Cardiff
1923–2000	Wembley Stadium (old)	2007 to date	Wembley Stadium (new)

THE FA CUP

1872	Wanderers v Royal Engineers	1-0
1873	Wanderers v Oxford University	2-0
1874	Oxford University v Royal Engineers	2-0
1875	Royal Engineers v Old Etonians	1-1*
Replay	Royal Engineers v Old Etonians	2-0
1876	Wanderers v Old Etonians	1-1*
Replay	Wanderers v Old Etonians	3-0
1877	Wanderers v Oxford University	2-1*
1878	Wanderers v Royal Engineers	3-1

Wanderers won the cup outright, but it was restored to the Football Association.

1879	Old Etonians v Clapham R	1-0
1880	Clapham R v Oxford University	1-0
1881	Old Carthusians v Old Etonians	3-0
1882	Old Etonians v Blackburn R	1-0
1883	Blackburn Olympic v Old Etonians	2-1*
1884	Blackburn R v Queen's Park, Glasgow	2-1
1885	Blackburn R v Queen's Park, Glasgow	2-0
1886	Blackburn R v WBA	0-0
Replay	Blackburn R v WBA	2-0
	(at Racecourse Ground, Derby Co)	

A special trophy was awarded to Blackburn R for third consecutive win.

1887	Aston Villa v WBA	2-0
1888	WBA v Preston NE	2-1
1889	Preston NE v Wolverhampton W	3-0
1890	Blackburn R v The Wednesday	6-1
1891	Blackburn R v Notts Co	3-1
1892	WBA v Aston Villa	3-0
1893	Wolverhampton W v Everton	1-0
1894	Notts Co v Bolton W	4-1
1895	Aston Villa v WBA	1-0
1896	The Wednesday v Wolverhampton W	2-1
1897	Aston Villa v Everton	3-2
1898	Nottingham F v Derby Co	3-1
1899	Sheffield U v Derby Co	4-1
1900	Bury v Southampton	4-0
1901	Tottenham H v Sheffield U	2-2
Replay	Tottenham H v Sheffield U	3-1
	(at Burnden Park, Bolton W)	
1902	Sheffield U v Southampton	1-1
Replay	Sheffield U v Southampton	2-1
1903	Bury v Derby Co	6-0
1904	Manchester C v Bolton W	1-0
1905	Aston Villa v Newcastle U	2-0
1906	Everton v Newcastle U	1-0
1907	The Wednesday v Everton	2-1
1908	Wolverhampton W v Newcastle U	3-1
1909	Manchester U v Bristol C	1-0
1910	Newcastle U v Barnsley	1-1
Replay	Newcastle U v Barnsley	2-0
	(at Goodison Park, Everton)	
1911	Bradford C v Newcastle U	0-0
Replay	Bradford C v Newcastle U	1-0
	(at Old Trafford, Manchester U)	
1912	Barnsley v WBA	0-0
Replay	Barnsley v WBA	1-0
	(at Bramall Lane, Sheffield U)	
1913	Aston Villa v Sunderland	1-0
1914	Burnley v Liverpool	1-0
1915	Sheffield U v Chelsea	3-0
1920	Aston Villa v Huddersfield T	1-0*

1921	Tottenham H v Wolverhampton W	1-0
1922	Huddersfield T v Preston NE	1-0
1923	Bolton W v West Ham U	2-0
1924	Newcastle U v Aston Villa	2-0
1925	Sheffield U v Cardiff C	1-0
1926	Bolton W v Manchester C	1-0
1927	Cardiff C v Arsenal	1-0
1928	Blackburn R v Huddersfield T	3-1
1929	Bolton W v Portsmouth	2-0
1930	Arsenal v Huddersfield T	2-0
1931	WBA v Birmingham	2-1
1932	Newcastle U v Arsenal	2-1
1933	Everton v Manchester C	3-0
1934	Manchester C v Portsmouth	2-1
1935	Sheffield W v WBA	4-2
1936	Arsenal v Sheffield U	1-0
1937	Sunderland v Preston NE	3-1
1938	Preston NE v Huddersfield T	1-0*
1939	Portsmouth v Wolverhampton W	4-1
1946	Derby Co v Charlton Ath	4-1*
1947	Charlton Ath v Burnley	1-0*
1948	Manchester U v Blackpool	4-2
1949	Wolverhampton W v Leicester C	3-1
1950	Arsenal v Liverpool	2-0
1951	Newcastle U v Blackpool	2-0
1952	Newcastle U v Arsenal	1-0
1953	Blackpool v Bolton W	4-3
1954	WBA v Preston NE	3-2
1955	Newcastle U v Manchester C	3-1
1956	Manchester C v Birmingham C	3-1
1957	Aston Villa v Manchester U	2-1
1958	Bolton W v Manchester U	2-0
1959	Nottingham F v Luton T	2-1
1960	Wolverhampton W v Blackburn R	3-0
1961	Tottenham H v Leicester C	2-0
1962	Tottenham H v Burnley	3-1
1963	Manchester U v Leicester C	3-1
1964	West Ham U v Preston NE	3-2
1965	Liverpool v Leeds U	2-1*
1966	Everton v Sheffield W	3-2
1967	Tottenham H v Chelsea	2-1
1968	WBA v Everton	1-0*
1969	Manchester C v Leicester C	1-0
1970	Chelsea v Leeds U	2-2*
Replay	Chelsea v Leeds U	2-1
	(at Old Trafford, Manchester U)	
1971	Arsenal v Liverpool	2-1*
1972	Leeds U v Arsenal	1-0
1973	Sunderland v Leeds U	1-0
1974	Liverpool v Newcastle U	3-0
1975	West Ham U v Fulham	2-0
1976	Southampton v Manchester U	1-0
1977	Manchester U v Liverpool	2-1
1978	Ipswich T v Arsenal	1-0
1979	Arsenal v Manchester U	3-2
1980	West Ham U v Arsenal	1-0
1981	Tottenham H v Manchester C	1-1*
Replay	Tottenham H v Manchester C	3-2
1982	Tottenham H v QPR	1-1*
Replay	Tottenham H v QPR	1-0
1983	Manchester U v Brighton & HA	2-2*
Replay	Manchester U v Brighton & HA	4-0
1984	Everton v Watford	2-0

1985	Manchester U v Everton	1-0*
1986	Liverpool v Everton	3-1
1987	Coventry C v Tottenham H	3-2*
1988	Wimbledon v Liverpool	1-0
1989	Liverpool v Everton	3-2*
1990	Manchester U v Crystal Palace	3-3*
Replay	Manchester U v Crystal Palace	1-0
1991	Tottenham H v Nottingham F	2-1*
1992	Liverpool v Sunderland	2-0
1993	Arsenal v Sheffield W	1-1*
Replay	Arsenal v Sheffield W	2-1*
1994	Manchester U v Chelsea	4-0

THE FA CUP SPONSORED BY LITTLEWOODS POOLS

1995	Everton v Manchester U	1-0
1996	Manchester U v Liverpool	1-0
1997	Chelsea v Middlesbrough	2-0
1998	Arsenal v Newcastle U	2-0

THE AXA-SPONSORED FA CUP

1999	Manchester U v Newcastle U	2-0
2000	Chelsea v Aston Villa	1-0
2001	Liverpool v Arsenal	2-1
2002	Arsenal v Chelsea	2-0

THE FA CUP

2003	Arsenal v Southampton	1-0
2004	Manchester U v Millwall	3-0
2005	Arsenal v Manchester U	0-0*
	Arsenal won 5-4 on penalties.	
2006	Liverpool v West Ham U	3-3*
	Liverpool won 3-1 on penalties.	

THE FA CUP SPONSORED BY E.ON

2007	Chelsea v Manchester U	1-0*
2008	Portsmouth v Cardiff C	1-0
2009	Chelsea v Everton	2-1
2010	Chelsea v Portsmouth	1-0
2011	Manchester C v Stoke C	1-0

THE FA CUP WITH BUDWEISER

2012	Chelsea v Liverpool	2-1
2013	Wigan Ath v Manchester C	1-0
2014	Arsenal v Hull C	3-2*

*After extra time.

FA CUP WINS

Arsenal 11, Manchester U 11, Tottenham H 8, Aston Villa 7, Chelsea 7, Liverpool 7, Blackburn R 6, Newcastle U 6, Everton 5, Manchester C 5, The Wanderers 5, WBA 5, Bolton W 4, Sheffield U 4, Wolverhampton W 4, Sheffield W 3, West Ham U 3, Bury 2, Nottingham F 2, Old Etonians 2, Portsmouth 2, Preston NE 2, Sunderland 2, Barnsley 1, Blackburn Olympic 1, Blackpool 1, Bradford C 1, Burnley 1, Cardiff C 1, Charlton Ath 1, Clapham R 1, Coventry C 1, Derby Co 1, Huddersfield T 1, Ipswich T 1, Leeds U 1, Notts Co 1, Old Carthusians 1, Oxford University 1, Royal Engineers 1, Southampton 1, Wigan Ath 1, Wimbledon 1.

APPEARANCES IN FINALS

Arsenal 18, Manchester U 18, Liverpool 14, Everton 13, Newcastle U 13, Chelsea 11, Aston Villa 10, Manchester C 10, WBA 10, Tottenham H 9, Blackburn R 8, Wolverhampton W 8, Bolton W 7, Preston NE 7, Old Etonians 6, Sheffield U 6, Sheffield W 6, Huddersfield T 5, Portsmouth 5, *The Wanderers 5, West Ham U 5, Derby Co 4, Leeds U 4, Leicester C 4, Oxford University 4, Royal Engineers 4, Southampton 4, Sunderland 4, Blackpool 3, Burnley 3, Cardiff C 3, Nottingham F 3, Barnsley 2, Birmingham C 2, *Bury 2, Charlton Ath 2, Clapham R 2, Notts Co 2, Queen's Park (Glasgow) 2, *Blackburn Olympic 1, *Bradford C 1, Brighton & HA 1, Bristol C 1, *Coventry C 1, Crystal Palace 1, Fulham 1, Hull C 1, *Ipswich T 1, Luton T 1, Middlesbrough 1, Millwall 1, *Old Carthusians 1, QPR 1, Stoke C 1, Watford 1, *Wigan Ath 1, *Wimbledon 1.
* Denotes undefeated in final.

APPEARANCES IN SEMI-FINALS

Manchester U 27, Arsenal 26, Everton 25, Liverpool 23, Chelsea 21, Aston Villa 20, WBA 20, Tottenham H 19, Blackburn R 18, Newcastle U 17, Sheffield W 16, Bolton W 14, Wolverhampton W 14, Derby Co 13, Sheffield U 13, Manchester C 12, Nottingham F 12, Sunderland 12, Southampton 11, Preston NE 10, Birmingham C 9, Burnley 8, Leeds U 8, Huddersfield T 7, Leicester C 7, Portsmouth 7, West Ham U 7, Old Etonians 6, Fulham 6, Oxford University 6, Millwall 5, Notts Co 5, The Wanderers 5, Watford 5, Cardiff C 4, Luton T 4, Queen's Park (Glasgow) 4, Royal Engineers 4, Stoke C 4, Barnsley 3, Blackpool 3, Clapham R 3, Crystal Palace (professional club) 3, Ipswich T 3, Middlesbrough 3, Norwich C 3, Old Carthusians 3, Oldham Ath 3, The Swifts 3, Blackburn Olympic 2, Bristol C 2, Bury 2, Charlton Ath 2, Grimsby T 2, Hull C 2, Swansea T 2, Swindon T 2, Wimbledon 2, Bradford C 1, Brighton & HA 1, Cambridge University 1, Chesterfield 1, Coventry C 1, Crewe Alex 1, Crystal Palace (amateur club) 1, Darwen 1, Derby Junction 1, Glasgow R 1, Marlow 1, Old Harrovians 1, Orient 1, Plymouth Arg 1, Port Vale 1, QPR 1, Reading 1, Shropshire W 1, Wigan Ath 1, Wycombe W 1, York C 1.

FA CUP ATTENDANCES 1969–2014

	1st Round	2nd Round	3rd Round	4th Round	5th Round	6th Round	Semi-finals & Final	Total	No. of matches	Average per match
1969–70	345,229	195,102	925,930	651,374	319,893	198,537	390,700	3,026,765	170	17,805
1970–71	329,687	230,942	956,683	757,852	360,687	304,937	279,644	3,220,432	162	19,879
1971–72	277,726	236,127	986,094	711,399	486,378	230,292	248,546	3,158,562	160	19,741
1972–73	259,432	169,114	938,741	735,825	357,386	241,934	226,543	2,928,975	160	18,306
1973–74	214,236	125,295	840,142	747,909	346,012	233,307	273,051	2,779,952	167	16,646
1974–75	283,956	170,466	914,994	646,434	393,323	268,361	291,369	2,968,903	172	17,261
1975–76	255,533	178,099	867,880	573,843	471,925	206,851	205,810	2,759,941	161	17,142
1976–77	379,230	192,159	942,523	631,265	373,330	205,379	258,216	2,982,102	174	17,139
1977–78	258,248	178,930	881,406	540,164	400,751	137,059	198,020	2,594,578	160	16,216
1978–79	243,773	185,343	880,345	537,748	243,683	263,213	249,897	2,604,002	166	15,687
1979–80	267,121	204,759	804,701	507,725	364,039	157,530	355,541	2,661,416	163	16,328
1980–81	246,824	194,502	832,578	534,402	320,530	288,714	339,250	2,756,800	169	16,312
1981–82	236,220	127,300	513,185	356,987	203,334	124,308	279,621	1,840,955	160	11,506
1982–83	191,312	150,046	670,503	452,688	260,069	193,845	291,162	2,209,625	154	14,348
1983–84	192,276	151,647	625,965	417,298	181,832	185,382	187,000	1,941,400	166	11,695
1984–85	174,604	137,078	616,229	320,772	269,232	148,690	242,754	1,909,359	157	12,162
1985–86	171,142	130,034	486,838	495,526	311,833	184,262	192,316	1,971,951	168	11,738
1986–87	209,290	146,761	593,520	349,342	263,550	119,396	195,533	1,877,400	165	11,378
1987–88	204,411	104,561	720,121	443,133	281,461	119,313	177,585	2,050,585	155	13,229
1988–89	212,775	121,326	690,199	421,255	206,781	176,629	167,353	1,966,318	164	12,173
1989–90	209,542	133,483	683,047	412,483	351,423	123,065	277,420	2,190,463	170	12,885
1990–91	194,195	121,450	594,592	530,279	276,112	124,826	196,434	2,038,518	162	12,583
1991–92	231,940	117,078	586,014	372,576	270,537	155,603	201,592	1,935,340	160	12,095
1992–93	241,968	174,702	612,494	377,211	198,379	149,675	293,241	2,047,670	161	12,718
1993–94	190,683	118,031	691,064	430,234	172,196	134,705	228,233	1,965,146	159	12,359
1994–95	219,511	125,629	640,017	438,596	257,650	159,787	174,059	2,015,249	161	12,517
1995–96	185,538	115,669	748,997	391,218	274,055	174,142	156,500	2,046,199	167	12,252
1996–97	209,521	122,324	651,139	402,293	199,873	67,035	191,813	1,843,998	151	12,211
1997–98	204,803	130,261	629,127	455,557	341,290	192,651	172,007	2,125,696	165	12,883
1998–99	191,954	132,341	609,486	431,613	359,398	181,005	202,150	2,107,947	155	13,599
1999–2000	181,485	127,728	514,030	374,795	182,511	105,443	214,921	1,700,913	158	10,765
2000–01	171,689	122,061	577,204	398,241	256,899	100,663	177,778	1,804,535	151	11,951
2001–02	198,369	119,781	566,284	330,434	249,190	173,757	171,278	1,809,093	148	12,224
2002–03	189,905	104,103	577,494	404,599	242,483	156,244	175,498	1,850,326	150	12,336
2003–04	162,738	117,967	624,732	347,964	292,521	156,780	167,401	1,870,103	149	12,551
2004–05	161,197	98,702	602,152	477,472	339,082	127,914	193,233	1,999,752	146	13,697
2005–06	188,876	107,456	654,570	388,339	286,225	163,449	177,723	1,966,638	160	12,291
2006–07	168,884	113,924	708,628	478,924	340,612	230,064	177,810	2,218,846	158	14,043
2007–08	175,195	99,528	704,300	356,404	276,903	142,780	256,210	2,011,320	152	13,232
2008–09	161,526	96,923	631,070	529,585	297,364	149,566	264,635	2,131,669	163	13,078
2009–10	147,078	100,476	613,113	335,426	288,604	144,918	254,806	1,884,421	151	12,480
2010–11	169,259	101,291	637,202	390,524	284,311	164,092	250,256	1,996,935	150	13,313
2011–12	155,858	92,267	640,700	391,214	250,666	194,971	262,064	1,987,740	151	13,164
2012–13	135,642	115,965	645,676	373,892	288,509	221,216	234,210	2,015,110	156	12,917
2013–14	144,709	75,903	668,242	346,706	254,084	156,630	243,350	1,889,624	149	12,682

THE FA CUP WITH BUDWEISER 2013–14
PRELIMINARY AND QUALIFYING ROUNDS

EXTRA PRELIMINARY ROUND

Darlington RA v Newton Aycliffe	1-5
Thackley v Guisborough T	1-3
Glasshoughton Welfare v Jarrow Roofing Boldon CA	2-3
Colne v South Shields	1-1, 1-2
Brighouse T v Seaham Red Star	3-1
Ashington v Pontefract Collieries	9-0
Dunston UTS v Pickering T	4-1
Garforth T v Shildon	1-4
Silsden v Bridlington T	1-2
Crook T v Billingham T	4-2
Northallerton T v Whitehaven	2-4
Morpeth T v Liversedge	6-0
Billingham Synthonia v West Allotment Celtic	4-0
Spennymoor T v Sunderland RCA	2-1
Team Northumbria v Whitley Bay	2-1
Bishop Auckland v Tadcaster Alb	0-0, 3-0
Albion Sports v North Shields	2-0
Hebburn T v Barnoldswick T	2-2, 2-0
Penrith v Newcastle Benfield	3-1
Marske U v Consett	3-1
Tow Law T v West Auckland T	0-5
Durham C v Hall Road Rangers	6-1
Runcorn T v Winterton Rangers	7-2
Stockport Sports v Winsford U	1-2
Worksop Parramore v AFC Blackpool	2-0
Maltby Main v Congleton T	1-4
Bacup & Rossendale Bor v Formby	1-4
Bootle v Squires Gate	2-1
Barton T OB's v Nostell MW	2-1
Maine Road v Runcorn Linnets	0-3
Parkgate v Shirebrook T	0-3
AFC Emley v Wigan Robin Park	3-2
AFC Liverpool v Cheadle T	1-0
Armthorpe Welfare v Glossop North End	1-4
Alsager T v Atherton Collieries	1-3
Staveley MW v Ashton T	2-1
West Didsbury & Chorlton v Abbey Hey	2-0
St Helens T v Ashton Ath	2-2, 0-1
Boldmere St Michaels v Tipton T	0-2
Bolehall Swifts v Causeway U	2-2, 4-0
Bewdley T v Coventry Sphinx	0-3
Rocester v Atherstone T	3-3, 0-1
Gornal Ath v Ellesmere Rangers	1-2
Westfields v Lye T	2-3
Studley v Stafford T	5-0
Heath Hayes v Black Country Rangers	1-3
Walsall Wood v Continental Star	4-1
Norton U v Southam U	7-1
Tividale v Alvechurch	3-0
Stourport Swifts v Coleshill T	3-1
AFC Wulfrunians v Earlswood T	4-1
Wolverhampton Casuals v Pegasus Juniors	7-1
Nuneaton Griff v Brocton	2-3
Shawbury U v Dudley T	0-0, 2-1
Thurnby Nirvana v Kirby Muxloe	0-0, 4-4
aet; Kirby Muxloe won 4-3 on penalties.	
Quorn v Holbrook Sports	5-1
Retford U v Heanor T	3-1
Graham St Prims v Shepshed Dynamo	1-3
Harborough T v Teversal	2-1
Dunkirk v Barrow T	4-0
Stewarts & Lloyds Corby v Arnold T	1-1, 1-2
Lincoln Moorlands Railway v Long Eaton U	2-4
Basford U v Holwell Sports	1-0
Borrowash Vic v Louth T	2-1
Desborough T v Oadby T	3-1
Blaby & Whetstone Ath v Heather St Johns	2-0
Hucknall T v Loughborough University	
Walkover for Loughborough University –	
Hucknall T removed.	
Gorleston v Deeping Rangers	2-1
Boston T v Great Yarmouth T	3-2
Godmanchester R v Blackstones	6-3
Holbeach U v Norwich U	2-1
Thetford T v Diss T	1-0
Ely C v Sleaford T	0-3
Yaxley v Peterborough Northern Star	0-3

Huntingdon T v Fakenham T	4-1
Spalding U v Eynesbury R	4-2
Swaffham T v Wisbech T	2-1
FC Clacton v Sporting Bengal U	3-1
Great Wakering R v Halstead T	5-0
Whitton U v London APSA	4-1
Kirkley & Pakefield v Brightlingsea Regent	2-2, 2-1
Stansted v Brantham Ath	0-0, 1-6
Clapton v Stanway R	0-0, 1-0
Sawbridgeworth T v Mildenhall T	1-6
Haverhill R v Eton Manor	3-1
Newmarket T v Ilford	3-1
Ipswich W v Wivenhoe T	0-0, 1-0
Barking v Bowers & Pitsea	3-1
Woodbridge T v Hullbridge Sports	0-2
Basildon U v Southend Manor	2-2, 2-1
Walsham Le Willows v Tower Hamlets	0-1
Takeley v Hadleigh U	0-2
Felixstowe & Walton U v Saffron Walden T	3-0
Berkhamsted v AFC Dunstable	2-1
Hadley v Oxhey Jets	1-1, 1-0
AFC Kempston R v Wembley	0-1
Wellingborough T v Greenhouse London	3-3, 3-5
aet.	
Hoddesdon T v St Margaretsbury	1-1, 1-4
Kings Langley v Long Buckby	3-1
Newport Pagnell T v Hatfield T	2-0
Hillingdon Bor v Leverstock Green	4-2
Cogenhoe U v Tring Ath	0-0, 0-3
London Lions v Stotfold	1-1, 0-1
Irchester U v Biggleswade U	0-2
Harefield U v Woodford U	3-0
Codicote v Crawley Green	1-1, 1-3
Holmer Green v Ampthill T	2-3
Hertford T v Colney Heath	2-1
Northampton Spencer v Bugbrooke St Michaels	2-0
Haringey Bor v Rushden & Higham U	6-0
Enfield 1893 v London Tigers	0-0, 1-2
Cockfosters v Hanwell T	1-1, 1-0
London Colney v AFC Rushden & Diamonds	1-1, 1-6
Sandhurst T v Farnham T	2-2, 1-4
Tadley Calleva v Ascot U	2-4
Walkover for Tadley Calleva – Ascot U removed.	
Bracknell T v Fairford T	2-1
Holyport v Hanworth Villa	2-7
Staines Lammas v Badshot Lea	0-2
Ardley U v Thame U	4-1
Camberley T v Chinnor	2-0
Reading T v Wantage T	0-5
Frimley Green v Ash U	3-2
Flackwell Heath v Binfield	0-0, 2-3
Bedfont Sports v Abingdon U	2-2, 1-0
Westfield v Shrivenham	2-1
Cheltenham Saracens v Slimbridge	0-0, 1-1
aet; Cheltenham Saracens won 4-1 on penalties.	
Cove v Carterton	5-0
Newbury v Windsor	1-4
Kidlington v Hartley Wintney	1-1, 2-5
Abingdon T v Highmoor Ibis	1-5
Dorking v Shoreham	1-4
Alton T v Selsey	3-1
Dorking W v Canterbury C	5-0
East Preston v Crowborough Ath	0-0, 3-2
Ashford U v Worthing U	0-0, 1-0
Sevenoaks T v Horley T	1-4
Sidley U v Erith T	
Walkover for Erith T – Sidley U removed.	
Whyteleafe v Epsom & Ewell	3-3, 6-1
Holmesdale v East Grinstead T	1-0
Horsham YMCA v Hassocks	2-3
Molesey v Hailsham T	8-1
Littlehampton T v St Francis Rangers	3-1
Chichester C v Chessington & Hook U	1-8
Pagham v Tunbridge Wells	2-4
Mole Valley SCR v South Park	0-1
Cray Valley (PM) v Lancing	1-1, 4-0
Arundel v Rye U	0-0, 1-2
Beckenham T v Corinthian	1-2

Epsom Ath v Croydon	1-3
Lordswood v Eastbourne U	1-4
Raynes Park Vale v Lingfield	2-1
Greenwich Bor v Ringmer	2-2, 3-1
Fisher v Deal T	1-2
Colliers Wood U v AFC Croydon Ath	6-2
Newport (IW) v Verwood T	4-1
Bournemouth v Highworth T	3-1
Team Solent v AFC Portchester	1-3
Bradford T v Longwell Green Sports	1-2
Horndean v Calne T	7-2
Cowes Sports v Fawley	4-1
Wootton Bassett T v Totton & Eling	0-2
Alresford v Winchester C	0-3
Downton v Sholing	1-3
Melksham T v Hamworthy U	3-3, 1-3
aet.	
Christchurch v Sherborne T	1-2
Bitton v Pewsey Vale	4-1
Winterbourne U v Folland Sports	1-4
(at Folland Sports FC)	
Moneyfields v Cadbury Heath	2-1
Hallen v Whitchurch U	1-1, 2-0
Corsham T v Gillingham T	3-1
Petersfield T v Blackfield & Langley	4-3
Bemerton Heath Harlequins v Fareham T	1-4
Romsey T v Brockenhurst	1-4
Bristol Manor Farm v Oldland Abbotonians	9-3
East Cowes Vic Ath v Lymington T	0-3
Hengrove Ath v Bridport	0-2
Willand R v Larkhall Ath	0-4
St Blazey v Tavistock	1-0
Bishop Sutton v Odd Down	1-1, 2-1
Shepton Mallet v Street	0-0, 0-2
AFC St Austell v Ilfracombe T	1-4
Buckland Ath v Wells C	0-3
Barnstable T v Brislington	0-2
Plymouth Parkway v Saltash U	2-1
Radstock T v Bodmin T	1-4

PRELIMINARY ROUND

Kendal T v Crook T	2-4
Billingham Synthonia v Brighouse T	1-1, 0-4
Jarrow Roofing Boldon CA v Dunston UTS	2-1
Whitehaven v Team Northumbria	0-2
Hebburn T v Marske U	1-2
Padiham v Clitheroe	3-1
Scarborough Ath v Ashington	4-1
Newton Aycliffe v Spennymoor T	3-3, 0-3
Farsley v Lancaster C	1-2
Albion Sports v South Shields	3-3, 2-1
Shildon v Penrith	0-2
Goole v Bishop Auckland	0-2
Guisborough T v Bridlington T	1-1, 4-2
Durham C v Morpeth T	1-1, 2-3
Harrogate RA v West Auckland T	2-2, 2-4
Formby v Northwich Vic	0-3
Bootle v Barton T OB's	4-1
Ossett T v AFC Emley	3-0
Mossley v Worksop Parramore	1-1, 2-3
Atherton Collieries v Radcliffe Bor	1-1, 1-2
Bamber Bridge v Staveley MW	1-0
Cammell Laird v Salford C	2-0
Prescot Cables v Congleton T	0-0, 1-0
Sheffield v Shirebrook T	1-1, 4-0
Curzon Ashton v Ashton Ath	4-0
Warrington T v Winsford U	5-1
Ossett Alb v Runcorn Linnets	1-3
Runcorn T v Glossop North End	0-1
Wakefield v New Mills	0-2
West Didsbury & Chorlton v Burscough	0-3
Ramsbottom U v AFC Liverpool	5-0
Newcastle T v Shawbury U	2-1
Rugby T v Norton U	1-1, 1-1
aet; Rugby T won 4-3 on penalties.	
Tividale v Wolverhampton Casuals	3-0
Stourport Swifts v AFC Wulfrunians	1-1, 1-4
aet.	
Black Country Rangers v Halesowen T	1-2
Chasetown v Romulus	3-1
Sutton Coldfield T v Bedworth U	1-0
Coventry Sphinx v Lye T	2-1
Leek T v Walsall Wood	2-2, 0-2
Atherstone T v Studley	3-1

Market Drayton T v Kidsgrove Ath	1-3
Evesham U v Bolehall Swifts	2-1
Brocton v Ellesmere Rangers	6-0
Tipton T v Stratford T	1-0
Loughborough Dynamo v Eastwood T	0-1
Kettering T v Gresley	0-2
Basford U v Quorn	2-2, 1-1
aet; Basford U won 5-3 on penalties.	
Dunkirk v Rainworth MW	1-1, 1-0
aet.	
Coalville T v Lincoln U	7-1
Desborough T v Loughborough University	2-4
Blaby & Whetstone Ath v Kirby Muxloe	2-0
(at Kirby Muxloe FC)	
Carlton T v Borrowash Vic	2-0
Arnold T v Brigg T	2-2, 2-4
Long Eaton U v Shepshed Dynamo	4-0
Mickleover Sports v Harborough T	8-0
Belper T v Retford U	5-0
Sleaford T v Godmanchester R	2-0
Swaffham T v Huntingdon T	0-2
Spalding U v Holbeach U	4-0
Gorleston v Thetford T	4-1
Peterborough Northern Star v Wroxham	2-4
St Ives T v Soham T Rangers	3-1
Boston T v Dereham T	1-3
Brantham Ath v Barkingside	1-0
Clapton v Mildenhall T	0-2
AFC Sudbury v Ipswich W	4-1
Waltham Abbey v Whitton U	1-1, 3-0
Basildon U v Heybridge Swifts	0-3
Harlow T v Tower Hamlets	4-1
Aveley v Waltham Forest	7-0
Tilbury v Kirkley & Pakefield	2-0
Witham T v Newmarket T	0-0, 2-0
Thurrock v Felixstowe & Walton U	3-0
Brentwood T v Great Wakering R	3-2
Needham Market v Haverhill R	3-2
FC Clacton v Hullbridge Sports	3-0
Redbridge v Burnham Ramblers	1-3
Hadleigh U v Romford	0-5
Maldon & Tiptree v Barking	1-1, 1-0
St Margaretsbury v London Tigers	1-0
Kings Langley v Newport Pagnell T	2-1
Uxbridge v Stotfold	5-1
Ware v Wembley	1-5
Crawley Green v Dunstable T	0-3
Barton R v Ampthill T	4-0
Haringey Bor v AFC Hayes	2-1
Potters Bar T v Greenhouse London	0-3
North Greenford U v Tring Ath	3-0
Royston T v Northampton Spencer	3-3, 3-2
Cockfosters v Hadley	2-1
Daventry T v Hillingdon Bor	1-0
Berkhamsted v Harefield U	4-1
Northwood v AFC Rushden & Diamonds	1-2
Hertford v Cheshunt	4-2
Leighton T v Biggleswade U	1-3
Bedfont Sports v North Leigh	1-3
Beaconsfield SYCOB v Bracknell T	5-3
Badshot Lea v Hartley Wintney	2-3
Wantage T v Didcot T	2-3
Marlow v Chertsey T	1-2
Slough T v Cirencester T	1-1, 0-1
Ashford T (Middlesex) v Bishop's Cleeve	0-0, 1-0
Binfield v Cheltenham Saracens	0-0, 7-1
Shortwood U v Egham T	2-1
Ardley v Hanworth Villa	1-0
Chalfont St Peter v Tadley Calleva	5-3
Fleet T v Westfield	0-1
Windsor v Highmoor Ibis	1-3
Aylesbury v Thatcham T	2-1
Frimley Green v Cove	0-2
Cinderford T v Aylesbury U	1-3
Farnham v Camberley T	0-3
Erith & Belvedere v Chatham T	0-5
Littlehampton T v Greenwich Bor	1-0
Raynes Park Vale v Alton T	4-4, 0-1
Eastbourne U v Herne Bay	2-2, 2-1
Guildford C v South Park	0-0
Folkestone Invicta v Molesey	3-3, 4-2
Colliers Wood U v East Preston	1-3
Merstham v Deal T	4-2
Croydon v Whyteleafe	0-2

Hastings U v Ramsgate	1-0
Leatherhead v Tooting & Mitcham U	1-0
Shoreham v Walton Casuals	2-1
Crawley Down Gatwick v Guernsey	1-3
Horley T v Holmesdale	5-3
Dorking W v Hassocks	0-0, 0-1
Walton & Hersham v Horsham	0-2
Chipstead v Rye U	3-2
Eastbourne T v Corinthian	1-0
Faversham T v Worthing	5-1
VCD Ath v Burgess Hill T	1-3
Chessington & Hook U v Sittingbourne	0-1
Corinthian Casuals v Erith T	3-0
Peacehaven & Telscombe v Ashford U	4-0
Three Bridges v Hythe T	2-1
Tunbridge Wells v Whitstable T	0-0, 2-0
Cray Valley (PM) v Redhill	0-2
Corsham T v Sherborne T	2-0
Moneyfields v Longwell Green Sports	2-2, 2-1
Godalming T v AFC Portchester	0-1
Bournemouth v Hallen	2-4
Winchester C v Swindon Supermarine	3-0
Yate T v Cowes Sports	2-1
Bristol Manor Farm v Lymington T	7-1
Petersfield T v Horndean	1-2
Wimborne T v Hamworthy U	1-3
Newport (IW) v Fareham T	0-2
Brockenhurst v Folland Sports	2-0
Totton & Eling v Sholing	0-0, 1-2
Mangotsfield U v Bitton	3-0
Taunton T v Bridgwater T	1-1, 1-2
Bridport v Merthyr T	2-3
Clevedon T v Bishop Sutton	4-1
Plymouth Parkway v Ilfracombe T	4-1
Street v Paulton R	1-0
Wells C v Bodmin T	3-2
Brislington v St Blazey	4-0
Larkhall Ath v Tiverton T	1-0

FIRST QUALIFYING ROUND

Marske U v Albion Sports	3-0
Blyth Spartans v AFC Fylde	1-3
Whitby T v West Auckland T	1-1, 1-4
Penrith v Padiham	3-1
Spennymoor T v Lancaster C	0-1
Team Northumbria v Scarborough Ath	0-4
Brighouse T v Crook T	4-1
Guisborough T v Bishop Auckland	2-2, 2-0
Jarrow Roofing Boldon CA v Morpeth T	1-0
Stocksbridge Park Steels v Ramsbottom U	2-2, 0-3
Marine v Curzon Ashton	2-4
Warrington T v New Mills	0-0, 1-0
Runcorn Linnets v Glossop North End	2-1
Prescot Cables v Buxton	0-1
FC United of Manchester v Chorley	0-1
Ashton U v Witton Alb	2-1
Ossett T v Bamber Bridge	2-2, 2-1
Frickley Ath v Sheffield	4-1
Worksop Parramore v Cammell Laird	1-3
Droylsden v Trafford	1-5
Worksop T v Bootle	1-1, 4-0
Burscough v Radcliffe Bor	2-1
Northwich Vic v Skelmersdale U	0-3
Tipton T v Kidsgrove Ath	2-0
Atherstone T v Redditch U	3-3, 2-1
AFC Wulfrunians v Walsall Wood	1-1, 4-3
aet.	
Evesham U v Stourbridge	0-3
Hinckley U v Rushall Olympic	0-3
Newcastle T v Sutton Coldfield T	2-2, 0-2
Chasetown v Stafford Rangers	0-0, 0-2
Halesowen T v Brocton	2-1
Coventry Sphinx v Tividale	2-1
Nantwich T v Rugby T	1-2
Coalville U v Long Eaton U	3-2
Stamford v Grantham T	0-0, 3-2
Corby T v Barwell	3-0
Mickleover Sports v Loughborough University	2-0
Carlton T v Brigg T	1-1, 2-1
Dunkirk v Blaby & Whetstone Ath	0-0, 1-2
Gresley v Eastwood T	3-2
Ilkeston v Belper T	1-2
Basford U v Matlock T	0-2

St Neots T v Wroxham	3-1
Sleaford T v Huntingdon T	2-1
Tie abandoned after 87 minutes due to player misconduct.	
King's Lynn T v Cambridge C	1-5
St Ives T v Dereham T	4-1
Spalding U v Gorleston	1-0
Billericay T v Leiston	2-0
Grays Ath v Romford	2-1
Witham T v Mildenhall T	1-1, 3-1
Harlow T v Lowestoft T	2-1
AFC Hornchurch v East Thurrock U	1-1, 2-1
Brentwood T v FC Clacton	3-3, 1-2
Needham Market v Brantham Ath	3-2
Bury T v Thurrock	0-2
Aveley v Canvey Island	2-5
Tilbury v Waltham Abbey	2-1
Maldon & Tiptree v Heybridge Swifts	0-2
Burnham Ramblers v AFC Sudbury	1-2
Hendon v Biggleswade U	7-1
Chesham U v Royston T	1-2
Cockfosters v AFC Rushden & Diamonds	2-2, 0-8
Daventry T v Berkhamsted	6-1
Greenhouse London v Bedford T	2-6
Wingate & Finchley v Biggleswade T	0-0, 3-4
Hitchin T v Arlesley T	1-1, 0-2
Uxbridge v Barton R	2-3
Harrow Bor v North Greenford U	2-2, 1-2
Wembley v Haringey Bor	0-2
St Albans C v Enfield T	6-1
Wealdstone v Kings Langley	6-1
Hertford T v Dunstable T	0-6
St Margaretsbury v Hemel Hempstead T	0-7
Westfield v Aylesbury U	1-1, 0-2
Beaconsfield SYCOB v Burnham	2-4
Chertsey T v Highmoor Ibis	4-0
Didcot T v North Leigh	2-1
Hampton & Richmond Bor v Ashford T (Middlesex)	4-2
Aylesbury v Shortwood U	1-5
Hungerford T v Cove	4-0
Chalfont St Peter v Metropolitan Police	0-0, 1-0
Ardley U v Binfield	2-2, 1-4
Hartley Wintney v Camberley T	0-0, 2-0
Banbury U v Cirencester T	1-2
Leatherhead v Carshalton Ath	2-1
Burgess Hill T v Alton T	8-1
South Park v Horsham	1-1, 2-5
Merstham v Corinthian Casuals	1-0
Peacehaven & Telscombe v Lewes	2-3
Three Bridges v Maidstone U	0-1
Thamesmead T v Redhill	2-0
Hastings U v Guernsey	2-3
Margate v Kingstonian	2-1
Folkestone Invicta v Eastbourne U	2-0
Sittingbourne v Littlehampton T	3-2
Dulwich Hamlet v Shoreham	6-0
Hassocks v Chipstead	1-2
Eastbourne T v Tunbridge Wells	3-2
Whyteleafe v Horley T	3-0
Cray W v Faversham T	0-3
Chatham T v East Preston	2-1
Poole T v Brockenhurst	2-0
Fareham T v Weymouth	0-1
Hallen v Hamworthy U	1-2
Sholing v AFC Totton	4-0
Frome T v Bognor Regis T	1-1, 0-4
Corsham T v Bristol Manor Farm	4-4, 0-1
Yate T v Chippenham T	3-2
Winchester C v Mangotsfield U	1-2
Horndean v AFC Portchester	0-5
Bashley v Moneyfields	2-0
Truro C v Street	1-0
Bridgwater T v Merthyr T	2-1
Bideford v Larkhall Ath	3-0
Wells C v Brislington	1-2
Clevedon T v Plymouth Parkway	1-0

SECOND QUALIFYING ROUND

Runcorn Linnets v Cammell Laird	1-0
Guiseley v Bradford (Park Avenue)	1-3
Frickley Ath v Marske U	1-3
Scarborough Ath v Penrith	1-1, 2-2
aet; Penrith won 4-3 on penalties.	

Jarrow Roofing Boldon CA v Guisborough T	3-3, 1-3
Curzon Ashton v Lancaster C	0-0, 2-1
Workington v Burscough	2-1
Stockport Co v Brighouse T	1-0
Ossett T v Warrington T	1-1, 3-1
aet.	
AFC Fylde v Ashton U	0-1
Colwyn Bay v Harrogate T	1-0
Vauxhall Motors v Chorley	4-0
Trafford v Altrincham	2-1
Stalybridge Celtic v Worksop T	3-5
Buxton v North Ferriby U	1-4
West Auckland T v Skelmersdale U	5-0
Barrow v Ramsbottom U	3-0
AFC Telford U v Hednesford T	1-3
Solihull Moors v Leamington	1-1, 2-1
Atherstone T v Coalville T	1-0
Stamford v AFC Wulfrunians	4-1
Stourbridge v Sutton Coldfield T	3-2
Brackley T v Gresley	1-1, 1-0
Gainsborough Trinity v Rushall Olympic	2-0
Walkover for Rushall Olympic – Gainsborough Trinity	
removed.	
Mickleover Sports v Corby T	3-3, 2-5
Worcester C v Coventry Sphinx	4-0
Belper T v Daventry T	1-3
Stafford Rangers v Boston U	0-4
Blaby & Whetstone Ath v Rugby T	0-6
Halesowen T v Tipton T	5-0
Carlton T v Matlock T	1-0
Grays Ath v Tilbury	3-0
Spalding U v AFC Hornchurch	1-4
Concord Rangers v St Ives T	4-3
Royston T v Histon	0-4
FC Clacton v North Greenford U	1-1, 1-3
Needham Market v Dunstable T	3-1
St Albans C v Billericay T	2-0
Hampton & Richmond Bor v Bedford T	1-0
Arlesey T v Thurrock	1-0
AFC Rushden & Diamonds v Cambridge C	3-2
Hemel Hempstead T v Witham T	1-1, 4-3
Barton R v Boreham Wood	0-0, 0-3
Biggleswade T v Chelmsford C	2-0
Harlow T v Heybridge Swifts	2-3
Wealdstone v Haringey Bor	4-1
Hendon v Bishop's Stortford	0-5
Sleaford T or Huntingdon T v AFC Sudbury	
Walkover for AFC Sudbury – Sleaford T and	
Huntingdon T removed.	
Canvey Island v St Neots T	2-2, 2-1
Whitehawk v Sutton U	0-1
Thamesmead T v Sittingbourne	1-2
Didcot T v Burnham	2-1
Merstham v Maidstone U	1-4
Bromley v Burgess Hill T	1-0
Horsham v Faversham T	2-0
Ebbsfleet U v Folkestone Invicta	1-0
Guernsey v Dover Ath	2-3
(at Sussex FA, Lancing)	
Oxford C v Maidenhead U	1-0
Eastbourne T v Hartley Wintney	1-5
Whyteleafe v Chatham T	1-2
Chertsey v Chipstead	1-2
Eastbourne Bor v Farnborough	0-0, 2-0
Margate v Dulwich Hamlet	1-2
Binfield v Leatherhead	1-2
Aylesbury U v Staines T	0-3
Hayes & Yeading U v Tonbridge Angels	0-0, 1-2
Chalfont St Peter v Lewes	0-1
Dorchester T v Shortwood U	0-1
Hamworthy U v Poole T	2-4
Cirencester T v AFC Portchester	2-0
Brislington v Truro C	3-2
Bristol Manor Farm v Bridgwater T	4-4, 1-2
Gloucester C v Havant & Waterlooville	1-1, 3-2
Eastleigh v Mangotsfield U	4-0
Basingstoke T v Weston Super Mare	1-3
Yate T v Bideford	2-1
Weymouth v Bognor Regis T	2-2, 4-1
Clevedon T v Sholing	2-0
Bath C v Gosport Bor	2-0
Bashley v Hungerford T	0-3

THIRD QUALIFYING ROUND

Worcester C v Rugby T	0-0, 2-0
Corby T v Trafford	4-2
Carlton T v Vauxhall Motors	1-3
Marske U v Halesowen T	3-2
Stockport Co v Rushall Olympic	0-1
Stourbridge v Curzon Ashton	3-0
Stamford v Ashton U	4-2
Solihull Moors v Worksop T	4-0
Colwyn Bay v Ossett T	2-1
Hednesford T v West Auckland T	2-2, 2-2
aet; Hednesford T won 4-2 on penalties.	
Atherstone T v Barrow	0-4
Brackley T v Boston U	2-0
North Ferriby U v Runcorn Linnets	2-0
Bradford (Park Avenue) v Penrith	2-1
Guisborough T v Workington	1-4
Maidstone U v Boreham Wood	0-2
Biggleswade T v Leatherhead	5-1
Dover Ath v AFC Rushden & Diamonds	3-1
Chipstead v Bishop's Stortford	1-6
Horsham v Chatham T	0-1
Concord Rangers v Histon	2-1
Hampton & Richmond Bor v Arlesey T	5-1
Needham Market v AFC Sudbury	2-1
Staines T v Sittingbourne	4-1
Lewes v Sutton U	0-1
St Albans C v Tonbridge Angels	2-1
Hemel Hempstead T v Dulwich Hamlet	3-1
AFC Hornchurch v Wealdstone	6-1
Canvey Island v North Greenford U	2-1
Ebbsfleet U v Eastbourne Bor	2-0
Bromley v Heybridge Swifts	1-2
Grays Ath v Daventry T	0-4
Cirencester T v Weymouth	1-2
Weston Super Mare v Brislington	2-3
Eastleigh v Oxford C	2-3
Hartley Wintney v Clevedon T	1-1, 4-3
Bridgwater T v Bath C	0-3
Poole T v Hungerford T	2-0
Didcot T v Shortwood U	0-1
Yate T v Gloucester C	2-2, 0-7

FOURTH QUALIFYING ROUND

Macclesfield T v Vauxhall Motors	7-0
Stamford v Hednesford T	0-2
Grimsby T v Rushall Olympic	3-0
Worcester C v Lincoln C	1-1, 0-3
Bradford (Park Avenue) v Kidderminster H	1-1, 1-2
Wrexham v Hyde	2-0
Workington v Stourbridge	1-3
Southport v Marske U	6-2
Colwyn Bay v Corby T	1-3
Tamworth v Solihull Moors	4-1
Nuneaton T v FC Halifax T	0-2
North Ferriby U v Alfreton T	1-3
Brackley T v Barrow	0-0, 1-0
aet.	
Chester FC v Gateshead	0-1
Hemel Hempstead T v Sutton U	3-3, 0-2
AFC Hornchurch v Hereford U	0-1
Ebbsfleet U v Dartford	1-1, 0-1
Barnet v Concord Rangers	3-0
Chatham T v St Albans C	0-2
Dover Ath v Oxford C	3-0
Boreham Wood v Heybridge Swifts	1-0
Bath C v Salisbury C	2-0
Gloucester C v Hampton & Richmond Bor	3-1
Weymouth v Braintree T	1-2
Forest Green R v Bishop's Stortford	0-1
Needham Market v Cambridge U	0-1
Biggleswade T v Canvey Island	1-0
Shortwood U v Aldershot T	1-1, 2-1
Woking v Luton T	0-1
Brislington v Welling U	0-1
Hartley Wintney v Daventry T	1-6
Staines T v Poole T	0-0, 1-0

THE BUDWEISER FA CUP 2013–14
COMPETITION PROPER

* *Denotes player sent off.*

FIRST ROUND
Friday, 8 November 2013
AFC Wimbledon (0) 1 *(Smith 54)*
Coventry C (0) 3 *(Wilson 57, Baker 60, Kennedy 70 (og))*
3379
AFC Wimbledon: (4141) Brown; Fuller, Bennett, Frampton, Kennedy; Moore S; Porter, Pell (Midson 73), Sweeney, Francomb (Moore L 70); Smith.
Coventry C: (442) Murphy; Christie, Clarke J, Webster, Adams; Baker, Thomas, Barton, Moussa (Phillips 86); Wilson, Clarke L.
Referee: Darren Drysdale.

Bristol R (1) 3 *(Richards 37, Harrold 59, Beardsley 75)*
York C (2) 3 *(Jarvis 35, Carson 41, Fletcher 86)*   4654
Bristol R: (451) Mildenhall; Smith, Lockyer, Parkes, Brown; Santos, Clucas, Norburn (Harrold 58), Clarke; Richards; Beardsley (Brunt 84).
York C: (442) Ingham; Oyebanjo, Smith, Parslow, Fyfield; Carson, Platt, Whitehouse, Puri (Brobbel 54); Jarvis (Fletcher 74), Bowman (Cresswell 88).
Referee: Trevor Kettle.

Saturday, 9 November 2013
Accrington S (0) 0
Tranmere R (0) 1 *(Lowe 90)*   1711
Accrington S: (442) Bettinelli; Hunt (Windass 46), Aldred, Winnard, Naylor; Mingoia, Joyce, Murphy, Naismith; Gray (Bowerman 76), Odejayi.
Tranmere R: (451) Fon Williams; Holmes, Taylor, McNulty, Ridehalgh; Bell-Baggie (Stockton 87), Atkinson, Koumas, Hateley (Akpa Akpro 59), Kirby; Lowe.
Referee: Seb Stockbridge.

Boreham Wood (0) 0
Carlisle U (0) 0   901
Boreham Wood: (4411) Russell; Nunn, O'Loughlin, Reynolds, Jones; Montgomery, Cox, Garrard, Morgan; Lipman (Ball 76), Moli (Sterling-Parker 76).
Carlisle U: (4141) Gillespie; Potts, O'Hanlon, Thirlwell, Townsend; Buaben (Gillies 75); Amoo, Berrett, Noble, Robson (Beck 61); Guy (Symington 54).
Referee: Brendan Malone.

Braintree T (1) 1 *(Isaac 9)*
Newport Co (0) 1 *(Naylor 50)*   1004
Braintree T: (442) Hamann; Peters, Wells, Massey, Carney; Isaac (Sparkes 90), Paine, Davis, Mulley; Marks, Holman (Cox 90).
Newport Co: (343) Pidgeley; Yakubu, Jones, Worley; Pipe, Naylor, Chapman, Flynn; Crow, Zebroski (Jackson 81), Jolley (Washington 71).
Referee: Graham Horwood.

Brentford (3) 5 *(McCormack 21 (pen), Reeves 35, Harris 38, Trotta 50, Donaldson 90)*
Staines T (0) 0   5263
Brentford: (442) Button; McCormack, Craig, Nugent, Bidwell; Douglas (Diagouraga 46), Saville, Reeves, Harris (El Alagui 73); Trotta (Grigg 52), Donaldson.
Staines T: (3511) Merson; Ifil, Ferrell, Brown; Ming, Ngamvoulou (Taylor 68), Lodge, Ferguson (Beadle 64), Worsfold; Pashaj (Felix 77); Theophanous.
Referee: Steven Rushton.

Bristol C (1) 3 *(Emmanuel-Thomas 35, 90, Elliott M 87)*
Dagenham & R (0) 0   5313
Bristol C: (442) Parish; Moloney, Flint, Williams, Cunningham; Reid (Elliott M 80), Wagstaff (Burns 90), Pack, Shorey (Wynter 87); Baldock, Emmanuel-Thomas.

Dagenham & R: (433) Lewington; Hoyte, Saah, Doe (Wilkinson 79), Connors; Howell (Dickson 66), Ogogo, Bingham; Elito (Obafemi 65), Hines, Murphy.
Referee: Andy Woolmer.

Chesterfield (0) 2 *(Roberts 69, Ryan 88)*
Daventry T (0) 0   5269
Chesterfield: (4231) Lee; Talbot, Hird, Evatt, Cooper; Banks, Ryan; Roberts, Doyle (Darikwa 81), McSheffrey (O'Shea 57); Richards (Gnanduillet 64).
Daventry T: (442) Morris; Wilkinson, Simpson, Dolman (Henderson 55), Blake; Oulton, Confue, Howell (Cross 78), Beckley (Murphy 64); Robinson, Lorraine.
Referee: Darren Handley.

Colchester U (0) 2 *(Bonne 48, Garbutt 64)*
Sheffield U (2) 3 *(Maguire 10, Walker 12 (og), Porter 81 (pen))*   2509
Colchester U: (442) Walker; Wilson, Okuonghae, Eastman, Garbutt; Bond (Dickson 46), Bean, Eastmond (Vose 79), Gilbey; Morrison, Bonne (Szmidics 87).
Sheffield U: (442) Long; McMahon, Maguire, Collins, Hill; Coady, McGinn (Flynn 68), Doyle, Lappin; Porter (Taylor 90), Miller (Baxter 75).
Referee: Phil Gibbs.

Corby (0) 1 *(Carruthers 90)*
Dover Ath (0) 2 *(Elder 57, Kinnear 66)*   1387
Corby: (451) Walker; Thomas, Malone, Gascoigne, Carruthers; Berwick, Hendrie L (Jelleyman 80), McGowan, Rooney (Ives 69), Hendrie S (Shariff 88); Wright.
Dover Ath: (451) Walker; Stone, Raggett, Forbes, Wynter; Modeste (Bellamy 45), Rogers, Kinnear, Murphy, Cogan; Elder.
Referee: Amy Fearn.

Gillingham (0) 0
Brackley T (0) 1 *(Martin 69 (og))*   3004
Gillingham: (442) Nelson; Harriman, Davies (Akinfenwa 66), Barrett, Martin; Weston (Dack 66), Whelpdale, Gregory, Lee (Mousinho 67); Kedwell, McDonald.
Brackley T: (442) Turley; Reid, Sharpe, Austin, McDonald (Nisevic 46); Sandy, Towers, Solkhon, Walker; Mulligan (Mills 70), Diggin (Jarvis 89).
Referee: Lee Collins.

Gloucester C (0) 0
Fleetwood T (1) 2 *(Ball 11, Parkin 84)*   1183
Gloucester C: (532) Green Mike; Green Michael (Morford 81), Mullings, Coupe, Harris, Weir; Goddard, Webb, Liddiard (Parker 54); Edwards, Wilson (Groves 67).
Fleetwood T: (4411) Davies; McLaughlin, Pond, Roberts, Taylor; Evans (Brown 87), Schumacher, Murdoch, Hughes J; Sarcevic (Parkin 65); Ball (Blair 86).
Referee: Fred Graham.

Grimsby T (0) 0
Scunthorpe U (0) 0   8306
Grimsby T: (442) McKeown; Hatton, McDonald, Pearson, Thomas; Colbeck, Disley, Kerr, Neilson (Rodman 83); John-Lewis, Hannah (Hearn 83).
Scunthorpe U: (442) Slocombe; Byrne, Waterfall, Mirfin, Dawson; Hawkridge, Collins, McAllister, Esajas (Sparrow 69 (Ribeiro 74)); Spencer (Burton 61), Winnall.
Referee: David Coote.

Hartlepool U (2) 3 *(Baldwin 16, James 42, 75)*
Notts Co (1) 2 *(Leacock 17, Murray 84)*   3313
Hartlepool U: (442) Flinders; Duckworth, Baldwin, Collins, Austin; Franks (Richards 86), Walton, Dolan, Monkhouse; Poole (Sweeney 86), James.
Notts Co: (442) Bialkowski; Sheehan, Liddle, Leacock, Grealish (Showunmi 61); McGregor, Arquin, Labadie (Boucaud 61), Campbell-Ryce; Thompson (Murray 77), Fotheringham.
Referee: Carl Boyeson.

Hednesford T (0) 1 *(Durrell 76 (pen))*
Crawley T (0) 2 *(Campion 61 (og), Sinclair 83)*   2231
Hednesford T: (442) Crane; Disney, Francis, Bailey, Campion (Rey 78); Osborne, Taylor, Thompson-Brown (Melbourne 59), Durrell; Lennon (Riley 75), Harvey.
Crawley T: (4141) Jones P; Hurst, Connolly M, Walsh, Sadler; Bulman; Adams, Simpson, Jones M (Sinclair 80), Drury (McFadzean 90); Proctor (Alexander 80).
Referee: Michael Bull.

Kidderminster H (2) 4 *(Morgan-Smith 13, Gittings 18, Lolley 60, Malbon 90)*
Sutton U (1) 1 *(Clough 10)*   2045
Kidderminster H: (4231) Lewis; Vaughan, Gowling, Dunkley, Jackman; Fowler (Dance 71), Storer; Gittings, Lolley (Blissett 86), Gash; Morgan-Smith (Malbon 74).
Sutton U: (4411) Lovelock; Rents (Scannell 67), Clough, Stuart (Nelson 70), Downer; McDonald (Folkes 68), Dundas, Fuseini, Riviere; Binns; Slabber.
Referee: Justin Amey.

Leyton Orient (3) 5 *(Batt 3, 56, Mooney 9, James 45, Cox 67)*
Southport (1) 2 *(George 21, Flynn 87)*   3014
Leyton Orient: (442) Larkins; Omozusi, Cuthbert, Clarke, Sawyer; Lasimant, Vincelot, Sutherland (James 38), Gorman; Mooney (Odubajo 75), Batt (Cox 61).
Southport: (433) Hurst (Stevenson 15); Challoner, Smith, Brown M (Flynn 15), Fitzpatrick; Brown S, George, Milligan; Rutherford, Hattersley, Ellington (Ledsham 35).
Referee: Kevin Johnson.

Lincoln C (0) 0
Plymouth Arg (0) 0   2924
Lincoln C: (433) Farman; Miller, Boyce, Brown, Newton; Power, Nolan (Fofana 75), Jordan; Jackson (Sheridan 71), Tomlinson, Wright (Dixon 79).
Plymouth Arg: (352) Cole; Blanchard, Trotman, Nelson; Berry, Young, Boco (Obadeyi 58), Hourihane, Reckord; Reid, Alessandra.
Referee: Scott Duncan.

Macclesfield T (1) 4 *(Jennings 26, 74, Boden 70, Winn 89)*
Swindon T (0) 0   1835
Macclesfield T: (442) Branagan; Halls, Williams, Martin, Andrew; Rowe (Connor 85), Whitaker, Turnbull, Winn; Boden, Jennings.
Swindon T: (433) Belford; Byrne, Hall, Ward, McEveley; Luongo, Mason (Harley 85), Kasim (Barthram 72); Pritchard, Ranger (Ajose 75), N'Guessan.
Referee: Andrew Madley.

Milton Keynes D (1) 4 *(McLeod 39, 70, Williams 53 (pen), Galloway 90)*
FC Halifax T (0) 1 *(Gregory 78)*   4049
Milton Keynes D: (451) McLoughlin; Hodson, Spence J, Williams, Lewington; Powell, Gleeson (Galloway 71), Bamford, Potter, Banton (Baldock 46); McLeod (Rasulo 71).
FC Halifax T: (4231) Glennon; Toulson (Worthington 26), Ainge, Roberts, Lowe; Pearson, Marshall, Maynard (Wilson 68), Gardner (Love 74), McManus; Gregory.
Referee: Darren Bond.

Morecambe (0) 0
Southend U (2) 3 *(Straker 7, 9, Leonard 90)*   1475
Morecambe: (433) Roche; Wright, McCready, Parrish (Diagne 90), Threlfall; Williams, Drummond, Fleming (Sampson 72); Amond, Marshall (Mwasile 77), Ellison.
Southend U: (433) Bentley; White, Kiernan, Prosser, Coker; Leonard, Atkinson, Timlin; Hurst, Corr, Straker.
Referee: Rob Lewis.

Oldham Ath (1) 1 *(Kusunga 2)*
Wolverhampton W (1) 1 *(Golbourne 37)*   3916
Oldham Ath: (442) Oxley; Kusunga, Grounds, Tarkowski, Mellor; Philliskirk (Montano 72), Smith, Wesolowski, Dayton; Rooney, Clarke-Harris (Millar 80).
Wolverhampton W: (4411) Ikeme; Ricketts, Stearman, Batth, Golbourne; Henry, Davis, Price (Doyle 90), Sako; Edwards; Cassidy (Griffiths 79).
Referee: Geoff Eltringham.

Oxford U (0) 2 *(Smalley 77, Rose 90)*
Gateshead (1) 2 *(Marwood 12, Chandler 51)*   3114
Oxford U: (433) Clarke; Hunt, Raynes, Wright (Ruffels 31), Newey (Constable 46); Davies (Williams 71), Mullins, Rose; Smalley, Kitson, Rigg.
Gateshead: (433) Bartlett; Baxter, Clark, Curtis, Sirrell; Oster (Tait 85), Turnbull, Chandler (Magnay 58); Larkin, Hatch, Marwood.
Referee: Jeremy Simpson.

Peterborough U (0) 2 *(Assombalonga 72, Mendez-Laing 79)*
Exeter C (0) 0   3379
Peterborough U: (352) Olejnik; Alcock, Brisley, Knight; Little, Swanson (Ephraim 46), Payne (Conlon 68), Newell, Nthle; Assombalonga, Barnett (Mendez-Laing 46).
Exeter C: (451) Krysiak; Bennett, Baldwin (Nichols 77), Coles, Woodman; Sercombe, Doherty (O'Flynn 47), Davies, Grimes, Gill (Wheeler 81); Parkin.
Referee: Graham Salisbury.

Preston NE (3) 6 *(Clarke 18, Garner 36, 82, Gallagher 45, 68, 79)*
Barnet (0) 0   5217
Preston NE: (442) Rudd; Keane, Clarke, Huntington (King 65), Laird; Holmes (Hayhurst 78), Welsh, Brownhill (Byrom 66), Gallagher; Beavon■, Garner.
Barnet: (451) Stack; Yiadom, Stephens, Saville, Vilhete; Abdulla (Fletcher 70), Byrne, Davids (Mengerink 76), Weston (Crawford 61), Cadogan; Marsh-Brown■.
Referee: Ross Joyce.

Rotherham U (0) 3 *(Agard 13, 71, Revell 62)*
Bradford C (0) 0   7667
Rotherham U: (442) Collin; Bradley (Brindley 84), Morgan, Arnason, Skarz; Agard, Frecklington, O'Connor (Milsom 76), Pringle (Tidser 89); Tubbs, Revell.
Bradford C: (442) McLaughlin; Darby, McArdle, Bates, Meredith; De Vita (Yeates 63), Jones, Doyle (Kennedy 74), Reid; Hanson, Wells (McBurnie 82).
Referee: James Adcock.

Salisbury C (3) 4 *(Fitchett 13, 77, Wright 18, Frear 45)*
Dartford (0) 2 *(Burns 68, Cornhill 90)*   1313
Salisbury C: (451) Puddy; Dutton, Clarke (MacDonald 64), Wilson, Wright; McPhee, Lewis (Thomson 80), Frear, Kamdjo, Sinclair; Fitchett (Wellard 81).
Dartford: (451) Julian; Burns, Clark, Mitchel-King, Fry; Hayes, Cornhill, Noble (Sterling 69), Woodyard, Collier (Ibemere 62); Harris (Prior 61).
Referee: Simon Bennett.

St Albans C (1) 1 *(Locke 8)*
Mansfield T (2) 8 *(Stevenson 43, Howell 45, Daniel 70, Clucas 74, 81, 86, 90, Palmer 77)*   3251
St Albans C: (442) Bastock; Hall, Locke, Kaloczi, Chappell; Graham (Henry 51), Marwa, Comley, Keenleyside; Frendo, Nwokeji (Bailey 78 (Watters 82)).
Mansfield T: (442) Marriott; Pilkington, McCombe, Sutton, Jennings (Black 89); Clucas, McGuire, Howell, Daniel; Stevenson (Meikle 78), Palmer (Poku 90).
Referee: Mark Heywood.

Stevenage (2) 2 *(Zoko 9, 39)*
Portsmouth (0) 1 *(Connolly 71)*   2829
Stevenage: (442) Day; Smith J, Ashton, Jones, Doughty; Morais (Deacon 85), Heslop, Freeman, Andrade (Tansey 68); Akins, Zoko (Burrow 90).
Portsmouth: (442) Carson; Moutaouakil (East 46), N'Gala, Devera, Bradley; Barcham, Ertl (Holmes 73), Mahon■, Bird; Agyemang (Connolly 46), Wallace.
Referee: Gary Sutton.

Stourbridge (2) 4 *(Rowe 12, 17, Richards 58, Benbow 85)*
Biggleswade T (1) 1 *(Key 14)*   1605
Stourbridge: (442) Coleman; Drake (Francis 57), Bennett, Richards, Oliver; Canavan, Geddes, Broadhurst, Fitzpatrick (Washbourne 73); Benbow, Rowe.
Biggleswade T: (442) Brown; York, Coulson, Mawer, Gentle; Allinson, Daniel, Reed L (Witham 60), Lewis (Donnelly 52); Key (Baidoo 75), Reed S.
Referee: Lee Swabey.

Tamworth (1) 1 *(Chadwick 20)*
Cheltenham T (0) 0 1566
Tamworth: (433) Belford; Thomas, Richards-Everton, Courtney, Capaldi; Hildreth, Todd, Morgan; Wright, Richards, Chadwick.
Cheltenham T: (41212) Brown S; Braham-Barrett, Lowe, Brown T, Richards; Deering (Kotwica 82); Penn (Elliott 46), Taylor; Gornell; Cureton, Harrison.
Referee: Richard Clark.

Torquay U (0) 0
Rochdale (0) 2 *(Hogan 85, Vincenti 89)* 1976
Torquay U: (442) Rice; Tonge, Downes, O'Connor, Nicholson; Chapell (Craig 78), Mansell, McCourt, Azeez (Cameron 78); Benyon (Hawley 78), McCallum.
Rochdale: (352) Lillis; Eastham, Lancashire, O'Connell; Lund, Rafferty (Done 81), Henderson, Tutte, Rose; Hogan, Vincenti.
Referee: Keith Hill.

Walsall (1) 3 *(Westcarr 29, 59, Sawyers 73)*
Shrewsbury T (0) 0 3004
Walsall: (4321) O'Donnell; Chambers J (Purkiss 85), Downing, Butler, Taylor (Benning 80); Baxendale, Mantom, Chambers A; Sawyers, Lalkovic (Hemmings 85); Westcarr.
Shrewsbury T: (451) Weale; Goldson, Mkandawire, Winfield, Woods; Taylor, Summerfield (McAllister 67), Reach (Parry 65), Wroe, Wildig; Bradshaw (Marsden 68).
Referee: Charles Breakspear.

Welling U (2) 2 *(Clarke 28, Healy 44)*
Luton T (0) 1 *(Benson 57)* 1555
Welling U: (442) Butcher; Fazakerley, Gallagher, Franks, Obersteller; Dyer (Beautyman 84), Clarke, Hudson, Healy; Guthrie (Hughes-Mason 84), Lafayette.
Luton T: (4141) Justham; Parry, McNulty, Lacey, Howells (Banton 90); Smith; Cullen, Guttridge (O'Donnell 80), Stevenson, Martin (Lawless 58); Benson.
Referee: Ben Toner.

Wrexham (1) 3 *(Bishop 24, 49, Harris 72)*
Alfreton T (0) 1 *(Speight 61 (pen))* 2415
Wrexham: (433) Coughlin; Carrington, Wright, Artell, Ashton; Harris (Hunt 89), Clarke, Keates; Ogleby (Bailey-Jones 76), Bishop, Ormerod (Cieslewicz 83).
Alfreton T: (442) Atkins; Wood (Akinde S 90), Westwood, Fenton, Rowe-Turner; Bradley, Shaw (Meadows 58), McGrath, Law; Akinde J (Franklin 88), Speight.
Referee: Darren England.

Wycombe W (1) 1 *(Cowan-Hall 37)*
Crewe Alex (1) 1 *(Grant 4)* 1929
Wycombe W: (442) Ingram; McCoy, Stewart, Hause, Wood; Cowan-Hall (Kretzschmar 46), Knott, Lewis, Spring; Morgan (Craig 90), McClure.
Crewe Alex: (442) Martin; Guthrie, Davis, Dugdale, Mellor; Aneke (Molyneux 75), Grant, Evans, Moore; Clayton (Osman 85), Oliver (Inman 59).
Referee: David Phillips.

Sunday, 10 November 2013
Bishop's Stortford (0) 1 *(Prestedge 81)*
Northampton T (0) 2 *(Emerton 62, Norris 68)* 2545
Bishop's Stortford: (532) Wright; Miller, Fletcher (Asante 77), Francis, McNaughton, Herd; Johnson, Symons (Baker 66), Prestedge; Vassell (Sykes 58), Akurang.
Northampton T: (442) Duke; Collins (Tozer 67), Reid, Kouo-Doumbe, Widdowson; Hackett, Ferdinand, Ravenhill, Emerton; Norris, Blyth (Morris 90).
Referee: Stephen Martin.

Burton Alb (1) 2 *(McGurk 37, Palmer 84)*
Hereford U (0) 0 2069
Burton Alb: (442) Lyness; Edwards, Diamond, Sharps, McCrory; Palmer, Weir, Bell, Hussey (Phillips 76); Kee (Knowles 82), McGurk.
Hereford U: (442) Evans; Leadbitter, McDonald, Collins, Purdie; Walker, O'Keefe, Artus, Krans (Smith 60); Rankine, Odhiambo (Brown 60).
Referee: Chris Kavanagh.

Monday, 11 November 2013
Shortwood U (0) 0
Port Vale (2) 4 *(Myrie-Williams 15, 89 (pen), Birchall 30, Lines 90)* 1247
Shortwood U: (451) King; Avery, Coates, Pritchett, Bennett (Axton 78); Baldwin, Hancock (Slack 67), Haddock, Parrott, Mann; Culley.
Port Vale: (442) Neal; Yates, Robertson, Chilvers, Dickinson; Birchall (Dodds 73), Lines, Griffith, Myrie-Williams; Pope (Hugill 81), Hughes (Williamson 66).
Referee: Dean Whitestone.

Tuesday, 19 November 2013
Bury (0) 0
Cambridge U (0) 0 1712
Bury: (442) Jensen; Beeley, Cameron, Edjenguele, Howell; Jones, Procter, Soares (Miller 62), Mayor; Harrad (Forrester 62), Hylton.
Cambridge U: (442) Maxwell; Tait, Coulson, Miller, Taylor; Hughes, Champion, Berry, Dunk; Cunnington (Sam-Yorke 74), Appiah.
Referee: Mark Brown.

FIRST ROUND REPLAYS

Monday, 18 November 2013
Brackley T (1) 1 *(Walker 21)*
Gillingham (0) 0 1772
Brackley T: (352) Worby; Sharpe, Austin, McDonald; Odhiambo, Sandy, Walker, Towers, Solkhon; Mulligan, Diggin.
Gillingham: (433) Nelson; Butcher (McDonald 66), Legge, Barrett, Martin; Lee, Mousinho, Dack; German (Whelpdale 66), Akinfenwa, Weston.
Referee: Lee Collins.

Tuesday, 19 November 2013
Carlisle U (0) 0 *(Miller 80, Beck 90)*
Boreham Wood (1) 1 *(Garrard 29 (pen))* 1484
Carlisle U: (442) Fleming; McSweeney (Berrett 55), O'Hanlon, Chimbonda, Townsend; Amoo (Symington 59), Thirlwell, Noble, Robson; Guy (Beck 66), Miller.
Boreham Wood: (442) Russell; Nunn, O'Loughlin, Reynolds, Jones; Montgomery, Cox, Garrard, Morgan; Moli (Sterling-Parker 89), Lipman (Ball 82).
Referee: Mark Haywood.

Crewe Alex (0) 0
Wycombe W (0) 2 *(Craig 50 (pen), Doherty 70)* 1695
Crewe Alex: (451) Garratt; Mellor, Ellis, Davis, Guthrie; Clayton (Oliver 59), Osman, Evans, Grant, Moore (Inman 67); Leitch-Smith.
Wycombe W: (442) Ingram; McCoy, Stewart, Doherty, Wood; Cowan-Hall, Lewis, Knott (Bloomfield 82), Scowen; McClure, Craig (Morias 90).
Referee: Kevin Wright.

Newport Co (1) 1 *(Willmott 45)*
Braintree T (0) 0 1406
Newport Co: (442) Pidgeley; Jackson, Yakubu, Naylor (Flynn 85), Oshilaja; Chapman, Crow, Willmott, Worley; Washington, Jolley (Minshull 69).
Braintree T: (442) Hamann; Habergham, Wells, Paine, Peters; Mulley (Cox 88), Isaac, Davis, Daley (Enver-Marum 68); Holman (Quinton 83), Marks.
Referee: Andy Davies.

Scunthorpe U (0) 1 *(Hawkridge 46)*
Grimsby T (1) 2 *(John-Lewis 10, McDonald 58)* 5699
Scunthorpe U: (442) Slocombe; Ribeiro, Mirfin, Canavan, Dawson; Spencer (Adelakun 70), McAllister, Collins, Hawkridge; Winnall, Burton (Iwelumo 78).
Grimsby T: (442) McKeown; Hatton, Pearson, McDonald, Thomas; Colbeck, Disley, Kerr, Neilson (McLaughlin 73); John-Lewis, Hannah (Rodman 89).
Referee: Stuart Atwell.

Wolverhampton W (0) 1 *(Griffiths 90)*
Oldham Ath (1) 2 *(Philliskirk 21, Rooney 73)*   4226
Wolverhampton W: (442) Ikeme; Ebanks-Landell (Ismail 46), Batth, Stearman, Elokobi (Ricketts 46); Sigurdarson (Evans 69), Price, McDonald, Golbourne; Cassidy, Griffiths.
Oldham Ath: (442) Oxley; Smith, Kusunga, Tarkowski, Mellor (Lanzoni 75); Dayton, Rodgers, Wesolowski, Montano (Schmeltz 62); Philliskirk, Clarke-Harris (Rooney 67).
Referee: Keith Stroud.

York C (0) 2 *(Fletcher 70 (pen), 71)*
Bristol R (2) 3 *(O'Toole 16, Norburn 45, Beardsley 50)*
     2051
York C: (442) Kettings; Oyebanjo, Smith (McGurk 46), Parslow, Fyfield; Clay (Chambers 46), Whitehouse, Montrose, Jarvis (Puri 46); Fletcher, Bowman.
Bristol R: (442) Mildenhall; Smith, Parkes, Lockyer, Brown; Norburn, O'Toole, Clarke, Richards; Clarkson, Beardsley (Harrold 78).
Referee: Andy Haines.

Wednesday, 20 November 2013

Plymouth Arg (4) 5 *(Reid 4, 24 (pen), 35, Alessandra 5, Boyce 65 (og))*
Lincoln C (0) 0   3324
Plymouth Arg: (352) Cole; Blanchard, Trotman, Nelson; Hourihane (Blizzard 65), Berry, Gurrieri, Alessandra (Boco 73); Young; Obadeyi, Reid (Harvey 58).
Lincoln C: (352) Farman; Boyce, Foster (Sheridan 58), Brown; Nolan, Miller, Fofana, Power, Newton; Tomlinson (Wright 86), Jackson.
Referee: Darren Deadman.

Tuesday, 3 December 2013

Cambridge U (0) 2 *(Berry 61, 87)*
Bury (0) 1 *(Harrad 63)*   3342
Cambridge U: (442) Maxwell; Tait, Miller, Coulson, Taylor; Hughes, Champion, Berry, Dunk; Cunnington, Appiah.
Bury: (442) Jensen; Cameron, Hinds (Mayor 89), Edjenguele, Howell; Jones, Procter, Soares (Holden 90), Sedgwick; Harrad, Hylton.
Referee: Mark Brown.

Thursday, 5 December 2013

Gateshead (0) 0
Oxford U (0) 1 *(Smalley 116 (pen))*   2632
Gateshead: (433) Bartlett; Baxter, Curtis, Clark, Sirrell; Oster (Tait 117), Turnbull, Chandler (Ramshaw 115); Walker (Hatch 118), Larkin, Marwood.
Oxford U: (442) Clarke; Bevans, Hunt, Newey, Lynn; Williams, Davies (Smalley 68), Rose (Long 99), Ruffels; Kitson (Marsh 106), Constable.
aet.
Referee: Paul Tierney.

SECOND ROUND

Friday, 6 December 2013

Port Vale (1) 4 *(Robertson 24, Pope 78, Taylor 81, Williamson 90)*
Salisbury C (0) 1 *(Fitchett 64)*   4658
Port Vale: (442) Johnson; Yates, Robertson, Duffy, Dickinson; Birchall, Lines, Griffith (Taylor 62), Myrie-Williams (Williamson 69); Pope, Tomlin (Dodds 82).
Salisbury C: (451) Puddy; Clarke, Wilson, MacDonald, Hart (Brett 82); Fitchett, Lewis, Kamdjo, Sinclair (Dutton 90), Frear; White (McPhee 46).
Referee: Darren Sheldrake.

Saturday, 7 December 2013

Bristol R (0) 0
Crawley T (0) 0   4623
Bristol R: (451) Mildenhall; Smith, Lockyer, Parkes, Brown; Clarkson (Santos 69), Norburn, Richards, Clarke, Harding; Harrold.
Crawley T: (442) Jones P; Connolly M, McFadzean, Walsh, Sadler; Bulman, Adams, Drury, Clarke; Sinclair (Proctor 80), Alexander.
Referee: Christopher Sarginson.

Carlisle U (1) 3 *(Berrett 45, Miller 73, 77 (pen))*
Brentford (0) 2 *(Chimbonda 63 (og), El Alagui 86)*   2581
Carlisle U: (433) Fleming; Chimbonda (Symington 82), O'Hanlon, Meppen-Walter, Robson; Berrett, Thirlwell, Buaben; Amoo, Miller, Lawrence (Potts 64).
Brentford: (433) Lee; McCormack, Craig, Dean, Bidwell; Diagouraga (Reeves 59), Forshaw, Saville (Saunders 84); Donaldson, Trotta (El Alagui 68), Grigg.
Referee: Andy Woolmer.

Chesterfield (1) 1 *(Darikwa 4)*
Southend U (2) 3 *(Laird 12, Straker 17, Hurst 85)*   4067
Chesterfield: (4231) Lee; Talbot, Hird, Evatt, McFadzean (Doyle 75); Ryan, Banks; Darikwa, O'Shea (Richards 69), Roberts (Humphreys 16); Gnanduillet.
Southend U: (433) Bentley; White, Kiernan (Phillips 64), Prosser, Coker; Clifford (Thompson 83), Laird, Timlin; Hurst, Corr, Straker.
Referee: Mick Russell.

Fleetwood T (0) 1 *(Hughes J 83)*
Burton Alb (0) 1 *(Kee 90)*   2119
Fleetwood T: (451) Davies; McLaughlin, Roberts, Pond, Taylor; Blair, Murdoch, Sarcevic (Brown 76), Hughes J, Evans (Crowther 83); Parkin.
Burton Alb: (442) Lyness; Edwards, Cansdell-Sherriff, Sharps, McCrory; MacDonald (Phillips 74), Weir, Bell, Hussey; Howe (Knowles 73), McGurk (Kee 34).
Referee: Eddie Ilderton.

Grimsby T (0) 2 *(Pearson 64, McLaughlin 90)*
Northampton T (0) 0   3828
Grimsby T: (442) McKeown; Hatton, McDonald, Pearson, Thomas; Rodman, Disley, Kerr, Neilson (Colbeck 68); John-Lewis, Hannah (McLaughlin 89).
Northampton T: (442) Duke; Amankwaah, Reid, Kouo-Doumbe, Widdowson (Norris 85); Emerton (Platt 59), Deegan (Demontagnac 85), Ravenhill, Morris; Hackett, Blyth.
Referee: Scott Mathieson.

Hartlepool U (0) 1 *(Monkhouse 78)*
Coventry C (1) 1 *(Baker 12)*   2898
Hartlepool U: (4411) Flinders; Duckworth, Baldwin, Burgess, Austin; Compton (Franks 63), Walton (Walker 83), Dolan, Monkhouse; Poole (Sweeney 46); James.
Coventry C: (4411) Murphy; Christie, Seaborne, Clarke J, Adams; Baker, Thomas, Webster, Moussa (Baker-Richardson 71); Fleck; Daniels.
Referee: Andrew Madley.

Kidderminster H (3) 4 *(Gash 19, 63, Gittings 28, 43)*
Newport Co (0) 2 *(Willmott 79, 83)*   2636
Kidderminster H: (4231) Lewis; Vaughan, Gowling, Dunkley, Jackman; Storer, Fowler; Lolley, Gittings (Byrne 73), Morgan-Smith (Johnson 70); Gash.
Newport Co: (352) Pidgeley; Oshilaja (Flynn 67), Worley, Hughes; Jackson, Naylor, Minshull (Jolley 46), Chapman, Willmott; Crow (Sandell 64), Washington.
Referee: Mark Heywood.

Leyton Orient (1) 1 *(Cox 41)*
Walsall (0) 0   2604
Leyton Orient: (442) Jones; Odubajo, Omozusi, Baudry, Sawyer; Lasimant (Gorman 75), Vincelot, James, Cox (Simpson 60); Mooney■, Batt (Lee 85).
Walsall: (433) O'Donnell; Purkiss, Downing, Butler, Taylor; Mantom, Featherstone (Sawyers 62), Chambers; Hemmings (Hewitt 82), Lalkovic (Baxendale 71), Westcarr.
Referee: Mark Brown.

Macclesfield T (1) 3 *(Andrew 17, Boden 50, Mackreth 81)*
Brackley T (0) 2 *(Diggin 58, Story 71)*   2438
Macclesfield T: (442) Taylor; Halls, Williams, Martin, Andrew; Mackreth, Whitaker, Turnbull, Rowe (Winn 77 (Connor 84)); Jennings, Boden.
Brackley T: (352) Turley; Solkhon, Sharpe, Austin; Reid, Sandy (Story 53), McDonald (Jarvis 87), Towers, Walker; Diggin, Mulligan (Mills 54).
Referee: Tony Harrington.

Milton Keynes D (0) 1 *(Reeves 51)*

Dover Ath (0) 0 4060

Milton Keynes D: (4231) Martin (McLoughlin 77); Hodson, Spence J, Williams, Lewington; Gleeson, Smith; Carruthers (Galloway 77), Reeves, Banton (Baldock 46); Bamford.
Dover Ath: (451) Walker; Stone, Forbes, Raggett, Wynter; Modeste (Bakare 57), Kinnear (Orlu 90), Cogan, Rogers, Murphy (Charles 86); Elder.
Referee: Lee Collins.

Oldham Ath (1) 1 *(Smith 28)*

Mansfield T (1) 1 *(Clucas 45)* 3429

Oldham Ath: (4411) Oxley; Lanzoni, Tarkowski, Grounds, Plummer; Schmeltz (Petrasso 57), Smith, Rodgers, Dayton (Clarke-Harris 57); Philliskirk; Rooney.
Mansfield T: (4411) Marriott; Westlake, Dempster, Riley, Daniel; Meikle (Palmer 78), Murray (Hutchinson 81), McGuire, Clucas; Howell; Dyer.
Referee: Iain Williamson.

Peterborough U (2) 5 *(Assombalonga 38, 64, 73, Jeffers 45, 90)*

Tranmere R (0) 0 3269

Peterborough U: (442) Olejnik; Little (Knight-Percival 74), Brisley, Bostwick, Ntlhe; Ephraim (Swanson 28), Anderson, Tomlin (Mendez-Laing 75), McCann; Jeffers, Assombalonga.
Tranmere R: (442) Fon Williams; Holmes, McNulty, Edwards, Ridehalgh; Kirby (Rowe 65), Wallace, Atkinson, Peterson; Akpa Akpro (Stockton 59), Lowe.
Referee: Michael Naylor.

Plymouth Arg (3) 3 *(Gurrieri 13, Nelson 18, Alessandra 21)*

Welling U (0) 1 *(Lafayette 53)* 4706

Plymouth Arg: (352) Cole (McCormick 73); Blanchard (Boco 64), Trotman, Nelson; Berry, Young (Blizzard 80), Hourihane, Gurrieri, Reckord; Alessandra, Reid.
Welling U: (4411) Butcher; Vanderhyde, Hudson, Franks, Cargill; Guthrie, Dyer, Gallagher (Beautyman 81), Healy (Cumbers 81); Clarke; Lafayette.
Referee: Steve Bratt.

Rotherham U (1) 1 *(Frecklington 6)*

Rochdale (0) 2 *(Lund 55, Vincenti 83)* 4957

Rotherham U: (442) Collin; Bradley, Morgan, Arnason, Skarz; Brindley (Davis 76), Frecklington, Tidser, Pringle; Revell, Agard.
Rochdale: (532) Lillis; Bennett, Eastham, Lancashire (Vincenti 22), O'Connell, Rose; Lund, Dicker, Done (Bunney 78); Henderson, Hogan (Allen 86).
Referee: Graham Scott.

Stevenage (1) 4 *(Zoko 44, Akins 49, Freeman 60, Morais 90 (pen))*

Stourbridge (0) 0 2160

Stevenage: (442) Day; Smith J, Ashton, Jones, Hartley; Morais, Heslop (Andrade 80), Doughty (Parrett 12), Freeman; Akins (Wedgbury 73), Zoko.
Stourbridge: (442) Coleman; Canavan (Washbourne 56), Geddes, Bennett, Richards; Rowe, Oliver (Knight 73), Broadhurst, Benbow; Francis (Drake 79), Billingham.
Referee: Tim Robinson.

Wycombe W (0) 0

Preston NE (1) 1 *(Davies K 34)* 2249

Wycombe W: (442) Ingram; McCoy, Stewart, Hause, Dunne (Wood 14); Cowan-Hall, Lewis, Scowen, Knott (Kretzschmar 71); McClure, Morgan (Craig 81).
Preston NE: (352) Rudd; Clarke, Huntington, Laird; Humphrey, Keane, Welsh, Brownhill (Byrom 90), Buchanan; Beavon, Davies K.
Referee: David Webb.

Sunday, 8 December 2013

Cambridge U (0) 0

Sheffield U (1) 2 *(Baxter 12, Murphy 58)* 4593

Cambridge U: (442) Maxwell; Tait, Coulson, Miller, Taylor; Hughes, Champion, Berry, Dunk (Arnold 82); Cunnington (Roberts 60); Appiah.
Sheffield U: (3511) Long; Maguire, Collins, Hill; Flynn, Doyle, Coady, McGinn (Murphy 22), Lappin; Baxter; Porter (Taylor 86).
Referee: Oliver Langford.

Tamworth (0) 1 *(Todd 90)*

Bristol C (1) 2 *(Emmanuel-Thomas 36, Baldock 83)* 2860

Tamworth: (442) Belford; Thomas, Courtney, Richards-Everton, Capaldi; Todd, Morgan (Kerry 73), Hildreth, Peniket (Woolery 87); Chadwick (Byfield 60), Richards.
Bristol C: (41212) Parish; Moloney, Flint, Williams, Cunningham; Elliott M; Wagstaff (Carey 90), Bryan; Emmanuel-Thomas; Baldock, Taylor (Pack 60).
Referee: Andy D'Urso.

Monday, 9 December 2013

Wrexham (1) 1 *(Clarke 29)*

Oxford U (0) 2 *(Constable 54, Williams 56)* 2906

Wrexham: (442) Coughlin; Carrington, Wright, Artell, Ashton; Harris, Keates (Morrell 83), Clarke, Hunt (Ogleby 64); Ormerod (Cieslewicz 64), Bishop.
Oxford U: (442) Clarke; Bevans, Hunt, Mullins, Newey; Williams (Smalley 87), Davies, Ruffels, Rose; Kitson, Constable (Long 89).
Referee: Gavin Ward.

SECOND ROUND REPLAYS

Tuesday, 17 December 2013

Burton Alb (1) 1 *(Kee 25)*

Fleetwood T (0) 0 1777

Burton Alb: (442) Lyness; Edwards, Cansdell-Sherriff, Sharps, McCrory; MacDonald (Palmer 84), Weir, Bell (Diamond 90), Hussey; Kee, Howe.
Fleetwood T: (4411) Davies; Taylor, Roberts, Cresswell, McLaughlin; Brown (Crowther 77), Murdoch (Ball 72), Schumacher, Evans; Hughes J (Sarcevic 34); Dieseruvwe.
Referee: Seb Stockbridge.

Coventry C (1) 2 *(Clarke L 36, 90)*

Hartlepool U (0) 1 *(Baldwin 88)* 1214

Coventry C: (442) Murphy; Christie, Clarke J, Seaborne, Adams; Baker (Webster 90), Thomas, Fleck, Moussa; Clarke L, Wilson (Daniels 84).
Hartlepool U: (451) Flinders; Duckworth, Baldwin, Burgess, Austin; Compton (James 56), Walton (Poole 69), Walker, Dolan, Monkhouse; Franks (Collins 83).
Referee: Keith Hill.

Mansfield T (1) 1 *(Dyer 12)*

Oldham Ath (0) 4 *(Philliskirk 57, Clarke-Harris 62, Lanzoni 75, Rooney 81 (pen))* 2836

Mansfield T: (4411) Marriott; Westlake, Dempster, Riley, Daniel; Meikle (Rhead 68), Murray (Palmer 67), McGuire, Clucas; Hutchinson (Clements 19); Dyer.
Oldham Ath: (4222) Oxley; Kusunga (Lanzoni 46), Tarkowski, Grounds, Mellor; Wesolowski (Winchester 24), Smith (Rodgers 82); Petrasso, Philliskirk; Clarke-Harris, Rooney.
Referee: Charles Breakspear.

Wednesday, 8 January 2014

Crawley T (1) 1 *(Proctor 15)*

Bristol R (0) 2 *(Richards 83, O'Toole 90)* 2435

Crawley T: (442) Jones P; Connolly M, McFadzean, Walsh, Sadler; Adams, Drury, Torres, Jones M; Proctor, Sinclair (Alexander 72).
Bristol R: (4321) Mildenhall; Smith, McChrystal, Parkes, Brown; Lockyer (Beardsley 63), Clarke, O'Toole; Clarkson (Harrison 72), Richards; Harrold.
Referee: Andy Davies.

THIRD ROUND

Saturday, 4 January 2014

Arsenal (1) 2 *(Cazorla 31, Rosicky 62)*

Tottenham H (0) 0 59,476

Arsenal: (4231) Fabianski; Sagna, Koscielny, Vermaelen (Mertesacker 46), Monreal; Wilshere (Flamini 71), Arteta (Ozil 75); Gnabry, Rosicky, Cazorla; Walcott.
Tottenham H: (442) Lloris; Walker, Dawson, Chiriches, Rose; Lennon, Bentaleb, Dembele, Eriksen; Adebayor, Soldado (Chadli 63).
Referee: Mark Clattenburg.

Aston Villa (0) 1 *(Helenius 75)*
Sheffield U (1) 2 *(Murphy 20, Flynn 81)*   24,038
Aston Villa: (433) Steer; Luna, Clark, Lowton, Tonev (Helenius 60); Bacuna, Westwood, Delph; Albrighton, Benteke, Weimann.
Sheffield U: (451) Long; McMahon, Collins, Maguire, Hill; Flynn, McGinn, Baxter (Coady 80), Doyle, Murphy (Miller 90); Porter (Kennedy 90).
Referee: David Coote.

Barnsley (1) 1 *(O'Brien 19)*
Coventry C (0) 2 *(Moussa 78, Clarke L 89)*   7439
Barnsley: (4411) Steele; Cranie, Ramage, Mvoto, Kennedy; O'Brien, Dawson, Perkins (Scotland 77), Cywka; Mellis; O'Grady (Pedersen 66).
Coventry C: (442) Murphy; Christie, Webster, Willis, Adams; Baker, Fleck, Daniels, Moussa; Clarke L, Slager (Barton 57).
Referee: Carl Boyeson.

Blackburn R (0) 1 *(Dann 55)*
Manchester C (1) 1 *(Negredo 45)*   18,813
Blackburn R: (451) Robinson; Henley, Dann, Hanley G, Spurr; Cairney, Lowe, Williamson (King 44), Taylor, Marshall (Campbell 81); Gestede (Rhodes 81).
Manchester C: (442) Pantilimon; Boyata▪, Lescott, Nastasic, Clichy; Milner, Fernandinho (Toure 64), Javi Garcia, Silva (Zabaleta 88); Negredo (Jesus Navas 74), Dzeko.
Referee: Michael Oliver.

Bolton W (1) 2 *(Ngog 10, Beckford 51)*
Blackpool (1) 1 *(Barkhuizen 45)*   11,180
Bolton W: (451) Lonergan; Baptiste, Mills, Knight, Ream; Danns, Medo, Ngog, Moritz (Pratley 80), Eagles (Vela 87); Beckford (Lee 71).
Blackpool: (451) Gilks; Bishop, MacKenzie, Cathcart, Robinson; Basham, Ferguson, Barkhuizen (Eccleston 66), Martinez (Chopra 81), Ince; Fuller.
Referee: Simon Hooper.

Brighton & HA (1) 1 *(Crofts 32)*
Reading (0) 0   20,696
Brighton & HA: (433) Brezovan; Calderon, Greer (Dunk 67), El-Abd, Chicksen; Crofts, Andrews, Agustien (Orlandi 64); March (LuaLua 79), Barnes, Forster-Caskey.
Reading: (433) Federici; Gunter, Kelly (Williams D 73), Pearce, Gorkss; Guthrie, Taylor, Obita; Blackman (Drenthe 57), Le Fondre, McCleary (Pogrebnyak 85).
Referee: Chris Foy.

Bristol C (0) 0 *(Emmanuel-Thomas 85)*
Watford (0) 1 *(Murray 84)*   10,165
Bristol C: (352) Parish; Osborne, Flint, Fontaine (Moloney 77); Wagstaff (Burns 71), Elliott M, Pack, Reid, Bryan (Cunningham 82); Baldock, Emmanuel-Thomas.
Watford: (352) Almunia; Nosworthy, Angella, Ekstrand; Cassetti (Smith 46), Murray, McGugan, Iriney, Battocchio; Fabbrini, Deeney.
Referee: Paul Tierney.

Doncaster R (0) 2 *(Forrester 72, Wakefield 90)*
Stevenage (0) 3 *(Zoko 49, Hartley 65, Charles 90)*   3899
Doncaster R: (4231) Turnbull; Wakefield, Quinn, McCullough, Stevens; Furman (Paynter 56), Woods; Duffy, Syers, Cotterill (Forrester 56); Brown (Bennett 73).
Stevenage: (442) Day; Jones, Ashton, Chorley, Hartley; Morais (Andrade 75), Doughty, Parrett (Wedgbury 75), Freeman; Zoko, Haber (Charles 78).
Referee: Scott Duncan.

Everton (2) 4 *(Barkley 35, Jelavic 44, 68, Coleman 76)*
QPR (0) 0   32,283
Everton: (4231) Robles; Coleman (Hibbert 82), Alcaraz, Stones, Oviedo; McCarthy, Barry (Heitinga 83); Naismith, Barkley (Mirallas 89), Osman; Jelavic.
QPR: (451) Julio Cesar; Simpson, Hill, Onuoha, Assou-Ekotto; Phillips, O'Neil, Henry (Johnson 58), Barton, Traore (Kranjcar 46); Austin (Benayoun 76).
Referee: Howard Webb.

Grimsby T (1) 2 *(Hannah 25, Disley 62)*
Huddersfield T (0) 3 *(Norwood 51, Paterson 86, Thomas 90 (og))*   6504
Grimsby T: (442) McKeown; Bignot, Pearson, Doig (Southwell 90), Thomas; Colbeck, Disley, Thanoj (McLaughlin 66), Neilson (Rodman 82); Cook, Hannah.
Huddersfield T: (352) Smithies; Smith, Gerrard, Wallace; Hammill (Lopez 77), Clayton, Hogg (Holmes 58), Norwood, Dixon; Paterson, Ward (Scannell 58).
Referee: Keith Stroud.

Ipswich T (1) 1 *(McGoldrick 38)*
Preston NE (1) 1 *(Davies K 42)*   13,534
Ipswich T: (532) Loach; Edwards, Chambers, Berra, Mings, Cresswell; Wordsworth (Tunnicliffe 78), Hyam, Tabb (Taylor 68); Ebanks-Blake (McGoldrick 29), Nouble.
Preston NE: (442) Rudd; Keane, Huntington, Wright, Buchanan (Laird 88); Holmes, Welsh, Kilkenny, Gallagher (Hayhurst 90); Hume (Garner 78), Davies K.
Referee: Michael Naylor.

Kidderminster H (0) 0
Peterborough U (0) 0   3858
Kidderminster H: (433) Lewis; Jackman, Vaughan, Gowling, Demetriou; Fowler (Byrne 63), Storer, Gittings (Dyer 52); Lolley, Gash, Morgan-Smith (Malbon 71).
Peterborough U: (41212) Olejnik; Little, Bostwick, Brisley, Ntlhe; Payne; Anderson, Newell; Tomlin; Assombalonga, Jeffers.
Referee: Jon Moss.

Macclesfield T (0) 1 *(Williams 72)*
Sheffield W (1) 1 *(Johnson Reda 25)*   5873
Macclesfield T: (442) Taylor; Halls, Williams, Connor, Andrew; Mackreth, Whitaker, Turnbull, Winn; Holroyd (Lewis 64), Boden (Martin 90).
Sheffield W: (4231) Martinez; Palmer, Loovens, Llera, Johnson Reda; McPhail (McCabe 73), Semedo; Maguire (Maghoma 87), Lee, Helan (Johnson J 74); Nuhiu.
Referee: Lee Mason.

Middlesbrough (0) 0
Hull C (1) 2 *(Mclean 10, Proschwitz 61)*   15,571
Middlesbrough: (4231) Konstantopoulos; Varga, Gibson, Williams R, Friend; Leadbitter, Whitehead; Ledesma (Adomah 46), Emnes (Butterfield 83), Williams L (Jutkiewicz 46); Main.
Hull C: (442) Harper; Rosenior, McShane (Chester 76), Faye, Figueroa; Boyd, Quinn (Jahraldo-Martin 83), Meyler, Gedo; Mclean (Elmohamady 80), Proschwitz.
Referee: Kevin Friend.

Newcastle U (0) 1 *(Cisse 62)*
Cardiff C (0) 2 *(Noone 73, Campbell 80)*   31,166
Newcastle U: (4411) Elliot; Santon, Taylor S, Yanga-Mbiwa, Haidara; Sissoko (Remy 85), Tiote, Anita, Gouffran (Obertan 63); Ben Arfa; Cisse (Ameobi 85).
Cardiff C: (442) Marshall; McNaughton, Hudson, Turner, John; Cowie, Gunnarsson, Kim (Smith 79), Whittingham; Odemwingie (Noone 72), Cornelius (Campbell 60).
Referee: Anthony Taylor.

Norwich C (1) 1 *(Snodgrass 45)*
Fulham (1) 1 *(Bent 40)*   21,703
Norwich C: (4411) Bunn; Martin, Bennett R, Whittaker, Olsson; Snodgrass, Elmander (Redmond 67), Garrido, Fox; Murphy Josh (Murphy Jacob 79); van Wolfswinkel.
Fulham: (4231) Stockdale; Zverotic, Burn, Hughes, Amorebieta (Riise 70); David, Boateng (Christensen 70); Kacaniklic (Duhamel 46), Kasami, Dempsey; Bent.
Referee: Craig Pawson.

Rochdale (1) 2 *(Hogan 45, Henderson 84)*
Leeds U (0) 0   8255
Rochdale: (433) Lillis; Bennett R, Lancashire, O'Connell, Done; Lund, Cavanagh, Henderson; Vincenti, Hogan, Bunney (Cummins 72).
Leeds U: (343) Kenny; Wootton (Hunt 76), Zaliukas, Pearce; Peltier (Poleon 85), Austin, Murphy, Pugh; Byram, Smith, McCormack.
Referee: Mike Jones.

Southampton (2) 4 *(Clyne 22, Lambert 28, Rodriguez 66, Lallana 73)*

Burnley (0) 3 *(Vokes 51, Ings 57, Long 87)*   15,077

Southampton: (4231) Davis K; Clyne, Hooiveld (Fonte 79), Yoshida, Shaw; Schneiderlin, Cork; Ward-Prowse, Davis S, Ramirez (Lallana 59); Lambert (Rodriguez 35).
Burnley: (4231) Heaton; Trippier, Long, Shackell, Lafferty; Jones, Marney; Treacy (Stanislas 64), Ings, Arfield; Vokes.
Referee: Robert Madley.

Southend U (2) 4 *(Corr 22, Atkinson 45, Timlin 57, Leonard 90)*

Millwall (0) 1 *(Woolford 64)*   7923

Southend U: (433) Bentley; White (Phillips 89), Thompson, Prosser, Coker; Clifford (Laird 70), Leonard, Timlin (Eastwood 84); Atkinson, Corr, Straker.
Millwall: (442) Forde; Dunne, Shittu, Lowry, Smith (Marquis 78); Chaplow (Onyedinma 62), Bailey, Abdou, Martin (Woolford 46); Morison, Easter▪.
Referee: James Adcock.

Stoke C (1) 2 *(Jones 16, Adam 55)*

Leicester C (0) 1 *(Nugent 77)*   16,844

Stoke C: (4231) Butland; Cameron, Shawcross, Wilson, Pieters; Whelan, Nzonzi; Arnautovic, Adam, Assaidi (Walters 80); Jones.
Leicester C: (433) Schmeichel; De Laet, Wasilewski, Miquel, Konchesky; James, Hammond, King (Dyer 68); Knockaert, Vardy (Waghorn 80), Schlupp (Nugent 68).
Referee: Lee Probert.

WBA (0) 0

Crystal Palace (1) 2 *(Gayle 23, Chamakh 90)*   12,700

WBA: (433) Foster; Lugano, Dawson (Amalfitano 61), McAuley, Popov; Morrison, Yacob (Sessegnon 82), Gera; Vydra (Sinclair 69), Long, Berahino.
Crystal Palace: (442) Speroni; Mariappa, Delaney, Gabbidon, Parr; Bolasie, Dikgacoi, Bannan (Puncheon 79), Williams (Chamakh 78); Gayle, Boateng (O'Keefe 68).
Referee: Phil Dowd.

Wigan Ath (2) 3 *(Espinoza 18, Gomez 27, McManaman 65)*

Milton Keynes D (2) 3 *(Reeves 45, 45, Bamford 84)*   6960

Wigan Ath: (442) Al Habsi; Boyce, Barnett, Perch, Beausejour; McManaman, McArthur, Espinoza, McClean (Dicko 75); Holt (Fortune 59), Gomez (McCann 46).
Milton Keynes D: (4231) Martin; Hodson (Baldock 35), Kay, Williams, Lewington; Gleeson, Potter; Carruthers (Galloway 71), Reeves, Alli (Powell 71); Bamford.
Referee: Roger East.

Yeovil T (1) 4 *(Hayter 12, 60, Grant 49, Moore 90)*

Leyton Orient (0) 0   3667

Yeovil T: (442) Stech; Edwards, Ayling, Duffy, Davis; Dawson, Webster (Upson 50), Lundstram, Foley (Morgan 72); Hayter (Moore 82), Grant.
Leyton Orient: (451) Larkins; Omozusi, Cuthbert, Clarke, Sawyer; Odubajo, James (Gorman 70), Ness, Baudry (Lee 80), Cox (Coulthirst 61); Lasimant.
Referee: Oliver Langford.

Sunday, 5 January 2014

Derby Co (0) 0

Chelsea (0) 2 *(Mikel 66, Oscar 71)*   32,110

Derby Co: (433) Grant; Wisdom, Keane, Buxton, Forsyth; Hughes, Eustace (Bennett 70), Hendrick; Ward (Sammon 69), Martin, Dawkins S (Bailey 83).
Chelsea: (4231) Schwarzer; Azpilicueta, Cahill, Luiz, Cole; Essien (Hazard 55), Mikel; Ramires, Oscar (Baker 87), Willian; Eto'o (Torres 64).
Referee: Andre Marriner.

Liverpool (0) 2 *(Aspas 55, Tarkowski 82 (og))*

Oldham Ath (0) 0   44,102

Liverpool: (4231) Jones; Kelly, Toure, Agger, Cissokho; Alberto (Lucas 46), Gerrard (Suarez 77); Moses (Coutinho 46), Henderson, Sterling; Aspas.

Oldham Ath: (4411) Oxley; Kusunga, Tarkowski, Grounds, Mellor (Rodgers 84); Rooney (Harkins 62), Wesolowski, Smith, Petrasso; Philliskirk; Clarke-Harris (Dayton 61).
Referee: Stuart Attwell.

Manchester U (1) 1 *(Hernandez 16)*

Swansea C (1) 2 *(Routledge 12, Bony 90)*   73,190

Manchester U: (442) Lindegaard; Smalling, Ferdinand (Da Silva F▪ 76), Evans, Buttner; Valencia (Januzaj 63), Fletcher, Cleverley, Kagawa; Welbeck, Hernandez.
Swansea C: (4231) Tremmel; Tiendalli, Chico, Amat, Taylor; Britton, de Guzman (Vazquez 85); Pozuelo, Shelvey (Canas 64), Routledge; Bony.
Referee: Mike Dean.

Nottingham F (1) 5 *(Abdoun 12 (pen), Paterson 65, 71, 79, Reid 90)*

West Ham U (0) 0   14,397

Nottingham F: (451) Darlow; Jara, Lascelles, Hobbs, Lichaj (Harding 58); Abdoun, Lansbury, Reid, Moussi, Paterson (Derbyshire 83); Halford (Cox 75).
West Ham U: (3511) Adrian; Driver, Diarra (Burke 55), Potts; Jarvis, Whitehead, Moncur (Fanimo 55), Lletget, Downing (Turgott 64); Morrison; Maiga.
Referee: Martin Atkinson.

Port Vale (2) 2 *(Tomlin 15, Pope 36)*

Plymouth Arg (0) 2 *(Reid 51, Purrington 74)*   5511

Port Vale: (442) Neal; Yates, Robertson, Duffy (Chilvers 40), Dickinson; Myrie-Williams (Hugill 71), Griffith, Loft, Dodds (Williamson 65); Pope, Tomlin.
Plymouth Arg: (442) Cole; Blanchard (Purrington 58), Trotman, Nelson, Berry; Gurrieri, Blizzard, Hourihane, Alessandra; Obadeyi (Thomas 67), Reid (Boco 88).
Referee: David Webb.

Sunderland (1) 3 *(Johnson 34, O'Hanlon 50 (og), Ba 90)*

Carlisle U (1) 1 *(Robson 43)*   21,973

Sunderland: (4411) Mannone; Gardner, Brown, Ki (Bardsley 63), Dossena; Johnson, Larsson (Ba 80), Celustka, Colback; Ji (Watmore 63); Altidore.
Carlisle U: (352) Fleming; Potts, O'Hanlon, Ehmer; Buaben, Berrett, Lawrence (Townsend 83), Noble (Symington 70), Robson; Guy (Miller 69), Amoo.
Referee: Neil Swarbrick.

Tuesday, 14 January 2014

Birmingham C (1) 3 *(Robinson 35, Burke 85, 87)*

Bristol R (0) 0   10,064

Birmingham C: (442) Doyle; Caddis, Mullins, Robinson, Hancox; Burke, Lee (Adams 89), Brown (Elliott 73), Ferguson (Gray 89); Novak, Zigic.
Bristol R: (4231) Mildenhall; Smith, Parkes, McChrystal, Brown; Norburn (Clarkson 83), Clarke (Woodards 76); Richards, O'Toole, Harrison (Beardsley 63); Harrold.
Referee: Michael Naylor.

Bournemouth (2) 4 *(Pitman 5, 88 (pen), Elphick 45, Fraser 86)*

Burton Alb (1) 1 *(Phillips 35)*   10,343

Bournemouth: (442) Allsop; Francis, Elphick, Cook, Daniels; Pugh (Surman 72), O'Kane, Arter, Ritchie (Fraser 55); Pitman, Rantie (Grabban 83).
Burton Alb: (4411) Lyness; Edwards, Diamond, Sharps, McCrory; Buxton (MacDonald 63), Palmer, Bell (Hussey 73), Phillips; McGurk; Kee (Knowles 80).
Referee: Iain Williamson.

Charlton Ath (0) 2 *(Morrison 54, Kermorgant 82)*

Oxford U (2) 2 *(Mullins 13, Davies 24)*   5566

Charlton Ath: (442) Hamer; Wilson, Morrison, Wood, Wiggins; Cook (Harriott 78), Cousins, Jackson, Pritchard (Green 67); Kermorgant, Church (Pigott 78).
Oxford U: (442) Clarke; Hunt, Raynes, Wright, Newey; Davies (Williams 87), Mullins, Ruffels, Rigg; Constable (Kitson 78), Marsh (Smalley 54).
Referee: Stephen Martin.

THIRD ROUND REPLAYS

Tuesday, 14 January 2014

Fulham (2) 3 *(Bent 16, Dejagah 41, Sidwell 68)*

Norwich C (0) 0   11,172

Fulham: (4231) Stekelenburg; Riether, Hangeland, Burn, Richardson; Karagounis, Sidwell (Christensen 84); Dejagah, Kasami, Kacaniklic (Tankovic 87); Bent (Dembele 79).
Norwich C: (4231) Bunn; Whittaker, Martin, Bassong, Garrido; Fox, Johnson; Redmond (van Wolfswinkel 46); Snodgrass, Murphy Jacob; Elmander (Becchio 68).
Referee: Lee Mason.

Milton Keynes D (1) 1 *(Chadwick 10)*

Wigan Ath (0) 3 *(Powell 79, 92, Fortune 105)*   8316

Milton Keynes D: (451) Martin; Hodson, Kay, Williams, Lewington; Carruthers (Smith 95), Gleeson, Chadwick (Bowditch 58), Potter, Reeves; Powell (Baldock 95).
Wigan Ath: (442) Al Habsi; Perch (Boyce 60), McCann, Barnett, Crainey; Espinoza, Watson, McArthur, McClean (Gomez 72); Fortune, Fyvie (Powell 60).
aet.
Referee: James Adcock.

Peterborough U (1) 2 *(Rowe 26, Assombalonga 74 (pen))*

Kidderminster H (0) 3 *(Gash 48, Byrne 52, Lolley 76)*
                                             3483

Peterborough U: (352) Olejnik; Bostwick, Brisley, Knight-Percival; Little, Payne, Anderson (McCann 54), Rowe (Newell 38), Kearns (Swanson 54); Assombalonga, Jeffers.
Kidderminster H: (433) Lewis; Vaughan, Demetriou, Gowling, Jackman; Storer, Fowler, Byrne; Lolley (Dyer 88), Gash, Morgan-Smith (Johnson 57).
Referee: Andy D'Urso.

Plymouth Arg (2) 2 *(Gurrieri 2, Hourihane 36)*

Port Vale (1) 3 *(Hugill 30, Williamson 63, Myrie-Williams 75)*   6474

Plymouth Arg: (442) Cole; Berry (Blanchard 46), Trotman, Nelson, Purrington; Gurrieri, Blizzard, Hourihane, Vassell (Thomas 75); Reid, Alessandra.
Port Vale: (442) Neal; Yates, Robertson, Dickinson, Loft; Myrie-Williams (Birchall 82), Lines*, Griffith (Shuker 61), Dodds; Pope, Hugill (Williamson 61).
Referee: Graham Scott.

Preston NE (0) 3 *(Garner 68, 68, 88)*

Ipswich T (0) 2 *(Nouble 58, McGoldrick 76)*   6088

Preston NE: (442) Rudd; Keane, Clarke, Huntington, Laird; Humphrey (Wright 90), Kilkenny, Garner (Holmes 79), Hayhurst (Garner 62); Gallagher, Davies K.
Ipswich T: (433) Loach; Edwards, Berra, Smith, Mings; Tunnicliffe, Hyam, Tabb (McGoldrick 74); Anderson (Taylor 73), Nouble, Hunt (Lee 90).
Referee: Keith Stroud.

Sheffield W (1) 4 *(Maguire 3, Maghoma 78, Johnson J 85, Llera 90)*

Macclesfield T (0) 1 *(Boden 65 (pen))*   12,302

Sheffield W: (442) Martinez; Palmer, Llera, Loovens, Johnson R (Mattock 46); Maguire, Semedo, Lee (McCabe 83), Helan (Johnson J 65); Maghoma, Nuhiu.
Macclesfield T: (442) Taylor; Connor, Turnbull (Rowe 61), Williams (Martin 88), Andrew; Kay, Boden, Whitaker, Winn (Holroyd 60); Mackreth, Halls.
Referee: Nigel Miller.

Watford (1) 2 *(Faraoni 29, McGugan 64)*

Bristol C (0) 0   7302

Watford: (352) Bond; Angella, Ekstrand, Hall; Anya (Pudil 86), Iriney, McGugan (Abdi 75), Battocchio, Faraoni; Deeney, Forestieri.
Bristol C: (352) Parish; Osborne, Flint, Fontaine; Moloney (Wagstaff 79), Reid, Pack, Elliott M, Bryan (Cunningham 78); Baldock (Burns 78), Emmanuel-Thomas.
Referee: Darren Drysdale.

Wednesday, 15 January 2014

Manchester C (1) 5 *(Negredo 45, 47, Dzeko 67, 79, Aguero 73)*

Blackburn R (0) 0   35,000

Manchester C: (442) Pantilimon; Richards (Huws 77), Lescott, Nastasic, Clichy; Jesus Navas, Javi Garcia, Fernandinho (Kolarov 46), Milner; Dzeko, Negredo (Aguero 72).
Blackburn R: (4141) Robinson (Eastwood 46); Henley, Hanley G, Kilgallon, Spurr; Williamson (Mahoney 89); Cairney, Lowe, Taylor, Marshall; Campbell (King 59).
Referee: Craig Pawson.

Tuesday, 21 January 2014

Oxford U (0) 0

Charlton Ath (2) 3 *(Kermorgant 35, 58, Green 38)*   3225

Oxford U: (442) Clarke; Hunt, Wright, Raynes, Newey; Davies, Ruffels, Mullins, Rigg (O'Dowda 80); Constable (Marsh 79), Smalley.
Charlton Ath: (442) Alnwick; Wilson, Morrison, Dervite, Evina; Green, Stephens (Poyet 81), Jackson, Harriott (Pritchard 69); Church, Kermorgant (Sordell 76).
Referee: David Coote.

FOURTH ROUND

Friday, 24 January 2014

Arsenal (2) 4 *(Podolski 15, 27, Giroud 84, Cazorla 89)*

Coventry C (0) 0   59,451

Arsenal: (4231) Fabianski; Jenkinson, Mertesacker, Koscielny, Gibbs; Oxlade-Chamberlain (Zelalem 71), Wilshere; Gnabry, Ozil, Podolski (Giroud 79); Bendtner (Cazorla 71).
Coventry C: (442) Murphy; Christie, Webster, Seaborne, Adams; Baker, Thomas, Fleck, Daniels; Moussa (Clarke J 88), Clarke L.
Referee: Robert Madley.

Nottingham F (0) 0

Preston NE (0) 0   26,465

Nottingham F: (433) Darlow; Jara, Halford, Collins, Lichaj; Majewski (Derbyshire 74), Vaughan, Reid; Mackie (Abdoun 60), Cox (Henderson 60), Paterson.
Preston NE: (433) Rudd; Wiseman, Clarke, Wright, Buchanan; Brownhill, Welsh, Kilkenny (Hume 82); Humphrey (Holmes 71), Garner (King 85), Gallagher.
Referee: Mike Dean.

Saturday, 25 January 2014

Birmingham C (1) 1 *(Novak 15)*

Swansea C (0) 2 *(Bony 67, 69)*   11,490

Birmingham C: (442) Doyle; Caddis, Packwood, Robinson, Hancox; Burke, Lee (Lovenkrands 81), Brown, Ferguson (Adeyemi 74); Novak, Rusnak.
Swansea C: (4231) Tremmel; Tiandalli, Chico, Williams, Taylor; Amat, Britton; Hernandez (Bony 46), Lamah, Pozuelo; Vazquez (Routledge 64).
Referee: Neil Swarbrick.

Bolton W (0) 0

Cardiff C (0) 1 *(Campbell 50)*   12,750

Bolton W: (4231) Lonergan; Baptiste, Knight, Mills, Ream; Medo (Odelusi 72), Spearing; Lee, Danns, Eagles (Moritz 72); Davies C.
Cardiff C: (442) Marshall; Theophile-Catherine, Hudson, Turner, McNaughton; Kim, Gunnarsson, Eikrem (Noone 46), Whittingham; Mason (Daehli 80), Cornelius (Campbell 46).
Referee: Jon Moss.

Bournemouth (0) 0

Liverpool (1) 2 *(Moses 26, Sturridge 60)*   11,475

Bournemouth: (4231) Camp; Francis, Elphick, Ward, Daniels; O'Kane, Arter (Pitman 78); Ritchie (Fraser 73), Surman, Pugh (Rantie 73); Grabban.
Liverpool: (4231) Jones; Kelly (Flanagan 73), Skrtel, Toure, Cissokho; Gerrard, Henderson; Sturridge, Coutinho (Alberto 84), Moses (Sterling 84); Suarez.
Referee: Lee Probert.

Huddersfield T (0) 0
Charlton Ath (0) 1 *(Church 54)* 10,120
Huddersfield T: (352) Smithies; Smith, Gerrard, Wallace; Hammill (Sinnott 35 (Scannell 55)), Gobern (Holmes 64), Norwood, Clayton, Dixon; Ward, Vaughan.
Charlton Ath: (442) Alnwick; Wilson, Morrison, Dervite, Evina (Lennon 35); Ajdarevic (Cousins 69), Stephens, Jackson, Harriott; Church, Sordell (Green 69).
Referee: Stuart Attwell.

Manchester C (0) 4 *(Aguero 60, 79, 90, Kolarov 87)*
Watford (2) 2 *(Forestieri 21, Deeney 30)* 46,514
Manchester C: (442) Pantilimon; Richards (Zabaleta 46), Demichelis, Lescott, Kolarov; Jesus Navas, Toure, Rodwell (Kompany 46), Lopes (Jovetic 57); Dzeko, Aguero.
Watford: (442) Bond; Angella, Ekstrand, Pudil, Doyley; Battocchio, Murray (Abdi 74), Faraoni (Fabbrini 84), Anya; Deeney, Forestieri (Cassetti 60).
Referee: Kevin Friend.

Port Vale (1) 1 *(Robertson 36)*
Brighton & HA (2) 3 *(Ince 27, March 43, Obika 78)* 7293
Port Vale: (442) Neal; Grimmer, Robertson, Davis, Taylor (Yates 46); Myrie-Williams (Williamson 66), Lines, Griffith, Loft; Pope, Tomlin (Hugill 75).
Brighton & HA: (4141) Brezovan; Calderon, Dunk, Upson, Chicksen; Ince; March (LuaLua 81), Forster-Caskey, Agustien (Andrews 70), Orlandi; Obika.
Referee: Paul Tierney.

Rochdale (0) 1 *(Rose 60)*
Sheffield W (0) 2 *(Mattock 51, Onyewu 57)* 8240
Rochdale: (451) Lillis; Bennett (Camps 75), Eastham, O'Connell, Done; Vincenti (Cummins 67), Allen (Donnelly 59), Lund, Rose, Henderson; Hogan.
Sheffield W: (442) Martinez; Palmer, Onyewu, Loovens, Mattock**; Maguire, Lee, Semedo, Maghoma (Coke 82); Nuhiu (Johnson J 78), Lavery (Helan 67).
Referee: Simon Hooper.

Southampton (1) 2 *(Do Prado 23 (pen), Gallagher 70)*
Yeovil T (0) 0 24,070
Southampton: (433) Davis K; Clyne, Yoshida, Hooiveld, Shaw; Ward-Prowse (Reed 84), Cork, Schneiderlin; Do Prado (Gallagher 55), Rodriguez, Lallana (Davis S 74).
Yeovil T: (442) Stech; Ayling, Duffy, Webster, McAllister; Grant (Upson 74), Edwards, Lundstram, Ralls; Hayter (Moore 62), Miller (Foley 85).
Referee: Phil Dowd.

Southend U (0) 0
Hull C (0) 2 *(Fryatt 63, 90)* 10,250
Southend U: (442) Bentley; Thompson, Phillips, Prosser, Coker; Hurst, Leonard, Timlin (Woodrow 70), Straker (Payne 80); Atkinson, Corr (Eastwood 88).
Hull C: (442) Harper; Rosenior, Faye, McShane, Figueroa; Boyd, Meyler, Quinn (Bruce 88), Sagbo (Livermore 82); Graham (Brady 73), Fryatt.
Referee: Lee Mason.

Stevenage (0) 0
Everton (2) 4 *(Naismith 5, 32, Heitinga 55, Gueye 84)* 6913
Stevenage: (442) Day; Jones (Parrett 72), Ashton, Charles, Hartley; Morais (Andrade 81), Heslop, Smith J, Freeman; Akins, Zoko (Deacon 85).
Everton: (4231) Robles; Hibbert, Stones, Jagielka (Heitinga 46), Baines; McCarthy, Barry; McGeady, Mirallas (Gueye 81), Oviedo (Osman 22); Naismith.
Referee: Anthony Taylor.

Sunderland (1) 1 *(Mavrias 5)*
Kidderminster H (0) 0 25,081
Sunderland: (4231) Ustari; Celustka, Vergini, Diakite, Roberge; Ba (Gardner 66), Cattermole (Colback 72); Larsson, Giaccherini (Borini 66), Mavrias; Altidore.
Kidderminster H: (4411) Lewis; Vaughan, Gowling, Demetriou, Jackman; Morgan-Smith (Ladapo 68), Storer, Dyer (Aloi 83), Johnson (Gittings 69); Byrne; Deeney.
Referee: Roger East.

Wigan Ath (1) 2 *(Watson 36, McClean 78)*
Crystal Palace (0) 1 *(Wilbraham 69)* 9542
Wigan Ath: (4231) Al Habsi; Perch, Boyce, Barnett, Beausejour; Watson, McArthur (McCann 80); McManaman (Fortune 74), Espinoza, McClean; Maynard (Powell 74).
Crystal Palace: (442) Speroni; Mariappa, McCarthy, Delaney, Parr (Moxey 45); Puncheon, O'Keefe, Guedioura, Bannan; Chamakh (Wilbraham 66), Jerome (Gayle 66).
Referee: Mike Jones.

Sunday, 26 January 2014
Chelsea (1) 1 *(Oscar 27)*
Stoke C (0) 0 40,845
Chelsea: (4231) Schwarzer; Ivanovic, Cahill, Luiz, Cole; Lampard, Matic; Schurrle (Ramires 70), Oscar (Willian 81), Hazard; Eto'o (Ba 85).
Stoke C: (4231) Begovic; Cameron, Shawcross, Wilson, Pieters (Muniesa 85); Palacios (Assaidi 72), Nzonzi; Arnautovic (Adam 83), Ireland, Walters; Crouch.
Referee: Chris Foy.

Sheffield U (1) 1 *(Porter 31)*
Fulham (0) 1 *(Rodallega 75)* 16,324
Sheffield U: (4411) Long; Brayford, Maguire (Harris 48), Collins, Hill; Flynn, Coady, Doyle**, Murphy; Baxter (McGinn 85); Porter (Scougall 46).
Fulham: (4411) Stockdale; Passley, Senderos, Hughes, Riise (Plumain 10 (Taarabt 67)); Duff, Karagounis, David (Bent 57), Kasami; Tankovic; Rodallega.
Referee: Andre Marriner.

FOURTH ROUND REPLAYS
Tuesday, 4 February 2014
Fulham (0) 0
Sheffield U (0) 1 *(Miller 120)* 10,139
Fulham: (4411) Stockdale; Passley, Hangeland, Burn, Amorebieta; Kasami, Parker (Sidwell 69), Tankovic, Kacaniklic (Duff 59); Dempsey; Rodallega (Dejagah 59).
Sheffield U: (451) Howard; Brayford, Maguire, Collins, Harris (Hill 91); Flynn, McGinn, Scougall (Miller 97), Coady, Murphy; Porter (Baxter 75).
aet.
Referee: Neil Swarbrick.

Wednesday, 5 February 2014
Preston NE (0) 0
Nottingham F (1) 2 *(Mackie 18, Henderson 90)* 9744
Preston NE: (451) Rudd; Wiseman, Clarke, Wright, Buchanan (Laird 77); Humphrey (Garner 66), Kilkenny, Welsh, Keane, Holmes (Gallagher 66); Davies K.
Nottingham F: (442) De Vries; Halford, Lascelles, Collins, Harding; Mackie, Moussi, Jara, Abdoun (Paterson 51); Cox (Henderson 67), Derbyshire (Majewski 51).
Referee: Jon Moss.

FIFTH ROUND
Saturday, 15 February 2014
Cardiff C (1) 1 *(Campbell 27)*
Wigan Ath (2) 2 *(McCann 18, Watson 40)* 17,123
Cardiff C: (4231) Marshall; Theophile-Catherine, Caulker, Cala, Taylor; Medel (Cowie 46), Eikrem (Kim 78); Daehli, Berget (Noone 61), Zaha; Campbell.
Wigan Ath: (3412) Al Habsi; Boyce, Ramis, McCann; Perch, Watson (McEachran 58), Espinoza, Beausejour; Gomez (Crainey 78); McManaman (McClean 67), Fortune.
Referee: Martin Atkinson.

Manchester C (1) 2 *(Jovetic 16, Nasri 67)*
Chelsea (0) 0 47,013
Manchester C: (442) Pantilimon; Zabaleta, Kompany, Lescott, Clichy; Milner, Javi Garcia, Toure, Silva (Jesus Navas 69); Dzeko (Negredo 81), Jovetic (Nasri 51).
Chelsea: (4231) Cech; Ivanovic, Cahill, Luiz, Azpilicueta; Mikel, Matic; Ramires (Torres 61), Willian (Oscar 71), Hazard; Eto'o (Salah 46).
Referee: Phil Dowd.

Sunderland (0) 1 *(Gardner 49)*
Southampton (0) 0 16,777
Sunderland: (433) Ustari; Celustka, Vergini, O'Shea, Dossena (Alonso 77); Larsson, Cattermole, Gardner (Colback 83); Giaccherini, Scocco (Wickham 69), Borini.
Southampton: (4231) Davis K; Clyne, Yoshida, Hooiveld, Shaw; Davis S, Wanyama; Ward-Prowse (Schneiderlin 62), Lallana (McQueen 82), Do Prado (Rodriguez 62); Lambert.
Referee: Mike Dean.

Sunday, 16 February 2014
Arsenal (1) 2 *(Oxlade-Chamberlain 16, Podolski 47)*
Liverpool (0) 1 *(Gerrard 59 (pen))* 59,801
Arsenal: (4231) Fabianski; Jenkinson, Mertesacker, Koscielny, Monreal; Flamini, Arteta; Oxlade-Chamberlain (Gibbs 76), Ozil, Podolski (Cazorla 69); Sanogo (Giroud 88).
Liverpool: (433) Jones; Flanagan, Skrtel, Agger, Cissokho (Henderson 62); Allen, Gerrard, Coutinho; Suarez, Sturridge, Sterling.
Referee: Howard Webb.

Everton (1) 3 *(Traore 4, Naismith 65, Baines 72 (pen))*
Swansea C (1) 1 *(de Guzman 15)* 31,498
Everton: (4231) Robles; Coleman, Jagielka, Distin, Baines; McCarthy, Barry; Mirallas (Deulofeu 87), Barkley (Osman 61), Pienaar; Traore (Naismith 61).
Swansea C: (4231) Tremmel; Richards, Bartley (Williams 31), Amat, Taylor; de Guzman, Canas; Hernandez, Routledge (Dyer 46), Lamah (Lita 69); Vazquez.
Referee: Kevin Friend.

Sheffield U (0) 3 *(Coady 66, Porter 90 (pen))*
Nottingham F (1) 1 *(Paterson 28)* 25,118
Sheffield U: (442) Howard; Brayford, Maguire, Collins, Harris (Hill 90); Flynn, Coady (McGinn 90), Doyle, Murphy; Scougall, Baxter (Porter 87).
Nottingham F: (41212) De Vries; Halford, Lascelles, Collins, Fox; Jara; Majewski (Abdoun 78), Paterson; Reid; Henderson (Djebbour 70), Cox (Mackie 67).
Referee: Michael Oliver.

Monday, 17 February 2014
Brighton & HA (1) 1 *(Ulloa 30)*
Hull C (0) 1 *(Sagbo 85)* 21,352
Brighton & HA: (433) Brezovan; Calderon, Dunk, Upson, Chicksen; Andrews, Ince, Forster-Caskey; Buckley (March 46), Ulloa (Obika 79), LuaLua (David Rodriguez 90).
Hull C: (442) McGregor; Elmohamady, Davies, Faye (Boyd 67), Figueroa; Koren, Huddlestone, Livermore (Meyler 82), Quinn (Fryatt 66); Sagbo, Aluko.
Referee: Lee Probert.

Monday, 24 February 2014
Sheffield W (0) 1 *(Best 57)*
Charlton Ath (1) 2 *(Harriott 22, Church 65)* 24,607
Sheffield W: (442) Martinez; Palmer, Loovens, Llera, Mattock; Maguire, Gardner (Nuhiu 58), Coke, Maghoma (Lavery 58); Afobe (Helan 74), Best.
Charlton Ath: (4411) Hamer; Wilson, Morrison, Wood (Dervite 90), Fox; Cousins, Poyet, Jackson, Harriott; Ajdarevic (Hughes 90); Church (Ghoochannejhad 85).
Referee: Mark Clattenburg.

FIFTH ROUND REPLAY

Monday, 24 February 2014
Hull C (2) 2 *(Davies 14, Koren 36)*
Brighton & HA (0) 1 *(Ulloa 68)* 10,795
Hull C: (433) Harper; Elmohamady, Chester, Davies, Figueroa; Koren, Livermore, Meyler (Quinn 84); Aluko (Boyd 76), Fryatt, Sagbo.
Brighton & HA: (4141) Brezovan; Calderon, Dunk, Upson, Ward; Ince (March 60); Lopez (Obika 89), Forster-Caskey, Andrews, David Rodriguez (LuaLua 46); Ulloa.
Referee: Andre Marriner.

SIXTH ROUND

Saturday, 8 March 2014
Arsenal (1) 4 *(Ozil 7, Arteta 68 (pen), Giroud 83, 85)*
Everton (1) 1 *(Lukaku 32)* 59,719
Arsenal: (4231) Fabianski; Sagna, Mertesacker, Vermaelen, Gibbs (Jenkinson 88); Flamini, Arteta; Oxlade-Chamberlain (Rosicky 78), Ozil, Cazorla; Sanogo (Giroud 61).
Everton: (4231) Robles; Coleman, Stones, Distin, Baines; McCarthy, Barry; Mirallas (McGeady 76), Barkley (Deulofeu 84), Pienaar (Osman 76); Lukaku.
Referee: Mark Clattenburg.

Sunday, 9 March 2014
Hull C (0) 3 *(Davies 68, Meyler 72, Fryatt 77)*
Sunderland (0) 0 20,047
Hull C: (4231) McGregor; Rosenior, Chester, Davies, Figueroa; Huddlestone, Meyler; Elmohamady (Quinn 81), Aluko (Koren 67), Sagbo (Boyd 58); Fryatt.
Sunderland: (433) Ustari; Bardsley, Vergini, O'Shea, Dossena; Larsson, Cattermole, Colback; Giaccherini (Johnson 67), Fletcher, Scocco (Borini 67).
Referee: Craig Pawson.

Manchester C (0) 1 *(Nasri 68)*
Wigan Ath (1) 2 *(Gomez 27 (pen), Perch 47)* 46,824
Manchester C: (442) Pantilimon; Richards, Demichelis, Lescott, Clichy; Jesus Navas (Dzeko 53), Toure (Silva 53), Javi Garcia, Nasri; Negredo (Milner 53), Aguero.
Wigan Ath: (541) Carson; Perch, Boyce, Ramis, McCann (Barnett 46); Crainey; McManaman (McClean 58), McArthur, McEachran (Espinoza 66), Gomez; Fortune.
Referee: Anthony Taylor.

Sheffield U (0) 2 *(Flynn 65, Brayford 67)*
Charlton Ath (0) 0 30,040
Sheffield U: (4411) Howard; Brayford, Maguire, Collins, Harris; Flynn (McGinn 90), Coady, Doyle, Murphy; Scougall (Porter 86); Baxter (Davies 81).
Charlton Ath: (4231) Hamer; Wilson (Ghoochannejhad 71), Morrison, Wood, Wiggins; Cousins, Poyet (Green 71), Jackson, Harriott; Tudgay, Church (Ajdarevic 65).
Referee: Lee Mason.

SEMI-FINALS (at Wembley)

Saturday, 12 April 2014
Wigan Ath (0) 1 *(Gomez 63 (pen))*
Arsenal (0) 1 *(Mertesacker 82)* 82,185
Wigan Ath: (343) Carson; Boyce, Ramis (Caldwell 86), Crainey; Perch, McEachran (Collison 64), McArthur, Beausejour; McManaman (Powell 68), Fortune, Gomez.
Arsenal: (4231) Fabianski; Sagna, Mertesacker, Vermaelen, Monreal (Gibbs 63); Arteta, Ramsey (Kallstrom 113); Oxlade-Chamberlain, Cazorla, Podolski (Giroud 68); Sanogo.
aet; Arsenal won 4-2 on penalties.
Referee: Michael Oliver.

Sunday, 13 April 2014
Hull C (1) 5 *(Sagbo 42, Fryatt 49, Huddlestone 54, Quinn 67, Meyler 90)*
Sheffield U (2) 3 *(Baxter 19, Scougall 44, Murphy 90)* 71,820
Hull C: (451) Harper; Rosenior, Chester, Davies, Figueroa (Aluko 46); Elmohamady, Huddlestone, Livermore, Meyler, Boyd (Fryatt 46); Sagbo (Quinn 64).
Sheffield U: (4231) Howard; Brayford, Maguire, Collins, Harris (Hill 90); Doyle, Coady; Flynn, Scougall (Porter 83), Murphy; Baxter (Davies 83).
Referee: Andre Marriner.

THE FA CUP FINAL
Saturday, 17 May 2014

(at Wembley Stadium, attendance 89,345)

Arsenal (1) 3   Hull C (2) 2 (aet)

Arsenal: (4231) Fabianski; Sagna, Mertesacker, Koscielny, Gibbs; Arteta, Ramsey; Cazorla (Wilshere 106), Ozil (Rosicky 106), Podolski (Sanogo 61); Giroud.
Scorers: Cazorla 17, Koscielny 71, Ramsey 109.

Hull C: (3511) McGregor; Chester, Bruce (McShane 67), Davies; Elmohamady, Livermore, Huddlestone, Meyler, Rosenior (Boyd 102); Quinn (Aluko 75); Fryatt.
Scorers: Chester 4, Davies 9.

Referee: Lee Probert.

Arsenal's Aaron Ramsay celebrates after scoring his team's decisive third goal against Hull City in the FA Cup final. The London club recovered from being 2-0 down inside the game's first ten minutes to win 3-2 after extra time.
(Adam Davy/EMPICS Sport)

SKRILL PREMIER 2013–14

(P) *Promoted into division at end of 2012–13 season.*   (R) *Relegated into division at end of 2012–13 season.*

				Total					Home					Away					
		P	W	D	L	F	A	W	D	L	F	A	W	D	L	F	A	GD	Pts
1	Luton T	46	30	11	5	102	35	18	3	2	64	16	12	8	3	38	19	67	101
2	Cambridge U¶	46	23	13	10	72	35	16	4	3	49	14	7	9	7	23	21	37	82
3	Gateshead	46	22	13	11	72	50	12	7	4	42	24	10	6	7	30	26	22	79
4	Grimsby T	46	22	12	12	65	46	11	7	5	40	26	11	5	7	25	20	19	78
5	FC Halifax T (P)	46	22	11	13	85	58	16	6	1	55	19	6	5	12	30	39	27	77
6	Braintree T	46	21	11	14	57	39	12	4	7	27	18	9	7	7	30	21	18	74
7	Kidderminster H	46	20	12	14	66	59	15	4	4	45	22	5	8	10	21	37	7	72
8	Barnet (R)	46	19	13	14	58	53	11	6	6	30	26	8	7	8	28	27	5	70
9	Woking	46	20	8	18	66	69	11	4	8	32	30	9	4	10	34	39	–3	68
10	Forest Green R	46	19	10	17	80	66	13	6	4	47	22	6	4	13	33	44	14	67
11	Alfreton T†	46	21	7	18	69	74	13	6	4	45	33	8	1	14	24	41	–5	67
12	Salisbury C‡ (P)	46	19	10	17	58	63	13	6	4	34	21	6	4	13	24	42	–5	67
13	Nuneaton T	46	18	12	16	54	60	12	4	7	29	25	6	8	9	25	35	–6	66
14	Lincoln C	46	17	14	15	60	59	10	7	6	30	19	7	7	9	30	40	1	65
15	Macclesfield T	46	18	7	21	62	63	11	5	7	35	27	7	2	14	27	36	–1	61
16	Welling U (P)	46	16	12	18	59	61	10	5	8	31	24	6	7	10	28	37	–2	60
17	Wrexham	46	16	11	19	61	61	11	5	7	31	21	5	6	12	30	40	0	59
18	Southport	46	14	11	21	53	71	13	5	5	33	23	1	6	16	20	48	–18	53
19	Aldershot T* (R)	46	16	13	17	69	62	11	6	6	48	32	5	7	11	21	30	7	51
20	Hereford U§	46	13	12	21	44	63	9	6	8	24	24	4	6	13	20	39	–19	51
21	Chester FC (P)	46	12	15	19	49	70	5	12	6	26	30	7	3	13	23	40	–21	51
22	Dartford	46	12	8	26	49	74	8	3	12	32	35	4	5	14	17	39	–25	44
23	Tamworth	46	10	9	27	43	81	6	7	10	25	31	4	2	17	18	50	–38	39
24	Hyde	46	1	7	38	38	119	1	4	18	20	57	0	3	20	18	62	–81	10

Aldershot T deducted 10 points for entering administration. †*Alfreton T deducted 3 points for fielding an ineligible player.* ¶*Cambridge U promoted via play-offs.* ‡*Salisbury C demoted to Conference South due to financial irregularities. Dartford retain place in league.* §*Hereford U expelled for financial irregularities, demoted to Southern Premier League. Chester FC retain their place in league.*

SKRILL PREMIER PLAY-OFFS 2013–14

■ *Denotes player sent off.*

SEMI-FINALS FIRST LEG

Wednesday, 30 April 2014

FC Halifax T (0) 1 *(Gregory 83 (pen))*

Cambridge U (0) 0   3668

FC Halifax T: (4411) Glennon; Bolton, Smith C, Roberts, Lowe; Smith A (Spencer 73), Marshall, Maynard, McManus; Pearson; Gregory.
Cambridge U: (442) Smith A; Roberts, Coulson, Miller, Taylor; Donaldson, Champion, Hughes, Chadwick (Dunk 72); Smith S (Barnes-Homer 90), Elliott.

Thursday, 1 May 2014

Grimsby T (1) 1 *(Disley 24)*

Gateshead (1) 1 *(Larkin 7)*   5234

Grimsby T: (442) McKeown; Hatton, Pearson, Boyce, Thomas; Neilson, Kerr, Disley, Rodman; John-Lewis (Cook 86), Hannah.
Gateshead: (433) Bartlett; Magnay, Curtis, Clark, Baxter; Walker, Turnbull, Oster; Maddison (Hatch 64), Larkin (O'Donnell 59), Marwood.

SEMI-FINALS SECOND LEG

Sunday, 4 May 2014

Cambridge U (2) 2 *(Sam-Yorke 11, 38)*

FC Halifax T (0) 0   6262

Cambridge U: (442) Smith A; Roberts, Miller, Coulson, Taylor; Donaldson, Champion, Berry (Chambers 80), Dunk (Hughes 69); Elliott, Sam-Yorke (Cunnington 72).
FC Halifax T: (4231) Glennon; Bolton, Roberts, Smith C (Ainge 46), Lowe (Crowther 80); Maynard, Marshall (Spencer 61); Smith A, Pearson, McManus; Gregory.
Cambridge U won 2-1 on aggregate.

Gateshead (1) 3 *(Marwood 22, 84, O'Donnell 90)*

Grimsby T (0) 1 *(Disley 60)*   8144

Gateshead: (433) Bartlett; Baxter, Curtis, Clark, Magnay; Chandler, Turnbull, Oster; Maddison (Hatch 72), Marwood, Larkin (O'Donnell 67).
Grimsby T: (442) McKeown; Hatton■, Doig (Cook 86), Boyce, Thomas; Neilson, Kerr (Thanoj 82), Disley, Rodman; Neilson■; Hannah (Fyfield 82), John-Lewis.
Gateshead won 4-2 on aggregate.

FINAL

Sunday, 18 May 2014

Cambridge U (0) 2 *(Hughes 51, Donaldson 71)*

Gateshead (0) 1 *(Lester 80)*   19,613

Cambridge U: (442) Smith A; Roberts, Miller, Coulson, Taylor; Champion, Berry (Chadwick 65), Donaldson, Elliott (Cunnington 76); Sam-Yorke (Dunk 45), Hughes.
Gateshead: (442) Bartlett; Magnay, Curtis, Clark, Baxter; Chandler (Lester 69), Turnbull, Maddison (O'Donnell 58), Marwood; Oster, Larkin (Hatch 58).
Referee: Peter Bankes.

SKRILL PREMIER PROMOTED TEAMS ROLL CALL 2013–14

LUTON T

Player	H	W	DOB
Benson, Paul (F)	6 1	11 00	12/10/79
Charles, Anthony (D)	6 0	13 00	12/3/81
Cullen, Mark (F)	5 9	11 11	21/4/92
Franks, Fraser (D)	6 2	10 12	22/11/90
Gray, Andre (F)	5 10	12 06	26/6/91
Griffiths, Scott (D)	5 9	11 08	27/11/85
Guttridge, Luke (M)	5 8	10 08	27/3/82
Henry, Ronnie (D)	5 11	11 09	2/1/84
Howells, Jake (D)	5 9	11 09	18/4/91
Lacey, Alex (D)	5 11	11 11	31/5/93
Lawless, Alex (M)	5 11	10 08	5/2/83
Martin, Dave (M)	5 11	11 07	3/6/85
McNulty, Steve (D)	6 1	13 12	26/9/83
Parry, Andy (D)			13/9/91
Robinson, Matt (M)	6 2	12 08	1/6/94
Rooney, Luke (M)	5 8	11 03	28/12/90
Shaw, Jon (F)	6 1	12 08	10/11/83
Smith, Jonathan (M)	5 5	10 01	17/10/86
Taiwo, Solomon (M)	6 1	13 02	29/4/85
Tyler, Mark (G)	5 11	13 01	2/4/77
Wall, Alex (F)	5 11	12 06	22/11/90

CAMBRIDGE U

Player	H	W	DOB
Arnold, Nathan (M)	5 7	10 03	26/7/87
Barnes-Homer, Matthew (F)	5 11	12 06	25/1/86
Berry, Luke (M)	5 10	11 05	12/7/92
Bonner, Tom (D)	6 0	11 07	6/2/88
Chadwick, Luke (M)	5 11	10 08	18/11/80
Champion, Tom (M)	6 3	12 04	15/5/86
Coulson, Josh (D)	6 3	11 11	28/1/89
Cunnington, Adam (F)	6 3	12 11	7/10/87
Donaldson, Ryan (M)	6 4	14 11	1/5/91
Dunk, Harrison (M)	6 0	11 07	25/10/90
Elliott, Tom (F)	6 3	12 00	9/11/90
Hughes, Liam (F)	6 4	13 08	10/8/92
Miller, Ian	6 2	12 02	23/11/83
Norris, Will (G)	6 5	11 09	12/8/93
Sam-Yorke, Delano (F)	6 2	13 05	20/1/89
Tait, Richard (D)	5 11	12 00	2/12/89
Taylor, Greg (D)	6 1	12 02	15/1/90

SKRILL PREMIER ATTENDANCES BY CLUB 2013–14

	Aggregate 2013–14	Average 2013–14	Highest Attendance 2013–14
Luton T	169,906	7,387	10,044 v Forest Green R
Grimsby T	82,057	3,568	5,484 v Lincoln C
Cambridge U	70,956	3,085	6,050 v Luton T
Wrexham	68,850	2,993	6,037 v Chester FC
Chester FC	54,420	2,366	4,326 v Wrexham
Lincoln C	54,135	2,354	5,421 v Grimsby T
Kidderminster H	46,794	2,035	3,420 v Hereford U
Aldershot T	44,775	1,947	3,593 v Hereford U
Hereford U	40,429	1,758	2,545 v Grimsby T
Barnet	39,228	1,706	3,608 v Luton T
Woking	36,832	1,601	4,728 v Aldershot T
FC Halifax T	36,734	1,597	3,586 v Luton T
Macclesfield T	34,780	1,512	2,207 v Aldershot T
Dartford	28,764	1,251	2,869 v Luton T
Nuneaton T	27,809	1,209	3,480 v Luton T
Forest Green R	27,474	1,195	1,858 v Luton T
Southport	24,125	1,049	2,210 v Luton T
Salisbury C	23,070	1,003	2,633 v Luton T
Braintree T	22,854	994	1,518 v Luton T
Tamworth	22,184	965	2,066 v Luton T
Gateshead	20,366	885	2,916 v Cambridge U
Welling U	18,567	807	2,650 v Luton T
Alfreton T	18,514	805	1,771 v Grimsby T
Hyde	15,837	689	2,729 v Luton T

SKRILL PREMIER LEADING GOALSCORERS 2013–14

Player	Club	League	FA Cup	FA Trophy	Play-Offs	Total
Lee Gregory	FC Halifax T	29	2	0	1	32
Andre Gray	Luton T	30	0	0		30
Brett Williams	Aldershot T	24	1	3		28
Scott Boden	Macclesfield T	18	4	0		22
Ben Tomlinson	Lincoln C	18	2	0		20
James Norwood	Forest Green R	19	0	0		19
Scott Rendell	Woking	17	0	2		19
Paul Benson	Luton T	17	1	0		18
Louis Moult	Nuneaton T	17	0	1		18
John Akinde	Alfreton T	17	1	0		18
Ross Lafayette	Welling U	16	1	0		17
Connor Jennings	Macclesfield T	14	3	0		17
Dan Fitchett	Salisbury C	13	3	0		16
Luke Berry	Cambridge U	12	2	2	0	16
Ross Hannah	Grimsby T	13	2	0	0	15
Michael Gash	Kidderminster H	11	3	1		15
Dan Holman	Braintree T	13	0	1		14
James Marwood	Gateshead	10	1	1	2	14
Luke Guttridge	Luton T	13	0	0		13
Jack Marriott	Woking	12	0	1		13

SKRILL NORTH 2013–14

(P) *Promoted into division at end of 2012–13 season.*   (R) *Relegated into division at end of 2012–13 season.*

			Total					Home					Away					
		P	W	D	L	F	A	W	D	L	F	A	W	D	L	F	A	GD	Pts
1	AFC Telford U (R)	42	25	10	7	82	53	16	2	3	46	20	9	8	4	36	33	29	85
2	North Ferriby U (P)	42	24	10	8	80	51	13	6	2	47	25	11	4	6	33	26	29	82
3	Altrincham¶	42	24	9	9	95	51	13	5	3	47	21	11	4	6	48	30	44	81
4	Hednesford T (P)	42	24	6	12	87	65	14	3	4	52	27	10	3	8	35	38	22	78
5	Guiseley	42	23	9	10	78	56	14	2	5	35	20	9	7	5	43	36	22	78
6	Boston U	42	20	12	10	85	60	15	4	2	54	21	5	8	8	31	39	25	72
7	Brackley T	42	17	16	9	66	45	8	8	5	30	23	9	8	4	36	22	21	67
8	Solihull Moors	42	17	14	11	63	52	7	9	5	29	27	10	5	6	34	25	11	65
9	Harrogate T*	42	19	9	14	75	59	12	6	3	47	24	7	3	11	28	35	16	63
10	Bradford PA	42	15	12	15	66	70	7	7	7	36	36	8	5	8	30	34	−4	57
11	Barrow (R)	42	14	14	14	50	56	6	8	7	20	28	8	6	7	30	28	−6	56
12	Colwyn Bay	42	14	13	15	63	67	5	9	7	26	32	9	4	8	37	35	−4	55
13	Leamington (P)	42	13	13	16	54	53	10	3	8	26	19	3	10	8	28	34	1	52
14	Stockport Co (R)	42	12	14	16	58	57	9	7	5	40	27	3	7	11	18	30	1	50
15	Worcester C	42	13	11	18	40	53	8	6	7	26	22	5	5	11	14	31	−13	50
16	Gainsborough Trinity	42	13	6	23	67	86	8	4	9	41	40	5	2	14	26	46	−19	45
17	Gloucester C	42	11	11	20	64	77	7	6	8	36	34	4	5	12	28	43	−13	44
18	Vauxhall Motors	42	12	8	22	43	74	9	3	9	27	36	3	5	13	16	38	−31	44
19	Stalybridge Celtic	42	10	9	23	57	88	6	6	9	34	45	4	3	14	23	43	−31	39
20	Oxford C†	42	9	13	20	50	70	7	6	8	29	26	2	7	12	21	44	−20	37
21	Histon	42	7	11	24	42	76	5	5	11	23	37	2	6	13	19	39	−34	32
22	Workington	42	6	10	26	39	85	6	5	10	25	38	0	5	16	14	47	−46	28

*Harrogate T deducted 3 points for fielding an ineligible player. †Oxford C deducted 3 points for fielding an ineligible player. ¶Altrincham promoted via play-offs.

SKRILL NORTH PLAY-OFFS 2013–14

SEMI-FINALS FIRST LEG

Wednesday 30 April 2014

Guiseley (1) 2 *(Boyes 37, Johnson O 49)*

North Ferriby U (0) 0   1164

Guiseley: Dickinson; Holdsworth, Parker, Hall, Ellis, Lawlor, Brooksby, Boshell, Boyes (Holsgrave 86), Johnson O (Potts 76), Rothery.
North Ferriby U: Nicklin; Robson, Wilde, King, Gray, Wilson M, Clark (Lisles 71), Fry, Kendall (Wilson A 60), Jarman, Emerton.
Referee: I. Hussin.

Wednesday 30 April 2014

Hednesford (1) 2 *(Melbourne 33, Glover 56)*

Altrincham (1) 2 *(Reeves 13, Walshaw 59)*   1209

Hednesford: Crane; Disney, Campion, Bailey, McCone, McPherson (Taylor 60), Riley (Sullivan 83), Johnson, Glover (Robinson 73), Melbourne, Thorley.
Altrincham: Coburn; Densmore, Griffin, Moult, Havern, Leather, Lawrie, Walshaw, Reeves (Marshall 90), Clee (Perry 90), Richman.
Referee: D. Richardson.

SEMI-FINALS SECOND LEG

Saturday 3 May 2014

North Ferriby U (0) 0

Guiseley (0) 1 *(Brooksby 60)*   924

Guiseley won 3-0 on aggregate.
North Ferriby U: Nicklin; Robson (Lisles 83), Peat, D'Laryea, Gray, Wilson M, Clark, Fry, Wilson A, Jarman, Emerton.
Guiseley: Dickinson; Holdsworth, Parker, Hall, Ellis, Lawlor, Brooksby (Meynell 88), Boshell (Potts 86), Boyes, Johnson O (Johnson A 58), Rothery.
Referee: G. Fyvie.

Saturday 3 May 2014

Altrincham (0) 2 *(Reeves 85, Lawrie 87)*

Hednesford (0) 1 *(Thorley 80)*   1974

Altrincham won 4-3 on aggregate.
Altrincham: Coburn; Densmore, Griffin (Marshall 82), Moult, Havern, Lawrie, Leather, Richman, Walshaw, Reeves (Perry 88), Clee.
Hednesford: Crane; Disney, Campion, Bailey, McCone, McPherson (Thompson-Brown 56), Taylor (Robinson 76), Johnson, Glover (Sullivan 89), Melbourne, Thorley.
Referee: R. Jones.

FINAL

Saturday 10 May 2014

Altrincham (0) 2 *(Lawrie 51, Wilkinson 119)*

Guiseley (0) 1 *(Forrest 70)*   4632

Altrincham: Coburn; Densmore, Havern, Leather, Griffin (Marshall 103), Lawrie, Moult, Richman, Clee, Walshaw (Perry 74), Reeves (Wilkson 120).
Guiseley: Drench; Holdsworth, Parker, Hall, Ellis, Lawlor, Potts, Johnson O (Holsgrove 86), Boyes, Johnson A (Forrest 57, Meynell 86), Rothery.
(aet)
Referee: J. Brookes.

SKRILL SOUTH 2013–14

(P) Promoted into division at end of 2012–13 season.   *(R) Relegated into division at end of 2012–13 season.*

			Total				Home					Away					
		P	W	D	L	F	A	W	D	L	F	A	W	D	L	F	A	GD	Pts
1	Eastleigh	42	26	8	8	71	40	17	2	2	40	16	9	6	6	31	24	31	86
2	Sutton U	42	23	12	7	77	39	15	3	3	44	16	8	9	4	33	23	38	81
3	Bromley	42	25	5	12	82	50	15	2	4	54	26	10	3	8	28	24	32	80
4	Ebbsfleet U (R)	42	21	11	10	67	40	13	5	3	34	14	8	6	7	33	26	27	74
5	Dover Ath¶	42	20	9	13	63	38	7	6	8	22	19	13	3	5	41	19	25	69
6	Havant & Waterlooville	42	19	12	11	57	43	13	2	6	36	23	6	10	5	21	20	14	69
7	Bath C	42	18	12	12	64	52	11	6	4	38	26	7	6	8	26	26	12	66
8	Staines T	42	18	9	15	56	57	13	5	3	33	22	5	4	12	23	35	–1	63
9	Concord Rangers (P)	42	17	10	15	58	59	7	5	9	33	34	10	5	6	25	25	–1	61
10	Eastbourne Bor	42	16	10	16	55	59	10	5	6	34	27	6	5	10	21	32	–4	58
11	Weston-super-Mare	42	16	9	17	50	55	11	4	6	31	25	5	5	11	19	30	–5	57
12	Gosport Bor (P)	42	16	7	19	46	51	9	4	8	25	22	7	3	11	21	29	–5	55
13	Boreham Wood	42	14	11	17	65	55	6	7	8	36	34	8	4	9	29	21	10	53
14	Basingstoke T	42	15	8	19	55	56	8	5	8	26	22	7	3	11	29	34	–1	53
15	Bishop's Stortford	42	13	13	16	63	68	8	7	6	31	27	5	6	10	32	41	–5	52
16	Farnborough	42	15	5	22	62	78	11	2	8	37	29	4	3	14	25	49	–16	50
17	Chelmsford C	42	14	7	21	57	77	10	4	7	32	30	4	3	14	25	47	–20	49
18	Maidenhead U	42	12	10	20	55	69	5	4	12	23	35	7	6	8	32	34	–14	46
19	Whitehawk (P)	42	12	10	20	56	71	5	8	8	25	34	7	2	12	31	37	–15	46
20	Hayes & Yeading U	42	13	6	23	45	52	6	3	12	23	25	7	3	11	22	27	–7	45
21	Tonbridge Angels	42	9	13	20	43	77	6	8	7	24	30	3	5	13	19	47	–34	40
22	Dorchester T	42	8	7	27	33	94	4	5	12	18	45	4	2	15	15	49	–61	31

¶*Dover Ath promoted via play-offs.*

SKRILL SOUTH PLAY-OFFS 2013–14

SEMI-FINALS FIRST LEG

Wednesday 30 April 2014

Dover Ath (1) 1 *(Ademola 43)*

Sutton U (1) 1 *(Dundas 1)*   1273

Dover Ath: Walker; Stone, Wynter, Kinnear, Raggett, Orlu, Modeste (Rogers 80), Davies, Elder (Murphy 76), Bellamy, Ademola (Goulding 76).
Sutton U: Brown; Sawyer, King (Sinclair 46), Spillane, Downer, Clough, Haysman (Williams 71), Scannell, Dundas, Taylor (McCallum 71), Binns.
Referee: D. Rock.

Wednesday 30 April 2014

Ebbsfleet U (2) 4 *(May 1, Bricknell 9 (pen), Howe 60, McMahon 80)*

Bromley (0) 0   1693

Ebbsfleet U: Edwards, Howe, Palmer, McMahon, Acheampong, Sankofa, Osborn (Sessegnon 88), Rance, May (Thalassitis 82), Bricknell (Long 69), Cook.
Bromley: Welch; Pooley, Anderson, Nicholls■, Swaine, Holland, Joseph-Dubois, Waldren (Buchanan 70), May (Higgins 83), Goldberg, Kiernan (Fuseini 70).
Referee: N. Lugg.

SEMI-FINALS SECOND LEG

Saturday 3 May 2014

Bromley (1) 1 *(Waldren 25)*

Ebbsfleet U (0) 0   1441

Ebbsfleet U won 4-1 on aggregate.
Bromley: Welch; Holland, Anderson, Waldren, Swaine, Bailey-Dennis (May 67), Joseph-Dubois, Buchanan, Higgins, Goldberg, Dennis (Reid 77).
Ebbsfleet U: Edwards; Howe, Palmer, McMahon, Acheampong (Hall 90), Huke, Osborn (Sankofa 86), Rance, May, Bricknell (Thalassitis 72), Cook.
Referee: S. Ross.

Saturday 3 May 2014

Sutton U (0) 0

Dover Ath (0) 3 *(Modeste 57, 77, Ademola 79)*   1671

Dover Ath won 4-1 on aggregate.
Sutton U: Brown; Sinclair, (McCallum 61), Spetch (King 18), Spillane, Downer, Clough, Sawyer, Scannell, Dundas, Taylor, Williams (Haysman 71).
Dover Ath: Walker; Stone, Wynter, Kinnear, Raggett, Orlu, Modeste (Forbes 83), Davies, Elder, Bellamy, Ademola (Rogers 86).
Referee: C. Powell.

SKRILL SOUTH PLAY-OFF FINAL 2014

Saturday 10 May 2014

Dover Ath (0) 1 *(Elder 56)*

Ebbsfleet U (0) 0   4294

Dover Ath: Walker; Stone, Wynter, Kinnear, Raggett, Orlu, Modeste (Forbes 90), Davies, Elder, Bellamy, Ademola.
Ebbsfleet U: Edwards; Howe, Lorraine, Huke, Palmer, Osborn (Long 71), McMahon, Corcoran, Cook, May, Bricknell (Thalassitis 64, Sessegnon 90).
Referee: M. Pottage.

ALDERSHOT TOWN

Ground: The EBB Stadium at the Recreation Ground, High Street, Aldershot, Hampshire GU11 1TW.
Tel: (01252) 320211.   *Fax:* (01252) 324347.   *Website:* www.theshots.co.uk   *Year Formed:* 1926.
Record Attendance: 19,138 v Carlisle U, FA Cup 4th rd (replay), 28 January 1970.   *Nickname:* 'The Shots'.
Manager: Andy Scott.   *Colours:* Red shirts with white trim, blue shorts with white trim, blue socks.

ALDERSHOT TOWN – SKRILL PREMIER 2013–14 LEAGUE RECORD

Match No.	Date	Venue	Opponents	Result		H/T Score	Lg Pos.	Goalscorers	Atten- dance
1	Aug 10	A	Grimsby T	D	1-1	0-0	24	Oastler [58]	4037
2	13	H	Dartford	W	3-0	1-0	24	Williams, B [18], Oyeleke [61], Wickham [87]	2138
3	17	H	Cambridge U	L	0-1	0-1	24		2022
4	24	A	Salisbury C	L	0-1	0-0	24		1175
5	26	H	Woking	W	2-1	2-0	24	Paterson [1], Williams, B [18]	3138
6	31	A	Southport	L	0-1	0-1	24		1012
7	Sept 7	H	Macclesfield T	W	1-0	0-0	24	Molesley [66]	1752
8	13	A	Hereford U	W	2-0	1-0	22	Williams, B 2 [14, 66]	1851
9	17	H	Barnet	D	3-3	1-0	22	Williams, B 2 [3, 69], Oyeleke [64]	1740
10	21	H	Wrexham	W	2-0	0-0	22	Molesley [61], Roberts [80]	1915
11	24	A	Welling U	L	0-1	0-1	23		837
12	27	A	Kidderminster H	D	0-0	0-0	21		2049
13	Oct 5	H	Grimsby T	L	0-3	0-2	23		2118
14	8	H	Luton T	D	3-3	3-2	23	Goodman [13], Roberts [24], Molesley [45]	2693
15	12	A	Lincoln C	W	1-0	0-0	23	Williams, B (pen) [48]	2748
16	19	H	Alfreton T	L	2-3	1-2	23	Gibbs [28], Williams, B [47]	1732
17	Nov 2	A	Chester FC	D	1-1	0-0	23	Gibbs [90]	2029
18	12	A	Cambridge U	L	0-4	0-1	23		3110
19	16	A	FC Halifax T	L	0-4	0-3	23		1418
20	23	H	Southport	W	5-1	4-0	23	Williams, B 3 (1 pen) [1, 24, 77 (p)], Smith (og) [12], Mekki [19]	1592
21	26	H	Braintree T	W	2-1	1-1	21	Williams, B [21], Paterson [90]	1215
22	Dec 21	H	Tamworth	W	6-0	2-0	19	Oyeleke [11], Molesley [33], Williams, B 2 (1 pen) [63 (p), 73], O'Brien [66], Roberts [77]	1598
23	26	A	Forest Green R	L	1-3	1-1	20	Roberts [42]	1676
24	28	H	Welling U	W	3-1	0-0	19	Williams, B (pen) [68], O'Brien 2 [78, 86]	2058
25	Jan 4	A	Wrexham	L	1-2	1-0	20	Williams, B [20]	2819
26	14	A	Gateshead	D	0-0	0-0	20		724
27	21	A	Barnet	W	3-1	1-1	19	Roberts [3], Bubb [48], Molesley [55]	1387
28	25	H	FC Halifax T	D	2-2	1-1	19	Roberts [45], Stanley [66]	1977
29	28	A	Nuneaton T	L	1-2	0-2	19	Plummer [84]	718
30	Feb 18	H	Forest Green R	D	2-2	0-0	19	Mekki [58], Bubb [61]	1407
31	22	A	Hyde	D	2-2	1-1	19	Williams, B [37], Partington [85]	520
32	25	A	Dartford	D	1-1	0-1	21	Williams, B [88]	1125
33	Mar 1	H	Lincoln C	L	2-3	1-2	21	Bubb [10], Scott [53]	1944
34	8	A	Tamworth	L	0-1	0-0	21		915
35	11	H	Chester FC	W	2-0	1-0	21	Williams, B 2 [20, 83]	1545
36	15	H	Nuneaton T	D	2-2	0-2	21	Scott [63], Rowlands [82]	1606
37	18	H	Kidderminster H	D	0-0	0-0	21		1558
38	22	A	Braintree T	L	0-1	0-1	21		1090
39	25	H	Gateshead	L	1-2	1-0	21	Scott [32]	1358
40	29	H	Hyde	W	1-0	1-0	21	Mekki [45]	1591
41	Apr 5	A	Luton T	L	0-1	0-0	21		8558
42	8	A	Alfreton T	W	4-1	2-0	21	Rowlands [11], Phillips [16], Oyeleke [57], Molesley [66]	620
43	12	A	Macclesfield T	D	1-1	0-0	20	Williams, B (pen) [90]	2207
44	18	H	Salisbury C	W	3-2	2-2	19	Williams, B 2 (1 pen) [16, 23 (p)], Oastler [48]	2485
45	21	A	Woking	W	2-1	0-0	19	Williams, B (pen) [65], Molesley [83]	4728
46	26	H	Hereford U	L	1-2	0-1	19	Oyeleke [76]	3593

Final League Position: 19

GOALSCORERS

League (69): Williams, B 24 (7 pens), Molesley 7, Roberts 6, Oyeleke 5, Bubb 3, Mekki 3, O'Brien 3, Scott 3, Gibbs 2, Oastler 2, Paterson 2, Rowlands 2, Goodman 1, Partington 1, Phillips 1, Plummer 1, Stanley 1, Wickham 1, own goal 1.
The Budweiser FA Cup (2): Paterson 1, Williams, B 1.
FA Trophy (14): O'Brien 4, Williams, B 3 (1 pen), Young 2, Oyeleke 1, Paterson 1, Roberts 1, Stanley 1, own goal 1.

Morris 31	Oastler 37 + 2	Goodman 20 + 1	Webster 24	Barker 41 + 1	Mekki 20 + 6	Stanley 46	Rowlands 25 + 11	Molesley 28 + 3	Williams B 42 + 1	Paterson 12 + 13	Oyeleke 32 + 3	Roberts 24 + 15	Wickham 1 + 6	Douglas — + 2	Brown — + 3	Maloney — + 2	Gibbs 24 + 7	Young 10 + 5	Pope 5	Henly 7	Butler 11 + 2	Tonkin 10 + 4	Strutton 1	O'Brien 5	Partington 8	Bubb 13 + 6	Scott 11 + 9	Plummer 2 + 4	Taiwo 6	Williams L — + 1	Martin 3	Phillips 7	Cornick — + 2	Match No.
1	2	3	4	5	6^1	7	8	9^2	10	11^3	12	13	14																					1
1	2^3	3	4	5		7	8^2	6	10	11^1	9	12	13	14																				2
1	2	3	4	5^3		8	7	6^2	10	11^1	9	13	12	14																				3
1	2	3	4	5		8	7	6^2	10		9^1	12	11^3	13	14																			4
1	2	3	4	5		8	7	6	11	10^1	9	12																						5
1	2	3	4	5		8	6	7^3	11	10^1	9^2	13			14	12																		6
1	2	3	4	5		8	7^1	9	10^2	11	6	12	13																					7
1	2	3	4	5		7	8	11	9	10^1	6	12																						8
1	2	4	5	3		7	6	8	11	10^1	9^2	12					13																	9
1		3	4	5	2	8	9	10	11^2	7	12						13	6^1																10
1	2^1	4	3	5		7	12	8	9	10^2	6	11					13																	11
		4	3	5	6	7	9	10	12	2	8						11		11^1	1														12
	2^2	3	4	5	6	7^1	8	11	13	10	12						14	9^1	1															13
	2	3	4			7		9	11	8	5^1	12					10	6	1															14
	3	4	5			7	12	6	11	13	2	10^2					9^1	8	1															15
	2^2	3	4	5		8	13	9^1	10	14	7	12					11^1	6	1															16
		4	3	5	6^3	8	14		11	12	2	7^2					13	9^1		1	10													17
	3	2	4	9^2	6	7^1		10	13	8	11^3						14	12		1	5													18
	3		4	6^1	8	7^2		10	11	2							9	12		1	5	13												19
	3		4^2	7^3	8	14		10	12	2	9						13	6		1	5	11^1												20
	3			9	7			11	12	8	5^4						2	6		1	4			10^1										21
	2		3	4	5	14	9^1	10	13	7^3	8						6	12		1				11^2										22
	2^1	12	3^3	4	5^2	6		10	14	9	7						8	13		1				11										23
1	2	3		4	12	8		10^2	13	6	9						5	7^1						11										24
1	2^1	3		5	12	7	8	10	13	9^2							6							11	4									25
1			4	5	12	8			6^1	10	13	7					2								9	3	11^2							26
1		3		5	13	7		8^3	6^2	10		14	9				2									4	11^1	12						27
1		3		5		7		8^1	6^3	10		12	9^2				2									4	11	14	13					28
1		3		5		6^2	7	14	10		8^3	9^1					2									4	11	12	13					29
1		3		5^3		6^2	8	10		9^1							2								14	4	11	13	12	7				30
1		3		5		9^1	7	8	10								2									4	11	12	6					31
1^1		3		5		7			10			9					2								12^3	4^1	11	14	6^2	8	13			32
	3		4	5		7	13		10		9						2									6	11	12	8^2			1		33
	3		4	12		8			10		9						2							5		6	11^1	7				1		34
	2^3	3	4	6^1	7	8		10	13	12	9^2						12				9^2	5				11	14				1			35
1	12	3^2	4	6^3	7	8	14	10									2				9^1	5				11	13							36
1	2		4	6^2	7		12	10	13								8				9^1	5				9	11		3					37
1	3		4	6^2	7	8	13	10									2				9^1	5				12	11							38
1	3		4	14	7	13	6	10^8				9^2					2					5				11^1	12		8^3					39
1	13		4^2	6	9	7		10	8^3			9^2					2					12		5^1		11					3	14		40
1	3		6	8	7^3	10^2		9	13			2					5					12				11^1					4	14		41
1	3		10	7	8^1	6		2	9			5					12					11									4			42
1	3		10^1	7	6^2	9^1	12	8	5			2					13					14				11					4			43
1	3		12	6	7	13	9^1	10	8			2^1					14					5				11					4^2			44
1	4		5	8	6^1	9	10^2	7	12			2					13									11					3			45
1	2		4^1	6^2	3	14	8^3	10	11	12		5					13									9					7			46

The Budweiser FA Cup

Fourth Qualifying	Shortwood U	(a)	1-1
Replay	Shortwood U	(h)	1-2

FA Trophy

First Round	Weston Super Mare	(h)	1-1
Replay	Weston Super Mare	(a)	5-2
Second Round	Worcester C	(h)	4-1
Third Round	Guiseley	(h)	3-0
Quarter-Finals	Havant & Waterlooville	(a)	1-4

ALFRETON TOWN

Ground: The Impact Arena, North Street, Alfreton, Derbyshire DE55 7FZ.   *Tel:* (01773) 830 277.
Fax: (01773) 836 164.   *Website:* www.alfretontownfc.com   *Year Formed:* 1959.
Record Attendance: 5,023 v Matlock T, Central Alliance League, 23 April 1960.   *Nickname:* 'The Reds'.
Manager: Nicky Law.   *Colours:* Red shirts with white trim, red shorts with white trim, red socks.

ALFRETON TOWN – SKRILL PREMIER 2013–14 LEAGUE RECORD

Match No.	Date	Venue	Opponents	Result	H/T Score	Lg Pos.	Goalscorers	Attendance
1	Aug 10	A	Dartford	L	0-1	0-1	17		1202
2	13	H	Kidderminster H	W	3-1	1-0	11	Bradley 2 [11, 70], Shaw [51]	722
3	17	H	Salisbury C	W	3-2	1-1	5	Akinde, J 3 [39, 63, 78]	463
4	24	A	Grimsby T	L	1-3	0-2	12	Fenton [90]	3245
5	26	H	Hereford U	W	2-1	1-1	8	Akinde, J [12], Law [90]	740
6	31	A	Forest Green R	L	1-3	0-3	13	Bradley [79]	1027
7	Sept 7	H	Woking	W	3-1	2-1	7	Shaw 2 [9, 43], Meadows [90]	628
8	14	A	Macclesfield T	W	1-0	1-0	5	Meadows [27]	1271
9	17	H	Cambridge U	D	1-1	1-0	7	Clayton [15]	731
10	21	H	Barnet	W	3-1	1-0	3	McGrath [13], Clayton 2 [54, 61]	783
11	24	A	Southport	L	1-2	0-0	6	Akinde, J [49]	726
12	28	A	Braintree T	L	1-3	0-0	11	Wood [89]	927
13	Oct 5	H	Forest Green R	W	3-2	2-2	8	Shaw [12], Wishart 2 [43, 51]	582
14	8	H	Chester FC	L	0-1	0-1	10		743
15	12	A	Gateshead	L	0-3	0-0	12		778
16	19	A	Aldershot T	W	3-2	2-1	12	Shaw [23], Law [31], Speight [56]	1732
17	Nov 2	H	FC Halifax T	W	3-0	2-0	9	Speight 2 [14, 31], Akinde, J [49]	900
18	12	A	Tamworth	L	0-1	0-1	10		716
19	16	H	Braintree T	W	3-1	2-0	6	Akinde, J [15], Shaw [42], Law [66]	904
20	23	A	Hyde	W	2-1	0-0	5	Bradley [74], Westwood [78]	448
21	26	A	Nuneaton T	L	0-3	0-2	6		715
22	Dec 7	H	Luton T	L	0-5	0-4	8		1279
23	14	A	Kidderminster H	W	3-1	0-1	6	Wylde 2 [52, 68], Akinde, J (pen) [89]	1834
24	21	H	Dartford	W	2-1	0-1	4	Clayton 2 [52, 60]	575
25	26	H	Wrexham	W	3-2	0-0	4	Wylde [73], Akinde, J [85], Westwood [90]	3371
26	28	H	Southport	W	2-1	2-0	3	Wylde [22], Meadows [30]	976
27	Jan 1	H	Wrexham	W	1-0	1-0	3	Akinde, J [45]	765
28	4	A	Barnet	L	0-1	0-1	3		1400
29	7	A	Lincoln C	L	1-4	0-2	3	Fenton [55]	1877
30	25	A	Welling U	W	2-1	1-1	3	Law [17], Harrad (pen) [58]	677
31	Feb 8	A	Salisbury C	D	0-0	0-0	3		623
32	11	A	Cambridge U	W	1-0	1-0	3	Wood [25]	2106
33	22	H	Gateshead	D	1-1	0-0	3	Shaw [71]	817
34	Mar 1	A	Luton T	L	0-3	0-1	4		8412
35	8	H	Lincoln C	D	1-1	0-0	3	Harrad [61]	1331
36	11	H	Hyde	W	3-0	1-0	3	Harrad 2 [19, 82], Akinde, J [50]	506
37	15	A	Chester FC	W	1-0	0-0	3	Harrad (pen) [66]	2042
38	18	H	Tamworth	W	4-2	2-1	3	Harrad (pen) [41], Shaw [45], Akinde, J [73], Clayton [83]	594
39	24	A	FC Halifax T	L	0-2	0-1	3		1454
40	29	H	Nuneaton T	D	1-1	1-0	4	Akinde, J [32]	789
41	Apr 5	H	Welling U	D	2-2	1-1	6	Fenton [19], Akinde, J [73]	599
42	8	A	Aldershot T	L	1-4	0-2	6	Akinde, J [56]	620
43	12	A	Woking	L	1-2	1-0	7	Akinde, J [20]	1485
44	18	H	Grimsby T	D	3-3	1-2	8	Law [25], Akinde, J (pen) [51], Clayton [80]	1771
45	21	A	Hereford U	L	2-3	1-1	9	Akinde, J [7], Harrad [87]	2445
46	26	H	Macclesfield T	L	0-1	0-0	11		696

Final League Position: 11

GOALSCORERS

League (69): Akinde, J 18 (2 pens), Shaw 8, Clayton 7, Harrad 7 (3 pens), Law 5, Bradley 4, Wylde 4, Fenton 3, Meadows 3, Speight 3, Westwood 2, Wishart 2, Wood 2, McGrath 1.
The Budweiser FA Cup (4): Speight 2 (1 pen), Akinde, J 1, McGrath 1.
FA Trophy (0).

Atkins 22	Wood 44 + 1	Westwood 24 + 2	Fenton 32	Franklin 22 + 4	McGrath 22 + 1	Shaw 34 + 7	Bradley 40 + 4	Law 33 + 6	Meadows 24 + 14	Clayton 19 + 13	Wishart 4 + 15	Ramsey-Dickson — + 1	Akinde J 42 + 1	Taylor 1 + 6	Wylde 26 + 2	Rowe-Turner 30	Akinde S — + 3	Kempson 13 + 6	Speight 4	Worsnop 23	Poku 15 + 2	Harrad 13 + 3	Jones 10	Hoganson 5 + 1	Whitehouse 3 + 1	Wildsmith 1 + 1	Match No.
1	2	3	4	5	6	7^2	8	9	10^1	11	12	13															1
1	2	3	4	5	9	7	8	6		10			11														2
1	2	3	4	5	8	7^2	9	6	12	10^1	13		11														3
1	2	3	4	5	6	8^3	9^1	7	12	10^2	13		11	14													4
1	2	3	4	5		7	8	6	9	12	10^1		11														5
1	2	3^1	4	5		7	8	6	9^2	14	10^3		11	13	12												6
1	2		4		7	8	9	6	12	10^1			11		3	5											7
1	2		4		6	7	8		9	11			10		3	5											8
1	2		4		7	8	6	12	9^1	11^2	13		10		3	5											9
1	2		4		6	9	7	12	8^1	11			10		3	5											10
1	2	13	4^2		7	6	8^1	12	10^3	11	14		9		3	5											11
1	2	12	3^1		7	8	14	6	9^2	11^3	13		10		4	5											12
1	2	4^2			7	9	8	6		10^1	12		11		3	5											13
1	2		3		8	7	6	13	9^2		10^1		11		4^3	5	12	14									14
1	2		3		6^1	8	7	5	9				11^1			12	4	10									15
1	2^1	3	12			7	9	8	6				10		4	5		11									16
1	2	3	4		8	7	6	9					11		5			10									17
1	2	4	3		9	8	7^1	6^2	12	13			11^2	14	5			10									18
1	2	4			7	6	8	9	11				10		3	5											19
1	2	4			7	8^1	6	9	11^3	13	12		10^2	14	3	5											20
1	5	3	4^3		8	7^1	6	9		12	10^2		11	13	14	2											21
1	2	4		5	8	7^2		6	10^1	14			11	9^1	3		13	12									22
	2	9^1	5	6		7	8		12				11		4	10		3		1							23
	2		5	6^1	13	9^2	8		7	11	12				3	10		4		1							24
	7	3			8^1	12	6		9	10^2	13		11		4	5		2		1							25
	7	2		13		8	9^2		6	10^1	12		11		3	5		4		1							26
	7	2		9		13	6^2		8	10^1	12		11		3	5		4		1							27
	7	2		10		13	6^3	14	8^2		12		11		3^1	5		4		1	9						28
	7^2	2	4			6^1	8^3	12	13	11	14		10			5		3		1	9						29
	7	2		13			9	8^2		12			10^1		3	5		4		1	6	11					30
	7^1	2	4	5		8	6	10	12	13			11^2		3					1	9						31
	6	2^1	3	5		12	7	8	14				10^3		4^2			13		1	9	11					32
	8^2		4	5		12	6	9^1	14	13			10		3					1	7	11^3	2				33
	8^1		3	5		7	6	10					12		4					1	9	11	2				34
	8		4	5		11	9	6							3					1	7	10	2				35
	13		3	5^1		7	9	2	12	14			10^3		4					1	8	11		6^2			36
	5		4			9	7	2	13	14			11^3		3^1			12		1	8	10		6^2			37
	6^1		3	12		7	13	2	9^2	14			11					4^3		1	8	10		5			38
	6		3	5		8^1	12	2		10^2			11		4					1	7^1	9		14	13		39
	7		3^1			9^1	13	2	14				10		4			12		1		11^2	6	5	8		40
	8		3			13	6	2	12				10		4					1	7	11^1		5	9^2		41
	8		3			9	2	10					11		5			4		1	7^1	12	6				42
	7		3^1	5		9^2		6	13	14			10		4			12		1		11^3	2		8		43
	5					12	8	7	6^1	11^3			10		4			3		1	13	14	2	9^2			44
		4				9^1	6	7	8^2				11					5		3	13	12	2	10		1	45
	2	3		5		8^1	6	9	13				11	12	4					1^2	7	10^3				14	46

The Budweiser FA Cup
Fourth Qualifying   North Ferriby U   (a)   3-1
First Round   Wrexham   (a)   1-3

FA Trophy
First Round   Nuneaton T   (h)   0-1

BARNET

Ground: The Hive Stadium, Camrose Avenue, Edgware HA8 6AG. *Tel:* (020) 831 3800. *Fax:* (020) 8447 0655.
Website: www.barnetfc.com *Year Formed:* 1888. *Record Attendance:* 11,026 v Wycombe W, FA Amateur Cup, 1951–52.
Nickname: 'The Bees'. *Manager:* Martin Allen. *Colours:* Amber shirts with black trim, black shorts, amber socks
with black trim.

BARNET – SKRILL PREMIER 2013–14 LEAGUE RECORD

Match No.	Date	Venue	Opponents	Result	H/T Score	Lg Pos.	Goalscorers	Atten- dance
1	Aug 10	H	Chester FC	W	3-0	0-0	2	Gambin [46], Hyde 2 [63, 73]	2543
2	13	A	Tamworth	D	0-0	0-0	3		1379
3	17	A	Gateshead	W	2-1	1-1	2	Marsh-Brown [37], Hyde [88]	639
4	24	H	Nuneaton T	D	1-1	1-1	4	Hyde [16]	1507
5	26	A	Braintree T	W	3-0	0-0	1	Marsh-Brown [46], Byrne [72], Hyde [90]	1480
6	31	H	Hyde	W	3-2	2-0	2	Marsh-Brown [5], Byrne [40], Crawford [84]	1669
7	Sept 7	A	FC Halifax T	L	1-2	0-1	3	Weston [65]	1651
8	14	H	Lincoln C	D	1-1	0-0	4	Marsh-Brown [56]	1913
9	17	A	Aldershot T	D	3-3	0-1	5	Weston [57], Mengerink [78], Crawford [88]	1740
10	21	A	Alfreton T	L	1-3	0-1	8	Marsh-Brown [49]	783
11	24	H	Macclesfield T	L	1-2	0-2	12	Vilhete [74]	1179
12	28	H	Salisbury C	W	3-1	0-1	10	Abdulla [72], Yiadom [74], Marsh-Brown [88]	1499
13	Oct 5	A	Welling U	D	1-1	0-1	10	Marsh-Brown (pen) [72]	1017
14	8	A	Woking	D	0-0	0-0	11		1413
15	13	H	Wrexham	D	1-1	1-0	9	Acheampong [7]	2143
16	19	A	Hereford U	W	1-0	1-0	8	Abdulla [36]	1632
17	Nov 2	H	Kidderminster H	W	1-0	1-0	7	Villa [25]	1557
18	12	H	Welling U	D	0-0	0-0	6		1274
19	16	H	Cambridge U	D	2-2	2-2	7	Villa [38], Weston [45]	2853
20	23	A	Grimsby T	L	1-2	0-0	11	Stephens [84]	3441
21	26	A	Dartford	W	2-0	2-0	7	Marsh-Brown [19], Villa [33]	803
22	Dec 7	H	Dartford	W	1-0	1-0	6	Nurse [30]	1461
23	21	A	Hyde	W	1-0	0-0	5	Nurse [57]	499
24	26	H	Luton T	L	1-2	0-2	7	Hyde [69]	3608
25	28	A	Salisbury C	L	1-2	1-1	9	Hyde [20]	1343
26	Jan 1	A	Luton T	L	1-2	0-2	9	Hyde [71]	7543
27	4	H	Alfreton T	W	1-0	1-0	6	Lopez [40]	1400
28	18	A	Chester FC	L	1-2	0-1	10	Hyde [84]	2179
29	21	H	Aldershot T	L	1-3	1-1	10	Vilhete [45]	1387
30	25	H	Southport	W	1-0	0-0	7	Vilhete [90]	1510
31	Feb 15	H	Tamworth	W	1-0	0-0	9	Villa [84]	1296
32	18	H	Grimsby T	W	2-1	1-0	6	Vilhete [3], Hyde [81]	1375
33	22	A	Wrexham	W	1-0	0-0	4	Hyde [79]	2925
34	25	A	Forest Green R	W	2-1	2-0	3	Byrne [1], Lopez [42]	869
35	Mar 1	A	Woking	L	1-3	1-2	3	Weston [26]	1708
36	8	H	Gateshead	L	0-1	0-0	4		1361
37	15	A	Kidderminster H	L	0-1	0-0	7		1950
38	18	A	Macclesfield T	L	0-2	0-0	9		1153
39	22	H	Hereford U	W	2-0	2-0	6	Marsh-Brown 2 [14, 23]	1497
40	29	A	Cambridge U	D	1-1	0-1	9	Dymond [69]	3386
41	Apr 5	H	Forest Green R	W	2-1	1-0	8	Gjokaj [19], Byrne [80]	1466
42	8	A	Southport	D	1-1	1-1	8	Byrne [45]	774
43	12	H	FC Halifax T	L	0-4	0-3	8		1683
44	19	A	Nuneaton T	W	1-0	0-0	8	Gjokaj [56]	852
45	21	H	Braintree T	D	1-1	1-0	8	Marsh-Brown [40]	1339
46	26	A	Lincoln C	D	3-3	1-1	8	Abdulla (pen) [6], Allen [57], Hyde [90]	2812

Final League Position: 8

GOALSCORERS

League (58): Hyde 12, Marsh-Brown 11 (1 pen), Byrne 5, Vilhete 4, Villa 4, Weston 4, Abdulla 3 (1 pen), Crawford 2,
Gjokaj 2, Lopez 2, Nurse 2, Acheampong 1, Allen 1, Dymond 1, Gambin 1, Mengerink 1, Stephens 1, Yiadom 1.
The Budweiser FA Cup (3): Lopez 2, Marsh-Brown 1.
FA Trophy (2): Marsh-Brown 1, Sykes 1.

Stack 31	Yiadom 42	Stephens 46	Saville 21 + 3	Johnson 27 + 3	Marsh-Brown 35 + 3	Byrne 32 + 4	Weston 39	Gambin 16 + 8	Hyde 25 + 2	Garcia Casabella 10 + 1	Villa 18 + 10	Mengerink 5 + 15	Crawford 12 + 17	Acheampong 13 + 8	Vilhete 18 + 12	Brown 3	Abdulla 15 + 8	Davids 8	Cadogan 16 + 6	Allen 2 + 3	Lopez 12 + 3	Fletcher 2 + 1	Nurse 9 + 9	Sykes 3 + 1	Jupp 15 + 2	Adams 3 + 2	Gjokaj 14	Dymond 2 + 4	Peterson 1	Harper 6	Muggleton 1 + 5	Lowe 2 + 1	Warren 2	Match No.
1	2	3	4	5	6¹	7	8	9²	10³	11	12	13	14																					1
1	2	3	4¹	5	9²	8	7	11³	10	6		13	14	12																				2
1	2	3		5	7³	9	6	10²	11	8¹		13	12	4	14																			3
1	2	3		5	9	8	7	11²	10	6¹		13	12	4																				4
1	2	3			9³	6²	7	11	10		12	8	4¹	14	5	13																		5
1	2	3			9²	7	8	10¹	11	6	12³	13	4	14	5																			6
1	2	4		5	6	7	8	9³	10	11²	13	12	3¹	14																				7
1	2	4		5	6³	8	7	9²	10¹		13	14	11	3			12																	8
1	8	2	14	3	6	7	5	9¹			12	13	11	4¹			10²																	9
1	2	3		5	9¹	7	6	11²			13	14	10	4³	12		8																	10
1	2	4		5		8²	7	12			11	9	13	3¹	6			10																11
1	2	3		5	6	7¹		9²			4	11³	10		14	13	12	8																12
1	2⁴	3	4		10		7		13	8¹		11²	12	14	6³		5	9																13
1		3	4	2	9		7			8	13	11¹	10²	5			6	12																14
1		3	4		5		7³		8¹	9²		2	14		12	6²	10	13	11															15
1		4	5		6³	12		10	13		3	2		7		9		11²	8¹	14														16
1	2	3		8³	6²			9¹	14	12	13	5		7		10	11¹																	17
1	2	3	4¹	5		9	7		8	12	10		6²	11			13																	18
1	6	4	3	5		13	7²		8		11	2¹		10	9			12																19
1	2	3	4	5			9	13		6		7²	8	10			12	11¹																20
1	5	2	3	4	7		6	8³			10¹			9	12		13	14	11³															21
1	2	3	5		6	14	7	9²			11³		8	4¹	13		12	10¹																22
1	2	5	4	3	6²	7	8		11¹	9³			14			13	12	10																23
1	2⁹	3	4	5		6	7		10	8¹		14	13		9²	12	11⁴																	24
1		3	5	6	2¹	9³	12	10		13	14	7²		8¹		11	4⁴																	25
1¹	2	4	5	3	10	6	8		11	7³	13		14		9²		12																	26
	2	3	4	5		7	6		10	8³	12		14	13	9²	11¹			1															27
	2⁹	4	3	5	6	7		9	12	11	8¹	13	14		10²				1															28
	2	4	3²	6	8	7		9¹	10		12	13	11	5³			14	1																29
	2	4	3		9³	7	6		10²	8	13		5	14			11¹	12			1													30
	2	4	3	14	6³	8	7		10	9²			5			13	11¹			1	12													31
	2	3		13	6³	7	8		10	9			5²			14	11¹			1	12	4												32
	2	3		5	6¹	7	9		11³	13	14					8	12			1	10¹	4												33
	2	3		14	12	8	7		11¹		13			5³	9		6	10²			1		4											34
	2	4			3	6	10¹	9			14			12	8²		11³	13		1	7	5												35
	2	3	4		6²	7	12			14	5	8	9³	10¹	13		1	11																36
1⁹	2	3		12		7	13		6	11	5	8¹	9²			10³	14	4																37
	2	3		6²		9	13		14	11	5	12	7²				1	4	8¹	10														38
	2	3	14	5¹	6²	7	12			10¹	9				11		1	4	13		8													39
	2	3		9	6¹	7		10		13	5³					11²	1	4	12		8	14												40
1	2	3	14	5²	6	7		10³			9	12			11¹		4				8	13												41
1	2	3		6³	7		10			5²	9¹					11		4	12		8	13	14											42
1	2	3		5	12	9	7	10			11					4	6¹				8²	13												43
	2	3			8		13³	10		12	7		9¹				1		4	14			5	6²	11									44
1	2	4		3³	9	6	8	11¹	13					12		10				5		7²	14											45
	2	3			13		9	14	12		11¹	5		7²	6		1		4					10³	8									46

The Budweiser FA Cup
Fourth Qualifying　Concord Rangers　(h)　3-0
First Round　Preston NE　(a)　0-6

FA Trophy
First Round　Hayes & Yeading U　(a)　1-0
Second Round　Grimsby T　(h)　1-2

BRAINTREE TOWN

Ground: The Amlin Stadium, Clockhouse Way, Braintree, Essex CM7 3RD.   *Tel:* (01376) 345 617.   *Fax:* (01376) 330 976.
Website: www.braintreetownfc.org.uk   *Year Formed:* 1898.
Record Attendance: 2,029 v Cambridge U, Blue Square Premier League, 1 January 2012.
Nickname: 'The Iron'.   *Manager:* Alan Devonshire.   *Colours:* Orange shirts with white trim, blue shorts, blue socks.

BRAINTREE TOWN – SKRILL PREMIER 2013–14 LEAGUE RECORD

Match No.	Date	Venue	Opponents	Result		H/T Score	Lg Pos.	Goalscorers	Atten- dance
1	Aug 10	A	Hereford U	D	1-1	1-0	9	Smith (og) [8]	2033
2	13	H	Woking	W	2-0	2-0	4	Holman [17], Marks [19]	995
3	17	H	Kidderminster H	L	0-1	0-0	12		874
4	24	A	Dartford	W	2-0	0-0	7	Massey [69], Enver-Marum [90]	1015
5	26	H	Barnet	L	0-3	0-0	13		1480
6	31	A	Macclesfield T	W	1-0	0-0	9	Enver-Marum [47]	1264
7	Sept 7	H	Forest Green R	D	1-1	1-1	12	Davis (pen) [45]	944
8	14	A	Grimsby T	L	0-1	0-1	13		3403
9	17	H	Salisbury C	D	1-1	1-1	14	Marks [28]	594
10	21	H	Southport	W	1-0	1-0	12	Marks [37]	924
11	24	A	Wrexham	W	3-2	2-2	9	Carrington (og) [3], Wells [21], Tomassen (og) [70]	2731
12	28	H	Alfreton T	W	3-1	0-0	5	Strutton [61], Marks [84], Sparkes [87]	927
13	Oct 5	A	Hyde	W	3-0	1-0	3	Strutton 2 [37, 57], Cox [67]	402
14	8	H	Welling U	L	2-3	1-1	4	Strutton [27], Cox [89]	1119
15	12	A	Nuneaton T	D	1-1	1-0	7	Paine [30]	1031
16	19	H	Chester FC	W	3-0	3-0	4	Strutton 2 [6, 7], Wells [28]	1132
17	Nov 2	A	Tamworth	D	0-0	0-0	6		716
18	12	H	Luton T	L	1-2	0-1	7	Holman [67]	1518
19	16	A	Alfreton T	L	1-3	0-2	10	Daley [47]	904
20	23	H	FC Halifax T	W	1-0	0-0	8	Davis (pen) [62]	943
21	26	A	Aldershot T	L	1-2	1-1	9	Davis (pen) [16]	1215
22	Dec 7	A	Chester FC	W	2-0	1-0	7	Holman 2 [34, 58]	1736
23	26	A	Cambridge U	L	0-1	0-1	11		4194
24	28	H	Tamworth	W	2-0	0-0	10	Peters [52], Mulley [76]	811
25	Jan 11	A	Woking	L	0-1	0-0	11		1270
26	Feb 22	A	Kidderminster H	D	2-2	0-0	17	Paine [53], Holman [67]	1653
27	25	A	Cambridge U	W	1-0	0-0	16	Sparkes [67]	1016
28	Mar 1	H	Hyde	W	2-1	1-1	16	Mensah [5], Holman [84]	754
29	8	H	Hereford U	D	1-1	1-1	17	Holman [34]	805
30	11	A	Wrexham	W	3-0	1-0	13	Marks [38], Holman [75], Jakubiak [90]	699
31	13	A	Forest Green R	W	2-0	1-0	11	Holman (pen) [36], Mensah [68]	841
32	15	A	Lincoln C	L	0-2	0-0	12		2002
33	18	H	Lincoln C	L	0-2	0-1	13		787
34	22	H	Aldershot T	W	1-0	1-0	12	Holman [3]	1090
35	25	A	Welling U	W	2-0	1-0	11	Davis 2 (1 pen) [35, 51 (p)]	403
36	27	H	Nuneaton T	W	2-1	2-0	5	Streete (og) [8], Holman [17]	802
37	29	A	Gateshead	L	0-1	0-0	8		859
38	Apr 1	A	Southport	W	4-0	1-0	6	Marks [6], Holman 2 [52, 77], Mulley [62]	714
39	3	H	FC Halifax T	D	0-0	0-0	4		1535
40	5	H	Salisbury C	L	0-1	0-1	7		905
41	8	H	Macclesfield T	L	0-1	0-0	7		739
42	12	A	Luton T	W	3-2	2-0	6	Wells [16], Mulley [21], Isaac [56]	10,020
43	15	H	Gateshead	D	0-0	0-0	6		901
44	18	H	Dartford	W	1-0	1-0	6	Davis [24]	1200
45	21	A	Barnet	D	1-1	0-1	6	Davis (pen) [58]	1339
46	26	H	Grimsby T	D	0-0	0-0	6		1489

Final League Position: 6

GOALSCORERS

League (57): Holman 13 (1 pen), Davis 7 (5 pens), Marks 6, Strutton 6, Mulley 3, Wells 3, Cox 2, Enver-Marum 2, Mensah 2, Paine 2, Sparkes 2, Daley 1, Isaac 1, Jakubiak 1, Massey 1, Peters 1, own goals 4.
The Budweiser FA Cup (3): Isaac 1, Marks 1, Paine 1.
FA Trophy (4): Cox 1, Holman 1, Marks 1, Sparkes 1.

McDonald 17 + 1	Peters 39	Habergham 42	Paine 44	Wells 42	Isaac 38 + 4	Davis 38	Massey 39	Mulley 35 + 1	Marks 38 + 1	Holman 26 + 9	Daley 13 + 17	Enver-Marum 5 + 12	Sparkes 19 + 17	Symons — + 1	Carney 3 + 5	Griffiths 5 + 1	Cox 8 + 19	Strutton 7	Hamann 29	Geoghaghon 1 + 2	Mensah 7 + 2	Laurent 9 + 7	Jakubiak 2 + 9	Match No.
1	2	3	4	5	6	7	8	9^1	10	11^2	12	13												1
1	2	5	7	3	9^1	8	4		10^2	11	6	13	12											2
1	2^1	6	4	3	9^3	8	5		10	11^2	7	14	13	12										3
1	2	5	7	3	6^3	8	4		11	10^2	9^1	13	12		14									4
1	2	5	7	3^4	9	8	$4^{\blacksquare}$		10^3	11^1	6^2	14	12			13								5
1	2	5	3		7	8		9			6	10^1	12			4	11							6
1	2	5	3		8	7	4	9	10		6^2		11^1		13		12							7
1	2	5^1	3		8	7	4	9	11^2	6^1	10				14		13							8
1	2	5	3	9	8	7	4	6	11		10^1						12							9
1	2	5	7	3	9	8	4		6^3	10^1		13			14		12	11^2						10
1	2	4	3	6	7	8	5		11^2	10^3		12	13			14	9^1							11
1		5	7	3	6	8^1	4	9	11			12			2	13	10^2							12
1		5	7	4	8		3	6^2	11^1	14		9			2	13	12	10^3						13
1		5	7	3	8		4	6^1		13		12	9^2		2	10	11							14
1	2	5	6	4	8	7	3		12		13	9				11^2	10^1							15
1		5	8	3	7		4	9^1	10^2	14	12		6		2	13	11^3							16
	2		7	4	9^1	8	3	6	10^3	11^2	12	14			5	13			1					17
	2	4	3	8	7		6^3	10	13	12	14	9^1			5	11^2			1					18
	2		3	8	7^1		6	10^2	9	11	13				5	12			1	4				19
	2	5	8	3		7	4	6	10	11^1	9					12			1					20
	2	5		4	8	7	3	6	11^1	10	9^2	13				12			1					21
	2	5	7	4	6	8	3		10^3	11^2	12		9^1			13			1	14				22
	2	5	8^3	3	6^2	7	4	9	10	11^1	14		12			13			1					23
	2	5	7	3	6^3	8	4		9^1	10	11^1	14			13					1	12			24
	2	5	7	3	6^3	8	4	9	10	11^1	14				12				1		13			25
	2	5	8	3		7	4	9	10^1	12	14	13							1		6^3	11^2		26
	2	5	8	3		7^1	4	9	10		12								1		11	6		27
	2	5	3		14	7^1	4	6	10	12	13	9^2							1		11^1	8		28
	2	5	8	3		7	4	6^1	10	11	12								1		9			29
	2	5	8	3	12	7^1	4		10	11^1		13							1		9^2	6	14	30
	2	5	7	4	8		3		13	10^2	9^1	11							1		6^1	14	12	31
	2	5^1	8	3	7^1		4	6	11	13		14							1		12	9	10^2	32
	2	5^1	4	3	14	7		8	10	9		12							1		11^2	6^3	13	33
	2		3	4	8	7		9	10	11^2	6^1	5							1			12	13	34
	2	5	3	4	8	7		6^1	11		12	9^2							1			10	13	35
	2	5	3	4	7	8		6	10	11^1		9							1				12	36
	2	5	3	7	8	4		9	10	11^1		12							1			6		37
	2	5	8	4	6^2	7^1	3	12	10^3	11	14	9							1			13		38
	2	5	8	4	7		3		11	10	6^2	9^1							1			12	13	39
		5	2	3	7	8	4		$11^{\blacksquare}$	9	13					12			1			6^3	10^1	40
		5	2	3	8^1	7	4	6		10	14	9^3				11^2			1			12	13	41
12	2	5	8	4	7^2		3	6		10^1		9				11^3		$1^{\blacksquare}$				13	14	42
1	2	5	7	3	8		4	6		11		9				10								43
	2	5	7	3	9^2	8	4	6	11		13		10^1			12			1					44
	2	5	8^2	4	7	9	3	6	10^3	11^1		14				12			1			13		45
	2	5	7^3	3	8	10	4	6^1	11	14	13	9^1				12			1					46

The Budweiser FA Cup

Fourth Qualifying	Weymouth	(a)	2-1
First Round	Newport Co	(h)	1-1
Replay	Newport Co	(a)	0-1

FA Trophy

| First Round | Welling U | (h) | 3-0 |
| Second Round | Lincoln C | (h) | 1-3 |

CAMBRIDGE UNITED

Ground: R Costings Abbey Stadium, Newmarket Road, Cambridge CB5 8LN.   *Tel:* (01223) 566 500.
Fax: (01223) 729 220.   *Website:* www.cambridge-united.co.uk   *Year Formed:* 1912.
Record Attendance: 14,000 v Chelsea, Friendly, 1 May 1970.   *Nickname:* 'The U's'.   *Head Coach:* Richard Money.
Colours: Amber shirts with black trim, black shorts, black socks with amber trim.

CAMBRIDGE UNITED – SKRILL PREMIER 2013–14 LEAGUE RECORD

Match No.	Date	Venue	Opponents	Result		H/T Score	Lg Pos.	Goalscorers	Attendance
1	Aug 11	H	FC Halifax T	W	5-1	2-1	2	Cunnington 2 (1 pen) [13 (p), 67], Donaldson [36], Sam-Yorke 2 [49, 71]	2780
2	14	A	Welling U	D	2-2	1-2	3	Donaldson [33], Arnold [68]	1010
3	17	A	Aldershot T	W	1-0	1-0	1	Oastler (og) [12]	2022
4	24	H	Lincoln C	W	1-0	1-0	1	Berry [41]	3022
5	26	A	Luton T	D	0-0	0-0	2		7517
6	31	H	Tamworth	W	3-0	1-0	1	Cunnington (pen) [38], Berry 2 [58, 66]	2527
7	Sept 7	A	Hyde	W	1-0	1-0	1	Cunnington [42]	766
8	14	A	Gateshead	W	1-0	1-0	1	Cunnington [16]	2599
9	17	A	Alfreton T	D	1-1	0-1	2	Donaldson [63]	731
10	21	H	Forest Green R	W	2-1	1-0	1	Berry [1], Champion [53]	2915
11	24	H	Nuneaton T	W	3-0	1-0	1	Berry [22], Appiah [74], Dunk [89]	3740
12	28	A	Wrexham	D	1-1	1-1	1	Appiah [17]	3136
13	Oct 5	H	Hereford U	W	1-0	1-0	1	Appiah [7]	3381
14	8	A	Grimsby T	W	1-0	0-0	1	Cunnington [68]	4386
15	12	A	Chester FC	D	0-0	0-0	1		2530
16	19	H	Salisbury C	W	2-0	0-0	1	Appiah 2 [49, 56]	3622
17	Nov 2	A	Southport	L	0-1	0-1	1		1006
18	12	H	Aldershot T	W	4-0	1-0	1	Berry [45], Appiah [51], Cunnington [56], Arnold [71]	3110
19	16	A	Barnet	D	2-2	2-2	1	Appiah 2 [29, 32]	2853
20	23	H	Woking	W	2-0	2-0	1	Dunk 2 [3, 15]	3515
21	Dec 1	H	Macclesfield T	W	3-0	2-0	1	Appiah 2 [18, 27], Gillies [81]	2284
22	21	A	Hereford U	L	0-1	0-1	1		1558
23	26	H	Braintree T	W	1-0	1-0	1	Berry [19]	4194
24	28	A	Nuneaton T	D	0-0	0-0	2		1478
25	Jan 18	A	FC Halifax T	D	1-1	0-0	2	Elliott [65]	1767
26	21	A	Tamworth	W	1-0	0-0	2	Hughes [64]	833
27	25	A	Dartford	D	3-3	2-2	2	Bird 2 [2, 16], Berry [79]	2023
28	28	H	Grimsby T	L	1-2	0-1	2	Berry [54]	3027
29	Feb 11	H	Alfreton T	L	0-1	0-1	2		2106
30	18	H	Wrexham	D	0-0	0-0	2		2231
31	25	A	Braintree T	L	0-1	0-0	2		1016
32	Mar 1	H	Kidderminster H	W	5-1	1-1	2	Coulson [42], Bird [53], Sam-Yorke [55], Berry (pen) [79], Pugh [90]	2528
33	8	A	Forest Green R	L	2-3	2-2	2	Coulson [8], Arnold [10]	1411
34	11	H	Luton T	D	1-1	0-1	2	Elliott [62]	6050
35	15	H	Dartford	D	1-1	0-0	2	Elliott [67]	2885
36	18	H	Welling U	W	2-1	0-0	2	Cunnington (pen) [64], Sam-Yorke [75]	2012
37	26	A	Salisbury C	W	3-0	1-0	2	Bird [42], Taylor [61], Donaldson [63]	695
38	29	H	Barnet	D	1-1	1-0	2	Gillies (pen) [23]	3386
39	Apr 1	A	Macclesfield T	W	1-0	0-0	2	Berry (pen) [87]	1278
40	5	H	Southport	W	3-1	1-1	2	Berry (pen) [25], Chadwick [51], Pugh [68]	2717
41	10	A	Woking	W	3-0	2-0	2	Sam-Yorke [17], Chadwick [25], Hughes [85]	1805
42	12	H	Hyde	W	7-2	4-1	2	Gillies [2], Pugh 4 [18, 20, 47, 51], Chambers [26], Barnes-Homer [90]	2804
43	15	A	Kidderminster H	L	0-2	0-0	2		1938
44	18	A	Lincoln C	L	0-1	0-1	2		2535
45	21	H	Chester FC	L	0-1	0-1	2		3521
46	26	A	Gateshead	L	0-2	0-1	2		2916

Final League Position: 2

GOALSCORERS

League (72): Berry 12 (3 pens), Appiah 10, Cunnington 8 (3 pens), Pugh 6, Sam-Yorke 5, Bird 4, Donaldson 4, Arnold 3, Dunk 3, Elliott 3, Gillies 3 (1 pen), Chadwick 2, Coulson 2, Hughes 2, Barnes-Homer 1, Chambers 1, Champion 1, Taylor 1, own goal 1.
The Budweiser FA Cup (3): Berry 2, Cunnington 1.
FA Trophy (14): Bird 4, Berry 2 (1 pen), Arnold 2, Chambers 2, Donaldson 2, Elliott 1, Pierre 1.
Skrill Premier League Play-Offs (4): Sam-Yorke 2, Donaldson 1, Hughes 1.

Maxwell 24	Tait 32 + 3	Miller 41	Bonner 9	Taylor 43 + 3	Arnold 14 + 21	Donaldson 29 + 1	Champion 43	Dunk 27 + 3	Elliott 14	Cunnington 22 + 2	Sam-Yorke 10 + 17	Berry 34 + 8	Hughes 30 + 10	McAuley 2	Austin 1 + 7	Spillane 6 + 10	Coulson 39	Roberts 12 + 4	Appiah 13 + 1	Gillies 4 + 8	Sullivan 3	Chambers 6 + 4	Barnes-Homer 9 + 5	Norris 15	Bird 8 + 1	Pugh 4 + 9	Chadwick 8	Siegrist 3	Smith A 1	Match No.
1	2	3	4	5[2]	6[3]	7	8	9	10[1]	11	12	13	14																	1
1	2	3		5	13	10	7	9		11[2]	12	8[1]	6	4																2
1	2	4		5	10	6	7	9			11	8	12	3[1]																3
1	2	3		12	9	6	7	5[2]		10[3]	11[1]	8	4		13	14														4
1	2	4		5	11[2]	6	7	9[3]		10[1]	12	8			14		13	3												5
1	2	3		5	10	6[2]	7	9[3]		11		8[1]	13		14		12	4												6
1	2	4		5	12	10		9[1]		11[2]		7[3]	6		13		8	3	14											7
1	2	4		13	9[1]	6	7	5		10[5]		8[1]	12		14		3		11											8
1		4		5	12	9	7	6		10[1]		13	2			8[2]	3		11											9
1	5	4		2	12	9[2]	6	8	10			7	13				3		11[1]											10
1	5	4		2	6[1]		8	7		11[2]	13	9[3]	12		14		3	10												11
1	2	4		5	12		7	9[2]		13	10[1]	8[1]	6		14		3		11											12
1	2	4		5			7	9		10[1]	12	8	6[2]				13	3	11											13
1	2	4		5			7	9		11			6				8	3	10											14
1	2	4		5	14		6	8	10[1]	12	13	7			9[3]		3		11[2]											15
1	2	3		5	6		7	9	11[1]	10[3]	14	13			8[2]		4		12											16
1	2	4		5[2]	12		7	14		10		13	6[1]	9	8[2]		3		11											17
1	2	3		5	12		7	9		10[1]	14	8[2]	6				4	13	11[1]											18
1	2	4		5	12		7	9		11[1]	13	8	6[2]				3	14	10[3]											19
1	2	3		5			7			10[1]	12	8[2]	6		13		4		11											20
1		3		5	12		7			10		8	6				4	2	11[1]	9										21
1	13	4[3]		5	10[1]		8	9		11	12	7			14		3	2[2]		6										22
1	2	4		5	11	6[2]	7	9		10	13	8[1]			12		3													23
1	2	4		5	13	12	7	9	11	10[1]		8	6[2]				3													24
	2	4		5	13	6[3]	7	8	10		12	14					3					1	9[2]	11[1]						25
14	3			5	12	6[1]	7	9[3]	10			8			2		4	13						11[2]	1					26
	2	4		5	12	8[3]	7			10	14		6[2]				3	13				1	9	11[1]						27
	2	3		5	13	9	7[3]		11			8	6[1]				4		12			1	10[3]	14						28
	3[1]			5	12		7	9		10		6	8[1]				4	2		14			11[2]	1	13					29
	3			5	13	9	7			10		8	6[2]				4	2					1	11[1]	12					30
		4		5	14		7					8[4]	9				3	2	13			12	11[3]	1	10	6[1]				31
2	3			5	6	9[3]	7[1]			10		8	12		13		4						1	11[2]	14					32
2	3			5	9[1]		7	8		10[2]	12	6[3]			14			13					1	11						33
		4		5		9	7			10		8	6				3	2					1	11						34
		4		5		9	7[3]			10	12	8	6		13		3	2[2]		14			1	11[1]						35
2	3			5	10[1]	9	7			11[3]	13	8[1]	12				4							1		14	6			36
	4	3		5	14	6	7				12	9[2]	8				2	13						11[1]		10[3]		1		37
2	3			5			10	7		11		6[2]					4	9[1]				13				12	8	1		38
14	4	3		5	13	6	7			10[1]		8[3]					2							11[2]		12	9	1		39
	3			5		9	7			10[1]		8[3]	14				4	2				13		11[2]	1	12	6			40
2	3			5		9	7			10[2]			6				4					13		11[1]	1	12	8			41
5			4	14	10[2]							13	7		6[3]		3	2		11[1]		8	12		1	9				42
	4			5			9	6[2]	12	10[1]	13	7					3	2				11[3]		1		14	8			43
2	4	3		5		6[4]						9	11[2]		12		7	8				10	13	1		11	9			44
2[2]	3			5			7	12	10[3]	8[1]	6						4					13	14	1		11	9			45
	4			5	12	6[2]	7	9				2[1]					3					13	10	11		14	8[2]		1	46

The Budweiser FA Cup

Fourth Qualifying	Needham Market	(a)	1-0
First Round	Bury	(a)	0-0
Replay	Bury	(h)	2-1
Second Round	Sheffield U	(h)	0-2

Skrill Premier Play-Offs

Semi-Finals 1st leg	Halifax T	(a)	0-1
Semi-Finals 2nd leg	Halifax T	(h)	2-0
Final	Gateshead	(Wembley)	2-1

FA Trophy

First Round	Salisbury	(a)	1-0
Second Round	St Albans C	(a)	2-1
Third Round	Luton T	(h)	2-2
Replay	Luton T	(a)	1-0
Quarter-Finals	Eastleigh	(a)	1-0
Semi-Finals 1st leg	Grimsby T	(h)	2-1
Semi-Finals 2nd leg	Grimsby T	(a)	1-1
Final	Gosport Borough	(h)	4-0

CHESTER FC

Ground: Swansway Chester Stadium, Bumpers Lane, Chester CH1 4LT. *Tel:* (01244) 371376.
Website: www.chesterfc.com   *Year Formed:* 1885.
Record Attendance: 20,500 v Chelsea, FA Cup 3rd rd (replay), 16 January 1952 (at Sealand Road).
Nickname: 'The Blues'.   *Manager:* Steve Burr.   *Colours:* Blue and white striped shirts, blue shorts, blue socks.

CHESTER FC – SKRILL PREMIER 2013–14 LEAGUE RECORD

Match No.	Date	Venue	Opponents	Result	H/T Score	Lg Pos.	Goalscorers	Atten- dance
1	Aug 10	A	Barnet	L	0-3	0-0	22		2543
2	13	H	Hereford U	L	0-2	0-1	22		2900
3	17	H	Woking	L	0-2	0-0	23		2016
4	24	A	Kidderminster H	L	1-3	1-2	23	Harrison [45]	2283
5	26	H	Forest Green R	L	1-2	0-1	23	Mills [80]	2083
6	31	A	Wrexham	W	2-0	2-0	22	Linwood [5], Turner, L [17]	6037
7	Sept 7	H	Dartford	D	0-0	0-0	21		2587
8	14	A	Salisbury C	L	1-3	1-1	21	Heath [14]	925
9	17	H	Macclesfield T	W	2-1	2-1	20	Chippendale [18], Seddon [30]	2012
10	21	H	Grimsby T	D	0-0	0-0	21		2363
11	24	A	Gateshead	L	2-3	1-1	22	Harrison [27], Higginbotham [74]	610
12	28	A	FC Halifax T	L	1-2	1-1	23	Seddon [18]	1805
13	Oct 5	A	Kidderminster H	D	0-0	0-0	22		2223
14	8	A	Alfreton T	W	1-0	1-0	22	Reed [33]	743
15	12	H	Cambridge U	D	0-0	0-0	22		2530
16	19	A	Braintree T	L	0-3	0-3	22		1132
17	Nov 2	H	Aldershot T	D	1-1	0-0	22	Wilkinson [68]	2029
18	9	A	Hyde	W	2-1	1-1	21	Lindfield [40], Mahon [47]	1232
19	12	A	Hereford U	D	2-2	2-2	20	Lindfield [18], Seddon [21]	1512
20	16	H	Luton T	D	1-1	1-1	21	Seddon [23]	3291
21	23	A	Nuneaton T	L	0-1	0-0	21		1221
22	Dec 7	H	Braintree T	L	0-2	0-1	22		1736
23	21	H	Lincoln C	D	3-3	2-1	21	Menagh 2 [8, 10], Rooney (pen) [50]	1850
24	26	A	Southport	D	0-0	0-0	21		1872
25	28	H	Gateshead	D	1-1	1-0	21	Killock [10]	2017
26	Jan 18	H	Barnet	W	2-1	1-0	21	Turner, L [34], Reed [85]	2179
27	21	A	Woking	W	1-0	1-0	20	Menagh [29]	1124
28	25	A	Forest Green R	L	0-3	0-1	20		1483
29	Feb 1	H	Welling U	L	1-3	0-2	20	Taylor [55]	2074
30	4	A	Macclesfield T	L	2-3	1-2	20	Seddon [19], Rooney [88]	1771
31	13	H	FC Halifax T	W	2-1	0-0	20	Mahon [55], Menagh [90]	2127
32	22	A	Lincoln C	D	1-1	0-1	21	Taylor [52]	2354
33	25	A	Tamworth	W	4-3	3-1	20	Taylor 3 [23, 33, 60], Rooney [30]	1036
34	Mar 1	A	Nuneaton T	D	3-3	2-2	21	Rooney [16], Taylor [35], Killock [70]	2214
35	7	A	Dartford	W	1-0	0-0	20	Seddon [51]	1610
36	11	A	Aldershot T	L	0-2	0-1	20		1545
37	15	H	Alfreton T	L	0-1	0-0	21		2042
38	18	H	Southport	D	2-2	1-0	21	Hobson [34], Mahon [49]	2274
39	22	A	Luton T	L	0-3	0-0	21		8475
40	25	H	Tamworth	W	2-0	0-0	18	Richards-Everton (og) [62], Carlton [67]	1731
41	29	A	Welling U	L	0-2	0-0	19		706
42	Apr 5	H	Hyde	W	3-2	2-0	18	Seddon [15], Brizell (og) [23], Hobson [50]	2228
43	12	A	Grimsby T	L	1-2	0-1	19	Caton [90]	4174
44	19	H	Wrexham	D	0-0	0-0	20		4326
45	21	H	Cambridge U	W	1-0	1-0	20	Carlton [12]	3521
46	26	A	Salisbury C	D	2-2	1-1	21	Carlton [14], Rooney [58]	3588

Final League Position: 21

GOALSCORERS

League (49): Seddon 7, Taylor 6, Rooney 5 (1 pen), Menagh 4, Carlton 3, Mahon 3, Harrison 2, Hobson 2, Killock 2, Lindfield 2, Reed 2, Turner, L 2, Caton 1, Chippendale 1, Heath 1, Higginbotham 1, Linwood 1, Mills 1, Wilkinson 1, own goals 2.
The Budweiser FA Cup (0).
FA Trophy (1): Seddon 1.

Danby 29 + 1	Kay 25 + 5	Linwood 24 + 4	Harrison 15 + 1	Horan 21	McIntyre 29 + 2	Mahon 18 + 9	Jarret 27 + 2	Reed 13 + 9	Lindfield 16 + 6	Seddon 25 + 10	Mills 6 + 5	Turner N 18 + 7	Williams M 1 + 1	Turner L 43	Heath 16 + 7	Titchiner 11 + 4	Williams A 6 + 2	Laidler 3	Chippendale 3 + 4	Fearon 1	Pugh 8	Higginbotham 15 + 2	McDonald — + 1	Killock 17	Lester 4 + 1	Wilkinson 3 + 1	Miller G 8	Miller S 1	Rooney 25	Peers 2 + 5	Menagh 10 + 9	Bond 17 + 2	Taylor 7	Mainwaring — + 2	Chapman 16	Brown 8	Bridge 2	Match No.
1	2	3	4	5	6	7³	8²	9¹	10	11	12	13	14																									1
1	4⁸	12	7	3	5	9¹	14	13	6⁹	10		8	11²	2																								2
1		4	6	3	9	12	7¹	14	10²	11		8		2	5³	13																						3
1	2	3	6		5			13		10¹	12	7		4		11	8³	9²	14																			4
	4		7	3	9		13	12		10	8		2		11²		6¹		1	5																		5
1	2	3	7		5				14	10	8		6		9³	12⁸	11¹	13			4²																	6
1	2	3	7		5		12	14	13	10²	8		6		9³			11¹			4																	7
1	2	3	9		6				12	10¹	7		4	5³	11²			14			8	13⁸																8
1	2	12	3	8					11¹	10	7		6	14	13			9²		5³	4																	9
1	2		8	3	7	13			11	10¹			6		12			9²		5	4																	10
1	2		8	3	10⁸				11⁸	14	7		6		13	9³		12		5¹	4																	11
1	2	12	5	4¹		14			6³	10²	13	8		7	3	11					9																	12
1	2	3	7		9			11²	8		13			6	12	10					5¹	4																13
1	2	4	7	3	8			10²	6³	13		14		9	12	11					5¹																	14
1	2	4	7	3⁸	8			10	9²	14		13		6		11³					5	12																15
1	2²	4⁸	7	3⁸	6			10		12	8		5		11³	14					9⁸	13																16
1				5		8		6				7	2	10							4			3	9	11												17
1	14			5	10²	8		9	12			7	2	13							4			3	6³	11¹												18
1	12			5	9	8	13	6	11³		7¹		2								3			4	14	10²												19
1	13			5	10⁸	8		9	11			2	12			7¹					4			3	6													20
1		12			5	10	7	14	9³	11²			2			8					4			3⁸	6	13												21
1	2	3⁸				13	12		10³			6	5	8²							4				7	9¹	11	14										22
1	2		3	13		7	10²	14	11⁸			5³									4				8	9	12	6¹										23
1	3		4	5		10	2						7												8	6	11	9										24
1			3	13		8	10¹				2	5	11								4				7	9	12	6²										25
1			4	5	13	7	10²	12			2	14									3				6	11	8²	9¹										26
1			3	5		7	11²	9			2	12									4				8	10	13	6¹										27
1			4	5	13	8²	10	7¹			2										3				9	11	14	6³	12									28
1	5		3	9¹		7	10		13			2									4⁸				8³	6		12	14	11								29
1	14	4		3³		12	7¹	10²		11			2		5										9				6	8	13							30
12					9²	7	14		10			2	5												4				6	13	8	11³			1¹	3		31
					9²	7			10			2	5¹												3				6	13	8	11	12		1	4		32
	4				9¹	8			10			5													2				6	12	7	11			1	3		33
	3				9	7⁸			10	12		2													4				6		8	11			1		5¹	34
	3				9¹			13	10		8	2	5	12											4				6		7	11²			1			35
	4				9			10¹	11		8²	2	5	12											3				6	13	7				1			36
	4				9				11³		8²	6	5	14			12								2¹				10	13	7			1	3		37
12	3¹				9	8			10		13	2					11²		14						6					7				1	4²	5	38
2	4				7					8	5	3		6											11				9	10				1			39
3	4¹				11²	8	14		13		2	5				10		12							6				9³	7				1			40
3	4				9	8⁸		11¹	14		2	5				10²	12								6				13	7				1			41
4	13			5	9²	8		10¹			2					11³						12			6	14	7						1	3⁸		42
	4				9	8		14			2¹					11²	13		5	10		12	6			7³				1	3		43
	3		2²	9	13	6			10		5³						11					4	12		8	14	7²					1		44
	4		3¹	5	13	8					6					14	11⁸			2⁸	12				10	9	7				1		45
	2	3²		5	13	7			12		6					14	10³							11	9¹	8			1	4		46

The Budweiser FA Cup
Fourth Qualifying   Gateshead   (h)   0-1

FA Trophy
First Round   Barrow   (h)   1-2

DARTFORD

Ground: Princes Park, Grassbanks, Darenth Road, Dartford, Kent DA1 1RT.
Tel: (01322) 299 990.   *Website:* www.dartfordfconline.co.uk   *Year Formed:* 1888.
Record Attendance: 4,097 v Horsham YMCA, Ryman League, 11 November 2006.
Nickname: 'The Darts'.   *Manager:* Tony Burman.   *Secretary:* Peter Martin.
Colours: White shirts with black trim, black shorts, white socks with black trim.

DARTFORD – SKRILL PREMIER 2013–14 LEAGUE RECORD

Match No.	Date	Venue	Opponents	Result	H/T Score	Lg Pos.	Goalscorers	Atten- dance
1	Aug 10	H	Alfreton T	W	1-0	1-0	5	Birchall [42]	1202
2	13	A	Aldershot T	L	0-3	0-1	15		2138
3	17	A	FC Halifax T	L	0-2	0-0	18		1296
4	24	H	Braintree T	L	0-2	0-0	19		1015
5	26	A	Tamworth	W	2-0	2-0	15	Harris [3], Clark [26]	864
6	31	H	Lincoln C	L	1-2	0-2	16	Bradbrook [59]	1386
7	Sept 7	A	Chester FC	D	0-0	0-0	18		2587
8	14	H	Nuneaton T	L	1-2	1-2	19	Bradbrook [28]	1155
9	17	A	Luton T	L	0-3	0-2	21		5433
10	21	H	Kidderminster H	W	3-0	1-0	18	Prior [34], Bradbrook [51], Harris [61]	1020
11	24	A	Grimsby T	L	2-5	1-3	19	Harris [24], Noble [55]	2503
12	28	H	Southport	W	1-0	1-0	17	Birchall [32]	1025
13	Oct 5	A	Gateshead	L	0-2	0-1	18		561
14	8	H	Salisbury C	D	1-1	1-1	20	Godden [29]	920
15	12	A	Hereford U	D	2-2	1-0	20	Noble [11], Ibemere [85]	1583
16	19	H	Hyde	W	4-3	2-2	18	Godden 3 [12, 15, 87], Monger [83]	1083
17	Nov 2	A	Forest Green R	L	0-1	0-1	18		960
18	12	A	Woking	L	0-3	0-0	21		1157
19	16	A	Macclesfield T	L	1-3	1-0	22	Godden (pen) [13]	1543
20	19	H	Wrexham	L	1-5	1-4	22	Burns [3]	816
21	23	H	Gateshead	L	0-1	0-0	22		975
22	26	H	Barnet	L	0-2	0-2	23		803
23	Dec 7	A	Barnet	L	0-1	0-1	23		1461
24	14	H	FC Halifax T	L	1-2	0-0	23	Essam [83]	952
25	21	A	Alfreton T	L	1-2	1-0	23	Bradbrook (pen) [16]	575
26	26	H	Welling U	L	1-2	1-0	23	Burns [29]	1758
27	Jan 10	A	Welling U	D	1-1	1-1	23	Stevenson [10]	1336
28	18	A	Salisbury C	L	0-1	0-1	23		850
29	21	A	Kidderminster H	W	2-1	2-0	23	Cornhill [3], Pugh [23]	1580
30	25	H	Cambridge U	D	3-3	2-2	23	Bradbrook (pen) [26], Cornhill [45], Harris [69]	2023
31	Feb 8	A	Wrexham	W	2-1	2-1	23	Pugh [10], Bradbrook [45]	2645
32	18	H	Woking	W	5-1	2-1	22	Wall 2 [5, 45], Cornhill 2 [56, 74], Noble [90]	1002
33	22	H	Hereford U	W	2-0	1-0	21	Wall [12], Noble [71]	1137
34	25	H	Aldershot T	D	1-1	1-0	22	Bradbrook (pen) [45]	1125
35	Mar 1	A	Southport	L	0-3	0-1	22		1041
36	7	H	Chester FC	L	0-1	0-0	22		1610
37	15	A	Cambridge U	D	1-1	0-0	22	Wall [90]	2885
38	22	A	Hyde	W	2-0	0-0	22	Wall 2 [57, 80]	358
39	29	H	Macclesfield T	W	2-1	0-1	22	Harris [47], Cornhill [81]	1105
40	Apr 1	H	Luton T	L	1-2	1-0	22	Suarez [34]	2869
41	5	A	Lincoln C	D	0-0	0-0	22		1947
42	10	H	Grimsby T	W	1-0	0-0	22	Cornhill [75]	1257
43	12	H	Forest Green R	L	0-1	0-0	22		1061
44	18	A	Braintree T	L	0-1	0-1	22		1200
45	21	H	Tamworth	L	2-3	1-0	22	Bradbrook 2 [30, 90]	1465
46	26	A	Nuneaton T	L	1-3	1-2	22	McAuley [17]	903

Final League Position: 22

GOALSCORERS

League (49): Bradbrook 9 (3 pens), Cornhill 6, Wall 6, Godden 5 (1 pen), Harris 5, Noble 4, Birchall 2, Burns 2, Pugh 2, Clark 1, Essam 1, Ibemere 1, McAuley 1, Monger 1, Prior 1, Stevenson 1, Suarez 1.
The Budweiser FA Cup (4): Bradbrook 1, Burns 1, Cornhill 1, Noble 1.
FA Trophy (1): Harris 1.

Julian 42	Burns 46	Clark 29+4	Mitchel-King 33	Fry 15	Hayes 13+3	Cornhill 29+7	Bradbrook 38+1	Noble 29+8	Prior 7+7	Birchall 22+1	Rogers 3+4	Harris 34+8	Woodyard 26+11	Collier 19+16	Sterling 30+4	Ibemere —+9	Godden 8+1	Hill —+2	Monger —+1	Forecast 1+1	Martin 9	Smith 3	Essam 4	Stevenson 23	Dembele —+3	Kamara —+5	Scantlebury —+1	McAuley 18	Pugh 4	Wall 11	Suarez 6+5	Swallow 4+7	Eisa —+1	Akinwande —+1	Adams —+1	Vint —+1	Match No.
1	2	3	4	5¹	6³	7	8	9	10²	11	12	13	14																								1
1	3	2	4		6²	5	8	7¹	11³	10		9	12	14	14	13																					2
1	3	2	4			5¹	8	7²	10	11		9	6	12	13																					3
1	2	3	4		6³	7	8	9²	11¹	10		12	14	13	5																					4
1	7	2	3¹	5		8	9		11	12	10²	6	13	4																						5
1	2	3		5	12	13	8	6²	14	10	9¹	11	7³		4																					6
1	2	4		5	6¹		8	9		10	12	11	7	3																						7
1	2	3		5⁴	6		8	7	12	11²		10	9¹	4	13	14																				8
1	11	3		5	6²		8	7	12	10	14	9²	13	2	4¹																					9
1	2	3		5	6³		8	9²	11¹	12		10	7	4	13	14																				10
1	11	3		4	6²	14	7	12		10		9	5³	8	2¹	13																				11
1	2	3		5	6¹	12	8	9	13	11²		10³	7	4		14																				12
1	2	3		5	13	8	7	9²	12	11¹		10	6³	4		14																				13
1	2	3	4		6²	14	8	9	10¹			12	7	5		13	11³																			14
1	5	4¹	3		13	9²	7	6¹				11	8	2		14	10	12																		15
1	2		4	5	6²	7		9¹				11	8	3		12	10	13																		16
1	8	2	3	4	11	5			9²			6	7¹			12	10	13																		17
1	2	3	4	5	6²	7		9	14	10		12	8¹	13		11³																				18
1¹	2	4	3	5		7			10			6	13	8	9²	11		12																		19
	2	4	3²	5¹		14		6		10		13	9³	7	12	11			1	8																20
	2	3				8	7⁴	12	10¹	11			6	5					9	1	4															21
	8²	3				5		10¹	11			9	12	6		2	13			7	1	4														22
	2	4					7	6		11		10²		12	5					9¹	1	3	8	13												23
1	2	3				13	8	6²		11¹		12			5	10				9		4	7													24
1	2	5		4³		13	7	6⁴		11		10¹		14	3					9²			8		12											25
1	2	3	4			7¹	10			11			13	6³	5					9			8²		12	14										26
1	2		4				8					10²	6	12	5					9			7		13		3	11¹								27
1	2		4				7					9⁴	8¹	12	5					6²			10		13		3	11								28
1	2		3				11	8					7		4					9			12			5	6	10¹								29
1	2	3	4				8	11	12			9	6¹		5					7					10											30
1	2	14	3				7	9	13			12	6²		5					8							4	10³	11¹							31
1	2		4				8	9	14			11²	6³		5					7					3			10¹	12	13						32
1	2	14	3				8	9	12			11³	6¹		5					7					4			10²		13						33
1	2		3				7	9	12			10	6¹		5					8					4			11²		13						34
1	5	12	3¹				9	8²	13			6	10³	2						7					4			11	14							35
1	2		3				8²	9	12			11	6¹	14	5					7¹					4			10	13							36
1	2	4¹	3				8¹	9	6			10²		14	5					7								11	12	13						37
1	2		4				8	9	6¹			10²	13	12	5					7					3			11								38
1	2		3				8	9	6¹			11		13	5					7					4			10²		12						39
1	2	8⁴	3				7	9	6			10		12	5					4								11¹								40
1	2		3				6	9¹				11²	7³	13	5					8	14				4			10	12							41
1	2		3				8		6			11		12	5					7					4			10²	9¹	13						42
1	2		3				8		9²			10³	13	12	5					7					4			11¹	6		14					43
1	2		3				8	12	9¹			6		11²	5					7					4			10	13							44
1	5	12	2¹				8	10	9			11	14		4³					7²					3			13	6							45
1	2²	3					7	10				6²	5							8	12				4			11	9¹			13	14			46

The Budweiser FA Cup

Fourth Qualifying	Ebbsfleet U	(a)	1-1
Replay	Ebbsfleet U	(h)	1-0
First Round	Salisbury	(a)	2-4

FA Trophy

First Round	Forest Green R	(h)	1-1
Replay	Forest Green R	(a)	0-1

FOREST GREEN ROVERS

Ground: The New Lawn, Another Way, Nailsworth, Gloucestershire GL6 0FG. *Tel:* (01453) 834 860.
Fax: (01453) 835 291. *Website:* www.forestgreenroversfc.com *Year Formed:* 1890.
Record Attendance: 4,836 v Derby Co, FA Cup 3rd rd, 3 January 2009.
Nickname: 'The Rovers'. *Manager:* Adrian Pennock.
Colours: Green shirts with black trim, black shorts with white trim, black socks with white trim.

FOREST GREEN ROVERS – SKRILL PREMIER 2013–14 LEAGUE RECORD

Match No.	Date	Venue	Opponents	Result	H/T Score	Lg Pos.	Goalscorers	Attendance
1	Aug 10	H	Hyde	W 8-0	4-0	1	Kelly 3 [25, 29, 76], Wright, D [33], Norwood [38], Taylor 2 [60, 72], Barnes-Homer [71]	1158
2	13	A	Nuneaton T	D 1-1	0-1	2	Hodgkiss [78]	1005
3	17	A	Lincoln C	L 1-2	1-1	11	Barry [20]	2290
4	24	H	Luton T	D 0-0	0-0	13		1858
5	26	A	Chester FC	W 2-1	1-0	10	Wright, D [6], Barnes-Homer [73]	2083
6	31	H	Alfreton T	W 3-1	3-0	6	Norwood 2 [7, 23], Wright, D [35]	1027
7	Sept 7	A	Braintree T	D 1-1	1-1	6	Klukowski [6]	944
8	14	H	FC Halifax T	W 2-1	0-1	3	Barry [90], Vieira [90]	1195
9	17	A	Welling U	L 2-5	1-2	8	Barry [45], Klukowski (pen) [62]	452
10	21	A	Cambridge U	L 1-2	0-1	10	Klukowski [57]	2915
11	24	H	Tamworth	L 1-2	1-1	14	Taylor [37]	829
12	28	H	Gateshead	W 1-0	1-0	12	Klukowski [15]	1149
13	Oct 5	A	Alfreton T	L 2-3	2-2	13	Vieira [20], Barnes-Homer [27]	582
14	8	A	Kidderminster H	L 1-4	1-1	14	Barnes-Homer [6]	2244
15	12	H	Macclesfield T	L 2-3	1-1	14	Barnes-Homer [10], Klukowski (pen) [68]	1181
16	19	A	Grimsby T	L 1-3	1-1	16	Klukowski [24]	3150
17	Nov 2	H	Dartford	W 1-0	1-0	15	Norwood [5]	960
18	12	H	Nuneaton T	W 1-0	1-0	14	Kelly [38]	933
19	16	H	Lincoln C	W 4-1	2-1	13	Norwood 2 [21, 73], Green [37], Turley [90]	1128
20	23	A	Wrexham	L 0-2	0-2	14		3083
21	26	A	Salisbury C	W 4-1	1-1	12	Norwood 2 [10, 86], Wright, D [68], Klukowski (pen) [82]	725
22	Dec 21	A	FC Halifax T	L 0-1	0-1	13		1262
23	26	H	Aldershot T	W 3-1	1-1	13	Kelly 2 [12, 77], Norwood [90]	1676
24	28	A	Hereford U	L 0-1	0-1	14		1848
25	Jan 9	A	Hereford U	D 1-1	0-0	14	Kelly [53]	1077
26	18	A	Hyde	W 6-2	4-1	14	Oshodi 2 [11, 67], Norwood 2 [13, 86], Kelly [15], Styche [24]	496
27	25	H	Chester FC	W 3-0	1-0	12	Hughes 2 [23, 73], Norwood [65]	1483
28	Feb 18	A	Aldershot T	D 2-2	0-0	15	Norwood [56], Hughes [64]	1407
29	22	H	Southport	W 3-1	2-0	11	Wright, D 2 [23, 30], Klukowski [73]	1118
30	25	H	Barnet	L 1-2	0-2	13	Kelly [90]	869
31	Mar 1	A	Gateshead	D 1-1	0-0	15	Hughes (pen) [75]	649
32	8	H	Cambridge U	W 3-2	2-2	12	Norwood [5], Hodgkiss [44], Wright, D [47]	1411
33	11	H	Salisbury C	W 4-0	2-0	12	Racine [39], Hodgkiss [42], Hughes [56], Klukowski [90]	918
34	13	H	Braintree T	L 0-2	0-1	13		841
35	15	A	Tamworth	W 2-1	2-0	11	Klukowski [11], Norwood [27]	736
36	18	A	Grimsby T	W 2-1	2-0	6	Hughes [3], Oshodi [30]	1219
37	22	H	Welling U	D 0-0	0-0	9		1338
38	27	A	Southport	L 0-2	0-0	11		1227
39	Apr 1	A	Woking	L 1-2	0-0	11	Hughes [63]	1315
40	5	A	Barnet	L 1-2	0-1	13	Norwood [61]	1466
41	8	H	Kidderminster H	D 1-1	1-0	13	Green [13]	1231
42	12	A	Dartford	W 1-0	0-0	12	Wright, D [83]	1061
43	15	A	Macclesfield T	W 2-1	2-0	9	Klukowski 2 [2, 19]	1142
44	19	H	Woking	D 2-2	1-0	10	Norwood [33], Hughes [90]	1245
45	21	A	Luton T	L 1-4	1-1	10	Klukowski (pen) [34]	10,044
46	26	H	Wrexham	D 1-1	1-0	10	Norwood [14]	1630

Final League Position: 10

GOALSCORERS

League (80): Norwood 18, Klukowski 13 (4 pens), Kelly 9, Hughes 8 (1 pen), Wright, D 8, Barnes-Homer 5, Barry 3, Hodgkiss 3, Oshodi 3, Taylor 3, Green 2, Vieira 2, Racine 1, Styche 1, Turley 1.
The Budweiser FA Cup (0).
FA Trophy (2): Barnes-Homer 1, Klukowski 1.

Russell 46	Hodgkiss 33+5	Bennett 31+1	Pilkington 8	Stokes 20	Bangura 35+3	Barry 34+2	Kelly 31+2	Taylor 17+8	Wright D 31+9	Norwood 40+5	Klukowski 23+13	Barnes-Homer 10+8	Asafu-Adjaye 13+4	Vieira 3+12	Williams S —+1	Koroma —+5	Oshodi 31+3	Mangan 3+6	Turley 19+2	Racine 13+2	Forbes 3+5	Green 20+3	Styche 1+5	Alabi —+2	Brogan —+3	Williams J 3	Hughes 18+3	Walker 1+2	Oliver 11	Rodgers 3+7	Jordan 5+1	Martin —+1	White —+1	Match No.
1	2	3	4	5^2	6	7	8	9	10^2	11^1	12	13	14																					1
1	2	3	4	5		7	6^2	8	9	10^1	11	13	12																					2
1	2	3	4	5		7	8^2	9			6^2	10	11^1	12	13	14																		3
1	2		4		3	6	8	9		10^1	7^3	12	11^2		13		14	5																4
1	2		4		5	7	6^2	8		9^1	11	10	12		13		3																	5
1	2		4		5	6	7^3	8	13	10^2	11^1	9	12		14		3																	6
1	2	3			5	6	8		11^1	10^2	9	7^3			14	4	12	13																7
1	5	4				7	6		9^1	10	11^3	8^2	12			13		3	14	2															8
1	5	2^1				7	6	8^1		10^2	11	12^3	9				4	14	3	13														9
1		5			2	8	6		7^1	10^3	13	12	9		14		3	11^2	4															10
1	12	4^1			2	6	7^3		11^2	10	9^1	8	13				5		3		14													11
1	2		4	3	7	6^2			10^3		8	11		9^1	14		12		5	13														12
1	2		4	5	7		12		10	14	8	11^3		9^2			13		3	6^1														13
1	2		3	5	8^1		9		11	14	6^2	10^3		13			12		4^1	7														14
1			3	5		7^3	8		9	12	13	11	2	6^2		14	4	10^1																15
1	12	4		5	7	8	6		10^3	13	9^1	14			3^3	11^2	2																	16
1	12	5		2^1	8		7		11	9^1	10				5		4			6														17
1	2	4			7		9		11	10^1	6			5	12^2		3			8	13													18
1	2	4			8^1		9	13	11	10^2	6			5			3		12	7														19
1	2^2	4			8^1		7	12	11	10	9^3			5			14	3^1			6	13												20
1	2	4			8^2			13	10	7^1	9	11^3		5				14	6	12														21
1	2	4					8	9	12	10^2	6^2		11^1	5			3		7^3	13	14													22
1	2^1	3			8^2	7	6	11	9	10				5			12		4	13														23
1		3			7	2	8^3	9^2	10^1	11		12	5				4	6		13	14													24
1		3^2			7	8	9		10^3	6		2				12	4^1		14	13	5^2	11												25
1					7	8	6^3		12	9	13	5		3	4				10^2	14	2	11^1												26
1	2				8	7^3	6		10^1	9		12		4	3			13			5	11^3	14											27
1	5	4			8	7	9		10^1	6^2	13			2								11	12	3										28
1	5	4			7	8	9		10	6^2	12		13	2								11^1		3										29
1	4	5			7^3	8	9		10^2	6	14	12	13	2								11		3^1										30
1	2	4^2			7	8	9^3		10	6^1		5	12	3			13		14			11												31
1	2				12	8^1	9		11	6^3	14			3		5	4		7			10^2			13									32
1	2				8	7^3	9	10		6^1	12			3		5	4		14			11^2			13									33
1	2				8^2	9	12	10^1	6	13		5		3			4		7			11												34
1	12			5^1	7^3	14	9	11		10	6^2			3		2	4^1		8			13												35
1	13	3		5		8^2	9	10^1		6^3			14	4		2			7			11			12									36
1	12	3		5		8	9^1	10^3	14	6				4		2			7			11^2			13									37
1				5	7	9^1		14	12	6^2	13			2		3	4		8			11			10^2									38
1				5^2	13			10^3	6	9				12		2	3^1		7			11	4	14	8									39
1	5^3				7^2	12		14	11	9				4		2^1			6			10	3	13	8									40
1	5	4				7		10^2		11	9			2					8			13	3	12	6^1									41
1	5	3			7			11^1	13	9	10			2					6			12	4		8^2									42
1	5	3			6		12	9^2	13	7	10^1			2					8			11	4											43
1	5	4^1			13^3	7		9^2	11	14	6			2					8			10	3		12^3									44
1	5					8		9	13	6	7			4					2				11^1	3	10^2		12							45
1^1	5	3				7^2		13	14	6				2					8			11^3		4	10	9		12						46

The Budweiser FA Cup

Fourth Qualifying	Bishop's Stortford		(h)	0-1

FA Trophy

First Round	Dartford	(a)	1-1
Replay	Dartford	(h)	1-0
Second Round	Chorley	(a)	0-0
Replay	Chorley	(h)	0-0
(aet; lost 1-3 on penalties)			

GATESHEAD

Ground: Gateshead International Stadium, Neilson Road, Gateshead NE10 0EF.   *Tel:* (0191) 478 3883.
Fax: (0191) 440 0404.   *Website:* www.gateshead-fc.com   *Year Formed:* 1889 (Reformed 1977).
Record Attendance: 20,752 v Lincoln C, Division 3N (at Redheugh Park), 25 September 1937.
Nickname: 'The Tynesiders', 'The Heed'.   *Manager:* Gary Mills.
Colours: White shirts, black shorts, black socks with white trim.

GATESHEAD – SKRILL PREMIER 2013–14 LEAGUE RECORD

Match No.	Date	Venue	Opponents	Result	H/T Score	Lg Pos.	Goalscorers	Atten-dance
1	Aug 10	A	Kidderminster H	L	1-3	1-1	21	Brodie [43]	2110
2	13	H	Grimsby T	L	1-2	1-1	20	Turnbull [20]	944
3	17	H	Barnet	L	1-2	1-1	21	Larkin [32]	639
4	24	A	Southport	L	1-2	0-2	22	Brodie [62]	915
5	26	H	Macclesfield T	D	2-2	0-2	22	Magnay [51], Hatch [70]	631
6	31	A	Woking	W	2-1	2-0	19	Brown [20], Chandler [30]	1230
7	Sept 7	H	Hereford U	W	2-1	2-0	17	Walker 2 [32, 42]	931
8	14	A	Cambridge U	L	0-1	0-1	18		2599
9	17	H	Wrexham	L	0-3	0-0	19		538
10	21	A	Tamworth	W	1-0	1-0	17·	Larkin (pen) [24]	738
11	24	H	Chester FC	W	3-2	1-1	16	Magnay [1], Hugill [54], Larkin [56]	610
12	28	A	Forest Green R	L	0-1	0-1	16		1149
13	Oct 5	A	Dartford	W	2-0	1-0	16	Marwood [43], Ramshaw [58]	561
14	8	A	Hyde	W	2-0	1-0	13	Marwood [10], Hugill [79]	409
15	12	A	Alfreton T	W	3-0	0-0	10	Larkin [63], Hugill 2 [78, 83]	778
16	19	A	Nuneaton T	W	4-1	2-0	10	Marwood [15], Hugill [20], Larkin (pen) [57], Ramshaw [59]	946
17	Nov 2	H	Luton T	D	0-0	0-0	11		1080
18	12	H	Wrexham	L	2-3	2-1	12	Marwood [36], Boyes [37]	2469
19	16	H	Salisbury C	W	3-2	1-0	11	Walker 2 [1, 58], Marwood [46]	839
20	23	A	Dartford	W	1-0	0-0	9	Brown [89]	975
21	Dec 10	A	Lincoln C	W	1-0	0-0	8	Walker [56]	1411
22	21	H	Luton T	L	2-4	0-3	10	Oster [70], Hatch [84]	6913
23	26	H	FC Halifax T	D	1-1	0-1	10	Chandler [57]	857
24	28	A	Chester FC	D	1-1	0-1	11	Marwood [68]	2017
25	Jan 1	A	FC Halifax T	D	3-3	0-2	12	Brown [46], Maddison [76], Marwood [82]	1624
26	4	H	Hyde	W	4-0	1-0	8	Maddison [12], Brown [58], Hatch [68], Chandler [73]	502
27	11	H	Nuneaton T	W	2-1	0-0	6	Brown [46], Marwood [80]	726
28	14	H	Aldershot T	D	0-0	0-0	4		724
29	18	A	Grimsby T	D	2-2	1-1	4	Larkin (pen) [14], Maddison [55]	3243
30	21	H	Welling U	D	1-1	0-1	4	Maddison (pen) [50]	621
31	Feb 1	H	Kidderminster H	W	3-1	0-0	4	Oster [52], Marwood [63], Maddison [70]	625
32	15	H	Woking	L	0-2	0-1	5		706
33	22	A	Alfreton T	D	1-1	0-0	7	Maddison [51]	817
34	25	A	Welling U	L	0-2	0-1	7		455
35	Mar 1	H	Forest Green R	D	1-1	0-0	8	Hatch [89]	649
36	8	A	Barnet	W	1-0	0-0	6	Chandler [71]	1361
37	15	A	Salisbury C	D	0-0	0-0	9		685
38	22	A	Lincoln C	W	3-1	2-0	7	Lester [34], Chandler [44], Noble [79]	804
39	25	A	Aldershot T	W	2-1	0-1	4	Lester [57], Marwood [82]	1358
40	29	H	Braintree T	W	1-0	0-0	3	O'Donnell [90]	859
41	Apr 5	H	Tamworth	W	5-0	1-0	4	Chandler [36], Ramshaw 2 [72, 90], Maddison 2 [89, 90]	705
42	12	A	Hereford U	W	1-0	1-0	4	Marwood [36]	1783
43	15	A	Braintree T	D	0-0	0-0	5		901
44	18	H	Southport	D	2-2	1-1	5	Chandler 2 [27, 88]	2121
45	21	A	Macclesfield T	W	2-0	1-0	5	Larkin [26], Maddison [51]	1628
46	26	H	Cambridge U	W	2-0	1-0	3	Larkin [18], Ramshaw [81]	2916

Final League Position: 3

GOALSCORERS
League (72): Marwood 11, Maddison 9 (1 pen), Chandler 8, Larkin 8 (3 pens), Brown 5, Hugill 5, Ramshaw 5, Walker 5, Hatch 4, Brodie 2, Lester 2, Magnay 2, Oster 2, Boyes 1, Noble 1, O'Donnell 1, Turnbull 1.
The Budweiser FA Cup (3): Chandler 1, Curtis 1, Marwood 1.
FA Trophy (4): Maddison 1, Marwood 1, Tait 1, Walker 1.
Skrill Premier League Play-Offs (5): Marwood 2, Larkin 1, Lester 1, O'Donnell 1.

Bartlett 46	Baxter 37 + 1	Tait 3 + 1	Clark 44	O'Brien 9	Chandler 33 + 7	Turnbull 45	Walker 21 + 9	Brodie 4 + 4	Boyes 6 + 6	Brown 22 + 10	Larkin 24 + 4	Magnay 24 + 6	Maddison 18 + 11	Marwood 36 + 1	Hatch 8 + 16	Curtis 41	Ramshaw 7 + 13	Cummins 5 + 10	Lelan 3 + 1	Hugill 4 + 3	Oster 31 + 1	Sirrell 18	Noble 1 + 8	O'Donnell 12 + 2	Lester 4 + 4	Holt — + 1	Match No.
1	2	3	4	5	6	7	8	9¹	10	11	12																1
1		3	4	5	6²	8	7	11	10¹	9	12	2	13														2
1	2	3	4	5	6	8	7²	10¹	13	11	9³		12	14													3
1	2		4	5	7	8	13	14	12		10	6	11²	9¹	3³												4
1			4	5	6	8	7	10²	11¹	12	9³	2			13	3	14										5
1	4		5	3	8	6	7	13	12	9²	11¹	2		10													6
1			4	5	8	6	7	13	12	10¹	11		9²		3		2										7
1			4	5	8³	6	7²		12	11	10	2	13	9¹		3		14									8
1			4	5	7	8	9¹		11²	10	6	2	14		13	3		12²									9
1			4		7¹	6				11	2		9	14	3	8²	13	5	10³	12							10
1			4			7				9¹	11	2	12	8	13	3		6	5	10²							11
1	12	3				7				14	11	2		9	13	4		8	5¹	10³	6²						12
1	2		4		13	8				9	5		11	10¹	3	6²				12	7						13
1	5		4			8	12			7	2³		6	11²	3	9¹		14	13	10							14
1	5		4			7	6¹			14	9		11³	10²	3	13				12	8	2					15
1	2		4	12	6		13		14	9³		10			3	7				11²	8¹	5					16
1	2		4		8³	7		13	12	11	14		10²	3	9¹					6	5						17
1	2		4		8	9		11²	13	6			7		3	12				10¹	5						18
1	2		4		11¹	7	8			10	12		9²		3	13				6	5						19
1	5		4		8²	7	10¹			13	9		12	11	3					6	2						20
1	3	14	6¹		7²	8	9			2	13³	10³	12	5						11	4						21
1	7			6	11³	10¹			9²	2	12		4	3	13	14				8	5						22
1	3	5		6	7	11¹				10²			12	8	13	4				9	2						23
1	2		4		6³	7	9²		14			11¹	10	12	3		13			8	5						24
1	2		4	13	7	10³			9		5	12	6	11¹	3		14			8²							25
1	2		4		8²	7³	6			10			11	9¹	12	3	13	14			5						26
1	2		4		8²	7	6			10	12	14	9¹	11		3		13				5¹					27
1	2		4		8³	7	6²			9	13		12	11		3		14				5	10¹				28
1	2		4		8	7	12			11	10¹		6²			3						5	13	9			29
1	2		4		8¹	7	13			10²			9		14	3				6³	5	12	11				30
1	2		4		14	7				12	10¹		9	11²		3				6	5	13	8³				31
1	2		4		13	7				10²			9	11	14	3				6³	5	12	8¹				32
1	2		4		12	7⁴				11¹		5	10²	6	13	3		9		8							33
1	5			7³		14				11¹		4	10	6	12	3		8²		9	2			13			34
1	2		4			7¹	8²			10³		5	9⁴	11	13	3				6		14	12				35
1	2		4		8	7				11		5¹	9²	13	3	6				10³		14		12			36
1	5		4		8	9	12			11			6¹		3	7				10²		2	13				37
1	2		4		8	7	11²			13		9		3	12					6¹		14	10³				38
1	2²		4		8¹	7	12			11³		13	9		3					6		14	5	10			39
1	5		4		13	7				6²		14	11¹	9		3	12			8³		2	10				40
1			4		8	6				12		2	9	11		3	13			7²		5	10¹				41
1	4		5		9	7						2	10	11		3				8		6					42
1	5		4		6	7	12					2	11¹	10		3	13			8²		9					43
1	2		4		6	7						5	9	10		3	14			8²		13	11¹	12³			44
1	2		4		6	7	14			10¹		5	9²	11³	12	3	13			8							45
1	5		4		6³	7				11¹		2	9²	10		3	12	14		8		13					46

The Budweiser FA Cup

First Qualifying	Chester	(a)	1-0
First Round	Oxford U	(a)	2-2
Replay	Oxford U	(h)	0-1
(aet)			

FA Trophy

First Round	Hednesford T	(h)	4-1
Second Round	Eastleigh	(a)	0-2

Skrill Premier Play-Offs

Semi-Finals 1st leg	Grimsby T	(a)	1-1
Semi-Finals 2nd leg	Grimsby T	(h)	3-1
Final	Cambridge U	(Wembley)	1-2

GRIMSBY TOWN

Ground: Blundell Park, Cleethorpes, NE Lincolnshire DN35 7PY. *Tel:* (01472) 605 050. *Fax:* (01472) 693 665.
Website: www.grimsby-townfc.co.uk *Year Formed:* 1878. *Record Attendance:* 31,651 v Wolverhampton W, FA Cup
5th rd, 20 February 1937. *Nickname:* 'The Mariners'. *Team Manager:* Paul Hurst.
Colours: Black and white striped shirts, black shorts with white trim, red socks with black stripes.

GRIMSBY TOWN – SKRILL PREMIER 2013–14 LEAGUE RECORD

Match No.	Date	Venue	Opponents	Result	H/T Score	Lg Pos.	Goalscorers	Atten- dance
1	Aug 10	H	Aldershot T	D 1-1	0-0	9	Hannah (pen) [81]	4037
2	13	A	Gateshead	W 2-1	1-1	6	Hearn [25], Doig [72]	944
3	17	A	Welling U	L 0-1	0-0	16		807
4	24	H	Alfreton T	W 3-1	2-0	9	Hearn [13], Colbeck [39], McLaughlin [57]	3245
5	26	H	Hyde	W 1-0	0-0	4	Rodman [72]	786
6	31	H	Nuneaton T	L 1-2	0-2	8	Cook [86]	3321
7	Sept 7	A	Luton T	D 0-0	0-0	11		6131
8	14	H	Braintree T	W 1-0	1-0	7	John-Lewis [13]	3403
9	17	A	FC Halifax T	L 0-4	0-3	10		1602
10	21	A	Chester FC	D 0-0	0-0	13		2363
11	24	H	Dartford	W 5-2	3-1	8	McLaughlin [32], Pearson [36], John-Lewis [43], Kerr [85], Disley [90]	2503
12	28	H	Tamworth	W 3-1	0-0	4	Pearson [56], Hannah (pen) [67], Hearn [83]	3105
13	Oct 5	A	Aldershot T	W 3-0	2-0	2	John-Lewis [4], Hannah [10], Hearn [54]	2118
14	8	H	Cambridge U	L 0-1	0-0	5		4386
15	12	A	Salisbury C	L 0-1	0-0	6		1313
16	19	H	Forest Green R	W 3-1	1-1	5	Hannah 2 (1 pen) [37, 64 (p)], Rodman [84]	3150
17	Nov 2	A	Woking	W 2-1	1-1	4	Hannah [1], Disley [90]	1432
18	16	A	Tamworth	W 2-0	0-0	4	Disley [51], Rodman [84]	1306
19	23	H	Barnet	W 2-1	0-0	4	Hannah [67], Hearn [81]	3441
20	Dec 10	H	Welling U	D 1-1	0-1	5	Southwell [90]	2487
21	19	H	Kidderminster H	W 3-1	2-1	3	Disley [17], Neilson 2 [30, 62]	3086
22	26	A	Lincoln C	W 2-0	2-0	3	Hannah [10], Disley [39]	5421
23	28	A	Macclesfield T	L 2-3	0-2	4	Williams (og) [56], Doig [61]	4002
24	Jan 1	H	Lincoln C	D 1-1	1-1	4	Disley [38]	5484
25	18	H	Gateshead	D 2-2	1-1	5	McDonald [8], Bignot [82]	3243
26	28	A	Cambridge U	W 2-1	1-0	4	John-Lewis [18], Neilson [56]	3027
27	Feb 8	H	Southport	D 0-0	0-0	6		3306
28	18	A	Barnet	L 1-2	0-1	8	Disley [59]	1375
29	25	A	Southport	L 1-2	1-1	9	John-Lewis [9]	812
30	Mar 1	A	Salisbury C	W 2-0	1-0	7	Disley [3], Rodman [83]	3269
31	8	A	Macclesfield T	D 1-1	1-0	9	Jennings [36]	2092
32	11	H	Hereford U	D 1-1	1-1	8	Hannah (pen) [17]	3007
33	15	H	Wrexham	W 3-1	1-1	6	Neilson [21], Disley [87], Cook [90]	3506
34	18	A	Forest Green R	L 1-2	0-2	8	Neilson [58]	1219
35	22	A	Nuneaton T	W 1-0	1-0	5	Rodman [8]	1585
36	25	H	Luton T	L 1-2	1-1	7	Neilson [19]	3789
37	29	A	Hereford U	W 1-0	0-0	6	Rodman [62]	2545
38	Apr 1	A	Wrexham	W 1-0	1-0	3	McLaughlin [11]	2019
39	5	A	Kidderminster H	W 1-0	1-0	3	Rodman [20]	2176
40	8	H	Woking	D 2-2	0-0	3	John-Lewis (pen) [90], Tounkara [90]	3507
41	10	A	Dartford	L 0-1	0-0	3		1257
42	12	H	Chester FC	W 2-1	1-0	3	Tounkara [16], Cook [84]	4174
43	15	H	FC Halifax T	L 0-1	0-0	4		4374
44	18	A	Alfreton T	D 3-3	2-1	3	Hannah 3 (1 pen) [7, 33, 70 (p)]	1771
45	21	H	Hyde	W 1-0	0-0	3	Hannah [76]	4232
46	26	A	Braintree T	D 0-0	0-0	4		1489

Final League Position: 4

GOALSCORERS
League (65): Hannah 13 (5 pens), Disley 9, Rodman 7, John-Lewis 6 (1 pen), Neilson 6, Hearn 5, Cook 3, McLaughlin 3, Doig 2, Pearson 2, Tounkara 2, Bignot 1, Colbeck 1, Jennings 1, Kerr 1, McDonald 1, Southwell 1, own goal 1.
The Budweiser FA Cup (9): Hannah 2 (1 pen), Pearson 2, Cook 1, Disley 1, John-Lewis 1, McDonald 1, McLaughlin 1.
FA Trophy (14): Southwell 4, Cook 2, John-Lewis 2, Colbeck 1, McLaughlin 1, Neilsen 1, Pearson 1, Rodman 1, Tounkara 1.
Skrill Premier League Play-Offs (2): Disley 2.

McKeown 45	Bignot 21+2	Pearson S 40	McDonald 18+2	Thomas 32+4	Disley 38+1	Kerr 36+1	McLaughlin 23+8	Colbeck 19+9	Hearn 6+8	Neilson 28+6	John-Lewis 35+3	Rodman 26+9	Hannah 23+10	Doig 21+1	Southwell —+8	Cook 9+21	Thanoi 16+6	Hatton 24+4	Walker 1+2	Goodall 7	Jones 4+2	Winfarrah —+4	Fyfield 6+3	Tounkara 5+7	Jennings 9+3	Boyce 13	Hedge 1	Charlesworth —+1	Match No.
1	2	3	4	5	6	7¹	8	9	10³	11¹	12	13	14																1
1	2	3		5	6	7	8	9	11¹		10			4		12													2
1	2		3	5	6	7³	8	9		13	10¹	11²		4	14	12													3
1	2³	3	4¹	5	6		8	9	11²		10	13		12			7	14											4
1	13	4		5	6		8	11	9¹		10³	12		3		14	7	2²											5
1	2	3		5¹	6		8¹	9²	12		10³	11		4		14	7	13											6
1	2	4			6³	7	8	9²		12	11	10¹		5		13	14	3											7
1	2	3	4			6	8	12		11¹	10³	9				14	7	13	5¹										8
1	2	4	3			7	8	14		11¹	10	9³	13			6²		5	12										9
1	2	3				7	9	6¹	13		10¹			11²	4	12		5	8										10
1	2	3	14	12	7	9		13	6³	11		10²	4			5	8¹												11
1		3	14	6	8	7		13	9¹	11¹		10²	4		12		2	5											12
1		3	12	7	8	6		13	9	10		11²	4			2²		5¹	14										13
1		3		5	7	8	9	14	11²	6¹	10³	12		4		13	2												14
1		3	5		8	9	6²	11³	13		12		4	14	10	2		7¹											15
1	3	12	5	7	8		6³	14	13		9	11³	4¹		10	2													16
1	4	6	5	7	3		8	12				11²		10¹		2		9	13										17
1	4	3	5	7	8	14	6		9¹	10²	12	11³		13		2													18
1	3	4	5	7	8	9	14	12³		10¹	6	11²		13		2													19
1	3	4³	5	7	8		12		9¹	10²	6	11	14	13		2													20
1	3	4	5	7	8	12			9¹	11²	6	10³	14	13		2													21
1	13	3²		5	7	8¹	12		9³	10	6	11	4		14	2													22
1	3		5	7		8	6		12	13	9¹	11³	4	14	10³	2													23
1	2	3	5	7			6¹		9	10²	12	11	4			8													24
1	2	3	4	5	7	8³	14	6¹		9	10	12	11	11²															25
1	2	4	3²	13	7	8		12		9¹	10³	6	11									5	14						26
1	2	3	4		7	8		12		9¹	11³	6	10²		14							5	13						27
1	5		4	3¹	7	8			9³	10	6	13	2		14							12	11²						28
1	2	3	4²		7	8¹		6³		9	11	14	10			12	13					5							29
1	2	3			7	13			9²	10	6	12	4			8³	14					5	11¹						30
1	2	3		5	7	6	14			10	9³	13	4¹			8	12						11²						31
1	2	3		5	7¹	8		12	10³	6	11²					14	9						13	4					32
1	3		5	7		14			9	10¹	6³	13				12	8	2					11²	4					33
1	3		5	7	6	14			9²			13				10¹	8³	2					12	11	4				34
1	2¹	3	12	5	6	7			9²	10³	8					14	13						11	4					35
1	3		5	6	7			9	10¹	8²	13					2							12	11	4				36
1	3		5	8	7⁴			9³	12	6	13				11	14	2						10²	4					37
1	3		5	7		9			10²	6	11¹					8	2						13	12	4				38
1	3		5	7	8	9			10	6	11¹						2						12	4					39
1	3		5²	7	8		12		9¹	10	6						2						14	13	11²	4			40
1	4				8	6				9²	3	12	10	7		2			13	5¹	11¹								41
1	3		7	8	5		6³			12	13	2				11	14		10¹	11²	4								42
1	3		5	7	8²	12	6²	9			13				11	14	2					10¹		4					43
1	3		5	7	6			9	10¹		11				12	8	2							4					44
1		5²		7	6	12		9³	10¹		11	3			8	2					14	13		4					45
	2	4		8¹			6³			9²		3	12	10	7				14	5	11				1	13			46

The Budweiser FA Cup

Fourth Qualifying	Rushall Olympic	(h)	3-0
First Round	Scunthorpe U	(h)	0-0
Replay	Scunthorpe U	(a)	2-1
Second Round	Northampton T	(h)	2-0
Third Round	Huddersfield T	(h)	2-3

Skrill Premier Play-Offs

Semi-Finals 1st leg	Gateshead	(h)	1-1
Semi-Finals 2nd leg	Gateshead	(a)	1-3

FA Trophy

First Round	Coalville T	(a)	1-1
Replay	Coalville T	(h)	0-0
Second Round	Barnet	(a)	2-1
Third Round	Maidenhead U	(h)	2-1
Quarter-Finals	Tamworth	(h)	4-1
Semi-Finals 1st leg	Cambridge U	(a)	1-2
Semi-Finals 2nd leg	Cambridge U	(h)	1-1

FC HALIFAX TOWN

Ground: The Shay Stadium, Halifax, West Yorkshire HX1 2 YT.   *Tel:* (01422) 341222.   *Fax:* (01422) 349487.
Website: www.halifaxafc.co.uk   *Year Formed:* 1911.
Record Attendance: 36,855 v Tottenham H, FA Cup 5th rd, 15 February 1953.   *Nickname:* 'The Shaymen'.
Manager: Neil Aspin.   *Colours:* Blue shirts with white trim, white shorts with blue trim, blue socks with white trim.

FC HALIFAX TOWN – SKRILL PREMIER 2013–14 LEAGUE RECORD

Match No.	Date	Venue	Opponents	Result	H/T Score	Lg Pos.	Goalscorers	Atten- dance
1	Aug 11	A	Cambridge U	L	1-5	1-2	22	Gregory [7]	2780
2	13	H	Wrexham	W	3-2	3-1	16	Maynard [34], Wilson (pen) [40], Gregory [45]	1674
3	17	H	Dartford	W	2-0	0-0	8	Gregory [49], Holsgrove [54]	1296
4	24	A	Macclesfield T	D	2-2	2-1	11	Gregory [16], Holsgrove [21]	1720
5	26	H	Southport	W	1-0	0-0	6	Holsgrove [86]	1583
6	31	A	Salisbury C	L	1-3	0-1	10	Brett (og) [87]	820
7	Sept 7	H	Barnet	W	2-1	1-0	5	McManus [21], Maynard [50]	1651
8	14	A	Forest Green R	L	1-2	1-0	10	Gardner (pen) [34]	1195
9	17	H	Grimsby T	W	4-0	3-0	6	Carver [19], Gardner 2 [27, 32], Smith, A [47]	1602
10	21	H	Hereford U	D	1-1	1-1	7	Smith (og) [31]	1362
11	24	A	Kidderminster H	L	0-2	0-1	11		1703
12	28	H	Chester FC	W	2-1	1-1	9	Gregory [4], Roberts [64]	1805
13	Oct 5	A	Luton T	L	3-4	3-3	11	Marshall [3], Ainge [19], Gardner [23]	6519
14	8	H	Nuneaton T	D	2-2	1-1	12	Gardner [40], Toulson [90]	1197
15	12	A	Woking	D	0-0	0-0	11		1552
16	19	H	Welling U	W	3-0	3-0	11	Gregory 3 [7, 24, 36]	1345
17	Nov 2	A	Alfreton T	L	0-3	0-2	12		900
18	12	H	Hyde	W	4-0	1-0	9	Maynard [5], Gregory 2 (1 pen) [72, 83 (p)], Wilson [76]	1037
19	16	H	Aldershot T	W	4-0	3-0	5	Gregory [18], Smith, A [27], McManus [41], Roberts [71]	1418
20	23	A	Braintree T	L	0-1	0-0	10		943
21	26	A	Hereford U	L	2-3	1-1	11	Wilson (pen) [20], Ironside [62]	1158
22	Dec 7	A	Woking	L	3-4	1-3	11	Love [2], Wilson [74], Gardner [81]	1033
23	14	A	Dartford	W	2-1	0-0	10	Ironside [63], Wilson [74]	952
24	21	H	Forest Green R	W	1-0	1-0	8	Roberts [28]	1262
25	26	A	Gateshead	D	1-1	1-0	8	Pearson [26]	857
26	28	H	Lincoln C	W	5-1	2-1	6	Gardner (pen) [13], Gregory [27], Smith, A [79], Worthington [85], Gray [90]	1979
27	Jan 1	H	Gateshead	D	3-3	2-0	5	Gregory 2 [10, 13], Ainge [61]	1624
28	4	A	Tamworth	L	0-2	0-1	5		890
29	11	A	Wrexham	D	0-0	0-0	7		3214
30	18	H	Cambridge U	D	1-1	0-0	7	Gregory [76]	1767
31	25	A	Aldershot T	D	2-2	1-1	6	Gregory 2 [34, 83]	1977
32	Feb 1	A	Lincoln C	L	1-3	0-2	9	Crowther [51]	2077
33	4	H	Salisbury C	W	5-1	2-0	7	Gregory 3 (1 pen) [3, 53, 72 (p)], Maynard [16], Wilson [90]	1003
34	13	A	Chester FC	L	1-2	0-0	8	Bolton [90]	2127
35	Mar 1	A	Tamworth	W	2-0	1-0	9	Pearson [14], Maynard [67]	1313
36	8	A	Hyde	W	5-1	2-0	7	Crowther [9], Gregory 3 [27, 60, 82], Marshall [50]	901
37	15	A	Welling U	W	1-0	0-0	5	Gregory (pen) [50]	645
38	24	H	Alfreton T	W	2-0	1-0	5	Gregory 2 [22, 50]	1454
39	29	A	Luton T	W	2-0	1-0	5	Roberts [18], Gregory [69]	3586
40	Apr 3	H	Braintree T	D	0-0	0-0	7		1535
41	5	A	Nuneaton T	W	1-0	0-0	5	Smith, C [85]	1041
42	12	A	Barnet	W	4-0	3-0	5	Spencer 2 [6, 32], Gregory [24], Maynard [53]	1683
43	15	A	Grimsby T	W	1-0	0-0	3	Maynard [52]	4374
44	19	H	Macclesfield T	W	2-1	2-1	3	Roberts [18], Smith, C [22]	2119
45	21	A	Southport	L	1-2	1-0	4	Gregory [5]	2043
46	26	H	Kidderminster H	D	1-1	1-1	5	Wilson [1]	2089

Final League Position: 5

GOALSCORERS
League (85): Gregory 29 (3 pens), Gardner 7 (2 pens), Maynard 7, Wilson 7 (2 pens), Roberts 5, Holsgrove 3, Smith, A 3, Ainge 2, Crowther 2, Ironside 2, Marshall 2, McManus 2, Pearson 2, Smith, C 2, Spencer 2, Bolton 1, Carver 1, Gray 1, Love 1, Toulson 1, Worthington 1, own goals 2.
The Budweiser FA Cup (3): Gregory 2, McManus 1.
FA Trophy (0).
Skrill Premier League Play-Offs (1): Gregory 1.

Glennon 45	Toulson 16	Roberts 44	Lowe 19 + 4	McManus 45	Pearson 43	Maynard 44 + 1	Smith A 38 + 2	Wilson 22 + 11	Holsgrove 9 + 9	Gregory 35 + 1	Ainge 40 + 1	Morgan — + 1	Briggs — + 2	Senior 1 + 1	Gardner 18 + 5	Johnson — + 5	Marshall 28 + 8	Williams — + 5	McReady 2 + 12	Carver 3 + 2	Ball — + 2	Worthington — + 10	Ironside 6 + 4	Love 3 + 3	Patterson — + 2	Anderson 1	Gray 2 + 5	Challinor 5	Clay 3 + 1	Jackson 2 + 12	Crowther 10 + 3	Bolton 11 + 1	Lenighan 1	Smith C 6 + 4	Spencer 4 + 3	Marie — + 1	Match No.
1*	2	3³	4*	5	6	7	8²	9	10¹	11	12	13	14																								1
	2	3		5	7	8	6¹	11³	9²	10	4		12	1	13		14																				2
1	2	3		5		7	8²	6	11	9¹	10		4				12	13																			3
1	2	3		5		7	8³	6	10²	9¹	11		4		13	14	12																				4
1	2	3	14	5	7	8	6³	10¹	9	11²	4						12	13																			5
1	2	3	4³	5		6²	8	11*	10*	9					7¹	13	12	14																			6
1	2	3	10	5	7	9	6³				4				8²	12	13	14	11¹																		7
1	2	4	10	5	7³	6*	8				3				9²	14	13	11¹	12																		8
1	2	4	10	5	6	8¹					3				9³	7	14	13	11²	12																	9
1	2	3	5¹	9	8	7		13		11³	4				10²	6			12	14																	10
1	2	3	5²	10	6	7¹	8	14		11	4				9³	12	13																				11
1	2	4		5	7	6¹	8		10²	11	3				9³	12	13	14																			12
1	2	5	12	3	6		8¹		13	11²	10				7	14	9³																				13
1	2	4	12	5	6	13			8	11¹	3				9	7	10²																				14
1	2	4		3	7	5	8²	14	12	11	6				9³	10¹	13																				15
1	2	3		9	5	8	7	6³	14	10²	4				11¹	13	12																				16
1	2	4	5	10²	6	7	8¹	14	13	11	3				9³		12																				17
1		4	5	9³	2	8	13	10		3	6¹				7							12	11²	14													18
1		3	5	9	2	8	6³	10	14	11¹	4						7²					12	13														19
1		3	5	9	2	6³	8	10		11	4						7²					12	13	14													20
1		3¹	4²	5	2	7	8³	9	10						14							12	11	6	13												21
1			5	2³	9	6	13				4				7				11²	8¹	14	3	10*														22
1		3	5	6	2	9	10	13			4				8¹		7					12	11²														23
1		4	5	7	2	6	11¹				3				9		8					13	10¹														24
1		4	5	7	2	6		11¹			3				9		8					12	10²	8													25
1		3	5	8	2	9	10	11³			4				6²		7¹					12	14				13										26
1		3	5	8	2	6³	10	11			4				9²		7¹					12	14				13										27
1		3	5	7	2	6	10	13		11	3						8¹					12			9²												28
1		3	5	7	2	6²	10	9¹	11		4										13	12	8														29
1		3	5*	7	8²	9	10	11			4				13														2	6¹	12						30
1		3	6²	5	9	13		10		4¹					8							12					14	2	7	11³							31
1		3	5	6	9	7²		11			4				8							12					2	8¹	13	10							32
1		4	5		8³	6¹	9	11			3				7												2¹	14	12	10	13						33
1		3	5		2	13	10*	11			4				6													12	8²	9	7¹						34
1		4	5		8	7	6²	11			3				9													12	10¹	2			13			35
1		4	5		8²	7	6¹	11			3				10			14										12	9³	2		13				36
1		3	5		9²	7	8¹	11			4				6													12	10	2		13				37
1		3	5		6	7	8²	11			4				10													12	9¹	2		13				38
1		3	5		8	7	6²	13		11	4				9													12	10¹	2						39
1	3²	13	5	10	7	6¹		11							8													14	9³	2				12		40
1		4	6	3	7		12	11							8¹													10²	9	2		5	13		41
1	5	3	4		7	8	12	13		10					9²												14		2	7		6³	11¹		42
1	5	3	4		7	8			10						9													12		2		6	11¹		43
1	3	9	5	10	7	6¹	14	11³			4				8²												13					2	12		44
1	3		5	9	10	7	14	11²							8³												12	13	2			4	6¹	45
1*		4	9	5²	7	8²	6	11					2			12	14																3	10	13	46

The Budweiser FA Cup

Fourth Qualifying	Nuneaton T	(a)	2-0
First Round	Milton Keynes D	(a)	1-4

FA Trophy

First Round	Guiseley AFC	(h)	0-1

Skrill Premier Play-Offs

Semi-Finals 1st leg	Cambridge U	(h)	1-0
Semi-Finals 2nd leg	Cambridge U	(a)	0-2

HEREFORD UNITED

Ground: Edgar Street Athletic Ground, Blackfriars Street, Hereford HR4 9JU
Tel: (08442) 761 939.   *Fax:* (08442) 761 982.   *Website:* www.herefordunited.co.uk   *Year Formed:* 1924.
Record Attendance: 18,114 v Sheffield W, FA Cup 3rd rd, 4 January 1958.   *Nickname:* 'The Bulls'.
Manager: John Taylor.   *Colours:* White shirts with black trim, black shorts with white trim, white socks.

HEREFORD UNITED – SKRILL PREMIER 2013–14 LEAGUE RECORD

Match No.	Date	Venue	Opponents	Result	H/T Score	Lg Pos.	Goalscorers	Attendance
1	Aug 10	H	Braintree T	D	1-1	0-1	9	Walker 79	2033
2	13	A	Chester FC	W	2-0	1-0	4	Graham 45, Smith 50	2900
3	17	A	Hyde	D	2-2	1-2	9	Bush 15, Rankine 70	509
4	24	H	Tamworth	W	1-0	0-0	5	Smith 51	1864
5	26	A	Alfreton T	L	1-2	1-1	12	Sharp 45	740
6	31	H	Welling U	W	2-1	0-0	7	Sharp 49, Rankine 84	1527
7	Sept 7	A	Gateshead	L	1-2	0-2	10	West 74	931
8	13	H	Aldershot T	L	0-2	0-1	12		1851
9	17	A	Nuneaton T	L	1-2	0-1	16	McDonald 53	1085
10	21	A	FC Halifax T	D	1-1	1-1	15	Brodie 8	1362
11	24	H	Lincoln C	W	1-0	0-0	15	Bush 85	1398
12	28	H	Luton T	D	0-0	0-0	14		2386
13	Oct 5	A	Cambridge U	L	0-1	0-1	15		3381
14	8	A	Macclesfield T	L	0-1	0-0	16		1329
15	12	H	Dartford	D	2-2	0-1	16	Krans 49, Dyer 60	1583
16	19	H	Barnet	L	0-1	0-1	19		1632
17	31	A	Salisbury C	L	1-4	0-2	19	Smith 59	1112
18	Nov 12	H	Chester FC	D	2-2	2-2	19	Dyer 2 17, 38	1512
19	16	A	Southport	W	3-0	1-0	17	Collins 23, Rankine 69, Dyer 89	876
20	23	A	Lincoln C	D	1-1	0-0	17	Artus 89	1874
21	26	H	FC Halifax T	W	3-2	1-1	17	O'Keefe 37, Collins 73, Odhiambo 77	1158
22	Dec 7	H	Nuneaton T	L	0-1	0-1	17		1292
23	21	H	Cambridge U	W	1-0	1-0	17	Rankine 24	1558
24	26	A	Kidderminster H	L	1-2	0-2	17	O'Keefe 49	3420
25	28	H	Forest Green R	W	1-0	1-0	16	Brown 26	1848
26	Jan 9	A	Forest Green R	D	1-1	0-0	16	Bush 76	1077
27	18	H	Southport	W	4-1	1-0	16	Brown 31, Rankine 2 53, 89, Walker 55	1569
28	25	H	Salisbury C	W	1-0	0-0	16	Collins 52	2016
29	28	H	Kidderminster H	D	1-1	0-0	15	O'Keefe 61	2014
30	Feb 3	A	Woking	L	0-3	0-2	15		1131
31	15	A	Luton T	L	0-7	0-1	17		7111
32	22	A	Dartford	L	0-2	0-1	18		1137
33	25	H	Macclesfield T	L	1-2	0-1	18	Collins 78	1013
34	Mar 1	A	Wrexham	L	0-2	0-2	18		1884
35	8	A	Braintree T	D	1-1	1-1	18	Walker 36	805
36	11	A	Grimsby T	D	1-1	1-1	18	McDonald 22	3007
37	15	H	Hyde	D	0-0	0-0	18		1378
38	18	A	Wrexham	L	0-2	0-1	18		2056
39	22	A	Barnet	L	0-2	0-2	19		1497
40	29	H	Grimsby T	L	0-1	0-0	20		2545
41	Apr 5	H	Woking	L	0-2	0-2	20		2140
42	8	A	Welling U	W	1-0	0-0	20	James 61	480
43	12	A	Gateshead	L	0-1	0-1	21		1783
44	18	A	Tamworth	L	0-1	0-0	21		1154
45	21	H	Alfreton T	W	3-2	1-1	21	James 29, Collins 61, Bowen 71	2445
46	26	A	Aldershot T	W	2-1	1-0	20	Smith 28, Rankine 88	3593

Final League Position: 20

GOALSCORERS

League (44): Rankine 7, Collins 5, Dyer 4, Smith 4, Bush 3, O'Keefe 3, Walker 3, Brown 2, James 2, McDonald 2, Sharp 2, Artus 1, Bowen 1, Brodie 1, Graham 1, Krans 1, Odhiambo 1, West 1.
The Budweiser FA Cup (1): O'Keefe 1.
FA Trophy (0).

Evans R 20	Leadbitter 30 + 8	Bush 39 + 3	McDonald 37	Graham 42	James 21 + 2	Purdie 21 + 8	O'Keefe 18	Walker 26 + 17	Smith 26 + 8	Rankine 25 + 6	Sharp 21 + 9	Pilkington 4 + 9	Artus 31 + 3	Edwards — + 4	Collins 32 + 2	West 7 + 1	Gwynne 4 + 1	Harris — + 1	Green 7	Brown 21 + 15	Brodie 6 + 2	Othiambo 2 + 5	Dyer 5	Krans 2 + 1	Lloyd-Weston 26 + 1	Lathrope 8	Evans M 6	Williams — + 10	Edge 7 + 5	Bowen 8	Murphy 4	Match No.
1	2	3	4	5	6	7¹	8	9	10²	11	12	13																				1
1	2	5	4	3		7	9²	8	6¹	11¹	10	12	14	13																		2
1	2	5	4	3		8	6	9²	11¹	10	12	13	7²	14																		3
1	2	5	4	3		8	6	10	11¹²	12	9¹	7			13																	4
1	2	5		3	12	7¹	9	10			11³		8		4	6²	13	14														5
1		2	3	4		6		9	11	12	10¹		13		5	7²			8													6
1	2	5	3	4		7²		6³	11	13	10¹		14		9				8	12												7
1	12	5²	4	3		7		6	10		13				2¹	9³			8	14	11											8
1	2	5	3	4	12	8²		9³	10			6¹			13				7	14	11											9
1	2	5	3	4	8			14	11³	12					6²				7	9	10¹	13										10
1	2	5	3	4	8			12	10			13			6²				7	9	11¹											11
1	2	5	3	4	8			12	11¹			13			9²				7	6	10³	14										12
1	2	5	3	4	7¹	12		13	10		14	9²				8³				6	11											13
1	2	5	4	3		7		6	10		12	14				8³				9²	13	11¹										14
1	2³	5	3	4		7		6		10¹		14			8				13	12	9	11²										15
1	2	5	3	4		7³		6²		10	14				8				12	13	11	9¹										16
1	5	9¹	2	3		6²	7	14	10	12	8³				4					11	13											17
	2	5	3		8			9¹	10				7²	13	4					12					1		6					18
	2	5	4					6¹	10²				7	13	3	11			9	12					1	8						19
	2	5	4			7		9	10²	11					3					12					1	8	6¹	13				20
	2	5²	3		8			9³	10	11					4					12		14			1	7	6¹	13				21
	2	5	3		8			9¹	10						4					12			11²		1	7	6	13				22
	2	5	4	3	8			9	10						2					12			11²		1	7	6¹					23
	2	5	4	3	8			9¹	10					13	2					12			11²		1	7	6					24
12	2¹	5	4	3	8			9	10³					13									11²		1	7	6	14				25
12	3	4	5			7		9	10	11				13	2²	8¹									1		6					26
12		5	4	3		7²		6	10	11			14		2¹	8³				9					1			13				27
13		5	4	3		7		6¹	10³	11			14		2²	8				9					1			12				28
13		5	4	3		7		6¹	10	11²					2	8				9					1			12				29
14		5	4	3	8			12	10	11²	13		7¹		2³					6					1			9				30
	2	5³	3	4		7¹		9	10	11²	12	13				8									1		6		14			31
1	2	13	5¹	4		7²		6	10³	11	12				3	8				9					1			14				32
1	2	12	5¹	4		7²		6	10³	11	13				3	8				9					1			14				33
1¹	2	5	3		8			6	10	11²	13				4	9				7³					1			14	12			34
	2¹	5	4	3	8			6	10	11					9	10				12					1				7			35
	6¹	5	3	4	7			10	13	11²					9	2				12					1				8			36
	5	2	4		8		14	11	13	12³	10²		9¹		3					6					1				7			37
	5	3	4		7³		14	10	9²	11	13				2					6					1			12	8¹			38
	5	3¹	4		8	12		14	11³		10	13	7		2					9					1				6²			39
13	5		4		7²	2		12	11		10¹		8		3					9					1			14	6¹			40
	2		4	7	5			6¹	11³	12		13	8		3					9²					1			14	10			41
	2		4	7	5			13	11²		10¹		8		3					12					1				6	9		42
	2		3	7	5			13	11		10¹		9²		4					12					1			14	6³	8		43
	2¹	12	3	7	5			14	10	11			9²		4					13					1				6³	8		44
	5		3	7	2			11	10¹				8		4					13					1			14	12	9²	6¹	45
	5		4	7	6			14	9²	10			8		3					12					1			13	2¹	11²		46

The Budweiser FA Cup
Fourth Qualifying	AFC Hornchurch	(a)	1-0
First Round	Burton	(a)	0-2

FA Trophy
First Round	Woking	(h)	0-3

HYDE

Ground: Ewen Fields, Walker Lane, Hyde, Cheshire SK14 5PL.
Tel: (0161) 367 7273.   *Fax:* (0161) 367 7273.   *Website:* www.hydefc.co.uk   *Year Formed:* 1919.
Record Attendance: 9,500 v Nelson, FA Cup 4th qualifying rd, 11 November 1950.   *Nickname:* 'The Tigers'.
Manager: Scott McNiven.   *Colours:* Red shirts, navy shorts, navy socks.

HYDE – SKRILL PREMIER 2013–14 LEAGUE RECORD

Match No.	Date	Venue	Opponents	Result		H/T Score	Lg Pos.	Goalscorers	Attendance
1	Aug 10	A	Forest Green R	L	0-8	0-4	23		1158
2	13	H	Southport	L	1-2	1-0	23	Collins [28]	769
3	17	H	Hereford U	D	2-2	2-1	20	Collins [21], Tomsett [42]	509
4	24	A	Wrexham	D	2-2	1-2	21	Collins (pen) [13], Spencer (pen) [90]	3304
5	26	H	Grimsby T	L	0-1	0-0	21		786
6	31	A	Barnet	L	2-3	0-2	23	Tomsett 2 [46, 78]	1669
7	Sept 7	H	Cambridge U	L	0-1	0-1	23		766
8	14	A	Kidderminster H	L	1-2	1-2	24	Collins [15]	1607
9	17	H	Woking	L	0-2	0-0	24		387
10	21	H	Welling U	L	0-1	0-1	24		427
11	24	A	Salisbury C	L	0-2	0-0	24		638
12	28	A	Lincoln C	L	0-3	0-0	24		2311
13	Oct 5	H	Braintree T	L	0-3	0-1	24		402
14	8	H	Gateshead	L	0-2	0-1	24		409
15	12	A	Luton T	L	1-4	1-1	24	McNulty (og) [45]	7081
16	19	A	Dartford	L	3-4	2-2	24	Spencer 2 (1 pen) [34 (p), 43], Almond [54]	1083
17	Nov 2	H	Nuneaton T	D	2-2	1-1	24	Almond [27], Spencer [90]	447
18	9	H	Chester FC	L	1-2	1-1	24	Almond [3]	1232
19	12	A	FC Halifax T	L	0-4	0-1	24		1037
20	16	A	Woking	L	2-3	2-1	24	Spencer [14], Gray [23]	1381
21	23	H	Alfreton T	L	1-2	0-0	24	Spencer [66]	448
22	Dec 21	H	Barnet	L	0-1	0-0	24		499
23	26	A	Macclesfield T	L	0-3	0-2	24		1882
24	28	H	Wrexham	L	2-5	2-2	24	Hughes [28], Spencer [33]	952
25	Jan 1	H	Macclesfield T	L	0-3	0-0	24		979
26	4	A	Gateshead	L	0-4	0-1	24		502
27	11	A	Southport	D	1-1	1-0	24	Spencer [38]	871
28	14	A	Welling U	W	2-0	0-0	24	Almond [58], Hughes [71]	436
29	18	H	Forest Green R	L	2-6	1-4	24	Blakeman [21], Carlton [50]	496
30	25	H	Tamworth	L	0-3	0-1	24		369
31	Feb 8	H	Lincoln C	L	3-4	1-2	24	Hughes 2 [41, 65], Brizell [68]	646
32	11	A	Tamworth	D	1-1	0-1	24	Brizell [70]	616
33	15	A	Nuneaton T	L	0-1	0-1	24		876
34	22	H	Aldershot T	D	2-2	1-1	24	Blakeman [39], Clark [75]	520
35	Mar 1	A	Braintree T	L	1-2	1-1	24	Brown [37]	754
36	8	H	FC Halifax T	L	1-5	0-2	24	Brown [56]	901
37	11	A	Alfreton T	L	0-3	0-1	24		506
38	15	A	Hereford U	D	0-0	0-0	24		1378
39	22	H	Dartford	L	0-2	0-0	24		358
40	29	A	Aldershot T	L	0-1	0-1	24		1591
41	Apr 5	A	Chester FC	L	2-3	0-2	24	Blakeman 2 [57, 64]	2228
42	8	H	Salisbury C	L	0-2	0-0	24		275
43	12	A	Cambridge U	L	2-7	1-4	24	Poole [13], Thurston [86]	2804
44	18	H	Kidderminster H	L	1-3	1-1	24	Blakeman [35]	531
45	21	A	Grimsby T	L	0-1	0-0	24		4232
46	26	H	Luton T	L	0-1	0-0	24		2729

Final League Position: 24

GOALSCORERS

League (38): Spencer 8 (2 pens), Blakeman 5, Almond 4, Collins 4 (1 pen), Hughes 4, Tomsett 3, Brizell 2, Brown 2, Carlton 1, Clark 1, Gray 1, Poole 1, Thurston 1, own goal 1.
The Budweiser FA Cup (0).
FA Trophy (1) O'Donnell 1.

Carnell 13	Brizell 36	Haining 26 + 1	Ashworth 21 + 1	Blakeman 40	Tomsett 39	Brown 35	Poole 21 + 5	Collins 11 + 7	Almond 21 + 7	Carlton 19 + 5	Fitzgerald 1 + 3	Spencer 22 + 9	Moses 1 + 3	Thurston 22 + 3	Dennis 4	Hughes 27 + 10	Griffin 15	Mainwaring 8 + 3	McQuade 10	Dieseruvwe 3 + 4	Liversedge 3	Whincop 1 + 1	McNiven — + 2	Walker 6	Devaney 2 + 9	Gray 9	Lazenbury — + 2	Belezika 4	Frith 1 + 1	Vigouroux 12	O'Connor 9 + 1	O'Donnell 5	Kiwanda — + 6	Day 10 + 4	Lomax 10 + 3	Kirby 2 + 10	Thornton 6 + 5	Manship — + 1	Pollard 1 + 5	Ketings 17	Clark 13 + 3	Match No.
1	2^4	3	4	5	6	7^1	8	9	10^3	11^2	12	13	14																													1
1		3^1	4	5	7	6^3	8	9^2	11	13	12	10	14		2																											2
1		3		5	8		7^1	6	10^2	11	9^5		13	12	2	4	14																									3
1		3		8			7^3	11	10	9		13	6^1	2^4	4	14	5	12																								4
1	2		5			6	8^1	7^2	10^1	11	14		9			4	13	3	12																							5
1	2	12	5			6	8		10^2	13	11		9			4^1	14	3	7^3																							6
1	2	3		8^1	7^1	6^2	12	13	11	10^2		9				14	5	4																							7
1	2	4	3	6		7	9^2	10^3	14			13				11	5	8^1	12																							8
1	2	3	4	8		7		9	11			12				6	5		10^1																							9
	2	4	5	6		8		10^2	7^3			12				11^1	3	13	9	1	14																					10
	2	3	4	9^1	7	8		14	12			11				5	6^1	10^1	1		13																					11
	2	3	4	8^1	7	6	14	11^2	13			10				5	12	1		9^3																					12
1	2	3	4		7	8^1	6^3	14	12			10				9^5	5	13			11																					13
1	2	3	4	8^1	7		6	12	13			11^3					5	14		9^2	10																					14
1	2	5	4^1	8	7		6	11^1	9			12				3				13	10^2																					15
1^1	2	3		5	7	6^3	8^2	14	11			9				13	10	4	12																						16
	2		3		6	7			11			10				12	5	8^1		9	4					1															17
	2		5		7	8	12	14	10			11^2				13	3	6^1		9^3	4					1																18
	2^1	3	4	8^1	7	6		11				10^3		14		13	5			12	9^2					1																19
		4	8	7		6^1		11				2				9^5	5			12	10	3	1																			20
		3	6^1	7	8	13		10	14			11		2^3		5				12	9^2					1	4															21
	3		5		7	6^2		11	10^1			9^3		2		13				12						1	4	8	14													22
5	3		9	8	7	6^3		13	11^1			12		2^2						14						1	4	10														23
2			5	7^3	8^1			10	13			11		12		9				14						1	4	6	3^2													24
2		3	8	7				10	13			11				6^1										1	5	9	4^2	12												25
2		5	8					11				10		7		9^1										1	4	6	13	3^2	12											26
5		9	7					6	10^2			11		2^1		8										1	3			12	4	13										27
2		7	8					9	10^3			11^2				6										1	3		4^1	5	13	12	14									28
2		3	6					7	10^1							11^2											1		5	13		8	9	4		12						29
2		3	6	8^1	7^2			10						9^3		11													14	13	4		5		12	1						30
2	3		5	7^1	8	10^2		11				12		9		6															4						1	13				31
2^9	3		5^1		6	8^2		10				9		7		11													14	4		12				1	13					32
2	4		3	6	7			11				9		8		10^1													5						1	12	13					33
2	3		6	8	7			11								10													4^1	5	12				1	9						34
2	4		5^1		6			10						8^4		11	3												7	12					1	9						35
2	3	5	6		9			11								7^2	4												13		8^1	12				1	10					36
2	3	4	10	8				11						7^1		6	5																	12	1	9	7					37
2	8^1	13	5	9				11^2	14			7				10	3												4^3	12					1	6						38
2			5	7	8	12						9^1				11	4		10^3											3^2	13	14			1	6						39
2	3^2		5^2	6	7	9^1						8				10	4		12													13	14		1	11						40
2	3^1		5	7	8							9^2				5	4							11							13		12		1	10						41
2	4^2		6^1	7	8^3							13				10	5							11							3		14	12	1	9						42
			2	6	7	9^3				8^1		5		13		3								11							12			4^2		14	1	10				43
			5	7	6^3	9^2						2^1		8							10		14							3	12	4		13	1	11					44
			5	7	6^1	9								8					13	10	12									3		2^2	4		1	11						45
			5	7		11						2		9	3					10										12			4		6^1	8						46

The Budweiser FA Cup
Fourth Qualifying   Wrexham   (a)   0-2   **FA Trophy**
First Round   North Ferriby U   (h)   1-2

KIDDERMINSTER HARRIERS

Ground: Aggborough Stadium, Hoo Road, Kidderminster DY10 1NB.   *Tel:* (01562) 823 931.   *Fax:* (01562) 827 329.
Website: www.harriers.co.uk   *Year Formed:* 1886.   *Record Attendance:* 9,155 v Hereford U, FA Cup 1st rd, 27 November 1948.
Nickname: 'The Harriers'.   *Manager:* Gary Whild.   *Colours:* Red shirts with white trim, red shorts with white trim,
white socks.

KIDDERMINSTER HARRIERS – SKRILL PREMIER 2013–14 LEAGUE RECORD

Match No.	Date	Venue	Opponents	Result	H/T Score	Lg Pos.	Goalscorers	Attendance
1	Aug 10	H	Gateshead	W 3-1	1-1	3	Gash 13, Gittings 60, Dunkley 81	2110
2	13	A	Alfreton T	L 1-3	0-1	13	Storer 79	722
3	17	A	Braintree T	W 1-0	0-0	6	Storer 89	874
4	24	H	Chester FC	W 3-1	2-1	2	Gowling 32, Johnson 45, Lolley 90	2283
5	26	A	Nuneaton T	L 1-2	1-0	7	Malbon 5	1481
6	31	H	Luton T	L 0-2	0-0	12		2866
7	Sept 7	A	Welling U	W 2-1	2-0	8	Dance 2 10, 25	911
8	14	H	Hyde	W 2-1	2-1	6	Malbon 3, Gash 34	1607
9	17	H	Tamworth	W 3-0	1-0	3	Dance 6, Gash 63, Malbon (pen) 90	874
10	21	A	Dartford	L 0-3	0-1	4		1020
11	24	H	FC Halifax T	W 2-0	1-0	3	Gash 21, Lolley 57	1703
12	27	H	Aldershot T	D 0-0	0-0	3		2049
13	Oct 5	A	Chester FC	D 0-0	0-0	6		2223
14	8	H	Forest Green R	W 4-1	1-1	2	Storer 12, Byrne 65, Morgan-Smith 2 (1 pen) 72, 88 (p)	2244
15	12	A	Southport	W 2-1	2-1	2	Lolley 8, Blissett 45	1018
16	19	H	Lincoln C	W 4-1	1-0	2	Gash 42, Boyce (og) 55, Storer 68, Malbon 90	2103
17	Nov 2	A	Barnet	L 0-1	0-1	2		1557
18	12	A	Macclesfield T	D 1-1	1-0	3	Gittings 27	1395
19	16	H	Wrexham	W 3-1	1-0	2	Lolley 2 31, 64, Dunkley 78	2532
20	23	H	Tamworth	W 5-3	2-0	2	Malbon 20, Lolley 22, Morgan-Smith 2 56, 77, Storer 83	1951
21	Dec 10	A	Woking	L 0-1	0-0	3		1166
22	14	H	Alfreton T	L 1-3	1-0	3	Gittings 17	1834
23	19	A	Grimsby T	L 1-3	1-2	4	Gash 8	3086
24	26	H	Hereford U	W 2-1	2-0	5	Gash 9, Jackman 29	3420
25	28	A	Luton T	L 0-6	0-1	5		8488
26	Jan 11	H	Salisbury C	W 3-0	1-0	4	Lolley 3 (2 pens) 18, 75 (p), 86 (p)	2034
27	21	H	Dartford	L 1-2	0-2	6	Gash 49	1580
28	28	A	Hereford U	D 1-1	0-0	7	Gowling 65	2014
29	Feb 1	A	Gateshead	L 1-3	0-0	7	Johnson 90	625
30	15	A	Lincoln C	L 0-2	0-1	10		2012
31	22	H	Braintree T	D 2-2	0-0	10	Morgan-Smith 2 78, 82	1653
32	25	H	Woking	W 2-0	1-0	8	Morgan-Smith 1, Storer 69	1448
33	Mar 1	A	Cambridge U	L 1-5	1-1	10	Malbon 30	2528
34	8	A	Wrexham	D 0-0	0-0	10		3159
35	11	H	Macclesfield T	W 2-1	2-1	9	Gittings 1, Morgan-Smith 39	1591
36	15	H	Barnet	W 1-0	0-0	8	Gash 60	1950
37	18	A	Aldershot T	D 0-0	0-0	5		1558
38	22	H	Southport	D 1-1	0-1	8	Byrne 77	1818
39	29	A	Salisbury C	D 1-1	1-0	10	Gittings 35	2217
40	Apr 5	H	Grimsby T	L 0-1	0-1	10		2176
41	8	A	Forest Green R	D 1-1	0-0	11	Wright 49	1231
42	12	A	Welling U	W 2-0	0-0	9	Gash 77, Blissett 84	1882
43	15	H	Cambridge U	W 2-0	0-0	7	Bell 67, Gash 77	1938
44	18	A	Hyde	W 3-1	1-1	7	Bell 6, Thornton (og) 74, Morgan-Smith 76	531
45	21	H	Nuneaton T	D 0-0	0-0	7		2022
46	26	A	FC Halifax T	D 1-1	1-1	7	Blissett 30	2089

Final League Position: 7

GOALSCORERS

League (66): Gash 11, Lolley 9 (2 pens), Morgan-Smith 9 (1 pen), Malbon 6 (1 pen), Storer 6, Gittings 5, Blissett 3,
Dance 3, Bell 2, Byrne 2, Dunkley 2, Gowling 2, Johnson 2, Jackman 1, Wright 1, own goals 2.
The Budweiser FA Cup (14): Gash 3, Gittings 3, Byrne 2, Lolley 2, Johnson 1, Malbon 1, Morgan-Smith 1, Smith 1.
FA Trophy (1): Gash 1.

Lewis 33	Vaughan L 43	Dunkley 28	Gowling 36	Demetriou 37 + 2	Gittings 27 + 6	Fowler 23 + 3	Storer 32 + 3	Johnson 9 + 16	Gash 35 + 1	Malbon 25 + 8	Byrne 23 + 11	Angus 1 + 5	Tolley — + 1	Dance 5 + 8	Lolley 15 + 6	Jackman 30 + 5	Vaughan N 13 + 1	Morgan-Smith 25 + 12	Blissett 8 + 8	Grimes 22	Dyer 1 + 1	Cieslewicz 8 + 6	Aloi 1 + 3	Ladapo 2 + 1	O'Keefe 12 + 5	Rowe — + 2	Wright 3 + 6	Bell 8 + 2	Verma 1 + 3	Match No.
1	2	3	4	5	6^3	7	8^1	9^2	10	11	12	13	14																	1
1	2	3	4	5	8^1	6	7	11	10	9^2		13		12																2
1	2	3	4	5	6^1	7	8	9^2	10	11^3	12					13	14													3
1	2	4	3	5	8	7^3	6	11	10	9^2						13	12	14												4
1	2	4	3	5		13	6		11	8^3	9	10^1				14	12	7^2												5
1	2	4	3	5	7		6	8^2	9^3	11	12	13				10^1	14													6
	2	4	3	5			7^3	8	14	11^1	10^2				6		9	1	12	13										7
	2	4	3	5	14		7	8	12	11^2	10^3				6^1		9	1	13											8
	2	4		5	7	8	6^2	14	10^3	11	13				9^1		1	12		3										9
	2		3	5	9^1	7		13	10	11	8^2				6^3	14	12	1		4										10
	2		3	5	9^1	6		14	11^2	8	12				10^3	7	1	13		4										11
	2		3	5	8	6^3	13	14	10	11					9^2	7^1	1	12		4										12
	2		3		8	7	6	11^2		9^1	13				12	5	1	10^3	14	4										13
	2		4		8^1	6	7			12	13	14^4			9^2	5	1	10^3	11	3										14
	2		3			7	6	12		13	8	14			9^3	5	1	10^1	11^2	4										15
1	2		3			8	7	14	12	13	6^2				9^3		5	11	10^1	4										16
1	2		3	5		6	7	11^2	10	12					9^1	13	8^1		14	4										17
1	2	4	3	14	9^1	7	6		10	12				13	8^3	5		11^2												18
1	2	4	3			6^1	7	13	10^3	8	12				9	5		11^2	14											19
1	2	4	3	13			8^2	7		11	10^1	12		14	6^3	5		9												20
1	2	5	4	3	7				12	11^1	8^2				9	6		10	13											21
1		4	3	5	2	6^1	7		10	12					9	8		11^4												22
1	2	4	3	5		7	8		10	11^1				12	9	6														23
1	2	3			5	7	12	4	10		6^1		13	11^2	8		9													24
1	2	4^4	5		8	12	7	13	11		6^3	14		9^1	3	10^2														25
1	2		3	4		6	7	12	10	13	8^2				9^3	5	11^1		14											26
1	2		3	4		7^2	6	11^3	10	13	8				5	9^1		12	14											27
1	2		4	3	13		7		11		9				5	12	6^2	10	8^1											28
1	2		3	4	8		7	13	10		6^3				5	11^2	9	14	12											29
	2	4	3	5	9^2		8	6	11^1		10^3					1	12		14	13	7									30
		3	4	5			6			10	13				2	1	12		9^3	8^2	11^1	7	14							31
		4	3	5	12		8			11	9^1				2	1	10		6		7									32
	2	4	3	13			7			10	9^1				5	1	11		6		8^2	12								33
1	2		3	5	7		6	13	10						8^1	11	4	9^2		12										34
1	2		3	5	7			12^3	10^2						8	11	4	9^1		6		13	14							35
1	2		3	5	8^3		14	9^2	10	12					7	11	4		6^1	13										36
1	2		4	5	8^3			9	6^2						7	10	11^1	3		13		12	14							37
1	2		3	5	8			10^2	11	6					7^1	9	13	4		12										38
1	2			5	8^1	7^4		10	11^1	6^2		13			9		3		12	14	4									39
	2	4		5				10^2	7						11	13	3	12	6	9^1	8^1	14								40
	2	4		5				10^3	6						11^2	14	3	13	7	9^1	8	12								41
	2	3		5^4	14			10	8						13	12	4	6^2	7	11^1	9									42
	2	3		5	9^2			10^3	6		12				11^1	4		7	14	8	13									43
1	2	3		5	9^3	13		10	7^2						12	11^1	4	14	6	8										44
1	2	3		5	9^2	14		11^1	7						12	10	4	13	6	8^3										45
1	2	3		5	13		7^2		8						10^3	9	4	14	12	11	6^1									46

The Budweiser FA Cup

Fourth Qualifying	Bradford (Park Avenue)	(a)	1-1	
Replay *(aet)*	Bradford (Park Avenue)	(h)	2-1	
First Round	Sutton U	(h)	4-1	
Second Round	Newport Co	(h)	4-2	
Third Round	Peterborough U	(h)	0-0	
Replay	Peterborough U	(a)	3-2	
Fourth Round	Sunderland	(a)	0-1	

FA Trophy

First Round	Bradford (Park Avenue)	(a)	1-2

LINCOLN CITY

Ground: Gelder Group Sincil Bank Stadium, Sincil Bank, Lincoln LN5 8LD. *Tel:* (01522) 880 011. *Fax:* (01522) 880 020. *Website:* www.redimps.com *Year Formed:* 1884. *Record Attendance:* 23,196 v Derby Co, League Cup 4th rd (replay), 15 November 1967. *Nickname:* 'The Red Imps'. *Manager:* Gary Simpson. *Colours:* Red shirts with white stripe, black shorts, red socks.

LINCOLN CITY – SKRILL PREMIER 2013–14 LEAGUE RECORD

Match No.	Date	Venue	Opponents	Result	H/T Score	Lg Pos.	Goalscorers	Attendance
1	Aug 10	A	Woking	D	0-0	0-0	12		1845
2	13	H	Macclesfield T	W	1-0	1-0	8	Rowe [27]	2386
3	17	H	Forest Green R	W	2-1	1-1	4	Fairhurst 2 [27, 86]	2290
4	24	A	Cambridge U	L	0-1	0-1	10		3022
5	26	H	Wrexham	W	2-0	1-0	5	Tomlinson 2 [38, 82]	2610
6	31	A	Dartford	W	2-1	2-0	4	Tomlinson [21], Boyce [33]	1386
7	Sept 7	H	Salisbury C	L	0-1	0-1	4		2646
8	14	A	Barnet	D	1-1	0-0	8	Nolan [90]	1913
9	17	H	Southport	W	1-0	1-0	4	Miller [26]	1879
10	21	A	Luton T	L	2-3	1-0	6	Power [20], Tomlinson [51]	6203
11	24	A	Hereford U	L	0-1	0-0	10		1398
12	28	H	Hyde	W	3-0	0-0	7	Tomlinson [48], Dixon 2 [79, 89]	2311
13	Oct 5	A	Nuneaton T	D	2-2	1-1	9	Miller [37], Nolan [47]	1634
14	8	H	Tamworth	D	0-0	0-0	9		2603
15	12	H	Aldershot T	L	0-1	0-0	9		2748
16	19	A	Kidderminster H	L	1-4	0-1	13	Wright [80]	2103
17	Nov 2	A	Welling U	L	0-1	0-0	13		746
18	12	H	Southport	W	1-0	0-0	13	Nolan [75]	818
19	16	A	Forest Green R	L	1-4	1-2	15	Sharp [39]	1128
20	23	H	Hereford U	D	1-1	0-0	16	Tomlinson [47]	1874
21	Dec 10	A	Gateshead	L	0-1	0-0	16		1411
22	21	A	Chester FC	D	3-3	1-2	18	Dixon [19], Power (pen) [47], Robinson [90]	1850
23	26	H	Grimsby T	L	0-2	0-2	18		5421
24	28	A	FC Halifax T	L	1-5	1-2	18	Tomlinson [25]	1979
25	Jan 1	A	Grimsby T	D	1-1	1-1	18	Thomas (og) [21]	5484
26	4	H	Luton T	D	0-0	0-0	18		2928
27	7	H	Alfreton T	W	4-1	2-0	16	Kempson (og) [8], Wright [21], Nolan [80], Sam-Yorke [87]	1877
28	21	A	Macclesfield T	L	1-3	1-0	17	Tomlinson [44]	1364
29	25	H	Woking	D	2-2	2-1	17	Brown [25], Tomlinson [40]	2017
30	Feb 1	H	FC Halifax T	W	3-1	2-0	17	Tomlinson 3 [3, 11, 53]	2077
31	4	H	Nuneaton T	L	1-2	0-1	18	Power [70]	1772
32	8	A	Hyde	W	4-3	2-1	16	Sam-Yorke [15], Audel [45], Tomlinson [76], Miller [90]	646
33	15	H	Kidderminster H	W	2-0	1-0	14	Tomlinson 2 [19, 78]	2012
34	22	H	Chester FC	D	1-1	1-0	15	Sam-Yorke [16]	2354
35	Mar 1	A	Aldershot T	W	3-2	2-1	14	Miller [5], Audel [26], Tomlinson [71]	1944
36	8	A	Alfreton T	D	1-1	0-0	16	Newton [90]	1331
37	11	H	Welling U	L	1-2	1-2	17	Bright [5]	1623
38	15	H	Braintree T	W	2-0	0-0	14	Miller [64], Audel [73]	2002
39	18	H	Braintree T	W	2-0	1-0	12	Foster [37], Sheridan [76]	787
40	22	A	Gateshead	L	1-3	0-2	15	Nolan [47]	804
41	29	A	Tamworth	D	0-0	0-0	15		979
42	Apr 5	A	Dartford	D	0-0	0-0	15		1947
43	12	A	Salisbury C	W	2-1	0-0	15	Newton [70], Rowe [90]	952
44	18	H	Cambridge U	W	1-0	1-0	14	Tomlinson (pen) [32]	2535
45	21	A	Wrexham	W	1-0	1-0	13	Rowe [31]	2714
46	26	H	Barnet	D	3-3	1-1	14	Brown [7], Bright [46], Tomlinson [54]	2812

Final League Position: 14

GOALSCORERS

League (60): Tomlinson 18 (1 pen), Miller 5, Nolan 5, Audel 3, Dixon 3, Power 3 (1 pen), Rowe 3, Sam-Yorke 3, Bright 2, Brown 2, Fairhurst 2, Newton 2, Wright 2, Boyce 1, Foster 1, Robinson 1, Sharp 1, Sheridan 1, own goals 2.
The Budweiser FA Cup (4): Tomlinson 2, Boyce 1, Dixon 1.
FA Trophy (8): Power 3, Fofana 1, Foster 1, Jackson 1, Sharp 1, own goal 1.

Farman 31	Gray 9 + 8	Brown 44	Boyce 19	Newton 45	Foster 25 + 6	Nolan 28 + 4	Fofana 19 + 3	Power 36 + 2	Wright 8 + 11	Tomlinson 39	Dixon 8 + 21	Rowe 15 + 8	Fairhurst 5 + 7	Miller 37 + 1	Sheridan 20 + 10	Jordan 29 + 3	Yussuf 1 + 1	Preece 1	Jackson 4	Sharp 3	Robinson 9 + 7	Everington — + 1	Sam-Yorke 9	Austin 4 + 2	Audel 14	Adams 14	Townsend 14	Bright 7	Mendy 7	Simmons — + 1	Arthur 2 + 4	Match No.
1	2	3	4	5	6	7	8	9	10[1]	11	12																					1
1	7	4	3	2	5	6	13	8	11[1]	9	12	10[2]																				2
1	2	4	3	5	12	9	8	7		11				10	6[1]																	3
1		4	3	5	6	8		7		10	13	12		2	9[2]	11[1]																4
1	2	4	3	5	13	7	6			11	12	10[1]		9[2]	14	8[3]																5
1		4	3	5	7	6	8	9		10	11[1]			2	12																	6
1		4	3	5	8[1]	6	7			10	13	11[2]	9[3]	2	12				14													7
1		4	3	5				9	7[3]	10	12	11[2]	14	13	2	6	8[1]															8
1		4	3	5	14	8	7	9[3]		12	11[1]	13		2	10[2]	6																9
1		5	4	3	9[2]	8	7	6	13	11		10[1]		2	12																	10
1		3	4	5[2]	7	8	10	12	11[1]	14	13			2	6[2]	9																11
1		4	3	5	13	9	6[2]	8	11[3]	10	12			2	14	7[1]																12
1		4	3	5	8	6	13	7[2]		10[1]	11	12		2	9																	13
1		4	3	5	6	7		9		10[1]	11	13		12	2	8[2]																14
1		4	3	5	6	8		9		13		12		10	2	7[1]	11[2]															15
1		4	3	5	6[2]	8[1]	13	9			12	11	14	2	7	10[1]																16
1		4	3	5	7[1]			9	13	11	10[2]	12		2	6																	17
1	2	4	3	5	14	7	6	10[1]	12	8	13				9[2]	11[1]																18
1	3	4	2	5		7	8[3]	6	12	10	13		14			11[1]	9[2]															19
1		4	5	3	9[1]	7	8	11[2]	10		13			2	12	6																20
1		4	5	3		6[2]	8	12			13			2	9	7					10		11[1]									21
1	3[2]	5	4		8[1]	7		10[2]	9	6	13			2	11	14					12											22
1	12	4	3		7			10	6	9	13			2[1]	8	5					11[2]											23
1	3	5	4		12	2[2]	7		6	8	11	13			9	10[1]																24
1		4	5	3	7	11	8	9		12				2	6								10[2]	13								25
1	13	4	3	5	7[2]	8		12						2	6						9				10	11[1]						26
1	12	4		5[1]	7	6		9		8			14	2[2]	13	3										11	10[3]					27
1	14	3	4	5	6[2]	7		10	9[1]		12			2											13	11	8[2]					28
1	12	3	4	5	8[1]	7		10						2	6						9					11						29
1		3		5			8	10[2]						2	13	6					9[1]					11	12	4	7			30
1		5		3			8	10						2	12	6					9[1]					11	13	4	7[2]			31
1[2]	13	4		5	14	9	8							2	12	6[3]										11	10[1]	3	7			32
		3		5			8				11			2	9	7					10					4	6	1				33
		3		5			8	9						2	11[1]	6					12					10	4	7	1			34
		4		5	7			9	12	10				2	8						11[1]					3	6	1				35
	2	4		5	13	7		11	9[1]	10[3]			14	8[2]							12					3	6	1				36
	2	3		5	6[2]		8			10				12	13						9[1]					4	7	1	11			37
		3		5			8	9	12					2	11[1]	7										4	6	1	10			38
				5				9			2		6[1]		13	11				3			8[2]	7		4		1	10		12	39
		3					8				12			11	13	5			10	4[2]							2	7	1	6	9[1]	40
	13	3		5[2]		4	8	12					14	2	11[3]	6[1]					9						7	1	10			41
		3		5			4	9[1]	10					2	6[2]						13					7		1	11	8	12	42
	14	3		5		7	4[3]				13			2	9						12				10			1	11	8[2]	6[1]	43
		3		5			8			10	13			2	9[1]										4	7[2]		1	11	6	12	44
		3		5		7		12	11[2]	10[3]				2	6						14					4		1	9[1]	8	13	45
		3		5	12	7	8	9[2]		10				2	6											4[1]		1	11		13	46

The Budweiser FA Cup

Fourth Qualifying	Worcester C	(a)	1-1
Replay	Worcester C	(h)	3-0
First Round	Plymouth Arg	(h)	0-0
Replay	Plymouth Arg	(a)	0-5

FA Trophy

First Round	Stalybridge	(h)	5-1
Second Round	Braintree T	(a)	3-1
Third Round	North Ferriby U	(h)	0-4

LUTON TOWN

Ground: Kenilworth Road Stadium, 1 Maple Road, Luton, Bedfordshire LU4 8AW. *Tel:* (01582) 411 622.
Fax: (01582) 405 070. *Website:* www.lutontown.co.uk *Year Formed:* 1885. *Nickname:* 'The Hatters'.
Record Attendance: 30,869 v Blackpool, FA Cup 6th rd (replay), 4 March 1959. *Manager:* John Still. *Colours:* Orange shirts, navy blue shorts with orange trim, white socks with orange trim.

LUTON TOWN – SKRILL PREMIER 2013–14 LEAGUE RECORD

Match No.	Date	Venue	Opponents	Result	H/T Score	Lg Pos.	Goalscorers	Attendance
1	Aug 10	A	Southport	L	0-1	0-1	17		2210
2	13	H	Salisbury C	W	2-0	0-0	12	Taiwo (pen) [64], Guttridge [81]	6520
3	17	H	Macclesfield T	D	1-1	0-0	12	Guttridge [90]	6216
4	24	A	Forest Green R	D	0-0	0-0	14		1858
5	26	H	Cambridge U	D	0-0	0-0	14		7517
6	31	A	Kidderminster H	W	2-0	0-0	11	Howells 2 (2 pens) [70, 81]	2866
7	Sept 7	H	Grimsby T	D	0-0	0-0	13		6131
8	13	A	Wrexham	L	0-2	0-1	13		3122
9	17	H	Dartford	W	3-0	2-0	11	Benson [30], Guttridge [33], Lawless [64]	5433
10	21	H	Lincoln C	W	3-2	0-1	9	Cullen 2 [46, 80], Guttridge [77]	6203
11	24	A	Woking	W	4-0	3-0	5	Cullen 2 [29, 45], Lacey [35], Gray [70]	1955
12	28	A	Hereford U	D	0-0	0-0	6		2386
13	Oct 5	H	FC Halifax T	W	4-3	3-3	5	Guttridge [16], Benson [33], Gray [39], Wall [83]	6519
14	8	A	Aldershot T	D	3-3	2-3	4	Gray [4], Parry [16], Whalley (pen) [80]	2693
15	12	H	Hyde	W	4-1	1-1	3	Gray 3 [16, 55, 79], Guttridge [51]	7081
16	19	A	Tamworth	W	4-3	2-1	3	Smith [31], Parry [41], Benson 2 [46, 54]	2066
17	Nov 2	A	Gateshead	D	0-0	0-0	3		1080
18	12	A	Braintree T	W	2-1	1-0	2	Benson [30], Parry [65]	1518
19	16	A	Chester FC	D	1-1	1-1	3	Gray [11]	3291
20	23	H	Welling U	W	2-1	1-0	3	Gray 2 [17, 79]	6592
21	26	H	Southport	W	3-0	1-0	2	McNulty [30], Smith [66], Gray [75]	6057
22	Dec 7	A	Alfreton T	W	5-0	4-0	2	Gray 2 [10, 14], Benson [13], Guttridge [18], Lawless [67]	1279
23	21	H	Gateshead	W	4-2	3-0	2	Benson [16], Lawless 2 [27, 60], Gray [30]	6913
24	26	A	Barnet	W	2-1	2-0	2	Benson [22], Lawless [34]	3608
25	28	H	Kidderminster H	W	6-0	1-0	1	Guttridge 2 [28, 86], Benson [52], Howells 2 (1 pen) [56 ipi, 70], Griffiths [79]	8488
26	Jan 1	A	Barnet	W	2-1	2-0	1	Gray [2], Benson [31]	7543
27	4	A	Lincoln C	D	0-0	0-0	1		2928
28	25	H	Nuneaton T	W	3-0	0-0	1	Gray 3 [50, 64, 77]	7310
29	Feb 11	A	Macclesfield T	W	2-1	1-1	1	Gray 2 [9, 82]	1705
30	15	H	Hereford U	W	7-0	1-0	1	Gray 3 [12, 68, 82], Benson [49], Howells (pen) [56], Ruddock [60], Lawless [90]	7111
31	22	A	Nuneaton T	W	5-0	1-0	1	Benson 2 [34, 81], Gray [64], Guttridge [70], Howells [85]	3480
32	25	H	Wrexham	W	5-0	4-0	1	Guttridge 2 [3, 17], Gray [9], Benson [38], Howells (pen) [70]	7526
33	Mar 1	H	Alfreton T	W	3-0	1-0	1	Guttridge [29], Gray [52], Benson [86]	8412
34	8	A	Salisbury C	D	0-0	0-0	1		2633
35	11	A	Cambridge U	D	1-1	0-0	1	Cullen [90]	6050
36	17	H	Woking	L	0-1	0-0	1		6683
37	22	H	Chester FC	W	3-0	0-0	1	Robinson [70], Gray [82], Benson [90]	8475
38	25	A	Grimsby T	W	2-1	1-1	1	Robinson [21], Benson [61]	3789
39	29	A	FC Halifax T	L	0-2	0-1	1		3586
40	Apr 1	A	Dartford	W	2-1	0-1	1	Ruddock [83], Gray [86]	2869
41	5	H	Aldershot T	W	1-0	0-0	1	McGeehan [85]	8558
42	8	H	Tamworth	W	2-0	0-0	1	McGeehan [49], Cullen [65]	8554
43	12	H	Braintree T	L	2-3	0-2	1	Howells (pen) [62], Wall [65]	10,020
44	19	A	Welling U	W	2-1	1-0	1	Cullen [28], Gray [72]	2650
45	21	H	Forest Green R	W	4-1	1-1	1	Gray 2 (1 pen) [45 ipi, 60], McGeehan [56], Cullen [90]	10,044
46	26	A	Hyde	W	1-0	0-0	1	Wall [70]	2729

Final League Position: 1

GOALSCORERS

League (102): Gray 30 (1 pen), Benson 17, Guttridge 13, Cullen 8, Howells 8 (6 pens), Lawless 6, McGeehan 3, Parry 3, Wall 3, Robinson 2, Ruddock 2, Smith 2, Griffiths 1, Lacey 1, McNulty 1, Taiwo 1 (1 pen), Whalley 1 (1 pen).
The Budweiser FA Cup (2): Benson 1, Cullen 1.
FA Trophy (6): Cullen 1, Inniss 1, Parry 1, Wall 1, Whalley 1, own goal 1.

Tyler 46	Smith 22 + 2	McNulty 46	Lacey 18 + 3	Griffiths 46	Whalley 8 + 8	Guttridge 31 + 1	Taiwo 3 + 2	Howells 28 + 7	Martin 3 + 4	Cullen 12 + 17	Gray 39 + 5	Charles 1 + 3	Parry 18 + 5	Shaw 4 + 7	Henry 43	Benson 36	Wall 1 + 9	Stevenson 3 + 2	Lawless 23 + 8	O'Donnell — + 2	Banton — + 1	Robinson 13 + 14	Mawson 1	Ruddock 18 + 3	Davis 5 + 1	Ferdinand — + 1	Inniss 1	McGeehan 18	Franks 17	Rooney 2 + 4	Match No.
1	2	3	4	5	6	7	8^3	9^1	10^2	11	12	13	14																		1
1	2	4	13	3	6	7	8	14	9^3	11^1	12	5^2			10																2
1	14	4	5	3^2	6	8	7^3			12	9^1	13	11		10	2															3
1	6	2	5	3	8	7				12	10^1	11			13	9^1	4														4
1	7	3	4	5	6	8				12	13	11^1	10			9^2	2														5
1	8	3	4	5^2	6					11	12		9		7	2		10^1	13												6
1	8	4	5^1	3	13	9^3		6			10^2				7	2	11	14	12												7
1	9	3		5	6^2	8				10^3	7	14		4	2	11		13	12												8
1	8	3		5	13	7		14		10^1	12			4	2	11			6^2												9
1	7	4		3^2		8		14		10	11^3		12	5	2			9^1	6			13									10
1	7	3	4	5	14	8^3				11^1	10		9^2		6	2						12	13								11
1	7	3	4	5	13	8		9^2		11^1	12				6	2		10													12
1	7	5	4	3	8					11			9		2^1	10		12	6^2			13									13
1	8	4	3	5	13	7		9^1		11					6^2	2		10	12												14
1	7	4	5	3	12	8^1		14		10			9^2		2	11			6^3			13									15
1	8	3	4	5	6	9^1				10^2		13			7	2		11	12												16
1	7	3	4	5	8					11^2	12		9^1		6	2		10	13												17
1	8	3^1	4	5				9		13		11			7	2	12	10^2	6												18
1	7	3	4	5	14	9^2		13		12	11				8	2		10^1	6^3												19
1		4	5	3		9^1		12		11					8	2		7^2	6			13									20
1	7	4	5^1	3	13	9		14		11^3					8	2		10	6^2												21
1	8	3		5		9				11					2	10			6			4^1		7	12						22
1	6	3		5	8^1					11					2	10			9			12		7	4						23
1	8^1	3		5		9		13		10^2					2	11			6			12		7	4						24
1	4	3				9		12		13	10				2	11^2			6			8		7^1	5						25
1	4	3	7			9				11					2	10			6			8			5						26
1		3	7^1	5		9				11					2	10			6			8			5	4		12			27
1	4	3	7			9^2		13		12	11				2	10^1						8					5	6			28
1	4	5	8			9^1				11					2	10			12					7				6	3		29
1	3	5	6			9^1					10		14		2	11^3			13					12				7	8^1	4	30
1	4	5	6^3			9				11^2	12				2	10^1			13					14				8	7	3	31
1	4	3	6^3			9				12	10^2				2	11^1			13					14				7	8	5	32
1	4	5	7^2			9				11				14	2	10^1			13					12				6	8^3	3	33
1	3	5				9		13		11					4	10						8^2		12				6	7^1	2	34
1	4	5				9^1		13		11^2				14	2	10			6					12				7^3	8	3	35
1	4	3				9^2		14		11					2	10	13		6			12		8^3				7^1	5		36
1	4	3				9^1				12	10		8^2		2	11			6			13		7^3				5		14	37
1	4	3									10				2	11			6			9		7				8	5		38
1	4	5								12			11^2		2	10			9			6		8^1				7	3	13	39
1	4	5				9				12	10				2	11^1			6					7^2	13			8	3	14	40
1	3	5						13			10			14	2	11			6^2			12		8^1				7	4	9^2	41
1	4	3				9				12	10^1			14	2	11^3						13		8				7	5	6^2	42
1	4	5				9					10				2	11	14		6^1					8^2	13			7	3	12^3	43
1	4^1	12	5					9		11		13		14	2^2	10^3								7	8			6	3		44
1	4^1	12	5			9^3				11^2	10			14	2							13		8				7	3		45
1	14	4	3	5	6					11	10^3	13			2^2							12		9				7^1	8		46

The Budweiser FA Cup

Fourth Qualifying	Woking	(a)	1-0
First Round	Welling U	(a)	1-2

FA Trophy

First Round	Staines T	(a)	0-0
Replay	Staines T	(h)	2-0
Second Round	Wrexham	(h)	2-0
Third Round	Cambridge U	(a)	2-2
Replay	Cambridge U	(h)	0-1

MACCLESFIELD TOWN

Ground: Moss Rose Stadium, London Road, Macclesfield, Cheshire SK11 7SP.   *Tel:* (01625) 264 686.
Fax: (01625) 264 692.   *Website:* www.mtfc.co.uk   *Year Formed:* 1874.
Record Attendance: 9,008 v Winsford U, Cheshire Senior Cup 2nd rd, 4 February 1948.
Nickname: 'The Silkmen'.   *Manager:* John Askey.   *Colours:* Blue shirts with white trim, white shorts, blue socks.

MACCLESFIELD TOWN – SKRILL PREMIER 2013–14 LEAGUE RECORD

Match No.	Date	Venue	Opponents	Result	H/T Score	Lg Pos.	Goalscorers	Atten- dance
1	Aug 10	H	Nuneaton T	L	0-1	0-1	17		1585
2	13	A	Lincoln C	L	0-1	0-1	19		2386
3	17	A	Luton T	D	1-1	0-0	19	Holroyd [63]	6216
4	24	H	FC Halifax T	D	2-2	1-2	20	Boden [38], Mackreth [82]	1720
5	26	A	Gateshead	D	2-2	2-0	20	Boden 2 [19, 41]	631
6	31	H	Braintree T	L	0-1	0-0	21		1264
7	Sept 7	A	Aldershot T	L	0-1	0-0	22		1752
8	14	H	Alfreton T	L	0-1	0-1	23		1271
9	17	H	Chester FC	L	1-2	1-2	23	Whitaker [44]	2012
10	21	H	Woking	W	3-2	2-0	23	Jennings 2 [12, 45], Mackreth [78]	1195
11	24	A	Barnet	W	2-1	2-0	20	Jennings 2 [27, 35]	1179
12	28	H	Welling U	W	2-1	0-0	18	Jennings [64], Holroyd [67]	1321
13	Oct 5	A	Tamworth	L	0-1	0-1	19		864
14	8	H	Hereford U	W	1-0	0-0	18	Jennings [62]	1329
15	12	A	Forest Green R	W	3-2	1-1	15	Williams [41], Whitaker [59], Lewis [90]	1181
16	17	H	Southport	D	2-2	1-0	14	Jennings 2 [10, 77]	1370
17	Nov 2	H	Wrexham	W	3-2	2-1	14	Jennings 3 (1 pen) [1 (pl), 40, 90]	1978
18	12	H	Kidderminster H	D	1-1	0-0	15	Turnbull [90]	1395
19	16	H	Dartford	W	3-1	0-1	14	Boden [66], Jennings 2 [68, 69]	1543
20	23	A	Salisbury C	L	2-3	1-1	15	Jennings (pen) [45], Turnbull [55]	843
21	Dec 10	A	Cambridge U	L	0-3	0-2	15		2284
22	14	A	Salisbury C	W	1-0	0-0	14	Rowe [85]	1235
23	26	H	Hyde	W	3-0	2-0	14	Turnbull [6], Andrew [29], Holroyd [88]	1882
24	28	A	Grimsby T	W	3-2	2-0	12	Boden [9], Holroyd [22], Andrew [84]	4002
25	Jan 1	A	Hyde	W	3-0	0-0	11	O'Connor (og) [60], Boden 2 (1 pen) [64, 76 (p)]	979
26	18	A	Nuneaton T	L	0-1	0-0	12		1002
27	21	H	Lincoln C	W	3-1	0-1	11	Boden [60], Mackreth [79], Holroyd [81]	1364
28	Feb 4	H	Chester FC	W	3-2	2-1	11	Boden [22], Williams [33], Holroyd [54]	1771
29	11	H	Luton T	L	1-2	1-1	11	Andrew [38]	1705
30	22	A	Woking	L	2-3	1-0	12	Boden [6], Pilkington [73]	1144
31	25	A	Hereford U	W	2-1	1-0	11	Pilkington [29], Boden [48]	1013
32	Mar 1	A	Welling U	L	0-1	0-0	12		701
33	8	H	Grimsby T	D	1-1	0-1	13	Boden (pen) [90]	2092
34	11	A	Kidderminster H	L	1-2	1-2	14	Whitaker [41]	1591
35	15	A	Southport	L	1-4	1-2	15	Andrew [16]	1045
36	18	H	Barnet	W	2-0	0-0	15	Holroyd [81], Whitaker [87]	1153
37	22	H	Tamworth	W	2-1	1-1	13	Andrew [9], Boden [57]	1352
38	29	A	Dartford	L	1-2	1-0	14	Turnbull [42]	1105
39	Apr 1	H	Cambridge U	L	0-1	0-0	15		1278
40	5	A	Wrexham	L	0-1	0-1	16		2402
41	8	A	Braintree T	W	1-0	0-0	15	Boden [62]	739
42	12	H	Aldershot T	D	1-1	0-0	14	Boden [77]	2207
43	15	H	Forest Green R	L	1-2	0-2	14	Boden [60]	1142
44	19	A	FC Halifax T	L	1-2	1-2	16	Boden [45]	2119
45	21	H	Gateshead	L	0-2	0-1	16		1628
46	26	A	Alfreton T	W	1-0	0-0	15	Boden [89]	696

Final League Position: 15

GOALSCORERS

League (62): Boden 18 (2 pens), Jennings 14 (2 pens), Holroyd 7, Andrew 5, Turnbull 4, Whitaker 4, Mackreth 3, Pilkington 2, Williams 2, Lewis 1, Rowe 1, own goal 1.
The Budweiser FA Cup (16): Boden 4 (1 pen), Jennings 3 (1 pen), Rowe 3, Andrew 1, Kay 1, Mackreth 1, Whittaker 1, Williams 1, Winn 1.
FA Trophy (0).

Taylor 45	Connor 27 + 5	Bolton 8 + 2	Williams 32 + 6	Andrew 46	Mackreth 32 + 11	Whitaker 43 + 1	Kay 20 + 7	Rowe 11 + 17	Kissock 7 + 5	Jennings 14 + 2	Holroyd 26 + 13	Winn 32 + 5	Gnahoua 3 + 7	Lewis 9 + 12	Boden 38 + 2	Halls 36 + 1	Sodje E 5 + 1	Turnbull 37	Martin 16 + 2	Chalmers — + 2	Fairhurst — + 2	Pilkington 15 + 1	Sodje A 2 + 3	Cowan 1 + 1	Branagan 1	Match No.
1	2	3	4	5	6³	7	8	9²	10¹	11	12	13	14													1
1	5	3¹	4	2	12	7	8			10	11				6	9										2
1		3	4	5		7	8		6	12	10²	9			13	11¹	2									3
1		3	4	5	14	7	8		6³	12⁴	10¹	9²			13	11	2									4
1		3	12	5		7		9	6		10²	13			11	2	4	8²								5
1		3	14	5	12		8	6³		11¹		13	9		10	2	4	7²								6
1		3		5	12	8	6	9²		11	13				10	2	4	7¹								7
1	6	3		5	12	7		8¹	13	14		11	9²		10	2	4									8
1	8		12	5	6²	7		9³	13		10	14			11	2	3¹		4							9
1	3			5	6	7				10	11¹	9			2		8	4	12							10
1	4			5	6	8		14	11	10²	9				2	12³	7		3¹	13						11
1	3	13	5	6	7		12		10	11²	9¹				2	8	4									12
1	3		5	6²	8		12		10	11	9				13	2	7	4								13
1	3	12	4	5	6	7			10	11¹	9				2	8										14
1	3	12	4	5	6	8			10³	11²	9	14	13	2¹	7											15
1	3		4	5	6²	7	13		10	11	9¹	12			2	8										16
1			4	5	13	7³	12	6		10	14	9¹		11²	2	8	3									17
1	14	3		5		7		6¹	10³	12	9²	13			11	2	8	4								18
1	14		4	5	13	7¹	12	6³		10	9²				11	2	8	3								19
1	13	8		5	6³	7⁸	12		10	14	9¹				11	2	4	3²								20
1	12	3		5	6	8	13	9²		10	14				11³	2	7	4¹								21
1	3		4	5	6	7	12			11²	9¹	13			10	2	8									22
1	3		4	5	6	7	13	9¹		11	12	14			10²	2	8³									23
1	4	3	5	6	8	7	12			11¹	9²	13			10	2										24
1	4	5³	3	6			9	10¹		13	12	7			11²	2	8	14								25
1	3		4	5	9	10²	13	6¹		12	8				7	2³	11	14								26
1	2	3	5	6	7¹	9		12	10		11				8	4										27
1	3		4	5	6	7	8		11³	9	14	10²	12		2¹	13										28
1	3		4	5	6	7	8³	14		10	9¹	13	11²	2	12											29
1	3	2	7	8		13		9	10²	14	11¹	4		6¹							5	12				30
1	3	13	5	6	7		12	9			10²	2			8						4	11¹				31
1	3	14	5	6²	7¹	9	13		12	10³		11		2	8					4						32
1	3			5	6²	7		13		12	9				11	2	8				4		10¹			33
1	3			5	14	8		6³	12		11²	9¹			10	2	7				4	13				34
1	4			5	12	6		7³	14		10²	9¹			11	2	8				3	13				35
1		3	5	6	7		9²			12	13	10¹	11		8	2			4							36
1		3	5	6	7		9¹	10²		12	13	11			8	4			2							37
1		3	5	6¹	8		13	10		9²	12	11			7	4			2							38
1		3	5	6	9			11		7	10				8	4			2							39
1			4	5	6¹	9		12		10		7	11	2	8				3							40
1	3		4	5	12	6	13	11		9¹		8	10²	2	7											41
1	3		4	5	6	10²		12		9¹		8	13	2												42
1	14	3	5	7¹	8	13	12		10	6²	11³	2	9	4												43
1	3		4	5	12	6	9	7²	6¹	10	13	11	8	2												44
1		3	5	6	7	8²	14	13	10³	11	2¹	9	4	12												45
	4	5	6	12	9¹	13	10	7²	11	8	3	2	1													46

The Budweiser FA Cup

Fourth Qualifying	Vauxhall Motors	(h)	7-0
First Round	Swindon T	(h)	4-0
Second Round	Brackley T	(h)	3-2
Third Round	Sheffield W	(h)	1-1
Replay	Sheffield W	(a)	1-4

FA Trophy

First Round	Tamworth	(a)	0-2

NUNEATON TOWN

Ground: Sperrin Brewery Stadium, Liberty Way, Nuneaton, Warwickshire CV11 6RR.
Tel: (0247) 638 5738.   *Fax:* (0247) 637 2995.   *Website:* nuneatontownfc.com   *Year Formed:* 1889.
Record Attendance: 22,114 v Rotherham U, FA Cup 3rd rd, 28 January 1967 (at Manor Park).
Nickname: 'Boro', 'The Nuns'.   *Manager:* Brian Reid.   *Colours:* Blue shirts with white trim, blue shorts, blue socks.

NUNEATON TOWN – SKRILL PREMIER 2013–14 LEAGUE RECORD

Match No.	Date	Venue	Opponents	Result	H/T Score	Lg Pos.	Goalscorers	Attendance
1	Aug 10	A	Macclesfield T	W 1-0	1-0	5	Moult [23]	1585
2	13	H	Forest Green R	D 1-1	1-0	7	Brown [18]	1005
3	17	H	Southport	W 3-1	2-1	3	Moult 2 [2, 10], Walker [83]	919
4	24	A	Barnet	D 1-1	1-1	5	Brown [43]	1507
5	26	H	Kidderminster H	W 2-1	0-1	3	Moult [83], Armson [90]	1481
6	31	A	Grimsby T	W 2-1	2-0	3	Cowan [26], Brown [33]	3321
7	Sept 7	H	Wrexham	W 2-0	0-0	2	Brown [75], Moult [90]	1561
8	14	A	Dartford	W 2-1	2-1	2	Moult 2 [4, 8]	1155
9	17	H	Hereford U	W 2-1	1-0	1	York [23], Moult [61]	1085
10	21	H	Salisbury C	L 1-2	0-0	2	Moult [73]	1355
11	24	A	Cambridge U	L 0-3	0-1	2		3740
12	28	A	Woking	L 0-2	0-1	2		1272
13	Oct 5	H	Lincoln C	D 2-2	1-1	4	York [3], Brown [84]	1634
14	8	A	FC Halifax T	D 2-2	1-1	3	York 2 [5, 90]	1197
15	12	A	Braintree T	D 1-1	0-1	5	Streete [64]	1031
16	19	H	Gateshead	L 1-4	0-2	6	Moult [73]	946
17	Nov 2	A	Hyde	D 2-2	1-1	10	Ladapo [18], Hibbert [90]	447
18	12	A	Forest Green R	L 0-1	0-1	11		933
19	16	A	Welling U	W 2-1	0-0	9	Armson [55], Ladapo [90]	807
20	23	H	Chester FC	W 1-0	0-0	7	Moult [84]	1221
21	26	H	Alfreton T	W 3-0	2-0	5	Walker [27], Hibbert [42], York [88]	715
22	Dec 7	A	Hereford U	W 1-0	1-0	4	Moult (pen) [40]	1292
23	21	H	Woking	L 0-2	0-0	7		895
24	26	A	Tamworth	D 1-1	0-1	6	Streete [69]	1347
25	28	A	Cambridge U	D 0-0	0-0	7		1478
26	Jan 4	A	Southport	L 0-1	0-0	9		811
27	11	A	Gateshead	L 1-2	0-0	9	Walker [55]	726
28	18	H	Macclesfield T	W 1-0	0-0	8	Brown [71]	1002
29	25	A	Luton T	L 0-3	0-0	9		7310
30	28	H	Aldershot T	W 2-1	2-0	6	Brown [38], Moult [44]	718
31	Feb 1	A	Salisbury C	L 1-2	1-1	6	Sleath [34]	740
32	4	A	Lincoln C	W 2-1	1-0	5	Walker [18], Streete [58]	1772
33	15	H	Hyde	W 1-0	1-0	4	Armson [2]	876
34	22	H	Luton T	L 0-5	0-1	6		3480
35	Mar 1	A	Chester FC	D 3-3	2-2	5	Moult [31], Brown 2 [45, 86]	2214
36	8	H	Welling U	W 2-0	0-0	5	Brown [62], Hibbert [87]	929
37	11	H	Tamworth	W 1-0	1-0	4	Delfouneso [12]	1097
38	15	A	Aldershot T	D 2-2	2-0	4	Cowan [27], Armson (pen) [42]	1606
39	22	H	Grimsby T	L 0-1	0-1	4		1585
40	27	A	Braintree T	L 1-2	0-2	6	Hibbert [70]	802
41	29	A	Alfreton T	D 1-1	0-1	7	Armson [84]	789
42	Apr 5	H	FC Halifax T	L 0-1	0-0	9		1041
43	12	A	Wrexham	L 0-3	0-0	13		2706
44	19	H	Barnet	L 0-1	0-0	13		852
45	21	A	Kidderminster H	D 0-0	0-0	14		2022
46	26	H	Dartford	W 3-1	2-1	13	Moult 3 [26, 37, 63]	903

Final League Position: 13

GOALSCORERS

League (54): Moult 17 (1 pen), Brown 10, Armson 5 (1 pen), York 5, Hibbert 4, Walker 4, Streete 3, Cowan 2, Ladapo 2, Delfouneso 1, Sleath 1.
The Budweiser FA Cup (0).
FA Trophy (1): Moult 1.

Evtimov 4	Streete 44	Cowan 31+1	Dean 45	Bell A 19	York 40+5	Armson 37+4	Adams 12+7	Walker 39+2	Brown 30+4	Moult 36+7	Taylor 3+19	Pearson 4+9	Belshaw 31	Sleath 39+2	Trainer 18+7	Bell M —+3	McNamee 3	Gordon 17+3	Richens —+4	Delfouneso 8+3	Briscoe 1+1	Hibbert 22+6	Ladapo 2+4	Roos 9	Barroilhet —+1	Akubuine 1	Magri 3+1	Eve 2	Cranston 6+1	Match No.
1	2	3	4	5	6^1	7	8	9	10	11^2	12	13																		1
	2	4	3	5	6^1	8	7	9	10	11	12		1																	2
	2	4	3	5	9^2	6^1		8	11	10		13	1	7	12															3
1	2	3	4	5	8	6	7	11	10	12				9^1																4
	2	4	3	5	9^1	7		8	11	10		12	1	6^2		13														5
1	2	4	3	5	6^1	8		7	11	10	12			9																6
	2	4	3		6^2	7		8	11	10	13		1	9				5^1	12											7
	2	4	3	5	6^1	7		8	10	11^3	14	13	1	9^2					12											8
1	2	4	3	5	6^1	7		8	11	10	12			9																9
	2	4	3			7		8	11	10	6^1	13	1	9^2		12	5													10
	2	4^3	5		11	8	13	7	9	10			1	6^2			3^1	14	12											11
	2	4	3	5^3	6^2	7		8	11	10		12	1	9^1				14	13											12
	2	4^2	3	5	6^3	7		8	11	10	14		1	12				13		9^1										13
	2		4	5	6	7	8	9		11	12	10^1	1				3					12								14
	2		4	5	6	7	8	9		10		11^1	1				3					12								15
	2		3	5	6	7	8^2	9		10			1	14				4^1	12		13	11^3								16
	2		3	5	8^2	6	7^1		11	13			1	14	9			4				12	10^3							17
	2		3	5	11	7			9				1	8	6			4				10								18
	2		4	5	12	6^1		8		11^2			1	9	7			3				10	13							19
	2^1		3	5	13	6		8^2		14				9	7			4	12			10	11^{13}	1						20
			4	5	12	6^1		8		10^1				9	7			3		2		11^2	14	1	13					21
	2		4	5	6^1	13		8		10^2				9	7			3				11	12	1						22
			4		6	7	12	9^2		10	13			5	8			3				11		1		2^1				23
	2		4		9^2	6	12	7		10				5	8^1			3				11	13	1						24
	2		4		9^3	6		7^1	8	13	10	14		5	12			3				11^2		1						25
	2	12	4^1		6	7	8	9	13	10^2				5				3				11^1		1						26
	2	3			6	8^2	7	9^3	12	10^1	13			5	14			4				11		1		2^1				27
	2	4	5		11		6	8	10	7^1	12			3								9		1						28
	2	5	4		9	12	7^1	8^3	11		6	13	1	3	14							10^2								29
	5	4	3		6	12	7^1	8	11	10			1	9				2												30
	5	4	3		6	7		8^1	11	10^2			1	9	12						2	13								31
	5	2	4		9	7		8	11		12		1	6							3	10^1								32
	5	3	4		6	7		8	11	10^1	12	1		9							2									33
	5	4	3		11	7		8^3	10	12	6^1		1	9	14						2^2	13								34
	5	4	3		6	7		8	11	10			1	9			2^1					12								35
	5	4	3		6	7	14	8^1	11^3	10^2			1	9	13						2	12								36
	5	4	3		6	7		12	10	13			1	9	8						2^1	11^2								37
	5	4	3		6	7			10				1	9	8							11				2				38
	5	4	3		6			8	10	12		13	1	9	7							11^2				2^1				39
	2	4	3		6	12	14	7^1			13	10^3		9^2	8							11						1	5	40
	2	3	4		6^1	8	13		11	12			1	9	7^2							10							5	41
	6	3	2		13	5		12	10	9^1			1	8^1	7							11						4		42
	2	4	3		8^2	6	13		11	14			1	9	7^3							10					12	5^1		43
	5	4	3		6^1			8	13	10	12		1	9^2	7^3							11					2	14		44
	2		4		13			7	10	12	6^2	11^1		9	8			3										1	5	45
	4		3		5^1			7	10^2	11^3	12	13	1	8	6			2		14									9	46

The Budweiser FA Cup
Fourth Qualifying   Halifax T   (h)   0-2

FA Trophy
First Round   Alfreton T   (a)   1-0
Second Round   Gosport Borough   (a)   0-0
Replay   Gosport Borough   (h)   0-0
(aet; lost 2-4 on penalties)

SALISBURY CITY

Ground: The Raymond McEnhill Stadium, Partridge Way, Old Sarum, Salisbury, Wiltshire SP4 6PU.
Tel: (01722) 776655. *Fax:* (01722) 323100. *Website:* www.salisburycity-fc.co.uk *Year Formed:* 1947.
Record Attendance: 3,408 v Dover Ath, Conference South Play-off semi-finals 2nd leg, 12 May 2013.
Nickname: 'The Whites'. *Manager:* Mikey Harris.
Colours: White shirts with black trim, white shorts with black trim, white socks.

SALISBURY CITY – SKRILL PREMIER 2013–14 LEAGUE RECORD

Match No.	Date	Venue	Opponents	Result		H/T Score	Lg Pos.	Goalscorers	Attendance
1	Aug 10	H	Tamworth	L	0-1	0-1	17		958
2	13	A	Luton T	L	0-2	0-0	21		6520
3	17	A	Alfreton T	L	2-3	1-1	22	Lewis [33], Wright [89]	463
4	24	H	Aldershot T	W	1-0	0-0	18	Lewis [69]	1175
5	26	A	Welling U	D	0-0	0-0	19		725
6	31	H	FC Halifax T	W	3-1	1-0	15	Frear [22], Ruddick [69], Wright [81]	820
7	Sept 7	A	Lincoln C	W	1-0	1-0	14	McPhee [40]	2646
8	14	H	Chester FC	W	3-1	1-1	9	Fitchett [29], Frear [67], Kamdjo [85]	925
9	17	H	Braintree T	D	1-1	1-1	9	Fitchett [13]	594
10	21	A	Nuneaton T	W	2-1	0-0	5	Wright (pen) [87], Frear [89]	1355
11	24	H	Hyde	W	2-0	0-0	4	Wright (pen) [78], McPhee [89]	638
12	28	A	Barnet	L	1-3	1-0	8	Fitchett [8]	1499
13	Oct 5	H	Wrexham	W	2-1	0-1	6	Fitchett [79], MacDonald [82]	986
14	8	A	Dartford	D	1-1	1-1	7	Lewis [17]	920
15	12	H	Grimsby T	W	1-0	0-0	4	Fitchett [48]	1313
16	19	A	Cambridge U	L	0-2	0-0	6		3622
17	31	H	Hereford U	W	4-1	2-0	4	Kamdjo [10], Fitchett 2 [28, 89], Wright [90]	1112
18	Nov 16	A	Gateshead	L	2-3	0-1	8	White [81], Frear [90]	839
19	23	H	Macclesfield T	W	3-2	1-1	6	Fitchett 2 (1 pen) [45, 72 (p)], White [82]	843
20	26	H	Forest Green R	L	1-4	1-1	8	Fitchett [45]	725
21	Dec 14	A	Macclesfield T	L	0-1	0-0	11		1235
22	21	H	Southport	D	1-1	0-0	11	Brett [72]	724
23	26	A	Woking	W	3-1	2-1	9	McPhee [17], Wellard [26], Harvey [90]	2112
24	28	H	Barnet	W	2-1	1-1	8	McPhee [17], White (pen) [76]	1343
25	Jan 11	A	Kidderminster H	L	0-3	0-1	10		2034
26	18	H	Dartford	W	1-0	1-0	9	White [15]	850
27	25	A	Hereford U	L	0-1	0-0	10		2016
28	Feb 1	H	Nuneaton T	W	2-1	1-1	8	White [43], Frear [55]	740
29	4	A	FC Halifax T	L	1-5	0-2	9	White [78]	1003
30	8	H	Alfreton T	D	0-0	0-0	8		623
31	11	H	Woking	W	2-0	0-0	5	Kamdjo [64], MacDonald [88]	624
32	15	A	Southport	L	1-3	1-2	6	Fitchett [36]	719
33	18	A	Tamworth	W	2-1	2-1	5	Fitchett 2 [16, 20]	564
34	Mar 1	A	Grimsby T	L	0-2	0-1	6		3269
35	8	H	Luton T	D	0-0	0-0	8		2633
36	11	A	Forest Green R	L	0-4	0-2	10		918
37	15	A	Gateshead	D	0-0	0-0	10		685
38	22	A	Wrexham	D	1-1	1-1	11	Kamdjo [45]	2850
39	26	H	Cambridge U	L	0-3	0-1	12		695
40	29	H	Kidderminster H	D	1-1	0-1	12	Sheringham (pen) [90]	2217
41	Apr 5	A	Braintree T	W	1-0	1-0	12	Sheringham [19]	905
42	8	A	Hyde	W	2-0	0-0	9	Sheringham [54], White [71]	275
43	12	H	Lincoln C	L	1-2	0-0	11	White [62]	952
44	18	A	Aldershot T	L	2-3	2-2	12	Brett [27], Sheringham [33]	2485
45	21	H	Welling U	W	3-0	3-0	11	McPhee [14], White 2 [17, 20]	895
46	26	A	Chester FC	D	2-2	1-1	12	Sheringham [36], White [86]	3588

Final League Position: 12

GOALSCORERS

League (58): Fitchett 13 (1 pen), White 11 (1 pen), Frear 5, McPhee 5, Sheringham 5 (1 pen), Wright 5 (2 pens), Kamdjo 4, Lewis 3, Brett 2, MacDonald 2, Harvey 1, Ruddick 1, Wellard 1.
The Budweiser FA Cup (6): Fitchett 3, Frear 1, Lewis 1, Wright 1.
FA Trophy (0).

Puddy 40	Wilson 46	Dutton 15+5	Clarke 36+1	Hart 13	Sinclair S 33+2	Sinclair R 13+8	Lewis 35+2	Wellard 16+15	Wright 8+12	Feeney 8+7	Fitchett 32+10	Frear 35+8	Kamdjo 34+3	Ruddick 10	McPhee 32+9	Brett 27+8	Belezika 5	Thomson 1+5	White 14+14	MacDonald 21+8	Storey 2+1	Bittner 6+1	Harvey 2+2	Amankwaah 14	Sheringham 8+1	Flint —+1	Roberts —+1	Match No.
1	2	3	4	5	6	7³	8	9²	10	11¹	12	13	14															1
1	3		4	5	8¹	7		9	10²	13	11³	14	6	2	12													2
1	4	3		5³		9	8¹	14	10²	11	13	6	2	7	12													3
1	4	3					8²	7	11¹	10	12	6	2	9	14	5												4
1	4	3					8⁴	7	13	12¹	11¹	10	6	2³	9	14	5											5
1	4	3				6³		8	13	10²	11	7	5	9	12	2¹	14											6
1	3		4	5²		7			9³		8¹	12	11³	10	6	2	9	13	14									7
1	3	14	4		7				9³		11¹	10	8	2²	6	5		12	13⁴									8
1	3		4		7¹		13	9¹	14		11	10	8	6³	2	5	12											9
1	4	3			9		8²		14		11	10	6	2²	7	12	5¹	13										10
1	4	3			9		7¹	13	12	14	11¹²	10	8	2	6³	5												11
1	4	3			9		7²	8¹		11	10	13	5¹	6	12			14		2								12
1	4	14	3		9		7		12	11³	10	8¹	6²	5					2	13								13
1	3	12	4	5¹	9		8		7		10²	13	6						2	11								14
1	3	4	2		6		8²	14	11³		9	7	5	12					13	10¹								15
1	2	4	3³		6		8²	7	10	13	11	9¹	12	5					14									16
1	3	4	2		7		8¹	12	13	10²	11	9³	6	5					14									17
1	4³	2	3		7			5	9²	10¹	11	8	6		12	13	14											18
	4	2	3		8		7		11¹		10	9	5	13	6²	12			1									19
1	3	5²	4		2		7³	14	12		11	9	8	6¹					10	13								20
1	3		4	8		7		14	13	11	9¹		6³	5		12	2			10²								21
1	3	9	4	8		7		10			6	5		12	2				11¹									22
1	4	5	2¹	10		7	9	13			6	11	8		3²				12									23
1	4	3	2¹	10		7	8¹	14		9³	6	5		13	11				12									24
1	4	3	5³	8	13	6	10¹		12	7		11	9²		14	2												25
1	4	5	3	2	8¹	14	9		6³	13	10	7	12						11²									26
1	3	2	12	5¹		13	8		10	14	9	7²		6					11³	4								27
1	4	3¹	2		12	6		14	11¹	13	9	7		8					10³	5								28
1	3	14	4³		12	8⁴	13		11	9	2¹		6²	7					10	5								29
1	4	3			8¹		12		11	13	9	7		6²	5				10	2								30
1	4	3			12	8³		14	11²	10	9	7		6¹	5				13	2								31
1	4	3⁴			12	8¹	6¹	14		11	9²	7		13	5				10	2								32
1	6				9²	8	13		11	7	2	12	5						10¹	4			3					33
1	3				6	10	7¹		11	9	8²	12	5						13	4			2					34
1	4	3			7	8²		12		11¹	10	9	6						13	5			2					35
1	4	14	5		8	7		12		10	9³	6¹	11²						13	3			2					36
1	4	3	5¹	10	8²	9	6		12	14		13	7		11³					2								37
1²	4	5	6						11	9	7	10¹	8		3					13			2	12				38
	4	5	3	10	7¹	14			13	12	6		8		11²	5²		1		2			9					39
	4	3			8		10		9²	6	13	7¹		12	5⁴			1		2			11					40
	4	3		8		6	12		13	9²	7¹	10	5							1		2	11					41
	4	2		7		8	13		6	9⁴		10¹	5		12					1		3	11²	14				42
	4	3²		6		8	13		12	9		5	7		10					1		2¹	11					43
1	3			8	13	7²	12		6	9	4¹		14	5		11³					2	10						44
1	4	3		8	12	7³			9		6¹	5		11	13						2³	10			14			45
1	4	3²		7	12	6		14	9		8¹	5		10	13						2³	11						46

The Budweiser FA Cup

Fourth Qualifying	Bath C	(a)	1-0
First Round	Dartford	(h)	4-2
Second Round	Port Vale	(a)	1-4

FA Trophy

| First Round | Cambridge U | (h) | 0-1 |

SOUTHPORT

Ground: Merseyrail Community Stadium, Haig Avenue, Southport PR8 6JZ.   *Tel:* (01704) 533 422.
Website: southportfc.net   *Year Formed:* 1881.   *Record Attendance:* 20,010 v Newcastle U, FA Cup 4th rd (replay),
26 January 1932.   *Nickname:* 'The Sandgrounders'.   *Manager:* Martin Foyle.   *Colours:* Yellow and black striped
shirts, yellow shorts, yellow socks.

SOUTHPORT – SKRILL PREMIER 2013–14 LEAGUE RECORD

Match No.	Date	Venue	Opponents	Result	H/T Score	Lg Pos.	Goalscorers	Attendance
1	Aug 10	H	Luton T	W	1-0	1-0	5	Milligan [22]	2210
2	13	A	Hyde	W	2-1	0-1	1	Hattersley [78], Tames [90]	769
3	17	A	Nuneaton T	L	1-3	1-2	7	Chalmers [8]	919
4	24	H	Gateshead	W	2-1	2-0	3	Ledsham 2 [34, 45]	915
5	26	A	FC Halifax T	L	0-1	0-0	9		1583
6	31	H	Aldershot T	W	1-0	1-0	5	Osawe [27]	1012
7	Sept 7	A	Tamworth	L	1-4	1-1	9	Osawe [20]	933
8	14	H	Welling U	D	2-2	0-0	11	Almond [51], Hattersley [62]	825
9	17	A	Lincoln C	L	0-1	0-1	12		1879
10	21	A	Braintree T	L	0-1	0-1	14		924
11	24	H	Alfreton T	W	2-1	0-0	13	Fenton (og) [68], Osawe [83]	726
12	28	A	Dartford	L	0-1	0-1	15		1025
13	Oct 5	A	Woking	D	1-1	1-1	14	Milligan [19]	873
14	8	A	Wrexham	L	0-1	0-0	15		2734
15	12	H	Kidderminster H	L	1-2	1-2	17	Smith [42]	1018
16	17	A	Macclesfield T	D	2-2	0-1	16	Hattersley [61], Milligan (pen) [90]	1370
17	Nov 2	H	Cambridge U	W	1-0	1-0	16	Brown, M [2]	1006
18	12	H	Lincoln C	L	0-1	0-0	17		818
19	16	H	Hereford U	L	0-3	0-1	18		876
20	23	A	Aldershot T	L	1-5	0-4	18	Irie-Bi [85]	1592
21	26	A	Luton T	L	0-3	0-1	18		6057
22	Dec 21	A	Salisbury C	D	1-1	0-0	20	Hattersley [64]	724
23	26	H	Chester FC	D	0-0	0-0	19		1872
24	28	A	Alfreton T	L	1-2	0-2	20	Brodie [76]	976
25	Jan 4	H	Nuneaton T	W	1-0	0-0	19	Hattersley [88]	811
26	11	A	Hyde	D	1-1	0-1	19	George [78]	871
27	18	A	Hereford U	L	1-4	0-1	19	Akrigg [60]	1569
28	21	H	Wrexham	L	1-2	1-1	21	Brown, S [4]	911
29	25	H	Barnet	L	0-1	0-0	22		1510
30	Feb 8	A	Grimsby T	D	0-0	0-0	21		3306
31	15	H	Salisbury C	W	3-1	2-1	20	Ledsham [3], Hattersley [29], Brown, S [88]	719
32	22	A	Forest Green R	L	1-3	0-2	22	O'Sullivan [48]	1118
33	25	H	Grimsby T	W	2-1	1-1	20	Brown, S [36], Osawe [68]	812
34	Mar 1	H	Dartford	W	3-0	1-0	19	Hattersley [12], Walker [71], Osawe [78]	1041
35	8	A	Woking	L	0-2	0-0	20		1504
36	15	H	Macclesfield T	W	4-1	2-1	19	Nsiala [13], Walker [34], Osawe [63], Hattersley [83]	1045
37	18	A	Chester FC	D	2-2	0-1	19	Ledsham 2 [56, 89]	2274
38	22	A	Kidderminster H	D	1-1	1-0	18	Hattersley [7]	1818
39	27	H	Forest Green R	W	2-0	0-0	18	Ledsham [49], O'Sullivan [62]	1227
40	Apr 1	H	Braintree T	L	0-4	0-1	18		714
41	5	A	Cambridge U	L	1-3	1-1	19	Walker [16]	2717
42	8	A	Barnet	D	1-1	1-1	18	Brown, S [3]	774
43	12	H	Tamworth	W	2-0	0-0	18	Walker 2 [50, 72]	1006
44	18	A	Gateshead	D	2-2	1-1	18	George [2], Walker [54]	2121
45	21	H	FC Halifax T	W	2-1	0-1	18	George [70], Fitzpatrick [79]	2043
46	26	A	Welling U	L	3-4	3-1	18	George [15], Mukendi [22], O'Sullivan [38]	521

Final League Position: 18

GOALSCORERS

League (53): Hattersley 9, Ledsham 6, Osawe 6, Walker 6, Brown, S 4, George 4, Milligan 3 (1 pen), O'Sullivan 3, Akrigg 1, Almond 1, Brodie 1, Brown, M 1, Chalmers 1, Fitzpatrick 1, Irie-Bi 1, Mukendi 1, Nsiala 1, Smith 1, Tames 1, own goal 1.
The Budweiser FA Cup (8): Hattersley 2, Brown, S 1, Ellington 1, Flynn 1, George 1, Ledsham 1, Milligan 1.
FA Trophy (1): Ellington 1.

Hurst 45	Challoner 27 + 3	Flynn 17 + 1	George 41	Fitzpatrick 41 + 2	Milligan 23 + 3	Chalmers 11 + 1	Rutherford 15 + 3	Brown S 42 + 2	Almond 12 + 2	Hattersley 30 + 9	Ledsham 27 + 7	Tames 3 + 10	Osawe 22 + 19	Akrigg 9 + 5	Irie-Bi 6 + 8	Smith 20	Ellington 3	Brown M 4	Stevenson 1	Willis 3 + 1	Logan 4	Brodie 11 + 6	Abataki 2 + 1	Hand 1	Jefford 3	O'Sullivan 21	Dillon 5 + 3	Nsiala 19	Daly 11	Joyce 2 + 4	O'Neil 4	Mukendi 5 + 9	Walker 10	Monthe 3 + 4	Boothman 3 + 3	Match No.
1	2	3	4	5	6	7^1	8^3	9	10	11^2	12	13	14																							1
1	2	3	4	5	7	8^2	9^2	6^1	11	10	13	14	12																							2
1	2	3	4	5	7^3	6	9^1	8	11^2	10	13	12				14																				3
1	2	4	3	5	12	6	9	8^1	10^2	7^3	13	11				14																				4
1	2	3	5	4	12	6	9^3	8^1	10	7^2	14	11				13																				5
1	2	3	4	5	6	7^3	11	13	10^1	8	12	9^2				14																				6
1	2	3^1	4	5	6	7	11	13	10^1	8^2	14	9				12																				7
1	2	3	4	5	9	7^2	13	8	6	11^1	12	10^3				14																				8
1	2		5	6	14			7	13	10^1	9	11	12	4^2	8^3	3																				9
1		3	4	5	6		9^1	8^2	10	13	11	12	7			2																				10
1	2		4	5	7	6		8	9^1	12	11		10^2	13		3																				11
1	5		4	9	7^3	6^2		8	12	14	11		10	2^1	13	3																				12
1	2		4	5	9^3	14	8	6		11^2	13	12	10		7^2	3																				13
1	2		4	5	9	6^2	13	8		14	10	11^3	12		7^1	3																				14
1	2		4	5	8	6	7	9^1		11	10	12				3																				15
1	5	3	4	6	8	7	9	12					10^1	13	2	11^2																				16
1	2		7	5	8	6		9			12		10^1			3	11	4																		17
	2		7	5	8^2		11^1	6		10		9	12			13	3	4	1																	18
1	2		5	7	9^1		6			11^2	10	12	13		8^3	3		4		14																19
1	2^3	12	5	8	6^2	7							14			13	3	4^1				9	10	11												20
1			4	3		7		13			12				2	5					6	9^1	11	10^2	8											21
1			4	9		8		7	13	12					2	3					6	10^1	5	11^2												22
1	3	12				7		8	9^2	10					2	4					5	6^1	11	13												23
1	6^2	12	4	10	8	7			9^3	14			13		2	3						5^1	11													24
1	3	8	5		7^2			6	11^1	9	12		13		2	4						10														25
1	4^3		7	8^2	9					11	12		14		3	2						10^1			5^1	6	13									26
1	3		9	5	7			8			12		4^1			2						11				10^1	6									27
1			4		7					11	12					2^2						10			5	9	6^1	3	8	13						28
1			4		8					10^1	12											11			5	6	9	3	7		2					29
1			4	5	7					11^2		8	12									10^1				6	3	2				9	13			30
1			4	5	7						10^1	9	14									11^3				6	3	2	13			8^2	12			31
1			4	5	7						10^1	9										11				6	3^2	2	13			8	12			32
1			4	5	7						10^1	9										11				6	3	2	13			8^2	12			33
1	12	2	4	5	7						10^2		8									9				6	3^1		14			13		11^2		34
1	12	2^1	4	5	7						10^2		8									9^3				6	3		14			13		11		35
1	14	12	4	5	7						11	8^3										9^1				6^2	3	2					13	10		36
1			4	5	7						10	8										9				6	3	2					11			37
1			4	5	8						10	7										9^2				6	3	2	13			12	11^1			38
1			4	5	7^3						10^1	8										9				6^1	3	2	14	13		11	12			39
1	4^1		5								11^2	7										9				6	3	2		8^1	14	10^3	13	12		40
1	2		5		7							9										11^2				6	3		13	12		10	4	8^1		41
1	2		4	5	8							7										12				6	3			11^2		10	13	9^1		42
1	2		4	5	7							8^1	14													6	3		13	10^1		11	12	9^2		43
1	2		5		8							7										11^2				6			9^1	13		4	10	3^2	12	44
1	3		4	5						11	9^1	7														6	8	2					10		12	45
1	3		4	5	7					11																6	8	2^2					10	9		46

The Budweiser FA Cup
Fourth Qualifying   Marske U   (h)   6-2
First Round   Leyton Orient   (a)   2-5

FA Trophy
First Round   Boston U   (h)   1-2

TAMWORTH

Ground: The Lamb Ground, Kettlebrook, Tamworth, Staffordshire B77 1AA.   *Tel:* (01827) 65798.
Fax: (01827) 62236.   *Website:* thelambs.co.uk   *Year Formed:* 1933.
Record Attendance: 4,920 v Atherstone T, Birmingham Combination, 3 April 1948.   *Nickname:* 'The Lambs'.
Manager: Dale Belford.   *Colours:* Red shirts with white trim, red shorts, red socks.

TAMWORTH – SKRILL PREMIER 2013–14 LEAGUE RECORD

Match No.	Date	Venue	Opponents	Result	H/T Score	Lg Pos.	Goalscorers	Attendance
1	Aug 10	A	Salisbury C	W 1-0	1-0	5	Thomas [32]	958
2	13	H	Barnet	D 0-0	0-0	8		1379
3	17	H	Wrexham	D 2-2	1-1	10	Jones [19], Byfield [84]	1128
4	24	A	Hereford U	L 0-1	0-0	16		1864
5	26	H	Dartford	L 0-2	0-2	17		864
6	31	A	Cambridge U	L 0-3	0-1	18		2527
7	Sept 7	H	Southport	W 4-1	1-1	16	Baker (pen) [12], George (og) [61], Peniket 2 [66, 78]	933
8	13	A	Woking	D 2-2	1-0	15	Baker [24], Peniket [84]	1264
9	17	H	Kidderminster H	L 0-3	0-1	17		874
10	21	H	Gateshead	L 0-1	0-1	19		738
11	24	A	Forest Green R	W 2-1	1-1	17	Baker (pen) [26], Wright [53]	829
12	28	A	Grimsby T	L 1-3	0-0	20	Todd [73]	3105
13	Oct 5	H	Macclesfield T	W 1-0	1-0	17	Elford-Alliyu [15]	864
14	8	A	Lincoln C	D 0-0	0-0	17		2603
15	12	A	Welling U	L 0-2	0-0	18		803
16	19	A	Luton T	L 3-4	1-2	20	Courtney 2 [13, 76], Elford-Alliyu (pen) [64]	2066
17	Nov 2	H	Braintree T	D 0-0	0-0	20		716
18	12	H	Alfreton T	W 1-0	1-0	18	Chadwick [23]	716
19	16	H	Grimsby T	L 0-2	0-0	20		1306
20	23	A	Kidderminster H	L 3-5	0-2	20	Peniket [49], Morgan [60], Chadwick [89]	1951
21	Dec 21	A	Aldershot T	L 0-6	0-2	22		1598
22	26	H	Nuneaton T	D 1-1	1-0	22	Chadwick [9]	1347
23	28	A	Braintree T	L 0-2	0-0	22		811
24	Jan 4	H	FC Halifax T	W 2-0	1-0	21	Kerry [45], Todd [59]	890
25	21	H	Cambridge U	L 0-1	0-0	22		833
26	25	A	Hyde	W 3-0	1-0	21	Peniket [10], Richards [60], Chadwick [77]	369
27	28	A	Wrexham	L 0-2	0-1	21		2160
28	Feb 11	H	Hyde	D 1-1	1-0	20	Byfield [44]	616
29	15	A	Barnet	L 0-1	0-0	22		1296
30	18	H	Salisbury C	L 1-2	1-2	23	Hildreth [32]	564
31	22	H	Welling U	D 1-1	0-1	23	Godden [84]	742
32	25	H	Chester FC	L 3-4	1-3	23	Godden 2 [43, 75], Peniket [82]	1036
33	Mar 1	A	FC Halifax T	L 0-2	0-1	23		1313
34	8	H	Aldershot T	W 1-0	0-0	23	Barnes-Homer [68]	915
35	11	A	Nuneaton T	L 0-1	0-1	23		1097
36	15	H	Forest Green R	L 1-2	0-2	23	Godden (pen) [89]	736
37	18	A	Alfreton T	L 2-4	1-2	23	Peniket [7], Godden (pen) [67]	594
38	22	A	Macclesfield T	L 1-2	1-1	23	Thornton [40]	1352
39	25	A	Chester FC	L 0-2	0-0	23		1731
40	29	H	Lincoln C	D 0-0	0-0	23		979
41	Apr 5	A	Gateshead	L 0-5	0-1	23		705
42	8	A	Luton T	L 0-2	0-0	23		8554
43	12	A	Southport	L 0-2	0-0	23		1006
44	18	H	Hereford U	W 1-0	0-0	23	Kerry [62]	1154
45	21	A	Dartford	W 3-2	0-1	23	Reindorf [60], Thornton 2 (1 pen) [73 (pl), 90]	1465
46	26	H	Woking	L 2-4	0-2	23	Reindorf 2 [51, 57]	788

Final League Position: 23

GOALSCORERS

League (43): Peniket 7, Godden 5 (2 pens), Chadwick 4, Baker 3 (2 pens), Reindorf 3, Thornton 3 (1 pen), Byfield 2, Courtney 2, Elford-Alliyu 2 (1 pen), Kerry 2, Todd 2, Barnes-Homer 1, Hildreth 1, Jones 1, Morgan 1, Richards 1, Thomas 1, Wright 1, own goal 1.
The Budweiser FA Cup (6): Chadwick 3, Lambs 1, Peniket 1, Todd 1.
FA Trophy (8): Chadwick 3 (1 pen), Todd 2, Richards 1, Richards-Everton 1, Thomas 1.

Above-line column headers (placed diagonally): **Aimson 3**, **Barnes-Homer 7**, **Caprice 11 + 1**, **Thornton 12**, **Hoban 2 + 2**, **Batis-Candé 1 + 1**, **Vanderhyde — +1**, **Baker-Richardson — +1**

Belford 46	Evans 36 + 1	Courtney 18 + 1	Thomas 22	Richards-Everton 37	Kerry 33 + 3	Baker 26 + 3	Capaldi 24	Jones 4 + 1	Richards 13 + 5	Peniket 38 + 4	Todd 16 + 19	Woolery 3 + 15	Byfield 4 + 9	Hendrie 1 + 1	Aimson 3	Harris 1 + 1	Barnes-Homer 7	Regan 1 + 1	Rose 2 + 2	Caprice 11 + 1	Lloyd 5 + 1	Wright 10 + 4	Thornton 12	Elford-Alliyu 11	Gudger 2 + 2	Hoban 2 + 2	Higgins 1	Hildreth 11 + 1	Chadwick 16 + 3	Keane 26 + 2	Morgan 9	Batis-Candé 1 + 1	Allen — +1	Croasdale 2	Haworth 6 + 5	Mahon 20	Vanderhyde — +1	Waldon 1 + 1	Palmer 2 + 3	Fenton 5	Townsend 5 + 1	Reindorf 4 + 8	Godden 9 + 1	Baker-Richardson — +1	Match No.
1	2	3	4	5	6¹	7	8	9³	10	11²	12	13	14																																1
1	2	6	4	3	7³	8	5	11²	9	10¹	14	12	13																																2
1	2	7	3	4	8	6²	5	11	9¹	10	13		12																																3
1	9	7*	3	4	6¹	8	5	2²		10	12	13	11³	14																															4
1	2		3	4	8	7²	5	12		11	13	14	10¹			9		6³																											5
1	2	4					12		7	5	9	8¹	13	10²	3				6¹	11																									6
1	2	3	4		8	7	5			11	12	13								9	6¹			10²																					7
1	2¹	12	3	4	6²	8	5			11	14	13								9³	10	7																							8
1	7	4	3	13	8²	5				10	14	12							2	9	6³	11																							9
1	2	4	3*	8	7	5				10	12	14	13							6²	9¹	11²																							10
1	2	3	4¹	7	8	5				10	9²	13										6						11	12																11
1	2	4	3	7¹	8	5				11	10											12						6	9																12
1	2	4	3	6	9	5				10	7¹	13																11	8²	12															13
1	2	3	4	8¹	7	5				11	9	13					12											6	10²																14
1	2¹	3	4²	7	6	5				10	8	12	13				14											11³	9																15
1		3		4	9	8²	5		14	10	7¹													6³				11		2	12	13													16
1		3		4			5			11³	6	13					14							9²				7	10	2		8¹	12*												17
1		3	2	4		12	5²		10³	9	6	14					8											11	13				7¹												18
1		3	2	4			5			11	9	6¹												12				8	10				7												19
1		3		4			5			11	9	6¹												12				7	10	8	2														20
1	3*		2	6			5			11	10	8¹	12															9		4	7														21
1	2	3		8			5			10	6	13					12											7	11¹	4			9²												22
1	4¹	3		8						10	9	12	13											6²				7*	11	2															23
1	2	3		9		6	5			11	8																	10¹	4				12	7											24
1	5	3	4	9						10	13													8¹				11	2			6²	7	12										25
1	12	3²	4		6		5¹		14	9	13													10				2		8³	7	11												26
1	5	4	3¹	6	13					11	9	8²	14															10	2			7	12												27
1	2	4		8						10	13	9²																11	3	6¹		7	12	5										28
1	2	4		8						10³	13	12																11²	3			7	9¹	5	6	14								29
1	2¹	3		8						10	6																	7³	11²	12			9	14	5	4	13								30
1			4	7						10	12																	9²		5		8³	2¹	6	3	14	11	13							31
1	2		4							9	13																	8³	10¹			12	7	5	3²	14	11								32
1	5		3	7						12	6¹					4			11										2			9²	8		13	10									33
1	2		5	7						12						3			11	6¹						8			4			9	8		13	14	10								34
1	2		4	7						12²						3¹			11					8					5			6¹	9		13	14	10								35
1	2		5	8						9		14							10³	12	6²								4				7		13	8				3¹	13	11			36
1	2		3	6¹	12				14	7									10¹	5	9²								4						13	8							11		37
1	2		3		7					14	9¹								10²	5	6			12				4						13	8³							11		38
1	2		4	9	6¹					10	12								11²	5	8							3				13	14	7³										39
1	2		4	6	7					11														3		8		5	10	4	6			8										40
1	2		3	7¹	9					11²									5¹	10								13	4	6			8						14	12				41
1	2		4		7				12		13								3	10								11¹	5	6			8							9²				42
1	2		4		7				14		13								3¹	9³								11	5	6			8						12	10²				43
1	2		3	7						9	11								5	8		12		13	4						6¹							10²						44
1	2		3	7¹	12					11	9								4	5	6	8		5														10						45
1	2		3	7						9	10								5	6	8			4														11						46

The Budweiser FA Cup

Fourth Qualifying	Solihull Moors	(h)	4-1
First Round	Cheltenham T	(h)	1-0
Second Round	Bristol C	(h)	1-2

FA Trophy

First Round	Macclesfield T	(h)	2-0
Second Round	Boston U	(h)	2-0
Third Round	Chorley	(h)	1-1
Replay	Chorley	(a)	2-2
(aet; won 6-5 on penalties)			
Quarter-Finals	Grimsby T	(a)	1-4

WELLING UNITED

Ground: Park View Road, Welling, Kent DA16 1SY.   *Tel:* (0208) 3011196.   *Fax:* (0208) 3015676.
Website: www.wellingunited.com   *Year Formed:* 1963.
Record Attendance: 4,100 v Gillingham, FA Cup 1st rd (replay), 22 November 1989.
Nickname: 'The Wings'.   *Manager:* Jamie Day.   *Colours:* Red shirts with white trim, red shorts, red socks.

WELLING UNITED – SKRILL PREMIER 2013–14 LEAGUE RECORD

Match No.	Date	Venue	Opponents	Result	H/T Score	Lg Pos.	Goalscorers	Atten- dance
1	Aug 10	A	Wrexham	L	1-2	1-1	16	Healy [43]	4011
2	14	H	Cambridge U	D	2-2	2-1	17	Lafayette [37], Clarke [43]	1010
3	17	H	Grimsby T	W	1-0	0-0	15	Lafayette [85]	807
4	24	A	Woking	W	4-2	3-1	8	Howe (og) [15], Bergqvist [19], Beautyman [29], Pires [67]	1430
5	26	H	Salisbury C	D	0-0	0-0	11		725
6	31	A	Hereford U	L	1-2	0-0	14	Lafayette [90]	1527
7	Sept 7	A	Kidderminster H	L	1-2	0-2	15	Fazakerley [81]	911
8	14	A	Southport	D	2-2	0-0	15	Clarke [48], Lafayette [76]	825
9	17	H	Forest Green R	W	5-2	2-1	13	Bergqvist [9], Pires [19], Lafayette (pen) [66], Clarke [69], Dyer [80]	452
10	21	A	Hyde	W	1-0	1-0	11	Healy [37]	427
11	24	H	Aldershot T	W	1-0	1-0	7	Dyer [15]	837
12	28	A	Macclesfield T	L	1-2	0-0	13	Lafayette [83]	1321
13	Oct 5	H	Barnet	D	1-1	1-0	12	Healy [29]	1017
14	8	A	Braintree T	W	3-2	1-1	8	Day [31], Clarke [72], Dyer [82]	1119
15	12	H	Tamworth	W	2-0	0-0	6	Clarke [63], Pires [82]	803
16	19	A	FC Halifax T	L	0-3	0-3	9		1345
17	Nov 2	H	Lincoln C	W	1-0	0-0	8	Gallagher [53]	746
18	12	A	Barnet	D	0-0	0-0	8		1274
19	16	H	Nuneaton T	L	1-2	0-0	12	Lafayette (pen) [53]	807
20	23	A	Luton T	L	1-2	0-1	12	Dyer [47]	6592
21	Dec 10	A	Grimsby T	D	1-1	1-0	13	Healy [11]	2487
22	21	H	Wrexham	D	1-1	1-1	12	Guthrie [29]	633
23	26	A	Dartford	W	2-1	0-1	12	Lafayette [74], Guthrie [80]	1758
24	28	A	Aldershot T	L	1-3	0-0	13	Lafayette [50]	2058
25	Jan 10	H	Dartford	D	1-1	1-1	14	Lafayette (pen) [18]	1336
26	14	H	Hyde	L	0-2	0-0	14		436
27	18	H	Woking	W	3-0	0-0	13	Healy 2 [62, 75], Clarke [83]	809
28	21	H	Gateshead	D	1-1	1-0	13	Healy [10]	621
29	25	H	Alfreton T	L	1-2	1-1	14	Guthrie [43]	677
30	Feb 1	A	Chester FC	W	3-1	2-0	12	Cornick [16], Lafayette [40], Healy [53]	2074
31	22	A	Tamworth	D	1-1	1-0	14	Guthrie [41]	742
32	25	H	Gateshead	W	2-0	1-0	12	Healy [7], Mawson [59]	455
33	Mar 1	H	Macclesfield T	W	1-0	0-0	11	Hudson [62]	701
34	8	A	Nuneaton T	L	0-2	0-0	11		929
35	11	A	Lincoln C	W	2-1	2-1	11	Wakefield [37], Beautyman [40]	1623
36	15	H	FC Halifax T	L	0-1	0-0	13		645
37	18	A	Cambridge U	L	1-2	0-0	14	Sho-Silva [71]	2012
38	22	A	Forest Green R	D	0-0	0-0	14		1338
39	25	H	Braintree T	L	0-2	0-1	14		403
40	29	H	Chester FC	W	2-0	0-0	13	Karagiannis [57], Lafayette [89]	706
41	Apr 5	A	Alfreton T	D	2-2	1-1	14	Taylor [2], Lafayette (pen) [62]	599
42	8	H	Hereford U	L	0-1	0-0	14		480
43	12	A	Kidderminster H	L	0-2	0-0	17		1882
44	19	A	Luton T	L	1-2	0-1	17	Lafayette [80]	2650
45	21	A	Salisbury C	L	0-3	0-3	17		895
46	26	H	Southport	W	4-3	1-3	16	Lafayette 2 (1 pen) [10, 73 (p)], Beautyman [49], Gallagher [57]	521

Final League Position: 16

GOALSCORERS
League (59): Lafayette 16 (5 pens), Healy 9, Clarke 6, Dyer 4, Guthrie 4, Beautyman 3, Pires 3, Bergqvist 2, Gallagher 2, Cornick 1, Day 1, Fazakerley 1, Hudson 1, Karagiannis 1, Mawson 1, Sho-Silva 1, Taylor 1, Wakefield 1, own goal 1.
The Budweiser FA Cup (4): Clarke 2, Healy 1, Lafayette 1.
FA Trophy (0).

Butcher 42	Fazakerley 33 + 4	Franks 26	Bergqvist 18 + 2	Hudson 35 + 1	Gallagher 33 + 2	Dyer 20	Clarke 28 + 5	Healy 43 + 3	Guthrie 26 + 5	Lafayette 37 + 2	Pires 6 + 11	Obersteller Jack 21 + 4	Beautyman 26 + 2	Obersteller Joe — + 3	Hughes-Mason 1 + 14	Ouani — + 3	Webb — + 2	Cargill 13	Day 8	Vanderhyde 4	Bassele — + 4	Cumbers 2 + 7	McLaren 7 + 4	Wakefield 13 + 5	Cornick 2 + 3	Sho-Silva 15 + 2	Ajala 11 + 4	Mawson 9	Bender 8 + 3	Turner 4	Karagiannis 1 + 4	Taylor 9	Williams 4	Ekim 1	Match No.
1	2	3	4	5	6	7	8	9²	10¹	11	12	13																							1
1	2	3	4		6	7¹	8	9	10	11	12	5																							2
1		2	4	3	7	6		9	10²	11	12	5	7¹	13																					3
1		3	2	4	8	6		9	10²	11	12	5	7¹	13																					4
1		3	2	4	6	8		9	10	11	7	5																							5
1		3	4	5	6	8	7	9		10	11¹	2	12																						6
1	14	3	2	4	6¹	7	8³	9	13	11	10²	5		12																					7
1	2	3	4		6	7	8¹	9	10²	11	12	5		13																					8
1	2	3	4¹		6	7	8	9	10³	11¹	12	5		13	14																				9
1	2	4		5	6	8	7	9²	11¹	10	13	3		12																					10
1	2	3		4	6	7	8	9²	10	11¹	12	5		13																					11
1	2	3		4¹	6	8	7	11	9²	10	12	5		13																					12
1	2	3		6²	8	7	11	9	10¹	12		5		13				4																	13
1	2	3			8	7	9	10		11	5							4	6																14
1	2	3			6	7¹	8	9	10		11	5		12				4																	15
1	2	3		4	7		6	9	11	10¹				12				5	8																16
1	2	3	13	4	7	8²	6	11	10	12		5		9¹																					17
1	2	3	4¹	12	7	9	8	10	13	11³		5²	6		14																				18
1	2	3		4	5	6	9	10	7²	11	12³		8¹		13	14																			19
1	2¹	4⁴		5	7	8	6	11	10	9					12			3																	20
1		3		4	9	8		10²	6¹	11										5	7	2	12	13											21
1		3	12	4	6¹		7	11	9²	10			8³							5		2	14	13											22
1		4	3		6		8	12	11			10³								5²	9	2	14	7¹	13										23
1		3	7	4⁴			11	9³	10			6²								5¹	8	2	13	14	12										24
1	13	3	4			6	10	9	11¹			8								5²	7			12	2										25
1	7³	3	6	4			13	8	11¹			9²	14	12						5				10	2										26
1	2		3	4			7	10	9¹	11²		8	13							5				12		6									27
1	13		4	3	12		8¹	9¹	6²	11		10								5			14	2	7										28
1	2²		4	5	6			9	10³	11		13	8¹										14	3	7	12									29
1		4	3	8			9	13	11			5	7	12										2¹		6²	10³	14							30
1	2		4	8			6	9¹	10			5	7											13		11²		3	12						31
1	2		4	7			8	10				6¹												13	12	9	11²	3	5						32
13			3	7			8	10				6²												2	12	9	11¹	4	5	1					33
1	2		4	7³		14	8	12	10			9²							8					13		11	6¹	3	5						34
2			3	7		12	8¹	13				6												10³		9	11²	4	5	1	14				35
2		3⁴				7	8					6												5¹	11	12	10	9	4		1				36
1	2					7	8	10¹						13										6	12	9	11²	3				4	5		37
1	2			13		12	8					6³												7	9¹	10	11²	3		14	4	5		38
1	9		3	8		7	11¹					13												6	10	5			12	4²	2			39
1	5		4	7⁴		8²	14	10				6³												13	9	12			11¹	3	2			40
1	2		3			14	9	10³				5²	7					8						11¹	12	6	13		4					41
1	2		4			7	12	10				6												8	9	11¹	5		3					42
1	2		3			8		10		5	6													7	9	11¹	12		4					43
1	2		4	7		11		10		12	6		14											8³	9³	13	5		3¹					44
1	2		3	7		13	11			5	6¹			9										14	12	10²	4	1				8³		45
1	2		4	7		8³		10		13	6													11	9¹	12	5²		14	3				46

The Budweiser FA Cup

Fourth Qualifying	Brislington	(a)	1-0
First Round	Luton T	(h)	2-1
Second Round	Plymouth Arg	(a)	1-3

FA Trophy

First Round	Braintree T	(a)	0-3

WOKING

Ground: Kingfield Stadium, Kingfield, Woking, Surrey GU22 9AA.   *Tel:* (01483) 722 470.   *Fax:* (01483) 888 423.
Website: wokingfc.co.uk   *Year Formed:* 1889.   *Record Attendance:* 6,064 v Coventry C, FA Cup 3rd rd, 4 February 1997.
Nickname: 'The Cardinals'.   *Manager:* Garry Hill.   *Colours:* Red shirts with white and black trim, black shorts with
white trim, white socks with black and red trim.

WOKING – SKRILL PREMIER 2013–14 LEAGUE RECORD

Match No.	Date	Venue	Opponents	Result		H/T Score	Lg Pos.	Goalscorers	Atten- dance
1	Aug 10	H	Lincoln C	D	0-0	0-0	12		1845
2	13	A	Braintree T	L	0-2	0-2	17		995
3	17	A	Chester FC	W	2-0	0-0	17	Williams 58, McNerney 63	2016
4	24	H	Welling U	L	2-4	1-3	17	Johnson 38, McNerney 69	1430
5	26	A	Aldershot T	L	1-2	0-2	18	Williams (pen) 74	3138
6	31	H	Gateshead	L	1-2	0-2	20	Williams (pen) 90	1230
7	Sept 7	A	Alfreton T	L	1-3	1-2	20	Williams (pen) 10	628
8	13	H	Tamworth	D	2-2	0-1	20	Rendell 70, Williams (pen) 78	1264
9	17	A	Hyde	W	2-0	0-0	18	Betsy 2 74, 87	387
10	21	A	Macclesfield T	L	2-3	0-2	20	Sole 80, Betsy 90	1195
11	24	H	Luton T	L	0-4	0-3	21		1955
12	28	H	Nuneaton T	W	2-0	1-0	21	Rendell 13, Payne 49	1272
13	Oct 5	A	Southport	D	1-1	1-1	21	Rendell 3	873
14	8	H	Barnet	D	0-0	0-0	21		1413
15	12	H	FC Halifax T	D	0-0	0-0	21		1552
16	19	A	Wrexham	L	0-2	0-1	21		3183
17	Nov 2	H	Grimsby T	L	1-2	1-1	21	Betsy 28	1432
18	12	H	Dartford	W	3-0	0-0	22	Marriott 63, Rendell 75, McNerney 77	1157
19	16	H	Hyde	W	3-2	1-2	19	Marriott 2 40, 74, Rendell 47	1381
20	23	A	Cambridge U	L	0-2	0-2	19		3515
21	Dec 7	A	FC Halifax T	W	4-3	3-1	18	Marriott 3 9, 13, 73, Rendell 16	1033
22	10	H	Kidderminster H	W	1-0	0-0	17	Rendell 64	1166
23	21	A	Nuneaton T	W	2-0	0-0	16	Marriott 50, Betsy 60	895
24	26	H	Salisbury C	L	1-3	1-2	16	Marriott 14	2112
25	Jan 11	H	Braintree T	W	1-0	0-0	17	McNerney 60	1270
26	18	A	Welling U	L	0-3	0-0	18		809
27	21	H	Chester FC	L	0-1	0-1	18		1124
28	25	A	Lincoln C	D	2-2	1-2	18	Betsy 19, Sole 73	2017
29	Feb 3	H	Hereford U	W	3-0	2-0	17	Marriott 24, Murtagh 26, Payne 88	1131
30	11	A	Salisbury C	L	0-2	0-0	18		624
31	15	A	Gateshead	W	2-0	1-0	16	Nutter 2, Goddard 70	706
32	18	A	Dartford	L	1-5	1-2	17	Rendell 4	1002
33	22	H	Macclesfield T	W	3-2	0-1	16	Marriott 61, Goddard 69, Rendell 78	1144
34	25	A	Kidderminster H	L	0-2	0-1	17		1448
35	Mar 1	A	Barnet	W	3-1	2-1	17	Payne 23, Rendell 2 (1 pen) 33 (p), 88	1708
36	8	H	Southport	W	2-0	0-0	14	Rendell 55, Murtagh 80	1504
37	17	A	Luton T	W	1-0	0-0	14	Sole 87	6683
38	29	H	Wrexham	W	2-1	1-1	16	Rendell 20, Jones 57	2117
39	Apr 1	H	Forest Green R	W	2-1	0-0	12	Rendell (pen) 68, Marriott 82	1315
40	5	A	Hereford U	W	2-0	2-0	11	Rendell 20, Newton 35	2140
41	8	A	Grimsby T	D	2-2	0-0	12	Betsy 84, Murtagh 90	3507
42	10	H	Cambridge U	L	0-3	0-2	12		1805
43	12	H	Alfreton T	W	2-1	0-1	10	Jones 80, Marriott 85	1485
44	19	A	Forest Green R	D	2-2	0-1	11	Johnson 68, Goddard 90	1245
45	21	H	Aldershot T	L	1-2	0-0	12	Johnson 72	4728
46	26	A	Tamworth	W	4-2	2-0	9	Sole 8, Rendell 2 13, 56, Betsy 90	788

Final League Position: 9

GOALSCORERS
League (66): Rendell 17 (2 pens), Marriott 12, Betsy 8, Williams 5 (4 pens), McNerney 4, Sole 4, Goddard 3, Johnson 3,
Murtagh 3, Payne 3, Jones 2, Newton 1, Nutter 1.
The Budweiser FA Cup (0).
FA Trophy (3): Rendell 2, Marriott 1.

Howe 13	Newton 33+4	Parkinson 19	Johnson 17+8	Nutter 42+1	Ricketts 41	Payne 40	Sawyer 9+1	Williams 15+1	Betsy 46	McCallum 4+2	McNerney 41+5	McNamee 3+16	Frith —+4	Sole 12+25	Ivey-Ward —+1	Ladapo 1+3	Bowerman 2	Cestor 20+10	Rendell 33+1	Beasant 31+1	Goddard 24+10	Murphy 3	Banya 8	Marriott 21+1	Murragh 20+1	Wright —+7	Beckles —+6	Springthorpe 2	Jones 6+6	Brice —+1	Match No.
1	2	3	4	5	6	7	8²	9³	10	11¹	12	13	14																		1
1	2	8	4	5⁴		7	9	11	10	6²	3¹	12		13⁴	14																2
1	2	3	4	5		7	9⁴	8³	10²	6	13	12		14		11¹															3
1	2	4¹	3	5¹		7	8	10²	9			13	11	14				6³	12												4
1	2			5³	6	8		7	11	9¹	3	12		14		13		10²	4												5
1	2³	4	3			8	7	9	6	10¹	11²	13		14		12			5												6
1		4	3¹	12	2	7³	8	9	6			10	14	13			11²		5												7
1	2	3	6	8¹		7	9	10	4			12		5					11												8
	2	7		5	3	8	6¹	11²	9³				14	12				4	10	1	13										9
	2¹	3		5²	7³	8	12		9				14	6		13		4	10	1	11										10
		4		5	2	7		9³	6		11	12	14	10¹				3		1	13	8²									11
		3		5	2	6		9³	8		4	10¹	14					13	11	1	12	7²									12
12		4		5	2	7		10²	6		3	13		14				9³	11	1		8¹									13
	2	4		5	6	7		9	8²		3	12						13	11	1	10¹										14
	2	5		3	7	8		10¹	6		4	12		13					11	1	9²										15
	2	4		5²	9	8		6	3		12	13						10	11	1	7¹										16
	2	4		5	7	8		9	3		11¹								10	1	12		6								17
	2	4		5	7	8		9	3		13							12	10	1	14			6³	11²						18
	2	4		5	8	7		6	3		13								10	1	12			9¹	11²						19
	2	4¹		5³	7²	8		13	6		3			14				12	10	1				9	11						20
	12		13	5	7	8			6		3							4	11	1				9¹	10²	2					21
	12		13	3	2¹	6		8	4									5	10	1				9	11²	7					22
	14			5	2³	7		6	3		13							4	10	1	12			9¹	11²	8					23
			3²	5¹	2	7		6	4		13							12	10	1	14			9³	11	8					24
	2		13	5	6	7			10		3			11				4		1	8²			9¹	12						25
	2		12	5²	6	7		8	3					11³				4		1	10¹			9⁴	14	13					26
	2		4³	5²	7	8		6	3	13				11			10				9¹					14	12	1			27
	2		4	5		7		10	3	13	13			11				8¹			9				6	12²		1			28
	2¹		4	5		8³		6	3					13					11	1	9			10²	7		14		12		29
			4	5	2²	7		6	3	14				13					11³		9¹			10	8				12		30
			4	5	8	7		6	3					12					11	1	9			10¹		13		2²			31
			4	5¹	2	7³		6	3					10²					11	1	9			12	13	14		8⁴			32
		12	2	5	7			6²	3					13				4	10	1	8			11¹	9						33
1				5	2	7		6	3²					12³		4¹	10			9				11	8		13			14	34
1	2			4	5	6		9	3					12					11		7²			10¹	8	13					35
1	2			4	5	6³		9	3	14				12					11		7²			10¹	8			13			36
1	2			3	5	8		6	4					12					10		9²			11¹	7			13			37
1¹	2		14	5	8			9	3					13				10	12	6				11²	7			4³			38
	2²		12	5	4			9	3					13			10		1	8				11¹	7			6			39
	2			5²	4	7¹		6³	3					14			13		10	1	9			11	8			12			40
	2			5	4	7		6	3					12			10		1	9²				11	8			13			41
	2		13	4²	7			9	3					10			5	14	1	12				11³	6¹			8			42
	2			4	5	8	7		9²		3¹			13					10	1	12			11				6			43
	2			4	5	6¹	7		9		3			11¹				12	10	1	8										44
	2			4	5²		7		6		3	12		11¹				9	10	1	8					13					45
	2			4¹	5		6		7		3			10²				12	11	1	9				8	13					46

The Budweiser FA Cup
Fourth Qualifying   Luton T   (h)   0-1

FA Trophy
First Round   Hereford U   (a)   3-0
Second Round   North Ferriby U   (a)   0-4

WREXHAM

Ground: Racecourse Ground, Mold Road, Wrexham LL11 2AH.   *Tel:* (01978) 262 129.   *Fax:* (01978) 357 821.
Website: wrexhamafc.co.uk   *Year Formed:* 1872.
Record Attendance: 34,445 v Manchester U, FA Cup 4th rd, 26 January 1957.
Nickname: 'Red Dragons'.   *Manager:* Kevin Wilkin.
Colours: Red shirts with white trim, white shorts with red trim, red socks with white trim.

WREXHAM – SKRILL PREMIER 2013–14 LEAGUE RECORD

Match No.	Date	Venue	Opponents	Result	H/T Score	Lg Pos.	Goalscorers	Attendance
1	Aug 10	H	Welling U	W 2-1	1-1	4	Clarke [17], Ogleby [83]	4011
2	13	A	FC Halifax T	L 2-3	1-3	13	Ainge (og) [22], Cieslewicz [80]	1674
3	17	A	Tamworth	D 2-2	1-1	14	Ormerod [37], Reid [79]	1128
4	24	H	Hyde	D 2-2	2-1	15	Thornton [24], Ntame [27]	3304
5	26	A	Lincoln C	L 0-2	0-1	16		2610
6	31	H	Chester FC	L 0-2	0-2	17		6037
7	Sept 7	A	Nuneaton T	L 0-2	0-0	19		1561
8	13	H	Luton T	W 2-0	1-0	17	Bishop [21], Hunt [58]	3122
9	17	A	Gateshead	W 3-0	0-0	15	Ormerod [55], Tomassen [65], Bishop [71]	538
10	21	A	Aldershot T	L 0-2	0-0	16		1915
11	24	H	Braintree T	L 2-3	2-2	18	Hunt [29], Harris [34]	2731
12	28	H	Cambridge U	D 1-1	1-1	19	Clowes [6]	3136
13	Oct 5	A	Salisbury C	L 1-2	1-0	20	Anyinsah [40]	986
14	8	H	Southport	W 1-0	0-0	19	Anyinsah [75]	2734
15	13	A	Barnet	D 1-1	0-1	18	Keates [90]	2143
16	19	H	Woking	W 2-0	1-0	14	Keates [21], Clarke [90]	3183
17	Nov 2	A	Macclesfield T	L 2-3	1-2	17	Anyinsah [13], Ormerod [80]	1978
18	12	A	Gateshead	W 3-2	1-2	16	Bishop 3 (1 pen) [23, 77 (p), 90]	2469
19	16	A	Kidderminster H	L 1-3	0-1	16	Cieslewicz [71]	2532
20	19	A	Dartford	W 5-1	4-1	15	Ormerod 2 [15, 34], Clarke [23], Ogleby [31], Hunt [76]	816
21	23	H	Forest Green R	W 2-0	2-0	13	Morrell [30], Hunt [36]	3083
22	Dec 21	A	Welling U	D 1-1	1-1	14	Hunt [38]	633
23	26	H	Alfreton T	L 2-3	0-0	15	Carrington [64], Clowes [87]	3371
24	28	A	Hyde	W 5-2	2-2	15	Ogleby 3 [12, 39, 71], Clarke [63], Artell [89]	952
25	Jan 1	A	Alfreton T	L 0-1	0-1	15		765
26	4	A	Aldershot T	W 2-1	1-1	13	Clarke [15], Harris [87]	2819
27	11	H	FC Halifax T	D 0-0	0-0	13		3214
28	21	A	Southport	W 2-1	1-1	12	Artell [14], Anyinsah [87]	911
29	28	H	Tamworth	W 2-0	1-0	11	Bishop [12], Hunt [90]	2160
30	Feb 8	H	Dartford	L 1-2	1-2	12	Clarke [21]	2645
31	18	A	Cambridge U	D 0-0	0-0	12		2231
32	22	H	Barnet	L 0-1	0-0	13		2925
33	25	A	Luton T	L 0-5	0-4	14		7526
34	Mar 1	A	Hereford U	W 2-0	2-0	13	Hunt [10], Ogleby [42]	1884
35	8	H	Kidderminster H	D 0-0	0-0	15		3159
36	11	A	Braintree T	L 0-3	0-1	16		699
37	15	A	Grimsby T	L 1-3	1-1	17	Pearson, S (og) [45]	3506
38	18	H	Hereford U	W 2-0	1-0	17	Graham (og) [1], Carrington [63]	2056
39	22	H	Salisbury C	D 1-1	1-1	16	Ashton (pen) [24]	2850
40	29	A	Woking	L 1-2	1-1	17	Hunt [22]	2117
41	Apr 1	H	Grimsby T	L 0-1	0-1	17		2019
42	5	H	Macclesfield T	W 1-0	1-0	17	Hunt [12]	2402
43	12	H	Nuneaton T	W 3-0	0-0	16	Hunt [54], Bishop [70], Ashton [90]	2706
44	19	A	Chester FC	D 0-0	0-0	15		4326
45	21	H	Lincoln C	L 0-1	0-1	15		2714
46	26	A	Forest Green R	D 1-1	0-1	17	Hunt (pen) [90]	1630

Final League Position: 17

GOALSCORERS

League (61): Hunt 11 (1 pen), Bishop 7 (1 pen), Clarke 6, Ogleby 6, Ormerod 5, Anyinsah 4, Artell 2, Ashton 2 (1 pen), Carrington 2, Cieslewicz 2, Clowes 2, Harris 2, Keates 2, Morrell 1, Ntame 1, Reid 1, Thornton 1, Tomassen 1, own goals 3.
The Budweiser FA Cup (6): Bishop 2, Ogleby 2, Clarke 1, Harris 1.
FA Trophy (2): Hunt 1, Morrell 1.

Mayebi 18	Tomassen 26 + 5	Wright 19	Creighton 2 + 2	Ashton 42	Harris 35 + 1	Clarke 43	Thornton 7 + 2	Cieslewicz 4 + 14	Bishop 33 + 5	Reid 5 + 4	Ogleby 17 + 16	Evans 9 + 7	Hunt 35 + 7	Clowes 11 + 4	Ormerod 26 + 9	Ntame 5 + 2	Anyinsah 24 + 10	Morrell — + 6	Artell 26 + 2	Bailey-Jones 11 + 10	Carrington 36 + 1	Coughlin 28	Keates 26 + 1	Colbeck — + 1	Parle — + 1	Livesey 16	Durrell 2 + 1	Reynolds — + 2	Williams — + 3	Match No.
1	2	3	4	5	6	7	8²	9¹	10	11³	12	13	14																	1
1	2²	3⁸		4	8	7	6³	9	10		11¹	13	5	12	14															2
1	2			7	6	8³	9¹	11	13	12	14	5	4	10²	3															3
1	2	3		5	6⁸	7	8²		10³	9		12	13		11¹	4	14													4
1	2	3¹		5		7	8²		10	9³		6	14	12	11	4	13													5
1	2		3¹	4		7	8³		10	9	14	6	5		11²	12	13													6
1	2			4		7	8²	12	10			6	5	3	11		9¹	13												7
1	2	3¹		5	6	7		13	10				8		9	12			4	11²										8
1	2			5	6	7		12	10²		13		8	14	9	3³			4	11¹										9
1	2			5	7	6		12	10		13		8³		11²	3			4	9¹	14									10
1	4³			5	6	7		12	10		13		8		9²		14		3	11¹	2									11
1				5	6	7		13			12		8²	4	9		10¹		3	11	2									12
				5		8		14	12		13	7	9	4	10¹		11²		3	6³	2	1								13
				5	6	7		10³		14		12	4¹	11²			9		3	13	2	1	8							14
13	2⁸		3	8²	7		10¹				14⁸		11³		5				4	12	6	1	9							15
3				5	6	7		9	12			4	10¹	11²						13	2	1	8							16
12				5	6	7		14	10²		9		3¹	13		11³			4	2	1	8								17
1		3		5	6	7		12	10		9¹				11²				4	13	2		8							18
1		3	13	5	8	6		12	10⁸		9³		14		11¹				4		2		7²							19
		3		5	8	6		12			9³		10		11²			14	4	13	2	1	7¹							20
		2	14	4	5	7		13			10²		9		11¹			12³	3		2	1	8							21
		3¹		5		7			10³		9	6	8	12	11²		13	14	4		2	1								22
	2			5					11³	7¹	8	3	10²		9	13	4	14	6	1				12						23
	14			6	7			12	9		10²	8³	5	3			11¹		4	13	2	1								24
	13			8	6			9	10¹			7	5	4	11		12	3		2⁸		1								25
	2			7	8		13	14			10²		5	3¹			9		4	11³	6	1			12					26
	3			5	7	6			12		11²		8		10⁸		9¹		4	13	2	1								27
	4			5	6	8			9			13	11¹				10		3	12	2	1	7²							28
	3			5	6	7			10			11					9¹		4	12	2	1	8							29
	3			5	6	7	14		10		9²		11¹				12			2	1	8⁸			4	13				30
	4			5	7	10		11		13		12		14	6²					2	1	8⁸			3	9¹				31
	4			5	6	7	14		10²		13			12	11¹					2	1	8			3	9³				32
	5			3		8		13		11²	6	10		9	12					2	1	7¹			4					33
	4	2		5				10¹		12	9			11						6	1	8			3					34
	2	4		5	7			10⁸		12		9¹	13	11²						6	1	8			3					35
	3	2		5	7³					13		9²	10	11		12				6	1	8			4¹		14		36
	2	3		5	13	7			11²		9		12	10¹		14				6	1	8³			4				37
	4			5	6	7					10²	12	11		9³					2	1	8¹			3		14		38
	4			5	6	7		12			10¹		11		9²		13			2	1	8			3				39
	3			5	7	6		11²	10¹			9		13	12					2	1	8			4				40
	4			5	6	7			10¹			9	12	11						2	1	8			3				41
1	13			5	6³	7			10	12	9		14	11¹		4		2		8						3²				42
1				5		7			10³	12	11¹	13	9						3	6	2	8²			4		14		43
1				5		7			10	12			9				11¹		3	6	2	8			4				44
1	4			5	8	7¹			10²				9				11		3	6	2	12			4		13		45
				5	7	6¹			12				11				10²		3	9	2	1	8			4		13		46

The Budweiser FA Cup

Fourth Qualifying	Hyde	(h)	2-0
First Round	Alfreton T	(h)	3-1
Second Round	Oxford U	(h)	1-2

FA Trophy

First Round	Gresley	(h)	2-1
Second Round	Luton T	(a)	0-2

SCOTTISH LEAGUE TABLES 2013–14

(P) *Promoted into division at end of 2012–13 season.*   (R) *Relegated into division at end of 2012–13 season.*

SCOTTISH PREMIER LEAGUE 2013–14

			Total				Home				Away					
		P	W	D	L	F	A	W	D	L	F	A	W	D	L	F	A	GD	Pts

		P	W	D	L	F	A	W	D	L	F	A	W	D	L	F	A	GD	Pts
1	Celtic	38	31	6	1	102	25	16	3	0	50	10	15	3	1	52	15	77	99
2	Motherwell	38	22	4	12	64	60	13	2	4	39	29	9	2	8	25	31	4	70
3	Aberdeen	38	20	8	10	53	38	10	3	5	20	13	10	5	5	33	25	15	68
4	Dundee U	38	16	10	12	65	50	11	2	6	40	23	5	8	6	25	27	15	58
5	Inverness CT	38	16	9	13	44	44	8	6	5	26	16	8	3	8	18	28	0	57
6	St Johnstone	38	15	8	15	48	42	10	4	5	35	16	5	4	10	13	26	6	53
7	Ross Co	38	11	7	20	44	62	8	2	9	25	29	3	5	11	19	33	–18	40
8	St Mirren	38	10	9	19	39	58	7	7	5	23	20	3	2	14	16	38	–19	39
9	Kilmarnock	38	11	6	21	45	66	7	3	9	25	30	4	3	12	20	36	–21	39
10	Partick Th (P)	38	8	14	16	46	65	2	8	9	21	37	6	6	7	25	28	–19	38
11	Hibernian†	38	8	11	19	31	51	4	7	9	20	29	4	4	10	11	22	–20	35
12	Hearts*	38	10	8	20	45	65	6	3	10	21	29	4	5	10	24	36	–20	23

*Top 6 teams split after 33 games. *Hearts deducted 15 points for entering administration. †Hibernian relegated after play-offs.*

SCOTTISH LEAGUE CHAMPIONSHIP 2013–14

		Total						Home					Away						

		P	W	D	L	F	A	W	D	L	F	A	W	D	L	F	A	GD	Pts
1	Dundee (R)	36	21	6	9	54	26	11	4	3	27	9	10	2	6	27	17	28	69
2	Hamilton A¶	36	19	10	7	68	41	12	3	3	43	21	7	7	4	25	20	27	67
3	Falkirk	36	19	9	8	59	33	12	4	2	38	13	7	5	6	21	20	26	66
4	Queen of the South (P)	36	16	7	13	53	39	9	4	5	28	17	7	3	8	25	22	14	55
5	Dumbarton	36	15	6	15	65	64	7	5	6	33	28	8	1	9	32	36	1	51
6	Livingston	36	13	7	16	51	56	7	4	7	27	24	6	3	9	24	32	–5	46
7	Raith R	36	11	9	16	48	61	7	4	7	29	33	4	5	9	19	28	–13	42
8	Alloa Ath (P)	36	11	7	18	34	51	7	1	10	15	24	4	6	8	19	27	–17	40
9	Cowdenbeath	36	11	7	18	50	72	7	3	8	32	30	4	4	10	18	42	–22	40
10	Greenock Morton	36	6	8	22	32	71	5	6	7	20	23	1	2	15	12	48	–39	26

¶Hamilton A promoted via play-offs. Cowdenbeath not relegated after play-offs.

SCOTTISH LEAGUE ONE 2013–14

		P	W	D	L	F	A	W	D	L	F	A	W	D	L	F	A	GD	Pts
1	Rangers (P)	36	33	3	0	106	18	16	2	0	60	12	17	1	0	46	6	88	102
2	Dunfermline Ath (R)	36	19	6	11	68	54	9	4	5	33	23	10	2	6	35	31	14	63
3	Stranraer	36	14	9	13	57	57	9	4	5	30	22	5	5	8	27	35	0	51
4	Ayr U	36	14	7	15	65	66	8	3	7	39	33	6	4	8	26	33	–1	49
5	Stenhousemuir	36	12	12	12	57	66	5	8	5	30	31	7	4	7	27	35	–9	48
6	Airdrieonians (R)	36	12	9	15	47	57	9	2	7	27	26	3	7	8	20	31	–10	45
7	Forfar Ath	36	12	7	17	55	62	6	4	8	27	24	6	3	9	28	38	–7	43
8	Brechin C	36	12	6	18	57	71	7	4	7	32	34	5	2	11	25	37	–14	42
9	East Fife†	36	9	5	22	31	69	5	2	11	15	33	4	3	11	16	36	–38	32
10	Arbroath	36	9	4	23	52	75	6	1	11	28	36	3	3	12	24	39	–23	31

No promoted team via play-offs. †East Fife relegated after play-offs.

SCOTTISH LEAGUE TWO 2013–14

		P	W	D	L	F	A	W	D	L	F	A	W	D	L	F	A	GD	Pts
1	Peterhead	36	23	7	6	74	38	11	6	1	37	16	12	1	5	37	22	36	76
2	Annan Ath	36	19	6	11	69	49	10	3	5	34	23	9	3	6	35	26	20	63
3	Stirling Alb¶	36	16	10	10	60	50	9	6	3	34	22	7	4	7	26	28	10	58
4	Clyde	36	17	6	13	50	48	9	3	6	29	24	8	3	7	21	24	2	57
5	Berwick Rangers	36	15	7	14	63	49	10	2	6	38	22	5	5	8	25	27	14	52
6	Montrose	36	12	10	14	44	56	7	4	7	21	24	5	6	7	23	32	–12	46
7	Albion R (R)	36	12	8	16	41	54	10	2	6	23	20	2	6	10	18	34	–13	44
8	East Stirlingshire	36	12	8	16	45	59	6	6	6	26	28	6	2	10	19	31	–14	44
9	Elgin C	36	9	9	18	62	73	6	3	9	37	33	3	6	9	25	40	–11	36
10	Queen's Park	36	5	9	22	36	68	2	5	11	17	36	3	4	11	19	32	–32	24

¶Stirling Alb promoted via play-offs.

SCOTTISH LEAGUE ATTENDANCES 2013–14

SCOTTISH PREMIER LEAGUE ATTENDANCES

	Average Gate			Season 2013–14	
	2012–13	2013–14	+/–%	Highest	Lowest
Aberdeen	9,611	13,085	+36.14	20,017	9,332
Celtic	46,917	47,079	+0.35	52,670	44,271
Dundee U	7,547	7,599	+0.69	12,601	5,808
Hearts	13,163	14,123	+7.29	16,873	11,950
Hibernian	10,489	11,027	+5.13	20,106	8,277
Inverness CT	4,038	3,558	–11.89	6,384	2,366
Kilmarnock	4,647	4,250	–8.54	7,495	3,035
Motherwell	5,362	5,175	–3.49	9,117	3,432
Partick Th	3,614	5,003	+38.43	7,978	2,719
Ross Co	4,430	3,787	–14.52	5,982	2,792
St Johnstone	3,712	3,806	+2.55	7,231	1,892
St Mirren	4,389	4,511	+2.77	6,311	2,817

SCOTTISH LEAGUE CHAMPIONSHIP ATTENDANCES

	Average Gate			Season 2013–14	
	2012–13	2013–14	+/–%	Highest	Lowest
Alloa Ath	551	876	+59.00	2,552	546
Cowdenbeath	791	623	–21.25	1,419	318
Dumbarton	927	938	+1.22	1,469	463
Dundee	5,943	4,738	–20.28	10,718	3,533
Falkirk	3,102	3,114	+0.38	4,183	2,489
Hamilton A	1,231	1,436	+16.64	4,529	817
Livingston	1,308	1,157	–11.56	1,759	709
Greenock Morton	2,137	1,686	–21.11	2,341	826
Queen of the South	1,659	1,724	+3.90	2,644	1,476
Raith R	1,829	1,659	–9.30	4,039	978

SCOTTISH LEAGUE ONE ATTENDANCES

	Average Gate			Season 2013–14	
	2012–13	2013–14	+/–%	Highest	Lowest
Airdrieonians	936	1,586	+69.43	8,930	579
Arbroath	684	1,054	+54.15	3,902	498
Ayr U	1,007	1,905	+89.21	8,968	643
Brechin C	549	900	+63.85	3,237	445
Dunfermline Ath	3,796	3,331	–12.26	10,089	1,983
East Fife	526	1,249	+137.47	4,700	561
Forfar Ath	539	865	+60.53	3,776	422
Rangers	45,744	42,657	–6.75	46,093	38,745
Stenhousemuir	543	826	+52.07	2,767	368
Stranraer	426	802	+88.22	3,473	326

SCOTTISH LEAGUE TWO ATTENDANCES

	Average Gate			Season 2013–14	
	2012–13	2013–14	+/–%	Highest	Lowest
Albion R	387	403	+4.16	718	286
Annan Ath	641	409	–36.12	560	277
Berwick Rangers	917	468	–49.02	778	227
Clyde	1,313	519	–60.46	751	173
East Stirlingshire	612	343	–43.93	584	218
Elgin C	1,030	574	–44.24	670	485
Montrose	831	363	–56.34	486	262
Peterhead	938	573	–38.93	852	423
Queen's Park	2,803	425	–84.84	704	251
Stirling Alb	897	616	–31.35	1,028	378

ABERDEEN

Year Formed: 1903. *Ground & Address:* Pittodrie Stadium, Pittodrie St, Aberdeen AB24 5QH. *Telephone:* 01224 650400. *Fax:* 01224 644173. *E-mail:* feedback@afc.co.uk *Website:* www.afc.co.uk
Ground Capacity: all seated: 21,421. *Size of Pitch:* 105m × 66m.
Chairman: Stewart Milne. *Chief Executive:* Duncan Fraser.
Manager: Derek McInnes. *Assistant Manager:* Tony Docherty. *U-20 Coach:* Paul Sheerin.
Club Nicknames: 'The Dons', 'The Reds', 'The Dandies'.
Previous Grounds: None.
Record Attendance: 45,061 v Hearts, Scottish Cup 4th rd, 13 Mar 1954.
Record Transfer Fee received: £1.75 million for Eoin Jess to Coventry City (February 1996).
Record Transfer Fee paid: £1m+ for Paul Bernard from Oldham Athletic (September 1995).
Record Victory: 13-0 v Peterhead, Scottish Cup 3rd rd, 10 Feb 1923.
Record Defeat: 0-9 v Celtic, Premier League, 6 Nov 2010.
Most Capped Player: Alex McLeish, 77 (Scotland).
Most League Appearances: 556: Willie Miller, 1973-90.
Most League Goals in Season (Individual): 38: Benny Yorston, Division I, 1929-30.
Most Goals Overall (Individual): 199: Joe Harper, 1969-72; 1976-81.

ABERDEEN – SCOTTISH PREMIER LEAGUE 2013–14 LEAGUE RECORD

Match No.	Date	Venue	Opponents	Result	H/T Score	Lg Pos.	Goalscorers	Attendance
1	Aug 3	H	Kilmarnock	W 2-1	1-0	2	Hayes [21], Flood [53]	13,149
2	11	A	Motherwell	W 3-1	0-1	2	McGinn 2 (2 pens) [62, 84], Reynolds [76]	6242
3	17	H	Celtic	L 0-2	0-1	4		20,017
4	24	A	Hearts	L 1-2	0-1	4	McGinn (pen) [68]	15,218
5	31	H	St Johnstone	D 0-0	0-0	6		9478
6	Sept 14	A	Partick Thistle	W 3-0	2-0	4	Zola [13], Pawlett [20], Magennis [70]	6193
7	21	A	Inverness CT	W 1-0	0-0	3	Vernon [81]	11,251
8	30	A	St Mirren	D 1-1	0-0	4	Pawlett [85]	4051
9	Oct 5	A	Ross Co	L 0-1	0-0	4		5290
10	19	H	Dundee U	W 1-0	0-0	4	Zola [54]	12,654
11	26	H	Hibernian	W 2-0	0-0	2	Vernon [80], Wylde [90]	12,810
12	Nov 4	H	Partick Thistle	W 4-0	2-0	2	McGinn 2 [25, 87], Zola [40], Hector [64]	10,057
13	9	H	Hearts	L 1-3	1-0	4	McGinn [26]	13,940
14	23	A	Celtic	L 1-3	1-1	5	McGinn [45]	49,683
15	Dec 7	A	St Johnstone	W 2-0	1-0	4	Pawlett [17], McGinn [85]	4741
16	14	H	St Mirren	W 2-0	1-0	4	Vernon [20], Robson [66]	9332
17	21	A	Inverness CT	W 4-3	4-0	3	Robson 2 (1 pen) [22 (p), 32], Pawlett [37], McGinn [44]	4810
18	26	H	Motherwell	L 0-1	0-0	5		12,494
19	29	H	Ross Co	W 1-0	1-0	3	Low [2]	11,602
20	Jan 1	A	Dundee U	W 2-1	0-0	3	Robson (pen) [64], Pawlett [90]	12,601
21	5	A	Kilmarnock	W 1-0	0-0	2	Reynolds [83]	4073
22	10	H	Hibernian	W 1-0	0-0	2	Flood [87]	12,734
23	18	A	Inverness CT	L 0-1	0-1	2		12,021
24	25	A	Motherwell	D 2-2	0-0	2	Rooney [67], Anderson [90]	5756
25	Feb 15	A	St Mirren	W 1-0	0-0	2	Rooney (pen) [80]	4073
26	22	A	Partick Thistle	L 1-3	0-0	2	Rooney [66]	4554
27	25	H	Celtic	W 2-1	2-0	2	Hayes [41], Rooney [45]	16,634
28	Mar 1	A	St Johnstone	W 1-0	1-0	2	Jack [8]	11,487
29	22	H	Kilmarnock	W 2-1	1-1	2	Rooney [17], Jack [72]	17,029
30	25	A	Ross Co	D 1-1	0-1	2	Rooney [77]	3775
31	29	H	Dundee U	D 1-1	0-1	2	McGinn [52]	14,627
32	Apr 2	A	Hearts	D 1-1	0-0	2	Flood [74]	13,913
33	7	A	Hibernian	W 2-0	1-0	2	McGinn 2 [14, 62]	9321
34	18	A	Inverness CT	D 0-0	0-0	2		4224
35	26	H	St Johnstone	D 1-1	1-1	2	Rooney [31]	10,003
36	May 3	A	Celtic	L 2-5	1-2	2	McGinn [28], Logan [56]	47,468
37	6	H	Dundee U	W 3-1	1-1	2	Vernon 3 [7, 55, 76]	8677
38	11	H	Motherwell	L 0-1	0-0	3		17,016

Final League Position: 3

Honours
League Champions: Division I 1954-55. Premier Division 1979-80, 1983-84, 1984-85; *Runners-up:* Division I 1910-11, 1936-37, 1955-56, 1970-71, 1971-72. Premier Division 1977-78, 1980-81, 1981-82, 1988-89, 1989-90, 1990-91, 1992-93, 1993-94.
Scottish Cup Winners: 1947, 1970, 1982, 1983, 1984, 1986, 1990; *Runners-up:* 1937, 1953, 1954, 1959, 1967, 1978, 1993, 2000.
League Cup Winners: 1955-56, 1976-77, 1985-86, 1989-90, 1995-96, 2013-14; *Runners-up:* 1946-47, 1978-79, 1979-80, 1987-88, 1988-89, 1992-93, 1999-2000.
Drybrough Cup Winners: 1971, 1980.

European: *European Cup:* 12 matches (1980-81, 1984-85, 1985-86); *Cup Winners' Cup:* 39 matches (1967-68, 1970-71, 1978-79, 1982-83 winners, 1983-84 semi-finals, 1986-87, 1990-91, 1993-94); *UEFA Cup:* 56 matches (*Fairs Cup:* 1968-69. *UEFA Cup:* 1971-72, 1972-73, 1973-74, 1977-78, 1979-80, 1981-82, 1987-88, 1988-89, 1989-90, 1991-92, 1994-95, 1996-97, 2000-01, 2002-03, 2007-08). *Europa League:* 2 matches (2009-10).

Club colours: All red with white trim.

Goalscorers: *League (53):* McGinn 13 (3 pens), Rooney 7 (1 pen), Vernon 6, Pawlett 5, Robson 4 (2 pens), Flood 3, Zola 3, Hayes 2, Jack 2, Reynolds 2, Anderson 1, Hector 1, Logan 1, Low 1, Magennis 1, Wylde 1.
William Hill Scottish FA Cup (5): Anderson 1, Considine 1, McGinn 1, Pawlett 1, Rooney 1.
Scottish Communities League Cup (11): Vernon 3 (1 pen), Hayes 3, Considine 1, Pawlett 1, Rooney 1, Shaughnessy 1, Smith 1.

Langfield J 37	Shaughnessy J 20+6	Robertson C 5+3	Flood W 31+2	Anderson R 27+3	Reynolds M 37	Jack R 34	Robson B 20+8	McGinn N 35+1	Zola C 11+9	Hayes J 28+3	Magennis J 1+17	Hector M 18+2	Pawlett P 33+2	Wylde G 3+5	Weaver N 1+1	Vernon S 14+11	Smith C 8+10	Murray C —+2	Considine A 21	Storie C —+1	Low N 3+9	Tate A 5+2	Rooney A 13	Logan S 13	McManus D —+3	Match No.
1	2	3³	4	5	6	7	8³	9	10²	11	12	13	14													1
1	2	12	8	3²	5	7		11	10¹	9	13	4	6³	14												2
1¹	2		7	3¹	5	8		11	10³	9	13	4	6²	14	12											3
	2	5²	6	4	7	11	12	9	14	3	8¹	13	1			10²										4
1	2¹	5	3	8	7	11	14	10	4³	6	9²					12	13									5
1	2	14	3	5		10¹	7	12	8	6	9		11³			4²	13									6
1	2		3	7		10¹	8	13	4	6	9²		14	11³		5	12									7
1	2		5	7		14	10³	6	13	3	9		11²	8¹		4	12									8
1	2	12	13	5	6		11		8	14	3	10	9²			7¹	4³									9
1	2¹		7	3	5	8²	12	10	11³	6	14	9				13	4									10
1	2	5	7	3	4	8	13	6	11¹	9²		10³	14			12										11
1		7	14	4	2	12	11	10²	9		3	6¹				13	8³	5								12
1		8¹	6	4	2	12▪	10	11²	7		3³	9				13	14	5								13
1	2³		3	5	7	10	11¹	8²	12	6	9	13				14	4									14
1		12	3	5	6	9²	7	10¹	13	2	8		11³			4	14									15
1	14	7³	3	5	6	8¹	11	12		2	9²		10			4	13									16
1	2		8	4	5¹	6	9	7		12	13	3	10			11²										17
1	2³		7	3		5	6¹	11	14	9	12	4	8			10²	13									18
1	2		7		4	8³	12	11		9	14	3	6²			10¹	13			5						19
1	13		7	3	4	6	8	10		5	12	2	9¹			11²										20
1	14		8	3	4	6	7	10		5³	12	2	9¹			11²			13▪							21
1	2		6	13	4	7	8	10²	12	5³	14		9			11¹					3					22
1	12		6	3	4	7	9²	10	13	14	8		11¹						5	13	10					23
1	2		7	3	4	8²	9¹	11		6	12								5		13	10				24
1	6		8	3	4		9						10						5		7¹	12	11	2		25
1	2		6	3	4	7¹	8	12	10		9								5²		13		11			26
1	12		6	13	4	7	8	10		9¹	14								5		3³	11	2²			27
1		7	4		6²	12	11³	9	8¹		13	5	14						3		10	2				28
1		7	3	4	8	12	6¹					10							5		9²	11	2	13		29
1	12		7	4	6	10	8³	14								13	9²	5▪			3¹	11	2			30
1	4		7	3	5	6	8	11									9¹				10	2	12			31
1		7	3	4	6	8¹	11						9²			13	12	5			10	2				32
1		6	3	5	7	9¹	11						8²			13	12	4	14		10³	2				33
1		7	3	4		8	9	13	6²				10			12		5			11¹	2				34
1	5¹	7	3	4	8	12	6¹	14	9				10²			13					11	2				35
1		7	4	3	8	5³	10	9					6²			12	13				11¹	2	14			36
1		7³	4	3	2	6	9¹	14	10				8			11¹	12				13		5			37
1		7	3	4	8	9	6						5			10	11					2				38

AIRDRIEONIANS

Year Formed: 2002. *Ground & Address:* Excelsior Stadium, New Broomfield, Craigneuk Avenue, Airdrie ML6 8QZ.
Telephone: (Stadium) 01236 622000. *Fax:* 01236 626002. *Postal Address:* 60 St Enoch Square, Glasgow G1 4AG.
E-mail: annmarie@ballantyneand.co.uk *Website:* www.airdriefc.com
Ground Capacity: 10,171 (all seated). *Size of Pitch:* 105m × 67m.
Chairman: Jim Ballantyne. *Secretary:* Ann Marie Ballantyne.
Manager: Gary Bollan. *Assistant Manager:* Stuart Balmer.
Club Nickname: 'The Diamonds'.
Record Attendance: 9,044 v Rangers, League 1, 23 Aug 2013.
Record Victory: 11-0 v Gala Fairydean, Scottish Cup 3rd rd, 19 Nov 2011.
Record Defeat: 0-7 v Partick Th, First Division, 20 Oct 2012.
Most League Appearances: 222, Paul Lovering 2004-12.
Most League Goals in Season (Individual): 19: Alan Russell, 2007-08.
Most Goals Overall (Individual): 33: Stephen McKeown, 2002-08.

AIRDRIEONIANS – SCOTTISH LEAGUE ONE 2013–14 LEAGUE RECORD

Match No.	Date	Venue	Opponents	Result	H/T Score	Lg Pos.	Goalscorers	Atten- dance
1	Aug 10	A	Forfar Ath	D	3-3	1-1	5	Lister [32], McLaren [48], Coult [65]	704
2	17	H	Stenhousemuir	L	0-1	0-0	7		722
3	23	H	Rangers	L	0-6	0-2	8		9044
4	31	A	Ayr U	D	2-2	2-2	8	Boyle [4], Blockley [37]	1339
5	Sept 14	H	Stranraer	W	3-2	1-1	7	Sinclair [12], Coult [72], Buchanan [89]	679
6	21	A	Dunfermline Ath	L	1-2	0-0	7	Coogans [57]	2607
7	28	A	East Fife	L	0-1	0-1	9		665
8	Oct 5	H	Brechin C	W	3-1	2-1	8	Hardie [22], Coogans [34], Coult [90]	606
9	12	A	Arbroath	L	2-3	0-1	8	McLaren [60], Coult [79]	747
10	19	H	Forfar Ath	L	0-2	0-1	10		579
11	26	H	Ayr U	L	0-1	0-0	10		1012
12	Nov 9	A	Rangers	L	0-2	0-0	10		43,158
13	16	H	Dunfermline Ath	L	0-3	0-1	10		1219
14	23	A	Stranraer	L	1-3	0-2	10	Hardie [52]	461
15	Dec 14	H	East Fife	L	1-3	1-1	10	Coult [18]	624
16	17	A	Brechin C	L	3-4	0-2	10	Lister [61], Coult [83], Blockley [90]	445
17	21	A	Stenhousemuir	D	1-1	1-0	10	Buchanan [6]	419
18	28	H	Arbroath	W	2-1	0-1	10	Buchanan [59], Parker [62]	641
19	Jan 2	H	Rangers	L	0-1	0-1	10		6522
20	11	A	Ayr U	L	0-3	0-0	10		1037
21	18	A	Dunfermline Ath	W	1-0	1-0	10	McAleer [19]	2711
22	25	H	Stranraer	D	1-1	1-0	10	Lister [39]	726
23	Feb 1	A	Forfar Ath	D	1-1	0-1	10	Lister [64]	542
24	15	H	Brechin C	W	2-1	1-1	9	Gilmour [18], Buchanan [90]	690
25	22	A	East Fife	D	0-0	0-0	9		815
26	25	H	Stenhousemuir	D	1-1	0-0	9	Lister [68]	586
27	Mar 1	A	Ayr U	W	3-0	1-0	8	Barr [30], Watt [69], Parker (pen) [75]	880
28	12	A	Rangers	L	0-3	0-3	8		41,343
29	15	A	Arbroath	W	1-0	1-0	8	Lister [33]	823
30	22	H	Forfar Ath	W	5-1	3-1	8	Buchanan [15], Bain [19], Baxter (og) [22], Dods (og) [52], Watt [82]	712
31	29	A	Stranraer	D	1-1	0-0	8	Rumsby (og) [88]	404
32	Apr 5	H	Dunfermline Ath	W	2-0	1-0	8	Parker [28], Lister [90]	1142
33	12	A	Brechin C	D	1-1	1-0	8	Lister [36]	646
34	19	H	East Fife	W	2-1	0-0	8	McAleer [52], Lister [78]	1033
35	26	A	Stenhousemuir	W	2-1	1-0	8	Stewart, S [28], Barr [63]	812
36	May 3	H	Arbroath	W	2-0	1-0	6	McAleer [45], Coogans [89]	1243

Final League Position: 6

Honours
League Champions: Second Division 2003-04; *Runners-up:* Second Division 2007-08.
League Challenge Cup Winners: 2008-09; *Runners-up:* 2003-04.

Club colours: Shirt: White with red diamond. Shorts: White. Socks: White.

Goalscorers: *League (47):* Lister 9, Coult 6, Buchanan 5, Coogans 3, McAleer 3, Parker 3 (1 pen), Barr 2, Blockley 2, Hardie 2, McLaren 2, Watt 2, Bain 1, Boyle 1, Gilmour 1, Sinclair 1, Stewart S 1, own goals 3.
William Hill Scottish FA Cup (0).
Scottish Communities League Cup (4): Blockley 1, Coult 1, O'Byrne 1, Sinclair 1.
Ramsdens Cup (2): Blockley 1, McLaren 1.

Stewart C 3	Evans G 10+3	McCormack D 34	O'Byrne M 6+3	Hay G 2+2	Blockley N 21+4	Sinclair D 12+2	Hardie M 11	McLaren W 7+6	Lister J 28+5	Coult L 14+7	Bain J 26+6	Coogans L 9+14	O'Neil C 6	Boyle P 30	Buchanan G 28+4	Duncan A 3	Watt L 24+1	Gallagher S 8	Drummond G 3+1	Stewart S 2+8	Pollock J 2+1	Cadden N 8+4	Grier J —+1	McAleer C 19+1	Rogers D 6	Gilmour R 11	Parker K 19+1	Milojevic S 17	Adam G 16	Barr C 11	Match No.
1	2	3	4	5	6	7	8¹	9	10	11²	12	13																			1
1		4	3	9²	6¹	7	8	13	10	11	12	14	2³	5																	2
1		3	12	13	8	7		9¹	10³	11	6²	14	2	5	4																3
		3²	4	14	7	8		9	10	11¹		13	2	5	12³	1	6														4
4		3			7	8		9	11²	10¹	6	12		5	2				1		13										5
4		3			9	8	7	12		11¹	6	10		5	2				1												6
4		3			8		10	12		13	6	11²		5	2¹		9	1	7												7
4		3	12		6	8	7²		11³	14	13	9	2¹	5			9²	1													8
4		3		6¹	7³	8	13		10	12	11	2³	5	14			9²	1													9
3	4			8²	7	12	10	9	6¹	11		5	2				1		13												10
3²	4			8	9	7	6¹	11	12	13	10		5	2			1														11
4			9	6²	7		11		8¹	10	5	2	1	13	3		12														12
	3	12		14		6		10³		8	9	8	5	2	1●			4²		7¹	11	13									13
	3	4¹		8	14	7		10²	11	12	13		5	2		1					9³	6									14
	3			7	14		12	10¹		13		5	4		8		11	9³	6²	1	2										15
	3		8	7³		13	10		6²	5¹	4	9			14	12	1	2	11												16
	3		8			11	10	2		4	7		9		6	1	5														17
	7	3			12	13	11¹	2		4	8		14	9³	6	1	5	10²													18
	9	3	8¹		10	11		5		4	7				6	1	2	12													19
	8		6		9	12	11¹	5		4	7					1	2	10	3												20
	6		9			10	2		8	3				7		5	11	4	1												21
	8		7			11	12	2		9	3				6		5	10¹	4	1											22
3			7			10		5	12	9		8			6		2	11¹	4	1											23
4²	9		12			11	14			5	13	7			10¹	6	2	8³	3	1											24
	8					10	12	9		5	3	7				6	2	11¹	4	1											25
	8					10		5		9	3	7				6	11	4	1	2											26
	8		12			11²		2	14	5	3	9			13	6¹	10	4	1	7³											27
	6					11²	10	14		5	3	8		12	13	7	9¹	4	1	2¹											28
12	9					10	7			5	3	8²		13		6●	11¹	4	1	7											29
13	8					10²	12	2	14	5³	3	9			6³		11	4	1	7											30
	8²					10		2	13	5	3	9		6	12		11¹	4	1	7											31
	8					11		2	13	5	3	8		12		6²	10¹	4	1	7											32
	9					10		7		5	3	8		12		6¹	11	4	1	2											33
12	9					11		7	5		3	8		13		6²	10¹	4	1	2											34
			7			13		5		11	12	3		4	10¹	6	9²	8	1	2											35
	8³		13			10		5	12	9	3	7		14		6¹	11²	4	1	2											36

ALBION ROVERS

Year Formed: 1882. *Ground & Address:* Cliftonhill Stadium, Main St, Coatbridge ML5 3RB. *Telephone/Fax:* 01236 606334.
E-mail: info@albionroversfc.com *Website:* albionroversfc.com
Ground capacity: 1,249 (seated: 489). *Size of Pitch:* 101m × 66m.
Chairman John Devlin. *Secretary:* Paul Reilly.
Manager: Darren Young. *Assistant Manager:* Sandy Clark.
Club Nickname: 'The Wee Rovers'.
Previous Grounds: Cowheath Park, Meadow Park, Whifflet.
Record Attendance: 27,381 v Rangers, Scottish Cup 2nd rd, 8 Feb 1936.
Record Transfer Fee received: £40,000 from Motherwell for Bruce Cleland.
Record Transfer Fee paid: £7000 for Gerry McTeague to Stirling Albion, September 1989.
Record Victory: 12-0 v Airdriehill, Scottish Cup 1st rd, 3 Sept 1887.
Record Defeat: 1-11 v Partick Thistle, League Cup 2nd rd, 11 Aug 1993.
Most Capped Player: Jock White, 1 (2), Scotland.
Most League Appearances: 399: Murdy Walls, 1921-36.
Most League Goals in Season (Individual): 41: Jim Renwick, Division II, 1932-33.
Most Goals Overall (Individual): 105: Bunty Weir, 1928-31.

ALBION ROVERS – SCOTTISH LEAGUE TWO 2013–14 LEAGUE RECORD

Match No.	Date	Venue	Opponents	Result	H/T Score	Lg Pos.	Goalscorers	Attendance
1	Aug 10	A	Elgin C	W 2-1	1-0	2	Walker [43], Crawford (pen) [53]	541
2	17	H	Clyde	W 3-0	3-0	2	Phillips 2 [8, 37], Walker [18]	528
3	24	A	Annan Ath	D 1-1	0-0	2	Crawford (pen) [48]	492
4	31	H	Montrose	L 0-2	0-1	4		311
5	Sept 14	H	Berwick R	L 0-2	0-0	6		322
6	21	A	East Stirling	W 4-1	3-0	3	Dunlop, M [3], Dallas 2 [29, 40], McGuigan [89]	336
7	28	H	Peterhead	L 1-2	0-1	6	Miller [49]	354
8	Oct 19	H	Elgin C	D 0-0	0-0	9		337
9	26	A	Queen's Park	D 1-1	0-1	9	Quinn (og) [88]	541
10	29	A	Stirling Alb	L 1-2	1-1	9	Dallas [15]	423
11	Nov 9	H	Annan Ath	W 2-0	0-0	6	Watson (og) [75], Shankland [90]	319
12	16	A	Montrose	L 1-2	1-1	7	McGuigan [24]	343
13	23	A	Berwick R	L 1-2	0-2	8	Hoskins (og) [73]	388
14	Dec 3	H	East Stirling	W 3-2	2-0	7	Phillips [22], Dallas [40], Chaplain [76]	323
15	7	H	Stirling Alb	W 2-1	2-0	7	Russell [25], Dallas [44]	396
16	14	A	Peterhead	D 1-1	0-0	5	McGuigan [83]	423
17	21	A	Clyde	D 2-2	1-0	5	Dunlop, M [45], Cusack [53]	508
18	28	H	Queen's Park	W 2-1	1-0	4	Cusack [45], Chaplain [70]	538
19	Jan 4	A	Annan Ath	L 0-2	0-1	5		403
20	11	H	Montrose	W 1-0	1-0	5	Chaplain (pen) [6]	718
21	18	A	East Stirling	D 1-1	0-0	5	Chaplain [59]	319
22	25	H	Berwick R	L 0-3	0-2	5		366
23	Feb 1	A	Elgin C	D 1-1	0-0	5	Chaplain (pen) [56]	519
24	15	A	Stirling Alb	L 0-2	0-0	7		541
25	22	H	Peterhead	D 0-0	0-0	7		442
26	25	H	Clyde	W 1-0	0-0	6	Chaplain (pen) [66]	423
27	Mar 1	A	Montrose	L 1-2	0-0	7	Phillips [52]	334
28	15	A	Queen's Park	L 0-4	0-2	8		361
29	22	H	Elgin C	W 5-2	3-0	8	Donnelly, C [4], Cusack [13], Phillips [45], Chaplain 2 (1 pen) [53 (p), 80]	286
30	25	H	Annan Ath	L 0-2	0-1	8		323
31	29	A	Berwick R	L 1-3	0-2	8	Donnelly, R [60]	471
32	Apr 5	H	East Stirling	W 2-1	1-0	6	Donnelly, R 2 [1, 57]	287
33	12	H	Stirling Alb	L 0-2	0-2	7		480
34	19	A	Peterhead	L 0-2	0-2	7		775
35	26	A	Clyde	L 0-4	0-1	8		620
36	May 3	H	Queen's Park	W 1-0	1-0	7	Chaplain (pen) [32]	503

Final League Position: 7

Scottish League Clubs – Albion Rovers

661

Honours
League Champions: Division II 1933-34, Second Division 1988-89; *Runners-up:* Division II 1913-14, 1937-38, 1947-48. *Promoted to Second Division:* 2010-11 (play-offs). *Scottish Cup Runners-up:* 1920.

Club colours: Shirt: Yellow with red trim. Shorts: Red. Socks: Red.

Goalscorers: *League (41):* Chaplain 9 (5 pens), Dallas 5, Phillips 5, Cusack 3, Donnelly R 3, McGuigan 3, Crawford 2 (2 pens), Dunlop M 2, Walker 2, Donnelly C 1, Miller 1, Russell 1, Shankland 1, own goals 3. *William Hill Scottish FA Cup (6):* McGuigan 2, Phillips 2, Donnelly 1, own goal 1. *Scottish Communities League Cup (0). Ramsdens Cup (0).*

Parry N 32	Reid A 34+1	Donnelly C 29+2	Dunlop M 32	Dunlop R 34	Crawford D 13+8	Innes P 5+2	Cusack L 30+2	Phillips G 31+4	McGuigan M 30+1	Walker P 9+7	Tiffney R 3+17	McGinley M 4+2	Flood J 11+12	Chaplain S 26+4	Nicoll K 2+2	Dallas C 18+5	Miller D 3+2	Maguire M 2+2	Russell B 21+2	Shankland M 3	Mercer S 1	Allan J —+5	Donnelly R 12+2	Kennedy D 9	Bosley L 1	Lamont M 1	Match No.
1*	2	3	4	5	6	7	8¹	9³	10	11²	12	13	14														1
	2	4	7	5	6¹	3	8³	9	10	11²	13	1	14	12													2
1	2	3	4	5	6	7	8	9	10	11¹					12												3
1	2	3	4	5	6	7³	8¹	9	10	11²					12	13	14										4
1	2	3	4	5	6		11³	9	10¹				14	12		7²	13	8									5
1	2	4	8	5	12	7		9	10	13				6²		11¹	3										6
1	2	3		4			9	5	10¹		12	13		6²	7	11³	8	14									7
1	2	7	3	4	13		11¹	5	10					8	6	9²	14	12³									8
1	2	6	4	3	8³		13	5	10				14	7²		11	9¹	12									9
1	2	4	8	5	14		12	9	10	7¹		13		11*		6³	3²										10
1	2²	3	4	5	6¹	7		9	10		12³		14	11		13		8									11
1	2	3	4	5	6	7		9		11	12			10¹		8											12
1	2	7¹	4	3			8	5	6				14	13		12			11		10³	9²					13
1	2	3	4	5	6			9	10	13				12		7		8²	11¹								14
1	2	3	4	5	12	6		9	10					8		11¹			7								15
1	2	3	4	5	6			9	10					12		8			11¹				7				16
1	2	7	4	5	13	6		9	10					8²		11¹			3				12				17
1	2	8	4	5	7		10³	6					14	9²		13	11¹		3				12				18
1	2	3	4	5	12		8	9	10	13				6³		11¹			7²				14				19
1	2	7	3	4	6		12		9¹					8		11			5				13	10²			20
1	2	4	8	5	6		13	12	9³	7						11²			3				14	10¹			21
1	2	7¹	3	4	13		12	9	6					8		10			5				11²				22
1	2	12	4	5	6		3²	9	10	11				13		7							8¹				23
1		4	5	12	14		8²	9	10	13				6		11			3		2¹		7³				24
1	2	7	4	5					10	6				8		11			3				9				25
1	2	7	4	3			12	9	10	13				6¹		8			5				11²				26
1	2	4	7	5			9		11				14	6¹		13	12		3				10³	8²			27
12	13	6³		7									14	11		8	1	9		3¹			10	4	2²	5	28
1	2	8	4	3	6		7	11						12		10²		9¹	5				13				29
1	2	3	4	5	10		7	11	6					9		8											30
1	2	7	4	3	6¹		11³	9	10		12		14	8					5²				13				31
1	5		2	3	14	6	9	10¹	13		12			8		7							11²	4¹			32
1	2		5	4			7	9	11		12			8					3				10	6¹			33
1*	2	3			6²		9	7³	10¹	14	12	13		8		13	8		5				11	4			34
	2	4			6		9	12	11		5¹	1	7			8							10	3			35
	2	4	3		10¹	12	6	14	13	1			9			8			5				11³	7²			36

ALLOA ATHLETIC

Year Formed: 1878. *Ground & Address:* Recreation Park, Clackmannan Rd, Alloa FK10 1RY. *Telephone:* 01259 722695. *Fax:* 01259 210886. *E-mail:* fcadmin@alloaatheltic.co.uk *Website:* www.alloaathletic.co.uk
Ground Capacity: 3,100 (seated: 919). *Size of Pitch:* 102m × 69m.
Honorary President: George Ormiston. *Chairman:* Mike Mulraney. *Secretary:* Ewen G. Cameron.
Manager: Barry Smith. *Assistant Manager:* Paddy Connolly. *Physio:* Niam Mohammed.
Club Nicknames: 'The Wasps', 'The Hornets'.
Previous Grounds: West End Public Park, Gabberston Park, Bellevue Park.
Record Attendance: 13,000 v Dunfermline Athletic, Scottish Cup 3rd rd replay, 26 Feb 1939.
Record Transfer Fee received: £100,000 for Martin Cameron to Bristol Rovers.
Record Transfer Fee paid: £26,000 for Ross Hamilton from Stenhousemuir.
Record Victory: 9-0 v Selkirk, Scottish Cup First Round, 28 November 2005.
Record Defeat: 0-10 v Dundee, Division II, 8 Mar 1947 v Third Lanark, League Cup, 8 Aug 1953.
Most Capped Player: Jock Hepburn, 1, Scotland.
Most League Appearances: 239: 1960-69.
Most League Goals in Season (Individual): 49: 'Wee' Willie Crilley, Division II, 1921-22.
Most Goals Overall (Individual): 91: Willie Irvine, 1996-2001.

ALLOA ATHLETIC – SCOTTISH CHAMPIONSHIP 2013–14 LEAGUE RECORD

Match No.	Date	Venue	Opponents	Result	H/T Score	Lg Pos.	Goalscorers	Attendance
1	Aug 10	H	Livingston	W 1-0	1-0	3	Simmons [42]	714
2	17	A	Dundee	L 0-1	0-0	7		4167
3	24	A	Cowdenbeath	W 3-1	0-0	3	Gordon [50], Kirk [79], Ferns [89]	611
4	31	A	Queen of the South	D 0-0	0-0	4		1607
5	Sept 14	H	Dumbarton	L 1-2	0-1	5	Simmons [54]	626
6	21	A	Raith R	L 2-4	1-1	6	Cawley [16], McCord (pen) [62]	1397
7	28	H	Hamilton A	W 1-0	1-0	5	McCord (pen) [45]	653
8	Oct 5	A	Greenock Morton	W 2-0	1-0	5	Holmes [41], Kirk [48]	1478
9	12	H	Falkirk	D 0-0	0-0	5		1625
10	19	A	Livingston	L 2-3	1-1	5	Cawley [8], Gordon [87]	869
11	26	H	Queen of the South	L 0-3	0-1	6		724
12	Nov 9	A	Cowdenbeath	W 2-0	2-0	5	Cawley [19], Kirk [32]	346
13	16	H	Raith R	W 1-0	0-0	4	Kirk [64]	858
14	Dec 4	A	Dumbarton	D 1-1	1-0	5	Cawley [24]	463
15	7	A	Hamilton A	W 1-0	0-0	5	Meggatt [47]	860
16	14	H	Greenock Morton	W 2-0	1-0	4	Kirk [43], McManus [85]	546
17	21	H	Dundee	L 0-1	0-0	5		1170
18	28	A	Falkirk	D 0-0	0-0	5		3417
19	Jan 2	H	Cowdenbeath	L 0-1	0-0	5		818
20	11	A	Queen of the South	L 1-3	0-2	6	Caldwell [62]	1476
21	18	H	Dumbarton	L 1-5	0-3	8	Cawley [71]	602
22	Feb 1	A	Dundee	D 1-1	0-0	7	Gordon [90]	4021
23	15	H	Livingston	L 0-3	0-1	8		605
24	22	A	Greenock Morton	W 1-0	1-0	7	McCord [18]	1628
25	25	A	Raith R	D 1-1	1-0	6	Ferns [24]	978
26	Mar 1	H	Hamilton A	L 0-3	0-3	7		656
27	8	A	Cowdenbeath	D 2-2	1-1	7	Holmes [6], McCord [59]	458
28	15	H	Queen of the South	L 0-1	0-1	8		644
29	22	H	Falkirk	W 3-0	0-0	7	Ferns [71], Cawley [78], McCord [87]	1025
30	25	A	Livingston	L 0-2	0-1	7		709
31	29	H	Raith R	L 0-1	0-0	8		726
32	Apr 5	A	Dumbarton	L 1-4	0-1	8	Caddis [88]	677
33	12	H	Greenock Morton	W 2-0	1-0	7	Cawley [15], McCord [53]	615
34	19	A	Hamilton A	L 1-2	0-1	8	Caldwell [83]	1087
35	26	H	Dundee	L 0-3	0-1	8		2552
36	May 3	A	Falkirk	L 1-3	1-1	8	Cawley [29]	3998

Final League Position: 8

Honours
League Champions: Division II 1921-22; Third Division 1997-98, 2011-12; *Runners-up:* Division II 1938-39.
Second Division 1976-77, 1981-82, 1984-85, 1988-89, 1999-2000, 2001-02, 2009-10; *Runners-up:* 2012-13 (promoted via play-offs).
League Challenge Cup Winners: 1999-2000; *Runners-up:* 2001-02.

Club colours: Shirt: Gold with black trim. Shorts: Black. Socks: Black.

Goalscorers: *League (34):* Cawley 8, McCord 6 (2 pens), Kirk 5, Ferns 3, Gordon 3, Caldwell 2, Holmes 2, Simmons 2, Caddis 1, McManus 1, Meggatt 1.
William Hill Scottish FA Cup (6): McCord 1 (1 pen), Cawley 1, Gordon 1, Holmes 1, Marr 1, Salmon 1.
Scottish Communities League Cup (2): McCord 1 (1 pen), Kirk 1.
Ramsdens Cup (0).

Bain S 35	Doyle M 36	Gordon B 35	Meggatt D 34	Creaney J 7+1	Cawley K 35	McCord R 34+1	Simmons S 29+1	McManus D 7+11	Kirk A 27+5	Holmes G 33+1	Tiffoney J 17+6	Robertson W 5+5	Ferns E 6+17	Salmon A 1+4	Young D 14+3	Marr J 13+1	Flannigan I 1+11	Gemmell R —+1	Caddis L 12+5	Caldwell R 4+8	Lindsay L 10	McDowall C 1	Riordan D —+2	Match No.
1	2	3	4	5	6	7	8	9	10	11[1]	12													1
1	2	3	4	5	6	7	9[1]	10	11[2]	13	12													2
1	2	3	4	5	6	8	7[1]	9[2]	11	10		13	12											3
1	2	3	4	5	8	9	7	11[1]	10[1]	6			13[3]	12	14									4
1	2	3	4	5[2]	6	8	7	13	11	10					9[1]	12								5
1	2	3	9	10	8	7	12	11[2]	6	5[1]				13										6
1	2	3	5		6	7	8	11[3]	10[1]	9[2]				13	14	4	12							7
1	2	3	5		8	6	7	11[1]	10[3]	9[2]				12	14	4	13							8
1	2	3	5		6	9	7	10[2]	11[1]	8				13	4	12								9
1	2	3	4	5	10	8[1]	7	13	11	9[3]			6[4]	14	12									10
1	2	3	4		6	7[1]	8	12	10	11	5		13		9[2]									11
1	2	3	5		11	8[1]	7	13	10[2]	9	6			12	4									12
1	2	3	5		11	6	8	13	10[1]	7	9[2]			12	4									13
1	2	3	5		10	8	7	12	11[1]	9	6				4									14
1	2	3	5		11	9[1]	7	10[1]	12	6			13	8	4									15
1	2	3	5		11	6[1]	7	13	10[2]	9	8[1]			12	4	14								16
1	2	3	5		11	8	13	10	7	9[2]				12	4	6[1]								17
1	2	3			11	8	12	10	5	7[1]				6	4	9								18
1	2	3	5		6	7	14	12	10[3]	11	13			8[1]	4	9[2]								19
1	2	3	5	14	10	7[1]	8[2]		11	6	13		4[3]		9	12								20
1	2	3[2]	4	5[1]	10	12	6[2]	13	8	9					14	7	11							21
1	2	3	5		7	8	10	11[1]	12	13				6	9[2]	4								22
	2	3	5		10	8	6[3]	14	11	12				7[1]	9[2]	4						1	13	23
1	2	3	5		10	9[1]	8	6	11[2]	7	13				4					12				24
1	2	3	5		10	9	6	13	8	7[1]	11[2]								12	4				25
1	2	3	5		10	9	6[2]	13	7	14	11[3]				8[1]				12	4				26
1	2	3	5		7	9	6	11[2]	8	13	10								12	4[1]				27
1	2	3	5		6	7	8	10[1]	11[3]	4	13			9[2]					12	14				28
1	2	3	5		10	8	7	11[3]	6[2]	12	9[1]				13				14	4				29
1	2	3	5		11	8	7[1]	14	12	6[2]	10				9[3]				13	4				30
1	2	3			6	7	11	8	5[3]	12	13				9[2]				10[1]	14				31
1	2	3	5		10	9	11[1]	8	7[2]	6	13								13	12	4			32
1	2	3	5		7	9	11[1]	8	4	6	13								10[2]	12				33
1	2	3	4		8	9	11	7	5	6[1]									10	12				34
1	2	3	4[8]		10	6	9[2]	11[1]	8	5	14				7[3]				13	12				35
1	2	3			10	6	4	13	8	5	12								9[2]	11	7[1]			36

ANNAN ATHLETIC

Year Formed: 1942. *Ground & Address:* Galabank, North Street, Annan DG12 5DQ. *Telephone:* 01461 204108.
E-mail: annanathleticfc1@btinternet.com *Website:* www.annanathleticfc.com
Ground capacity: 2,517 (seated: 500). *Size of Pitch:* 100m × 62m.
Chairman: Henry McClelland.
Secretary: Alan Irving.
Manager: Jim Chapman.
Assistant Manager: John Joyce.
Coaches: Bill Bentley.
Club Nicknames: 'Galabankies', 'Black and Golds'.
Record attendance: 2,517, v Rangers, Third Division, 15 Sept 2012.
Most League Appearances: 154: Steven Sloan, 2008-14.
Most League Goals in Season (Individual): 15: Mike Jack, 2008-09.
Most Goals Overall (Individual): 23: Graeme Bell, 2008-13.

ANNAN ATHLETIC – SCOTTISH LEAGUE TWO 2013–14 LEAGUE RECORD

Match No.	Date	Venue	Opponents	Result		H/T Score	Lg Pos.	Goalscorers	Attendance
1	Aug 10	A	Peterhead	D	2-2	1-0	5	Hopkirk 2 [24, 57]	504
2	17	H	Montrose	W	2-1	0-0	4	Mackay [61], Black [76]	286
3	24	H	Albion R	D	1-1	0-0	5	Davidson [85]	492
4	31	A	Berwick R	L	2-4	2-3	7	Hopkirk [23], Love (pen) [38]	448
5	Sept14	A	Stirling Alb	W	2-0	1-0	5	Love [6], Hopkirk [53]	608
6	21	H	Clyde	L	1-2	1-1	8	Weatherson [40]	483
7	28	A	Queen's Park	W	5-2	3-0	4	Mackay 2 [21, 50], Todd 2 [37, 65], Love [43]	413
8	Oct 26	A	Elgin C	W	3-2	1-2	3	Weatherson [33], Todd [74], Mackay [90]	648
9	29	H	East Stirling	L	1-2	0-1	4	Hopkirk [49]	301
10	Nov 5	H	Peterhead	W	2-0	0-0	2	Todd [62], McGeever (og) [72]	277
11	9	A	Albion R	L	0-2	0-0	2		319
12	16	H	Berwick R	W	3-2	1-2	2	McNiff [6], Davidson [67], Brannan [90]	395
13	23	H	Stirling Alb	D	4-4	2-1	2	Davidson [2], Mitchell, Andrew [37], Mackay [67], Love (pen) [90]	384
14	Dec 3	A	Clyde	L	1-2	1-0	4	Mackay [43]	422
15	7	A	East Stirling	D	1-1	0-0	4	Mitchell, Andrew [58]	218
16	26	A	Montrose	W	2-0	0-0	3	Mackay [90], Todd [90]	350
17	28	H	Elgin C	W	2-1	0-0	3	Davidson (pen) [78], Mackay [84]	401
18	Jan 4	H	Albion R	W	2-0	1-0	2	Todd [35], Mackay [53]	403
19	11	A	Berwick R	W	4-1	3-0	2	Flynn [19], Swinglehurst [29], Todd 2 [36, 61]	429
20	18	H	Clyde	L	0-1	0-1	2		456
21	25	A	Stirling Alb	D	1-1	1-0	3	Davidson [14]	509
22	Feb 8	H	Montrose	W	1-0	0-0	2	Todd [48]	354
23	15	A	East Stirling	L	2-3	1-1	2	Davidson (pen) [43], Mitchell, Andrew [48]	401
24	22	A	Queen's Park	W	1-0	1-0	2	Mackay [28]	356
25	25	H	Queen's Park	W	3-2	0-1	2	McNiff [50], Davidson 2 [75, 80]	345
26	Mar 1	H	Berwick R	W	4-0	1-0	2	Love (pen) [38], Mackay 2 [56, 71], Watson [89]	473
27	4	A	Peterhead	L	1-3	1-2	2	Ross (og) [37]	607
28	15	A	Elgin C	W	3-2	3-0	2	Love [29], Swinglehurst [33], Henderson [36]	485
29	22	H	Peterhead	W	2-1	0-1	2	Mitchell, Andrew [47], Love [55]	452
30	25	A	Albion R	W	2-0	1-0	2	Todd [36], Mackay [54]	323
31	29	H	Stirling Alb	L	1-2	0-1	2	Henderson (pen) [76]	479
32	Apr 5	A	Clyde	W	3-0	1-0	2	Davidson [41], Todd 2 [48, 65]	516
33	12	A	East Stirling	L	1-2	1-1	2	Henderson [26]	253
34	19	H	Queen's Park	D	1-1	0-0	2	Mitchell, Andrew (pen) [60]	560
35	26	A	Montrose	L	1-2	0-1	2	Hopkirk [74]	264
36	May 3	H	Elgin C	W	2-0	1-0	2	Hopkirk [33], McNiff [61]	428

Final League Position: 2

Honours
League Two Runners-up: 2013-14.
East of Scotland Premier League: Winners (4).
East of Scotland League Cup: Winners (1).
East of Scotland Div 1: Winners (1).
South of Scotland League: Winners (2).
South of Scotland League Cup: Winners (4).
Scottish Challenge Cup South: Winners (1).
Scottish Qualifying Cup South: Winners (1).

Club colours: Shirt: Gold with black trim. Shorts: Black with gold trim. Socks: Gold with black and white rings.

Goalscorers: *League (69):* Mackay 13, Todd 12, Davidson 9 (2 pens), Hopkirk 7, Love 7 (3 pens), Mitchell, Andrew 5 (1 pen), Henderson 3 (1 pen), McNiff 3, Swinglehurst 2, Weatherson 2, Black 1, Brannan 1, Flynn 1, Watson 1, own goals 2.
William Hill Scottish FA Cup (8): Flynn 2, Brannon 1, Hopkirk 1, Love 1, Mackay 1, McNiff 1, Todd 1.
Scottish Communities League Cup (0).
Ramsdens Cup (8): Mackay 3, Hopkirk 2, Love 1 (1 pen), Brannan 1, Weatherson 1.
League 1 Play-Offs (4): Davidson 1, Hopkirk 1, Love 1, McNiff 1.

Mitchell Alex 3	Watson P 31	Weatherson P 11	Black S 15 + 2	Chisholm I 20 + 1	Flynn M 19 + 5	Sloan S 23 + 3	Love A 28 + 5	Bradley P 14 + 3	Hopkirk D 15 + 4	Mackay K 26 + 2	Jardine C 11 + 1	Arthur K 33	McCrudden K — + 1	Davidson S 18 + 14	Brannan K 14 + 16	Moffat J — + 9	McNiff M 31 + 1	Mitchell Andrew 25 + 1	Logan S 1 + 1	Todd J 23 + 4	Swinglehurst S 24 + 1	Wood D — + 2	McAnespie M 1	Orsi D 1 + 7	Henderson B 8 + 3	Match No.
1	2	3	4	5	6	7	8	9	10	11^1	12															1
	3	4	2	6	7	8	9	5	11^1	10^2		1	12	13												2
	4	3	2^3		8	7	9^1	5^2	11	10		1		13	12	14										3
	4	3	2^3	6	8		9^1	5^2	11	10		1		12	13	14	7									4
	3	4		6	5^3	7	10	8	11	9^2		1		13	14			12	2^1							5
		4	2		8^1	7^3	9	5^3	11	10		1		14			3	6	12	13						6
	4	3		5			7		10^2	11		1	14	12			9	2		6^3	8^1	13				7
	4	10	2^3		8^3	12	9	14	11	6		1		7^1			5	3		13						8
	3	4			7		6	5^2	10	11		1		13	12		8	2		9^1						9
	3	4				6	9		10^2	11^1	7	1		13			8	2		12	5					10
	2	4				5	9^2		11		6	1		12	13		8	7		10^1	3					11
1	3			13	7	12		5^1	11		8			10^3	14			9	2	6^2	4					12
1	3			13	5	9		11^2	12	6^3				10	14			8	2	7^1	4					13
	3	7^2		13	2	9^3	12		11			1		10^1	6			5	4			8	14			14
	4	7		6	2	9			10			1		5	3			11	8							15
	3			7	2	9			10			1		6^1	8	12	5			11	4					16
	2			7	6	8^2	13		11			1		10^1	5	12	4			9	3					17
	2			7	6	8			11			1		10^1	5	12	4			9	3					18
	2			7	6	8			11			1		10^2	5	12		9^1	3	13	4					19
	2	14		6^2	7	8^1			11			1		10^3	5	13	4	12	9	3						20
8^6			3	5			9					1		6^1	7^2	13	4	10		11	2			12		21
		9			7	8		5				1		10	6^1			4	2	11	3			12		22
		3		7	8	14	9^1					1		11^3	6	12	5	2^2		10	4			13		23
	3			13	7	2	6		10^2			1		9^1	12		5	8		11^3	4			14		24
	3	12	6	8^2	7	9^1			11			1		13	14		5	2			4^8			10^3		25
	3	7	5	12	6	9^3		10^2	8^1			1		11	13		4	2						14		26
	4	3	2		7	9^2		10	8^3			1		11^1	14		5	6						13	12	27
	7	4	2		12	9		10^3				1		6^2			5	8		13	3		14		11^1	28
	3	8	2				9^1		10			1		13	12		6	7		5	4				11^2	29
	3	7	2				9^2		10			1		12	13		5	8		6	4				11^1	30
	6	4	5		8^1		14	10^3				1		12	13		2	7^2		9	3				11	31
	6		5	14			13			3^3		1		7^2	9		4	8		11	2			12	10^1	32
	3^6		2		13		12			8		1		6^2	11		5	7		10	4				9^1	33
			2	13		14		4	12	6^3		1		10^2	7		8	5		9	3				11^1	34
			2		8	3	11^1	12	7			1		13	9		5			6	4				10^2	35
	2	3	5		14		4	11^2	10^3	6^1		1		12			7	9		8					13	36

ARBROATH

Year Formed: 1878. *Ground & Address:* Gayfield Park, Arbroath DD11 1QB. *Telephone:* 01241 872157. *Fax:* 01241 431125. *E-mail:* afc@gayfield.fsnet.co.uk *Website:* www.arbroathfc.co.uk
Ground Capacity: 4,165 (seated: 860). *Size of Pitch:* 105m × 65m.
Chairman: John Christison. *Secretary:* Dr Gary Callon. *Administrator:* Mike Cargill.
Manager: Allan Moore. *Assistant Manager:* Todd Lumsden. *Physio:* Becky Dunphy.
Club Nickname: 'The Red Lichties'.
Previous Grounds: Lesser Gayfield.
Record Attendance: 13,510 v Rangers, Scottish Cup 3rd rd, 23 Feb 1952.
Record Transfer Fee received: £120,000 for Paul Tosh to Dundee (Aug 1993).
Record Transfer Fee paid: £20,000 for Douglas Robb from Montrose (1981).
Record Victory: 36-0 v Bon Accord, Scottish Cup 1st rd, 12 Sept 1885.
Record Defeat: 1-9 v Celtic, League Cup 3rd rd, 25 Aug 1993.
Most Capped Player: Ned Doig, 2 (5), Scotland.
Most League Appearances: 445: Tom Cargill, 1966-81.
Most League Goals in Season (Individual): 45: Dave Easson, Division II, 1958-59.
Most Goals Overall (Individual): 120: Jimmy Jack, 1966-71.

ARBROATH – SCOTTISH LEAGUE ONE 2013–14 LEAGUE RECORD

Match No.	Date	Venue	Opponents	Result	H/T Score	Lg Pos.	Goalscorers	Attendance
1	Aug 10	H	Ayr U	L 0-3	0-2	10		775
2	17	A	Dunfermline Ath	W 3-2	3-2	6	Milne [8], Cook 2 (1 pen) [44 (p), 45]	3242
3	24	A	East Fife	L 1-2	1-2	7	Cook [41]	809
4	31	H	Brechin C	W 2-1	2-0	6	Erwin 2 [15, 30]	801
5	Sept 14	A	Rangers	L 1-5	0-0	6	Cook [48]	43,562
6	21	H	Stenhousemuir	L 3-4	1-1	6	Erwin [34], Hamilton [69], Cook [82]	596
7	28	H	Forfar Ath	W 3-0	1-0	6	Cook [11], Sibanda [69], Erwin [83]	855
8	Oct 5	A	Stranraer	L 2-3	0-3	6	Erwin [59], Cook (pen) [90]	334
9	12	H	Airdrieonians	W 3-2	1-0	5	Linn [20], Banjo [77], Erwin (pen) [89]	747
10	19	A	Ayr U	L 0-2	0-1	6		990
11	26	A	Brechin C	L 1-3	0-1	7	Cook [79]	765
12	Nov 9	H	East Fife	D 2-2	0-0	7	Cook [55], Erwin (pen) [78]	603
13	16	A	Stenhousemuir	L 2-3	0-0	8	Travis [64], Erwin [83]	469
14	25	H	Rangers	L 0-3	0-3	8		3902
15	Dec 7	A	Stranraer	L 1-2	0-1	9	Doris [47]	521
16	14	A	Forfar Ath	D 1-1	0-0	8	Travis [84]	609
17	21	H	Dunfermline Ath	L 0-3	0-2	9		967
18	28	A	Airdrieonians	L 1-2	1-0	9	Donaldson [25]	641
19	Jan 2	A	East Fife	L 0-1	0-1	9		910
20	11	A	Brechin C	L 0-1	0-1	9		777
21	18	H	Stenhousemuir	W 2-1	1-1	9	Scott [19], Robertson [87]	498
22	25	A	Rangers	L 2-3	1-1	9	Banjo [2], Linn [50]	41,207
23	Feb 1	H	Ayr U	L 2-3	0-3	9	Linn [63], McIntosh [79]	605
24	15	A	Stranraer	D 1-1	1-0	10	McManus [14]	377
25	22	H	Forfar Ath	L 2-3	0-1	10	Cook [69], McIntosh [82]	823
26	25	A	Dunfermline Ath	L 0-3	0-1	10		1983
27	Mar 1	A	Brechin C	W 4-2	2-0	10	Linn 2 [7, 22], Travis [53], McManus [84]	668
28	8	A	East Fife	W 2-1	1-1	10	Travis [22], McManus [77]	679
29	15	H	Airdrieonians	L 0-1	0-1	10		823
30	22	A	Ayr U	L 1-2	1-2	10	Deuchar [38]	766
31	29	H	Rangers	L 1-2	0-1	10	McManus [61]	3400
32	Apr 5	A	Stenhousemuir	D 2-2	1-1	10	McManus [30], Linn [71]	518
33	12	H	Stranraer	W 4-2	1-0	10	McManus [45], Cook 2 [46, 49], Sheerin [80]	528
34	19	A	Forfar Ath	W 2-0	2-0	10	Sheerin [24], Deuchar [26]	833
35	26	H	Dunfermline Ath	L 1-2	0-1	10	Travis [56]	1079
36	May 3	A	Airdrieonians	L 0-2	0-1	10		1243

Final League Position: 10

Honours
League Champions: Third Division 2010-11; *Runners-up:* Division II 1934-35, 1958-59, 1967-68, 1971-72; Second Division 2000-01; Third Division 1997-98, 2007-08. *Promoted to Second Division:* 2007-08 (play-offs).
Scottish Cup: Quarter-finals 1993.

Club colours: Shirt: Maroon with white trim. Shorts: White. Socks: Maroon with white tops.

Goalscorers: *League (52):* Cook 12 (2 pens), Erwin 8 (2 pens), Linn 6, McManus 6, Travis 5, Banjo 2, Deuchar 2, McIntosh 2, Sheerin 2, Donaldson 1, Doris 1, Hamilton 1, Milne 1, Robertson 1, Scott 1, Sibanda 1.
William Hill Scottish FA Cup (0).
Scottish Communities League Cup (0).
Ramsdens Cup (4): Milne 2, Banjo 1, Linn 1.

Morrison S 28	Hamilton C 35	Travis M 34	Keddie A 27+1	Lindsay J 7+2	Smith D 16+2	Linn R 36	Chisholm R 28+3	Yao L 1+8	Bayne G 3+11	Milne S 6+5	Cook A 30+5	Sheerin P 30+4	Martin P —+2	Banjo D 23+8	Scott C 8+4	Sibanda L 1+12	Donaldson B 9+1	Erwin L 11	McWalter K 1+2	Rosscraig J 1	Doris S 2	Robertson D 2+10	Nicoll K 16	Little R 8+2	McManus P 12+3	McIntosh L 4+4	Wood S 8	Deuchar K 4+5	Adams S —+1	McGeever R 5	Match No.
1	2	3	4	5	6	7	8^3	9^1	10	11^{12}	12	13	14																		1
1	5	3	4^3	12	7	11	14				10	9^2	8	2	6^1	13															2
1	4^a	3			5	7	8^2	12	13	14	11	9		10^1	2	6^2															3
1	5		4		7	6	8				14	11^3	12	9^1	2		13	3	10^2												4
1	5	4			8^2	6^1	9		13	12	11	7		2	14			3	10^3												5
1	5	3^a			7	6	8		13	11	12	9^1		2				4	10												6
1	5	4	3		7^3	11	8	14		6^2	9	10^1		2	12	13															7
1	5^3	3	4	12	8	10^1	7		13	6	9^2			2	14	11															8
1	5	3	4		7	6^3	8		11^2	9^1	12			2	13	14	10														9
1	5	3	4		6	7	8	13		12	11^3	9^1		2^2	14		10														10
1	5	3^a	4		7	6				12	13		9	8	2		11	10^2													11
1	5		4		7^1	10	8			12	9	13		2	6^2			3	11												12
1	7	4		5^3	6	9		14	13		8	10^1		3^2	12		2	11													13
1	5	3		13	6	8				12	14	11	9^2	2	7^1			4	10^3												14
1	4	3		5	8	6	7	13	12		9^1			11^2	2		10														15
1	5	3	4		7^1	6	8		12^a		11	9^2		2	13		10														16
1	5	4	9		6		8^3		10				14	2		13	12	3				7^2	11^1								17
1	5	3	4		8	6			13		11	9^2		2			12						7^1		10						18
1	5	3	4		7^2	6	8		10		11^3	9		2^1	13	14							12								19
1	5	3	4		6	8			10		11	9		2			12						7^1								20
1	5	3	4	12	6	8^2					10^1	9		2			11					13	7^3	14							21
1	5	3	4			11	8^1	14			10	12	7^3	9^2									6	2	13						22
1	5		4		6	8		13			11^3	9		2^1									14	7^2	3	12	10				23
	5	3	4		6	7					9^2	13	12	8	2							11	1	10^3	14						24
	5^2	3	4		6	8					13	9^1		7	2							11	1	10	12						25
	5	3	4		6	8			10^2		12	9^1		7	2							13	1	11^3	14						26
	5	3	4		6^1	9			10^2		8	14										13	1	7	2	11^3	12				27
	5	3	4		6^2				11		9	7		8	2							13	1		12			10^1			28
	5	3^2			10	7					9^1	8		2									1	13	6	4^a		11		12	29
	5	3	4		6	8^2					12	9		2^1								13	1	14	7	11^1		10			30
	5	2	4	3^2	6	7	8^1		10		12	9										11	1		13						31
1	8	2	14	5^2	6	7					11^3	9				13							4^1		10			12		3	32
1	5	2	4		6	8	14		11^2		9^1	12											13	7	10^1					3	33
1	5	2	4		6^3	7	8^1				9	12												14	10	13		11^2		3	34
1	5	2	4		6	13					8^3	9^2		14										7	10	12		11^1		3	35
1	5	2	4		11						8^2	9		13										7	6	12		10^1		3	36

AYR UNITED

Year Formed: 1910. *Ground & Address:* Somerset Park, Tryfield Place, Ayr KA8 9NB. *Telephone:* 01292 263435.
Fax: 01292 281314. *E-mail:* info@ayrunitedfc.co.uk *Website:* ayrunitedfc.co.uk
Ground Capacity: 10,185 (seated: 1,597). *Size of Pitch:* 101m × 66m.
Chairman: Lachlan Cameron.
Managing Director: Lewis Grant.
Manager: Mark Roberts. *Assistant Manager:* David White. *Physio:* Steven Maguire.
Club Nickname: 'The Honest Men'.
Previous Grounds: None.
Record Attendance: 25,225 v Rangers, Division I, 13 Sept 1969.
Record Transfer Fee received: £300,000 for Steven Nicol to Liverpool (Oct 1981).
Record Transfer Fee paid: £90,000 for Mark Campbell from Stranraer (March 1999).
Record Victory: 11-1 v Dumbarton, League Cup, 13 Aug 1952.
Record Defeat: 0-9 in Division I v Rangers (1929); v Hearts (1931); B Division v Third Lanark (1954).
Most Capped Player: Jim Nisbet, 3, Scotland.
Most League Appearances: 459: John Murphy, 1963-78.
Most League League and Cup Goals in Season (Individual): 66: Jimmy Smith, 1927-28.
Most League and Cup Goals Overall (Individual): 213: Peter Price, 1955-61.

AYR UNITED – SCOTTISH LEAGUE ONE 2013–14 LEAGUE RECORD

Match No.	Date	Venue	Opponents	Result	H/T Score	Lg Pos.	Goalscorers	Attendance
1	Aug 10	A	Arbroath	W 3-0	2-0	2	Moffat 2 [13, 17], Forrest [62]	775
2	17	H	Forfar Ath	W 2-0	1-0	2	Malcolm [41], Moffat (pen) [75]	1056
3	24	A	Stranraer	D 1-1	1-1	2	McGowan [37]	845
4	31	H	Airdrieonians	D 2-2	2-2	4	Moffat 2 [12, 17]	1339
5	Sept 14	A	Stenhousemuir	D 1-1	1-0	4	Roberts [42]	657
6	21	H	Brechin C	D 2-2	2-0	4	Moffat [43], McGowan [46]	987
7	28	A	Dunfermline Ath	L 1-5	1-4	4	Moffat [3]	2743
8	Oct 6	H	Rangers	L 0-2	0-0	4		8968
9	12	A	East Fife	W 4-1	2-1	4	Donald 2 [29, 90], Moffat [36], McLaughlin [53]	753
10	19	H	Arbroath	W 2-0	1-0	3	Kyle [45], Hunter [74]	990
11	26	A	Airdrieonians	W 1-0	0-0	2	Marenghi [53]	1012
12	Nov 12	H	Stranraer	L 3-6	2-3	4	Moffat 3 (1 pen) [15, 17, 57 (p)]	986
13	16	A	Brechin C	D 1-1	1-0	4	Marenghi [44]	518
14	23	H	Stenhousemuir	W 4-3	2-2	3	Moffat 2 (2 pens) [5, 72], Donald [33], Kyle [85]	986
15	Dec 7	A	Rangers	L 0-3	0-2	4		45,227
16	14	H	Dunfermline Ath	L 2-4	2-1	4	Gilmour [17], Moffat [27]	643
17	21	A	Forfar Ath	W 1-0	0-0	4	Kyle [62]	473
18	28	H	East Fife	W 2-0	1-0	4	Moffat 2 [32, 68]	1059
19	Jan 4	A	Stranraer	L 0-4	0-2	4		1097
20	11	H	Airdrieonians	W 3-0	0-0	4	Kyle [59], Moffat [76], Forrest [79]	1037
21	18	H	Brechin C	L 1-3	0-2	4	Pope [79]	1018
22	25	A	Stenhousemuir	D 1-1	1-0	4	Malcolm [27]	467
23	Feb 1	A	Arbroath	W 3-2	3-0	3	Moffat 2 [4, 29], Donald [18]	605
24	15	H	Rangers	L 0-2	0-0	4		8449
25	22	A	Dunfermline Ath	L 0-3	0-2	4		2773
26	Mar 1	A	Airdrieonians	L 0-3	0-1	4		880
27	4	H	Forfar Ath	L 2-3	1-2	4	Malcolm [34], Campbell [62]	656
28	8	A	Stranraer	W 5-0	3-0	4	Moffat 2 (1 pen) [8 (p), 59], Malcolm [20], Donald [30], Forrest [76]	1141
29	15	A	East Fife	W 5-0	3-0	4	Moffat 2 (1 pen) [36 (p), 39], Kyle [45], Donald [51], Forrest [90]	647
30	22	H	Arbroath	W 2-1	2-1	4	Malcolm [4], Moffat [40]	766
31	29	H	Stenhousemuir	L 2-3	0-1	4	Moffat [66], Forrest [68]	992
32	Apr 5	A	Brechin C	L 1-2	0-1	4	Forrest [75]	507
33	19	A	Dunfermline Ath	D 1-1	0-0	4	Forrest [55]	1272
34	22	A	Rangers	L 1-2	0-0	4	Forrest [69]	40,651
35	26	A	Forfar Ath	L 2-4	0-2	4	Moffat (pen) [60], Gilmour [90]	532
36	May 3	H	East Fife	W 4-1	1-0	4	Malcolm 3 [42, 53, 63], Gilmour [75]	1952

Final League Position: 4

Honours
League Champions: Division II 1911-12, 1912-13, 1927-28, 1936-37, 1958-59, 1965-66. Second Division 1987-88, 1996-97; *Runners-up:* Division II 1910-11, 1955-56, 1968-69. Second Division 2008-09. *Promoted to First Division:* 2008-09 (play-offs). *Promoted to First Division:* 2010-11 (play-offs).
Scottish Cup: Semi-finals 2002.
League Cup: Runners-up: 2001-02.
B&Q Cup Runners-up: 1990-91, 1991-92.

Club colours: Shirt: White with vertical black stripe. Shorts: Black. Socks: Black.

Goalscorers: *League (65):* Moffat 26 (7 pens), Forrest 8, Malcolm 8, Donald 6, Kyle 5, Gilmour 3, Marenghi 2, McGowan 2, Campbell 1, Hunter 1, McLaughlin 1, Pope 1, Roberts 1.
William Hill Scottish FA Cup (4): Donald 1, Lithgow 1, Malcolm 1, Marenghi 1.
Scottish Communities League Cup (1): Shankland 1.
Ramsdens Cup (3): Forrest 1, Malcolm 1, Moffat 1.
Championship Play-Offs (2): Donald 1, Pope 1.

Hutton D 36	Hunter A 28 + 1	Lithgow A 34	McArthur J 1	Pope G 32	McGowan M 17 + 7	McLaughlin S 35	Marenghi A 16 + 5	Donald M 34	Moffat M 32	Malcolm C 28 + 5	Forrest A 11 + 16	Shankland M — + 12	Campbell M 18 + 1	Crawford R 12 + 3	Roberts M 5 + 2	Kyle K 22 + 4	Wyllie A — + 1	Longridge J 2 + 2	McAusland K 12 + 5	Gilmour B 21 + 1	Wardrobe M — + 1	Match No.
1	2	3	4^2	5	6	7	8^1	9	10	11	12	13										1
1	2	4		5	6^1	7	8	9	10	11^2	12		14	3^3	13							2
1	2	4		5	6^3	7	8^1	9	10	11^2	13			3	12	14						3
1	2	4		5^4	6^3	7	8^1	9	10	11	12^8		14	3^2	13							4
1	2	3			6	4	8	5	10	11						7	9^1	12				5
1	2	4			6^2	3	8	5	10	11						7	9^1	12	13			6
1	2	4	3		6^3	8		5	10	11	9^2					7^1	12	14	13			7
1	2	3		5		9	12	10	6	13	14			4		7^1	8^3		11^2			8
1	2	4		5	12		8	9	10	13				3	6	7^2			11^1			9
1	2	4		5		7	13	9	10	14	12			8^1	6^3	11^2			3			10
1	2	4		5	8	6		9	10^1	12						7			11	3^8		11
1	2	4	3		6^1	7	9	5	10	13	8^2					11			12			12
1	2	5		4	6	9		10	8	11				3		7						13
1	2	4		5	6	7		9	10	12	8^1					11			3			14
1	2^2	3		5	12	4		9	11	8	6^1	13				10^3			7	14		15
1	2	4		5	3	13		9	10	8	6^2					11^1		12	7			16
1		4		5	3	6		9	11^1	8	10	12							2	7		17
1		4		5	3	6		9	10	8		12				11^1			2	7		18
1		4		5	3	6^1		9^2	10	7		12		13		11			2	8		19
1		4		5	13	6		9^1	10	8		12		3^2		11			2	7^2		20
1	12	4		5		6		9	11	8		13		3^2		10			2	7^1		21
1	2	4		5	12	3		8^1	11	9	7					10			6			22
1	2	4		5	12	7	13	9^1	10	8	6^1					11			3			23
1	2	3		5	13	4		9	8	11	12			6^1		10^2			7			24
1	2	3		5	13	4	14	9	7	10^3	12			6^2		11			8			25
1	2^8				6	7	8	9	10	12	3					11^1		5	4^8			26
1	2	4			6	7^2	8^1	9	10	12	13			3		11		5				27
1	7	4		5	6			9	10	11	12			3^1					2	8		28
1	7	3		5	2	6		9	11	12	13			4^2		10^1				8		29
1	8	4		5	2	6^1		9^8	10	11	12			3					13	7^2		30
1	8	4		5	2	6		9^2	10	11^1	12			3					13	7		31
1	8^1	4		5	2	6		10	9	12				3		11^2			13	7		32
1		4		5	8			9	10	11	6			3					2	7		33
1		4		5	2	7		9	10	11	6			3						8		34
1		4		5	2^2	8		9	10	11	6^1	13		3					12	7		35
1	2	4		5		8		9	10	11^1	6	13		3^2					12	7		36

BERWICK RANGERS

Year Formed: 1884. *Ground & Address:* Shielfield Park, Tweedmouth, Berwick-upon-Tweed TD15 2EF. *Telephone:* 01289 307424. *Fax:* 01289 309424. *Email:* club@berwickrangersfc.co.uk *Website:* berwickrangersfc.co.uk
Ground Capacity: 4,131 (seated: 1,366). *Size of Pitch:* 101m × 64m.
Chairman: Brian Porteous. *Vice-Chairman:* John Bell. *Football Secretary:* Dennis McCleary.
Manager: Colin Cameron. *Assistant Manager:* Robbie Horn. *Physio:* Jamie Dougall.
Club Nicknames: 'The Borderers', 'Black and Gold', 'The Wee Gers'.
Previous Grounds: Bull Stob Close, Pier Field, Meadow Field, Union Park, Old Shielfield.
Record Transfer Fee received: £80,000 for John Hughes to Swansea City (Nov 1989).
Record Transfer Fee paid: £27,000 for Sandy Ross from Cowdenbeath (Mar 1991).
Record Attendance: 13,283 v Rangers, Scottish Cup 1st rd, 28 Jan 1967.
Record Victory: 8-1 v Forfar Ath, Division II, 25 Dec 1965; v Vale of Leithen, Scottish Cup, Dec 1966.
Record Defeat: 1-9 v Hamilton A, First Division, 9 Aug 1980.
Most League Appearances: 439: Eric Tait, 1970-87.
Most League Goals in Season (Individual): 33: Ken Bowron, Division II, 1963-64.
Most Goals Overall (Individual): 114: Eric Tait, 1970-87.

BERWICK RANGERS – SCOTTISH LEAGUE TWO 2013–14 LEAGUE RECORD

Match No.	Date	Venue	Opponents	Result	H/T Score	Lg Pos.	Goalscorers	Atten- dance
1	Aug 10	A	Clyde	L 0-1	0-0	9		469
2	17	H	Queen's Park	W 4-0	2-0	5	Keenan (og) [28], Dalziel [33], Lavery 2 [68, 75]	439
3	24	A	Montrose	D 1-1	0-0	6	Lavery [68]	285
4	31	H	Annan Ath	W 4-2	3-2	3	Dalziel 2 [3, 34], O'Brien [14], Lavery [59]	448
5	Sept 14	A	Albion R	W 2-0	0-0	2	O'Brien [63], Dalziel [90]	322
6	21	H	Stirling Alb	D 1-1	0-0	2	Lavery [89]	491
7	28	A	East Stirling	L 0-1	0-1	2		301
8	Oct 12	H	Elgin C	L 2-3	2-0	4	Lavery [26], Hoskins [42]	495
9	19	H	Clyde	L 0-1	0-0	6		472
10	26	A	Peterhead	D 1-1	1-0	8	Tulloch [18]	503
11	Nov 16	A	Annan Ath	L 2-3	2-1	9	Lavery 2 [40, 42]	395
12	20	H	Montrose	D 1-1	0-1	8	Currie, L [66]	227
13	23	H	Albion R	W 2-1	2-0	7	Gielty [2], Currie, L [43]	388
14	Dec 3	A	Stirling Alb	L 1-3	0-1	9	Currie, L [48]	378
15	7	A	Elgin C	L 0-2	0-2	9		543
16	14	H	East Stirling	W 2-0	1-0	9	Lavery [10], Currie, L [89]	361
17	21	A	Queen's Park	W 4-0	1-0	6	Dalziel 3 [21, 65, 90], Lavery [48]	302
18	28	H	Peterhead	L 1-3	1-1	8	Notman [44]	778
19	Jan 2	A	Montrose	D 0-0	0-0	8		456
20	11	H	Annan Ath	L 1-4	0-3	8	Currie, L (pen) [67]	429
21	18	A	Stirling Alb	W 4-0	2-0	7	Lavery [1], Hoskins [35], Currie, L (pen) [54], Currie, P [59]	464
22	25	A	Albion R	W 3-0	2-0	7	Currie, P [4], Currie, L 2 (1 pen) [15, 65 (p)]	366
23	Feb 1	A	Clyde	D 3-3	3-1	7	Dunlop [2], Morris [19], Currie, P [38]	467
24	8	H	Queen's Park	W 1-0	0-0	5	Lavery [76]	443
25	15	H	Elgin C	L 2-3	1-1	6	Currie, L [42], Fairburn [75]	412
26	22	A	East Stirling	D 1-1	1-0	6	Currie, L [42]	341
27	Mar 1	A	Annan Ath	L 0-4	0-1	8		473
28	8	H	Montrose	W 5-0	3-0	6	Lavery [6], Notman [24], Currie, L 2 (1 pen) [25, 61 (p)], Dalziel [90]	410
29	15	A	Peterhead	L 0-3	0-1	7		497
30	22	H	Clyde	W 3-0	0-0	6	Lavery [57], Currie, L 2 [76, 82]	519
31	29	H	Albion R	W 3-1	2-0	5	Currie, P [4], Gray [33], Dalziel [50]	471
32	Apr 5	A	Stirling Alb	L 1-2	1-0	5	Lavery [39]	665
33	12	A	Elgin C	W 3-1	0-1	5	Currie, L (pen) [50], Russell [87], Morris [88]	602
34	19	H	East Stirling	W 1-0	0-0	5	Russell [44]	582
35	26	A	Queen's Park	W 3-1	0-1	5	Currie, L [56], Dunlop [68], Russell [79]	420
36	May 3	H	Peterhead	L 1-2	1-0	5	Currie, L [33]	586

Final League Position: 5

Honours
League Champions: Second Division 1978-79. Third Division 2006-07; *Runners-up:* Second Division 1993-94. Third Division 1999-2000, 2005-06 (not promoted).
Scottish Cup: Quarter-finals 1953-54, 1979-80.
League Cup: Semi-finals 1963-64.
League Challenge Cup: Quarter-finals 2004-05.

Club colours: Shirt: Black with gold vertical stripes. Shorts: Black. Socks: Black.

Goalscorers: *League (63):* Currie L 17 (5 pens), Lavery 15, Dalziel 9, Currie P 4, Russell 3, Dunlop 2, Hoskins 2, Morris 2, Notman 2, O'Brien 2, Fairburn 1, Gielty 1, Gray 1, Tulloch 1, own goal 1.
William Hill Scottish FA Cup (7): Lavery 2, O'Brien 2, Currie L 1, Dalziel 1, Notman 1.
Scottish Communities League Cup (0).
Ramsdens Cup (3): Gray 1, Morris 1, Ronald 1.

Grant P 15	Turner L 1+2	Pullock S 3	Hoskins D 25+5	Notman S 25	Brydon D 1	Gray R 26+7	Currie L 36	Lavery R 32+2	Dalziel S 28+7	Ronald O 3+6	Gielty D 15+11	O'Brien K 16+8	Morris J 6+19	Jacobs D 32+2	Fairburn J 15+2	Miller B 5+6	Dunlop M 26	Tulloch S 16	Janczyk N 8+1	Carse D —+8	Bald W 13	Andrews M 8	Currie P 12+3	Cameron C 10	Downie J —+2	Drummond R 11	Russell A 8+3	Match No.
1	2	3	4	5	6	7^1	8	9	10	11^2	12	13	14															1
1			4			7^1	12	8	11	10^3	14	5	9^2	6	2	3	13											2
1			4	8		7	12	11^1	10	13		5	6	9^2	2	3												3
1				5	6		8	9^2	10^3	13	14	11^1	12	2			3	4	7									4
1			4	5	6		12	8	11^1	10	13		9^2	2			3		7									5
1			4	5	6		13	8	9	10^1	12	11^2		2			3		7^3	14								6
1			5	8			12	6	9	10^1		11^3	13	2			3	4	7^2	14								7
1			4	6^2		11^1	8	9^1	10		5	12	13	2			3		7	14								8
1			4	6^2		12	8	9	10	14	5	11^2	13	2		3^1			7									9
1			5	6		9^1	8		10		13	11^3	12	2^2	14		3	4	7									10
1			5	7		6^3	9	11^2	12		13	10^1		2			3	4	8	14								11
1			5	6		9	7	10	11^1		8^2	13	12	2			3	4										12
1			5	6		9	7	12	13		8	11^2	10^1	2			3	4										13
1			5^2	7		9	6	10	12	13	8	11^1		2			3	4										14
			12	8		14	7	13	10	9	5	11^1	6^2				3	4^2			1							15
			4	6		8	7	9	11^2	10^1	5	12	13	2			3				1							16
			3	7^2		9	8	11^3	10	12	5	6^1	13	2		14	4		13		1							17
			4	7		6^2	8	10^1	11		5	9	12	2			3		13		1							18
1	12			8		9	7	11	10		5	6^1		2	4		3											19
			5	6^2		9	7	11	10^1	12		14		2^3	3		4		13		1	8						20
	12		4			9	8	11^1	10^3			14	13	2			3	5			1	6	7^2					21
			4			6^2	8	9^1	10	14	12	13		2	5		3				1	11	7^3					22
			4				8	9	10		12	6^2	13	2	5	3^1					1	11	7					23
			4			9^1	8	11^2	10		5	12	14	2			3				1	6	7^3		13			24
			4			9^1	8	11	10^2		13	14	12	2	5		3				1	6	7^3					25
			8			9	11^1		10	3	6		13	2	13	4					1		7^2			5	12	26
			4			6	9		10^1	8		14		2	13	7^2	3^3				1		12			5	11	27
			6^1			9	8	11			13	14		2			3				1	12	7^1			5	10^2	28
			12			6	10	9			13			2^3	3	4^1					1		7	8		5	11^2	29
						9^2	8	11	12		14			2	3		4		13		1	6	7^3			5	10^1	30
						9^1	8	11	10^2					2	3		4		13		1	6	7			5	12	31
						6^2	7	11	10					2	4	12	8				1		9^1	3^1		5	13	32
						6^2	8	9	11		12			2^1	4	7	3				1				13	5	10	33
		14				6	8	9	10^2	13				2^3	3	7^1	4				1	12				5	11	34
		13				6^2	8	11	12		14			2^3	4	7	3				1		9^1			5	10	35
		12				6^1	8	9	11^2		13			2^3	3	7	4		14		1					5	10	36

BRECHIN CITY

Year Formed: 1906. *Ground & Address:* Glebe Park, Trinity Rd, Brechin, Angus DD9 6BJ. *Telephone:* 01356 622856.
Fax: 01382 206331. *E-mail:* secretary@brechincityfc.com *Website:* www.brechincity.com
Ground Capacity: 3,960 (seated: 1,519). *Size of Pitch:* 101m × 61m.
Chairman: Kenneth Ferguson. *Vice-Chairman:* Martin Smith. *Secretary:* Gus Fairlie.
Manager: Ray McKinnon. *Assistant Manager:* Grant Johnson. *Coach:* Darren Taylor.
Club Nicknames: 'The City', 'The Hedgemen'.
Previous Grounds: Nursery Park.
Record Attendance: 8,122 v Aberdeen, Scottish Cup 3rd rd, 3 Feb 1973.
Record Transfer Fee received: £100,000 for Scott Thomson to Aberdeen (1991) and Chris Templeman to Morton (2004).
Record Transfer Fee paid: £16,000 for Sandy Ross from Berwick Rangers (1991).
Record Victory: 12-1 v Thornhill, Scottish Cup 1st rd, 28 Jan 1926.
Record Defeat: 0-10 v Airdrieonians, Albion R and Cowdenbeath, all in Division II, 1937-38.
Most League Appearances: 459: David Watt, 1975-89.
Most League Goals in Season (Individual): 26: Ronald McIntosh, Division II, 1959-60.
Most Goals Overall (Individual): 131: Ian Campbell, 1977-85.

BRECHIN CITY – SCOTTISH LEAGUE ONE 2013–14 LEAGUE RECORD

Match No.	Date	Venue	Opponents	Result	H/T Score	Lg Pos.	Goalscorers	Atten- dance
1	Aug 10	A	Rangers	L 1-4	0-2	9	Jackson, S [65]	44,380
2	17	H	East Fife	W 2-0	0-0	5	Donnelly [66], Trouten [83]	543
3	24	H	Forfar Ath	W 2-1	1-0	5	Molloy [19], Trouten [54]	724
4	31	A	Arbroath	L 1-2	0-2	5	Barr [62]	801
5	Sept 14	H	Dunfermline Ath	D 1-1	0-1	5	Jackson, A [76]	923
6	21	A	Ayr U	D 2-2	0-2	5	Trouten [68], McLean [90]	987
7	28	H	Stranraer	D 1-1	1-0	5	Trouten (pen) [37]	455
8	Oct 5	A	Airdrieonians	L 1-3	1-2	5	Jackson, A [38]	606
9	12	A	Stenhousemuir	L 2-3	1-0	7	McLean [14], Jackson, A [79]	415
10	19	H	Rangers	L 3-4	3-1	9	Hay [5], Brown [10], Trouten [35]	3237
11	26	H	Arbroath	W 3-1	1-0	6	Hay (pen) [39], Ryan [61], Carcary [90]	765
12	Nov 9	A	Forfar Ath	L 0-2	0-1	8		663
13	16	H	Ayr U	D 1-1	0-1	7	Jackson, A [75]	518
14	23	A	Dunfermline Ath	L 1-3	0-2	7	McLean [80]	2569
15	Dec 14	A	Stranraer	L 0-3	0-1	9		357
16	17	H	Airdrieonians	W 4-3	2-0	8	Donnelly [26], Trouten 2 [29, 90], Jackson, A [57]	445
17	21	A	East Fife	W 3-1	1-0	7	Jackson, A [30], Barr [54], Carcary [89]	745
18	28	H	Stenhousemuir	L 0-1	-0-1	7		507
19	Jan 2	H	Forfar Ath	L 1-5	0-4	8	Barr [75]	812
20	11	A	Arbroath	W 1-0	1-0	7	Barr [39]	777
21	18	A	Ayr U	W 3-1	2-0	6	McLauchlan [12], McAusland (og) [33], Hay (pen) [90]	1018
22	25	H	Dunfermline Ath	W 3-2	0-1	5	Carcary [57], Jackson, A [61], Petrie [89]	854
23	Feb 1	A	Rangers	L 1-2	0-2	5	Robb [52]	40,377
24	8	H	East Fife	W 3-0	2-0	5	Barr [27], Jackson, A [42], Thomson [62]	523
25	15	A	Airdrieonians	L 1-2	1-1	5	Thomson [15]	690
26	22	H	Stranraer	L 1-3	0-3	5	Jackson, A [59]	452
27	Mar 1	H	Arbroath	L 2-4	0-2	6	Jackson, A [57], Thomson [61]	668
28	8	A	Forfar Ath	D 1-1	0-0	7	Jackson, A [73]	641
29	15	A	Stenhousemuir	L 2-4	1-2	7	Trouten 2 (1 pen) [36, 70 (p)]	512
30	23	H	Rangers	L 1-2	0-1	7	Thomson [49]	3070
31	29	A	Dunfermline Ath	L 1-2	0-0	7	Thomson [60]	2241
32	Apr 5	H	Ayr U	W 2-1	1-0	7	Thomson [6], Molloy [67]	507
33	12	A	Airdrieonians	D 1-1	0-1	7	Molloy [52]	646
34	19	A	Stranraer	W 2-1	1-1	7	Trouten (pen) [5], Thomson [67]	407
35	26	A	East Fife	W 2-1	1-0	7	Jackson, A [20], Trouten [88]	591
36	May 3	H	Stenhousemuir	L 1-3	0-1	8	Trouten (pen) [53]	543

Final League Position: 8

Honours
League Champions: Second Division 1982-83, 1989-90, 2004-05. Third Division 2001-02. C Division 1953-54; *Runners-up:* Second Division 1992-93, 2002-03. Third Division 1995-96.
League Challenge Cup Runners-up: 2002-03.

Club colours: Red with white trim.

Goalscorers: *League (57):* Jackson A 12, Trouten 12 (4 pens), Thomson 7, Barr 5, Carcary 3, Hay 3 (2 pens), McLean 3, Molloy 3, Donnelly 2, Brown 1, Jackson S 1, McLauchlan 1, Petrie 1, Robb 1, Ryan 1, own goal 1.
William Hill Scottish FA Cup (6): Trouten 3 (1 pen), Jackson A 2, Walker 1.
Scottish Communities League Cup (3): Donnelly 2, Barr 1.
Ramsdens Cup (1): own goal 1.

Smith G 31	McLean P 26 + 3	Jackson S 18 + 9	McLauchlan G 24 + 1	Brown J 22 + 3	Trouten A 24 + 2	Molloy C 24 + 7	Anderson S 10 + 2	Barr R 23 + 11	Donnelly R 8 + 6	Carcary D 7 + 15	Jackson A 32 + 1	Cameron G 11 + 7	Moyes E 17 + 1	Hay G 31	Robb S 13 + 8	Walker A 11 + 5	Tobin C 1 + 1	Connolly A 1 + 3	Petrie D 23 + 1	Ryan A 4	Nelson C 1	Antell C 4	Ferguson R 13 + 3	Thomson R 12 + 2	Kenneth G 5	Match No.
1	2	3	4	5[1]	6	7[1]	8	9	10[3]	11	12	13	14													1
1	2[4]		4	13	6	7	9	12	11[3]	10	14				3	5	8[1]									2
1	2		4	5	9	6	7	11[2]	12	10	13				3	8[1]										3
1	2	6	4	5		7[2]	8[3]	9	11		10	13			3[1]			12	14							4
1	2	14	4	5	6	8[2]		12	11[3]		10				3	13	7		9[1]							5
1	2	12	4	5	6	13		10			11				3	9[3]	7[1]		8[2]	14						6
1	2	3	5	9	6[1]	7	8	11[2]		10			4			12		13								7
1	2	13	3	5	6		7	9	10[2]		11		4			8	12									8
1	7	6	4[3]	9[2]	10		5	12	14	13	11		2	3		8[1]										9
1	2[2]	14	3	6	8[1]	13	7[1]	12			10		5	4					9	11[3]						10
1	2		14	5		6	7[3]	12		13	11		4	3	10[1]				9	8[2]						11
1	2			5	8	12		14		13	9	6[2]	4	3	10[1]				7	11[3]						12
1		5		2[1]	9	8		12	13		10		4	3	6				7	11[2]						13
1	5	2			6	7[1]	12[▪]		14	10[1]	11		4	3	9[2]	13			8							14
	2	4[2]	5	6	13	8[3]	12	14	9	10	11[1]	3							7[▪]		1					15
	5			2	9	6	12	13	8[2]	11[1]	10	7[▪]	4	3								1				16
	5	2	7[2]		6	8		12	11[1]	13	10		4	3	9							1				17
	5[2]	2		14	9	6		7	10[3]	12	11		4	3	13				8[1]			1				18
12	2		5	6	8[3]		9		11[2]	10	14		4	3	13				7[1]			1				19
1	2	5			9		7		10[1]	11			4	3	6	12			8							20
1	2	14	6	5		8		9[2]	12	11			4[3]	3	13				10				7[1]			21
1	2	5[1]	6		8[2]	10		12	11				4	3	14	13			9				7[2]			22
1	2		4	5		13		10		12	11			3	9[3]	8[2]			7				6[1]	14		23
1	2	13	4	5				10		12	9			3	7[2]	6							8	11[1]		24
1	2		5[3]		13		9		12	11				3	8	7[2]			14				6[1]	10	4	25
1	2[▪]			13		12		10		14	11			3	5[1]	6			7[3]				8[2]	9	4	26
1		5	2	9[1]	14	6		7		10	13	4[3]							8				12	11	3[2]	27
1		2	4		12	8		13			10	9[2]		3		7			5				6	11[1]		28
1	14	2	4		10	7		13			11	6[3]		3[▪]		8			5				9[1]	12		29
1	2[3]	5	4	6[2]	7	9		10[1]		14		12		3					8				13	11		30
1	2	3		6	8	11[1]		12		4		7							5				9	10		31
1	2	3		7	8	10				9		4		7					5				6	11		32
1	12	7[1]	4		8	6		14	10[3]	9[1]		3	13						5				2	11		33
1	2	12	4[1]		6	8		7[2]		10	9		3						5				13	11		34
1	2	13			8	6			14	9[3]	7		3	12					5				10[1]	11	4[2]	35
1	2	13			6			9		10	7[1]		3	12					5				8	11[2]	4[▪]	36

CELTIC

Year Formed: 1888. *Ground & Address:* Celtic Park, Glasgow G40 3RE. *Telephone:* 0871 226 1888. *Fax:* 0141 551 4223.
E-mail: customerservices@celticfc.co.uk *Website:* www.celticfc.net
Ground Capacity: 60,355 (all seated). *Size of Pitch:* 105m × 68m.
Chairman: Ian Bankier. *Chief Executive:* Peter Lawwell. *Secretary:* Michael Nicholson.
Manager: Ronny Deila. *Assistant Manager:* John Collins. *First Team Coach:* Garry Parker. *Physio:* Graham Parsons.
Club Nicknames: 'The Bhoys', 'The Hoops', 'The Celts'. *Previous Grounds:* None.
Record Attendance: 92,000 v Rangers, Division I, 1 Jan 1938.
Record Transfer Fee received: £6,500,000 for Stilian Petrov to Aston Villa (August 2007).
Record Transfer Fee paid: £6,000,000 for Chris Sutton from Chelsea (July 2000).
Record Victory: 11-0 Dundee, Division I, 26 Oct 1895.
Record Defeat: 0-8 v Motherwell, Division I, 30 Apr 1937.
Most Capped Player: Pat Bonner 80, Republic of Ireland.
Most League Appearances: 486: Billy McNeill, 1957-75.
Most League Goals in Season (Individual): 50: James McGrory, Division I, 1935-36.
Most Goals Overall (Individual): 397: James McGrory, 1922-39.

Honours
League Champions: (45 times) Division I 1892-93, 1893-94, 1895-96, 1897-98, 1904-05, 1905-06, 1906-07, 1907-08, 1908-09, 1909-10, 1913-14, 1914-15, 1915-16, 1916-17, 1918-19, 1921-22, 1925-26, 1935-36, 1937-38, 1953-54, 1965-66, 1966-67, 1967-68, 1968-69, 1969-70, 1970-71, 1971-72, 1972-73, 1973-74. Premier Division 1976-77, 1978-79, 1980-81, 1981-82, 1985-86, 1987-88, 1997-98, 2000-01, 2001-02, 2003-04, 2005-06, 2006-07, 2007-08, 2011-12, 2012-13; Premiership 2013-14.
Runners-up: 31 times.
Scottish Cup Winners: (36 times) 1892, 1899, 1900, 1904, 1907, 1908, 1911, 1912, 1914, 1923, 1925, 1927, 1931, 1933, 1937, 1951, 1954, 1965, 1967, 1969, 1971, 1972, 1974, 1975, 1977, 1980, 1985, 1988, 1989, 1995, 2001, 2004, 2005, 2007, 2011, 2013.
Runners-up: 18 times.

CELTIC – SCOTTISH PREMIER LEAGUE 2013–14 LEAGUE RECORD

Match No.	Date	Venue	Opponents	Result	H/T Score	Lg Pos.	Goalscorers	Attendance
1	Aug 3	H	Ross Co	W 2-1	1-1	2	Stokes 2 [28, 87]	45,705
2	17	A	Aberdeen	W 2-0	1-0	3	Commons (pen) [45], Forrest [87]	20,017
3	24	H	Inverness CT	D 2-2	1-2	2	Mulgrew [42], Matthews [82]	45,160
4	31	H	Dundee U	W 1-0	0-0	2	Stokes [87]	10,586
5	Sept 14	A	Hearts	W 3-1	1-0	2	Commons (pen) [19], Stokes [65], Pukki [86]	15,928
6	21	H	St Johnstone	W 2-1	2-0	2	Pukki [11], Mulgrew [26]	45,220
7	28	A	Kilmarnock	W 5-2	3-2	2	Commons [20], Samaras 3 [24, 27, 88], Balde [90]	6149
8	Oct 5	H	Motherwell	W 2-0	1-0	1	Stokes [26], Commons [49]	46,608
9	19	A	Hibernian	D 1-1	0-1	1	Forrest [77]	14,220
10	27	A	Partick Thistle	W 2-1	1-0	1	Samaras [34], Balde [75]	7978
11	Nov 2	H	Dundee U	D 1-1	0-1	1	Mulgrew [90]	47,386
12	9	A	Ross Co	W 4-1	1-0	1	van Dijk 2 [41, 53], Ledley 2 [70, 73]	5982
13	23	A	Aberdeen	W 3-1	1-1	1	Commons 2 [36, 90], Boerrigter [90]	49,683
14	Dec 6	A	Motherwell	W 5-0	1-0	1	Commons 2 [44, 76], Ambrose [54], Stokes [78], Atajic [90]	9117
15	14	H	Hibernian	W 1-0	1-0	1	Pukki [29]	46,065
16	21	H	Hearts	W 2-0	0-0	1	Commons [64], Forrest [90]	46,058
17	26	A	St Johnstone	W 1-0	1-0	1	van Dijk [5]	7034
18	29	A	Inverness CT	W 1-0	1-0	1	Commons [3]	6384
19	Jan 1	H	Partick Thistle	W 1-0	1-0	1	Ledley [39]	52,670
20	5	A	St Mirren	W 4-0	0-0	1	Mulgrew [53], Stokes [58], Commons 2 [70, 72]	5778
21	18	H	Motherwell	W 3-0	2-0	1	Commons 2 (1 pen) [5, 39 ipi], McManus (og) [68]	47,489
22	26	A	Hibernian	W 4-0	1-0	1	Commons 2 (1 pen) [9, 90 ipi], van Dijk [77], Pukki [83]	12,542
23	29	H	Kilmarnock	W 4-0	2-0	1	Ledley [11], Ashcroft (og) [21], Mulgrew [68], Balde [90]	44,271
24	Feb 2	H	St Mirren	W 1-0	1-0	1	Commons [6]	45,014
25	16	H	St Johnstone	W 3-0	1-0	1	Stokes 3 [16, 64, 66]	45,239
26	22	A	Hearts	W 2-0	0-0	1	Griffiths [58], Pukki [90]	15,801
27	25	A	Aberdeen	L 1-2	0-2	1	Forrest [62]	16,634
28	Mar 1	H	Inverness CT	W 5-0	2-0	1	Griffiths 3 [12, 57, 85], Mulgrew [22], Commons [78]	46,552
29	14	A	Kilmarnock	W 3-0	0-0	1	Commons 3 [57, 59, 86]	7495
30	22	H	St Mirren	W 3-0	1-0	1	Johansen [44], Griffiths [61], Stokes [90]	46,536
31	26	A	Partick Thistle	W 5-1	1-0	1	Stokes 2 [4, 90], Henderson [49], Johansen [53], Commons [90]	7549
32	29	H	Ross Co	D 1-1	1-1	1	Commons [35]	49,270
33	Apr 5	A	Dundee U	W 2-0	2-0	1	Samaras [5], Stokes [24]	11,033
34	19	A	Motherwell	D 3-3	1-2	1	Stokes [45], Samaras [56], Griffiths [86]	7493
35	27	H	Inverness CT	W 6-0	2-0	1	Stokes 3 (1 pen) [34, 45, 53 ipi], Griffiths [68], Ambrose [78], Pukki [78]	45,712
36	May 3	H	Aberdeen	W 5-2	2-1	1	Brown 2 [25, 44], Stokes [53], Commons 2 [69, 87]	47,468
37	7	A	St Johnstone	D 3-3	0-1	1	Commons (pen) [53], Pukki [73], van Dijk [77]	4624
38	11	H	Dundee U	W 3-1	0-0	1	Stokes [64], Samaras (pen) [76], Commons [82]	52,400

Final League Position: 1

League Cup Winners: (14 times) 1956-57, 1957-58, 1965-66, 1966-67, 1967-68, 1968-69, 1969-70, 1974-75, 1982-83, 1997-98, 1999-2000, 2000-01, 2005-06, 2008-09; *Runners-up:* 15 times.

European: *European Cup/Champions League:* 164 matches (1966-67 winners, 1967-68, 1968-69, 1969-70 runners-up, 1970-71, 1971-72, 1972-73, 1973-74 semi-finals, 1974-75, 1977-78, 1979-80, 1981-82, 1982-83, 1986-87, 1988-89, 1998-99, 2001-02, 2002-03, 2003-04, 2004-05, 2005-06, 2006-07, 2007-08, 2008-09, 2009-10, 2010-11, 2012-13, 2013-14). *Cup Winners' Cup:* 38 matches (1963-64 semi-finals, 1965-66 semi-finals, 1975-76, 1980-81, 1984-85, 1985-86, 1989-90, 1995-96). *UEFA Cup:* 75 matches (*Fairs Cup:* 1962-63, 1964-65). *UEFA Cup:* 1976-77, 1983-84, 1987-88, 1991-92, 1992-93, 1993-94, 1996-97, 1997-98, 1998-99, 1999-2000, 2000-01, 2001-02, 2002-03 runners-up, 2003-04 quarter-finals). *Europa League:* 16 matches (2009-10, 2010-11, 2011-12).

Club colours: Shirt: Green and white hoops. Shorts: White. Socks: White.

Goalscorers: *League (102):* Commons 27 (5 pens), Stokes 20 (1 pen), Griffiths 7, Pukki 7, Samaras 7 (1 pen), Mulgrew 6, van Dijk 5, Forrest 4, Ledley 4, Balde 3, Ambrose 2, Brown 2, Johansen 2, Atajic 1, Boerrigter 1, Henderson 1, Matthews 1, own goals 2.
William Hill Scottish FA Cup (8): Commons 3, Brown 2, Ledley 1, Lustig 1, Stokes 1.
Scottish Communities League Cup (0).
UEFA Champions League (12): Samaras 4, Forrest 3 (1 pen), Commons 2, Ambrose 1, Kayal 1, Lustig 1.

Forster F 37	Lustig M 9+7	Izaguirre E 34	Brown S 37+1	Ambrose E 37+1	Mulgrew C 27+1	Forrest J 10+6	Ledley J 18+2	Stokes A 30+3	Commons K 32+2	Boerrigter D 5+10	Watt T 1+1	Matthews A 21+2	Kayal B 7+6	Mouyokolo S 1+1	Samaras G 10+10	van Dijk V 35+1	Rogic T 1+2	Atajic B —+3	Pukki T 13+12	Biton N 8+7	Fisher D 10+2	McGeouch D —+1	Henderson L 4+4	Johansen S 13+3	Griffiths L 11+2	O'Connell E 1	Herron J 1	Zaluska L 1	Twardzik F 1	Match No.
1	2¹	3	4	5	6	7²	8	9	10	11³	12	13	14																	1
1	12	5	6	4¹	9	13	8		10			2³	7²	3	11	14														2
1	13	5	7	3	9		12					10	2	6³		4²	8¹	11	14											3
1	9²	5	7	3		8	10	11	6¹			2			4	13	12													4
1	2	5	7	3	13		8²	11	10³	9		6¹			12	4			14											5
1		5	7	3	8		10	6¹	9			2²			13	4		14	11³	12										6
1	12	5	7	3	8		11	6				2¹			9²	4		13	14	10²										7
1	2	5³	7	3	8	12			6²							4		14	11¹	13										8
1		8	3	5	12	13	10	7³				9¹			11	4		14	6¹	2										9
1	2	5³	7	3			9	11				8²			10	4		12	6¹	14	13									10
1	12	5	6	3	7	9	8²	11		14						4		10³	13	2¹										11
1		5	9	3	10	8¹	7²	12		14					4	13		11	6³	2										12
1	13	5	7	3	6		8¹		9	12					11	4		14	10³	2²										13
1	2	5	7¹	3	9		8	10	6³	13						4		12	11²		14									14
1	2¹	5	6	3			8	10	9			13				12	4		11²	7										15
1		5	6	3		12	8	10	9						13	4			11²	7¹	2									16
1		5	7	3		12	8	10	9¹			6³			11²	4		14		13	2									17
1		5	7	3		6¹	8	11³	10			2			9	4			12	13										18
1		5	6	3	7³	9	8	13	10¹			2			12	4			11²	14										19
1		5	7³	3	9¹	6²	8	11	10	12		2				4		14		13										20
1		5	6	3²	8	9	7	11¹	10¹							4		13	12	2										21
1		5	7	4	9³		8		10			11¹	3			13		12	6²	2		14								22
1		5	6	3	7²	9¹	8		11	13						4		12	10³	2		14								23
1		5	6	3	8	9²		10	11¹	12						4		13		2		7								24
1	5²	6¹	3				10²	9	13			2				4		14	7	12		8	11							25
1		7	3	5			10¹	9	13			2				4		14	12	6			8³	11²						26
1	5²	6	3	9	12		10	8¹				2			13	4⁴	14		7					11³						27
1	5	6³	3	8	9		10¹	12				2²				4				7	13		14	11						28
1	5	7	3	4			11	9	14			2	13									8²	6¹	10³						29
1	5	6	12	4			11	9³				2			14	3						8²	7	10¹						30
1	5	7	3	8¹			10	6				2²	13			14	4						12	9	11³					31
1	5	7	2				11	9³					13	12	4		14						6	8	10¹	3²				32
1	5	2	3				10	9					6	14	11¹	4		13					8³	7²	12					33
1	5	6	3				10	9					7¹		11	4		13					8	12	2²					34
1	12	5	6	3	8¹		10²	9				2³				4			13			14	7	11						35
1	13	5	6	3	8		10	9²				2	12			4		13					14	7¹	11³					36
	2	13	3	5			14	12	9¹			6³	7			4	10²		11				8				1			37
1	2²		6	3	5		10	9					13			12	4						14	7	11³				8¹	38

CLYDE

Year Formed: 1877. *Ground & Address:* Broadwood Stadium, Cumbernauld, G68 9NE. *Telephone:* 01236 451511.
Fax: 01236 733490. *E-mail:* info@clydefc.co.uk *Website:* www.clydefc.co.uk
Ground Capacity: 8,006 (all seated). *Size of Pitch:* 100m × 68m.
Chairman: John Alexander. *Secretary:* John Taylor.
Manager: Barry Ferguson. *Assistant Manager:* Malky Thomson. *Physio:* Iain McKinlay.
Club Nickname: 'The Bully Wee'.
Previous Grounds: Barrowfield Park 1877-98, Shawfield Stadium 1898-1986, Firhill Stadium 1986-91, Douglas Park 1991-94.
Record Attendance: 52,000 v Rangers, Division I, 21 Nov 1908.
Record Transfer Fee received: £200,000 from Blackburn R for Gordon Greer (May 2001).
Record Transfer Fee paid: £14,000 for Harry Hood from Sunderland (1966).
Record Victory: 11-1 v Cowdenbeath, Division II, 6 Oct 1951.
Record Defeat: 0-11 v Dumbarton, Scottish Cup 4th rd, 22 Nov, 1879; v Rangers, Scottish Cup 4th rd, 13 Nov 1880.
Most Capped Player: Tommy Ring, 12, Scotland.
Most League Appearances: 420: Brian Ahern, 1971-81; 1987-88.
Most League Goals in Season (Individual): 32: Bill Boyd, 1932-33.
Most Goals Overall (Individual): 124: Tommy Ring, 1950-60.

CLYDE – SCOTTISH LEAGUE TWO 2013–14 LEAGUE RECORD

Match No.	Date	Venue	Opponents	Result		H/T Score	Lg Pos.	Goalscorers	Attendance
1	Aug 10	H	Berwick R	W	1-0	0-0	4	Daly [73]	469
2	17	A	Albion R	L	0-3	0-3	6		528
3	24	H	Queen's Park	W	3-0	0-0	4	MacDonald [50], Ferguson [52], Brough (og) [71]	621
4	31	A	Elgin C	L	0-1	0-0	5		544
5	Sept 14	H	East Stirling	L	1-2	0-0	7	Sweeney [76]	497
6	21	A	Annan Ath	W	2-1	1-1	5	Frances [26], Sweeney (pen) [49]	483
7	28	H	Montrose	L	0-3	0-0	9		464
8	Oct 12	A	Peterhead	D	1-1	0-1	8	MacDonald (pen) [90]	562
9	19	A	Berwick R	W	1-0	0-0	4	Frances [48]	472
10	26	H	Stirling Alb	W	2-1	2-0	2	Marsh [17], Ferguson [40]	676
11	Nov 9	A	Queen's Park	D	1-1	0-0	4	McColm [58]	704
12	16	H	Elgin C	W	2-1	0-0	4	McCluskey [74], Scullion [77]	533
13	23	A	East Stirling	W	1-0	0-0	1	McCluskey [72]	452
14	Dec 3	A	Annan Ath	W	2-1	0-1	1	McColm 2 [50, 85]	422
15	7	H	Peterhead	L	1-3	1-2	2	Ferguson [11]	498
16	14	A	Montrose	W	2-0	2-0	1	Watt [30], Ferguson [33]	410
17	21	A	Albion R	D	2-2	0-1	2	Daly [68], Ferguson [73]	508
18	28	A	Stirling Alb	D	1-1	1-0	2	Sweeney [44]	859
19	Jan 4	H	Queen's Park	L	1-2	1-0	3	McCluskey [25]	751
20	11	A	Elgin C	L	1-3	0-1	4	Ferguson [63]	585
21	18	A	Annan Ath	W	1-0	1-0	3	McCluskey [15]	456
22	25	H	East Stirling	W	1-0	0-0	2	MacDonald [54]	173
23	Feb 1	H	Berwick R	D	3-3	1-3	2	Daly [37], Ferguson [77], McQueen [90]	467
24	15	A	Peterhead	L	0-2	0-1	3		511
25	22	H	Montrose	D	1-1	1-0	4	McCluskey [31]	418
26	25	A	Albion R	L	0-1	0-0	4		423
27	Mar 1	H	Elgin C	W	4-0	1-0	3	Daly 2 [33, 80], Ferguson [65], Young [89]	504
28	8	A	Queen's Park	W	3-1	3-0	3	McQueen [16], McCluskey [19], Daly [33]	608
29	15	H	Stirling Alb	W	1-0	1-0	3	McCluskey [44]	673
30	22	A	Berwick R	L	0-3	0-0	3		519
31	29	A	East Stirling	W	4-2	3-1	3	MacDonald [6], McCluskey 2 [16, 51], Daly [43]	449
32	Apr 5	H	Annan Ath	L	0-3	0-1	3		516
33	12	H	Peterhead	L	0-2	0-1	4		534
34	19	A	Montrose	W	2-0	2-0	3	Daly [21], McCluskey (pen) [27]	422
35	26	H	Albion R	W	4-0	1-0	3	McCluskey [24], Daly [54], Sweeney [62], Watt [90]	620
36	May 3	A	Stirling Alb	L	1-4	1-1	4	McKinnon (pen) [28]	1028

Final League Position: 4

Honours
League Champions: Division II 1904-05, 1951-52, 1956-57, 1961-62, 1972-73. Second Division 1977-78, 1981-82, 1992-93, 1999-2000; *Runners-up:* Division II 1903-04, 1905-06, 1925-26, 1963-64. First Division 2002-03, 2003-04.
Scottish Cup Winners: 1939, 1955, 1958; *Runners-up:* 1910, 1912, 1949.
League Challenge Cup Runners-up: 2006-07.

Club colours: Shirt: White with black trim. Shorts: Black. Socks: Red.

Goalscorers: *League (50):* McCluskey 11 (1 pen), Daly 9, Ferguson 8, MacDonald 4 (1 pen), Sweeney 4 (1 pen), McColm 3, Frances 2, McQueen 2, Watt 2, Marsh 1, McKinnon 1 (1 pen), Scullion 1, Young 1, own goal 1.
William Hill Scottish FA Cup (7): Watt 3, Daly 1, MacDonald 1, McCluskey 1, McColm 1.
Scottish Communities League Cup (0).
Ramsdens Cup (1): McCluskey 1
League 1 Play-Offs (2): Ferguson 2.

Barclay J 25	Brown G 12 + 1	Marsh D 29	Frances R 12 + 5	MacDonald K 34	MacBeth R 3 + 3	Scullion P 19 + 10	Sweeney J 36	McColm S 31 + 1	Daly M 23 + 8	McCluskey S 26 + 4	McQueen B 31 + 2	Orrick P — + 2	McGachie K — + 3	Monaghan H 3	Watt K 7 + 10	Ferguson S 28 + 5	Gray I 24 + 3	Dickie G — + 5	Capuano G 16 + 7	Fitzharris S — + 1	Rajovic N 8	McGhee F 8 + 3	McGovern J 3	Coyne B — + 4	Janczyk N 12 + 2	Currie J — + 1	McKinnon R 4 + 3	Young G 2 + 3	Match No.
1	2	3²	4	5¹	6	7	8	9	10	11¹	12	13	14																1
1	2¹		3	5	6	10³	7	9	11		4		14		8²	12	13												2
1			4	5	12		7	9	11²		3		14		8	10³	6¹	2	13										3
1			4	5			14	8	9	10¹		3		12	7³	11²	6	2	13										4
1	2		4³	5		7¹	13	10	9	11²	12	3			14	6	8												5
1	2²		4	5			13	8	9	10	11¹	3				6³	12	14	7										6
1			4	5	14	7		9¹	12	10¹	3					11²	6	2	13	8									7
1	2	3	4	5			14	8	9	10	11¹					12	13	7³			6²								8
1	2	3	4¹	5			11	8	9²	13	14	12				10³	6⁴		7										9
1	2⁴	3		5		10¹	8	9	12	11	4					6²		13	7										10
1		3		5		10¹	7	9	12²	11	4					6		2	13	8									11
9²		3	14	5²			10	8		11¹	4			12		6	2		7	1	13								12
	2²		4	5		11	7	9	10¹	8		13		12		6	3		1										13
	2	3	5³			10¹	7	9	12	11	4					6²	13	8	14	1									14
14	4		5			11¹	8	9²	13	10	3					12	6	2³	7	1									15
2	4		8			10	7			5						11	6	3	12	1									16
2	3⁴	14		5		10	8	9¹	13	12	4					11	6²	7		1									17
	4			5		12	7	9	10¹	11	8					6	2	3		1									18
	3			5		10¹	8	9		11	4					13	6	2²	7			12	1						19
	3			5		10¹	8	12	9	11	4					6²	2	7				1	13						20
	4²	12		5			6	10	11¹	9	3					9³	2	7				1	14	13					21
1	3			5		13	8	10	9¹	11²	4					6	2					12	7						22
1	4			5		6²	7	9	11	12	3					8	2²	7¹				13		9³	12				23
1	4			5		6²	7	9	11	12	3					13								10		8¹			24
1	4			5			9	10	11	7	3					8	2		12					6¹					25
1	3	13		5			8		10	11	4					6	2		7²					12	9¹				26
1	4			5			8	9	10	11	3					6¹					2			7			12		27
1	3			5		13	8	9¹	10²	11	4					6					2			7	12				28
1	3			5		12	8	9¹	10	11³	4					6¹	14				2			7	13				29
1	3	4	5			10	8	9		11						6	2							7¹	12				30
1	4		5			7	9	11	10	8						6¹	2		12					3²			13		31
1	4	8	5			13	7	9¹	11	10²						6	14		2					3³	12				32
1	3²	13	5			11¹	7	9	12	10	4					6	14		2					8³					33
1	3						7	8	9	10	11	4				6¹	12		2							5			34
1	3						7	8		10	11²	4			12	6¹	13		2			14		5	9¹				35
		4	9²	14		11	7¹		10³		8					12	13		3	1	2			5	6				36

COWDENBEATH

Year Formed: 1882. *Ground & Address:* Central Park, Cowdenbeath KY4 9QQ. *Telephone:* 01383 610166. *Fax:* 01383 512132.
E-mail: office@cowdenbeathfc.com *Website:* www.cowdenbeathfc.com
Ground Capacity: 4,370 (seated: 1,431). *Size of Pitch:* 98m × 59m.
Chairman: Donald Findlay QC. *Vice-Chairman:* John Lints. *Operations:* John Cameron.
Club Nicknames: 'The Blue Brazil', 'Cowden', 'The Miners'.
Manager: Jimmy Nichol. *Assistant Manager:* Lee Makel. *Physio:* Pablo Jorda.
Previous Grounds: North End Park.
Record Attendance: 25,586 v Rangers, League Cup quarter-final, 21 Sept 1949.
Record Transfer Fee received: £30,000 for Nicky Henderson to Falkirk (March 1994).
Record Victory: 12-0 v Johnstone, Scottish Cup 1st rd, 21 Jan 1928.
Record Defeat: 1-11 v Clyde, Division II, 6 Oct 1951.
Most Capped Player: Jim Paterson, 3, Scotland.
Most League and Cup Appearances: 491, Ray Allan 1972-75, 1979-89.
Most League Goals in Season (Individual): 54, Rab Walls, Division II, 1938-39.
Most Goals Overall (Individual): 127, Willie Devlin, 1922-26, 1929-30.

COWDENBEATH – SCOTTISH CHAMPIONSHIP 2013–14 LEAGUE RECORD

Match No.	Date	Venue	Opponents	Result	H/T Score	Lg Pos.	Goalscorers	Attendance
1	Aug 10	A	Greenock Morton	L	0-2	0-1	10		1817
2	17	H	Raith R	L	3-4	2-2	10	Morton [9], Adamson [43], Stewart, G [65]	837
3	24	A	Alloa Ath	L	1-3	0-0	10	Hemmings [55]	611
4	31	H	Dumbarton	W	3-2	1-0	9	Stevenson [21], Robertson [72], Hemmings [90]	384
5	Sept 14	H	Falkirk	W	1-0	0-0	7	Stewart, G [89]	644
6	21	A	Hamilton A	L	0-1	0-0	8		817
7	28	A	Livingston	L	1-5	1-1	9	Hemmings [17]	894
8	Oct 5	H	Dundee	L	0-2	0-1	9		1013
9	12	A	Queen of the South	D	1-1	1-0	9	Stewart, G [11]	1514
10	19	H	Greenock Morton	W	5-1	3-1	8	Morton [2], Hemmings 3 [4, 39, 79], Stewart, G [72]	543
11	26	A	Dumbarton	D	0-0	0-0	9		700
12	Nov 9	H	Alloa Ath	L	0-2	0-2	9		346
13	16	H	Hamilton A	L	2-4	2-0	9	Wedderburn [18], Milne [37]	401
14	23	A	Falkirk	L	0-4	0-0	9		2550
15	Dec 7	H	Livingston	L	2-3	0-0	9	Hemmings 2 [56, 69]	363
16	14	A	Dundee	W	2-1	0-0	9	Hemmings [52], Morton [70]	3533
17	21	A	Raith R	D	3-3	1-1	9	Stewart, G [11], Hemmings 2 (1 pen) [74 (p), 90]	1597
18	28	H	Queen of the South	L	0-2	0-1	9		556
19	Jan 2	A	Alloa Ath	W	1-0	0-0	9	Hemmings [73]	818
20	11	H	Dumbarton	L	2-4	2-2	9	Miller [3], Stevenson [27]	434
21	18	A	Falkirk	L	0-2	0-0	9		566
22	25	A	Hamilton A	W	4-3	3-0	9	Stewart, G 2 [5, 46], Hemmings 2 [9, 20]	944
23	Feb 1	H	Raith R	W	1-0	0-0	9	Hemmings [70]	961
24	15	A	Greenock Morton	D	1-1	1-0	9	Armstrong [13]	2087
25	22	H	Dundee	W	2-0	1-0	9	McKeown [33], Stewart, G [81]	1419
26	Mar 1	A	Livingston	L	0-1	0-0	9		980
27	8	H	Alloa Ath	D	2-2	1-1	9	Stewart, G 2 [37, 73]	458
28	15	A	Dumbarton	L	1-5	0-1	9	Armstrong [63]	687
29	22	A	Queen of the South	L	1-2	0-2	9	Stewart, S [90]	1619
30	25	H	Greenock Morton	W	3-0	1-0	9	Miller 2 [6, 70], Stewart, G [63]	318
31	29	H	Hamilton A	D	1-1	0-0	9	O'Brien [90]	497
32	Apr 5	A	Falkirk	L	0-5	0-3	9		2830
33	12	A	Dundee	L	0-4	0-2	9		4751
34	19	H	Livingston	W	4-0	1-0	9	Armstrong 2 [45, 73], Hemmings 2 [51, 65]	420
35	26	A	Raith R	W	2-1	1-0	9	McKeown [19], Milne [81]	1760
36	May 3	H	Queen of the South	D	1-1	0-0	9	Hemmings [76]	1053

Final League Position: 9

Honours
League Champions: Division II 1913-14, 1914-15, 1938-39. Second Division 2011-12. Third Division 2005-06. *Runners-up:* Division II 1921-22, 1923-24, 1969-70. Second Division 1991-92. Third Division 2000-01, 2008-09. *Promoted to First Division:* 2009-10 (play-offs).
Scottish Cup: Quarter-finals 1931.
League Cup: Semi-finals 1959-60, 1970-71.

Club colours: Shirt: Royal blue. Shorts: White. Socks: Red.

Goalscorers: *League (50):* Hemmings 18 (1 pen), Stewart G 11, Armstrong 4, Miller 3, Morton 3, McKeown 2, Milne 2, Stevenson 2, Adamson 1, O'Brien 1, Robertson 1, Stewart S 1, Wedderburn 1.
William Hill Scottish FA Cup (1): Stevenson 1.
Scottish Communities League Cup (6): Hemmings 4, Miller 1, Stewart G 1.
Ramsdens Cup (1): Wedderburn 1.
Championship Play-Offs (9): Stewart G 4, O'Brien 3, Hemmings 2.

Adam G 11	Brett D 31 + 1	Wedderburn N 33 + 1	Armstrong J 36	Adamson K 24 + 1	Russell A 4 + 8	O'Brien T 22 + 2	Miller K 14 + 10	McKenzie M 8 + 6	Morton J 7 + 17	Hemmings K 30 + 1	Stevenson J 21 + 6	Stewart G 27 + 6	Milne L 25 + 3	Flynn T 20 + 1	Robertson J 24 + 6	Cowan D 7	Anthony B — + 3	Gold D 3 + 2	Brownlie D 11	Fowler J 10	Kane C 7 + 3	McKeown R 12	Stewart S 4 + 2	Usai S 5	Johnston C — + 1	Match No.
1	2	3¹	4	5	6²	7*	8	9	10	11	12	13	14													1
1*	2	3¹	4	5	13	7		9	6²	11	8	10¹	12	14												2
	2	8	3	5	12	4		6	10²	11	9	13	7¹	1												3
1	2	7²	3	5	4	6	12	11	8¹	13	9	10														4
1	2	6²	3	5	10¹	4	7	12	11	13	8	9														5
1	2	8	3	5	4	10¹	13	11	7	12	6²	9														6
1	2	9	3	5	12	4	8¹	13	11	7	6²	10														7
	4	6	2	3		8	13	10¹	12	9	5²	11		1	7											8
	6	4	5	3	12	13		9¹	11²	8	10			1	7	2										9
	12	8	3	5	13	4	14	9	10	6¹	11³			1	7											10
	7	3	5	4	12	13	6²	11	9	10				1	8¹	2										11
	7	4	5	3	13	12	6²	11	8¹	10				1	9	2										12
	2	3	4	5	11¹		8²	13	12	6	10	9		1	7											13
1	2	3	4	5	10¹		8²	13	11	6	12	9			7											14
1	7	3²	5	12	9	13	11	8¹	10	6	4	2														15
1	6	4³	3	5	14	12	8	13	11	10¹	7	9²			2											16
1	6		4	5	14	3	10	13	9	12	11¹	7		8³	2²											17
1	2³	8	3	5	13	4¹	7	14	11	9	10²	6	12													18
	8	6	3	4		12	2	10	11¹	5²	7			1	9	13										19
	2	4	3	5	6	8¹	13	11	7					1	10	12	9²									20
	2		3	5	13	12	10	7¹	11	8²				1		14		9³	4	6						21
	2	8	3²	5		13	10³	11	9					1	6	14		4	7	12						22
	2	6	4	5	11		10		8					1	7			3	9							23
	2	7	3	5	11	12	10¹	6						1	9			4	8							24
	2	8	3			10¹	12	11	6²					1	9			4			7	13	5			25
	6	5	3			12	10	11						1	8			4			7	9¹	2			26
	2	8	3			12	10¹	11	6					1				4			7		5	9		27
	2	4	3			12	7²	11	9					1	10¹			5			8		6	13		28
	2¹	4	3			14	12	9²	10	7	11³		8		6			5			13				1	29
	2	4	3		7²	11	13		10		12	8	6¹								5	9	1			30
	5	4	3	2	7	11²		10¹	12	13		6									9	8			1	31
	2	6¹	3	4²	9	13		10	11	8	14	12³									5	7			1	32
	2	12	4	3	8³	13		11	14	10¹	6	7²		9							5					33
	5	4	3	13	8		11³	12	10	6	1		2¹		7	9²								14		34
	5²	4	3	2³	13		11		10	6	1	12		14	8	7¹	9									35
	5	4	3		8	13		11¹		10	7	1	12		2	6²	9									36

DUMBARTON

Year Formed: 1872. *Ground:* Bet Butler Stadium, Castle Road, Dumbarton G82 1JJ. *Telephone/Fax:* 01389 762569.
E-mail: enquiries@dumbartonfc.com *Website:* www.dumbartonfootballclub.com
Ground Capacity: total: 2,025. *Size of Pitch:* 104m × 69m.
Chairman: Alan Jardine. *Club Secretary:* David Prophet. *Chief Executive Officer:* Gilbert Lawrie.
Player-Manager: Ian Murray. *Assistant Manager:* Jack Ross. *Physio:* Ahmed Habib.
Club Nickname: 'The Sons', 'Sons of the Rock'.
Previous Grounds: Broadmeadow, Ropework Lane, Townend Ground, Boghead Park, Cliftonhill Stadium.
Record Attendance: 18,000 v Raith Rovers, Scottish Cup, 2 Mar 1957.
Record Transfer Fee received: £125,000 for Graeme Sharp to Everton (March 1982).
Record Transfer Fee paid: £50,000 for Charlie Gibson from Stirling Albion (1989).
Record Victory: 13-1 v Kirkintilloch Central, Scottish Cup 1st rd, 1 Sept 1888.
Record Defeat: 1-11 v Albion Rovers, Division II, 30 Jan 1926: v Ayr United, League Cup, 13 Aug 1952.
Most Capped Player: James McAulay, 9, Scotland.
Most League Appearances: 297: Andy Jardine, 1957-67.
Most Goals in Season (Individual): 38: Kenny Wilson, Division II, 1971-72. *(League and Cup):* 46 Hughie Gallacher, 1955-56.
Most Goals Overall (Individual): 202: Hughie Gallacher, 1954-62

DUMBARTON – SCOTTISH CHAMPIONSHIP 2013–14 LEAGUE RECORD

Match No.	Date	Venue	Opponents	Result		H/T Score	Lg Pos.	Goalscorers	Attendance
1	Aug 10	H	Falkirk	D	1-1	0-0	5	Prunty [84]	1224
2	17	A	Hamilton A	L	1-4	0-2	9	Agnew (pen) [67]	995
3	24	A	Greenock Morton	W	3-1	2-1	7	Megginson [18], Nish [42], McDougall [84]	1171
4	31	A	Cowdenbeath	L	2-3	0-1	7	Turner 2 [51, 64]	384
5	Sept 14	A	Alloa Ath	W	2-1	1-0	6	Graham [45], Agnew (pen) [71]	626
6	21	H	Livingston	L	1-2	1-0	7	Megginson [44]	759
7	28	A	Queen of the South	W	2-1	1-1	6	Turner [19], Fleming [87]	1693
8	Oct 5	H	Raith R	L	2-4	0-1	6	Prunty 2 (1 pen) [89, 90 (p)]	843
9	12	H	Dundee	L	1-4	0-0	6	Fleming [78]	1175
10	19	A	Falkirk	W	2-1	2-1	6	Fleming [7], Megginson [24]	2704
11	26	H	Cowdenbeath	D	0-0	0-0	7		700
12	Nov 9	A	Greenock Morton	L	0-2	0-0	7		1687
13	16	A	Livingston	W	3-1	1-1	6	Megginson [43], Turner (pen) [52], Prunty [74]	1039
14	Dec 4	H	Alloa Ath	D	1-1	0-1	6	Prunty [78]	463
15	7	A	Queen of the South	L	0-1	0-1	8		824
16	14	A	Raith R	L	1-2	0-0	8	McDougall [90]	1351
17	21	H	Hamilton A	W	2-1	1-1	7	Fleming [11], Graham [71]	642
18	28	A	Dundee	L	0-3	0-0	8		4489
19	Jan 4	H	Greenock Morton	W	2-0	1-0	7	Prunty (pen) [45], Kane [82]	1469
20	11	A	Cowdenbeath	W	4-2	2-2	7	Nish [4], Megginson 2 [22, 83], Kane [51]	434
21	18	A	Alloa Ath	W	5-1	3-0	4	McLaughlin [9], Turner [30], Kane 2 (1 pen) [42 (p), 76], Kirkpatrick [81]	602
22	Feb 1	A	Hamilton A	D	3-3	1-1	5	Kirkpatrick [27], Hendrie (og) [69], Kane [89]	1061
23	5	H	Livingston	D	2-2	0-0	5	Nish [72], Kane [90]	562
24	15	H	Falkirk	W	2-1	0-1	5	Megginson [63], Kirkpatrick [73]	1003
25	22	H	Raith R	D	3-3	2-1	4	Nish [24], Kane [37], Agnew [64]	786
26	Mar 1	A	Queen of the South	L	1-3	0-2	5	Miller [71]	1604
27	15	H	Cowdenbeath	W	5-1	1-0	5	Megginson [22], Miller [55], Kirkpatrick [73], Fleming [81], Kane [90]	687
28	22	H	Dundee	L	0-1	0-0	5		1222
29	25	A	Falkirk	L	0-2	0-1	6		2489
30	29	A	Livingston	W	2-1	0-1	6	Turner (pen) [86], Kane [88]	949
31	Apr 1	A	Greenock Morton	L	0-3	0-2	6		826
32	5	H	Alloa Ath	W	4-1	1-0	5	Gilhaney [25], Fleming [48], Agnew [80], Kane [83]	677
33	12	H	Raith R	W	3-1	2-0	5	Gilhaney [22], Megginson [28], Nish [50]	1602
34	19	H	Queen of the South	L	0-3	0-1	5		1263
35	26	H	Hamilton A	W	4-1	1-1	5	Agnew [32], Nish [77], Megginson [85], Kirkpatrick [87]	1420
36	May 3	A	Dundee	L	1-2	0-2	5	Agnew (pen) [69]	10,718

Final League Position: 5

Honours
League Champions: Division I 1890-91 (shared with Rangers), 1891-92. Division II 1910-11, 1971-72. Second Division 1991-92. Third Division 2008-09; *Runners-up:* First Division 1983-84. Division II 1907-08. Second Division 1994-95. Third Division 2001-02.
Scottish Cup Winners: 1883; *Runners-up:* 1881, 1882, 1887, 1891, 1897.

Club colours: Shirt: White with yellow and black horizontal stripe. Shorts: White. Socks: White.

Goalscorers: *League (65):* Kane 10 (1 pen), Megginson 10, Agnew 6 (3 pens), Fleming 6, Nish 6, Prunty 6 (2 pens), Turner 6 (2 pens), Kirkpatrick 5, Gilhaney 2, Graham 2, McDougall 2, Miller 2, McLaughlin 1, own goal 1.
William Hill Scottish FA Cup (6): Kirkpatrick 2, Prunty 1 (1 pen), Linton 1, Megginson 1, Nish 1.
Scottish Communities League Cup (3): Gilhaney 1, Megginson 1, Smith K 1.
Ramsdens Cup (2): Fleming 1, Smith K 1.

Ewings J 27	McGinn P 35	Graham A 36	Barry A 18	Smith S 5+1	Gilhaney M 31+3	Turner C 30	Agnew S 18+7	McDougall S 4+14	Fleming G 12+16	Smith K 3+7	Megginson M 32+4	Prunty B 13+17	Kirkpatrick J 24+8	Murray I 2	Nish C 23+10	Murray H 10+4	McKerracher A —+2	Linton S 29	Phinn N —+1	Grindlay S 9	McLaughlin M 13	Kane C 13+5	Miller M 9+3	Match No.
1	2	3	4	5	6	7	8	9¹	10²	11	12	13												1
1	2	3	4	5³	8	6	7		10¹	13	11²	9	14		12									2
1	2	3	4	5	9	6	8²	12	13		10¹	14		7	11³									3
1	2	3	4	5		6	8¹	11²		13	9	14			10³	7	12							4
1	2	3	4		6		7²	9		13	11²	10¹	14		12	8		5						5
1	2	4	3		6		8	9³		12	14	10	13		11	7¹		5²						6
1	2	3	4		6		7	9		12	10²	13	14		11¹	8³		5						7
1	2	3	4		8	6	7²		11¹	13	10	9	14		12			5¹						8
1	2	3	4	7³	6	8		12	14	9	11²	13			10⁴			5¹						9
1	2	3	4		6	8		9²	12	11¹	10	7					13	5						10
1	2	3	4		7	6		11²		10	9¹	8			12			5	13					11
1	2	3	4		7	9	13		14	10	12	8²			11	6¹		5¹						12
1	2	3	4	6²	7	12	14		10	13	9		11³	8¹				5						13
1	2	3	4		6	8		13		11²	10	9	7¹	12				5						14
1	2	3	4		6	7		14		11¹	10³	12	9²		13	8		5						15
1	2	3	4		7	9		14	13		12	11²	8¹		10	6³		5						16
1	2	3	4	14	6			13	8¹		11	10³	9		12	7²		5						17
1	2	3	4		6	7²		12		8¹	14	10³	11	9		13		5						18
	2	3			6	8		14			10²	7¹	9³		11	13		5		1	4	12		19
	2	3			6	7	12		13		9	14	8¹		11²			5		1	4	10³		20
	2	3			6³	8	13		12		10	14	7²		11¹			5		1	4	9		21
		3			6		7¹	14	12		9³	13	8		10²			5		1	4	11	2	22
	2	3			13	7¹	8³	6⁴			12	10²	9		14			5		1		11	4	23
	2	4			7		9	13			8¹		6		10²			5		1	3	11	12	24
	2	3			6		7		13		9²		8		10¹			5		1	4	11	12	25
1	2	3			7²		6	12	13		8¹		9³		10			5			4	11	14	26
	2	3			5	6	7²	14	13		9³		8		10¹	12			1			11	4	27
5	2				12	6²		13			9	14	7³		11		8¹			1	3	10	4	28
1	2	3			7	4²	9³	8			14		12		13	6⁴		5¹				11	10	29
1	2	3			12	5		9¹	13		7³	14	6		11²						4	10	8	30
1	2	3				5¹	8³		14		9	13	6		10²	12					4	11	7	31
1	2	3			7²		13	14	10³		8	9¹	6		11			5			4	12		32
1	2	3			6	8	12		7³		11		9²		10¹	14		5			4	13		33
1	2	3			6	7	12	14			9¹	13	8³		10			5²			4	11		34
1	2	3			7	6	9²		11¹		8	10³	13		12			5				14	4	35
1	2	4			6	3³	8		9¹		11²	13	14		10			5				12	7	36

DUNDEE

Year Formed: 1893. *Ground & Address:* Dens Park Stadium, Sandeman St, Dundee DD3 7JY. *Telephone:* 01382 889966.
Fax: 01382 832284. *E-mail:* laura@dundeefc.co.uk *Website:* www.dundeefc.co.uk
Ground Capacity: 11,850 (all seated). *Size of Pitch:* 101m × 66m.
Chairmain: Bill Covlin. *Chief Executive:* Scot Gardiner. *Club Secretary:* Laura Hayes.
Manager: Paul Hartley. *Assistant Manager:* Gerry McCabe. *Youth Development Coach:* Gordon Wallace.
Physio: Karen Gibson.
Club Nicknames: 'The Dark Blues' or 'The Dee'.
Previous Grounds: Carolina Port 1893-98.
Record Attendance: 43,024 v Rangers, Scottish Cup 2nd rd, 7 Feb 1953.
Record Transfer Fee received: £1,200,000 for Robert Douglas to Celtic (2000).
Record Transfer Fee paid: £600,000 for Fabian Caballero from Sol de América (Paraguay) (July 2000).
Record Victory: 10-0 Division II v Alloa, 9 Mar 1947 and v Dunfermline Ath, 22 Mar 1947.
Record Defeat: 0-11 v Celtic, Division I, 26 Oct 1895.
Most Capped Player: Alex Hamilton, 24, Scotland.
Most League Appearances: 400: Barry Smith, 1995-2006.
Most League Goals in Season (Individual): 52: Alan Gilzean, 1960-64.
Most Goals Overall (Individual): 113: Alan Gilzean 1960-64.

DUNDEE – SCOTTISH CHAMPIONSHIP 2013–14 LEAGUE RECORD

Match No.	Date	Venue	Opponents	Result	H/T Score	Lg Pos.	Goalscorers	Atten- dance
1	Aug 10	A	Queen of the South	L 3-4	1-1	7	MacDonald [7], Gallacher [80], Davidson [89]	2644
2	17	H	Alloa Ath	W 1-0	0-0	4	McBride (pen) [90]	4167
3	24	A	Raith R	D 0-0	0-0	4		2603
4	30	H	Livingston	W 3-0	1-0	3	Monti (pen) [33], Gallacher [58], MacDonald [83]	3955
5	Sept 14	H	Hamilton A	D 0-0	0-0	2		4155
6	21	A	Falkirk	L 1-3	0-1	4	Conroy [74]	3349
7	28	A	Greenock Morton	W 3-1	0-1	4	MacDonald 2 [47, 50], Beattie [71]	3870
8	Oct 5	A	Cowdenbeath	W 2-0	1-0	4	Beattie [36], Conroy [82]	1013
9	12	A	Dumbarton	W 4-1	0-0	2	MacDonald 2 (1 pen) [49, 71 (p)], Conroy [68], Rae [88]	1175
10	19	H	Queen of the South	W 2-1	0-0	2	MacDonald [78], Beattie [89]	4357
11	26	A	Livingston	L 1-2	0-0	2	MacDonald [54]	1597
12	Nov 9	H	Raith R	W 2-0	1-0	2	Conroy [28], Wighton [49]	5064
13	16	H	Falkirk	D 1-1	1-0	2	Conroy (pen) [24]	4661
14	23	A	Hamilton A	W 3-0	1-0	2	Davidson [16], Gallacher [57], MacDonald [90]	2077
15	Dec 7	H	Greenock Morton	W 2-1	2-0	1	Beattie [17], Gallacher [45]	1536
16	14	H	Cowdenbeath	L 1-2	0-0	2	McAlister [66]	3533
17	21	A	Alloa Ath	W 1-0	0-0	1	MacDonald [68]	1170
18	28	H	Dumbarton	W 3-0	0-0	1	MacDonald 2 [47, 90], McBride [82]	4489
19	Jan 2	A	Raith R	W 2-0	0-0	1	McAlister 2 [90, 90]	4039
20	11	H	Livingston	L 0-1	0-1	1		4367
21	25	A	Falkirk	L 0-2	0-1	2		4183
22	Feb 1	H	Alloa Ath	D 1-1	0-0	2	Conroy (pen) [69]	4021
23	8	H	Hamilton A	W 1-0	1-0	2	Boyle [6]	5206
24	15	A	Queen of the South	W 1-0	1-0	2	Conroy (pen) [45]	2152
25	22	A	Cowdenbeath	L 0-2	0-1	1		1419
26	Mar 1	H	Greenock Morton	W 2-0	1-0	1	Nade [13], MacDonald [86]	4488
27	15	A	Livingston	W 2-0	1-0	1	MacDonald [8], Benedictus [55]	1759
28	18	H	Raith R	D 0-0	0-0	1		4561
29	22	A	Dumbarton	W 1-0	0-0	1	MacDonald [83]	1222
30	25	H	Queen of the South	W 1-0	0-0	1	Davidson [58]	3999
31	29	H	Falkirk	L 0-1	0-1	2		4919
32	Apr 5	A	Hamilton A	D 1-1	1-0	2	Boyle [37]	4529
33	12	H	Cowdenbeath	W 4-0	2-0	1	Wighton [6], Boyle 2 [45, 66], McAlister [60]	4751
34	19	A	Greenock Morton	L 0-1	0-0	2		2117
35	26	A	Alloa Ath	W 3-0	1-0	1	Nade [42], MacDonald (pen) [71], Beattie [88]	2552
36	May 3	H	Dumbarton	W 2-1	2-0	1	Nade [25], MacDonald [36]	10,718

Final League Position: 1

Honours

League Champions: Division I 1961-62. First Division 1978-79, 1991-92, 1997-98. Division II 1946-47; Championship 2013-14.
Runners-up: Division I 1902-03, 1906-07, 1908-09, 1948-49. First Division 1980-81, 2007-08, 2009-10, 2011-12.
Scottish Cup Winners: 1910; *Runners-up:* 1925, 1952, 1964, 2003.
League Cup Winners: 1951-52, 1952-53, 1973-74; *Runners-up:* 1967-68, 1980-81, 1995-96.
League Challenge Cup Winners: 1990-91, 2009-10.
B&Q (Centenary) Cup Winners: 1990-91; *Runners-up:* 1994-95.

European: European Cup: 8 matches (1962-63 semi-finals). *Cup Winners' Cup:* 2 matches: (1964-65).
UEFA Cup: 22 matches: (*Fairs Cup:* 1967-68 semi-finals. *UEFA Cup:* 1971-72, 1973-74, 1974-75, 2003-04).

Club colours: Shirt: Navy blue. Shorts: White. Socks: Navy blue.

Goalscorers: *League (54):* MacDonald 17 (2 pens), Conroy 7 (3 pens), Beattie 5, Boyle 4, Gallacher 4, McAlister 4, Davidson 3, Nade 3, McBride 2 (1 pen), Wighton 2, Benedictus 1, Monti 1 (1 pen), Rae 1.
William Hill Scottish FA Cup (0).
Scottish Communities League Cup (2): MacDonald 1, McAlister 1.
Ramsdens Cup (5): MacDonald 3 (1 pen), Monti 1 (1 pen), McBride 1.

Letheren K 35	Gallacher D 36	Davidson J 25 + 1	Benedictus K 15 + 2	Lockwood M 17	Rae G 34 + 2	McBride K 19 + 6	Conroy R 20 + 12	McAlister J 36	Monti C 7 + 7	MacDonald P 33 + 2	Doris S 2 + 10	Boyle M 18 + 11	Irvine G 33	Reid J — + 4	Dyer W 21	Riley N 18 + 9	Beattie C 8 + 10	Wighton C 7 + 6	McIntosh L — + 2	O'Donnell S — + 1	Gibson J — + 1	Kerr C 2 + 1	Hughes S 1	Nade C 6 + 7	Twardzik D 1 + 1	Cummins A 2 + 1	Match No.
1	2	3	4	5^2	6	7	8	9	10^1	11	12	13															1
1	2	3	4		7	6	8^1	9	11^3	10^2	13	12	5	14													2
1	3		4		8	7	9^1	6	11^3	10^2	12	13	2	14	5												3
1	3	13	4		8	7^1	9^2	6	11^3	10			2	14	5	12											4
1	5	4	3		8	7^1	14	9		10	13		2		6^3	12	11^2										5
1	3	4			8		9	7	10^3	12	11^1	14	2			5	6^3	13									6
1	3	4			8	13	9	7	12	10^1	14		2			5	6^3	11^2									7
1	3	4		5	8	13	9	7		11^2	14		2			6^1	10^3	12									8
1	4	3		5	7		9	8		10^1	13		2	14		6^1	11^2	12									9
1	4	3		5	7		9	8		10	14	13	2			6^3	12	11^2									10
1	8				3	7	4	5	9		10	12	13			2	6^1	11^2									11
1	3	4		5^2	7	13	9	8		10^1			2			6^3	14	11^1									12
1	4	3		5	7	12	9	8	13	10			2			6^2		11^1									13
1	4	3		5	7	13	9	8		10^1			2			6^3	14	11^2									14
1	4	3		5	7	12	9^1	8		10			13		2	6		11^2									15
1	3	4			5	7	9^1	8	14	10^3			2			6	11^2		13								16
1	4	3^4	14		5	8	7^2	12	9	13	10^1	11^3				6											17
1	3		4		5	7	8^1	12	9	13	11		10^1			6^2					14						18
1	4		3		5	8	7	9	6	10			11^2						13		12						19
1	3	4		5	8^2	9	6	13		11^1			2						10^2	12		14					20
1	3	6	4	5^2	13			9	10	14			2	7						8^3	11^1	12					21
	4	3			8	7	12	9	10^1	11^3			6^2		2	5					14			13	1		22
	4	3			8	7^1	9	6		10			11		2	5					12			13			23
1	3		4		6	7	10^2	9	12	11^1			8		2	5								13			24
1	3		4		7	6^1	10	9^2		11^3			8		2	5	14							13			25
1	4	12	3		6^2	7		8		9			10		2	5	13							11^1			26
1	3	7	4		8		14	9		10^3	12	6^2	2			5	13							11^1			27
1	4	8	3		7		12	9		10	11^2	6^1	2			5	13										28
1	3	7	4		12	6^2	10^1	9		13			2			5	8	14						11^3			29
1	4	7			6		13	9		11^1			8		2	5	10^2							12		3	30
1	3	8			7^3		12	6^2		10			9		2	5	14	11^1						13		4	31
1	4	3^3			6	7	14	10		11^2			8		2	5	9^1	13								12	32
1	3	4			7		13	8		11^3			9			5	6^1	14	10^2			2		12			33
1	3	4			7		8	11		6			9			5	13	10^2			2^1			12			34
1	3	4			7	8^2	13	6^3		11			9	2		5	14	12						10^1			35
1	3		4		7	8	12	9		11^2			6^2	2		5	13	14						10^1			36

DUNDEE UNITED

Year Formed: 1909 (1923). *Ground & Address:* Tannadice Park, Tannadice St, Dundee DD3 7JW. *Telephone:* 01382 833166. *Fax:* 01382 889398. *E-mail:* enquiries@dundeeunited.co.uk *Website:* www.dundeeunitedfc.co.uk
Ground Capacity: 14,223 (all seated). *Size of Pitch:* 100m × 66m.
Chairman: Stephen Thompson, OBE. *Vice-Chair:* Justine Mitchell. *Secretary:* Spence Anderson.
Manager: Jackie McNamara. *Assistant Manager:* Simon Donnelly. *First Team Coach:* Darren Jackson. *Physio:* Jeff Clarke.
Club Nicknames: 'The Terrors', 'The Arabs'.
Previous Grounds: None.
Record Attendance: 28,000 v Barcelona, Fairs Cup, 16 Nov 1966.
Record Transfer Fee received: £4,000,000 for Duncan Ferguson from Rangers (July 1993).
Record Transfer Fee paid: £750,000 for Steven Pressley from Coventry C (July 1995).
Record Victory: 14-0 v Nithsdale Wanderers, Scottish Cup 1st rd, 17 Jan 1931.
Record Defeat: 1-12 v Motherwell, Division II, 23 Jan 1954.
Most Capped Player: Maurice Malpas, 55, Scotland.
Most League Appearances: 618, Maurice Malpas, 1980-2000.
Most Appearances in European Matches: 76, Dave Narey (record for Scottish player).
Most League Goals in Season (Individual): 40: John Coyle, Division II, 1955-56.
Most Goals Overall (Individual): 199: Peter McKay, 1947-54.

DUNDEE UNITED – SCOTTISH PREMIER LEAGUE 2013–14 LEAGUE RECORD

Match No.	Date		Venue	Opponents	Result	H/T Score	Lg Pos.	Goalscorers	Attendance
1	Aug	2	A	Partick Thistle	D	0-0	0-0	1		7822
2		10	H	Inverness CT	L	0-1	0-1	7		6664
3		17	H	Hibernian	D	1-1	1-0	8	Armstrong [29]	9171
4		24	H	St Johnstone	W	4-0	3-0	6	Watson [4], Goodwillie [25], Mackay-Steven [40], Armstrong [53]	6992
5		31	H	Celtic	L	0-1	0-0	7		10,586
6	Sept	15	A	Ross Co	W	4-2	3-0	5	Mackay-Steven (pen) [18], Armstrong [20], Gauld [40], Ciftci [65]	3005
7		22	H	Motherwell	D	2-2	0-1	6	Ciftci [54], Robertson [57]	5808
8		28	A	Hearts	D	0-0	0-0	6		13,970
9	Oct	5	H	Kilmarnock	W	1-0	0-0	6	Ciftci [56]	5850
10		19	A	Aberdeen	L	0-1	0-0	6		12,654
11		26	H	St Mirren	W	4-0	2-0	5	Ciftci 2 (1 pen) [27, 34 (p)], Gauld [59], Erskine [83]	6331
12	Nov	2	A	Celtic	D	1-1	1-0	6	Armstrong [38]	47,386
13		9	A	Motherwell	W	4-0	2-0	6	Gauld 2 [16, 64], Paton [19], Robertson [90]	5103
14		23	H	Partick Thistle	W	4-1	1-0	4	Mackay-Steven 2 [2, 77], Robertson [70], Graham [85]	6700
15	Dec	7	H	Hearts	W	4-1	1-1	3	Armstrong [16], Graham [49], Mackay-Steven [85], Rankin [90]	7808
16		14	A	Kilmarnock	W	4-1	0-0	3	Watson [60], Armstrong [75], Gauld [77], Goodwillie [90]	3452
17		21	H	Ross Co	W	1-0	0-0	2	Mackay-Steven [69]	8029
18		26	A	St Mirren	L	1-4	1-2	4	Ciftci [36]	4780
19		29	A	St Johnstone	L	0-3	0-1	5		7231
20	Jan	1	A	Aberdeen	L	1-2	0-0	5	Souttar [51]	12,601
21		5	H	Hibernian	D	2-2	0-1	4	Goodwillie [83], Graham [90]	7862
22		12	A	Inverness CT	D	1-1	1-1	4	Watson [10]	2980
23		18	A	Ross Co	L	0-3	0-1	5		3609
24	Feb	1	H	Partick Thistle	D	1-1	1-0	5	El Alagui [29]	3748
25		15	H	Kilmarnock	W	3-2	1-1	4	Mackay-Steven [10], Good [65], Rankin [71]	6038
26		21	H	Motherwell	W	3-1	2-0	4	Dow [22], Gunning 2 [42, 47]	7029
27		28	A	Hibernian	W	3-1	1-1	4	Ciftci [43], Gunning [56], El Alagui [83]	9608
28	Mar	12	A	St Johnstone	L	0-1	0-0	5		6720
29		15	H	St Mirren	W	3-2	0-2	4	Graham [79], Armstrong [84], Ciftci [90]	6524
30		21	A	Hearts	W	2-1	1-0	4	Graham [35], Ciftci [70]	13,448
31		26	H	Inverness CT	W	2-1	0-0	4	Gauld [49], Dow [76]	6754
32		29	A	Aberdeen	D	1-1	1-0	4	Paton [6]	14,627
33	Apr	5	A	Celtic	L	0-2	0-2	4		11,033
34		19	A	St Johnstone	L	0-2	0-1	4		5223
35		26	H	Motherwell	W	5-1	2-0	4	Ciftci 2 [8, 41], Armstrong [61], Dow [72], Graham [81]	6383
36	May	3	A	Inverness CT	D	1-1	0-1	4	El Alagui [71]	3428
37		6	H	Aberdeen	L	1-3	1-1	4	Dillon [34]	8677
38		11	A	Celtic	L	1-3	0-0	4	Twardzik (og) [79]	52,400

Final League Position: 4

Honours
League Champions: Premier Division 1982-83.
Division II 1924-25, 1928-29.
Runners-up: Division II 1930-31, 1959-60. First Division 1995-96.
Scottish Cup Winners: 1994, 2010; *Runners-up:* 1974, 1981, 1985, 1987, 1988, 1991, 2005, 2014.
League Cup Winners: 1979-80, 1980-81; *Runners-up:* 1981-82, 1984-85, 1997-98, 2007-08.
League Challenge Cup Runners-up: 1995-96.

European: *European Cup:* 8 matches (1983-84, semi-finals). *Cup Winners' Cup:* 10 matches (1974-75, 1988-89, 1994-95).
UEFA Cup: 86 matches (*Fairs Cup:* 1966-67, 1969-70, 1970-71. *UEFA Cup:* 1975-76, 1977-78, 1978-79, 1979-80, 1980-81, 1981-82, 1982-83, 1984-85, 1985-86, 1986-87 runners-up, 1987-88, 1989-90, 1990-91, 1993-94, 1997-98, 2005-06). *Europa League:* 6 matches (2010-2011, 2011-12, 2012-13).

Club colours: Shirt: Tangerine with black trim. Shorts: Black. Socks: Tangerine with black hoop.

Goalscorers: *League (65):* Ciftci 11 (1 pen), Armstrong 8, Mackay-Steven 7 (1 pen), Gauld 6, Graham 6, Dow 3, El Alagui 3, Goodwillie 3, Gunning 3, Robertson 3, Watson 3, Paton 2, Rankin 2, Dillon 1, Erskine 1, Good 1, Souttar 1, own goal 1.
William Hill Scottish FA Cup (14): Ciftci 4, Armstrong 3, Mackay-Steven 2, Robertson 2, Graham 1 (1 pen), Gunning 1 (1 pen), Gauld 1.
Scottish Communities League Cup (8): Goodwillie 3, Ciftci 2, Dow 1, Gauld 1, Watson 1.

Cierzniak R 37	Watson K 24 + 1	Robertson A 36	Paton P 36 + 1	Dillon S 22 + 1	Butcher C 6	Dow R 16 + 10	Armstrong S 32 + 4	Goodwillie D 9 + 10	Gauld R 21 + 10	Mackay-Steven G 27 + 8	Erskine C 4 + 4	Graham B 11 + 19	Rankin J 35	Gunning G 26 + 1	Souttar J 21 + 1	Oyenuga K — +1	Wilson M 14	Gomis M 5 + 11	El Alagui F 4 + 9	Good C 4	Connolly A — +2	Smith S — +2	McCallum M 1	Fraser S — +1	Match No.
1	2	3	4	5	6	7³	8	9	10¹	11²	12	13	14												1
1	2	3	8	5	4	13	6	11³	14		9	10²	12	7¹											2
1		5	6	3	4	10	7²	11³		13	8¹	14	12	9	2⁸										3
1	2	5	7	4	3	8²	6¹	11³	12	13	10	14		9											4
1	2	5	7	4		9	10¹	11	12	6			8	3											5
1	2	5	6	3		12	9¹	13	10²	11³	8		14	7		4									6
1	2	5	6	3		8³	9	12	11²	10¹			13	7		4	14								7
1	2	5	3			9	11	10	6¹	12			7		8										8
1	2³	5	7	4		14	8²	11	10¹	9	13			6	12	3									9
1	2	5	7	3		14	9¹	11³	8	10²	12		13	6	4										10
1		5	7³			14		10¹	9²	6	13	11	8	4	3		2	12							11
1		5	12			14	10	13	9		8²		11¹	6	4	3	2	7³							12
1		5	9				8³	13	11¹	6²	10		12	7	4	3	2	14							13
1		5	7²				8³	13	11¹	9	10		14	6	4	3	2	12							14
1	13	5¹	6	3			9	12		8	10		11³	7		4	2²	14							15
1	2	5	6				9	14	12	8²	10¹		11³	7	4	3		13							16
1		5	6				10	12	13	9¹	8		11²	7	4	3	2								17
1	2⁸	5	6				10¹	12	11	9²	8		13	7	4	3									18
1		5	6	4	3⁸	10¹	13	9²			14		8³	11			12		2	7					19
1		5	7¹			10		11	9²	8			12	6	4	3		2	13						20
1		5	7	13		10	14	11²	9³	8			12	6	4	3	2¹								21
1	2	5	7			9²			13	10	8	11¹	6	4	3			12							22
1	2	5	6	4	3		13		12	10	8¹		7					9²	11						23
1		5	6			14	8¹		9³	13	10		12	7		3	2	11²	4						24
1	2	5	6			12	8³		11¹	10²	9		7		4		14	13	3						25
1	2	5	6			10¹	9²		11	8			7	3			12	4	13						26
1	2	5	7			10	9¹		11³		8²		13	6	3		14	12	4						27
1	2	5	6	3⁸		9²	8¹		11	12	10		14	7	4			13							28
1	2	5	6¹			12	13		11	9³	8		14	7	4			10³							29
1		5	7	3		9	6³		11²	12			10¹	8	4		2	13			14				30
1		5	7	3		8	10³		11²	9¹	12		13	6	4		2	14							31
1	2		7	3		6	9²			12	10¹		11	8	5	4		13							32
1	2	5	6	3		9¹	10		8³	13	12		11²	7	4				14						33
1	2	5	6			12	10		11	9²	8¹		13	7	3	4									34
1	2	5	6¹	3		10	9³		11²	13	8		12	7	4		14								35
1	2	5	6	3		10²			11	8¹	9³		12	7	4				13		14				36
	5		2			9¹	6	11					10		4	3		7⁸	8	12		13	1		37
1	3		6	5		9¹	13		10³	12			7²	4		2	8	11						14	38

DUNFERMLINE ATHLETIC

Year Formed: 1885. *Ground & Address:* East End Park, Halbeath Road, Dunfermline KY12 7RB.
Telephone: 01383 724295. *Fax:* 01383 745 959. *E-mail:* enquiries@dafc.co.uk
Website: www.dafc.co.uk
Ground Capacity: 11,380 (all seated). *Size of Pitch:* 105m × 65m.
Chairman: Bob Garmony. *Football matters:* Craig McWhirter.
Manager: Jim Jefferies. *First Team Coach:* Neil McCann. *Physio:* Kenny Murray.
Club Nickname: 'The Pars'.
Previous Grounds: None.
Record Attendance: 27,816 v Celtic, Division I, 30 Apr 1968.
Record Transfer Fee received: £650,000 for Jackie McNamara to Celtic (Oct 1995).
Record Transfer Fee paid: £540,000 for Istvan Kozma from Bordeaux (Sept 1989).
Record Victory: 11-2 v Stenhousemuir, Division II, 27 Sept 1930.
Record Defeat: 1-13 v St. Bernard's, Scottish Cup, 1st rd; 15 Sept 1883.
Most Capped Player: Colin Miller 16 (61), Canada.
Most League Appearances: 497: Norrie McCathie, 1981-96.
Most League Goals in Season (Individual): 53: Bobby Skinner, Division II, 1925-26.
Most Goals Overall (Individual): 212: Charles Dickson, 1954-64.

DUNFERMLINE ATHLETIC – SCOTTISH LEAGUE ONE 2013–14 LEAGUE RECORD

Match No.	Date	Venue	Opponents	Result	H/T Score	Lg Pos.	Goalscorers	Atten-dance
1	Aug 10	A	East Fife	W 1-0	1-0	3	Wallace (pen) [2]	1927
2	17	H	Arbroath	L 2-3	2-3	4	Morris [27], Byrne [41]	3242
3	24	A	Stenhousemuir	W 5-4	0-2	3	Moore 2 (1 pen) [57, 86 (p)], Geggan 2 [63, 89], Smith [84]	968
4	31	H	Stranraer	W 3-1	1-1	2	Geggan [24], Johnston [82], Smith [86]	2585
5	Sept 14	A	Brechin C	D 1-1	1-0	2	Thomson, Robert [39]	923
6	21	H	Airdrieonians	W 2-1	0-0	2	Husband [56], Geggan [86]	2607
7	28	H	Ayr U	W 5-1	4-1	2	Wallace 2 (1 pen) [21 (p), 65], Whittle [31], Geggan [39], Falkingham [41]	2743
8	Oct 5	A	Forfar Ath	L 0-4	0-2	2		968
9	19	H	East Fife	L 1-2	1-0	4	Moore [42]	3131
10	26	A	Stranraer	W 2-1	0-1	3	Husband [49], Falkingham [70]	622
11	Nov 6	A	Rangers	L 1-3	0-0	3	Falkingham [81]	43,082
12	9	H	Stenhousemuir	W 3-2	1-1	2	Byrne [37], Wallace (pen) [67], Smith [90]	2517
13	16	A	Airdrieonians	W 3-0	1-0	2	Byrne [17], Smith [69], Dargo [90]	1219
14	23	H	Brechin C	W 3-1	2-0	2	Wallace 2 [3, 87], Moyes (og) [22]	2569
15	Dec 7	H	Forfar Ath	D 1-1	0-1	2	Moore [90]	2469
16	14	A	Ayr U	W 4-2	1-2	2	Husband [44], Wallace 2 (1 pen) [60 (p), 69], Moore [90]	643
17	21	A	Arbroath	W 3-0	2-0	2	Geggan [12], Thomson, Ryan [36], Falkingham [65]	967
18	30	H	Rangers	L 0-4	0-1	2		10,089
19	Jan 2	A	Stenhousemuir	W 2-1	1-0	2	El Bakhtaoui [14], Geggan [90]	1556
20	11	A	Stranraer	W 3-2	1-1	2	Thomson, Ryan [34], Byrne [58], Shankland [75]	2952
21	18	A	Airdrieonians	L 0-1	0-1	2		2711
22	25	A	Brechin C	L 2-3	1-0	2	Shankland [31], Wallace [54]	854
23	Feb 1	A	East Fife	W 3-1	1-0	2	Forbes [44], Wallace [75], Grainger [77]	1872
24	15	A	Forfar Ath	W 4-2	1-1	2	El Bakhtaoui [4], Husband [69], Dods (og) [71], Shankland [89]	833
25	22	H	Ayr U	W 3-0	2-0	2	Forbes [8], Shankland 2 [45, 78]	2773
26	25	A	Arbroath	W 3-0	1-0	2	Husband [27], Forbes [60], Falkingham [72]	1983
27	Mar 1	A	Stranraer	L 1-3	0-2	2	Grainger (pen) [78]	704
28	8	H	Stenhousemuir	D 0-0	0-0	2		2510
29	15	A	Rangers	L 0-2	0-1	2		44,110
30	22	H	East Fife	L 1-2	1-0	2	Shankland [22]	2858
31	29	H	Brechin C	W 2-1	0-0	2	Shankland [48], Millen (pen) [90]	2241
32	Apr 5	A	Airdrieonians	L 0-2	0-1	2		1142
33	12	H	Forfar Ath	D 0-0	0-0	2		2364
34	19	A	Ayr U	D 1-1	1-0	2	Thomson, Ryan [50]	1272
35	26	A	Arbroath	W 2-1	1-0	2	Thomson, Ryan [14], Geggan [79]	1079
36	May 3	H	Rangers	D 1-1	0-0	2	Martin [71]	7605

Final League Position: 2

Honours
League Champions: First Division 1988-89, 1995-96, 2010-11. Division II 1925-26. Second Division 1985-86;
Runners-up: First Division 1986-87, 1993-94, 1994-95, 1999-2000. Division II 1912-13, 1933-34, 1954-55, 1957-58, 1972-73.
Second Division 1978-79. League One 2013-14.
Scottish Cup Winners: 1961, 1968; *Runners-up:* 1965, 2004, 2007.
League Cup Runners-up: 1949-50, 1991-92, 2005-06.
League Challenge Cup Runners-up: 2007-08.

European: *Cup Winners' Cup:* 14 matches (1961-62, 1968-69 semi-finals). *UEFA Cup:* 32 matches (*Fairs Cup:* 1962-63, 1964-65, 1965-66, 1966-67, 1969-70. *UEFA Cup:* 2004-05, 2007-08).

Club colours: Shirt: Black and white stripes. Shorts: White. Socks: White.

Goalscorers: *League (68):* Wallace 10 (4 pens), Geggan 8, Shankland 7, Falkingham 5, Husband 5, Moore 5 (1 pen), Byrne 4, Smith 4, Thomson, Ryan 4, Forbes 3, El Bakhtaoui 2, Grainger 2 (1 pen), Dargo 1, Johnston 1, Martin 1, Millen 1 (1 pen), Morris 1, Thomson, Robert 1, Whittle 1, own goals 2.
William Hill Scottish FA Cup (7): Moore 2 (1 pen), Wallace 2, Geggan 1, Thomson Ryan 1, Whittle 1.
Scottish Communities League Cup (3): Wallace 1 (1 pen), Dargo 1, Moore 1.
Ramsdens Cup (3): Ferguson 1, Morris 1, Thomson Ryan 1.
Championship Play-Offs (5): Geggan 3, El Bakhtaoul 2.

Scully R 34	Millen R 22	Young K 17+1	Morris C 27+1	Whittle A 27+3	Ferguson R 1+7	Geggan A 32+1	Kane C 2+1	Byrne S 25+6	Wallace R 23+4	Thomson Ryan 14+10	Falkingham J 28+2	Dargo C 2+6	Moore J 9+7	Williamson R 15+3	Husband S 22+9	Smith A 7+15	Johnston L 5	Thomson Robert 7+2	El Bakhtaoui F 12+2	Goodfellow R 2+2	Martin L 13	Spence L 2+4	Drummond R 1+1	Shankland L 11+2	O'Kane D —+1	Page J 12+1	Grainger D 11	Forbes R 11+2	Potter J 1	Graham F 1	Mercer S —+1	Match No.
1	2	3	4	5	6^2	7	8	9^1	10	11	12	13																				1
1	2^3	3	4	5	13	8	7^1	6^2	10	11^1	9			12	14																	2
1	2	3	4	5		6		9^1	12	7^1	8		11^2	10		13	14															3
1	2		4	5		6	14	9^1	13	8	10^1			7	12	3	11^2															4
1	2		4	5	14	6		9^1	13	8	11^3			7^2	12	3	10															5
1	2		4	5		9	8^2	13	14	6	11^3			7	12	3	10^1															6
1	2	12	4	5^2		8^3		6	10	14	9			7^1		3	11	13														7
1	2		4	5		6^1	10	12	8	14				7^3	13	3	11^2															8
1	2	3	4	5^2	14	8		6	10^3	12	9			11^1		7		13														9
1	2	3	4	5	14	8		6^1	10^2	11^3	9			7	12			13														10
1	2	3	4	5		8		6	9^2		7			11^8		13	12		10^1													11
1	2	3	4	5	12	6		11		8	13			7^1	10			9^2														12
1^1	2	3	4	5	14	6		11^3		8	13	10^2		9							12											13
1		3	4	5	13	7		6	11	10^1	8	12				2		9^2														14
1		3	4	5		7		6^1	9	11^3	8	13	12		2	14	10^2															15
1			4	5		7		6	11	9	10		12		2	8^1						3										16
1		4		5		7		6^1	10^2	11	9		12		2	8			13		3											17
1		3		5		6		7^2	10		9			11	2^1	8	12				4	13										18
1		3		5^1		8	14	6	10					11^3	2	7^2	13		9		4		12									19
1		3				7		6	10^2	11^1	8				2	13			9^8		4		5	12								20
1		4^1		5		6		7^2	9		8			13	2	12	10^3				3			11	14							21
1		4		5		7		6^3	10	14	9			13	2	8^2					3	12		11^1								22
1	6							7^2	10	9^5	12				2	13					3			11		4	5	8				23
1		4				6^1			10^2	8					5	12		11		3				13		2	9	7				24
1	2		4	14		7		13	12	9					6^1			11^2						10		3	5	8^3				25
1	2^2		4			7		13			9	14		12	6			10^1						11		3	5	8^3				26
1			4	12		7				13	9^1			2	6			10^2						11		3	5	8				27
1	2^2		4			9		6	13					14	8	12		10^1						11^1		3	5	7				28
1^2	2	3	8^3			7		13						6	14			10^1	12					11		4	5^8	9				29
1		3	5			7		6	9^2	14				2	8	12							13	10^1		4		11^3				30
1	2	3	8			7				9^2	6^1			14	12			10	5^3					11		4		13				31
1	2		4	12		7					6^2			8	13			10^1						11		3	5	9				32
1		12	9		6			13	11	8				2	7^1	10^2						4				3		5^3	14			33
	2	4		6^1		13		8	11						12			10	1	3	7^2							5	9			34
1	2		4		8			13	14	11	7			10^3				9^2					12			3	5	6^1				35
	3		6			8				11^3		2	12	10			1	5	9					13				4^1		7^2	14	36

EAST FIFE

Year Formed: 1903. *Ground & Address:* Bayview Stadium, Harbour View, Methil, Fife KY8 3RW. *Telephone:* 01333 426323. *Fax:* 01333 426376. *E-mail:* office@eastfife.org. *Website:* www.eastfifefc.info
Ground Capacity: 1,992. *Size of Pitch:* 105m × 65m.
Chairman: Lee Murray. *Vice-Chairman:* David Hamilton. *Secretary:* Jim Stevenson.
Manager: Gary Naysmith. *Coach:* Douglas Anderson. *Physio:* Brian McNeill.
Club Nickname: 'The Fifers'.
Previous Ground: Bayview Park.
Record Attendance: 22,515 v Raith Rovers, Division I, 2 Jan 1950 (Bayview Park); 4,700 v Rangers, League One, 26 Oct 2013 (Bayview Stadium).
Record Transfer Fee received: £150,000 for Paul Hunter from Hull C (March 1990).
Record Transfer Fee paid: £70,000 for John Sludden from Kilmarnock (July 1991).
Record Victory: 13-2 v Edinburgh City, Division II, 11 Dec 1937.
Record Defeat: 0-9 v Hearts, Division I, 5 Oct 1957.
Most Capped Player: George Aitken, 5 (8), Scotland.
Most League Appearances: 517: David Clarke, 1968-86.
Most League Goals in Season (Individual): 41: Jock Wood, Division II; 1926-27 and Henry Morris, Division II, 1947-48.
Most Goals Overall (Individual): 225: Phil Weir, 1922-35.

EAST FIFE – SCOTTISH LEAGUE ONE 2013–14 LEAGUE RECORD

Match No.	Date	Venue	Opponents	Result	H/T Score	Lg Pos.	Goalscorers	Attendance
1	Aug 10	H	Dunfermline Ath	L 0-1	0-1	7		1927
2	17	A	Brechin C	L 0-2	0-0	9		543
3	24	A	Arbroath	W 2-1	2-1	6	Durie [10], Buchanan (pen) [31]	809
4	31	A	Rangers	L 0-5	0-3	7		42,870
5	Sept 14	H	Forfar Ath	L 1-3	1-1	9	Durie [36]	796
6	21	A	Stranraer	L 0-2	0-1	10		349
7	28	H	Airdrieonians	W 1-0	1-0	7	McBride [12]	665
8	Oct 5	A	Stenhousemuir	D 1-1	1-1	10	Johnstone [45]	567
9	12	H	Ayr U	L 1-4	1-2	10	Buchanan (pen) [43]	753
10	19	A	Dunfermline Ath	W 2-1	0-1	8	Brown [81], Buchanan [84]	3131
11	26	H	Rangers	L 0-4	0-0	9		4700
12	Nov 9	A	Arbroath	D 2-2	0-0	9	Buchanan 2 [71, 76]	603
13	16	H	Stranraer	L 1-2	1-1	9	Buchanan [42]	713
14	23	A	Forfar Ath	L 0-2	0-0	9		556
15	Dec 7	H	Stenhousemuir	W 1-0	1-0	7	Fisher [40]	561
16	14	A	Airdrieonians	W 3-1	1-1	7	Buchanan (og) [43], Brown [70], Hughes [76]	624
17	21	H	Brechin C	L 1-3	0-1	8	Stewart, R [71]	745
18	28	A	Ayr U	L 0-2	0-1	8		1059
19	Jan 2	H	Arbroath	W 1-0	1-0	7	Austin [27]	910
20	11	A	Rangers	L 0-2	0-1	8		42,182
21	25	H	Forfar Ath	W 2-1	0-1	8	McKenzie [48], O'Neill [73]	685
22	Feb 1	H	Dunfermline Ath	L 1-3	0-1	8	Willis [78]	1872
23	8	A	Brechin C	L 0-3	0-2	8		523
24	15	A	Stenhousemuir	D 1-1	0-0	8	Buchanan [46]	465
25	22	H	Airdrieonians	D 0-0	0-0	8		815
26	Mar 1	H	Rangers	L 0-1	0-0	9		4020
27	4	A	Stranraer	L 0-2	0-1	9		407
28	8	A	Arbroath	L 1-2	1-1	9	Buchanan [17]	679
29	15	H	Ayr U	L 0-5	0-3	9		647
30	22	A	Dunfermline Ath	W 2-1	0-1	9	Buchanan (pen) [56], Austin [82]	2858
31	29	A	Forfar Ath	W 2-1	2-1	9	Buchanan [35], Austin [45]	539
32	Apr 5	H	Stranraer	D 1-1	1-0	9	Austin [22]	636
33	12	A	Stenhousemuir	L 1-2	1-0	9	Hughes [44]	639
34	19	A	Airdrieonians	L 1-2	0-0	9	Campbell [63]	1033
35	26	H	Brechin C	L 1-2	0-1	9	Clarke [90]	591
36	May 3	A	Ayr U	L 1-4	0-1	9	Buchanan [82]	1952

Final League Position: 9

Honours
League Champions: Division II 1947-48. Third Division 2007-08.
Runners-up: Division II 1929-30, 1970-71. Second Division 1983-84, 1995-96. Third Division 2002-03.
Scottish Cup Winners: 1938; *Runners-up:* 1927, 1950.
League Cup Winners: 1947-48, 1949-50, 1953-54.

Club colours: Shirt: Gold and black stripes. Shorts: White. Socks: White.

Goalscorers: *League (31):* Buchanan 11 (3 pens), Austin 4, Brown 2, Durie 2, Hughes 2, Campbell 1, Clarke 1, Fisher 1, Johnstone 1, McBride 1, McKenzie 1, O'Neill 1, Stewart R 1, Willis 1, own goal 1.
William Hill Scottish FA Cup (1): Johnstone 1.
Scottish Communities League Cup (2): Buchanan 2.
Ramsdens Cup (1): Buchanan 1 (1 pen).
League 1 Play-Offs (4): McBride 2, Austin 1, Smith 1.

Andrews M 4	Durie S 25+5	Mbu J 24+1	Thom G 18+2	Tuta C 5+4	Stewart J 19+7	Dutot A 6+1	Brown R 14+4	Fotheringham G 1	Buchanan L 34+1	Willis P 6+5	McBride S 14+5	Austin N 11+11	Johnstone C 26+3	Moosari C 4+4	Stewart R 8+10	Naysmith G 10	Neilson R 5	Paterson G 30	Campbell S 25+1	Hughes S 18+1	Smith J 2+2	Barr L 7+6	Holmes D —+1	Thomson J 3	Fisher G 12+1	Henderson B 1+2	Lennie R —+1	Rutkiewicz K 13+1	McKenzie M 9+3	O'Neill S 10+2	Smith K 15	Cowan D 7+2	Inkango B —+4	Hamilton J 2	Match No.
1	2	3	4	5²	6³	7¹	8	9	10	11	12	13	14																						1
1	2	4	3	10²	7¹		14		12	11	6	9			5³	8	13																		2
1	2⁴	4	3	11¹	8	6			12	10	13	14	9²	7³	5																				3
1	5		3	11³	9	2¹	7		14	10²	8	12	13	6		4																			4
8	4	3³	11¹	12	6²	14			10	7	9			5	2	1	13																		5
	3	14	7³	12		11¹	10	8	6	13	9			5²	2	1	4																		6
12	14	3		7		11	10	6¹	8¹		9	13		5	2²	1	4																		7
6	3	14	7³			10¹	11		9	13	8	12		5	2²	1	4																		8
2	3	13	7²	14		11	10		8¹		9	6³	12	5		1	4																		9
12	4	3	13		2	8	14	11	9²		10		6³	5		1		7¹																	10
	4	3	12		2	8		11	9		10		6²	5		1		7¹	13																11
14	4	3⁸		8³	2			11	5⁴			7¹	10⁷			1	6	9	12	13															12
2	3		6³		7	12	11		8²	5	13			1	4	9	10¹	14																	13
12	4	3⁸		6		11		5	9³	14				1	2	8	10²	7¹	13																14
	4		8		6²	10	11¹		14	5		12		1	2		9		3	7³	13														15
	4		8	6	11			10³	5		13			1	2	12	9¹	3	7²		14														16
		7		6¹	11³	13		10²	5		12			1	4	8	9	3	2	14															17
2	4		7		8³	13	11	12	10	14	5²	6¹		1	3		9																		18
2	3			14	10	6²	5¹	11¹	13	9			1	4	7	12		8																	19
12	3	4		10²	13³	9		5	7			1	2	6	14		8	11¹																	20
	2	4		13		10	12		9¹	5	1						7²					3	6	8	11										21
	2	4		13		10	12		9¹	5	1						8					3	6	7²11											22
5	4	13		14	10	9¹		12	1	8							7²					3³	6		11	2									23
5²	4		9		11		13	14	1	3¹						7				12	8	6	10	2³											24
5	4	12	8³		11	13	9		1			14				7				3²	6	10¹	2												25
5	4		13	10¹		14			1	8	9					7³				3	6	12	11¹²	2											26
5	4			14	10³		13	12	1	8²	9									3	6³	7	11¹	2											27
5	4			14	10		13	8	12	1	7	9²								3	6³		11	2¹											28
5	4¹	7		11		12	10		1	2	9								3	8	6														29
2	4	13		10¹		6	5	14	1	3	7²	9					4			8	11³			12											30
2	13	14		11		7³	5		4²	9	8						3	12	6¹	10					1										31
2		7²		11		8³	5¹	14	4	9							3		6	10	13	12		1											32
2		6¹		11		14	8	5³	1	4	9²						12	3	7	10	13														33
5		7¹		11		6²	10		1	3	8						4	12	14	9	2¹	13													34
2²	4	3				13	11	6	8¹	5						1	7	9	—			12		10⁵	14										35
6	4	2	8²				14	10	9¹	12	5					1	3			13		7³ 11													36

EAST STIRLINGSHIRE

Year Formed: 1880. *Grounds:* Ochilview Park (with Stenhousemuir). *Contact address:* 81d Main Street, Bainsford, Falkirk FK2 7NZ. *Telephone/Fax:* 01324 629 942.
E-mail: fceaststirlingshire@gmail.com *Website:* www.eaststirlingshirefc.com
Ground Capacity: 3,776 (626 seated). *Size of Pitch:* 100m × 66m.
Chairman: Tony Ford. *Secretary:* Tadek Kopszywa.
Head Coach: Craig Tully. *Assistant Head Coach:* George Shaw.
Club Nickname: 'The Shire'.
Previous Grounds: Burnhouse, Randyford Park, Merchiston Park, New Kilbowie Park, Firs Park.
Record Attendance: 12,000 v Partick Thistle, *Scottish Cup* 3rd rd, 21 Feb 1921.
Record Transfer Fee received: £35,000 for Jim Docherty to Chelsea (1978).
Record Transfer Fee paid: £6,000 for Colin McKinnon from Falkirk (March 1991).
Record Victory: 11-2 v Vale of Bannock, *Scottish Cup* 2nd rd, 22 Sept 1888.
Record Defeat: 1-12 v Dundee United, Division II, 13 Apr 1936.
Most Capped Player: Humphrey Jones, 5 (14), Wales.
Most League Appearances: 415: Gordon Russell, 1983-2001.
Most League Goals in Season (Individual): 36: Malcolm Morrison, Division II, 1938-39.

EAST STIRLINGSHIRE – SCOTTISH LEAGUE TWO 2013–14 LEAGUE RECORD

Match No.	Date	Venue	Opponents	Result	H/T Score	Lg Pos.	Goalscorers	Attendance
1	Aug 10	A	Queen's Park	W 3-1	2-1	1	Thomson (pen) [26], Townsley 2 [43, 50]	476
2	17	H	Elgin C	W 3-0	2-0	1	Greenhill 2 [30, 37], McMullan (og) [90]	254
3	24	A	Stirling Alb	W 3-1	2-0	1	Bolochoweckyj [6], Quinn [24], McKechnie [54]	735
4	31	H	Peterhead	L 1-4	1-0	1	Quinn (pen) [5]	286
5	Sept 14	A	Clyde	W 2-1	0-0	1	Wright 2 [49, 78]	497
6	21	H	Albion R	L 1-4	0-3	1	Quinn (pen) [51]	336
7	28	H	Berwick R	W 1-0	1-0	1	Bolochoweckyj [5]	301
8	Oct 19	A	Queen's Park	D 1-1	0-0	1	McGowan [51]	339
9	26	A	Montrose	L 0-2	0-1	1		338
10	29	A	Annan Ath	W 2-1	1-0	1	Thomson (pen) [28], McKechnie [51]	301
11	Nov 9	H	Stirling Alb	D 2-2	1-2	1	White (og) [42], Bolochoweckyj [72]	541
12	16	A	Peterhead	D 1-1	0-0	1	McKechnie [90]	545
13	23	H	Clyde	L 0-1	0-0	4		452
14	Dec 3	A	Albion R	L 2-3	0-2	5	Quinn 2 (1 pen) [74, 78 (p)]	323
15	7	H	Annan Ath	D 1-1	0-0	6	Turner [88]	218
16	14	A	Berwick R	L 0-2	0-1	7		361
17	21	A	Elgin C	W 1-0	0-0	3	Glasgow [79]	502
18	28	H	Montrose	D 2-2	1-1	5	Gallagher [7], Thomson [51]	244
19	Jan 4	A	Stirling Alb	L 1-2	1-0	6	Wright [41]	639
20	11	H	Peterhead	W 2-0	1-0	6	Townsley [14], Greenhill [52]	310
21	18	H	Albion R	D 1-1	0-0	6	Gallagher [90]	319
22	25	A	Clyde	L 0-1	0-0	6		173
23	Feb 1	A	Queen's Park	D 0-0	0-0	6		337
24	8	H	Elgin C	W 3-0	1-0	4	Maxwell [38], Bolochoweckyj [79], Wright [83]	309
25	15	A	Annan Ath	W 3-2	1-1	4	Wright [21], Greenhill [74], Shepherd [87]	401
26	22	H	Berwick R	D 1-1	0-1	5	Quinn (pen) [68]	341
27	Mar 1	A	Peterhead	L 0-4	0-3	5		554
28	8	H	Stirling Alb	W 1-0	1-0	4	Thomson (pen) [45]	584
29	15	A	Montrose	L 0-2	0-2	5		333
30	22	H	Queen's Park	L 1-4	1-2	5	Quinn [11]	376
31	29	H	Clyde	L 2-4	1-3	6	McQueen (og) [20], Turner [90]	449
32	Apr 5	A	Albion R	L 1-2	0-1	7	Maxwell [81]	287
33	12	A	Annan Ath	W 2-1	1-1	6	Wright [29], Turner [90]	253
34	19	A	Berwick R	L 0-1	0-1	6		582
35	26	A	Elgin C	L 0-5	0-1	6		588
36	May 3	H	Montrose	L 1-2	1-2	8	Bolochoweckyj [42]	265

Final League Position: 8

Honours
League Champions: Division II 1931-32; C Division 1947-48.
Runners-up: Division II 1962-63. Second Division 1979-80. Division Three 1923-24.

Club colours: Shirt: Black and white hoops. Shorts: Black. Socks: Red.

Goalscorers: *League (45):* Quinn 7 (4 pens), Wright 6, Bolochoweckyj 5, Greenhill 4, Thomson 4 (3 pens), McKechnie 3, Townsley 3, Turner 3, Gallagher 2, Maxwell 2, Glasgow 1, McGowan 1, Shepherd 1, own goals 3.
William Hill Scottish FA Cup (6): Greenhill 2, Glasgow 1, Maxwell 1, McKechnie 1, Turner 1.
Scottish Communities League Cup (0).
Ramsdens Cup (0).

Hay G 33	MacGregor G 26 + 6	Bolochoweckyj M 30	Townsley C 35	McGowan M 16	Thomson I 30	Greenhill D 31 + 3	O'Donoghue R 19 + 6	Maxwell S 28 + 2	Turner K 18 + 9	Wright M 25 + 4	Glasgow J 10 + 19	McKechnie J 17 + 6	Quinn P 15 + 10	Kelly C — + 2	Miller R 14 + 4	McCaughie D — + 3	Herd M 14 + 7	Devlin R 7 + 4	Tapping J 10 + 3	Gallagher C 3 + 1	Watt J 2 + 3	Shepherd N 6 + 5	Lamie R 4	Gordon C 3	Match No.
1	2	3	4	5	6	7	8	9	10¹	11²	12³	13	14												1
1	2	4	3	5	9	7	6²		11³	8	10¹	13	12	14											2
1	2	4	3	5	8	7¹		10³	9²		6	11	12	13	14										3
1	2	4	3	5	6	8²	14	12	7	10³	13	9³	11		14										4
1	2	4	3	5	8	9¹		10³	12	6	13	7	11²		14										5
1	2¹	4	3	5	9	7	14	10³	12	8	13	6²	11▪												6
1	2	4	3	5	7	8²	6³	12	10	9	11¹	13			14										7
1	2	4	3	5	9	7	6	8	11	10¹					14		12								8
1	2	4	3	5	8	7³	6¹	9	10				11²		13	12	14								9
1	2	3	4	5	7	8	6	11	10¹		9				12										10
1	2²	4	3	5	8	7	6	9	10		13	11			12										11
1	2	4	3	5			7²	9¹	10		12	11	13		14	6³	8								12
1	2	4	3	5			7	6	8¹	11		12	10	13			9²								13
1	2	3		5			8	6	9¹	10		11	7	13					4	12					14
1	2³	4	3	5	7	8	6²		12	13	9¹	10	11				14								15
1	2	4▪	3	5	8²	6▪	7		10¹	13	12	9	11³						14						16
1		3		8			7	5	10²	6¹	11		9	13			2		4	12					17
1	14	4	3		7	13	8²	5	12	9		6¹	11³				2		10						18
1	12	4	3		8	7	6¹			11	13	5		9			2²		10						19
1	6	4	3		8	7¹	5		9	10¹	14		11²				2	13				12			20
1	7	4	3		8	6²	5		9	13		14	10²				2¹		11	12					21
1	12		3		7	10¹	5		9	11³	14	13	8²				2		4	6					22
1	12	3	4		6	9	5		10¹	11			7³				2	14	13	8²					23
1	4	3		7	8	9³			11²	13		10¹	6		2			5			12	14			24
1		3		7	8			5	11	13	9³	10¹	4		2			6			12				25
1	6	3		9	7	14	5		10	12	9³	11²	4¹				13	2							26
1	6	3			9	8³	5		11	13	14	10	4					7²	2¹			12			27
1	10	4¹	3		8	9	12	5	13	11			7						2			6²			28
1	11²	4	3		8	9		5	14	10			13		7³		12	2				6¹			29
1	10¹	4	3		6	8		5	13	7	14		11³				2	9²				12			30
1		3	2		7¹	9²	14	8	13	11			10³		6	5						12	4		31
1	5	3			7	14	9	10³	13	12			11¹		6²		8	2					4		32
	5	3	2		12	7	8	13	10	11¹			6²	14						2³		9	4³	1	33
13	4	3		6	9	7²	8	10¹	11	12		14								2³		5		1	34
	5	3	2¹		7	13		10	12	14			11³		6		8²					9	4	1	35
1	12	4	3²		7	9³	6¹	5	11	8	13		14		2							10			36

ELGIN CITY

Year Formed: 1893. *Ground and Address:* Borough Briggs, Borough Briggs Road, Elgin IV30 1AP.
Telephone: 01343 551114. *Fax:* 01343 547921. *E-mail:* accountsecfc@btconnect.com *Website:* www.elgincity.com
Ground Capacity: 3,927 (seated: 478). *Size of pitch:* 102m × 68m.
Chairman: Graham Tatters. *Secretary:* Kate Taylor.
Manager: Barry Wilson. *Physio:* Kerry Hendry.
Previous names: 1893-1900 Elgin City, 1900-03 Elgin City United, 1903- Elgin City.
Club Nicknames: 'City', 'The Black & Whites'.
Previous Grounds: Association Park 1893-95; Milnfield Park 1895-1909; Station Park 1909-19; Cooper Park 1919-21.
Record Attendance: 12,608 v Arbroath, Scottish Cup, 17 Feb 1968.
Record Transfer Fee received: £32,000 for Michael Teasdale to Dundee (Jan 1994).
Record Transfer Fee paid: £10,000 for Russell McBride from Fraserburgh (July 2001).
Record Victory: 18-1 v Brora Rangers, North of Scotland Cup, 6 Feb 1960.
Record Defeat: 1-14 v Hearts, Scottish Cup, 4 Feb 1939.
Most League Appearances: 224: David Hind, 2001-09.
Most League Goals in Season (Individual): 19: Martin Johnston, 2005-06.
Most Goals Overall (Individual): 74: Craig Gunn, 2009-14.

ELGIN CITY – SCOTTISH LEAGUE TWO 2013–14 LEAGUE RECORD

Match No.	Date	Venue	Opponents	Result	H/T Score	Lg Pos.	Goalscorers	Attendance
1	Aug 10	H	Albion R	L 1-2	0-1	7	Gunn [87]	541
2	17	A	East Stirling	L 0-3	0-2	9		254
3	24	A	Peterhead	D 2-2	1-0	9	Wyness [13], Gunn [77]	543
4	31	H	Clyde	W 1-0	0-0	9	Wyness [61]	544
5	Sept 14	H	Montrose	D 3-3	0-1	9	Niven [59], McKinnon [61], Crighton [79]	577
6	21	A	Queen's Park	D 3-3	3-2	9	Wyness [14], Gunn [20], Harkins [39]	342
7	28	H	Stirling Alb	W 4-0	2-0	8	Sutherland [20], Gunn 2 [43, 48], Cameron [79]	623
8	Oct 12	A	Berwick R	W 3-2	0-2	2	Sutherland 2 [55, 61], Harkins (pen) [74]	495
9	19	A	Albion R	D 0-0	0-0	2		337
10	26	H	Annan Ath	L 2-3	2-1	6	Gunn [4], Cameron [15]	648
11	Nov 9	H	Peterhead	L 2-4	0-1	8	Gunn [85], Urqhart [90]	622
12	16	A	Clyde	L 1-2	0-0	8	McHardy [88]	533
13	23	A	Montrose	D 3-3	2-1	9	Wyness 2 [20, 45], Gunn [52]	398
14	30	H	Queen's Park	W 3-2	1-2	7	Gunn 2 [43, 70], McKinnon (pen) [53]	608
15	Dec 7	H	Berwick R	W 2-0	2-0	8	Sutherland 2 [37, 45]	543
16	21	H	East Stirling	L 0-1	0-0	9		502
17	28	A	Annan Ath	L 1-2	0-0	9	Sutherland [64]	401
18	Jan 2	A	Peterhead	L 1-2	1-0	9	Niven [13]	737
19	11	H	Clyde	W 3-1	1-0	9	Gunn [42], Sutherland 2 [49, 52]	585
20	18	A	Queen's Park	L 0-2	0-1	9		346
21	25	H	Montrose	L 2-3	0-2	9	Masson [48], Sutherland [74]	550
22	Feb 1	H	Albion R	D 1-1	0-0	9	Duff [70]	519
23	8	A	East Stirling	L 0-3	0-1	9		309
24	15	A	Berwick R	W 3-2	1-1	9	Gunn (pen) [30], Wyness [46], Nicolson (pen) [85]	412
25	22	H	Stirling Alb	L 2-3	2-0	9	Crighton [30], Wyness [39]	576
26	Mar 1	A	Clyde	L 0-4	0-1	9		504
27	8	H	Peterhead	L 2-3	2-1	9	Mckenzie [6], Sutherland [43]	670
28	11	A	Stirling Alb	D 1-1	0-0	9	Gunn [85]	641
29	15	H	Annan Ath	L 2-3	0-3	9	Sutherland [60], Harkins [90]	485
30	22	A	Albion R	L 2-5	0-3	9	Wyness [47], Sutherland [69]	286
31	29	A	Montrose	W 3-0	0-0	9	Sutherland [53], MacLeod 2 [75, 86]	262
32	Apr 5	H	Queen's Park	D 1-1	0-1	9	Wyness [53]	555
33	12	H	Berwick R	L 1-3	1-0	9	Currie, L (og) [40]	602
34	19	A	Stirling Alb	D 2-2	1-1	9	Sutherland [14], Gunn [54]	640
35	26	H	East Stirling	W 5-0	1-0	9	Gunn [37], Bayne [57], Urqhart [64], Duff [86], Harkins [90]	588
36	May 3	A	Annan Ath	L 0-2	0-1	9		428

Final League Position: 9

Honours
Scottish Cup: Quarter-finals 1968.
Highland League Champions: winners 15 times.
Scottish Qualifying Cup (North): winners 7 times.
North of Scotland Cup: winners 17 times.
Highland League Cup: winners 5 times.
Inverness Cup: winners twice.

Club colours: Shirt: Black and white stripes. Shorts: Black. Socks: Red.

Goalscorers: *League (62):* Gunn 15 (1 pen), Sutherland 14, Wyness 9, Harkins 4 (1 pen), Cameron 2, Crighton 2, Duff 2, MacLeod 2, McKinnon 2 (1 pen), Niven 2, Urqhart 2, Bayne 1, Masson 1, McHardy 1, Mckenzie 1, Nicolson 1 (1 pen), own goal 1.
William Hill Scottish FA Cup (7): Gunn 2, Mckenzie 2, Duff 1, Khutsishvili 1, Wyness 1.
Scottish Communities League Cup (1): Crighton 1.
Ramsdens Cup (3): Crighton 1, Gunn 1, Sutherland 1.

Jellema R 26	McLean C 5+4	Crighton S 33	Duff J 33+1	McMullan P 19+2	Cameron B 10+1	Harkins P 23+4	McKinnon R 11+4	Beveridge G 23+6	Gunn C 36	Sutherland S 36	Wyness D 32+3	Mckenzie A 24+7	Urqhart S 6+18	Niven D 19+1	Khutsishvili D 2+4	Black S 4+1	Nicolson M 19+1	McHardy D —+8	Masson J 9	MacCauley C 1+1	MacLeod A —+9	Finlayson G 13	MacDonald C 2+3	Bayne G 3+3	Kaczan P 1	Murray C —+2	Gibson J 6	Match No.
1	2¹	3*	4	5²	6	7³	8	9	10	11	12	13	14															1
1	3¹		4	5	11	7³	8²	9	6	10	12	14	13	2														2
1		4	3		6		8	7	9	11	10			2	5													3
1		3	4	12	8		5²	2	10	11	9	13		6	7¹													4
	2	4	3	5	7		8¹		10	9	11	12			6¹	1												5
1	2¹	4	3		7	8	9	12	6³	10	11²	5	14		13													6
1		3	4	13	6	7¹	5³	2	8	9	11	10²	12		14													7
1		3	4	5	7	6		12	11	8	10	9			2¹													8
1	12	3	4	5¹		7	8²	6	9	11		10	13	2														9
1	12	3¹	4	5		7²	6¹	14	10	8	11	9		2	13													10
1			4	5		6	14	2¹	10	8	11²	9³	12	3			7	13										11
1		3	4	5		6¹	12		11	8	10	9³	13	2			7³	14										12
1		4	3	5		6¹	12	10	8	11	9			2			7											13
1		4	3	5		9¹		10	8	11²	6	12		2			7	13										14
1		3	4	5	12	9¹		10	7	11²	6	13		2			8											15
1		3	4	5¹		9²		10	7	11	6	13		2	12		8											16
1*	7	3	5		8¹		11	6	10²	13	9	2	12	4														17
1		4	3	5	8		6	10	11		9	2					7											18
		3	4	5		12	6	11	10²	9	13	2¹		1			8	7										19
1		3	5	13	12	2¹	6	11	10	9²							7	8										20
1		3	4	5	12	13	2	6	10	11¹	9³						8*	7										21
1		3	4	5²	9		2	11¹	8	10	6	13						7	12									22
1		3	4		2	7¹	9	11	10²	12	6						5	8	13									23
1		3	4	7²	2	8³	11	9	10¹	13						6			14	5	12							24
1		3	4	6¹	2	8	11	10²	9	13						7				5	12							25
1	8	3		7	2	6	11	10	9¹	4²						5			12	13								26
1	12	3	4*	8	2	10	7	11¹	9²	6³						14			13	5								27
1		3		8	2	6	11	10	9³	7²								13	5	12	4¹	14						28
	14	3	4	8	2¹	6	7	11	9³	10²			1		13	5	12											29
		4	3	8	2	6²	11	10	9³	13			1	12		7¹	14	5										30
1		3			7	9¹	6	8	11³	13	14		4		12	5	2	10²		1								31
		3	12		7¹	6	10	9	11			4¹	13	8	14	5	2²		1									32
7	4¹	3*		14	5	8	10	9³	13		2²			6²		12	2	11¹		1								33
	3	4		10³	8	6	11	13	9¹	2²		12	7	14	5			1										34
	3	4		14	13	8	10	9²		12	2¹	7	6		5	11³	1											35
		3	5		7³	2	6²	11	10¹		9			8	12		13	4				14	1					36

FALKIRK

Year Formed: 1876. *Ground & Address:* The Falkirk Stadium, Westfield, Falkirk FK2 9DX. *Telephone:* 01324 624121.
Fax: 01324 612418. *Email:* post@falkirkfc.co.uk *Website:* www.falkirkfc.co.uk
Ground Capacity: 8,750 (all seated). *Size of Pitch:* 105m × 68m.
Chairman: Martin Ritchie. *Secretary:* Robert Bateman.
Manager: Peter Houston. *Assistant Manager:* Dale Brooks.
Club Nickname: 'The Bairns'.
Previous Grounds: Randyford 1876-81; Blinkbonny Grounds 1881-83; Brockville Park 1883-2003.
Record Attendance: 23,100 v Celtic, Scottish Cup 3rd rd, 21 Feb 1953.
Record Transfer Fee received: £380,000 for John Hughes to Celtic (Aug 1995).
Record Transfer Fee paid: £225,000 to Chelsea for Kevin McAllister (Aug 1991).
Record Victory: 11-1 v Tillicoultry, Scottish Cup 1st rd, 7 Sep 1889.
Record Defeat: 1-11 v Airdrieonians, Division I, 28 Apr 1951.
Most Capped Player: Alex Parker, 14 (15), Scotland.
Most League Appearances: 451: Tom Ferguson, 1919-32.
Most League Goals in Season (Individual): 43: Evelyn Morrison, Division I, 1928-29.
Most Goals Overall (Individual): 154: Kenneth Dawson, 1935-51.

FALKIRK – SCOTTISH CHAMPIONSHIP 2013–14 LEAGUE RECORD

Match No.	Date	Venue	Opponents	Result	H/T Score	Lg Pos.	Goalscorers	Attendance
1	Aug 10	A	Dumbarton	D 1-1	0-0	5	McGrandles [61]	1224
2	17	H	Greenock Morton	W 3-1	2-0	2	Loy 2 [40, 45], Roberts [48]	3058
3	24	A	Livingston	W 3-0	2-0	2	Roberts 3 [30, 41, 54]	1416
4	31	H	Hamilton A	L 1-2	0-0	2	Fulton [50]	3266
5	Sept 14	A	Cowdenbeath	L 0-1	0-0	4		644
6	21	H	Dundee	W 3-1	1-0	3	Loy 2 [12, 65], Fulton [55]	3349
7	28	A	Raith R	D 1-1	0-1	3	Faulds [90]	1715
8	Oct 5	H	Queen of the South	W 2-1	1-0	3	Loy 2 (1 pen) [33 (p), 85]	3189
9	12	A	Alloa Ath	D 0-0	0-0	3		1625
10	19	H	Dumbarton	L 1-2	1-2	4	Roberts [39]	2704
11	26	A	Hamilton A	L 0-2	0-1	4		1340
12	Nov 9	H	Livingston	W 4-1	1-0	4	Vaulks [37], Loy 2 [52, 69], Sibbald [60]	2878
13	16	A	Dundee	D 1-1	0-1	5	Leahy [90]	4661
14	23	H	Cowdenbeath	W 4-0	0-0	4	Millar 2 [51, 84], Loy [75], Shepherd [87]	2550
15	Dec 7	H	Raith R	W 3-1	2-0	4	Sibbald [4], McGrandles [25], Kingsley [51]	2934
16	21	A	Greenock Morton	W 2-0	0-0	4	Duffie [51], Loy (pen) [69]	1873
17	28	H	Alloa Ath	D 0-0	0-0	3		3417
18	Jan 4	A	Livingston	W 1-0	1-0	3	Loy (pen) [26]	1585
19	11	H	Hamilton A	D 0-0	0-0	3		3099
20	18	A	Cowdenbeath	W 2-0	0-0	3	Millar [54], Loy [56]	566
21	25	H	Dundee	W 2-0	1-0	1	McGrandles [16], Loy [73]	4183
22	Feb 1	H	Greenock Morton	D 1-1	0-1	1	Millar (pen) [63]	3120
23	8	A	Queen of the South	L 0-2	0-0	2		1818
24	15	A	Dumbarton	L 1-2	1-0	3	Loy [29]	1003
25	22	H	Queen of the South	W 1-0	0-0	3	Millar (pen) [90]	2862
26	Mar 1	A	Raith R	W 4-2	1-2	3	Hill (og) [18], McCracken [47], Loy [71], Millar [87]	1729
27	8	H	Livingston	D 1-1	0-1	3	Alston [82]	2924
28	15	A	Hamilton A	L 1-3	0-1	3	Beck [71]	1706
29	22	A	Alloa Ath	L 0-3	0-0	3		1025
30	25	H	Dumbarton	W 2-0	1-0	3	McCracken [25], Loy [73]	2489
31	29	A	Dundee	W 1-0	1-0	3	Beck [19]	4919
32	Apr 5	H	Cowdenbeath	W 5-0	3-0	3	Loy 3 [16, 28, 54], Alston [40], Sibbald [48]	2830
33	12	A	Queen of the South	W 2-1	0-0	3	Alston [59], Beck [61]	1863
34	19	H	Raith R	W 2-1	2-1	3	Loy [19], McGrandles [23]	3200
35	26	A	Greenock Morton	D 1-1	1-0	3	McGrandles [41]	1921
36	May 3	H	Alloa Ath	W 3-1	1-1	3	Beck 2 [23, 90], Sibbald [61]	3998

Final League Position: 3

Honours

League Champions: Division II 1935-36, 1969-70, 1974-75. First Division 1990-91, 1993-94, 2002-03, 2004-05. Second Division 1979-80;
Runners-up: Division I 1907-08, 1909-10. First Division 1985-86, 1988-89, 1997-98, 1998-99. Division II 1904-05, 1951-52, 1960-61.
Scottish Cup Winners: 1913, 1957; *Runners-up:* 1997, 2009. *League Cup Runners-up:* 1947-48. *B&Q Cup Winners:* 1993-94. *League Challenge Cup Winners:* 1997-98, 2004-05, 2011-12.

European: *Europa League:* 2 matches (2009-10).

Club colours: Shirt: Navy blue with white seams. Shorts: White. Socks: White.

Goalscorers: *League (59):* Loy 20 (3 pens), Millar 6 (2 pens), Beck 5, McGrandles 5, Roberts 5, Sibbald 4, Alston 3, Fulton 2, McCracken 2, Duffie 1, Faulds 1, Kingsley 1, Leahy 1, Shepherd 1, Vaulks 1, own goal 1.
William Hill Scottish FA Cup (0).
Scottish Communities League Cup (5): Alston 1, Fulton 1, Grant 1, Roberts 1, own goal 1.
Ramsdens Cup (4): Alston 1, Loy 1, McGrandles 1, Shepherd 1.
Premiership Play-Offs (5): Alston 2, Beck 1, Loy 1, Sibbald 1.

McGovern M 34	Duffie K 26	Vaulks W 33	Kingsley S 35	Turnbull K 4 + 1	Fulton J 19 + 2	Durojaiye S 7 + 10	Alston B 23 + 6	McGrandles C 36	Roberts P 24 + 2	Loy R 34	Grant T — + 4	Sibbald C 29 + 5	Dick L 1 + 3	Shepherd S 1 + 13	Leahy L 1 + 18	Flynn J 14 + 8	Bingham R 2 + 9	McCracken D 24 + 1	Faulds K — + 2	Bowman G 2	Small L — + 5	Millar M 24	Beck M 13 + 2	Chalmers J 10 + 1	Hogg C — + 2	Match No.
1	2	3	4	5	6^1	7	8^2	9	10	11	12	13														1
1	2	4	5^1	3	6^2	8	7	9^2	10	11	14	13	12													2
1	2	3	4	5	9^3	7	6	8	11^1	10^2	12	13			14											3
1	2	4	5	3^1	6	7	9	10	11	8^2	12	13														4
1	2	3	5	12	9	6	7^1	8	11	10		13						4^1								5
1	2	4^1	5	7	9	6	10	11^3	8^2		14	13			12			4								6
1	2	3	5	9^1	7^2	10	11^3	8			14	13			12			4				6				7
1	2	5	8^1	9	6	10^2	11^3	13	7		14				12			4				3				8
	2	5	7^3	6	9	11	10	8^1	12		4	13	3^2	14	1											9
1	2	4	5	6^3	7	9	11^8	10	13		12	14	3^1	8^2												10
1	2	3		6^1	7	9	11	8^2	5	13	12	10^3	4		14											11
1	2	3	5	9^1	13	7	10^3	11	8^2		14	12	4									6				12
1	2^1	3	5	6	13	9	11	10	8^2		14	12	4^3									7				13
1	2	3	5	6	14	9	11^1	10^2	8		13	4	12									7^3				14
1	2	3^1	5	8^2	14	7	10^3	11	9		13	12	4									6				15
1	2	3	5	6	14	9	10^1	11^3	8^2		12	13	4									7				16
1	2	4	5	9^1	13	7	12	11	8		10^2	3										6				17
1	2	3	5	6^3	13	8	10^2	11	9		14	12	4^1									7				18
1	2	3	5	7^1	14	6	11^3	10	9		13	12	4^2									8				19
1	2	4	5	13	14	7^2	6	11	10^3		9	12	3									8				20
1	2	3	5	12	6^1	9	11^2	10	8^3		14	13	4									7				21
1	2	4	5	11	8	9^2	10	6^1		13	3											7	12			22
1	2	3	4	12	9^2	6	11	10	8													7^1	13	5		23
1	2	3	5	9	6^2	10	8^1	12	13			4										7	11			24
1	2	4	5	6	12	11	8^2	14	13		3											7	10^3	9^1		25
1		2	5	14	6	9^1	11	13	12		4	3										7^3	10	8^2		26
1		2	5^3	14	7	6^8	11	13	9^2		3	4										8	10^1	12		27
1		2	5	8^3	6^1	7	11^2	9	13		3	4			12	10						7	11		14	28
		2	5	6^1	8	10^8	9	13	3		3^2	1	12	7	11	4										29
1		2	4	8^3	6	11^2	9^1	12	13		7				13	7						10	5		14	30
1		2	5	13	8^2	9^3	11^1	6	12	14	3											7	10	4		31
1		2	5	12	8	6^2	11	9^1	13	3				14	7	10^3								5		32
1		2	5	7	8	9		10	12	3^8	4											6	11^1			33
1		3	5	7	9	11	10			4												6	8	2		34
1	2		4	12	6^2	7	10	9	13		3											8^1	11	5		35
1		3	5	13	7	10	11^3	9	12	14	4	4^1										6^2	8	2		36

FORFAR ATHLETIC

Year Formed: 1885. *Ground & Address:* Station Park, Carseview Road, Forfar DD8 3BT. *Telephone:* 01307 463576.
Fax: 01307 466956. *E-mail:* pat@ramsayladders.co.uk *Website:* www.forfarathletic.co.uk
Ground Capacity: 4,602 (seated: 739). *Size of Pitch:* 103m × 64m.
Chairman: Alastair Donald. *Vice-Chairman:* Jim Farquhar. *Secretary:* David McGregor.
Manager: Dick Campbell. *Coach:* John Young. *Physios:* Duncan Sangster and Donald Ritchie.
Club Nicknames: 'The Loons', 'The Sky Blues'.
Previous Grounds: None.
Record Attendance: 10,780 v Rangers, Scottish Cup 2nd rd, 2 Feb 1970.
Record Transfer Fee received: £65,000 for David Bingham to Dunfermline Ath (September 1995).
Record Transfer Fee paid: £50,000 for Ian McPhee from Airdrieonians (1991).
Record Victory: 14-1 v Lindertis, Scottish Cup 1st rd, 1 Sept 1888.
Record Defeat: 2-12 v King's Park, Division II, 2 Jan 1930.
Most League Appearances: 463: Ian McPhee, 1978-88 and 1991-98.
Most League Goals in Season (Individual): 46: Dave Kilgour, Division II, 1929-30.
Most Goals Overall: 125: John Clark, 1978-91.

FORFAR ATHLETIC – SCOTTISH LEAGUE ONE 2013–14 LEAGUE RECORD

Match No.	Date	Venue	Opponents	Result	H/T Score	Lg Pos.	Goalscorers	Attendance
1	Aug 10	H	Airdrieonians	D 3-3	1-1	5	Malin [17], McManus 2 [53, 54]	704
2	17	A	Ayr U	L 0-2	0-1	8		1056
3	24	A	Brechin C	L 1-2	0-1	8	Campbell, I (pen) [90]	724
4	31	H	Stenhousemuir	L 1-2	0-2	9	Campbell, I (pen) [59]	483
5	Sept 14	A	East Fife	W 3-1	1-1	8	Dale [16], Hilson [51], Swankie [82]	796
6	22	H	Rangers	L 0-1	0-1	8		3776
7	28	A	Arbroath	L 0-3	0-1	10		855
8	Oct 5	H	Dunfermline Ath	W 4-0	2-0	9	McManus [2], Malcolm [15], Malin [74], Hilson [82]	968
9	12	H	Stranraer	L 1-2	1-2	9	Templeman [4]	449
10	19	A	Airdrieonians	W 2-0	1-0	7	McCluskey [13], Campbell, R (pen) [90]	579
11	26	A	Stenhousemuir	D 1-1	1-1	8	Hilson [36]	408
12	Nov 9	H	Brechin C	W 2-0	1-0	5	Hilson [39], Campbell, R [87]	663
13	23	H	East Fife	W 2-0	0-0	6	Templeman [68], Campbell, R [80]	556
14	Dec 3	A	Rangers	L 1-6	1-4	6	Swankie [25]	38,745
15	7	A	Dunfermline Ath	D 1-1	1-0	6	Dods [19]	2469
16	14	H	Arbroath	D 1-1	0-0	6	McManus [47]	609
17	21	H	Ayr U	L 0-1	0-0	6		473
18	Jan 2	A	Brechin C	W 5-1	4-0	6	Fotheringham [7], Templeman 2 [17, 81], Dods [31], Hilson [35]	812
19	11	H	Stenhousemuir	W 3-0	3-0	5	Swankie [4], Fotheringham 2 (1 pen) [28 (p), 39]	485
20	20	H	Rangers	L 0-2	0-0	5		2067
21	25	A	East Fife	L 1-2	1-0	7	Swankie [30]	685
22	Feb 1	H	Airdrieonians	D 1-1	1-0	7	Kader [28]	542
23	15	H	Dunfermline Ath	L 2-4	1-1	7	Dale [36], Swankie [60]	833
24	22	A	Arbroath	W 3-2	1-0	6	Hilson [13], Swankie 2 [50, 58]	823
25	Mar 1	H	Stenhousemuir	L 1-4	0-1	7	Malcolm [59]	368
26	4	A	Ayr U	W 3-2	2-1	6	Swankie 2 [13, 67], Templeman [45]	656
27	8	H	Brechin C	D 1-1	0-0	6	Hilson [52]	641
28	11	A	Stranraer	W 4-0	2-0	5	Hilson [8], Kader [36], Fotheringham (pen) [61], Swankie [68]	342
29	15	H	Stranraer	W 1-0	1-0	5	Hilson [15]	422
30	22	A	Airdrieonians	L 1-5	1-3	5	Hilson [40]	712
31	29	H	East Fife	L 1-2	1-2	6	Duggan [32]	539
32	Apr 12	A	Dunfermline Ath	D 0-0	0-0	6		2364
33	15	A	Rangers	L 0-3	0-0	6		39,704
34	19	H	Arbroath	L 0-2	0-2	6		833
35	26	H	Ayr U	W 4-2	2-0	6	McCluskey [2], Hilson 2 [25, 73], Kader [52]	532
36	May 3	A	Stranraer	L 1-3	1-1	7	Swankie [5]	501

Final League Position: 7

Honours
League Champions: Second Division 1983-84. Third Division 1994-95; C Division 1948-49.
Runners-up: Third Division 1996-97, 2009-10. *Promoted to Second Division:* 2009-10 (play-offs).
Scottish Cup: Semi-finals 1982.
League Cup: Semi-finals 1977-78.
League Challenge Cup: Semi-finals 2004-05.

Club colours: Shirt: Sky blue with navy trim. Shorts: Navy. Socks: Navy.

Goalscorers: *League (55):* Hilson 12, Swankie 11, Templeman 5, Fotheringham 4 (2 pens), McManus 4, Campbell R 3 (1 pen), Kader 3, Campbell I 2 (2 pens), Dale 2, Dods 2, Malcolm 2, Malin 2, McCluskey 2, Duggan 1.
William Hill Scottish FA Cup (6): Templeman 3, Fotheringham 1, Hilson 1, Malin 1.
Scottish Communities League Cup (3): Swankie 2, Campbell I 1 (1 pen).
Ramsdens Cup (3): Malcolm 2, Kader 1.

Hill D 19	McCabe N 14+3	Andrews M 15+2	Dods D 32+1	Baxter M 30+2	Kader D 20+10	Malin G 11+17	Dale J 18+11	Deasley B 2	Templeman C 35+1	Swankie G 27+2	McManus P 5+8	Fusco G 26+5	Campbell R 8+19	Dunlop M 1	Campbell I 30+1	Fotheringham M 13+7	Malcolm S 23	Hilson D 28+1	Smith C —+2	Keiller L —+2	McCluskey J 8+6	Douglas R 17	Storie C 4	Faero O 6	McLelland P —+2	Duggan C 4+2	Match No.
1	2	3	4	5	6	7	8²	9¹	10	11³	12	13	14														1
1	7	4	3⁴	5	12	8³	6		10¹	14	11	13	9	2²													2
1	3	4	2	6³	12				9¹	13	11	10	8	14	5	7²											3
1	9¹	3	2	13	14	12			10	11			8²		5	7³	4	6									4
1	7³	3	4	2	6	12	8²		10	11	13	14			5			9¹									5
1	2	3	4	5	6¹	13	7³		11²	10	14		12		9		8										6
1	2³	4	3	5	6²	12	7¹		11	10	14		8		9	13											7
1		4	2	12	8³	6¹			10		11²	7	13		5		3	9			14						8
1	3	4	2	14	12	6²			10	9	11¹	7			5		8³				13						9
1	5²	3	4	2	13	7			10	9		12	14		8¹		11				6³						10
1		4	3	2		7²	12		10	11	13	8			5		9				6¹						11
1	3	2²	12	14					10	9		8	13		5	4	11¹				6³	1	7				12
14		4	2						10	9		7	13		5	12	3	11¹			6³	1	8²				13
1	3¹	4	2				13		11³	9	12	14	6		5			10²					8	7			14
13		3	2	6¹			8		10	11³	14	4			5²	12					10²		8	7			15
7³		4	2	6¹	9	8²			10		11		13		5	12	3				14	1					16
12		3					11	8	10		13	2	14		5²	7¹	4	9			6³	1					17
		4	2³	12	9²	7¹			11			6	14		5	8	3	10			13	1					18
	3			6¹	13	12			10	11³		2			5	8²	4	9				1			7	14	19
	3	12		6¹	13				11	9		2³	14		5	8²	4	10				1			7		20
	3	2		6	14	13			10²	9		7³	12		5	8¹	4	11				1					21
2³		4	13	6		8¹			10²	11		5	9		14	7	3	12				1					22
	4	2		9²	6¹	8			10	11		7	13		5	12	3					1					23
	14	4	2				13		10²	11		8	12		5	6¹	3	9²				1			7		24
	4	5		6²	12	8³			10	9¹		2	14				3	11			13	1			7		25
8		4	2	12					10	11		7	6¹		5		3	9				1					26
8¹	12				14				10	9		7	6		5	13³	3²11				13	1				14	27
	3	4¹	2	8¹	14	12			10	9²		7			5	6²		11			13	1					28
	3		2	6¹	12	14			10	9²		7			5	8¹	4	11	13			1					29
1	7	3²	12	2	9¹				10			6			5¹	8	4	11¹			13					14	30
1	4²		5	6¹	12	8			11³	13		2	14			7	3	9								10	31
1	3		5	12	14	8			10	9		2	13			4	11²				6³					7¹	32
1		4	2	6	12	7			11³			8²	13		5	14	3	9¹								10	33
1		4	2	12	13	8¹			10	9		7³	14		5	3	6									11²	34
1	3	4		6	8	12			10¹			2	11		5		9¹				7²				14	13	35
1	3	4		6	8³	12			10	9¹			11		5	13	2			14	7²						36

GREENOCK MORTON

Year Formed: 1874. *Ground & Address:* Cappielow Park, Sinclair St, Greenock PA15 2TY. *Telephone:* 01475 723571.
Fax: 01475 781084. *E-mail:* info@gmfc.net *Website:* www.gmfc.net
Ground Capacity: 11,612 (seated: 6,062). *Size of Pitch:* 100m × 65m.
Chairman: Douglas Rae. *Chief Executive:* Gillian Donaldson. *Company Secretary:* Mary Davidson.
Manager: Jim Duffy. *Assistant Manager:* Craig McPherson. *Physio:* Alyson Hendry.
Club Nickname: 'The Ton'.
Previous Grounds: Grant Street 1874, Garvel Park 1875, Cappielow Park 1879, Ladyburn Park 1882, Cappielow Park 1883.
Record Attendance: 23,500 v Celtic, 29 April 1922.
Record Transfer Fee received: £500,000 for Derek Lilley to Leeds United (March 1997).
Record Transfer Fee paid: £250,000 for Janne Lindberg and Marko Rajamäki from MyPa, Finland (Nov 1994).
Record Victory: 11-0 v Carfin Shamrock, Scottish Cup 4th rd, 13 Nov 1886.
Record Defeat: 1-10 v Port Glasgow Ath, Division II, 5 May, 1894 and v St Bernards, Division II, 14 Oct 1933.
Most Capped Player: Jimmy Cowan, 25, Scotland.
Most League Appearances: 534: Derek Collins, 1987-98, 2001-05.
Most League Goals in Season (Individual): 58: Allan McGraw, Division II, 1963-64.
Most Goals Overall (Individual): 136: Andy Ritchie, 1976-83.

GREENOCK MORTON – SCOTTISH CHAMPIONSHIP 2013–14 LEAGUE RECORD

Match No.	Date	Venue	Opponents	Result	H/T Score	Lg Pos.	Goalscorers	Attendance
1	Aug 10	H	Cowdenbeath	W 2-0	1-0	1	Hands [27], Campbell [65]	1817
2	17	A	Falkirk	L 1-3	0-2	6	Hands [90]	3058
3	24	A	Dumbarton	L 1-3	1-2	8	Imrie (pen) [19]	1171
4	31	H	Raith R	D 1-1	1-0	8	Imrie (pen) [39]	1545
5	Sept 14	A	Livingston	D 2-2	2-2	8	Hands [34], Cham [45]	1077
6	21	H	Queen of the South	L 0-2	0-1	9		1826
7	28	A	Dundee	L 1-3	1-0	10	Peciar [23]	3870
8	Oct 5	H	Alloa Ath	L 0-2	0-1	10		1478
9	12	H	Hamilton A	D 1-1	0-1	10	Habai [69]	2106
10	19	A	Cowdenbeath	L 1-5	1-3	10	Imrie [45]	543
11	26	A	Raith R	L 1-2	0-1	10	Novo [70]	1569
12	Nov 9	H	Dumbarton	W 2-0	0-0	10	McLaughlin [60], Peciar [88]	1687
13	16	A	Queen of the South	L 0-2	0-2	10		1685
14	23	H	Livingston	L 1-5	1-3	10	Cham [26]	1460
15	Dec 7	H	Dundee	L 1-2	0-2	10	Imrie [59]	1536
16	14	A	Alloa Ath	L 0-2	0-1	10		546
17	21	H	Falkirk	L 0-2	0-0	10		1873
18	28	A	Hamilton A	L 0-1	0-1	10		1472
19	Jan 4	A	Dumbarton	L 0-2	0-1	10		1469
20	11	A	Raith R	D 0-0	0-0	10		1745
21	18	A	Livingston	W 1-0	1-0	10	McKay [45]	1245
22	29	H	Queen of the South	D 1-1	0-1	10	Campbell [86]	2341
23	Feb 1	A	Falkirk	D 1-1	1-0	10	Imrie [45]	3120
24	15	H	Cowdenbeath	D 1-1	0-1	10	Campbell [85]	2087
25	22	H	Alloa Ath	L 0-1	0-1	10		1628
26	Mar 1	A	Dundee	L 0-2	0-1	10		4488
27	15	A	Raith R	L 1-2	1-0	10	Vine [18]	1308
28	22	H	Hamilton A	L 3-4	1-1	10	Vine [23], Fitzpatrick [60], O'Connor [84]	1345
29	25	A	Cowdenbeath	L 0-3	0-1	10		318
30	29	A	Queen of the South	L 0-3	0-1	10		1487
31	Apr 1	H	Dumbarton	W 3-0	2-0	10	Vine [14], O'Ware [38], McKay [57]	826
32	5	A	Livingston	W 2-0	2-0	10	Imrie [14], McKay [45]	1009
33	12	A	Alloa Ath	L 0-2	0-1	10		615
34	19	H	Dundee	W 1-0	0-0	10	Imrie [78]	2117
35	26	H	Falkirk	D 1-1	0-1	10	Vine [60]	1921
36	May 3	A	Hamilton A	L 2-10	1-5	10	Imrie 2 [22, 73]	2034

Final League Position: 10

Honours
League Champions: First Division 1977-78, 1983-84, 1986-87. Division II 1949-50, 1963-64, 1966-67. Second Division 1994-95, 2006-07. Third Division 2002-03.
Runners-up: Division 1 1916-17. First Division 2012-13. Division II 1899-1900, 1928-29, 1936-37.
Scottish Cup Winners: 1922; *Runners-up:* 1948. *League Cup Runners-up:* 1963-64.
B&Q Cup Runners-up: 1992-93.

European: *UEFA Cup:* 2 matches (*Fairs Cup:* 1968-69).

Club colours: Shirt: Blue and white hoops. Shorts: White with blue trim. Socks: White.

Goalscorers: *League (32):* Imrie 9 (2 pens), Vine 4, Campbell 3, Hands 3, McKay 3, Cham 2, Peciar 2, Fitzpatrick 1, Habai 1, McLaughlin 1, Novo 1, O'Connor 1, O'Ware 1.
William Hill Scottish FA Cup (0).
Scottish Communities League Cup (11): Imrie 2 (1 pen), Campbell 2, Cham 1, Fitzpatrick 1, Fulton 1, Habai 1, Hands 1, McLaughlin 1, McNeil 1.
Ramsdens Cup (0).

Gaston D 17+1	Taggart S 29	Habai M 14+1	McLaughlin M 12	Fitzpatrick M 29	Imrie D 33	Hands R 9+1	Bachirou F 35	McKee J 6+8	Campbell A 11+19	Cham K 7+2	McNeil D 2+8	Wallace A 8+6	Fulton A 2+12	O'Brien D 3+3	Peciar T 15+2	Page J 10+2	Caraux N 19+1	Stirling S 8+3	Novo N 8	Reid C 9	Russell M 4+8	Nicholson J 3+1	O'Ware T 10+1	Ferris A —+1	Cole D 18	McKay B 14+4	McCormack J 10	Robertson D 14+2	O'Connor G 9+2	Sampayo B —+2	Findlay S 14	Vine R 12	Smith J —+2	Knight C 2+1	Cairnie J —+1	Match No.
1	2	3	4	5	6³	7	8	9¹	10	11²	12	13	14																							1
1	2	3	4	5	6	8	7	9²	10¹	11³		13	14	12																						2
1	2	4²	3			9	7	8		12	10		6³	14	11¹	5	13																			3
	2	7²	4³	5	10	9	6		13	11¹	14		8		12	3	1																			4
	2	6³	4¹	5	10	9	7		13	11		8²		14	12	3	1																			5
	2	6	4¹	5	10²	9	7		13	11		8		12		3	1																			6
	2	6²		5	10		7		11¹		13	8	9		4	3	1	12																		7
	2	7		5	10		8	12	11³		14	13	9¹		4	3²	1	6																		8
	2	11	4	9	6		8	12							5	3	1	7¹	10																	9
3¹	11		9	6		7	12	13							5	4	1	8	10²	2																10
	11	3	5	9		8	7	14			13				4¹	12	1	6³	10²	2																11
1		4		9³	8	7	10²	12		6					5	3		13	11	2	14															12
1		4		9³	7	8²	10	14		6¹					5	3		13	11	2	12															13
		8	4²	5	9	7	13	10ᵇ							3	1		11	2³	14	6¹	12														14
	14	4⁷	7	10	6			12			5			1	9¹	11	2	13	8	3³																15
	2	7²		5	10		8	14	12	13			3		1	9	11¹	4	8²																	16
	3			5¹	8	9	6	10²	13	11				4	1	7	2	12																		17
				5³	8	9	6	11¹	13		14		4		1	7²	2	12							3	10										18
8				5¹	10²	7	13	11		12			4	1			14								3	9³	2⁵	8¹¹								19
7				5	10	6	14		13	12		4	1												3	9³	2⁵	9³ 11								20
12	6			5	10	13	7			14		4	1²												3	8¹	2	9³ 11								21
7				5	8	6	13			12			1					4¹							3	10	2³	9³ 11	14							22
1	7			5	10	6	12	13					3		9	2	8²	11¹		4					3	9	2	8² 11¹	4							23
1	7			5	10	6¹	13						3		8⁷	2³	14	11	12	4	9				3	8²	2³ 14 11	12	4	9						24
1	6²			5	8ᵇ	7	10						3		2¹	12	11³	4	9	14					3	2¹ 12	11³		4	9 14						25
1	6			5		8	12			13	10		3		7	2²	11	4	9¹						3	7	2²	11	4	9¹						26
1	4		8	5¹			10			12	7		3		11²	6	13	2	9						3	11²	6 13		2	9						27
1	7			5	9¹	8	10						3		12	6	13	4	11³		14				3	12	6 13		4	11³	2⁴					28
1	8			5		6	13		10	14		7	3²		12	11³	4	9⁴	2¹				7		3² 12	11³			4	9⁴	2¹					29
1	8			5	9	7	10¹						4		13	2	6²	11³						4	13	2	6² 11³	3	12	12	14					30
1	8			5	9¹	7	13									12	2	3	10²		6³				3	10²	6³		4	11	14					31
1	6			5¹	10	7	14	13					12		2	3	9¹	8²	4	11					3	9¹	8²		4	11						32
1	6¹			8		7	12³	13			14		5		2	3	10	9²	4	11					3	10	9²		4	11						33
1³	6				10	7	13	14					12		5	2	3	9¹	8	4	11²				3	9¹	8		4	11²						34
	7				10	6							1		5	2	3	9	8	4	11				3	9	8		4	11						35
	6				10	7	12						1		5	2	3	9	8⁵	4	11				3	9	8⁵		4	11						36

HAMILTON ACADEMICAL

Year Formed: 1874. *Ground:* New Douglas Park, Cadzow Avenue, Hamilton ML3 0FT. *Telephone:* 01698 368652.
Fax: 01698 285422. *E-mail:* scott@acciesfc.co.uk *Website:* www.acciesfc.co.uk
Ground Capacity: 6,078 (all seated). *Size of Pitch:* 105m × 68m.
Chairman: Les Gray. *Secretary:* Scott Struthers.
Player Manager: Alex Neil. *Assistant Manager:* Frank MacAvoy. *Physio:* Victoria McIntyre.
Club Nickname: 'The Accies'.
Previous Grounds: Bent Farm, South Avenue, South Haugh, Douglas Park, Cliftonhill Stadium, Firhill Stadium.
Record Attendance: 28,690 v Hearts, Scottish Cup 3rd rd, 3 Mar 1937 (at Douglas Park); 5,895 v Rangers, 28 Feb 2009
(at New Douglas Park).
Record Transfer Fee received: £1,200,000 for James McCarthy to Wigan Ath (July 2009).
Record Transfer Fee paid: £180,000 for Tomas Cerny from Sigma Olomouc (July 2009).
Record Victory: 10-2 v Greenock Morton, Scottish Championship, 3 May 2014.
Record Defeat: 1-11 v Hibernian, Division I, 6 Nov 1965.
Most Capped Player: Colin Miller, 29 (61), Canada, 1988-94.
Most League Appearances: 452: Rikki Ferguson, 1974-88.
Most League Goals in Season (Individual): 35: David Wilson, Division I; 1936-37.
Most Goals Overall (Individual): 246: David Wilson, 1928-39.

HAMILTON ACADEMICAL – SCOTTISH CHAMPIONSHIP 2013–14 LEAGUE RECORD

Match No.	Date	Venue	Opponents	Result	H/T Score	Lg Pos.	Goalscorers	Attendance
1	Aug 10	A	Raith R	W 1-0	0-0	3	Keatings [68]	1652
2	17	H	Dumbarton	W 4-1	2-0	1	Keatings 2 (1 pen) [28 (p), 30], Gillespie [72], Andreu [77]	995
3	24	H	Queen of the South	W 2-0	1-0	1	Mackinnon [39], Ryan [80]	1367
4	31	A	Falkirk	W 2-1	0-0	1	Antoine-Curier [72], Crawford [75]	3266
5	Sept 14	A	Dundee	D 0-0	0-0	1		4155
6	21	H	Cowdenbeath	W 1-0	0-0	1	Gordon [51]	817
7	28	A	Alloa Ath	L 0-1	0-1	1		653
8	Oct 5	H	Livingston	W 2-0	1-0	1	Keatings 2 (1 pen) [33 (p), 65]	1059
9	12	A	Greenock Morton	D 1-1	1-0	1	Andreu [33]	2106
10	19	H	Raith R	D 1-1	1-0	1	Keatings [31]	1113
11	26	H	Falkirk	W 2-0	1-0	1	Andreu [21], Longridge [89]	1340
12	Nov 9	A	Queen of the South	W 1-0	1-0	1	Antoine-Curier [16]	1557
13	16	A	Cowdenbeath	W 4-2	0-2	1	Garcia Tena [66], Mackinnon [69], Gordon [71], Andreu [90]	401
14	23	H	Dundee	L 0-3	0-1	1		2077
15	Dec 7	H	Alloa Ath	L 0-1	0-0	2		860
16	14	A	Livingston	D 0-0	0-0	1		794
17	21	A	Dumbarton	L 1-2	1-1	2	Keatings [33]	642
18	28	H	Greenock Morton	W 1-0	1-0	2	Antoine-Curier [24]	1472
19	Jan 4	H	Queen of the South	W 3-1	2-1	2	Longridge [4], Antoine-Curier [9], Crawford [58]	1366
20	11	A	Falkirk	D 0-0	0-0	2		3099
21	25	H	Cowdenbeath	L 3-4	0-3	3	Andreu 2 [66, 86], Keatings (pen) [81]	944
22	Feb 1	H	Dumbarton	D 3-3	1-1	3	Keatings 2 [4, 71], Scotland [88]	1061
23	8	A	Dundee	L 0-1	0-1	3		5206
24	15	A	Raith R	W 4-2	4-0	2	Andreu 2 [4, 32], Longridge [39], Keatings (pen) [43]	1436
25	21	H	Livingston	W 2-0	1-0	2	Scotland [28], Antoine-Curier [90]	1063
26	Mar 1	A	Alloa Ath	W 3-0	3-0	2	Longridge [1], Keatings (pen) [11], Andreu [20]	656
27	8	A	Queen of the South	D 1-1	0-0	2	Canning [56]	1703
28	15	H	Falkirk	W 3-1	1-0	2	Scotland [4], Mackinnon [74], Longridge [90]	1706
29	22	A	Greenock Morton	W 4-3	1-1	2	Scotland [13], Longridge 2 [54, 64], Antoine-Curier [87]	1345
30	25	H	Raith R	W 3-2	0-1	2	Andreu [65], Keatings [68], Scotland [90]	954
31	29	A	Cowdenbeath	D 1-1	0-0	1	Antoine-Curier [90]	497
32	Apr 5	H	Dundee	D 1-1	0-1	1	Antoine-Curier [71]	4529
33	12	A	Livingston	D 1-1	0-0	2	Scotland [86]	1133
34	19	H	Alloa Ath	W 2-1	1-0	1	Scotland [4], Ryan [46]	1087
35	26	A	Dumbarton	L 1-4	1-1	2	Scotland [41]	1420
36	May 3	H	Greenock Morton	W 10-2	5-1	2	Antoine-Curier 4 [5, 56, 76, 86], Andreu 3 (1 pen) [8, 32, 45 (p)], Longridge [35], Devlin [49], Findlay (og) [85]	2034

Final League Position: 2

Honours
League Champions: Division II 1903-04. First Division 1985-86, 1987-88, 2007-08; Third Division 2000-01.
Runners-up: Division II 1952-53, 1964-65; Second Division 1996-97, 2003-04; Championship 2013-14 (promoted via play-offs).
Scottish Cup Runners-up: 1911, 1935. *League Cup:* Semi-finalists three times. *League Challenge Cup Runners-up:* 2005-06, 2011-12. *B&Q Cup Winners:* 1991-92, 1992-93.

Club colours: Shirt: Red and white hoops. Shorts: White. Socks: White.

Goalscorers: *League (68):* Andreu 13 (1 pen), Keatings 13 (5 pens), Antoine-Curier 12, Longridge 8, Scotland 8, Mackinnon 3, Crawford 2, Gordon 2, Ryan 2, Canning 1, Devlin 1, Garcia Tena 1, Gillespie 1, own goal 1.
William Hill Scottish FA Cup (0).
Scottish Communities League Cup (4): Keatings 2, Antoine-Curier 1, own goal 1.
Ramsdens Cup (1): Longridge 1.
Premiership Play-Offs (2): Andreu 1, MacKinnon 1.

Cuthbert K 34	Gordon Z 34	Kilday L 8+2	Devlin M 25+2	Hendrie S 19+3	Neil A 10	Crawford A 33+3	Mackinnon D 30+1	Gillespie G 31+2	Keatings J 29+1	McShane J 8+5	Ryan A 1+18	Andreu A 28+7	Brophy E 1+6	Canning M 34	McGrath J —+4	Watson C —+5	Antoine-Curier M 17+12	Longridge L 17+10	Finnie R —+1	Garcia Tena J 15+3	Docherty G —+3	Currie B 2+1	Scotland J 14+1	George P 1+5	Routledge J 5+6	Lyon D —+1	Match No.
1	2	3	4	5	6	7³	8	9	10²	11¹	12	13	14														1
1	5		4	2		7	9²	6	8	10¹	11³	12	13		3	14											2
1	2		3	5	8²	9¹	6	7	10³	11	13	12		4		14											3
1	2		3	5	8	9	7	6³	10¹	14	12	13		3		11²											4
1	2		4	5	8	9	6	7³	10¹	14	12	13		3		11²											5
1	2³		4	5	6	9	7²	8	10¹		13	12		3	11	14											6
1	2		3	5²	7³	9	6	8		11¹	14	12		4	10	13											7
1	2		4		8	9	6	10²	12	7³	14		3	13	11¹												8
1	5		4		8	9¹	6	2	10¹	12	7	3	14	13	11²												9
1	2		4	5		9	7³	8	10	14	6²	3	13	11¹	12												10
1	2		3	5		8	9	6	10¹		7³	14	4	12	11²	13											11
1	2		3	5		9	8	7	10¹		6	13	4	11²	12												12
1	2		3	5		9¹	6	8		11²	7	10	4³	14	12	13											13
1	2	12	4	6¹		8	7	5²	10³	11	9	3			13	14											14
1	2	3				9³	6¹	8	10		12	7	14	4	11²		5	13									15
1	2	3				9¹	6	8	10²	11³	14	7		4	12	13		5									16
1	2		5			9	8²	7	10		13	6		3	11¹	12		4									17
	2	5	4			9	7	8	10²		13	6¹		3	11	12		1									18
	2³	14	4	5		7	·	6	10¹		12	9²		3	11	8		13	1								19
1	2		4	5		7		6	11²		12	9	13	3	10¹	8											20
1	2		4	5		7²		6³	9		8			12	10¹					11	13	14					21
1	2		3¹	5		13	12		9		8		4	11²			14			10	7³	6					22
1	2⁴		3	12⁴		9	6	13	10¹		7		4			14	8²			11		5³					23
1		3¹				8	7	2	10²		6		4	12	14	9	5			11³					13		24
1	2		12			8	7	5	11²		6³		3	13	9¹	4				10			14				25
1	2					8	7	5	11³		6¹		3	13	9	4				10²	14		12				26
1	2	14				9	6	5	11¹		8		3	13	7	4²				10³	12						27
1	2		12			8²	6	5³	10		7		3	14	9	4				11¹		13					28
1	5	12				6	9	2	10²		13		3	14	8	4¹				11³		7					29
1	2		4			8¹	7	5	10²		6³		3	11	9					12	13	14					30
1	2	5	3			14	7		10¹		13	9	4	12	8²					11³		6					31
1	2	4¹				6	8	14	9²		13	7	3	12	10	5				11³							32
1	2		5¹			9	7		12		6	4		10¹	8	3				11							33
1		2				6²	8	9¹	5		12		10	3	14	7	4	13		11³							34
1	2		4			8⁴	9³		6² 12		10		3	13	7¹	5				11		14					35
1³	2	5	3			14		9¹	10² 7			11	8	4				12		13	6						36

HEART OF MIDLOTHIAN

Year Formed: 1874. *Ground & Address:* Tynecastle Stadium, McLeod Street, Edinburgh EH11 2NL. *Telephone:* 0871 663 1874. *Fax:* 0131 200 7222. *E-mail:* hearts@homplc.co.uk *Website:* www.heartsfc.co.uk
Ground Capacity: 17,402. *Size of Pitch:* 100m × 64m.
Administrators: Bryan Jackson, James Stephen and Trevor Birch.
Head Coach: Robbie Neilson. *Assistant Head Coach:* Stevie Crawford. *Physio:* Rob Marshall.
Club Nicknames: 'Hearts', 'Jambos'.
Previous Grounds: The Meadows 1874, Powderhall 1878, Old Tynecastle 1881 Tynecastle Park, 1886.
Record Attendance: 53,396 v Rangers, Scottish Cup 3rd rd, 13 Feb 1932 (57,857 v Barcelona, 28 July 2007 at Murrayfield).
Record Transfer Fee received: £9,000,000 for Craig Gordon to Sunderland (August 2008).
Record of Transfer paid: £850,000 for Mirsad Beslija to Genk (January 2006).
Record Victory: 15-0 v King's Park, Scottish Cup 2nd rd, 13 Feb 1937 (21-0 v Anchor, EFA Cup, 30 Oct 1880).
Record Defeat: 1-8 v Vale of Leven, Scottish Cup 3rd rd, 1883.
Most Capped Player: Steven Pressley, 32, Scotland.
Most League Appearances: 515: Gary Mackay, 1980-97.
Most League Goals in Season (Individual): 44: Barney Battles, 1930-31.
Most Goals Overall (Individual): 214: John Robertson, 1983-98.

HEART OF MIDLOTHIAN – SCOTTISH PREMIER LEAGUE 2013–14 LEAGUE RECORD

Match No.	Date	Venue	Opponents	Result	H/T Score	Lg Pos.	Goalscorers	Atten- dance
1	Aug 4	A	St Johnstone	L	0-1	0-1	12		6174
2	11	H	Hibernian	W	1-0	0-0	12	Paterson 72	16,621
3	16	A	Partick Thistle	D	1-1	0-0	12	Walker 88	6540
4	24	H	Aberdeen	W	2-1	1-0	12	Walker 18, McGhee 88	15,218
5	31	A	Inverness CT	L	0-2	0-2	12		4034
6	Sept 14	H	Celtic	L	1-3	0-1	12	Holt 58	15,928
7	21	A	Ross Co	L	1-2	1-0	12	Paterson 24	4059
8	28	H	Dundee U	D	0-0	0-0	12		13,970
9	Oct 5	H	St Mirren	L	0-2	0-1	12		14,769
10	19	A	Motherwell	L	1-2	0-0	12	Stevenson 62	5350
11	26	A	Kilmarnock	L	0-2	0-1	12		5090
12	Nov 2	H	St Johnstone	L	0-2	0-1	12		13,175
13	9	A	Aberdeen	W	3-1	0-1	12	Walker 66, Paterson 74, Stevenson 90	13,940
14	23	H	Ross Co	D	2-2	1-1	12	Paterson 28, Wilson 89	12,508
15	Dec 7	A	Dundee U	L	1-4	1-1	12	Hamill (pen) 20	7808
16	14	H	Inverness CT	L	0-2	0-0	12		11,950
17	21	A	Celtic	L	0-2	0-0	12		46,058
18	26	H	Kilmarnock	L	0-4	0-2	12		13,684
19	29	A	St Mirren	D	1-1	0-1	12	Hamill 48	4568
20	Jan 2	A	Hibernian	L	1-2	0-0	12	Smith 72	20,106
21	5	H	Partick Thistle	L	0-2	0-2	12		13,763
22	11	H	Motherwell	L	0-1	0-1	12		12,888
23	18	A	St Johnstone	D	3-3	0-1	12	Carrick 58, Nicholson 89, Wilson 90	3395
24	25	A	Ross Co	W	2-1	1-1	12	Paterson 37, Robinson 80	4016
25	29	H	St Mirren	W	2-1	1-1	12	Paterson 5, Hamill (pen) 52	12,422
26	Feb 15	A	Inverness CT	D	0-0	0-0	12		3392
27	22	H	Celtic	L	0-2	0-0	12		15,801
28	Mar 1	A	Motherwell	L	1-4	0-2	12	Paterson 69	4914
29	8	A	Kilmarnock	L	2-4	1-1	12	Carrick 30, Nicholson 69	3510
30	21	H	Dundee U	L	1-2	0-1	12	Wilson 78	13,448
31	30	H	Hibernian	W	2-0	1-0	12	Carrick 7, King, B 90	16,873
32	Apr 2	H	Aberdeen	D	1-1	0-0	12	Hamill (pen) 87	13,913
33	5	A	Partick Thistle	W	4-2	1-1	12	Carrick 44, King, B 50, Stevenson 2 61, 68	4262
34	19	A	Ross Co	W	2-0	0-0	12	Hamill (pen) 65, Carrick 90	13,692
35	27	A	Hibernian	W	2-1	2-0	12	Paterson 2 37, 41	14,806
36	May 4	H	Kilmarnock	W	5-0	3-0	12	Stevenson 3 11, 24, 45, King, B 56, Paterson 60	13,656
37	7	H	Partick Thistle	L	2-4	2-1	12	Paterson 16, Wilson 41	14,059
38	10	A	St Mirren	D	1-1	0-1	12	Carrick 48	6311

Final League Position: 12

Honours
League Champions: Division I 1894-95, 1896-97, 1957-58, 1959-60. First Division 1979-80;
Runners-up: Division I 1893-94, 1898-99, 1903-04, 1905-06, 1914-15, 1937-38, 1953-54, 1956-57, 1958-59, 1964-65. Premier Division 1985-86, 1987-88, 1991-92, 2005-06. First Division 1977-78, 1982-83.
Scottish Cup Winners: 1891, 1896, 1901, 1906, 1956, 1998, 2006, 2012; *Runners-up:* 1903, 1907, 1968, 1976, 1986, 1996.
League Cup Winners: 1954-55, 1958-59, 1959-60, 1962-63; *Runners-up:* 1961-62, 1996-97, 2012-13.

European: *European Cup:* 8 matches (1958-59, 1960-61, 2006-07). *Cup Winners' Cup:* 10 matches (1976-77, 1996-97, 1998-99). *UEFA Cup:* 46 matches (*Fairs Cup:* 1961-62, 1963-64, 1965-66. *UEFA Cup:* 1984-85, 1986-87, 1988-89, 1990-91, 1992-93, 1993-94, 2000-01, 2003-04, 2004-05, 2006-07). *Europa League:* 8 matches (2010-11, 2011-12, 2012-13).

Club colours: Shirt: Maroon with white trim. Shorts: White with maroon trim. Socks: Maroon with white tops.

Goalscorers: *League (45):* Paterson 11, Stevenson 7, Carrick 6, Hamill 5 (4 pens), Wilson 4, King B 3, Walker 3, Nicholson 2, Holt 1, McGhee 1, Robinson 1, Smith 1.
William Hill Scottish FA Cup (0).
Scottish Communities League Cup (7): Hamill 4 (2 pens), McHattie 1, Stevenson 1, Wilson 1.

MacDonald J 37	Hamill J 34 + 1	McHattie K 35	Tapping C 13 + 6	McKay D 23 + 5	Wilson D 32	Stevenson R 25 + 1	McGowan D 37	Robinson S 31 + 5	Paterson C 36 + 1	Walker J 21 + 5	Holt J 18 + 5	King B 7 + 25	Smith D 18 + 14	McGhee J 14 + 3	Oliver G 1 + 7	Nicholson S 15 + 10	Carrick D 14 + 11	King A 2	McCallum P 4 + 2	Ridgers M 1	Match No.
1	2	3	4^2	5	6	7	8	9^1	10	11^3	12	13	14								1
1	7	5		3	4	9^1	2	8	11	12	10	13	6^2								2
1	7	5	13	3	4		2	8^1	11	9	10	12	6^1								3
1	7	5^1	13	3^1	4		2	9	11	6^2	8	10^3	14	12							4
1	5^1		6^2	4		3	7	8	10^3	9	12	11^1	2	13	14						5
1	8	5		3	4		2	7	11	9^1	6^3	10^1	12		14		13				6
1	7	5		3	4		2	9	10	11^1	6	12	9^2			13					7
1	9	5	12		3	14	4	8^1	6	10	7^2	13	11^3	2							8
1	7	5	13		4	9^2	3^1	6^2	11	10	8	12		2		14					9
1	8		7^2	3	4	10	2	12	6^1	11	13		9^3	5		14					10
1	7	5	8^1	4	3	11^3		6	12	10			9^2	2		14	13				11
1	7	5			4	11	3	6^1	8^3	10^4	9		14	2		12	13				12
1	7	5	13		4	11	3	6^1	10	9^2	8^2	14	12	2							13
1	6	5	7^1		4	10	3	8^2	11	9		13	12	2							14
1	2	5	8^2		3	6^1	4	10	11	7		12		9			13				15
1	2	5	7		4		3	6	10	9^1		13	12		11^2	8^1	14				16
1	2	5	6^1	3	4		7		11	8^2		10				13	12	9			17
1	2	5	8^2	3	4		7	12	11	9		13	6^3				14	10^1			18
1	6	5	8	3	4	11	2	7^1	9	10		12									19
1	8	5	6^1	3		10	4	7	11	9		12	2								20
1		5	7	3		10	4	8	11^3	9^2		12	6^1	2		14	13				21
1	7	5^1		3		10	4	8	11	12		14	9^2	2		13	6^3				22
1	7	5	8^1	2	3	10^4	4^2		11			14	9^3		13	12	6				23
1	7	2	13	5	3		4	10	11			12	6			9^2	8^1				24
1	7	5		3	4		2^1	8	11			12	9	14	13	6^2	10^2				25
1	6		3	4	9	2	7			12		5		10	8^1				11		26
1	9	5		3	4	7^2	2	10^2	6			13	14			8	12		11^1		27
1	8	5		3^3	4	6	2	7^3	11			14	13			9	12		10^1		28
1	8^1	5		14	3	10	4	7	6^2			12			2^2		11		13		29
1	8	5		14	4	6^1	3	7	2			12	13	9^3		11	10^2				30
1	7	5			4	10	3	14	2			8^1	13	6^3		9	11^2		12		31
1	6	5		14	4^4	9	3	12	2			7	13	8^1		10^2			11^3		32
1	7	5		4		10	3	6^2	2			8	11^2	12		14	13		9^3		33
1	7^1	5		4		10^1	3	13	2	12	8	9^3	14			11^1	6				34
1		5		14	4	10	3	8	2	13	7	6^1	12			9^2	11^1				35
1	14	5		4	10^2	3	7	2		8	9^1	12		13	11	6^1					36
	8	5	14	4		3	9^2	2^3	13	7	6^1	12			10	11			1		37
1		5		4		3	7	2	9^2	6	13	11^3	12	14		8	10^1				38

HIBERNIAN

Year Formed: 1875. *Ground & Address:* Easter Road Stadium, 12 Albion Place, Edinburgh EH7 5QG. *Telephone:* 0131 661 2159. *Fax:* 0131 659 6488. *E-mail:* club@hibernianfc.co.uk *Website:* www.hibernianfc.co.uk
Ground Capacity: 20,421 (all seated). *Size of Pitch:* 102m × 67m.
Chairman: Rod Petrie. *Chief Executive:* Leean Dempster. *Club Secretary:* Garry O'Hagan.
Head Coach: Alan Stubbs. *Assistant Head Coach:* TBC. *Physio:* Calum Rea.
Club Nickname: 'Hibs', 'Hibees'.
Previous Grounds: Meadows 1875-78, Powderhall 1878-79, Mayfield 1879-80, First Easter Road 1880-92, Second Easter Road 1892-.
Record Attendance: 65,860 v Hearts, Division I, 2 Jan 1950.
Record Transfer Fee received: £4,400,000 for Scott Brown from Celtic (2007).
Record of Transfer paid: £700,000 for Ulises de la Cruz to LDU Quito (2001).
Record Victory: 15-1 v Pebbles Rovers, Scottish Cup 2nd rd, 11 Feb 1961.
Record Defeat: 0-10 v Rangers, Division I, 24 Dec 1898.
Most Capped Player: Lawrie Reilly, 38, Scotland.
Most League Appearances: 446: Arthur Duncan.
Most League Goals in Season (Individual): 42: Joe Baker, 1959-60.
Most Goals Overall (Individual): 233: Lawrie Reilly, 1945-58.

HIBERNIAN – SCOTTISH PREMIER LEAGUE 2013–14 LEAGUE RECORD

Match No.	Date		Venue	Opponents	Result		H/T Score	Lg Pos.	Goalscorers	Atten- dance
1	Aug	4	H	Motherwell	L	0-1	0-0	10		9237
2		11	A	Hearts	L	0-1	0-0	9		16,621
3		17	H	Dundee U	D	1-1	0-1	9	Robertson [81]	9171
4		24	A	Kilmarnock	W	2-1	0-1	8	Craig 2 [47, 80]	3807
5		31	H	Ross Co	D	0-0	0-0	8		9569
6	Sept	14	A	St Johnstone	W	2-1	1-1	6	Heffernan [35], Collins [59]	4095
7		21	H	St Mirren	W	2-0	1-0	5	Collins [10], Heffernan [61]	9417
8		28	A	Inverness CT	L	0-3	0-1	5		4261
9	Oct	7	A	Partick Thistle	W	1-0	0-0	5	Craig [69]	4521
10		19	H	Celtic	D	1-1	1-0	5	Heffernan [18]	14,220
11		26	H	Aberdeen	L	0-2	0-0	6		12,810
12	Nov	3	A	Motherwell	L	0-1	0-1	7		3864
13		9	H	Inverness CT	L	0-2	0-2	7		8750
14		23	A	St Mirren	D	0-0	0-0	7		4451
15	Dec	7	H	Partick Thistle	D	1-1	0-0	7	Collins [90]	10,431
16		14	A	Celtic	L	0-1	0-1	7		46,065
17		21	H	St Johnstone	D	0-0	0-0	7		8776
18		26	A	Ross Co	W	2-0	1-0	7	Nelson [18], Forster [56]	3383
19		29	H	Kilmarnock	W	3-0	1-0	7	Hanlon [12], Cairney [77], Stevenson [90]	9683
20	Jan	2	H	Hearts	W	2-1	0-0	6	Collins [61], Craig (pen) [83]	20,106
21		5	A	Dundee U	D	2-2	1-0	6	Craig 2 (1 pen) [38, 61 (p)]	7862
22		10	A	Aberdeen	L	0-1	0-0	6		12,734
23		18	H	St Mirren	L	2-3	0-3	7	Collins 2 [63, 89]	9610
24		26	H	Celtic	L	0-4	0-1	7		12,542
25	Feb	15	H	Ross Co	W	2-1	2-0	7	Stanton [10], Taiwo [24]	8411
26		22	A	Kilmarnock	D	1-1	0-1	7	Haynes [56]	4036
27		28	H	Dundee U	L	1-3	1-1	7	Forster [45]	9608
28	Mar	8	H	Motherwell	D	3-3	1-2	7	Forster [43], Nelson [76], Heffernan [79]	8277
29		12	A	Inverness CT	D	0-0	0-0	7		2537
30		15	A	Partick Thistle	L	1-3	0-1	7	Watmore [62]	4448
31		22	A	St Johnstone	L	0-2	0-1	7		3553
32		30	A	Hearts	L	0-2	0-1	7		16,873
33	Apr	7	H	Aberdeen	L	0-2	0-1	7		9321
34		19	A	St Mirren	L	0-2	0-2	7		5287
35		27	H	Hearts	L	1-2	0-2	8	Forster [69]	14,806
36	May	3	H	Partick Thistle	D	1-1	0-1	8	Stanton [88]	10,740
37		6	A	Ross Co	L	0-1	0-0	9		3850
38		10	A	Kilmarnock	L	0-1	0-1	11		15,057

Final League Position: 11

Honours
League Champions: Division I 1902-03, 1947-48, 1950-51, 1951-52. First Division 1980-81, 1998-99. Division II 1893-94, 1894-95, 1932-33; *Runners-up:* Division I 1896-97, 1946-47, 1949-50, 1952-53, 1973-74, 1974-75.
Scottish Cup Winners: 1887, 1902; *Runners-up:* 1896, 1914, 1923, 1924, 1947, 1958, 1972, 1979, 2001, 2012, 2013.
League Cup Winners: 1972-73, 1991-92, 2006-07; *Runners-up:* 1950-51, 1968-69, 1974-75, 1985-86, 1993-94, 2003-04.
Drybrough Cup Winners: 1972-73, 1973-74.

European: *European Cup:* 6 matches (1955-56 semi-finals). *Cup Winners' Cup:* 6 matches (1972-73). *UEFA Cup:* 64 matches (*Fairs Cup:* 1960-61 semi-finals, 1961-62, 1962-63, 1965-66, 1967-68, 1968-69, 1970-71. *UEFA Cup:* 1973-74, 1974-75, 1975-76, 1976-77, 1978-79, 1989-90, 1992-93, 2001-02, 2005-06. *Europa League:* 4 matches 2010-11, 2012-13).

Club colours: Shirt: Green with white sleeves. Shorts: White. Socks: Green.

Goalscorers: *League (31):* Collins 6, Craig 6 (2 pens), Forster 4, Heffernan 4, Nelson 2, Stanton 2, Cairney 1, Hanlon 1, Haynes 1, Robertson 1, Stevenson 1, Taiwo 1, Watmore 1.
William Hill Scottish FA Cup (3): Handling 1, Nelson 1, Stanton 1.
Scottish Communities League Cup (5): Craig 3 (1 pen), Zoubir 1, own goal 1.
Premiership Play-Offs (0).
UEFA Europa League (0).

Williams B 37	Mullen F 3	Stevenson L 33+2	Robertson S 24	Nelson M 32+1	Hanlon P 28	Harris A 10+5	Thomson K 15+3	Collins J 27+9	Tudur Jones O 8+6	Craig L 31+3	Stanton S 15+13	Taiwo T 17+5	Handling D 10+9	Vine R 4+6	McGivern R 31+2	Caldwell R —+3	Horribine D —+1	Heffernan P 13+6	Maybury A 14	McPake J 1+2	Zoubir A 3+10	Forster J 26	Cummings J 9+7	Cairney P 14+4	Haynes D 7+2	Boateng D 1+2	Watmore D 4+5	Murdoch S 1	Match No.
1	2	3	4¹	5	6	7³	8²	9	10	11	12	13	14																1
1	2³	5	7²	3	4			9	11	8¹	10	14	13	6	12														2
1	2³	5	6¹	3	4		8¹	11		9	13	14	7	10²	12														3
1	2		3	4		10²	7	9	13	8¹	6	11³	5	12	14														4
1	2		3	4		11³	8	9	13	7	6²	10¹	5	12		14													5
1	5	6	3	4		7	11³	9²	14	8					10	2	12	13											6
1	5	6		3	4	8	11³	9	12	7²		14				10¹	2	13											7
1	2	6		3	4	8²	10	9	14	7³			13	5		11¹		12											8
1	2	6¹	4	3		8	10²	12	9	14	7²			5		11		13											9
1	2	10	3	4		9		7	8¹	14	13	5³			11		12	6²											10
1	2	6		4		8	12	7²	9		14	13	5		11³	3	10¹												11
1	8	6		4		7	14	9		10²		13	5³		11	2¹		12	3										12
1	9	6		4		8	10²			7¹		12	5³		11	2		13	3	14									13
1	9	7		4			12		8		13	10¹		5	14	11²	2				3		6²						14
1	8¹	14	4			11	7	9		10²			5					2³	12	13	13	6							15
1	9²	7	3	4		14	11	8		10¹			5					13	2	12	6³								16
1	9²	7¹	3	4		12	10	8					5					13	2	11	6								17
1	9	7	3	4		11²	13	8				12	5					2	10¹	6									18
1	9	7	3	4		10	13	8				12	5					2	11²	6¹									19
1	9	7²	3	4		10	13	8	14				5		12			2	11³	6¹									20
1	9	7	3	4		11	13	8	12				5		10¹			2		6²									21
1	9	7²	4	3	14	10		8	12				5		11¹			2	13	6²									22
1	9	7	4		12		8	13					5³			2	14	3	11²	6¹									23
1	5		3		10		11		9	8	6¹				12	2	7	4											24
1	8		3	4	9¹		13			11	7	6³	5					2		12	10²	14							25
1	9³		3	4	6		14			12	8	7	10¹	5				2			13	11²							26
1	9		3	4³	6		14			8¹	10	7⁴	12	5				2				11²	13						27
1	9¹		3	4	12		10			7	8	14	5		13			2			6³	11²							28
1	12		3	4			11			13	8	7¹	5		14			2			6	10³		9²					29
1			3	4		10¹	13	8	7				5		12			2			11²	6¹	14	9					30
1	14		3		9¹			10	8²	7³	12		5		11			2			13	6⁴		4				1	31
1	9		3	4			12	13	11		8	7³	10¹	5			2⁸				3	14		6²					32
1	5		3		6		10²		8	11	7³	12	4				2			14	9¹			13					33
1	5		4		6	8	10¹	7²	9						2						3	12		11			13		34
1		7¹	4		6	9	13	10	8				5					2			3	11²					12		35
1	5	7³	3⁴		11¹	8²	12	9	10			14		4			2				6			13					36
1	5	6			8³		13	7		9		4¹		3			2				10	11²	14	12					37
1		8³	4		13		10	12		6	9²			5			11	2			3	14		7¹					38

INVERNESS CALEDONIAN THISTLE

Year Formed: 1994. *Ground & Address:* Tulloch Caledonian Stadium, Stadium Road, Inverness IV1 1FF. *Telephone:* 01463 222880. *Fax:* 01463 227479. *E-mail:* jim.falconer@ictfc.co.uk *Website:* www.ictfc.co.uk
Ground Capacity: 7,780 (all seated). *Size of Pitch:* 105m × 68m.
Chairman: Kenny Cameron. *Club Secretary:* Jim Falconer.
Club Nicknames: 'Caley Thistle', 'Caley Jags', 'ICT'.
Manager: John Hughes. *Physios:* John McCreadie and Stuart Phin.
Record Attendance: 7,753 v Rangers, SPL, 20 January 2008.
Record Transfer Fee received: £400,000 for Marius Niculae to Dinamo Bucharest (July 2008).
Record of Transfer paid: £65,000 for John Rankin from Ross County (July 2006).
Record Victory: 8-1 v Annan Ath, Scottish Cup 3rd rd, 24 January 1998.
Record Defeats: 0-6 v Airdrieonians, First Division, 21 Sep 2000; 0-6 v Celtic, League Cup 3rd rd, 22 Sep 2010; 0-6 v Celtic Scottish Premiership, 27 April 2014.
Most Capped Player: Richard Hastings, 38 (59), Canada.
Most League Appearances: 490: Ross Tokely, 1995-2012.
Most League Goals in Season: 27: Iain Stewart, 1996-97; Denis Wyness, 2002-03.
Most Goals Overall (Individual): 118: Denis Wyness, 2000-03, 2005-08.

INVERNESS CALEDONIAN THISTLE –
SCOTTISH PREMIER LEAGUE 2013–14 LEAGUE RECORD

Match No.	Date	Venue	Opponents	Result		H/T Score	Lg Pos.	Goalscorers	Attendance
1	Aug 3	H	St Mirren	W	3-0	0-0	1	Vincent (pen) [48], Doran [49], McKay [59]	3215
2	10	A	Dundee U	W	1-0	1-0	1	McKay [20]	6664
3	17	H	Motherwell	W	2-0	2-0	1	Foran [4], McKay [36]	3031
4	24	A	Celtic	D	2-2	2-1	1	Doran [14], Foran [35]	45,160
5	31	H	Hearts	W	2-0	2-0	1	McKay 2 [10, 32]	4034
6	Sept 14	A	Kilmarnock	W	2-1	1-0	1	Foran [6], McKay [56]	3063
7	21	A	Aberdeen	L	0-1	0-0	1		11,251
8	28	H	Hibernian	W	3-0	1-0	1	McKay 2 [11, 61], Foran [59]	4261
9	Oct 5	A	St Johnstone	L	0-4	0-2	2		3020
10	20	H	Partick Thistle	L	1-2	0-1	2	Warren [47]	3154
11	Nov 2	H	Kilmarnock	W	2-1	1-0	2	Doran [7], Shinnie [52]	2948
12	9	A	Hibernian	W	2-0	2-0	2	Ross (pen) [14], McKay [18]	8750
13	23	H	St Johnstone	W	1-0	1-0	2	McKay [4]	3255
14	Dec 7	A	St Mirren	D	0-0	0-0	2		3305
15	14	A	Hearts	W	2-0	0-0	2	McKay 2 [59, 83]	11,950
16	21	H	Aberdeen	L	3-4	0-4	4	McKay 2 [47, 57], Shinnie [90]	4810
17	26	A	Partick Thistle	D	0-0	0-0	3		2887
18	29	H	Celtic	L	0-1	0-1	4		6384
19	Jan 1	H	Ross Co	L	1-2	0-2	4	Doran [89]	4332
20	12	H	Dundee U	D	1-1	1-1	5	McKay [5]	2980
21	18	A	Aberdeen	W	1-0	1-0	4	Williams [22]	12,021
22	25	A	Kilmarnock	L	0-2	0-1	4		3035
23	Feb 15	H	Hearts	D	0-0	0-0	5		3392
24	22	A	St Johnstone	W	1-0	1-0	5	Warren [42]	2415
25	25	A	Ross Co	W	3-0	2-0	4	Raven [8], McKay [40], Watkins [78]	4805
26	Mar 1	A	Celtic	L	0-5	0-2	5		46,552
27	12	H	Hibernian	D	0-0	0-0	4		2537
28	19	A	Motherwell	L	0-2	0-2	5		3432
29	22	H	Partick Thistle	W	1-0	0-0	5	McKay [62]	3093
30	26	A	Dundee U	L	1-2	0-0	5	Polworth [81]	6754
31	29	H	St Mirren	D	2-2	2-1	5	Draper [16], Tansey [34]	3032
32	Apr 1	H	Motherwell	L	1-2	0-1	5	Christie [74]	2366
33	4	A	Ross Co	W	2-1	1-0	5	Doran [45], McKay [79]	4433
34	18	H	Aberdeen	D	0-0	0-0	5		4224
35	27	A	Celtic	L	0-6	0-2	5		45,712
36	May 3	H	Dundee U	D	1-1	1-0	5	Christie [7]	3428
37	7	A	Motherwell	L	1-2	0-2	5	Shinnie [55]	4482
38	11	H	St Johnstone	W	2-0	0-0	5	Christie [59], Tansey [90]	3121

Final League Position: 5

Honours
League Champions: First Division 2003-04, 2009-10. Third Division 1996-97.
Scottish Cup: Semi-finals 2003, 2004; Quarter-finals 1996; *Runners-up:* Second Division 1998-99.
League Cup Runners-up: 2013-14.
League Challenge Cup Winners: 2003-04; *Runners-up:* 1999-2000, 2009-10.

Club colours: Shirt: Blue with red trim. Shorts: Blue. Socks: Blue.

Goalscorers: *League (44):* McKay 18, Doran 5, Foran 4, Christie 3, Shinnie 3, Tansey 2, Warren 2, Draper 1, Polworth 1, Raven 1, Ross 1 (1 pen), Vincent 1 (1 pen), Watkins 1, Williams 1.
William Hill Scottish FA Cup (8): Doran 3 (1 pen), McKay 3, Ross 2 (1 pen).
Scottish Communities League Cup (5): Draper 1, McKay 1, Ross 1, Tansey 1, Warren 1.

Brill D 37	Raven D 25 + 1	Shinnie G 36	Foran R 23 + 1	Meekings J 34	Warren G 34	Doran A 33	Draper R 33 + 1	McKay B 38	Vincent J 19 + 2	Ross N 25 + 8	Polworth L 7 + 12	Agdestein T — + 13	Williams D 11 + 9	Devine D 8 + 5	Watkins M 15 + 11	Greenhalgh B 1 + 5	Tremarco C 20 + 1	Christie R 3 + 12	Tansey G 15 + 1	Evans A — + 2	Esson R 1	Match No.
1	2	3	4	5	6	7²	8³	9	10¹	11	12	13	14									1
1	2²	3	11	5	4	6¹	7	10	9	8	13				12							2
1	2	5	8	4	3	6¹	7	10³	11¹	9	12	13	14									3
1	2	5	7	4	3	8²	6	11	9	10		13		12								4
1	2	5	8	4	3	9	7	11²	10¹	6		12				13						5
1	2	5	7	4	3	10	6	11²	9¹	8	13		12									6
1	2	5	8	4	3	9	7	11²	10¹	6	13	12										7
1	2	5	7	4	3	10	6¹	11	9²	8³	13	14					12					8
1		3	9¹	5	4	6	7	11		10³	8²	13	14	2	12							9
1	2	5	8	4	3	6	7	11¹	10³	12	14				13	9²						10
1		2	7	4	3	9	8	11		10³	13	12	14				6¹	5²				11
1	2	10	4	3	6	7	11	9		12							8¹		5			12
1	2	8	4	3	9²	7	11	10¹						12			6	13	5			13
1	2	7	4	3	10	6	11	9									8		5			14
1	2	7	4	3	9¹	8	11	10			12	13					6²		5			15
1	12	2	7²	4	3	9	8	11	10¹				13				6		5			16
1	2		4	3		9	6	11	10¹	7				12			8		5			17
1	2		4	3		9	7	11	10²		12					8	6¹		5	13		18
1	2		4	3		9	7¹	11	10		13	12				8	6¹		5²			19
1	2	7	4	3	6		11	9¹	10²							8		13	5	12		20
1	2	6		3	7²	11³	8	10¹	9	13	4							5	12	14		21
1	2²	6	3¹	4		7	14	11	10³				13			8	9	12	5			22
1	2	5	12	4	3	9	7	11	10¹								6	8				23
1	2	5	10	4	3	6	7	11²	13	12							9¹	8				24
1	2	5	10³	4	3	9²	7	11	6	14							12	13	8			25
1	2	5	8	4	3²	9¹	11³	7	6							12	13	14	10			26
1		6	2	4	10²		11	7¹	8	9	3						5	13		12		27
1	2	5	8	4		11¹	7	10	6²	3								13	12	9		28
1	2	5	7²	4	3		8	11	10¹		12					9³	14	13	6			29
1	2	5	7¹	4	3	8¹	11	10	14	12							9²	13	6			30
1	2	5	4¹	3	8	11	9	12	7		13	14					10³	6²				31
	2¹	10		3		8	11	7	6²		4	13						5	12	9	1	32
1	2	9	4	3	10		11	8¹									6	5	12	7		33
1	2		4	3	6		8	11	10²				13			9¹		5	12	7		34
1	2		4	3	6	7¹	11	10²				13				9	5	12	8			35
1	2			9	8	11	13	12			5	3		6²	4	10¹	7					36
1	2	5			3	11¹	8	10			12	7	6²	4	13		9					37
1	2	9		6	3	11³	8¹	14				13	4	12		5	10²	7				38

KILMARNOCK

Year Formed: 1869. *Ground & Address:* Rugby Park, Kilmarnock KA1 2DP. *Telephone:* 01563 545300. *Fax:* 01563 522181. *Email:* kirstencallaghan@kilmarnockfc.co.uk *Website:* www.kilmarnockfc.co.uk
Ground Capacity: 18,128 (all seated). *Size of Pitch:* 102m × 67m.
Chairman: Michael Johnston. *Secretary:* Kirsten Callaghan.
Manager: Allan Johnston. *U-20 Coach:* Alan Robertson. *Physio:* Alex MacQueen.
Club Nickname: 'Killie'.
Previous Grounds: Rugby Park (Dundonald Road); The Grange; Holm Quarry; Rugby Park 1899.
Record Attendance: 35,995 v Rangers, Scottish Cup Quarter-final, 10 Mar 1962.
Record Transfer Fee received: £1,900,000 for Stephen Naismith to Rangers (2007).
Record Transfer Fee paid: £340,000 for Paul Wright from St Johnstone (1995).
Record Victory: 11-1 v Paisley Academical, Scottish Cup 1st rd, 18 Jan 1930.
Record Defeat: 1-9 v Celtic, Division I, 13 Aug 1938.
Most Capped Player: Joe Nibloe, 11, Scotland.
Most League Appearances: 481: Alan Robertson, 1972-88.
Most League Goals in Season (Individual): 34: Harry 'Peerie' Cunningham 1927-28; Andy Kerr 1960-61.
Most Goals Overall (Individual): 148: Willy Culley, 1912-23.

KILMARNOCK – SCOTTISH PREMIER LEAGUE 2013–14 LEAGUE RECORD

Match No.	Date	Venue	Opponents	Result	H/T Score	Lg Pos.	Goalscorers	Attendance
1	Aug 3	A	Aberdeen	L 1-2	0-1	9	Boyd [64]	13,149
2	11	H	St Johnstone	D 0-0	0-0	7		3550
3	17	A	St Mirren	D 1-1	0-0	7	Boyd [49]	4625
4	24	H	Hibernian	L 1-2	1-0	10	Nicholson [23]	3807
5	31	A	Motherwell	L 1-2	1-2	10	McManus (og) [17]	4353
6	Sept 14	H	Inverness CT	L 1-2	0-1	10	Nicholson [51]	3063
7	21	A	Partick Thistle	D 1-1	0-1	10	Boyd [48]	4310
8	28	H	Celtic	L 2-5	2-3	10	Clingan [35], Clohessy [42]	6149
9	Oct 5	A	Dundee U	L 0-1	0-0	11		5850
10	19	H	Ross Co	W 2-0	1-0	11	Boyd [17], Irvine [71]	3582
11	26	A	Hearts	W 2-0	1-0	10	Boyd 2 [16, 64]	5090
12	Nov 2	A	Inverness CT	L 1-2	0-1	10	Barr [76]	2948
13	9	A	St Johnstone	L 1-3	0-2	11	Clohessy [69]	2855
14	23	H	Motherwell	L 0-2	0-0	11		3704
15	Dec 7	A	Ross Co	W 2-1	2-1	10	Johnston [7], Boyd [43]	2937
16	14	H	Dundee U	L 1-4	0-0	10	Boyd [89]	3452
17	21	H	Partick Thistle	W 2-1	1-0	9	Johnston [42], Boyd [73]	3865
18	26	A	Hearts	W 4-0	2-0	9	Boyd 2 [13, 48], Johnston [40], McKenzie [90]	13,684
19	29	A	Hibernian	L 0-3	0-1	9		9683
20	Jan 2	H	St Mirren	W 2-1	1-1	8	McKenzie [29], Boyd [90]	5410
21	5	H	Aberdeen	L 0-1	0-0	8		4073
22	18	A	Partick Thistle	D 1-1	0-1	9	Muirhead [90]	4092
23	25	H	Inverness CT	W 2-0	1-0	8	Ashcroft [16], Boyd [74]	3035
24	29	A	Celtic	L 0-4	0-2	8		44,271
25	Feb 1	H	Ross Co	D 2-2	0-2	8	Boyd 2 [48, 90]	3372
26	15	A	Dundee U	L 2-3	1-1	8	Eremenko [40], Boyd [64]	6038
27	22	H	Hibernian	D 1-1	1-0	8	McKenzie [20]	4036
28	Mar 1	A	St Mirren	L 0-2	0-0	8		4650
29	8	H	Hearts	W 4-2	1-1	8	Wilson (og) [27], Boyd 2 [49, 51], Gardyne [72]	3510
30	14	H	Celtic	L 0-3	0-0	8		7495
31	22	A	Aberdeen	L 1-2	1-1	8	Boyd [11]	17,029
32	29	A	Motherwell	W 2-1	0-1	8	McKenzie [66], Slater [90]	4467
33	Apr 5	A	St Johnstone	L 1-2	1-2	8	Muirhead [5]	3665
34	19	H	Partick Thistle	L 1-2	0-0	9	Maksimenko [54]	4980
35	26	A	Ross Co	L 1-2	0-1	11	Boyd [88]	3401
36	May 4	A	Hearts	L 0-5	0-3	11		13,656
37	7	H	St Mirren	W 1-0	1-0	10	Boyd [21]	4911
38	10	A	Hibernian	W 1-0	1-0	9	Boyd [44]	15,057

Final League Position: 9

Honours
League Champions: Division I 1964-65. Division II 1897-98, 1898-99; *Runners-up:* Division I 1959-60, 1960-61, 1962-63, 1963-64. First Division 1975-76, 1978-79, 1981-82, 1992-93. Division II 1953-54, 1973-74. Second Division 1989-90.
Scottish Cup Winners: 1920, 1929, 1997; *Runners-up:* 1898, 1932, 1938, 1957, 1960.
League Cup Winners: 2011-12; *Runners-up:* 1952-53, 1960-61, 1962-63, 2000-01, 2006-07.

European: *European Cup:* 4 matches (1965-66). *Cup Winners' Cup:* 4 matches (1997-98). *UEFA Cup:* 32 matches (*Fairs Cup:* 1964-65, 1966-67 semi-finals, 1969-70, 1970-71. *UEFA Cup:* 1998-99, 1999-2000, 2001-02).

Club colours: Shirts: White and dark blue stripes. Shorts: White. Socks: Dark blue with yellow tops.

Goalscorers: *League (45):* Boyd 22, McKenzie 3, Johnston 3, Clohessy 2, Muirhead 2, Nicholson 2, Ashcroft 1, Barr 1, Clingan 1, Eremenko 1, Gardyne 1, Irvine 1, Maksimenko 1, Slater 1, own goals 2.
William Hill Scottish FA Cup (2): Barr 1, Johnston 1.
Scottish Communities League Cup (0).

Samson C 38	Tesselaar J 36	McKenzie R 28 + 5	Fowler J 6 + 3	Barr D 12	Fisher G 1	Johnston C 15 + 6	Jacobs K 5	Heffernan P 4	Gros W 4 + 10	McKeown R 6 + 3	Boyd K 35 + 1	Ibrahim R 6 + 4	Slater C 20 + 2	O'Hara M 11 + 3	Pascali M 29 + 2	Clohessy S 24	Nicholson B 14 + 9	Irvine J 25 + 2	Stewart M 1 + 3	Gardyne M 17 + 6	Bouzid I 4	Clingan S 13 + 5	David Silva M 1 + 2	Muirhead R 10 + 11	Ashcroft L 23 + 2	Winchester J — + 4	Gabriel R 2	Kiltie G 3 + 2	Eremenko A 9 + 4	Moberg Karlsson D 2 + 2	Maksimenko V 8	Barbour R 6 + 1	Match No.
1	2	3	4	5	6²	7³	8	9	10¹	11	12	13	14																				1
1	4	6³	8	3²		12	7	11	13	5	10	9¹		2	14																		2
1	4	13	3			7	11³			5	10⁴	9¹		14	2	6²	8	12															3
1	5		8¹	3		13	11⁴		12		9		4		2	6	7	10															4
1	5	9²	7	3		8	11¹				10		13	2	6			4	12														5
1	4	7³	8¹	9²		5	11		12		13		2	6	3	14	10																6
1	5¹	3	14			12	10		9²		8		2	6	7	13	11²	4															7
1	14	3		5		11	9³		12		7¹		2	6²	10		4	8	13													8
1	10	12		3		11	13		5		7²		2	6¹	14		4	8	9³													9
1	5	13		4		11					10²			6	2		8	7		9¹		3		12									10
1	5	13		4¹			11²						2	6	8³		7		10	3	12			14								11
1	5	6¹		3		11	9¹				13		2	4	8		7		10²	12	14											12
1	5	12		4			9				10		2	8	7²	3	11¹		6		13											13
1	5	12				8	9		13		10		2	4	6³	3	11²		7¹				14									14
1	5	13				7	11¹				8		2	9	12	6³	4		10²				14	3				6³				15
1	5	10²				7¹	11				13		2	9	8	6⁴	12							4	3							16
1	5	11				9²					10			8	2	6¹	4		7		12		13	3								17
1	5	6				9	11¹				13		7	3²	2		8		10³		12		14	4								18
1	5	6				9					11		2	7	4		8		10¹		12			3								19
1	5	6				9¹					11		2	7	4	13	8		10²				12	3								20
1	5	8²		10¹		11							2	6	4		12		13		9		7	3								21
1	5	8²		10¹		11					13			7	4	6	2		9					3		12						22
1	5	10				11					8			7	2	6	4		9					3								23
1	5	6				11					8		13	4	2²		12		7		10³		14	3				9¹				24
1	5²	10				11					13		2	6	4				7				8¹	3		12		9				25
1	5	8				11					10		2	6	4				7				12	3¹				9				26
1	5	8				11					10¹		2	6	4				7				13	3		12		9²				27
1	5	8				11					10³		2	6					7²			12	13	4	14			9¹				28
1	5	8²				11							14	7	2		6		10²			12	13	3		4		9¹				29
1	5	8²				11							2	7	4		6		10³				13	3	14			9¹	12			30
1	5	6				9²					11		2	8	4				10¹				13	3				7	12			31
1	5	9²									10		2¹	6			8		7				13	3				11	12	4		32
1	5	10				11					13			9²					7			12	8¹	3	14			6³		4	2	33
1	5	9²				11					10			8					7¹			12	13	3				6		4	2	34
1	5	8				11					10¹			6³					7			12	13	3	14			9²		4	2	35
1	5	6²				11¹					10³			9			8		7				13	3	14				12	4	2	36
1	5	10¹				11²								6			8		7			12	13	3				9		4	2	37
1	5	10¹				11								6			8		7²			12	13	3	14			9		4¹	2	38

LIVINGSTON

Year Formed: 1974. *Ground:* The Braidwood Motor Company Stadium, Almondvale Stadium, Alderstone Road, Livingston EH54 7DN. *Telephone:* 01506 417000. *Fax:* 01506 429 948.
Email: lfcreception@livingstonfc.co.uk *Website:* www.livingstonfc.co.uk
Ground Capacity: 10,005 (all seated). *Size of Pitch:* 98m × 69m.
Chairman: Gordon McDougall. *Vice-Chairman:* Robert Wilson.
Manager: John McGlynn. *Assistant Manager:* Mark Burchill. *Physio:* Andy Mackenzie.
Club Nickname: 'Livi Lions'.
Previous Grounds: Meadowbank Stadium (as Meadowbank Thistle).
Record Attendance: 10,024 v Celtic, Premier League, 18 Aug 2001.
Record Transfer Fee received: £1,000,000 for David Fernandez to Celtic (June 2002).
Record Transfer Fee paid: £120,000 for Wes Hoolahan from Shelbourne (December 2005).
Record Victory: 7-0 v Queen of the South, Scottish Cup, 29 Jan 2000.
Record Defeat: 0-8 v Hamilton A. Division II, 14 Dec 1974.
Most Capped Player (under 18): Ian Little.
Most League Appearances: 446: Walter Boyd, 1979-89.
Most League Goals in Season (Individual): 22: Leigh Griffiths, 2008-09; Iain Russell, 2010-11.
Most Goals Overall (Individual): 64: David Roseburgh, 1986-93.

LIVINGSTON – SCOTTISH CHAMPIONSHIP 2013–14 LEAGUE RECORD

Match No.	Date	Venue	Opponents	Result	H/T Score	Lg Pos.	Goalscorers	Attendance
1	Aug 10	A	Alloa Ath	L 0-1	0-1	8		714
2	17	H	Queen of the South	D 3-3	1-2	9	Denholm [12], Fordyce [58], Mullen [80]	1149
3	24	H	Falkirk	L 0-3	0-2	9		1416
4	30	A	Dundee	L 0-3	0-1	9		3955
5	Sept 14	H	Greenock Morton	D 2-2	2-2	10	Mensing [4], McNulty [14]	1077
6	21	A	Dumbarton	W 2-1	0-1	10	McNulty 2 [49, 76]	759
7	28	H	Cowdenbeath	W 5-1	1-1	8	Fordyce 3 [42, 60, 87], Barrowman [72], Burchill [82]	894
8	Oct 5	A	Hamilton A	L 0-2	0-1	8		1059
9	19	H	Alloa Ath	W 3-2	1-1	7	Scougall [2], Donaldson [69], Barrowman [90]	869
10	26	H	Dundee	W 2-1	0-0	5	Jacobs, Keaghan [55], Scott [88]	1597
11	29	A	Raith R	L 0-1	0-1	6		1304
12	Nov 9	A	Falkirk	L 1-4	0-1	6	Vaulks (og) [72]	2878
13	16	H	Dumbarton	L 1-3	1-1	8	McNulty [20]	1039
14	23	A	Greenock Morton	W 5-1	3-1	6	McNulty 3 (1 pen) [7, 64 (p), 90], Barrowman [28], Scott [37]	1460
15	Dec 7	A	Cowdenbeath	W 3-2	0-0	6	McNulty 2 [77, 90], Barrowman [87]	363
16	14	H	Hamilton A	D 0-0	0-0	6		794
17	21	A	Queen of the South	D 2-2	1-2	6	McNulty 2 [4, 77]	1523
18	28	H	Raith R	W 3-0	2-0	6	Thomson (og) [8], Scott [45], Scougall [62]	1322
19	Jan 4	H	Falkirk	L 0-1	0-1	6		1585
20	11	A	Dundee	W 1-0	1-0	5	Burchill [11]	4367
21	18	H	Greenock Morton	L 0-1	0-1	7		1245
22	Feb 1	H	Queen of the South	L 1-2	1-0	8	McNulty (pen) [40]	1041
23	5	A	Dumbarton	D 2-2	0-0	7	Jacobs, Keaghan [66], Barrowman [79]	562
24	15	A	Alloa Ath	W 3-0	1-0	6	Mensing [20], Scott [81], Jacobs, Keaghan [86]	605
25	21	H	Hamilton A	L 0-2	0-1	6		1063
26	Mar 1	H	Cowdenbeath	W 1-0	0-0	6	Talbot [63]	980
27	8	A	Falkirk	D 1-1	1-0	5	McNulty [35]	2924
28	15	H	Dundee	L 0-2	1-0	6		1759
29	22	A	Raith R	W 4-2	1-0	6	Sives 2 [5, 54], McNulty 2 (1 pen) [50 (p), 90]	1329
30	25	H	Alloa Ath	W 2-0	1-0	5	McNulty (pen) [21], Jacobs, Keaghan [86]	709
31	29	H	Dumbarton	L 1-2	1-0	5	Mevlja [28]	949
32	Apr 5	A	Greenock Morton	L 0-2	0-2	6		1009
33	12	H	Hamilton A	D 1-1	0-0	6	Jacobs, Kyle [64]	1133
34	19	A	Cowdenbeath	L 0-4	0-1	6		420
35	26	A	Queen of the South	L 0-2	0-1	6		1923
36	May 3	H	Raith R	W 2-0	1-0	6	Mullen [8], McNulty [80]	1265

Final League Position: 6

Honours
League Champions: First Division 2000-01. Second Division 1986-87, 1998-99, 2010-11. Third Division 1995-96, 2009-10;
Runners-up: Second Division 1982-83. First Division 1987-88.
Scottish Cup: Semi-finals 2001, 2004.
League Cup Winners: 2003-04. Semi-finals 1984-85. *B&Q Cup:* Semi-finals 1992-93, 1993-94, 2001.
League Challenge Cup Runners-up: 2000-01.

European: *UEFA Cup:* 4 matches (2002-03).

Club colours: Shirt: Yellow with black trim. Shorts: Black with yellow trim. Socks: Yellow.

Goalscorers: *League (51):* McNulty 17 (4 pens), Barrowman 5, Fordyce 4, Jacobs, Keaghan 4, Scott 4, Burchill 2, Mensing 2, Mullen 2, Scougall 2, Sives 2, Denholm 1, Donaldson 1, Jacobs, Kyle 1, Mevlja 1, Talbot 1, own goals 2.
William Hill Scottish FA Cup (0).
Scottish Communities League Cup (6): Barrowman 1, Denholm 1, Fordyce 1, McNulty 1, Scott 1, Wilkie 1.
Ramsdens Cup (2): Mensing 1 (1 pen), McNulty 1.

Jamieson D 31	Donaldson C 19	Mensing S 27	Fordyce C 35	Talbot J 27 + 2	Wilkie K 8 + 12	Docherty R 5 + 3	Scott M 26 + 7	Beaumont J 3	McNulty M 32 + 3	McDonald C 8 + 2	Mullen D 8 + 15	Denholm D 10 + 17	Mampuya M 14 + 1	Hastings N — + 1	Burchill M 6 + 14	Barrowman A 16 + 3	Lander K — + 5	Walker K 5	O'Brien B 30	Scougall S 16	Jacobs Keaghan 28 + 4	Twardzik P — + 1	Habai M 4 + 3	Mevlja N 12 + 1	Jacobs Kyle 13	Sives C 11 + 1	Praprotnik N 2 + 3	Rutherford S — + 1	Match No.
1	2	3	4^1	5	6	7■	8	9^2	10	11	12	13																	1
1	3	4	9	5		7	8^2	11	6^2	13	10	2^1	12■	14															2
1	2	4	3	5	6	7	10^1	9^2	12	8	11	13																	3
6	3	4	5	8		7	9^1	12	10^2	2								1	11	13									4
	3	4	5	6^2	7^3		11	14	13	2	10							1	8	9^1	12								5
1	3	4	5^3	8			10^1	6	14	2	13	11							7	9^2	12								6
1	4	3	5	14	9	11^3	2	13	12	10									8	7^2	6^1								7
1	4	3	2	9^2	8	5	14	13	12	11^1									6	10^3	7								8
1	3	4	2	5			9^1	10^2	13	12	11								7	8	6								9
1	2	3	4	5			9^1	13	11^3	14	12	10							7	8^3	6								10
1	2	3	4	5			9^3	12	11^2	14	8^4	13							7	10^1	6								11
1	9^1	3	4	5			12	2	8^2	13	14	11							7	10^3	6								12
	3	4	5	13			6^1	10	9	12	11^2					2			1	7	8								13
	3	4	2	5			14	8^2	11	12	10^3	13				7			1	6	9^1								14
9	3	2	4				13	6^2	10	12	11								8	7	5^1								15
1	3	4	2	5			12	13	11^3	9	14	10							7	8^1	6^2								16
1	2	4	3	5^1			14	12	11	9^1	13	10							7	8^2	6								17
1	3	4	2^3	5			9	10^2	13	14	12	11^1							7	8	6								18
3■	4	2	5				14	9^3	10	12	13	11^2							7	8	6^1								19
1	3	5	13	2			9	11^1	14	12	4	10^2							7	8^3	6								20
1	4	3	5	12			9^1	7	10	14	13	2							11^3	8^2	6								21
1	4	3	5	9^2			8^1	10	12	2	11^3	13							7		6		14						22
	4	3	5^1	13			10^2	12	2	14	11								1	9	6		7^3	8					23
1	3■	4	5	12			7	13	11^1	2^2									9		6		8	10^3	14				24
		2	9				11^3	12	10	14	5^1								7		6^2		13	3	8	4			25
	4	3	5				8	10^1	13							12			7		6		11^1	9	8	2			26
	4	3	5				7	11							13	12^2					6		10^1	9	8	8	2		27
	4	2	9^2				8	10			14				13						6		11^1	5	7^3	3	12		28
		3					13	10	11^1	6^2	2	12							8		7^2			5	9	4	14		29
		3	13				12	10	11^1	6^2	2^3	14							7		9			5	8	4			30
		2	5^1	12			10	11^2	9^1		13								7		6			4	8	3			31
	3	4		13			12	11	10^2	9^3	14								8		6^1			5	7	2			32
	3		9^2	8^1			10	13	2		11^3								7		12			5	6	4	14		33
	3	13	9^2	8			11			2^3	10	12							7		14			5^1	6	4			34
	3	5	14				7^3	11	10^2										6		2	13			8	4	9^1		35
	2	5					9	10^3	11^2	13									7		6			12	8	3■	4^1	14	36

MONTROSE

Year Formed: 1879. *Ground & Address:* Links Park, Wellington St, Montrose DD10 8QD. *Telephone:* 01674 673200.
Fax: 01674 677311. *E-mail:* glynis@montrosefc.co.uk *Website:* www.montrosefc.co.uk
Ground Capacity: total: 4,936, (seated: 1,338). *Size of Pitch:* 100m × 64m.
Chairman: Derek Sim. *Vice-Chairman:* John Crawford. *Secretary:* Malcolm J. Watters.
Manager: George Shields. *Assistant Manager:* Lee Wilkie. *Physio:* Sarah Richardson.
Club Nickname: 'The Gable Endies'.
Previous Grounds: None.
Record Attendance: 8,983 v Dundee, Scottish Cup 3rd rd, 17 Mar 1973.
Record Transfer Fee received: £50,000 for Gary Murray to Hibernian (Dec 1980).
Record Transfer Fee paid: £17,500 for Jim Smith from Airdrieonians (Feb 1992).
Record Victory: 12-0 v Vale of Leithen, Scottish Cup 2nd rd, 4 Jan 1975.
Record Defeat: 0-13 v Aberdeen, 17 Mar 1951.
Most Capped Player: Alexander Keillor, 2 (6), Scotland.
Most League Appearances: 432: David Larter, 1987-98.
Most League Goals in Season (Individual): 28: Brian Third, Division II, 1972-73.

MONTROSE – SCOTTISH LEAGUE TWO 2013–14 LEAGUE RECORD

Match No.	Date	Venue	Opponents	Result	H/T Score	Lg Pos.	Goalscorers	Atten-dance
1	Aug 10	H	Stirling Alb	L 1-2	1-1	7	Webster [38]	486
2	17	A	Annan Ath	L 1-2	0-0	8	Wood (pen) [87]	286
3	24	H	Berwick R	D 1-1	0-0	8	Watson [84]	285
4	31	A	Albion R	W 2-0	1-0	8	Young [29], Deasley [64]	311
5	Sept 14	A	Elgin C	D 3-3	1-0	8	Deasley 2 [19, 67], Young [64]	577
6	21	H	Peterhead	W 2-1	1-1	7	Deasley 2 [29, 80]	434
7	28	A	Clyde	W 3-0	0-0	3	Wood [50], Rodger [54], Johnston, S [61]	464
8	Oct 19	A	Stirling Alb	L 1-3	1-1	8	Deasley [16]	481
9	26	H	East Stirling	W 2-0	1-0	4	McGowan (og) [35], Masson [51]	338
10	29	A	Queen's Park	L 1-2	0-1	5	Masson [87]	358
11	Nov 16	A	Albion R	W 2-1	1-1	5	Deasley 2 [9, 74]	343
12	20	A	Berwick R	D 1-1	1-0	5	Webster [24]	227
13	23	H	Elgin C	D 3-3	1-2	6	Watson 2 [30, 90], Johnston, S [87]	398
14	30	A	Peterhead	L 0-3	0-0	6		473
15	Dec 7	A	Queen's Park	W 1-0	0-0	5	Johnston, S [51]	357
16	14	H	Clyde	L 0-2	0-2	6		410
17	26	H	Annan Ath	L 0-2	0-0	6		350
18	28	A	East Stirling	D 2-2	1-1	7	Wood [26], Webster [59]	244
19	Jan 2	A	Berwick R	D 0-0	0-0	7		456
20	11	A	Albion R	L 0-1	0-1	7		718
21	18	H	Peterhead	L 2-3	1-0	8	Wood [21], Masson [90]	424
22	25	A	Elgin C	W 3-2	2-0	8	Webster [5], Johnston, S [28], Watson [77]	550
23	Feb 1	H	Stirling Alb	D 0-0	0-0	8		333
24	8	A	Annan Ath	L 0-1	0-0	8		354
25	15	H	Queen's Park	W 1-0	0-0	8	Watson [61]	301
26	22	A	Clyde	D 1-1	0-1	8	Johnston, S [82]	418
27	Mar 1	H	Albion R	W 2-1	0-0	6	Johnston, S [54], Masson [56]	334
28	8	A	Berwick R	L 0-5	0-3	8		410
29	15	H	East Stirling	W 2-0	2-0	6	Gray [15], Deasley [45]	333
30	22	A	Stirling Alb	D 2-2	0-0	7	Watson [79], Wood (pen) [90]	529
31	29	H	Elgin C	L 0-3	0-0	7		262
32	Apr 5	A	Peterhead	L 0-4	0-0	8		671
33	12	A	Queen's Park	D 1-1	0-0	8	Watson [58]	251
34	19	H	Clyde	L 0-2	0-2	8		422
35	26	H	Annan Ath	W 2-1	1-0	7	Deasley [29], Wood [76]	264
36	May 3	A	East Stirling	W 2-1	2-1	6	Wood [16], Watson [32]	265

Final League Position: 6

Honours
League Champions: Second Division 1984-85; *Runners-up:* Second Division 1990-91. Third Division 1994-95.
Scottish Cup: Quarter-finals 1973, 1976.
League Cup: Semi-finals 1975-76.
B&Q Cup: Semi-finals 1992-93.
League Challenge Cup: Semi-finals 1996-97.

Club colours: Shirt: Blue with white trim. Shorts: Blue with white trim. Socks: Blue.

Goalscorers: *League (44):* Deasley 10, Watson 8, Wood 7 (2 pens), Johnston S 6, Masson 4, Webster 4, Young 2, Gray 1, Rodger 1, own goal 1.
William Hill Scottish FA Cup (2): McCord 1, Wilson 1.
Scottish Communities League Cup (1): McCord 1.
Ramsdens Cup (0).

McKenzie S 36	McNally S 18	Campbell A 27	Wilson C 16 + 3	McIntosh R 25 + 6	Webster G 23 + 7	Masson T 28 + 3	McCord R 16 + 8	Johnston S 28 + 7	Sturrock K 3 + 10	Bonar L 3 + 9	Bell C 9 + 3	Young L 4 + 3	Winter J —+ 1	Watson P 32	Wood G 32 + 2	Crawford J 24 + 3	Rae D 1 + 1	Gray D 17 + 6	Deasley B 33	Rodger G 4	Reid J 8 + 2	Johnston L 6	Ferguson C 3 + 1	Match No.
1	2	3	4	5^1	6^3	7	8	9	10^2	11^1	12	13	14											1
1	2	3	4		6	8^3	7^2	9^1	13	11	12		14	5	10									2
1	2		4	5	7^1	6^2	8	11^3	13				14	9	10	3	12							3
1	2		4	5	14	13	7^3	12					9^1	8	10	3		6^2	11					4
1	2	3^1		5			7	13					9^1	8	11	12		6	10	4				5
1	2		3^1	5		7		13	12				9	8	10			6^2	11	4				6
1	2		3	5	13	7		12	14				9^2	8	10			6^3	11^1	4				7
1	2		3	8	13	7^1	12	9^2					14	5	10	4		6^3	11					8
1	2		4	5	12	7		9						8	10	3		6^1	11					9
1	2		4^1	5		7	12	9^1	13				14	8	10	3		6^2	11					10
1	2				9^1	6	7^2	12			5			8	10	3		13	11	4				11
1	2		3	13	9^1	7	8	11		12	5			4			6^2	10						12
1	2		4		9^2	6^1	7	13	12		5			8	10^3	3		14	11					13
1	2			5	9^1	6	7	10	12					8	4	3			11					14
1	2	3	4^1	5		7	8^3	12					14	6	10^2	13		9			11			15
1	2	3		5^2	12	6	7^1	10					14	8^2	13			11			9^1	4		16
1		3	12	7	2		6				5			8	10			11			9^1	4		17
1		3	14	7^3	2^4		6				9			5	10	12		13	11		8^1	4^2		18
1	2	3		13	7^2		12	6			5^1			8^1	10			9	11		4			19
1		4	14		7		8	9^3	13	12	5^1				10	3		6^2	11		2			20
1	2	3		5	7^1	13		6^2					14	8	10	3		9^1	11		12	4		21
1		3	12	5^1	8	7		6						4	10	2		11			9			22
1		3	5	6^1	7		10							8	4	2		11			9	12		23
1		3	5	6		12	8	13						7	4	2		11			9^2	10^1		24
1		3	5		7	12	9							8	4	2		13	10		6^1	11^2		25
1		3	5	9^1	7	13	6							8	4	2		12	10			11^2		26
1		3	5	8^1	6		11							7	4	2		10	9		12			27
1		3	5	8^1	6	13	11	12						7	4	2		9^2	10					28
1		4	3	5	10	6	12	11^1						7		2		8	9					29
1		4	3	5	6^1	8		12						9	10	2		7	11					30
1		4	3	5^2	6^1	7		10			13			8	12	2		9	11					31
1		5	3	12	6	7		10						8	4	2		9^1	11					32
1		3		5	12		7	10	13	9^2				8	4	2		6^1	11					33
1		4	3	5	8	12	7	6	11^1						10	2		9						34
1		4	3^1	13		6	7	9			5^2			8	10	2		12	11					35
1		4	13		12	6	7	9	11^1		5^2			8	3	2		10						36

MOTHERWELL

Year Formed: 1886. *Ground & Address:* Fir Park Stadium, Motherwell ML1 2QN. *Telephone:* 01698 333333. *Fax:* 01698 338001.
E-mail: mfcenquiries@motherwellfc.co.uk *Website:* www.motherwellfc.co.uk
Ground Capacity: 13,742 (all seated). *Size of Pitch:* 100m × 68m.
Manager: Stuart McCall. *Assistant Manager:* Kenny Black. *Physio:* John Porteous.
Club Nicknames: 'The Well', 'The Steelmen'.
Previous Grounds: The Meadows, Dalziel Park.
Record Attendance: 35,632 v Rangers, Scottish Cup 4th rd replay, 12 Mar 1952.
Record Transfer Fee received: £1,750,000 for Phil O'Donnell to Celtic (September 1994).
Record Transfer Fee paid: £500,000 for John Spencer from Everton (Jan 1999).
Record Victory: 12-1 v Dundee U, Division II, 23 Jan 1954.
Record Defeat: 0-8 v Aberdeen, Premier Division, 26 Mar 1979.
Most Capped Player: Stephen Craigan, 54, Northern Ireland.
Most League Appearances: 626: Bobby Ferrier, 1918-37.
Most League Goals in Season (Individual): 52: Willie McFadyen, Division I, 1931-32.
Most Goals Overall (Individual): 283: Hugh Ferguson, 1916-25.

MOTHERWELL – SCOTTISH PREMIER LEAGUE 2013–14 LEAGUE RECORD

Match No.	Date	Venue	Opponents	Result	H/T Score	Lg Pos.	Goalscorers	Atten-dance
1	Aug 4	A	Hibernian	W 1-0	0-0	4	Anier [83]	9237
2	11	H	Aberdeen	L 1-3	1-0	6	Anier [1]	6242
3	17	A	Inverness CT	L 0-2	0-2	6		3031
4	24	H	Partick Thistle	W 1-0	1-0	5	Sutton [21]	5527
5	31	H	Kilmarnock	W 2-1	2-1	3	Anier [20], Sutton [45]	4353
6	Sept 14	A	St Mirren	W 1-0	1-0	3	Sutton [38]	4012
7	22	A	Dundee U	D 2-2	1-0	4	Anier [30], Ainsworth [76]	5808
8	28	H	Ross Co	W 3-1	0-1	3	Sutton 2 [54, 68], McHugh [77]	4263
9	Oct 5	A	Celtic	L 0-2	0-1	3		46,608
10	19	H	Hearts	W 2-1	0-0	3	Moore [69], Hutchinson [83]	5350
11	27	A	St Johnstone	L 0-2	0-0	4		2449
12	Nov 3	H	Hibernian	W 1-0	1-0	3	McManus [23]	3864
13	9	H	Dundee U	L 0-4	0-2	4		5103
14	23	A	Kilmarnock	W 2-0	0-0	3	Sutton [55], Anier [88]	3704
15	Dec 6	H	Celtic	L 0-5	0-1	3		9117
16	14	A	Ross Co	W 2-1	2-0	5	Sutton 2 [15, 27]	2792
17	21	H	St Mirren	W 3-0	2-0	5	Anier 2 [31, 64], Ainsworth [42]	3867
18	26	A	Aberdeen	W 1-0	0-0	2	Ainsworth [49]	12,494
19	29	A	Partick Thistle	W 5-1	3-1	2	Lasley [15], Francis-Angol [21], McFadden [36], Ainsworth [57], Sutton [65]	4588
20	Jan 1	H	St Johnstone	W 4-0	1-0	2	Sutton [22], Vigurs [49], Ainsworth [73], McFadden [87]	3763
21	11	A	Hearts	W 1-0	1-0	3	Sutton [40]	12,888
22	18	A	Celtic	L 0-3	0-2	3		47,489
23	25	H	Aberdeen	D 2-2	0-0	3	McManus [47], Francis-Angol [69]	5756
24	Feb 15	H	Partick Thistle	W 4-3	1-1	3	Lasley [43], Ainsworth [52], Sutton [85], McManus [88]	5048
25	21	A	Dundee U	L 1-3	0-2	3	Sutton (pen) [57]	7029
26	25	A	St Johnstone	L 0-3	0-2	3		1892
27	Mar 1	H	Hearts	W 4-1	2-0	3	Vigurs [18], Ainsworth [37], Sutton [65], McFadden [74]	4914
28	8	A	Hibernian	D 3-3	2-1	3	Sutton 2 [12, 90], Ainsworth [29]	8277
29	19	H	Inverness CT	W 2-0	2-0	3	Ainsworth [26], Sutton [34]	3432
30	22	H	Ross Co	W 2-1	0-0	3	McFadden [48], Sutton [60]	4080
31	29	H	Kilmarnock	L 1-2	1-0	3	Vigurs [41]	4467
32	Apr 1	A	Inverness CT	W 2-1	1-0	2	Anier [40], Vigurs [83]	2366
33	5	A	St Mirren	L 2-3	2-1	3	Anier [17], Sutton [27]	4377
34	19	H	Celtic	D 3-3	2-1	3	Sutton 2 [5, 90], Francis-Angol [44]	7493
35	26	A	Dundee U	L 1-5	0-2	3	Ainsworth [88]	6383
36	May 3	H	St Johnstone	W 2-1	2-1	3	Ainsworth [21], McManus [36]	7201
37	7	H	Inverness CT	W 2-1	2-0	3	Sutton (pen) [4], Warren (og) [32]	4482
38	11	A	Aberdeen	W 1-0	0-0	2	Reid [90]	17,016

Final League Position: 2

Honours
League Champions: Division I 1931-32. First Division 1981-82, 1984-85. Division II 1953-54, 1968-69.
Runners-up: Premier Division 1994-95, 2012-13. Premiership 2013-14. Division I 1926-27, 1929-30, 1932-33, 1933-34. Division II 1894-95, 1902-03.
Scottish Cup: 1952, 1991; *Runners-up:* 1931, 1933, 1939, 1951, 2011.
League Cup Winners: 1950-51; *Runners-up:* 1954-55, 2004-05.

European: *Champions League:* 2 matches (2012-13). *Cup Winners' Cup:* 2 matches (1991-92). *UEFA Cup:* 8 matches (1994-95, 1995-96, 2008-09). *Europa League:* 16 matches (2009-10, 2010-11, 2012-13, 2013-14).

Club colours: Shirt: Amber with maroon band. Shorts: Amber. Socks: Amber.

Goalscorers: *League (64):* Sutton 22 (2 pens), Ainsworth 11, Anier 9, McFadden 4, McManus 4, Vigurs 4, Francis-Angol 3, Lasley 2, Hutchinson 1, McHugh 1, Moore 1, Reid 1, own goal 1.
William Hill Scottish FA Cup (0).
Scottish Communities League Cup (2): McFadden 1, McHugh 1.
UEFA Europa League (0).

Hollis L 14	Ramsden S 18	Hammell S 34	Lawson P 5 + 12	Hutchinson S 35	McManus S 37	McFadden J 21 + 6	Lasley K 37	McHugh B 3 + 5	Sutton J 37 + 1	Vigurs I 33 + 3	Anier H 19 + 14	Francis-Angol Z 21 + 12	Carswell S 24 + 4	Kerr F 10 + 9	Ainsworth L 22 + 7	Cummins A 1 + 2	Nielsen G 19	Moore C 3 + 14	Murray E 1 + 2	Twardzik D 5	Leitch J 6 + 3	Reid C 13 + 1	Shirkie D — + 1	Cadden C — + 3	Match No.
1	2	3	4¹	5	6	7²	8	9³	10	11	12	13	14												1
1	2	5		3	4	6³	7²	14	10	8	11		9¹	13	12										2
1	2	5	7³	3	4	8²	6	9	11	10	12	14	13												3
1	2	5	12	3	4	6	7		11	14	10¹	8²	9³	13											4
1	2⁴	5	14	3	4	9¹	7		10	8³	11²	13	6		12										5
	2	13		3	4	6²	7	12	10	9	11³	5¹	8				14								6
1	2	5		3	4	13	7		10	8²	11¹	9	6		12										7
1	2	5		3	4	6²	7	13	10	14	11¹	9²	8		12										8
1	2	5	14	3	4		7¹		11	8³	12	10	9	13	6²										9
	2	5	12	3	4		7	14	10	6	11²	9³	8¹				1	13							10
	2	5	7	3	4		9	10	11	6²		12	8¹				1	13							11
	2¹	5²		3⁴	4	9³	7		10	14	11	13	8	12	6		1								12
			4	12	7		10	8	11³	5	6²	3	9	2¹	1	14	13								13
		8	3	4	6²	7		11	9	13	5			2	12		1	10¹							14
4	6		3	5		8		10	9	13		7	2¹	12	1	11²									15
	2	5	14	3	4	13	8		10	9¹	11³		7	6²		12	1								16
	2	5	14	3	4		7¹		10	9	11²		8	13	6³	12	1								17
4	5	9	3			8		10		11²	13	7	2	6¹	12	1									18
3	2	13		4	11²	8	14	12	9	10³	5	7¹	6			1									19
	2	5	14	3	4	13	7³		11²	9	10¹	8	6		12	1									20
	2	5	14	3	4	10³	8		11	9¹	13	12	7	6²		1									21
		5		3	4	10	8	11¹	9	13	6	2	12	7²		1									22
		5	12	3	4	11¹	7	10	13	9	8	2³	6²	1							14				23
		5	13	3	4	11	7	10	8¹	12	6	2	9²	1											24
	2		3	4	10	7	11	9¹	13	5	8	6²	1									12			25
	5²	3	4	13	7	11	9¹	6³	10	8	12	1										2	14		26
1		3	4	11	7²	10	9	5³	13	6¹			12	8	2							14			27
1		4	3	10²	8	11	9	6¹			12	5	7	2	13										28
	5	3	4	11¹	7	10	8	12	6	9	1	2													29
	5	3	4	10¹	8	11	9	13	7	6²	1	12	2												30
	5	3	4	7	10	8	12	9³	14	6¹	1	11²	13	2											31
	5	3	4	7	10	8	11¹	12	6	1	13	9³	2²	14											32
	5		4	7	10	9	11¹	13	3	6²	1	12	8	2											33
	5	3	4	10	8	11²	9	7	12	1	13	6¹	2												34
	5	3	4	8	10	9²	11³	14	6¹	12	1	13	7	2											35
1	5	3	4	11¹	7	10	8	12	9²	13	6	2													36
1	5	3	4	11¹	7	10	8	13	9¹	12	6³	14	2												37
1	5	3	4³	14	7	11	8²	12	9	10	6¹	13	2												38

PARTICK THISTLE

Year Formed: 1876. *Ground & Address:* Firhill Stadium, 80 Firhill Rd, Glasgow G20 7AL. *Telephone:* 0141 579 1971.
Fax: 0141 945 1525. *E-mail:* mail@ptfc.co.uk *Website:* www.ptfc.co.uk
Ground Capacity: 10,102 (all seated). *Size of Pitch:* 105m × 69m.
Chairman: David Beattie. *General Manager:* Ian Maxwell.
Manager: Alan Archibald. *Assistant Manager:* Scott Paterson. *Head of Youth Development:* Gerry Britton.
Club Nickname: 'The Jags'.
Previous Grounds: Overnewton Park; Jordanvale Park; Muirpark; Inchview; Meadowside Park.
Record Attendance: 49,838 v Rangers, Division I, 18 Feb 1922. *Ground Record:* 54,728, Scotland v Ireland, 25 Feb 1928.
Record Transfer Fee received: £200,000 for Mo Johnston to Watford (July 1981).
Record Transfer Fee paid: £85,000 for Andy Murdoch from Celtic (Feb 1991).
Record Victory: 16-0 v Royal Albert, Scottish Cup 1st rd, 17 Jan 1931.
Record Defeat: 0-10 v Queen's Park, Scottish Cup 5th rd, 3 Dec 1881.
Most Capped Player: Alan Rough, 51 (53), Scotland.
Most League Appearances: 410: Alan Rough, 1969-82.
Most League Goals in Season (Individual): 41: Alex Hair, Division I, 1926-27.
Most Goals Overall (Individual): 229: Willie Sharp, 1939-57.

PARTICK THISTLE – SCOTTISH PREMIER LEAGUE 2013–14 LEAGUE RECORD

Match No.	Date		Venue	Opponents	Result		H/T Score	Lg Pos.	Goalscorers	Atten- dance
1	Aug	2	H	Dundee U	D	0-0	0-0	1		7822
2		10	A	Ross Co	W	3-1	1-0	2	Doolan [18], Lawless 2 [53, 59]	3331
3		16	H	Hearts	D	1-1	0-0	3	Muirhead (pen) [86]	6540
4		24	A	Motherwell	L	0-1	0-1	7		5527
5		31	A	St Mirren	W	2-1	0-0	4	Higginbotham [81], Forbes [84]	5601
6	Sept	14	H	Aberdeen	L	0-3	0-2	7		6193
7		21	H	Kilmarnock	D	1-1	1-0	6	Muirhead (pen) [11]	4310
8		28	A	St Johnstone	D	1-1	1-1	7	Doolan [6]	3248
9	Oct	7	H	Hibernian	L	0-1	0-0	8		4521
10		20	A	Inverness CT	W	2-1	1-0	7	Doolan 2 [20, 83]	3154
11		27	H	Celtic	L	1-2	0-1	8	Doolan [67]	7978
12	Nov	4	A	Aberdeen	L	0-4	0-2	8		10,057
13		9	H	St Mirren	L	0-3	0-1	8		4946
14		23	A	Dundee U	L	1-4	0-1	9	Muirhead (pen) [57]	6700
15	Dec	7	A	Hibernian	D	1-1	0-0	9	Doolan [49]	10,431
16		21	H	Kilmarnock	L	1-2	0-1	10	Doolan [49]	3865
17		26	H	Inverness CT	D	0-0	0-0	10		2887
18		29	H	Motherwell	L	1-5	1-3	10	Lawless [8]	4588
19	Jan	1	A	Celtic	L	0-1	0-1	10		52,670
20		5	A	Hearts	W	2-0	2-0	10	Taylor [14], Sinclair [40]	13,763
21		11	H	Ross Co	D	3-3	2-1	10	Taylor 2 [28, 39], Lawless [47]	3539
22		18	A	Kilmarnock	D	1-1	1-0	11	Higginbotham [3]	4092
23		21	A	St Johnstone	L	0-1	0-1	11		2719
24		25	A	St Mirren	D	0-0	0-0	11		4660
25	Feb	1	H	Dundee U	D	1-1	0-1	11	Fraser [75]	3748
26		15	A	Motherwell	L	3-4	1-1	11	Erskine [37], Higginbotham 2 (1 pen) [66 (p), 72]	5048
27		22	H	Aberdeen	W	3-1	0-0	10	Balatoni [59], Taylor 2 [64, 72]	4554
28	Mar	1	A	Ross Co	D	1-1	1-1	10	Higginbotham [9]	3441
29		15	H	Hibernian	W	3-1	1-0	9	Erskine [43], Mair [60], Higginbotham [90]	4448
30		22	A	Inverness CT	L	0-1	0-0	9		3093
31		26	H	Celtic	L	1-5	0-1	10	Elliot [85]	7549
32		29	A	St Johnstone	D	1-1	0-1	10	Doolan [90]	2999
33	Apr	5	H	Hearts	L	2-4	1-1	11	Doolan [5], McMillan [88]	4262
34		19	A	Kilmarnock	W	2-1	0-0	10	Higginbotham [57], Sinclair [85]	4980
35		25	H	St Mirren	D	1-1	1-1	9	Doolan [26]	5971
36	May	3	A	Hibernian	D	1-1	1-0	9	Doolan [8]	10,740
37		7	A	Hearts	W	4-2	1-2	7	Taylor [31], Fraser [51], Mair [68], Higginbotham [73]	14,059
38		10	A	Ross Co	L	2-3	0-1	10	Taylor [51], Moncur [73]	4390

Final League Position: 10

Honours
League Champions: First Division 1975-76, 2001-02, 2012-13; Division II 1896-97, 1899-1900, 1970-71; Second Division 2000-01; *Runners-up:* First Division 1991-92, 2008-09. Division II 1901-02. *Promoted to First Division:* 2005-06 (play-offs).
Scottish Cup Winners: 1921; *Runners-up:* 1930.
League Cup Winners: 1971-72; *Runners-up:* 1953-54, 1956-57, 1958-59.
League Challenge Cup Runners-up: 2012-13.

European: *Fairs Cup:* 4 matches (1963-64). *UEFA Cup:* 2 matches (1972-73). *Intertoto Cup:* 4 matches (1995-96).

Club colours: Shirt: Yellow and red stripes. Shorts: Black. Socks: Black.

Goalscorers: *League (46):* Doolan 11, Higginbotham 8 (1 pen), Taylor 7, Lawless 4, Muirhead 3 (3 pens), Erskine 2, Fraser 2, Mair 2, Sinclair 2, Balatoni 1, Elliot 1, Forbes 1, McMillan 1, Moncur 1.
William Hill Scottish FA Cup (0).
Scottish Communities League Cup (6): Elliott 2, Muirhead 1 (1 pen), Balatoni 1, Lawless 1, O'Donnell 1.

Fox S 21	O'Donnell S 23 + 4	Sinclair A 36	Welsh S 10	Muirhead A 18 + 2	Balatoni C 31	Fraser G 18 + 1	Bannigan S 33	Doolan K 22 + 14	Lawless S 17 + 11	Craigen J 26 + 5	Elliot C 11 + 19	Baird J 2 + 11	Forbes R 1 + 15	Higginbotham K 33 + 3	Osbourne I 11 + 1	Piccolo G 15 + 2	Gallacher P 17 + 1	McMillan J 16	Lindsay L — + 1	Taylor J 17 + 3	Wilson D — + 1	Mair L 17	Erskine C 14 + 1	Buaben P 9 + 2	Moncur G — + 2	Match No.
1	2	3	4	5	6	7³	8	9²	10	11¹	12	13	14													1
1	2	5	7	4	3	6	10¹	11²	8	9				12	13											2
1	2	5	7²	3	4	6	10	11¹	8	9				13	12											3
1	2	5		3	4	7²	10	11¹	8	9				13	14	12	6³									4
1	2	5		3	4	7	12	10¹	6	14	11³	13		8	9²											5
1	2	5	6²	3		7	14	9	8¹	10³	13	11		12			4									6
1	2	5	7	3	4		9	11	6³	14	12	13		10²	8¹											7
	2	5	9	3	4		10	11		12	8			6¹	7		1									8
1	2	5	6	4	3		9²	11	8³	12	13	14		10¹	7											9
1	2	5	6	3	4		9	11	13	8¹	12			10²	7											10
1	2	5	7	3	4		9¹	11	10²	12	13			8	6											11
1	2	5	7	3	8		11¹	9³	13	14	12			10²	6	4										12
1	7¹	5	14	3	2¹		11	10³	9	12	13			8	4	6²										13
1		5	4	3⁴			10⁴	11	12	8	13			7¹	9²	6				2						14
1		5	3				10¹	9³	11	7	13	12		6²	8	4				2	14					15
1	13	5		3			7	11	9²	6	10³	12	14	8¹		4	2									16
1	12	5		4			7	11	8³	6	10	14	13	9¹		3	2²									17
1	2	5		3			7	11	9¹	6	8²	13	12	10		4										18
1	2	5	3³	4			9	12	13	6	8			10¹		7				11²	14					19
1	2	5	6	3			8⁴	13	7³	9	12	14		10²		4				11¹						20
1	2	5	7	4			13	9²	6	10¹		12	8			3				11						21
	2	5⁴	12	3	7¹		9	8²	6	13				10		1				11	4					22
	2		4	6			12	8¹	7³	13		14		9²		1	5			11		3	10			23
	5		7	4			9	13	12	6	14			10²		1	2			11³		3	8¹			24
12	5		4	7	10		13		14	8				9²		1	2¹			11		3		6³		25
	5		4	10	7		12		14	13				8³		1	2			11²		3	6¹	9		26
13	5		4	6	10		12			8						1	2			11²		3	9	7¹		27
2	5		4	6	10		12			8						1	11¹					3	9	7		28
2	5		3	7			11	13		12				9		1				10²		4	6¹	8		29
2	5		6¹	7	10	13								8	4	1				11²		3	9³	12	14	30
2	5		7	10	14	13				12				8¹	3	1				11²		4	6³	9		31
	5			7	8	12	13		6					6	4	1	2			11		3	10¹	9²		32
	5			6¹	7	9	13	14						8²	3	1	2			11		4	10³	12		33
	5		3		10	11¹	14	7	13					8²		1	2			12		4	9³	6		34
	5			4	12	7	11¹		9	13				10		1	2			14		3	8³	6²		35
	5		3	7	8	10³	11	14	6		13			6	13	1	2			12		4²	9¹			36
	5		4	7	8²	13	10		6		9¹	14		9	14	1	2			11³		3	12			37
1²		5	6			13	8	7		9				9	4³	12	2			11		3	10¹		14	38

PETERHEAD

Year Formed: 1891. *Ground and Address:* Balmoor Stadium, Balmoor Terrace, Peterhead AB42 1EQ.
Telephone: 01779 478256. *Fax:* 01779 490682. *E-mail:* office@peterheadfc.co.uk *Website:* www.peterheadfc.com
Ground Capacity: 4,000 (seated: 1,000). *Size of Pitch:* 101m × 64m.
Chairman: Rodger Morrison. *Vice-Chairman:* Ian Grant. *Secretary:* Brian McCombie.
Manager: Jim McInally. *Assistant coaches:* David Nicholls and Craig Tully. *Physio:* Greig Smith.
Club Nickname: 'Blue Toon'.
Previous Ground: Recreation Park.
Record Attendance: 8,643 v Raith R, Scottish Cup 4th rd replay, 25 Feb 1987 (Recreation Park); 4,855 v Rangers, Third Division, 19 Jan 2013 (at Balmoor).
Record Victory: 8-0 v Forfar Athletic, Second Division, 30 Sep 2006.
Record Defeat: 0-13 v Aberdeen, Scottish Cup 3rd rd, 10 Feb 1923.
Most League Appearances: 275: Martin Bavidge, 2003-13.
Most League Goals in Season (Individual): 32: Rory McAllister, 2013-14.
Most Goals Overall (Individual): 98: Martin Bavidge, 2003-13.

PETERHEAD – SCOTTISH LEAGUE TWO 2013–14 LEAGUE RECORD

Match No.	Date	Venue	Opponents	Result	H/T Score	Lg Pos.	Goalscorers	Attendance
1	Aug 10	H	Annan Ath	D	2-2	0-1	5	Gilfillan 56, Cox 85	504
2	17	A	Stirling Alb	L	0-2	0-1	7		573
3	24	H	Elgin C	D	2-2	0-1	7	McGeever 79, Gilfillan 84	543
4	31	A	East Stirling	W	4-1	0-1	6	Brown 58, Redman 66, O'Neill 76, McGeever 81	286
5	Sept 14	H	Queen's Park	W	2-1	1-1	4	McAllister 43, McLaren 50	491
6	21	A	Montrose	L	1-2	1-1	6	McAllister 14	434
7	28	A	Albion R	W	2-1	1-0	5	Ross 19, McAllister (pen) 61	354
8	Oct 12	A	Clyde	D	1-1	1-0	3	McLaren 10	562
9	26	H	Berwick R	D	1-1	0-1	5	McAllister (pen) 51	503
10	Nov 5	A	Annan Ath	L	0-2	0-0	7		277
11	9	A	Elgin C	W	4-2	1-0	5	Rodgers 22, McAllister 2 47, 48, Cowie 52	622
12	16	H	East Stirling	D	1-1	0-0	6	Rodgers 76	545
13	23	A	Queen's Park	W	5-0	2-0	5	Rodgers 2 25, 56, Sharp 37, Gilfillan 58, McAllister 84	447
14	30	H	Montrose	W	3-0	0-0	1	McAllister 2 64, 81, McLaren 69	473
15	Dec 7	A	Clyde	W	3-1	2-1	1	Rodgers 2 9, 13, Donaldson 66	498
16	14	H	Albion R	D	1-1	0-0	2	McCann 86	423
17	21	A	Stirling Alb	W	3-1	2-0	1	McAllister 3 (1 pen) 4, 33, 72 (p)	521
18	28	A	Berwick R	W	3-1	1-1	1	McAllister 2 5, 62, Cowie 76	778
19	Jan 2	H	Elgin C	W	2-1	0-1	1	Sharp 63, Redman 90	737
20	11	A	East Stirling	L	0-2	0-1	1		310
21	18	A	Montrose	W	3-2	0-1	1	McNally (og) 52, McAllister 2 55, 83	424
22	25	H	Queen's Park	W	1-0	1-0	1	Ross 35	542
23	Feb 8	A	Stirling Alb	W	2-1	1-0	1	McAllister 23, McLaren 67	498
24	15	H	Clyde	W	2-0	1-0	1	Rodgers 3, McLaren 86	511
25	22	A	Albion R	D	0-0	0-0	1		442
26	Mar 1	H	East Stirling	W	4-0	3-0	1	Brown 19, Tapping (og) 27, McAllister (pen) 45, Rodgers 50	554
27	4	H	Annan Ath	W	3-1	2-1	1	Strachan 8, McAllister 25, Noble 50	607
28	8	A	Elgin C	W	3-2	1-2	1	Rodgers 16, McAllister 2 58, 75	670
29	15	H	Berwick R	W	3-0	1-0	1	Gilfillan 13, McAllister 67, Brown 90	497
30	22	A	Annan Ath	L	1-2	1-0	1	McAllister 16	452
31	29	H	Queen's Park	W	2-0	0-0	1	McAllister 2 (1 pen) 59 (p), 66	387
32	Apr 5	H	Montrose	W	4-0	0-0	1	Strachan 59, McAllister 2 63, 86, McIntosh (og) 77	671
33	12	A	Clyde	W	2-0	1-0	1	Rodgers 29, McAllister 69	534
34	19	A	Albion R	W	2-0	2-0	1	McAllister 2 (1 pen) 21 (p), 23	775
35	26	H	Stirling Alb	L	0-4	0-2	1		852
36	May 3	A	Berwick R	W	2-1	0-1	1	McAllister 2 (1 pen) 62, 79 (p)	586

Final League Position: 1

Honours
League Champions League Two: 2013-14.
Third Division Runners up: 2004-05, 2012-13.
Scottish Cup: Quarter-finals 2001.

Club colours: Shirt: Royal blue shirts with white trim. Shorts: White. Socks: Royal blue.

Goalscorers: *League (74):* McAllister 32 (7 pens), Rodgers 10, McLaren 5, Gilfillan 4, Brown 3, Cowie 2, McGeever 2, Redman 2, Ross 2, Sharp 2, Strachan 2, Cox 1, Donaldson 1, McCann 1, Noble 1, O'Neill 1, own goals 3.
William Hill Scottish FA Cup (1): McAllister 1.
Scottish Communities League Cup (0).
Ramsdens Cup (3): Cox 2, Brown 1.

Smith G 36	Sharp S 30	Ross S 30	Noble S 36	McGlinchey C 5+10	Redman J 35	Brown J 21+14	Cowie D 26+2	Cox D 9+4	Gilfillan B 29+3	McAllister R 32	McLaren F 12+19	Rodgers A 23+9	Richardson D 3+6	Strachan R 22+2	McCann R 11+15	McGeever R 7+1	O'Neill S 3+1	Buchan K —+8	Tully C 5	Donaldson R 7	Smith R 10+1	Low T —+3	Match No.
1	2	3[1]	4[3]	5[2]	6	7	8	9	10	11	12	13	14										1
1	2	3	5	14	8	11	7[2]	6[3]	9		12	13[4]		4	10[1]								2
1	2	3	5		7	10[1]		9	8	11	6					4	12						3
1		4	5	2	8	10		9[2]		11[2]	6[1]	12	14			3	7	13					4
1	2	3	5	14	6	8[3]	12	9[1]		11	10[2]	13				4	7						5
1	2[1]	4	5		7	8[3]	13	9[1]	14	10	11	12				3	6						6
1	2	3	5	14	6		7	9[3]	8	10[1]	11[2]	12			13	4							7
1	2		4	5[4]	6	13		12	7	10[3]	9	11[2]	14		8[1]	3							8
1	2		4		6	8[1]	7	9[2]	3	11	10[4]			5	13	12							9
1	2	3	13		8	9	7	11	10		5[2]	6	4[1]			12							10
1	2	3	13		7	9	8	11[1]	10		6[3]	5[2]	12				14	4					11
1	5	4		6	8	7	11[3]	12	10[2]	9[1]		13					14	3	2				12
1	5	2	9		8	12	7	6[1]	11	13	10[3]	14					3	4[2]					13
1	5	2	9		7	14	6	8[1]	11	13	10[2]	12					3[2]	4					14
1	2	3	5		7	13	9	8[3]	10[2]	12	11	14			6[1]	4							15
1	5	4	9		6	8[1]	7				10			3	11		12		2				16
1	5[3]	4	9		6	7[2]	8		13	10	14	11[1]		3	12				2				17
1		4	9		6	13	8	7[1]	10	12	11[2]			3	5				2				18
1	2	3	5	13	6	12	8		7	11[2]		10[3]		4	9[1]				14				19
1	2	4	3	13	7	12	8		11[1]	10	6[2]	9		5[3]	14								20
1	2	3	5	9	7	14	6		8[2]	11[3]	12	10[1]		4	13								21
1	5	2	4	9[1]	6[1]	14	8		7	10	13	11[1]		3	12								22
1	2[1]	3	5	14	7	8			6[2]	11	13	10[3]		9	12					4			23
1	5	2	9	14	6	7[3]	8[1]		11	12	10[2]			3	13					4			24
1	5	3	9		8	4[1]			10	11	12	7		6					2				25
1	2		5	12	6	8	7[3]		3	10[2]	9	11[1]	13	4					4			14	26
1	5	2	9		6	13	8		7[2]	10[1]	12	11[3]		3	14					4			27
1	5	2	9		6	12	8[2]		7[3]	11	13	10[1]		3	14					4			28
1	5	4	9		8	13	6		7[3]	11[1]	12	10[2]		3	14					2			29
1	2	3	5		6	12	8[2]		7[1]	11	13	10		4							9[8]		30
1	2[1]	4	5		7	3	6		8	10[3]	13	11[12]		9	12							14	31
1	2[2]	3	5		6	7	8	14	9[3]	11	13	10[1]		4	12								32
1	2	3	5		6	7	8		9[2]	11[1]	13	10[3]		4	12				14				33
1	5[3]	4	9[1]		8	7[2]		12		11	10		13	3	6						2	14	34
1	5	2	9		6[2]	8[3]	7	13	14		10	12		3[1]	11						4		35
1	5	2	9			14	8	6[1]	7	11[3]	10[2]	12		3	13						4		36

QUEEN OF THE SOUTH

Year Formed: 1919. *Ground & Address:* Palmerston Park, Dumfries DG2 9BA. *Telephone:* 01387 254853.
Fax: 01387 240470. *E-mail:* admin@qosfc.com *Website:* www.qosfc.com
Ground Capacity: 7,620 (seated: 3,509) *Size of Pitch:* 102m × 66m.
Chairman: Billy Hewitson. *Vice-Chairman:* Craig Paterson. *Assistant Club Secretary:* Susan Grierson.
Manager: Jim McIntyre. *Coach:* Billy Dodds. *Physio:* Ross Goodwin.
Club Nickname: 'The Doonhamers'.
Previous Grounds: None.
Record Attendance: 26,552 v Hearts, Scottish Cup 3rd rd, 23 Feb 1952.
Record Transfer Fee received: £250,000 for Andy Thomson to Southend U (July 1994).
Record Transfer Fee paid: £30,000 for Jim Butter from Alloa Athletic (1995).
Record Victory: 11-1 v Stranraer, Scottish Cup 1st rd, 16 Jan 1932.
Record Defeat: 2-10 v Dundee, Division I, 1 Dec 1962.
Most Capped Player: Billy Houliston, 3, Scotland.
Most League Appearances: 731: Allan Ball, 1963-82.
Most League Goals in Season (Individual): 37: Jimmy Gray, Division II, 1927-28.
Most Goals in Season: 41: Jimmy Rutherford, 1931-32; Nicky Clark, 2012-13.
Most Goals Overall (Individual): 251: Jim Patterson, 1949-63.

QUEEN OF THE SOUTH – SCOTTISH CHAMPIONSHIP 2013–14 LEAGUE RECORD

Match No.	Date	Venue	Opponents	Result	H/T Score	Lg Pos.	Goalscorers	Atten- dance
1	Aug 10	H	Dundee	W 4-3	1-1	2	Lyle [45], McGuffie (pen) [59], Russell [63], Paton [70]	2644
2	17	A	Livingston	D 3-3	2-1	3	Russell [38], McGuffie (pen) [44], Reilly [86]	1149
3	24	A	Hamilton A	L 0-2	0-1	6		1367
4	31	H	Alloa Ath	D 0-0	0-0	6		1607
5	Sept14	H	Raith R	L 0-1	0-1	6		1620
6	21	A	Greenock Morton	W 2-0	1-0	5	Russell [45], Lyle [59]	1826
7	28	H	Dumbarton	L 1-2	1-1	7	Russell [26]	1693
8	Oct 5	A	Falkirk	L 1-2	0-1	7	Russell [57]	3189
9	12	H	Cowdenbeath	D 1-1	0-1	7	Dowie [85]	1514
10	19	A	Dundee	L 1-2	0-0	9	Lyle [80]	4357
11	26	A	Alloa Ath	W 3-0	1-0	8	Russell 2 [16, 71], Reilly [75]	724
12	Nov 9	H	Hamilton A	L 0-1	0-1	8		1557
13	16	H	Greenock Morton	W 2-0	2-0	7	Reilly [6], McShane [18]	1685
14	23	A	Raith R	L 1-2	0-0	8	Reilly [62]	1497
15	Dec 7	A	Dumbarton	W 1-0	1-0	7	Russell [15]	824
16	21	H	Livingston	D 2-2	2-1	8	Paton [17], Durnan [45]	1523
17	28	A	Cowdenbeath	W 2-0	1-0	7	Burns [45], Russell [64]	556
18	Jan 4	A	Hamilton A	L 1-3	1-2	8	Russell [22]	1366
19	11	H	Alloa Ath	W 3-1	2-0	8	Paton [30], Reilly [34], Lyle [56]	1476
20	18	H	Raith R	W 1-0	1-0	6	McShane [25]	1538
21	29	A	Greenock Morton	D 1-1	1-0	6	Russell [44]	2341
22	Feb 1	A	Livingston	W 2-1	0-1	4	Durnan [55], Lyle [79]	1041
23	8	H	Falkirk	W 2-0	0-0	4	Reilly 2 [81, 86]	1818
24	15	H	Dundee	L 0-1	0-1	4		2152
25	22	A	Falkirk	L 0-1	0-0	5		2862
26	Mar 1	H	Dumbarton	W 3-1	2-0	4	Durnan [30], Reilly [45], McHugh [66]	1604
27	8	H	Hamilton A	D 1-1	0-0	4	Reilly [63]	1703
28	15	A	Alloa Ath	W 1-0	1-0	4	Dowie [18]	644
29	22	H	Cowdenbeath	W 2-1	2-0	4	Higgins [16], Reilly [33]	1619
30	25	A	Dundee	L 0-1	0-0	4		3999
31	29	H	Greenock Morton	W 3-0	1-0	4	Higgins [9], Lyle [49], Reilly [81]	1487
32	Apr 12	A	Falkirk	L 1-2	0-0	4	Reilly [67]	1863
33	15	A	Raith R	L 2-3	2-2	4	Durnan 2 [37, 45]	993
34	19	A	Dumbarton	W 3-0	1-0	4	Russell [17], Lyle [52], Holt [66]	1263
35	26	H	Livingston	W 2-0	1-0	4	McShane [25], Russell [54]	1923
36	May 3	A	Cowdenbeath	D 1-1	0-0	4	Carmichael [90]	1053

Final League Position: 4

Honours

League Champions: Division II 1950-51. Second Division 2001-02, 2012-13.
Runners-up: Division II 1932-33, 1961-62, 1974-75. Second Division 1980-81, 1985-86.
Scottish Cup Runners-up: 2007-08.
League Cup: semi-finals 1950-51, 1960-61.
League Challenge Cup Winners: 2002-03, 2012-13; *Runners-up:* 1997-98, 2010-11. *B&Q Cup:* semi-finals 1991-92.

European: *UEFA Cup:* 2 matches (2008-09).

Club colours: Shirt: Royal blue with white trim. Shorts: Royal blue. Socks: Royal blue.

Goalscorers: *League (53):* Russell 13, Reilly 12, Lyle 7, Durnan 5, McShane 3, Paton 3, Dowie 2, Higgins 2, McGuffie 2 (2 pens), Burns 1, Carmichael 1, Holt 1, McHugh 1.
William Hill Scottish FA Cup (3): Lyle 1, Paton 1, Russell 1.
Scottish Communities League Cup (8): Lyle 3, Paton 2, Higgins 1, McGuffie 1, McKenna 1.
Ramsdens Cup (6): Lyle 3, McKenna 2, Holt 1.
Premiership Play-Offs (3): McHugh 3.

Antell C 9+1	Mitchell C 31	Dowie A 27+1	Higgins C 25+1	Holt K 28+2	McGuffie R 9+1	McKenna S 17+6	Burns P 22+3	Russell I 28+6	Lyle D 25+10	Paton M 24+6	Carmichael D 9+17	Reilly G 19+15	Durnan M 28	Young D 12+4	Dzierzawski K 10+4	McShane J 24+4	Orsi D —+1	Clark A 24	Atkinson J 3+1	McHugh B 10+3	Kerr M 10+1	Kidd L 1+3	Hooper S 1	Match No.
1	2	3	4	5	6	7	8	9	10^2	11^1	12	13												1
1	2	3	4	5	7	6^2	8	11^1	10	9	12	13												2
1	2	4	14	5^2	7^2	6	8	11^1	10			9	13	3	12									3
1	2	3^1	5	12	6^2	7		13	10	11^2	9	14	4	8										4
1	2^1	3	5		8	6	11^2	10	14	9	12	4^8	7^3	13										5
1		3	4	5	2			9	10^1	11^2	12	13				7	8	6						6
1		3	4	5	2		13	9	10^3	11		12				7^1	8	6	14					7
1	4	3	5	2				9	10	11^2	12	13				8	7	6						8
1	3	4	5	2					10^2	11	9	6	12			8^1	13	7						9
	2		4	5				11	13	9^1	12	10^2	3	7	6	8		1						10
	2		7	5				11	13	9	10^2	4	6	3	8^1			1						11
	2		4	5		12		9	10	13	6^2	11	3	8^1	7^3	14		1						12
	2		4	5		13	12	8	11^2	14	7	10^1	3	6	9^3			1						13
	2		4	5		12	13	10^1	11^2	14	9	8	3	7^3	6			1						14
	2		4	5		8	6	10	11^1	9^2		13	3	12	7			1						15
	2	4				8	6	9	13	11^1	12	10^3	3		7^2	14		1						16
	2	4	5			7	6	9^2	10^1	11	13	12	3		8			1						17
	2	4	5				6^2	9^1	10	11	8	14	12	3	7^3	13		1						18
	2	4	5	13	7	6		9^1	11	8	12	10	3					1						19
	2	4	5		7			9	10^1	6	13	11	3		12	8^2		1						20
	2	13	4^8	5		7	6	11	10	8^3		9^1	3			14			1^2	12				21
	2	3		5		6	7	12	11^1	13	8^2	4		9					1	10				22
	2	4		5		8	6	10	9	13	3		7^2					1	1	11^1	12			23
12	2	4		5		7		13	14	9	10^2				8^1				1^8	11^3	6			24
	2	4		5			6	12	10	11^2	13	14	3		7				1		9^1	8^3		25
	2	4		5			7	8^2	13		12	11^1	3	14	9				1		10	6^1		26
	2	4		5			6	9	13		12	11	3		7^1				1		10^2	8		27
	2	8		5			6	9	12			11^1		4	3				1		10	7		28
	2	3	4	5				9	6^1		13	12	11		7				1		10^2	8		29
	2	5	3				6	12	10	9^3	13	11^1	4		7^2				1		14	8		30
	2	3		5			13	6^1	14	10^2	9	11	4		8^3				1		12	7		31
	2	4		5			7	6	13	12	8^1	11	3		9^1				1		10^3		14	32
	2	4	5^3	14		7^2	6	9^1	10	13		11	3		8				1				12	33
	2	4		5	14	9	6	10^2	11	13			3	12	8^1				1			7^3		34
	2	4		5			6	11	10^3	9^2			3	13	8^1				1		12	7	14	35
	3	4		5				13	9^1	10		12^2		7	8				1		11	6	2	36

QUEEN'S PARK

Year Formed: 1867. *Ground & Address:* Hampden Park, Mount Florida, Glasgow G42 9BA. *Telephone:* 0141 632 1275.
Fax: 0141 636 1612. *E-mail:* secretary@queensparkfc.co.uk *Website:* queensparkfc.co.uk
Ground Capacity: 52,025 (all seated). *Size of Pitch:* 105m × 68m.
President: Ron Jack. *Secretary:* Christine Wright. *Treasurer:* David Gordon.
Head Coach: Gus MacPherson. *Assistant Head Coach:* Chris Hillcoat.
Club Nickname: 'The Spiders'.
Previous Grounds: 1st Hampden (Recreation Ground); (Titwood Park was used as an interim measure between 1st &
2nd Hampdens); 2nd Hampden (Cathkin); 3rd Hampden.
Record Attendance: 95,772 v Rangers, Scottish Cup 1st rd, 18 Jan 1930.
Record for Ground: 149,547 Scotland v England, 1937.
Record Transfer Fee received: Not applicable due to amateur status.
Record Transfer Fee paid: Not applicable due to amateur status.
Record Victory: 16-0 v St. Peter's, Scottish Cup 1st rd, 12 Sep 1885.
Record Defeat: 0-9 v Motherwell, Division I, 26 Apr 1930.
Most Capped Player: Walter Arnott, 14, Scotland.
Most League Appearances: 532: Ross Caven, 1982-2002.
Most League Goals in Season (Individual): 30: William Martin, Division I, 1937-38.
Most Goals Overall (Individual): 163: James B. McAlpine, 1919-33.

QUEEN'S PARK – SCOTTISH LEAGUE TWO 2013–14 LEAGUE RECORD

Match No.	Date		Venue	Opponents	Result		H/T Score	Lg Pos.	Goalscorers	Attendance
1	Aug	10	H	East Stirling	L	1-3	1-2	10	Spittal [45]	476
2		17	A	Berwick R	L	0-4	0-2	10		439
3		24	A	Clyde	L	0-3	0-0	10		621
4		31	H	Stirling Alb	L	0-2	0-0	10		527
5	Sept	14	A	Peterhead	L	1-2	1-1	10	Quinn [24]	491
6		21	H	Elgin C	D	3-3	2-3	10	Quinn 2 (1 pen) [31 (pl, 43], Vitoria [77]	342
7		28	A	Annan Ath	L	2-5	0-3	10	Vitoria [51], Gormley [81]	413
8	Oct	19	A	East Stirling	D	1-1	0-0	10	Spittal [90]	339
9		26	H	Albion R	D	1-1	1-0	10	Davison [36]	541
10		29	A	Montrose	W	2-1	1-0	10	Spittal [25], Gormley [90]	358
11	Nov	9	H	Clyde	D	1-1	0-0	10	Spittal [90]	704
12		16	A	Stirling Alb	L	0-3	0-1	10		681
13		23	H	Peterhead	L	0-5	0-2	10		447
14		30	A	Elgin C	L	2-3	2-1	10	Spittal [5], Quinn (pen) [36]	608
15	Dec	7	H	Montrose	L	0-1	0-0	10		357
16		21	H	Berwick R	L	0-4	0-1	10		302
17		28	A	Albion R	L	1-2	0-1	10	Dunlop, M (og) [84]	538
18	Jan	4	A	Clyde	W	2-1	0-1	10	Spittal (pen) [58], Collins [72]	751
19		11	H	Stirling Alb	L	0-1	0-1	10		472
20		18	H	Elgin C	W	2-0	1-0	10	Gallacher [6], Vitoria [90]	346
21		25	A	Peterhead	L	0-1	0-1	10		542
22	Feb	1	H	East Stirling	D	0-0	0-0	10		337
23		8	A	Berwick R	L	0-1	0-0	10		443
24		15	A	Montrose	L	0-1	0-0	10		301
25		22	H	Annan Ath	L	0-1	0-1	10		356
26		25	A	Annan Ath	L	2-3	1-0	10	Wallace 2 [4, 90]	345
27	Mar	1	A	Stirling Alb	D	2-2	2-1	10	Spittal [18], Mitchell [33]	656
28		8	H	Clyde	L	1-3	0-3	10	Brophy [52]	608
29		15	H	Albion R	W	4-0	2-0	10	Brough 2 [2, 26], Spittal [67], Gormley [86]	361
30		22	A	East Stirling	W	4-1	2-1	10	Brophy 2 [12, 37], Quinn (pen) [73], Burns [80]	376
31		29	H	Peterhead	L	0-2	0-0	10		387
32	Apr	5	A	Elgin C	D	1-1	1-0	10	Brophy [3]	555
33		12	H	Montrose	D	1-1	0-0	10	Brophy [50]	251
34		19	A	Annan Ath	D	1-1	0-0	10	Brophy [65]	560
35		26	H	Berwick R	L	1-3	1-0	10	Brophy [19]	420
36	May	3	A	Albion R	L	0-1	0-1	10		503

Final League Position: 10

Honours
League Champions: Division II 1922-23. B Division 1955-56. Second Division 1980-81. Third Division 1999-2000.
Runners-up: Third Division 2011-12. *Promoted to Second Division:* 2006-07 (play-offs).
Scottish Cup Winners: 1874, 1875, 1876, 1880, 1881, 1882, 1884, 1886, 1890, 1893; *Runners-up:* 1892, 1900.
FA Cup Runners-up: 1884, 1885.

Club colours: Shirt: Black and white thin hoops. Shorts: White. Socks: Black.

Goalscorers: *League (36):* Spittal 8 (1 pen), Brophy 7, Quinn 5 (3 pens), Gormley 3, Vitoria 3, Brough 2, Wallace 2, Burns 1, Collins 1, Davison 1, Gallacher 1, Mitchell 1, own goal 1.
William Hill Scottish FA Cup (6): Spittal 4, Brough 1, Lamie 1.
Scottish Communities League Cup (0).
Ramsdens Cup (1): Quinn 1 (1 pen).

Brown M 4	Rooney S 5+3	Brough J 24	Lamie R 12+1	Coll B 21+2	Spittal B 35+1	Quinn A 25+4	McVey C 14+10	Burns S 23+5	Winters D 1	Keenan M 29+3	Grier A —+1	Davison L 6+17	Fisher R 22+1	Mosson G 5	Anderson D 21	Baty J 12+1	Vitoria J 7+11	Mitchell G 16+2	McComish M 5	Lochhead B 14	Gold D 11	McLean E —+1	Gormley L 7+19	Brinsinfil L 18	Gallacher P 19+1	Collins T 4+10	Gibson S 13+2	Wallace A 10	Brophy E 8+1	Sutherland C 4	Marr J 1	Chalmers K —+1	Match No.
1	2	3	4⁴	5²	6	7	8¹	9	10	11	12	13																					1
1	14	3		5²	11	8	13	12		7²			2	4	6³	9¹	10																2
1	7	3			6	10²	12	9²		8		13	4				8	11¹	2	5													3
1		3			7	6		10		9		12	4				8	11¹	2	5													4
		3	4		9	8	6	11¹		10²					13	2	5	1					7	12									5
	14	3	4		9	10	8³	12		11¹					6²	13	2	5	1				7										6
	14	3	4		6	11³	8	9¹		10²					12	2	5	1					7		13								7
		8		11	7²	9³	5	10¹		12	4		6		14			3					13	1	2								8
			4		9	10	12	5		11		6¹	2		7²			13					1	3									9
		3	4		11	12	10²	5		8		9¹	2		7			6					13		1								10
		3	4	14	9	10¹	5¹	11²		6		2	7		12²	8		13					1										11
		3⁴	4		9		5	10		6²		2	7		11¹	8		12					1		13								12
			4²	5	6	11¹		9²		7		13	3		8	2					10		1	12	14								13
	12				9	11¹	6³	5		10	14		4		7			13					3		1	2	8²						14
		4	8		9	10³	6²	5		11¹					13	2		7	12		1		3		14								15
		3	4	14	9	7	5¹	8		6²			2¹		10	11				1			13		12								16
		3		5	6	12	8	14		2			11²		7³						10		1		9¹	13	4						17
		3		5	9	12	8			2		7	11²				7³				11		1		6	10¹	4						18
		3		5	9	14	8	13		2		7			12			11¹			1		6³		10²	4							19
		3			9	8	10²	14		7¹	12		2		6	13	15				1		5³		11³	4							20
5					9	7	10³	8¹	14				2		6	12		13			1		3		11²	4							21
5¹					9	11	12	6				8²	14		4		7	10³			1		2	13	3								22
					9	11	10	8⁹	13			7¹			2	4²	6				14		1	5¹	12	3							23
		3			5	6³	11			10²	14		7¹		4	9	8	12					13	1	2								24
		3			5	8		13	10			12	4		6²	7		11			1		2²	14		9¹							25
		3			5	7		10²		9		6¹	12	13				11			1		2	14	4³	8							26
					10	7	11	12						5	9²	6		4			13		1	2	3	8¹							27
					9	11	10	7				14	4⁷		6		5		1				13	2¹	3	8	12⁹						28
	8			5	6	10	12	9		14					4¹	3		2		1			13				7³	11²					29
		3		5	6	10	12	9		13	14				8³	4²		2		1			13				7¹	11					30
	4			5²	9	3⁸	8	11³		7¹			12			6		2		1			13			14	10						31
		2			8		12	9		6	14					5				1			13		4	3¹	7³	11	10²				32
	4			5	6¹		3	9³		7	12				2					1			13		14		8	11	10²				33
				5	11	4	14			8			3			6		1			12		2³	13		7²	10	9¹					34
				5	6	4		9		8²	13	3				2		1			12		7				10¹	11					35
6					13	3				7¹						5		1			11		8²	12	4		10	9³	2	14			36

RAITH ROVERS

Year Formed: 1883. *Ground & Address:* Stark's Park, Pratt St, Kirkcaldy KY1 1SA. *Telephone:* 01592 263514. *Fax:* 01592 642833. *E-mail:* info@raithrovers.net *Website:* www.raithrovers.net
Ground Capacity: 8,473 (all seated). *Size of Pitch:* 103m × 64m.
Chairman: Turnbull Hutton. *Secretary:* Eric Drysdale.
Manager: Grant Murray. *Assistant Manager:* Paul Smith.
Club Nickname: 'Rovers'.
Previous Grounds: Robbie's Park.
Record Attendance: 31,306 v Hearts, Scottish Cup 2nd rd, 7 Feb 1953.
Record Transfer Fee received: £900,000 for Steve McAnespie to Bolton Wanderers (Sept 1995).
Record Transfer Fee paid: £225,000 for Paul Harvey from Airdrieonians (July 1996).
Record Victory: 10-1 v Coldstream, Scottish Cup 2nd rd, 13 Feb 1954.
Record Defeat: 2-11 v Morton, Division II, 18 Mar 1936.
Most Capped Player: David Morris, 6, Scotland.
Most League Appearances: 430: Willie McNaught, 1946-51.
Most League Goals in Season (Individual): 38: Norman Haywood, Division II, 1937-38.
Most Goals Overall (Individual): 154: Gordon Dalziel (League), 1987-94.

RAITH ROVERS – SCOTTISH CHAMPIONSHIP 2013–14 LEAGUE RECORD

Match No.	Date	Venue	Opponents	Result	H/T Score	Lg Pos.	Goalscorers	Atten- dance
1	Aug 10	H	Hamilton A	L 0-1	0-0	8		1652
2	17	A	Cowdenbeath	W 4-3	2-2	4	Spence 3 (2 pens) [3, 81 (p), 90 (p)], Cardle [26]	837
3	24	H	Dundee	D 0-0	0-0	4		2603
4	31	A	Greenock Morton	D 1-1	0-1	5	Anderson [78]	1545
5	Sept 14	A	Queen of the South	W 1-0	1-0	3	Spence [18]	1620
6	21	H	Alloa Ath	W 4-2	1-1	2	Cardle 2 [28, 90], Anderson [48], Elliot [79]	1397
7	28	H	Falkirk	D 1-1	1-0	2	Anderson [3]	1715
8	Oct 5	A	Dumbarton	W 4-2	1-0	2	Elliot [17], Spence (pen) [56], Hill [61], Vaughan [90]	843
9	19	A	Hamilton A	D 1-1	0-1	3	Elliot (pen) [70]	1113
10	26	H	Greenock Morton	W 2-1	1-0	3	Moon [44], Smith [90]	1569
11	29	H	Livingston	W 1-0	1-0	2	Smith [22]	1304
12	Nov 9	A	Dundee	L 0-2	0-1	3		5064
13	16	A	Alloa Ath	L 0-1	0-0	3		858
14	23	H	Queen of the South	W 2-1	0-0	3	Elliot 2 [63, 87]	1497
15	Dec 7	A	Falkirk	L 1-3	0-2	4	Spence [73]	2934
16	14	H	Dumbarton	W 2-1	0-0	3	Vaughan [51], Thomson [74]	1351
17	21	H	Cowdenbeath	D 3-3	1-1	3	Hill [32], Elliot [60], Booth (pen) [83]	1597
18	28	A	Livingston	L 0-3	0-2	4		1322
19	Jan 2	H	Dundee	L 0-2	0-0	4		4039
20	11	A	Greenock Morton	D 0-0	0-0	4		1745
21	18	A	Queen of the South	L 0-1	0-1	5		1538
22	Feb 1	A	Cowdenbeath	L 0-1	0-0	6		961
23	15	H	Hamilton A	L 2-4	0-4	7	Cardle [82], Baird [89]	1436
24	22	A	Dumbarton	D 3-3	1-2	8	Smith 2 [29, 61], Baird [57]	786
25	25	H	Alloa Ath	D 1-1	0-1	8	Hill [54]	978
26	Mar 1	H	Falkirk	L 2-4	2-1	8	Baird [23], Booth (pen) [28]	1729
27	15	H	Greenock Morton	W 2-1	0-1	7	Spence 2 (1 pen) [68 (p), 80]	1308
28	18	A	Dundee	D 0-0	0-0	7		4561
29	22	H	Livingston	L 2-4	0-1	8	Baird [48], Thomson [85]	1329
30	25	A	Hamilton A	L 2-3	1-0	8	Baird 2 [45, 69]	954
31	29	A	Alloa Ath	W 1-0	0-0	7	Booth [49]	726
32	Apr 12	H	Dumbarton	L 1-3	0-2	8	Smith [59]	1602
33	15	H	Queen of the South	W 3-2	2-2	7	Cardle [4], Watson [7], Baird [81]	993
34	19	A	Falkirk	L 1-2	1-2	7	Vaulks (og) [32]	3200
35	26	H	Cowdenbeath	L 1-2	0-1	7	Spence [88]	1760
36	May 3	A	Livingston	L 0-2	0-1	7		1265

Final League Position: 7

Honours

League Champions: First Division 1992-93, 1994-95. Second Division 2002-03, 2008-09. Division II 1907-08, 1909-10 (shared), 1937-38, 1948-49; *Runners-up:* Division II 1908-09, 1926-27, 1966-67. Second Division 1975-76, 1977-78, 1986-87.
Scottish Cup Runners-up: 1913.
League Cup Winners: 1994-95. *Runners-up:* 1948-49.
League Challenge Cup Winners: 2013-14.

European: *UEFA Cup:* 6 matches (1995-96).

Club colours: Shirt: White with navy blue trim. Shorts: White. Socks: White.

Goalscorers: *League (48):* Spence 9 (4 pens), Baird 7, Elliot 6 (1 pen), Cardle 5, Smith 5, Anderson 3, Booth 3 (2 pens), Hill 3, Thomson 2, Vaughan 2, Moon 1, Watson 1, own goal 1.
William Hill Scottish FA Cup (7): Anderson 1, Cardle 1, Hill 1, Moon 1, Smith 1, own goals 2.
Scottish Communities League Cup (7): Elliot 2, Cardle 1, Fox 1, Smith 1, Spence 1, Vaughan 1.
Ramsdens Cup (9): Elliot 2, Fox 1 (1 pen), Baird 1, Cardle 1, Hill 1, Moon 1, Spence 1, own goal 1.

McGurn D 10	Thomson J 33	Watson P 22	Hill D 30	Booth C 35	Anderson G 29+4	Fox L 29+1	Moon K 29+1	Cardle J 33	Smith G 16+17	Elliot C 28+2	Spence G 14+13	Vaughan L 5+16	Callachan R 16+12	Donaldson R 8+2	Ellis L 11+2	Laidlaw R 12+1	McCann K 1+3	Matthews R —+1	Mullen R 7+3	Baird J 14+1	Robinson L 14	Match No.
1	2	3	4	5	6	7	8	9	10^1	11	12											1
1	2	3	4	5	6^1	7	8	9	12	11	10											2
1	2	3	4	5	6		8	9	10	11			7									3
1	2	3	4	5	6	8	7^1	9	11^2	10		12	13									4
1	2	3	4	5	6^2	8	7	9	12^3	11	10^1	13	14									5
1	2	3	4	5	6^2	8	7^3	9	14	11	10^1	13	12									6
1	2	3	4	5	6	8	7	9	12	11	10^1	13										7
1	2	4	3^2	5	9	7	8	6^2	13	10	11^1	14		12^4								8
1	2	3^4		5	6^1	7	8	9^3	13	11	10^2	14	12		4							9
1^1	2	3		5	6	7	8^3	9	14	10	11^2		12		4	13						10
	2	3		5	6^2	7	8	9	10^1	11	12		13		4	1						11
	2	3		5^1	7	4^1	8	11^3	10^2	9	13		14	6		1	12					12
	2	4	3		9^2	8	7	6	11^3	10	12	13	14			1	5					13
	2	3	4^1	5	6		7	9	12	11	10^2		8		13	1						14
	2	3		5	6		8	9^1	11^2	10	12	13	7		4	1						15
	2		4	5	6^2	12	8	9^4	13	10	11^1		7		3	1						16
	2		4	5		7	8		12	10	11^1	9	6		3^2	1	13					17
	2		4	5		8	6		10	11^1		9^2	7		3	1	12	13				18
		3^4	4	5	13	7	8	9	10^1	11			6^2	2	12	1						19
			4	5	10^2	7	8	9	12	11^1		13		6	3	1			2			20
	2		4	5	6	8^1	7	10^2	14	11	12	13	9	3		1						21
		3	4	5	12	7^2	8	9	14	10^3		13		6	2	1				11^1		22
		3	4	5	7	9^2	6	10	13	11^1	8								2	12	1	23
	2			5	6	7		9	10		8	3^1	4						12	11	1	24
	2	3		5	6		8	9	11^1	12			7		4					10	1	25
	2		4	5	6	8		9^1	12		13	10^2	7		3					11	1	26
	2	3	4	5	6^1	8	7	9	10^2		12	13								11	1	27
	2	3^4	4	5	6	8	7^2	9	14	10^1		13								11	1	28
	2		4	5	6^2	8	7^3	9	14	10^1	13	12	3							11	1	29
	2	4	3	5	6^2	7		9	13	10^3	14	12		8						11^1	1	30
	2	3	4	5	9	7	12	6^2	10	14	13		8^3							11^1	1	31
	2	3	4^4	5	9^1	7	11	8^2	13	12		6								10	1	32
	2	3		5		7	8^2	9	6	10	12		4^4		13					11^1	1	33
	2	3	4	5	12	8		9^2	7^1	11	14	13	6		10^3						1	34
		3		5	12	7		8^2	11^1	10	13		6	4					2	9	1	35
		3	4	5	9	7		6	11	12	8^1								2	10	1	36

RANGERS

Year Formed: 1873. *Ground & Address:* Ibrox Stadium, 150 Edmiston Drive, Glasgow G51 2XD.
Telephone: 0871 702 1972. *Fax:* 0870 600 1978. *Website:* www.rangers.co.uk
Ground Capacity: 51,082 (all seated). *Size of Pitch:* 105m × 68m.
Manager: Ally McCoist. *Assistant Manager:* Kenny McDowall. *Coach:* Ian Durrant. *Head of Football Administration:*
Andrew Dickson.
Club Nickname: 'The Gers', 'The Teddy Bears'.
Previous Grounds: Flesher's Haugh, Burnbank, Kinning Park, Old Ibrox.
Record Attendance: 118,567 v Celtic, Division I, 2 Jan 1939.
Record Transfer Fee received: £8,500,000 for Giovanni van Bronckhorst to Arsenal (July 2001).
Record Transfer Fee paid: £12,000,000 for Tore Andre Flo from Chelsea (November 2000).
Record Victory: 14-2 v Blairgowrie, Scottish Cup 1st rd, 20 Jan, 1934.
Record Defeat: 1-7 v Celtic, League Cup Final, 19 Oct 1957.
Most Capped Player: Ally McCoist, 60, Scotland.
Most League Appearances: 496: John Greig, 1962-78.
Most League Goals in Season (Individual): 44: Sam English, Division I, 1931-32.
Most Goals Overall (Individual): 355: Ally McCoist; 1985-98.

Honours
League Champions: (54 times) Division I 1890-91 (shared), 1898-99, 1899-1900, 1900-01, 1901-02, 1910-11, 1911-12, 1912-13,
1917-18, 1919-20, 1920-21, 1922-23, 1923-24, 1924-25, 1926-27, 1927-28, 1928-29, 1929-30, 1930-31, 1932-33, 1933-34, 1934-35,
1936-37, 1938-39, 1946-47, 1948-49, 1949-50, 1952-53, 1955-56, 1956-57, 1958-59, 1960-61, 1962-63, 1963-64, 1974-75. Premier
Division: 1975-76, 1977-78, 1986-87, 1988-89, 1989-90, 1990-91, 1991-92, 1992-93, 1993-94, 1994-95, 1995-96, 1996-97, 1998-99,
1999-2000, 2002-03, 2004-05, 2008-09, 2009-10, 2010-11. Third Division 2012-13. League One 2013-14. *Runners-up:* 30 times.

RANGERS – SCOTTISH LEAGUE ONE 2013–14 LEAGUE RECORD

Match No.	Date	Venue	Opponents	Result	H/T Score	Lg Pos.	Goalscorers	Attendance
1	Aug 10	H	Brechin C	W 4-1	2-0	1	Hegarty [2], Law [40], Black [81], Shiels [85]	44,380
2	17	A	Stranraer	W 3-0	3-0	1	Little [7], Macleod [23], McCulloch [30]	3473
3	23	A	Airdrieonians	W 6-0	2-0	1	Macleod [19], Little [37], Crawford [49], Daly 2 [66, 71], Law [69]	8930
4	31	H	East Fife	W 5-0	3-0	1	Clark [1], McCulloch 3 [17, 36, 63], Macleod [54]	42,870
5	Sept 14	H	Arbroath	W 5-1	0-0	1	Mohsni [57], McCulloch 3 [65, 75, 90], Little [88]	43,562
6	22	A	Forfar Ath	W 1-0	1-0	1	Little [43]	3776
7	28	H	Stenhousemuir	W 8-0	3-0	1	Daly 4 [3, 17, 50, 83], Little [38], Wallace [60], Templeton [87], Mohsni [90]	43,877
8	Oct 6	A	Ayr U	W 2-0	0-0	1	Mohsni [56], Macleod [59]	8968
9	19	A	Brechin C	W 4-3	1-3	1	Daly [25], Mohsni [53], Law [66], Clark [85]	3237
10	26	A	East Fife	W 4-0	0-0	1	Thom (og) [49], Daly 3 [52, 57, 66]	4700
11	Nov 6	H	Dunfermline Ath	W 3-1	0-0	1	McCulloch (pen) [71], Daly [78], Mohsni [90]	43,082
12	9	H	Airdrieonians	W 2-0	0-0	1	Daly [46], McCulloch (pen) [64]	43,158
13	25	A	Arbroath	W 3-0	3-0	1	Daly [3], Donaldson (og) [27], Clark [41]	3902
14	Dec 3	H	Forfar Ath	W 6-1	4-1	1	Clark 4 [6, 27, 44, 66], Wallace [37], McCulloch (pen) [71]	38,745
15	7	H	Ayr U	W 3-0	2-0	1	Daly [12], Aird [23], Mohsni [86]	45,227
16	26	H	Stranraer	D 1-1	1-0	1	McCulloch (pen) [37]	45,462
17	30	A	Dunfermline Ath	W 4-0	1-0	1	Aird [22], Clark [52], Law [70], Crawford [90]	10,089
18	Jan 2	A	Airdrieonians	W 1-0	1-0	1	Macleod [18]	6522
19	5	A	Stenhousemuir	W 2-0	1-0	1	Law 2 [36, 90]	2546
20	11	H	East Fife	W 2-0	1-0	1	Shiels 2 [5, 64]	42,182
21	20	A	Forfar Ath	W 2-0	0-0	1	Mohsni [75], Templeton [90]	2067
22	25	H	Arbroath	W 3-2	1-1	1	Daly [21], Templeton [72], McCulloch (pen) [78]	41,207
23	Feb 1	H	Brechin C	W 2-1	2-0	1	Shiels [14], Daly [25]	40,377
24	15	A	Ayr U	W 2-0	0-0	1	Law [46], Daly [72]	8449
25	22	H	Stenhousemuir	D 3-3	1-1	1	Law [36], McMillan (og) [69], Daly [72]	41,794
26	25	A	Stranraer	W 2-0	1-0	1	Wallace [5], Daly [89]	3024
27	Mar 1	A	East Fife	W 1-0	0-0	1	McCulloch (pen) [90]	4020
28	12	A	Airdrieonians	W 3-0	3-0	1	McCulloch 3 (2 pens) [3 (pl), 21 (pl), 41]	41,343
29	15	H	Dunfermline Ath	W 2-0	1-0	1	Smith [45], Gallagher, C [90]	44,110
30	23	A	Brechin C	W 2-1	1-0	1	Aird [23], Clark [67]	3070
31	29	A	Arbroath	W 2-1	1-0	1	Daly [19], Aird [87]	3400
32	Apr 15	H	Forfar Ath	W 3-0	0-0	1	Black [67], Mohsni [75], Shiels [85]	39,704
33	19	A	Stenhousemuir	W 4-0	2-0	1	Smith [32], Shiels [36], McCulloch (pen) [65], Law [78]	2767
34	22	H	Ayr U	W 2-1	0-0	1	Mohsni 2 [54, 82]	40,651
35	26	H	Stranraer	W 3-0	1-0	1	Aird [37], Peralta [60], Shiels [66]	46,093
36	May 3	A	Dunfermline Ath	D 1-1	0-0	1	Shiels [46]	7605

Final League Position: 1

Scottish Cup Winners: (33 times) 1894, 1897, 1898, 1903, 1928, 1930, 1932, 1934, 1935, 1936, 1948, 1949, 1950, 1953, 1960, 1962, 1963, 1964, 1966, 1973, 1976, 1978, 1979, 1981, 1992, 1993, 1996, 1999, 2000, 2002, 2003, 2008, 2009; *Runners-up:* 17 times.
League Cup Winners: (27 times) 1946-47, 1948-49, 1960-61, 1961-62, 1963-64, 1964-65, 1970-71, 1975-76, 1977-78, 1978-79, 1981-82, 1983-84, 1984-85, 1986-87, 1987-88, 1988-89, 1990-91, 1992-93, 1993-94, 1996-97, 1998-99, 2001-02, 2002-03, 2004-05, 2007-08, 2009-10, 2010-11; *Runners-up:* 7 times.
League Challenge Cup Runners-up: 2013-14.

European: *European Cup:* 161 matches (1956-57, 1957-58, 1959-60 semi-finals, 1961-62, 1963-64, 1964-65, 1975-76, 1976-77, 1978-79, 1987-88, 1989-90, 1990-91, 1991-92, 1992-93 final pool, 1993-94, 1994-95, 1995-96; 1996-97, 1997-98, 1999-2000, 2000-01, 2001-02, 2003-04, 2004-05, 2005-06, 2007-08, 2008-09, 2009-10, 2010-11, 2011-12).
Cup Winners' Cup: 54 matches (1960-61 runners-up, 1962-63, 1966-67 runners-up, 1969-70, 1971-72 winners, 1973-74, 1977-78, 1979-80, 1981-82, 1983-84).
UEFA Cup: 88 matches (*Fairs Cup:* 1967-68, 1968-69 semi-finals, 1970-71. *UEFA Cup:* 1982-83, 1984-85, 1985-86, 1986-87, 1988-89, 1997-98, 1998-99, 1999-2000, 2000-01, 2001-02, 2002-03, 2004-05, 2006-07, 2007-08 runners-up). *Europa League:* 6 matches (2010-11, 2011-12).

Club colours: Shirt: Royal blue with red trim. Shorts: White. Socks: Black with red tops.

Goalscorers: *League (106):* Daly 20, McCulloch 17 (9 pens), Mohsni 10, Clark 9, Law 9, Shiels 8, Aird 5, Little 5, Macleod 5, Templeton 5, Wallace 3, Black 2, Crawford 2, Smith 2, Gallagher C 1, Hegarty 1, Peralta 1, own goals 3.
William Hill Scottish FA Cup (13): Daly 3, Shiels 3, Templeton 3, Aird 1, Law 1, Mohsni 1, Smith 1.
Scottish Communities League Cup (1): Aird 1.
Ramsdens Cup (10): Daly 2, Law 2, Black 1, Little 1, McCulloch 1, McKay 1, Mohsni 1, Templeton 1.

Gallagher S 3	Hegarty C 1	Emilson Cribari S 4 + 3	Faure S 22 + 4	Wallace L 28	Little A 13 + 8	Crawford R 6 + 14	Black I 32	Law N 32	Macleod L 16 + 2	Daly J 34	McAusland K 3 + 1	Shiels D 13 + 5	McCulloch L 34	Templeton D 9 + 11	Aird F 22 + 5	Bell C 31	Clark N 13 + 10	McKay B — + 2	Murdoch A — + 1	Mohsni B 28	Smith S 11 + 2	Peralta A 17 + 3	Foster R 19 + 4	Hutton K 2 + 8	Simonsen S 2	Gallagher C 1 + 3	Telfer C — + 1	Match No.
1	2	3^1	4	5	6	7^2	8	9	10	11	12	13																1
1			4	5	6	13	7^2	9	8	11	2	10^1	3	12														2
1			4	5	11^1	7	6^2	10	9^3	8	2	14	3	13	12													3
		3	4	5	6	7^3	8	2	11	9^2	14					1	10^1	12	13									4
		2	9	13	8	7^1	10	3	12							1	11^2	4	5	6								5
		12	5	6	8	11	3	10^2								1	13	4	9^1	7	2							6
		5	10^2	14	7	8	9^3	11	3	13						1	12	4	6^1	2								7
		5	10^1	13	6	8	9	11	4	12						1	3	7^2	2									8
		10^1	6^2	8	9	7^3	11	4	13							1	12	3	5	2	14							9
		5^3	13	7^2	9	8	11^1	4								1	10	3	14	6	2	12						10
		13	5	10^3	7	8	11	3	9							1	12	4	6^2	2^1	14							11
		2	5	14	7	8	12	11	3	9^2	13					1	10^3	4	6^1									12
		2	5	12	7^2	8	9	10	3	6^1						1	11	4	13									13
		14	2	5	6	8^1	9	11^3	13	4^2	12	7				1	10	3										14
		2	5	13	7^2	8	10	3	12	9^1						1	11	4	6									15
		2	3	13	8	9	10^2	11	4	14	12					1	6^1	5	7^3									16
		2	5	14	6^1	8	12	11	3	7						1	9^3	4	10^2	13								17
		2	5	13	7	8	9^2	11	4	6						1	10^1	3	12									18
		4	5	6^1	12	7^2	9	10	3	11						1	13	8^4	2									19
		2	5	9	12	7	8	11	10^1	3	6					1	4											20
		2	5	8	9	11	10^1	3	12	6	4	7				1												21
		2	5	13	7	8	9^1	11	10^3	3	12	6				1	4											22
		2	5	7	8	11	10^1	4	9^3	6^2						1	3^4	14	12									23
		4	3	5	12	7	8	10	11^1	9^2	6					1	13	2										24
		4	2^1	5	11^2	7	8	10	13	3	9	6				1	12											25
		5	12	13	7	11	10	4	6^1							1	3	9	8^2	2								26
		5	12	13	7	9	10	11^2	3	6	8^1					1	4	2										27
		5	10^2	7	8	11	3	9^1	6							1	12	4	13	2								28
		12	4	6	7	10^3	9									1	11	3^2	5^1	8	2	13	14					29
		12	5	7^2	9^1	10	11	3	6							1	13	4	2	8								30
		4	5	6^1	10^1	13	3	9^2								1	11	14	8	2	7	12						31
		14	7^2	8	10	11	3	12	9^1	4	5	6^2	2	13											1			32
		12	8^1	9	11^3	10^2	3	6								1	14	4	5	2	7	13						33
		6	10^1	11	9^3	3	8									1	13	4	5	7^2	2	14	12					34
		14	6^2	10	11^2	9	3	8								1	12	4^1	5	7	2	13						35
		2	12	7	10	11	9^1	3	8							1	13	4	5	6^2								36

ROSS COUNTY

Year Formed: 1929. *Ground & Address:* The Global Energy Stadium, Victoria Park, Dingwall IV15 9QZ. *Telephone:* 01349 860860. *Fax:* 01349 866277. *E-mail:* donnie.macbean@rosscountyfootballclub.co.uk
Website: www.rosscountyfootballclub.co.uk
Ground Capacity: 6,700 (all seated). *Size of Ground:* 105 × 68m.
Chairman: Rory MacGregor. *Secretary:* Donnie MacBean.
Manager: Derek Adams. *Assistant Manager:* Neale Cooper. *Director of Football:* George Adams.
Club Nickname: 'The Staggies'.
Record Attendance: 6,110 v Celtic, Premier League, 18 August 2012.
Record Transfer Fee received: £200,000 for Neil Tarrant to Aston Villa (April 1999).
Record Transfer Fee paid: £50,000 for Derek Holmes from Hearts (1999).
Record Victory: 11-0 v St Cuthbert Wanderers, Scottish Cup 1st rd, 11 Dec 1993.
Record Defeat: 0-7 v Kilmarnock, Scottish Cup 3rd rd, 17 Feb 1962.
Most League Appearances: 230: Mark McCulloch, 2002-09.
Most League Goals in Season: 24: Andrew Barrowman, 2007-08.
Most League Goals (Overall): 47: Sean Higgins, 2002-09.

ROSS COUNTY – SCOTTISH PREMIER LEAGUE 2013–14 LEAGUE RECORD

Match No.	Date	Venue	Opponents	Result		H/T Score	Lg Pos.	Goalscorers	Attendance
1	Aug 3	A	Celtic	L	1-2	1-1	9	Maatsen [3]	45,705
2	10	H	Partick Thistle	L	1-3	0-1	10	Carey [71]	3331
3	17	A	St Johnstone	L	0-4	0-2	11		2833
4	24	H	St Mirren	W	3-0	2-0	9	Kettlewell [9], Brittain 2 [24, 57]	3142
5	31	A	Hibernian	D	0-0	0-0	9		9569
6	Sept15	H	Dundee U	L	2-4	0-3	9	Sproule [72], Quinn [77]	3005
7	21	H	Hearts	W	2-1	0-1	9	De Leeuw [89], Brittain [90]	4059
8	28	A	Motherwell	L	1-3	1-0	9	De Leeuw [30]	4263
9	Oct 5	H	Aberdeen	W	1-0	0-0	9	Quinn [52]	5290
10	19	A	Kilmarnock	L	0-2	0-1	9		3582
11	Nov 9	H	Celtic	L	1-4	0-1	10	Sproule [68]	5982
12	17	A	St Mirren	L	1-2	0-1	10	Saunders [67]	4205
13	23	A	Hearts	D	2-2	1-1	10	Carey [23], De Leeuw [50]	12,508
14	Dec 7	H	Kilmarnock	L	1-2	1-2	11	Kettlewell [33]	2937
15	14	H	Motherwell	L	1-2	0-2	11	De Leeuw [62]	2792
16	21	A	Dundee U	L	0-1	0-0	11		8029
17	26	H	Hibernian	L	0-2	0-1	11		3383
18	29	A	Aberdeen	L	0-1	0-1	11		11,602
19	Jan 1	A	Inverness CT	W	2-1	2-0	11	Boyd [15], Cooper [17]	4332
20	4	H	St Johnstone	W	1-0	0-0	10	Carey [88]	3305
21	11	A	Partick Thistle	D	3-3	1-2	10	Kiss 2 [23, 76], Gordon [50]	3539
22	18	H	Dundee U	W	3-0	1-0	10	Kiss 2 [42, 74], Arquin [69]	3609
23	25	H	Hearts	L	1-2	1-1	10	Songo'o [45]	4016
24	Feb 1	A	Kilmarnock	D	2-2	2-0	10	Arquin [30], Songo'o [36]	3372
25	15	A	Hibernian	L	1-2	0-2	10	Brittain [59]	8411
26	22	H	St Mirren	W	2-1	1-0	9	Arquin [38], De Leeuw [83]	3394
27	25	H	Inverness CT	L	0-3	0-2	10		4805
28	Mar 1	H	Partick Thistle	D	1-1	1-1	11	Brittain [14]	3441
29	15	A	St Johnstone	W	1-0	1-0	10	De Leeuw [29]	2213
30	22	A	Motherwell	L	1-2	0-0	10	Songo'o [82]	4080
31	25	H	Aberdeen	D	1-1	1-0	9	De Leeuw [35]	3775
32	29	A	Celtic	D	1-1	1-1	9	De Leeuw [16]	49,270
33	Apr 4	H	Inverness CT	L	1-2	0-1	9	Kiss [50]	4433
34	19	A	Hearts	L	0-2	0-0	11		13,692
35	26	H	Kilmarnock	W	2-1	1-0	9	Kiss [41], Brittain (pen) [77]	3401
36	May 3	A	St Mirren	L	0-1	0-0	10		4414
37	6	H	Hibernian	W	1-0	0-0	8	Brittain (pen) [63]	3850
38	10	A	Partick Thistle	W	3-2	1-0	7	Siew [22], Arquin [48], De Leeuw [77]	4390

Final League Position: 7

Honours
League Champions: First Division 2011-12. Second Division 2007-08. Third Division 1998-99.
Scottish Cup Runners-up: 2009-10.
League Challenge Cup Winners: 2006-07, 2010-11; *Runners-up:* 2004-05, 2008-09.

Club colours: Shirt: Navy blue with white trim. Shorts: Navy blue. Socks: Navy blue.

Goalscorers: *League (44):* De Leeuw 9, Brittain 7 (2 pens), Kiss 6, Arquin 4, Carey 3, Songo'o 3, Kettlewell 2, Quinn 2, Sproule 2, Boyd 1, Cooper 1, Gordon 1, Maatsen 1, Saunders 1, Slew 1.
William Hill Scottish FA Cup (0).
Scottish Communities League Cup (2): Brittain 1 (1 pen), Mustafi 1.

Brown M 28	Kovacevic M 13	Gordon B 25+3	Quinn R 20+9	McLean B 25+1	Munro G 5+1	Kettlewell S 22+3	Maatsen D 2+8	Luckassen K 9+5	Micic B 8+1	Carey G 31+5	Cooper A 5+12	Saunders S 4+8	Mustafi O 2+5	De Leeuw M 19+14	Ross S 5+5	Glen G 4+11	Boyd S 27+1	Sproule 17+3	Brittain R 34	Kiok M 4+2	Fraser M 10	Slew J 17+3	Ikonomou E 15	Tidser M 15+1	Kiss F 17	Songo'o Y 17	Arquin Y 14+2	Cikos E 14	Match No.
1	2	3	4	5	6	7	8²	9¹	10	11³	12	13	14																1
1	2	5	9	4	3	6	7²		8¹	10				11³	12	13	14												2
1		5	9			13			2	10		4		12		7¹	11²	3	6	8									3
1	2	5	8¹	3	4	7	14	11³		10				13	12				9²	6									4
1	2	5	9²	3	4	8	13	11		10				12			6¹	7											5
1	2³	5¹	9	3	4²	6		11		10				12	13	14	7	8											6
1	2	5	9²	3		6				10				12	11	13	4	7¹	8										7
1	2	5	9	4²	12	6				10				11³	7¹	14	3	13	8										8
1	2	5	8¹	3		6				12			7	10³	11²		4	13	9										9
1	2	5	9	3			8	12	13					11	10¹	14	4	6³	7²										10
1	5²		7	3			8	13		2	9²		14	10			4	12	6	11¹									11
	13	9	4				8²		11³	5	12		2⁴	10¹	14		3	6²	7										12
		8	3				5	13	10	4	7			9²		11¹	2		6²	12									13
1	2	5	9			7		11¹	4³					14	10	13	12	3		6²									14
	2	5	8	4		6		12		10²				11	13	12	9	7¹	1										15
	2	5	8³	4		6	14	7¹		10				11²	13	12	3	9	1										16
		5²	8	4		7		11¹	2	9	13		14	10³		12	3	6	1										17
		5		4		8	14			10		7³	2⁴	11¹	13	12	3	6	9		1								18
		5	14	4		7³		13	12	9	8	2¹		11²			3	6			1	10							19
		5		4		7				8	9			12	10²	3		6			1	11¹	2	13					20
	2	14	3			13⁴				9	12				11¹	4		6			1	10	5	8¹	7²				21
	2	12	4							9¹	14			13				6			1	10	5	8	7²	3	11³		22
	2¹		3							9	13			12				7			1	10	4	8¹	6	5	11		23
	2	14	3							9	12			13				7			1	10¹	4	8³	6⁶	5	11²		24
1	14	7²	3					13		9	12						6					11	5³	8		4	10	2	25
1		14	4							9²	12			13			6					11¹	5	7³	8	3	10	2	26
1			4							12	9			13			6²					11	5¹	8	7	3³		2	27
1			4			7				13				12			4	6				11²	5	9¹	8	3	10	2	28
1		12								14				9²	13	3	7					11	5	6³	8	4	10	2	29
1										12	14			10¹	13	3	7					9	5	8	6³	4	11	2²	30
1										10	13			9²		4	6					12	5	8	7	3	11¹	2	31
1	14									9		13		10¹		3	7					12	5	8⁶	6	4	11³	2	32
1		12								9				10		4	6					13	5¹	8²	7	3	11	2	33
1		9²	14							6	12	13				4	8					11	5	10¹	7	3³		2	34
1	5							12		9²	13			10¹		4	6					11		8³	7	3	14	2	35
1	5	14					8			9²	12			10³		3	6¹					11			7	4	13	2	36
1	3	12					8²			14	13			7³		5	6					11¹			9	4	10	2	37
1	5	7						13		9	6¹			12		3				14		10²		8		4	11¹	2	38

ST JOHNSTONE

Year Formed: 1884. *Ground & Address:* McDiarmid Park, Crieff Road, Perth PH1 2SJ. *Telephone:* 01738 459090. *Fax:* 01738 625 771. *Email:* karin@perthsaints.co.uk *Website:* www.perthstjohnstonefc.co.uk
Ground Capacity: 10,673 (all seated). *Size of Pitch:* 105m × 68m.
Chairman: Steve Brown.
Manager: Tommy Wright. *U20 Coach:* Alec Cleland. *Youth Coach:* Alistair Stevenson. *Physio:* Nick Summersgill.
Club Nickname: 'Saints'.
Previous Grounds: Recreation Grounds, Muirton Park.
Record Attendance: 29,972 v Dundee, Scottish Cup 2nd rd, 10 Feb 1951 (Muirton Park): 10,545 v Dundee, Premier Division, 23 May 1999 (McDiarmid Park).
Record Transfer Fee received: £1,750,000 for Callum Davidson to Blackburn R (March 1998).
Record Transfer Fee paid: £400,000 for Billy Dodds from Dundee (1994).
Record Victory: 9-0 v Albion R, League Cup, 9 Mar 1946.
Record Defeat: 1-10 v Third Lanark, Scottish Cup 1st rd, 24 Jan 1903.
Most Capped Player: Nick Dasovic, 26, Canada.
Most League Appearances: 298: Drew Rutherford, 1976-85.
Most League Goals in Season (Individual): 36: Jimmy Benson, Division II, 1931-32.
Most Goals Overall (Individual): 140: John Brogan, 1977-83.

ST JOHNSTONE – SCOTTISH PREMIER LEAGUE 2013–14 LEAGUE RECORD

Match No.	Date	Venue	Opponents	Result		H/T Score	Lg Pos.	Goalscorers	Attendance
1	Aug 4	H	Hearts	W	1-0	1-0	4	May [25]	6174
2	11	A	Kilmarnock	D	0-0	0-0	4		3550
3	17	H	Ross Co	W	4-0	2-0	2	Hasselbaink [14], Wotherspoon [16], May [50], Mackay [62]	2833
4	24	A	Dundee U	L	0-4	0-3	3		6992
5	31	A	Aberdeen	D	0-0	0-0	5		9478
6	Sept 14	H	Hibernian	L	1-2	1-1	5	May [17]	4095
7	21	A	Celtic	L	1-2	0-2	8	Caddis [81]	45,220
8	28	H	Partick Thistle	D	1-1	1-1	8	MacLean [42]	3248
9	Oct 5	H	Inverness CT	W	4-0	2-0	6	May [18], Mackay [27], MacLean 2 [73, 82]	3020
10	19	A	St Mirren	L	3-4	1-1	7	MacLean [17], Hasselbaink [61], Fallon [84]	3739
11	27	H	Motherwell	W	2-0	0-0	6	May [49], Hasselbaink [64]	2449
12	Nov 2	H	Hearts	W	2-0	1-0	5	Hasselbaink [29], May [53]	13,175
13	9	H	Kilmarnock	W	3-1	2-0	5	Hasselbaink [24], May 2 (1 pen) [31, 54 (p)]	2855
14	23	A	Inverness CT	L	0-1	0-1	6		3255
15	Dec 7	H	Aberdeen	L	0-2	0-1	6		4741
16	21	A	Hibernian	D	0-0	0-0	6		8776
17	26	H	Celtic	L	0-1	0-1	6		7034
18	29	H	Dundee U	W	3-0	1-0	6	May 3 (1 pen) [20 (p), 57, 87]	7231
19	Jan 1	A	Motherwell	L	0-4	0-1	6		3763
20	4	A	Ross Co	L	0-1	0-0	7		3305
21	11	H	St Mirren	W	2-0	0-0	6	Davidson [71], May [74]	2329
22	18	H	Hearts	D	3-3	1-0	6	May 3 (2 pens) [39 (p), 49, 92 (p)]	3395
23	22	A	Partick Thistle	W	1-0	1-0	6	May [27]	2719
24	Feb 16	A	Celtic	L	0-3	0-1	6		45,239
25	22	H	Inverness CT	L	0-1	0-1	6		2415
26	25	H	Motherwell	W	3-0	2-0	6	MacLean 2 [6, 35], Miller [87]	1892
27	Mar 1	A	Aberdeen	L	0-1	0-1	6		11,487
28	12	A	Dundee U	W	1-0	0-0	6	May [48]	6720
29	15	H	Ross Co	L	0-1	0-1	6		2213
30	22	H	Hibernian	W	2-0	1-0	6	MacLean [18], McGivern (og) [55]	3553
31	25	A	St Mirren	W	1-0	1-0	6	MacLean [39]	2817
32	29	A	Partick Thistle	D	1-1	1-0	6	May [9]	2999
33	Apr 5	A	Kilmarnock	W	2-1	2-1	6	Wright [31], Anderson [44]	3665
34	19	H	Dundee U	W	2-0	1-0	6	Anderson [32], May [76]	5223
35	26	A	Aberdeen	D	1-1	1-1	6	May [8]	10,003
36	May 3	A	Motherwell	L	1-2	1-2	6	Mackay [27]	7201
37	7	H	Celtic	D	3-3	1-0	6	Clancy [9], Brown [84], O'Halloran [86]	4624
38	11	A	Inverness CT	L	0-2	0-0	6		3121

Final League Position: 6

Honours
League Champions: First Division 1982-83, 1989-90, 1996-97, 2008-09. Division II 1923-24, 1959-60, 1962-63;
Runners-up: Division II 1931-32. First Division 2005-06, 2006-07. Second Division 1987-88.
Scottish Cup Winners: 2014.
League Cup Runners-up: 1969-70, 1998-99.
League Challenge Cup Winners: 2007-08; *Runners-up:* 1996-97.

European: *UEFA Cup:* 16 matches (1971-72, 1999-2000, 2012-13, 2013-14).

Club colours: Shirt: Blue. Short: White. Socks: Blue.

Goalscorers: *League (48):* May 20 (4 pens), MacLean 8, Hasselbaink 5, Mackay 3, Anderson 2, Brown 1, Caddis 1, Clancy 1, Davidson 1, Fallon 1, Miller 1, O'Halloran 1, Wotherspoon 1, Wright 1, own goal 1.
William Hill Scottish FA Cup (13): May 4, Anderson 2, Dunne 1, Hasselbaink 1, Jahic 1, MacLean 1, McDonald 1, O'Halloran 1, Wright 1.
Scottish Communities League Cup (7): May 3, Edwards 1, MacLean 1, McDonald 1, Wright 1.

Mannus A 34	Miller G 18 + 7	Scobbie T 18 + 3	Cregg P 13 + 7	Mackay D 36	Anderson S 29	Millar C 26 + 6	McDonald G 26 + 3	May S 34 + 4	MacLean S 18 + 3	Wotherspoon D 32 + 6	Davidson M 18 + 3	Hasselbaink N 20 + 10	Fallon R 1 + 7	Wright F 25 + 1	Easton B 22 + 1	Edwards G 4 + 9	Banks S 4	Caddis L — + 8	Brown S 2 + 2	Jahic S 3 + 2	Kane C — + 2	Croft L 10 + 9	O'Halloran M 9 + 5	Dunne J 13	Ivelumo C — + 6	Clancy T 3 + 1	Thomson C — + 1	Match No.
1	2	3	4¹	5	6	7	8	9²	10³	11	12	13	14															1
1	5		2	3	6	13	10	14	12	7		11²	4	8¹	9³													2
	5	8	2	3	12		10³	11	6¹	7²	9	14	4		14	1	13											3
	5	7³	2	3	12	13	9	10	6	8¹	11²		4		14	1												4
	5		2	3	8	9	12	11²	6	7	10¹		4		1	13												5
1	12	5	8	2	3		11	10¹	6	7	9²	13	4³		14													6
1		6¹	2	4	7	9	12	11	10²	8³	14		3	5		13												7
1	12	7¹	2	3³	9		11	10	6²	8	13		4	5		14												8
1	2		3		7	8¹	10	11	6³	13	9²		4	5	12		14											9
1	4	12	14	2		7	8³	10	11²	6		9¹	13	3⁴	5													10
1	2	4	7²	3		6	8	11		9¹	12	10³		5	14	13												11
1	2	4		3		6	7¹	10		9¹	8	11²		5	13	14		13										12
1	2	4		3		6	8	10³		9²	7	11¹		5	13	12		14										13
1	2¹	4		3		6²	9	10		7	8	11		5	12			13										14
1		5		2		6¹	8²	10		9	7	11³	13⁴	4		12		14		3								15
1	13	5	12⁴	2		6²	8	10		9	7²			4	14	11¹		3										16
1	7¹		2			9	11			6³	8	10²		4	5	12			3	14	13							17
1	2	12	8³		3		9	11		6²	7	13		4	5¹	10		14										18
1		5		2	4	14	9³	11		10¹	8	12	13	3		7			6²									19
1		5		2	4	6²	7	10		9³	8	11¹	13	3									14	12				20
1		5		2	3	6	7	11		9²	8	10¹		4									12	13				21
1⁺	12	5	14	2	3⁴	6	7	10		13	8²	11³		4									9¹					22
	13	5	7²	2	3	6	8	10		11				4			1						9¹	12				23
1		4	14	2	3	7¹	8	11		10		12		5									6³	13	9²			24
1		12	9¹	2	3	7²	10	11		6		8		4³	5								14			13		25
1	2		3	4	14	7	10	11³	12		9¹			5									6²		8	13		26
1	2		4	3		6¹	11	12⁴	10³		14			5									9²	8	7	13		27
1	2²	14	3	4	9	7	11		10					5³									13	8¹	6		12	28
1	2		3	4	14	8	10	11	12		9¹						/						6²	7¹³	13	5		29
1	2		5	3	12	7	10	11	6²					4									13	9	8¹			30
1	2	13	5	4	8		14	11²	9¹					12									6	10	7	3³		31
1		13	2	3	8		10	11¹	12					4	5								6	9²	7			32
1			2	3	8		10¹	11	9					4	5								6	12	7			33
1	13		8	2	3		11²	10	6³		12			4	5								9¹	7			14	34
1	14		8³	2	3	9¹	11	13	6		10²			4	5								12	7				35
1	2		3	4	6	14	10	11	7²		13			5									12	9⁹	8¹			36
1	2³	8		3		9	11¹	13	12		4			7								6²	10		14	5		37
1	2		3	4	7	14	11³	6¹	10²		5												12	9	8	13		38

ST MIRREN

Year Formed: 1877. *Ground & Address:* St Mirren Park, Greenhill Road, Paisley PA3 1RU. *Telephone:* 0141 889 2558.
Fax: 0141 848 6444. *E-mail:* info@saintmirren.net *Website:* www.saintmirren.net
Ground Capacity: 8,023 (all seated). *Size of Pitch:* 100m × 64m.
Chairman: Stewart Gilmour. *Vice-Chairman:* George Campbell. *Secretary:* Chris Stewart.
Manager: Tommy Craig. *Player Coaches:* Jim Goodwin and Gary Teale. *Youth Development Officer:* David Longwell.
Physio: Gerry Docherty.
Club Nickname: 'The Buddies'.
Previous Grounds: Shortroods 1877-79, Thistle Park Greenhill 1879-83, Westmarch 1883-94, Love Street 1894-2009.
Record Attendance: 47,438 v Celtic, League Cup, 20 Aug 1949.
Record Transfer Fee received: £850,000 for Ian Ferguson to Rangers (Feb 1988).
Record Transfer Fee paid: £400,000 for Thomas Stickroth from Bayer Uerdingen (March 1990).
Record Victory: 15-0 v Glasgow University, Scottish Cup 1st rd, 30 Jan 1960.
Record Defeat: 0-9 v Rangers, Division I, 4 Dec 1897.
Most Capped Player: Godmundor Torfason, 29, Iceland.
Most League Appearances: 399: Hugh Murray, 1997-2012.
Most League Goals in Season (Individual): 45: Dunky Walker, Division I, 1921-22.
Most Goals Overall (Individual): 221: David McCrae, 1923-34.

ST MIRREN – SCOTTISH PREMIER LEAGUE 2013–14 LEAGUE RECORD

Match No.	Date	Venue	Opponents	Result	H/T Score	Lg Pos.	Goalscorers	Attendance
1	Aug 3	A	Inverness CT	L 0-3	0-0	11		3215
2	17	H	Kilmarnock	D 1-1	0-0	10	Harkins [65]	4625
3	24	A	Ross Co	L 0-3	0-2	11		3142
4	31	H	Partick Thistle	L 1-2	0-0	11	McLean [50]	5601
5	Sept14	H	Motherwell	L 0-1	0-1	11		4012
6	21	A	Hibernian	L 0-2	0-1	11		9417
7	30	H	Aberdeen	D 1-1	0-0	11	Thompson [54]	4051
8	Oct 5	H	Hearts	W 2-0	1-0	10	McGinn [42], McGowan [58]	14,769
9	19	H	St Johnstone	W 4-3	1-1	10	McLean 2 (1 pen) [8, 76 (p)], McGowan [60], Thompson [89]	3739
10	26	A	Dundee U	L 0-4	0-2	11		6331
11	Nov 9	A	Partick Thistle	W 3-0	1-0	9	Thompson 2 [15, 90], Newton [72]	4946
12	17	H	Ross Co	W 2-1	1-0	8	Thompson [35], Newton [51]	4205
13	23	H	Hibernian	D 0-0	0-0	8		4451
14	Dec 7	H	Inverness CT	D 0-0	0-0	8		3305
15	14	A	Aberdeen	L 0-2	0-1	8		9332
16	21	A	Motherwell	L 0-3	0-2	8		3867
17	26	H	Dundee U	W 4-1	2-1	8	Thompson 2 [12, 88], McGinn [35], Naismith [71]	4780
18	29	H	Hearts	D 1-1	1-0	8	Thompson [3]	4568
19	Jan 2	A	Kilmarnock	L 1-2	1-1	9	Campbell [18]	5410
20	5	H	Celtic	L 0-4	0-0	9		5778
21	11	A	St Johnstone	L 0-2	0-0	9		2329
22	18	A	Hibernian	W 3-2	3-0	8	Williams (og) [5], Campbell [24], Thompson [26]	9610
23	25	H	Partick Thistle	D 0-0	0-0	9		4660
24	29	A	Hearts	L 1-2	1-1	9	Thompson [1]	12,422
25	Feb 2	A	Celtic	L 0-1	0-1	9		45,014
26	15	H	Aberdeen	L 0-1	0-0	9		4073
27	22	A	Ross Co	L 1-2	0-1	11	McGinn [66]	3394
28	Mar 1	H	Kilmarnock	W 2-0	0-0	9	Newton [79], Wylde [88]	4650
29	15	A	Dundee U	L 2-3	2-0	11	McGowan [20], Thompson [40]	6524
30	22	A	Celtic	L 0-3	0-1	11		46,561
31	25	H	St Johnstone	L 0-1	0-1	11		2817
32	29	A	Inverness CT	D 2-2	1-2	11	Naismith [3], Kelly [62]	3032
33	Apr 5	H	Motherwell	W 3-2	1-2	10	Thompson 2 [42, 87], McLean (pen) [86]	4377
34	19	H	Hibernian	W 2-0	2-0	8	McLean [1], McGowan [15]	5287
35	25	A	Partick Thistle	D 1-1	1-1	7	McLean (pen) [45]	5971
36	May 3	H	Ross Co	W 1-0	0-0	7	Wylde [79]	4414
37	7	A	Kilmarnock	L 0-1	0-1	8		4911
38	10	H	Hearts	D 1-1	1-0	8	Newton [28]	6311

Final League Position: 8

Honours
League Champions: First Division 1976-77, 1999-2000, 2005-06. Division II 1967-68;
Runners-up: First Division 2004-05; Division II 1935-36.
Scottish Cup Winners: 1926, 1959, 1987; *Runners-up:* 1908, 1934, 1962.
League Cup Winners: 2012-13; *Runners-up:* 1955-56, 2009-10.
League Challenge Cup Winners: 2005-06.
B&Q Cup Runners-up: 1993-94. *Anglo-Scottish Cup:* 1979-80.

European: *Cup Winners' Cup:* 4 matches (1987-88). *UEFA Cup:* 10 matches (1980-81, 1983-84, 1985-86).

Club colours: Shirt: Thin black and white vertical stripes with yellow trim. Shorts: White. Socks: Black with yellow tops.

Goalscorers: *League (39):* Thompson 13, McLean 6 (3 pens), McGowan 4, Newton 4, McGinn 3, Campbell 2, Naismith 2, Wylde 2, Harkins 1, Kelly 1, own goal 1.
William Hill Scottish FA Cup (6): Thompson 2, McLean 1 (1 pen), Harkins 1, Kelly 1, Newton 1.
Scottish Communities League Cup (1): Thompson 1.

Cornell D 5	van Zanten D 8+8	Grainger D 10+3	Reilly T 1+7	Goodwin J 31+1	McAusland M 30+2	Teale G 6+10	McGinn J 31+4	Thompson S 37	McGowan P 33+3	Harkins G 7+8	Kelly S 32+1	Robertson J —+1	McGregor D 35	Newton C 36+1	McLean K 28+2	Bahoken S 2+3	Caprice J —+6	Dilo C 12+1	Mair L 5+1	Kello M 21	Naismith J 26+1	Campbell A 7+4	Brady A —+1	Wylde G 6+11	Magennis J 7+6	Djemba-Djemba E 2	Match No.
1	2⁴	3	4	5	6	7	8²	9	10¹	11	12	13															1
1		5²	12	4	2	6	13	11	8	10			3	7	9¹												2
1	13	5	12	4	3	6	11	7	10¹				2²	8	9												3
1		4	5	3	2	12	6	10	13	8³				9	7²	11¹	14										4
1		5²	12	4	3	7		10	8	9³			2	6	14	11¹	13										5
	5³	4⁴		3	2	10	14	11	8²	9¹				6	7	13	12	1									6
	5			3		13	6¹	11²	10		9		2	7	8		12	1	4								7
	2			9¹	12	7	11	10			5		3	6	8			1	4								8
	2²			7¹		8	11	10	13		5		3	6	9	12		1	4								9
	2²			6³		10¹	11	9	14		5		3	8	7	13		4	1	12							10
	12	14		7³	4		9	11	10¹	13	5		3	6	8				1	2²							11
			12	7	3		9	11	10¹		5		4	6	8				1	2							12
	7¹				4		9	11	10		5		3	6	8	12			1	2							13
				3	4		9	10	11¹	12	5		7	6	8				1	2							14
				9	3		10¹	11	7	12	5		4	6	8				1	2							15
	14		13	6²			12	11	8	10¹	2		3	7¹	9			4	1	5							16
	12	13		6¹	3		8	11	10	14	5³		4	7	9²				1	2							17
	12	5		7	3²		8	11	10¹	13	9		4	6						1	2						18
	9	12		4			7²	10¹	8	13	5		3	6						1	2	11					19
	9	14		4			8	11³	7		5		3	6	12					1	2	10²	13				20
		9		7	3		10	8			5		4	6	12					1	2	11¹					21
	13	14		8²	4		7	10	9³		5		3	6						1	2	11¹		12			22
		7		4			8	11	6		5		3	12						1	2	9¹		10			23
	13			7	3⁴		9	10	11²		5		4	8						1	2	6¹		12			24
		7²	3				8	11¹			5		4	6	12					1	2	13		9	10		25
		4		13			6	11	10²		5		3	2	7					1		12		9	8¹		26
		3²	13				6	11	12		5		4	2	8					1				9	10	7¹	27
		4					9	11	10¹		5		3	7	8					1	2	13		12	6²		28
		3	13				9	11	10¹		5		4	7	8					1	2²	12		6			29
		13	3				8	11²	7³		5		4	6¹	9					1	2	12		14	10		30
		4	14				9	11	10³		5		3	7²	8	12				1¹	2			13	6		31
		3	12	13			6²	10			5		4	7	8			1			2	9¹		11¹	14		32
		7²	4	14			9	11	10¹		5		3	6⁴	8			1			2			12	13		33
		6⁴	4	14			10¹	11²	9³		5		3	7	8			1			2			13	12		34
		7	3				8¹	11	10²		5		4	6	9			1			2			13	12		35
		6	4				10¹¹	9²			5		3	7	8			1			2			13	12		36
		7	3	14			10³	11	8¹		5		4	6	9			1			2			12	13		37
	14		7	4			8³	13		12	5		3	6¹	9			1			2²			10	11		38

STENHOUSEMUIR

Year Formed: 1884. *Ground & Address:* Ochilview Park, Gladstone Rd, Stenhousemuir FK5 4QL. *Telephone:* 01324 562992. *Fax:* 01324 562980. *E-mail:* info@stenhousemuirfc.com *Website:* www.stenhousemuirfc.com
Ground Capacity: 3,776 (seated: 626). *Size of Pitch:* 101m × 66m.
Chairman: Bill Darroch. *Vice-Chairman:* Gordon Thompson. *Secretary/General Manager:* Margaret Kilpatrick.
Manager: Scott Booth. *Assistant Manager:* Brown Ferguson. *Physio:* Louise Wilson.
Club Nickname: 'The Warriors'.
Previous Grounds: Tryst Ground 1884-86, Goschen Park 1886-90.
Record Attendance: 12,500 v East Fife, Scottish Cup Quarter-final, 11 Mar 1950.
Record Transfer Fee received: £70,000 for Euan Donaldson to St Johnstone (May 1995).
Record Transfer Fee paid: £20,000 to Livingston for Ian Little (June 1995); £20,000 to East Fife for Paul Hunter (September 1995).
Record Victory: 9-2 v Dundee U, Division II, 16 Apr 1937.
Record Defeat: 2-11 v Dunfermline Ath, Division II, 27 Sept 1930.
Most League Appearances: 434: Jimmy Richardson, 1957-73.
Most League Goals in Season (Individual): 32: Robert Taylor, Division II, 1925-26.

STENHOUSEMUIR – SCOTTISH LEAGUE ONE 2013–14 LEAGUE RECORD

Match No.	Date	Venue	Opponents	Result	H/T Score	Lg Pos.	Goalscorers	Attendance
1	Aug 10	H	Stranraer	W	1-0	1-0	3	Gemmell [31]	483
2	17	A	Airdrieonians	W	1-0	0-0	3	McNeil [90]	722
3	24	H	Dunfermline Ath	L	4-5	2-0	4	Gemmell [12], Smith, R [23], Lynch [51], Higgins [72]	968
4	31	A	Forfar Ath	W	2-1	2-0	3	Higgins [30], Smith, D [31]	483
5	Sept 14	H	Ayr U	D	1-1	0-1	3	Smith, D [71]	657
6	21	A	Arbroath	W	4-3	1-1	3	Hodge [21], Higgins [48], Gemmell [53], Dickson [64]	596
7	28	A	Rangers	L	0-8	0-3	3		43,877
8	Oct 5	H	East Fife	D	1-1	1-1	3	Gemmell (pen) [23]	567
9	12	H	Brechin C	W	3-2	0-1	2	Gemmell 2 [47, 64], Dickson [53]	415
10	19	A	Stranraer	L	0-1	0-1	2		326
11	26	H	Forfar Ath	D	1-1	1-1	4	Gemmell [10]	408
12	Nov 9	A	Dunfermline Ath	L	2-3	1-1	4	McKinlay [24], Smith, D [50]	2517
13	16	H	Arbroath	W	3-2	0-0	3	Lynch [49], Malone [73], Douglas [79]	469
14	23	A	Ayr U	L	3-4	2-2	5	Gemmell (pen) [14], Dickson [19], McNeil [59]	986
15	Dec 7	A	East Fife	L	0-1	0-1	5		561
16	21	H	Airdrieonians	D	1-1	0-1	5	Dickson [82]	419
17	28	A	Brechin C	W	1-0	1-0	5	Hodge [38]	507
18	Jan 2	H	Dunfermline Ath	L	1-2	0-1	5	Lynch [85]	1556
19	5	H	Rangers	L	0-2	0-1	5		2546
20	11	A	Forfar Ath	L	0-3	0-3	6		485
21	18	A	Arbroath	L	1-2	1-1	7	Smith, D [13]	498
22	25	H	Ayr U	D	1-1	0-1	6	McNeil [89]	467
23	Feb 1	H	Stranraer	D	1-1	0-0	6	Malone [90]	466
24	15	H	East Fife	D	1-1	0-0	6	Malone [90]	465
25	22	A	Rangers	D	3-3	1-1	7	Dickson [16], Higgins 2 (1 pen) [58, 75 (p)]	41,794
26	25	A	Airdrieonians	D	1-1	0-0	6	Greacen [86]	586
27	Mar 1	H	Forfar Ath	W	4-1	1-0	5	Smith, D 2 [14, 88], Dickson 2 [62, 74]	368
28	8	A	Dunfermline Ath	D	0-0	0-0	5		2510
29	15	H	Brechin C	W	4-2	2-1	6	Smith, D [3], Dickson [7], Watt [53], Gemmell [76]	512
30	22	A	Stranraer	D	1-1	0-1	6	Rowson [90]	403
31	29	A	Ayr U	W	3-2	1-0	5	Greenhalgh [20], Higgins 2 (1 pen) [87 (p), 90]	992
32	Apr 5	H	Arbroath	D	2-2	1-1	5	Greenhalgh [39], Higgins [86]	518
33	12	A	East Fife	W	2-1	0-1	5	Dickson [68], Higgins (pen) [90]	639
34	19	H	Rangers	L	0-4	0-2	5		2767
35	26	A	Airdrieonians	L	1-2	0-1	5	Dickson [64]	812
36	May 3	A	Brechin C	W	3-1	1-0	5	Gemmell 2 (2 pens) [12, 61], Greenhalgh [70]	543

Final League Position: 5

Honours

League Champions: Third Division runners-up: 1998-99. *Promoted to Second Division:* 2008-09 (play-offs).
Scottish Cup: Semi-finals 1902-03. Quarter-finals 1948-49, 1949-50, 1994-95.
League Cup: Quarter-finals 1947-48, 1960-61, 1975-76.
League Challenge Cup Winners: 1995-96.

Club colours: Shirt: Maroon with white trim. Shorts: White. Socks: Maroon.

Goalscorers: *League (57):* Gemmell 11 (4 pens), Dickson 10, Higgins 9 (3 pens), Smith D 7, Greenhalgh 3, Lynch 3, Malone 3, McNeil 3, Hodge 2, Douglas 1, Greacen 1, McKinlay 1, Rowson 1, Smith R 1, Watt 1.
William Hill Scottish FA Cup (9): McNeil 3, Gemmell 2 (1 pen), Douglas 2, Dickson 1, Lynch 1.
Scottish Communities League Cup (3): Dickson 1, McMillan 1, Smith D 1.
Ramsdens Cup (8): Gemmell 3 (1 pen), Higgins 2, Douglas 1, McNeil 1, Smith D 1.

Smith C 36	Devlin N 29 + 1	Smith R 14	McMillan R 28	McKinlay K 25 + 3	Ferguson B 9 + 3	Anderson C 2 + 4	Dickson S 33 + 3	Smith D 20 + 7	Gemmell J 18 + 8	Higgins S 29 + 1	McNeil R 7 + 17	Douglas E 1 + 18	Lawson A 2 + 3	Malone E 24 + 4	Lynch S 26 + 4	Rowson D 22 + 4	Hodge B 26 + 1	Brash R 1 + 3	Nimmo D — + 1	Faulds K 5 + 4	Kouider-Aisser S — + 1	Greacen S 18	Watt J 8 + 3	Greenhalgh B 6	Duncan R 3	Summers C 4	Shaw D — + 1	Match No.
1	2	3	4	5	6	7	8^1	9	10^3	11^2	12	13	14															1
1	2	3	4*	5	6^2	7	9^1	8	10	11^3	14			12	13													2
1	2	3		5	10^1	13	9	6	11	7^2	14			4	8^3	12												3
1		3	4	5	7		6	9^1	10	11^2	13			2	12	8												4
1	2	3	4^1	5	6	12	9	8	10	11^3	14			13	7^2													5
1	2	3	4	5^2	8	14	6	9^1	10	11^2	13			12			7											6
1	2	3	4	5	10^2		8	9	11^1	7^3	14			13	12	6												7
1	12	3	4	5^1			9	6	11	10^2			14	2	7^3	8	13											8
1	2^2	3		5	12	13	6^1		11	10^3	9			4	8	7			14									9
1	2	3		5	14		6	12	10	11	9^2	13		4^1	8^3	7												10
1	2	3		5			9^1	6	11	10		13		4		7^2	8	12										11
1	2	3		5	6^2		10	7^1	11			13		4	9		8	12										12
1	2		4	5	14		9^2		10	11^3		13		3	6	7	12	8^1										13
1	2	3		5			8		10	11^1	12			4	9	6	7											14
1	2	4	3	5			8		11		10	12			7		6^2					9^1	13					15
1	2	4	5	6^2			12	10^3	13	9^1	14			3	11	7	8											16
1	2	4	5	6^2			12	11^3	14	10^1				3	9	8	7			13								17
1	2	4	5	6			12	10						3	11	7	8			9^1								18
1	2		4	9			6^1	13	12	10				5	11	7	8^2					3						19
1	2	7*	4				6	12	10^1	11^2		13		5	9	8						3						20
1	5		2^2				6	11^1	10	13				4	9	12	7			8		3						21
1	2						9	11	10	13	12			5	6^1	3	8			7^2		4						22
1	2	3					9	11^1	10	12	13			5	6^2	7	8					4						23
1	2	4					9^3	11^1	10	14	13			5	6^2	7	8					3	12					24
1	2	3					9^1	6^3	12	11^2	14			5	10	7	8					4	13					25
1	2	3					11^1	6^2	12	10	14			5	7	8	9^3					4	13					26
1	2	4	14				8	6^2	11^1		13			5	12	9	7					3	10^3					27
1	2	4	13				9^3	6^1	10	14	12			5	11^2	7	8					3						28
1	2	4					6	10	12	11^2				5	8^3	14	7			13		3	9^1					29
1	2	4	13				6	11	12	10	14			5^1	7^1	8						3	9^2					30
1	2	4^3	5				6^1	13	11		14		12	8^2	7							3	9	10				31
1	2^1		5^1	12	6		11	14					4	7^2	13	8						3	9	10				32
1			4	12			9					13		8^1	7	6^2						5	10	11	2	3		33
1			4				8	13	14	10^1				6^2	7					12		3	11^3	9		2*	5	34
1	2		4^2				6	13	14	11	12			9		8				7^2		3	10^1			5		35
1*							8^3	6^2	10			14	4	7						13		3	9	11^1	2	5	12	36

STIRLING ALBION

Year Formed: 1945. *Ground & Address:* Forthbank Stadium, Springkerse, Stirling FK7 7UJ. *Telephone:* 01786 450399.
Fax: 01786 448592. *Email:* admin@stirlingalbionfc.co.uk *Website:* www.stirlingalbionfc.co.uk
Ground Capacity: 3,808 (seated: 2,508). *Size of Pitch:* 101m × 68m.
Chairman: Stuart Brown.
Manager: Greig McDonald. *Assistant Manager:* Marc McCulloch. *Physio:* Jenna Orr.
Club Nickname: 'The Binos'.
Previous Grounds: Annfield 1945-92.
Record Attendance: 26,400 v Celtic, Scottish Cup 4th rd, 14 Mar 1959 (Annfield); 3,808 v Aberdeen, Scottish Cup 4th rd, 15 February 1996 (Forthbank).
Record Transfer Fee received: £90,000 for Stephen Nicholas to Motherwell (Mar 1999).
Record Transfer Fee paid: £25,000 for Craig Taggart from Falkirk (Aug 1994).
Record Victory: 20-0 v Selkirk, Scottish Cup 1st rd, 8 Dec 1984.
Record Defeat: 0-9 v Dundee U, Division I, 30 Dec 1967; 0-9 v Ross Co Scottish Cup 5th rd, 6 Feb 2010.
Most League Appearances: 504: Matt McPhee, 1967-81.
Most League Goals in Season (Individual): 27: Joe Hughes, Division II, 1969-70.
Most Goals Overall (Individual): 129: Billy Steele, 1971-83.

STIRLING ALBION – SCOTTISH LEAGUE TWO 2013–14 LEAGUE RECORD

Match No.	Date	Venue	Opponents	Result	H/T Score	Lg Pos.	Goalscorers	Attendance
1	Aug 10	A	Montrose	W 2-1	1-1	2	Fulton [6], Ferry [75]	486
2	17	H	Peterhead	W 2-0	1-0	3	Fulton [27], Johnston [75]	573
3	24	H	East Stirling	L 1-3	0-2	3	White [78]	735
4	31	A	Queen's Park	W 2-0	0-0	2	Cunningham [83], Ferry [90]	527
5	Sept 14	H	Annan Ath	L 0-2	0-1	3		608
6	21	A	Berwick R	D 1-1	0-0	4	Weatherston [60]	491
7	28	A	Elgin C	L 0-4	0-2	7		623
8	Oct 19	H	Montrose	W 3-1	1-1	3	Smith, C [2], White [49], Cunningham [78]	481
9	26	A	Clyde	L 1-2	0-2	7	Coyne [56]	676
10	29	H	Albion R	W 2-1	1-1	2	Johnston [10], Fulton [63]	423
11	Nov 9	A	East Stirling	D 2-2	2-1	3	White 2 [30, 45]	541
12	16	H	Queen's Park	W 3-0	1-0	3	Fulton [44], Cunningham [76], Coyne [83]	681
13	23	A	Annan Ath	D 4-4	1-2	3	McAnespie [11], Cunningham [51], White [70], Forsyth [74]	384
14	Dec 3	H	Berwick R	W 3-1	1-0	2	White [9], Notman (og) [52], Forsyth [63]	378
15	7	A	Albion R	L 1-2	0-2	3	Bishop [61]	396
16	21	A	Peterhead	L 1-3	0-2	4	Forsyth [55]	521
17	28	H	Clyde	D 1-1	0-1	5	Weir [69]	859
18	Jan 4	H	East Stirling	W 2-1	0-1	4	Comrie [90], Ferry [90]	639
19	11	A	Queen's Park	W 1-0	1-0	3	Ferry [3]	472
20	18	A	Berwick R	L 0-4	0-2	4		464
21	25	H	Annan Ath	D 1-1	0-1	4	White [90]	509
22	Feb 1	A	Montrose	D 0-0	0-0	4		333
23	8	H	Peterhead	L 1-2	0-1	6	White [53]	498
24	15	H	Albion R	W 2-0	0-0	5	Weatherston [67], White [82]	541
25	22	A	Elgin C	W 3-2	0-2	3	White 2 [77, 86], McAnespie [83]	576
26	Mar 1	H	Queen's Park	D 2-2	1-2	4	Gibson (og) [36], Comrie [57]	656
27	8	A	East Stirling	L 0-1	0-1	5		584
28	11	A	Elgin C	D 1-1	0-0	4	Cunningham [50]	641
29	15	A	Clyde	L 0-1	0-1	4		673
30	22	H	Montrose	D 2-2	0-0	4	Comrie [51], McClune [83]	529
31	29	A	Annan Ath	W 2-1	1-0	4	Weatherston 2 [36, 63]	479
32	Apr 5	H	Berwick R	W 2-1	0-1	4	Weatherston [89], Cunningham [90]	665
33	12	A	Albion R	W 2-0	2-0	3	White [30], Weatherston [42]	480
34	19	H	Elgin C	D 2-2	1-1	4	White [37], Comrie [81]	640
35	26	A	Peterhead	W 4-0	2-0	4	Comrie 2 [35, 75], Weatherston [41], Weir [54]	852
36	May 3	H	Clyde	W 4-1	1-1	3	White 2 (1 pen) [14, 84], Forsyth [88], Johnston [90]	1028

Final League Position: 3

Honours
League Champions: Division II 1952-53, 1957-58, 1960-61, 1964-65. Second Division 1976-77, 1990-91, 1995-96, 2009-10;
Runners-up: Division II 1948-49, 1950-51. Second Division 2006-07. Third Division 2003-04. *Promoted to First Division:* 2006-07 (play-offs). *Promoted to League One:* 2013-14 (play-offs).
League Cup: Semi-finals 1961-62.

Club colours: All red with white trim.

Goalscorers: *League (60):* White 15 (1 pen), Weatherston 7, Comrie 6, Cunningham 6, Ferry 4, Forsyth 4, Fulton 4, Johnston 3, Coyne 2, McAnespie 2, Weir 2, Bishop 1, McClune 1, Smith C 1, own goals 2.
William Hill Scottish FA Cup (9): White 3, Cunningham 1, Ferry 1, Forsyth 1, McAnespie 1, Weir 1, own goal 1.
Scottish Communities League Cup (0).
Ramsdens Cup (1): White 1 (1 pen).
League 1 Play-Offs (11): White 4, Weatherston 2, Comrie 1, Cunningham 1, Forsyth 1, McClune 1, Weir 1.

Crawford D 34	McCunnie J 1+1	Bishop J 27+2	Smith C 20	Forsyth R 25+1	Johnston P 25+7	Ferry M 17+10	Fulton D 18+6	McAnespie K 14+3	Weir G 27+6	White J 35+1	McClune D 22+4	Coyne B 4+9	Weatherston D 21+9	McGeachie R 19+4	Clark J 1	Day S 8+8	Cunningham A 10+17	Ashe D 19+4	Paton C —+1	Reidford C 2+1	Munn B 1+1	Gasparotto L 3	Comrie C 15+3	O'Byrne M 11	Smith D 7+2	Hamilton L 10+1	Boyle R —+1	Match No.
1	2	3	4	5	6	7	8³	9	10	11²	12	13	14															1
1	14	3⁴	4	5	6	7²	10⁵	8	9¹	11	13		12	2														2
1			4	5	6	7	11	8²	9	10			14	12	2³	3¹	13											3
1			4	5		12	8	3	10	11	7²	14	6³	2		9¹	13											4
1		3	5	12	7	6¹	4²	9	10		13	11³	2			8	14											5
1		3	4	5	6	8		7	10		11	2¹		9		12												6
1		3	4	5	6	7	14		9²	10¹	2	13	11		8³	12												7
1		3	4	9	6³	8		13	10³	7	11¹		2		12	5	14											8
1		4	3	9	6¹	8	13		12	10³	7²	11		2		14	5											9
1		3	4		6³	9	7		11	12	8	10¹		2²		14	13	5										10
1³		3	4	9	6¹	7	8		13	10	2	14			11²	5		12										11
1		3		8	6¹	9³	7	4	12	10	2	14		13	11²	5												12
1		3		8	6	9¹	7³	4	13	10	2	14	12		11²	5		1										13
1		3		8	6²		7¹	4	11	10	2	12	9⁵		13		5		14									14
1		3		7	12		8¹	4	6⁴	11	2¹	10²	9	13		14	5											15
1		3		8	6	12	7¹	5		10	2		9		13	11²					4⁴							16
1		3		8¹	6	14	13	4	10	11	7³		9²	2		12	5											17
1		3		8	6	13	7³	5	9	10		12			11¹	2²							4	14				18
1		3		7	6³	9²	8		10	11	2¹		12		13	5							4	14				19
1		3		7	12	9²	8⁴	4	11	10	13		6¹	2		14	5											20
1		3			6	14	7²		9¹	10	2		13		11	5		8³					12	4				21
1		3		5			8		9	10	2²		6³		14	11¹	12						7	4	13			22
	3²		5	12³			7¹		10	11			9	13		14	2	1					6	4	8			23
1		3			8				10		11²	2	9¹	13	5								6	4	7³	12	14	24
1				8		14	12	10		11¹	3		9²	13	5								6³	4	7	2		25
1	4		13	8		14		11		10	2		12		5²								6³	3	7	9¹		26
1		3		14			8⁴	9	10	12⁴		11¹	2		13								6	4	7²	5³		27
1	4		6		13		8	10		12	2		9	11¹	5								7²	3				28
1	3	7		13		12	6	10		14	2		9	11	5²								8	4³				29
1	3	4		6			9	10	8	12			11¹										7	2		5		30
1	3	4	14	6		13	8¹	10	5	11³	12												7	2²		9		31
1	3	4		5	14		8²	10	6³	11	2	12	13										7			9¹		32
1		3	5	6	14		9²	10	7	11³	4		12										8¹		13	2		33
1		4	5	6	13		9¹	10	8	11²	3		12	14									7			2¹		34
1	12	4	5	6	13	14		9	10	3			11³										7¹		8²	2		35
1	13	3	4	5	14			9	10²	7			11¹										6²		8	2		36

STRANRAER

Year Formed: 1870. *Ground & Address:* Stair Park, London Rd, Stranraer DG9 8BS. *Telephone and Fax:* 01776 703271.
E-mail: secretary@stranraerfc.org *Website:* www.stranraerfc.org
Ground Capacity: 6,250 (seated: 1,830). *Size of Pitch:* 103m × 64m.
Chairman: Robert Rice. *Vice-Chairman:* Iain Dougan. *Secretary:* David Broadfoot.
Manager: Stephen Aitken. *Assistant Manager:* Stephen Farrell. *Physio:* Walter Cannon.
Club Nicknames: 'The Blues', 'The Clayholers'.
Previous Grounds: None.
Record Attendance: 6,500 v Rangers, Scottish Cup 1st rd, 24 Jan 1948.
Record Transfer Fee received: £90,000 for Mark Campbell to Ayr U (1999).
Record Transfer Fee paid: £35,000 for Michael Moore from St Johnstone (Mar 2005).
Record Victory: 9-0 v St Cuthbert Wanderers, Scottish Cup 2nd rd, 23 Oct 2010; 9-0 v Wigtown & Bladnoch, Scottish Cup 2nd rd, 22 Oct 2011.
Record Defeat: 1-11 v Queen of the South, Scottish Cup 1st rd, 16 Jan 1932.
Most League Appearances: 301: Keith Knox, 1986-90; 1999-2001.
Most League Goals in Season (Individual): 27: Derek Frye, 1977-78.
Most Goals Overall (Individual): 115: Jim Campbell, 1965-75.

STRANRAER – SCOTTISH LEAGUE ONE 2013–14 LEAGUE RECORD

Match No.	Date	Venue	Opponents	Result	H/T Score	Lg Pos.	Goalscorers	Attendance
1	Aug 10	A	Stenhousemuir	L 0-1	0-1	7		483
2	17	H	Rangers	L 0-3	0-3	9		3473
3	24	H	Ayr U	D 1-1	1-1	10	Longworth [8]	845
4	31	A	Dunfermline Ath	L 1-3	1-1	10	Grehan [22]	2585
5	Sept 14	A	Airdrieonians	L 2-3	1-1	10	Aitken (pen) [39], Grehan [56]	679
6	21	H	East Fife	W 2-0	1-0	9	Grehan [22], Longworth [61]	349
7	28	A	Brechin C	D 1-1	0-1	8	Corcoran [54]	455
8	Oct 5	H	Arbroath	W 3-2	3-0	7	Grehan 2 [11, 39], Longworth [30]	334
9	12	A	Forfar Ath	W 2-1	2-1	6	Longworth [18], Aitken [36]	449
10	19	H	Stenhousemuir	W 1-0	1-0	5	Aitken (pen) [32]	326
11	26	H	Dunfermline Ath	L 1-2	1-0	5	Longworth [12]	622
12	Nov 2	H	Ayr U	W 6-3	3-2	5	Longworth 3 [11, 24, 41], Aitken 2 (2 pens) [48, 86], McKenna [77]	986
13	16	A	East Fife	W 2-1	1-1	5	Longworth [1], Bell [90]	713
14	23	H	Airdrieonians	W 3-1	2-0	4	Grehan [8], Winter [45], Stirling, A [58]	461
15	Dec 7	A	Arbroath	W 2-1	1-0	3	Longworth [2], Aitken [82]	521
16	14	H	Brechin C	W 3-0	1-0	3	Longworth [27], Grehan [59], Gallagher [90]	357
17	26	A	Rangers	D 1-1	0-1	3	Longworth [90]	45,462
18	Jan 4	H	Ayr U	W 4-0	2-0	3	Winter [14], Grehan 2 (1 pen) [33 (p), 47], Stirling, A [49]	1097
19	11	A	Dunfermline Ath	L 2-3	1-1	3	Bell [16], McKeown [51]	2952
20	25	A	Airdrieonians	D 1-1	0-1	3	McKeown [70]	726
21	Feb 1	A	Stenhousemuir	D 1-1	0-0	4	Stirling, A [88]	466
22	15	H	Arbroath	D 1-1	1-1	3	Gallagher [79]	377
23	22	A	Brechin C	W 3-1	3-0	3	Grehan 3 (1 pen) [26, 35 (p), 41]	452
24	25	H	Rangers	L 0-2	0-1	3		3024
25	Mar 1	H	Dunfermline Ath	W 3-1	2-0	3	Grehan (pen) [7], McKenna 2 [39, 73]	704
26	4	H	East Fife	W 2-0	1-0	3	McKenna [36], Stirling, S [61]	407
27	8	A	Ayr U	L 0-5	0-3	3		1141
28	11	A	Forfar Ath	L 0-4	0-2	3		342
29	15	A	Forfar Ath	L 0-1	0-1	3		422
30	22	H	Stenhousemuir	D 1-1	1-0	3	Longworth [9]	403
31	29	H	Airdrieonians	D 1-1	0-0	3	Longworth [50]	404
32	Apr 5	A	East Fife	D 1-1	0-1	3	Robertson [77]	636
33	12	A	Arbroath	L 2-4	0-1	3	Winter [51], Forde [90]	528
34	19	H	Brechin C	L 1-2	1-1	3	Stirling, A [22]	407
35	26	A	Rangers	L 0-3	0-1	3		46,093
36	May 3	H	Forfar Ath	W 3-1	1-1	3	Winter [41], Rumsby [54], McKeown [72]	501

Final League Position: 3

Honours
League Champions: Second Division 1993-94, 1997-98. Third Division 2003-04.
Runners-up: Second Division 2004-05, Third Division 2007-08. Promoted to Second Division 2011-12 (play-offs).
Scottish Cup: Quarter-finals 2003
League Challenge Cup Winners: 1996-97.
Qualifying Cup Winners: 1937.

Club colours: Shirt: Blue with black trim. Shorts: Blue. Socks: Blue.

Goalscorers: *League (57):* Longworth 14, Grehan 13 (3 pens), Aitken 6 (4 pens), McKenna 4, Stirling A 4, Winter 4, McKeown 3, Bell 2, Gallagher 2, Corcoran 1, Forde 1, Robertson 1, Rumsby 1, Stirling S 1.
William Hill Scottish FA Cup (12): Longworth 7, Grehan 2 (1 pen), Gallagher 1, Longworth 1, McKeown 1, Stirling A 1.
Scottish Communities League Cup (10): Aitken 3 (2 pens), Borris 1, Grehan 1, Longworth 1, McKenna 1, Robertson 1, Winter 1, own goal 1.
Ramsdens Cup (6): Aitken 3 (2 pens), Grehan 2, Winter 1.
Championship Play-Offs (2): Bell 1, Grehan 1.

Mitchell D 36	Kinnaird L 5 + 9	Robertson S 35	McKeown F 34	Docherty M 30 + 2	Winter S 28 + 4	Aitken C 15	Gallagher G 34	Borris R 5 + 17	Grehan M 32 + 3	McKenna D 14 + 20	Stirling A 31 + 5	Longworth J 28 + 8	Corcoran M 7 + 5	MacGregor D 13 + 3	Rumsby S 27	Forde A — + 14	Bell S 14 + 7	Stirling S 8 + 4	Match No.
1	2	3	4	5	6¹	7	8³	9²	10	11	12	13	14						1
1		4	3	5	6¹	7*	8	12	11³	14	13	10	9²	2					2
1		3	4		6		7	9	10³	12	8²	11³	13	5	2	14			3
1	5	3	4		6³	7¹	8	12	10	13	14	11³	9		2				4
1		3	4		6³	8	7	13	11	10³	12	14	9¹	5	2				5
1	14	3	4		5²	7	6	12	10³	11	8	13	9¹		2				6
1	5	3	4	14		7	8	13	10	11²	6¹	12	9³		2				7
1		2	4	12		8	7	14	10³	13	6²	11	9¹	5	3				8
1		3	4	5	12	8	7		11	13	6¹	10⁴	9²	2		14			9
1		3	4	5		7	8	13	10	14	6³	11³	12	2		9²			10
1		2	4	5		8³	7	14	10	12	9	11¹	13	3		6²			11
1	2	3	4	5	6¹	7	8		11³	12	9	10²	13	14					12
1		2	3	5	6¹	7	8	14	12	10²	9	11³		4		13			13
1		2	4	5	9²	8³	7	13	10¹	12	6	11		3		14			14
1	14	2²	4	5	6	8	7	13		10³	9¹	11		3	12				15
1	13	2¹	4	5	6	8²		11	14	9	10¹			3	12				16
1	14	2	4	5	6¹		8	12	11³	12	9	10		3		7²			17
1	14	2	4	5	6¹		8	12	10	13	9³	11²		3		7			18
1		2	4	5	6		8²	7	10¹	12	9	11		3		7	13		19
1		2	4	5	6²	7		11		9	10			3	13	12	8¹		20
1		2	4	5	12	8		10	6¹	9	11³			3	13	14	7²		21
1		2	4	5	12	7		10¹	13	9	11			3	14	8²	6³		22
1		2	4	5	6¹	8		10²	11³	9	13			3	14	7	12		23
1		2	4	5	6¹	7		10²	12	9	11			3	13	8			24
1	14	2	4	5	12	7		10	11²	9³	13			3		8	6¹		25
1	12	2	4	5	6	8		13	11³	9	10⁵			3	14		7⁷		26
1	13	2	4⁴	5	6			10¹	11	9	7	12		3³	14		8²		27
1	2⁷			5	6	8		10¹	11	9	12	4	3	13					28
1		4	5		6¹	8	12	10		9	11²			3	2	13	7		29
1		2	3	5	6	8	12	10³	13	9¹	11²	14	4				7*		30
1		2	4	5	6		7	12	10²	13	9¹	11		3		8			31
1		2	4	5	6		7	12	10²	13	9¹	11		3		8			32
1		2		5	9		7	6¹	12	10¹	13	11²		4	3	14	8		33
1		2	4	5	6		8		10	13	9	11²		3¹	14	7³	12		34
1	14	2²	4	5¹	6		8	9	11¹	12	7	10		3			13		35
1		2	4	5	8²		6	10³	11	9¹	12			3	14	13	7		36

SCOTTISH LEAGUE HONOURS 1890–2014

=Until 1921–22 season teams were equal if level on points, unless a play-off took place. §Not promoted after play-offs.
*Won or placed on goal average (ratio), goal difference or most goals scored (goal average from 1921–22 until 1971–72
when it was replaced by goal difference). No official competition during 1939–46; Regional Leagues operated.

DIVISION 1 (1898–99 to 1974–75) – TIER 1

Tier	Season	Max Pts	First	Pts	Second	Pts	Third	Pts
1	1890–91	36	Dumbarton=	29	Rangers=	29	Celtic	21
	Dumbarton and Rangers held title jointly after indecisive play-off ended 2-2. Celtic deducted 4 points for fielding an ineligible player.							
1	1891–92	44	Dumbarton	37	Celtic	35	Hearts	34
1	1892–93	36	Celtic	29	Rangers	28	St Mirren	20
1	1893–94	36	Celtic	29	Hearts	26	St Bernard's	23
1	1894–95	36	Hearts	31	Celtic	26	Rangers	22
1	1895–96	36	Celtic	30	Rangers	26	Hibernian	24
1	1896–97	36	Hearts	28	Hibernian	26	Rangers	25
1	1897–98	36	Celtic	33	Rangers	29	Hibernian	22
1	1898–99	36	Rangers	36	Hearts	26	Celtic	24
1	1899–1900	36	Rangers	32	Celtic	25	Hibernian	24
1	1900–01	40	Rangers	35	Celtic	29	Hibernian	25
1	1901–02	36	Rangers	28	Celtic	26	Hearts	22
1	1902–03	44	Hibernian	37	Dundee	31	Rangers	29
1	1903–04	52	Third Lanark	43	Hearts	39	Celtic / Rangers=	38
1	1904–05	52	Celtic=	41	Rangers=	41	Third Lanark	35
	Celtic won title after beating Rangers 2-1 in play-off.							
1	1905–06	60	Celtic	49	Hearts	43	Airdrieonians	38
1	1906–07	68	Celtic	55	Dundee	48	Rangers	45
1	1907–08	68	Celtic	55	Falkirk	51	Rangers	45
1	1908–09	68	Celtic	51	Dundee	50	Clyde	48
1	1909–10	68	Celtic	54	Falkirk	52	Rangers	46
1	1910–11	68	Rangers	52	Aberdeen	48	Falkirk	44
1	1911–12	68	Rangers	51	Celtic	45	Clyde	42
1	1912–13	68	Rangers	53	Celtic	49	Hearts / Airdrieonians=	41
1	1913–14	76	Celtic	65	Rangers	59	Hearts / Morton=	54
1	1914–15	76	Celtic	65	Hearts	61	Rangers	50
1	1915–16	76	Celtic	67	Rangers	56	Morton	51
1	1916–17	76	Celtic	64	Morton	54	Rangers	53
1	1917–18	68	Rangers	56	Celtic	55	Kilmarnock / Morton=	43
1	1918–19	68	Celtic	58	Rangers	57	Morton	47
1	1919–20	84	Rangers	71	Celtic	68	Motherwell	57
1	1920–21	84	Rangers	76	Celtic	66	Hearts	50
1	1921–22	84	Celtic	67	Rangers	66	Raith R	51
1	1922–23	76	Rangers	55	Airdrieonians	50	Celtic	46
1	1923–24	76	Rangers	59	Airdrieonians	50	Celtic	46
1	1924–25	76	Rangers	60	Airdrieonians	57	Hibernian	52
1	1925–26	76	Celtic	58	Airdrieonians*	50	Hearts	50
1	1926–27	76	Rangers	56	Motherwell	51	Celtic	49
1	1927–28	76	Rangers	60	Celtic*	55	Motherwell	55
1	1928–29	76	Rangers	67	Celtic	51	Motherwell	50
1	1929–30	76	Rangers	60	Motherwell	55	Aberdeen	53
1	1930–31	76	Rangers	60	Celtic	58	Motherwell	56
1	1931–32	76	Motherwell	66	Rangers	61	Celtic	48
1	1932–33	76	Rangers	62	Motherwell	59	Hearts	50
1	1933–34	76	Rangers	66	Motherwell	62	Celtic	47
1	1934–35	76	Rangers	55	Celtic	52	Hearts	50
1	1935–36	76	Celtic	66	Rangers*	61	Aberdeen	61
1	1936–37	76	Rangers	61	Aberdeen	54	Celtic	52
1	1937–38	76	Celtic	61	Hearts	58	Rangers	49
1	1938–39	76	Rangers	59	Celtic	48	Aberdeen	46
1	1946–47	60	Rangers	46	Hibernian	44	Aberdeen	39
1	1947–48	60	Hibernian	48	Rangers	46	Partick Thistle	36
1	1948–49	60	Rangers	46	Dundee	45	Hibernian	39
1	1949–50	60	Rangers	50	Hibernian	49	Hearts	43
1	1950–51	60	Hibernian	48	Rangers*	38	Dundee	38
1	1951–52	60	Hibernian	45	Rangers	41	East Fife	37
1	1952–53	60	Rangers*	43	Hibernian	43	East Fife	39
1	1953–54	60	Celtic	43	Hearts	38	Partick Thistle	35
1	1954–55	60	Aberdeen	49	Celtic	46	Rangers	41
1	1955–56	68	Rangers	52	Aberdeen	46	Hearts*	45
1	1956–57	68	Rangers	55	Hearts	53	Kilmarnock	42
1	1957–58	68	Hearts	62	Rangers	49	Celtic	46
1	1958–59	68	Rangers	50	Hearts	48	Motherwell	44
1	1959–60	68	Hearts	54	Kilmarnock	50	Rangers*	42
1	1960–61	68	Rangers	51	Kilmarnock	50	Third Lanark	42
1	1961–62	68	Dundee	54	Rangers	51	Celtic	46

1	1962–63	68	Rangers	57	Kilmarnock	48	Partick Thistle	46
1	1963–64	68	Rangers	55	Kilmarnock	49	Celtic*	47
1	1964–65	68	Kilmarnock*	50	Hearts	50	Dunfermline Ath	49
1	1965–66	68	Celtic	57	Rangers	55	Kilmarnock	45
1	1966–67	68	Celtic	58	Rangers	55	Clyde	46
1	1967–68	68	Celtic	63	Rangers	61	Hibernian	45
1	1968–69	68	Celtic	54	Rangers	49	Dunfermline Ath	45
1	1969–70	68	Celtic	57	Rangers	45	Hibernian	44
1	1970–71	68	Celtic	56	Aberdeen	54	St Johnstone	44
1	1971–72	68	Celtic	60	Aberdeen	50	Rangers	44
1	1972–73	68	Celtic	57	Rangers	56	Hibernian	45
1	1973–74	68	Celtic	53	Hibernian	49	Rangers	48
1	1974–75	68	Rangers	56	Hibernian	49	Celtic*	45

PREMIER DIVISION (1975–76 to 1997–98)

1	1975–76	72	Rangers	54	Celtic	48	Hibernian	43
1	1976–77	72	Celtic	55	Rangers	46	Aberdeen	43
1	1977–78	72	Rangers	55	Aberdeen	53	Dundee U	40
1	1978–79	72	Celtic	48	Rangers	45	Dundee U	44
1	1979–80	72	Aberdeen	48	Celtic	47	St Mirren	42
1	1980–81	72	Celtic	56	Aberdeen	49	Rangers*	44
1	1981–82	72	Celtic	55	Aberdeen	53	Rangers	43
1	1982–83	72	Dundee U	56	Celtic*	55	Aberdeen	55
1	1983–84	72	Aberdeen	57	Celtic	50	Dundee U	47
1	1984–85	72	Aberdeen	59	Celtic	52	Dundee U	47
1	1985–86	72	Celtic*	50	Hearts	50	Dundee U	47
1	1986–87	88	Rangers	69	Celtic	63	Dundee U	60
1	1987–88	88	Celtic	72	Hearts	62	Rangers	60
1	1988–89	72	Rangers	56	Aberdeen	50	Celtic	46
1	1989–90	72	Rangers	51	Aberdeen*	44	Hearts	44
1	1990–91	72	Rangers	55	Aberdeen	53	Celtic*	41
1	1991–92	88	Rangers	72	Hearts	63	Celtic	62
1	1992–93	88	Rangers	73	Aberdeen	64	Celtic	60
1	1993–94	88	Rangers	58	Aberdeen	55	Motherwell	54
1	1994–95	108	Rangers	69	Motherwell	54	Hibernian	53
1	1995–96	108	Rangers	87	Celtic	83	Aberdeen*	55
1	1996–97	108	Rangers	80	Celtic	75	Dundee U	60
1	1997–98	108	Celtic	74	Rangers	72	Hearts	67

PREMIER LEAGUE (1998–99 to 2012–13)

1	1998–99	108	Rangers	77	Celtic	71	St Johnstone	57
1	1999–2000	108	Rangers	90	Celtic	69	Hearts	54
1	2000–01	114	Celtic	97	Rangers	82	Hibernian	66
1	2001–02	114	Celtic	103	Rangers	85	Livingston	58
1	2002–03	114	Rangers*	97	Celtic	97	Hearts	63
1	2003–04	114	Celtic	98	Rangers	81	Hearts	68
1	2004–05	114	Rangers	93	Celtic	92	Hibernian*	61
1	2005–06	114	Celtic	91	Hearts	74	Rangers	73
1	2006–07	114	Celtic	84	Rangers	72	Aberdeen	65
1	2007–08	114	Celtic	89	Rangers	86	Motherwell	60
1	2008–09	114	Rangers	86	Celtic	82	Hearts	59
1	2009–10	114	Rangers	87	Celtic	81	Dundee U	63
1	2010–11	114	Rangers	93	Celtic	92	Hearts	63
1	2011–12	114	Celtic	93	Rangers	73	Motherwell	62

Rangers deducted 10 points for entering administration.

1	2012–13	114	Celtic	79	Motherwell	63	St Johnstone	56

SPFL SCOTTISH PREMIERSHIP

Tier	Season	Max Pts	First	Pts	Second	Pts	Third	Pts
1	2013–14	114	Celtic	99	Motherwell	70	Aberdeen	68

DIVISION 2 (1893–93 to 1974–75) – TIER 2

2	1893–94	36	Hibernian	29	Cowlairs	27	Clyde	24
2	1894–95	36	Hibernian	30	Motherwell	22	Port Glasgow Ath	20
2	1895–96	36	Abercorn	27	Leith Ath	23	Renton / Kilmarnock=	21
2	1896–97	36	Partick Thistle	31	Leith Ath	27	Airdrieonians / Kilmarnock=	21
2	1897–98	36	Kilmarnock	29	Port Glasgow Ath	25	Morton	22
2	1898–99	36	Kilmarnock	32	Leith Ath	27	Port Glasgow Ath	25
2	1899–1900	36	Partick Thistle	29	Morton	28	Port Glasgow Ath	20
2	1900–01	36	St Bernard's	26	Airdrieonians	23	Abercorn	21
2	1901–02	44	Port Glasgow Ath	32	Partick Thistle	30	Motherwell	26
2	1902–03	44	Airdrieonians	35	Motherwell	28	Ayr U / Leith Ath=	27
2	1903–04	44	Hamilton A	37	Clyde	29	Ayr U	28

2	1904–05	44	Clyde	32	Falkirk	28	Hamilton A	27
2	1905–06	44	Leith Ath	34	Clyde	31	Albion R	27
2	1906–07	44	St Bernard's	32	Vale of Leven=	27	Arthurlie=	27
2	1907–08	44	Raith R	30	Dumbarton=	27	Ayr U=	27

Dumbarton deducted 2 points for registration irregularities.

2	1908–09	44	Abercorn	31	Raith R=	28	Vale of Leven=	28
2	1909–10	44	Leith Ath=	33	Raith R=	33	St Bernard's	27

Leith Ath and Raith R held title jointly, no play-off game played.

2	1910–11	44	Dumbarton	31	Ayr U	27	Albion R	25
2	1911–12	44	Ayr U	35	Abercorn	30	Dumbarton	27
2	1912–13	52	Ayr U	34	Dunfermline Ath	33	East Stirling	32
2	1913–14	44	Cowdenbeath	31	Albion R	27	Dunfermline Ath / Dundee U=	26
2	1914–15	52	Cowdenbeath=	37	St Bernard's=	37	Leith Ath=	37

Cowdenbeath won title after a round robin tournament between the three tied clubs.

2	1921–22	76	Alloa Ath	60	Cowdenbeath	47	Armadale	45
2	1922–23	76	Queen's Park	57	Clydebank	50	St Johnstone	48

Clydebank and St Johnstone both deducted 2 points for fielding an ineligible player.

2	1923–24	76	St Johnstone	56	Cowdenbeath	55	Bathgate	44
2	1924–25	76	Dundee U	50	Clydebank	48	Clyde	47
2	1925–26	76	Dunfermline Ath	59	Clyde	53	Ayr U	52
2	1926–27	76	Bo'ness	56	Raith R	49	Clydebank	45
2	1927–28	76	Ayr U	54	Third Lanark	45	King's Park	44
2	1928–29	72	Dundee U	51	Morton	50	Arbroath	47
2	1929–30	76	Leith Ath*	57	East Fife	57	Albion R	54
2	1930–31	76	Third Lanark	61	Dundee U	50	Dunfermline Ath	47
2	1931–32	76	East Stirling*	55	St Johnstone	55	Raith R*	46
2	1932–33	68	Hibernian	54	Queen of the South	49	Dunfermline Ath	47

Armadale and Bo'ness were expelled for failing to meet match guarantees. Their records were expunged.

2	1933–34	68	Albion R	45	Dunfermline Ath*	44	Arbroath	44
2	1934–35	68	Third Lanark	52	Arbroath	50	St Bernard's	47
2	1935–36	68	Falkirk	59	St Mirren	52	Morton	48
2	1936–37	68	Ayr U	54	Morton	51	St Bernard's	48
2	1937–38	68	Raith R	59	Albion R	48	Airdrieonians	47
2	1938–39	68	Cowdenbeath	60	Alloa Ath*	48	East Fife	48
2	1946–47	52	Dundee	45	Airdrieonians	42	East Fife	31
2	1947–48	60	East Fife	53	Albion R	42	Hamilton A	40
2	1948–49	60	Raith R*	42	Stirling Alb	42	Airdrieonians*	41
2	1949–50	60	Morton	47	Airdrieonians	44	Dunfermline Ath*	36
2	1950–51	60	Queen of the South*	45	Stirling Alb	45	Ayr U*	36
2	1951–52	60	Clyde	44	Falkirk	43	Ayr U	39
2	1952–53	60	Stirling Alb	44	Hamilton A	43	Queen's Park	37
2	1953–54	60	Motherwell	45	Kilmarnock	42	Third Lanark*	36
2	1954–55	60	Airdrieonians	46	Dunfermline Ath	42	Hamilton A	39
2	1955–56	72	Queen's Park	54	Ayr U	51	St Johnstone	49
2	1956–57	72	Clyde	64	Third Lanark	51	Cowdenbeath	45
2	1957–58	72	Stirling Alb	55	Dunfermline Ath	53	Arbroath	47
2	1958–59	72	Ayr U	60	Arbroath	51	Stenhousemuir	46
2	1959–60	72	St Johnstone	53	Dundee U	50	Queen of the South	49
2	1960–61	72	Stirling Alb	55	Falkirk	54	Stenhousemuir	50
2	1961–62	72	Clyde	54	Queen of the South	53	Morton	44
2	1962–63	72	St Johnstone	55	East Stirling	49	Morton	48
2	1963–64	72	Morton	67	Clyde	53	Arbroath	46
2	1964–65	72	Stirling Alb	59	Hamilton A	50	Queen of the South	45
2	1965–66	72	Ayr U	53	Airdrieonians	50	Queen of the South	47
2	1966–67	76	Morton	69	Raith R	58	Arbroath	57
2	1967–68	72	St Mirren	62	Arbroath	53	East Fife	49
2	1968–69	72	Motherwell	64	Ayr U	53	East Fife*	48
2	1969–70	72	Falkirk	56	Cowdenbeath	55	Queen of the South	50
2	1970–71	72	Partick Thistle	56	East Fife	51	Arbroath	46
2	1971–72	72	Dumbarton*	52	Arbroath	52	Stirling Alb*	50
2	1972–73	72	Clyde	56	Dumfermline Ath	52	Raith R*	47
2	1973–74	72	Airdrieonians	60	Kilmarnock	58	Hamilton A	55
2	1974–75	76	Falkirk	54	Queen of the South*	53	Montrose	53

Elected to First Division: 1894 Clyde; 1895 Hibernian; 1896 Abercorn; 1897 Partick Thistle; 1899 Kilmarnock; 1900 Morton and Partick Thistle; 1902 Port Glasgow and Partick Thistle; 1903 Airdrieonians and Motherwell; 1905 Falkirk and Aberdeen; 1906 Clyde and Hamilton A; 1910 Raith R; 1913 Ayr U and Dumbarton.

FIRST DIVISION (1975–76 to 2012–13)

2	1975–76	52	Partick Thistle	41	Kilmarnock	35	Montrose	30
2	1976–77	78	St Mirren	62	Clydebank	58	Dundee	51
2	1977–78	78	Morton*	58	Hearts	58	Dundee	57
2	1978–79	78	Dundee	55	Kilmarnock*	54	Clydebank	54
2	1979–80	78	Hearts	53	Airdrieonians	51	Ayr U*	44
2	1980–81	78	Hibernian	57	Dundee	52	St Johnstone	51
2	1981–82	78	Motherwell	61	Kilmarnock	51	Hearts	50

2	1982–83	78	St Johnstone	55	Hearts	54	Clydebank	50
2	1983–84	78	Morton	54	Dumbarton	51	Partick Thistle	46
2	1984–85	78	Motherwell	50	Clydebank	48	Falkirk	45
2	1985–86	78	Hamilton A	56	Falkirk	45	Kilmarnock*	44
2	1986–87	88	Morton	57	Dunfermline Ath	56	Dumbarton	53
2	1987–88	88	Hamilton A	56	Meadowbank Th	52	Clydebank	49
2	1988–89	78	Dunfermline Ath	54	Falkirk	52	Clydebank	48
2	1989–90	78	St Johnstone	58	Airdrieonians	54	Clydebank	44
2	1990–91	78	Falkirk	54	Airdrieonians	53	Dundee	52
2	1991–92	88	Dundee	58	Partick Thistle*	57	Hamilton A	57
2	1992–93	88	Raith R	65	Kilmarnock	54	Dunfermline Ath	52
2	1993–94	88	Falkirk	66	Dunfermline Ath	65	Airdrieonians	54
2	1994–95	108	Raith R	69	Dunfermline Ath*	68	Dundee	68
2	1995–96	108	Dunfermline Ath	71	Dundee U*	67	Greenock Morton	67
2	1996–97	108	St Johnstone	80	Airdrieonians	60	Dundee*	58
2	1997–98	108	Dundee	70	Falkirk	65	Raith R*	60
2	1998–99	108	Hibernian	89	Falkirk	66	Ayr U	62
2	1999–2000	108	St Mirren	76	Dunfermline Ath	71	Falkirk	68
2	2000–01	108	Livingston	76	Ayr U	69	Falkirk	56
2	2001–02	108	Partick Thistle	66	Airdrieonians	56	Ayr U*	52
2	2002–03	108	Falkirk	81	Clyde	72	St Johnstone	67
2	2003–04	108	Inverness CT	70	Clyde	69	St Johnstone	57
2	2004–05	108	Falkirk	75	St Mirren*	60	Clyde	60
2	2005–06	108	St Mirren	76	St Johnstone	66	Hamilton A	59
2	2006–07	108	Gretna	66	St Johnstone	65	Dundee*	53
2	2007–08	108	Hamilton A	76	Dundee	69	St Johnstone	58
2	2008–09	108	St Johnstone	65	Partick Thistle	55	Dunfermline Ath	51
2	2009–10	108	Inverness CT	73	Dundee	61	Dunfermline Ath	58
2	2010–11	108	Dunfermline Ath	70	Raith R	60	Falkirk	58
2	2011–12	108	Ross Co	79	Dundee	55	Falkirk	52
2	2012–13	108	Partick Thistle	78	Greenock Morton	67	Falkirk	53

SPFL SCOTTISH CHAMPIONSHIP

Tier	Season	Max Pts	First	Pts	Second	Pts	Third	Pts
2	2013–14	108	Dundee	69	Hamilton A	67	Falkirk§	66

SECOND DIVISION (1975–76 to 2012–13) – TIER 3

3	1975–76	52	Clydebank*	40	Raith R	40	Alloa Ath	35
3	1976–77	78	Stirling Alb	55	Alloa Ath	51	Dunfermline Ath	50
3	1977–78	78	Clyde*	53	Raith R	53	Dunfermline Ath*	48
3	1978–79	78	Berwick R	54	Dunfermline Ath	52	Falkirk	50
3	1979–80	78	Falkirk	50	East Stirling	49	Forfar Ath	46
3	1980–81	78	Queen's Park	50	Queen of the South	46	Cowdenbeath	45
3	1981–82	78	Clyde	59	Alloa Ath*	50	Arbroath	50
3	1982–83	78	Brechin C	55	Meadowbank Th	54	Arbroath	49
3	1983–84	78	Forfar Ath	63	East Fife	47	Berwick R	43
3	1984–85	78	Montrose	53	Alloa Ath	50	Dunfermline Ath	49
3	1985–86	78	Dunfermline Ath	57	Queen of the South	55	Meadowbank Th	49
3	1986–87	78	Meadowbank Th	55	Raith R*	52	Stirling Alb*	52
3	1987–88	78	Ayr U	61	St Johnstone	59	Queen's Park	51
3	1988–89	78	Albion R	50	Alloa Ath	45	Brechin C	43
3	1989–90	78	Brechin C	49	Kilmarnock	48	Stirling Alb	47
3	1990–91	78	Stirling Alb	54	Montrose	46	Cowdenbeath	45
3	1991–92	78	Dumbarton	52	Cowdenbeath	51	Alloa Ath	50
3	1992–93	78	Clyde	54	Brechin C*	53	Stranraer	53
3	1993–94	78	Stranraer	56	Berwick R	48	Stenhousemuir*	47
3	1994–95	108	Greenock Morton	64	Dumbarton	60	Stirling Alb	58
3	1995–96	108	Stirling Alb	81	East Fife	67	Berwick R	60
3	1996–97	108	Ayr U	77	Hamilton A	74	Livingston	64
3	1997–98	108	Stranraer	61	Clydebank	60	Livingston	59
3	1998–99	108	Livingston	77	Inverness CT	72	Clyde	53
3	1999–2000	108	Clyde	65	Alloa Ath	64	Ross Co	62
3	2000–01	108	Partick Thistle	75	Arbroath	58	Berwick R*	54
3	2001–02	108	Queen of the South	67	Alloa Ath	59	Forfar Ath	53
3	2002–03	108	Raith R	59	Brechin C	55	Airdrie U	54
3	2003–04	108	Airdrie U	70	Hamilton A	62	Dumbarton	60
3	2004–05	108	Brechin C	72	Stranraer	63	Greenock Morton	62
3	2005–06	108	Gretna	88	Greenock Morton§	70	Peterhead*§	57
3	2006–07	108	Greenock Morton	77	Stirling Alb	69	Raith R§	62
3	2007–08	108	Ross Co	73	Airdrie U	66	Raith R§	60
3	2008–09	108	Raith R	76	Ayr U	74	Brechin C§	62
3	2009–10	108	Stirling Alb*	65	Alloa Ath§	65	Cowdenbeath	59
3	2010–11	108	Livingston	82	Ayr U*	59	Forfar Ath§	59
3	2011–12	108	Cowdenbeath	71	Arbroath§	63	Dumbarton	58
3	2012–13	108	Queen of the South	92	Alloa Ath	67	Brechin C	61

SPFL SCOTTISH LEAGUE ONE

Tier	Season	Max Pts	First	Pts	Second	Pts	Third	Pts
3	2013–14	108	Rangers	102	Dunfermline Ath§	63	Stranraer§	51

THIRD DIVISION (1994–95 to 2012–13) – TIER 4

4	1994–95	108	Forfar Ath	80	Montrose	67	Ross Co	60
4	1995–96	108	Livingston	72	Brechin C	63	Inverness CT	57
4	1996–97	108	Inverness CT	76	Forfar Ath*	67	Ross Co	67
4	1997–98	108	Alloa Ath	76	Arbroath	68	Ross Co	67
4	1998–99	108	Ross Co	77	Stenhousemuir	64	Brechin C	59
4	1999–2000	108	Queen's Park	69	Berwick R	66	Forfar Ath	61
4	2000–01	108	Hamilton A*	76	Cowdenbeath	76	Brechin C	72
4	2001–02	108	Brechin C	73	Dumbarton	61	Albion R	59
4	2002–03	108	Greenock Morton	72	East Fife	71	Albion R	70
4	2003–04	108	Stranraer	79	Stirling Alb	77	Gretna	68
4	2004–05	108	Gretna	98	Peterhead	78	Cowdenbeath	51
4	2005–06	108	Cowdenbeath*	76	Berwick R§	76	Stenhousemuir§	73
4	2006–07	108	Berwick R	75	Arbroath§	70	Queen's Park	68
4	2007–08	108	East Fife	88	Stranraer	65	Montrose§	59
4	2008–09	108	Dumbarton	67	Cowdenbeath	63	East Stirling§	61
4	2009–10	108	Livingston	78	Forfar Ath	63	East Stirling§	61
4	2010–11	108	Arbroath	66	Albion R	61	Queen's Park*§	59
4	2011–12	108	Alloa Ath	77	Queen's Park§	63	Stranraer	58
4	2012–13	108	Rangers	83	Peterhead§	59	Queen's Park§	56

SPFL SCOTTISH LEAGUE TWO

Tier	Season	Max Pts	First	Pts	Second	Pts	Third	Pts
4	2013–14	108	Peterhead	76	Annan Ath§	63	Stirling Alb	57

RELEGATED CLUBS

RELEGATED FROM DIVISION I (1921–22 to 1973–74)

1921–22 *Dumbarton, Queen's Park, Clydebank
1922–23 Albion R, Alloa Ath
1923–24 Clyde, Clydebank
1924–25 Ayr U, Third Lanark
1925–26 Raith R, Clydebank
1926–27 Morton, Dundee U
1927–28 Bo'ness, Dunfermline Ath
1928–29 Third Lanark, Raith R
1929–30 Dundee U, St Johnstone
1930–31 Hibernian, East Fife
1931–32 Dundee U, Leith Ath
1932–33 Morton, East Stirling
1933–34 Third Lanark, Cowdenbeath
1934–35 St Mirren, Falkirk
1935–36 Airdrieonians, Ayr U
1936–37 Dunfermline Ath, Albion R
1937–38 Dundee, Morton
1938–39 Queen's Park, Raith R
1946–47 Kilmarnock, Hamilton A
1947–48 Airdrieonians, Queen's Park
1948–49 Morton, Albion R
1949–50 Queen of the South, Stirling Alb
1950–51 Clyde, Falkirk

1951–52 Morton, Stirling Alb
1952–53 Motherwell, Third Lanark
1953–54 Airdrieonians, Hamilton A
1954–55 *No clubs relegated as league extended to 18 teams*
1955–56 Clyde, Stirling Alb
1956–57 Dunfermline Ath, Ayr U
1957–58 East Fife, Queen's Park
1958–59 Falkirk, Queen of the South
1959–60 Stirling Alb, Arbroath
1960–61 Clyde, Ayr U
1961–62 St Johnstone, Stirling Alb
1962–63 Clyde, Raith R
1963–64 Queen of the South, East Stirling
1964–65 Airdrieonians, Third Lanark
1965–66 Morton, Hamilton A
1966–67 St Mirren, Ayr U
1967–68 Motherwell, Stirling Alb
1968–69 Falkirk, Arbroath
1969–70 Raith R, Partick Thistle
1970–71 St Mirren, Cowdenbeath
1971–72 Clyde, Dunfermline Ath
1972–73 Kilmarnock, Airdrieonians
1973–74 East Fife, Falkirk

Season 1921–22 – only 1 club promoted, 3 clubs relegated.

RELEGATED FROM PREMIER DIVISION (1974–75 to 1997–98)

1974–75 *No relegation due to League reorganization*
1975–76 Dundee, St Johnstone
1976–77 Hearts, Kilmarnock
1977–78 Ayr U, Clydebank
1978–79 Hearts, Motherwell
1979–80 Dundee, Hibernian
1980–81 Kilmarnock, Hearts
1981–82 Partick Thistle, Airdrieonians
1982–83 Morton, Kilmarnock
1983–84 St Johnstone, Motherwell
1984–85 Dumbarton, Morton
1985–86 *No relegation due to League reorganization*

1986–87 Clydebank, Hamilton A
1987–88 Falkirk, Dunfermline Ath, Morton
1988–89 Hamilton A
1989–90 Dundee
1990–91 *No clubs relegated*
1991–92 St Mirren, Dunfermline Ath
1992–93 Falkirk, Airdrieonians
1993–94 *See footnote.* St Johnstone, Raith R, Dundee
1994–95 Dundee U
1995–96 Partick Thistle, Falkirk
1996–97 Raith R
1997–98 Hibernian

RELEGATED FROM PREMIER LEAGUE (1998–99 to 2012–13)

1998–99 Dunfermline Ath
1999–2000 *No relegation due to League reorganization*
2000–01 St Mirren
2001–02 St Johnstone
2002–03 *No clubs relegated*
2003–04 Partick Thistle
2005–06 Livingston
2006–07 Dunfermline Ath

2007–08 Gretna
2008–09 Inverness CT
2009–10 Falkirk
2010–11 Hamilton A
2011–12 Dunfermline Ath, Rangers (demoted to third division)
2012–13 Dundee

RELEGATED FROM SPFL SCOTTISH PREMIERSHIP (2013–14)

2013–14 Hibernian, Hearts

RELEGATED FROM FIRST DIVISION (1975–76 to 2013–14)

1975–76 Dunfermline Ath, Clyde	1994–95 Ayr U, Stranraer
1976–77 Raith R, Falkirk	1995–96 Hamilton A, Dumbarton
1977–78 Alloa Ath, East Fife	1996–97 Clydebank, East Fife
1978–79 Montrose, Queen of the South	1997–98 Partick Thistle, Stirling Alb
1979–80 Arbroath, Clyde	1998–99 Hamilton A, Stranraer
1980–81 Stirling Alb, Berwick R	1999–2000 Clydebank
1981–82 East Stirling, Queen of the South	2000–01 Morton, Alloa Ath
1982–83 Dunfermline Ath, Queen's Park	2001–02 Raith R
1983–84 Raith R, Alloa Ath	2002–03 Alloa Ath, Arbroath
1984–85 Meadowbank Th, St Johnstone	2003–04 Ayr U, Brechin C
1985–86 Ayr U, Alloa Ath	2004–05 Partick Thistle, Raith R
1986–87 Brechin C, Montrose	2005–06 Stranraer, Brechin C
1987–88 East Fife, Dumbarton	2006–07 Airdrie U, Ross Co
1988–89 Kilmarnock, Queen of the South	2007–08 Stirling Alb
1989–90 Albion R, Alloa Ath	2008–09 Livingstone *(for breaching rules)*, Clyde
1990–91 Clyde, Brechin C	2009–10 Airdrie U, Ayr U
1991–92 Montrose, Forfar Ath	2010–11 Cowdenbeath, Stirling Alb
1992–93 Meadowbank Th, Cowdenbeath	2011–12 Ayr U, Queen of the South
1993–94 *See footnote.* Dumbarton, Stirling Alb, Clyde, Morton, Brechin C	2012–13 Dunfermline Ath, Airdrie U

RELEGATED FROM SPFL SCOTTISH CHAMPIONSHIP (2013–14)

2013–14 Greenock Morton

RELEGATED FROM SECOND DIVISION

1993–94 *See footnote.* Alloa Ath, Forfar Ath, East Stirlingshire, Montrose, Queen's Park, Arbroath, Albion R, Cowdenbeath

1994–95 Meadowbank Th, Brechin C	2004–05 Arbroath, Berwick R
1995–96 Forfar Ath, Montrose	2005–06 Dumbarton
1996–97 Dumbarton, Berwick R	2006–07 Stranraer, Forfar Ath
1997–98 Stenhousemuir, Brechin C	2007–08 Cowdenbeath, Berwick R
1998–99 East Fife, Forfar Ath	2008–09 Queen's Park, Stranraer
1999–2000 Hamilton A *(after being deducted 15 points)*	2009–10 Arbroath, Clyde
2000–01 Queen's Park, Stirling Alb	2010–11 Alloa Ath, Peterhead
2001–02 Morton	2011–12 Stirling Alb
2002–03 Stranraer, Cowdenbeath	2012–13 Albion R
2003–04 East Fife, Stenhousemuir	

RELEGATED FROM SPFL SCOTTISH LEAGUE ONE (2013–14)

2013–14 East Fife, Arbroath

SCOTTISH LEAGUE CHAMPIONSHIP WINS

Rangers 54, Celtic 45, Aberdeen 4, Hearts 4, Hibernian 4, Dumbarton 2, Dundee 1, Dundee U 1, Kilmarnock 1, Motherwell 1, Third Lanark 1.

The totals for Rangers and Dumbarton each include the shared championship of 1890–91.

Footnote: From 1946–47 to 1955–56 the two divisions were known as A and B. A division 3 had existed for three years from 1923–24 and was revived for three more seasons from 1946–47 as Division C when it included reserve teams.

At the end of the 1993–94 season four divisions were created assisted by the admission of two new clubs Ross County and Inverness Caledonian Thistle. Only one club was promoted from Division 1 and Division 2. The three relegated from the Premier joined with teams finishing second to seventh in Division 1 to form the new First Division. Five relegated from Division 1 combined with those who finished second to sixth to form a new Second Division and the bottom eight in Division 2 linked with the two newcomers to form a new Third Division.

At the end of the 1997–98 season the nine clubs remaining in the Premier Division plus the promoted team from the First Division formed a breakaway Premier League.

At the end of the 1999–2000 season two teams were added to the Scottish League. There was no relegation from the Premier League but two promoted from the First Division and three from each of the Second and Third Divisions. One team was relegated from the First Division and one from the Second Division, leaving 12 teams in each division. In season 2002–03, Falkirk were not promoted to the Premier League due to the failure of their ground to meet League rules. Inverness Caledonian Thistle were promoted after a previous refusal in 2003–04 because of ground sharing.

At the end of 2005–06 the Scottish League introduced play-offs for the team finishing second from the bottom of the First Division against the second, third and fourth finishing teams in the Second Division and with a similar procedure for the Second Division and the Third Division.

SCOTTISH LEAGUE PLAY-OFFS 2013–14

Denotes player sent off.

SCOTTISH PREMIER QUARTER-FINAL FIRST LEG

Tuesday, 6 May 2014

Queen of the South (0) 2 *(McHugh 56, 90)*

Falkirk (1) 1 *(Alston 8)*   1996

Queen of the South: (442) Clark; Mitchell, Durnan, Dowie, Holt; Burns, Kerr, McShane (Young 87), Russell (Kidd 90); Lyle (Carmichael 82), McHugh.
Falkirk: (442) McGovern; Vaulks, McCracken (Dick 76), Flynn, Kingsley; Alston, Millar, Sibbald, McGrandles; Beck, Shepherd (Bia Bi 83).
Referee: John McKendrick.

SCOTTISH PREMIER QUARTER-FINAL SECOND LEG

Saturday, 10 May 2014

Falkirk (0) 3 *(Loy 53, Sibbald 70, Alston 118)*

Queen of the South (1) 1 *(McHugh 36)*   4427

Falkirk: (41212) McGovern; Vaulks, McCracken, Flynn, Kingsley (Dick 94); Millar (Durojaiye 97); Alston, Sibbald; McGrandles; Beck (Shepherd 109), Loy.
Queen of the South: (4231) Clark; Dowie (Young 73), Durnan, Higgins, Holt; Kerr, McShane; Kidd (Dzierzawski 119), Carmichael, Russell; McHugh (Lyle 94).
aet; Falkirk won 4-3 on aggregate.
Referee: Calum Murray.

SCOTTISH PREMIER SEMI-FINAL FIRST LEG

Tuesday, 13 May 2014

Falkirk (0) 1 *(Beck 80)*

Hamilton A (0) 1 *(Mackinnon 61)*   4194

Falkirk: (442) Vaulks, Flynn, Kingsley, Dick; McGrandles, Millar, Alston, Sibbald (Shepherd 73); Beck, Loy.
Hamilton A: (41212) Cuthbert; Gordon, Canning, Garcia Tena, Gillespie (Kilday 82); Routledge; Andreu, Crawford (Ryan 87); Mackinnon; Longridge, Scotland (Antoine-Curier 64).
Referee: John Beaton.

SCOTTISH PREMIER SEMI-FINAL SECOND LEG

Sunday, 18 May 2014

Hamilton A (1) 1 *(Andreu 16)*

Falkirk (0) 0   4678

Hamilton A: (4411) Cuthbert; Gillespie, Canning, Garcia Tena, Gordon; Andreu, Routledge, Mackinnon, Crawford (Ryan 68); Longridge (Keatings 90); Scotland (Antoine-Curier 69).
Falkirk: (4411) McGovern; Vaulks, Flynn, McCracken (Leahy 82), Kingsley; McGrandles, Millar, Alston (Shepherd 67), Sibbald; Loy; Beck.
Hamilton A win 2-1 on aggregate.
Referee: Kevin Clancy.

SCOTTISH PREMIER FINAL FIRST LEG

Wednesday, 21 May 2014

Hamilton A (0) 0

Hibernian (1) 2 *(Cummings 39, 55)*   5322

Hamilton A: (4411) Cuthbert; Gillespie, Canning, Garcia Tena, Gordon; Andreu, Routledge (Crawford 84), Mackinnon, Keatings (Ryan 52); Longridge (Scotland 73); Antoine-Curier.
Hibernian: (4231) Williams; Maybury, Nelson, McGivern, Stevenson; Robertson (Tudur Jones 90), Craig; Harris, Stanton, Heffernan; Cummings (Cairney 85).
Referee: Bobby Madden.

SCOTTISH PREMIER FINAL SECOND LEG

Sunday, 25 May 2014

Hibernian (0) 0

Hamilton A (1) 2 *(Scotland 13, Andreu 90)*   18,031

Hibernian: (4231) Williams; Maybury, Nelson, McGivern, Stevenson; Robertson, Craig; Heffernan (Tudur Jones 83), Stanton, Cummings; Haynes (Harris 8 (Thomson 68)).
Hamilton A: (442) Cuthbert; Gordon, Canning, Garcia Tena, Mackinnon; Longridge (Antoine-Curier 67), Routledge (Neil 81), Gillespie, Crawford (Ryan 81); Scotland, Andreu.
aet; Hamilton A won 4-3 on penalties.
Referee: William Collum.

SCOTTISH CHAMPIONSHIP SEMI-FINALS FIRST LEG

Wednesday, 7 May 2014

Ayr U (0) 1 *(Pope 79)*

Cowdenbeath (2) 2 *(Stewart G 15, 37)*   1495

Ayr U: (442) Hutton; Hunter, McAusland, Lithgow, Pope; Forrest (Shankland 71), Gilmour, McLaughlin, Marenghi (Kyle 60); Moffat, Malcolm.
Cowdenbeath: (442) Flynn; McKeown, Armstrong (Kane 46), Wedderburn, O'Brien; Brett, Milne, Robertson, Brownlie; Stewart G, Hemmings.
Referee: Don Robertson.

Stranraer (1) 2 *(Grehan 12, Bell 88)*

Dunfermline Ath (1) 1 *(El Bakhtaoui 41)*   867

Stranraer: (442) Mitchell; Robertson, Rumsby, MacGregor, Docherty; Winter (Borris 78), Gallagher, Bell (Stirling S 90), Stirling A; Grehan (McKenna 61), Longworth.
Dunfermline Ath: (442) Scully; Millen, Page*, Morris, Grainger; Falkingham (Husband 70), Geggan (Forbes 42), Byrne, Spence; El Bakhtaoui, Thomson Ryan (Martin 86).
Referee: Bobby Madden.

SCOTTISH CHAMPIONSHIP SEMI-FINALS SECOND LEG

Saturday, 10 May 2014

Cowdenbeath (2) 3 *(Stewart G 1, 30, O'Brien 52)*

Ayr U (1) 1 *(Donald 35)*   933

Cowdenbeath: (352) Flynn; Brownlie, Armstrong, Wedderburn; Brett, Milne (Stevenson 64), Robertson, O'Brien (Kane 76), McKeown; Stewart G (Gold 88), Hemmings.
Ayr U: (442) Hutton; Hunter, McAusland (Forrest 57), Lithgow, Pope (McGowan 67); McLaughlin, Malcolm, Gilmour, Donald; Moffat, Kyle.
Cowdenbeath won 5-2 on aggregate.
Referee: John Beaton.

Dunfermline Ath (0) 3 *(Geggan 59, 98, El Bakhtaoui 103)*

Stranraer (0) 0   4525

Dunfermline Ath: (3412) Scully; Young, Martin, Grainger; Williamson, Geggan (Byrne 112), Falkingham, Whittle; Husband (Forbes 55); El Bakhtaoui, Thomson Ryan (Smith 76).
Stranraer: (442) Mitchell; Robertson (Stirling S 74), MacGregor, Rumsby, Docherty; Gallagher, Bell, Winter, Stirling A; Grehan (McKenna 46), Longworth (Forde 83).
aet; Dunfermline Ath won 4-2 on aggregate.
Referee: Crawford Allan.

SCOTTISH CHAMPIONSHIP FINAL FIRST LEG

Wednesday, 14 May 2014

Cowdenbeath (0) 1 *(O'Brien 83)*

Dunfermline Ath (0) 1 *(Geggan 77)* 3379

Cowdenbeath: (352) Flynn; Brownlie, Armstrong, Wedderburn; Brett, Robertson, O'Brien, Milne, McKeown; Hemmings, Stewart G.
Dunfermline Ath: (352) Scully; Martin, Young, Grainger; Williamson, Geggan, Husband (Forbes 63), Falkingham, Whittle; El Bakhtaoui (Smith 59), Thomson Ryan (Morris 82).
Referee: Stephen Finnie.

SCOTTISH CHAMPIONSHIP FINAL SECOND LEG

Sunday, 18 May 2014

Dunfermline Ath (0) 0

Cowdenbeath (1) 3 *(Hemmings 1, O'Brien 67, Stewart G 77)* 8288

Dunfermline Ath: (352) Scully; Martin, Young, Grainger; Williamson, Byrne (Forbes 46), Geggan, Falkingham, Whittle (Husband 67); El Bakhtaoui, Thomson Ryan (Dargo 75).
Cowdenbeath: (352) Flynn; Brownlie (Stevenson 81), Armstrong, Wedderburn; Brett (Miller 61), Robertson, O'Brien, Milne, McKeown (Adamson 90); Hemmings, Stewart G.
Cowdenbeath won 4-1 on aggregate.
Referee: Steven McLean.

SCOTTISH LEAGUE ONE SEMI-FINALS FIRST LEG

Wednesday, 7 May 2014

Clyde (1) 1 *(Ferguson 38)*

East Fife (0) 0 1005

Clyde: (442) Barclay; McGhee, Marsh, McQueen, McKinnon; Ferguson (Watt 90), Capuano, Sweeney, MacDonald; Daly, McCluskey.
East Fife: (442) Paterson; Cowan, Mbu, Campbell, Durie; McKenzie (McBride 75), Barr (Hughes 65), Smith, Johnstone; Buchanan (Austin 65), Clarke.
Referee: Euan Anderson.

Stirling Alb (3) 3 *(Weir 12, Weatherston 26, 30)*

Annan Ath (0) 1 *(Hopkirk 70)* 972

Stirling Alb: (352) Crawford; Hamilton, Smith C, Forsyth; Johnston, Comrie, McClune, Smith D (Bishop 64), Weir (Cunningham 89); White, Weatherston (Ashe 78).
Annan Ath: (433) Arthur; Chisholm, Bradley, Watson, McNiff (Henderson 78); Brannan (Sloan 57), Mitchell Andrew, Black; Hopkirk, Mackay, Todd.
Referee: Greg Aitken.

SCOTTISH LEAGUE ONE SEMI-FINALS SECOND LEG

Saturday, 10 May 2014

Annan Ath (1) 3 *(McNiff 40, Love 50, Davidson 90)*

Stirling Alb (2) 5 *(McClune 9, White 23, 79, 83, Comrie 56)* 912

Annan Ath: (3412) Arthur; Watson (Jardine 67), Swinglehurst, McNiff◾; Chisholm, Sloan (Davidson 72), Mitchell, Love; Todd (Henderson 73); Mackay, Hopkirk.
Stirling Alb: (442) Crawford; Hamilton, Smith C, McClune, Forsyth; Johnston (McGeachie 36), Comrie (Fulton 70), Smith D, Weir; White, Weatherston (Ferry 80).
Stirling Alb won 8-4 on aggregate.
Referee: George Salmond.

East Fife (1) 2 *(McBride 12, Smith 85)*

Clyde (1) 1 *(Ferguson 45)* 1018

East Fife: (442) Paterson (Rooney 46); Cowan, Campbell, Mbu, Johnstone; McKenzie (Buchanan 61), Barr (Brown 72), Hughes, McBride; Austin, Smith.
Clyde: (442) Barclay; McGhee, Marsh, McQueen, McKinnon (Watt 91); Ferguson, Scullion (Capuano 101), Sweeney, MacDonald; Daly, McCluskey.
aet; East Fife won 7-6 on penalties.
Referee: Brian Colvin.

SCOTTISH LEAGUE ONE FINAL FIRST LEG

Wednesday, 14 May 2014

Stirling Alb (1) 1 *(Forsyth 42)*

East Fife (2) 2 *(McBride 70, Austin 89)* 1501

Stirling Alb: (352) Crawford; Hamilton (McGeachie 81), Bishop, Forsyth; Johnston, McClune, Comrie (Ferry 79), Smith D, Weir; White, Weatherston (Cunningham 75).
East Fife: (451) Rooney; Cowan, Campbell, Thom, Johnstone; McKenzie (Austin 65), Barr, Brown (McBride 47), Stewart, Smith (Buchanan 76); Clarke.
Referee: Craig Charleston.

SCOTTISH LEAGUE ONE FINAL SECOND LEG

Sunday, 18 May 2014

East Fife (0) 0

Stirling Alb (0) 2 *(White 74, Cunningham 81)* 1516

East Fife: (442) Rooney; Cowan, Thom, Campbell, Johnstone; Stewart (Brown 65), Barr, Smith (Buchanan 71), McBride (Durie 53); Clarke, Austin.
Stirling Alb: (352) Crawford; Hamilton, Smith C, Forsyth; Johnston (Ferry 90), McClune, Comrie (Bishop 89), Smith D, Weir; White, Weatherston (Cunningham 71).
Stirling Alb won 3-2 on aggregate.
Referee: Calum Murray.

SCOTTISH COMMUNITIES
LEAGUE CUP 2013–14

■ *Denotes player sent off.*

FIRST ROUND

Saturday, 3 August 2013

Airdrieonians (3) 4 *(Sinclair 33, Blockley 44, O'Byrne 45, Coult 77)*

Stenhousemuir (2) 3 *(Dickson 16, Smith D 24, McMillan 88)*   647

Airdrieonians: (442) Stewart C; O'Neil■, Evans, Hardie, O'Byrne; McCormack, Blockley (Bain 69), Sinclair, Coult (Coogans 81); Lister, McLaren.
Stenhousemuir: (4231) Smith C; Devlin, Malone■, Lynch (Douglas 38), McMillan; McKinlay, Smith D; Brash (Anderson 22), Gemmell, Higgins; Dickson.
Referee: Andrew Dallas.

Arbroath (0) 0

Montrose (0) 1 *(McCord 76)*   903

Arbroath: (4411) Morrison; Banjo (Sheerin 83), Hamilton, Chisholm, Travis; Keddie, Linn, Smith, Bayne; Milne; Cook (Yao 75).
Montrose: (442) McKenzie; Masson, McIntosh, Webster, Wilson; Campbell, McCord, Watson■, Bonar (Winter 67); Wood, Johnston S.
Referee: Alan Muir.

Berwick R (0) 0

Cowdenbeath (2) 5 *(Hemmings 36, 38, 88, Miller 50, Stewart G 73)*   465

Berwick R: (442) Grant; Turner, Gielty, Notman, Tulloch; Hoskins, Ronald (O'Brien 60), Currie L, Lavery; Dalziel (Morris 71), Gray (Miller 74).
Cowdenbeath: (442) Adam; Cowan (Dunn 87), Brett, McKenzie, Adamson; Armstrong, Miller, Russell (Stewart G 72), Hemmings; Morton (Callaghan 66), Cameron.
Referee: Crawford Allan.

Dumbarton (1) 1 *(Gilhaney 42)*

Albion R (0) 0   505

Dumbarton: (4411) Ewings; McGinn, Linton, Turner, Graham; Barry, Megginson, Agnew, Prunty (Smith K 62); McDougall (Fleming 70); Gilhaney.
Albion R: (4231) Parry; Reid, Dunlop R, Nicoll, Donnelly C; Dunlop M, Crawford; Innes, McGuigan, Chaplain (Phillips 77); Cusack (Dallas 77).
Referee: Barry Cook.

East Fife (0) 2 *(Buchanan 85, 90)*

Greenock Morton (0) 6 *(McLaughlin 55, Habai 81, McNeil 93, Campbell 99, 119, Imrie 104)*   727

East Fife: (442) Andrews; Durie, Johnstone■, Stewart J (Grieve 73), Dutot; Mbu, Willis (Stewart R 90), Brown, Moosari; Buchanan, Clarke (Austin 84).
Greenock Morton: (4231) Gaston; Taggart, Fitzpatrick, Hands, Habai; McLaughlin, Imrie; Bachirou (Fulton 106), Cham (McNeil 89), McKee (Wallace 79); Campbell.
aet.
Referee: Craig Charleston.

East Stirling (0) 0

Dunfermline Ath (1) 2 *(Wallace 10 (pen), Dargo 88)* 1043

East Stirling: (4141) Hay; MacGregor, McGowan, Thomson Ryan, Miller; Bolochoweckyj; O'Donoghue, Greenhill, Turner■, Maxwell (McKechnie 74); Wright (McCaughie 84).
Dunfermline Ath: (442) Scully; Millen, Whittle, Byrne, Young; Morris, Ferguson (Dargo 74), Falkingham (Geggan 27), Thomson; Wallace (Moore 87), Kane.
Referee: Matt Northcroft.

Elgin C (1) 1 *(Crighton 45)*

Livingston (2) 3 *(Scott 15, Fordyce 39, McNulty 62)* 563

Elgin C: (442) Jellema; McLean (Wyness 79), McMullan, Niven (Urqhart 74), Crighton; Duff, Cameron, Harkins (Mckenzie 64), Sutherland; Gunn, Beveridge.
Livingston: (442) Jamieson; Donaldson, Talbot, Scott (Mullen 90), Mensing; Fordyce, Beaumont, Docherty (Downie 90), Wilkie (Denholm 78); McNulty, McDonald.
Referee: Don Robertson.

Falkirk (0) 3 *(Alston 73, Roberts 79, Grant 81)*

Clyde (0) 0   1154

Falkirk: (442) McGovern; Duffie, Kingsley, Turnbull, Durojaiye; Vaulks, Grant (Martin 82), Sibbald (Alston 60), Loy; Roberts, McGrandles (Fulton 83).
Clyde: (442) Rajovic; Brown, MacDonald, Gray, Frances; Marsh (Ferguson 82), MacBeth, Sweeney, Watt (McGachie 83); Daly, McColm (McCluskey 65).
Referee: Brian Colvin.

Forfar Ath (1) 2 *(Swankie 9, 115)*

Rangers (0) 1 *(Aird 84)*   4079

Forfar Ath: (442) Hill; Baxter, McCulloch, Fotheringham (Campbell R 47), Malcolm (Campbell I 33); Andrews, Kader, McCabe (Dale 91), Swankie; Templeman, Malin.
Rangers: (4141) Gallagher S; Hegarty, Wallace, Black, Faure; McCulloch; Mitchell (Aird 46), Crawford, Little, Macleod (McAusland 74); Templeton (McKay 100).
aet. Referee: Calum Murray.

Peterhead (0) 0

Alloa Ath (0) 2 *(McCord 52 (pen), Kirk 83)*   429

Peterhead: (433) Smith; Sharp, McGlinchey, Cowie (Gilfillan 63), Strachan; Noble, Brown, Redman; McAllister, McCann (Rodgers 63), Cox (Buchan 79).
Alloa Ath: (442) Bain; Doyle, Creaney, Simmons, Meggatt; Gordon, Holmes (Tiffoney 65), Cawley, McManus; Kirk, McCord.
Referee: David Somers.

Queen of the South (0) 3 *(Lyle 59, 67, 69)*

Annan Ath (0) 0   1588

Queen of the South: (433) Antell; Mitchell, Holt, McGuffie, Dowie; Higgins, McKenna (McShane 81), Burns; Lyle (Reilly 72), Paton, Russell (Orsi 78).
Annan Ath: (442) Mitchell Alex; Watson■, Bradley, Sloan, Weatherson; Swinglehurst, Chisholm, Flynn (Jardine 72), Love (Moffat 80); Mackay (Davidson 69), Hopkirk.
Referee: Paul Robertson.

Raith R (2) 6 *(Smith 15, Cardle 34, Elliot 57, 67, Spence 70, Vaughan 86)*

Queen's Park (0) 0   1219

Raith R: (442) McGurn; Thomson, Booth, Fox, Watson; Hill, Anderson, Moon (Vaughan 71), Elliot (Callachan 76); Smith (Spence 63), Cardle.
Queen's Park: (4141) Brown; Gebbie, Spittal, Quinn, Keenan; Grier; Rooney (Davison 90), Anderson (McVey 79), Vitoria, Capuano■; Burns.
Referee: Stephen Finnie.

Stirling Alb (0) 0

Hamilton A (2) 3 *(Keatings 32, 65, Smith C 41 (og))* 556

Stirling Alb: (4141) Crawford; McGeachie, Forsyth, McCunnie (Coyne 57), Bishop; Smith C; Johnston, Ferry (McAnespie 68), White, Weir; Day.
Hamilton A: (442) Cuthbert; Gordon, Gillespie, Routledge, Devlin (Kilday 87); Canning, Keatings, Neil (Andreu 74), Mackinnon; Longridge (McShane 69), Crawford.
Referee: John McKendrick.

Stranraer (3) 4 *(Borris 10, Robertson 24, Aitken 33 (pen), McKenna 48)*

Brechin C (0) 3 *(Donnelly 55, 83, Barr 86)*   291

Stranraer: (442) Mitchell; MacGregor, Docherty, Gallagher, Robertson; McKeown, Winter, Aitken, McKenna (Forde 83); Grehan, Borris (Corcoran 76).
Brechin C: (442) Smith; McLean, Brown, Anderson (Barr 46), Hay; Molloy, Trouten, Walker (Donnelly 46), Carcary; Jackson A, Jackson S.
Referee: Kevin Graham.

Tuesday, 6 August 2013

Partick Thistle (1) 2 *(O'Donnell 13, Balatoni 83)*

Ayr U (0) 1 *(Shankland 89)*   2145

Partick Thistle: (4231) Fox; O'Donnell, Sinclair, Osbourne (Welsh 64), Balatoni; Piccolo, Lawless; Kerr, Baird, Forbes (Mukendi 70); Elliot (Bannigan 59).

Ayr U: (442) Hutton; Hunter, Pope, Marenghi, Campbell (McArthur 22); Lithgow, McGowan (Forrest 51), McLaughlin, Malcolm (Shankland 85); Moffat, Donald.
Referee: Iain Brines.

SECOND ROUND

Tuesday, 27 August 2013

Aberdeen (0) 0

Alloa Ath (0) 0 4897

Aberdeen: (442) Langfield; Murray, Anderson, Reynolds, Robertson (Vernon 67); Pawlett, Flood (Low 55), Jack, Hayes (Wylde 67); Zola, McGinn.
Alloa Ath: (442) Bain; Doyle, Marr, Meggatt, Gordon; Holmes, Simmons (Young 83), McCord, Creaney; Cawley, Kirk (Ferns 77).
aet; Aberdeen won 6-5 on penalties.
Referee: Stevie O'Reilly.

Airdrieonians (0) 0

Livingston (1) 2 *(Barrowman 38, Wilkie 67)* 483

Airdrieonians: (442) Stewart C; Evans, McCormack, Buchanan, Boyle; Blockley, Sinclair, Hardie (Bain 39), Hay (McLaren 64); Lister, Coult (Coogans 74).
Livingston: (4231) Walker; Mampuya, Fordyce, Mensing, Talbot; Donaldson, Docherty (Beaumont 69); Denholm (Wilkie 59), Scott, McDonald (Mullen 81); Barrowman.
Referee: Greg Aitken.

Dundee (0) 2 *(McAlister 51, MacDonald 120)*

Forfar Ath (1) 1 *(Campbell I 43 (pen))* 2027

Dundee: (442) Letheren; Irvine, Lockwood, Gallacher, Dyer; McAlister, McBride■, Rae, Conroy; MacDonald, Monti (Boyle 75).
Forfar Ath: (442) Hill; Baxter, Malcolm■, Dods, Campbell I; Kader, Fusco, Malin (Dale 97), Hilson (McManus 86); Templeman (Campbell R 97), Swankie.
aet. Referee: Barry Cook.

Falkirk (2) 2 *(Morris 19 (og), Fulton 33)*

Dunfermline Ath (1) 1 *(Moore 28)* 3663

Falkirk: (442) McGovern; Duffie, Vaulks, Kingsley, Dick (Flynn 88); Alston (Leahy 80), Durojaiye, Sibbald (McGrandles 68), Fulton; Roberts, Loy.
Dunfermline Ath: (442) Scully; Millen (Dargo 90), Johnston, Morris, Whittle; Geggan, Thomson Ryan (Smith 63), Falkingham, Wallace; Moore, Husband (Byrne 84).
Referee: Steven McLean.

Kilmarnock (0) 0

Hamilton A (1) 1 *(Antoine-Curier 42)* 2033

Kilmarnock: (442) Samson; Clohessy, Barr, O'Hara, Tesselaar; McKeown (Fowler 46), Jacobs, Irvine, Gros; Ibrahim (Heffernan 64), Stewart (McKenzie 74).
Hamilton A: (442) Cuthbert; Gordon, Devlin, Canning, Hendrie; Mackinnon, Gillespie (Neil 74), Andreu, Crawford; Keatings (McShane 70), Antoine-Curier (Ryan 70).
Referee: Calum Murray.

Greenock Morton (0) 4 *(Cham 50, Fitzpatrick 69, Hands 90, Fulton 90)*

Montrose (0) 0 918

Greenock Morton: (4231) Caraux; Taggart, Page, McLaughlin, Fitzpatrick; Bachirou, Habai (McNeil 82); Wallace, Hands, Imrie (Fulton 80); Cham (Campbell 73).
Montrose: (451) McKenzie; McNally, Crawford (Bonar 77), Campbell, McIntosh; Gray, Masson, Johnston S, McCord (Webster 64), Young (Sturrock 72); Wood.
Referee: Andrew Dallas.

Partick Thistle (0) 3 *(Elliot 92, Lawless 103, Muirhead 114 (pen))*

Cowdenbeath (0) 1 *(Hemmings 93)* 1544

Partick Thistle: (4231) Fox; O'Donnell, Muirhead, Piccolo, Sinclair; Kerr (Doolan 71), Forbes; Craigen (Lawless 62), Higginbotham (Elliot 84), Bannigan; Baird.
Cowdenbeath: (442) Adam; Brett, Armstrong, Wedderburn, Adamson; McKenzie (Morton 78), O'Brien, Stevenson, Milne; Stewart G (Miller 95), Russell (Hemmings 72).
aet. Referee: John McKendrick.

Queen of the South (0) 2 *(McKenna 103, Paton 115)*

St Mirren (0) 1 *(Thompson 95)* 2073

Queen of the South: (433) Antell; Mitchell, Dowie, Durnan, Holt; McKenna, Young (Reilly 70), Burns (McGuffie 18); Paton, Lyle, Carmichael (Russell 83).
St Mirren: (4411) Cornell; van Zanten, McAusland, Goodwin, Grainger; Teale (Caprice 104), McGinn, Newton (McGowan 76), McLean; Harkins; Thompson.
aet. Referee: Craig Charleston.

Raith R (0) 1 *(Fox 50)*

Hearts (0) 1 *(Hamill 62 (pen))* 3668

Raith R: (442) McGurn; Thomson, Watson, Hill■, Booth; Anderson (Vaughan 85), Fox, Moon (Callachan 99), Cardle; Elliot, Smith (Ellis 75).
Hearts: (442) MacDonald (Ridgers 25); McGowan, McKay, Wilson, McHattie; King B (Smith 77), Hamill, Holt, Walker; Robinson (Oliver 55), Paterson.
aet; Hearts won 5-4 on penalties.
Referee: Brian Colvin.

Stranraer (0) 3 *(Winter 65, Aitken 71 (pen), Grehan 82)*

Ross Co (1) 2 *(Brittain 45 (pen), Mustafi 79)* 215

Stranraer: (442) Mitchell; Robertson, Rumsby, McKeown, Kinnaird; Winter (MacGregor 90), Gallagher, Aitken, Corcoran (Borris 84); Grehan, McKenna (Longworth 73).
Ross Co: (442) Brown; Kovacevic, McLean, Munro, Gordon; Brittain, Quinn, Kettlewell, Carey (Maatsen 85); Sproule (De Leeuw 85), Luckassen (Mustafi 60).
Referee: Stephen Finnie.

Wednesday, 28 August 2013

Dumbarton (1) 2 *(Smith K 34, Megginson 87)*

Dundee U (0) 3 *(Ciftci 69, 89, Gauld 77)* 1045

Dumbarton: (4411) Ewings; McGinn, Graham, Barry, Smith S (McKerracher 79); Fleming (Megginson 67), Turner, Murray, McDougall (Nish 79); Smith K; Prunty.
Dundee U: (3412) Cierzniak; Souttar, Dillon, Butcher; Wilson (Ciftci 63), Paton, Gauld (Millar 83), Robertson; Rankin; Graham, Goodwillie (Erskine 76).
Referee: Alan Muir.

THIRD ROUND

Tuesday, 24 September 2013

Celtic (0) 0

Greenock Morton (0) 1 *(Imrie 97 (pen))* 14,900

Celtic: (4411) Zaluska; Lustig, Ambrose, van Dijk, Mulgrew; McGeouch (Matthews 74), Brown, Biton, Boerrigter (Commons 83); Rogic (Stokes 65); Pukki.
Greenock Morton: (4231) Caraux; Taggart, Page, Peciar, Fitzpatrick; Habai, Bachirou; Imrie, Hands, O'Brien (Wallace 39); Cham (Campbell 78 (McLaughlin 120)).
aet. Referee: Bobby Madden.

Dundee (0) 0

Inverness CT (1) 1 *(McKay 11)* 1682

Dundee: (442) Letheren; Irvine, Gallacher, Davidson, Dyer; Riley, McAlister, Rae, Conroy; MacDonald, Beattie (Doris 68).
Inverness CT: (4231) Brill; Raven, Meekings, Devine, Shinnie; Draper, Foran (Agdestein 90); Doran (Polworth 62), Vincent, Ross; McKay.
Referee: Stephen Finnie.

Hamilton A (0) 0

St Johnstone (1) 3 *(May 4, 90, Edwards 86)* 1059

Hamilton A: (41212) Cuthbert; Gordon, Canning, Devlin, Hendrie; Neil; Mackinnon, Andreu (Longridge 81); Crawford; McShane (Ryan 61), Antoine-Curier.
St Johnstone: (442) Mannus; Mackay, Anderson, Wright, Easton; Millar, McDonald (Wotherspoon 90), Cregg (Miller 90), Hasselbaink (Edwards 75); MacLean, May.
Referee: John Beaton.

Hibernian (3) 5 *(Craig 8, 47, 61 (pen), Zoubir 34, Rumsby 36 (og))*

Stranraer (1) 3 *(Longworth 3, Aitken 48, Nelson 52 (og))* 6431

Hibernian: (442) Williams; Stevenson, Nelson, Hanlon, Maybury (McGivern 46); Robertson, Taiwo, Craig, Vine (Caldwell 79); Zoubir (Stanton 83), Collins.
Stranraer: (442) Mitchell; Rumsby, Robertson, McKeown, Kinnaird; Gallagher (Docherty 80), Aitken, Stirling A, Longworth (McKenna 73); Grehan, Borris (Corcoran 57).
Referee: Crawford Allan.

Wednesday, 25 September 2013
Dundee U (2) 4 *(Goodwillie 33, 45, 90, Dow 87)*
Partick Thistle (0) 1 *(Elliot 89)* 3778
Dundee U: (433) Cierzniak; Wilson, Butcher, Gunning, Robertson; Paton (Souttar 90), Rankin, Armstrong; Goodwillie, Graham (Dow 51), Ciftci (Gauld 76).
Partick Thistle: (4231) Fox; O'Donnell, Piccolo, Balatoni, Sinclair; Welsh, Kerr; Higginbotham (Craigen 76), Forbes (Lawless 65), Elliot; Doolan (Baird 51).
Referee: Calum Murray.

Falkirk (0) 0
Aberdeen (2) 5 *(Shaughnessy 23, Smith 36,*
Vernon 54, 55, 75 (pen)) 2838
Falkirk: (4231) McGovern; Duffie, Vaulks, Flynn, Kingsley; McGrandles, Alston (Bingham 56); Sibbald, Fulton, Loy; Roberts (Leahy 66).
Aberdeen: (4141) Langfield; Shaughnessy, Hector, Reynolds, Robertson; Jack; Hayes (Murray 67), Smith (Magennis 80), Pawlett, Low; Zola (Vernon 33).
Referee: Steven McLean.

Hearts (1) 3 *(McHattie 14, Hamill 51 (pen), Wilson 93)*
Queen of the South (1) 3 *(McGuffie 20, Paton 62,*
Higgins 116) 8381
Hearts: (433) MacDonald; McGowan, McKay (McGhee 68), Wilson, McHattie; Robinson (Carrick 91), Hamill, Holt; Paterson, Oliver (King 68), Walker.
Queen of the South: (4231) Antell; McGuffie (Mitchell 87), Dzierzawski, Dowie, Holt; Higgins, Young (Reilly 97); McShane, Paton, Russell (Carmichael 79); Lyle.
aet; Hearts won 4-2 on penalties.
Referee: John McKendrick.

Livingston (0) 1 *(Denholm 90)*
Motherwell (1) 2 *(McHugh 16, McFadden 73)* 1660
Livingston: (442) Jamieson; Donaldson, Mensing, Fordyce, Talbot; Jacobs Keaghan (McDonald 70), O'Brien, Scougall (Denholm 77), Scott; McNulty, Barrowman (Burchill 82).
Motherwell: (442) Nielsen; Ramsden, Hutchinson, McManus, Hammell (Moore 81); Ainsworth, Lawson, Carswell, Francis-Angol; McFadden, McHugh (Sutton 70).
Referee: Brian Colvin.

QUARTER-FINALS
Tuesday, 29 October 2013
Inverness CT (0) 2 *(Warren 54, Draper 120)*
Dundee U (1) 1 *(Watson 5)* 2133
Inverness CT: (4411) Brill; Shinnie, Warren, Meekings, Tremarco (Polworth 107); Watkins (Williams 85), Draper, Foran, Doran; Ross (Agdestein 100); McKay.
Dundee U: (4231) Cierzniak; Watson, Dillon, Gunning, Robertson (Butcher 80); Paton, Rankin; Gauld, Armstrong (Graham 46), Mackay-Steven (Gomis 46); Ciftci■.
aet. Referee: Kevin Clancy.

Wednesday, 30 October 2013
Hibernian (0) 0
Hearts (1) 1 *(Stevenson 34)* 16,797
Hibernian: (442) Williams; Stevenson, McPake■, Hanlon, McGivern; Robertson, Taiwo (Zoubir 76), Thomson, Craig; Collins (Caldwell 64), Vine.
Hearts: (4411) MacDonald; McGhee, Robinson (Tapping 90), McGowan, Wilson; McHattie, Stevenson, Hamill, Walker; Holt; Paterson.
Referee: William Collum.

Greenock Morton (0) 0
St Johnstone (0) 1 *(McDonald 90)* 2619
Greenock Morton: (4231) Caraux; Reid, McLaughlin, Peciar, Fitzpatrick (Page 36); Bachirou, Habai; Wallace, McKee (Stirling 58), Imrie; Novo.
St Johnstone: (442) Mannus; Miller, Mackay, Wright (Scobbie 46), Easton; Millar, McDonald, Cregg (Davidson 64), Wotherspoon; Hasselbaink (Fallon 79), May.
Referee: John McKendrick.

Motherwell (0) 0
Aberdeen (0) 2 *(Considine 83, Hayes 90)* 6995
Motherwell: (442) Nielsen; Ramsden, Hutchinson, McManus, Hammell; Carswell, Lasley, Lawson (Ainsworth 46), Francis-Angol; Sutton, Anier (McHugh 68).
Aberdeen: (442) Langfield; Shaughnessy■, Anderson, Reynolds, Robertson (Vernon 45); Hayes, Flood, Jack, Pawlett (Robson 85); Zola (Considine 21), McGinn.
Referee: John Beaton.

SEMI-FINALS
Saturda, 1 February 2014
Aberdeen (2) 4 *(Hayes 3, 79, Pawlett 32, Rooney 63)*
St Johnstone (0) 0 16,761
Aberdeen: (442) Langfield; Logan, Anderson (Tate 81), Reynolds, Considine; Pawlett (Low 87), Flood, Robson (Vernon 82); Hayes; Rooney, McGinn.
St Johnstone: (442) Banks; Mackay, Wright, Anderson, Easton (Miller 88); Wotherspoon, McDonald, Croft (O'Halloran 72), Millar; Hasselbaink (Iwelumo 61), May.
Referee: Bobby Madden.

Sunday, 2 February 2014
Hearts (0) 2 *(Hamill 68, 70)*
Inverness CT (0) 2 *(Tansey 54, Ross 90)* 12,762
Hearts: (4411) MacDonald; McKay, McGowan (McCallum 64), Wilson, McHattie; Smith (Stevenson 46), Hamill, Robinson, Nicholson (Tapping 85); Paterson; Carrick.
Inverness CT: (4411) Brill; Raven (Ross 87), Warren■, Meekings■, Shinnie; Watkins, Vincent (Tremarco 91), Tansey, Doran (Devine 69); Draper; McKay.
aet; Inverness CT won 4-2 on penalties.
Referee: John Beaton.

Aberdeen's players are jubilant after winning the penalty shoot-out against Inverness Caledonian Thistle in the Scottish Communities League Cup final at Celtic Park. The Dons won 4-2 on penalties following a 0-0 scoreline after extra time.
(Jeff Holmes/PA Wire/Press Association Images)

SCOTTISH COMMUNITIES LEAGUE CUP FINAL 2014

Sunday, 16 March 2014

(at Celtic Park, attendance 51,143)

Aberdeen (0) 0   Inverness CT (0) 0

Aberdeen: (442) Langfield; Logan, Anderson, Reynolds, Considine (Vernon 108); Robson, Jack, Flood, Hayes (Smith 6 (Low 70)); McGinn, Rooney.

Inverness CT: (4411) Brill; Raven, Devine, Meekings, Shinnie; Watkins (Ross 80), Draper, Tansey, Vincent (Doran 63); Foran (Christie 100); McKay.

aet; Aberdeen won 4-2 on penalties.

Referee: Steven McLean.

SCOTTISH LEAGUE CUP FINALS 1946–2014

SCOTTISH LEAGUE CUP

1946–47	Rangers v Aberdeen	4-0
1947–48	East Fife v Falkirk	0-0*
Replay	East Fife v Falkirk	4-1
1948–49	Rangers v Raith R	2-0
1949–50	East Fife v Dunfermline Ath	3-0
1950–51	Motherwell v Hibernian	3-0
1951–52	Dundee v Rangers	3-2
1952–53	Dundee v Kilmarnock	2-0
1953–54	East Fife v Partick Thistle	3-2
1954–55	Hearts v Motherwell	4-2
1955–56	Aberdeen v St Mirren	2-1
1956–57	Celtic v Partick Thistle	0-0*
Replay	Celtic v Partick Thistle	3-0
1957–58	Celtic v Rangers	7-1
1958–59	Hearts v Partick Thistle	5-1
1959–60	Hearts v Third Lanark	2-1
1960–61	Rangers v Kilmarnock	2-0
1961–62	Rangers v Hearts	1-1*
Replay	Rangers v Hearts	3-1
1962–63	Hearts v Kilmarnock	1-0
1963–64	Rangers v Morton	5-0
1964–65	Rangers v Celtic	2-1
1965–66	Celtic v Rangers	2-1
1966–67	Celtic v Rangers	1-0
1967–68	Celtic v Dundee	5-3
1968–69	Celtic v Hibernian	6-2
1969–70	Celtic v St Johnstone	1-0
1970–71	Rangers v Celtic	1-0
1971–72	Partick Thistle v Celtic	4-1
1972–73	Hibernian v Celtic	2-1
1973–74	Dundee v Celtic	1-0
1974–75	Celtic v Hibernian	6-3
1975–76	Rangers v Celtic	1-0
1976–77	Aberdeen v Celtic	2-1*
1977–78	Rangers v Celtic	2-1*
1978–79	Rangers v Aberdeen	2-1

BELL'S LEAGUE CUP

1979–80	Dundee U v Aberdeen	0-0*
Replay	Dundee U v Aberdeen	3-0
1980–81	Dundee U v Dundee	3-0

SCOTTISH LEAGUE CUP

1981–82	Rangers v Dundee U	2-1
1982–83	Celtic v Rangers	2-1
1983–84	Rangers v Celtic	3-2*

SKOL CUP

1984–85	Rangers v Dundee U	1-0
1985–86	Aberdeen v Hibernian	3-0
1986–87	Rangers v Celtic	2-1
1987–88	Rangers v Aberdeen	3-3*
	Rangers won 5-3 on penalties.	
1988–89	Rangers v Aberdeen	3-2
1989–90	Aberdeen v Rangers	2-1*
1990–91	Rangers v Celtic	2-1*
1991–92	Hibernian v Dunfermline Ath	2-0
1992–93	Rangers v Aberdeen	2-1*

SCOTTISH LEAGUE CUP

1993–94	Rangers v Hibernian	2-1

COCA-COLA CUP

1994–95	Raith R v Celtic	2-2*
	Raith R won 6-5 on penalties.	
1995–96	Aberdeen v Dundee	2-0
1996–97	Rangers v Hearts	4-3
1997–98	Celtic v Dundee U	3-0

SCOTTISH LEAGUE CUP

1998–99	Rangers v St Johnstone	2-1

CIS INSURANCE CUP

1999–2000	Celtic v Aberdeen	2-0
2000–01	Celtic v Kilmarnock	3-0
2001–02	Rangers v Ayr U	4-0
2002–03	Rangers v Celtic	2-1
2003–04	Livingston v Hibernian	2-0
2004–05	Rangers v Motherwell	5-1
2005–06	Celtic v Dunfermline Ath	3-0
2006–07	Hibernian v Kilmarnock	5-1
2007–08	Rangers v Dundee U	2-2*
	Rangers won 3-2 on penalties.	

CO-OPERATIVE INSURANCE CUP

2008–09	Celtic v Rangers	2-0*
2009–10	Rangers v St Mirren	1-0
2010–11	Rangers v Celtic	2-1*

SCOTTISH COMMUNITIES CUP

2011–12	Kilmarnock v Celtic	1-0
2012–13	St Mirren v Hearts	3-2
2013–14	Aberdeen v Inverness CT	0-0*
	Aberdeen won 4-2 on penalties.	

*After extra time.

SCOTTISH LEAGUE CUP WINS

Rangers 27, Celtic 14, Aberdeen 6, Hearts 4, Dundee 3, East Fife 3, Hibernian 3, Dundee U 2, Kilmarnock 1, Livingston 1, Motherwell 1, Partick Thistle 1, Raith R 1, St Mirren 1.

APPEARANCES IN FINALS

Rangers 34, Celtic 29, Aberdeen 13, Hibernian 9, Hearts 7, Dundee 6, Dundee U 6, Kilmarnock 6, Partick Thistle 4, Dunfermline Ath 3, East Fife 3, Motherwell 3, St Mirren 3, Raith R 2, St Johnstone 2, Ayr U 1, Falkirk 1, Inverness CT 1, Livingston 1, Morton 1, Third Lanark 1.

RAMSDENS LEAGUE CHALLENGE CUP 2013–14

▪ *Denotes player sent off.*

PRELIMINARY ROUND FIRST LEG

Saturday, 13 July 2013

Spartans (0) 4 *(Ross 48, 55, Motion 84, Anderson 90 (pen))*
Threave R (0) 2 *(Milligan 71 (pen), Wilby 74)*   321
Spartans: (442) Bennett; Main, Cennerazzo, Sivewright, Whatley; Motion, Beesley, Ross (Anderson 84), MacKinnon; Brown (Henretty 78), Beacher.
Threave R: (442) Parker V; Wilby, Kerr, Cooksley, Patterson; Fyfe, Degnan, Nicholl (Milligan 89), Parker G; Kay (Roan 51), Parker R.
Referee: Nick Walsh.

PRELIMINARY ROUND SECOND LEG

Saturday, 20 July 2013

Threave R (0) 1 *(Fyfe 75)*
Spartans (0) 0   252
Threave R: (442) Parker V; Kerr, Patterson, Cooksley, Baty; Wilby, Milligan, Nicholl, Fyfe; McClymont, Degnan.
Spartans: (442) Bennett; Main, Cennerazzo, Sivewright, Whatley; Motion, Beesley, Blaikie (Anderson 80), MacKinnon; Beacher, Ross.
Spartans won 4-3 on aggregate.
Referee: Kevin Graham.

FIRST ROUND NORTH-EAST

Saturday, 27 July 2013

Alloa Ath (0) 0
Dundee (0) 1 *(Monti 60 (pen))*   880
Alloa Ath: (442) Bain; Doyle, Creaney, Simmons, Gordon; Meggatt, Tiffoney, Holmes, Cawley; Kirk, McCord (Ferns 69).
Dundee: (352) Letheren; Irvine, Conroy (Riley 79), Gallacher; Davidson, Benedictus, Rae, McAlister, Monti (Doris 69); MacDonald, McBride (Dyer 79).
Referee: Kevin Clancy.

Cowdenbeath (1) 1 *(Wedderburn 15)*
Dunfermline Ath (1) 3 *(Morris 36, Ferguson 64, Thomson Ryan 80)*   1161
Cowdenbeath: (442) Flynn; Cowan (Brett 70), Adamson, Milne▪, Armstrong; Wedderburn, McKenzie (Miller 81), O'Brien, Morton; Stewart G (Hemmings 62), Russell.
Dunfermline Ath: (442) Scully; Millen, Whittle, O'Kane, Young; Morris, Ferguson (Dargo 71), Byrne, Thomson Ryan; Wallace (El Bakhtaoui 88), Falkingham.
Referee: Bobby Madden.

Elgin C (0) 2 *(Gunn 57, Sutherland 84)*
Montrose (0) 0   505
Elgin C: (433) Jellema; McLean, Niven, Duff, Crighton; McMullan, Beveridge, Cameron; Harkins (Mckenzie 87), Gunn, Sutherland.
Montrose: (442) McKenzie; Masson, McIntosh, McCord, Wilson; Campbell, Webster, Winter (Gray 86), Johnston S (Sturrock 77); Wood, Watson (Bell 71).
Referee: Barry Cook.

Forfar Ath (2) 2 *(Kader 25, Malcolm 30)*
East Fife (1) 1 *(Buchanan 40 (pen))*   545
Forfar Ath: (442) Hill; McCabe, Baxter, Fotheringham, Malcolm; McCulloch, Kader (Dale 70), Malin, Swankie; McManus (McLelland 85), Deasley (Campbell R 70).
East Fife: (442) Andrews; Durie, Johnstone, McBride (Austin 85), Thom▪; Mbu, Willis (Fotheringham 80), Stewart J, Buchanan; Clarke, Wilson (Stewart R 44).
Referee: Andrew Dallas.

Formartine U (2) 2 *(Park 26, Keith 42)*
East Stirling (0) 0   186
Formartine U: (433) Shearer; Jeffrey, Hamill, McKeown, Smith M; Smith S, Clark, Bagshaw; Napier, Park (Jarosiewicz 82), Keith.
East Stirling: (442) Hay; MacGregor, Bolochoweckyj, Miller, McGowan; O'Donoghue, Thomson, Greenhill, Maxwell (Wright 62); Quinn (Kelly 85), McKechnie (Glasgow 63).
Referee: Colin Steven.

Peterhead (1) 2 *(Cox 8, Brown 73)*
Brechin C (1) 1 *(Strachan 45 (og))*   546
Peterhead: (433) Smith; Sharp, Ross (McGlinchey 49), Strachan, Noble; Redman, Cowie (Buchan 81), Brown; McCann (Rodgers 60), McAllister, Cox.
Brechin C: (4231) Smith; Jackson S, Hay (Brown 86), McLauchlan, McLean; Anderson (Molloy 74), Walker; Trouten, Jackson A, Barr; Carcary.
Referee: Des Roache.

Raith R (0) 2 *(Moon 74, Cardle 90)*
Stirling Alb (0) 1 *(White 88 (pen))*   1111
Raith R: (442) McGurn; Thomson, Booth, Fox, Watson; Hill, Anderson, Moon, Elliot; Smith C (Spence 64), Cardle.
Stirling Alb: (442) Crawford; McGeachie (Cunningham 32), Forsyth, McCunnie, Bishop; Smith, Johnston, McAnespie, Weir (Day 83); White, Ferry.
Referee: Euan Norris.

Stenhousemuir (1) 4 *(Higgins 25, Gemmell 68, 119 (pen), Douglas 97)*
Arbroath (2) 4 *(Linn 21, Banjo 36, Milne 95, 120)*   280
Stenhousemuir: (433) Smith C; Devlin▪, Malone, Rowson (Anderson 49), McMillan; McKinlay, Brash, Dickson (Douglas 64); Gemmell, Smith D, Higgins (McNeil 89).
Arbroath: (442) Morrison; Banjo, Lindsay, Chisholm, Travis; Little (Sibanda 7), Linn, Smith (Sheerin 73), Milne; Bayne, Cook (Yao 100).
aet; Stenhousemuir won 3-2 on penalties.
Referee: David Somers.

FIRST ROUND SOUTH-WEST

Saturday, 27 July 2013

Airdrieonians (1) 2 *(McLaren 24, Blockley 59)*
Hamilton A (1) 1 *(Longridge 18)*   807
Airdrieonians: (442) Stewart C; O'Neil, Evans, Sinclair, O'Byrne; McCormack, Bain (Hardie 67), Blockley, Coult (Coogans 77); Lister, McLaren (Watt 83).
Hamilton A: (4231) Cuthbert; Gordon, Hendrie, Routledge, Devlin; Kilday, Crawford; Gillespie (McShane 67), Longridge (Andreu 44), Mackinnon; Keatings (Brophy 83).
Referee: Calum Murray.

Annan Ath (0) 1 *(Weatherson 71)*
Greenock Morton (0) 0   732
Annan Ath: (4141) Mitchell Alex; Chisholm, Bradley, Sloan, Weatherson; Hopkirk (Anderson 81), Watson, Mackay (Davidson 86), Flynn; Love (Brannan 67).
Greenock Morton: (4231) Caraux; Taggart, Fitzpatrick, Hands (Campbell 67), Peciar; Imrie, Bachirou; Cham (Wallace 75), McKee, O'Brien (Fulton 75); Irvine.
Referee: Crawford Allan.

Berwick R (1) 3 *(Gray 26, Morris 99, Ronald 105)*
Livingston (0) 2 *(McNulty 90, Mensing 105 (pen))*   460
Berwick R: (442) Grant; Gielty, Turner, Notman, Tulloch; Hoskins, Gray (O'Brien 74), Currie L, Lavery (Morris 82); Dalziel (Miller 86), Ronald.
Livingston: (433) Jamieson; Mampuya, Talbot▪, Fordyce (Docherty 71), Donaldson; Mensing, Scott, Beaumont (Wilkie 57); McNulty, Burchill, McDonald (Mullen 77).
aet.
Referee: George Salmond.

Clyde (0) 1 *(McCluskey 61)*

Falkirk (0) 2 *(Alston 49, McGrandles 64)* 935

Clyde: (442) Barclay; Scullion (Ferguson 70), MacDonald, Francis, Marsh; Gray, MacBeth, McCluskey (Watt 77), Daly; Sweeney, McColm.

Falkirk: (442) McGovern; Duffie, Turnbull, Kingsley, Vaulks; Durojaiye, McGrandles, Leahy, Fulton (Grant 68); Roberts, Alston (Sibbald 78).

Referee: Iain Brines.

Queen of the South (3) 4 *(McKenna 12, 23, Lyle 18, Holt 68)*

Spartans (0) 0 1224

Queen of the South: (4141) Antell; Mitchell, Dowie, Higgins, Holt; Young (McShane 69); Paton (Russell 51), McKenna, Burns, Carmichael (Reilly 59); Lyle.

Spartans: (442) Bennett; Cennerazzo, Sivewright, Blaikie, Main; Brown (Anderson 74), Whatley, Motion, Beacher (O'Donnell 82); Beesley, Ross (Henretty 66).

Referee: Don Robertson.

Queen's Park (1) 1 *(Quinn 28 (pen))*

Ayr U (0) 2 *(Moffat 53, Forrest 89)* 887

Queen's Park: (4141) Brown; Gallacher, Coll, Quinn, Grier; Brough; Spittal, Rooney, Vitoria, Anderson; Burns (Davison 69).

Ayr U: (442) Hutton; Hunter, Pope, McLaughlin, Campbell; Lithgow, McGowan (Forrest 79), Malcolm (Shankland 90), Moffat; Crawford, Donald.

Referee: Paul Robertson.

Stranraer (1) 4 *(Winter 10, Grehan 67, Aitken 83, 88 (pen))*

Dumbarton (2) 2 *(Fleming 26, Smith K 45)* 333

Stranraer: (442) Mitchell; MacGregor, Docherty, Aitken, Robertson (Kinnaird 89); McKeown, Winter, Gallacher, Longworth (McKenna 71); Grehan, Borris (Corcoran 82).

Dumbarton: (442) Ewings; McGinn, Linton, Graham, Smith S; Phinn (McKerracher 85), Gilhaney, Agnew, McDougall (Prunty 79); Smith K, Fleming (Megginson 60).

Referee: John McKendrick.

Sunday, 28 July 2013

Albion R (0) 0

Rangers (2) 4 *(Law 26, 44, Black 71, Templeton 74)* 5345

Albion R: (442) Parry; Reid, Donnelly C, Dunlop M, Dunlop R; Crawford, Innes (Tiffney 64), Nicoll (Miller 73), Phillips; McGuigan, Flood (Chaplain 46).

Rangers: (433) Gallagher S; McAusland, McCulloch, Faure, Wallace; Crawford (Aird 77), Black, Law; Macleod (Templeton 66), Little, Daly.

Referee: John Beaton.

SECOND ROUND NORTH-EAST

Tuesday, 20 August 2013

Dundee (0) 3 *(McBride 80, MacDonald 97, 120)*

Forfar Ath (0) 1 *(Malcolm 52)* 2052

Dundee: (442) Letheren; Irvine, Davidson, Gallacher, Dyer; Reid, Rae (Conroy 46), McBride, McAlister; Doris (Monti 63), Boyle (MacDonald 46).

Forfar Ath: (442) Douglas; Baxter, Malcolm, Dods, McCulloch (McCabe 46); Kader, Fusco, Campbell I, Deasley (Templeman 82); McManus (Campbell R 82), Swankie.

aet.

Referee: Crawford Allan.

Dunfermline Ath (0) 0

Raith R (1) 2 *(Hill 2, Fox 64 (pen))* 3765

Dunfermline Ath: (442) Scully; Geggan, Young, Morris, Whittle; Ferguson (Husband 46), Byrne, Falkingham, Thomson Ryan; Wallace (Dargo 72), Moore.

Raith R: (442) McGurn; Thomson, Watson, Hill, Booth; Anderson (Vaughan 84), Fox, Moon, Cardle; Spence (Smith 46), Elliot.

Referee: Greg Aitken.

Peterhead (1) 1 *(Cox 23)*

Stenhousemuir (0) 3 *(Gemmell 63, Smith D 93, McNeil 120)* 427

Peterhead: (442) Smith; Sharp, Ross, Strachan, Noble; Redman, Cowie (McGlinchey 70), Brown, Gilfillan (Buchan 79); McLaren, Cox (McCann 79).

Stenhousemuir: (4321) Smith C; Ferguson (Duncan 112), Smith R[x], Malone, Lawson (Nimmo 91); Lynch, Anderson (McNeil 47), Dickson; Higgins, Smith D; Gemmell.

aet.

Referee: Matt Northcroft.

Wednesday, 21 August 2013

Formartine U (1) 5 *(Ewen 15, Keith 52 (pen), 57, 61, McKeown 90)*

Elgin C (1) 1 *(Crighton 6)* 480

Formartine U: (442) Shearer; Jeffrey, Clark (Napier 81), Smith M (Munro 72), Smith S; Park, McKeown, McVitie (Bagshaw 65), Hamill; Ewen, Keith.

Elgin C: (442) Jellema; Cameron, Duff, Niven, Beveridge (Mckenzie 72); Gunn (McHardy 84), Harkins (MacLeod 89), Crighton[x], McKinnon; Wyness, Sutherland.

Referee: David Somers.

SECOND ROUND SOUTH-WEST

Tuesday, 20 August 2013

Airdrieonians (0) 0

Queen of the South (1) 2 *(Lyle 45, 64)* 637

Airdrieonians: (442) Stewart C; Evans, Buchanan (O'Byrne 67), Drummond, Hay; Bain, Watt, Barclay (Higgins 23), McLaren; Coogans, Richford (McMillan 73).

Queen of the South: (451) Antell; Mitchell, Dowie, Durnan, Holt; McKenna, McGuffie, Paton (Carmichael 24), McShane (Slattery 84), Russell (Reilly 70); Lyle.

Referee: John McKendrick.

Ayr U (1) 1 *(Malcolm 41)*

Falkirk (0) 2 *(Loy 63, Shepherd 111)* 921

Ayr U: (442) Hutton; Wyllie (Shankland 114), Lithgow, Campbell, Pope; Forrest (McGowan 67), Marenghi (Crawford 82), McLaughlin, Donald; Malcolm, Moffat.

Falkirk: (442) McGovern; Duffie, Vaulks, Dick, Turnbull; McGrandles (Fulton 56), Durojaiye, Grant (Shepherd 96), Sibbald; Loy, Leahy (Alston 56).

aet.

Referee: Craig Charleston.

Stranraer (1) 2 *(Aitken 41 (pen), Grehan 85)*

Annan Ath (2) 3 *(Mackay 19, 36, Hopkirk 86)* 290

Stranraer: (442) Mitchell; MacGregor, Robertson, McKeown, Docherty (Winter 46); Stirling A, Gallacher, Aitken, Corcoran (Grehan 46); McKenna, Longworth.

Annan Ath: (442) Arthur; Black, Watson, Weatherson, Bradley; Chisholm (Brannan 46), Flynn (Swinglehurst 69), Sloan, Love (Davidson 78); Mackay, Hopkirk.

Referee: Stevie O'Reilly.

Tuesday, 27 August 2013

Rangers (0) 2 *(McKay 60, Little 62)*

Berwick R (0) 0 16,097

Rangers: (442) Gallagher S; Faure, McCulloch, Emilson Cribari, Wallace; Crawford, Black, Macleod, Templeton (McAusland 77); Little (Aird 72), Shiels (McKay 59).

Berwick R: (4141) Grant; Jacobs, Dunlop, Pullock, Hoskins; Currie L; Gray (Morris 56), Janczyk (Dalziel 70), Notman, O'Brien (Gielty 70); Lavery.

Referee: Euan Norris.

QUARTER-FINALS

Saturday, 7 September 2013

Annan Ath (0) 4 *(Love 53 (pen), Brannan 73, Mackay 79, Hopkirk 86)*

Formartine U (0) 0 506

Annan Ath: (442) Arthur; Chisholm, Watson, Weatherson, Bradley; Sloan, Flynn (Todd 76), Davidson (Brannan 69), Love (Moffat 84); Hopkirk, Mackay.

Formartine U: (442) Shearer■; Jeffrey, McKeown, Munro (Bagshaw 77), Smith S; Park, Clark (Calder 52), McVitie, Hamill; Keith, Ewen.
Referee: Euan Anderson.

Dundee (0) 1 *(MacDonald 52 (pen))*
Stenhousemuir (0) 1 *(Higgins 63)* 1615
Dundee: (442) Letheren; Irvine, Lockwood, Gallacher, Dyer; McAlister, Rae, McBride, Conroy (Boyle 75); Monti (Riley 7 (Benedictus 97)), MacDonald.
Stenhousemuir: (442) Smith C; Devlin, Rowson, McMillan, McKinlay; Dickson, Ferguson, Anderson (Douglas 66), Smith D (Lynch 66); Gemmell, Higgins (McNeil 105).
aet; Stenhousemuir won 5-4 on penalties.
Referee: John McKendrick.

Raith R (0) 1 *(Spence 86)*
Falkirk (0) 0 1565
Raith R: (4411) McGurn; Thomson, Watson, Ellis, Booth; Anderson, Fox, Moon, Cardle; Vaughan (Spence 61); Elliot.
Falkirk: (4321) Bowman; Duffie, Vaulks, Flynn, Kingsley; McGrandles, Fulton (Grant 77), Sibbald; Bingham (Shepherd 89), Roberts; Loy.
Referee: Crawford Allan.

Tuesday, 17 September 2013
Queen of the South (0) 0
Rangers (1) 3 *(Mohsni 7, Daly 75, McCulloch 83)* 6155
Queen of the South: (451) Antell; McGuffie, Dowie, Higgins■, Holt; Russell, Young, McShane (Reilly 69), McKenna (Dzierzawski 58), Paton; Lyle.
Rangers: (442) Bell; Foster, Mohsni, McCulloch, Wallace (Templeton 85); Crawford, Peralta (Faure 68), Law, Smith; Daly, Little (Clark 80).
Referee: Calum Murray.

SEMI-FINALS

Sunday, 13 October 2013
Raith R (1) 3 *(Weatherson 1 (og), Elliot 73, 89)*
Annan Ath (0) 0 2119
Raith R: (442) McGurn; Thomson, Watson (Donaldson 46), Hill, Booth; Anderson (Callachan 83), Moon, Fox, Cardle; Spence, Elliot (Smith 90).
Annan Ath: (343) Arthur; Watson, Weatherson, Swinglehurst (Bradley 80); Mitchell Andrew, Black, Flynn, Chisholm; Hopkirk, Davidson (Todd 61), Brannan (Moffat 90).
Referee: Kevin Clancy.

Tuesday, 29 October 2013
Stenhousemuir (0) 0
Rangers (0) 1 *(Daly 74)* 2338
Stenhousemuir: (4231) Smith C; Devlin, Malone, McMillan, McKinlay; Rowson, Hodge (Ferguson 14); Dickson, Lynch, Smith D; Higgins (Douglas 84).
Rangers: (442) Bell; Foster, McCulloch, Mohsni, Wallace; Peralta (Templeton 66), Black, Law, Macleod; Clark (Little 74), Daly.
Referee: Bobby Madden.

RAMSDENS CUP FINAL 2014

Sunday, 6 April 2014

(at Easter Road, attendance 19,983)

Raith R (0) 1   Rangers (0) 0

Raith R: (442) Robinson; Thomson, Watson, Hill, Booth; Anderson, Moon (Mullen 78), Fox, Cardle (Spence 90); Baird, Elliot (Smith 86).
Scorer: Baird 117.

Rangers: (442) Bell; Foster, McCulloch, Mohsni, Wallace (Faure 66); Aird, Black, Hutton (Clark 61), Smith (Gallagher C 111); Daly, Law.

aet.

Referee: Kevin Clancy.

LEAGUE CHALLENGE FINALS 1991–2014

B&Q CENTENARY CUP

1990–91	Dundee v Ayr U	3-2*
1991–92	Hamilton A v Ayr U	1-0
1992–93	Hamilton A v Morton	3-2
1993–94	Falkirk v St Mirren	3-0
1994–95	Airdrieonians v Dundee	3-2*

SCOTTISH LEAGUE CHALLENGE CUP

1995–96	Stenhousemuir v Dundee U	0-0*
	Stenhousemuir won 5-4 on penalties.	
1996–97	Stranraer v St Johnstone	1-0
1997–98	Falkirk v Queen of the South	1-0
1998–99	No competition.	
	Suspended due to lack of sponsorship.	

BELL'S CHALLENGE CUP

1999–2000	Alloa Ath v Inverness CT	4-4*
	Alloa Ath won 5-4 on penalties.	
2000–01	Airdrieonians v Livingston	2-2*
	Airdrieonians won 3-2 on penalties.	
2001–02	Airdrieonians v Alloa Ath	2-1
2002–03	Queen of the South v Brechin C	2-0
2003–04	Inverness CT v Airdrie U	2-0
2004–05	Falkirk v Ross Co	2-1
2005–06	St Mirren v Hamilton A	2-1

SCOTTISH LEAGUE CHALLENGE CUP

2006–07	Ross Co v Clyde	1-1*
	Ross Co won 5-4 on penalties.	
2007–08	St Johnstone v Dunfermline Ath	3-2

ALBA CHALLENGE CUP

2008–09	Airdrie U v Ross Co	2-2*
	Airdrie U won 3-2 on penalties.	
2009–10	Dundee v Inverness CT	3-2
2010–11	Ross Co v Queen of the South	2-0

RAMSDENS CUP

2011–12	Falkirk v Hamilton A	1-0
2012–13	Queen of the South v Partick Thistle	1-1*
	Queen of the South won 6-5 on penalties.	
2013–14	Raith R v Rangers	1-0*

*After extra time.

SCOTTISH CUP FINALS 1874–2014

SCOTTISH FA CUP

1874	Queen's Park v Clydesdale	2-0
1875	Queen's Park v Renton	3-0
1876	Queen's Park v Third Lanark	1-1
Replay	Queen's Park v Third Lanark	2-0
1877	Vale of Leven v Rangers	1-1
Replay	Vale of Leven v Rangers	1-1
2nd Replay	Vale of Leven v Rangers	3-2
1878	Vale of Leven v Third Lanark	1-0
1879	Vale of Leven v Rangers	1-1
	Vale of Leven awarded cup, Rangers failing to appear for replay.	
1880	Queen's Park v Thornliebank	3-0
1881	Queen's Park v Dumbarton	2-1
Replay	Queen's Park v Dumbarton	3-1
	After Dumbarton protested the first game.	
1882	Queen's Park v Dumbarton	2-2
Replay	Queen's Park v Dumbarton	4-1
1883	Dumbarton v Vale of Leven	2-2
Replay	Dumbarton v Vale of Leven	2-1
1884	Queen's Park v Vale of Leven	
	Queen's Park awarded cup, Vale of Leven failing to appear.	
1885	Renton v Vale of Leven	0-0
Replay	Renton v Vale of Leven	3-1
1886	Queen's Park v Renton	3-1
1887	Hibernian v Dumbarton	2-1
1888	Renton v Cambuslang	6-1
1889	Third Lanark v Celtic	3-0
Replay	Third Lanark v Celtic	2-1
	Replay by order of Scottish FA because of playing conditions in first match.	
1890	Queen's Park v Vale of Leven	1-1
Replay	Queen's Park v Vale of Leven	2-1
1891	Hearts v Dumbarton	1-0
1892	Celtic v Queen's Park	1-0
Replay	Celtic v Queen's Park	5-1
	After mutually protested first match.	
1893	Queen's Park v Celtic	0-1
Replay	Queen's Park v Celtic	2-1
	Replay by order of Scottish FA because of playing conditions in first match.	
1894	Rangers v Celtic	3-1
1895	St Bernard's v Renton	2-1
1896	Hearts v Hibernian	3-1
1897	Rangers v Dumbarton	5-1
1898	Rangers v Kilmarnock	2-0
1899	Celtic v Rangers	2-0
1900	Celtic v Queen's Park	4-3
1901	Hearts v Celtic	4-3
1902	Hibernian v Celtic	1-0
1903	Rangers v Hearts	1-1
Replay	Rangers v Hearts	0-0
2nd Replay	Rangers v Hearts	2-0
1904	Celtic v Rangers	3-2
1905	Third Lanark v Rangers	0-0
Replay	Third Lanark v Rangers	3-1
1906	Hearts v Third Lanark	1-0
1907	Celtic v Hearts	3-0
1908	Celtic v St Mirren	5-1
1909	Celtic v Rangers	2-2
Replay	Celtic v Rangers	1-1
	Owing to riot, the cup was withheld.	
1910	Dundee v Clyde	2-2
Replay	Dundee v Clyde	0-0*
2nd Replay	Dundee v Clyde	2-1
1911	Celtic v Hamilton A	0-0
Replay	Celtic v Hamilton A	2-0
1912	Celtic v Clyde	2-0
1913	Falkirk v Raith R	2-0
1914	Celtic v Hibernian	0-0
Replay	Celtic v Hibernian	4-1
1920	Kilmarnock v Albion R	3-2
1921	Partick Thistle v Rangers	1-0
1922	Morton v Rangers	1-0
1923	Celtic v Hibernian	1-0
1924	Airdrieonians v Hibernian	2-0
1925	Celtic v Dundee	2-1
1926	St Mirren v Celtic	2-0
1927	Celtic v East Fife	3-1
1928	Rangers v Celtic	4-0
1929	Kilmarnock v Rangers	2-0
1930	Rangers v Partick Thistle	0-0
Replay	Rangers v Partick Thistle	2-1
1931	Celtic v Motherwell	2-2
Replay	Celtic v Motherwell	4-2
1932	Rangers v Kilmarnock	1-1
Replay	Rangers v Kilmarnock	3-0
1933	Celtic v Motherwell	1-0
1934	Rangers v St Mirren	5-0
1935	Rangers v Hamilton A	2-1
1936	Rangers v Third Lanark	1-0
1937	Celtic v Aberdeen	2-1
1938	East Fife v Kilmarnock	1-1
Replay	East Fife v Kilmarnock	4-2*
1939	Clyde v Motherwell	4-0
1947	Aberdeen v Hibernian	2-1
1948	Rangers v Morton	1-1*
Replay	Rangers v Morton	1-0*
1949	Rangers v Clyde	4-1
1950	Rangers v East Fife	3-0
1951	Celtic v Motherwell	1-0
1952	Motherwell v Dundee	4-0
1953	Rangers v Aberdeen	1-1
Replay	Rangers v Aberdeen	1-0
1954	Celtic v Aberdeen	2-1
1955	Clyde v Celtic	1-1
Replay	Clyde v Celtic	1-0
1956	Hearts v Celtic	3-1
1957	Falkirk v Kilmarnock	1-1
Replay	Falkirk v Kilmarnock	2-1*
1958	Clyde v Hibernian	1-0
1959	St Mirren v Aberdeen	3-1
1960	Rangers v Kilmarnock	2-0
1961	Dunfermline Ath v Celtic	0-0
Replay	Dunfermline Ath v Celtic	2-0
1962	Rangers v St Mirren	2-0
1963	Rangers v Celtic	1-1
Replay	Rangers v Celtic	3-0
1964	Rangers v Dundee	3-1
1965	Celtic v Dunfermline Ath	3-2
1966	Rangers v Celtic	0-0
Replay	Rangers v Celtic	1-0
1967	Celtic v Aberdeen	2-0
1968	Dunfermline Ath v Hearts	3-1
1969	Celtic v Rangers	4-0
1970	Aberdeen v Celtic	3-1
1971	Celtic v Rangers	1-1
Replay	Celtic v Rangers	2-1
1972	Celtic v Hibernian	6-1
1973	Rangers v Celtic	3-2
1974	Celtic v Dundee U	3-0
1975	Celtic v Airdrieonians	3-1
1976	Rangers v Hearts	3-1
1977	Celtic v Rangers	1-0
1978	Rangers v Aberdeen	2-1
1979	Rangers v Hibernian	0-0
Replay	Rangers v Hibernian	0-0*
2nd Replay	Rangers v Hibernian	3-2*
1980	Celtic v Rangers	1-0*
1981	Rangers v Dundee U	0-0*
Replay	Rangers v Dundee U	4-1
1982	Aberdeen v Rangers	4-1*
1983	Aberdeen v Rangers	1-0*
1984	Aberdeen v Celtic	2-1*
1985	Celtic v Dundee U	2-1
1986	Aberdeen v Hearts	3-0
1987	St Mirren v Dundee U	1-0*
1988	Celtic v Dundee U	2-1
1989	Celtic v Rangers	1-0

TENNENTS SCOTTISH CUP

1990	Aberdeen v Celtic	0-0*
	Aberdeen won 9-8 on penalties.	
1991	Motherwell v Dundee U	4-3*
1992	Rangers v Airdrieonians	2-1
1993	Rangers v Aberdeen	2-1
1994	Dundee U v Rangers	1-0
1995	Celtic v Airdrieonians	1-0
1996	Rangers v Hearts	5-1
1997	Kilmarnock v Falkirk	1-0
1998	Hearts v Rangers	2-1
1999	Rangers v Celtic	1-0
2000	Rangers v Aberdeen	4-0
2001	Celtic v Hibernian	3-0
2002	Rangers v Celtic	3-2
2003	Rangers v Dundee	1-0
2004	Celtic v Dunfermline Ath	3-1
2005	Celtic v Dundee U	1-0
2006	Hearts v Gretna	1-1*
	Hearts won 4-2 on penalties.	
2007	Celtic v Dunfermline Ath	1-0

SCOTTISH FA CUP

2008	Rangers v Queen of the South	3-2

HOMECOMING SCOTTISH CUP

2009	Rangers v Falkirk	1-0

ACTIVE NATION SCOTTISH CUP

2010	Dundee U v Ross Co	3-0

SCOTTISH FA CUP

2011	Celtic v Motherwell	3-0

WILLIAM HILL SCOTTISH CUP

2012	Hearts v Hibernian	5-1
2013	Celtic v Hibernian	3-0
2014	St Johnstone v Dundee U	2-0

*After extra time.

SCOTTISH CUP WINS

Celtic 36, Rangers 33, Queen's Park 10, Hearts 8, Aberdeen 7, Clyde 3, Kilmarnock 3, St Mirren 3, Vale of Leven 3, Dundee U 2, Dunfermline Ath 2, Falkirk 2, Hibernian 2, Motherwell 2, Renton 2, Third Lanark 2, Airdrieonians 1, Dumbarton 1, Dundee 1, East Fife 1, Morton 1, Partick Thistle 1, St Bernard's 1, St Johnstone 1.

APPEARANCES IN FINAL

Celtic 54, Rangers 50, Aberdeen 15, Hearts 14, Hibernian 13, Queen's Park 12, Dundee U 10, Kilmarnock 8, Motherwell 7, Vale of Leven 7, Clyde 6, Dumbarton 6, St Mirren 6, Third Lanark 6, Dundee 5, Dunfermline Ath 5, Renton 5, Airdrieonians 4, Falkirk 4, East Fife 3, Hamilton A 2, Morton 2, Partick Thistle 2, Albion R 1, Cambuslang 1, Clydesdale 1, Gretna 1, Queen of the South 1, Raith R 1, Ross Co 1, St Bernard's 1, St Johnstone 1, Thornliebank 1.

WILLIAM HILL SCOTTISH CUP 2013–14

▪ *Denotes player sent off.*

FIRST ROUND

Brora Rangers v Vale of Leithen	1-0
Coldstream v Wick Academy	0-6
Deveronvale v Clachnacuddin	5-0
Edinburgh Univ v Spartans	0-2
Forres Mechanics v Keith	4-5
Fort William v Newton Stewart	0-0, 1-3
Fraserburgh v Civil Service Strollers	4-0
Gala Fairydean v Glasgow Univ	3-1
Girvan v Auchinleck Talbot	1-5
Golspie Sutherland v Edinburgh C	0-4
Hawick Royal Albert v St Cuthbert W	0-1
Huntly v Preston Ath	3-4
Inverurie Loco Works v Burntisland Shipyard	3-0
Linlithgow Rose v Nairn Co	2-0
Lossiemouth v Culter	0-0, 1-3
Selkirk v Turriff U	1-3
Threave R v Rothes	3-0
Wigtown & Bladnoch v Buckie Th	3-4

SECOND ROUND

Albion R v Spartans	1-0
Auchinleck Talbot v St Cuthbert W	4-0
Berwick R v Peterhead	2-1
Brora Rangers v Cove Rangers	1-1, 3-0
Buckie Th v Annan Ath	0-0, 0-4
Dalbeattie Star v Montrose	0-1
Deveronvale v Linlithgow Rose	2-2, 3-1
Edinburgh C v Fraserburgh	4-4, 0-2
Formartine U v Inverurie Loco Works	0-2
Gala Fairydean v Clyde	0-3
Keith v Elgin C	0-4
Newton Stewart v Culter	0-6
Queen's Park v Preston Ath	2-2, 2-1
Stirling Alb v Whitehill Welfare	2-2, 2-1
Turriff U v Wick Academy	4-2
East Stirling v Threave R	6-0

THIRD ROUND

Friday, 1 November 2013

Rangers (0) 3 *(Daly 49, 53, Templeton 80)*
Airdrieonians (0) 0   22,533

Rangers: (442) Bell; Foster, McCulloch, Mohsni, Wallace; Peralta (Aird 81), Hutton, Macleod (Templeton 66), Law; Daly, Clark (Little 70).
Airdrieonians: (451) Bullock; Buchanan, Drummond, McCormack, Boyle; Bain (Coogans 86), Sinclair, Hardie, Blockley, Lister; Coult (Watt 57).
Referee: John Beaton.

Saturday, 2 November 2013

Albion R (0) 1 *(McGuigan 73)*
Deveronvale (0) 0   484

Albion R: (442) Parry; Reid, Dunlop R, Dunlop M, Phillips; Crawford (Maguire 90), Tiffney (Flood 79), Donnelly C, Cusack; McGuigan, Dallas.
Deveronvale: (451) McConnachie; Rae (Scott 72), Rennie, Henry, Adams; Cowie, Urquhart, Charlesworth C (Wardrop 46), Rodger, Watt (Simpson 84); Charlesworth M.
Referee: David Somers.

Alloa Ath (0) 3 *(Cawley 58, Gordon 69, Salmon 87)*
Inverurie Loco Works (0) 0   403

Alloa Ath: (442) Jamie; Tiffoney, Gordon, Meggatt, Wilson; Holmes (Salmon 64), Simmons (Young 78), McCord, Flannigan (Ferns 46); Cawley, Kirk.
Inverurie Loco Works: (451) Reid; Mitchell (Forsyth 73), Adams, Anderson, Matiland; Ross (Gauld 66), Souter (Young 80), Donaldson, Begg, McLean; Bavidge.
Referee: Matt Northcroft.

Arbroath (0) 0
Brechin C (0) 2 *(Jackson S 57, Trouten 88)*   634

Arbroath: (442) Morrison; Banjo (Yao 85), Travis, Keddie, Hamilton; Linn, Smith, Chisholm (Cook 64), Sibanda (McWalter 90); Bayne, Milne.
Brechin C: (442) Smith; McLean, Hay, Moyes, Brown; Trouten, Anderson (Carcary 65), Molloy, Robb (Jackson S 74); Jackson A, Petrie.
Referee: Des Roache.

Ayr U (1) 3 *(Marenghi 39, Lithgow 50, Malcolm 60)*
Queen's Park (1) 2 *(Brough 27, Spittal 67)*   879

Ayr U: (442) Hutton; Hunter, Pope, Lithgow, Donald; Marenghi, McLaughlin, Crawford, Roberts (McGowan 69); Moffat (Kyle 79), Malcolm.
Queen's Park: (4411) Birinstinfil; Fisher, Brough, Lamie, Burns; Davison (Gormley 58), Gold, Anderson, Spittal; Keenan (Gallacher 82); Quinn (Vitoria 73).
Referee: Euan Anderson.

Clyde (1) 2 *(McCluskey 14, Watt 74)*
Brora Rangers (1) 1 *(Sutherland 3)*   686

Clyde: (442) Barclay; Brown, Marsh, McQueen, MacDonald; Ferguson, Capuano, Sweeney, McColm (Watt 73); Scullion, McCluskey.
Brora Rangers: (442) Malin; Hind, Munro, Tokely, Mackay D; Houston, Morrison, Hart, Greig (Watson 79); Sutherland (Dey 90), Mackay S.
Referee: Stevie O'Reilly.

Culter (0) 1 *(Dunlop 62 (og))*
Berwick R (0) 1 *(Notman 53)*   639

Culter: (442) Duffy; Sim, Reid, Kelly, Robertson; Greig, McArthur (Rintoul 53), Youngson (Taylor S 76), Leith; McAllister, McBain (Taylor M 90).
Berwick R: (442) Bald; Jacobs, Dunlop, Tulloch, Hoskins; Currie L, Janczyk, Notman, Gielty; Dalziel, Lavery (Morris 68).
Referee: Gavin Ross.

Dumbarton (1) 2 *(Kirkpatrick 19, 64)*
Cowdenbeath (0) 1 *(Stevenson 61)*   450

Dumbarton: (41212) Ewings; McGinn, Graham, Barry, Linton; Murray (Agnew 75); Gilhaney, Kirkpatrick; Megginson; Fleming (Prunty 29), Nish.
Cowdenbeath: (442) Flynn; Cowan, Armstrong, O'Brien, Adamson; Morton (McKenzie 67), Milne, Wedderburn (Miller 82), Stevenson; Hemmings (Russell 72), Stewart G.
Referee: Iain Brines.

Elgin C (1) 3 *(Duff 16, Wyness 82, Khutsishvili 84)*
Dunfermline Ath (2) 5 *(Wallace 19, 28, Moore 63 (pen), 64, Whittle 73)*   1108

Elgin C: (442) Jellema; McLean (Harkins 46), Duff, Nicolson (Khutsishvili 71), McMullan; Beveridge, Niven, Sutherland, Mckenzie; Gunn (Urqhart 53), Wyness.
Dunfermline Ath: (442) Scully; Millen, Young, Morris, Whittle; Byrne, Husband (Ferguson 61), Falkingham, Geggan; Wallace (Smith 77), Thomson Ryan (Moore 55).
Referee: Barry Cook.

Forfar Ath (1) 2 *(Hilson 45, Templeman 69)*
East Fife (0) 1 *(Johnstone 74)*   485

Forfar Ath: (442) Douglas; Baxter, Andrews (Malcolm 65), Dods, Campbell I; McCluskey (Campbell R 78), Fusco, Main (Dale 73), Hilson; Templeman, Swankie.
East Fife: (541) Andrews; Durie, Thom, Mbu, Campbell (Clarke 66), McBride; Stewart R, Hughes, Brown (Stewart J 17), Johnstone (Austin 84); Buchanan.
Referee: Andrew Dallas.

Fraserburgh (0) 2 *(Johnston 73, Noble 90)*
Montrose (1) 1 *(McCord 37)* 565
Fraserburgh: (433) Leask; Dickson, McBride, Hay, Main; Cowie M, Fowlie (Noble 63), West; Johnston (Davidson 90), Barbour, Bruce.
Montrose: (442) McKenzie; McNally, Crawford, Rodger, McIntosh (Sturrock 90); McCord, Masson (Bonar 90), Watson, Johnston S (Webster 80); Wood, Deasley.
Referee: Colin Steven.

Queen of the South (0) 1 *(Lyle 64)*
Hamilton A (0) 0 1324
Queen of the South: (442) Clark; Mitchell, Durnan, Higgins, Holt; McShane (Lyle 57), Dzierzawski, Young, Carmichael; Reilly (Paton 84), Russell.
Hamilton A: (442) Cuthbert; Gordon, Canning, Devlin, Hendrie; Brophy (Longridge 68), Gillespie, Andreu (Antoine-Curier 74), Crawford (McGrath 68); McShane, Mackinnon.
Referee: Stephen Finnie.

Stenhousemuir (0) 2 *(Douglas 51, Gemmell 58)*
Annan Ath (1) 2 *(McNiff 26, Brannan 90)* 309
Stenhousemuir: (442) Smith C; Devlin, Malone, McMillan, McKinlay; Smith D, Ferguson, Lynch, Dickson; Gemmell, Douglas (Watt 72).
Annan Ath: (442) Arthur; Sloan (Todd 70), Watson, Swinglehurst, McNiff; Mackay, Mitchell Andrew, Jardine (Brannan 88), Love (Davidson 88); Weatherson, Hopkirk.
Referee: Greg Aitken.

Stranraer (1) 2 *(Longworth 35, 90)*
Auchinleck Talbot (2) 2 *(Young 6, Milligan 31)* 1170
Stranraer: (442) Mitchell; Robertson (McKenna 82), MacGregor, McKeown, Docherty; Bell (Borris 69), Gallagher, Aitken, Stirling A; Grehan, Longworth.
Auchinleck Talbot: (442) Leishman; Lyle, Pettigrew, McGoldrick, Park; White (Faulds 89), Young, Spence, Latta; Milligan (McCann 78), Gormley (Mackenzie 79).
Referee: Craig Charleston.

Turriff U (0) 0
Stirling Alb (2) 3 *(Forsyth 8, Cumming 12 (og), Ferry 61)* 490
Turriff U: (442) Coutts; Davidson, Cumming, Bowden, McKibben (Allan R 46); McKenna, Young, Brownie (Shand 68), McGowan; Harris, Beagrie (McKenzie 80).
Stirling Alb: (442) Crawford; Forsyth, Bishop, Smith C, Ashe; Johnston (Day 86), McClune, Fulton (McAnespie 75), Ferry; White, Cunningham (Coyne 69).
Referee: Alan Newlands.

Sunday, 3 November 2013

East Stirling (0) 0
Raith R (0) 2 *(Smith 48, McGowan 80 (og))* 716
East Stirling: (4141) Hay; MacGregor, Townsley, Bolochoweckyj, McGowan; Thomson; Herd (O'Donoghue 78), Greenhill, McKechnie (Wright 69), Maxwell (Devlin 78); Turner.
Raith R: (442) Laidlaw; Thomson, Watson, Fox, Booth; Moon, Elliot, McCann, Ellis; Anderson, Smith (Spence 69).
Referee: Don Robertson.

THIRD ROUND REPLAYS

Saturday, 9 November 2013

Auchinleck Talbot (0) 2 *(Latta 59, Gormley 77)*
Stranraer (2) 3 *(Longworth 5, 31, Gallagher 88)* 1386
Auchinleck Talbot: (442) Leishman; Lyle (Mackenzie 88), Pettigrew, McGoldrick, Park; Young, Spence (Faulds 80), White, Latta; Milligan, Gormley.
Stranraer: (442) Mitchell; Kinnaird, Robertson, McKeown, Docherty; Winter (Borris 86), Gallagher, Aitken, Stirling A (Corcoran 90); Grehan (McKenna 90), Longworth.
Referee: Craig Charleston.

Berwick R (1) 3 *(O'Brien 17, Dalziel 51, Lavery 85)*
Culter (0) 1 *(Youngson 82 (pen))* 411
Berwick R: (433) O'Connor; Jacobs, Dunlop, Tulloch, Hoskins; Notman, Janczyk (Gielty 70), Currie L; Lavery, Dalziel (Carse 77), O'Brien (Gray 61).
Culter: (4411) Duffy; Sim, Reid, Kelly, Robertson; Greig (Taylor M 65), Leith, Rintoul (McArthur 77), Youngson; McAllister; McBain.
Referee: Gavin Ross.

Tuesday, 12 November 2013

Annan Ath (1) 2 *(Todd 32, Hopkirk 50)*
Stenhousemuir (0) 4 *(Gemmell 77 (pen), Dickson 90, Lynch 105, McNeil 107)* 421
Annan Ath: (442) Mitchell Alex; Mitchell Andrew, Watson, Weatherson (Davidson 101), Swinglehurst; Sloan, Jardine (Black 84), McNiff, Love; Todd (Mackay 84), Hopkirk.
Stenhousemuir: (442) Smith C; Devlin (Smith R 88), Malone, McMillan, McKinlay; Lynch, Rowson, Brash, Dickson (Ferguson 104); Gemmell, Douglas (McNeil 62). aet.
Referee: Des Roache.

FOURTH ROUND

Friday, 29 November 2013

Dundee U (1) 5 *(Robertson 27, 76, Armstrong 64, Graham 82 (pen), Mackay-Steven 84)*
Kilmarnock (0) 2 *(Barr 48, Johnston 50)* 6979
Dundee U: (4231) Cierzniak; Wilson, Souttar, Gunning, Robertson; Rankin (Gomis 87), Paton; Armstrong, Gauld (Goodwillie 85), Mackay-Steven; Ciftci (Graham 68).
Kilmarnock: (442) Samson; Clohessy (O'Hara 46), Irvine, Barr, Tesselaar; Gabriel (Gros 83), Pascali, Johnston, Slater; Boyd, McKenzie.
Referee: Calum Murray.

Saturday, 30 November 2013

Albion R (0) 1 *(Phillips 90)*
Motherwell (0) 0 2950
Albion R: (442) Parry; Reid, Donnelly C, Russell, Dunlop R; Cusack (Flood 82), Chaplain, Dunlop M, Phillips; McGuigan, Dallas (Tiffney 71).
Motherwell: (442) Nielsen; Kerr, Hutchinson, McManus, Hammell; McFadden (Leitch 71), Lawson, Carswell, Francis-Angol (Lasley 71); McHugh (Sutton 46), Anier.
Referee: Euan Anderson.

Alloa Ath (0) 3 *(McCord 51 (pen), Holmes 59, Marr 90)*
Stirling Alb (1) 2 *(White 10, Weir 90)* 1278
Alloa Ath: (4411) Bain; Doyle, Gordon, Marr, Meggatt; Tiffoney, Simmons, Holmes, McCord (Robertson 74); Cawley; Kirk (Salmon 71).
Stirling Alb: (442) Crawford; McClune, Bishop, McAnespie, Ashe; Johnston, Forsyth (Coyne 80), Fulton (Day 71), Weatherston (Weir 56); White, Cunningham.
Referee: Stevie O'Reilly.

Ayr U (0) 1 *(Donald 59)*
Dunfermline Ath (1) 1 *(Geggan 14)* 1391
Ayr U: (442) Hutton; Hunter, McLaughlin, Lithgow, Pope; Marenghi, Gilmour, Crawford (Forrest 64), Donald; Moffat, Kyle.
Dunfermline Ath: (41212) Scully; Millen, Young, Morris, Whittle; Geggan; Byrne, Falkingham; Wallace; Smith (Dargo 71), Thomson Ryan.
Referee: Stephen Finnie.

Berwick R (1) 1 *(Currie L 8)*
Dumbarton (2) 3 *(Prunty 30 (pen), Megginson 43, Linton 56)* 406
Berwick R: (433) Bald; Jacobs, Dunlop, Tulloch, Hoskins; Notman, Janczyk (Dalziel 61), Currie L; Gray (O'Brien 71), Lavery (Morris 69), Gielty.
Dumbarton: (433) Ewings; McGinn, Graham, Barry, Linton; Gilhaney (McDougall 83), Kirkpatrick, Turner; Megginson (McKerracher 87), Prunty (Nish 74), Smith K.
Referee: Des Roache.

Brechin C (0) 1 *(Trouten 53)*
Forfar Ath (0) 1 *(Fotheringham 90)* 724
Brechin C: (433) Smith; McLean, Hay, Moyes■, Brown; Molloy (Walker 59), Petrie, Jackson S; Trouten, Jackson A, Carcary (Donnelly 75).
Forfar Ath: (442) Douglas; Baxter■, Malcolm■, Dods, Campbell I; McCluskey (McCabe 79), Fusco, Faero, Hilson (Fotheringham 80); Templeman (Campbell R 81), Swankie.
Referee: John McKendrick.

Clyde (1) 1 *(MacDonald 15)*
Stranraer (1) 1 *(Longworth 44)* 681
Clyde: (442) Rajovic; Brown (Capuano 71), Marsh, McQueen, MacDonald; Ferguson (Daly 81), Gray, Sweeney, McColm; Scullion (Watt 74), McCluskey.
Stranraer: (442) Mitchell; MacGregor, McKeown, Robertson, Docherty; Winter (Borris 66), Aitken (Bell 90), Gallagher, Stirling A; Longworth, Grehan (McKenna 66).
Referee: Alan Muir.

Dundee (0) 0
Raith R (1) 1 *(Irvine 8 (og))* 3184
Dundee: (442) Letheren; Irvine, Gallacher, Davidson, Lockwood (Monti 83); Riley, Rae, McAlister, Conroy (Beattie 62); MacDonald, Wighton (Boyle 46).
Raith R: (442) Laidlaw; Thomson, Ellis, Hill, Booth; Anderson (McCann 89), Moon, Callachan, Cardle; Smith (Spence 69), Elliot.
Referee: Steven McLean.

Falkirk (0) 0
Rangers (0) 2 *(Law 89, Templeton 90)* 6228
Falkirk: (4141) McGovern; Duffie, McCracken■, Vaulks, Kingsley; Millar; McGrandles, Sibbald, Fulton (Alston 73), Roberts (Flynn 60); Loy (Shepherd 82).
Rangers: (442) Bell; Faure, McCulloch, Mohsni, Wallace; Peralta (Aird 67), Black, Law, Macleod; Clark (Templeton 67), Daly.
Referee: Brian Colvin.

Inverness CT (1) 4 *(Ross 45 (pen), McKay 71, 90, Doran 90 (pen))*
Greenock Morton (0) 0 2453
Inverness CT: (4231) Brill; Shinnie, Meekings, Warren, Tremarco; Draper (Williams 90), Polworth; Watkins, Ross (Agdestein 90), Doran; McKay.
Greenock Morton: (4141) Caraux; Taggart■, O'Ware, Reid, Fitzpatrick; Stirling (McKee 84); Nicholson (O'Brien 75), Bachirou, Imrie, Russell (Campbell 61); Novo.
Referee: Don Robertson.

Queen of the South (1) 2 *(Russell 35, Paton 72)*
St Mirren (1) 2 *(Newton 9, Thompson 51)* 2176
Queen of the South: (4231) Clark; Mitchell, Durnan, Higgins, Holt; McKenna, McShane; Burns, Paton, Russell; Reilly (Lyle 67).
St Mirren: (4411) Kello; Naismith, McGregor, McAusland, Kelly; Newton, Goodwin, McLean, McGinn; McGowan (Reilly 21); Thompson.
Referee: Kevin Clancy.

Ross Co (0) 0
Hibernian (1) 1 *(Handling 31)* 2213
Ross Co: (352) Brown; Boyd, McLean, Micic (Saunders 43); Kettlewell, De Leeuw, Brittain, Quinn (Kovacevic 67), Glen (Maatsen 64); Luckassen, Carey.
Hibernian: (442) Williams; Maybury, Forster, Hanlon, McGivern; Cairney■, Robertson (Tudur Jones 67), Craig, Stevenson; Handling (Caldwell 80 (Taiwo 90)), Collins.
Referee: Craig Thomson.

St Johnstone (1) 2 *(May 24, Jahic 62)*
Livingston (0) 0 2294
St Johnstone: (442) Mannus; Mackay, Jahic, Scobbie, Easton; Millar, Davidson (Caddis 85), McDonald, Wotherspoon; May, Hasselbaink (Fallon 77).
Livingston: (442) Walker; Fordyce, Mensing, Donaldson, Talbot (Twardzik 69); Jacobs Keaghan, Scott (Denholm 75), O'Brien, Scougall; Barrowman (Burchill 83), McNulty.
Referee: Andrew Dallas.

Stenhousemuir (0) 3 *(McNeil 63, 88, Douglas 90)*
Fraserburgh (0) 0 487
Stenhousemuir: (442) Smith C; Devlin, Malone, Smith R, McKinlay; Dickson (Watt 90), Faulds, Hodge, McNeil; Gemmell (Douglas 81), Lynch (Ferguson 86).
Fraserburgh: (442) Leask; Paterson, Cowie R, Cowie M, McBride; Fowlie (Main 77), West, Dickson, Barbour; Bruce, Noble (Cooper 67).
Referee: Kevin Graham.

Sunday, 1 December 2013
Hearts (0) 0
Celtic (5) 7 *(Commons 3, 21, 59 (pen), Brown 34, 75, Ledley 42, Lustig 44)* 10,636
Hearts: (4411) MacDonald; McGhee, McGowan, Wilson, McHattie; Robinson, Hamill (King A 79), Smith (McKay 46), Walker; Stevenson (Carrick 68); Paterson.
Celtic: (4411) Forster; Lustig (Fisher 73), Ambrose, van Dijk, Izaguirre; Brown, Biton, Ledley, Mulgrew (Pukki 59); Commons (Boerrigter 77); Stokes.
Referee: William Collum.

Partick Thistle (0) 0
Aberdeen (1) 1 *(Considine 5)* 3642
Partick Thistle: (4231) Fox; Osbourne, Balatoni, Piccolo, Sinclair; Kerr (Welsh 62), Forbes (Lawless 76); Elliot, Craigen, Higginbotham; Doolan (Baird 80).
Aberdeen: (4141) Langfield; Hector, Anderson, Considine, Reynolds; Jack; McGinn, Pawlett (Vernon 86), Robson, Wylde (Smith 61); Zola (Magennis 61).
Referee: Bobby Madden.

FOURTH ROUND REPLAYS

Wednesday, 4 December 2013
Dunfermline Ath (0) 1 *(Thomson Ryan 60)*
Ayr U (0) 0 1932
Dunfermline Ath: (442) Scully; Millen, Young, Morris, Whittle; Geggan, Byrne, Falkingham, Thomson Ryan; Smith (Dargo 74), Wallace (Husband 90).
Ayr U: (442) Hutton; Hunter, McLaughlin, Lithgow, Pope; Marenghi (Malcolm 68), Gilmour, Crawford (Forrest 60), Donald; Moffat, Kyle.
Referee: Stephen Finnie.

Tuesday, 10 December 2013
Forfar Ath (1) 3 *(Templeman 19, 108, Malin 85)*
Brechin C (1) 3 *(Jackson 7, Trouten 50 (pen), Walker 95)* 811
Forfar Ath: (442) Douglas; McCabe (Malin 58), Faero, Dods, Campbell I; Kader, Fusco, Dale, Fotheringham (McManus 72); Templeman, Swankie (Smith 54).
Brechin C: (433) Smith; Jackson S, Hay, McLauchlan, Brown; Petrie, Molloy, Robb (Walker 69); Trouten, Jackson A (Donnelly 112), Carcary (Barr 80).
aet; Forfar won 4-3 on penalties.
Referee: John McKendrick.

St Mirren (1) 3 *(Harkins 19, Thompson 74, Kelly 87)*
Queen of the South (0) 0 2775
St Mirren: (4411) Kello; van Zanten, McAusland, McGregor, Grainger; Newton, Goodwin, McLean, McGinn (Kelly 77); Harkins (Brady 88); Thompson (Reilly 86).
Queen of the South: (4141) Clark; Mitchell, Higgins, Durnan, Holt; McKenna; Burns, Carmichael, McShane, Russell; Lyle.
Referee: John Beaton.

Stranraer (0) 4 *(Stirling A 60, McKeown 61, Longworth 88, Grehan 90)*
Clyde (0) 1 *(Watt 54)* 454
Stranraer: (442) Mitchell; Robertson, Rumsby, McKeown, Docherty; Borris (Winter 61), Aitken, Gallagher, Stirling A; McKenna (Grehan 55), Longworth (Forde 89).
Clyde: (4141) Rajovic; Brown, McQueen, Gray, MacDonald; Frances; McCluskey (Ferguson 68), Capuano (MacBeth 82), Sweeney (Scullion 76), Watt; Daly.
Referee: Alan Muir.

FIFTH ROUND

Friday, 7 February 2014

Rangers (3) 4 *(Shiels 8, 24, 47, Templeton 37)*

Dunfermline Ath (0) 0   19,396

Rangers: (442) Bell; Faure, McCulloch, Mohsni, Wallace; Aird (Peralta 72), Black, Law (Crawford 82), Templeton; Daly, Shiels (Little 76).
Dunfermline Ath: (442) Scully; Millen (Thomson Ryan 46), Morris, Martin, Whittle; Williamson, Byrne (El Bakhtaoui 46), Geggan, Falkingham; Shankland (Moore 76), Wallace.
Referee: Bobby Madden.

Saturday, 8 February 2014

Albion R (1) 2 *(McMillan 24 (og), Phillips 67)*

Stenhousemuir (0) 0   748

Albion R: (442) Parry; Reid, Dunlop M, Dunlop R, Russell; Cusack, Donnelly C, Chaplain, Phillips; McGuigan (Crawford 90), Dallas (Tiffney 77).
Stenhousemuir: (433) Smith C; Devlin, McMillan, Malone, McKinlay (Nimmo 84); Lynch (McNeil 46), Faulds, Rowson; Smith D (Douglas 72), Higgins, Dickson.
Referee: Brian Colvin.

Alloa Ath (0) 0

Dumbarton (1) 1 *(Nish 31)*   749

Alloa Ath: (4411) Bain (McDowall 46); Doyle, Gordon, Lindsay, Meggatt; Cawley, Simmons, McCord, Young (Tiffoney 67); Holmes; Kirk (Ferns 61).
Dumbarton: (433) Grindlay; McGinn, Graham, McLaughlin (Miller 80), Linton; Gilhaney, Agnew (Fleming 86), Kirkpatrick; Megginson, Kane (Prunty 90), Nish.
Referee: Calum Murray.

Celtic (1) 1 *(Stokes 9)*

Aberdeen (1) 2 *(Anderson 38, Pawlett 50)* 30,413

Celtic: (4411) Forster; Matthews, Ambrose, van Dijk, Izaguirre; Forrest, Brown, Johansen, Samaras (Griffiths 63); Commons (Boerrigter 84); Stokes (Balde 76).
Aberdeen: (4411) Langfield; Logan, Anderson, Reynolds, Considine; McGinn (Shaughnessy 90), Flood, Robson, Hayes; Pawlett (Vernon 77); Rooney.
Referee: William Collum.

Forfar Ath (0) 0

St Johnstone (2) 4 *(May 27, Wright 42, O'Halloran 64, Dunne 80)*   1803

Forfar Ath: (442) Douglas; Baxter, Malcolm, Dods, Campbell I; Kader (Campbell R 69), Fotheringham (Hilson 46), Fusco, Faero (Malin 72); Templeman, Swankie.
St Johnstone: (442) Banks; Mackay, Wright, Anderson, Easton; Croft, Cregg, McDonald (Brown 82), Wotherspoon (Dunne 69); May (Iwelumo 77), O'Halloran.
Referee: John Beaton.

Hibernian (2) 2 *(Stanton 14, Nelson 45)*

Raith R (2) 3 *(Moon 6, Hill 45, Anderson 63)* 10,503

Hibernian: (442) Williams; Forster, Nelson, Hanlon, Stevenson; Watmore, Taiwo (Heffernan 71), Craig, Harris (Haynes 61); Stanton, Collins (Zoubir 61).
Raith R: (451) Laidlaw; Thomson, Hill (Ellis 73), Donaldson (Mullen 41), Booth; Anderson, Callachan, Moon, Fox, Cardle; Spence (Smith 64).
Referee: Steven McLean.

Stranraer (1) 2 *(Grehan 45 (pen), Longworth 72)*

Inverness CT (1) 2 *(Doran 40, McKay 74)* 722

Stranraer: (442) Mitchell; Robertson, Rumsby, McKeown, Docherty; Winter, Bell, Gallagher, Stirling A (McKenna 82); Grehan, Longworth (Forde 87).
Inverness CT: (451) Brill; Raven, Warren, Meekings, Shinnie; Watkins (Foran 58), Draper, Vincent, Tansey, Doran (Williams 68); McKay.
Referee: Kevin Clancy.

Sunday, 9 February 2014

Dundee U (1) 2 *(Gauld 21, Ciftci 51)*

St Mirren (1) 1 *(McLean 26 (pen))*   4952

Dundee U: (4231) Cierzniak; Wilson, Souttar, Good, Robertson; Paton, Rankin; Mackay-Steven, Gauld (Gomis 88), Armstrong (Dow 75); Ciftci (El Alagui 88).
St Mirren: (442) Kello; Kelly, McAusland, McGregor, Naismith; Goodwin, Newton (Campbell 85), Djemba-Djemba (Teale 71), McLean; McGowan, Thompson.
Referee: Craig Thomson.

FIFTH ROUND REPLAY

Tuesday, 18 February 2014

Inverness CT (1) 2 *(Ross 3, Doran 90)*

Stranraer (0) 0   1458

Inverness CT: (4141) Brill; Raven, Warren, Meekings, Shinnie; Foran; Draper (Doran 67), Tansey, Vincent, Ross (Watkins 80); McKay.
Stranraer: (4231) Mitchell; Robertson, Rumsby, McKeown, Docherty; Gallagher, Bell; Winter (McKenna 67), Longworth (Forde 75), Stirling A; Grehan.
Referee: Alan Muir.

QUARTER-FINALS

Saturday, 8 March 2014

Aberdeen (0) 1 *(Rooney 53)*

Dumbarton (0) 0   10,600

Aberdeen: (4411) Langfield; Logan, Anderson, Reynolds, Considine; Jack, Flood, Robson (Low 87), Hayes; Smith (McGinn 70); Rooney (Vernon 83).
Dumbarton: (442) Grindlay; McGinn, Graham, Miller, Linton (Smith 63); Gilhaney, Agnew (Prunty 70), Kane, Kirkpatrick; Nish (Fleming 60), Megginson.
Referee: Kevin Clancy.

Raith R (1) 1 *(Cardle 21)*

St Johnstone (1) 3 *(McDonald 4, Hasselbaink 49, Anderson 79)*   3767

Raith R: (4411) Robinson; Thomson, Watson, Hill, Booth; Anderson, Fox, Moon, Cardle; Callachan (Vaughan 75); Smith (Spence 83).
St Johnstone: (442) Mannus; Miller, Mackay, Anderson, Easton; Croft (Millar 86), Dunne, McDonald, Hasselbaink (Wotherspoon 76); MacLean, May (O'Halloran 82).
Referee: Craig Thomson.

Sunday, 9 March 2014

Inverness CT (0) 0

Dundee U (3) 5 *(Ciftci 16, 28, Gunning 36 (pen), Mackay-Steven 49, Armstrong 57)* 3164

Inverness CT: (4411) Brill; Raven, Warren, Meekings, Shinnie; Watkins■, Vincent, Tansey■, Doran (Williams 60); Foran (Polworth 60); McKay (Christie 87).
Dundee U: (4231) Cierzniak; Watson, Gunning, Dillon, Robertson; Paton, Rankin (Gomis 59); Armstrong, Dow (El Alagui 54), Mackay-Steven; Ciftci (Graham 60).
Referee: William Collum.

Rangers (0) 1 *(Mohsni 78)*

Albion R (1) 1 *(Donnelly C 14)*   23,976

Rangers: (442) Bell; Foster, McCulloch, Mohsni, Wallace; Aird, Black, Law, Templeton; Shiels (Little 63), Daly (Faure 75).
Albion R: (4141) Parry; Reid, Dunlop M, Dunlop R, Russell (Flood 75); Donnelly C; Phillips, Chaplain, Cusack (Kennedy 69), McGuigan; Dallas (Crawford 21).
Referee: John Beaton.

QUARTER-FINAL REPLAY

Monday, 17 March 2014

Albion R (0) 0

Rangers (1) 2 *(Aird 18, Daly 57)*   5354

Albion R: (451) Parry; Reid, Dunlop R, Dunlop M, Russell; McGuigan, Chaplain, Donnelly C, Cusack (Flood 78), Phillips (Tiffney 81); Crawford (Walker 60).
Rangers: (4141) Bell; Foster, McCulloch, Mohsni, Wallace; Hutton (Faure 81); Gallagher C (Clark 71), Black, Law, Aird; Daly.
Referee: John Beaton.

SEMI-FINALS (at Ibrox)

Saturday, 12 April 2014

Rangers (1) 1 *(Smith 42)*

Dundee U (2) 3 *(Armstrong 23, Mackay-Steven 36, Ciftci 83)* 41,059

Rangers: (4231) Simonsen; Foster, McCulloch, Mohsni, Smith; Peralta, Black; Aird (Clark 63), Shiels, Law; Daly.
Dundee U: (4231) Cierzniak; Wilson (Watson 61), Souttar, Gunning, Robertson (Gomis 85); Paton, Rankin; Gauld (Dow 67), Armstrong, Mackay-Steven; Ciftci.
Referee: Bobby Madden.

Sunday, 13 April 2014

St Johnstone (0) 2 *(May 61, 84)*

Aberdeen (1) 1 *(McGinn 15)* 19,057

St Johnstone: (442) Mannus; Mackay, Anderson, Wright, Easton; Wotherspoon, Millar, Dunne, O'Halloran (Cregg 89); MacLean, May.
Aberdeen: (442) Langfield; Logan, Anderson, Considine (Vernon 90), Reynolds; Jack, Flood, Robson, Pawlett; McGinn, Rooney.
Referee: William Collum.

WILLIAM HILL SCOTTISH CUP FINAL

Saturday, 17 May 2014

(at Celtic Park, attendance 47,345)

St Johnstone (1) 2   Dundee U (0) 0

St Johnstone: (442) Mannus; Mackay, Wright, Anderson, Easton; Millar, Wotherspoon (McDonald 85), Dunne, O'Halloran (Croft 73); MacLean, May.
Scorers: Anderson 45, MacLean 84.

Dundee U: (4231) Cierzniak; Watson, Dillon, Gunning, Robertson; Paton (Graham 77), Rankin; Dow, Armstrong, Mackay-Steven (Gauld 64); Clifci.
Referee: Craig Thomson.

Steve May of St Johnstone and Andrew Robertson of Dundee United in action during the William Hill Scottish FA Cup final at Celtic Park. The Perth club won its first ever Scottish FA Cup by defeating Tayside rivals United 2-0.
(Action Images/Ed Sykes)

WELSH FOOTBALL 2013–14

CORBETT SPORTS WELSH PREMIER LEAGUE 2013–14

				Total				Home					Away					
		P	W	D	L	F	A	W	D	L	F	A	W	D	L	F	A	GD	Pts
1	The New Saints	32	22	7	3	86	20	13	3	0	53	7	9	4	3	33	13	66	73
2	Airbus UK Broughton*	32	17	9	6	56	34	9	3	4	29	14	8	6	2	27	20	22	59
3	Carmarthen T	32	14	6	12	54	51	8	3	5	28	20	6	3	7	26	31	3	48
4	Bangor C	32	14	6	12	47	50	8	1	7	27	29	6	5	5	20	21	–3	48
5	Newtown	32	12	6	14	46	58	7	4	5	23	23	5	2	9	23	35	–12	42
6	Rhyl	32	11	5	16	43	49	7	3	6	25	24	4	2	10	18	25	–6	38
7	Aberystwyth T	32	15	9	8	72	48	9	5	2	46	25	6	4	6	26	23	24	51
8	Bala T	32	13	6	13	61	45	7	3	6	29	18	6	3	7	32	27	16	45
9	Port Talbot T	32	10	8	14	45	53	5	5	6	20	17	5	3	8	25	36	–8	38
10	Gap Connah's Quay	32	10	8	14	47	65	5	4	7	19	28	5	4	7	28	37	–18	38
11	Prestatyn T	32	9	8	15	42	47	4	6	6	25	21	5	2	9	17	26	–5	35
12	Afan Lido	32	3	6	23	21	100	2	2	12	14	56	1	4	11	7	44	–79	15

Airbus UK Broughton deducted 1 point. †Aberystwyth T deducted 3 points. Top 6 teams split after 22 games.

PREVIOUS WELSH LEAGUE WINNERS

1993	Cwmbran Town	1999	Barry Town	2005	TNS	2011	Bangor C
1994	Bangor City	2000	TNS	2006	TNS	2012	The New Saints
1995	Bangor City	2001	Barry Town	2007	TNS	2013	The New Saints
1996	Barry Town	2002	Barry Town	2008	Llanelli	2014	The New Saints
1997	Barry Town	2003	Barry Town	2009	Rhyl		
1998	Barry Town	2004	Rhyl	2010	The New Saints		

NATHANIEL CARS WELSH LEAGUE 2013–14

				Total				Home					Away					
		P	W	D	L	F	A	W	D	L	F	A	W	D	L	F	A	GD	Pts
1	Monmouth T	30	21	2	7	78	33	12	2	1	44	13	9	0	6	34	20	45	65
2	Taff's Well	30	19	6	5	63	30	10	3	2	32	11	9	3	3	31	19	33	63
3	Penybont*	30	17	4	9	77	44	10	2	3	45	23	7	2	6	32	21	33	55
4	Haverfordwest Co	30	16	7	7	59	37	9	2	4	32	19	7	5	3	27	18	22	55
5	Goytre	30	15	9	6	49	43	7	5	3	29	23	8	4	3	20	20	6	54
6	Cambrian & Clydach Vale	30	15	5	10	60	44	9	1	5	30	19	6	4	5	30	25	16	50
7	Caerau Ely	30	12	10	8	52	51	6	6	3	26	21	6	4	5	26	30	1	46
8	Aberdare T	30	13	5	12	49	48	8	2	5	26	20	5	3	7	23	28	1	44
9	Goytre U	30	11	6	13	56	43	6	4	5	33	20	5	2	8	23	23	13	39
10	AFC Porth	30	10	9	11	48	49	3	7	5	20	20	7	2	6	28	29	–1	39
11	Ton Pentre	30	9	11	10	36	47	5	4	6	13	19	4	7	4	23	28	–11	38
12	Pontardawe T	30	9	6	15	34	60	6	3	6	21	31	3	3	9	13	29	–26	33
13	Cwmbran Celtic	30	7	5	18	40	58	6	1	8	24	27	1	4	10	16	31	–18	26
14	Tata Steel	30	6	7	17	29	65	3	4	8	16	28	3	3	9	13	37	–36	25
15	Aberbargoed Buds	30	4	8	18	35	65	2	5	8	23	30	2	3	10	12	35	–30	20
16	West End	30	5	2	23	36	84	4	0	11	21	42	1	2	12	15	42	–48	17

Bridgend T and Bryntirion Ath merged to form Penybont.

HUWS GRAY CYMRU ALLIANCE LEAGUE 2013–14

				Total				Home					Away					
		P	W	D	L	F	A	W	D	L	F	A	W	D	L	F	A	GD	Pts
1	Cefn Druids	30	22	7	1	90	20	10	4	1	49	8	12	3	0	41	12	70	73
2	Conwy Bor	30	19	6	5	66	35	11	1	3	34	16	8	5	2	32	19	31	63
3	Caernarfon T	30	18	8	4	79	33	10	3	2	47	19	8	5	2	32	14	46	62
4	Caersws	30	17	10	3	56	32	7	7	1	24	15	10	3	2	32	17	24	61
5	Llandudno	30	12	9	9	55	42	7	4	4	34	16	5	5	5	21	26	13	45
6	Guilsfield	30	10	12	8	44	41	4	7	4	23	24	6	5	4	21	17	3	42
7	Porthmadog	30	12	6	12	55	53	7	2	6	30	25	5	4	6	25	28	2	42
8	Flint Town U	30	12	5	13	46	53	8	3	4	26	16	4	2	9	20	37	–7	41
9	Holyhead Hotspur	30	9	10	11	53	57	4	7	4	34	32	5	3	7	19	25	–4	37
10	Penycae	30	10	4	16	47	64	6	1	8	25	28	4	3	8	22	36	–17	34
11	Rhayader T	30	8	9	13	41	60	5	5	5	21	27	3	4	8	20	33	–19	33
12	Buckley T	30	6	13	11	41	54	2	8	5	21	28	4	5	6	20	26	–13	31
13	Llanidloes T	30	8	6	16	44	63	6	3	6	29	27	2	3	10	15	36	–19	30
14	Rhydymwyn	30	8	4	18	32	64	4	1	10	8	28	4	3	8	24	36	–32	28
15	Penrhyncoch	30	5	8	17	35	58	3	3	9	19	28	2	5	8	16	30	–23	23
16	Llanrhaeadr	30	5	1	24	32	87	1	0	14	13	42	4	1	10	19	45	–55	13

WELSH CUP 2013–14

After extra time.

FIRST QUALIFYING ROUND – CENTRAL

Llandrindod Wells v Newbridge on Wye	5-0
Llanfair U v Kerry	9-1
Machynlleth v Hay St Mary	6-3
Presteigne St Andrews v Llanfyllin T	7-0

FIRST QUALIFYING ROUND – NORTH

Brickfield Rangers v New Brighton Villa	
New Brighton Villa withdrew.	
FC Nomads of Connah's Quay v Halkyn U	3-2
Greenfield v Connah's Quay T	
Connah's Quay T withdrew.	
Kinmel Bay Sports v St Asaph C	3-4
Lex XI v Castell Alun Colts	2-2
Lex XI won 4-2 on penalties.	
Llandudno Junction v Gaerwen	7-2
Llandyrnog U v Llanuwchllyn	1-3
Llangefni T v Blaenau Amateur	1-2
Llannerch ym Medd v Amlwch T	4-1
Llanystumdwy v Penmaenmawr Phoenix	3-4
Meliden v Dyffryn Nantlle Vale	0-2
Nefyn U v Trearddur Bay U	4-3
Penrhyndeudraeth v Llanfairpwll	3-1
Rhos Aelwyd v Llay Miners Welfare	A-A
Match abandoned after 49 minutes, with score 9-1.	
Both teams removed from competition.	
Venture Community v Caerwys	2-5

FIRST QUALIFYING ROUND – SOUTH

Aber Valley YMCA v Cardiff Grange Harlequins	0-5
AFC Llwydcoed v Carnetown	10-0
AFC Rumney Juniors v Tonyrefail Welfare	3-2
Barry Town U v Treforest	8-0
Bettws v Rhoose	0-4
Blaenrhondda v Treharris Athletic Western	0-5
Butetown v Aberfan	3-1
Cardiff Corinthians v Brecon Corinthians	1-3
Chepstow T v Clwb Cymric	3-0
Cwmbran T v Cardiff Metropolitan	2-3
Dafen Welfare v Sully Sports	1-8
Garw v Kenfig Hill	7-1
Llanharry v Canton Rangers	2-2*
Canton Rangers won 4-2 on penalties.	
Llantwit Fardre v Bridgend Street	0-1
Llantwit Major v Penrhiwfer	3-1
Lliswerry v Fairfield U	2-3
Merthyr Saints v Cwmaman Institute	8-1
Nelson Cavaliers v Cardiff Hibernian	1-2
Newcastle Emlyn v Llanelli T	4-1
Penygraig v Pontyclun	2-1
Pontllotyn v Newport Civil Service	1-5
Risca U v Llanwern	1-4
Splott Alb v RTB Ebbw Vale Ladies	3-0*
Tredegar Ath v Cefn Fforest	1-3
Tredegar T v Trelewis Welfare	0-1
Trefelin v Porthcawl Town Ath	3-1
Trethomas Bluebirds v Graig y Rhacca	6-0
Ynysddu Welfare v Abertillery Bluebirds	3-2
Ely Rangers v Sporting Marvels	8-0
Ely Valley v Pontypridd T	0-6

SECOND QUALIFYING ROUND – CENTRAL

Aberaeron v Bow Street	3-0
Builth Wells v Llanfair U	3-7
Carno v Barmouth & Dyffryn U	1-2
Llandrindod Wells v Waterloo R	5-3
Llansantffraid Village v Berriew	1-5
Machynlleth v Montgomery T	3-0
Presteigne St Andrews v Four Crosses	3-2
Welshpool T v Tywyn Bryncrug	
Welshpool T unable to field a team. Tywyn Bryncrug	
advance.	

SECOND QUALIFYING ROUND – NORTH

Brickfield Rangers v Llandudno Junction	3-1
Brymbo v Chirk AAA	0-4
Corwen v Caerwys	0-1
FC Nomads of Connah's Quay v	
Penmaenmawr Phoenix	3-0
Greenfield v Mold Alexandra	1-3

Gresford Ath v Coedpoeth U	2-2*
Coedpoeth U won 4-2 on penalties.	
Holywell T v Llannerch ym Medd	8-1
Lex XI v Denbigh T	0-1
Llanberis v Hawarden Rangers	3-2
Llanllyfni v Llangollen T	0-6
Llanrug U v St Asaph C	5-0
Llanrwst U v Llanuwchllyn	4-2
Nefyn U v Blaenau Amateur	7-3
Overton Recreational v Gwalchmai	1-3
Penyffordd v Glan Conwy	3-4
Pwllheli v Dyffryn Nantlle Vale	3-1
Ruthin T v Glantraeth	1-3
Saltney T v Penrhyndeudraeth	1-3
Bye: Bodedern Ath.	

SECOND QUALIFYING ROUND – SOUTH

AFC Llwydcoed v Penrhiwceiber Rangers	2-1
AFC Rumney Juniors v Barry Town U	0-3
Brecon Corinthians v Cardiff Metropolitan	1-4
Butetown v Cardiff Grange Harlequins	2-1
Caerau v Trefelin	0-11
Caerleon v Briton Ferry Llansawel	1-5
Caldicot T v Newport YMCA	5-0
Canton Rangers v Cardiff Hibernian	0-6
Croesyceiliog v Splott Alb	0-1
Fairfield U v Cefn Fforest	8-4
Garden Village v Ammanford	4-3*
Llantwit Major v Trelewis Welfare	6-2
Llanwern v Treowen Stars	2-3
Newcastle Emlyn v Ely Rangers	1-0
Newport Civil Service v Garw	3-2
Penygraig v Sully Sports	2-4
Pontypridd T v Bridgend Street	1-1*
Bridgend Street won 4-1 on penalties.	
Rhoose v Merthyr Saints	5-1
Treharris Athletic Western v Dinas Powys	2-1
Undy Ath v Trethomas Bluebirds	2-1
Ynysddu Welfare v Chepstow T	0-3

FIRST ROUND – NORTH

Bodedern Ath v Glantraeth	3-2*
Caernarfon T v Llanrug U	4-1
Caersws v Denbigh T	2-0
Coedpoeth U v Barmouth & Dyffryn U	2-6
FC Nomads of Connah's Quay v Pwllheli	3-0
Flint Town U v Llanberis	3-1
Glan Conwy v Llanidloes T	1-3
Guilsfield Ath v Machynlleth	6-1*
Holyhead Hotspur v Cefn Druids	0-3
Holywell T v Penrhyncoch	3-0
Llandudno v Llanrhaeadr	5-1
Llanfair U v Gwalchmai	3-2
Llangollen T v Buckley T	0-2
Llanrwst U v Conwy Bor	3-4
Nefyn U v Penrhyndeudraeth	3-4
Penycae v Brickfield Rangers	7-4*
Porthmadog v Mold Alexandra	1-0
Rhayader T v Chirk AAA	1-0
Rhydymwyn v Caerwys	2-1
Tywyn Bryncrug v Berriew	2-2*
Tywyn Bryncrug won 5-4 on penalties.	

FIRST ROUND – SOUTH

AFC Porth v Monmouth T	1-2
Barry Town U v Taff's Well	1-0
Bridgend Street v Tata Steel	1-3
Briton Ferry Llansawel v Aberbargoed Buds	3-1*
Caerau Ely v Cardiff Hibernian	4-0
Caldicot T v Splott Alb	2-1
Cambrian & Clydach Vale v Butetown	4-0
Cardiff Metropolitan v Aberaeron	4-1
Cwmbran Celtic v Penybont	0-1
Garden Village v Rhoose	1-2
Goytre (Gwent) v Pontardawe T	1-2
Goytre U v Trefelin	3-1
Llandrindod Wells v Newport Civil Service	3-0
Llantwit Major v Treharris Athletic Western	2-3
Newcastle Emlyn v Chepstow T	1-2*
Sully Sports v AFC Llwydcoed	3-1
Ton Pentre v Fairfield U	3-0

Treowen Stars v Aberdare T	2-4
Undy Ath v Presteigne St Andrews	5-2
West End v Haverfordwest Co	2-3

SECOND ROUND – NORTH

Barmouth & Dyffryn U v Cefn Druids	1-3
Bodedern Ath v Tywyn Bryncrug	5-1
Buckley T v Rhayader T	1-0
Conwy Bor v Flint Town U	3-2
Holywell T v Penycae	3-0
Llanfair U v Guilsfield Ath	2-1
Llanidloes T v Llandudno	2-0
Nefyn U v Caersws	1-3*
Rhydymwyn v FC Nomads of Connah's Quay	4-1
Caernarfon T v Porthmadog	1-2

SECOND ROUND – SOUTH

Barry Town U v Undy Ath	4-3*
Caldicot T v Penybont	3-0

Caldicot disqualified for fielding an ineligible player. Penybont advance.

Cardiff Metropolitan v Haverfordwest Co	6-1
Llandrindod Wells v Caerau Ely	3-3*

Llandrindod Wells won 4-3 on penalties.

Briton Ferry Llansawel v Aberdare T	2-3
Cambrian & Clydach Vale v Pontardawe T	2-0
Goytre U v Chepstow T	0-1
Ton Pentre v Sully Sports	0-1
Treharris Athletic Western v Monmouth T	1-7
Rhoose v Tata Steel	1-0

THIRD ROUND

Aberdare T v Prestatyn T	4-2
Afan Lido v Rhydymwyn	2-0
Bodedern Ath v Buckley T	2-0*
Caersws v Gap Connah's Quay	2-1*
Cambrian & Clydach Vale v Chepstow T	3-1
Carmarthen T v Port Talbot T	2-1
Cefn Druids v Barry Town U	5-2
Llandrindod Wells v Holywell T	1-3
Llanfair U v Aberystwyth T	2-4

Monmouth T v Llanidloes T	2-1
Newtown v Cardiff Metropolitan	2-1
Penybont v Airbus UK Broughton	0-2
Porthmadog v Sully Sports	2-1
Rhoose v Bala T	1-6
Rhyl v Bangor C	1-2
Conwy Bor v The New Saints	1-2*

FOURTH ROUND

Newtown v Holywell T	2-3
Carmarthen T v The New Saints	0-2
Monmouth T v Porthmadog	2-3*
Bala T v Cefn Druids	5-0
Airbus UK Broughton v Bangor C	2-0
Aberdare T v Bodedern Ath	4-1
Aberystwyth T v Afan Lido	5-1
Caersws v Cambrian & Clydach Vale	4-3*

QUARTER-FINALS

Aberdare T v Bala T	1-2
Aberystwyth T v Caersws	2-1
Holywell T v Porthmadog	2-1
The New Saints v Airbus UK Broughton	2-0

SEMI-FINALS

Aberystwyth T v Holywell T	3-1
The New Saints v Bala T	2-1

THE FAW WELSH CUP FINAL
Wrexham, Saturday 3 May 2014

The New Saints (0) 3 *(Draper 74 (pen), 79, Wilde 87)*

Aberystwyth T (2) 2 *(Venables 10, 12 (pen))* 1273

The New Saints: Harrison; Edwards, Marriott, Baker, Jones (Mullan 46), Edwards, Seargeant (Spender 68), Finley, Wilde, Williams (Draper 60), Fraughan.
Aberystwyth T: Lewis; Corbisiero, Hoy, Jones S, Venables, Jones M, Kellaway, Davies, Sherbon, Williams (Nalborski 82), Thomas.
Referee: Brian James.

PREVIOUS WELSH CUP WINNERS

1878	Wrexham	1910	Wrexham	1952	Rhyl	1984	Shrewsbury Town
1879	Newtown White Star	1911	Wrexham	1953	Rhyl	1985	Shrewsbury Town
1880	Druids	1912	Cardiff City	1954	Flint Town United	1986	Wrexham
1881	Druids	1913	Swansea Town	1955	Barry Town	1987	Merthyr Tydfil
1882	Druids	1914	Wrexham	1956	Cardiff City	1988	Cardiff City
1883	Wrexham	1915	Wrexham	1957	Wrexham	1989	Swansea City
1884	Oswestry White Stars	1920	Cardiff City	1958	Wrexham	1990	Hereford United
1885	Druids	1921	Wrexham	1959	Cardiff City	1991	Swansea City
1886	Druids	1922	Cardiff City	1960	Wrexham	1992	Cardiff City
1887	Chirk	1923	Cardiff City	1961	Swansea Town	1993	Cardiff City
1888	Chirk	1924	Wrexham	1962	Bangor City	1994	Barry Town
1889	Bangor	1925	Wrexham	1963	Borough United	1995	Wrexham
1890	Chirk	1926	Ebbw Vale	1964	Cardiff City	1996	TNS
1891	Shrewsbury Town	1927	Cardiff City	1965	Cardiff City	1997	Barry Town
1892	Chirk	1928	Cardiff City	1966	Swansea Town	1998	Bangor City
1893	Wrexham	1929	Connah's Quay	1967	Cardiff City	1999	Inter Cable-Tel
1894	Chirk	1930	Cardiff City	1968	Cardiff City	2000	Bangor City
1895	Newtown	1931	Wrexham	1969	Cardiff City	2001	Barry Town
1896	Bangor	1932	Swansea Town	1970	Cardiff City	2002	Barry Town
1897	Wrexham	1933	Chester	1971	Cardiff City	2003	Barry Town
1898	Druids	1934	Bristol City	1972	Wrexham	2004	Rhyl
1899	Druids	1935	Tranmere Rovers	1973	Cardiff City	2005	TNS
1900	Aberystwyth Town	1936	Crewe Alexandra	1974	Cardiff City	2006	Rhyl
1901	Oswestry United	1937	Crewe Alexandra	1975	Wrexham	2007	Carmarthen Town
1902	Wellington Town	1938	Shrewsbury Town	1976	Cardiff City	2008	Bangor City
1903	Wrexham	1939	South Liverpool	1977	Shrewsbury Town	2009	Bangor City
1904	Druids	1940	Wellington Town	1978	Wrexham	2010	Bangor City
1905	Wrexham	1947	Chester	1979	Shrewsbury Town	2011	Llanelli
1906	Wellington Town	1948	Lovell's Athletic	1980	Newport County	2012	The New Saints
1907	Oswestry United	1949	Merthyr Tydfil	1981	Swansea City	2013	Prestatyn Town
1908	Chester	1950	Swansea Town	1982	Swansea City	2014	The New Saints
1909	Wrexham	1951	Merthyr Tydfil	1983	Swansea City		

WELSH THEWORD LEAGUE CUP 2013–14

FIRST ROUND

Aberystwyth T v Cambrian & Clydach Vale	2-3
Afan Lido v Taffs Well	4-3
Bala T v Bangor C	3-1
Buckley T v Conwy Borough	1-2
Gap Connah's Quay v Prestatyn T	2-1
Haverfordwest County v Aberdare T	0-3
Newtown AFC v Port Talbot T	1-2
Rhyl v Cefn Druids	2-0

SECOND ROUND

Aberdare T v Port Talbot T	0-2
Afan Lido v Cambrian & Clydach Vale	1-2
Conwy Borough v Bala T	2-4
Rhyl v Gap Connah's Quay	2-0

THIRD ROUND

Caersws FC v Carmarthen T	0-5
Cambrian & Clydach Vale v Port Talbot T	2-1
Rhyl v Bala T	2-3
Airbus UK Broughton v The New Saints	2-1

SEMI-FINALS

Carmarthen T v Cambrian & Clydach Vale	3-2
Bala T v Airbus UK Broughton	2-1

WELSH THEWORD CUP FINAL 2013–14

Aberystwyth, 11 January 2014

Carmarthen T (0) 0

Bala T (0) 0

Carmarthen T: Cann; Thomas Corey, Thomas Chris, Evans, Hanford, Collins, Fowler, Bowen, Thomas L (Reffel 69), Doidge, Bassett (Jenkins 78).
Bala T: Morris; Jones S, Valentine, Morley, Davies, Murtagh, Connolly, Jones M, Brown, Sheridan, Smith (Codling 118).
aet; Carmarthen T won 3-1 on penalties.
Referee: Huw Jones.

THE FAW TROPHY 2013–14

THIRD ROUND – NORTH

FC Nomads of Connah's Quay v Dyffryn Banw	5-0
Barmouth & Dyffryn U v Glantraeth	2-1
Blaenau Amateur v St Asaph C	0-2
Brickfield Rangers v Overton Recreational	3-0
Castell Alun Colts v Llandudno Junction	1-3
Chirk AAA v Four Crosses	4-1
Kinmel Bay Sports v Denbigh T	3-1
Llanrug U v Bodedern Ath	4-1
Llanystumdwy v Holywell T	0-6
Mold Alexandra v Llandyrnog U	2-1
Nefyn U v Penrhyndeudraeth	1-3
Pwllheli v Saltney T	3-3*
Saltney T won 5-3 on penalties.	
Ruthin T v Llanrwst U	1-1*
Ruthin T won 3-2 on penalties.	
Trearddur Bay U v Corwen	2-3
Tywyn Bryncrug v Rhos Aelwyd	3-2
Venture Community v Berriew	0-9
Welshpool T v Llangollen T	1-2

THIRD ROUND – SOUTH

Treowen Stars v Cwm Welfare	3-2
Fairfield U v Ton & Gelli	1-2
Baglan Dragons v Race	4-0
Blaenavon Blues v Cwmbach Royal Stars	1-1*
Blaenavon Blues won 3-2 on penalties.	
Cwmmaman U v Clydach Wasps	5-2
Cwmfelin Press v Bridgend Street	1-0
Dafen Welfare v Penlan	2-2*
Penlan won 7-6 on penalties.	
Kilvey Fords v Trefelin	1-8
Llanelli T v Bonymaen Colts	6-1
Machynlleth v Creigiau	3-0
Maltsters Sports v Cardiff Metropolitan	0-4
Penrhiwceiber Constitutional Ath v Abercarn U	2-3
Rhoose v Tredegar Ath	0-1
Sully Sports v Lliswerry	2-1
Garden Village v Ystradgynlais	4-1

FOURTH ROUND – NORTH

Berriew v Ruthin T	1-3
Tywyn Bryncrug v St Asaph C	1-2
Brickfield Rangers v Chirk AAA	0-4
FC Nomads of Connah's Quay v Barmouth & Dyffryn U	4-3
Llangollen T v Corwen	1-0
Llanrug U v Kinmel Bay Sports	2-1
Machynlleth v Llandudno Junction	3-2
Penrhyndeudraeth v Holywell T	2-0
Saltney T v Mold Alexandra	1-5

FOURTH ROUND – SOUTH

Cardiff Metropolitan v Llanelli T	4-2
Cwmamman U v Garden Village	1-7
Penlan v Abercarn U	2-0
Ton & Gelli v Baglan Dragons	4-1
Tredegar Ath v Blaenavon Blues	0-2
Trefelin v Cwmfelin Press	5-2
Treowen Stars v Sully Sports	5-4*

FIFTH ROUND

Llanrug U v Ruthin T	3-1
Ton & Gelli v Machynlleth	2-1
Penlan v Garden Village	2-1
FC Nomads of Connah's Quay v Llangollen T	3-0
Penrhyndeudraeth v Mold Alexandra	3-3*
Penrhyndeudraeth won 4-2 on penalties.	
St Asaph C v Chirk AAA	0-1
Trefelin v Blaenavon Blues	2-0
Treowen Stars v Cardiff Metropolitan	0-8

QUARTER-FINALS

Llanrug U v FC Nomads of Connah's Quay	3-2
Trefelin v Penrhyndeudraeth	1-2
Chirk AAA v Penlan	9-0
Ton & Gelli v Cardiff Metropolitan	3-2

SEMI-FINALS

Chirk AAA v Ton & Gelli	6-1
Llanrug U v Penrhyndeudraeth	2-0

THE FAW TROPHY FINAL 2013–14

Rhyl, 12 April 2014

Chirk AAA (0) 2 *(Phil Pearce 60, Jamie Foulkes 90)*

Llanrug U (0) 3 *(David Noel Williams 56, Kevin Lloyd 58, 81)*

Chirk AAA: Roberts; Foulkes, Jones, Williams J, Pearce, Morris A (Morris S 27), Williams N, Bennion, Blackwell (Jones B 72), Jones N (Jones K,72'), Jones A.
Llanrug U: Roberts; Phillips D (Garlick 85), Phillips M, Jones T, Williams E, Owen, Roberts (Jones JP 77), Williams DN, Pritchard (Pyrs 34), Lloyd, Griffiths.
Referee: Aled Jones (Lampeter).

NORTHERN IRISH FOOTBALL 2013–14

NORTHERN IRISH DANSKE BANK PREMIER LEAGUE 2013–14

		Total					Home					Away						
		P	W	D	L	F	A	W	D	L	F	A	W	D	L	F	A	GD	Pts
1	Cliftonville	38	26	7	5	88	39	12	2	4	40	16	14	5	1	48	23	49	85
2	Linfield	38	24	7	7	81	46	11	5	3	45	23	13	2	4	36	23	35	79
3	Crusaders	38	18	12	8	67	42	11	5	3	43	21	7	7	5	24	21	25	66
4	Portadown	38	18	8	12	77	53	12	3	5	43	20	6	5	7	34	33	24	62
5	Glentoran	38	16	11	11	54	42	5	8	6	23	20	11	3	5	31	22	12	59
6	Glenavon	38	15	6	17	75	79	8	3	8	40	41	7	3	9	35	38	-4	51
7	Ballymena U	38	13	8	17	48	59	8	3	8	32	35	5	5	9	16	24	-11	47
8	Dungannon Swifts	38	12	8	18	49	66	5	3	10	18	30	7	5	8	31	36	-17	44
9	Coleraine	38	10	12	16	51	61	6	6	7	31	31	4	6	9	20	30	-10	42
10	Ballinamallard U	38	10	9	19	35	70	7	4	8	21	26	3	5	11	14	44	-35	39
11	Warrenpoint T	38	10	6	22	43	72	4	4	12	20	34	6	2	10	23	38	-29	36
12	Ards	38	6	6	26	44	83	5	4	10	26	33	1	2	16	18	50	-39	24

Top 6 split after 33 games.
No promotion/relegation play-off as Bangor, runners-up in the Belfast Telegraph Championship, would not accept a place in the Premier League for the 2014–15 season.

LEADING GOALSCORERS (League goals only)

Joe Gormley	Cliftonville	27 (1 pen)
Darren Murray	Portadown	23 (4 pens)
Andrew Waterworth	Linfield	22 (1 pen)
Liam Boyce	Cliftonville	21 (2 pens)
Gary Twigg	Portadown	19
Darren Boyce	Ballymena U	16 (4 pens)
Jordan Owens	Crusaders	16
Guy Bates	Glenavon	14 (1 pen)
Paul Heatley	Crusaders	14
Daniel Hughes	Warrenpoint T	12
Gary McCutcheon	Crusaders	10
William Faulkner	Ards	10
Eoin Bradley	Coleraine	9 (2 pens)
Gary Liggett	Dungannon Swifts	9
Stephen Hughes	Warrenpoint T	9 (3 pens)

IRISH LEAGUE CHAMPIONSHIP WINNERS

1891	Linfield	1913	Glentoran	1940	Belfast Celtic	1970	Glentoran	1993	Linfield
1892	Linfield	1914	Linfield	1948	Belfast Celtic	1971	Linfield	1994	Linfield
1893	Linfield	1915	Belfast Celtic	1949	Linfield	1972	Glentoran	1995	Crusaders
1894	Glentoran	1920	Belfast Celtic	1950	Linfield	1973	Crusaders	1996	Portadown
1895	Linfield	1921	Glentoran	1951	Glentoran	1974	Coleraine	1997	Crusaders
1896	Distillery	1922	Linfield	1952	Glenavon	1975	Linfield	1998	Cliftonville
1897	Glentoran	1923	Linfield	1953	Glentoran	1976	Crusaders	1999	Glentoran
1898	Linfield	1924	Queen's Island	1954	Linfield	1977	Glentoran	2000	Linfield
1899	Distillery	1925	Glentoran	1955	Linfield	1978	Linfield	2001	Linfield
1900	Belfast Celtic	1926	Belfast Celtic	1956	Linfield	1979	Linfield	2002	Portadown
1901	Distillery	1927	Belfast Celtic	1957	Glentoran	1980	Linfield	2003	Glentoran
1902	Linfield	1928	Belfast Celtic	1958	Ards	1981	Glentoran	2004	Linfield
1903	Distillery	1929	Belfast Celtic	1959	Linfield	1982	Linfield	2005	Glentoran
1904	Linfield	1930	Linfield	1960	Glenavon	1983	Linfield	2006	Linfield
1905	Glentoran	1931	Glentoran	1961	Linfield	1984	Linfield	2007	Linfield
1906	Cliftonville	1932	Linfield	1962	Linfield	1985	Linfield	2008	Linfield
	Distillery	1933	Belfast Celtic	1963	Distillery	1986	Linfield	2009	Glentoran
1907	Linfield	1934	Linfield	1964	Glentoran	1987	Linfield	2010	Linfield
1908	Linfield	1935	Linfield	1965	Derry City	1988	Glentoran	2011	Linfield
1909	Linfield	1936	Belfast Celtic	1966	Linfield	1989	Linfield	2012	Linfield
1910	Cliftonville	1937	Belfast Celtic	1967	Glentoran	1990	Portadown	2013	Cliftonville
1911	Linfield	1938	Belfast Celtic	1968	Glentoran	1991	Portadown	2014	Cliftonville
1912	Glentoran	1939	Belfast Celtic	1969	Linfield	1992	Glentoran		

BELFAST TELEGRAPH CHAMPIONSHIP ONE 2013–14

				Total					Home					Away						
		P	W	D	L	F	A	W	D	L	F	A	W	D	L	F	A	GD	Pts
1	Institute	26	15	9	2	72	35	10	3	0	42	13	5	6	2	30	22	37	54
2	Bangor	26	16	5	5	65	39	10	1	2	36	14	6	4	3	29	25	26	53
3	Knockbreda	26	14	4	8	57	36	9	2	2	35	15	5	2	6	22	21	21	46
4	Dundela	26	14	4	8	65	47	7	3	3	26	14	7	1	5	39	33	18	46
5	Carrick Rangers	26	14	4	8	52	34	7	1	5	26	19	7	3	3	26	15	18	46
6	H&W Welders	26	11	8	7	46	34	4	4	5	22	20	7	4	2	24	14	12	41
7	Ballyclare Comrades	26	10	4	12	53	50	6	2	5	27	21	4	2	7	26	29	3	34
8	Loughgall	26	9	6	11	48	56	5	4	4	31	28	4	2	7	17	28	–8	33
9	Larne	26	9	5	12	32	47	5	2	6	20	26	4	3	6	12	21	–15	32
10	Lisburn Distillery	26	8	7	11	43	49	6	2	5	21	20	2	5	6	22	29	–6	31
11	Donegal Celtic	26	8	5	13	41	55	5	3	5	22	28	3	2	8	19	27	–14	29
12	Dergview	26	6	8	12	30	46	3	6	4	18	22	3	2	8	12	24	–16	26
13	Coagh U	26	5	6	15	38	74	2	4	7	21	35	3	2	8	17	39	–36	21
14	Limavady U	26	4	3	19	19	59	4	2	7	12	27	0	1	12	7	32	–40	15

BELFAST TELEGRAPH CHAMPIONSHIP (Previously First Division)

1996	Coleraine	2003	Dungannon Swifts	2010	Loughgall	
1997	Ballymena United	2004	Loughgall	2011	Carrick Rangers	
1998	Newry Town	2005	Armagh City	2012	Ballinamallard U	
1999	Distillery	2006	Crusaders	2013	Ards	
2000	Omagh Town	2007	Institute	2014	Institute	
2001	Ards	2008	Loughgall			
2002	Lisburn Distillery	2009	Portadown			

BELFAST TELEGRAPH CHAMPIONSHIP TWO 2013–14

				Total					Home					Away						
		P	W	D	L	F	A	W	D	L	F	A	W	D	L	F	A	GD	Pts
1	Armagh C	30	25	2	3	90	26	15	0	0	57	8	10	2	3	33	18	64	77
2	PSNI	30	20	6	4	84	28	11	2	2	46	15	9	4	2	38	13	56	66
3	Queen's University	30	19	6	5	47	32	8	5	2	24	17	11	1	3	23	15	15	63
4	Newington Youth	30	15	9	6	56	32	10	4	1	29	10	5	5	5	27	22	24	54
5	Annagh U	30	15	7	8	75	53	11	2	2	49	20	4	5	6	26	33	22	52
6	Banbridge T	30	16	2	12	60	44	10	2	3	33	18	6	0	9	27	26	16	50
7	Moyola Park	30	14	4	12	61	53	7	2	6	33	27	7	2	6	28	26	8	46
8	Portstewart	30	12	7	11	52	46	5	3	7	21	22	7	4	4	31	24	6	43
9	Ballymoney U	30	11	6	13	61	59	5	4	6	32	31	6	4	5	29	28	2	39
10	Tobermore U	30	10	4	16	47	63	5	3	7	23	24	5	1	9	24	39	–16	34
11	Glebe Rangers	30	10	3	17	48	64	5	1	9	25	35	5	2	8	23	29	–16	33
12	Lurgan Celtic	30	9	6	15	41	67	5	3	7	22	28	4	3	8	19	39	–26	33
13	Wakehurst	30	7	6	17	47	75	4	3	8	23	29	3	3	9	24	46	–28	27
14	Chimney Corner	30	7	2	21	38	75	5	1	9	19	26	2	1	12	19	49	–37	23
15	Sport & Leisure Swifts	30	5	7	18	37	70	3	4	8	24	34	2	3	10	13	36	–33	22
16	Killymoon Rangers	30	5	3	22	33	90	3	3	9	24	49	2	0	13	9	41	–57	18

IFA YOUTH LEAGUE 2013–14

SECTION A

	P	W	D	L	F	A	GD	Pts
Linfield Rangers	22	16	4	2	72	17	55	52
Crusaders Colts	22	14	5	3	53	27	26	47
Glenavon III	22	12	5	5	59	45	14	41
Cliftonville Strollers	22	10	5	7	48	37	11	35
Ballinamallard U III	22	11	0	11	49	44	5	33
Dungannon Swifts Youth	22	10	3	9	46	43	3	33
Limavady U Youth	22	9	4	9	36	44	–8	31
Ballymena U III	22	7	6	9	37	36	1	27
Coleraine Colts	22	7	3	12	38	64	–26	24
Glentoran Colts	22	6	3	13	40	55	–15	21
Newington YC U18	22	4	7	11	24	45	–21	19
Donegal Celtic Youth	22	1	5	16	28	73	–45	8

SECTION B

	P	W	D	L	F	A	GD	Pts
Institute Colts	21	17	1	3	85	27	58	52
Lisburn Distillery III	21	14	2	5	71	31	40	44
Ards Youth	21	12	2	7	59	44	15	38
Carrick Rangers Colts	21	11	2	8	46	39	7	35
Portadown III	21	8	5	8	59	59	0	29
Ballymoney U Colts	21	5	2	14	35	77	–42	17
St Oliver Plunkett	21	3	14		34	79	–45	15
Ballyclare Comrades Colts	21	4	1	16	37	70	–33	13

IFA RESERVE LEAGUE 2013–14

	P	W	D	L	F	A	GD	Pts
Cliftonville Olympic	33	22	7	4	98	35	63	73
Linfield Swifts	33	23	3	7	115	44	71	72
Crusaders Res	33	21	5	7	108	44	64	68
Coleraine Res	33	19	4	10	79	68	11	61
Ballinamallard United II	33	18	5	10	79	48	31	59
Glentoran II	33	16	4	13	79	62	17	52
Ards II	33	17	1	15	87	95	–8	52
Ballymena U Res	33	15	6	12	77	58	19	51
Glenavon Res	33	12	4	17	60	88	–28	40
Portadown Res	33	5	3	25	33	109	–76	18
Dungannon Swifts Res	33	4	4	25	40	108	–68	16
Warrenpoint T Res	33	1	4	28	29	125	–96	7

IRISH CUP 2013–14

After extra time. ■ Denotes player sent off.

FIRST ROUND

1st Bangor v Newtowne	2-3
18th Newtownabbey v Lurgan T	4-2
Ardstraw v Richhill	0-1
Bangor Amateurs v Ballynahinch U	2-3
Bangor Swifts v Groomsport	6-1
Bloomfield v Shankill U	0-1
Brantwood v Ardglass	2-3
Carniny Amateurs v Wellington Rec	2-0
Comber Rec v Kilmore Rec	1-3
Crewe U v Dollingstown	2-5
Crumlin U v Draperstown Celtic	8-1
Crumlin Star v Newcastle	3-0
Derriaghy CC v Lower Maze	6-2
Donard Hospital v UU Jordanstown	0-5
Downpatrick v Saintfield U	5-2
Dromara Village v Ballynure	2-1
Dromore Amateurs v Banbridge Rangers	0-7
Drumaness Mills v Valley Rangers	6-0
Dunmurry Rec v Newry C	0-1
Immaculata v Ballynure OB	3-1
Islandmagee v St. Mary's	3-2
Iveagh U v Mountjoy U	2-4
Killyleagh YC v Ballymacash Rangers	1-0
Lisanally Rangers v Newbuildings U	0-6
Lisburn Rangers v Dunmurry YM	3-1
Magherafelt Sky Blues v Camlough R	2-3
Moneyslane v Kilroot Rec.	6-2
Mossley v Downshire YM	1-4
Nortel v Malachians	5-3
Rathfern Rangers v Broomhill	3-0
Rathfriland Rangers v Abbey Villa	2-1
Roe R v Bryansburn Rangers	1-2
Seagoe v Tandragee R	3-0
Sirocco Works v Larne Tech. OB	3-1
St Patrick's YM v Oxford U Stars	2-2

Oxford U Stars won 5-3 on penalties.
Strabane Athletic walkover Holywood withdrawn.
Byes: Ards Rangers, Albert Foundry, Ballywalter Rec, Barn U, Dungiven, Oxford Sunnyside, Shorts.

SECOND ROUND

Albert Foundry v Shankill U	1-0

Albert Foundry ejected for fielding ineligible player.

Ardglass v Banbridge Rangers	4-3
Ballynahinch U v Sirocco Works	0-1
Ballywalter Rec v Rathfriland Rangers	2-3
Carniny Amateurs v Oxford U Stars	1-0
Crumlin Star v Dollingstown	2-1
Crumlin U v Islandmagee	4-4

Crumlin U won 3-2 on penalties.

Derriaghy CC v Ards Rangers	7-5
Downpatrick v UU Jordanstown	5-0
Downshire YM v Mountjoy U	1-0
Dromara Village v Kilmore Rec	1-4
Dungiven v Newbuildings U	0-1

Immaculate walkover Camlough R withdrawn.

Lisburn Rangers v Barn U	2-2

Lisburn Rangers won 3-2 on penalties.

Nortel v Moneyslane	2-0
Richhill v Newry C	1-3
Oxford Sunnyside v Drumaness Mills	1-5
Rathfern Rangers v Killyleagh YC	3-1
Seagoe v Bryansburn Rangers	0-2
Shorts v Bangor Swifts	0-3
Strabane Athletic v Newtowne	6-2

Bye: 18th Newtownabbey.

THIRD ROUND

Carniny Amateurs v Ardglass	3-5
Derriaghy CC v 18th Newtownabbey	3-0
Downshire YM v Shankill U	2-2

Downshire YM won 4-2 on penalties.

Kilmore Rec v Immaculata	0-0

Kilmore Rec won 4-2 on penalties.

Lisburn Rangers v Bryansburn Rangers	3-1
Newbuildings U v Crumlin Star	1-2
Newry C v Downpatrick	0-0

Newry C won 4-3 on penalties.

Nortel v Drumaness Mills	0-2
Rathfern Rangers v Sirocco Works	1-2
Rathfriland Rangers v Bangor Swifts	4-1

Strabane Athletic v Crumlin U	2-0

FOURTH ROUND

Armagh C v Loughgall	2-0
Ballyclare Comrades v Larne	4-1
Banbridge T v Rathfriland Rangers	4-2
Bangor v Knockbreda	5-2
Chimney Corner v Wakehurst	3-0
Coagh U v Carrick Rangers	0-2
Crumlin Star v Newry C	4-1
Dergview v Drumaness Mills	2-0
Downshire YM v Kilmore Rec	1-3
Glebe Rangers v Ardglass	3-2
HW Welders v Killymoon Rangers	8-1
Institute v Lisburn Distillery	1-1

Lisburn Distillery won 5-4 on penalties.

Limavady U v Derriaghy CC	2-1
Moyola Park v Annagh U	2-0
Newington YC v Ballymoney U	1-3
Portstewart v Dundela	2-5
PSNI v Tobermore U	2-1
Queen's University v Lurgan Celtic	5-0
Sport & Leisure Swifts v Sirocco Works	2-1
Strabane Athletic v Lisburn Rangers	2-0

FIFTH ROUND

Ards v Armagh C	2-2
Ballinamallard U v Strabane Athletic	0-0
Ballyclare Comrades v Kilmore Rec	3-0
Ballymoney U v Banbridge T	1-0
Bangor v Glebe Rangers	7-1
Carrick Rangers v Dundela	3-2
Cliftonville v Coleraine	2-2
Crusaders v Crumlin Star	2-1
Glenavon v Sport & Leisure Swifts	7-0
HW Welders v Ballymena U	2-2
Linfield v Dergview	5-0
Lisburn Distillery v PSNI	0-0
Moyola Park v Dungannon Swifts	1-5
Portadown v Glentoran	1-3
Queen's University v Limavady U	1-0
Warrenpoint T v Chimney Corner	2-0

FIFTH ROUND REPLAYS

Armagh C v Ards	3-1
Ballinamallard U v Strabane Athletic	1-0
Ballymena U v HW Welders	1-0
Coleraine v Cliftonville	4-3
PSNI v Lisburn Distillery	0-2

SIXTH ROUND

Armagh C v Glentoran	1-1
Ballyclare Comrades v Carrick Rangers	2-1
Ballinamallard U v Glenavon	0-3
Coleraine v Dungannon Swifts	2-3
Crusaders v Ballymoney U	4-0
Linfield v Ballymena U	1-2
Lisburn Distillery v Queen's University	0-2
Warrenpoint T v Bangor	0-0

SIXTH ROUND REPLAYS

Bangor v Warrenpoint T	1-0
Glentoran v Armagh C	2-1

QUARTER-FINALS

Ballymena U v Dungannon Swifts	4-1
Crusaders v Ballyclare Comrades	5-0
Queen's University v Bangor	3-2
Glentoran v Glenavon	1-2

SEMI-FINALS

Ballymena U v Queen's University	3-0
Glenavon v Crusaders	3-1

NORTHERN IRISH FA CUP FINAL
Windsor Park, Belfast, Saturday 3 May 2014

Ballymena U (1) 1 *(Neil 34)*
Glenavon (0) 2 *(Jenkins 70, Patton 75)*
Ballymena U: Shanahan; Ervin, McBride, Taylor, Munster, Kane■, Thompson, Jenkins, Teggart, Cushley, Boyce.
Glenavon: McGrath; Marshall, Lindsay, McKeown■, Singleton, McGrory, Martyn, McCabe, Neill, Bates, Mulvenna.
Referee: Raymond Crangle.

IRISH CUP FINALS (from 1946–47)

1946–47 Belfast Celtic 1, Glentoran 0	1982–83 Glentoran 1:2, Linfield 1:1
1947–48 Linfield 3, Coleraine 0	1983–84 Ballymena U 4, Carrick Rangers 1
1948–49 Derry City 3, Glentoran 1	1984–85 Glentoran 1:1, Linfield 1:0
1949–50 Linfield 2, Distillery 1	1985–86 Glentoran 2, Coleraine 1
1950–51 Glentoran 3, Ballymena U 1	1986–87 Glentoran 1, Larne 0
1951–52 Ards 1, Glentoran 0	1987–88 Glentoran 1, Glenavon 0
1952–53 Linfield 5, Coleraine 0	1988–89 Ballymena U 1, Larne 0
1953–54 Derry City 1, Glentoran 0	1989–90 Glentoran 3, Portadown 0
1954–55 Dundela 3, Glenavon 0	1990–91 Portadown 2, Glenavon 1
1955–56 Distillery 1, Glentoran 0	1991–92 Glenavon 2, Linfield 1
1956–57 Glenavon 2, Derry City 0	1992–93 Bangor 1:1:1, Ards 1:1:0
1957–58 Ballymena U 2, Linfield 0	1993–94 Linfield 2, Bangor 0
1958–59 Glenavon 2, Ballymena U 0	1994–95 Linfield 3, Carrick Rangers 1
1959–60 Linfield 5, Ards 1	1995–96 Glentoran 1, Glenavon 0
1960–61 Glenavon 5, Linfield 1	1996–97 Glenavon 1, Cliftonville 0
1961–62 Linfield 4, Portadown 0	1997–98 Glentoran 1, Glenavon 0
1962–63 Linfield 2, Distillery 1	1998–99 *Portadown awarded trophy after Cliftonville*
1963–64 Derry City 2, Glentoran 0	*were eliminated for using an ineligible player in*
1964–65 Coleraine 2, Glenavon 1	*semi-final.*
1965–66 Glentoran 2, Linfield 0	1999–2000 Glentoran 1, Portadown 0
1966–67 Crusaders 3, Glentoran 1	2000–01 Glentoran 1, Linfield 0
1967–68 Crusaders 2, Linfield 0	2001–02 Linfield 2, Portadown 1
1968–69 Ards 4, Distillery 2	2002–03 Coleraine 1, Glentoran 0
1969–70 Linfield 2, Ballymena U 1	2003–04 Glentoran 1, Coleraine 0
1970–71 Distillery 3, Derry City	2004–05 Portadown 5, Larne 1
1971–72 Coleraine 2, Portadown 1	2005–06 Linfield 2, Glentoran 1
1972–73 Glentoran 3, Linfield 2	2006–07 Linfield 2, Dungannon Swifts 2
1973–74 Ards 2, Ballymena U 1	*(aet; Linfield won 3-2 on penalties).*
1974–75 Coleraine 1:0:1, Linfield 1:0:0	2007–08 Linfield 2, Coleraine 1
1975–76 Carrick Rangers 2, Linfield 1	2008–09 Crusaders 1, Cliftonville 0
1976–77 Coleraine 4, Linfield 1	2009–10 Linfield 2, Portadown 1
1977–78 Linfield 3, Ballymena U 1	2010–11 Linfield 2, Crusaders 1
1978–79 Cliftonville 3, Portadown 2	2011–12 Linfield 4, Crusaders 1
1979–80 Linfield 2, Crusaders 0	2012–13 Glentoran 3, Cliftonville 1
1980–81 Ballymena U 1, Glenavon 0	2013–14 Glenavon 2, Balymena U 1
1981–82 Linfield 2, Coleraine 1	

SETANTA SPORTS CUP 2013–14

QUARTER-FINALS FIRST LEG

Crusaders v Sligo R	1-4
Dundalk v Coleraine	2-3
Shamrock R v Glentoran	5-1
Ballinamallard U v St Patrick's Ath	0-1

QUARTER-FINALS SECOND LEG

Sligo R v Crusaders	5-0
Sligo R won 9-1 on aggregate.	
Coleraine v Dundalk	0-2
Dundalk won 4-3 on aggregate.	
Glentoran v Shamrock R	0-0
Shamrock R won 5-1 on aggregate.	
St Patrick's Ath v Ballinamallard U	5-0
St Patrick's Ath won 6-0 on aggregate.	

SEMI-FINALS FIRST LEG

Shamrock R v Dundalk	1-2
Sligo R v St Patrick's Ath	2-0

SEMI-FINALS SECOND LEG

Dundalk v Shamrock R	1-0
Dundalk won 3-1 on aggregate.	
St Patrick's Ath v Sligo R	1-5
Sligo won 7-1 on aggregate.	

SETANTA CUP FINAL 2014

Tallagh Stadium, Dublin, Saturday 10 May 2014

Sligo R (1) 1 *(O'Conor 13)*

Dundalk (0) 0 2,600

Sligo R: Rogers; Conneely, McMillan E, Henderson, Gaynor, Cawley, O'Conor, Russell, Ndo (Ledwith 35), Greene, North.
Dundalk: Cherrie; Gannon, Gartland, Boyle, Massey, Shields (Higgins 74), Meenan (McMillan 80), Towell, Mountney (Byrne 67), Horgan, Hoban.
Referee: Arnold Hunter.

SETANTA SPORTS CUP WINNERS

2004–05 Linfield	2007–08 Cork C	2011–12 Crusaders
2005–06 Drogheda U	2009–10 Bohemians	2012–13 Shamrock R
2006–07 Drogheda U	2010–11 Shamrock R	2013–14 Sligo R

ULSTER CUP WINNERS

1949 Linfield	1962 Linfield	1975 Coleraine	1988 Glentoran	2001 *No competition*
1950 Larne	1963 Crusaders	1976 Glentoran	1989 Glentoran	2002 *No competition*
1951 Glentoran	1964 Linfield	1977 Linfield	1990 Portadown	2003 Dungannon Swifts
1952 *No competition*	1965 Coleraine	1978 Linfield	1991 Bangor	*(Confined to*
1953 Glentoran	1966 Glentoran	1979 Linfield	1992 Linfield	*First Division clubs)*
1954 Crusaders	1967 Linfield	1980 Ballymena U	1993 Crusaders	2004–14 *No competition*
1955 Glenavon	1968 Coleraine	1981 Glentoran	1994 Bangor	
1956 Linfield	1969 Coleraine	1982 Glentoran	1995 Portadown	
1957 Linfield	1970 Linfield	1983 Glentoran	1996 Portadown	
1958 Distillery	1971 Linfield	1984 Linfield	1997 Coleraine	
1959 Glenavon	1972 Coleraine	1985 Coleraine	1998 Ballyclare Comrades	
1960 Linfield	1973 Ards	1986 Coleraine	1999 Distillery	
1961 Ballymena U	1974 Linfield	1987 Larne	2000 *No competition*	

ROLL OF HONOUR SEASON 2013–14

Competition	Winner	Runner-up
Northern Irish Danske Bank Premier League	Cliftonville	Linfield
Northern Irish FA Cup	Glenavon	Ballymena U
Belfast Telegraph Irish Championship Division One	Institute	Bangor
Belfast Telegraph Irish Championship Division Two	Armagh C	PSNI
Wasp Solutions League Cup	Cliftonville	Crusaders
County Antrim Shield	Linfield	Crusaders
Steel & Sons Cup	Dundela	Immaculata
Co Antrim Junior Shield	St Paul's	St Luke's
Setanta Sports Cup	Sligo R	Dundalk
Coca-Cola Irish Junior Cup	Harryville Homers	Lisbellaw U
Mid Ulster Cup (Senior)	Dungannon Swifts	Annagh U
Harry Cavan Youth Cup	Portadown III	Crusaders Colts
George Wilson Memorial Cup	Glentoran II	Ballinamallard U II
North West Senior Cup	Newbuildings U	Institute
The Fermanagh Mulhern Cup	Enniskillen Town U	Beragh Swifts
Britton Rose Bowl	Northern Irish AFL	Scottish AFA
Coca-Cola Intermediate Cup	Bangor	Armagh C

NORTHERN IRELAND FOOTBALL WRITERS ASSOCIATION AWARDS

MANAGER OF THE YEAR
Tommy Breslin (Cliftonville)

PLAYER OF THE YEAR
Joe Gormley (Cliftonville)

CHAMPIONSHIP PLAYER OF THE YEAR
Michael McCrudden (Institute)

YOUNG PLAYER OF THE YEAR
Rhys Marshall (Glenavon)

INTERNATIONAL PERSONALITY OF THE YEAR
Steve Davis (Southampton)

JUNIOR TEAM OF THE YEAR
Harryville Homers

MERIT AWARD
Don Stirling (Ballymena U secretary)

DR MALCOLM BRODIE HALL OF FAME
David Healy

TEAM OF THE SEASON
Elliott Morris (Glentoran)
Rhys Marshall (Glenavon)
Sean Ward (Linfield)
Paul Leeman (Crusaders)
Craig McClean (Crusaders)
Chris Curran (Cliftonville)
Ryan Catney (Cliftonville)
Barry Johnston (Cliftonville)
Paul Heatley (Crusaders)
Liam Boyce (Cliftonville)
Joe Gormley (Cliftonville)

NIFWA @BTSPORT PREMIERSHIP PLAYER OF THE MONTH 2013–14

Month	Player	Team
August	Joe Gormley	Cliftonville
September	Gary Twigg	Portadown
October	Darren Murray	Portadown
November	Darren Boyce	Dungannon Swifts
December	Marty Donnelly	Cliftonville
January	Eugene Ferry	Coleraine
February	Philip Lowry	Linfield
March	Liam Boyce	Cliftonville
April	Chris Curran	Cliftonville

NIFWA MANAGER OF THE MONTH 2013–14

August	Ronnie McFall	Portadown
September	David Jeffrey	Linfield
October	Stephen Baxter	Crusaders
November	Stephen Baxter	Crusaders
December	David Jeffrey	Linfield
January	Oran Kearney	Coleraine
February	Tommy Breslin	Cliftonville
March	Tommy Breslin	Cliftonville
April	Tommy Breslin	Cliftonville

NIFWA CHAMPIONSHIP PLAYER OF THE MONTH 2013–14

August	Owain Beggs	Dundela
September	Darren McCauley	Institute
October	Michael Halliday	Dundela
November	Kyle Cherry	Dundela
December	Carl McComb	Dundela
January	Mark Cooling	Bangor
February	Stephen O'Flynn	Institute
March	Miguel Chines	Knockbreda
April	Ben Roy	Dundela

EUROPEAN CUP FINALS

EUROPEAN CUP FINALS 1956–1992

Year	Winners v Runners-up		Venue	Attendance	Referee
1956	Real Madrid v Reims	4-3	Paris	38,239	A. Ellis (England)
1957	Real Madrid v Fiorentina	2-0	Madrid	124,000	L. Horn (Netherlands)
1958	Real Madrid v AC Milan	3-2*	Brussels	67,000	A. Alsteen (Belgium)
1959	Real Madrid v Reims	2-0	Stuttgart	72,000	A. Dutsch (West Germany)
1960	Real Madrid v Eintracht Frankfurt	7-3	Glasgow	127,621	J. Mowat (Scotland)
1961	Benfica v Barcelona	3-2	Berne	26,732	G. Dienst (Switzerland)
1962	Benfica v Real Madrid	5-3	Amsterdam	61,257	L. Horn (Netherlands)
1963	AC Milan v Benfica	2-1	Wembley	45,715	A. Holland (England)
1964	Internazionale v Real Madrid	3-1	Vienna	71,333	J. Stoll (Austria)
1965	Internazionale v Benfica	1-0	Milan	89,000	G. Dienst (Switzerland)
1966	Real Madrid v Partizan Belgrade	2-1	Brussels	46,745	R. Kreitlein (West Germany)
1967	Celtic v Internazionale	2-1	Lisbon	45,000	K. Tschenscher (West Germany)
1968	Manchester U v Benfica	4-1*	Wembley	92,225	C. Lo Bello (Italy)
1969	AC Milan v Ajax	4-1	Madrid	31,782	J. Ortiz de Mendibil (Spain)
1970	Feyenoord v Celtic	2-1*	Milan	53,187	C. Lo Bello (Italy)
1971	Ajax v Panathinaikos	2-0	Wembley	90,000	J. Taylor (England)
1972	Ajax v Internazionale	2-0	Rotterdam	61,354	R. Helies (France)
1973	Ajax v Juventus	1-0	Belgrade	89,484	M. Guglovic (Yugoslavia)
1974	Bayern Munich v Atletico Madrid	1-1	Brussels	48,722	V. Loraux (Belgium)
Replay	Bayern Munich v Atletico Madrid	4-0	Brussels	23,325	A. Delcourt (Belgium)
1975	Bayern Munich v Leeds U	2-0	Paris	48,374	M. Kitabdjian (France)
1976	Bayern Munich v St Etienne	1-0	Glasgow	54,864	K. Palotai (Hungary)
1977	Liverpool v Moenchengladbach	3-1	Rome	52,078	R. Wurtz (France)
1978	Liverpool v FC Brugge	1-0	Wembley	92,500	C. Corver (Netherlands)
1979	Nottingham F v Malmo	1-0	Munich	57,500	E. Linemayr (Austria)
1980	Nottingham F v Hamburg	1-0	Madrid	51,000	A. Garrido (Portugal)
1981	Liverpool v Real Madrid	1-0	Paris	48,360	K. Palotai (Hungary)
1982	Aston Villa v Bayern Munich	1-0	Rotterdam	46,000	G. Konrath (France)
1983	Hamburg v Juventus	1-0	Athens	73,500	N. Rainea (Romania)
1984	Liverpool v Roma	1-1*	Rome	69,693	E. Fredriksson (Sweden)
	(Liverpool won 4-2 on penalties)				
1985	Juventus v Liverpool	1-0	Brussels	58,000	A. Daina (Switzerland)
1986	Steaua Bucharest v Barcelona	0-0*	Seville	70,000	M. Vautrot (France)
	(Steaua won 2-0 on penalties)				
1987	Porto v Bayern Munich	2-1	Vienna	57,500	A. Ponnet (Belgium)
1988	PSV Eindhoven v Benfica	0-0*	Stuttgart	68,000	L. Agnolin (Italy)
	(PSV won 6-5 on penalties)				
1989	AC Milan v Steaua Bucharest	4-0	Barcelona	97,000	K.-H. Tritschler (West Germany)
1990	AC Milan v Benfica	1-0	Vienna	57,500	H. Kohl (Austria)
1991	Red Star Belgrade v Marseille	0-0*	Bari	56,000	T. Lanese (Italy)
	(Red Star won 5-3 on penalties)				
1992	Barcelona v Sampdoria	1-0*	Wembley	70,827	A. Schmidhuber (Germany)

UEFA CHAMPIONS LEAGUE FINALS 1993–2014

1993	Marseille† v AC Milan	1-0	Munich	64,400	K. Rothlisberger (Switzerland)
1994	AC Milan v Barcelona	4-0	Athens	70,000	P. Don (England)
1995	Ajax v AC Milan	1-0	Vienna	49,730	I. Craciunescu (Romania)
1996	Juventus v Ajax	1-1*	Rome	70,000	M. D. Vega (Spain)
	(Juventus won 4-2 on penalties)				
1997	Borussia Dortmund v Juventus	3-1	Munich	59,000	S. Puhl (Hungary)
1998	Real Madrid v Juventus	1-0	Amsterdam	48,500	H. Krug (Germany)
1999	Manchester U v Bayern Munich	2-1	Barcelona	90,245	P. Collina (Italy)
2000	Real Madrid v Valencia	3-0	Paris	80,000	S. Braschi (Italy)
2001	Bayern Munich v Valencia	1-1*	Milan	79,000	D. Jol (Netherlands)
	(Bayern Munich won 5-4 on penalties)				
2002	Real Madrid v Leverkusen	2-1	Glasgow	50,499	U. Meier (Switzerland)
2003	AC Milan v Juventus	0-0*	Manchester	62,315	M. Merk (Germany)
	(AC Milan won 3-2 on penalties)				
2004	Porto v Monaco	3-0	Gelsenkirchen	53,053	K. M. Nielsen (Denmark)
2005	Liverpool v AC Milan	3-3*	Istanbul	65,000	M. M. González (Spain)
	(Liverpool won 3-2 on penalties)				
2006	Barcelona v Arsenal	2-1	Paris	79,610	T. Hauge (Norway)
2007	AC Milan v Liverpool	2-1	Athens	74,000	H. Fandel (Germany)
2008	Manchester U v Chelsea	1-1*	Moscow	67,310	L. Michel (Slovakia)
	(Manchester U won 6-5 on penalties)				
2009	Barcelona v Manchester U	2-0	Rome	62,467	M. Busacca (Switzerland)
2010	Internazionale v Bayern Munich	2-0	Madrid	73,490	H. Webb (England)
2011	Barcelona v Manchester U	3-1	Wembley	87,695	V. Kassai (Hungary)
2012	Chelsea v Bayern Munich	1-1*	Munich	62,500	P. Proença (Portugal)
	(Chelsea won 4-3 on penalties)				
2013	Bayern Munich v Borussia Dortmund	2-1	Wembley	86,298	N. Rizzoli (Italy)
2014	Real Madrid v Atletico Madrid	4-1*	Lisbon	60,000	B. Kuipers (Netherlands)

†*Subsequently stripped of title.*
*After extra time.

UEFA CHAMPIONS LEAGUE 2013-14

■ *Denotes player sent off.*

FIRST QUALIFYING ROUND FIRST LEG

Tuesday, 2 July 2013

Lusitanos (2) 2 *(Martinez Alejo 24 (pen), 29)*
EB/Streymur (0) 2 *(Hansen A 67, Hanssen 69 (pen))* 750
Lusitanos: (442) Fernandez; Brito, Sonejee, Soto, Reis (Pedro 59); Pinheiro, Martinez Alejo, Machado (Soares 82), Bruno Filipe; Jimenez (Zarioh 87), Antunes.
EB/Streymur: (442) Gango; Hansen G■, Jacobsen, Hanssen, Bo; Zachariasen (Hansen A 46), Samuelsen, Djurhuus, Nielsen; Dam, Niclasen (Danielsen 90).

Shirak (1) 3 *(Fofana 36, 55, 64)*
Tre Penne (0) 0 2600
Shirak: (442) Harutyunian; Kadio, Hakobian (Panosyan 63), Kyere (Marikyan 78), Fofana; Aleksanyan, Muradyan, Hovanisian, Odhiambo (Mkrtchyan 73); Diop, Davoyan.
Tre Penne: (442) Pazzini; Valentini C, Baschetti, Mikhaylovsky, Rossi A; Cibelli, Pignieri (Cardini 79), Chiaruzzi, Valli; Capicchioni (Menin 71), Rossi M (Tamburini 88).

FIRST QUALIFYING ROUND SECOND LEG

Tuesday, 9 July 2013

EB/Streymur (2) 5 *(Hansen 3, Hanssen 38, 85, Zachariasen 72, Niclasen 90)*
Lusitanos (0) 1 *(Reis 66)* 1200
EB/Streymur: (433) Torgard; Jacobsen (Zachariasen 69 (Olsen B 88)), Hanssen, Bo, Samuelsen; Djurhuus, Nielsen, Davidsen; Dam, Hansen A (Danielsen 72), Niclasen.
Lusitanos: (433) Pol; Brito, Sonejee, Soto, Reis; Pinheiro (Zarioh 58), Martinez Alejo, Machado■; Bruno Filipe, Jimenez (Fuente 65), Maciel (Soares 80).

Tre Penne (1) 1 *(Kyere 2 (og))*
Shirak (0) 0 453
Tre Penne: (442) Valentini F; Valentini C, Gasperoni, Mikhaylovsky, Rossi; Cibelli, Cardini, Pignieri (Menin 62), Chiaruzzi; Valli (Tamburini 85), Capicchioni (Nanni 87).
Shirak: (442) Harutyunian; Kadio, Fofana, Hakobian, Barikian (Odhiambo 65); Kyere (Marikyan■ 67), Aleksanyan, Hovhannisian, Davoyan (Davtyan 60); Diop, Muradyan.

SECOND QUALIFYING ROUND FIRST LEG

Tuesday, 16 July 2013

BATE (0) 0
Shakhter Karagandy (0) 1 *(Khizhnichenko 48)* 5207
BATE: (433) Gorbunov; Polyakov, Gajduchik, Filipenko, Yurevich; Sivakov, Aleksievich (Krivets 60), Pavlov; Nekhaychik (Kontsevoy 76), Rodionov, Hleb (Volodjko 46).
Shakhter Karagandy: (442) Mokin; Simcevic, Dzidic, Vasiljevic, Maliy (Tarasov 76); Khizhnichenko (Gabyshev 90), Canas, Vicius, Poryvaev; Zenkovich (Murtazaev 74), Finonchenko.

Birkirkara (0) 0
Maribor (0) 0 1419
Birkirkara: (442) Haber; Herrera, Sciberras, Fenech, Camenzuli; Shodiya (Toure 68), Temile (Zerafa 80), Vucanac, Moreno; Muscat R (Triganza 83), Muscat Z.
Maribor: (442) Handanovic; Filipovic, Milec, Mejac, Mezga; Tavares (Fajic 84), Ibraimi, Cvijanovic, Rajcevic; Arghus, Mertelj (Bohar 69).

Dinamo Tbilisi (2) 6 *(Ustaritz 40, Dvali 43, Grigalashvili 72, Xisco 75, Vouho 77, 81)*
EB/Streymur (1) 1 *(Glisic 42 (og))* 9425
Dinamo Tbilisi: (442) Loria; Ustaritz, Kvaratskhelia, Seturidze, Khmaladze; Dvali (Vouho 71), Merebashvili, Kvirkvelia, Xisco (Khocholava 88); Glisic, Dzaria (Grigalashvili 24).
EB/Streymur: (442) Torgard; Hansen G, Jacobsen, Hanssen, Djurhuus; Nielsen (Hansen J 90), Davidsen, Danielsen (Olsen B 76); Dam; Hansen A, Niclasen.

Ekranas (0) 0
FH Hafnarfjordur (1) 1 *(Vidarsson 30)* 1753
Ekranas: (442) Kauneckas; Varnas, Norvilas (Buinickij 46), Djenic (Ribokas 77), Reyes; Vucetic, Umeh, Tomkevicius (Kozlovs 76), Pilotas; Slavickas, Girdvainis.
FH Hafnarfjordur: (442) Oskarsson R; Tillen, Vidarsson P, Palsson (Thorisson 72), Sverrisson; Gudnason, Emilsson, Ingason (Bjornsson 79), Jonsson; Snorrason, Gudmundsson (Oskarsson I 89).

Fola Esch (0) 0
Dinamo Zagreb (0) 5 *(Soudani 59, 63, Cop 64, Ademi 74, Ivo Pinto 79)* 1489
Fola Esch: (433) Hym; Jans, Klein, Bernard, Kirch; Ronny, Payal, Dallevedove (Hadji 76); Laterza (Rani 78), Bensi, Hornuss (Mace 69).
Dinamo Zagreb: (433) Migliore; Ivo Pinto, Addy, Simunic, Ibanez; Pamic (Antolic 58), Ademi, Husejinovic; Soudani (Halilovic 65), Cop (Kramaric 76), Fernandes.

Sheriff (1) 1 *(Luvannor 45)*
Sutjeska (0) 1 *(Pejovic 54)* 6153
Sheriff: (442) Stajila; Markovski (Pesic 82), Ricardinho (Isa 68), Metoua, Fernando (Pascenco 57); Cadu, Paye, Samardzic, William; Stanojevic, Luvannor.
Sutjeska: (442) Janjusevic; Becelic, Ognjanovic, Jovovic (Pocek 83), Stevovic; Isidorovic (Stefanovic 73), Karadzic D, Nikolic, Nikola; Pejovic (Karadzic V 86), Cukovic.

Steau Bucharest (3) 3 *(Tanase 12, Pintilii 21, Pavlovic 45 (og))*
Vardar (0) 0 36,433
Steau Bucharest: (4231) Tatarusanu; Georgievski, Szukala, Chiriches, Latovlevici; Bourceanu, Pintilii; Popa, Stanciu (Iancu 57), Tanase (Tatu 68); Nikolic (Piovaccari 60).
Vardar: (4231) Pavlovic; Reljic, Tanevski, Bojovic, Cikarski; Temelkov, Petrovic; Stojkov (Georgiev 79), Petrov (Dimitrovski 90), Gimenez (Manevski 54); Kostovski.

Viktoria Plzen (0) 4 *(Cisovsky 63, Kolar 66, 76, Rajtoral 81)*
Zeljeznicar Sarajevo (0) 3 *(Tomic 52, Selimovic 78, Bucan 84)* 10,381
Viktoria Plzen: (4231) Kozacik; Reznik, Cisovsky, Prochazka, Limbersky; Horvath, Darida; Rajtoral, Kolar (Duris 83), Petrzela (Kovarik 55); Tecl (Wagner 55).
Zeljeznicar Sarajevo: (4231) Hadzic; Zeljkovic, Kerla, Skaljic, Urdinov; Hasanovic (Sadikovic 26), Tomic; Selimovic (Hodzic 87), Jamak, Bucan; Adilovic (Bajic 77).

Wednesday, 17 July 2013

Cliftonville (0) 0
Celtic (2) 3 *(Lustig 25, Samaras 31, Forrest 84)* 5442
Cliftonville: (4141) Devlin; McGovern, Scannell, Johnston, Caldwell (Donnelly 73); McMullan; Garrett (Curran 79), Smyth, Catney, Gormley (O'Carroll 69); Boyce.
Celtic: (442) Forster; Izaguirre, Ambrose, Wilson, Brown; Samaras (Watt 76), Stokes, Commons (Rogic 81), Lustig; Kayal, Forrest (McGeouch 86).

Gyor ETO (0) 0
Maccabi Tel Aviv (0) 2 *(Yitzhaki 76, Alberman 90)* 8175
Gyor ETO: (433) Kamenar; Svec, Takacs, Liptak, Volgyi; Patkai, Kamber, Strestik (Trajkovic 54); Kink (Andric 46), Koltai (Martinez 69), Varga.
Maccabi Tel Aviv: (433) Juan Pablo; Yeyni, Tibi, Carlos Garcia, Ziv; Radi, Alberman, Zahavi; Yitzhaki (Ben Haim 88), Prica (Micha 74), Altman (Lugasi 83).

HJK Helsinki (0) 0
Nomme Kalju (0) 0 7011
HJK Helsinki: (532) Wallen; Kansikas, Moren, Heikkila, Zeneli (Alho 80), Tainio; Pohjanpalo (Forssell 56), Sumusalo, Mattila (Perovuo 75); Savage, Schuller.
Nomme Kalju: (442) Teles; Koogas, Barengrub, Puri (Toomet 90), Ceesay; Quintieri (Dupikov 89), Kimbaloula, Kallaste, Sisov; Voskoboinikov (Neemelo 63), Wakui.

IF Elfsborg (1) 7 *(Rohden 21, 62, Sokolovs 48 (og), Nilsson 60, Bangura 68, Claesson 89, Holmen 90)*
Daugava Daugavpils (0) 1 *(Babatunde 78)* 3342
IF Elfsborg: (442) Stuhr-Ellegaard; Larsson J, Holmen, Mobaeck, Klarstrom; Ishizaki, Svensson, Hauger (Jorgensen 80), Rohden; Nilsson (Keene 68), Bangura (Claesson 73).
Daugava Daugavpils: (4231) Nerugals; Sokolovs, Savcenkovs, Chikhradze, Japalau (Solovjovs 71); Iizuka (Silagailis 80), Ola; Kovalovs, Volkovs, Ibe; Gongadze (Babatunde 56).

Neftchi (0) 0
Skenderbeu (0) 0 10,200
Neftchi: (442) Stamenkovic; Silva, Mitreski, Sadygov, Abdullayev (Imamverdiyev 69); Flavinho, Wobay (Nasimov 86), Platje, Ramos; Bertucci, Shukurov.
Skenderbeu: (442) Shehi; Arapi, Orelesi, Shkembi, Lika (Nimaga 86); Ademir, Pejic, Sefa (Abazi 81), Radas; Gvozdenovi C, Lilaj.

Shirak (0) 1 *(Hakobyan 48)*
Partizan Belgrade (0) 1 *(Volkov 90)* 2860
Shirak: (442) Harutyunian; Kadio, Davtyan, Fofana, Hakobyan (Apau 69); Barikian (Odhiambo 62), Kyere, Aleksanyan, Muradyan; Hovanisian, Diop (Mkrtchyan 80).
Partizan Belgrade: (442) Lukac; Volkov, Stankovic, Luka (Brasanac 46), Kojic; Ninkovic (Scepovic 46), Aksentijevic, Markovic, Ilic (Malbasic 77); Jojic, Ostojic.

Sligo R (0) 0
Molde (1) 1 *(Chukwa 42)* 3840
Sligo R: (442) Rogers; Henderson (Keane 72), McMillan E, Peers, Davoren (Martin 79); Lynch, Ndo, Conneely, Gaynor; McMillan D (Djilali 60), Elding.
Molde: (442) Nyland; Linnes, Toivio, Forren, Simonsen; Mostrom (Tripic 77), Berg Hestad, Ekpo, Chukwa; Coly (Agnaldo 62), Berget (Hovland 84).

Slovan Bratislava (0) 2 *(Halenar 87, 90)*
Ludogorets (0) 1 *(Mantyla 65)* 8126
Slovan Bratislava: (4231) Putnocky; Bagayoko, Kolcak, Gorosito, Josimov; Zofcak (Hlohovsky 6 (Peltier 69)), Kladrubsky; Grendel■, Meszaros, Milinkovic; Fort (Halenar 75).
Ludogorets: (4231) Stoyanov V; Junior Caicara, Mantyla, Moti, Minev; Zlatinski, Dyakov; Dani Abalo (Aleksandrov 52), Fabio Espinho, Stoyanov I (Bakalov 76); Michel Platini (Bezjak 8).

The New Saints (1) 1 *(Fraughan 11)*
Legia Warsaw (0) 3 *(Kucharczyk 47, Saganowski 57, Kosecki 74)* 2925
The New Saints: (433) Harrison; Marriott, Edwards K, Baker, Spender; Seargeant, Darlington (Williams 80), Edwards A; Mullan, Wilde, Fraughan (Finley 64).
Legia Warsaw: (442) Kuciak; Bereszynski, Rzezniczak, Dossa Junior, Wawrzyniak; Kosecki (Żyro 80), Vrdoljak, Pinto (Furman 46), Radovic (Kucharczyk 46); Dvalishvili, Saganowski.

Tuesday, 23 July 2013

Celtic (1) 2 *(Ambrose 16, Samaras 70)*
Cliftonville (0) 0 29,758
Celtic: (4312) Forster; Lustig, Wilson, Ambrose, Izaguirre; Forrest (Balde 76), Kayal (Rogic 65), Brown; Commons; Samaras, Stokes (Hooper 65).
Cliftonville: (451) Devlin; Cosgrove (O'Carroll 76), Smyth, McGovern, Seydak; Caldwell (Curran 58), Catney, McMullan, Johnston, Garrett; Boyce (Gormley 85).

Daugava Daugavpils (0) 0
IF Elfsborg (1) 4 *(Keene 41, Claesson 61, Hult 66, Andersson 86 (pen))* 350
Daugava Daugavpils: (343) Vlasovs; Savcenkovs, Chikhradze, Jermolajevs; Ibe, Ola, Babatunde (Kovalovs 75), Sevelovs; Japalau, Gongadze (Zizilevs 46), Militaru.
IF Elfsborg: (532) Hassan; Larsson S, Jorgensen, Mobaeck (Andersson 77), Keene, Klarstrom; Claesson, Hedlund, Hult; Rohden (Ishizaki 68), Soderberg (Lans 77).

Dinamo Zagreb (0) 1 *(Kramaric 78 (pen))*
Fola Esch (0) 0 8995
Dinamo Zagreb: (433) Zelenika; Simunic, Simunovic, Ivo Pinto, Pivaric; Sare, Antolic (Ademi 61), Husejinovic (Pamic 61); Halilovic (Rukavina 71), Kramaric, Fernandes.
Fola Esch: (433) Hym; Keita, Laterza, Klein, Dallevedove; Ronny, Hadji, Kirch; Payal (Alunni 86), Rani (Guerenne 82), Bensi (Hornuss 73).

EB/Streymur (1) 1 *(Danielsen 27)*
Dinamo Tbilisi (2) 3 *(Xisco 7 (pen), Dvali 12, Glisic 84)* 317
EB/Streymur: (442) Torgard; Hansen G, Jacobsen, Nielsen (Olsen A 80), Davidsen; Danielsen (Olsen H 84), Zachariasen (Olsen B 70), Hanssen, Hansen J; Hansen A, Niclasen.
Dinamo Tbilisi: (442) Loria; Ustaritz, Kvaratskhelia, Kvirkvelia, Khmaladze; Merebashvili, Grigalashvili, Seturidze (Khurtsilava 53); Papava (Glisic 70); Dvali, Xisco (Vouho 71).

FH Hafnarfjordur (1) 2 *(Sverrisson 38, Bjornsson 90)*
Ekranas (1) 1 *(Buinickij 26 (pen))* 1623
FH Hafnarfjordur: (433) Oskarsson R; Tillen, Emilsson, Thorisson, Gudmundsson (Bjarnason 45); Palsson, Sverrisson, Snorrason; Jonsson, Vidarsson P (Bjornsson 46), Gudnason (Oskarsson I 88).
Ekranas: (343) Kauneckas; Pilotas, Slavickas, Girdvainis; Vucetic, Tomkevicius, Djenic (Kozlovs 16 (Kavaliauskas 60)), Buinickij (Ribokas 67); Varnas, Umeh, Reyes■.

Maccabi Tel Aviv (1) 2 *(Ben Haim 25, Zahavi 79)*
Gyor ETO (0) 1 *(Martinez 86)* 12,732
Maccabi Tel Aviv: (433) Juan Pablo; Yeyni, Tibi, Carlos Garcia, Ziv; Radi, Alberman, Zahavi; Ben Haim (Lugasi 74), Yitzhaki (Micha 66), Altman (Mane 81).
Gyor ETO: (442) Kamenar; Wolfe, Liptak, Takacs, Dinjar; Kronaveter (Koltai 59), Kamber, Mevoungou, Varga; Strestik (Trajkovic 64), Andric (Martinez 46).

Molde (1) 2 *(Linnes 5, Coly 78)*
Sligo R (0) 0 5765
Molde: (433) Nyland; Hovland, Toivio, Mostrom, Berget (Coly 46); Linnes, Hussain (Hoseth 76), Forren; Chukwa, Ekpo, Tripic (Hestad 46).
Sligo R: (442) Rogers; Keane, Peers, McMillan E, Cawley; Elding (Cretaro 59), Gaynor, McMillan D (North 74), Djilali; Ndo (Lynch 80), Conneely.

Nomme Kalju (2) 2 *(Ceesay 28, Quintieri 35)*
HJK Helsinki (0) 1 *(Savage 64)* 4220
Nomme Kalju: (532) Teles; Koogas, Barengrub, Puri (Maehara 66), Ceesay, Quintieri (Rodrigues 76); Kimbaloula, Kallaste, Voskoboinikov (Neemelo 69); Wakui, Sisov.
HJK Helsinki: (442) Wallen; Kansikas (Lindstrom 76), Moren, Heikkila, Zeneli (Alho 46); Pohjanpalo, Sumusalo, Perovuo (Forssell 56), Mattila; Savage, Schuller.

Shakhter Karagandy (0) 1 *(Zenkovich 82)*
BATE (0) 0 21,800
Shakhter Karagandy: (541) Mokin; Vicius, Vasiljevic, Finonchenko (Gabyshev 87), Poryvaev, Dzidic; Maliy, Ghazaryan (Zenkovich 70), Simcevic, Canas (Baizhanov 90); Khizhnichenko.
BATE: (433) Gorbunov; Likhtarovich (Pavlov 53), Volodjko, Aleksievich, Krivets; Hleb (Kontsevoy 75), Radkov, Bordachev (Yurevich 81); Rodionov, Filipenko, Polyakov.

Skenderbeu (0) 1 *(Orelesi 116)*
Neftchi (0) 0 3,500
Skenderbeu: (442) Shehi; Arapi, Orelesi, Shkembi, Lika (Morina 77); Ademir, Pejic, Sefa (Abazi 57), Radas; Gvozdenovi C, Lilaj (Tomic 82).
Neftchi: (442) Stamenkovic; Carlos Cardoso (Sadygov 36), Silva, Mitreski■, Flavinho; Wobay, Platje (Yunuszade 91), Ramos, Bertucci; Shukurov, Imamverdiyev (Abdullayev 72).
aet.

Sutjeska (0) 0
Sheriff (1) 5 *(Cadu 14, Ricardinho 47, Fernando 52, 65, Scripcenco 86)* 5100
Sutjeska: (442) Janjusevic; Becelic■, Ognjanovic, Jovovic (Nedeljkovic 68), Stevovic; Isidorovic (Karadzic V 56), Karadzic D, Nikolic, Nikola; Pejovic (Stefanovic 58), Cukovic.
Sheriff: (442) Stajila; Ricardinho, Metoua, Fernando, Cadu (Pascenco 66); Paye, Samardzic (Scripcenco 67), Isa, William; Stanojevic, Luvannor (Pesic 78).

Vardar (1) 1 *(Kostovski 45)*
Steaua Bucharest (1) 2 *(Piovaccari 24, Bourceanu 72)* 3450
Vardar: (4141) Pavlovic; Reljic, Bojovic, Tanevski, Cikarski; Petrovic (Manevski 80); Temelkov, Gimenez (Simjanoski 89), Stojkov (Georgiev 67), Petrov; Kostovski.
Steaua Bucharest: (4141) Tatarusanu; Georgievski, Szukala, Gardos, Latovlevici; Pintilii (Radut 77); Bourceanu, Popa, Parvulescu (Iancu 54), Stanciu; Piovaccari (Nikolic 46).

Zeljeznicar Sarajevo (1) 1 *(Jamak 45)*
Viktoria Plzen (2) 2 *(Wagner 5, Petrzela 30)* 15,000
Zeljeznicar Sarajevo: (4231) Hadzic; Colic (Zeljkovic 12), Kerla, Skaljic (Bajic 67), Urdinov; Tomic, Svraka (Hodzic 59); Selimovic, Jamak, Bucan; Adilovic.
Viktoria Plzen: (4141) Kozacik; Reznik, Cisovsky, Prochazka■, Limbersky; Petrzela (Tecl 67); Horvath, Darida, Kovarik, Kolar (Rajtoral 87); Wagner (Hejda 25).

Wednesday, 24 July 2013

Legia Warsaw (0) 1 *(Dvalishvili 53)*
The New Saints (0) 0 11,712
Legia Warsaw: (442) Kuciak; Dossa Junior, Jodlowiec, Wawrzyniak, Bereszynski; Vrdoljak (Rzezniczak 65), Radovic, Furman, Saganowski (Pinto 71); Dvalishvili, Zyro (Brzyski 75).
The New Saints: (442) Harrison; Spender, Marriott, Baker, Edwards K; Fraughan (Finley 57), Seargeant, Mullan, Edwards A; Wilde (Draper 72), Darlington (Williams 82).

Ludogorets (2) 3 *(Stoyanov I 3, Dani Abalo 13, 78)*
Slovan Bratislava (0) 0 3890
Ludogorets: (442) Stoyanov V; Mantyla, Minev, Moti, Junior Caicara; Dyakov, Zlatinski, Dani Abalo (Aleksandrov 83), Stoyanov I (Bakalov 72); Marcelinho (Fabio Espinho 62), Bezjak.
Slovan Bratislava: (442) Putnocky; Josimov, Gorosito, Bagayoko, Kolcak; Zofcak, Milinkovic, Jakubek (Soumah 76), Kladrubsky; Peltier (Fort 71), Halenar.

Maribor (1) 2 *(Cvijanovic 28, Viler 47)*
Birkirkara (0) 0 9036
Maribor: (4231) Handanovic; Milec, Rajcevic, Arghus (Potokar 71), Viler; Cvijanovic, Filipovic; Ibraimi, Tavares, Mezga (Bohar 21); Fajic (Mendy 86).
Birkirkara: (352) Haber; Moreno, Vucanac (Maciel 79), Muscat Z; Sciberras, Fenech, Camenzuli (Toure 46), Muscat R (Triganza 82), Herrera; Shodiya, Temile.

Partizan Belgrade (0) 0
Shirak (0) 0 15,742
Partizan Belgrade: (433) Lukac; Volkov■, Luka (Ivkovic 60), Aksentijevic, Ivanov; Markovic, Ilic, Malbasic (Kojic 46); Jojic, Ostojic (Stankovic 46), Scepovic.
Shirak: (433) Harutyunian; Kadio, Davtyan, Fofana, Hakobian (Odhiambo 62); Barikian (Apau 76), Kyere, Aleksanyan; Muradyan, Hovanisian, Diop.
Partizan won on away goals rule.

THIRD QUALIFYING ROUND FIRST LEG

Tuesday, 30 July 2013

Austria Vienna (1) 1 *(Royer 25)*
FH Hafnarfjordur (0) 0 8075
Austria Vienna: (4231) Lindner; Koch, Rotpuller, Ortlechner, Suttner; Mader, Grunwald; Royer (Murg 80), Stankovic, Jun (Spiridonovic 76); Hosiner (Okotie 83).
FH Hafnarfjordur: (4231) Oskarsson R; Gudmundsson (Jonsson 76), Thorisson, Bjarnason, Tillen; Palsson, Sverrisson; Snorrason, Emilsson, Gudnason (Oskarsson I 86); Bjornsson (Ingvarsson 71).

Dinamo Tbilisi (0) 0
Steaua Bucharest (0) 2 *(Iancu 64, 80)* 20,728
Dinamo Tbilisi: (442) Loria; Seturidze, Kvaratskhelia, Ustaritz, Glisic; Merebashvili (Khocholava 87), Grigalashvili, Khmaladze, Kvirkvelia; Xisco (Vouho 67), Dvali (Goga 79).
Steaua Bucharest: (4321) Tatarusanu; Georgievski, Szukala, Chiriches, Latovlevici; Bourceanu, Pintilii (Gardos 84), Stanciu (Iancu 46); Tanase, Popa; Nikolic (Piovaccari 57).

Dinamo Zagreb (0) 1 *(Rukavina 89)*
Sheriff (0) 0 10,347
Dinamo Zagreb: (442) Zelenika; Simunic, Ivo Pinto, Addy, Ademi (Sare 49); Husejinovic, Pivaric, Pamic, Soudani (Rukavina 74); Fernandes, Cop (Kramaric 88).
Sheriff: (442) Tomic; Metoua, Paye, Samardzic, William; Luvannor (Pesic 81), Fernando, Cadu (Pascenco 84), Stanojevic; Markovski (Isa 57), Ricardinho.

FC Basel (1) 1 *(Stocker 38)*
Maccabi Tel Aviv (0) 0 12,353
FC Basel: (442) Sommer; Degen, Schar, Ajeti, Safari; Salah (Andrist 87), Frei, Diaz (Xhaka 62), Stocker; El-Nenny (Bobadilla 76), Streller.
Maccabi Tel Aviv: (433) Juan Pablo; Yeyni, Tibi, Carlos Garcia, Ziv; Radi, Alberman, Zahavi (Lugasi 90); Yitzhaki (Ben Haroush 82), Prica, Altman (Ben Haim 62).

Lyon (0) 1 *(Bisevac 64)*
Grasshoppers (0) 0 27,331
Lyon: (4231) Lopes; Miguel Lopes, Bisevac, Umtiti, Dabo (Kone B 61); Malbranque (Fofana 69), Gonalons; Lacazette, Grenier, Danic (Gourcuff 79); Lopez.
Grasshoppers: (4231) Burki; Lang, Vilotic, Grichting, Pavlovic; Abrashi, Salatic; Hajrovic, Toko, Gashi (Feltscher 78); Ngamukol (Vonlanthen 69).

Nomme Kalju (0) 0
Viktoria Plzen (1) 4 *(Cisovsky 2, 52, 90, Duris 77)* 4400
Nomme Kalju: (442) Teles; Sisov, Barengrub, Koogas, Kallaste; Puri (Maehara 78), Ceesay, Wakui, Kimbaloula; Voskoboinikov (Neemelo 69), Quintieri.
Viktoria Plzen: (4231) Kozacik; Reznik, Hejda, Cisovsky, Limbersky; Darida (Horava 85), Horvath; Petrzela (Rajtoral 80), Kolar (Duris 65), Kovarik; Wagner.

Nordsjaelland (0) 0
Zenit St Petersburg (0) 1 *(Kerzhakov 49)* 5417
Nordsjaelland: (343) Hansen M; Gregor, Runje, Jakobsen; Larsen, Stokholm, Christiansen (Nordstrand 62), Mtiliga; Thychosen (Hansen E 82), Vingaard, Ticinovic (Aabech 77).
Zenit St Petersburg: (4231) Lodigin; Hubocan, Luis Neto, Lombaerts, Tymoschuk; Zyryanov, Witsel; Arshavin (Kerzhakov 46), Faitzulin, Danny (Bystrov 90); Hulk (Lukovic 83).

PAOK Salonika (0) 0
Metalist Kharkiv (1) 2 *(Devic 42 (pen), 71)*
PAOK Salonika: (442) Jacobo; Kitsiou, Katsouranis, Miguel Vitor, Lino; Lucas (Oliseh 54), Tziolis, Lazar, Georgiadis (Vukic 67); Salpingidis, Athanasiadis (Necid 78).
Metalist Kharkiv: (4231) Disljenkovic; Villagra, Gueye, Rodrigo Moledo, Marcio Azevedo; Edmar, Torres; Marlos, De Souza Carballo (Blanco 61), Sosa (Krasnopyorov 90); Devic (Cristaldo 76).
Behind closed doors.

PSV Eindhoven (0) 2 *(Depay 61, Locadia 75)*
Zulte Waregem (0) 0   35,000
PSV Eindhoven: (4321) Zoet; Rekik, Bruma, Willems, Brenet; Maher, Schaars, Wijnaldum; Matavz (Locadia 72), Bakkali (Jozefzoon 81); Depay.
Zulte Waregem: (442) Bossut; De Fauw, Colpaert, Verboom (Duplus 46), D'Haene; N'Diaye, Skulason, Hazard, Berrier (Conte 67); Habibou (Naessens 74), Leye.

Shakhter Karagandy (1) 3 *(Dzidic 8, Murtazaev 77, Khizhnichenko 90)*
Skenderbeu (0) 0   21,800
Shakhter Karagandy: (442) Mokin; Simcevic, Dzidic, Vasiljevic, Poryvaev; Finonchenko (Darabayev 85), Canas (Baizhanov 90), Vicius, Ghazaryan; Khizhnichenko, Zenkovich (Murtazaev 72).
Skenderbeu: (442) Shehi; Ademir, Radas, Gvozdenovic (Dimo 79), Vrapi; Sefa, Orelesi, Shkembi, Lilaj; Pejic (Nimaga 46), Tomic (Abazi 72).

Wednesday, 31 July 2013

Apoel Nicosia (1) 1 *(Goncalves 21)*
Maribor (0) 1 *(Tavares 64)*   17,387
Apoel Nicosia: (4321) Urko; Mario Sergio, Joao Guilherme, Marcelo Oliveira, Japones (Benachour 85); Gomes, Manduca, Morais; Charalambidis (Budimir 73), Alexandrou (Aloneftis 73); Goncalves.
Maribor: (4231) Handanovic; Milec, Rajcevic, Arghus, Viler; Filipovic, Cvijanovic; Ibraimi (Mejac 71), Tavares (Potokar 83), Bohar; Fajic (Mendy 65).

Celtic (0) 1 *(Commons 76)*
IF Elfsborg (0) 0   40,153
Celtic: (442) Forster; Lustig, Ambrose, Wilson, Izaguirre; Forrest, Kayal (Ledley 66), Brown, Commons; Samaras (Mulgrew 86), Stokes.
IF Elfsborg: (4321) Stuhr-Ellegaard; Larsson J, Jonsson, Klarstrom, Mobaeck; Hauger, Ishizaki (Jorgensen 85), Keene (Hult 80); Svensson, Rohden; Bangura (Nilsson 81).

Ludogorets (0) 2 *(Marcelinho 54, Aleksandrov 67)*
Partizan Belgrade (0) 1 *(Markovic 49)*   7000
Ludogorets: (433) Stoyanov V; Junior Caicara, Barthe, Moti, Minev; Dyakov, Marcelinho (Hernandez 90), Zlatinski; Dani Abalo (Aleksandrov 58), Bezjak (Fabio Espinho 81), Stoyanov I.
Partizan Belgrade: (433) Lukac; Aksentijevic, Ivanov, Obradovic, Gulan; Jojic■, Ilic (Kojic 82), Markovic; Grbic (Malbasic 59), Scepovic, Ninkovic (Djemba-Djemba 64).

Molde (1) 1 *(Chukwa 29)*
Legia Warsaw (0) 1 *(Dvalishvili 68)*   6063
Molde: (442) Nyland; Linnes, Toivio, Forren, Rindaroy; Mostrom (Tripic 79), Ekpo (Hoseth 87), Berg Hestad, Chukwa; Berget (Hoiland 77), Gulbrandsen■.
Legia Warsaw: (4231) Kuciak; Bereszynski, Dossa Junior, Jodlowiec, Brzyski; Vrdoljak, Furman; Radovic, Dvalishvili, Kosecki (Zyro 85); Saganowski (Ojamaa 46).

Red Bull Salzburg (0) 1 *(Alan 68)*
Fenerbahce (0) 1 *(Baroni 90 (pen))*   28,640
Red Bull Salzburg: (442) Gulacsi; Schwegler, Andre Ramalho, Hinteregger, Ulmer; Meilinger (Hierlander 75), Kampl, Ilsanker, Mane (Berisha 82); Jonathan, Alan (Reyna 72).
Fenerbahce: (442) Demirel; Topal, Yobo, Kadlec, Bruno Alves; Topuz, Potuk (Sow 58), Emre (Baroni 68); Meireles (Sahin 90); Webo, Kuyt.

THIRD QUALIFYING ROUND SECOND LEG

Tuesday, 6 August 2013

Fenerbahce (3) 3 *(Meireles 8, Sow 17, Webo 34)*
Red Bull Salzburg (1) 1 *(Jonathan 4)*   32,669
Fenerbahce: (433) Demirel; Topuz, Yobo, Bruno Alves, Kadlec; Topal (Sahin 88), Meireles (Potuk 44), Baroni; Kuyt (Erkin 77), Webo, Sow.
Red Bull Salzburg: (442) Gulacsi; Klein, Andre Ramalho, Hinteregger, Ulmer; Meilinger (Jantscher 54), Kampl, Ilsanker, Mane; Jonathan, Alan (Hierlander 79).

Grasshoppers (0) 0
Lyon (0) 1 *(Grenier 82)*   9500
Grasshoppers: (4321) Burki; Grichting, Vilotic, Lang, Pavlovic; Salatic, Abrashi, Gashi; Feltscher (Ngamukol 70), Hajrovic (Brahimi 79); Toko (Vonlanthen 69).
Lyon: (4321) Lopes; Kone B, Bisevac, Umtiti, Grenier; Malbranque (Fofana 75), Miguel Lopes, Danic (Gourcuff 56); Gonalons, Lopez; Lacazette (Benzia 80).

Maccabi Tel Aviv (2) 3 *(Schar 34 (og), Zahavi 37, Radi 55)*
FC Basel (3) 3 *(Schar 5 (pen), Salah 21, Diaz 32)*   13,100
Maccabi Tel Aviv: (442) Juan Pablo; Ziv (Micha 35), Tibi, Carlos Garcia, Alberman; Radi, Yeyni, Zahavi (Margolis 63), Yitzhaki; Ben Haim (Einbinder 74), Prica.
FC Basel: (442) Sommer; Degen (Voser 61), Ajeti, Schar, Safari; Stocker, Frei, Diaz, Salah (El-Nenny 75); Xhaka, Streller (Sauro 55).

Maribor (0) 0
Apoel Nicosia (0) 0   12,100
Maribor: (4231) Handanovic; Milec, Rajcevic, Arghus (Mejac 73), Viler; Mertelj, Filipovic; Bohar, Cvijanovic, Ibraimi (Dervisevic 84); Tavares (Fajic 81).
Apoel Nicosia: (4231) Urko; Mario Sergio, Marcelo Oliveira, Joao Guilherme, Japones; Gomes (Aloneftis 82), Morais; Manduca, Benachour (Charalambidis 72), Alexandrou (Budimir 66); Goncalves■.
Maribor won on away goals rule.

Partizan Belgrade (0) 0
Ludogorets (0) 1 *(Zlatinski 88 (pen))*   22,312
Partizan Belgrade: (4411) Lukac (Zivkovic 45); Ivanov, Obradovic, Ostojic, Djemba-Djemba; Ninkovic, Markovic, Ilic (Scepovic 68), Grbic (Luka 81); Gulan■; Mitrovic.
Ludogorets: (433) Stoyanov V; Mantyla, Barthe, Minev, Junior Caicara; Dyakov, Zlatinski, Aleksandrov (Vitinha 85); Stoyanov I (Dani Abalo 54), Marcelinho (Fabio Espinho 64), Bezjak.

Skenderbeu (3) 3 *(Tomic 8, Shkembi 18 (pen), 27 (pen))*
Shakhter Karagandy (1) 2 *(Khizhnichenko 38, Baizhanov 66)*   2500
Skenderbeu: (4312) Shehi; Ademir (Fagu 85), Radas, Gvozdenovic, Arapi; Tomic (Abazi 61), Lilaj, Orelesi; Shkembi; Pejic■, Morina (Ejupi 64).
Shakhter Karagandy: (541) Mokin; Poryvaev (Tarasov 61), Dzidic, Maliy (Baizhanov 46), Vasiljevic, Ghazaryan; Khizhnichenko (Zenkovich 72), Vicius, Canas, Simcevic; Finonchenko.

Steau Bucharest (1) 1 *(Latovlevici 6)*
Dinamo Tbilisi (0) 1 *(Ustaritz 48)*   37,249
Steau Bucharest: (4231) Tatarusanu; Georgievski, Szukala (Gardos 46), Chiriches, Latovlevici; Pintilii (Stanciu 46), Bourceanu; Popa, Iancu (Prepelita 56), Tanase; Piovaccari.
Dinamo Tbilisi: (442) Loria; Seturidze, Kvaratskhelia, Ustaritz, Kvirkvelia; Grigalashvili, Khmaladze, Papava (Goga 60), Merebashvilli; Dvali (Vouho 71), Xisco.

Wednesday, 7 August 2013

FH Hafnarfjordur (0) 0
Austria Vienna (0) 0   2647
FH Hafnarfjordur: (433) Oskarsson R; Tillen, Sverrisson, Emilsson, Thorisson; Bjarnason, Palsson (Bjornsson 68), Gudmundsson; Gudnason, Jonsson, Snorrason (Oskarsson I 76).
Austria Vienna: (442) Lindner; Rogulj, Ortlechner, Suttner■, Koch; Mader, Holland (Dilaver 66), Royer, Jun; Stankovic, Hosiner (Okotie 61).

IF Elfsborg (0) 0
Celtic (0) 0   9040

IF Elfsborg: (451) Stuhr-Ellegaard; Larsson J, Jonsson, Mobaeck (Soderberg 33), Klarstrom (Elm 84); Keene, Svensson, Ishizaki, Hauger (Hedlund 75), Rohden; Bangura.
Celtic: (4411) Forster; Lustig, Ambrose, Wilson, Izaguirre; Forrest, Brown, Ledley, Mulgrew (Matthews 74); Commons; Samaras (Stokes 69).

Legia Warsaw (0) 0
Molde (0) 0   23,379

Legia Warsaw: (4231) Kuciak; Bereszynski, Dossa Junior, Rzezniczak, Wawrzyniak; Vrdoljak, Jodlowiec; Ojamaa (Kucharczyk 70), Radovic, Zyro (Kosecki 61); Dvalishvili.
Molde: (442) Nyland; Toivio, Hovland (Coly 74), Forren, Rindaroy; Linnes, Ekpo■, Berg Hestad, Mostrom (Tripic 74); Berget (Hussain 84), Chukwa.
Legia Warsaw won on away goals rule.

Metalist Kharkiv (0) 1 *(Blanco 72)*

PAOK Salonika (0) 1 *(Necid 83)*   39,286

Metalist Kharkiv: (4231) Disljenkovic; Villagra, Rodrigo Moledo, Gueye, Marcio Azevedo; Edmar (Berezovchuk 90), Krasnopyorov; Blanco, De Souza Carballo (Marlos 62), Sosa; Devic (Cristaldo 76).
PAOK Salonika: (442) Jacobo; Kitsiou, Katsouranis, Miguel Vitor, Lino; Lucas, Tziolis (Necid 82), Lazar, Georgiadis (Lawrence 75); Oliseh, Salpingidis (Athanasiadis 67).

Sheriff (0) 0

Dinamo Zagreb (2) 3 *(Fernandes 10, Soudani 27, Cop 61)*
                                                             10,234
Sheriff: (4231) Tomic; Metoua, Samardzic, William, Paye; Fernando, Stanojevic (Pascenco 14); Ricardinho (Isa 63), Cadu, Luvannor; Jhulliam (Balima 81).
Dinamo Zagreb: (4141) Zelenika; Ivo Pinto, Addy (Simunovic 72), Simunic, Pivaric; Pamic; Fernandes, Ademi (Sare 59), Husejinovic, Soudani (Halilovic 79); Cop.

Viktoria Plzen (2) 6 *(Horvath 20 (pen), 44, 62, Tecl 58, Horava 71, Wagner 82)*
Nomme Kalju (1) 2 *(Quintieri 10, 69)*   9482

Viktoria Plzen: (4231) Kozacik; Reznik, Cisovsky, Prochazka, Limbersky; Darida, Horvath (Horava 69); Petrzela, Kolar (Rajtoral 46), Duris; Tecl (Wagner 59).
Nomme Kalju: (4411) Teles; Sisov, Barengrub, Kallaste, Koogas; Puri (Kirss 71), Ceesay (Soares 75), Wakui, Quintieri; Kimbaloula; Voskoboinikov (Neemelo 65).

Zenit St Petersburg (1) 5 *(Shirokov 26, 90, Hulk 50, Danny 62, Arshavin 68)*
Nordsjaelland (0) 0   20,072

Zenit St Petersburg: (433) Lodigin; Aniukov (Tymoschuk 53), Lombaerts, Luis Neto■, Khodzhaniyazov; Witsel, Shirokov, Zyryanov (Faitzulin 81); Hulk, Bukharov (Arshavin 67), Danny.
Nordsjaelland: (343) Hansen M; Gregor, Runje, Jakobsen; Larsen (O'Brien 71), Christiansen, Stokholm, Ticinovic; Thychosen (Hansen E 38), Nordstrand (Johannesen 56), Vingaard.

Zulte Waregem (0) 0

PSV Eindhoven (0) 3 *(Matavz 56 (pen), Bakkali 73, Godeau 90 (og))*   6189

Zulte Waregem: (442) Bossut; De Fauw, D'Haene, Colpaert■, Godeau; Conte, Skulason, Malanda, Hazard (N'Diaye 72); Habibou (Naessens 30), Leye (Trajkovski 72).
PSV Eindhoven: (433) Zoet; Brenet, Rekik (Marcelo 80), Bruma, Willems; Maher, Schaars (Hiljemark 84), Wijnaldum; Bakkali (Jozefzoon 76), Matavz, Depay.

Tuesday, 20 August 2013

Lyon (0) 0
Real Sociedad (1) 2 *(Griezmann 17, Seferovic 50)* 38,156

Lyon: (4231) Lopes; Bedimo, Bisevac■, Fofana, Miguel Lopes; Gonalons, Malbranque (Bahlouli 57); Grenier, Gourcuff, Benzia (Danic 58); Lacazette.
Real Sociedad: (433) Bravo; Carlos Martinez, Cadamuro, De la Bella, Markel; Martinez, Prieto, Zurutuza (Pardo 81); Griezmann (Castro 70), Seferovic (Granero 64), Vela.

Pacos Ferreira (0) 1 *(Andre Leao 58)*
Zenit St Petersburg (1) 4 *(Shirokov 27, 60, 90, Degra 84 (og))*   4466

Pacos Ferreira: (4231) Degra; Rodrigo Antonio, Filipe Anunciacao, Ricardo, Nuno Santos; Romeu, Andre Leao; Rui Miguel (Vitor 50), Sergio Oliveira (Manuel Jose 80), Hurtado; Irobiso (Carlao 64).
Zenit St Petersburg: (433) Lodigin; Aniukov, Lombaerts, Hubocan, Smolnikov; Witsel, Zyryanov (Tymoschuk 70), Shirokov; Bystrov (Arshavin 61), Kerzhakov, Danny (Mogilevets 80).

PSV Eindhoven (0) 1 *(Matavz 60)*
AC Milan (1) 1 *(El Shaarawy 15)*   35,000

PSV Eindhoven: (433) Zoet; Brenet, Bruma, Rekik, Willems; Wijnaldum, Schaars (Hiljemark 89); Maher; Park (Jozefzoon 68), Matavz (Locadia 76), Depay.
AC Milan: (433) Abbiati; Abate, Zapata, Mexes, Emanuelson; Muntari, De Jong (Poli 78), Montolivo; Boateng (Niang 84), Balotelli, El Shaarawy.

Shakhter Karagandy (1) 2 *(Finonchenko 12, Khizhnichenko 77)*
Celtic (0) 0   29,950

Shakhter Karagandy: (541) Mokin; Simcevic, Maliy, Vasiljevic, Dzidic, Poryvaev; Finonchenko (Zenkovich 82), Canas, Vicius, Ghazaryan; Khizhnichenko.
Celtic: (442) Forster; van Dijk, Mouyokolo, Mulgrew, Izaguirre (Balde 83); Lustig (Matthews 67), Brown, Commons, Forrest; Samaras, Ledley.

Viktoria Plzen (1) 3 *(Cisovsky 8, Darida 58, Duris 89)*
Maribor (0) 1 *(Mejac 66)*   11,158

Viktoria Plzen: (451) Kozacik; Limbersky, Reznik, Prochazka, Cisovsky; Horava, Horvath, Petrzela (Rajtoral 77), Darida (Tecl 87), Kovarik; Wagner (Duris 63).
Maribor: (442) Handanovic; Mejac, Potokar, Rajcevic, Viler; Milec (Dervisevic 85), Cvijanovic, Mertelj, Bohar; Ibraimi (Mendy 88), Tavares.

Wednesday, 21 August 2013

Dinamo Zagreb (0) 0
Austria Vienna (0) 2 *(Leovac 68, Stankovic 75)* 21,729

Dinamo Zagreb: (433) Zelenika; Ivo Pinto, Addy, Simunic, Pivaric; Husejinovic (Sammir 62), Ademi, Pamic (Brozovic 83); Soudani, Cop (Rukavina■ 71), Fernandes.
Austria Vienna: (433) Lindner; Koch, Rogulj, Ortlechner, Leovac; Stankovic, Holland, Mader; Royer (Murg 90), Hosiner (Okotie 82), Jun (Grunwald 85).

Fenerbahce (0) 0
Arsenal (0) 3 *(Gibbs 51, Ramsey 64, Giroud 77 (pen))*
                                                            40,375
Fenerbahce: (433) Demirel; Irtegun (Gonul 46), Yobo, Bruno Alves, Kadlec; Topal, Meireles (Potuk 82), Emre; Sow, Webo (Emenike 62), Kuyt.
Arsenal: (433) Szczesny; Sagna, Mertesacker, Koscielny (Jenkinson 33), Gibbs; Rosicky, Wilshere, Ramsey; Cazorla, Giroud (Podolski 82), Walcott (Monreal 87).

Ludogorets (1) 2 *(Marcelinho 23, Stoyanov I 50)*
FC Basel (1) 4 *(Salah 12, 59, Sio 64, Schar 84 (pen))* 11,927

Ludogorets: (4231) Stoyanov V; Junior Caicara■, Barthe, Moti, Minev; Zlatinski, Dyakov; Dani Abalo (Misidjan 63), Marcelinho (Fabio Espinho 72), Stoyanov I; Bezjak (Michel Platini 56).
FC Basel: (433) Sommer; Voser, Schar, Ajeti, Safari; El-Nenny, Frei, Diaz; Salah (Delgado 88), Sio (Xhaka 65), Stocker (Sauro 86).

Schalke 04 (1) 1 *(Farfan 32)*
PAOK Salonika (0) 1 *(Stoch 73)*   52,444
Schalke 04: (4231) Hildebrand; Uchida, Matip, Howedes, Fuchs; Hoger (Goretzka 78), Jones; Meyer (Clemens 69), Draxler, Farfan (Pukki 87); Szalai.
PAOK Salonika: (433) Jacobo; Miguel Vitor, Lino, Kitsiou, Katsouranis; Tziolis, Lawrence (Kace 62), Lazar; Stoch, Salpingidis (Athanasiadis 62), Lucas (Oliseh 90).

Steau Bucharest (1) 1 *(Piovaccari 34)*
Legia Warsaw (0) 1 *(Kosecki 53)*   50,655
Steau Bucharest: (4231) Tatarusanu; Georgievski, Szukala, Gardos, Latovlevici; Bourceanu, Pintilii (Prepelita 46); Popa, Stanciu (Iancu 61), Tanase; Piovaccari (Cristea 70).
Legia Warsaw: (4231) Kuciak; Rzezniczak, Jodlowiec (Broz 27), Dossa Junior, Wawrzyniak; Furman, Vrdoljak; Kucharczyk (Zyro 75), Radovic, Kosecki; Saganowski (Dvalishvili 81).

PLAY-OFF ROUND SECOND LEG

Tuesday, 27 August 2013
Arsenal (1) 2 *(Ramsey 25, 72)*
Fenerbahce (0) 0   56,271
Arsenal: (433) Szczesny; Jenkinson, Sagna, Mertesacker, Monreal; Wilshere, Ramsey, Cazorla; Walcott (Miyaichi 74), Giroud (Sanogo 60), Podolski (Gibbs 49).
Fenerbahce: (433) Demirel; Gonul, Bruno Alves, Korkmaz, Erkin; Sahin, Baroni (Potuk 67), Meireles; Kuyt (Webo 66), Emenike, Sow (Topuz 83).

Austria Vienna (1) 2 *(Mader 4, Kienast 82)*
Dinamo Zagreb (2) 3 *(Brozovic 34, Fernandes 44, Beqiraj 71)*   10,500
Austria Vienna: (442) Lindner; Rogulj, Ortlechner, Suttner, Koch; Mader, Holland (Kienast 81), Royer, Jun (Grunwald 68); Hosiner (Leovac 85), Stankovic.
Dinamo Zagreb: (442) Sandomierski; Simunic, Ivo Pinto, Addy, Pivaric; Ademi, Sammir (Antolic 73), Husejinovic (Beqiraj 59), Brozovic; Soudani (Leko 75), Fernandes.

FC Basel (1) 2 *(Frei 11, Degen 79)*
Ludogorets (0) 0   15,733
FC Basel: (4231) Sommer; Voser, Schar (Sauro 55), Ajeti, Safari (Degen 77); Xhaka, Frei; Salah (Delgado 70), Diaz, Stocker; Sio.
Ludogorets: (4231) Stoyanov V; Choco, Mantyla, Moti, Minev; Zlatinski (Fabio Espinho 59), Dyakov; Stoyanov I (Vitinha 86), Marcelinho, Misidjan (Aleksandrov 73); Bezjak.

Legia Warsaw (1) 2 *(Radovic 27, Rzezniczak 90)*
Steaua Bucharest (2) 2 *(Stanciu 7, Piovaccari 9)*   21,514
Legia Warsaw: (4231) Kuciak; Wawrzyniak, Dossa Junior, Rzezniczak, Bereszynski; Furman (Zyro 75), Vrdoljak; Kosecki, Radovic, Kucharczyk (Ojamaa 63); Saganowski (Mikita 79).
Steaua Bucharest: (4231) Tatarusanu; Latovlevici, Szukala, Gardos, Georgievski; Filip, Bourceanu; Tanase (Tatu 71), Stanciu (Cristea 59), Popa; Piovaccari (Iancu 89).
Steaua Bucharest won on away goals rule.

PAOK Salonika (0) 2 *(Athanasiadis 53, Katsouranis 79)*
Schalke 04 (1) 3 *(Szalai 43, 90, Draxler 67)*
PAOK Salonika: (442) Jacobo; Kitsiou, Katsouranis, Miguel Vitor, Skondras; Lucas (Georgiadis 80), Kace, Tziolis, Stoch; Athanasiadis (Necid 73), Salpingidis (Oliseh 74).
Schalke 04: (4231) Hildebrand; Uchida, Felipe Santana, Howedes, Fuchs; Hoger, Jones■; Farfan (Matip 83), Draxler, Clemens (Meyer 60 (Neustadter 70)); Szalai.
Behind closed doors.

Wednesday, 28 August 2013
AC Milan (1) 3 *(Boateng 9, 77, Balotelli 55)*
PSV Eindhoven (0) 0   51,598
AC Milan: (433) Abbiati; Abate, Zapata, Mexes, De Sciglio; Montolivo, De Jong, Muntari (Nocerino 82); Boateng (Robinho 86), Balotelli, El Shaarawy (Poli 74).
PSV Eindhoven: (433) Zoet; Brenet, Bruma, Rekik, Willems; Wijnaldum, Schaars, Maher (Toivonen 69); Park (Jozefzoon 61), Matavz, Depay (Locadia 74).

Celtic (1) 3 *(Commons 45, Samaras 48, Forrest 90)*
Shakhter Karagandy (0) 0   50,063
Celtic: (4411) Forster; Matthews, Mulgrew, Ambrose, Lustig; Commons (Boerrigter 79), Ledley, Brown, Forrest (van Dijk 90); Stokes; Samaras.
Shakhter Karagandy: (541) Mokin; Dzidic, Poryvaev, Vasiljevic, Maliy, Simcevic; Ghazaryan, Vicius, Canas, Finonchenko (Zenkovich 83); Khizhnichenko.

Maribor (0) 0
Viktoria Plzen (1) 1 *(Tecl 3)*   12,306
Maribor: (4411) Handanovic; Milec, Rajcevic, Arghus (Filipovic 46), Viler; Cvijanovic, Mertelj, Ibraimi, Bohar (Mejac 75); Tavares (Mendy 65); Fajic.
Viktoria Plzen: (4231) Kozacik; Reznik (Petrzela 28), Prochazka, Cisovsky, Limbersky; Horava, Horvath; Rajtoral, Kovarik (Kolar 85), Darida; Tecl (Duris 74).

Real Sociedad (0) 2 *(Vela 67, 90)*
Lyon (0) 0   28,955
Real Sociedad: (433) Bravo; Ansotegui, Estrada, De la Bella, Markel (Elustondo 84); Martinez, Prieto (Castro 78), Zurutuza; Griezmann (Granero 72), Seferovic, Vela.
Lyon: (433) Lopes; Bedimo, Kone B, Fofana, Miguel Lopes; UGrmtiti, Grenier, Gourcuff (Bahlouli 77); Gonalons (Ferri 84), Lacazette, Benzia (Fekir 46).

Zenit St Petersburg (1) 4 *(Danny 29, 48, Bukharov 66, Arshavin 78 (pen))*
Pacos Ferreira (0) 2 *(Manuel Jose 67, Carlao 83)*   21,507
Zenit St Petersburg: (4231) Lodigin; Aniukov, Luis Neto, Lombaerts, Smolnikov; Tymoschuk, Witsel (Zyryanov 69); Mogilevets, Shirokov (Arshavin 46), Danny (Kerzhakov 73); Bukharov.
Pacos Ferreira: (433) Degra; Nuno Santos (Rodrigo Antonio 64), Gregory, Ricardo, Helder Lopes; Romeu, Andre Leao, Vitor; Manuel Jose (Caetano 80), Carlao, Hurtado (Rui Miguel 56).

GROUP STAGE

GROUP A

Tuesday, 17 September 2013
Manchester U (1) 4 *(Rooney 22, 70, van Persie 59, Valencia 79)*
Bayer Leverkusen (0) 2 *(Rolfes 54, Toprak 88)*   74,000
Manchester U: (442) De Gea; Smalling, Ferdinand, Vidic, Evra; Valencia, Carrick, Fellaini (Cleverley 81), Kagawa (Young 71); Rooney (Hernandez 84), van Persie.
Bayer Leverkusen: (433) Leno; Donati, Spahic, Toprak, Boenisch; Can, Reinartz, Rolfes; Sam (Kruse 78), Kiessling (Derdiyok 78), Son (Bender 64).

Real Sociedad (0) 0
Shakhtar Donetsk (0) 2 *(Alex Teixeira 65, 87)*   27,902
Real Sociedad: (433) Bravo; Estrada, Mikel Gonzalez, Martinez, De la Bella; Markel, Prieto, Pardo (Granero 83); Vela, Seferovic (Agirretxe 69), Griezmann (Castro 74).
Shakhtar Donetsk: (4231) Pyatov; Srna, Rakitskiy, Kucher, Shevchuk; Fernando (Fred 86), Hubschman (Stepanenko 67); Douglas Costa (Bernard 76), Alex Teixeira, Taison; Luiz Adriano.

Wednesday, 2 October 2013
Bayer Leverkusen (1) 2 *(Rolfes 45, Hegeler 90)*
Real Sociedad (0) 1 *(Vela 51)*   27,462
Bayer Leverkusen: (442) Leno; Hilbert, Wollscheid, Toprak, Boenisch (Can 69); Bender, Reinartz, Rolfes, Sam (Hegeler 84); Kiessling, Son (Kruse 68).
Real Sociedad: (433) Bravo; Carlos Martinez, Mikel Gonzalez, Martinez, De la Bella; Markel, Elustondo, Zurutuza (Ros 90); Vela, Seferovic (Agirretxe 68), Griezmann (Castro 83).

Shakhtar Donetsk (0) 1 *(Taison 76)*
Manchester U (1) 1 *(Welbeck 18)*   51,555
Shakhtar Donetsk: (4231) Pyatov; Srna, Kucher, Rakitskiy, Shevchuk; Fernando (Ilsinho 84), Hubschman; Taison (Bernard 90), Alex Teixeira, Douglas Costa; Luiz Adriano (Ferreyra 89).
Manchester U: (442) De Gea; Da Silva R, Smalling, Vidic, Evra; Valencia, Carrick, Fellaini (Giggs 66), Cleverley; Welbeck (Jones 90), van Persie.

Wednesday, 23 October 2013
Bayer Leverkusen (1) 4 *(Kiessling 23, 72, Rolfes 51 (pen), Sam 57)*
Shakhtar Donetsk (0) 0   25,184
Bayer Leverkusen: (442) Leno; Castro, Spahic (Wollscheid 56), Boenisch, Toprak; Donati, Rolfes, Can, Sam; Son (Hegeler 71), Kiessling (Derdiyok 76).
Shakhtar Donetsk: (442) Pyatov; Kucher, Shevchuk, Rakitskiy, Hubschman; Fernando (Ilsinho 61), Douglas Costa, Srna, Luiz Adriano (Ferreyra 78); Alex Teixeira, Taison (Bernard 46).

Manchester U (1) 1 *(Martinez 2 (og))*
Real Sociedad (0) 0   74,500
Manchester U: (442) De Gea; Da Silva R (Smalling 59), Jones, Evans, Evra; Valencia, Carrick, Giggs, Kagawa; Hernandez (Young 80), Rooney.
Real Sociedad: (451) Bravo; Carlos Martinez, Mikel Gonzalez, Martinez, De la Bella; Vela, Zurutuza (Castro 75), Markel, Prieto (Pardo 68), Griezmann; Seferovic (Agirretxe 75).

Tuesday, 5 November 2013
Real Sociedad (0) 0
Manchester U (0) 0   30,998
Real Sociedad: (433) Bravo; Carlos Martinez, Mikel Gonzalez, Martinez, De la Bella; Pardo (Prieto 72), Markel, Zurutuza; Vela, Agirretxe (Castro 64), Griezmann (Seferovic 79).
Manchester U: (442) De Gea; Smalling, Ferdinand, Vidic, Evra; Valencia, Fellaini■, Giggs, Kagawa (Jones 90); Rooney (van Persie 63), Hernandez (Young 64).

Shakhtar Donetsk (0) 0
Bayer Leverkusen (0) 0   50,115
Shakhtar Donetsk: (4231) Pyatov; Srna, Kucher, Rakitskiy, Shevchuk; Fernando, Hubschman; Douglas Costa (Taison 78), Alex Teixeira, Bernard (Ilsinho 64); Ferreyra (Luiz Adriano 78).
Bayer Leverkusen: (433) Leno; Donati, Spahic, Toprak, Boenisch; Bender, Rolfes, Castro (Can 69); Son (Hegeler 77), Kiessling, Sam (Kruse 90).

Wednesday, 27 November 2013
Bayer Leverkusen (0) 0
Manchester U (2) 5 *(Valencia 22, Spahic 30 (og), Evans 66, Smalling 77, Nani 88)*   29,412
Bayer Leverkusen: (433) Leno; Donati, Spahic, Toprak, Can; Bender (Kohr 81), Reinartz (Hegeler 70), Rolfes; Castro, Kiessling, Son (Derdiyok 70).
Manchester U: (4231) De Gea; Smalling, Ferdinand, Evans, Evra (Buttner 69); Giggs, Jones; Valencia (Young 80), Nani, Kagawa; Rooney (Anderson 80).

Shakhtar Donetsk (1) 4 *(Luiz Adriano 37, Alex Teixeira 48, Douglas Costa 68, 87)*
Real Sociedad (0) 0   44,384
Shakhtar Donetsk: (4231) Pyatov; Srna, Rakitskiy, Kucher, Shevchuk; Fred, Stepanenko; Douglas Costa, Alex Teixeira (Eduardo 75), Bernard (Taison 68); Luiz Adriano (Ferreyra 71).

Real Sociedad: (442) Bravo; Cadamuro, Ansotegui, Martinez, De la Bella; Pardo (Ros 68), Elustondo, Prieto, Castro; Vela (Seferovic 74), Griezmann (Agirretxe 74).

Tuesday, 10 December 2013
Manchester U (0) 1 *(Jones 67)*
Shakhtar Donetsk (0) 0   74,506
Manchester U: (4231) De Gea; Da Silva R, Ferdinand, Evans, Buttner (Valencia 88); Jones, Giggs (Cleverley 63); Young (van Persie 63), Kagawa, Januzaj; Rooney.
Shakhtar Donetsk: (4231) Pyatov; Srna, Kucher, Rakitskiy, Shevchuk; Fred (Fernando 81), Stepanenko; Douglas Costa, Alex Teixeira, Taison (Bernard 63); Luiz Adriano (Ferreyra 88).

Real Sociedad (0) 0
Bayer Leverkusen (0) 1 *(Toprak 49)*   23,408
Real Sociedad: (433) Zubikarai; Markel, Carlos Martinez, Mikel Gonzalez (Gazta 66), Ansotegui; Jose Angel, Elustondo (Prieto 62), Pardo; Griezmann, Agirretxe (Seferovic 80), Vela.
Bayer Leverkusen: (433) Leno; Castro, Spahic, Toprak, Donati; Rolfes, Hegeler (Kruse 46), Bender; Can, Son (Kohr 90), Kiessling (Derdiyok 86).

Group A Table	P	W	D	L	F	A	GD	Pts
Manchester U	6	4	2	0	12	3	9	14
Bayer Leverkusen	6	3	1	2	9	10	–1	10
Shakhtar Donetsk	6	2	2	2	7	6	1	8
Real Sociedad	6	0	1	5	1	10	–9	1

GROUP B

Tuesday, 17 September 2013
FC Copenhagen (1) 1 *(Jorgensen 14)*
Juventus (0) 1 *(Quagliarella 54)*   36,524
FC Copenhagen: (442) Wiland; Jacobsen, Mellberg, Sigurdsson, Bengtsson; Bolanos (Toutouh 79), Claudemir (Margreitter 86), Delaney, Braaten; Adi (Gislason 69), Jorgensen.
Juventus: (352) Buffon; Ogbonna, Bonucci, Chiellini; Lichtsteiner (Isla 87), Vidal, Pirlo, Pogba, Peluso (De Ceglie 73); Tevez, Quagliarella (Giovinco 77).

Galatasaray (0) 1 *(Bulut 84)*
Real Madrid (1) 6 *(Isco 33, Benzema 54, 81, Ronaldo 63, 66, 90)*   47,669
Galatasaray: (433) Muslera; Eboue, Chedjou, Nounkeu, Riera; Inan, Felipe Melo, Baytar (Bruma 62); Yilmaz B (Bulut 78), Sneijder, Drogba (Amrabat 46).
Real Madrid: (4231) Casillas (Diego Lopez 14); Carvajal, Sergio Ramos, Pepe, Arbeloa; Modric (Illarramendi 72), Khedira; Di Maria, Isco (Bale 64), Ronaldo; Benzema.

Wednesday, 2 October 2013
Juventus (0) 2 *(Vidal 78 (pen), Quagliarella 87)*
Galatasaray (1) 2 *(Drogba 36, Bulut 88)*   33,466
Juventus: (352) Buffon; Barzagli, Bonucci (Llorente 68), Chiellini; Lichtsteiner (Isla 46); Pirlo, Asamoah, Vidal, Pogba; Tevez, Vucinic (Quagliarella 25).
Galatasaray: (4231) Muslera; Eboue, Kaya (Zan 26), Chedjou, Riera (Amrabat 60); Felipe Melo, Inan; Balta, Sneijder (Bulut 74), Bruma; Drogba.

Real Madrid (1) 4 *(Ronaldo 21, 66, Di Maria 71, 90)*
FC Copenhagen (0) 0   69,347
Real Madrid: (442) Casillas; Carvajal, Pepe, Varane, Marcelo; Di Maria, Modric (Isco 67), Khedira (Morata 74), Illarramendi; Benzema (Jese 81), Ronaldo.
FC Copenhagen: (442) Wiland; Jacobsen, Mellberg, Sigurdsson, Bengtsson; Gislason, Delaney, Claudemir, Toutouh (Bolanos 63); Braaten (Adi 67), Jorgensen (Kristensen 72).

Wednesday, 23 October 2013
Galatasaray (3) 3 *(Felipe Melo 10, Sneijder 38, Drogba 45)*
FC Copenhagen (0) 1 *(Claudemir 88)*   42,798
Galatasaray: (442) Muslera; Eboue, Kaya, Chedjou, Nounkeu; Bruma, Inan, Felipe Melo (Gulselam 76), Sneijder (Amrabat 80); Yilmaz B, Drogba (Bulut 85).

FC Copenhagen: (442) Wiland; Jacobsen, Mellberg, Sigurdsson, Bengtsson; Gislason (Bolanos 46), Claudemir, Delaney, Jorgensen; Braaten (Toutouh 84), Vetokele (Adi 46).

Real Madrid (2) 2 *(Ronaldo 4, 28 (pen))*
Juventus (1) 1 *(Llorente 23)* 77,856
Real Madrid: (4231) Casillas; Arbeloa, Sergio Ramos, Pepe, Marcelo; Khedira, Illarramendi (Isco 72); Di Maria (Morata 79), Modric, Ronaldo; Benzema (Bale 67).
Juventus: (433) Buffon; Caceres, Barzagli, Chiellini■, Ogbonna (Giovinco 69); Vidal, Pirlo (Asamoah 59), Pogba; Tevez, Llorente (Bonucci 50), Marchisio.

Tuesday, 5 November 2013
FC Copenhagen (1) 1 *(Braaten 6)*
Galatasaray (0) 0 36,204
FC Copenhagen: (442) Wiland; Jacobsen, Mellberg, Sigurdsson, Bengtsson (Bolanos 56), Claudemir (Margreitter 87), Delaney, Braaten; Jorgensen, Toutouh (Kristensen 75).
Galatasaray: (442) Iscan; Eboue, Kaya (Bulut 76), Chedjou, Riera; Bruma, Inan, Felipe Melo, Yilmaz A (Gulselam 62); Yilmaz B (Amrabat 86), Drogba.

Juventus (1) 2 *(Vidal 42 (pen), Llorente 65)*
Real Madrid (0) 2 *(Ronaldo 52, Bale 60)* 40,696
Juventus: (433) Buffon; Caceres, Barzagli, Bonucci, Asamoah; Vidal, Pirlo, Pogba; Tevez (Quagliarella 81), Marchisio, Llorente (Giovinco 88).
Real Madrid: (433) Casillas; Sergio Ramos, Pepe, Varane, Marcelo; Khedira, Alonso (Illarramendi 71), Bale (Di Maria 75); Modric, Ronaldo, Benzema (Jese 81).

Wednesday, 27 November 2013
Juventus (1) 3 *(Vidal 29 (pen), 61 (pen), 63)*
FC Copenhagen (0) 1 *(Mellberg 56)* 39,506
Juventus: (4411) Buffon; Caceres, Bonucci, Chiellini, Asamoah; Padoin (Marchisio 69), Vidal (Ogbonna 83), Pirlo, Pogba; Tevez (Vucinic 81); Llorente.
FC Copenhagen: (451) Wiland; Jacobsen, Mellberg, Sigurdsson, Bengtsson; Gislason, Claudemir, Delaney (Amankwaa 76), Bolanos (Kristensen 61), Toutouh (Pourie 80); Jorgensen.

Real Madrid (1) 4 *(Bale 37, Arbeloa 51, Di Maria 63, Isco 80)*
Galatasaray (1) 1 *(Bulut 38)* 67,728
Real Madrid: (4231) Casillas; Arbeloa, Sergio Ramos■, Pepe, Marcelo (Carvajal 74); Casemiro (Alonso 58), Illarramendi; Bale, Isco, Di Maria; Jese (Nacho 28).
Galatasaray: (4231) Iscan; Eboue, Zan, Chedjou, Nounkeu; Felipe Melo (Gulselam 88), Inan; Bruma (Sneijder 64), Bulut, Amrabat (Riera 67); Drogba.

Tuesday, 10 December 2013
FC Copenhagen (0) 0
Real Madrid (1) 2 *(Modric 25, Ronaldo 48)* 37,241
FC Copenhagen: (442) Wiland; Jacobsen, Mellberg, Sigurdsson, Bengtsson; Gislason, Delaney, Claudemir, Toutouh (Pourie 79); Jorgensen (Bolanos 9 (Remmer 77)), Vetokele.
Real Madrid: (4231) Casillas; Arbeloa, Nacho, Pepe, Marcelo; Alonso (Illarramendi 77), Modric (Casemiro 82); Bale, Isco (Di Maria 67), Ronaldo; Benzema.

Wednesday, 11 December 2013
Galatasaray (0) 1 *(Sneijder 85)*
Juventus (0) 0 37,375
Galatasaray: (3412) Muslera; Chedjou, Kaya, Zan; Eboue (Bulut 86), Felipe Melo, Inan, Riera; Sneijder (Gulselam 90); Yilmaz B, Drogba.
Juventus: (352) Buffon; Barzagli, Bonucci (Giovinco 90), Chiellini; Lichtsteiner, Vidal, Pogba, Marchisio (Quagliarella 86), Asamoah; Llorente, Tevez.

Group B Table	P	W	D	L	F	A	GD	Pts
Real Madrid	6	5	1	0	20	5	15	16
Galatasaray	6	2	1	3	8	14	–6	7
Juventus	6	1	3	2	9	9	0	6
FC Copenhagen	6	1	1	4	4	13	–9	4

GROUP C

Tuesday, 17 September 2013
Benfica (2) 2 *(Djuricic 4, Luisao 30)*
Anderlecht (0) 0 29,393
Benfica: (433) Artur Moraes; Siqueira, Garay, Luisao, Andre Almeida; Matic, Fejsa, Perez (John 69); Djuricic (Maxi Pereira 75), Cardozo (Lima 87), Markovic.
Anderlecht: (433) Proto; N'Sakala, Mbemba, Kouyate, Gillet; De Zeeuw (Acheampong 45), Milivojevic, Kljestan; Bruno (Praet 79), Mitrovic (Cyriac 76), Suarez.

Olympiacos (1) 1 *(Weiss 25)*
Paris St Germain (1) 4 *(Cavani 20, Thiago Motta 68, 73, Marquinhos 86)* 31,253
Olympiacos: (4231) Roberto; Maniatis, Medjani, Siovas, Bong Songo; Paulo Machado, Samaris; David Fuster (Saviola 74), Dominguez (Campbell 60), Weiss (Yatabare 84); Mitroglou.
Paris St Germain: (41212) Sirigu; Van Der Wiel, Marquinhos, Thiago Silva, Maxwell; Thiago Motta; Verratti (Rabiot 79), Matuidi; Lucas Moura (Lavezzi 46); Ibrahimovic, Cavani (Menez 89).

Wednesday, 2 October 2013
Anderlecht (0) 0
Olympiacos (1) 3 *(Mitroglou 17, 56, 72)* 15,918
Anderlecht: (442) Proto; Gillet, Kouyate, Nuytinck, N'Sakala; Bruno, Tielemans, Praet (Acheampong 74), Kljestan; Suarez, Mitrovic.
Olympiacos: (4231) Roberto; Maniatis, Manolas, Siovas, Bong Songo; Ndinga, Samaris; Olaitan (David Fuster 57), Saviola (Dominguez 65 (Holebas 78)), Weiss; Mitroglou.

Paris St Germain (3) 3 *(Ibrahimovic 5, 30, Marquinhos 25)*
Benfica (0) 0 44,732
Paris St Germain: (433) Sirigu; Van Der Wiel, Alex (Camara 78), Marquinhos, Maxwell; Verratti (Rabiot 70), Thiago Motta, Matuidi; Cavani, Ibrahimovic, Lavezzi (Lucas Moura 70).
Benfica: (433) Artur Moraes; Andre Almeida, Luisao, Garay, Siqueira; Fejsa (Gomes 29), Matic; Perez, Djuricic (Markovic 46), Gaitan (Sulejmani 66); Cardozo.

Wednesday, 23 October 2013
Anderlecht (0) 0
Paris St Germain (3) 5 *(Ibrahimovic 17, 22, 36, 62, Cavani 52)* 18,465
Anderlecht: (4231) Kaminski; Mbemba, Kouyate, Nuytinck, N'Sakala; Tielemans, Kljestan; Gillet, Praet (Milivojevic 72), Suarez (Acheampong 46); Mitrovic (Cyriac 72).
Paris St Germain: (433) Sirigu; Van Der Wiel, Alex (Camara 55), Marquinhos, Maxwell; Verratti, Thiago Motta, Matuidi (Rabiot 64); Cavani, Ibrahimovic, Lavezzi (Lucas Moura 71).

Benfica (0) 1 *(Cardozo 83)*
Olympiacos (1) 1 *(Dominguez 29)* 38,149
Benfica: (442) Artur Moraes; Luisao, Siqueira, Garay, Andre Almeida; Gaitan (Rodrigo 83), Matic, Perez (Ruben Amorim 82), Cardozo; Lima, John (Ivan Cavaleiro 46).
Olympiacos: (442) Roberto; Maniatis, Holebas, Manolas, Leandro Salino; Samaris, David Fuster (Yatabare 68), Siovas, Dominguez (Medjani 88); Weiss (Ndinga 56), Mitroglou.

Tuesday, 5 November 2013
Olympiacos (1) 1 *(Manolas 13)*
Benfica (0) 0 31,461
Olympiacos: (442) Roberto; Leandro Salino, Manolas, Siovas, Holebas; Yatabare (Ndinga 56), Maniatis, Samaris, David Fuster (Bong Songo 74); Saviola (Dominguez 46), Mitroglou.
Benfica: (4231) Artur Moraes; Maxi Pereira, Luisao, Garay, Silvio; Perez, Matic; Ruben Amorim (Ivan Cavaleiro 80), Gaitan, Markovic (Djuricic 74); Cardozo (Lima 70).

Paris St Germain (0) 1 *(Ibrahimovic 70)*
Anderlecht (0) 1 *(De Zeeuw 68)* 43,091
Paris St Germain: (4141) Sirigu; Van Der Wiel, Alex, Marquinhos (Thiago Silva 62), Maxwell; Thiago Motta; Lucas Moura, Matuidi, Verratti (Menez 75), Lavezzi (Pastore 75); Ibrahimovic.
Anderlecht: (4231) Kaminski; Vanden Borre, Mbemba, Kouyate, Deschacht; Kljestan■, Milivojevic; Praet (Acheampong 78), De Zeeuw (Nuytinck 90), N'Sakala; Mitrovic.

Wednesday, 27 November 2013
Anderlecht (1) 2 *(Mbemba 18, Bruno 76)*
Benfica (1) 3 *(Matic 34, Mbemba 53 (og), Rodrigo 90)*
16,780
Anderlecht: (451) Proto; Vanden Borre, Mbemba, Nuytinck (Vargas 73), Deschacht (Acheampong 55); Bruno, Gillet, Kouyate, Praet, N'Sakala; Mitrovic.
Benfica: (442) Artur Moraes; Maxi Pereira, Luisao, Garay, Andre Almeida; Gaitan (Sulejmani 71), Matic, Perez (Rodrigo 87), Markovic (Ivan Cavaleiro 89); Fejsa, Lima.

Paris St Germain (1) 2 *(Ibrahimovic 7, Cavani 90)*
Olympiacos (0) 1 *(Manolas 80)* 44,466
Paris St Germain: (433) Sirigu; Van Der Wiel, Alex, Thiago Silva, Maxwell; Verratti■, Thiago Motta, Matuidi (Lucas Moura 86); Cavani, Lavezzi (Rabiot 50), Ibrahimovic (Marquinhos 78).
Olympiacos: (4231) Roberto; Leandro Salino (Dominguez 57), Manolas, Siovas, Bong Songo (Weiss 46); Maniatis, Samaris; Campbell (Saviola 77), David Fuster, Holebas; Mitroglou.

Tuesday, 10 December 2013
Benfica (1) 2 *(Lima 45 (pen), Gaitan 58)*
Paris St Germain (1) 1 *(Cavani 37)* 30,089
Benfica: (442) Artur Moraes; Maxi Pereira, Luisao, Garay, Silvio; Fejsa, Matic, Perez (Gomes 89), Gaitan (Sulejmani 76); Markovic (Ivan Cavaleiro 69), Lima.
Paris St Germain: (4231) Sirigu; Traore, Marquinhos, Camara, Digne; Thiago Motta (Matuidi 61), Rabiot; Lucas Moura, Pastore, Menez; Cavani (Lavezzi 61).

Olympiacos (1) 3 *(Saviola 33, 58, Dominguez 90 (pen))*
Anderlecht (1) 1 *(Kljestan 39)* 31,444
Olympiacos: (4411) Roberto; Leandro Salino, Manolas, Siovas, Holebas; David Fuster (Ndinga 88), Samaris, Paulo Machado (Weiss 53); Campbell; Saviola (Dominguez 61); Olaitan.
Anderlecht: (433) Proto■; Vanden Borre (Acheampong 72), Kouyate■, Mbemba, N'Sakala■; Gillet, Milivojevic (Nuytinck 53), Kljestan; Najar, Mitrovic, Praet (Tielemans 83).

Group C Table	P	W	D	L	F	A	GD	Pts
Paris St Germain	6	4	1	1	16	5	11	13
Olympiacos	6	3	1	2	10	8	2	10
Benfica	6	3	1	2	8	8	0	10
Anderlecht	6	0	1	5	4	17	–13	1

GROUP D

Tuesday, 17 September 2013
Bayern Munich (2) 3 *(Alaba 3, Mandzukic 41, Robben 68)*
CSKA Moscow (0) 0 68,000
Bayern Munich: (4141) Neuer; Rafinha, Boateng, Dante, Alaba; Lahm; Robben (Shaqiri 79), Muller, Kroos (Schweinsteiger 71), Ribery; Mandzukic (Pizarro 75).
CSKA Moscow: (4231) Akinfeev; Nababkin, Berezutsky V, Ignashevich, Shchennikov; Cauna, Wernbloom; Zuber (Milanov 77), Honda, Vitinho (Tosic 46); Musa (Bazelyuk 73).

Viktoria Plzen (0) 0
Manchester C (0) 3 *(Dzeko 48, Toure 53, Aguero 58)*
11,281
Viktoria Plzen: (4231) Kozacik; Rajtoral, Hejda (Hubnik 66), Prochazka, Limbersky; Horava, Horvath; Petrzela, Kolar (Duris 61), Kovarik; Bakos (Tecl 84).

Manchester C: (4231) Hart; Zabaleta, Kompany, Nastasic, Kolarov; Toure (Javi Garcia 80), Fernandinho; Jesus Navas (Milner 67), Aguero, Nasri; Dzeko (Negredo 83).

Wednesday, 2 October 2013
CSKA Moscow (2) 3 *(Tosic 19, Honda 29, Reznik 78 (og))*
Viktoria Plzen (1) 2 *(Rajtoral 4, Bakos 90)* 6000
CSKA Moscow: (4231) Akinfeev; Nababkin, Berezutsky A, Ignashevich, Shchennikov; Elm (Milanov 72), Wernbloom; Tosic, Honda, Zuber (Gonzalez 63); Musa (Vitinho 88).
Viktoria Plzen: (4231) Kozacik; Rajtoral, Hubnik, Prochazka, Reznik (Pospisil 84); Horvath, Horava (Duris 76); Petrzela, Kolar, Kovarik (Tecl 70); Bakos.

Manchester C (0) 1 *(Negredo 80)*
Bayern Munich (1) 3 *(Ribery 7, Muller 56, Robben 60)*
45,021
Manchester C: (4231) Hart; Richards, Kompany, Nastasic, Clichy; Toure, Fernandinho; Jesus Navas, Aguero (Silva 70), Nasri (Milner 70); Dzeko (Negredo 57).
Bayern Munich: (4141) Neuer; Rafinha, Boateng■, Dante, Alaba; Lahm; Robben (Shaqiri 78), Schweinsteiger (Kirchhoff 76), Kroos, Ribery (Gotze 85); Muller.

Wednesday, 23 October 2013
Bayern Munich (2) 5 *(Ribery 25 (pen), 61, Alaba 37, Schweinsteiger 64, Gotze 90)*
Viktoria Plzen (0) 0 68,000
Bayern Munich: (4141) Neuer; Rafinha, Van Buyten, Contento, Alaba; Lahm (Gotze 63); Robben, Schweinsteiger, Kroos, Ribery (Muller 67); Mandzukic (Pizarro 71).
Viktoria Plzen: (4231) Kozacik; Reznik, Cisovsky, Hubnik, Limbersky (Kovarik 75); Prochazka, Horvath (Duris 63); Horava, Rajtoral, Petrzela (Tecl 86); Kolar.

CSKA Moscow (1) 1 *(Tosic 32)*
Manchester C (2) 2 *(Aguero 34, 42)* 14,000
CSKA Moscow: (4231) Akinfeev; Nababkin, Berezutsky V (Berezutsky A 6), Ignashevich, Shchennikov; Milanov, Wernbloom; Tosic, Honda, Zuber (Musa 50); Doumbia.
Manchester C: (352) Hart; Zabaleta, Nastasic, Kolarov; Jesus Navas, Fernandinho, Toure, Javi Garcia, Silva (Nasri 79); Aguero (Clichy 89); Negredo (Dzeko 71).

Tuesday, 5 November 2013
Manchester C (3) 5 *(Aguero 3 (pen), 20, Negredo 30, 51, 90)*
CSKA Moscow (1) 2 *(Doumbia 45, 71 (pen))* 38,512
Manchester C: (4411) Pantilimon; Zabaleta, Demichelis, Nastasic, Clichy; Nasri (Jesus Navas 76), Fernandinho (Milner 46), Toure, Silva (Kolarov 65); Aguero; Negredo.
CSKA Moscow: (4231) Akinfeev; Nababkin, Berezutsky A, Ignashevich, Shchennikov; Milanov (Elm 46), Wernbloom; Musa (Zuber 45), Honda (Vitinho 78), Tosic; Doumbia.

Viktoria Plzen (0) 0
Bayern Munich (0) 1 *(Mandzukic 66)* 11,360
Viktoria Plzen: (451) Kozacik; Rajtoral, Cisovsky, Prochazka, Hubnik (Reznik 71); Petrzela, Horava, Horvath, Duris (Pospisil 83), Kolar; Tecl (Bakos 87).
Bayern Munich: (4141) Neuer; Rafinha, Van Buyten, Alaba, Contento; Lahm; Muller (Mandzukic 59), Schweinsteiger (Javi Martinez 59), Kroos, Ribery; Gotze (Weiser 87).

Wednesday, 27 November 2013
CSKA Moscow (0) 1 *(Honda 62 (pen))*
Bayern Munich (1) 3 *(Robben 17, Gotze 56, Muller 65 (pen))* 14,000
CSKA Moscow: (4231) Akinfeev; Nababkin, Berezutsky A, Ignashevich, Shchennikov; Wernbloom, Milanov (Vitinho 90); Zuber (Elm 68), Honda, Tosic; Musa (Bazelyuk 80).
Bayern Munich: (4141) Neuer; Rafinha, Boateng, Dante, Alaba; Lahm (Thiago 29); Muller, Javi Martinez (Kirchhoff 80), Kroos, Robben; Gotze (Green 88).

Manchester C (1) 4 *(Aguero 33 (pen), Nasri 65, Negredo 78, Dzeko 89)*
Viktoria Plzen (1) 2 *(Horava 43, Tecl 69)* 37,742
Manchester C: (442) Hart; Richards, Demichelis, Lescott, Kolarov; Milner, Javi Garcia, Fernandinho (Toure 64), Nasri (Negredo 75); Aguero (Jesus Navas 46), Dzeko.
Viktoria Plzen: (4411) Kozacik; Rajtoral, Cisovsky, Prochazka, Hubnik; Petrzela (Kovarik 73), Horava, Horvath, Duris (Wagner 89); Kolar (Bakos 85); Tecl.

Tuesday, 10 December 2013
Bayern Munich (2) 2 *(Muller 5, Gotze 12)*
Manchester C (1) 3 *(Silva 28, Kolarov 59 (pen), Milner 62)* 68,000
Bayern Munich: (4141) Neuer; Lahm, Boateng, Dante, Alaba; Thiago; Muller, Gotze (Javi Martinez 55), Kroos, Ribery; Mandzukic (Shaqiri 68).
Manchester C: (4231) Hart; Richards (Zabaleta 15), Demichelis, Lescott, Kolarov; Javi Garcia, Fernandinho; Jesus Navas, Silva (Negredo 73), Milner; Dzeko (Rodwell 88).

Viktoria Plzen (0) 2 *(Kolar 77, Wagner 90)*
CSKA Moscow (0) 1 *(Musa 65)* 11,205
Viktoria Plzen: (451) Kozacik; Rajtoral, Cisovsky, Prochazka, Limbersky; Horava, Horvath, Petrzela (Bakos 70), Kolar, Duris (Kovarik 58); Tecl (Wagner 82).
CSKA Moscow: (451) Akinfeev; Karavev, Berezutsky A, Ignashevich, Shchennikov; Elm, Wernbloom*, Milanov (Zuber 74), Dzagoev*, Tosic (Honda 52); Musa (Vitinho 90).

Group D Table	P	W	D	L	F	A	GD	Pts
Bayern Munich	6	5	0	1	17	5	12	15
Manchester C	6	5	0	1	18	10	8	15
Viktoria Plzen	6	1	0	5	6	17	–11	3
CSKA Moscow	6	1	0	5	8	17	–9	3

GROUP E

Wednesday, 18 September 2013
Chelsea (1) 1 *(Oscar 45)*
FC Basel (0) 2 *(Salah 71, Streller 82)* 40,358
Chelsea: (433) Cech; Ivanovic, Cahill, Luiz, Cole; Oscar, van Ginkel (Mikel 75), Lampard (Ba 76); Willian (Mata 67), Eto'o, Hazard.
FC Basel: (442) Sommer; Voser, Schar, Ivanov, Safari; Salah (Xhaka 88), Diaz, Frei, Stocker (Ajeti 83); Sio (Delgado 65), Streller.

Schalke 04 (0) 3 *(Uchida 67, Boateng 78, Draxler 85)*
Steaua Bucharest (0) 0 49,358
Schalke 04: (4231) Hildebrand; Uchida, Howedes, Matip, Aogo; Hoger (Goretzka 88), Neustadter; Farfan (Clemens 88), Boateng, Draxler; Szalai (Fuchs 82).
Steaua Bucharest: (4231) Tatarusanu; Georgievski, Szukala, Gardos, Latovlevici; Pintilii, Bourceanu; Popa, Stanciu (Tatu 60 (Cristea 72)), Tanase; Kapetanos (Piovaccari 64).

Tuesday, 1 October 2013
FC Basel (0) 0
Schalke 04 (0) 1 *(Draxler 54)* 33,251
FC Basel: (433) Sommer; Voser, Schar, Ivanov, Safari (Delgado 84); Diaz, Frei (Degen 84), Xhaka (Sio 62); Salah, Streller, Stocker.
Schalke 04: (4231) Hildebrand; Uchida, Howedes, Felipe Santana, Aogo (Kolasinac 78); Hoger, Neustadter; Farfan (Szalai 45), Meyer (Hoogland 84), Draxler; Boateng.

Steau Bucharest (0) 0
Chelsea (2) 4 *(Ramires 19, 55, Georgievski 44 (og), Lampard 90)* 36,713
Steau Bucharest: (4231) Tatarusanu; Georgievski (Varela 71), Szukala, Gardos, Latovlevici; Bourceanu, Filip; Popa (Tatu 46), Stanciu, Tanase; Piovaccari (Kapetanos 46).
Chelsea: (433) Cech; Ivanovic, Terry, Luiz, Cole; Oscar (Azpilicueta 78), Ramires, Lampard; Mata (Willian 80), Torres (Eto'o 11), Schurrle.

Tuesday, 22 October 2013
Schalke 04 (0) 0
Chelsea (1) 3 *(Torres 5, 69, Hazard 87)* 54,442
Schalke 04: (4231) Hildebrand; Uchida, Howedes, Matip, Aogo; Jones (Kolasinac 70), Neustadter; Clemens, Meyer (Goretzka 78), Draxler; Boateng (Szalai 70).
Chelsea: (433) Cech; Azpilicueta, Terry, Cahill, Ivanovic; Oscar (Luiz 83), Ramires, Lampard; Schurrle (Mikel 72), Torres, Hazard (Eto'o 88).

Steau Bucharest (0) 1 *(Tatu 88)*
FC Basel (0) 1 *(Diaz 48)* 23,899
Steau Bucharest: (4231) Tatarusanu; Georgievski, Szukala, Gardos, Latovlevici; Bourceanu, Pintilii (Filip 59); Popa, Stanciu (Tatu 55), Tanase; Piovaccari (Kapetanos 46).
FC Basel: (433) Sommer; Voser, Schar, Ivanov, Safari (Xhaka 68); Diaz, Die (Ajeti 86), Frei; Salah, Streller (El-Nenny 74), Stocker.

Wednesday, 6 November 2013
Chelsea (1) 3 *(Eto'o 31, 54, Ba 83)*
Schalke 04 (0) 0 41,194
Chelsea: (433) Cech; Ivanovic, Cahill, Terry, Azpilicueta; Ramires, Oscar (Lampard 81), Mikel; Willian, Schurrle (De Bruyne 78), Eto'o (Ba 76).
Schalke 04: (451) Hildebrand; Aogo, Howedes, Uchida, Fuchs (Meyer 66); Matip, Boateng (Kolasinac 76), Draxler (Clemens 61), Jones, Neustadter; Szalai.

FC Basel (0) 1 *(Sio 90)*
Steaua Bucharest (1) 1 *(Piovaccari 17)* 30,704
FC Basel: (4231) Sommer; Voser, Schar, Ivanov, Xhaka; Die, Frei (Diaz 78); Salah (Degen 84), Delgado (Sio 66), Stocker; Streller.
Steaua Bucharest: (4231) Tatarusanu; Georgievski, Szukala, Gardos, Latovlevici; Bourceanu, Pintilii (Filip 46); Popa, Stanciu (Chipciu 63), Tanase; Piovaccari (Kapetanos 76).

Tuesday, 26 November 2013
FC Basel (0) 1 *(Salah 87)*
Chelsea (0) 0 35,208
FC Basel: (451) Sommer; Voser, Schar, Ivanov, Xhaka (Ajeti 71); Salah, El-Nenny, Die, Frei, Stocker (Sauro 90); Streller (Sio 78).
Chelsea: (4411) Cech; Ivanovic, Cahill, Terry, Azpilicueta; Ramires, Mikel, Lampard, Willian (De Bruyne 86); Oscar (Hazard 55); Eto'o (Torres 42).

Steau Bucharest (0) 0
Schalke 04 (0) 0 50,633
Steau Bucharest: (4231) Tatarusanu; Prepelita (Stanciu 82), Szukala, Gardos, Latovlevici; Neagu (Varela 46), Bourceanu; Popa, Chipciu (Iancu 77), Tanase; Piovaccari.
Schalke 04: (4231) Fahrmann; Uchida, Howedes, Felipe Santana; Aogo; Jones, Neustadter; Farfan, Meyer (Draxler 73), Fuchs (Obasi Ogbuke 88); Szalai.

Wednesday, 11 December 2013
Chelsea (1) 1 *(Ba 11)*
Steaua Bucharest (0) 0 41,181
Chelsea: (433) Schwarzer; Ivanovic, Luiz, Terry, Cole; Oscar (Schurrle 66), Mikel (Ramires 74), Lampard; Willian (De Bruyne 80), Ba, Hazard.
Steaua Bucharest: (451) Tatarusanu; Georgievski, Szukala, Gardos, Latovlevici; Chipciu, Iancu, Pintilii (Tatu 64), Stanciu (Prepelita 60), Parvulescu; Kapetanos (Piovaccari 71).

Schalke 04 (0) 2 *(Draxler 51, Matip 57)*
FC Basel (0) 0 52,093
Schalke 04: (4231) Fahrmann; Uchida, Howedes (Szalai 30), Felipe Santana, Kolasinac; Matip, Neustadter; Farfan, Meyer (Goretzka 88), Draxler (Fuchs 66); Boateng.
FC Basel: (451) Sommer; Voser, Schar, Ivanov*, Xhaka; Salah, El-Nenny (Sio 61), Frei, Die (Ajeti 72), Stocker (Delgado 72); Streller.

Group E Table

	P	W	D	L	F	A	GD	Pts
Chelsea	6	4	0	2	12	3	9	12
Schalke 04	6	3	1	2	6	6	0	10
FC Basel	6	2	2	2	5	6	-1	8
Steaua Bucharest	6	0	3	3	2	10	-8	3

GROUP F

Wednesday, 18 September 2013

Marseille (0) 1 *(Ayew J 90 (pen))*

Arsenal (0) 2 *(Walcott 65, Ramsey 84)*   38,380

Marseille: (4231) Mandanda; Fanni, N'Koulou, Lucas Mendes, Morel; Romao, Imbula (Thauvin 79); Payet (Ayew J 73), Valbuena (Khelifa 90), Ayew A; Gignac.
Arsenal: (4231) Szczesny; Sagna, Mertesacker, Koscielny, Gibbs; Flamini (Miyaichi 90), Ramsey; Walcott (Monreal 78), Wilshere, Ozil; Giroud.

Napoli (1) 2 *(Higuain 29, Insigne 67)*

Borussia Dortmund (0) 1 *(Zuniga 88 (og))*   55,766

Napoli: (4231) Reina; Maggio, Albiol, Britos, Zuniga; Behrami, Inler; Callejon, Hamsik (Mesto 90), Insigne (Mertens 73); Higuain (Pandev 77).
Borussia Dortmund: (4231) Weidenfeller■; Grosskreutz, Subotic, Hummels (Aubameyang 45), Schmelzer; Sahin, Bender; Blaszczykowski (Langerak 45), Mkhitaryan (Hofmann 76), Reus; Lewandowski.

Tuesday, 1 October 2013

Arsenal (2) 2 *(Ozil 8, Giroud 15)*

Napoli (0) 0   59,536

Arsenal: (433) Szczesny; Sagna, Mertesacker, Koscielny, Gibbs; Arteta, Flamini, Ramsey (Monreal 88); Rosicky (Wilshere 63), Giroud, Ozil.
Napoli: (4231) Reina; Mesto, Albiol (Fernandez 82), Britos, Zuniga; Behrami, Inler; Callejon (Zapata 76), Hamsik, Insigne; Pandev (Mertens 60).

Borussia Dortmund (1) 3 *(Lewandowski 19, 80 (pen), Reus 52)*

Marseille (0) 0   65,829

Borussia Dortmund: (4231) Langerak; Grosskreutz, Subotic, Hummels, Durm; Sahin, Bender; Aubameyang (Blaszczykowski 71), Mkhitaryan (Papastathopoulos 88), Reus (Hofmann 82); Lewandowski.
Marseille: (4231) Mandanda; Fanni, N'Koulou, Lucas Mendes, Mendy; Romao, Imbula; Payet (Lemina 73), Valbuena (Ayew J 81), Ayew A; Khelifa (Thauvin 81).

Tuesday, 22 October 2013

Arsenal (1) 1 *(Giroud 41)*

Borussia Dortmund (1) 2 *(Mkhitaryan 16, Lewandowski 82)*   60,011

Arsenal: (4231) Szczesny; Sagna, Mertesacker, Koscielny, Gibbs; Ramsey (Bendtner 86), Arteta; Wilshere (Cazorla 58), Ozil, Rosicky (Gnabry 89); Giroud.
Borussia Dortmund: (4231) Weidenfeller; Grosskreutz, Subotic, Hummels, Schmelzer; Bender, Sahin; Blaszczykowski (Aubameyang 67), Mkhitaryan (Hofmann 66), Reus (Papastathopoulos 87); Lewandowski.

Marseille (0) 1 *(Ayew A 86)*

Napoli (1) 2 *(Callejon 42, Zapata 67)*   39,790

Marseille: (4231) Mandanda; Fanni (Abdallah 52), N'Koulou, Diawara, Morel; Romao, Cheyrou; Payet (Thauvin 70), Valbuena, Ayew A; Gignac (Ayew J 76).
Napoli: (4231) Reina; Maggio, Fernandez, Albiol, Armero; Behrami, Inler; Callejon, Hamsik (Insigne 83), Mertens (Mesto 76); Higuain (Zapata 58).

Wednesday, 6 November 2013

Borussia Dortmund (0) 0

Arsenal (0) 1 *(Ramsey 62)*   65,829

Borussia Dortmund: (4231) Weidenfeller; Grosskreutz, Papastathopoulos, Subotic, Schmelzer; Sahin, Bender (Hofmann 75); Blaszczykowski (Aubameyang 74), Mkhitaryan, Reus (Schieber 86); Lewandowski.
Arsenal: (4231) Szczesny; Sagna, Mertesacker, Koscielny, Gibbs; Ramsey, Arteta; Cazorla (Monreal 75), Ozil, Rosicky (Vermaelen 90); Giroud (Bendtner 90).

Napoli (2) 3 *(Inler 22, Higuain 25, 75)*

Marseille (1) 2 *(Ayew A 10, Thauvin 64)*   39,148

Napoli: (4231) Reina; Maggio, Albiol, Fernandez, Armero; Dzemaili (Behrami 90), Inler; Callejon, Pandev (Hamsik 66), Mertens (Insigne 83); Higuain.
Marseille: (4231) Mandanda; Abdallah, N'Koulou, Morel, Diawara; Cheyrou, Romao (Lemina 83); Thauvin, Valbuena (Payet 56), Ayew A; Ayew J (Gignac 67).

Tuesday, 26 November 2013

Arsenal (1) 2 *(Wilshere 1, 65)*

Marseille (0) 0   59,912

Arsenal: (4231) Szczesny; Sagna, Mertesacker, Koscielny, Monreal; Ramsey, Flamini; Wilshere (Walcott 75), Ozil (Arteta 81), Rosicky (Cazorla 75); Giroud.
Marseille: (4231) Mandanda; Abdallah, N'Koulou, Lucas Mendes, Morel; Lemina (Cheyrou 82), Romao; Ayew J (Valbuena 56), Imbula (Thauvin 56), Khelifa; Gignac.

Borussia Dortmund (1) 3 *(Reus 10 (pen), Blaszczykowski 60, Aubameyang 78)*

Napoli (0) 1 *(Insigne 71)*   65,829

Borussia Dortmund: (4231) Weidenfeller; Grosskreutz, Bender, Papastathopoulos, Durm; Sahin, Kehl; Blaszczykowski (Aubameyang 68), Mkhitaryan, Reus (Piszczek 81); Lewandowski (Schieber 89).
Napoli: (4231) Reina; Maggio, Albiol, Fernandez, Armero; Behrami, Dzemaili (Inler 62); Callejon (Insigne 66), Pandev (Zapata 76), Mertens; Higuain.

Wednesday, 11 December 2013

Marseille (1) 1 *(Diawara 14)*

Borussia Dortmund (1) 2 *(Lewandowski 4, Grosskreutz 86)*   36,655

Marseille: (442) Mandanda; Fanni, Lucas Mendes (Abdallah 46), Diawara, Mendy; Thauvin (Imbula 79), Cheyrou, Lemina, Payet■; Khelifa (Morel 54), Gignac.
Borussia Dortmund: (4231) Weidenfeller; Grosskreutz, Papastathopoulos, Sarr, Durm; Kehl (Piszczek 77), Sahin; Blaszczykowski (Hofmann 66), Mkhitaryan, Reus (Schieber 78); Lewandowski.

Napoli (0) 2 *(Higuain 73, Callejon 90)*

Arsenal (0) 0   34,027

Napoli: (4231) Rafael Cabral; Maggio, Fernandez, Albiol, Armero; Dzemaili, Behrami; Callejon, Pandev (Insigne 57), Mertens; Higuain.
Arsenal: (4231) Szczesny; Jenkinson, Mertesacker, Koscielny, Gibbs; Flamini, Arteta■; Rosicky (Monreal 74), Ozil, Cazorla (Ramsey 67); Giroud.

Group F Table

	P	W	D	L	F	A	GD	Pts
Borussia Dortmund	6	4	0	2	11	6	5	12
Arsenal	6	4	0	2	8	5	3	12
Napoli	6	4	0	2	10	9	1	12
Marseille	6	0	0	6	5	14	-9	0

GROUP G

Wednesday, 18 September 2013

Atletico Madrid (1) 3 *(Miranda 40, Turan 64, Leo Baptistao 80)*

Zenit St Petersburg (0) 1 *(Hulk 58)*   33,855

Atletico Madrid: (4231) Courtois; Juanfran, Miranda, Godin, Filipe Luis; Mario Suarez, Gabi; Koke (Rodriguez 88), Adrian (Leo Baptistao 79), Turan (Raul Garcia 86); Villa.
Zenit St Petersburg: (523) Lodigin; Smolnikov, Lombaerts, Luis Neto (Shatov 46), Hubocan, Ansaldi; Zyryanov (Arshavin 74), Witsel; Hulk (Bystrov 85), Kerzhakov, Danny.

Austria Vienna (0) 0

FC Porto (0) 1 *(Gonzalez 55)*   37,500

Austria Vienna: (451) Lindner; Koch, Rogulj, Ortlechner, Suttner; Royer, Stankovic, Holland (Okotie 84), Mader, Jun (Simkovic 68); Hosiner (Kienast 84).
FC Porto: (433) Helton; Alex Sandro, Mangala, Otamendi, Danilo; Josue, Gonzalez (Quintero 87), Fernando; Lica (Izmailov 67), Martinez, Varela (Herrera 79).

Tuesday, 1 October 2013
FC Porto (1) 1 *(Martinez 16)*
Atletico Madrid (0) 2 *(Godin 58, Turan 87)* 33,989
FC Porto: (442) Helton; Danilo, Otamendi, Mangala (Ghilas 89), Alex Sandro; Defour, Fernando, Gonzalez (Quintero 68), Josue (Lica 60); Martinez, Varela.
Atletico Madrid: (442) Courtois; Juanfran, Miranda, Godin, Filipe Luis; Raul Garcia (Torres 79), Turan, Tiago, Gabi; Villa (Rodriguez 46), Leo Baptistao (Koke 74).

Zenit St Petersburg (0) 0
Austria Vienna (0) 0 18,785
Zenit St Petersburg: (4231) Lodigin; Aniukov (Criscito 87), Hubocan, Lombaerts, Smolnikov; Faitzulin, Witsel**; Shatov (Shirokov 49), Danny; Kerzhakov (Arshavin 64).
Austria Vienna: (4231) Lindner; Koch, Ramsebner, Ortlechner, Suttner; Holland, Mader, Royer (Murg 57), Simkovic, Leovac (Okotie 81); Hosiner (Kienast 90).

Tuesday, 22 October 2013
Austria Vienna (0) 0
Atletico Madrid (2) 3 *(Raul Garcia 8, Diego Costa 20, 53)* 45,675
Austria Vienna: (451) Lindner; Dilaver, Rogulj, Ortlechner, Suttner; Royer (Leovac 86), Stankovic (Kienast 14), Holland, Mader, Jun (Spiridonovic 76); Hosiner.
Atletico Madrid: (4231) Courtois; Juanfran, Miranda, Alderweireld, Filipe Luis (Insua 46); Tiago, Gabi; Turan, Raul Garcia (Adrian 80), Koke; Diego Costa (Rodriguez 59).

FC Porto (0) 0
Zenit St Petersburg (0) 1 *(Kerzhakov 86)* 31,109
FC Porto: (433) Helton; Danilo, Otamendi, Mangala, Alex Sandro; Fernando, Gonzalez (Ghilas 86), Herrera**; Lica (Varela 53), Martinez, Josue (Defour 75).
Zenit St Petersburg: (4231) Lodigin; Ansaldi, Luis Neto, Lombaerts, Smolnikov (Criscito 81); Shatov, Faitzulin; Arshavin (Zyryanov 65), Shirokov (Kerzhakov 73), Danny; Hulk.

Wednesday, 6 November 2013
Atletico Madrid (3) 4 *(Miranda 11, Raul Garcia 25, Filipe Luis 45, Diego Costa 82)*
Austria Vienna (0) 0 29,841
Atletico Madrid: (442) Courtois; Juanfran, Miranda, Godin, Filipe Luis; Adrian (Torres 46), Tiago (Guilavogui 56), Gabi, Koke (Rodriguez 66); Diego Costa, Raul Garcia.
Austria Vienna: (4141) Lindner; Koch, Ramsebner, Ortlechner, Leovac; Holland; Royer, Mader (Dilaver 68), Simkovic (Hosiner 52), Murg (Suttner 52); Kienast.

Zenit St Petersburg (1) 1 *(Hulk 28)*
FC Porto (1) 1 *(Gonzalez 23)* 17,786
Zenit St Petersburg: (4321) Lodigin; Ansaldi, Hubocan, Lombaerts, Criscito; Shirokov (Arshavin 67), Witsel (Zyryanov 81), Faitzulin; Shatov, Danny (Kerzhakov 28); Hulk.
FC Porto: (433) Helton; Danilo, Otamendi, Mangala, Alex Sandro; Fernando, Gonzalez (Ghilas 86), Defour; Josue (Lica 76), Martinez, Varela.

Tuesday, 26 November 2013
FC Porto (0) 1 *(Martinez 49)*
Austria Vienna (1) 1 *(Kienast 11)* 24,809
FC Porto: (433) Helton; Danilo, Maicon, Mangala, Alex Sandro; Fernando, Gonzalez, Defour (Varela 46); Josue (Quintero 72), Martinez, Lica (Ricardo 65).
Austria Vienna: (4231) Lindner; Koch, Rogulj, Ortlechner, Suttner (Okotie 82); Holland, Dilaver (Mader 69); Royer, Kienast, Murg (Leovac 64); Hosiner.

Zenit St Petersburg (0) 1 *(Alderweireld 74 (og))*
Atletico Madrid (0) 1 *(Adrian 53)* 17,885
Zenit St Petersburg: (433) Lodigin; Smolnikov, Hubocan, Lombaerts, Criscito; Witsel, Faitzulin (Bystrov 64), Shirokov (Arshavin 64); Shatov, Hulk, Kerzhakov.

Atletico Madrid: (4411) Courtois; Juanfran, Alderweireld, Miranda, Insua; Rodriguez (Torres 79), Guilavogui, Gabi, Koke; Raul Garcia; Adrian.

Wednesday, 11 December 2013
Atletico Madrid (2) 2 *(Raul Garcia 14, Diego Costa 37)*
FC Porto (0) 0 24,629
Atletico Madrid: (4231) Aranzubia; Manquillo, Alderweireld, Miranda, Insua; Gabi, Koke; Torres (Turan 62), Raul Garcia, Adrian (Leo Baptistao 82); Diego Costa (Villa 46).
FC Porto: (433) Helton; Danilo, Maicon, Mangala, Alex Sandro; Fernando, Gonzalez (Ghilas 64), Defour (Herrera 78); Varela, Martinez, Josue (Lica 46).

Austria Vienna (1) 4 *(Hosiner 44, 52, Jun 48, Kienast 90)*
Zenit St Petersburg (1) 1 *(Kerzhakov 35)* 37,500
Austria Vienna: (4141) Lindner; Dilaver, Rogulj, Ortlechner, Suttner; Holland; Murg (Royer 60), Stankovic (Simkovic 68), Mader, Jun (Kienast 83); Hosiner.
Zenit St Petersburg: (451) Lodigin; Ansaldi (Smolnikov 83), Hubocan, Lombaerts, Criscito; Witsel, Zyryanov (Arshavin 63), Faitzulin (Bystrov 83), Shirokov, Hulk; Kerzhakov.

Group G Table	P	W	D	L	F	A	GD	Pts
Atletico Madrid	6	5	1	0	15	3	12	16
Zenit St Petersburg	6	1	3	2	5	9	–4	6
FC Porto	6	1	2	3	4	7	–3	5
Austria Vienna	6	1	2	3	5	10	–5	5

GROUP H

Wednesday, 18 September 2013
AC Milan (0) 2 *(Izaguirre 82 (og), Muntari 85)*
Celtic (0) 0 54,623
AC Milan: (433) Abbiati; Zaccardo, Zapata, Mexes, Constant (Robinho 75); Muntari, De Jong, Nocerino; Matri (Poli 87), Birsa (Emanuelson 63), Balotelli.
Celtic: (442) Forster; van Dijk, Lustig, Ambrose, Izaguirre; Brown, Matthews (Boerrigter 75), Mulgrew (Biton 89), Commons (Pukki 77); Samaras, Stokes.

Barcelona (1) 4 *(Messi 21, 55, 75, Pique 69)*
Ajax (0) 0 79,412
Barcelona: (433) Valdes; Dani Alves, Pique (Bartra 79), Mascherano, Adriano; Busquets, Fabregas (Xavi 71), Iniesta; Alexis, Messi, Neymar (Pedro 72).
Ajax: (433) Vermeer; Van Rhijn, Denswil, Moisander (van der Hoorn 73), Blind (Schone 78); Poulsen, De Jong (Serero 59), Duarte; Bojan, Sigthorsson, Boilesen.

Tuesday, 1 October 2013
Ajax (0) 1 *(Denswil 90)*
AC Milan (0) 1 *(Balotelli 90 (pen))* 51,692
Ajax: (433) Cillessen; Van Rhijn, Moisander (van der Hoorn 78), Blind, Denswil; Poulsen, Duarte (Schone 59), De Jong; Fischer, Sigthorsson, De Sa (Andersen 64).
AC Milan: (433) Abbiati; Mexes, Zapata, Abate, Constant; Muntari, Montolivo, De Jong; Poli (Emanuelson 84), Robinho (Matri 80), Balotelli.

Celtic (0) 0
Barcelona (0) 1 *(Fabregas 76)* 58,128
Celtic: (4411) Forster; Lustig (Forrest 69), van Dijk, Ambrose, Izaguirre; Matthews, Brown**, Mulgrew, Samaras; Commons (Pukki 86); Stokes (Kayal 70).
Barcelona: (4312) Valdes; Dani Alves, Pique, Bartra, Adriano; Xavi, Busquets, Iniesta (Song 89); Fabregas (Tello 78); Pedro (Alexis 75), Neymar.

Tuesday, 22 October 2013
AC Milan (1) 1 *(Robinho 10)*
Barcelona (1) 1 *(Messi 23)* 74,487
AC Milan: (433) Amelia; Abate, Zapata, Mexes, Constant; Montolivo, De Jong, Muntari; Birsa (Poli 80), Robinho (Balotelli 64), Kaka (Emanuelson 71).
Barcelona: (433) Valdes; Dani Alves, Pique, Mascherano, Adriano; Iniesta, Busquets, Xavi; Alexis (Fabregas 74), Messi, Neymar (Pedro 81).

Celtic (1) 2 *(Forrest 45 (pen), Kayal 54)*
Ajax (0) 1 *(Schone 90)*   58,719
Celtic: (442) Forster; Ambrose, Lustig (Biton▪ 77), van Dijk, Mulgrew; Samaras, Pukki (Balde 90), Kayal (Ledley 70), Izaguirre; Stokes, Forrest.
Ajax: (433) Cillessen; Van Rhijn (Schone 80), Veltman, Denswil, Blind; De Jong, Poulsen (Boilesen 68), Serero; Andersen, Sigthorsson, Fischer (De Sa 72).

Wednesday, 6 November 2013
Ajax (0) 1 *(Schone 51)*
Celtic (0) 0   59,908
Ajax: (433) Cillessen; Van Rhijn, Veltman, Denswil, Boilesen; Klaassen (Poulsen 83), Blind, Serero (Fischer 72); Schone, De Jong, Sigthorsson (van der Hoorn 90).
Celtic: (4411) Forster; Lustig, Ambrose, van Dijk, Mulgrew; Stokes (Boerrigter 73), Commons (Pukki 81), Kayal (Ledley 77), Izaguirre; Forrest; Samaras.

Barcelona (2) 3 *(Messi 30 (pen), 83, Busquets 39)*
AC Milan (1) 1 *(Pique 45 (og))*   80,517
Barcelona: (433) Valdes; Dani Alves, Pique, Mascherano, Adriano; Xavi (Song 88), Busquets, Iniesta (Fabregas 78); Alexis, Messi, Neymar (Pedro 85).
AC Milan: (4411) Abbiati; Abate, Zapata, Mexes, Emanuelson; Muntari, Montolivo, De Jong, Poli (Birsa 74); Kaka (Matri 84); Robinho (Balotelli 46).

Tuesday, 26 November 2013
Ajax (2) 2 *(Serero 19, Hoesen 42)*
Barcelona (0) 1 *(Xavi 49 (pen))*   53,000
Ajax: (433) Cillessen; Van Rhijn, Veltman▪, Moisander, Boilesen (Poulsen 35); Klaassen, Blind, Serero; Schone (Denswil 51), Hoesen (Duarte 83), Fischer.
Barcelona: (433) Pinto; Puyol (Patric Gil 68), Mascherano, Pique, Montoya; Xavi (Sergi Roberto 73), Song, Iniesta; Pedro, Fabregas (Traore 81), Neymar.

Celtic (0) 0
AC Milan (1) 3 *(Kaka 12, Zapata 49, Balotelli 59)*   58,619
Celtic: (4411) Forster; Lustig, Ambrose, van Dijk, Izaguirre; Boerrigter, Mulgrew, Kayal (Ledley 30), Forrest (Rogic 80); Commons (Stokes 65); Samaras.
AC Milan: (4321) Abbiati; Abate (Nocerino 48), Zapata, Bonera, Emanuelson; Montolivo, De Jong, Poli; Birsa (Constant 72), Kaka (Robinho 80); Balotelli.

Wednesday, 11 December 2013
AC Milan (0) 0
Ajax (0) 0   61,744
AC Milan: (433) Abbiati; De Sciglio, Bonera, Zapata, Constant; Montolivo▪, De Jong, Muntari; Kaka (Mexes 80), Balotelli, El Shaarawy (Poli 24).
Ajax: (433) Cillessen; Van Rhijn, Moisander, Denswil, Blind; Klaassen, Poulsen (Hoesen 46), Serero (van der Hoorn 81); Schone, Bojan (Sigthorsson 72), Fischer.

Barcelona (3) 6 *(Pique 7, Pedro 39, Neymar 44, 48, 58, Tello 72)*
Celtic (0) 1 *(Samaras 89)*   54,342
Barcelona: (433) Pinto; Montoya, Mascherano, Pique, Adriano; Sergi Roberto, Busquets (Song 74), Xavi; Alexis (Tello 63), Neymar (Dongou 79), Pedro.
Celtic: (4411) Forster; Lustig, Ambrose, van Dijk, Matthews (Stokes 82); Brown, Biton (Commons 70), Ledley, Boerrigter; Pukki (Mulgrew 47); Samaras.

Group H Table	P	W	D	L	F	A	GD	Pts
Barcelona	6	4	1	1	16	5	11	13
AC Milan	6	2	3	1	8	5	3	9
Ajax	6	2	2	2	5	8	–3	8
Celtic	6	1	0	5	3	14	–11	3

KNOCK-OUT STAGE

ROUND OF 16 FIRST LEG

Tuesday, 18 February 2014
Bayer Leverkusen (0) 0
Paris St Germain (3) 4 *(Matuidi 3, Ibrahimovic 39 (pen), 42, Cabaye 88)*   29,412
Bayer Leverkusen: (433) Leno; Hilbert, Spahic▪, Toprak, Guardado; Bender, Rolfes (Reinartz 46), Castro; Sam (Wollscheid 61), Kiessling, Son (Brandt 46).
Paris St Germain: (433) Sirigu; Van Der Wiel, Alex, Thiago Silva, Maxwell; Verratti, Thiago Motta, Matuidi (Cabaye 67); Lucas Moura, Ibrahimovic, Lavezzi (Pastore 76).

Manchester C (0) 0
Barcelona (0) 2 *(Messi 54 (pen), Dani Alves 90)*   46,033
Manchester C: (4411) Hart; Zabaleta, Kompany, Demichelis▪, Clichy; Jesus Navas (Nasri 57), Fernandinho, Toure, Kolarov (Lescott 57); Silva; Negredo (Dzeko 74).
Barcelona: (433) Valdes; Dani Alves, Pique, Mascherano, Jordi Alba; Xavi, Busquets, Fabregas (Sergi Roberto 86); Alexis (Neymar 73), Messi, Iniesta.

Wednesday, 19 February 2014
AC Milan (0) 0
Atletico Madrid (0) 1 *(Diego Costa 83)*   65,890
AC Milan: (4231) Abbiati; De Sciglio (Abate 25), Bonera, Rami, Emanuelson; Essien, De Jong; Poli (Constant 85), Kaka, Taarabt; Balotelli (Pazzini 77).
Atletico Madrid: (4411) Courtois; Juanfran, Miranda, Godin, Insua; Turan (Rodriguez 74), Mario Suarez, Gabi, Koke; Raul Garcia (Adrian 80); Diego Costa.

Arsenal (0) 0
Bayern Munich (0) 2 *(Kroos 54, Muller 88)*   59,911
Arsenal: (4231) Szczesny▪; Sagna, Mertesacker, Koscielny, Gibbs (Monreal 31); Flamini, Wilshere; Oxlade-Chamberlain (Rosicky 74), Ozil, Cazorla (Fabianski 38); Sanogo.
Bayern Munich: (4231) Neuer; Lahm, Boateng (Rafinha 46), Dante, Alaba; Thiago (Pizarro 79), Javi Martinez; Robben, Kroos, Gotze; Mandzukic (Muller 64).

Tuesday, 25 February 2014
Olympiacos (1) 2 *(Dominguez 38, Campbell 54)*
Manchester U (0) 0   29,815
Olympiacos: (4231) Roberto; Leandro Salino, Manolas, Marcano, Holebas; Maniatis, Ndinga; Campbell (David Fuster 67), Dominguez (Paulo Machado 76), Perez (Haedo Valdez 85); Olaitan.
Manchester U: (4231) De Gea; Smalling, Ferdinand, Vidic, Evra; Cleverley (Kagawa 60), Carrick; Valencia (Welbeck 60), Rooney, Young; van Persie.

Zenit St Petersburg (0) 2 *(Shatov 58, Hulk 70 (pen))*
Borussia Dortmund (2) 4 *(Mkhitaryan 4, Reus 5, Lewandowski 61, 71)*   15,099
Zenit St Petersburg: (4231) Lodigin; Aniukov (Smolnikov 83), Luis Neto, Lombaerts, Criscito; Witsel, Faitzulin (Kerzhakov 83); Hulk, Shatov, Arshavin (Tymoschuk 15); Rondon.
Borussia Dortmund: (4231) Weidenfeller; Friedrich, Schmelzer, Papastathopoulos, Piszczek; Kehl, Sahin; Grosskreutz (Durm 90), Mkhitaryan (Aubameyang 70), Reus (Hofmann 85); Lewandowski.

Wednesday, 26 February 2014
Galatasaray (0) 1 *(Chedjou 64)*
Chelsea (1) 1 *(Torres 9)*   49,194
Galatasaray: (442) Muslera; Alex, Balta (Kaya 46), Chedjou, Eboue; Sneijder, Inan, Felipe Melo, Hajrovic (Kurtulus 31); Drogba (Bulut 79), Yilmaz B.
Chelsea: (442) Cech; Azpilicueta, Cahill, Terry, Ivanovic; Hazard (Oscar 90), Lampard, Ramires, Willian; Schurrle (Mikel 66), Torres (Eto'o 68).

Schalke 04 (0) 1 *(Huntelaar 90)*
Real Madrid (2) 6 *(Benzema 13, 57, Bale 21, 69, Ronaldo 52, 89)*   54,442
Schalke 04: (4231) Fahrmann; Howedes, Matip, Felipe Santana, Kolasinac (Fuchs 76); Boateng (Goretzka 59), Neustadter; Farfan (Obasi Ogbuke 72), Meyer, Draxler; Huntelaar.

Real Madrid: (433) Casillas; Carvajal, Pepe, Sergio Ramos, Marcelo; Modric, Alonso (Illarramendi 73), Di Maria (Isco 68); Bale (Jese 80), Benzema, Ronaldo.

ROUND OF 16 SECOND LEG

Tuesday, 11 March 2014

Atletico Madrid (2) 4 *(Diego Costa 3, 85, Turan 40, Raul Garcia 71)*

AC Milan (1) 1 *(Kaka 27)* 49,186

Atletico Madrid: (433) Courtois; Juanfran, Miranda, Godin, Filipe Luis; Turan (Rodriguez 78), Gabi, Mario Suarez; Koke (Diego 81), Raul Garcia (Sosa 72), Diego Costa.
AC Milan: (4411) Abbiati; Abate, Rami, Bonera, Emanuelson; Essien (Pazzini 68), Poli, De Jong (Muntari 78), Kaka; Taarabt (Robinho 46); Balotelli.

Bayern Munich (0) 1 *(Schweinsteiger 55)*

Arsenal (0) 1 *(Podolski 57)* 68,000

Bayern Munich: (451) Neuer; Lahm, Javi Martinez, Dante, Alaba; Robben, Schweinsteiger, Thiago, Ribery (Muller 85), Gotze (Kroos 60); Mandzukic.
Arsenal: (451) Fabianski; Sagna, Mertesacker, Koscielny, Vermaelen; Cazorla, Arteta (Gnabry 77), Oxlade-Chamberlain (Flamini 84), Podolski, Ozil (Rosicky 46); Giroud.

Wednesday, 12 March 2014

Barcelona (0) 2 *(Messi 67, Dani Alves 90)*

Manchester C (0) 1 *(Kompany 89)* 85,957

Barcelona: (433) Valdes; Dani Alves, Pique, Mascherano, Jordi Alba; Xavi, Busquets, Iniesta; Messi, Fabregas (Sergi Roberto 86), Neymar (Alexis 79).
Manchester C: (4411) Hart; Zabaleta■, Kompany, Lescott, Kolarov; Silva (Negredo 72), Fernandinho, Milner, Nasri (Jesus Navas 74); Toure; Aguero (Dzeko 46).

Paris St Germain (1) 2 *(Marquinhos 13, Lavezzi 53)*

Bayer Leverkusen (1) 1 *(Sam 6)* 45,596

Paris St Germain: (433) Sirigu; Jallet, Marquinhos, Thiago Silva, Digne; Pastore, Cabaye, Rabiot; Cavani (Camara 85), Ibrahimovic (Menez 72), Lavezzi (Lucas Moura 62).
Bayer Leverkusen: (433) Leno; Donati, Wollscheid, Toprak, Guardado; Rolfes, Reinartz (Wagener 78), Can■; Sam (Brandt 66), Derdiyok, Castro (Son 66).

Tuesday, 18 March 2014

Chelsea (2) 2 *(Eto'o 4, Cahill 43)*

Galatasaray (0) 0 38,038

Chelsea: (4231) Cech; Ivanovic, Cahill, Terry, Azpilicueta; Ramires, Lampard; Oscar (Schurrle 81), Hazard, Willian (Kalas 90); Eto'o (Torres 85).
Galatasaray: (442) Muslera; Alex, Chedjou, Kaya, Eboue (Hajrovic 77); Felipe Melo, Inan, Sneijder, Kurtulus (Balta 67); Drogba, Yilmaz B (Bulut 53).

Real Madrid (1) 3 *(Ronaldo 22, 74, Morata 76)*

Schalke 04 (1) 1 *(Hoogland 31)* 65,148

Real Madrid: (442) Casillas; Varane, Sergio Ramos (Carvajal 69), Fabio Coentrao, Nacho; Alonso (Casemiro 46), Isco, Illarramendi, Ronaldo; Jese (Bale 8), Morata.
Schalke 04: (442) Fahrmann; Howedes (Papadopoulos 57), Matip, Kolasinac, Hoogland; Meyer, Draxler, Ayhan (Annan 81), Neustadter; Obasi Ogbuke, Huntelaar (Szalai 45).

Wednesday, 19 March 2014

Borussia Dortmund (0) 1 *(Kehl 39)*

Zenit St Petersburg (1) 2 *(Hulk 16, Rondon 73)* 65,929

Borussia Dortmund: (4231) Weidenfeller; Piszczek, Papastathopoulos, Hummels, Schmelzer (Durm 76); Sahin, Kehl; Aubameyang (Hofmann 90), Mkhitaryan (Jojic 68), Grosskreutz; Lewandowski.
Zenit St Petersburg: (4231) Malafeev; Aniukov, Hubocan, Lombaerts (Luis Neto 46); Criscito; Witsel, Faitzulin (Smolnikov 84); Hulk, Shatov, Danny; Kerzhakov (Rondon 62).

Manchester U (2) 3 *(van Persie 25 (pen), 45, 52)*

Olympiacos (0) 0 75,000

Manchester U: (4411) De Gea; Da Silva R, Jones, Ferdinand, Evra; Welbeck (Fletcher 81), Giggs, Carrick, Valencia (Young 77); Rooney; van Persie (Fellaini 90).
Olympiacos: (451) Roberto; Leandro Salino (Paulo Machado 74), Manolas, Marcano, Holebas; Perez (Haedo Valdez 57), Ndinga, Dominguez, Maniatis, David Fuster (Vergos 82); Campbell.

QUARTER-FINALS FIRST LEG

Tuesday, 1 April 2014

Barcelona (0) 1 *(Neymar 71)*

Atletico Madrid (0) 1 *(Diego 57)* 79,941

Barcelona: (433) Pinto; Dani Alves, Pique (Bartra 12), Mascherano, Jordi Alba; Xavi, Busquets, Fabregas (Alexis 68); Neymar, Messi, Iniesta.
Atletico Madrid: (4411) Courtois; Juanfran, Godin, Miranda, Filipe Luis; Turan (Rodriguez 77), Gabi, Tiago, Koke; Villa (Sosa 70); Diego Costa (Diego 29).

Manchester U (0) 1 *(Vidic 58)*

Bayern Munich (0) 1 *(Schweinsteiger 67)* 75,199

Manchester U: (442) De Gea; Jones, Ferdinand, Vidic, Buttner (Young 74); Valencia, Carrick, Fellaini, Giggs (Kagawa 46); Rooney, Welbeck (Hernandez 84).
Bayern Munich: (4411) Neuer; Rafinha, Javi Martinez, Boateng, Alaba; Robben, Lahm, Schweinsteiger■, Ribery; Kroos (Gotze 74); Muller (Mandzukic 63).

Wednesday, 2 April 2014

Paris St Germain (1) 3 *(Lavezzi 4, Luiz 62 (og), Pastore 90)*

Chelsea (1) 1 *(Hazard 27 (pen))* 45,517

Paris St Germain: (433) Sirigu; Jallet, Alex, Thiago Silva, Maxwell; Verratti (Cabaye 76), Thiago Motta, Matuidi; Cavani, Ibrahimovic (Lucas Moura 68), Lavezzi (Pastore 84).
Chelsea: (4231) Cech; Ivanovic, Cahill, Terry, Azpilicueta; Ramires, Luiz; Willian, Oscar (Lampard 72), Hazard; Schurrle (Torres 59).

Real Madrid (2) 3 *(Bale 3, Isco 27, Ronaldo 57)*

Borussia Dortmund (0) 0 70,089

Real Madrid: (433) Casillas; Carvajal, Pepe, Sergio Ramos, Fabio Coentrao; Modric, Alonso, Isco (Illarramendi 71); Bale, Benzema (Morata 75), Ronaldo (Casemiro 80).
Borussia Dortmund: (4231) Weidenfeller; Piszczek (Schieber 67), Hummels, Papastathopoulos, Durm; Kehl (Jojic 74), Sahin; Grosskreutz, Mkhitaryan (Hofmann 64), Reus; Aubameyang.

QUARTER-FINALS SECOND LEG

Tuesday, 8 April 2014

Borussia Dortmund (2) 2 *(Reus 24, 37)*

Real Madrid (0) 0 65,829

Borussia Dortmund: (4231) Weidenfeller; Piszczek (Aubameyang 81), Friedrich, Hummels, Durm; Jojic, Kirch; Grosskreutz, Mkhitaryan, Reus; Lewandowski.
Real Madrid: (433) Casillas; Carvajal, Pepe, Sergio Ramos, Fabio Coentrao; Illarramendi (Isco 46), Alonso, Modric; Di Maria (Casemiro 73), Benzema (Varane 90), Bale.

Chelsea (1) 2 *(Schurrle 32, Ba 87)*

Paris St Germain (0) 0 38,080

Chelsea: (4231) Cech; Ivanovic, Cahill, Terry, Azpilicueta; Luiz, Lampard (Ba 66); Willian, Oscar (Torres 81), Hazard (Schurrle 18); Eto'o.
Paris St Germain: (433) Sirigu; Jallet, Alex, Thiago Silva, Maxwell; Verratti (Cabaye 54), Thiago Motta, Matuidi; Lucas Moura (Marquinhos 84), Cavani, Lavezzi (Pastore 72).
Chelsea won on away goals rule.

Wednesday, 9 April 2014
Atletico Madrid (1) 1 *(Koke 6)*
Barcelona (0) 0   53,592
Atletico Madrid: (442) Courtois; Godin, Filipe Luis; Juanfran, Miranda; Tiago, Koke, Raul Garcia, Gabi; Adrian (Diego 61), Villa (Rodriguez 79).
Barcelona: (451) Pinto; Mascherano, Bartra, Jordi Alba, Dani Alves; Fabregas (Alexis 61), Xavi, Iniesta (Pedro 72), Busquets, Messi; Neymar.

Bayern Munich (0) 3 *(Mandzukic 59, Muller 67, Robben 76)*
Manchester U (0) 1 *(Evra 57)*   67,300
Bayern Munich: (433) Neuer; Lahm, Boateng, Dante, Alaba; Muller (Pizarro 84), Kroos, Gotze (Rafinha 65); Robben, Mandzukic, Ribery.
Manchester U: (4231) De Gea; Jones, Smalling, Vidic, Evra; Carrick, Fletcher (Hernandez 75); Valencia, Kagawa, Welbeck (Januzaj 81); Rooney.

SEMI-FINALS FIRST LEG
Tuesday, 22 April 2014
Atletico Madrid (0) 0
Chelsea (0) 0   52,560
Atletico Madrid: (442) Courtois; Juanfran, Miranda, Godin, Filipe Luis; Raul Garcia (Villa 86), Gabi, Mario Suarez (Sosa 80), Koke; Diego (Turan 60), Diego Costa.
Chelsea: (433) Cech (Schwarzer 18); Azpilicueta, Cahill, Terry (Schurrle 73), Cole; Mikel, Luiz, Lampard; Ramires, Torres, Willian (Ba 90).

Wednesday, 23 April 2014
Real Madrid (1) 1 *(Benzema 19)*
Bayern Munich (0) 0   80,354
Real Madrid: (433) Casillas; Carvajal, Sergio Ramos, Pepe (Varane 73), Fabio Coentrao; Modric, Alonso, Di Maria; Isco (Illarramendi 81), Benzema, Ronaldo (Bale 73).

Bayern Munich: (4231) Neuer; Rafinha (Javi Martinez 66), Boateng, Dante, Alaba; Lahm, Schweinsteiger (Muller 73); Robben, Kroos, Ribery (Gotze 72); Mandzukic.

SEMI-FINALS SECOND LEG
Tuesday, 29 April 2014
Bayern Munich (0) 0
Real Madrid (3) 4 *(Sergio Ramos 16, 20, Ronaldo 34, 90)*
                                                       68,000
Bayern Munich: (442) Neuer; Alaba, Dante, Boateng, Lahm; Ribery (Gotze 72), Muller (Pizarro 72), Schweinsteiger, Kroos; Robben, Mandzukic (Javi Martinez 46).
Real Madrid: (4231) Casillas; Carvajal, Sergio Ramos (Varane 75), Pepe, Fabio Coentrao; Alonso, Modric, Bale, Di Maria (Casemiro 84), Ronaldo; Benzema (Isco 79).

Wednesday, 30 April 2014
Chelsea (1) 1 *(Torres 36)*
Atletico Madrid (1) 3 *(Adrian 44, Diego Costa 60 (pen), Turan 72)*   37,918
Chelsea: (4231) Schwarzer; Ivanovic, Cahill, Terry, Cole (Eto'o 54); Ramires, Luiz; Willian (Schurrle 76), Azpilicueta, Hazard; Torres (Ba 67).
Atletico Madrid: (442) Courtois; Juanfran, Miranda, Godin, Filipe Luis; Koke, Tiago, Mario Suarez, Turan (Rodriguez 83); Diego Costa (Sosa 76), Adrian (Raul Garcia 66).

CHAMPIONS LEAGUE FINAL 2014
Saturday, 24 May 2014
(in Lisbon, 60,976)

Real Madrid (0) 4 *(Sergio Ramos 90, Bale 110, Marcelo 118, Ronaldo 120 (pen))*   **Atletico Madrid (1) 1** *(Godin 36)*
Real Madrid: (433) Casillas; Carvajal, Varane, Sergio Ramos, Fabio Coentrao (Marcelo 59); Modric, Khedira (Isco 59), Di Maria; Bale, Benzema (Morata 79), Ronaldo.

Atletico Madrid: (442) Courtois; Juanfran, Miranda, Godin, Filipe Luis (Alderweireld 83); Raul Garcia (Sosa 66), Gabi, Tiago, Koke; Villa, Diego Costa (Adrian 9).

aet; Referee: Bjorn Kuipers.

Real's Sergio Ramos heads his side's 93rd-minute equaliser against rivals Atletico in the all-Madrid UEFA Champions League final in the Estadio da Luz in Lisbon. Real went on to win 4-1 in extra time, in the process claiming the club's tenth European Cup triumph (*La Decima*). (David Klein/Landov/Press Association Images)

EUROPEAN CUP-WINNERS' CUP
FINALS 1961–99

Year	Winners v Runners-up		Venue	Attendance	Referee
1961	1st Leg Fiorentina v Rangers	2-0	Glasgow	80,000	C. E. Steiner (Austria)
	2nd Leg Fiorentina v Rangers	2-1	Florence	50,000	V. Hernadi (Hungary)
1962	Atletico Madrid v Fiorentina	1-1	Glasgow	27,389	T. Wharton (Scotland)
Replay	Atletico Madrid v Fiorentina	3-0	Stuttgart	38,000	K. Tschenscher (West Germany)
1963	Tottenham Hotspur v Atletico Madrid	5-1	Rotterdam	49,000	A. van Leuwen (Netherlands)
1964	Sporting Lisbon v MTK Budapest	3-3*	Brussels	3,208	L. van Nuffel (Belgium)
Replay	Sporting Lisbon v MTK Budapest	1-0	Antwerp	13,924	G. Versyp (Belgium)
1965	West Ham U v Munich 1860	2-0	Wembley	7,974	I. Zsolt (Hungary)
1966	Borussia Dortmund v Liverpool	2-1*	Glasgow	41,657	P. Schwinte (France)
1967	Bayern Munich v Rangers	1-0*	Nuremberg	69,480	C. Lo Bello (Italy)
1968	AC Milan v Hamburg	2-0	Rotterdam	53,000	J. Ortiz de Mendibil (Spain)
1969	Slovan Bratislava v Barcelona	3-2	Basle	19,000	L. van Ravens (Netherlands)
1970	Manchester C v Gornik Zabrze	2-1	Vienna	7,968	P. Schiller (Austria)
1971	Chelsea v Real Madrid	1-1*	Athens	45,000	R. Scheurer (Switzerland)
Replay	Chelsea v Real Madrid	2-1*	Athens	19,917	R. Scheurer (Switzerland)
1972	Rangers v Moscow Dynamo	3-2	Barcelona	24,701	J. Ortiz de Mendibil (Spain)
1973	AC Milan v Leeds U	1-0	Salonika	40,154	C. Mihas (Greece)
1974	Magdeburg v AC Milan	2-0	Rotterdam	4,641	A. van Gemert (Netherlands)
1975	Dynamo Kiev v Ferencvaros	3-0	Basle	13,000	R. Davidson (Scotland)
1976	Anderlecht v West Ham U	4-2	Brussels	51,296	R. Wurtz (France)
1977	Hamburg v Anderlecht	2-0	Amsterdam	66,000	P. Partridge (England)
1978	Anderlecht v Austria/WAC	4-0	Paris	48,679	H. Adlinger (West Germany)
1979	Barcelona v Fortuna Dusseldorf	4-3*	Basle	58,000	K. Palotai (Hungary)
1980	Valencia v Arsenal	0-0*	Brussels	40,000	V. Christov (Czechoslovakia)
	(Valencia won 5-4 on penalties)				
1981	Dynamo Tbilisi v Carl Zeiss Jena	2-1	Dusseldorf	4,750	R. Lattanzi (Italy)
1982	Barcelona v Standard Liege	2-1	Barcelona	80,000	W. Eschweiler (West Germany)
1983	Aberdeen v Real Madrid	2-1*	Gothenburg	17,804	G. Menegali (Italy)
1984	Juventus v Porto	2-1	Basle	55,000	A. Prokop (Egypt)
1985	Everton v Rapid Vienna	3-1	Rotterdam	38,500	P. Casarin (Italy)
1986	Dynamo Kiev v Atletico Madrid	3-0	Lyon	50,000	P. Wohrer (Austria)
1987	Ajax v Lokomotiv Leipzig	1-0	Athens	35,107	L. Agnolin (Italy)
1988	Mechelen v Ajax	1-0	Strasbourg	39,446	D. Pauly (West Germany)
1989	Barcelona v Sampdoria	2-0	Berne	42,707	G. Courtney (England)
1990	Sampdoria v Anderlecht	2-0*	Gothenburg	20,103	B. Galler (Switzerland)
1991	Manchester U v Barcelona	2-1	Rotterdam	43,500	B. Karlsson (Sweden)
1992	Werder Bremen v Monaco	2-0	Lisbon	16,000	P. D'Elia (Italy)
1993	Parma v Antwerp	3-1	Wembley	37,393	K.-J. Assenmacher (Germany)
1994	Arsenal v Parma	1-0	Copenhagen	33,765	V. Krondl (Czech Republic)
1995	Zaragoza v Arsenal	2-1	Paris	42,424	P. Ceccarini (Italy)
1996	Paris St Germain v Rapid Vienna	1-0	Brussels	37,000	P. Pairetto (Italy)
1997	Barcelona v Paris St Germain	1-0	Rotterdam	52,000	M. Merk (Germany)
1998	Chelsea v Stuttgart	1-0	Stockholm	30,216	S. Braschi (Italy)
1999	Lazio v Mallorca	2-1	Villa Park	33,021	G. Benko (Austria)

INTER-CITIES FAIRS CUP FINALS 1958–71

Year	1st Leg		Attendance	2nd Leg	Attendance		Agg	Winner
1958	London XI v Barcelona		45,466	0-6	70,000		2-8	Barcelona
1960	Birmingham C v Barcelona	0-0	40,524	1-4	70,000		1-4	Barcelona
1961	Birmingham C v Roma	2-2	21,005	0-2	60,000		2-4	Roma
1962	Valencia v Barcelona	6-2	65,000	1-1	60,000		7-3	Valencia
1963	Dynamo Zagreb v Valencia	1-2	40,000	0-2	55,000		1-4	Valencia
1964	Zaragoza v Valencia	2-1	50,000	(in Barcelona, one match only)				
1965	Ferencvaros v Juventus	1-0	25,000	(in Turin, one match only)				
1966	Barcelona v Zaragoza	0-1	70,000	4-2*	70,000		4-3	Barcelona
1967	Dynamo Zagreb v Leeds U	2-0	40,000	0-0	35,604		2-0	Dynamo Zagreb
1968	Leeds U v Ferencvaros	1-0	25,368	0-0	70,000		1-0	Leeds U
1969	Newcastle U v Ujpest Dozsa	3-0	60,000	3-2	37,000		6-2	Newcastle U
1970	Anderlecht v Arsenal	3-1	37,000	0-3	51,612		3-4	Arsenal
1971	Juventus v Leeds U	0-0	*(abandoned 51 minutes)*		42,000			
	Juventus v Leeds U	2-2	42,000	1-1	42,483		3-3	Leeds U
	Leeds U won on away goals rule.							

Trophy Play-Off – *between first and last winners to decide who would have possession of the original trophy*

1971	Barcelona v Leeds U	2-1	50,000	(in Barcelona, one match only)

*After extra time.

UEFA CUP FINALS 1972–97

Year	1st Leg		Attendance	2nd Leg	Attendance	Agg	Winner
1972	Wolverhampton W v Tottenham H	1-2	38,562	1-1	54,303	2-3	Tottenham H
1973	Liverpool v Moenchengladbach	0-0	*(abandoned after 27 minutes)*		44,967		
	Liverpool v Moenchengladbach	3-0	41,169	0-2	35,000	3-2	Liverpool
1974	Tottenham H v Feyenoord	2-2	46,281	0-2	59,317	2-4	Feyenoord
1975	Moenchengladbach v Twente	0-0	42,368	5-1	21,767	5-1	Moenchengladbach
1976	Liverpool v FC Brugge	3-2	49,981	1-1	29,423	4-3	Liverpool
1977	Juventus v Athletic Bilbao	1-0	66,000	1-2	39,700	2-2	Juventus
	Juventus won on away goals rule.						
1978	Bastia v PSV Eindhoven	0-0	8,006	0-3	28,000	0-3	PSV Eindhoven
1979	RS Belgrade v Moenchengladbach	1-1	65,000	0-1	45,000	1-2	Moenchengladbach
1980	Moenchengladbach v E. Frankfurt	3-2	25,000	0-1	59,000	3-3	E. Frankfurt
	Eintracht Frankfurt won on away goals rule.						
1981	Ipswich T v AZ 67 Alkmaar	3-0	27,532	2-4	22,291	5-4	Ipswich T
1982	Gothenburg v Hamburg	1-0	42,548	3-0	57,312	4-0	Gothenburg
1983	Anderlecht v Benfica	1-0	55,000	1-1	70,000	2-1	Anderlecht
1984	Anderlecht v Tottenham H	1-1	33,000	1-1*	46,258	2-2	Tottenham H
	Tottenham H won 4-3 on penalties.						
1985	Videoton v Real Madrid	0-3	30,000	1-0	80,000	1-3	Real Madrid
1986	Real Madrid v Cologne	5-1	60,000	0-2	22,000	5-3	Real Madrid
1987	Gothenburg v Dundee U	1-0	48,614	1-1	20,900	2-1	Gothenburg
1988	Espanol v Bayer Leverkusen	3-0	31,180	0-3*	21,600	3-3	B. Leverkusen
	Bayer Leverkusen won 3-2 on penalties.						
1989	Napoli v Stuttgart	2-1	81,093	3-3	64,000	5-4	Napoli
1990	Juventus v Fiorentina	3-1	47,519	0-0	30,999	3-1	Juventus
1991	Internazionale v Roma	2-0	68,887	0-1	70,901	2-1	Internazionale
1992	Torino v Ajax	2-2	65,377	0-0	40,000	2-2	Ajax
	Ajax won on away goals rule.						
1993	Borussia Dortmund v Juventus	1-3	37,000	0-3	62,781	1-6	Juventus
1994	Salzburg v Internazionale	0-1	43,000	0-1	80,345	0-2	Internazionale
1995	Parma v Juventus	1-0	22,057	1-1	80,000	2-1	Parma
1996	Bayern Munich v Bordeaux	2-0	63,000	3-1	30,000	5-1	Bayern Munich
1997	Schalke v Internazionale	1-0	57,000	0-1*	81,675	1-1	Schalke
	Schalke won 4-1 on penalties.						

UEFA CUP FINALS 1998–2009

Year	Winners v Runners-up		Venue	Attendance	Referee
1998	Internazionale v Lazio	3-0	Paris	44,412	A. L. Nieto (Spain)
1999	Parma v Marseille	3-0	Moscow	61,000	H. Dallas (Scotland)
2000	Galatasaray v Arsenal	0-0*	Copenhagen	38,919	A. L. Nieto (Spain)
	Galatasaray won 4-1 on penalties.				
2001	Liverpool v Alaves	5-4*	Dortmund	48,050	G. Veissiere (France)
	Liverpool won on sudden death 'golden goal'.				
2002	Feyenoord v Borussia Dortmund	3-2	Rotterdam	45,611	V. M. M. Pereira (Portugal)
2003	Porto v Celtic	3-2*	Seville	52,140	L. Michel (Slovakia)
2004	Valencia v Marseille	2-0	Gothenburg	39,000	P. Collina (Italy)
2005	CSKA Moscow v Sporting Lisbon	3-1	Lisbon	47,085	G. Poll (England)
2006	Sevilla v Middlesbrough	4-0	Eindhoven	32,100	H. Fandel (Germany)
2007	Sevilla v Espanyol	2-2*	Glasgow	47,602	M. Busacca (Switzerland)
	Sevilla won 3-1 on penalties.				
2008	Zenit St Petersburg v Rangers	2-0	Manchester	43,878	P. Fröjdfeldt (Sweden)
2009	Shakhtar Donetsk v Werder Bremen	2-1*	Istanbul	37,357	L. M. Chantalejo (Spain)

UEFA EUROPA LEAGUE FINALS 2010–14

Year	Winners v Runners-up		Venue	Attendance	Referee
2010	Atletico Madrid v Fulham	2-1*	Hamburg	49,000	N. Rizzoli (Italy)
2011	Porto v Braga	1-0	Dublin	45,391	V. Carballo (Spain)
2012	Atletico Madrid v Athletic Bilbao	3-0	Bucharest	52,347	W. Stark (Germany)
2013	Chelsea v Benfica	2-1	Amsterdam	46,163	B. Kuipers (Netherlands)
2014	Sevilla v Benfica	0-0*	Turin	33,120	F. Brych (Germany)
	Sevilla won 4-2 on penalties.				

*After extra time.

UEFA EUROPA LEAGUE 2013–14

■ *Denotes player sent off.*

FIRST QUALIFYING ROUND FIRST LEG

Tuesday, 2 July 2013

Bala T (1) 1 *(Sheridan 4)*

Levadia Tallinn (0) 0   1287

Bala T: (442) Morris; Valentine, Collins, Davies (Codling 46), Jones S; Murtagh, Connolly (Edwards 82), Jones M, Sheridan (Lewis 90); Brown, Lunt.
Levadia Tallinn: (442) Smishko; Artjunin, Podholjuzin, Jahhimovits, Kulinits; Antonov, Subbotin, Pikk, Raudsepp; Hunt (Teever 84), Kaljumae (Rattel 46).

Metalurg Skopje (0) 0

Qarabag (0) 1 *(Reynaldo 64)*   425

Metalurg Skopje: (442) Efremov; Dalceski (Krstev 67), Georgievski, Ljamcevski, Peev; Simonovski (Alomerovic 63), Mitrev, Radeski (Curlinov 46), Mitrevski; Stefanovic, Ignatov.
Qarabag: (442) Varvodic; Qarayev, Medvedev, Reynaldo, Muarem (Yusifov 46); Gelashvili (George 84), Sadyqov, Nadirov (Sattarly 70), Almeida; Teli, Agoli.

Sliema Wanderers (0) 1

Khazar Lankaran (1) 1 *(Nildo 14)*   394

Sliema Wanderers: (442) Zammit; Muscat A, Mintoff (Martinelli 84), Scerri, Ohawuchi; Baldacchino, Cilia (Laudisi 53), Barbetti, Muchard; Muscat G (Timotic 90), Bianciardi.
Khazar Lankaran: (442) Doblas; Scarduelli (Pit 59), Silva, Allahverdiyev■, Tounkara; Abdullayev, Benouahi, Nildo (Gligorov 50); Todorov; Skarlatake, Orsulic (Ramaldanov 66).

Trans Narva (0) 0

Gefle (1) 3 *(Dubokin 43 (og), Dahlberg 57, Lantto 90)*   263

Trans Narva: (4231) Smelkov; Kulikov, Kitto, Nesterovski, Dubokin; Elysee, Kazakov (Plotnikov 63); Pereplotkins (Lvov 82), Taar, Shesterkov; Jogi (Skinjov 46).
Gefle: (442) Hedvall; Apr, Fallman, Wikstrom, Portin; Lundevall (Phekezela 66), Faltsetas (Abdullai 73), Hansson, Lantto; Orlov, Dahlberg (Oremo 83).

Wednesday, 3 July 2013

Fuglafjordur (0) 0

Linfield (0) 2 *(Waterworth 68, Lowry 74)*   411

Fuglafjordur: (433) Hansen; Madsen (Kristiansen 90), Ellingsgaard J, Thorleifsson (Jovevic 28), Eliasen; Petersen B, Nesa, Lambanum; Saric (Johnsen 73), Dalbuo, Ellingsgaard A.
Linfield: (4312) Tuffey; Burns A, Ervin, Burns B, Clarke; McCaul (Mulgrew 60), Gault, Knowles (Thompson 64); Waterworth (Lowry 71); Tipton, Carvill.

Thursday, 4 July 2013

Airbus UK Broughton (0) 1 *(Budrys 80)*

Ventspils (0) 1 *(Paulius 48)*   1451

Airbus UK Broughton: (442) Coates; Owens, Pearson, Kearney, Short; Riley, Rule, Field (Ward 71), Wade (Jones 57); Abbott (Hart 75), Budrys.
Ventspils: (442) Melnicenko; Kurakins, Smirnovs, Dubra, Timofejevs; Tarkhnishvili (Turkovs 44), Tarasovs, Paulius (Zatkins 70), Sukhanov; Abdultaofik (Ignatans 90), Yanchuk.

Astana (0) 0

Botev Plovdiv (1) 1 *(Jirsak 44)*   5670

Astana: (442) Eric; Korobkin, Nurdauletov, Konysbaev (Kojasevic 46), Dmitrenko; Kethevoama, Islamkhan (Kuat 62), Igumanovic, Beisebekov; Nuserbaev, Zelao.
Botev Plovdiv: (442) Stachowiak; Grncarov, Ognyanov, Vander (Nedelev 89), Hristov; Minev, Abel (Kostov 90), Jirsak, Kortzorg (Dyakov 74); Galchev, Sprockel.

Breidablik (3) 4 *(Hreidarsson 19, Hreinsson 23, 25, Lydsson 61 (pen))*

FC Santa Coloma (0) 0   848

Breidablik: (442) Hreidarsson (Sigurgeirsson 67); Hreinsson (Rohde 73), Lydsson (Vilhjalmsson 67), Gunnleifsson, Margeirsson; Troost, Adalsteinsson, Ingason, Jonsson; Gardarsson, Yeoman.
FC Santa Coloma: (442) Casals; Fite Castillo, Rebes, Romero (Wagner 71), Blanco; Mercade, Ribolleda, Quinones, Sanchez; Garcia (Bousenine 42), Juanfer.

Celik Niksic (1) 1 *(Radovic 16)*

Budapest Honved (2) 4 *(Delczeg 38, Holender 41, 62, Diaby 52)*   1300

Celik Niksic: (442) Banovic; Dubljevic, Vukovic, Radovic (Bakoc 66), Adrovic; Ivanovic (Kasalica 89), Zoric (Simic 46), Vidakanic, Jovovic; Racic, Bulajic.
Budapest Honved: (442) Kemenes; Ignjatovic (Alcibiade 54), Ikenne, Lovric, Zivanovic; Nagy, Hidi, Holender (Mancini 75), Diaby; Vecsei (Diarra 55), Delczeg.

Chikhura Sachkhere (0) 0

Vaduz (0) 0   1200

Chikhura Sachkhere: (442) Somkhishvili; Tchelidze, Jigauri, Kvaskhvadze (Gogatishvili 11 (Kimadze 36)), Tsinamdzgvrishvili; Datunaishvili, Bechvaia, Kashia, Odikadze; Dekanoidze (Lomashvili 71), Rekhviashvili.
Vaduz: (442) Jehle; Pergl, Sara, Baron (Ciccone 86), Burgmeier (Milosevic 50); Schurpf, Maccoppi, Pak, Hasler; Neumayr (Sutter 76), Niederhausen.

Crusaders (1) 1 *(Owens 22)*

Rosenborg (1) 2 *(Chibuike 45, Svensson 78)*   948

Crusaders: (442) O'Neill; Robinson, Magowan, Coates, McClean; McAllister, Cleary (Watson 68), Heatley (McMaster 83), Morrow; Snoddy (McCutcheon 78), Owens.
Rosenborg: (442) Hansen; Gamboa, Reginiussen, Ronning, Dorsin; Berntsen (Mikkelsen 90), Selnaes (Strandberg 85), Svensson (Jensen 83), Chibuike; Bille Nielsen, Dockal.

Domzale (0) 0

Astra Giurgiu (0) 1 *(Budescu 83)*   1000

Domzale: (451) Vidmar; Kous (Dobrovoljc 70), Skubic, Ljubovic, Janza (Balkovec 84); Parker, Majer, Stankovic, Bozovic, Gabric (Vuk S 67); Vuk G.
Astra Giurgiu: (4231) Lung Jr; Matel, Ben Youssef, Muresan, Junior Morais; Yahaya (Barboianu 90), Seto; Enache, Bukari, Budescu; Ivanovski (William Amorim 62).

Drogheda U (0) 0

Malmo (0) 0   1496

Drogheda U: (442) Sava; Daly, McNally, Prendergast, Brennan G; Brennan R■, O'Conor, Byrne, Cassidy; O'Neill (O'Brien 67), Hynes (Gannon 79).
Malmo: (442) Dahlin; Albornoz, Jansson, Johansson, Ricardinho; Hamad, Friberg (Petrovic 84), Halsti, Forsberg (Thern 55); Rantie, Eriksson.

Flora Tallinn (1) 1 *(Post 11)*

Kukesi (0) 1 *(Progni 79)*   2400

Flora Tallinn: (442) Meerits; Mets, Jurgenson, Palatu, Post; Van der Streek, Luigend (Logua 74), Laabus (Sappinen 85), Frolov; Alliku (Prosa 80), Mikadze.
Kukesi: (442) Halili; Peqini, Hallaci, Brahja, Malacarne; Alikaj (Malota 66), Musolli, Allmuca, Progni; Hoxha (Manuka 78), Popovic (Malindi 82).

Gandzasar Kapan (0) 1 *(Dashyan 90)*

Aktobe (0) 2 *(Davydov 61, Tagybergen 78)*   2100

Gandzasar Kapan: (442) Beglaryan A; Barseghyan (Zakaryan 65), Vukomanovic (Avagyan H 72), Avagyan A, Obradovic; Grigoryan, Khachatrian, Jikia (Petrosyan 86), Dashyan; Beglaryan N, Melkonyan.

Aktobe: (442) Sidelnikov; Muldarov, Badlo, Primus, Kenzhisariev (Davydov 46); Khayrullin, Tagybergen, Kharabara, Kovalchuk (Logvinenko 71); Geynrikh (Gridin 84), Kapadze.

Hibernians (0) 1 *(Obiefule 78)*
Vojvodina (2) 4 *(Skuletic 40, Soares 43 (og),*
Oumarou 50, Kosovic 82)   638
Hibernians: (442) Muscat; Kristensen, Tabone (Lima 65), Dias (Chetcuti 66), Failla; Pearson, Soares, Edison, Obiefule (Farrugia 78); Camilleri, Cohen.
Vojvodina: (442) Kordic; Radoja, Trajkovic, Djuric■, Baric; Alivodic (Gacinovic 88), Vranjes (Kosovic 71), Poletanovic, Vulicevic; Oumarou, Skuletic (Bilbija 58).

IBV Vestmannaeyjar (1) 1 *(Gudmundsson 16)*
HB Torshavn (0) 1 *(Jogvan Davidsen 66)*   950
IBV Vestmannaeyjar: (442) James; Gudjonsson, Sigurbjornsson, Olafsson, Garner; Gudmundsson, Thorvardarson, Mawejje, Jeffs; Thorsteinsson (Bergsson 81), Spear (Simmonds 81).
HB Torshavn: (442) Gestson; Davidsen Johan, Alex, Vatnsdal (Jensen 82), Benjaminsen; Mouritsen C, Haraldsen, Davidsen Jogvan, Olsen; Heinesen (Joensen 69), Mouritsen K.

Inter Baku (1) 1 *(Mamedov 7)*
Mariehamn (0) 1 *(Adlam 72)*   2300
Inter Baku: (442) Lomaia; Alejandro, Georgievski, Amiraslanov, Abdoulaye; Dashdemirov, Tskhadadze (Mansurov 83), Abasiyev, Mamedov (Mikel Alvaro 46); Lashvili, Javadov (Genov 76).
Mariehamn: (442) Enckelman; Thompson, Orgill (Bright 18), Lagerblom, Lyyski; Wirtanen, Andersson, Ostlind, Adlam; Diego Assis (Jokihaara 33), Byskata.

Jeunesse d'Esch (1) 2 *(Benichou 21, Wang 52)*
TPS Turku (0) 0   1157
Jeunesse d'Esch: (442) Oberweis; Moreira (Kintziger 66), Hoffmann, Portier, Benichou; Wang (Piskor 74), Ibrahimovic, Vitali, Ramdedovic; Collette (Deidda 88), Delgado.
TPS Turku: (442) Lehtovaara; Tanska, Lahde, Nyberg (Lehtonen 86), Rahmonen; Brown (Ristola 66), Hyyrynen (Hradecky 43), Pennanen, Aaritalo; Riski, Hurme.

KR Reykjavik (0) 0
Glentoran (0) 0   967
KR Reykjavik: (442) Halldorsson; Hauksson H, Sigurdsson G, Gunnarsson GT, Gunnarsson GR; Gudjonsson, Sigurdsson B, Saevarsson, Finnbogason; Martin (Sigurjonsson 70), Hauksson O.
Glentoran: (451) Morris; Bradley, Magee, Birney (Garrett 79), Hill; Howland, Clarke M (O'Hanlon 67), McAlorum, Kane (McCullough 79), Clarke R; Miskimmon.

Kruoja (0) 0
Dinamo Minsk (0) 3 *(Figueredo 63, Politevich 72,*
Rassadkin 84)   760
Kruoja: (442) Eltermanis; Poceviciu5, ■tmanavicius (Sidlauskas 71), Paulauskas, Lunskis; Tsishkevich (Lipskis 59), Maciulis, Soblirov (Bagocius 81), Strockis; Slavickas, Beniusis.
Dinamo Minsk: (442) Gutor; Plaskonny, Veretilo, Politevich, Bychenok (Coccaro 62); Simovic, Khatskevitch (Rassadkin 82), Korzun, Figueredo; Stasevich, Sychev (Bykov 73).

La Fiorita (0) 0
Valletta (1) 3 *(Denni 30 (pen), 50, Zammit 90)*   374
La Fiorita: (442) Montanari; Rinaldi D (Guidi 85), Confalone, Ceci, Mazzola; Bollini G, Rinaldi F, Bollini F (Silva Bahiano 83), Sorbera; Selva (Gualtieri 65), Bucchi.
Valletta: (442) Marino; Caruana (Bajada 46), Azzopardi, Camilleri, Dimech; Vandelannoite, Fenech, Briffa, Hamza; Denni (Zammit 85), Falzon (Cremona 83).

Laci (0) 0
Differdange 03 (0) 1 *(Lebresne 84)*   300
Laci: (442) Bakaj; Ndreka, Doku, Ofoyen, Kastrati; Buljan, Nimani, Shazivari (Sefgjinaj 40), Vucaj; Zefi, Rovcanin (Ajazi 70).
Differdange 03: (442) Weber; Bukvic, Janisch, Caillet, Rodrigues (Bastos 68); May, Ribeiro (Meligner 75), Bisevac (Kettenmeyer 82), Lebresne; Franzoni, Er Rafik.

Levski Sofia (0) 0
Irtysh Pavlodar (0) 0   5945
Levski Sofia: (442) Iliev; Mulder, Angelov, Silva (De Carvalho 53), Mendes Rodrgues; Vezalov, Cristovao (Lopes 81), Nuno Pinto, Gadzhev (Vutov 60); Bru, Velev.
Irtysh Pavlodar: (442) Kotlyar; Kucera, Khalmuratov, Govedarica, Coulibaly; Yurin, Shomko, Mukhutdinov, Murzoev (Strukov 90); Shabalin (Chichulin 21), Bakaev (Chernyshov 90).

Milsami (1) 1 *(Andronic 35)*
F91 Dudelange (0) 0   2500
Milsami: (442) Negai; Rhaili, Gheti, Shedrack, Patras (Leuca 90); Boghiu (Iavorschi 76), de Paula (Ciofu 90), Rassulov, Andronic; Gheorghiu, Soporan.
F91 Dudelange: (442) Joubert; Prempeh, Ney, Martino, Fernandes (Wang 80); Benzouien, Steinmetz, Da Mota Alves (Karapetyan 67), Kitenge; Pedro (Benajiba 46), Maurv.

Prestatyn T (1) 1 *(Parkinson 45)*
Liepajas Metalurgs (1) 2 *(Kalns 16, Sadcins 62)*   1017
Prestatyn T: (532) Roberts; Davies, Hayes (Murray 81), Hessey, Lewis, Stephens; Stones, Gibson, Parker; Hunt, Parkinson.
Liepajas Metalurgs: (532) Varazinskis; Jemelins, Otankis (Sadcins 46), Kirilins, Zirnis, Slampe I; Savalnieks■, Afanasjevs (Ikaunieks D 58), Hmizs; Prohorenkovs, Kalns.

Rudar Pljevlja (1) 1 *(Damjanovic 16)*
Mika (0) 0   600
Rudar Pljevlja: (442) Vuklis; Nestorovic, Sljivancanin, Petrovic, Jeknic (Bambur 85); Vlahovic, Brnovic, Jovanovic, Stojanovic (Cosovic 74); Kaludjerovic (Sekulic 69), Damjanovic.
Mika: (442) Fishyan; Alex, Petrosyan, Voskanyan, Ghazaryan (Arakelyan 71); Mkrtchyan (Adamyan 78), Poghosian (Shahinyan 54), Poghosyan, Muradyan; Movsisyan, Satunyan.

Sarajevo (1) 1 *(Melunovic 19)*
Libertas (0) 0   6500
Sarajevo: (442) Melunovic; Bandovic, Radulovic, Huseinbasic (Radovac 57), Haurdic; Tatomirovic, Dzakmic, Cimirot, Tadejevic (Sunjevaric 85); Dupovac, Suljic (Aganspahic 82).
Libertas: (442) Simoncini A; Rocchi, Molinari, Simoncini D, Rosti (Zennaro 66); Facondini (Morelli 60), Antonelli, Benvenuti (Polidori 83), Camillini; Bacciocchi, Dall'Ara.

Suduva (1) 2 *(Basic 23, Valskis 85)*
Turnovo (2) 2 *(Baldovaliev 30, Blazevski 45 (pen))*   1500
Suduva: (442) Davidovs; Basic, Radzius, Isoda, Leimonas; Brokas (Chvedukas 46), Baranovskij, Soblinskas (Kiselevskis 81), Ugge; Radzinevicius, Valskis.
Turnovo: (442) Dimovski; Tasev, Petrov, Mitrev, Mavrov; Tenekedziev (Iliev 87), Mitrov (Stoilov 68), Vasilev, Blazevski; Varelovski, Baldovaliev (Jasharoski 90).

Teteks (0) 1 *(Iseni 90)*
Pyunik (0) 1 *(Ayvazyan 81)*   1200
Teteks: (442) Mancevski; Krsteski, Bejtulai, Kralevski, Jovanoski (Ristovski 77); Bozinovski, Micevski (Tosevski 87), Nachevski, Iseni; Angelov (Petkovski 82), Despotovski.
Pyunik: (442) Manukyan; Minasian, Haroyan, Poghosyan Gagik, Poghosyan Ghukas; Manoyan, Hovhannisyan K, Papikyan (Zakaryan 66), Sardaryan (Malakyan 72); Baloyan (Ayvazyan 75), Voskanyan.

Teuta (1) 3 *(Xhafaj 29, Dosti 68, Mancaku 73)*
Dacia (1) 1 *(Pavlov 38)*   1000
Teuta: (442) Rizvani; Idrizaj, Buiu, Nika (Cyrbja 73), Dosti; Osmani, Jakupi, Xhafaj, Hyshmeri (Cekici 81); Mado (Hoxha 85), Mancaku.
Dacia: (442) Matiughin; Posmac, Ilescu, Soppo (Cociuc 76), Grosu; Orbu (Dragovozov 76), Mihaliov, Stoleru, Ogada; Lapushenko, Pavlov (Shevel 80).

Tiraspol (0) 0
Skonto (0) 1 *(Mingazov 51)*   3575
Tiraspol: (442) Livsit; Popovici D, Novikov, Zarichinyuk, Shapoval; Popovici A (Nevuche 73), Josan, Karaneychev (Grosu 57), Boestean; Bulat (Gheorghiev 80), Khachaturov.
Skonto: (442) Grybauskas; Gabovs, Rode, Bulvitis, Fertovs; Isajevs, Laizans, Mingazov (Klimiashvili 85), Sinelnikovs (Osipovs 79); Sabala, Dvali.

Torpedo Kutaisi (0) 0
Zilina (0) 3 *(Majtan 58, 84, Pich 77)*   4150
Torpedo Kutaisi: (442) Migineishvili; Tabatadze, Chiteishvili, Pirtskhalava (Pantsulaia 53), Tsintsadze; Gigauri, Kukhianidze (Kapanadze 73), Tchanturia, Gorozia (Tughushi 64); Chelidze, Barabadze.
Zilina: (442) Dubravka; Akakpo, Majtan, Pecovsky, Babatounde (Kacer 90); Piacek, Pich, Ceesay, Mihalik (Zilak 73); Paur (Skvarka 88), Mabouka.

Tromso (1) 1 *(Koppinen 30)*
Celje (0) 2 *(Zurej 75, Gobec 84 (pen))*   1582
Tromso: (442) Sahlman; Fojut, Koppinen, Bendiksen, Drage (Moldskred 55); Ondrasek (Pritchard 81), Norbye■, Andersen (Kristiansen 69), Johansen; Ciss, Prijovic.
Celje: (442) Kotnik; Vrhovec, Krajcer, Verbic, Jugovic; Bajde (Zagar-Knez 66), Cebara (Korosec 46), Gobec, Zitko; Zajc (Plesec 13), Zurej.

UE Santa Coloma (1) 1 *(Bernat 45)*
Zrinjski Mostar (0) 3 *(Crnov 63, Popovic 66, Djuric 77)*   215
UE Santa Coloma: (442) Perianes Meca; Maneiro, Martinez (Marc Blazquez 83), Roca, Anton; Bernat (Vall 67), Bousenine, Pereira, Crespo; Rubio (Triquell 77), Do Nascimento.
Zrinjski Mostar: (442) Dujkovic; Radeljic, Simeunovic, Crnov, Popovic (Bekic 83); Stojkic, Brkovic, Muminovic (Barisic 79), Savic (Scepanovic 70); Ancic, Djuric.

Videoton (2) 2 *(Vinicius 35, Gyurcso 41)*
Mladost Podgorica (1) 1 *(Markovic 3 (pen))*   6520
Videoton: (442) Vinicius; Gyurcso (Kleinheisler 80), Tujvel, Gomes, Oliveira; Nikolic, Szekeres, Alvarez (Paraiba 54), Mamadu; Toth (Enete 66), Kovacs.
Mladost Podgorica: (442) Markovic (Knezevic 87); Vujadinovic, Zivkovic, Sankovic, Sofranac; Mitrovic, Kaljevic (Kalezic 90), Savicevic (Pavicevic 84), Seratlic; Tomic, Taku.

Vikingur (0) 1 *(Justinussen 75)*
Inter Turku (1) 1 *(Nikkari 20)*   280
Vikingur: (442) Turi; Jacobsen H, Gregersen A, Petersen (Hansen Hjartvard 86), Djordjevic (Olsen 90); Bartalstovu, Hansen B, Jacobsen E, Djurhuus; Justinussen, Vatnhamar■.
Inter Turku: (442) Bahne; Hamalainen, Aspegren, Gruborovics, Nyman; Sirbiladze, Gnabouyou (Tumanto 71), Paajanen, Kauppi (Bouwman 7); Nikkari, Lehtonen.

VMFD Zalgiris (1) 2 *(Komolov 23, Bilinski 70)*
St Patrick's Ath (0) 2 *(Byrne 55, O'Brien 87)*   4200
VMFD Zalgiris: (433) Vitkauskas; Vaitkunas, Peric, Skerla, Silenas; Svrljuga, Zulpa (Janusauskas 62), Radavicius (Velicka 60); Komolov (Gerc 83), Kuklys, Bilinski.
St Patrick's Ath: (433) Clarke; O'Brien, Kenna, Browne, Bermingham; Forrester, Bolger, Byrne; Russell, Brennan (McFaul 85), Fagan (Hughes 88).

FIRST QUALIFYING ROUND SECOND LEG

Tuesday, 9 July 2013

Differdange 03 (0) 2 *(Er Rafik 55, 75)*
Laci (1) 1 *(Nimani 38)*   952
Differdange 03: (442) Weber; Rodrigues, Caillet, Bukvic, Janisch; Ribeiro (Bastos 84), Bisevac (Kettenmeyer 90), Lebresne, Er Rafik (Luisi 90); May, Franzoni.
Laci: (442) Bakaj; Doku, Buljan, Ndreka■, Kastrati; Shazivari (Rovcanin 85), Vucaj■, Sefgjinaj■, Nimani; Zefi, Danaj.

Mika (1) 1 *(Ghazaryan 45)*
Rudar Pljevlja (0) 1 *(Stojanovic 85)*   2760
Mika: (442) Khachatryan; Ghazaryan, Petrosyan, Voskanyan, Mkrtchyan; Satunyan, Poghosian (Adamyan 88), Movsisyan, Arakelyan (Shahinyan 53); Alex, Hakobyan (Muradyan 46).
Rudar Pljevlja: (442) Vuklis; Kaludjerovic (Sekulic 74), Sljivancanin (Bambur 51), Stojanovic, Petrovic; Damjanovic, Jeknic, Brnovic (Rustemovic 90), Jovanovic; Nestorovic, Vlahovic.

TPS Turku (1) 2 *(Vitali 38 (og), Riski 88)*
Jeunesse d'Esch (0) 1 *(Wang 80)*   2189
TPS Turku: (442) Lehtovaara; Tanska, Hurme, Nyberg (Makinen 67), Rahmonen; Pennanen, Hradecky (Brown 29), Lahde, Aaritalo; Riski, Ristola (Hyyrynen 60).
Jeunesse d'Esch: (442) Oberweis; Moreira, Hoffmann, Kintziger (Albanese 86), Benichou; Wang (Agovic 84), Portier, Ibrahimovic, Collette; Vitali, Delgado.

Wednesday, 10 July 2013

Linfield (1) 3 *(Gault 40, Mulgrew 55, Lowry 60)*
Fuglafjordur (0) 0   2500
Linfield: (442) Tuffey; Burns B, Burns A (McAllister 45), Clarke, Ervin; Gault, Lowry, Knowles, Mulgrew; Thompson, Carvill.
Fuglafjordur: (442) Mikkelsen J; Mikkelsen P (Lambanum 67), Nesa, Ellingsgaard J, Eliasen; Saric, Madsen (Johansen 70), Jovevic, Petersen B; Ellingsgaard A, Dalbuo (Petersen A 89).

Thursday, 11 July 2013

Aktobe (1) 2 *(Kapadze 2, 54)*
Gandzasar Kapan (1) 1 *(Beglaryan N 35)*   12,800
Aktobe: (442) Sidelnikov; Badlo, Kenzhisariev, Logvinenko, Primus; Muldarov, Kharabara, Khayrullin, Kapadze (Tagybergen 86); Davydov (Kovalchuk 39), Geynrikh (Gridin 81).
Gandzasar Kapan: (442) Beglaryan A; Tatintsian (Avagyan H 86), Vukomanovic (Petrosyan 74), Avagyan A, Obradovic; Jikia (Barseghyan 63), Khachatrian, Dashyan, Grigoryan; Melkonyan, Beglaryan N.

Astra Giurgiu (0) 2 *(Vidmar 50 (og), Bukari 62)*
Domzale (0) 0   1513
Astra Giurgiu: (442) Lung Jr; Ben Youssef, Junior Morais, Matel, Yahaya (Barboianu 72); Seto, Enache (William Amorim 66), Bukari (Ivanovski 78), Muresan; Budescu, Fatai.
Domzale: (442) Vidmar; Skubic, Bozovic, Dobrovoljc, Majer (Pozeg 69); Janza, Stankovic, Gabric, Kous (Pihler 84); Vuk G (Parker 65), Vuk S.

Botev Plovdiv (0) 5 *(Ognyanov 54, Vander 56 (pen), Nedelev 58, 75, Grncarov 71)*
Astana (0) 0   7400
Botev Plovdiv: (442) Stachowiak; Sprockel, Minev, Abel, Grncarov; Ognyanov, Hristov, Jirsak, Galchev (Pedro 76); Vander (Dyakov 61), Kortzorg (Nedelev 46).
Astana: (442) Eric; Korobkin, Nurdauletov, Zelao, Dmitrenko; Kethevoama (Pasichnik 76), Igumanovic, Kojasevic (Nuserbaev 64), Kuat■; Beisebekov, Shakhmetov (Konysbaev 60).

Budapest Honved (3) 9 *(Holender 14, Diaby 23, Diarra 36, Delczeg 49 (pen), Testardi 66 (pen), 75, 87, Alcibiade 67, Kozma 81)*

Celik Niksic (0) 0   1800

Budapest Honved: (442) Kemenes; Ignjatovic, Barath, Zivanovic (Mancini 46), Alcibiade; Diarra, Lovric, Hidi, Holender (Kozma 55); Delczeg, Diaby (Testardi 61).
Celik Niksic: (442) Banovic; Dubljevic (Bakoc 20), Vukovic, Ivanovic (Vilotijevic 69), Radovic (Bulatovic 46); Bulajic, Adrovic, Jovovic, Zoric; Vidakanic, Racic.

Celje (0) 0

Tromso (2) 2 *(Andersen 4, Moldskred 16)*   2800

Celje: (442) Kotnik; Gobec, Korosec, Zitko, Vidmajer; Jugovic, Plesec (Zajc 46), Zurej, Verbic; Bajde (Zagar-Knez 46), Krajcer.
Tromso: (442) Sahlman; Fojut, Causevic, Koppinen, Kristiansen; Ciss■, Bendiksen (Moldskred 15), Andersen (Drage 73), Johansen; Pritchard, Prijovic.

Dacia (1) 2 *(Stoleru 20, Pavlov 75)*

Teuta (0) 0   2561

Dacia: (442) Matiughin; Posmac, Ilescu, Grosu (Molla 83), Orbu; Mihaliov, Stoleru, Ogada, Cociuc (Ovseannicov 56); Lapushenko, Pavlov (Orlovski 85).
Teuta: (442) Rizvani; Idrizaj (Sakaj 46), Buiu, Nika, Dosti (Deliallisi 83); Osmani, Jakupi, Xhafaj, Hyshmeri (Cyrbja 80); Mado, Mancaku.

Dinamo Minsk (4) 5 *(Bykov 5, Figueredo 14, Sychev 16, 17, Khvashchinski 70)*

Kruoja (0) 0   2900

Dinamo Minsk: (442) Gutor; Plaskonny, Veretilo, Simovic, Politevich; Bykov, Danilov (Shetilovski 57), Figueredo (Bychenok 64), Stasevich; Khvashchinski, Sychev (Rassadkin 70).
Kruoja: (442) Malinauskas; Pocevicius, Strockis, Lunskis, Tsishkevich; Maciulis, Lipskis, Sidlauskas (Bagocius 46), Slavickas; Atmanavicius (Balasauskas 88), Beniusis (Kochanauskas 83).

F91 Dudelange (0) 0

Milsami (0) 0   952

F91 Dudelange: (442) Joubert; Prempeh, Martino (Beltorangal 82), Benzouien, Ney; Fernandes, Louadj (Karapetyan 56), Maurv, Steinmetz; Da Mota Alves, Kitenge (Benajiba 67).
Milsami: (442) Negai; Rhaili (Ciofu 13), Gheorghiu, Rassulov, Gheti; Andronic (Stadiiciuc 89), Bolohan, Patras (Leuca 88), Boghiu; Guillherme, Soporan.

FC Santa Coloma (0) 0

Breidablik (0) 0   190

FC Santa Coloma: (442) Casals; Wagner, Fite Castillo, Rebes, Blanco; Mercade (Romero 74), Ribolleda, Quinones■, Sanchez (Garcia 63); Juanfer, Smith (Mota 70).
Breidablik: (442) Gunnleifsson; Margeirsson, Troost, Adalsteinsson (Yeoman 64), Lydsson; Sigurgeirsson, Ingason, Elisabetarson, Jonsson; Rohde (Hreinsson 87), Vilhjalmsson.

Gefle (1) 5 *(Hansson 17, Oremo 47, 90, Dahlberg 50, Tornros 71)*

Trans Narva (0) 0 *(Lvov 82)*   444

Gefle: (442) Hedvall; Mard, Olsson J, Wikstrom, Faltsetas; Oremo, Phekezela (Adukor 33), Portin, Dahlberg (Tornros 65); Lantto (Lundevall 56), Hansson.
Trans Narva: (442) Ponyatovski; Nesterovski, Kazakov, Pereplotkins (Lvov 55), Shesterkov■; Dubokin, Kitto, Taar, Kulikov (Kutuzov 84); Elysee, Jogi (Skinjov 46).

Glentoran (0) 0

KR Reykjavik (1) 3 *(Martin 24, Saevarsson 65, 90)*   1700

Glentoran: (442) Morris; Bradley, Magee, Clarke R, Kane; Callacher, McAlorum (Gordon 86), Howland, Clarke M; O'Hanlon (Hughes 70), Miskimmon (McComb 70).
KR Reykjavik: (442) Halldorsson; Gunnarsson GR, Hauksson H, Sigurdsson G, Gudjonsson; Hauksson O, Saevarsson, Atlason (Olafsson 87), Sigurdsson B (Ragnarsson 73); Finnbogason, Martin.

HB Torshavn (0) 0

IBV Vestmannaeyjar (0) 1 *(Bergsson 90 (pen))*   1608

HB Torshavn: (442) Gestson; Alex, Davidsen Johan, Vatnsdal, Benjaminsen; Samuelsen (Joensen 76), Mouritsen C, Haraldsen, Davidsen Jogvan (Slaetarlid 90); Olsen, Heinesen (Mouritsen K 68).
IBV Vestmannaeyjar: (442) James; Gudjonsson (Bergsson 56), Garner, Gudmundsson, Thorsteinsson (Hreidarsson 75); Spear (Leosson 69), Thorvardarson, Mawejje, Olafsson; Sigurbjornsson, Jeffs.

Inter Turku (0) 0

Vikingur (0) 1 *(Jacobsen H 78 (pen))*   1781

Inter Turku: (442) Bahne; Aspegren, Gruborovics (Duah 46), Nyman, Bouwman; Sirbiladze, Gnabouyou, Paajanen, Nikkari; Tumanto (Camara 76), Lehtonen.
Vikingur: (442) Turi; Jacobsen H, Gregersen A, Lervig (Hansen Hjartvard 67), Petersen; Djordjevic, Bartalstovu, Hansen B, Jacobsen E; Djurhuus, Justinussen.

Irtysh Pavlodar (2) 2 *(Murzoev 6, Bakaev 13 (pen))*

Levski Sofia (0) 0   9500

Irtysh Pavlodar: (442) Kotlyar; Chernyshov, Govedarica (Chichulin 58), Coulibaly, Bakaev; Ivanov, Yurin (Shabalin 73), Shomko, Kucera; Mukhutdinov, Murzoev (Ayaganov 90).
Levski Sofia: (442) Iliev; Mulder, Angelov, Starokin, Lopes (De Carvalho 46); Silva (Velev 46), Mendes Rodrgues, Vezalov, Cristovao; Dimov■, Bru (Vutov 73).

Khazar Lankaran (1) 1 *(Amirquliev 29)*

Sliema Wanderers (0) 0   11,055

Khazar Lankaran: (442) Doblas; Ramaldanov, Tounkara, Bonfim, Benouahi (Silva 69); Nildo, Amirquliev, Todorov, Gligorov (Pit 61); Skarlatake, Orsulic (Abdullayev■ 80).
Sliema Wanderers: (442) Zammit; Muscat A, Mintoff, Muchard, Scerri; Ohawuchi, Laudisi (Woods 70), Baldaccchino■, Barbetti; Muscat G, Bonello.

Kukesi (0) 0

Flora Tallinn (0) 0   4000

Kukesi: (442) Halili; Brahja, Peqini, Malacarne, Progni; Hallaci, Allmuca, Alikaj (Malota 66), Musolli■; Popovic (Malindi 83), Hoxha (Manuka 90).
Flora Tallinn: (442) Meerits; Mets, Frolov, Palatu, Mikadze (Adou 86); Van de Streek, Jurgenson, Luigend, Prosa (Logua 64); Alliku, Laabus (Post 64).
Kukesi won on away goals rule.

Levadia Tallinn (2) 3 *(Hunt 6, 21, 50)*

Bala T (0) 1 *(Jones R 89)*   2567

Levadia Tallinn: (442) Smishko; Kulinits, Jahhimovits, Artjunin, Pikk; Subbotin, Antonov, Dmitrijev, Raudsepp; Hunt (Kaljumae 78), Rattel.
Bala T: (4411) Morris; Connolly, Jones S, Valentine, Collins; Brown (Pierce 89), Murtagh (Jones R 64), Lunt, Sheridan; Jones M; Codling (Edwards 75).

Libertas (1) 1 *(Morelli 28)*

Sarajevo (2) 2 *(Haurdic 2, Todorovic 45)*   665

Libertas: (442) Simoncini A; Rocchi, Molinari (Benvenuti 65), Morelli (Polidori 84), Simoncini D; Facondini, Zennaro, Antonelli, Camillini; Bacciocchi (Macerata 46), Dall'Ara.
Sarajevo: (442) Bandovic; Radovac (Culov 70), Haurdic, Melunovic (Aganspahic 76), Todorovic; Tatomirovic, Dzakmic, Cimirot, Tadejevic; Dupovac, Suljic (Osmanagic 82).

Liepajas Metalurgs (1) 1 *(Afanasjevs 17)*

Prestatyn T (0) 2 *(Stephens 77, Gibson 90)*   2500

Liepajas Metalurgs: (541) Varazinskis; Hmizs (Slampe E 46), Slampe I, Zirnis■, Jemelins, Sadcins; Afanasjevs (Kirilins 96), Ikaunieks J (Zuntners 65), Prohorenkovs, Kalns; Ikaunieks D.
Prestatyn T: (433) Roberts; Davies (Murray 113), Hayes, Hessey, Lewis; Parker, Gibson, Stones; Holmes (Owen 75), Parkinson, Stephens.
aet; Prestatyn T won 4-3 on penalties.

Malmo (1) 2 *(Forsberg 45, Kroon 90)*
Drogheda U (0) 0   5689

Malmo: (442) Dahlin; Albornoz, Jansson, Johansson, Ricardinho; Hamad, Thern (Friberg 70), Halsti, Forsberg (Kroon 79); Rantie (Olsen 86), Eriksson.
Drogheda U: (442) Sava; Daly, Prendergast, McNally (Rusk 74), Brennan G; O'Neill, O'Conor, Cassidy, Byrne; O'Brien (Hand 86), Hynes.

Mariehamn (0) 0
Inter Baku (1) 2 *(Tskhadadze 21 (pen), Javadov 86)* 1532

Mariehamn: (442) Enckelman; Thompson, Lagerblom, Amani (Wiklof 61), Lyyski; Andersson, Ostlind, Adlam, Bright; Byskata, Wirtanen.
Inter Baku: (442) Lomaia; Alejandro, Georgievski, Amirjanov, Mikel Alvaro; Lashvili (Spicic 69), Abdoulaye, Dashdemirov, Tskhadadze (Genov 73); Abasiyev (Alakbarov 90), Javadov.

Mladost Podgorica (0) 1 *(Knezevic 90 (pen))*
Videoton (0) 0   2700

Mladost Podgorica: (442) Vujadinovic; Zivkovic, Sankovic, Sofranac, Mitrovic; Kaljevic (Knezevic 70), Markovic■, Savicevic, Seratlic; Tomic (Pavicevic 88), Taku.
Videoton: (442) Tujvel; Vinicius, Caneira, Gomes, Oliveira (Paraiba 55); Nikolic, Stopira, Toth, Szolnoki; Kovacs, Gyurcso (Kleinheisler 79).
Mladost Podgorica won on away goals rule.

Pyunik (0) 1 *(Ayvazyan 90)*
Teteks (0) 0   2900

Pyunik: (442) Manukyan; Hovhannisyan A, Haroyan, Poghosyan Gagik, Manoyan; Papikyan (Poghosyan Ghukas 70), Minasian, Sardaryan (Malakyan 86), Baloyan (Ayvazyan 59); Voskanian, Yuspashyan.
Teteks: (442) Mancevski; Krsteski, Bejtulai, Kralevski, Jovanoski (Iseni 59 (Tosevski 84)); Bozinovski, Micevski, Angelov (Ristovski 76), Petkovski; Despotovski, Nachevski.

Qarabag (0) 1 *(George 85)*
Metalurg Skopje (0) 0   5000

Qarabag: (442) Varvodic; Teli, Qarayev, Medvedev, Yusifov (George 79); Reynaldo, Sadyqov, Almeida, Agoli; Gelashvili (Kapolongo 89), Nadirov (Sattarly 90).
Metalurg Skopje: (442) Efremov; Ljamcevski, Mitrevski, Berisha, Krstev; Peev, Simonovski (Gjorgievski 68), Mitrev, Radeski (Maznov 46); Siskov (Curlinov 46), Dalceski.

Rosenborg (2) 7 *(Hoiland 15, Chibuike 35, 50, Dockal 57, Mikkelsen 60, Sorloth 72, Svensson 90)*
Crusaders (0) 2 *(Leeman 49, Owens 68)*   4003

Rosenborg: (433) Hansen; Hoiland, Ronning, Moe, Dorsin (Gamboa 46); Berntsen (Svensson 73), Selnaes, Jensen; Dockal, Chibuike (Sorloth 60), Mikkelsen.
Crusaders: (4141) O'Neill; Robinson (McMaster 64), Leeman, Coates, McClean; Watson (King 64); McAllister, Snoddy, Morrow, Heatley (McCutcheon 63); Owens.

Skonto (0) 0
Tiraspol (0) 1 *(Zarichnyuk 80)*   3000

Skonto: (442) Grybauskas; Gabovs, Rode, Laizans, Fertovs; Mingazov, Sinelnikovs (Osipovs 100), Sabala, Bulvitis; Karasauskas (Isajevs 80), Dvali.
Tiraspol: (442) Livsit; Zarichnyuk, Popovici D, Novikov, Shapoval; Popovici A (Nevuche 56), Josan, Hausi, Boestean; Bulat (Grosu 70), Nelson (Gheorghiev 17).
aet; Skonto FC won 4-2 on penalties.

St Patrick's Ath (0) 1 *(Brennan 85 (pen))*
VMFD Zalgiris (1) 2 *(Kuklys 45, Bilinski 52)* 2700

St Patrick's Ath: (433) Clarke; O'Brien, Kenna, Browne, Bermingham; Russell (Kelly 86), Bolger, Brennan; Byrne (Price 60), Fagan, Forrester (Flood 59).
VMFD Zalgiris: (4141) Vitkauskas; Vaitkunas, Peric, Skerla, Silenas (Janusauskas 67); Zulpa; Svrljuga, Komolov (Zagurskas 78), Kuklys, Radavicius (Leliuga 46); Bilinski.

Turnovo (0) 2 *(Mitrov 47, Blazevski 90 (pen))*
Suduva (1) 2 *(Valskis 43, Radzinevicius 52)* 1558

Turnovo: (442) Dimovski; Iliev, Petrov (Tasev 82), Mitrev (Stoilov 71), Mavrov; Tenekedziev, Blazevski, Mitrov, Vasilev (Najdenov 90); Varelovski, Baldovaliev.
Suduva: (442) Davidovs; Radzius, Isoda, Leimonas, Chvedukas (Urba 90); Valskis (Brokas 90), Baranovskij (Bagdanavicius 81), Basic, Radzinevicius■; Soblinskas, Ugge.
aet; Turnovo won 5-4 on penalties.

Vaduz (1) 1 *(Sutter 29)*
Chikhura Sachkhere (1) 1 *(Jigauri 2)*   1124

Vaduz: (442) Jehle; Pergl, Sara, Niederhausen, Burgmeier (Cecchini 87); Schurpf, Hasler, Baron (Tighazaoui 63), Pak; Sutter, Neumayr.
Chikhura Sachkhere: (442) Somkhishvili; Kashia, Rekhviashvili, Lomashvili, Chikvaidze; Datunaishvili, Jigauri, Odikadze, Dekanoidze (Kimadze 90); Tsinamdzgvrishvili (Gogatishvili 83), Bechvaia.
Chikhura Sachkere won on away goals rule.

Valletta (0) 1 *(Zammit 90 (pen))*
La Fiorita (0) 0   998

Valletta: (442) Marino (Cini 60); Azzopardi, Fenech, Briffa, Hamza; Bajada, Denni, Falzon (Zammit 57), Vandelannoite; Cremona (Agius 70), Dimech.
La Fiorita: (442) Montanari; Confalone, Ceci (Pedrelli 90), Mazzola, Cavalli (Guidi 83); Bollini G, Rinaldi F, Rinaldi D (Franklin 70), Sorbera; Selva, Piccioni.

Ventspils (0) 0
Airbus UK Broughton (0) 0   1100

Ventspils: (442) Uvarenko; Kurakins, Smirnovs, Dubra, Timofejevs; Kozlovs, Tarasovs, Paulius, Sukhanov; Abdultaofik (Turkovs 82), Yanchuk.
Airbus UK Broughton: (4411) Coates; Owens, Pearson, Kearney, Short; Riley (Johnson 89), Rule, Field (Ward 74); Jones; Abbott; Budrys (Wade 85).
FK Ventspils win on Away Goal Rule

Vojvodina (1) 3 *(Alivodic 40, Skuletic 62, 67)*
Hibernians (1) 2 *(Obiefule 42, Failla 47 (pen))*   4582

Vojvodina: (442) Kordic; Alivodic, Skuletic (Gacinovic 86), Radoja, Trajkovic; Vranjes, Baric (Kosovic 67), Poletanovic (Nastic 79), Bilbija; Kovacevic, Vulicevic.
Hibernians: (442) Balzan; Obiefule, Failla, Camilleri, Pearson; Lima (Farrugia 85), Soares, Dias (Edison■ 70), Cohen; Kristensen, Chetcuti.

Zilina (2) 3 *(Majtan 17, Pich 23, 62)*
Torpedo Kutaisi (1) 3 *(Kapanadze 29, 61, Mzevashvili 79)*
    3197

Zilina: (442) Dubravka; Majtan, Pich (Zilak 87), Akakpo, Pecovsky; Babatounde, Piacek (Vavro 77), Ceesay, Skvarka (Paur 63); Mihalik, Mabouka.
Torpedo Kutaisi: (442) Migineishvili; Kapanadze, Mzevashvili (Jikia 81), Tabatadze, Tsintsadze (Pirtskhalava 69); Gigauri, Kukhianidze, Tchanturia, Gabadze; Chelidze, Sabanadze (Gorozia 60).

Zrinjski Mostar (0) 1 *(Djuric 76)*
UE Santa Coloma (0) 0   2000

Zrinjski Mostar: (442) Dujkovic; Bekic (Popovic 60), Crnov (Djuric 68), Pehar (Simeunovic 82), Scepanovic; Stojkic, Brkovic, Savic, Anicic; Graovac, Kantar.
UE Santa Coloma: (442) Godswill; Maneiro, Martinez, Roca, Anton; Vall (Pereira 78), Bernat (Do Nascimento 73), Bousenine, Triquell; Crespo, Rubio.

SECOND QUALIFYING ROUND FIRST LEG

Tuesday, 16 July 2013
Levadia Tallinn (0) 0
Panduri Targu Jiu (0) 0   2848

Levadia Tallinn: (442) Smishko; Kulinits, Jahhimovits, Pikk, Kaljumae; Raudsepp (Pebre 79), Dmitrijev, Subbotin, Antonov; Hunt (Rattel 65), Volchkov.
Panduri Targu Jiu: (442) Mingote; Momcilovic, Christou, Ungurusan, Erico; Anton (Buleica 66), Pereira, Breeveld, Nistor; Ciucur (Brata 66), Matulevicius (Lemnaru 77).

Thursday, 18 July 2013
Anorthosis Famagusta (2) 3 *(Garcia 12 (pen), Colautti 33, 84)*
Gefle (0) 0
Anorthosis Famagusta: (451) Valverde; Andic, Paulo Jorge, Pavicevic, Galamaz; Alexa, Garcia (Makos 80), Fofana (Avraam 70), Ohayon, Marangos; Colautti (Okkas 86).
Gefle: (442) Hedvall; Asp, Fallman, Wikstrom, Portin; Adukor (Olsson 54), Hansson, Faltsetas, Lundevall (Olsson E 87); Orlov (Oremo 75), Dahlberg.
Behind closed doors.

Astra Giurgiu (1) 1 *(Tembo 8)*
Omonia Nicosia (0) 1 *(Joao Paulo 66)* 2164
Astra Giurgiu: (442) Lung Jr; Ben Youssef, Yahaya (Barboianu 87), Tembo (William Amorim 65), Seto; Enache (Fatai 72), Budescu, Junior Morais, Bukari; Muresan, Matel.
Omonia Nicosia: (442) Moreira; Alabi, Cervera, Scaramozzino, Nuno Assis (Margaca 88); Joao Paulo, Leandro, Marco Soares, Schembri (Platini 90); Gikiewicz, Taylor (Efrem 63).

Beroe Stara Zagora (1) 1 *(Hristov 25)*
Hapoel Tel Aviv (2) 4 *(Lucas Sasha 5, Damari 9, 54, Shechter 60)* 9500
Beroe Stara Zagora: (4411) Karadzhov; Krumov, Stoychev, Zafirov, Penev; Iliev (Goranov 64), Elias, Djoman (Sayoud 58), Caiado; Andonov; Hristov.
Hapoel Tel Aviv: (4411) Amos; Dgani, Ilic, Colin, Harush; Gordana (Abutbul 82), Gerzycich, Lucas Sasha, Zaguri (Safuri 67); Shechter; Damari (Toama 74).

Breidablik (0) 0
SK Sturm Graz (0) 0 1052
Breidablik: (442) Gunnleifsson; Troost, Ingason, Jonsson, Rohde (Hreinsson 78); Gardarsson, Margeirsson, Hreidarsson, Yeoman; Lydsson, Adalsteinsson.
SK Sturm Graz: (442) Gratzei; Vuyadinovich, Todorovski, Klem, Hadzic; Weber, Hoelzl (Offenbacher 65), Kainz, Madl; Djuricin (Szabics 77), Beric.

Chornomorets (0) 2 *(Gai 46, Antonov 90)*
Dacia (0) 0 20,230
Chornomorets: (433) Bezotosny; Kutas, Fontanello, Berger, Kovalchuk K; Gai, Bobko, Samodin; Bakaj (Sito Riera 65), Djadjedje, Antonov.
Dacia: (433) Matiughin; Posmac, Ilescu, Soppo, Krkotic (Odia 53); Mihaliov, Stoleru (Dragovozov 65), Ogada; Ovseannicov, Camara (Shevel 72), Lapushenko.

Differdange 03 (1) 2 *(Er Rafik 26, 57)*
Utrecht (1) 1 *(Mulenga 2)* 2591
Differdange 03: (4231) Weber; Franzoni, Bukvic, Caillet, Janisch; May, Lebresne; Bastos (Luisi 78), Bisevac (Bettmer 63), Rodrigues; Er Rafik (Kettenmeyer 88).
Utrecht: (4132) Ruiter; Van der Maarel, Markiet, Heerings, Teijsse; Martensson (Diemers 67); Duplan (Schepers 77), Toornstra, Oar; Takagi (Van der Gun 59), Mulenga.

Dila Gori (0) 3 *(Modebadze 61, Gorelishvili 68, 90)*
Aalborg (0) 0 3500
Dila Gori: (442) Revishvili; Tomashvili, Khizaneishvili, Kobakhidze, Bolkvadze; Guruli, Aladashvili, Dolidze (Gorelishvili 63), Modebadze (Aleksidze 74); Gvalia, Iluridze (Aburdjania 84).
Aalborg: (442) Larsen; Kristensen (Wichmann 71), Thelander, Ahlmann, Nielsen; Thomsen, Due (Kusk 62), Wurtz, Curth; Frederiksen (Toft 76), Dalsgaard.

Dinamo Minsk (0) 1 *(Veselinovic 62)*
Lokomotiva Zagreb (2) 2 *(Situm 11, Misic 41)* 4850
Dinamo Minsk: (442) Gutor; Simovic■, Politevich, Nikolic (Khvashchinski 61), Veselinovic; Bykov, Veretilo, Figueredo (Kontsevoj 84), Stasevich; Trubilo, Adamovic (Coto 61).
Lokomotiva Zagreb: (442) Picak; Matas, Musa, Barbaric, Mesaric; Brucic (Martinac 82), Mrzljak, Chago, Situm (Miskic 90); Misic (Pjaca 69), Trebotic.

Hajduk Split (1) 2 *(Bencun 8, Maloca 79)*
Turnovo (1) 1 *(Blazevski 45 (pen))*
Hajduk Split: (442) Kalinic; Milkanovic, Milic, Jozinovic, Maloca; Andjelkovic, Pasalic (Maglica 62), Caktas, Susic; Bencun (Mujan 36), Kouassi (Kis 88).
Turnovo: (442) Dimovski; Tasev, Iliev, Petrov (Pandev 87), Mitev; Mavrov, Blazevski, Mitrov (Mutafchyiski 62), Stoilov (Najdenov 79); Vasilev, Baldovaliev.
Behind closed doors.

Hodd (1) 1 *(Standal 28)*
Aktobe (0) 0 2019
Hodd: (442) Lie; Moltu, Tornqvist, Sandal, Helland (Rekdal 90); Magnussen, Standal (Ertsas 78), Brandal, Nilsen; Aursnes, Latifu.
Aktobe: (442) Sidelnikov; Muldarov, Kharabara, Badlo, Davydov (Lisenkov 82); Khayrullin, Primus, Tagybergen (Miroshchnichenko 46), Kenzhisariev; Logvinenko, Kovalchuk.

Honka (1) 1 *(Vasara 17)*
Lech Poznan (1) 3 *(Ubiparip 11, Teodorczyk 53, Kaminski 71)* 3126
Honka: (442) Viitala; Koskinen, Baah, Aalto, Meite; Vasara, Makijarvi (Aijala 75), Yaghoubi, Palazuelos; Porokara (Kastrati 75), Vayrynen.
Lech Poznan: (442) Kotorowski; Arboleda, Wolakiewicz, Kaminski, Drewniak; Hamalainen, Tralka, Mozdzen, Teodorczyk (Slusarski 86); Lovrencsics (Pawlowski 83), Ubiparip (Formella 90).

IFK Gothenburg (0) 0
Trencin (0) 0 4282
IFK Gothenburg: (442) Alvbage; Salomonsson, Dyrestam, Jonsson, Johansson A; Vibe, Haglund, Johansson J, Larsson (Daniel Sobralense 60); Soder, Hysen.
Trencin: (442) Volesak; Ramon, Klescik, Mazan R■, Cogley; Baez, Mondek (Mazan P 70), Stefanik (Baris 90), Holubek; Willian (Duriska 78), Adi.

Irtysh Pavlodar (2) 3 *(Shomko 14, Yurin 41, Suyumbayev 86)*
Siroki Brijeg (0) 2 *(Kordic 56, Silic 64)* 10,000
Irtysh Pavlodar: (442) Kotlyar; Chernyshov, Kucera, Govedarica, Coulibaly; Averchenko (Suyumbayev 76), Yurin (Shabalin 69), Shomko, Mukhutdinov; Bakaev, Murzoev.
Siroki Brijeg: (442) Bilobrk; Markovic, Ljubic, Dzidic, Jese; Blaic (Silic 60), Zakaric (Maric 71), Landeka, Plazonic; Wagner (Coric 90), Kordic.

Jagodina (0) 2 *(Damjanovic 72, Lepovic 90)*
Rubin Kazan (2) 3 *(Prudnikov 12, Natcho 21, Rondon 87)* 4000
Jagodina: (442) Djuricic; Tomic, Djuric, Mihajlovic, Hadzibulic (Stojanovic 65); Damjanovic, Lepovic, Gogic, Dukic; Cvetkovic (Stojkov 90), El Monir (Projic 85).
Rubin Kazan: (442) Arlauskis; Ansaldi, Sharonov (Karadeniz 59), Marcano, Ryazantsev; Kisliak, Eremenko (Kulik 85), Natcho, M'Vila; Rondon, Prudnikov (Cesar Navas 59).

KR Reykjavik (1) 1 *(Finnbogason 35)*
Standard Liege (1) 3 *(Kanu 44, Batshuayi 62, M'Poku 90)* 1410
KR Reykjavik: (433) Halldorsson; Gunnarsson GT, Gunnarsson GR, Sigurdsson G, Gudjonsson; Sigurdsson B (Atlason 73), Hauksson O, Saevarsson (Gunnarsson B 59); Sigurdsson H (Martin 67), Finnbogason, Hauksson H.
Standard Liege: (442) Kawashima; Opare, Kanu, Arslanagic, Van Damme; Buyens, M'Poku, Mujangi Bia (Bulot 65), Vainqueur (Cisse 73); Batshuayi, Ezekiel (Biton 81).

Kukesi (2) 3 *(Hoxha 24, Popovic 45, Allmuca 58)*
Sarajevo (2) 2 *(Popovic 32 (og), Todorovic 33)* 4500
Kukesi: (334) Halili; Brahja, Malacarne, Peqini; Malota, Progni, Allmuca; Alikaj (Mziu 90), Karabeci, Hoxha (Manuka 78), Popovic (Malindi 76).
Sarajevo: (442) Bandovic; Radovac (Karic 81), Haurdic, Melunovic, Todorovic (Sunjevaric 72); Tatomirovic, Dzakmic, Cimirot, Tadejevic; Dupovac, Suljic.

Maccabi Haifa (1) 2 *(Ezra 37, Turgeman 55)*
Khazar Lankaran (0) 0   9520
Maccabi Haifa: (433) Saranov; Twatha, Keinan, Cocalic, Meshumar; Boccoli, Ezra, Katan (Golasa 74); Rayo, Turgeman (Pylyavskyi 83), Abuhatzira (Sallalich 66).
Khazar Lankaran: (343) Doblas; Ramaldanov, Tounkara, Bonfim (Allahverdiyev 71); Benouahi, Franca, Amirquliev, Todorov (Scarduelli 66); Gligorov, Skarlatake, Orsulic (Pit 46).

Malmo (2) 2 *(Hamad 11, Eriksson 13)*
Hibernian (0) 0   8628
Malmo: (442) Dahlin; Albornoz, Jansson, Johansson, Ricardinho; Hamad, Halsti, Thern (Friberg 68), Forsberg (Kroon 78); Rantie (Cibicki 68), Eriksson.
Hibernian: (442) Williams; Stevenson, McPake, Hanlon, Forster; Taiwo, Tudur Jones (Robertson 55), Thomson (Harris 77), Handling; Craig, Vine (Caldwell 84).

Mladost Podgorica (0) 2 *(Knezevic 54 (pen), Taku 85)*
Senica (1) 2 *(Kalabiska 33, Diarrassouba 76)*   4500
Mladost Podgorica: (442) Vujadinovic; Sankovic, Zivkovic, Sofranac, Mitrovic; Kaljevic (Novovic 70), Savicevic, Tomic, Taku; Knezevic, Seratlic.
Senica: (442) Sulla; Krizko, Cermak (Zeman 52), Brabec, Cristovam Roberto; Diarrassouba, Jirasek (Opiela 60), Kalabiska, Kona; Divis (Hiago 90), Piroska.

Olimpija Ljubljana (2) 3 *(Sporar 19, Djurkovic 26, Ivelja 90)*
Zilina (0) 1 *(Skvarka 82)*   1400
Olimpija Ljubljana: (433) Dzafic; Delamea-Mlinar■, Jovic, Zarifovic, Zeba (Mbatama 73); Ivelja, Bagaric, Omladic; Trifkovic, Sporar (Valencic 77), Djurkovic (Mitrovic 46).
Zilina: (433) Dubravka; Piacek, Mabouka, Akakpo, Majtan; Pecovsky, Babatounde■, Paur (Skvarka 46); Hucko, Mihalik (Guba 63), Pich.

Petrolul Ploiesti (1) 3 *(De Lucas 26, Grozav 49, 68)*
Vikingur (0) 0   9854
Petrolul Ploiesti: (442) Pecanha; Alves (Naziri 82), Mustivar (Romatio 71), Grozav, Boudjemaa; Younes, Hoban, Guilherme, Achim; Teixeira (Enza-Yamissi 62), De Lucas.
Vikingur: (442) Turi; Jacobsen H (Bartalstovu 75), Lervig, Petersen (Hansen Hjartvard 90), Djordjevic; Hansen B, Jacobsen E, Djurhuus (Sorensen 90), Justinussen; Vatnhamar, Jacobsen S.

Qarabag (1) 2 *(Almeida 40, Reynaldo 83)*
Piast Gliwice (1) 1 *(Robak 19)*   11,000
Qarabag: (442) Varvodic; Almeida, Reynaldo, Qarayev, Medvedev; Yusifov (George 46), Sadygov, Nadyrov (Sattarly 90), Agolli; Gelashvili (Kapolongo 75), Teli.
Piast Gliwice: (442) Szumski; Robak (Murawski 83), Matras, Izvolt (Wilczek 68), Jurado (Cicman 46); Zbozien, Horvath, Polak, Klepczynski; Podgorski, Hanzel.

Red Star Belgrade (1) 2 *(Pecnik 12, Mijailovic 76)*
IBV Vestmannaeyjar (0) 0   32,886
Red Star Belgrade: (442) Bajkovic; Lazic, Mijailovic (Miric 90), Krneta, Milijas (Savicevic 71); Vesovic, Kovacevic, Ninkovic, Dauda; Pecnik, Kasalica (Mladenovic 25).
IBV Vestmannaeyjar: (442) James; Gudjonsson, Garner, Olafsson, Sigurbjornsson; Hreidarsson (Petursson 72), Thorsteinsson, Thorvardarson (Ingason 87), Mawejje; Gudmundsson, Jeffs (Bergsson 90).

Rijeka (2) 5 *(Benko 19, 23, 59, Jugovic 67, Zlomislic 85)*
Prestatyn T (0) 0   6660
Rijeka: (442) Vargic; Knezevic, Tomecak, Leskovic, Boras; Alispahic (Krstanovic 50), Males (Zlomislic 59), Brezovec, Jugovic; Goodness, Benko (Culina 69).
Prestatyn T: (451) Roberts (Hill-Dunt 87); Davies, Hessey, Stones, Holmes; Hayes, Parker, Gibson, Owen (Kemp 69), Parkinson; Stephens.

Rosenborg (0) 0
St Johnstone (1) 1 *(Wright 19)*   5952
Rosenborg: (433) Orlund; Gamboa, Reginiussen, Strandberg, Dorsin; Svensson, Jensen, Berntsen (Selnaes 82); Chibuike, Bille Nielsen (Soderlund 57), Mikkelsen (Dockal 46).
St Johnstone: (4231) Mannus; Mackay, Anderson, Wright, Scobbie; Cregg, Millar; Wotherspoon (Miller 82), McDonald, Hasselbaink (Edwards 66); MacLean.

Shakhtyor Soligorsk (1) 1 *(Sitko 16)*
Milsami (0) 1 *(Leuca 56)*   2700
Shakhtyor Soligorsk: (433) Tsygalko; Balanovich (Kovalev 86), Kolomyts, Postnikov, Kashevski; Leonchik, Soro, Yanush; Sitko (Rios 69), Matveychik, Osipenko.
Milsami: (532) Negai; Gheti, Bolohan (Ciofu 82), Shedrack, Patras, Leuca; Guillherme (Stadiiciuc 90), Rassulov (Furdui 84), Andronic; Gheorghiu, Soporan.

Skoda Xanthi (0) 0
Linfield (1) 1 *(Burns A 25)*   2117
Skoda Xanthi: (451) Chema; Paito, Komesidis, Vallas, Goutas; Marcelinho (Triadis 69), Vassilakakis (Ranos 63), Mantalos, Marin, Die (Fliskas 79); Soltani.
Linfield: (442) Tuffey; Burns B, Ervin, Ward, Clarke; Burns A (McCaul 79), Gault, Lowry, Knowles (Mulgrew 65); Thompson (McAllister 71), Carvill.

Skonto (1) 2 *(Sabala 39, Karasauskas 47)*
Slovan Liberec (1) 1 *(Grybauskas 8 (og))*   2300
Skonto: (442) Grybauskas; Gabovs, Rode, Laizans, Rugins (Osipovs 84); Fertovs, Mingazov, Sinelnikovs (Isajevs 89), Sabala; Bulvitis, Karasauskas (Klimiashvili 68).
Slovan Liberec: (442) Kovar; Kelic, Husek, Pavelka, Kalitvintsev (Delarge 64); Rybalka (Szabo 81), Frydek, Kusnir, Kovac; Rabusic, Fleisman.

Slask Wroclaw (2) 4 *(Paixao 5, 9, Sobota 56, Plaku 70)*
Rudar Pljevlja (0) 0   14,700
Slask Wroclaw: (442) Gikiewicz; Ostrowski, Kokoszka, Sobota, Patejuk (Plaku 68); Mila, Paraiba, Stevanovic (Holota 85), Pawelec; Paixao (Wiezik 81), Kazmierczak.
Rudar Pljevlja: (442) Vuklis; Sljivancanin (Bambur 57), Petrovic, Damjanovic, Kaludjerovic (Sekulic 77); Jeknic, Stojanovic (Rustemovic 84), Brnovic, Jovanovic; Nestorovic, Vlahovic.

Sparta Prague (1) 2 *(Lafata 33, 66)*
Hacken (0) 2 *(Mohammed 69, Makondele 77)*   7434
Sparta Prague: (4141) Vaclik; Vacha, Prikryl (Skalak 80), Matejovsky, Pauschek (Nhamoinesu 90); Kadlec; Kaderabek, Lafata, Husbauer (Vacek 67), Holek; Polom.
Hacken: (4231) Kallqvist; Bjorck, El Kabir, Lewicki, Ericsson; Arkivuo, Joza; Anklev, Chatto, Mohammed (Ojala 90); Gustafsson (Makondele 60).

Stromsgodset (0) 2 *(Horn 53, Kovacs 90)*
Debrecen (1) 2 *(Sidibe 36, 55 (pen))*   3582
Stromsgodset: (433) Stubhaug; Storbaek, Madsen, Horn, Hamoud; Ibrahim, Johansen, Boateng (Sveen 82); Olsen (Ovenstad 46), Storflor (Nuhu 46), Kovacs.
Debrecen: (4231) Verpecz; Nagy, Morozov, Mate, Korhut; Bodi■, Damahou (Zsidai 12); Czvitkovics, Bouadla (Kulcsar 86), Szakaly (Trninic 71); Sidibe.

Thun (2) 2 *(Sanogo 12, Schirinzi 38)*
Chikhura Sachkhere (0) 0   3114
Thun: (442) Moser; Sulmoni, Reinmann, Luthi, Schirinzi; Hediger, Wittwer, Salamand (Gasser 83), Sanogo; Schneuwly M (Sadik 59), Martinez (Cassio 68).
Chikhura Sachkhere: (4231) Somkhishvili; Kashia, Rekhviashvili, Jigauri, Lomashvili; Chikvaidze (Kimadze 46), Datunaishvili, Odikadze, Dekanoidze; Tsinamdzgvrishvili (Gogatishvili 86), Bechvaia.

Trabzonspor (3) 4 *(Mierzejewski 10, Paulo Henrique 15, Molloy 39 (og), Kacar 52)*
Derry C (2) 2 *(McDaid 24, Kavanagh 32)*　　　17,213
Trabzonspor: (451) Kivrak; Yumlu, Kacar, Celustka, Yavru; Sen (Oztekin 80), Mierzejewski (Alanzinho 68), Akgun, Colman, Adin; Paulo Henrique (Gural 75).
Derry C: (442) Doherty; Greacen, McEleney S, Madden, Osbourne; Molloy, Higgins, Kavanagh (McBride 63), McNamee; McEleney P (Duffy 73), McDaid (Griffin 86).

Tromso (1) 2 *(Ondrasek 43, Andersen 62)*
Inter Baku (0) 0　　　1998
Tromso: (4411) Sahlman; Kristiansen, Fojut, Koppinen, Norbye (Causevic 46); Bendiksen, Drage (Moldskred 60), Andersen, Johansen; Pritchard (Johnsen 83); Ondrasek.
Inter Baku: (4312) Lomaia; Ivan Benitez, Amirjanov, Abdoulaye, Spicic; Georgievski, Mikel Alvaro, Abasiyer (Genov 76); Iashvili; Tskhadadze, Javadov (Zargarov 78).

Valletta (1) 1 *(Fenech 45)*
FK Minsk (1) 1 *(Sachivko 6)*　　　1104
Valletta: (442) Marino; Camilleri, Fenech (Zammit 90), Briffa, Hamza; Conde (James Obaje 59), Bajada (Caruana 70), Denni, Falzon; Vandelannoite, Dimech.
FK Minsk: (442) Bushma; Begunov, Sosnovski, Sverchinski, Kozeka; Vasilyuk, Sachivko, Gorbushin (Rozhok 46), Belevich (Ostroukh 75); Makas (Kibuk 55), Rnic.

Ventspils (1) 1 *(Hoffmann 10 (og))*
Jeunesse d'Esch (0) 0　　　1300
Ventspils: (442) Uvarenko; Dubra, Kurakins, Smirnovs, Turkovs; Paulius, Zigajevs (Sukhanov 62), Tarasovs, Yanchuk (Kozlovs 79); Abdultaofik, Timofejevs.
Jeunesse d'Esch: (442) Hoffmann; Oberweis, Moreira (Piskor 86), Portier, Benichou; Wang (Albanese 90), Ibrahimovic, Collette, Vitali; Delgado, Ramdedovic (Kintziger 53).

VMFD Zalgiris (0) 2 *(Bilinski 46, Leliuga 66)*
Pyunik (0) 0　　　4500
VMFD Zalgiris: (442) Vitkauskas; Skerla, Vaitkunas, Leliuga (Zagurskas 74), Komolov (Freidgeimas 83); Svrljuga, Peric, Bilinski, Silenas; Zulpa (Janusauskas 68), Kuklys.
Pyunik: (442) Manukyan; Hovhannisyan A, Haroyan, Poghosyan Gagik (Ayvazyan 69), Poghosyan Ghukas (Zakaryan 81); Manoyan, Yuspashyan, Papikyan, Minasyan; Sardaryan (Hovhannisyan K 45), Voskanyan.

Vojvodina (1) 2 *(Trajkovic 19, Vranjes 71 (pen))*
Budapest Honved (0) 0　　　5000
Vojvodina: (433) Delac; Radoja, Trajkovic, Alivodic (Bilbija 90), Skuletic (Baric 26); Vranjes, Oumarou (Ivanic 89), Nastic■; Poletanovic, Vulicevic, Djuric.
Budapest Honved: (433) Kemenes; Ignjatovic, Alcibiade, Holender (Ikenne 65), Testardi; Lovric, Hidi, Vecsei (Diarra 55); Zivanovic, Barath, Nagy (Delczeg 46).

Zrinjski Mostar (1) 1 *(Simeunovic 21)*
Botev Plovdiv (0) 1 *(Kortzorg 48)*　　　1998
Zrinjski Mostar: (442) Dujkovic; Radeljic, Simeunovic, Crnov (Kantar 64), Popovic (Bekic 74); Stojkic■, Brkovic, Muminovic, Savic (Milicevic 54); Anicic, Djuric.
Botev Plovdiv: (433) Stachowiak; Grncarov, Ognyanov, Nedelev, Vander (Kostov 79); Hristov (Kortzorg 46), Minev, Abel (Domovchiyski■ 34); Jirsak, Galchev, Sprockel.

SECOND QUALIFYING ROUND SECOND LEG
Thursday, 25 July 2013
Aalborg (0) 0
Dila Gori (0) 0　　　5472
Aalborg: (442) Larsen; Thelander, Pedersen (Kristensen 46), Nielsen, Wurtz (Toft 78); Wichmann, Thomsen, Kusk, Frederiksen (Due 63); Dalsgaard, Curth.
Dila Gori: (442) Revishvili; Gongadze, Tomashvili, Khizaneishvili, Kobakhidze; Guruli, Gorelishvili (Aladashvili 53), Bolkvadze (Aleksidze 82), Aburdjania (Dolidze 50); Iluridze, Gvalia.

Aktobe (1) 2 *(Davydov 6, 61)*
Hodd (0) 0　　　12,200
Aktobe: (433) Sidelnikov; Badlo, Primus, Kenzhisariev, Logvinenko; Khayrullin, Muldarov, Kovalchuk; Kapadze (Kharabara 77), Davydov (Tagybergen 85), Geynrikh (Gridin 90).
Hodd: (433) Lie; Brandal, Moltu, Vibe (Torset 64), Sandal; Helland, Rekdal, Aursnes; Standal (Ertsas 64), Tornqvist, Magnussen (Hjelmeseth 85).

Botev Plovdiv (0) 2 *(Ognyanov 80, Nedelev 88)*
Zrinjski Mostar (0) 0　　　8000
Botev Plovdiv: (532) Stachowiak; Grncarov, Sprockel, Abel (Kostov 68), Minev (Henrique 90), Ognyanov; Nedelev, Hristov, Jirsak; Kortzorg (Pedro 58), Galchev.
Zrinjski Mostar: (433) Dujkovic; Radeljic, Simeunovic, Crnov (Popovic 86), Milicevic; Kantar, Brkovic, Muminovic (Bekic 59); Savic (Scepanovic 70), Ancic, Djuric.

Budapest Honved (1) 1 *(Diarra 44)*
Vojvodina (2) 3 *(Bilbija 27, Alivodic 41, Vranjes 64)* 2750
Budapest Honved: (433) Kemenes; Ignjatovic (Alcibiade 46), Barath, Zivanovic, Lovric; Ikenne, Diarra, Hidi; Kozma (Testardi 46), Delczeg, Diaby (Vernes 66).
Vojvodina: (433) Delac; Vulicevic, Radoja, Djuric, Trajkovic; Alivodic, Vranjes (Mitosevic 89), Baric; Poletanovic, Bilbija (Kosovic 79), Skuletic (Ilic 85).

Chikhura Sachkhere (1) 1 *(Rekhviashvili 6)*
Thun (1) 3 *(Lomashvili 45 (og), Martinez 49, Schneuwly M 84)*　　　1400
Chikhura Sachkhere: (433) Somkhishvili; Dekanoidze, Rekhviashvili, Kashia, Lomashvili; Chikvaidze, Datunaishvili (Demetrashvili 78), Odikadze; Jigauri, Bechvaia, Tsinamdzgvrishvili (Kimadze 78).
Thun: (433) Moser; Schirinzi (Frey 72), Luthi, Reinmann, Schenkel; Hediger, Wittwer, Sanogo (Gasser 60); Cassio, Sadik, Martinez (Schneuwly M 76).

Dacia (1) 2 *(Orlovski 45, Orbu 64)*
Chornomorets (1) 1 *(Gai 26)*　　　3720
Dacia: (532) Matiughin; Posmac, Ilescu, Orlovski (Pavlov 50), Soppo, Krkotic; Orbu (Odia 77), Mihaliov, Stoleru (Barakhoev 63); Ogada, Ovseannicov.
Chornomorets: (433) Bezotosny; Anderson Mineiro, Berger, Fontanello, Kutas; Gai (Valeyev 75), Bobko, Samodin (Didenko 68); Djadjedje, Antonov, Sito Riera (Bakaj 46).

Debrecen (0) 0
Stromsgodset (1) 3 *(Kovacs 34, Boateng 50, Storflor 57)*　　　6300
Debrecen: (4231) Verpecz; Trninic (Kulcsar 56), Meszaros, Mate, Nagy (Ferenczi 75); Korhut, Zsidai; Bouadla, Szakaly, Czvitkovics (Volas 56); Sidibe.
Stromsgodset: (433) Kwarasey; Horn, Storbaek■, Boateng (Brenne 84), Vilsvik; Ibrahim (Sveen 72), Storflor (Ovenstad 72), Hamoud; Johansen, Kovacs, Wikheim.

Derry C (0) 0
Trabzonspor (0) 3 *(Paulo Henrique 56, 82, Ozdemir 90)*　　　2150
Derry C: (442) Doherty; Greacen, McEleney S, McBride (Houston 79), Madden; Osbourne, Molloy, Higgins, Kavanagh (Duffy 73); McEleney P (McNamee 63), McDaid.
Trabzonspor: (442) Kivrak; Yumlu, Kacar (Demir 46), Celustka, Yavru; Sen, Mierzejewski (Aydogdu 83), Akgun, Colman (Ozdemir 46); Adin, Paulo Henrique.

FK Minsk (0) 2 *(Vasilyuk 53, Kibuk 60)*
Valletta (0) 0　　　1500
FK Minsk: (433) Bushma; Begunov, Sosnovski, Sverchinski, Kozeka; Vasilyuk (Makas 89), Sachivko, Gorbushin (Buloychik 57); Rnic, Kibuk (Rozhok 78), Bukatkin.
Valletta: (433) Marino; Caruana (Antoneli 69), Azzopardi (Bajada 46), Fenech, Briffa; Hamza, Denni, Falzon; James Obaje (Zammit 77), Vandelannoite, Dimech.

Gefle (1) 4 *(Orlov 25, 85, Faltsetas 67, Dahlberg 87)*
Anorthosis Famagusta (0) 0   304
Gefle: (442) Hedvall; Mard■, Olsson J, Asp, Portin; Faltsetas, Lundevall (Adukor 90), Hansson, Oremo; Orlov (Abdullai 90), Dahlberg.
Anorthosis Famagusta: (433) Valverde; Paulo Jorge, Pavicevic, Galamaz, Laifis; Alexa, Marangos (Ohayon 46), Makos (Okkas 88); Garcia, Fofana (Avraam 61), Colautti.

Hacken (0) 1 *(Ericsson 86)*
Sparta Prague (0) 0   2618
Hacken: (433) Kallqvist; Bjorck, Lewicki, Arkivuo, Joza; Anklev, Mohammed, Ericsson (Khan 90); Chatto, Makondele (Gustafsson 89), El Kabir.
Sparta Prague: (442) Vaclik; Svejdik, Nhamoinesu, Vacha, Matejovsky; Kaderabek (Pauschek 41 (Bednar 68)), Husbauer, Krejci (Prikryl 82), Holek; Kadlec, Lafata.

Hapoel Tel Aviv (1) 2 *(Damari 22 (pen), 61)*
Beroe Stara Zagora (1) 2 *(Krumov 45, Caiado 71)*   6400
Hapoel Tel Aviv: (442) Amos; Colin, Ilic, Dgani, Harush; Gordana, Zaguri (Vermouth 76), Lucas Sasha (Abutbul 81), Gerzycich; Damari (Safuri 67), Shechter.
Beroe Stara Zagora: (442) Karadzhov; Iliev, Stoychev, Ivanov, Krumov; Elias (Rainov 68), Djoman, Penev, Hristov (Atanasov 87); Andonov, Caiado (Goranov 78).

Hibernian (0) 0
Malmo (4) 7 *(Eriksson 21, Forsberg 26, Halsti 30, Albornoz 41, Rantie 61, Hamad 65, Kroon 72)*   16,018
Hibernian: (442) Williams; Stevenson, McPake (Mullen 24), Forster, Hanlon; Harris (Stanton 75), Taiwo (Robertson 54), Thomson, Craig; Vine, Handling.
Malmo: (442) Dahlin; Albornoz, Jansson, Johansson, Ricardinho; Hamad, Halsti (Friberg 63), Thern, Forsberg (Kroon 46); Eriksson (Cibicki 60), Rantie.

IBV Vestmannaeyjar (0) 0
Red Star Belgrade (0) 0   950
IBV Vestmannaeyjar: (433) James; Gudjonsson, Garner, Sigurbjornsson, Gudmundsson; Thorsteinsson (Hreidarsson 73), Bergsson (Simmonds 63), Thorvardarson (Spear 80); Mawejje, Jeffs, Olsen.
Red Star Belgrade: (442) Bajkovic; Krneta, Mladenovic, Lazic, Milijas; Vesovic, Ninkovic (Savicevic 68), Kovacevic, Dauda (Mihajlovic■ 61); Pecnik, Kasalica (Milivojevic 86).

Inter Baku (0) 1 *(Tskhadadze 76)*
Tromso (0) 0   2100
Inter Baku: (442) Lomaia; Salukvadze, Amirjanov, Abdoulaye, Georgievski; Mikel Alvaro, Mammadov (Genov 61), Dashdemirov, Flavio Beck; Iashvili (Zargarov 84), Javadov (Tskhadadze 45).
Tromso: (442) Sahlman; Kristiansen, Fojut (Drage 79), Causevic (Norbe 78), Koppinen; Ciss, Bendiksen, Andersen, Johansen; Pritchard (Johnsen 67), Ondrasek.

Jeunesse d'Esch (1) 1 *(Benichou 39)*
Ventspils (1) 4 *(Paulius 33, Zigajevs 47, Yanchuk 51, Turkovs 65)*   1249
Jeunesse d'Esch: (433) Oberweis; Moreira, Hoffmann, Kintziger, Portier; Benichou, Wang, Ibrahimovic (Deidda 84); Vitali (Piskor 46), Ramdedovic■, Collette (Albanese 50).
Ventspils: (433) Uvarenko; Dubra, Kurakins, Smirnovs, Timofejevs; Paulius (Tarkhnishvili 71), Zigajevs, Tarasovs; Yanchuk (Sukhanov 66), Abdultaofik (Kozlovs 57), Turkovs.

Khazar Lankaran (0) 0
Maccabi Haifa (6) 8 *(Turgeman 7, Katan 10, Rayo 13 (pen), 62, Abuhatzira 26, 44, Ezra 41, Golasa 76)*   9000
Khazar Lankaran: (442) Doblas (Sadigli 45); Allahverdiyev, Ramaldanov, Pamuk, Benouahi (Gligorov 91); Franca, Amirquliev, Pit; Todorov, Skarlatake (Silva 46), Orsulic.
Maccabi Haifa: (433) Saranov; Twatha, Keinan, Cocalic, Gabai; Boccoli (Yadin 73), Ezra (Raiyan 77), Rayo (Golasa 67); Turgeman, Abuhatzira, Katan.

Lech Poznan (2) 2 *(Teodorczyk 6, Kedziora 40)*
Honka (1) 1 *(Koskinen 8)*   15,103
Lech Poznan: (442) Buric; Wolakiewicz, Kaminski, Kedziora, Tralka (Drygas 61); Pawlowski (Lovrencsics 61), Drewniak, Hamalainen (Slusarski 71), Mozdzen; Teodorczyk, Ubiparip.
Honka: (442) Viitala; Palazuelos, Koskinen, Baah, Aalto; Vasara (Aijala 77), Makijarvi (Mombilo 36), Yaghoubi, Meite; Porokara, Vayrynen (Kastrati 69).

Linfield (0) 1 *(Gault 99)*
Skoda Xanthi (1) 2 *(Marcelinho 27, 105)*   2494
Linfield: (442) Tuffey; Burns B, Burns A (McAllister 71), Ward, Clarke; Ervin, Gault, Lowry (McCaul 91), Knowles (Mulgrew 46); Thompson, Carvill.
Skoda Xanthi: (442) Kiriakidis; Paito, Komesidis (Bertos 57), Vallas, Goutas; Marcelinho, Vassilakakis (Gohouri 98), Mantalos (Baxevanidis 57), Fliskas■; Marin, Die.
aet; Skoda Xanthi won on away goals rule.

Lokomotiva Zagreb (0) 2 *(Misic 68, Situm 72)*
Dinamo Minsk (1) 3 *(Veselinovic 41, 82, Figueredo 59)*   3950
Lokomotiva Zagreb: (532) Picak; Matas, Musa (Pjaca 26), Barbaric, Mesaric, Brucic; Mrzljak (Martinac 65), Misic, Chago; Trebotic, Situm.
Dinamo Minsk: (433) Sulima; Veretilo, Politevich, Veselinovic (Plaskonny 90), Kontsevoj; Nikolic, Bykov, Danilov; Figueredo (Korzun 86), Coto, Stasevich (Adamovic 74).
Dinamo Minsk won on away goals rule.

Milsami (1) 1
Shakhtyor Soligorsk (1) 1 *(Kashevski 30)*   2500
Milsami: (433) Negai■; Shedrack, Gheorghiu, Rassulov, Gheti; Bolohan (Iavorschi 119), Patras, Andronic (Bantis 90); Soporan, Leuca (Ciofu 102), Guillherme.
Shakhtyor Soligorsk: (334) Tsygalko; Kolomyts, Postnikov, Kashevski; Soro (Vergeychik■ 106), Sitko, Leonchik; Balanovich (Kovalev 81), Matveychik, Yanush, Osipenko (Rios 64).
aet; Milsami won 4-2 on penalties.

Omonia Nicosia (0) 1 *(Gikiewicz 55)*
Astra Giurgiu (1) 2 *(Budescu 39, 69)*   18,271
Omonia Nicosia: (433) Moreira; Alabi, Cervera (Platini 75), Gikiewicz, Scaramozzino; Nuno Assis, Joao Paulo, Schembri; Leandro, Marco Soares, Taylor (Efrem 46).
Astra Giurgiu: (433) Lung Jr; Ben Youssef, Tembo (Enache 75), Seto, Budescu; Junior Morais, Laban■, Fatai (Bukari 59 (Barboianu 86)); Gaman, Matel, William Amorim.

Pandurii Targu Jiu (3) 4 *(Matulevicius 7, Erico 35, 57, Breeveld 39)*
Levadia Tallinn (0) 0   4270
Pandurii Targu Jiu: (442) Stanca; Momcilovic, Christou, Buleica, Nistor; Ungurusan (Brata 60), Anton, Erico, Pereira (Ciucur 73); Breeveld, Matulevicius (Lemnaru 55).
Levadia Tallinn: (442) Smishko; Antonov, Subbotin, Dmitrijev, Podholjuzin; Jahhimovits, Pikk, Kaljumae (Rattel 46), Raudsepp (Pebre 75); Hunt (Jakovlev 82), Volchkov.

Piast Gliwice (2) 2 *(Matras 29, Robak 36)*
Qarabag (1) 2 *(George 8, Kapolongo 108)*   8534
Piast Gliwice: (433) Szumski; Horvath, Matras, Robak, Klepczynski; Podgorski, Izvolt (Cicman 95), Hanzel (Docekal 74); Jurado (Lazdins 68), Krol, Zbozien.
Qarabag: (433) Varvodic; Qarayev, Medvedev, Reynaldo, Gelashvili (Kapolongo 85); Sadygov, George (Yusifov 63), Nadyrov (Guseynov 76); Almeida, Teli, Agolli.
aet.

Prestatyn T (0) 0
Rijeka (2) 3 *(Mocinic 36, Boras 40, Mujanovic 66)*   930
Prestatyn T: (442) Hill-Dunt; Davies, Lewis, Hessey, Holmes; Hayes (France 90), Parker, Gibson, Owen (Kemp 85); Parkinson, Stephens (Hunt 74).
Rijeka: (442) Mance; Datkovic, Leskovic, Boras (Skrabot 78), Bertosa; Mujanovic, Mocinic, Males (Zlomislic 57), Pokrivac; Tadic, Krstanovic (Pilcic 57).

Pyunik (0) 1 *(Ayvazyan 55)*
VMFD Zalgiris (0) 1 *(Kuklys 88 (pen))* 3500
Pyunik: (442) Manukyan; Hovhannisyan A (Baloyan 86), Haroyan, Poghosyan Gagik, Manoyan; Yuspashyan, Papikyan, Minasyan, Zakaryan (Ayvazyan 46); Sardaryan (Poghosyan Ghukas 55), Voskanyan.
VMFD Zalgiris: (442) Vitkauskas; Skerla, Vaitkunas, Leliuga (Janusauskas 78), Komolov; Svrljuga, Peric, Bilinski (Velicka 67), Silenas (Freidgeimas 55); Zulpa, Kuklys.

Rubin Kazan (0) 1 *(Karadeniz 52)*
Jagodina (0) 0 5986
Rubin Kazan: (442) Arlauskis; Ryazantsev, Kisliak, Galiulin, Marcano; Getigezhev, Cesar Navas, Karadeniz (Azmoun 73), Natcho (Kulik 64); M'Vila, Rondon (Prudnikov 64).
Jagodina: (442) Djuricic; Djuric, Tomic, Stojanovic, Mihajlovic; Damjanovic, Lepovic (Hadzibulic 75), Dukic■, Cvetkovic; El Monir (Projic 66), Arsenijevic (Stojkov 89).

Rudar Pljevlja (0) 2 *(Jovanovic 57, Bambur 90)*
Slask Wroclaw (2) 2 *(Sobota 31, Paixao 34)* 367
Rudar Pljevlja: (442) Vuklis; Vukovic, Bambur, Mijuskovic (Damjanovic 64), Petrovic; Kaludjerovic (Sekulic 17), Stojanovic (Cosovic 46), Brnovic, Jovanovic; Nestorovic, Vlahovic.
Slask Wroclaw: (442) Gikiewicz; Ostrowski, Kokoszka, Sobota (Holota 46), Patejuk; Mila (Plaku 46), Paraiba, Stevanovic, Pawelec; Paixao, Kazmierczak (Socha 62).

Sarajevo (0) 0
Kukesi (0) 0 14,000
Sarajevo: (433) Bandovic; Suljic (Huseinbasic 75), Melunovic (Karic 69), Todorovic, Dupovac; Tatomirovic, Dzakmic, Cimirot; Tadejevic, Sunjevaric (Osmanagic 74), Hadzic.
Kukesi: (433) Halili; Brahja, Malota, Peqini, Malacarne; Progni (Alikaj 90), Malindi (Popovic 70), Hallaci; Allmuca, Karabeci, Hoxha (Manuka 84).

Senica (0) 0
Mladost Podgorica (1) 1 *(Kaljevic 38)* 3908
Senica: (442) Sulla; Kona, Brabec, Krizko, Hiago (Divis 46); Cristovam Roberto (Cermak 56), Diarrassouba, Kalabiska, Zeman; Opiela (Jakubov 79), Piroska.
Mladost Podgorica: (442) Vujadinovic; Zivkovic, Markovic (Knezevic 90), Sofranac, Mitrovic; Sankovic, Tomic, Taku, Savicevic (Pavicevic 68); Kaljevic (Novovic 77), Seratlic.

Siroki Brijeg (1) 2 *(Jese 20, Ivankovic 74)*
Irtysh Pavlodar (0) 0 4000
Siroki Brijeg: (442) Bilobrk; Dzidic, Barisic, Coric (Silic 77), Jese; Plazonic, Kordic, Zakaric (Ivankovic 65), Landeka (Ljubic 65); Wagner, Blaic.
Irtysh Pavlodar: (442) Kotlyar; Govedarica, Coulibaly, Bakaev, Mukhutdinov; Chichulin, Averchenko (Strukov 86), Yurin (Begalyn 75), Shomko; Kucera, Murzoev (Shabalin 65).

Slovan Liberec (1) 1 *(Delarge 14)*
Skonto (0) 0 5707
Slovan Liberec: (433) Kovar; Kovac, Frydek, Kelic, Husek; Pavelka, Kalitvintsev (Fleisman 90), Rybalka (Sural 72); Kusnir, Rabusic (Sackey 81), Delarge.
Skonto: (433) Grybauskas; Gabovs, Bulvitis, Fertovs (Blanks 84), Rode; Laizans, Mingazov, Sinelnikovs (Rugins 39); Sabala, Osipovs (Klimiashvili 82), Karasauskas.
Slovan Liberec won on away goals rule.

St Johnstone (1) 1 *(May 21)*
Rosenborg (1) 1 *(Soderlund 4)* 7850
St Johnstone: (442) Mannus; Mackay, Anderson (Miller 78), Wright, Scobbie; Wotherspoon, McDonald, Cregg, May (Fallon 78); Hasselbaink (Edwards 64), MacLean.
Rosenborg: (433) Orlund; Gamboa, Ronning (Hoiland 23), Reginiussen, Dorsin; Svensson, Berntsen (Chibuike 75), Jensen; Soderlund, Bille Nielsen, Mikkelsen (Dockal 59).

Standard Liege (1) 3 *(Bulot 26, Ezekiel 68, 73)*
KR Reykjavik (0) 1 *(Atlason 69)* 21,288
Standard Liege: (442) Kawashima; Opare, Ciman, Arslanagic, Van Damme; Bulot, Cisse, Buyens, M'Poku (Mujangi Bia 62); Batshuayi (Ezekiel 57), Biton (Nagai 80).
KR Reykjavik: (442) Runarsson; Josepsson, Sigurdsson G, Gunnarsson B (Saevarsson 22), Gunnarsson GT; Hauksson, Gudjonsson, Sigurdsson B (Finnbogason 71), Martin (Atlason 46); Sigurjonsson, Ragnarsson.

Sturm Graz (0) 0
Breidablik (1) 1 *(Hreinsson 39)* 7903
Sturm Graz: (433) Gratzei; Todorovski (Hoelzl 83), Weber (Beichler 46), Hadzic, Szabics; Vuyadinovich, Kainz, Madl; Offenbacher (Djuricin 59), Beric, Klem.
Breidablik: (433) Gunnleifsson; Margeirsson, Hreidarsson, Troost, Adalsteinsson■; Ingason, Jonsson, Rohde (Lydsson 71); Hreinsson (Vilhjalmsson 90), Gardarsson, Yeoman.

Trencin (1) 2 *(Adi 15, 71)*
IFK Gothenburg (0) 1 *(Haglund 82)* 4150
Trencin: (352) Volesak; Cogley, Klescik, Ramon; Baez (Bednarik 83), Holubek, Mazan P (Frimmel 66), Mondek, Stefanik; Willian (Baris 89), Adi.
IFK Gothenburg: (442) Alvbage; Jonsson, Johansson A (Engvall 84), Dyrestam, Salomonsson; Haglund, Vibe, Johansson J, Larsson (Farnerud 45); Hysen, Soder.

Turnovo (0) 1 *(Pandev 70)*
Hajduk Split (0) 1 *(Caktas 60)* 2973
Turnovo: (433) Dimovski; Iliev (Pandev 68), Petrov, Mitev, Mavrov; Tenekedziev (Mitrov 43), Blazevski, Stoilov (Tasev 46); Vasilev, Varelovski, Baldovaliev.
Hajduk Split: (532) Kalinic; Milic, Jozinovic, Maloca, Mikanovic, Andjelkovic; Pasalic (Kouassi 46), Caktas, Susic (Milovic 81); Mujan, Maglica (Tomicic 89).

Utrecht (1) 3 *(Mulenga 45, 49, 54)*
Differdange 03 (1) 3 *(Er Rafik 26, Franzoni 64 (pen), Bastos 72)* 16,437
Utrecht: (433) Ruiter; Van der Maarel, Bulthuis, Heerings (de Kogel 70), Markiet; Toornstra, Martensson, Duplan (Takagi 81); Schepers (Van der Gun 46), Mulenga, Oar.
Differdange 03: (433) Weber; Lebresne, Caillet, Rodrigues (Kettenmeyer 75), Bukvic; Bisevac (Caron 71), Bastos (Luisi 84), Janisch; Franzoni, May, Er Rafik.

Vikingur (0) 0
Petrolul Ploiesti (2) 4 *(Gregersen A 5 (og), Younes 11, 63, Grozav 77)* 288
Vikingur: (433) Turi; Gregersen A, Jacobsen H, Gregersen P, Lervig; Petersen (Djordjevic 65), Hansen B, Jacobsen E; Justinussen, Vatnhamar (Hansen Hjartvard 78), Jacobsen S (Hansen Hedin 85).
Petrolul Ploiesti: (433) Bornescu; Enza-Yamissi, Younes (Grozav 65), Boudjemaa (Mustivar 46), Naziri; Hoban, Guilherme, Romario; De Lucas, Teixeira (Achim 46), Morar.

Zilina (1) 2 *(Paur 38, 55)*
Olimpija Ljubljana (0) 0 4137
Zilina: (433) Dubravka; Hucko, Akakpo, Majtan (Mravec 90), Pecovsky; Piacek, Pich, Skvarka; Mihalik (Gaba 73), Paur (Zilak 78), Mabouka.
Olimpija Ljubljana: (433) Dzafic; Eteme (Trifkovic 11), Jovic, Zarifovic, Djurkovic (Valencic 74); Sporar, Ivelja, Omladic; Bagaric, Mitrovic, Zeba (Zorc 67).
Zilina won on away goals rule.

THIRD QUALIFYING ROUND FIRST LEG

Thursday, 1 August 2013

Aktobe (0) 1 *(Khayrullin 90 (pen))*
Breidablik (0) 0 12,700
Aktobe: (442) Sidelnikov; Muldarov, Badlo, Primus, Arzumanyan (Kenzhisariev 61); Logvinenko, Kharabara, Khayrullin, Kovalchuk (Geynrikh 73); Kapadze, Davydov (Gridin 79).
Breidablik: (442) Gunnleifsson; Troost, Ingason, Jonsson, Margeirsson; Hreidarsson, Gardarsson (Sigurdsson 64), Lydsson (Elisabetarson 79), Yeoman; Rohde, Hreinsson (Vilhjalmsson 87).

Asteras Tripolis (1) 1 *(Zisopoulos 27)*
Rapid Vienna (1) 1 *(Boyd 32 (pen))*   5000
Asteras Tripolis: (442) Bantis; Zaradoukas (Caffa 46),
Ximo Navarro (Grazzini 72), Lisgaras, Pipinis; Usero,
Zisopoulos, Kourbelis, De Blasis; Barrales (Delgado 61),
Tsambouris.
Rapid Vienna: (433) Novota; Behrendt, Schrammel,
Dibon (Hofmann M 46), Sonnleitner; Petsos, Trimmel,
Hofmann S (Sabitzer 68); Schaub (Grozurek 85), Boyd,
Burgstaller.

Botev Plovdiv (0) 1 *(Domovchiyski 73)*
VfB Stuttgart (0) 1 *(Ibisevic 67)*   10,000
Botev Plovdiv: (442) Stachowiak; Grncarov, Minev,
Sprockel, Ognyanov (Domovchiyski 88); Hristov,
Nedelev, Abel (Sarmov 72), Jirsak; Galchev, Kortzorg
(Dyakov 87).
VfB Stuttgart: (442) Ulreich; Schwaab, Tasci, Boka,
Rausch; Rudiger, Leitner, Traore, Torun (Cacau 56);
Ibisevic (Abdellaoue 68), Werner (Maxim 67).

Chornomorets (2) 3 *(Sito Riera 32, Djadjedje 38,*
Antonov 78 (pen))
Red Star Belgrade (0) 1 *(Savicevic 59)*   28,862
Chornomorets: (442) Bezotosny; Berger, Fontanello,
Anderson Mineiro (Vangieli 84), Kutas; Kovalchuk K,
Gai, Bobko, Sito Riera (Priyomov 82); Djadjedje,
Antonov (Samodin 82).
Red Star Belgrade: (442) Bajkovic; Mijailovic
(Mladenovic 45), Krneta, Milijas, Lazic; Savicevic,
Vesovic, Ninkovic, Kovacevic; Pecnik (Dauda 46),
Kasalica (Milunovic 85).

Dinamo Minsk (0) 0
Trabzonspor (1) 1 *(Paulo Henrique 41)*   7500
Dinamo Minsk: (4321) Sulima; Veretilo, Politevich,
Kontsevoj, Danilov; Simovic (Bykov 65), Nikolic,
Stasevich (Khvashchinski 85); Coto (Adamovic 65),
Figueredo; Veselinovic*.
Trabzonspor: (4321) Kivrak; Yavru, Yumlu, Kacar,
Celustka (Malouda 59); Sen, Akgun, Adin; Colman*,
Mierzejewski (Alanzinho 65); Paulo Henrique (Gural 82).

Estoril (0) 0
Hapoel Ramat Gan (0) 0   2584
Estoril: (442) Vagner; Tavares, Bruno Miguel, Anderson
Luis, Goncalo Santos; Babanco, Filipe Goncalves
(Gladestony 85), Joao Pedro, Evandro; Seba (Leal 52),
Carlitos (Gerso 73).
Hapoel Ramat Gan: (442) Straus; Maabi, Levy (Cohen
83), Soffer, Roman; Hazum (Addo 70), Lingane,
Buksenbaum, Brossou (Buzaglo 33); Asayag, Diamant.

FK Minsk (0) 0
St Johnstone (0) 1 *(MacLean 69)*   2900
FK Minsk: (442) Bushma; Sverchinski, Sosnovskiy,
Sachivko, Rnic; Begunov (Makas 78), Bukatkin, Kazeka
(Buloychik 86), Gorbushin (Belevich 70); Kibuk,
Vasilyuk.
St Johnstone: (442) Mannus; Mackay, Anderson, Wright,
Scobbie; Wotherspoon (Easton 85), McDonald (Davidson
50), Cregg, Caddis; Hasselbaink (May 68), MacLean.

Hacken (0) 1 *(Ericsson 65)*
Thun (1) 2 *(Zuffi 33, 64)*   2802
Hacken: (442) Kallqvist; Bjorck, Arkivuo, Joza, Anklev
(Frolund 83); Ericsson, Chatto, Makondele, Gustafsson
(Bjurstrom 83); El Kabir, Mohammed (Strandberg 45).
Thun: (442) Faivre; Schenkel (Reinmann 6), Sulmoni,
Wittwer, Luthi; Zuffi (Schirinzi 68), Hediger, Frey,
Sanogo; Martinez (Siegfried 80), Schneuwly M.

Hajduk Split (0) 0
Dila Gori (1) 1 *(Iluridze 24)*   28,000
Hajduk Split: (442) Kalinic; Mikanovic, Milovic,
Jozinovic*, Maloca; Vrsajevic, Pasalic (Bencun 73),
Andjelkovic (Kis 46), Caktas; Susic (Mujan 87), Maglica.
Dila Gori: (442) Revishvili; Tomashvili, Khizaneishvili*,
Gongadze, Kobakhidze; Guruli, Aladashvili (Gorelishvili
85), Dolidze (Modebadze 66), Bolkvadze (Aburdjania
89); Iluridze, Gvalia.

Jablonec (1) 2 *(Pitak 17 (pen), Vosahlik 90)*
Stromsgodset (1) 1 *(Benes 39 (og))*   4285
Jablonec: (4321) Spit; Kysela, Benes, Zoubele, Novak;
Cizek (Kopic 60), Loucka, Jablonsky; Pitak (Vosahlik
59), Vanek (Kubista 83); Hubnik.
Stromsgodset: (433) Kwarasey; Vilsvik, Horn, Madsen,
Nuhu (Hamoud 45); Ibrahim, Johansen, Boateng
(Brenne 72); Storflor (Wikheim 77), Kovacs, Kamara.

Kukesi (1) 2 *(Malacarne 6, Malota 84)*
Metallurg Donetsk (0) 0   7000
Kukesi: (442) Halili; Brahja, Hallici, Malacarne (Alikaj
46), Peqini; Malota, Progni, Allmuca (Manuka 83),
Karabeci; Popovic (Malindi 74), Hoxha.
Metallurg Donetsk: (442) Pankiv; Checher, Polevoy,
O'Dea (Nelson 34 (Alexandre 62)), Mkrtchyan; Lazic,
Makridis, Morozyuk*, Danilo; Dimitrov, Junior Moraes
(Degtiarov 69).

Motherwell (0) 0
Kuban Krasnodar (0) 2 *(Popov 52, 78)*   6748
Motherwell: (4321) Hollis; Ramsden, Hutchinson,
McManus, Hammell; Francis-Angol, Lasley, Vigurs;
McFadden (Kerr 82), Lawson (Anier 80); Sutton.
Kuban Krasnodar: (4321) Belenov; Kozlov, Xandao,
Dealbert, Bugaev; Popov, Tsoraev (Fidler 79), Sosnin;
Bucur (Urena 85), Kabore; Ibra (Cisse 82).

Pandurii Targu Jiu (1) 1 *(Nistor 4)*
Hapoel Tel Aviv (1) 1 *(Lucas Sasha 29)*   4996
Pandurii Targu Jiu: (451) Stanca; Christou, Nicoara (Buleica
34), Ungurusan, Erico; Momcilovic, Nistor (Lemnaru 86),
Anton (Brata 63), Pereira, Breeveld; Matulevicius.
Hapoel Tel Aviv: (433) Amos; Dgani, Colin, Ben Shimon,
Ilic; Gordana (Abutbul 79), Zaguri (Safuri 71), Lucas
Sasha (Vermouth 71); Gerzycich, Shechter, Damari.

Petrolul Ploiesti (0) 1 *(Grozav 83)*
Vitesse (0) 1 *(Reis 52 (pen))*   11,887
Petrolul Ploiesti: (433) Pecanha; Alcenat, Geraldo, Benga,
Guilherme; Hoban, Younes (Abel Camara 69), De Lucas;
Boudjemaa (Morar 72), Dore (Teixeira 63), Grozav.
Vitesse: (433) Velthuizen; Leerdam, Kashia, Van Der
Heijden, Van Aanholt; Vejinovic (Van Der Struijk 75),
Qazaishvili, Janssen; Ibarra, Reis, Kakuta (Chanturia 23).

Qarabag (0) 1 *(Reynaldo 89)*
Gefle (0) 0   22,000
Qarabag: (433) Varvodic; Yusifov (Reynaldo 69), Garayev,
Medvedev, Teli; Sadygov, Agolli, Muarem (Chumbinho
46); Almeida, Karimov, Gelashvili (Kapolongo 46).
Gefle: (352) Hugosson; Mard, Wikstrom, Asp; Portin,
Fallman, Faltsetas, Lundevall (Oremo 46), Hansson
(Abdullai 78); Orlov (Olsson J 90), Dahlberg.

Randers (0) 1 *(Borring 60)*
Rubin Kazan (2) 2 *(Torbinsky 11, Rondon 42)*   3153
Randers: (442) Andersen; Thomsen, Agesen, Fenger,
Tamboura; Bjarnason (Davids 79), Svensson, Borring
(Kamper 81), Keller; Schwartz, Brock-Madsen.
Rubin Kazan: (442) Arlauskis; Ansaldi, Marcano, Cesar
Navas, Kulik (Sharonov 86); Ryazantsev, Torbinsky (Natcho
72), Kisliak, M'Vila; Prudnikov (Kuzmin 63), Rondon.

Rijeka (1) 2 *(Sharbini 3, Kvrzic 59)*
Zilina (0) 1 *(Majtan 74)*   7000
Rijeka: (442) Vargic; Skarabot, Knezevic, Tomecak,
Maric; Alispahic (Kvrzic 51), Mocinic (Pokrivac 74),
Males, Jugovic; Benko (Krstanovic 83), Sharbini.
Zilina: (442) Dubravka; Akakpo, Piacek, Mabouka,
Nunes; Pecovsky, Skvarka, Paur (Jelic 70), Majtan
(Skriniar 86); Pich, Mihalik (Zilak 63).

Sevilla (1) 3 *(Bacca 19, Perotti 82 (pen), Carrico 90)*
Mladost Podgorica (0) 0   27,548
Sevilla: (442) Beto; Fazio, Coke, Pareja, Carrico; Moreno,
Rakitic, Rabello (Perotti 59), Vitolo (Rusescu 76); Bacca,
Reyes (Jairo 19).
Mladost Podgorica: (433) Vujadinovic; Zivkovic,
Sofranac, Mitrovic, Markovic (Kascelan 80); Novovic,
Bozovic, Sankovic; Savicevic (Pavicevic 72), Kaljevic
(Knezevic 63), Seratlic.

Siroki Brijeg (0) 1 *(Coric 77)*
Udinese (3) 3 *(Di Natale 16, Muriel 31, 39)*   4500
Siroki Brijeg: (442) Bilobrk; Blaic, Spikic, Jese, Markovic; Ivankovic, Landenka, Coric, Wagner (Maric 46); Zakaric (Silic 70), Kordic (Barisic 46).
Udinese: (3142) Kelava; Domizzi, Danilo, Heurtaux; Allan; Basta (Widmer 46), Pinzi, Pereyra (Lazzari 73), Silva; Muriel, Di Natale (Maicosuel 85).

Skoda Xanthi (1) 1 *(Die 36)*
Standard Liege (1) 2 *(Mujangi Bia 18, Ciman 74)*   3500
Skoda Xanthi: (442) Kiriakidis; Paito, Bertos■, Vallas, Goutas; Baxevanidis (Marin 56), Komesidis, Marcelinho, Vassilakakis; Mantalos (De Guzman 56), Die (Solari 87).
Standard Liege: (442) Kawashima; Iandoli, Opare, Ciman, Arslanagic; Bulot, Cisse (Buyens 46), Marquet, Mujangi Bia (Ghoochannejhad 76); De Camargo, Ezekiel (Batshuayi 62).

Slask Wroclaw (0) 1 *(Plaku 64)*
Club Brugge (0) 0   17,132
Slask Wroclaw: (352) Gikiewicz; Kokoszka, Dudu Paraiba, Pawelec; Ostrowski (Socha 60), Sobota, Mila, Stevanovic, Kazmierczak; Plaku, Paixao (Patejuk 88).
Club Brugge: (442) Ryan; Hogli, Duarte, De Bock (Bolingoli Mbombo 45), Mechele; Simons, Rafaelov (Gudjohnsen 65), Blondel, Verstraete; Wang (Dierckx 78), De Sutter.

Slovan Liberec (0) 2 *(Rabusic 67, Frydek 81)*
FC Zurich (1) 1 *(Chiumiento 5 (pen))*   7780
Slovan Liberec: (442) Kovar; Kelic, Frydek (Kolar 90), Kovac, Husek (Sural 58); Pavelka, Kusnir, Rybalka, Fleisman; Rabusic, Delarge (Kalitvintsev 58).
FC Zurich: (433) Da Costa; Djimsiti, Nef■, Koch P, Benito; Henrique, Schonbachler (Koch R 87), Chiumiento; Gavranovic (Etoundi 80), Chermiti (Buff 87), Rikan.

St Etienne (2) 3 *(Brandao 3, 81, Cohade 20)*
Milsami (0) 0   24,671
St Etienne: (433) Ruffier; Clerc, Bayal Sall, Perrin, Brison; Lemoine, Guilavogui (Clement 75), Cohade (Corgnet 64); Hamouma, Brandao, Tabanou (Nicolita 80).
Milsami: (4231) Bantis; Rassulov■, Soporan, Shedrack, Gheorghiu (Rhaili 90); Bolohan, Gheti; Patras, Andronic (Leuca 90), Ciofu (Iavorschi 88); Guillherme.

Swansea C (1) 4 *(Michu 37, Bony 55, 60, Pozuelo 86)*
Malmo (0) 0   16,176
Swansea C: (442) Vorm; Rangel, Williams, Amat, Davies; Dyer (Pozuelo 73), Britton (Canas 80), Shelvey, Routledge; Michu (de Guzman 66), Bony.
Malmo: (442) Dahlin; Albornoz, Jansson, Helander, Ricardinho; Hamad (Kroon 82), Halsti, Thern, Friberg (Forsberg 67); Rantie, Eriksson (Johansson 76).

Trencin (0) 1 *(Holubek 82)*
Astra Giurgiu (1) 3 *(Budescu 8, Tembo 49, Fatai 51)* 4271
Trencin: (442) Volesak; Cogley, Klescik, Ramon, Mazan R; Baez (Baris■ 60), Holubek, Mondek (Frimmel 79), Stefanik; Willian, Adi (Malek 81).
Astra Giurgiu: (433) Lung Jr; Ben Youssef, Junior Morais, Gaman, Matel; Tembo, Seto, Cristescu (Barboianu 87); William Amorim (Enache 63) Budescu, Fatai (Ivanovski 78).

Tromso (0) 1 *(Ondrasek 77)*
Differdange 03 (0) 0   2135
Tromso: (541) Sahlman; Causevic, Koppinen, Norbye, Kristiansen (Drage 58), Ciss (Frantzen 88); Bendiksen, Andersen, Johansen, Pritchard (Johnsen 73); Ondrasek.
Differdange 03: (433) Weber; Rodrigues, Janisch, Bukvic, Caillet; Bisevac (Bettmer 69), Lebresne, Meligner (Caron 48); May, Er Rafik, Franzoni (Siebenaler 74).

Ventspils (0) 0
Maccabi Haifa (0) 0   2800
Ventspils: (442) Uvarenko; Kurakins, Smirnovs, Dubra, Timofejevs; Zigajevs (Turkovs 75), Paulius, Tarasovs, Freidgeimas (Ignatans 90); Yanchuk, Sukhanov (Tarkhnishvili 83).

Maccabi Haifa: (433) Saranov; Twatha, Keinan, Cocalic, Meshumar; Rayo (Abukarat 90), Boccoli, Katan; Ezra (Golasa 81), Turgeman (Sallalich 63), Abuhatzira.

VMFD Zalgiris (1) 1 *(Kuklys 44)*
Lech Poznan (0) 0   4300
VMFD Zalgiris: (442) Vitkauskas; Skerla, Vaitkunas, Peric, Kuklys; Leliuga (Freidgeimas 45), Komolov (Velicka 77), Svrljuga (Janusauskas 50), Silenas; Zulpa, Bilinski.
Lech Poznan: (442) Kotorowski; Kedziora, Arboleda, Ceesay, Kaminski; Tralka, Drewniak, Hamalainen, Pawlowski (Lovrencsics 61); Teodorczyk (Slusarski 70), Ubiparip (Formella 87).

Vojvodina (0) 2 *(Vulicevic 71, Oumarou 81)*
Bursaspor (1) 2 *(Batalla 36 (pen), Taiwo 90)*   6500
Vojvodina: (532) Delac; Radoja, Trajkovic, Djuric, Vulicevic, Lekovic; Vranjes, Alivodic, Poletanovic (Tumbasevic 70); Skuletic (Kaludjerovic 60), Oumarou.
Bursaspor: (433) Frey; Civelli, Taiwo, Ozbayrakli, Ozturk; Cinaz (Yildirim 88), Belluschi, Batalla; Sanli (Kiraz 73), Sestak, Pinto (Unal 85).

THIRD QUALIFYING ROUND SECOND LEG

Thursday, 8 August 2013
Astra Giurgiu (0) 2 *(Ivanovski 86, Tembo 89)*
Trencin (0) 2 *(Adi 83, Van Kessel 88)*   1440
Astra Giurgiu: (442) Lung Jr; Ben Youssef, Junior Morais, Gaman, Matel; Tembo, Seto (Barboianu 90), Laban, William Amorim (Enache 75); Budescu (Cristescu 63), Ivanovski.
Trencin: (442) Volesak; Cogley, Klescik, Bero (Hajradinovic 71), Ramon; Mazan R, Holubek, Mondek (Van Kessel 61), Stefanik (Malek 80); Willian, Adi.

Breidablik (1) 1 *(Margeirsson 27)*
Aktobe (0) 0   2449
Breidablik: (442) Gunnleifsson; Hreidarsson, Ingason, Troost, Gardarsson (Rohde 73); Jonsson, Lydsson, Margeirsson, Yeoman (Vilhjalmsson 104); Adalsteinsson (Helgason 83), Hreinsson.
Aktobe: (451) Sidelnikov; Muldarov, Badlo, Primus, Arzumanyan (Baltaev 104); Kenzhisariev, Kharabara, Khayrullin, Kovalchuk, Kapadze; Lisenkov (Geynrikh 82).
aet; Aktobe won 2-1 on penalties.

Bursaspor (0) 0
Vojvodina (2) 3 *(Oumarou 9, Vranjes 29, Kaludjerovic 83)*   19,130
Bursaspor: (442) Frey; Taiwo, Civelli, Ozbayrakli, Ozturk; Cinaz (Unal 35), Batalla, Yildirim, Kiraz (Deniz 70); Sestak, Pinto (Sanli 46).
Vojvodina: (442) Delac; Radoja, Trajkovic, Djuric, Vulicevic; Vranjes, Lekovic, Alivodic, Poletanovic (Nastic 90); Skuletic (Tumbasevic 62), Oumarou (Kaludjerovic 69).

Club Brugge (0) 3 *(Rafaelov 58, Duarte 80, De Sutter 90)*
Slask Wroclaw (1) 3 *(Sobota 9, 76, Paixao 60)* 25,945
Club Brugge: (433) Ryan; Hogli, Duarte, Mechele, De Bock; Vazquez (Gudjohnsen 77), Simons, Blondel (Rafaelov 46); Wang, De Sutter, Lestienne.
Slask Wroclaw: (4231) Gikiewicz; Ostrowski (Socha 55), Pawelec, Kokoszka, Dudu Paraiba; Kazmierczak, Stevanovic; Sobota, Mila, Plaku; Paixao (Patejuk 83).

Differdange 03 (0) 1 *(Er Rafik 46)*
Tromso (0) 0   1960
Differdange 03: (4231) Weber; Franzoni, Caillet, Bukvic, Janisch; Lebresne, May; Bisevac (Caron 114), Bastos (Ribeiro 104), Rodrigues (Luisi 99); Er Rafik.
Tromso: (433) Sahlman; Ciss, Koppinen, Fojut, Kristiansen; Johansen, Bendiksen (Nystrom 82), Pritchard; Andersen (Moldskred 23), Ondrasek, Drage.
aet; Tromso won 4-3 on penalties.

Dila Gori (0) 1 *(Dolidze 83)*
Hajduk Split (0) 0　　　　　　　　　　13,891
Dila Gori: (3331) Revishvili; Kobakhidze, Tomashvili, Kvakhadze; Gongadze, Guruli, Aladashvili (Dolidze 79); Gvalia, Bolkvadze (Aburdjania 86), Iluridze; Modebadze (Gorelishvili 77).
Hajduk Split: (442) Kalinic; Maloca, Milovic, Mikanovic, Bradaric; Susic (Andrijasevic 45), Andjelkovic (Kis 85), Vrsajevic, Caktas; Bencun (Mujan 63), Maglica.

FC Zurich (1) 1 *(Chermiti 17)*
Slovan Liberec (0) 2 *(Frydek 64, Rybalka 85)*　　5915
FC Zurich: (433) Da Costa; Koch P, Koch R, Djimsiti, Benito; Schonbachler (Kukuruzovic 85), Rikan (Buff 75), Chiumiento; Henrique, Gavranovic (Etoundi 75), Chermiti.
Slovan Liberec: (433) Kovar; Kusnir, Kovac, Kelic (Sural 53), Fleisman; Frydek (Kalitvintsev 75), Sackey (Karisik 71), Pavelka; Rybalka, Delarge, Rabusic.

Gefle (0) 0
Qarabag (1) 2 *(Chumbinho 41, Reynaldo 50)*　　1137
Gefle: (4312) Hugosson; Olsson J, Fallman, Wikstrom, Portin; Hansson (Abdullai 60), Faltsetas (Phekezela 74), Lundevall; Oremo; Dahlberg, Orlov (Bellander 60).
Qarabag: (4231) Varvodic; Medvedev, Teli, Sadygov, Agolli; Garayev, Yusifov; George (Muarem 74), Chumbinho (Sattarly 85), Reynaldo; Kapolongo (Gelashvili 66).

Hapoel Ramat Gan (0) 0
Estoril (1) 1 *(Evandro 11 (pen))*　　　　　　1360
Hapoel Ramat Gan: (442) Straus; Levy, Soffer■, Hazum, Maabi; Buksenbaum, Lingane, Roman (Cohen 90); Luzon (Gabai 58); Asayag (Buzaglo 45), Diamant.
Estoril: (4132) Vagner; Anderson Luis, Bruno Miguel, Tavares, Babanco; Goncalo Santos (Diogo Amado 81); Filipe Goncalves, Evandro, Joao Coimbra (Lopes 89); Leal, Carlitos (Gerso 66).

Hapoel Tel Aviv (1) 1 *(Damari 21 (pen))*
Pandurii Targu Jiu (1) 2 *(Pereira 34, Ciucur 50)*　　6700
Hapoel Tel Aviv: (442) Amos; Dgani, Ilic, Colin, Harush; Gerzycich, Lucas Sasha (Abutbul 69), Safuri (Gordana 46), Zaguri (Vermouth 57); Damari, Shechter.
Pandurii Targu Jiu: (442) Mingote; Ungurusan, Mamele, Christou, Momcilovic; Nistor, Anton, Buleica (Ciucur 46), Nicoara (Brata 65 (Rada 86)); Matulevicius, Pereira.

Kuban Krasnodar (0) 1 *(McManus 50 (og))*
Motherwell (0) 0　　　　　　　　　　　31,754
Kuban Krasnodar: (4231) Belenov; Kozlov, Dealbert, Xandao, Bugaev; Kabore, Tlisov; Tsoraev (Bezlikhotnov 83), Sosnin, Urena (Zhavnerchik 61); Ibra (Cisse 76).
Motherwell: (4231) Nielsen; Ramsden, McManus, Hutchinson, Hammell; Kerr, Lasley (Moore 79); Carswell, Lawson (Cummins 71), Francis-Angol; Anier (McHugh 71).

Lech Poznan (0) 2 *(Teodorczyk 87, Ubiparip 90)*
VMFD Zalgiris (1) 1 *(Bilinski 29)*　　　　16,326
Lech Poznan: (4321) Kotorowski; Wolakiewicz, Arboleda, Kaminski, Henriquez; Drewniak (Slusarski 61), Tralka, Hamalainen; Mozdzen (Lovrencsics 53), Pawlowski (Teodorczyk■ 53); Ubiparip.
VMFD Zalgiris: (451) Vitkauskas; Skerla, Peric, Vaitkunas, Freidgeimas; Zulpa, Komolov, Kuklys, Leliuga (Kanai 88), Silenas (Janusauskas 64); Bilinski (Velicka■ 69).
VMFD Zalgiris won on away goals rule.

Maccabi Haifa (2) 3 *(Smirnovs 35 (og), Rayo 41, 53)*
Ventspils (0) 0　　　　　　　　　　　10,800
Maccabi Haifa: (433) Saranov; Meshumar (Gabai 58), Cocalic, Keinan, Twatha; Katan, Boccoli, Rayo (Abukarat 63); Ezra, Abuhatzira, Turgeman (Raiyan 68).
Ventspils: (433) Uvarenko; Timofejevs, Dubra, Smirnovs, Kurakins; Sukhanov, Tarasovs, Paulius (Zigajevs 63); Freidgeimas, Yanchuk (Kozlovs 72), Tarkhnishvili (Zatkins 85).

Malmo (0) 0
Swansea C (0) 0　　　　　　　　　　　11,538
Malmo: (442) Dahlin; Albornoz, Jansson, Helander, Ricardinho; Hamad (Petrovic 55), Rakip, Friberg (Halsti 68), Forsberg; Cibicki, Eriksson (Rantie 74).
Swansea C: (4141) Tremmel; Richards (Rangel 84), Taylor, Chico, Williams; de Guzman; Pozuelo, Canas, Michu (Ki 73), Routledge (Dyer 66); Bony.

Metallurg Donetsk (1) 1 *(Dimitrov 27)*
Kukesi (0) 0　　　　　　　　　　　　3000
Metallurg Donetsk: (4231) Pankiv; Nasonov (Golaydo 69), Checher, Prijma, Polevoy (Oliveira 84); Mkrtchyan, Makridis; Nelson (Alexandre 59), Dimitrov, Lazic; Junior Moraes.
Kukesi: (433) Halili; Peqini, Brahja, Malota, Hallici; Allmuca (Mziu 90), Karabeci, Alikaj (Popovic 69); Progni, Malindi■, Hoxha (Manuka 81).

Milsami (0) 0
St Etienne (2) 3 *(Brandao 29, Hamouma 39, Nicolita 69)*　　　3027
Milsami: (442) Negai; Gheti, Soporan, Rhaili, Bolohan; Patras (Paseciniuc 90), Andronic, Calugher (Stadiiciuc 84), Iavorschi; Leuca (Ciofu 73), Guillherme.
St Etienne: (4141) Ruffier; Clerc, Bayal Sall, Zouma, Brison; Guilavogui; Hamouma (Nicolita 59), Corgnet, Cohade (Clement 54), Tabanou; Brandao (Saadi 46).

Mladost Podgorica (0) 1 *(Pavicevic 90)*
Sevilla (5) 6 *(Vitolo 10, Rusescu 23, 38, Rabello 33, Coke 37, 60)*　　　4000
Mladost Podgorica: (4231) Vujadinovic; Zivkovic, Sofranac, Mitrovic, Novovic; Bozovic, Kalezic (Cetkovic 89); Savicevic, Kaljevic (Pavicevic 46), Seratlic; Markovic (Knezevic 62).
Sevilla: (4312) Javi Varas; Coke, Pareja (Moreno 60), Cala, Fernando Navarro; Rabello, Maduro, Vitolo (Marin 64); Rakitic (Cotan 46); Jairo, Rusescu.

Rapid Vienna (1) 3 *(Petsos 26, Schaub 62, 85)*
Asteras Tripolis (0) 1 *(Grazzini 57)*　　　15,300
Rapid Vienna: (4231) Novota; Trimmel, Sonnleitner, Behrendt, Schrammel; Petsos, Boskovic; Hofmann S (Grozurek 80), Burgstaller (Pavelic 88), Boyd; Sabitzer (Schaub 61).
Asteras Tripolis: (4231) Bantis; Tsambouris, Kourbelis, Goian, Pipinis; Usero, Zisopoulos (Grazzini 46); Ximo Navarro (Bakasetas 70), De Blasis, Caffa; Barrales (Delgado 68).

Red Star Belgrade (0) 0
Chornomorets (0) 0　　　　　　　　　39,730
Red Star Belgrade: (451) Bajkovic; Vesovic, Martinovic, Lazic, Mladenovic; Pecnik, Milijas (Kasalica 45), Ninkovic, Kovacevic, Savicevic (Milunovic 78); Dauda (Mihajlovic 67).
Chornomorets: (442) Bezotosny; Kutas, Berger, Fontanello, Anderson Mineiro; Djadjedje (Priyomov 69), Kovalchuk K, Bobko, Sito Riera (Zubeyko 88); Antonov, Samodin (Didenko 80).

Rubin Kazan (1) 2 *(Cesar Navas 18, Eremenko 86)*
Randers (0) 0　　　　　　　　　　　5012
Rubin Kazan: (4411) Ryzhikov; Kuzmin, Marcano, Cesar Navas, Getigezhev; Torbinsky (Karadeniz 69), Natcho (Kulik 69), M'Vila (Abishov 88), Ryazantsev; Eremenko; Rondon.
Randers: (442) Andersen; Fenger, Sorensen, Agesen, Tamboura; Svensson (Poulsen 76), Keller (Bjarnason 63), Davids, Borring; Schwartz (Brock-Madsen 46), Lundberg.

St Johnstone (0) 1 *(Rnic 75)*
FK Minsk (0) 0　　　　　　　　　　　8594
St Johnstone: (442) Mannus; Mackay, Anderson, Wright, Scobbie; Wotherspoon (Edwards 104), McDonald, Cregg, Hasselbaink (Millar 66); MacLean, May (Fallon 108).
FK Minsk: (442) Bushma; Sverchinski, Sosnovskiy■, Sachivko, Rnic; Begunov, Bukatkin (Kazeka 77), Mayevskiy (Makas 72), Gorbushin (Razin 54); Kibuk, Vasilyuk.
aet; FK Minsk won 3-2 on penalties.

Standard Liege (0) 2 *(Bulot 53, De Camargo 70)*
Skoda Xanthi (0) 1 *(De Guzman 83)*   24,706
Standard Liege: (442) Kawashima; Ngawa, Ben Haim,
Arslanagic, Van Damme; Bulot (Mujangi Bia 60),
Buyens (Ozturk 60), Marquet, M'Poku; Ghoochannejhad
(De Camargo 67), Batshuayi.
Skoda Xanthi: (4141) Kiriakidis; Baxevanidis, Goutas,
Vallas, Paito (Mantalos 59); Komesidis; Marin (Triadis 67),
Die, De Guzman, Marcelinho (Solari 74); Vassilakakis.

Stromsgodset (0) 1 *(Kamara 71)*
Jablonec (1) 3 *(Hubnik 16, Vanek 81, Pitak 90)*   4439
Stromsgodset: (442) Kwarasey; Vilsvik, Horn, Madsen
(Diomande 46), Hamoud; Boateng, Johansen, Ibrahim,
Storflor; Kovacs (Keita 65), Wikheim (Kamara 46).
Jablonec: (442) Spit; Zoubele (Vanek 46), Benes, Kysela,
Cizek; Kopic, Pitak, Loucka, Kubista; Vosahlik
(Jablonsky 87), Hubnik (Tresnak 68).

Thun (0) 1 *(Sanogo 69)*
Hacken (0) 0   5027
Thun: (442) Faivre; Sulmoni, Schirinzi, Reinmann
(Siegfried 46), Luthi; Wittwer, Zuffi, Hediger, Sanogo;
Martinez (Frey 72), Schneuwly M (Sadik 84).
Hacken: (442) Kallqvist; Wahlstrom, Lewicki (Ojala 85),
Bjorck, Arkivuo (Zuta 76); Anklev, Chatto, Makondele,
Gustafsson (Strandberg 63); Ericsson, Williams.

Trabzonspor (0) 0
Dinamo Minsk (0) 0   22,803
Trabzonspor: (4141) Kivrak; Yavru, Kacar (Demir 61),
Yumlu, Celustka; Akgun; Sen (Erdogan 85), Aydogdu,
Mierzejewski (Malouda 67), Adin; Paulo Henrique.
Dinamo Minsk: (4231) Sulima; Veretilo (Trubilo 84),
Politevich (Bykov 67), Kontsevoj, Danilov; Simovic,
Nikolic; Coto (Khvashchinski 60), Figueredo, Stasevich;
Adamovic.

Udinese (1) 4 *(Di Natale 9, Lazzari 82, Basta 86, Vydra 90)*
Siroki Brijeg (0) 0   4326
Udinese: (352) Kelava; Naldo, Danilo, Domizzi; Basta,
Pinzi, Allan, Pereyra (Lazzari 79), Silva; Di Natale
(Maicosuel 67), Muriel (Vydra 87).
Siroki Brijeg: (4231) Bilobrk; Blaic, Jese, Spikic,
Markovic; Landenka, Plazonic (Ivankovic 53); Coric
(Ljubic 76), Maric, Zakaric (Silic 63); Barisic.

VfB Stuttgart (0) 0
Botev Plovdiv (0) 0   7000
VfB Stuttgart: (4231) Ulreich; Schwaab, Tasci,
Niedermaier (Rudiger 62), Sakai; Gentner, Boka; Cacau,
Maxim (Harnik 46), Traore; Abdellaoue (Ibisevic 79).
Botev Plovdiv: (442) Stachowiak; Hristov, Sprockel,
Grncarov, Minev; Abel (Domovchiyski 68), Galchev,
Jirsak, Kortzorg (Pedro 85); Ognyanov (Kostov 81),
Nedelev.
VfB Stuttgart won on away goals rule.

Vitesse (0) 1 *(Van Der Heijden 72)*
Petrolul Ploiesti (1) 2 *(Boudjemaa 21, Grozav 90)* 10,088
Vitesse: (433) Velthuizen; Van Der Struijk, Kashia, Van
Der Heijden, Van Aanholt; Leerdam (Propper 67),
Qazaishvili (Havenaar 46), Janssen; Ibarra, Pedersen,
Chanturia.
Petrolul Ploiesti: (433) Pecanha; Alcenat■, Geraldo,
Enza-Yamissi, Guilherme; Hoban, Boudjemaa, De
Lucas; Dore (Abel Camara 74), Younes (Mustivar 63),
Grozav.

Zilina (0) 1 *(Mihalik 89)*
Rijeka (0) 1 *(Pokrivac 50)*   6319
Zilina: (433) Dubravka; Mabouka, Vavro, Akakpo,
Hucko (Nunes 81); Skvarka, Pecovsky, Paur
(Babatounde 66); Mihalik, Majtan, Pich (Jelic 67).
Rijeka: (361) Vargic; Tomecak, Knezevic■, Maric;
Skarabot, Alispahic (Mocinic 77), Males, Pokrivac,
Benko, Jugovic (Kvrzic 20); Sharbini (Zlomislic 60).

PLAY-OFF ROUND FIRST LEG

Thursday, 22 August 2013
Aktobe (1) 2 *(Tremoulinas 37 (og), Khayrullin 66)*
Dynamo Kyiv (1) 3 *(Yarmolenko 13, Ideye 51,
Belhanda 57)*   12,500
Aktobe: (4231) Sidelnikov; Badlo, Arzumanyan,
Muldarov, Kharabara (Primus 60); Logvinenko,
Kapadze; Kovalchuk (Lisenkov 60), Geynrikh,
Khayrullin; Davydov (Tagybergen 86).
Dynamo Kyiv: (442) Shovkovskiy; Vida, Dragovic,
Khacheridi, Tremoulinas; Yarmolenko (Gusev 67),
Haruna, Vukojevic, Dudu Rodrigues (Lens 52);
Belhanda (Bezus 81), Ideye.

Apollon Limassol (0) 2 *(Sangoy 54, 63)*
Nice (0) 0   7157
Apollon Limassol: (442) Bruno Vale; Merkis, Dananae,
Karipidis, Gullon; Robert (Kyriakou 73), Hamdani,
Vasilou, Roberto; Sangoy (Haber 90), Papoulis
(Konstantinou 82).
Nice: (442) Ospina; Kolodzieczak, Gomis, Genevois
(Bautheac 58), Palun; Mendy, Digard, Traore, Eysseric
(Bosetti 80); Pied (Cvitanich 58), Constant.

Atromitos (0) 1 *(Papadopoulos 75 (pen))*
AZ Alkmaar (0) 3 *(Gudmundsson 51, 90, Johannsson 74)*
          8500
Atromitos: (433) Sifakis; Nastos, Fitanidis, Lazaridis,
Giannoulis; Ballas (Karamanos 84), Pitu, Dimoutsos
(Brito 70); Umbides, Papadopoulos, Karagounis
(Napoleoni 61).
AZ Alkmaar: (433) Alvarado; Johansson, Gouweleeuw,
Wuytens, Viergever; Gudelj, Henriksen, Elm (Overtoom
71); Beerens (Martens 86), Johannsson (Berghuis 90),
Gudmundsson.

Chornomorets (0) 1 *(Gai 75)*
Skenderbeu (0) 0   34,000
Chornomorets: (451) Bezotosny; Kutas, Fontanello,
Berger, Anderson Mineiro; Samodin (Priyomov 73), Gai,
Antonov (Didenko 84), Kovalchuk K, Djadjedje (Leo
Matos 79); Sito Riera.
Skenderbeu: (451) Shehi; Ademir, Gvozdenovic, Radas,
Arapi; Tomic (Bicaj 90), Lilaj, Orelesi, Nimaga (Fagu
65), Muzaka (Abazi 71); Ribaj.

Dinamo Tbilisi (0) 0
Tottenham H (2) 5 *(Townsend 12, Paulinho 44,
Soldado 58, 67, Rose 64)*   22,500
Dinamo Tbilisi: (4312) Loria; Khurtsilava, Gvelesiani,
Kvaratskhelia, Glisic (Papava 46); Grigalashvili, Dzaria
(Goga 81), Kvirkvelia; Merebashvilli; Xisco (Vouho 42),
Dvali.
Tottenham H: (4231) Lloris; Naughton, Dawson, Kaboul,
Rose; Paulinho (Carroll 71), Dembele; Capoue,
Sigurdsson (Chadli 61), Townsend; Soldado (Kane 71).

Esbjerg (1) 4 *(Ankersen P 26, 80, van Buren 64,
Andreasen 75)*
St Etienne (2) 3 *(Tabanou 22, Hamouma 42, Perrin 70)*
          11,478
Esbjerg: (442) Ronnow; Ankersen P, Hansen K, Drobo-
Ampem, Knudsen; Ankersen J, Andreasen, Lekven
(Berthel Askou 90), Lyng (Rasmussen 61); Diouf, van
Buren.
St Etienne: (442) Ruffier; Brison, Zouma, Perrin, Clerc;
Clement (Cohade 67), Lemoine, Tabanou (Sissoko 84),
Guilavogui; Hamouma, Brandao.

Estoril (2) 2 *(Evandro 10, Carlitos 40)*
Pasching (0) 0   2178
Estoril: (4231) Vagner; Anderson Luis, Tavares, Bruno
Miguel, Mano; Goncalo Santos (Diogo Amado 68),
Filipe Goncalves; Carlitos, Evandro, Joao Pedro (Gerso
80); Leal (Seba 73).
Pasching: (433) Berger; Kerschbaumer, Grasegger,
Kablar, Prettenthaler; Perchtold, Sobkova (Pfennich 69),
Krammer (Mossner 78); Schobesherger (Hamdemir 46),
Nacho Casanova, Petrovic.

FH Hafnarfjordur (0) 0
Genk (1) 2 *(Vossen 44, Tillen 79 (og))* 2700
FH Hafnarfjordur: (4231) Oskarsson R; Jonsson, Vidarsson P, Bjarnason, Tillen; Snorrason (Palsson 69), Gudmundsson; Vidarsson D, Gudnason (Ingason 81), Sverrisson; Emilsson (Bjornsson 62).
Genk: (433) Koteles; Ngcongca, Koulibaly, Mbodji, Hamalainen; Kumordzi, Camus (Limbombe 83), Gorius; M'Boyo (De Ceulaer 73), Vossen, Buffel.

FK Minsk (0) 0
Standard Liege (0) 2 *(Batshuayi 56, Bulot 83)* 2467
FK Minsk: (442) Bushma; Begunov, Sverchinski, Sachivko[#], Rnic; Razin (Kazeka 40), Rozhok, Gorbushin, Mayevskiy; Kibuk (Ostroukh 79), Vasilyuk (Makas 87).
Standard Liege: (442) Kawashima; Opare, Ben Haim, Arslanagic, Van Damme; Bulot, Cisse, De Sart, M'Poku (Mujangi Bia 59); De Camargo (Biton 69), Batshuayi (Ezekiel 79).

Grasshoppers (0) 1 *(Ngamukol 64)*
Fiorentina (1) 2 *(Cuadrado 13, Grichting 46 (og))* 15,000
Grasshoppers: (4231) Burki; Lang, Vilotic, Grichting, Pavlovic; Abrashi (Caio 77), Salatic; Hajrovic (Feltscher 82), Toko, Gashi (Ben Khalifa 57); Ngamukol.
Fiorentina: (352) Neto; Roncaglia, Rodriguez, Savic; Cuadrado, Valero (Fernandez 82), Ambrosini, Aquilani, Pasqual (Alonso 76); Rossi (Ljajic 67), Gomez.

IF Elfsborg (0) 1 *(Larsson J 74)*
Nordsjaelland (1) 1 *(Nordstrand 34)* 5330
IF Elfsborg: (442) Stuhr-Ellegaard; Larsson J, Mobaeck, Jonsson, Klarstrom; Ishizaki, Rohden, Svensson, Hult; Beckmann (Claesson 89), Bangura (Keene 72).
Nordsjaelland: (4231) Hansen M; Ticinovic, Runje, Jakobsen, Mtiliga; Stokholm, Petry; Larsen (Gregor 85), Christiansen (Lindberg 71), Vingaard; Nordstrand (Hansen E 63).

Jablonec (1) 1 *(Kopic 43)*
Real Betis (1) 2 *(Jorge Molina 21, Cedrick 86)* 5850
Jablonec: (4321) Spit; Elias, Kysela, Benes, Novak; Kopic (Jablonsky 84), Loucka, Cizek (Tresnak 74); Pitak (Vosahlik 89), Vanek; Hubnik.
Real Betis: (433) Sara; Steinhofer, Perquis, Paulao, Nacho; Igiebor, Verdu, Torres (Matilla 70); Vadillo (Chuli 67), Jorge Molina (Juan Carlos 80), Cedrick.

Kuban Krasnodar (0) 1 *(Ibra 60)*
Feyenoord (0) 0 32,275
Kuban Krasnodar: (4231) Belenov; Kozlov, Xandao, Dealbert, Bugaev; Tlisov, Kabore; Tsoraev, Popov, Bucur (Sosnin 87); Ibra (Cisse 90).
Feyenoord: (433) Mulder; van Beek, De Vrij, Mathijsen, Martins Indi; Immers, Clasie, Trindade de Vilhena (Vormer 75); Schaken (Manu 65), Pelle, Armenteros.

Kukesi (0) 0
Trabzonspor (1) 2 *(Mierzejewski 31 (pen),*
Paulo Henrique 68) 17,000
Kukesi: (442) Halili; Peqini (Smajlaj 46), Malota, Musolli, Brahja; Allmuca (Cikalleshi 63), Karabeci, Hallici, Progni; Hoxha, Popovic (Alikaj 78).
Trabzonspor: (4321) Kivrak; Adin, Yavru, Demir, Yumlu; Zokora, Sen (Alanzinho 89), Akgun; Aydogdu (Erdogan 90), Mierzejewski (Karadeniz 82); Paulo Henrique.

Maccabi Haifa (1) 2 *(Rayo 30, Turgeman 61)*
Astra Giurgiu (0) 0 11,900
Maccabi Haifa: (442) Saranov; Twatha (Scheimann 85), Keinan, Meshumar, Cocalic; Boccoli, Ezra, Rayo (Ndlovu 78), Turgeman (Kozar 70); Abuhatzira, Katan.
Astra Giurgiu: (442) Lung Jr; Ben Youssef, Junior Morais, Matel, Muresan; Tembo (Fatai 55), Laban, Cristescu, William Amorim (Enache 85); Budescu (Seto 77), Ivanovski.

Molde (0) 0
Rubin Kazan (1) 2 *(Rondon 21, 89)* 4384
Molde: (442) Haskjold; Toivio (Tripic 86), Hovland, Forren, Rindaroy; Linnes, Berg Hestad, Hussain, Daehli (Chukwu 68); Gulbrandsen, Berget (Agnaldo 76).
Rubin Kazan: (442) Ryzhikov; Kuzmin, Cesar Navas, Marcano, Getigezhev; Torbinsky (Natcho 62), M'Vila, Kulik (Prudnikov 87), Ryazantsev; Eremenko (Karadeniz 62), Rondon.

Nomme Kalju (0) 1 *(Toomet 54)*
Dnipro (2) 3 *(Seleznyov 21 (pen), Giuliano 35,*
Zozulya 53) 2462
Nomme Kalju: (442) Teles; Koogas, Rodrigues, Barengrub, Kallaste; Puri (Soares 90), Wakui, Ceesay (Toomet 41), Kimbaloula; Quintieri, Voskoboinikov (Neemelo 81).
Dnipro: (442) Lastuvka; Fedetskiy, Mazuch, Cheberyachko, Vlad; Giuliano (Kobakhidze 68), Kankava, Rotan, Konoplyanka; Seleznyov (Politylo 75), Zozulya.

Pandurii Targu Jiu (0) 0
Braga (0) 1 *(Yazalde 51)* 11,500
Pandurii Targu Jiu: (442) Stanca; Christou, Mamele (Sipo Bohale 56), Ungurusan, Erico; Nicoara (Buleica 55), Momcilovic, Anton, Pereira; Breeveld (Adrovic 80), Matulevicius.
Braga: (442) Eduardo; Nuno Andre, Joaozinho, Baiano, Aderlan Santos; Luiz Carlos, Ruben Micael (Joao Pedro 90), Alan (Custodio 73), Mauro; Yazalde, Salvador Agra (Pardo 64).

Partizan Belgrade (0) 1 *(Jojic 70)*
Thun (0) 0 12,500
Partizan Belgrade: (4231) Stojkovic; Aksentijevic, Obradovic, Petrovic, Stankovic; Djemba-Djemba (Malbasic 45), Markovic; Grbic (Ninkovic 57), Ilic, Jojic; Mitrovic.
Thun: (4231) Faivre; Luthi, Siegfried, Sulmoni, Wittwer; Sanogo, Hediger; Martinez (Cassio 79), Zuffi, Schneuwly C (Ferreira 69); Schneuwly M (Sadik 86).

Qarabag (0) 0
Eintracht Frankfurt (1) 2 *(Meier 6, 75)* 30,500
Qarabag: (4231) Varvodic; Medvedev, Teli, Sadygov, Agolli; Garayev (Yusifov 61), Almeida; George, Chumbinho, Muarem (Nadirov 69); Gelashvili (Kapolongo 62).
Eintracht Frankfurt: (4231) Trapp; Celozzi, Zambrano, Bamba Anderson, Oczipka; Flum (Russ 80), Rode (Djakpa 85); Aigner, Meier, Inui (Lanig 69); Lakic.

Rapid Vienna (1) 1 *(Schaub 42)*
Dila Gori (0) 0 14,500
Rapid Vienna: (4231) Novota; Trimmel, Sonnleitner, Dibon, Schrammel; Petsos (Behrendt 71); Boskovic; Schaub, Hofmann S (Sabitzer 81), Grozurek (Denner 88); Burgstaller.
Dila Gori: (4141) Revishvili; Tomashvili (Bolkvadze 50), Khizaneishvili, Guruli, Kvakhadze; Gvalia; Dolidze (Gabashvili 68), Aladashvili (Maisuradze 54), Gongadze, Kobakhidze; Iluridze.

Red Bull Salzburg (3) 5 *(Jonathan 29, 37, 63, Mane 40,*
Hinteregger 68)
VMFD Zalgiris (0) 0 7827
Red Bull Salzburg: (442) Gulacsi; Klein, Andre Ramalho, Hinteregger, Ulmer; Kampf (Leitgeb 89), Hierlander, Ilsanker, Mane (Meilinger 78); Alan, Jonathan (Berisha 67).
VMFD Zalgiris: (4141) Vitkauskas; Freidgeimas, Peric, Skerla, Vaitkunas; Zulpa; Leliuga (Janusauskas 46), Komolov, Kuklys (Zagurskas 79), Silenas (Nyuiadzi 46); Bilinski.

Rijeka (0) 2 *(Benko 75, Kvrzic 87)*
VfB Stuttgart (0) 1 *(Ibisevic 89)* 11,000
Rijeka: (4321) Vargic; Tomecak, Leskovic, Maric, Skarabot (Boras 78); Zlomislic, Males, Kvrzic; Alispahic (Pokrivac 69), Sharbini (Mocinic 61); Benko.
VfB Stuttgart: (4321) Ulreich; Sakai, Schwaab, Rudiger, Molinaro; Leitner, Boka, Gentner; Harnik (Abdellaoue 84), Cacau (Maxim 69); Ibisevic.

Sevilla (1) 4 *(Rakitic 36, Marin 67, 88, Gameiro 85)*
Slask Wroclaw (1) 1 *(Paixao 17)* 16,758
Sevilla: (442) Beto; Diogo Figueiras, Fazio, Fernando Navarro, Moreno; Rabello (Perotti 75), Rakitic, Kondogbia (Iborra 17), Jairo; Marin, Gameiro.
Slask Wroclaw: (442) Gikiewicz; Kokoszka, Dudu Paraiba[a], Pawelec, Ostrowski; Sobota, Mila, Stevanovic (Holota 79), Kazmierczak; Plaku, Paixao.

St Gallen (0) 1 *(Mathys 47)*
Spartak Moscow (1) 1 *(Movsisyan 37)* 18,000
St Gallen: (442) Lopar; Mutsch, Montandon, Besle, Nushi (Wuthrich 64); Nater, Mathys, Lenjani, Janjatovic; Rodriguez (Vitkieviez 80), Karanovic (Keita 66).
Spartak Moscow: (433) Pesiakov; Insaurralde, Makeev, Tino Costa (Suchy 74), Rafael Carioca; Kombarov, Bilyaletdinov, Timofeev (Glushakov 46); Movsisyan (Barrios 58), Yakovlev, Krotov.

Swansea C (3) 5 *(Routledge 14, 25, Michu 22, Pecanha 58 (og), Pozuelo 70)*
Petrolul Ploiesti (0) 1 *(Grozav 87)* 12,500
Swansea C: (442) Vorm; Rangel, Williams (Amat 71), Chico, Taylor; Hernandez, Britton, Shelvey (de Guzman 69), Routledge (Pozuelo 60); Michu, Bony.
Petrolul Ploiesti: (4141) Pecanha; Achim, Geraldo, Benga, Guilherme; Mustivar; Hoban (Abel Camara 46), Boudjemaa (Priso 57), Grozav, Teixeira; Younes (Dore 58).

Tromso (0) 2 *(Bendiksen 49 (pen), Pritchard 68)*
Besiktas (1) 1 *(Almeida 9)* 4528
Tromso: (4231) Sahlman; Ciss, Koppinen, Fojut, Kristiansen; Bendiksen, Johansen; Andersen (Drage 90), Pritchard (Causevic 90), Moldskred; Ondrasek.
Besiktas: (4231) Zengin; Kurtulus, Sivok, Escude, Gulum; Kavlak (Eneramo 83), Fernandes; Hutchinson, Dentinho (Tore 60), Sahan (Ozyakup 73); Almeida.

Udinese (1) 1 *(Silva 35)*
Slovan Liberec (1) 3 *(Rybalka 16, Delarge 49, Kusnir 83)* 10,000
Udinese: (442) Kelava; Danilo, Basta, Domizzi, Silva; Heurtaux, Allan, Lazzari (Maicosuel 63), Pinzi (Zielinski 63); Muriel, Di Natale.
Slovan Liberec: (442) Kovar; Kelic, Frydek (Sural 65), Kovac, Kusnir; Pavelka, Rybalka, Sackey (Husek 84), Fleisman; Rabusic, Delarge (Hadascok 90).

Vojvodina (0) 1 *(Skuletic 54)*
Sheriff (1) 1 *(Isa 36)* 11,000
Vojvodina: (4411) Delac; Lekovic, Trajkovic, Djuric, Vulicevic; Radoja (Tumbasevic 84), Poletanovic (Vukcevic 45), Vranjes, Gacinovic (Kaludjerovic 45); Alivodic; Skuletic.
Sheriff: (4141) Tomic; Metoua, Samardzic, Paye, Luvannor[a]; Balima; Fernando, Cadu (William 84), Moyal (Pascenco 79), Ricardinho; Isa (Jhulliam 76).

Zulte Waregem (1) 1 *(Malanda 21)*
Apoel Nicosia (0) 1 *(Alexandrou 88)* 5095
Zulte Waregem: (4231) Bossut; De Fauw, D'Haene, Duplus, Verboom; Malanda, Skulason; Hazard (Trajkovski 74), Naessens, Conte; Leye.
Apoel Nicosia: (4231) Urko; Mario Sergio, Marcelo Oliveira, Joao Guilherme, Japones; Gomes (Benachour 60), Morais; Charalambidis (Alexandrou 79), Vinicius, Aloneftis; Sheridan (Budimir 73).

PLAY-OFF ROUND SECOND LEG
Thursday, 29 August 2013
Apoel Nicosia (0) 1 *(Aloneftis 52)*
Zulte Waregem (1) 2 *(Habibou 12, Naessens 90)* 18,959
Apoel Nicosia: (442) Urko; Morais, Mario Sergio, Marcelo Oliveira, Joao Guilherme; Gomes (Charalambidis 78), Vinicius (Sotiriou 68), Japones, Aloneftis; Manduca (Alexandrou 46), Sheridan.
Zulte Waregem: (442) Bossut; De Fauw, Conte, Duplus, D'Haene; Malanda, Colpaert, Hazard (N'Diaye 90), Skulason; Trajkovski (Naessens 67), Habibou (Berrier 77).

Astra Giurgiu (1) 1 *(Gaman 26)*
Maccabi Haifa (1) 1 *(Rayo 34)* 1512
Astra Giurgiu: (4231) Lung Jr; Barboianu, Gaman, Muresan, Junior Morais; Laban, Cristescu; Enache, Ivanovski, William Amorim; Fatai.
Maccabi Haifa: (433) Saranov; Meshumar (Pylyavskyi 72), Cocalic, Keinan, Twatha (Scheimann 19); Rayo, Boccoli, Katan; Ezra, Abuhatzira, Turgeman (Ndlovu 61).

Besiktas (0) 2 *(Almeida 51, Ozyakup 54)*
Tromso (0) 0 44,578
Besiktas: (4231) Zengin; Kurtulus, Sivok, Escude, Gulum (Ozyakup 46); Hutchinson, Kavlak; Tore (Demirci 84), Fernandes, Sahan; Almeida (Eneramo 61).
Tromso: (433) Sahlman; Norbye, Causevic (Koppinen 57), Fojut, Kristiansen; Johnsen (Johansen 59), Bendiksen, Helmke (Ondrasek 71); Drage, Moldskred, Andersen.

Braga (0) 0
Pandurii Targu Jiu (1) 2 *(Buleica 15, Ciucur 117)* 11,312
Braga: (433) Eduardo; Baiano, Nuno Andre, Aderlan Santos, Joaozinho; Ruben Micael, Mauro, Luiz Carlos; Alan (Salvador Agra 65), Edinho (Pardo 65), Yazalde (Eder 81).
Pandurii Targu Jiu: (4231) Mingote; Ungurusan, Erico, Christou, Momcilovic; Anton, Breeveld; Nicoara (Ciucur 84), Pereira (Cristea 70), Buleica (Mamele 120); Matulevicius.
aet.

Dila Gori (0) 0
Rapid Vienna (1) 3 *(Schaub 45, Sabitzer 64, Behrendt 90)* 19,012
Dila Gori: (442) Revishvili; Kobakhidze, Khizaneishvili, Tomashvili (Kvakhadze 59), Guruli (Gorelishvili 46); Gongadze, Gvalia, Bolkvadze, Maisuradze (Modebadze 46); Dolidze, Iluridze.
Rapid Vienna: (4231) Novota; Trimmel, Sonnleitner, Dibon, Schrammel; Petsos, Pichler; Schaub (Grozurek 66), Hofmann S (Behrendt 81), Sabitzer; Burgstaller (Palla 75).

Dnipro (1) 2 *(Kobakhidze 39, Zozulya 70)*
Nomme Kalju (0) 0 12,831
Dnipro: (3421) Boyko; Vlad, Mandzyuk, Douglas; Cheberyachko (Lobjanidze 46), Kravchenko, Kulakov, Kobakhidze; Politylo, Shakhov; Seleznyov (Zozulya 53).
Nomme Kalju: (451) Teles; Koogas (Puri 7), Barengrub, Kallaste, Rodrigues; Ceesay, Quintieri (Kirss 85), Soares, Wakui (Toomet 56), Kimbaloula; Voskoboinikov.

Dynamo Kyiv (3) 5 *(Lens 8, Bezus 30, Mbokani 35, Ideye 52 (pen), Gusev 73)*
Aktobe (1) 1 *(Geynrikh 37 (pen))*
Dynamo Kyiv: (4231) Koval; Gusev (Vida 76), Khacheridi, Dragovic, Tremoulinas; Vukojevic, Veloso; Yarmolenko (Dudu Rodrigues 46), Bezus, Lens; Mbokani (Ideye 46).
Aktobe: (532) Sidelnikov; Baltaev, Arzumanyan, Muldarov (Kharabara 58), Primus, Badlo; Geynrikh, Tagybergen, Kapadze (Gridin 72); Khayrullin, Davydov (Lisenkov 58).
Behind closed doors.

Eintracht Frankfurt (1) 2 *(Meier 10, Inui 75)*
Qarabag (0) 1 *(Reynaldo 58)* 48,400
Eintracht Frankfurt: (4231) Trapp; Celozzi, Zambrano, Bamba Anderson, Oczipka; Flum, Schwegler (Russ 63); Aigner, Rode (Rosenthal 63), Inui; Meier (Joselu 70).
Qarabag: (4231) Varvodic; Medvedev, Sadygov, Teli, Agolli; Yusifov (Garayev 68), Almeida; George, Chumbinho, Nadirov (Reynaldo 57); Gelashvili (Kapolongo 79).

Feyenoord (1) 1 *(Pelle 7)*
Kuban Krasnodar (1) 2 *(Popov 18, Bucur 50)* 45,000
Feyenoord: (433) Mulder; Janmaat, De Vrij, Martins Indi, Nelom; Clasie (Vormer 53), Immers, Trindade de Vilhena; Schaken (Manu 59), Pelle, Armenteros (Verhoek 76).
Kuban Krasnodar: (4231) Belenov; Kozlov, Xandao, Dealbert, Bugaev; Tlisov, Kabore; Tsoraev (Sosnin 69), Popov (Fidler 83), Bucur; Ibra (Cisse 90).

Fiorentina (0) 0

Grasshoppers (1) 1 *(Ben Khalifa 41)* 22,227

Fiorentina: (3142) Neto; Tomovic, Rodriguez, Savic; Pizarro; Cuadrado (Ilicic 46), Valero, Fernandez (Bakic 86), Pasqual; Joaquin (Aquilani 62), Gomez.
Grasshoppers: (3142) Burki; Lang, Grichting, Vilotic; Salatic; Gashi (Hajrovic 75), Toko, Abrashi, Pavlovic; Ngamukol (Caio 84), Ben Khalifa (Vonlanthen 84).
Fiorentina won on away goals rule.

Genk (1) 5 *(Vossen 5, Mbodji 52, Limbombe 57, Camus 59, 78)*

FH Hafnarfjordur (1) 2 *(Snorrason 27, Sverrisson 48)*
7285

Genk: (4231) Koteles; Mbodji, Koulibaly, Hamalainen, Simaeys; Hyland, Gorius (Kumordzi 79); Camus, Buffel (Schrijvers 59), Vossen; De Ceulaer (Limbombe 17).
FH Hafnarfjordur: (4231) Oskarsson R; Tillen, Bjarnason, Emilsson (Gudnason 60), Thorisson; Sverrisson, Vidarsson D; Snorrason, Oskarsson I (Palsson 60), Jonsson; Bjornsson (Ingason 70).

Nice (1) 1 *(Cvitanich 4)*

Apollon Limassol (0) 0 12,219

Nice: (4231) Ospina; Genevois, Gomis (Puel 66), Kolodzieczak, Amavi; Digard, Mendy; Pied (Bosetti 76), Eysseric, Bautheac; Cvitanich.
Apollon Limassol: (4231) Bruno Vale; Dananae, Merkis, Karipidis, Vasilou; Hamdani, Gullon; Papoulis (Kyriakou 72 (Haber 90)), Sangoy, Robert (Konstantinou 90); Roberto.

Nordsjaelland (0) 0

IF Elfsborg (0) 1 *(Beckmann 71)* 4629

Nordsjaelland: (433) Hansen; Mtiliga, Jakobsen, Runje, Ticinovic; Petry (Jensen 82), Stokholm, Christiansen; Vingaard (Jradi 82), Nordstrand, Larsen (Lindberg 60).
IF Elfsborg: (433) Stuhr-Ellegaard; Jonsson (Holmen 33), Mobaeck, Klarstrom, Larsson J; Hauger, Svensson, Ishizaki (Jorgensen 79); Hult, Nilsson, Keene (Beckmann 46).

Pasching (0) 1 *(Sobkova 57)*

Estoril (1) 2 *(Leal 21, 52)* 1350

Pasching: (433) Berger; Kerschbaumer, Grasegger, Kablar, Prettenthaler; Krammer (Mossner 59), Perchtold, Hamdemir; Petrovic (Schobesherger 74), Nacho Casanova, Sobkova (Pfennich 77).
Estoril: (4231) Vagner; Mano, Bruno Miguel, Tavares, Ruben Fernandes; Filipe Goncalves, Goncalo Santos (Diogo Amado 46); Balboa, Joao Pedro (Evandro 70), Leal (Lopes 66); Seba.

Petrolul Ploiesti (0) 2 *(Priso 73, Younes 83)*

Swansea C (0) 1 *(Lamah 74)* 12,880

Petrolul Ploiesti: (4231) Bornescu; Alcenat, Alves, Hoban, Guilherme; Mustivar (Romario 66), De Lucas (Teixeira 46); Priso, Younes, Boudjemaa; Dore (Abel Camara 46).
Swansea C: (4411) Tremmel; Rangel, Chico, Amat, Davies; Hernandez (Lamah 67), Britton■, de Guzman (Ki 60), Pozuelo; Michu (Canas 76); Donnelly.

Real Betis (2) 6 *(Ruben Castro 18, Benes 28 (og), Matila 49, Jorge Molina 58, Rodriguez 74, Torres 81)*

Jablonec (0) 0 27,371

Real Betis: (442) Andersen; Chica, Amaya, Jordi, Nacho (Chuli 74); Juanfran, Sevilla, Matilla, Torres; Jorge Molina (Rodriguez 60), Ruben Castro (Cedrick 52).
Jablonec: (442) Spit; Novak, Benes, Vanek, Cizek (Kopic 46); Daniel Rossi, Elias, Loucka, Pitak (Kubista 74); Vosahlik (Tresnak 46), Hubnik.

Rubin Kazan (1) 3 *(Prudnikov 33, Eremenko 50, Azmoun 84)*

Molde (0) 0 7500

Rubin Kazan: (4231) Ryzhikov; Kuzmin, Cesar Navas, Marcano, Mavinga (Kvirkvelia 70); Natcho (Abishov 64), Kulik; Ryazantsev, Eremenko, Torbinsky; Prudnikov (Azmoun 64).
Molde: (4411) Haskjold; Vatshaug, Toivio, Forren (Hovland 65), Rindaroy; Ekpo, Hoseth, Berg Hestad (Berget 56), Chukwa; Agnaldo, Coly (Tripic 56).

Sheriff (0) 2 *(Jhulliam 59, Fernando 67)*

Vojvodina (0) 1 *(Lekovic 90)* 6839

Sheriff: (4231) Tomic; Balima, Metoua, Samardzic, Paye; William, Moyal (Pascenco 75); Ricardinho, Fernando (Bolsacov 90), Isa; Jhulliam (Paireli 90).
Vojvodina: (4231) Delac; Vulicevic, Djuric (Denkovich 71), Trajkovic, Lekovic; Radoja, Poletanovic (Tumbasevic 71); Alivodic, Vranjes, Vukcevic; Skuletic (Kaludjerovic 49).

Skenderbeu (1) 1 *(Ribaj 19)*

Chornomorets (0) 0 7500

Skenderbeu: (442) Shehi; Arapi, Gvozdenovic, Radas, Ademir (Bicaj 84); Lilaj, Orelesi, Shkembi, Muzaka (Nimaga 85); Ribaj, Morina (Abazi 74).
Chornomorets: (433) Bezotosny; Kutas, Fontanello, Berger, Anderson Mineiro; Sito Riera (Leo Matos 36), Gai, Kovalchuk K; Djadjedje (Priyomov 79), Antonov (Didenko 110), Samodin.
aet; Chornomorets won 7-6 on penalties.

Slask Wroclaw (0) 0

Sevilla (2) 5 *(Rakitic 22, Bacca 38, 87, Jairo 71, Perotti 78)*
41,955

Slask Wroclaw: (442) Gikiewicz; Spahic (Wiezik 46), Kokoszka, Pawelec (Gavish 70), Ostrowski; Kazmierczak, Holota, Patejuk (Socha 71), Mila; Sobota, Plaku.
Sevilla: (442) Beto; Cala, Fernando Navarro, Diogo Figueiras, Moreno; Iborra, Rakitic (Cotan 57), Vitolo, Rabello (Perotti 63); Jairo, Bacca.

Slovan Liberec (1) 1 *(Delarge 23)*

Udinese (1) 1 *(Lazzari 42)* 9700

Slovan Liberec: (4231) Kovar; Frydek, Kovac, Kelic, Fleisman; Delarge, Sackey; Pavelka, Sural (Kolar 84), Rybalka (Husek 90); Rabusic (Kalitvintsev 86).
Udinese: (3142) Kelava; Domizzi (Maicosuel 31), Danilo, Heurtaux; Lazzari; Basta, Allan, Pereyra■, Silva; Muriel, Di Natale (Lopez 80).

Spartak Moscow (1) 2 *(Ozbiliz 1, Movsisyan 83)*

St Gallen (3) 4 *(Karanovic 17, 32, Rodriguez 36, Janjatovic 88)* 8134

Spartak Moscow: (433) Pesiakov; Parshivlyuk, Suchy, Makeev, Kombarov; Jurado, Rafael Carioca, Tino Costa (Kallstrom 77); Ozbiliz, Barrios (Yakovlev 55), Majeed (Movsisyan 46).
St Gallen: (4231) Lopar; Mutsch, Montandon, Besle, Lenjani; Nater (Schonenberger 68), Janjatovic; Vitkieviez (Martic 77), Mathys, Rodriguez; Karanovic (Keita 71).

St Etienne (0) 0

Esbjerg (0) 1 *(Bayal Sall 73 (og))* 24,321

St Etienne: (4231) Ruffier; Clerc, Bayal Sall, Perrin, Zouma; Lemoine (Mignot 86), Guilavogui; Hamouma, Cohade (Saint-Maximin 75), Tabanou (Corgnet 78); Brandao.
Esbjerg: (442) Ronnow; Ankersen P, Hansen K, Berthel Askou, Knudsen; Ankersen J, Andreasen, Lekven (Drobo-Ampem 89), Lyng; van Buren (Bergvold 86), Diouf (Rasmussen 70).

Standard Liege (3) 3 *(M'Poku 3, De Camargo 6, Mujangi Bia 35)*

FK Minsk (1) 1 *(Kibuk 8)* 25,684

Standard Liege: (442) Kawashima; Iandoli, Opare, Ben Haim, Arslanagic; De Sart, M'Poku (Bulot 66), Mujangi Bia, Ozturk (Marquet 62); Ghoochannejhad, De Camargo (Cisse 84).
FK Minsk: (442) Bushma; Begunov, Ostroukh, Sachivko, Pushnyakov (Kazeka 71); Gorbushin (Evdokimov 66), Belevich (Rozhok 46), Mayevskiy, Kibuk; Bukatkin, Vasilyuk.

Thun (1) 3 *(Schneuwly C 15, Schneuwly M 48, Zuffi 75)*

Partizan Belgrade (0) 0 8150

Thun: (4231) Faivre; Schirinzi, Sulmoni, Siegfried, Luthi; Sanogo, Hediger; Wittwer (Ferreira 90), Zuffi, Schneuwly C (Martinez 76); Schneuwly M (Sadik 82).
Partizan Belgrade: (442) Stojkovic; Volkov, Stankovic, Obradovic, Aksentijevic■; Jojic, Ilic (Zivkovic 64), Markovic, Malbasic (Brasanac 82); Ninkovic, Mitrovic (Grbic 67).

Tottenham H (2) 3 *(Defoe 40, 45, Holtby 69)*
Dinamo Tbilisi (0) 0   26,189
Tottenham H: (451) Friedel; Walker (Fryers 56), Kaboul, Vertonghen, Naughton; Townsend (Kane 46), Carroll, Sandro, Sigurdsson, Holtby (Dembele 76); Defoe.
Dinamo Tbilisi: (4312) Loria; Khurtsilava, Gvelesiani, Kvaratskhelia, Kvirkvelia (Glisic 34); Grigalashvili (Seturidze 86), Dzaria, Khmaladze; Merebashvilli (Khocholava 79); Vouho, Goga.

Trabzonspor (1) 3 *(Paulo Henrique 14, 64, Malouda 54)*
Kukesi (1) 1 *(Popovic 11)*   23,500
Trabzonspor: (433) Kivrak; Yavru, Demir, Kacar, Adin; Akgun, Zokora, Mierzejewski (Alanzinho 77); Erdogan (Karadeniz 60), Paulo Henrique, Malouda (Ozdemir 87).
Kukesi: (433) Halili; Smajlaj, Brahja, Malota, Hallici; Karabeci, Musolli, Allmuca (Cikalleshi 68); Hoxha (Manuka 60), Popovic, Progni.

VfB Stuttgart (1) 2 *(Gentner 34, Traore 75)*
Rijeka (1) 2 *(Benko 29, Mujanovic 90)*   30,200
VfB Stuttgart: (4231) Ulreich; Schwaab, Rudiger, Rocker, Boka; Kvist Jorgensen, Gentner; Harnik (Werner 55), Cacau (Abdellaoue 73), Traore; Ibisevic.
Rijeka: (4231) Vargic; Tomecak, Leskovic, Maric, Skarabot; Males, Pokrivac; Kvrzic (Krstanovic 90), Alispahic (Mocinic 68), Sharbini (Mujanovic 70); Benko.

VMFD Zalgiris (0) 0
Red Bull Salzburg (0) 2 *(Kampl 60, Meilinger 74)*   5400
VMFD Zalgiris: (4231) Vitkauskas; Vaitkunas, Skerla, Jankauskas, Freidgeimas (Leliuga 68); Zulpa (Nyuiadzi 74), Janusauskas; Komolov, Kuklys, Svrljuga; Bilinski (Silenas 84).
Red Bull Salzburg: (343) Gulacsi; Rodnei, Ulmer, Andre Ramalho; Ilsanker, Klein, Kampl (Berisha 66), Meilinger; Mane (Reyna 74), Jonathan (Hierlander 89), Nielsen.

Friday, 30 August 2013
AZ Alkmaar (0) 0
Atromitos (0) 2 *(Papadopoulos 53, Karagounis 74)*   11,569
AZ Alkmaar: (433) Alvarado; Johansson, Gouweleeuw, Wuytens, Viergever; Gudelj, Henriksen■, Elm; Johannsson (Berghuis 53), Beerens, Gudmundsson.
Atromitos: (4231) Cennamo; Fitanidis, Tavlaridis (Brito 84), Lazaridis, Papoutsogiannopoulos (Giannoulis 46); Iglesias, Dimoutsos (Pitu 60); Karagounis, Papadopoulos, Umbides; Napoleoni.
AZ Alkmaar won on away goals rule. The match on 29.8.13 was abandoned due to fire and resumed on 30.8.2013 from the point of abandonment.

GROUP STAGE

GROUP A

Thursday, 19 September 2013
St Gallen (0) 2 *(Karanovic 56, Mathys 77)*
Kuban Krasnodar (0) 0   12,551
St Gallen: (442) Lopar; Montandon, Besle, Mutsch, Martic; Mathys, Lenjani, Janjatovic, Rodriguez (Nushi 73); Karanovic (Keita 86), Vitkieviez (Wuthrich 83).
Kuban Krasnodar: (442) Belenov; Xandao, Dealbert, Kozlov, Bugaev; Tsoraev (Melgarejo 69), Kabore■, Rabiu (Tlisov 20), Popov (Ibra 63); Cisse, Bucur.

Valencia (0) 0
Swansea C (1) 3 *(Bony 14, Michu 58, de Guzman 62)*
                                                     32,305
Valencia: (442) Guaita; Barragan, Rami■, Feghouli (Pabon 59), Mathieu; Ever, Javi Fuego, Guardado, Canales (Bernat 66); Cartabia (Ricardo Costa 14), Postiga.
Swansea C: (4411) Vorm; Rangel (Davies 55), Amat, Chico, Tiendalli; de Guzman, Canas, Pozuelo, Dyer (Lamah 65); Michu (Shelvey 76); Bony.

Thursday, 3 October 2013
Kuban Krasnodar (0) 0
Valencia (0) 2 *(Alcacer 73, Feghouli 81)*   29,300
Kuban Krasnodar: (4411) Belenov; Kozlov, Xandao, Dealbert, Melgarejo; Khubulov (Tsoraev 59), Fidler, Tlisov, Bueno (Bucur 68); Popov; Cisse (Ibra 80).
Valencia: (442) Guaita; Barragan, Ricardo Costa, Victor Ruiz, Guardado; Feghouli, Parejo (Romeu 76), Javi Fuego, Bernat; Canales (Cartabia 59), Piatti (Alcacer 66).

Swansea C (0) 1 *(Routledge 52)*
St Gallen (0) 0   15,397
Swansea C: (4141) Tremmel; Tiendalli, Chico, Amat, Davies; Britton; Pozuelo (Shelvey 83), de Guzman, Michu, Routledge (Dyer 61); Bony (Vazquez 70).
St Gallen: (4231) Lopar; Martic, Montandon (Russo 73), Besle, Lenjani; Mutsch, Janjatovic; Vitkieviez, Mathys, Rodriguez (Nater 62); Karanovic (Keita 46).

Thursday, 24 October 2013
Swansea C (0) 1 *(Michu 68)*
Kuban Krasnodar (1) 1 *(Cisse 90 (pen))*   14,964
Swansea C: (442) Tremmel; Tiendalli (Rangel 59), Chico, Amat, Taylor; Dyer (Lamah 77), Canas, Shelvey, Pozuelo; Michu, Bony (Vazquez 59).
Kuban Krasnodar: (442) Belenov; Kozlov, Xandao, Armas, Zhavnerchik; Khubulov (Ignatiev 70), Kabore, Fidler, Melgarejo (Bucur 63); Popov (Ibra 76); Cisse.

Valencia (4) 5 *(Alcacer 12, Cartabia 21, 30, Ricardo Costa 33, Canales 71)*
St Gallen (0) 1 *(Nater 74)*   26,645
Valencia: (4231) Guaita; Joao Pereira (Michel 56), Ricardo Costa, Victor Ruiz, Bernat; Parejo, Romeu; Cartabia (Pabon 64), Canales, Piatti; Alcacer (Postiga 76).
St Gallen: (4231) Lopar; Mutsch, Montandon, Besle, Lenjani; Janjatovic (Demiri 46), Nater; Vitkieviez (Wuthrich 64), Mathys, Rodriguez (Nushi 56); Karanovic.

Thursday, 7 November 2013
Kuban Krasnodar (0) 1 *(Ibra 90)*
Swansea C (1) 1 *(Bony 9)*   27,843
Kuban Krasnodar: (433) Belenov; Bugaev, Xandao■, Dealbert, Kozlov; Melgarejo (Ibra 73), Kabore, Tlisov (Fidler 78); Popov, Cisse, Khubulov (Ignatiev 66).
Swansea C: (4231) Vorm; Tiendalli, Amat, Williams, Davies; de Guzman, Canas; Dyer (Rangel 62), Pozuelo, Lamah (Routledge 61); Bony (Vazquez 71).

St Gallen (1) 2 *(Besle 38, Karanovic 65)*
Valencia (1) 3 *(Piatti 30, 75, Canales 85)*   16,951
St Gallen: (4411) Lopar; Martic, Montandon■, Besle, Lenjani; Vitkieviez (Wuthrich 72), Nater, Mutsch, Rodriguez (Stocklasa 59); Mathys; Karanovic (Keita 77).
Valencia: (4231) Guaita; Barragan, Ricardo Costa, Victor Ruiz, Bernat; Cartabia (Piatti 24), Romeu; Michel (Parejo 62), Canales, Jonas (Alcacer 68); Postiga.

Thursday, 28 November 2013
Kuban Krasnodar (1) 4 *(Melgarejo 3, 72, Ignatiev 55, Kabore 90)*
St Gallen (0) 0   19,032
Kuban Krasnodar: (4141) Belenov; Melgarejo (Bueno 79), Armas, Dealbert, Kozlov; Popov (Ibra 76); Ignatiev (Khubulov 62), Sosnin, Kabore, Zhavnerchik; Cisse.
St Gallen: (4231) Lopar; Mutsch, Besle (Russo 46), Stocklasa, Lenjani; Nater, Demiri; Vitkieviez (Wuthrich 73), Mathys (Keita 60), Rodriguez; Karanovic.

Swansea C (0) 0
Valencia (1) 1 *(Parejo 21)*   17,896
Swansea C: (4411) Tremmel; Rangel, Chico, Amat, Taylor; Dyer (Hernandez 66), Britton, Shelvey, Lamah (de Guzman 46); Pozuelo; Bony (Vazquez 42).
Valencia: (442) Diego Alves; Joao Pereira, Victor Ruiz, Mathieu, Guardado; Feghouli (Piatti 68), Parejo, Romeu, Bernat; Jonas (Postiga 76), Canales (Javi Fuego 84).

Thursday, 12 December 2013
St Gallen (0) 1 *(Mathys 80)*
Swansea C (0) 0 15,298
St Gallen: (442) Herzog; Mutsch, Besle, Russo, Lenjani; Wuthrich, Janjatovic, Demiri, Rodriguez (Nushi 59); Mathys (Franin 88), Karanovic (Keita 13).
Swansea C: (4231) Tremmel; Tiendalli, Chico (Canas 62), Amat, Taylor; Shelvey, de Guzman; Pozuelo, Routledge (Williams 64), Lamah; Bony (Hernandez 77).

Valencia (0) 1 *(Alcacer 67)*
Kuban Krasnodar (0) 1 *(Melgarejo 85)* 14,581
Valencia: (442) Diego Alves; Victor Ruiz■, Joao Pereira, Ricardo Costa, Ever; Javi Fuego, Michel, Cartabia (Piatti 75), Gaya; Postiga (Alcacer 66), Pabon (Feghouli 81).
Kuban Krasnodar: (451) Belenov; Armas, Dealbert, Kozlov, Melgarejo; Bugaev (Lobkarev 79), Kabore, Ignatiev, Sosnin, Khubulov (Bueno 28); Ibra (Cisse 46).

Group A Table	P	W	D	L	F	A	GD	Pts
Valencia	6	4	1	1	12	7	5	13
Swansea C	6	2	2	2	6	4	2	8
Kuban Krasnodar	6	1	3	2	7	7	0	6
St Gallen	6	2	0	4	6	13	-7	6

GROUP B

Thursday, 19 September 2013
Dinamo Zagreb (1) 1 *(Fernandes 43)*
Chornomorets (0) 2 *(Antonov 62, Djadjedje 65)* 12,522
Dinamo Zagreb: (442) Zelenika; Ivo Pinto, Simunic, Simunovic, Ruben Lima; Brozovic (Beqiraj 74), Ademi, Pamic (Husejinovic 62), Sammir; Cop (Halilovic 86), Fernandes.
Chornomorets: (4411) Bezotosny; Kutas, Berger, Fontanello, Anderson Mineiro; Leo Matos (Sito Riera 46), Kovalchuk K, Gai, Djadjedje (Bobko 69); Priyomov; Antonov (Samodin 85).

PSV Eindhoven (0) 0
Ludogorets (0) 2 *(Bezjak 60, Misidjan 75)* 11,000
PSV Eindhoven: (433) Zoet; Bruma, Arias, Willems (Jorgensen 44), Hendrix; Maher, Hiljemark (Schaars 76), Toivonen; Matavz, Bakkali (Park 61), Depay.
Ludogorets: (433) Stoyanov V; Mantyla, Barthe, Choco, Junior Caicara; Fabio Espinho, Dani Abalo (Aleksandrov 75), Dyakov; Marcelinho, Bezjak (Zlatinski 80), Misidjan (Stoyanov I 89).

Thursday, 3 October 2013
Chornomorets (0) 0
PSV Eindhoven (1) 2 *(Depay 13, Jozefzoon 89)* 33,839
Chornomorets: (4231) Bezotosny; Djadjedje, Berger, Fontanello, Anderson Mineiro; Bobko, Kovalchuk K; Sito Riera (Priyomov 82), Gai (Samodin 84), Bakaj (Leo Matos 56); Antonov.
PSV Eindhoven: (433) Tyton; Arias, Bruma, Hendrix, Willems; Toivonen, Schaars, Maher (Hiljemark 81); Bakkali (Jozefzoon 74), Locadia, Depay.

Ludogorets (2) 3 *(Quixada 11, Misidjan 34, Dyakov 61)*
Dinamo Zagreb (0) 0 6900
Ludogorets: (4231) Stoyanov V; Choco, Moti, Barthe, Junior Caicara; Dyakov, Fabio Espinho; Aleksandrov, Marcelinho (Zlatinski 63), Misidjan (Dani Abalo 89); Quixada (Bezjak 71).
Dinamo Zagreb: (4231) Zelenika; Ivo Pinto, Simunic, Simunovic, Pivaric; Ademi, Sare (Cop 39); Brozovic (Pamic 88), Sammir (Halilovic 67), Fernandes; Soudani.

Thursday, 24 October 2013
Chornomorets (0) 0
Ludogorets (1) 1 *(Zlatinski 45)* 20,084
Chornomorets: (4231) Bezotosny; Kutas, Berger, Fontanello, Anderson Mineiro; Kovalchuk K, Bobko; Priyomov (Leo Matos 81), Gai (Djadjedje 47), Sito Riera; Antonov (Didenko 47).
Ludogorets: (4231) Stoyanov V; Junior Caicara, Moti, Barthe, Minev; Zlatinski, Dyakov; Stoyanov I (Dani Abalo 63), Marcelinho (Michel Platini 78), Misidjan; Quixada (Fabio Espinho 69).

Dinamo Zagreb (0) 0
PSV Eindhoven (0) 0
Dinamo Zagreb: (4231) Zelenika; Ivo Pinto, Addy (Simunovic 81), Simunic, Pivaric; Antolic (Ruben Lima 86), Ademi; Soudani, Brozovic, Fernandes; Sammir (Cop 53).
PSV Eindhoven: (4231) Tyton; Arias, Bruma, Hendrix, Willems (Tamata 58); Maher (Hiljemark 86), Schaars; Jozefzoon, Toivonen, Depay; Locadia (Matavz 75).
Behind closed doors.

Thursday, 7 November 2013
Ludogorets (0) 1 *(Quixada 47)*
Chornomorets (0) 1 *(Gai 65)* 6113
Ludogorets: (442) Stoyanov V; Barthe, Minev, Moti, Junior Caicara; Aleksandrov (Stoyanov I 57), Fabio Espinho, Zlatinski, Marcelinho (Bezjak 86); Quixada (Burgzorg 79), Misidjan.
Chornomorets: (433) Bezotosny; Berger, Fontanello, Anderson Mineiro (Leo Matos 59), Kutas; Kovalchuk K, Gai, Bobko; Sito Riera, Djadjedje, Antonov (Didenko 87).

PSV Eindhoven (1) 2 *(Maher 29, Toivonen 57)*
Dinamo Zagreb (0) 0 10,500
PSV Eindhoven: (433) Tyton; Arias, Bruma, Hendrix (Jorgensen 69), Willems; Maher, Schaars (Hiljemark 80), Toivonen; Narsingh (Jozefzoon 76), Locadia, Depay.
Dinamo Zagreb: (433) Zelenika; Ivo Pinto, Addy, Simunic, Pivaric; Brozovic, Antolic, Ruben Lima (Rukavina 46); Soudani (Cop 63), Sammir (Halilovic 78), Fernandes.

Thursday, 28 November 2013
Chornomorets (0) 2 *(Antonov 78, Didenko 90)*
Dinamo Zagreb (1) 1 *(Beqiraj 20)* 14,182
Chornomorets: (451) Bezotosny; Zubeyko, Berger, Fontanello, Kutas (Priyomov 27); Kovalchuk K, Bobko, Sito Riera (Leo Matos 46), Gai, Djadjedje (Didenko 74); Antonov.
Dinamo Zagreb: (442) Zelenika; Ivo Pinto (Ademi 46), Simunovic, Addy, Ruben Lima; Pamic (Brozovic 76), Leko, Antolic, Halilovic (Fernandes 64); Rukavina, Beqiraj.

Ludogorets (1) 2 *(Bezjak 38, 79)*
PSV Eindhoven (0) 0 3012
Ludogorets: (4231) Stoyanov V; Junior Caicara, Barthe, Moti, Minev; Zlatinski, Dyakov (Fabio Espinho 89); Aleksandrov, Marcelinho, Misidjan (Stoyanov I 90); Bezjak (Quixada 82).
PSV Eindhoven: (433) Zoet; Arias, Bruma■, Rekik, Hendrix; Schaars, Toivonen, Maher; Narsingh (Jorgensen 63), Locadia (Jozefzoon 75), Depay (Bakkali 81).

Thursday, 12 December 2013
Dinamo Zagreb (1) 1 *(Cop 45)*
Ludogorets (1) 2 *(Dani Abalo 27, Bezjak 72)* 3120
Dinamo Zagreb: (451) Sandomierski; Ivo Pinto, Simunic, Calusic, Ruben Lima; Soudani (Beqiraj 80), Brozovic, Ademi, Pamic (Halilovic 73), Fernandes; Cop.
Ludogorets: (4231) Cvorovich; Choco, Moti, Terziev, Junior Caicara; Dyakov, Zlatinski; Dani Abalo (Stoyanov I 90), Marcelinho (Fabio Espinho 80), Aleksandrov; Bezjak (Quixada 89).

PSV Eindhoven (0) 0
Chornomorets (0) 1 *(Djadjedje 59)* 13,500
PSV Eindhoven: (433) Zoet; Arias, Rekik, Jorgensen, Willems (Park 66); Maher, Hendrix, Hiljemark (Toivonen 75); Narsingh (Bakkali 80), Locadia, Depay.
Chornomorets: (433) Bezotosny; Zubeyko, Kovalchuk P, Fontanello, Anderson Mineiro; Kovalchuk K, Gai (Didenko 79), Bobko; Sito Riera■, Antonov (Kutas 90), Djadjedje (Leo Matos 81).

Group B Table	P	W	D	L	F	A	GD	Pts
Ludogorets	6	5	1	0	11	2	9	16
Chornomorets	6	3	1	2	6	0	6	10
PSV Eindhoven	6	2	1	3	4	5	-1	7
Dinamo Zagreb	6	0	1	5	3	11	-8	1

GROUP C

Thursday, 19 September 2013

Red Bull Salzburg (2) 4 *(Alan 36, Jonathan 45 (pen), 69, 79)*

IF Elfsborg (0) 0 7879

Red Bull Salzburg: (442) Gulacsi; Schwegler, Ulmer, Rodnei (Hinteregger 64), Andre Ramalho; Ilsanker, Hierlander, Kampl (Berisha 72), Mane; Jonathan (Nielsen 81), Alan.
IF Elfsborg: (442) Stuhr-Ellegaard; Jonsson, Holmen, Klarstrom, Jorgensen (Rohden 45); Larsson J, Beckmann, Svensson, Hult (Bangura 72); Ishizaki, Nilsson (Keene 77).

Standard Liege (0) 1 *(Mujangi Bia 73)*

Esbjerg (0) 2 *(van Buren 63, Bakenga 90)* 11,871

Standard Liege: (442) Kawashima; Opare, Ben Haim, Arslanagic, Van Damme; Bulot, De Sart, M'Poku, Ozturk (Vainqueur 62); Ghoochannejhad (Mujangi Bia 71), De Camargo (Batshuayi 26).
Esbjerg: (442) Ronnow; Hansen K, Berthel Askou, Ankersen P, Knudsen; Diouf (Bakenga 59), Lekven (Bergvold 85), Ankersen J, Andreasen; van Buren (Rasmussen 84), Lyng.

Esbjerg (0) 1 *(Diouf 89)*

Red Bull Salzburg (2) 2 *(Alan 6, 38)* 11,298

Esbjerg: (433) Ronnow; Hansen, Ankersen P, Berthel Askou, Knudsen; Lekven (Bergvold 83), Ankersen J, Andreasen; van Buren (Rasmussen 58), Bakenga, Lyng (Diouf 55).
Red Bull Salzburg: (442) Gulacsi; Schwegler, Rodnei, Ulmer, Andre Ramalho; Hinteregger, Berisha (Hierlander 86), Kampl, Mane (Ilsanker 62); Jonathan, Alan (Leitgeb 71).

Thursday, 3 October 2013

IF Elfsborg (1) 1 *(Claesson 23)*

Standard Liege (0) 1 *(Mujangi Bia 62)* 3778

IF Elfsborg: (4141) Stuhr-Ellegaard; Larsson J, Jonsson, Holmen, Klarstrom; Svensson; Ishizaki, Rohden, Claesson (Jorgensen 70), Nilsson (Hedlund 86); Beckmann (Bangura 75).
Standard Liege: (442) Kawashima; Stam, Arslanagic, Kanu, Van Damme; Mujangi Bia, Ozturk, Buyens (Vainqueur 46), Carcela-Gonzalez (M'Poku 63); Batshuayi (Ghoochannejhad 79), Ezekiel.

Thursday, 24 October 2013

IF Elfsborg (0) 1 *(Jonsson 69)*

Esbjerg (1) 2 *(Andreasen 6, 66)* 3142

IF Elfsborg: (4141) Stuhr-Ellegaard; Larsson J, Jonsson, Holmen, Klarstrom (Keene 74); Svensson; Ishizaki, Claesson, Rohden (Bangura 64), Hult; Nilsson.
Esbjerg: (442) Ronnow; Ankersen P, Hansen, Berthel Askou, Knudsen; Ankersen J, Lekven (Bergvold 49), Andreasen, Lyng; Bakenga (Diouf 89), van Buren (Rasmussen 78).

Red Bull Salzburg (0) 2 *(Jonathan 53, Andre Ramalho 85)*

Standard Liege (0) 1 *(Mujangi Bia 88 (pen))* 14,856

Red Bull Salzburg: (442) Gulacsi; Schwegler, Andre Ramalho, Hinteregger, Ulmer; Kampl, Ilsanker, Leitgeb (Schiemer 82), Mane■; Alan (Nielsen 87), Jonathan (Berisha 61).
Standard Liege: (442) Kawashima; Opare, Kanu■, Ciman, Van Damme; Bulot, Buyens, Vainqueur (Mujangi Bia 76), Carcela-Gonzalez■; M'Poku (Batshuayi 59), Ezekiel (Ben Haim 70).

Thursday, 7 November 2013

Esbjerg (0) 1 *(Rohden 71 (og))*

IF Elfsborg (0) 0 10,049

Esbjerg: (4411) Ronnow; Ankersen P, Hansen K, Drobo-Ampem, Knudsen; Ankersen J, Bergvold (Berthel Askou 88), Andersen, Lyng; Andreasen (van Buren 50); Bakenga (Diouf 62).
IF Elfsborg: (4231) Stuhr-Ellegaard; Larsson J, Jonsson, Mobaeck, Klarstrom; Svensson, Lundqvist (Hedlund 65); Rohden (Jorgensen 77), Claesson, Nilsson (Ishizaki 46); Beckmann.

Standard Liege (0) 1 *(M'Poku 55)*

Red Bull Salzburg (2) 3 *(Svento 42, Kampl 45, Alan 58)* 12,005

Standard Liege: (442) Thuram-Ulien; Stam, Ben Haim, Ciman, Opare; M'Poku (Mujangi Bia 65), Buyens (Cisse 75), Vainqueur, Bulot (Ghoochannejhad 80); Batshuayi, Ezekiel.
Red Bull Salzburg: (442) Gulacsi; Schwegler, Andre Ramalho, Hinteregger, Ulmer; Kampl, Ilsanker, Leitgeb, Svento (Teigl 65); Berisha (Meilinger 59), Alan (Schiemer 88).

Esbjerg (1) 2 *(van Buren 18, 79)*

Standard Liege (0) 1 *(De Camargo 53)* 9184

Esbjerg: (442) Ronnow; Ankersen P, Drobo-Ampem, Berthel Askou, Knudsen; Andreasen (Hansen K 76), Lucena (Diouf 84), van Buren, Bakenga; Lyng (Nielsen 46), Hojbjerg.
Standard Liege: (442) Thuram-Ulien; Iandoli, Ciman (Vainqueur 56), Arslanagic, Ben Haim; Carcela-Gonzalez (Biton 85), Cisse, M'Poku, Ozturk; De Camargo, Ghoochannejhad (Batshuayi 67).

Thursday, 28 November 2013

IF Elfsborg (0) 0

Red Bull Salzburg (1) 1 *(Meilinger 39)* 2456

IF Elfsborg: (4411) Stuhr-Ellegaard (Hassan 46); Larsson S (Hedlund 51), Jonsson, Larsson J, Svensson; Mobaeck, Hauger, Hult, Ishizaki; Rohden (Claesson 78); Keene.
Red Bull Salzburg: (442) Gulacsi; Schwegler, Schiemer, Ulmer, Hinteregger; Klein, Ilsanker, Meilinger (Teigl 70), Berisha (Reyna 90); Mane (Alan 81), Nielsen.

Thursday, 12 December 2013

Red Bull Salzburg (1) 3 *(Mane 20, 63, Kampl 58)*

Esbjerg (0) 0 6890

Red Bull Salzburg: (442) Gulacsi; Klein, Schiemer, Hinteregger, Ulmer; Andre Ramalho, Leitgeb, Kampl (Meilinger 69), Berisha (Nielsen 71); Mane (Reyna 78), Alan.
Esbjerg: (4141) Ronnow; Laursen, Berthel Askou, Drobo-Ampem, Knudsen; Hansen K (Andreasen J 72 (Maigaard 83)); Andreasen, Lucena (Nielsen 46), Andersen, van Buren; Hojbjerg.

Standard Liege (1) 1 *(Mbombo 31)*

IF Elfsborg (1) 3 *(Nilsson 41, 46, Beckmann 52)* 6466

Standard Liege: (442) Thuram-Ulien; Stam, Ciman (Arslanagic 54), Ben Haim, Iandoli; Buyens, Cisse, Marquet (Biton 64), Bulot (Milosevic 76); De Camargo, Mbombo.
IF Elfsborg: (433) Stuhr-Ellegaard; Larsson J, Holmen, Lans, Klarstrom; Rohden, Claesson (Mobaeck 90), Svensson; Hedlund, Beckmann (Bangura 62), Nilsson (Lundqvist 78).

Group C Table	P	W	D	L	F	A	GD	Pts
Red Bull Salzburg	6	6	0	0	15	3	12	18
Esbjerg	6	4	0	2	8	8	0	12
IF Elfsborg	6	1	1	4	5	10	−5	4
Standard Liege	6	0	1	5	6	13	−7	1

GROUP D

Thursday, 19 September 2013

Maribor (1) 2 *(Milec 35, Fajic 74)*

Rubin Kazan (2) 5 *(Karadeniz 23, Marcano 27, Eremenko 69, Rondon 90, Ryazantsev 90)* 7500

Maribor: (4231) Handanovic; Milec, Rajcevic, Arghus (Trajkovski 43), Mejac; Mertelj, Filipovic; Bohar, Tavares, Cvijanovic (Crnic 76); Mendy (Fajic 64).
Rubin Kazan: (4231) Ryzhikov; Kuzmin, Cesar Navas, Marcano, Mavinga; Natcho, M'Vila; Wakaso (Eremenko 63), Ryazantsev, Karadeniz; Rondon.

Zulte Waregem (0) 0

Wigan Ath (0) 0 7041

Zulte Waregem: (442) Bossut; De Fauw, Conte, Malanda, Duplus; D'Haene, Hazard, Kums, Skulason; Habibou (Caceres 72), Naessens.
Wigan Ath: (433) Carson; Shotton, Boyce, Perch, Crainey; McArthur, McCann, McManaman (Fortune 66); Gomez (Watson 66), McClean, Powell (Dicko 83).

Thursday, 3 October 2013
Rubin Kazan (0) 4 *(Duplus 60 (og), Karadeniz 74,*
Ryazantsev 81, Natcho 89)
Zulte Waregem (0) 0   4057
Rubin Kazan: (4231) Ryzhikov; Kuzmin, Cesar Navas,
Marcano, Abishov (Mavinga 76); Ryazantsev, M'Vila;
Natcho, Karadeniz (Torbinsky 77), Eremenko;
Mukhametshin (Prudnikov 62).
Zulte Waregem: (4231) Bossut; De Fauw, D'Haene,
Malanda, Duplus; Conte (Sylla 71), Kums; Skulason,
Naessens, Hazard (N'Diaye 84); Habibou (Caceres 71).

Wigan Ath (2) 3 *(Powell 22, 90, Watson 33)*
Maribor (0) 1 *(Tavares 60)*   12,753
Wigan Ath: (4411) Carson; Boyce, Shotton, Barnett,
Perch; McManaman (McClean 67), Watson (McCann
77), McArthur, Beausejour; Gomez; Powell (Dicko 90).
Maribor: (4231) Handanovic; Milec, Rajcevic, Arghus,
Mejac (Viler 83); Filipovic, Mertelj; Bohar (Fajic 83),
Tavares, Cvijanovic (Mezga 76); Mendy.

Thursday, 24 October 2013
Wigan Ath (1) 1 *(Powell 39)*
Rubin Kazan (1) 1 *(Prudnikov 15)*   14,723
Wigan Ath: (4231) Carson; Boyce, Shotton, Barnett,
Crainey; Watson, McCann; Gomez (McManaman 76),
Powell, Beausejour (McClean 68); Holt (Fortune 63).
Rubin Kazan: (4231) Ryzhikov; Kuzmin, Sharonov
(Cesar Navas 67), Marcano, Mavinga; Kisliak, M'Vila;
Torbinsky (Wakaso 58), Ryazantsev, Eremenko;
Prudnikov (Karadeniz 74).

Zulte Waregem (1) 1 *(De Fauw 13)*
Maribor (2) 3 *(Crnic 21, Mertelj 34, Mezga 49)*   5023
Zulte Waregem: (4231) Bossut; De Fauw, D'Haene,
Colpaert, Duplus (Sylla 46); Kums, Malanda; Naessens,
Hazard (Caceres 46), Conte (N'Diaye 71); Habibou.
Maribor: (442) Handanovic; Milec**■**, Rajcevic, Arghus,
Viler; Crnic (Cvijanovic 59), Mertelj, Filipovic, Mezga
(Moravac 85); Mendy, Tavares (Dervisevic 89).

Thursday, 7 November 2013
Maribor (0) 0
Zulte Waregem (1) 1 *(Hazard 30 (pen))*   8500
Maribor: (442) Handanovic; Rajcevic, Crnic, Arghus,
Viler; Filipovic, Mezga (Moravac 79), Cvijanovic (Bohar
55), Mertelj (Dervisevic 74); Tavares, Fajic.
Zulte Waregem: (532) Bossut; De Fauw, Colpaert,
Godeau, D'Haene, Conte; Malanda, Kums (N'Diaye 85),
Hazard; Habibou, Caceres.

Rubin Kazan (1) 1 *(Kuzmin 22)*
Wigan Ath (0) 0   5579
Rubin Kazan: (4231) Ryzhikov; Kuzmin, Sharonov,
Cesar Navas, Mavinga (Kisliak 46); M'Vila, Natcho;
Eremenko, Torbinsky (Wakaso 76), Ryazantsev;
Mukhametshin (Prudnikov 84).
Wigan Ath: (433) Nicholls; Shotton, Rogne, Barnett,
Crainey; McArthur, Perch (Powell 60), Espinoza;
McManaman (Gomez 74), Holt (Fortune 71), McClean.

Thursday, 28 November 2013
Rubin Kazan (1) 1 *(Natcho 43)*
Maribor (0) 1 *(Mezga 87)*   2754
Rubin Kazan: (3331) Ryzhikov; Sharonov, Marcano,
Mavinga; Natcho, Kisliak, Torbinsky; Kulik, Ryazantsev
(Rondon 62), Eremenko (M'Vila 75); Prudnikov
(Mukhametshin 61).
Maribor: (451) Handanovic; Milec, Rajcevic, Arghus,
Viler; Mertelj (Cvijanovic 77), Filipovic, Mezga,
Dervisevic (Crnic 65), Bohar (Zahovic 84); Fajic.

Wigan Ath (1) 1 *(Barnett 7)*
Zulte Waregem (1) 2 *(Hazard 37, Malanda 88)*   15,543
Wigan Ath: (451) Nicholls; Boyce, Rogne, Barnett,
Crainey; McManaman (Espinoza 84), McArthur (Holt
90), Gomez (Fortune 64), McCann, McClean; Powell.
Zulte Waregem: (4231) Bossut; De Fauw, D'Haene,
Colpaert, Duplus; Skulason (N'Diaye 80), Malanda,
Conte (Sylla 73), Kums (Caceres 90), Hazard; Habibou.

Thursday, 12 December 2013
Maribor (1) 2 *(Mezga 43, Filipovic 59)*
Wigan Ath (1) 1 *(Gomez 41 (pen))*   9035
Maribor: (424) Handanovic; Milec, Rajcevic, Arghus,
Viler; Filipovic, Mertelj**■**; Mezga (Crnic 81), Fajic (Mendy
85), Tavares (Cvijanovic 77), Bohar.
Wigan Ath: (4231) Carson; Perch, Rogne, Barnett,
Beausejour; McArthur (Boyce 75), McCann**■**;
McManaman (Watson 46), Gomez, Espinoza; Powell
(Fortune 65).

Zulte Waregem (0) 0
Rubin Kazan (0) 2 *(Natcho 79 (pen), Rondon 86)*   6083
Zulte Waregem: (4411) Bossut; De Fauw, D'Haene,
Colpaert, Duplus (Naessens 81); Conte (Caceres 81),
Malanda, Skulason, Hazard; Kums; Sylla.
Rubin Kazan: (3331) Arlauskis; Sharonov, Cesar Navas,
Marcano; Kuzmin, Abishov (Rondon 46), Mavinga
(Dzhalilov 86); M'Vila, Natcho, Kulik (Kisliak 66);
Mukhametshin.

Group D Table	P	W	D	L	F	A	GD	Pts
Rubin Kazan	6	4	2	0	14	4	10	14
Maribor	6	2	1	3	9	12	–3	7
Zulte Waregem	6	2	1	3	4	10	–6	7
Wigan Ath	6	1	2	3	6	7	–1	5

GROUP E
Thursday, 19 September 2013
Fiorentina (1) 3 *(Rodriguez 30, Ryder 67, Rossi 76)*
Pacos Ferreira (0) 0   7577
Fiorentina: (4312) Neto; Tomovic, Rodriguez, Compper,
Alonso; Ambrosini (Aquilani 58), Pizarro, Fernandez;
Valero; Joaquin (Ryder 66), Rossi (Bakic 77).
Pacos Ferreira: (442) Degra; Tony (Rodrigo Antonio 69),
Filipe Anunciacao, Ricardo, Nuno Santos; Hurtado,
Andre Leao, Seri (Romeu 70), Ruben Ribeiro (Rui
Miguel 75); Bebe, Irobiso.

Pandurii Targu Jiu (0) 0
Dnipro (1) 1 *(Rotan 38)*   8000
Pandurii Targu Jiu: (442) Stanca; Momcilovic, Christou,
Ungurusan (Paulinho 76), Erico; Buleica, Anton, Pereira,
Breeveld (Distefano 64); Adrovic, Nicoara (Ciucur 55).
Dnipro: (442) Boyko; Vlad, Mazuch, Cheberyachko,
Fedetskiy; Kankava, Bruno Gama (Seleznyov 46), Rotan,
Zozulya (Kulakov 89); Matheus, Konoplyanka (Shakhov
84).

Thursday, 3 October 2013
Dnipro (0) 1 *(Seleznyov 57 (pen))*
Fiorentina (0) 2 *(Rodriguez 53 (pen), Ambrosini 73)*
                                                     25,837
Dnipro: (442) Boyko; Mandzyuk (Bruno Gama 78),
Mazuch, Cheberyachko, Strinic; Fedetskiy (Matheus 58),
Rotan, Kankava, Konoplyanka; Seleznyov, Zozulya.
Fiorentina: (352) Neto; Roncaglia, Rodriguez, Compper;
Cuadrado (Joaquin 76), Bakic (Valero 54), Pizarro**■**,
Ambrosini, Alonso; Ryder, Fernandez (Tomovic 85).

Pacos Ferreira (0) 1 *(Rui Miguel 49)*
Pandurii Targu Jiu (1) 1 *(Momcilovic 5)*   1314
Pacos Ferreira: (442) Antonio Filipe; Tiago Valente,
Gregory, Helder Lopes, Rui Miguel (Sergio Oliveira 81);
Rodrigo Antonio, Seri, Filipe Anunciacao, Manuel Jose
(Ruben Ribeiro 74); Caetano (Hurtado 65), Bebe.
Pandurii Targu Jiu: (442) Mingote; Momcilovic,
Christou, Ungurusan, Buleica; Erico, Anton, Pereira
(Distefano 58), Breeveld; Ciucur (Cristea 66),
Matulevicius (Grigoras 73).

Thursday, 24 October 2013
Fiorentina (2) 3 *(Joaquin 26, Ryder 34, Cuadrado 69)*
Pandurii Targu Jiu (0) 0   14,834
Fiorentina: (433) Neto; Rodriguez (Roncaglia 64),
Compper, Tomovic, Alonso; Bakic, Valero (Aquilani 73),
Fernandez; Joaquin, Ryder (Cuadrado 60), Yakovenko.
Pandurii Targu Jiu: (442) Stanca; Erico, Christou,
Ungurusan, Momcilovic; Anton, Breeveld, Pereira
(Distefano 80), dos Santos (Nicoara 46); Ciucur (Buleica
46), Matulevicius.

Pacos Ferreira (0) 0
Dnipro (0) 2 *(Rotan 83, Konoplyanka 86)* 1137
Pacos Ferreira: (433) Antonio Filipe; Tony, Ricardo, Tiago Valente, Nuno Santos; Andre Leao, Seri, Manuel Jose (Ruben Ribeiro 64); Sergio Oliveira, Rui Miguel (Irobiso 82), Bebe.
Dnipro: (4411) Boyko; Mazuch, Mandzyuk, Cheberyachko, Strinic; Kankava (Giuliano 52), Rotan, Zozulya, Konoplyanka; Bruno Gama (Matheus 67); Kalinic (Seleznyov 58).

Thursday, 7 November 2013
Dnipro (1) 2 *(Matheus 44, Konoplyanka 66)*
Pacos Ferreira (0) 0 14,039
Dnipro: (4411) Boyko; Fedetskiy, Mazuch, Cheberyachko, Vlad; Bruno Gama (Zozulya 46), Kankava, Rotan (Politylo 72), Konoplyanka; Kalinic; Matheus (Giuliano 66).
Pacos Ferreira: (433) Antonio Filipe; Rodrigo Antonio, Ricardo, Tiago Valente, Nuno Santos; Andre Leao, Rui Miguel (Seri 60), Filipe Anunciacao; Manuel Jose, Irobiso, Ruben Ribeiro (Sergio Oliveira 80).

Pandurii Targu Jiu (1) 1 *(Pereira 32)*
Fiorentina (0) 2 *(Ryder 86, Valero 90)* 11,750
Pandurii Targu Jiu: (4231) Stanca (Mingote 24); Ungurusan, Erico (Mamele 42), Christou, Momcilovic; Breeveld, Anton; Buleica, Pereira, Distefano (Sipo Bohale 87); dos Santos.
Fiorentina: (433) Munua; Roncaglia (Capezzi 80), Rodriguez, Compper, Alonso; Cuadrado, Aquilani, Fernandez (Ilicic 65); Joaquin, Ryder, Yakovenko (Valero 45).

Thursday, 28 November 2013
Dnipro (1) 4 *(Kalinic 12, Zozulya 56, Shakhov 86, Kravchenko 89)*
Pandurii Targu Jiu (0) 1 *(Pereira 70 (pen))* 5157
Dnipro: (4411) Boyko; Kulakov, Mandzyuk, Cheberyachko (Svatok 64), Vlad; Bruno Gama (Blyznychenko 46), Kravchenko, Politylo, Kobakhidze; Kalinic (Shakhov 63); Zozulya.
Pandurii Targu Jiu: (4231) Mingote; Pleasca, Christou, Rada, Momcilovic; Breeveld, Cristea (dos Santos 59); Buleica (Pitian 81), Pereira, Ciucur (Distefano 57); Adrovic.

Pacos Ferreira (0) 0
Fiorentina (0) 0 1347
Pacos Ferreira: (4411) Antonio Filipe; Tiago Valente, Tony, Ricardo, Helder Lopes; Andre Leao, Ruben Ribeiro (Sergio Oliveira 71), Manuel Jose, Filipe Anunciacao; Seri (Romeu 90); Bebe (Hurtado 58).
Fiorentina: (4411) Munua; Alonso, Roncaglia, Compper, Tomovic; Bakic (Pizarro 46), Aquilani, Fernandez, Ambrosini (Cuadrado 62); Ilicic (Yakovenko 74); Ryder.

Thursday, 12 December 2013
Fiorentina (1) 2 *(Joaquin 42, Cuadrado 77)*
Dnipro (1) 1 *(Konoplyanka 13)* 12,486
Fiorentina: (4411) Neto; Rodriguez, Roncaglia, Pasqual, Cuadrado (Aquilani 80); Savic, Fernandez (Pizarro 70), Joaquin, Valero; Ambrosini; Ryder (Ilicic 76).
Dnipro: (442) Boyko; Vlad (Kalinic 76), Fedetskiy, Mandzyuk, Cheberyachko; Kankava, Bruno Gama (Kulakov 63), Rotan, Politylo (Seleznyov 69); Zozulya, Konoplyanka.

Pandurii Targu Jiu (0) 0
Pacos Ferreira (0) 0 1213
Pandurii Targu Jiu: (41212) Stanca; Pleasca, Mamele, Christou, Momcilovic; Erico; Ciucur (Paulinho 71), Nicoara (Cristea 83); Pereira; dos Santos (Buleica 57), Breeveld.
Pacos Ferreira: (433) Degra; Tony, Tiago Valente, Ricardo, Helder Lopes; Andre Leao[*], Manuel Jose (Bebe 73), Filipe Anunciacao; Seri (Sergio Oliveira 46), Hurtado, Carlao (Romeu 90).

Group E Table	P	W	D	L	F	A	GD	Pts
Fiorentina	6	5	1	0	12	3	9	16
Dnipro	6	4	0	2	11	5	6	12
Pacos Ferreira	6	0	3	3	1	8	-7	3
Pandurii Targu Jiu	6	0	2	4	3	11	-8	2

GROUP F

Thursday, 19 September 2013
Eintracht Frankfurt (2) 3 *(Kadlec 4, Russ 16, Djakpa 52)*
Bordeaux (0) 0 44,000
Eintracht Frankfurt: (4141) Trapp; Jung, Zambrano, Bamba Anderson, Djakpa; Russ; Aigner, Rode (Celozzi 68), Barnetta, Inui (Flum 46); Kadlec (Lakic 80).
Bordeaux: (442) Carasso; Faubert (Chalme 46), Henrique, Brechet, Orban[*]; Traore, Biyogo Poko (Ben Khalfallah 69), Sertic, Maurice-Belay (Poundje 64); Rolan, Jussie.

Maccabi Tel Aviv (0) 0
Apoel Nicosia (0) 0 11,772
Maccabi Tel Aviv: (442) Juan Pablo; Mane (Ben Haroush 44), Tibi, Carlos Garcia, Radi (Yitzhaki 69); Micha, Yeyni, Mitrovic, Zahavi; Ben Haim (Dabbur 77), Prica.
Apoel Nicosia: (442) Urko; Morais, Joao Guilherme, Marcelo Oliveira, Mario Sergio; Charalambidis (Sheridan 78), Vinicius, Aritz Borda, Japones; Aloneftis (Gomes 90), Goncalves (Helder Cabral 85).

Thursday, 3 October 2013
Apoel Nicosia (0) 0
Eintracht Frankfurt (1) 3 *(Alexandrou 27 (og), Lakic 57, Jung 67)* 13,729
Apoel Nicosia: (4411) Urko; Joao Guilherme, Marcelo Oliveira, Morais, Mario Sergio; Helder Cabral, Aritz Borda, Gomes (Vinicius 78), Alexandrou (Sotiriou 65); Aloneftis (Benachour 78); Goncalves.
Eintracht Frankfurt: (4411) Trapp; Russ, Zambrano, Oczipka, Bamba Anderson; Jung, Lakic, Flum, Rode (Celozzi 68); Barnetta (Lanig 81); Kadlec (Joselu 74).

Bordeaux (0) 1 *(Jussie 48)*
Maccabi Tel Aviv (0) 2 *(Yitzhaki 71, Micha 79)* 7329
Bordeaux: (433) Olimpa; Chalme, Brechet, Poundje, Sane; N'Guemo (Ben Khalfallah 77), Traore, Rolan; Sacko (Obraniak 46), Jussie, Maurice-Belay (Saivet 62).
Maccabi Tel Aviv: (433) Juan Pablo; Tibi, Carlos Garcia, Ben Haroush, Yeyni; Radi (Micha 66), Alberman, Altman (Mitrovic 46); Zahavi, Yitzhaki (Einbinder 88), Prica.

Thursday, 24 October 2013
Bordeaux (1) 2 *(Sane 24, Henrique 89)*
Apoel Nicosia (1) 1 *(Goncalves 45)* 10,404
Bordeaux: (4231) Carasso; Chalme, Henrique, Brechet, Poundje; Sane, Sertic (Diabate 46); Obraniak (Sacko 71), Saivet (Faubert 71), Traore; Rolan.
Apoel Nicosia: (433) Urko; Mario Sergio, Joao Guilherme, Marcelo Oliveira, Alexandrou (Manduca 61); Morais, Japones, Vinicius; Charalambidis, Aloneftis (Gomes 79), Goncalves (Budimir 70).

Eintracht Frankfurt (1) 2 *(Kadlec 12, Meier 53)*
Maccabi Tel Aviv (0) 0 40,800
Eintracht Frankfurt: (433) Trapp; Jung, Zambrano, Bamba Anderson, Oczipka; Rode, Russ (Aigner 46); Flum; Kadlec, Barnetta (Inui 68), Meier (Lakic 77).
Maccabi Tel Aviv: (433) Juan Pablo; Yeyni, Tibi, Carlos Garcia, Ben Haroush; Mitrovic, Alberman (Margolis 55), Radi; Zahavi (Altman 74), Prica (Dabbur 65), Ben Haim[*].

Thursday, 7 November 2013
Apoel Nicosia (1) 2 *(Alexandrou 13, Morais 54)*
Bordeaux (1) 1 *(Sane 45)* 11,853
Apoel Nicosia: (4411) Urko; Mario Sergio, Marcelo Oliveira, Aritz Borda, Helder Cabral; Charalambidis (Sotiriou 56), Morais, Vinicius, Aloneftis (Solomou 88); Alexandrou (Benachour 38); Budimir[*].
Bordeaux: (4312) Carasso; Faubert, Brechet, Sane, Poundje; N'Guemo[*], Sertic, Maurice-Belay; Obraniak (Bellion 70); Jussie (Sacko 70), Rolan (Saivet 70).

Maccabi Tel Aviv (3) 4 *(Zahavi 14, 90 (pen),*
Yitzhaki 30, 35)
Eintracht Frankfurt (0) 2 *(Lakic 63, Meier 67 (pen))*
13,232
Maccabi Tel Aviv: (4141) Juan Pablo; Yeyni, Tibi, Carlos
Garcia, Ben Haroush; Zahavi; Mitrovic, Altman
(Margolis 66), Yitzhaki (Radi 70), Einbinder; Dabbur
(Prica 83).
Eintracht Frankfurt: (4141) Trapp; Schrock, Zambrano,
Bamba Anderson, Djakpa (Oczipka 86); Meier; Russ,
Aigner (Kadlec 67), Inui, Flum; Lakic (Joselu 78).

Thursday, 28 November 2013
Apoel Nicosia (0) 0
Maccabi Tel Aviv (0) 0 13,052
Apoel Nicosia: (4411) Urko; Marcelo Oliveira, Morais,
Mario Sergio, Helder Cabral; Charalambidis (Sheridan
74), Vinicius, Aritz Borda, Aloneftis; Solomou
(Alexandrou 45); Manduca (Goncalves 62).
Maccabi Tel Aviv: (4411) Juan Pablo; Ben Haroush,
Carlos Garcia, Tibi, Radi (Alberman 85); Einbinder,
Yeyni, Mitrovic, Ben Haim; Yitzhaki (Altman 80); Prica
(Dabbur 68).

Bordeaux (0) 0
Eintracht Frankfurt (0) 1 *(Lanig 81)* 19,013
Bordeaux: (442) Carasso; Henrique, Poundje, Planus
(Sertic 46), Faubert; Sane, Diabate, Traore (Obraniak
74), Rolan; Saivet, Maurice-Belay (Jussie 63).
Eintracht Frankfurt: (442) Trapp; Zambrano, Oczipka,
Kempf, Jung; Flum, Rode (Lanig 65), Barnetta,
Schwegler; Kadlec (Lakic 78), Joselu (Schrock 46).

Thursday, 12 December 2013
Eintracht Frankfurt (0) 2 *(Schrock 67, Djakpa 77)*
Apoel Nicosia (0) 0 32,400
Eintracht Frankfurt: (442) Wiedwald; Celozzi, Russ, Bamba
Anderson, Djakpa; Schrock, Flum, Barnetta (Kittel 61),
Inui (Bakalorz 78); Lakic (Joselu 68), Rosenthal.
Apoel Nicosia: (4141) Chiotis; Solomou, Aritz Borda,
Joao Guilherme, Antoniades (Japones 64); Morais
(Vinicius 46); Sotiriou, Charalambidis (Manduca 46),
Artymatas, Alexandrou; Sheridan.

Maccabi Tel Aviv (0) 1 *(Zahavi 74 (pen))*
Bordeaux (0) 0 11,742
Maccabi Tel Aviv: (4231) Juan Pablo; Yeyni, Carlos
Garcia, Tibi, Ben Haroush; Alberman, Radi; Yitzhaki
(Mitrovic 66), Zahavi (Ziv 78), Altman (Ben Haim 74);
Dabbur.
Bordeaux: (4231) Olimpa; Chalme■, Planus, Brechet,
Poundje; Savic, D'Almeida (Pellenard 75); Rolan,
Bellion, Ben Khalfallah; Sacko.

Group F Table	P	W	D	L	F	A	GD	Pts
Eintracht Frankfurt	6	5	0	1	13	4	9	15
Maccabi Tel Aviv	6	3	2	1	7	5	2	11
Apoel Nicosia	6	1	2	3	3	8	−5	5
Bordeaux	6	1	0	5	4	10	−6	3

GROUP G
Thursday, 19 September 2013
Dynamo Kyiv (0) 0
Genk (0) 1 *(Gorius 62)* 30,345
Dynamo Kyiv: (4231) Koval; Danilo Silva, Khacheridi,
Vida, Tremoulinas; Haruna (Gusev 72), Vukojevic;
Yarmolenko, Belhanda (Bezus 46), Lens; Ideye
(Mbokani 56).
Genk: (4231) Koteles; Ngcongca, Mbodji, Koulibaly,
Tshimanga; Kumordzi, Hyland; Buffel, Vossen (Monrose
79), Camus (Limbombe 90); M'Boyo (Gorius 31).

Thun (1) 1 *(Schneuwly C 35)*
Rapid Vienna (0) 0 7022
Thun: (4231) Faivre; Luthi, Reinmann, Sulmoni,
Schirinzi; Hediger, Sanogo; Schneuwly C, Zuffi, Wittwer
(Ferreira 72); Schneuwly M (Sadik 79).
Rapid Vienna: (433) Novota; Trimmel, Sonnleitner,
Dibon, Schrammel; Petsos, Hofmann S (Boyd 63),
Boskovic (Grozurek 80); Schaub, Sabitzer, Burgstaller
(Behrendt 80).

Thursday, 3 October 2013
Genk (0) 2 *(Gorius 55, Vossen 63)*
Thun (0) 1 *(Martinez 90)* 11,559
Genk: (442) Koteles; Ngcongca, Mbodji, Koulibaly,
Tshimanga; Buffel (Limbombe 73), Kumordzi, Gorius,
De Ceulaer (Masika 64); Vossen, Camus (Schrijvers 87).
Thun: (4231) Faivre; Wittwer, Schenkel, Reinmann,
Luthi; Hediger, Siegfried; Ferreira (Krstic 71), Martinez,
Cassio (Schneuwly C 64); Schneuwly M (Sadik 60).

Rapid Vienna (0) 2 *(Burgstaller 53, Trimmel 90)*
Dynamo Kyiv (2) 2 *(Yarmolenko 30, Dibon 34 (og))*
34,800
Rapid Vienna: (4231) Novota; Trimmel, Sonnleitner,
Dibon, Palla; Petsos, Behrendt; Burgstaller (Grozurek
74), Schaub, Sabitzer; Boyd.
Dynamo Kyiv: (4231) Koval; Danilo Silva, Dragovic,
Khacheridi, Tremoulinas; Veloso, Sydorchuk (Vukojevic
46); Lens (Gusev 87), Belhanda (Haruna 74),
Yarmolenko; Mbokani.

Thursday, 24 October 2013
Dynamo Kyiv (1) 3 *(Yarmolenko 35, Mbokani 59,*
Gusev 78)
Thun (0) 0 26,042
Dynamo Kyiv: (442) Shovkovskiy; Danilo Silva,
Dragovic, Khacheridi, Makarenko; Veloso, Haruna
(Sydorchuk 69), Belhanda, Yarmolenko (Gusev 68
(Bezus 81)); Lens, Mbokani.
Thun: (442) Faivre; Schenkel, Reinmann, Luthi, Schirinzi;
Sanogo, Zuffi, Hediger, Schneuwly C (Salamand 75);
Martinez (Ferreira 65), Schneuwly M (Sadik 60).

Genk (1) 1 *(Gorius 20)*
Rapid Vienna (0) 1 *(Sabitzer 82)* 14,142
Genk: (4231) Koteles; Ngcongca, Mbodji, Koulibaly,
Tshimanga; Gorius, Kumordzi; Buffel (Masika 69),
Camus (Hyland 76), De Ceulaer; Vossen.
Rapid Vienna: (4231) Novota; Trimmel, Sonnleitner,
Dibon, Palla (Schrammel 61); Petsos, Boskovic
(Behrendt 73); Hofmann S (Starkl 81), Schaub, Sabitzer;
Boyd.

Thursday, 7 November 2013
Rapid Vienna (2) 2 *(Boyd 40, 45)*
Genk (1) 2 *(Mbodji 29 (pen), Buffel 60)* 34,300
Rapid Vienna: (4231) Novota; Trimmel, Sonnleitner,
Dibon, Schrammel; Petsos, Boskovic (Behrendt 81);
Hofmann S (Starkl 87), Schaub, Sabitzer (Burgstaller 77);
Boyd.
Genk: (442) Koteles; Ngcongca, Mbodji, Koulibaly,
Tshimanga; De Ceulaer, Gorius, Hyland, Buffel; Camus
(Kumordzi 90), Vossen.

Thun (0) 0
Dynamo Kyiv (1) 2 *(Schenkel 29 (og), Yarmolenko 68)*
6523
Thun: (4231) Faivre; Luthi, Reinmann, Schenkel,
Wittwer (Zuffi 73); Hediger, Sanogo; Cassio (Schneuwly
M 70), Martinez, Schneuwly C (Ferreira 69); Sadik.
Dynamo Kyiv: (4231) Shovkovskiy; Danilo Silva,
Khacheridi, Dragovic (Vida 59), Tremoulinas; Veloso,
Sydorchuk (Vukojevic 46); Yarmolenko, Belhanda,
Gusev (Makarenko 88); Mbokani■.

Thursday, 28 November 2013
Genk (3) 3 *(Vossen 17 (pen), Kumordzi 37, De Ceulaer 40)*
Dynamo Kyiv (1) 1 *(Yarmolenko 9)* 13337
Genk: (442) Koteles; Ngcongca (Simaeys 52), Mbodji,
Koulibaly, Tshimanga; Buffel, Hyland, Kumordzi
(Gerkens 87), Gorius; Camus (De Ceulaer 18), Vossen.
Dynamo Kyiv: (4411) Koval; Gusev, Khacheridi,
Dragovic, Tremoulinas; Lens (Bezus 55), Sydorchuk,
Veloso, Yarmolenko; Belhanda (Makarenko 72); Ideye.

Rapid Vienna (1) 2 *(Boyd 17, Boskovic 64)*
Thun (0) 1 *(Sadik 61)* 34,300
Rapid Vienna: (4231) Novota; Trimmel, Sonnleitner,
Dibon, Schrammel; Petsos, Boskovic (Behrendt 65);
Hofmann S (Starkl 86), Sabitzer (Schaub 80), Burgstaller;
Boyd.

Thun: (4231) Faivre; Luthi, Reinmann (Schenkel 46), Sulmoni, Schirinzi; Hediger, Siegfried; Ferreira (Martinez 59), Zuffi (Sadik 59), Wittwer; Schneuwly M.

Thursday, 12 December 2013

Dynamo Kyiv (2) 3 *(Lens 22, Gusev 28, Veloso 71)*

Rapid Vienna (1) 1 *(Boyd 6)*   18,762

Dynamo Kyiv: (4231) Shovkovskiy; Gusev, Khacheridi, Dragovic, Makarenko; Vukojevic, Veloso; Yarmolenko, Belhanda (Bezus 83), Lens (Dudu Rodrigues 71); Ideye.
Rapid Vienna: (4231) Novota; Trimmel, Sonnleitner, Dibon, Schrammel; Petsos, Boskovic (Behrendt 68); Hofmann S (Schaub 68), Burgstaller, Sabitzer (Starkl 46); Boyd.

Thun (0) 0

Genk (1) 1 *(Vossen 31)*   5185

Thun: (4231) Moser; Luthi, Schenkel, Sulmoni, Wittwer; Hediger, Siegfried; Schneuwly C (Martinez 59), Krstic (Sadik 59), Ferreira (Cassio 71); Schneuwly M.
Genk: (442) Van Hout; Walsh, Simaeys, Mbodji, Tshimanga; Masika, Gerkens, Kumordzi (Ngcongca 84), Limbombe; Schrijvers (Gorius 76), Vossen (Makraou 63).

Group G Table	P	W	D	L	F	A	GD	Pts
Genk	6	4	2	0	10	5	5	14
Dynamo Kyiv	6	3	1	2	11	7	4	10
Rapid Vienna	6	1	3	2	8	10	–2	6
Thun	6	1	0	5	3	10	–7	3

GROUP H

Thursday, 19 September 2013

Estoril (0) 1 *(Bruno Miguel 61)*

Sevilla (0) 2 *(Vitolo 59, Gameiro 77)*   4154

Estoril: (442) Vagner; Tavares, Bruno Miguel, Babanco, Mano (Anderson Luis 72); Goncalo Santos, Filipe Goncalves (Joao Pedro 79), Evandro, Balboa (Gerso 64); Leal, Seba.
Sevilla: (442) Javi Varas; Fernando Navarro, Cala, Diogo Figueiras, Moreno; Mbia, Marin, Rabello (Jairo 72), Vitolo; Bacca (Gameiro 65), Iborra (Rakitic 66).

Freiburg (2) 2 *(Schuster 23 (pen), Mehmedi 35)*

Slovan Liberec (0) 2 *(Kalitvintsev 66, Rabusic 73)*   14,100

Freiburg: (4231) Baumann; Sorg, Krmas, Ginter, Gunter; Fernandes, Schuster; Schmid, Mehmedi (Coquelin 89), Kerk (Guede■ 65); Hanke (Freis 79).
Slovan Liberec: (4231) Kovar; Kusnir, Kovac, Kelic, Fleisman; Sackey (Kalitvintsev 61), Rybalka■; Delarge, Pavelka, Frydek (Sural 46); Rabusic.

Thursday, 3 October 2013

Sevilla (0) 2 *(Perotti 63 (pen), Bacca 90)*

Freiburg (0) 0   17,041

Sevilla: (451) Javi Varas; Cala, Diogo Figueiras, Moreno, Pareja; Rakitic (Cristoforo 88), Trochowski (Marin 54), Jairo, Bacca, Iborra; Perotti (Rabello 76).
Freiburg: (451) Baumann; Diagne■, Coquelin (Kerk 59), Sorg, Ginter; Gunter, Fernandes, Hofler, Albutat (Mehmedi 60), Hanke; Klaus (Freis 67).

Slovan Liberec (1) 2 *(Sural 15, Kovac 63)*

Estoril (1) 1 *(Leal 45)*   7500

Slovan Liberec: (4141) Kovar; Coufal, Kovac, Kelic, Fleisman; Sackey■; Sural (Hadascok 90), Pavelka, Frydek, Delarge (Kalitvintsev 76); Rabusic (Pimpara 90).
Estoril: (433) Vagner; Anderson Luis (Balboa 83), Bruno Miguel■, Ruben Fernandes, Mano; Goncalo Santos, Evandro, Filipe Goncalves (Gerso 70); Joao Pedro (Tavares 62), Leal, Seba.

Thursday, 24 October 2013

Freiburg (1) 1 *(Darida 11)*

Estoril (0) 1 *(Seba 53)*   14,500

Freiburg: (442) Baumann; Hedenstad (Pilar 66), Ginter, Hohn, Lorenzoni; Schmid, Schuster, Fernandes (Hofler 46), Coquelin; Darida (Hanke 76), Mehmedi.
Estoril: (4231) Vagner; Mano, Tavares, Ruben Fernandes, Babanco; Filipe Goncalves, Goncalo Santos; Seba (Lopes 89), Evandro, Joao Pedro (Carlitos 69); Leal (Balboa 79).

Slovan Liberec (1) 1 *(Rabusic 20)*

Sevilla (0) 1 *(Vitolo 88)*   7700

Slovan Liberec: (4141) Kovar■; Husek (Kalitvintsev 64 (Kolar 90)), Kelic, Kovac, Kusnir; Fleisman; Pavelka, Rybalka, Rabusic, Sural; Delarge (Hroso 79).
Sevilla: (4411) Javi Varas; Fernando Navarro (Moreno 75), Cala, Pareja, Coke; Cristoforo, Iborra, Rabello (Bacca 56), Perotti; Gameiro; Reyes (Vitolo 56).

Thursday, 7 November 2013

Estoril (0) 0

Freiburg (0) 0   2014

Estoril: (433) Vagner; Tavares, Mano, Goncalo Santos, Ruben Fernandes; Babanco, Filipe Goncalves (Joao Pedro 81), Evandro; Leal (Lopes 81), Seba, Carlitos (Balboa 66).
Freiburg: (4231) Baumann; Krmas, Diagne, Coquelin (Gunter 69), Sorg; Lorenzoni, Darida (Freis 66); Pilar, Hofler■, Guede■; Kerk (Mehmedi 45).

Sevilla (1) 1 *(Perotti 29)*

Slovan Liberec (0) 1 *(Pavelka 71)*   15,178

Sevilla: (4231) Javi Varas; Fazio, Fernando Navarro, Cala, Coke; Cristoforo, Mbia; Reyes, Rabello (Rakitic 69), Perotti (Vitolo 80); Rusescu (Bacca 77).
Slovan Liberec: (4231) Hroso; Frydek, Kovac, Kelic, Fleisman; Sackey, Rybalka (Coufal 70); Sural, Pavelka, Delarge (Kalitvintsev 63); Rabusic (Husek 90).

Thursday, 28 November 2013

Sevilla (1) 1 *(Gameiro 7)*

Estoril (0) 1 *(Ruben Fernandes 90)*   12,557

Sevilla: (4231) Javi Varas; Coke, Cala, Fazio, Moreno; Cristoforo, Mbia (Iborra 61); Reyes (Jairo 81), Rakitic, Perotti (Vitolo 67); Gameiro.
Estoril: (4231) Vagner; Tavares, Mano, Ruben Fernandes, Babanco; Filipe Goncalves (Joao Pedro 62), Evandro (Balboa 76); Goncalo Santos, Carlitos, Seba (Lopes 83); Leal.

Slovan Liberec (0) 1 *(Rybalka 81)*

Freiburg (1) 2 *(Ginter 23, Coquelin 73)*   8800

Slovan Liberec: (433) Kovar; Kusnir (Pimpara 72), Kovac, Kelic, Fleisman; Sackey, Pavelka, Rybalka; Sural (Kalitvintsev 77), Rabusic, Delarge (Frydek 58).
Freiburg: (4141) Baumann; Sorg, Diagne, Krmas, Gunter; Ginter (Albutat 89); Coquelin, Fernandes, Kerk (Freis 60), Lorenzoni (Hohn 90); Hanke.

Thursday, 12 December 2013

Estoril (0) 1 *(Seba 82)*

Slovan Liberec (1) 2 *(Sural 18, Rabusic 70)*   1247

Estoril: (451) Vagner (Ricardo Ribeiro 27); Tavares, Mano, Joao Pedro S, Babanco; Filipe Goncalves (Evandro 62), Joao Pedro G, Diogo Amado, Balboa, Gerso (Seba 62); Lopes.
Slovan Liberec: (4231) Hroso; Karisik, Frydek, Kovac, Fleisman; Pavelka, Kalitvintsev (Kolar 71); Rybalka, Sackey (Husek 81), Rabusic (Pimpara 89); Sural.

Freiburg (0) 0

Sevilla (1) 2 *(Iborra 40, Rusescu 90)*   15,700

Freiburg: (442) Baumann; Sorg, Krmas, Hohn, Gunter; Fernandes (Pilar 75), Ginter, Hofler, Lorenzoni (Kerk 58); Darida, Mehmedi.
Sevilla: (4231) Javi Varas; Coke, Cala, Carrico, Fernando Navarro; Iborra, Cristoforo (Fazio 78); Jairo, Rakitic, Perotti (Trochowski 86); Bacca (Rusescu 73).

Group H Table	P	W	D	L	F	A	GD	Pts
Sevilla	6	3	3	0	9	4	5	12
Slovan Liberec	6	2	3	1	9	8	1	9
Freiburg	6	1	3	2	5	8	–3	6
Estoril	6	0	3	3	5	8	–3	3

GROUP I

Thursday, 19 September 2013
Guimaraes (1) 4 *(Ba 36, Plange 48, Maazou 68 (pen), Andre Andre 81)*
Rijeka (0) 0 9794
Guimaraes: (433) Douglas; Pedro Correia, Paulo Oliveira, Ba, Luis Rocha; Moreno, Andre Santos (Tiago Rodrigues 75), Andre Andre; Plange (Marco Matias 72), Maazou (Ricardo Gomes 82), Malonga Ntsayi.
Rijeka: (4231) Vargic; Tomecak (Brezovec 75), Leskovic (Bertosa 18), Maric, Boras; Males, Pokrivac; Kvrzic, Mocinic, Kramaric (Mujanovic 51); Benko.

Real Betis (0) 0
Lyon (0) 0 22,463
Real Betis: (4231) Andersen; Steinhofer, Perquis (Amaya 77), Jordi, Didac; Igiebor, Reyes; Vadillo (Juanfran 54), Verdu (Sevilla 66), Cedrick; Chuli.
Lyon: (4231) Lopes; Dabo (Fofana 78), Kone B, Umtiti, Bedimo; Ferri, Gonalons; Briand, Grenier (Mvuemba 89), Lacazette; Gomis (Fekir 68).

Thursday, 3 October 2013
Lyon (0) 1 *(Gonalons 53)*
Guimaraes (1) 1 *(Maazou 39)* 30,061
Lyon: (433) Lopes; Kone B, Gonalons, Umtiti (Zeffane 35), Fofana; Ferri, Mvuemba (Danic 83), Malbranque (Grenier 62); Lacazette, Gomis, Plea.
Guimaraes: (4231) Douglas; Paulo Oliveira, Ba, Pedro Correia, Luis Rocha; Andre Santos (Andre Andre 75), Leonel; Tiago Rodrigues (Moreno 89), Marco Matias, Malonga Ntsayi (Plange 66); Maazou■.

Rijeka (1) 1 *(Benko 10)*
Real Betis (1) 1 *(Cedrick 14)* 7313
Rijeka: (442) Vargic; Tomecak (Boras 62), Knezevic, Maric, Bertosa; Brezovec (Sharbini 84), Males, Mocinic, Kvrzic (Mujanovic 65); Krstanovic, Benko.
Real Betis: (442) Andersen; Steinhofer, Perquis, Jordi, Didac; Juanfran, Reyes (Igiebor 57), Torres, Cedrick; Rodriguez (Jorge Molina 84), Sevilla (Verdu 69).

Thursday, 24 October 2013
Lyon (0) 1 *(Grenier 66)*
Rijeka (0) 0 30,461
Lyon: (433) Lopes; Zeffane, Bisevac, Fofana, Dabo (Tolisso 69); Malbranque (Mvuemba 84), Gonalons, Ferri; Grenier, Lacazette (Benzia 76), Briand.
Rijeka: (433) Vargic; Mujanovic, Maric, Knezevic, Bertosa; Mocinic, Males, Pokrivac (Sharbini 74); Kvrzic (Brezovec 65), Benko, Alispahic (Krstanovic 81).

Real Betis (0) 1 *(Vadillo 50)*
Guimaraes (0) 0 17,100
Real Betis: (4411) Andersen; Juanfran, Perquis, Amaya, Didac; Vadillo (Steinhofer 76), Igiebor (Nono 63), Reyes, Verdu; Chuli; Jorge Molina (Cedrick 69).
Guimaraes: (442) Douglas; Kanu (Tomane 83), Paulo Oliveira, Ba, Addy; Leonel, Andre Santos (Andre Andre 61), Marco Matias, Malonga Ntsayi (Plange 61); Tiago Rodrigues, Fernando Russi.

Thursday, 7 November 2013
Guimaraes (0) 0
Real Betis (0) 1 *(Chuli 90)* 22,602
Guimaraes: (433) Douglas; Pedro Correia, Paulo Oliveira, Ba, Addy; Andre Santos (Tiago Rodrigues 56), Leonel, Andre Andre; Plange (Ricardo Gomes 72), Maazou, Barrientos (Tomane 84).
Real Betis: (4231) Andersen; Juanfran, Caro, Jordi, Nacho; Nono, Torres; Vadillo (Cedrick 84), Verdu, Juan Carlos (Chuli 79); Rodriguez (Jorge Molina 60).

Rijeka (1) 1 *(Kramaric 21)*
Lyon (1) 1 *(Plea 14)* 7300
Rijeka: (4231) Vargic; Tomecak, Knezevic, Maric, Bertosa; Mocinic, Males; Kvrzic (Mujanovic 88), Kramaric (Pokrivac 83), Sharbini (Alispahic 58); Benko.
Lyon: (4231) Gorgelin; Miguel Lopes (Kone S 81), Kone B, Sarr, Zeffane; Ferri, Mvuemba; Plea, Gourcuff, Danic (Tolisso 65); Briand.

Thursday, 28 November 2013
Lyon (0) 1 *(Gomis 66)*
Real Betis (0) 0 24,112
Lyon: (4312) Vercoutre; Miguel Lopes, Bisevac, Umtiti (Kone B 80), Bedimo; Malbranque, Gonalons, Fofana; Grenier (Gourcuff 59); Lacazette, Briand (Gomis 45).
Real Betis: (4231) Andersen; Juanfran, Paulao, Jordi, Nacho; Nono (Torres 80), Reyes; Cedrick (Steinhofer 63), Verdu, Sevilla (Pepelu 74); Chuli.

Rijeka (0) 0
Guimaraes (0) 0 7138
Rijeka: (442) Vargic; Tomecak, Knezevic, Maric, Bertosa; Kvrzic, Males, Mocinic, Alispahic (Brezovec 80); Kramaric (Sharbini 71), Benko (Krstanovic 85).
Guimaraes: (442) Douglas; Joao Amorim, Paulo Oliveira, Ba, Addy; Barrientos (Fernando Russi 78), Leonel, Andre Andre, Tomane; Maazou, Andre Santos (Marco Matias 68).

Thursday, 12 December 2013
Guimaraes (1) 1 *(Tomane 11)*
Lyon (0) 2 *(Gomis 63 (pen), Ferri 65)* 5845
Guimaraes: (433) Douglas; Pedro Correia■, Paulo Oliveira, Freire, Addy; Moreno, Andre Andre, Rafael Crivellaro (Maazou 78); Malonga Ntsayi (Plange 71), Marco Matias, Tomane (Andre Santos 81).
Lyon: (4231) Lopes; Tolisso, Bisevac, Kone B, Zeffane; Mvuemba, Ferri (Kone S 81), Plea (N'Jie 74), Gourcuff, Danic; Gomis (Benzia 64).

Real Betis (0) 0
Rijeka (0) 0 14,556
Real Betis: (4231) Sara; Steinhofer, Amaya, Jordi, Nacho; Reyes, Torres (Ruben Castro 56); Juanfran, Sevilla (Verdu 66), Juan Carlos; Chuli (Nono 66).
Rijeka: (442) Vargic; Mujanovic, Knezevic, Datkovic, Bertosa; Brezovec (Tomecak 63), Males, Mocinic, Jugovic (Kvrzic 31); Krstanovic (Kramaric 70), Benko.

Group I Table	P	W	D	L	F	A	GD	Pts
Lyon	6	3	3	0	6	3	3	12
Real Betis	6	2	3	1	3	2	1	9
Guimaraes	6	1	2	3	6	5	1	5
Rijeka	6	0	4	2	2	7	–5	4

GROUP J

Thursday, 19 September 2013
Apollon Limassol (1) 1 *(Sangoy 18 (pen))*
Trabzonspor (1) 2 *(Malouda 20, Erdogan 86)* 10,204
Apollon Limassol: (4231) Bruno Vale; Stylianou, Merkis, Karipidis, Vasilou; Gullon, Hamdani; Sangoy, Papoulis (Robert 82), Konstantinou (Roberto 70); Guie Guie (Meriem 63).
Trabzonspor: (4231) Kivrak; Bosingwa (Yavru 80), Yumlu, Bamba, Demir; Zokora, Colman (Akgun 46); Adin, Mierzejewski, Malouda; Paulo Henrique (Erdogan 76).

Lazio (0) 1 *(Hernanes 53)*
Legia Warsaw (0) 0 11,769
Lazio: (442) Marchetti; Ciani, Konko, Cavanda, Hernanes (Lulic 75); Ederson (Ledesma 69), Gonzalez, Onazi, Cana; Keita Balde (Novaretti 83), Floccari.
Legia Warsaw: (442) Skaba; Dossa Junior, Rzeczniczak, Broz, Vrdoljak (Jodlowiec 70); Brzyski, Radovic, Furman, Kosecki; Ojamaa, Saganowski (Kucharczyk 68).

Thursday, 3 October 2013
Legia Warsaw (0) 0
Apollon Limassol (0) 1 *(Sangoy 56)*
Legia Warsaw: (442) Skaba; Rzeczniczak, Jodlowiec, Dossa Junior (Wawrzyniak); Ojamaa (Kucharczyk 85); Pinto (Furman 82), Vrdoljak, Zyro (Brzyski 85); Radovic, Dvalishvili.
Apollon Limassol: (433) Hidi; Rojas Mena, Merkis, Karipidis, Vasilou (Catala 89); Hamdani, Meriem, Gullon; Papoulis, Roberto, Sangoy (Konstantinou 86).
Behind closed doors.

Trabzonspor (3) 3 *(Erdogan 12, Mierzejewski 22, Paulo Henrique 35)*
Lazio (1) 3 *(Onazi 29, Floccari 84, 85)* 13,002
Trabzonspor: (4231) Kivrak; Bosingwa, Demir, Yumlu, Adin; Zokora, Colman (Akgun 57); Erdogan, Mierzejewski, Malouda (Alanzinho 64); Paulo Henrique.
Lazio: (4231) Marchetti; Cavanda, Ciani, Cana, Lulic; Hernanes (Ederson 74), Biglia; Candreva (Floccari 61), Onazi, Felipe Anderson (Keita Balde 80); Perea.

Thursday, 24 October 2013
Apollon Limassol (0) 0
Lazio (0) 0 8943
Apollon Limassol: (4231) Bruno Vale; Stylianou, Merkis, Karipidis, Vasilou; Hamdani, Gullon; Sangoy (Konstantinou 88), Meriem (Grigorie 90), Papoulis (Haber 90); Roberto.
Lazio: (4411) Marchetti; Cavanda, Cana, Novaretti, Radu; Gonzalez (Onazi 87), Hernanes, Ledesma, Keita Balde (Felipe Anderson 81); Ederson; Floccari (Perea 70).

Trabzonspor (1) 2 *(Janko 7, Adin 83)*
Legia Warsaw (0) 0 12,871
Trabzonspor: (4231) Kivrak; Bosingwa, Yumlu, Bamba, Demir; Malouda, Zokora; Adin, Paulo Henrique (Gural 80), Mierzejewski (Aydogdu 81); Janko (Erdogan 70).
Legia Warsaw: (4231) Skaba; Broz, Rzezniczak, Dossa Junior, Brzyski; Vrdoljak (Furman 65), Jodlowiec; Kosecki (Kucharczyk 74), Pinto, Zyro (Ojamaa 8); Dvalishvili.

Thursday, 7 November 2013
Lazio (2) 2 *(Floccari 14, 36)*
Apollon Limassol (1) 1 *(Papoulis 39)* 6498
Lazio: (433) Berisha; Konko (Novaretti 67), Cana, Ciani, Cavanda; Onazi, Hernanes, Keita Balde (Perea 82); Candreva, Floccari, Ederson (Ledesma 76).
Apollon Limassol: (4411) Bruno Vale; Stylianou, Merkis, Karipidis, Vasilou; Sangoy, Hamdani, Gullon (Konstantinou 86), Papoulis (Haber 90); Meriem; Roberto.

Legia Warsaw (0) 0
Trabzonspor (0) 2 *(Dossa Junior 72 (og), Adin 79)* 14,088
Legia Warsaw: (4231) Skaba; Bereszynski, Rzezniczak, Dossa Junior, Brzyski; Jodlowiec, Furman (Mikita 85); Kucharczyk (Ojamaa 73), Pinto, Kosecki; Dvalishvili.
Trabzonspor: (4231) Kivrak (Ayvaz 53); Bosingwa, Yumlu, Bamba (Kacar 51), Demir; Colman, Zokora; Adin, Mierzejewski (Alanzinho 84), Malouda; Paulo Henrique.

Thursday, 28 November 2013
Legia Warsaw (0) 0
Lazio (1) 2 *(Perea 24, Felipe Anderson 57)* 12,000
Legia Warsaw: (433) Kuciak; Bereszynski, Rzezniczak, Jodlowiec, Wawrzyniak; Vrdoljak, Furman (Astiz 64), Radovic; Pinto (Ojamaa 46), Brzyski, Dvalishvili (Mikita 75).
Lazio: (442) Berisha; Gonzalez (Lulic 81), Ciani, Radu, Cavanda; Felipe Anderson (Floccari 77), Biglia, Cana, Keita Balde (Onazi 73); Hernanes, Perea.

Trabzonspor (2) 4 *(Adin 23, 61, 83, Aydogdu 25)*
Apollon Limassol (0) 2 *(Guie Guie 68, Sangoy 80 (pen))* 11,151
Trabzonspor: (4141) Kivrak; Bosingwa, Yumlu, Bamba, Keles; Zokora; Adin, Colman, Aydogdu (Alanzinho 73), Malouda (Ozdemir 90); Paulo Henrique (Janko 65).
Apollon Limassol: (4231) Hidi; Dananae, Merkis, Charalambous, Vasilou; Kyriakou (Sangoy 60), Gullon; Konstantinou, Grigorie (Meriem 67), Robert; Roberto (Guie Guie 60).

Thursday, 12 December 2013
Apollon Limassol (0) 0
Legia Warsaw (1) 2 *(Jodlowiec 8, Brzyski 63)* 1681
Apollon Limassol: (4411) Bruno Vale; Rojas Mena, Merkis, Catala (Charalambous 61), Dananae; Papoulis (Grigorie 23), Gullon, Kyriakou (Meriem 70), Robert; Sangoy■; Roberto.
Legia Warsaw: (4411) Kuciak; Bereszynski■, Rzezniczak, Dossa Junior, Brzyski (Wawrzyniak 79); Kucharczyk, Jodlowiec, Furman, Ojamaa (Mikita 87); Pinto (Astiz 71); Dvalishvili.

Lazio (0) 0
Trabzonspor (0) 0 7732
Lazio: (442) Berisha; Biava, Radu, Cavanda, Novaretti; Felipe Anderson (Candreva 59), Ederson (Klose 75), Onazi (Hernanes 65), Ledesma; Keita Balde, Floccari.
Trabzonspor: (442) Kivrak; Bosingwa, Demir, Bamba, Yumlu; Malouda, Akgun, Colman, Alanzinho (Erdogan 65); Adin, Paulo Henrique (Gural 86).

Group J Table	P	W	D	L	F	A	GD	Pts
Trabzonspor	6	4	2	0	13	6	7	14
Lazio	6	3	3	0	8	4	4	12
Apollon Limassol	6	1	1	4	5	10	–5	4
Legia Warsaw	6	1	0	5	2	8	–6	3

GROUP K

Thursday, 19 September 2013
Sheriff (0) 0
Anzhi Makhachkala (0) 0 8882
Sheriff: (4141) Tomic; Metoua, Samardzic, Melli, Paye; Moyal; Ricardinho (Balima 53), Fernando, Cadu, Luvannor; Jhulliam (Isa 46).
Anzhi Makhachkala: (442) Kerzhakov; Angbwa, Adeleye, Epureanu (Grigalava 25), Gadzhibekov; Agalarov, Ahmedov, Jucilei, Burmistrov; Abdulavov (Gatagov 85), Traore (Solomatin 40).

Tottenham H (2) 3 *(Defoe 21, 29, Eriksen 86)*
Tromso (0) 0 26,681
Tottenham H: (4231) Lloris; Naughton, Kaboul, Dawson, Rose (Vertonghen 39); Sandro, Dembele (Eriksen 64); Sigurdsson, Holtby (Paulinho 71), Lamela; Defoe.
Tromso: (442) Sahlman; Kristiansen, Fojut, Koppinen (Antonsen 61), Causevic; Bendiksen (Johnsen 46), Johansen, Drage (Andersen 78), Pritchard; Moldskred, Ondrasek.

Thursday, 3 October 2013
Anzhi Makhachkala (0) 0
Tottenham H (2) 2 *(Defoe 34, Chadli 39)* 5662
Anzhi Makhachkala: (442) Pomazan; Angbwa (Gadzhibekov 78), Tagirbekov, Adeleye, Ewerton; Jucilei, Ahmedov, Razak, Solomatin; Serderov (Yeschenko 56), Abdulavov (Traore 46).
Tottenham H: (442) Lloris; Walker, Kaboul (Dawson 71), Chiriches, Fryers; Holtby (Eriksen 78), Dembele, Chadli, Sandro; Lamela (Sigurdsson 71), Defoe.

Tromso (0) 1 *(Ondrasek 65)*
Sheriff (0) 1 *(Ricardinho 87)* 3710
Tromso: (442) Sahlman; Fojut, Causevic, Norbye, Kristiansen; Bendiksen, Drage, Andersen (Nystrom 67), Helmke (Pritchard 77); Moldskred, Ondrasek (Johansen 88).
Sheriff: (442) Tomic; Melli■, Metoua, Paye, Luvannor; Samardzic, Balima, Cadu (William 75), Moyal; Isa (Fernando 62), Ricardinho.

Thursday, 24 October 2013
Anzhi Makhachkala (1) 1 *(Burmistrov 19)*
Tromso (0) 0 2797
Anzhi Makhachkala: (4231) Kerzhakov; Yeschenko, Ewerton, Adeleye, Angbwa; Jucilei, Razak (Abdulavov 90); Ahmedov, Gatagov (Agalarov 62), Burmistrov (Gadzhibekov 83); Solomatin.
Tromso: (442) Lekstrom; Norbye, Causevic, Fojut, Kristiansen; Johansen (Antonsen 59), Bendiksen, Helmke, Drage (Espejord 74); Nystrom, Ondrasek (Moldskred 46).

Sheriff (0) 0
Tottenham H (1) 2 *(Vertonghen 12, Defoe 75)* 11,725
Sheriff: (4231) Tomic; Balima, Metoua, Samardzic, Paye; Moyal (Furdui 70), Stanojevic; Ricardinho, Cadu (Fernando 84), Luvannor; Isa (Paireli 88).
Tottenham H: (4231) Lloris; Naughton, Chiriches, Vertonghen, Fryers (Dawson 34); Dembele, Sandro (Holtby 76); Lamela (Chadli 61), Eriksen, Lennon; Defoe.

Thursday, 7 November 2013
Tottenham H (0) 2 *(Lamela 60, Defoe 67 (pen))*
Sheriff (0) 1 *(Isa 72)*   32,225
Tottenham H: (4231) Friedel; Walker, Kaboul, Vertonghen, Naughton; Capoue (Paulinho 57), Dembele; Lamela, Eriksen (Holtby 81), Sigurdsson (Kane 69); Defoe.
Sheriff: (433) Tomic; Balima, Samardzic, Metoua, Paye; Stanojevic, Cadu (Pascenco 73), Moyal (Furdui 61); Ricardinho, Isa, Luvannor (Jhulliam 87).

Tromso (0) 0
Anzhi Makhachkala (0) 1 *(Mkrtchyan 90)*   3673
Tromso: (433) Sahlman; Frantzen, Fojut, Pritchard, Antonsen; Johnsen, Helmke, Zakari (Moldskred 66); Nystrom, Espejord (Johansen 78), Drage (Bendiksen 59).
Anzhi Makhachkala: (4231) Pomazan; Angbwa, Demidov, Ewerton, Grigalava; Epureanu, Jucilei; Razak (Sobolev 77), Gatagov (Serderov 80), Mkrtchyan; Solomatin (Ahmedov 57).

Thursday, 28 November 2013
Anzhi Makhachkala (0) 1 *(Epureanu 58)*
Sheriff (0) 1 *(Isa 52)*   2760
Anzhi Makhachkala: (4231) Kerzhakov; Agalarov, Adeleye, Ewerton, Grigalava; Ahmedov, Epureanu (Mkrtchyan 59); Sobolev (Yeschenko 83), Maksimov, Burmistrov; Serderov (Solomatin 57).
Sheriff: (451) Tomic; Balima, Samardzic, Metoua, Paye; Ricardinho■, Cadu, Moyal, Stanojevic (Jhulliam 76), Luvannor; Isa.

Tromso (0) 0
Tottenham H (0) 2 *(Causevic 63 (og), Dembele 75)*   5868
Tromso: (442) Lekstrom; Frantzen (Norbye 68), Fojut, Causevic, Kristiansen; Andersen, Johansen, Bendiksen (Helmke 78), Drage; Moldskred (Espejord 71), Ondrasek.
Tottenham H: (4231) Friedel; Naughton, Dawson, Chiriches, Fryers (Vertonghen 72); Capoue, Dembele; Townsend, Chadli (Holtby 72), Sigurdsson (Lamela 78); Soldado.

Thursday, 12 December 2013
Sheriff (2) 2 *(Cadu 4, Isa 36)*
Tromso (0) 0   1211
Sheriff: (4231) Tomic (Stajila 60); Metoua, Samardzic, Melli, Paye; Moyal (Stanojevic 55), Furdui; Balima (Pascenco 68), Cadu, Luvannor; Isa.
Tromso: (442) Lekstrom; Norbye (Frantzen 74), Causevic, Antonsen, Kristiansen; Andersen (Johnsen 81), Johansen, Bendiksen, Drage; Moldskred, Ondrasek (Espejord 57).

Tottenham H (2) 4 *(Soldado 7, 16, 70 (pen), Holtby 54)*
Anzhi Makhachkala (1) 1 *(Ewerton 44)*   23,101
Tottenham H: (442) Friedel; Naughton, Fryers, Rose (Fredericks 46), Holtby; Capoue, Townsend, Sigurdsson, Lamela; Soldado (Coulthirst 77), Dembele (Eriksen 64).
Anzhi Makhachkala: (442) Pomazan; Grigalava, Epureanu, Agalarov (Angbwa 80), Ewerton; Jucilei, Sobolev, Razak (Gatagov 84), Maksimov; Serderov, Burmistrov.

Group K Table	P	W	D	L	F	A	GD	Pts
Tottenham H	6	6	0	0	15	2	13	18
Anzhi Makhachkala	6	2	2	2	4	7	–3	8
Sheriff	6	1	3	2	5	6	–1	6
Tromso	6	0	1	5	1	10	–9	1

GROUP L

Thursday, 19 September 2013
Maccabi Haifa (0) 0
AZ Alkmaar (0) 1 *(Gudmundsson 71)*   10,000
Maccabi Haifa: (433) Saranov; Meshumar (Vered 83), Cocalic, Keinan, Scheimann; Katan (Ndlovu 69), Boccoli, Rayo; Abuhatzira, Turgeman (Yadin 69), Ezra.
AZ Alkmaar: (433) Alvarado; Johansson, Gouweleeuw, Wuytens, Viergever (Gorter 80); Gudelj, Ortiz, Elm (Overtoom 63); Beerens (Martens 62), Johannsson, Gudmundsson.

PAOK Salonika (0) 2 *(Athanasiadis 75, Vukic 90)*
Shakhter Karagandy (0) 1 *(Canas 50 (pen))*
PAOK Salonika: (442) Jacobo; Kitsiou, Miguel Vitor, Katsouranis, Tzavelas (Lino 65); Tziolis, Lazar (Salpingidis 58), Lucas, Stoch; Ninis (Vukic 85), Athanasiadis.
Shakhter Karagandy: (343) Mokin; Maliy, Dzidic, Tarasov; Simcevic, Canas, Vicius, Poryavev■; Finonchenko (Baizhanov 81), Khizhnichenko (Zenkovich 88), Ghazaryan.
Behind closed doors

Thursday, 3 October 2013
AZ Alkmaar (0) 1 *(Gouweleeuw 82)*
PAOK Salonika (0) 1 *(Salpingidis 90)*   10,761
AZ Alkmaar: (442) Alvarado; Johansson, Viergever, Gouweleeuw, Wuytens; Martens, Gudelj, Elm (Overtoom 81), Ortiz; Beerens (Gudmundsson 69), Johannsson (Avdic 90).
PAOK Salonika: (433) Jacobo; Tzavelas, Miguel Vitor, Tziolis, Lazar (Salpingidis 84); Katsouranis, Kitsiou, Ninis (Lawrence 76); Stoch, Lucas (Oliseh 72), Athanasiadis.

Shakhter Karagandy (2) 2 *(Finonchenko 40, Tarasov 45)*
Maccabi Haifa (0) 2 *(Ezra 54, Turgeman 78)*   19,100
Shakhter Karagandy: (541) Mokin; Simcevic, Maliy, Vasiljevic, Dzidic, Tarasov (Baizhanov 66); Finonchenko (Darabayev 81), Canas, Vicius, Ghazaryan (Murtazaev 90); Khizhnichenko.
Maccabi Haifa: (4141) Saranov; Gabai, Cocalic, Pylyavskyi, Twatha; Yadin; Raiyan (Ezra 46), Golasa, Rayo, Abuhatzira (Vered 78); Ndlovu (Turgeman 46).

Thursday, 24 October 2013
PAOK Salonika (2) 3 *(Miguel Vitor 35, Ninis 40, Salpingidis 66)*
Maccabi Haifa (2) 2 *(Ndlovu 14, Golasa 22)*   14,211
PAOK Salonika: (433) Jacobo; Miguel Vitor, Lino, Tziolis, Lazar; Katsouranis, Kitsiou, Ninis (Lucas 60); Salpingidis (Vukic 78), Athanasiadis, Stoch (Lawrence 87).
Maccabi Haifa: (442) Saranov; Twatha, Meshumar (Azulay 73), Pylyavskyi, Cocalic; Boccoli, Ezra, Rayo, Golasa; Yadin (Katan 67), Ndlovu (Abuhatzira 45).

Shakhter Karagandy (1) 1 *(Finonchenko 11)*
AZ Alkmaar (1) 1 *(Gudmundsson 26)*   10,500
Shakhter Karagandy: (541) Mokin; Simcevic, Maliy (Tarasov 75), Vasiljevic, Dzidic, Poryavev; Finonchenko, Canas (Baizhanov 89), Vicius, Ghazaryan; Khizhnichenko (Zenkovich 86).
AZ Alkmaar: (433) Alvarado; Johansson, Gouweleeuw, Wuytens, Viergever; Gudelj, Ortiz, Martens; Beerens, Johannsson, Gudmundsson.

Thursday, 7 November 2013
AZ Alkmaar (0) 1 *(Ortiz 55)*
Shakhter Karagandy (0) 0   9778
AZ Alkmaar: (433) Alvarado; Johansson, Gouweleeuw, Wuytens, Viergever; Gudelj, Ortiz, Martens; Beerens, Johannsson (Avdic 46), Gudmundsson (Henriksen 83).
Shakhter Karagandy: (541) Pokatilov; Simcevic, Maliy, Vasiljevic, Tarasov, Borantaev; Darabayev, Baizhanov, Canas, Ghazaryan; Zenkovich (Murtazaev 72).

Maccabi Haifa (0) 0
PAOK Salonika (0) 0   10,000
Maccabi Haifa: (451) Saranov; Meshumar, Keinan, Falach, Twatha; Ndlovu (Raiyan 79), Abukarat, Boccoli, Vered (Rayo 58); Ezra; Gozlan (Abuhatzira 46).
PAOK Salonika: (442) Jacobo; Skondras, Katsouranis, Katsikas, Tzavelas; Lucas (Lino 90), Tziolis, Stoch (Oliseh 68); Ninis (Salpingidis 62), Athanasiadis.

Thursday, 28 November 2013
AZ Alkmaar (1) 2 *(Gudelj 37, Gudmundsson 90)*
Maccabi Haifa (0) 0   11,211
AZ Alkmaar: (433) Alvarado; Viergever, Wuytens, Gouweleeuw, Johansson; Martens, Ortiz, Gudelj; Gudmundsson, Johannsson (Avdic 80), Beerens (Elm 67).
Maccabi Haifa: (433) Saranov; Twatha, Keinan, Cocalic, Gabai; Abukarat, Yadin (Boccoli 78), Rayo; Abuhatzira (Ndlovu 69), Turgeman, Vered (Azulay 62).

Shakhter Karagandy (0) 0
PAOK Salonika (0) 2 *(Dzidic 54 (og), Kitsiou 90)*   7556
Shakhter Karagandy: (541) Mokin; Simcevic, Maliy, Dzidic, Tarasov, Poryvaev (Baizhanov 83); Finonchenko, Vicius, Canas, Ghazaryan (Lunin 66); Khizhnichenko (Zenkovich 76).
PAOK Salonika: (4231) Glykos; Kitsiou, Katsouranis, Tzavelas, Lino; Tziolis, Lazar; Lucas (Necid 90), Ninis (Salpingidis 83), Stoch (Vukic 78); Athanasiadis.

Thursday, 12 December 2013
Maccabi Haifa (0) 2 *(Gozlan 73, Abuhatzira 81)*
Shakhter Karagandy (1) 1 *(Canas 44 (pen))*   2100
Maccabi Haifa: (433) Edri; Scheimann, Twatha (Rayo 60), Gabai, Pylyavskyi; Abukarat, Cocalic, Azulay (Turgeman 53); Vered, Raiyan (Abuhatzira 72), Gozlan.
Shakhter Karagandy: (433) Pokatilov; Poryvaev, Tarasov (Canas 39), Dzidic, Maliy; Simcevic, Vicius, Baizhanov; Ghazaryan (Lunin 84), Finonchenko, Khizhnichenko (Zenkovich 85).

PAOK Salonika (1) 2 *(Lucas 38 (pen), Pozoglou 90)*
AZ Alkmaar (1) 2 *(Lam 31, Gorter 71 (pen))*   10,000
PAOK Salonika: (442) Glykos; Miguel Vitor, Lino, Konstantinidis (Skondras 56), Tziolis; Stoch (Pozoglou 74), Lazar, Katsouranis, Kitsiou; Lucas, Athanasiadis (Necid 64).
AZ Alkmaar: (442) De Winter; Reijnen, Lam, Hoedt, Gorter; Gudelj, Berghuis, Overtoom (Johannsson 73), Haps; Lewis (Gudmundsson 54), Avdic.

Group L Table	P	W	D	L	F	A	GD	Pts
AZ Alkmaar	6	3	3	0	8	4	4	12
PAOK Salonika	6	3	3	0	10	6	4	12
Maccabi Haifa	6	1	2	3	6	9	-3	5
Shakhter Karagandy	6	0	2	4	5	10	-5	2

KNOCK-OUT STAGE

ROUND OF 32 FIRST LEG
Thursday, 20 February 2014
Ajax (0) 0
Red Bull Salzburg (3) 3 *(Jonathan 14 (pen), 35, Mane 21)*   51,240
Ajax: (433) Cillessen; Van Rhijn, Veltman, Moisander, Blind; Duarte (Poulsen 59), De Jong, Sigthorsson (Kishna 59); Fischer, Bojan, Klaassen (Andersen 81).
Red Bull Salzburg: (442) Gulacsi; Schwegler, Hinteregger, Andre Ramalho, Ulmer; Mane, Ilsanker, Leitgeb (Berisha 83), Kampl (Svento 88); Jonathan (Zulj 77), Alan.

Anzhi Makhachkala (0) 0
Genk (0) 0   3168
Anzhi Makhachkala: (532) Kerzhakov; Yeschenko, Grigalava, Epureanu, Tagirbekov (Ewerton 86), Gadzhibekov; Ahmedov, Maksimov■, Aliyev; Bukharov, Smolov (Abdulavov 73).
Genk: (4141) Koteles; Mbodji, Koulibaly, Simaeys, Hamalainen; Hyland; Gorius, Buffel (Camus 81), Kumordzi (M'Boyo 70), Vossen; Cisse (De Ceulaer 64).

Chornomorets (0) 0
Lyon (0) 0   28,456
Chornomorets: (4411) Past; Zubeyko, Berger, Fontanello, Anderson Mineiro; Leo Matos (Rebenok 66), Kovalchuk K, Bobko, Djadjedje (Okriashvili 86); Gai (Didenko 90); Antonov.
Lyon: (442) Vercoutre; Bisevac, Kone B, Sarr, Zeffane; Tolisso, Mvuemba, Ferri, Malbranque; Danic, Briand (Fekir 84).

Dnipro (0) 1 *(Konoplyanka 81 (pen))*
Tottenham H (0) 0   22,356
Dnipro: (4411) Boyko; Fedetskiy, Mazuch, Cheberyachko, Strinic; Kankava, Rotan, Zozulya, Giuliano (Politylo 76); Konoplyanka; Matheus (Kulakov 89).
Tottenham H: (451) Friedel; Naughton, Dawson, Vertonghen, Rose; Townsend (Eriksen 63), Paulinho, Capoue, Bentaleb, Chadli; Soldado (Kane 85).

Dynamo Kyiv (0) 0
Valencia (0) 2 *(Vargas 80, Feghouli 90)*   3711
Dynamo Kyiv: (4231) Shovkovskiy (Rybka 54); Danilo Silva, Vida, Dragovic, Makarenko; Veloso, Vukojevic; Gusev, Belhanda (Garmash 73), Lens (Kravets 83); Ideye.
Valencia: (442) Diego Alves; Joao Pereira, Ricardo Costa, Mathieu, Bernat; Michel (Feghouli 67), Keita, Javi Fuego, Parejo; Alcacer (Vargas 59), Jonas (Barragan 88).

Esbjerg (1) 1 *(Pusic 10)*
Fiorentina (3) 3 *(Matri 8, Ilicic 15, Aquilani 37 (pen))*   11,033
Esbjerg: (4411) Dubravka; Ankersen P, Drobo-Ampem, Jakobsen, Knudsen; Ankersen J, Lekven (Rasmussen 72), Andreasen (Bergvold 83), Lyng (Andersen 46); Fellah; Pusic.
Fiorentina: (433) Neto; Roncaglia, Savic, Compper, Pasqual; Fernandez (Bakic 65), Aquilani (Pizarro 75), Valero; Ilicic, Matri (Gomez 55), Ryder.

FC Porto (1) 2 *(Quaresma 45, Varela 68)*
Eintracht Frankfurt (0) 2 *(Joselu 72, Alex Sandro 78 (og))*   25,107
FC Porto: (4231) Helton; Danilo, Maicon, Mangala, Alex Sandro; Fernando (Ghilas 82), Herrera; Quaresma, Josue (Carlos Eduardo 67), Varela; Martinez.
Eintracht Frankfurt: (4231) Trapp; Jung, Zambrano, Madlung, Oczipka; Schwegler, Russ; Rode (Barnetta 71), Meier, Flum (Lanig 88); Joselu (Aigner 90).

Juventus (1) 2 *(Osvaldo 15, Pogba 90)*
Trabzonspor (0) 0   35,436
Juventus: (352) Buffon; Caceres, Bonucci, Ogbonna; Isla (Vidal 66), Pogba, Pirlo, Marchisio (Giovinco 76), Peluso; Tevez, Osvaldo (Llorente 66).
Trabzonspor: (451) Kivrak; Bosingwa, Yumlu, Demir, Keles; Adin, Zokora, Bourceanu (Erdogan 67), Colman, Hurmaci (Mierzejewski 81); Gural (Paulo Henrique 56).

Lazio (0) 0
Ludogorets (1) 1 *(Bezjak 45)*   7459
Lazio: (343) Berisha; Ciani, Cana, Radu; Cavanda■, Onazi, Biglia, Lulic (Kakuta 68); Felipe Anderson (Candreva 58), Klose (Perea 78), Keita Balde.
Ludogorets: (4231) Stoyanov V; Junior Caicara, Mantyla, Moti, Minev; Zlatinski, Dyakov■; Aleksandrov, Marcelinho (Quixada 88), Misidjan (Lumu 81); Bezjak (Fabio Espinho 59).

Maccabi Tel Aviv (0) 0
FC Basel (0) 0   13,519
Maccabi Tel Aviv: (433) Juan Pablo; Yeyni, Carlos Garcia, Tibi, Ben Haroush; Radi, Mitrovic (Prica 58), Alberman (Einbinder 82); Zahavi, Yitzhaki, Micha.
FC Basel: (541) Sommer; Degen P, Sauro, Suchy, Ajeti Arlind, Safari; El-Nenny, Die (Diaz 84), Delgado (Frei 63), Xhaka; Sio (Stocker 79).

Maribor (1) 2 *(Tavares 33, Vrsic 81)*
Sevilla (0) 2 *(Gameiro 47, Fazio 71)*   12,700
Maribor: (442) Handanovic; Milec, Rajcevic, Arghus, Viler; Mezga (Vrsic 75), Filipovic, Dervisevic (Cvijanovic 86), Bohar; Tavares, Mendy (Tajic 85).
Sevilla: (442) Javi Varas; Diogo Figueiras, Fazio, Pareja (Iborra 58), Fernando Navarro; Carrico, Cristoforo (Trochowski 83); Vitolo, Rakitic, Cheryshev (Marin 40); Gameiro.

PAOK Salonika (0) 0
Benfica (0) 1 *(Lima 59)* 24,670
PAOK Salonika: (433) Glykos; Kitsiou, Katsouranis, Insaurralde, Lino; Kace, Lazar (Salpingidis 82), Maduro; Ninis (Lucas 63), Athanasiadis, Oliseh (Stoch 76).
Benfica: (433) Artur Moraes; Maxi Pereira, Luisao, Jardel, Silvio; Gomes (Markovic 66), Ruben Amorim, Perez (Fejsa 63); Djuricic, Lima, Sulejmani (Salvio 75).

Real Betis (1) 1 *(Didac 4)*
Rubin Kazan (0) 1 *(Eremenko 74 (pen))* ⁻ 11,825
Real Betis: (4231) Adan; Juanfran, N'Diaye, Didac, Perquis; Reyes (Jorge Molina 78), Igiebor (Nono 68); Leo Baptistao, Sevilla, Cedrick; Chuli (Ruben Castro 53).
Rubin Kazan: (4231) Ryzhikov; Kuzmin, Sharonov, Burlak, Kisliak; M'Vila, Kulik (Mullin 67 (Kvirkvelia 90)); Karadeniz, Eremenko, Torbinsky; Prudnikov■.

Slovan Liberec (0) 0
AZ Alkmaar (0) 1 *(Viergever 89)* 6719
Slovan Liberec: (4411) Kovar; Coufal, Kovac, Rajnoch, Fleisman; Sural, Sackey, Rybalka, Frydek; Pavelka; Budnik (Pimpara 86).
AZ Alkmaar: (442) Alvarado; Reijnen, Gouweleeuw, Wuytens, Viergever; Gudelj, Ortiz, Elm, Gudmundsson; Johannsson, Beerens.

Swansea C (0) 0
Napoli (0) 0 19,567
Swansea C: (4231) Vorm; Rangel, Chico, Williams, Davies; Canas (Shelvey 71), Britton; Dyer (Emnes 78), Routledge, Hernandez (de Guzman 56); Bony.
Napoli: (4231) Rafael Cabral (Reina 46); Maggio, Henrique, Britos, Reveillere; Dzemaili, Inler; Callejon, Hamsik, Insigne (Mertens 74); Higuain (Pandev 83).

Viktoria Plzen (0) 1 *(Tecl 62)*
Shakhtar Donetsk (0) 1 *(Luiz Adriano 66)* 11,170
Viktoria Plzen: (4231) Kozacik; Reznik, Cisovsky, Prochazka, Limbersky; Horava, Horvath; Petrzela, Kolar (Bakos 87), Duris; Tecl (Wagner 81).
Shakhtar Donetsk: (4231) Pyatov; Srna, Kucher, Rakitskiy, Ismaily; Fred, Hubschman; Douglas Costa (Eduardo 87), Alex Teixeira, Taison (Bernard 68); Luiz Adriano (Ferreyra 85).

ROUND OF 32 SECOND LEG

Thursday, 27 February 2014

AZ Alkmaar (1) 1 *(Viergever 19)*
Slovan Liberec (0) 1 *(Budnik 72)* 10,166
AZ Alkmaar: (433) Alvarado; Viergever, Reijnen, Gouweleeuw, Wuytens; Gudelj, Elm, Ortiz; Gudmundsson, Johannsson (Lewis 75), Beerens (Poulsen 87).
Slovan Liberec: (4231) Hroso; Coufal, Frydek (Djika 31), Kovac, Rajnoch; Fleisman, Pavelka; Rybalka, Jarolim (Pimpara 69), Sural; Budnik (Kolar 82).

Benfica (0) 3 *(Gaitan 70, Lima 79 (pen), Markovic 80)*
PAOK Salonika (0) 0 31,058
Benfica: (442) Artur Moraes; Maxi Pereira, Luisao, Garay, Silvio; Gomes, Ruben Amorim, Gaitan, Djuricic (Rodrigo 79); Cardozo (Lima 60), Salvio (Markovic 60).
PAOK Salonika: (442) Glykos; Kitsiou, Insaurralde, Maduro, Katsouranis■; Lino, Lazar, Kace, Lucas (Vukic 74); Oliseh (Stoch 46 (Ninis 83)), Athanasiadis.

Eintracht Frankfurt (1) 3 *(Aigner 37, Meier 52, 76)*
FC Porto (0) 3 *(Mangala 58, 71, Ghilas 86)* 48,000
Eintracht Frankfurt: (4231) Trapp; Jung, Madlung, Zambrano, Oczipka; Flum, Schwegler; Aigner (Rosenthal 69), Meier, Barnetta; Joselu (Lanig 85).
FC Porto: (433) Helton; Danilo, Maicon, Mangala, Alex Sandro; Fernando, Carlos Eduardo, Herrera (Ghilas 54); Varela (Lica 78), Martinez (Reyes 90), Quaresma.
FC Porto won on away goals rule.

FC Basel (1) 3 *(Stocker 18, Streller 60, 71)*
Maccabi Tel Aviv (0) 0 15,212
FC Basel: (442) Sommer; Degen P, Ajeti Arlind, Safari, Suchy; Sauro, Die, Stocker (Xhaka 73), Frei (Delgado 80); El-Nenny, Streller (Sio 77).
Maccabi Tel Aviv: (442) Juan Pablo; Ben Haroush, Ziv, Tibi, Mareval (Ben Haim 63); Alberman, Radi (Micha 59), Yeyni, Altman (Mitrovic 43); Zahavi, Prica.

Fiorentina (0) 1 *(Ilicic 47)*
Esbjerg (0) 1 *(Vestergaard 90)* 13,815
Fiorentina: (433) Rosati; Roncaglia, Rodriguez (Tomovic 59), Compper, Pasqual (Vargas 78); Ambrosini (Bakic 65), Pizarro, Valero; Ilicic, Gomez, Ryder.
Esbjerg: (4411) Dubravka; Laursen, Lucena, Drobo-Ampem, Knudsen; Rasmussen (Vestergaard 42), Bergvold, Andersen (Lekven 68), Nielsen; Pusic (Ankersen J 56); van Buren.

Genk (0) 0
Anzhi Makhachkala (0) 2 *(Tshimanga 64 (og), Aliyev 71)* 10,176
Genk: (442) Van Hout; Koulibaly (Ngcongca 68), Simaeys, Mbodji, Tshimanga; De Ceulaer, Kumordzi, Gorius (Cisse 72), Camus; Vossen, M'Boyo (Buffel 57).
Anzhi Makhachkala: (4231) Kerzhakov; Yeschenko, Grigalava, Epureanu, Tagirbekov■; Gadzhibekov, Mkrtchyan (Agalarov 90); Ahmedov, Aliyev (Angbwa 88), Bukharov (Serderov 46); Smolov.

Ludogorets (0) 3 *(Bezjak 67, Zlatinski 78, Quixada 89)*
Lazio (1) 3 *(Keita Balde 1, Perea 54, Klose 83)* 28,742
Ludogorets: (4411) Stoyanov V; Mantyla (Quixada 85), Minev, Moti, Junior Caicara; Aleksandrov (Lumu 57), Fabio Espinho, Zlatinski, Marcelinho (Michel Platini 77); Bezjak; Misidjan.
Lazio: (433) Marchetti; Ciani, Biava, Radu, Konko; Biglia, Onazi, Ledesma; Candreva (Lulic 64), Perea (Klose 71), Keita Balde (Gonzalez 84).

Lyon (0) 1 *(Lacazette 80)*
Chornomorets (0) 0 25,039
Lyon: (433) Lopes; Miguel Lopes, Bisevac, Umtiti, Bedimo; Ferri, Fofana, Malbranque (Tolisso 85); Grenier, Lacazette (Kone B 86), Gomis (Briand 81).
Chornomorets: (4231) Past; Zubeyko■, Berger, Fontanello, Anderson Mineiro; Kovalchuk (Didenko 85), Bobko; Leo Matos, Gai (Okriashvili 89), Djadjedje; Antonov.

Napoli (1) 3 *(Insigne 17, Higuain 78, Inler 90)*
Swansea C (1) 1 *(de Guzman 30)* 31,121
Napoli: (4231) Reina; Maggio, Albiol, Henrique, Ghoulam; Inler, Behrami; Callejon (Britos 84), Pandev (Hamsik 59), Insigne (Mertens 68); Higuain.
Swansea C: (4231) Vorm; Tiendalli, Williams, Chico, Davies; Canas, de Guzman (Pozuelo 82); Routledge (Dyer 62), Emnes (Taylor 70), Hernandez; Bony.

Red Bull Salzburg (0) 3 *(van der Hoorn 56 (og), Mane 66, Jonathan 77)*
Ajax (0) 1 *(Klaassen 82)* 29,320
Red Bull Salzburg: (433) Gulacsi; Schwegler (Klein 88), Ulmer (Svento 79), Hinteregger, Andre Ramalho; Ilsanker, Leitgeb, Kampl; Alan (Zulj 73), Mane, Jonathan.
Ajax: (4312) Cillessen; Van Rhijn, van der Hoorn, Blind, Denswil; Poulsen (Riedewald 62), Duarte (Andersen 79), De Jong (Bojan 62); Klaassen; Sigthorsson, De Sa.

Rubin Kazan (0) 0
Real Betis (1) 2 *(Nono 45, Ruben Castro 64)* 5102
Rubin Kazan: (343) Ryzhikov; Kvirkvelia, Burlak, Sharonov (Cesar Navas 73); Kisliak, Eremenko, M'Vila (Abishov 76), Mavinga; Mukhametshin (Wakaso 46), Mullin, Karadeniz.
Real Betis: (4231) Adan; Juanfran, Perquis, Jordi, Didac; N'Diaye, Reyes; Leo Baptistao, Nono (Caro 79), Cedrick (Sevilla 70); Ruben Castro (Varela 81).

Sevilla (1) 2 *(Reyes 42, Gameiro 59)*
Maribor (0) 1 *(Vrsic 90)* 21,562
Sevilla: (4231) Javi Varas; Diogo Figueiras, Pareja (Iborra 46), Fazio, Moreno; Carrico, Trochowski; Reyes (Marin 73), Rakitic, Vitolo; Gameiro (Bacca 81).
Maribor: (4231) Handanovic; Milec, Rajcevic, Arghus, Viler; Filipovic, Mertelj (Vrsic 60); Mezga (Cvijanovic 53), Dervisevic, Bohar; Mendy (Fajic 68).

Shakhtar Donetsk (0) 1 *(Luiz Adriano 89)*
Viktoria Plzen (2) 2 *(Kolar 29, Petrzela 33)* 36,729
Shakhtar Donetsk: (4231) Pyatov; Srna, Kucher, Kryvtsov, Shevchuk; Stepanenko, Ilsinho (Ferreyra 67); Douglas Costa, Alex Teixeira, Bernard (Taison 67); Luiz Adriano.
Viktoria Plzen: (4231) Bolek; Reznik, Prochazka, Cisovsky, Hubnik; Horvath, Horava; Petrzela (Bakos 68), Kolar, Duris (Kovarik 79); Tecl (Hejda 90).

Tottenham H (0) 3 *(Eriksen 56, Adebayor 65, 69)*
Dnipro (0) 1 *(Zozulya 48)* 34,815
Tottenham H: (442) Lloris; Naughton, Dawson, Vertonghen, Fryers; Townsend (Lennon 85), Sandro (Bentaleb 76), Dembele, Eriksen; Soldado (Kane 88), Adebayor.
Dnipro: (4411) Boyko; Fedetskiy (Kulakov 84), Mazuch, Cheberyachko, Strinic; Matheus, Kankava (Seleznyov 70), Rotan, Konoplyanka; Giuliano; Zozulya■.

Trabzonspor (0) 0
Juventus (2) 2 *(Vidal 19, Osvaldo 34)* 20,686
Trabzonspor: (451) Kivrak; Bosingwa (Osmanpasa 46), Demir, Yumlu, Mierzejewski (Bourceanu 72); Malouda, Zokora, Hurmaci, Adin, Keles (Yavru 37); Janko.
Juventus: (451) Buffon; Caceres (Barzagli 58), Ogbonna, Peluso, Bonucci; Pogba (Padoin 38), Marchisio (Pirlo 72), Vidal, Isla, Giovinco; Osvaldo.

Valencia (0) 0
Dynamo Kyiv (0) 0 26,261
Valencia: (352) Diego Alves; Joao Pereira, Ricardo Costa (Senderos 66), Mathieu; Bernat, Michel (Barragan 74), Parejo, Keita, Cartabia (Portu 81); Alcacer, Vargas.
Dynamo Kyiv: (442) Rybka; Danilo Silva, Khacheridi, Dragovic, Makarenko; Lens (Gusev 76), Veloso, Vukojevic, Yarmolenko; Haruna (Bezus 65), Ideye (Mbokani 70).

ROUND OF 16 FIRST LEG
Thursday, 13 March 2014
AZ Alkmaar (1) 1 *(Johannsson 29 (pen))*
Anzhi Makhachkala (0) 0 9653
AZ Alkmaar: (433) Alvarado; Johansson, Gouweleeuw, Viergever, Poulsen (Wuytens 46); Gudelj, Ortiz, Elm; Berghuis (Gudmundsson 24), Johannsson, Beerens.
Anzhi Makhachkala: (4231) Kerzhakov; Angbwa, Ewerton (Burmistrov 46), Gadzhibekov, Yeschenko; Mkrtchyan, Epureanu; Aliyev (Serderov 71), Ahmedov, Smolov; Bukharov (Abdulavov 86).

FC Basel (0) 0
Red Bull Salzburg (0) 0 17,027
FC Basel: (4411) Sommer; Degen P, Sauro, Suchy, Ajeti Arlind; Die (Embolo 90), Frei, Stocker, Degen D; Delgado (El-Nenny 71); Sio (Ajeti Albian 90).
Red Bull Salzburg: (442) Gulacsi; Schwegler (Klein 46), Andre Ramalho, Hinteregger, Svento; Kampl (Lazaro 90), Ilsanker, Leitgeb, Mane; Zulj (Berisha 85), Jonathan.

FC Porto (0) 1 *(Martinez 57)*
Napoli (0) 0 25,520
FC Porto: (451) Helton; Danilo, Maicon, Mangala, Alex Sandro; Quaresma, Defour (Herrera 87), Fernando, Carlos Eduardo (Quintero 67), Varela (Ghilas 71); Martinez.
Napoli: (4411) Reina; Reveillere, Albiol, Britos, Ghoulam; Callejon (Pandev 79), Henrique, Behrami, Insigne; Hamsik (Mertens 74); Higuain (Zapata 83).

Juventus (1) 1 *(Vidal 3)*
Fiorentina (0) 1 *(Gomez 79)* 39,610
Juventus: (352) Buffon; Caceres, Chiellini, Ogbonna; Isla (Padoin 82), Vidal, Pirlo, Marchisio, Asamoah; Giovinco (Llorente 63), Osvaldo (Pogba 74).
Fiorentina: (4231) Neto; Roncaglia, Rodriguez, Savic, Tomovic; Aquilani (Vargas 76), Pizarro, Valero, Fernandez (Ambrosini 50); Ilicic, Matri (Gomez 67).

Ludogorets (0) 0
Valencia (2) 3 *(Barragan 5, Cartabia 34, Senderos 59)* 41,085
Ludogorets: (4231) Stoyanov V; Junior Caicara, Barthe (Terziev 46), Mantyla (Quixada■ 62), Minev; Fabio Espinho, Dyakov; Aleksandrov, Marcelinho, Misidjan; Bezjak (Michel Platini 73).
Valencia: (442) Diego Alves; Joao Pereira, Senderos, Mathieu, Bernat; Barragan (Feghouli 65), Javi Fuego, Keita■, Cartabia (Jonas 87); Alcacer (Victor Ruiz 56), Vargas.

Lyon (1) 4 *(Fofana 12, 70, Lacazette 53, Mvuemba 61)*
Viktoria Plzen (1) 1 *(Horava 3)* 28,248
Lyon: (433) Lopes; Miguel Lopes, Bisevac, Umtiti, Dabo (Kone B 85); Fofana, Gonalons, Mvuemba; Lacazette (Gomis 83), Malbranque (Tolisso 69), Briand.
Viktoria Plzen: (4231) Bolek; Hubnik, Cisovsky, Prochazka, Limbersky; Horava, Horvath (Hejda 73); Petrzela (Duris 81), Kolar, Kovarik; Tecl.

Sevilla (0) 0
Real Betis (1) 2 *(Leo Baptistao 15, Sevilla 77)* 35,506
Sevilla: (4231) Beto; Coke (Diogo Figueiras 46), Fazio, Fernando Navarro, Moreno; Cristoforo (Gameiro 46), Iborra; Vitolo (Marin 66), Rakitic, Reyes; Bacca.
Real Betis: (541) Adan; Juanfran, Perquis, N'Diaye, Jordi, Didac; Leo Baptistao, Caro, Reyes (Amaya 80), Cedrick (Vadillo 74); Ruben Castro (Sevilla 67).

Tottenham H (0) 1 *(Eriksen 63)*
Benfica (1) 3 *(Rodrigo 29, Luisao 58, 84)* 34,283
Tottenham H: (442) Lloris; Walker (Rose 76), Kaboul, Vertonghen, Naughton; Lennon, Paulinho, Sandro (Bentaleb 82), Eriksen; Adebayor, Kane (Soldado 75).
Benfica: (433) Oblak; Silvio; Luisao, Garay, Siqueira; Fejsa, Ruben Amorim, Sulejmani (Perez 66); Rodrigo (Lima 87), Cardozo (Gaitan 65), Markovic.

ROUND OF 16 SECOND LEG
Thursday, 20 March 2014
Anzhi Makhachkala (0) 0
AZ Alkmaar (0) 0 3896
Anzhi Makhachkala: (442) Kerzhakov; Grigalava, Epureanu, Agalarov (Abdulavov 85), Gadzhibekov; Mkrtchyan■, Sobolev (Serderov 71), Aliyev, Bukharov; Burmistrov (Yeschenko 67), Smolov.
AZ Alkmaar: (442) Alvarado; Johansson, Viergever, Reijnen, Poulsen; Wuytens, Gudelj, Elm, Berghuis; Johannsson, Beerens.

Benfica (1) 2 *(Garay 34, Lima 90 (pen))*
Tottenham H (0) 2 *(Chadli 78, 79)* 40,990
Benfica: (433) Oblak; Maxi Pereira, Luisao, Garay, Siqueira; Salvio, Gomes, Ruben Amorim; Djuricic (Perez 71), Cardozo (Lima 75), Sulejmani (Markovic 90).
Tottenham H: (4231) Friedel; Naughton, Sandro, Fryers, Rose; Sigurdsson, Bentaleb; Lennon, Chadli, Townsend (Eriksen 75); Soldado (Kane 71).

Fiorentina (0) 0
Juventus (0) 1 *(Pirlo 71)* 32,633
Fiorentina: (352) Neto; Tomovic, Rodriguez■, Savic; Cuadrado, Aquilani, Pizarro (Ambrosini 47), Valero, Vargas; Ilicic (Roncaglia 72), Gomez (Matri 63).
Juventus: (352) Buffon; Caceres, Bonucci, Chiellini; Isla (Lichtsteiner 76), Vidal, Pirlo, Pogba, Asamoah; Llorente (Osvaldo 87), Tevez.

Napoli (1) 2 *(Pandev 21, Zapata 90)*
FC Porto (0) 2 *(Ghilas 69, Quaresma 76)*   54,145
Napoli: (4411) Reina; Henrique, Fernandez, Albiol, Ghoulam; Mertens (Callejon 83), Inler, Behrami, Insigne; Pandev (Hamsik 68); Higuain (Zapata 78).
FC Porto: (4141) Fabiano; Danilo, Mangala, Reyes, Ricardo; Fernando; Varela (Ghilas 66), Carlos Eduardo (Josue 63), Defour, Quaresma (Lica 80); Martinez.

Real Betis (0) 0
Sevilla (1) 2 *(Reyes 20, Bacca 75)*   38,799
Real Betis: (541) Adan; Juanfran, Perquis (Nono 14), Amaya, Jordi, Juan Carlos; N'Diaye, Reyes (Jorge Molina 90), Leo Baptistao (Sevilla 73), Cedrick; Ruben Castro.
Sevilla: (4231) Beto; Diogo Figueiras, Fazio, Pareja, Moreno; Mbia (Vitolo 76), Rakitic; Reyes (Coke 50), Gameiro, Marin; Bacca (Jairo 105).
aet; Sevilla won 4-3 on penalties.

Red Bull Salzburg (1) 1 *(Jonathan 22)*
FC Basel (0) 2 *(Streller 51, Sauro 60)*   29,320
Red Bull Salzburg: (442) Gulacsi; Klein, Rodnei, Andre Ramalho, Svento (Meilinger 82); Kampl, Leitgeb, Ilsanker (Zulj 72), Mane; Jonathan (Berisha 78), Alan■.
FC Basel: (343) Sommer; Ajeti Arlind (Embolo 87), Suchy■, Sauro; Degen P, Frei, El-Nenny, Degen D (Aliji 45); Sio (Xhaka 57), Stocker, Streller.

Valencia (0) 1 *(Alcacer 59)*
Ludogorets (0) 0   18,429
Valencia: (4231) Diego Alves; Joao Pereira, Victor Ruiz, Mathieu, Gaya (Bernat 71); Javi Fuego, Michel (Barragan 57); Vargas, Parejo, Cartabia; Alcacer (Jonas 65).
Ludogorets: (4231) Stoyanov V; Junior Caicara, Terziev, Moti, Minev; Zlatinski, Dyakov; Misidjan, Marcelinho (Hernandez 67), Aleksandrov (Lumu 76); Bezjak (Michel Platini 79).

Viktoria Plzen (0) 2 *(Kolar 60, Tecl 62)*
Lyon (1) 1 *(Gomis 45)*   10,352
Viktoria Plzen: (442) Bolek; Reznik, Prochazka, Cisovsky, Limbersky; Hrosovsky, Kolar (Bakos 74), Duris (Koncal 84), Petrzela (Wagner 78); Horava, Tecl.
Lyon: (442) Lopes; Kone B, Bisevac, Dabo, Miguel Lopes (Bedimo 62); Gourcuff, Ferri, Gonalons, Tolisso (Mvuemba 77); Gomis (Malbranque 83), Briand.

QUARTER-FINALS FIRST LEG
Thursday, 3 April 2014
AZ Alkmaar (0) 0
Benfica (0) 1 *(Salvio 49)*   16,906
AZ Alkmaar: (433) Alvarado; Johansson, Gouweleeuw, Viergever, Poulsen (Gudmundsson 49); Gudelj (Henriksen 81), Ortiz, Elm; Beerens, Johannsson, Berghuis.
Benfica: (442) Artur Moraes; Maxi Pereira, Luisao, Garay, Siqueira; Salvio, Ruben Amorim (Andre Almeida 38), Gaitan, Gomes; Cardozo (Lima 64), Rodrigo (Markovic 77).

FC Basel (2) 3 *(Delgado 34, 38, Stocker 90)*
Valencia (0) 0
FC Basel: (433) Sommer; Degen P (Frei 46), Schar (Embolo 72), Sauro, Aliji; Xhaka, Die, Diaz; Degen D, Delgado (El-Nenny 58), Stocker.
Valencia: (442) Guaita; Joao Pereira, Senderos (Barragan 25), Mathieu, Bernat; Feghouli, Keita, Parejo, Cartabia (Piatti 70); Alcacer, Vargas.
Behind closed doors.

FC Porto (1) 1 *(Mangala 31)*
Sevilla (0) 0   31,122
FC Porto: (4321) Fabiano; Danilo, Reyes, Mangala, Alex Sandro; Defour (Herrera 70), Fernando■, Carlos Eduardo (Quintero 57); Varela (Ghilas 76), Quaresma; Martinez.
Sevilla: (4411) Beto; Coke, Pareja, Fernando Navarro, Moreno; Reyes (Vitolo 74), Iborra (Diogo Figueiras 63), Carrico, Marin (Gameiro 63); Rakitic; Bacca.

Lyon (0) 0
Juventus (0) 1 *(Bonucci 85)*   37,084
Lyon: (4231) Lopes; Tolisso, Kone B, Umtiti, Bedimo; Ferri, Gonalons; Malbranque (Fekir 87), Lacazette (Gomis 74), Mvuemba; Briand (N'Jie 89).
Juventus: (3142) Buffon; Caceres, Bonucci, Chiellini; Pirlo, Isla (Lichtsteiner 78), Pogba, Marchisio, Asamoah; Osvaldo (Giovinco 62), Tevez (Vucinic 55).

QUARTER-FINALS SECOND LEG
Thursday, 10 April 2014
Benfica (1) 2 *(Rodrigo 39, 72)*
AZ Alkmaar (0) 0   35,723
Benfica: (451) Artur Moraes; Silvio (Andre Almeida 3), Luisao, Garay, Siqueira; Rodrigo, Salvio, Fejsa (Perez 64), Gomes, Sulejmani (Markovic 70); Cardozo.
AZ Alkmaar: (433) Alvarado; Johansson, Gouweleeuw, Wuytens, Viergever; Gudelj, Ortiz (Henriksen 79), Elm; Berghuis (Haye 77), Johannsson, Beerens (Gudmundsson 77).

Juventus (1) 2 *(Pirlo 4, Umtiti 68 (og))*
Lyon (1) 1 *(Briand 18)*   40,710
Juventus: (352) Buffon; Caceres, Bonucci, Chiellini; Isla, Vidal (Pogba 75), Pirlo, Marchisio, Asamoah; Tevez (Giovinco 77), Vucinic (Llorente 60).
Lyon: (442) Lopes; Abenzoar, Kone B, Umtiti, Bedimo; Malbranque (Danic 76), Ferri, Gonalons, Mvuemba; Briand (N'Jie 70), Lacazette (Gomis 70).

Sevilla (3) 4 *(Rakitic 5 (pen), Vitolo 26, Bacca 30, Gameiro 79)*
FC Porto (0) 1 *(Quaresma 90)*   31,422
Sevilla: (4231) Beto; Coke■, Pareja, Fazio, Fernando Navarro; Carrico, Mbia; Reyes (Diogo Figueiras 56), Rakitic (Trochowski 86), Vitolo; Bacca (Gameiro 69).
FC Porto: (433) Fabiano; Danilo (Kelvin 64), Reyes, Mangala, Alex Sandro; Carlos Eduardo (Quintero 46), Defour, Herrera; Varela (Ricardo 46), Ghilas, Quaresma.

Valencia (2) 5 *(Alcacer 38, 70, 113, Vargas 43, Bernat 118)*
FC Basel (0) 0   33,152
Valencia: (442) Guaita; Joao Pereira (Piatti 110), Javi Fuego, Mathieu (Ricardo Costa 81), Bernat; Feghouli, Parejo, Keita, Cartabia (Jonas 76); Alcacer, Vargas.
FC Basel: (442) Sommer; Xhaka, Schar, Sauro■, Safari (Embolo 116); El-Nenny, Die, Diaz■, Degen D (Aliji 60); Frei, Delgado (Sio 53).
aet.

SEMI-FINALS FIRST LEG

Thursday, 24 April 2014

Benfica (1) 2 *(Garay 2, Lima 84)*

Juventus (0) 1 *(Tevez 73)*   55,779

Benfica: (433) Artur Moraes; Maxi Pereira, Luisao, Garay, Siqueira; Markovic, Perez, Gomes (Ivan Cavaleiro 82); Rodrigo, Cardozo (Lima 62), Sulejmani (Andre Almeida 60).

Juventus: (4231) Buffon; Caceres, Bonucci, Chiellini, Pirlo; Lichtsteiner, Pogba; Marchisio, Asamoah, Tevez (Osvaldo 83); Vucinic (Giovinco 65).

SEMI-FINALS SECOND LEG

Thursday, 1 May 2014

Juventus (0) 0

Benfica (0) 0   40,775

Juventus: (352) Buffon; Caceres, Bonucci (Giovinco 72), Chiellini; Lichtsteiner, Pogba, Vidal (Marchisio 78), Pirlo, Asamoah; Llorente (Osvaldo 78), Tevez.

Benfica: (433) Oblak; Maxi Pereira, Luisao, Garay, Siqueira; Perez■, Ruben Amorim, Gaitan (Salvio 76); Markovic (Sulejmani 85), Lima, Rodrigo (Andre Almeida 68).

Sevilla (2) 2 *(Mbia 33, Bacca 36)*

Valencia (0) 0   33,496

Sevilla: (4411) Beto; Fazio, Fernando Navarro, Diogo Figueiras, Carrico; Pareja, Mbia, Rakitic, Vitolo (Iborra 90); Bacca (Gameiro 72); Reyes (Marin 58).

Valencia: (442) Guaita; Joao Pereira, Mathieu, Feghouli (Jonas 74); Bernat (Gaya 46); Javi Fuego, Parejo, Cartabia (Piatti 57), Keita; Alcacer, Vargas.

Valencia (2) 3 *(Feghouli 14, Beto 26 (og), Mathieu 69)*

Sevilla (0) 1 *(Mbia 90)*   45,938

Valencia: (442) Diego Alves; Joao Pereira, Ricardo Costa, Mathieu, Bernat; Feghouli, Parejo (Javi Fuego 78), Keita, Piatti (Cartabia 61); Vargas, Jonas (Barragan 84).

Sevilla: (4231) Beto; Coke, Fazio, Pareja, Fernando Navarro (Moreno 72); Mbia, Carrico; Vitolo, Rakitic, Reyes (Marin 79); Bacca (Gameiro 66).

Sevilla won on away goals rule.

UEFA EUROPA LEAGUE FINAL 2014

Wednesday, 14 May 2014

(in Turin, 33,120)

Sevilla (0) 0   **Benfica (0) 0**

(aet; Sevilla won 4-2 on penalties)

Sevilla: (4231) Beto; Coke, Pareja, Fazio, Moreno; Mbia, Carrico; Reyes (Marin 78 (Gameiro 104)), Rakitic, Vitolo (Diogo Figueiras 110); Bacca.

Benfica: (433) Oblak; Maxi Pereira, Luisao, Garay, Siqueira (Cardozo 99); Ruben Amorim, Gomes, Gaitan (Ivan Cavaleiro 118); Sulejmani (Andre Almeida 24), Lima, Rodrigo.

Referee: Felix Brych.

Benfica's Rodrigo shoots during the Portuguese club's UEFA Europa League final against Sevilla at the Juventus Stadium in Turin. The game finished 0-0 after extra time, with the Spanish club winning the penalty shoot-out 4-2 to achieve their third trophy in this competition in eight years. (John Walton/EMPICS Sport)

UEFA CHAMPIONS LEAGUE 2014–15

PARTICIPATING CLUBS

The list below is provisional and is subject to pending legal proceedings and final confirmation from UEFA.

UEFA CHAMPIONS LEAGUE GROUP STAGE
Real Madrid (ESP) – holders
Barcelona (ESP)
Bayern Munich (GER)
Chelsea (ENG)
Benfica (POR)
Atletico Madrid (ESP)
Schalke 04 (GER)
Borussia Dortmund (GER)
Juventus (ITA)
Paris Saint Germain (FRA)
Shakhtar Donetsk (UKR)
FC Basel (SUI)
Manchester C (ENG)
Olympiacos (GRE)
CSKA Moscow (RUS)
Ajax (NED)
Liverpool (ENG)
Sporting Lisbon (POR)
Galatasaray (TUR)
Anderlecht (BEL)
Roma (ITA)
Monaco (FRA)

UEFA CHAMPIONS LEAGUE PLAY-OFF – LEAGUE ROUTE
Arsenal (ENG)
Porto (POR)
Bayer Leverkusen (GER)
Napoli (ITA)
Athletic Bilbao (ESP)

UEFA CHAMPIONS LEAGUE THIRD QUALIFYING ROUND – LEAGUE ROUTE
Zenit St Petersburg (RUS)
Lille (FRA)
FC Copenhagen (DEN)
Standard Liege (BEL)
Besiktas (TUR)
Dnipro Dnipropetrovsk (UKR)
Panathinaikos (GRE)
Feyenoord (NED)
Grasshoppers (SUI)
AEL Limassol (CYP)

UEFA CHAMPIONS LEAGUE THIRD QUALIFYING ROUND – CHAMPIONS ROUTE
Salzburg (AUT)
APOEL (CYP)
Aalborg (DEN)

UEFA CHAMPIONS LEAGUE SECOND QUALIFYING ROUND
Steaua Bucharest (ROU)
Celtic (SCO)
BATE Borisov (BLR)
Sparta Prague (CZE)
Dinamo Zagreb (CRO)
Ludogorets Razgrad (BUL)
Maccabi Tel Aviv (ISR)
Sheriff (MDA)
Maribor (SVN)
Legia Warsaw (POL)
Partizan Belgrade (SRB)
Debrecen (HUN)
Slovan Bratislava (SVK)
Aktobe (KAZ)
Ventspils (LVA)
Qarabag (AZE)
HJK Helsinki (FIN)
Dinamo Tbilisi (GEO)
Malmo (SWE)
KR Reykjavik (ISL)
F91 Dudelange (LUX)
Stromsgodset (NOR)
The New Saints (WAL)
Saint Patrick's Ath (IRL)
Skenderbeu (ALB)
Rabotnicki (MKD)
Valletta (MLT)
Zrinjski (BIH)
Cliftonville (NIR)
Zalgiris (LTU)
Sutjeska (MNE)

UEFA CHAMPIONS LEAGUE FIRST QUALIFYING ROUND
Levadia Tallinn (EST)
Torshavn (FRO)
Santa Coloma (AND)
Banants (ARM)
La Fiorita (SMR)
Lincoln (GIB)

UEFA EUROPA LEAGUE 2014–15

PARTICIPATING CLUBS
The list below is provisional and is subject to pending legal proceedings and final confirmation from UEFA.

UEFA EUROPA LEAGUE GROUP STAGE
Sevilla (ESP) - Holders
Dynamo Kyiv (UKR)*
Fiorentina (ITA)
Wolfsburg (GER)
Everton (ENG)
Estoril Praia (POR)
Guingamp (FRA)*

UEFA EUROPA LEAGUE PLAY-OFFS
Inter Milan (ITA)
Tottenham H (ENG)

Villarreal (ESP)
FC Twente (NED)
Metalist Kharkiv (UKR)
PAOK (GRE)
Trabzonspor (TUR)
Borussia Mounchengladbach (GER)
Lokomotiv Moscow (RUS)
Rapid Vienna (AUT)
FC Zurich (SUI)*
Nacional (POR)
Saint Etienne (FRA)
Dynamo Moscow (RUS)
Zwolle (NED)*
Lokeren (BEL)*
Apollon Limassol (CYP)
Midtjylland (DEN)

**UEFA EUROPA LEAGUE
THIRD QUALIFYING ROUND**
Olympique Lyonnais (FRA)
PSV Eindhoven (NED)
Viktoria Plzen (CZE)
Club Brugge (BEL)
Real Sociedad (ESP)
Young Boys (SUI)
Mainz 05 (GER)
Hull C (ENG)§
Chornomorets Odesa (UKR)
Torino (ITA)
Rio Ave (POR)§
Atromitos (GRE)
Krasnodar (RUS)
Brondby (DEN)
Hapoel Kiryat Shmona (ISR)*
Astra Giurgiu (ROU)*
Kardemir Karabukspor (TUR)
Ermis Aradippou (CYP)§

**UEFA EUROPA LEAGUE
SECOND QUALIFYING ROUND**
Spartak Moscow (RUS)
Hapoel Tel Aviv (ISR)
Cluj (ROU)
Lech Poznan (POL)
Slovan Liberec (CZE)
Bursaspor (TUR)
Esbjerg (DEN)
Zulte Waregem (BEL)
Elfsborg (SWE)*
Omonia (CYP)
Hajduk Split (CRO)
Molde (NOR)*
Luzern (SUI)
CSKA Sofia (BUL)
HNK Rijeka (CRO)*
FC Groningen (NED)
Asteras Tripolis (GRE)
Motherwell (SCO)
Zorya Luhansk (UKR)
Mlada Boleslav (CZE)
AIK Solna (SWE)
Neftchi (AZE)*
Petrolul Ploiesti (ROU)
Vojvodina (SRB)*
Dinamo Minsk (BLR)
Grodig (AUT)
SKN St Pölten (AUT)§
Zestafoni (GEO)
Ruch Chorzow (POL)
Sarajevo (BIH)*
Hapoel Beer Sheva (ISR)
Shakhtyor Soligorsk (BLR)*
Gyori ETO (HUN)
St Johnstone (SCO)*
Zawisza Bydgoszcz (POL)*
Neman Grodno (BLR)
MFK Kosice (SVK)*
Jagodina (SRB)
Trencin (SVK)
Gorica (SVN)*
RoPS Rovaniemi (FIN)*

UEFA EUROPA LEAGUE FIRST QUALIFYING ROUND
Rosenborg (NOR)
Tromso (NOR)¶
Litex Lovech (BUL)
Ekranas (LTU)
Hafnarfjordur (ISL)
IFK Gothenburg (SWE)

Zeljeznicar (BIH)
Shakhter Karagandy (KAZ)
Spartak Trnava (SVK)
Differdange 03 (LUX)*
Hajduk Split (CRO)
Linfield (NIR)
Inter Baku (AZE)
Pyunik (ARM)*
Aberdeen (SCO)
Siroki Brijeg (BIH)
Botev Plovdiv (BUL)§
Honka Espoo (FIN)
Sligo R (IRL)*
Birkirkara (MLT)
Buducnost Podgorica (MNE)
Vaduz (LIE)*
Koper (SVN)
Bangor C (WAL)
Brommapojkarna (SWE)¶
Zimbru Chisinau (MDA)*
Myllykosken Pallo-47 (FIN)¶
Haugesund (NOR)
Nomme Kalju (EST)
Cukaricki (SRB)
Ferencvaros (HUN)
Daugava Daugavpils (LVA)
Jeunesse Esch (LUX)
Rudar Velenje (SVN)
Kukesi (ALB)
Metalurg Skopje (MKD)
Derry C (IRL)
Chikhura Sachkhere (GEO)§
Flamurtari (ALB)*
Tiraspol (MDA)
Diosgyori (HUN)§
Skendija (MKD)
Fola Esch (LUX)
Crusaders (NIR)
Sant Julia (AND)*
Shirak (ARM)
Veris (MDA)
Gabala (AZE)
Mika (ARM)
Sioni Bolnisi (GEO)
Hibernians (MLT)
Sliema Wanderers (MLT)§
Celik Niksic (MNE)
Astana (KAZ)
Fram Reykjavík (ISL)*
Jelgava (LVA)*
Víkingur (FRO)*
Kairat (KAZ)
Laci (ALB)
Turnovo (MKD)
Dundalk (IRL)
Vaasa (FIN)
Stjarnan (ISL)
Banga (LTU)
Daugava Riga (LVA)
Lovcen (MNE)*
B36 Torshavn (FRO)
Santa Coloma (AND)
Sillamae Kalev (EST)
Atlantas (LTU)
Fuglafjordur (FRO)
AUK Broughton (WAL)
Glenavon (NIR)*
Libertas (SMR)*
Aberystwyth T (WAL)§
Santos Tartu (EST)§
Folgore/Falciano (SMR)
College Europa (GIB)§

---

* – cup winners; † – league cup winners; § – losing cup finalists; ¶ – Fair Play winners.

BRITISH AND IRISH CLUBS IN EUROPE

SUMMARY OF APPEARANCES

EUROPEAN CUP AND CHAMPIONS LEAGUE (1955–2014)

(Winners in brackets) (SE = seasons entered).

	SE	P	W	D	L	F	A
ENGLAND							
Manchester U (3)	25	253	141	62	50	469	240
Liverpool (5)	20	175	99	39	37	317	144
Arsenal	18	175	88	39	48	280	176
Chelsea (1)	12	136	69	38	29	222	117
Leeds U	4	40	22	6	12	76	41
Manchester C	4	22	8	5	9	36	33
Nottingham F (2)	3	20	12	4	4	32	14
Newcastle U	3	24	11	3	10	33	33
Everton	3	10	2	5	3	14	10
Tottenham H	2	20	9	4	7	46	32
Aston Villa (1)	2	15	9	3	3	24	10
Derby Co	2	12	6	2	4	18	12
Wolverhampton W	2	8	2	2	4	12	16
Ipswich T	1	4	3	0	1	16	5
Burnley	1	4	2	0	2	8	8
Blackburn R	1	6	1	1	4	5	8
SCOTLAND							
Rangers	30	161	62	40	59	232	218
Celtic (1)	28	164	78	26	60	241	183
Aberdeen	3	12	5	4	3	14	12
Hearts	3	8	2	1	5	8	16
Dundee U	1	8	5	1	2	14	5
Dundee	1	8	5	0	3	20	14
Hibernian	1	6	3	1	2	9	5
Kilmarnock	1	4	1	2	1	4	7
Motherwell	1	2	0	0	2	0	5
WALES							
The New Saints	7	16	2	2	12	12	32
Barry T	6	14	4	1	9	11	38
Rhyl	2	4	0	0	4	1	19
Cwmbran T	1	2	1	0	1	4	4
Llanelli	1	2	1	0	1	1	4
Bangor C	1	2	0	0	2	0	13
NORTHERN IRELAND							
Linfield	27	63	6	22	35	55	112
Glentoran	12	28	3	7	18	20	59
Portadown	3	6	0	1	5	3	24
Crusaders	3	6	0	0	6	2	27
Cliftonville	2	4	0	0	4	1	18
Glenavon	1	2	0	1	1	0	3
Lisburn Distillery	1	2	0	1	1	3	8
Ards	1	2	0	0	2	3	10
Coleraine	1	2	0	0	2	1	11
REPUBLIC OF IRELAND							
Shamrock R	9	20	1	6	13	9	33
Dundalk	7	18	3	4	11	13	41
Shelbourne	6	20	4	8	8	21	31
Bohemians	6	18	4	4	10	13	29
Waterford U	6	14	3	0	11	15	47
Derry C	4	9	1	1	7	9	26
St Patrick's Ath	3	6	0	2	4	1	17
Dublin C	3	6	1	0	5	3	25
Cork C	2	8	2	1	5	7	12
Athlone T	2	4	0	2	2	7	14
Sligo R	2	4	0	0	4	0	9
Limerick	2	4	0	0	4	4	16
Drogheda U	1	4	2	1	1	6	5
Cork Hibernians	1	2	0	0	2	1	7
Cork Celtic	1	2	0	0	2	1	7

UEFA CUP AND EUROPA LEAGUE 1971–2014

	SE	P	W	D	L	F	A
ENGLAND							
Aston Villa	13	56	24	14	18	77	60
Liverpool (3)	12	107	59	27	21	166	80
Tottenham H (2)	12	118	68	30	20	244	98
Ipswich T (1)	10	52	30	10	12	98	53
Newcastle U	8	72	42	17	13	123	60
Manchester C	8	52	28	13	11	84	51
Leeds U	8	46	20	10	16	66	48
Everton	7	32	17	4	11	54	37
Manchester U	7	24	7	10	7	25	23
Arsenal	6	25	12	4	9	45	32
Blackburn R	6	22	7	8	7	27	26
Southampton	5	12	2	6	4	11	14
Chelsea (1)	4	17	10	2	5	28	20
Wolverhampton W	4	20	13	3	4	41	23
Fulham	3	39	21	10	8	64	31
Nottingham F	3	20	10	5	5	18	16
Stoke C	3	16	8	4	4	21	16
WBA	3	12	5	2	5	15	13
West Ham U	2	6	2	1	3	6	7
Leicester C	2	4	0	1	3	3	8
Middlesbrough	2	25	13	4	8	36	24
Bolton W	2	18	6	10	2	18	14
QPR	2	12	8	1	3	39	18
Derby Co	2	10	5	2	3	32	17
Birmingham C	1	8	4	2	2	11	8
Norwich C	1	6	2	2	2	6	4
Portsmouth	1	6	2	2	2	11	10
Watford	1	6	2	1	3	10	12
Wigan Ath	1	6	1	2	3	6	7
Sheffield W	1	4	2	1	1	13	7
Millwall	1	2	0	1	1	2	4
SCOTLAND							
Dundee U	19	82	33	25	24	134	89
Celtic	17	85	38	19	28	134	85
Rangers	16	76	31	23	22	99	77
Aberdeen	16	54	15	18	21	63	77
Hearts	13	46	19	9	18	54	57
Hibernian	11	32	11	9	12	40	51
Motherwell	7	24	8	1	15	29	29
St Johnstone	4	16	6	4	6	18	20
Dundee	4	14	6	0	8	24	24
Kilmarnock	3	12	4	2	6	7	14
St Mirren	3	10	2	3	5	9	12
Dunfermline Ath	2	4	0	2	2	4	6
Raith R	1	6	2	1	3	10	8
Livingston	1	4	1	2	1	7	9
Falkirk	1	2	1	0	1	1	2
Gretna	1	2	0	1	1	3	7
Queen of the South	1	2	0	0	2	2	4
Partick Th	1	2	0	0	2	0	4
WALES							
Bangor C	8	18	2	2	14	10	49
The New Saints	8	18	1	2	15	12	49
Llanelli	5	12	3	3	6	12	24
Rhyl	3	8	2	1	5	9	12
UWIC Inter Cardiff	3	6	1	0	5	1	18
Cwmbran T	3	6	0	0	6	0	21
Barry T	2	8	2	2	4	10	16
Carmarthen T	2	6	1	0	5	8	21
Newtown	2	4	0	1	3	1	14
Prestatyn T	1	4	1	0	3	3	11
Bala T	1	2	1	0	1	2	3
Air UK Broughton	1	2	0	2	0	1	1
Afan Lido	1	2	0	1	1	1	2
Cefn Druids	1	2	0	1	1	0	5
Port Talbot T	1	2	0	0	2	1	7
Neath	1	2	0	0	2	1	6
Haverfordwest Co	1	2	0	0	2	1	4
Swansea C	1	12	4	4	4	17	10
NORTHERN IRELAND							
Glentoran	17	38	3	8	27	21	90
Portadown	11	28	3	7	18	16	62
Linfield	9	24	6	6	12	25	48
Coleraine	7	14	1	3	10	8	36
Crusaders	7	14	1	2	11	10	38
Glenavon	5	12	1	2	9	3	24
Cliftonville	4	10	2	2	6	4	22
Ards	1	2	1	0	1	4	8
Ballymena U	1	2	1	0	1	2	4
Dungannon Swifts	1	2	1	0	1	1	4
Lisburn Distillery	1	2	0	0	2	1	11
Bangor	1	2	0	0	2	0	6

REPUBLIC OF IRELAND

Bohemians	14	30	3	9	18	16	56
St Patrick's Ath	8	32	9	6	17	30	49
Derry C	6	18	4	5	9	16	26
Cork C	6	16	2	4	10	8	26
Shelbourne	6	12	0	2	10	8	28
Shamrock R	5	20	4	2	14	17	43
Dundalk	5	12	1	2	9	5	31
Drogheda U	4	12	3	4	5	10	24

Longford T	3	6	1	1	4	6	12
Sligo R	3	6	0	3	3	4	9
Finn Harps	3	6	0	0	6	3	33
Athlone T	1	4	1	2	1	4	5
Limerick	1	2	0	1	1	1	4
Sporting Fingal	1	2	0	0	2	4	6
Galway U	1	2	0	0	2	2	8
Bray W	1	2	0	0	2	0	8

EUROPEAN CUP WINNERS' CUP 1960–1999

ENGLAND	SE	P	W	D	L	F	A
Tottenham H (1)	6	33	20	5	8	65	34
Chelsea (2)	5	39	23	10	6	81	28
Liverpool	5	29	16	5	8	57	29
Manchester U (1)	5	31	16	9	6	55	35
West Ham U (1)	4	30	15	6	9	58	42
Arsenal (1)	3	27	15	10	2	48	20
Everton (1)	3	17	11	4	2	25	9
Manchester C (1)	2	18	11	2	5	32	13
Ipswich T	1	6	3	2	1	6	3
Leeds U	1	9	5	3	1	13	3
Leicester C	1	4	2	1	1	8	5
Newcastle U	1	2	1	0	1	2	2
Southampton	1	6	4	0	2	16	8
Sunderland	1	4	3	0	1	5	3
WBA	1	6	2	2	2	8	5
Wolverhampton W	1	4	1	1	2	6	5

SCOTLAND							
Rangers (1)	10	54	27	11	16	100	62
Aberdeen (1)	8	39	22	5	12	79	37
Celtic	8	38	21	4	13	75	37
Dundee U	3	10	3	3	4	9	10
Hearts	3	10	3	3	4	16	14
Dunfermline Ath	2	14	7	2	5	34	14
Airdrieonians	1	2	0	0	2	1	3
Dundee	1	2	0	1	1	3	4
Hibernian	1	6	3	1	2	19	10
Kilmarnock	1	4	1	2	1	5	6
Motherwell	1	2	1	0	1	3	3
St Mirren	1	4	1	2	1	1	2

WALES							
Cardiff C	14	49	16	14	19	67	61
Wrexham	8	28	10	8	10	34	35
Swansea C	7	18	3	4	11	32	37
Bangor C	3	9	1	2	6	5	12
Barry T	1	2	0	0	2	0	7
Borough U	1	4	1	1	2	2	4
Cwmbran T	1	2	0	0	2	2	12
Merthyr Tydfil	1	2	1	0	1	2	3
Newport Co	1	6	2	3	1	12	3
The New Saints (Llansantffraid)	1	2	0	1	1	1	6

NORTHERN IRELAND							
Glentoran	9	22	3	7	12	18	46
Glenavon	5	10	1	3	6	11	25
Ballymena U	4	8	0	0	8	1	25
Coleraine	4	8	0	1	7	7	34
Crusaders	3	6	0	2	4	5	18
Derry C	3	6	1	1	4	1	11
Linfield	3	6	2	0	4	6	11
Ards	2	4	0	1	3	2	17
Bangor	2	4	0	1	3	2	8
Carrick Rangers	1	4	1	0	3	7	12
Cliftonville	1	2	0	0	2	0	8
Distillery	1	2	0	0	2	1	7
Portadown	1	2	1	0	1	4	7

REPUBLIC OF IRELAND							
Shamrock R	6	16	5	2	9	19	27
Shelbourne	4	10	1	1	8	9	20
Bohemians	3	8	2	2	4	6	13
Dundalk	3	8	2	1	5	7	14
Limerick U	3	6	0	1	5	2	11
Waterford U	3	8	1	1	6	6	14
Cork C	2	4	1	0	3	2	9
Cork Hibernians	2	6	2	1	3	7	8
Galway U	2	4	0	0	4	2	11
Sligo R	2	6	1	1	4	5	11
Bray W	1	2	0	1	1	1	3
Cork Celtic	1	2	0	1	1	1	3
Finn Harps	1	2	0	1	1	2	4
Home Farm	1	2	0	1	1	1	7
St Patrick's Ath	1	2	0	0	2	1	8
University College Dublin	1	2	0	1	1	0	1

INTER-CITIES FAIRS CUP 1955–1970

ENGLAND	SE	P	W	D	L	F	A
Leeds U (2)	5	53	28	17	8	92	40
Birmingham C	4	25	14	6	5	51	38
Liverpool	4	22	12	4	6	46	15
Arsenal (1)	3	24	12	5	7	46	19
Chelsea	3	20	10	5	5	33	24
Everton	3	12	7	2	3	22	15
Newcastle U (1)	3	24	13	6	5	37	21
Nottingham F	2	6	3	0	3	8	9
Sheffield W	2	10	5	0	5	25	18
Burnley	1	8	4	3	1	16	5
Coventry C	1	4	3	0	1	9	8
London XI	1	8	4	1	3	14	13
Manchester U	1	11	6	3	2	29	10
Southampton	1	6	2	3	1	11	6
WBA	1	4	1	1	2	7	9

SCOTLAND							
Hibernian	7	36	18	5	13	66	60
Dunfermline Ath	5	28	16	3	9	49	31
Kilmarnock	4	20	8	3	9	34	32
Dundee U	3	10	5	1	4	11	12
Hearts	3	12	4	4	4	20	20
Rangers	3	18	8	4	6	27	17
Celtic	2	6	1	3	2	9	10
Aberdeen	1	4	2	1	1	4	4
Dundee	1	8	5	1	2	14	6
Morton	1	2	0	0	2	3	9
Partick Th	1	4	3	0	1	10	7

NORTHERN IRELAND							
Glentoran	4	8	1	1	6	7	22
Coleraine	2	8	2	1	5	15	23
Linfield	2	4	1	0	3	3	11

REPUBLIC OF IRELAND							
Drumcondra	2	6	2	0	4	8	19
Dundalk	2	6	1	1	4	4	25
Shamrock R	2	4	0	2	2	4	6
Cork Hibernians	1	2	0	0	2	1	6
Shelbourne	1	5	1	2	2	3	4
St Patrick's Ath	1	2	0	0	2	4	9

FIFA CLUB WORLD CUP 2013

Formerly known as the FIFA Club World Championship, this tournament is played annually between the champion clubs from all 6 continental confederations, although since 2007 the champions of Oceania must play a qualifying play-off against the champion club of the host country.

(Finals in Morocco)

■ *Denotes player sent off.*

PLAY-OFF FOR QUARTER FINALS
Wednesday 11 December 2013
Raja Casablanca (1) 2 *(Iajour 39, Hafidi 90)*
Auckland City (0) 1 *(Krishna 63)*   34,875
Raja Casablanca: Askri; Oulhaj, Karrouchy, Belmaalem, El Hachimi, Raki, Moutouali, Guehi, Chtibi (Kanda 74), Hafidi (Rahmani 90), Iajour (Mabide 85).
Auckland City: Williams; Vicelich, Irving (Pritchett 86), Angel Berlanga, Iwata, Koprivcic (Browne 82), Bilen, Cristobal, Bale, Krishna, Dickinson (Tade 64).
Referee: B. Gassama.

QUARTER-FINALS
Saturday 14 December 2013
Guangzhou Evergrande (0) 2 *(Elkeson 49, Conca 67)*
Al Ahly (0) 0   34,579
Guangzhou Evergrande: Zeng Cheng; Sun Xiang (Zhao Xuri 79), Feng Xiaoting, Young-Gwon Kim, Zhang Linpeng, Zheng Zhi, Huang Bowen, Conca, Elkeson, Gao Lin (Rong Hao 63), Muriqui.
Al Ahly: Sherif Ekramy; Ahmed Fathy, Ahmed Shedid, Mohamed Naguib, Saad Samir, Rami Rabia, Hossam Ashour (Trezeguet 78), Abdalla El Said, Waleed Soliman, Mohamed Abo Trika (Da Sylva 46), Emad Moteab (Al Sayed Hamdy 64).
Referee: Sandro Meira Ricci.

Raja Casablanca (1) 2 *(Chtibi 25, Guehi 95)*
Monterrey (0) 1 *(Basanta 53)*   34,579
aet.
Raja Casablanca: Askri; Oulhaj, Karrouchy, Belmaalem, El Hachimi, Raki, Moutouali, Guehi, Chtibi (Mabide 67), Hafidi (Salhi 81), Iajour (Coulibaly 109).
Monterrey: Orozco; Basanta, Leobardo Lopez, Meza, Juarez (Chavez 101), Osorio, Cardozo, Zavala (de Jesus 99), Lucas Silva, Suazo, Delgado (Arellano 76).
Referee: A. Faghani.

SEMI-FINALS
Tuesday 17 December 2013
Guangzhou Evergrande (0) 0
Bayern Munich (2) 3 *(Ribery 40, Mandzukic 44, Gotze 47)*
                                                          27,311
Guangzhou Evergrande: Zeng Cheng; Sun Xiang, Feng Xiaoting, Young-Gwon Kim, Zhang Linpeng, Zheng Zhi, Zhao Xuri (Feng Junyan 76), Huang Bowen (Rong Hao 46), Conca, Elkeson, Muriqui (Gao Lin 72).
Bayern Munich: Neuer; Lahm, Rafinha, Van Buyten, Boateng, Alaba, Ribery (Shaqiri 72), Kroos (Javi Martinez 58), Thiago Alcantara, Gotze, Mandzukic (Pizarro 75).
Referee: B. Gassama.

Wednesday 18 December 2013
Raja Casablanca (0) 3 *(Iajour 51, Moutouali 84 (pen), Mabide 90)*
Atletico Mineiro (0) 1 *(Ronaldinho Gaucho 64)*   35,219
Raja Casablanca: Askri; Oulhaj, Karrouchy, Belmaalem, El Hachimi, Raki, Moutouali, Guehi, Chtibi (Mabide 55), Hafidi (Kanda 76), Iajour (Coulibaly 87).
Atletico Mineiro: Victor; Leonardo Silva, Rever, Marcos Rocha (Luan 63), Ronaldinho Gaucho, Pierre, Josue (Leandro Donizete 58), Lucas Candido (Alecsandro 85), Diego Tardelli, Jo, Fernandinho.
Referee: Carlos Velasco.

MATCH FOR FIFTH PLACE
Wednesday 18 December 2013
Al Ahly (1) 1 *(Emad Moteab 8)*
Monterrey (4) 5 *(Cardozo 3, Delgado 22, 65, Leobardo Lopez 27, Suazo 45 (pen))*   35,219
Al Ahly: Sherif Ekramy; Ahmed Fathy, Wael Gomaa, Ahmed Shedid (Saad Samir 46), Mohamed Naguib, Rami Rabia, Abdalla El Said, Waleed Soliman (Ahmed Shokri 66), Shehab Ahmed, Trezeguet, Emad Moteab (Amr Gamal 68).
Monterrey: Ibarra; Basanta, Leobardo Lopez, Meza, Chavez, Juarez (Garcia 86), Osorio, Cardozo (Arellano 78), Lucas Silva (Zavala 89), Suazo, Delgado.
Referee: M. Geiger.

MATCH FOR THIRD PLACE
Saturday 21 December 2013
Guangzhou Evergrande (2) 2 *(Muriqui 9, Conca 15 (pen))*
Atletico Mineiro (2) 3 *(Diego Tardelli 2, Ronaldinho Gaucho 45, Luan 90)*   37,774
Guangzhou Evergrande: Li Shuai; Sun Xiang (Rong Hao 64), Feng Xiaoting, Young-Gwon Kim, Zhang Linpeng, Zheng Zhi (Zhao Xuri 85), Huang Bowen, Conca, Elkeson (Feng Junyan 77), Gao Lin, Muriqui.
Atletico Mineiro: Victor; Leonardo Silva, Rever, Marcos Rocha, Ronaldinho Gaucho■, Pierre, Josue (Leandro Donizete 79), Lucas Candido (Junior Cesar 34), Diego Tardelli, Jo (Luan 60), Fernandinho.
Referee: A. Faghani.

FIFA CLUB WORLD CUP FINAL 2013

Marrakesh, Wednesday 21 December 2013 (attendance 37,774)

Bayern Munich (2) 2 *(Dante 7, Thiago Alcantara 22)*   **Raja Casablanca (0) 0**

Bayern Munich: Neuer; Lahm, Rafinha, Boateng, Alaba, Dante, Ribery, Kroos (Javi Martinez 60), Thiago Alcantara, Shaqiri (Gotze 80), Muller (Mandzukic 76).
Raja Casablanca: Askri; Oulhaj, Karrouchy, Belmaalem, El Hachimi, Raki, Moutouali, Guehi, Chtibi (Mabide 50), Hafidi (Kachani 88), Iajour (Soulaimani 78).
Referee: Sandro Meira Ricci.

PREVIOUS FINALS

2000 Corinthians beat Vaso de Gama 4-3 on penalties after 0-0 draw
2005 Sao Paulo beat Liverpool 1-0
2006 Internacional beat Barcelona 1-0
2007 AC Milan beat Boca Juniors 4-2
2008 Manchester U beat Liga De Quito 1-0

2009 Barcelona beat Estudiantes 2-1
2010 Internazionale beat TP Mazembe Englebert 3-0
2011 Barcelona beat Santos 4-0
2012 Corinthians beat Chelsea 1-0
2013 Bayern Munich beat Raja Casablanca 2-0

WORLD CLUB CHAMPIONSHIP

Played annually up to 1974 and intermittently since then between the winners of the European Cup and the winners of the South American Champions Cup — known as the Copa Libertadores. In 1980 the winners were decided by one match arranged in Tokyo in February 1981 which remained the venue until 2004, when the match was superseded by the FIFA Club World Championship. AC Milan replaced Marseille who had been stripped of their European Cup title in 1993.

1960 Real Madrid beat Penarol 0-0, 5-1
1961 Penarol beat Benfica 0-1, 5-0, 2-1
1962 Santos beat Benfica 3-2, 5-2
1963 Santos beat AC Milan 2-4, 4-2, 1-0
1964 Inter-Milan beat Independiente 0-1, 2-0, 1-0
1965 Inter-Milan beat Independiente 3-0, 0-0
1966 Penarol beat Real Madrid 2-0, 2-0
1967 Racing Club beat Celtic 0-1, 2-1, 1-0
1968 Estudiantes beat Manchester United 1-0, 1-1
1969 AC Milan beat Estudiantes 3-0, 1-2
1970 Feyenoord beat Estudiantes 2-2, 1-0
1971 Nacional beat Panathinaikos* 1-1, 2-1
1972 Ajax beat Independiente 1-1, 3-0
1973 Independiente beat Juventus* 1-0
1974 Atlético Madrid* beat Independiente 0-1, 2-0
1975 Independiente and Bayern Munich could not agree dates; no matches.
1976 Bayern Munich beat Cruzeiro 2-0, 0-0
1977 Boca Juniors beat Borussia Moenchengladbach* 2-2, 3-0
1978 Not contested
1979 Olimpia beat Malmö* 1-0, 2-1
1980 Nacional beat Nottingham Forest 1-0
1981 Flamengo beat Liverpool 3-0
1982 Penarol beat Aston Villa 2-0
1983 Gremio Porto Alegre beat SV Hamburg 2-1
1984 Independiente beat Liverpool 1-0

1985 Juventus beat Argentinos Juniors 4-2 on penalties after a 2-2 draw
1986 River Plate beat Steaua Bucharest 1-0
1987 FC Porto beat Penarol 2-1 after extra time
1988 Nacional (Uru) beat PSV Eindhoven 7-6 on penalties after 1-1 draw
1989 AC Milan beat Atletico Nacional (Col) 1-0 after extra time
1990 AC Milan beat Olimpia 3-0
1991 Red Star Belgrade beat Colo Colo 3-0
1992 Sao Paulo beat Barcelona 2-1
1993 Sao Paulo beat AC Milan 3-2
1994 Velez Sarsfield beat AC Milan 2-0
1995 Ajax beat Gremio Porto Alegre 4-3 on penalties after 0-0 draw
1996 Juventus beat River Plate 1-0
1997 Borussia Dortmund beat Cruzeiro 2-0
1998 Real Madrid beat Vasco da Gama 2-1
1999 Manchester U beat Palmeiras 1-0
2000 Boca Juniors beat Real Madrid 2-1
2001 Bayern Munich beat Boca Juniors 1-0 after extra time
2002 Real Madrid beat Olimpia 2-0
2003 Boca Juniors beat AC Milan 3-1 on penalties after 1-1 draw
2004 Porto beat Once Caldas 8-7 on penalties after 0-0 draw

*European Cup runners-up; winners declined to take part.

EUROPEAN SUPER CUP 2013

Played annually between the winners of the European Champions' Cup and the European Cup-Winners' Cup (UEFA Cup from 2000; UEFA Europa League from 2010). AC Milan replaced Marseille in 1993–94.

■ *Denotes player sent off.*

Stadion Eden, Prague, Friday 30 August 2013, attendance 20,000
Bayern Munich (0) 2 *(Ribery 47, Martinez 120)*   **Chelsea (1) 2** *(Torres 8, Hazard 93)*
aet; Bayern Munich won 5-4 on penalties.
Bayern Munich: (4141) Neuer; Rafinha (Martinez 56), Boateng, Dante, Alaba; Lahm; Robben (Shaqiri 95), Muller (Gotze 71), Kroos, Ribery; Mandzukic.
Chelsea: (4231) Cech; Ivanovic, Cahill, Luiz, Cole; Ramires■, Lampard; Shurrle (Mikel 87), Oscar, Hazard (Terry 113); Torres (Lukaku 97).
Referee: J. Eriksson.

PREVIOUS MATCHES

1972 Ajax beat Rangers 3-1, 3-2
1973 Ajax beat AC Milan 0-1, 6-0
1974 Not contested
1975 Dynamo Kiev beat Bayern Munich 1-0, 2-0
1976 Anderlecht beat Bayern Munich 4-1, 1-2
1977 Liverpool beat Hamburg 1-1, 6-0
1978 Anderlecht beat Liverpool 3-1, 1-2
1979 Nottingham F beat Barcelona 1-0, 1-1
1980 Valencia beat Nottingham F 1-0, 1-2
1981 Not contested
1982 Aston Villa beat Barcelona 0-1, 3-0
1983 Aberdeen beat Hamburg 0-0, 2-0
1984 Juventus beat Liverpool 2-0
1985 Juventus v Everton not contested due to UEFA ban on English clubs
1986 Steaua Bucharest beat Dynamo Kiev 1-0
1987 FC Porto beat Ajax 1-0, 1-0
1988 KV Mechelen beat PSV Eindhoven 3-0, 0-1
1989 AC Milan beat Barcelona 1-1, 1-0
1990 AC Milan beat Sampdoria 1-1, 2-0
1991 Manchester U beat Red Star Belgrade 1-0
1992 Barcelona beat Werder Bremen 1-1, 2-1

1993 Parma beat AC Milan 0-1, 2-0
1994 AC Milan beat Arsenal 0-0, 2-0
1995 Ajax beat Zaragoza 1-1, 4-0
1996 Juventus beat Paris St Germain 6-1, 3-1
1997 Barcelona beat Borussia Dortmund 2-0, 1-1
1998 Chelsea beat Real Madrid 1-0
1999 Lazio beat Manchester U 1-0
2000 Galatasaray beat Real Madrid 2-1
2001 Liverpool beat Bayern Munich 3-2
2002 Real Madrid beat Feyenoord 3-1
2003 AC Milan beat Porto 1-0
2004 Valencia beat Porto 2-1
2005 Liverpool beat CSKA Moscow 3-1
2006 Sevilla beat Barcelona 3-0
2007 AC Milan beat Sevilla 3-1
2008 Zenit beat Manchester U 2-1
2009 Barcelona beat Shakhtar Donetsk 1-0
2010 Atletico Madrid beat Internazionale 2-0
2011 Barcelona beat Porto 2-0
2012 Atletico Madrid beat Chelsea 4-1
2013 Bayern Munch beat Chelsea 5-4 on penalties after 2-2 draw

INTERNATIONAL DIRECTORY

The latest available information has been given regarding numbers of clubs and players registered with FIFA, the world governing body. Where known, official colours are listed. With European countries, League tables show a number of signs: * team relegated, *+ team relegated after play-offs, ┴ team not relegated after play-offs.

There are 209 member associations. The four home countries, England, Scotland, Northern Ireland and Wales, are dealt with elsewhere in the Yearbook; but basic details appear in this directory. The following countries are not members of FIFA: Gibraltar (now a full UEFA member), Kosovo, and Northern Cyprus. *N.B. In this edition international results for 2013–14 include matches played from 1 July 2013 to 13 July 2014.*

There are a number of associate members and others who have affiliation to their confederations, but there is only one recent official addition and that is South Sudan. Of the many affiliated countries, they include Northern Mariana Islands, Reunion, Zanzibar, French Guiana, Saint-Martin, Sint Maarten, Kiribati, Niue and Tuvalu.

EUROPE

ALBANIA

Football Association of Albania, Rruga e Elbasanit, 1000 Tirana.
Founded: 1930; *National Colours:* Red shirts, black shorts, red socks.

International matches 2013–14
Armenia (h) 2-0, Slovenia (a) 0-1, Iceland (a) 1-2, Switzerland (h) 1-2, Cyprus (a) 0-0, Belarus (n) 0-0, Malta (h) 2-0, Romania (n) 0-1, Hungary (a) 0-1, San Marino (a) 3-0.

League Championship wins (1930–37; 1945–2013)
KF Tirana 24 (formerly SK Tirana; includes 17 Nentori 8); Dinamo Tirana 18; Partizani Tirana 15; Vllaznia 9; Skenderbeu 5; Elbasan 2 (including Labinoti 1); Flamurtari 1; Teuta 1.

Cup wins (1948–2014)
Partizani Tirana 15; KF Tirana 15 (formerly SK Tirana; includes 17 Nentori 8); Dinamo Tirana 13; Vllaznia 6; Flamurtari 4; Teuta 3; Elbasan 2 (including Labinoti 1); Besa 2; Apolonia 1; Laci 1.

Final League Table 2013–14

	P	W	D	L	F	A	GD	Pts
Skenderbeu	33	18	7	8	52	32	20	61
Kukesi	33	16	9	8	46	34	12	57
Laci	33	16	6	11	41	28	13	54
Teuta	33	14	12	7	46	35	11	54
Partizani	33	15	8	10	33	26	7	53
Tirana	33	14	8	11	36	31	5	50
Flamurtari (–3)	33	14	9	10	45	40	5	48
Vllaznia	33	12	9	12	42	36	6	45
Besa* (–3)	33	11	9	13	34	32	2	39
Kastrioti*	33	8	5	20	26	46	–20	29
Lushnja*	33	7	5	21	32	59	–27	26
Bylis*	33	5	9	19	20	54	–34	24

Top scorer: Pejic (Skenderbeu) 20.
Cup Final: Flamurtari 1, Kukesi 0.

ANDORRA

Federacio Andorrana de Futbol, Avda Carlemany 67, 3er Pis, Apartado postal 65, Escaldes-Engordany.
Founded: 1994; *National Colours:* All red.

International matches 2013–14
Moldova (a) 1-1, Turkey (a) 0-5, Netherlands (h) 0-2, Romania (h) 0-4, Hungary (a) 0-2, Moldova (h) 0-3, Indonesia (n) 0-1.

League Championship wins (1996–2014)
FC Santa Coloma 7; Principat 3; Encamp 2; Ranger's 2; Sant Julia 2; Lusitanos 2; Constelacio 1.

Cup wins (1991–2014)
FC Santa Coloma 9; Principat 6; Sant Julia 4; Constelacio 1; Lusitanos 1; UE Santa Coloma 1.

Qualifying League Table 2013–14

	P	W	D	L	F	A	GD	Pts
FC Santa Coloma	14	10	2	2	41	7	34	32
Lusitanos	14	10	0	4	50	11	39	30
Sant Julia	14	9	3	2	41	14	27	30
UE Santa Coloma	14	9	2	3	35	17	18	29
Ordino	14	6	2	6	26	27	–1	20
Encamp	14	4	1	9	21	47	–26	13
Inter Club	14	2	1	11	11	41	–30	7
Principat	14	0	1	13	1	62	–61	1

Championship Round

	P	W	D	L	F	A	GD	Pts
FC Santa Coloma	20	13	3	4	50	12	38	42
UE Santa Coloma	20	12	3	5	40	24	16	39
Sant Julia	20	11	5	4	46	19	27	38
Lusitans	20	11	2	7	57	20	37	35

Relegation Round

	P	W	D	L	F	A	GD	Pts
Ordino	20	9	5	6	41	34	7	32
Encamp	20	7	4	9	34	53	–19	25
Inter Club+	20	3	2	15	16	55	–39	11
Principat*	20	1	2	17	8	75	–67	5

Top scorer: Dos Reis (Lusitanos) 13.
Cup Final: Sant Julia 2, Lusitanos 1.

ARMENIA

Football Federation of Armenia, Khanjyan 27, 0010 Yerevan, Armenia.
Founded: 1992; *National Colours:* Red shirts, red shorts, red and yellow socks.

International matches 2013–14
Albania (a) 0-2, Czech Republic (a) 2-1, Denmark (h) 0-1, Bulgaria (h) 2-1, Italy (a) 2-2, Russia (a) 0-2, UAE (n) 4-3, Algeria (n) 1-3, Germany (a) 1-6.

League Championship wins (1992–2014)
Pyunik 13 (including Homenetmen); Shirak 5*; Ararat Yerevan 2*; Araks 2 (including Tsement); FC Yerevan 1; Ulisses 1; Banants 1.
*Includes one unofficial title.

Cup wins (1992–2014)
Mika 6; Pyunik 6; Ararat Yerevan 5; Banants 2; Tsement 2; Pyunik (including Homenetmen) 1; Shirak 1.

Final League Table 2013–14

	P	W	D	L	F	A	GD	Pts
Banants	28	14	8	6	38	23	15	50
Shirak	28	13	8	7	48	31	17	47
Mika	28	12	11	5	36	27	9	47
Ararat	28	12	8	8	30	23	7	44
Gandzasar	28	8	11	9	36	31	5	35
Pyunik	28	8	8	12	41	39	2	32
Ulisses	28	7	4	17	21	45	–24	25
Alashkert*	28	6	6	16	38	69	–31	24

Top scorer: Manasyan (Alashkert) 17.
Cup Final: Pyunik 2, Gandzasar 1.

AUSTRIA

Oesterreichischer Fussball-Bund, Ernst-Happel Stadion – Sektor A/F, Postfach 340, Meierestrasse 7, Wien 1021.
Founded: 1904; *National Colours:* White shirts, black shorts, white socks.

International matches 2013–14
Greece (h) 0-2, Germany (a) 0-3, Republic of Ireland (h) 1-0, Sweden (a) 1-2, Faroe Islands (a) 3-0, USA (h) 1-0, Uruguay (h) 1-1, Iceland (h) 1-1, Czech Republic (a) 2-1.

League Championship wins (1912–2014)
Rapid Vienna 32; FK Austria Vienna (formerly Amateure) 24; Wacker Innsbruck 10 (incl. Svarowski Tirol 2, Tirol Innsbruck 3); Admira Vienna (now Admira Wacker Modling) 9 (incl. Wacker Vienna 1); Red Bull Salzburg 8 (incl. Austria Salzburg 3); First Vienna 6; Wiener Sportklub 3; Sturm Graz 3; WAF 1; WAC 1; Florisdorfer 1; Hakoah 1; Linz ASK 1; Voest Linz 1; Graz 1.

Cup wins (1919–2013)
FK Austria Vienna (formerly Amateure) 27; Rapid Vienna 14; Wacker Innsbruck 7 (incl. Svarowski Tirol 1, Tirol Innsbruck); Admira Vienna 6 (including Wacker Vienna 1); Graz 4; Sturm Graz 4; First Vienna 3; WAC 2; Ried 2; Red Bull Salzburg 2; Linz ASK 1; WAF 1; Wiener Sportklub 1; Kremser 1; Stockerau 1; Karnten 1; Kremser 1; Horn 1; Pasching 1.

Final League Table 2013–14

	P	W	D	L	F	A	GD	Pts
Red Bull Salzburg	36	25	5	6	110	35	75	80
Rapid Vienna	36	17	11	8	63	40	23	62
Grodig	36	15	9	12	68	71	–3	54
FK Austria Vienna	36	14	11	11	58	44	14	53
Sturm Graz	36	13	9	14	55	55	0	48
Ried	36	10	13	13	55	66	–11	43
Wolfsberger	36	11	8	17	50	63	–13	41
Wiener Neustadt	36	10	9	17	43	84	–41	39
Admira (–5)	36	11	9	16	51	67	–16	37
Wacker Innsbruck*	36	5	14	17	42	70	–28	29

Top scorer: Soriano (Red Bull Salzburg) 31.
Cup Final: Red Bull Salzburg 4, St Polten 2.

AZERBAIJAN

Association of Football Federations of Azerbaijan, 2208 Nobel prospekti, 1025 Baku.
Founded: 1992; *National Colours:* White shirts, blue shorts, white socks.

International matches 2013–14
Malta (h) 3-0, Israel (a) 1-1, Northern Ireland (h) 2-0, Russia (h) 1-1, Estonia (a) 1-2, Kyrgyzstan (a) 0-0, Philippines (n) 1-0, USA (a) 0-2.

League Championship wins (1992–2014)
Neftchi 8; Kapaz 3; Shamkir 3; Qarabag 2; FK Baku 2; Inter Baku 2; Turan 1; Khazar Lankaran 1.
Includes one unofficial title for Shamkir in 2002.

Cup wins (1992–2013)
Neftchi 7; Kapaz 4; Qarabag 3; Khazar Lankaran 3; FK Baku 3; Inshatchi 1; Shafa 1.
Includes one title awarded by forfeit to Neftchi in 2002.

Final League Table 2013–14

	P	W	D	L	F	A	GD	Pts
Qarabag	36	21	9	6	66	21	45	72
Inter Baku	36	20	7	9	60	37	23	67
Gabala	36	18	7	11	48	36	12	61
Neftchi	36	17	9	10	48	42	6	60
FK Baku	36	16	9	11	53	43	10	57
Khazar Lankaran	36	12	13	11	44	49	–5	49
Simurq	36	11	13	12	35	28	7	46
Olimpik Suvalan	36	6	13	17	29	49	–20	31
Sumgayit	36	5	10	21	27	61	–34	25
Ravan Baku*	36	4	10	22	22	66	–44	22

Top scorer: Reynaldo (Qarabag) 22.
Cup Final: Neftchi 1, Gabala 1.
aet; Neftchi won 3-2 on penalties.

BELARUS

Belarus Football Federation, Prospekt Pobeditelei 20/3, Minsk 220020.
Founded: 1992; *National Colours:* All red.

International matches 2013–14
Montenegro (h) 1-1, Kyrgyzstan (h) 3-1, France (h) 2-4, Spain (a) 1-2, Japan (h) 1-0, Albania (n) 0-0, Turkey (a) 1-2, Bulgaria (a) 1-2, Iran (n) 0-0, Liechtenstein (a) 5-1.

League Championship wins (1992–2013)
BATE Borisov 9; Dinamo Minsk 7; Slavia Mozyr (formerly MPKC Mozyr) 2; Shakhtyor Soligorsk 2; Dnepr Mogilev 1; Belshina Bobruisk 1; Gomel 1.

Cup wins (1992–2014)
Dinamo Minsk 3; Belshina Bobruisk 3; Slavia Mozyr (formerly MPKC Mozyr) 2; Gomel 2; Shakhtyor Soligorsk 2; MTZ-RIPA 2; BATE Borisov 2; Naftan Novopolotsk 2; Neman Grodno 1; Dinamo 93 Minsk 1; Lokomotiv 96 1; Dinamo Brest 1; FK Minsk 1.

Qualifying League Table 2013

	P	W	D	L	F	A	GD	Pts
Shakhtyor Soligorsk	22	15	4	3	35	13	22	49
BATE Borisov	22	15	3	4	46	17	29	48
Dinamo Minsk	22	9	7	6	30	26	4	34
Gomel	22	9	7	6	25	20	5	34
Neman Grodno	22	8	6	8	23	23	0	30
Torpedo Zhodino	22	8	4	10	26	28	–2	28
Belshina	22	7	7	8	24	28	–4	28
Minsk	22	6	7	9	21	27	–6	25
Dinamo Brest	22	6	6	10	18	30	–12	24
Dnepr Mogilev	22	6	5	11	20	29	–9	23
Naftan Novopolotsk	22	4	9	9	19	29	–10	21
Slavia Mozyr	22	3	7	12	16	33	–17	16

Championship Round

	P	W	D	L	F	A	GD	Pts
BATE Borisov	32	21	4	7	61	25	36	67
Shakhtyor Soligorsk	32	17	7	8	44	26	18	58
Dinamo Minsk	32	15	9	8	44	33	11	54
Neman Grodno	32	13	8	11	34	30	4	47
Torpedo Zhodino	32	12	6	14	33	38	–5	42
Gomel	32	11	7	14	34	40	–6	40

Relegation Round

	P	W	D	L	F	A	GD	Pts
Belshina	32	15	8	9	42	38	4	53
Dinamo Brest	32	11	7	14	32	41	–9	40
Minsk	32	10	8	14	36	40	–4	38
Naftan	32	9	10	13	29	41	–12	37
Dnepr Mogilev+	32	9	6	17	28	42	–14	33
Slavia Mozyr*	32	5	8	19	24	47	–23	23

Top scorer: Rodionov (BATE Borisov) 14.
Cup Final: Shakhtyor Soligorsk 1, Neman Grodno 0.

BELGIUM

Union Royale Belge des Societes de Football-Association, 145 Avenue Houba de Strooper, B-1020 Bruxelles.
Founded: 1895; *National Colours:* All red.

International matches 2013–14
France (h) 0-0, Scotland (a) 2-0, Croatia (a) 2-1, Wales (h) 1-1, Colombia (h) 0-2, Japan (h) 2-3, Ivory Coast (h) 2-2, Luxembourg (h) 5-1, Sweden (a) 2-0, Tunisia (h) 1-0, Algeria (n) 2-1, Russia (n) 1-0, Korea Republic (n) 1-0, USA (n) 2-1, Argentina (n) 0-1.

League Championship wins (1896–2014)
Anderlecht 33; Club Brugge 13; Union St Gilloise 11; Standard Liege 10; Beerschot VAC (became Germinal) 7; RC Brussels 6; FC Liege 5; Daring Brussels 5; Antwerp 4; Mechelen 4; Lierse 4; Cercle Brugge 3; Genk 3; Beveren 2; RWD Molenbeek 1.

Cup wins (1912–14; 1927; 1935; 1954–2014)
Club Brugge 10; Anderlecht 9; Standard Liege 6; Genk 4; KAA Gent 3; Beerschot VAC (became Germinal) 2; Waterschei (became Racing Genk) 2; Beveren 2; Antwerp 2; Lierse 2; Union St Gilloise 2; Cercle Brugge 2; Beerschot Antwerpen Club (incl. Germinal Ekeren) 2; Lokeren 2; Mechelen 1; FC Liege 1; Westerlo 1; La Louviere 1; Zulte-Waregem 1; Daring 1; Tournai 1; Racing 1; Waregem 1.

Qualifying League Table 2013–14

	P	W	D	L	F	A	GD	Pts
Standard Liege	30	20	7	3	59	17	42	67
Club Brugge	30	19	6	5	54	28	26	63
Anderlecht	30	18	3	9	61	31	30	57
Zulte Waregem	30	14	11	5	51	38	13	53
Lokeren	30	15	6	9	48	31	17	51
Genk	30	14	3	13	42	39	3	45
Gent	30	12	8	10	39	37	2	44
Kortrijk	30	10	9	11	42	44	–2	39
Oostende	30	9	7	14	28	46	–18	34
Charleroi	30	8	10	12	36	41	–5	34
Cercle Brugge	30	9	6	15	29	55	–26	33
Lierse	30	9	5	16	36	53	–17	32
Mechelen	30	3	8	15	34	51	–17	31
Waasland-Beveren	30	6	9	15	28	35	–7	27
Oud-Heverlee Leuven	30	6	9	15	30	47	–17	27
Mons	30	6	4	20	29	53	–24	22

NB: Points earned in Qualifying phase are halved and rounded up at start of Championship play-off phase.

Championship Play-off

	P	W	D	L	F	A	GD	Pts
Anderlecht	10	7	1	2	17	6	11	51
Standard Liege	10	4	3	3	14	11	3	49
Club Brugge	10	5	1	4	16	11	5	48
Zulte Waregem	10	4	2	4	16	15	1	41
Lokeren	10	2	2	6	14	25	–11	34
KRC Genk	10	2	3	5	10	19	–9	32

Europa League Qualifying Table A

	P	W	D	L	F	A	GD	Pts
Oostende	6	4	2	0	7	1	6	14
Gent	6	3	1	2	11	6	5	10
Lierse	6	2	0	4	5	12	-7	6
Waasland-Beveren	6	1	1	4	7	11	-4	4

Europa League Qualifying Table B

	P	W	D	L	F	A	GD	Pts
Kortrijk	6	4	1	1	16	5	11	13
Charleroi	6	4	1	1	13	5	8	13
Mechelen	6	3	0	3	6	10	-4	9
Cercle Brugge	6	0	0	6	2	17	-15	0

Europa League Qualifying Play-off
Kortrijk 2, 2, Oostende 2, 2*
aet; Oostende won 7-6 on penalties.

Europa League Testmatch
Not played as Oostende not licensed for European football, so Zulte Waregem enter Europa League 2014–15.

Relegation Table

	P	W	D	L	F	A	GD	Pts
Oud–Heverlee Leuven*+	3	2	1	0	5	1	4	10
Mons*	3	0	1	2	1	5	-4	1

Top scorer: Harbaoui (Lokeren) 22.
Cup Final: Lokeren 1, Zulte Waregem 0.

Bosnia & HERZEGOVINA

Football Federation of Bosnia & Herzegovina, Ferhadija 30, Sarajevo 71000.
Founded: 1992; *National Colours:* White shirts, blue shorts, white socks.

International matches 2013–14
USA (h) 3-4, Slovakia (h) 0-1, Slovakia (a) 2-1, Liechtenstein (h) 4-1, Lithuania (a) 1-0, Argentina (n) 0-2, Egypt (n) 0-2, Ivory Coast (n) 2-1, Mexico (n) 1-2, Argentina (n) 1-2, Nigeria (n) 1-0, Iran (n) 3-1.

League Championship wins (1998; 2000–14)
Zeljeznicar 6; Zrinjski 3; Siroki Brijeg 2; Sarajevo 2; Brotnjo 1; Leotar 1; Modrica 1; Borac Banja Luka 1.

Cup wins (1998; 2000–14)
Zeljeznicar 5; Sarajevo 4; Siroki Brijeg 2; Modrica 1; Orasje 1; Zrinjski 1; Slavija 1; Borac Banja Luka 1.

Final League Table 2013–14

	P	W	D	L	F	A	GD	Pts
Zrinjski	30	18	7	5	56	21	35	61
Siroki Brijeg	30	17	8	5	66	23	43	59
Sarajevo	30	16	10	4	45	21	24	58
Zeljeznicar	30	16	9	5	51	29	22	57
Velez	30	15	9	6	42	23	19	54
Borac Banja Luka	30	13	6	11	39	32	7	45
Celik Zenica	30	10	13	7	35	32	3	43
Olimpik	30	10	11	9	39	30	9	41
Vitez	30	10	6	14	34	39	-5	36
Radnik	30	10	6	14	34	50	-16	36
Mladost Velika Obarska	30	8	9	13	24	38	-14	33
Travnik	30	7	10	13	31	44	-13	31
Slavija (–3)	30	9	7	14	43	-16	31	
Zvijezda	30	9	4	17	25	49	-24	31
Rudar Prijedor*	30	5	12	13	24	39	-15	27
Leotar*	30	2	3	25	11	70	-59	9

Top scorer: Wagner (Siroki Brijeg) 18.
Cup Final: Celik Zenica 0, 1, Sarajevo 2, 3 (agg. 1-5).

BULGARIA

Bulgarian Football Union, 26 Tzar Ivan Assen II Str., 1124 Sofia.
Founded: 1923; *National Colours:* White shirts, green shorts, red socks.

International matches 2013–14
FYR Macedonia (a) 0-2, Italy (a) 0-1, Malta (a) 2-1, Armenia (a) 1-2, Czech Republic (h) 0-1, Belarus (h) 2-1, Canada (n) 1-1.

League Championship wins (1925–2014)
CSKA Sofia 31; Levski Sofia 26; Slavia Sofia 7; Lokomotiv Sofia 4; Litex Sofia 4; Vladislav Varna 3; Ludogorets Razgrad 3; Botev Plovdiv (includes Trakija) 2; AC 23 Sofia 1; Sokol (Spartak) Varna 1; Sportklub Sofia 1; Ticha Varna 1; Spartak Plovdiv 1; Beroe Stara Zagora 1; Etar 1; Lokomotiv Plovdiv 1.

Cup wins (1946–2014)
Levski Sofia 24; CSKA Sofia 19; Slavia Sofia 7; Lokomotiv Sofia 4; Litex Lovech 4; Botev Plovdiv (includes Trakija) 2; Beroe Stara Zagora 2; Ludogorets Razgrad 2; Spartak Plovdiv 1; Septemvri Sofia 1; Spartak Sofia 1; Marek Dupnica 1; Sliven 1.

Final League Table 2013–14

	P	W	D	L	F	A	GD	Pts
Ludogorets Razgrad	38	25	9	4	74	20	54	84
CSKA Sofia	38	21	9	8	56	20	36	72
Litex Lovech	38	21	9	8	74	37	37	72
Botev Plovdiv	38	18	11	9	57	32	25	65
Levski Sofia	38	19	5	14	59	39	20	62
Cherno More Varna	38	14	12	12	40	33	-7	54
Lokomotiv Plovdiv	38	15	5	18	49	55	-6	50
Beroe Stara Zagora	38	21	7	10	58	29	29	70
Slavia Sofia	38	16	7	15	57	46	11	55
Lokomotiv Sofia	38	16	6	16	46	52	-6	54
Chernomorets Burgas*38		13	5	20	56	62	-6	44
Neftochimic Burgas*	38	7	4	27	26	92	-66	25
Pirin Gotse Delchev*	38	4	4	28	35	91	-56	22
Lyubimets 2007*	38	6	3	29	25	104	-79	21

Top scorers (equal): Jordan (Litex Lovech), Kamburov (Lokomotiv Plovdiv) 20.
Cup Final: Ludogorets Razgrad 1, Botev Plovdiv 0.

CHANNEL ISLANDS

Guernsey

League Championship wins (1894–2014)
Northerners 30; Rangers 17; Vale Recreation 15; St Martin's 13; Sylvans 10; Belgrave Wanderers 8; 2nd Bn Manchesters 3; 2nd Bn Royal Irish Regt 2; 2nd Bn Wiltshires 2; 10th Comp W Div Royal Artillery 1; 2nd Bn Leicesters 1; 2nd Bn PA Somerset Light Infantry 1; 2nd Middlesex Regt 1; Athletics 1; Band Comp 2nd Bn Royal Fusiliers 1; G&H Comp Royal Fusiliers 1; Grange 1; Yorkshire Regt (Green Howards) 1.

Final League Table 2013–14

	P	W	D	L	F	A	GD	Pts
Belgrave Wanderers	24	17	6	1	88	29	59	57
Northerners	24	14	4	6	68	44	24	46
Rangers	24	9	7	8	41	44	-3	35
Vale Recreation	24	10	3	11	39	53	-14	33
Sylvans	24	8	4	12	34	50	-16	28
Rovers	24	7	2	15	31	61	-30	23
St Martins	24	4	4	16	30	50	-20	16

Jersey

League Championship wins (1894–2014)
Jersey Wanderers 20; First Tower United 19; St Paul's 15; Jersey Scottish 10; Beeches Old Boys 5; Magpies 4; 2nd Bn King's Own Regt 3; Oaklands 3; St Peter 3; 1st Batt Devon Regt 2; 1st Bn East Surrey Regt 2; Georgetown 2; Mechanics 2; YMCA 2; 2nd Bn East Surrey Regt 1; 20th Comp Royal Garrison Artillery 1; National Rovers 1; Sporting Academics 1; Trinity 1.

Final League Table 2013–14

	P	W	D	L	F	A	GD	Pts
St Paul's	16	13	3	0	56	14	42	42
Jersey Scottish	16	12	3	1	63	15	48	39
Jersey Wanderers	16	8	2	6	35	27	8	26
Trinity	16	8	1	7	43	35	8	25
St Peter	16	6	2	8	29	36	-7	20
St Clement	16	5	4	7	21	38	-17	19
St Ouen	16	3	5	8	28	39	-11	14
St Brelade (–3)	16	4	1	11	25	50	-25	10
Grouville (+3)	16	2	1	13	11	57	-46	10

Upton Park Trophy 2014 (For Guernsey & Jersey League Champions)
Belgrave Wanderers 0, St Paul's 3

Upton Park Trophy wins (1907–2014)
Northerners 18; First Tower United 12; Jersey Wanderers 11; St Martin's 11; St Paul's 7; Jersey Scottish 6; Rangers 5; Vale Recreation 4; Belgrave Wanderers 4; Sylvans 3; Beeches Old Boys 3; Old St Paul's 3; Magpies 3; St Peter 2; Jersey Mechanics 1; Jersey YMCA 1; National Rovers 1; Sporting Academics 1; Trinity 1.

CROATIA

Croatian Football Federation, Rusanova 13, 10 000 Zagreb.
Founded: 1912; *National Colours:* Red and white check shirts, white shorts, blue socks.

International matches 2013–14
Liechtenstein (a) 3-2, Serbia (a) 1-1, Korea Republic (a) 2-1, Belgium (h) 1-2, Scotland (a) 0-2, Iceland (a) 0-0, Iceland (h) 2-0, Switzerland (a) 2-2, Mali (h) 2-1, Australia (n) 1-0, Brazil (a) 1-3, Cameroon (n) 4-0, Mexico (a) 1-3.

League Championship wins (1941–46; 1992–2014)
Dinamo Zagreb (formerly Croatia Zagreb) 16; Hajduk Split 8; Concordia 1; Gradjanski 1; NK Zagreb 1.

Cup wins (1992–2014)
Dinamo Zagreb (formerly Croatia Zagreb) 12; Hajduk Split 6; Rijeka 3, Inter Zapresic 1; Osijek 1.

Final League Table 2013–14

	P	W	D	L	F	A	GD	Pts
Dinamo Zagreb	36	26	6	4	81	26	55	84
Rijeka	36	21	10	5	72	35	37	73
Hajduk Split	36	17	11	8	58	42	16	62
Split	36	14	10	12	41	41	0	52
Lokomotiva Zagreb	36	15	7	14	57	59	–2	52
Istra	36	12	8	16	45	56	–11	44
Zadar	36	10	5	21	35	67	–32	35
Osijek	36	8	9	19	38	62	–24	33
Slaven Koprivnica+	36	7	11	18	46	65	–19	32
Hrvatski Dragovoljac*	36	7	9	20	41	61	–20	30

Top scorer: Cop (Dinamo Zagreb) 22.
Cup Final: Dinamo Zagreb 0, 0, Rijeka 1, 2 (agg. 0-3).

CYPRUS

Cyprus Football Association, 10 Achaion Street, 2413 Engomi, PO Box 25071, 1306 Nicosia.
Founded: 1934; *National Colours:* All blue.

International matches 2013–14
Norway (a) 0-2, Slovenia (h) 0-2, Iceland (a) 0-2, Albania (h) 0-0, Northern Ireland (h) 0-0, Japan (a) 0-1.

League Championship wins (1935–2014)
APOEL 23; Omonia 20; Anorthosis 13; AEL 6; EPA 3; Olympiakos 3; Apollon 3; Pezoporikos 2; Trast 1; Cetinkaya 1.

Cup wins (1935–2014)
APOEL 20; Omonia 14; Anorthosis 10; Apollon 7; AEL 6; EPA 5; Trast 3; Cetinkaya 2; Olympiakos 1; Pezoporikos 1; Nea Salamis 1; AEK 1; APOP 1.

Qualifying League Table 2013–14

	P	W	D	L	F	A	GD	Pts
AEL Limassol	26	19	5	2	48	16	32	62
Apollon Limassol	26	19	2	5	47	19	28	59
APOEL	26	18	5	3	56	18	38	59
Ermis Aradippou	26	15	7	4	44	28	16	52
Omonia	26	13	8	5	45	22	23	47
Anorthosis Famagusta	26	11	5	10	46	36	10	38
AEK Larnaca	26	10	7	9	37	28	9	37
Nea Salamis Famagusta (–3)	26	12	2	12	26	31	–5	35
Doxa Katokopia	26	7	7	12	33	45	–12	28
Ethnikos Achnas	26	6	5	15	27	38	–11	23
AEK Kouklia	26	6	3	17	27	64	–37	21
Aris Limassol	26	3	11	12	29	40	–11	20
Enosis Neon Paralimni* (–3)	26	5	7	14	29	45	–16	19
Alki Larnaca* (–41)	26	0	2	24	14	78	–64	–39

Championship Round

	P	W	D	L	F	A	GD	Pts
APOEL	36	25	6	5	80	25	55	81
AEL Limassol	36	25	6	5	68	29	39	81
Apollon Limassol	36	24	5	7	66	29	37	77
Ermis Aradippou	36	18	8	10	55	54	1	62
Omonia	36	16	11	9	59	37	22	59
Anorthosis Famagusta	36	12	6	18	57	64	–7	42

Relegation Round

	P	W	D	L	F	A	GD	Pts
Nea Salamis Famagusta	36	17	3	16	43	49	–6	51
AEK Larnaca	36	13	11	12	49	36	13	50
Ethnikos Achnas	36	12	8	16	48	45	3	44
Doxa Katokopia	36	11	9	16	50	61	–11	42
Aris Limassol*	36	8	13	15	51	57	–6	37
AEK Kouklia*	36	6	5	25	34	94	–60	23

Top scorers (equal): Monteiro (AEL), Sangoy (Apollon), Tagbajumi (Ermis) 18.
Cup Final: Ermis Aradippou 0, APOEL 2.

CZECH REPUBLIC

Fotbalova Asociace Ceske Republiky, Diskarska 2431/4, PO Box 11, Praha 6 16017.
Founded: 1901; *National Colours:* All red.

International matches 2013–14
Hungary (a) 1-1, Armenia (h) 1-2, Italy (a) 1-2, Malta (a) 4-1, Bulgaria (a) 1-0, Canada (h) 2-0, Norway (h) 2-2, Finland (a) 2-2, Austria (h) 1-2.

League Championship wins – Czechoslovakia (1925–93)
Sparta Prague 21; Slavia Prague 13; Dukla Prague (prev. UDA, now Marila Pribram) 11; Slovan Bratislava (formerly NV Bratislava) 8; Spartak Trnava 5; Banik Ostrava 3; Viktoria Zizkov 1; Inter-Bratislava 1; Spartak Hradec Kralove 1; Zbrojovka Brno 1; Bohemians 1; Vitkovice 1.

Cup wins – Czechoslovakia (1961–93)
Dukla Prague 8; Sparta Prague 8; Slovan Bratislava 5; Spartak Trnava 4; Banik Ostrava 3; Lokomotiva Kosice 2; TJ Gottwaldov 1; Lokomotiva Kosice 1; Dunajska Streda 1.

League Championship wins – Czech Republic (1994–2014)
Sparta Prague 12; Slavia Prague 3; Slovan Liberec 3; Viktoria Plzen 2; Banik Ostrava 1.

Cup wins – Czech Republic (1994–2014)
Sparta Prague 6; Slavia Prague 3; Viktoria Zizkov 2; Jablonec 2; Teplice 2; Hradec Kralove (formerly Spartak) 1; Slovan Liberec 1; Banik Ostrava 1; Viktoria Plzen 1; Mlada Boleslav 1; Sigma Olomouc 1.

Final League Table 2013–14

	P	W	D	L	F	A	GD	Pts
Sparta Prague	30	25	4	1	78	19	59	79
Viktoria Plzen	30	19	9	2	64	21	43	66
Mlada Boleslav	30	14	8	8	54	38	16	50
Slovan Liberec	30	14	6	10	37	46	–9	48
Teplice	30	13	7	10	51	35	16	46
Slovacko	30	11	7	12	43	40	3	40
Dukla Prabue	30	10	8	12	35	37	–2	38
Vysocina Jihlava	30	10	7	13	46	50	–5	37
Zbrojovka Brno	30	10	7	13	32	42	–10	37
Banik Ostrava	30	8	11	11	33	43	–10	35
Jablonec	30	9	7	14	43	53	–10	34
Pribram	30	9	7	14	34	49	–15	34
Slavia Prague	30	8	6	16	24	51	–27	30
Bohemians 1905	30	7	9	14	26	40	–14	30
Sigma Olomouc*	30	7	8	15	42	60	–18	29
Znojmo*	30	6	9	15	32	49	–17	27

Top scorer: Husbauer (Sparta Prague) 18.
Cup Final: Sparta Prague 1, Viktoria Plzen 1.
Sparta Prague won 8-7 on penalties.

DENMARK

Dansk Boldspil-Union, Idraettens Hus, DBU Alle 1, DK-2605, Brondby.
Founded: 1889; *National Colours:* Red shirts, white shorts, red socks.

International matches 2013–14
Poland (a) 2-3, Malta (a) 2-1, Armenia (a) 1-0, Italy (h) 2-2, Malta (h) 6-0, Norway (h) 2-1, England (a) 0-1, Hungary (a) 2-2, Sweden (h) 1-0.

League Championship wins (1913–2014)
KB Copenhagen 15; Brondby 10; FC Copenhagen 10; B 93 Copenhagen 9; AB (Akademisk) 9; B 1903 Copenhagen 7; Frem 6; Esbjerg 5; Vejle 5; AGF Aarhus 5; AaB Aalborg 4; Hvidovre 3; OB Odense 3; B 1909 Odense 2; Koge 2; Lyngby 2; Silkeborg 1; Herfolge 1; Nordsjaelland 1.

Cup wins (1955–2014)
AGF Aarhus 9; Vejle 6; Brondby 6; OB Odense 5; FC Copenhagen 5; Esbjerg 3; AaB Aalborg 3; Randers Freja 3; Lyngby 3; B 1909 Odense 2; Frem 2; B 1903 Copenhagen 2; Nordsjaelland 2; B 93 Copenhagen 1; KB Copenhagen 1; Vanlose 1; Hvidovre 1; B 1913 Odense 1; AB (Akademisk) 1; Viborg 1; Silkeborg 1.

Final League Table 2013–14

	P	W	D	L	F	A	GD	Pts
AaB Aalborg	33	18	8	7	60	38	22	62
FC Copenhagen	33	15	11	7	54	38	16	56
Midtjylland	33	16	7	10	61	38	23	55
Brondby	33	13	13	7	47	38	9	52
Esbjerg	33	13	9	11	47	38	9	48

Nordsjaelland	33	13	7	13	38	44	−6	46
Randers	33	9	14	10	41	45	−4	41
Odense BK	33	10	10	13	47	46	1	40
Vestsjaelland	33	8	14	11	31	42	−11	38
SonderjyskE	33	10	8	15	41	53	−12	38
AGF Aarhus*	33	9	5	19	38	60	−22	32
Viborg*	33	6	10	17	38	63	−25	28

Top scorer: Dalgaard (Viborg) 18.
Cup Final: AaB Aalborg 4, FC Copenhagen 2.

ENGLAND

The Football Association, Wembley Stadium, PO Box 1966, London SW1P 9EQ.
Founded: 1863; *National Colours:* All white.

ESTONIA

Eesti Jalgpalli Liit, A. Le Coq Arena, Asula 4c, 11312 Tallinn.
Founded: 1921; *National Colours:* Blue shirts, black shorts, white socks.

International matches 2013–14
Latvia (h) 1-1, Netherlands (h) 2-2, Hungary (a) 1-5, Turkey (h) 0-2, Romania (h) 0-2, Azerbaijan (h) 2-1, Liechtenstein (a) 3-0, Gibraltar (a) 2-0, Gibraltar (h) 1-1, Latvia (a) 0-0 (2-4p), Finland (n) 0-2, Iceland (a) 0-1,Tajikistan (h) 2-1.

League Championship wins (1921–40; 1992–2013)
Sport 9; Flora 9; Levadia Tallinn (formerly Levadia Maardu) 8; Estonia 5; Tallinn JK 2; Norma 2; Lantana (formerly Nikol) 2; Sillamae Kalev 2; Olimpia Tartu 1; TVMK Tallinn 1; Nomme Kalju 1.

Cup wins (1993–2014)
Levadia Tallinn (formerly Levadia Maardu) 8; Flora 6; Sadam 2; TVMK Tallinn 2; Lantana (formerly Nikol) 1; Norma 1; Trans Narva 1; Levadia Tallinn (pre-2004) 1.

Final League Table 2013
	P	W	D	L	F	A	GD	Pts
Levadia	36	30	1	5	69	24	45	91
Nomme Kalju	36	26	6	4	78	23	55	84
Sillamae Kalev	36	23	6	7	75	22	53	75
Flora	36	21	5	10	83	40	43	68
Paide	36	15	2	19	43	58	−15	47
Tallinna Infonet	36	10	8	18	36	56	−20	38
Trans	36	11	3	22	39	55	−16	36
Tallinna Kalev	36	10	4	22	35	77	−42	34
Tammeka+	36	8	8	20	30	68	−38	32
Kuressaare*	36	2	5	29	22	87	−65	11

Top scorer: Voskoboinikov (Nome Kalju) 23.
Cup Final: Levadia 4, Santos Tartu 0.

FAROE ISLANDS

Faroe Islands Football Association, Gundadalur, PO Box 3028, 110 Torshavn.
Founded: 1979; *National Colours:* White shirts, blue shorts, white socks.

International matches 2013–14
Iceland (a) 0-1, Kazakhstan (a) 1-2, Germany (h) 0-3, Kazakhstan (h) 1-1, Austria (a) 0-3, Malta (a) 2-3, Gibraltar (a) 4-1.

League Championship wins (1942–2014)
HB Torshavn 22; KI Klaksvik 17; B36 Torshavn 9; TB Tvoroyri 7; GI Gota 6; B68 Toftir 3; EB/Streymur 2; SI Sorvag 1; IF Fuglafjordur 1; B71 Sandur 1; VB Vagur 1; NSI Runavik 1.

Cup wins (1955–2013)
HB Torshavn 26; GI Gota 6; TB Tvoroyri 5; B36 Torshavn 5; KI Klaksvik 5; EB/Streymur 4; Vikingur 3; NSI Runavik 2; VB Vagur 1; B71 Sandur 1.

Final League Table 2013
	P	W	D	L	F	A	GD	Pts
HB Torshavn	27	16	6	5	68	34	34	54
IF Fuglafjordur	27	14	7	6	55	48	7	49
B36 Torshavn	27	12	10	5	48	35	13	46
NSI Runavik	27	13	6	8	54	47	7	45
EB/Streymur	27	12	5	10	55	36	19	41
Vikingur	27	12	5	10	41	42	−1	41
AB Argir	27	9	4	14	36	48	−12	31
KI Klaksvik	27	6	10	11	54	55	−1	28
TB Tvoroyri*	27	5	8	14	27	48	−21	23
07 Vestur*	27	3	5	19	25	70	−45	14

Top scorer: Olsen (NSI Runavik) 21.
Cup Final: EB/Streymur 0, Vikingur 2.

FINLAND

Suomen Palloliitto Finlands Bollfoerbund, Urheilukatu 5, PO Box 191, 00251 Helsinki.
Founded: 1907; *National Colours:* White shirts, blue shorts, white socks.

International matches 2013–14
Slovenia (h) 2-0, Spain (h) 0-2, Georgia (a) 1-0, France (a) 0-3, Wales (a) 1-1, Oman (a) 0-0, Hungary (a) 2-1, Czech Republic (h) 2-2, Lithuania (n) 0-1, Estonia (n) 2-0.

League Championship wins (1908–2013)
HJK Helsinki 26; Haka Valkeakoski 9; HPS Helsinki 9; TPS Turku 8; HIFK Helsinki 7; Tampere United (includes Ilves) 5; KuPS Kuopio 5; Kuusysi Lahti 5; KIF Helsinki 4; AIFK Turku 3; Reipas Lahti 3; VIFK Vaasa 3; Jazz Pori 2; KTP Kotka 2; OPS Oulu 2; VPS Vaasa 2; Unitas Helsinki 1; PUS Helsinki 1; Sudet Viipuri 1; HT Helsinki 1; Pyrkiva Turku 1; KPV Kokkola 1; TPV Tampere 1; MyPa Anjalankoski (renamed MYPA-47) 1; Inter Turku 1.

Cup wins (1955–2013)
Haka Valkeakoski 12; HJK Helsinki 11; Reipas Lahti 7; KTP Kotka 4; Tampere United (includes Ilves) 3; TPS Turku 3; MyPa Anjalankoski (renamed MYPA-47) 3; KuPS Kuopio 2; Mikkeli 2; Kuusysi Lahti 2; RoPS Rovaniemi 2; Pallo-Pojat 1; Drott (renamed Jaro) 1; HPS Helsinki 1; AIFK Turku 1; Jokerit (formerly PK-35) 1; Allianssi (formerly Atlantis) 1; Inter Turku1 1; FC Honka 1.

Final League Table 2013
	P	W	D	L	F	A	GD	Pts
HJK Helsinki	33	22	7	4	78	25	53	73
FC Honka	33	18	7	8	51	37	14	61
VPS Vaasa	33	14	9	10	41	39	2	51
IFK Mariehamn	33	14	7	12	57	62	−5	49
FC Lahti	33	15	3	15	47	49	−2	48
MYPA-47	33	14	5	14	42	37	5	47
KuPS Kuopio	33	11	8	14	43	42	1	41
TPS Turku	33	10	11	12	42	46	−4	41
Inter Turku	33	9	13	11	31	38	−7	40
FF Jaro	33	9	10	14	41	50	−9	37
RoPS Rovaniemi	33	8	10	15	25	36	−11	34
JJK Jyvaskyla*	33	4	10	19	27	64	−37	22

Top scorer: Vayrinen (FC Honka) 17.
Cup Final: RoPS Rovaniemi 2, KuPS Kuopio 1.

FRANCE

Federation Francaise de Football, 87 Boulevard de Grenelle, 75738 Paris Cedex 15.
Founded: 1919; *National Colours:* Blue shirts, white shorts, red socks.

International matches 2013–14
Belgium (a) 0-0, Georgia (a) 0-0, Belarus (a) 4-2, Australia (h) 6-0, Finland (h) 3-0, Ukraine (a) 0-2, Ukraine (h) 3-0 Netherlands (h) 2-0, Norway (h) 4-0, Paraguay (h) 1-1, Jamaica (h) 8-0, Honduras (n) 3-0, Switzerland (n) 5-2, Ecuador (n) 0-0, Nigeria (n) 2-0, Germany (n) 0-1.

League Championship wins (1933–2014)
Saint-Etienne 10; Olympique Marseille 9; Nantes 8; AS Monaco 7; Olympique Lyonnais 7; Stade de Reims 6; Bordeaux 6; OGC Nice 4; Paris Saint-Germain 4; Lille OSC (includes Olympique Lillois) 4; FC Sete 2; Sochaux 2; Racing Club Paris 1; Roubaix-Tourcoing 1; Strasbourg 1; Auxerre 1; Lens 1; Montpellier 1.

Cup wins (1918–2014)
Olympique Marseille 10; Paris Saint-Germain 8; Lille OSC 6; Saint-Etienne 6; Red Star 5; Racing Club Paris 5; AS Monaco 5; Olympique Lyonnais 5; Bordeaux 4; Auxerre 4; Strasbourg 3; OGC Nice 3; Nantes 3; CAS Genereaux 2; Montpellier 2; FC Sete 2; Sochaux 2; Stade de Reims 2; Sedan 2; Stade Rennais 2; Metz 2; Guingamp 2; Olympique de Pantin 1; CA Paris 1; Club Français 1; AS Cannes 1; Excelsior Roubaix 1; EF Nancy-Lorraine 1; Toulouse 1; Le Havre 1; AS Nancy 1; Bastia 1; Lorient 1.

Final League Table 2013–14
	P	W	D	L	F	A	GD	Pts
Paris Saint-Germain	38	27	8	3	84	23	61	89
Monaco	38	23	11	4	63	31	32	80
Lille OSC	38	20	11	7	46	26	20	71
Saint-Etienne	38	20	9	9	56	34	22	69

	P	W	D	L	F	A	GD	Pts
Olympique Lyonnais	38	17	10	11	56	44	12	61
Olympique Marseille	38	16	12	10	53	40	13	60
Bordeaux	38	13	14	11	49	43	6	53
Lorient	38	13	10	15	48	53	-5	49
Toulouse	38	12	13	13	46	53	-7	49
Bastia	38	13	10	15	42	56	-14	49
Stade de Reims	38	12	12	14	44	52	-8	48
Stade Rennais	38	11	13	14	47	45	2	46
Nantes	38	12	10	16	38	43	-5	46
Evian	38	11	11	16	39	51	-12	44
Montpellier	38	8	18	12	45	53	-8	42
Guingamp	38	11	9	18	34	42	-8	42
Nice	38	12	6	20	30	44	-14	42
Sochaux*	38	10	10	18	37	61	-24	40
Valenciennes*	38	7	8	23	37	65	-28	29
Ajaccio*	38	4	11	23	37	72	-35	23

Top scorer: Ibrahimovic (Paris Saint-Germain) 26.
Cup Final: Stade Rennais 0, Guingamp 2.

FYR MACEDONIA

Football Federation of the Former Yugoslav Republic of Macedonia, VIII-ma Udarna Brigada 31-A, PO Box 84, 1000 Skopje.
Founded: 1948; *National Colours:* All red.

International matches 2013–14
Bulgaria (h) 2-0, Wales (h) 2-1, Scotland (h) 1-2, Wales (a) 0-1, Serbia (a) 1-5, Latvia (h) 2-1, Cameroon (n) 0-2, Qatar (n) 0-0, China PR (a) 0-2, China PR (a) 0-0.

League Championship wins (1992–2014)
Vardar 7; Rabotnicki 4; Sileks 3; Sloga Jugomagnat 3; Pobeda 2; Makedonija 1; Renova 1; Shkendija 1.

Cup wins (1992–2014)
Vardar 5; Sloga Jugomagnat 3; Rabotnicki 3; Sileks 2; Teteks 2; Pelister 1; Pobeda 1; Cementarnica 55 1; Bashkimi 1; Makedonija 1; Metalurg 1; Renova 1.

Final League Table 2013–14

	P	W	D	L	F	A	GD	Pts
Rabotnicki	33	18	8	7	66	35	31	62
Turnovo	33	18	6	9	61	33	28	60
Metalurg	33	16	11	6	48	29	19	59
Shkendija	33	16	9	8	53	32	21	57
Vardar	33	15	11	7	55	32	23	56
Pelister	33	14	10	9	40	40	0	52
Bregalnica Stip	33	11	11	11	34	34	0	44
Renova	33	10	14	9	42	46	-4	44
Gorno Lisice*	33	9	12	12	34	37	-3	39
Makedonija*	33	9	5	19	40	56	-16	32
Napredok*	33	3	9	21	27	75	-48	18
Gostivar*	33	3	6	24	19	70	-51	15

Top scorer: Blazevski (Turnovo) 19.
Cup Final: Rabotnicki 2, Metalurg 0.

GEORGIA

Georgian Football Federation, 76a Chavchavadze Avenue, 0162 Tbilisi.
Founded: 1990; *National Colours:* All white.

International matches 2013–14
Kazakhstan (a) 0-1, France (h) 0-0, Finland (h) 0-1, Spain (a) 0-2, Liechtenstein (h) 2-0, Saudi Arabia (n) 2-0, UAE (n) 0-1.

League Championship wins (1990–2014)
Dinamo Tbilisi 15; Torpedo Kutaisi 3; WIT Georgia 2; Metalurgi Rustavi (formerly Olimpi) 2; Zestafoni 2; Sioni 1.

Cup wins (1990–2014)
Dinamo Tbilisi 11; Lokomotivi 3; Torpedo Kutaisi 2; Ameri 2; Guria Lanchkhuti 1; Dinamo Batumi 1; Zestafoni 1; WIT Georgia 1; Gagra 1; Dila Gori 1.

Qualifying League Table 2013–14

	P	W	D	L	F	A	GD	Pts
Dinamo Tbilisi	22	15	3	4	51	17	34	48
Zestafoni	22	12	4	6	30	15	15	40
Chikhura Sachkhere	22	11	5	6	40	13	7	38
Sioni Bolnisi	22	9	6	7	27	23	4	33
Metalurgi Rustavi	22	9	6	9	26	25	1	33
Guria Lanchkhuti	22	11	0	11	25	29	-4	33
Torpedo Kutaisi	22	8	8	6	28	22	6	32
WIT Georgia	22	8	5	9	28	29	-1	29
Dila Gori	22	8	5	9	24	30	-6	29
Spartaki Tskhinvali	22	6	2	14	19	32	-13	20
Zugdidi	22	5	5	12	12	30	-18	20
Merani Martvili	22	4	3	15	16	41	-25	15

Championship Round

	P	W	D	L	F	A	GD	Pts
Dinamo Tbilisi	32	21	5	6	67	23	44	68
Zestafoni	32	19	5	8	48	23	25	62
Sioni Bolnisi	32	16	7	9	41	33	8	55
Chikhura Sachkhere	32	13	7	12	56	50	6	46
Metalurgi Rustavi	32	13	6	13	35	40	-5	45
Guria Lanchkhuti	32	12	0	20	31	53	-22	36

Relegation Round

	P	W	D	L	F	A	GD	Pts
Torpedo Kutaisi	32	14	6	12	43	44	-1	48
WIT Georgia	32	13	6	13	41	45	-4	45
Dila Gori	32	11	8	13	44	36	8	41
Spartaki Tskhinvali	32	12	4	16	33	38	-5	40
Zugdidi*	32	10	6	16	26	42	-16	36
Merani Martvili*	32	6	4	22	21	60	-39	22

Top scorer: Xisco (Dinamo Tbilisi) 19.
Cup Final: Dinamo Tbilisi 2, Chikhura Sachkhere 1.

GERMANY

Deutscher Fussball-Bund, Otto-Fleck-Schneise 6, Postfach 710265, 60492 Frankfurt Am Main.
Founded: 1900; *National Colours:* White shirts, black shorts, white socks.

International matches 2013–14
Paraguay (h) 3-3, Austria (h) 3-0, Faroe Islands (a) 3-0, Republic of Ireland (h) 3-0, Sweden (a) 5-3, Italy (a) 1-1, England (a) 1-0, Chile (h) 1-0, Poland (h) 0-0, Cameroon (h) 2-2, Armenia (h) 6-1, Portugal (n) 4-0, Ghana (n) 2-2, USA (n) 1-0, Algeria (n) 2-1, France (n) 1-0, Brazil (a) 7-1, Argentina (n) 1-0.

League Championship wins (1903–2014)
Bayern Munich 24; 1.FC Nuremberg 9; Borussia Dortmund 8; Schalke 04 7; Hamburger SV 6; VfB Stuttgart 5; Borussia Moenchengladbach 5; 1.FC Kaiserslautern 4; Werder Bremen 4; VfB Leipzig 3; SpVgg Greuther Furth 3; 1.FC Cologne 3; Viktoria Berlin 2; Hertha Berlin 2; Hannover 96 2; Dresden SC 2; Union Berlin 1; Freiburger FC 1; Phoenix Karlsruhe 1; Karlsruher FV 1; Holstein Kiel 1; Fortuna Dusseldorf 1; Rapid Vienna 1; VfR Mannheim 1; Rot-Weiss Essen 1; Eintracht Frankfurt 1; Munich 1860 1; Eintracht Braunschweig 1; Wolfsburg 1.

Cup wins (1935–2014)
Bayern Munich 17; Werder Bremen 6; Schalke 04 5; 1.FC Nuremberg 4; 1.FC Cologne 4; Eintracht Frankfurt 4; Hamburger SV 3; VfB Stuttgart 3; Borussia Moenchengladbach 3; Borussia Dortmund 3; Dresden SC 2; Munich 1860 2; Fortuna Dusseldorf 2; Karlsruhe SC 2; 1.FC Kaiserslautern 2; VfB Leipzig 1; Rapid Vienna 1; First Vienna 1; Rot-Weiss Essen 1; SW Essen 1; Kickers Offenbach 1; Bayer Uerdingen 1; Bayer Leverkusen 1; Hannover 96 1.

Final League Table 2013–14

	P	W	D	L	F	A	GD	Pts
Bayern Munich	34	29	3	2	94	23	71	90
Borussia Dortmund	34	22	5	7	80	38	42	71
Schalke 04	34	19	7	8	63	43	20	64
Bayer Leverkusen	34	19	4	11	60	41	19	61
VfL Wolfsburg	34	18	6	10	63	50	13	60
Borussia M'gladbach	34	16	7	11	59	43	16	55
1.FSV Mainz 05	34	16	5	13	52	54	-2	53
Augsburg	34	15	7	12	47	47	0	52
TSG 1899 Hoffenheim	34	11	11	12	72	70	2	44
Hannover 96	34	12	6	16	46	59	-13	42
Hertha Berlin	34	11	8	15	40	48	-8	41
Werder Bremen	34	10	9	15	42	66	-24	39
Eintracht Frankfurt	34	9	9	16	40	57	-17	36
Freiburg	34	9	9	16	43	61	-18	36
VfB Stuttgart	34	8	8	18	49	62	-13	32
Hamburger SV+	34	7	6	21	51	75	-24	27
1.FC Nuremberg*	34	5	11	18	37	70	-33	26
Eintracht Braunschweig*	34	6	7	21	29	60	-31	25

Top scorer: Lewandowski (Borussia Dortmund) 20.
Cup Final: Borussia Dortmund 0, Bayern Munich 2.

GIBRALTAR

Gibraltar Football Association, 32A Rosia Road, PO Box 515, Gibraltar.
Founded: 1895. *National Colours:* Red shirts with white trim, red shorts, red socks.

International matches 2013–14
Faroe Islands (h) 1-4, Estonia (h) 0-2, Estonia (a) 1-1, Malta (n) 1-0.

League Championship wins (1896–2014)
Lincoln 20 (incl. Newcastle United 5; 1 title shared); Prince of Wales 19; Glacis United 17 (incl. 1 shared); Britannia 14; Gibraltar United 11; Manchester United 7; Europa 6; St Theresas 3; Chief Construction 2; Jubilee 2; Exiles 2; South United 2; Gibraltar FC 2; Albion 1; Athletic 1; Royal Sovereign 1; Commander of the Yard 1; St Joseph's 1.

Cup wins (1895–2014)
Lincoln (incl. Newcastle United 4) 14; St Joseph's 9; Europa 5; Glacis United 5; Britannia 3; Gibraltar United 3; Manchester United 3; Gibraltar FC 1; HMS Hood 1; 2nd Bn The King's Regt 1; AARA 1; RAF New Camp 1; 4th Bn Royal Scots 1; Prince of Wales 1; Manchester United Reserves 1; 2nd Bn Royal Green Jackets 1; RAF Gibraltar 1; Lincoln Reliance 1; St Theresas 1.

Final League Table 2013–14

	P	W	D	L	F	A	GD	Pts
Lincoln	14	11	3	0	66	6	60	36
Manchester 62	14	9	3	2	37	10	27	30
Lynx	14	9	2	3	36	18	18	29
College Europa	14	5	4	5	31	20	11	19
Glacis United	14	6	1	7	18	32	–14	19
Lions Gibraltar	14	4	2	8	23	33	–10	14
St Joseph's+	14	4	1	9	23	30	–7	13
Gibraltar Phoenix*	14	0	0	14	9	94	–85	0

Top scorer: Duarte (Lincoln) 15.
Cup Final: Lincoln 1, College Europa 0.

GOZO
Gozo Football Association. GFA Headquarters, Mgarr Road, Xewkija, XWK 9014, Malta.
Founded: 1936.

League Championship wins (1938–2014)
Victoria Hotspurs 11; Nadur Youngsters 11; Sannat Lions 10; Xaghra United 6 (incl. Xaghra Blue Stars 1, Xaghra Young Stars 1); Salesian Youths (renamed Oratory Youths) 6; Ghajnsielem 6; Xewkija Tigers 6; Victoria Athletics 4; Victoria Stars 1; Victoria City 1; Calypcians 1; Victoria United 1; Kercem Ajax 1; Zebbug Rovers 1.

Cup wins (1972–2014)
Sannat Lions 9; Nadur Youngsters 8; Xewkija Tigers 8; Ghajnsielem 5; Xaghra United 4; Kercem Ajax 2; Calypsians 1; Calypsians Bosco Youths 1; Victoria Hotspurs 1; Victoria Wanderers 1; Qala St Joseph 1.

Qualifying League Table 2013–14

	P	W	D	L	F	A	GD	Pts
Xewkija Tigers	14	10	3	1	36	10	26	33
Victoria Wanderers	14	10	1	3	32	13	13	31
Nadur Youngsters	14	9	2	3	34	15	19	29
Victoria Hotspurs	14	8	2	4	28	13	15	26
Kercem Ajax	14	7	3	4	31	15	16	24
Oratory Youths	14	4	1	9	18	26	–8	13
Xaghra United	14	1	0	13	8	44	–36	3
Munxar Falcons	14	1	0	13	8	59	–51	3

Championship Round

	P	W	D	L	F	A	GD	Pts
Xewkija Tigers	20	15	4	1	58	21	37	49
Victoria Wanderers	20	12	3	5	44	22	22	39
Nadur Youngsters	20	11	3	6	47	30	17	36
Victoria Hotspurs	20	8	4	8	34	31	3	28

Relegation Round

	P	W	D	L	F	A	GD	Pts
Kercem Ajax	20	10	6	4	31	15	16	36
Oratory Youths	20	5	5	10	18	26	–8	20
Munxar Falcons*+	20	3	1	16	8	44	–36	10
Xaghra United*	20	2	2	16	8	59	–51	8

Cup Final: Nadur Youngsters 3, Oratory Youths 0.

GREECE
Hellenic Football Federation, Singrou Avenue 137, 17121 Athens.
Founded: 1926; National Colours: All white.

International matches 2013–14
Austria (a) 2-0, Liechtenstein (a) 1-0, Latvia (h) 1-0, Slovakia (h) 1-0, Liechtenstein (h) 2-0, Romania (h) 3-1, Romania (a) 1-1, Korea Republic (h) 0-2, Portugal (a) 0-0, Nigeria (n) 0-0, Bolivia (n) 2-1, Colombia (n) 0-3,

Japan (n) 0-0, Ivory Coast (n) 2-1, Costa Rica (n) 1-1 (5-3p).

League Championship wins (1928–2014)
Olympiacos 41; Panathinaikos 20; AEK Athens 11; Aris Salonika 3; PAOK Salonika 2; Larissa 1.

Cup wins (1932–2014)
Olympiacos 26; Panathinaikos 18; AEK Athens 14; PAOK Salonika 4; Panionios 2; Larissa 2; Ethnikos 1; Aris Salonika 1; Iraklis 1; Kastoria 1; OFI Crete 1.

Final League Table 2013–14

	P	W	D	L	F	A	GD	Pts
Olympiacos	34	28	2	4	88	19	69	86
PAOK	34	21	6	7	68	37	31	69
Atromitos	34	19	9	6	54	25	29	66
Panathinaikos	34	20	6	8	57	28	29	66
Asteras Tripolis	34	16	10	8	46	35	11	58
OFI Crete	34	11	11	12	30	39	–9	44
Ergotelis	34	11	11	12	39	40	–1	44
Panaitolikos	34	11	9	14	32	33	–1	42
Levadiakos	34	13	3	18	42	61	–19	42
Panthrakikos	34	11	8	15	39	52	–13	41
PAS Giannina	34	12	5	17	34	43	–9	41
Kalloni	34	12	3	19	31	62	–31	39
Panionios GSS	34	10	9	15	33	42	–9	39
Platanias	34	10	8	16	39	48	–9	38
Veria	34	9	11	14	31	51	–20	38
Xanthi+	34	11	5	18	44	54	–10	38
Apollon Smyrnis*	34	9	9	16	43	54	–11	36
Aris Thessaloniki*	34	3	13	18	26	53	–27	22

Top scorer: Solari (Xanthi) 16.
Cup Final: PAOK 1, Panathinaikos 4.

HUNGARY
Hungarian Football Federation, Koerberek Tovaros Kanai ut 314/24 hrsz., 1112 Budapest.
Founded: 1901; *National Colours:* Red shirts, white shorts, green socks.

International matches 2013–14
Czech Republic (h) 1-1, Romania (a) 0-3, Estonia (h) 5-1, Netherlands (a) 1-8, Andorra (h) 2-0, Finland (h) 1-2, Denmark (h) 2-2, Albania (h) 1-0, Kazakhstan (h) 3-0.

League Championship wins (1901–2014)
Ferencvaros 28; MTK-Hungaria Budapest 23; Ujpest 20; Budapest Honved 13 (incl. Kispest Honved); Debrecen 7; Vasas Budapest 6; Csepel 4; Gyori ETO 4; BTC 2; Nagyvarad 1; Vac 1; Dunaferr (renamed Dunaujvaros) 1; Zalaegerszeg 1; Videoton 1.

Cup wins (1910–2014)
Ferencvaros 20; MTK-Hungaria Budapest 12; Ujpest 9; Budapest Honved 7 (inc. Kispest Honved); Debrecen 6; Vasas Budapest 4; Gyori ETO 4; Diosgyor 2; Bocskai 1; III Ker 1; Soroksar 1; Szolnoki MAV 1; Siofoki Banyasz 1; Bekescsaba 1; Pecsi 1; Sopron 1; Fehervar (renamed Videoton) 1; Kecskemet 1.
Cup not regularly held until 1964.

Final League Table 2013–14

	P	W	D	L	F	A	GD	Pts
Debrecen	30	18	8	4	66	33	33	62
Gyori ETO	30	18	8	4	58	32	26	62
Ferencvaros	30	17	6	7	47	33	14	57
Videoton	30	15	8	7	52	31	21	53
Diosgyor	30	12	11	7	45	38	7	47
Szombathelyi Haladas	30	12	10	8	37	31	6	46
Pecs	30	12	9	9	41	38	3	45
MTK Budapest	30	11	7	12	42	36	6	40
Budapest Honved	30	10	6	14	37	39	–2	36
Kecskemet	30	9	9	12	36	51	–15	36
Paks	30	8	10	12	39	42	–3	34
Lombard-Papa	30	9	6	15	32	50	–18	33
Ujpest	30	8	8	14	46	51	–5	32
Puskas Akademia	30	8	7	15	36	51	–15	31
Mezokovesdi-Zsory*	30	6	6	18	27	52	–25	24
Kaposvari Rakoczi*	30	4	7	19	21	54	–33	19

Top scorers (equal): Nikolic (Videoton), Simon (Paks) 18.
Cup Final: Ujpest 1, Diosgyor 1.
aet; Ujpest won 4-3 on penalties.

ICELAND

Knattspyrnusamband Islands, Laugardal, 104 Reykjavik.
Founded: 1929; *National Colours:* All blue.

International matches 2013–14

Faroe Islands (h) 1-0, Switzerland (a) 4-4, Albania (h) 2-1, Cyprus (h) 2-0, Norway (a) 1-1, Croatia (h) 0-0, Croatia (a) 0-2, Sweden (n) 0-2, Wales (a) 1-3, Austria (a) 1-1, Estonia (h) 1-0.

League Championship wins (1912–2013)

KR Reykjavik 26; Valur 20; Fram 18; IA Akranes 18; FH Hafnarfjordur 6; Vikingur 5; IBK Keflavik 4; IBV Vestmannaeyjar 3; KA Akureyri 1; Breidablik 1.

Cup wins (1960–2013)

KR Reykjavik 13; Valur 9; IA Akranes 9; Fram 8; IBV Vestmannaeyjar 4; IBK Keflavik 4; Fylkir 2; FH Hafnarfjordur 2; IBA Akureyri 1; Vikingur 1; Breidablik 1.

Final League Table 2013

	P	W	D	L	F	A	GD	Pts
KR Reykjavik	22	17	1	4	50	27	23	52
FH Hafnarfjordur	22	14	5	3	47	22	25	47
Stjarnan	22	13	4	5	34	25	9	43
Breidablik	22	11	6	5	37	27	10	39
Valur	22	8	9	5	45	31	14	33
IBV Vestmannaeyjar	22	8	5	9	26	28	–2	29
Fylkir	22	7	5	10	33	33	0	26
Thor	22	6	6	10	31	44	–13	24
Keflavik	22	7	3	12	33	47	–14	24
Fram	22	6	4	12	26	37	–11	22
Vikingur Olafsvik*	22	3	8	11	21	35	–14	17
IA Akranes*	22	3	2	17	29	56	–27	11

Top scorers (equal): Bjornsson (FH), Kjartansson (Fylkir), Martin (KR) 13.
Cup Final: Stjarnan 3, Fram 3.
aet; Fram won 3-1 on penalties.

REPUBLIC OF IRELAND

Football Association of Ireland (Cumann Peile na hEireann), National Sports Campus, Abbotstown, Dublin 15.
Founded: 1921; *National Colours:* Green shirts, white shorts, green socks.

League Championship wins (1922–2013)

Shamrock Rovers 17; Shelbourne 13; Bohemians 11; Dundalk 9; St Patrick's Athletic 8; Cork Athletic (formerly Cork United) 7; Waterford United 6; Drumcondra 5; Sligo Rovers 3; St James's Gate 2; Limerick 2; Athlone Town 2; Derry City 2; Cork City 2; Dolphin 1; Cork Hibernians 1; Cork Celtic 1; Drogheda United 1.

Cup wins (1922–2013)

Shamrock Rovers 24; Dundalk 9; Bohemians 7; Shelbourne 7; Drumcondra 5; Sligo Rovers 5; Derry City 5; Cork Athletic (formerly Cork United) 4; St James's Gate 2; Waterford United 2; St Patrick's Athletic 2; Limerick 2; Cork Hibernians 2; Bray Wanderers 2; Cork City 2; Longford Town 1; Alton United 1; Athlone Town 1; Fordsons 1; Cork 1; Transport 1; Finn Harps 1; Home Farm 1; UC Dublin 1; Galway United 1; Drogheda United 1; Sporting Fingal 1.

Final League Table 2013

	P	W	D	L	F	A	GD	Pts
St Patrick's Athletic	33	21	8	4	56	20	36	71
Dundalk	33	21	5	7	55	30	25	68
Sligo Rovers	33	19	9	5	53	22	31	66
Derry City	33	17	5	11	57	39	18	56
Shamrock Rovers	33	13	13	7	43	28	15	52
Cork City	33	13	7	13	47	50	–3	46
Limerick	33	11	9	13	38	46	–8	42
Drogheda United	33	8	14	11	44	46	–2	38
UCD Dublin	33	8	6	19	45	73	–28	30
Bohemians	33	7	8	18	27	47	–20	29
Bray Wanderers+	33	7	6	20	33	66	–33	27
Shelbourne*	33	5	6	22	25	56	–31	21

Top scorer: Patterson (Derry City) 18.
Cup Final: Drogheda United 2, Sligo Rovers 3.

ISRAEL

Israel Football Association, Ramat-Gan Stadium, 299 Aba Hilell Street, Ramat-Gan 52134.
Founded: 1948; *National Colours:* Blue shirts, white shorts, blue socks.

International matches 2013–14

Ukraine (a) 0-2, Azerbaijan (h) 1-1, Russia (a) 1-3, Portugal (a) 1-1, Northern Ireland (h) 1-1, Slovakia (h) 1-3, Mexico (a) 0-3, Honduras (n) 4-2.

League Championship wins (1932–2014)

Maccabi Tel Aviv 20; Hapoel Tel Aviv 13; Maccabi Haifa 12; Hapoel Petah Tikva 6; Beitar Jerusalem 6; Maccabi Netanya 5; Hakoah Ramat Gan 2; Hapoel Beersheba 2; British Police 1; Hapoel Ramat Gan 1; Hapoel Kfar Saba 1; Bnei Yehuda 1; Hapoel Haifa 1; Ironi Kiryat Shmona 1.

Cup wins (1928–2014)

Maccabi Tel Aviv 22; Hapoel Tel Aviv 15; Beitar Jerusalem 7; Maccabi Haifa 5; Hapoel Haifa 3; Hapoel Kfar Saba 3; Maccabi Petah Tikva 2; Beitar Tel Aviv 2; Hapoel Petah Tikva 2; Bnei Yehuda 2; Hakoah Ramat Gan 2; Hapoel Ramat Gan 2; Maccabi Hashmonai Jerusalem 1; British Police 1; Hapoel Jerusalem 1; Maccabi Netanya 1; Hapoel Yehud 1; Hapoel Lod 1; Hapoel Beersheba 1; Bnei Sakhnin 1; Ironi Kiryat Shmona 1.

Qualifying League Table 2013–14

	P	W	D	L	F	A	GD	Pts
Maccabi Tel Aviv	26	21	3	2	58	18	40	66
Hapoel Beer Sheva	26	18	5	3	48	19	29	59
Ironi Kiryat Shmona	26	12	8	6	38	26	12	44
Maccabi Haifa	26	13	5	8	39	30	9	44
Bnei Sakhnin	26	11	7	8	30	25	5	40
Hapoel Tel Aviv	26	11	6	9	51	38	13	39
FC Ashdod	26	8	7	11	28	35	–7	31
Hapoel Haifa	26	8	7	11	27	34	–7	31
Beitar Jerusalem	26	8	6	12	21	28	–7	30
Hapoel Ironi Akko	26	6	9	11	24	37	–13	27
Hapoel Ra'anana	26	6	8	12	20	33	–13	26
Maccabi Petah Tikva	26	5	8	13	28	45	–17	23
Bnei Yehuda Tel Aviv	26	8	14	26	39	–13	20	
Hapoel Nir Ramat HaSharon	26	5	5	16	21	52	–31	20

Championship Round

	P	W	D	L	F	A	GD	Pts
Maccabi Tel Aviv	36	26	6	4	76	30	46	84
Hapoel Beer Sheva	36	20	8	8	56	33	23	68
Hapoel Kiryat Shmona	36	18	10	8	59	38	21	64
Hapoel Tel Aviv	36	16	10	10	72	47	25	58
Maccabi Haifa	36	15	8	13	49	46	3	53
Bnei Sakhnin	36	13	8	15	37	47	–10	47

Relegation Round

	P	W	D	L	F	A	GD	Pts
Beitar Jerusalem	33	12	6	15	31	32	–1	42
FC Ashdod	33	10	9	14	35	45	–10	39
Hapoel Ra'anana	33	9	11	13	31	40	–9	38
Hapoel Ironi Akko	33	8	12	13	30	42	–12	36
Hapoel Haifa	33	9	7	17	30	45	–15	34
Maccabi Petah Tikva	33	8	9	16	39	57	–18	33
Hapoel Nir Ramat HaSharon*	33	9	6	18	29	59	–30	33
Bnei Yehuda Tel Aviv*	33	7	10	16	32	45	–13	31

Top scorer: Zahavi (Maccabi Tel Aviv) 29.
Cup Final: Maccabi Netanya 0, Ironi Kiryat Shmona 1

ITALY

Federazione Italiana Giuoco Calcio, Via Gregorio Allegri 14, CP 2450, 00198 Roma.
Founded: 1898; *National Colours:* Blue shirts, white shorts, blue socks.

International matches 2013–14

Argentina (h) 1-2, Bulgaria (h) 1-0, Czech Republic (h) 2-1, Denmark (a) 2-2, Armenia (h) 2-2, Germany (h) 1-1, Nigeria (n) 2-2, Spain (a) 0-1, Republic of Ireland (n) 0-0, Luxembourg (h) 1-1, England (n) 2-1, Costa Rica (n) 0-1, Uruguay (n) 0-1.

League Championship wins (1898–2014)

Juventus 30 (excludes two titles revoked); AC Milan 18; Internazionale 18 (includes one title awarded); Genoa 9; Pro Vercelli 7; Bologna 7; Torino 7 (excludes one title revoked); Roma 3; Fiorentina 2; Lazio 2; Napoli 2; Casale 1; Novese 1; Cagliari 1; Verona 1; Sampdoria 1.

Cup wins (1928–2014)

Juventus 9; Roma 9; Internazionale 7; Fiorentina 6; Lazio 6; Torino 5; Napoli 5; AC Milan 5; Sampdoria 4; Parma 3; Bologna 2; Vado 1; Genoa 1; Venezia 1; Atalanta 1; Vicenza 1.

Qualifying League Table 2013–14

	P	W	D	L	F	A	GD	Pts
Juventus	38	33	3	2	80	23	57	102
Roma	38	26	7	5	72	25	47	85
Napoli	38	23	9	6	77	39	38	78
Fiorentina	38	19	8	11	65	44	21	65
Internazionale	38	15	15	8	62	39	23	60
Parma	38	15	13	10	58	46	12	58
Torino	38	15	12	11	58	48	10	57
AC Milan	38	16	9	13	57	49	8	57
Lazio	38	15	11	12	54	54	0	56
Hellas Verona	38	16	6	16	62	68	–6	54
Atalanta	38	15	5	18	43	51	–8	50
Sampdoria	38	12	9	17	48	62	–14	45
Udinese	38	12	8	18	46	57	–11	44
Genoa	38	11	11	16	41	50	–9	44
Cagliari	38	9	12	17	34	53	–19	39
Chievo	38	10	6	22	34	54	–20	36
Sassuolo	38	9	7	22	43	72	–29	34
Catania*	38	8	8	22	34	66	–32	32
Bologna*	38	5	14	19	28	58	–30	29
Livorno*	38	6	7	25	39	77	–38	25

Top scorer: Immobile (Torino) 22.
Cup Final: Fiorentina 1, Napoli 3.

KAZAKHSTAN

Football Federation of Kazakhstan, 29 Syganak Str., 14th floor, 010000 Astana.
Founded: 1914; *National Colours:* All blue.

International matches 2013–14
Georgia (h) 1-0, Faroe Islands (h) 2-1, Sweden (h) 0-1, Faroe Islands (a) 1-1, Republic of Ireland (a) 1-3, Lithuania (n) 1-1, Hungary (a) 3-0.

League Championship wins (1992–2013)
Irtysh (includes Ansat) 5; Aktobe 5; Yelimay (renamed Spartak Semey) 3; FC Astana-64 (incl. Zhenis) 3; Kairat 2; Shakhter Karagandy 2; Taraz 1; Tobol 1.

Cup wins (1992–2013)
Kairat 5; FC Astana-64 (incl. Zhenis) 3; Astana (incl. Lokomotiv) 2; Dostyk 1; Vostok 1; Yelimay (renamed Spartak Semey) 1; Irtysh 1; Kaisar 1; Taraz 1; Almaty 1; Tobol 1; Aktobe 1; Atirau 1; Ordabasy 1; Shakhter Karagandy 1.

Final League Table 2013

	P	W	D	L	F	A	GD	Pts
Aktobe	22	14	5	3	30	12	18	47
Astana	22	12	5	5	35	24	11	41
Shakhter Karagandy	22	10	5	7	31	23	8	35
Irtysh	22	9	7	6	24	20	4	34
Kairat	22	7	10	5	28	24	4	31
Ordabasy	22	8	6	8	20	20	0	30
Atyrau	22	7	6	9	18	28	–10	27
Tobol	22	7	5	10	30	27	3	26
Vostok	22	5	8	9	12	24	–12	23
Zhetysu (–3)	22	4	12	6	20	25	–5	21
Taraz	22	4	6	12	19	29	–10	18
Akzhayik (–6)	22	4	7	11	24	35	–11	13

Championship Round

	P	W	D	L	F	A	GD	Pts
Aktobe	32	20	6	6	46	22	24	43
Astana	32	19	5	8	54	35	19	42
Kairat	32	12	12	8	44	38	6	33
Irtysh	32	12	8	12	41	39	2	27
Shakhter Karagandy	32	12	7	13	43	45	–2	26
Ordabasy	32	11	8	13	33	34	–1	23

Relegation Round

	P	W	D	L	F	A	GD	Pts
Tobol	32	14	6	12	48	33	15	35
Atyrau	32	10	11	11	26	38	–12	28
Zhetysu	32	6	17	9	22	32	–10	22
Taraz	32	7	9	16	30	38	–8	21
Vostok*+	32	6	13	13	20	37	–17	20
Akzhayik*	32	7	10	15	37	50	–13	19

Top scorer: Zenkovich (Shakhter Karagandy) 15.
Cup Final: Shakhter Karagandy 1, Taraz 0.

KOSOVO

Football Federation of Kosovo, Agim Ramadani 45, Prishtina, Kosovo 10000.
Founded: 1948; *National Colours:* Blue shirts, white shorts, blue socks.

League Championship wins (1945–2014)
Prishtina 14; Vellaznimi 9; KF Trepca 7; Liria 5; Buduqnosti 4; Rudari 3; Red Star 3; Besa 3; Jedinstvo 2; Kosova Prishtina 2; Slloga 2; Obiliqi 2; Fushe-Kosova 2; Proletari 1; KXEK Kosova 1; Rudniku 1; KNI Ramiz Sadiku 1; Dukagjini 1; Besiana 1; Drita 1; Hysi 1; Kosova Vushtrri 1.

Cup wins (1992–2014)
Liria 3; Flamurtari 2; Besa 2; Prishtina 2; KF Trepca 1; KF 2 Korriku 1; Gjilani 1; Drita 1; Besiana 1; KEK-u 1; Kosova Prishtina 1; Vellaznimi 1; Hysi 1; Trepca'89 1; Feronikeli 1.

Final League Table 2013–14

	P	W	D	L	F	A	GD	Pts
Kosova Vushtrri	33	19	7	7	48	22	26	64
Prishtina	33	17	6	10	39	26	13	57
Trepca'89	33	16	5	12	45	31	14	53
Ferizaj	33	15	6	12	43	35	8	51
Besa	33	15	4	14	37	36	1	49
Hajvalia	33	13	8	12	40	32	8	47
Drita	33	12	11	10	43	37	6	47
Drenica Skenderaj	33	12	9	12	45	42	3	45
Feronikeli+	33	10	11	12	28	33	–5	41
Trepca Mitrovice+	33	9	9	15	25	32	–7	36
Fushe Kosova*	33	8	8	17	29	49	–20	32
Hysi‡	33	8	4	21	21	68	–47	28

‡*Hysi withdrew from league during season; remaining opponents awarded 3-0 wins.*
Top scorer: Zenkovich (Shakhter Karagandy) 15.
Cup Final: Hajvalia 1, Feronikeli 2.

LATVIA

Latvijas Futbola Federacija, Olympic Sports Centre, Grostonas Street 6b, 1013 Riga.
Founded: 1921; *National Colours:* All carmine red.

International matches 2013–14
Estonia (a) 1-1, Lithuania (h) 2-1, Greece (a) 0-1, Lithuania (a) 2-0, Slovakia (h) 2-2, Republic of Ireland (a) 0-3, Macedonia 1-2, Estonia (h) 0-0 (4-2p), Lithuania (h) 1-0.

League Championship wins (1922–2013)
Skonto Riga 15; ASK Riga (incl. AVN 2) 11; RFK Riga 8; Sarkanais Metalurgs Liepaja 7; Olympija Liepaya 7; VEF Riga 6; Ventspils 5; Energija Riga (incl. ESR Riga 2) 4; Elektrons Riga (incl. Alfa 1) 4; Torpedo Riga 3; Keisermezhs Riga 2; Khimikis Daugavpils 2; RAF Yelgava 2; Daugava Liepaja 2; Liepajas Metalurgs 2; Dinamo Riga 1; Zhmilyeva Team 1; Darba Rezervi 1; RER Riga 1; Starts Brotseni 1; Venta Ventspils 1; Jumieks Riga 1; Gauja Valmiera 1; Daugava Daugavpils 1.

Cup wins (1937–2014)
Skonto Riga 8; Elektrons Riga 7; Ventspils 6; Sarkanais Metalurgs Liepaja 5; VEF Riga 3; ASK Riga 3; Tseltnieks Riga 3; RAF Yelgava 3; RFK Riga 2; Daugava Liepaja 2; Starts Brotseni 2; Selmash Liepaya 2; Yurnieks Riga 2; Khimikis Daugavpils 2; Jelgava 2; Rigas Vilki 1; Dinamo Liepaya 1; Dinamo Riga 1; RER Riga 1; Voulkan Kouldiga 1; Baltika Liepaja 1; Venta Ventspils 1; Pilots Riga 1; Lielupe Yurmala 1; Energija Riga (formerly ESR Riga)1; Torpedo Riga 1; Daugava SKIF Riga 1; Tseltnieks Daugavpils 1; Olympija Riga 1; FK Riga 1; Liepajas Metalurgs 1; Daugava Daugavpils 1.

Final League Table 2013

	P	W	D	L	F	A	GD	Pts
Ventspils	27	14	5	8	65	19	46	67
Skonto	27	18	8	1	68	11	57	62
Daugava Daugavpils	27	15	7	5	44	19	25	52
Daugava Riga	27	14	6	7	44	21	23	48
Liepajas Metalurgs	27	11	7	9	54	35	19	40
Jurmala	27	7	5	15	20	52	–32	26
Spartaks	27	7	4	16	30	49	–19	25
Jelgava	27	5	8	14	26	46	–20	23
Metta/LU+	27	4	7	16	15	47	–32	19
Ilukstes*	27	2	6	19	26	93	–67	12

Top scorers (equal): Karasausks (Skonto), Kovalovs (Daugava) 16.
Cup Final: Jelgava 0, Skonto 0.
aet; Jelgava won 5-3 on penalties.

LIECHTENSTEIN

Liechtensteiner Fussballverband, Landstrasse 149, 9494 Schaan.
Founded: 1934; *National Colours:* Blue shirts, red shorts, blue socks.

International matches 2013–14
Croatia (h) 2-3, Greece (h) 0-1, Lithuania (a) 0-2, Bosnia & Herzogovina (a) 1-4, Greece (a) 0-2, Estonia (h) 0-3, Georgia (a) 0-2, Belarus (h) 1-5.
Liechtenstein has no national league. Teams compete in Swiss regional leagues.

Cup wins (1937–2014)
Vaduz 42; Balzers 11; Triesen 8; 5; Schaan 3.
Cup Final: Vaduz 6, USV Eschen/Mauren 0.

LITHUANIA

Lithuanian Football Federation, Stadiono g. 2, 02106 Vilnius.
Founded: 1922; *National Colours:* Yellow shirts, green shorts, yellow socks.

International matches 2013–14
Luxembourg (a) 1-2, Latvia (a) 1-2, Liechtenstein (h) 2-0, Latvia (h) 2-0, Bosnia & Herzogovina (h) 0-1, Moldova (a) 1-1, Kazakhstan (n) 1-1 Finland (n) 1-0. Latvia (a) 0-1, Poland (a) 1-2.

League Championship wins (1990–2013)
FBK Kaunas 8 (including Zalgiris Kaunas 1); Ekranas 7; Zalgiris Vilnius (renamed VMFD Zalgiris) 4; Inkaras Kaunas 2; Kareda 2; Sirijus Klaipeda 1; Mazeikiai 1.

Cup wins (1990–2014)
Zalgiris Vilnius (renamed VMFD Zalgiris) 8; Ekranas 4; FBK Kaunas 4; Kareda 2; Atlantas 2; Suduva 2; Sirijus Klaipeda 1; Lietuvos Makabi Vilnius 1; Inkaras Kaunas 1.

Final League Table 2013
	P	W	D	L	F	A	GD	Pts
Zalgiris	32	22	7	3	77	19	58	73
Atlantas	32	22	5	5	64	23	41	71
Ekranas	32	20	4	8	58	34	24	64
Suduva	32	18	8	6	73	33	40	62
Kruoja	32	13	9	10	46	47	−1	48
Banga	32	10	5	17	39	56	−17	35
Siauliai	32	6	7	19	34	65	−31	25
Dainava	32	4	5	23	27	74	−47	17
Tauras*	32	3	2	27	25	92	−67	11

Top scorer: Valskis (Suduva) 27.
Cup Final: VMFD Zalgiris 2, Banga 1.

LUXEMBOURG

Federation Luxembourgeoise de Football, BP 5 Rue de Limpach, 3901 Mondercange.
Founded: 1908; *National Colours:* All white.

International matches 2013–14
Lithuania (h) 2-1, Russia (a) 1-4, Northern Ireland (h) 3-2, Russia (h) 0-4, Portugal (a) 0-3, Montenegro (h) 1-4, Cape Verde Islands (h) 0-0, Belgium (a) 1-5, Italy (a) 1-1.

League Championship wins (1910–2014)
Jeunesse Esch 28; F91 Dudelange 11; Spora Luxembourg 11; Stade Dudelange 10; Fola Esch 6; Red Boys Differdange (now Differdange 03) 6; Union Luxembourg 6; Avenir Beggen 6; US Hollerich-Bonnevoie 5; Progres Niedercorn 3; Aris Bonnevoie 3; Sporting Club 2; Racing Club 1; National Schifflange 1; Grevenmacher 1.

Cup wins (1922–2014)
Red Boys Differdange (now Differdange 03) 16; Jeunesse Esch 13; Union Luxembourg 10; Spora Luxembourg 8; Avenir Beggen 7; F91 Dudelange 5; Progres Niedercorn 4; Stade Dudelange 4; Grevenmacher 3; Fola Esch 3; Alliance Dudelange 2; US Rumelange 2; Differdange 03 2; Racing Club 1; US Dudelange 1; SC Tetange 1; National Schifflange 1; Aris Bonnevoie 1; Jeunesse Hautcharage 1; Swift Hesperange 1; Etzella Ettelbruck 1; CS Petange 1.

Final League Table 2013–14
	P	W	D	L	F	A	GD	Pts
F91 Dudelange	26	19	4	3	64	21	43	61
Fola Esch	26	18	5	3	53	19	34	59
Differdange 03	26	17	0	9	53	23	30	51
Jeunesse Esch	26	11	10	5	47	35	12	43
Progres Niedercorn	26	11	9	6	33	26	7	42
Etzella Ettelbruck	26	9	5	12	44	46	−2	32

UN Kaerjeng 97	26	9	5	12	32	35	−3	32
Grevenmacher	26	8	8	10	27	34	−7	32
Wiltz	26	9	4	13	40	53	−13	31
Jeunesse Canach	26	8	6	12	27	42	−15	30
Rumelange	26	6	10	10	25	36	−11	28
RM Hamm Benfica*+	26	6	6	14	32	46	−14	24
Swift Hesper*	26	4	8	14	22	51	−29	20
Racing Luxembourg*	26	4	6	16	22	54	−32	18

Top scorer: Ibrahimovic (Jeunesse Esch) 22.
Cup Final: Differdange 03 2, F91 Dudelange 0.

MALTA

Malta Football Association, Millennium Stand, Floor 2 National Stadium, Ta'Qali ATD4000.
Founded: 1900; *National Colours:* Red shirts, white shorts, red socks.

International matches 2013–14
Azerbaijan (a) 0-3, Denmark (h) 1-2, Bulgaria (h) 1-2, Czech Republic (h) 1-4, Denmark (a) 0-6, Faroe Islands (h) 3-2, Albania (a) 0-2, Gibraltar (n) 0-1.

League Championship wins (1910–2014)
Sliema Wanderers 26; Floriana 25; Valletta 22; Hibernians 10; Hamrun Spartans 7; Birkirkara 4; Rabat Ajax 2; St George's 1; KOMR 1; Marsaxlokk 1.

Cup wins (1935–2014)
Sliema Wanderers 20; Floriana 19; Valletta 13; Hibernians 10; Hamrun Spartans 6; Birkirkara 4; Melita 1; Gzira United 1; Zurrieq 1; Rabat Ajax 1.

Qualifying League Table 2013–14
	P	W	D	L	F	A	GD	Pts
Birkirkara	22	18	2	2	51	19	32	56
Valletta	22	17	2	3	51	13	38	53
Hibernians	22	15	2	5	57	27	30	47
Sliema Wanderers	22	12	7	3	43	24	19	43
Mosta	22	12	2	8	44	35	9	38
Balzan Youths	22	8	4	10	24	31	−7	28
Naxxar Lions	22	8	3	11	27	39	−12	27
Floriana (−6)	22	8	4	10	30	36	−6	22
Vittoriosa Stars	22	5	3	14	24	47	−23	18
Qormi	22	4	4	14	45	45	−17	16
Tarxien Rainbows	22	4	4	14	45	45	−19	16
Rabat Ajax	22	1	3	18	61	61	−44	4

NB: Points earned in Qualifying phase are halved at start of Championship and Relegation phase.

Championship Round
	P	W	D	L	F	A	GD	Pts
Valletta	32	24	5	3	74	21	53	51
Birkirkara	32	25	3	4	76	25	51	50
Hibernians	32	18	4	10	77	51	26	35
Mosta	32	15	6	11	58	57	1	32
Sliema Wanderers	32	14	10	8	54	42	12	31
Balzan Youths	32	9	5	18	36	58	−22	18

Relegation Round
	P	W	D	L	F	A	GD	Pts
Floriana	32	14	5	13	50	48	2	30
Tarxien Rainbows	32	10	6	16	51	55	−4	28
Qormi	32	10	4	18	51	62	−11	26
Naxxar Lions	32	11	6	15	40	55	−15	26
Vittoriosa Stars*	32	9	6	17	41	66	−25	24
Rabat Ajax*	32	1	4	27	23	91	−68	4

Top scorers (equal): Edison (Hibernians), Jhonnattan (Birkirkara) 21.
Cup Final: Valletta1, Sliema Wanderers 0.

MOLDOVA

Federatia Moldoveneasca de Fotbal, 39 Tricorolului Str, 2012 Chisinau.
Founded: 1990; *National Colours:* All blue.

International matches 2013–14
Andorra (h) 1-1, England (a) 0-4, San Marino (h) 3-0, Montenegro (a) 5-2, Lithuania (h) 1-1, Norway (n) 1-2, Sweden (n) 1-2, Poland (n) 0-1, Andorra (a) 3-0, Saudi Arabia (n) 0-4, Canada (n) 1-1, Cameroon (n) 0-1.

League Championship wins (1992–2014)
Sheriff 13; Zimbru Chisinau 8; Constructorul 1; Dacia Chisinau 1.

Cup wins (1992–2014)
Sheriff 7; Zimbru Chisinau 5; Tiligul 3; Tiraspol 3 (incl. Constructorul 2); Comrat 1; Nistru Otaci 1; Iskra-Stal 1; Milsami (formerly Milsami-Ursidos) 1.

Final League Table 2013–14

	P	W	D	L	F	A	GD	Pts
Sheriff	33	28	3	2	98	16	82	87
Tiraspol	33	21	9	3	60	27	33	72
Veris	33	21	8	4	74	25	49	71
Zimbru Chisinau	33	18	7	8	56	24	32	61
Dacia Chisinau	33	18	7	8	68	29	39	61
Milsami Orhei	33	17	5	11	54	32	22	56
Costuleni	33	16	4	13	43	33	10	52
Dinamo-Auto	33	9	4	20	37	72	–35	31
Rapid Ghidighici‡ (–2)	33	6	4	23	27	75	–48	20
Academia Chisinau	33	5	4	24	26	88	–62	19
Olimpia Balti	33	5	3	25	26	77	–51	18
Sperant* (–3)	33	4	2	27	20	91	–71	11

‡*Rapid Ghidighici demoted for financial irregularities.*
Top scorer: Luvanor (Sheriff) 26.
Cup Final: Zimbru Chisinau 3, Sheriff 1.

MONTENEGRO

Football Association of Montenegro, Ulica 19. Decembra 13, PO Box 275, 81000 Podgorica.
Founded: 1931; *National Colours:* Red and gold shirts, red shorts, red socks.

International matches 2013–14
Belarus (a) 1-1, Poland (a) 1-1, England (a) 1-4, Moldova (h) 2-5, Luxembourg (a) 4-1, Ghana (h) 1-0, Slovakia (a) 0-2, Iran (n) 0-0.

League Championship wins (2006–14)
Buducnost Podgorica 2; Mogren 2; Sutjeska 2; Zeta 1; Rudar Pljevlja 1.

Cup wins (2006–14)
Rudar Pljevlja 3; Mogren 1; Petrovac 1; Celik 1; Buducnost Podgorica 1; Lovcen 1.

Final League Table 2013–14

	P	W	D	L	F	A	GD	Pts
Sutjeska	33	17	12	4	46	21	25	63
Lovcen	33	17	8	8	52	31	21	59
Celik Niksic	33	15	9	9	47	28	19	54
Buducnost Podgorica	33	16	6	11	36	26	10	54
Petrovac	33	11	13	9	37	31	6	46
Rudar Pljevlja	33	11	9	13	32	31	1	42
Grbalj (–3)	33	11	10	12	36	40	–4	40
Zeta	33	12	4	17	39	57	–18	40
Mladost Podgorica	33	11	6	16	38	46	–8	39
Mogren+ (–3)	33	11	9	13	45	56	–11	39
Mornar*+	33	9	9	15	35	47	–12	36
Decic*	33	5	9	19	32	61	–29	24

Top scorer: Mugosa (Mladost), 15.
Cup Final: Mladost 0, Lovcen 1.

NETHERLANDS

Koninklijke Nederlandse Voetbalbond, Woudenbergseweg 56–58, Postbus 515, 3700 AM Zeist.
Founded: 1889; *National Colours:* All orange.

International matches 2013–14
Portugal (a) 1-1, Estonia (a) 2-2, Andorra (a) 2-0, Hungary (h) 8-1, Turkey (a) 2-0, Japan (n) 2-2, Colombia (h) 0-0, France (a) 0-2, Ecuador (h) 1-1, Ghana (h) 1-0, Wales (h) 2-0, Spain (n) 5-1, Australia (n) 3-2, Chile (n) 2-0, Mexico (n) 2-1, Costa Rica (n) 0-0 (4-3p), Argentina (n) 0-0 (2-4p), Brazil (a) 3-0.

League Championship wins (1889–2014)
Ajax Amsterdam 33; PSV Eindhoven 21; Feyenoord 14; HVV The Hague 8; Sparta Rotterdam 6; RAP Amsterdam 5; Go Ahead Eagles Deventer 4; HFC Haarlem 3; HBS Craeyenhout 3; Willem II Tilburg 3; RCH Heemstede 2; Heracles 2; ADO The Hague 2; AZ 67 Alkmaar 2; VV Concordia 1; Quick The Hague 1; Be Quick Groningen 1; NAC Breda 1; SC Enschede 1; Volewijckers Amsterdam 1; Haarlem 1; BVV Den Bosch 1; Schiedam 1; Limburgia 1; EVV Eindhoven 1; SVV Rapid JC Den Heerlen 1; DOS Utrecht 1; DWS Amsterdam 1; FC Twente 1.

Cup wins (1899–2014)
Ajax Amsterdam 18; Feyenoord 11; PSV Eindhoven 9; Quick The Hague 4; AZ 67 Alkmaar 4; HFC Haarlem 3; Sparta Rotterdam 3; Twente 3; Utrecht 3; Haarlem 2; VOC 2; HBS Craeyenhout 2; DFC 2; RCH Haarlem 2; Wageningen 2; Willem II Tilburg 2; Fortuna 54 2; FC Den Haag (includes ADO) 2; Roda JC 2; RAP Amsterdam 1; Velocitas Breda 1; HVV The Hague 1; Concordia Delft 1; CVV 1; Schoten 1; ZFC Zaandam 1;

Longa 1; VUC 1; Velocitas Groningen 1; Roermond 1; FC Eindhoven 1; VSV 1; Quick 1888 Nijmegen 1; VVV Groningen 1; NAC Breda 1; Heerenveen 1; PEC Zwolle 1.

Final League Table 2013–14

	P	W	D	L	F	A	GD	Pts
Ajax	34	20	11	3	69	28	41	71
Feyenoord	34	20	7	7	76	40	36	67
FC Twente	34	17	12	5	72	37	35	63
PSV Eindhoven	34	18	5	11	60	45	15	59
Heerenveen	34	16	9	9	72	51	21	57
Vitesse	34	15	10	9	65	49	16	55
FC Groningen	34	14	9	11	57	53	4	51
AZ Alkmaar	34	13	8	13	54	50	4	47
ADO Den Haag	34	12	7	15	45	64	–19	43
Utrecht	34	11	8	15	46	65	–19	41
PEC Zwolle	34	9	13	12	47	49	–2	40
Cambuur	34	10	9	15	40	50	–10	39
Go Ahead Eagles	34	10	8	16	45	69	–24	38
Heracles Almelo	34	10	7	17	45	59	–14	37
NAC Breda	34	8	11	15	43	54	–11	35
RKC Waalwijk*+	34	8	8	18	44	64	–20	32
NEC Nijmegen*+	34	5	15	14	54	82	–28	30
Roda JC*	34	7	8	19	44	69	–25	29

Top scorer: Finnbogason (Heerenveen) 29.
Cup Final: PEC Zwolle 5, Ajax 1.

NORTHERN CYPRUS

Turkish Republic of Northern Cyprus Football Federation. (Not a member of FIFA or UEFA.)
Founded: 1955; *National Colours:* Red shirts with white trim, red shorts, red socks.

League Championship wins (1956–63; 1969–74; 1976–2014)
Cetinkaya 14; Gonyeli 9; Magusa 7; Dogan 6; Yenicami Agdelen 6; BAF Ulku 4; Kucuk 4; Akincilar 1; Binatli 1.

Cup wins (1956–2014)
Cetinkaya 17; Gonyeli 8; Kucuk 6; Yenicami Agdelen 6; Magusa 5; Turk Ocagi 4; Dogan 2; Lefke 2; Genclik 1; Yalova 1; Binatli 1.

Final League Table 2013–14

	P	W	D	L	F	A	GD	Pts
Yenicami Agdelen	26	20	3	3	76	16	60	63
Kaymakli	26	20	2	4	82	23	59	62
Lefke	26	15	6	5	60	25	35	51
Cetinkaya	26	13	5	8	36	30	6	44
Dogan	26	12	6	8	51	45	6	42
Cihangir	26	10	6	10	44	38	6	36
Magusa	26	11	3	12	35	40	–5	36
Bostanci Bagcil	26	10	6	10	43	43	0	36
Serdarli+	26	9	8	9	33	36	–3	35
Mormenekse+	26	11	2	13	34	41	–7	35
Hamitkoy*+	26	8	6	12	34	51	–17	30
Yeni Bogazici+	26	6	3	17	30	57	–27	21
Yalova*	26	5	5	16	30	61	–31	20
Genclik*	26	1	1	24	21	103	–82	4

Top scorer: Sonay (Kaymakli) 28.
Cup Final: Lefke 3, Yenicami Agdelen 1.

NORTHERN IRELAND

Irish Football Association Ltd, 20 Windsor Avenue, Belfast BT9 6EE.
Founded: 1880; *National Colours:* Green shirts, white shorts, green socks.

NORWAY

Norges Fotballforbund, Ullevaal Stadion, Serviceboks 1, 0840 Oslo.
Founded: 1902; *National Colours:* Red shirts, white shorts, red socks.

International matches 2013–14
Sweden (a) 2-4, Cyprus (h) 2-0, Switzerland (h) 0-2, Slovenia (a) 0-3, Iceland (h) 1-1, Denmark (a) 1-2, Scotland (h) 0-1, Moldova (n) 2-1, Poland (n) 0-3, Czech Republic (a) 2-2, France (a) 0-4, Russia (h) 1-1.

League Championship wins (1938–2013)
Rosenborg 22; Fredrikstad 9; Viking Stavanger 8; Lillestrom 5; Valerenga 5; Larvik Turn 3; Brann 3; Lyn Oslo 2; IK Start 2; Molde 2; Stromsgodset 2; Freidig 1; Fram 1; Skeid 1; Moss 1; Stabaek 1.

Cup wins (1902–2013)
Odd Grenland 12; Fredrikstad 11; Rosenborg 9; Lyn Oslo

8; Skeid 8; Sarpsborg 6; Brann 6; Viking Stavanger 5; Stromsgodset 5; Lillestrom 5; Orn-Horten 4; Valerenga 4; Frigg 3; Mjondalen 3; Molde 3; Mercantile 2; Bodo/Glimt 2; Tromso 2;Aalesund 2; Grane Nordstrand 1; Kvik Haldøn 1; Sparta 1; Gjovik/Lyn 1; Moss 1; Bryne 1; Stabaek 1; Hodd 1.
(Known as the Norwegian Championship for HM The King's Trophy.)

Final League Table 2013

	P	W	D	L	F	A	GD	Pts
Stromsgodset	30	19	6	5	66	26	40	63
Rosenborg	30	18	8	4	50	25	25	62
Haugesund	30	15	6	9	41	39	2	51
Aalesund	30	14	7	9	55	44	11	49
Viking	30	12	10	8	41	36	5	46
Molde	30	12	8	10	47	38	9	44
Odd	30	11	7	12	43	39	4	40
Brann	30	11	6	13	46	46	0	39
Start	30	10	8	12	43	46	-3	38
Lillestrom	30	9	9	12	37	44	-7	36
Valerenga	30	10	6	14	41	50	-9	36
Sogndal	30	8	9	13	33	48	-15	33
Sandnes Ulf	30	9	6	15	36	58	-22	33
Sarpsborg 08+	30	8	7	15	40	58	-18	31
Tromso*	30	7	8	15	41	50	-9	29
Honefoss*	30	6	11	13	34	47	-13	29

Top scorer: Johnsen (Odd) 16.
Cup Final: Molde 4, Rosenborg 2.

POLAND

Polish Football Association, Bitwy Warszawskiej 1920 r. 7, 02-366 Warsaw.
Founded: 1919; *National Colours:* White shirts, red shorts, white socks.

International matches 2013–14
Denmark (h) 3-2, Montenegro (h) 1-1, San Marino (a) 5-1, Ukraine (a) 0-1, England (a) 0-2, Slovakia (h) 0-2, Republic of Ireland (h) 0-0, Norway (n) 3-0, Moldova (n) 1-0, Scotland (h) 0-1, Germany (a) 0-0, Lithuania (h) 2-1.

League Championship wins (1921–2014)
Gornik Zabrze 14; Ruch Chorzow 14; Wisla Krakow 13; Legia Warsaw 10; Lech Poznan 6; Cracovia 5; Pogon Lwow 4; Widzew Lodz 4; Warta Poznan 2; Polonia Warsaw 2; Polonia Bytom 2; LKS Lodz 2; Stal Mielec 2; Zaglebie Lubin 2; Slask Wroclaw 2; Garbarnia Krakow 1; Szombierki Bytom 1.

Cup wins (1926; 1951–2014)
Legia Warsaw 16; Gornik Zabrze 6; Lech Poznan 5; Wisla Krakow 4; Zaglebie Sosnowiec 4; Ruch Chorzow 3; GKS Katowice 3; Amica Wronki 3; Polonia Warsaw 2; Slask Wroclaw 2; Dyskobolia Grodzisk 2; Gwardia Warsaw 1; LKS Lodz 1; Stal Rzeszow 1; Arka Gdynia 1; Lechia Gdansk 1; Widzew Lodz 1; Miedz Legnica 1; Wisla Plock 1; Jagiellonia Bialystok 1; Zawisza Bydgoszcz 1.

Qualifying League Table 2013–14

	P	W	D	L	F	A	GD	Pts
Legia Warsaw	30	20	3	7	60	30	30	63
Lech Poznan	30	15	8	7	56	34	22	53
Ruch Chorzow	30	14	8	8	40	38	2	50
Pogon Szczecin	30	11	14	5	47	38	9	47
Wisla Krakow	30	12	9	9	38	30	8	45
Zawisza Bydgoszcz	30	11	9	10	43	37	6	42
Gornik Zabrze	30	11	9	10	42	46	-4	42
Lechia Gdansk	30	10	10	10	38	37	1	40
Cracovia	30	11	6	13	37	43	-6	39
Jagiellonia Bialystok	30	10	9	11	46	43	3	39
Korona Kielce	30	9	10	11	36	41	-5	37
Slask Wroclaw	30	7	13	10	38	40	-2	34
GKS Piast Gliwice	30	8	10	12	29	47	-18	34
Podbeskidzie Bielsko-Biala	30	6	13	11	27	39	-12	31
Zaglebie Lubin	30	7	8	15	31	40	-9	29
Widzew Lodz	30	5	7	18	26	51	-25	22

Championship Round

	P	W	D	L	F	A	GD	Pts
Legia Warsaw	37	26	3	8	75	34	41	50
Lech Poznan	37	19	9	9	68	40	28	40
Ruch Chorzow	37	16	11	10	47	48	-1	34
Lechia Gdansk	37	13	13	11	46	41	5	32
Wisla Krakow	37	14	11	12	51	46	5	31
Gornik Zabrze	37	14	10	13	53	57	-4	31

| Pogon Szczecin | 37 | 11 | 17 | 9 | 50 | 50 | 0 | 27 |
| Zawisza Bydgoszcz | 37 | 12 | 10 | 15 | 48 | 48 | 0 | 25 |

Relegation Round

	P	W	D	L	F	A	GD	Pts
Slask Wroclaw	37	12	15	10	49	41	8	34
Podbeskidzie Bielsko-Biala	37	10	15	12	39	45	-6	30
Jagiellonia Bialystok	37	12	13	59	58	1	29
GKS Piast Gliwice	37	11	12	14	43	56	-13	28
Korona Kielce	37	10	14	13	47	56	-9	26
Cracovia	37	12	8	17	43	56	-13	25
Widzew Lodz*	37	7	10	20	36	62	-26	20
Zagl bie Lubin*	37	7	10	20	35	51	-16	17

Top scorer: Robak (Pogon Szczecin) 22 (incl. 1 for Piast Gliwice).
Cup Final: Zaglebie Lubin 0, Zawisza Bydgoszcz 0.
aet; Zawisza Bydgoszcz won 6-5 on penalties.

PORTUGAL

Federacao Portuguesa de Futebol, Rua Alexandre Herculano No. 58, Apartado postal 24013, Lisboa 1251-977.
Founded: 1914; *National Colours:* Red shirts, red shorts, red and green socks.

International matches 2013–14
Netherlands (h) 1-1, Northern Ireland (a) 4-2, Brazil (n) 1-3, Israel (h) 1-1, Luxembourg (h) 3-0, Sweden (h) 1-0, Sweden (a) 3-2, Cameroon (h) 5-1, Greece (h) 0-0, Mexico (n) 1-0, Republic of Ireland (n) 5-1, Germany (n) 0-4, USA (n) 2-2, Ghana (n) 2-1.

League Championship wins (1935–2014)
Benfica 33; FC Porto 27; Sporting Lisbon 18; Belenenses 1; Boavista 1.

Cup wins (1939–2014)
Benfica 25; FC Porto 16; Sporting Lisbon 15; Boavista 5; Belenenses 3; Vitoria de Setubal 3; Academica de Coimbra 2; Leixoes 1; Braga 1; Estrela da Amadora 1; Beira Mar 1; Vitoria de Guimaraes 1.

Final League Table 2013–14

	P	W	D	L	F	A	GD	Pts
Benfica	30	23	5	2	58	18	40	74
Sporting Lisbon	30	20	7	3	54	20	34	67
FC Porto	30	19	4	7	57	25	32	61
Estoril	30	15	9	6	42	26	16	54
Nacional	30	11	12	7	43	33	10	45
Maritimo	30	11	8	11	40	44	-4	41
Vitoria Setubal	30	10	9	11	41	41	0	39
Academica de Coimbra	30	9	10	11	25	35	-10	37
Braga	30	10	7	13	39	37	2	37
Vitoria de Guimaraes	30	10	5	15	30	35	-5	35
Rio Ave	30	8	8	14	21	35	-14	32
Arouca	30	8	7	15	28	42	-14	31
Gil Vicente	30	8	7	15	23	37	-14	31
Belenenses	30	6	10	14	19	33	-14	28
Pacos de Ferreira+	30	6	6	18	28	59	-31	24
Olhanense*	30	6	6	18	21	49	-28	24

Top scorer: Jackson Martinez (Porto) 20.
Cup Final: Benfica 1, Rio Ave 0.

ROMANIA

Federatia Romana de Fotbal, House of Football, Str. Serg. Serbanica Vasile 12, 22186 Bucuresti.
Founded: 1909; *National Colours:* All yellow.

International matches 2013–14
Slovakia (h) 1-1, Hungary (h) 3-0, Turkey (h) 0-2, Andorra (a) 4-0, Estonia (h) 2-0, Greece (a) 1-3, Greece (h) 1-1, Argentina (n) 0-0, Albania (n) 1-0, Algeria (n) 1-2.

League Championship wins (1910–2014)
Steaua Bucharest 25; Dinamo Bucharest 18; Venus Bucharest 8; Chinezul Timisoara 6; UT Arad 6; Universitatea Craiova 5; Ripensia Timisoara 4; Rapid Bucharest 4; Petrolul Ploiesti 3; CFR Cluj 3; Olimpia Bucharest 2; Colentina Bucharest 2; Arges Pitesti 2; United Ploiesti 1; Romano-Americana Bucharest 1; Prahova Ploiesti 1; Coltea Brasov 1; Juventus Bucharest 1; Metalochimia Resita 1; Unirea Tricolor 1; ICO Oradea 1; Unirea Urziceni 1; Otelul Galati 1.

Cup wins (1934–2014)
Steaua Bucharest 22; Rapid Bucharest 13; Dinamo Bucharest 13; Uni Craiova 6; Petrolul Ploiesti 3; CFR Cluj 3; Ripensia Timisoara 2; UT Arad 2; Politehnica

Timisoara 2; CFR Turnu Severin 1; Metalochimia Resita 1; Universitata Cluj (includes Stiinta) 1; Progresul Oradea (formerly ICO) 1; Progresul Bucharest 1; Ariesul Turda 1; Chimia Ramnicu Vilcea 1; Jiul Petrosani 1; Gloria Bistrita 1; Astra Giurgiu 1.

Final League Table 2013–14

	P	W	D	L	F	A	GD	Pts
Steaua Bucharest	34	22	11	1	71	20	51	77
Astra Giurgiu	34	22	6	6	70	28	42	72
Petrolul Ploiesti	34	18	14	2	53	20	33	68
Dinamo Bucharest	34	17	8	9	52	34	18	59
Vaslui	34	15	6	13	38	32	6	51
CFR Cluj	34	13	12	9	44	33	11	51
Pandurii Targu Jiu	34	14	8	12	59	39	20	50
Botosani	34	12	7	15	36	52	–16	43
Ceahlaul Piatra Neam	34	10	11	13	27	31	–4	41
Otelul Galati	34	12	5	17	43	52	–9	41
Universitatea Cluj	34	11	7	16	29	46	–17	40
Viitorul Constanta	34	10	10	14	29	50	–21	40
Gaz Metan Medias	34	10	9	15	32	38	–6	39
Concordia Chiajna	34	10	9	15	34	47	–13	39
Brasov*	34	9	11	14	32	40	–8	38
Politehnica Timisoara*	34	10	8	16	26	42	–16	38
Sageata Navodari*	34	10	8	16	32	54	–22	38
Corona Brasov*	34	2	8	24	20	69	–49	14

Top scorer: Antal (Vaslui) 15.
Cup Final: Steaua Bucharest 0, Astra Giurgiu 0.
aet; Astra Giurgiu won 4-2 on penalties.

RUSSIA

Football Union of Russia, Ulitsa Narodnaya 7, 115 172 Moscow.
Founded: 1912; *National Colours:* All brick red.

International matches 2013–14
Northern Ireland (a) 0-1, Luxembourg (h) 4-1, Israel (h) 3-1, Luxembourg (a) 4-0, Azerbaijan (a) 1-1, Serbia (n) 1-1, Korea Republic (n) 2-1, Armenia (h) 2-0, Slovakia (h) 1-0, Norway (a) 1-1, Morocco (n) 2-0, Korea Republic (n) 1-1, Belgium (n) 0-1, Algeria (n) 1-1.

League Championship wins (1936–2014)
Spartak Moscow 21; Dynamo Kiev 13; CSKA Moscow 12; Dynamo Moscow 11; Zenit St Petersburg (formerly Zenit Leningrad) 4; Torpedo Moscow 3; Dinamo Tbilisi 2; Dnepr Dnepropetrovsk 2; Lokomotiv Moscow 2; Rubin Kazan 2; Saria Voroshilovgrad 1; Ararat Erevan 1; Dynamo Minsk 1; Spartak Vladikavkaz (renamed Alania) 1.

Cup wins (1936–2013)
Spartak Moscow 13; Dynamo Kiev 9; Torpedo Moscow 7; Dynamo Moscow 7; Lokomotiv Moscow 7; Shakhtar Donetsk 4; Zenit St Petersburg (formerly Zenit Leningrad) 3; Dinamo Tbilisi 2; Ararat Erevan 2; Karpaty Lvov 1; SKA Rostov-on-Don 1; Metalist Kharkov 1; Dnepr 1; Terek Grozny 1; Rubin Kazan 1; Rostov 1.

First Stage Final League Table 2013–14

	P	W	D	L	F	A	GD	Pts
CSKA Moscow	30	20	4	6	49	26	23	64
Zenit St Petersburg	30	19	6	5	63	32	31	63
Lokomotiv Moscow	30	17	8	5	51	23	28	59
Dinamo Moscow	30	15	7	8	54	37	17	52
Krasnodar	30	15	5	10	46	39	7	50
Spartak Moscow	30	15	5	10	46	36	10	50
Rostov	30	10	9	11	40	40	0	39
Kuban Krasnodar	30	10	8	12	40	42	–2	38
Rubin Kazan	30	9	11	10	36	30	6	38
Amkar Perm	30	9	11	10	36	37	–1	38
Ural Sverdlovsk Oblast	30	9	7	14	28	46	–18	34
Terek Grozny	30	8	9	13	27	33	–6	33
Tom Tomsk*+	30	7	5	15	23	39	–16	31
Krylya Sovetov Samara*+	30	6	11	13	27	46	–19	29
Volga Nizhny Novgorod*	30	6	3	21	22	65	–43	21
Anzhi Makhachkala*	30	3	11	16	25	42	–17	20

Top scorer: Doumbia (CSKA Moscow) 18.
Cup Final: Krasnodar 1, Rostov 1.
aet; Rostov won 6-5 on penalties.

SAN MARINO

Federazione Sammarinese Giuoco Calcio, Strada di Montecchio 17, 47890 San Marino.
Founded: 1931; *National Colours:* All cobalt blue.

International matches 2013–14
Ukraine (a) 0-9, Poland (h) 1-5, Moldova (a) 0-3, Ukraine (h) 0-8, Albania (h) 0-3.

League Championship wins (1986–2014)
Tre Fiori 7; Domagnano 4; Faetano 3; Folgore/Falciano 3; La Fiorita 3; Murata 3; Tre Penne 2; Montevito 1; Libertas 1; Cosmos 1; Pennarossa 1.

Cup wins (1937–2014)
Libertas 11; Domagnano 8; Tre Fiori 6; Juvenes 5; Tre Penne 5; Cosmos 4; La Fiorita 3; Faetano 3; Murata 3; Dogana 2; Pennarossa 2; Juvenes/Dogana 2.

Qualifying League Table 2013–14

Group A

	P	W	D	L	F	A	GD	Pts
Tre Fiori	21	12	5	4	34	20	14	41
Tre Penne	21	10	7	4	25	15	10	37
Faetano	21	10	6	5	35	27	8	36
Libertas	21	8	7	6	26	18	8	31
Virtus	21	3	7	11	21	35	–14	16
Fiorentino	21	4	4	13	25	45	–20	16
Murata	21	4	3	15	13	34	–21	12
Domagnano	21	2	3	16	16	46	–30	9

Group B

	P	W	D	L	F	A	GD	Pts
La Fiorita	20	14	4	2	47	19	29	46
Cosmos	20	12	2	6	44	26	18	38
Folgore/Falciano	20	11	5	4	36	18	18	38
Juvenes-Dogana	20	10	7	3	35	20	15	37
Pennarossa	20	10	4	6	28	19	9	34
Cailungo	20	5	5	10	27	42	–15	20
San Giovanni	20	3	5	12	23	52	–29	14

Play-offs
(Double-elimination format; Group winners receive byes in first two rounds.)
Rnd 1: Cosmos 0, Faetano 0 (4-3p); Tre Penne 1, Folgore 1 (4-5p)
Rnd 2: Faetano 2, Tre Penne 1; Cosmos 0, Folgore 2
Rnd 3: La Fiorita 0, Tre Fiori 0 (1-4p); Faetano 0, Cosmos 1
Rnd 4: Tre Fiore 0, Folgore 1; Cosmos 1, La Fiorita 2
Rnd 5: La Fiorita 4, Tre Fiori 1; Final: Folgore 0, La Fiorita 2
Top scorer: Gualtieri (La Fiorita) 21.
Cup Final: Faetano 0, Libertas 2.

SCOTLAND

The Scottish Football Association Ltd, Hampden Park, Glasgow G42 9AY.
Founded: 1873; *National Colours:* Dark blue shirts, white shorts, dark blue socks.

SERBIA

Football Association of Serbia, Terazije 35, PO Box 263, 11000 Beograd.
Founded: 1919; *National Colours:* Red shirts, blue shorts, white socks.

International matches 2013–14
Colombia (n) 0-1, Croatia (h) 1-1, Wales (a) 3-0, Japan (h) 2-0, FYR Macedonia (h) 5-1, Russia (a) 1-1, Republic of Ireland (a) 2-1, Jamaica (n) 2-1, Panama (n) 1-1, Brazil (a) 0-1.

League Championship wins (1923–2014)
Red Star Belgrade 26; Partizan Belgrade 25; Hajduk Split 9; Gradjanski Zagreb 5; BSK Belgrade (renamed OFK) 5; Dinamo Zagreb 4; Jugoslavija Belgrade 2; Concordia Zagreb 2; FC Sarajevo 2; Vojvodina Novi Sad 2; HASK Zagreb 1; Zeljeznicar 1; Obilic 1.

Cup wins (1947–2014)
Red Star Belgrade 24; Partizan Belgrade 12; Hajduk Split 9; Dinamo Zagreb 8; BSK Belgrade (incl. OFK 2) 4; Rijeka 2; Velez Mostar 2; Vardar Skopje 1; Borac Banjaluka 1; Sartid 1; Zeleznik 1; Jagodina 1; Vojvodina 1.

Final League Table 2013–14

	P	W	D	L	F	A	GD	Pts
Red Star Belgrade	30	23	3	4	66	27	39	72
Partizan Belgrade	30	22	5	3	64	20	44	71
Jagodina	30	13	9	8	40	30	10	48
Vojvodina	30	11	12	7	38	32	6	45
Cukaricki	30	12	8	10	30	31	–1	44
Radnicki Nis	30	10	13	7	28	22	6	43

Vozdovac	30	12	6	12	34	35	–1	42
Novi Pazar	30	11	6	13	32	34	–2	39
Napredak	30	9	8	13	42	44	–2	35
Spartak Subotica	30	8	10	12	24	37	–13	34
OFK Beograd	30	10	3	17	31	43	–12	33
Donji Srem	30	7	11	12	29	40	–11	32
Radnicki 1923	30	7	11	12	30	49	–19	32
Rad+	30	8	5	17	19	37	–18	29
Javor*	30	6	11	13	29	38	–9	29
Sloboda Uzice*	30	7	7	16	21	38	–17	28

Top scorer: Mrda (Red Star Belgrade) 14.
Cup Final: Vojvodina 2, Jagodina 0.

SLOVAKIA

Slovensky Futbalovy Zvaz, Trnavska cesta 100, 821 01 Bratislava.
Founded: 1993; *National Colours:* White shirts with blue trim, white shorts, white socks with blue trim.

International matches 2013–14
Romania (a) 1-1, Bosnia & Herzogovina (a) 1-0, Bosnia & Herzogovina (h) 1-2, Greece (a) 0-1, Latvia (a) 2-2, Poland (a) 2-0, Israel (a) 3-1, Montenegro (h) 2-0, Russia (a) 0-1.

League Championship wins (1939–44; 1994–2014)
Slovan Bratislava 12; Zilina 6; Kosice 2; Inter Bratislava 2; Artmedia Petrzalka 2; Bystrica 1; OAP Bratislava 1; Ruzomberok 1.

Cup wins (1994–2014)
Slovan Bratislava 6; Inter Bratislava 3; Artmedia Petrzalka 2; Kosice 2; Humenne 1; Spartak Trnava 1; Koba Senec 1; Matador Puchov 1; Bystrica 1; Ruzomberok 1; ViOn Zlate Moravce 1; Zilina 1.

Final League Table 2013–14
	P	W	D	L	F	A	GD	Pts
Slovan Bratislava	33	24	3	6	63	32	31	75
Trencín	33	19	6	8	74	35	39	63
Spartak Trnava	33	16	5	12	47	42	5	53
Ruzomberok	33	15	5	13	56	51	5	50
Kosice	33	13	7	13	41	40	1	46
Senica	33	13	7	13	45	47	–2	46
Spartak Myjava	33	13	6	14	45	54	–9	45
Dukla Banks Bystrica	33	11	9	13	48	48	0	42
Zilina	33	11	7	15	49	50	–1	40
ViOn Zlate Moravce	33	11	5	17	36	47	–11	38
Dunajska Streda (–6)	33	8	8	17	29	57	–28	26
Nitra*	33	6	8	19	33	63	–30	26

Top scorer: Malec (Trencin) 14.
Cup Final: Slovan Bratislava 1, Kosice 2.

SLOVENIA

Nogometna Zveza Slovenije, Cerinova 4, PO Box 3986, 1001 Ljubljana.
Founded: 1920; *National Colours:* White shirts with blue/green trim, white shorts, white stockings with blue/green trim.

International matches 2013–14
Finland (a) 0-2, Albania (h) 1-0, Cyprus (a) 2-0, Norway (h) 3-0, Switzerland (a) 0-1, Canada (h) 1-0, Algeria (h) 0-2, Uruguay (a) 0-2, Argentina (a) 0-2.

League Championship wins (1992–2014)
Maribor 12; Olimpija Ljubljana (pre-2005) 4; Gorica 4; Domzale 2; Koper 1.

Cup wins (1992–2014)
Maribor 8; Olimpija Ljubljana (pre-2005) 4; Gorica 3; Koper 2; Interblock 2; Mura (pre-2004) 1; Rudar Velenje 1; Celje 1; Domzale 1.

Final League Table 2013–14
	P	W	D	L	F	A	GD	Pts
Maribor	36	24	5	7	78	31	47	77
Koper	36	21	6	9	52	36	16	69
Rudar Velenje	36	18	9	9	55	33	22	63
Gorica	36	16	10	10	60	32	28	58
Zavrc	36	16	5	15	58	63	–5	53
Domzale	36	10	15	11	47	36	11	45
Olimpija Ljubljana	36	12	6	18	38	56	–18	42
Celje	36	10	7	19	30	58	–28	37
Krka	36	8	7	21	31	64	–33	31
Triglav*	36	6	8	22	34	74	–40	26

Top scorer: Eterovic (Rudar) 19.
Cup Final: Maribor 0, Gorica 2.

SPAIN

Real Federacion Espanola de Futbol, Ramon y Cajal s/n, Apartado postale 385, 28230 Las Rozas (Madrid).
Founded: 1913; *National Colours:* Red shirts, blue shorts, red socks.

International matches 2013–14
Ecuador (a) 2-0, Finland (a) 2-0, Chile (n) 2-2, Belarus (h) 2-1, Georgia (h) 2-0, Equatorial Guinea (a) 2-1, South Africa (a) 0-1, Italy (h) 1-0, Bolivia (h) 2-0, El Salvador (n) 2-0, Netherlands (n) 1-5, Chile (n) 0-2, Australia (n) 3-0.

League Championship wins (1929–36; 1940–2014)
Real Madrid 32; Barcelona 22; Atletico Madrid 10; Athletic Bilbao 8; Valencia 6; Real Sociedad 2; Real Betis 1; Sevilla 1; Deportivo La Coruna 1.

Cup wins (1903–2014)
Barcelona 26; Athletic Bilbao (includesVizcaya Bilbao 1) 23; Real Madrid 19; Atletico Madrid 10; Valencia 7; Real Zaragoza 6; Sevilla 5; Espanyol 4; Real Union de Irun 3; Real Betis 2; Real Sociedad (includes Ciclista) 2; Deportivo La Coruna 2; Arenas 1; Racing de Irun 1; Mallorca 1.

Final League Table 2013–14
	P	W	D	L	F	A	GD	Pts
Atletico Madrid	38	28	6	4	77	26	51	90
Barcelona	38	27	6	5	100	33	67	87
Real Madrid	38	27	6	5	104	38	66	87
Athletic Bilboa	38	20	10	8	66	39	27	70
Sevilla	38	18	9	11	69	52	17	63
Villarreal	38	17	8	13	60	44	16	59
Real Sociedad	38	16	11	11	62	55	7	59
Valencia	38	13	10	15	51	53	–2	49
Celta Vigo	38	14	7	17	49	54	–5	49
Levante	38	12	12	14	35	43	–8	48
Malaga	38	12	9	17	39	46	–7	45
Rayo Vallecano	38	13	4	21	46	80	–34	43
Getafe	38	11	9	18	35	54	–19	42
Espanyol	38	11	9	18	41	51	–10	42
Granada	38	12	5	21	32	56	–24	41
Elche	38	9	13	16	30	50	–20	40
Almeria	38	11	7	20	43	71	–28	40
Osasuna*	38	10	9	19	32	62	–30	39
Real Valladolid*	38	7	15	16	38	60	–22	36
Real Betis*	38	6	7	25	36	78	–42	25

Top scorer: Ronaldo (Real Madrid) 31.
Cup Final: Real Madrid 2, Barcelona 1.

SWEDEN

Svenska Fotbollfoerbundet, Evenemangsgatan 31, PO Box 1216, SE-171 23 Solna.
Founded: 1904; *National Colours:* Yellow shirts, blue shorts, yellow socks.

International matches 2013–14
Norway (h) 4-2, Republic of Ireland (a) 2-1, Kazakhstan (a) 1-0, Austria (h) 2-1, Germany (h) 3-5, Portugal (a) 0-1, Portugal (h) 2-3, Moldova (n) 2-1, Iceland (n) 2-0, Turkey (a) 1-2, Denmark (a) 0-1, Belgium (h) 0-2.

League Championship wins (1896–2013)
IFK Gothenburg 18; Malmo 17; Orgryte 14; IFK Norrkoping 12; Djurgaarden 11; AIK Stockholm 11; Helsingborg 7; GAIS Gothenburg 6; IF Elfsborg 6; Oster Vaxjo 4; Halmstad 4; Atvidaberg 2; IF Gothenburg 1; IFK Eskilstuna 1; Fassbergs 1; IF Gavic Brynas 1; IK Sleipner 1; Hammarby 1; Kalmar 1.

Cup wins (1941–2014)
Malmo 14; AIK Stockholm 8; IFK Norrkoping 6; IFK Gothenburg 6; Djurgaarden 4; Kalmar 3; IF Elfsborg 3; Atvidaberg 2; GAIS Gothenburg 1; IF Raa 1; Landskrona 1; Oster Vaxjo 1; Degerfors 1; Halmstad 1; Orgryte 1.

Final League Table 2013
	P	W	D	L	F	A	GD	Pts
Malmo	30	19	6	5	56	30	26	63
AIK Solna	30	17	7	6	54	32	22	58
IFK Gothenburg	30	16	6	8	49	31	18	54
Kalmar	30	14	10	6	35	26	9	52
Helsingborg	30	14	7	9	61	41	20	49
Elfsborg	30	12	10	8	49	34	15	46
Djurgarden	30	12	8	10	38	44	–6	44
Atvidaberg	30	11	7	12	37	37	0	40
Norrkoping	30	11	6	13	45	47	–2	39

Hacken	30	10	7	13	37	41	-4	37
Mjallby	30	10	6	14	46	47	-1	36
Gefle	30	7	13	10	34	42	-8	34
Brommapojkarna	30	8	8	14	33	54	-21	32
Halmstad+	30	7	10	13	32	46	-14	31
Oster*	30	6	10	14	27	43	-16	28
Syrianska*	30	3	5	22	26	64	-38	14

Top scorer: Khalili (Helsingborg) 15 (incl. 7 for Norrkoping).
Cup Final: Helsingborg 0, Elfsborg 1.

SWITZERLAND

Schweizerisher Fussballverband, Worbstrasse 48, Postfach 3000, Berne 15.
Founded: 1895; *National Colours:* Red shirts, white shorts, red socks.

International matches 2013–14
Brazil (h) 1-0, Iceland (h) 4-4, Norway (a) 2-0, Albania (a) 2-1, Slovenia (h) 1-0, Korea Republic (a) 1-2, Croatia (h) 2-2, Jamaica (h) 1-0, Peru (h) 2-0, Ecuador (n) 2-1, France (n) 2-5, Honduras (n) 3-0, Argentina (n) 0-1.

League Championship wins (1897–2014)
Grasshoppers 27; Servette 17; FC Basel 17; FC Zurich 12; Young Boys 11; Lausanne-Sport 7; La Chaux-de-Fonds 3; Lugano 3; Winterthur 3; Aarau 3; Neuchatel Xamax 2; Sion 2; St Gallen 2; Anglo-American Club 1; Brühl 1; Cantonal-Neuchatel 1; Biel-Bienne 1; Bellinzona 1; Etoile La Chaux-de-Fonds 1; Luzern 1.

Cup wins (1926–2014)
Grasshoppers 19; Sion 12; FC Basel 11; Lausanne-Sport 9; FC Zurich 8; Servette 7; Young Boys 6; La Chaux-de-Fonds 6; Lugano 3; Luzern 2; FC Grenchen 1; St Gallen 1; Urania Geneva 1; Young Fellows Zurich 1; Aarau 1; Wil 1.

Final League Table 2013–14

	P	W	D	L	F	A	GD	Pts
FC Basel	36	19	15	2	70	34	36	72
Grasshoppers	36	19	8	9	67	43	24	65
Young Boys	36	17	8	11	59	50	9	59
Luzern	36	15	6	15	48	54	-6	51
FC Zurich	36	14	8	14	51	52	-1	50
Thun	36	13	9	14	57	53	4	48
St Gallen	36	11	12	13	37	47	-10	45
Sion	36	12	7	17	38	45	-7	43
Aarau	36	12	6	18	55	71	-16	42
Lausanne-Sport*	36	7	3	26	38	71	-33	24

Top scorer: Gashi (Grasshoppers) 19.
Cup Final: FC Zurich 2, FC Basel 0.

TURKEY

Turkiye Futbol Federasyonu, Mahallesi Darussafaka Caddesi No. 45, Kat. 2–3, 34330 Istinye, Istanbul.
Founded: 1923; *National Colours:* All red.

International matches 2013–14
Ghana (h) 2-2, Andorra (h) 5-0, Romania (a) 2-0, Estonia (a) 2-0, Netherlands (h) 0-2, Northern Ireland (h) 1-0, Belarus (h) 2-1, Sweden (h) 2-1, Republic of Ireland (a) 2-1, Honduras (n) 2-0, Niger (n) 1-2.

League Championship wins (1959–2014)
Galatasaray 19; Fenerbahce 19; Besiktas 11; Trabzonspor 6; Bursa 1.

Cup wins (1963–2014)
Galatasaray 15; Besiktas 9; Trabzonspor 8; Fenerbahce 6; Altay Izmir 2; Goztepe Izmir 2; Ankaragucu 2; Genclerbirligi 2; Kocaelispor 2; Eskisehirspor 1; Bursapor 1; Sakaryaspor 1; Kayseri 1.

Final League Table 2013–14

	P	W	D	L	F	A	GD	Pts
Fenerbahce	34	23	5	6	74	33	41	74
Galatasaray	34	18	11	5	59	32	27	65
Besiktas	34	17	11	6	53	33	20	62
Trabzonspor	34	14	11	9	53	41	12	53
Sivasspor	34	16	5	13	60	55	5	53
Kasimpasa	34	13	12	9	56	39	17	51
Kardemir Karabuükspor	34	13	11	10	33	34	-1	50
Bursaspor	34	12	10	12	40	46	-6	46
Genclerbirligi	34	13	6	15	39	43	-4	45
Akhisar Belediyespor	34	12	8	14	44	55	-11	44
Konyaspor	34	11	9	14	48	45	3	42
Eskisehirspor	34	10	12	12	33	35	-2	42
Rizespor	34	10	12	12	43	43	0	42
Kayseri Erciyesspor	34	10	7	17	34	50	-16	37

Gaziantepspor	34	10	7	17	38	58	-20	37
Elazigspor*	34	10	4	20	38	62	-24	34
Antalyaspor*	34	6	13	15	34	47	-13	31
Kayserispor*	34	7	8	19	30	58	-28	29

Top scorer: Chahechouhe (Sivasspor) 17.
Cup Final: Galatasaray 1, Eskisehirspor 0.

UKRAINE

Football Federation of Ukraine, Provulok Laboratornyi 7-A, PO Box 55, 01133 Kiev.
Founded: 1991; *National Colours:* Yellow shirts with blue trim, yellow shorts with blue trim, yellow socks.

International matches 2013–14
Israel (h) 2-0, San Marino (h) 9-0, England (h) 0-0, Poland (h) 1-0, San Marino (a) 8-0, France (h) 2-0, France (a) 0-3, USA (n) 0-2, Niger (h) 2-1.

League Championship wins (1992–2014)
Dynamo Kyiv 13; Shakhtar Donetsk 9; Tavriya Simferopol 1.

Cup wins (1992–2014)
Dynamo Kyiv 10; Shakhtar Donetsk 9; Chornomorets Odessa 2; Vorskla 1; Tavriya Simferopol 1.

Final League Table 2013–14

	P	W	D	L	F	A	GD	Pts
Shakhtar Donetsk	28	21	2	5	62	23	39	65
Dnipro Dnipropetrovsk	28	18	5	5	56	28	28	59
Metalist Kharkiv	28	16	9	3	54	29	25	57
Dynamo Kyiv	28	16	5	7	55	33	22	53
Chornomorets Odesa	28	12	10	6	30	22	8	46
Metalurh Donetsk	28	12	7	9	45	42	3	43
Zorya Luhansk	28	11	9	8	35	30	5	42
Vorskla Poltava	28	10	10	8	36	38	-2	40
Sevastopol‡	28	10	5	13	32	43	-11	35
Illychivets Mariupil	28	10	4	14	27	33	-6	34
Karpaty Lviv	28	7	11	10	33	39	-6	32
Hoverla Uzhhorod	28	7	5	16	26	39	-13	26
Volyn Lutsk (–3)	28	7	6	15	25	51	-26	24
Metalurh Zaporizhya	28	6	2	20	19	54	-35	12
Tavriya Simferopol‡	28	2	4	22	15	46	-31	10
Arsenal Kyiv	0	0	0	0	0	0	0	0

‡ *Clubs disbanded due to political turmoil in Crimea.*
Arsenal Kyiv expelled due to financial difficulties, results annulled.
Top scorer: Luiz Adriano (Shakhtar Donetsk) 20.
Cup Final: Dynamo Kyiv 2, Shakhtar Donetsk 1.

WALES

The Football Association of Wales Limited, 11/12 Neptune Court, Vanguard Way, Cardiff CF24 5PJ.
Founded: 1876; *National Colours:* All red.

SOUTH AMERICA

ARGENTINA

Asociacion Del Futbol Argentina, Viamonte 1366/76, 1053 Buenos Aires.
Founded: 1893; *National Colours:* Light blue and white vertical striped shirts, dark blue shorts, white socks.
International matches 2013–14
Italy (a) 2-1, Paraguay (a) 5-2, Peru (h) 3-1, Uruguay (a) 2-3, Ecuador (n) 0-0, Bosnia & Herzegovina (n) 2-0, Romania (a) 0-0, Trinidad & Tobago (h) 3-0, Slovenia (h) 2-0, Bosnia & Herzegovina (n) 2-1, Iran (n) 1-0, Nigeria (n) 3-2, Switzerland (n) 1-0, Belgium (n) 1-0, Netherlands (n) 0-0 (4-2p), Germany (n) 0-1.

BOLIVIA

Federacion Boliviana De Futbol, Av. Libertador Bolivar No. 1168, Casilla de Correo 484, Cochabamba, Bolivia.
Founded: 1925; *National Colours:* Green shirts, white shorts, green socks.
International matches 2013–14
Venezuela (a) 2-2, Paraguay (a) 0-4, Ecuador (h) 1-1, Peru (a) 1-1, Spain (a) 0-2, Greece (n) 1-2.

BRAZIL

Confederacao Brasileira De Futebol, Rua Victor Civita 66, Bloco 1-Edificio 5-5 Andar, Barra da Tijuca, Rio De Janeiro 22775-040.

Founded: 1914; *National Colours:* Yellow shirts with green collar and cuffs, blue shorts, white socks with green and yellow border.
International matches 2013–14
Switzerland (a) 0-1, Australia (h) 6-0, Portugal (h) 3-1, Korea Republic (a) 2-0, Zambia (n) 2-0, Honduras (n) 5-0, Chile (n) 2-1, South Africa (a) 5-0, Panama (h) 4-0, Serbia (h) 1-0, Croatia (h) 3-1, Mexico (h) 0-0, Cameroon (h) 4-1, Chile (h) 1-1 (3-2p), Colombia (h) 2-1, Germany (h) 1-7, Netherlands (h) 0-3.

CHILE
Federacion De Futbol De Chile, Avda. Quillin No. 5635, Casilla postal 3733, Correo Central, Santiago de Chile.
Founded: 1895; *National Colours:* Red shirts with blue collar and cuffs, blue shorts, white socks.
International matches 2013–14
Iraq (n) 6-0, Venezuela (h) 3-0, Spain (n) 2-2, Colombia (a) 3-3, Ecuador (h) 2-1, England (a) 2-0, Brazil (n) 1-2, Costa Rica (h) 4-0, Germany (a) 0-1, Egypt (h) 3-2, Northern Ireland (h) 2-0, Australia (n) 3-1, Spain (n) 2-0, Netherlands (n) 0-2, Brazil (a) 1-1 (2-3p).

COLOMBIA
Federacion Colombiana De Futbol, Avenida 32, No. 16–22 piso 4o. Apartado Aereo 17602, Santafe de Bogota.
Founded: 1924; *National Colours:* Yellow shirts, blue shorts, red socks.
International matches 2013–14
Serbia (n) 1-0, Ecuador (h) 1-0, Uruguay (a) 0-2, Chile (h) 3-3, Paraguay (a) 2-1, Belgium (a) 2-0, Netherlands (a) 0-0, Tunisia (n) 1-1, Senegal (n) 2-2, Jordan (n) 3-0, Greece (n) 3-0, Ivory Coast (n) 2-1, Japan (n) 4-1, Uruguay (n) 2-0, Brazil (a) 1-2.

ECUADOR
Federacion Ecuatoriana del Futbol, km 4 1/2 via a la Costa (Avda. del Bombero), PO Box 09-01-7447 Guayaquil.
Founded: 1925; *National Colours:* Yellow shirts, blue shorts, red socks.
International matches 2013–14
Spain (h) 0-2, Colombia (a) 0-1, Bolivia (a) 1-1, Uruguay (h) 1-0, Chile (a) 1-2, Argentina (n) 0-0, Honduras (n) 2-2, Australia (n) 4-3, Netherlands (a) 1-1, Mexico (n) 1-3, England (n) 2-2, Switzerland (n) 1-2, Honduras (n) 2-1, France (n) 0-0.

PARAGUAY
Asociacion Paraguaya de Futbol, Estadio De Los Defensores del Chaco, Calles Mayor Martinez 1393, Asuncion.
Founded: 1906; *National Colours:* Red and white shirts, blue shorts, blue socks.
International matches 2013–14
Germany (a) 3-3, Bolivia (h) 4-0, Argentina (h) 2-5, Venezuela (a) 1-1, Colombia (h) 1-2, Costa Rica (a) 1-2, Cameroon (n) 2-1, France (a) 1-1.

PERU
Federacion Peruana De Futbol, Av. Aviacion 2085, San Luis, Lima 30.
Founded: 1922; *National Colours:* White shirts with red stripe, white shorts with red lines, white socks with red line.
International matches 2013–14
Korea Republic (a) 0-0, Uruguay (h) 1-2, Venezuela (a) 2-3, Argentina (a) 1-3, Bolivia (h) 1-1, England (a) 0-3, Switzerland (a) 0-2.

URUGUAY
Asociacion Uruguaya De Futbol, Guayabo 1531, 11200 Montevideo.
Founded: 1900; *National Colours:* Sky blue shirts with white collar/cuffs, black shorts and socks with sky blue borders.

International matches 2013–14
Japan (a) 4-2, Peru (a) 2-1, Colombia (h) 2-0, Ecuador (a) 0-1, Argentina (h) 3-2, Jordan (a) 5-0, Jordan (h) 0-0, Austria (a) 1-1, Northern Ireland (h) 1-0, Slovenia (h) 2-0, Costa Rica (n) 1-3, England (n) 2-1, Italy (n) 1-0, Colombia (a) 0-2.

VENEZUELA
Federacion Venezolana De Futbol, Avda. Santos Erminy Ira, Calle las Delicias Torre Mega II, P.H. Sabana Grande, Caracas 1050.
Founded: 1926; *National Colours:* Burgundy shirts, white shorts and socks.
International matches 2013–14
Bolivia (h) 2-2, Chile (a) 0-3, Peru (h) 3-2, Paraguay (h) 1-1, Honduras (a) 1-2.

ASIA

AFGHANISTAN
Afghanistan Football Federation, PO Box 128, Kabul.
Founded: 1933; *National Colours:* All white with red lines.
International matches 2013–14
Tajikistan (a) 2-3*, Pakistan (h) 3-0, Bhutan (n) 3-0, Sri Lanka (n) 3-1, Maldives (n) 0-0, Nepal (a) 1-0, India (n) 2-0, Kyrgyzstan (n) 0-0, Tajikistan (a) 0-1, Kyrgyzstan (n) 1-0, Kuwait (a) 2-3, Philippines (n) 0-0, Turkmenistan (n) 3-1, Laos (n) 0-0, Palestine (n) 2-0, Maldives (n) 0-0 (7-8p).
* *Played 04.06.2013, result omitted from last edition.*

AUSTRALIA
Soccer Australia Ltd, Level 3, East Stand, Stadium Australia, Edwin Flack Avenue, Homebush, NSW 2127.
Founded: 1961; *National Colours:* All green with gold trim.
International matches 2013–14
Korea Republic (a) 0-0, Japan (n) 2-3, China PR (n) 3-4, Brazil (a) 0-6, France (a) 0-6, Canada (n) 3-0, Costa Rica (h) 1-0, Ecuador (n) 3-4, South Africa (h) 1-1, Croatia (n) 0-1, Chile (n) 1-3, Netherlands (n) 2-3, Spain (n) 0-3.

BAHRAIN
Bahrain Football Association, PO Box 5464, Manama.
Founded: 1957; *National Colours:* All red.
International matches 2013–14
Kuwait (a) 1-2, Thailand (a) 0-1, Malaysia (a) 1-1, Lebanon (h) 1-0, Malaysia (h) 1-0, Yemen (h) 2-0, Qatar (a) 1-1, Oman (n) 0-0, Iraq (n) 0-1, Jordan (n) 0-1, Kuwait (n) 0-0 (3-2p), Qatar (h) 0-0.

BANGLADESH
Bangladesh Football Federation, Bangabandhu National Stadium-1, Dhaka 1000.
Founded: 1972; *National Colours:* Orange shirts, white shorts, green socks.
International matches 2013–14
Pakistan (h) 0-0, Nepal (a) 0-2, India (n) 1-1, Pakistan (n) 1-2, India (a) 2-2.

BHUTAN
Bhutan Football Federation, PO Box 365, Thimphu.
National Colours: All yellow and red.
International matches 2013–14
Afghanistan (n) 0-3, Maldives (n) 2-8, Sri Lanka (n) 2-5.

BRUNEI DARUSSALAM
Football Association of Brunei Darussalam, PO Box 2010, 1920 Bandar Seri Begawan BS 8674.
Founded: 1959; *National Colours:* Yellow shirts, black shorts, black and white socks.
International matches 2013–14
None played.

CAMBODIA
Cambodian Football Federation, Chaeng Maeng Village, Rd. Kab Srov, Sangkat Samrong Krom, Khan Dangkor, Phnom-Penh.
Founded: 1933; *National Colours:* All blue.
International matches 2013–14
Guam (h) 0-2, Singapore (a) 0-1.

CHINA PR
Football Association of The People's Republic of China, Dongjiudasha Mansion, Xizhaosi Street, Dongcheng 100061, Beijing.
Founded: 1924; *National Colours:* All white.
International matches 2013–14
Japan (n) 3-3, Korea Republic (a) 0-0, Australia (n) 4-3, Singapore (h) 6-1, Malaysia (h) 2-0, Indonesia (a) 1-1, Indonesia (h) 1-0, Saudi Arabia (h) 0-0, Iraq (n) 1-3, FYR Macedonia (h) 2-0, FYR Macedonia (h) 0-0, Mali (h) 1-3.

CHINESE TAIPEI
Chinese Taipei Football Association, Room 210, 2F, 55 Chang Chi Street, Tatung 10363, Taipei.
Founded: 1936; *National Colours:* Blue shirts and shorts, white socks.
International matches 2013–14
Philippines (a) 2-1, Pakistan (n) 0-1.

GUAM
Guam Football Association, PO Box 5093, 96932 Hagatna, Guam.
Founded: 1975; *National Colours:* Blue shirts, white shorts, blue socks.
International matches 2013–14
Laos (a) 1-1, Cambodia (a) 2-0, Aruba (a) 2-2), Aruba (a) 0-2.

HONG KONG
Hong Kong Football Association Ltd, 55 Fat Kwong Street, Homantin, Kowloon, Hong Kong.
Founded: 1914; *National Colours:* All red.
International matches 2013–14
Myanmar (a) 0-1, Singapore (h) 1-0, UAE (h) 0-4, UAE (a) 0-4, Uzbekistan (h) 0-2, Vietnam (a) 1-3.

INDIA
All India Football Federation, Football House, Sector 19, Phase 1 Dwarka 110075, New Delhi.
Founded: 1937; *National Colours:* Sky blue shirts, navy blue shorts, sky and navy blue socks.
International matches 2013–14
Tajikistan (a) 0-3, Pakistan (n) 1-0, Bangladesh (n) 1-1, Nepal (a) 1-2, Maldives (n) 1-0, Afghanistan (n) 0-2, Philippines (h) 1-1, Nepal (h) 2-0, Bangladesh (h) 2-2.

INDONESIA
Football Association of Indonesia, Gelora Bung Karno, Pintu X-XI, Senayan, 10270 Jakarta.
Founded: 1930; *National Colours:* Red shirts, white shorts, red socks.
International matches 2013–14
Philippines (h) 2-0, China PR (h) 1-1, Kyrgyzstan (h) 4-0, China PR (a) 0-1, Iraq (h) 0-2, Saudi Arabia (a) 0-1, Andorra (n) 1-0, Cuba (n) 0-1, Dominican Republic (h) 1-1, Pakistan (h) 4-0, Nepal (h) 2-0.

IRAN
IR Iran Football Federation, No. 2/2 Third St. Seoul Avenue, 19958-73591 Teheran.
Founded: 1920; *National Colours:* All white.
International matches 2013–14
Thailand (h) 2-1, Thailand (a) 3-0, Lebanon (a) 4-1, Kuwait (h) 3-2, Guinea (h) 1-2, Belarus (n) 0-0, Montenegro (n) 0-0, Angola (n) 1-1, Trinidad & Tobago (n) 2-0, Nigeria (n) 0-0, Argentina (n) 0-1, Bosnia & Herzegovina (n) 1-3.

IRAQ
Iraqi Football Association, Olympic Committee Building, Palestine Street, PO Box 484, Baghdad.
Founded: 1948; *National Colours:* All black.
International matches 2013–14
Chile (n) 0-6, Yemen (n) 3-2, Lebanon (a) 1-1, Saudi Arabia (n) 0-2, Saudi Arabia (a) 1-2, Indonesia (a) 2-0, Bahrain (n) 0-0, Oman (n) 0-0, Korea DPR (n) 2-0, China PR (n) 3-1.

JAPAN
Japan Football Association, JFA House, 3-10-15, Hongo, Bunkyo-ku, Tokyo 113-0033.
Founded: 1921; *National Colours:* Blue shirts, white shorts, blue socks.
International matches 2013–14
China PR (n) 3-3, Australia (n) 3-2, Korea Republic (a) 2-1, Uruguay (n) 2-4, Guatemala (h) 3-0, Ghana (h) 3-1, Serbia (a) 0-2, Belarus (a) 0-1, Netherlands (a) 2-2, Belgium (a) 3-2, New Zealand (h) 4-2, Cyprus (h) 1-0, Costa Rica (n) 3-1, Zambia (n) 4-3, Ivory Coast (n) 1-2, Greece (n) 0-0, Colombia (n) 1-4.

JORDAN
Jordan Football Association, PO Box 962024 Al-Hussein Sports City, 11196 Amman.
Founded: 1949; *National Colours:* All white and red.
International matches 2013–14
Palestine (h) 4-1, Libya (h) 2-1, Syria (n) 1-1, Uzbekistan (h) 1-1, Uzbekistan (a) 1-1 (8-7p), Kuwait (h) 1-1, Oman (h) 0-0, Nigeria (h) 1-0, Zambia (n) 1-0, Uruguay (h) 0-5, Uruguay (a) 0-0, Lebanon (n) 0-0, Kuwait (n) 2-1, Bahrain (n) 1-0, Qatar (a) 0-2, Oman (a) 0-0, Singapore (a) 3-1, Syria (h) 2-1, Colombia (n) 0-3.

KOREA DPR
Football Association of The Democratic People's Rep. of Korea, Kumsong-dong, Kwangbok Street, Mangyongdae Distr, PO Box 56, Pyongyang FNJ-PRK.
Founded: 1945; *National Colours:* All white.
International matches 2013–14
Kuwait (a) 1-2, Iraq (n) 0-2.

KOREA REPUBLIC
Korea Football Association, 1-131 Sinmunno, 2-ga, Jongno-Gu, Seoul 110-062.
Founded: 1928; *National Colours:* Red shirts, blue shorts, red socks.
International matches 2013–14
Australia (h) 0-0, China PR (h) 0-0, Japan (h) 1-2, Peru (h) 0-0, Haiti (h) 4-1, Croatia (h) 1-2, Brazil (h) 0-2, Mali (h) 3-1, Switzerland (h) 2-1, Russia (n) 1-2, Costa Rica (n) 1-0, Mexico (n) 0-4, USA (a) 0-2, Greece (a) 2-0, Tunisia (h) 0-1, Ghana (n) 0-4, Russia (n) 1-1, Algeria (n) 2-4, Belgium (n) 0-1.

KUWAIT
Kuwait Football Association, PO Box 2029, Udiliya, Block 4 Al-Ittihad Street, Safat 13021.
Founded: 1952; *National Colours:* All blue.
International matches 2013–14
Korea DPR (h) 2-1, Bahrain (h) 2-1, Jordan (a) 1-1, Kyrgyzstan (a) 0-3, Lebanon (a) 1-1, Malaysia (h) 3-0, Lebanon (h) 0-0, Thailand (h) 3-1, Lebanon (n) 2-0, Jordan (n) 1-2, Qatar (a) 0-3, Bahrain (n) 0-0 (2-3p), Iran (a) 2-3, Afghanistan (h) 3-2, Kyrgyzstan (h) 2-2, Thailand (a) 1-1.

KYRGYZSTAN
Football Federation of Kyrgyz Republic, PO Box 1484, Kurenkeeva Street 195, Bishkek 720040.
Founded: 1992; *National Colours:* Red shirts, white shorts, red socks.
International matches 2013–14
Belarus (a) 1-3, Kuwait (h) 3-0, Tajikistan (h) 1-4, Indonesia (a) 0-4, Azerbaijan (h) 0-0, Afghanistan (n) 0-0, Afghanistan (n) 0-1, Kuwait (a) 2-2, Palestine (n) 0-1, Maldives (a) 0-2, Myanmar (n) 1-0.

LAOS
Federation Lao de Football, National Stadium, Kounboulo Street, PO Box 3777, Vientiane 856-21.
Founded: 1951; *National Colours:* All red.
International matches 2013–14
Singapore (a) 0-1, Guam (h) 1-1, Maldives (a) 1-7, Turkmenistan (n) 1-5, Philippines (n) 0-2, Afghanistan (n) 0-0.

LEBANON
Federation Libanaise De Football-Association, PO Box 4732, Verdun Street, Bristol, Radwan Centre Building, Beirut.
Founded: 1933; *National Colours:* Red shirts, white shorts, red socks.
International matches 2013–14
Syria (h) 2-0, Qatar (a) 1-1, Iraq (h) 1-1, Kuwait (h) 1-1, Bahrain (a) 0-1, Kuwait (a) 0-0, Iran (h) 1-4, Jordan (n) 0-0, Kuwait (n) 0-2, Pakistan (h) 3-1, Thailand (a) 5-2.

MACAO
Associacao De Futebol De Macau (AFM), Ave. da Amizade 405, Seng Vo Kok, 13 Andar 'A', Macau.
Founded: 1939; *National Colours:* All green.
International matches 2013–14
None played.

MALAYSIA
Football Association of Malaysia, 3rd Floor, Wisma Fam, Jalan, SSA/9, Kelana Jaya Selangor Darul Ehsan 47301.
Founded: 1933; *National Colours:* All yellow and black.
International matches 2013–14
China PR (a) 0-2, Bahrain (h) 1-1, Kuwait (a) 0-3, Bahrain (a) 0-1, Qatar (h) 0-1, Philippines (h) 0-0, Yemen (n) 2-1, Philippines (a) 0-0.

MALDIVES
Football Association of Maldives, FAM House, Ujaalahingun 20388, Male.
Founded: 1982; *National Colours:* Red shirts, Green shorts, white socks.
International matches 2013–14
Sri Lanka (n) 10-0, Bhutan (n) 8-2, Afghanistan (n) 0-0, India (n) 0-1, Seychelles (a) 1-3, Seychelles (a) 1-2, Laos (h) 7-1, Myanmar (h) 2-3, Kyrgyzstan (h) 2-0, Palestine (h) 0-0, Philippines (h) 2-3, Afghanistan (h) 1-1 (8-7p).

MONGOLIA
Mongolia Football Federation, PO Box 259, 210646 Ulan Bator.
National Colours: White shirts, red shorts, white socks.
International matches 2013–14
None played.

MYANMAR
Myanmar Football Federation, Wai Za Yan Tar Road, Thingangyun Township, 11072 Yangon.
Founded: 1947; *National Colours:* Red shirts, white shorts, red socks.
International matches 2013–14
Hong Kong (h) 0-0, Maldives (a) 3-2, Palestine (n) 0-2, Kyrgyzstan (n) 0-1, Vietnam (a) 0-6.

NEPAL
All-Nepal Football Association, AMFA House, Ward No. 4, Bishalnagar, PO Box 12582, Kathmandu.
Founded: 1951; *National Colours:* All red.
International matches 2013–14
Bangladesh (h) 2-0, Pakistan (h) 1-1, India (h) 2-1, Afghanistan (h) 0-1, India (a) 0-2, Yemen (n) 0-2, Philippines (n) 0-3, Indonesia (a) 0-2.

OMAN
Oman Football Association, PO Box 3462, 112 Ruwi.
Founded: 1978; *National Colours:* All white.
International matches 2013–14
Singapore (a) 2-0, Mauritania (h) 0-0, Jordan (a) 0-0, Syria (n) 1-0, Bahrain (n) 0-0, Iraq (n) 0-0, Finland (h) 0-0, Jordan (h) 0-0, Singapore (h) 3-1, Uzbekistan (a) 1-0, Uzbekistan (a) 1-0.

PAKISTAN
Pakistan Football Federation, 6 National Hockey Stadium, Ferozepur Road, 54600 Lahore.
Founded: 1948; *National Colours:* All green and white.
International matches 2013–14
Bangladesh (a) 0-0, Afghanistan (a) 0-3, India (n) 0-1, Nepal (n) 1-1, Bangladesh (n) 2-1, Chinese Taipei (n) 1-0, Philippines (a) 1-3, Lebanon (a) 1-3, Indonesia (a) 0-4.

PALESTINE
Palestinian Football Federation, PO Box 4373, Ramallah, Al Bireh, Palestine.
Founded: 1928; *National Colours:* White shirts, black shorts, white socks.
International matches 2013–14
Jordan (a) 1-4, Qatar (a) 0-1, Saudi Arabia (n) 0-0, Kyrgyzstan (n) 1-0, Myanmar (n) 2-0, Maldives (a) 0-0, Afghanistan (n) 2-0, Philippines (n) 1-0.

PHILIPPINES
Philippine Football Federation, Room 405, Building V, Philsports Complex, Meralco Avenue, Pasig City, Metro Manila.
Founded: 1907; *National Colours:* All blue.
International matches 2013–14
Turkmenistan (h) 1-0*, Hong Kong (a) 1-0*, Indonesia (a) 0-2, Chinese Taipei (h) 1-2, Pakistan (h) 3-1, UAE (a) 0-4, India (a) 1-1, Malaysia (a) 0-0, Azerbaijan (n) 0-1, Nepal (n) 3-0, Malaysia (h) 0-0, Afghanistan (n) 0-0, Laos (n) 2-0, Turkmenistan (n) 2-0, Maldives (a) 3-2, Palestine (n) 0-1.
**Played in 2012–13 season, results omitted in last edition.*

QATAR
Qatar Football Association, 7th Floor, QNOC Building, Cornich, PO Box 5333, Doha.
Founded: 1960; *National Colours:* All white.
International matches 2013–14
Mauritius (h) 3-0, Lebanon (h) 1-1, Vietnam (h) 1-2, Yemen (h) 6-0, Yemen (n) 4-1, Malaysia (a) 1-0, Bahrain (h) 1-1, Palestine (h) 1-0, Saudi Arabia (n) 4-1, Kuwait (h) 3-0, Jordan (h) 2-0, Bahrain (h) 0-0, FYR Macedonia (n) 0-0.

SAUDI ARABIA
Saudi Arabian Football Federation, Al Mather Quarter (Olympic Complex), Prince Faisal Bin Fahad Street, PO Box 5844, 11432 Riyadh.
Founded: 1959; *National Colours:* White shirts, green shorts, white socks.
International matches 2013–14
New Zealand (h) 0-1, Trinidad & Tobago (h) 1-3, Iraq (n) 2-0, Iraq (h) 2-1, China PR (a) 0-0, Palestine (n) 0-0, Qatar (a) 1-4, Indonesia (h) 1-0, Moldova (n) 0-4, Georgia (n) 0-2.

SINGAPORE
Football Association of Singapore, Jalan Besar Stadium, 100 Tyrwhitt Road, 207542 Singapore.
Founded: 1892; *National Colours:* All red.
International matches 2013–14
Oman (h) 0-2, China PR (a) 1-6, Hong Kong (a) 0-1, Laos (h) 1-0, Syria (h) 2-1, Syria (n) 0-4, Cambodia (h) 1-0, Jordan (h) 1-3, Oman (a) 1-3.

SRI LANKA
Football Federation of Sri Lanka, 100/9, Independence Avenue, Colombo 07.
Founded: 1939; *National Colours:* All white.
International matches 2013–14
Maldives (n) 0-10, Afghanistan (n) 1-3, Bhutan (n) 5-2.

SYRIA
Syrian Football Federation, PO Box 421, Maysaloon Street, Damascus.
Founded: 1936; *National Colours:* All red.
International matches 2013–14
Jordan (n) 1-1, Lebanon (a) 0-2, Singapore (a) 1-2, Singapore (n) 4-0, Oman (n) 0-1, Jordan (a) 1-2.

TAJIKISTAN
Tajikistan Football Federation, 22 Shotemur Ave., Dushanbe 734 025.
Founded: 1991; *National Colours:* All white.
International matches 2013–14
India (h) 3-0, Kyrgyzstan (a) 4-1, Afghanistan (h) 1-0, Estonia (a) 1-2.

THAILAND
Football Association of Thailand, Gate 3, Rama I Road, Patumwan, Bangkok 10330.
Founded: 1916; *National Colours:* All red.
International matches 2013–14
Bahrain (h) 1-0, Iran (a) 1-2, Iran (h) 0-3, Kuwait (a) 1-3, Lebanon (h) 2-5, Kuwait (h) 1-1.

TIMOR-LESTE
Federacao Futebol Timor-Leste, Rua 12 de Novembro Str., Cruz, Dili.
Founded: 2002; *National Colours:* Red shirts, black shorts, red socks.
International matches 2013–14
None played.

TURKMENISTAN
Football Association of Turkmenistan, 32 Belinskiy Street, Stadium Kopetdag, 744 001 Ashgabat.
Founded: 1992; *National Colours:* Green shirts, white shorts, green socks.
International matches 2013–14
Laos (n) 5-1, Afghanistan (n) 1-3, Philippines (n) 0-2.

UNITED ARAB EMIRATES
United Arab Emirates Football Association, PO Box 961, Abu Dhabi.
Founded: 1971; *National Colours:* All white.
International matches 2013–14
Trinidad & Tobago (n) 3-3 (7-6p), New Zealand (n) 2-0, Hong Kong (a) 4-0, Philippines (h) 4-0, Hong Kong (h) 4-0, Vietnam (h) 5-0, Uzbekistan (a) 1-1, Armenia (n) 3-4, Georgia (n) 1-0.

UZBEKISTAN
Uzbekistan Football Federation, Massiv Almazar Furkat Street 15/1, 700 003 Tashkent.
Founded: 1946; *National Colours:* All white.
International matches 2013–14
Jordan (a) 1-1, Jordan (h) 1-1 (7-8p), Vietnam (h) 3-1, Vietnam (a) 3-0, Hong Kong (a) 2-0, UAE (h) 1-1, Oman (h) 0-1, Oman (h) 0-1.

VIETNAM
Vietnam Football Federation, 18 Ly van Phuc, Dong Da District, Hanoi 844.
Founded: 1962; *National Colours:* All red.
International matches 2013–14
Qatar (a) 2-1, Uzbekistan (a) 1-3, Uzbekistan (h) 0-3, UAE (a) 0-5, Hong Kong (h) 3-1, Myanmar (h) 6-0.

YEMEN
Yemen Football Association, Quarter of Sport – Al Jeraf, Behind the Stadium of Ali Muhsen Al-Moreisi in the Sport, Al-Thawra City.
Founded: 1962; *National Colours:* All green.
International matches 2013–14
Iraq (n) 2-3, Qatar (a) 0-6, Qatar (n) 1-4, Bahrain (a) 0-2, Malaysia (n) 1-2, Nepal (n) 2-0, Chad (n) 0-0.

CONCACAF

ANGUILLA
Anguilla Football Association, Albert Lake Drive, PO Box 1318, 2640 The Valley, Anguilla, BWI.
National Colours: Turquoise, white, orange and blue shirts and shorts, turquoise and orange socks.
International matches 2013–14
None played.

ANTIGUA & BARBUDA
The Antigua/Barbuda Football Association, Newgate Street, PO Box 773, St John's.
Founded: 1928; *National Colours:* Red, black, yellow and blue shirts, black shorts and socks.
International matches 2013–14
None played.

ARUBA
Arubaanse Voetbal Bond, Ferguson Street, Z/N PO Box 376, Oranjestad, Aruba.
Founded: 1932; *National Colours:* Yellow shirts, blue shorts, yellow and blue socks.
International matches 2013–14
Curacao (a) 0-2, Guam (h) 2-2, Guam (h) 2-0, Turks & Caicos Islands (h) 1-0, British Virgin Islands (h) 7-0, French Guiana (h) 0-2.

BAHAMAS
Bahamas Football Association, Plaza on the Way, West Bay Street, PO Box N-8434, Nassau, NP.
Founded: 1967; *National Colours:* Yellow shirts, black shorts, yellow socks.
International matches 2013–14
None played.

BARBADOS
Barbados Football Association, Hildor No. 4, 10th Avenue, PO Box 1362, Belleville-St. Michael, Barbados.
Founded: 1910; *National Colours:* Royal blue and gold shirts, gold shorts, white, gold and blue socks.
International matches 2013–14
Jamaica (h) 0-2.

BELIZE
Belize National Football Association, 26 Hummingbird Highway, Belmopan, PO Box 1742, Belize City.
Founded: 1980; *National Colours:* Red, white and black shirts, black shorts, red and black socks.
International matches 2013–14
USA (a) 1-6, Costa Rica (n) 0-1, Cuba (n) 0-4.

BERMUDA
The Bermuda Football Association, 48 Cedar Avenue, Hamilton HM12.
Founded: 1928; *National Colours:* All blue.
International matches 2013–14
None played.

BRITISH VIRGIN ISLANDS
British Virgin Islands Football Association, PO Box 29, Road Town, Tortola, BVI.
National Colours: Gold and green shirts, green shorts, and socks.
International matches 2013–14
French Guiana (n) 0-6, Aruba (n) 0-7, Turks & Caicos Islands (n) 0-2.

US VIRGIN ISLANDS
USVI Soccer Federation Inc., 54, Castle Coakley, PO Box 2346, Kingshill, St Croix 00851.
National Colours: Royal blue and gold shirts, royal blue shorts and socks.
International matches 2013–14
Montserrat (a) 0-1, Bonaire (n) 1-2.

CANADA
The Canadian Soccer Association, Place Soccer Canada, 237 Metcalfe Street, Ottawa, ONT K2P 1R2.
Founded: 1912; *National Colours:* All red.
International matches 2013–14
Martinique (n) 0-1, Mexico (n) 0-2, Panama (n) 0-0, Mauritania (n) 0-0, Mauritania (n) 0-1, Australia (n) 0-3, Czech Republic (a) 0-2, Slovenia (a) 0-1, Bulgaria (n) 1-1, Moldova (n) 1-1.

CAYMAN ISLANDS

Cayman Islands Football Association, PO Box 178 GT, Truman Bodden Sports Complex, Olympic Way Off Walkers Rd, George Town, Grand Cayman, Cayman Islands WI.
Founded: 1966; *National Colours:* Red and white shirts, blue and white shorts, white and red socks.
International matches 2013–14
None played.

COSTA RICA

Federacion Costarricense De Futbol, Costado Norte Estatua Leon Cortes, San Jose 670-1000.
Founded: 1921; *National Colours:* Red shirts, blue shorts, white socks.
International matches 2013–14
Cuba (h) 3-0, Belize (n) 1-0, USA (a) 0-1, Honduras (n) 0-1, Dominican Republic (a) 4-0, USA (h) 3-1, Jamaica (a) 1-1, Honduras (a) 0-1, Mexico (h) 2-1, Australia (a) 0-1, Chile (a) 0-4, Korea Republic (n) 0-1, Paraguay (h) 2-1, Japan (n) 1-3, Republic of Ireland (n) 1-1, Uruguay (n) 3-1, Italy (n) 1-0, England (n) 0-0, Greece (n) 1-1 (5-3p), Netherlands (n) 0-0 (3-4p).

CUBA

Asociacion de Futbol de Cuba, Calle 13 No. 661, Esq. C. Vedado, ZP 4, La Habana.
Founded: 1924; *National Colours:* All red, white and blue.
International matches 2013–14
Costa Rica (a) 0-3, USA (a) 1-4, Belize (n) 4-0, Panama (n) 1-6, Indonesia (n) 1-0.

CURACAO

Curacao Football Federation, Bonamweg 49, PO Box 341, Willemstad, Curacao.
Founded: 1921; *National Colours:* Blue shirts, red shorts and socks.
International matches 2013–14
Aruba (h) 2-0, Suriname (h) 1-3.

DOMINICA

Dominica Football Association, 33 Great Marlborough Street, Roseau.
Founded: 1970; *National Colours:* Emerald green shirts, black shorts, green socks.
International matches 2013–14
St Lucia (h) 0-1, St Lucia (h) 1-0, St Vincent/Grenadines (a) 2-3, St Vincent/Grenadines (a) 0-0, St Lucia (h) 0-2, St Vincent/Grenadines (h) 2-3, Grenada (h) 3-5.

DOMINICAN REPUBLIC

Federacion Dominicana De Futbol, Centro Olimpico Juan Pablo Duarte, Ensanche Miraflores, Apartado De Correos No. 1953, Santo Domingo.
Founded: 1953; *National Colours:* Navy blue shirts, white shorts, red socks.
International matches 2013–14
Costa Rica (h) 0-4, Indonesia (a) 1-1.

EL SALVADOR

Federacion Salvadorena De Futbol, Primera Calle Poniente No. 2025, San Salvador CA1029.
Founded: 1935; *National Colours:* All blue.
International matches 2013–14
Trinidad & Tobago (n) 2-2, Honduras (n) 0-1, Haiti (n) 1-0, USA (a) 1-5, Ivory Coast (n) 1-2, Spain (n) 0-2.

GRENADA

Grenada Football Association, PO Box 326, National Stadium, Queens Park, St George's, Grenada.
Founded: 1924; *National Colours:* Green and yellow striped shirts, red shorts, yellow socks.
International matches 2013–14
St Vincent/Grenadines (n) 0-0, St Lucia (n) 0-1, Dominica (a) 5-3.

GUADELOUPE

Ligue Guadeloupeenne de Football, Rue de la Ville D'Orly, Bergevin, 97110, Pointe-a-Pitre.
Not affiliated to FIFA.
International matches 2013–14
French Guiana (h) 3-2, Martinique (h) 0-1.

GUATEMALA

Federacion Nacional de Futbol de Guatemala, 2a Calle 15-57, Zona 15, Boulevard Vista Hermosa, 01009 Guatemala City.
Founded: 1946; *National Colours:* Blue shirts, white shorts, blue socks.
International matches 2013–14
Japan (a) 0-3.

GUYANA

Guyana Football Federation, 159 Rupununi Street, Bel Air Park, PO Box 10727, Georgetown.
Founded: 1902; *National Colours:* Green shirts and shorts, yellow socks.
International matches 2013–14
None played.

HAITI

Federation Haitienne De Football, 128 Avenue Christophe, PO Box 2258, Port-Au-Prince.
Founded: 1904; *National Colours:* Blue shirts, red shorts, blue socks.
International matches 2013–14
Honduras (n) 0-2, Trinidad & Tobago (n) 2-0, El Salvador (n) 0-1, Korea Republic (n) 1-4.

HONDURAS

Federacion Nacional Autonoma De Futbol De Honduras, Colonia Florencia Norte, Ave Roble, Edificio Plaza America, Ave. Roble 1 y 2 Nivel, Tegucigalpa, D.C.
Founded: 1951; *National Colours:* All white.
International matches 2013–14
Haiti (n) 2-0, El Salvador (n) 1-0, Trinidad & Tobago (n) 0-2, Costa Rica (n) 1-0, USA (a) 1-3, Mexico (a) 2-1, Panama (h) 2-2, Costa Rica (h) 1-0, Jamaica (a) 2-2, Brazil (n) 0-5, Ecuador (h) 2-2, Venezuela (h) 2-1, Turkey (n) 0-2, Israel (n) 2-4, England (n) 0-0, France (n) 0-3, Ecuador (n) 1-2, Switzerland (n) 0-3.

JAMAICA

Jamaica Football Federation Ltd, 20 St Lucia Crescent, Kingston 5.
Founded: 1910; *National Colours:* Gold shirts, black shorts, gold socks.
International matches 2013–14
Panama (a) 0-0, Costa Rica (h) 1-1, USA (a) 0-2, Honduras (h) 2-2, Trinidad & Tobago (h) 0-1, Trinidad & Tobago (a) 0-2, Barbados (a) 2-0, St Lucia (a) 5-0, Serbia (n) 1-2, Switzerland (a) 0-1, Egypt (n) 2-2, France (a) 0-8.

MARTINIQUE

2, Rue Saint John Perse, Nome Tartenson, BP 307, 97203 Fort de France.
Not affiliated to FIFA.
International matches 2013–14
Canada (n) 1-0, Panama (n) 0-1, Mexico (n) 1-3, St Lucia (a) 0-0, Guadeloupe (a) 1-0.

MEXICO

Federacion Mexicana De Futbol Asociacion, A.C., Colima No. 373, Colonia Roma, Mexico DF 06700.
Founded: 1927; *National Colours:* Green shirts with white collar, white shorts, red socks.
International matches 2013–14
Panama (n) 1-2, Canada (n) 2-0, Martinique (n) 3-1, Trinidad & Tobago (n) 1-0, Panama (n) 1-2, Ivory Coast (n) 4-1, Honduras (h) 1-2, USA (a) 0-2, Panama (h) 2-1, Costa Rica (a) 1-2, New Zealand (h) 5-1, New Zealand (a) 4-2, Korea Republic (n) 4-0, Nigeria (n) 0-0, USA (a) 2-2, Israel (h) 3-0, Ecuador (n) 3-1, Bosnia & Herzegovina (n) 0-1, Portugal (n) 0-1, Cameroon (n) 1-0, Brazil (a) 0-0, Croatia (n) 3-1, Netherlands (n) 1-2.

MONTSERRAT

Montserrat Football Association Inc., PO Box 505, Woodlands, Montserrat.
National Colours: Green shirts with black and white stripes, green shorts with white stripes, green socks with black and white stripes.
International matches 2013–14
US Virgin Islands (h) 1-0, Bonaire (h) 0-0.

NICARAGUA

Federacion Nicaraguense De Futbol, Hospital Pautista 1, Cuadra avajo, 1 cuada al Sur y 1/2, Cuadra Abajo, Managua 976.
Founded: 1931; *National Colours:* Blue shirts, white shorts, blue socks.
International matches 2013–14
None played.

PANAMA

Federacion Panamena De Futbol, Estadio Rommel Fernandez, Puerta 24, Ave. Jose Agustin Araneo, Apartado Postal 8-391, Zona 8, Panama.
Founded: 1937; *National Colours:* All red.
International matches 2013–14
Mexico (n) 2-1, Martinique (n) 1-0, Canada (n) 0-0, Cuba (n) 6-1, Mexico (n) 2-1, USA (a) 0-1, Jamaica (h) 0-0, Honduras (a) 2-2, Mexico (a) 1-2, USA (h) 2-3, Serbia (n) 1-1, Brazil (a) 0-4.

PUERTO RICO

Federacion Puertorriquena De Futbol, PO Box 193590, 00919 San Juan.
Founded: 1940; *National Colours:* Red, blue and white shirts and shorts, red and blue socks.
International matches 2013–14
None played.

ST KITTS & NEVIS

St Kitts & Nevis Football Association, PO Box 465, Warner Park, Basseterre, St Kitts.
Founded: 1932; *National Colours:* Green and yellow shirts, red shorts, yellow socks.
International matches 2013–14
None played.

ST LUCIA

St Lucia National Football Association, PO Box 255, Sans Souci, Castries, St Lucia.
Founded: 1979; *National Colours:* White shirts and shorts with yellow, blue and black stripes, white, blue and yellow socks.
International matches 2013–14
Dominica (a) 1-0, Dominica (a) 0-1, Jamaica (h) 0-5, Martinique (h) 0-0, Dominica (a) 2-0, Grenada (n) 1-0, St Vincent/Grenadines (n) 0-0.

ST VINCENT & THE GRENADINES

St Vincent & The Grenadines Football Federation, PO Box 1278, Nichols Building (2nd Floor), Bentinck Square, Victoria Park, St George.
Founded: 1979; *National Colours:* Green shirts with yellow border, yellow shorts, blue socks.
International matches 2013–14
Dominica (h) 3-2 Dominica (h) 0-0, Grenada (n) 0-0, Dominica (a) 3-2, St Lucia (n) 0-0.

SURINAME

Surinaamse Voetbal Bond, Letitia Vriesde Laan 7, PO Box 1223, Paramaribo.
Founded: 1920; *National Colours:* White, green and red shirts, green and white shirts and socks.
International matches 2013–14
Curacao (a) 3-1, French Guiana (a) 0-0, French Guiana (h) 1-0.

TRINIDAD & TOBAGO

Trinidad & Tobago Football Federation, 24–26 Dundonald Street, PO Box 400, Port of Spain.
Founded: 1908; *National Colours:* Red shirts, black shorts, white socks.
International matches 2013–14
El Salvador (n) 2-2, Haiti (n) 0-2, Honduras (n) 2-0, Mexico (n) 0-1, UAE (n) 3-3 (6-7p), Saudi Arabia (a) 3-1, New Zealand (h) 0-0, Jamaica (a) 1-0, Jamaica (h) 2-0, Argentina (a) 0-3, Iran (n) 0-2.

TURKS & CAICOS ISLANDS

Turks & Caicos Islands Football Association, PO Box 626, Tropicana Plaza, Leeward Highway, Providenciales.
National Colours: All white.
International matches 2013–14
Aruba (a) 0-1, French Guiana (n) 0-6, British Virgin Islands (n) 2-0.

USA

US Soccer Federation, US Soccer House, 1801–1811 S. Prairie Avenue, Chicago, Illinois 60616.
Founded: 1913; *National Colours:* White shirts, blue shorts, white socks.
International matches 2013–14
Guatemala (h) 6-0, Belize (h) 6-1, Cuba (h) 4-1, Costa Rica (h) 1-0, El Salvador (h) 5-1, Honduras (h) 3-1, Panama (h) 1-0, Bosnia & Herzegovina (a) 4-3, Costa Rica (a) 1-3, Mexico (h) 2-0, Jamaica (h) 2-0, Panama (a) 3-2, Scotland (a) 0-0, Austria (a) 0-1, Korea Republic (h) 2-0, Ukraine (n) 0-2, Mexico (h) 2-2, Azerbaijan (h) 2-0, Turkey (h) 2-1, Nigeria (h) 2-1, Ghana (n) 2-1, Portugal (n) 2-2, Germany (n) 0-1, Belgium (n) 1-2.

OCEANIA

AMERICAN SAMOA

American Samoa Football Association, PO Box 282, AS 96799 Pago Pago.
National Colours: Navy blue shirts, white shorts, red socks.
International matches 2013–14
None played.

COOK ISLANDS

Cook Islands Football Association, Victoria Road, Tupapa, PO Box 29, Avarua, Rarotonga.
Founded: 1971; *National Colours:* Green shirts with white sleeves, green shorts, white socks.
International matches 2013–14
None played.

FIJI

Fiji Football Association, PO Box 2514, Government Buildings, Suva.
Founded: 1938; *National Colours:* White shirts, blue shorts and socks.
International matches 2013–14
None played.

NEW CALEDONIA

Federation Caledonienne de Football, 7 bis, Rue Suffren Quartien latin, BP 560, 99845 Noumea.
Founded: 1928; *National Colours:* Grey shirts, red shorts, grey socks.
International matches 2013–14
None played.

NEW ZEALAND

New Zealand Soccer Inc., PO Box 301 043, Albany, Auckland.
Founded: 1891; *National Colours:* All white.
International matches 2013–14
Saudi Arabia (a) 1-0, UAE (n) 0-2, Trinidad & Tobago (a) 0-0, Mexico (a) 1-5, Mexico (h) 2-4, Japan (a) 2-4, South Africa (h) 0-0.

PAPUA NEW GUINEA

Papua New Guinea Football Association, PO Box 957, Room II Level I, Haus Tisa, Lae.
Founded: 1962; *National Colours:* Red and yellow shirts, black shorts, yellow socks.
International matches 2013–14
None played.

SAMOA

The Samoa Football Soccer Federation, PO Box 960, Apia.
Founded: 1968; *National Colours:* Blue, white and red shirts, blue and white shorts, red and blue socks.
International matches 2013–14
None played.

SOLOMON ISLANDS

Solomon Islands Football Federation, PO Box 854, Honiara, Solomon Islands.
Founded: 1978; *National Colours:* Gold and blue shirts, blue and white shorts, white and blue socks.
International matches 2013–14
None played.

TAHITI

Federation Tahitienne de Football, Rue Coppenrath Stade de Fautana, PO Box 50858 Pirae 98716.
Founded: 1989; *National Colours:* Red shirts, white shorts, red socks.
International matches 2013–14
None played.

TONGA

Tonga Football Association, Tungi Arcade, Taufa'Ahau Road, PO Box 852, Nuku'Alofa.
Founded: 1965; *National Colours:* Red shirts, white shorts, red socks.
International matches 2013–14
None played.

VANUATU

Vanuatu Football Federation, PO Box 266, Port Vila.
Founded: 1934; *National Colours:* Gold and black shirts, black shorts, gold and black socks.
International matches 2013–14
None played.

AFRICA

ALGERIA

Federation Algerienne De Foot-ball, Chemin Ahmed Ouaked, Boite Postale No. 39, Dely-Ibrahim-Alger.
Founded: 1962; *National Colours:* Green shirts, white shorts, green socks.
International matches 2013–14
Guinea (h) 2-2, Mali (h) 1-0, Burkina Faso (a) 2-3, Burkina Faso (h) 1-0, Slovenia (h) 2-0, Armenia (n) 3-1, Romania (n) 2-1, Belgium (n) 1-2, Korea Republic (n) 4-2, Russia (n) 1-1, Germany (h) 1-2.

ANGOLA

Federation Angolaise De Football, Compl. da Cidadela Desportiva, BP 3449, Luanda.
Founded: 1979; *National Colours:* Red shirts, black shorts, red socks.
International matches 2013–14
Swaziland (a) 1-0*, Swaziland (h) 1-0*, Lesotho (n) 1-1 (3-5p), Malawi (n) 3-2, Mozambique (n) 0-1, Mozambique (a) 0-0, Mozambique (h) 1-1, Liberia (h) 4-1, Mozambique (a) 1-1, Morocco (n) 2-0, Iran (n) 1-1.
* *Played in 2012–13, results omitted from last edition.*

BENIN

Federation Beninoise De Football, Stade Rene Pleven d'Akpakpa, BP 965, Cotonou 01.
Founded: 1962; *National Colours:* Green shirts, Yellow shorts, red socks.
International matches 2013–14
Rwanda (h) 2-0, Sao Tome & Principe (a) 2-0, Sao Tome & Principe (h) 2-0.

BOTSWANA

Botswana Football Association, PO Box 1396, Gaborone.
Founded: 1970; *National Colours:* Blue, white and black striped shirts, blue, white and black shorts and socks.
International matches 2013–14
Swaziland (n) 0-0, Lesotho (n) 3-3, Kenya (n) 2-1, Zambia (h) 1-1, Zambia (a) 0-2, Uganda (h) 1-3, Malawi (h) 1-0, South Africa (a) 1-4, Burkina Faso (h) 1-0, South Sudan (h) 3-0, Swaziland (h) 1-4, Burundi (a) 0-0, Burundi (h) 1-0, Tanzania (h) 4-2.

BURKINA FASO

Federation Burkinabe De Foot-Ball, 01 BP 57, Ouagadougou 01.
Founded: 1960; *National Colours:* All green, red and white.
International matches 2013–14
Niger (h) 1-0, Niger (a) 1-0 (6-5p), Morocco (a) 2-1, South Africa (a) 0-2, Gabon (h) 1-0, Nigeria (a) 1-4, Botswana (a) 1-4, Algeria (h) 3-2, Algeria (a) 0-1, Uganda (n) 1-2, Morocco (n) 1-1, Zimbabwe (n) 0-1, Comoros (n) 1-1, Senegal (h) 1-1.

BURUNDI

Federation De Football Du Burundi, Bulding Nyogozi, Boulevard de l'Uprona, BP 3426, Bujumbura.
Founded: 1948; *National Colours:* Red and white shirts, white and red shorts, green socks.
International matches 2013–14
Sudan (h) 1-1, Sudan (a) 1-1 (4-3p), Somalia (n) 2-0, Zambia (n) 0-1, Tanzania (n) 0-1, Zambia (n) 0-0 (3-4p), Gabon (n) 0-0, Mauritania (n) 3-2, Congo DR (n) 1-2, Rwanda (h) 1-1, Tanzania (a) 3-0, Botswana (h) 0-0, Botswana (h) 0-1.

CAMEROON

Federation Camerounaise De Football, BP 1116, Yaounde.
Founded: 1959; *National Colours:* Green shirts, red shorts, yellow socks.
International matches 2013–14
Gabon (h) 1-0, Gabon (a) 0-1 (5-6p), Congo DR (h) 0-1, Congo DR (a) 1-1, Libya (h) 1-0, Tunisia (a) 0-0, Tunisia (h) 4-1, Portugal (a) 1-5, FYR Macedonia (n) 2-0, Paraguay (n) 1-2, Germany (a) 2-2, Moldova (h) 1-0, Mexico (n) 0-1, Croatia (n) 0-4, Brazil (h) 1-4.

CAPE VERDE ISLANDS

Federacao Cabo-Verdiana De Futebol, Praia Cabo Verde, FCF CX, PO Box 234, Praia.
Founded: 1982; *National Colours:* Blue and white shirts and shorts, blue and red socks.
International matches 2013–14
Gabon (n) 1-1, Tunisia (a) 0-3, Luxembourg (a) 0-0.

CENTRAL AFRICAN REPUBLIC

Federation Centrafricaine De Football, Immeuble Soca Constructa, BP 344, Bangui.
Founded: 1937; *National Colours:* Blue and white shirts, white shorts, blue socks.
International matches 2013–14
Libya (a) 0-0, Ethiopia (n) 1-2, Guinea-Bissau (h) 0-0, Guinea-Bissau (a) 1-3,

CHAD

Federation Tchadienne de Football, BP 886, N'Djamena.
Founded: 1962; *National Colours:* Blue shirts, yellow shorts, red socks.
International matches 2013–14
Yemen (n) 0-0, Malawi (a) 0-2, Malawi (h) 3-1.

COMOROS

Comoros FA, BP 798, Moroni.
Founded: 1979.
International matches 2013–14
Burkina Faso (n) 1-1, Kenya (a) 0-1, Kenya (h) 1-1.

CONGO

Federation Congolaise De Football, 80 Rue Eugene-Etienne, Centre Ville, PO Box 11, Brazzaville.
Founded: 1962; *National Colours:* Green shirts, yellow shorts, red socks.
International matches 2013–14
Congo DR (a) 1-2, Congo DR (h) 1-0, Tunisia (a) 0-3, Niger (a) 2-2, Ghana (n) 0-1, Ethiopia (n) 1-0, Libya (n) 2-2, Libya (n) 0-0, Namibia (a) 0-1, Namibia (h) 3-0.

CONGO DR

Federation Congolaise De Football-Association, Av. de l'Enseignement 210, C/Kasa-Vubu, Kinshasa 1.
Founded: 1919; *National Colours:* Blue and yellow shirts, yellow and blue shorts, white and blue socks.
International matches 2013–14
Congo (h) 2-1, Congo (a) 0-1, Cameroon (a) 1-0, Cameroon (h) 1-1, Togo (a) 1-2, Mauritania (n) 1-0, Gabon (n) 0-1, Burundi (n) 2-1, Ghana (n) 0-1.

DJIBOUTI

Federation Djiboutienne de Football, Stade el Haoj Hassan Gouled, BP 2694, Djibouti.
Founded: 1977; *National Colours:* Green shirts, white shorts, blue socks.
International matches 2013–14
None played.

EGYPT

Egyptian Football Association, 5 Gabalaya Street, Guezira, El Borg Post Office, Cairo.
Founded: 1921; *National Colours:* Red shirts, white shorts, black socks.
International matches 2013–14
Uganda (h) 3-0, Guinea (h) 4-2, Uganda (h) 2-0, Uganda (h) 3-0, Ghana (a) 1-6, Zambia (h) 2-0, Ghana (a) 2-1, Bosnia & Herzegovina (n) 2-0, Chile (a) 2-3, Jamaica (n) 2-2.

ERITREA

The Eritrean National Football Federation, Sematat Avenue 29–31, PO Box 3665, Asmara.
National Colours: Blue shirts, red shorts, green socks.
International matches 2013–14
Sudan (n) 0-3, Uganda (n) 0-3, Rwanda (n) 0-1.

ETHIOPIA

Ethiopia Football Federation, Addis Ababa Stadium, PO Box 1080, Addis Ababa.
Founded: 1943; *National Colours:* Green shirts, yellow shorts, red socks.
International matches 2013–14
Botswana (a) 2-1, Rwanda (h) 1-0, Rwanda (a) 0-1 (6-5p), Central African Republic (n) 2-1, Nigeria (h) 1-2, Nigeria (a) 0-2, Kenya (h) 0-0, Zanzibar (n) 3-1, South Sudan (n) 2-0, Sudan (n) 0-2, Libya (n) 0-2, Congo (n) 0-1, Ghana (n) 0-1.

GABON

Federation Gabonaise De Football, BP 181, Libreville.
Founded: 1962; *National Colours:* Green, yellow and blue shirts, blue and yellow shorts, white socks with tricolour trims.
International matches 2013–14
Cameroon (a) 0-1, Cameroon (h) 1-0 (6-5p), Cape Verde Islands (h) 1-1, Burkina Faso (a) 0-1, Zimbabwe (a) 0-2, Burundi (n) 0-0, Congo DR (n) 1-0, Mauritania (n) 4-2, Libya (n) 1-1 (2-4p), Morocco (a) 1-1.

GAMBIA

Gambia Football Association, Independence Stadium, Bakau, PO Box 523, Banjul.
Founded: 1952; *National Colours:* All red, blue and white.
International matches 2013–14
Tanzania (h) 2-0.

GHANA

Ghana Football Association, National Sports Council, PO Box 1272, Accra.
Founded: 1957; *National Colours:* All yellow.
International matches 2013–14
Turkey (a) 2-2, Libya (n) 0-1, Zambia (h) 2-1, Japan (a) 1-3, Egypt (h) 6-1, Egypt (a) 1-2, Namibia (a) 1-0, Congo (n) 1-0, Libya (n) 1-1, Ethiopia (n) 1-0, Congo DR (n) 1-0, Nigeria (n) 0-0 (4-1p), Libya (n) 0-0 (3-4p), Montenegro (a) 0-1, Netherlands (a) 0-1, Korea Republic (n) 4-0, USA (n) 1-2, Germany (n) 2-2, Portugal (n) 1-2.

GUINEA

Federation Guineenne De Football, PO Box 3645, Conakry.
Founded: 1959; *National Colours:* Red shirts, yellow shorts, green socks.
International matches 2013–14
Mali (a) 1-3, Mali (h) 1-0, Algeria (a) 2-2, Egypt (a) 2-4, Iran (a) 2-1, Mali (n) 2-1.

GUINEA-BISSAU

Federacao De Football Da Guinea-Bissau, Alto Bandim (Nova Sede), PO Box 375, 1035 Bissau.
Founded: 1974; *National Colours:* Red, green and yellow shirts, green and yellow shorts, red, green and yellow socks.
International matches 2013–14
Central African Republic (a) 0-0, Central African Republic (h) 3-1.

GUINEA, EQUATORIAL

Federacion Ecuatoguineana De Futbol, c/P Patricio Lumumba (Estadio La Paz), 1071 Malabo.
Founded: 1986; *National Colours:* All red.
International matches 2013–14
Libya (h) 1-1, Sierra Leone (a) 2-3, Spain (h) 1-2, Mauritania (a) 0-1, Mauritania (h) 3-0.

IVORY COAST

Federation Ivorienne De Football, PO Box 1202, Abidjan 01.
Founded: 1960; *National Colours:* Orange shirts, black shorts, green socks.
International matches 2013–14
Nigeria (a) 1-4, Nigeria (h) 2-0, Mexico (n) 1-4, Morocco (h) 1-1, Senegal (h) 3-1, Senegal (a) 1-1, Belgium (a) 2-2, Bosnia & Herzegovina (n) 1-2, El Salvador (n) 2-1, Japan (n) 2-1, Colombia (n) 1-2, Greece (n) 1-2.

KENYA

Kenya Football Federation, Nyayo National Stadium, PO Box 40234, Nairobi.
Founded: 1960; *National Colours:* All red.
International matches 2013–14
Lesotho (n) 2-2, Swaziland (n) 2-0, Botswana (n) 1-2, Namibia (h) 1-0, Ethiopia (h) 0-0, South Sudan (h) 3-1, Zanzibar (h) 2-0, Rwanda (h) 1-0, Tanzania (h) 1-0, Sudan (h) 2-0, Comoros (h) 1-0, Comoros (a) 1-1.

LESOTHO

Lesotho Football Association, PO Box 1879, Maseru-100, Lesotho.
Founded: 1932; *National Colours:* Blue shirts, green shorts, white socks.
International matches 2013–14
Kenya (n) 2-2, Botswana (n) 3-3, Swaziland (n) 2-0, Angola (h) 1-1 (5-3p), Zimbabwe (n) 1-2, South Africa (n) 1-2, Sudan (a) 3-1, Swaziland (h) 0-1, Swaziland (h) 0-0, Liberia (a) 0-1, Liberia (h) 2-0.

LIBERIA

Liberia Football Association, Broad and Center Streets, PO Box 10-1066, 1000 Monrovia.
Founded: 1936; *National Colours:* Blue shirts, white shorts, red socks.
International matches 2013–14
Angola (a) 1-4, Lesotho (h) 1-0, Lesotho (a) 0-2.

LIBYA

Libyan Football Federation, Asayadi Street, Near Janat Al-Areet, PO Box 5137, Tripoli.
Founded: 1963; *National Colours:* Green and black shirts, black shorts and socks.
International matches 2013–14
Jordan (a) 1-2, Central African Republic (h) 0-0, Ghana (n) 1-0, Equatorial Guinea (a) 1-1, Cameroon (a) 0-1, Niger (n) 1-1, Ethiopia (n) 2-0, Ghana (n) 1-1, Congo (n) 2-2, Gabon (n) 1-1 (4-2p), Zimbabwe (n) 0-0 (5-4p), Ghana (n) 0-0 (4-3p), Congo (n) 0-0, Rwanda (h) 0-0, Rwanda (a) 0-3.

MADAGASCAR

Federation Malagasy de Football, Immeuble Preservatrice Vie-Lot IBF-9B, Rue Rabearivelo-Antsahavola, PO Box 4409, Antananarivo 101.
Founded: 1961; *National Colours:* Red and green shirts, white and green shorts, green and white socks.
International matches 2013–14
Uganda (h) 2-1, Uganda (a) 0-1.

MALAWI

Football Association of Malawi, Mpira House, Old Chileka Road, PO Box 865, Blantyre.
Founded: 1966; *National Colours:* Red shirts, white shorts, red and black socks.
International matches 2013–14
Zimbabwe (n) 1-1 (1-3p), Angola (n) 2-3, Rwanda (a) 1-0, Botswana (a) 0-1, Nigeria (a) 0-2, Zimbabwe (h) 1-4, Tanzania (a) 0-0, Chad (h) 2-0, Tanzania (a) 0-1, Chad (a) 1-3, Mozambique (h) 1-1.

MALI

Federation Malienne De Football, Avenue du Mali, Hamdallaye ACI 2000, PO Box 1020, Bamako 12582.
Founded: 1960; *National Colours:* Green shirts, yellow shorts, red socks.
International matches 2013–14
Guinea (h) 3-1, Guinea (a) 0-1, Algeria (a) 0-1, Korea Republic (a) 1-3, Nigeria (n) 2-1, South Africa (a) 1-1, Mozambique (n) 2-1, Zimbabwe (n) 1-2, Senegal (n) 1-1, Guinea (n) 1-2, Croatia (a) 1-2, China PR (a) 3-1.

MAURITANIA

Federation De Foot-Ball De La Rep. Islamique. De Mauritanie, BP 566, Nouakchott.
Founded: 1961; *National Colours:* Green and yellow shirts, yellow shorts, green socks.
International matches 2013–14
Senegal (a) 0-1, Senegal (h) 2-0, Canada (n) 0-0, Canada (n) 1-0, Oman (a) 0-0, Mozambique (n) 3-2, Congo DR (n) 0-1, Burundi (a) 2-3, Gabon (n) 2-4, Niger (h) 1-1, Mauritius (h) 1-0, Mauritius (a) 2-0, Equatorial Guinea (h) 1-0, Equatorial Guinea (a) 0-3.

MAURITIUS

Mauritius Football Association, Chancery House, 2nd Floor Nos. 303–305, 14 Lislet Geoffroy Street, Port Louis.
Founded: 1952; *National Colours:* All red.
International matches 2013–14
Namibia (n) 1-2, Seychelles (n) 4-0, Zimbabwe (h) 0-3, Zimbabwe (a) 1-1, Qatar (n) 0-3, Mauritania (a) 0-1, Mauritania (h) 0-2.

MOROCCO

Federation Royale Marocaine De Football, 51 Bis Av. Ibn Sina, PO Box 51, Agdal, 10 000 Rabat.
Founded: 1955; *National Colours:* All green, white and red.
International matches 2013–14
Tunisia (a) 1-0, Tunisia (h) 0-0, Burkina Faso (h) 1-2, Ivory Coast (a) 1-1, South Africa (h) 1-1, Zimbabwe (n) 0-0, Burkina Faso (n) 1-1, Uganda (n) 3-1, Nigeria (n) 3-4, Gabon (h) 1-1, Mozambique (n) 4-0, Angola (n) 0-2, Russia (a) 0-2.

MOZAMBIQUE

Federacao Mocambicana De Futebol, Av. Samora Machel 11-2, Caixa Postal 1467, Maputo.
Founded: 1978; *National Colours:* Red shirts, black shorts, red and black socks.
International matches 2013–14
Zambia (a) 1-3, Namibia (n) 1-0, Angola (n) 1-0, Namibia (h) 3-0, Namibia (a) 0-3 (5-4p), Angola (h) 0-0, Angola (a) 1-1, Zimbabwe (a) 1-1, Namibia (a) 0-0, Zimbabwe (a) 1-2, Mauritania (n) 2-3, South Africa (a) 1-3, Nigeria (n) 2-4, Mali (n) 1-2, Angola (h) 1-1, South Sudan (h) 5-0, Morocco (n) 0-4, South Sudan (n) 0-0, Malawi (a) 1-1.

NAMIBIA

Namibia Football Association, Abraham Mashego Street 8521, Katurua Council of Churches in Namibia, PO Box 1345, 9000 Windhoek.
Founded: 1990; *National Colours:* All red.
International matches 2013–14
Mauritius (n) 2-1, Seychelles (n) 4-2, South Africa (n) 1-2, Mozambique (n) 0-1, Mozambique (a) 0-3, Mozambique (h) 3-0 (4-5p), Kenya (n) 0-1, Mozambique (h) 0-0, Ghana (h) 0-1, Tanzania (h) 1-1, Congo (h) 1-0, Congo (a) 0-3.

NIGER

Federation Nigerienne De Football, Rue de la Tapoa, PO Box 10299, Niamey.
Founded: 1967; *National Colours:* Orange shirts, white shorts, green socks.
International matches 2013–14
Burkina Faso (a) 0-1, Burkina Faso (h) 1-0 (5-6p), Congo (h) 2-2, Libya (n) 1-1, Mauritania (a) 1-1, Ukraine (a) 1-2.

NIGERIA

Nigeria Football Association, Plot 2033, Olusegun, Obasanjo Way, Zone 7, Wuse Abuja, PO Box 5101 Garki, Abuja.
Founded: 1945; *National Colours:* All green and white.
International matches 2013–14
Ivory Coast (h) 4-1, Ivory Coast (a) 0-2, South Africa (a) 2-0, Malawi (h) 2-0, Burkina Faso (h) 4-1, Ethiopia (a) 2-1, Jordan (a) 0-1, Ethiopia (h) 2-0, Italy (n) 2-2, Mali (n) 1-2, Mozambique (n) 4-2, South Africa (a) 3-1, Morocco (n) 4-3, Ghana (n) 0-0 (1-4p), Zimbabwe (n) 1-0, Mexico (n) 0-0, Scotland (n) 2-2, Greece (n) 0-0, USA (a) 1-2, Iran (n) 0-0, Bosnia & Herzegovina (n) 1-0, Argentina (n) 2-3, France (n) 0-2.

RWANDA

Federation Rwandaise De Football Amateur, BP 2000, Kigali.
Founded: 1972; *National Colours:* Red, green and yellow shirts, green shorts, red socks.
International matches 2013–14
Ethiopia (a) 0-1, Ethiopia (h) 1-0 (5-6p), Malawi (h) 0-1, Benin (h) 0-2, Uganda (a) 0-0, Uganda (n) 0-1, Sudan (n) 0-1, Eritrea (n) 2-1, Kenya (a) 0-1, Burundi (a) 1-1, Libya (a) 0-0, Libya (h) 3-0.

SAO TOME & PRINCIPE

Federation Santomense De Futebol, Rua Ex-Joao de Deus No. QXXIII-426/26, PO Box 440, Sao Tome.
Founded: 1975; *National Colours:* Green and red shirts, yellow shorts, green socks.
International matches 2013–14
Benin (h) 0-2, Benin (a) 0-2.

SENEGAL

Federation Senegalaise De Football, Stade Leopold Sedar Senghor, Route De L'Aeroport De Yoff, BP 13021, Dakar.
Founded: 1960; *National Colours:* All white and green.
International matches 2013–14
Mauritania (h) 1-0, Mauritania (a) 0-2, Zambia (n) 1-1, Uganda (h) 1-0, Ivory Coast (a) 1-3, Ivory Coast (h) 1-1, Mali (n) 1-1, Burkina Faso (n) 1-1, Colombia (n) 2-2.

SEYCHELLES
Seychelles Football Federation, PO Box 843, People's Stadium, Victoria-Mahe.
Founded: 1979; *National Colours:* Red and green shirts and shorts, red socks.
International matches 2013–14
Namibia (n) 2-4, Mauritius (n) 0-4, Maldives (h) 3-1, Maldives (h) 2-1.

SIERRA LEONE
Sierra Leone Football Association, 21 Battery Street, Kingtorn, PO Box 672, National Stadium, Brookfields, Freetown.
Founded: 1967; *National Colours:* Green and blue shirts, green, blue and white shorts and socks.
International matches 2013–14
Equatorial Guinea (h) 3-2, Swaziland (a) 1-1, Swaziland (a) 1-0.

SOMALIA
Somali Football Federation, PO Box 222, Mogadishu BN 03040.
Founded: 1951; *National Colours:* Sky blue and white shirts and shorts, white and sky blue socks.
International matches 2013–14
Burundi (n) 0-2, Tanzania (n) 0-1, Zambia (n) 0-4.

SOUTH AFRICA
South African Football Association, First National Bank Stadium, PO Box 910, Johannesburg 2000.
Founded: 1991; *National Colours:* White shirts with yellow striped sleeves, white shorts with yellow stripes, white socks.
International matches 2013–14
Namibia (n) 2-1, Zambia (n) 0-0 (3-5p), Lesotho (n) 2-1, Nigeria (h) 0-2, Burkina Faso (h) 2-0, Botswana (h) 4-1, Zimbabwe (h) 1-2, Morocco (a) 1-1, Swaziland (a) 3-0, Spain (h) 1-0, Mozambique (h) 3-1, Mali (h) 1-1, Nigeria (h) 1-3, Brazil (h) 0-5, Australia (a) 1-1, New Zealand (a) 0-0.

SOUTH SUDAN
South Sudan Football Association, Juba National Stadium, Hai Himra, Talata, Juba.
Founded: 2011; *National Colours:* All white.
International matches 2013–14
Uganda (h) 2-2*, Ethiopia (n) 0-1*, Kenya (n) 0-2*, Uganda (n) 0-4*, Zanzibar (n) 1-2, Kenya (a) 1-3, Ethiopia (n) 0-2, Botswana (a) 0-3, Mozambique (a) 0-5, Mozambique (n) 0-0.
* *Played in 2012, results omitted from last edition.*

SUDAN
Sudan Football Association, Bladia Street, Khartoum.
Founded: 1936; *National Colours:* Red shirts, white shorts, black socks.
International matches 2013–14
Burundi (a) 1-1, Burundi (h) 1-1 (3-4p), Lesotho (n) 1-3, Eritrea (n) 3-0, Rwanda (n) 1-0, Uganda (n) 0-1, Ethiopia (n) 2-0, Zambia (n) 2-1, Kenya (a) 0-2.

SWAZILAND
National Football Association of Swaziland, Sigwaca House, Plot 582, Sheffield Road, PO Box 641, Mbabane H100.
Founded: 1968; *National Colours:* Blue shirts, gold shorts, red socks.
International matches 2013–14
Angola (h) 0-1*, Angola (a) 0-1*, Botswana (n) 0-0, Kenya (n) 0-2, Lesotho (n) 0-2, South Africa (h) 0-3, Lesotho (a) 1-0, Lesotho (a) 0-0, Botswana (a) 4-1, Sierra Leone (h) 1-1, Sierra Leone (a) 1-0.
* *Played in 2012–13, results omitted from last edition.*

TANZANIA
Football Association of Tanzania, Uhuru/Shaurimoyo Road, Karume Memorial Stadium, PO Box 1574, Ilala/Dar Es Salaam.
Founded: 1930; *National Colours:* Green, yellow and blue shirts, black shorts, green socks with horizontal stripe.
International matches 2013–14
Uganda (h) 0-1, Uganda (a) 1-3, Gambia (a) 0-2, Zimbabwe (h) 0-0, Zambia (n) 1-1, Somalia (n) 1-0, Burundi (n) 1-0, Uganda (n) 2-2 (3-2p), Kenya (a) 0-1, Zambia (n) 1-1 (5-6p), Namibia (a) 1-1, Burundi (h) 0-3, Malawi (h) 0-0, Zimbabwe (h) 1-0, Malawi (h) 1-0, Zimbabwe (a) 2-2, Botswana (a) 2-4.

TOGO
Federation Togolaise De Football, C.P. 5, Lome.
Founded: 1960; *National Colours:* White shirts, green shorts, red socks with yellow and green stripes.
International matches 2013–14
Congo DR (h) 2-1.

TUNISIA
Federation Tunisienne De Football, Maison des Federations Sportives, Cite Olympique, Tunis 1003.
Founded: 1956; *National Colours:* Red shirts, white shorts, red socks.
International matches 2013–14
Morocco (h) 0-1, Morocco (a) 0-0, Congo (h) 3-0, Cape Verde Islands (h) 3-0, Cameroon (h) 0-0, Cameroon (a) 1-4, Colombia (n) 1-1, Korea Republic (a) 1-0, Belgium (a) 0-0.

UGANDA
Federation of Uganda Football Associations, Plot No. 879, Kyadondo Block 8, Mengo Wakaliga Road, PO Box 22518, Kampala.
Founded: 1924; *National Colours:* All yellow, red and white.
International matches 2013–14
Tanzania (a) 1-0, Tanzania (h) 3-1, Egypt (a) 0-3, Botswana (a) 3-1, Senegal (n) 0-1, Egypt (a) 0-2, Egypt (n) 0-3, Rwanda (h) 0-0, Rwanda (n) 1-0, Eritrea (n) 3-0, Sudan (n) 1-0, Tanzania (n) 2-2 (2-3p), Burkina Faso (n) 2-1, Zimbabwe (n) 0-0, Morocco (n) 1-3, Zambia (a) 1-2, Madagascar (a) 1-2, Madagascar (h) 1-0.

ZAMBIA
Football Association of Zambia, Football House, Alick Nkhata Road, PO Box 34751, Lusaka.
Founded: 1929; *National Colours:* White and green shirts, green and white shorts, white and green socks.
International matches 2013–14
Mozambique (h) 3-1, South Africa (h) 0-0 (5-3p), Zimbabwe (h) 2-0, Botswana (a) 1-1, Botswana (h) 2-0, Senegal (n) 1-1, Zimbabwe (a) 0-0, Zimbabwe (h) 0-1, Ghana (a) 1-2, Brazil (n) 0-2, Jordan (n) 0-1, Egypt (a) 0-2, Tanzania (n) 0-1, Burundi (n) 1-0, Somalia (n) 4-0, Burundi (n) 0-0 (4-3p), Sudan (n) 1-2, Tanzania (n) 1-1 (6-5p), Uganda (h) 2-1, Japan (n) 3-4.

ZIMBABWE
Zimbabwe Football Association, PO Box CY 114, Causeway, Harare.
Founded: 1965; *National Colours:* All green and gold.
International matches 2013–14
Malawi (n) 1-1 (3-1p), Lesotho (n) 2-1, Zambia (n) 0-2, Mauritius (a) 3-0, Mauritius (h) 1-1, Zambia (h) 0-0, Zambia (a) 1-0, Mozambique (h) 1-1, South Africa (a) 2-1, Tanzania (a) 0-0, Mozambique (h) 2-1, Gabon (h) 2-0, Morocco (n) 0-0, Uganda (n) 0-0, Burkina Faso (n) 1-0, Mali (n) 2-1, Libya (n) 0-0 (4-5p), Nigeria (n) 0-1, Malawi (a) 4-1, Tanzania (a) 0-1, Tanzania (h) 2-2.

WORLD CUP 2014 QUALIFYING COMPETITION

EUROPE

* *Denotes player sent off.*

GROUP A

Friday, 7 September 2012

Croatia (0) 1 *(Jelavic 68)*

FYR Macedonia (0) 0   15,150

Croatia: (352) Pletikosa; Strinic, Simunic, Corluka (Vida 81); Rakitic (Kranjcar 46), Vukojevic, Modric, Srna, Perisic; Mandzukic, Eduardo (Jelavic 63).
FYR Macedonia: (442) Bogatinov; Georgievski, Popov, Noveski, Sikov; Gligorov (Tasevski 83), Demiri, Trickovski (Georgiev 73), Ristic (Ivanovski 80); Pandev, Ibraimi.
Referee: Alon Yefet.

Wales (0) 0

Belgium (1) 2 *(Kompany 42, Vertonghen 82)*   20,201

Wales: (352) Myhill; Blake, Collins*, Williams A; Gunter, Edwards (King 79), Ramsey, Bale, Matthews; Church (Robson-Kanu 71), Morison (Vokes 71).
Belgium: (442) Courtois; Gillet G, Vermaelen, Kompany, Vertonghen; Witsel, Dembele (De Bruyne 64), Hazard, Mertens; Mirallas (Lukaku 46), Fellaini.
Referee: Stefan Johannesson.

Saturday, 8 September 2012

Scotland (0) 0

Serbia (0) 0   47,473

Scotland: (4141) McGregor; Hutton, Webster, Berra, Dixon; Caldwell; Naismith, Snodgrass (Forrest 69), Adam, Morrison (Mackie 81); Miller (Rhodes 81).
Serbia: (4141) Stojkovic; Ivanovic, Bisevac, Nastasic, Kolarov; Mijailovic (Fejsa 46); Tosic, Ninkovic, Ignjovski, Djuricic (Lekic 83); Lazovic (Tadic 58).
Referee: Jonas Eriksson.

Tuesday, 11 September 2012

Belgium (1) 1 *(Gillet G 45)*

Croatia (1) 1 *(Perisic 6)*   43,430

Belgium: (442) Courtois; Gillet G, Vermaelen, Kompany, Vertonghen; Defour (Fellaini 67), Witsel, Mertens (Mirallas 81), Hazard; Benteke, Dembele (De Bruyne 72).
Croatia: (442) Pletikosa; Strinic, Vida, Simunic, Schildenfeld; Radosevic (Vukojevic 78), Modric, Srna, Perisic; Mandzukic (Kalinic 88), Jelavic (Olic 59).
Referee: Alberto Undiano Mallenco.

Scotland (1) 1 *(Miller 43)*

FYR Macedonia (1) 1 *(Noveski 11)*   32,324

Scotland: (4141) McGregor; Hutton, Webster, Berra, Dixon; Caldwell; Forrest, Maloney, Morrison (Rhodes 66), Mackie (Naismith 77); Miller (Adam 58).
FYR Macedonia: (4411) Bogatinov; Georgievski, Sikov, Noveski, Popov; Ibraimi (Tasevski 89), Gligorov (Sumulikoski 70), Demiri, Trickovski (Hasani 37); Pandev; Ivanovski.
Referee: Sergei Karasev.

Serbia (3) 6 *(Kolarov 16, Tosic 24, Djuricic 39, Tadic 55, Ivanovic 80, Sulejmani 90)*

Wales (1) 1 *(Bale 31)*   11,113

Serbia: (4141) Stojkovic; Ivanovic, Bisevac, Nastasic, Kolarov; Ignjovski (Mijailovic 85); Tadic, Fejsa, Djuricic (Lekic 81), Tosic (Sulejmani 71); Markovic.
Wales: (442) Myhill; Gunter, Williams A, Blake, Matthews (Ricketts 46); Edwards (Vaughan 46), Allen (King 72), Ramsey, Bale; Morison, Church.
Referee: Duarte Gomes.

Friday, 12 October 2012

FYR Macedonia (1) 1 *(Ibraimi 16)*

Croatia (1) 2 *(Corluka 33, Rakitic 60)*   33,330

FYR Macedonia: (442) Bogatinov; Georgievski, Popov (Hasani 82), Noveski, Sikov (Grncarov 77); Sumulikoski (Gligorov 54), Demiri, Trickovski, Ristic; Pandev, Ibraimi.

Croatia: (442) Pletikosa; Strinic, Simunic, Corluka, Rakitic; Vukojevic, Modric (Badelj 83), Srna, Perisic; Jelavic (Sammir 64), Mandzukic (Kalinic 72).
Referee: Peter Rasmussen.

Serbia (0) 0

Belgium (1) 3 *(Benteke 34, De Bruyne 68, Mirallas 90)*
                                          22,220

Serbia: (442) Brkic; Bisevac, Nastasic, Ivanovic, Tosic (Stevanovic 67); Tadic (Lekic 80), Kolarov, Mijailovic, Ignjovski; Djuricic (Scepovic 56), Markovic.
Belgium: (442) Courtois; Alderweireld, Vermaelen, Kompany, Vertonghen; Witsel, De Bruyne (Mirallas 87), Dembele, Benteke; Hazard (Mertens 55), Chadli.
Referee: Pavel Kralovec.

Wales (0) 2 *(Bale 81 (pen), 89)*

Scotland (1) 1 *(Morrison 27)*   23,232

Wales: (451) Price; Gunter, Blake, Williams, Davies B; Bale, Allen, Vaughan, Ramsey, Ledley (Robson-Kanu 71); Morison (Davies C 64).
Scotland: (451) McGregor; Hutton, Caldwell, Berra, Fox; Maloney, Morrison (Miller 84), Fletcher D, Brown (Adam 46), Commons (Mackie 84); Fletcher S.
Referee: Florian Meyer.

Tuesday, 16 October 2012

Belgium (0) 2 *(Benteke 69, Kompany 71)*

Scotland (0) 0   44,440

Belgium: (442) Courtois; Alderweireld, Vermaelen, Kompany, Vertonghen; De Bruyne, Witsel, Chadli, Mertens (Mirallas 55); Dembele (Hazard 46), Benteke (M'Boyo 86).
Scotland: (451) McGregor; Hutton, Berra, Caldwell, Fox; Maloney, Morrison (Phillips 79), Fletcher D, McArthur, Commons (Mackie 46); Fletcher S (Miller 76).
Referee: Mauricio Morales.

Croatia (1) 2 *(Mandzukic 27, Eduardo 58)*

Wales (0) 0   18,180

Croatia: (442) Pletikosa; Strinic, Simunic, Lovren (Schildenfeld 46), Srna; Badelj, Perisic (Vida 85), Rakitic, Modric; Mandzukic, Eduardo (Kranjcar 78).
Wales: (442) Price; Williams, Davies B, Gunter, Blake; King (Vokes 72), Vaughan, Bale, Allen; Ledley (Robson-Kanu 82), Morison (Church 61).
Referee: Alexandru Dan Tudor.

FYR Macedonia (0) 1 *(Ibraimi 61 (pen))*

Serbia (0) 0   31,310

FYR Macedonia: (433) Pacovski; Lazevski, Noveski, Grncarov, Georgievski; Gligorov, Demiri (Sumulikoski 86), Tasevski (Trickovski 73); Hasani, Ibraimi, Ivanovski (Ristovski 90).
Serbia: (442) Brkic; Tomovic*, Bisevac, Nastasic, Kolarov; Ignjovski, Fejsa, Tosic, Tadic (Ivanovic 68); Markovic (Sulejmani 74), Djuricic (Lekic 63).
Referee: Bas Nijhuis.

Friday, 22 March 2013

Croatia (2) 2 *(Mandzukic 23, Olic 37)*

Serbia (0) 0   36,360

Croatia: (442) Pletikosa; Srna, Simunic, Corluka, Strinic (Lovren 82); Kovacic, Modric, Rakitic, Kranjcar (Vida 63); Mandzukic, Olic (Vukojevic 83).
Serbia: (442) Brkic; Ivanovic, Subotic, Nastasic, Kolarov; Radovanovic, Ignjovski (Petrovic 75), Tosic, Stevanovic (Tadic 57); Scepovic (Djordjevic 9), Djuricic.
Referee: Cuneyt Cakir.

FYR Macedonia (0) 0

Belgium (1) 2 *(De Bruyne 26, Hazard 62 (pen))* 20,200

FYR Macedonia: (442) Pacovski; Todorovski, Noveski, Grncarov, Lazevski; Demiri, Trickovski (Tasevski 81), Jahovic (Ivanovski 57); Pandev; Hasani (Trajkovski 81), Ibraimi.

Belgium: (442) Courtois; Alderweireld, Vermaelen, Vertonghen, Van Buyten; Witsel, Fellaini, Hazard, De Bruyne; Dembele, Benteke (Chadli 85).
Referee: Deniz Aytekin.

Scotland (1) 1 *(Hanley 45)*
Wales (0) 2 *(Ramsey 73 (pen), Robson-Kanu 74)* 39,393
Scotland: (4411) McGregor; Hutton, Caldwell, Hanley, Mulgrew; Burke (Rhodes 86), McArthur, Dorrans (Adam 63), Snodgrass■; Maloney; Fletcher S (Miller 4).
Wales: (433) Myhill; Gunter, Ricketts, Williams A, Davies B; Collison (King 58), Ramsey■, Ledley (Church 89); Bale (Williams J 46), Robson-Kanu, Bellamy.
Referee: Antony Gautier.

Tuesday, 26 March 2013
Belgium (0) 1 *(Hazard 62)*
FYR Macedonia (0) 0 45,450
Belgium: (442) Courtois; Alderweireld, Vermaelen, Vertonghen; Witsel, Dembele (Chadli 55), Mertens (Mirallas 46), De Bruyne; Hazard (Fellaini 90), Benteke.
FYR Macedonia: (442) Pacovski; Georgievski, Noveski, Sikov, Ristovski (Todorovski 70); Gligorov, Tasevski (Hasani 46), Ibraimi, Trickovski (Trajkovski 64); Pandev, Ivanovski.
Referee: Olegario Benquerenca.

Serbia (0) 2 *(Djuricic 59, 65)*
Scotland (0) 0 10,100
Serbia: (442) Stojkovic; Ivanovic, Nastasic, Subotic, Tomovic; Basta, Fejsa (Petrovic 85), Milivojevic, Tosic (Stevanovic 90); Tadic (Djordjevic 69), Djuricic.
Scotland: (4411) Marshall; Hutton, Caldwell, Hanley, Whittaker; Boyd, McArthur (Adam 46), Bridcutt, Maloney (Burke 79); Naismith; Rhodes (Miller 80).
Referee: Istvan Vad.

Wales (1) 1 *(Bale 21 (pen))*
Croatia (0) 2 *(Lovren 77, Eduardo 87)* 12,125
Wales: (433) Myhill; Gunter, Williams A, Collins, Davies B; Ledley, Williams J (Church 83), King; Bellamy, Robson-Kanu (Richards 63), Bale.
Croatia: (442) Pletikosa; Strinic (Olic 73), Corluka, Lovren, Srna; Rakitic, Modric, Sammir (Kovacic 61), Badelj (Schildenfeld 46); Mandzukic, Eduardo.
Referee: Luca Banti.

Friday, 7 June 2013
Belgium (1) 2 *(De Bruyne 13, Fellaini 60)*
Serbia (0) 1 *(Kolarov 87)* 45,458
Belgium: (4141) Courtois; Alderweireld, Kompany, Van Buyten, Vertonghen; Witsel; De Bruyne (Lukaku 82), Fellaini (Dembele 71), Chadli, Mirallas (Hazard 64); Benteke.
Serbia: (4231) Stojkovic; Ivanovic, Bisevac, Subotic, Kolarov; Milivojevic (Petrovic 68), Fejsa; Tadic, Basta, Markovic; Mitrovic (Scepovic 69).
Referee: Stephane Lannoy.

Croatia (0) 0
Scotland (1) 1 *(Snodgrass 26)* 28,280
Croatia: (442) Pletikosa; Strinic (Kalinic 70), Simunic, Schildenfeld, Srna; Rakitic, Kovacic, Perisic (Eduardo 55), Sammir; Mandzukic (Kranjcar 87), Olic.
Scotland: (451) McGregor; Hutton, Martin R, Hanley, Whittaker; Maloney (Conway 75), Morrison, McArthur, Bannan (Naismith 63), Snodgrass; Griffiths (Rhodes 64).
Referee: David Fernandez Borbalan.

Friday, 6 September 2013
FYR Macedonia (1) 2 *(Trickovski 21, Trajkovski 80)*
Wales (1) 1 *(Ramsey 39 (pen))* 13,000
FYR Macedonia: (433) Pacovski; Georgievski (Lazevski 77), Sikov, Noveski, Ristovski; Gligorov, Pandev, Tasevski; Ibraimi (Trajkovski 60), Kostovski, Trickovski (Mojsov 85).
Wales: (433) Myhill; Gunter, Williams A, Ricketts, Davies B; Collison (Matthews 78), Vaughan (Vokes 85), Ledley; Williams J (Crofts 62), Bellamy, Ramsey.
Referee: Sascha Kever.

Scotland (0) 0
Belgium (1) 2 *(Defour 38, Mirallas 89)* 36,000
Scotland: (442) Marshall; Hutton, Hanley, Martin R, Whittaker; Mulgrew, Brown, Maloney, Forrest (McCormack 86); Griffiths (Rhodes 68), Snodgrass (Anya 59).
Belgium: (433) Courtois; Alderweireld, Lombaerts (Pocognoli 76), Van Buyten, Vertonghen; Fellaini (Mirallas 68), Witsel, Chadli; De Bruyne, Benteke, Defour (Dembele 87).
Referee: Paolo Tagliavento.

Serbia (0) 1 *(Mitrovic 66)*
Croatia (0) 1 *(Mandzukic 53)* 35,000
Serbia: (442) Stojkovic; Nastasic, Ivanovic, Kolarov, Subotic; Tosic (Sulejmani 56), Matic■, Fejsa, Mitrovic; Djuricic (Tadic 56), Markovic (Petrovic 79).
Croatia: (442) Pletikosa; Simunic■, Corluka, Lovren, Srna; Rakitic (Jelavic 76), Vukojevic, Modric, Mandzukic; Olic (Perisic 56), Eduardo (Kovacic 63).
Referee: Felix Brych.

Tuesday, 10 September 2013
FYR Macedonia (0) 1 *(Kostovski 83)*
Scotland (0) 2 *(Anya 59, Maloney 88)* 16,000
FYR Macedonia: (442) Pacovski; Georgievski, Ristovski, Noveski, Sikov; Trickovski, Babunski (Tasevski 41), Jahovic (Kostovski 82), Pandev; Trajkovski (Ivanovski 56), Stjepanovic.
Scotland: (433) Marshall (Gilks 45); Hutton, Martin R, Hanley, Whittaker (Wallace 79); Mulgrew, Brown, Bannan (McArthur 77); Maloney, Naismith, Anya.
Referee: Fredy Fautrel.

Wales (0) 0
Serbia (2) 3 *(Djordjevic 9, Kolarov 38, Markovic 55)* 7500
Wales: (4231) Myhill; Gunter, Gabbidon, Davies, Matthews; Crofts (Vaughan 58), King (Bale 58); Bellamy, Ramsey, Ledley (Robson-Kanu 75); Vokes.
Serbia: (4231) Stojkovic; Ivanovic, Bisevac, Nastasic, Kolarov; Fejsa (Petrovic 90), Radovanovic (Milivojevic 67); Djordjevic, Tadic (Krsticic 88), Markovic; Djuricic.
Referee: Szymon Marciniak.

Friday, 11 October 2013
Croatia (0) 1 *(Kranjcar 84)*
Belgium (2) 2 *(Lukaku 15, 38)* 30,000
Croatia: (442) Pletikosa; Strinic, Corluka, Lovren, Vrsaljko; Vida, Perisic (Kalinic 45), Rakitic (Kranjcar 75), Modric; Kovacic (Vukojevic 65), Mandzukic.
Belgium: (442) Courtois; Alderweireld, Van Buyten, Lombaerts, Vertonghen; Witsel, De Bruyne (Mirallas 64), Fellaini, Hazard; Defour (Dembele 85), Lukaku (Chadli 68).
Referee: Howard Webb.

Wales (0) 1 *(Church 67)*
FYR Macedonia (0) 0 5000
Wales: (442) Hennessey; Taylor, Gunter, Collins, John; Vaughan, Ramsey, King, Robson-Kanu; Church (Easter 90), Bellamy.
FYR Macedonia: (433) Pacovski; Ristovski, Alioski, Noveski, Sikov; Stjepanovic (Tasevski 75), Demiri (Kostovski 86), Randjelovic; Ibraimi, Pandev, Ivanovski (Trajkovski 80).
Referee: Suren Baliyan.

Tuesday, 15 October 2013
Belgium (0) 1 *(De Bruyne 64)*
Wales (0) 1 *(Ramsey 88)* 25,000
Belgium: (433) Courtois; Alderweireld, Van Buyten (Vertonghen 72); Vermaelen, Pocognoli; Witsel, Dembele, Chadli (Hazard 57); De Bruyne, Mirallas (Bakkali 77), Lukaku.
Wales: (442) Hennessey; Richards, Gunter, Collins (Wilson H 56), Taylor; Vaughan, King, Ramsey, Bellamy; Robson-Kanu (Wilson J 87), Church (Vokes 70).
Referee: Vitaliy Meshkov.

Scotland (1) 2 *(Snodgrass 28, Naismith 73)*
Croatia (0) 0 45,000
Scotland: (442) McGregor; Hutton, Martin R, Hanley, Mulgrew; Morrison, Bannan (Burke 89), Brown, Anya (Dorrans 77); Snodgrass (McArthur 82), Naismith.
Croatia: (442) Pletikosa; Vida, Corluka, Lovren, Strinic; Kranjcar (Perisic 68), Vukojevic, Modric, Srna; Kalinic (Eduardo 59), Mandzukic (Jelavic 80).
Referee: Ovidiu Alin Hategan.

Serbia (3) 5 *(Ristovski 17 (og), Basta 19, Kolarov 38 (pen), Tadic 54, Scepovic 73)*
FYR Macedonia (0) 1 *(Jahovic 83)* 12,000
Serbia: (433) Stojkovic; Basta, Rukavina (Trajkovic 84), Nastasic, Ivanovic; Kolarov, Matic, Milivojevic (Petrovic 76); Tosic, Tadic, Djordjevic (Scepovic 61).
FYR Macedonia: (433) Pacovski; Ristovski, Alioski, Noveski, Grncarov; Demiri (Babunski 56), Randjelovic, Stjepanovic; Ibraimi (Trajkovski 45), Kostovski, Ivanovski (Jahovic 81).
Referee: Richard Trutz.

Group A Table	P	W	D	L	F	A	GD	Pts
Belgium	10	8	2	0	18	4	14	26
Croatia	10	5	2	3	12	9	3	17
Serbia	10	4	2	4	18	11	7	14
Scotland	10	3	2	5	8	12	–4	11
Wales	10	3	1	6	9	20	–11	10
FYR Macedonia	10	2	1	7	7	16	–9	7

GROUP B

Friday, 7 September 2012
Bulgaria (1) 2 *(Manolev 30, Milanov G 66)*
Italy (2) 2 *(Osvaldo 37, 40)* 25,250
Bulgaria: (442) Mihailov; Bodurov, Minev I, Minev V, Ivanov; Manolev, Milanov G, Gadzhev (Sarmov 79), Dyakov; Gargorov (Mitsanski 62), Popov (Tonev 81).
Italy: (442) Buffon; Maggio, Ogbonna (Peluso 68), Barzagli, Bonucci; Marchisio, Giaccherini (Diamanti 64), De Rossi, Pirlo; Osvaldo, Giovinco (Destro 73).
Referee: Martin Atkinson.

Malta (0) 0
Armenia (0) 1 *(Sarkisov 70)* 4000
Malta: (352) Hogg; Muscat A, Borg, Agius A; Dimech, Schembri, Sciberras, Briffa (Bajada 85), Bogdanovic; Mifsud, Cohen (Caruana 74).
Armenia: (442) Kasparov; Hovsepyan, Hayrapetyan, Arzumanyan (Aleksanyan 79), Mkoyan; Yedigaryan Artak (Manoyan 52), Mkhitaryan, Mkrtchyan, Ozbiliz; Pizelli (Sarkisov 64), Movsisyan.
Referee: Rene Eisner.

Saturday, 8 September 2012
Denmark (0) 0
Czech Republic (0) 0 24,240
Denmark: (442) Andersen; Jacobsen, Kjaer, Agger, Wass; Kristensen (Andreasen 58), Kvist Jorgensen, Eriksen, Krohn-Delhi; Rommedahl (Mikkelsen 80), Jorgensen (Cornelius 71).
Czech Republic: (442) Cech; Gebre Selassie, Sivok, Suchy, Kadlec M; Hubschman, Plasil (Darida 75), Jiracek, Rezek (Husbauer 89); Pekhart, Vydra (Rajtoral 73).
Referee: Wolfgang Stark.

Tuesday, 11 September 2012
Bulgaria (1) 1 *(Manolev 44)*
Armenia (0) 0 10,100
Bulgaria: (442) Mihailov; Bodurov, Ivanov, Minev V, Minev I; Dyakov[■], Manolev, Gadzhev (Sarmov 59), Milanov G; Mitsanski (Rangelov 65), Popov (Gargorov 82).
Armenia: (4231) Berezovsky; Arzumanyan, Hayrapetyan (Yedigaryan Artak 45), Hovsepyan, Mkoyan; Mkhitaryan, Ozbiliz (Pizelli[■] 54); Mkrtchyan, Yedigaryan Artur (Sarkisov 77), Ghazaryan[■]; Movsisyan.
Referee: Stephan Studer.

Italy (1) 2 *(Destro 5, Peluso 90)*
Malta (0) 0 18,180
Italy: (442) Buffon; Peluso, Cassani, Barzagli, Bonucci; Marchisio, Nocerino, Diamanti (Insigne 46), Pirlo; Destro (Giovinco 82), Osvaldo (Pazzini 69).

Malta: (442) Hogg; Muscat A (Camilleri 85), Herrera, Agius A, Dimech; Borg, Briffa, Schembri, Sciberras; Bogdanovic (Cohen 69), Mifsud.
Referee: Antti Munukka.

Friday, 12 October 2012
Armenia (1) 1 *(Mkhitaryan 27)*
Italy (1) 3 *(Pirlo 11 (pen), De Rossi 64, Osvaldo 81)* 32,320
Armenia: (442) Berezovsky; Aleksanyan, Mkoyan, Arzumanyan, Yedigaryan Artak; Ozbiliz, Mkrtchyan, Yedigaryan Artur (Manucharyan 65), Mkhitaryan; Manoyan (Sarkisov 76), Movsisyan.
Italy: (442) Buffon; Maggio, Barzagli, Bonucci, Criscito; De Rossi, Pirlo (Giaccherini 74), Marchisio, Montolivo (Candreva 89); Giovinco (El Shaarawy 61), Osvaldo.
Referee: Marijo Strahonja.

Bulgaria (1) 1 *(Rangelov 7)*
Denmark (1) 1 *(Bendtner 40)* 30,300
Bulgaria: (442) Mihailov; Bodurov, Minev I, Bandalovski[■], Ivanov; Manolev, Milanov G, Gadzhev, Iliev (Milanov I 35); Rangelov (Tonev 61), Popov (Bojinov 85).
Denmark: (442) Andersen; Kristensen (Cornelius 36), Kjaer, Agger, Wass (Mtiglia 54); Jacobsen, Kvist Jorgensen, Eriksen (Poulsen J 90), Krohn-Delhi; Rommedahl, Bendtner.
Referee: Tony Chapron.

Czech Republic (1) 3 *(Gebre Selassie 34, Pekhart 51, Rezek 67)*
Malta (1) 1 *(Briffa 38)* 10,103
Czech Republic: (442) Cech; Gebre Selassie, Sivok, Kadlec M, Limbersky; Rajtoral (Petrzela 61), Hubschman, Plasil, Jiracek (Darida 73); Rezek, Pekhart (Lafata 82).
Malta: (451) Hogg; Borg, Dimech, Agius A, Muscat A; Herrera, Sciberras, Bajada (Azzopardi 88), Briffa, Schembri (Fenech P 87); Mifsud.
Referee: Anar Salmanov.

Tuesday, 16 October 2012
Czech Republic (0) 0
Bulgaria (0) 0 16,161
Czech Republic: (442) Cech; Gebre Selassie, Sivok, Limbersky; Rajtoral (Darida 58), Rezek (Lafata 80), Plasil, Hubschman; Jiracek, Pekhart (Vydra 58).
Bulgaria: (442) Mihailov; Zanev (Milanov I 41), Bodurov, Minev I, Ivanov; Manolev, Milanov G, Gadzhev (Bojinov 61), Dyakov; Iliev, Popov (Tonev 75).
Referee: Vladislav Bezborodov.

Italy (2) 3 *(Montolivo 33, De Rossi 37, Balotelli 54)*
Denmark (1) 1 *(Kvist Jorgensen 45)* 37,370
Italy: (4312) De Sanctis; Balzaretti, Barzagli, Chiellini, Abate; De Rossi, Pirlo, Marchisio (Candreva 74); Montolivo (Giaccherini 85); Osvaldo[■], Balotelli (Destro 89).
Denmark: (4231) Andersen; Kjaer, Agger, Jacobsen, Silberbauer (Lorentzen 72); Kvist Jorgensen (Kahlenberg 59), Stokholm; Eriksen, Krohn-Delhi (Poulsen J 83), Rommedahl; Bendtner.
Referee: Damir Skomina.

Friday, 22 March 2013
Bulgaria (2) 6 *(Tonev 6, 38, 68, Popov 47, Gargorov 55, Ivanov 78)*
Malta (0) 0 0
Bulgaria: (442) Mihailov; Bodurov, Minev V, Ivanov, Minev I (Dimitrov 63); Milanov G, Gadzhev (Sarmov 70), Iliev, Gargorov (Bojinov 56); Popov, Tonev.
Malta: (442) Hogg; Caruana, Herrera, Agius A (Camilleri 56), Dimech; Briffa, Failla, Fenech P (Muscat R 70); Mifsud; Schembri, Fenech R.
Referee: Eitan Shmuelevitz.

Czech Republic (0) 0
Denmark (0) 3 *(Cornelius 57, Kjaer 67, Zimling 82)* 12,120
Czech Republic: (4231) Cech; Gebre Selassie, Sivok, Kadlec M, Limbersky; Darida, Plasil (Kozak 74); Jiracek (Rosicky 61), Krejci (Dockal 64), Vydra; Lafata.
Denmark: (4231) Andersen; Jacobsen, Kjaer, Agger, Poulsen S; Zimling, Stokholm; Eriksen, Krohn-Delhi, Jorgensen (Rommedahl 66); Cornelius (Makienok 85).
Referee: Manuel Ricardo Neves.

Tuesday, 26 March 2013
Armenia (0) 0
Czech Republic (0) 3 *(Vydra 47, 81, Kolar 90)*   15,150
Armenia: (433) Berezovsky; Arzumanyan, Voskanyan, Hovhannisyan, Aleksanyan; Pizzelli, Mkhitaryan, Muradyan (Manoyan 78); Ghazaryan (Sarkisov 60), Manucharyan (Ozbiliz 50), Movsisyan.
Czech Republic: (433) Cech; Gebre Selassie, Kadlec M, Sivok (Suchy 43), Limbersky; Rosicky, Plasil, Hubschman; Darida (Jiracek 84), Lafata (Kolar 74), Vydra.
Referee: Pavel Balaj.

Denmark (0) 1 *(Agger 63 (pen))*
Bulgaria (0) 1 *(Manolev 52)*   22,221
Denmark: (433) Andersen; Jacobsen, Kjaer, Agger, Poulsen S; Zimling (Makienok 85), Stokholm, Eriksen; Krohn-Delhi (Schone 69), Rommedahl (Jorgensen 54), Cornelius.
Bulgaria: (442) Mihailov; Bodurov (Dimitrov 23), Minev V, Ivanov, Milanov I; Manolev (Gargorov 87), Milanov G, Gadzhev, Dyakov; Tonev, Popov (Iliev 71).
Referee: Firat Aydinus.

Malta (0) 0
Italy (2) 2 *(Balotelli 8 (pen), 45)*   18,180
Malta: (451) Haber; Caruana, Muscat A, Dimech, Herrera; Camilleri, Sciberras, Failla (Cohen 82), Briffa, Mifsud (Vella 88); Schembri.
Italy: (433) Buffon; De Sciglio, Abate, Barzagli, Bonucci; Marchisio, El Shaarawy (Cerci 75), Montolivo; Pirlo, Giaccherini (Candreva 61), Balotelli (Gilardino 86).
Referee: Serdar Gozubuyuk.

Friday, 7 June 2013
Armenia (0) 0
Malta (1) 1 *(Mifsud 7)*   9000
Armenia: (442) Berezovsky; Hovhannisyan, Arzumanyan, Voskanyan, Aleksanyan; Ozbiliz, Manoyan (Sarkisov 66), Mkrtchyan, Pizzelli; Mkhitaryan, Manucharyan (Movsisyan 46).
Malta: (433) Haber; Caruana, Sciberras (Fenech P 56), Camilleri, Dimech; Briffa (Muscat R 84), Muscat A, Failla; Herrera, Schembri, Mifsud (Vella 90).
Referee: Arnold Hunter.

Czech Republic (0) 0
Italy (0) 0   18,182
Czech Republic: (4231) Cech; Gebre Selassie, Sivok, Kadlec M, Limbersky (Suchy 20); Darida (Kadlec V 75), Hubschman; Jiracek (Kolar 86), Rosicky, Plasil; Kozak.
Italy: (4312) Buffon; Abate, Bonucci, Barzagli, Chiellini; Marchisio, Pirlo (Aquilani 77), De Rossi; Montolivo; Balotelli, El Shaarawy (Giovinco 46).
Referee: Svein Oddvar Moen.

Tuesday, 11 June 2013
Denmark (0) 0
Armenia (2) 4 *(Movsisyan 1, 59, Ozbiliz 19, Mkhitaryan 82)*   14,147
Denmark: (442) Andersen; Kjaer, Bjelland (Okore 46), Poulsen S, Jacobsen; Zimling (Pedersen 28 (Christiansen 53)), Kvist Jorgensen, Eriksen, Krohn-Delhi; Rommedahl, Cornelius.
Armenia: (442) Berezovsky; Arzumanyan, Hovhannisyan, Aleksanyan, Haroyan; Ozbiliz (Aslanyan 90), Yedigaryan Artur (Pizzelli 86), Mkhitaryan; Movsisyan (Sarkisov 84), Ghazaryan.
Referee: Aleksei Nikolaev.

Friday, 6 September 2013
Czech Republic (0) 1 *(Rosicky 70)*
Armenia (1) 2 *(Mkrtchyan 31, Ghazaryan 90)*   20,000
Czech Republic: (442) Cech; Gebre Selassie, Kadlec M, Sivok, Limbersky (Suchy 64); Husbauer, Rosicky, Plasil, Jiracek (Vanek 62); Rabusic (Kolaf 56), Kozak.
Armenia: (442) Berezovsky (Kasparov 69); Haroyan, Arzumanyan, Mkoyan, Hovhannisyan (Pizzelli 76); Mkrtchyan, Yedigaryan Artur, Ghazaryan, Ozbiliz (Hayrapetyan 28); Mkhitaryan, Movsisyan.
Referee: Antony Gautier.

Italy (1) 1 *(Gilardino 38)*
Bulgaria (0) 0   28,662
Italy: (442) Buffon; Abate (Maggio 80), Bonucci, Chiellini, Antonelli (Astori 62); De Rossi, Pirlo, Thiago Motta, Candreva; Insigne (Giaccherini 62), Gilardino.
Bulgaria: (442) Mihailov; Minev V, Bodurov, Ivanov, Minev I; Dyakov (Delev 76), Manolev (Iliev 55), Nedelev, Gadzhev; Popov, Tonev (Rangelov 61).
Referee: Carlos Velasco Carballo.

Malta (1) 1 *(Failla 38)*
Denmark (1) 2 *(Andreasen 2, Camilleri 53 (og))*   3000
Malta: (4141) Haber; Agius A, Briffa, Herrera (Cohen 89), Camilleri; Sciberras; Failla, Mintoff (Fenech R 75), Muscat R, Schembri; Mifsud (Vella 80).
Denmark: (433) Andersen; Kjaer, Agger, Boilesen, Jacobsen; Andreasen (Sloth 72), Kvist Jorgensen, Eriksen; Braithwaite (Fischer 83), Pedersen, Falk (Krohn-Delhi 46).
Referee: Anastasios Sidiropoulos.

Tuesday, 10 September 2013
Armenia (0) 0
Denmark (0) 1 *(Agger 74 (pen))*   25,000
Armenia: (442) Kasparov; Haroyan■, Mkoyan, Hayrapetyan, Hovhannisyan; Yedigaryan Artur, Mkrtchyan (Sarkisov 27 (Adamyan 45)), Mkhitaryan, Ghazaryan; Ozbiliz, Pizzelli (Manoyan 70).
Denmark: (442) Andersen; Bjelland, Agger, Boilesen, Ankersen; Kvist Jorgensen, Zimling (Sloth 45), Eriksen, Krohn-Delhi; Bille Nielsen (Makienok 83), Braithwaite (Fischer 66),
Referee: Bas Nijhuis.

Italy (0) 2 *(Chiellini 52, Balotelli 55 (pen))*
Czech Republic (1) 1 *(Kozak 19)*   35,299
Italy: (343) Buffon; Bonucci, De Rossi, Chiellini; Maggio, Pirlo, Montolivo (Thiago Motta 86), Pasqual (Ogbonna 78); Candreva, Balotelli, Giaccherini (Osvaldo 45).
Czech Republic: (4141) Cech; Gebre Selassie (Rabusic 77), Sivok, Suchy, Limbersky; Prochazka; Plasil, Darida (Vanek 55), Rosicky (Kolaf■ 37), Jiracek; Kozak.
Referee: Jonas Eriksson.

Malta (0) 1 *(Herrera 78)*
Bulgaria (1) 2 *(Haber 10 (og), Gargorov 59)*   4844
Malta: (442) Haber; Agius A, Dimech, Muscat A, Herrera; Camilleri (Caruana 82), Sciberras, Failla (Fenech R 66), Muscat R; Mifsud (Vella 76), Schembri.
Bulgaria: (442) Mihailov; Bodurov, Minev V, Ivanov, Dimitrov; Nedelev (Delev 66), Milanov G (Zlatinski 81), Gadzhev, Dyakov; Gargorov (Rangelov 61), Popov.
Referee: Alexandru Dan Tudor.

Friday, 11 October 2013
Armenia (1) 2 *(Ozbiliz 45, Movsisyan 87)*
Bulgaria (0) 1 *(Popov 61)*   10,500
Armenia: (4231) Berezovsky; Hovhannisyan, Arzumanyan (Aleksanyan 12), Mkoyan, Hayrapetyan; Mkhitaryan, Mkrtchyan; Ozbiliz (Pizzelli 54), Sarkisov (Manoyan 90), Ghazaryan; Movsisyan.
Bulgaria: (4231) Stoyanov; Minev I, Ivanov, Bodurov■, Zanev; Gadzhev, Dyakov■; Manolev (Tonev 59), Milanov G (Hristov 76), Popov; Gargorov (Zlatinski 69).
Referee: Felix Brych.

Denmark (1) 2 *(Bendtner 45, 78)*
Italy (1) 2 *(Osvaldo 27, Aquilani 90)*   35,000
Denmark: (442) Andersen; Bjelland, Agger, Boilesen, Jacobsen; Zimling (Andreasen 82), Kvist Jorgensen, Eriksen, Krohn-Delhi; Braithwaite (Larsen 45), Bendtner (Makienok 83).
Italy: (442) Buffon; De Silvestri, Chiellini, Balzaretti, Ranocchia; Thiago Motta, Marchisio (Aquilani 68), Candreva, Montolivo (Gilardino 81); Diamanti (Cerci 76), Osvaldo.
Referee: Stephane Lannoy.

Malta (0) 1 *(Mifsud 47)*
Czech Republic (2) 4 *(Muscat R 3 (og), Lafata 33,*
Kadlec V 51, Pekhart 90) 3000
Malta: (4141) Haber; Muscat A, Dimech, Caruana (Agius A 57), Failla (Fenech R 87); Camilleri (Fenech P 80); Mintoff, Cohen, Muscat R, Briffa; Mifsud.
Czech Republic: (4141) Cech; Kadlec M, Sivok, Suchy, Rajtoral; Hubschman; Dockal, Plasil, Lafata (Jiracek 85), Husbauer; Kadlec V (Pekhart 73 (Vanek 90)).
Referee: Matej Jug.

Tuesday, 15 October 2013
Bulgaria (0) 0
Czech Republic (0) 1 *(Dockal 51)* 25,000
Bulgaria: (442) Stoyanov; Zanev■, Minev I, Ivanov, Milanov I; Manolev, Milanov G (Rangelov 45), Gadzhev, Gargorov (Marquinhos 56); Popov, Hristov (Slavchev 72).
Czech Republic: (442) Cech; Kadlec M, Suchy, Mazuch, Rajtoral; Dockal (Vanek 84), Plasil, Hubschman, Jiracek (Husbauer 90); Kozak, Kadlec V (Lafata 90).
Referee: Viktor Kassai.

Denmark (4) 6 *(Rasmussen 8, 74, Agger 11 (pen), 39 (pen),*
Bjelland 28, Bille Nielsen 84)
Malta (0) 0 11,478
Denmark: (442) Schmeichel; Ankersen, Bjelland, Agger, Delaney; Sloth (Andreasen 64), Kvist Jorgensen, Eriksen (Kuski 53), Larsen; Krohn-Delhi, Rasmussen (Bille Nielsen 75).
Malta: (442) Haber; Herrera (Fenech R 82), Muscat A, Agius A, Briffa; Camilleri, Failla, Mintoff, Muscat R; Mifsud, Schembri.
Referee: Alexsander Stavrev.

Italy (1) 2 *(Florenzi 25, Balotelli 76)*
Armenia (1) 2 *(Movsisyan 5, Mkhitaryan 70)* 22,000
Italy: (442) Marchetti; Abate, Astori, Bonucci, Pasqual; Florenzi (Candreva 60), Montolivo, Aquilani (Rossi 73), Pirlo; Insigne, Osvaldo (Balotelli 54).
Armenia: (442) Berezovsky; Haroyan, Arzumanyan, Mkoyan, Hayrapetyan (Hovhannisyan 62); Mkrtchyan, Ghazaryan, Mkhitaryan, Yedigaryan Artur (Pizzelli 90); Ozbiliz (Sarkisov 78), Movsisyan.
Referee: Michael Oliver.

Group B Table	P	W	D	L	F	A	GD	Pts
Italy	10	6	4	0	19	9	10	22
Denmark	10	4	4	2	17	12	5	16
Czech Republic	10	4	3	3	13	9	4	15
Bulgaria	10	3	4	3	14	9	5	13
Armenia	10	4	1	5	12	13	–1	13
Malta	10	1	0	9	5	28	–23	3

GROUP C

Friday, 7 September 2012
Germany (1) 3 *(Gotze 28, Ozil 54, 71)*
Faroe Islands (0) 0 32,327
Germany: (4141) Neuer; Lahm, Mertesacker, Hummels, Badstuber; Khedira; Muller (Schurrle 68), Ozil, Gotze (Draxler 87), Reus; Klose (Podolski 75).
Faroe Islands: (4231) Nielsen; Naes, Faeroe, Baldvinsson, Justinussen; Benjaminsen, Hansson, Samuelsen S (Elttor 64), Holst, Udsen (Olsen S 46); Edmundsson (Olsen K 84).
Referee: Bobby Madden.

Kazakhstan (1) 1 *(Nurdauletov 38)*
Rep of Ireland (0) 2 *(Keane 89 (pen), Doyle 90)* 9500
Kazakhstan: (442) Sidelnikov; Kirov, Kislitsyn, Mukhtarov, Nurdauletov; Konysbayev (Gridin 84), Bogdanov, Ostapenko, Schmidtgal; Nusrbayev (Dzholchiyev 68), Rozhkov.
Rep of Ireland: (442) Westwood; O'Shea, St Ledger, O'Dea, Ward; McGeady, Whelan, McCarthy, Cox (Doyle 57); Keane, Walters (Long 70).
Referee: Ionut Avram.

Tuesday, 11 September 2012
Austria (0) 1 *(Junuzovic 57)*
Germany (1) 2 *(Reus 44, Ozil 52 (pen))* 50,500
Austria: (451) Almer; Garics, Prodl, Pogatetz, Fuchs; Ivanschitz (Jantscher 75), Baumgartlinger (Janko 85), Kavlak, Junuzovic, Harnik (Burgstaller 55); Arnautovic.
Germany: (4141) Neuer; Lahm, Schmelzer, Hummels, Badstuber; Khedira; Muller, Kroos, Ozil, Reus (Gotze 46); Klose (Podolski 75).
Referee: Bjorn Kuipers.

Sweden (1) 2 *(Elm 38, Berg 90)*
Kazakhstan (0) 0 20,204
Sweden: (433) Isaksson; Lustig, Olsson J, Granqvist, Safari; Larsson, Elm (Svensson 64), Wernbloom; Elmander (Berg 85), Ibrahimovic, Toivonen (Bajrami 56).
Kazakhstan: (442) Sidelnikov; Kirov, Rozhkov, Nurdauletov, Kislitsyn; Nusrbayev (Gridin 68), Schmidtgal, Shabalin (Islamkhan 84), Dmitrenko; Ostapenko (Shakmetov 46), Bogdanov.
Referee: Sergiy Boiko.

Friday, 12 October 2012
Faroe Islands (0) 1 *(Baldvinsson 57)*
Sweden (0) 2 *(Kacaniklic 65, Ibrahimovic 75)* 5100
Faroe Islands: (4411) Nielsen; Naes, Justinussen, Faeroe, Baldvinsson; Hansson (Olsen S 83), Benjaminsen, Holst (Hansen 71), Samuelsen S; Udsen (Elttor 86); Edmundsson.
Sweden: (442) Isaksson; Lustig, Olsson J, Granqvist, Olsson M; Larsson, Kallstrom (Svensson 62), Wernbloom, Wilhelmsson (Kacaniklic 62); Ibrahimovic, Ranegie (Berg 77).
Referee: Anastasios Sidiropoulos.

Kazakhstan (0) 0
Austria (0) 0 10,100
Kazakhstan: (442) Sidelnikov; Kirov, Nurdauletov, Dmitrenko, Rozhkov; Korobkin, Konysbayev (Gridin 90), Khairullin M (Mukhtarov 90), Bogdanov; Ostapenko, Nusrbayev (Nurgaliev 86).
Austria: (442) Almer; Garics, Pogatetz, Fuchs, Prodl; Ivanschitz (Jantscher 73), Junuzovic, Baumgartlinger (Janko 63), Kavlak; Arnautovic, Harnik (Weimann 84).
Referee: Tamas Bognar.

Rep of Ireland (0) 1 *(Keogh A 90)*
Germany (2) 6 *(Reus 32, 40, Ozil 55 (pen), Klose 58,*
Kroos 61, 83) 51,517
Rep of Ireland: (442) Westwood; Coleman, O'Shea, O'Dea, Ward; McGeady (Keogh A 69), McCarthy, Andrews, Fahey (Long 51); Cox (Brady 84), Walters.
Germany: (4231) Neuer; Boateng, Mertesacker, Badstuber; Schmelzer; Khedira (Kroos 46), Schweinsteiger; Ozil, Muller, Reus (Podolski 66); Klose (Schurrle 72).
Referee: Nicola Rizzoli.

Tuesday, 16 October 2012
Austria (1) 4 *(Janko 23, 64, Alaba 71, Harnik 90)*
Kazakhstan (0) 0 40,400
Austria: (442) Almer; Pogatetz, Prodl (Dragovic 59), Fuchs, Harnik; Klein, Kavlak, Alaba (Leitgeb 81), Junuzovic; Arnautovic, Janko (Jantscher 81).
Kazakhstan: (442) Sidelnikov; Kirov, Mukhtarov, Nurdauletov, Dmitrenko (Gorman 74); Korobkin, Konysbayev, Nurgaliev (Khairullin M 83), Shakmetov (Islamkhan 70); Bogdanov, Gridin.
Referee: Jakob Kehlet.

Faroe Islands (0) 1 *(Hansen 68)*
Rep of Ireland (0) 4 *(Wilson 46, Walters 53,*
Justinussen 73 (og), O'Dea 88) 4400
Faroe Islands: (442) Nielsen; Naes, Justinussen, Faeroe (Jacobsen 61), Baldvinsson; Hansson, Benjaminsen, Samuelsen S, Udsen (Hansen 61); Holst, Edmundsson (Elttor 79).
Rep of Ireland: (442) Westwood; Coleman, O'Shea, O'Dea, Wilson; Brady (Cox 46), Andrews (Meyler 90), McCarthy, McGeady; Keane (Long 80), Walters.
Referee: Lorenc Jemini.

Germany (3) 4 *(Klose 8, 15, Mertesacker 39, Ozil 55)*
Sweden (0) 4 *(Ibrahimovic 62, Lustig 64, Elmander 76, Elm 90)*   70,700
Germany: (451) Neuer; Boateng, Mertesacker, Badstuber, Lahm; Schweinsteiger, Kroos, Muller (Gotze 67), Ozil, Reus (Podolski 87); Klose.
Sweden: (442) Isaksson; Lustig, Granqvist, Olsson J, Safari; Holmen (Kacaniklic 46), Wernbloom (Kallstrom 47), Larsson (Sana 80), Ibrahimovic; Elm, Elmander.
Referee: Pedro Proenca.

Friday, 22 March 2013

Austria (3) 6 *(Hosiner 8, 20, Ivanschitz 28, Junuzovic 77, Alaba 78, Garics 82)*
Faroe Islands (0) 0   24,242
Austria: (442) Lindner; Garics, Dragovic, Pogatetz, Fuchs (Suttner 70); Ivanschitz (Weimann 61), Alaba, Junuzovic, Kavlak (Leitgeb 55); Arnautovic, Hosiner.
Faroe Islands: (442) Nielsen; Naes, Justinussen, Faeroe, Baldvinsson; Hansson, Benjaminsen, Elttor (Gregersen 86), Holst; Samuelsen S (Jacobsen 70), Edmundsson (Hansen 78).
Referee: Oleksandr Derdo.

Kazakhstan (0) 0
Germany (2) 3 *(Muller 20, 74, Gotze 22)*   28,280
Kazakhstan: (442) Sidelnikov; Kirov, Logvinenko, Gorman, Nurdauletov; Dmitrenko, Khairullin M (Konysbayev 65), Baizhanov (Korobkin 36), Schmidtgal; Dzholchiev, Ostapenko (Khairullin K 84).
Germany: (442) Neuer; Schmelzer, Howedes, Lahm, Mertesacker; Khedira (Gundogan 82), Schweinsteiger, Ozil, Draxler (Podolski 19); Muller (Schurrle 82), Gotze.
Referee: Anastassios Kakos

Sweden (0) 0
Rep of Ireland (0) 0   49,494
Sweden: (4231) Isaksson; Lustig (Antonsson 46), Olsson J, Granqvist, Safari; Elm, Larsson (Durmaz 87); Kallstrom, Ibrahimovic, Hysen (Toivonen 72); Kacaniklic.
Rep of Ireland: (442) Forde; Coleman, Clark, O'Shea, Wilson; McCarthy, McClean (Keogh A 83), Green, Walters; Keane (Hoolahan 76), Long (Sammon 87).
Referee: Alberto Undiano Mallenco.

Tuesday, 26 March 2013

Germany (3) 4 *(Reus 23, 90, Gotze 28, Gundogan 31)*
Kazakhstan (0) 1 *(Schmidtgal 47)*   40,400
Germany: (4231) Neuer; Schmelzer, Boateng, Mertesacker, Lahm; Khedira, Ozil; Muller, Gundogan, Reus (Jansen 90); Gotze.
Kazakhstan: (442) Sidelnikov; Kirov, Korobkin, Mukhtarov, Engel; Gorman, Nurdauletov (Dzholchiev 47), Dmitrenko, Konysbayev (Shomko 78); Schmidtgal, Ostapenko (Kukeev 63).
Referee: Halis Ozkahya.

Rep of Ireland (2) 2 *(Walters 25 (pen), 45)*
Austria (1) 2 *(Harnik 11, Alaba 90)*   50,500
Rep of Ireland: (442) Forde; Coleman, O'Shea, Clark (St Ledger 72); Wilson; Walters, Whelan, McCarthy, McClean; Sammon, Long (Green 83).
Austria: (442) Lindner; Garics, Dragovic, Pogatetz, Fuchs; Kavlak (Weimann 69), Alaba, Harnik, Junuzovic (Baumgartlinger 25); Arnautovic, Hosiner (Janko 62).
Referee: Marijo Strahonja.

Friday, 7 June 2013

Austria (2) 2 *(Alaba 26 (pen), Janko 32)*
Sweden (0) 1 *(Elmander 82)*   48,485
Austria: (433) Almer; Dragovic, Pogatetz (Prodl 29), Fuchs, Garics; Alaba, Junuzovic (Schiemer 75), Baumgartlinger; Arnautovic, Harnik, Janko (Weimann 46).
Sweden: (442) Isaksson; Lustig, Olsson J, Granqvist, Wendt; Elm (Svensson 60), Larsson, Kallstrom (Toivonen 70), Kacaniklic; Ibrahimovic, Elmander (Durmaz 84).
Referee: Gianluca Rocchi.

Rep of Ireland (1) 3 *(Keane 5, 55, 81)*
Faroe Islands (0) 0   19,190
Rep of Ireland: (442) Forde; Coleman, O'Shea, St. Ledger, Wilson (Kelly 82); McGeady (McClean 76), Whelan, Hoolahan, Walters (Sammon 73); Keane, Cox.
Faroe Islands: (4231) Nielsen; Frederiksberg, Gregersen, Baldvinsson, Jonsson; Olsen S, Vatnsdal; Samuelsen S, Holst (Samuelsen H 84), Justinussen; Klettskaro (Edmundsson 64).
Referee: Mattias Gestranius.

Tuesday, 11 June 2013

Sweden (1) 2 *(Ibrahimovic 35, 82 (pen))*
Faroe Islands (0) 0   32,328
Sweden: (442) Hansson; Lustig, Granqvist, Nilsson P, Bengtsson P; Larsson (Durmaz 63), Kallstrom (Svensson 57), Ekdal, Kacaniklic; Toivonen (Olsson J 83), Ibrahimovic.
Faroe Islands: (442) Nielsen; Naes, Davidsen V, Gregersen, Davidsen J; Edmundsson, Justinussen, Hansson (Klettskaro 86), Benjaminsen; Holst (Samuelsen S 59), Olsen (Vatnsdal 40).
Referee: Nikolay Yordanov.

Friday, 6 September 2013

Germany (1) 3 *(Klose 33, Kroos 51, Muller 88)*
Austria (0) 0   68,000
Germany: (451) Neuer; Lahm, Boateng, Mertesacker, Schmelzer (Howedes 46); Kroos, Khedira, Muller, Ozil, Reus (Draxler 90); Klose (Bender S 82).
Austria: (4231) Almer; Garics (Klein 78), Dragovic, Pogatetz, Fuchs; Alaba, Kavlak; Ivanschitz (Burgstaller 67), Harnik, Arnautovic (Sabitzer 67); Weimann.
Referee: Milorad Mazic.

Kazakhstan (0) 2 *(Zhumaskaliyev 50 (pen), Finonchenko 63)*
Faroe Islands (1) 1 *(Benjaminsen 23)*   7000
Kazakhstan: (442) Sidelnikov; Logvinenko, Kislitsyn (Ostapenko 84), Nurdauletov, Dmitrenko; Korobkin, Zhumaskaliyev (Khairullin M 90), Shomko, Bogdanov; Khizhnichenko, Shchetkin (Finonchenko 46).
Faroe Islands: (442) Nielsen; Naes, Davidsen V, Baldvinsson, Davidsen J; Olsen S, Benjaminsen, Hansson (Vatnsdal 80), Holst; Edmundsson (Klettskard 80), Mouritsen.
Referee: Johnny Casanova.

Rep of Ireland (1) 1 *(Keane 21)*
Sweden (1) 2 *(Elmander 33, Svensson 57)*   49,500
Rep of Ireland: (442) Forde; Coleman, O'Shea, Dunne, Wilson; Whelan, McCarthy, Long, Keane; McClean (Pilkington 74), Walters (Cox 68).
Sweden: (442) Isaksson; Lustig (Johansson 46), Nilsson P, Olsson M, Antonsson; Ekdal, Larsson, Svensson (Wernbloom 68), Kacaniklic; Ibrahimovic, Elmander (Olsson J 90).
Referee: Damir Skomina.

Tuesday, 10 September 2013

Austria (0) 1 *(Alaba 84)*
Rep of Ireland (0) 0   48,500
Austria: (442) Almer; Garics, Dragovic, Fuchs, Alaba; Weimann (Janko 73), Harnik, Baumgartlinger, Prodl; Burgstaller (Arnautovic 60), Kavlak (Leitgeb 45).
Rep of Ireland: (442) Forde; Coleman, Dunne, O'Shea (Clark 49), Wilson; Walters, Green, McCarthy, Pilkington (McClean 73); Keane, Long (Sammon 81).
Referee: Olegario Benquerenca.

Faroe Islands (0) 0
Germany (1) 3 *(Mertesacker 23, Ozil 74 (pen), Muller 84)*   4100
Faroe Islands: (4141) Nielsen; Davidsen J, Gregersen, Baldvinsson, Davidsen V; Benjaminsen, Udsen (Mouritsen 67), Holst (Hansson 76), Olsen S, Justinussen; Edmundsson (Klettskard 68).
Germany: (433) Neuer; Lahm, Boateng, Mertesacker, Schmelzer; Kroos, Khedira, Ozil; Muller (Sam 85), Klose (Kruse 78), Draxler (Schurrle 75).
Referee: Gediminas Mazeika.

Kazakhstan (0) 0
Sweden (1) 1 *(Ibrahimovic 1)*   20,000
Kazakhstan: (442) Sidelnikov; Nurdauletov, Gorman, Kislitsyn, Dmitrenko; Shomko, Baizhanov (Khairullin M 77), Korobkin, Bogdanov; Khizhnichenko, Finonchenko.
Sweden: (442) Isaksson; Johansson, Antonsson, Nilsson P, Olsson M; Larsson (Durmaz 69), Svensson (Kallstrom 87), Ekdal, Kacaniklic; Ibrahimovic, Elmander (Hysen 80).
Referee: Miroslav Zelinka.

Friday, 11 October 2013
Faroe Islands (1) 1 *(Hansson 42)*
Kazakhstan (0) 1 *(Finonchenko 55)*   1800
Faroe Islands: (442) Nielsen; Davidsen V, Naes, Justinussen, Davidsen J; Baldvinsson, Benjaminsen, Hansson, Holst; Udsen (Olsen S 77), Edmundsson (Klettskard 77).
Kazakhstan: (442) Sidelnikov; Gorman, Engel, Kislitsyn, Muldarov (Logvinenko 80); Zhumaskaliyev (Baizhanov 71), Shomko, Bogdanov, Korobkin; Finonchenko (Chshyotkin 90), Khizhnichenko.
Referee: Dumitri Muntean.

Germany (1) 3 *(Khedira 12, Schurrle 58, Ozil 90)*
Rep of Ireland (0) 0   46,237
Germany: (4231) Neuer; Jansen, Mertesacker, Boateng, Lahm; Khedira (Kruse 82), Schweinsteiger; Kroos, Ozil, Schurrle (Gotze 86); Muller (Sam 88).
Rep of Ireland: (4231) Forde; Coleman, Clark, Delaney, Kelly; Gibson, Wilson; Whelan, McCarthy, Doyle; Stokes.
Referee: Serge Gumienny.

Sweden (0) 2 *(Olsson M 56, Ibrahimovic 86)*
Austria (1) 1 *(Harnik 29)*   49,416
Sweden: (442) Isaksson; Lustig (Durmaz 65), Nilsson P, Antonsson, Olsson M; Larsson, Elm (Kallstrom 72), Svensson (Wernbloom 80), Kacaniklic; Elmander, Ibrahimovic.
Austria: (433) Almer; Garics, Dragovic, Pogatetz, Fuchs; Prodl, Alaba, Junuzovic (Leitgeb 63); Arnautovic[■], Janko (Ivanschitz 79), Harnik (Weimann 73).
Referee: Cuneyt Cakir.

Tuesday, 15 October 2013
Faroe Islands (0) 0
Austria (1) 3 *(Ivanschitz 16, Prodl 64, Alaba 67 (pen))*
        3100
Faroe Islands: (442) Nielsen; Justinussen, Naes, Davidsen V, Davidsen J; Baldvinsson, Olsen S (Edmundsson 82), Benjaminsen, Hansson; Holst (Mouritsen 71), Klettskard (Olsen K 74).
Austria: (442) Lindner; Prodl (Ortlechner 80), Klein, Dragovic, Pogatetz; Fuch (Suttner 72), Ivanschitz, Alaba, Kavlak; Harnik (Sabitzer 73), Hosiner.
Referee: Liran Liany.

Rep of Ireland (2) 3 *(Keane 17 (pen), O'Shea 27, Finonchenko 78 (og))*
Kazakhstan (1) 1 *(Shomko 13)*   20,000
Rep of Ireland: (442) Forde; Wilson, O'Shea, Dunne, Coleman; Reid (McGeady 75), McCarthy, Gibson (Whelan 37), Keane; Doyle, Stokes (Hoolahan 87).
Kazakhstan: (442) Sidelnikov; Korobkin, Dmitrenko, Kislitsyn (Finonchenko 32), Gorman; Karpovich (Shabalin 84), Baizhanov, Engel, Shomko; Khizhnichenko, Shchetkin (Yurin 61).
Referee: Vadim Direktorenko.

Sweden (2) 3 *(Hysen 6, 69, Kacaniklic 42)*
Germany (1) 5 *(Ozil 45, Gotze 53, Schurrle 57, 66, 76)*
        49,251
Sweden: (442) Wiland; Antonsson, Nilsson P, Olsson M, Bengtsson; Elm (Svensson 58), Larsson, Kallstrom, Kacaniklic (Durmaz 72); Hysen, Toivonen (Wernbloom 83).
Germany: (442) Neuer; Lahm, Boateng, Hummels, Jansen; Kroos, Schweinsteiger, Ozil (Draxler 82), Schurrle; Muller (Gotze 47), Kruse (Howedes 75).
Referee: William Collum.

Group C Table

	P	W	D	L	F	A	GD	Pts
Germany	10	9	1	0	36	10	26	28
Sweden	10	6	2	2	19	14	5	20
Austria	10	5	2	3	20	10	10	17
Republic of Ireland	10	4	2	4	16	17	–1	14
Kazakhstan	10	1	2	7	6	21	–15	5
Faroe Islands	10	0	1	9	4	29	–25	1

GROUP D

Friday, 7 September 2012
Andorra (0) 0
Hungary (2) 5 *(Juhasz 12, Gera 33 (pen), Szalai 54, Priskin 68, Koman 82)*   600
Andorra: (4231) Gomez J; Garcia E, Lima, Rodrigues, Vales[■]; Pujol, Clemente (Lorenzo 72); Vieira, Silva, Garcia M (Maneiro 80); Moreno (Gomez S 69).
Hungary: (442) Bogdan; Vanczak, Juhasz, Liptak, Laczko; Korcsmar, Koman, Hajnal (Elek 75), Dzsudzsak; Gera (Priskin 46), Szalai (Nemeth 82).
Referee: Emer Aleckovic.

Estonia (0) 0
Romania (0) 2 *(Torje 55, Marica 75)*   7936
Estonia: (442) Pareiko; Jaager, Morozov, Klavan, Teniste; Puri (Kink 77), Dmitrijev, Vunk (Voskoboinikov 61), Vassiljev; Ojamaa (Lindpere 46), Oper.
Romania: (442) Lobont; Chiriches, Goian (Gaman 90), Matel, Rat; Bourceanu, Grozav, Lazar (Pintilii 66), Tanase; Torje, Marica (Niculae 87).
Referee: Milorad Mazic.

Netherlands (1) 2 *(van Persie 16, Narsingh 90)*
Turkey (0) 0   53,530
Netherlands: (442) Krul; Janmaat (Van Rhijn 46), Heitinga (Vlaar 86), Martins Indi, Willems; Clasie (Fer 50), Strootman, Sneijder, Narsingh; van Persie, Robben.
Turkey: (442) Zengin; Ali Kaldirim, Kaya, Toprak, Emre (Sahin 60); Altintop, Torun (Erdinc 81), Turan, Topal; Bulut, Sararer (Yilmaz 70).
Referee: Carlos Velasco Carballo.

Tuesday, 11 September 2012
Hungary (1) 1 *(Dzsudzsak 8 (pen))*
Netherlands (2) 4 *(Lens 3, Martins Indi 19, Lens 53, Huntelaar 74)*   22,220
Hungary: (4231) Bogdan; Liptak, Vanczak, Juhasz, Korcsmar; Varga, Elek (Gyurcso 61); Dzsudzsak, Gera (Nemeth 80), Koman (Hajnal 46); Priskin.
Netherlands: (433) Stekelenburg; Van Rhijn, Vlaar, Martins Indi (Mathijsen 64), Willems; Clasie, Strootman (Maher 78), Sneijder; Narsingh, van Persie (Huntelaar 46), Lens.
Referee: Pedro Proenca.

Romania (2) 4 *(Torje 29, Lazar 44, Gaman 90, Maxim 90)*
Andorra (0) 0   25,250
Romania: (451) Lobont (Tatarusanu 46); Matel, Rat, Chiriches, Gaman; Bourceanu, Grozav, Lazar, Tanase (Maxim 80), Torje; Marica (Rusescu 54).
Andorra: (334) Gomez J; Garcia E, Lima, Rodrigues; Pujol (Peppe 79), Clemente (Moreno 86), Ayala; Gomez S (Maneiro 70), Lorenzo, Vieira, Garcia M.
Referee: Pavle Radovanovic.

Turkey (1) 3 *(Emre 44, Bulut 60, Inan 75)*
Estonia (0) 0   48,485
Turkey: (433) Zengin; Ali Kaldirim, Kaya, Gonul, Toprak; Turan, Emre (Sahin 82), Topal; Yilmaz, Bulut (Inan 68), Sararer (Torun 68).
Estonia: (532) Pareiko; Rahn, Kruglov, Klavan, Jaager[■], Teniste; Lindpere (Puri 56), Vunk, Vassiljev; Oper (Purje 56), Kink (Saag 77).
Referee: Marcin Borski.

Friday, 12 October 2012
Estonia (0) 0
Hungary (0) 1 *(Hajnal 46)*   3500
Estonia: (442) Pareiko; Sisov, Rahn, Morozov, Kruglov; Puri (Mosnikov 69), Lindpere, Vassiljev, Oper; Kink (Vunk 86), Ojamaa (Purje 52).
Hungary: (442) Bogdan; Korcsmar (Elek 61), Varga, Kadar, Juhasz; Meszaros, Dzsudzsak, Gera (Szabics 79), Koltai (Gyurcso 84); Hajnal, Szalai.
Referee: Liran Liany.

Netherlands (2) 3 *(Van der Vaart 7, Huntelaar 15, Schaken 50)*
Andorra (0) 0   38,380
Netherlands: (442) Stekelenburg; Janmaat, Heitinga, Vlaar, Martins Indi; De Jong, Strootman (Emanuelson 74), Van der Vaart (Afellay 70), Schaken; Huntelaar, Lens (Kuyt 70).
Andorra: (442) Gomez J; Rodrigues (San Nicolas 52), Lima, Vieira, Pujol; Moreira (Bernaus 82), Ayala, Vales, Gomez S (Moreno 74); Lorenzo, Garcia M.
Referee: Aliaksei Kulbakou.

Turkey (0) 0
Romania (1) 1 *(Grozav 45)*   51,510
Turkey: (4231) Demirel; Gonul, Kaya, Toprak, Ali Kaldirim; Emre (Sahin 81), Topal; Altintop (Erdinc 62), Turan, Sararer (Colak 68); Bulut.
Romania: (442) Tatarusanu; Tamas, Chiriches, Goian, Rat; Bourceanu, Pintilii, Torje, Grozav (Cocis 49); Stancu (Mutu 82), Marica (Chipciu 79).
Referee: Howard Webb.

Tuesday, 16 October 2012
Andorra (0) 0
Estonia (0) 1 *(Oper 57)*   216
Andorra: (442) Gomez; San Nicolas, Lima, Pujol, Vieira; Vales, Moreira (Clemente 69), Ayala (Riera 77), Lorenzo; Garcia M, Silva (Garcia E 80).
Estonia: (442) Pareiko; Sisov, Rahn, Kruglov, Klavan; Lindpere (Puri 69), Vassiljev, Purje, Neemelo (Vunk 46); Oper, Kink (Ojamaa 82).
Referee: Dimitar Meckarovski.

Hungary (1) 3 *(Koman 31, Szalai 50, Gera 58 (pen))*
Turkey (1) 1 *(Erdinc 22)*   26,260
Hungary: (442) Bogdan; Vanczak, Kadar, Elek (Patkai 46), Varga; Szalai, Gera, Koman (Koltai 73), Meszaros; Hajnal (Pinter 77), Korcsmar.
Turkey: (442) Demirel; Korkmaz, Ali Kaldirim, Emre, Altintop; Ekici (Sararer 64), Sahin, Torun (Yilmaz 46); Erdinc; Erkin (Bulut 74), Toprak.
Referee: Daniele Orsato.

Romania (1) 1 *(Marica 40)*
Netherlands (3) 4 *(Lens 10, Martins Indi 29, Van der Vaart 45 (pen), van Persie 86)*   53,533
Romania: (4231) Tatarusanu; Rat, Goian, Chiriches, Tamas; Bourceanu (Lazar 61), Torje (Popa 66); Pintilii, Marica, Grozav (Mutu 74); Stancu.
Netherlands: (4231) Stekelenburg; Van Rhijn, Heitinga, Vlaar, Martins Indi; De Jong, Strootman; Van der Vaart (Afellay 76), van Persie, Narsingh; Lens (Elia 89).
Referee: Craig Thomson.

Friday, 22 March 2013
Andorra (0) 0
Turkey (2) 2 *(Inan 30, Yilmaz 45)*   700
Andorra: (4231) Gomez J; Lima, San Nicolas, Martinez (Clemente 69), Vieira; Vales, Peppe (Garcia E 82); Moreira, Ayala (Andorra 77), Gomez S; Garcia M.
Turkey: (4132) Kivrak; Irtegun, Ali Kaldirim, Kaya, Gonul; Inan; Sahin (Frei 90), Turan, Bulut (Sahan 81); Yilmaz, Sararer (Potuk 57).
Referee: Nerijus Dunauskas.

Netherlands (0) 3 *(Van der Vaart 47, van Persie 72, Schaken 84)*
Estonia (0) 0   49,490
Netherlands: (442) Vermeer; Janmaat, De Vrij, Martins Indi, Blind; de Guzman (Clasie 85), Strootman, Sneijder (Van der Vaart 36), van Persie; Lens (Schaken 73), Robben.
Estonia: (442) Pareiko; Kruglov (Kink 62), Jaager, Morozov, Klavan; Teniste, Puri, Vassiljev, Vunk; Ojamaa (Lindpere 77), Oper (Zenjov 46).
Referee: Vitaliy Meshkov.

Hungary (1) 2 *(Vanczak 16, Dzsudzsak 71 (pen))*
Romania (0) 2 *(Mutu 68 (pen), Chipciu 90)*   400
Hungary: (442) Kiraly; Meszaros, Vanczak, Kadar, Korcsmar; Dzsudzsak (Halmosi 90), Koman, Pinter, Hajnal (Kovacs 80); Szabics (Varga 58), Szalai.

Romania: (442) Tatarusanu; Tamas, Goian, Chiriches, Radu; Pintilii (Chipciu 86), Torje (Maxim 66), Bourceanu, Mutu; Grozav (Rusescu 71), Stancu.
Referee: Wolfgang Stark.

Tuesday, 26 March 2013
Estonia (1) 2 *(Anier 45, Lindpere 61)*
Andorra (0) 0   5237
Estonia: (433) Pareiko; Morozov, Piiroja, Teniste, Jaager; Vassiljev, Mosnikov, Purje (Zenjov 76); Kink, Ahjupera (Oper 55), Anier (Lindpere 55).
Andorra: (442) Gomez J; Lima, Martinez, San Nicolas, Vieira; Vales, Peppe (Garcia E 66), Moreira (Bernaus 79), Ayala; Gomez S (Silva 85), Garcia M.
Referee: Jan Valasek.

Netherlands (1) 4 *(Van der Vaart 11, van Persie 55, 65 (pen), Lens 90)*
Romania (0) 0   48,480
Netherlands: (433) Vermeer; Janmaat, De Vrij, Martins Indi, Blind; de Guzman (Maher 73), Strootman, Van der Vaart (Clasie 79); Lens, van Persie (De Jong 86), Robben.
Romania: (442) Pantilimon; Rat, Tamas, Gardos, Chiriches; Bourceanu, Popa (Torje 62), Pintilii, Tanase (Chipciu 59); Stancu, Grozav (Mutu 67).
Referee: Mark Clattenburg.

Turkey (0) 1 *(Yilmaz 63)*
Hungary (0) 1 *(Bode 71)*   46,460
Turkey: (442) Kivrak; Gonul, Irtegun, Ali Kaldirim, Kaya; Potuk (Altintop 70), Inan, Sahin (Frei 90), Turan; Yilmaz, Bulut (Erdinc 80).
Hungary: (451) Kiraly; Varga, Meszaros, Korcsmar (Guzmics 46), Vanczak; Kadar, Dzsudzsak, Koman, Pinter, Hajnal (Bode 68); Szalai (Elek 78).
Referee: Milorad Mazic.

Friday, 6 September 2013
Estonia (2) 2 *(Vassiljev 18, 57)*
Netherlands (1) 2 *(Robben 2, van Persie 90 (pen))* 10,210
Estonia: (442) Pareiko; Jaager, Klavan, Kruglov, Piiroja[a]; Lindpere (Kams 85), Dmitrijev, Vassiljev, Vunk; Anier (Zenjov 55), Ojamaa (Reintam 90).
Netherlands: (433) Vorm; Janmaat, De Vrij (Bruma 67), Martins Indi, Willems (de Guzman 75); Schaars, Strootman, Sneijder; Lens (Kuyt 67), van Persie, Robben.
Referee: Sergiy Boiko.

Romania (2) 3 *(Marica 2, Pintilii 31, Tanase 88)*
Hungary (0) 0   45,000
Romania: (442) Tatarusanu; Matel, Rat, Chiriches, Goian; Bourceanu, Pintilii, Torje (Tanase 58), Maxim (Popa 64); Marica (Hoban 79), Stancu.
Hungary: (442) Bogdan; Guzmics, Vanczak, Kadar, Korcsmar (Hajnal 34); Liptak, Dzsudzsak, Varga (Lovrencsics 68), Koman (Szabics 85); Bode, Szalai.
Referee: Alberto Undiano Mallenco.

Turkey (2) 5 *(Bulut 35, 39, 68, Yilmaz 63, Turan 90)*
Andorra (0) 0   29,000
Turkey: (442) Demirel; Gonul, Kaya, Toprak, Erkin; Topal, Sahin (Sahan 65), Turan, Tore (Calhanoglu 82); Bulut, Yilmaz (Altintop 78).
Andorra: (442) Pol; Garcia E, Lima, San Nicolas, Martinez; Vales, Pujol, Ayala (Peppe 80), Lorenzo (Vieira 61); Gomez M (Riera 69), Garcia.
Referee: Sven Bindels.

Tuesday, 10 September 2013
Andorra (0) 0
Netherlands (0) 2 *(van Persie 50, 55)*   500
Andorra: (442) Pol; San Nicolas, Lima, Garcia E, Martinez; Vales, Pujol (Ayala 85), Vieira, Riera (Moreira 71); Lorenzo (Moreno 59), Garcia M.
Netherlands: (442) Vorm; Janmaat, De Vrij, Vlaar, Willems (Maher 47); Schaars, Strootman, Sneijder (Kuyt 79), Schaken; van Persie, Lens.
Referee: Ante Vucemilovic.

Hungary (3) 5 *(Klavan 11 (og), Hajnal 21, Bode 41,*
Nemeth 70, Dzsudzsak 85)
Estonia (0) 1 *(Kink 48)*   15,000
Hungary: (442) Bogdan; Guzmics, Vanczak, Kadar,
Laczko (Devecseri 62); Elek (Gyomber 75), Dzsudzsak,
Koman, Nemeth (Szakaly 85); Bode, Hajnal.
Estonia: (442) Pareiko; Reintam, Jaager, Teniste, Klavan;
Vunk, Mosnikov, Purje (Ojamaa 45), Anier; Kink (Kams
76), Ahjupera (Zenjov 45).
Referee: Aleksei Kulbakov.

Romania (0) 0
Turkey (1) 2 *(Yilmaz 22, Erdinc 90)*   44,537
Romania: (4231) Tatarusanu; Matel, Goian, Chiriches,
Rat; Hoban, Pintilii; Torje (Popa 45), Tanase (Bucur 77),
Stancu; Marica (Maxim 45).
Turkey: (442) Demirel; Kaya, Gonul, Toprak, Inan;
Turan, Topal, Erkin, Tore (Erdinc 84); Bulut (Gulum
90), Yilmaz (Sahan 72).
Referee: Kim Thomas Haglund.

Friday, 11 October 2013

Andorra (0) 0
Romania (1) 4 *(Keseru 43, Stancu 54, Torje 63 (pen),*
Lazar 85)   700
Andorra: (442) Pol; Garcia E, Rodrigues (Lorenzo 80),
Martinez, Vales (Sonejee 64); Pujol (Peppe 47), Vieira,
Ayala, Riera; Moreno, Garcia M.
Romania: (442) Lobont; Matel, Latovlevici, Chiriches,
Goian; Bourceanu, Lazar, Torje, Maxim (Tanase 70);
Keseru (Marica 59), Stancu (Grozav 83).
Referee: Stephan Klossner.

Estonia (0) 0
Turkey (1) 2 *(Bulut 22, Yilmaz 47)*   8572
Estonia: (442) Pareiko; Piiroja (Reintam 33), Kruglov,
Klavan, Kams (Kink 66); Teniste, Dmitrijev, Vunk,
Vassiljev; Zenjov, Ojamaa (Puri 75).
Turkey: (442) Demirel; Kaya, Gonul, Toprak, Inan;
Turan (Adin 87), Topal, Erkin, Tore (Potuk 82); Bulut,
Yilmaz (Sahan 79).
Referee: Nicola Rizzoli.

Netherlands (4) 8 *(van Persie 16, 44, 53, Strootman 25,*
Lens 38, Devecseri 65 (og), Van der Vaart 86, Robben
90)
Hungary (0) 1 *(Dzsudzsak 47 (pen))*   50,000
Netherlands: (433) Vorm; Janmaat, Bruma, Vlaar, Blind;
Van der Vaart, Strootman (Fer 81), De Jong; Robben,
van Persie (Kuyt 61), Lens.
Hungary: (442) Bogdan; Guzmics, Korcsmar, Vanczak,
Kadar (Devecseri 45); Dzsudzsak, Hajnal (Elek 45),
Varga, Koman; Nemeth (Nikolic 79), Bode.
Referee: Martin Atkinson.

Tuesday, 15 October 2013

Hungary (0) 2 *(Nikolic 52, Lima 79 (og))*
Andorra (0) 0   7000
Hungary: (442) Kiraly; Vanczak, Devecseri (Varga 48),
Meszaros, Liptak (Korcsmar 48); Elek, Dzsudzsak,
Koman, Stieber; Szalai (Nemeth 76), Nikolic.
Andorra: (442) Pol; San Nicolas■, Garcia, Lima,
Martinez; Sonejee, Vieira, Peppe (Viera 80), Riera
(Moreira 62); Lorenzo (Clemente 86), Garcia M.
Referee: Daniel Stefanski.

Romania (1) 2 *(Marica 30 (pen), 81)*
Estonia (0) 0   20,000
Romania: (4231) Tatarusanu; Matel, Goian, Gardos, Rat;
Bourceanu, Lazar (Hoban 79); Bucur (Torje 57), Stancu
(Grozav 47), Tanase; Marica.
Estonia: (442) Pareiko; Jaager, Klavan, Reintam, Teniste;
Puri (Ojamaa 58), Dmitrijev, Vassiljev, Kink; Lindpere
(Kruglov 75), Zenjov (Anier 46).
Referee: Mario Strahonja.

Turkey (0) 0
Netherlands (1) 2 *(Robben 9, Sneijder 47)*   52,000
Turkey: (4132) Demirel; Gonul, Kaya, Toprak, Ali
Kaldirim; Inan (Tosun 74); Turan, Topal, Adin (Tore 55);
Yilmaz (Sahan 56), Bulut.

Netherlands: (4231) Cillessen; Janmaat, Vlaar, Martins
Indi (Bruma 45), Blind; Clasie, Fer; Sneijder, Robben,
Lens (Depay 89); van Persie (Kuyt 45).
Referee: Olegario Bartolo Benquerenca.

Group D Table

	P	W	D	L	F	A	GD	Pts
Netherlands	10	9	1	0	34	5	29	28
Romania	10	6	1	3	19	12	7	19
Hungary	10	5	2	3	21	20	1	17
Turkey	10	5	1	4	16	9	7	16
Estonia	10	2	1	7	6	20	–14	7
Andorra	10	0	0	10	0	30	–30	0

GROUP E

Friday, 7 September 2012

Albania (1) 3 *(Sadiku 36, Cani 84, Bogdani 86)*
Cyprus (1) 1 *(Laban 45)*   6000
Albania: (442) Ujkani; Lila, Dallku, Cana, Sadiku (Hyka
57); Bulku, Vila (Bogdani 71), Mavraj, Salihi (Cani 81);
Meha, Kukeli.
Cyprus: (442) Georgallides (Mastrou 46); Junior,
Charalambous E, Merkis, Aloneftis; Charalambidis
(Christofi 55), Konstantinou (Avraam 75), Makridis,
Demetriou; Laban, Nicolaou.
Referee: Artyom Kuchin.

Iceland (1) 2 *(Arnason 21, Finnbogason 81)*
Norway (0) 0   8451
Iceland: (442) Halldorsson; Sigurdsson R, Eiriksson,
Steinsson, Bjarnason B; Sigurdsson G, Gislason
(Finnbogason 73), Arnason (Ottesen 50), Danielsson;
Gunnarsson, Hallfredsson (Jonsson 90).
Norway: (433) Pettersen; Ruud, Waehler, Hangeland, Riise
J; Nordtveit, Riise B (Henriksen 90), Eikrem; Braaten
(Soderlund 67), Abdellaoui (King 67), Elyounoussi.
Referee: Antony Gautier.

Slovenia (0) 0
Switzerland (1) 2 *(Xhaka 20, Inler 51)*   13,132
Slovenia: (442) Handanovic J; Brecko, Suler, Cesar,
Jokic; Birsa (Ilicic 61), Radosavljevic (Kurtic 80),
Bacinovic, Kirm; Dedic (Ljubijankic 55), Matavz.
Switzerland: (442) Benaglio; Lichtsteiner, Von Bergen,
Barnetta■, Inler; Derdiyok, Xhaka (Fernandes 85),
Behrami, Rodriguez; Djourou, Shaqiri (Dzemaili 74).
Referee: Paolo Tagliavento.

Tuesday, 11 September 2012

Cyprus (0) 1 *(Makridis 57)*
Iceland (0) 0   2000
Cyprus: (442) Kissas; Merkis, Junior, Charalambous E,
Solomou; Nicolaou, Laban, Makridis (Demetriou 90),
Dobrasinovic (Sielis 77); Konstantinou (Aloneftis 65),
Christofi.
Iceland: (442) Halldorsson; Sigurdsson R, Eiriksson
(Skulason A 63), Saevarsson, Ottesen■; Bjarnason B,
Gislason, Sigurdsson G, Danielsson (Gudmundsson 77);
Gunnarsson, Hallfredsson (Finnbogason 46).
Referee: Sebastien Delferiere.

Norway (1) 2 *(Henriksen 27, Riise J 90 (pen))*
Slovenia (1) 1 *(Suler 17)*   11,111
Norway: (442) Jarstein; Waehler, Henriksen, Hangeland,
Ruud; Riise J, Nordtveit (Riise B 53), Abdellaoui (King
46), Jenssen; Braaten, Elyounoussi (Soderlund 88).
Slovenia: (433) Oblak; Brecko, Suler, Cesar, Jokic;
Kurtic, Ilicic, Bacinovic (Matic 60); Ljubijankic (Kelhar
90), Birsa (Pecnik 7), Matavz.
Referee: Firat Aydinus.

Switzerland (1) 2 *(Shaqiri 22, Inler 69 (pen))*
Albania (0) 0   38,385
Switzerland: (442) Benaglio; Lichtsteiner, Von Bergen,
Rodriguez, Djourou; Inler, Xhaka (Drmic 90), Stocker
(Mehmedi 78), Behrami (Dzemaili 73); Shaqiri,
Derdiyok.
Albania: (442) Ujkani; Dallku, Mavraj, Lila, Meha;
Agolli, Cana, Kukeli (Hyka 73), Vila (Roshi 55); Bulku,
Bogdani (Cani 55).
Referee: Ovidiu Alin Hategan.

Friday, 12 October 2012

Albania (1) 1 *(Cani 29)*

Iceland (1) 2 *(Bjarnason B 19, Sigurdsson G 81)*   4000

Albania: (451) Ujkani; Lila, Dallku, Mavraj, Cana; Bulku, Sadiku, Lika (Salihi 74), Meha (Roshi 46), Kukeli; Cani (Bogdani 85).
Iceland: (451) Halldorsson; Steinsson, Arnason, Skulason A, Sigurdsson R; Gunnarsson, Hallfredsson, Gislason (Saevarsson 68), Bjarnason B (Gudmundsson 85), Sigurdsson G; Finnbogason (Jonsson 90).
Referee: Tony Asumaa.

Slovenia (1) 2 *(Matavz 38, 61)*

Cyprus (0) 1 *(Aloneftis 83)*   7988

Slovenia: (442) Handanovic S; Brecko, Suler, Cesar■, Jokic; Ilicic (Cvijanovic 84), Kirm, Kurtic, Radosavljevic (Maroh 90); Dedic (Kampl 68), Matavz.
Cyprus: (442) Kissas; Charalambous E, Sielis, Charalambous A, Christou; Demetriou, Dobrasinovic, Charalambidis (Aloneftis 79), Marangos (Artymatas 46); Christofi, Konstantinou (Efrem 64).
Referee: Ivan Kruzliak.

Switzerland (0) 1 *(Gavranovic 79)*

Norway (0) 1 *(Hangeland 81)*   31,315

Switzerland: (442) Benaglio; Lichtsteiner, Von Bergen, Rodriguez, Djourou; Barnetta (Gavranovic 70), Inler, Xhaka, Behrami (Dzemaili 90); Shaqiri, Derdiyok.
Norway: (442) Jarstein; Hangeland, Riise J, Ruud, Forren; Henriksen, Nordtveit, Jenssen, Soderlund (King 71); Braaten, Elyounoussi (Parr 90).
Referee: David Fernandez Borbalan.

Tuesday, 16 October 2012

Albania (1) 1 *(Roshi 37)*

Slovenia (0) 0   10,100

Albania: (442) Berisha; Mavraj, Lila, Cana, Agolli; Bulku, Vila (Dallku 84), Sadiku (Salihi 46), Kukeli; Roshi, Cani (Curri 75).
Slovenia: (442) Handanovic S; Brecko, Suler, Jokic, Maroh; Kirm, Radosavljevic (Kampl 79), Ilicic (Sisic 73), Mertelj; Matavz, Dedic (Cavusevic 58).
Referee: Martin Hansson.

Cyprus (1) 1 *(Aloneftis 42)*

Norway (1) 3 *(Hangeland 45, Elyounoussi 81 (pen), King 83)*   3500

Cyprus: (442) Kissas (Georgallides 55); Junior, Charalambous E, Charalambous A (Demetriou 46), Aloneftis (Mitidis 88); Solomou, Nicolaou, Dobrasinovic, Laban; Efrem, Christofi.
Norway: (442) Jarstein; Forren, Ruud, Hangeland, Riise J; Eikrem (Gashi 90), Jenssen (Berisha 75), Henriksen, Elyounoussi; Braaten, Soderlund (King 46).
Referee: Pawel Gil.

Iceland (0) 0

Switzerland (0) 2 *(Barnetta 65, Gavranovic 79)*   8369

Iceland: (451) Halldorsson; Skulason A, Steinsson, Arnason, Sigurdsson R; Jonsson (Baldvinsson 82), Bjarnason B, Sigurdsson G, Gislason (Gudmundsson 70), Hallfredsson; Finnbogason.
Switzerland: (442) Benaglio; Rodriguez, Djourou, Lichtsteiner, Von Bergen; Barnetta (Klose 90), Inler, Xhaka, Behrami; Gavranovic (Mehmedi 83), Shaqiri (Dzemaili 80).
Referee: Alan Kelly.

Friday, 22 March 2013

Norway (0) 0

Albania (0) 1 *(Salihi 67)*   11,112

Norway: (433) Jarstein; Hogli, Hangeland, Riise J, Forren; Jenssen, Henriksen, Nordtveit; Elyounoussi (King 61), Soderlund (Berisha 73), Abdellaoui.
Albania: (433) Berisha; Lila■, Dallku (Hisaj 78), Mavraj, Cana; Agolli, Bulku, Basha; Cani (Bogdani 73), Salihi (Curri 89), Roshi.
Referee: Kevin Blom.

Slovenia (1) 1 *(Novakovic 34)*

Iceland (0) 2 *(Sigurdsson G 55, 78)*   5500

Slovenia: (442) Handanovic S; Brecko, Cesar, Ilic, Jokic; Krhin (Dedic 80), Kurtic, Radosavljevic, Birsa (Lazarevic 51); Ljubijankic (Matavz 65), Novakovic.
Iceland: (442) Halldorsson; Sigurdsson R, Skulason A, Saevarsson, Jonsson; Bjarnason B, Sigurdsson G, Gunnarsson, Hallfredsson (Gudjohnsen 76); Sigthorsson (Danielsson 90), Finnbogason (Gudmundsson 47).
Referee: Stavros Tritsonis.

Saturday, 23 March 2013

Cyprus (0) 0

Switzerland (0) 0   3572

Cyprus: (442) Georgallides; Junior, Theophilou, Charalambous E, Solomou (Efrem 53); Charalambidis (Alexandrou 74), Makridis, Dobrasinovic, Laban; Nicolaou, Christofi (Sotiriou 90).
Switzerland: (442) Sommer; Von Bergen, Lichtsteiner, Djourou (Senderos 52), Rodriguez; Behrami (Derdiyok 76), Inler, Stocker, Shaqiri; Emeghara (Xhaka 46), Seferovic.
Referee: Manuel Graefe.

Friday, 7 June 2013

Albania (1) 1 *(Rama 41)*

Norway (0) 1 *(Hogli 87)*   15,150

Albania: (442) Berisha E; Teli, Mavraj, Dallku, Agolli; Rama, Bulku (Hisaj 90), Vila (Kace 85), Basha; Cani, Salihi (Osmani 77).
Norway: (442) Jarstein; Hogli, Ruud, Reginiussen, Hangeland; Henriksen, Jenssen (Skjelbred 84), Nordtveit, Elyounoussi (Berisha 46); King (Soderlund 71), Braaten.
Referee: William Collum.

Iceland (2) 2 *(Bjarnason B 22, Finnbogason 27 (pen))*

Slovenia (2) 4 *(Kirm 11, Birsa 31 (pen), Cesar 61, Krhin 85)*   9202

Iceland: (442) Halldorsson; Saevarsson (Thorvaldsson 83), Sigurdsson R, Arnason, Skulason A; Bjarnason B, Gunnarsson (Gudjohnsen 52), Danielsson, Hallfredsson (Gislason 63); Finnbogason, Sigthorsson.
Slovenia: (451) Handanovic S; Brecko, Ilic, Cesar, Jokic; Krhin, Birsa (Struna 90), Kampl (Radosavljevic 72), Kurtic, Kirm; Novakovic (Matavz 86).
Referee: Felix Zwayer.

Saturday, 8 June 2013

Switzerland (0) 1 *(Seferovic 90)*

Cyprus (0) 0   16,169

Switzerland: (442) Benaglio; Lichtsteiner, Djourou, Rodriguez, Von Bergen; Shaqiri, Inler, Behrami (Dzemaili 67), Stocker (Barnetta 77); Gavranovic, Drmic (Seferovic 73).
Cyprus: (442) Georgallides; Theophilou (Dobrasinovic 90), Charalambous E, Merkis, Charalambous A; Aloneftis (Kyriakou 61), Alexandrou, Makridis, Laban; Nicolaou, Sotiriou.
Referee: Paolo Mazzoleni.

Friday, 6 September 2013

Norway (1) 2 *(Elyounoussi 43, King 66)*

Cyprus (0) 0   11,295

Norway: (433) Jarstein; Hogli, Hangeland, Ruud, Gashi; Eikrem, Johansen (Jenssen 74), Bjordal; Braaten (Soderlund 81), Elyounoussi (King 63), Abdellaoue.
Cyprus: (442) Georgallides; Merkis, Theophilou, Junior, Dobrasinovic (Artymatas 73); Alexandrou, Nicolaou (Sotiriou 52), Aloneftis, Charalambidis (Demetriou 54); Laban, Mitidis.
Referee: Kenn Hansen.

Slovenia (1) 1 *(Kampl 19)*

Albania (0) 0   14,000

Slovenia: (442) Handanovic S; Brecko, Ilic, Kelhar, Jokic; Krhin, Kurtic, Kirm, Kampl (Ljubijankic 90); Birsa (Mertelj 75), Novakovic (Matavz 82).
Albania: (442) Berisha; Lila, Teli, Cana, Bulku (Salihi 53); Basha, Kace, Rama (Abrashi 81), Agolli; Cani (Mehmeti 71), Roshi.
Referee: Istvan Vad.

Switzerland (3) 4 *(Lichtsteiner 14, 30, Schar 27, Dzemaili 54 (pen))*
Iceland (1) 4 *(Gudmundsson 3, 67, 90, Sigthorsson 55)*
26,000
Switzerland: (442) Benaglio; Lichtsteiner, Von Bergen, Schar, Rodriguez; Xhaka (Drmic 76), Behrami, Stocker (Barnetta 78), Dzemaili; Shaqiri (Klose 89), Seferovic.
Iceland: (442) Halldorsson; Saevarsson (Skulason O 81), Sigurdsson R, Skulason A, Arnason; Gudmundsson, Bjarnason B, Sigurdsson G, Danielsson (Gudjohnsen 45); Gunnarsson, Sigthorsson.
Referee: Sergei Karasev.

Tuesday, 10 September 2013
Cyprus (0) 0
Slovenia (1) 2 *(Novakovic 13, Ilicic 80)*
700
Cyprus: (442) Georgallides; Theophilou (Demetriou 45), Merkis, Junior, Charalambous E; Dobrasinovic (Nicolaou 68), Laban, Eleftheriou (Charalambidis 33), Makridis; Alexandrou, Sotiriou.
Slovenia: (442) Handanovic S; Brecko, Ilic, Cesar, Struna; Kampl, Mertelj, Birsa (Ilicic 59), Novakovic (Filipovic 90); Kirm, Ljubijankic (Matavz 89).
Referee: Ruddy Buquet.

Iceland (1) 2 *(Bjarnason B 13, Sigthorsson 47)*
Albania (1) 1 *(Rama 9)*
9768
Iceland: (442) Halldorsson; Arnason, Skulason A, Saevarsson (Jonasson 90), Sigurdsson R; Gudmundsson, Bjarnason B, Sigurdsson G, Gunnarsson; Gudjohnsen (Skulason O 78), Sigthorsson.
Albania: (442) Berisha; Lila, Teli, Dallku (Gjasula 82), Basha (Bulku 63); Cana, Rama, Kace, Cani (Januzi 63); Salihi, Roshi.
Referee: Andre Marriner.

Norway (0) 0
Switzerland (1) 2 *(Schar 12, 51)*
16,631
Norway: (451) Jarstein; Ruud, Bjordal, Hangeland, Hogli (Elabdellaoui 70); Stocker, Johansen, Nordtveit, Eikrem (Jenssen 64), Elyounoussi; Pedersen Marcus (King 22).
Switzerland: (451) Benaglio; Lichtsteiner, Von Bergen, Rodriguez, Schar; Xhaka (Senderos 90), Behrami, Stocker (Fernandes 74), Inler, Shaqiri (Dzemaili 90); Seferovic.
Referee: Howard Webb.

Friday, 11 October 2013
Albania (0) 1 *(Salihi 89 (pen))*
Switzerland (0) 2 *(Shaqiri 48, Lang 78)*
18,000
Albania: (442) Berisha; Mavraj, Lila, Cana, Agolli; Bulku, Gashi (Roshi 55), Kace, Rama (Mehmeti 84); Abrashi (Hyka 64), Salihi.
Switzerland: (442) Benaglio; Schar, Rodriguez, Von Bergen, Lang; Inler, Xhaka, Behrami, Stocker (Fernandes 68); Shaqiri (Mehmedi 54), Seferovic (Dzemaili 89).
Referee: Pedro Proenca.

Iceland (0) 2 *(Sigthorsson 60, Sigurdsson G 77)*
Cyprus (0) 0
9767
Iceland: (442) Halldorsson; Arnason, Skulason A, Saevarsson, Sigurdsson R; Gudmundsson, Bjarnason B, Sigurdsson G (Gislason 82), Gunnarsson (Danielsson 78); Gudjohnsen (Finnbogason 66), Sigthorsson.
Cyprus: (442) Georgallides; Demetriou, Merkis, Mertakkas, Charalambous A; Aloneftis, Charalambidis (Efrem 67), Alexandrou (Pavlou 84), Laban; Mitidis (Sotiriou 75), Vasilou.
Referee: Istvan Vad.

Slovenia (2) 3 *(Novakovic 13, 15, 49)*
Norway (0) 0
11,000
Slovenia: (451) Handanovic S; Brecko, Ilic, Cesar, Struna; Kampl (Krhin 81), Mertelj, Kurtic, Kirm, Pecnik (Ljubijankic 70); Novakovic (Bezjak 90).
Norway: (451) Jarstein; Hogli, Bjordal, Hangeland, Elabdellaoui; Johansen, Eikrem (Storflor 73), Skjelbred, Elyounoussi, Abdellaoue (Johnsen 80); Braaten (Kamara 60).
Referee: Carlos Velasco Carballo.

Tuesday, 15 October 2013
Cyprus (0) 0
Albania (0) 0
300
Cyprus: (442) Georgallides; Junior, Charalambous A, Demetriou, Alexandrou (Aloneftis 45); Laban, Nicolaou, Mitidis (Pavlou 64), Sotiriou (Avraam 85); Vasilou, Efrem.
Albania: (442) Berisha; Lila, Mavraj, Cana, Agolli; Bulku (Abrashi 72), Hyka (Mehmeti 72), Kace, Rama; Salihi (Balaj 87), Roshi.
Referee: Ivan Bebek.

Norway (1) 1 *(Braaten 30)*
Iceland (1) 1 *(Sigthorsson 12)*
6796
Norway: (442) Jarstein; Elabdellaoui, Hogli, Reginiussen, Hangeland; Tettey, Skjelbred (Johnsen 85), Johansen, Elyounoussi; Kamara (Berisha 55), Braaten (Abdellaoue 74).
Iceland: (442) Halldorsson; Skulason A, Arnason, Saevarsson, Sigurdsson R; Bjarnason, Sigurdsson G, Gunnarsson, Gudmundsson (Gislason 90); Sigthorsson, Gudjohnsen (Finnbogason 58).
Referee: Paolo Tagliavento.

Switzerland (0) 1 *(Xhaka 74)*
Slovenia (0) 0
25,000
Switzerland: (4231) Sommer; Lang, Djourou, Senderos, Ziegler; Inler, Dzemaili; Xhaka, Mehmedi (Fernandes 87), Barnetta (Kasami 71); Seferovic (Derdiyok 71).
Slovenia: (4231) Handanovic S; Brecko, Ilic, Cesar, Struna, Mertelj (Ljubijankic 79), Kurtic; Pecnik (Matavz 43), Kampl (Lazarevic 86), Kirm; Novakovic.
Referee: Bjorn Kuipers.

Group E Table	P	W	D	L	F	A	GD	Pts
Switzerland	10	7	3	0	17	6	11	24
Iceland	10	5	2	3	17	15	2	17
Slovenia	10	5	0	5	14	11	3	15
Norway	10	3	3	4	10	13	–3	12
Albania	10	3	2	5	9	11	–2	11
Cyprus	10	1	2	7	4	15	–11	5

GROUP F

Friday, 7 September 2012
Azerbaijan (0) 1 *(Abishov 65)*
Israel (0) 1 *(Natcho 50)*
15,150
Azerbaijan: (442) Agayev K; Shukurov, Sadygov, Abishov, Medvedev; Allahverdiev, Gokdemir (Ismayilov 59), Chertoganov (Amirquliev 76), Javadov; Subasic, Aliyev (Azkara 58).
Israel: (442) Aouate; Spungin, Ziv, Mori, Tibi; Melikson (Hzra 71), Natcho, Alberman, Vermouth; Hemed (Damari 67), Shechter (Benayoun 74).
Referee: Matej Jug.

Luxembourg (1) 1 *(Da Mota Alves 14)*
Portugal (1) 2 *(Ronaldo 28, Postiga 54)*
9000
Luxembourg: (442) Joubert; Blaise, Schnell, Bukvic, Mutsch; Janisch, Payal, Bettmer, Joachim; Krogh Gerson, Da Mota Alves (Deville 79).
Portugal: (442) Rui Patricio; Joao Pereira, Bruno Alves, Pepe, Fabio Coentrao; Veloso (Varela 46), Joao Moutinho, Meireles (Custodio 67), Nani (Ruben Micael 81); Ronaldo, Postiga.
Referee: Kristo Tohver.

Russia (1) 2 *(Faitzulin 30, Shirokov 78 (pen))*
Northern Ireland (0) 0
12,120
Russia: (433) Akinfeev; Aniukov, Berezutsky V, Ignashevich, Kombarov; Denisov, Shirokov, Faitzulin (Glushakov 85); Dzagoev (Kokorin 58), Kerzhakov, Bystrov.
Northern Ireland: (442) Carroll; Hughes, Evans J, McAuley, Cathcart; Evans C (Shiels 84), Davis, Baird, Ward (Little 76); Brunt, Lafferty K.
Referee: Antonio Miguel Mateu Lahoz.

Tuesday, 11 September 2012
Israel (0) 0
Russia (2) 4 *(Kerzhakov 6, 64, Kokorin 18, Faitzulin 77)*
30,300
Israel: (442) Aouate; Tibi, Ben Haim, Spungin, Ziv; Natcho, Radi, Cohen (Ben Basat 46), Benayoun (Vermouth 73); Shechter (Sahar 46), Hzra.
Russia: (442) Akinfeev; Aniukov (Yeschenko 50), Ignashevich, Berezutsky V, Denisov; Glushakov, Shirokov, Bystrov (Samedov 22), Kombarov; Kokorin (Faitzulin 35), Kerzhakov.
Referee: Mark Clattenburg.

Northern Ireland (1) 1 *(Shiels 14)*
Luxembourg (0) 1 *(Da Mota Alves 86)* 11,114
Northern Ireland: (4411) Carroll; Hughes, McGivern, McAuley, Ferguson (Ward 74); Evans J, Baird, Davis, Brunt; Shiels (Norwood 83); Lafferty K.
Luxembourg: (451) Joubert; Blaise, Schnell, Janisch, Payal; Bukvic, Mutsch, Bettmer (Hoffmann 90), Krogh Gerson (Philipps 50), Da Mota Alves; Joachim (Deville 46).
Referee: Vlado Glodjovic.

Portugal (0) 3 *(Varela 63, Postiga 85, Bruno Alves 88)*
Azerbaijan (0) 0 29,299
Portugal: (442) Rui Patricio; Fabio Coentrao, Joao Pereira, Bruno Alves, Pepe; Veloso (Varela 62), Joao Moutinho, Meireles, Nani (Ruben Amorim 77); Postiga (Eder 87), Ronaldo.
Azerbaijan: (442) Agayev K; Levin, Medvedev, Shukurov, Allahverdiev; Sadygov, Abishov, Gokdemir (Chertoganov 89), Huseynov (Ismayilov 59); Amirquliev, Ozkara (Subasic 72).
Referee: Szymon Marciniak.

Friday, 12 October 2012
Luxembourg (0) 0
Israel (3) 6 *(Radi 4, Ben Basat 12, Hemed 27, 73, 90, Melikson 60)* 2631
Luxembourg: (442) Joubert; Schnell (Leweck 18), Bukvic, Philipps, Mutsch; Janisch, Bettmer, Payal (Hoffmann 78), Krogh Gerson; Da Mota Alves, Joachim (Deville 61).
Israel: (442) Aouate; Shish (Ziv 57), Mori, Tibi (Keinan 55), Spungin; Alberman, Melikson, Radi, Natcho (Biton 77); Ben Basat, Hemed.
Referee: Leontios Trattou.

Russia (1) 1 *(Kerzhakov 6)*
Portugal (0) 0 75,750
Russia: (4231) Akinfeev; Aniukov, Ignashevich, Berezutsky V, Kombarov; Denisov, Shirokov, Bystrov (Samedov 83), Faitzulin (Glushakov 46), Kokorin; Kerzhakov (Yeschenko 65).
Portugal: (4231) Rui Patricio; Joao Pereira, Bruno Alves, Pepe, Fabio Coentrao (Miguel Lopes 20); Veloso, Joao Moutinho; Nani, Ruben Micael (Varela 66), Ronaldo; Postiga (Eder 75).
Referee: Viktor Kassai.

Tuesday, 16 October 2012
Israel (2) 3 *(Hemed 13, 48, Ben Basat 35)*
Luxembourg (0) 0 15,150
Israel: (442) Aouate; Keinan, Mori, Gabai, Ziv; Melikson (Abuhatzira 81), Natcho, Alberman, Radi (Vermouth 56 (Ezra 71)); Ben Basat, Hemed.
Luxembourg: (442) Joubert; Mutsch, Blaise, Hoffmann, Peters (Philipps 81); Bettmer, Payal, Jans, Leweck; Da Mota Alves (Laterza 86), Joachim (Deville 46).
Referee: Harald Lechner.

Portugal (0) 1 *(Postiga 79)*
Northern Ireland (1) 1 *(McGinn 30)* 48,487
Portugal: (4231) Rui Patricio; Joao Pereira (Eder 73), Bruno Alves, Pepe, Miguel Lopes (Ruben Amorim 47); Veloso, Ruben Micael (Varela 61); Ronaldo, Joao Moutinho, Nani; Postiga.
Northern Ireland: (451) Carroll; McGivern, Cathcart, Evans J, Hughes; Baird, Davis, Evans C, McGinn, Norwood; Lafferty K.
Referee: Thorsten Kinhoefer.

Russia (0) 1 *(Shirokov 84 (pen))*
Azerbaijan (0) 0 15,150
Russia: (442) Akinfeev; Yeschenko, Berezutsky V, Ignashevich, Kombarov; Shirokov, Denisov, Faitzulin (Glushakov 46), Samedov (Bystrov 62); Kerzhakov (Dzagoev 78), Kokorin.
Azerbaijan: (442) Agayev K; Shukurov, Abishov, Medvedev, Levin; Chertoganov (Aliyev 84), Gokdemir, Javadov, Ozkara; Subasic (Amirquliev 62), Nadirov (Huseynov 46).
Referee: Aleksandar Stavrev.

Wednesday, 14 November 2012
Northern Ireland (0) 1 *(Healy 90)*
Azerbaijan (1) 1 *(Aliyev 5)* 12,123
Northern Ireland: (442) Carroll; Hughes, Cathcart (Healy 81), McAuley, Lafferty D; McGinn (Brunt 66), Davis, Baird, Ferguson; Shiels (McCourt 55), Lafferty K.
Azerbaijan: (451) Agayev S; Ramaldanov (Naziri 72), Abishov, Levin, Medvedev; Aliyev, Huseynov, Gokdemir (Guseynov 63), Amirquliev, Nadirov; Ozkara (Javadov 78).
Referee: Victor Shvetsov.

Friday, 22 March 2013
Israel (2) 3 *(Hemed 24, Ben Basat 40, Gershon 70)*
Portugal (1) 3 *(Bruno Alves 2, Postiga 72, Fabio Coentrao 90)* 40,400
Israel: (442) Aouate; Spungin, Ben Haim, Gershon, Yeini; Tibi, Natcho, Melikson (Refaelov 73), Kayal; Hemed (Atar 63), Ben Basat (Benayoun 81).
Portugal: (442) Rui Patricio; Bruno Alves (Almeida 74), Joao Pereira, Pepe, Fabio Coentrao; Veloso (Carlos Martins 61), Joao Moutinho, Meireles, Ronaldo; Varela (Vieirinha 61), Postiga.
Referee: Stephane Lannoy.

Luxembourg (0) 0
Azerbaijan (0) 0 1324
Luxembourg: (4141) Joubert; Hoffmann, Janisch, Schnell, Philipps; Mutsch (Bettmer 90); Jans, Krogh Gerson, Joachim (Deville 90), Da Mota Alves (Laterza 67); Bensi.
Azerbaijan: (442) Agayev K; Ramaldanov, Shukurov, Sadygov, Abishov; Ismailov, Sadyqov (Huseynov 87), Fardjad-Azad (Ozkara 71); Aliyev, Javadov (Nadirov 59).
Referee: Padraigh Sutton.

Tuesday, 26 March 2013
Azerbaijan (0) 0
Portugal (0) 2 *(Bruno Alves 63, Almeida 79)* 30,300
Azerbaijan: (442) Agayev K; Medvedev, Sadygov, Abishov, Ramaldanov; Shukurov, Mammadov E (Fardjad-Azad 69), Ismailov, Huseynov; Nadirov (Levin 62), Aliyev.
Portugal: (442) Rui Patricio; Joao Pereira, Pepe, Bruno Alves, Fabio Coentrao; Joao Moutinho, Meireles (Almeida 58), Veloso, Danny (Varela 73); Vieirinha, Postiga (Custodio 82).
Referee: Andre Marriner.

Northern Ireland (0) 0
Israel (0) 2 *(Refaelov 77, Ben Basat 84)* 7300
Northern Ireland: (4231) Carroll; Hughes, McAuley, Evans J, Lafferty D; Brunt, Clingan (McCourt 79); McGinn, Davis, Ferguson (Magennis 72); Paterson (Healy 83).
Israel: (442) Aouate; Spungin, Tibi, Ben Haim, Gershon; Yeini, Natcho, Radi (Zahavi 60), Melikson (Refaelov 69); Shechter (Benayoun 86), Ben Basat.
Referee: Hannes Kaasik.

Friday, 7 June 2013
Azerbaijan (0) 1 *(Abishov 71)*
Luxembourg (0) 1 *(Bensi 80)* 6000
Azerbaijan: (4231) Agayev K; Shukurov, Sadygov, Ramaldanov, Abdullayev E; Amirquliev (Subasic 62), Abishov; Abdullayev A (Mammadov E 84), Sadyqov, Javadov; Dadasov.
Luxembourg: (433) Joubert; Jans, Chanot, Hoffmann, Martino; Mutsch, Philipps (Payal 46), Krogh Gerson; Deville (Laterza 27 (Da Mota Alves 78)), Joachim, Bensi.
Referee: Mihaly Fabian.

Portugal (1) 1 *(Postiga 9)*
Russia (0) 0   55,550
Portugal: (433) Rui Patricio; Bruno Alves, Fabio Coentrao, Luis Neto, Joao Pereira; Veloso, Joao Moutinho, Meireles (Ruben Amorim 73); Ronaldo, Vieirinha (Custodio 90), Postiga (Nani 66).
Russia: (4141) Akinfeev; Aniukov (Kozlov 31), Berezutsky V, Ignashevich, Zhirkov; Denisov; Shirokov, Bystrov, Faitzulin (Glushakov 21), Kombarov; Kerzhakov (Smolov 67).
Referee: Damir Skomina.

Wednesday, 14 August 2013
Northern Ireland (1) 1 *(Paterson 43)*
Russia (0) 0   11,805
Northern Ireland: (442) Carroll; McAuley, Hughes, Cathcart, Lafferty D; Ferguson, McGinn (Evans C 82), Davis, Norwood; Ward, Paterson (Grigg 86).
Russia: (451) Akinfeev; Aniukov, Ignashevich, Berezutsky V, Dzagoev (Cheryshev 45 (Samedov 52)); Shirokov, Denisov, Bystrov, Faitzulin, Kombarov; Kerzhakov (Dzjuba 46).
Referee: Tom Harald Hagen.

Friday, 6 September 2013
Northern Ireland (1) 2 *(McAuley 36, Ward 52)*
Portugal (1) 4 *(Bruno Alves 21, Ronaldo 68, 77, 83)* 12,001
Northern Ireland: (442) Carroll; Hodson, McAuley, Evans J, Ferguson (Baird 76); McGinn (Lafferty K[*] 67), Davis, Brunt[*], Norwood; Ward (Evans C 71), Paterson.
Portugal: (433) Rui Patricio; Joao Pereira, Bruno Alves, Pepe, Fabio Coentrao; Veloso, Meireles (Nani 55), Joao Moutinho; Vieirinha (Nelson Oliveira 64), Postiga[*], Ronaldo (Ruben Amorim 90).
Referee: Danny Makkelie.

Russia (2) 4 *(Kokorin 1, 36, Kerzhakov 59, Samedov 90)*
Luxembourg (0) 1 *(Joachim 90)*   18,000
Russia: (442) Akinfeev; Shirokov (Ryazantsev 82), Granat, Kozlov, Ignashevich; Kombarov, Denisov, Bystrov (Samedov 68), Faitzulin; Kokorin (Smolov 45), Kerzhakov.
Luxembourg: (442) Joubert; Philipps, Laterza, Janisch, Payal; Krogh Gerson (Peters 66), Jans, Bensi (Luisi 77), Joachim; Turpel (Bastos 60), Da Mota Alves.
Referee: Manuel Grafe.

Saturday, 7 September 2013
Israel (0) 1 *(Shechter 73)*
Azerbaijan (0) 1 *(Amirquliev 61)*   21,250
Israel: (442) Aouate; Davidadze, Yeini, Tibi, Ben Haim; Alberman (Radi 72), Natcho, Zahavi (Barda 62), Ezra (Rafaelov 62); Melikson, Shechter.
Azerbaijan: (442) Agayev K; Ramaldanov (Levin 70), Abishov (Huseynov 78), Sadygov, Shukurov; Allahverdiev, Abdullayev A (Garayev 46), Amirquliev, Ozkara; Dadasov, Aliyev.
Referee: Stefan Johannesson.

Tuesday, 10 September 2013
Luxembourg (1) 3 *(Joachim 45, Bensi 78, Janisch 87)*
Northern Ireland (1) 2 *(Paterson 14, McAuley 82)*   1114
Luxembourg: (442) Joubert; Laterza, Mutsch, Philipps, Janisch; Krogh Gerson, Jans, Bensi, Da Mota Alves (Bukvic 89); Turpel (Luisi 68), Joachim.
Northern Ireland: (442) Carroll; Hodson, McAuley, Lafferty D (Grigg 80), Evans J; Ferguson (McKay 60), McGinn (O'Connor 35), Davis, Norwood; Paterson, Ward.
Referee: Robert Malek.

Russia (0) 3 *(Berezutsky V 49, Kokorin 52, Glushakov 74)*
Israel (0) 1 *(Zahavi 90)*   21,000
Russia: (442) Akinfeev; Kozlov, Ignashevich, Berezutsky V, Kombarov; Denisov (Glushakov 45), Faitzulin (Dzagoev 45); Shirokov, Samedov; Kokorin (Bystrov 77), Kerzhakov.
Israel: (442) Aouate; Ben Haim, Yeini, Keinan, Davidadze; Zahavi, Alberman (Radi 71), Natcho, Rafaelov; Melikson (Ezra 45), Barda (Shechter 64).
Referee: Manuel Graefe.

Friday, 11 October 2013
Azerbaijan (0) 2 *(Dadasov 58, Shukurov 90)*
Northern Ireland (0) 0   7000
Azerbaijan: (4231) Agayev K; Shukurov, Ramaldanov, Sadygov, Allahverdiev; Garayev, Amirquliev; Abdullayev A (Ozkara 82), Aliyev, Nadirov (Huseynov 45); Dadasov (Guseynov 90).
Northern Ireland: (352) Carroll; Cathcart, Evans J[*], McAuley; Hodson (McGinn 66), Norwood, Davis, Brunt (McKay 74), Ferguson; Paterson, Ward (Grigg 84).
Referee: Andrea De Marco.

Luxembourg (0) 0
Russia (3) 4 *(Samedov 9, Faitzulin 39, Glushakov 45, Kerzhakov 73)*   5354
Luxembourg: (433) Joubert; Laterza, Mutsch, Philipps, Janisch; Krogh Gerson, Jans, Bensi; Da Mota Alves (Bastos 62), Turpel (Payal 32), Luisi (Martino 75).
Russia: (442) Akinfeev; Kozlov, Berezutsky V, Granat, Glushakov; Kombarov (Shchennikov 85), Faitzulin, Shirokov, Samedov; Kokorin (Zhirkov 45 (Bystrov 65)), Kerzhakov.
Referee: Stephan Studer.

Portugal (1) 1 *(Ricardo Costa 28)*
Israel (0) 1 *(Ben Basat 85)*   48,317
Portugal: (433) Rui Patricio; Antunes, Pepe, Ricardo Costa, Andre Almeida; Veloso (Diego 87), Ruben Micael (Josue 69), Joao Moutinho; Nani, Ronaldo, Almeida (Nelson Oliveira 69).
Israel: (541) Aouate; Meshumar, Ben Haim, Ben Haroush, Tibi, Natcho; Yeini, Radi (Rafaelov 67), Zahavi (Damari 83), Ben Basat; Barda (Ben Haim T 60).
Referee: Tom Harald Hagen.

Tuesday, 15 October 2013
Azerbaijan (0) 1 *(Javadov 90)*
Russia (1) 1 *(Shirokov 16)*   11,000
Azerbaijan: (541) Agayev K; Shukurov, Levin, Sadygov, Allahverdiev, Medvedev[*]; Abishov, Ismailov (Garayev 46), Aliyev, Abdullayev A (Amirquliev 79); Dadasov (Javadov 83).
Russia: (433) Akinfeev; Kozlov, Ignashevich, Berezutsky V, Kombarov; Shirokov, Glushakov, Faitzulin (Shatov 46); Samedov (Mamaev 82), Kerzhakov, Kokorin.
Referee: Milorad Mazic.

Israel (1) 1 *(Ben Basat 43)*
Northern Ireland (0) 1 *(Davis 73)*   13,115
Israel: (442) Aouate; Meshumar, Ben Haim (Keinan 45), Melikson, Natcho; Zahavi (Ben Chaim 71), Ben Basat, Rafaelov (Shechter 78), Yeini; Davidadze, Tibi.
Northern Ireland: (442) Carroll; Hodson, Lafferty D (Ferguson 78), Baird, McGinn (Ward 65); Davis, Paterson, Evans C (Brunt 24), Clingan; McArdle, Cathcart.
Referee: Laurent Duhamel.

Portugal (2) 3 *(Varela 30, Nani 36, Postiga 78)*
Luxembourg (0) 0   18,900
Portugal: (442) Rui Patricio; Veloso (Almeida 58), Fabio Coentrao (Antunes 75), Joao Moutinho, Ricardo Costa (Sereno 59); Luis Neto, Nani, Josue, Andre Almeida; Postiga, Varela.
Luxembourg: (442) Joubert; Janisch, Krogh Gerson, Da Mota Alves (Martino 82), Payal (Peters 61); Bensi (Luisi 45), Joachim[*], Laterza, Philipps; Mutsch, Jans.
Referee: Bulent Yildirim.

Group F Table	P	W	D	L	F	A	GD	Pts
Russia	10	7	1	2	20	5	15	22
Portugal	10	6	3	1	20	9	11	21
Israel	10	3	5	2	19	14	5	14
Azerbaijan	10	1	6	3	7	11	-4	9
Northern Ireland	10	1	4	5	9	17	-8	7
Luxembourg	10	1	3	6	7	26	-19	6

GROUP G

Friday, 7 September 2012

Latvia (1) 1 *(Cauna 43 (pen))*

Greece (0) 2 *(Spyropoulos 57, Gekas 70)* 7956

Latvia: (442) Vanins; Klava, Krjauklis, Laizans (Gauracs 89), Ivanovs; Cauna, Visnjakovs (Verpakovskis 75), Lukjanovs, Gorkss; Rudnevs, Fertovs (Rugins 76).
Greece: (442) Karnezis; Maniatis, Spyropoulos, Papadopoulos, Tziolis; Mitroglou (Samaras 46 (Ninis 69)), Torosidis, Gekas, Papastathopoulos; Katsouranis, Fortounis (Holebas 80).
Referee: Ivan Bebek.

Liechtenstein (0) 1 *(Christen M 61)*

Bosnia & Herzegovina (4) 8 *(Misimovic 26, 32, Ibisevic 34, 40, 83, Dzeko 46, 64, 81)* 5900

Liechtenstein: (442) Jehle; Oehri, Stocklasa, Quintans, Kaufmann; Polverino, Burgmeier, Flatz (Christen M 46), Erne (Beck 71); Hasler N (Eberle 89), Hasler D.
Bosnia & Herzegovina: (442) Begovic; Spahic, Sunjic, Vranjes, Vrsajevic; Pjanic (Vrancic 79), Misimovic (Svraka 78), Zahirovic (Ibricic 78), Salihovic; Ibisevic, Dzeko.
Referee: Marco Borg.

Lithuania (1) 1 *(Zaliukas 18)*

Slovakia (1) 1 *(Sapara 41)* 3000

Lithuania: (442) Karcemarskas; Semberas, Radavicius, Andriuskevicius, Zaliukas; Cesnauskis (Novikovas 58), Sernas, Mikoliunas (Labukas 74), Vicius (Cesnauskis D 67); Klimavicius, Borovskij.
Slovakia: (433) Mucha; Pekarik, Skrtel, Zabavnik, Stoch (Breznanik 60); Sapara, Bakos (Jakubko 78), Hubocan; Hamsik (Kucka 86), Pecovsky, Duris.
Referee: Carlos Clos Gomez.

Tuesday, 11 September 2012

Bosnia & Herzegovina (2) 4 *(Misimovic 13 (pen), 54, Pjanic 44, Dzeko 90)*

Latvia (1) 1 *(Gorkss 5)* 12,120

Bosnia & Herzegovina: (442) Begovic; Spahic, Mujdza, Vranjes, Pjanic; Lulic (Vrsajevic 30), Misimovic, Zahirovic, Salihovic (Sunjic 90); Ibisevic (Medunjanin 87), Dzeko.
Latvia: (442) Vanins; Klava, Krjauklis, Gorkss, Ivanovs; Rugins, Laizans, Cauna, Visnjakovs (Kamess 61); Lukjanovs (Zjuzins 80), Rudnevs (Verpakovskis 61).
Referee: Deniz Aytekin.

Greece (0) 2 *(Ninis 56, Mitroglou 72)*

Lithuania (0) 0 22,220

Greece: (442) Karnezis; Torosidis, Spyropoulos, Papastathopoulos, Papadopoulos; Katsouranis, Tziolis, Maniatis (Mitroglou 46), Ninis; Fortounis (Holebas 68), Gekas (Mavrias 80).
Lithuania: (442) Karcemarskas; Zaliukas, Borovskij (Cesnauskis D 46), Semberas, Cesnauskis E; Mikoliunas, Vicius, Klimavicius, Sernas (Rimkevicius 57); Velicka (Novikovas 76), Vaitkunas.
Referee: Mark Courtney.

Slovakia (1) 2 *(Sapara 36, Jakubko 78)*

Liechtenstein (0) 0 3500

Slovakia: (442) Kuciak; Pekarik, Skrtel, Zabavnik, Salata; Weiss (Breznanik 63), Stoch, Sapara, Hamsik (Kucka 82); Guldan, Bakos (Jakubko 60).
Liechtenstein: (442) Jehle; Oehri, Kaufmann, Stocklasa, Burgmeier; Erne, Polverino, Hasler N, Christen M (Flatz 84); Hasler D, Beck (Eberle 70).
Referee: Simon Evans.

Friday, 12 October 2012

Greece (0) 0

Bosnia & Herzegovina (0) 0 28,280

Greece: (442) Karnezis; Torosidis, Spyropoulos, Malezas (Karagounis 66), Papastathopoulos; Katsouranis, Fortounis, Tziolis, Maniatis (Mitroglou 79); Samaras, Gekas (Salpingidis 57).
Bosnia & Herzegovina: (442) Begovic; Spahic, Vranjes, Mujdza, Salihovic; Lulic (Stevanovic 75), Zahirovic, Medunjanin (Ibricic 75), Misimovic; Ibisevic, Dzeko.
Referee: Antonio Damato.

Liechtenstein (0) 0

Lithuania (0) 2 *(Cesnauskis E 51, 75)* 700

Liechtenstein: (442) Buchel; Oehri, Kaufmann, Quintans, Stocklasa; Burgmeier, Erne (Ospelt 87), Hasler N (Kieber 73), Wieser (Eberle 84); Polverino, Beck.
Lithuania: (442) Karcemarskas; Kijanskas, Zaliukas, Klimavicius, Semberas; Radavicius (Stankevicius 90), Cesnauskis D (Sernas 58), Cesnauskis E, Mikoliunas; Danilevicius (Rimkevicius 87), Novikovas.
Referee: Slavko Vincic.

Slovakia (2) 2 *(Hamsik 6 (pen), Sapara 9)*

Latvia (0) 1 *(Verpakovskis 85 (pen))* 4012

Slovakia: (352) Kuciak; Pekarik, Skrtel (Durica 90), Salata; Breznanik, Weiss (Duris 42), Stoch, Sapara, Hamsik; Pecovsky, Bakos (Holosko 61).
Latvia: (442) Vanins; Klava, Krjauklis, Gorkss, Ivanovs; Laizans (Rugins 69), Cauna (Verpakovskis 76), Visnjakovs, Fertovs; Lukjanovs (Gauracs 53), Rudnevs.
Referee: Danny Makkelie.

Tuesday, 16 October 2012

Bosnia & Herzegovina (3) 3 *(Ibisevic 29, Dzeko 35, Pjanic 41)*

Lithuania (0) 0 15,150

Bosnia & Herzegovina: (352) Begovic; Spahic, Mujdza (Vrsajevic 59), Vranjes; Pjanic (Stevanovic 67), Misimovic, Zahirovic, Salihovic, Lulic (Zukanovic 75); Ibisevic, Dzeko.
Lithuania: (532) Karcemarskas; Kijanskas, Zaliukas, Klimavicius, Borovskij, Stankevicius; Semberas, Radavicius (Sernas 51), Panka (Pilibaitis 85); Labukas (Rimkevicius 66), Novikovas.
Referee: Miroslav Zelinka.

Latvia (1) 2 *(Kamess 29, Gauracs 77)*

Liechtenstein (0) 0 4073

Latvia: (433) Vanins; Bulvitis, Rugins, Ivanovs, Gorkss; Laizans (Gauracs 66), Fertovs, Cauna; Verpakovskis (Zjuzins 85), Rudnevs, Kamess (Visnjakovs 74).
Liechtenstein: (451) Bicer; Oehri, Kaufmann, Quintans, Stocklasa; Burgmeier, Erne (Kieber 80), Hasler N (Eberle 85), Wieser, Polverino; Christen M.
Referee: Istvan Kovacs.

Slovakia (0) 0

Greece (0) 1 *(Salpingidis 63)* 7694

Slovakia: (442) Kuciak; Skrtel, Zabavnik, Salata, Breznanik; Stoch (Weiss 69), Sapara, Hamsik, Pecovsky; Kucka (Guede 82), Duris (Holosko 71).
Greece: (442) Karnezis; Spyropoulos, Siovas (Fotakis 75), Torosidis, Papastathopoulos; Ninis (Karagounis 66), Tziolis, Katsouranis, Samaras; Salpingidis, Gekas (Mitroglou 59).
Referee: William Collum.

Friday, 22 March 2013

Bosnia & Herzegovina (2) 3 *(Dzeko 30, 54, Ibisevic 36)*

Greece (0) 1 *(Gekas 90)* 15,150

Bosnia & Herzegovina: (442) Begovic; Spahic, Vranjes, Mujdza (Vrsajevic 84), Zukanovic; Lulic, Zahirovic, Medunjanin (Rahimic 78), Misimovic; Dzeko, Ibisevic (Stevanovic 84).
Greece: (442) Karnezis; Papadopoulos (Gekas 47), Torosidis (Maniatis 58), Papastathopoulos, Tzavelas; Tziolis, Karagounis (Christodoulopoulos 73), Holebas, Katsouranis; Samaras, Salpingidis.
Referee: Bjorn Kuipers.

Liechtenstein (1) 1 *(Polverino 17)*

Latvia (1) 1 *(Cauna 30)* 1150

Liechtenstein: (442) Jehle; Oehri (Quintans 46), Stocklasa, Burgmeier, Erne (Gur 90); Hasler N, Wieser, Polverino, Hasler D; Frick, Christen M (Beck 72).
Latvia: (442) Vanins; Klava, Ivanovs, Gorkss, Rugins; Laizans (Visnjakovs 46), Cauna, Lazdins, Kamess (Zigajevs 56); Verpakovskis (Gauracs 66), Rudnevs.
Referee: Kevin Clancy.

Slovakia (1) 1 *(Durica 40)*
Lithuania (1) 1 *(Sernas 19)* 4560
Slovakia: (451) Kuciak; Skrtel, Durica, Hubocan, Pecovsky (Bakos 70); Sapara, Hamsik, Svento, Kucka, Mak (Duris 64); Jakubko.
Lithuania: (442) Karcemarskas (Arlauskis 46); Kijanskas, Mikuckis, Cesnauskis E, Semberas; Mikoliunas, Ivaskevicius, Kalonas (Novikovas 69), Panka; Matulevicius, Sernas (Luksa 90).
Referee: Michael Oliver.

Friday, 7 June 2013
Latvia (0) 0
Bosnia & Herzegovina (0) 5 *(Lulic 47, Ibisevic 53, Medunjanin 62, Pjanic 80, Dzeko 81)* 7787
Latvia: (442) Vanins; Mihadjuks, Klava, Bulvitis, Ivanovs; Gorkss, Fertovs■, Sinelnikovs, Gauracs (Sabala 81); Kamess (Gabovs 59), Verpakovskis (Lazdins 15).
Bosnia & Herzegovina: (442) Begovic; Mujdza, Spahic, Zukanovic, Lulic; Salihovic (Ibricic 79), Medunjanin (Stevanovic 69), Rahimic (Visca 69), Pjanic; Ibisevic, Dzeko.
Referee: Mike Dean.

Liechtenstein (1) 1 *(Buchel 13)*
Slovakia (0) 1 *(Durica 73)* 1623
Liechtenstein: (4411) Jehle; Oehri, Kaufmann, Frick (Vogt 25), Quintans; Buchel, Christen A, Hasler N, Wieser (Gubser 90); Christen M (Beck 90); Hasler D.
Slovakia: (4411) Kuciak; Hubocan (Pauschek 46), Cisovsky, Durica, Svento; Lasik (Dubek 24), Stoch, Sapara, Mak; Hamsik; Holosko (Bakos 70).
Referee: Martin Strombergsson.

Lithuania (0) 0
Greece (1) 1 *(Christodoulopoulos 20)* 8500
Lithuania: (433) Zubas; Kijanskas, Mikuckis, Borovskij, Stankevicius; Matulevicius (Cesnauskis D 86), Kalonas, Mikoliunas (Zulpa 73); Ivaskevicius (Eliosius 86), Panka, Cesnauskis E.
Greece: (433) Karnezis; Maniatis, Manolas, Torosidis, Papastathopoulos; Holebas (Tzavelas 46), Karagounis, Katsouranis (Tziolis 84); Samaras, Gekas (Salpingidis 64), Christodoulopoulos.
Referee: Olegario Benquerenca.

Friday, 6 September 2013
Bosnia & Herzegovina (0) 0
Slovakia (0) 1 *(Pecovsky 77)* 15,000
Bosnia & Herzegovina: (442) Begovic; Pjanic, Spahic, Vrsajevic (Visca 65), Salihovic; Bicakcic, Lulic, Misimovic (Stevanovic 79), Medunjanin (Hajrovic 82); Dzeko, Ibisevic.
Slovakia: (451) Mucha; Skrtel, Durica, Pekarik, Hubocan; Kucka, Pecovsky, Sestak (Jendrisek 60), Hamsik (Guede 72), Weiss; Nemec (Jakubko 86).
Referee: Nicola Rizzoli.

Latvia (2) 2 *(Laizans 20, Zjuzins 42)*
Lithuania (1) 1 *(Matulevicius 44)* 7306
Latvia: (442) Vanins; Bulvitis, Gorkss, Maksimenko, Sinelnikovs; Rugins (Lazdins 75), Zjuzins (Cauna 63), Laizans, Gabovs; Rudnevs (Rode 90), Sabala.
Lithuania: (442) Karcemarskas; Mikuckis, Kijanskas, Stankevicius, Vicius; Kalonas (Cesnauskis E 86), Panka, Mikoliunas (Razulis 73), Novikovas (Cesnauskis D 50); Matulevicius, Sernas.
Referee: Sebastien Delferiere.

Liechtenstein (0) 0
Greece (0) 1 *(Mitroglou 73)* 2680
Liechtenstein: (442) Jehle; Oehri, Quintans, Stocklasa, Frick (Christen A 28); Burgmeier, Hasler N, Wieser (Yildiz 86), Polverino; Hasler D■, Christen M (Gubser 90).
Greece: (442) Karnezis; Holebas■, Papastathopoulos, Siovas, Torosidis; Kone (Ninis 47), Katsouranis, Maniatis, Tachtsidis (Karagounis 67); Christodoulopoulos (Papadopoulos 84), Mitroglou.
Referee: Stanislav Todorov.

Tuesday, 10 September 2013
Greece (0) 1 *(Salpingidis 58)*
Latvia (0) 0 70,000
Greece: (442) Karnezis; Torosidis, Tzavelas (Karagounis 73), Papastathopoulos, Siovas; Katsouranis■, Maniatis, Ninis, Salpingidis (Christodoulopoulos 64); Samaras (Fetfatzidis 88), Mitroglou.
Latvia: (442) Kolinko; Rugins■, Gabovs, Bulvitis, Gorkss; Maksimenko, Lazdins (Sinelnikovs 61), Laizans, Zjuzins (Karasausks 68); Cauna, Verpakovskis (Rakels 79).
Referee: Kristinn Jakobsson.

Lithuania (2) 2 *(Matulevicius 18, Kijanskas 40)*
Liechtenstein (0) 0 2700
Lithuania: (4231) Karcemarskas; Mikoliunas, Kijanskas, Mikuckis, Andriuskevicius; Ivaskevicius, Vicius; Cesnauskis D, Kalonas (Kuklys 72), Cesnauskis E (Sernas 79); Matulevicius (Sirgedas 90).
Liechtenstein: (541) Jehle; Quintans, Kaufmann, Christen A, Stocklasa, Oehri; Christen M, Burgmeier, Polverino, Gubser (Erne 75); Wieser.
Referee: Lasha Silagava.

Slovakia (1) 1 *(Hamsik 42)*
Bosnia & Herzegovina (0) 2 *(Bicakcic 70, Hajrovic 78)* 9438
Slovakia: (442) Mucha; Pekarik, Skrtel, Durica, Hubocan; Weiss (Jakubko 83), Hamsik, Pecovsky, Kucka; Sestak (Jendrisek 62), Nemec (Mak 82).
Bosnia & Herzegovina: (442) Begovic; Bicakcic, Spahic, Mujdza (Zahirovic 48), Lulic; Pjanic, Misimovic (Hajrovic 77), Salihovic (Visca 69), Medunjanin; Ibisevic, Dzeko.
Referee: David Fernandez Borbalan.

Friday, 11 October 2013
Bosnia & Herzegovina (4) 4 *(Dzeko 27, 39, Misimovic 34, Ibisevic 38)*
Liechtenstein (0) 1 *(Hasler N 61)* 15,000
Bosnia & Herzegovina: (442) Begovic; Vrsajevic, Bicakcic, Spahic, Lulic (Kvrzic 62); Misimovic, Pjanic (Hajrovic 62), Medunjanin (Ibricic 62), Salihovic; Ibisevic, Dzeko.
Liechtenstein: (4231) Jehle; Christen A, Quintans (Erne 57), Stocklasa, Oehri; Polverino, Kaufmann; Hasler D (Eris 80), Christen M (Yildiz 64), Gubser; Hasler N.
Referee: Richard Liesveld.

Greece (1) 1 *(Skrtel 44 (og))*
Slovakia (0) 0 21,067
Greece: (442) Karnezis; Torosidis, Manolas, Papastathopoulos, Holebas; Salpingidis (Karagounis 76), Maniatis, Tziolis, Christodoulopoulos (Ninis 57); Samaras, Mitroglou (Fetfatzidis 89).
Slovakia: (451) Mucha; Pekarik, Skrtel, Durica, Hubocan; Sestak (Jakubko 63), Kucka, Stoch, Pecovsky (Guede 63), Weiss; Nemec (Duris 76).
Referee: Deniz Aytekin.

Lithuania (1) 2 *(Cernych 8, Mikoliunas 67)*
Latvia (0) 0 2900
Lithuania: (442) Arlauskis; Vaitkunas, Zaliukas, Kijanskas, Borovskij; Kalonas, Ivaskevicius, Mikoliunas (Sirgedas 75), Cernych (Valskis 72); Panka, Matulevicius (Razulis 58).
Latvia: (442) Vanins; Bulvitis, Gorkss, Maksimenko, Gabovs (Kovalovs 73); Rakels (Lukjanovs 66), Zjuzins, Laizans, Fertovs; Sabala, Verpakovskis (Visnakovs 76).
Referee: Petur Reinert.

Tuesday, 15 October 2013
Greece (1) 2 *(Salpingidis 7, Karagounis 81)*
Liechtenstein (0) 0 16,086
Greece: (442) Karnezis; Vyntra, Holebas, Siovas, Tziolis; Kone (Samaris 45), Karagounis, Katsouranis, Samaras (Christodoulopoulos 69); Mitroglou (Athanasiadis 86), Salpingidis.
Liechtenstein: (442) Jehle; Stocklasa, Oehri, Kaufmann, Burgmeier; Hasler N, Christen A, Polverino, Wieser; Hasler D (Yildiz 90), Christen M (Erne 82).
Referee: Libor Kovank.

Latvia (0) 2 *(Sabala 47, Rode 90)*
Slovakia (2) 2 *(Jakubko 9, Salata 16)*   3813
Latvia: (442) Kolinko; Rode, Bulvitis, Gorkss, Maksimenko; Laizans (Zjuzins 53), Lazdins, Fertovs, Kovalovs; Sabala, Visnakovs (Verpakovskis 85).
Slovakia: (442) Kozacik; Pekarik, Durica, Salata, Svento; Kona, Kucka (Pecovsky 86), Sestak (Guede 62), Jakubko (Bakos 55); Jendrisek, Duris.
Referee: Yevhen Aranovskiy.

Lithuania (0) 0
Bosnia & Herzegovina (0) 1 *(Ibisevic 68)*   8000
Lithuania: (4411) Arlauskis; Kijanskas, Zaliukas, Vaitkunas, Borovskij; Mikoliunas (Valskis 69), Vicius, Panka, Kalonas; Cernych (Sirgedas 85); Matulevicius (Razulis 78).
Bosnia & Herzegovina: (442) Begovic; Vrsajevic (Zahirovic 71), Bicakcic, Spahic, Salihovic; Pjanic, Misimovic, Medunjanin, Lulic; Ibisevic, Dzeko.
Referee: Felix Zwayer.

Group G Table	P	W	D	L	F	A	GD	Pts
Bosnia & Herzegovina	10	8	1	1	30	6	24	25
Greece	10	8	1	1	12	4	8	25
Slovakia	10	3	4	3	11	10	1	13
Lithuania	10	3	2	5	9	11	–2	11
Latvia	10	2	2	6	10	20	–10	8
Liechtenstein	10	0	2	8	4	25	–21	2

GROUP H

Friday, 7 September 2012
Moldova (0) 0
England (3) 5 *(Lampard 3 (pen), 29, Defoe 32, Milner 74, Baines 83)*   10,102
Moldova: (451) Namasco; Armas, Epureanu, Bulgaru, Golovatenco; Kovalchuk, Gatcan, Onica, Suvorov (Dedov 46), Patras; Picusciac (Sidorenco 76 (Ovseanicov 85)).
England: (4411) Hart; Johnson G, Lescott, Terry, Baines; Milner, Lampard, Cleverley, Oxlade-Chamberlain (Walcott 58); Gerrard (Carrick 46); Defoe (Welbeck 68).
Referee: Paul van Boekel.

Montenegro (2) 2 *(Drincic 27, Vucinic 45)*
Poland (1) 2 *(Blaszczykowski 5 (pen), Mierzejewski 54)*   5000
Montenegro: (442) Bozovic M; Pavicevic■, Basa, Jovanovic (Kasalica 65), Volkov; Savic, Vukcevic (Pekovic 71), Zverotic, Drincic (Djudovic 84); Jovetic, Vucinic.
Poland: (442) Tyton; Glik, Piszczek, Wasilewski, Wawrzyniak; Polanski, Obraniak■, Blaszczykowski, Grosicki (Mierzejewski 46); Borysiuk (Murawski 69), Lewandowski R (Saganowski 90).
Referee: Kristinn Jakobsson.

Tuesday, 11 September 2012
England (0) 1 *(Lampard 87 (pen))*
Ukraine (1) 1 *(Konoplianka 39)*   68,681
England: (4231) Hart; Johnson G, Jagielka, Lescott, Baines (Bertrand 73); Lampard, Gerrard■; Milner, Cleverley (Welbeck 62), Oxlade-Chamberlain (Sturridge 69); Defoe.
Ukraine: (4231) Pyatov; Gusev, Khacheridi, Rakitskiy, Selin (Shevchuk 75); Tymoschuk, Rotan (Nazarenko 90); Yarmolenko, Garmash, Konoplianka; Zozulya (Devic 89).
Referee: Cuneyt Cakir.

Poland (1) 2 *(Blaszczykowski 33 (pen), Wawrzyniak 81)*
Moldova (0) 0   38,380
Poland: (442) Tyton; Glik, Piszczek, Wasilewski, Wawrzyniak; Polanski, Borysiuk (Krychowiak 76), Blaszczykowski, Mierzejewski (Sobiech 71); Saganowski (Sobota 46), Lewandowski R.
Moldova: (451) Namasco; Armas, Epureanu, Racu, Golovatenco; Kovalchuk, Gatcan, Suvorov (Alexeev 82), Ivanov (Onica 73), Patras (Ovseanicov 46); Picusciac.
Referee: Ilias Spathas.

San Marino (0) 0
Montenegro (2) 6 *(Djordjevic 25, Beqiraj 26, 52, Zverotic 69, Delibasic 78, 82)*   1947
San Marino: (442) Simoncini A; Brolli (Vannucci 83), Cervellini, Simoncini D, Vitaioli F; Gasperoni, Della Valle, Coppini, Rinaldi; Marani (Cibelli 64), Vitaioli M (Mazza 79).
Montenegro: (442) Bozovic M; Basa, Savic, Volkov, Djudovic; Vukcevic (Zverotic 65), Jovetic, Pekovic, Beqiraj (Kasalica 75); Damjanovic, Djordjevic (Delibasic 65).
Referee: Neil Doyle.

Friday, 12 October 2012
England (2) 5 *(Rooney 35 (pen), 69, Welbeck 38, 71, Oxlade-Chamberlain 77)*
San Marino (0) 0   85,856
England: (442) Hart; Walker, Cahill, Jagielka, Baines; Walcott (Lennon 10); Carrick (Shelvey 66), Cleverley, Oxlade-Chamberlain; Welbeck, Rooney (Carroll 73).
San Marino: (442) Simoncini A; Vitaioli F (Bacciocchi 83), Simoncini D, Brolli, Palazzi; Cibelli, Coppini (Buscarini 75), Rinaldi (Selva 78), Della Valle Alessandro; Gasperoni, Cervellini.
Referee: Gediminas Mazeika.

Moldova (0) 0
Ukraine (0) 0   10,100
Moldova: (442) Namasco; Bulgaru, Golovatenco, Racu, Epureanu; Onica, Kovalchuk (Pascenco A 60), Gatcan, Suvorov (Ovseanicov 78); Dedov, Picusciac (Doros 84).
Ukraine: (442) Pyatov; Butko, Mykhalyk, Selin, Khacheridi; Tymoschuk, Garmash (Seleznyov 60), Zozulya (Milevskiy 74), Gusev (Devic 79); Yarmolenko, Rotan.
Referee: Clement Turpin.

Tuesday, 16 October 2012
San Marino (0) 0
Moldova (0) 2 *(Dadu 73 (pen), Epureanu 78)*   736
San Marino: (442) Simoncini A; Vitaioli F, Palazzi (Vannucci 46), Bollini, Simoncini D; Della Valle Alessandro, Cervellini, Buscarini, Mazza (Cibelli 60); Marani (Selva 67), Vitaioli M.
Moldova: (442) Namasco; Golovatenco, Epureanu, Bulgaru, Bordiyan; Onica, Gatcan, Suvorov (Patras 58), Picusciac (Cebotaru 81); Dedov (Dadu 71), Alexeev.
Referee: Marios Panayi.

Ukraine (0) 0
Montenegro (1) 1 *(Damjanovic 45)*   50,505
Ukraine: (442) Pyatov; Selin, Kucher, Mykhalyk, Butko (Yarmolenko 62); Tymoschuk, Gusev, Konoplianka, Rotan; Seleznyov (Nazarenko 82), Devic (Zozulya 52).
Montenegro: (442) Bozovic M; Basa, Jovanovic, Volkov, Djudovic; Savic, Pekovic, Zverotic (Novakovic 88), Drincic; Jovetic (Vucinic 85), Damjanovic (Vukcevic 72).
Referee: Michail Koukoulakis.

Wednesday, 17 October 2012
Poland (0) 1 *(Glik 70)*
England (1) 1 *(Rooney 31)*   43,430
Poland: (4231) Tyton; Piszczek, Wasilewski, Wawrzyniak, Glik; Polanski, Krychowiak; Wszolek (Mierzejewski 63), Grosicki (Milik 82), Obraniak (Borysiuk 90); Lewandowski R.
England: (442) Hart; Johnson G, Jagielka, Lescott, Cole; Milner, Carrick, Gerrard, Cleverley; Rooney (Oxlade-Chamberlain 73), Defoe (Welbeck 67).
Referee: Gianluca Rocchi.

Wednesday, 14 November 2012
Montenegro (2) 3 *(Delibasic 15, 32, Zverotic 69)*
San Marino (0) 0   7000
Montenegro: (433) Bozovic M; Pavicevic, Basa (Kecojevic 71), Savic (Djordjevic 46), Volkov; Vukcevic, Novakovic, Zverotic; Kasalica (Igumanovic 77), Beqiraj, Delibasic.
San Marino: (532) Simoncini A; Palazzi, Cervellini, Benedettini (Della Valle Alex 83), Della Valle Alessandro, Bollini G; Vannucci, Cibelli (Gasperoni 89), Coppini; Rinaldi, Vitaioli (Buscarini 73).
Referee: Sandor Szabo.

Friday, 22 March 2013

Moldova (0) 0
Montenegro (0) 1 *(Vucinic 78)*   9000
Moldova: (442) Pascenco S; Golovatenco, Bulgaru, Bordiyan, Epureanu; Gatcan■, Dedov, Ionita, Gheorghiev (Josan 77); Pascenco A, Sidorenco.
Montenegro: (442) Bozovic M; Basa, Savic, Volkov, Pavicevic; Zverotic, Pekovic■, Bozovic V (Vukcevic 64), Jovetic; Kasalica (Damjanovic 45), Vucinic (Novakovic 80).
Referee: Daniele Orsato.

Poland (1) 1 *(Piszczek 18)*
Ukraine (3) 3 *(Yarmolenko 2, Gusev 7, Zozulya 45)*
     55,550
Poland: (451) Boruc; Boenisch, Piszczek, Wasilewski, Glik; Lukasik (Obraniak 59), Krychowiak, Blaszczykowski, Majewski (Teodorczyk 76), Rybus (Kosecki 46); Lewandowski R.
Ukraine: (451) Pyatov; Fedetskiy, Khacheridi, Kucher, Shevchuk; Gusev (Morozyuk 90), Rotan, Stepanenko (Tymoschuk 60), Yarmolenko, Garmash (Bezus 90); Zozulya.
Referee: Pavel Kralovec.

San Marino (0) 0
England (5) 8 *(Della Valle Alessandro 12 (og), Oxlade-Chamberlain 28, Defoe 35, 77, Young 39, Lampard 42, Rooney 54, Sturridge 70)*   4900
San Marino: (442) Simoncini A; Vitaioli F, Palazzi, Della Valle Alessandro, Simoncini D; Cervellini, Gasperoni, Cibelli (Buscarini 67), Bollini F (Valentini C 81); Selva (Rinaldi 74), Vitaioli M.
England: (442) Hart; Walker, Smalling, Lescott, Baines; Oxlade-Chamberlain, Lampard (Parker 66) Cleverley (Osman 56), Young; Rooney (Sturridge 55), Defoe.
Referee: Alain Bieri.

Tuesday, 26 March 2013

Montenegro (0) 1 *(Damjanovic 77)*
England (1) 1 *(Rooney 6)*   12,120
Montenegro: (442) Bozovic M; Basa, Savic, Volkov, Djudovic; Zverotic, Vukcevic (Krkotic 62), Bozovic V (Delibasic 76), Novakovic (Damjanovic 46); Jovetic, Vucinic.
England: (4231) Hart; Johnson G, Smalling, Lescott, Cole; Gerrard, Carrick; Milner, Cleverley (Young 78), Welbeck; Rooney.
Referee: Jonas Eriksson.

Poland (2) 5 *(Lewandowski R 21 (pen), 50 (pen), Piszczek 28, Teodorczyk 61, Kosecki 90)*
San Marino (0) 0   45,450
Poland: (442) Boruc; Salamon (Wasilewski 86), Piszczek, Glik (Kosecki 46), Wawrzyniak; Polanski, Krychowiak, Grosicki, Mierzejewski; Milik (Teodorczyk 59), Lewandowski R.
San Marino: (541) Simoncini A; Della Valle Alex (Buscarini 80), Palazzi, Vitaioli F, Della Valle Alessandro, Bollini G (Bacciocchi 57); Vitaioli M, Bollini F, Coppini, Selva (Rinaldi 51); Gasperoni.
Referee: Ken Henry Johnsen.

Ukraine (0) 2 *(Yarmolenko 61, Khacheridi 70)*
Moldova (0) 1 *(Suvorov 80)*   31,310
Ukraine: (442) Pyatov; Shevchuk, Fedetskiy, Khacheridi, Kucher; Stepanenko■, Tymoschuk, Yarmolenko, Gusev (Grechyshkin 90); Seleznyov (Bezus 62), Zozulya.
Moldova: (442) Namasco; Golovatenco, Bulgaru, Bordiyan, Epureanu; Ionita, Dedov (Suvorov 78), Gheorghiev, Pascenco A (Onica 67); Sidorenco, Bugaev (Doros 69).
Referee: Kenn Hansen.

Friday, 7 June 2013

Moldova (1) 1 *(Sidorenco 37)*
Poland (1) 1 *(Blaszczykowski 7)*   10,105
Moldova: (442) Namasco; Armas, Golovatenco, Bordiyan (Cebotaru 71), Epureanu; Ionita, Gatcan, Antoniuc (Ovseannicov 81), Dedov; Suvorov (Pascenco A 74), Sidorenco.

Poland: (442) Boruc; Jedrzejczyk, Komorowski, Salamon, Wawrzyniak; Krychowiak, Polanski (Sobiech 79), Blaszczykowski, Mierzejewski (Zielinski 62); Rybus (Kosecki 64), Lewandowski R.
Referee: Fernando Teixeira Vitienes.

Montenegro (0) 0
Ukraine (0) 4 *(Garmash 51, Konoplianka 77, Fedetskiy 84, Bezus 90)*   13,130
Montenegro: (442) Bozovic M; Pavicevic■, Basa, Kecojevic, Bozovic V (Delibasic 62); Volkov■, Zverotic, Pekovic, Jovetic (Damjanovic 43); Vucinic, Kasalica (Beqiraj 76).
Ukraine: (442) Pyatov; Fedetskiy, Rakitskiy, Tymoschuk, Yarmolenko (Kovpak 90); Gusev, Konoplianka, Rotan (Bezus 90), Garmash (Kravchenko 69); Edmar, Zozulya■.
Referee: Manuel Graefe.

Friday, 6 September 2013

England (3) 4 *(Gerrard 12, Lambert 26, Welbeck 45, 50)*
Moldova (0) 0   61,607
England: (433) Hart; Walker, Cahill, Jagielka, Cole (Baines 45); Lampard, Gerrard, Wilshere (Barkley 59); Walcott, Lambert (Milner 70), Welbeck.
Moldova: (541) Namasco; Armas, Golovatenco, Bordiyan, Bulgaru (Suvorov 57); Epureanu; Ionita (Onica 19), Antoniuc, Dedov, Gheorghiev (Pascenco A 84); Sidorenco.
Referee: Ivan Kruzliak.

Poland (1) 1 *(Lewandowski R 16)*
Montenegro (1) 1 *(Damjanovic 12)*   25,652
Poland: (442) Boruc; Jedrzejczyk, Wawrzyniak (Sobiech 27), Glik, Szukala; Sobota (Wszolek 62), Krychowiak, Zielinski (Mierzejewski 75), Blaszczykowski, Klich; Lewandowski R.
Montenegro: (442) Bozovic M; Bozovic V, Basa, Zverotic, Djudovic; Savic, Krkotic (Vukcevic 45), Drincic, Boskovic; Vucinic (Kasalica 37), Damjanovic (Beqiraj 85).
Referee: Bjorn Kuipers.

Ukraine (4) 9 *(Devic 11, Seleznyov 27, Edmar 33, Khacheridi 45, 54, Konoplyanka 51, Bezus 64, Fedetskiy 75, Rakitskiy 90)*
San Marino (0) 0   34,915
Ukraine: (442) Pyatov; Khacheridi, Shevchuk (Gusev 60), Fedetskiy, Rakitskiy; Tymoschuk (Bezus 60), Yarmolenko (Khomchenovskiy 76), Konoplyanka, Edmar; Seleznyov, Devic.
San Marino: (442) Valentini F; Valentini C (Bollini G 57), Palazzi, Vitaioli F, Simoncini D; Genghini, Coppini (Buscarini 69), Cervellini, Gasperoni (Rinaldi 88); Vitaioli M, Selva.
Referee: Neil Doyle.

Tuesday, 10 September 2013

San Marino (1) 1 *(Della Valle Alessandro 22)*
Poland (3) 5 *(Zielinski 11, 66, Blaszczykowski 24, Sobota 34, Mierzejewski 76)*   1597
San Marino: (433) Simoncini A; Palazzi (Cibelli 70), Vitaioli F, Della Valle Alessandro, Bollini G; Calzolari, Gasperoni (Cervellini 43), Buscarini; Vitaioli M, Selva, Rinaldi (Bianchi 80).
Poland: (451) Boruc; Boenisch, Celeban, Salamon, Jedrzejczyk; Sobota, Krychowiak (Wszolek 79), Zielinski, Klich, Blaszczykowski (Mierzejewski 72); Brozek (Robak 55).
Referee: Marco Borg.

Ukraine (0) 0
England (0) 0   69,890
Ukraine: (4231) Pyatov; Fedetskiy, Khacheridi, Kucher, Shevchuk; Stepanenko, Edmar; Gusev (Bezus 68), Yarmolenko (Khomchenovskiy 90), Konoplyanka; Zozulya (Seleznyov 90).
England: (433) Hart; Walker, Cahill, Jagielka, Cole; Lampard, Gerrard, Wilshere (Young 67); Walcott (Cleverley 87), Lambert, Milner.
Referee: Pedro Proenca.

Friday, 11 October 2013

England (0) 4 *(Rooney 49, Boskovic 62 (og), Townsend 78, Sturridge 90 (pen))*

Montenegro (0) 1 *(Damjanovic 72)* 83,807

England: (442) Hart; Walker, Cahill, Jagielka, Baines; Townsend (Wilshere 80), Gerrard (Milner 87), Lampard (Carrick 65), Welbeck; Rooney, Sturridge.
Montenegro: (442) Poleksic; Pavicevic (Beqiraj 57), Jovanovic, Savic, Kecojevic; Volkov (Vukcevic 73), Boskovic, Zverotic, Drincic; Jovetic (Kasalica 81), Damjanovic.
Referee: Alberto Undiano Mallenco.

Moldova (0) 3 *(Frunza 55, Sidorenco 59, 89)*

San Marino (0) 0 5000

Moldova: (352) Cebanu; Armas, Golovatenco, Bordiyan; Gatcan (Cojocari 86), Ionita, Doros (Antoniuc 46), Dedov, Andronic (Suvorov 72); Sidorenco, Frunza.
San Marino: (442) Simoncini A; Vitaioli F, Palazzi, Berretti (Battistini 64), Simoncini D; Della Valle Alessandro, Valentini C (Gasperoni L 79), Gasperoni A, Rinaldi (Bianchi 82); Cibelli, Cervellini.
Referee: Ignasi Villamayor.

Ukraine (0) 1 *(Yarmolenko 64)*

Poland (0) 0 39,126

Ukraine: (433) Pyatov; Khacheridi, Shevchuk, Fedetskiy, Rakitskiy; Stepanenko, Yarmolenko (Gusev 90), Konoplyanka; Rotan, Edmar (Bezus 90), Zozulya (Devic 61).
Poland: (4231) Boruc; Wojtkowiak, Jedrzejczyk, Szukala, Glik; Sobota (Peszko 61), Lewandowski M (Zielinski 76); Krychowiak, Blaszczykowski, Klich (Mierzejewski 66); Lewandowski R.
Referee: Jonas Eriksson.

Tuesday, 15 October 2013

England (1) 2 *(Rooney 41, Gerrard 88)*

Poland (0) 0 85,186

England: (4231) Hart; Smalling, Cahill, Jagielka, Baines; Carrick (Lampard 71), Gerrard; Townsend (Milner 86), Rooney, Welbeck; Sturridge (Wilshere 82).
Poland: (451) Szczesny; Wojtkowiak, Jedrzejczyk, Glik, Celeban; Blaszczykowski, Mierzejewski (Zielinski 76); Krychowiak, Sobota (Peszko 64), Lewandowski M (Klich 45); Lewandowski R.
Referee: Damir Skomina.

Montenegro (0) 2 *(Jovetic 56 (pen), 90)*

Moldova (1) 5 *(Antoniuc 28, 89, Armas 62, Sidorenco 64, Ionita 73)* 11,000

Montenegro: (433) Poleksic; Pavicevic, Jovanovic (Krkotic 4), Kecojevic, Bozovic V; Zverotic, Drincic, Boskovic (Kasalica 45); Beqiraj (Vesovic 77), Damjanovic, Jovetic.
Moldova: (442) Cebanu; Armas, Golovatenco, Racu, Bordiyan; Ionita, Gatcan, Antoniuc, Dedov; Gheorghiev, Sidorenco (Frunza 84).
Referee: Robert Schorgenhofer.

San Marino (0) 0

Ukraine (3) 8 *(Seleznyov 13 (pen), 19, Devic 15, 51, 58 (pen), Yarmolenko 55, Bezus 65, Mandzyuk 90)* 1268

San Marino: (442) Simoncini A; Vitaioli F (Genghini 85), Palazzi[■], Simoncini D, Della Valle Alessandro[■]; Valentini (Benedettini 73), Berretti (Della Valle Alex 60), Battistini, Rinaldi; Vitaioli M, Cervellini.
Ukraine: (442) Pyatov; Mandzyuk, Shevchuk, Kucher, Konoplyanka (Morozyuk 77); Tymoschuk, Yarmolenko (Fedetskiy 66); Rotan, Gusev; Seleznyov (Bezus 64), Devic.
Referee: Harald Lechner.

Group H Table	P	W	D	L	F	A	GD	Pts
England	10	6	4	0	31	4	27	22
Ukraine	10	6	3	1	28	4	24	21
Montenegro	10	4	3	3	18	17	1	15
Poland	10	3	4	3	18	12	6	13
Moldova	10	3	2	5	12	17	–5	11
San Marino	10	0	0	10	1	54	–53	0

GROUP I

Friday, 7 September 2012

Finland (0) 0

France (1) 1 *(Diaby 20)* 35,351

Finland: (442) Hradecky; Halsti, Arkivuo, Moisander, Toivio; Eremenko R, Hetemaj (Eremenko A 64), Sparv, Ring; Hamalainen (Kuqi 77), Pukki.
France: (442) Lloris; Reveillere, Yanga-Mbiwa, Evra, Sakho; Cabaye (Matuidi 72), Diaby, Mavuba, Ribery (Gomis 88); Benzema, Menez (Valbuena 62).
Referee: Craig Thomson.

Georgia (0) 1 *(Okriashvili 51)*

Belarus (0) 0 10,100

Georgia: (442) Loria; Grigalava, Kashia, Amisulashvili, Khizanishvili; Kankava, Daushvili, Okriashvili (Sirbiladze 83), Targamadze; Ananidze (Gorgiashvili 74), Mchedlidze (Kvirkvelia D 56).
Belarus: (442) Veremko; Zhavnerchik (Balanovich 34), Polyakov, Martynovich, Tigorev (Dragun 62); Verkhovtsov, Bressan, Nekhaychik (Bardachov 30), Putsila; Kulchy, Kornilenko.
Referee: Stanislav Todorov.

Tuesday, 11 September 2012

France (0) 3 *(Capoue 49, Jallet 68, Ribery 80)*

Belarus (0) 1 *(Putsila 72)* 55,550

France: (433) Lloris; Yanga-Mbiwa, Evra, Sakho, Cabaye (Matuidi 75); Mavuba, Jallet, Capoue; Ribery (Menez 90), Giroud (Valbuena 61), Benzema.
Belarus: (451) Veremko; Martynovich, Polyakov, Radkov, Verkhovtsov (Balanovich 70); Bardachov, Dragun, Kisliak, Bressan (Kulchy 46), Putsila; Rodionov (Kornilenko 62).
Referee: Huseyin Gocek.

Georgia (0) 0

Spain (0) 1 *(Soldado 86)* 32,320

Georgia: (442) Loria (Kvaskhvadze 73); Lobjanidze, Kashia, Amisulashvili, Khizanishvili; Kankava, Kvirkvelia D, Daushvili, Targamadze (Dzalamidze 64); Okriashvili, Mchedlidze (Sirbiladze 79).
Spain: (433) Casillas; Jordi Alba, Arbeloa (Fabregas 80), Pique, Sergio Ramos; Busquets (Pedro 57), Alonso, Xavi; Iniesta, Silva (Cazorla 64), Soldado.
Referee: Svein Oddvar Moen.

Friday, 12 October 2012

Belarus (0) 0

Spain (2) 4 *(Jordi Alba 12, Pedro 20, 69, 72)* 30,300

Belarus: (4231) Veremko; Filipenko, Plaskonny, Shitov, Martynovich; Bardachov, Dragun (Chukhley 79); Tigorev, Volodko (Kisliak 46), Hleb; Rodionov (Bressan 65).
Spain: (433) Casillas; Arbeloa, Sergio Ramos (Albiol 72), Busquets, Jordi Alba; Xavi (Villa 75), Alonso, Cazorla; Pedro, Fabregas, Silva (Iniesta 56).
Referee: Serge Gumienny.

Finland (0) 1 *(Hamalainen 62)*

Georgia (0) 1 *(Kashia 57)* 12,126

Finland: (442) Maenpaa; Moisander, Raitala, Uronen, Ojala J; Eremenko R, Sparv, Ring, Hamalainen; Pukki (Hetemaj 62), Eremenko A[■].
Georgia: (442) Revishvili; Grigalava, Kashia, Khizanishvili, Amisulashvili; Kobakhidze, Daushvili, Targamadze (Kenia 80); Okriashvili (Ananidze 67), Mchedlidze (Devdariani 59).
Referee: Yevhen Aranovskiy.

Tuesday, 16 October 2012

Belarus (2) 2 *(Bressan 6, Dragun 28)*

Georgia (0) 0 22,220

Belarus: (442) Veremko; Verkhovtsov, Bardachov, Polyakov, Filipenko; Tigorev, Dragun, Pavlov (Kisliak 82), Hleb; Bressan (Volodko 85), Rodionov (Chukhley 90).
Georgia: (442) Revishvili; Kashia, Khizanishvili, Amisulashvili, Grigalava; Kankava, Daushvili, Kobakhidze, Targamadze (Kenia 74); Okriashvili (Ananidze 48), Devdariani (Mchedlidze 46).
Referee: Robert Schoergenhofer.

Spain (1) 1 *(Sergio Ramos 25)*
France (0) 1 *(Giroud 90)*   46,460
Spain: (442) Casillas; Sergio Ramos, Arbeloa (Juanfran 51), Jordi Alba, Iniesta (Torres 75); Xavi, Fabregas, Alonso, Busquets; Silva (Cazorla 13), Pedro.
France: (442) Lloris; Koscielny, Debuchy, Evra, Sakho; Valbuena, Cabaye, Gonalons (Matuidi 57), Ribery; Benzema (Giroud 87), Menez (Sissoko 68).
Referee: Felix Brych.

Friday, 22 March 2013
France (1) 3 *(Giroud 45, Valbuena 47, Ribery 61)*
Georgia (0) 1 *(Kobakhidze 70)*   77,770
France: (442) Lloris; Varane, Clichy, Jallet, Sakho; Valbuena (Remy 66), Matuidi (Sissoko 67), Pogba, Ribery (Menez 78); Benzema, Giroud.
Georgia: (442) Loria; Lobjanidze, Kvirkvelia D, Kashia, Amisulashvili, Khizanishvili, Kobakhidze, Daushvili, Targamadze (Gelashvili 84); Ananidze (Kenia 46), Vatsadze (Dvalishvili 74).
Referee: Ivan Bebek.

Spain (0) 1 *(Sergio Ramos 49)*
Finland (0) 1 *(Pukki 79)*   28,280
Spain: (4231) Valdes; Arbeloa, Pique, Sergio Ramos, Jordi Alba; Fabregas (Mata 76), Busquets; Silva, Cazorla (Pedro 46), Iniesta; Villa (Negredo 65).
Finland: (451) Maenpaa; Moisander, Toivio, Arkivuo, Raitala; Eremenko R, Hetemaj, Tainio (Sparv 69), Ring, Hamalainen; Pukki (Halsti 90).
Referee: Ovidiu Alin Hategan.

Tuesday, 26 March 2013
France (0) 0
Spain (0) 1 *(Pedro 58)*   80,800
France: (451) Lloris; Jallet (Giroud 90), Koscielny, Varane, Evra; Cabaye (Menez 70), Matuidi, Pogba■, Valbuena, Ribery; Benzema (Sissoko 82).
Spain: (433) Valdes; Arbeloa, Pique, Sergio Ramos, Monreal; Alonso, Busquets, Xavi; Iniesta (Mata 90), Villa (Jesus Navas 61), Pedro (Fabregas 76).
Referee: Viktor Kassai.

Friday, 7 June 2013
Finland (0) 1 *(Shitov 58 (og))*
Belarus (0) 0   24,249
Finland: (442) Maenpaa; Raitala, Pasanen, Arkivuo (Hurme 53), Halsti; Eremenko R, Hetemaj, Tainio (Sparv 68), Ring; Hamalainen, Pukki (Forssell 77).
Belarus: (442) Veremko; Martynovich, Shitov (Kalachev 78), Filipenko, Bardachov; Dragun (Pavlov 66), Hleb, Putsila, Kisliak; Balanovich (Nekhaychik■ 17), Rodionov.
Referee: Eli Hacmon.

Tuesday, 11 June 2013
Belarus (0) 1 *(Verkhovtsov 85)*
Finland (1) 1 *(Pukki 24)*   5000
Belarus: (4231) Veremko; Veretilo (Kisliak 46), Martynovich (Sitko 79), Verkhovtsov, Olekhnovich; Trubila, Dragun; Kalachev, Hleb, Putsila (Bressan 64); Rodionov.
Finland: (442) Maenpaa; Raitala, Pasanen, Moisander, Hurme; Eremenko R, Hetemaj, Sparv, Ring; Hamalainen (Arajuuri 82), Pukki (Furuholm 75).
Referee: Libor Kovarik.

Friday, 6 September 2013
Finland (0) 0
Spain (1) 2 *(Jordi Alba 18, Negredo 86)*   35,000
Finland: (442) Maenpaa; Pasanen, Moisander, Toivio, Halsti; Arkivuo, Eremenko R, Tainio (Riski 69), Ring (Hamalainen 69); Schuller, Pukki (Zeneli 81).
Spain: (442) Casillas; Albiol, Sergio Ramos, Jordi Alba, Koke; Mario Suarez, Iniesta, Fabregas (Negredo 71); Xavi; Pedro (Cazorla 81), Villa (Jesus Navas 55).
Referee: Ivan Bebek.

Georgia (0) 0
France (0) 0   25,000
Georgia: (442) Loria; Grigalava, Lobjanidze, Kashia, Amisulashvili; Khubutia, Kankava, Ananidze (Targamadze 69), Okriashvili; Kobakhidze (Grigalashvili 60), Gelashvili (Dvalishvili 79).
France: (442) Lloris; Evra, Sagna, Koscielny, Abidal; Valbuena, Sissoko, Guilavogui (Nasri 78), Ribery; Giroud, Benzema (Gignac 62).
Referee: Firat Aydinus.

Tuesday, 10 September 2013
Belarus (1) 2 *(Filipenko 32, Kalachev 57)*
France (0) 4 *(Ribery 47 (pen), 64, Nasri 70, Pogba 74)*
                                                  12,203
Belarus: (442) Veremko; Martynovich, Verkhovtsov (Rodionov 77), Bordachev, Filipenko; Dragun (Olekhnovich 71), Hleb, Putsila, Balanovich; Tigorev (Bressan 83), Kalachev.
France: (442) Lloris; Sagna, Koscielny, Abidal, Clichy; Valbuena (Guilavogui 90), Matuidi, Pogba, Ribery (Sissoko 79); Giroud, Payet (Nasri 60).
Referee: Daniele Orsato.

Georgia (0) 0
Finland (0) 1 *(Eremenko R 75 (pen))*   29,000
Georgia: (442) Revishvili; Lobjanidze, Khubutia, Amisulashvili, Grigalashvili; Ananidze (Dvalishvili 83), Kashia, Kankava■, Okriashvili; Gelashvili (Grigalava 57), Kobakhidze (Targamadze 45).
Finland: (442) Maenpaa; Lampi, Arkivuo, Moisander, Ojala J; Tainio, Eremenko R, Hetemaj, Hamalainen (Riski 89); Ring (Sparv 71), Pukki (Schuller 90).
Referee: Michael Soteriou.

Friday, 11 October 2013
Spain (0) 2 *(Xavi 61, Negredo 78)*
Belarus (0) 1 *(Kornilenko 89)*   21,000
Spain: (433) Valdes; Arbeloa, Pique, Sergio Ramos, Monreal (Iniesta 46); Xavi, Busquets, Fabregas (Koke 83); Silva, Pedro, Michu (Negredo 57).
Belarus: (442) Gutor; Martynovich (Kisliak 81), Verkhovtsov, Bordachev, Filipenko; Dragun, Putsila (Kornilenko 76), Balanovich, Tigorev; Kalachev, Rodionov (Krivets 55).
Referee: Bas Nijhuis.

Tuesday, 15 October 2013
France (1) 3 *(Ribery 8, Toivio 77 (og), Benzema 87)*
Finland (0) 0   65,000
France: (442) Lloris; Debuchy, Abidal, Evra, Koscielny; Valbuena, Nasri (Remy 71), Matuidi (Cabaye 71); Pogba, Ribery, Giroud (Benzema 81).
Finland: (451) Maenpaa; Arkivuo, Halsti, Pasanen, Lampi; Eremenko R, Hetemaj, Tainio (Toivio 64), Ring, Hamalainen (Riski 79); Pukki (Furuholm 86).
Referee: Michail Koukoulakis.

Spain (1) 2 *(Negredo 26, Mata 61)*
Georgia (0) 0   14,000
Spain: (442) Casillas; Juanfran, Pique, Sergio Ramos, Moreno; Iniesta (Isco 81), Jesus Navas, Xavi (Koke 66), Busquets; Negredo, Pedro (Mata 57).
Georgia: (442) Loria; Lobjanidze, Grigalava, Kashia, Amisulashvili; Khubutia, Kankava (Dolidze 70), Ananidze, Okriashvili (Dzaria 76); Kobakhidze, Gelashvili (Modebadze 87).
Referee: Florian Meyer.

Group I Table	P	W	D	L	F	A	GD	Pts
Spain	8	6	2	0	14	3	11	20
France	8	5	2	1	15	6	9	17
Finland	8	2	3	3	5	9	-4	9
Georgia	8	1	2	5	3	10	-7	5
Belarus	8	1	1	6	7	16	-9	4

EUROPEAN PLAY-OFFS

FIRST LEG

Friday, 15 November 2013
Greece (2) 3 *(Mitroglou 14, 67, Salpingidis 21)*
Romania (1) 1 *(Stancu 19)* 28,200
Greece: (433) Karnezis; Holebas, Papastathopoulos, Torosidis, Maniatis (Karagounis 77); Siovas, Tziolis, Katsouranis (Samaris 86); Mitroglou (Gekas 80), Salpingidis, Samaras.
Romania: (442) Lobont; Gardos, Goian, Rat, Matel; Tanase (Maxim 86), Cocis, Bourceanu (Lazar■ 74), Torje (Grozav 75); Stancu, Marica.
Referee: Pedro Proenca.

Iceland (0) 0
Croatia (0) 0 9768
Iceland: (442) Halldorsson; Skulason O■, Arnason, Sigurdsson R, Skulason A; Gudmundsson, Gunnarsson, Sigurdsson G, Bjarnason B; Finnbogason (Gislason 63), Sigthorsson (Gudjohnsen 45).
Croatia: (442) Pletikosa; Srna, Simunic, Corluka, Pranjic; Perisic, Rakitic, Modric, Ilicevic (Olic 45); Mandzukic (Benko 87), Eduardo (Rebic 72).
Referee: Alberto Undiano Mallenco.

Portugal (0) 1 *(Ronaldo 82)*
Sweden (0) 0 64,000
Portugal: (433) Rui Patricio; Fabio Coentrao, Bruno Alves, Pepe, Joao Pereira; Veloso, Joao Moutinho, Meireles (Josue 78); Nani, Ronaldo, Postiga (Almeida 65).
Sweden: (442) Isaksson; Lustig, Nilsson P, Antonsson, Olsson M; Larsson, Elm (Wernbloom 72), Kallstrom (Svensson 78), Kacaniklic; Elmander (Gerndt 88), Ibrahimovic.
Referee: Nicola Rizzoli.

Ukraine (0) 2 *(Zozulya 61, Yarmolenko 83 (pen))*
France (0) 0 67,732
Ukraine: (4141) Pyatov; Khacheridi, Shevchuk, Fedetskiy, Kucher■; Yarmolenko; Stepanenko, Konoplyanka (Gusev 90), Rotan, Edmar (Bezus 76); Zozulya (Seleznyov 86).
France: (4231) Lloris; Debuchy, Abidal, Koscielny■, Evra; Nasri (Valbuena 80), Matuidi; Pogba, Giroud (Benzema 70), Ribery; Remy (Sissoko 64).
Referee: Cuneyt Cakir.

SECOND LEG

Tuesday, 19 November 2013
Croatia (1) 2 *(Mandzukic 27, Srna 47)*
Iceland (0) 0 25,000
Croatia: (442) Pletikosa; Srna, Simunic, Corluka, Pranjic; Kovacic (Rebic 74), Rakitic, Modric (Lovren 89), Perisic; Mandzukic■, Olic (Jelavic 80).
Iceland: (442) Halldorsson; Saevarsson, Arnason, Sigurdsson R, Skulason A; Gunnarsson (Hallfredsson 72), Gudmundsson, Sigurdsson G, Bjarnason B; Gudjohnsen (Gislason 64), Finnbogason.
Referee: Bjorn Kuipers.

France (2) 3 *(Sakho 22, Benzema 33, Gusev 74 (og))*
Ukraine (0) 0 77,000
France: (442) Lloris; Debuchy (Sagna 78), Evra, Varane, Sakho; Cabaye, Matuidi, Valbuena, Pogba; Ribery, Benzema (Giroud 82).
Ukraine: (442) Pyatov; Shevchuk, Khacheridi■, Mandzyuk, Rakitskiy; Yarmolenko, Konoplyanka, Rotan, Bezus (Gusev 64 (Stepanenko 76)); Edmar, Zozulya.
Referee: Damir Skomina.

Romania (0) 1 *(Holebas 55 (og))*
Greece (1) 1 *(Mitroglou 23)* 53,174
Romania: (442) Tatarusanu; Matel, Goian, Chiriches, Rat (Latovlevici 26); Hoban, Tanase, Torje (Niculae 56), Maxim; Marica, Stancu (Grozav 86).
Greece: (442) Karnezis; Siovas (Manolas 80), Torosidis (Vyntra 72), Papastathopoulos, Holebas; Karagounis (Samaris 73), Tziolis, Maniatis, Mitroglou; Samaras, Salpingidis.
Referee: Milorad Mazic.

Sweden (0) 2 *(Ibrahimovic 68, 72)*
Portugal (0) 3 *(Ronaldo 50, 77, 79)* 49,766
Sweden: (442) Isaksson; Lustig, Nilsson P, Antonsson, Olsson; Larsson (Gerndt 90), Elm (Svensson 46), Kallstrom, Kacaniklic (Durmaz 82); Elmander, Ibrahimovic.
Portugal: (433) Rui Patricio; Joao Pereira, Pepe, Bruno Alves, Fabio Coentrao (Antunes 52); Meireles (William Carvalho 73), Veloso, Joao Moutinho; Nani, Almeida (Ricardo Costa 81), Ronaldo.
Referee: Howard Webb.

Belgium, Italy, Germany, Netherlands, Switzerland, Russia, Bosnia & Herzegovina, England, Spain, Portugal, France, Greece and Croatia qualify for World Cup 2014 in Brazil.

SOUTH AMERICA

■ *Denotes player sent off.*

Friday, 7 October 2011

Argentina (2) 4 *(Higuain 7, 52, 63, Messi 25)*

Chile (0) 1 *(Fernandez M 59)*   26,161

Argentina: Andujar; Zabaleta, Burdisso, Rojo, Otamendi, Di Maria (Gutierrez 85), Sosa (Salvio 79), Higuain, Messi, Banega (Rinaudo 72), Brana.
Chile: Bravo; Ponce, Isla, Carmona, Vidal, Suazo, Valdivia, Pinilla (Gonzalez Marcos 54), Fernandez M (Jorquera 81), Beausejour (Vargas 54), Jara.
Referee: Roldan (Colombia).

Ecuador (2) 2 *(Ayovi J 15, Benitez 28)*

Venezuela (0) 0   32,278

Ecuador: Banguera; Erazo, Paredes J, Noboa (Arroyo 76), Ayovi W, Benitez (Mendez 83), Campos, Valencia A, Ayovi J, Saritama.
Venezuela: Vega; Granados, Rey■, Velazquez, Flores F (Flores A 57), Di Giorgi, Meza, Maldonado (Feltscher F 72), Seijas, Lucena, Aristeguieta (Moreno 46).
Referee: Osses (Chile).

Peru (0) 2 *(Guerrero 46, 71)*

Paraguay (0) 0   39,600

Peru: Fernandez; Rodriguez, Acasiete, Guizasola, Balbin, Vargas, Guerrero P (Advincula 90), Farfan, Pizarro, Cruzado (Lobaton 89), Yotun.
Paraguay: Barreto D; Piris, Marecos (Samudio 25), Veron, Barreto E, Santa Cruz R, Estigarribia, Da Silva, Riveros, Pirez (Cardozo O 66), Ramirez (Pittoni 55).
Referee: Pezzotta (Argentina).

Uruguay (3) 4 *(Suarez 3, Lugano 25, 71, Cavani 34)*

Bolivia (1) 2 *(Cardozo 17, Martins 87 (pen))*   25,500

Uruguay: Muslera; Lugano, Godin, Suarez, Forlan, Pereira A (Fucile 56), Pirez, Pereira M, Arevalo, Cavani (Rodriguez C 70), Caceres.
Bolivia: Arias; Gutierrez, Rivero, Flores (Chavez 81), Rojas (Vaca 60), Martins, Vargas, Robles, Raldes, Saucedo (Pena 46), Cardozo.
Referee: Carrillo (Peru).

Tuesday, 11 October 2011,

Bolivia (0) 1 *(Flores 85)*

Colombia (0) 2 *(Pabon 48, Falcao 90)*   33,155

Bolivia: Vaca; Gutierrez (Campos J 70), Alvarez (Chavez 77), Rivero, Flores, Martins (Andaveris 71), Robles, Raldes, Arce, Escobar, Cardozo.
Colombia: Ospina; Rodriguez, Sanchez, Armero, Aguilar, Pabon (Moreno 62), Guarin F (Chara 70), Perea, Zuniga, Gutierrez (Falcao 79), Mosquera.
Referee: Amarilla (Paraguay).

Chile (2) 4 *(Ponce 2, Vargas 18, Medel 47, Suazo 63 (pen))*

Peru (0) 2 *(Pizarro 49, Farfan 59)*   39,000

Chile: Bravo; Ponce, Isla, Gonzalez Marcos, Vidal, Suazo (Paredes 72), Valdivia (Carmona 90), Beausejour, Medel, Jara, Vargas (Fernandez M 84).
Peru: Fernandez; Rodriguez, Acasiete (Chiroque 87), Balbin (Guizasola 46), Vargas, Guerrero P, Farfan, Revoredo, Pizarro, Cruzado, Yotun (Lobaton 46).
Referee: Orosco (Bolivia).

Paraguay (0) 1 *(Ortiz 90)*

Uruguay (0) 1 *(Forlan 67)*   12,922

Paraguay: Barreto D; Veron, Bonet (Perez 79), Cardozo O (Caballero 67), Barreto E, Estigarribia, Da Silva, Caceres (Santa Cruz R 77), Riveros, Valdez, Ortiz.
Uruguay: Muslera; Lugano, Godin, Suarez, Forlan (Rodriguez C 83), Pereira A (Gonzalez 64), Perez (Eguren 58), Pereira M, Arevalo, Cavani, Caceres.
Referee: Seneme (Brazil).

Venezuela (0) 1 *(Amorebieta 61)*

Argentina (0) 0   37,000

Venezuela: Vega; Vizcarrondo, Amorebieta, Cichero, Fedor (Moreno 89), Rincon, Gonzalez C (Alvarez 83), Lucena, Rosales, Arango, Rondon J (Feltscher F 76).

Argentina: Andujar; Demichelis, Zabaleta (Banega 66), Burdisso, Rojo, Otamendi, Di Maria (Pastore 84), Sosa (Palacio R 74), Higuain, Messi, Mascherano.
Referee: Silvera (Uruguay).

Friday, 11 November 2011

Argentina (0) 1 *(Lavezzi 60)*

Bolivia (0) 1 *(Martins 56)*   27,592

Argentina: Romero; Burdisso, Demichelis, Zabaleta, Rodriguez C, Mascherano (Sosa 82), Gago, Pastore, Alvarez (Lavezzi 59), Messi, Higuain.
Bolivia: Arias; Gutierrez, Mendez, Vargas, Rivero, Flores, Robles, Cardozo, Martins (Andaveris 77), Escobar (Chavez 84), Rojas (Segovia 54).
Referee: Vera (Ecuador).

Uruguay (2) 4 *(Suarez 42, 45, 68, 74)*

Chile (0) 0   40,500

Uruguay: Muslera; Lugano, Caceres, Godin, Pereira A, Perez, Gonzalez (Eguren 70), Arevalo, Ramirez (Abreu 58), Suarez (Rodriguez C 77), Cavani.
Chile: Bravo; Gonzalez Marcos, Contreras, Isla, Ponce, Diaz (Mirosevic 61), Fernandez M, Medel, Suazo (Paredes 61), Vargas (Canales 72), Campos.
Referee: Baldassi (Argentina).

Saturday, 12 November 2011

Colombia (1) 1 *(Guarin F 11)*

Venezuela (0) 1 *(Feltscher F 79)*   49,612

Colombia: Ospina; Yepes, Perea, Vallejo, Armero, Bolivar, Guarin F, Rodriguez (Moreno 90), Gutierrez (Quintero 85), Martinez J, Pabon (Marrugo 77).
Venezuela: Vega; Amorebieta, Vizcarrondo, Rosales, Cichero, Arango, Gonzalez C, Flores A, Rincon (Guerra 84), Moreno (Feltscher F 71), Fedor (Rondon J 58).
Referee: Ponce (Ecuador).

Paraguay (0) 2 *(Riveros 47, Veron 57)*

Ecuador (0) 1 *(Rojas 90)*   11,173

Paraguay: Barreto D; Da Silva, Veron, Bonet, Riveros, Estigarribia (Samudio 80), Caceres, Ayala, Ortiz, Haedo Valdez (Caballero 74), Barrios (Dos Santos 64).
Ecuador: Banguera; Achilier, Erazo, Saritama (Rojas 78), Valencia A, Noboa, Ayovi W, Morante, Borja (Mendez 71), Suarez (Montero 59), Ayovi J.
Referee: Buitrago (Colombia).

Tuesday, 15 November 2011

Chile (1) 2 *(Contreras 28, Campos 86)*

Paraguay (0) 0   44,726

Chile: Bravo; Gonzalez Marcos, Contreras, Isla, Ponce, Fernandez M (Mirosevic 87), Medel, Aranguiz, Sanchez, Suazo (Campos 71), Vargas (Paredes 78).
Paraguay: Barreto D; Manzur, Veron, Bonet (Hernan Perez 46), Samudio, Barreto E, Dos Santos (Benitez 62), Riveros, Estigarribia (Cardozo O 75), Aquino, Haedo Valdez.
Referee: Lopes (Brazil).

Colombia (1) 1 *(Pabon 45)*

Argentina (0) 2 *(Messi 61, Aguero 85)*   49,600

Colombia: Ospina; Yepes, Zuniga, Mosquera, Armero, Aguilar (Arias 77), Bolivar, Rodriguez, Ramos, Martinez J (Quintero 77), Pabon (Moreno 62).
Argentina: Romero; Burdisso (Desabato 38), Zabaleta, Rodriguez C, Fernandez F, Mascherano, Brana, Guinazu (Aguero 46), Sosa, Messi, Higuain (Gago 86).
Referee: Filho (Brazil).

Ecuador (0) 2 *(Mendez 70, Benitez 89)*

Peru (0) 0   34,481

Ecuador: Banguera; Campos, Erazo (Morante 37), Castillo, Saritama (Minda 81), Valencia A, Ayovi W, Paredes P, Benitez, Rojas (Mendez 46), Ayovi J.
Peru: Fernandez; Acasiete, Vilchez, Revoredo, Ramos, Vargas, Lobaton (Guevara 46), Retamoso, Guerrero P, Pizarro (Chiroque 63), Farfan (Advincula 66).
Referee: Larrionda (Uruguay).

Venezuela (1) 1 *(Vizcarrondo 26)*
Bolivia (0) 0 33,351
Venezuela: Vega; Amorebieta, Vizcarrondo, Rosales, Cichero, Arango, Gonzalez C (Feltscher F 63), Rincon, Julio Alvarez (Lucena 72), Maldonado (Feltscher R 78), Rondon J.
Bolivia: Arias; Raldes, Gutierrez, Christian Vargas, Rivero, Robles, Chavez, Cardozo (Andaveris 78), Marcelo Martins, Escobar (Campos J 59), Segovia (Arce 59).
Referee: Buckley (Peru).

Saturday, 2 June 2012
Argentina (3) 4 *(Aguero 19, Higuain 29, Messi 31, Di Maria 76)*
Ecuador (0) 0 50,000
Argentina: Romero; Garay, Zabaleta, Gago, Di Maria (Rodriguez M 82), Higuain (Lavezzi 73), Messi, Mascherano, Rodriguez C, Aguero (Sosa 62), Fernandez F.
Ecuador: Dominguez; Guagua, Noboa, Ayovi W, Benitez (Ibarra 84), Suarez (Montero 46), Quinonez, Valencia A, Saritama (Ayovi J 39), Achilier, Campos.
Referee: Rivera (Peru).

Bolivia (0) 0
Chile (1) 2 *(Aranguiz 45, Vidal 83)* 34,389
Bolivia: Vaca; Mendez, Gutierrez, Vargas, Rivero, Flores, Arce, Campos J (Cardozo 56), Chumacero, Pedriel (Andaveris 70), Escobar (Pena 73).
Chile: Bravo; Contreras, Gonzalez O, Sanchez, Vidal, Suazo (Vargas 78), Rojas, Fernandez M (Figueroa 73), Mena, Aranguiz (Leal 87), Diaz.
Referee: Intriago (Ecuador).

Uruguay (1) 1 *(Forlan 38)*
Venezuela (0) 1 *(Rondon J 84)* 57,000
Uruguay: Muslera; Lugano (Coates 78), Godin, Suarez, Forlan (Abreu 88), Pereira A, Perez (Gonzalez 75), Pereira M, Arevalo, Cavani, Caceres.
Venezuela: Vega; Vizcarrondo, Amorebieta, Cichero, Rincon, Seijas (Perozo 88), Di Giorgi (Orozco 75), Rosales, Arango, Feltscher F (Fedor 55), Rondon J.
Referee: Arias (Paraguay).

Sunday, 3 June 2012
Peru (0) 0
Colombia (0) 1 *(Rodriguez 51)* 35,724
Peru: Penny; Galliquio, Carrillo (Farfan 85), Guerrero P, Revoredo (Rui Diaz 68), Ramos, Lobaton (Chiroque 57), Cruzado, Votun, Ramirez, Alvarez.
Colombia: Ospina; Yepes, Cuadrado (Ramirez 72), Sanchez, Armero, Falcao, Rodriguez (Martinez J 90), Pabon, Guarin F (Mejia 86), Perea, Mosquera.
Referee: Pitana (Argentina).

Bolivia (1) 3 *(Pena 10, Escobar 70, 80)*
Paraguay (0) 1 *(Riveros 83)* 17,320
Bolivia: Galarza; Valverde, Vargas, Jimenez, Flores, Martins (Andaveris 84), Escobar (Cardozo 85), Pena, Chumacero, Mojica (Chavez 73), Barba.
Paraguay: Villar; Roman, Aranda (Perez 74), Zeballos, Mazacotte, Da Silva, Ramos (Benitez 58), Riveros, Torres, Valdez, Martinez.
Referee: Silvera (Uruguay).

Saturday, 9 June 2012
Venezuela (0) 0
Chile (0) 2 *(Fernandez M 85, Aranguiz 90)* 35,000
Venezuela: Vega; Vizcarrondo, Chicero, Fedor (Del Valle 63), Seijas (Orozco 82), Di Giorgi, Rosales, Arango, Perozo, Rondon J, Alvarez (Guerra 63).
Chile: Bravo; Contreras (Figueroa 65), Gonzalez O, Sanchez, Vidal, Suazo (Pinto 79), Rojas (Gonzalez Marcos 30), Fernandez M, Mena, Aranguiz, Diaz.
Referee: Buitrago (Colombia).

Sunday, 10 June 2012
Ecuador (0) 1 *(Benitez 54)*
Colombia (0) 0 37,353
Ecuador: Dominguez; Erazo, Paredes J, Noboa■, Rojas (Mendez 72), Montero (Saritama 78), Ayovi W, Benitez (Minda 90), Castillo, Valencia A, Campos.

Colombia: Ospina; Yepes, Sanchez, Armero, Falcao, Rodriguez, Pabon, Guarin F (Cuadrado 66), Perea (Zuniga 35), Soto (Muriel 73), Mosquera.
Referee: Seneme (Brazil).

Montevideo, 10 June 2012,
Uruguay (2) 4 *(Coates 15, Pereira M 30, Rodriguez C 63, Eguren 90)*
Peru (1) 2 *(Godin 40 (og), Guerrero P 48)* 55,000
Uruguay: Muslera; Godin, Coates, Suarez (Eguren 90), Forlan (Rodriguez C 60), Pereira A (Ramirez 60), Perez, Pereira M, Arevalo, Cavani, Caceres.
Peru: Penny; Galliquio, Gonzales (Lobaton 46), Guerrero P, Fernandez (Carrillo 76), Ramos, Advincula (Cueva 68), Cruzado, Yotun, Ramirez, Alvarez.
Referee: Pedro (Brazil).

Friday, 7 September 2012
Colombia (1) 4 *(Falcao 3, Gutierrez 49, 53, Zuniga 90)*
Uruguay (0) 0 40000
Colombia: (442) Ospina, Zuniga, Valdes, Perea, Armero, Rodriguez (Sanchez Moreno 84), Valencia, Torres, Aguilar (Ramirez 49), Falcao, Gutierrez (Quintero 80).
Uruguay: (442) Muslera, Pereira M (Ramirez 60), Lugano, Godin, Victorino (Gonzalez 47), Rodriguez C, Pereira, Perez, Arevalo Rios (Gargano 74), Forlan, Cavani.
Referee: Heber Roberto Lopes.

Ecuador (0) 1 *(Caicedo 75 (pen))*
Bolivia (0) 0 32,322
Ecuador: (442) Dominguez; Paredes J, Campos, Erazo, Ayovi W; Castillo, Saritama, Valencia A, Montero (Arroyo 47); Mina (Quinonez 87), Ayovi J (Caicedo 57).
Bolivia: (442) Suarez; Mendez, Raldes, Vargas, Gutierrez; Barba Paz, Azogue, Chavez (Chumacero 78), Mojica (Cabrera 85); Saucedo (Pena 47), Martins.
Referee: Juan Soto Arevalo.

Saturday, 8 September 2012
Argentina (2) 3 *(Di Maria 3, Higuain 31, Messi 64)*
Paraguay (1) 1 *(Fabbro 18 (pen))* 48,480
Argentina: (442) Romero; Garay, Fernandez F, Campagnaro, Rojo; Gago, Di Maria (Guinazu 79), Brana (Biglia 88), Higuain; Messi, Lavezzi (Palacio R 65).
Paraguay: (442) Villar; Piris, Alcaraz, Da Silva, Ayala; Estigarribia (Benitez 73), Caceres, Riveros, Fabbro (Cardozo O 58); Ortiz, Santa Cruz R (Haedo Valdez 59).
Referee: Wilson Seneme.

Peru (0) 2 *(Farfan 47, 60)*
Venezuela (1) 1 *(Arango 43)* 39,393
Peru: (442) Fernandez; Revoredo (Guizasola 73), Vargas, Zambrano, Rodriguez; Yotun, Ramirez, Cruzado, Farfan (Lobaton 80); Pizarro, Guerrero P (Carrillo 49).
Venezuela: (442) Vega; Vizcarrondo, Rosales, Cichero■, Tunez; Feltscher, Flores, Flores F (Gonzalez C 64), Arango; Seijas (Feltscher A 75), Miku (Rondon J 70).
Referee: Martin Vazquez Broquetas.

Tuesday, 11 September 2012
Chile (1) 1 *(Fernandez M 43)*
Colombia (0) 3 *(Rodriguez 60, Falcao 75, Gutierrez 78)* 38,380
Chile: (442) Bravo; Jara Reyes, Gonzalez Marcos, Isla (Fernandez J 68), Vidal; Fernandez M, Mena, Medel■, Diaz; Sanchez (Pinilla 83), Suazo (Pinto 72).
Colombia: (442) Ospina; Zuniga, Perea, Yepes (Cuadrado 47); Armero, Aguilar■, Rodriguez (Sanchez Moreno 81), Torres (Ramirez 70), Valencia; Gutierrez, Falcao.
Referee: Vitor Hugo Carrillo.

Uruguay (0) 1 *(Cavani 68)*
Ecuador (1) 1 *(Caicedo 9 (pen))* 52,520
Uruguay: (433) Muslera; Pereira M, Lugano, Godin, Pereira (Gargano 47); Perez (Rodriguez C 60), Ramirez, Alfaro (Gonzalez 47); Suarez, Forlan, Cavani.
Ecuador: (442) Dominguez; Campos, Ayovi W, Erazo, Paredes J; Minda, Castillo, Valencia A■, Saritama (Ibarra 84); Benitez (Achilier 90), Caicedo (Ayovi J 58).
Referee: Carlos Amarilla.

Wednesday, 12 September 2012

Paraguay (0) 0
Venezuela (1) 2 *(Rondon J 46, 68)*   20,200
Paraguay: (442) Villar; Alcaraz (Ayala 71), Veron, Bonet, Samudio (Estigarribia 41); Da Silva, Caceres (Dos Santos 65), Riveros, Fabbro; Haedo Valdez, Cardozo O.
Venezuela: (4411) Hernandez D; Gonzalez, Vizcarrondo, Tunez, Rosales; Gonzalez A (Perez Greco E 81), Lucena, Seijas (Flores A 87), Arango; Martinez (Blanco 74); Rondon J.
Referee: Enrique Osses.

Peru (1) 1 *(Zambrano 22)*
Argentina (1) 1 *(Higuain 39)*   39,393
Peru: (442) Fernandez; Zambrano, Rodriguez, Yotun, Advincula; Ramirez (Guerrero P 87), Cruzado, Lobaton (Ballon 47), Farfan; Pizarro, Carrillo (Hurtado 77).
Argentina: (433) Romero; Campagnaro, Garay, Fernandez F, Rojo; Gago (Guinazu 61), Mascherano, Di Maria (Rodriguez M 85); Messi, Higuain, Lavezzi (Perez 75).
Referee: Wilmar Roldan Perez.

Friday, 12 October 2012

Bolivia (0) 1 *(Chumacero 52)*
Peru (1) 1 *(Marino 23)*   35,350
Bolivia: (442) Suarez; Mendez, Raldes, Valverde, Vargas (Segovia 47); Flores, Chumacero, Cardozo, Campos J; Arce (Suarez 75), Pena (Martins 47).
Peru: (442) Carvallo; Acasiete, Ramos, Farfan, Sanchez; Herrera, Retamoso, Cominges (Ampuero 60), Marino (Cueva 79); Chiroque, Avila (Aguirre 61).
Referee: Carlos Vera.

Colombia (0) 2 *(Falcao 52, 89)*
Paraguay (0) 0   40,404
Colombia: (4312) Ospina; Zuniga, Valdes, Yepes, Armero; Valencia (Soto 84), Ramirez (Cuadrado 47), Torres (Benitez 75); Rodriguez; Falcao, Gutierrez.
Paraguay: (442) Barreto D; Piris, Ortiz, Da Silva, Aguilar; Ayala, Caceres, Riveros, Estigarribia (Benitez 67); Nunez (Fabbro 80), Haedo Valdez (Caballero 61).
Referee: Sergio Pezzotta.

Ecuador (1) 3 *(Caicedo 33, 56 (pen), Castillo 90)*
Chile (1) 1 *(Paredes J 26 (og))*   33,330
Ecuador: (433) Dominguez; Paredes J, Achilier, Erazo, Ayovi; Castillo, Saritama, Ibarra (Montero 78); Rojas (Gonzalez 74), Caicedo (Ayovi 63), Benitez.
Chile: (451) Pinto; Contreras**, Gonzalez O, Jara Reyes, Seymour (Gonzalez Mark 63); Diaz, Isla, Vidal**, Beausejour (Vargas 78), Fernandez M (Fernandez J 61); Sanchez.
Referee: Heber Roberto Lopes.

Saturday, 13 October 2012

Argentina (0) 3 *(Messi 66, 80, Aguero 75)*
Uruguay (0) 0   42,425
Argentina: (433) Romero; Zabaleta, Fernandez F, Garay, Rojo (Campagnaro 68); Mascherano, Gago, Di Maria; Aguero (Guinazu 79), Messi, Higuain (Barcos 84).
Uruguay: (433) Muslera; Pereira M, Godin, Lugano (Scotti 65), Caceres; Gonzalez (Rodriguez C 68), Arevalo Rios, Gargano; Suarez, Forlan, Cavani.
Referee: Leandro Pedro Vauden.

Tuesday, 16 October 2012

Bolivia (2) 4 *(Saucedo 6, 50, 55, Mojica 27)*
Uruguay (0) 1 *(Suarez 81)*   9500
Bolivia: (442) Galarza; Zenteno, Raldes, Gutierrez, Bejarano M; Cardozo, Azogue (Melean 74), Chumacero, Mojica (Campos J 68); Saucedo, Martins (Arce 57).
Uruguay: (442) Muslera; Scotti, Victorino, Pereira M (Cavani 37), Pereira; Gonzalez, Arevalo Rios, Gargano (Lodeiro 37), Rodriguez C; Forlan (Fernandez 66), Suarez.
Referee: Victor Hugo Rivera.

Paraguay (0) 1 *(Aguilar 53)*
Peru (0) 0   13,130
Paraguay: (442) Barreto D; Piris, Da Silva, Aguilar, Samudio; Oviedo, Dos Santos, Riveros, Benitez (Fabbro 82); Nunez (Caceres 75), Haedo Valdez (Caballero 47).

Peru: (442) Fernandez; Rodriguez (Ramos 16), Zambrano, Yotun (Ruidiaz 82), Vargas; Cruzado, Ramirez, Advincula, Farfan; Pizarro, Guerrero P (Carrillo 67).
Referee: Pablo Lunati.

Venezuela (1) 1 *(Arango 6)*
Ecuador (1) 1 *(Castillo 25)*   34,345
Venezuela: (442) Hernandez D; Gonzalez A (Cichero 82), Perozo, Amorebieta, Rosales; Hernandez G, Lucena, Perez Greco E (Vargas 57), Arango; Martinez (Miku 68), Rondon J.
Ecuador: (442) Dominguez; Paredes J, Achilier, Erazo, Ayovi W; Castillo, Noboa (Montero 80), Valencia A, Arroyo (Rojas 87); Ayovi J (Minda 72), Benitez.
Referee: Nestor Pitana.

Wednesday, 17 October 2012

Chile (0) 1 *(Gutierrez 90)*
Argentina (2) 2 *(Messi 28, Higuain 31)*   51,510
Chile: (442) Pinto; Gonzalez Marcos, Jara Reyes, Isla, Gonzalez Mark (Gutierrez 75); Fernandez M, Beausejour, Medel, Diaz; Pinto (Vargas 56), Sanchez.
Argentina: (442) Romero; Zabaleta, Garay, Campagnaro, Fernandez F; Gago, Di Maria (Sosa 78), Mascherano, Messi; Aguero (Barcos 87), Higuain (Guinazu 62).
Referee: Antonio Arias.

Friday, 22 March 2013

Colombia (1) 5 *(Torres 21, Valdes 50, Gutierrez 62, Falcao 87, Armero 90)*
Bolivia (0) 0   40,478
Colombia: (4312) Ospina; Valdes, Yepes, Zuniga, Cuadrado (Armero 79); Valencia, Aguilar, Rodriguez (Guarin F 83); Torres (Ramirez 86); Falcao, Gutierrez.
Bolivia: (442) Arias (Galarza 47); Jimenez, Zenteno, Bejarano M, Gutierrez; Bejarano, Chumacero, Veizaga, Garcia (Arce 58); Saucedo (Cardozo 47), Martins.
Referee: Carlos Vera.

Uruguay (0) 1 *(Suarez 82)*
Paraguay (0) 1 *(Benitez 86)*   30,300
Uruguay: (442) Muslera; Maxi Pereira (Ramirez 69), Lugano, Godin, Pereira; Gonzalez, Perez (Arevalo Rios 47), Lodeiro, Rodriguez C (Cavani 47); Suarez, Forlan.
Paraguay: (442) Barreto D; Piris, Aguilar, Da Silva, Samudio; Ayala, Oviedo, Riveros, Ortiz (Benitez 66); Haedo Valdez (Fabbro 80), Cardozo O (Caballero 66).
Referee: Wilmar Roldan Perez.

Saturday, 23 March 2013

Argentina (2) 3 *(Higuain 29, 59, Messi 46 (pen))*
Venezuela (0) 0   55,550
Argentina: (433) Romero; Zabaleta, Fernandez F, Garay, Rojo; Gago (Ever 62), Mascherano, Montillo; Lavezzi (Rodriguez M 84), Messi, Higuain (Palacio R 80).
Venezuela: (4231) Hernandez D; Gonzalez A, Vizcarrondo, Tunez, Cichero; Lucena, Rincon; Feltscher F, Arango (Gonzalez C 75), Seijas (Otero 58); Rondon J (Miku 82).
Referee: Vitor Hugo Carrillo.

Peru (0) 1 *(Farfan 87)*
Chile (0) 0   50,000
Peru: (433) Fernandez; Herrera, Ramos (Alvarez 25), Rodriguez, Yotun; Lobaton (Marino 47), Ramirez, Cruzado; Farfan, Pizarro (Reyna 80), Hurtado.
Chile: (433) Bravo; Medel, Gonzalez Marcos, Rojas, Mena; Isla, Aranguiz (Silva 54), Carmona; Beausejour (Castillo 71), Sanchez, Vargas (Fernandez J 75).
Referee: Diego Abal.

Tuesday, 26 March 2013

Bolivia (1) 1 *(Martins 25)*
Argentina (1) 1 *(Ever 45)*   38,380
Bolivia: (532) Galarza; Torrico (Bejarano M 46), Raldes, Zenteno, Gutierrez, Bejarano D (Arce 66); Veizaga, Chumacero, Cardozo (Mojica 74); Saucedo, Martins.
Argentina: (532) Romero; Peruzzi, Dominguez, Rodriguez C, Basanta, Campagnaro; Ever (Di Santo 63), Mascherano, Di Maria (Guinazu 91); Messi, Palacio R (Ponzio 87).
Referee: Enrique Osses.

Chile (1) 2 *(Paredes 11, Vargas 79)*
Uruguay (0) 0 45,450
Chile: (343) Bravo; Medel, Rojas, Jara Reyes; Isla (Gonzalez Marcos 85), Aranguiz (Fernandez 59), Diaz, Mena; Vargas, Beausejour (Carmona 69), Paredes.
Uruguay: (442) Muslera; Aguirregaray (Silva 47), Lugano, Godin, Pereira; Gonzalez, Arevalo Rios, Lodeiro (Rodriguez C 83), Ramirez (Forlan 70); Suarez, Cavani.
Referee: Nestor Pitana.

Ecuador (1) 4 *(Caicedo 39, Montero 51, 76, Benitez 54)*
Paraguay (1) 1 *(Caballero 16)* 35,357
Ecuador: (442) Dominguez; Achilier, Erazo, Ayovi W, Quinonez (Saritama 72); Noboa, Paredes J, Valencia A, Montero (Ibarra 83); Benitez, Caicedo (Rojas 80).
Paraguay: (442) Barreto D; Piris (Haedo Valdez 61), Da Silva, Aguilar, Samudio; Oviedo, Riveros, Ayala, Ortiz (Caceres 46); Caballero (Velazquez 78), Benitez.
Referee: Ricci Sandro.

Wednesday, 27 March 2013

Venezuela (1) 1 *(Rondon 14)*
Colombia (0) 0 40,400
Venezuela: (442) Hernandez D; Gonzalez C, Vizcarrondo, Tunez (Flores A 63), Cichero (Feltscher R 84); Gonzalez A, Rincon, Lucena, Arango; Aristeguieta (Miku 68), Rondon J.
Colombia: (4231) Ospina; Zuniga, Valdes, Perea, Armero; Valencia, Aguilar; Cuadrado (Gutierrez 66), Rodriguez, Torres (Bacca 75); Falcao.
Referee: Antonio Arias.

Friday, 7 June 2013

Argentina (0) 0
Colombia (0) 0 60,600
Argentina: (442) Romero; Zabaleta, Fernandez F, Garay, Rojo; Mascherano, Biglia, Montillo (Messi 58), Di Maria; Higuain*, Aguero (Lavezzi 82).
Colombia: (442) Ospina; Armero, Yepes, Zapata*, Zuniga; Aguilar (Mejia 62), Sanchez C, Ramirez, Rodriguez (Cuadrado 34); Martinez J (Perea 47), Falcao.
Referee: Marlon Escalante.

Bolivia (0) 1 *(Campos J 87)*
Venezuela (0) 1 *(Arango 59)* 14,140
Bolivia: (442) Galarza; Raldes (Campos J 73), Zenteno, Eguino, Veizaga; Chumacero, Chavez (Mojica 47), Cardozo, Arce; Saucedo, Martins (Fierro 62).
Venezuela: (442) Vega; Rosales, Perozo, Cichero, Rincon; Flores A, Gonzalez C (Gonzalez A 71), Seijas, Arango (Feltscher R 82); Martinez, Blanco (Hernandez E 66).
Referee: Patricio Loustau.

Saturday, 8 June 2013

Paraguay (0) 1 *(Santa Cruz R 88)*
Chile (1) 2 *(Vargas 41, Vidal 57)* 15,150
Paraguay: (433) Villar; Caceres, Da Silva, Samudio, Candia; Riveros (Ortiz 57), Oviedo, Dos Santos (Caballero 80); Benitez, Lopez (Santa Cruz R 59), Cardozo O.
Chile: (343) Bravo; Medel, Gonzalez Marcos, Rojas; Isla, Vidal, Diaz, Mena; Sanchez (Pinto 90), Paredes (Fernandez M 60), Vargas (Gutierrez 86).
Referee: Leandro Pedro Vauden.

Saturday, 8 June 2013

Peru (1) 1 *(Pizarro 11)*
Ecuador (0) 0 39,393
Peru: (442) Fernandez; Rodriguez, Herrera, Zambrano, Vargas (Ampuero 80); Yotun, Farfan (Advincula 88), Retamoso, Ramiez; Guerrero P, Pizarro (Ramos 90).
Ecuador: (442) Dominguez; Guagua, Erazo, Ayovi W, Paredes J (Ibarra 74); Castillo, Noboa, Valencia A, Montero; Rojas (Caicedo 54), Benitez (de Jesus 86).
Referee: Marcelo De Lima.

Tuesday, 11 June 2013

Colombia (2) 2 *(Falcao 13 (pen), Gutierrez 45)*
Peru (0) 0 42,265
Colombia: (442) Ospina; Perea, Yepes, Armero, Zuniga; Cuadrado (Guarin F 77), Sanchez, Aguilar (Mejia 86), Torres; Gutierrez (Muriel 80), Falcao.
Peru: (442) Fernandez; Rodriguez, Herrera (Farfan 33), Zambrano*, Vargas; Yotun (Carrillo 32), Advincula, Retamoso (Lobaton 63), Ballon; Guerrero P, Pizarro.
Referee: Sandro Meira Ricci.

Ecuador (1) 1 *(Castillo 15)*
Argentina (1) 1 *(Aguero 5 (pen))* 32,320
Ecuador: (442) Dominguez; Guagua, Erazo, Ayovi W, Paredes J (Ibarra 72); Castillo, Noboa (Saritama 71), Valencia A, Montero; Rojas (Anangono 89), Caicedo.
Argentina: (442) Romero; Garay, Rojo, Fernandez F, Peruzzi; Basanta, Di Maria, Mascherano*, Ever (Biglia 78); Palacio R (Brana 90), Aguero (Messi 62).
Referee: Enrique Caceres.

Wednesday, 12 June 2013

Chile (2) 3 *(Vargas 16, Sanchez 18, Vidal 91)*
Bolivia (1) 1 *(Martins 32)* 45,000
Chile: (433) Bravo; Medel, Gonzalez Marcos, Rojas, Mena (Beausejour 75); Diaz, Pizarro, Vidal; Sanchez, Paredes (Jara Reyes 55), Vargas.
Bolivia: (451) Galarza; Zenteno, Raldes, Gutierrez, Bejarano D; Mojica, Veizaga, Chumacero (Rojas 47), Chavez (Cardozo 47), Arze (Campos J 70); Martins.
Referee: Dario Ubriaco.

Venezuela (0) 0
Uruguay (1) 1 *(Cavani 28)* 36,297
Venezuela: (442) Hernandez D; Tunez, Vizcarrondo, Cichero (Seijas 59), Rosales; Rincon*, Gonzalez C (Blanco 78), Lucena, Arango; Feltscher F (Aristeguieta 57), Rondon J.
Uruguay: (442) Muslera; Lugano, Godin, Pereira M, Caceres; Gargano, Rodriguez C (Pereira A 86), Perez (Eguren 76), Ramirez (Gonzalez 60); Forlan, Cavani.
Referee: Paulo Cesar Oliveira.

Friday, 6 September 2013

Colombia (1) 1 *(Rodriguez 30)*
Ecuador (0) 0 47,000
Colombia: (442) Ospina; Zuniga, Valdes, Perea, Armero; Sanchez Moreno, Aguilar (Cuadrado 46), Rodriguez, Torres (Mejia 72); Gutierrez (Martinez J 81), Falcao.
Ecuador: (442) Banguera; Paredes J, Achilier*, Erazo, Ayovi W; Castillo, Noboa, Mendez (Guagua 46), Valencia A; Montero (Ibarra 76), Valencia E (Rojas 69).
Referee: Heber Roberto Lopes.

Paraguay (1) 4 *(Fabbro 16, Santa Cruz R 47, Ortiz 80, Gomez 83)*
Bolivia (0) 0 15,000
Paraguay: (442) Silva; Samudio, Candia, Da Silva, Gomez; Ayala, Pittoni (Aquino 70), Ortiz, Fabbro (Sanabria 65); Santa Cruz R, Romero A (Romero O 65).
Bolivia: (442) Galarza; Zenteno (Arce 46), Raldes, Cabrera, Gutierrez; Rodriguez, Bejarano, Azogue, Chavez (Maygua Rios 68); Arze (Cardozo 46), Martins.
Referee: Victor Carillo.

Saturday, 7 September 2013

Chile (2) 3 *(Vargas 10, Gonzalez Marcos 29, Vidal 84)*
Venezuela (0) 0 46,500
Chile: (442) Bravo; Isla, Medel, Gonzalez Marcos, Mena; Diaz, Vidal, Valdivia (Beausejour 72), Aranguiz (Pizarro 57); Alexis, Vargas (Henriquez 83).
Venezuela: (442) Hernandez D; Rosales, Vizcarrondo, Perozo, Cichero (Gonzalez A 44); Lucena, Seijas (Flores A 79), Arango, Gonzalez C (Orozco 69); Martinez, Rondon J.
Referee: Sandro Meira Ricci.

Peru (0) 1 *(Farfan 83)*
Uruguay (1) 2 *(Suarez 42 (pen), 66)* 39,305
Peru: (442) Fernandez; Advincula (Herrera 65), Ramos, Rodriguez, Yotun*; Ramirez (Hurtado 65), Ballon (Vargas 46), Cruzado, Farfan; Pizarro, Guerrero P.
Uruguay: (442) Muslera; Pereira M, Lugano, Godin, Caceres (Fucile 81); Gargano (Gonzalez 69), Arevalo Rios, Rodriguez C, Cavani; Forlan (Stuani 25), Suarez.
Referee: Patricio Loustau.

Tuesday, 10 September 2013

Bolivia (0) 1 *(Arrascaita 47)*
Ecuador (0) 1 *(Caicedo 58 (pen))* 5000
Bolivia: (442) Quinonez; Zenteno, Raldes, Cabrera, Bejarano D; Bejarano M (Arrascaita 46), Veizaga, Chumacero (Maygua Rios 71), Azogue (Martins 46); Cardozo, Arce.
Ecuador: (442) Dominguez; Ayovi W, Guagua, Erazo, Paredes J; Castillo (Noboa 64), Montero, Valencia A, Caicedo (Guerron 70); Ayovi J (Ibarra 51), Saritama.
Referee: Paulo Cesar Oliveira.

Uruguay (0) 2 *(Cavani 78, Stuani 81)*
Colombia (0) 0 51,000
Uruguay: (442) Muslera; Gimenez, Pereira M, Scotti, Fucile;
Rodriguez C (Ramirez 72), Lodeiro (Stuani 46), Arevalo
Rios, Gonzalez (Gargano 46); Suarez, Cavani.
Colombia: (442) Ospina; Perea, Zuniga, Yepes, Medina;
Aguilar (Ramirez 80), Rodriguez, Sanchez Moreno
(Martinez J 86), Guarin F; Gutierrez (Cuadrado 69), Falcao.
Referee: Antonio Arias.

Wednesday, 11 September 2013

Paraguay (1) 2 *(Nunez 17, Santa Cruz R 85)*
Argentina (2) 5 *(Messi 11 (pen), 52 (pen), Aguero 31,*
Di Maria 49, Rodriguez M 89) 35,000
Paraguay: (442) Fernandez; Caceres, Da Silva, Ayala,
Samudio; Riveros, Ortiz (Aquino 20 (Romero O 46)),
Fabbro (Rojas 54), Nunez; Santa Cruz R, Silva.
Argentina: (442) Romero; Zabaleta, Campagnaro,
Basanta, Coloccini; Biglia, Gago (Rodriguez M 86), Di
Maria, Aguero (Ever 76); Messi, Palacio R (Lavezzi 65).
Referee: Enrique Osses.

Venezuela (1) 3 *(Rondon J 37, Gonzalez C 62 (pen), Otero 77)*
Peru (1) 2 *(Hurtado 20, Zambrano 88)* 20,049
Venezuela: (442) Hernandez D; Gonzalez A,
Amorebieta, Vizcarrondo, Rosales; Arango (Aristeguieta
88), Gonzalez C (Otero 68), Rincon, Orozco; Martinez
(Lucena 75), Rondon J.
Peru: (442) Fernandez; Rodriguez, Zambrano, Herrera
(Advincula 13), Vargas; Lobaton, Cruzado (Ramirez 63),
Retamoso, Pizarro (Guerrero P 63); Hurtado, Carrillo.
Referee: Nestor Pittana.

Friday, 11 October 2013

Colombia (0) 3 *(Gutierrez 69, Falcao 73 (pen), 83 (pen))*
Chile (3) 3 *(Vidal 19 (pen), Alexis 22, 29)* 40,388
Colombia: (442) Ospina; Yepes, Armero, Perea, Medina
(Guarin F 46); Cuadrado, Sanchez Moreno (Bacca 67),
Aguilar (Torres 46), Rodriguez; Gutierrez, Falcao.
Chile: (442) Bravo; Mena, Jara, Gonzalez Marcos, Isla
(Rojas 53); Carmona**■**, Vidal, Valdivia (Beausejour 60);
Medel; Alexis, Vargas (Silva 68).
Referee: Paulo De Oliveira.

Ecuador (1) 1 *(Montero 23)*
Uruguay (0) 0 32,996
Ecuador: (442) Dominguez; Erazo, Guagua, Paredes J,
Ayovi W; Valencia A, Noboa, Valencia E (Rojas 70
(Bolanos 89)), Montero (Ibarra 81); Castillo, Caicedo.
Uruguay: (442) Muslera; Pereira M (Forlan 64), Godin,
Lugano, Fucile; Gimenez, Gargano (Silva 72), Arevalo
Rios, Rodriguez C (Ramirez 78); Suarez, Cavani.
Referee: Sandro Meira Ricci.

Venezuela (0) 1 *(Seijas 83)*
Paraguay (1) 1 *(Benitez 28)* 27,227
Venezuela: (442) Hernandez D; Rosales, Vizcarrondo,
Gonzalez A (Seijas 76), Amorebieta; Lucena, Arango,
Otero (Aristeguieta 64), Orozco; Miku, Martinez (Pena 70).
Paraguay: (442) Villar; Bonet, Alonso, Da Silva, Gomez;
Ayala, Caceres, Mino, Cardozo O (Oviedo 66); Santa
Cruz R, Benitez (Romero O 57).
Referee: Victor Carrillo.

Saturday, 12 October 2013

Argentina (2) 3 *(Lavezzi 23, 34, Palacio R 46)*
Peru (1) 1 *(Pizarro 21)* 30,000
Argentina: (442) Romero; Zabaleta, Fernandez F, Rojo,
Garay; Biglia, Di Maria (Somoza 90), Ever, Lavezzi
(Rodriguez M 87); Aguero, Palacio R (Lamela 80).
Peru: (442) Penny; Aparicio, Duarte, Gambetta, Gomez
(Benavente 46); Ballon, Hurtado, Ramirez (Reyna 83),
Vargas; Carrillo (Vilchez 68), Pizarro.
Referee: Carlos Vera.

Wednesday, 16 October 2013

Chile (2) 2 *(Alexis 35, Medel 38)*
Ecuador (0) 1 *(Caicedo 66)* 47,548
Chile: (442) Bravo; Mena, Gonzalez Marcos, Isla, Vidal;
Valdivia (Pinilla 90), Medel, Aranguiz (Fernandez M 76),
Diaz; Alexis, Vargas (Beausejour 86).

Ecuador: (442) Dominguez; Guagua, Erazo, Paredes J,
Ayovi W; Noboa, Montero (Martinez 84), Valencia E,
Castillo; Valencia A (Ayovi J 72), Caicedo (Ibarra 90).
Referee: Leandro Vuaden.

Paraguay (1) 1 *(Rojas 7)*
Colombia (1) 2 *(Yepes 38, 56)* 3000
Paraguay: (442) Villar; Bonet (Cardozo O 46), Gomez,
Da Silva, Candia; Aquino, Oviedo, Rojas, Romero O
(Mendieta 76); Santa Cruz R, Nunez (Sanabria 62).
Colombia: (442) Ospina; Arias, Zapata, Yepes, Armero;
Torres (Ramirez 37), Sanchez Moreno, Guarin F**■**,
Rodriguez; Martinez J, Bacca (Quintero 66).
Referee: Diego Abal.

Peru (1) 1 *(Yotun 19)*
Bolivia (1) 1 *(Bejarano D 45)* *(Behind closed doors)*
Peru: (433) Penny; Duarte, Zambrano, Yotun, Vargas;
Benavente (Reyna 46), Advincula, Ballon; Lobaton,
Avila (Carrillo 60), Pizarro.
Bolivia: (442) Quinonez; Zenteno, Raldes, Bejarano D
(Rodriguez 86), Gutierrez; Bejarano M, Veizaga, Chavez,
Rojas Hermoza (Arrascaita 74); Bejarano D (Arce 40),
Martins.
Behind closed doors.
Referee: Enrique Caceres.

Uruguay (2) 3 *(Rodriguez C 5, Suarez 34 (pen), Cavani 49)*
Argentina (2) 2 *(Rodriguez M 15, 42)* 55,000
Uruguay: (442) Muslera; Pereira M (Ramirez 46),
Lugano, Godin, Fucile; Stuani (Gimenez 89), Perez,
Arevalo Rios, Rodriguez C; Suarez, Cavani.
Argentina: (442) Romero; Campagnaro, Fernandez F,
Dominguez, Basanta; Fernandez A (Icardi 82), Biglia, Ever
(Somoza 67), Rodriguez M; Lamela (Sosa 76), Palacio R.
Referee: Marcelo de Lima Henrique.

South America

Group Matches Table	P	W	D	L	F	A	GD	Pts
Argentina	16	9	5	2	35	15	20	32
Colombia	16	9	3	4	27	13	14	30
Chile	16	9	1	6	29	25	4	28
Ecuador	16	7	4	5	20	16	4	25
Uruguay	16	7	4	5	25	25	0	25
Venezuela	16	5	5	6	14	20	–6	20
Peru	16	4	3	9	17	26	–9	15
Bolivia	16	2	6	8	17	30	–13	12
Paraguay	16	3	3	10	17	31	–14	12

SOUTH AMERICA/ASIA PLAY-OFF 1ST LEG
Wednesday, 13 November 2013

Jordan (0) 0
Uruguay (2) 5 *(Pereira M 16, Stuani 42, Lodeiro 69,*
Rodriguez C 78, Cavani 90) 19,000
Jordan: (442) Shatnawi; Adnan, Khattab, Zahran (Bawab
53), Bani Attiah (Al-Khalidi 65); Aqel, Al Shaqran,
Adous, Murjan; Al-Saify (Al-Laham 59), Hayel.
Uruguay: (433) Silva; Pereira M, Lugano, Godin,
Caceres; Arevalo Rios, Rodriguez C, Lodeiro (Pereira
70); Stuani (Ramirez 70), Cavani, Suarez (Forlan 81).
Referee: Svein Oddvar Moen.

SOUTH AMERICA/ASIA PLAY-OFF 2ND LEG
Wednesday, 20 November 2013

Uruguay (0) 0
Jordan (0) 0 65,000
Uruguay: (433) Silva; Pereira M, Godin, Lugano,
Caceres; Arevalo Rios, Lodeiro (Ramirez 60), Rodriguez
C; Stuani (Forlan 60), Suarez, Cavani (Hernandez 81).
Jordan: (442) Shatnawi; Adnan, Khattab, Al-Saify (Bani
Attiah 59), Adous; Hayel (Bawab 90), Zahran, Deeb
(Samir 86), Abu-Hashhash; Aqel, Al-Rawshdeh.
Referee: Jonas Eriksson.

Argentina, Colombia, Chile, Ecuador and Uruguay
qualify for World Cup 2014 in Brazil.

AFRICA

ROUND 1 – FIRST LEG

Sao Tome & Principe v Congo	0-5
Djibouti v Namibia	0-4
Comoros v Mozambique	0-1
Eritrea v Rwanda	1-1
Swaziland v DR Congo	1-3
Equatorial Guinea v Madagascar	2-0
Chad v Tanzania	1-2
Guinea-Bissau v Togo	1-1
Seychelles v Kenya	0-3
Lesotho v Burundi	1-0
Somalia v Ethiopia	0-0

ROUND 1 – SECOND LEG

Congo v Sao Tome & Principe	1-1
Namibia v Djibouti	4-0
Mozambique v Comoros	4-1
Rwanda v Eritrea	3-1
DR Congo v Swaziland	5-1
Madagascar v Equatorial Guinea	2-1
Tanzania v Chad	0-1
Togo v Guinea-Bissau	1-0
Kenya v Seychelles	4-0
Burundi v Lesotho	2-2
Ethiopia v Somalia	5-0

ROUND 2

GROUP A

Central African Republic v Botswana	2-0
South Africa v Ethiopia	1-1
Botswana v South Africa	1-1
Ethiopia v Central African Republic	2-0
South Africa v Central African Republic	2-0
Ethiopia v Botswana	1-0
Central African Republic v South Africa	3-0
Botswana v Ethiopia	3-0

Match awarded 3-0 to Botswana; Ethiopia fielded an ineligible player. Original result 2-1 to Ethiopia.

Botswana v Central African Republic	3-2
Ethiopia v South Africa	2-1
Central African Republic v Ethiopia	1-2
South Africa v Botswana	4-1

Group A Table	P	W	D	L	F	A	Pts
Ethiopia	6	4	1	1	8	6	13
South Africa	6	3	2	1	12	5	11
Botswana	6	2	1	3	8	10	7
Central African Republic	6	1	0	5	5	12	3

GROUP B

Sierra Leone v Cape Verde Islands	2-1
Tunisia v Equatorial Guinea	3-1
Cape Verde Islands v Tunisia	1-2
Equatorial Guinea v Sierra Leone	2-2
Tunisia v Sierra Leone	2-1
Equatorial Guinea v Cape Verde Islands	0-3

Match awarded 3-0 to Cape Verde Islands; Equatorial Guinea fielded an ineligible player. Original result 4-3 to Equatorial Guinea.

Cape Verde Islands v Equatorial Guinea	3-0

Match awarded 3-0 to Cape Verde Islands; Equatorial Guinea fielded an ineligible player. Original result 2-1 to Cape Verde Islands.

Sierra Leone v Tunisia	2-2
Cape Verde Islands v Sierra Leone	1-0
Equatorial Guinea v Tunisia	1-1
Sierra Leone v Equatorial Guinea	3-2
Tunisia v Cape Verde Islands	3-0

Match awarded 3-0 to Tunisia; Cape Verde Islands fielded an ineligible player. Original result 2-0 to Cape Verde Islands.

Group B Table	P	W	D	L	F	A	Pts
Tunisia	6	4	2	0	13	6	14
Cape Verde Islands	6	3	0	3	9	7	9
Sierra Leone	6	2	2	2	10	10	8
Equatorial Guinea	6	0	2	4	6	15	2

GROUP C

Gambia v Morocco	1-1
Ivory Coast v Tanzania	2-0
Morocco v Ivory Coast	2-2
Tanzania v Gambia	2-1
Ivory Coast v Gambia	3-0
Tanzania v Morocco	3-1
Gambia v Ivory Coast	0-3
Morocco v Tanzania	2-1
Morocco v Gambia	2-0
Tanzania v Ivory Coast	2-4
Gambia v Tanzania	2-0
Ivory Coast v Morocco	1-1

Group C Table	P	W	D	L	F	A	Pts
Ivory Coast	6	4	2	0	15	5	14
Morocco	6	2	3	1	9	8	9
Tanzania	6	2	0	4	8	12	6
Gambia	6	1	1	4	4	11	4

GROUP D

Ghana v Lesotho	7-0
Sudan v Zambia	0-3

Match awarded 0-3 to Zambia; Sudan fielded an ineligible player. Original result 2-0 to Sudan.

Zambia v Ghana	1-0
Lesotho v Sudan	0-0
Lesotho v Zambia	1-1
Ghana v Sudan	4-0
Sudan v Ghana	1-3
Zambia v Lesotho	4-0
Zambia v Sudan	1-1
Lesotho v Ghana	0-2
Ghana v Zambia	2-1
Sudan v Lesotho	1-3

Group D Table	P	W	D	L	F	A	Pts
Ghana	6	5	0	1	18	3	15
Zambia	6	3	2	1	11	4	11
Lesotho	6	1	2	3	4	15	5
Sudan	6	0	2	4	3	14	2

GROUP E

Burkina Faso v Congo	0-3

Match awarded 0-3 to Congo; Burkino Faso fielded an ineligible player. Original result 0-0.

Niger v Gabon	3-0

Match awarded 3-0 to Niger; Gabon fielded an ineligible player. Original result 0-0.

Gabon v Burkina Faso	1-0
Congo v Niger	1-0
Congo v Gabon	1-0
Burkina Faso v Niger	4-0
Gabon v Congo	0-0
Niger v Burkina Faso	0-1
Congo v Burkina Faso	0-1
Gabon v Niger	4-1
Burkina Faso v Gabon	1-0
Niger v Congo	2-2

Group E Table	P	W	D	L	F	A	Pts
Burkina Faso	6	4	0	2	7	4	12
Congo	6	3	2	1	7	3	11
Gabon	6	2	1	3	5	6	7
Niger	6	1	1	4	6	12	4

GROUP F

Kenya v Malawi	0-0
Nigeria v Namibia	1-0
Malawi v Nigeria	1-1
Namibia v Kenya	1-0
Nigeria v Kenya	1-1
Namibia v Malawi	0-1
Malawi v Namibia	0-0
Kenya v Nigeria	0-1
Malawi v Kenya	2-2
Namibia v Nigeria	1-1
Nigeria v Malawi	2-0
Kenya v Namibia	1-0

Group F Table	P	W	D	L	F	A	Pts
Nigeria	6	3	3	0	7	3	12
Malawi	6	1	4	1	4	5	7
Kenya	6	1	3	2	4	5	6
Namibia	6	1	2	3	2	4	5

GROUP G

Egypt v Mozambique	2-0
Zimbabwe v Guinea	0-1
Mozambique v Zimbabwe	0-0
Guinea v Egypt	2-3

Mozambique v Guinea	0-0
Egypt v Zimbabwe	2-1
Zimbabwe v Egypt	2-4
Guinea v Mozambique	6-1
Mozambique v Egypt	0-1
Guinea v Zimbabwe	1-0
Zimbabwe v Mozambique	1-1
Egypt v Guinea	4-2

Group G Table	P	W	D	L	F	A	Pts
Egypt	6	6	0	0	16	7	18
Guinea	6	3	1	2	12	8	10
Mozambique	6	0	3	3	2	10	3
Zimbabwe	6	0	2	4	4	9	2

GROUP H

Algeria v Rwanda	4-0
Benin v Mali	1-0
Rwanda v Benin	1-1
Mali v Algeria	2-1
Rwanda v Mali	1-2
Algeria v Benin	3-1
Benin v Algeria	1-3
Mali v Rwanda	1-1
Rwanda v Algeria	0-1
Mali v Benin	2-2
Benin v Rwanda	2-0
Algeria v Mali	1-0

Group H Table	P	W	D	L	F	A	Pts
Algeria	6	5	0	1	13	4	15
Mali	6	2	2	2	7	7	8
Benin	6	2	2	2	8	9	8
Rwanda	6	0	2	4	3	11	2

GROUP I

Cameroon v Congo DR	1-0
Togo v Libya	1-1
Congo DR v Togo	2-0
Libya v Cameroon	2-1
Cameroon v Togo	2-1
Congo DR v Libya	0-0
Libya v Congo DR	0-0
Togo v Cameroon	0-3

Match awarded 3-0 to Cameroon; Togo fielded an ineligible player. Original result 2-0 to Togo.

Libya v Togo	2-0
Congo DR v Cameroon	0-0

Togo v Congo DR	2-1
Cameroon v Libya	1-0

Group I Table	P	W	D	L	F	A	Pts
Cameroon	6	4	1	1	8	3	13
Libya	6	2	3	1	5	3	9
Congo DR	6	1	3	2	3	3	6
Togo	6	1	1	4	4	11	4

GROUP J

Senegal v Liberia	3-1
Angola v Uganda	1-1
Uganda v Senegal	1-1
Liberia v Angola	0-0
Senegal v Angola	1-1
Liberia v Uganda	2-0
Angola v Senegal	1-1
Uganda v Liberia	1-0
Uganda v Angola	2-1
Liberia v Senegal	0-2
Angola v Liberia	3-0

Match awarded 3-0 to Angola; Liberia fielded an ineligible player. Original result 4-1 to Angola.

Senegal v Uganda	1-0

Group J Table	P	W	D	L	F	A	Pts
Senegal	6	3	3	0	9	4	12
Uganda	6	2	2	2	5	6	8
Angola	6	1	4	1	8	6	7
Liberia	6	1	1	4	10	4

ROUND 3 FIRST LEG

Burkina Faso v Algeria	3-2
Ivory Coast v Senegal	3-1
Ethiopia v Nigeria	1-2
Tunisia v Cameroon	0-0
Ghana v Egypt	6-1

ROUND 3 SECOND LEG

	(agg)
Algeria v Burkina Faso	1-0 (3-3)

Algeria won on away goals

Senegal v Ivory Coast	1-1 (2-4)
Nigeria v Ethiopia	2-0 (4-1)
Cameroon v Tunisia	4-1 (4-1)
Egypt v Ghana	2-1 (3-7)

Algeria, Ivory Coast, Nigeria, Cameroon and Ghana qualify for World Cup 2014 in Brazil.

OCEANIA

ROUND 1

American Samoa v Tonga	2-1
Cook Islands v Samoa	2-3
American Samoa v Cook Islands	1-1
Samoa v Tonga	1-1
Samoa v American Samoa	1-0
Tonga v Cook Islands	2-1

Round 1 Table	P	W	D	L	F	A	Pts
Samoa	3	2	1	0	5	3	7
Tonga	3	1	1	1	4	4	4
American Samoa	3	1	1	1	3	3	4
Cook Islands	3	0	1	2	4	6	1

ROUND 2
GROUP A

Vanuatu v New Caledonia	2-5
Samoa v Tahiti	1-10
Tahiti v New Caledonia	4-3
Vanuatu v Samoa	5-0
Tahiti v Vanuatu	4-1
New Caledonia v Samoa	9-0

Group A Table	P	W	D	L	F	A	Pts
Tahiti	3	3	0	0	18	5	9
New Caledonia	3	2	0	1	17	6	6
Vanuatu	3	1	0	2	8	9	3
Samoa	3	0	0	3	1	24	0

GROUP B

Fiji v New Zealand	0-1
Solomon Islands v Papua New Guinea	1-0
Fiji v Solomon Islands	0-0

Papua New Guinea v New Zealand	1-2
New Zealand v Solomon Islands	1-1
Papua New Guinea v Fiji	1-1

Group B Table	P	W	D	L	F	A	Pts
New Zealand	3	2	1	0	4	2	7
Solomon Islands	3	1	2	0	2	1	5
Fiji	3	0	2	1	1	2	2
Papua New Guinea	3	0	1	2	2	4	1

ROUND 3

New Caledonia v New Zealand	0-2
Solomon Islands v Tahiti	2-0
Tahiti v New Caledonia	0-4
New Zealand v Solomon Islands	6-1
Tahiti v New Zealand	0-2
Solomon Islands v New Caledonia	2-6
New Zealand v Tahiti	3-0
New Caledonia v Solomon Islands	5-0
New Zealand v New Caledonia	2-1
Tahiti v Solomon Islands	2-0
Solomon Islands v New Zealand	0-2
New Caledonia v Tahiti	1-0

Round 3 Table	P	W	D	L	F	A	Pts
New Zealand	6	6	0	0	17	2	18
New Caledonia	6	4	0	2	17	6	12
Tahiti	6	1	0	5	2	12	3
Solomon Islands	6	1	0	5	5	21	3

New Zealand qualify for Intercontinental Play-off.

INTERCONTINENTAL PLAY-OFF
The Intercontinental play-off is played between the fourth-placed team in Concacaf (Mexico) and the winner of Oceania (New Zealand).

FIRST LEG
Mexico v New Zealand   5-1

SECOND LEG   (agg)
New Zealand v Mexico   2-4 (3-9)

No team qualify from Oceania for World Cup 2014 in Brazil after New Zealand lost to Mexico in Intercontinental play-off.

CONCACAF

ROUND 2

GROUP A
Suriname v Cayman Islands	1-0
El Salvador v Dominican Republic	3-2
Dominican Republic v Suriname	1-1
Cayman Islands v El Salvador	1-4
Dominican Republic v El Salvador	1-2
Cayman Islands v Suriname	0-1
Suriname v Dominican Republic	1-3
El Salvador v Cayman Islands	4-0
Dominican Republic v Cayman Islands	4-0
Suriname v El Salvador	1-3
Cayman Islands v Dominican Republic	1-1
El Salvador v Suriname	4-0

Group A Table	P	W	D	L	F	A	Pts
El Salvador	6	6	0	0	20	5	18
Dominican Republic	6	2	2	2	12	8	8
Suriname	6	2	1	3	5	11	7
Cayman Islands	6	0	1	5	2	15	1

GROUP B
Trinidad & Tobago v Bermuda	1-0
Guyana v Barbados	2-0
Barbados v Trinidad & Tobago	0-2
Guyana v Bermuda	2-1
Barbados v Guyana	0-2
Bermuda v Trinidad & Tobago	2-1
Trinidad & Tobago v Barbados	4-0
Bermuda v Guyana	1-1
Bermuda v Barbados	2-1
Guyana v Trinidad & Tobago	2-1
Barbados v Bermuda	1-2
Trinidad & Tobago v Guyana	3-0
Match awarded 3-0 to Trinidad & Tobago; Guyana fielded an ineligible player. Original result 2-0.	

Group B Table	P	W	D	L	F	A	Pts
Guyana	6	4	1	1	9	6	13
Trinidad & Tobago	6	4	0	2	12	4	12
Bermuda	6	3	1	2	8	7	10
Barbados	6	0	0	6	2	14	0

GROUP C
Dominica v Nicaragua	0-2
Nicaragua v Panama	1-2
Dominica v Panama	0-5
Panama v Nicaragua	5-1
Nicaragua v Dominica	1-0
Panama v Dominica	3-0
Bahamas withdrew.	

Group C Table	P	W	D	L	F	A	Pts
Panama	4	4	0	0	15	2	12
Nicaragua	4	2	0	2	5	7	6
Dominica	4	0	0	4	0	11	0

GROUP D
St Kitts & Nevis v Puerto Rico	0-0
Canada v St Lucia	4-1
St Lucia v St Kitts & Nevis	2-4
Puerto Rico v Canada	0-3
St Lucia v Canada	0-7
Match awarded 0-7 to Canada. Original result 0-7.	
Puerto Rico v St Kitts & Nevis	1-1
Canada v Puerto Rico	0-0
St Kitts & Nevis v St Lucia	1-1
St Lucia v Puerto Rico	0-4
Match awarded 0-4 to Puerto Rico. Original result 0-4.	
St Kitts & Nevis v Canada	0-0
Puerto Rico v St Lucia	3-0
Canada v St Kitts & Nevis	4-0

Group D Table	P	W	D	L	F	A	Pts
Canada	6	4	2	0	18	1	14
Puerto Rico	6	2	3	1	8	4	9
St Kitts & Nevis	6	1	4	1	6	8	7
St Lucia	6	0	1	5	4	23	1

GROUP E
Grenada v Belize	0-3
Guatemala v St Vincent & the Grenadines	4-0
Belize v Guatemala	1-2
St Vincent & the Grenadines v Grenada	2-1
St Vincent & the Grenadines v Guatemala	0-3
Belize v Grenada	1-4
Guatemala v Belize	3-1
Grenada v St Vincent & the Grenadines	1-1
Belize v St Vincent & the Grenadines	1-1
Guatemala v Grenada	3-0
Grenada v Guatemala	1-4
St Vincent & the Grenadines v Belize	0-2

Group E Table	P	W	D	L	F	A	Pts
Guatemala	6	6	0	0	19	3	18
Belize	6	2	1	3	9	10	7
St Vincent & the Grenadines	6	1	2	3	4	12	5
Grenada	6	1	1	4	7	14	4

GROUP F
Haiti v US Virgin Islands	6-0
Antigua & Barbuda v Curacao	5-2
US Virgin Islands v Antigua & Barbuda	1-8
Curacao v Haiti	2-4
US Virgin Islands v Haiti	0-7
Curacao v Antigua & Barbuda	0-3
Match awarded 0-3 to Antigua & Barbuda. Original result 0-1.	
Haiti v Curacao	2-2
Antigua & Barbuda v US Virgin Islands	10-0
US Virgin Islands v Curacao	0-3
Antigua & Barbuda v Haiti	1-0
Haiti v Antigua & Barbuda	2-1
Curacao v US Virgin Islands	6-1

Group F Table	P	W	D	L	F	A	Pts
Antigua & Barbuda	6	5	0	1	28	5	15
Haiti	6	4	1	1	21	6	13
Curacao	6	2	1	3	15	15	7
US Virgin Islands	6	0	0	6	2	40	0

ROUND 3

GROUP A
USA v Antigua & Barbuda	3-1
Jamaica v Guatemala	2-1
Antigua & Barbuda v Jamaica	0-0
Guatemala v USA	1-1
Jamaica v USA	2-1
Guatemala v Antigua & Barbuda	3-1
Antigua & Barbuda v Guatemala	0-1
USA v Jamaica	1-0
Antigua & Barbuda v USA	1-2
Guatemala v Jamaica	2-1
Jamaica v Antigua & Barbuda	4-1
USA v Guatemala	3-1

Group A Table	P	W	D	L	F	A	Pts
USA	6	4	1	1	11	6	13
Jamaica	6	3	1	2	9	6	10
Guatemala	6	3	1	2	9	8	10
Antigua & Barbuda	6	0	1	5	4	13	1

GROUP B
Mexico v Guyana	3-1
Costa Rica v El Salvador	2-2
El Salvador v Mexico	1-2
Guyana v Costa Rica	0-4
El Salvador v Guyana	2-2

Costa Rica v Mexico	0-2
Guyana v El Salvador	2-3
Mexico v Costa Rica	1-0
El Salvador v Costa Rica	0-1
Guyana v Mexico	0-5
Costa Rica v Guyana	7-0
Mexico v El Salvador	2-0

Group B Table	P	W	D	L	F	A	Pts
Mexico	6	6	0	0	15	2	18
Costa Rica	6	3	1	2	14	5	10
El Salvador	6	1	2	3	8	11	5
Guyana	6	0	1	5	5	24	1

GROUP C

Cuba v Canada	0-1
Honduras v Panama	0-2
Canada v Honduras	0-0
Panama v Cuba	1-0
Cuba v Honduras	0-3
Canada v Panama	1-0
Honduras v Cuba	1-0
Panama v Canada	2-0
Canada v Cuba	3-0
Panama v Honduras	0-0
Honduras v Canada	8-1
Cuba v Panama	1-1

Group C Table	P	W	D	L	F	A	Pts
Honduras	6	3	2	1	12	3	11
Panama	6	3	2	1	6	2	11
Canada	6	3	1	2	6	10	10
Cuba	6	0	1	5	1	10	1

ROUND 4

Honduras v USA	2-1
Mexico v Jamaica	0-0
Panama v Costa Rica	2-2
Honduras v Mexico	2-2
USA v Costa Rica	1-0
Jamaica v Panama	1-1
Costa Rica v Jamaica	2-0
Mexico v USA	0-0
Panama v Honduras	2-0

Jamaica v Mexico	0-1
Costa Rica v Honduras	1-0
Jamaica v USA	1-2
Panama v Mexico	0-0
Honduras v Jamaica	2-0
Mexico v Costa Rica	0-0
USA v Panama	2-0
USA v Honduras	1-0
Costa Rica v Panama	2-0
Costa Rica v USA	3-1
Mexico v Honduras	1-2
Panama v Jamaica	0-0
Honduras v Panama	2-2
Jamaica v Costa Rica	1-1
USA v Mexico	2-0
Honduras v Costa Rica	1-0
USA v Jamaica	2-0
Mexico v Panama	2-1
Costa Rica v Mexico	2-1
Panama v USA	2-3
Jamaica v Honduras	2-2

Round 4 Table	P	W	D	L	F	A	Pts
USA	10	7	1	2	15	8	22
Costa Rica	10	5	3	2	13	7	18
Honduras	10	4	3	3	13	12	15
Mexico	10	2	5	3	7	9	11
Panama	10	1	5	4	10	14	8
Jamaica	10	0	5	5	5	13	5

Mexico qualify for Intercontinental Play-off.

INTERCONTINENTAL PLAY-OFF

The Intercontinental play-off is played between the fourth-placed team in Concacaf (Mexico) and the winner of Oceania (New Zealand).

FIRST LEG

| Mexico v New Zealand | 5-1 |

| **SECOND LEG** | | (agg) |
| New Zealand v Mexico | 2-4 | (3-9) |

USA, Costa Rica, Honduras and Mexico qualify for World Cup 2014 in Brazil.

ASIA

ROUND 1 – FIRST LEG

Cambodia v Laos	4-2
Nepal v Timor-Leste	2-1
Afghanistan v Palestine	0-2
Sri Lanka v Philippines	1-1
Bangladesh v Pakistan	3-0
Mongolia v Myanmar	1-0
Vietnam v Macau	6-0
Malaysia v Chinese Taipei	2-1

ROUND 1 – SECOND LEG

Laos v Cambodia	6-2
Timor-Leste v Nepal	0-5
Palestine v Afghanistan	1-1
Philippines v Sri Lanka	4-0
Pakistan v Bangladesh	0-0
Myanmar v Mongolia	2-0
Macau v Vietnam	1-7
Chinese Taipei v Malaysia	3-2

Malaysia won on away goals rule.

ROUND 2 – FIRST LEG

China PR v Laos	7-2
Lebanon v Bangladesh	4-0
Thailand v Palestine	1-0
Turkmenistan v Indonesia	1-1
Iraq v Yemen	2-0
Syria v Tajikistan	0-3
Match awarded 0-3 to Tajikistan. Syria fielded an ineligible player. Original result 2-1.	
Uzbekistan v Kyrgyzstan	4-0
Jordan v Nepal	9-0
Qatar v Vietnam	3-0
Singapore v Malaysia	5-3
Kuwait v Philippines	3-0
Iran v Maldives	4-0
Oman v Myanmar	2-0
Match abandoned, awarded to Oman.	

ROUND 2 – SECOND LEG

United Arab Emirates v India	3-0
Saudi Arabia v Hong Kong	3-0
Laos v China PR	1-6
Bangladesh v Lebanon	2-0
Palestine v Thailand	2-2
Indonesia v Turkmenistan	4-3
Yemen v Iraq	0-0
Tajikistan v Syria	3-0
Match awarded 3-0 to Tajikistan. Syria fielded an ineligible player. Original result 0-4.	
Kyrgyzstan v Uzbekistan	0-3
Nepal v Jordan	1-1
Vietnam v Qatar	2-1
Malaysia v Singapore	1-1
Philippines v Kuwait	1-2
Maldives v Iran	0-1
Myanmar v Oman	0-2
India v United Arab Emirates	2-2
Hong Kong v Saudi Arabia	0-5

ROUND 3

GROUP A

Iraq v Jordan	0-2
China PR v Singapore	2-1
Jordan v China PR	2-1
Singapore v Iraq	0-2
Singapore v Jordan	0-3
China PR v Iraq	0-1
Iraq v China PR	1-0
Jordan v Singapore	2-0
Jordan v Iraq	1-3
Singapore v China PR	0-4
China PR v Jordan	3-1
Iraq v Singapore	7-1

Group A Table	P	W	D	L	F	A	Pts
Iraq	6	5	0	1	14	4	15
Jordan	6	4	0	2	11	7	12
China PR	6	3	0	3	10	6	9
Singapore	6	0	0	6	2	20	0

GROUP B

United Arab Emirates v Kuwait	2-3
Korea Republic v Lebanon	6-0
Lebanon v United Arab Emirates	3-1
Kuwait v Korea Republic	1-1
Lebanon v Kuwait	2-2
Korea Republic v United Arab Emirates	2-1
United Arab Emirates v Korea Republic	0-2
Kuwait v Lebanon	0-1
Lebanon v Korea Republic	2-1
Kuwait v United Arab Emirates	2-1
United Arab Emirates v Lebanon	4-2
Korea Republic v Kuwait	2-0

Group B Table	P	W	D	L	F	A	Pts
Korea Republic	6	4	1	1	14	4	13
Lebanon	6	3	1	2	10	14	10
Kuwait	6	2	2	2	8	9	8
United Arab Emirates	6	1	0	5	9	14	3

GROUP C

Tajikistan v Uzbekistan	0-1
Japan v Korea DPR	1-0
Korea DPR v Tajikistan	1-0
Uzbekistan v Japan	1-1
Korea DPR v Uzbekistan	0-1
Japan v Tajikistan	8-0
Tajikistan v Japan	0-4
Uzbekistan v Korea DPR	1-0
Korea DPR v Japan	1-0
Uzbekistan v Tajikistan	3-0
Tajikistan v Korea DPR	1-1
Japan v Uzbekistan	0-1

Group C Table	P	W	D	L	F	A	Pts
Uzbekistan	6	5	1	0	8	1	16
Japan	6	3	1	2	14	3	10
Korea DPR	6	2	1	3	3	4	7
Tajikistan	6	0	1	5	1	18	1

GROUP D

Oman v Saudi Arabia	0-0
Australia v Thailand	2-1
Thailand v Oman	3-0
Saudi Arabia v Australia	1-3
Thailand v Saudi Arabia	0-0
Australia v Oman	3-0
Oman v Australia	1-0
Saudi Arabia v Thailand	3-0
Thailand v Australia	0-1
Saudi Arabia v Oman	0-0
Oman v Thailand	2-0
Australia v Saudi Arabia	4-2

Group D Table	P	W	D	L	F	A	Pts
Australia	6	5	0	1	13	5	15
Oman	6	2	2	2	3	6	8
Saudi Arabia	6	1	3	2	6	7	6
Thailand	6	1	1	4	4	8	4

GROUP E

Iran v Indonesia	3-0
Bahrain v Qatar	0-0
Indonesia v Bahrain	0-2
Qatar v Iran	1-1
Indonesia v Qatar	2-3
Iran v Bahrain	6-0
Bahrain v Iran	1-1
Qatar v Indonesia	4-0
Qatar v Bahrain	0-0
Indonesia v Iran	1-4
Bahrain v Indonesia	10-0
Iran v Qatar	2-2

Group E Table	P	W	D	L	F	A	Pts
Iran	6	3	3	0	17	5	12
Qatar	6	2	4	0	10	5	10
Bahrain	6	2	3	1	13	7	9
Indonesia	6	0	0	6	3	26	0

ROUND 4

GROUP A

Lebanon v Qatar	0-1
Uzbekistan v Iran	0-1
Qatar v Korea Republic	1-4
Lebanon v Uzbekistan	1-1
Korea Republic v Lebanon	3-0
Iran v Qatar	0-0
Uzbekistan v Korea Republic	2-2
Lebanon v Iran	1-0
Iran v Korea Republic	1-0
Qatar v Uzbekistan	0-1
Iran v Uzbekistan	0-1
Qatar v Lebanon	1-0
Uzbekistan v Lebanon	1-0
Korea Republic v Qatar	2-1
Qatar v Iran	0-1
Lebanon v Korea Republic	1-1
Iran v Lebanon	4-0
Korea Republic v Uzbekistan	1-0
Korea Republic v Iran	0-1
Uzbekistan v Qatar	5-1

Group A Table	P	W	D	L	F	A	Pts
Iran	8	5	1	2	8	2	16
Korea Republic	8	4	2	2	13	7	14
Uzbekistan	8	4	2	2	11	6	14
Qatar	8	2	1	5	5	13	7
Lebanon	8	1	2	5	3	12	5

GROUP B

Japan v Oman	3-0
Jordan v Iraq	1-1
Japan v Jordan	6-0
Oman v Australia	0-0
Australia v Japan	1-1
Iraq v Oman	1-1
Japan v Iraq	1-0
Jordan v Australia	2-1
Iraq v Australia	1-2
Oman v Jordan	2-1
Iraq v Jordan	1-0
Oman v Japan	1-2
Jordan v Japan	2-1
Australia v Oman	2-2
Japan v Australia	1-1
Oman v Iraq	1-0
Iraq v Japan	0-1
Australia v Jordan	4-0
Australia v Iraq	1-0
Jordan v Oman	1-0

Group B Table	P	W	D	L	F	A	Pts
Japan	8	5	2	1	16	5	17
Australia	8	3	4	1	12	7	13
Jordan	8	3	1	4	7	16	10
Oman	8	2	3	3	7	10	9
Iraq	8	1	2	5	4	8	5

ROUND 5 – CONTINENTAL PLAY-OFF
The two third-placed teams from Group A (Uzbekistan) and Group B (Jordan) of Round 4 contest the Continental play-off.

FIRST LEG

Jordan v Uzbekistan	1-1

SECOND LEG   (agg)

Uzbekistan v Jordan	1-1 (2-2)

Jordan won 9-8 on penalties.

INTERCONTINENTAL PLAY-OFF
The Intercontinental play-off is played between the Round 5 winner from Asia (Jordan) and the fifth-placed team in South America (Uruguay).

FIRST LEG

Jordan v Uruguay	0-5

SECOND LEG   (agg)

Uruguay v Jordan	0-0 (0-5)

Iran, Korea Republic, Japan and Australia qualify for World Cup 2014 in Brazil.

FIFA WORLD CUP 2014

FINALS IN BRAZIL

GROUP A

Sao Paulo, Thursday 12 June 2014
Brazil (1) 3 *(Neymar 29, 71 (pen), Oscar 90)*
Croatia (1) 1 *(Marcelo 11 (og))*   62,103
Brazil: (4231) Julio Cesar; Dani Alves, Thiago Silva,
Luiz, Marcelo; Paulinho (Hernanes 63), Gustavo; Hulk
(Bernard 68), Oscar, Neymar (Ramires 88); Fred.
Croatia: (4231) Pletikosa; Srna, Corluka, Lovren,
Vrsaljko; Modric, Rakitic; Perisic, Kovacic (Brozovic 61),
Olic; Jelavic (Rebic 78).
Referee: Yuichi Nishimura (Japan).

Natal, Friday 13 June 2014
Mexico (0) 1 *(Peralta 61)*
Cameroon (0) 0   44,000
Mexico: (532) Ochoa; Layun, Moreno, Marquez,
Rodriguez, Aguilar; Guardado (Fabian 69), Herrera
(Salcido 90); Giovani, Peralta (Hernandez 73).
Cameroon: (433) Itandje; Djeugoue (Nounkeu 46),
N'Koulou, Chedjou, Assou-Ekotto; Song (Webo 79),
Mbia, Enoh; Moukandjo, Eto'o, Choupo-Moting.
Referee: Wilmar Roldan Perez (Colombia).

Fortaleza, Tuesday 17 June 2014
Brazil (0) 0
Mexico (0) 0   60,342
Brazil: (4231) Julio Cesar; Dani Alves, Thiago Silva,
Luiz, Marcelo; Paulinho, Gustavo; Ramires (Bernard 46),
Oscar (Willian 84), Neymar; Fred (Jo 68).
Mexico: (532) Ochoa; Aguilar, Rodriguez, Marquez,
Moreno, Layun; Herrera (Fabian 76), Vazquez,
Guardado; Giovani (Jimenez 84), Peralta (Hernandez 73).
Referee: Cuneyt Cakir (Turkey).

Manaus, Wednesday 18 June 2014
Cameroon (0) 0
Croatia (1) 4 *(Olic 11, Perisic 48, Mandzukic 61, 73)*
     36,000
Cameroon: (433) Itandje; Mbia, Chedjou (Nounkeu 46),
N'Koulou, Assou-Ekotto; Song , Matip, Enoh; Choupo-
Moting (Salli 75), Aboubakar (Webo 70), Moukandjo.
Croatia: (4231) Pletikosa; Srna, Corluka, Lovren, Pranjic;
Modric, Rakitic; Perisic (Rebic 78), Sammir (Kovacic 72),
Olic (Eduardo 68); Mandzukic.
Referee: Pedro Proenca (Portugal).

Brasilia, Monday 23 June 2014
Cameroon (1) 1 *(Matip 26)*
Brazil (2) 4 *(Neymar 17, 34, Fred 49, Fernandinho 84)*
     69,112
Cameroon: (4141) Itandje; Nyom, Matip, N'Koulou,
Bedimo; Enoh; Moukandjo (Salli 58), Mbia, N'Guemo,
Choupo-Moting (Makoun 81); Aboubakar (Webo 72).
Brazil: (4231) Julio Cesar; Dani Alves, Thiago Silva,
Luiz, Marcelo; Paulinho (Fernandinho 46), Gustavo;
Hulk (Ramires 63), Oscar, Neymar (Willian 71); Fred.
Referee: Jonas Eriksson (Sweden).

Recife, Monday 23 June 2014
Croatia (0) 1 *(Perisic 87)*
Mexico (0) 3 *(Marquez 72, Guardado 75, Hernandez 82)*
     41,212
Croatia: (4231) Pletikosa; Srna, Corluka, Lovren,
Vrsaljko (Kovacic 58); Rakitic, Pranjic (Jelavic 74);
Perisic, Modric, Olic (Rebic 69); Mandzukic.
Mexico: (532) Ochoa; Aguilar, Rodriguez, Marquez,
Moreno, Layun; Herrera, Vazquez, Guardado (Fabian
84); Giovani (Hernandez 62), Peralta (Pena 79).
Referee: Ravshan Irmatov (Uzbekistan).

GROUP B

Salvador, Friday 13 June 2014
Spain (1) 1 *(Alonso 27 (pen))*
Netherlands (1) 5 *(van Persie 44, 72, Robben 53, 80,*
De Vrij 64)   50,000
Spain: (433) Casillas; Azpilicueta, Sergio Ramos, Pique,
Jordi Alba; Alonso (Pedro 62), Xavi, Busquets; Silva
(Fabregas 78), Diego Costa (Torres 62), Iniesta.
Netherlands: (532) Cillessen; Janmaat, Vlaar, De Vrij
(Veltman 77), Martins Indi, Blind; de Guzman (Wijnaldum
62), Sneijder, De Jong; van Persie (Lens 79), Robben.
Referee: Nicola Rizzoli (Italy).

Cuiaba, Friday 13 June 2014
Chile (2) 3 *(Alexis 12, Valdivia 14, Beausejour 90)*
Australia (1) 1 *(Cahill 35)*   35,000
Chile: (433) Bravo; Isla, Medel, Jara, Mena; Aranguiz,
Diaz, Vidal (Gutierrez 60); Alexis, Valdivia (Beausejour
68), Vargas (Pinilla 88).
Australia: (4411) Ryan; Franjic (McGowan 49),
Wilkinson, Spiranovic, Davidson; Leckie, Jedinak,
Milligan, Oar (Halloran 68); Bresciano (Troisi 78); Cahill.
Referee: Noumandiez Doue (Ivory Coast).

Porto Alegre, Wednesday 18 June 2014
Australia (1) 2 *(Cahill 21, Jedinak 54 (pen))*
Netherlands (1) 3 *(Robben 20, van Persie 58, Depay 68)*
     45,000
Australia: (4411) Ryan; McGowan, Wilkinson,
Spiranovic, Davidson; Leckie, Jedinak, McKay, Oar
(Taggart 77); Bresciano (Bozanic 51); Cahill (Halloran
70).
Netherlands: (343) Cillessen; Martins Indi (Depay 45),
Vlaar, De Vrij; Janmaat, De Jong, Blind, de Guzman
(Wijnaldum 78); Sneijder, van Persie (Lens 87), Robben.
Referee: Djamel Haimoudi (Algeria).

Rio de Janeiro, Wednesday 18 June 2014
Spain (0) 0
Chile (2) 2 *(Vargas 20, Aranguiz 43)*   72,000
Spain: (4231) Casillas; Azpilicueta, Javi Martinez, Sergio
Ramos, Jordi Alba; Alonso (Koke 46), Busquets; Silva,
Iniesta, Pedro (Cazorla 76); Diego Costa (Torres 64).
Chile: (352) Bravo; Medel, Silva, Jara; Isla, Aranguiz
(Gutierrez 64), Diaz, Mena, Vidal (Carmona 88); Alexis,
Vargas (Valdivia 84).
Referee: Mark Geiger (USA).

Curitiba, Monday 23 June 2014
Australia (0) 0
Spain (1) 3 *(Villa 36, Torres 69, Mata 82)*   39,375
Australia: (433) Ryan; McGowan, Spiranovic, Wilkinson,
Davidson; McKay, Jedinak, Bozanic (Bresciano 72);
Leckie, Taggart (Halloran 46), Oar (Troisi 61).
Spain: (4231) Reina; Juanfran, Albiol, Sergio Ramos,
Jordi Alba; Alonso (Silva 83), Koke; Cazorla (Fabregas
68), Iniesta, Villa (Mata 57); Torres.
Referee: Nawaf Shukralla (Bahrain).

Sao Paulo, Monday 23 June 2014
Netherlands (0) 2 *(Fer 77, Depay 90)*
Chile (0) 0   62,996
Netherlands: (3412) Cillessen; Blind, Vlaar, De Vrij; Kuyt
(Kongolo 89), De Jong, Wijnaldum, Janmaat; Sneijder
(Fer 75); Lens (Depay 69), Robben.
Chile: (3412) Bravo; Silva (Valdivia 70), Medel, Jara; Isla,
Aranguiz, Diaz, Mena; Gutierrez (Beausejour 46);
Vargas (Pinilla 81), Alexis.
Referee: Bakary Gassama (Gambia).

Group A Table	P	W	D	L	F	A	GD	Pts
Brazil	3	2	1	0	7	2	5	7
Mexico	3	2	1	0	4	1	3	7
Croatia	3	1	0	2	6	6	0	3
Cameroon	3	0	0	3	1	9	-8	0

Group B Table	P	W	D	L	F	A	GD	Pts
Netherlands	3	3	0	0	10	3	7	9
Chile	3	2	0	1	5	3	2	6
Spain	3	1	0	2	4	7	-3	3
Australia	3	0	0	3	3	9	-6	0

GROUP C

Belo Horizonte, Saturday 14 June 2014
Colombia (1) 3 *(Armero 5, Gutierrez 58, Rodriguez J 90)*
Greece (0) 0   57,174
Colombia: (442) Ospina; Zuniga, Zapata, Yepes, Armero (Arias 74); Sanchez Moreno, Aguilar (Mejia 69), Rodriguez J, Cuadrado; Gutierrez (Martinez J 76), Ibarbo.
Greece: (433) Karnezis; Manolas, Torosidis, Papastathopoulos, Holebas; Maniatis, Katsouranis, Kone (Karagounis 78); Salpingidis (Fetfatzidis 57), Gekas (Mitroglou 64), Samaras.
Referee: Mark Geiger (USA).

Recife, Sunday 15 June 2014
Ivory Coast (0) 2 *(Bony 64, Gervinho 66)*
Japan (1) 1 *(Honda 16)*   40,000
Ivory Coast: (433) Barry; Aurier, Bamba, Zokora, Boka (Djakpa 75); Tiote, Toure Y, Die (Drogba 62); Gervinho, Bony (Konan 77), Kalou.
Japan: (4231) Kawashima; Uchida, Morishige, Yoshida, Nagatomo; Yamaguchi, Hasebe (Endo 53); Okazaki, Honda, Kagawa (Kakitani 86); Osako (Okubo 68).
Referee: Enrique Osses (Chile).

Brasilia, Thursday 19 June 2014
Colombia (0) 2 *(Rodriguez J 64, Quintero 70)*
Ivory Coast (0) 1 *(Gervinho 73)*   68,748
Colombia: (4231) Ospina; Armero (Arias 72), Yepes, Zapata, Zuniga; Sanchez Moreno, Aguilar (Mejia 79); Ibarbo (Quintero 53), Rodriguez J, Cuadrado; Gutierrez.
Ivory Coast: (4231) Barry; Boka, Bamba, Zokora, Aurier; Die (Bolly 73), Tiote; Gervinho, Toure Y, Gradel (Kalou 67); Bony (Drogba 60).
Referee: Howard Webb (England).

Natal, Thursday 19 June 2014
Japan (0) 0
Greece (0) 0   39,485
Japan: (4231) Kawashima; Uchida, Konno, Yoshida, Nagatomo; Yamaguchi, Hasebe (Endo 46); Okazaki, Honda, Okubo; Osako (Kagawa 57).
Greece: (433) Karnezis; Torosidis, Papastathopoulos, Manolas, Holebas; Maniatis, Katsouranis[■], Kone (Salpingidis 80); Fetfatzidis (Karagounis 41), Mitroglou (Gekas 35), Samaras.
Referee: Joel Aguilar (El Salvador).

Fortaleza, Tuesday 24 June 2014
Greece (1) 2 *(Samaris 42, Samaras 90 (pen))*
Ivory Coast (0) 1 *(Bony 74)*   58,000
Greece: (433) Karnezis (Glykos 24); Torosidis, Papastathopoulos, Manolas, Holebas; Christodoulopoulos, Maniatis, Karagounis (Gekas 77); Kone (Samaris 12), Salpingidis, Samaras.
Ivory Coast: (4231) Barry; Aurier, Toure K, Bamba, Boka; Die, Tiote (Bony 61); Kalou, Toure Y, Gervinho (Sio 83); Drogba (Diomande 78).
Referee: Carlos Vera Rodriguez (Ecuador).

Cuiaba, Tuesday 24 June 2014
Japan (1) 1 *(Okazaki 45)*
Colombia (1) 4 *(Cuadrado 17 (pen), Martinez J 55, 82, Rodriguez J 89)*   41,112
Japan: (4411) Kawashima; Uchida, Yoshida, Konno, Nagatomo; Okazaki (Kakitani 69), Aoyama (Yamaguchi 62), Hasebe, Kagawa (Kiyotake 85); Honda; Okubo.
Colombia: (442) Ospina (Mondragon 85); Arias, Valdes, Balanta, Armero; Cuadrado (Carbonero 46), Mejia, Guarin F, Quintero (Rodriguez J 46); Martinez J, Ramos.
Referee: Pedro Proenca (Portugal).

Group C Table	P	W	D	L	F	A	GD	Pts
Colombia	3	3	0	0	9	2	7	9
Greece	3	1	1	1	2	4	-2	4
Ivory Coast	3	1	0	2	4	5	-1	3
Japan	3	0	1	2	2	6	-4	1

GROUP D

Fortaleza, Saturday 14 June 2014
Uruguay (1) 1 *(Cavani 24 (pen))*
Costa Rica (0) 3 *(Campbell 54, Duarte 57, Urena 84)*
                                                      58,679
Uruguay: (442) Muslera; Pereira[■] M, Lugano, Godin, Caceres; Stuani, Arevalo Rios, Gargano (Gonzalez 60), Rodriguez C (Hernandez 76); Forlan (Lodeiro 60), Cavani.
Costa Rica: (532) Navas; Gamboa, Duarte, Gonzalez, Umana, Diaz; Borges, Tejeda (Cubero 74), Bolanos (Barrantes 88); Ruiz (Urena 82), Campbell.
Referee: Felix Brych (Germany).

Manaus, Saturday 14 June 2014
England (1) 1 *(Sturridge 37)*
Italy (1) 2 *(Marchisio 35, Balotelli 50)*   40,000
England: (4231) Hart; Johnson, Cahill, Jagielka, Baines; Gerrard, Henderson (Wilshere 73); Sterling, Rooney, Welbeck (Barkley 61); Sturridge (Lallana 79).
Italy: (433) Sirigu; Darmian, Paletta, Barzagli, Chiellini; Verratti (Thiago Motta 57), Pirlo, De Rossi; Candreva (Parolo 79), Balotelli (Immobile 73), Marchisio.
Referee: Bjorn Kuipers (Netherlands).

Sao Paulo, Thursday 19 June 2014
Uruguay (1) 2 *(Suarez 39, 85)*
England (0) 1 *(Rooney 75)*   62,575
Uruguay: (442) Muslera; Gimenez, Godin, Caceres, Pereira A; Lodeiro (Stuani 67), Gonzalez (Fucile 79), Arevalo Rios, Rodriguez C; Cavani, Suarez (Coates 87).
England: (4231) Hart; Baines, Cahill, Jagielka, Johnson; Gerrard, Henderson (Lambert 87); Sterling (Barkley 64), Rooney, Welbeck (Lallana 71); Sturridge.
Referee: Carlos Velasco Carballo (Spain).

Recife, Friday 20 June 2014
Italy (0) 0
Costa Rica (1) 1 *(Ruiz 44)*   38,000
Italy: (4231) Buffon; Darmian, Barzagli, Chiellini, Abate; Thiago Motta (Cassano 46), De Rossi; Candreva (Insigne 57), Pirlo, Marchisio (Cerci 70); Balotelli.
Costa Rica: (4141) Navas; Gamboa, Umana, Duarte, Diaz; Gonzalez; Ruiz (Brenes 81), Borges, Tejeda (Cubero 67), Bolanos; Campbell (Urena 74).
Referee: Enrique Osses (Chile).

Belo Horizonte, Tuesday 24 June 2014
Costa Rica (0) 0
England (0) 0   57,823
Costa Rica: (541) Navas; Gamboa, Duarte, Gonzalez, Miller, Diaz; Ruiz, Borges (Barrantes 78), Tejeda, Brenes (Bolanos 59); Campbell (Urena 65).
England: (4231) Foster; Jones, Smalling, Cahill, Shaw; Lampard, Wilshere (Gerrard 73); Milner (Rooney 76), Barkley, Lallana (Sterling 62); Sturridge.
Referee: Djamel Haimoudi (Algeria).

Belo Horizonte, Tuesday 24 June 2014
Italy (0) 0
Uruguay (0) 1 *(Godin 81)*   39,706
Italy: (352) Buffon; Chiellini, Bonucci, Barzagli; De Sciglio, Marchisio[■], Pirlo, Verratti (Thiago Motta 75), Darmian; Immobile (Cassano 71), Balotelli (Parolo 46).
Uruguay: (4312) Muslera; Caceres, Gimenez, Godin, Pereira A (Stuani 63); Gonzalez, Arevalo Rios, Rodriguez C (Ramirez 78); Lodeiro (Pereira M 46); Cavani, Suarez.
Referee: Marco Rodriguez Moreno (Mexico).

Group D Table	P	W	D	L	F	A	GD	Pts
Costa Rica	3	2	1	0	4	1	3	7
Uruguay	3	2	0	1	4	4	0	6
Italy	3	1	0	2	2	3	-1	3
England	3	0	1	2	2	4	-2	1

GROUP E

Brasilia, Sunday 15 June 2014
Switzerland (0) 2 *(Mehmedi 48, Seferovic 90)*
Ecuador (1) 1 *(Valencia E 22)*   35,000
Switzerland: (4231) Benaglio; Lichtsteiner, Djourou, von Bergen, Rodriguez; Behrami, Inler; Shaqiri, Xhaka, Stocker (Mehmedi 46); Drmic (Seferovic 75).
Ecuador: (442) Dominguez; Paredes J, Erazo, Guagua, Ayovi W; Valencia A, Gruezo, Noboa, Montero (Rojas 76); Caicedo (Arroyo 70), Valencia E.
Referee: Ravshan Irmatov (Uzbekistan).

Porto Alegre, Sunday 15 June 2014
France (1) 3 *(Benzema 45 (pen), 72, Valladares 48 (og))*
Honduras (0) 0   40,000
France: (433) Lloris; Debuchy, Varane, Sakho, Evra; Pogba (Sissoko 57), Cabaye (Mavuba 65), Matuidi; Valbuena (Giroud 78), Benzema, Griezmann.
Honduras: (442) Valladares; Beckeles, Bernardez (Chavez O 46), Figueroa, Izaguirre; Najar (Claros 58), Palacios W■, Garrido, Espinoza; Bengtson (Garcia O 46), Costly.
Referee: Sandro Meira Ricci (Brazil).

Salvador, Friday 20 June 2014
Switzerland (0) 2 *(Dzemaili 81, Xhaka 87)*
France (3) 5 *(Giroud 17, Matuidi 18, Valbuena 40, Benzema 67, Sissoko 73)*   48,000
Switzerland: (4231) Benaglio; Lichtsteiner, Djourou, von Bergen (Senderos 9), Rodriguez; Behrami (Dzemaili 46); Inler; Shaqiri, Xhaka, Mehmedi; Seferovic (Drmic 69).
France: (433) Lloris; Debuchy, Varane, Sakho (Koscielny 66), Evra; Sissoko, Cabaye, Matuidi; Valbuena (Griezmann 82), Giroud (Pogba 63), Benzema.
Referee: Bjorn Kuipers (Netherlands).

Curitiba, Friday 20 June 2014
Honduras (1) 1 *(Costly 31)*
Ecuador (1) 2 *(Valencia E 34, 65)*   39,224
Honduras: (442) Valladares; Beckeles, Bernardez, Figueroa, Izaguirre (Garcia J 46); Garcia O (Chavez M 82), Garrido (Martinez 71), Claros, Espinoza; Bengtson, Costly.
Ecuador: (442) Dominguez; Paredes J, Guagua, Erazo, Ayovi W; Valencia A, Minda (Gruezo 83), Noboa, Montero (Achilier 90); Caicedo (Mendez 82), Valencia E.
Referee: Benjamin Williams (Australia).

Rio de Janeiro, Wednesday 25 June 2014
Ecuador (0) 0
France (0) 0   73,749
Ecuador: (442) Dominguez; Paredes J, Guagua, Erazo, Ayovi W; Valencia A■, Minda, Noboa (Caicedo 89), Montero (Ibarra 63); Arroyo (Achilier 81), Valencia E.
France: (451) Lloris; Sagna, Koscielny, Sakho (Varane 61), Digne; Griezmann (Remy 79), Pogba, Schneiderlin, Matuidi (Giroud 67); Sissoko; Benzema.
Referee: Noumandiez Doue (Ivory Coast).

Manaus, Wednesday 25 June 2014
Honduras (0) 0
Switzerland (2) 3 *(Shaqiri 6, 31, 71)*   40,332
Honduras: (442) Valladares; Beckeles, Bernardez, Figueroa, Garcia J; Garcia O (Najar 77), Palacios W, Claros, Espinoza (Chavez M 46); Bengtson, Costly (Palacios J 40).
Switzerland: (4231) Benaglio; Lichtsteiner, Djourou, Schar, Rodriguez; Behrami, Inler; Shaqiri (Dzemaili 87), Xhaka (Lang 76), Mehmedi; Drmic (Seferovic 73).
Referee: Nestor Pitana (Argentina).

Group E Table	P	W	D	L	F	A	GD	Pts
France	3	2	1	0	8	2	6	7
Switzerland	3	2	0	1	7	6	1	6
Ecuador	3	1	1	1	3	3	0	4
Honduras	3	0	0	3	1	8	-7	0

GROUP F

Rio de Janeiro, Sunday 15 June 2014
Argentina (1) 2 *(Kolasinac 3 (og), Messi 65)*
Bosnia & Herzegovina (0) 1 *(Ibisevic 84)*   50,000
Argentina: (532) Romero; Zabaleta, Campagnaro (Gago 46), Fernandez F, Garay, Rojo; Maxi Rodriguez (Higuain 46), Mascherano, Di Maria; Messi, Aguero (Biglia 87).
Bosnia & Herzegovina: (4231) Begovic; Mujdza (Ibisevic 69), Bicakcic, Spahic, Kolasinac; Besic, Hajrovic (Visca 71); Pjanic, Misimovic (Medunjanin 74), Lulic; Dzeko.
Referee: Joel Aguilar (El Salvador).

Curitiba, Monday 16 June 2014
Iran (0) 0
Nigeria (0) 0   38,081
Iran: (4231) Haghighi A; Montazeri, Hosseini, Sadeghi, Pouladi; Teymourian, Nekounam; Heydari (Shojaei 89), Dejagah (Jahanbakhsh 78), Hajsafi; Ghoochannejhad.
Nigeria: (4231) Enyeama; Ambrose, Oboabona (Yobo 29), Omeruo, Oshaniwa; Onazi, Mikel; Moses (Ameobi 52), Musa, Azeez (Odemwingie 69); Emenike.
Referee: Carlos Vera Rodriguez (Ecuador).

Belo Horizonte, Saturday 21 June 2014
Argentina (0) 1 *(Messi 90)*
Iran (0) 0   57,698
Argentina: (433) Romero; Zabaleta, Garay, Fernandez F, Rojo; Gago, Mascherano, Di Maria (Biglia 90); Aguero (Lavezzi 77), Messi, Higuain (Palacio R 77).
Iran: (451) Haghighi A; Montazeri, Hosseini, Sadeghi, Pouladi; Shojaei (Heydari 76), Teymourian, Nekounam, Hajsafi (Haghighi R 88), Dejagah (Jahanbakhsh 85); Ghoochannejhad.
Referee: Milorad Mazic.

Cuiaba, Saturday 21 June 2014
Nigeria (1) 1 *(Odemwingie 29)*
Bosnia & Herzegovina (0) 0   40,499
Nigeria: (442) Enyeama; Ambrose, Yobo, Omeruo, Oshaniwa; Musa (Ameobi 65), Mikel, Onazi, Babatunde (Uzoenyi 75); Emenike, Odemwingie.
Bosnia & Herzegovina: (4231) Begovic; Mujdza, Spahic, Sunjic, Lulic (Salihovic 58); Besic, Pjanic; Hajrovic (Ibisevic 57), Misimovic, Medunjanin (Susic 64); Dzeko.
Referee: Peter O'Leary (New Zealand).

Salvador, 25 June 2014
Bosnia & Herzegovina (1) 3 *(Dzeko 23, Pjanic 59, Vrsajevic 83)*
Iran (0) 1 *(Ghoochannejhad 82)*   48,011
Bosnia & Herzegovina: (442) Begovic; Vrsajevic, Sunjic, Spahic, Kolasinac; Hadzic (Vranjes 61), Pjanic, Besic, Susic (Salihovic 79); Dzeko (Visca 84), Ibisevic.
Iran: (4231) Haghighi A; Hosseini, Sadeghi, Montazeri, Pouladi; Teymourian, Nekounam; Dejagah (Ansarifard 68), Shojaei (Heydari 46), Hajsafi (Jahanbakhsh 63); Ghoochannejhad.
Referee: Carlos Velasco Carballo (Spain).

Porto Alegre, 25 June 2014
Nigeria (1) 2 *(Musa 4, 47)*
Argentina (2) 3 *(Messi 3, 45, Rojo 50)*   43,285
Nigeria: (433) Enyeama; Ambrose, Yobo, Omeruo, Oshaniwa; Onazi, Mikel, Babatunde (Uchebo 65); Odemwingie (Nwofor 80), Emenike, Musa.
Argentina: (433) Romero; Zabaleta, Fernandez F, Garay, Rojo; Gago, Mascherano, Di Maria; Messi (Alvarez 63), Higuain (Biglia 90), Aguero (Lavezzi 38).
Referee: Nicola Rizzoli (Italy).

Group F Table	P	W	D	L	F	A	GD	Pts
Argentina	3	3	0	0	6	3	3	9
Nigeria	3	1	1	1	3	3	0	4
Bosnia & Herzegovina	3	1	0	2	4	4	0	3
Iran	3	0	1	2	1	4	-3	1

GROUP G

Salvador, Monday 16 June 2014
Germany (3) 4 *(Muller 12 (pen), 45, 78, Hummels 32)*
Portugal (0) 0   45,392
Germany: (433) Neuer; Boateng, Mertesacker, Hummels (Mustafi 73), Howedes; Lahm, Khedira, Kroos; Ozil (Schurrle 62), Muller (Podolski 81), Gotze.
Portugal: (433) Rui Patricio; Joao Pereira, Pepe■, Bruno Alves, Fabio Coentrao (Andre Almeida 65); Veloso (Ricardo Costa 46), Joao Moutinho, Meireles; Nani, Almeida (Eder 28), Ronaldo.
Referee: Milorad Mazic (Serbia).

Natal, Monday 16 June 2014
Ghana (0) 1 *(Ayew A 82)*
USA (1) 2 *(Dempsey 21, Brooks 86)*   39,760
Ghana: (4411) Kwarasey; Opare, Mensah, Boye, Asamoah; Atsu (Adomah 77), Rabiu (Essien 71), Muntari, Ayew A; Ayew J (Boateng 58); Gyan.
USA: (4411) Howard; Johnson, Cameron, Besler (Brooks 46), Beasley; Bedoya (Zusi 77), Jones, Bradley, Beckerman; Dempsey; Altidore (Johannsson 23).
Referee: Jonas Eriksson (Sweden).

Fortaleza, Saturday 21 June 2014
Germany (0) 2 *(Gotze 51, Klose 71)*
Ghana (0) 2 *(Ayew A 54, Gyan 63)*   59,621
Germany: (433) Neuer; Boateng (Mustafi 46), Mertesacker, Hummels, Howedes; Lahm, Khedira (Schweinsteiger 70), Kroos; Muller, Ozil, Gotze (Klose 69).
Ghana: (4231) Dauda; Afful, Boye, Mensah, Asamoah; Muntari, Rabiu (Agyemang-Badu 78); Atsu (Wakaso 73), Boateng (Ayew J 53), Ayew A; Gyan.
Referee: Sandro Meira Ricci (Brazil).

Manaus, Sunday 22 June 2014
USA (0) 2 *(Jones 64, Dempsey 81)*
Portugal (1) 2 *(Nani 5, Varela 90)*   39,000
USA: (4312) Howard; Johnson, Cameron, Besler, Beasley; Bedoya (Yedlin 71), Beckerman, Jones; Bradley; Zusi (Gonzalez 90), Dempsey (Wondolowski 87).
Portugal: (433) Beto; Joao Pereira, Bruno Alves, Ricardo Costa, Andre Almeida (William Carvalho 46); Joao Moutinho, Veloso, Meireles (Varela 68); Nani, Postiga (Eder 16), Ronaldo.
Referee: Nestor Pittana (Argentina).

Brasilia, Thursday 26 June 2014
Portugal (1) 2 *(Boye 30 (og), Ronaldo 80)*
Ghana (0) 1 *(Gyan 57)*   67,540
Portugal: (433) Beto (Eduardo 89); Joao Pereira (Varela 61), Pepe, Bruno Alves, Veloso; Joao Moutinho, William Carvalho, Ruben Amorim; Nani, Ronaldo, Eder (Vieirinha 69).
Ghana: (442) Dauda; Afful, Boye, Mensah, Asamoah; Atsu, Rabiu (Afriyie 76), Agyemang-Badu, Ayew A (Wakaso 81); Waris (Ayew J 71), Gyan.
Referee: Nawaf Shukralla (Bahrain).

Recife, Thursday 26 June 2014
USA (0) 0
Germany (0) 1 *(Muller 55)*   41,876
USA: (4231) Howard; Johnson, Gonzalez, Besler, Beasley; Beckerman, Jones; Zusi (Yedlin 83), Bradley, Davis (Bedoya 59); Dempsey.
Germany: (433) Neuer; Boateng, Mertesacker, Hummels, Howedes; Schweinsteiger (Gotze 76), Lahm, Kroos; Ozil (Schurrle 89), Muller, Podolski (Klose 46).
Referee: Ravshan Irmatov (Uzbekistan).

Group G Table	P	W	D	L	F	A	GD	Pts
Germany	3	2	1	0	7	2	5	7
USA	3	1	1	1	4	4	0	4
Portugal	3	1	1	1	4	7	–3	4
Ghana	3	0	1	2	4	6	–2	1

GROUP H

Belo Horizonte, Tuesday 17 June 2014
Belgium (0) 2 *(Fellaini 70, Mertens 80)*
Algeria (1) 1 *(Feghouli 25 (pen))*   56,800
Belgium: (4231) Courtois; Alderweireld, Kompany, Van Buyten, Vertonghen; Witsel, Dembele (Fellaini 65); Chadli (Mertens 46), De Bruyne, Hazard; Lukaku (Origi 58).
Algeria: (433) M'Bolhi; Halliche, Bougherra, Medjani (Ghilas 84), Ghoulam; Bentaleb, Mostefa, Taider; Mahrez (Lacen 71), Soudani (Slimani 66), Feghouli.
Referee: Marco Rodriguez Moreno (Mexico).

Cuiaba, Tuesday 17 June 2014
Russia (0) 1 *(Kerzhakov 74)*
Korea Republic (0) 1 *(Lee K 68)*   37,603
Russia: (433) Akinfeev; Eshchenko, Ignashevich, Berezutski V, Kombarov; Fayzulin, Glushakov (Denisov 72), Zhirkov (Kerzhakov 71); Samedov, Kokorin, Shatov (Dzagoev 59).
Korea Republic: (442) Jung; Lee Y, Kim Y, Hong (Hwang 73), Yun; Ki, Han, Lee C, Koo; Park (Lee K 56), Son (Kim B 84).
Referee: Nestor Pitana (Argentina).

Rio de Janeiro, Sunday 22 June 2014
Belgium (0) 1 *(Origi 88)*
Russia (0) 0   74,738
Belgium: (4231) Courtois; Alderweireld, Van Buyten, Kompany, Vermaelen (Vertonghen 31); Witsel, Fellaini; De Bruyne, Hazard, Mertens (Mirallas 75); Lukaku (Origi 57).
Russia: (4231) Akinfeev; Kozlov (Eshchenko 62), Berezutski V, Ignashevich, Kombarov; Glushakov, Fayzulin; Samedov (Kerzhakov 90), Shatov (Dzagoev 83), Kanunnikov; Kokorin.
Referee: Felix Brych (Germany).

Porto Alegre, Sunday 22 June 2014
Korea Republic (0) 2 *(Son 50, Koo 72)*
Algeria (3) 4 *(Slimani 26, Halliche 28, Djabou 37, Brahimi 62)*   43,394
Korea Republic: (4231) Jung; Lee Y, Hong, Kim Y, Yun; Han (Ji 78), Lee C (Lee K 64); Ki, Park (Shin-Wook Kim 57), Koo; Son.
Algeria: (541) M'Bolhi; Mandi, Medjani, Bougherra (Belkalem 89), Halliche, Mesbah; Feghouli, Brahimi (Lacen 77), Djabou (Ghilas 73), Bentaleb; Slimani.
Referee: Wilmar Roldan Perez (Colombia).

Curitiba, Thursday 26 June 2014
Algeria (0) 1 *(Slimani 60)*
Russia (1) 1 *(Kokorin 6)*   39,311
Algeria: (4231) M'Bolhi; Mandi, Belkalem, Halliche, Mesbah; Medjani, Bentaleb; Feghouli, Brahimi (Yebda 71), Djabou (Ghilas 76); Slimani (Soudani 90).
Russia: (4231) Akinfeev; Kozlov, Berezutski V, Ignashevich, Kombarov; Glushakov (Denisov 46), Fayzulin; Samedov, Kokorin, Shatov (Dzagoev 67); Kerzhakov (Kanunnikov 81).
Referee: Cuneyt Cakir (Turkey).

Sao Paulo, Thursday 26 June 2014
Korea Republic (0) 0
Belgium (0) 1 *(Vertonghen 78)*   61,397
Korea Republic: (4231) Seung-Gyu Kim; Lee Y, Hong, Kim Y, Yun; Han (Lee K 46), Ki; Lee C, Koo, Son (Ji 73); Shin-Wook Kim (Kim B 66).
Belgium: (433) Courtois; Vanden Borre, Van Buyten, Lombaerts, Vertonghen; Fellaini, Defour■, Dembele; Mertens (Origi 60), Mirallas (Hazard 88), Januzaj (Chadli 60).
Referee: Benjamin Williams (Australia).

Group H Table	P	W	D	L	F	A	GD	Pts
Belgium	3	3	0	0	4	1	3	9
Algeria	3	1	1	1	6	5	1	4
Russia	3	0	2	1	2	3	–1	2
Korea Republic	3	0	1	2	3	6	–3	1

SECOND ROUND

Belo Horizonte, Saturday 28 June 2014

Brazil (1) 1 *(Luiz 18)*

Chile (1) 1 *(Alexis 32)*   57,714

Brazil: (4231) Julio Cesar; Dani Alves, Thiago Silva, Luiz, Marcelo; Fernandinho (Ramires 72), Gustavo; Hulk, Oscar (Willian 106), Neymar; Fred (Jo 64).
Chile: (3412) Bravo; Mena, Isla, Silva; Alexis, Vidal (Pinilla 87), Vargas (Gutierrez 57), Medel (Rojas 108); Jara; Aranguiz, Diaz.
aet; Brazil won 3-2 on penalties: Brazil first – Luiz 1-0, Pinilla 1-0, Willian 1-0, Sanchez 1-0, Marcelo 2-0, Aranguiz 2-1, Hulk 2-1, Dia 2-2, Neymar 3-2, Jara 3-2.
Referee: Howard Webb (England).

Rio de Janeiro, Saturday 28 June 2014

Colombia (1) 2 *(Rodriguez J 28, 50)*

Uruguay (0) 0   73,804

Colombia: (4231) Ospina; Zuniga, Zapata, Yepes, Armero; Aguilar, Sanchez Moreno; Cuadrado (Guarin F 81), Rodriguez J (Ramos 85), Martinez; Gutierrez (Mejia 68).
Uruguay: (532) Muslera; Pereira M, Gimenez, Godin, Caceres, Pereira A (Ramirez 53); Gonzalez (Hernandez 67), Arevalo Rios, Rodriguez C; Cavani, Forlan (Stuani 53).
Referee: Bjorn Kuipers (Germany).

Recife, Sunday 29 June 2014

Costa Rica (0) 1 *(Ruiz 52)*

Greece (0) 1 *(Papastathopoulos 90)*   41,242

Costa Rica: (541) Navas; Gamboa (Acosta 76), Duarte■, Gonzalez, Umana, Diaz; Ruiz, Borges, Tejeda (Cubero 65), Bolanos (Brenes 83); Campbell.
Greece: (4141) Karnezis; Torosidis, Manolas, Papastathopoulos, Holebas; Karagounis; Salpingidis (Gekas 69), Maniatis (Katsouranis 77), Christodoulopoulos, Samaris (Mitroglou 58); Samaras.
aet; Costa Rica won 5-3 on penalties: Costa Rica first – Borges 1-0, Mitroglou 1-1, Ruiz 2-1, Christodoulopoulos 2-2, Gonzalez 3-2, Holebas 3-3, Campbell 4-3, Gekas 4-3, Umana 5-3.
Referee: Benjamin Williams (Australia).

Fortaleza, Sunday 29 June 2014

Netherlands (0) 2 *(Sneijder 88, Huntelaar 90 (pen))*

Mexico (0) 1 *(Giovani 48)*   58,817

Netherlands: (3412) Cillessen; Vlaar, De Vrij, Verhaegh (Depay 56); Kuyt, Wijnaldum, De Jong (Martins Indi 9), Blind; Sneijder; Robben, van Persie (Huntelaar 76).
Mexico: (532) Ochoa; Aguilar, Rodriguez, Marquez, Moreno (Reyes 46), Layun; Salcido, Herrera, Guardado; Giovani (Aquino 61), Peralta (Hernandez 75).
Referee: Pedro Proenca (Portugal).

Brasilia, Monday 30 June 2014

France (0) 2 *(Pogba 79, Yobo 90 (og))*

Nigeria (0) 0   68,009

France: (433) Lloris; Debuchy, Varane, Koscielny, Evra; Pogba, Cabaye, Matuidi; Valbuena (Sissoko 90), Giroud (Griezmann 62), Benzema.
Nigeria: (442) Enyeama; Ambrose, Yobo, Oshaniwa, Omeruo; Musa, Onazi (Gabriel 59), Mikel, Moses (Nwofor 89); Odemwingie, Emenike.
Referee: Mark Geiger (USA).

Porto Alegre, Monday 30 June 2014

Germany (0) 2 *(Schurrle 92, Ozil 119)*

Algeria (0) 1 *(Djabou 120)*   51,300

Germany: (4141) Neuer; Mustafi (Khedira 70), Mertesacker, Boateng, Howedes; Lahm; Ozil, Schweinsteiger (Kramer 109), Kroos, Gotze (Schurrle 46); Muller.
Algeria: (4231) M'Bolhi; Mandi, Belkalem, Halliche (Bougherra 97), Ghoulam; Lacen, Mostefa; Feghouli, Soudani (Djabou 100), Taider (Brahimi 78); Slimani.
aet.
Referee: Sandro Meira Ricci (Brazil).

Sao Paulo, Tuesday 1 July 2014

Argentina (0) 1 *(Di Maria 118)*

Switzerland (0) 0   63,255

Argentina: (433) Romero; Fernandez F, Zabaleta, Garay, Rojo (Basanta 105); Gago (Biglia 106), Mascherano, Di Maria; Higuain, Messi, Lavezzi (Palacio R 74).
Switzerland: (433) Benaglio; Lichtsteiner, Schar, Djourou, Rodriguez; Inler, Behrami, Xhaka (Fernandes 65); Shaqiri, Mehmedi (Dzemaili 113), Drmic (Seferovic 82).
aet.
Referee: Jonas Eriksson (Sweden).

Salvadore, Tuesday 1 July 2014

Belgium (0) 2 *(De Bruyne 93, Lukaku 105)*

USA (0) 1 *(Green 107)*   51,227

Belgium: (4231) Courtois; Alderweireld, Van Buyten, Kompany, Vertonghen; Fellaini, Witsel; Mertens (Mirallas 60), De Bruyne, Hazard (Chadli 111); Origi (Lukaku 91).
USA: (4141) Howard; Johnson (Yedlin 32), Gonzalez, Besler, Beasley; Cameron; Zusi (Wondolowski 72), Jones, Bradley, Bedoya (Green 105); Dempsey.
aet.
Referee: Djamel Haimoudi (Algeria).

QUARTER-FINALS

Fortaleza, Friday 4 July 2014

Brazil (1) 2 *(Thiago Silva 7, Luiz 68)*

Colombia (0) 1 *(Rodriguez J 80 (pen))*   67,037

Brazil: (4231) Julio Cesar; Maicon, Thiago Silva, Luiz, Marcelo; Fernandinho, Paulinho (Hernanes 86); Oscar, Neymar (Henrique 88), Hulk (Ramires 82); Fred.
Colombia: (4231) Ospina; Zuniga, Zapata, Yepes, Armero; Guarin F, Sanchez Moreno; Cuadrado (Quintero 80), Rodriguez J, Ibarbo (Ramos 46); Gutierrez (Bacca 70).
Referee: Carlos Velasco Carballo (Spain).

Rio de Janeiro, Friday 4 July 2014

France (0) 0

Germany (1) 1 *(Hummels 12)*   78,838

France: (451) Lloris; Debuchy, Varane, Sakho (Koscielny 71), Evra; Valbuena (Giroud 85), Pogba, Cabaye (Remy 73), Matuidi; Griezmann; Benzema.
Germany: (451) Neuer; Lahm, Hummels, Boateng, Howedes; Ozil (Gotze 38), Kroos (Kramer 90), Schweinsteiger, Khedira, Muller; Klose (Schurrle 69).
Referee: Nestor Pitana (Argentina).

Brasilia, Saturday 5 July 2014

Argentina (1) 1 *(Higuain 8)*

Belgium (0) 0   68,551

Argentina: (4231) Romero; Zabaleta, Demichelis, Garay, Basanta; Biglia, Mascherano; Lavezzi (Palacio 71), Messi, Di Maria (Perez 33); Higuain (Gago 81).
Belgium: (4231) Courtois; Alderweireld, Van Buyten, Kompany, Vertonghen; Fellaini, Witsel; Mirallas (Mertens 59), De Bruyne, Hazard (Chadli 75); Origi (Lukaku 59).
Referee: Nicola Rizzoli (Italy).

Salvadore, Saturday 5 July 2014

Netherlands (0) 0

Costa Rica (0) 0   45,000

Netherlands: (352) Cillessen (Krul 120); De Vrij, Vlaar, Martins Indi (Huntelaar 105); Depay (Lens 76), Wijnaldum, Blind, Kuyt, Sneijder; van Persie, Robben.
Costa Rica: (4141) Navas; Gamboa (Myrie 79), Acosta, Gonzalez, Umana; Diaz; Tejeda (Cubero 97), Borges, Ruiz, Campbell (Urena 66); Bolanos.
aet; Holland won 4-3 on penalties: Costa Rica first – Borges 1-0, van Persie 1-1, Ruiz 1-1, Robben 1-2, Gonzalez 2-2, Sneijder 2-3, Bolanos 3-3, Kuyt 3-4, Umana 3-4.
Referee: Ravshan Irmatov (Uzbekistan).

Lionel Messi scores his country's second goal, and his second of the game, during Argentina's 3-2 victory in Group F against Nigeria in Porto Alegre. (Getty Images/Jeff Gross)

SEMI-FINALS

Belo Horizonte, Tuesday 8 July 2014

Brazil (0) 1 *(Oscar 90)*

Germany (5) 7 *(Muller 11, Klose 23, Kroos 24, 26, Khedira 29, Schurrle 69, 79)*   58,141

Brazil: (4231) Julio Cesar; Maicon, Dante, Luiz, Marcelo; Gustavo, Fernandinho (Paulinho 46); Hulk (Ramires 46), Oscar, Bernard; Fred (Willian 70).
Germany: (4231) Neuer; Lahm, Boateng, Hummels (Mertesacker 46), Howedes; Schweinsteiger, Khedira (Draxler 76); Muller, Kroos, Ozil; Klose (Schurrle 58).
Referee: Marco Rodriguez (Mexico).

Sao Paulo, Wednesday 9 July 2014

Netherlands (0) 0

Argentina (0) 0   63,267

Netherlands: (352) Cillessen; De Vrij, Vlaar, Martins Indi (Janmaat 46); Kuyt, De Jong (Clasie 62), Sneijder, Wijnaldum, Blind; Robben, van Persie (Huntelaar 96).
Argentina: (4231) Romero; Zabaleta, Demichelis, Garay, Rojo; Biglia, Mascherano; Lavezzi (Maxi Rodriguez 100), Messi, Perez (Palacio R 81); Higuain (Aguero 82).
aet; Argentina won 4-2 on penalties: Netherlands first – Vlaar 0-0, Messi 0-1, Robben 1-1, Garay 1-2, Sneijder 1-2, Aguero 1-3, Kuyt 2-3, Rodriguez 2-4.
Referee: Cuneyt Cakir (Turkey).

THIRD PLACE PLAY-OFF

Saturday 12 July 2014

(at Brasilia, attendance 68,034)

Brazil (0) 0   Netherlands (2) 3

Brazil: (4231) Julio Cesar; Maicon, Luiz, Thiago Silva, Maxwell; Paulinho (Hernanes 57), Gustavo (Fernandinho 46); Ramires (Hulk 73), Oscar, Willian; Jo.

Netherlands: (352) Cillessen (Vorm 90); De Vrij, Vlaar, Martins Indi; Kuyt, Wijnaldum, de Guzman, Clasie (Veltman 90), Blind (Janmaat 70); Robben, van Persie.
Scorers: van Persie 3 (pen), Blind 16, Wijnaldum 90.

Referee: Djamel Haimoudi (Algeria).

WORLD CUP FINAL 2014

Sunday 13 July 2014

(at Rio de Janeiro, attendance 74,738)

Germany (0) 1   Argentina (0) 0 (aet)

Germany: (4231) Neuer; Lahm, Boateng, Hummels, Howedes; Kramer (Schurrle 32), Schweinsteiger; Muller, Kroos, Ozil (Mertesacker 120); Klose (Gotze 88).
Scorer: Gotze 113.

Argentina: (433) Romero; Zabaleta, Demichelis, Garay, Rojo; Biglia, Mascherano, Perez (Gago 86); Higuain (Palacio R 78), Messi, Lavezzi (Aguero 46).

Referee: Nicola Rizzoli (Italy).

Germany's Mario Gotze volleys the winning goal past Sergio Romero of Argentina during extra time in the FIFA World Cup final at the Maracana on July 13. (Getty Images/Laurence Griffiths)

FIFA WORLD CUP 2014 – STATISTICS

- The Golden Ball for the best player at the FIFA World Cup 2014 was awarded to Lionel Messi of Argentina for his outstanding displays in Brazil.
- The Golden Boot for the top scorer at the FIFA World Cup 2014 was awarded to James Rodriguez of Colombia. He scored in each of his first five career World Cup appearances, scoring six goals in the five matches helping Colombia to the quarter-finals for the first time in their history.
- The Golden Glove for the tournament's most outstanding goalkeeper was awarded to Germany's Manuel Neuer.
- The Young Player Award was awarded to Paul Pogba of France.
- The Fair Play Award for the team with the best disciplinary record went to Colombia. Only teams reaching the knockout phase were eligible.
- Miroslav Klose of Germany became the World Cup Finals all-time top goalscorer with his goal in the semi-final match against Brazil. His 16th strike at World Cup Finals eclipsed the previous top scorer Ronaldo of Brazil.
- All eight group stage winners progressed to the quarter-finals stage for the first time in World Cup history.
- Germany become the first European team to win the World Cup in Latin America. It was the third World Cup in succession won by a European team – the first time a single confederation has won three in a row. Germany also recorded the biggest victory in a World Cup semi-final with their 7-1 demolition of Brazil and were 5-0 up in 29 minutes which is faster than any other team in World Cup history. They ended the tournament as the top-scoring nation in World Cup history with 224 goals overtaking Brazil.
- Mario Gotze who scored the winning goal for Germany in the final against Argentina became the first substitute to score the winning goal in a World Cup Final.
- Neymar scored the 100th goal of the 2014 World Cup Brazil in the Group A match with Cameroon. It was Brazil's 100th game in World Cup Finals history.
- Oliver Giroud scored France's 100th World Cup Finals goal in the 17th minute of the Group E match against Switzerland.
- More goals were scored by substitutes in Brazil 2014 than in any other World Cup Finals (32).
- The total number of goals scored at Brazil 2014 was 171 equalling the previous record of France 1998.
- England managed only one point in the group stage and were eliminated at this stage for the first time since 1958.
- Xherdan Shaqiri of Switzerland scored the 50th hat-trick in World Cup Finals history in the Group E match against Honduras.
- Faryd Mondragon became the oldest player to play in World Cup Finals at 43 years and 3 days. He appeared as an 85th minute substitute for Colombia in the match against Japan in Group C.
- Luke Shaw of England was the youngest player to play at Brazil 2014 when he started for England in the Group D match against Cost Rica aged 18 years and 348 days.

THE WORLD CUP 1930–2014

Year	Winners v Runners-up		Venue	Attendance	Referee
1930	Uruguay v Argentina	4-2	Montevideo	68,346	J. Langenus (Belgium)
1934	Italy v Czechoslovakia	2-1*	Rome	55,000	I. Eklind (Sweden)
1938	Italy v Hungary	4-2	Paris	45,000	G. Capdeville (France)
1950	Uruguay v Brazil	2-1	Rio de Janeiro	173,850	G. Reader (England)
1954	West Germany v Hungary	3-2	Berne	62,500	W. Ling (England)
1958	Brazi v Sweden	5-2	Stockholm	49,737	M. Guigue (France)
1962	Brazil v Czechoslovakia	3-1	Santiago	68,679	N. Latychev (USSR)
1966	England v West Germany	4-2*	Wembley	96,924	G. Dienst (Sweden)
1970	Brazil v Italy	4-1	Mexico City	107,412	R. Glockner (East Germany)
1974	West Germany v Netherlands	2-1	Munich	78,200	J. Taylor (England)
1978	Argentina v Netherlands	3-1*	Buenos Aires	71,483	S. Gonella (Italy)
1982	Italy v West Germany	3-1	Madrid	90,000	A. C. Coelho (Brazil)
1986	Argentina v West Germany	3-2	Mexico City	114,600	R. A. Filho (Brazil)
1990	West Germany v Argentina	1-0	Rome	73,603	E. C. Mendez (Mexico)
1994	Brazil v Italy	0-0*	Los Angeles	94,194	S. Puhl (Hungary)
	Brazil won 3-2 on penalties.				
1998	France v Brazil	3-0	St-Denis	80,000	S. Belqola (Morocco)
2002	Brazil v Germany	2-0	Yokohama	69,029	P. Collina (Italy)
2006	Italy v France	1-1*	Berlin	69,000	H. Elizondo (Argentina)
	Italy won 5-3 on penalties.				
2010	Spain v Netherlands	1-0	Johannesburg	84,490	H. Webb (England)
2014	Germany v Argentina	1-0*	Rio de Janeiro	74,738	N. Rizzoli (Italy)

(*After extra time)

GOALSCORING AND ATTENDANCES IN WORLD CUP FINAL ROUNDS

Year	Venue	Matches	Goals (av)	Attendance (av)
1930	Uruguay	18	70 (3.9)	590,549 (32,808)
1934	Italy	17	70 (4.1)	363,000 (21,352)
1938	France	18	84 (4.7)	375,700 (20,872)
1950	Brazil	22	88 (4.0)	1,045,246 (47,511)
1954	Switzerland	26	140 (5.4)	768,607 (29,562)
1958	Sweden	35	126 (3.6)	819,810 (23,423)
1962	Chile	32	89 (2.8)	893,172 (27,912)
1966	England	32	89 (2.8)	1,563,135 (48,848)
1970	Mexico	32	95 (3.0)	1,603,975 (50,124)
1974	West Germany	38	97 (2.6)	1,865,753 (49,098)
1978	Argentina	38	102 (2.7)	1,545,791 (40,678)
1982	Spain	52	146 (2.8)	2,109,723 (40,571)
1986	Mexico	52	132 (2.5)	2,394,031 (46,039)
1990	Italy	52	115 (2.2)	2,516,215 (48,388)
1994	USA	52	141 (2.7)	3,587,538 (68,991)
1998	France	64	171 (2.7)	2,785,100 (43,517)
2002	Japan/S. Korea	64	161 (2.5)	2,705,197 (42,268)
2006	Germany	64	147 (2.3)	3,359,439 (52,491)
2010	South Africa	64	145 (2.3)	3,178,856 (49,669)
2014	Brazil	64	171 (2.7)	3,367,727 (52,621)
Total		836	2379 (2.8)	37,438,564 (44,783)

LEADING GOALSCORERS

Year	Player	Goals
1930	Guillermo Stabile (Argentina)	8
1934	Oldrich Nejedly (Czechoslovakia)	5
1938	Leonidas da Silva (Brazil)	7
1950	Ademir (Brazil)	8
1954	Sandor Kocsis (Hungary)	11
1958	Just Fontaine (France)	13
1962	Valentin Ivanov (USSR), Leonel Sanchez (Chile), Garrincha (Brazil), Vava (Brazil), Florian Albert (Hungary), Drazen Jerkovic (Yugoslavia)	4
1966	Eusebio (Portugal)	9
1970	Gerd Muller (West Germany)	10
1974	Grzegorz Lato (Poland)	7
1978	Mario Kempes (Argentina)	6
1982	Paolo Rossi (Italy)	6
1986	Gary Lineker (England)	6
1990	Salvatore Schillaci (Italy)	6
1994	Oleg Salenko (Russia), Hristo Stoichkov (Bulgaria)	6
1998	Davor Suker (Croatia)	6
2002	Ronaldo (Brazil)	8
2006	Miroslav Klose (Germany)	5
2010	Thomas Muller (Germany), David Villa (Spain), Wesley Sneijder (Netherlands), Diego Forlan (Uruguay)	5
2014	James Rodriguez (Colombia)	6

EUROPEAN FOOTBALL CHAMPIONSHIP 1960–2012

(formerly EUROPEAN NATIONS' CUP)

Year	Winners v Runners-up		Venue	Attendance	Referee
1960	USSR v Yugoslavia	2-1*	Paris	17,966	A. E. Ellis (England)
1964	Spain v USSR	2-1	Madrid	79,115	A. E. Ellis (England)
1968	Italy v Yugoslavia	1-1	Rome	68,817	G. Dienst (Switzerland)
Replay	Italy v Yugoslavia	2-0	Rome	32,866	J. M. O. de Mendibil (Spain)
1972	West Germany v USSR	3-0	Brussels	43,066	F. Marschall (Austria)
1976	Czechoslovakia v West Germany	2-2	Belgrade	30,790	S. Gonella (Italy)
	Czechoslovakia won 5-3 on penalties.				
1980	West Germany v Belgium	2-1	Rome	47,860	N. Rainea (Romania)
1984	France v Spain	2-0	Paris	47,368	V. Christov (Slovakia)
1988	Netherlands v USSR	2-0	Munich	62,770	M. Vautrot (France)
1992	Denmark v Germany	2-0	Gothenburg	37,800	B. Galler (Switzerland)
1996	Germany v Czech Republic	2-1*	Wembley	73,611	P. Pairetto (Italy)
	Germany won on sudden death 'golden goal'.				
2000	France v Italy	2-1*	Rotterdam	48,200	A. Frisk (Sweden)
	France won on sudden death 'golden goal'.				
2004	Greece v Portugal	1-0	Lisbon	62,865	M. Merk (Germany)
2008	Spain v Germany	1-0	Vienna	51,428	R. Rosetti (Italy)
2012	Spain v Italy	4-0	Kiev	63,170	P. Proenca (Portugal)

BRITISH AND IRISH INTERNATIONAL RESULTS 1872–2014

Note: In the results that follow, wc=World Cup, ec=European Championship, ui=Umbro International Trophy. tf = Tournoi de France. nc = Nations Cup. Northern Ireland played as Ireland before 1921. *After extra time.

ENGLAND v SCOTLAND

Played: 111; England won 46, Scotland won 41, Drawn 24. Goals: England 195, Scotland 171.

			E	S				E	S
1872	30 Nov	Glasgow	0	0	1932	9 Apr	Wembley	3	0
1873	8 Mar	Kennington Oval	4	2	1933	1 Apr	Glasgow	1	2
1874	7 Mar	Glasgow	1	2	1934	14 Apr	Wembley	3	0
1875	6 Mar	Kennington Oval	2	2	1935	6 Apr	Glasgow	0	2
1876	4 Mar	Glasgow	0	3	1936	4 Apr	Wembley	1	1
1877	3 Mar	Kennington Oval	1	3	1937	17 Apr	Glasgow	1	3
1878	2 Mar	Glasgow	2	7	1938	9 Apr	Wembley	0	1
1879	5 Apr	Kennington Oval	5	4	1939	15 Apr	Glasgow	2	1
1880	13 Mar	Glasgow	4	5	1947	12 Apr	Wembley	1	1
1881	12 Mar	Kennington Oval	1	6	1948	10 Apr	Glasgow	2	0
1882	11 Mar	Glasgow	1	5	1949	9 Apr	Wembley	1	3
1883	10 Mar	Sheffield	2	3	wc1950	15 Apr	Glasgow	1	0
1884	15 Mar	Glasgow	0	1	1951	14 Apr	Wembley	2	3
1885	21 Mar	Kennington Oval	1	1	1952	5 Apr	Glasgow	2	1
1886	31 Mar	Glasgow	1	1	1953	18 Apr	Wembley	2	2
1887	19 Mar	Blackburn	2	3	wc1954	3 Apr	Glasgow	4	2
1888	17 Mar	Glasgow	5	0	1955	2 Apr	Wembley	7	2
1889	13 Apr	Kennington Oval	2	3	1956	14 Apr	Glasgow	1	1
1890	5 Apr	Glasgow	1	1	1957	6 Apr	Wembley	2	1
1891	6 Apr	Blackburn	2	1	1958	19 Apr	Glasgow	4	0
1892	2 Apr	Glasgow	4	1	1959	11 Apr	Wembley	1	0
1893	1 Apr	Richmond	5	2	1960	9 Apr	Glasgow	1	1
1894	7 Apr	Glasgow	2	2	1961	15 Apr	Wembley	9	3
1895	6 Apr	Everton	3	0	1962	14 Apr	Glasgow	0	2
1896	4 Apr	Glasgow	1	2	1963	6 Apr	Wembley	1	2
1897	3 Apr	Crystal Palace	1	2	1964	11 Apr	Glasgow	0	1
1898	2 Apr	Glasgow	3	1	1965	10 Apr	Wembley	2	2
1899	8 Apr	Birmingham	2	1	1966	2 Apr	Glasgow	4	3
1900	7 Apr	Glasgow	1	4	ec1967	15 Apr	Wembley	2	3
1901	30 Mar	Crystal Palace	2	2	ec1968	24 Jan	Glasgow	1	1
1902	3 Mar	Birmingham	2	2	1969	10 May	Wembley	4	1
1903	4 Apr	Sheffield	1	2	1970	25 Apr	Glasgow	0	0
1904	9 Apr	Glasgow	1	0	1971	22 May	Wembley	3	1
1905	1 Apr	Crystal Palace	1	0	1972	27 May	Glasgow	1	0
1906	7 Apr	Glasgow	1	2	1973	14 Feb	Glasgow	5	0
1907	6 Apr	Newcastle	1	1	1973	19 May	Wembley	1	0
1908	4 Apr	Glasgow	1	1	1974	18 May	Glasgow	0	2
1909	3 Apr	Crystal Palace	2	0	1975	24 May	Wembley	5	1
1910	2 Apr	Glasgow	0	2	1976	15 May	Glasgow	1	2
1911	1 Apr	Everton	1	1	1977	4 June	Wembley	1	2
1912	23 Mar	Glasgow	1	1	1978	20 May	Glasgow	1	0
1913	5 Apr	Chelsea	1	0	1979	26 May	Wembley	3	1
1914	14 Apr	Glasgow	1	3	1980	24 May	Glasgow	2	0
1920	10 Apr	Sheffield	5	4	1981	23 May	Wembley	0	1
1921	9 Apr	Glasgow	0	3	1982	29 May	Glasgow	1	0
1922	8 Apr	Aston Villa	0	1	1983	1 June	Wembley	2	0
1923	14 Apr	Glasgow	2	2	1984	26 May	Glasgow	1	1
1924	12 Apr	Wembley	1	1	1985	25 May	Glasgow	0	1
1925	4 Apr	Glasgow	0	2	1986	23 Apr	Wembley	2	1
1926	17 Apr	Manchester	0	1	1987	23 May	Glasgow	0	0
1927	2 Apr	Glasgow	2	1	1988	21 May	Wembley	1	0
1928	31 Mar	Wembley	1	5	1989	27 May	Glasgow	2	0
1929	13 Apr	Glasgow	0	1	ec1996	15 June	Wembley	2	0
1930	5 Apr	Wembley	5	2	ec1999	13 Nov	Glasgow	2	0
1931	28 Mar	Glasgow	0	2	ec1999	17 Nov	Wembley	0	1
					2013	14 Aug	Wembley	3	2

ENGLAND v WALES

Played: 101; England won 66, Wales won 14, Drawn 21. Goals: England 245, Wales 90.

			E	W				E	W
1879	18 Jan	Kennington Oval	2	1	1887	26 Feb	Kennington Oval	4	0
1880	15 Mar	Wrexham	3	2	1888	4 Feb	Crewe	5	1
1881	26 Feb	Blackburn	0	1	1889	23 Feb	Stoke	4	1
1882	13 Mar	Wrexham	3	5	1890	15 Mar	Wrexham	3	1
1883	3 Feb	Kennington Oval	5	0	1891	7 May	Sunderland	4	1
1884	17 Mar	Wrexham	4	0	1892	5 Mar	Wrexham	2	0
1885	14 Mar	Blackburn	1	1	1893	13 Mar	Stoke	6	0
1886	29 Mar	Wrexham	3	1	1894	12 Mar	Wrexham	5	1

			E	W
1895	18 Mar	Queen's Club, Kensington	1	1
1896	16 Mar	Cardiff	9	1
1897	29 Mar	Sheffield	4	0
1898	28 Mar	Wrexham	3	0
1899	20 Mar	Bristol	4	0
1900	26 Mar	Cardiff	1	1
1901	18 Mar	Newcastle	6	0
1902	3 Mar	Wrexham	0	0
1903	2 Mar	Portsmouth	2	1
1904	29 Feb	Wrexham	2	2
1905	27 Mar	Liverpool	3	1
1906	19 Mar	Cardiff	1	0
1907	18 Mar	Fulham	1	1
1908	16 Mar	Wrexham	7	1
1909	15 Mar	Nottingham	2	0
1910	14 Mar	Cardiff	1	0
1911	13 Mar	Millwall	3	0
1912	11 Mar	Wrexham	2	0
1913	17 Mar	Bristol	4	3
1914	16 Mar	Cardiff	2	0
1920	15 Mar	Highbury	1	2
1921	14 Mar	Cardiff	0	0
1922	13 Mar	Liverpool	1	0
1923	5 Mar	Cardiff	2	2
1924	3 Mar	Blackburn	1	2
1925	28 Feb	Swansea	2	1
1926	1 Mar	Crystal Palace	1	3
1927	12 Feb	Wrexham	3	3
1927	28 Nov	Burnley	1	2
1928	17 Nov	Swansea	3	2
1929	20 Nov	Chelsea	6	0
1930	22 Nov	Wrexham	4	0
1931	18 Nov	Liverpool	3	1
1932	16 Nov	Wrexham	0	0
1933	15 Nov	Newcastle	1	2
1934	29 Sept	Cardiff	4	0
1936	5 Feb	Wolverhampton	1	2
1936	17 Oct	Cardiff	1	2
1937	17 Nov	Middlesbrough	2	1
1938	22 Oct	Cardiff	2	4
1946	13 Nov	Manchester	3	0
1947	18 Oct	Cardiff	3	0
1948	10 Nov	Aston Villa	1	0
wc1949	15 Oct	Cardiff	4	1
1950	15 Nov	Sunderland	4	2
1951	20 Oct	Cardiff	1	1
1952	12 Nov	Wembley	5	2
wc1953	10 Oct	Cardiff	4	1
1954	10 Nov	Wembley	3	2
1955	27 Oct	Cardiff	1	2
1956	14 Nov	Wembley	3	1
1957	19 Oct	Cardiff	4	0
1958	26 Nov	Aston Villa	2	2
1959	17 Oct	Cardiff	1	1
1960	23 Nov	Wembley	5	1
1961	14 Oct	Cardiff	1	1
1962	21 Oct	Wembley	4	0
1963	12 Oct	Cardiff	4	0
1964	18 Nov	Wembley	2	1
1965	2 Oct	Cardiff	0	0
EC1966	16 Nov	Wembley	5	1
EC1967	21 Oct	Cardiff	3	0
1969	7 May	Wembley	2	1
1970	18 Apr	Cardiff	1	1
1971	19 May	Wembley	0	0
1972	20 May	Cardiff	3	0
wc1972	15 Nov	Cardiff	1	0
wc1973	24 Jan	Wembley	1	1
1973	15 May	Wembley	3	0
1974	11 May	Cardiff	2	0
1975	21 May	Wembley	2	2
1976	24 Mar	Wrexham	2	1
1976	8 May	Cardiff	1	0
1977	31 May	Wembley	0	1
1978	3 May	Cardiff	3	1
1979	23 May	Wembley	0	0
1980	17 May	Wrexham	1	4
1981	20 May	Wembley	0	0
1982	27 Apr	Cardiff	1	0
1983	23 Feb	Wembley	2	1
1984	2 May	Wrexham	0	1
wc2004	9 Oct	Old Trafford	2	0
wc2005	3 Sept	Cardiff	1	0
EC2011	26 Mar	Cardiff	2	0
EC2011	6 Sept	Wembley	1	0

ENGLAND v NORTHERN IRELAND

Played: 98; England won 75, Northern Ireland won 7, Drawn 16. Goals: England 323, Northern Ireland 81.

			E	NI
1882	18 Feb	Belfast	13	0
1883	24 Feb	Liverpool	7	0
1884	23 Feb	Belfast	8	1
1885	28 Feb	Manchester	4	0
1886	13 Mar	Belfast	6	1
1887	5 Feb	Sheffield	7	0
1888	31 Mar	Belfast	5	1
1889	2 Mar	Everton	6	1
1890	15 Mar	Belfast	9	1
1891	7 Mar	Wolverhampton	6	1
1892	5 Mar	Belfast	2	0
1893	25 Feb	Birmingham	6	1
1894	3 Mar	Belfast	2	2
1895	9 Mar	Derby	9	0
1896	7 Mar	Belfast	2	0
1897	20 Feb	Nottingham	6	0
1898	5 Mar	Belfast	3	2
1899	18 Feb	Sunderland	13	2
1900	17 Mar	Dublin	2	0
1901	9 Mar	Southampton	3	0
1902	22 Mar	Belfast	1	0
1903	14 Feb	Wolverhampton	4	0
1904	12 Mar	Belfast	3	1
1905	25 Feb	Middlesbrough	1	1
1906	17 Feb	Belfast	5	0
1907	16 Feb	Everton	1	0
1908	15 Feb	Belfast	3	1
1909	13 Feb	Bradford	4	0
1910	12 Feb	Belfast	1	1
1911	11 Feb	Derby	2	1
1912	10 Feb	Dublin	6	1
1913	15 Feb	Belfast	1	2
1914	14 Feb	Middlesbrough	0	3
1919	25 Oct	Belfast	1	1
1920	23 Oct	Sunderland	2	0
1921	22 Oct	Belfast	1	1
1922	21 Oct	West Bromwich	2	0
1923	20 Oct	Belfast	1	2
1924	22 Oct	Everton	3	1
1925	24 Oct	Belfast	0	0
1926	20 Oct	Liverpool	3	3
1927	22 Oct	Belfast	0	2
1928	22 Oct	Everton	2	1
1929	19 Oct	Belfast	3	0
1930	20 Oct	Sheffield	5	1
1931	17 Oct	Belfast	6	2
1932	17 Oct	Blackpool	1	0
1933	14 Oct	Belfast	3	0
1935	6 Feb	Everton	2	1
1935	19 Oct	Belfast	3	1
1936	18 Nov	Stoke	3	1
1937	23 Oct	Belfast	5	1
1938	16 Nov	Manchester	7	0
1946	28 Sept	Belfast	7	2
1947	5 Nov	Everton	2	2
1948	9 Oct	Belfast	6	2
wc1949	16 Nov	Manchester	9	2
1950	7 Oct	Belfast	4	1
1951	14 Nov	Aston Villa	2	0
1952	4 Oct	Belfast	2	2
wc1953	11 Nov	Everton	3	1
1954	2 Oct	Belfast	2	0
1955	2 Nov	Wembley	3	0
1956	10 Oct	Belfast	1	1

			E	NI
1957	6 Nov	Wembley	2	3
1958	4 Oct	Belfast	3	3
1959	18 Nov	Wembley	2	1
1960	8 Oct	Belfast	5	2
1961	22 Nov	Wembley	1	1
1962	20 Oct	Belfast	3	1
1963	20 Nov	Wembley	8	3
1964	3 Oct	Belfast	4	3
1965	10 Nov	Wembley	2	1
EC1966	20 Oct	Belfast	2	0
EC1967	22 Nov	Wembley	2	0
1969	3 May	Belfast	3	1
1970	21 Apr	Wembley	3	1
1971	15 May	Belfast	1	0
1972	23 May	Wembley	0	1
1973	12 May	Everton	2	1
1974	15 May	Wembley	1	0

			E	NI
1975	17 May	Belfast	0	0
1976	11 May	Wembley	4	0
1977	28 May	Belfast	2	1
1978	16 May	Wembley	1	0
EC1979	7 Feb	Wembley	4	0
1979	19 May	Belfast	2	0
EC1979	17 Oct	Belfast	5	1
1980	20 May	Wembley	1	1
1982	23 Feb	Wembley	4	0
1983	28 May	Belfast	0	0
1984	24 Apr	Wembley	1	0
wc1985	27 Feb	Belfast	1	0
wc1985	13 Nov	Wembley	0	0
EC1986	15 Oct	Wembley	3	0
EC1987	1 Apr	Belfast	2	0
wc2005	26 Mar	Old Trafford	4	0
wc2005	7 Sept	Belfast	0	1

SCOTLAND v WALES

Played: 107; Scotland won 61, Wales won 23, Drawn 23. Goals: Scotland 243, Wales 124.

			S	W
1876	25 Mar	Glasgow	4	0
1877	5 Mar	Wrexham	2	0
1878	23 Mar	Glasgow	9	0
1879	7 Apr	Wrexham	3	0
1880	3 Apr	Glasgow	5	1
1881	14 Mar	Wrexham	5	1
1882	25 Mar	Glasgow	5	0
1883	12 Mar	Wrexham	3	0
1884	29 Mar	Glasgow	4	1
1885	23 Mar	Wrexham	8	1
1886	10 Apr	Glasgow	4	1
1887	21 Mar	Wrexham	2	0
1888	10 Mar	Easter Road	5	1
1889	15 Apr	Wrexham	0	0
1890	22 Mar	Paisley	5	0
1891	21 Mar	Wrexham	4	3
1892	26 Mar	Tynecastle	6	1
1893	18 Mar	Wrexham	8	0
1894	24 Mar	Kilmarnock	5	2
1895	23 Mar	Wrexham	2	2
1896	21 Mar	Dundee	4	0
1897	20 Mar	Wrexham	2	2
1898	19 Mar	Motherwell	5	2
1899	18 Mar	Wrexham	6	0
1900	3 Feb	Aberdeen	5	2
1901	2 Mar	Wrexham	1	1
1902	15 Mar	Greenock	5	1
1903	9 Mar	Cardiff	1	0
1904	12 Mar	Dundee	1	1
1905	6 Mar	Wrexham	1	3
1906	3 Mar	Tynecastle	0	2
1907	4 Mar	Wrexham	0	1
1908	7 Mar	Dundee	2	1
1909	1 Mar	Wrexham	2	3
1910	5 Mar	Kilmarnock	1	0
1911	6 Mar	Cardiff	2	2
1912	2 Mar	Tynecastle	1	0
1913	3 Mar	Wrexham	0	0
1914	28 Feb	Glasgow	0	0
1920	26 Feb	Cardiff	1	1
1921	12 Feb	Aberdeen	2	1
1922	4 Feb	Wrexham	1	2
1923	17 Mar	Paisley	2	0
1924	16 Feb	Cardiff	0	2
1925	14 Feb	Tynecastle	3	1
1925	31 Oct	Cardiff	3	0
1926	30 Oct	Glasgow	3	0
1927	29 Oct	Wrexham	2	2
1928	27 Oct	Glasgow	4	2
1929	26 Oct	Cardiff	4	2
1930	25 Oct	Glasgow	1	1
1931	31 Oct	Wrexham	3	2
1932	26 Oct	Tynecastle	2	5
1933	4 Oct	Cardiff	2	3

			S	W
1934	21 Nov	Aberdeen	3	2
1935	5 Oct	Cardiff	1	1
1936	2 Dec	Dundee	1	2
1937	30 Oct	Cardiff	1	2
1938	9 Nov	Tynecastle	3	2
1946	19 Oct	Wrexham	1	3
1947	12 Nov	Glasgow	1	2
1948	23 Oct	Cardiff	3	1
wc1949	9 Nov	Glasgow	2	0
1950	21 Oct	Cardiff	3	1
1951	14 Nov	Glasgow	0	1
1952	18 Oct	Cardiff	2	1
wc1953	4 Nov	Glasgow	3	3
1954	16 Oct	Cardiff	1	0
1955	9 Nov	Glasgow	2	0
1956	20 Oct	Cardiff	2	2
1957	13 Nov	Glasgow	1	1
1958	18 Oct	Cardiff	3	0
1959	4 Nov	Glasgow	1	1
1960	20 Oct	Cardiff	0	2
1961	8 Nov	Glasgow	2	0
1962	20 Oct	Cardiff	3	2
1963	20 Nov	Glasgow	2	1
1964	3 Oct	Cardiff	2	3
EC1965	24 Nov	Glasgow	4	1
EC1966	22 Oct	Cardiff	1	1
1967	22 Nov	Glasgow	3	2
1969	3 May	Wrexham	5	3
1970	22 Apr	Glasgow	0	0
1971	15 May	Cardiff	0	0
1972	24 May	Glasgow	1	0
1973	12 May	Wrexham	2	0
1974	14 May	Glasgow	2	0
1975	17 May	Cardiff	2	2
1976	6 May	Glasgow	3	1
wc1976	17 Nov	Glasgow	1	0
1977	28 May	Wrexham	0	0
wc1977	12 Oct	Liverpool	2	0
1978	17 May	Glasgow	1	1
1979	19 May	Cardiff	0	3
1980	21 May	Glasgow	1	0
1981	16 May	Swansea	0	2
1982	24 May	Glasgow	1	0
1983	28 May	Cardiff	2	0
1984	28 Feb	Glasgow	2	1
wc1985	27 Mar	Glasgow	0	1
wc1985	10 Sept	Cardiff	1	1
1997	27 May	Kilmarnock	0	1
2004	18 Feb	Cardiff	0	4
2009	14 Nov	Cardiff	0	3
NC2011	25 May	Dublin	3	1
wc2012	12 Oct	Cardiff	1	2
wc2013	22 Mar	Glasgow	1	2

SCOTLAND v NORTHERN IRELAND

Played: 95; Scotland won 63, Northern Ireland won 15, Drawn 17. Goals: Scotland 260, Northern Ireland 81.

Year	Date	Venue	S	NI		Year	Date	Venue	S	NI
1884	26 Jan	Belfast	5	0		1935	13 Nov	Tynecastle	2	1
1885	14 Mar	Glasgow	8	2		1936	31 Oct	Belfast	3	1
1886	20 Mar	Belfast	7	2		1937	10 Nov	Aberdeen	1	1
1887	19 Feb	Glasgow	4	1		1938	8 Oct	Belfast	2	0
1888	24 Mar	Belfast	10	2		1946	27 Nov	Glasgow	0	0
1889	9 Mar	Glasgow	7	0		1947	4 Oct	Belfast	0	2
1890	29 Mar	Belfast	4	1		1948	17 Nov	Glasgow	3	2
1891	28 Mar	Glasgow	2	1		wc1949	1 Oct	Belfast	8	2
1892	19 Mar	Belfast	3	2		1950	1 Nov	Glasgow	6	1
1893	25 Mar	Glasgow	6	1		1951	6 Oct	Belfast	3	0
1894	31 Mar	Belfast	2	1		1952	5 Nov	Glasgow	1	1
1895	30 Mar	Glasgow	3	1		wc1953	3 Oct	Belfast	3	1
1896	28 Mar	Belfast	3	3		1954	3 Nov	Glasgow	2	2
1897	27 Mar	Glasgow	5	1		1955	8 Oct	Belfast	1	2
1898	26 Mar	Belfast	3	0		1956	7 Nov	Glasgow	1	0
1899	25 Mar	Glasgow	9	1		1957	5 Oct	Belfast	1	1
1900	3 Mar	Belfast	3	0		1958	5 Nov	Glasgow	2	2
1901	23 Feb	Glasgow	11	0		1959	3 Oct	Belfast	4	0
1902	1 Mar	Belfast	5	1		1960	9 Nov	Glasgow	5	2
1902	9 Aug	Belfast	3	0		1961	7 Oct	Belfast	6	1
1903	21 Mar	Glasgow	0	2		1962	7 Nov	Glasgow	5	1
1904	26 Mar	Dublin	1	1		1963	12 Oct	Belfast	1	2
1905	18 Mar	Glasgow	4	0		1964	25 Nov	Glasgow	3	2
1906	17 Mar	Dublin	1	0		1965	2 Oct	Belfast	2	3
1907	16 Mar	Glasgow	3	0		1966	16 Nov	Glasgow	2	1
1908	14 Mar	Dublin	5	0		1967	21 Oct	Belfast	0	1
1909	15 Mar	Glasgow	5	0		1969	6 May	Glasgow	1	1
1910	19 Mar	Belfast	0	1		1970	18 Apr	Belfast	1	0
1911	18 Mar	Glasgow	2	0		1971	18 May	Glasgow	0	1
1912	16 Mar	Belfast	4	1		1972	20 May	Glasgow	2	0
1913	15 Mar	Dublin	2	1		1973	16 May	Glasgow	1	2
1914	14 Mar	Belfast	1	1		1974	11 May	Glasgow	0	1
1920	13 Mar	Glasgow	3	0		1975	20 May	Glasgow	3	0
1921	26 Feb	Belfast	2	0		1976	8 May	Glasgow	3	0
1922	4 Mar	Glasgow	2	1		1977	1 June	Glasgow	3	0
1923	3 Mar	Belfast	1	0		1978	13 May	Glasgow	1	1
1924	1 Mar	Glasgow	2	0		1979	22 May	Glasgow	1	0
1925	28 Feb	Belfast	3	0		1980	17 May	Belfast	0	1
1926	27 Feb	Glasgow	4	0		wc1981	25 Mar	Glasgow	1	1
1927	26 Feb	Belfast	2	0		1981	19 May	Glasgow	2	0
1928	25 Feb	Glasgow	0	1		wc1981	14 Oct	Belfast	0	0
1929	23 Feb	Belfast	7	3		1982	28 Apr	Belfast	1	1
1930	22 Feb	Glasgow	3	1		1983	24 May	Glasgow	0	0
1931	21 Feb	Belfast	0	0		1983	13 Dec	Belfast	0	2
1931	19 Sept	Glasgow	3	1		1992	19 Feb	Glasgow	1	0
1932	12 Sept	Belfast	4	0		2008	20 Aug	Glasgow	0	0
1933	16 Sept	Glasgow	1	2		NC2011	9 Feb	Dublin	3	0
1934	20 Oct	Belfast	1	2						

WALES v NORTHERN IRELAND

Played: 94; Wales won 44, Northern Ireland won 27, Drawn 23. Goals: Wales 189, Northern Ireland 131.

Year	Date	Venue	W	NI		Year	Date	Venue	W	NI
1882	25 Feb	Wrexham	7	1		1905	18 Apr	Belfast	2	2
1883	17 Mar	Belfast	1	1		1906	2 Apr	Wrexham	4	4
1884	9 Feb	Wrexham	6	0		1907	23 Feb	Belfast	3	2
1885	11 Apr	Belfast	8	2		1908	11 Apr	Aberdare	0	1
1886	27 Feb	Wrexham	5	0		1909	20 Mar	Belfast	3	2
1887	12 Mar	Belfast	1	4		1910	11 Apr	Wrexham	4	1
1888	3 Mar	Wrexham	11	0		1911	28 Jan	Belfast	2	1
1889	27 Apr	Belfast	3	1		1912	13 Apr	Cardiff	2	3
1890	8 Feb	Shrewsbury	5	2		1913	18 Jan	Belfast	1	0
1891	7 Feb	Belfast	2	7		1914	19 Jan	Wrexham	1	2
1892	27 Feb	Bangor	1	1		1920	14 Feb	Belfast	2	2
1893	8 Apr	Belfast	3	4		1921	9 Apr	Swansea	2	1
1894	24 Feb	Swansea	4	1		1922	4 Apr	Belfast	1	1
1895	16 Mar	Belfast	2	2		1923	14 Apr	Wrexham	0	3
1896	29 Feb	Wrexham	6	1		1924	15 Mar	Belfast	1	0
1897	6 Mar	Belfast	3	4		1925	18 Apr	Wrexham	0	0
1898	19 Feb	Llandudno	0	1		1926	13 Feb	Belfast	0	3
1899	4 Mar	Belfast	0	1		1927	9 Apr	Cardiff	2	2
1900	24 Feb	Llandudno	2	0		1928	4 Feb	Belfast	2	1
1901	23 Mar	Belfast	1	0		1929	2 Feb	Wrexham	2	2
1902	22 Mar	Cardiff	0	3		1930	1 Feb	Belfast	0	7
1903	28 Mar	Belfast	0	2		1931	22 Apr	Wrexham	3	2
1904	21 Mar	Bangor	0	1		1931	5 Dec	Belfast	0	4

			W	NI
1932	7 Dec	Wrexham	4	1
1933	4 Nov	Belfast	1	1
1935	27 Mar	Wrexham	3	1
1936	11 Mar	Belfast	2	3
1937	17 Mar	Wrexham	4	1
1938	16 Mar	Belfast	0	1
1939	15 Mar	Wrexham	3	1
1947	16 Apr	Belfast	1	2
1948	10 Mar	Wrexham	2	0
1949	9 Mar	Belfast	2	0
wc1950	8 Mar	Wrexham	0	0
1951	7 Mar	Belfast	2	1
1952	19 Mar	Swansea	3	0
1953	15 Apr	Belfast	3	2
wc1954	31 Mar	Wrexham	1	2
1955	20 Apr	Belfast	3	2
1956	11 Apr	Cardiff	1	1
1957	10 Apr	Belfast	0	0
1958	16 Apr	Cardiff	1	1
1959	22 Apr	Belfast	1	4
1960	6 Apr	Wrexham	3	2
1961	12 Apr	Belfast	5	1
1962	11 Apr	Cardiff	4	0
1963	3 Apr	Belfast	4	1

			W	NI
1964	15 Apr	Swansea	2	3
1965	31 Mar	Belfast	5	0
1966	30 Mar	Cardiff	1	4
EC1967	12 Apr	Belfast	0	0
EC1968	28 Feb	Wrexham	2	0
1969	10 May	Belfast	0	0
1970	25 Apr	Swansea	1	0
1971	22 May	Belfast	0	1
1972	27 May	Wrexham	0	0
1973	19 May	Everton	0	1
1974	18 May	Wrexham	1	0
1975	23 May	Belfast	0	1
1976	14 May	Swansea	1	0
1977	3 June	Belfast	1	1
1978	19 May	Wrexham	1	0
1979	25 May	Belfast	1	1
1980	23 May	Cardiff	0	1
1982	27 May	Wrexham	3	0
1983	31 May	Belfast	1	0
1984	22 May	Swansea	1	1
wc2004	8 Sept	Cardiff	2	2
wc2005	8 Oct	Belfast	3	2
2007	6 Feb	Belfast	0	0
NC2011	27 May	Dublin	2	0

OTHER BRITISH INTERNATIONAL RESULTS 1908–2013

ENGLAND

		v ALBANIA	E	A
wc1989	8 Mar	Tirana	2	0
wc1989	26 Apr	Wembley	5	0
wc2001	28 Mar	Tirana	3	1
wc2001	5 Sept	Newcastle	2	0

		v ALGERIA	E	A
wc2010	18 June	Cape Town	0	0

		v ANDORRA	E	A
EC2006	2 Sept	Old Trafford	5	0
EC2007	28 Mar	Barcelona	3	0
wc2008	6 Sept	Barcelona	2	0
wc2009	10 June	Wembley	6	0

		v ARGENTINA	E	A
1951	9 May	Wembley	2	1
1953	17 May	Buenos Aires	0	0
(abandoned after 21 mins)				
wc1962	2 June	Rancagua	3	1
1964	6 June	Rio de Janeiro	0	1
wc1966	23 July	Wembley	1	0
1974	22 May	Wembley	2	2
1977	12 June	Buenos Aires	1	1
1980	13 May	Wembley	3	1
wc1986	22 June	Mexico City	1	2
1991	25 May	Wembley	2	2
wc1998	30 June	St Etienne	2	2
2000	23 Feb	Wembley	0	0
wc2002	7 June	Sapporo	1	0
2005	12 Nov	Geneva	3	2

		v AUSTRALIA	E	A
1980	31 May	Sydney	2	1
1983	11 June	Sydney	0	0
1983	15 June	Brisbane	1	0
1983	18 June	Melbourne	1	1
1991	1 June	Sydney	1	0
2003	12 Feb	West Ham	1	3

		v AUSTRIA	E	A
1908	6 June	Vienna	6	1
1908	8 June	Vienna	11	1
1909	1 June	Vienna	8	1
1930	14 May	Vienna	0	0
1932	7 Dec	Chelsea	4	3
1936	6 May	Vienna	1	2
1951	28 Nov	Wembley	2	2
1952	25 May	Vienna	3	2
wc1958	15 June	Boras	2	2
1961	27 May	Vienna	1	3
1962	4 Apr	Wembley	3	1
1965	20 Oct	Wembley	2	3

			E	A
1967	27 May	Vienna	1	0
1973	26 Sept	Wembley	7	0
1979	13 June	Vienna	3	4
wc2004	4 Sept	Vienna	2	2
wc2005	8 Oct	Old Trafford	1	0
2007	16 Nov	Vienna	1	0

		v AZERBAIJAN	E	A
wc2004	13 Oct	Baku	1	0
wc2005	30 Mar	Newcastle	2	0

		v BELARUS	E	B
wc2008	15 Oct	Minsk	3	1
wc2009	14 Oct	Wembley	3	0

		v BELGIUM	E	B
1921	21 May	Brussels	2	0
1923	19 Mar	Highbury	6	1
1923	1 Nov	Antwerp	2	2
1924	8 Dec	West Bromwich	4	0
1926	24 May	Antwerp	5	3
1927	11 May	Brussels	9	1
1928	19 May	Antwerp	3	1
1929	11 May	Brussels	5	1
1931	16 May	Brussels	4	1
1936	9 May	Brussels	2	3
1947	21 Sept	Brussels	5	2
1950	18 May	Brussels	4	1
1952	26 Nov	Wembley	5	0
wc1954	17 June	Basle	4	4*
1964	21 Oct	Wembley	2	2
1970	25 Feb	Brussels	3	1
EC1980	12 June	Turin	1	1
wc1990	27 June	Bologna	1	0*
1998	29 May	Casablanca	0	0
1999	10 Oct	Sunderland	2	1
2012	2 June	Wembley	1	0

		v BOHEMIA	E	B
1908	13 June	Prague	4	0

		v BRAZIL	E	B
1956	9 May	Wembley	4	2
wc1958	11 June	Gothenburg	0	0
1959	13 May	Rio de Janeiro	0	2
wc1962	10 June	Vina del Mar	1	3
1963	8 May	Wembley	1	1
1964	30 May	Rio de Janeiro	1	5
1969	12 June	Rio de Janeiro	1	2
wc1970	7 June	Guadalajara	0	1
1976	23 May	Los Angeles	0	1
1977	8 June	Rio de Janeiro	0	0

			E	B
1978	19 Apr	Wembley	1	1
1981	12 May	Wembley	0	1
1984	10 June	Rio de Janeiro	2	0
1987	19 May	Wembley	1	1
1990	28 Mar	Wembley	1	0
1992	17 May	Wembley	1	1
1993	13 June	Washington	1	1
UI1995	11 June	Wembley	1	3
TF1997	10 June	Paris	0	1
2000	27 May	Wembley	1	1
wc2002	21 June	Shizuoka	1	2
2007	1 June	Wembley	1	1
2009	14 Nov	Doha	0	1
2013	6 Feb	Wembley	2	1
2013	2 June	Rio de Janeiro	2	2

v BULGARIA

			E	B
wc1962	7 June	Rancagua	0	0
1968	11 Dec	Wembley	1	1
1974	1 June	Sofia	1	0
EC1979	6 June	Sofia	3	0
EC1979	22 Nov	Wembley	2	0
1996	27 Mar	Wembley	1	0
EC1998	10 Oct	Wembley	0	0
EC1999	9 June	Sofia	1	1
EC2010	3 Sept	Wembley	4	0
EC2011	2 Sept	Sofia	3	0

v CAMEROON

			E	C
wc1990	1 July	Naples	3	2*
1991	6 Feb	Wembley	2	0
1997	15 Nov	Wembley	2	0
2002	26 May	Kobe	2	2

v CANADA

			E	C
1986	24 May	Burnaby	1	0

v CHILE

			E	C
wc1950	25 June	Rio de Janeiro	2	0
1953	24 May	Santiago	2	1
1984	17 June	Santiago	0	0
1989	23 May	Wembley	0	0
1998	11 Feb	Wembley	0	2
2013	15 Nov	Wembley	0	2

v CHINA

			E	C
1996	23 May	Beijing	3	0

v CIS

			E	C
1992	29 Apr	Moscow	2	2

v COLOMBIA

			E	C
1970	20 May	Bogota	4	0
1988	24 May	Wembley	1	1
1995	6 Sept	Wembley	0	0
wc1998	26 June	Lens	2	0
2005	31 May	New Jersey	3	2

v COSTA RICA

			E	C
wc2014	26 June	Belo Horizonte	0	0

v CROATIA

			E	C
1996	24 Apr	Wembley	0	0
2003	20 Aug	Ipswich	3	1
EC2004	21 June	Lisbon	4	2
EC2006	11 Oct	Zagreb	0	2
EC2007	21 Nov	Wembley	2	3
wc2008	10 Sept	Zagreb	4	1
wc2009	9 Sept	Wembley	5	1

v CYPRUS

			E	C
EC1975	16 Apr	Wembley	5	0
EC1975	11 May	Limassol	1	0

v CZECHOSLOVAKIA

			E	C
1934	16 May	Prague	1	2
1937	1 Dec	Tottenham	5	4
1963	29 May	Bratislava	4	2
1966	2 Nov	Wembley	0	0
wc1970	11 June	Guadalajara	1	0
1973	27 May	Prague	1	1
EC1974	30 Oct	Wembley	3	0
EC1975	30 Oct	Bratislava	1	2
1978	29 Nov	Wembley	1	0
wc1982	20 June	Bilbao	2	0
1990	25 Apr	Wembley	4	2
1992	25 Mar	Prague	2	2

v CZECH REPUBLIC

			E	C
1998	18 Nov	Wembley	2	0
2008	20 Aug	Wembley	2	2

v DENMARK

			E	D
1948	26 Sept	Copenhagen	0	0
1955	2 Oct	Copenhagen	5	1
wc1956	5 Dec	Wolverhampton	5	2
wc1957	15 May	Copenhagen	4	1
1966	3 July	Copenhagen	2	0
EC1978	20 Sept	Copenhagen	4	3
EC1979	12 Sept	Wembley	1	0
EC1982	22 Sept	Copenhagen	2	2
EC1983	21 Sept	Wembley	0	1
1988	14 Sept	Wembley	1	0
1989	7 June	Copenhagen	1	1
1990	15 May	Wembley	1	0
EC1992	11 June	Malmo	0	0
1994	9 Mar	Wembley	1	0
wc2002	15 June	Niigata	3	0
2003	16 Nov	Old Trafford	2	3
2005	17 Aug	Copenhagen	1	4
2011	9 Feb	Copenhagen	2	1
2014	5 Mar	Wembley	1	0

v ECUADOR

			E	Ec
1970	24 May	Quito	2	0
wc2006	25 June	Stuttgart	1	0
2014	4 June	Miami	2	2

v EGYPT

			E	Eg
1986	29 Jan	Cairo	4	0
wc1990	21 June	Cagliari	1	0
2010	3 Mar	Wembley	3	1

v ESTONIA

			E	Es
EC2007	6 June	Tallinn	3	0
EC2007	13 Oct	Wembley	3	0

v FIFA

			E	FIFA
1938	26 Oct	Highbury	3	0
1953	21 Oct	Wembley	4	4
1963	23 Oct	Wembley	2	1

v FINLAND

			E	F
1937	20 May	Helsinki	8	0
1956	20 May	Helsinki	5	1
1966	26 June	Helsinki	3	0
wc1976	13 June	Helsinki	4	1
wc1976	13 Oct	Wembley	2	1
1982	3 June	Helsinki	4	1
wc1984	17 Oct	Wembley	5	0
wc1985	22 May	Helsinki	1	1
1992	3 June	Helsinki	2	1
wc2000	11 Oct	Helsinki	0	0
wc2001	24 Mar	Liverpool	2	1

v FRANCE

			E	F
1923	10 May	Paris	4	1
1924	17 May	Paris	3	1
1925	21 May	Paris	3	2
1927	26 May	Paris	6	0
1928	17 May	Paris	5	1
1929	9 May	Paris	4	1
1931	14 May	Paris	2	5
1933	6 Dec	Tottenham	4	1
1938	26 May	Paris	4	2
1947	3 May	Highbury	3	0
1949	22 May	Paris	3	1
1951	3 Oct	Highbury	2	2
1955	15 May	Paris	0	1
1957	27 Nov	Wembley	4	0
EC1962	3 Oct	Sheffield	1	1
EC1963	27 Feb	Paris	2	5
wc1966	20 July	Wembley	2	0
1969	12 Mar	Wembley	5	0
wc1982	16 June	Bilbao	3	1
1984	29 Feb	Paris	0	2
1992	19 Feb	Wembley	2	0
EC1992	14 June	Malmo	0	0
TF1997	14 June	Montpellier	1	0
1999	10 Feb	Wembley	0	2
2000	2 Sept	Paris	1	1
EC2004	13 June	Lisbon	1	2
2008	26 Mar	Paris	0	1
2010	17 Nov	Wembley	1	2
EC2012	11 June	Donetsk	1	1

v GEORGIA

			E	G
wc1996	9 Nov	Tbilisi	2	0
wc1997	30 Apr	Wembley	2	0

v GERMANY

			E	G
1930	10 May	Berlin	3	3
1935	4 Dec	Tottenham	3	0
1938	14 May	Berlin	6	3
1991	11 Sept	Wembley	0	1
1993	19 June	Detroit	1	2
EC1996	26 June	Wembley	1	1*
EC2000	17 June	Charleroi	1	0
wc2000	7 Oct	Wembley	0	1
wc2001	1 Sept	Munich	5	1
2007	22 Aug	Wembley	1	2
2008	19 Nov	Berlin	2	1
wc2010	27 June	Bloemfontein	1	4
2013	19 Nov	Wembley	0	1

v EAST GERMANY

			E	EG
1963	2 June	Leipzig	2	1
1970	25 Nov	Wembley	3	1
1974	29 May	Leipzig	1	1
1984	12 Sept	Wembley	1	0

v WEST GERMANY

			E	WG
1954	1 Dec	Wembley	3	1
1956	26 May	Berlin	3	1
1965	12 May	Nuremberg	1	0
1966	23 Feb	Wembley	1	0
wc1966	30 July	Wembley	4	2*
1968	1 June	Hanover	0	1
wc1970	14 June	Leon	2	3*
EC1972	29 Apr	Wembley	1	3
EC1972	13 May	Berlin	0	0
1975	12 Mar	Wembley	2	0
1978	22 Feb	Munich	1	2
wc1982	29 June	Madrid	0	0
1982	13 Oct	Wembley	1	2
1985	12 June	Mexico City	3	0
1987	9 Sept	Dusseldorf	1	3
wc1990	4 July	Turin	1	1*

v GHANA

			E	G
2011	29 Mar	Wembley	1	1

v GREECE

			E	G
EC1971	21 Apr	Wembley	3	0
EC1971	1 Dec	Piraeus	2	0
EC1982	17 Nov	Salonika	3	0
EC1983	30 Mar	Wembley	0	0
1989	8 Feb	Athens	2	1
1994	17 May	Wembley	5	0
wc2001	6 June	Athens	2	0
wc2001	6 Oct	Old Trafford	2	2
2006	16 Aug	Old Trafford	4	0

v HONDURAS

			E	H
2014	7 June	Miami	0	0

v HUNGARY

			E	H
1908	10 June	Budapest	7	0
1909	29 May	Budapest	4	2
1909	31 May	Budapest	8	2
1934	10 May	Budapest	1	2
1936	2 Dec	Highbury	6	2
1953	25 Nov	Wembley	3	6
1954	23 May	Budapest	1	7
1960	22 May	Budapest	0	2
wc1962	31 May	Rancagua	1	2
1965	5 May	Wembley	1	0
1978	24 May	Wembley	4	1
wc1981	6 June	Budapest	3	1
wc1982	18 Nov	Wembley	1	0
EC1983	27 Apr	Wembley	2	0
EC1983	12 Oct	Budapest	3	0
1988	27 Apr	Budapest	0	0
1990	12 Sept	Wembley	1	0
1992	12 May	Budapest	1	0
1996	18 May	Wembley	3	0
1999	28 Apr	Budapest	1	1
2006	30 May	Old Trafford	3	1
2010	11 Aug	Wembley	2	1

v ICELAND

			E	I
1982	2 June	Reykjavik	1	1
2004	5 June	City of Manchester	6	1
EC2007	24 Mar	Tel Aviv	0	0

v REPUBLIC OF IRELAND

			E	RI
1946	30 Sept	Dublin	1	0
1949	21 Sept	Everton	0	2
wc1957	8 May	Wembley	5	1
wc1957	19 May	Dublin	1	1
1964	24 May	Dublin	3	1
1976	8 Sept	Wembley	1	1
EC1978	25 Oct	Dublin	1	1
EC1980	6 Feb	Wembley	2	0
1985	26 Mar	Wembley	2	1
EC1988	12 June	Stuttgart	0	1
wc1990	11 June	Cagliari	1	1
EC1990	14 Nov	Dublin	1	1
EC1991	27 Mar	Wembley	1	1
1995	15 Feb	Dublin	0	1
		(abandoned after 27 mins)		
2013	29 May	Wembley	1	1

v ISRAEL

			E	I
1986	26 Feb	Ramat Gan	2	1
1988	17 Feb	Tel Aviv	0	0
EC2007	24 Mar	Tel Aviv	0	0
EC2007	8 Sept	Wembley	3	0

v ITALY

			E	I
1933	13 May	Rome	1	1
1934	14 Nov	Highbury	3	2
1939	13 May	Milan	2	2
1948	16 May	Turin	4	0
1949	30 Nov	Tottenham	2	0
1952	18 May	Florence	1	1
1959	6 May	Wembley	2	2
1961	24 May	Rome	3	2
1973	14 June	Turin	0	2
1973	14 Nov	Wembley	0	1
1976	28 May	New York	3	2
wc1976	17 Nov	Rome	0	2
wc1977	16 Nov	Wembley	2	0
EC1980	15 June	Turin	0	1
1985	6 June	Mexico City	1	2
1989	15 Nov	Wembley	0	0
wc1990	7 July	Bari	1	2
wc1997	12 Feb	Wembley	0	1
TF1997	4 June	Nantes	2	0
wc1997	11 Oct	Rome	0	0
2000	15 Nov	Turin	0	1
2002	27 Mar	Leeds	1	2
EC2012	24 June	Kiev	0	0
2012	15 Aug	Berne	2	1
wc2014	14 June	Manaus	1	2

v JAMAICA

			E	J
2006	3 June	Old Trafford	6	0

v JAPAN

			E	J
U11995	3 June	Wembley	2	1
2004	1 June	City of Manchester	1	1
2010	30 May	Graz	2	1

v KAZAKHSTAN

			E	K
wc2008	11 Oct	Wembley	5	1
wc2009	6 June	Almaty	4	0

v KOREA REPUBLIC

			E	KR
2002	21 May	Seoguipo	1	1

v KUWAIT

			E	K
wc1982	25 June	Bilbao	1	0

v LIECHTENSTEIN

			E	L
EC2003	29 Mar	Vaduz	2	0
EC2003	10 Sept	Old Trafford	2	0

v LUXEMBOURG

			E	L
1927	21 May	Esch-sur-Alzette	5	2
wc1960	19 Oct	Luxembourg	9	0
wc1961	28 Sept	Highbury	4	1
wc1977	30 Mar	Wembley	5	0
wc1977	12 Oct	Luxembourg	2	0
EC1982	15 Dec	Wembley	9	0
EC1983	16 Nov	Luxembourg	4	0
EC1998	14 Oct	Luxembourg	3	0
EC1999	4 Sept	Wembley	6	0

v MACEDONIA

			E	M
EC2002	16 Oct	Southampton	2	2
EC2003	6 Sept	Skopje	2	1
EC2006	6 Sept	Skopje	1	0
EC2006	7 Oct	Old Trafford	0	0

v MALAYSIA

			E	M
1991	12 June	Kuala Lumpur	4	2

v MALTA

			E	M
EC1971	3 Feb	Valletta	1	0
EC1971	12 May	Wembley	5	0
2000	3 June	Valletta	2	1

v MEXICO

			E	M
1959	24 May	Mexico City	1	2
1961	10 May	Wembley	8	0
wc1966	16 July	Wembley	2	0
1969	1 June	Mexico City	0	0
1985	9 June	Mexico City	0	1
1986	17 May	Los Angeles	3	0
1997	29 Mar	Wembley	2	0
2001	25 May	Derby	4	0
2010	24 May	Wembley	3	1

v MOLDOVA

			E	M
wc1996	1 Sept	Chisinau	3	0
wc1997	10 Sept	Wembley	4	0
wc2012	7 Sept	Chisinau	5	0
wc2013	6 Sept	Wembley	4	0

v MONTENEGRO

			E	M
EC1989	8 Mar	Tirana	2	0
2010	12 Oct	Wembley	0	0
EC2011	7 Oct	Podgorica	2	2
wc2013	26 Mar	Podgorica	1	1
wc2013	11 Oct	Wembley	4	1

v MOROCCO

			E	M
wc1986	6 June	Monterrey	0	0
1998	27 May	Casablanca	1	0

v NETHERLANDS

			E	N
1935	18 May	Amsterdam	1	0
1946	27 Nov	Huddersfield	8	2
1964	9 Dec	Amsterdam	1	1
1969	5 Nov	Amsterdam	1	0
1970	14 Jun	Wembley	0	0
1977	9 Feb	Wembley	0	2
1982	25 May	Wembley	2	0
1988	23 Mar	Wembley	2	2
EC1988	15 June	Dusseldorf	1	3
wc1990	16 June	Cagliari	0	0
2005	9 Feb	Villa Park	0	0
wc1993	28 Apr	Wembley	2	2
wc1993	13 Oct	Rotterdam	0	2
EC1996	18 June	Wembley	4	1
2001	15 Aug	Tottenham	0	2
2002	13 Feb	Amsterdam	1	1
2006	15 Nov	Amsterdam	1	1
2009	12 Aug	Amsterdam	2	2
2012	29 Feb	Wembley	2	3

v NEW ZEALAND

			E	NZ
1991	3 June	Auckland	1	0
1991	8 June	Wellington	2	0

v NIGERIA

			E	N
1994	16 Nov	Wembley	1	0
wc2002	12 June	Osaka	0	0

v NORWAY

			E	N
1937	14 May	Oslo	6	0
1938	9 Nov	Newcastle	4	0
1949	18 May	Oslo	4	1
1966	29 June	Oslo	6	1
wc1980	10 Sept	Wembley	4	0
wc1981	9 Sept	Oslo	1	2
wc1992	14 Oct	Wembley	1	1
wc1993	2 June	Oslo	0	2
1994	22 May	Wembley	0	0
1995	11 Oct	Oslo	0	0
2012	26 May	Oslo	1	0

v PARAGUAY

			E	P
wc1986	18 June	Mexico City	3	0
2002	17 Apr	Liverpool	4	0
wc2006	10 June	Frankfurt	1	0

v PERU

			E	P
1959	17 May	Lima	1	4
1962	20 May	Lima	4	0
2014	30 May	Wembley	3	0

v POLAND

			E	P
1966	5 Jan	Everton	1	1
1966	5 July	Chorzow	1	0
wc1973	6 June	Chorzow	0	2
wc1973	17 Oct	Wembley	1	1
wc1986	11 June	Monterrey	3	0
wc1989	3 June	Wembley	3	0
wc1989	11 Oct	Katowice	0	0
EC1990	17 Oct	Wembley	2	0
EC1991	13 Nov	Poznan	1	1
wc1993	29 May	Katowice	1	1
wc1993	8 Sept	Wembley	3	0
wc1996	9 Oct	Wembley	2	1
wc1997	31 May	Katowice	2	0
EC1999	27 Mar	Wembley	3	1
EC1999	8 Sept	Warsaw	0	0
wc2004	8 Sept	Katowice	2	1
wc2005	12 Oct	Old Trafford	2	1
wc2012	17 Oct	Warsaw	1	1
wc2013	15 Oct	Wembley	2	0

v PORTUGAL

			E	P
1947	25 May	Lisbon	10	0
1950	14 May	Lisbon	5	3
1951	19 May	Everton	5	2
1955	22 May	Oporto	1	3
1958	7 May	Wembley	2	1
wc1961	21 May	Lisbon	1	1
wc1961	25 Oct	Wembley	2	0
1964	17 May	Lisbon	4	3
1964	4 June	São Paulo	1	1
wc1966	26 July	Wembley	2	1
1969	10 Dec	Wembley	1	0
1974	3 Apr	Lisbon	0	0
EC1974	20 Nov	Wembley	0	0
EC1975	19 Nov	Lisbon	1	1
wc1986	3 June	Monterrey	0	1
1995	12 Dec	Wembley	1	1
1998	22 Apr	Wembley	3	0
EC2000	12 June	Eindhoven	2	3
2002	7 Sept	Villa Park	1	1
2004	18 Feb	Faro	1	1
EC2004	24 June	Lisbon	2	2*
wc2006	1 July	Gelsenkirchen	0	0

v ROMANIA

			E	R
1939	24 May	Bucharest	2	0
1968	6 Nov	Bucharest	0	0
1969	15 Jan	Wembley	1	1
wc1970	2 June	Guadalajara	1	0
wc1980	15 Oct	Bucharest	1	2
wc1981	29 April	Wembley	0	0
wc1985	1 May	Bucharest	0	0
wc1985	11 Sept	Wembley	1	1
1994	12 Oct	Wembley	1	1
wc1998	22 June	Toulouse	1	2
EC2000	20 June	Charleroi	2	3

v RUSSIA

			E	R
EC2007	12 Sept	Wembley	3	0
EC2007	17 Oct	Moscow	1	2

v SAN MARINO

			E	SM
wc1992	17 Feb	Wembley	6	0
wc1993	17 Nov	Bologna	7	1
wc2012	12 Oct	Wembley	5	0
wc2013	22 Mar	Serravalle	8	0

v SAUDI ARABIA

			E	SA
1988	16 Nov	Riyadh	1	1
1998	23 May	Wembley	0	0

v SERBIA-MONTENEGRO

			E	S-M
2003	3 June	Leicester	2	1

v SLOVAKIA

			E	S
EC2002	12 Oct	Bratislava	2	1
EC2003	11 June	Middlesbrough	2	1
2009	28 Mar	Wembley	4	0

v SLOVENIA

			E	S
2009	5 Sept	Wembley	2	1
wc2010	23 June	Port Elizabeth	1	0

v SOUTH AFRICA

			E	SA
1997	24 May	Old Trafford	2	1
2003	22 May	Durban	2	1

v SPAIN

			E	S
1929	15 May	Madrid	3	4
1931	9 Dec	Highbury	7	1
wc1950	2 July	Rio de Janeiro	0	1
1955	18 May	Madrid	1	1
1955	30 Nov	Wembley	4	1
1960	15 May	Madrid	0	3
1960	26 Oct	Wembley	4	2
1965	8 Dec	Madrid	2	0
1967	24 May	Wembley	2	0
EC1968	3 Apr	Wembley	1	0
EC1968	8 May	Madrid	2	1
1980	26 Mar	Barcelona	2	0
EC1980	18 June	Naples	2	1
1981	25 Mar	Wembley	1	2
wc1982	5 July	Madrid	0	0
1987	18 Feb	Madrid	4	2
1992	9 Sept	Santander	0	1
EC 1996	22 June	Wembley	0	0
2001	28 Feb	Villa Park	3	0
2004	17 Nov	Madrid	0	1
2007	7 Feb	Old Trafford	0	1
2009	11 Feb	Seville	0	2
2011	12 Nov	Wembley	1	0

v SWEDEN

			E	S
1923	21 May	Stockholm	4	2
1923	24 May	Stockholm	3	1
1937	17 May	Stockholm	4	0
1947	19 Nov	Highbury	4	2
1949	13 May	Stockholm	1	3
1956	16 May	Stockholm	0	0
1959	28 Oct	Wembley	2	3
1965	16 May	Gothenburg	2	1
1968	22 May	Wembley	3	1
1979	10 June	Stockholm	0	0
1986	10 Sept	Stockholm	0	1
wc1988	19 Oct	Wembley	0	0
wc1989	6 Sept	Stockholm	0	0
EC1992	17 June	Stockholm	1	2
UI1995	8 June	Leeds	3	3
EC1998	5 Sept	Stockholm	1	2
EC1999	5 June	Wembley	0	0
2001	10 Nov	Old Trafford	1	1
wc2002	2 June	Saitama	1	1
2004	31 Mar	Gothenburg	0	1
wc2006	20 June	Cologne	2	2
2011	15 Nov	Wembley	1	0
EC2012	15 June	Kiev	3	2
2012	14 Nov	Stockholm	2	4

v SWITZERLAND

			E	S
1933	20 May	Berne	4	0
1938	21 May	Zurich	1	2
1947	18 May	Zurich	0	1
1948	2 Dec	Highbury	6	0
1952	28 May	Zurich	3	0
wc1954	20 June	Berne	2	0
1962	9 May	Wembley	3	1
1963	5 June	Basle	8	1
EC1971	13 Oct	Basle	3	2
EC1971	10 Nov	Wembley	1	1
1975	3 Sept	Wembley	2	1
1977	7 Sept	Wembley	0	0
wc1980	19 Nov	Wembley	2	1
wc1981	30 May	Basle	1	2
1988	28 May	Lausanne	1	0
1995	15 Nov	Wembley	3	1
EC1996	8 June	Wembley	1	1
1998	25 Mar	Berne	1	1
EC2004	17 June	Coimbra	3	0
2008	6 Feb	Wembley	2	1
EC1989	8 Mar	Tirana	2	0
EC2010	7 Sept	Basle	3	1
EC2011	4 June	Wembley	2	2

v TRINIDAD & TOBAGO

			E	TT
wc2006	15 June	Nuremberg	2	0
2008	2 June	Port of Spain	3	0

v TUNISIA

			E	T
1990	2 June	Tunis	1	1
wc1998	15 June	Marseilles	2	0

v TURKEY

			E	T
wc1984	14 Nov	Istanbul	8	0
wc1985	16 Oct	Wembley	5	0
EC1987	29 Apr	Izmir	0	0
EC1987	14 Oct	Wembley	8	0
EC1991	1 May	Izmir	1	0
EC1991	16 Oct	Wembley	1	0
wc1992	18 Nov	Wembley	4	0
wc1993	31 Mar	Izmir	2	0
EC2003	2 Apr	Sunderland	2	0
EC2003	11 Oct	Istanbul	0	0

v UKRAINE

			E	U
2000	31 May	Wembley	2	0
2004	18 Aug	Newcastle	3	0
wc2009	1 Apr	Wembley	2	1
wc2009	10 Oct	Dnepr	0	1
EC2012	19 June	Donetsk	1	0
wc2012	11 Sept	Wembley	1	1
wc2013	10 Sept	Kiev	0	0

v URUGUAY

			E	U
1953	31 May	Montevideo	1	2
wc1954	26 June	Basle	2	4
1964	6 May	Wembley	2	1
wc1966	11 July	Wembley	0	0
1969	8 June	Montevideo	2	1
1977	15 June	Montevideo	0	0
1984	13 June	Montevideo	0	2
1990	22 May	Wembley	1	2
1995	29 Mar	Wembley	0	0
2006	1 Mar	Liverpool	2	1
wc2014	19 June	Sao Paulo	1	2

v USA

			E	USA
wc1950	29 June	Belo Horizonte	0	1
1953	8 June	New York	6	3
1959	28 May	Los Angeles	8	1
1964	27 May	New York	10	0
1985	16 June	Los Angeles	5	0
1993	9 June	Foxboro	0	2
1994	7 Sept	Wembley	2	0
2005	28 May	Chicago	2	1
2008	28 May	Wembley	2	0
wc2010	12 June	Rustenburg	1	1

v USSR

			E	USSR
1958	18 May	Moscow	1	1
wc1958	8 June	Gothenburg	2	2
wc1958	17 June	Gothenburg	0	1
1958	22 Oct	Wembley	5	0
1967	6 Dec	Wembley	2	2
EC1968	8 June	Rome	2	0
1973	10 June	Moscow	2	1
1984	2 June	Wembley	0	2
1986	26 Mar	Tbilisi	1	0
EC1988	18 June	Frankfurt	1	3
1991	21 May	Wembley	3	1

v YUGOSLAVIA

			E	Y
1939	18 May	Belgrade	1	2
1950	22 Nov	Highbury	2	2
1954	16 May	Belgrade	0	1
1956	28 Nov	Wembley	3	0
1958	11 May	Belgrade	0	5
1960	11 May	Wembley	3	3
1965	9 May	Belgrade	1	1
1966	4 May	Wembley	2	0
EC1968	5 June	Florence	0	1
1972	11 Oct	Wembley	1	1
1974	5 June	Belgrade	2	2
EC1986	12 Nov	Wembley	2	0
EC1987	11 Nov	Belgrade	4	1
1989	13 Dec	Wembley	2	1

SCOTLAND

v ARGENTINA

			S	A
1977	18 June	Buenos Aires	1	1
1979	2 June	Glasgow	1	3
1990	28 Mar	Glasgow	1	0
2008	19 Nov	Glasgow	0	1

v AUSTRALIA

			S	A
wc1985	20 Nov	Glasgow	2	0
wc1985	4 Dec	Melbourne	0	0
1996	27 Mar	Glasgow	1	0
2000	15 Nov	Glasgow	0	2
2012	15 Aug	Easter Road	3	1

v AUSTRIA

			S	A
1931	16 May	Vienna	0	5
1933	29 Nov	Glasgow	2	2
1937	9 May	Vienna	1	1
1950	13 Dec	Glasgow	0	1
1951	27 May	Vienna	0	4
wc1954	16 June	Zurich	0	1
1955	19 May	Vienna	4	1
1956	2 May	Glasgow	1	1
1960	29 May	Vienna	1	4
1963	8 May	Glasgow	4	1
(abandoned after 79 mins)				
wc1968	6 Nov	Glasgow	2	1
wc1969	5 Nov	Vienna	0	2
EC1978	20 Sept	Vienna	2	3
EC1979	17 Oct	Glasgow	1	1
1994	20 Apr	Vienna	2	1
wc1996	31 Aug	Vienna	0	0
wc1997	2 Apr	Celtic Park	2	0
2003	30 Apr	Glasgow	0	2
2005	17 Aug	Graz	2	2
2007	30 May	Vienna	1	0

v BELARUS

			S	B
wc1997	8 June	Minsk	1	0
wc1997	7 Sept	Aberdeen	4	1
wc2005	8 June	Minsk	0	0
wc2005	8 Oct	Glasgow	0	1

v BELGIUM

			S	B
1946	23 Jan	Glasgow	2	2
1947	18 May	Brussels	1	2
1948	28 Apr	Glasgow	2	0
1951	20 May	Brussels	5	0
EC1971	3 Feb	Liege	0	3
EC1971	10 Nov	Aberdeen	1	0
1974	1 June	Brussels	1	2
EC1979	21 Nov	Brussels	0	2
EC1979	19 Dec	Glasgow	1	3
EC1982	15 Dec	Brussels	2	3
EC1983	12 Oct	Glasgow	1	1
EC1987	1 Apr	Brussels	1	4
EC1987	14 Oct	Glasgow	2	0
wc2001	24 Mar	Glasgow	2	2
wc2001	5 Sept	Brussels	0	2
wc2012	16 Oct	Brussels	0	2
wc2013	6 Sept	Glasgow	0	2

v BOSNIA

			S	B
EC1999	4 Sept	Sarajevo	2	1
EC1999	5 Oct	Ibrox	1	0

v BRAZIL

			S	B
1966	25 June	Glasgow	1	1
1972	5 July	Rio de Janeiro	0	1
1973	30 June	Glasgow	0	1
wc1974	18 June	Frankfurt	0	0
1977	23 June	Rio de Janeiro	0	2
wc1982	18 June	Seville	1	4
1987	26 May	Glasgow	0	2
wc1990	20 June	Turin	0	1
wc1998	10 June	St Denis	1	2
2011	27 Mar	Emirates	0	2

v BULGARIA

			S	B
1978	22 Feb	Glasgow	2	1
EC1986	10 Sept	Glasgow	0	0
EC1987	11 Nov	Sofia	1	0
EC1990	14 Nov	Sofia	1	1
EC1991	27 Mar	Glasgow	1	1
2006	11 May	Kobe	5	1

v CANADA

			S	C
1983	12 June	Vancouver	2	0
1983	16 June	Edmonton	3	0
1983	20 June	Toronto	2	0
1992	21 May	Toronto	3	1
2002	15 Oct	Easter Road	3	1

v CHILE

			S	C
1977	15 June	Santiago	4	2
1989	30 May	Glasgow	2	0

v CIS

			S	C
EC1992	18 June	Norrkoping	3	0

v COLOMBIA

			S	C
1988	17 May	Glasgow	0	0
1996	29 May	Miami	0	1
1998	23 May	New York	2	2

v COSTA RICA

			S	CR
wc1990	11 June	Genoa	0	1

v CROATIA

			S	C
wc2000	11 Oct	Zagreb	1	1
wc2001	1 Sept	Glasgow	0	0
2008	26 Mar	Glasgow	1	1
wc2013	7 June	Zagreb	1	0
wc2013	15 Oct	Glasgow	2	0

v CYPRUS

			S	C
wc1968	11 Dec	Nicosia	5	0
wc1969	17 May	Glasgow	8	0
wc1989	8 Feb	Limassol	3	2
wc1989	26 Apr	Glasgow	2	1
2011	11 Nov	Larnaca	2	1

v CZECHOSLOVAKIA

			S	C
1937	15 May	Prague	3	1
1937	8 Dec	Glasgow	5	0
wc1961	14 May	Bratislava	0	4
wc1961	26 Sept	Glasgow	3	2
wc1961	29 Nov	Brussels	2	4*
1972	2 July	Porto Alegre	0	0
wc1973	26 Sept	Glasgow	2	1
wc1973	17 Oct	Bratislava	0	1
wc1976	13 Oct	Prague	0	2
wc1977	21 Sept	Glasgow	3	1

v CZECH REPUBLIC

			S	C
EC1999	31 Mar	Glasgow	1	2
EC1999	9 June	Prague	2	3
2008	30 May	Prague	1	3
2010	3 Mar	Glasgow	1	0
EC2010	8 Oct	Prague	0	1
EC2011	3 Sept	Glasgow	2	2

v DENMARK

			S	D
1951	12 May	Glasgow	3	1
1952	25 May	Copenhagen	2	1
1968	16 Oct	Copenhagen	1	0
EC1970	11 Nov	Glasgow	1	0
EC1971	9 June	Copenhagen	0	1
wc1972	18 Oct	Copenhagen	4	1
wc1972	15 Nov	Glasgow	2	0
EC1975	3 Sept	Copenhagen	1	0
EC1975	29 Oct	Glasgow	3	1
wc1986	4 June	Nezahualcoyotl	0	1
1996	24 Apr	Copenhagen	0	2
1998	25 Mar	Ibrox	0	1
2002	21 Aug	Glasgow	0	1
2004	28 Apr	Copenhagen	0	1
2011	10 Aug	Glasgow	2	1

v ECUADOR

			S	E
1995	24 May	Toyama	2	1

v EGYPT

			S	E
1990	16 May	Aberdeen	1	3

v ESTONIA

			S	E
wc1993	19 May	Tallinn	3	0
wc1993	2 June	Aberdeen	3	1
wc1997	11 Feb	Monaco	0	0
wc1997	29 Mar	Kilmarnock	2	0
EC1998	10 Oct	Tynecastle	3	2
EC1999	8 Sept	Tallinn	0	0

			S	E
2004	27 May	Tallinn	1	0
2013	6 Feb	Aberdeen	1	0

v FAROE ISLANDS			S	F
EC1994	12 Oct	Glasgow	5	1
EC1995	7 June	Toftir	2	0
EC1998	14 Oct	Aberdeen	2	1
EC1999	5 June	Toftir	1	1
EC2002	7 Sept	Toftir	2	2
EC2003	6 Sept	Glasgow	3	1
EC2006	2 Sept	Celtic Park	6	0
EC2007	6 June	Toftir	2	0
2010	16 Nov	Aberdeen	3	0

v FINLAND			S	F
1954	25 May	Helsinki	2	1
wc1964	21 Oct	Glasgow	3	1
wc1965	27 May	Helsinki	2	1
1976	8 Sept	Glasgow	6	0
1992	25 Mar	Glasgow	1	1
EC1994	7 Sept	Helsinki	2	0
EC1995	6 Sept	Glasgow	1	0
1998	22 Apr	Easter Road	1	1

v FRANCE			S	F
1930	18 May	Paris	2	0
1932	8 May	Paris	3	1
1948	23 May	Paris	0	3
1949	27 Apr	Glasgow	2	0
1950	27 May	Paris	1	0
1951	16 May	Glasgow	1	0
wc1958	15 June	Orebro	1	2
1984	1 June	Marseilles	0	2
wc1989	8 Mar	Glasgow	2	0
wc1989	11 Oct	Paris	0	3
1997	12 Nov	St Etienne	1	2
2000	29 Mar	Glasgow	0	2
2002	27 Mar	Paris	0	5
EC2006	7 Oct	Glasgow	1	0
EC2007	12 Sept	Paris	1	0

v GEORGIA			S	G
EC2007	24 Mar	Glasgow	2	1
EC2007	17 Oct	Tblisi	0	2

v GERMANY			S	G
1929	1 June	Berlin	1	1
1936	14 Oct	Glasgow	2	0
EC1992	15 June	Norrkoping	0	2
1993	24 Mar	Glasgow	0	1
1999	28 Apr	Bremen	1	0
EC2003	7 June	Glasgow	1	1
EC2003	10 Sept	Dortmund	1	2

v EAST GERMANY			S	EG
1974	30 Oct	Glasgow	3	0
1977	7 Sept	East Berlin	0	1
EC1982	13 Oct	Glasgow	2	0
EC1983	16 Nov	Halle	1	2
1985	16 Oct	Glasgow	0	0
1990	25 Apr	Glasgow	0	1

v WEST GERMANY			S	WG
1957	22 May	Stuttgart	3	1
1959	6 May	Glasgow	3	2
1964	12 May	Hanover	2	2
wc1969	16 Apr	Glasgow	1	1
wc1969	22 Oct	Hamburg	2	3
1973	14 Nov	Glasgow	1	1
1974	27 Mar	Frankfurt	1	2
wc1986	8 June	Queretaro	1	2

v GREECE			S	G
EC1994	18 Dec	Athens	0	1
EC1995	16 Aug	Glasgow	1	0

v HONG KONG XI			S	HK
†2002	23 May	Hong Kong	4	0

†match not recognised by FIFA

v HUNGARY			S	H
1938	7 Dec	Ibrox	3	1
1954	8 Dec	Glasgow	2	4
1955	29 May	Budapest	1	3
1958	7 May	Glasgow	1	1
1960	5 June	Budapest	3	3
1980	31 May	Budapest	1	3

			S	B
1987	9 Sept	Glasgow	2	0
2004	18 Aug	Glasgow	0	3

v ICELAND			S	I
wc1984	17 Oct	Glasgow	3	0
wc1985	28 May	Reykjavik	1	0
EC2002	12 Oct	Reykjavik	2	0
EC2003	29 Mar	Glasgow	2	1
wc2008	10 Sept	Reykjavik	2	1
wc2009	1 Apr	Glasgow	2	1

v IRAN			S	I
wc1978	7 June	Cordoba	1	1

v REPUBLIC OF IRELAND			S	RI
wc1961	3 May	Glasgow	4	1
wc1961	7 May	Dublin	3	0
1963	9 June	Dublin	0	1
1969	21 Sept	Dublin	1	1
EC1986	15 Oct	Dublin	0	0
EC1987	18 Feb	Glasgow	0	1
2000	30 May	Dublin	2	1
2003	12 Feb	Glasgow	0	2
NC2011	29 May	Dublin	0	1

v ISRAEL			S	I
wc1981	25 Feb	Tel Aviv	1	0
wc1981	28 Apr	Glasgow	3	1
1986	28 Jan	Tel Aviv	1	0

v ITALY			S	I
1931	20 May	Rome	0	3
wc1965	9 Nov	Glasgow	1	0
wc1965	7 Dec	Naples	0	3
1988	22 Dec	Perugia	0	2
wc1992	18 Nov	Ibrox	0	0
wc1993	13 Oct	Rome	1	3
wc2005	26 Mar	Milan	0	2
wc2005	3 Sept	Glasgow	1	1
EC2007	28 Mar	Bari	0	2
EC2007	17 Nov	Glasgow	1	2

v JAPAN			S	J
1995	21 May	Hiroshima	0	0
2006	13 May	Saitama	0	0
2009	10 Oct	Yokohama	0	2

v KOREA REPUBLIC			S	KR
2002	16 May	Busan	1	4

v LATVIA			S	L
wc1996	5 Oct	Riga	2	0
wc1997	11 Oct	Celtic Park	2	0
wc2000	2 Sept	Riga	1	0
wc2001	6 Oct	Glasgow	2	1

v LIECHTENSTEIN			S	L
EC2010	7 Sept	Glasgow	2	1
EC2011	8 Oct	Vaduz	1	0

v LITHUANIA			S	L
EC1998	5 Sept	Vilnius	0	0
EC1999	9 Oct	Glasgow	3	0
EC2003	2 Apr	Kaunas	0	1
EC2003	11 Oct	Glasgow	1	0
EC2006	6 Sept	Kaunas	2	1
EC2007	8 Sept	Glasgow	3	1
EC2010	3 Sept	Kaunas	0	0
EC2011	6 Sept	Glasgow	1	0

v LUXEMBOURG			S	L
1947	24 May	Luxembourg	6	0
EC1986	12 Nov	Glasgow	3	0
EC1987	2 Dec	Esch	0	0
2012	14 Nov	Luxembourg	2	1

v MACEDONIA			S	M
wc2008	6 Sept	Skopje	0	1
wc2009	5 Sept	Glasgow	2	0
wc2012	11 Sept	Glasgow	1	1
wc2013	10 Sept	Skopje	2	1

v MALTA			S	M
1988	22 Mar	Valletta	1	1
1990	28 May	Valletta	2	1
wc1993	17 Feb	Ibrox	3	0
wc1993	17 Nov	Valletta	2	0
1997	1 June	Valletta	3	2

v MOLDOVA		S	M
wc2004	13 Oct	Chisinau	1	1
wc2005	4 June	Glasgow	2	0

v MOROCCO		S	M
wc1998	23 June	St Etienne	0	3

v NETHERLANDS		S	N
1929	4 June	Amsterdam	2	0
1938	21 May	Amsterdam	3	1
1959	27 May	Amsterdam	2	1
1966	11 May	Glasgow	0	3
1968	30 May	Amsterdam	0	0
1971	1 Dec	Amsterdam	1	2
wc1978	11 June	Mendoza	3	2
1982	23 Mar	Glasgow	2	1
1986	29 Apr	Eindhoven	0	0
EC1992	12 June	Gothenburg	0	1
1994	23 Mar	Glasgow	0	1
1994	27 May	Utrecht	1	3
EC1996	10 June	Villa Park	0	0
2000	26 Apr	Arnhem	0	0
EC2003	15 Nov	Glasgow	1	0
EC2003	19 Nov	Amsterdam	0	6
wc2009	28 Mar	Amsterdam	0	3
wc2009	9 Sept	Glasgow	0	1

v NEW ZEALAND		S	NZ
wc1982	15 June	Malaga	5	2
2003	27 May	Tynecastle	1	1

v NIGERIA		S	N
2002	17 Apr	Aberdeen	1	2
2014	28 May	Craven Cottage	2	2

v NORWAY		S	N
1929	26 May	Oslo	7	3
1954	5 May	Glasgow	1	0
1954	19 May	Oslo	1	1
1963	4 June	Bergen	3	4
1963	7 Nov	Glasgow	6	1
1974	6 June	Oslo	2	1
EC1978	25 Oct	Glasgow	3	2
EC1979	7 June	Oslo	4	0
wc1988	14 Sept	Oslo	2	1
wc1989	15 Nov	Glasgow	1	1
1992	3 June	Oslo	0	0
wc1998	16 June	Bordeaux	1	1
2003	20 Aug	Oslo	0	0
wc2004	9 Oct	Glasgow	0	1
wc2005	7 Sept	Oslo	2	1
wc2008	11 Oct	Glasgow	0	0
wc2009	12 Aug	Oslo	0	4
2013	19 Nov	Molde	1	0

v PARAGUAY		S	P
wc1958	11 June	Norrkoping	2	3

v PERU		S	P
1972	26 Apr	Glasgow	2	0
wc1978	3 June	Cordoba	1	3
1979	12 Sept	Glasgow	1	1

v POLAND		S	P
1958	1 June	Warsaw	2	1
1960	4 May	Glasgow	2	3
wc1965	23 May	Chorzow	1	1
wc1965	13 Oct	Glasgow	1	2
1980	28 May	Poznan	0	1
1990	19 May	Glasgow	1	1
2001	25 Apr	Bydgoszcz	1	1
2014	5 Mar	Warsaw	1	0

v PORTUGAL		S	P
1950	21 May	Lisbon	2	2
1955	4 May	Glasgow	3	0
1959	3 June	Lisbon	0	1
1966	18 June	Glasgow	0	1
EC1971	21 Apr	Lisbon	0	2
EC1971	13 Oct	Glasgow	2	1
1975	13 May	Glasgow	1	0
EC1978	29 Nov	Lisbon	0	1
EC1980	26 Mar	Glasgow	4	1
wc1980	15 Oct	Glasgow	0	0
wc1981	18 Nov	Lisbon	1	2
wc1992	14 Oct	Ibrox	0	0
wc1993	28 Apr	Lisbon	0	5
2002	20 Nov	Braga	0	2

v ROMANIA		S	R
EC1975	1 June	Bucharest	1	1
EC1975	17 Dec	Glasgow	1	1
1986	26 Mar	Glasgow	3	0
EC1990	12 Sept	Glasgow	2	1
EC1991	16 Oct	Bucharest	0	1
2004	31 Mar	Glasgow	1	2

v RUSSIA		S	R
EC1994	16 Nov	Glasgow	1	1
EC1995	29 Mar	Moscow	0	0

v SAN MARINO		S	SM
EC1991	1 May	Serravalle	2	0
EC1991	13 Nov	Glasgow	4	0
EC1995	26 Apr	Serravalle	2	0
EC1995	15 Nov	Glasgow	5	0
wc2000	7 Oct	Serravalle	2	0
wc2001	28 Mar	Glasgow	4	0

v SAUDI ARABIA		S	SA
1988	17 Feb	Riyadh	2	2

v SERBIA		S	Se
wc2012	8 Sept	Glasgow	0	0
wc2013	26 Mar	Novi Sad	0	2

v SLOVENIA		S	Sl
wc2004	8 Sept	Glasgow	0	0
wc2005	12 Oct	Celje	3	0
2012	29 Feb	Koper	1	1

v SOUTH AFRICA		S	SA
2002	20 May	Hong Kong	0	2
2007	22 Aug	Aberdeen	1	0

v SPAIN		S	Sp
wc1957	8 May	Glasgow	4	2
wc1957	26 May	Madrid	1	4
1963	13 June	Madrid	6	2
1965	8 May	Glasgow	0	0
EC1974	20 Nov	Glasgow	1	2
EC1975	5 Feb	Valencia	1	1
1982	24 Feb	Valencia	0	3
wc1984	14 Nov	Glasgow	3	1
wc1985	27 Feb	Seville	0	1
1988	27 Apr	Madrid	0	0
2004	3 Sept	Valencia	1	1

Match abandoned after 60 minutes; floodlight failure.

EC2010	12 Oct	Glasgow	2	3
EC2011	11 Oct	Alicante	1	3

v SWEDEN		S	Sw
1952	30 May	Stockholm	1	3
1953	6 May	Glasgow	1	2
1975	16 Apr	Gothenburg	1	1
1977	27 Apr	Glasgow	3	1
wc1980	10 Sept	Stockholm	1	0
wc1981	9 Sept	Glasgow	2	0
wc1990	16 June	Genoa	2	1
1995	11 Oct	Stockholm	0	2
wc1996	10 Nov	Ibrox	1	0
wc1997	30 Apr	Gothenburg	1	2
2004	17 Nov	Easter Road	1	4
2010	11 Aug	Stockholm	0	3

v SWITZERLAND		S	Sw
1931	24 May	Geneva	3	2
1946	15 May	Glasgow	3	1
1948	17 May	Berne	1	2
1950	26 Apr	Glasgow	3	1
wc1957	19 May	Basle	2	1
wc1957	6 Nov	Glasgow	3	2
1973	22 June	Berne	0	1
1976	7 Apr	Glasgow	1	0
EC1982	17 Nov	Berne	0	2
EC1983	30 May	Glasgow	2	2
EC1990	17 Oct	Glasgow	2	1
EC1991	11 Sept	Berne	2	2
wc1992	9 Sept	Berne	1	3
wc1993	8 Sept	Aberdeen	1	1
wc1996	18 June	Villa Park	1	0
2006	1 Mar	Glasgow	1	3

v TRINIDAD & TOBAGO		S	TT
2004	30 May	Easter Road	4	1

v TURKEY		S	T
1960	8 June	Ankara	2	4

v UKRAINE		S	U
EC2006	11 Oct	Kiev	0	2
EC2007	13 Oct	Glasgow	3	1

v URUGUAY		S	U
wc1954	19 June	Basle	0	7
1962	2 May	Glasgow	2	3
1983	21 Sept	Glasgow	2	0
wc1986	13 June	Nezahualcoyotl	0	0

v USA		S	USA
1952	30 Apr	Glasgow	6	0
1992	17 May	Denver	1	0
1996	26 May	New Britain	1	2
1998	30 May	Washington	0	0
2005	12 Nov	Glasgow	1	1

			S	USA
2012	26 May	Jacksonville	1	5
2013	15 Nov	Glasgow	0	0

v USSR		S	USSR
1967	10 May	Glasgow	0	2
1971	14 June	Moscow	0	1
wc1982	22 June	Malaga	2	2
1991	6 Feb	Ibrox	0	1

v YUGOSLAVIA		S	Y
1955	15 May	Belgrade	2	2
1956	21 Nov	Glasgow	2	0
wc1958	8 June	Vasteras	1	1
1972	29 June	Belo Horizonte	2	2
wc1974	22 June	Frankfurt	1	1
1984	12 Sept	Glasgow	6	1
wc1988	19 Oct	Glasgow	1	1
wc1989	6 Sept	Zagreb	1	3

v ZAIRE		S	Z
wc1974	14 June	Dortmund	2	0

WALES

v ALBANIA		W	A
EC1994	7 Sept	Cardiff	2	0
EC1995	15 Nov	Tirana	1	1

v ARGENTINA		W	A
1992	3 June	Tokyo	0	1
2002	13 Feb	Cardiff	1	1

v ARMENIA		W	A
wc2001	24 Mar	Erevan	2	2
wc2001	1 Sept	Cardiff	0	0

v AUSTRALIA		W	A
2011	10 Aug	Cardiff	1	2

v AUSTRIA		W	A
1954	9 May	Vienna	0	2
1955	23 Nov	Wrexham	1	2
EC1974	4 Sept	Vienna	1	2
1975	19 Nov	Wrexham	1	0
1992	29 Apr	Vienna	1	1
EC2005	26 Mar	Cardiff	0	2
EC2005	30 Mar	Vienna	0	1
2013	6 Feb	Swansea	2	1

v AZERBAIJAN		W	A
EC2002	20 Nov	Baku	2	0
EC2003	29 Mar	Cardiff	4	0
wc2004	4 Sept	Baku	1	1
wc2005	12 Oct	Cardiff	2	0
wc2008	6 Sept	Cardiff	1	0
wc2009	6 June	Baku	1	0

v BELARUS		W	B
EC1998	14 Oct	Cardiff	3	2
EC1999	4 Sept	Minsk	2	1
wc2000	2 Sept	Minsk	1	2
wc2001	6 Oct	Cardiff	1	0

v BELGIUM		W	B
1949	22 May	Liege	1	3
1949	23 Nov	Cardiff	5	1
EC1990	17 Oct	Cardiff	3	1
EC1991	27 Mar	Brussels	1	1
wc1992	18 Nov	Brussels	0	2
wc1993	31 Mar	Cardiff	2	0
wc1997	29 Mar	Cardiff	1	2
wc1997	11 Oct	Brussels	2	3
wc2012	7 Sept	Cardiff	0	2
wc2013	15 Oct	Brussels	1	1

v BOSNIA		W	B
2003	12 Feb	Cardiff	2	2
2012	15 Aug	Llanelli	0	2

v BRAZIL		W	B
wc1958	19 June	Gothenburg	0	1
1962	12 May	Rio de Janeiro	1	3
1962	16 May	São Paulo	1	3
1966	14 May	Rio de Janeiro	1	3

			W	B
1966	18 May	Belo Horizonte	0	1
1983	12 June	Cardiff	1	1
1991	11 Sept	Cardiff	1	0
1997	12 Nov	Brasilia	0	3
2000	23 May	Cardiff	0	3
2006	5 Sept	Cardiff	0	2

v BULGARIA		W	B
EC1983	27 Apr	Wrexham	1	0
EC1983	16 Nov	Sofia	0	1
EC1994	14 Dec	Cardiff	0	3
EC1995	29 Mar	Sofia	1	3
2006	15 Aug	Swansea	0	0
2007	22 Aug	Burgas	1	0
EC2010	8 Oct	Cardiff	0	1
EC2011	12 Oct	Sofia	1	0

v CANADA		W	C
1986	10 May	Toronto	0	2
1986	20 May	Vancouver	3	0
2004	30 May	Wrexham	1	0

v CHILE		W	C
1966	22 May	Santiago	0	2
2014	4 June	Valparaiso	0	2

v COSTA RICA		W	CR
1990	20 May	Cardiff	1	0
2012	29 Feb	Cardiff	0	1

v CROATIA		W	C
2002	21 Aug	Varazdin	1	1
2010	23 May	Osijek	0	2
wc2012	16 Oct	Osijek	0	2
wc2013	26 Mar	Swansea	1	2

v CYPRUS		W	C
wc1992	14 Oct	Limassol	1	0
wc1993	13 Oct	Cardiff	2	0
2005	16 Nov	Limassol	0	1
EC2006	11 Oct	Cardiff	3	1
EC2007	13 Oct	Nicosia	1	3

v CZECHOSLOVAKIA		W	C
wc1957	1 May	Cardiff	1	0
wc1957	26 May	Prague	0	2
EC1971	21 Apr	Swansea	1	3
EC1971	27 Oct	Prague	0	1
wc1977	30 Mar	Wrexham	3	0
wc1977	16 Nov	Prague	0	1
wc1980	19 Nov	Cardiff	1	0
wc1981	9 Sept	Prague	0	2
EC1987	29 Apr	Wrexham	1	1
EC1987	11 Nov	Prague	0	2
wc1993	28 Apr	Ostrava†	1	1
wc1993	8 Sept	Cardiff†	2	2

†Czechoslovakia played as RCS (Republic of Czechs and Slovaks).

		v CZECH REPUBLIC	W	CR
2002	27 Mar	Cardiff	0	0
EC2006	2 Sept	Teplice	1	2
EC2007	2 June	Cardiff	0	0

		v DENMARK	W	D
wc1964	21 Oct	Copenhagen	0	1
wc1965	1 Dec	Wrexham	4	2
EC1987	9 Sept	Cardiff	1	0
EC1987	14 Oct	Copenhagen	0	1
1990	11 Sept	Copenhagen	0	1
EC1998	10 Oct	Copenhagen	2	1
EC1999	9 June	Liverpool	0	2
2008	19 Nov	Brondby	1	0

		v ESTONIA	W	E
1994	23 May	Tallinn	2	1
2009	29 May	Llanelli	1	0

		v FAROE ISLANDS	W	F
wc1992	9 Sept	Cardiff	6	0
wc1993	6 June	Toftir	3	0

		v FINLAND	W	F
EC1971	26 May	Helsinki	1	0
EC1971	13 Oct	Swansea	3	0
EC1987	10 Sept	Helsinki	1	1
EC1987	1 Apr	Wrexham	4	0
wc1988	19 Oct	Swansea	2	2
wc1989	6 Sept	Helsinki	0	1
2000	29 Mar	Cardiff	1	2
EC2002	7 Sept	Helsinki	2	0
EC2003	10 Sept	Cardiff	1	1
wc2009	28 Mar	Cardiff	0	2
wc2009	10 Oct	Helsinki	1	2
2013	16 Nov	Cardiff	1	1

		v FRANCE	W	F
1933	25 May	Paris	1	1
1939	20 May	Paris	1	2
1953	14 May	Paris	1	6
1982	2 June	Toulouse	1	0

		v GEORGIA	W	G
EC1994	16 Nov	Tbilisi	0	5
EC1995	7 June	Cardiff	0	1
2008	20 Aug	Swansea	1	2

		v GERMANY	W	G
EC1995	26 Apr	Dusseldorf	1	1
EC1995	11 Oct	Cardiff	1	2
2002	14 May	Cardiff	1	0
EC2007	8 Sept	Cardiff	0	2
EC2007	21 Nov	Frankfurt	0	0
wc2008	15 Oct	Moenchengladbach	0	1
wc2009	1 Apr	Cardiff	0	2

		v EAST GERMANY	W	EG
wc1957	19 May	Leipzig	1	2
wc1957	25 Sept	Cardiff	4	1
wc1969	16 Apr	Dresden	1	2
wc1969	22 Oct	Cardiff	1	3

		v WEST GERMANY	W	WG
1968	8 May	Cardiff	1	1
1969	26 Mar	Frankfurt	1	1
1976	6 Oct	Cardiff	0	2
1977	14 Dec	Dortmund	1	1
EC1979	2 May	Wrexham	0	2
EC1979	17 Oct	Cologne	1	5
wc1989	31 May	Cardiff	0	0
wc1989	15 Nov	Cologne	1	2
EC1991	5 June	Cardiff	1	0
EC1991	16 Oct	Nuremberg	1	4

		v GREECE	W	G
wc1964	9 Dec	Athens	0	2
wc1965	17 Mar	Cardiff	4	1

		v HUNGARY	W	H
wc1958	8 June	Sanviken	1	1
wc1958	17 June	Stockholm	2	1
1961	28 May	Budapest	2	3
EC1962	7 Nov	Budapest	1	3
EC1963	20 Mar	Cardiff	1	1
EC1974	30 Oct	Cardiff	2	0
EC1975	16 Apr	Budapest	2	1

			W	H
1985	16 Oct	Cardiff	0	3
2004	31 Mar	Budapest	2	1
2005	9 Feb	Cardiff	2	0

		v ICELAND	W	I
wc1980	2 June	Reykjavik	4	0
wc1981	14 Oct	Swansea	2	2
wc1984	12 Sept	Reykjavik	0	1
wc1984	14 Nov	Cardiff	2	1
1991	1 May	Cardiff	1	0
2008	28 May	Reykjavik	1	0
2014	5 Mar	Cardiff	3	1

		v IRAN	W	I
1978	18 Apr	Teheran	1	0

		v REPUBLIC OF IRELAND	W	RI
1960	28 Sept	Dublin	3	2
1979	11 Sept	Swansea	2	1
1981	24 Feb	Dublin	3	1
1986	26 Mar	Dublin	1	0
1990	28 Mar	Dublin	0	1
1991	6 Feb	Wrexham	0	3
1992	19 Feb	Dublin	1	0
1993	17 Feb	Dublin	1	2
1997	11 Feb	Cardiff	0	0
EC2007	24 Mar	Dublin	0	1
EC2007	17 Nov	Cardiff	2	2
NC2011	8 Feb	Dublin	0	3
2013	14 Aug	Cardiff	0	0

		v ISRAEL	W	I
wc1958	15 Jan	Tel Aviv	2	0
wc1958	5 Feb	Cardiff	2	0
1984	10 June	Tel Aviv	0	0
1989	8 Feb	Tel Aviv	3	3

		v ITALY	W	I
1965	1 May	Florence	1	4
wc1968	23 Oct	Cardiff	0	1
wc1969	4 Nov	Rome	1	4
1988	4 June	Brescia	1	0
1996	24 Jan	Terni	0	3
EC1998	5 Sept	Liverpool	0	2
EC1999	5 June	Bologna	0	4
EC2002	16 Oct	Cardiff	2	1
EC2003	6 Sept	Milan	0	4

		v JAMAICA	W	J
1998	25 Mar	Cardiff	0	0

		v JAPAN	W	J
1992	7 June	Matsuyama	1	0

		v KUWAIT	W	K
1977	6 Sept	Wrexham	0	0
1977	20 Sept	Kuwait	0	0

		v LATVIA	W	L
2004	18 Aug	Riga	2	0

		v LIECHTENSTEIN	W	L
2006	14 Nov	Swansea	4	0
wc2008	11 Oct	Cardiff	2	0
wc2009	14 Oct	Vaduz	2	0

		v LUXEMBOURG	W	L
EC1974	20 Nov	Swansea	5	0
EC1975	1 May	Luxembourg	3	1
EC1990	14 Nov	Luxembourg	1	0
EC1991	13 Nov	Cardiff	1	0
2008	26 Mar	Luxembourg	2	0
2010	11 Aug	Llanelli	5	1

		v MALTA	W	M
EC1978	25 Oct	Wrexham	7	0
EC1979	2 June	Valletta	2	0
1988	1 June	Valletta	3	2
1998	3 June	Valletta	3	0

		v MACEDONIA	W	M
wc2013	6 Sept	Skopje	1	2
wc2013	11 Oct	Cardiff	1	0

v MEXICO

			W	M
wc1958	11 June	Stockholm	1	1
1962	22 May	Mexico City	1	2
2012	27 May	New Jersey	0	2

v MOLDOVA

			W	M
EC1994	12 Oct	Kishinev	2	3
EC1995	6 Sept	Cardiff	1	0

v MONTENEGRO

			W	M
2009	12 Aug	Podgorica	1	2
EC2010	3 Sept	Podgorica	0	1
EC2011	2 Sept	Cardiff	2	1

v NETHERLANDS

			W	N
wc1988	14 Sept	Amsterdam	0	1
wc1989	11 Oct	Wrexham	1	2
1992	30 May	Utrecht	0	4
wc1996	5 Oct	Cardiff	1	3
wc1996	9 Nov	Eindhoven	1	7
2008	1 June	Rotterdam	0	2
2014	4 June	Amsterdam	0	2

v NEW ZEALAND

			W	NZ
2007	26 May	Wrexham	2	2

v NORWAY

			W	N
EC1982	22 Sept	Swansea	1	0
EC1983	21 Sept	Oslo	0	0
1984	6 June	Trondheim	0	1
1985	26 Feb	Wrexham	1	1
1985	5 June	Bergen	2	4
1994	9 Mar	Cardiff	1	3
wc2000	7 Oct	Cardiff	1	1
wc2001	5 Sept	Oslo	2	3
2004	27 May	Oslo	0	0
2008	6 Feb	Wrexham	3	0
2011	12 Nov	Cardiff	4	1

v PARAGUAY

			W	P
2006	1 Mar	Cardiff	0	0

v POLAND

			W	P
wc1973	28 Mar	Cardiff	2	0
wc1973	26 Sept	Katowice	0	3
1991	29 May	Radom	0	0
wc2000	11 Oct	Warsaw	0	0
wc2001	2 June	Cardiff	1	2
wc2004	13 Oct	Cardiff	2	3
wc2005	7 Sept	Warsaw	0	1
2009	11 Feb	Vila Real	0	1

v PORTUGAL

			W	P
1949	15 May	Lisbon	2	3
1951	12 May	Cardiff	2	1
2000	2 June	Chaves	0	3

v QATAR

			W	Q
2000	23 Feb	Doha	1	0

v ROMANIA

			W	R
EC1970	11 Nov	Cardiff	0	0
EC1971	24 Nov	Bucharest	0	2
1983	12 Oct	Wrexham	5	0
wc1992	20 May	Bucharest	1	5
wc1993	17 Nov	Cardiff	1	2

v RUSSIA

			W	R
EC2003	15 Nov	Moscow	0	0
EC2003	19 Nov	Cardiff	0	1
wc2008	10 Sept	Moscow	1	2
wc2009	9 Sept	Cardiff	1	3

v SAN MARINO

			W	SM
wc1996	2 June	Serravalle	5	0
wc1996	31 Aug	Cardiff	6	0
EC2007	28 Mar	Cardiff	3	0
EC2007	17 Oct	Serravalle	2	1

v SAUDI ARABIA

			W	SA
1986	25 Feb	Dahran	2	1

v SERBIA

			W	S
wc2012	11 Sept	Novi Sad	1	6
wc2013	10 Sept	Cardiff	0	3

v SERBIA-MONTENEGRO

			W	SM
EC2003	20 Aug	Belgrade	0	1
EC2003	11 Oct	Cardiff	2	3

v SLOVAKIA

			W	S
EC2006	7 Oct	Cardiff	1	5
EC2007	12 Sept	Trnava	5	2

v SLOVENIA

			W	SI
2005	17 Aug	Swansea	0	0

v SPAIN

			W	S
wc1961	19 Apr	Cardiff	1	2
wc1961	18 May	Madrid	1	1
1982	24 Mar	Valencia	1	1
wc1984	17 Oct	Seville	0	3
wc1985	30 Apr	Wrexham	3	0

v SWEDEN

			W	S
wc1958	15 June	Stockholm	0	0
1988	27 Apr	Stockholm	1	4
1989	26 Apr	Wrexham	0	2
1990	25 Apr	Stockholm	2	4
1994	20 Apr	Wrexham	0	2
2010	3 Mar	Swansea	0	1

v SWITZERLAND

			W	S
1949	26 May	Berne	0	4
1951	16 May	Wrexham	3	2
1996	24 Apr	Lugano	0	2
EC1999	31 Mar	Zurich	0	2
EC1999	9 Oct	Wrexham	0	2
EC2010	12 Oct	Basle	1	4
EC2011	8 Oct	Swansea	2	0

v TRINIDAD & TOBAGO

			W	TT
2006	27 May	Graz	2	1

v TUNISIA

			W	T
1998	6 June	Tunis	0	4

v TURKEY

			W	T
EC1978	29 Nov	Wrexham	1	0
EC1979	21 Nov	Izmir	0	1
wc1980	15 Oct	Cardiff	4	0
wc1981	25 Mar	Ankara	1	0
wc1996	14 Dec	Cardiff	0	0
wc1997	20 Aug	Istanbul	4	6

v REST OF UNITED KINGDOM

			W	
1951	5 Dec	Cardiff	3	2
1969	28 July	Cardiff	0	1

v UKRAINE

			W	U
wc2001	28 Mar	Cardiff	1	1
wc2001	6 June	Kiev	1	1

v URUGUAY

			W	U
1986	21 Apr	Wrexham	0	0

v USA

			W	USA
2003	27 May	San Jose	0	2

v USSR

			W	USSR
wc1965	30 May	Moscow	1	2
wc1965	27 Oct	Cardiff	2	1
wc1981	30 May	Wrexham	0	0
wc1981	18 Nov	Tbilisi	0	3
1987	18 Feb	Swansea	0	0

v YUGOSLAVIA

			W	Y
1953	21 May	Belgrade	2	5
1954	22 Nov	Cardiff	1	3
EC1976	24 Apr	Zagreb	0	2
EC1976	22 May	Cardiff	1	1
EC1982	15 Dec	Titograd	4	4
EC1983	14 Dec	Cardiff	1	1
1988	23 Mar	Swansea	1	2

NORTHERN IRELAND

v ALBANIA			NI	A
wc1965	7 May	Belfast	4	1
wc1965	24 Nov	Tirana	1	1
EC1982	15 Dec	Tirana	0	0
EC1983	27 Apr	Belfast	1	0
wc1992	9 Sept	Belfast	3	0
wc1993	17 Feb	Tirana	2	1
wc1996	14 Dec	Belfast	2	0
wc1997	10 Sept	Zurich	0	1
2010	3 Mar	Tirana	0	1

v ALGERIA			NI	A
wc1986	3 June	Guadalajara	1	1

v ARGENTINA			NI	A
wc1958	11 June	Halmstad	1	3

v ARMENIA			NI	A
wc1996	5 Oct	Belfast	1	1
wc1997	30 Apr	Erevan	0	0
EC2003	29 Mar	Erevan	0	1
EC2003	10 Sept	Belfast	0	1

v AUSTRALIA			NI	A
1980	11 June	Sydney	2	1
1980	15 June	Melbourne	1	1
1980	18 June	Adelaide	2	1

v AUSTRIA			NI	A
wc1982	1 July	Madrid	2	2
EC1982	13 Oct	Vienna	0	2
EC1983	21 Sept	Belfast	3	1
EC1990	14 Nov	Vienna	0	0
EC1991	16 Oct	Belfast	2	1
EC1994	12 Oct	Vienna	2	1
EC1995	15 Nov	Belfast	5	3
wc2004	13 Oct	Belfast	3	3
wc2005	12 Oct	Vienna	0	2

v AZERBAIJAN			NI	A
wc2004	9 Oct	Baku	0	0
wc2005	3 Sept	Belfast	2	0
wc2012	14 Nov	Belfast	1	1
wc2013	11 Oct	Baku	0	2

v BARBADOS			NI	B
2004	30 May	Waterford	1	1

v BELGIUM			NI	B
wc1976	10 Nov	Liege	0	2
wc1977	16 Nov	Belfast	3	0
1997	11 Feb	Belfast	3	0

v BRAZIL			NI	B
wc1986	12 June	Guadalajara	0	3

v BULGARIA			NI	B
wc1972	18 Oct	Sofia	0	3
wc1973	26 Sept	Sheffield	0	0
EC1978	29 Nov	Sofia	2	0
EC1979	2 May	Belfast	2	0
wc2001	28 Mar	Sofia	3	4
wc2001	2 June	Belfast	0	1
2008	6 Feb	Belfast	0	1

v CANADA			NI	C
1995	22 May	Edmonton	0	2
1999	27 Apr	Belfast	1	1
2005	9 Feb	Belfast	0	1

v CHILE			NI	C
1989	26 May	Belfast	0	1
1995	25 May	Edmonton	1	2
2010	30 May	Chillan	0	1
2014	4 June	Valparaiso	0	2

v COLOMBIA			NI	C
1994	4 June	Boston	0	2

v CYPRUS			NI	C
EC1971	3 Feb	Nicosia	3	0
EC1971	21 Apr	Belfast	5	0

			NI	C
wc1973	14 Feb	Nicosia	0	1
wc1973	8 May	London	3	0
2002	21 Aug	Belfast	0	0
2014	5 Mar	Nicosia	0	0

v CZECHOSLOVAKIA			NI	C
wc1958	8 June	Halmstad	1	0
wc1958	17 June	Malmo	2	1*

*After extra time

v CZECH REPUBLIC			NI	C
wc2001	24 Mar	Belfast	0	1
wc2001	6 June	Teplice	1	3
wc2008	10 Sept	Belfast	0	0
wc2009	14 Oct	Prague	0	0

v DENMARK			NI	D
EC1978	25 Oct	Belfast	2	1
EC1979	6 June	Copenhagen	0	4
1986	26 Mar	Belfast	1	1
EC1990	17 Oct	Belfast	1	1
EC1991	13 Nov	Odense	1	2
wc1992	18 Nov	Belfast	0	1
wc1993	13 Oct	Copenhagen	0	1
wc2000	7 Oct	Belfast	1	1
wc2001	1 Sept	Copenhagen	1	1
EC2006	7 Oct	Copenhagen	0	0
EC2007	17 Nov	Belfast	2	1

v ESTONIA			NI	E
2004	31 Mar	Tallinn	1	0
2006	1 Mar	Belfast	1	0
EC2011	6 Sept	Tallinn	1	4
EC2011	7 Oct	Belfast	1	2

v FAROE ISLANDS			NI	F
EC1991	1 May	Belfast	1	1
EC1991	11 Sept	Landskrona	5	0
EC2010	12 Oct	Toftir	1	1
EC2011	10 Aug	Belfast	4	0

v FINLAND			NI	F
wc1984	27 May	Pori	0	1
wc1984	14 Nov	Belfast	2	1
EC1998	10 Oct	Belfast	1	0
EC1998	9 Oct	Helsinki	1	4
2003	12 Feb	Belfast	0	1
2006	16 Aug	Helsinki	2	1
2012	15 Aug	Belfast	3	3

v FRANCE			NI	F
1928	21 Feb	Paris	0	4
1951	12 May	Belfast	2	2
1952	11 Nov	Paris	1	3
wc1958	19 June	Norrkoping	0	4
1982	24 Mar	Paris	0	4
wc1982	4 July	Madrid	1	4
1986	26 Feb	Paris	0	0
1988	27 Apr	Belfast	0	0
1999	18 Aug	Belfast	0	1

v GEORGIA			NI	G
2008	26 Mar	Belfast	4	1

v GERMANY			NI	G
1992	2 June	Bremen	1	1
1996	29 May	Belfast	1	1
wc1996	9 Nov	Nuremberg	1	1
wc1997	20 Aug	Belfast	1	3
EC1999	27 Mar	Belfast	0	3
EC1999	8 Sept	Dortmund	0	4
2005	4 June	Belfast	1	4

v WEST GERMANY			NI	WG
wc1958	15 June	Malmo	2	2
wc1960	26 Oct	Belfast	3	4
wc1961	10 May	Hamburg	1	2
1966	7 May	Belfast	0	2
1977	27 Apr	Cologne	0	5

			NI	WG
EC1982	17 Nov	Belfast	1	0
EC1983	16 Nov	Hamburg	1	0

		v GREECE	NI	G
wc1961	3 May	Athens	1	2
wc1961	17 Oct	Belfast	2	0
1988	17 Feb	Athens	2	3
EC2003	2 Apr	Belfast	0	2
EC2003	11 Oct	Athens	0	1

		v HONDURAS	NI	H
wc1982	21 June	Zaragoza	1	1

		v HUNGARY	NI	H
wc1988	19 Oct	Budapest	0	1
wc1989	6 Sept	Belfast	1	2
2000	26 Apr	Belfast	0	1
2008	19 Nov	Belfast	0	2

		v ICELAND	NI	I
wc1977	11 June	Reykjavik	0	1
wc1977	21 Sept	Belfast	2	0
wc2000	11 Oct	Reykjavik	0	1
wc2001	5 Sept	Belfast	3	0
EC2006	2 Sept	Belfast	0	3
EC2007	12 Sept	Reykjavik	1	2

		v REPUBLIC OF IRELAND	NI	RI
EC1978	20 Sept	Dublin	0	0
EC1979	21 Nov	Belfast	1	0
wc1988	14 Sept	Belfast	0	0
wc1989	11 Oct	Dublin	0	3
wc1993	31 Mar	Dublin	0	3
wc1993	17 Nov	Belfast	1	1
EC1994	16 Nov	Belfast	0	4
EC1995	29 Mar	Dublin	1	1
1999	29 May	Dublin	1	0
NC2011	24 May	Dublin	0	5

		v ISRAEL	NI	I
1968	10 Sept	Jaffa	3	2
1976	3 Mar	Tel Aviv	1	1
wc1980	26 Mar	Tel Aviv	0	0
wc1981	18 Nov	Belfast	1	0
1984	16 Oct	Belfast	3	0
1987	18 Feb	Tel Aviv	1	1
2009	12 Aug	Belfast	1	1
wc2013	26 Mar	Belfast	0	2
wc2013	15 Oct	Tel Aviv	1	1

		v ITALY	NI	I
wc1957	25 Apr	Rome	0	1
1957	4 Dec	Belfast	2	2
wc1958	15 Jan	Belfast	2	1
1961	25 Apr	Bologna	2	3
1997	22 Jan	Palermo	0	2
2003	3 June	Campobasso	0	2
2009	6 June	Pisa	0	3
EC2010	8 Oct	Belfast	0	0
EC2011	11 Oct	Pescara	0	3

		v LATVIA	NI	L
wc1993	2 June	Riga	2	1
wc1993	8 Sept	Belfast	2	0
EC1995	26 Apr	Riga	1	0
EC1995	7 June	Belfast	1	2
EC2006	11 Oct	Belfast	1	0
EC2007	8 Sept	Riga	0	1

		v LIECHTENSTEIN	NI	L
EC1994	20 Apr	Belfast	4	1
EC1995	11 Oct	Eschen	4	0
2002	27 Mar	Vaduz	0	0
EC2007	24 Mar	Vaduz	4	1
EC2007	22 Aug	Belfast	3	1

		v LITHUANIA	NI	L
wc1992	28 Apr	Belfast	2	2
wc1993	25 May	Vilnius	1	0

		v LUXEMBOURG	NI	L
2000	23 Feb	Luxembourg	3	1
wc2012	11 Sept	Belfast	1	1
wc2013	10 Sept	Luxembourg	2	3

		v MALTA	NI	M
wc1988	21 May	Belfast	3	0
wc1989	26 Apr	Valletta	2	0
2000	28 Mar	Valletta	3	0
wc2000	2 Sept	Belfast	1	0
wc2001	6 Oct	Valletta	1	0
2005	17 Aug	Ta'Qali	1	1
2013	6 Feb	Ta'Qali	0	0

		v MEXICO	NI	M
1966	22 June	Belfast	4	1
1994	11 June	Miami	0	3

		v MOLDOVA	NI	M
EC1998	18 Nov	Belfast	2	2
EC1999	31 Mar	Chisinau	0	0

		v MONTENEGRO	NI	M
2010	11 Aug	Podgorica	0	2

		v MOROCCO	NI	M
1986	23 Apr	Belfast	2	1
2010	17 Nov	Belfast	1	1

		v NETHERLANDS	NI	N
1962	9 May	Rotterdam	0	4
wc1965	17 Mar	Belfast	2	1
wc1965	7 Apr	Rotterdam	0	0
wc1976	13 Oct	Rotterdam	2	2
wc1977	12 Oct	Belfast	0	1
2012	2 June	Amsterdam	0	6

		v NORWAY	NI	N
1922	25 May	Bergen	1	2
EC1974	4 Sept	Oslo	1	2
EC1975	29 Oct	Belfast	3	0
1990	27 Mar	Belfast	2	3
1996	27 Mar	Belfast	0	2
2001	28 Feb	Belfast	0	4
2004	18 Feb	Belfast	1	4
2012	29 Feb	Belfast	0	3

		v POLAND	NI	P
EC1962	10 Oct	Katowice	2	0
EC1962	28 Nov	Belfast	2	0
1988	23 Mar	Belfast	1	1
1991	5 Feb	Belfast	3	1
2002	13 Feb	Limassol	1	4
EC2004	4 Sept	Belfast	0	3
EC2005	30 Mar	Warsaw	0	1
wc2009	28 Mar	Belfast	3	2
wc2009	5 Sept	Chorzow	1	1

		v PORTUGAL	NI	P
wc1957	16 Jan	Lisbon	1	1
wc1957	1 May	Belfast	3	0
wc1973	28 Mar	Coventry	1	1
wc1973	14 Nov	Lisbon	1	1
wc1980	19 Nov	Lisbon	0	1
wc1981	29 Apr	Belfast	1	0
EC1994	7 Sept	Belfast	1	2
EC1995	3 Sept	Lisbon	1	1
wc1997	29 Mar	Belfast	0	0
wc1997	11 Oct	Lisbon	0	1
2005	15 Nov	Belfast	1	1
wc2012	16 Oct	Porto	1	1
wc2013	6 Sept	Belfast	2	4

		v ROMANIA	NI	R
wc1984	12 Sept	Belfast	3	2
wc1985	16 Oct	Bucharest	1	0
1994	23 Mar	Belfast	2	0
2006	27 May	Chicago	0	2

v RUSSIA

			NI	R
wc2012	7 Sept	Moscow	0	2
wc2013	14 Aug	Belfast	1	0

v SAN MARINO

			NI	SM
wc2008	15 Oct	Belfast	4	0
wc2009	11 Feb	Serravalle	3	0

v ST KITTS & NEVIS

			NI	SK
2004	2 June	Basseterre	2	0

v SERBIA

			NI	S
2009	14 Nov	Belfast	0	1
EC2011	25 Mar	Belgrade	1	2
EC2011	2 Sept	Belfast	0	1

v SERBIA-MONTENEGRO

			NI	SM
2004	28 Apr	Belfast	1	1

v SLOVAKIA

			NI	S
1998	25 Mar	Belfast	1	0
wc2008	6 Sept	Bratislava	1	2
wc2009	9 Sept	Belfast	0	2

v SLOVENIA

			NI	S
wc2008	11 Oct	Maribor	0	2
wc2009	1 Apr	Belfast	1	0
EC2010	3 Sept	Maribor	1	0
EC2011	29 Mar	Belfast	0	0

v SOUTH AFRICA

			NI	SA
1924	24 Sept	Belfast	1	2

v SPAIN

			NI	S
1958	15 Oct	Madrid	2	6
1963	30 May	Bilbao	1	1
1963	30 Oct	Belfast	0	1
EC1970	11 Nov	Seville	0	3
EC1972	16 Feb	Hull	1	1
wc1982	25 June	Valencia	1	0
1985	27 Mar	Palma	0	0
wc1986	7 June	Guadalajara	1	2
wc1988	21 Dec	Seville	0	4
wc1989	8 Feb	Belfast	0	2
wc1992	14 Oct	Belfast	0	0
wc1993	28 Apr	Seville	1	3
1998	2 June	Santander	1	4
2002	17 Apr	Belfast	0	5
EC2002	12 Oct	Albacete	0	3
EC2003	11 June	Belfast	0	0
EC2006	6 Sept	Belfast	3	2
EC2007	21 Nov	Las Palmas	0	1

v SWEDEN

			NI	S
EC1974	30 Oct	Solna	2	0
EC1975	3 Sept	Belfast	1	2
wc1980	15 Oct	Belfast	3	0
wc1981	3 June	Solna	0	1
1996	24 Apr	Belfast	1	2
			NI	S
EC2007	28 Mar	Belfast	2	1
EC2007	17 Oct	Stockholm	1	1

v SWITZERLAND

			NI	S
wc1964	14 Oct	Belfast	1	0
wc1964	14 Nov	Lausanne	1	2
1998	22 Apr	Belfast	1	0
2004	18 Aug	Zurich	0	0

v THAILAND

			NI	T
1997	21 May	Bangkok	0	0

v TRINIDAD & TOBAGO

			NI	TT
2004	6 June	Bacolet	3	0

v TURKEY

			NI	T
wc1968	23 Oct	Belfast	4	1
wc1968	11 Dec	Istanbul	3	0
2013	15 Nov	Adana	0	1
EC1983	30 Mar	Belfast	2	1
EC1983	12 Oct	Ankara	0	1
wc1985	1 May	Belfast	2	0
wc1985	11 Sept	Izmir	0	0
EC1986	12 Nov	Izmir	0	0
EC1987	11 Nov	Belfast	1	0
EC1998	5 Sept	Istanbul	0	3
EC1999	4 Sept	Belfast	0	3
2010	26 May	New Britain	0	2
2013	15 Nov	Adana	0	1

v UKRAINE

			NI	U
wc1996	31 Aug	Belfast	0	1
wc1997	2 Apr	Kiev	1	2
EC2002	16 Oct	Belfast	0	0
EC2003	6 Sept	Donetsk	0	0

v URUGUAY

			NI	U
1964	29 Apr	Belfast	3	0
1990	18 May	Belfast	1	0
2006	21 May	New Jersey	0	1
2014	30 May	Montevideo	0	1

v USSR

			NI	USSR
wc1969	19 Sept	Belfast	0	0
wc1969	22 Oct	Moscow	0	2
EC1971	22 Sept	Moscow	0	1
EC1971	13 Oct	Belfast	1	1

v YUGOSLAVIA

			NI	Y
EC1975	16 Mar	Belfast	1	0
EC1975	19 Nov	Belgrade	0	1
wc1982	17 June	Zaragoza	0	0
EC1987	29 Apr	Belfast	1	2
EC1987	14 Oct	Sarajevo	0	3
EC1990	12 Sept	Belfast	0	2
EC1991	27 Mar	Belgrade	1	4
2000	16 Aug	Belfast	1	2

REPUBLIC OF IRELAND

v ALBANIA

			RI	A
wc1992	26 May	Dublin	2	0
wc1993	26 May	Tirana	2	1
EC2003	2 Apr	Tirana	0	0
EC2003	7 June	Dublin	2	1
			RI	A
1998	22 Apr	Dublin	0	2
2010	11 Aug	Dublin	0	1

†Not considered a full international.

v ALGERIA

			RI	A
1982	28 Apr	Algiers	0	2
2010	28 May	Dublin	3	0

v ARMENIA

			RI	A
EC2010	3 Sept	Erevan	1	0
EC2011	11 Oct	Dublin	2	1

v ANDORRA

			RI	A
wc2001	28 Mar	Barcelona	3	0
wc2001	25 Apr	Dublin	3	1
EC2010	7 Sept	Dublin	3	1
EC2011	7 Oct	Andorra La Vella	2	0

v AUSTRALIA

			RI	A
2003	19 Aug	Dublin	2	1
2009	12 Aug	Limerick	0	3

v ARGENTINA

			RI	A
1951	13 May	Dublin	0	1
†1979	29 May	Dublin	0	0
1980	16 May	Dublin	0	1

v AUSTRIA

			RI	A
1952	7 May	Vienna	0	6
1953	25 Mar	Dublin	4	0
1958	14 Mar	Vienna	1	3
wc2013	10 Sept	Vienna	0	1
1962	8 Apr	Dublin	2	3
EC1963	25 Sept	Vienna	0	0

			RI	A
EC1963	13 Oct	Dublin	3	2
1966	22 May	Vienna	0	1
1968	10 Nov	Dublin	2	2
EC1971	30 May	Dublin	1	4
EC1971	10 Oct	Linz	0	6
EC1995	11 June	Dublin	1	3
EC1995	6 Sept	Vienna	1	3
wc2013	26 Mar	Dublin	2	2
wc2013	10 Sept	Vienna	0	1

		v BELGIUM	RI	B
1928	12 Feb	Liege	4	2
1929	30 Apr	Dublin	4	0
1930	11 May	Brussels	3	1
wc1934	25 Feb	Dublin	4	4
1949	24 Apr	Dublin	0	2
1950	10 May	Brussels	1	5
1965	24 Mar	Dublin	0	2
1966	25 May	Liege	3	2
wc1980	15 Oct	Dublin	1	1
wc1981	25 Mar	Brussels	0	1
EC1986	10 Sept	Brussels	2	2
EC1987	29 Apr	Dublin	0	0
wc1997	29 Oct	Dublin	1	1
wc1997	16 Nov	Brussels	1	2

		v BOLIVIA	RI	B
1994	24 May	Dublin	1	0
1996	15 June	New Jersey	3	0
2007	26 May	Boston	1	1

		v BOSNIA	RI	B
2012	26 May	Dublin	1	0

		v BRAZIL	RI	B
1974	5 May	Rio de Janeiro	1	2
1982	27 May	Uberlandia	0	7
1987	23 May	Dublin	1	0
2004	18 Feb	Dublin	0	0
2008	6 Feb	Dublin	0	1
2010	2 Mar	Emirates	0	2

		v BULGARIA	RI	B
wc1977	1 June	Sofia	1	2
wc1977	12 Oct	Dublin	0	0
EC1979	19 May	Sofia	0	1
EC1979	17 Oct	Dublin	3	0
wc1987	1 Apr	Sofia	1	2
wc1987	14 Oct	Dublin	2	0
2004	18 Aug	Dublin	1	1
wc2009	28 Mar	Dublin	1	1
wc2009	6 June	Sofia	1	1

		v CAMEROON	RI	C
wc2002	1 June	Niigata	1	1

		v CANADA	RI	C
2003	18 Nov	Dublin	3	0

		v CHILE	RI	C
1960	30 Mar	Dublin	2	0
1972	21 June	Recife	1	2
1974	12 May	Santiago	2	1
1982	22 May	Santiago	0	1
1991	22 May	Dublin	1	1
2006	24 May	Dublin	0	1

		v CHINA	RI	C
1984	3 June	Sapporo	1	0
2005	29 Mar	Dublin	1	0

		v COLOMBIA	RI	C
2008	29 May	Fulham	1	0

		v COSTA RICA	RI	C
2014	6 June	Philadephia	1	1

		v CROATIA	RI	C
1996	2 June	Dublin	2	2
EC1998	5 Sept	Dublin	2	0
EC1999	4 Sept	Zagreb	0	1
2001	15 Aug	Dublin	2	2
2004	16 Nov	Dublin	1	0

			RI	C
2011	10 Aug	Dublin	0	0
EC2012	10 June	Poznan	1	3

		v CYPRUS	RI	C
wc1980	26 Mar	Nicosia	3	2
wc1980	19 Nov	Dublin	6	0
wc2001	24 Mar	Nicosia	4	0
wc2001	6 Oct	Dublin	4	0
wc2004	4 Sept	Dublin	3	0
wc2005	8 Oct	Nicosia	1	0
EC2006	7 Oct	Nicosia	2	5
EC2007	17 Oct	Dublin	1	1
2008	15 Oct	Dublin	1	0
wc2009	5 Sept	Nicosia	2	1

		v CZECHOSLOVAKIA	RI	C
1938	18 May	Prague	2	2
EC1959	5 Apr	Dublin	2	0
EC1959	10 May	Bratislava	0	4
wc1961	8 Oct	Dublin	1	3
wc1961	29 Oct	Prague	1	7
EC1967	21 May	Dublin	0	2
EC1967	22 Nov	Prague	2	1
wc1969	4 May	Dublin	1	2
wc1969	7 Oct	Prague	0	3
1979	26 Sept	Prague	1	4
1981	29 Apr	Dublin	3	1
1986	27 May	Reykjavik	1	0

		v CZECH REPUBLIC	RI	C
1994	5 June	Dublin	1	3
1996	24 Apr	Prague	0	2
1998	25 Mar	Olomouc	1	2
2000	23 Feb	Dublin	3	2
2004	31 Mar	Dublin	2	1
EC2006	11 Oct	Dublin	1	1
EC2007	12 Sept	Prague	0	1
2012	29 Feb	Dublin	1	1

		v DENMARK	RI	D
wc1956	3 Oct	Dublin	2	1
wc1957	2 Oct	Copenhagen	2	0
wc1968	4 Dec	Dublin	1	1
(abandoned after 51 mins)				
wc1969	27 May	Copenhagen	0	2
wc1969	15 Oct	Dublin	1	1
EC1978	24 May	Copenhagen	3	3
EC1979	2 May	Dublin	2	0
wc1984	14 Nov	Copenhagen	0	3
wc1985	13 Nov	Dublin	1	4
wc1992	14 Oct	Copenhagen	0	0
wc1993	28 Apr	Dublin	1	1
2002	27 Mar	Dublin	3	0
2007	22 Aug	Copenhagen	4	0

		v ECUADOR	RI	E
1972	19 June	Natal	3	2
2007	23 May	New Jersey	1	1

		v EGYPT	RI	E
wc1990	17 June	Palermo	0	0

		v ENGLAND	RI	E
1946	30 Sept	Dublin	0	1
1949	21 Sept	Everton	2	0
wc1957	8 May	Wembley	1	5
wc1957	19 May	Dublin	1	1
1964	24 May	Dublin	1	3
1976	8 Sept	Wembley	1	1
EC1978	25 Oct	Dublin	1	1
EC1980	6 Feb	Wembley	0	2
1985	26 Mar	Wembley	1	2
EC1988	12 June	Stuttgart	1	0
wc1990	11 June	Cagliari	1	1
EC1990	14 Nov	Dublin	1	1
EC1991	27 Mar	Wembley	1	1
1995	15 Feb	Dublin	1	0
(abandoned after 27 mins)				
2013	29 May	Wembley	1	1

		v ESTONIA	RI	E
wc2000	11 Oct	Dublin	2	0
wc2001	6 June	Tallinn	2	0
EC2011	11 Nov	Tallinn	4	0
EC2011	15 Nov	Dublin	1	1

		v FAROE ISLANDS	RI	F
EC2004	13 Oct	Dublin	2	0
EC2005	8 June	Toftir	2	0
wc2012	16 Oct	Torshavn	4	1
wc2013	7 June	Dublin	3	0

		v FINLAND	RI	F
wc1949	8 Sept	Dublin	3	0
wc1949	9 Oct	Helsinki	1	1
1990	16 May	Dublin	1	1
2000	15 Nov	Dublin	3	0
2002	21 Aug	Helsinki	3	0

		v FRANCE	RI	F
1937	23 May	Paris	2	0
1952	16 Nov	Dublin	1	1
wc1953	4 Oct	Dublin	3	5
wc1953	25 Nov	Paris	0	1
wc1972	15 Nov	Dublin	2	1
wc1973	19 May	Paris	1	1
wc1976	17 Nov	Paris	0	2
wc1977	30 Mar	Dublin	1	0
wc1980	28 Oct	Paris	0	2
wc1981	14 Oct	Dublin	3	2
1989	7 Feb	Dublin	0	0
wc2004	9 Oct	Paris	0	0
wc2005	7 Sept	Dublin	0	1
wc2009	14 Nov	Dublin	0	1
wc2009	18 Nov	Paris	1	1

		v GEORGIA	RI	G
EC2003	29 Mar	Tbilisi	2	1
EC2003	11 June	Dublin	2	0
wc2008	6 Sept	Mainz	2	1
wc2009	11 Feb	Dublin	2	1
2013	2 June	Dublin	3	0

		v GERMANY	RI	G
1935	8 May	Dortmund	1	3
1936	17 Oct	Dublin	5	2
1939	23 May	Bremen	1	1
1994	29 May	Hanover	2	0
wc2002	5 June	Ibaraki	1	1
EC2006	2 Sept	Stuttgart	0	1
EC2007	13 Oct	Dublin	0	0
wc2012	12 Oct	Dublin	1	6
wc2013	11 Oct	Cologne	0	3

		v WEST GERMANY	RI	WG
1951	17 Oct	Dublin	3	2
1952	4 May	Cologne	0	3
1955	28 May	Hamburg	1	2
1956	25 Nov	Dublin	3	0
1960	11 May	Dusseldorf	1	0
1966	4 May	Dublin	0	4
1970	9 May	Berlin	1	2
1975	1 Mar	Dublin	1	0†
1979	22 May	Dublin	1	3
1981	21 May	Bremen	0	3†
1989	6 Sept	Dublin	1	1

†*v West Germany 'B'*

		v GREECE	RI	G
2000	26 Apr	Dublin	0	1
2002	20 Nov	Athens	0	0
2012	14 Nov	Dublin	0	1

		v HUNGARY	RI	H
1934	15 Dec	Dublin	2	4
1936	3 May	Budapest	3	3
1936	6 Dec	Dublin	2	3
1939	19 Mar	Cork	2	2
1939	18 May	Budapest	2	2
wc1969	8 June	Dublin	1	2
wc1969	5 Nov	Budapest	0	4

			RI	H
wc1989	8 Mar	Budapest	0	0
wc1989	4 June	Dublin	2	0
1991	11 Sept	Gyor	2	1
2012	4 June	Budapest	0	0

		v ICELAND	RI	I
EC1962	12 Aug	Dublin	4	2
EC1962	2 Sept	Reykjavik	1	1
EC1982	13 Oct	Dublin	2	0
EC1983	21 Sept	Reykjavik	3	0
1986	25 May	Reykjavik	2	1
wc1996	10 Nov	Dublin	0	0
wc1997	6 Sept	Reykjavik	4	2

		v IRAN	RI	I
1972	18 June	Recife	2	1
wc2001	10 Nov	Dublin	2	0
wc2001	15 Nov	Tehran	0	1

		v N. IRELAND	RI	NI
EC1978	20 Sept	Dublin	0	0
EC1979	21 Nov	Belfast	0	1
wc1988	14 Sept	Belfast	0	0
wc1989	11 Oct	Dublin	3	0
wc1993	31 Mar	Dublin	3	0
wc1993	17 Nov	Belfast	1	1
EC1994	16 Nov	Belfast	4	0
EC1995	29 Mar	Dublin	1	1
1999	29 May	Dublin	0	1
NC2011	24 May	Dublin	5	0

		v ISRAEL	RI	I
1984	4 Apr	Tel Aviv	0	3
1985	27 May	Tel Aviv	0	0
1987	10 Nov	Dublin	5	0
EC2005	26 Mar	Tel Aviv	1	1
EC2005	4 June	Dublin	2	2

		v ITALY	RI	I
1926	21 Mar	Turin	0	3
1927	23 Apr	Dublin	1	2
EC1970	8 Dec	Rome	0	3
EC1971	10 May	Dublin	1	2
1985	5 Feb	Dublin	1	2
wc1990	30 June	Rome	0	1
1992	4 June	Foxboro	0	2
wc1994	18 June	New York	1	0
2005	17 Aug	Dublin	1	2
wc2009	1 Apr	Bari	1	1
wc2009	10 Oct	Dublin	2	2
2011	7 June	Liege	2	0
EC2012	18 June	Poznan	0	2
2014	31 May	Craven Cottage	0	0

		v JAMAICA	RI	J
2004	2 June	Charlton	1	0

		v KAZAKHSTAN	RI	K
wc2012	7 Sept	Astana	2	1
wc2013	15 Oct	Dublin	3	1

		v LATVIA	RI	L
wc1992	9 Sept	Dublin	4	0
wc1993	2 June	Riga	2	1
EC1994	7 Sept	Riga	3	0
EC1995	11 Oct	Dublin	2	1
2013	15 Nov	Dublin	3	0

		v LIECHTENSTEIN	RI	L
EC1994	12 Oct	Dublin	4	0
EC1995	3 June	Eschen	0	0
wc1996	31 Aug	Eschen	5	0
wc1997	21 May	Dublin	5	0

		v LITHUANIA	RI	L
wc1993	16 June	Vilnius	1	0
wc1993	8 Sept	Dublin	2	0
wc1997	20 Aug	Dublin	0	0
wc1997	10 Sept	Vilnius	2	1

v LUXEMBOURG			RI	L
1936	9 May	Luxembourg	5	1
wc1953	28 Oct	Dublin	4	0
wc1954	7 Mar	Luxembourg	1	0
EC1987	28 May	Luxembourg	2	0
EC1987	9 Sept	Dublin	2	1

v MACEDONIA			RI	M
wc1996	9 Oct	Dublin	3	0
wc1997	2 Apr	Skopje	2	3
EC1999	9 June	Dublin	1	0
EC1999	9 Oct	Skopje	1	1
EC2011	26 Mar	Dublin	2	1
EC2011	4 June	Podgorica	2	0

v MALTA			RI	M
EC1983	30 Mar	Valletta	1	0
EC1983	16 Nov	Dublin	8	0
wc1989	28 May	Dublin	2	0
wc1989	15 Nov	Valletta	2	0
1990	2 June	Valletta	3	0
EC1998	14 Oct	Dublin	5	0
EC1999	8 Sept	Valletta	3	2

v MEXICO			RI	M
1984	8 Aug	Dublin	0	0
wc1994	24 June	Orlando	1	2
1996	13 June	New Jersey	2	2
1998	23 May	Dublin	0	0
2000	4 June	Chicago	2	2

v MONTENEGRO			RI	M
wc2008	10 Sept	Podgorica	0	0
wc2009	14 Oct	Dublin	0	0

v MOROCCO			RI	M
1990	12 Sept	Dublin	1	0

v NETHERLANDS			RI	N
1932	8 May	Amsterdam	2	0
1934	8 Apr	Amsterdam	2	5
1935	8 Dec	Dublin	3	5
1955	1 May	Dublin	1	0
1956	10 May	Rotterdam	4	1
wc1980	10 Sept	Dublin	2	1
wc1981	9 Sept	Rotterdam	2	2
EC1982	22 Sept	Rotterdam	1	2
EC1983	12 Oct	Dublin	2	3
EC1988	18 June	Gelsenkirchen	0	1
wc1990	21 June	Palermo	1	1
1994	20 Apr	Tilburg	1	0
wc1994	4 July	Orlando	0	2
EC1995	13 Dec	Liverpool	0	2
1996	4 June	Rotterdam	1	3
wc2000	2 Sept	Amsterdam	2	2
wc2001	1 Sept	Dublin	1	0
2004	5 June	Amsterdam	1	0
2006	16 Aug	Dublin	0	4

v NIGERIA			RI	N
2002	16 May	Dublin	1	2
2004	29 May	Charlton	0	3
2009	29 May	Fulham	1	1

v NORWAY			RI	N
wc1937	10 Oct	Oslo	2	3
wc1937	7 Nov	Dublin	3	3
1950	26 Nov	Dublin	2	2
1951	30 May	Oslo	3	2
1954	8 Nov	Dublin	2	1
1955	25 May	Oslo	3	1
1960	6 Nov	Dublin	3	1
1964	13 May	Oslo	4	1
1973	6 June	Oslo	1	1
1976	24 Mar	Dublin	3	0
1978	21 May	Oslo	0	0
wc1984	17 Oct	Oslo	0	1
wc1985	1 May	Dublin	0	0
1988	1 June	Oslo	0	0

			RI	N
wc1994	28 June	New York	0	0
2003	30 Apr	Dublin	1	0
2008	20 Aug	Oslo	1	1
2010	17 Nov	Dublin	1	2

v OMAN			RI	O
2012	11 Sept	London	4	1

v PARAGUAY			RI	P
1999	10 Feb	Dublin	2	0
2010	25 May	Dublin	2	1

v POLAND			RI	P
1938	22 May	Warsaw	0	6
1938	13 Nov	Dublin	3	2
1958	11 May	Katowice	2	2
1958	5 Oct	Dublin	2	2
1964	10 May	Kracow	1	3
1964	25 Oct	Dublin	3	2
1968	15 May	Dublin	2	2
1968	30 Oct	Katowice	0	1
1970	6 May	Dublin	1	2
1970	23 Sept	Dublin	0	2
1973	16 May	Wroclaw	0	2
1973	21 Oct	Dublin	1	0
1976	26 May	Poznan	2	0
1977	24 Apr	Dublin	0	0
1978	12 Apr	Lodz	0	3
1981	23 May	Bydgoszcz	0	3
1984	23 May	Dublin	0	0
1986	12 Nov	Warsaw	0	1
1988	22 May	Dublin	3	1
EC1991	1 May	Dublin	0	0
EC1991	16 Oct	Poznan	3	3
2004	28 Apr	Bydgoszcz	0	0
2013	19 Nov	Poznan	0	0
2008	19 Nov	Dublin	2	3
2013	6 Feb	Dublin	2	0
2013	19 Nov	Poznan	0	0

v PORTUGAL			RI	P
1946	16 June	Lisbon	1	3
1947	4 May	Dublin	0	2
1948	23 May	Lisbon	0	2
1949	22 May	Dublin	1	0
1972	25 June	Recife	1	2
1992	7 June	Boston	2	0
EC1995	26 Apr	Dublin	1	0
EC1995	15 Nov	Lisbon	0	3
1996	29 May	Dublin	0	1
wc2000	7 Oct	Lisbon	1	1
wc2001	2 June	Dublin	1	1
2005	9 Feb	Dublin	1	0
2014	10 June	New Jersey	1	5

v ROMANIA			RI	R
1988	23 Mar	Dublin	2	0
wc1990	25 June	Genoa	0	0*
wc1997	30 Apr	Bucharest	0	1
wc1997	11 Oct	Dublin	1	1
2004	27 May	Dublin	1	0

v RUSSIA			RI	R
1994	23 Mar	Dublin	0	0
1996	27 Mar	Dublin	0	2
2002	13 Feb	Dublin	2	0
EC2002	7 Sept	Moscow	2	4
EC2003	6 Sept	Dublin	1	1
EC2010	8 Oct	Dublin	2	3
EC2011	6 Sept	Moscow	0	0

v SAN MARINO			RI	SM
EC2006	15 Nov	Dublin	5	0
EC2007	7 Feb	Serravalle	2	1

v SAUDI ARABIA			RI	SA
wc2002	11 June	Yokohama	3	0

v SERBIA

			RI	S
2008	24 May	Dublin	1	1
2012	15 Aug	Belgrade	0	0
2014	5 Mar	Dublin	1	2

v SCOTLAND

			RI	S
wc1961	3 May	Glasgow	1	4
wc1961	7 May	Dublin	0	3
1963	9 June	Dublin	1	0
1969	21 Sept	Dublin	1	1
EC1986	15 Oct	Dublin	0	0
EC1987	18 Feb	Glasgow	1	0
2000	30 May	Dublin	1	2
2003	12 Feb	Glasgow	2	0
NC2011	29 May	Dublin	1	0

v SLOVAKIA

			RI	S
EC2007	28 Mar	Dublin	1	0
EC2007	8 Sept	Bratislava	2	2
EC2010	12 Oct	Zilina	1	1
EC2011	2 Sept	Dublin	0	0

v SOUTH AFRICA

			RI	SA
2000	11 June	New Jersey	2	1
2009	8 Sept	Limerick	1	0

v SPAIN

			RI	S
1931	26 Apr	Barcelona	1	1
1931	13 Dec	Dublin	0	5
1946	23 June	Madrid	1	0
1947	2 Mar	Dublin	3	2
1948	30 May	Barcelona	1	2
1949	12 June	Dublin	1	4
1952	1 June	Madrid	0	6
1955	27 Nov	Dublin	2	2
EC1964	11 Mar	Seville	1	5
EC1964	8 Apr	Dublin	0	2
wc1965	5 May	Dublin	1	0
wc1965	27 Oct	Seville	1	4
wc1965	10 Nov	Paris	0	1

v SPAIN

			RI	S
EC1966	23 Oct	Dublin	0	0
EC1966	7 Dec	Valencia	0	2
1977	9 Feb	Dublin	0	1
EC1982	17 Nov	Dublin	3	3
EC1983	27 Apr	Zaragoza	0	2
1985	26 May	Cork	0	0
wc1988	16 Nov	Seville	0	2
wc1989	26 Apr	Dublin	1	0
wc1992	18 Nov	Seville	0	0
wc1993	13 Oct	Dublin	1	3
wc2002	16 June	Suwon	1	1
EC2012	14 June	Gdansk	0	4
2013	11 June	New York	0	2

v SWEDEN

			RI	S
wc1949	2 June	Stockholm	1	3
wc1949	13 Nov	Dublin	1	3
1959	1 Nov	Dublin	3	2
1960	18 May	Malmo	1	4
EC1970	14 Oct	Dublin	1	1
EC1970	28 Oct	Malmo	0	1
1999	28 Apr	Dublin	2	0
2006	1 Mar	Dublin	3	0
wc2013	22 Mar	Stockholm	0	0
wc2013	6 Sept	Dublin	1	2

v SWITZERLAND

			RI	S
1935	5 May	Basle	0	1
1936	17 Mar	Dublin	1	0
1937	17 May	Berne	1	0
1938	18 Sept	Dublin	4	0
1948	5 Dec	Dublin	0	1
EC1975	11 May	Dublin	2	1
EC1975	21 May	Berne	0	1
1980	30 Apr	Dublin	2	0
wc1985	2 June	Dublin	3	0
wc1985	11 Sept	Berne	0	0
1992	25 Mar	Dublin	2	1
EC2002	16 Oct	Dublin	1	2
EC2003	11 Oct	Basle	0	2
wc2004	8 Sept	Basle	1	1
wc2005	12 Oct	Dublin	0	0

v TRINIDAD & TOBAGO

			RI	TT
1982	30 May	Port of Spain	1	2

v TUNISIA

			RI	T
1988	19 Oct	Dublin	4	0

v TURKEY

			RI	T
EC1966	16 Nov	Dublin	2	1
EC1967	22 Feb	Ankara	1	2
EC1974	20 Nov	Izmir	1	1
EC1975	29 Oct	Dublin	4	0
2014	25 May	Dublin	1	2
1976	13 Oct	Ankara	3	3
1978	5 Apr	Dublin	4	2
1990	26 May	Izmir	0	0
EC1990	17 Oct	Dublin	5	0
EC1991	13 Nov	Istanbul	3	1
EC2000	13 Nov	Dublin	1	1
EC2000	17 Nov	Bursa	0	0
2003	9 Sept	Dublin	2	2
2014	25 May	Dublin	1	2

v URUGUAY

			RI	U
1974	8 May	Montevideo	0	2
1986	23 Apr	Dublin	1	1
2011	29 Mar	Dublin	2	3

v USA

			RI	USA
1979	29 Oct	Dublin	3	2
1991	1 June	Boston	1	1
1992	29 Apr	Dublin	4	1
1992	30 May	Washington	1	3
1996	9 June	Boston	1	2
2000	6 June	Boston	1	1
2002	17 Apr	Dublin	2	1

v USSR

			RI	USSR
wc1972	18 Oct	Dublin	1	2
wc1973	13 May	Moscow	0	1
EC1974	30 Oct	Dublin	3	0
EC1975	18 May	Kiev	1	2
wc1984	12 Sept	Dublin	1	0
wc1985	16 Oct	Moscow	0	2
EC1988	15 June	Hanover	1	1
1990	25 Apr	Dublin	1	0

v WALES

			RI	W
1960	28 Sept	Dublin	2	3
1979	11 Sept	Swansea	1	2
1981	24 Feb	Dublin	1	3
1986	26 Mar	Dublin	0	1
1990	28 Mar	Dublin	1	0
1991	6 Feb	Wrexham	3	0
1992	19 Feb	Dublin	0	1
1993	17 Feb	Dublin	2	1
1997	11 Feb	Cardiff	0	0
EC2007	24 Mar	Dublin	1	0
EC2007	17 Nov	Cardiff	2	2
NC2011	8 Feb	Dublin	3	0
2013	14 Aug	Cardiff	0	0

v YUGOSLAVIA

			RI	Y
1955	19 Sept	Dublin	1	4
1988	27 Apr	Dublin	2	0
EC1998	18 Nov	Belgrade	0	1
EC1999	1 Sept	Dublin	2	1

OTHER BRITISH AND IRISH
INTERNATIONAL MATCHES 2013–14

FRIENDLIES

∎ *Denotes player sent off.*

ENGLAND

Wednesday, 14 August 2013
England (1) 3 *(Walcott 29, Welbeck 53, Lambert 70)*
Scotland (1) 2 *(Morrison 11, Miller 49)*   80,485
England: (433) Hart; Walker, Cahill, Jagielka (Jones 84), Baines; Cleverley (Milner 67), Gerrard (Oxlade-Chamberlain 62), Wilshere (Lampard 46); Walcott (Zaha 75), Rooney (Lambert 67), Welbeck.
Scotland: (4411) McGregor; Hutton, Martin R, Hanley, Whittaker; Snodgrass (Conway 66), Morrison (Rhodes 82), Brown, Forrest (Mulgrew 67); Maloney (Naismith 86); Miller (Griffiths 73).

Friday, 15 November 2013
England (0) 0
Chile (1) 2 *(Alexis 7, 90)*   62,963
England: (442) Forster; Johnson, Jones (Smalling 57), Cahill, Baines; Milner (Defoe 65), Wilshere (Cleverley 71), Lampard (Henderson 71), Lallana (Barkley 77); Rooney, Rodriguez (Townsend 57).
Chile: (442) Bravo; Mena, Gonzalez Marcos, Isla (Jara 59), Fernandez M (Carmona 46); Beausejour (Fuenzalida 82), Medel, Aranguiz (Gutierrez 46), Diaz; Alexis, Vargas (Munoz 71).

Tuesday, 19 November 2013
England (0) 0
Germany (1) 1 *(Mertesacker 39)*   85,934
England: (442) Hart; Walker, Smalling, Jagielka, Cole (Gibbs 52); Townsend, Gerrard (Henderson 56), Cleverley (Wilshere 64), Lallana (Lambert 76); Sturridge, Rooney (Barkley 71).
Germany: (451) Weidenfeller; Schmelzer (Jansen 46), Westermann (Draxler 66), Mertesacker, Boateng (Hummels 46 (Howedes 66)); Bender S, Kruse (Sam 56), Bender L, Kroos, Reus (Schurrle 82); Gotze.

Wednesday, 5 March 2014
England (0) 1 *(Sturridge 82)*
Denmark (0) 0   68,573
England: (433) Hart; Johnson, Cahill, Smalling, Cole (Shaw 46); Wilshere (Lallana 59), Henderson (Oxlade-Chamberlain 77), Gerrard; Sterling (Townsend 86), Rooney (Welbeck 60), Sturridge (Milner 88).
Denmark: (4411) Schmeichel; Sloth (Zimling 62), Agger, Kjaer (Bjelland 62), Ankersen; Kvist Jorgensen, Jacobsen (Juelsgaard 46); Poulsen J (Olsen 81), Krohn-Delhi; Larsen (Kusk 46); Bendtner (Rasmussen 62).

Friday, 30 May 2014
England (1) 3 *(Sturridge 32, Cahill 65, Jagielka 70)*
Peru (0) 0   83,578
England: (4231) Hart; Johnson, Cahill, Jagielka (Smalling 73), Baines (Stones 75); Gerrard (Wilshere 64), Henderson; Lallana (Milner 73), Rooney (Sterling 66), Welbeck; Sturridge (Barkley 82).
Peru: (532) Fernandez; Rodriguez, Callens, Ramos (Riojas 68), Advincula (Velarde 78), Yotun; Cruzado, Ballon, Ramirez (Hurtado 60); Deza (Ruidiaz 66), Carrillo (Flores 86).

Wednesday, 4 June 2014
England (1) 2 *(Rooney 29, Lambert 51)*
Ecuador (1) 2 *(Valencia E 8, Arroyo 70)*   ·18,327
England: (4231) Foster; Milner, Smalling, Jones, Shaw (Stones 74); Wilshere (Lallana 87), Lampard; Oxlade-Chamberlain (Flanagan 63), Barkley (Henderson 83), Rooney (Sterling∎ 65); Lambert (Welbeck 83).
Ecuador: (442) Banguera; Paredes J (Achilier 90), Guagua, Erazo, Ayovi; Valencia A∎, Noboa (Mendez 50), Montero (Arroyo 68), Valencia E (Ibarra 83); Gruezo (Saritama 89), Caicedo (Rojas 46).

Saturday, 7 June 2014
England (0) 0
Honduras (0) 0   18,000
England: (433) Hart (Forster 75); Johnson, Cahill, Jagielka, Baines; Gerrard (Wilshere 47), Henderson (Lampard 83), Lallana; Sturridge, Rooney (Barkley 47), Welbeck (Lambert 79).
Honduras: (442) Valladares; Beckeles∎, Figueroa, Bernardez, Izaguirre (Martinez 90); Espinoza (Garcia J 87), Palacios W, Garrido (Claros 46), Chavez M (Najar 60); Costly (Delgado 68), Bengtson (Palacios J 74).

SCOTLAND

Friday, 15 November 2013
Scotland (0) 0
USA (0) 0   30,000
Scotland: (442) Marshall; Hutton, Whittaker (Wallace 69), Hanley, Greer; Bannan (Naismith 81), Mulgrew, Brown, Fletcher S; Snodgrass (McCormack 69), Conway (Mackay-Steven 84).
USA: (4231) Howard; Evans (Lichaj 72), Gonzalez, Cameron, Beasley; Bradley, Jones (Diskerud 63); Bedoya (Wondolowski 81), Kljestan (Johannsson 63), Johnson (Shea 62); Altidore (Boyd 90).

Tuesday, 19 November 2013
Norway (0) 0
Scotland (0) 1 *(Brown 61)*   20,000
Norway: (442) Nyland; Hogli, Reginiussen (Strandberg 65), Elabdellaoui (Linnes 60), Forren; Pedersen Morten Gamst, Eikrem (Konradsen 80), Skjelbred (Daehli 61), Jenssen; Pedersen Marcus (Elyounoussi 86), Kamara (Abdellaoue 46).
Scotland: (451) Marshall; Hutton, Martin R, Greer, Whittaker; Anya (Conway 51), Adam (McArthur 64), Brown, Bryson (Bannan 46), Snodgrass; Naismith (Berra 90).

Wednesday, 5 March 2014
Poland (0) 0
Scotland (0) 1 *(Brown 77)*   41,000
Poland: (451) Szczesny; Piszczek, Szukala, Glik, Brzyski (Kowalcyzk 90); Sobota (Maslowski 88), Klich (Teodorczyk 82), Krychowiak (Jodlowiec 88), Peszko (Polanski 74), Obraniak (Robak 74); Milik.
Scotland: (442) Marshall; Hutton (Bardsley 67), Mulgrew, Martin R, Greer; Bannan (Robertson 67), Morrison (Fletcher D 46), Brown, Anya (Burke 90); Fletcher S (Naismith 46), McCormack (Adam 77).

Wednesday, 28 May 2014
Scotland (1) 2 *(Mulgrew 10, Egwuekwe 54 (og))*
Nigeria (1) 2 *(Uchebo 41, Nwofor 90)*   24,000
Scotland: (442) McGregor; Hutton, Greer, Hanley, Robertson (Forsyth 76); Brown, Morrison (Boyd 63), Mulgrew, Anya (Whittaker 84); Maloney, Naismith (Martin C 46).
Nigeria: (442) Ejide; Yobo, Echiejile, Egwuekwe, Odunlami (Ambrose 75); Obi (Igiebor 54), Uzoenyi (Moses 62), Gabriel, Babatunde (Oduamadi 66); Ameobi (Nwofor 61), Uchebo (Odemwingie 54).

WALES

Wednesday, 14 August 2013
Wales (0) 0
Republic of Ireland (0) 0   20,000
Wales: (433) Myhill; Gunter, Williams A, Ricketts, Davies B; Ledley (King 60), Allen (Crofts 86), Bellamy (Vokes 59); Collison (Davies C 82), Williams J, Robson-Kanu (Taylor 74).
Republic of Ireland: (442) Westwood; Coleman, Clark, O'Shea (O'Dea 60), Wilson; Walters (Sammon 84), McCarthy, Whelan (Green 60), Brady (McClean 46); Hoolahan (Madden 69), Long (Keogh A 74).

Saturday, 16 November 2013
Wales (0) 1 *(King 58)*
Finland (0) 1 *(Riski 90)*   11,809
Wales: (4231) Hennessey; Gunter (Richards 72), Ricketts, Williams A, Taylor (Davies B 72); Ledley, Allen (Tudur Jones 90); Robson-Kanu (Cotterill 84), King, Bale; Church (Vokes 63).
Finland: (442) Hradecky; Uronen, Moisander (Pasanen 63), Ojala J (Toivio 46), Arkivuo (Lampi 46 (Raitala 70)); Eremenko, Riski, Sparv, Schuller (Hetemaj 70); Ring, Pukki (Hamalainen 63).

Wednesday, 5 March 2014
Wales (1) 3 *(Collins 12, Vokes 64, Bale 70)*
Iceland (1) 1 *(Williams A (og) 26)*   13,219
Wales: (451) Hennessey; Gunter, Collins (Gabbidon 46), Williams A (Ricketts 65), Taylor; Huws, Allen, Robson-Kanu (Davies B 87), King (Collison 76), Bale (Williams J 72); Vokes.
Iceland: (442) Halldorsson; Skulason A (Jonsson 84), Bjarnason T, Sigurdsson R (Bjarnason B 46), Arnason; Gudmundsson, Sigurdsson G, Gunnarsson, Hallfredsson; Sigthorsson (Sverrisson 76), Finnbogason (Ottesen 46).

Wednesday, 4 June 2014
Netherlands (1) 2 *(Robben 32, Lens 76)*
Wales (0) 0   50,000
Netherlands: (433) Cillessen; Vlaar, De Vrij, Martins Indi, Blind; Janmaat, De Jong (Huntelaar 78), Sneijder; Fer (Wijnaldum 46), van Persie (Lens 46), Robben.
Wales: (451) Hennessey; Gunter, Taylor (Dummett 83), Gabbidon, Chester; Ledley (Huws 62), Allen, Robson-Kanu (John 60), King (Vaughan 77), Williams J (Williams G 70); Church (Easter 67).

NORTHERN IRELAND
Friday, 15 November 2013
Turkey (1) 1 *(Erdinc 45)*
Northern Ireland (0) 0   14,000
Turkey: (442) Zengin; Gonul (Camdal 72), Kaya, Gulum, Erkin; Topal, Ozyakup (Yilmaz 46), Turan (Dogan 89), Kisa (Sahan 83); Buyuk (Ucan 67), Erdinc (Tore 77).
Northern Ireland: (442) Carroll (Mannus 46); Baird, Hughes, Evans J, Hodson; Norwood, Clingan (McKay 75), McGinn (Steele 67), Davis; Lafferty D (McGivern 76), Paterson.

Wednesday, 5 March 2014
Cyprus (0) 0
Northern Ireland (0) 0   400
Cyprus: (433) Georgallides; Charis Kyriakou, Junior, Merkis, Antoniades; Nicolaou (Artymatas 58), Laban (Charalambos Kyriakou 66), Makridis (Charalambidis 63); Christofi (Makris 85), Aloneftis (Efrem 50), Mitidis (Papathanasiou 77).
Northern Ireland: (442) Mannus (Carroll 46); Cathcart, McGivern, McAuley■, Bruce; Davis, Norwood (McCourt 73), McGinn (Ferguson 73), Brunt; Ward (McKay 62 (McArdle 79)), Paterson (Lafferty K 46).

Saturday, 31 May 2014
Uruguay (0) 1 *(Stuani 62)*
Northern Ireland (0) 0   55,000
Uruguay: (442) Muslera; Pereira M, Lugano, Coates (Gimenez 46), Caceres (Pereira A 72); Ramirez (Lodeiro 65), Gargano (Perez 74), Arevalo Rios, Rodriguez C; Cavani (Hernandez 65), Forlan (Stuani 46).
Northern Ireland: (442) Carroll; Baird, McCullough, Hughes, Evans C (McLaughlin R 87); Clingan (Paton 74), Ferguson (Lafferty D 80), Davis, McGinn (Magennis 61); Norwood (Steele 85), McKay (McLaughlin C 81).

Thursday, 5 June 2014
Chile (0) 2 *(Vargas 79, Pinilla 82)*
Northern Ireland (0) 0   20,000
Chile: (343) Herrera; Medel (Pinilla 77), Silva, Rojas; Isla, Diaz (Gutierrez 85), Carmona (Aranguiz 59), Mena; Valdivia (Vidal 77), Orellana (Alexis 59), Paredes E (Vargas 61).
Northern Ireland: (352) Carroll; McLaughlin R, McLaughlin C (McGinn 70), Hughes; Norwood (Steele 88), Evans C (Donnelly 89), Davis, Clingan, Ferguson (Lafferty D 77); McKay (Magennis 63), McCullough.

REPUBLIC OF IRELAND
Friday, 15 November 2013
Republic of Ireland (1) 3 *(Keane 22, McGeady 67, Long 79)*
Latvia (0) 0   42,000
Republic of Ireland: (442) Westwood; Coleman, O'Shea, Wilson, Ward; McGeady (Reid 72), Whelan, McCarthy (Doyle 80), McClean (Stokes 80); Hoolahan (Long 73), Keane (Walters 72).
Latvia: (442) Vanins; Gabovs, Bulvitis, Gorkss, Maksimenko; Rode, Rugins (Fertovs 27), Laizans (Sinelnikovs 72), Lazdins; Sabala (Turkovs 62), Verpakovskis (Visnakovs 46).

Tuesday, 19 November 2013
Poland (0) 0
Republic of Ireland (0) 0   3500
Poland: (442) Szczesny; Celeban, Szukala, Kowalcyzk, Marciniak; Cwielong (Olkowski 81), Pazdan, Maczynski (Jodlowiec 60), Sobota (Brzyski 81); Blaszczykowski (Robak 89), Lewandowski R (Teodorczyk 57).
Republic of Ireland: (442) Forde; Kelly, St. Ledger (O'Shea 32), Wilson (Whelan 76), Ward; Walters, McCarthy (McClean 64), Green, McGeady (Pearce 65); Stokes (Doyle 68), Long (Hoolahan 73).

Wednesday, 5 March 2014
Republic of Ireland (1) 1 *(Long 8)*
Serbia (0) 2 *(McCarthy 48 (og), Djordjevic 60)*   30,000
Republic of Ireland: (442) Forde; Coleman, Keogh R, Wilson, Ward (Clark 63); McGeady (Murphy 72), McCarthy (Meyler 63), Whelan (Quinn 80), Hoolahan (Pilkington 64); McClean, Long (Walters 72).
Serbia: (442) Stojkovic; Rukavina (Gudelj 89), Kolarov, Ivanovic, Bisevac; Matic, Fejsa, Basta (Tosic 59), Tadic (Ljajic 80); Markovic (Sulejmani 75), Djordjevic (Scepovic 86).

Sunday, 25 May 2014
Republic of Ireland (0) 1 *(Walters 78)*
Turkey (1) 2 *(Ozek 17, Camdal 75)*   15,000
Republic of Ireland: (4231) Elliot; Coleman, O'Shea, Delaney (Meyler 65), Ward; Whelan (Quinn 82), Wilson; McGeady (Walters 66), Hoolahan, McClean; Long (Murphy 66).
Turkey: (442) Kivrak; Gonul, Toprak, Balta, Erkin; Ozek (Camdal 70), Calhanoglu (Adin 63), Inan (Ozyakup 21), Sahin (Dogan 84); Kisa (Tufan 46), Erdinc (Pektemek 81).

Saturday, 31 May 2014
Italy (0) 0
Republic of Ireland (0) 0   22,879
Italy: (442) Sirigu; De Sciglio, Bonucci, Paletta, Darmian (Abate 88); Thiago Motta (De Rossi 62), Marchisio, Montolivo (Aquilani 15 (Parolo 37)), Verratti; Immobile (Cassano 56), Rossi (Cerci 71).
Republic of Ireland: (451) Forde; Coleman, O'Shea, Pearce, Ward; McGeady, Meyler (Green 85), Pilkington (McClean 58), Hoolahan (Quinn 67), Hendrick; Long (Cox 73).

Saturday, 7 June 2014
Costa Rica (0) 1 *(Borges 63)*
Republic of Ireland (1) 1 *(Doyle 17)*   7000
Costa Rica: (433) Navas (Pemberton 46); Diaz, Borges, Duarte, Gonzalez■; Umana, Mora, Cubero; Ruiz (Bolanos 74), Campbell (Calvo 86), Urena (Brenes 78).
Republic of Ireland: (442) Forde; Kelly, Keogh R, Duffy, Wilson (McClean 40); Green, Whelan, Pilkington (McGeady 65), Quinn (Cox 83); Keane (Hoolahan 83), Doyle (Long 65).

Wednesday, 11 June 2014
Republic of Ireland (0) 1 *(McClean 52)*
Portugal (3) 5 *(Almeida 2, 37, Keogh R 20 (og), Vieirinha 77, Fabio Coentrao 83)*   40,000
Republic of Ireland: (4231) Forde; Kelly (Cox 75), Keogh R, Ward (Quinn 67), Pearce; McGeady (Doyle 76), Hendrick; Meyler, Hoolahan (Keane 64), McClean (Pilkington 67); Walters (Long 63).
Portugal: (433) Rui Patricio; Ruben Amorim (Veloso 81), Ricardo Costa, Luis Neto (Pepe 65), Fabio Coentrao; William Carvalho, Meireles (Andre Almeida 66), Joao Moutinho; Varela (Vieirinha 73), Almeida (Postiga 66), Ronaldo (Nani 65).

BRITISH AND IRISH INTERNATIONAL APPEARANCES 1872–2014

This is a list of full international appearances by Englishmen, Irishmen, Scotsmen and Welshmen in matches against the Home Countries and against foreign nations. It does not include unofficial matches against Commonwealth and Empire countries. The year indicated refers to the player's international debut season; i.e. 2014 is the 2013–14 season. **Bold** type indicates players who have made an international appearance in season 2013–14.

As at July 2014.

ENGLAND

Abbott, W. 1902 (Everton)	1
A'Court, A. 1958 (Liverpool)	5
Adams, T. A. 1987 (Arsenal)	66
Adcock, H. 1929 (Leicester C)	5
Agbonlahor, G. 2009 (Aston Villa)	3
Alcock, C. W. 1875 (Wanderers)	1
Alderson, J. T. 1923 (Crystal Palace)	1
Aldridge, A. 1888 (WBA, Walsall Town Swifts)	2
Allen, A. 1888 (Aston Villa)	1
Allen, A. 1960 (Stoke C)	3
Allen, C. 1984 (QPR, Tottenham H)	5
Allen, H. 1888 (Wolverhampton W)	5
Allen, J. P. 1934 (Portsmouth)	2
Allen, R. 1952 (WBA)	5
Alsford, W. J. 1935 (Tottenham H)	1
Amos, A. 1885 (Old Carthusians)	2
Anderson, R. D. 1879 (Old Etonians)	1
Anderson, S. 1962 (Sunderland)	2
Anderson, V. A. 1979 (Nottingham F, Arsenal, Manchester U)	30
Anderton, D. R. 1994 (Tottenham H)	30
Angus, J. 1961 (Burnley)	1
Armfield, J. C. 1959 (Blackpool)	43
Armitage, G. H. 1926 (Charlton Ath)	1
Armstrong, D. 1980 (Middlesbrough, Southampton)	3
Armstrong, K. 1955 (Chelsea)	1
Arnold, J. 1933 (Fulham)	1
Arthur, J. W. H. 1885 (Blackburn R)	7
Ashcroft, J. 1906 (Woolwich Arsenal)	3
Ashmore, G. S. 1926 (WBA)	1
Ashton, C. T. 1926 (Corinthians)	1
Ashton, D. 2008 (West Ham U)	1
Ashurst, W. 1923 (Notts Co)	5
Astall, G. 1956 (Birmingham C)	2
Astle, J. 1969 (WBA)	5
Aston, J. 1949 (Manchester U)	17
Athersmith, W. C. 1892 (Aston Villa)	12
Atyeo, P. J. W. 1956 (Bristol C)	6
Austin, S. W. 1926 (Manchester C)	1
Bach, P. 1899 (Sunderland)	1
Bache, J. W. 1903 (Aston Villa)	7
Baddeley, T. 1903 (Wolverhampton W)	5
Bagshaw, J. J. 1920 (Derby Co)	1
Bailey, G. R. 1985 (Manchester U)	2
Bailey, H. P. 1908 (Leicester Fosse)	5
Bailey, M. A. 1964 (Charlton Ath)	2
Bailey, N. C. 1878 (Clapham R)	19
Baily, E. F. 1950 (Tottenham H)	9
Bain, J. 1877 (Oxford University)	1
Baines, L. J. 2010 (Everton)	**26**
Baker, A. 1928 (Arsenal)	1
Baker, B. H. 1921 (Everton, Chelsea)	2
Baker, J. H. 1960 (Hibernian, Arsenal)	8
Ball, A. J. 1965 (Blackpool, Everton, Arsenal)	72
Ball, J. 1928 (Bury)	1
Ball, M. J. 2001 (Everton)	1
Balmer, W. 1905 (Everton)	1
Bamber, J. 1921 (Liverpool)	1
Bambridge, A. L. 1881 (Swifts)	3
Bambridge, E. C. 1879 (Swifts)	18
Bambridge, E. H. 1876 (Swifts)	1
Banks, G. 1963 (Leicester C, Stoke C)	73
Banks, H. E. 1901 (Millwall)	1
Banks, T. 1958 (Bolton W)	6
Bannister, W. 1901 (Burnley, Bolton W)	2
Barclay, R. 1932 (Sheffield U)	3
Bardsley, D. J. 1993 (QPR)	2
Barham, M. 1983 (Norwich C)	2

Barkas, S. 1936 (Manchester C)	5
Barker, J. 1935 (Derby Co)	11
Barker, R. 1872 (Herts Rangers)	1
Barker, R. R. 1895 (Casuals)	1
Barkley, R. 2013 (Everton)	**9**
Barlow, R. J. 1955 (WBA)	1
Barmby, N. J. 1995 (Tottenham H, Middlesbrough, Everton, Liverpool)	23
Barnes, J. 1983 (Watford, Liverpool)	79
Barnes, P. S. 1978 (Manchester C, WBA, Leeds U)	22
Barnet, H. H. 1882 (Royal Engineers)	1
Barrass, M. W. 1952 (Bolton W)	3
Barrett, A. F. 1930 (Fulham)	1
Barrett, E. D. 1991 (Oldham Ath, Aston Villa)	3
Barrett, J. W. 1929 (West Ham U)	1
Barry, G. 2000 (Aston Villa, Manchester C)	53
Barry, L. 1928 (Leicester C)	5
Barson, F. 1920 (Aston Villa)	1
Barton, J. 1890 (Blackburn R)	1
Barton, J. 2007 (Manchester C)	1
Barton, P. H. 1921 (Birmingham)	7
Barton, W. D. 1995 (Wimbledon, Newcastle U)	3
Bassett, W. I. 1888 (WBA)	16
Bastard, S. R. 1880 (Upton Park)	1
Bastin, C. S. 1932 (Arsenal)	21
Batty, D. 1991 (Leeds U, Blackburn R, Newcastle U, Leeds U)	42
Baugh, R. 1886 (Stafford Road, Wolverhampton W)	2
Bayliss, A. E. J. M. 1891 (WBA)	1
Baynham, R. L. 1956 (Luton T)	3
Beardsley, P. A. 1986 (Newcastle U, Liverpool, Newcastle U)	59
Beasant, D. J. 1990 (Chelsea)	2
Beasley, A. 1939 (Huddersfield T)	1
Beats, W. E. 1901 (Wolverhampton W)	2
Beattie, J. S. 2003 (Southampton)	5
Beattie, T. K. 1975 (Ipswich T)	9
Beckham, D. R. J. 1997 (Manchester U, Real Madrid, LA Galaxy)	115
Becton, F. 1895 (Preston NE, Liverpool)	2
Bedford, H. 1923 (Blackpool)	2
Bell, C. 1968 (Manchester C)	48
Bennett, W. 1901 (Sheffield U)	2
Benson, R. W. 1913 (Sheffield U)	1
Bent, D. A. 2006 (Charlton Ath, Tottenham H, Sunderland, Aston Villa)	13
Bentley, D. M. 2008 (Blackburn R, Tottenham H)	7
Bentley, R. T. F. 1949 (Chelsea)	12
Beresford, J. 1934 (Aston Villa)	1
Berry, A. 1909 (Oxford University)	1
Berry, J. J. 1953 (Manchester U)	4
Bertrand, R. 2013 (Chelsea)	2
Bestall, J. G. 1935 (Grimsby T)	1
Betmead, H. A. 1937 (Grimsby T)	1
Betts, M. P. 1877 (Old Harrovians)	1
Betts, W. 1889 (Sheffield W)	1
Beverley, J. 1884 (Blackburn R)	3
Birkett, R. H. 1879 (Clapham R)	1
Birkett, R. J. E. 1936 (Middlesbrough)	1
Birley, F. H. 1874 (Oxford University, Wanderers)	2
Birtles, G. 1980 (Nottingham F)	3
Bishop, S. M. 1927 (Leicester C)	4
Blackburn, F. 1901 (Blackburn R)	3
Blackburn, G. F. 1924 (Aston Villa)	1
Blenkinsop, E. 1928 (Sheffield W)	26
Bliss, H. 1921 (Tottenham H)	1
Blissett, L. L. 1983 (Watford, AC Milan)	14
Blockley, J. P. 1973 (Arsenal)	1
Bloomer, S. 1895 (Derby Co, Middlesbrough)	23

Blunstone, F. 1955 (Chelsea)	5
Bond, R. 1905 (Preston NE, Bradford C)	8
Bonetti, P. P. 1966 (Chelsea)	7
Bonsor, A. G. 1873 (Wanderers)	2
Booth, F. 1905 (Manchester C)	1
Booth, T. 1898 (Blackburn R, Everton)	2
Bothroyd, J. 2011 (Cardiff C)	1
Bould, S. A. 1994 (Arsenal)	2
Bowden, E. R. 1935 (Arsenal)	6
Bower, A. G. 1924 (Corinthians)	5
Bowers, J. W. 1934 (Derby Co)	3
Bowles, S. 1974 (QPR)	5
Bowser, S. 1920 (WBA)	1
Bowyer, L. D. 2003 (Leeds U)	1
Boyer, P. J. 1976 (Norwich C)	1
Boyes, W. 1935 (WBA, Everton)	3
Boyle, T. W. 1913 (Burnley)	1
Brabrook, P. 1958 (Chelsea)	3
Bracewell, P. W. 1985 (Everton)	3
Bradford, G. R. W. 1956 (Bristol R)	1
Bradford, J. 1924 (Birmingham)	12
Bradley, W. 1959 (Manchester U)	3
Bradshaw, F. 1908 (Sheffield W)	1
Bradshaw, T. H. 1897 (Liverpool)	1
Bradshaw, W. 1910 (Blackburn R)	4
Brann, G. 1886 (Swifts)	3
Brawn, W. F. 1904 (Aston Villa)	2
Bray, J. 1935 (Manchester C)	6
Brayshaw, E. 1887 (Sheffield W)	1
Bridge W. M. 2002 (Southampton, Chelsea, Manchester C)	36
Bridges, B. J. 1965 (Chelsea)	4
Bridgett, A. 1905 (Sunderland)	11
Brindle, T. 1880 (Darwen)	2
Brittleton, J. T. 1912 (Sheffield W)	5
Britton, C. S. 1935 (Everton)	9
Broadbent, P. F. 1958 (Wolverhampton W)	7
Broadis, I. A. 1952 (Manchester C, Newcastle U)	14
Brockbank, J. 1872 (Cambridge University)	1
Brodie, J. B. 1889 (Wolverhampton W)	3
Bromilow, T. G. 1921 (Liverpool)	5
Bromley-Davenport, W. E. 1884 (Oxford University)	2
Brook, E. F. 1930 (Manchester C)	18
Brooking, T. D. 1974 (West Ham U)	47
Brooks, J. 1957 (Tottenham H)	3
Broome, F. H. 1938 (Aston Villa)	7
Brown, A. 1882 (Aston Villa)	3
Brown, A. 1971 (WBA)	1
Brown, A. S. 1904 (Sheffield U)	2
Brown, G. 1927 (Huddersfield T, Aston Villa)	9
Brown, J. 1881 (Blackburn R)	5
Brown, J. H. 1927 (Sheffield W)	6
Brown, K. 1960 (West Ham U)	1
Brown, W. 1924 (West Ham U)	1
Brown, W. M. 1999 (Manchester U)	23
Bruton, J. 1928 (Burnley)	3
Bryant, W. I. 1925 (Clapton)	1
Buchan, C. M. 1913 (Sunderland)	6
Buchanan, W. S. 1876 (Clapham R)	1
Buckley, F. C. 1914 (Derby Co)	1
Bull, S. G. 1989 (Wolverhampton W)	13
Bullock, F. E. 1921 (Huddersfield T)	1
Bullock, N. 1923 (Bury)	3
Burgess, H. 1904 (Manchester C)	4
Burgess, H. 1931 (Sheffield W)	4
Burnup, C. J. 1896 (Cambridge University)	1
Burrows, H. 1934 (Sheffield W)	3
Burton, F. E. 1889 (Nottingham F)	1
Bury, L. 1877 (Cambridge University, Old Etonians)	2
Butcher, T. 1980 (Ipswich T, Rangers)	77
Butland, J. 2013 (Birmingham C)	1
Butler, J. D. 1925 (Arsenal)	1
Butler, W. 1924 (Bolton W)	1
Butt, N. 1997 (Manchester U, Newcastle U)	39
Byrne, G. 1963 (Liverpool)	2
Byrne, J. J. 1962 (Crystal Palace, West Ham U)	11
Byrne, R. W. 1954 (Manchester U)	33
Cahill, G. J. 2011 (Bolton W, Chelsea)	**26**
Callaghan, I. R. 1966 (Liverpool)	4
Calvey, J. 1902 (Nottingham F)	1
Campbell, A. F. 1929 (Blackburn R, Huddersfield T)	8
Campbell, F. L. 2012 (Sunderland)	1
Campbell, S. 1996 (Tottenham H, Arsenal, Portsmouth)	
	73
Camsell, G. H. 1929 (Middlesbrough)	9
Capes, A. J. 1903 (Stoke)	1
Carr, J. 1905 (Newcastle U)	2
Carr, J. 1920 (Middlesbrough)	2
Carr, W. H. 1875 (Owlerton, Sheffield)	1
Carragher, J. L. 1999 (Liverpool)	38
Carrick, M. 2001 (West Ham U, Tottenham H, Manchester U)	**32**
Carroll, A. T. 2011 (Newcastle U, Liverpool)	9
Carson, S. P. 2008 (Liverpool, WBA)	4
Carter, H. S. 1934 (Sunderland, Derby Co)	13
Carter, J. H. 1926 (WBA)	3
Catlin, A. E. 1937 (Sheffield W)	5
Caulker, S. A. 2013 (Tottenham H)	1
Chadwick, A. 1900 (Southampton)	2
Chadwick, E. 1891 (Everton)	7
Chamberlain, M. 1983 (Stoke C)	8
Chambers, H. 1921 (Liverpool)	8
Channon, M. R. 1973 (Southampton, Manchester C)	46
Charles, G. A. 1991 (Nottingham F)	2
Charlton, J. 1965 (Leeds U)	35
Charlton, R. 1958 (Manchester U)	106
Charnley, R. O. 1963 (Blackpool)	1
Charsley, C. C. 1893 (Small Heath)	1
Chedgzoy, S. 1920 (Everton)	8
Chenery, C. J. 1872 (Crystal Palace)	3
Cherry, T. J. 1976 (Leeds U)	27
Chilton, A. 1951 (Manchester U)	2
Chippendale, H. 1894 (Blackburn R)	1
Chivers, M. 1971 (Tottenham H)	24
Christian, E. 1879 (Old Etonians)	1
Clamp, E. 1958 (Wolverhampton W)	4
Clapton, D. R. 1959 (Arsenal)	1
Clare, T. 1889 (Stoke)	4
Clarke, A. J. 1970 (Leeds U)	19
Clarke, H. A. 1954 (Tottenham H)	1
Clay, T. 1920 (Tottenham H)	4
Clayton, R. 1956 (Blackburn R)	35
Clegg, J. C. 1872 (Sheffield W)	1
Clegg, W. E. 1873 (Sheffield W, Sheffield Alb)	2
Clemence, R. N. 1973 (Liverpool, Tottenham H)	61
Clement, D. T. 1976 (QPR)	5
Cleverley, T. W. 2013 (Manchester U)	**13**
Clough, B. H. 1960 (Middlesbrough)	2
Clough, N. H. 1989 (Nottingham F)	14
Coates, R. 1970 (Burnley, Tottenham H)	4
Cobbold, W. N. 1883 (Cambridge University, Old Carthusians)	9
Cock, J. G. 1920 (Huddersfield T, Chelsea)	2
Cockburn, H. 1947 (Manchester U)	13
Cohen, G. R. 1964 (Fulham)	37
Cole, A. 2001 (Arsenal, Chelsea)	**107**
Cole, A. A. 1995 (Manchester U)	15
Cole, C. 2009 (West Ham U)	7
Cole, J. J. 2001 (West Ham U, Chelsea)	56
Colclough, H. 1914 (Crystal Palace)	1
Coleman, E. H. 1921 (Dulwich Hamlet)	1
Coleman, J. 1907 (Woolwich Arsenal)	1
Collymore, S. V. 1995 (Nottingham F, Aston Villa)	3
Common, A. 1904 (Sheffield U, Middlesbrough)	3
Compton, L. H. 1951 (Arsenal)	2
Conlin, J. 1906 (Bradford C)	1
Connelly, J. M. 1960 (Burnley, Manchester U)	20
Cook, T. E. R. 1925 (Brighton)	1
Cooper, C. T. 1995 (Nottingham F)	2
Cooper, N. C. 1893 (Cambridge University)	1
Cooper, T. 1928 (Derby Co)	15
Cooper, T. 1969 (Leeds U)	20
Coppell, S. J. 1978 (Manchester U)	42
Copping, W. 1933 (Leeds U, Arsenal, Leeds U)	20
Corbett, B. O. 1901 (Corinthians)	1
Corbett, R. 1903 (Old Malvernians)	1
Corbett, W. S. 1908 (Birmingham)	3
Corrigan, J. T. 1976 (Manchester C)	9
Cottee, A. R. 1987 (West Ham U, Everton)	7
Cotterill, G. H. 1891 (Cambridge University, Old Brightonians)	4
Cottle, J. R. 1909 (Bristol C)	1
Cowan, S. 1926 (Manchester C)	3

Cowans, G. S. 1983 (Aston Villa, Bari, Aston Villa) 10
Cowell, A. 1910 (Blackburn R) 1
Cox, J. 1901 (Liverpool) 3
Cox, J. D. 1892 (Derby Co) 1
Crabtree, J. W. 1894 (Burnley, Aston Villa) 14
Crawford, J. F. 1931 (Chelsea) 1
Crawford, R. 1962 (Ipswich T) 2
Crawshaw, T. H. 1895 (Sheffield W) 10
Crayston, W. J. 1936 (Arsenal) 8
Creek, F. N. S. 1923 (Corinthians) 1
Cresswell, W. 1921 (South Shields, Sunderland, Everton) 7
Crompton, R. 1902 (Blackburn R) 41
Crooks, S. D. 1930 (Derby Co) 26
Crouch, P. J. 2005 (Southampton, Liverpool, Portsmouth, Tottenham H) 42
Crowe, C. 1963 (Wolverhampton W) 1
Cuggy, F. 1913 (Sunderland) 2
Cullis, S. 1938 (Wolverhampton W) 12
Cunliffe, A. 1933 (Blackburn R) 2
Cunliffe, D. 1900 (Portsmouth) 1
Cunliffe, J. N. 1936 (Everton) 1
Cunningham, L. 1979 (WBA, Real Madrid) 6
Curle, K. 1992 (Manchester C) 3
Currey, E. S. 1890 (Oxford University) 2
Currie, A. W. 1972 (Sheffield U, Leeds U) 17
Cursham, A. W. 1876 (Notts Co) 6
Cursham, H. A. 1880 (Notts Co) 8

Daft, H. B. 1889 (Notts Co) 5
Daley, A. M. 1992 (Aston Villa) 7
Danks, T. 1885 (Nottingham F) 1
Davenport, P. 1985 (Nottingham F) 1
Davenport, J. K. 1885 (Bolton W) 2
Davies, K. C. 2011 (Bolton W) 1
Davis, G. 1904 (Derby Co) 2
Davis, H. 1903 (Sheffield W) 3
Davison, J. E. 1922 (Sheffield W) 1
Dawson, J. 1922 (Burnley) 2
Dawson, M. R. 2011 (Tottenham H) 4
Day, S. H. 1906 (Old Malvernians) 3
Dean, W. R. 1927 (Everton) 16
Deane, B. C. 1991 (Sheffield U) 3
Deeley, N. V. 1959 (Wolverhampton W) 2
Defoe, J. C. 2004 (Tottenham H, Portsmouth, Tottenham H) **55**
Devey, J. H. G. 1892 (Aston Villa) 2
Devonshire, A. 1980 (West Ham U) 8
Dewhurst, F. 1886 (Preston NE) 9
Dewhurst, G. P. 1895 (Liverpool Ramblers) 1
Dickinson, J. W. 1949 (Portsmouth) 48
Dimmock, J. H. 1921 (Tottenham H) 3
Ditchburn, E. G. 1949 (Tottenham H) 6
Dix, R. W. 1939 (Derby Co) 1
Dixon, J. A. 1885 (Notts Co) 1
Dixon, K. M. 1985 (Chelsea) 8
Dixon, L. M. 1990 (Arsenal) 22
Dobson, A. T. C. 1882 (Notts Co) 4
Dobson, C. F. 1886 (Notts Co) 1
Dobson, J. M. 1974 (Burnley, Everton) 5
Doggart, A. G. 1924 (Corinthians) 1
Dorigo, A. R. 1990 (Chelsea, Leeds U) 15
Dorrell, A. R. 1925 (Aston Villa) 4
Douglas, B. 1958 (Blackburn R) 36
Downing, S. 2005 (Middlesbrough, Aston Villa, Liverpool) 34
Downs, R. W. 1921 (Everton) 1
Doyle, M. 1976 (Manchester C) 5
Drake, E. J. 1935 (Arsenal) 5
Dublin, D. 1998 (Coventry C, Aston Villa) 4
Ducat, A. 1910 (Woolwich Arsenal, Aston Villa) 6
Dunn, A. T. B. 1883 (Cambridge University, Old Etonians) 4
Dunn, D. J. I. 2003 (Blackburn R) 1
Duxbury, M. 1984 (Manchester U) 10
Dyer, K. C. 2000 (Newcastle U, West Ham U) 33

Earle, S. G. J. 1924 (Clapton, West Ham U) 2
Eastham, G. 1963 (Arsenal) 19
Eastham, G. R. 1935 (Bolton W) 1
Eckersley, W. 1950 (Blackburn R) 17
Edwards, D. 1955 (Manchester U) 18

Edwards, J. H. 1874 (Shropshire Wanderers) 1
Edwards, W. 1926 (Leeds U) 16
Ehiogu, U. 1996 (Aston Villa, Middlesbrough) 4
Ellerington, W. 1949 (Southampton) 2
Elliott, G. W. 1913 (Middlesbrough) 3
Elliott, W. H. 1952 (Burnley) 5
Evans, R. E. 1911 (Sheffield U) 4
Ewer, F. H. 1924 (Casuals) 2

Fairclough, P. 1878 (Old Foresters) 1
Fairhurst, D. 1934 (Newcastle U) 1
Fantham, J. 1962 (Sheffield W) 1
Fashanu, J. 1989 (Wimbledon) 2
Felton, W. 1925 (Sheffield W) 1
Fenton, M. 1938 (Middlesbrough) 1
Fenwick, T. W. 1984 (QPR, Tottenham H) 20
Ferdinand, L. 1993 (QPR, Newcastle U, Tottenham H) 17
Ferdinand, R. G. 1998 (West Ham U, Leeds U, Manchester U) 81
Field, E. 1876 (Clapham R) 2
Finney, T. 1947 (Preston NE) 76
Flanagan, J. P. 2014 (Liverpool) **1**
Fleming, H. J. 1909 (Swindon T) 11
Fletcher, A. 1889 (Wolverhampton W) 2
Flowers, R. 1955 (Wolverhampton W) 49
Flowers, T. D. 1993 (Southampton, Blackburn R) 11
Forman, Frank 1898 (Nottingham F) 9
Forman, F. R. 1899 (Nottingham F) 3
Forrest, J. H. 1884 (Blackburn R) 11
Forster, F. G. 2013 (Celtic) **2**
Fort, J. 1921 (Millwall) 1
Foster, B. 2007 (Manchester U, Birmingham C, WBA) **8**
Foster, R. E. 1900 (Oxford University, Corinthians) 5
Foster, S. 1982 (Brighton & HA) 3
Foulke, W. J. 1897 (Sheffield U) 1
Foulkes, W. A. 1955 (Manchester U) 1
Fowler, R. B. 1996 (Liverpool, Leeds U) 26
Fox, F. S. 1925 (Millwall) 1
Francis, G. C. J. 1975 (QPR) 12
Francis, T. 1977 (Birmingham C, Nottingham F, Manchester C, Sampdoria) 52
Franklin, C. F. 1947 (Stoke C) 27
Freeman, B. C. 1909 (Everton, Burnley) 5
Froggatt, J. 1950 (Portsmouth) 13
Froggatt, R. 1953 (Sheffield W) 4
Fry, C. B. 1901 (Corinthians) 1
Furness, W. I. 1933 (Leeds U) 1

Galley, T. 1937 (Wolverhampton W) 2
Gardner, A. 2004 (Tottenham H) 1
Gardner, T. 1934 (Aston Villa) 2
Garfield, B. 1898 (WBA) 1
Garraty, W. 1903 (Aston Villa) 1
Garrett, T. 1952 (Blackpool) 3
Gascoigne, P. J. 1989 (Tottenham H, Lazio, Rangers, Middlesbrough) 57
Gates, E. 1981 (Ipswich T) 2
Gay, L. H. 1893 (Cambridge University, Old Brightonians) 3
Geary, F. 1890 (Everton) 2
Geaves, R. L. 1875 (Clapham R) 1
Gee, C. W. 1932 (Everton) 3
Geldard, A. 1933 (Everton) 4
George, C. 1977 (Derby Co) 1
George, W. 1902 (Aston Villa) 3
Gerrard, S. G. 2000 (Liverpool) **114**
Gibbins, W. V. T. 1924 (Clapton) 2
Gibbs, K. J. R. 2011 (Arsenal) **3**
Gidman, J. 1977 (Aston Villa) 1
Gillard, I. T. 1975 (QPR) 3
Gilliat, W. E. 1893 (Old Carthusians) 1
Goddard, P. 1982 (West Ham U) 1
Goodall, F. R. 1926 (Huddersfield T) 25
Goodall, J. 1888 (Preston NE, Derby Co) 14
Goodhart, H. C. 1883 (Old Etonians) 3
Goodwyn, A. G. 1873 (Royal Engineers) 1
Goodyer, A. C. 1879 (Nottingham F) 1
Gosling, R. C. 1892 (Old Etonians) 5
Gosnell, A. A. 1906 (Newcastle U) 1
Gough, H. C. 1921 (Sheffield U) 1
Goulden, L. A. 1937 (West Ham U) 14
Graham, L. 1925 (Millwall) 2

Graham, T. 1931 (Nottingham F)	2
Grainger, C. 1956 (Sheffield U, Sunderland)	7
Gray, A. A. 1992 (Crystal Palace)	1
Gray, M. 1999 (Sunderland)	3
Greaves, J. 1959 (Chelsea, Tottenham H)	57
Green, F. T. 1876 (Wanderers)	1
Green, G. H. 1925 (Sheffield U)	8
Green, R. P. 2005 (Norwich C, West Ham U)	12
Greenhalgh, E. H. 1872 (Notts Co)	2
Greenhoff, B. 1976 (Manchester U, Leeds U)	18
Greenwood, D. H. 1882 (Blackburn R)	2
Gregory, J. 1983 (QPR)	6
Grimsdell, A. 1920 (Tottenham H)	6
Grosvenor, A. T. 1934 (Birmingham)	3
Gunn, W. 1884 (Notts Co)	2
Guppy, S. 2000 (Leicester C)	1
Gurney, R. 1935 (Sunderland)	1
Hacking, J. 1929 (Oldham Ath)	3
Hadley, H. 1903 (WBA)	1
Hagan, J. 1949 (Sheffield U)	1
Haines, J. T. W. 1949 (WBA)	1
Hall, A. E. 1910 (Aston Villa)	1
Hall, G. W. 1934 (Tottenham H)	10
Hall, J. 1956 (Birmingham C)	17
Halse, H. J. 1909 (Manchester U)	1
Hammond, H. E. D. 1889 (Oxford University)	1
Hampson, J. 1931 (Blackpool)	3
Hampton, H. 1913 (Aston Villa)	4
Hancocks, J. 1949 (Wolverhampton W)	3
Hapgood, E. 1933 (Arsenal)	30
Hardinge, H. T. W. 1910 (Sheffield U)	1
Hardman, H. P. 1905 (Everton)	4
Hardwick, G. F. M. 1947 (Middlesbrough)	13
Hardy, H. 1925 (Stockport Co)	1
Hardy, H. 1907 (Liverpool, Aston Villa)	21
Harford, M. G. 1988 (Luton T)	2
Hargreaves, F. W. 1880 (Blackburn R)	3
Hargreaves, J. 1881 (Blackburn R)	2
Hargreaves, O. 2002 (Bayern Munich, Manchester U)	42
Harper, E. C. 1926 (Blackburn R)	1
Harris, G. 1966 (Burnley)	1
Harris, P. P. 1950 (Portsmouth)	2
Harris, S. S. 1904 (Cambridge University, Old Westminsters)	6
Harrison, A. H. 1893 (Old Westminsters)	2
Harrison, G. 1921 (Everton)	2
Harrow, J. H. 1923 (Chelsea)	2
Hart, C. J. J. 2008 (Manchester C)	**43**
Hart, E. 1929 (Leeds U)	8
Hartley, F. 1923 (Oxford C)	1
Harvey, A. 1881 (Wednesbury Strollers)	1
Harvey, J. C. 1971 (Everton)	1
Hassall, H. W. 1951 (Huddersfield T, Bolton W)	5
Hateley, M. 1984 (Portsmouth, AC Milan, Monaco, Rangers)	32
Hawkes, R. M. 1907 (Luton T)	5
Haworth, G. 1887 (Accrington)	5
Hawtrey, J. P. 1881 (Old Etonians)	2
Haygarth, E. B. 1875 (Swifts)	1
Haynes, J. N. 1955 (Fulham)	56
Healless, H. 1925 (Blackburn R)	2
Hector, K. J. 1974 (Derby Co)	2
Hedley, G. A. 1901 (Sheffield U)	1
Hegan, K. E. 1923 (Corinthians)	4
Hellawell, M. S. 1963 (Birmingham C)	2
Henderson, J. B. 2011 (Sunderland, Liverpool)	**13**
Hendrie, L. A. 1999 (Aston Villa)	1
Henfrey, A. G. 1891 (Cambridge University, Corinthians)	5
Henry, R. P. 1963 (Tottenham H)	1
Heron, F. 1876 (Wanderers)	1
Heron, G. H. 1873 (Uxbridge, Wanderers)	5
Heskey, E. W. I. 1999 (Leicester C, Liverpool, Birmingham C, Wigan Ath, Aston Villa)	62
Hibbert, W. 1910 (Bury)	1
Hibbs, H. E. 1930 (Birmingham)	25
Hill, F. 1963 (Bolton W)	2
Hill, G. A. 1976 (Manchester U)	6
Hill, J. H. 1925 (Burnley, Newcastle U)	11
Hill, R. 1983 (Luton T)	3
Hill, R. H. 1926 (Millwall)	1

Hillman, J. 1899 (Burnley)	1
Hills, A. F. 1879 (Old Harrovians)	1
Hilsdon, G. R. 1907 (Chelsea)	8
Hinchcliffe, A. G. 1997 (Everton, Sheffield W)	7
Hine, E. W. 1929 (Leicester C)	6
Hinton, A. T. 1963 (Wolverhampton W, Nottingham F)	3
Hirst, D. E. 1991 (Sheffield W)	3
Hitchens, G. A. 1961 (Aston Villa, Internazionale)	7
Hobbis, H. H. F. 1936 (Charlton Ath)	2
Hoddle, G. 1980 (Tottenham H, Monaco)	53
Hodge, S. B. 1986 (Aston Villa, Tottenham H, Nottingham F)	24
Hodgetts, D. 1888 (Aston Villa)	6
Hodgkinson, A. 1957 (Sheffield U)	5
Hodgson, G. 1931 (Liverpool)	3
Hodkinson, J. 1913 (Blackburn R)	3
Hogg, W. 1902 (Sunderland)	3
Holdcroft, G. H. 1937 (Preston NE)	2
Holden, A. D. 1959 (Bolton W)	5
Holden, G. H. 1881 (Wednesbury OA)	4
Holden-White, C. 1888 (Corinthians)	2
Holford, T. 1903 (Stoke)	1
Holley, G. H. 1909 (Sunderland)	10
Holliday, E. 1960 (Middlesbrough)	3
Hollins, J. W. 1967 (Chelsea)	1
Holmes, R. 1888 (Preston NE)	7
Holt, J. 1890 (Everton, Reading)	10
Hopkinson, E. 1958 (Bolton W)	14
Hossack, A. H. 1892 (Corinthians)	2
Houghton, W. E. 1931 (Aston Villa)	7
Houlker, A. E. 1902 (Blackburn R, Portsmouth, Southampton)	5
Howarth, R. H. 1887 (Preston NE, Everton)	5
Howe, D. 1958 (WBA)	23
Howe, J. R. 1948 (Derby Co)	3
Howell, L. S. 1873 (Wanderers)	1
Howell, R. 1895 (Sheffield U, Liverpool)	2
Howey, S. N. 1995 (Newcastle U)	4
Huddlestone, T. A. 2010 (Tottenham H)	4
Hudson, A. A. 1975 (Stoke C)	2
Hudson, J. 1883 (Sheffield)	1
Hudspeth, F. C. 1926 (Newcastle U)	1
Hufton, A. E. 1924 (West Ham U)	6
Hughes, E. W. 1970 (Liverpool, Wolverhampton W)	62
Hughes, L. 1950 (Liverpool)	3
Hulme, J. H. A. 1927 (Arsenal)	9
Humphreys, P. 1903 (Notts Co)	1
Hunt, G. S. 1933 (Tottenham H)	3
Hunt, Rev. K. R. G. 1911 (Leyton)	2
Hunt, R. 1962 (Liverpool)	34
Hunt, S. 1984 (WBA)	2
Hunter, J. 1878 (Sheffield Heeley)	7
Hunter, N. 1966 (Leeds U)	28
Hurst, G. C. 1966 (West Ham U)	49
Ince, P. E. C. 1993 (Manchester U, Internazionale, Liverpool, Middlesbrough)	53
Iremonger, J. 1901 (Nottingham F)	2
Jack, D. N. B. 1924 (Bolton W, Arsenal)	9
Jackson, E. 1891 (Oxford University)	1
Jagielka, P. N. 2008 (Everton)	**28**
James, D. B. 1997 (Liverpool, Aston Villa, West Ham U, Manchester C, Portsmouth)	53
Jarrett, B. G. 1876 (Cambridge University)	3
Jarvis, M. T. 2011 (Wolverhampton W)	1
Jefferis, F. 1912 (Everton)	2
Jeffers, F. 2003 (Arsenal)	1
Jenas, J. A. 2003 (Newcastle U, Tottenham H)	21
Jenkinson, C. D. 2013 (Arsenal)	1
Jezzard, B. A. G. 1954 (Fulham)	2
Johnson, A. 2005 (Crystal Palace, Everton)	8
Johnson, A. 2010 (Manchester C)	12
Johnson, D. E. 1975 (Ipswich T, Liverpool)	8
Johnson, E. 1880 (Saltley College, Stoke)	2
Johnson, G. M. C. 2004 (Chelsea, Portsmouth, Liverpool)	**54**
Johnson, J. A. 1937 (Stoke C)	5
Johnson, S. A. M. 2001 (Derby Co)	1
Johnson, T. C. F. 1926 (Manchester C, Everton)	5
Johnson, W. H. 1900 (Sheffield U)	6
Johnston, H. 1947 (Blackpool)	10

Morse, H. 1879 (Notts Co)	1
Mort, T. 1924 (Aston Villa)	3
Morten, A. 1873 (Crystal Palace)	1
Mortensen, S. H. 1947 (Blackpool)	25
Morton, J. R. 1938 (West Ham U)	1
Mosforth, W. 1877 (Sheffield W, Sheffield Alb, Sheffield W)	9
Moss, F. 1922 (Aston Villa)	5
Moss, F. 1934 (Arsenal)	4
Mosscrop, E. 1914 (Burnley)	2
Mozley, B. 1950 (Derby Co)	3
Mullen, J. 1947 (Wolverhampton W)	12
Mullery, A. P. 1965 (Tottenham H)	35
Murphy, D. B. 2002 (Liverpool)	9
Neal, P. G. 1976 (Liverpool)	50
Needham, E. 1894 (Sheffield U)	16
Neville, G. A. 1995 (Manchester U)	85
Neville, P. J. 1996 (Manchester U, Everton)	59
Newton, K. R. 1966 (Blackburn R, Everton)	27
Nicholls, J. 1954 (WBA)	2
Nicholson, W. E. 1951 (Tottenham H)	1
Nish, D. J. 1973 (Derby Co)	5
Norman, M. 1962 (Tottenham H)	23
Nugent, D. J. 2007 (Preston NE)	1
Nuttall, H. 1928 (Bolton W)	3
Oakley, W. J. 1895 (Oxford University, Corinthians)	16
O'Dowd, J. P. 1932 (Chelsea)	3
O'Grady, M. 1963 (Huddersfield T, Leeds U)	2
Ogilvie, R. A. M. M. 1874 (Clapham R)	1
Oliver, L. F. 1929 (Fulham)	1
Olney, B. A. 1928 (Aston Villa)	2
Osborne, F. R. 1923 (Fulham, Tottenham H)	4
Osborne, R. 1928 (Leicester C)	1
Osgood, P. L. 1970 (Chelsea)	4
Osman, L. 2013 (Everton)	1
Osman, R. 1980 (Ipswich T)	11
Ottaway, C. J. 1872 (Oxford University)	2
Owen, J. R. B. 1874 (Sheffield)	1
Owen, M. J. 1998 (Liverpool, Real Madrid, Newcastle U)	89
Owen, S. W. 1954 (Luton T)	3
Oxlade-Chamberlain, A. M. D. 2012 (Arsenal)	**15**
Page, L. A. 1927 (Burnley)	7
Paine, T. L. 1963 (Southampton)	19
Pallister, G. A. 1988 (Middlesbrough, Manchester U)	22
Palmer, C. L. 1992 (Sheffield W)	18
Pantling, H. H. 1924 (Sheffield U)	1
Paravicini, P. J. de 1883 (Cambridge University)	3
Parker, P. A. 1989 (QPR, Manchester U)	19
Parker, S. M. 2004 (Charlton Ath, Chelsea, Newcastle U, West Ham U, Tottenham H)	18
Parker, T. R. 1925 (Southampton)	1
Parkes, P. B. 1974 (QPR)	1
Parkinson, J. 1910 (Liverpool)	2
Parlour, R. 1999 (Arsenal)	10
Parr, P. C. 1882 (Oxford University)	1
Parry, E. H. 1879 (Old Carthusians)	3
Parry, R. A. 1960 (Bolton W)	2
Patchitt, B. C. A. 1923 (Corinthians)	2
Pawson, F. W. 1883 (Cambridge University, Swifts)	2
Payne, J. 1937 (Luton T)	1
Peacock, A. 1962 (Middlesbrough, Leeds U)	6
Peacock, J. 1929 (Middlesbrough)	3
Pearce, S. 1987 (Nottingham F, West Ham U)	78
Pearson, H. F. 1932 (WBA)	1
Pearson, J. H. 1892 (Crewe Alex)	1
Pearson, J. S. 1976 (Manchester U)	15
Pearson, S. C. 1948 (Manchester U)	8
Pease, W. H. 1927 (Middlesbrough)	1
Pegg, D. 1957 (Manchester U)	1
Pejic, M. 1974 (Stoke C)	4
Pelly, F. R. 1893 (Old Foresters)	3
Pennington, J. 1907 (WBA)	25
Pentland, F. B. 1909 (Middlesbrough)	5
Perry, C. 1890 (WBA)	3
Perry, T. 1898 (WBA)	1
Perry, W. 1956 (Blackpool)	3
Perryman, S. 1982 (Tottenham H)	1
Peters, M. 1966 (West Ham U, Tottenham H)	67

Phelan, M. C. 1990 (Manchester U)	1
Phillips, K. 1999 (Sunderland)	8
Phillips, L. H. 1952 (Portsmouth)	3
Pickering, F. 1964 (Everton)	3
Pickering, J. 1933 (Sheffield U)	1
Pickering, N. 1983 (Sunderland)	1
Pike, T. M. 1886 (Cambridge University)	1
Pilkington, B. 1955 (Burnley)	1
Plant, J. 1900 (Bury)	1
Platt, D. 1990 (Aston Villa, Bari, Juventus, Sampdoria, Arsenal)	62
Plum, S. L. 1923 (Charlton Ath)	1
Pointer, R. 1962 (Burnley)	3
Porteous, T. S. 1891 (Sunderland)	1
Powell, C. G. 2001 (Charlton Ath)	5
Priest, A. E. 1900 (Sheffield U)	1
Prinsep, J. F. M. 1879 (Clapham R)	1
Puddefoot, S. C. 1926 (Blackburn R)	2
Pye, J. 1950 (Wolverhampton W)	1
Pym, R. H. 1925 (Bolton W)	3
Quantrill, A. 1920 (Derby Co)	4
Quixall, A. 1954 (Sheffield W)	5
Radford, J. 1969 (Arsenal)	2
Raikes, G. B. 1895 (Oxford University)	4
Ramsey, A. E. 1949 (Southampton, Tottenham H)	32
Rawlings, A. 1921 (Preston NE)	1
Rawlings, W. E. 1922 (Southampton)	2
Rawlinson, J. F. P. 1882 (Cambridge University)	1
Rawson, H. E. 1875 (Royal Engineers)	1
Rawson, W. S. 1875 (Oxford University)	2
Read, A. 1921 (Tufnell Park)	1
Reader, J. 1894 (WBA)	1
Reaney, P. 1969 (Leeds U)	3
Redknapp, J. F. 1996 (Liverpool)	17
Reeves, K. P. 1980 (Norwich C, Manchester C)	2
Regis, C. 1982 (WBA, Coventry C)	5
Reid, P. 1985 (Everton)	13
Revie, D. G. 1955 (Manchester C)	6
Reynolds, J. 1892 (WBA, Aston Villa)	8
Richards, C. H. 1898 (Nottingham F)	1
Richards, G. H. 1909 (Derby Co)	1
Richards, J. P. 1973 (Wolverhampton W)	1
Richards, M. 2007 (Manchester C)	13
Richardson, J. R. 1933 (Newcastle U)	2
Richardson, K. 1994 (Aston Villa)	1
Richardson, K. E. 2005 (Manchester U)	8
Richardson, W. G. 1935 (WBA)	1
Rickaby, S. 1954 (WBA)	1
Ricketts, M. B. 2002 (Bolton W)	1
Rigby, A. 1927 (Blackburn R)	5
Rimmer, E. J. 1930 (Sheffield W)	4
Rimmer, J. J. 1976 (Arsenal)	1
Ripley, S. E. 1994 (Blackburn R)	2
Rix, G. 1981 (Arsenal)	17
Robb, G. 1954 (Tottenham H)	1
Roberts, C. 1905 (Manchester U)	3
Roberts, F. 1925 (Manchester C)	4
Roberts, G. 1983 (Tottenham H)	6
Roberts, H. 1931 (Arsenal)	1
Roberts, H. 1931 (Millwall)	1
Roberts, R. 1887 (WBA)	3
Roberts, W. T. 1924 (Preston NE)	2
Robinson, J. 1937 (Sheffield W)	4
Robinson, J. W. 1897 (Derby Co, New Brighton Tower, Southampton)	11
Robinson, P. W. 2003 (Leeds U, Tottenham H, Blackburn R)	41
Robson, B. 1980 (WBA, Manchester U)	90
Robson, R. 1958 (WBA)	20
Rocastle, D. 1989 (Arsenal)	14
Rodriguez, J. E. 2013 (Southampton)	**1**
Rodwell, J. 2012 (Everton)	3
Rooney, W. 2003 (Everton, Manchester U)	**95**
Rose, W. C. 1884 (Swifts, Preston NE, Wolverhampton W)	5
Rostron, T. 1881 (Darwen)	2
Rowe, A. 1934 (Tottenham H)	1
Rowley, J. F. 1949 (Manchester U)	6
Rowley, W. 1889 (Stoke)	2
Royle, J. 1971 (Everton, Manchester C)	6

Ruddlesdin, H. 1904 (Sheffield W)	3
Ruddock, N. 1995 (Liverpool)	1
Ruddy, J. T. G. 2013 (Norwich C)	1
Ruffell, J. W. 1926 (West Ham U)	6
Russell, B. B. 1883 (Royal Engineers)	1
Rutherford, J. 1904 (Newcastle U)	11
Sadler, D. 1968 (Manchester U)	4
Sagar, C. 1900 (Bury)	2
Sagar, E. 1936 (Everton)	4
Salako, J. A. 1991 (Crystal Palace)	5
Sandford, E. A. 1933 (WBA)	1
Sandilands, R. R. 1892 (Old Westminsters)	5
Sands, J. 1880 (Nottingham F)	1
Sansom, K. G. 1979 (Crystal Palace, Arsenal)	86
Saunders, F. E. 1888 (Swifts)	1
Savage, A. H. 1876 (Crystal Palace)	1
Sayer, J. 1887 (Stoke)	1
Scales, J. R. 1995 (Liverpool)	3
Scattergood, E. 1913 (Derby Co)	1
Schofield, J. 1892 (Stoke)	3
Scholes, P. 1997 (Manchester U)	66
Scott, L. 1947 (Arsenal)	17
Scott, W. R. 1937 (Brentford)	1
Seaman, D. A. 1989 (QPR, Arsenal)	75
Seddon, J. 1923 (Bolton W)	6
Seed, J. M. 1921 (Tottenham H)	5
Settle, J. 1899 (Bury, Everton)	6
Sewell, J. 1952 (Sheffield W)	6
Sewell, W. R. 1924 (Blackburn R)	1
Shackleton, L. F. 1949 (Sunderland)	5
Sharp, J. 1903 (Everton)	2
Sharpe, L. S. 1991 (Manchester U)	8
Shaw, G. E. 1932 (WBA)	1
Shaw, G. L. 1959 (Sheffield U)	5
Shaw, L. P. H. 2014 (Southampton)	**3**
Shawcross, R. J. 2013 (Stoke C)	1
Shea, D. 1914 (Blackburn R)	2
Shearer, A. 1992 (Southampton, Blackburn R, Newcastle U)	63
Shellito, K. J. 1963 (Chelsea)	1
Shelton A. 1889 (Notts Co)	6
Shelton, C. 1888 (Notts Rangers)	1
Shelvey, J. 2013 (Liverpool)	1
Shepherd, A. 1906 (Bolton W, Newcastle U)	2
Sheringham, E. P. 1993 (Tottenham H, Manchester U, Tottenham H)	51
Sherwood, T. A. 1999 (Tottenham H)	3
Shilton, P. L. 1971 (Leicester C, Stoke C, Nottingham F, Southampton, Derby Co)	125
Shimwell, E. 1949 (Blackpool)	1
Shorey, N. 2007 (Reading)	2
Shutt, G. 1886 (Stoke)	1
Silcock, J. 1921 (Manchester U)	3
Sillett, R. P. 1955 (Chelsea)	3
Simms, E. 1922 (Luton T)	1
Simpson, J. 1911 (Blackburn R)	8
Sinclair, T. 2002 (West Ham U, Manchester C)	12
Sinton, A. 1992 (QPR, Sheffield W)	12
Slater, W. J. 1955 (Wolverhampton W)	12
Smalley, T. 1937 (Wolverhampton W)	1
Smalling, C. 2012 (Manchester U)	**13**
Smart, T. 1921 (Aston Villa)	5
Smith, A. 1891 (Nottingham F)	3
Smith, A. 2001 (Leeds U, Manchester U, Newcastle U)	19
Smith, A. K. 1872 (Oxford University)	1
Smith, A. M. 1989 (Arsenal)	13
Smith, B. 1921 (Tottenham H)	2
Smith, C. E. 1876 (Crystal Palace)	1
Smith, G. O. 1893 (Oxford University, Old Carthusians, Corinthians)	20
Smith, H. 1905 (Reading)	4
Smith, J. 1920 (WBA)	2
Smith, Joe 1913 (Bolton W)	5
Smith, J. C. R. 1939 (Millwall)	2
Smith, J. W. 1932 (Portsmouth)	3
Smith, Leslie 1939 (Brentford)	1
Smith, Lionel 1951 (Arsenal)	6
Smith, R. A. 1961 (Tottenham H)	15
Smith, S. 1895 (Aston Villa)	1
Smith, S. C. 1936 (Leicester C)	1
Smith, T. 1960 (Birmingham C)	2
Smith, T. 1971 (Liverpool)	1
Smith, W. H. 1922 (Huddersfield T)	3
Sorby, T. H. 1879 (Thursday Wanderers, Sheffield)	1
Southgate, G. 1996 (Aston Villa, Middlesbrough)	57
Southworth, J. 1889 (Blackburn R)	3
Sparks, F. J. 1879 (Herts Rangers, Clapham R)	3
Spence, J. W. 1926 (Manchester U)	2
Spence, R. 1936 (Chelsea)	2
Spencer, C. W. 1924 (Newcastle U)	2
Spencer, H. 1897 (Aston Villa)	6
Spiksley, F. 1893 (Sheffield W)	7
Spilsbury, B. W. 1885 (Cambridge University)	3
Spink, N. 1983 (Aston Villa)	1
Spouncer, W. A. 1900 (Nottingham F)	1
Springett, R. D. G. 1960 (Sheffield W)	33
Sproston, B. 1937 (Leeds U, Tottenham H, Manchester C)	11
Squire, R. T. 1886 (Cambridge University)	3
Stanbrough, M. H. 1895 (Old Carthusians)	1
Staniforth, R. 1954 (Huddersfield T)	8
Starling, R. W. 1933 (Sheffield W, Aston Villa)	2
Statham, D. J. 1983 (WBA)	3
Steele, F. C. 1937 (Stoke C)	6
Stein, B. 1984 (Luton T)	1
Stephenson, C. 1924 (Huddersfield T)	1
Stephenson, G. T. 1928 (Derby Co, Sheffield W)	3
Stephenson, J. E. 1938 (Leeds U)	2
Stepney, A. C. 1968 (Manchester U)	1
Sterland, M. 1989 (Sheffield W)	1
Sterling, R. S. 2013 (Liverpool)	**7**
Steven, T. M. 1985 (Everton, Rangers, Marseille)	36
Stevens, G. A. 1985 (Tottenham H)	7
Stevens, M. G. 1985 (Everton, Rangers)	46
Stewart, J. 1907 (Sheffield W, Newcastle U)	3
Stewart, P. A. 1992 (Tottenham H)	3
Stiles, N. P. 1965 (Manchester U)	28
Stoker, J. 1933 (Birmingham)	3
Stone, S. B. 1996 (Nottingham F)	9
Stones, J. 2014 (Everton)	**2**
Storer, H. 1924 (Derby Co)	2
Storey, P. E. 1971 (Arsenal)	19
Storey-Moore, I. 1970 (Nottingham F)	1
Strange, A. H. 1930 (Sheffield W)	20
Stratford, A. H. 1874 (Wanderers)	1
Streten, B. 1950 (Luton T)	1
Sturgess, A. 1911 (Sheffield U)	2
Sturridge, D. 2012 (Chelsea, Liverpool)	**15**
Summerbee, M. G. 1968 (Manchester C)	8
Sunderland, A. 1980 (Arsenal)	1
Sutcliffe, J. W. 1893 (Bolton W, Millwall)	5
Sutton, C. R. 1998 (Blackburn R)	1
Swan, P. 1960 (Sheffield W)	19
Swepstone, H. A. 1880 (Pilgrims)	6
Swift, F. V. 1947 (Manchester C)	19
Tait, G. 1881 (Birmingham Excelsior)	1
Talbot, B. 1977 (Ipswich T, Arsenal)	6
Tambling, R. V. 1963 (Chelsea)	3
Tate, J. T. 1931 (Aston Villa)	3
Taylor, E. 1954 (Blackpool)	1
Taylor, E. H. 1923 (Huddersfield T)	8
Taylor, J. G. 1951 (Fulham)	2
Taylor, P. H. 1948 (Liverpool)	3
Taylor, P. J. 1976 (Crystal Palace)	4
Taylor, T. 1953 (Manchester U)	19
Temple, D. W. 1965 (Everton)	1
Terry, J. G. 2003 (Chelsea)	78
Thickett, H. 1899 (Sheffield U)	2
Thomas, D. 1975 (QPR)	8
Thomas, D. 1983 (Coventry C)	2
Thomas, G. R. 1991 (Crystal Palace)	9
Thomas, M. L. 1989 (Arsenal)	2
Thompson, A. 2004 (Celtic)	1
Thompson, P. 1964 (Liverpool)	16
Thompson, P. B. 1976 (Liverpool)	42
Thompson T. 1952 (Aston Villa, Preston NE)	2
Thomson, R. A. 1964 (Wolverhampton W)	8
Thornewell, G. 1923 (Derby Co)	4
Thornley, I. 1907 (Manchester C)	1
Tilson, S. F. 1934 (Manchester C)	4
Titmuss, F. 1922 (Southampton)	2
Todd, C. 1972 (Derby Co)	27
Toone, G. 1892 (Notts Co)	2

Topham, A. G. 1894 (Casuals) 1
Topham, R. 1893 (Wolverhampton W, Casuals) 2
Towers, M. A. 1976 (Sunderland) 3
Townley, W. J. 1889 (Blackburn R) 2
Townrow, J. E. 1925 (Clapton Orient) 2
Townsend, A. D. 2013 (Tottenham H) **5**
Tremelling, D. R. 1928 (Birmingham) 1
Tresadern, J. 1923 (West Ham U) 2
Tueart, D. 1975 (Manchester C) 6
Tunstall, F. E. 1923 (Sheffield U) 7
Turnbull, R. J. 1920 (Bradford) 1
Turner, A. 1900 (Southampton) 1
Turner, H. 1931 (Huddersfield T) 2
Turner, J. A. 1893 (Bolton W, Stoke, Derby Co) 3
Tweedy, G. J. 1937 (Grimsby T) 1

Ufton, D. G. 1954 (Charlton Ath) 1
Underwood, A. 1891 (Stoke C) 2
Unsworth, D. G. 1995 (Everton) 1
Upson, M. J. 2003 (Birmingham C, West Ham U) 21
Urwin, T. 1923 (Middlesbrough, Newcastle U) 4
Utley, G. 1913 (Barnsley) 1

Vassell, D. 2002 (Aston Villa) 22
Vaughton, O. H. 1882 (Aston Villa) 5
Veitch, C. C. M. 1906 (Newcastle U) 6
Veitch, J. G. 1894 (Old Westminsters) 1
Venables, T. F. 1965 (Chelsea) 2
Venison, B. 1995 (Newcastle U) 2
Vidal, R. W. S. 1873 (Oxford University) 1
Viljoen, C. 1975 (Ipswich T) 2
Viollet, D. S. 1960 (Manchester U) 2
Von Donop 1873 (Royal Engineers) 2

Wace, H. 1878 (Wanderers) 3
Waddle, C. R. 1985 (Newcastle U, Tottenham H, Marseille) 62
Wadsworth, S. J. 1922 (Huddersfield T) 9
Wainscoat, W. R. 1929 (Leeds U) 1
Waiters, A. K. 1964 (Blackpool) 5
Walcott, T. J. 2006 (Arsenal) **36**
Walden, F. I. 1914 (Tottenham H) 2
Walker, D. S. 1989 (Nottingham F, Sampdoria, Sheffield W) 59
Walker, I. M. 1996 (Tottenham H, Leicester C) 4
Walker, K. A. 2012 (Tottenham H) **10**
Walker, W. H. 1921 (Aston Villa) 18
Wall, G. 1907 (Manchester U) 7
Wallace, C. W. 1913 (Aston Villa) 3
Wallace, D. L. 1986 (Southampton) 1
Walsh, P. A. 1983 (Luton T) 5
Walters, A. M. 1885 (Cambridge University, Old Carthusians) 9
Walters, K. M. 1991 (Rangers) 1
Walters, P. M. 1885 (Oxford University, Old Carthusians) 13
Walton, N. 1890 (Blackburn R) 1
Ward, J. T. 1885 (Blackburn Olympic) 1
Ward, P. 1980 (Brighton & HA) 1
Ward, T. V. 1948 (Derby Co) 2
Waring, T. 1931 (Aston Villa) 5
Warner, C. 1878 (Upton Park) 1
Warnock, S. 2008 (Blackburn R, Aston Villa) 2
Warren, B. 1906 (Derby Co, Chelsea) 22
Waterfield, G. S. 1927 (Burnley) 1
Watson, D. 1984 (Norwich C, Everton) 12
Watson, D. V. 1974 (Sunderland, Manchester C, Werder Bremen, Southampton, Stoke C) 65
Watson, V. M. 1923 (West Ham U) 5
Watson, W. 1913 (Burnley) 3
Watson, W. 1950 (Sunderland) 4
Weaver, S. 1932 (Newcastle U) 3
Webb, G. W. 1911 (West Ham U) 2
Webb, N. J. 1988 (Nottingham F, Manchester U) 26
Webster, M. 1930 (Middlesbrough) 3
Wedlock, W. J. 1907 (Bristol C) 26
Weir, D. 1889 (Bolton W) 2
Welbeck, D. 2011 (Manchester U) **26**
Welch, R. de C. 1872 (Wanderers, Harrow Chequers) 2
Weller, K. 1974 (Leicester C) 4
Welsh, D. 1938 (Charlton Ath) 3
West, G. 1969 (Everton) 3

Westwood, R. W. 1935 (Bolton W) 6
Whateley, O. 1883 (Aston Villa) 2
Wheeler, J. E. 1955 (Bolton W) 1
Wheldon, G. F. 1897 (Aston Villa) 4
White, D. 1993 (Manchester C) 1
White, T. A. 1933 (Everton) 1
Whitehead, J. 1893 (Accrington, Blackburn R) 2
Whitfeld, H. 1879 (Old Etonians) 1
Whitham, M. 1892 (Sheffield U) 1
Whitworth, S. 1975 (Leicester C) 7
Whymark, T. J. 1978 (Ipswich T) 1
Widdowson, S. W. 1880 (Nottingham F) 1
Wignall, F. 1965 (Nottingham F) 2
Wilcox, J. M. 1996 (Blackburn R, Leeds U) 3
Wilkes, A. 1901 (Aston Villa) 5
Wilkins, R. C. 1976 (Chelsea, Manchester U, AC Milan) 84
Wilkinson, B. 1904 (Sheffield U) 1
Wilkinson, L. R. 1891 (Oxford University) 1
Williams, B. F. 1949 (Wolverhampton W) 24
Williams, O. 1923 (Clapton Orient) 2
Williams, S. 1983 (Southampton) 6
Williams, W. 1897 (WBA) 6
Williamson, E. C. 1923 (Arsenal) 2
Williamson, R. G. 1905 (Middlesbrough) 7
Willingham, C. K. 1937 (Huddersfield T) 12
Willis, A. 1952 (Tottenham H) 1
Wilshaw, D. J. 1954 (Wolverhampton W) 12
Wilshere, J. A. 2011 (Arsenal) **20**
Wilson, C. P. 1884 (Hendon) 2
Wilson, C. W. 1879 (Oxford University) 2
Wilson, G. 1921 (Sheffield W) 12
Wilson, G. P. 1900 (Corinthians) 2
Wilson, R. 1960 (Huddersfield T, Everton) 63
Wilson, T. 1928 (Huddersfield T) 1
Winckworth, W. N. 1892 (Old Westminsters) 2
Windridge, J. E. 1908 (Chelsea) 8
Wingfield-Stratford, C. V. 1877 (Royal Engineers) 1
Winterburn, N. 1990 (Arsenal) 2
Wise, D. F. 1991 (Chelsea) 21
Withe, P. 1981 (Aston Villa) 11
Wollaston, C. H. R. 1874 (Wanderers) 4
Wolstenholme, S. 1904 (Everton, Blackburn R) 3
Wood, H. 1890 (Wolverhampton W) 3
Wood, R. E. 1955 (Manchester U) 3
Woodcock, A. S. 1978 (Nottingham F, Cologne, Arsenal) 42
Woodgate, J. S. 1999 (Leeds U, Newcastle U, Real Madrid, Tottenham H) 8
Woodger, G. 1911 (Oldham Ath) 1
Woodhall, G. 1888 (WBA) 2
Woodley, V. R. 1937 (Chelsea) 19
Woods, C. C. E. 1985 (Norwich C, Rangers, Sheffield W) 43
Woodward, V. J. 1903 (Tottenham H, Chelsea) 23
Woosnam, M. 1922 (Manchester C) 1
Worrall, F. 1935 (Portsmouth) 2
Worthington, F. S. 1974 (Leicester C) 8
Wreford-Brown, C. 1889 (Oxford University, Old Carthusians) 4
Wright, E. G. D. 1906 (Cambridge University) 1
Wright, I. E. 1991 (Crystal Palace, Arsenal, West Ham U) 33
Wright, J. D. 1939 (Newcastle U) 1
Wright, M. 1984 (Southampton, Derby Co, Liverpool) 45
Wright, R. I. 2000 (Ipswich T, Arsenal) 2
Wright, T. J. 1968 (Everton) 11
Wright, W. A. 1947 (Wolverhampton W) 105
Wright-Phillips, S. C. 2005 (Manchester C, Chelsea, Manchester C) 36
Wylie, J. G. 1878 (Wanderers) 1

Yates, J. 1889 (Burnley) 1
York, R. E. 1922 (Aston Villa) 2
Young, A. 1933 (Huddersfield T) 9
Young, A. S. 2008 (Aston Villa, Manchester U) **30**
Young, G. M. 1965 (Sheffield W) 1
Young, L. P. 2005 (Charlton Ath) 7

Zaha, D. W. A. 2013 (Manchester U) **2**
Zamora, R. L. 2011 (Fulham) 2

NORTHERN IRELAND

Addis, D. J. 1922 (Cliftonville)	1
Aherne, T. 1947 (Belfast Celtic, Luton T)	4
Alexander, T. E. 1895 (Cliftonville)	1
Allan, C. 1936 (Cliftonville)	1
Allen, J. 1887 (Limavady)	1
Anderson, J. 1925 (Distillery)	1
Anderson, T. 1973 (Manchester U, Swindon T, Peterborough U)	22
Anderson, W. 1898 (Linfield, Cliftonville)	4
Andrews, W. 1908 (Glentoran, Grimsby T)	3
Armstrong, G. J. 1977 (Tottenham H, Watford, Real Mallorca, WBA, Chesterfield)	63
Baird, C. P. 2003 (Southampton, Fulham)	**65**
Baird, G. 1896 (Distillery)	3
Baird, H. C. 1939 (Huddersfield T)	1
Balfe, J. 1909 (Shelbourne)	2
Bambrick, J. 1929 (Linfield, Chelsea)	11
Banks, S. J. 1937 (Cliftonville)	1
Barr, H. H. 1962 (Linfield, Coventry C)	3
Barron, J. H. 1894 (Cliftonville)	7
Barry, J. 1888 (Cliftonville)	3
Barry, J. 1900 (Bohemians)	1
Barton, A. J. 2011 (Preston NE)	1
Baxter, R. A. 1887 (Distillery)	1
Baxter, S. N. 1887 (Cliftonville)	1
Bennett, L. V. 1889 (Dublin University)	1
Best, G. 1964 (Manchester U, Fulham)	37
Bingham, W. L. 1951 (Sunderland, Luton T, Everton, Port Vale)	56
Black, K. T. 1988 (Luton T, Nottingham F)	30
Black, T. 1901 (Glentoran)	1
Blair, H. 1928 (Portadown, Swansea T)	4
Blair, J. 1907 (Cliftonville)	5
Blair, R. V. 1975 (Oldham Ath)	5
Blanchflower, J. 1954 (Manchester U)	12
Blanchflower, R. D. 1950 (Barnsley, Aston Villa, Tottenham H)	56
Blayney, A. 2006 (Doncaster R, Linfield)	5
Bookman, L. J. O. 1914 (Bradford C, Luton T)	4
Bothwell, A. W. 1926 (Ards)	5
Bowler, G. C. 1950 (Hull C)	3
Boyce, L. 2011 (Werder Bremen)	4
Boyle, P. 1901 (Sheffield U)	5
Braithwaite, R. M. 1962 (Linfield, Middlesbrough)	10
Braniff, K. R. 2010 (Portadown)	2
Breen, T. 1935 (Belfast Celtic, Manchester U)	9
Brennan, B. 1912 (Bohemians)	1
Brennan, R. A. 1949 (Luton T, Birmingham C, Fulham)	5
Briggs, W. R. 1962 (Manchester U, Swansea T)	2
Brisby, D. 1891 (Distillery)	1
Brolly, T. H. 1937 (Millwall)	4
Brookes, E. A. 1920 (Shelbourne)	1
Brotherston, N. 1980 (Blackburn R)	27
Brown, J. 1921 (Glenavon, Tranmere R)	3
Brown, J. 1935 (Wolverhampton W, Coventry C, Birmingham C)	10
Brown, N. M. 1887 (Limavady)	1
Brown, W. G. 1926 (Glenavon)	1
Browne, F. 1887 (Cliftonville)	5
Browne, R. J. 1936 (Leeds U)	6
Bruce, A. 1925 (Belfast Celtic)	1
Bruce, A. S. 2013 (Hull C)	**2**
Bruce, W. 1961 (Glentoran)	2
Brunt, C. 2005 (Sheffield W, WBA)	**46**
Bryan, M. A. 2010 (Watford)	2
Buckle, H. R. 1903 (Cliftonville, Sunderland, Bristol R)	3
Buckle, J. 1882 (Cliftonville)	1
Burnett, J. 1894 (Distillery, Glentoran)	5
Burnison, J. 1901 (Distillery)	2
Burnison, S. 1908 (Distillery, Bradford, Distillery)	8
Burns, J. 1923 (Glenavon)	1
Burns, W. 1925 (Glentoran)	1
Butler, M. P. 1939 (Blackpool)	1
Camp, L. M. J. 2011 (Nottingham F)	9
Campbell, A. C. 1963 (Crusaders)	2
Campbell, D. A. 1986 (Nottingham F, Charlton Ath)	10
Campbell, James 1897 (Cliftonville)	14
Campbell, John 1896 (Cliftonville)	1
Campbell, J. P. 1951 (Fulham)	2

Campbell, R. M. 1982 (Bradford C)	2
Campbell, W. G. 1968 (Dundee)	6
Capaldi, A. C. 2004 (Plymouth Arg, Cardiff C)	22
Carey, J. J. 1947 (Manchester U)	7
Carroll, E. 1925 (Glenavon)	1
Carroll, R. E. 1997 (Wigan Ath, Manchester U, West Ham U, Olympiacos)	**35**
Carson, J. G. 2011 (Ipswich T)	4
Carson, S. 2009 (Coleraine)	1
Casement, C. 2009 (Ipswich T)	1
Casey, T. 1955 (Newcastle U, Portsmouth)	12
Caskey, W. 1979 (Derby Co, Tulsa Roughnecks)	8
Cassidy, T. 1971 (Newcastle U, Burnley)	24
Cathcart, C. G. 2011 (Blackpool)	**18**
Caughey, M. 1986 (Linfield)	2
Chambers, R. J. 1921 (Distillery, Bury, Nottingham F)	12
Chatton, H. A. 1925 (Partick Th)	3
Christian, J. 1889 (Linfield)	1
Clarke, C. J. 1986 (Bournemouth, Southampton, QPR, Portsmouth)	38
Clarke, R. 1901 (Belfast Celtic)	2
Cleary, J. 1982 (Glentoran)	5
Clements, D. 1965 (Coventry C, Sheffield W, Everton, New York Cosmos)	48
Clingan, S. G. 2006 (Nottingham F, Norwich C, Coventry C, Kilmarnock)	**38**
Clugston, J. 1888 (Cliftonville)	14
Clyde, M. G. 2005 (Wolverhampton W)	3
Coates, C. 2009 (Crusaders)	6
Cochrane, D. 1939 (Leeds U)	12
Cochrane, G. 1903 (Cliftonville)	1
Cochrane, G. T. 1976 (Coleraine, Burnley, Middlesbrough, Gillingham)	26
Cochrane, M. 1898 (Distillery, Leicester Fosse)	8
Collins, F. 1922 (Celtic)	1
Collins, R. 1922 (Cliftonville)	1
Condy, J. 1882 (Distillery)	3
Connell, T. E. 1978 (Coleraine)	1
Connor, J. 1901 (Glentoran, Belfast Celtic)	13
Connor, M. J. 1903 (Brentford, Fulham)	3
Cook, W. 1933 (Celtic, Everton)	15
Cooke, S. 1889 (Belfast YMCA, Cliftonville)	3
Coote, A. 1999 (Norwich C)	6
Coulter, J. 1934 (Belfast Celtic, Everton, Grimsby T, Chelmsford C)	11
Cowan, J. 1970 (Newcastle U)	1
Cowan, T. S. 1925 (Queen's Island)	1
Coyle, F. 1956 (Coleraine, Nottingham F)	4
Coyle, L. 1989 (Derry C)	1
Coyle, R. I. 1973 (Sheffield W)	5
Craig, A. B. 1908 (Rangers, Morton)	9
Craig, D. J. 1967 (Newcastle U)	25
Craigan, S. J. 2003 (Partick Th, Motherwell)	54
Crawford, A. 1889 (Distillery, Cliftonville)	7
Croft, T. 1922 (Queen's Island)	3
Crone, R. 1889 (Distillery)	4
Crone, W. 1882 (Distillery)	12
Crooks, W. J. 1922 (Manchester U)	1
Crossan, E. 1950 (Blackburn R)	3
Crossan, J. A. 1960 (Sparta-Rotterdam, Sunderland, Manchester C, Middlesbrough)	24
Crothers, C. 1907 (Distillery)	1
Cumming, L. 1929 (Huddersfield T, Oldham Ath)	3
Cunningham, W. 1892 (Ulster)	4
Cunningham, W. E. 1951 (St Mirren, Leicester C, Dunfermline Ath)	30
Curran, S. 1926 (Belfast Celtic)	4
Curran, J. J. 1922 (Glenavon, Pontypridd, Glenavon)	5
Cush, W. W. 1951 (Glenavon, Leeds U, Portadown)	26
Dallas, S. 2011 (Crusaders)	1
Dalrymple, J. 1922 (Distillery)	1
Dalton, W. 1888 (YMCA, Linfield)	11
D'Arcy, S. D. 1952 (Chelsea, Brentford)	5
Darling, J. 1897 (Linfield)	22
Davey, H. H. 1926 (Reading, Portsmouth)	5
Davis, S. 2005 (Aston Villa, Fulham, Rangers, Southampton)	**68**
Davis, T. L. 1937 (Oldham Ath)	1
Davison, A. J. 1996 (Bolton W, Bradford C, Grimsby T)	3
Davison, J. R. 1882 (Cliftonville)	8

Dennison, R. 1988 (Wolverhampton W) 18
Devine, A. O. 1886 (Limavady) 4
Devine, J. 1990 (Glentoran) 1
Dickson, D. 1970 (Coleraine) 4
Dickson, T. A. 1957 (Linfield) 1
Dickson, W. 1951 (Chelsea, Arsenal) 12
Diffin, W. J. 1931 (Belfast Celtic) 2
Dill, A. H. 1882 (Knock, Down Ath, Cliftonville) 9
Doherty, I. 1901 (Belfast Celtic) 1
Doherty, J. 1928 (Portadown) 1
Doherty, J. 1933 (Cliftonville) 2
Doherty, L. 1985 (Linfield) 2
Doherty, M. 1938 (Derry C) 1
Doherty, P. D. 1935 (Blackpool, Manchester C, Derby
 Co, Huddersfield T, Doncaster R) 16
Doherty, T. E. 2003 (Bristol C) 9
Donaghey, B. 1903 (Belfast Celtic) 1
Donaghy, M. M. 1980 (Luton T, Manchester U, Chelsea) 91
Donnelly, L. 1913 (Distillery) 1
Donnelly, L. F. P. 2014 (Fulham) **1**
Donnelly, M. 2009 (Crusaders) 1
Doran, J. F. 1921 (Brighton) 3
Dougan, A. D. 1958 (Portsmouth, Blackburn R,
 Aston Villa, Leicester C, Wolverhampton W) 43
Douglas, J. P. 1947 (Belfast Celtic) 1
Dowd, H. O. 1974 (Glenavon, Sheffield W) 3
Dowie, I. 1990 (Luton T, West Ham U, Southampton,
 C Palace, West Ham U, QPR) 59
Duff, M. J. 2002 (Cheltenham T, Burnley) 24
Duggan, H. A. 1930 (Leeds U) 8
Dunlop, G. 1985 (Linfield) 4
Dunne, J. 1928 (Sheffield U) 7

Eames, W. L. E. 1885 (Dublin University) 3
Eglington, T. J. 1947 (Everton) 6
Elder, A. R. 1960 (Burnley, Stoke C) 40
Elleman, A. R. 1889 (Cliftonville) 2
Elliott, S. 2001 (Motherwell, Hull C) 39
Elwood, J. H. 1929 (Bradford) 2
Emerson, W. 1920 (Glentoran, Burnley) 11
English, S. 1933 (Rangers) 2
Enright, J. 1912 (Leeds C) 1
Evans, C. J. 2009 (Manchester U, Hull C, Blackburn R) **23**
Evans, J. G. 2007 (Manchester U) **38**

Falloon, E. 1931 (Aberdeen) 2
Farquharson, T. G. 1923 (Cardiff C) 7
Farrell, P. 1901 (Distillery) 2
Farrell, P. 1938 (Hibernian) 1
Farrell, P. D. 1947 (Everton) 7
Feeney, J. M. 1947 (Linfield, Swansea T) 2
Feeney, W. 1976 (Glentoran) 1
Feeney, W. J. 2002 (Bournemouth, Luton T, Cardiff C,
 Oldham Ath, Plymouth Arg) 46
Ferguson, G. 1999 (Linfield) 5
Ferguson, S. 2009 (Newcastle U) **16**
Ferguson, W. 1966 (Linfield) 2
Ferris, J. 1920 (Belfast Celtic, Chelsea, Belfast Celtic) 6
Ferris, R. O. 1950 (Birmingham C) 3
Fettis, A. W. 1992 (Hull C, Nottingham F, Blackburn R)
 25
Finney, T. 1975 (Sunderland, Cambridge U) 14
Fitzpatrick, J. C. 1896 (Bohemians) 2
Flack, H. 1929 (Burnley) 1
Fleming, J. G. 1987 (Nottingham F, Manchester C,
 Barnsley) 31
Forbes, G. 1888 (Limavady, Distillery) 3
Forde, J. T. 1959 (Ards) 4
Foreman, T. A. 1899 (Cliftonville) 1
Forsythe, J. 1888 (YMCA) 2
Fox, W. T. 1887 (Ulster) 2
Frame, T. 1925 (Linfield) 1
Fulton, R. P. 1928 (Larne, Belfast Celtic) 21

Gaffikin, G. 1890 (Linfield Ath) 15
Galbraith, W. 1890 (Distillery) 1
Gallagher, P. 1920 (Celtic, Falkirk) 11
Gallogly, C. 1951 (Huddersfield T) 2
Gara, A. 1902 (Preston NE) 3
Gardiner, A. 1930 (Cliftonville) 5
Garrett, J. 1925 (Distillery) 1
Garrett, R. 2009 (Linfield) 5

Gaston, R. 1969 (Oxford U) 1
Gaukrodger, G. 1895 (Linfield) 1
Gault, M. 2008 (Linfield) 1
Gaussen, A. D. 1884 (Moyola Park, Magherafelt) 6
Geary, J. 1931 (Glentoran) 2
Gibb, J. T. 1884 (Wellington Park, Cliftonville) 10
Gibb, T. J. 1936 (Cliftonville) 1
Gibson W. K. 1894 (Cliftonville) 14
Gillespie, K. R. 1995 (Manchester U, Newcastle U,
 Blackburn R, Leicester C, Sheffield U) 86
Gillespie, S. 1886 (Hertford) 6
Gillespie, W. 1889 (West Down) 1
Gillespie, W. 1913 (Sheffield U) 25
Goodall, A. L. 1899 (Derby Co, Glossop) 10
Goodbody, M. F. 1889 (Dublin University) 2
Gordon, H. 1895 (Linfield) 3
Gordon R. W. 1891 (Linfield) 7
Gordon, T. 1894 (Linfield) 2
Gorman, R. J. 2010 (Wolverhampton W) 9
Gorman, W. C. 1947 (Brentford) 4
Gough, J. 1925 (Queen's Island) 1
Gowdy, J. 1920 (Glentoran, Queen's Island, Falkirk) 6
Gowdy, W. A. 1932 (Hull C, Sheffield W, Linfield,
 Hibernian) 6
Graham, W. G. L. 1951 (Doncaster R) 14
Gray, P. 1993 (Luton T, Sunderland, Nancy, Luton T,
 Burnley, Oxford U) 26
Greer, W. 1909 (QPR) 3
Gregg, H. 1954 (Doncaster R, Manchester U) 25
Griffin, D. J. 1996 (St Johnstone, Dundee U,
 Stockport Co) 29
Grigg, W. D. 2012 (Walsall, Brentford) **5**

Hall, G. 1897 (Distillery) 1
Halligan, W. 1911 (Derby Co, Wolverhampton W) 2
Hamill, M. 1912 (Manchester U, Belfast Celtic,
 Manchester C) 7
Hamill, R. 1999 (Glentoran) 1
Hamilton, B. 1969 (Linfield, Ipswich T, Everton,
 Millwall, Swindon T) 50
Hamilton, G. 2003 (Portadown) 5
Hamilton, J. 1882 (Knock) 2
Hamilton, R. 1928 (Rangers) 5
Hamilton, W. D. 1885 (Dublin Association) 1
Hamilton, W. J. 1885 (Dublin Association) 1
Hamilton, W. J. 1908 (Distillery) 1
Hamilton, W. R. 1978 (QPR, Burnley, Oxford U) 41
Hampton, H. 1911 (Bradford C) 9
Hanna, J. 1912 (Nottingham F) 2
Hanna, J. D. 1899 (Royal Artillery, Portsmouth) 1
Hannon, D. J. 1908 (Bohemians) 6
Harkin, J. T. 1968 (Southport, Shrewsbury T) 5
Harland, A. I. 1922 (Linfield) 2
Harris, J. 1921 (Cliftonville, Glenavon) 2
Harris, V. 1906 (Shelbourne, Everton) 20
Harvey, M. 1961 (Sunderland) 34
Hastings, J. 1882 (Knock, Ulster) 7
Hatton, S. 1963 (Linfield) 2
Hayes, W. E. 1938 (Huddersfield T) 4
Healy, D. J. 2000 (Manchester U, Preston NE, Leeds U,
 Fulham, Sunderland, Rangers, Bury) 95
Healy, P. J. 1982 (Coleraine, Glentoran) 4
Hegan, D. 1970 (WBA, Wolverhampton W) 7
Henderson, J. 1885 (Ulster) 3
Hewison, G. 1885 (Moyola Park) 2
Hill, C. F. 1990 (Sheffield U, Leicester C, Trelleborg,
 Northampton T) 27
Hill, M. J. 1959 (Norwich C, Everton) 7
Hinton, E. 1947 (Fulham, Millwall) 7
Hodson, L. J. S. 2011 (Watford, Milton Keynes D) **14**
Holmes, S. P. 2002 (Wrexham) 1
Hopkins, J. 1926 (Brighton) 1
Horlock, K. 1995 (Swindon T, Manchester C) 32
Houston, J. 1912 (Linfield, Everton) 6
Houston, W. 1933 (Linfield) 1
Houston, W. J. 1885 (Moyola Park) 2
**Hughes, A. W. 1998 (Newcastle U, Aston Villa, Fulham,
 QPR)** **90**
Hughes, J. 2006 (Lincoln C) 2
Hughes, M.A. 2006 (Oldham Ath) 2
Hughes, M. E. 1992 (Manchester C, Strasbourg,
 West Ham U, Wimbledon, Crystal Palace) 71

Hughes, P. A. 1987 (Bury) 3
Hughes, W. 1951 (Bolton W) 1
Humphries, W. M. 1962 (Ards, Coventry C, Swansea T) 14
Hunter, A. 1905 (Distillery, Belfast Celtic) 8
Hunter, A. 1970 (Blackburn R, Ipswich T) 53
Hunter, B. V. 1995 (Wrexham, Reading) 15
Hunter, R. J. 1884 (Cliftonville) 3
Hunter, V. 1962 (Coleraine) 2

Ingham, M. G. 2005 (Sunderland, Wrexham) 3
Irvine, R. J. 1962 (Linfield, Stoke C) 8
Irvine, R. W. 1922 (Everton, Portsmouth, Connah's Quay, Derry C) 15
Irvine, W. J. 1963 (Burnley, Preston NE, Brighton & HA) 23
Irving, S. J. 1923 (Dundee, Cardiff C, Chelsea) 18

Jackson, T. A. 1969 (Everton, Nottingham F, Manchester U) 35
Jamison, J. 1976 (Glentoran) 1
Jenkins, I. 1997 (Chester C, Dundee U) 6
Jennings, P. A. 1964 (Watford, Tottenham H, Arsenal, Tottenham H) 119
Johnson, D. M. 1999 (Blackburn R, Birmingham C) 56
Johnston, H. 1927 (Portadown) 1
Johnston, R. S. 1882 (Distillery) 5
Johnston, R. S. 1905 (Distillery) 1
Johnston, S. 1890 (Linfield) 4
Johnston, W. 1885 (Oldpark) 2
Johnston, W. C. 1962 (Glenavon, Oldham Ath) 2
Jones, J. 1930 (Linfield, Hibernian, Glenavon) 23
Jones, J. 1956 (Glenavon) 3
Jones, S. 1934 (Distillery, Blackpool) 2
Jones, S. G. 2003 (Crewe Alex, Burnley) 29
Jordan, T. 1895 (Linfield) 2

Kavanagh, P. J. 1930 (Celtic) 1
Keane, T. R. 1949 (Swansea T) 1
Kearns, A. 1900 (Distillery) 6
Kee, P. V. 1990 (Oxford U, Ards) 9
Keith, R. M. 1958 (Newcastle U) 23
Kelly, H. R. 1950 (Fulham, Southampton) 4
Kelly, J. 1896 (Glentoran) 1
Kelly, J. 1932 (Derry C) 11
Kelly, P. J. 1921 (Manchester C) 1
Kelly, P. M. 1950 (Barnsley) 1
Kennedy, A. L. 1923 (Arsenal) 2
Kennedy, P. H. 1999 (Watford, Wigan Ath) 20
Kernaghan, N. 1936 (Belfast Celtic) 3
Kirk, A. R. 2000 (Hearts, Boston U, Northampton T, Dunfermline Ath) 11
Kirkwood, H. 1904 (Cliftonville) 1
Kirwan, J. 1900 (Tottenham H, Chelsea, Clyde) 17

Lacey, W. 1909 (Everton, Liverpool, New Brighton) 23
Lafferty, D. P. 2012 (Burnley) **10**
Lafferty, K. 2006 (Burnley, Rangers, FC Sion, Palermo) **37**
Lawrie, J. 2009 (Port Vale) 3
Lawther, R. 1888 (Glentoran) 2
Lawther, W. I. 1960 (Sunderland, Blackburn R) 4
Leatham, J. 1939 (Belfast Celtic) 1
Ledwidge, J. J. 1906 (Shelbourne) 2
Lemon, J. 1886 (Glentoran, Belfast YMCA) 3
Lennon, N. F. 1994 (Crewe Alex, Leicester C, Celtic) 40
Leslie, W. 1887 (YMCA) 1
Lewis, J. 1899 (Glentoran, Distillery) 4
Little, A. 2009 (Rangers) 9
Lockhart, H. 1884 (Rossall School) 1
Lockhart, N. H. 1947 (Linfield, Coventry C, Aston Villa) 8
Lomas, S. M. 1994 (Manchester C, West Ham U) 45
Loyal, J. 1891 (Clarence) 1
Lutton, R. J. 1970 (Wolverhampton W, West Ham U) 6
Lynas, R. 1925 (Cliftonville) 1
Lyner, D. R. 1920 (Glentoran, Manchester U, Kilmarnock) 6
Lytle, J. 1898 (Glentoran) 1

McAdams, W. J. 1954 (Manchester C, Bolton W, Leeds U) 15
McAlery, J. M. 1882 (Cliftonville) 2

McAlinden, J. 1938 (Belfast Celtic, Portsmouth, Southend U) 4
McAllen, J. 1898 (Linfield) 9
McAlpine, S. 1901 (Cliftonville) 1
McArdle, R. A. 2010 (Rochdale, Aberdeen, Bradford C) **7**
McArthur, A. 1886 (Distillery) 1
McAuley, G. 2005 (Lincoln C, Leicester C, Ipswich T, WBA) **47**
McAuley, J. L. 1911 (Huddersfield T) 6
McAuley, P. 1900 (Belfast Celtic) 1
McBride, S. D. 1991 (Glenavon) 4
McCabe, J. J. 1949 (Leeds U) 6
McCabe, W. 1891 (Ulster) 1
McCambridge, J. 1930 (Ballymena, Cardiff C) 4
McCandless, J. 1912 (Bradford) 5
McCandless, W. 1920 (Linfield, Rangers) 9
McCann, G. S. 2002 (West Ham U, Cheltenham T, Barnsley, Scunthorpe U, Peterborough U) 39
McCann, P. 1910 (Belfast Celtic, Glentoran) 7
McCarthy, J. D. 1996 (Port Vale, Birmingham C) 18
McCartney, A. 1903 (Ulster, Linfield, Everton, Belfast Celtic, Glentoran) 15
McCartney, G. 2002 (Sunderland, West Ham U, Sunderland) 34
McCashin, J. W. 1896 (Cliftonville) 5
McCavana, W. T. 1955 (Coleraine) 3
McCaw, J. H. 1927 (Linfield) 6
McClatchey, J. 1886 (Distillery) 3
McClatchey, T. 1895 (Distillery) 1
McCleary, J. W. 1955 (Cliftonville) 1
McCleery, W. 1922 (Cliftonville, Linfield) 10
McClelland, J. 1980 (Mansfield T, Rangers, Watford, Leeds U) 53
McClelland, J. T. 1961 (Arsenal, Fulham) 6
McCluggage, A. 1922 (Cliftonville, Bradford, Burnley) 13
McClure, G. 1907 (Cliftonville, Distillery) 4
McConnell, E. 1904 (Cliftonville, Glentoran, Sunderland, Sheffield W) 12
McConnell, P. 1928 (Doncaster R, Southport) 2
McConnell, W. G. 1912 (Bohemians) 6
McConnell, W. H. 1925 (Reading) 8
McCourt, F. J. 1952 (Manchester C) 6
McCourt, P. J. 2002 (Rochdale, Celtic, Barnsley) **14**
McCoy, R. K. 1987 (Coleraine) 1
McCoy, S. 1896 (Distillery) 1
McCracken, E. 1928 (Barking) 1
McCracken, R. 1921 (Crystal Palace) 4
McCracken, R. 1922 (Linfield) 1
McCracken, W. R. 1902 (Distillery, Newcastle U, Hull C) 16
McCreery, D. 1976 (Manchester U, QPR, Tulsa Roughnecks, Newcastle U, Hearts) 67
McCrory, S. 1958 (Southend U) 1
McCullough, K. 1935 (Belfast Celtic, Manchester C) 5
McCullough, L. 2014 (Doncaster R) **2**
McCullough, W. J. 1961 (Arsenal, Millwall) 10
McCurdy, C. 1980 (Linfield) 1
McDonald, A. 1986 (QPR) 52
McDonald, R. 1930 (Rangers) 2
McDonnell, J. 1911 (Bohemians) 4
McElhinney, G. M. A. 1984 (Bolton W) 6
McEvilly, L. R. 2002 (Rochdale) 1
McFaul, W. S. 1967 (Linfield, Newcastle U) 6
McGarry, J. K. 1951 (Cliftonville) 3
McGaughey, M. 1985 (Linfield) 1
McGibbon, P. C. G. 1995 (Manchester U, Wigan Ath) 7
McGinn, N. 2009 (Celtic, Aberdeen) **31**
McGivern, R. 2009 (Manchester C, Hibernian) **21**
McGovern, M. 2010 (Ross Co) 1
McGrath, R. C. 1974 (Tottenham H, Manchester U) 21
McGregor, S. 1921 (Glentoran) 1
McGrillen, J. 1924 (Clyde, Belfast Celtic) 2
McGuire, E. 1907 (Distillery) 1
McGuire, J. 1928 (Linfield) 1
McIlroy, H. 1906 (Cliftonville) 1
McIlroy, J. 1952 (Burnley, Stoke C) 55
McIlroy, S. B. 1972 (Manchester U, Stoke C, Manchester C) 88
McIlvenny, P. 1924 (Distillery) 1
McIlvenny, R. 1890 (Distillery, Ulster) 2
McKay, W. R. 2013 (Inverness CT) **7**
McKeag, W. 1968 (Glentoran) 2

McKeague, T. 1925 (Glentoran) 1
McKee, F. W. 1906 (Cliftonville, Belfast Celtic) 5
McKelvey, H. 1901 (Glentoran) 2
McKenna, J. 1950 (Huddersfield T) 7
McKenzie, H. 1922 (Distillery) 2
McKenzie, R. 1967 (Airdrieonians) 1
McKeown, N. 1892 (Linfield) 7
McKie, H. 1895 (Cliftonville) 3
Mackie, J. A. 1923 (Arsenal, Portsmouth) 3
McKinney, D. 1921 (Hull C, Bradford C) 2
McKinney, V. J. 1966 (Falkirk) 1
McKnight, A. D. 1988 (Celtic, West Ham U) 10
McKnight, J. 1912 (Preston NE, Glentoran) 2
McLaughlin, C. G. 2012 (Preston NE, Fleetwood T) 3
McLaughlin, J. C. 1962 (Shrewsbury T, Swansea T) 12
McLaughlin, R. 2014 (Liverpool) 2
McLean, B. S. 2006 (Rangers) 1
McLean, T. 1885 (Limavady) 1
McMahon, G. J. 1995 (Tottenham H, Stoke C) 17
McMahon, J. 1934 (Bohemians) 1
McMaster, G. 1897 (Glentoran) 3
McMichael, A. 1950 (Newcastle U) 40
McMillan, G. 1903 (Distillery) 2
McMillan, S. T. 1963 (Manchester U) 2
McMillen, W. S. 1934 (Manchester U, Chesterfield) 7
McMordie, A. S. 1969 (Middlesbrough) 21
McMorran, E. J. 1947 (Belfast Celtic, Barnsley,
Doncaster R) 15
McMullan, D. 1926 (Liverpool) 3
McNally, B. A. 1986 (Shrewsbury T) 5
McNinch, J. 1931 (Ballymena) 3
McPake, J. 2012 (Coventry C) 1
McParland, P. J. 1954 (Aston Villa, Wolverhampton W) 34
McQuoid, J. J. B. 2011 (Millwall) 5
McShane, J. 1899 (Cliftonville) 4
McVeigh, P. M. 1999 (Tottenham H, Norwich C) 20
McVicker, J. 1888 (Linfield, Glentoran) 2
McWha, W. B. R. 1882 (Knock, Cliftonville) 7
Madden, O. 1938 (Norwich C) 1
Magee, G. 1885 (Wellington Park) 3
Magennis, J. B. D. 2010 (Cardiff C, Aberdeen) 7
Magill, E. J. 1962 (Arsenal, Brighton & HA) 26
Magilton, J. 1991 (Oxford U, Southampton, Sheffield W,
Ipswich T) 52
Maginnis, H. 1900 (Linfield) 8
Mahood, J. 1926 (Belfast Celtic, Ballymena) 9
Mannus, A. 2004 (Linfield, St Johnstone) 7
Manderson, R. 1920 (Rangers) 5
Mansfield, J. 1901 (Dublin Freebooters) 1
Martin, C. 1882 (Cliftonville) 3
Martin, C. 1925 (Bo'ness) 1
Martin, C. J. 1947 (Glentoran, Leeds U, Aston Villa) 6
Martin, D. K. 1934 (Belfast Celtic, Wolverhampton W,
Nottingham F) 10
Mathieson, A. 1921 (Luton T) 2
Maxwell, J. 1902 (Linfield, Glentoran, Belfast Celtic) 7
Meek, H. L. 1925 (Glentoran) 1
Mehaffy, J. A. C. 1922 (Queen's Island) 1
Meldon, P. A. 1899 (Dublin Freebooters) 1
Mercer, H. V. A. 1908 (Linfield) 1
Mercer, J. T. 1898 (Distillery, Linfield, Distillery,
Derby Co) 12
Millar, W. 1932 (Barrow) 2
Miller, J. 1929 (Middlesbrough) 3
Milligan, D. 1939 (Chesterfield) 1
Milne, R. G. 1894 (Linfield) 28
Mitchell, E. J. 1933 (Cliftonville, Glentoran) 2
Mitchell, W. 1932 (Distillery, Chelsea) 15
Molyneux, T. B. 1883 (Ligoniel, Cliftonville) 11
Montgomery, F. J. 1955 (Coleraine) 1
Moore, C. 1949 (Glentoran) 1
Moore, P. 1933 (Aberdeen) 1
Moore, R. 1891 (Linfield Ath) 3
Moore, R. L. 1887 (Ulster) 1
Moore, W. 1923 (Falkirk) 1
Moorhead, F. W. 1885 (Dublin University) 1
Moorhead, G. 1923 (Linfield) 4
Moran, J. 1912 (Leeds C) 1
Moreland, V. 1979 (Derby Co) 6
Morgan, G. F. 1922 (Linfield, Nottingham F) 8
Morgan, S. 1972 (Port Vale, Aston Villa, Brighton & HA,
Sparta Rotterdam) 18

Morrison, R. 1891 (Linfield Ath) 2
Morrison, T. 1895 (Glentoran, Burnley) 7
Morrogh, D. 1896 (Bohemians) 1
Morrow, S. J. 1990 (Arsenal, QPR) 39
Morrow, W. J. 1883 (Moyola Park) 3
Muir, R. 1885 (Oldpark) 2
Mulgrew, J. 2010 (Linfield) 2
Mulholland, T. S. 1906 (Belfast Celtic) 2
Mullan, G. 1983 (Glentoran) 4
Mulligan, J. 1921 (Manchester C) 1
Mulryne, P. P. 1997 (Manchester U, Norwich C,
Cardiff C) 27
Murdock, C. J. 2000 (Preston NE, Hibernian,
Crewe Alex, Rotherham U) 34
Murphy, J. 1910 (Bradford C) 3
Murphy, N. 1905 (QPR) 3
Murray, J. M. 1910 (Motherwell, Sheffield W) 3

Napier, R. J. 1966 (Bolton W) 1
Neill, W. J. T. 1961 (Arsenal, Hull C) 59
Nelis, P. 1923 (Nottingham F) 1
Nelson, S. 1970 (Arsenal, Brighton & HA) 51
Nicholl, C. J. 1975 (Aston Villa, Southampton,
Grimsby T) 51
Nicholl, H. 1902 (Belfast Celtic) 3
Nicholl, J. M. 1976 (Manchester U, Toronto Blizzard,
Sunderland, Toronto Blizzard, Rangers,
Toronto Blizzard, WBA) 73
Nicholson, J. J. 1961 (Manchester U, Huddersfield T) 41
Nixon, R. 1914 (Linfield) 1
Nolan, I. R. 1997 (Sheffield W, Bradford C, Wigan Ath)
18
Nolan-Whelan, J. V. 1901 (Dublin Freebooters) 5
Norwood, O. J. 2011 (Manchester U, Huddersfield T) 17

O'Boyle, G. 1994 (Dunfermline Ath, St Johnstone) 13
O'Brien, M. T. 1921 (QPR, Leicester C, Hull C,
Derby Co) 10
O'Connell, P. 1912 (Sheffield W, Hull C) 5
**O'Connor, M. J. 2008 (Crewe Alex, Scunthorpe U,
Rotherham U) 11**
O'Doherty, A. 1970 (Coleraine) 2
O'Driscoll, J. F. 1949 (Swansea T) 3
O'Hagan, C. 1905 (Tottenham H, Aberdeen) 11
O'Hagan, W. 1920 (St Mirren) 2
O'Hehir, J. C. 1910 (Bohemians) 1
O'Kane, W. J. 1970 (Nottingham F) 20
O'Mahoney, M. T. 1939 (Bristol R) 1
O'Neill, C. 1989 (Motherwell) 3
O'Neill, J. 1962 (Sunderland) 1
O'Neill, J. P. 1980 (Leicester C) 39
O'Neill, M. A. M. 1988 (Newcastle U, Dundee U,
Hibernian, Coventry C) 31
O'Neill, M. H. M. 1972 (Distillery, Nottingham F,
Norwich C, Manchester C, Norwich C, Notts Co) 64
O'Reilly, H. 1901 (Dublin Freebooters) 3
Owens, J. 2011 (Crusaders) 1

Parke, J. 1964 (Linfield, Hibernian, Sunderland) 14
**Paterson, M. A. 2008 (Scunthorpe U, Burnley,
Huddersfield T) 22**
Paton, P. R. 2014 (Dundee U) 1
Patterson, D. J. 1994 (Crystal Palace, Luton T,
Dundee U) 17
Patterson, R. 2010 (Coleraine, Plymouth Arg) 5
Peacock, R. 1952 (Celtic, Coleraine) 31
Peden, J. 1887 (Linfield, Distillery) 24
Penney, S. 1985 (Brighton & HA) 17
Percy, J. C. 1889 (Belfast YMCA) 1
Platt, J. A. 1976 (Middlesbrough, Ballymena U,
Coleraine) 23
Pollock, W. 1928 (Belfast Celtic) 1
Ponsonby, J. 1895 (Distillery) 9
Potts, R. M. C. 1883 (Cliftonville) 2
Priestley, T. J. M. 1933 (Coleraine, Chelsea) 2
Pyper, Jas. 1897 (Cliftonville) 7
Pyper, John 1897 (Cliftonville) 9
Pyper, M. 1932 (Linfield) 1

Quinn, J. M. 1985 (Blackburn R, Swindon T, Leicester C,
Bradford C, West Ham U, Bournemouth, Reading) 46

Quinn, S. J. 1996 (Blackpool, WBA, Willem II,
   Sheffield W, Peterborough U, Northampton T)   50

Rafferty, P. 1980 (Linfield)   1
Ramsey, P. C. 1984 (Leicester C)   14
Rankine, J. 1883 (Alexander)   2
Rattray, D. 1882 (Avoniel)   3
Rea, R. 1901 (Glentoran)   1
Redmond, R. 1884 (Cliftonville)   1
Reid, G. H. 1923 (Cardiff C)   1
Reid, J. 1883 (Ulster)   6
Reid, S. E. 1934 (Derby Co)   3
Reid, W. 1931 (Hearts)   1
Reilly, M. M. 1900 (Portsmouth)   2
Renneville, W. T. J. 1910 (Leyton, Aston Villa)   4
Reynolds, J. 1890 (Distillery, Ulster)   5
Reynolds, R. 1905 (Bohemians)   1
Rice, P. J. 1969 (Arsenal)   49
Roberts, F. C. 1931 (Glentoran)   1
Robinson, P. 1920 (Distillery, Blackburn R)   2
Robinson, S. 1997 (Bournemouth, Luton T)   7
Rogan, A. 1988 (Celtic, Sunderland, Millwall)   18
Rollo, D. 1912 (Linfield, Blackburn R)   16
Roper, E. O. 1886 (Dublin University)   1
Rosbotham, A. 1887 (Cliftonville)   7
Ross, W. E. 1969 (Newcastle U)   1
Rowland, K. 1994 (West Ham U, QPR)   19
Rowley, R. W. M. 1929 (Southampton, Tottenham H)   6
Rushe, F. 1925 (Distillery)   1
Russell, A. 1947 (Linfield)   1
Russell, S. R. 1930 (Bradford C, Derry C)   3
Ryan, R. A. 1950 (WBA)   1

Sanchez, L. P. 1987 (Wimbledon)   3
Scott, E. 1920 (Liverpool, Belfast Celtic)   31
Scott, J. 1958 (Grimsby)   2
Scott, J. E. 1901 (Cliftonville)   1
Scott, L. J. 1895 (Dublin University)   1
Scott, P. W. 1975 (Everton, York C, Aldershot)   10
Scott, T. 1894 (Cliftonville)   13
Scott, W. 1903 (Linfield, Everton, Leeds C)   25
Scraggs, M. J. 1921 (Glentoran)   1
Seymour, H. C. 1914 (Bohemians)   1
Seymour, J. 1907 (Cliftonville)   2
Shanks, T. 1903 (Woolwich Arsenal, Brentford)   3
Sharkey, P. G. 1976 (Ipswich T)   1
Sheehan, Dr G. 1899 (Bohemians)   1
Sheridan, J. 1903 (Everton, Stoke C)   6
Sherrard, J. 1885 (Limavady)   3
Sherrard, W. C. 1895 (Cliftonville)   3
Sherry, J. J. 1906 (Bohemians)   2
Shields, R. J. 1957 (Southampton)   1
Shiels, D. 2006 (Hibernian, Doncaster R, Kilmarnock)   14
Silo, M. 1888 (Belfast YMCA)   1
Simpson, W. J. 1951 (Rangers)   12
Sinclair, J. 1882 (Knock)   2
Slemin, J. C. 1909 (Bohemians)   1
Sloan, A. S. 1925 (London Caledonians)   1
Sloan, D. 1969 (Oxford U)   2
Sloan, H. A. de B. 1903 (Bohemians)   8
Sloan, J. W. 1947 (Arsenal)   1
Sloan, T. 1926 (Cardiff C, Linfield)   11
Sloan, T. 1979 (Manchester U)   3
Small, J. M. 1887 (Clarence, Cliftonville)   4
Smith, A. W. 2003 (Glentoran, Preston NE)   18
Smith, E. E. 1921 (Cardiff C)   4
Smith, J. E. 1901 (Distillery)   2
Smyth, R. H. 1886 (Dublin University)   1
Smyth, S. 1948 (Wolverhampton W, Stoke C)   9
Smyth, W. 1949 (Distillery)   4
Snape, A. 1920 (Airdrieonians)   1
Sonner, D. J. 1998 (Ipswich T, Sheffield W,
   Birmingham C, Nottingham F, Peterborough U)   13
Spence, D. W. 1975 (Bury, Blackpool, Southend U)   29
Spencer, S. 1890 (Distillery)   6
Spiller, E. A. 1883 (Cliftonville)   5
Sproule, I. 2006 (Hibernian, Bristol C)   11
Stanfield, O. M. 1887 (Distillery)   30
Steele, A. 1926 (Charlton Ath, Fulham)   4
Steele, J. 2013 (New York Red Bulls)   **3**
Stevenson, A. E. 1934 (Rangers, Everton)   17
Stewart, A. 1967 (Glentoran, Derby Co)   7

Stewart, D. C. 1978 (Hull C)   1
Stewart, I. 1982 (QPR, Newcastle U)   31
Stewart, R. K. 1890 (St Columb's Court, Cliftonville)   11
Stewart, T. C. 1961 (Linfield)   1
Swan, S. 1899 (Linfield)   1

Taggart, G. P. 1990 (Barnsley, Bolton W, Leicester C)   51
Taggart, J. 1899 (Walsall)   1
Taylor, M. S. 1999 (Fulham, Birmingham C, unattached)
      88
Thompson, A. L. 2011 (Watford)   2
Thompson, F. W. 1910 (Cliftonville, Linfield, Bradford
   C, Clyde)   12
Thompson, J. 1897 (Distillery)   1
Thompson, P. 2006 (Linfield, Stockport Co)   8
Thompson, R. 1928 (Queen's Island)   1
Thompson, W. 1889 (Belfast Ath)   1
Thunder, P. J. 1911 (Bohemians)   1
Todd, S. J. 1966 (Burnley, Sheffield W)   11
Toner, C. 2003 (Leyton Orient)   2
Toner, J. 1922 (Arsenal, St Johnstone)   8
Torrans, R. 1893 (Linfield)   1
Torrans, S. 1889 (Linfield)   26
Trainor, D. 1967 (Crusaders)   1
Tuffey, J. 2009 (Partick T, Inverness CT)   8
Tully, C. P. 1949 (Celtic)   10
Turner, A. 1896 (Cliftonville)   1
Turner, E. 1896 (Cliftonville)   1
Turner, W. 1886 (Cliftonville)   3
Twomey, J. F. 1938 (Leeds U)   2

Uprichard, W. N. M. C. 1952 (Swindon T, Portsmouth)   18

Vernon, J. 1947 (Belfast Celtic, WBA)   17

Waddell, T. M. R. 1906 (Cliftonville)   1
Walker, J. 1955 (Doncaster R)   1
Walker, T. 1911 (Bury)   1
Walsh, D. J. 1947 (WBA)   9
Walsh, W. 1948 (Manchester C)   5
Ward, J. J. 2012 (Derby Co)   **10**
Waring, J. 1899 (Cliftonville)   1
Warren, P. 1913 (Shelbourne)   2
Watson, J. 1883 (Ulster)   9
Watson, P. 1971 (Distillery)   1
Watson, T. 1926 (Cardiff C)   1
Wattie, J. 1899 (Distillery)   1
Webb, C. G. 1909 (Brighton & HA)   3
Webb, S. M. 2006 (Ross Co)   4
Weir, E. 1939 (Clyde)   1
Welsh, E. 1966 (Carlisle U)   4
Whiteside, N. 1982 (Manchester U, Everton)   38
Whiteside, T. 1891 (Distillery)   1
Whitfield, E. R. 1886 (Dublin University)   1
Whitley, Jeff 1997 (Manchester C, Sunderland, Cardiff C)
      20
Whitley, Jim 1998 (Manchester C)   3
Williams, J. R. 1886 (Ulster)   2
Williams, M. S. 1999 (Chesterfield, Watford, Wimbledon,
   Stoke C, Wimbledon, Milton Keynes D)   36
Williams, P. A. 1991 (WBA)   1
Williamson, J. 1890 (Cliftonville)   1
Willighan, J. 1933 (Burnley)   2
Willis, G. 1906 (Linfield)   4
Wilson, D. J. 1987 (Brighton & HA, Luton T,
   Sheffield W)   24
Wilson, H. 1925 (Linfield)   2
Wilson, K. J. 1987 (Ipswich T, Chelsea, Notts Co,
   Walsall)   42
Wilson, M. 1884 (Distillery)   3
Wilson, R. 1888 (Cliftonville)   1
Wilson, S. J. 1962 (Glenavon, Falkirk, Dundee)   12
Wilton, J. M. 1888 (St Columb's Court, Cliftonville, St
   Columb's Court)   7
Winchester, C. 2011 (Oldham Ath)   1
Wood, T. J. 1996 (Walsall)   1
Worthington, N. 1984 (Sheffield W, Leeds U, Stoke C)   66
Wright, J. 1906 (Cliftonville)   6
Wright, T. J. 1989 (Newcastle U, Nottingham F,
   Manchester C)   31

Young, S. 1907 (Linfield, Airdrieonians, Linfield)   9

SCOTLAND

Adam, C. G. 2007 (Rangers, Blackpool, Liverpool, Stoke C) 25
Adams, J. 1889 (Hearts) 3
Agnew, W. B. 1907 (Kilmarnock) 3
Aird, J. 1954 (Burnley) 4
Aitken, A. 1901 (Newcastle U, Middlesbrough, Leicester Fosse) 14
Aitken, G. G. 1949 (East Fife, Sunderland) 8
Aitken, R. 1886 (Dumbarton) 2
Aitken, R. 1980 (Celtic, Newcastle U, St Mirren) 57
Aitkenhead, W. A. C. 1912 (Blackburn R) 1
Albiston, A. 1982 (Manchester U) 14
Alexander, D. 1894 (East Stirlingshire) 2
Alexander, G. 2002 (Preston NE, Burnley) 40
Alexander, N. 2006 (Cardiff C) 3
Allan, D. S. 1885 (Queen's Park) 3
Allan, G. 1897 (Liverpool) 1
Allan, H. 1902 (Hearts) 1
Allan, J. 1887 (Queen's Park) 2
Allan, T. 1974 (Dundee) 2
Ancell, R. F. D. 1937 (Newcastle U) 2
Anderson, A. 1933 (Hearts) 23
Anderson, F. 1874 (Clydesdale) 1
Anderson, G. 1901 (Kilmarnock) 1
Anderson, H. A. 1914 (Raith R) 1
Anderson, J. 1954 (Leicester C) 1
Anderson, K. 1896 (Queen's Park) 3
Anderson, R. 2003 (Aberdeen, Sunderland) 11
Anderson, W. 1882 (Queen's Park) 6
Andrews, P. 1875 (Eastern) 1
Anya, I. 2013 (Watford) 6
Archibald, A. 1921 (Rangers) 8
Archibald, S. 1980 (Aberdeen, Tottenham H, Barcelona) 27
Armstrong, M. W. 1936 (Aberdeen) 3
Arnott, W. 1883 (Queen's Park) 14
Auld, J. R. 1887 (Third Lanark) 3
Auld, R. 1959 (Celtic) 3

Baird, A. 1892 (Queen's Park) 2
Baird, D. 1890 (Hearts) 3
Baird, H. 1956 (Airdrieonians) 1
Baird, J. C. 1876 (Vale of Leven) 3
Baird, S. 1957 (Rangers) 7
Baird, W. U. 1897 (St Bernard) 1
Bannan, B. 2011 (Aston Villa, Crystal Palace) 17
Bannon, E. J. 1980 (Dundee U) 11
Barbour, A. 1885 (Renton) 1
Bardsley, P. A. 2011 (Sunderland) 13
Barker, J. B. 1893 (Rangers) 2
Barr, D. 2009 (Falkirk) 1
Barrett, F. 1894 (Dundee) 2
Battles, B. 1901 (Celtic) 3
Battles, B. jun. 1931 (Hearts) 1
Bauld, W. 1950 (Hearts) 3
Baxter, J. C. 1961 (Rangers, Sunderland) 34
Baxter, R. D. 1939 (Middlesbrough) 3
Beattie, A. 1937 (Preston NE) 7
Beattie, C. 2006 (Celtic, WBA) 7
Beattie, R. 1939 (Preston NE) 1
Begbie, I. 1890 (Hearts) 4
Bell, A. 1912 (Manchester U) 1
Bell, C. 2011 (Kilmarnock) 1
Bell, J. 1890 (Dumbarton, Everton, Celtic) 10
Bell, M. 1901 (Hearts) 1
Bell, W. J. 1966 (Leeds U) 2
Bennett, A. 1904 (Celtic, Rangers) 11
Bennie, R. 1925 (Airdrieonians) 3
Bernard, P. R. J. 1995 (Oldham Ath) 2
Berra, C. 2008 (Hearts, Wolverhampton W, Ipswich T) 28
Berry, D. 1894 (Queen's Park) 3
Berry, W. H. 1888 (Queen's Park) 4
Bett, J. 1982 (Rangers, Lokeren, Aberdeen) 25
Beveridge, W. W. 1879 (Glasgow University) 3
Black, A. 1938 (Hearts) 3
Black, D. 1889 (Hurlford) 1
Black, E. 1988 (Metz) 2
Black, I. 2013 (Rangers) 1
Black, I. H. 1948 (Southampton) 1
Blackburn, J. E. 1873 (Royal Engineers) 1

Blacklaw, A. S. 1963 (Burnley) 3
Blackley, J. 1974 (Hibernian) 7
Blair, D. 1929 (Clyde, Aston Villa) 8
Blair, J. 1920 (Sheffield W, Cardiff C) 8
Blair, J. 1934 (Motherwell) 1
Blair, J. A. 1947 (Blackpool) 1
Blair, W. 1896 (Third Lanark) 1
Blessington, J. 1894 (Celtic) 4
Blyth, J. A. 1978 (Coventry C) 2
Bone, J. 1972 (Norwich C) 2
Booth, S. 1993 (Aberdeen, Borussia Dortmund, Twente) 21
Bowie, J. 1920 (Rangers) 2
Bowie, W. 1891 (Linthouse) 1
Bowman, D. 1992 (Dundee U) 6
Bowman, G. A. 1892 (Montrose) 1
Boyd, G. I. 2013 (Peterborough U, Hull C) 2
Boyd, J. M. 1934 (Newcastle U) 1
Boyd, K. 2006 (Rangers, Middlesbrough) 18
Boyd, R. 1889 (Mossend Swifts) 2
Boyd, T. 1991 (Motherwell, Chelsea, Celtic) 72
Boyd, W. G. 1931 (Clyde) 2
Bradshaw, T. 1928 (Bury) 1
Brand, R. 1961 (Rangers) 8
Brandon, T. 1896 (Blackburn R) 1
Brazil, A. 1980 (Ipswich T, Tottenham H) 13
Breckenridge, T. 1888 (Hearts) 1
Bremner, D. 1976 (Hibernian) 1
Bremner, W. J. 1965 (Leeds U) 54
Brennan, F. 1947 (Newcastle U) 7
Breslin, B. 1897 (Hibernian) 1
Brewster, G. 1921 (Everton) 1
Bridcutt, L. 2013 (Brighton & HA) 1
Broadfoot, K. 2009 (Rangers) 4
Brogan, J. 1971 (Celtic) 4
Brown, A. 1890 (St Mirren) 2
Brown, A. 1904 (Middlesbrough) 1
Brown, A. D. 1950 (East Fife, Blackpool) 14
Brown, G. C. P. 1931 (Rangers) 19
Brown, H. 1947 (Partick Th) 3
Brown, J. B. 1939 (Clyde) 1
Brown, J. G. 1975 (Sheffield U) 1
Brown, R. 1884 (Dumbarton) 2
Brown, R. 1890 (Cambuslang) 1
Brown, R. 1947 (Rangers) 3
Brown, R. jun. 1885 (Dumbarton) 1
Brown, S. 2006 (Hibernian, Celtic) 38
Brown, W. D. F. 1958 (Dundee, Tottenham H) 28
Browning, J. 1914 (Celtic) 1
Brownlie, J. 1909 (Third Lanark) 16
Brownlie, J. 1971 (Hibernian) 7
Bruce, D. 1890 (Vale of Leven) 1
Bruce, R. F. 1934 (Middlesbrough) 1
Bryson, C. 2011 (Kilmarnock, Derby Co) 2
Buchan, M. M. 1972 (Aberdeen, Manchester U) 34
Buchanan, J. 1889 (Cambuslang) 1
Buchanan, J. 1929 (Rangers) 2
Buchanan, P. S. 1938 (Chelsea) 1
Buchanan, R. 1891 (Abercorn) 1
Buckley, P. 1954 (Aberdeen) 3
Buick, A. 1902 (Hearts) 2
Burchill, M. J. 2000 (Celtic) 6
Burke, C. 2006 (Rangers, Birmingham C) 7
Burley, C. W. 1995 (Chelsea, Celtic, Derby Co) 46
Burley, G. E. 1979 (Ipswich T) 11
Burns, F. 1970 (Manchester U) 1
Burns, K. 1974 (Birmingham C, Nottingham F) 20
Burns, T. 1981 (Celtic) 8
Busby, M. W. 1934 (Manchester C) 1

Cairns, T. 1920 (Rangers) 8
Calderhead, D. 1889 (Q of S Wanderers) 1
Calderwood, C. 1995 (Tottenham H) 36
Calderwood, R. 1885 (Cartvale) 3
Caldow, E. 1957 (Rangers) 40
Caldwell, G. 2002 (Newcastle U, Hibernian, Celtic, Wigan Ath) 55
Caldwell, S. 2001 (Newcastle U, Sunderland, Burnley, Wigan Ath) 12
Callaghan, P. 1900 (Hibernian) 1

Callaghan, W. 1970 (Dunfermline Ath) 2
Cameron, C. 1999 (Hearts, Wolverhampton W) 28
Cameron, J. 1886 (Rangers) 1
Cameron, J. 1896 (Queen's Park) 1
Cameron, J. 1904 (St Mirren, Chelsea) 2
Campbell, C. 1874 (Queen's Park) 13
Campbell, H. 1889 (Renton) 1
Campbell, Jas 1913 (Sheffield W) 1
Campbell, J. 1880 (South Western) 1
Campbell, J. 1891 (Kilmarnock) 2
Campbell, John 1893 (Celtic) 12
Campbell, John 1899 (Rangers) 4
Campbell, K. 1920 (Liverpool, Partick Th) 8
Campbell, P. 1878 (Rangers) 2
Campbell, P. 1898 (Morton) 1
Campbell, R. 1947 (Falkirk, Chelsea) 5
Campbell, W. 1947 (Morton) 5
Canero, P. 2004 (Leicester C) 1
Carabine, J. 1938 (Third Lanark) 3
Carr, W. M. 1970 (Coventry C) 6
Cassidy, J. 1921 (Celtic) 4
Chalmers, S. 1965 (Celtic) 5
Chalmers, W. 1885 (Rangers) 1
Chalmers, W. S. 1929 (Queen's Park) 1
Chambers, T. 1894 (Hearts) 1
Chaplin, G. D. 1908 (Dundee) 1
Cheyne, A. G. 1929 (Aberdeen) 5
Christie, A. J. 1898 (Queen's Park) 3
Christie, R. M. 1884 (Queen's Park) 1
Clark, J. 1966 (Celtic) 4
Clark, R. B. 1968 (Aberdeen) 17
Clarke, S. 1988 (Chelsea) 6
Clarkson, D. 2008 (Motherwell) 2
Cleland, J. 1891 (Royal Albert) 1
Clements, R. 1891 (Leith Ath) 1
Clunas, W. L. 1924 (Sunderland) 2
Collier, W. 1922 (Raith R) 1
Collins, J. 1988 (Hibernian, Celtic, Monaco, Everton) 58
Collins, R. Y. 1951 (Celtic, Everton, Leeds U) 31
Collins, T. 1909 (Hearts) 1
Colman, D. 1911 (Aberdeen) 4
Colquhoun, E. P. 1972 (Sheffield U) 9
Colquhoun, J. 1988 (Hearts) 2
Combe, J. R. 1948 (Hibernian) 3
Commons, K. 2009 (Derby Co, Celtic) 12
Conn, A. 1956 (Hearts) 1
Conn, A. 1975 (Tottenham H) 2
Connachan, E. D. 1962 (Dunfermline Ath) 2
Connelly, G. 1974 (Celtic) 2
Connolly, J. 1973 (Everton) 1
Connor, J. 1886 (Airdrieonians) 1
Connor, J. 1930 (Sunderland) 4
Connor, R. 1986 (Dundee, Aberdeen) 4
Conway, C. 2010 (Dundee U, Cardiff C) 7
Cook, W. L. 1934 (Bolton W) 3
Cooke, C. 1966 (Dundee, Chelsea) 16
Cooper, D. 1980 (Rangers, Motherwell) 22
Cormack, P. B. 1966 (Hibernian, Nottingham F) 9
Cowan, J. 1896 (Aston Villa) 3
Cowan, J. 1948 (Morton) 25
Cowan, W, D. 1924 (Newcastle U) 1
Cowie, D. 1953 (Dundee) 20
Cowie, D. M. 2010 (Watford, Cardiff C) 10
Cox, C. J. 1948 (Hearts) 1
Cox, S. 1949 (Rangers) 24
Craig, A. 1929 (Motherwell) 3
Craig, J. 1977 (Celtic) 1
Craig, J. P. 1968 (Celtic) 1
Craig, T. 1927 (Rangers) 8
Craig, T. B. 1976 (Newcastle U) 1
Crainey, S. D. 2002 (Celtic, Southampton, Blackpool) 12
Crapnell, J. 1929 (Airdrieonians) 9
Crawford, D. 1894 (St Mirren, Rangers) 3
Crawford, J. 1932 (Queen's Park) 5
Crawford, S. 1995 (Raith R, Dunfermline Ath, Plymouth Arg) 25
Crerand, P. T. 1961 (Celtic, Manchester U) 16
Cringan, W. 1920 (Celtic) 5
Crosbie, J. A. 1920 (Ayr U, Birmingham) 2
Croal, J. A. 1913 (Falkirk) 3
Cropley, A. J. 1972 (Hibernian) 2
Cross, J. H. 1903 (Third Lanark) 1

Cruickshank, J. 1964 (Hearts) 6
Crum, J. 1936 (Celtic) 2
Cullen, M. J. 1956 (Luton T) 1
Cumming, D. S. 1938 (Middlesbrough) 1
Cumming, J. 1955 (Hearts) 9
Cummings, G. 1935 (Partick Th, Aston Villa) 9
Cummings, W. 2002 (Chelsea) 1
Cunningham, A. N. 1920 (Rangers) 12
Cunningham, W. C. 1954 (Preston NE) 8
Curran, H. P. 1970 (Wolverhampton W) 5

Dailly, C. 1997 (Derby Co, Blackburn R, West Ham U, Rangers) 67
Dalglish, K. 1972 (Celtic, Liverpool) 102
Davidson, C. I. 1999 (Blackburn R, Leicester C, Preston NE) 19
Davidson, D. 1878 (Queen's Park) 5
Davidson, J. A. 1954 (Partick Th) 8
Davidson, M. 2013 (St Johnstone) 1
Davidson, S. 1921 (Middlesbrough) 1
Dawson, A. 1980 (Rangers) 5
Dawson, J. 1935 (Rangers) 14
Deans, J. 1975 (Celtic) 2
Delaney, J. 1936 (Celtic, Manchester U) 13
Devine, A. 1910 (Falkirk) 1
Devlin, P. J. 2003 (Birmingham C) 10
Dewar, G. 1888 (Dumbarton) 2
Dewar, N. 1932 (Third Lanark) 3
Dick, J. 1959 (West Ham U) 1
Dickie, M. 1897 (Rangers) 3
Dickov, P. 2001 (Manchester C, Leicester C, Blackburn R) 10
Dickson, W. 1888 (Dundee Strathmore) 1
Dickson, W. 1970 (Kilmarnock) 5
Divers, J. 1895 (Celtic) 1
Divers, J. 1939 (Celtic) 1
Dixon, P. A. 2013 (Huddersfield T) 3
Dobie, R. S. 2002 (WBA) 6
Docherty, T. H. 1952 (Preston NE, Arsenal) 25
Dodds, D. 1984 (Dundee U) 2
Dodds, J. 1914 (Celtic) 3
Dodds, W. 1997 (Aberdeen, Dundee U, Rangers) 26
Doig, J. E. 1887 (Arbroath, Sunderland) 5
Donachie, W. 1972 (Manchester C) 35
Donaldson, A. 1914 (Bolton W) 6
Donnachie, J. 1913 (Oldham Ath) 3
Donnelly, S. 1997 (Celtic) 10
Dorrans, G. 2010 (WBA) 10
Dougal, J. 1939 (Preston NE) 1
Dougall, C. 1947 (Birmingham C) 1
Dougan, R. 1950 (Hearts) 1
Douglas, A. 1911 (Chelsea) 1
Douglas, J. 1880 (Renfrew) 1
Douglas, R. 2002 (Celtic, Leicester C) 19
Dowds, P. 1892 (Celtic) 1
Downie, R. 1892 (Third Lanark) 1
Doyle, D. 1892 (Celtic) 8
Doyle, J. 1976 (Ayr U) 1
Drummond, J. 1892 (Falkirk, Rangers) 14
Dunbar, M. 1886 (Cartvale) 1
Duncan, A. 1975 (Hibernian) 6
Duncan, D. 1933 (Derby Co) 14
Duncan, D. M. 1948 (East Fife) 3
Duncan, J. 1878 (Alexandra Ath) 2
Duncan, J. 1926 (Leicester C) 1
Duncanson, J. 1947 (Rangers) 1
Dunlop, J. 1890 (St Mirren) 1
Dunlop, W. 1906 (Liverpool) 1
Dunn, J. 1925 (Hibernian, Everton) 6
Durie, G. S. 1988 (Chelsea, Tottenham H, Rangers) 43
Durrant, I. 1988 (Rangers, Kilmarnock) 20
Dykes, J. 1938 (Hearts) 8

Easson, J. F. 1931 (Portsmouth) 3
Elliott, M. S. 1998 (Leicester C) 18
Ellis, J. 1892 (Mossend Swifts) 1
Evans, A. 1982 (Aston Villa) 4
Evans, R. 1949 (Celtic, Chelsea) 48
Ewart, J. 1921 (Bradford C) 1
Ewing, T. 1958 (Partick Th) 2

Farm, G. N. 1953 (Blackpool) 10

Ferguson, B. 1999 (Rangers, Blackburn R, Rangers) 45
Ferguson, D. 1988 (Rangers) 2
Ferguson, D. 1992 (Dundee U, Everton) 7
Ferguson, I. 1989 (Rangers) 9
Ferguson, J. 1874 (Vale of Leven) 6
Ferguson, R. 1966 (Kilmarnock) 7
Fernie, W. 1954 (Celtic) 12
Findlay, R. 1898 (Kilmarnock) 1
Fitchie, T. T. 1905 (Woolwich Arsenal, Queen's Park) 4
Flavell, R. 1947 (Airdrieonians) 2
Fleck, R. 1990 (Norwich C) 4
Fleming, C. 1954 (East Fife) 1
Fleming, J. W. 1929 (Rangers) 3
Fleming, R. 1886 (Morton) 1
Fletcher, D. B. 2004 (Manchester U) **62**
Fletcher, S. 2008 (Hibernian, Burnley,
Wolverhampton W, Sunderland) **14**
Forbes, A. R. 1947 (Sheffield U, Arsenal) 14
Forbes, J. 1884 (Vale of Leven) 5
Ford, D. 1974 (Hearts) 3
Forrest, J. 1958 (Motherwell) 1
Forrest, J. 1966 (Rangers, Aberdeen) 5
Forrest, J. 2011 (Celtic) **9**
Forsyth, A. 1972 (Partick Th, Manchester U) 10
Forsyth, C. 2014 (Derby Co) **1**
Forsyth, R. C. 1964 (Kilmarnock) 4
Forsyth, T. 1971 (Motherwell, Rangers) 22
Fox, D. J. 2010 (Burnley, Southampton) 4
Foyers, R. 1893 (St Bernards) 2
Fraser, D. M. 1968 (WBA) 2
Fraser, J. 1891 (Moffat) 1
Fraser, M. J. E. 1880 (Queen's Park) 5
Fraser, J. 1907 (Dundee) 1
Fraser, W. 1955 (Sunderland) 2
Freedman, D. A. 2002 (Crystal Palace) 2
Fulton, W. 1884 (Abercorn) 1
Fyfe, J. H. 1895 (Third Lanark) 1

Gabriel, J. 1961 (Everton) 2
Gallacher, H. K. 1924 (Airdrieonians, Newcastle U,
Chelsea, Derby Co) 20
Gallacher, K. W. 1988 (Dundee U, Coventry C,
Blackburn R, Newcastle U) 53
Gallacher, P. 1935 (Sunderland) 1
Gallacher, P. 2002 (Dundee U) 8
Gallagher, P. 2004 (Blackburn R) 1
Galloway, M. 1992 (Celtic) 1
Galt, J. H. 1908 (Rangers) 2
Gardiner, I. 1958 (Motherwell) 1
Gardner, D. R. 1897 (Third Lanark) 1
Gardner, R. 1872 (Queen's Park, Clydesdale) 5
Gemmell, T. 1955 (St Mirren) 2
Gemmell, T. 1966 (Celtic) 18
Gemmill, A. 1971 (Derby Co, Nottingham F,
Birmingham C) 43
Gemmill, S. 1995 (Nottingham F, Everton) 26
Gibb, W. 1873 (Clydesdale) 1
Gibson, D. W. 1963 (Leicester C) 7
Gibson, J. D. 1926 (Partick Th, Aston Villa) 8
Gibson, N. 1895 (Rangers, Partick Th) 14
Gilchrist, J. E. 1922 (Celtic) 1
Gilhooley, M. 1922 (Hull C) 1
Gilks, M. 2013 (Blackpool) **3**
Gillespie, G. 1880 (Rangers, Queen's Park) 7
Gillespie, G. T. 1988 (Liverpool) 13
Gillespie, Jas 1898 (Third Lanark) 1
Gillespie, John 1896 (Queen's Park) 1
Gillespie, R. 1927 (Queen's Park) 4
Gillick, T. 1937 (Everton) 5
Gilmour, J. 1931 (Dundee) 1
Gilzean, A. J. 1964 (Dundee, Tottenham H) 22
Glass, S. 1999 (Newcastle U) 1
Glavin, R. 1977 (Celtic) 1
Glen, A. 1956 (Aberdeen) 2
Glen, R. 1895 (Renton, Hibernian) 3
Goodwillie, D. 2011 (Dundee U, Blackburn R) 3
Goram, A. L. 1986 (Oldham Ath, Hibernian, Rangers) 43
Gordon, C. S. 2004 (Hearts, Sunderland) 40
Gordon, J. E. 1912 (Rangers) 10
Gossland, J. 1884 (Rangers) 1
Goudle, J. 1884 (Abercorn) 1
Gough, C. R. 1983 (Dundee U, Tottenham H, Rangers) 61

Gould, J. 2000 (Celtic) 2
Gourlay, J. 1886 (Cambuslang) 2
Govan, J. 1948 (Hibernian) 6
Gow, D. R. 1888 (Rangers) 1
Gow, J. J. 1885 (Queen's Park) 1
Gow, J. R. 1888 (Rangers) 1
Graham, A. 1978 (Leeds U) 11
Graham, G. 1972 (Arsenal, Manchester U) 12
Graham, J. 1884 (Annbank) 1
Graham, J. A. 1921 (Arsenal) 1
Grant, J. 1959 (Hibernian) 2
Grant, P. 1989 (Celtic) 2
Gray, A. 1903 (Hibernian) 1
Gray, A. D. 2003 (Bradford C) 2
Gray, A. M. 1976 (Aston Villa, Wolverhampton W,
Everton) 20
Gray, D. 1929 (Rangers) 10
Gray, E. 1969 (Leeds U) 12
Gray, F. T. 1976 (Leeds U, Nottingham F, Leeds U) 32
Gray, W. 1886 (Pollokshields Ath) 1
Green, A. 1971 (Blackpool, Newcastle U) 6
Greer, G. 2013 (Brighton & HA) **4**
Greig, J. 1964 (Rangers) 44
Griffiths, L. 2013 (Hibernian, Celtic) **4**
Groves, W. 1888 (Hibernian, Celtic) 3
Gulliland, W. 1891 (Queen's Park) 4
Gunn, B. 1990 (Norwich C) 6

Haddock, H. 1955 (Clyde) 6
Haddow, D. 1894 (Rangers) 1
Haffey, F. 1960 (Celtic) 2
Hamilton, A. 1885 (Queen's Park) 4
Hamilton, A. W. 1962 (Dundee) 24
Hamilton, G. 1906 (Port Glasgow Ath) 1
Hamilton, G. 1947 (Aberdeen) 5
Hamilton, J. 1892 (Queen's Park) 3
Hamilton, J. 1924 (St Mirren) 1
Hamilton, R. C. 1899 (Rangers, Dundee) 11
Hamilton, T. 1891 (Hurlford) 1
Hamilton, T. 1932 (Rangers) 1
Hamilton, W. M. 1965 (Hibernian) 1
Hammell, S. 2005 (Motherwell) 1
Hanley, G. 2011 (Blackburn R) **13**
Hannah, A. B. 1888 (Renton) 1
Hannah, J. 1889 (Third Lanark) 1
Hansen, A. D. 1979 (Liverpool) 26
Hansen, J. 1972 (Partick Th) 2
Harkness, J. D. 1927 (Queen's Park, Hearts) 12
Harper, J. M. 1973 (Aberdeen, Hibernian, Aberdeen) 4
Harper, W. 1923 (Hibernian, Arsenal) 11
Harris, J. 1921 (Partick Th) 2
Harris, N. 1924 (Newcastle U) 1
Harrower, W. 1882 (Queen's Park) 3
Hartford, R. A. 1972 (WBA, Manchester C, Everton,
Manchester C) 50
Hartley, P. J. 2005 (Hearts, Celtic, Bristol C) 25
Harvey, D. 1973 (Leeds U) 16
Hastings, A. C. 1936 (Sunderland) 2
Haughney, M. 1954 (Celtic) 1
Hay, D. 1970 (Celtic) 27
Hay, J. 1905 (Celtic, Newcastle U) 11
Hegarty, P. 1979 (Dundee U) 8
Heggie, C. 1886 (Rangers) 1
Henderson, G. H. 1904 (Rangers) 1
Henderson, J. G. 1953 (Portsmouth, Arsenal) 7
Henderson, W. 1963 (Rangers) 29
Hendry, E. C. J. 1993 (Blackburn R, Rangers,
Coventry C, Bolton W) 51
Hepburn, J. 1891 (Alloa Ath) 1
Hepburn, R. 1932 (Ayr U) 1
Herd, A. C. 1935 (Hearts) 1
Herd, D. G. 1959 (Arsenal) 5
Herd, G. 1958 (Clyde) 5
Herriot, J. 1969 (Birmingham C) 8
Hewie, J. D. 1956 (Charlton Ath) 19
Higgins, A. 1885 (Kilmarnock) 1
Higgins, A. 1910 (Newcastle U) 4
Highet, T. C. 1875 (Queen's Park) 4
Hill, D. 1881 (Rangers) 3
Hill, D. A. 1906 (Third Lanark) 1
Hill, F. R. 1930 (Aberdeen) 3
Hill, J. 1891 (Hearts) 2

McBain, N. 1922 (Manchester U, Everton) 3
McBride, J. 1967 (Celtic) 2
McBride, P. 1904 (Preston NE) 6
McCall, A. 1888 (Renton) 1
McCall, A. S. M. 1990 (Everton, Rangers) 40
McCall, J. 1886 (Renton) 5
McCalliog, J. 1967 (Sheffield W, Wolverhampton W) 5
McCallum, N. 1888 (Renton) 1
McCann, N. 1999 (Hearts, Rangers, Southampton) 26
McCann, R. J. 1959 (Motherwell) 5
McCartney, W. 1902 (Hibernian) 1
McClair, B. 1987 (Celtic, Manchester U) 30
McClory, A. 1927 (Motherwell) 3
McCloy, P. 1924 (Ayr U) 2
McCloy, P. 1973 (Rangers) 4
McCoist, A. 1986 (Rangers, Kilmarnock) 61
McColl, I. M. 1950 (Rangers) 14
McColl, R. S. 1896 (Queen's Park, Newcastle U,
   Queen's Park) 13
McColl, W. 1895 (Renton) 1
McCombie, A. 1903 (Sunderland, Newcastle U) 4
McCorkindale, J. 1891 (Partick Th) 1
McCormack, R. 2008 (Motherwell, Cardiff C, Leeds U) 11
McCormick, R. 1886 (Abercorn) 1
McCrae, D. 1929 (St Mirren) 2
McCreadie, A. 1893 (Rangers) 2
McCreadie, E. G. 1965 (Chelsea) 23
McCulloch, D. 1935 (Hearts, Brentford, Derby Co) 7
McCulloch, L. 2005 (Wigan Ath, Rangers) 18
MacDonald, A. 1976 (Rangers) 1
McDonald, J. 1886 (Edinburgh University) 1
McDonald, J. 1956 (Sunderland) 2
MacDougall, E. J. 1975 (Norwich C) 7
McDougall, J. 1877 (Vale of Leven) 5
McDougall, J. 1926 (Airdrieonians) 1
McDougall, J. 1931 (Liverpool) 2
McEveley, J. 2008 (Derby Co) 3
McFadden, J. 2002 (Motherwell, Everton,
   Birmingham C) 48
McFadyen, W. 1934 (Motherwell) 2
Macfarlane, A. 1904 (Dundee) 5
Macfarlane, W. 1947 (Hearts) 1
McFarlane, R. 1896 (Greenock Morton) 1
McGarr, E. 1970 (Aberdeen) 2
McGarvey, F. P. 1979 (Liverpool, Celtic) 7
McGeoch, A. 1876 (Dumbreck) 4
McGhee, J. 1886 (Hibernian) 1
McGhee, M. 1983 (Aberdeen) 4
McGinlay, J. 1994 (Bolton W) 13
McGonagle, W. 1933 (Celtic) 6
McGrain, D. 1973 (Celtic) 62
McGregor, A. 2007 (Rangers, Besiktas, Hull C) 32
McGregor, J. C. 1877 (Vale of Leven) 4
McGrory, J. 1928 (Celtic) 7
McGrory, J. E. 1965 (Kilmarnock) 3
McGuire, W. 1881 (Beith) 2
McGurk, F. 1934 (Birmingham) 1
McHardy, H. 1885 (Rangers) 1
McInally, A. 1989 (Aston Villa, Bayern Munich) 8
McInally, J. 1987 (Dundee U) 10
McInally, T. B. 1926 (Celtic) 2
McInnes, D. 2003 (WBA) 2
McInnes, T. 1889 (Cowlairs) 1
McIntosh, W. 1905 (Third Lanark) 1
McIntyre, A. 1878 (Vale of Leven) 2
McIntyre, H. 1880 (Rangers) 1
McIntyre, J. 1884 (Rangers) 1
MacKay, D. 1959 (Celtic) 14
Mackay, D. C. 1957 (Hearts, Tottenham H) 22
Mackay, G. 1988 (Hearts) 4
Mackay, M. 2004 (Norwich C) 5
McKay, J. 1924 (Blackburn R) 1
McKay, R. 1928 (Newcastle U) 1
McKean, R. 1976 (Rangers) 1
McKenzie, D. 1938 (Brentford) 1
Mackenzie, J. A. 1954 (Partick Th) 9
McKeown, M. 1889 (Celtic) 2
McKie, J. 1898 (East Stirling) 1
McKillop, T. R. 1938 (Rangers) 1
McKimmie, S. 1989 (Aberdeen) 40
McKinlay, D. 1922 (Liverpool) 2
McKinlay, T. 1996 (Celtic) 22

McKinlay, W. 1994 (Dundee U, Blackburn R) 29
McKinnon, A. 1874 (Queen's Park) 1
McKinnon, R. 1966 (Rangers) 28
McKinnon, R. 1994 (Motherwell) 3
MacKinnon, W. 1883 (Dumbarton) 4
MacKinnon, W. W. 1872 (Queen's Park) 9
McLaren, A. 1929 (St Johnstone) 5
McLaren, A. 1947 (Preston NE) 4
McLaren, A. 1992 (Hearts, Rangers) 24
McLaren, A. 2001 (Kilmarnock) 1
McLaren, J. 1888 (Hibernian, Celtic) 3
McLean, A. 1926 (Celtic) 4
McLean, D. 1896 (St Bernards) 2
McLean, D. 1912 (Sheffield W) 1
McLean, G. 1968 (Dundee) 1
McLean, T. 1969 (Kilmarnock) 6
McLeish, A. 1980 (Aberdeen) 77
McLeod, D. 1905 (Celtic) 4
McLeod, J. 1888 (Dumbarton) 5
MacLeod, J. M. 1961 (Hibernian) 4
MacLeod, M. 1985 (Celtic, Borussia Dortmund,
   Hibernian) 20
McLeod, W. 1886 (Cowlairs) 1
McLintock, A. 1875 (Vale of Leven) 3
McLintock, F. 1963 (Leicester C, Arsenal) 9
McLuckie, J. S. 1934 (Manchester C) 1
McMahon, A. 1892 (Celtic) 6
McManus, S. 2007 (Celtic, Middlesbrough) 26
McMenemy, J. 1905 (Celtic) 12
McMenemy, J. 1934 (Motherwell) 1
McMillan, I. L. 1952 (Airdrieonians, Rangers) 6
McMillan, J. 1897 (St Bernards) 1
McMillan, T. 1887 (Dumbarton) 1
McMullan, J. 1920 (Partick Th, Manchester C) 16
McNab, A. 1921 (Morton) 2
McNab, A. 1937 (Sunderland, WBA) 2
McNab, C. D. 1931 (Dundee) 6
McNab, J. S. 1923 (Liverpool) 1
McNair, A. 1906 (Celtic) 15
McNamara, J. 1997 (Celtic, Wolverhampton W) 33
McNamee, D. 2004 (Livingston) 4
McNaught, W. 1951 (Raith R) 5
McNaughton, K. 2002 (Aberdeen, Cardiff C) 4
McNeill, W. 1961 (Celtic) 29
McNiel, H. 1874 (Queen's Park) 10
McNiel, M. 1876 (Rangers) 2
McPhail, J. 1950 (Celtic) 5
McPhail, R. 1927 (Airdrieonians, Rangers) 17
McPherson, D. 1892 (Kilmarnock) 1
McPherson, D. 1989 (Hearts, Rangers) 27
McPherson, J. 1875 (Clydesdale) 1
McPherson, J. 1879 (Vale of Leven) 8
McPherson, J. 1888 (Kilmarnock, Cowlairs, Rangers) 9
McPherson, J. 1891 (Hearts) 1
McPherson, R. 1882 (Arthurlie) 1
McQueen, G. 1974 (Leeds U, Manchester U) 30
McQueen, M. 1890 (Leith Ath) 2
McRorie, D. M. 1931 (Morton) 1
McSpadyen, A. 1939 (Partick Th) 2
McStay, P. 1984 (Celtic) 76
McStay, W. 1921 (Celtic) 13
McSwegan, G. 2000 (Hearts) 2
McTavish, J. 1910 (Falkirk) 1
McWattie, G. C. 1901 (Queen's Park) 2
McWilliam, P. 1905 (Newcastle U) 8
Mackay-Steven, G. 2013 (Dundee U) 1
Mackail-Smith, C. 2011 (Peterborough U,
   Brighton & HA) 7
Mackie, J. C. 2011 (QPR) 9
Madden, J. 1893 (Celtic) 2
Maguire, C. 2011 (Aberdeen) 2
Main, F. R. 1938 (Rangers) 1
Main, J. 1909 (Hibernian) 1
Maley, W. 1893 (Celtic) 2
**Maloney, S. R. 2006 (Celtic, Aston Villa, Celtic,
   Wigan Ath) 32**
Malpas, M. 1984 (Dundee U) 55
Marshall, D. J. 2005 (Celtic, Cardiff C) 11
Marshall, G. 1992 (Celtic) 1
Marshall, H. 1899 (Celtic) 2
Marshall, J. 1885 (Third Lanark) 4
Marshall, J. 1921 (Middlesbrough, Llanelly) 7

Marshall, J. 1932 (Rangers) 3
Marshall, R. W. 1892 (Rangers) 2
Martin, B. 1995 (Motherwell) 2
Martin, C. H. 2014 (Derby Co) **1**
Martin, F. 1954 (Aberdeen) 6
Martin, N. 1965 (Hibernian, Sunderland) 3
Martin, R. K. A. 2011 (Norwich C) **11**
Martis, J. 1961 (Motherwell) 1
Mason, J. 1949 (Third Lanark) 7
Massie, A. 1932 (Hearts, Aston Villa) 18
Masson, D. S. 1976 (QPR, Derby Co) 17
Mathers, D. 1954 (Partick Th) 1
Matteo, D. 2001 (Leeds U) 6
Maxwell, W. S. 1898 (Stoke C) 1
May, J. 1906 (Rangers) 5
Meechan, P. 1896 (Celtic) 1
Meiklejohn, D. D. 1922 (Rangers) 15
Menzies, A. 1906 (Hearts) 1
Mercer, R. 1912 (Hearts) 2
Middleton, R. 1930 (Cowdenbeath) 1
Millar, J. 1897 (Rangers) 3
Millar, J. 1963 (Rangers) 2
Miller, A. 1939 (Hearts) 1
Miller, C. 2001 (Dundee U) 1
Miller, J. 1931 (St Mirren) 5
Miller, K. 2001 (Rangers, Wolverhampton W, Celtic,
Derby Co, Rangers, Bursaspor, Cardiff C, Vancouver
Whitecaps) **69**
Miller, L. 2006 (Dundee U, Aberdeen) 3
Miller, P. 1882 (Dumbarton) 3
Miller, T. 1920 (Liverpool, Manchester U) 3
Miller, W. 1876 (Third Lanark) 1
Miller, W. 1947 (Celtic) 6
Miller, W. 1975 (Aberdeen) 65
Mills, W. 1936 (Aberdeen) 3
Milne, J. V. 1938 (Middlesbrough) 2
Mitchell, D. 1890 (Rangers) 5
Mitchell, J. 1908 (Kilmarnock) 3
Mitchell, R. C. 1951 (Newcastle U) 2
Mochan, N. 1954 (Celtic) 3
Moir, W. 1950 (Bolton W) 1
Moncur, R. 1968 (Newcastle U) 16
Morgan, H. 1898 (St Mirren, Liverpool) 2
Morgan, W. 1968 (Burnley, Manchester U) 21
Morris, D. 1923 (Raith R) 6
Morris, H. 1950 (East Fife) 1
Morrison, J. C. 2008 (WBA) **31**
Morrison, T. 1927 (St Mirren) 1
Morton, A. L. 1920 (Queen's Park, Rangers) 31
Morton, H. A. 1929 (Kilmarnock) 2
Mudie, K. 1957 (Blackpool) 17
Muir, W. 1907 (Dundee) 1
Muirhead, T. A. 1922 (Rangers) 8
Mulgrew, C. 2012 (Celtic) **13**
Mulhall, G. 1960 (Aberdeen, Sunderland) 3
Munro, A. D. 1937 (Hearts, Blackpool) 3
Munro, F. M. 1971 (Wolverhampton W) 9
Munro, I. 1979 (St Mirren) 7
Munro, N. 1888 (Abercorn) 2
Murdoch, J. 1931 (Motherwell) 1
Murdoch, R. 1966 (Celtic) 12
Murphy, F. 1938 (Celtic) 1
Murray, I. 2003 (Hibernian, Rangers) 6
Murray, J. 1895 (Renton) 1
Murray, J. 1958 (Hearts) 5
Murray, J. W. 1890 (Vale of Leven) 1
Murray, P. 1896 (Hibernian) 2
Murray, S. 1972 (Aberdeen) 1
Murty, G. S. 2004 (Reading) 4
Mutch, G. 1938 (Preston NE) 1

Naismith, S. J. 2007 (Kilmarnock, Rangers, Everton) **29**
Napier, C. E. 1932 (Celtic, Derby Co) 5
Narey, D. 1977 (Dundee U) 35
Naysmith, G. A. 2000 (Hearts, Everton, Sheffield U) 46
Neil, R. G. 1896 (Hibernian, Rangers) 2
Neill, R. W. 1876 (Queen's Park) 5
Neilson, R. 2007 (Hearts) 1
Nellies, P. 1913 (Hearts) 2
Nelson, J. 1925 (Cardiff C) 4
Nevin, P. K. F. 1986 (Chelsea, Everton, Tranmere R) 28
Niblo, T. D. 1904 (Aston Villa) 1

Nibloe, J. 1929 (Kilmarnock) 11
Nicholas, C. 1983 (Celtic, Arsenal, Aberdeen) 20
Nicholson, B. 2001 (Dunfermline Ath) 3
Nicol, S. 1985 (Liverpool) 27
Nisbet, J. 1929 (Ayr U) 3
Niven, J. B. 1885 (Moffat) 1

O'Connor, G. 2002 (Hibernian, Lokomotiv Moscow,
    Birmingham C) 16
O'Donnell, F. 1937 (Preston NE, Blackpool) 6
O'Donnell, P. 1994 (Motherwell) 1
Ogilvie, D. H. 1934 (Motherwell) 1
O'Hare, J. 1970 (Derby Co) 13
O'Neil, B. 1996 (Celtic, Wolfsburg, Derby Co,
    Preston NE) 7
O'Neil, J. 2001 (Hibernian) 1
Ormond, W. E. 1954 (Hibernian) 6
O'Rourke, F. 1907 (Airdrieonians) 1
Orr, J. 1892 (Kilmarnock) 1
Orr, R. 1902 (Newcastle U) 2
Orr, T. 1952 (Morton) 2
Orr, W. 1900 (Celtic) 3
Orrock, R. 1913 (Falkirk) 1
Oswald, J. 1889 (Third Lanark, St Bernards, Rangers) 3

Parker, A. H. 1955 (Falkirk, Everton) 15
Parlane, D. 1973 (Rangers) 12
Parlane, R. 1878 (Vale of Leven) 3
Paterson, G. D. 1939 (Celtic) 1
Paterson, J. 1920 (Leicester C) 1
Paterson, J. 1931 (Cowdenbeath) 3
Paton, A. 1952 (Motherwell) 2
Paton, D. 1896 (St Bernards) 1
Paton, M. 1883 (Dumbarton) 5
Paton, R. 1879 (Vale of Leven) 2
Patrick, J. 1897 (St Mirren) 2
Paul, H. McD. 1909 (Queen's Park) 3
Paul, W. 1888 (Partick Th) 3
Paul, W. 1891 (Dykebar) 1
Pearson, S. P. 2004 (Motherwell, Celtic, Derby Co) 10
Pearson, T. 1947 (Newcastle U) 2
Penman, A. 1966 (Dundee) 1
Pettigrew, W. 1976 (Motherwell) 5
Phillips, J. 1877 (Queen's Park) 3
Phillips, M. 2012 (Blackpool) 1
Plenderleith, J. B. 1961 (Manchester C) 1
Porteous, W. 1903 (Hearts) 1
Pressley, S. J. 2000 (Hearts) 32
Pringle, C. 1921 (St Mirren) 1
Provan, D. 1964 (Rangers) 5
Provan, D. 1980 (Celtic) 10
Pursell, P. 1914 (Queen's Park) 1

Quashie, N. F. 2004 (Portsmouth, Southampton, WBA) 14
Quinn, J. 1905 (Celtic) 11
Quinn, P. 1961 (Motherwell) 4

Rae, G. 2001 (Dundee, Rangers, Cardiff C) 14
Rae, J. 1889 (Third Lanark) 2
Raeside, J. S. 1906 (Third Lanark) 1
Raisbeck, A. G. 1900 (Liverpool) 8
Rankin, G. 1890 (Vale of Leven) 2
Rankin, R. 1929 (St Mirren) 3
Redpath, W. 1949 (Motherwell) 9
Reid, J. G. 1914 (Airdrieonians) 3
Reid, R. 1938 (Brentford) 2
Reid, W. 1911 (Rangers) 9
Reilly, L. 1949 (Hibernian) 38
Rennie, H. G. 1900 (Hearts, Hibernian) 13
Renny-Tailyour, H. W. 1873 (Royal Engineers) 1
Rhind, A. 1872 (Queen's Park) 1
Rhodes, J. L. 2012 (Huddersfield T, Blackburn R) **11**
Richmond, A. 1906 (Queen's Park) 1
Richmond, J. T. 1877 (Clydesdale, Queen's Park) 3
Ring, T. 1953 (Clyde) 12
Rioch, B. D. 1975 (Derby Co, Everton, Derby Co) 24
Riordan, D. G. 2006 (Hibernian) 3
Ritchie, A. 1891 (East Stirlingshire) 1
Ritchie, H. 1923 (Hibernian) 2
Ritchie, J. 1897 (Queen's Park) 1
Ritchie, P. S. 1999 (Hearts, Bolton W, Walsall) 7
Ritchie, W. 1962 (Rangers) 1

Robb, D. T. 1971 (Aberdeen) 5
Robb, W. 1926 (Rangers, Hibernian) 2
Robertson, A. 1955 (Clyde) 5
Robertson, A. 2014 (Dundee U) **2**
Robertson, D. 1992 (Rangers) 3
Robertson, G. 1910 (Motherwell, Sheffield W) 4
Robertson, G. 1938 (Kilmarnock) 1
Robertson, H. 1962 (Dundee) 1
Robertson, J. 1931 (Dundee) 2
Robertson, J. 1991 (Hearts) 16
Robertson, J. N. 1978 (Nottingham F, Derby Co) 28
Robertson, J. G. 1965 (Tottenham H) 1
Robertson, J. T. 1898 (Everton, Southampton, Rangers) 16
Robertson, P. 1903 (Dundee) 1
Robertson, S. 2009 (Dundee U) 2
Robertson, T. 1889 (Queen's Park) 4
Robertson, T. 1898 (Hearts) 1
Robertson, W. 1887 (Dumbarton) 2
Robinson, R. 1974 (Dundee) 4
Robson, B. G. G. 2008 (Dundee U, Celtic,
  Middlesbrough) 17
Ross, M. 2002 (Rangers) 13
Rough, A. 1976 (Partick Th, Hibernian) 53
Rougvie, D. 1984 (Aberdeen) 1
Rowan, A. 1880 (Caledonian, Queen's Park) 2
Russell, D. 1895 (Hearts, Celtic) 6
Russell, J. 1890 (Cambuslang) 1
Russell, W. F. 1924 (Airdrieonians) 2
Rutherford, E. 1948 (Rangers) 1

St John, I. 1959 (Motherwell, Liverpool) 21
Saunders, S. 2011 (Motherwell) 1
Sawers, W. 1895 (Dundee) 1
Scarff, P. 1931 (Celtic) 1
Schaedler, E. 1974 (Hibernian) 1
Scott, A. S. 1957 (Rangers, Everton) 16
Scott, J. 1966 (Hibernian) 1
Scott, J. 1971 (Dundee) 2
Scott, M. 1898 (Airdrieonians) 1
Scott, R. 1894 (Airdrieonians) 1
Scoular, J. 1951 (Portsmouth) 9
Sellar, W. 1885 (Battlefield, Queen's Park) 9
Semple, W. 1886 (Cambuslang) 1
Severin, S. D. 2002 (Hearts, Aberdeen) 15
Shankly, W. 1938 (Preston NE) 5
Sharp, G. M. 1985 (Everton) 12
Sharp, J. 1904 (Dundee, Woolwich Arsenal, Fulham) 5
Shaw, D. 1947 (Hibernian) 8
Shaw, F. W. 1884 (Pollokshields Ath) 2
Shaw, J. 1947 (Rangers) 4
Shearer, D. 1994 (Aberdeen) 7
Shearer, R. 1961 (Rangers) 4
Shinnie, A. M. 2013 (Inverness CT) 1
Sillars, D. C. 1891 (Queen's Park) 5
Simpson, J. 1895 (Third Lanark) 3
Simpson, J. 1935 (Rangers) 14
Simpson, N. 1983 (Aberdeen) 5
Simpson, R. C. 1967 (Celtic) 5
Sinclair, G. L. 1910 (Hearts) 3
Sinclair, J. W. E. 1966 (Leicester C) 1
Skene, L. H. 1904 (Queen's Park) 1
Sloan, T. 1904 (Third Lanark) 1
Smellie, R. 1887 (Queen's Park) 6
Smith, A. 1898 (Rangers) 20
Smith, D. 1966 (Aberdeen, Rangers) 2
Smith, G. 1947 (Hibernian) 18
Smith, H. G. 1988 (Hearts) 3
Smith, J. 1924 (Ayr U) 1
Smith, J. 1935 (Rangers) 2
Smith, J. 1968 (Aberdeen, Newcastle U) 4
Smith, J. 2003 (Celtic) 2
Smith, J. E. 1959 (Celtic) 2
Smith, Jas 1872 (Queen's Park) 1
Smith, John 1877 (Mauchline, Edinburgh University,
  Queen's Park) 10
Smith, N. 1897 (Rangers) 12
Smith, R. 1872 (Queen's Park) 2
Smith, T. M. 1934 (Kilmarnock, Preston NE) 2
Snodgrass, R. 2011 (Leeds U, Norwich C) **15**
Somers, P. 1905 (Celtic) 4
Somers, W. S. 1879 (Third Lanark, Queen's Park) 3
Somerville, G. 1886 (Queen's Park) 1

Souness, G. J. 1975 (Middlesbrough, Liverpool,
  Sampdoria) 54
Speedie, D. R. 1985 (Chelsea, Coventry C) 10
Speedie, F. 1903 (Rangers) 3
Speirs, J. H. 1908 (Rangers) 1
Spencer, J. 1995 (Chelsea, QPR) 14
Stanton, P. 1966 (Hibernian) 16
Stark, J. 1909 (Rangers) 2
Steel, W. 1947 (Morton, Derby Co, Dundee) 30
Steele, D. M. 1923 (Huddersfield) 3
Stein, C. 1969 (Rangers, Coventry C) 21
Stephen, J. F. 1947 (Bradford) 2
Stevenson, G. 1928 (Motherwell) 12
Stewart, A. 1888 (Queen's Park) 2
Stewart, A. 1894 (Third Lanark) 1
Stewart, D. 1888 (Dumbarton) 1
Stewart, D. 1893 (Queen's Park) 3
Stewart, D. S. 1978 (Leeds U) 1
Stewart, G. 1906 (Hibernian, Manchester C) 4
Stewart, J. 1977 (Kilmarnock, Middlesbrough) 2
Stewart, M. J. 2002 (Manchester U, Hearts) 4
Stewart, R. 1981 (West Ham U) 10
Stewart, W. G. 1898 (Queen's Park) 2
Stockdale, R. K. 2002 (Middlesbrough) 5
Storrier, D. 1899 (Celtic) 3
Strachan, G. D. 1980 (Aberdeen, Manchester U,
  Leeds U) 50
Sturrock, P. 1981 (Dundee U) 20
Sullivan, N. 1997 (Wimbledon, Tottenham H) 28
Summers, W. 1926 (St Mirren) 1
Symon, J. S. 1939 (Rangers) 1

Tait, T. S. 1911 (Sunderland) 1
Taylor, J. 1872 (Queen's Park) 6
Taylor, J. D. 1892 (Dumbarton, St Mirren) 4
Taylor, W. 1892 (Hearts) 1
Teale, G. 2006 (Wigan Ath, Derby Co) 13
Telfer, P. N. 2000 (Coventry C) 1
Telfer, W. 1933 (Motherwell) 2
Telfer, W. D. 1954 (St Mirren) 1
Templeton, R. 1902 (Aston Villa, Newcastle U,
  Woolwich Arsenal, Kilmarnock) 11
Thompson, S. 2002 (Dundee U, Rangers) 16
Thomson, A. 1886 (Arthurlie) 1
Thomson, A. 1889 (Third Lanark) 1
Thomson, A. 1909 (Airdrieonians) 1
Thomson, A. 1926 (Celtic) 3
Thomson, C. 1904 (Hearts, Sunderland) 21
Thomson, C. 1937 (Sunderland) 1
Thomson, D. 1920 (Dundee) 1
Thomson, J. 1930 (Celtic) 4
Thomson, J. J. 1872 (Queen's Park) 3
Thomson, J. R. 1933 (Everton) 1
Thomson, K. 2009 (Rangers, Middlesbrough) 3
Thomson, R. 1932 (Celtic) 1
Thomson, R. W. 1927 (Falkirk) 1
Thomson, S. 1884 (Rangers) 2
Thomson, W. 1892 (Dumbarton) 4
Thomson, W. 1896 (Dundee) 1
Thomson, W. 1980 (St Mirren) 7
Thornton, W. 1947 (Rangers) 7
Toner, W. 1959 (Kilmarnock) 2
Townsley, T. 1926 (Falkirk) 1
Troup, A. 1920 (Dundee, Everton) 5
Turnbull, E. 1948 (Hibernian) 8
Turner, T. 1884 (Arthurlie) 1
Turner, W. 1885 (Pollokshields Ath) 2

Ure, J. F. 1962 (Dundee, Arsenal) 11
Urquhart, D. 1934 (Hibernian) 1

Vallance, T. 1877 (Rangers) 7
Venters, A. 1934 (Cowdenbeath, Rangers) 3

Waddell, T. S. 1891 (Queen's Park) 6
Waddell, W. 1947 (Rangers) 17
Wales, H. M. 1933 (Motherwell) 1
Walker, A. 1988 (Celtic) 3
Walker, F. 1922 (Third Lanark) 1
Walker, G. 1930 (St Mirren) 4
Walker, J. 1895 (Hearts, Rangers) 5
Walker, J. 1911 (Swindon T) 9

WALES

Coyne, D. 1996 (Tranmere R, Grimsby T, Leicester C, Burnley, Tranmere R) 16
Crofts, A. L. 2006 (Gillingham, Brighton & HA, Norwich C, Brighton & HA, Bolton W) **27**
Crompton, W. 1931 (Wrexham) 3
Cross, E. A. 1876 (Wrexham) 2
Crosse, K. 1879 (Druids) 3
Crossley, M. G. 1997 (Nottingham F, Middlesbrough, Fulham) 8
Crowe, V. H. 1959 (Aston Villa) 16
Cumner, R. H. 1939 (Arsenal) 3
Curtis, A. T. 1976 (Swansea C, Leeds U, Swansea C, Southampton, Cardiff C) 35
Curtis, E. R. 1928 (Cardiff C, Birmingham) 3

Daniel, R. W. 1951 (Arsenal, Sunderland) 21
Darvell, S. 1897 (Oxford University) 2
Davies, A. 1876 (Wrexham) 2
Davies, A. 1904 (Druids, Middlesbrough) 2
Davies, A. 1983 (Manchester U, Newcastle U, Swansea C, Bradford C) 13
Davies, A. O. 1885 (Barmouth, Swifts, Wrexham, Crewe Alex) 9
Davies, A. R. 2006 (Yeovil T) 1
Davies, A. T. 1891 (Shrewsbury T) 1
Davies, B. T. 2013 (Swansea C) **10**
Davies, C. 1972 (Charlton Ath) 1
Davies, C. M. 2006 (Oxford U, Verona, Oldham Ath, Barnsley) **7**
Davies, D. 1904 (Bolton W) 3
Davies, D. C. 1899 (Brecon, Hereford) 2
Davies, D. W. 1912 (Treharris, Oldham Ath) 2
Davies, E. Lloyd 1904 (Stoke, Northampton T) 16
Davies, E. R. 1953 (Newcastle U) 6
Davies, G. 1980 (Fulham, Manchester C) 16
Davies, Rev. H. 1928 (Wrexham) 1
Davies, Idwal 1923 (Liverpool Marine) 1
Davies, J. E. 1885 (Oswestry) 1
Davies, Jas 1878 (Wrexham) 1
Davies, John 1879 (Wrexham) 1
Davies, Jos 1888 (Newton Heath, Wolverhampton W) 7
Davies, Jos 1889 (Everton, Chirk, Ardwick, Sheffield U, Manchester C, Millwall, Reading) 11
Davies, J. P. 1883 (Druids) 2
Davies, Ll. 1907 (Wrexham, Everton, Wrexham) 13
Davies, L. S. 1922 (Cardiff C) 23
Davies, O. 1890 (Wrexham) 1
Davies, R. 1883 (Wrexham) 3
Davies, R. 1885 (Druids) 1
Davies, R. O. 1892 (Wrexham) 2
Davies, R. T. 1964 (Norwich C, Southampton, Portsmouth) 29
Davies, R. W. 1964 (Bolton W, Newcastle U, Manchester C, Manchester U, Blackpool) 34
Davies, S. 2001 (Tottenham H, Everton, Fulham) 58
Davies, S. I. 1996 (Manchester U) 1
Davies, Stanley 1920 (Preston NE, Everton, WBA, Rotherham U) 18
Davies, T. 1886 (Oswestry) 1
Davies, T. 1903 (Druids) 4
Davies, W. 1884 (Wrexham) 1
Davies, W. 1924 (Swansea T, Cardiff C, Notts Co) 17
Davies, William 1903 (Wrexham, Blackburn R) 11
Davies, W. C. 1908 (Crystal Palace, WBA, Crystal Palace) 4
Davies, W. D. 1975 (Everton, Wrexham, Swansea C) 52
Davies, W. H. 1876 (Oswestry) 4
Davis, G. 1978 (Wrexham) 3
Davis, W. O. 1913 (Millwall Ath) 5
Day, A. 1934 (Tottenham H) 1
Deacy, N. 1977 (PSV Eindhoven, Beringen) 12
Dearson, D. J. 1939 (Birmingham) 3
Delaney, M. A. 2000 (Aston Villa) 36
Derrett, S. C. 1969 (Cardiff C) 4
Dewey, F. T. 1931 (Cardiff Corinthians) 2
Dibble, A. 1986 (Luton T, Manchester C) 3
Dorman, A. 2010 (St Mirren, Crystal Palace) 3
Doughty, J. 1886 (Druids, Newton Heath) 8
Doughty, R. 1888 (Newton Heath) 2
Duffy, R. M. 2006 (Portsmouth) 13
Dummett, P. 2014 (Newcastle U) **1**
Durban, A. 1966 (Derby Co) 27

Dwyer, P. J. 1978 (Cardiff C) 10

Eardley, N. 2008 (Oldham Ath, Blackpool) 16
Earnshaw, R. 2002 (Cardiff C, WBA, Norwich C, Derby Co, Nottingham F, Cardiff C) 59
Easter, J. M. 2007 (Wycombe W, Plymouth Arg, Milton Keynes D, Crystal Palace, Millwall) **12**
Eastwood, F. 2008 (Wolverhampton W, Coventry C) 11
Edwards, C. 1878 (Wrexham) 1
Edwards, C. N. H. 1996 (Swansea C) 1
Edwards, D. 2008 (Luton T, Wolverhampton W) 26
Edwards, G. 1947 (Birmingham C, Cardiff C) 12
Edwards, H. 1878 (Wrexham Civil Service, Wrexham) 8
Edwards, J. H. 1876 (Wanderers) 1
Edwards, J. H. 1895 (Oswestry) 3
Edwards, J. H. 1898 (Aberystwyth) 1
Edwards, L. T. 1957 (Charlton Ath) 2
Edwards, R. I. 1978 (Chester, Wrexham) 4
Edwards, R. O. 2003 (Aston Villa, Wolverhampton W) 15
Edwards, R. W. 1998 (Bristol C) 4
Edwards, T. 1932 (Linfield) 1
Egan, W. 1892 (Chirk) 1
Ellis, B. 1932 (Motherwell) 6
Ellis, E. 1931 (Nunhead, Oswestry) 3
Emanuel, W. J. 1973 (Bristol C) 2
England, H. M. 1962 (Blackburn R, Tottenham H) 44
Evans, B. C. 1972 (Swansea C, Hereford U) 7
Evans, C. M. 2008 (Manchester C, Sheffield U) 13
Evans, D. G. 1926 (Reading, Huddersfield T) 4
Evans, H. P. 1922 (Cardiff C) 6
Evans, I. 1976 (Crystal Palace) 13
Evans, J. 1893 (Oswestry) 3
Evans, J. 1912 (Cardiff C) 8
Evans, J. H. 1922 (Southend U) 4
Evans, Len 1927 (Aberdare Ath, Cardiff C, Birmingham) 4
Evans, M. 1884 (Oswestry) 1
Evans, P. S. 2002 (Brentford, Bradford C) 1
Evans, R. 1902 (Clapton) 1
Evans, R. E. 1906 (Wrexham, Aston Villa, Sheffield U) 10
Evans, R. O. 1902 (Wrexham, Blackburn R, Coventry C) 10
Evans, R. S. 1964 (Swansea T) 1
Evans, S. J. 2007 (Wrexham) 7
Evans, T. J. 1927 (Clapton Orient, Newcastle U) 4
Evans, W. 1933 (Tottenham H) 6
Evans, W. A. W. 1876 (Oxford University) 2
Evans, W. G. 1890 (Bootle, Aston Villa) 3
Evelyn, E. C. 1887 (Crusaders) 1
Eyton-Jones, J. A. 1883 (Wrexham) 4

Farmer, G. 1885 (Oswestry) 2
Felgate, D. 1984 (Lincoln C) 1
Finnigan, R. J. 1930 (Wrexham) 1
Fletcher, C. N. 2004 (Bournemouth, West Ham U, Crystal Palace) 36
Flynn, B. 1975 (Burnley, Leeds U, Burnley) 66
Ford, T. 1947 (Swansea T, Aston Villa, Sunderland, Cardiff C) 38
Foulkes, H. E. 1932 (WBA) 1
Foulkes, W. I. 1952 (Newcastle U) 11
Foulkes, W. T. 1884 (Oswestry) 2
Fowler, J. 1925 (Swansea T) 6
Freestone, R. 2000 (Swansea C) 1

Gabbidon, D. L. 2002 (Cardiff C, West Ham U, QPR, Crystal Palace) **49**
Garner, G. 2006 (Leyton Orient) 1
Garner, J. 1896 (Aberystwyth) 1
Giggs, R. J. 1992 (Manchester U) 64
Giles, D. C. 1980 (Swansea C, Crystal Palace) 12
Gillam, S. G. 1889 (Wrexham, Shrewsbury, Clapton) 5
Glascodine, G. 1879 (Wrexham) 1
Glover, E. M. 1932 (Grimsby T) 7
Godding, G. 1923 (Wrexham) 2
Godfrey, B. C. 1964 (Preston NE) 3
Goodwin, U. 1881 (Ruthin) 1
Goss, J. 1991 (Norwich C) 9
Gough, R. T. 1883 (Oswestry White Star) 1
Gray, A. 1924 (Oldham Ath, Manchester C, Manchester Central, Tranmere R, Chester) 24
Green, A. W. 1901 (Aston Villa, Notts Co, Nottingham F) 8

Green, C. R. 1965 (Birmingham C) 15
Green, G. H. 1938 (Charlton Ath) 4
Green, R. M. 1998 (Wolverhampton W) 2
Grey, Dr W. 1876 (Druids) 2
Griffiths, A. T. 1971 (Wrexham) 17
Griffiths, F. J. 1900 (Blackpool) 2
Griffiths, G. 1887 (Chirk) 1
Griffiths, J. H. 1953 (Swansea T) 1
Griffiths, L. 1902 (Wrexham) 1
Griffiths, M. W. 1947 (Leicester C) 11
Griffiths, P. 1884 (Chirk) 6
Griffiths, P. H. 1932 (Everton) 1
Griffiths, T. P. 1927 (Everton, Bolton W, Middlesbrough, Aston Villa) 21
Gunter, C. R. 2007 (Cardiff C, Tottenham H, Nottingham F, Reading) 53

Hall, G. D. 1988 (Chelsea) 9
Hallam, J. 1889 (Oswestry) 1
Hanford, H. 1934 (Swansea T, Sheffield W) 7
Harrington, A. C. 1956 (Cardiff C) 11
Harris, C. S. 1976 (Leeds U) 24
Harris, W. C. 1954 (Middlesbrough) 6
Harrison, W. C. 1899 (Wrexham) 5
Hartson, J. 1995 (Arsenal, West Ham U, Wimbledon, Coventry C, Celtic) 51
Haworth, S. O. 1997 (Cardiff C, Coventry C) 5
Hayes, A. 1890 (Wrexham) 2
Hennessey, W. R. 2007 (Wolverhampton W, Crystal Palace) 43
Hennessey, W. T. 1962 (Birmingham C, Nottingham F, Derby Co) 39
Hersee, A. M. 1886 (Bangor) 2
Hersee, R. 1886 (Llandudno) 1
Hewitt, R. 1958 (Cardiff C) 5
Hewitt, T. J. 1911 (Wrexham, Chelsea, South Liverpool) 8
Heywood, D. 1879 (Druids) 1
Hibbott, H. 1880 (Newtown Excelsior, Newtown) 3
Higham, G. G. 1878 (Oswestry) 2
Hill, M. R. 1972 (Ipswich T) 2
Hockey, T. 1972 (Sheffield U, Norwich C, Aston Villa) 9
Hoddinott, T. F. 1921 (Watford) 2
Hodges, G. 1984 (Wimbledon, Newcastle U, Watford, Sheffield U) 18
Hodgkinson, A. V. 1908 (Southampton) 1
Holden, A. 1984 (Chester C) 1
Hole, B. G. 1963 (Cardiff C, Blackburn R, Aston Villa, Swansea C) 30
Hole, W. J. 1921 (Swansea T) 9
Hollins, D. M. 1962 (Newcastle U) 11
Hopkins, I. J. 1935 (Brentford) 12
Hopkins, J. 1983 (Fulham, Crystal Palace) 16
Hopkins, M. 1956 (Tottenham H) 34
Horne, B. 1988 (Portsmouth, Southampton, Everton, Birmingham C) 59
Howell, E. G. 1888 (Builth) 3
Howells, R. G. 1954 (Cardiff C) 2
Hugh, A. R. 1930 (Newport Co) 1
Hughes, A. 1894 (Rhos) 2
Hughes, A. 1907 (Chirk) 1
Hughes, C. M. 1992 (Luton T, Wimbledon) 8
Hughes, E. 1899 (Everton, Tottenham H) 14
Hughes, E. 1906 (Wrexham, Nottingham F, Wrexham, Manchester C) 16
Hughes, F. W. 1882 (Northwich Victoria) 6
Hughes, I. 1951 (Luton T) 4
Hughes, J. 1877 (Cambridge University, Aberystwyth) 2
Hughes, J. 1905 (Liverpool) 3
Hughes, J. I. 1935 (Blackburn R) 1
Hughes, L. M. 1984 (Manchester U, Barcelona, Manchester U, Chelsea, Southampton) 72
Hughes, P. W. 1887 (Bangor) 3
Hughes, W. 1891 (Bootle) 3
Hughes, W. A. 1949 (Blackburn R) 5
Hughes, W. M. 1938 (Birmingham) 10
Humphreys, J. V. 1947 (Everton) 1
Humphreys, R. 1888 (Druids) 1
Hunter, A. H. 1887 (FA of Wales Secretary) 1
Huws, E. W. 2014 (Manchester C) 2

Jackett, K. 1983 (Watford) 31

Jackson, W. 1899 (St Helens Rec) 1
James, E. 1893 (Chirk) 8
James, E. G. 1966 (Blackpool) 9
James, L. 1972 (Burnley, Derby Co, QPR, Burnley, Swansea C, Sunderland) 54
James, R. M. 1979 (Swansea C, Stoke C, QPR, Leicester C, Swansea C) 47
James, W. 1931 (West Ham U) 2
Jarrett, R. H. 1889 (Ruthin) 2
Jarvis, A. L. 1967 (Hull C) 3
Jenkins, E. 1925 (Lovell's Ath) 1
Jenkins, J. 1924 (Brighton & HA) 8
Jenkins, R. W. 1902 (Rhyl) 1
Jenkins, S. R. 1996 (Swansea C, Huddersfield T) 16
Jenkyns, C. A. L. 1892 (Small Heath, Woolwich Arsenal, Newton Heath, Walsall) 8
Jennings, W. 1914 (Bolton W) 11
John, D. C. 2013 (Cardiff C) 2
John, R. F. 1923 (Arsenal) 15
John, W. R. 1931 (Walsall, Stoke C, Preston NE, Sheffield U, Swansea T) 14
Johnson, A. J. 1999 (Nottingham F, WBA) 15
Johnson, M. G. 1964 (Swansea T) 1
Jones, A. 1987 (Port Vale, Charlton Ath) 6
Jones, A. F. 1877 (Oxford University) 1
Jones, A. T. 1905 (Nottingham F, Notts Co) 2
Jones, Bryn 1935 (Wolverhampton W, Arsenal) 17
Jones, B. S. 1963 (Swansea T, Plymouth Arg, Cardiff C) 15
Jones, Charlie 1926 (Nottingham F, Arsenal) 8
Jones, Cliff 1954 (Swansea T, Tottenham H, Fulham) 59
Jones, C. W. 1935 (Birmingham) 2
Jones, D. 1888 (Chirk, Bolton W, Manchester C) 14
Jones, D. E. 1976 (Norwich C) 8
Jones, D. O. 1934 (Leicester C) 7
Jones, Evan 1910 (Chelsea, Oldham Ath, Bolton W) 7
Jones, F. R. 1885 (Bangor) 3
Jones, F. W. 1893 (Small Heath) 1
Jones, G. P. 1907 (Wrexham) 2
Jones, H. 1902 (Aberaman) 1
Jones, Humphrey 1885 (Bangor, Queen's Park, East Stirlingshire, Queen's Park) 14
Jones, Ivor 1920 (Swansea T, WBA) 10
Jones, Jeffrey 1908 (Llandrindod Wells) 3
Jones, J. 1876 (Druids) 1
Jones, J. 1883 (Berwyn Rangers) 3
Jones, J. 1925 (Wrexham) 1
Jones, J. L. 1895 (Sheffield U, Tottenham H) 21
Jones, J. Love 1906 (Stoke, Middlesbrough) 2
Jones, J. O. 1901 (Bangor) 2
Jones, J. P. 1976 (Liverpool, Wrexham, Chelsea, Huddersfield T) 72
Jones, J. T. 1912 (Stoke, Crystal Palace) 15
Jones, K. 1950 (Aston Villa) 1
Jones, Leslie J. 1933 (Cardiff C, Coventry C, Arsenal) 11
Jones, M. A. 2007 (Wrexham) 2
Jones, M. G. 2000 (Leeds U, Leicester C) 13
Jones, P. L. 1997 (Liverpool, Tranmere R) 2
Jones, P. S. 1997 (Stockport Co, Southampton, Wolverhampton W, QPR) 50
Jones, P. W. 1971 (Bristol R) 1
Jones, R. 1887 (Bangor, Crewe Alex) 3
Jones, R. 1898 (Leicester Fosse) 1
Jones, R. 1899 (Druids) 1
Jones, R. 1900 (Bangor) 2
Jones, R. 1906 (Millwall) 2
Jones, R. A. 1884 (Druids) 4
Jones, R. A. 1994 (Sheffield W) 1
Jones, R. S. 1894 (Everton) 1
Jones, S. 1887 (Wrexham, Chester) 2
Jones, S. 1893 (Wrexham, Burton Swifts, Druids) 6
Jones, T. 1926 (Manchester U) 1
Jones, T. D. 1908 (Aberdare) 1
Jones, T. G. 1938 (Everton) 17
Jones, T. J. 1932 (Sheffield W) 2
Jones, V. P. 1995 (Wimbledon) 9
Jones, W. E. A. 1947 (Swansea T, Tottenham H) 4
Jones, W. J. 1901 (Aberdare, West Ham U) 4
Jones, W. Lot 1905 (Manchester C, Southend U) 20
Jones, W. P. 1889 (Druids, Wynnstay) 4
Jones, W. R. 1897 (Aberystwyth) 1

Keenor, F. C. 1920 (Cardiff C, Crewe Alex) 32

Phillips, C. 1931 (Wolverhampton W, Aston Villa)   13
Phillips, D. 1984 (Plymouth Arg, Manchester C,
    Coventry C, Norwich C, Nottingham F)   62
Phillips, L. 1971 (Cardiff C, Aston Villa, Swansea C,
    Charlton Ath)   58
Phillips, T. J. S. 1973 (Chelsea)   4
Phoenix, H. 1882 (Wrexham)   1
Pipe, D. R. 2003 (Coventry C)   1
Poland, G. 1939 (Wrexham)   2
Pontin, K. 1980 (Cardiff C)   2
Powell, A. 1947 (Leeds U, Everton, Birmingham C)   8
Powell, D. 1968 (Wrexham, Sheffield U)   11
Powell, I. V. 1947 (QPR, Aston Villa)   8
Powell, J. 1878 (Druids, Bolton W, Newton Heath)   15
Powell, Seth 1885 (Oswestry, WBA)   7
Price, H. 1907 (Aston Villa, Burton U, Wrexham)   5
Price, J. 1877 (Wrexham)   12
Price, L. P. 2006 (Ipswich T, Derby Co,
    Crystal Palace)   11
Price, P. 1980 (Luton T, Tottenham H)   25
Pring, K. D. 1966 (Rotherham U)   3
Pritchard, H. K. 1985 (Bristol C)   1
Pryce-Jones, A. W. 1895 (Newtown)   1
Pryce-Jones, W. E. 1887 (Cambridge University)   5
Pugh, A. 1889 (Rhostyllen)   1
Pugh, D. H. 1896 (Wrexham, Lincoln C)   7
Pugsley, J. 1930 (Charlton Ath)   1
Pullen, W. J. 1926 (Plymouth Arg)   1

Ramsey, A. 2009 (Arsenal)   30
Rankmore, F. E. J. 1966 (Peterborough U)   1
Ratcliffe, K. 1981 (Everton, Cardiff C)   59
Rea, J. C. 1894 (Aberystwyth)   9
Ready, K. 1997 (QPR)   5
Reece, G. I. 1966 (Sheffield U, Cardiff C)   29
Reed, W. G. 1955 (Ipswich T)   2
Rees, A. 1984 (Birmingham C)   1
Rees, J. M. 1992 (Luton T)   1
Rees, R. R. 1965 (Coventry C, WBA, Nottingham F)   39
Rees, W. 1949 (Cardiff C, Tottenham H)   4
Ribeiro, C. M. 2010 (Bristol C)   2
Richards, A. 1932 (Barnsley)   1
Richards, A. D. J. 2012 (Swansea C)   4
Richards, D. 1931 (Wolverhampton W, Brentford,
    Birmingham)   21
Richards, G. 1899 (Druids, Oswestry, Shrewsbury T)   6
Richards, R. W. 1920 (Wolverhampton W, West Ham U,
    Mold)   9
Richards, S. V. 1947 (Cardiff C)   1
Richards, W. E. 1933 (Fulham)   1
**Ricketts, S. D. 2005 (Swansea C, Hull C, Bolton W,
    Wolverhampton W)   52**
Roach, J. 1885 (Oswestry)   1
Robbins, W. W. 1931 (Cardiff C, WBA)   11
Roberts, A. M. 1993 (QPR)   2
Roberts, D. F. 1973 (Oxford U, Hull C)   17
Roberts, G. W. 2000 (Tranmere R)   9
Roberts, I. W. 1990 (Watford, Huddersfield T,
    Leicester C, Norwich C)   15
Roberts, Jas 1913 (Wrexham)   2
Roberts, J. 1879 (Corwen, Berwyn R)   7
Roberts, J. 1881 (Ruthin)   2
Roberts, J. 1906 (Bradford C)   2
Roberts, J. G. 1971 (Arsenal, Birmingham C)   22
Roberts, J. H. 1949 (Bolton W)   1
Roberts, N. W. 2000 (Wrexham, Wigan Ath)   4
Roberts, P. S. 1974 (Portsmouth)   4
Roberts, R. 1884 (Druids, Bolton W, Preston NE)   9
Roberts, R. 1886 (Wrexham)   2
Roberts, R. 1891 (Rhos, Crewe Alex)   2
Roberts, R. L. 1890 (Chester)   1
Roberts, S. W. 2005 (Wrexham)   1
Roberts, W. 1879 (Llangollen, Berwyn R)   6
Roberts, W. 1883 (Rhyl)   4
Roberts, W. 1886 (Wrexham)   4
Roberts, W. H. 1882 (Ruthin, Rhyl)   6
Robinson, C. P. 2000 (Wolverhampton W, Portsmouth,
    Sunderland, Norwich C, Toronto Lynx)   52
Robinson, J. R. C. 1996 (Charlton Ath)   30
Robson-Kanu, T. H. 2010 (Reading)   21
Rodrigues, P. J. 1965 (Cardiff C, Leicester C, Sheffield W)   40
Rogers, J. P. 1896 (Wrexham)   3

Rogers, W. 1931 (Wrexham)   2
Roose, L. R. 1900 (Aberystwyth, London Welsh, Stoke,
    Everton, Stoke, Sunderland)   24
Rouse, R. V. 1959 (Crystal Palace)   1
Rowlands, A. C. 1914 (Tranmere R)   1
Rowley, T. 1959 (Tranmere R)   1
Rush, I. 1980 (Liverpool, Juventus, Liverpool)   73
Russell, M. R. 1912 (Merthyr T, Plymouth Arg)   23

Sabine, H. W. 1887 (Oswestry)   1
Saunders, D. 1986 (Brighton & HA, Oxford U,
    Derby Co, Liverpool, Aston Villa, Galatasaray,
    Nottingham F, Sheffield U, Benfica, Bradford C)   75
Savage, R. W. 1996 (Crewe Alex, Leicester C,
    Birmingham C)   39
Savin, G. 1878 (Oswestry)   1
Sayer, P. A. 1977 (Cardiff C)   7
Scrine, F. H. 1950 (Swansea T)   2
Sear, C. R. 1963 (Manchester C)   1
Shaw, E. G. 1882 (Oswestry)   3
Sherwood, A. T. 1947 (Cardiff C, Newport Co)   41
Shone, W. W. 1879 (Oswestry)   1
Shortt, W. W. 1947 (Plymouth Arg)   12
Showers, D. 1975 (Cardiff C)   2
Sidlow, C. 1947 (Liverpool)   7
Sisson, H. 1885 (Wrexham Olympic)   3
Slatter, N. 1983 (Bristol R, Oxford U)   22
Smallman, D. P. 1974 (Wrexham, Everton)   7
Southall, N. 1982 (Everton)   92
Speed, G. A. 1990 (Leeds U, Everton, Newcastle U,
    Bolton W)   85
Sprake, G. 1964 (Leeds U, Birmingham C)   37
Stansfield, F. 1949 (Cardiff C)   1
Stevenson, B. 1978 (Leeds U, Birmingham C)   15
Stevenson, N. 1982 (Swansea C)   4
Stitfall, R. F. 1953 (Cardiff C)   2
Stock, B. B. 2010 (Doncaster R)   3
Sullivan, D. 1953 (Cardiff C)   17
Symons, C. J. 1992 (Portsmouth, Manchester C, Fulham,
    Crystal Palace)   37

Tapscott, D. R. 1954 (Arsenal, Cardiff C)   14
Taylor, G. K. 1996 (Crystal Palace, Sheffield U, Burnley,
    Nottingham F)   15
Taylor, J. 1898 (Wrexham)   1
Taylor, N. J. 2010 (Wrexham, Swansea C)   16
Taylor, O. D. S. 1893 (Newtown)   4
Thatcher, B. D. 2004 (Leicester C, Manchester C)   7
Thomas, C. 1899 (Druids)   2
Thomas, D. A. 1957 (Swansea T)   2
Thomas, D. S. 1948 (Fulham)   4
Thomas, E. 1925 (Cardiff Corinthians)   1
Thomas, G. 1885 (Wrexham)   2
Thomas, H. 1927 (Manchester U)   1
Thomas, Martin R. 1987 (Newcastle U)   1
Thomas, Mickey 1977 (Wrexham, Manchester U,
    Everton, Brighton & HA, Stoke C, Chelsea, WBA)   51
Thomas, R. J. 1967 (Swindon T, Derby Co, Cardiff C)   50
Thomas, T. 1898 (Bangor)   2
Thomas, W. R. 1931 (Newport Co)   2
Thomson, D. 1876 (Druids)   1
Thomson, G. F. 1876 (Druids)   2
Toshack, J. B. 1969 (Cardiff C, Liverpool, Swansea C)   40
Townsend, W. 1887 (Newtown)   2
Trainer, H. 1895 (Wrexham)   3
Trainer, J. 1887 (Bolton W, Preston NE)   20
Trollope, P. J. 1997 (Derby Co, Fulham, Coventry C,
    Northampton T)   9
**Tudur-Jones, O. 2008 (Swansea C, Norwich C,
    Hibernian)   7**
Turner, H. G. 1937 (Charlton Ath)   8
Turner, J. 1892 (Wrexham)   1
Turner, R. E. 1891 (Wrexham)   2
Turner, W. H. 1887 (Wrexham)   5

Van Den Hauwe, P. W. R. 1985 (Everton)   13
**Vaughan, D. O. 2003 (Crewe Alex, Real Sociedad,
    Blackpool, Sunderland, Nottingham F)   38**
Vaughan, Jas 1893 (Druids)   4
Vaughan, John 1879 (Oswestry, Druids, Bolton W)   11
Vaughan, J. O. 1885 (Rhyl)   4
Vaughan, N. 1983 (Newport Co, Cardiff C)   10

Vaughan, T. 1885 (Rhyl) 1
Vearncombe, G. 1958 (Cardiff C) 2
Vernon, T. R. 1957 (Blackburn R, Everton, Stoke C) 32
Villars, A. K. 1974 (Cardiff C) 3
Vizard, E. T. 1911 (Bolton W) 22
Vokes, S. M. 2008 (Bournemouth, Wolverhampton W, Burnley) **31**

Walley, J. T. 1971 (Watford) 1
Walsh, I. P. 1980 (Crystal Palace, Swansea C) 18
Ward, D. 1959 (Bristol R, Cardiff C) 2
Ward, D. 2000 (Notts Co, Nottingham F) 5
Warner, J. 1937 (Swansea T, Manchester U) 2
Warren, F. W. 1929 (Cardiff C, Middlesbrough, Hearts) 6
Watkins, A. E. 1898 (Leicester Fosse, Aston Villa, Millwall) 5
Watkins, W. M. 1902 (Stoke, Aston Villa, Sunderland, Stoke) 10
Webster, C. 1957 (Manchester U) 4
Weston, R. D. 2000 (Arsenal, Cardiff C) 7
Whatley, W. J. 1939 (Tottenham H) 2
White, P. F. 1896 (London Welsh) 1
Wilcock, A. R. 1890 (Oswestry) 1
Wilding, J. 1885 (Wrexham Olympians, Bootle, Wrexham) 9
Williams, A. 1994 (Reading, Wolverhampton W, Reading) 13
Williams, A. E. 2008 (Stockport Co, Swansea C) **45**
Williams, A. L. 1931 (Wrexham) 1
Williams, A. P. 1998 (Southampton) 2
Williams, B. 1930 (Bristol C) 1
Williams, B. D. 1928 (Swansea T, Everton) 10
Williams, D. G. 1988 (Derby Co, Ipswich T) 13
Williams, D. M. 1986 (Norwich C) 5
Williams, D. R. 1921 (Merthyr T, Sheffield W, Manchester U) 8

Williams, E. 1893 (Crewe Alex) 2
Williams, E. 1901 (Druids) 5
Williams, G. 1893 (Chirk) 6
Williams, G. C. 2014 (Fulham) **1**
Williams, G. E. 1960 (WBA) 26
Williams, G. G. 1961 (Swansea T) 5
Williams, G. J. 2006 (West Ham U, Ipswich T) 2
Williams, G. J. J. 1951 (Cardiff C) 1
Williams, G. O. 1907 (Wrexham) 1
Williams, H. J. 1965 (Swansea T) 3
Williams, H. T. 1949 (Newport Co, Leeds U) 4
Williams, J. H. 1884 (Oswestry) 1
Williams, J. J. 1939 (Wrexham) 1
Williams, J. T. 1925 (Middlesbrough) 1
Williams, J. P. 2013 (Crystal Palace) **6**
Williams, J. W. 1912 (Crystal Palace) 2
Williams, R. 1935 (Newcastle U) 2
Williams, R. P. 1886 (Caernarvon) 1
Williams, S. G. 1954 (WBA, Southampton) 43
Williams, W. 1876 (Druids, Oswestry, Druids) 11
Williams, W. 1925 (Northampton T) 1
Wilson, H. 2013 (Liverpool) **1**
Wilson, J. S. 2013 (Bristol C) **1**
Witcomb, D. F. 1947 (WBA, Sheffield W) 3
Woosnam, A. P. 1959 (Leyton Orient, West Ham U, Aston Villa) 17
Woosnam, G. 1879 (Newtown Excelsior) 1
Worthington, T. 1894 (Newtown) 1
Wynn, G. A. 1909 (Wrexham, Manchester C) 11
Wynn, W. 1903 (Chirk) 1

Yorath, T. C. 1970 (Leeds U, Coventry C, Tottenham H, Vancouver Whitecaps) 59
Young, E. 1990 (Wimbledon, Crystal Palace, Wolverhampton W) 21

REPUBLIC OF IRELAND

Aherne, T. 1946 (Belfast Celtic, Luton T) 16
Aldridge, J. W. 1986 (Oxford U, Liverpool, Real Sociedad, Tranmere R) 69
Ambrose, P. 1955 (Shamrock R) 5
Anderson, J. 1980 (Preston NE, Newcastle U) 16
Andrews, K. J. 2009 (Blackburn R, WBA) 35
Andrews, P. 1936 (Bohemians) 1
Arrigan, T. 1938 (Waterford) 1

Babb, P. A. 1994 (Coventry C, Liverpool, Sunderland) 35
Bailham, E. 1964 (Shamrock R) 1
Barber, E. 1966 (Shelbourne, Birmingham C) 2
Barrett, G. 2003 (Arsenal, Coventry C) 6
Barry, P. 1928 (Fordsons) 2
Beglin, J. 1984 (Liverpool) 15
Bennett, A. J. 2007 (Reading) 2
Bermingham, J. 1929 (Bohemians) 1
Bermingham, P. 1935 (St James' Gate) 1
Best, L. J. B. 2009 (Coventry C, Newcastle U) 7
Bonner, P. 1981 (Celtic) 80
Brady, R. 2013 (Hull C) **6**
Braddish, S. 1978 (Dundalk) 2
Bradshaw, P. 1939 (St James' Gate) 5
Brady, F. 1926 (Fordsons) 2
Brady, T. R. 1964 (QPR) 6
Brady, W. L. 1975 (Arsenal, Juventus, Sampdoria, Internazionale, Ascoli, West Ham U) 72
Branagan, K. G. 1997 (Bolton W) 1
Breen, G. 1996 (Birmingham C, Coventry C, West Ham U, Sunderland) 63
Breen, T. 1937 (Manchester U, Shamrock R) 5
Brennan, F. 1965 (Drumcondra) 1
Brennan, S. A. 1965 (Manchester U, Waterford) 19
Brown, J. 1937 (Coventry C) 2
Browne, W. 1964 (Bohemians) 3
Bruce, A. S. 2007 (Ipswich T) 2
Buckley, L. 1984 (Shamrock R, Waregem) 2
Burke, F. 1952 (Cork Ath) 1
Burke, J. 1929 (Shamrock R) 1
Burke, J. 1934 (Cork) 1
Butler, P. J. 2000 (Sunderland) 1
Butler, T. 2003 (Sunderland) 2

Byrne, A. B. 1970 (Southampton) 14
Byrne, D. 1929 (Shelbourne, Shamrock R, Coleraine) 3
Byrne, J. 1928 (Bray Unknowns) 1
Byrne, J. 1985 (QPR, Le Havre, Brighton & HA, Sunderland, Millwall) 23
Byrne, J. 2004 (Shelbourne) 2
Byrne, P. 1931 (Dolphin, Shelbourne, Drumcondra) 3
Byrne, P. 1984 (Shamrock R) 8
Byrne, S. 1931 (Bohemians) 1

Campbell, A. 1985 (Santander) 3
Campbell, N. 1971 (St Patrick's Ath, Fortuna Cologne) 11
Cannon, H. 1926 (Bohemians) 2
Cantwell, N. 1954 (West Ham U, Manchester U) 36
Carey, B. P. 1992 (Manchester U, Leicester C) 3
Carey, J. J. 1938 (Manchester U) 29
Carolan, J. 1960 (Manchester U) 2
Carr, S. 1999 (Tottenham H, Newcastle U) 44
Carroll, B. 1949 (Shelbourne) 2
Carroll, T. R. 1968 (Ipswich T, Birmingham C) 17
Carsley, L. K. 1998 (Derby Co, Blackburn R, Coventry C, Everton) 39
Cascarino, A. G. 1986 (Gillingham, Millwall, Aston Villa, Celtic, Chelsea, Marseille, Nancy) 88
Chandler, J. 1980 (Leeds U) 2
Chatton, H. A. 1931 (Shelbourne, Dumbarton, Cork) 3
Clark, C. 2011 (Aston Villa) **10**
Clarke, C. R. 2004 (Stoke C) 2
Clarke, J. 1978 (Drogheda U) 1
Clarke, K. 1948 (Drumcondra) 1
Clarke, M. 1950 (Shamrock R) 1
Clinton, T. J. 1951 (Everton) 3
Coad, P. 1947 (Shamrock R) 11
Coffey, T. 1950 (Drumcondra) 1
Coleman, S. 2011 (Everton) **23**
Colfer, M. D. 1950 (Shelbourne) 2
Colgan, N. 2002 (Hibernian, Barnsley) 9
Collins, F. 1927 (Jacobs) 1
Conmy, O. M. 1965 (Peterborough U) 5
Connolly, D. J. 1996 (Watford, Feyenoord, Wolverhampton W, Excelsior, Feyenoord, Wimbledon, West Ham U, Wigan Ath) 41

Connolly, H. 1937 (Cork)	1
Connolly, J. 1926 (Fordsons)	1
Conroy, G. A. 1970 (Stoke C)	27
Conway, J. P. 1967 (Fulham, Manchester C)	20
Corr, P. J. 1949 (Everton)	4
Courtney, E. 1946 (Cork U)	1
Cox, S. R. 2011 (WBA, Nottingham F)	**30**
Coyle, O. C. 1994 (Bolton W)	1
Coyne, T. 1992 (Celtic, Tranmere R, Motherwell)	22
Crowe, G. 2003 (Bohemians)	2
Cummins, G. P. 1954 (Luton T)	19
Cuneen, T. 1951 (Limerick)	1
Cunningham, G. R. 2010 (Manchester C, Bristol C)	4
Cunningham, K. 1996 (Wimbledon, Birmingham C)	72
Curtis, D. P. 1957 (Shelbourne, Bristol C, Ipswich T, Exeter C)	17
Cusack, S. 1953 (Limerick)	1
Daish, L. S. 1992 (Cambridge U, Coventry C)	5
Daly, G. A. 1973 (Manchester U, Derby Co, Coventry C, Birmingham C, Shrewsbury T)	48
Daly, J. 1932 (Shamrock R)	2
Daly, M. 1978 (Wolverhampton W)	2
Daly, P. 1950 (Shamrock R)	1
Davis, T. L. 1937 (Oldham Ath, Tranmere R)	4
Deacy, E. 1982 (Aston Villa)	4
Delaney, D. F. 2008 (QPR, Ipswich T, Crystal Palace)	**9**
Delap, R. J. 1998 (Derby Co, Southampton)	11
De Mange, K. J. P. P. 1987 (Liverpool, Hull C)	2
Dempsey, J. T. 1967 (Fulham, Chelsea)	19
Dennehy, J. 1972 (Cork Hibernians, Nottingham F, Walsall)	11
Desmond, P. 1950 (Middlesbrough)	4
Devine, J. 1980 (Arsenal, Norwich C)	13
Doherty, G. M. T. 2000 (Luton T, Tottenham H, Norwich C)	34
Donnelly, J. 1935 (Dundalk)	10
Donnelly, T. 1938 (Drumcondra, Shamrock R)	2
Donovan, D. C. 1955 (Everton)	5
Donovan, T. 1980 (Aston Villa)	2
Douglas, J. 2004 (Blackburn R, Leeds U)	8
Dowdall, C. 1928 (Fordsons, Barnsley, Cork)	3
Doyle, C. 1959 (Shelbourne)	1
Doyle, Colin 2007 (Birmingham C)	1
Doyle, D. 1926 (Shamrock R)	1
Doyle, K. E. 2006 (Reading, Wolverhampton W)	**59**
Doyle, L. 1932 (Dolphin)	1
Doyle, M. P. 2004 (Coventry C)	1
Duff, D. A. 1998 (Blackburn R, Chelsea, Newcastle U, Fulham)	100
Duffy, B. 1950 (Shamrock R)	1
Duffy, S. P. M. 2014 (Everton)	**1**
Duggan, H. A. 1927 (Leeds U, Newport Co)	5
Dunne, A. P. 1962 (Manchester U, Bolton W)	33
Dunne, J. 1930 (Sheffield U, Arsenal, Southampton, Shamrock R)	15
Dunne, J. C. 1971 (Fulham)	1
Dunne, L. 1935 (Manchester C)	2
Dunne, P. A. J. 1965 (Manchester U)	5
Dunne, R. P. 2000 (Everton, Manchester C, Aston Villa, QPR)	**80**
Dunne, S. 1953 (Luton T)	15
Dunne, T. 1956 (St Patrick's Ath)	3
Dunning, P. 1971 (Shelbourne)	2
Dunphy, E. M. 1966 (York C, Millwall)	23
Dwyer, N. M. 1960 (West Ham U, Swansea T)	14
Eccles, P. 1986 (Shamrock R)	1
Egan, R. 1929 (Dundalk)	1
Eglington, T. J. 1946 (Shamrock R, Everton)	24
Eliot, R. 2014 (Newcastle U)	**1**
Elliott, S. W. 2005 (Sunderland)	9
Ellis, P. 1935 (Bohemians)	7
Evans, M. J. 1998 (Southampton)	1
Fagan, E. 1973 (Shamrock R)	1
Fagan, F. 1955 (Manchester C, Derby Co)	8
Fagan, J. 1926 (Shamrock R)	1
Fahey, K. D. 2010 (Birmingham C)	16

Fairclough, M. 1982 (Dundalk)	2
Fallon, S. 1951 (Celtic)	8
Fallon, W. J. 1935 (Notts Co, Sheffield W)	9
Farquharson, T. G. 1929 (Cardiff C)	4
Farrell, P. 1937 (Hibernian)	2
Farrell, P. D. 1946 (Shamrock R, Everton)	28
Farrelly, G. 1996 (Aston Villa, Everton, Bolton W)	6
Feenan, J. J. 1937 (Sunderland)	2
Finnan, S. 2000 (Fulham, Liverpool, Espanyol)	53
Finucane, A. 1967 (Limerick)	11
Fitzgerald, F. J. 1955 (Waterford)	2
Fitzgerald, P. J. 1961 (Leeds U, Chester)	5
Fitzpatrick, K. 1970 (Limerick)	1
Fitzsimons, A. G. 1950 (Middlesbrough, Lincoln C)	26
Fleming, C. 1996 (Middlesbrough)	10
Flood, J. J. 1926 (Shamrock R)	5
Fogarty, A. 1960 (Sunderland, Hartlepools U)	11
Folan, C. C. 2009 (Hull C)	7
Foley, D. J. 2000 (Watford)	6
Foley, J. 1934 (Cork, Celtic)	7
Foley, K. P. 2009 (Wolverhampton W)	8
Foley, M. 1926 (Shelbourne)	1
Foley, T. C. 1964 (Northampton T)	9
Forde, D. 2011 (Millwall)	**19**
Foy, T. 1938 (Shamrock R)	2
Fullam, J. 1961 (Preston NE, Shamrock R)	11
Fullam, R. 1926 (Shamrock R)	2
Gallagher, C. 1967 (Celtic)	2
Gallagher, M. 1954 (Hibernian)	1
Gallagher, P. 1932 (Falkirk)	1
Galvin, A. 1983 (Tottenham H, Sheffield W, Swindon T)	29
Gamble, J. 2007 (Cork C)	2
Gannon, E. 1949 (Notts Co, Sheffield W, Shelbourne)	14
Gannon, M. 1972 (Shelbourne)	1
Gaskins, P. 1934 (Shamrock R, St James' Gate)	7
Gavin, J. T. 1950 (Norwich C, Tottenham H, Norwich C)	7
Geoghegan, M. 1937 (St James' Gate)	2
Gibbons, A. 1952 (St Patrick's Ath)	4
Gibson, D. T. D. 2008 (Manchester U, Everton)	**21**
Gilbert, R. 1966 (Shamrock R)	1
Giles, C. 1951 (Doncaster R)	1
Giles, M. J. 1960 (Manchester U, Leeds U, WBA, Shamrock R)	59
Given, S. J. J. 1996 (Blackburn R, Newcastle U, Manchester C, Aston Villa)	125
Givens, D. J. 1969 (Manchester U, Luton T, QPR, Birmingham C, Neuchatel X)	56
Gleeson, S. M. 2007 (Wolverhampton W)	2
Glen, W. 1927 (Shamrock R)	8
Glynn, D. 1952 (Drumcondra)	2
Godwin, T. F. 1949 (Shamrock R, Leicester C, Bournemouth)	13
Golding, J. 1928 (Shamrock R)	2
Goodman, J. 1997 (Wimbledon)	4
Goodwin, J. 2003 (Stockport Co)	1
Gorman, W. C. 1936 (Bury, Brentford)	13
Grace, J. 1926 (Drumcondra)	1
Grealish, A. 1976 (Orient, Luton T, Brighton & HA, WBA)	45
Green, P. J. 2010 (Derby Co, Leeds U)	**20**
Gregg, E. 1978 (Bohemians)	8
Griffith, R. 1935 (Walsall)	1
Grimes, A. A. 1978 (Manchester U, Coventry C, Luton T)	18
Hale, A. 1962 (Aston Villa, Doncaster R, Waterford)	14
Hamilton, T. 1959 (Shamrock R)	2
Hand, E. K. 1969 (Portsmouth)	20
Harrington, W. 1936 (Cork)	5
Harte, I. P. 1996 (Leeds U, Levante)	64
Hartnett, J. B. 1949 (Middlesbrough)	2
Haverty, J. 1956 (Arsenal, Blackburn R, Millwall, Celtic, Bristol R, Shelbourne)	32
Hayes, A. W. P. 1979 (Southampton)	1
Hayes, W. E. 1947 (Huddersfield T)	2
Hayes, W. J. 1949 (Limerick)	1

Healey, R. 1977 (Cardiff C) 2
Healy, C. 2002 (Celtic, Sunderland) 13
Heighway, S. D. 1971 (Liverpool, Minnesota K) 34
Henderson, B. 1948 (Drumcondra) 2
Henderson, W. C. P. 2006 (Brighton & HA, Preston NE)
6
Hendrick, J. P. 2013 (Derby Co) 7
Hennessy, J. 1965 (Shelbourne, St Patrick's Ath) 5
Herrick, J. 1972 (Cork Hibernians, Shamrock R) 3
Higgins, J. 1951 (Birmingham C) 1
Holland, M. R. 2000 (Ipswich T, Charlton Ath) 49
Holmes, J. 1971 (Coventry C, Tottenham H,
Vancouver Whitecaps) 30
Hoolahan, W. 2008 (Blackpool, Norwich C) 15
Horlacher, A. F. 1930 (Bohemians) 7
Houghton, R. J. 1986 (Oxford U, Liverpool, Aston Villa,
Crystal Palace, Reading) 73
Howlett, G. 1984 (Brighton & HA) 1
Hoy, M. 1938 (Dundalk) 6
Hughton, C. 1980 (Tottenham H, West Ham U) 53
Hunt, N. 2009 (Reading) 3
Hunt, S. P. 2007 (Reading, Hull C, Wolverhampton W)
39
Hurley, C. J. 1957 (Millwall, Sunderland, Bolton W) 40
Hutchinson, F. 1935 (Drumcondra) 2

Ireland S J. 2006 (Manchester C) 6
Irwin, D. J. 1991 (Manchester U) 56

Jordan, D. 1937 (Wolverhampton W) 2
Jordan, W. 1934 (Bohemians) 2

Kavanagh, G. A. 1998 (Stoke C, Cardiff C, Wigan Ath)
16
Kavanagh, P. J. 1931 (Celtic) 2
Keane, R. D. 1998 (Wolverhampton W, Coventry C,
Internazionale, Leeds U, Tottenham H, Liverpool,
Tottenham H, LA Galaxy) 133
Keane, R. M. 1991 (Nottingham F, Manchester U) 67
Keane, T. R. 1949 (Swansea T) 4
Kearin, M. 1972 (Shamrock R) 1
Kearns, F. T. 1954 (West Ham U) 1
Kearns, M. 1971 (Oxford U, Walsall, Wolverhampton W)
18
Kelly, A. T. 1993 (Sheffield U, Blackburn R) 34
Kelly, D. T. 1988 (Walsall, West Ham U, Leicester C,
Newcastle U, Wolverhampton W, Sunderland,
Tranmere R) 26
Kelly, G. 1994 (Leeds U) 52
Kelly, J. 1932 (Derry C) 4
Kelly, J. A. 1957 (Drumcondra, Preston NE) 47
Kelly, J. P. V. 1961 (Wolverhampton W) 5
Kelly, M. J. 1988 (Portsmouth) 4
Kelly, N. 1954 (Nottingham F) 1
Kelly, S. M. 2006 (Tottenham H, Birmingham C,
Fulham, Reading) 38
Kendrick, J. 1927 (Everton, Dolphin) 4
Kenna, J. J. 1995 (Blackburn R) 27
Kennedy, M. F. 1986 (Portsmouth) 2
Kennedy, M. J. 1996 (Liverpool, Wimbledon,
Manchester C, Wolverhampton W) 34
Kennedy, W. 1932 (St James' Gate) 3
Kenny, P. 2004 (Sheffield U) 7
Keogh, A. D. 2007 (Wolverhampton W, Millwall) 30
Keogh, J. 1966 (Shamrock R) 1
Keogh, R. J. 2013 (Derby Co) 5
Keogh, S. 1959 (Shamrock R) 1
Kernaghan, A. N. 1993 (Middlesbrough, Manchester C)
22
Kiely, D. L. 2000 (Charlton Ath, WBA) 11
Kiernan, F. W. 1951 (Shamrock R, Southampton) 5
Kilbane, K. D. 1998 (WBA, Sunderland, Everton,
Wigan Ath, Hull C) 110
Kinnear, J. P. 1967 (Tottenham H, Brighton & HA) 26
Kinsella, J. 1928 (Shelbourne) 1
Kinsella, M. A. 1998 (Charlton Ath, Aston Villa, WBA)
48
Kinsella, O. 1932 (Shamrock R) 2
Kirkland, A. 1927 (Shamrock R) 1

Lacey, W. 1927 (Shelbourne) 3
Langan, D. 1978 (Derby Co, Birmingham C, Oxford U)
26
Lapira, J. 2007 (Notre Dame) 1
Lawler, J. F. 1953 (Fulham) 8
Lawlor, J. C. 1949 (Drumcondra, Doncaster R) 3
Lawlor, M. 1971 (Shamrock R) 5
Lawrence, L. 2009 (Stoke C, Portsmouth) 15
Lawrenson, M. 1977 (Preston NE, Brighton & HA,
Liverpool) 39
Lee, A. D. 2003 (Rotherham U, Cardiff C, Ipswich T) 10
Leech, M. 1969 (Shamrock R) 8
Lennon, C. 1935 (St James' Gate) 3
Lennox, G. 1931 (Dolphin) 2
Long, S. P. 2007 (Reading, WBA, Hull C) 47
Lowry, D. 1962 (St Patrick's Ath) 1
Lunn, R. 1939 (Dundalk) 2
Lynch, J. 1934 (Cork Bohemians) 1

McAlinden, J. 1946 (Portsmouth) 2
McAteer, J. W. 1994 (Bolton W, Liverpool, Blackburn
R, Sunderland) 52
McCann, J. 1957 (Shamrock R) 1
McCarthy, J. 1926 (Bohemians) 3
McCarthy, J. 2010 (Wigan Ath, Everton) 23
McCarthy, M. 1932 (Shamrock R) 1
McCarthy, M. 1984 (Manchester C, Celtic, Lyon,
Millwall) 57
McClean, J. 2012 (Sunderland, Wigan Ath) 23
McConville, T. 1972 (Dundalk, Waterford) 6
McDonagh, Jacko 1984 (Shamrock R) 3
McDonagh, J. 1981 (Everton, Bolton W, Notts Co,
Wichita Wings) 25
McEvoy, M. A. 1961 (Blackburn R) 17
McGeady, A. 2004 (Celtic, Spartak Moscow, Everton) 68
McGee, P. 1978 (QPR, Preston NE) 15
McGoldrick, E. J. 1992 (Crystal Palace, Arsenal) 15
McGowan, D. 1949 (West Ham U) 3
McGowan, J. 1947 (Cork U) 1
McGrath, M. 1958 (Blackburn R, Bradford) 22
McGrath, P. 1985 (Manchester U, Aston Villa,
Derby Co) 83
McGuire, W. 1936 (Bohemians) 1
Macken, A. 1977 (Derby Co) 1
Macken J. P. 2005 (Manchester C) 1
McKenzie, G. 1938 (Southend U) 9
Mackey, G. 1957 (Shamrock R) 3
McLoughlin, A. F. 1990 (Swindon T, Southampton,
Portsmouth) 42
McLoughlin, F. 1930 (Fordsons, Cork) 2
McMillan, W. 1946 (Belfast Celtic) 2
McNally, J. B. 1959 (Luton T) 3
McPhail, S. 2000 (Leeds U) 10
McShane, P. D. 2007 (WBA, Sunderland, Hull C) 31
Madden, O. 1936 (Cork) 1
Madden, P. 2013 (Scunthorpe U) 1
Maguire, J. 1929 (Shamrock R) 1
Mahon, A. J. 2000 (Tranmere R) 2
Malone, G. 1949 (Shelbourne) 1
Mancini, T. J. 1974 (QPR, Arsenal) 5
Martin, C. 1927 (Bo'ness) 1
Martin, C. J. 1946 (Glentoran, Leeds U,
Aston Villa) 30
Martin, M. P. 1972 (Bohemians, Manchester U,
WBA, Newcastle U) 52
Maybury, A. 1998 (Leeds U, Hearts, Leicester C) 10
Meagan, M. K. 1961 (Everton, Huddersfield T,
Drogheda) 17
Meehan, P. 1934 (Drumcondra) 1
Meyler, D. 2013 (Sunderland, Hull C) 8
Miller, L. W. P. 2004 (Celtic, Manchester U, Sunderland,
Hibernian) 21
Milligan, M. J. 1992 (Oldham Ath) 1
Monahan, J. 1935 (Sligo R) 2
Mooney, J. 1965 (Shamrock R) 2
Moore, A. 1996 (Middlesbrough) 8
Moore, P. 1931 (Shamrock R, Aberdeen, Shamrock R) 9
Moran, K. 1980 (Manchester U, Sporting Gijon,
Blackburn R) 71

Moroney, T. 1948 (West Ham U, Evergreen U)   12
Morris, C. B. 1988 (Celtic, Middlesbrough)   35
Morrison, C. H. 2002 (Crystal Palace, Birmingham C,
    Crystal Palace)   36
Moulson, C. 1936 (Lincoln C, Notts Co)   5
Moulson, G. B. 1948 (Lincoln C)   3
Muckian, C. 1978 (Drogheda U)   1
Muldoon, T. 1927 (Aston Villa)   1
Mulligan, P. M. 1969 (Shamrock R, Chelsea,
    Crystal Palace, WBA, Shamrock R)   50
Munroe, L. 1954 (Shamrock R)   1
Murphy, A. 1956 (Clyde)   1
Murphy, B. 1986 (Bohemians)   1
Murphy, D. 2007 (Sunderland, Ipswich T)   **11**
Murphy, J. 1980 (Crystal Palace)   3
Murphy, J. 2004 (WBA, Scunthorpe U)   2
Murphy, P. M. 2007 (Carlisle U)   1
Murray, T. 1950 (Dundalk)   1

Newman, W. 1969 (Shelbourne)   1
Nolan, E. W. 2009 (Preston NE)   3
Nolan, R. 1957 (Shamrock R)   10

O'Brien, A. 2007 (Newcastle U)   5
O'Brien, A. J. 2001 (Newcastle U, Portsmouth)   26
O'Brien, F. 1980 (Philadelphia F)   3
O'Brien J. M. 2006 (Bolton W, West Ham U)   5
O'Brien, L. 1986 (Shamrock R, Manchester U,
    Newcastle U, Tranmere R)   16
O'Brien, M. T. 1927 (Derby Co, Walsall, Norwich C,
    Watford)   4
O'Brien, R. 1976 (Notts Co)   5
O'Byrne, L. B. 1949 (Shamrock R)   1
O'Callaghan, B. R. 1979 (Stoke C)   6
O'Callaghan, K. 1981 (Ipswich T, Portsmouth)   21
O'Cearuill, J. 2007 (Arsenal)   2
O'Connell, A. 1967 (Dundalk, Bohemians)   2
O'Connor, T. 1950 (Shamrock R)   4
O'Connor, T. 1968 (Fulham, Dundalk, Bohemians)   7
O'Dea, D. 2010 (Celtic, Toronto, Metalurh Donetsk)   **20**
O'Driscoll, J. F. 1949 (Swansea T)   3
O'Driscoll, S. 1982 (Fulham)   3
O'Farrell, F. 1952 (West Ham U, Preston NE)   9
O'Flanagan, K. P. 1938 (Bohemians, Arsenal)   10
O'Flanagan, M. 1947 (Bohemians)   1
O'Halloran, S. E. 2007 (Aston Villa)   2
O'Hanlon, K. G. 1988 (Rotherham U)   1
O'Kane, P. 1935 (Bohemians)   3
O'Keefe, E. 1981 (Everton, Port Vale)   5
O'Keefe, T. 1934 (Cork, Waterford)   3
O'Leary, D. 1977 (Arsenal)   68
O'Leary, P. 1980 (Shamrock R)   7
O'Mahoney, M. T. 1938 (Bristol R)   6
O'Neill, F. S. 1962 (Shamrock R)   20
O'Neill, J. 1952 (Everton)   17
O'Neill, J. 1961 (Preston NE)   1
O'Neill, K. P. 1996 (Norwich C, Middlesbrough)   13
O'Neill, W. 1936 (Dundalk)   11
O'Regan, K. 1984 (Brighton & HA)   4
O'Reilly, J. 1932 (Brideville, Aberdeen, Brideville,
    St James' Gate)   20
O'Reilly, J. 1946 (Cork U)   2
O'Shea, J. F. 2002 (Manchester U, Sunderland)   **96**

Pearce, A. J. 2013 (Reading)   **4**
Peyton, G. 1977 (Fulham, Bournemouth, Everton)   33
Peyton, N. 1957 (Shamrock R, Leeds U)   6
Phelan, T. 1992 (Wimbledon, Manchester C, Chelsea,
    Everton, Fulham)   42
Pilkington, A. N. J. 2013 (Norwich C)   **6**
Potter, D. M. 2007 (Wolverhampton W)   5

Quinn, A. 2003 (Sheffield W, Sheffield U)   8
Quinn, B. S. 2000 (Coventry C)   4
Quinn, N. J. 1986 (Arsenal, Manchester C, Sunderland)   91
Quinn, S. 2013 (Hull C)   **7**

Randolf, D. E. 2013 (Motherwell)   2

**Reid, A. M. 2004 (Nottingham F, Tottenham H,
    Charlton Ath, Sunderland, Nottingham F)**   **29**
Reid, C. 1931 (Brideville)   1
Reid, S. J. 2002 (Millwall, Blackburn R)   23
Richardson, D. J. 1972 (Shamrock R, Gillingham)   3
Rigby, A. 1935 (St James' Gate)   3
Ringstead, A. 1951 (Sheffield U)   20
Robinson, J. 1928 (Bohemians, Dolphin)   2
Robinson, M. 1981 (Brighton & HA, Liverpool, QPR)   24
Roche, P. J. 1972 (Shelbourne, Manchester U)   8
Rogers, E. 1968 (Blackburn R, Charlton Ath)   19
Rowlands, M. C. 2004 (QPR)   5
Ryan, G. 1978 (Derby Co, Brighton & HA)   18
Ryan, R. A. 1950 (WBA, Derby Co)   16

Sadlier, R. T. 2002 (Millwall)   1
Sammon, C. 2013 (Derby Co)   **9**
Savage, D. P. T. 1996 (Millwall)   5
Saward, P. 1954 (Millwall, Aston Villa, Huddersfield T)
    18
Scannell, T. 1954 (Southend U)   1
Scully, P. J. 1989 (Arsenal)   1
Sheedy, K. 1984 (Everton, Newcastle U)   46
Sheridan, C. 2010 (Celtic, CSKA Sofia)   3
Sheridan, J. J. 1988 (Leeds U, Sheffield W)   34
Slaven, B. 1990 (Middlesbrough)   7
Sloan, J. W. 1946 (Arsenal)   2
Smyth, M. 1969 (Shamrock R)   1
Squires, J. 1934 (Shelbourne)   1
Stapleton, F. 1977 (Arsenal, Manchester U, Ajax,
    Le Havre, Blackburn R)   71
Staunton, S. 1989 (Liverpool, Aston Villa, Liverpool,
    Aston Villa)   102
St Ledger-Hall, S. P. 2009 (Preston NE, Leicester C)   **37**
Stevenson, A. E. 1932 (Dolphin, Everton)   7
Stokes, A. 2007 (Sunderland, Celtic)   **8**
Strahan, F. 1964 (Shelbourne)   5
Sullivan, J. 1928 (Fordsons)   1
Swan, M. M. G. 1960 (Drumcondra)   1
Synnott, N. 1978 (Shamrock R)   3

Taylor, T. 1959 (Waterford)   1
Thomas, P. 1974 (Waterford)   2
Thompson, J. 2004 (Nottingham F)   1
Townsend, A. D. 1989 (Norwich C, Chelsea, Aston Villa,
    Middlesbrough)   70
Traynor, T. J. 1954 (Southampton)   8
Treacy, K. 2011 (Preston NE, Burnley)   6
Treacy, R. C. P. 1966 (WBA, Charlton Ath, Swindon T,
    Preston NE, WBA, Shamrock R)   42
Tuohy, L. 1956 (Shamrock R, Newcastle U, Shamrock
    R)
    8
Turner, C. J. 1936 (Southend U, West Ham U)   10
Turner, P. 1963 (Celtic)   2

Vernon, J. 1946 (Belfast Celtic)   2

Waddock, G. 1980 (QPR, Millwall)   21
Walsh, D. J. 1946 (Linfield, WBA, Aston Villa)   20
Walsh, J. 1982 (Limerick)   1
Walsh, M. 1976 (Blackpool, Everton, QPR, Porto)   21
Walsh, M. 1982 (Everton)   4
Walsh, W. 1947 (Manchester C)   9
Walters, J. R. 2011 (Stoke C)   **27**
Ward, S. R. 2011 (Wolverhampton W)   **24**
Waters, J. 1977 (Grimsby T)   2
Watters, F. 1926 (Shelbourne)   1
Weir, E. 1939 (Clyde)   3
Westwood, K. 2009 (Coventry C, Sunderland)   **17**
Whelan, G. D. 2008 (Stoke C)   **58**
Whelan, R. 1964 (St Patrick's Ath)   2
Whelan, R. 1981 (Liverpool, Southend U)   53
Whelan, W. 1956 (Manchester U)   4
White, J. J. 1928 (Bohemians)   1
Whittaker, R. 1959 (Chelsea)   1
Williams, J. 1938 (Shamrock R)   1
Wilson, M. D. 2011 (Stoke C)   **17**

BRITISH AND IRISH INTERNATIONAL GOALSCORERS 1872–2014

Where two players with the same surname and initials have appeared for the same country, and one or both have scored, they have been distinguished by reference to the club which appears *first* against their name in the international appearances section.
Bold type indicates players who have scored international goals in season 2013–14.

ENGLAND

Player	Goals
A'Court, A.	
Adams, T. A.	5
Adcock, H.	1
Alcock, C. W.	1
Allen, A.	3
Allen, R.	2
Amos, A.	1
Anderson, V.	2
Anderton, D. R.	7
Astall, G.	1
Athersmith, W. C.	3
Atyeo, P. J. W.	5
Bache, J. W.	4
Bailey, N. C.	2
Baily, E. F.	5
Baines, L. J.	1
Baker, J. H.	3
Ball, A. J.	8
Bambridge, A. L.	1
Bambridge, E. C.	11
Barclay, R.	2
Barmby, N. J.	4
Barnes, J.	11
Barnes, P. S.	4
Barry, G.	3
Barton, J.	1
Bassett, W. I.	8
Bastin, C. S.	12
Beardsley, P. A.	9
Beasley, A.	1
Beattie, T. K.	1
Beckham, D. R. J.	17
Becton, F.	2
Bedford, H.	1
Bell, C.	9
Bent, D. A.	4
Bentley, R. T. F.	9
Bishop, S. M.	1
Blackburn, F.	1
Blissett, L.	3
Bloomer, S.	28
Bond, R.	2
Bonsor, A. G.	1
Bowden, E. R.	1
Bowers, J. W.	2
Bowles, S.	1
Bradford, G. R. W.	
Bradford, J.	7
Bradley, W.	2
Bradshaw, F.	3
Brann, J.	1
Bridge, W. M.	
Bridges, B. J.	1
Bridgett, A.	3
Brindle, T.	1
Britton, C. S.	1
Broadbent, P. F.	2
Broadis, I. A.	8
Brodie, J. B.	1
Bromley-Davenport, W.	2
Brook, E. F.	10
Brooking, T. D.	5
Brooks, J.	2
Broome, F. H.	3
Brown, A.	4
Brown, A. S.	1
Brown, G.	5
Brown, J.	3
Brown, W.	1
Brown, W. M.	1
Buchan, C. M.	4
Bull, S. G.	4
Bullock, N.	2
Burgess, H.	4
Butcher, T.	3
Byrne, J. J.	8
Cahill, G.	**3**
Campbell, S. J.	1
Camsell, G. H.	18
Carroll, A. T.	2
Carter, H. S.	7
Carter, J. H.	4
Caulker, S. A.	1
Chadwick, E.	3
Chamberlain, M.	1
Chambers, H.	5
Channon, M. R.	21
Charlton, J.	6
Charlton, R.	49
Chenery, C. J.	1
Chivers, M.	13
Clarke, A. J.	10
Cobbold, W. N.	6
Cock, J. G.	2
Cole, A.	1
Cole, J. J.	10
Common, A.	2
Connelly, J. M.	7
Coppell, S. J.	7
Cotterill, G. H.	2
Cowans, G.	2
Crawford, R.	1
Crawshaw, T. H.	1
Crayston, W. J.	1
Creek, F. N. S.	1
Crooks, S. D.	7
Crouch, P. J.	22
Currey, E. S.	2
Currie, A. W.	3
Cursham, A. W.	2
Cursham, H. A.	5
Daft, H. B.	3
Davenport, J. K.	2
Davis, G.	1
Davis, H.	1
Day, S. H.	2
Dean, W. R.	18
Defoe, J. C.	19
Devey, J. H. G.	1
Dewhurst, F.	11
Dix, W. R.	1
Dixon, K. M.	4
Dixon, L. M.	1
Dorrell, A. R.	1
Douglas, B.	11
Drake, E. J.	6
Ducat, A.	1
Dunn, A. T. B.	2
Eastham, G.	2
Edwards, D.	5
Ehiogu, U.	1
Elliott, W. H.	3
Evans, R. E.	1
Ferdinand, L.	5
Ferdinand, R. G.	3
Finney, T.	30
Fleming, H. J.	9
Flowers, R.	10
Forman, Frank	1
Forman, Fred	3
Foster, R. E.	3
Fowler, R. B.	7
Francis, G. C. J.	3
Francis, T.	12
Freeman, B. C.	3
Froggatt, J.	2
Froggatt, R.	2
Galley, T.	1
Gascoigne, P. J.	10
Geary, F.	3
Gerrard, S. G.	**21**
Gibbins, W. V. T.	3
Gilliatt, W. E.	3
Goddard, P.	1
Goodall, J.	12
Goodyer, A. C.	1
Gosling, R. C.	2
Goulden, L. A.	4
Grainger, C.	3
Greaves, J.	44
Grovesnor, A. T.	2
Gunn, W.	1
Haines, J. T. W.	2
Hall, G. W.	9
Halse, H. J.	2
Hampson, J.	5
Hampton, H.	2
Hancocks, J.	2
Hardman, H. P.	1
Harris, S. S.	2
Hassall, H. W.	4
Hateley, M.	9
Haynes, J. N.	18
Hegan, K. E.	4
Henfrey, A. G.	2
Heskey, E. W.	7
Hilsdon, G. R.	14
Hine, E. W.	2
Hinton, A. T.	1
Hirst, D. E.	1
Hitchens, G. A.	5
Hobbis, H. H. F.	1
Hoddle, G.	8
Hodgetts, D.	1
Hodgson, G.	1
Holley, G. H.	8
Houghton, W. E.	5
Howell, R.	1
Hughes, E. W.	1
Hulme, J. H. A.	4
Hunt, G. S.	1
Hunt, R.	18
Hunter, N.	2
Hurst, G. C.	24
Ince, P. E. C.	2
Jack, D. N. B.	3
Jagielka, P. N.	**2**
Jeffers, F.	1
Jenas, J. A.	1
Johnson, A.	2
Johnson, D. E.	6
Johnson, E.	2
Johnson, G. M. C.	1
Johnson, J. A.	2
Johnson, T. C. F.	5
Johnson, W. H.	1
Kail, E. I. L.	2
Kay, A. H.	1
Keegan, J. K.	21
Kelly, R.	8
Kennedy, R.	3
Kenyon-Slaney, W. S.	2
Keown, M. R.	2
Kevan, D. T.	8
Kidd, B.	1
King, L. B.	2
Kingsford, R. K.	1
Kirchen, A. J.	2
Kirton, W. J.	1
Lambert, R. L.	**3**
Lampard, F. J.	29
Langton, R.	1
Latchford, R. D.	5
Latheron, E. G.	1
Lawler, C.	1
Lawton, T.	22
Lee, F.	10
Lee, J.	1
Lee, R. M.	2
Lee, S.	2
Lescott, J.	1
Le Saux, G. P.	1
Lindley, T.	14
Lineker, G.	48
Lofthouse, J. M.	3
Lofthouse, N.	30
Hon. A. Lyttelton	1
Mabbutt, G.	1
Macdonald, M.	6
Mannion, W. J.	11
Mariner, P.	13
Marsh, R. W.	1
Matthews, S.	11
Matthews, V.	1
McCall, J.	1
McDermott, T.	3
McManaman, S.	3
Medley, L. D.	1
Melia, J.	1
Mercer, D. W.	1
Merson, P. C.	3
Milburn, J. E. T.	10
Miller, H. S.	1
Mills, G. R.	3
Milner, J. P.	1
Milward, A.	3
Mitchell, C.	5
Moore, J.	1
Moore, R. F.	2
Moore, W. G. B.	2
Morren, T.	1
Morris, F.	1
Morris, J.	3
Mortensen, S. H.	23
Morton, J. R.	1
Mosforth, W.	3
Mullen, J.	6
Mullery, A. P.	1
Murphy, D. B	1
Neal, P. G.	5
Needham, E.	3

Name	
Pyper, James	2
Pyper, John	1
Quinn, J. M.	12
Quinn, S. J.	4
Reynolds, J.	1
Rowland, K.	1
Rowley, R. W. M.	2
Rushe, F.	1
Sheridan, J.	2
Sherrard, J.	1
Sherrard, W. C.	2
Shields, D.	1
Simpson, W. J.	5
Sloan, H. A. de B.	4
Smyth, S.	5
Spence, D. W.	3
Sproule, I.	1
Stanfield, O. M.	11
Stevenson, A. E.	5
Stewart, I.	2
Taggart, G. P.	7
Thompson, F. W.	2
Torrans, S.	1
Tully, C. P.	3
Turner, A.	1
Walker, J.	1
Walsh, D. J.	5
Welsh, E.	1
Whiteside, N.	9
Whiteside, T.	1
Whitley, Jeff	2
Williams, J. R.	1
Williams, M. S.	1
Williamson, J.	1
Wilson, D. J.	1
Wilson, K. J.	6
Wilson, S. J.	7
Wilton, J. M.	2
Young, S.	1

N.B. In 1914 Young goal should be credited to Gillespie W v Wales

SCOTLAND

Name	
Aitken, R. *(Celtic)*	1
Aitken, R. *(Dumbarton)*	1
Aitkenhead, W. A. C.	2
Alexander, D.	1
Allan, D. S.	4
Allan, J.	2
Anderson, F.	1
Anderson, W.	4
Andrews, P.	1
Anya, I.	**1**
Archibald, A.	1
Archibald, S.	4
Baird, D.	2
Baird, J. C.	2
Baird, S.	2
Bannon, E.	1
Barbour, A.	1
Barker, J. B.	4
Battles, B. Jr	1
Bauld, W.	2
Baxter, J. C.	3
Beattie, C.	1
Bell, J.	5
Bennett, A.	2
Berra, C.	2
Berry, D.	1
Bett, J.	1
Beveridge, W. W.	1
Black, A.	3
Black, D.	1
Bone, J.	1
Booth, S.	6

Name	
Boyd, K	7
Boyd, R.	2
Boyd, T.	1
Boyd, W. G.	1
Brackenridge, T.	1
Brand, R.	8
Brazil, A.	1
Bremner, W. J.	3
Broadfoot, K.	1
Brown, A. D.	6
Brown, S.	**4**
Buchanan, P. S.	1
Buchanan, R.	1
Buckley, P.	1
Buick, A.	2
Burke, C.	2
Burley, C. W.	3
Burns, K.	1
Cairns, T.	1
Caldwell, G.	2
Calderwood, C.	1
Calderwood, R.	2
Caldow, E.	4
Cameron, C.	2
Campbell, C.	1
Campbell, John *(Celtic)*	5
Campbell, John *(Rangers)*	4
Campbell, J. (South Western)	1
Campbell, P.	2
Campbell, R.	1
Cassidy, J.	1
Chalmers, S.	3
Chambers, T.	1
Cheyne, A. G.	4
Christie, A. J.	1
Clarkson, D.	1
Clunas, W. L.	1
Collins, J.	12
Collins, R. Y.	10
Combe, J. R.	1
Commons, K.	2
Conn, A.	1
Cooper, D.	6
Craig, J.	1
Craig, T.	1
Crawford, S.	4
Cunningham, A. N.	5
Curran, H. P.	1
Dailly, C.	6
Dalglish, K.	30
Davidson, D.	1
Davidson, J. A.	1
Delaney, J.	3
Devine, A.	1
Dewar, G.	1
Dewar, N.	4
Dickov, P.	1
Dickson, W.	4
Divers, J.	1
Dobie, R. S.	1
Docherty, T. H.	1
Dodds, D.	1
Dodds, W.	7
Donaldson, A.	1
Donnachie, J.	1
Dougall, J.	1
Drummond, J.	2
Dunbar, M.	1
Duncan, D.	7
Duncan, D. M.	1
Duncan, J.	1
Dunn, J.	2
Durie, G. S.	7
Easson, J. F.	1
Elliott, M. S.	1
Ellis, J.	1

Name	
Ferguson, B.	3
Ferguson, J.	6
Fernie, W.	1
Fitchie, T. T.	1
Flavell, R.	2
Fleming, C.	2
Fleming, J. W.	3
Fletcher, D.	5
Fletcher, S.	1
Fraser, M. J. E.	3
Freedman, D. A.	1
Gallacher, H. K.	23
Gallacher, K. W.	9
Gallacher, P.	1
Galt, J. H.	1
Gemmell, T. *(St Mirren)*	1
Gemmell, T. *(Celtic)*	1
Gemmill, A.	8
Gemmill, S.	1
Gibb, W.	1
Gibson, D. W.	3
Gibson, J. D.	1
Gibson, N.	1
Gillespie, Jas.	3
Gillick, T.	3
Gilzean, A. J.	12
Goodwillie, D.	1
Gossland, J.	2
Goudie, J.	1
Gough, C. R.	6
Gourlay, J.	1
Graham, A.	2
Graham, G.	3
Gray, A.	7
Gray, E.	3
Gray, F.	1
Greig, J.	3
Groves, W.	4
Hamilton, G.	4
Hamilton, J. (Queen's Park)	3
Hamilton, R. C.	15
Hanley, G.	1
Harper, J. M.	2
Hartley, P. J.	1
Harrower, W.	5
Hartford, R. A.	4
Heggie, C. W.	4
Henderson, J. G.	1
Henderson, W.	5
Hendry, E. C. J.	3
Herd, D. G.	3
Herd, G.	1
Hewie, J. D.	2
Higgins, A. *(Newcastle U)*	
Higgins, A. *(Kilmarnock)*	4
Highet, T. C.	1
Holt, G.J.	1
Holton, J. A.	2
Hopkin, D.	2
Houliston, W.	2
Howie, H.	1
Howie, J.	2
Hughes, J.	1
Hunter, W.	1
Hutchison, D.	6
Hutchison, T.	1
Hutton, J.	1
Hyslop, T.	1
Imrie, W. N.	1
Jackson, A.	8
Jackson, C.	1
Jackson, D.	4
James, A. W.	4
Jardine, A.	1
Jenkinson, T.	1

Name	
Jess, E.	2
Johnston, A.	2
Johnston, L. H.	1
Johnston, M.	14
Johnstone, D.	2
Johnstone, J.	4
Johnstone, Jas.	1
Johnstone, R.	10
Johnstone, W.	1
Jordan, J.	11
Kay, J. L.	5
Keillor, A.	3
Kelly, J.	1
Kelso, R.	1
Ker, G.	10
King, A.	1
King, J.	1
Kinnear, D.	1
Kyle, K.	1
Lambert, P.	1
Lambie, J.	1
Lambie, W. A.	5
Lang, J. J.	2
Latta, A.	2
Law, D.	30
Leggat, G.	8
Lennie, W.	1
Lennox, R.	3
Liddell, W.	6
Lindsay, J.	6
Linwood, A. B.	1
Logan, J.	1
Lorimer, P.	4
Love, A.	1
Low, J. *(Cambuslang)*	1
Lowe, J. *(St Bernards)*	1
Macari, L.	5
MacDougall, E. J.	3
MacFarlane, A.	1
MacLeod, M.	1
Mackay, D. C.	4
Mackay, G.	1
MacKenzie, J. A.	1
Mackail-Smith, C.	1
Mackie, J. C.	2
MacKinnon, W. W.	5
Madden, J.	5
Maloney, S.	**2**
Marshall, H.	1
Marshall, J.	1
Mason, J.	4
Massie, A.	1
Masson, D. S.	5
McAdam, J.	1
McAllister, G.	5
McArthur, J.	1
McAulay, J. D.	1
McAvennie, F.	1
McCall, J.	1
McCall, S. M.	1
McCalliog, J.	1
McCallum, N.	1
McCann, N.	3
McClair, B. J.	2
McCoist, A.	19
McColl, R. S.	13
McCormack, R.	2
McCulloch, D.	3
McCulloch, C.	1
McDougall, J.	4
McFadden, J.	15*
McFadyen, W.	2
McGhee, M.	2
McGinlay, J.	4
McGregor, J.	1
McGrory, J.	6
McGuire, W.	1
McInally, A.	3
McInnes, T.	2
McKie, J.	2

* The Scottish FA officially changed Robsons's goal against Iceland on 10 September 2008 to McFadden.

Name	
McKimmie, S.	1
McKinlay, W.	4
McKinnon, A.	1
McKinnon, R.	1
McLaren, A.	4
McLaren, J.	1
McLean, A.	1
McLean, T.	1
McLintock, F.	1
McMahon, A.	6
McManus, S.	2
McMenemy, J.	5
McMillan, I. L.	2
McNeill, W.	3
McNiel, H.	5
McPhail, J.	3
McPhail, R.	7
McPherson, J. *(Kilmarnock)*	7
McPherson, J. *(Vale of Leven)*	1
McPherson, R.	1
McQueen, G.	5
McStay, P.	9
McSwegan, G.	1
Meiklejohn, D. D.	3
Millar, J.	2
Miller, K.	**18**
Miller, T.	2
Miller, W.	1
Mitchell, R. C.	1
Morgan, W.	1
Morris, D.	1
Morris, H.	3
Morrison, J. C.	**3**
Morton, A. L.	5
Mudie, J. K.	9
Mulgrew, C.	**2**
Mulhall, G.	1
Munro, A. D.	1
Munro, N.	2
Murdoch, R.	5
Murphy, F.	1
Murray, J.	1
Napier, C. E.	3
Narey, D.	1
Naismith, S.	**3**
Naysmith, G. A.	1
Neil, R. G.	2
Nevin, P. K. F.	5
Nicholas, C.	5
Nisbet, J.	2
O'Connor, G.	4
O'Donnell, F.	2
O'Hare, J.	5
Ormond, W. E.	2
O'Rourke, F.	1
Orr, R.	1
Orr, T.	1
Oswald, J.	1
Own goals	**21**
Parlane, D.	1
Paul, H. McD.	2
Paul, W.	5
Pettigrew, W.	2
Provan, D.	1
Quashie, N. F.	1
Quinn, J.	7
Quinn, P.	1
Rankin, G.	2
Rankin, R.	2
Reid, W.	4
Reilly, L.	22
Renny-Tailyour, H. W.	1
Rhodes, J. L.	3
Richmond, J. T.	1
Ring, T.	2
Rioch, B. D.	6
Ritchie, J.	1

Name	
Ritchie, P. S.	1
Robertson, A.	2
Robertson, J.	3
Robertson, J. N.	8
Robertson, J. T.	2
Robertson, T.	1
Robertson, W.	1
Russell, D.	1
Scott, A. S.	5
Sellar, W.	4
Sharp, G.	1
Shaw, F. W.	1
Shearer, D.	2
Simpson, J.	1
Smith, A.	5
Smith, G.	4
Smith, J.	1
Smith, John	13
Snodgrass, R.	**3**
Somerville, G.	1
Souness, G. J.	4
Speedie, F.	2
St John, I.	9
Steel, W.	12
Stein, C.	10
Stevenson, G.	4
Stewart, A.	1
Stewart, R.	1
Stewart, W. E.	1
Strachan, G.	5
Sturrock, P.	3
Taylor, J. D.	1
Templeton, R.	1
Thompson, S.	3
Thomson, A.	1
Thomson, C.	4
Thomson, R.	1
Thomson, W.	1
Thornton, W.	1
Waddell, T. S.	1
Waddell, W.	6
Walker, J.	2
Walker, R.	7
Walker, T.	9
Wallace, I. A.	1
Wark, J.	7
Watson, J. A. K.	1
Watt, F.	2
Watt, W. W.	1
Webster, A.	1
Weir, A.	1
Weir, D.	1
Weir, J. B.	2
White, J. A.	3
Wilkie, L.	1
Wilson, A. *(Sheffield W)*	2
Wilson, A. N. *(Dunfermline Ath)*	13
Wilson, D. *(Liverpool)*	1
Wilson, D. *(Queen's Park)*	2
Wilson, D. *(Rangers)*	9
Wilson, H.	1
Wylie, T. G.	1
Young, A.	5

WALES

Name	
Allchurch, I. J.	23
Allen, M.	3
Astley, D. J.	12
Atherton, R. W.	2
Bale, G.	**12**
Bamford, T.	1
Barnes, W.	1
Bellamy, C. D.	19
Blackmore, C. G.	1
Blake, D.	1
Blake, N. A.	4
Bodin, P. J.	3

Name	
Boulter, L. M.	1
Bowdler, J. C. H.	3
Bowen, D. L.	1
Bowen, M.	3
Boyle, T.	1
Bryan, T.	1
Burgess, W. A. R.	1
Burke, T.	1
Butler, W. T.	1
Chapman, T.	2
Charles, J.	1
Charles, M.	6
Charles, W. J.	15
Church, S. R.	**2**
Clarke, R. J.	5
Coleman, C.	4
Collier, D. J.	1
Collins, J.	**3**
Cotterill, D.	1
Crosse, K.	1
Cumner, R. H.	1
Curtis, A.	6
Curtis, E. R.	3
Davies, D. W.	1
Davies, E. Lloyd	1
Davies, G.	2
Davies, L. S.	6
Davies, R. T.	9
Davies, R. W.	6
Davies, Simon	6
Davies, Stanley	5
Davies, W.	6
Davies, W. H.	1
Davies, William	5
Davis, W. O.	1
Deacy, N.	4
Doughty, J.	6
Doughty, R.	2
Durban, A.	2
Dwyer, P.	2
Earnshaw, R.	16
Eastwood, F.	4
Edwards, D.	3
Edwards, G.	2
Edwards, R. I.	4
England, H. M.	4
Evans, C.	2
Evans, I.	1
Evans, J.	1
Evans, R. E.	2
Evans, W.	1
Eyton-Jones, J. A.	1
Fletcher, C.	1
Flynn, B.	7
Ford, T.	23
Foulkes, W. I.	1
Fowler, J.	3
Giles, D.	2
Giggs, R. J.	12
Glover, E. M.	7
Godfrey, B. C.	2
Green, A. W.	3
Griffiths, A. T.	6
Griffiths, M. W.	2
Griffiths, T. P.	3
Harris, C. S.	1
Hartson, J.	14
Hersee, R.	1
Hewitt, R.	1
Hockey, T.	1
Hodges, G.	2
Hole, W. J.	1
Hopkins, I. J.	2
Horne, B.	2
Howell, E. G.	3
Hughes, L. M.	16
James, E.	2

Name	
James, L.	10
James, R.	7
Jarrett, R. H.	3
Jenkyns, C. A.	1
Jones, A.	1
Jones, Bryn	6
Jones, B. S.	2
Jones, Cliff	16
Jones, C. W.	1
Jones, D. E.	1
Jones, Evan	1
Jones, H.	1
Jones, I.	1
Jones, J. L.	1
Jones, J. O.	1
Jones, J. P.	1
Jones, Leslie J.	1
Jones, R. A.	2
Jones, W. L.	6
Keenor, F. C.	2
King, A.	**2**
Koumas, J.	10
Krzywicki, R. L.	1
Ledley, J.	3
Leek, K.	5
Lewis, B.	4
Lewis, D. M.	2
Lewis, W.	8
Lewis, W. L.	3
Llewelyn, C. M	1
Lovell, S.	1
Lowrie, G.	2
Mahoney, J. F.	1
Mays, A. W.	1
Medwin, T. C.	6
Melville, A. K	3
Meredith, W. H.	11
Mills, T. J.	1
Moore, G.	1
Morgan, J. R.	2
Morgan-Owen, H.	1
Morgan-Owen, M. M.	1
Morison, S.	1
Morris, A. G.	9
Morris, H.	1
Morris, R.	1
Morris, S.	2
Nicholas, P.	2
O'Callaghan, E.	3
O'Sullivan, P. A.	1
Owen, G.	2
Owen, W.	4
Owen, W. P.	6
Own goals	14
Palmer, D.	3
Parry, P. I.	1
Parry, T. D.	3
Paul, R.	1
Peake, E.	1
Pembridge, M.	6
Perry, E.	1
Phillips, C.	5
Phillips, D.	2
Powell, A.	1
Powell, D.	1
Price, J.	1
Price, P.	1
Pryce-Jones, W. E.	3
Pugh, D. H.	2
Ramsay, A.	**8**
Reece, G. I.	2
Rees, R. R.	3
Richards, R. W.	1
Roach, J.	2
Robbins, W. W.	4
Roberts, J. (Corwen)	1
Roberts, Jas.	1

Roberts, P. S.	1	Brady, L.	9	Giles, J.	5	Mooney, J.	1

BRITISH AND IRISH INTERNATIONAL MANAGERS

England

Walter Winterbottom 1946–1962 (after period as coach); Alf Ramsey 1963–1974; Joe Mercer (caretaker) 1974; Don Revie 1974–1977; Ron Greenwood 1977–1982; Bobby Robson 1982–1990; Graham Taylor 1990–1993; Terry Venables (coach) l994–1996; Glenn Hoddle 1996–1999; Kevin Keegan 1999–2000; Sven-Goran Eriksson 2001–2006; Steve McClaren 2006–2007; Fabio Capello 2008–2012; Roy Hodgson from May 2012.

Northern Ireland

Peter Doherty 1951–1952; Bertie Peacock 1962–1967; Billy Bingham 1967–1971; Terry Neill 1971–1975; Dave Clements (player-manager) 1975–1976; Danny Blanchflower 1976–1979; Billy Bingham 1980–1994; Bryan Hamilton 1994–1998; Lawrie McMenemy 1998–1999; Sammy McIlroy 2000–2003; Lawrie Sanchez 2004–2007; Nigel Worthington 2007–2011; Michael O'Neill from December 2011.

Scotland (since 1967)

Bobby Brown 1967–1971; Tommy Docherty 1971–1972; Willie Ormond 1973–1977; Ally MacLeod 1977–1978; Jock Stein 1978–1985; Alex Ferguson (caretaker) 1985–1986 Andy Roxburgh (coach) 1986–1993; Craig Brown 1993–2001; Berti Vogts 2002–2004; Walter Smith 2004–2007; Alex McLeish 2007; George Burley 2008–2009; Craig Levein 2009–2012; Gordon Strachan from February 2013.

Wales (since 1974)

Mike Smith 1974–1979; Mike England 1980–1988; David Williams (caretaker) 1988; Terry Yorath 1988–1993; John Toshack 1994 for one match; Mike Smith 1994–1995; Bobby Gould 1995–1999; Mark Hughes 1999–2004; John Toshack 2004–2010; Gary Speed 2010–2011; Chris Coleman from January 2012.

Republic of Ireland

Liam Tuohy 1971–1972; Johnny Giles 1973–1980 (after period as player-manager); Eoin Hand 1980–1985; Jack Charlton 1986–1996; Mick McCarthy 1996–2002; Brian Kerr 2003–2006; Steve Staunton 2006–2007; Giovanni Trapattoni 2008–2013; Martin O'Neill from November 2013.

Martin O'Neill, the new manager of the Republic of Ireland, looks on during his side's friendly against Latvia at the Aviva Stadium in Dublin in November 2013. O'Neill marked his first game in charge with a 3-0 victory.
(Reuters/Cathal McNaughton)

SOUTH AMERICA

COPA SUDAMERICANA 2013

FIRST ROUND – FIRST LEG

Inti Gas v Atletico Nacional	0-1
LDU Loja v Deportivo Lara	2-0
Itagui v Juan Aurich	3-0
Nacional Asuncion v The Strongest	0-0
Real Potosi v Universidad Chile	3-1
Trujillanos v La Equidad	0-1
Sport Huancayo v Emelec	1-3
El Tanque Sisley v Colo Colo	0-1
Blooming v River Plate	0-1
Deportivo Pasto v Melgar	3-0
Universidad Catolica v Cerro Porteno	1-1
Independiente del Valle v Deportivo Anzoategui	0-0
Wanderers v Libertad	1-2
Cobreloa v Penarol	0-0
Mineros de Guayana v Barcelona	2-2
Guarani v Oriente Petrolero	0-0

FIRST ROUND – SECOND LEG

	(agg)
Atletico Nacional v Inti Gas	4-0 (5-0)
Deportivo Lara v LDU Loja	1-1 (1-3)
Juan Aurich v Itagui	2-3 (2-6)
The Strongest v Nacional Asuncion	1-1 (1-1)
Nacional Asuncion won on away goals rule.	
Universidad Chile v Real Potosi	5-0 (6-3)
La Equidad v Trujillanos	0-0 (1-0)
Emelec v Sport Huancayo	4-0 (7-1)
Colo Colo v El Tanque Sisley	2-0 (3-0)
River Plate v Blooming	4-0 (5-0)
Melgar v Deportivo Pasto	2-0 (2-3)
Cerro Porteno v Universidad Catolica	0-1 (1-2)
Deportivo Anzoategui v Independiente del Valle	0-2 (0-2)
Libertad v Wanderers	0-0 (2-1)
Penarol v Cobreloa	0-2 (0-2)
Barcelona v Mineros de Guayana	0-2 (2-4)
Oriente Petrolero v Guarani	1-4 (1-4)

SECOND ROUND – FIRST LEG

Belgrano v Velez Sarsfield	1-0
Racing Club v Lanus	1-2
Sport Recife v Nautico	2-0
Universidad Catolica v Emelec	4-0
Guarani v Atletico Nacional	0-2
La Equidad v Cobreloa	0-0
Itagui v River Plate	1-0
Libertad v Mineros de Guayana	2-0
Criciuma v Ponte Preta	1-2
Vitoria v Coritiba	1-0
Universidad Chile v Independiente del Valle	1-1
LDU Loja v Nacional Asuncion	0-0
San Lorenzo v River Plate	0-1
Portuguesa v Bahia	1-2
Deportivo Pasto v Colo Colo	1-0

SECOND ROUND – SECOND LEG

	(agg)
Velez Sarsfield v Belgrano	2-0 (2-1)
Lanus v Racing Club	2-0 (4-1)
Nautico v Sport Recife	2-0 (2-2)
Sport Recife won 3-1 on penalties.	
Emelec v Universidad Catolica	2-3 (2-7)

Atletico Nacional v Guarani	0-0 (2-0)
Cobreloa v La Equidad	1-1 (1-1)
La Equidad won on away goals rule.	
River Plate v Itagui	0-0 (1-0)
Mineros de Guayana v Libertad	1-2 (1-4)
Ponte Preta v Criciuma	0-0 (2-1)
Coritiba v Vitoria	1-0 (1-1)
Coritiba won 4-3 on penalties.	
Independiente del Valle v Universidad Chile	1-3 (2-4)
Nacional Asuncion v LDU Loja	0-1 (0-1)
River Plate v San Lorenzo	0-0 (1-0)
Bahia v Portuguesa	0-0 (2-1)
Colo Colo v Deportivo Pasto	0-2 (0-3)

ROUND OF 16 – FIRST LEG

Lanus v Universidad Chile	4-0
La Equidad v Velez Sarsfield	1-2
LDU Loja v River Plate	2-1
Coritiba v Itagui	0-1
Ponte Preta v Deportivo Pasto	2-0
Libertad v Sport Recife	2-0
Sao Paulo v Universidad Catolica	1-1
Atletico Nacional v Bahia	1-0

ROUND OF 16 – SECOND LEG

	(agg)
Universidad Chile v Lanus	1-0 (1-4)
Velez Sarsfield v La Equidad	2-1 (4-2)
River Plate v LDU Loja	2-0 (3-2)
Itagui v Coritiba	2-1 (3-1)
Deportivo Pasto v Ponte Preta	1-0 (1-2)
Sport Recife v Libertad	1-2 (1-4)
Universidad Catolica v Sao Paulo	3-4 (4-5)
Bahia v Atletico Nacional	1-0 (1-1)
Atletico Nacional won 4-3 on penalties.	

QUARTER-FINALS – FIRST LEG

Lanus v River Plate	0-0
Sao Paulo v Atletico Nacional	3-2
Ponte Preta v Velez Sarsfield	0-0
Libertad v Itagui	2-0

QUARTER-FINALS – SECOND LEG

	(agg)
River Plate v Lanus	1-3 (1-3)
Atletico Nacional v Sao Paulo	0-0 (2-3)
Velez Sarsfield v Ponte Preta	0-2 (0-2)
Itagui v Libertad	1-0 (1-2)

SEMI-FINALS – FIRST LEG

Sao Paulo v Ponte Preta	1-3
Libertad v Lanus	1-2

SEMI-FINALS – SECOND LEG

	(agg)
Ponte Preta v Sao Paulo	1-1 (4-2)
Lanus v Libertad	2-1 (4-2)

FINAL – FIRST LEG

Ponte Preta v Lanus	1-1

FINAL – SECOND LEG

	(agg)
Lanus v Ponte Preta	2-0 (3-1)

RECOPA SUDAMERICANA 2013

FINAL – FIRST LEG

Sao Paulo v Corinthians	1-2

FINAL – SECOND LEG

	(agg)
Corinthians v Sao Paulo	2-0 (4-1)

COPA SANTANDER LIBERTADORES 2013

SEMI-FINALS – FIRST LEG

Olimpia v Santa Fe	2-0
Newell's Old Boys v Atletico Mineiro	2-0

SEMI-FINALS – SECOND LEG

	(agg)
Santa Fe v Olimpia	1-0 (1-2)
Atletico Mineiro v Newell's Old Boys	2-0 (2-2)
Atletico Mineiro won 3-2 on penalties.	

FINAL – FIRST LEG

Olimpia v Atletico Mineiro	2-0

FINAL – SECOND LEG

	(agg)
Atletico Mineiro v Olimpia	2-0 (2-2)
Atletico Mineiro won 4-3 on penalties.	

COPA SANTANDER LIBERTADORES 2014

FIRST ROUND FIRST LEG

Oriente Petrolero v Nacional	1-0
Monarcas Morelia v Santa Fe	2-1
Sporting Cristal v Atletico Paranaense	2-1
Deportivo Quito v Botafogo	1-0
Universidad de Chile v Guarani	1-0
Caracas v Lanus	0-2

FIRST ROUND SECOND LEG (agg)

Nacional v Oriente Petrolero	2-0 (2-1)
Santa Fe v Monarcas Morelia	1-0 (2-2)
(Santa Fe won on away goals.)	
Atletico Paranaense v Sporting Cristal	2-1 (3-3)
(Atletico Parnaense won 5-4 on penalties.)	
Botafogo v Deportivo Quito	4-0 (4-1)
Guarani v Universidad de Chile	2-3 (2-4)
Lanus v Caracas	1-0 (3-0)

GROUP 1

Universitario v Velez Sarsfield	0-1
Atletico Paranaense v The Strongest	1-0
The Strongest v Universitario	1-0
Velez Sarsfield v Atletico Paranaense	2-0
The Strongest v Velez Sarsfield	2-0
Universitario v Atletico Paranaense	0-1
Velez Sarsfield v The Strongest	2-0
Atletico Paranaense v Universitario	3-0
Atletico Paranaense v Velez Sarsfield	1-3
Universitario v The Strongest	3-3
Velez Sarsfield v Universitario	1-0
The Strongest v Atletico Paranaense	2-1

GROUP 2

Botafogo v San Lorenzo	2-0
Independiente del Valle v Union Espanola	2-2
Union Espanola v Botafogo	1-1
San Lorenzo v Independiente del Valle	1-0
San Lorenzo v Union Espanola	1-1
Independiente del Valle v Botafogo	2-1
Botafogo v Independiente del Valle	1-0
Union Espanola v San Lorenzo	1-0
Independiente del Valle v San Lorenzo	1-1
Botafogo v Union Espanola	0-1
Union Espanola v Independiente del Valle	4-5
San Lorenzo v Botafogo	3-0

GROUP 3

Deportivo Cali v Cerro Porteno	1-0
Lanus v O'Higgins	0-0
O'Higgins v Deportivo Cali	1-0
Cerro Porteno v Lanus	3-1
O'Higgins v Cerro Porteno	2-2
Deportivo Cali v Lanus	2-1
Cerro Porteno v O'Higgins	2-1
Lanus v Deportivo Cali	2-0
Deportivo Cali v O'Higgins	1-1
Lanus v Cerro Porteno	2-0
Cerro Porteno v Deportivo Cali	3-2
O'Higgins v Lanus	0-0

GROUP 4

Zamora v Atletico Mineiro	0-1
Santa Fe v Club Nacional (Par)	3-1
Club Nacional (Par) v Zamora	1-0
Atletico Mineiro v Santa Fe	2-1
Club Nacional (Par) v Atletico Mineiro	2-2
Zamora v Santa Fe	2-1
Santa Fe v Zamora	2-2
Atletico Mineiro v Club Nacional (Par)	1-1
Zamora v Club Nacional (Par)	2-0
Santa Fe v Atletico Mineiro	1-1
Atletico Mineiro v Zamora	1-0
Club Nacional (Par) v Santa Fe	3-2

GROUP 5

Real Garcilaso v Cruzeiro	2-1
Universidad de Chile v Defensor Sporting	1-0
Defensor Sporting v Real Garcilaso	4-1
Cruzeiro v Universidad de Chile	5-1
Defensor Sporting v Cruzeiro	2-0
Real Garcilaso v Universidad de Chile	1-2
Universidad de Chile v Real Garcilaso	1-0
Cruzeiro v Defensor Sporting	2-2
Real Garcilaso v Defensor Sporting	0-2
Universidad de Chile v Cruzeiro	0-2
Cruzeiro v Real Garcilaso	3-0
Defensor Sporting v Universidad de Chile	1-1

GROUP 6

Nacional (Uru) v Gremio	0-1
Atletico Nacional (Col) v Newell's Old Boys	1-0
Gremio v Atletico Nacional (Col)	3-0
Newell's Old Boys v Nacional (Uru)	4-0
Atletico Nacional (Col) v Nacional (Uru)	2-2
Gremio v Newell's Old Boys	0-0
Nacional (Uru) v Atletico Nacional (Col)	0-1
Newell's Old Boys v Gremio	1-1
Nacional (Uru) v Newell's Old Boys	2-4
Atletico Nacional (Col) v Gremio	0-2
Newell's Old Boys v Atletico Nacional (Col)	1-3
Gremio v Nacional (Uru)	1-0

GROUP 7

Leon v Flamengo	2-1
Emelec v Bolivar	2-1
Bolivar v Leon	1-1
Flamengo v Emelec	3-1
Emelec v Leon	2-1
Flamengo v Bolivar	2-2
Bolivar v Flamengo	1-0
Leon v Emelec	3-0
Leon v Bolivar	0-1
Emelec v Flamengo	1-2
Bolivar v Emelec	2-1
Flamengo v Leon	2-3

GROUP 8

Santos Laguna v Arsenal	1-0
Deportivo Anzoategui v Penarol	1-1
Penarol v Santos Laguna	0-2
Arsenal v Deportivo Anzoategui	3-0
Deportivo Anzoategui v Santos Laguna	1-1
Arsenal v Penarol	1-0
Santos Laguna v Deportivo Anzoategui	3-0
Penarol v Arsenal	2-1
Santos Laguna v Penarol	4-1
Deportivo Anzoategui v Arsenal	1-3
Penarol v Deportivo Anzoategui	1-1
Arsenal v Santos Laguna	3-0

ROUND OF 16 FIRST LEG

Lanus v Santos Laguna	2-1
Leon v Bolivar	2-2
Cruzeiro v Cerro Porteno	1-1
The Strongest v Defensor Sporting	2-0
Nacional (Par) v Velez Sarsfield	1-0
San Lorenzo v Gremio	1-0
Atletico Nacional v Atletico Mineiro	1-0
Arsenal v Union Espanola	0-0

ROUND OF 16 SECOND LEG (agg)

Bolivar v Leon	1-1 (3-3)
(Bolivar won on away goals.)	
Santos Laguna v CA Lanus	0-2 (1-4)
Defensor Sporting v The Strongest	2-0 (2-2)
(Defensor Sporting won 4-2 on penalties.)	
Velez Sarsfield v Club Nacional (Par)	2-2 (2-3)
Union Espanola v Arsenal	0-1 (0-1)
Gremio v San Lorenzo	1-0 (1-1)
(San Lorenzo won 4-2 on penalties.)	
Cerro Porteno v Cruzeiro	0-2 (1-3)
Atletico Mineiro v Atletico Nacional	1-1 (1-2)

QUARTER-FINALS FIRST LEG

Club Nacional (Par) v Arsenal FC	1-0
San Lorenzo v Cruzeiro	1-0
Lanus v Bolivar	1-1
Atletico Nacional (Col) v Defensor Sporting	0-2

QUARTER-FINALS SECOND LEG (agg)

Arsenal v Club Nacional	0-0 (0-1)
Cruzeiro EC v San Lorenzo	1-1 (1-2)
Bolivar v CA Lanus	1-0 (2-1)
Defensor Sporting v Atletico Nacional (Col)	1-0 (3-0)
Competition still being played.	

AFRICA

AFRICAN CUP OF NATIONS 2013

GROUP A

South Africa v Mozambique	3-1
Mali v Nigeria	2-1
South Africa v Mali	1-1
Nigeria v Mozambique	4-2
Nigeria v South Africa	3-1
Mozambique v Mali	1-2

Group A Table	P	W	D	L	F	A	Pts
Mali	3	2	1	0	5	3	7
Nigeria	3	2	0	1	8	5	6
South Africa	3	1	1	1	5	5	4
Mozambique	3	0	0	3	4	9	0

GROUP B

Zimbabwe v Morocco	0-0
Uganda v Burkina Faso	2-1
Zimbabwe v Uganda	0-0
Burkina Faso v Morocco	1-1
Burkina Faso v Zimbabwe	0-1
Morocco v Uganda	3-1

Group B Table	P	W	D	L	F	A	Pts
Morocco	3	1	2	0	4	2	5
Zimbabwe	3	1	2	0	1	0	5
Uganda	3	1	1	1	3	4	4
Burkina Faso	3	0	1	2	2	4	1

GROUP C

Ghana v Congo	1-0
Libya v Ethiopia	2-0
Ghana v Libya	1-1
Ethiopia v Congo	0-1
Ethiopia v Ghana	0-1
Congo v Libya	2-2

Group C Table	P	W	D	L	F	A	Pts
Ghana	3	2	1	0	3	1	7
Libya	3	1	2	0	5	3	5
Congo	3	1	1	1	3	3	4
Ethiopia	3	0	0	3	0	4	0

GROUP D

DR Congo v Mauritania	1-0
Gabon v Burundi	0-0
DR Congo v Gabon	0-1
Burundi v Mauritania	3-2
Burundi v DR Congo	1-2
Mauritania v Gabon	2-4

Group D Table	P	W	D	L	F	A	Pts
Gabon	3	2	1	0	3	1	7
DR Congo	3	2	0	1	5	3	6
Burundi	3	1	1	0	3	2	4
Mauritania	3	0	0	3	4	8	0

QUARTER-FINALS

Morocco v Nigeria	3-4
Mali v Zimbabwe	1-2
Gabon v Libya	3-5
Ghana v DR Congo	1-0

SEMI-FINALS

| Zimbabwe v Libya | 4-5 |
| Ghana v Nigeria | 4-1 |

THIRD PLACE

| Zimbabwe v Nigeria | 0-1 |

FINAL

| Libya v Ghana | 4-3 |

NORTH AMERICA

MAJOR LEAGUE SOCCER 2013

EASTERN CONFERENCE	P	W	D	L	F	A	GD	Pts
New York Red Bulls	34	17	8	9	58	41	17	59
Sporting Kansas City	34	17	7	10	47	30	17	58
NE Revolution	34	14	9	11	49	38	11	51
Houston Dynamo	34	14	9	11	41	41	0	51
Montreal Impact	34	14	7	13	50	49	1	49
Chicago Fire	34	14	7	13	47	52	–5	49
Philadelphia Union	34	12	10	12	42	44	–2	46
Columbus Crew	34	12	5	17	42	46	–4	41
Toronto FC	34	6	11	17	30	47	–17	29
DC United	34	3	7	24	22	59	–37	16

WESTERN CONFERENCE	P	W	D	L	F	A	GD	Pts
Portland Timbers	34	14	15	5	54	33	21	57
Real Salt Lake	34	16	8	10	57	41	16	56
Los Angeles Galaxy	34	15	8	11	53	38	15	53
Seattle Sounders	34	15	7	12	42	42	0	52
Colorado Rapids	34	14	9	11	45	38	7	51
San Jose Earthquakes	34	14	9	11	35	42	–7	51
Vancouver Whitecaps	34	13	9	12	53	45	8	48
FC Dallas	34	11	11	12	48	52	–4	44
Chivas USA	34	6	8	20	30	67	–37	26

EASTERN KNOCKOUT ROUND

| Houston Dynamo v Montreal Impact | 3-0 |

WESTERN KNOCKOUT ROUND

| Seattle Sounders v Colorado Rapids | 2-0 |

EASTERN SEMI-FINALS – FIRST LEG

| Houston Dynamo v New York Red Bulls | 2-2 |
| NE Revolution v Sporting Kansas City | 2-1 |

EASTERN SEMI-FINALS – SECOND LEG

| New York Red Bulls v Houston Dynamo | 1-2 (3-4) |
| Sporting Kansas City v NE Revolution | 3-1 (4-3) |

WESTERN SEMI-FINALS – FIRST LEG

| Seattle Sounders v Portland Timbers | 1-2 |
| Real Salt Lake v Los Angeles Galaxy | 2-0 |

WESTERN SEMI-FINALS – SECOND LEG

| Portland Timbers v Seattle Sounders | 3-2 (5-3) |
| Los Angeles Galaxy v Real Salt Lake | 1-0 (1-2) |

EASTERN CHAMPIONSHIP – FIRST LEG

| Houston Dynamo v Sporting Kansas City | 0-0 |

EASTERN CHAMPIONSHIP – SECOND LEG

| Sporting Kansas City v Houston Dynamo | 2-1 (2-1) |

WESTERN CHAMPIONSHIP – FIRST LEG

| Real Salt Lake v Portland Timbers | 4-2 |

WESTERN CHAMPIONSHIP – SECOND LEG

| Portland Timbers v Real Salt Lake | 0-1 (2-5) |

MLS CUP FINAL 2013
Saturday 7 December 2013

Sporting Kansas City (0) 1 *(Collin 76)*

Real Salt Lake (0) 1 *(Saborio 52)*

Sporting Kansas City: Nielsen; Myers, Collin, Besler, Sinovic, Nagamura, Rosell (Olum 8), Feilhaber, Zusi, Dwyer (Bieler 72); Sapong.
Real Salt Lake: Rimando; Beltran, Borchers, Schuler Wingert (Palmer 72), Beckerman, Gil (Velasquez 87), Grabavoy, Morales, Saborio, Findley (Plata 112).
Referee: Hilario Grajeda.
aet; Sporting Kansas City won 7-6 on penalties.

UEFA UNDER-21 CHAMPIONSHIP 2013–15

QUALIFYING ROUND

GROUP 1

Wales v Moldova	1-0
Lithuania v San Marino	2-1
Finland v Lithuania	2-2
San Marino v Moldova	0-3
Wales v Finland	1-5
San Marino v Lithuania	0-1
Lithuania v Finland	0-1
England v Moldova	1-0
San Marino v Wales	1-0
Finland v England	1-1
Moldova v Wales	0-0
San Marino v England	0-4
Wales v Lithuania	2-0
Wales v San Marino	4-0
Moldova v Finland	1-0
England v Lithuania	5-0
England v Finland	3-0
Moldova v San Marino	2-0
Moldova v Lithuania	3-0
England v San Marino	9-0
England v Wales	1-0
San Marino v Finland	0-0
Wales v England	1-3
Finland v Moldova	1-0
Lithuania v Moldova	0-3

Group 1 Table	P	W	D	L	F	A	GD	Pts
England	8	7	1	0	27	2	25	22
Moldova	9	5	1	3	12	3	9	16
Finland	8	3	3	2	10	8	2	12
Wales	8	3	1	4	9	10	-1	10
Lithuania	8	2	1	5	5	17	-12	7
San Marino	9	1	1	7	2	25	-23	4

GROUP 2

Andorra v Russia	0-3
Bulgaria v Andorra	3-0
Andorra v Bulgaria	0-3
Estonia v Denmark	0-1
Estonia v Andorra	1-1
Slovenia v Estonia	0-1
Russia v Slovenia	2-1
Bulgaria v Estonia	1-1
Denmark v Andorra	6-0
Russia v Bulgaria	3-1
Slovenia v Denmark	2-2
Bulgaria v Russia	3-3
Denmark v Slovenia	2-2
Russia v Denmark	0-2
Slovenia v Bulgaria	2-1
Slovenia v Russia	0-1
Andorra v Estonia	0-2
Bulgaria v Denmark	2-3
Bulgaria v Slovenia	1-5
Andorra v Denmark	0-2
Russia v Estonia	1-0
Denmark v Estonia	8-0
Andorra v Slovenia	0-5
Estonia v Russia	1-2

Group 2 Table	P	W	D	L	F	A	GD	Pts
Denmark	8	6	2	0	26	6	20	20
Russia	8	6	1	1	15	8	7	19
Slovenia	8	3	2	3	17	10	7	11
Estonia	8	2	2	4	6	14	-8	8
Bulgaria	8	2	2	4	15	17	-2	8
Andorra	8	0	1	7	1	25	-24	1

GROUP 3

Scotland v Luxembourg	3-0
Luxembourg v Slovakia	1-7
Luxembourg v Georgia	0-3
Netherlands v Scotland	4-0
Luxembourg v Netherlands	0-1
Slovakia v Georgia	1-0
Georgia v Netherlands	0-6
Scotland v Slovakia	2-1

Georgia v Scotland	2-1
Slovakia v Luxembourg	3-0
Slovakia v Netherlands	2-2
Scotland v Georgia	1-1
Georgia v Slovakia	1-3
Georgia v Luxembourg	1-1
Awarded as forfeit win 3-0 to Luxembourg	
Scotland v Netherlands	1-6
Netherlands v Luxembourg	3-1

Group 3 Table	P	W	D	L	F	A	GD	Pts
Netherlands	6	5	1	0	22	4	18	16
Slovakia	6	4	1	1	17	6	11	13
Georgia	7	2	1	4	7	15	-8	7
Scotland	6	2	1	3	8	14	-6	7
Luxembourg	7	1	0	6	5	20	-15	3

GROUP 4

Albania v Hungary	1-2
Bosnia & Herzegovina v Albania	4-1
Albania v Austria	0-1
Hungary v Bosnia & Herzegovina	4-1
Austria v Spain	2-6
Bosnia & Herzegovina v Austria	0-2
Spain v Albania	4-0
Hungary v Austria	0-2
Spain v Bosnia & Herzegovina	3-2
Spain v Hungary	1-0
Albania v Bosnia & Herzegovina	0-1
Hungary v Albania	0-2
Bosnia & Herzegovina v Spain	1-6
Albania v Spain	0-2
Austria v Hungary	4-2
Austria v Albania	1-3

Group 4 Table	P	W	D	L	F	A	GD	Pts
Spain	6	6	0	0	22	5	17	18
Austria	6	4	0	2	12	11	1	12
Albania	8	2	0	6	7	15	-8	6
Bosnia & Herzegovina	6	2	0	4	9	16	-7	6
Hungary	6	2	0	4	8	11	-3	6

GROUP 5

Latvia v Liechtenstein	4-0
Liechtenstein v Croatia	0-5
Latvia v Switzerland	0-2
Ukraine v Croatia	0-2
Liechtenstein v Switzerland	0-6
Croatia v Liechtenstein	4-0
Latvia v Ukraine	1-5
Switzerland v Croatia	0-2
Croatia v Switzerland	0-2
Liechtenstein v Latvia	0-2
Switzerland v Ukraine	1-2
Croatia v Latvia	3-1
Switzerland v Liechtenstein	5-1
Croatia v Ukraine	1-1
Liechtenstein v Ukraine	2-5
Ukraine v Latvia	2-1

Group 5 Table	P	W	D	L	F	A	GD	Pts
Croatia	7	5	1	1	17	4	13	16
Ukraine	6	4	1	1	15	8	7	13
Switzerland	6	4	0	2	16	5	11	12
Latvia	6	2	0	4	9	12	-3	6
Liechtenstein	7	0	0	7	3	31	-28	0

GROUP 6

Faroe Islands v Romania	2-2
Montenegro v Faroe Islands	3-0
Faroe Islands v Republic of Ireland	1-4
Faroe Islands v Germany	0-3
Republic of Ireland v Germany	0-4
Montenegro v Romania	3-2
Germany v Montenegro	2-0
Romania v Republic of Ireland	0-0
Republic of Ireland v Romania	0-1
Germany v Faroe Islands	3-2
Republic of Ireland v Faroe Islands	5-2
Montenegro v Germany	1-1

Montenegro v Republic of Ireland   0-0
Romania v Germany   2-2
Romania v Faroe Islands   3-1
Republic of Ireland v Montenegro   1-2

Group 6 Table	P	W	D	L	F	A	GD	Pts
Germany	6	4	2	0	15	5	10	14
Montenegro	6	3	2	1	9	6	3	11
Romania	6	2	3	1	10	8	2	9
Republic of Ireland	7	2	2	3	10	10	0	8
Faroe Islands	7	0	1	6	8	23	–15	1

GROUP 7
Poland v Malta   2-0
Poland v Turkey   3-1
Turkey v Malta   4-0
Sweden v Poland   3-1
Greece v Malta   5-0
Turkey v Sweden   2-2
Turkey v Greece   1-0
Poland v Sweden   2-0
Malta v Greece   0-4
Turkey v Poland   1-0
Greece v Sweden   5-1
Malta v Poland   1-5
Poland v Greece   3-1
Sweden v Malta   5-0
Malta v Sweden   1-2
Greece v Turkey   2-1

Group 7 Table	P	W	D	L	F	A	GD	Pts
Poland	7	5	0	2	16	7	9	15
Greece	6	4	0	2	17	6	11	12
Sweden	6	3	1	2	13	11	2	10
Turkey	6	3	1	2	10	7	3	10
Malta	7	0	0	7	2	27	–25	0

GROUP 8
Azerbaijan v Macedonia   0-0
Portugal v Norway   5-1
Israel v Azerbaijan   7-2
Norway v Macedonia   2-1
Norway v Azerbaijan   1-3
Portugal v Israel   3-0
Azerbaijan v Portugal   0-2
Norway v Israel   1-3
Israel v Norway   4-1
Macedonia v Azerbaijan   1-0
Israel v Portugal   3-4
Macedonia v Norway   1-3
Portugal v Macedonia   2-0
Macedonia v Portugal   0-1
Azerbaijan v Norway   0-1

Group 8 Table	P	W	D	L	F	A	GD	Pts
Portugal	6	6	0	0	17	4	13	18
Israel	5	3	0	2	17	11	6	9
Norway	7	3	0	4	10	17	–7	9
Azerbaijan	6	1	1	4	5	12	–7	4
Macedonia	6	1	1	4	3	8	–5	4

GROUP 9
Belgium v Cyprus   2-0
Cyprus v Northern Ireland   3-0
Serbia v Cyprus   2-1
Italy v Belgium   1-3
Cyprus v Italy   0-2
Belgium v Northern Ireland   1-0
Northern Ireland v Belgium   0-1
Cyprus v Serbia   2-1
Belgium v Italy   0-1
Serbia v Northern Ireland   3-1
Italy v Northern Ireland   3-0
Serbia v Belgium   2-2
Serbia v Italy   1-0
Northern Ireland v Cyprus   1-0
Northern Ireland v Italy   0-2
Belgium v Serbia   0-3

Group 9 Table	P	W	D	L	F	A	GD	Pts
Serbia	6	4	1	1	12	6	6	13
Belgium	7	4	1	2	9	7	2	13
Italy	6	4	0	2	9	4	5	12
Cyprus	6	2	0	4	6	8	–2	6
Northern Ireland	7	1	0	6	2	13	–11	3

GROUP 10
Belarus v Iceland   1-2
Armenia v Iceland   1-2
Belarus v Kazakhstan   0-1
Kazakhstan v Armenia   0-1
Iceland v Belarus   4-1
France v Kazakhstan   5-0
Iceland v Kazakhstan   2-0
Kazakhstan v Belarus   1-2
Armenia v France   1-4
Armenia v Kazakhstan   1-2
Iceland v France   3-4
France v Armenia   6-0
Belarus v Armenia   0-1
France v Belarus   1-0
Kazakhstan v Iceland   3-2

Group 10 Table	P	W	D	L	F	A	GD	Pts
France	6	6	0	0	22	5	17	18
Iceland	6	4	0	2	15	10	5	12
Kazakhstan	7	3	0	4	7	13	–6	9
Armenia	6	2	0	4	5	14	–9	6
Belarus	7	1	0	6	5	12	–7	3

Competition still being played.

FIFA UNDER-20 WORLD CUP 2013

FINALS IN TURKEY

GROUP A

France v Ghana	3-1
USA v Spain	1-4
France v USA	1-1
Spain v Ghana	1-0
Spain v France	2-1
Ghana v USA	4-1

Group A Table	P	W	D	L	F	A	Pts
Spain	3	3	0	0	7	2	9
France	3	1	1	1	5	4	4
Ghana	3	1	0	2	5	5	3
USA	3	0	1	2	3	9	1

GROUP B

Cuba v Korea Republic	1-2
Nigeria v Portugal	2-3
Cuba v Nigeria	0-3
Portugal v Korea Republic	2-2
Korea Republic v Nigeria	0-1
Portugal v Cuba	5-0

Group B Table	P	W	D	L	F	A	Pts
Portugal	3	2	1	0	10	4	7
Nigeria	3	2	0	1	6	3	6
Korea Republic	3	1	1	1	4	4	4
Cuba	3	0	0	3	1	10	0

GROUP C

Colombia v Australia	1-1
Turkey v El Salvador	3-0
Australia v El Salvador	1-2
Turkey v Colombia	0-1
Australia v Turkey	1-2
El Salvador v Colombia	0-3

Group C Table	P	W	D	L	F	A	Pts
Colombia	3	2	1	0	5	1	7
Turkey	3	2	0	1	5	2	6
El Salvador	3	1	0	2	2	7	3
Australia	3	0	1	2	3	5	1

GROUP D

Mexico v Greece	1-2
Paraguay v Mali	1-1
Mexico v Paraguay	0-1
Mali v Greece	0-0
Greece v Paraguay	1-1
Mali v Mexico	1-4

Group D Table	P	W	D	L	F	A	Pts
Greece	3	1	2	0	3	2	5
Paraguay	3	1	2	0	3	2	5
Mexico	3	1	0	2	5	4	3
Mali	3	0	2	1	2	5	2

GROUP E

Chile v Egypt	2-1
England v Iraq	2-2
Chile v England	1-1
Iraq v Egypt	2-1
Iraq v Chile	2-1
Egypt v England	2-0

Group E Table	P	W	D	L	F	A	Pts
Iraq	3	2	1	0	6	4	7
Chile	3	1	1	1	4	4	4
Egypt	3	1	0	2	4	4	3
England	3	0	2	1	3	5	2

GROUP F

New Zealand v Uzbekistan	0-3
Uruguay v Croatia	0-1
New Zealand v Uruguay	0-2
Croatia v Uzbekistan	1-1
Uzbekistan v Uruguay	0-4
Croatia v New Zealand	2-1

Group F Table	P	W	D	L	F	A	Pts
Croatia	3	2	1	0	4	2	7
Uruguay	3	2	0	1	6	1	6
Uzbekistan	3	1	1	1	4	5	4
New Zealand	3	0	0	3	1	7	0

ROUND OF 16

Spain v Mexico	2-1
Greece v Uzbekistan	1-3
Nigeria v Uruguay	1-2
France v Turkey	4-1
Portugal v Ghana	2-3
Croatia v Chile	0-2
Colombia v Korea Republic	1-1
Korea Republic won 8-7 on penalties.	
Iraq v Paraguay	1-0
aet.	

QUARTER-FINALS

France v Uzbekistan	4-0
Uruguay v Spain	1-0
aet.	
Iraq v Korea Republic	3-3
aet; Iraq won 5-4 on penalties.	
Ghana v Chile	4-3
aet.	

SEMI-FINALS

France v Ghana	2-1
Iraq v Uruguay	1-1
aet; Uruguay won 7-6 on penalties.	

FINAL

France v Uruguay	0-0
aet; France won 4-1 on penalties.	

UEFA UNDER-19 CHAMPIONSHIP 2012–13

FINALS IN LITHUANIA

GROUP A

Lithuania v Netherlands	2-3
Spain v Portugal	1-0
Netherlands v Portugal	1-4
Lithuania v Spain	0-2
Portugal v Lithuania	4-2
Netherlands v Spain	2-3

Group A Table	P	W	D	L	F	A	GD	Pts
Spain	3	3	0	0	6	2	4	9
Portugal	3	2	0	1	8	4	4	6
Netherlands	3	1	0	2	6	9	–3	3
Lithuania	3	0	0	3	4	9	–5	0

GROUP B

Serbia v Turkey	2-1
Georgia v France	0-0
Serbia v Georgia	1-0
Turkey v France	1-2
France v Serbia	1-1
Turkey v Georgia	4-2

Group B Table	P	W	D	L	F	A	GD	Pts
Serbia	3	2	1	0	4	2	2	7
France	3	1	2	0	3	2	1	5
Turkey	3	1	0	2	6	6	0	3
Georgia	3	0	1	2	2	5	–3	1

SEMI-FINALS

Serbia v Portugal	2-2
Serbia win 3-2 on penalties.	
Spain v France	1-2
aet.	

FINAL

France v Serbia	0-1

UEFA UNDER-19 CHAMPIONSHIP 2013–14

QUALIFYING ROUND

GROUP 1 (CZECH REPUBLIC)
Croatia v Gibraltar	7-0
Czech Republic v Cyprus	4-1
Gibraltar v Czech Republic	0-3
Croatia v Cyprus	2-2
Czech Republic v Croatia	3-0
Cyprus v Gibraltar	7-0

Group 1 Table	P	W	D	L	F	A	GD	Pts
Czech Republic	3	3	0	0	10	1	9	9
Cyprus	3	1	1	1	10	6	4	4
Croatia	3	1	1	1	9	5	4	4
Gibraltar	3	0	0	3	0	17	–17	0

GROUP 2 (POLAND)
Romania v Armenia	1-1
Poland v Lithuania	1-1
Romania v Lithuania	1-0
Armenia v Poland	1-0
Poland v Romania	1-1
Lithuania v Armenia	1-0

Group 2 Table	P	W	D	L	F	A	GD	Pts
Romania	3	1	2	0	3	2	1	5
Lithuania	3	1	1	1	2	2	0	4
Armenia	3	1	1	1	2	2	0	4
Poland	3	0	2	1	2	3	–1	2

GROUP 3 (SWEDEN)
Republic of Ireland v Azerbaijan	2-0
Bosnia & Herzegovina v Sweden	1-4
Azerbaijan v Bosnia & Herzegovina	0-0
Republic of Ireland v Sweden	1-0
Bosnia & Herzegovina v Republic of Ireland	1-1
Sweden v Azerbaijan	5-1

Group 3 Table	P	W	D	L	F	A	GD	Pts
Republic of Ireland	3	2	1	0	4	1	3	7
Sweden	3	2	0	1	9	3	6	6
Bosnia & Herzegovina	3	0	2	1	2	5	–3	2
Azerbaijan	3	0	1	2	1	7	–6	1

GROUP 4 (BELGIUM)
France v Iceland	2-2
Belgium v Northern Ireland	2-0
Belgium v Iceland	2-0
Northern Ireland v France	1-1
France v Belgium	2-2
Iceland v Northern Ireland	1-0

Group 4 Table	P	W	D	L	F	A	GD	Pts
Belgium	3	2	1	0	6	2	4	7
Iceland	3	1	1	1	3	4	–1	4
France	3	0	3	0	5	5	0	3
Northern Ireland	3	0	1	2	1	4	–3	1

GROUP 5 (BELARUS)
Scotland v Latvia	1-1
Germany v Belarus	2-1
Germany v Latvia	5-0
Belarus v Scotland	0-1
Scotland v Germany	1-1
Latvia v Belarus	2-1

Group 5 Table	P	W	D	L	F	A	GD	Pts
Germany	3	2	1	0	8	2	6	7
Scotland	3	1	2	0	3	2	1	5
Latvia	3	1	1	1	3	7	–4	4
Belarus	3	0	0	3	2	5	–3	0

GROUP 6 (BULGARIA)
Slovakia v Bulgaria	1-2
Greece v Albania	1-0
Greece v Bulgaria	1-1
Albania v Slovakia	1-1
Slovakia v Greece	3-3
Bulgaria v Albania	1-1

Group 6 Table	P	W	D	L	F	A	GD	Pts
Greece	3	1	2	0	5	4	1	5
Bulgaria	3	1	2	0	4	3	1	5
Slovakia	3	0	2	1	5	6	–1	2
Albania	3	0	2	1	2	3	–1	2

GROUP 7 (SERBIA)
Serbia v Kazakhstan	3-0
Austria v Finland	6-0
Serbia v Finland	1-0
Kazakhstan v Austria	1-3
Austria v Serbia	0-1
Finland v Kazakhstan	0-0

Group 7 Table	P	W	D	L	F	A	GD	Pts
Serbia	3	3	0	0	5	0	5	9
Austria	3	2	0	1	9	2	7	6
Kazakhstan	3	0	1	2	1	6	–5	1
Finland	3	0	1	2	0	7	–7	1

GROUP 8 (PORTUGAL)
Norway v San Marino	2-0
Portugal v Luxembourg	3-0
Luxembourg v Norway	1-5
Portugal v San Marino	6-0
Norway v Portugal	2-3
San Marino v Luxembourg	0-4

Group 8 Table	P	W	D	L	F	A	GD	Pts
Portugal	3	3	0	0	12	2	10	9
Norway	3	2	0	1	9	4	5	6
Luxembourg	3	1	0	2	5	8	–3	3
San Marino	3	0	0	3	0	12	–12	0

GROUP 9 (SLOVENIA)
Switzerland v Andorra	4-0
England v Slovenia	1-1
Switzerland v Slovenia	3-1
Andorra v England	0-7
England v Switzerland	1-0
Slovenia v Andorra	7-0

Group 9 Table	P	W	D	L	F	A	GD	Pts
England	3	2	1	0	9	1	8	7
Switzerland	3	2	0	1	7	2	5	6
Slovenia	3	1	1	1	9	4	5	4
Andorra	3	0	0	3	0	18	–18	0

GROUP 10 (ISRAEL)
Italy v Israel	0-2
Denmark v Liechtenstein	2-0
Italy v Liechtenstein	5-0
Israel v Denmark	1-3
Denmark v Italy	0-2
Liechtenstein v Israel	0-9

Group 10 Table	P	W	D	L	F	A	GD	Pts
Denmark	3	2	0	1	5	3	2	6
Israel	3	2	0	1	12	3	9	6
Italy	3	2	0	1	7	2	5	6
Liechtenstein	3	0	0	3	0	16	–16	0

GROUP 11 (GEORGIA)
Georgia v Wales	5-1
Netherlands v Moldova	3-0
Moldova v Georgia	0-2
Netherlands v Wales	0-0
Georgia v Netherlands	2-1
Wales v Moldova	6-0

Group 11 Table	P	W	D	L	F	A	GD	Pts
Georgia	3	3	0	0	9	2	7	9
Wales	3	1	1	1	7	5	2	4
Netherlands	3	1	1	1	4	2	2	4
Moldova	3	0	0	3	0	11	–11	0

GROUP 12 (MACEDONIA)

Turkey v Macedonia	4-1
Montenegro v Faroe Islands	5-0
Turkey v Faroe Islands	2-0
Macedonia v Montenegro	2-1
Montenegro v Turkey	2-1
Faroe Islands v Macedonia	0-5

Group 12 Table	P	W	D	L	F	A	GD	Pts
Turkey	3	2	0	1	7	3	4	6
Montenegro	3	2	0	1	8	3	5	6
Macedonia	3	2	0	1	8	5	3	6
Faroe Islands	3	0	0	3	0	12	–12	0

GROUP 13 (RUSSIA)

Ukraine v Estonia	3-1
Russia v Malta	4-0
Malta v Ukraine	0-4
Russia v Estonia	5-1
Ukraine v Russia	1-1
Estonia v Malta	2-2

Group 13 Table	P	W	D	L	F	A	GD	Pts
Russia	3	2	1	0	10	2	8	7
Ukraine	3	2	1	0	8	2	6	7
Estonia	3	0	1	2	4	10	–6	1
Malta	3	0	1	2	2	10	–8	1

ELITE ROUND

GROUP 1 (ENGLAND)

England v Montenegro	6-0
Ukraine v Scotland	0-0
Montenegro v Ukraine	0-4
England v Scotland	2-1
Ukraine v England	1-0
Scotland v Montenegro	0-1

Group 1 Table	P	W	D	L	F	A	GD	Pts
Ukraine	3	2	1	0	5	0	5	7
England	3	2	0	1	8	2	6	6
Montenegro	3	1	0	2	1	10	–9	3
Scotland	3	0	1	2	1	3	–2	1

GROUP 2 (BULGARIA)

Czech Republic v Italy	1-0
Sweden v Bulgaria	1-2
Czech Republic v Bulgaria	0-2
Italy v Sweden	1-3
Sweden v Czech Republic	3-0
Bulgaria v Italy	1-1

Group 2 Table	P	W	D	L	F	A	GD	Pts
Bulgaria	3	2	1	0	5	2	3	7
Sweden	3	2	0	1	7	3	4	6
Czech Republic	3	1	0	2	1	5	–4	3
Italy	3	0	1	2	2	5	–3	1

GROUP 3 (SWITZERLAND)

Israel v Cyprus	4-0
Georgia v Switzerland	2-0
Georgia v Cyprus	5-1
Switzerland v Israel	0-1
Israel v Georgia	1-0
Cyprus v Switzerland	0-2

Group 3 Table	P	W	D	L	F	A	GD	Pts
Israel	3	3	0	0	6	0	6	9
Georgia	3	2	0	1	7	2	5	6
Switzerland	3	1	0	2	2	3	–1	3
Cyprus	3	0	0	3	1	11	–10	0

GROUP 4 (REPUBLIC OF IRELAND)

Serbia v Turkey	1-1
Republic of Ireland v Iceland	2-1
Serbia v Iceland	6-0
Turkey v Republic of Ireland	2-1
Republic of Ireland v Serbia	1-3
Iceland v Turkey	3-4

Group 4 Table	P	W	D	L	F	A	GD	Pts
Serbia	3	2	1	0	10	2	8	7
Turkey	3	2	1	0	7	5	2	7
Republic of Ireland	3	1	0	2	4	6	–2	3
Iceland	3	0	0	3	4	12	–8	0

GROUP 5 (SPAIN)

Germany v Lithuania	2-0
Spain v Denmark	3-1
Denmark v Germany	0-4
Spain v Lithuania	2-0
Germany v Spain	3-1
Lithuania v Denmark	1-3

Group 5 Table	P	W	D	L	F	A	GD	Pts
Germany	3	3	0	0	9	1	8	9
Spain	3	2	0	1	6	4	2	6
Denmark	3	1	0	2	4	8	–4	3
Lithuania	3	0	0	3	1	7	–6	0

GROUP 6 (ROMANIA)

Russia v Norway	3-0
Austria v Romania	5-0
Russia v Romania	3-1
Norway v Austria	1-3
Austria v Russia	0-0
Romania v Norway	3-0

Group 6 Table	P	W	D	L	F	A	GD	Pts
Austria	3	2	1	0	8	1	7	7
Russia	3	2	1	0	6	1	5	7
Romania	3	1	0	2	4	8	–4	3
Norway	3	0	0	3	1	9	–8	0

GROUP 7 (PORTUGAL)

Belgium v Wales	1-1
Portugal v Greece	3-0
Greece v Belgium	2-4
Portugal v Wales	3-2
Belgium v Portugal	2-3
Wales v Greece	3-0

Group 7 Table	P	W	D	L	F	A	GD	Pts
Portugal	3	3	0	0	9	4	5	9
Wales	3	1	1	1	6	4	2	4
Belgium	3	1	1	1	7	6	1	4
Greece	3	0	0	3	2	10	–8	0

Finals in Hungary 19–31 July 2014.

FIFA UNDER-17 WORLD CUP 2013

FINALS IN UNITED ARAB EMIRATES

GROUP A

Brazil v Slovakia	6-1
United Arab Emirates v Honduras	1-2
Slovakia v Honduras	2-2
United Arab Emirates v Brazil	1-6
Slovakia v United Arab Emirates	2-0
Honduras v Brazil	0-3

Group A Table	P	W	D	L	F	A	GD	Pts
Brazil	3	3	0	0	15	2	13	9
Honduras	3	1	1	1	4	6	-2	4
Slovakia	3	1	1	1	5	8	-3	4
United Arab Emirates	3	0	0	3	2	10	-8	0

GROUP B

Uruguay v New Zealand	7-0
Ivory Coast v Italy	0-1
Uruguay v Ivory Coast	1-1
Italy v New Zealand	1-0
New Zealand v Ivory Coast	0-3
Italy v Uruguay	1-2

Group B Table	P	W	D	L	F	A	GD	Pts
Uruguay	3	2	1	0	10	2	8	7
Italy	3	2	0	1	3	2	1	6
Ivory Coast	3	1	1	1	4	2	2	4
New Zealand	3	0	0	3	0	11	-11	0

GROUP C

Croatia v Morocco	1-3
Panama v Uzbekistan	0-2
Croatia v Panama	1-0
Uzbekistan v Morocco	0-0
Uzbekistan v Croatia	2-1
Morocco v Panama	4-2

Group C Table	P	W	D	L	F	A	GD	Pts
Morocco	3	2	1	0	7	3	4	7
Uzbekistan	3	2	1	0	4	1	3	7
Croatia	3	1	0	2	3	5	-2	3
Panama	3	0	0	3	2	7	-5	0

GROUP D

Tunisia v Venezuela	2-1
Russia v Japan	0-1
Tunisia v Russia	1-0
Japan v Venezuela	3-1
Venezuela v Russia	0-4
Japan v Tunisia	2-1

Group D Table	P	W	D	L	F	A	GD	Pts
Japan	3	3	0	0	6	2	4	9
Tunisia	3	2	0	1	4	3	1	6
Russia	3	1	0	2	4	2	2	3
Venezuela	3	0	0	3	2	9	-7	0

GROUP E

Canada v Austria	2-2
Iran v Argentina	1-1
Canada v Iran	1-1
Argentina v Austria	3-2
Argentina v Canada	3-0
Austria v Iran	0-1

Group E Table	P	W	D	L	F	A	GD	Pts
Argentina	3	2	1	0	7	3	4	7
Iran	3	1	2	0	3	2	1	5
Canada	3	0	2	1	3	6	-3	2
Austria	3	0	1	2	4	6	-2	1

GROUP F

Mexico v Nigeria	1-6
Iraq v Sweden	1-4
Mexico v Iraq	3-1
Sweden v Nigeria	3-3
Nigeria v Iraq	5-0
Sweden v Mexico	0-1

Group F Table	P	W	D	L	F	A	GD	Pts
Nigeria	3	2	1	0	14	4	10	7
Mexico	3	2	0	1	5	7	-2	6
Sweden	3	1	1	1	7	5	2	4
Iraq	3	0	0	3	2	12	-10	0

ROUND OF 16

Italy v Mexico	0-2
Japan v Sweden	1-2
Brazil v Russia	3-1
Honduras v Uzbekistan	1-0
Uruguay v Slovakia	4-2
Morocco v Ivory Coast	1-2
Argentina v Tunisia	3-1
Nigeria v Iran	4-1

QUARTER-FINALS

Brazil v Mexico	1-1
Mexico won 11-10 on penalties.	
Honduras v Sweden	1-2
Uruguay v Nigeria	0-2
Argentina v Ivory Coast	2-1

SEMI-FINALS

| Sweden v Nigeria | 0-3 |
| Argentina v Mexico | 0-3 |

PLAY-OFF FOR THIRD PLACE

| Sweden v Argentina | 4-1 |

FINAL

| Nigeria v Mexico | 3-0 |

UEFA REGIONS' CUP 2013–14

FINALS IN ITALY

GROUP A

Veneto v Eastern Region	4-1
Qarachala v Keleti Regio	0-2
Veneto v Qarachala	1-0
Eastern Region v Keleti Regio	2-2
Keleti Regio v Veneto	0-1
Eastern Region v Qarachala	5-2

Group A Table	P	W	D	L	F	A	GD	Pts
Veneto	3	3	0	0	6	1	5	9
Keleti Regio	3	1	1	1	4	3	1	4
Eastern Region	3	1	1	1	8	8	0	4
Qarachala	3	0	0	3	2	8	-6	0

GROUP B

Isloch v Seleccion Catalana	0-2
Olimp v Yugoiztochen Region	0-0
Isloch v Olimp	1-0
Seleccion Catalana v Yugoiztochen Region	2-2
Yugoiztochen Region v Isloch	0-1
Seleccion Catalana v Olimp	1-0

Group B Table	P	W	D	L	F	A	GD	Pts
Seleccion Catalana	3	2	1	0	5	2	3	7
Isloch	3	2	0	1	2	2	0	6
Yugoiztochen Region	3	0	2	1	2	3	-1	2
Olimp	3	0	1	2	0	2	-2	1

FINAL

| Veneto v Seleccion Catalana | 0-0 |
| *aet; Veneto won 5-4 on penalties.* | |

UEFA UNDER-17 CHAMPIONSHIP 2013–14

QUALIFYING ROUND

GROUP 1 (ALBANIA)
Belarus v Finland	1-0
Romania v Albania	1-0
Finland v Romania	0-1
Belarus v Albania	1-2
Romania v Belarus	2-0
Albania v Finland	0-0

GROUP 1 TABLE	P	W	D	L	F	A	GD	Pts
Romania	3	3	0	0	4	0	4	9
Albania	3	1	1	1	2	2	0	4
Belarus	3	1	0	2	2	4	–2	3
Finland	3	0	1	2	0	2	–2	1

GROUP 2 (LITHUANIA)
Italy v Ukraine	2-1
Sweden v Lithuania	3-0
Italy v Lithuania	0-0
Ukraine v Sweden	0-0
Sweden v Italy	0-3
Lithuania v Ukraine	1-1

GROUP 2 TABLE	P	W	D	L	F	A	GD	Pts
Italy	3	2	1	0	5	1	4	7
Sweden	3	1	1	1	3	3	0	4
Ukraine	3	0	2	1	2	3	–1	2
Lithuania	3	0	2	1	1	4	–3	2

GROUP 3 (ISRAEL)
Czech Republic v Israel	4-2
France v Liechtenstein	2-0
Czech Republic v Liechtenstein	3-0
Israel v France	2-2
France v Czech Republic	3-0
Liechtenstein v Israel	0-8

GROUP 3 TABLE	P	W	D	L	F	A	GD	Pts
France	3	2	1	0	7	2	5	7
Czech Republic	3	2	0	1	7	5	2	6
Israel	3	1	1	1	12	6	6	4
Liechtenstein	3	0	0	3	0	13	–13	0

GROUP 4 (SLOVENIA)
Scotland v Slovenia	3-1
Hungary v Wales	5-5
Scotland v Wales	0-0
Slovenia v Hungary	4-2
Hungary v Scotland	1-2
Wales v Slovenia	3-0

GROUP 4 TABLE	P	W	D	L	F	A	GD	Pts
Scotland	3	2	1	0	5	2	3	7
Wales	3	1	2	0	8	5	3	5
Slovenia	3	1	0	2	5	8	–3	3
Hungary	3	0	1	2	8	11	–3	1

GROUP 5 (BOSNIA & HERZEGOVINA)
Croatia v Montenegro	1-0
Portugal v Bosnia & Herzegovina	2-0
Croatia v Bosnia & Herzegovina	0-2
Montenegro v Portugal	1-2
Portugal v Croatia	1-0
Bosnia & Herzegovina v Montenegro	0-0

GROUP 5 TABLE	P	W	D	L	F	A	GD	Pts
Portugal	3	3	0	0	5	1	4	9
Bosnia & Herzegovina	3	1	1	1	2	2	0	4
Croatia	3	1	0	2	1	3	–2	3
Montenegro	3	0	1	2	1	3	–2	1

GROUP 6 (SERBIA)
Greece v Estonia	3-1
Serbia v Andorra	6-0
Greece v Andorra	1-0
Estonia v Serbia	1-4
Serbia v Greece	0-0
Andorra v Estonia	0-2

GROUP 6 TABLE	P	W	D	L	F	A	GD	Pts
Serbia	3	2	1	0	10	1	9	7
Greece	3	2	1	0	4	1	3	7
Estonia	3	1	0	2	4	7	–3	3
Andorra	3	0	0	3	0	9	–9	0

GROUP 7 (ARMENIA)
England v Armenia	4-0
Republic of Ireland v Gibraltar	4-1
Gibraltar v England	0-8
Republic of Ireland v Armenia	2-0
England v Republic of Ireland	6-0
Armenia v Gibraltar	2-1

GROUP 7 TABLE	P	W	D	L	F	A	GD	Pts
England	3	3	0	0	18	0	18	9
Republic of Ireland	3	2	0	1	6	7	–1	6
Armenia	3	1	0	2	2	7	–5	3
Gibraltar	3	0	0	3	2	14	–12	0

GROUP 8 (CYPRUS)
Norway v Cyprus	4-2
Spain v Moldova	3-0
Norway v Moldova	1-1
Cyprus v Spain	0-1
Spain v Norway	2-0
Moldova v Cyprus	0-2

GROUP 8 TABLE	P	W	D	L	F	A	GD	Pts
Spain	3	3	0	0	6	0	6	9
Norway	3	1	1	1	5	5	0	4
Cyprus	3	1	0	2	4	5	–1	3
Moldova	3	0	1	2	1	6	–5	1

GROUP 9 (NORTHERN IRELAND)
Turkey v Luxembourg	2-2
Northern Ireland v Latvia	0-1
Latvia v Turkey	0-1
Northern Ireland v Luxembourg	3-1
Turkey v Northern Ireland	2-0
Luxembourg v Latvia	0-2

GROUP 9 TABLE	P	W	D	L	F	A	GD	Pts
Turkey	3	2	1	0	5	2	3	7
Latvia	3	2	0	1	3	1	2	6
Northern Ireland	3	1	0	2	3	4	–1	3
Luxembourg	3	0	1	2	3	7	–4	1

GROUP 10 (RUSSIA)
Iceland v Azerbaijan	3-3
Russia v Slovakia	2-1
Slovakia v Iceland	2-4
Russia v Azerbaijan	1-0
Iceland v Russia	2-1
Azerbaijan v Slovakia	2-4

GROUP 10 TABLE	P	W	D	L	F	A	GD	Pts
Iceland	3	2	1	0	9	6	3	7
Russia	3	2	0	1	4	3	1	6
Slovakia	3	1	0	2	7	8	–1	3
Azerbaijan	3	0	1	2	5	8	–3	1

GROUP 11 (GEORGIA)
Netherlands v Faroe Islands	4-0
Georgia v San Marino	3-1
San Marino v Netherlands	0-12
Georgia v Faroe Islands	2-0
Netherlands v Georgia	1-0
Faroe Islands v San Marino	1-0

GROUP 11 TABLE	P	W	D	L	F	A	GD	Pts
Netherlands	3	3	0	0	17	0	17	9
Georgia	3	2	0	1	5	2	3	6
Faroe Islands	3	1	0	2	1	6	–5	3
San Marino	3	0	0	3	1	16	–15	0

GROUP 12 (DENMARK)
Denmark v Kazakhstan	1-0
Switzerland v Austria	4-0
Kazakhstan v Switzerland	0-3
Denmark v Austria	0-2
Switzerland v Denmark	0-0
Austria v Kazakhstan	2-0

GROUP 12 TABLE	P	W	D	L	F	A	GD	Pts
Switzerland	3	2	1	0	7	0	7	7
Austria	3	2	0	1	4	0	4	6
Denmark	3	1	1	1	1	2	–1	4
Kazakhstan	3	0	0	3	0	6	–6	0

GROUP 13 (MACEDONIA)

Belgium v Bulgaria	2-0
Poland v Macedonia	3-2
Belgium v Macedonia	5-0
Bulgaria v Poland	0-3
Poland v Belgium	2-0
Macedonia v Bulgaria	2-1

GROUP 13 TABLE	P	W	D	L	F	A	GD	Pts
Poland	3	3	0	0	8	2	6	9
Belgium	3	2	0	1	7	2	5	6
Macedonia	3	1	0	2	4	9	–5	3
Bulgaria	3	0	0	3	1	7	–6	0

ELITE ROUND

GROUP 1 (RUSSIA)

Switzerland v Wales	1-0
Spain v Russia	1-1
Spain v Wales	1-0
Russia v Switzerland	1-1
Switzerland v Spain	1-0
Wales v Russia	0-2

GROUP 1 TABLE	P	W	D	L	F	A	GD	Pts
Switzerland	3	2	1	0	3	1	2	7
Russia	3	1	2	0	4	2	2	5
Spain	3	1	1	1	2	2	0	4
Wales	3	0	0	3	0	4	–4	0

GROUP 2 (GREECE)

Poland v Greece	2-1
Turkey v Norway	3-2
Poland v Norway	2-1
Greece v Turkey	0-1
Turkey v Poland	0-0
Norway v Greece	0-3

GROUP 2 TABLE	P	W	D	L	F	A	GD	Pts
Poland	3	2	1	0	4	2	2	7
Turkey	3	2	1	0	4	2	2	7
Greece	3	1	0	2	4	3	1	3
Norway	3	0	0	3	3	8	–5	0

GROUP 3 (NETHERLANDS)

France v Sweden	3-0
Netherlands v Austria	2-1
Austria v France	1-2
Netherlands v Sweden	2-0
France v Netherlands	1-3
Sweden v Austria	0-1

GROUP 3 TABLE	P	W	D	L	F	A	GD	Pts
Netherlands	3	3	0	0	7	2	5	9
France	3	2	0	1	6	4	2	6
Austria	3	1	0	2	3	4	–1	3
Sweden	3	0	0	3	0	6	–6	0

GROUP 4 (CZECH REPUBLIC)

Italy v Albania	2-1
England v Czech Republic	1-0
England v Albania	1-0
Czech Republic v Italy	2-1
Italy v England	1-2
Albania v Czech Republic	0-2

GROUP 4 TABLE	P	W	D	L	F	A	GD	Pts
England	3	3	0	0	4	1	3	9
Czech Republic	3	2	0	1	4	2	2	6
Italy	3	1	0	2	4	5	–1	3
Albania	3	0	0	3	1	5	–4	0

GROUP 5 (SERBIA)

Germany v Georgia	4-0
Serbia v Republic of Ireland	2-1
Germany v Republic of Ireland	3-0
Georgia v Serbia	0-2
Republic of Ireland v Georgia	2-2
Serbia v Germany	1-1

GROUP 5 TABLE	P	W	D	L	F	A	GD	Pts
Germany	3	2	1	0	8	1	7	7
Serbia	3	2	1	0	5	2	3	7
Republic of Ireland	3	0	1	2	3	7	–4	1
Georgia	3	0	1	2	2	8	–6	1

GROUP 6 (SCOTLAND)

Romania v Belgium	0-0
Scotland v Bosnia & Herzegovina	2-0
Romania v Bosnia & Herzegovina	0-1
Belgium v Scotland	1-3
Scotland v Romania	1-0
Bosnia & Herzegovina v Belgium	3-0

GROUP 6 TABLE	P	W	D	L	F	A	GD	Pts
Scotland	3	3	0	0	6	1	5	9
Bosnia & Herzegovina	3	2	0	1	4	2	2	6
Romania	3	0	1	2	0	2	–2	1
Belgium	3	0	1	2	1	6	–5	1

GROUP 7 (PORTUGAL)

Iceland v Ukraine	0-2
Portugal v Latvia	3-0
Latvia v Iceland	0-0
Portugal v Ukraine	3-0
Iceland v Portugal	0-3
Ukraine v Latvia	5-1

GROUP 7 TABLE	P	W	D	L	F	A	GD	Pts
Portugal	3	3	0	0	9	0	9	9
Ukraine	3	2	0	1	7	4	3	6
Iceland	3	0	1	2	0	5	–5	1
Latvia	3	0	1	2	1	8	–7	1

FINAL TOURNAMENT (MALTA)

GROUP STAGE

GROUP A

Netherlands v Turkey	3-2
Malta v England	0-3
England v Turkey	4-1
Malta v Netherlands	2-5
Turkey v Malta	4-0
England v Netherlands	0-2

GROUP A TABLE	P	W	D	L	F	A	GD	Pts
Netherlands	3	3	0	0	10	4	6	9
England	3	2	0	1	7	3	4	6
Turkey	3	1	0	2	7	7	0	3
Malta	3	0	0	3	2	12	–10	0

GROUP B

Germany v Switzerland	1-1
Scotland v Portugal	0-2
Switzerland v Portugal	0-1
Germany v Scotland	0-1
Portugal v Germany	1-0
Switzerland v Scotland	1-3

GROUP B TABLE	P	W	D	L	F	A	GD	Pts
Portugal	3	3	0	0	4	0	4	9
Scotland	3	2	0	1	4	3	1	6
Germany	3	0	1	2	1	3	–2	1
Switzerland	3	0	1	2	2	5	–3	1

SEMI-FINALS

Portugal v England	0-2
Netherlands v Scotland	5-0

FINAL

Netherlands v England	1-1

England won 4-1 on penalties.

ENGLAND UNDER-21 RESULTS 1976–2014

EC *UEFA Competition for Under-21 Teams*

Year	Date		Venue	Eng	Alb
			v ALBANIA	*Eng*	*Alb*
EC1989	Mar	7	Shkroda	2	1
EC1989	April	25	Ipswich	2	0
EC2001	Mar	27	Tirana	1	0
EC2001	Sept	4	Middlesbrough	5	0
			v ANGOLA	*Eng*	*Ang*
1995	June	10	Toulon	1	0
1996	May	28	Toulon	0	2
			v ARGENTINA	*Eng*	*Arg*
1998	May	18	Toulon	0	2
2000	Feb	22	Fulham	1	0
			v AUSTRIA	*Eng*	*Aus*
1994	Oct	11	Kapfenberg	3	1
1995	Nov	14	Middlesbrough	2	1
EC2004	Sept	3	Krems	2	0
EC2005	Oct	7	Leeds	1	2
2013	June	26	Brighton	4	0
			v AZERBAIJAN	*Eng*	*Az*
EC2004	Oct	12	Baku	0	0
EC2005	Mar	29	Middlesbrough	2	0
2009	June	8	Milton Keynes	7	0
EC2011	Sept	1	Watford	6	0
EC2012	Sept	6	Baku	2	0
			v BELGIUM	*Eng*	*Bel*
1994	June	5	Marseille	2	1
1996	May	24	Toulon	1	0
EC2011	Nov	14	Mons	1	2
EC2012	Feb	29	Middlesbrough	4	0
			v BRAZIL	*Eng*	*B*
1993	June	11	Toulon	0	0
1995	June	6	Toulon	0	2
1996	June	1	Toulon	1	2
			v BULGARIA	*Eng*	*Bul*
EC1979	June	5	Pernik	3	1
EC1979	Nov	20	Leicester	5	0
1989	June	5	Toulon	2	3
EC1998	Oct	9	West Ham	1	0
EC1999	June	8	Vratsa	1	0
EC2007	Sept	11	Sofia	2	0
EC2007	Nov	16	Milton Keynes	2	0
			v CROATIA	*Eng*	*Cro*
1996	Apr	23	Sunderland	0	1
2003	Aug	19	West Ham	0	3
			v CZECHOSLOVAKIA	*Eng*	*Cz*
1990	May	28	Toulon	2	1
1992	May	26	Toulon	1	2
1993	June	9	Toulon	1	1
			v CZECH REPUBLIC	*Eng*	*CzR*
1998	Nov	17	Ipswich	0	1
EC2007	June	11	Arnhem	0	0
2008	Nov	18	Bramall Lane	2	0
EC2011	June	19	Viborg	1	2
			v DENMARK	*Eng*	*Den*
EC1978	Sept	19	Hvidovre	2	1
EC1979	Sept	11	Watford	1	0
EC1982	Sept	21	Hvidovre	4	1
EC1983	Sept	20	Norwich	4	1
EC1986	Mar	12	Copenhagen	1	0
EC1986	Mar	26	Manchester	1	1
1988	Sept	13	Watford	0	0
1994	Mar	8	Brentford	1	0
1999	Oct	8	Bradford	4	1
2005	Aug	16	Herning	1	0
2011	Mar	24	Viborg	4	0
			v EQUADOR	*Eng*	*E*
2009	Feb	10	Malaga	2	3
			v FINLAND	*Eng*	*Fin*
EC1977	May	26	Helsinki	1	0
EC1977	Oct	12	Hull	8	1
EC1984	Oct	16	Southampton	2	0
EC1985	May	21	Mikkeli	1	3
EC2000	Oct	10	Valkeakoski	2	2
EC2001	Mar	23	Barnsley	4	0
EC2009	June	15	Halmstad	2	1
EC2013	Sept	9	Tampere	1	1
EC2013	Nov	14	Milton Keynes	3	0
			v FRANCE	*Eng*	*Fra*
EC1984	Feb	28	Sheffield	6	1
EC1984	Mar	28	Rouen	1	0
1987	June	11	Toulon	0	2
EC1988	April	13	Besancon	2	4
EC1988	April	27	Highbury	2	2
1988	June	12	Toulon	2	4
1990	May	23	Toulon	7	3
1991	June	3	Toulon	1	0
1992	May	28	Toulon	0	0
1993	June	15	Toulon	1	0
1994	May	31	Aubagne	0	3
1995	June	10	Toulon	0	2
1998	May	14	Toulon	1	1
1999	Feb	9	Derby	2	1
EC2005	Nov	11	Tottenham	1	1
EC2005	Nov	15	Nancy	1	2
2009	Mar	31	Nottingham	0	2
			v GEORGIA	*Eng*	*Geo*
EC1996	Nov	8	Batumi	1	0
EC1997	April	29	Charlton	0	0
2000	Aug	31	Middlesbrough	6	1
			v GERMANY	*Eng*	*Ger*
1991	Sept	10	Scunthorpe	2	1
EC2000	Oct	6	Derby	1	1
EC2001	Aug	31	Frieburg	2	1
2005	Mar	25	Hull	2	2
2005	Sept	6	Mainz	1	1
EC2006	Oct	6	Coventry	1	0
EC2006	Oct	10	Leverkusen	2	0
EC2009	June	22	Halmstad	1	1
EC2009	June	29	Malmo	0	4
2010	Nov	16	Wiesbaden	0	2
			v EAST GERMANY	*Eng*	*EG*
EC1980	April	16	Sheffield	1	2
EC1980	April	23	Jena	0	1
			v WEST GERMANY	*Eng*	*WG*
EC1982	Sept	21	Sheffield	3	1
EC1982	Oct	12	Bremen	2	3
1987	Sept	8	Ludenscheid	0	2
			v GREECE	*Eng*	*Gre*
EC1982	Nov	16	Piraeus	0	1
EC1983	Mar	29	Portsmouth	2	1
1989	Feb	7	Patras	0	1
EC1997	Nov	13	Heraklion	0	2
EC1997	Dec	17	Norwich	4	2
EC2001	June	5	Athens	1	3
EC2001	Oct	5	Ewood Park	2	1
EC2009	Sept	8	Tripoli	1	1
EC2010	Mar	3	Doncaster	1	2
			v HUNGARY	*Eng*	*Hun*
EC1981	June	5	Keszthely	2	1
EC1981	Nov	17	Nottingham	2	0
EC1983	April	26	Newcastle	1	0
EC1983	Oct	11	Nyiregyhaza	2	0
1990	Sept	11	Southampton	3	1
1992	May	12	Budapest	2	2
1999	April	27	Budapest	2	2

v ICELAND			Eng	Ice
2011	Mar	28	Preston	1	2
EC2011	Oct	6	Reykjavik	3	0
EC2011	Nov	10	Colchester	5	0

v REPUBLIC OF IRELAND			Eng	RoI
1981	Feb	25	Liverpool	1	0
1985	Mar	25	Portsmouth	3	2
1989	June	9	Toulon	0	0
EC1990	Nov	13	Cork	3	0
EC1991	Mar	26	Brentford	3	0
1994	Nov	15	Newcastle	1	0
1995	Mar	27	Dublin	2	0
EC2007	Oct	16	Cork	3	0
EC2008	Feb	5	Southampton	3	0

v ISRAEL			Eng	Isr
1985	Feb	27	Tel Aviv	2	1
2011	Sept	5	Barnsley	4	1
EC2013	June	11	Jerusalem	0	1

v ITALY			Eng	Italy
EC1978	Mar	8	Manchester	2	1
EC1978	April	5	Rome	0	0
EC1984	April	18	Manchester	3	1
EC1984	May	2	Florence	0	1
EC1986	April	9	Pisa	0	2
EC1986	April	23	Swindon	1	1
EC1997	Feb	12	Bristol	1	0
EC1997	Oct	10	Rieti	1	0
EC2000	May	27	Bratislava	0	2
2000	Nov	14	Monza*	0	0
2002	Mar	26	Valley Parade	1	1
EC2002	May	20	Basle	1	2
2003	Feb	11	Pisa	0	1
2007	Mar	24	Wembley	3	3
EC2007	June	14	Arnhem	2	2
2011	Feb	8	Empoli	0	1
EC2013	June	5	Tel Aviv	0	1

Abandoned 11 mins; fog.

v LATVIA			Eng	Lat
1995	April	25	Riga	1	0
1995	June	7	Burnley	4	0

v LITHUANIA			Eng	Lith
EC2009	Nov	17	Vilnius	0	0
EC2010	Sept	7	Colchester	3	0
EC2013	Oct	15	Ipswich	5	0

v LUXEMBOURG			Eng	Lux
EC1998	Oct	13	Greven Macher	5	0
EC1999	Sept	3	Reading	5	0

v MACEDONIA			Eng	M
EC2002	Oct	15	Reading	3	1
EC2003	Sept	5	Skopje	1	1
EC2009	Sept	4	Prilep	2	1
EC2009	Oct	9	Coventry	6	3

v MALAYSIA			Eng	Mal
1995	June	8	Toulon	2	0

v MEXICO			Eng	Mex
1988	June	5	Toulon	2	1
1991	May	29	Toulon	6	0
1992	May	25	Toulon	1	1
2001	May	24	Leicester	3	0

v MOLDOVA			Eng	Mol
EC1996	Aug	31	Chisinau	2	0
EC1997	Sept	9	Wycombe	1	0
EC2006	Aug	15	Ipswich	2	2
EC2013	Sept	5	Reading	1	0

v MONTENEGRO			Eng	M
EC2007	Sept	7	Podgorica	3	0
EC2007	Oct	12	Leicester	1	0

v MOROCCO			Eng	Mor
1987	June	7	Toulon	2	0
1988	June	9	Toulon	1	0

v NETHERLANDS			Eng	H
EC1993	April	27	Portsmouth	3	0
EC1993	Oct	12	Utrecht	1	1
2001	Aug	14	Reading	4	0
EC2001	Nov	9	Utrecht	2	2
EC2001	Nov	13	Derby	1	0
2004	Feb	17	Hull	3	2
2005	Feb	8	Derby	1	2
2006	Nov	14	Alkmaar	1	0
EC2007	June	20	Heerenveen	1	1
2009	Aug	11	Groningen	0	0

v NORTHERN IRELAND			Eng	NI
2012	Nov	13	Blackpool	2	0

v NORWAY			Eng	Nor
EC1977	June	1	Bergen	2	1
EC1977	Sept	6	Brighton	6	0
1980	Sept	9	Southampton	3	0
1981	Sept	8	Drammen	0	0
EC1992	Oct	13	Peterborough	0	2
EC1993	June	1	Stavanger	1	1
1995	Oct	10	Stavanger	2	2
2006	Feb	28	Reading	3	1
2009	Mar	27	Sandefjord	5	0
2011	June	5	Southampton	2	0
EC2011	Oct	10	Drammen	2	1
EC2012	Sept	10	Chesterfield	1	0
EC2013	June	8	Petah Tikva	1	3

v POLAND			Eng	Pol
EC1982	Mar	17	Warsaw	2	1
EC1982	April	7	West Ham	2	2
EC1989	June	2	Plymouth	2	1
EC1989	Oct	10	Jastrzebie	3	1
EC1990	Oct	16	Tottenham	0	1
EC1991	Nov	12	Pila	1	2
EC1993	May	28	Zdroj	4	1
EC1993	Sept	7	Millwall	1	2
EC1996	Oct	8	Wolverhampton	0	0
EC1997	May	30	Katowice	1	1
EC1999	Mar	26	Southampton	5	0
EC1999	Sept	7	Plock	1	3
EC2004	Sept	7	Rybnik	3	1
EC2005	Oct	11	Hillsborough	4	1
2008	Mar	25	Wolverhampton	0	0

v PORTUGAL			Eng	Por
1987	June	13	Toulon	0	0
1990	May	21	Toulon	0	1
1993	June	7	Toulon	2	0
1994	June	7	Toulon	2	0
EC1994	Sept	6	Leicester	0	0
1995	Sept	2	Lisbon	0	2
1996	May	30	Toulon	1	3
2000	Apr	16	Stoke	0	1
EC2002	May	22	Zurich	1	3
EC2003	Mar	28	Rio Major	2	4
EC2003	Sept	9	Everton	1	2
EC2008	Nov	20	Agueda	1	1
2008	Sept	5	Wembley	2	0
EC2009	Nov	14	Wembley	1	0
EC2010	Sept	3	Barcelos	1	0

v ROMANIA			Eng	Rom
EC1980	Oct	14	Ploesti	0	4
EC1981	April	28	Swindon	3	0
EC1985	April	30	Brasov	0	0
EC1985	Sept	10	Ipswich	3	0
2007	Aug	21	Bristol	1	1
EC2010	Oct	8	Norwich	2	1
EC2010	Oct	12	Botosani	0	0
2013	Mar	21	Wycombe	3	0

v RUSSIA			Eng	Rus
1994	May	30	Bandol	2	0

v SAN MARINO				Eng	SM
EC1993	Feb	16	Luton	6	0
EC1993	Nov	17	San Marino	4	0
EC2013	Oct	10	San Marino	4	0
EC2013	Nov	19	Shrewsbury	9	0

v SCOTLAND				Eng	Sco
1977	April	27	Sheffield	1	0
EC1980	Feb	12	Coventry	2	1
EC1980	Mar	4	Aberdeen	0	0
EC1982	April	19	Glasgow	1	0
EC1982	April	28	Manchester	1	1
EC1988	Feb	16	Aberdeen	1	0
EC1988	Mar	22	Nottingham	1	0
1993	June	13	Toulon	1	0
2013	Aug	13	Sheffield	6	0

v SENEGAL				Eng	Sen
1989	June	7	Toulon	6	1
1991	May	27	Toulon	2	1

v SERBIA				Eng	Ser
EC2007	June	17	Nijmegen	2	0
EC2012	Oct	12	Norwich	1	0
EC2012	Oct	16	Krusevac	1	0

v SERBIA-MONTENEGRO				Eng	S-M
2003	June	2	Hull	3	2

v SLOVAKIA				Eng	Slo
EC2002	June	1	Bratislava	0	2
EC2002	Oct	11	Trnava	4	0
EC2003	June	10	Sunderland	2	0
2007	June	5	Norwich	5	0

v SLOVENIA				Eng	Slo
2000	Feb	12	Nova Gorica	1	0
2008	Aug	19	Hull	2	1

v SOUTH AFRICA				Eng	SA
1998	May	16	Toulon	3	1

v SPAIN				Eng	Spa
EC1984	May	17	Seville	1	0
EC1984	May	24	Sheffield	2	0
1987	Feb	18	Burgos	2	1
1992	Sept	8	Burgos	1	0
2001	Feb	27	Birmingham	0	4
2004	Nov	16	Alcala	0	1
2007	Feb	6	Derby	2	2
EC2009	June	18	Gothenburg	2	0
EC2011	June	12	Herning	1	1

v SWEDEN				Eng	Swe
1979	June	9	Vasteras	2	1
1986	Sept	9	Ostersund	1	1
EC1988	Oct	18	Coventry	1	1
EC1989	Sept	5	Uppsala	0	1
EC1998	Sept	4	Sundvall	2	0
EC1999	June	4	Huddersfield	3	0
2004	Mar	30	Kristiansund	2	2
EC2009	June	26	Gothenburg	3	3
2013	Feb	5	Walsall	4	0

v SWITZERLAND				Eng	Swit
EC1980	Nov	18	Ipswich	5	0
EC1981	May	31	Neuenburg	0	0
1988	May	28	Lausanne	1	1
1996	April	1	Swindon	0	0
1998	Mar	24	Brugglifeld	0	2
EC2002	May	17	Zurich	2	1
EC2006	Sept	6	Lucerne	3	2

v TURKEY				Eng	Tur
EC1984	Nov	13	Bursa	0	0
EC1985	Oct	15	Bristol	3	0
EC1987	April	28	Izmir	0	0
EC1987	Oct	13	Sheffield	1	1
EC1991	April	30	Izmir	2	2
1991	Oct	15	Reading	2	0
EC1992	Nov	17	Orient	0	1
EC1993	Mar	30	Izmir	0	0
EC2000	May	29	Bratislava	6	0
EC2003	April	1	Newcastle	1	1
EC2003	Oct	10	Istanbul	0	1

v UKRAINE				Eng	Uk
2004	Aug	17	Middlesbrough	3	1
EC2011	June	15	Herning	0	0

v USA				Eng	USA
1989	June	11	Toulon	0	2
1994	June	2	Toulon	3	0

v USSR				Eng	USSR
1987	June	9	Toulon	0	0
1988	June	7	Toulon	1	0
1990	May	25	Toulon	2	1
1991	May	31	Toulon	2	1

v UZBEKISTAN				Eng	Uzb
2010	Aug	10	Bristol	2	0

v WALES				Eng	Wales
1976	Dec	15	Wolverhampton	0	0
1979	Feb	6	Swansea	1	0
1990	Dec	5	Tranmere	0	0
EC2004	Oct	8	Blackburn	2	0
EC2005	Sept	2	Wrexham	4	0
2008	May	5	Wrexham	2	0
EC2008	Oct	10	Cardiff	3	2
EC2008	Oct	14	Villa Park	2	2
EC2013	Mar	5	Derby	1	0
EC2013	May	19	Swansea	3	1

v YUGOSLAVIA				Eng	Yugo
EC1978	April	19	Novi Sad	1	2
EC1978	May	2	Manchester	1	1
EC1986	Nov	11	Peterborough	1	1
EC1987	Nov	10	Zemun	5	1
EC2000	Mar	29	Barcelona	3	0
2002	Sept	6	Bolton	1	1

ENGLAND C 2013–14

FRIENDLIES

Woking, 19 November 2013
England C (0) 2 *(Franks 85, Norwood 90 (pen))*
Czech Republic U21 (0) 2 *(Krmencik 6, Stratil 45) Janos*
England C: Belshaw (Walker 80); MacDonald, Turley (Parry 57), Franks, Demetriou (Fitzpatrick 71), Marsh-Brown (Lolley 57), Armson, Pearson (Payne 57), Frear, Gray (Fitchett 71), Norwood.

Amman, 4 March 2014
Jordan U23 (0) 0
England C (1) 1 *(Berry 32)*
England C: Coughlin (Lloyd-Weston 73); Macdonald, Holland (Turley 64), Franks, Demetriou, Marsh-Brown (Pearson 59), Berry, Payne (Gallagher 55), Frear, Gray (Fitchett 46), Norwood.

Budapest, 28 May 2014
Hungary (2) 4 *(Bobal 37, Mervo 44, Varga 60, Toth 85)*
England C (0) 2 *(Pearson 52, Taylor 70)*
England C: Coughlin; Macdonald, Fitzpatrick, Roberts, Payne, Franks, Marwood, Gallagher, Taylor; Bradley, Maddison.

INTERNATIONAL CHALLENGE TROPHY GROUP A

Proprad, 24 May 2014
Slovakia U23 (0) 1 *(Vrablec 81)*
England C (0) 0
England C: Walker; Yiadom, Roberts, Franks, Demetriou, Bradley (Marwood 86), Payne, Pearson, (Gallagher 80), Marsh-Brown (Maddison 70), Norwood (Taylor 86), Frear (Fitzpatrick 90).

BRITISH AND IRISH UNDER-21 TEAMS 2013–14

■ *Denotes player sent off.*

ENGLAND

FRIENDLY

Tuesday, 13 August 2013

England (2) 6 *(Redmond 3, Sterling 38, Wickham 50, Barkley 55, Shelvey 56, Carroll 61)*

Scotland (0) 0   26,942

England: (433) Butland; Stones, Wisdom (Thorpe 72), Keane, Robinson; Shelvey (Carroll 58), Chalobah (Barkley 44), Hughes (Dier 72); Redmond (Lingard 65), Wickham (Kane 57), Sterling (Ameobi 65).
Scotland: (442) Archer; Jack (Duffie 46), McHattie, Robertson C, McKay; Fyvie, McGeouch, Bannigan (Macleod 78), Armstrong (Smith 62); Feruz (May 62), Watt (Holt 72).

UEFA UNDER-21 CHAMPIONSHIP QUALIFYING

Thursday, 5 September 2013

England (1) 1 *(Berahino 13)*

Moldova (0) 0   5268

England: (433) Butland; Stones, Keane, Wisdom, Shaw; Carroll, Chalobah, Ward-Prowse (Hughes 66); Zaha, Berahino (Kane 86), Redmond (Ameobi 75).

Monday, 9 September 2013

Finland (1) 1 *(Yaghoubi 15)*

England (0) 1 *(Berahino 67)*   4455

England: (433) Butland; Stones, Wisdom■, Keane, Shaw; Ward-Prowse, Chalobah (Kane 57), Carroll; Redmond (Ameobi 57), Berahino, Zaha (Dier 76).

Thursday, 10 October 2013

San Marino (0) 0

England (2) 4 *(Keane 5, Kane 45 (pen), 66, 89)*   150

England: (4231) Butland; Stones, Dier, Keane, Jenkinson; Carroll, Ward-Prowse; Sterling (Ings 66), Morrison (Lingard 56), Ince (Redmond 72); Kane.

Tuesday, 15 October 2013

England (2) 5 *(Morrison 2, 71, Ward-Prowse 27, Berahino 63, 76 (pen))*

Lithuania (0) 0   17,067

England: (4231) Butland; Stones, Keane, Chalobah, Robinson; Ward-Prowse, Carroll (Jenkinson 16); Zaha, Morrison, Ince (Redmond 76); Berahino (Powell 76).

Thursday, 14 November 2013

England (2) 3 *(Keane 21, Berahino 37, 90)*

Finland (0) 0   19,807

England: (442) Butland; Jenkinson, Shaw, Stones, Keane; Chalobah (Hughes 64), Ward-Prowse, Morrison (Lingard 83), Sterling (Ince 65); Berahino, Zaha.

Tuesday, 19 November 2013

England (5) 9 *(Keane 13, Sterling 15, 59, Ings 18, 48, Ward-Prowse 24, Ince 42, Jenkinson 60, Hughes 78)*

San Marino (0) 0   9264

England: (433) Butland (Bond 46); Jenkinson, Stones (Dier 61), Keane, Robinson; Hughes, Lingard, Ward-Prowse; Ince (Bamford 65), Ings, Sterling.

Wednesday, 5 March 2014

England (0) 1 *(Redmond 56)*

Wales (0) 0   6000

England: (433) Butland; Jenkinson, Stones, Chalobah (Moore 72), Robinson; Carroll, Morrison (Hughes 74), Ward-Prowse; Ince, Berahino (Ings 67), Redmond.
Wales: (451) Roberts; Freeman, Walsh, Tancock, John; Lawrence, Pritchard (Williams 83), O'Sullivan (Evans 66), Lucas, Isgrove; Burns (Ogleby 78).

Monday, 19 May 2014

Wales (1) 1 *(Edwards 20)*

England (2) 3 *(Redmond 18, 38, 90)*   5000

Wales: (451) Roberts; Freeman (Alfei 46), Ray, Walsh, John; Isgrove (Williams 40), Evans, Lucas, Pritchard (O'Sullivan 42), Edwards; Burns.
England: (4231) Butland; Jenkinson, Keane, Moore, Garbutt; Chalobah, Ward-Prowse; Ince (Kane 79 (Forster-Caskey 85)), Lingard, Redmond; Ings (Berahino 56).

NORTHERN IRELAND

FRIENDLY

Wednesday, 14 August 2013

N Ireland (1) 1 *(Thompson 24)*

Denmark (1) 4 *(Jensen P 17, Brock-Madsen 57, 63, Jradi 62)*   343

N Ireland: (442) Brennan; McCullough, Thompson, McKeown, Sendles-White; Carson, Tempest, Millar, Brobbel; Donnelly R, Gray.

UEFA UNDER-21 CHAMPIONSHIP QUALIFYING

Monday, 9 September 2013

Belgium (1) 1 *(Batshuayi 44)*

N Ireland (0) 0   2949

N Ireland: (442) Brennan; Donnelly L■, Sharpe, Thompson, Sendles-White; Millar (Shields 46), Ball (Reid 81), Winchester (McElroy 63), Brobbel; Carson, Gray.

Friday, 11 October 2013

N Ireland (0) 0

Belgium (1) 1 *(Batshuayi 44)*   150

N Ireland: (442) Brennan; Sendles-White, McCullough, McKeown, Winchester; Tempest (Millar 54), Sharpe, Brobbel (McCartan 71), Clucas; Gray, Carson.

Tuesday, 15 October 2013

Serbia (0) 3 *(Morgan 63 (og), Milunovic 64, Vitas 74)*

N Ireland (0) 1 *(Gray 54)*

N Ireland: (433) Brennan; Donnelly L, McKeown, McCullough, Sharpe; Morgan, Brobbel (Conlan 84), Winchester (Tempest 70); Gray, McCartan (Gorman 62), Millar.

Thursday, 14 November 2013

Italy (1) 3 *(Viviani 26, Rozzi 86, Belotti 88)*

N Ireland (0) 0   14,026

N Ireland: (442) Brennan; Thompson, McCullough, Sendles-White, McKeown; Donnelly L, Morgan (Tempest 67 (Brobbel 72)), Winchester, Carson; Millar, Gray (Lavery 79).

Tuesday, 19 November 2013

N Ireland (0) 1 *(Gorman 85)*

Cyprus (0) 0   300

N Ireland: (442) Brennan; Donnelly L, Conlan, McCullough, Sendles-White; Tempest, Winchester, Brobbel, Lavery (McCartan 75); Millar (Gorman 66), Carson (McGeehan 66).

Wednesday, 5 March 2014

N Ireland (0) 0

Italy (0) 2 *(Rugani 59, Trotta 89)*   230

N Ireland: (442) Brennan; Donnelly L, Conlan, McCullough, Sendles-White; Clucas (McNair 77), Winchester, McGeehan (Nolan 62), Brobbel; Millar (Gray 66), Lavery.

SCOTLAND

FRIENDLY

Wednesday, 5 March 2014
Scotland (2) 2 *(McGregor 25, Fraser R 38)*
Hungary (0) 2 *(Rado 68 (pen), 87)* 4537
Scotland: (442) Archer (Kettings 46); Fraser M, Findlay, Kelly (Chalmers 46), McGhee; Armstrong (Stanton 46), Slater (Grimmer 57), McLean (McGinn 58), McGregor; Paterson (Herron 76), Fraser R (Handling 76).

UEFA UNDER-21 CHAMPIONSHIP QUALIFYING

Thursday, 5 September 2013
Netherlands (0) 4 *(Trindade de Vilhena 52, Castaignos 69, van der Hoorn 74, Drost 78)*
Scotland (0) 0 5700
Scotland: (442) Archer; Jack, McGhee, Findlay, Robertson C; Fyvie (Macleod 77), McGeouch, Holt, Watt (May 54); Armstrong, Fraser R (Paterson 77).

Thursday, 10 October 2013
Scotland (2) 2 *(Armstrong 31, May 36)*
Slovakia (0) 1 *(Malec 68)* 2014
Scotland: (4231) Archer; Jack, Robertson C, Findlay, McGhee; Macleod (Holt 82), Fyvie (Robertson A 75); McGregor (Paterson 87), Armstrong, McGeouch; May.

Monday, 14 October 2013
Georgia (1) 2 *(Qazaishvili 39, Jigauri 70)*
Scotland (0) 1 *(Macleod 81)* 2000
Scotland: (451) Archer; Jack, Findlay, McGhee, Robertson C; Holt (Paterson 58), Fyvie (Macleod 72), Armstrong, McGeouch (Robertson A 72), McGregor; May.

Thursday, 14 November 2013
Scotland (0) 1 *(Paterson 84)*
Georgia (1) 1 *(Chanturia 35)* 1737
Scotland: (433) Archer; Jack, McGhee, Findlay, Robertson A; Macleod, Armstrong, Gauld; McGeouch (McLean 56), May, McGregor (Paterson 69).

Wednesday, 28 May 2014
Scotland (0) 1 *(May 85)*
Netherlands (3) 6 *(Promes 26, 40, 42, Rekik 50, Ziyech 76, 79)* 3002
Scotland: (433) Archer; Paterson, McGhee, Findlay, McHattie; McGinn (Slater 87), McLean, Armstrong; Fraser R (Scougall 75), May, McGregor (McKenzie 60).

WALES

UEFA UNDER-21 CHAMPIONSHIP QUALIFYING

Wednesday, 14 August 2013
Wales (0) 1 *(Huws 47 (pen))*
Finland (4) 5 *(Kastrati 7, Vayrynen 11, 30, 58, Yaghoubi 39)* 2000
Wales: (442) Ward; Walsh, Tancock, Hewitt, Freeman; Lucas, Bodin (Burns 46), Huws, Lawrence (Dawson 68); Isgrove, Cassidy.

Friday, 6 September 2013
San Marino (1) 1 *(Biordi 21)*
Wales (0) 0 221
Wales: (442) Ward; Freeman, Fox, Evans, Tancock; Walsh, Burns (Bodin 83), Huws (Ogleby 65), Cassidy (Bradshaw 56); Lawrence, Isgrove.

Tuesday, 10 September 2013
Moldova (0) 0
Wales (0) 0 523
Wales: (442) Roberts; Hewitt, Ray, Walsh, Fox; Lucas, Huws, Lawrence, Isgrove; Ogleby (Bradshaw 80), Burns (Bodin 73).

Friday, 11 October 2013
Wales (2) 2 *(Lawrence 22 (pen), 40 (pen))*
Lithuania (0) 0 403
Wales: (442) Roberts; Freeman, Ray, Walsh, Fox; Lucas, Bodin, Lawrence, Pritchard; Burns, Harrison (Edwards 79).

Tuesday, 15 October 2013
Wales (4) 4 *(Harrison 44, Lucas 50, Burns 64, Bodin 84)*
San Marino (0) 0 278
Wales: (442) Roberts; Hewitt, Ray, Tancock, Fox; Bodin, O'Sullivan (Ogleby 79), Lucas, Lawrence; Harrison (Edwards 73), Burns (Evans 79).

REPUBLIC OF IRELAND

UEFA UNDER-21 CHAMPIONSHIP QUALIFYING

Wednesday, 14 August 2013
Faroe Islands (1) 1 *(Sorensen 14)*
Rep of Ireland (1) 4 *(Carruthers 23, O'Brien 68, 90, Doherty 88)* 349
Rep of Ireland: (451) McCarey; Shaughnessy, McGinty, O'Connor, Duffy; Doherty, Harriman (Grealish 90), Carruthers, Murray (Sutherland 90), Reilly; O'Brien.

Monday, 9 September 2013
Rep of Ireland (0) 0
Germany (3) 4 *(Leitner 12, Volland 22, 24, Hofmann 83)* 1936
Rep of Ireland: (451) McCarey; Harriman, Duffy, O'Connor, McGinty; Murray, Carruthers[1], Reilly (Grealish 78), Doherty, Forde (Smith 46); O'Brien (Burke 82).

Friday, 11 October 2013
Romania (0) 0
Rep of Ireland (0) 0 998
Rep of Ireland: (451) McCarey; O'Connor, Williams, Duffy, McGinty; Smith (Sutherland 77), Doherty, Murray, Reilly, Forde; O'Brien.

Tuesday, 15 October 2013
Rep of Ireland (0) 0
Romania (0) 1 *(Madalin 54)* 2000
Rep of Ireland: (433) McCarey; O'Connor, Duffy, Williams, McGinty; Carruthers, Murray, Sutherland (Hayhurst 70); Smith (Reilly 78), O'Brien (Burke 68), Forde.

Friday, 15 November 2013
Rep of Ireland (5) 5 *(Carruthers 17, O'Brien 20, 42, Grealish 25, Forde 39)*
Faroe Islands (2) 2 *(Zachariasen 26, 37 (pen))* 320
Rep of Ireland: (442) McDermott; O'Connor, Duffy, Williams (Dunne 63), McGinty; Carruthers, Reilly, Grealish, Forde; O'Brien (Hayhurst 82), Murray (O'Sullivan 74).

Tuesday, 19 November 2013
Montenegro (0) 0
Rep of Ireland (0) 0 1000
Rep of Ireland: (4321) McDermott; Harriman, Williams, Duffy, McGinty; Carruthers, Reilly, Grealish; Murray, Forde; O'Brien.

Wednesday, 5 March 2014
Rep of Ireland (1) 1 *(Doherty 11)*
Montenegro (0) 2 *(Djordjevic 75, Mugosa 77)* 1304
Rep of Ireland: (433) McDermott; Doherty, Egan, Duffy, McGinty[1]; Smith, Hendrick, Murray (McAlinden 78); Grealish, O'Brien (Drennan 78), Forde (McEvoy 82).

BRITISH UNDER-21 APPEARANCES 1976–2014

Bold type indicates players who made an international appearance in season 2013–14 (includes 2014 Toulon Tournament).

ENGLAND

Ablett, G. 1988 (Liverpool)	1	Bridges, M. 1997 (Sunderland, Leeds U)	3
Adams, N. 1987 (Everton)	1	Briggs, M. 2012 (Fulham)	2
Adams, T. A. 1985 (Arsenal)	5	Brightwell, I. 1989 (Manchester C)	4
Addison, M. 2010 (Derby Co)	1	Briscoe, L. S. 1996 (Sheffield W)	5
Afobe, B. T. 2012 (Arsenal)	2	Brock, K. 1984 (Oxford U)	4
Agbonlahor, G. 2007 (Aston Villa)	16	Broomes, M. C. 1997 (Blackburn R)	2
Albrighton, M. K. 2011 (Aston Villa)	8	Brown, M. R. 1996 (Manchester C)	4
Allen, B. 1992 (QPR)	8	Brown, W. M. 1999 (Manchester U)	8
Allen, C. 1980 (QPR, Crystal Palace)	3	**Browning, T. (Everton)**	**5**
Allen, C. A. 1995 (Oxford U)	2	Bull, S. G. 1989 (Wolverhampton W)	5
Allen, M. 1987 (QPR)	2	Bullock, M. J. 1998 (Barnsley)	1
Allen, P. 1985 (West Ham U, Tottenham H)	3	Burrows, D. 1989 (WBA, Liverpool)	7
Allen, R. W. 1998 (Tottenham H)	3	Butcher, T. I. 1979 (Ipswich T)	7
Alnwick, B. R. 2008 (Tottenham H)	1	**Butland, J. 2012 (Birmingham C, Stoke C)**	**23**
Ambrose, D. P. F. 2003 (Ipswich T, Newcastle U,		Butt, N. 1995 (Manchester U)	7
Charlton Ath)	10	Butters, G. 1989 (Tottenham H)	3
Ameobi, S. 2012 (Newcastle U)	**5**	Butterworth, I. 1985 (Coventry C, Nottingham F)	8
Amos, B. P. 2012 (Manchester U)	3	Bywater, S. 2001 (West Ham U)	6
Anderson, V. A. 1978 (Nottingham F)	1		
Anderton, D. R. 1993 (Tottenham H)	12	Cadamarteri, D. L. 1999 (Everton)	3
Andrews, I. 1987 (Leicester C)	1	Caesar, G. 1987 (Arsenal)	3
Ardley, N. C. 1993 (Wimbledon)	10	Cahill, G. J. 2007 (Aston Villa)	3
Ashcroft, L. 1992 (Preston NE)	1	Callaghan, N. 1983 (Watford)	9
Ashton, D. 2004 (Crewe Alex, Norwich C)	9	Camp, L. M. J. 2005 (Derby Co)	5
Atherton, P. 1992 (Coventry C)	1	Campbell, A. P. 2000 (Middlesbrough)	4
Atkinson, B. 1991 (Sunderland)	6	Campbell, F. L. 2008 (Manchester U)	14
Awford, A. T. 1993 (Portsmouth)	9	Campbell, K. J. 1991 (Arsenal)	4
		Campbell, S. 1994 (Tottenham)	11
Bailey, G. R. 1979 (Manchester U)	14	Carbon, M. P. 1996 (Derby Co)	4
Baines, L. J. 2005 (Wigan Ath)	16	Carr, C. 1985 (Fulham)	1
Baker, G. E. 1981 (Southampton)	2	Carr, F. 1987 (Nottingham F)	9
Baker, N. L. 2011 (Aston Villa)	3	Carragher, J. L. 1997 (Liverpool)	27
Ball, M. J. 1999 (Everton)	7	Carroll, A. T. 2010 (Newcastle U)	5
Bamford, P. J. 2013 (Chelsea)	**1**	**Carroll, T. J. 2013 (Tottenham H)**	**7**
Bannister, G. 1982 (Sheffield W)	1	Carlisle, C. J. 2001 (QPR)	3
Barker, S. 1985 (Blackburn R)	4	Carrick, M. 2001 (West Ham U)	14
Barkley, R. 2012 (Everton)	**5**	Carson, S. P. 2004 (Leeds U, Liverpool)	29
Barmby, N. J. 1994 (Tottenham H, Everton)	4	Casper, C. M. 1995 (Manchester U)	1
Barnes, J. 1983 (Watford)	2	Caton, T. 1982 (Manchester C)	14
Barnes, P. S. 1977 (Manchester C)	9	Cattermole, L. B. 2008 (Middlesbrough, Wigan Ath,	
Barrett, E. D. 1990 (Oldham Ath)	4	Sunderland)	16
Barry, G. 1999 (Aston Villa)	27	Caulker, S. R. 2011 (Tottenham H)	10
Barton, J. 2004 (Manchester C)	2	Chadwick, L. H. 2000 (Manchester U)	13
Bart-Williams, C. G. 1993 (Sheffield W)	16	Challis, T. M. 1996 (QPR)	2
Batty, D. 1988 (Leeds U)	7	**Chalobah, N. N. 2012 (Chelsea)**	**18**
Bazeley, D. S. 1992 (Watford)	1	Chamberlain, M. 1983 (Stoke C)	4
Beagrie, P. 1988 (Sheffield U)	2	Chaplow, R. D. 2004 (Burnley)	1
Beardsmore, R. 1989 (Manchester U)	5	Chapman, L. 1981 (Stoke C)	1
Beattie, J. S. 1999 (Southampton)	5	Charles, G. A. 1991 (Nottingham F)	4
Beckham, D. R. J. 1995 (Manchester U)	9	Chettle, S. 1988 (Nottingham F)	12
Berahino, S. 2013 (WBA)	**9**	Chopra, R. M. 2004 (Newcastle U)	1
Bennett, J. 2011 (Middlesbrough)	3	Clark, L. R. 1992 (Newcastle U)	11
Bennett, R. 2012 (Norwich C)	2	Clarke, P. M. 2003 (Everton)	8
Bent, D. A. 2003 (Ipswich T, Charlton Ath)	14	Christie, M. N. 2001 (Derby Co)	11
Bent, M. N. 1994 (Crystal Palace)	2	Clegg, M. J. 1998 (Manchester U)	2
Bentley, D. M. 2004 (Arsenal, Blackburn R)	8	Clemence, S. N. 1999 (Tottenham H)	1
Beeston, C 1988 (Stoke C)	1	Cleverley, T. W. 2010 (Manchester U)	16
Benjamin, T. J. 2001 (Leicester C)	1	Clough, N. H. 1986 (Nottingham F)	15
Bertrand, R. 2009 (Chelsea)	16	Clyne, N. E. 2012 (Crystal Palace)	8
Bertschin, K. E. 1977 (Birmingham C)	3	Cole, A. 2001 (Arsenal)	4
Birtles, G. 1980 (Nottingham F)	2	Cole, A. A. 1992 (Arsenal, Bristol C, Newcastle U)	8
Blackstock, D. A. 2008 (QPR)	2	Cole, C. 2003 (Chelsea)	19
Blackwell, D. R. 1991 (Wimbledon)	6	Cole, J. J. 2000 (West Ham U)	8
Blake, M. A. 1990 (Aston Villa)	8	Coney, D. 1985 (Fulham)	4
Blissett, L. L. 1979 (Watford)	4	Connor, T. 1987 (Brighton & HA)	1
Bond, J. H. 2013 (Watford)	**3**	Cooke, R. 1986 (Tottenham H)	1
Booth, A. D. 1995 (Huddersfield T)	3	Cooke, T. J. 1996 (Manchester U)	4
Bothroyd, J. 2001 (Coventry C)	1	Cooper, C. T. 1988 (Middlesbrough)	8
Bowyer, L. D. 1996 (Charlton Ath, Leeds U)	13	Cork, J. F. P. 2009 (Chelsea)	13
Bracewell, P. 1983 (Stoke C)	13	Corrigan, T. J. 1978 (Manchester C)	3
Bradbury, L. M. 1997 (Portsmouth, Manchester C)	3	Cort, C. E. R. 1999 (Wimbledon)	12
Bramble, T. M. 2001 (Ipswich T, Newcastle U)	10	Cottee, A. R. 1985 (West Ham U)	8
Branch, P. M. 1997 (Everton)	4	**Cousins, J. P. (Charlton Ath)**	**3**
Bradshaw, P. W. 1977 (Wolverhampton W)	4	Couzens, A. J. 1995 (Leeds U)	3
Breacker, T. 1986 (Luton T)	2	Cowans, G. S. 1979 (Aston Villa)	5
Brennan, M. 1987 (Ipswich T)	5	Cox, N. J. 1993 (Aston Villa)	6
Bridge, W. M. 1999 (Southampton)	8	Cranie, M. J. 2008 (Portsmouth)	16
		Cranson, I. 1985 (Ipswich T)	5

Cresswell, R. P. W. 1999 (York C, Sheffield W)   4
Croft, G. 1995 (Grimsby T)   4
Crooks, G. 1980 (Stoke C)   4
Crossley, M. G. 1990 (Nottingham F)   3
Crouch, P. J. 2002 (Portsmouth, Aston Villa)   5
Cundy, J. V. 1991 (Chelsea)   3
Cunningham, L. 1977 (WBA)   6
Curbishley, L. C. 1981 (Birmingham C)   1
Curtis, J. C. K. 1998 (Manchester U)   16

Daniel, P. W. 1977 (Hull C)   7
Dann, S. 2008 (Coventry C)   2
Davenport, C. R. P. 2005 (Tottenham H)   8
Davies, A. J. 2004 (Middlesbrough)   1
Davies, C. E. 2006 (WBA)   3
Davies, K. C. 1998 (Southampton, Blackburn R, Southampton)   3
Davis, K. G. 1995 (Luton T)   3
Davis, P. 1982 (Arsenal)   11
Davis, S. 2001 (Fulham)   11
Dawson, C. 2012 (WBA)   15
Dawson, M. R. 2003 (Nottingham F, Tottenham H)   13
Day, C. N. 1996 (Tottenham H, Crystal Palace)   6
D'Avray, M. 1984 (Ipswich T)   2
Deehan, J. M. 1977 (Aston Villa)   7
Defoe, J. C. 2001 (West Ham U)   23
Delfouneso, N. 2010 (Aston Villa)   17
Delph, F. 2009 (Leeds U, Aston Villa)   8
Dennis, M. E. 1980 (Birmingham C)   3
Derbyshire, M. A. 2007 (Blackburn R)   14
Dichio, D. S. E. 1996 (QPR)   1
Dickens, A. 1985 (West Ham U)   1
Dicks, J. 1988 (West Ham U)   4
Dier, E. J. E. 2013 (Sporting Lisbon)   **7**
Digby, F. 1987 (Swindon T)   5
Dillon, K. P. 1981 (Birmingham C)   1
Dixon, K. M. 1985 (Chelsea)   1
Dobson, A. 1989 (Coventry C)   4
Dodd, J. R. 1991 (Southampton)   8
Donowa, L. 1985 (Norwich C)   3
Dorigo, A. R. 1987 (Aston Villa)   11
Downing, S. 2004 (Middlesbrough)   8
Dozzell, J. 1987 (Ipswich T)   9
Draper, M. A. 1991 (Notts Co)   3
Driver, A. 2009 (Hearts)   1
Duberry, M. W. 1997 (Chelsea)   5
Dunn, D. J. I. 1999 (Blackburn R)   20
Duxbury, M. 1981 (Manchester U)   7
Dyer, B. A. 1994 (Crystal Palace)   10
Dyer, C. 1998 (Ipswich T, Newcastle U)   11
Dyson, P. I. 1981 (Coventry C)   4

Eadie, D. M. 1994 (Norwich C)   7
Ebanks-Blake, S. 2009 (Wolverhampton W)   1
Ebbrell, J. 1989 (Everton)   14
Edghill, R. A. 1994 (Manchester C)   3
Ehiogu, U. 1992 (Aston Villa)   15
Elliott, P. 1985 (Luton T)   3
Elliott, R. J. 1996 (Newcastle U)   2
Elliott, S. W. 1998 (Derby Co)   3
Etherington, N, 2002 (Tottenham H)   3
Euell, J. J. 1998 (Wimbledon)   6
Evans, R. 2003 (Chelsea)   2

Fairclough, C. 1985 (Nottingham F, Tottenham H)   7
Fairclough, D. 1977 (Liverpool)   1
Fashanu, J. 1980 (Norwich C, Nottingham F)   11
Fear, P. 1994 (Wimbledon)   3
Fenton, G. A. 1995 (Aston Villa)   1
Fenwick, T. W. 1981 (Crystal Palace, QPR)   11
Ferdinand, A. 2005 (West Ham U)   17
Ferdinand, R. G. 1997 (West Ham U)   5
Fereday, W. 1985 (QPR)   5
Fielding, F. D. 2009 (Blackburn R)   12
Flanagan, J. 2012 (Liverpool)   3
Flitcroft, G. W. 1993 (Manchester C)   10
Flowers, T. D. 1987 (Southampton)   3
Ford, M. 1996 (Leeds U)   2
Forster, N. M. 1995 (Brentford)   4
Forsyth, M. 1988 (Derby Co)   1
Forster-Caskey, J. D. 2014 (Brighton & HA)   **6**
Foster, S. 1980 (Brighton & HA)   1
Fowler, R. B. 1994 (Liverpool)   8
Fox, D. J. 2008 (Coventry C)   1
Froggatt, S. J. 1993 (Aston Villa)   2
Futcher, P. 1977 (Luton T, Manchester C)   11

Gabbiadini, M. 1989 (Sunderland)   2
Gale, A. 1982 (Fulham)   1
Gallen, K. A. 1995 (QPR)   4
Garbutt, L. S. 2014 (Everton)   **5**
Gardner, A. 2002 (Tottenham H)   1
Gardner, C. 2008 (Aston Villa)   14
Gardner, G. 2012 (Aston Villa)   5
Gascoigne, P. J. 1987 (Newcastle U)   13
Gayle, H. 1984 (Birmingham C)   3
Gernon, T. 1983 (Ipswich T)   1
Gerrard, P. W. 1993 (Oldham Ath)   18
Gerrard, S. G. 2000 (Liverpool)   4
Gibbs, K. J. R. 2009 (Arsenal)   15
Gibbs, N. 1987 (Watford)   5
Gibson, B. J. (Middlesbrough)   **4**
Gibson, C. 1982 (Aston Villa)   1
Gilbert, W. A. 1979 (Crystal Palace)   11
Goddard, P. 1981 (West Ham U)   8
Gordon, D. 1987 (Norwich C)   4
Gordon, D. D. 1994 (Crystal Palace)   13
Gosling, D. 2010 (Everton, Newcastle U)   3
Grant, A. J. 1996 (Everton)   1
Grant, L. A. 2003 (Derby Co)   4
Granville, D. P. 1997 (Chelsea)   3
Gray, A. 1988 (Aston Villa)   2
Greening, J. 1999 (Manchester U, Middlesbrough)   18
Griffin, A. 1999 (Newcastle U)   3
Guppy, S. A. 1998 (Leicester C)   1

Haigh, P. 1977 (Hull C)   1
Hall, M. T. J. 1997 (Coventry C)   8
Hall, R. A. 1992 (Southampton)   11
Hamilton, D. V. 1997 (Newcastle U)   1
Hammill, A. 2010 (Wolverhampton W)   1
Harding, D. A. 2005 (Brighton & HA)   4
Hardyman, P. 1985 (Portsmouth)   2
Hargreaves, O. 2001 (Bayern Munich)   3
Harley, J. 2000 (Chelsea)   3
Hart, C. 2007 (Manchester C)   21
Hateley, M. 1982 (Coventry C, Portsmouth)   10
Hayes, M. 1987 (Arsenal)   3
Hazell, R. J. 1979 (Wolverhampton W)   1
Heaney, N. A. 1992 (Arsenal)   6
Heath, A. 1981 (Stoke C, Everton)   8
Heaton, T. D. 2008 (Manchester U)   3
Henderson, J. B. 2011 (Sunderland, Liverpool)   27
Hendon, I. M. 1992 (Tottenham H)   7
Hendrie, L. A. 1996 (Aston Villa)   13
Hesford, I. 1981 (Blackpool)   7
Heskey, E. W. I. 1997 (Leicester C, Liverpool)   16
Hilaire, V. 1980 (Crystal Palace)   9
Hill, D. R. L. 1995 (Tottenham H)   4
Hillier, D. 1991 (Arsenal)   1
Hinchcliffe, A. 1989 (Manchester C)   1
Hines, Z. 2010 (West Ham U)   2
Hinshelwood, P. A. 1978 (Crystal Palace)   2
Hirst, D. E. 1988 (Sheffield W)   7
Hislop, N. S. 1998 (Newcastle U)   1
Hoddle, G. 1977 (Tottenham H)   12
Hodge, S. B. 1983 (Nottingham F, Aston Villa)   8
Hodgson, D. J. 1981 (Middlesbrough)   6
Holdsworth, D. 1989 (Watford)   1
Holland, C. J. 1995 (Newcastle U)   10
Holland, P. 1995 (Mansfield T)   4
Holloway, D. 1998 (Sunderland)   1
Horne, B. 1989 (Millwall)   5
Howe, E. J. F. 1998 (Bournemouth)   2
Howson, J. M. 2011 (Leeds U)   1
Hoyte, J. R. 2004 (Arsenal)   18
Hucker, P. 1984 (QPR)   2
Huckerby, D. 1997 (Coventry C)   4
Huddlestone, T. A. 2005 (Derby Co, Tottenham H)   33
Hughes, S. J. 1997 (Arsenal)   8
Hughes, W. J. 2012 (Derby Co)   **7**
Humphreys, R. J. 1997 (Sheffield W)   3
Hunt, N. B. 2004 (Bolton W)   10

Impey, A. R. 1993 (QPR)   1
Ince, P. E. C. 1989 (West Ham U)   2
Ince, T. C. 2012 (Blackpool)   **14**
Ings, D. W. J. 2013 (Burnley)   **4**

Jackson, M. A. 1992 (Everton)   10
Jagielka, P. N. 2003 (Sheffield U)   6
James, D. B. 1991 (Watford)   10

James, J. C. 1990 (Luton T) 2
Jansen, M. B. 1999 (Crystal Palace, Blackburn R) 6
Jeffers, F. 2000 (Everton, Arsenal) 16
Jemson, N. B. 1991 (Nottingham F) 1
Jenas, J. A. 2002 (Newcastle U) 9
Jenkinson, C. D. 2013 (Arsenal) **6**
Jerome, C. 2006 (Cardiff C, Birmingham C) 10
Joachim, J. K. 1994 (Leicester C) 9
Johnson, A. 2008 (Middlesbrough) 19
Johnson, G. M. C. 2003 (West Ham U, Chelsea) 14
Johnson, M. 2008 (Manchester C) 2
Johnson, S. A. M. 1999 (Crewe Alex, Derby Co,
  Leeds U) 15
Johnson, T. 1991 (Notts Co, Derby Co) 7
Johnston, C. P. 1981 (Middlesbrough) 2
Jones, D. R. 1977 (Everton) 1
Jones, C. H. 1978 (Tottenham H) 1
Jones, D. F. L. 2004 (Manchester U) 1
Jones, P. A. 2011 (Blackburn R) 9
Jones, R. 1993 (Liverpool) 2

Kane, H. E. 2013 (Tottenham H) **5**
Keane, M. V. 2013 (Manchester U) **12**
Keane, W. D. 2012 (Manchester U) **6**
Keegan, G. A. 1977 (Manchester C) 1
Kelly, M. R. 2011 (Liverpool) 8
Kenny, W. 1993 (Everton) 1
Keown, M. R. 1987 (Aston Villa) 8
Kerslake, D. 1986 (QPR) 1
Kightly, M. J. 2008 (Wolverhampton W) 7
Kilcline, B. 1983 (Notts C) 2
Kilgallon, M. 2004 (Leeds U) 5
King, A. E. 1977 (Everton) 2
King, L. B. 2000 (Tottenham H) 12
Kirkland, C. E. 2001 (Coventry C, Liverpool) 8
Kitson, P. 1991 (Leicester C, Derby Co) 7
Knight, A. 1983 (Portsmouth) 2
Knight, I. 1987 (Sheffield W) 2
Knight, Z. 2002 (Fulham) 4
Konchesky, P. M. 2002 (Charlton Ath) 15
Kozluk, R. 1998 (Derby Co) 2

Lake, P. 1989 (Manchester C) 5
Lallana, A. D. 2009 (Southampton) 1
Lampard, F. J. 1998 (West Ham U) 19
Langley, T. W. 1978 (Chelsea) 1
Lansbury, H. G. 2010 (Arsenal, Nottingham F) 16
Leadbitter, G. 2008 (Sunderland) 3
Lee, D. J. 1990 (Chelsea) 10
Lee, R. M. 1986 (Charlton Ath) 2
Lee, S. 1981 (Liverpool) 6
Lees, T. J. 2012 (Leeds U) 6
Lennon, A. J. 2006 (Tottenham H) 5
Le Saux, G. P. 1990 (Chelsea) 4
Lescott, J. P. 2003 (Wolverhampton W) 2
Lewis, J. P. 2008 (Peterborough U) 5
Lingard, J. E. 2013 (Manchester U) **5**
Lita, L. H. 2005 (Bristol C, Reading) 9
Loach, S. J. 2009 (Watford) 14
Lowe, D. 1988 (Ipswich T) 2
Lowe, J. J. 2012 (Blackburn R) 11
Lukic, J. 1981 (Leeds U) 7
Lund, G. 1985 (Grimsby T) 3

McCall, S. H. 1981 (Ipswich T) 6
McCarthy, A. S. 2011 (Reading) 3
McDonald, N. 1987 (Newcastle U) 5
McEachran, J. M. 2011 (Chelsea) **15**
McEveley, J. 2003 (Blackburn R) 1
McGrath, L. 1986 (Coventry C) 1
MacKenzie, S. 1982 (WBA) 3
McLeary, A. 1988 (Millwall) 1
McLeod, I. M. 2006 (Milton Keynes D) 1
McMahon, S. 1981 (Everton, Aston Villa) 6
McManaman, S. 1991 (Liverpool) 7
Mabbutt, G. 1982 (Bristol R, Tottenham H) 7
Maguire, J. H. 2012 (Sheffield U) 1
Makin, C. 1994 (Oldham Ath) 5
Mancienne, M. I. 2008 (Chelsea) 30
March, S. B. (Brighton & HA) **4**
Marney, D. E. 2005 (Tottenham H) 1
Marriott, A. 1992 (Nottingham F) 1
Marsh, S. T. 1998 (Oxford U) 1
Marshall, A. J. 1995 (Norwich C) 4
Marshall, B. 2012 (Leicester C) 2
Marshall, L. K. 1999 (Norwich C) 1

Martin, L. 1989 (Manchester U) 2
Martyn, A. N. 1988 (Bristol R) 11
Matteo, D. 1994 (Liverpool) 4
Mattock, J. W. 2008 (Leicester C) 5
Matthew, D. 1990 (Chelsea) 9
May, A. 1986 (Manchester C) 1
Mee, B. 2011 (Manchester C) 2
Merson, P. C. 1989 (Arsenal) 4
Middleton, J. 1977 (Nottingham F, Derby Co) 3
Miller, A. 1988 (Arsenal) 4
Mills, D. J. 1999 (Charlton Ath, Leeds U) 14
Mills, G. R. 1981 (Nottingham F) 2
Milner, J. P. 2004 (Leeds U, Newcastle U, Aston Villa) 46
Mimms, R. 1985 (Rotherham U, Everton) 3
Minto, S. C. 1991 (Charlton Ath) 6
Moore, I. 1996 (Tranmere R, Nottingham F) 7
Moore, L. 2012 (Leicester C) **7**
Moore, L. I. 2006 (Aston Villa) 5
Moran, S. 1982 (Southampton) 2
Morgan, S. 1987 (Leicester C) 2
Morris, J. 1997 (Chelsea) 7
Morrison, R. R. 2013 (West Ham U) **4**
Mortimer, P. 1989 (Charlton Ath) 2
Moses, A. P. 1997 (Barnsley) 2
Moses, R. M. 1981 (WBA, Manchester U) 8
Moses, V. 2011 (Wigan Ath) 1
Mountfield, D. 1984 (Everton) 1
Muamba, F. N. 2008 (Birmingham C, Bolton W) 33
Muggleton, C. D. 1990 (Leicester C) 1
Mullins, H. I. 1999 (Crystal Palace) 3
Murphy, D. B. 1998 (Liverpool) 4
Murray, P. 1997 (QPR) 4
Murray, M. W. 2003 (Wolverhampton W) 5
Mutch, A. 1989 (Wolverhampton W) 1
Mutch, J. J. E. S. 2011 (Birmingham C) 1
Myers. A. 1995 (Chelsea) 4

Naughton, K. 2009 (Sheffield U, Tottenham H) 9
Naylor, L. M. 2000 (Wolverhampton W) 3
Nethercott, S. H. 1994 (Tottenham H) 8
Neville, P. J. 1995 (Manchester U) 7
Newell, M. 1986 (Luton T) 4
Newton, A. L. 2001 (West Ham U) 1
Newton, E. J. I. 1993 (Chelsea) 2
Newton, S. O. 1997 (Charlton Ath) 3
Nicholls, A. 1994 (Plymouth Arg) 1
Noble, M. J. 2007 (West Ham U) 20
Nolan, K. A. J. 2003 (Bolton W) 1
Nugent, D. J. 2006 (Preston NE) 14

Oakes, M. C. 1994 (Aston Villa) 6
Oakes, S. J. 1993 (Luton T) 1
Oakley, M. 1997 (Southampton) 4
Obita, J. J. (Reading) **2**
O'Brien, A. J. 1999 (Bradford C) 1
O'Connor, J. 1996 (Everton) 3
O'Hara, J. D. 2008 (Tottenham H) 7
Oldfield, D. 1989 (Luton T) 1
Olney, I. A. 1990 (Aston Villa) 10
O'Neil, G. P. 2005 (Portsmouth) 9
Onuoha, C. 2006 (Manchester C) 21
Ord, R. J. 1991 (Sunderland) 3
Osman, R. C. 1979 (Ipswich T) 7
Owen, G. A. 1977 (Manchester C, WBA) 22
Owen, M. J. 1998 (Liverpool) 1
Oxlade-Chamberlain, A. M. D. 2011 (Southampton,
  Arsenal) 8

Painter, I. 1986 (Stoke C) 1
Palmer, C. L. 1989 (Sheffield W) 4
Parker, G. 1986 (Hull C, Nottingham F) 6
Parker, P. A. 1985 (Fulham) 8
Parker, S. M. 2001 (Charlton Ath) 12
Parkes, P. B. F. 1979 (QPR) 1
Parkin, S. 1987 (Stoke C) 5
Parlour, R. 1992 (Arsenal) 12
Parnaby, S. 2003 (Middlesbrough) 4
Peach, D. S. 1977 (Southampton) 6
Peake, A. 1982 (Leicester C) 1
Pearce, I. A. 1995 (Blackburn R) 3
Pearce, S. 1987 (Nottingham F) 1
Pennant, J. 2001 (Arsenal) 24
Pickering N. 1983 (Sunderland, Coventry C) 15
Platt, D. 1988 (Aston Villa) 3
Plummer, C. S. 1996 (QPR) 5
Pollock, J. 1995 (Middlesbrough) 3

Porter, G. 1987 (Watford)	12
Potter, G. S. 1997 (Southampton)	1
Powell, N. E. 2012 (Manchester U)	**2**
Pressman, K. 1989 (Sheffield W)	1
Proctor, M. 1981 (Middlesbrough, Nottingham F)	4
Prutton, D. T. 2001 (Nottingham F, Southampton)	25
Purse, D. J. 1998 (Birmingham C)	2
Quashie, N. F. 1997 (QPR)	4
Quinn, W. R. 1998 (Sheffield U)	2
Ramage, C. D. 1991 (Derby Co)	3
Ranson, R. 1980 (Manchester C)	10
Redknapp, J. F. 1993 (Liverpool)	19
Redmond, N. D. J. 2013 (Birmingham C, Norwich C)	**14**
Redmond, S. 1988 (Manchester C)	14
Reeves, K. P. 1978 (Norwich C, Manchester C)	10
Regis, C. 1979 (WBA)	6
Reid, N. S. 1981 (Manchester C)	6
Reid, P. 1977 (Bolton W)	6
Reo-Coker, N. S. A. 2004 (Wimbledon, West Ham U)	23
Richards, D. I. 1995 (Wolverhampton W)	4
Richards, J. P. 1977 (Wolverhampton W)	2
Richards, M. 2007 (Manchester C)	15
Richards, M. L. 2005 (Ipswich T)	1
Richardson, K. E. 2005 (Manchester U)	12
Rideout, P. 1985 (Aston Villa, Bari)	5
Ridgewell, L. M. 2004 (Aston Villa)	8
Riggott, C. M. 2001 (Derby Co)	8
Ripley, S. E. 1988 (Middlesbrough)	8
Ritchie, A. 1982 (Brighton & HA)	1
Rix, G. 1978 (Arsenal)	7
Roberts, A. J. 1995 (Millwall, Crystal Palace)	5
Roberts, B. J. 1997 (Middlesbrough)	1
Robins, M. G. 1990 (Manchester U)	6
Robinson, J. 2012 (Liverpool)	**9**
Robinson, P. P. 1999 (Watford)	3
Robinson, P. W. 2000 (Leeds U)	11
Robson, B. 1979 (WBA)	7
Robson, S. 1984 (Arsenal, West Ham U)	8
Rocastle, D. 1987 (Arsenal)	14
Roche, L. P. 2001 (Manchester U)	1
Rodger, G. 1987 (Coventry C)	1
Rodriguez, J. E. 2011 (Burnley)	1
Rodwell, J. 2009 (Everton)	21
Rogers, A. 1998 (Nottingham F)	3
Rosario, R. 1987 (Norwich C)	4
Rose, D. L. 2009 (Tottenham H)	29
Rose, M. 1997 (Arsenal)	2
Rosenior, L. J. 2005 (Fulham)	9
Routledge, W. 2005 (Crystal Palace, Tottenham H)	12
Rowell, G. 1977 (Sunderland)	1
Rudd, D. T. 2013 (Norwich C)	1
Ruddock, N. 1989 (Southampton)	4
Rufus, R. R. 1996 (Charlton Ath)	6
Ryan, J. 1983 (Oldham Ath)	1
Ryder, S. H. 1995 (Walsall)	3
Samuel, J. 2002 (Aston Villa)	7
Samways, V. 1988 (Tottenham H)	5
Sansom, K. G. 1979 (Crystal Palace)	8
Scimeca, R. 1996 (Aston Villa)	9
Scowcroft, J. B. 1997 (Ipswich T)	5
Seaman, D. A. 1985 (Birmingham C)	10
Sears, F. D. 2010 (West Ham U)	3
Sedgley, S. 1987 (Coventry C, Tottenham H)	11
Sellars, S. 1988 (Blackburn R)	3
Selley, I. 1994 (Arsenal)	3
Serrant, C. 1998 (Oldham Ath)	2
Sharpe, L. S. 1989 (Manchester U)	8
Shaw, L. P. H. 2013 (Southampton)	**3**
Shaw, G. R. 1981 (Aston Villa)	7
Shawcross, R. J. 2008 (Stoke C)	2
Shearer, A. 1991 (Southampton)	11
Shelton, G. 1985 (Sheffield W)	1
Shelvey, J. 2012 (Liverpool, Swansea C)	**13**
Sheringham, E. P. 1988 (Millwall)	1
Sheron, M. N. 1992 (Manchester C)	16
Sherwood, T. A. 1990 (Norwich C)	4
Shipperley, N. J. 1994 (Chelsea, Southampton)	7
Sidwell, S. J. 2003 (Reading)	5
Simonsen, S. P. A. 1998 (Tranmere R, Everton)	4
Simpson, P. 1986 (Manchester C)	5
Sims, S. 1977 (Leicester C)	10
Sinclair, S. A. 2011 (Swansea C)	7
Sinclair, T. 1994 (QPR, West Ham U)	5

Sinnott, L. 1985 (Watford)	1
Slade, S. A. 1996 (Tottenham H)	4
Slater, S. I. 1990 (West Ham U)	3
Small, B. 1993 (Aston Villa)	12
Smalling, C. L. 2010 (Fulham, Manchester U)	14
Smith, A. 2000 (Leeds U)	10
Smith, A. J. 2012 (Tottenham H)	11
Smith, B. S. (Liverpool)	**3**
Smith, D. 1988 (Coventry C)	10
Smith, M. 1981 (Sheffield W)	5
Smith, M. 1995 (Sunderland)	1
Smith, T. W. 2001 (Watford)	1
Snodin, I. 1985 (Doncaster R)	4
Soares, T. J. 2006 (Crystal Palace)	4
Sordell, M. A. 2012 (Watford, Bolton W)	14
Spence, J. 2011 (West Ham U)	1
Stanislaus, F. J. 2010 (West Ham U)	2
Statham, B. 1988 (Tottenham H)	3
Statham, D. J. 1978 (WBA)	6
Stead, J. G. 2004 (Blackburn R, Sunderland)	4
Stearman, R. J. 2009 (Wolverhampton W)	11
Steele, J. 2011 (Middlesbrough)	7
Stein, B. 1984 (Luton T)	3
Sterland, M. 1984 (Sheffield W)	7
Sterling, R. S. 2012 (Liverpool)	**8**
Steven, T. M. 1985 (Everton)	2
Stevens, G. A. 1983 (Brighton & HA, Tottenham H)	8
Stewart, J. 2003 (Leicester C)	1
Stewart, P. 1988 (Manchester C)	1
Stockdale, R. K. 2001 (Middlesbrough)	1
Stones, J. 2013 (Everton)	**8**
Stuart, G. C. 1990 (Chelsea)	5
Stuart, J. C. 1996 (Charlton Ath)	4
Sturridge, D. A. 2010 (Chelsea)	15
Suckling, P. 1986 (Coventry C, Manchester C, Crystal Palace)	10
Summerbee, N. J. 1993 (Swindon T)	3
Sunderland, A. 1977 (Wolverhampton W)	1
Surman, A. R. E. 2008 (Southampton)	4
Sutch, D. 1992 (Norwich C)	4
Sutton, C. R. 1993 (Norwich C)	13
Swindlehurst, D. 1977 (Crystal Palace)	1
Talbot, B. 1977 (Ipswich T)	1
Taylor, A. D. 2007 (Middlesbrough)	13
Taylor, M. 2001 (Blackburn R)	1
Taylor, M. S. 2003 (Portsmouth)	3
Taylor, R. A. 2006 (Wigan Ath)	4
Taylor, S. J. 2002 (Arsenal)	3
Taylor, S. V. 2004 (Newcastle U)	29
Terry, J. G. 2001 (Chelsea)	9
Thatcher, B. D. 1996 (Millwall, Wimbledon)	4
Thelwell, A. A. 2001 (Tottenham H)	1
Thirlwell, P. 2001 (Sunderland)	1
Thomas, D. 1981 (Coventry C, Tottenham H)	7
Thomas, J. W. 2006 (Charlton Ath)	2
Thomas, M. 1986 (Luton T)	3
Thomas, M. L. 1988 (Arsenal)	12
Thomas, R. E. 1990 (Watford)	1
Thompson, A. 1995 (Bolton W)	2
Thompson, D. A. 1997 (Liverpool)	7
Thompson, G. L. 1981 (Coventry C)	6
Thorn, A. 1988 (Wimbledon)	5
Thornley, B. L. 1996 (Manchester U)	3
Thorpe, T. J. 2013 (Manchester U)	**1**
Tiler, C. 1990 (Barnsley, Nottingham F)	13
Tomkins, J. O. C. 2009 (West Ham U)	10
Tonge, M. W. E. 2004 (Sheffield U)	2
Townsend, A. D. 2012 (Tottenham H)	3
Trippier, K. J. 2011 (Manchester C)	2
Unsworth, D. G. 1995 (Everton)	6
Upson, M. J. 1999 (Arsenal)	11
Vassell, D. 1999 (Aston Villa)	11
Vaughan, J. O. 2007 (Everton)	4
Venison, B. 1983 (Sunderland)	10
Vernazza, P. A. P. 2001 (Arsenal, Watford)	2
Vinnicombe, C. 1991 (Rangers)	12
Waddle, C. R. 1985 (Newcastle U)	1
Waghorn, M. T. 2012 (Leicester C)	5
Walcott, T. J. 2007 (Arsenal)	21
Wallace, D. L. 1983 (Southampton)	14
Wallace, Ray 1989 (Southampton)	4
Wallace, Rod 1989 (Southampton)	11

Walker, D. 1985 (Nottingham F)	7
Walker, I. M. 1991 (Tottenham H)	9
Walker, K. 2010 (Tottenham H)	7
Walsh, G. 1988 (Manchester U)	2
Walsh, P. A. 1983 (Luton T)	4
Walters, K. 1984 (Aston Villa)	9
Ward, P. 1978 (Brighton & HA)	2
Ward-Prowse, J. M. E. 2013 (Southampton)	**12**
Warhurst, P. 1991 (Oldham Ath, Sheffield W)	8
Watson, B. 2007 (Crystal Palace)	1
Watson, D. 1984 (Norwich C)	7
Watson, D. N. 1994 (Barnsley)	5
Watson, G. 1991 (Sheffield W)	2
Watson, S. C. 1993 (Newcastle U)	12
Weaver, N. J. 2000 (Manchester C)	10
Webb, N. J. 1985 (Portsmouth, Nottingham F)	3
Welbeck, D. 2009 (Manchester U)	14
Welsh, J. J. 2004 (Liverpool, Hull C)	8
Wheater, D. J. 2008 (Middlesbrough)	11
Whelan, P. J. 1993 (Ipswich T)	3
Whelan, N. 1995 (Leeds U)	2
Whittingham, P. 2004 (Aston Villa, Cardiff C)	17
White, D. 1988 (Manchester C)	6
Whyte, C. 1982 (Arsenal)	4
Wickham, C. N. R. 2011 (Ipswich T, Sunderland)	**17**
Wicks, S. 1982 (QPR)	1
Wilkins, R. C. 1977 (Chelsea)	1
Wilkinson, P. 1985 (Grimsby T, Everton)	4

Williams, D. 1998 (Sunderland)	2
Williams, P. 1989 (Charlton Ath)	4
Williams, P. D. 1991 (Derby Co)	6
Williams, S. C. 1977 (Southampton)	14
Wilshere, J. A. 2010 (Arsenal)	7
Wilson, M. A. 2001 (Manchester U, Middlesbrough)	6
Winterburn, N. 1986 (Wimbledon)	1
Wisdom, A. 2012 (Liverpool)	**10**
Wise, D. F. 1988 (Wimbledon)	1
Woodcook, A. S. 1978 (Nottingham F)	2
Woodgate, J. S. 2000 (Leeds U)	1
Woodhouse, C. 1999 (Sheffield U)	4
Woodrow, C. (Fulham)	**5**
Woods, C. C. E. 1979 (Nottingham F, QPR, Norwich C)	6
Wright, A. G. 1993 (Blackburn R)	2
Wright, M. 1983 (Southampton)	4
Wright, R. I. 1997 (Ipswich T)	15
Wright, S. J. 2001 (Liverpool)	10
Wright, W. 1979 (Everton)	6
Wright-Phillips, S. C. 2002 (Manchester C)	6
Yates, D. 1989 (Notts Co)	5
Young, A. S. 2007 (Watford, Aston Villa)	10
Young, L. P. 1999 (Tottenham H, Charlton Ath)	12
Zaha, D. W. A. 2012 (Crystal Palace, Manchester U)	**13**
Zamora, R. L. 2002 (Brighton & HA)	6

NORTHERN IRELAND

Allen, C. 2009 (Lisburn Distillery)	1
Armstrong, D. T. 2007 (Hearts)	1
Bagnall, L. 2011 (Sunderland)	1
Bailie, N. 1990 (Linfield)	2
Baird, C. P. 2002 (Southampton)	6
Ball, D. 2013 (Tottenham H)	**2**
Ball, M. 2011 (Norwich C)	5
Beatty, S. 1990 (Chelsea, Linfield)	2
Black, J. 2003 (Tottenham H)	1
Black, K. T. 1990 (Luton T)	1
Black, R. Z. 2002 (Morecambe)	1
Blackledge, G. 1978 (Portadown)	1
Blake, R. G. 2011 (Brentford)	2
Blayney, A. 2003 (Southampton)	4
Boyce, L. 2010 (Cliftonville, Werder Bremen)	8
Boyle, W. S. 1998 (Leeds U)	7
Braniff, K. R. 2002 (Millwall)	11
Breeze, J. 2011 (Wigan Ath)	4
Brennan, C. 2013 (Kilmarnock)	**7**
Brobbel, R. 2013 (Middlesbrough)	**8**
Brotherston, N. 1978 (Blackburn R)	1
Browne, G. 2003 (Manchester C)	5
Brunt, C. 2005 (Sheffield W)	2
Bryan, M. A. 2010 (Watford)	4
Buchanan, D. T. H. 2006 (Bury)	15
Buchanan, W. B. 2002 (Bolton W, Lisburn Distillery)	4
Burns, L. 1998 (Port Vale)	13
Callaghan, A. 2006 (Limavady U, Ballymena U,	
Derry C)	15
Campbell, S. 2003 (Ballymena U)	1
Capaldi, A. C. 2002 (Birmingham C, Plymouth Arg)	14
Carlisle, W. T. 2000 (Crystal Palace)	9
Carroll, R. E. 1998 (Wigan Ath)	11
Carson, J. G. 2011 (Ipswich T, York C)	**12**
Carson, S. 2000 (Rangers, Dundee U)	2
Carson, T. 2007 (Sunderland)	15
Carvill, M. D. 2008 (Wrexham, Linfield)	8
Casement, C. 2007 (Ipswich T, Dundee)	18
Cathcart, C. 2007 (Manchester U)	15
Catney, R. 2007 (Lisburn Distillery)	1
Chapman, A. 2008 (Sheffield U, Oxford U)	7
Clarke, L. 2003 (Peterborough U)	5
Clarke, R. 2006 (Newry C)	7
Clarke, R. D. J. 1999 (Portadown)	5
Clingan, S. G. 2003 (Wolverhampton W, Nottingham F)	11
Close, B. 2002 (Middlesbrough)	10
Clucas, M. S. 2011 (Preston NE, Bristol R)	**11**
Clyde, M. G. 2002 (Wolverhampton W)	5
Colligan, L. 2009 (Ballymena U)	1
Conlan, L. 2013 (Burnley)	**3**
Connell, T. E. 1978 (Coleraine)	1

Coote, A. 1998 (Norwich C)	12
Convery, J. 2000 (Celtic)	4
Dallas, S. 2012 (Crusaders, Brentford)	2
Davey, H. 2004 (UCD)	3
Davis, S. 2004 (Aston Villa)	3
Devine, D. 1994 (Omagh T)	1
Devine, D. G. 2011 (Preston NE)	2
Devine, J. 1990 (Glentoran)	1
Devlin, C. 2011 (Manchester U, unattached,	
Cliftonville)	11
Dickson, H. 2002 (Wigan Ath)	1
Doherty, M. 2007 (Hearts)	2
Dolan, J. 2000 (Millwall)	6
Donaghy, M. M. 1978 (Larne)	1
Donnelly, L. 2012 (Fulham)	**6**
Donnelly, M. 2007 (Sheffield U, Crusaders)	5
Donnelly, R. 2013 (Swansea C)	**1**
Dowie, I. 1990 (Luton T)	1
Drummond, W. 2011 (Rangers)	2
Dudgeon, J. P. 2010 (Manchester U)	4
Duff, S. 2003 (Cheltenham T)	1
Duffy, S. P. M. 2010 (Everton)	3
Elliott, S. 1999 (Glentoran)	3
Ervin, J. 2005 (Linfield)	2
Evans, C. J. 2009 (Manchester U)	10
Evans, J. 2006 (Manchester U)	3
Feeney, L. 1998 (Linfield, Rangers)	8
Feeney, W. 2002 (Bournemouth)	8
Ferguson, M. 2000 (Glentoran)	2
Ferguson, S. 2009 (Newcastle U)	11
Fitzgerald, D. 1998 (Rangers)	4
Flanagan, T. M. 2012 (Milton Keynes D)	1
Flynn, J. J. 2009 (Blackburn R, Ross Co)	11
Fordyce, D. T. 2007 (Portsmouth, Glentoran)	12
Friars, E. C. 2005 (Notts Co)	7
Friars, S. M. 1998 (Liverpool, Ipswich T)	21
Garrett, R. 2007 (Stoke C, Linfield)	14
Gault, M. 2005 (Linfield)	2
Gibb, S. 2009 (Falkirk, Drogheda U)	2
Gilfillan, B. J. 2005 (Gretna, Peterhead)	9
Gillespie, K. R. 1994 (Manchester U)	1
Glendinning, M. 1994 (Bangor)	1
Glendinning, R. 2012 (Linfield)	3
Gorman, R. J. 2012 (Wolverhampton W, Leyton Orient)	**4**
Graham, G. L. 1999 (Crystal Palace)	5
Graham, R. S. 1999 (QPR)	15
Gray, J. P. 2012 (Accrington S)	**10**
Gray, P. 1990 (Luton T)	1
Griffin, D. J. 1998 (St Johnstone)	10

Grigg, W. D. 2011 (Walsall) — 10

Hamilton, G. 2000 (Blackburn R, Portadown) — 12
Hamilton, W. R. 1978 (Linfield) — 1
Hanley, N. 2011 (Linfield) — 1
Harkin, M. P. 2000 (Wycombe W) — 9
Harvey, J. 1978 (Arsenal) — 1
Hawe, S. 2001 (Blackburn R) — 2
Hayes, T. 1978 (Luton T) — 1
Hazley, M. 2007 (Stoke C) — 3
Healy, D. J. 1999 (Manchester U) — 8
Hegarty, C. 2011 (Rangers) — 7
Herron, C. J. 2003 (QPR) — 2
Higgins, R. 2006 (Derry C) — 1
Hodson, G. J. S. 2010 (Watford) — 10
Holmes, S. 2000 (Manchester C, Wrexham) — 13
Howland, D. 2007 (Birmingham C) — 4
Hughes, J. 2006 (Lincoln C) — 7
Hughes, M. A. 2003 (Tottenham H, Oldham Ath) — 12
Hughes, M. E. 1990 (Manchester C) — 1
Hunter, M. 2002 (Glentoran) — 1

Ingham, M. G. 2001 (Sunderland) — 4

Jarvis, D. 2010 (Aberdeen) — 2
Johnson, D. M. 1998 (Blackburn R) — 11
Johnston, B. 1978 (Cliftonville) — 1
Julian, A. A. 2005 (Brentford) — 1

Kane, A. M. 2008 (Blackburn R) — 5
Kane, M. 2012 (Glentoran) — 1
Kee, B. R. 2010 (Leicester C, Torquay U, Burton Alb) — 10
Kee, P. V. 1990 (Oxford U) — 1
Kelly, D. 2000 (Derry C) — 11
Kelly, N. 1990 (Oldham Ath) — 1
Kirk, A. R. 1999 (Hearts) — 9
Knowles, J. 2012 (Blackburn R) — 2

Lafferty, D. 2009 (Celtic) — 6
Lafferty, K. 2006 (Burnley) — 2
Lavery, C. 2011 (Ipswich T, Sheffield W) — **7**
Lawrie, J. 2009 (Port Vale, AFC Telford U) — 9
Lennon, N. F. 1990 (Manchester C, Crewe Alex) — 2
Lester, C. 2013 (Bolton W) — 1
Lindsay, K. 2006 (Larne) — 1
Little, A. 2009 (Rangers) — 6
Lowry, P. 2009 (Institute, Linfield) — 6
Lund, M. 2011 (Stoke C) — 6
Lyttle, G. 1998 (Celtic, Peterborough U) — 8

Magee, J. 1994 (Bangor) — 1
Magee, J. 2009 (Lisburn Distillery) — 1
Magennis, J. B. D. 2010 (Cardiff C, Aberdeen) — 16
Magilton, J. 1990 (Liverpool) — 1
Magnay, C. 2010 (Chelsea) — 1
Matthews, N. P. 1990 (Blackpool) — 1
McAlinden, L. J. 2012 (Wolverhampton W) — 3
McAllister, M. 2007 (Dungannon Swifts) — 4
McArdle, R. A. 2006 (Sheffield W, Rochdale) — 19
McAreavey, P. 2000 (Swindon T) — 7
McBride, J. 1994 (Glentoran) — 1
McCaffrey, D. 2006 (Hibernian) — 8
McCallion, E. 1998 (Coleraine) — 1
McCann, G. S. 2000 (West Ham U) — 11
McCann, P. 2003 (Portadown) — 1
McCann, R. 2002 (Rangers, Linfield) — 2
McCartan, S. V. 2013 (Accrington S) — **3**
McCartney, G. 2001 (Sunderland) — 5
McCashin, S. 2011 (Jerez Industrial, unattached) — 2
McChrystal, M. 2005 (Derry C) — 9
McClean, J. 2010 (Derry C) — 1
McClure, M. 2012 (Wycombe W) — 1
McCourt, P. J. 2002 (Rochdale, Derry C) — 8
McCoy, R. K. 1990 (Coleraine) — 1
McCreery, D. 1978 (Manchester U) — 1
McCullough, L. 2013 (Doncaster R) — **6**
McEleney, S. 2012 (Derry C) — 2
McElroy, P. 2013 (Hull C) — **1**
McEvilly, L. R. 2003 (Rochdale) — 9
McFlynn, T. M. 2000 (QPR, Woking, Margate) — 19
McGeehan, C. 2013 (Norwich C) — **2**
McGibbon, P. C. G. 1994 (Manchester U) — 1
McGivern, R. 2010 (Manchester C) — 6
McGlinchey, B. 1998 (Manchester C, Port Vale,
   Gillingham) — 14

McGovern, M. 2005 (Celtic) — 10
McGowan, M. V. 2006 (Clyde) — 2
McGurk, A. 2010 (Aston Villa) — 1
McIlroy, T. 1994 (Linfield) — 1
McKay, W. 2009 (Leicester C, Northampton T) — 7
McKenna, K. 2007 (Tottenham H) — 6
McKeown, R. 2012 (Kilmarnock) — **12**
McKnight, P. 1998 (Rangers) — 3
McLaughlin, C. G. 2010 (Preston NE, Fleetwood T) — 7
McLaughlin, P. 2010 (Newcastle U, York C) — 10
McLaughlin, R. 2012 (Liverpool) — 1
McLean, B. S. 2006 (Rangers) — 1
McLean, J. 2009 (Derry C) — 4
McLellan, M. 2012 (Preston NE) — 1
McMahon, G. J. 2002 (Tottenham H) — 1
McMenamin, L. A. 2009 (Sheffield W) — 4
McNair, P. J. C. 2014 (Manchester U) — **1**
McNally, P. 2013 (Celtic) — 1
McQuilken, J. 2009 (Tescoma Zlin) — 1
McQuoid, J. J. B. 2009 (Bournemouth) — 8
McVeigh, A. 2002 (Ayr U) — 1
McVeigh, P. M. 1998 (Tottenham H) — 11
McVey, K. 2006 (Coleraine) — 8
Meenan, D. 2007 (Finn Harps, Monaghan U) — 3
Melaugh, G. M. 2002 (Aston Villa, Glentoran) — 11
Millar, K. S. 2011 (Oldham Ath) — **10**
Millar, W. P. 1990 (Port Vale) — 1
Miskelly, D. T. 2000 (Oldham Ath) — 10
Mitchell, A. 2012 (Rangers) — 3
Moreland, V. 1978 (Glentoran) — 1
Morgan, D. 2012 (Nottingham F) — **4**
Morgan, M. P. T. 1999 (Preston NE) — 1
Morris, E. J. 2002 (WBA, Glentoran) — 8
Morrison, O. 2001 (Sheffield W, Sheffield U) — 7
Morrow, A. 2001 (Northampton T) — 1
Morrow, S. 2005 (Hibernian) — 4
Mulgrew, J. 2007 (Linfield) — 10
Mulryne, P. P. 1999 (Manchester U, Norwich C) — 5
Murray, W. 1978 (Linfield) — 1
Murtagh, C. 2005 (Hearts) — 1

Nicholl, J. M. 1978 (Manchester U) — 1
Nixon, C. 2000 (Glentoran) — 1
Nolan, L. J. 2014 (Crewe Alex) — **1**
Norwood, O. J. 2010 (Manchester U) — 11

O'Connor, M. J. 2008 (Crewe Alex) — 3
O'Hara, G. 1994 (Leeds U) — 1
O'Kane, E. 2009 (Everton, Torquay U) — 4
O'Neill, J. P. 1978 (Leicester C) — 1
O'Neill, M. A. M. 1994 (Hibernian) — 1
O'Neill, S. 2009 (Ballymena U) — 4

Paterson, M. A. 2007 (Stoke C) — 2
Paterson, D. J. 1994 (Crystal Palace) — 1

Quinn, S. J. 1994 (Blackpool) — 1

Ramsey, C. 2011 (Portadown) — 3
Ramsey, K. 2006 (Institute) — 1
Reid, J. T. 2013 (Exeter C) — **2**
Robinson, S. 1994 (Tottenham H) — 1

Scullion, D. 2006 (Dungannon Swifts) — 8
Sendles-White J. 2013 (QPR) — **7**
Sharpe, R. 2013 (Derby Co) — **3**
Shiels, D. 2005 (Hibernian) — 6
Shields, S. P. 2013 (Dagenham & R) — **2**
Shroot, R. 2009 (Harrow B, Birmingham C) — 4
Simms, G. 2001 (Hartlepool U) — 14
Skates, G. 2000 (Blackburn R) — 4
Sloan, T. 1978 (Ballymena U) — 1
Smylie, D. 2006 (Newcastle U, Livingston) — 6
Stewart, S. 2009 (Aberdeen) — 1
Stewart, T. 2006 (Wolverhampton W, Linfield) — 19

Taylor, J. 2007 (Hearts, Glentoran) — 10
Taylor, M. S. 1998 (Fulham) — 1
Teggart, N. 2005 (Sunderland) — 1
Tempest, G. 2013 (Notts Co) — **6**
Thompson, A. L. 2011 (Watford) — **11**
Thompson, P. 2006 (Linfield) — 4
Toner, C. 2000 (Tottenham H, Leyton Orient) — 17
Tuffey, J. 2007 (Partick Th) — 13
Turner, C. 2007 (Sligo R, Bohemians) — 12

Ward, J. J. 2006 (Aston Villa, Chesterfield) 7
Ward, M. 2006 (Dungannon Swifts) 1
Ward, S. 2005 (Glentoran) 10
Waterman, D. G. 1998 (Portsmouth) 14
Waterworth, A. 2008 (Lisburn Distillery, Hamilton A) 7
Webb, S. M. 2004 (Ross Co, St Johnstone, Ross Co) 6

Weir, R. J. 2009 (Sunderland) 8
Wells, D. P. 1999 (Barry T) 1
Whitley, J. 1998 (Manchester C) 17
Willis, P. 2006 (Liverpool) 1
Winchester, C. 2011 (Oldham Ath) **12**
Winchester, J. 2013 (Kilmarnock) 1

SCOTLAND

Adam, C. G. 2006 (Rangers) 5
Adam, G. 2011 (Rangers) 6
Adams, J. 2007 (Kilmarnock) 1
Aitken, R. 1977 (Celtic) 16
Albiston, A. 1977 (Manchester U) 5
Alexander, N. 1997 (Stenhousemuir, Livingston) 10
Allan, S. 2012 (WBA) 10
Anderson, I. 1997 (Dundee, Toulouse) 15
Anderson, R. 1997 (Aberdeen) 15
Andrews, M. 2011 (East Stirling) 1
Anthony, M. 1997 (Celtic) 3
Archdeacon, O. 1987 (Celtic) 1
Archer, J. G. 2012 (Tottenham H) **13**
Archibald, A. 1998 (Partick Th) 5
Archibald, S. 1980 (Aberdeen, Tottenham H) 5
Arfield, S. 2008 (Falkirk, Huddersfield T) 17
Armstrong, S. 2011 (Dundee U) **20**

Bagen, D. 1997 (Kilmarnock) 4
Bain, K. 1993 (Dundee) 4
Baker, M. 1993 (St Mirren) 10
Baltacha, S. S. 2000 (St Mirren) 3
Bannan, B. 2009 (Aston Villa) 10
Bannigan, S. 2013 (Partick Th) **3**
Bannon, E. J. 1979 (Hearts, Chelsea, Dundee U) 7
Barclay, J. 2011 (Falkirk) 1
Beattie, C. 2004 (Celtic) 7
Beattie, J. 1992 (St Mirren) 4
Beaumont, D. 1985 (Dundee U) 1
Bell, D. 1981 (Aberdeen) 2
Bernard, P. R. J. 1992 (Oldham Ath) 15
Berra, C. 2005 (Hearts) 6
Bett, J. 1981 (Rangers) 7
Black, E. 1983 (Aberdeen) 8
Blair, A. 1980 (Coventry C, Aston Villa) 5
Bollan, G. 1992 (Dundee U, Rangers) 17
Bonar, P. 1997 (Raith R) 4
Booth, C. 2011 (Hibernian) 4
Booth, S. 1991 (Aberdeen) 14
Bowes, M. J. 1992 (Dunfermline Ath) 1
Bowman, D. 1985 (Hearts) 1
Boyack, S. 1997 (Rangers) 1
Boyd, K. 2003 (Kilmarnock) 8
Boyd, T. 1987 (Motherwell) 5
Brazil, A. 1978 (Hibernian) 1
Brazil, A. 1979 (Ipswich T) 8
Brebner, G. I. 1997 (Manchester U, Reading, Hibernian) 18
Brighton, T. 2005 (Rangers, Clyde) 7
Broadfoot, K. 2005 (St Mirren) 5
Brough, J. 1981 (Hearts) 1
Brown, A. H. 2004 (Hibernian) 1
Brown, S. 2005 (Hibernian) 10
Browne, P. 1997 (Raith R) 1
Bryson, C. 2006 (Clyde) 1
Buchan, J. 1997 (Aberdeen) 13
Burchill, M. J. 1998 (Celtic) 15
Burke, A. 1997 (Kilmarnock) 4
Burke, C. 2004 (Rangers) 3
Burley, C. W. 1992 (Chelsea) 7
Burley, G. E. 1977 (Ipswich T) 5
Burns, H. 1985 (Rangers) 2
Burns, T. 1977 (Celtic) 5

Caddis, P. 2008 (Celtic, Dundee U, Celtic, Swindon T) 13
Cairney, T. 2011 (Hull C) 6
Caldwell, G. 2000 (Newcastle U) 19
Caldwell, S. 2001 (Newcastle U) 4
Cameron, G. 2008 (Dundee U) 3
Campbell, R. 2008 (Hibernian) 6
Campbell, S. 1989 (Dundee) 3
Campbell, S. P. 1998 (Leicester C) 15
Canero, P. 2000 (Kilmarnock) 17
Carey, L. A. 1998 (Bristol C) 1

Carrick, D. 2012 (Hearts) 1
Casey, J. 1978 (Celtic) 1
Chalmers, J. 2014 (Celtic) **1**
Christie, M. 1992 (Dundee) 3
Clark, R. B. 1977 (Aberdeen) 3
Clarke, S. 1984 (St Mirren) 8
Clarkson, D. 2004 (Motherwell) 13
Cleland, A. 1990 (Dundee U) 11
Cole, D. 2011 (Rangers) 2
Collins, J. 1988 (Hibernian) 8
Collins, N. 2005 (Sunderland) 7
Connolly, P. 1991 (Dundee U) 3
Connor, R. 1981 (Ayr U) 2
Conroy, R. 2007 (Celtic) 4
Considine, A. 2007 (Aberdeen) 5
Cooper, D. 1977 (Clydebank, Rangers) 6
Cooper, N. 1982 (Aberdeen) 13
Coutts, P. A. 2009 (Peterborough U, Preston NE) 7
Crabbe, S. 1990 (Hearts) 2
Craig, M. 1998 (Aberdeen) 2
Craig, T. 1977 (Newcastle U) 1
Crainey, S. D. 2000 (Celtic) 7
Crainie, D. 1983 (Celtic) 1
Crawford, S. 1994 (Raith R) 19
Creaney, G. 1991 (Celtic) 11
Cummings, W. 2000 (Chelsea) 8
Cuthbert, S. 2007 (Celtic, St Mirren) 13

Dailly, C. 1991 (Dundee U) 34
Dalglish, P. 1999 (Newcastle U, Norwich C) 6
Dargo, C. 2008 (Raith R) 10
Davidson, C. I. 1997 (St Johnstone) 2
Davidson, H. N. 2000 (Dundee U) 3
Davidson, M. 2011 (St Johnstone) 1
Dawson, A. 1979 (Rangers) 8
Deas, P. A. 1992 (St Johnstone) 2
Dempster, J. 2004 (Rushden & D) 1
Dennis, S. 1992 (Raith R) 1
Diamond, A. 2004 (Aberdeen) 12
Dickov, P. 1992 (Arsenal) 4
Dixon, P. 2008 (Dundee) 2
Dodds, D. 1978 (Dundee U) 1
Dods, D. 1997 (Hibernian) 5
Doig, C. R. 2000 (Nottingham F) 13
Donald, G. S. 1992 (Hibernian) 3
Donnelly, S. 1994 (Celtic) 11
Dorrans, G. 2007 (Livingston) 6
Dow, A. 1993 (Dundee, Chelsea) 3
Dowie, A. J. 2003 (Rangers, Partick Th) 14
Duff, J. 2009 (Inverness CT) 1
Duff, S. 2003 (Dundee U) 9
Duffie, K. 2011 (Falkirk) **6**
Duffy, D. A. 2005 (Falkirk, Hull C) 8
Duffy, J. 1987 (Dundee) 1
Durie, G. S. 1987 (Chelsea) 4
Durrant, I. 1987 (Rangers) 4
Doyle, J. 1981 (Partick Th) 2

Easton, B. 2009 (Hamilton A) 3
Easton, C. 1997 (Dundee U) 21
Edwards, M. 2012 (Rochdale) 1
Elliot, B. 1998 (Celtic) 2
Elliot, C. 2006 (Hearts) 9
Esson, R. 2000 (Aberdeen) 7

Fagan, S. M. 2005 (Motherwell) 1
Ferguson, B. 1997 (Rangers) 12
Ferguson, D. 1987 (Rangers) 5
Ferguson, D. 1992 (Dundee U) 7
Ferguson, D. 1992 (Manchester U) 5
Ferguson, I. 1983 (Dundee) 4
Ferguson, I. 1987 (Clyde, St Mirren, Rangers) 6
Ferguson, R. 1977 (Hamilton A) 1
Feruz, I. 2012 (Chelsea) **4**

Findlay, S. 2012 (Celtic) 7
Findlay, W. 1991 (Hibernian) 5
Fitzpatrick, A. 1977 (St Mirren) 5
Fitzpatrick, M. 2007 (Motherwell) 4
Flannigan, C. 1993 (Clydebank) 1
Fleck, J. 2009 (Rangers) 4
Fleck, R. 1987 (Rangers, Norwich C) 6
Fleming, G. 2008 (Gretna) 1
Fletcher, D. B. 2003 (Manchester U) 2
Fletcher, S. 2007 (Hibernian) 7
Forrest, J. 2011 (Celtic) 4
Foster, R. M. 2005 (Aberdeen) 5
Fotheringham, M. M. 2004 (Dundee) 3
Fowler, J. 2002 (Kilmarnock) 3
Foy, R. A. 2004 (Liverpool) 5
Fraser, M. 2012 (Celtic) 2
Fraser, R. 2013 (Aberdeen, Bournemouth) 4
Fraser, S. T. 2000 (Luton T) 4
Freedman, D. A. 1995 (Barnet, Crystal Palace) 8
Fridge, L. 1989 (St Mirren) 2
Fullarton, J. 1993 (St Mirren) 17
Fulton, M. 1980 (St Mirren) 5
Fulton, S. 1991 (Celtic) 7
Fyvie, F. 2012 (Wigan Ath) 8

Gallacher, K. W. 1987 (Dundee U) 7
Gallacher, P. 1999 (Dundee U) 7
Gallacher, S. 2009 (Rangers) 2
Gallagher, P. 2003 (Blackburn R) 11
Galloway, M. 1989 (Hearts, Celtic) 2
Gardiner, J. 1993 (Hibernian) 1
Gauld, R. 2013 (Dundee U) 1
Geddes, R. 1982 (Dundee) 5
Gemmill, S. 1992 (Nottingham F) 4
Germaine, G. 1997 (WBA) 1
Gilles, R. 1997 (St Mirren) 7
Gillespie, G. T. 1979 (Coventry C) 8
Glass, S. 1995 (Aberdeen) 11
Glover, L. 1988 (Nottingham F) 3
Goodwillie, D. 2009 (Dundee U) 9
Goram, A. L. 1987 (Oldham Ath) 1
Gordon, C. S. 2003 (Hearts) 5
Gough, G. C. 1983 (Dundee U) 5
Graham, D. 1998 (Rangers) 8
Grant, P. 1985 (Celtic) 10
Gray, D. P. 2009 (Manchester U) 3
Gray, S. 1987 (Aberdeen) 1
Gray S. 1995 (Celtic) 7
Griffiths, L. 2010 (Dundee, Wolverhampton W) 11
Grimmer, J. 2014 (Fulham) 1
Gunn, B. 1984 (Aberdeen) 9

Hagen, D. 1992 (Rangers) 8
Hamill, J. 2008 (Kilmarnock) 11
Hamilton, B. 1989 (St Mirren) 4
Hamilton, J. 1995 (Dundee, Hearts) 14
Hammell, S. 2001 (Motherwell) 11
Handling, D. 2014 (Hibernian) 1
Handyside, P. 1993 (Grimsby T) 7
Hanley, R. 2011 (Blackburn R) 1
Hanlon, P. 2009 (Hibernian) 23
Hannah, D. 1993 (Dundee U) 16
Harper, K. 1995 (Hibernian) 3
Hartford, R. A. 1977 (Manchester C) 1
Hartley, P. J. 1997 (Millwall) 1
Hegarty, P. 1987 (Dundee U) 6
Hendry, J. 1992 (Tottenham H) 1
Herron, J. 2012 (Celtic) 2
Hetherston, B. 1997 (St Mirren) 1
Hewitt, J. 1982 (Hibernian) 6
Hogg, G. 1984 (Manchester U) 4
Holt, J. 2012 (Hearts) 7
Hood, G. 1993 (Ayr U) 3
Horn, R. 1997 (Hearts) 6
Howie, S. 1993 (Cowdenbeath) 5
Hughes, D. R. 1999 (Bournemouth) 9
Hughes, S. 2002 (Rangers) 12
Hunter, G. 1987 (Hibernian) 3
Hunter, P. 1989 (East Fife) 3
Hutton, A. 2004 (Rangers) 7
Hutton, K. 2011 (Rangers) 1

Inman, B. 2011 (Newcastle U) 2
Irvine, G. 2006 (Celtic) 2

Jack, R. 2012 (Aberdeen) 17
James, K. F. 1997 (Falkirk) 1
Jardine, I. 1979 (Kilmarnock) 1
Jess, E. 1990 (Aberdeen) 14
Johnson, G. I. 1992 (Dundee U) 6
Johnston, A. 1994 (Hearts) 3
Johnston, F. 1993 (Falkirk) 1
Johnston, M. 1984 (Partick Th, Watford) 3
Jordan, A. J. 2000 (Bristol C) 3
Jupp, D. A. 1995 (Fulham) 9

Kelly, L. 2012 (Kilmarnock) 9
Kelly, S. 2014 (St Mirren) 1
Kennedy, J. 2003 (Celtic) 15
Kennedy, M. 2012 (Kilmarnock) 1
Kenneth, G. 2008 (Dundee U) 8
Kerr, B. 2003 (Newcastle U) 14
Kerr, F. 2012 (Birmingham C) 3
Kerr, M. 2001 (Kilmarnock) 1
Kerr, S. 1993 (Celtic) 10
Kettings, C. D. 2012 (Blackpool) 3
Kinniburgh, W. D. 2004 (Motherwell) 3
Kirkwood, D. 1990 (Hearts) 1
Kyle, K. 2001 (Sunderland) 12

Lambert, P. 1991 (St Mirren) 11
Langfield, J. 2000 (Dundee) 2
Lappin, S. 2004 (St Mirren) 10
Lauchlan, J. 1998 (Kilmarnock) 11
Lavety, B. 1993 (St Mirren) 9
Lavin, G. 1993 (Watford) 7
Lawson, P. 2004 (Celtic) 10
Leighton, J. 1982 (Aberdeen) 1
Lennon, S. 2008 (Rangers) 6
Levein, C. 1985 (Hearts) 2
Leven, P. 2005 (Kilmarnock) 2
Liddell, A. M. 1994 (Barnsley) 12
Lindsey, J. 1979 (Motherwell) 1
Locke, G. 1994 (Hearts) 10
Love, G. 1995 (Hibernian) 1
Loy, R. 2009 (Dunfermline Ath, Rangers) 5
Lynch, S. 2003 (Celtic, Preston NE) 13

McAllister, G. 1990 (Leicester C) 1
McAllister, R. 2008 (Inverness CT) 2
McAlpine, H. 1983 (Dundee U) 5
McAnespie, K. 1998 (St Johnstone) 4
McArthur, J. 2008 (Hamilton A) 2
McAuley, S. 1993 (St Johnstone) 1
McAvennie, F. 1982 (St Mirren) 5
McBride, J. 1981 (Everton) 1
McBride, J. P. 1998 (Celtic) 2
McCabe, R. 2012 (Rangers, Sheffield W) 3
McCall, A. S. M. 1988 (Bradford C, Everton) 2
McCann, K. 2008 (Hibernian) 4
McCann, N. 1994 (Dundee) 9
McClair, B. 1984 (Celtic) 8
McCluskey, G. 1979 (Celtic) 6
McCluskey, S. 1997 (St Johnstone) 14
McCoist, A. 1984 (Rangers) 1
McConnell, I. 1997 (Clyde) 1
McCormack, D. 2008 (Hibernian) 1
McCormack, R. 2006 (Rangers, Motherwell, Cardiff C) 13
McCracken, D. 2002 (Dundee U) 5
McCulloch, A. 1981 (Kilmarnock) 1
McCulloch, I. 1982 (Notts Co) 2
McCulloch, L. 1997 (Motherwell) 14
McCunnie, J. 2001 (Dundee U, Ross Co, Dunfermline Ath) 20
MacDonald, A. 2011 (Burnley) 6
MacDonald, J. 1980 (Rangers) 8
MacDonald, J. 2007 (Hearts) 11
McDonald, C. 1995 (Falkirk) 3
McDonald, K. 2008 (Dundee, Burnley) 14
McEwan, C. 1997 (Clyde, Raith R) 17
McEwan, D. 2003 (Livingston) 2
McFadden, J. 2003 (Motherwell) 7
McFarlane, D. 1997 (Hamilton A) 3
McGarry, S. 1997 (St Mirren) 3
McGarvey, F. P. 1977 (St Mirren, Celtic) 3
McGarvey, S. 1982 (Manchester U) 4
McGeough, D. 2012 (Celtic) 10
McGhee, J. 2013 (Hearts) 6
McGhee, M. 1981 (Aberdeen) 1
McGinn, J. 2014 (St Mirren) 2

McGinn, S. 2009 (St Mirren, Watford) 8
McGinnis, G. 1985 (Dundee U) 1
McGlinchey, M. R. 2007 (Celtic) 1
McGregor, A. 2003 (Rangers) 6
McGregor, C. W. 2013 (Celtic) 5
McGrillen, P. 1994 (Motherwell) 2
McGuire, D. 2002 (Aberdeen) 2
McHattie, K. 2012 (Hearts) 6
McInally, J. 1989 (Dundee U) 1
McKay, B. 2012 (Rangers) 1
McKay, B. 2013 (Hearts) 1
McKean, K. 2011 (St Mirren) 1
McKenzie, R. 2013 (Kilmarnock) 2
McKenzie, R. 1997 (Hearts) 2
McKimmie, S. 1985 (Aberdeen) 3
McKinlay, T. 1984 (Dundee) 6
McKinlay, W. 1989 (Dundee U) 6
McKinnon, R. 1991 (Dundee U) 6
McLaren, A. 1989 (Hearts) 11
McLaren, A. 1993 (Dundee U) 4
McLaughlin, B. 1995 (Celtic) 8
McLaughlin, J. 1981 (Morton) 10
McLean, E. 2008 (Dundee U, St Johnstone) 2
McLean, S. 2003 (Rangers) 4
McLeish, A. 1978 (Aberdeen) 6
McLean, K. 2012 (St Mirren) 11
MacLeod, A. 1979 (Hibernian) 3
McLeod, J. 1989 (Dundee U) 2
MacLeod, L. 2012 (Rangers) 6
MacLeod, M. 1979 (Dumbarton, Celtic) 5
McManus, T. 2001 (Hibernian) 14
McMillan, S. 1997 (Motherwell) 4
McNab, N. 1978 (Tottenham H) 1
McNally, M. 1991 (Celtic) 2
McNamara, J. 1994 (Dunfermline Ath, Celtic) 12
McNaughton, K. 2002 (Aberdeen) 1
McNeil, A. 2007 (Hibernian) 1
McNichol, J. 1979 (Brentford) 7
McNiven, D. 1977 (Leeds U) 3
McNiven, S. A. 1996 (Oldham Ath) 1
McParland, A. 2003 (Celtic) 1
McPhee, S. 2002 (Port Vale) 1
McPherson, D. 1984 (Rangers, Hearts) 4
McQuilken, J. 1993 (Celtic) 2
McStay, P. 1983 (Celtic) 5
McWhirter, N. 1991 (St Mirren) 1
Mackay-Steven, G. 2012 (Dundee U) 3
Maguire, C. 2009 (Aberdeen) 12
Main, A. 1988 (Dundee U) 3
Malcolm, R. 2001 (Rangers) 1
Maloney, S. 2002 (Celtic) 21
Malpas, M. 1983 (Dundee U) 8
Marr, B. 2011 (Ross Co) 1
Marshall, D. J. 2004 (Celtic) 10
Marshall, S. R. 1995 (Arsenal) 5
Martin, A. 2009 (Leeds U, Ayr U) 12
Mason, G. R. 1999 (Manchester C, Dunfermline Ath) 2
Mathieson, D. 1997 (Queen of the South) 3
May, E. 1989 (Hibernian) 2
May, S. 2013 (St Johnstone) 6
Meldrum, C. 1996 (Kilmarnock) 6
Melrose, J. 1977 (Partick Th) 8
Millar, M, 2009 (Celtic) 1
Miller, C. 1995 (Rangers) 8
Miller, J. 1987 (Aberdeen, Celtic) 7
Miller, K. 2000 (Hibernian, Rangers) 7
Miller, W. 1991 (Hibernian) 7
Miller, W. F. 1978 (Aberdeen) 2
Milne, K. 2000 (Hearts) 1
Milne, R. 1982 (Dundee U) 3
Mitchell, C. 2008 (Falkirk) 7
Money, I. C. 1987 (St Mirren) 3
Montgomery, N. A. 2003 (Sheffield U) 2
Morrison, S. A. 2004 (Aberdeen, Dunfermline Ath) 12
Muir, L. 1977 (Hibernian) 1
Mulgrew, C. P. 2006 (Celtic, Wolverhampton W, Aberdeen) 14
Murphy J. 2009 (Motherwell) 13
Murray, H. 2000 (St Mirren) 3
Murray, I. 2001 (Hibernian) 15
Murray, N. 1993 (Rangers) 16
Murray, R. 1993 (Bournemouth) 1
Murray, S. 2004 (Kilmarnock) 2

Narey, D. 1977 (Dundee U) 4
Naismith, S. J. 2006 (Kilmarnock, Rangers) 15
Naysmith, G. A. 1997 (Hearts) 22
Neilson, R. 2000 (Hearts) 1
Ness, J, 2011 (Rangers) 2
Nevin, P. 1985 (Chelsea) 5
Nicholas, C. 1981 (Celtic, Arsenal) 6
Nicholson, B. 1999 (Rangers) 7
Nicol, S. 1981 (Ayr U, Liverpool) 14
Nisbet, S. 1989 (Rangers) 5
Noble, D. J. 2003 (West Ham U) 2
Notman, A. M. 1999 (Manchester U) 10

O'Brien, B. 1999 (Blackburn R, Livingston) 6
O'Connor, G. 2003 (Hibernian) 8
O'Donnell, P. 1992 (Motherwell) 8
O'Donnell, S. 2013 (Partick Th) 1
O'Halloran, M. 2012 (Bolton W) 2
O'Leary, R. 2008 (Kilmarnock) 2
O'Neil, B. 1992 (Celtic) 7
O'Neil, J. 1991 (Dundee U) 1
O'Neill, M. 1995 (Clyde) 6
Orr, N. 1978 (Morton) 7

Palmer, L. J. 2011 (Sheffield W) 8
Park, C. 2012 (Middlesbrough) 1
Parker, K. 2001 (St Johnstone) 1
Parlane, D. 1977 (Rangers) 1
Paterson, C. 1981 (Hibernian) 2
Paterson, C. 2012 (Hearts) 7
Paterson, J. 1997 (Dundee U) 9
Pawlett, P. 2012 (Aberdeen) 7
Payne, G. 1978 (Dundee U) 3
Peacock, L. A. 1997 (Carlisle U) 1
Pearce, A. J. 2008 (Reading) 2
Pearson, S. P. 2003 (Motherwell) 8
Perry, R. 2010 (Rangers, Falkirk, Rangers) 16
Pressley, S. J. 1993 (Rangers, Coventry C, Dundee U) 26
Provan, D. 1977 (Kilmarnock) 1
Prunty, B. 2004 (Aberdeen) 6

Quinn, P. C. 2004 (Motherwell) 3
Quinn, R. 2006 (Celtic) 9

Rae, A. 1991 (Millwall) 8
Rae, G. 1999 (Dundee) 6
Redford, I. 1981 (Rangers) 6
Reid, B. 1991 (Rangers) 4
Reid, C. 1993 (Hibernian) 3
Reid, M. 1982 (Celtic) 2
Reid, R. 1977 (St Mirren) 3
Reilly, A. 2004 (Wycombe W) 1
Renicks, S. 1997 (Hamilton A) 1
Reynolds, M. 2007 (Motherwell) 9
Rhodes, J. L. 2011 (Huddersfield T) 8
Rice, B. 1985 (Hibernian) 1
Richardson, L. 1980 (St Mirren) 2
Ridgers, M. 2012 (Hearts) 5
Riordan, D. G. 2004 (Hibernian) 5
Ritchie, A. 1980 (Morton) 1
Ritchie, P. S. 1996 (Hearts) 7
Robertson, A. 1991 (Rangers) 1
Robertson, A. 2013 (Dundee U) 3
Robertson, C. 1977 (Rangers) 1
Robertson, C. 2012 (Aberdeen) 9
Robertson, D. 1987 (Aberdeen) 7
Robertson, D. 2007 (Dundee U) 4
Robertson, G. A. 2004 (Nottingham F, Rotherham U) 15
Robertson, H. 1994 (Aberdeen) 2
Robertson, J. 1985 (Hearts) 2
Robertson, L. 1993 (Rangers) 3
Robertson, S. 1998 (St Johnstone) 2
Roddie, A. 1992 (Aberdeen) 5
Ross, G. 2007 (Dunfermline Ath) 1
Ross, N. 2011 (Inverness CT) 2
Ross, T. W. 1977 (Arsenal) 1
Rowson, D. 1997 (Aberdeen) 5
Russell, J. 2011 (Dundee U) 11
Russell, R. 1978 (Rangers) 3

Salton, D. B. 1992 (Luton T) 6
Samson, C. I. 2004 (Kilmarnock) 6
Saunders, S. 2011 (Motherwell) 2
Scobbie, T. 2008 (Falkirk) 12
Scott, M. 2006 (Livingston) 1

Scott, P. 1994 (St Johnstone)	4
Scougall, S. 2012 (Livingston, Sheffield U)	2
Scrimgour, D. 1997 (St Mirren)	3
Seaton, A. 1998 (Falkirk)	1
Severin, S. D. 2000 (Hearts)	10
Shannon, R. 1987 (Dundee)	7
Sharp, G. M. 1982 (Everton)	1
Sharp, R. 1990 (Dunfermline Ath)	4
Sheerin, P. 1996 (Southampton)	1
Shields, G. 1997 (Rangers)	2
Shinnie, A. 2009 (Dundee, Rangers)	3
Shinnie, G. 2012 (Inverness CT)	2
Simmons, S. 2003 (Hearts)	1
Simpson, N. 1982 (Aberdeen)	11
Sinclair, G. 1977 (Dumbarton)	1
Skilling, M. 1993 (Kilmarnock)	2
Slater, C. 2014 (Kilmarnock)	1
Smith, B. M. 1992 (Celtic)	5
Smith, C. 2008 (St Mirren)	2
Smith, D. 2012 (Hearts)	4
Smith, D. L. 2006 (Motherwell)	2
Smith, G. 1978 (Rangers)	1
Smith, G. 2004 (Rangers)	8
Smith, H. G. 1987 (Hearts)	2
Smith, S. 2007 (Rangers)	1
Sneddon, A. 1979 (Celtic)	1
Snodgrass, R. 2008 (Livingston)	2
Soutar, D. 2003 (Dundee)	11
Speedie, D. R. 1985 (Chelsea)	1
Spencer, J. 1991 (Rangers)	3
Stanton, P. 1977 (Hibernian)	1
Stanton, S. 2014 (Hibernian)	1
Stark, W. 1985 (Aberdeen)	1
Stephen, R. 1983 (Dundee)	1
Stevens, G. 1977 (Motherwell)	1
Stevenson, L. 2008 (Hibernian)	8
Stewart, C. 2002 (Kilmarnock)	1
Stewart, J. 1978 (Kilmarnock, Middlesbrough)	3
Stewart, M. J. 2000 (Manchester U)	17
Stewart, R. 1979 (Dundee U, West Ham U)	12
Stillie, D. 1995 (Aberdeen)	14
Strachan, G. D. 1998 (Coventry C)	7
Sturrock, P. 1977 (Dundee U)	9
Sweeney, P. H. 2004 (Millwall)	8
Sweeney, S. 1991 (Clydebank)	7
Tapping, C. 2013 (Hearts)	1
Tarrant, N. K. 1999 (Aston Villa)	5
Teale, G. 1997 (Clydebank, Ayr U)	6

Telfer, P. N. 1993 (Luton T)	3
Templeton, D. 2011 (Hearts)	2
Thomas, K. 1993 (Hearts)	8
Thompson, S. 1997 (Dundee U)	12
Thomson, C. 2011 (Hearts)	2
Thomson, K. 2005 (Hibernian)	6
Thomson, W. 1977 (Partick Th, St Mirren)	10
Tolmie, J. 1980 (Morton)	1
Tortolano, J. 1987 (Hibernian)	2
Toshney, L. 2012 (Celtic)	5
Turner, I. 2005 (Everton)	6
Tweed, S. 1993 (Hibernian)	3
Wales, G. 2000 (Hearts)	1
Walker, A. 1988 (Celtic)	1
Walker, J. 2013 (Hearts)	1
Wallace, I. A. 1978 (Coventry C)	1
Wallace, L. 2007 (Hearts)	10
Wallace, M. 2012 (Huddersfield T)	4
Wallace, R. 2004 (Celtic, Sunderland)	4
Walsh, C. 1984 (Nottingham F)	5
Wark, J. 1977 (Ipswich T)	8
Watson, A. 1981 (Aberdeen)	4
Watson, K. 1977 (Rangers)	2
Watt, A. 2012 (Celtic)	9
Watt, M. 1991 (Aberdeen)	12
Watt, S. M. 2005 (Chelsea)	5
Webster, A. 2003 (Hearts)	2
Whiteford, A. 1997 (St Johnstone)	1
Whittaker, S. G. 2005 (Hibernian)	18
Whyte, D. 1987 (Celtic)	9
Wilkie, L. 2000 (Dundee)	6
Will, J. A. 1992 (Arsenal)	3
Williams, G. 2002 (Nottingham F)	9
Wilson, D. 2011 (Liverpool, Hearts)	13
Wilson, M. 2004 (Dundee U, Celtic)	19
Wilson, S. 1999 (Rangers)	7
Wilson, T. 1983 (St Mirren)	1
Wilson, T. 1988 (Nottingham F)	4
Winnie, D. 1988 (St Mirren)	1
Woods, M. 2006 (Sunderland)	2
Wotherspoon, D. 2011 (Hibernian)	16
Wright, P. 1989 (Aberdeen, QPR)	3
Wright, S. 1991 (Aberdeen)	14
Wright, T. 1987 (Oldham Ath)	1
Wylde, G. 2011 (Rangers)	7
Young, Darren 1997 (Aberdeen)	8
Young, Derek 2000 (Aberdeen)	5

WALES

Adams, N. W. 2008 (Bury, Leicester C)	5
Alfei, D. M. 2010 (Swansea C)	13
Aizlewood, M. 1979 (Luton T)	2
Allen, J. M. 2008 (Swansea C)	13
Anthony, B. 2005 (Cardiff C)	8
Baddeley, L. M. 1996 (Cardiff C)	2
Balcombe, S. 1982 (Leeds U)	1
Bale, G. 2006 (Southampton, Tottenham H)	4
Barnhouse, D. J. 1995 (Swansea C)	3
Basey, G. W. 2009 (Charlton Ath)	1
Bater, P. T. 1977 (Bristol R)	2
Beevers, L. J. 2005 (Boston U, Lincoln C)	7
Bellamy, C. D. 1996 (Norwich C)	8
Bender, P. J. 2011 (Colchester U)	4
Birchall, A. S. 2003 (Arsenal, Mansfield T)	12
Bird, A. 1993 (Cardiff C)	6
Blackmore, C. 1984 (Manchester U)	3
Blake, D. J. 2007 (Cardiff C)	14
Blake, N. A. 1991 (Cardiff C)	5
Blaney, S. D. 1997 (West Ham U)	3
Bloom, J. 2011 (Falkirk)	1
Bodin, B. P. 2010 (Swindon T, Torquay U)	21
Bodin, P. J. 1983 (Cardiff C)	1
Bond, J. H. 2011 (Watford)	1
Bowen, J. P. 1993 (Swansea C)	5
Bowen, M. R. 1983 (Tottenham H)	3
Boyle, T. 1982 (Crystal Palace)	1
Brace, D. P. 1995 (Wrexham)	6
Bradley, M. S. 2007 (Walsall)	17
Bradshaw, T. 2012 (Shrewsbury T)	8
Brough, M. 2003 (Notts Co)	3
Brown, J. D. 2008 (Cardiff C)	6

Brown, J. R. 2003 (Gillingham)	7
Brown, T. A. F. 2011 (Ipswich T, Rotherham U, Aldershot T)	10
Burns, W. 2013 (Bristol C)	9
Byrne, M. T. 2003 (Bolton W)	1
Calliste, R. T. 2005 (Manchester U, Liverpool)	15
Carpenter, R. E. 2005 (Burnley)	1
Cassidy, J. A. 2011 (Wolverhampton W)	8
Cegielski, W. 1977 (Wrexham)	2
Chamberlain, E. C. 2010 (Leicester C)	9
Chapple, S. R. 1992 (Swansea C)	8
Charles, J. M. 1979 (Swansea C)	2
Church, S. R. 2008 (Reading)	15
Clark, J. 1978 (Manchester U, Derby Co)	2
Coates, J. S. 1996 (Swansea C)	5
Coleman, C. 1990 (Swansea C)	3
Collins, J. M. 2003 (Cardiff C)	7
Collins, M. J. 2007 (Fulham, Swansea C)	2
Collison, J. D. 2008 (West Ham U)	7
Cornell, D. J. 2010 (Swansea C)	4
Cotterill, D. R. G. B. 2005 (Bristol C, Wigan Ath)	11
Coyne, D. 1992 (Tranmere R)	7
Craig, N. L. 2009 (Everton)	4
Critchell, K. A. R. 2005 (Southampton)	3
Crofts, A. L. 2005 (Gillingham)	10
Crowell, M. T. 2004 (Wrexham)	7
Curtis, A. T. 1977 (Swansea C)	1
Davies, A. 1982 (Manchester U)	6
Davies, A. G. 2006 (Cambridge U)	6
Davies, A. R. 2005 (Southampton, Yeovil T)	14
Davies, C. M. 2005 (Oxford U, Verona, Oldham Ath)	9

Davies, D. 1999 (Barry T)	1
Davies, G. M. 1993 (Hereford U, Crystal Palace)	7
Davies, I. C. 1978 (Norwich C)	1
Davies, L. 2005 (Bangor C)	1
Davies, R. J. 2006 (WBA)	4
Davies, S. 1999 (Peterborough U, Tottenham H)	10
Dawson, C. 2013 (Leeds U)	**2**
Day, R. 2000 (Manchester C, Mansfield T)	11
Deacy, N. 1977 (PSV Eindhoven)	1
De-Vulgt, L. S. 2002 (Swansea C)	2
Dibble, A. 1983 (Cardiff C)	3
Doble, R. A. 2010 (Southampton)	10
Doughty, M. E. 2012 (QPR)	1
Doyle, S. C. 1979 (Preston NE, Huddersfield T)	2
Duffy, R. M. 2005 (Portsmouth)	7
Dummett, P. 2011 (Newcastle U)	3
Dwyer, P. J. 1979 (Cardiff C)	1
Eardley, N. 2007 (Oldham Ath, Blackpool)	11
Earnshaw, R. 1999 (Cardiff C)	10
Easter, D. J. 2006 (Cardiff C)	1
Ebdon, M. 1990 (Everton)	2
Edwards, C. N. H. 1996 (Swansea C)	7
Edwards, D. A. 2006 (Shrewsbury T, Luton T, Wolverhampton W)	9
Edwards, G. D. R. 2012 (Swansea C)	**4**
Edwards, R. I. 1977 (Chester)	2
Edwards, R. W. 1991 (Bristol C)	13
Evans, A. 1977 (Bristol R)	1
Evans, C. 2007 (Manchester C, Sheffield U)	13
Evans, K. 1999 (Leeds U, Cardiff C)	4
Evans, L. 2013 (Wolverhampton W)	**4**
Evans, P. S. 1996 (Shrewsbury T)	1
Evans, S. J. 2001 (Crystal Palace)	2
Evans, T. 1995 (Cardiff C)	3
Fish, N. 2005 (Cardiff C)	2
Fleetwood, S. 2005 (Cardiff C)	5
Flynn, C. P. 2007 (Crewe Alex)	1
Folland, R. W. 2000 (Oxford U)	1
Foster, M. G. 1993 (Tranmere R)	1
Fowler, L. A. 2003 (Coventry C, Huddersfield T)	9
Fox, M. A. 2013 (Charlton Ath)	**4**
Freeman, K. 2012 (Nottingham F, Derby Co)	**15**
Freestone, R. 1990 (Chelsea)	1
Gabbidon, D. L. 1999 (WBA, Cardiff C)	17
Gale, D. 1983 (Swansea C)	2
Gall, K. A. 2002 (Bristol R, Yeovil T)	8
Gibson, N. D. 1999 (Tranmere R, Sheffield W)	11
Giggs, R. J. 1991 (Manchester U)	1
Gilbert, P. 2005 (Plymouth Arg)	12
Giles, D. C. 1977 (Cardiff C, Swansea C, Crystal Palace)	4
Giles, P. 1982 (Cardiff C)	3
Graham, D. 1991 (Manchester U)	1
Green, R. M. 1998 (Wolverhampton W)	16
Griffith, C. 1990 (Cardiff C)	1
Griffiths, C. 1991 (Shrewsbury T)	1
Grubb, D. 2007 (Bristol C)	1
Gunter, C. 2006 (Cardiff C, Tottenham H)	8
Haldane, L. O. 2007 (Bristol R)	1
Hall, G. D. 1990 (Chelsea)	1
Harrison, E. W. 2013 (Bristol R)	**2**
Hartson, J. 1994 (Luton T, Arsenal)	9
Haworth, S. O. 1997 (Cardiff C, Coventry C, Wigan Ath)	12
Henley, A. 2012 (Blackburn R)	3
Hennessey, W. R. 2006 (Wolverhampton W)	6
Hewitt, E. J. 2012 (Macclesfield T, Ipswich T)	**9**
Hillier, I. M. 2001 (Tottenham H, Luton T)	5
Hodges, G. 1983 (Wimbledon)	5
Holden, A. 1984 (Chester C)	1
Holloway, C. D. 1999 (Exeter C)	2
Hopkins, J. 1982 (Fulham)	5
Hopkins, S. A. 1999 (Wrexham)	1
Howells, J. 2012 (Luton T)	5
Huggins, D. S. 1996 (Bristol C)	1
Hughes, D. 2005 (Kaiserslautern, Regensburg)	3
Hughes, D. R. 1994 (Southampton)	1
Hughes, I. 1992 (Bury)	11
Hughes, L. M. 1983 (Manchester U)	5
Hughes, R. D. 1996 (Aston Villa, Shrewsbury T)	13
Hughes, W. 1977 (WBA)	3

Huws, E. W. 2012 (Manchester C)	**6**
Isgrove, L. J. 2013 (Southampton)	**6**
Jackett, K. 1981 (Watford)	2
Jacobson, J. M. 2006 (Cardiff C, Bristol R)	15
James, L. R. S. 2006 (Southampton)	10
James, R. M. 1977 (Swansea C)	3
Jarman, L. 1996 (Cardiff C)	10
Jeanne, L. C. 1999 (QPR)	8
Jelleyman, G. A. 1999 (Peterborough U)	1
Jenkins, L. D. 1998 (Swansea C)	9
Jenkins, S. R. 1993 (Swansea C)	2
John, D. C. 2014 (Cardiff C)	**2**
Jones, C. T. 2007 (Swansea C)	1
Jones, E. P. 2000 (Blackpool)	1
Jones, F. 1981 (Wrexham)	1
Jones, J. A. 2001 (Swansea C)	3
Jones, L. 1982 (Cardiff C)	3
Jones, M. A. 2004 (Wrexham)	4
Jones, M. G. 1998 (Leeds U)	7
Jones, P. L. 1992 (Liverpool)	12
Jones, R. 2011 (AFC Wimbledon)	1
Jones, R. A. 1994 (Sheffield W)	3
Jones, S. J. 2005 (Swansea C)	1
Jones, V. 1979 (Bristol R)	2
Kendall, L. M. 2001 (Crystal Palace)	2
Kendall, M. 1978 (Tottenham H)	1
Kenworthy, J. R. 1994 (Tranmere R)	3
King, A. 2008 (Leicester C)	11
Knott, G. R. 1996 (Tottenham H)	1
Law, B. J. 1990 (QPR)	2
Lawless, A. 2006 (Torquay U)	1
Lawrence, T. 2013 (Manchester U)	**8**
Ledley, J. C. 2005 (Cardiff C)	5
Letheran, G. 1977 (Leeds U)	2
Letheran, K. C. 2006 (Swansea C)	1
Lewis, D. 1982 (Swansea C)	9
Lewis, J. 1983 (Cardiff C)	1
Llewellyn, C. M. 1998 (Norwich C)	14
Loveridge, J. 1982 (Swansea C)	3
Low, J. D. 1999 (Bristol R, Cardiff C)	1
Lowndes, S. R. 1979 (Newport Co, Millwall)	4
Lucas, L. P. 2011 (Swansea C)	**19**
MacDonald, S. B. 2006 (Swansea C)	25
McCarthy, A. J. 1994 (QPR)	3
McDonald, C. 2006 (Cardiff C)	3
Mackin, L. 2006 (Wrexham)	1
Maddy, P. 1982 (Cardiff C)	2
Margetson, M. W. 1992 (Manchester C)	7
Martin, A. P. 1999 (Crystal Palace)	1
Martin, D. A. 2006 (Notts Co)	1
Marustik, C. 1982 (Swansea C)	7
Matthews, A. J. 2010 (Cardiff C)	5
Maxwell, C. 2009 (Wrexham)	16
Maxwell, L. J. 1999 (Liverpool, Cardiff C)	14
Meades, J. 2012 (Cardiff C)	4
Meaker, M. J. 1994 (QPR)	2
Melville, A. K. 1990 (Swansea C, Oxford U)	2
Micallef, C. 1982 (Cardiff C)	3
Morgan, A. M. 1995 (Tranmere R)	4
Morgan, C. 2004 (Wrexham, Milton Keynes D)	12
Morris, A. J. 2009 (Cardiff C, Aldershot T)	8
Moss, D. M. 2003 (Shrewsbury T)	6
Mountain, P. D. 1997 (Cardiff C)	2
Mumford, A. O. 2003 (Swansea C)	4
Nardiello, D. 1978 (Coventry C)	1
Neilson, A. B. 1993 (Newcastle U)	7
Nicholas, P. 1978 (Crystal Palace, Arsenal)	3
Nogan, K. 1990 (Luton T)	2
Nogan, L. M. 1991 (Oxford U)	1
Nyatanga, L. J. 2005 (Derby Co)	10
Oakley, A. 2013 (Swindon T)	1
Ogleby, R. 2011 (Hearts, Wrexham)	**12**
Oster, J. M. 1997 (Grimsby T, Everton)	9
O'Sullivan, T. P. 2013 (Cardiff C)	**3**
Owen, G. 1991 (Wrexham)	8
Page, R. J. 1995 (Watford)	4
Parslow, D. 2005 (Cardiff C)	4

Partington, J. M. 2009 (Bournemouth) — 8
Partridge, D. W. 1997 (West Ham U) — 1
Pascoe, C. 1983 (Swansea C) — 4
Pearce, S. 2006 (Bristol C) — 3
Pejic, S. M. 2003 (Wrexham) — 6
Pembridge, M. A. 1991 (Luton T) — 1
Peniket, R. 2012 (Fulham) — 1
Perry, J. 1990 (Cardiff C) — 3
Peters, M. 1992 (Manchester C, Norwich C) — 3
Phillips, D. 1984 (Plymouth Arg) — 3
Phillips, G. R. 2001 (Swansea C) — 3
Phillips, L. 1979 (Swansea C, Charlton Ath) — 2
Pipe, D. R. 2003 (Coventry C, Notts Co) — 12
Pontin, K. 1978 (Cardiff C) — 1
Powell, L. 1991 (Southampton) — 4
Powell, L. 2004 (Leicester C) — 3
Powell, R. 2006 (Bolton W) — 1
Price, J. J. 1998 (Swansea C) — 7
Price, L. P. 2005 (Ipswich T) — 10
Price, M. D. 2001 (Everton, Hull C, Scarborough) — 13
Price, P. 1981 (Luton T) — 1
Pritchard, J. P. 2013 (Fulham) — **3**
Pritchard, M. O. 2006 (Swansea C) — 4
Pugh, D. 1982 (Doncaster R) — 2
Pugh, S. 1993 (Wrexham) — 2
Pulis, A. J. 2006 (Stoke C) — 5

Ramasut, M. W. T. 1997 (Bristol R) — 4
Ramsey, A. J. 2008, (Cardiff C, Arsenal) — 12
Ratcliffe, K. 1981 (Everton) — 2
Ray, G. E. 2013 (Crewe Alex) — **4**
Ready, K. 1992 (QPR) — 5
Rees, A. 1984 (Birmingham C) — 1
Rees, J. M. 1990 (Luton T) — 3
Rees, M. R. 2003 (Millwall) — 4
Ribeiro, C. M. 2008 (Bristol C) — 8
Richards, A. D. J. 2010 (Swansea C) — 16
Richards, E. A. 2012 (Bristol R) — 1
Roberts, A. M. 1991 (QPR) — 2
Roberts, C. 2013 (Cheltenham T) — **6**
Roberts, C. J. 1999 (Cardiff C) — 1
Roberts, G. 1983 (Hull C) — 1
Roberts, G. W. 1997 (Liverpool, Panionios, Tranmere R) — 11
Roberts, I. G. 1977 (Wrexham) — 1
Roberts, N. W. 1999 (Wrexham) — 3
Roberts, P. 1997 (Porthmadog) — 1
Roberts, S. I. 1999 (Swansea C) — 13
Roberts, S. W. 2000 (Wrexham) — 3
Robinson, C. P. 1996 (Wolverhampton W) — 6
Robinson, J. R. C. 1992 (Brighton & HA, Charlton Ath) — 5
Robson-Kanu, K. H. 2010 (Reading) — 4
Rowlands, A. J. R. 1996 (Manchester C) — 5
Rush, I. 1981 (Liverpool) — 2

Savage, R. W. 1995 (Crewe Alex) — 3
Sayer, P. A. 1977 (Cardiff C) — 2
Searle, D. 1991 (Cardiff C) — 6
Slatter, D. 2000 (Chelsea) — 6
Slatter, N. 1983 (Bristol R) — 6
Somner, M. J. 2004 (Brentford) — 2
Speed, G. A. 1990 (Leeds U) — 3
Spender, S. 2005 (Wrexham) — 6

Stephens, D. 2011 (Hibernian) — 7
Stevenson, N. 1982 (Swansea C) — 2
Stevenson, W. B. 1977 (Leeds U) — 3
Stock, B. B. 2003 (Bournemouth) — 4
Symons, C. J. 1991 (Portsmouth) — 2

Tancock, S. 2013 (Swansea C) — **6**
Taylor, A. J. 2012 (Tranmere R) — 3
Taylor, G. K. 1995 (Bristol R) — 4
Taylor, J. W. T. 2010 (Reading) — 12
Taylor, N. J. 2008 (Wrexham, Swansea C) — 13
Taylor, R. F. 2008 (Chelsea) — 5
Thomas, C. E. 2010 (Swansea C) — 3
Thomas, D. G. 1977 (Leeds U) — 3
Thomas, D. J. 1998 (Watford) — 2
Thomas, J. A. 1996 (Blackburn R) — 21
Thomas, Martin R. 1979 (Bristol R) — 2
Thomas, Mickey R. 1977 (Wrexham) — 2
Thomas, S. 2001 (Wrexham) — 5
Tibbott, L. 1977 (Ipswich T) — 2
Tipton, M. J. 1998 (Oldham Ath) — 6
Tolley, J. C. 2001 (Shrewsbury T) — 12
Tudur-Jones, O. 2006 (Swansea C) — 3
Twiddy, C. 1995 (Plymouth Arg) — 3

Valentine, R. D. 2001 (Everton, Darlington) — 8
Vaughan, D. O. 2003 (Crewe Alex) — 8
Vaughan, N. 1982 (Newport Co) — 2
Vokes, S. M. 2007 (Bournemouth, Wolverhampton W) — 14

Walsh, D. 2000 (Wrexham) — 8
Walsh, I. P. 1979 (Crystal Palace, Swansea C) — 2
Walsh, J. 2012 (Swansea C, Crawley T) — **9**
Walton, M. 1991 (Norwich C.) — 1
Ward, D. 1996 (Notts Co) — 2
Ward, D. 2013 (Liverpool) — **4**
Warlow, O. J. 2007 (Lincoln C) — 2
Weston, R. D. 2001 (Arsenal, Cardiff C) — 4
Whitfield, P. M. 2003 (Wrexham) — 1
Wiggins, R. 2006 (Crystal Palace) — 9
Williams, A. P. 1998 (Southampton) — 9
Williams, A. S. 1996 (Blackburn R) — 16
Williams, D. 1983 (Bristol R) — 1
Williams, D. I. L. 1998 (Liverpool, Wrexham) — 9
Williams, D. T. 2006 (Yeovil T) — 1
Williams, E. 1997 (Caernarfon T) — 2
Williams, G. 1983 (Bristol R) — 2
Williams, G. A. 2003 (Crystal Palace) — 5
Williams, G. C. 2014 (Fulham) — **2**
Williams, J. P. 2011 (Crystal Palace) — 8
Williams, M. 2001 (Manchester U) — 10
Williams, M. P. 2006 (Wrexham) — 14
Williams, M. R. 2006 (Wrexham) — 6
Williams, O. fon 2007 (Crewe Alex, Stockport Co) — 11
Williams, R. 2007 (Middlesbrough) — 10
Williams, S. J. 1995 (Wrexham) — 4
Wilmot, R. 1982 (Arsenal) — 6
Wilson, J. S. 2009 (Bristol C) — 3
Worgan, L. J. 2005 (Milton Keynes D, Rushden & D) — 5
Wright, A. A. 1998 (Oxford U) — 3

Young, S. 1996 (Cardiff C) — 5

FA SCHOOLS AND YOUTH GAMES 2013–14

ENGLAND UNDER-16

SKY SPORTS VICTORY SHIELD
Kidderminster, 4 October 2013

England (1) 1 *(Wakefield 35)* **Wales (0) 0**   2702
England: Sandford; Yates, Cull (Johnson 65); Davies, Williams, Oxford (Collinge 55), Wakefield, Patching (Sheaf 40), Hinds, Phillips (Leko 55), Bell (Ndukwu 40).
Wales: Absalom; Coxe, Abbruzzese, Harrington, Challis, Williams, Chilekwa (Cullen 65), McNulty, Roberts, Broadhead (Keating 60), Mwamuka (Evans 40).

Bournemouth, 8 November 2013

England (0) 0   Northern Ireland (0) 1 *(Conaty 71)*   2810
England: McCulloch; Arnold, Coulson, Diallo (Murray 40 (Muskwe 63)), Assiana (Kane 40), Johnson, Maddox (Edwards K 63), Gribbin, Hector-Ingram, Edwards M, Green (Nmecha 63).
Northern Ireland: McDermott; Kerr, Mulligan, Smyth, King, Henry (Olali 68), McClean (Kerr 79), Crowe (Francis 62), Conaty, Gordon, Walker (Caulfield 40).

Kirkcaldy, 29 November 2013

Scotland (1) 1 *(Miller 28)* **England (0) 0**   2294
Scotland: McCrorie Robby; McCrorie Ross, Jones, Higgins, Harvie, McKirdy, Archibald, Hill (Ross 75), Miller (Norris 64), Heaney, Coote (Stirling 80).
England: Whiteman (King 73); Yates, Ndukwu, Davies, Humphreys, Collinge, Willock (Hinds 40), Kane (Maddox 64), Leko (Cull 64), Nabay, Nmecha (Hepburn-Murphy 40).

USA NIKE INTERNATIONAL TOURNAMENT
Lakewood Ranch, 9 December 2013

Brazil (2) 2 *(Marcelo 36, Rafael 41)*
England (1) 1 *(Hinds 18)*   500
England: Whiteman; Da Silva, Williams (Oxford 45), Humphreys, Naby (Wakefield 45), Hinds, Willock (Gribbin 66), Collinge (Arnold 45), Patching (Edwards M 58), Philips, Sheaf (Hepburn-Murphy 70).

Lakewood Ranch, 11 December 2013

USA (2) 5 *(Gallardo 13, 16, 85, Wright 72, 80)*
England (0) 1 *(Edwards M 47)*   1200
England: Sandford; Arnold, Gribbin (Patching 68), Williams (Humphreys 72), Wakefield, Nabay, Hepburn-Murphy (Hinds 46), Collinge, Philips (Da Silva 46), Ndukwu, Edwards M (Willock 68).

Lakewood Ranch, 13 December 2013

Portugal (1) 3 *(Sambu 9 (pen), 76, Centeno 48)*
England (1) 4 *(Phillips 41, Patching 53, Hinds 68, Willock 73)*
England: King; Arnold (Nabay 57), Da Silva, Humphreys, Wakefield (Hepburn-Murphy 46), Hinds, Willock (Ndukwu 82), Patching (Williams 90), Oxford, Phillips, Edwards M (Gribbin 36).

UEFA DEVELOPMENT TOURNAMENT
Burton, 9 February 2014

England (0) 1 *(Hinds 80)*
Spain (1) 3 *(Villanueva 6, Perez 60, Villalba 70)*
England: Sandford; Yates, Coulson, Gribbin (Hector-Ingram 72), Johnson, Collinge, Davies, Hinds, Leko (Diallo 40), Willock (Green 58), Kane.

Burton, 11 February 2014

England (2) 4 *(Dearnley 11, Dhanda 22 (pen), 62, Hector-Ingram 41)*
Denmark (0) 1 *(Christensen 58)*
England: Oxborough; Yates (Kane 40), Collinge, Dearnley (Green 55), Davies (Coulson 40), Arnold (Johnson 47), Dhanda, Williams, Edwards M (Gribbin 67), Diallo, Hector-Ingram (Leko 55).

Burton, 14 February 2014

England (2) 3 *(Hinds 17, 48, Hector-Ingram 38)*
Belgium (0) 2 *(Azzaoui 44, Janssens 57)*
England: Oxborough (Sandford 40); Arnold, Coulson, Williams (Yates 54), Gribbin (Dhanda 40), Johnson (Collinge 40), Davies (Kane 40), Hinds, Willock (Dearnley 54), Green (Leko 49), Hector-Ingram (Edwards M 40).

MONTAIGU TOURNAMENT
GROUP B
Mareuil Sur Lay, 15 April 2014

Saudi Arabia (2) 2 *(19, 26)* **England (0) 0**
England: Oxborough; Williams (Collinge 40), Humphreys, Suliman, Coulson, Maddox (Ndukwu 63), Davies (Nabay 63), Dearnley (Patching 40), Dhanda, Holland (Phillips 40), Hector-Ingram.

Mareuil Sur Lay, 17 April 2014

England (0) 1 *(Hector-Ingram 46)*
South Korea (0) 1 *(Lee Seunwoo 56)*
England: Whiteman; Nabay, Collinge, Suliman, Ndukwu (Holland 80), Davies, Patching (Maddox 73), Phillips (Williams 68), 17 Dearnley, Hector-Ingram, Dhanda (Coulson 68).

Chateu d'Olonne, 19 April 2014

England (0) 1 *(Phillips 80)*   **Portugal (0) 0**
England: Oxborough; Collinge, Coulson, Patching (Davies 69), Wakefield (Hector-Ingram 53), Phillips, Maddox (Dearnley 69), Holland (Dhanda 59), Nabay (Suliman 59), Williams, Ndukwu.

THIRD PLACE PLAY-OFF
Montaigu, 21 April 2014

England (1) 2 *(Hector-Ingram 33, Davies 51)*
France (1) 2 *(Karamoh 21, 41)*
England won 5-3 on penalties.
England: Whiteman; Williams (Collinge 41), Humphreys (Phillips 41), Suliman, Ndukwu, Nabay, Davies, Dearnley, Maddox (Patching 59), Wakefield (Holland 55), Hector-Ingram (Dhanda 45).

ENGLAND UNDER-17

FRIENDLIES
Burton, 28 January 2014

England (0) 2 *(Solanke 67, 80)*
Belgium (0) 1 *(Bertaccini 60)*
England: Henderson; Moore, O'Connor, Brewitt (Fry 58), Lowe, Ledson (Dowell 67), Christie-Davies (Kenny 76), Cooke (Cook 58), Maitland-Niles, Solanke, Fox (Mitchell 67).

Burton, 30 January 2014

England (0) 1 *(Mitchell 43)*
Belgium (1) 2 *(Damraoui 19, Verreth 72)*
England: Howes; Kenny (Moore Tafari 67), Lowe (Ledson 53), Brewitt (O'Connor 16), Fry, Borthwick-Jackson, Cooke, Fox (Maitland-Niles 63), Cook, Mitchell, Mahoney.

NORDIC TOURNAMENT
Brumunddal, 5 August 2013

England (1) 1 *(Boadu 35)*
Faroe Islands (0) 0
England: Henderson; Helm (Elsdon 56), Pybus, Suliman, Boadu (Rasulo 56), Da Silva, Logan, Humphreys, Ali (Drennan 63), Nabay (Cooke 56), Taylor.

Vang, 6 August 2013

Finland (0) 1 *(63)*

England (0) 1 *(Rasulo 76 (pen)*

England: Whiteman; Edwards, Elsdon, Drennan, Cooke, Rasulo, Da Silva, Humphreys, Ali, Nabay (Logan 64), Taylor (Boadu 64).
England won 5-4 on penalties.

Brumunddal, 8 August 2013

Norway (0) 1 *(72)*   **England (0) 1** *(Taylor 68)*

England: Whiteman; Edwards (Da Silva 62), Pybus, Elsdon, Suliman, Drennan (Rasulo 55), Cooke, Boadu, Fox (Ali 62), Logan (Taylor 55), Humphreys.

Hamar, 10 August 2013

Norway (0) 0   England (3) 4 *(Boadu 18, 32, 71, Taylor 21)*

England: Henderson; Helm, Edwards (Da Silva 41), Elsdon (Pybus 41), Suliman, Cooke, Boadu, Fox (Drennan 65), Ali, Nabay, Taylor.

FA INTERNATIONAL TOURNAMENT

Burton, 28 August 2013

England (0) 1 *(Roberts 45)*

Portugal (1) 3 *(Silva 3, 49, Buta 80)*   671

England: Moore Tafari (Egbo 73), Lowe, Ledson (Onomah 73), Adarabayio, Roberts, Brown, Crowley, Borthwick-Jackson, Solanke (Mitchell 62), Dowell (Cook 62).

Burton, 30 August 2013

England (0) 1 *(Armstrong 50)*   **Turkey (0) 0**   629

England: Huddart; Lowe (Ledson 75), Gomez, Onomah, Mitchell, Egbo, Cook (Moore Tafari 75), Borthwick-Jackson (Adarabayio 40), Solanke (Roberts 67), Armstrong (Crowley 67), Dowell (Brown 58).

Burton, 1 September 2013

England (1) 1 *(Ledson 26)*

Italy (1) 2 *(De Santis 6, Trani 45)*   722

England: Woodman (Huddart 45); Moore Tafari, Lowe (Borthwick-Jackson 19), Ledson, Adarabayio (Cook 45), Roberts (Mitchell 39), Onomah, Brown (Solanke 58), Crowley (Dowell 64), Egbo, Armstrong.

ALGARVE TOURNAMENT

Lagos, 26 February 2014

England (0) 2 *(Sims 43, Onomah 74)*

Netherlands (0) 0

England: Woodman; Egbo, Edwards (Lowe 39), Gomez, Fry, Cook, Roberts (Ojo 56), Onomah (Grant 76), Sims, Dowell (Moore Taylor 49), Mitchell (Rasulo 56).

Faro, 28 February 2014

Portugal (0) 2 *(Goncalves 43, Oliveira 72)*

England (1) 2 *(Cooke 33, 77)*

England: Howes; Egbo (Gomez 40), Lowe, Brewitt (Fry 33), Connolly, Ojo, Moore Taylor (Sims 50), Cooke, Mitchell (Roberts 40), Rasulo (Dowell 50), Grant (Cook 70).

Lagos, 2 March 2014

Germany (0) 1 *(Gimber 72)*   **England (0) 0**

England: Woodman; Connolly, Edwards (Moore Taylor 56), Gomez (Egbo 40), Fry, Cook (Dowell 56), Onomah, Cooke, Roberts (Grant 51), Sims (Rasulo 64), Mitchell (Ojo 51).

2014 EUROPEAN CHAMPIONSHIP

QUALIFYING ROUND

Yerevan, 24 October 2013

Armenia (0) 0

England (2) 4 *(Roberts 3, Armstrong 32, 80, Solanke 75)*

England: Henderson; Kenny, Ledson, Gomez, Brewitt, Roberts, Rossiter (Christie-Davies 68), Brown (Solanke 58), Onomah (Ojo 58), Borthwick-Jackson, Armstrong.

Yerevan, 26 October 2013

Gibraltar (0) 0

England (3) 8 *(Armstrong 29, 34, Ojo 36, Solanke 42, 74, Brewitt 48, Brown 52, Roberts 62)*

England: Huddart; Kenny (Roberts 53), Brewitt, Onomah (Ledson 53), Ojo, Egbo, Borthwick-Jackson, Cooke, Armstrong (Brown 41), Solanke, Christie-Davies.

Yerevan, 29 October 2013

England (2) 6 *(Brown 18, 52, Armstrong 37, 44, Roberts 57, Ledson 80 (pen))*

Republic of Ireland (0) 0

England: Henderson; Kenny, Lowe, Ledson, Gomez, Brewitt (Christie-Davies 59), Roberts, Rossiter, Brown, Armstrong (Ojo 48), Solanke (Cooke 58).

ELITE ROUND (CZECH REPUBLIC)

Uherske Hradiste, 26 March 2014

Czech Republic (0) 0   England (0) 1 *(Solanke 53)*

England: Woodman; Connolly, Moore Tafari, Gomez, Fry, Ledson, Cook, Sims (Mitchell 58), Brown (Cooke 74), Armstrong, Solanke.

Uherske Hradiste, 28 March 2014

England (0) 1 *(Brown 50)*   **Albania (0) 0**

England: Woodman; Egbo, Gomez, Moore Taylor, Moore Tafari, Ledson, Onomah, Maitland-Niles (Solanke 56), Brown (Cooke 67), Sims, Armstrong (Mitchell 71).

Zlin, 31 March 2014

Italy (0) 1 *(Trani 52)*

England (1) 2 *(Armstrong 20, Solanke 71)*

England: Woodman, Connolly, Gomez, Moore Taylor, Moore Tafari, Ledson, Cook (Cooke 76), Brown (Mitchell 80), Onomah, Solanke (Sims 78), Armstrong.

FINALS (MALTA)

GROUP A

Ta'Qali, 9 May 2014

Malta (0) 0   England (2) 3 *(Roberts 15, 48, Armstrong 25)*

England: Woodman; Kenny, Moore Tafari, Ledson, Gomez, Fry, Onomah (Cook 69), Armstrong, Solanke (Cooke 59), Sims, Roberts (Mitchell 50).

Gozo, 12 May 2014

England (1) 4 *(Solanke 21, 49, Kenny 58, Armstrong 64)*

Turkey (1) 1 *(Unal 14)*   1631

England: Kenny; Gomez, Moore Taylor, Moore Tafari (Egbo 65), Ledson, Cook, Roberts, Brown, Solanke (Cooke 65), Armstrong (Mitchell 70).

Paolo, 15 May 2014

England (0) 0   Netherlands (0) 2 *(Verdonk 45, van der Moot (68)*   1420

England: Howes; Egbo, Gomez, Fry, Kenny, Ledson, Onomah, Cooke (Roberts 74), Sims (Armstrong 47), Mitchell (Moore Taylor 74), Brown.

SEMI-FINALS

Ta'Qali, 18 May 2014

Portugal (0) 0

England (0) 2 *(Solanke 52, Roberts 74)*   2107

England: Woodman; Kenny, Gomez, Moore Taylor, Moore Tafari (Egbo 72), Ledson, Cook, Roberts (Cooke 75), Brown, Solanke, Armstrong (Onomah 35).

FINAL

Ta'Qali, 21 May 2014

England (1) 1 *(Solanke 25)*

Netherlands (1) 1 *(Shuurman 40)*   9432

England: Woodman; Kenny, Gomez, Moore Taylor, Moore Tafari, Ledson, Cook (Cooke 74), Roberts, Onomah, Brown, Solanke.
England won 4-1 on penalties.

ENGLAND UNDER-18

FRIENDLIES

Burton, 14 October 2013

England (4) 4 *(Fewster 19, 41, Kent 26, 38)*   **Hungary (0) 0**
England: Smith (Burton 88); Knoyle, O'Hanlon, Aina (Burke), Galloway, Morris, Kent (Barker 67), Miller (Green 60), Fewster (Kiwoma 80), Palmer (Smith-Brown 71), Iwobi.

Burton, 18 February 2014

England (1) 4 *(Fewster 22 (pen), 62, 72 (pen), Rittenberg 84)*
Belgium (0) 0
England: Smith; Knoyle (O'Hanlon 65), Burke, Galloway, Chilwell, Morris, Winks, Miller (Gilliead 85), Gray, Fewster (Rittenberg 72), Oduwa.

Burton, 3 March 2014

England (1) 1 *(Kiwomya 8)*
Croatia (0) 2 *(Stolnik 59, Vlasic 65)*
England: Burton; Knoyle, Burke (Brown 66), Smith-Brown, Chilwell, Morris, Alli (Anderson 87), Brannagan, Gray (Sonupe 76), Kiwomya, Barker (Rittenburg 68).

Burton, 5 March 2014

England (1) 1 *(Sonupe 38)*
Croatia (1) 2 *(Brodic 39, Lulic 73)*
England: Grainger; Smith-Brown, Chilwell, Whatmough, Morris, Colkett (Alli 72), Brown (Brannagan 86), Anderson, Sonupe (Gray 78), Rittenburg (Barker 59), Kiwomya.

Rotherham, 16 April 2014

England (0) 0 *(Rittenberg 74, Winks 82)*
Germany (1) 0 *(Pflucke 38)*
England: Smith; Birch (Burke 74), Dickie, Galloway, Smith-Brown, Morris, Gilliead (Winks 66), Kent (Miller 87), Oduwa (Brown 87), Barker (Rittenberg 74), Fewster.

ENGLAND UNDER-19

FRIENDLIES

Tallinn, 5 September 2013

Estonia (1) 1 *(Liivak 38)*
England (3) 6 *(Wilson 12, Ibe 30, Chambers 40, Morris 64, Baker 88, 90)*
England: Beeney (Coddington 46); Chambers C (Aina 46), Toffolo (Cooper 58), Pearson, Chambers L, Hayden, Ibe, Loftus-Cheek (Baker 58), Wilson (Akpom 54), Campbell (Morris 46), Murphy Joshua (Digby 58).

Telhi, 14 November 2013

Hungary (0) 1 *(Talaber 73)*
England (2) 4 *(Murphy Joshua 5, Digby 32, Bennett 57, Robinson 88)*
England: Coddington; Chambers C, Targett, Baker, Aina (Swift 75), Facey, Ibe (Williams 63), Rothwell (Long 63), Bennett (Robinson 63), Digby (Pearson 75), Murphy Joshua (Murphy Jacob 63).

Chester, 5 March 2014

England (1) 3 *(Cole 22, Baker 59 (pen), Robinson 63)*
Turkey (0) 0   3412
England: Beeney (Walton 76); Aina, Chambers C (Reed 46), Facey, Targett (Ormonde-Ottewill 67), Hayden, Swift (Ball 58), Baker, Murphy Joshua (Digby 67), Gallagher (Mowatt 67), Cole (Robinson 68).

2014 EUROPEAN CHAMPIONSHIP

QUALIFYING ROUND (SLOVENIA)

Ptuj, 10 October 2013

Slovenia (1) 1 *(Barisic 13)*   **England (0) 1** *(Baker 85)*
England: Beeney; Chambers C, Toffolo, Baker, Webster, Hayden (Facey 64), Swift, Pearson, Wilson (Bennett 76), Akpom, Ibe (Murphy Joshua 83).

Ptuj, 12 October 2013

Andorra (0) 0
England (4) 7 *(Bennett 17, 78, Loftus-Cheek 20, 48, Pearson 41, 45, Morris 57)*
England: Coddington; Chambers C (Swift 64), Baker, Pearson, Ibe, Bennett, Loftus-Cheek, Facey, Cooper (Hayden 68), Morris (Akpom 64), Murphy Joshua.

Ptuj, 15 October 2013

England (1) 1 *(Bennett 34)*   **Switzerland (0) 0**
England: Beeney; Chambers C, Toffolo, Webster, Hayden, Swift (Pearson 79), Wilson, Akpom (Morris 46), Bennett, Loftus-Cheek (Baker 60), Facey.

ELITE ROUND (ENGLAND)

Walsall, 24 May 2014

England (1) 6 *(Ibe 27, 58, 65, Baker 52 (pen), Gallagher 62, Robinson 90)*
Montenegro (0) 0   1,897
England: Walton; Chambers C, Targett, Baker, Jones (Galloway 63), Facey, Ibe, Swift (Robinson 63), Gallagher (Akpom 71), Murphy Joshua, Aina.

Burton, 26 May 2014

England (0) 2 *(Baker 76, 82)*
Scotland (0) 1 *(Souttar 51)*   835
England: Walton; Chambers C, Targett, Jones (Loftus-Cheek 71), Facey, Aina, Baker, Reed (Robinson 58), Ibe, Murphy Joshua (Galloway 85), Akpom.
Scotland: Fulton; McLennan, Souttar, Hyam, Hendrie (Sinnamon 81), King, Lindsay, Gauld, Henderson, Nicholson (Telfer 52), Johnstone (Cardwell 69).

Burton, 29 May 2014

England (0) 0   **Ukraine (0) 1** *(Chambers 90 (og))*   735
England: Walton, Aina, Chambers C, Jones, Targett (Galloway 56), Swift, Baker, Loftus-Cheek (Reed 85), Robinson, Akpom, Cole (Gallagher 80).

ENGLAND UNDER-20

TOULON TOURNAMENT

Toulon, 22 May 2014

England (1) 0 *(Obita 30, Forster-Caskey 54, Cousins 80)*
Qatar (0) 0
England: Bond; Browning, Moore, Gibson, Garbutt (Smith 74), Ward-Prowse (Dier 69), McEachran (Cousins 59), March, Forster-Caskey, Obita, Berahino (Woodrow 59).

St Raphael, 26 May 2014

England (0) 1 *(Ward-Prowse 71)*
Brazil (1) 2 *(Allison 7, Lucas Silva 46)*
England: Butland; Browning, Moore, Keane M, Garbutt (Smith 60), Ward-Prowse, Chalobah, Cousins (March 80), Forster-Caskey (Woodrow 51), Redmond, Berahino.

Aubagne, 28 May 2014

England (1) 1 *(Woodrow 3)*
Korea Republic (0) 1 *(Lee Changmin 54)*
England: Bond; Dier (Browning 67), Keane M, Gibson, Garbutt, Ward-Prowse, Redmond, Forster-Caskey (Keane W 64), Chalobah, Smith (March 40), Woodrow.

Toulon, 30 May 2014

England (1) 1 *(Woodrow 15)*
Colombia (0) 1 *(Jhoao Rodriguez 69)*
England: Butland; Dier (Keane M 32), Moore, Gibson, Browning, McEachran (Forster-Caskey 19), Cousins, March, Keane W (Chalobah 74), Obita, Woodrow (Redmond 67).

THIRD PLACE PLAY-OFF

Toulon, 1 June 2014

England (0) 0
Portugal (0) 1 *(Horta 56)*
England: Butland; Browning, Gibson, Moore, Garbutt, Chalobah, Ward-Prowse, Redmond, Forster-Caskey (Keane W 65), Berahino, Woodrow.

SCHOOLS FOOTBALL 2013–14

BOODLES INDEPENDENT SCHOOLS FA CUP 2012–13

After extra time.

PRELIMINARY ROUND

Bedales v ACS Cobham	0-9
Claremont Fan Court v Whitgift	0-10
Frensham Heights v Haberdashers' Aske's	3-2*
Royal Russell v St James School, Ashford	8-2

FIRST ROUND

Ackworth v St Columba's College	2-3*
ACS Cobham v LVS Ascot	6-3*
Birkdale v Ardingly	1-0
Box Hill v Stockport GS	1-5
Bradfield v Sherborne	5-0
Bury GS v Whitgift	0-6
Charterhouse v John Lyon	3-1
Cheadle Hulme v Hampton	0-2
Colfe's v Kimbolton	1-1*
(Kimbolton won 5-4 on penalties)	
Dover College v Bede's	2-4*
Dulwich College v City of London	4-2
Eton v Lancing	4-1
Frensham Heights v Lingfield Notre Dame	2-1
Grammar School at Leeds v Millfield	1-9
Grange v Forest	5-0
Haileybury v The Harrodian	2-3
(The Harrodian disqualified for fielding ineligible player)	
Highgate v Aldenham	2-0
Hurstpierpoint v Latymer Upper	0-3
KES Witley v Tonbridge	3-4
Malvern v Chigwell	2-3
Manchester GS v Bolton	2-0
Norwich v Ibstock Place	3-2
Oldham Hulme GS v Bedford Modern	0-4
QEGS Blackburn v St Bede's College	0-2
Repton v St Edmund's, Canterbury	14-0
RGS Guildford v Alleyn's	0-4
RGS Newcastle v King's School, Chester	0-5
Royal Russell v Brentwood	2-3*
Solihull v Winchester	1-2
Trinity v Harrow	1-3
University College School v Shrewsbury	1-0
Westminster v Wolverhampton GS	2-1*

SECOND ROUND

Charterhouse v Bede's	2-5
Frensham Heights v Dulwich College	1-11
Grange v Birkdale	5-1
Haileybury v Whitgift	2-4
Harrow v Alleyn's	0-3
Highgate v ACS Cobham	2-0
Kimbolton v Chigwell	2-1
King's School, Chester v St Columba's College	8-0
Manchester GS v Hampton	2-1

Millfield v Brentwood	9-0
Norwich v Bradfield	0-3
St Bede's College v Eton	0-3
Stockport GS v Bedford Modern	4-3
Tonbridge v Winchester	2-4
University College School v Latymer Upper	1-1*
(Latymer won 4-3 on penalties)	
Westminster v Repton	2-1*

THIRD ROUND

Alleyn's v Grange	2-0
Bradfield v Dulwich College	5-1
Kimbolton v Eton	0-3
King's School, Chester v Bede's	3-2
Millfield v Highgate	10-0
Westminster v Stockport GS	2-2*
(Westminster won 5-3 on penalties)	
Whitgift v Manchester GS	1-3
Winchester v Latymer Upper	0-2

FOURTH ROUND

Alleyn's v Eton	2-0
Bradfield v Latymer Upper	3-0
King's School, Chester v Manchester GS	1-2
Millfield v Westminster	4-1

SEMI-FINALS

Manchester GS v Bradfield	2-5
Millfield v Alleyn's	3-1

FINAL

Milton Keynes Dons, 6 March 2014

Millfield (0) 6 *(Duffy 2, Golby 2, Whelan (pen), Kadir)*

Bradfield (0) 1 *(Joslin)*

Millfield: J. Symes; K. McConnachie, T. Street, G. Hankins, T. Whelan, B. Downing, S. Holden, A. Kadir, M. Golby, C. Rey, E. Duffy.
Substitutes: D. Ramsaran, J. Lewis, T. Stevenson, S. Takker, N. Tomlin.
Bradfield: P. Rynne-Coleman; G. Knight, L. Williams, E. Ogilvie, F. Bloem, T. Robertson, M. Micaletto, M. Hemmings, N. Watts, T. Joslin.
Substitutes: R. King, K. Robinson, S. Iglesias, S. Clements, D. Hodgkinson.
Referee: H. Webb (Yorkshire).

INVESTEC ISFA U15 CUP FINAL

Ardingly College v Manchester Grammar School	3-0
(at Burton Albion FC)	

INVESTEC ISFA U13 CUP FINAL

Chigwell v Whitgift	3-0
(at Burton Albion FC)	

UNIVERSITY FOOTBALL 2014

130th UNIVERSITY MATCH

(Sunday 6 April, at Fulham's Craven Cottage, attendance 3341)

Cambridge (0) 0   Oxford (0) 0

Cambridge won 4-2 on penalties

Cambridge: Fergus Kent; Simon Court, Solomon Elliott, James May, Michael Smith, James Day, Daniel Forde, Anthony Childs (c), Haitham Sherif, Chris Hutton, Rory Griffiths.
Substitutes: Zac Baynham-Herd, John Gorringe, Henry Warne, Rich Wolstenhulme, Chris Fountain.

Oxford: Jamie Farmer; Tom Hobkinson, Aidan Barry, Alias Adrianessens, Mike Moneke, Ben May, Brook Tozer, Jack Fletcher (c), Peder Beck-Friis, Ezra Rubenstein, Mike Essman.
Substitutes: Alex Tsaptinos, Dan Ginger, Adam Heardman, Matt Smith, Ben Szreter.

Referee: Jon Moss.

Oxford have won 50 games, Cambridge 50 and 30 drawn.   *Oxford have scored 205 goals, Cambridge 204 goals.*

WOMEN'S SUPER LEAGUE 2013

WOMEN'S SUPER LEAGUE TABLE 2013

			Total				Home						Away					
	W	D	L	F	A	P	W	D	L	F	A	W	D	L	F	A	GD	Pts
1 Liverpool Ladies	12	0	2	46	19	14	6	0	1	19	11	6	0	1	27	8	27	36
2 Bristol Academy Ladies	10	1	3	30	20	14	5	0	2	17	12	5	1	1	13	8	10	31
3 Arsenal Ladies*	10	3	1	31	11	14	4	2	1	12	6	6	1	0	19	5	20	30
4 Birmingham C Ladies	5	3	6	16	21	14	3	1	3	9	12	2	2	3	7	9	–5	18
5 Everton Ladies	4	3	7	23	30	14	2	2	3	10	13	2	1	4	13	17	–7	15
6 Lincoln Ladies	2	4	8	10	15	14	1	2	4	4	7	1	2	4	6	8	–5	10
7 Chelsea Ladies	3	1	10	20	27	14	2	1	4	9	12	1	0	6	11	15	–7	10
8 Doncaster R Belles	1	3	10	9	42	14	1	1	5	5	27	0	2	5	4	15	–33	6

Arsenal Ladies deducted 3 points for fielding ineligible player.

WOMEN'S SUPER LEAGUE RESULTS 2013	Arsenal	Birmingham C	Bristol Academy	Chelsea	Doncaster R Belles	Everton	Liverpool	Lincoln
Arsenal Ladies	—	2–0	0–0	2–1	3–1	5–0	0–4	0–0
Birmingham C Ladies	1–3	—	0–2	2–1	1–0	2–1	2–4	1–1
Bristol Academy Ladies	2–3	1–0	—	2–0	3–1	4–3	3–4	2–1
Chelsea Ladies	0–1	1–1	1–3	—	4–0	1–4	2–1	0–2
Doncaster R Belles	0–6	0–3	3–4	0–4	—	1–1	0–9	1–0
Everton Ladies	1–2	0–0	2–3	3–2	2–2	—	1–4	1–0
Liverpool Ladies	0–3	4–1	2–0	4–3	2–0	4–2	—	3–2
Lincoln Ladies	1–1	1–2	0–1	2–0	0–0	0–2	0–1	—

WOMEN'S SUPER LEAGUE CONTINENTAL CUP

GROUP A

Bristol Academy Ladies v Birmingham C Ladies	0-2
Lincoln Ladies v Arsenal Ladies	1-1
Bristol Academy Ladies v Lincoln Ladies	0-1
Arsenal Ladies v Birmingham C Ladies	2-1
Arsenal Ladies v Bristol Academy Ladies	4-2
Birmingham C Ladies v Lincoln Ladies	1-1

Group A Table	P	W	D	L	F	A	GD	Pts
Arsenal Ladies	3	2	1	0	7	4	3	7
Lincoln Ladies	3	1	2	0	3	2	1	5
Birmingham C Ladies	3	1	1	1	4	3	1	4
Bristol Academy Ladies	3	0	0	3	2	7	–5	0

GROUP B

Liverpool Ladies v Everton Ladies	1-1
Doncaster R Belles v Chelsea Ladies	1-1
Liverpool Ladies v Doncaster R Belles	1-0
Everton Ladies v Chelsea Ladies	2-1
Doncaster R Belles v Everton Ladies	1-3
Chelsea Ladies v Liverpool Ladies	0-4

Group B Table	P	W	D	L	F	A	GD	Pts
Liverpool Ladies	3	2	1	0	6	1	5	7
Everton Ladies	3	2	1	0	6	3	3	7
Doncaster R Belles	3	0	1	2	2	5	–3	1
Chelsea Ladies	3	0	1	2	2	7	–5	1

SEMI-FINALS

Liverpool Ladies v Lincoln Ladies	1-1
(aet; Liverpool won 4-2 on penalties)	
Arsenal Ladies v Everton Ladies	4-0

WSL CONTINENTAL CUP FINAL 2013

Friday 4 October 2013

(at Barnet, attendance 3421)

Lincoln Ladies (0) 0

Arsenal Ladies (0) 2 *(White 76, Little 86)*

Lincoln Ladies: Bardsley; Bradley, Stoney, Turner, Whelan (Sargeant 63), Allen, Horwood (Roberts 81), Walton, Harris Martha, Sweetman-Kirk (Harris Megan 81), Clarke.
Arsenal Ladies: Byrne; Scott, Houghton, Flaherty, Mitchell, Little, Nobbs, Chapman, Yankey, White, Carter (Davison 81).
Referee: Helen Byrne.

FA WOMEN'S PREMIER LEAGUE 2013–14

FA WOMEN'S PREMIER LEAGUE NORTHERN DIVISION 2013–14

			Total					Home					Away					
		P	W	D	L	F	A	W	D	L	F	A	W	D	L	F	A	GD	Pts
1	Sheffield Ladies	20	17	2	1	74	15	9	1	0	43	5	8	1	1	31	10	59	53
2	Preston NE	20	12	1	7	49	39	7	0	3	25	17	5	1	4	24	22	10	37
3	Bradford C	20	11	2	7	36	33	5	2	3	21	18	6	0	4	15	15	3	35
4	Nottingham F	20	10	3	7	44	24	2	2	6	16	19	8	1	1	28	5	20	33
5	Stoke C	20	10	3	7	51	45	5	1	4	27	23	5	2	3	24	22	6	33
6	Sporting Club Alb	20	8	4	8	36	34	5	3	2	21	13	3	1	6	15	21	2	28
7	Derby Co	20	7	4	9	45	51	5	1	4	21	20	2	3	5	24	31	-6	25
8	Wolverhampton W	20	6	2	12	28	48	3	1	6	11	20	3	1	6	17	28	-20	20
9	Blackburn R	20	5	3	12	29	51	4	0	6	19	27	1	3	6	10	24	-22	18
10	Newcastle U	20	5	2	13	33	66	4	1	5	18	32	1	1	8	15	34	-33	17
11	Leeds United	20	4	4	12	37	56	2	3	5	19	27	2	1	7	18	29	-19	16

FA WOMEN'S PREMIER LEAGUE SOUTHERN DIVISION 2013–14

			Total					Home					Away					
		P	W	D	L	F	A	W	D	L	F	A	W	D	L	F	A	GD	Pts
1	Coventry C	20	14	4	2	42	14	6	2	2	19	8	8	2	0	23	6	28	46
2	Gillingham	20	14	2	4	58	21	8	1	1	29	9	6	1	3	29	12	37	44
3	Cardiff C	20	12	4	4	55	24	6	3	1	31	12	6	1	3	24	12	31	40
4	Portsmouth FC Ladies	20	12	1	7	42	29	8	0	2	28	11	4	1	5	14	18	13	37
5	Charlton Ath	20	9	5	6	39	35	6	2	2	20	17	3	3	4	19	18	4	32
6	Lewes	20	9	4	7	31	32	7	2	1	21	13	2	2	6	10	19	-1	31
7	Brighton & HA	20	7	2	11	32	31	3	1	6	15	12	4	1	5	17	19	1	23
8	Tottenham H	20	6	4	10	27	36	3	1	6	15	19	3	3	4	12	17	-9	22
9	Keynsham T	20	6	1	13	40	52	4	1	5	25	28	2	0	8	15	24	-12	19
10	West Ham U	20	4	3	13	25	48	3	2	5	12	18	1	1	8	13	30	-23	15
11	Chesham U	20	2	0	18	15	84	2	0	8	7	37	0	0	10	8	47	-69	6

WOMEN'S PREMIER LEAGUE CUP 2014

QUARTER-FINALS
Cardiff C v Lewes	1-0
Coventry C v Gillingham	1-0
Preston NE v Nottingham F	1-0
Bradford C v Sheffield Ladies	1-2

SEMI-FINALS
Cardiff C v Coventry C	1-0
Preston NE v Sheffield Ladies	1-4

FA WOMEN'S PREMIER LEAGUE CUP FINAL 2014

Sunday 4 May 2014
(at Burton, attendance 405)

Cardiff C (1) 2 *(Lloyd 41, Townsend 87 (pen))*
Sheffield Ladies (3) 6 *(Ward 12 (pen), 34, 74, Davis 45, Michalska 51, Giampala 75)*

Cardiff C: Sophie Dando; Cousins, Townsend, Williams (Atkins 63), Hutton (Mills 71), Green K, Aldridge, Green M, Lloyd, Isaac (Daley 80), Clipston.
Sheffield Ladies: Wallhead; Richardson, Cooke, Lee (Hayes 68), Gilliatt (Johnson 80), Giampala, Ward, Parkin, Goodman, Davies, Michalska (De Silva 73).
Referee: Sian Piret.

Arsenal's Alex Scott and Everton's Nikita Parris side-by-side during the FA Women's Cup final at Stadium MK. Arsenal won the trophy for the thirteenth time following a 2-0 victory. (Action Images/Paul Childs Livepic)

THE WOMEN'S FA CUP 2013–14

After extra time.

FIRST ROUND QUALIFYING

Whitley Bay v Middlesbrough Lionesses	2-1
Boldon v Lowick U	5-1
Rutherford v F Hall	5-0
Workington Reds v Tynedale	0-5
Kendal T v Birtley St Joseph	3-5
Willington v Seaton Carew	0-5
Peterlee St Francis v York C	3-2*
Prudhoe T v Kader FC Ladies	0-2
Birtley T v Abbeytown	1-2*
Whickham Fellside v Penrith AFC Ladies	2-2*
(Penrith won 3-0 on penalties)	
Sheffield W v Nettleham	1-6
Handsworth v Lepton Highlanders	1-0
Hull C v Brighouse Sports	4-1
Ossett Alb v Bradford Park Avenue	3-2
Farsley AFC Ladies v Steel C W	0-4
Hemsworth MW v Malet Lambert	3-5
Blackpool FC Ladies v Burnley FC Ladies	0-3
Brighouse T v CMB Ladies	4-1
Morecambe v Padiham FC Ladies	10-1
Middleton Ath v Blackpool Wren R	2-3
Chester C *(walkover)* v Preston NE	
Birkenhead v Crewe Alexandra	3-4
Bury Girls & Ladies v Woolton	1-2*
City of Manchester v Accrington Girls & Ladies	5-5*
(City of Manchester won 2-1 on penalties)	
Asfordby Amateurs v Arnold T	1-4
Sandiacre T v West Bridgford	7-1
Dronfield T v Ruddington Village	2-4
Teversal v Oadby & Wigston Dynamo	0-4
Rise Park v Ellistown	2-3
St George's v Long Eaton U	1-3
Coventrians v Malvern T	2-2*
(Malvern T won on penalties)	
Walsall v Pelsall Villa	7-6*
Crusaders v FC Reedswood Ladies	1-2
Allscott v TNS	0-4
Pegasus v Folly Lane	4-0
Cottage Farm Rangers v Kenilworth T KH	1-7
Bilbrook v Lye T	4-2
Netherton U v Peterborough Northern Star	0-15
Rothwell Corinthians v Raunds T	1-4
(First match abandoned after 15 mins due to serious injury to a Raunds T player, 0-0)	
Bar Hill v Moulton	2-1*
Peterborough Sports v Brackley Sports	9-0
Kettering T v Bedford	2-6
Southendian v Brandon	5-0
Colchester T v Haverhill R	5-0
Assandun Vikings v Waveney W	0-2
Lowestoft T v AFC Sudbury Ladies	6-1
Bungay T v West Billericay	2-3
FC Clacton Ladies v Billericay T	0-15
Sawbridgeworth T v St Albans C	1-2
KIKK U v Haringey Borough	7-0
Barking v Flitwick	6-0
Stevenage Borough v Hoddesdon Owls	5-2
Royston T v Wootton Blue Cross	2-1
Maidenhead U v Newbury	6-2
Tower Hill v Leverstock Green	0-7
Colne Valley v Old Actonians	1-4*
Oxford C v Marlow	2-0
Leighton U Vixens v Wealdstone	5-1
AFC Dunstable Ladies v Ascot U	4-0
Hemel Hempstead T v Banbury U	7-0
Headington v Bracknell T	0-3
Herne Bay v Anchorians	3-1
Rusthall v Rottingdean Village	4-1
London Corinthians v Maidstone U	2-0
Aylesford v Regents Park Rangers	5-0
Dartford YMCA v Haywards Heath T	2-6
Bexhill U *(walkover)* v Sheppey & Sheerness U	
Eastbourne v Eastbourne T	0-6
Prince Of Wales *(walkover)* v Tunbridge Wells Ridgewaye	
Crystal Palace v Parkwood Rangers	7-4
Fulham Compton v South Park	3-0
Battersea & Wandsworth v Abbey Rangers	8-1
AFC Wimbledon Ladies v Worthing T	5-1
Crawley Wasps v Milford & Witley	9-0

Westfield v Knaphill	11-0
Chertsey T v AFC Wimbledon Ladies Dev	0-3
Andover New Street v Basingstoke T	0-1
Southampton Women v New Forest	2-2*
(Southampton Women won 5-3 on penalties)	
Poole T v Fleet T	6-1
Gosport Borough v Weymouth	6-0
Aldershot T v Parley Sports	0-3
Cirencester T v Bitton	2-1
Quedgeley W v Swindon Spitfires	0-18
Downend Flyers v Forest of Dean	3-1
Bristol Ladies Union v Wootton Bassett T	11-0
Cheltenham T v Pen Mill	9-0
Brislington v Stoke Lane Ath	2-1
Frome T v Ilminster T	5-5*
(Ilminster T won 3-0 on penalties)	
Gloucester C v Longlevens	10-2
Bridgwater T v St Nicholas	1-5
Truro C v Launceston	4-0
Torquay U v Bude T	4-0

SECOND ROUND QUALIFYING

Boldon v Rutherford	4-1
Tynedale v Seaton Carew	4-1
Birtley St Joseph v Whitley Bay	0-2
Penrith AFC Ladies v Kader FC Ladies	2-2*
(Kader FC Ladies won 4-3 on penalties)	
Abbeytown v Peterlee St Francis	1-8
Brighouse T v Woolton	4-1
Burnley FC Ladies v City of Manchester	4-5*
Ossett Alb v Malet Lambert	0-3
Nettleham v Crewe Alexandra	6-0
Blackpool Wren R v Chester C	1-1*
(Blackpool Wren R won 5-4 on penalties)	
Morecambe v Steel C W	5-3*
Hull C v Handsworth	3-0
Walsall v Bilbrook	4-2
Malvern T v Raunds T	0-4
Oadby & Wigston Dynamo v Long Eaton U	4-5
Arnold T v Kenilworth T KH	4-3*
TNS v Pegasus	3-1
FC Reedswood Ladies v Ellistown	4-3
Ruddington Village v Sandiacre T	1-8
Bar Hill v Billericay T	0-4
Bedford v Stevenage Borough	5-2
AFC Dunstable Ladies v Royston	3-1
Southendian v Peterborough Northern Star	1-3
Lowestoft T v Peterborough Sports	4-0
Barking v West Billericay	3-1
Colchester T v Leighton U Vixens	1-3
Hemel Hempstead T v Leverstock Green	1-8
KIKK U v Battersea & Wandsworth	9-0
St Albans C v Waveney W	5-0
AFC Wimbledon Ladies v Oxford C	1-1*
(Oxford C won 3-2 on penalties)	
London Corinthians v Herne Bay	5-1
Maidenhead U v Eastbourne T	5-1
Bracknell T v Crawley Wasps	3-1
Prince of Wales v AFC Wimbledon Ladies Dev	1-2
Haywards Heath T v Rusthall	2-3
Crystal Palace v Old Actonians	2-1*
Westfield v Aylesford	7-2
Fulham Compton v Bexhill U	3-1
Gosport Borough v Bristol Ladies Union	2-0
St Nicholas v Southampton Women	11-0
Torquay U v Swindon Spitfires	0-4
Cirencester T v Parley Sports	2-4
Truro C v Poole T	4-0
Cheltenham T v Ilminster T	2-1
Gloucester C v Brislington	4-1
Downend Flyers v Basingstoke T	0-1

THIRD ROUND QUALIFYING

Boldon v Peterlee St Francis	1-3
Chester-le-Street T v Kader FC Ladies	10-1
Leeds C Vixens v Whitley Bay	2-2*
(Whitley Bay won 3-1 on penalties)	
Tynedale v Middlesbrough	2-6
Brighouse T v City of Manchester	8-8*
(Brighouse T won 5-4 on penalties)	
Tranmere R v Wakefield FC Ladies	6-0
Chorley v Morecambe	2-1

Huddersfield T v Stockport Co	2-1*
Liverpool Feds *(walkover)* v Malet Lambert	
Blackpool Wren R v Mossley Hill	4-2
Sheffield U Community v Cheadle Heath Nomads	3-2
Hull C v Curzon Ashton	4-2
Nettleham v Rotherham U	3-1
Arnold T v Loughborough Foxes	0-1
Raunds T v TNS	3-3*
(TNS won 4-3 on penalties)	
Walsall v Sandiacre T	1-4
Loughborough Students v Leafield Ath	7-2
Leicester C Ladies v Leicester C Women	2-2*
(Leicester C Ladies won 3-2 on penalties)	
FC Reedswood Ladies v Mansfield T	3-2
Copsewood Coventry v Long Eaton U	7-0
Cambridge Women's v Lowestoft T	5-1
Barking v Leverstock Green	1-4
KIKK U v Luton T	2-2*
(KIKK U won 3-1 on penalties)	
Norwich C v Peterborough Northern Star	7-1
C&K Basildon v Brentwood T	4-0
Ebbsfleet U v Ipswich T	5-3
Leighton U Vixens v Milton Keynes D	2-2*
(Milton Keynes D won 4-2 on penalties)	
Enfield T v St Albans C	6-2
AFC Dunstable Ladies v Denham U	1-5
Billericay T v Bedford	0-0*
(Bedford won 5-4 on penalties)	
Rusthall v University of Portsmouth	1-3
Bracknell T v Crystal Palace	2-2*
(Crystal Palace won 4-2 on penalties)	
Maidenhead U v Fulham Compton	2-1
Oxford C v Queens Park Rangers	0-5
Shanklin v Gosport Borough	0-1
Westfield v London Corinthians	4-1
Chichester C v AFC Wimbledon Ladies Development	8-0
Truro C v Plymouth Arg	0-8
Swindon Spitfires v Cheltenham T	3-2
St Nicholas v Basingstoke T	3-2
Swindon T v Forest Green R	0-3
Keynsham T Development v Larkhall Ath	1-2
Gloucester C v Southampton Saints	1-0
Exeter C v Parley Sports	6-0

FIRST ROUND

Chester-le-Street T v Tranmere R	0-1
Middlesbrough v Sheffield U Community	3-2
Whitley Bay v Brighouse T	2-1
Chorley v Huddersfield T	1-6
Blackpool Wren R v Hull C	1-0
Liverpool Feds v Peterlee St Francis	6-0
TNS v Sandiacre T	4-0
FC Reedswood v Leicester C Ladies	2-1*
Loughborough Students v Cambridge Women's	5-2
Copsewood Coventry v Nettleham	1-0
Loughborough Foxes v Milton Keynes D	1-3*
Crystal Palace v Maidenhead U	2-0
C&K Basildon v KIKK U	2-1
Bedford *(walkover)* v Westfield	
Leverstock Green v Queens Park Rangers	0-5
Ebbsfleet U v Denham U	2-5*
Enfield T v Norwich C	3-2
Exeter C v Gosport Borough	3-1
Forest Green R v St Nicholas	0-1
Plymouth Arg *(walkover)* v University of Portsmouth	
Larkhall Ath v Swindon Spitfires	3-0
Chichester C v Gloucester C	6-0

SECOND ROUND

TNS v Stoke C	0-7
FC Reedswood v Copsewood Coventry	1-2

Loughborough Students v Leeds U	1-4
Preston NE *(walkover)* v Sporting Club Alb	
Huddersfield T v Coventry C	1-4
Derby Co v Newcastle U	2-0
Middlesbrough v Tranmere R	4-0
Nottingham F v Wolverhampton W	3-0
Whitley Bay v Blackburn R	0-1
Sheffield FC Ladies v Liverpool Feds	10-0
Bradford C v Blackpool Wren R	7-0
Chichester C v Enfield T	6-0
Lewes v Denham U	1-0
Portsmouth FC Ladies v Keynsham T	4-0
Charlton Ath v Milton Keynes D	3-0
Queens Park Rangers v Gillingham	1-2*
Chesham U v Larkhall Ath	1-2
Exeter C v Plymouth Arg	1-6
C&K Basildon v West Ham U	3-3*
(West Ham U won 4-2 on penalties)	
Brighton & HA v Tottenham H	3-2
Cardiff C v St Nicholas	3-0
Bedford v Crystal Palace	2-3

THIRD ROUND

Plymouth Arg v Brighton & HA	0-4
Charlton Ath v Sheffield FC Ladies	0-6
Nottingham F v Gillingham	0-1
Preston NE v Yeovil T	3-0
Bradford C v Cardiff C	0-1
Portsmouth FC Ladies v Lewes	3-0
West Ham U v Watford	1-5
Durham Women's v Chichester C	4-0
Crystal Palace v Derby Co	2-0
Coventry C v Stoke C	3-1
Leeds U v London Bees	1-3
Blackburn R v Middlesbrough	3-0
Copsewood Coventry v Larkhall Ath	3-2*
Aston Villa v Doncaster R Belles	0-2
Millwall Lionesses v Reading Women	1-2
Sunderland v Oxford U	5-1

FOURTH ROUND

Cardiff C v London Bees	1-0
Coventry C v Brighton & HA	2-0
Sunderland v Watford	4-1
Gillingham v Preston NE	1-0
Reading Women v Blackburn R	2-0*
Crystal Palace v Portsmouth FC Ladies	2-3
Durham Women's v Sheffield FC Ladies	3-1
Doncaster R Belles v Copsewood Coventry	4-1

FIFTH ROUND

Manchester C v Reading Women	2-1
Notts Co v Coventry C	2-1
Arsenal v Gillingham	2-0
Birmingham C v Doncaster R Belles	3-1
Portsmouth FC Ladies v Durham Women's	2-1
Chelsea v Bristol Academy	2-1*
Cardiff C v Everton	1-3
Sunderland v Liverpool	0-2

SIXTH ROUND

Portsmouth FC Ladies v Notts Co	0-2
Liverpool v Everton	0-2
Manchester C v Chelsea	1-3
Birmingham C v Arsenal	1-2

SEMI-FINALS

Chelsea v Arsenal	3-5
Notts Co v Everton	1-2

WOMEN'S FA CUP FINAL

Sunday 1 June 2014
(at Milton Keynes, attendance 15,098)

Arsenal (1) 2　　　Everton (0) 0

Arsenal: Byrne; Scott, Mitchell, Kinga, Stoney, Ohno, Carter, Smith, Yankey, Fahey, Bailey (Williamson 76).
Scorers: Smith 15, Kinga 61.

Everton: Brown-Finnis; Jones V (Murphy 62), Alex Greenwood, Chaplen, Johnson, Hinnigan, Parris, Jones K, Turner D (Whelan 82), George, Turner M (Magill 71).

Referee: Martin Atkinson.

UEFA WOMEN'S CHAMPIONS LEAGUE 2013–14

*After extra time.

QUALIFYING ROUND

GROUP 1 (in Bosnia & Herzegovina)

SFK 2000 Sarajevo v Cardiff C								3-0
NSA Sofia v Konak Belediyespor								0-2
SFK 2000 Sarajevo v Konak Belediyespor								1-2
Cardiff C v NSA Sofia								0-2
NSA Sofia v SFK 2000 Sarajevo								2-3
Konak Belediyespor v Cardiff C								1-0

Group 1 Table	P	W	D	L	F	A	GD	Pts
Konak Belediyespor	3	3	0	0	5	1	4	9
SFK 2000 Sarajevo	3	2	0	1	7	4	3	6
NSA Sofia	3	1	0	2	4	5	–1	3
Cardiff C	3	0	0	3	0	6	–6	0

GROUP 2 (in Romania)

Spartak Subotica v Liepajas Metalurgs	10-0
Olimpia Cluj v Gintra Universitatis	3-0
Gintra Universitatis v Spartak Subotica	0-6
Olimpia Cluj v Liepajas Metalurgs	7-0
Liepajas Metalurgs v Gintra Universitatis	0-2
Spartak Subotica v Olimpia Cluj	8-3

Group 2 Table	P	W	D	L	F	A	GD	Pts
Spartak Subotica	3	3	0	0	24	3	21	9
Olimpia Cluj	3	2	0	1	13	8	5	6
Gintra Universitatis	3	1	0	2	2	9	–7	3
Liepajas Metalurgs	3	0	0	3	0	19	–19	0

GROUP 3 (in Northern Ireland)

MTK Hungaria v Raheny U	3-2
Kharkiv v Crusaders Strikers	5-0
Raheny U v Kharkiv	1-2
MTK Hungaria v Crusaders Strikers	2-0
Kharkiv v MTK Hungaria	0-1
Crusaders Strikers v Raheny U	1-2

Group 3 Table	P	W	D	L	F	A	GD	Pts
MTK Hungaria	3	3	0	0	6	2	4	9
Kharkiv	3	2	0	1	7	2	5	6
Raheny U	3	1	0	2	5	6	–1	3
Crusaders Strikers	3	0	0	3	1	9	–8	0

GROUP 4 (in Portugal)

Zurich v Clube Atletico Ouriense	5-0
Klaksvik v Ekonomist	1-1
Zurich v Ekonomist	4-1
Clube Atletico Ouriense v Klaksvik	2-1
Klaksvik v Zurich	0-3
Ekonomist v Clube Atletico Ouriense	1-1

Group 4 Table	P	W	D	L	F	A	GD	Pts
Zurich	3	3	0	0	12	1	11	9
Clube Atletico Ouriense	3	1	1	1	3	7	–4	4
Ekonomist	3	0	2	1	3	6	–3	2
Klaksvik	3	0	1	2	2	6	–4	1

GROUP 5 (in Slovenia)

Bobruichanka v Ada Velipoje	3-1
Unia Raciborz v Pomurje Beltinci	3-1
Pomurje Beltinci v Bobruichanka	3-1
Unia Raciborz v Ada Velipoje	7-0
Bobruichanka v Unia Raciborz	0-0
Ada Velipoje v Pomurje Beltinci	0-13

Group 5 Table	P	W	D	L	F	A	GD	Pts
Unia Raciborz	3	2	1	0	10	1	9	7
Pomurje Beltinci	3	2	0	1	17	4	13	6
Bobruichanka	3	1	1	1	4	4	0	4
Ada Velipoje	3	0	0	3	1	23	–22	0

GROUP 6 (in Finland)

PAOK Thessaloniki v Parnu	1-3
PK-35 Vantaa v Biljanini Izvori	13-1
PAOK Thessaloniki v Biljanini Izvori	5-0
Parnu v PK-35 Vantaa	0-0
PK-35 Vantaa v PAOK Thessaloniki	2-1
Biljanini Izvori v Parnu	1-3

Group 6 Table	P	W	D	L	F	A	GD	Pts
PK-35 Vantaa	3	2	1	0	15	2	13	7
Parnu	3	2	1	0	6	2	4	7
PAOK Thessaloniki	3	1	0	2	7	5	2	3
Biljanini Izvori	3	0	0	3	2	21	–19	0

GROUP 7 (in Cyprus)

Apollon Limassol v Nove Zamky	2-0
ASA Tel-Aviv v Goliador-SS11	6-0
Nove Zamky v ASA Tel-Aviv	0-0
Apollon Limassol v Goliador-SS11	1-0
ASA Tel-Aviv v Apollon Limassol	0-3
Goliador-SS11 v Nove Zamky	0-6

Group 7 Table	P	W	D	L	F	A	GD	Pts
Apollon Limassol	3	3	0	0	6	0	6	9
Nove Zamky	3	1	1	1	6	2	4	4
ASA Tel-Aviv	3	1	1	1	6	3	3	4
Goliador-SS11	3	0	0	3	0	13	–13	0

GROUP 8 (in the Netherlands)

Glasgow C v Osijek	7-0
Twente v Birkirkara	6-0
Glasgow City v Birkirkara	9-0
Osijek v Twente	0-4
Twente v Glasgow City	0-2
Birkirkara v Osijek	1-7

Group 8 Table	P	W	D	L	F	A	GD	Pts
Glasgow C	3	3	0	0	18	0	18	9
Twente	3	2	0	1	10	2	8	6
Osijek	3	1	0	2	7	12	–5	3
Birkirkara	3	0	0	3	1	22	–21	0

ROUND OF 32 FIRST LEG

CSHVSM-Kairat v Arsenal	1-7
Spartak Subotica v Rossiyanka	2-4
Parnu v Wolfsburg	0-14
PK-35 Vantaa v Birmingham C	0-3
Thor/KA v Zorky	1-2
Barcelona v Brondby	0-0
Zurich v Sparta Prague	2-1
Twente v Lyon	0-4
Spratzern v Torres	2-2
Standard v Glasgow C	2-2
Tyreso v PSG	2-1
Tavagnacco v Fortuna	3-2
MTK Hungaria v Potsdam	0-5
Apollon Limassol v Neulengbach	1-2
Konak Belediyespor v Unia Raciborz	2-1
LSK v Malmo	1-3

ROUND OF 32 SECOND LEG

		Agg
Torres v Spratzern	3-1	5-3
Birmingham C v PK-35 Vantaa	1-0	4-0
Zorky v Thor/KA	4-1	6-2
Wolfsburg v Pärnu	13-0	27-0
Brondby v Barcelona	2-2	2-2
Barcelona won on away goals.		
Fortuna v Tavagnacco	2-0	4-3
Malmo v LSK	5-0	8-1
Lyon v Twente	6-0	10-0
Neulengbach v Apollon Limassol	1-1	3-2
Potsdam v MTK Hungaria	6-0	11-0
Sparta Prague v Zurich	1-1	2-3
PSG v Tyreso	0-0	1-2
Rossiyanka v Spartak Subotica	1-1	5-3
Unia Raciborz v Konak Belediyespor	0-0	1-2
Arsenal v CSHVSM-Kairat	11-1	18-2
Glasgow C v Standard	3-1	5-3

ROUND OF 16 FIRST LEG

Rossiyanka v Torres	1-0
Zorky v Birmingham C	0-2
Arsenal v Glasgow C	3-0
Fortuna v Tyreso	1-2
Malmo v Wolfsburg	1-2
Barcelona v Zurich	3-0
Konak Belediyespor v Neulengbach	0-3
Potsdam v Lyon	0-1

ROUND OF 16 SECOND LEG

		Agg
Zurich v Barcelona	1-3	1-6
Wolfsburg v Malmo	3-1	5-2
Glasgow C v Arsenal	2-3	2-6
Birmingham C v Zorky	5-2	7-2
Torres v Rossiyanka	2-0	2-1
Neulengbach v Konak Belediyespor	3-0	6-0
Tyreso v Fortuna	4-0	6-1

Lyon v Potsdam 1-2 2-2
Potsdam won on away goals.

QUARTER-FINALS FIRST LEG
Tyreso v Neulengbach 8-1
Torres v Potsdam 0-8
Wolfsburg v Barcelona 3-0
Birmingham C v Arsenal 1-0

QUARTER-FINALS SECOND LEG *Agg*
Neulengbach v Tyreso 0-0 1-8
Potsdam v Torres 4-1 12-1
Barcelona v Wolfsburg 0-2 0-5
Arsenal v Birmingham C 0-2 0-3

SEMI-FINALS FIRST LEG
Potsdam v Wolfsburg 0-0
Birmingham v Tyreso 0-0

SEMI-FINALS SECOND LEG *Agg*
Wolfsburg v Potsdam 4-2 4-2
Tyreso v Birmingham 3-0 3-0

WOMEN'S UEFA CHAMPIONS LEAGUE FINAL 2013–14

Thursday 22 May 2014

(in Lisbon, attendance 10,000)

Tyreso (2) 3 *(Marta 28, 56, Boquete 30)*
Wolfsburg (0) 4 *(Popp 47, Muller 53, 80, Faisst 68)*

Tyreso: Soberg; Engen, Roddik, Dahlkvist (Thaisa 83), Boquete, Marta, Diaz (Edlund 67), Press, Seger, Sembrant, Klingenberg (Klinga 69).
Wolfsburg: Schult; Wensing, Fischer, Blasse, Wagner (Faisst 46), Popp, Kessler, Bunte, Muller, Henning, Goessling (Hartmann 90).
Referee: Kateryna Monzul.

WOMEN'S EUROPEAN CHAMPIONSHIP 2011–13

FINALS IN SWEDEN

GROUP STAGE

GROUP A
Italy v Finland 0-0
Sweden v Denmark 1-1
Italy v Denmark 2-1
Finland v Sweden 0-5
Sweden v Italy 3-1
Denmark v Finland 1-1

Group A Table	P	W	D	L	F	A	GD	Pts
Sweden	3	2	1	0	9	2	7	7
Italy	3	1	1	1	3	4	–1	4
Denmark	3	0	2	1	3	4	–1	2
Finland	3	0	2	1	1	6	–5	2

Denmark qualified for quarter finals after drawing lots.

GROUP B
Norway v Iceland 1-1
Germany v Netherlands 0-0
Norway v Netherlands 1-0
Iceland v Germany 0-3
Germany v Norway 0-1
Netherlands v Iceland 0-1

Group B Table	P	W	D	L	F	A	GD	Pts
Norway	3	2	1	0	3	1	2	7
Germany	3	1	1	1	3	1	2	4
Iceland	3	1	1	1	2	4	–2	4
Netherlands	3	0	1	2	0	2	–2	1

GROUP C
France v Russia 3-1
England v Spain 2-3
England v Russia 1-1
Spain v France 0-1
France v England 3-0
Russia v Spain 1-1

Group C Table	P	W	D	L	F	A	GD	Pts
France	3	3	0	0	7	1	6	9
Spain	3	1	1	1	4	4	0	4
Russia	3	0	2	1	3	5	–2	2
England	3	0	1	2	3	7	–4	1

QUARTER-FINALS
Sweden v Iceland 4-0
Italy v Germany 0-1
Norway v Spain 3-1
France v Denmark 1-1
aet; Denmark won 4-2 on penalties.

SEMI-FINALS
Sweden v Germany 0-1
Norway v Denmark 1-1
aet; Norway won 4-2 on penalties.

FINAL
Germany v Norway 1-0

WOMEN'S WORLD CUP CANADA 2015

EUROPEAN QUALIFICATION

Malta, Albania, Faroe Islands and Montenegro qualified from a Preliminary Round.

GROUP 1
Germany v Russia 9-0
Republic of Ireland v Slovakia 2-0
Croatia v Republic of Ireland 1-1
Slovakia v Slovenia 1-3
Croatia v Slovakia 0-1
Slovenia v Germany 0-13
Slovenia v Republic of Ireland 0-3
Germany v Croatia 4-0
Slovakia v Russia 0-2
Slovakia v Germany 0-6
Croatia v Germany 0-8
Russia v Slovenia 4-1
Republic of Ireland v Germany 2-3
Russia v Croatia 1-0
Germany v Slovenia 4-0
Republic of Ireland v Russia 1-3
Germany v Slovakia 9-1
Slovenia v Croatia 0-3
Slovenia v Russia 1-2
Republic of Ireland v Croatia 1-0
Russia v Republic of Ireland 0-0
Slovakia v Croatia 1-1

Group 1 Table	P	W	D	L	F	A	GD	Pts
Germany	8	8	0	0	56	3	53	24
Russia	7	5	1	1	12	12	0	16
Republic of Ireland	7	3	2	2	10	7	3	11
Croatia	8	1	2	5	5	17	–12	5
Slovakia	7	1	1	5	4	23	–19	4
Slovenia	7	1	0	6	5	30	–25	3

GROUP 2
Macedonia v Romania 1-9
Estonia v Italy 1-5
Italy v Romania 1-0
Macedonia v Czech Republic 1-3
Spain v Estonia 6-0
Macedonia v Estonia 0-2
Romania v Czech Republic 0-0
Spain v Italy 2-0
Spain v Romania 1-0
Spain v Czech Republic 3-2
Italy v Czech Republic 6-1
Spain v Macedonia 12-0
Italy v Spain 0-0
Macedonia v Spain 0-10
Romania v Italy 1-2
Czech Republic v Estonia 6-0
Czech Republic v Romania 0-0

Macedonia v Italy	0-11
Estonia v Spain	0-5
Czech Republic v Italy	0-4
Estonia v Macedonia	1-1
Czech Republic v Macedonia	5-2
Estonia v Romania	0-2

Group 2 Table	P	W	D	L	F	A	GD	Pts
Spain	8	7	1	0	39	2	37	22
Italy	8	6	1	1	29	5	24	19
Czech Republic	8	3	2	3	17	16	1	11
Romania	7	2	2	3	12	5	7	8
Estonia	7	1	1	5	4	25	–21	4
Macedonia	8	0	1	7	5	53	–48	1

GROUP 3

Switzerland v Serbia	9-0
Iceland v Switzerland	0-2
Serbia v Denmark	1-1
Israel v Malta	2-0
Serbia v Iceland	1-2
Denmark v Switzerland	0-1
Malta v Denmark	0-5
Israel v Serbia	3-1
Israel v Switzerland	0-5
Malta v Serbia	0-3
Switzerland v Malta	11-0
Israel v Iceland	0-1
Malta v Iceland	0-8
Switzerland v Denmark	1-1
Malta v Israel	0-2
Switzerland v Iceland	3-0
Denmark v Serbia	3-1
Switzerland v Israel	9-0
Serbia v Malta	5-0
Denmark v Iceland	1-1
Israel v Denmark	0-5
Serbia v Switzerland	0-7
Iceland v Malta	5-0

Group 3 Table	P	W	D	L	F	A	GD	Pts
Switzerland	9	8	1	0	48	1	47	25
Iceland	7	4	1	2	17	7	10	13
Denmark	7	3	3	1	16	5	11	12
Israel	7	3	0	4	8	21	–13	9
Serbia	8	2	1	5	12	25	–13	7
Malta	8	0	0	8	0	42	–42	0

GROUP 4

Sweden v Poland	2-0
Faroe Islands v Scotland	2-7
Poland v Faroe Islands	6-0
Scotland v Bosnia & Herzegovina	7-0
Bosnia & Herzegovina v Sweden	0-1
Scotland v Northern Ireland	2-0
Northern Ireland v Bosnia & Herzegovina	0-0
Poland v Scotland	0-4
Sweden v Faroe Islands	5-0
Northern Ireland v Poland	0-3
Scotland v Poland	2-0
Faroe Islands v Bosnia & Herzegovina	1-1
Northern Ireland v Sweden	0-4
Bosnia & Herzegovina v Scotland	1-3
Faroe Islands v Northern Ireland	0-0
Faroe Islands v Poland	0-3
Sweden v Northern Ireland	3-0
Bosnia & Herzegovina v Northern Ireland	1-0
Scotland v Sweden	1-3
Bosnia & Herzegovina v Poland	1-1
Faroe Islands v Sweden	0-5
Northern Ireland v Scotland	0-2

Group 4 Table	P	W	D	L	F	A	GD	Pts
Scotland	8	7	0	1	28	6	22	21
Sweden	7	7	0	0	23	1	22	21
Poland	7	3	1	3	13	9	4	10
Bosnia & Herzegovina	7	1	3	3	4	13	–9	6
Faroe Islands	7	0	2	5	3	27	–24	2
Northern Ireland	8	0	2	6	0	15	–15	2

GROUP 5

Belgium v Albania	2-0
Norway v Belgium	4-1
Greece v Portugal	1-5
Albania v Netherlands	0-4
Greece v Belgium	1-7
Norway v Albania	7-0
Portugal v Netherlands	0-7
Albania v Greece	1-0
Netherlands v Norway	1-2

Belgium v Portugal	4-1
Netherlands v Greece	7-0
Netherlands v Belgium	1-1
Portugal v Albania	7-1
Greece v Norway	0-5
Albania v Belgium	0-6
Greece v Netherlands	0-6
Portugal v Greece	1-0
Netherlands v Albania	10-1
Belgium v Norway	1-2
Norway v Portugal	2-0
Belgium v Netherlands	0-2
Norway v Greece	6-0
Albania v Portugal	0-3

Group 5 Table	P	W	D	L	F	A	GD	Pts
Norway	8	8	0	0	30	3	27	24
Netherlands	8	6	1	1	38	4	34	19
Belgium	8	4	1	3	22	11	11	13
Portugal	8	4	0	4	17	17	0	12
Albania	8	1	0	7	3	39	–36	3
Greece	8	0	0	8	2	38	–36	0

GROUP 6

England v Belarus	6-0
Wales v Belarus	1-0
England v Turkey	8-0
Belarus v Montenegro	3-1
England v Wales	2-0
Montenegro v Ukraine	1-4
Turkey v England	0-4
Montenegro v Wales	0-3
Turkey v Montenegro	3-1
Turkey v Ukraine	0-1
Turkey v Wales	1-5
England v Montenegro	9-0
Wales v Ukraine	1-1
Montenegro v Belarus	1-7
Belarus v Turkey	1-2
Wales v Montenegro	4-0
England v Ukraine	4-0
Wales v Turkey	1-0
Belarus v England	0-3
Ukraine v Montenegro	7-0
Montenegro v Turkey	2-3
Ukraine v England	1-2
Belarus v Wales	0-3

Group 6 Table	P	W	D	L	F	A	GD	Pts
England	8	8	0	0	38	1	37	24
Wales	8	6	1	1	18	4	14	19
Ukraine	6	3	1	2	14	8	6	10
Turkey	8	3	0	5	9	23	–14	9
Belarus	7	2	0	5	11	17	–6	6
Montenegro	9	0	0	9	6	43	–37	0

GROUP 7

Kazakhstan v Finland	0-2
Austria v Bulgaria	4-0
Kazakhstan v France	0-4
Finland v Austria	2-1
Bulgaria v Kazakhstan	1-1
Hungary v Austria	0-3
Hungary v Bulgaria	4-0
Finland v Kazakhstan	1-0
Austria v France	1-3
Hungary v Kazakhstan	4-1
Bulgaria v France	0-10
France v Bulgaria	14-0
Bulgaria v Austria	1-6
Hungary v Finland	0-4
France v Kazakhstan	7-0
France v Austria	3-1
Finland v Hungary	4-0
Kazakhstan v Bulgaria	4-1
France v Hungary	4-0
Kazakhstan v Hungary	1-2
Austria v Finland	3-1
Finland v Bulgaria	4-0
Kazakhstan v Austria	0-3

Group 7 Table	P	W	D	L	F	A	GD	Pts
France	7	7	0	0	45	2	43	21
Finland	7	6	0	1	18	4	14	18
Austria	8	5	0	3	22	10	12	15
Hungary	7	3	0	4	10	17	–7	9
Kazakhstan	9	1	1	7	7	25	–18	4
Bulgaria	8	0	1	7	3	47	–44	1

ENGLAND WOMEN'S INTERNATIONALS 2013-14

FRIENDLY

Uddevalla, 4 July 2013

Sweden (2) 4 *(Goransson 29, Schelin 33, 68, Seger 51)*
England (1) 1 *(White 12)*   4524

England: Bardsley (Brown-Finnis 46); Scott A, Houghton (Bassett 46), Scott J (Nobbs 64), Bradley, Stoney (Carney 46), Aluko, Asante, White (Duggan 46), Williams, Yankey (Susi 46).

EUROPEAN CHAMPIONSHIP FINALS – SWEDEN 2013

Linköping, 12 July 2013

England (1) 2 *(Aluko 8, Bassett 89)*
Spain (1) 3 *(Boquete 5, Hermoso 85, Putellas 90)*   5190

England: Bardsley; Scott A, Houghton, Scott J, Stoney, Aluko (Carney 72), Asante, White, Williams, Yankey (Clarke 90), Bassett.

Linköping, 15 July 2013

England (0) 1 *(Duggan 90)*
Russia (1) 1 *(Korovkina 38)*   3629

England: Bardsley; Scott, Houghton (Duggan 64), Scott J, Stoney, Aluko (Smith 79), Asante, White, Williams, Yankey (Carney 18), Bassett.

Linköping, 18 July 2013

France (1) 3 *(Sommer 9, Necib 62, Renard 64)*
England (0) 0   7332

England: Bardsley; Scott A, Houghton, Bradley, Stoney, Aluko (Smith 61), Asante (Scott J 46), White, Williams, Carney (Clarke 73), Duggan.

WORLD CUP CANADA 2015 EUROPEAN QUALIFICATION

GROUP 6

Bournemouth, 21 September 2013

England (4) 6 *(Carney 3, 25, 40, White 13, Dowie 60, Aluko 62)*
Belarus (0) 0   6818

England: Brown-Finnis; Scott A, Bronze, Williams (Moore 72), Bradley, Stoney, Aluko, Nobbs, White, Carney (Scott J 56), Duggan (Dowie 56).

Portsmouth, 26 September 2013

England (6) 8 *(Duggan 1, 2, 37, White 29, 43, Aluko 33, 49, Dowie 67)*
Turkey (0) 0   6293

England: Chamberlain; Scott A, Bronze, Williams, Bonner, Stoney (Houghton 75), Aluko (Dowie 59), Nobbs, White, Carney (Scott J 63), Duggan.

Millwall, 26 October 2013

England (0) 2 *(Nobbs 48, Duggan 57)*
Wales (0) 0   5764

England: Bardsley; Scott A, Bronze, Williams, Houghton, Stoney, Aluko (Scott J 62), Nobbs, White (Dowie 74), Carney, Duggan (Clarke 74).
Wales: Davies N; Dykes, Bleazard, Davies K, Ingle, Fishlock (Green 58), James, Ladd, Evans, Wiltshire (Keryakoplis 78), Harding (Hawkins 46).

Adana, 31 October 2013

Turkey (0) 0   784
England (0) 4 *(Aluko 10, Williams 17 (pen), Duggan 48, Nobbs 60)*

England: Bardsley; Scott A, Bronze, Williams (Moore 61), Bonner, Bradley, Aluko (Dowie 79), Scott J, White (Clarke 69), Nobbs, Duggan.

Brighton, 5 April 2014

England (4) 9 *(Duggan 1, 13, 71, Aluko 37, Scott J 39, Carney 49, Sanderson 55, Stokes 69, Dowie 83)*
Montenegro (0) 0   8908

England: Chamberlain; Scott A, Houghton, Bronze, Stokes, Williams, Scott J, Carney (Dowie 59), Aluko (Moore 64), Sanderson (White 72), Duggan.

Shrewsbury, 8 May 2014

England (1) 4 *(Dowie 40, 53, Aluko 49, 63)*
Ukraine (0) 0   5818

England: Chamberlain; Scott A, Houghton, Bronze, Stokes, Williams, Scott J (Bassett 62), Moore, Sanderson (Smith 62), Aluko (Clarke 79), Dowie.

Minsk, 14 June 2014

Belarus (0) 0
England (1) 3 *(Aluko 30, Houghton 36, Bronze 90)*

England: Bardsley; Scott A, Houghton, Bronze, Stokes (Bradley 62), Moore, Williams, Bassett, Carney, Aluko (Sanderson 78), Dowie (Clarke 66).

Lviv, 19 June 2014

Ukraine (0) 1 *(Ovdiychuk 63)*
England (2) 2 *(Stoney 10, Aluko 14)*

England: Bardsley; Scott A, Houghton, Stoney, Bronze, Moore, Williams, Scott J (Sanderson 69), Bassett, Aluko (Clarke 79), Carney (Greenwood 90).

CYPRUS CUP

GROUP A

Larnaca, 5 March 2014

England (1) 2 *(Carney 45 (pen), Duggan 62)*
Italy (0) 0

England: Chamberlain; Scott A, Houghton, Bronze, Stokes (Greenwood 80), Williams, Carney, Nobbs (Aluko 85), White (Bassett 86), Sanderson (Scott J 76), Duggan.

Larnaca, 7 March 2014

Finland (0) 0
England (1) 3 *(Asante 30, Bonner 67, Aluko 72)*

England: Telford (Durack 84); Moore, Bradley, Bonner, Greenwood, Asante (Scott A 62), Bassett, Davison (Duggan 70), Scott J (Carney 70), Aluko (White 76), Dowie.

Nicosia, 10 March 2014

England (2) 2 *(Sanderson 1, 32)*
Canada (0) 0

England: Chamberlain; Scott A, Houghton, Bronze, Stokes, Williams, Carney, Nobbs (Scott J 80), Duggan (Davison 86), Sanderson (Asante 64), White (Dowie 72).

CYPRUS CUP FINAL

Nicosia, 12 March 2014

England (0) 0
France (0) 2 *(Thiney 6, Abily 18)*

England: Chamberlain; 2 Scott A, Houghton, Bronze, Stokes, Williams, Carney (Sanderson 66), Asante (Scott J 51), Duggan, Dowie (Smith 66), Davison (Aluko 58).

NON-LEAGUE TABLES 2013–14

EVO-STIK NORTHERN PREMIER LEAGUE 2013–14

				Total				Home					Away						
		P	W	D	L	F	A	W	D	L	F	A	W	D	L	F	A	GD	Pts
1	Chorley	46	29	10	7	107	39	17	3	3	64	17	12	7	4	43	22	68	97
2	FC United of Manchester	46	29	9	8	108	52	15	4	4	58	26	14	5	4	50	26	56	96
3	AFC Fylde¶	46	28	9	9	97	41	15	2	6	46	21	13	7	3	51	20	56	93
4	Worksop T	46	27	7	12	120	87	16	0	7	66	45	11	7	5	54	42	33	88
5	Ashton U	46	24	8	14	92	62	14	4	5	52	31	10	4	9	40	31	30	80
6	Skelmersdale U	46	24	5	17	92	79	17	1	5	53	31	7	4	12	39	48	13	77
7	Rushall Olympic	46	21	12	13	79	65	10	10	3	38	22	11	2	10	41	43	14	75
8	Blyth Spartans	46	20	12	14	79	78	14	4	5	49	37	6	8	9	30	41	1	72
9	Whitby T	46	18	16	12	82	64	9	10	4	42	30	9	6	8	40	34	18	70
10	Trafford	46	20	8	18	77	73	11	2	10	35	38	9	6	8	42	35	4	68
11	King's Lynn T	46	20	8	18	76	77	12	6	5	49	30	8	2	13	27	47	-1	68
12	Matlock T	46	18	13	15	61	53	12	8	3	32	16	6	5	12	29	37	8	67
13	Buxton	46	16	14	16	63	60	8	6	9	40	36	8	8	7	23	24	3	62
14	Barwell	46	17	11	18	62	67	8	8	7	30	30	9	3	11	32	37	-5	62
15	Grantham T	46	17	10	19	77	78	12	4	7	42	31	5	6	12	35	47	-1	61
16	Witton Alb	46	17	9	20	77	80	11	2	10	44	39	6	7	10	33	41	-3	60
17	Ilkeston	46	17	8	21	81	77	7	5	11	37	34	10	3	10	44	43	4	59
18	Stamford	46	17	7	22	75	85	10	4	9	48	42	7	3	13	27	43	-10	58
19	Nantwich T	46	14	14	18	77	71	9	9	5	41	30	5	5	13	36	41	6	56
20	Marine	46	13	14	19	68	76	7	5	11	37	35	6	9	8	31	41	-8	53
21	Frickley Ath	46	12	13	21	62	80	8	8	7	32	30	4	5	14	30	50	-18	49
22	Stafford Rangers	46	9	8	29	56	112	5	6	12	32	48	4	2	17	24	64	-56	35
23	Stocksbridge PS	46	5	8	33	60	130	3	5	15	33	58	2	3	18	27	72	-70	23
24	Droylsden (R)	46	2	3	41	40	182	1	2	20	21	90	1	1	21	19	92	-142	9

¶AFC Fylde promoted via play-offs.

NORTHERN PREMIER LEAGUE DIVISION 1 NORTH

				Total				Home					Away						
		P	W	D	L	F	A	W	D	L	F	A	W	D	L	F	A	GD	Pts
1	Curzon Ashton	42	31	6	5	92	36	13	5	3	44	19	18	1	2	48	17	56	99
2	Darlington 1883	42	28	6	8	101	37	13	3	5	51	18	15	3	3	50	19	64	90
3	Warrington T	42	27	6	9	86	47	14	2	5	44	26	13	4	4	42	21	39	87
4	Bamber Bridge	42	26	5	11	81	45	14	2	5	44	19	12	3	6	37	26	36	83
5	Ramsbottom U*¶	42	25	8	9	112	57	13	5	3	65	24	12	3	6	47	33	55	80
6	Lancaster C	42	24	8	10	75	52	13	6	3	34	21	12	2	7	41	31	23	80
7	Farsley	42	21	12	9	76	51	10	6	5	42	28	11	6	4	34	23	25	75
8	Ossett T	42	19	8	15	66	63	8	5	8	28	29	11	3	7	38	34	3	65
9	Northwich Victoria	42	16	15	11	73	52	11	5	5	45	24	5	10	6	28	28	21	63
10	Kendal T	42	17	5	20	83	84	11	3	7	51	38	6	2	13	32	46	-1	56
11	Cammell Laird	42	15	9	18	65	64	8	4	9	32	29	7	5	9	33	35	1	54
12	Salford C	42	15	7	20	68	80	7	4	10	39	41	8	3	10	29	39	-12	52
13	Harrogate Railway Ath	42	14	6	22	52	66	9	2	10	33	30	5	4	12	19	36	-14	48
14	Burscough	42	13	9	20	58	82	5	5	11	26	39	8	4	9	32	43	-24	48
15	Mossley	42	13	8	21	73	90	9	4	8	41	38	4	4	13	32	52	-17	47
16	New Mills	42	12	9	21	68	95	8	3	10	38	42	4	6	11	30	53	-27	45
17	Clitheroe	42	12	7	23	55	81	10	3	8	40	35	2	4	15	15	46	-26	43
18	Radcliffe Bor	42	12	7	23	57	93	6	5	10	30	37	6	2	13	27	56	-36	43
19	Padiham	42	12	6	24	61	92	5	4	12	32	43	7	2	12	29	49	-31	42
20	Prescot Cables	42	10	10	22	63	86	9	2	10	38	37	1	8	12	25	49	-23	40
21	Ossett Alb	42	7	8	27	40	80	2	3	16	18	39	5	5	11	22	41	-40	29
22	Wakefield	42	7	7	28	55	127	2	5	14	27	62	5	2	14	28	65	-72	28

*Ramsbottom U deducted 3 points for fielding an ineligible player. ¶Ramsbottom U promoted via play-offs.

NORTHERN PREMIER LEAGUE DIVISION 1 SOUTH

				Total				Home					Away						
		P	W	D	L	F	A	W	D	L	F	A	W	D	L	F	A	GD	Pts
1	Halesowen T	40	29	4	7	80	38	15	1	4	41	17	14	3	3	39	21	42	91
2	Coalville T	40	27	8	5	101	36	13	3	4	50	18	14	5	1	51	17	66	89
3	Leek T	40	28	4	8	86	35	16	2	2	41	13	12	2	6	45	22	51	88
4	Belper T¶	40	24	9	7	98	50	12	2	5	50	18	11	7	2	48	32	48	81
5	Mickleover Sports	40	22	7	11	82	62	11	4	5	42	33	11	3	6	40	29	20	73
6	Sutton Coldfield T	40	19	7	14	74	53	11	2	7	45	28	8	5	7	29	25	21	64
7	Scarborough Ath	40	18	7	15	73	57	11	3	6	41	23	7	4	9	32	34	16	61
8	Newcastle T	40	18	5	17	66	65	11	3	6	38	29	7	2	11	28	36	1	59
9	Gresley	40	17	5	18	66	67	10	5	5	35	26	7	0	13	31	41	-1	56
10	Carlton T	40	15	10	15	58	55	9	4	7	33	25	6	6	8	25	30	3	55
11	Romulus	40	16	7	17	66	64	11	3	6	42	30	5	4	11	24	34	2	55
12	Chasetown	40	14	10	16	52	59	11	3	6	28	23	3	7	10	24	36	-7	52
13	Goole	40	15	6	19	61	76	8	3	9	29	38	7	3	10	32	38	-15	51
14	Loughborough Dynamo	40	12	10	18	52	77	6	4	10	32	44	7	4	9	30	33	-25	46
15	Rainworth MW	40	12	10	18	52	72	5	7	8	23	34	7	3	10	29	38	-20	46
16	Sheffield	40	12	8	20	69	80	5	7	8	36	39	7	1	12	33	41	-11	44
17	Lincoln U	40	10	6	24	55	88	6	2	12	34	49	4	4	12	21	39	-33	36
18	Brigg T	40	9	8	23	49	94	6	3	11	24	42	3	5	12	25	52	-45	35
19	Market Drayton T	40	8	11	21	56	105	5	5	10	33	53	3	6	11	23	52	-49	35
20	Bedworth U	40	9	7	24	48	83	3	4	13	19	39	6	3	11	29	44	-35	34
21	Kidsgrove Ath	40	7	9	24	41	80	6	8	6	28	30	1	1	18	13	50	-39	30

Eastwood T record expunged. ¶Belper T promoted via play-offs.

EVO-STIK SOUTHERN PREMIER LEAGUE 2013–14

		P	W	D	L	F	A	W	D	L	F	A	W	D	L	F	A	GD	Pts
				Total					*Home*					*Away*					
1	Hemel Hempstead T	44	32	6	6	128	38	18	3	1	74	14	14	3	5	54	24	90	102
2	Chesham U	44	29	5	10	102	47	14	3	5	50	23	15	2	5	52	24	55	92
3	Cambridge C	44	27	7	10	95	49	15	4	3	53	25	12	3	7	42	24	46	88
4	St Albans C¶	44	25	10	9	89	49	14	4	4	45	22	11	6	5	44	27	40	85
5	Stourbridge	44	26	6	12	114	54	13	2	7	56	29	13	4	5	58	25	60	84
6	Hungerford T	44	26	6	12	83	45	13	3	6	42	24	13	3	6	41	21	38	84
7	Poole T*	44	25	10	9	82	48	14	4	4	44	24	11	6	5	38	24	34	82
8	Bideford	44	18	13	13	75	64	11	7	4	42	26	7	6	9	33	38	11	67
9	Biggleswade T	44	16	16	12	85	61	9	9	4	39	27	7	7	8	46	34	24	64
10	Redditch U	44	20	3	21	68	85	11	2	9	35	38	9	1	12	33	47	–17	63
11	Corby T (R)	44	18	6	20	65	68	10	2	10	36	36	8	4	10	29	32	–3	60
12	Weymouth	44	18	6	20	69	80	10	3	9	35	40	8	3	11	34	40	–11	60
13	Hitchin T	44	16	11	17	63	52	10	5	7	37	24	6	6	10	26	28	11	59
14	Frome T	44	16	9	19	63	74	7	5	10	32	38	9	4	9	31	36	–11	57
15	Arlesey T	44	15	10	19	68	79	6	8	8	35	39	9	2	11	33	40	–11	55
16	St Neots T	44	15	9	20	74	76	10	4	8	47	36	5	5	12	27	40	–2	54
17	Truro C (R)	44	15	9	20	68	84	7	5	10	34	38	8	4	10	34	46	–16	54
18	Chippenham T	44	14	6	24	59	87	9	3	10	31	42	5	3	14	28	45	–28	48
19	Banbury U	44	14	5	25	64	116	8	4	10	34	50	6	1	15	30	66	–52	47
20	Burnham	44	12	8	24	60	91	8	2	12	30	39	4	6	12	30	52	–31	44
21	AFC Totton	44	10	7	27	58	119	6	4	12	32	57	4	3	15	26	62	–61	37
22	Bedford T	44	6	6	32	46	114	3	2	17	21	56	3	4	15	25	58	–68	24
23	Bashley	44	4	4	36	33	131	1	1	20	16	64	3	3	16	17	67	–98	16

*Hinckley U (R) record expunged. *Poole T deducted 3 points for fielding an ineligible player.
¶St Albans C promoted via play-offs.*

CALOR SOUTHERN LEAGUE DIVISION 1 CENTRAL

1	Dunstable T	42	28	6	8	94	44	15	3	3	51	23	13	3	5	43	21	50	90
2	Rugby T	42	27	8	7	100	45	14	5	2	52	21	13	3	5	48	24	55	89
3	Kettering T	42	27	7	8	86	41	15	3	3	49	20	12	4	5	37	21	45	88
4	Daventry T	42	27	5	10	82	40	15	3	3	53	16	12	2	7	29	24	42	86
5	Slough T¶	42	26	5	11	101	51	14	0	7	49	28	12	5	4	52	23	50	83
6	Barton R	42	24	8	10	79	48	13	3	5	50	27	11	5	5	29	21	31	80
7	Royston T	42	21	10	11	80	58	9	7	5	38	26	12	3	6	42	32	22	73
8	Beaconsfield SYCOB	22	22	7	13	79	60	10	4	7	40	34	12	3	6	39	26	19	73
9	Northwood	42	21	6	15	72	62	10	3	8	37	32	11	3	7	35	30	10	69
10	Uxbridge	42	18	7	17	84	70	9	3	9	41	42	9	4	8	43	28	14	61
11	Egham T	42	17	9	16	80	58	7	4	10	37	33	10	5	6	43	25	22	60
12	Aylesbury U	42	16	9	17	64	72	6	7	8	22	28	10	2	9	42	44	–8	57
13	St Ives T	42	16	8	18	68	77	7	3	11	30	41	9	5	7	38	36	–9	56
14	Chalfont St Peter	42	14	8	20	49	60	5	3	13	22	32	9	5	7	27	28	–11	50
15	Potters Bar T	42	13	10	19	61	86	7	7	7	34	30	6	3	12	27	56	–25	49
16	Aylesbury	42	14	6	22	56	73	9	3	9	35	33	5	3	13	21	40	–17	48
17	Marlow	42	12	11	19	73	84	8	5	8	42	42	4	6	11	31	42	–11	47
18	AFC Hayes	42	12	8	22	51	74	5	4	12	19	40	7	4	10	32	34	–23	44
19	Leighton T	42	6	13	23	45	85	3	7	11	23	33	3	6	12	22	52	–40	31
20	North Greenford U	42	7	5	30	52	114	4	1	16	27	62	3	4	14	25	52	–62	26
21	Chertsey T	42	6	4	32	38	117	1	2	18	16	61	5	2	14	22	56	–79	22
22	Ashford T (Middlesex)	42	5	6	31	32	107	3	3	15	13	42	2	3	16	19	65	–75	21

¶Slough T promoted via play-offs.

CALOR SOUTHERN LEAGUE DIVISION 1 SOUTH & WEST

1	Cirencester T	42	29	5	8	95	45	13	5	3	53	22	16	0	5	42	23	50	92
2	Merthyr T	42	28	5	9	111	58	18	3	0	76	22	10	2	9	35	36	53	89
3	Tiverton T	42	26	8	8	80	51	15	3	3	42	22	11	5	5	38	29	29	86
4	Paulton R¶	42	24	9	9	102	54	12	3	6	51	25	12	6	3	51	29	48	81
5	Swindon Supermarine	42	24	7	11	91	52	16	1	4	60	23	8	6	7	31	29	39	79
6	Shortwood U	42	23	9	10	91	44	13	5	3	47	19	10	4	7	44	25	47	78
7	North Leigh	42	22	6	14	84	46	14	2	5	45	21	8	4	9	39	25	38	72
8	Taunton T	42	21	7	14	71	58	11	5	5	35	22	10	2	9	36	36	13	69
9	Yate T	42	20	8	14	81	69	13	1	7	46	32	7	7	7	35	37	12	68
10	Stratford T	42	19	5	18	103	86	9	3	9	49	43	10	2	9	54	43	17	62
11	Mangotsfield U	42	18	7	17	65	62	10	4	7	33	24	8	3	10	32	38	3	61
12	Didcot T	42	17	6	19	70	85	9	3	9	39	40	8	3	10	31	45	–15	57
13	Wimborne T	42	16	7	19	78	70	11	3	7	48	28	5	4	12	30	42	8	55
14	Bridgwater T	42	14	11	17	62	64	7	9	5	36	31	7	2	12	26	33	–2	53
15	Cinderford T	42	13	10	19	69	79	5	3	13	30	42	8	7	6	39	37	–10	49
16	Evesham U	42	12	11	19	66	80	7	6	8	42	42	5	5	11	24	38	–14	47
17	Clevedon T	42	12	5	25	48	96	6	3	12	27	47	6	2	13	21	49	–48	41
18	Godalming T	42	10	9	23	47	79	6	4	11	26	37	4	5	12	21	42	–32	39
19	Thatcham T	42	11	6	25	41	99	6	4	11	20	36	5	2	14	21	63	–58	39
20	Bishops Cleeve	42	11	1	30	52	94	6	0	15	25	48	5	1	15	27	46	–42	34
21	Fleet T	42	7	8	27	43	90	5	3	13	24	43	2	5	14	19	47	–47	29
22	Guildford C	42	7	6	29	45	134	4	3	14	22	50	3	1	17	23	84	–89	27

Taunton T deducted 1 point for fielding an ineligible player. ¶Paulton R promoted via play-offs.

RYMAN ISTHMIAN PREMIER LEAGUE 2013–14

		P	W	D	L	F	A	W	D	L	F	A	W	D	L	F	A	GD	Pts
									Total						Home			Away	
1	Wealdstone	46	28	12	6	99	43	13	7	3	52	24	15	5	3	47	19	56	96
2	Kingstonian	46	25	10	11	80	44	15	2	6	47	24	10	8	5	33	20	36	85
3	Bognor Regis T	46	26	7	13	95	65	16	3	4	59	27	10	4	9	36	38	30	85
4	Lowestoft T¶	46	24	12	10	76	40	15	4	4	53	18	9	8	6	23	22	36	84
5	AFC Hornchurch (R)	46	24	11	11	83	53	11	5	7	36	25	13	6	4	47	28	30	83
6	Dulwich Hamlet	46	25	7	14	96	65	15	3	5	49	29	10	4	9	47	36	31	82
7	Maidstone U	46	23	12	11	92	57	12	10	1	53	22	11	2	10	39	35	35	81
8	Hendon	46	21	7	18	84	69	8	4	11	39	38	13	3	7	45	31	15	70
9	Leiston	46	19	10	17	73	71	10	5	8	37	28	9	5	9	36	43	2	67
10	Billericay T (R)	46	19	9	18	66	64	9	3	11	36	34	10	6	7	30	30	2	66
11	Margate	46	18	10	18	70	67	9	6	8	37	32	9	4	10	33	35	3	64
12	Hampton & Richmond Bor	46	18	10	18	72	70	9	3	11	36	31	9	7	7	36	39	2	64
13	Canvey Island	46	17	11	18	65	65	10	6	7	35	30	7	5	11	30	35	0	62
14	Grays Ath	46	17	10	19	74	82	9	6	8	38	39	8	4	11	36	43	–8	61
15	Bury T	46	17	9	20	60	65	8	5	10	23	32	9	4	10	37	33	–5	60
16	Lewes	46	14	17	15	67	67	9	8	6	36	30	5	9	9	31	37	0	59
17	Metropolitan Police	46	15	13	18	58	59	9	3	11	31	29	6	10	7	27	30	–1	58
18	Harrow Bor	46	15	13	18	66	72	7	9	7	32	30	8	4	11	34	42	–6	58
19	Enfield T	46	13	12	21	64	90	9	6	8	38	40	4	6	13	26	50	–26	51
20	East Thurrock U	46	13	10	23	66	84	8	4	11	39	37	5	6	12	27	47	–18	49
21	Wingate & Finchley	46	14	7	25	57	84	8	4	11	33	39	6	3	14	24	45	–27	49
22	Thamesmead T	46	12	10	24	61	90	7	7	9	32	36	5	3	15	29	54	–29	46
23	Carshalton Ath	46	8	6	32	40	101	3	3	17	16	51	5	3	15	24	50	–61	30
24	Cray W	46	7	5	34	40	137	3	4	16	24	68	4	1	18	16	69	–97	26

¶*Lowestoft T promoted via play-offs.*

RYMAN ISTHMIAN LEAGUE DIVISION 1 NORTH

		P	W	D	L	F	A	W	D	L	F	A	W	D	L	F	A	GD	Pts
1	VCD Ath	46	32	3	11	116	54	16	1	6	65	31	16	2	5	51	23	62	99
2	Witham T¶	46	30	8	8	109	54	17	5	1	58	20	13	3	7	51	34	55	98
3	Heybridge Swifts	46	28	9	9	108	59	15	4	4	57	29	13	5	5	51	30	49	93
4	Harlow T	46	27	10	9	105	59	14	6	3	59	30	13	4	6	46	29	46	91
5	Needham Market	46	25	12	9	85	44	14	6	3	44	21	11	6	6	41	23	41	87
6	Thurrock	46	26	9	11	99	60	16	2	5	59	29	10	7	6	40	31	39	87
7	Dereham T	46	22	11	13	98	65	13	4	6	59	29	9	7	7	39	36	33	77
8	Soham T Rangers	46	24	4	18	92	75	14	0	9	60	40	10	1	12	32	35	17	76
9	Maldon & Tiptree	46	21	13	12	82	68	15	4	4	52	30	6	9	8	30	38	14	76
10	AFC Sudbury	46	21	13	12	76	63	11	7	5	34	25	10	6	7	42	38	13	76
11	Romford	46	21	5	20	76	69	12	3	8	47	31	9	2	12	29	38	7	68
12	Chatham T	46	20	8	18	74	76	9	6	8	35	32	11	2	10	39	44	–2	68
13	Aveley	46	20	5	21	81	81	12	3	8	46	33	8	2	13	35	48	0	65
14	Redbridge	46	16	11	19	78	84	9	8	6	40	29	7	3	13	38	55	–6	59
15	Cheshunt	46	12	17	17	74	75	6	9	8	34	35	6	8	9	40	40	–1	53
16	Tilbury	46	14	11	21	56	74	11	4	8	33	29	3	7	13	23	45	–18	53
17	Burnham Ramblers	46	14	10	22	69	100	6	6	11	35	49	8	4	11	34	51	–31	52
18	Waltham Abbey	46	14	8	24	71	90	7	6	10	33	35	7	2	14	38	55	–19	50
19	Brentwood T	46	11	13	22	71	92	8	3	12	34	41	3	10	10	37	51	–21	46
20	Barkingside	46	12	10	24	76	120	6	6	11	40	58	6	4	13	36	62	–44	46
21	Ware	46	12	9	25	73	93	8	5	10	38	45	4	4	15	35	48	–20	45
22	Wroxham	46	10	6	30	77	123	8	1	14	53	55	2	5	16	24	68	–46	36
23	Waltham Forest	46	6	7	33	43	118	2	4	17	20	59	4	3	16	23	59	–75	25
24	Erith & Belvedere	46	6	4	36	44	137	4	2	17	22	61	2	2	19	22	76	–93	22

¶*Witham T promoted via play-offs.*

RYMAN ISTHMIAN LEAGUE DIVISION 1 SOUTH

		P	W	D	L	F	A	W	D	L	F	A	W	D	L	F	A	GD	Pts
1	Peacehaven & Telscombe	46	33	8	5	128	55	18	4	1	79	24	15	4	4	49	31	73	107
2	Folkestone Invicta	46	27	8	11	102	59	17	3	3	61	24	10	5	8	41	35	43	89
3	Leatherhead*¶	46	28	8	10	93	46	17	2	4	50	17	11	6	6	43	29	47	86
4	Guernsey	46	23	12	11	93	65	14	4	5	53	27	9	8	6	40	38	28	81
5	Hastings U	46	24	7	15	72	61	16	4	3	42	23	8	3	12	30	38	11	79
6	Burgess Hill T	46	22	11	13	88	67	15	5	3	52	24	7	6	10	36	43	21	77
7	Merstham	46	23	7	16	81	63	13	2	8	49	33	10	5	8	32	30	18	76
8	Hythe T	46	22	7	17	87	71	10	6	7	45	31	12	1	10	42	40	16	73
9	Walton Casuals	46	22	4	20	89	93	11	3	9	48	48	11	1	11	41	45	–4	70
10	Faversham T	46	18	14	14	78	69	11	6	6	42	30	7	8	8	36	39	9	68
11	Tooting & Mitcham U	46	17	12	17	79	75	12	5	6	50	33	5	7	11	29	42	4	63
12	Ramsgate	46	18	8	20	84	79	12	3	8	50	32	6	5	12	34	47	5	62
13	Chipstead	46	18	8	20	79	83	8	5	10	38	40	10	3	10	41	43	–4	62
14	Sittingbourne	46	16	13	17	69	75	10	7	6	37	28	6	6	11	32	47	–6	61
15	Worthing	46	17	8	21	80	98	13	5	5	57	43	4	3	16	23	55	–18	59
16	Horsham	46	15	11	20	66	78	9	6	8	35	36	6	5	12	31	42	–12	56
17	Corinthian–Casuals	46	15	10	21	69	73	6	7	10	33	33	9	3	11	36	40	–4	55
18	Herne Bay	46	15	9	22	69	72	10	3	10	32	28	5	6	12	37	44	–3	54
19	Three Bridges	46	15	8	23	71	88	8	4	11	39	42	7	4	12	32	46	–17	53
20	Whitstable T	46	14	11	21	60	77	8	7	8	35	35	6	4	13	25	42	–17	53
21	Walton & Hersham	46	14	9	23	75	92	5	3	15	32	52	9	6	8	43	40	–17	51
22	Redhill	46	13	6	27	72	96	6	4	13	35	46	7	2	14	37	50	–24	45
23	Crawley Down Gatwick	46	9	6	31	51	139	4	4	15	30	61	5	2	16	21	78	–88	33
24	Eastbourne T	46	6	11	29	60	121	4	6	13	30	51	2	5	16	30	70	–61	29

Leatherhead deducted 6 points for registration irregularity. ¶Leatherhead promoted via play-offs.

THE FA TROPHY 2013–14
IN PARTNERSHIP WITH CARLSBERG

After extra time.

PRELIMINARY ROUND

Brigg T v Bamber Bridge	2-1
Northwich Vic v Salford C	3-1
Prescot Cables v Scarborough Ath	0-1
Warrington T v Ramsbottom U	1-2
Goole v Burscough	1-5
Kendal T v Farsley	3-2
Wakefield v Harrogate RA	2-1
Clitheroe v Radcliffe Bor	3-3, 0-3
Ossett T v Darlington 1883	1-6
Padiham v Sheffield	1-2
Ossett Alb v Curzon Ashton	1-3
Lancaster C v New Mills	6-0
Lincoln C v Cammell Laird	1-2
Soham Town Rangers v Newcastle T	1-0
Kettering T v Romulus	1-1, 2-1
Carlton T v Gresley	2-2, 0-2
Stratford T v Coalville T	2-2, 1-3
Eastwood T v Halesowen T	0-3
Chasetown v Rugby T	2-1
Evesham U v Market Drayton T	3-1
Daventry T v Sutton Coldfield T	1-0
Belper T v Loughborough Dynamo	2-0
Kidsgrove Ath v Bedworth U	3-1
Rainworth MW v St Ives T	0-1
VCD Ath v Aylesbury	2-2, 1-2
Redbridge v Chatham T	2-3
Ware v Witham T	1-1, 2-4
Sittingbourne v Whitstable T	1-5
Leighton v North Greenford U	0-3
Redhill v Burnham Ramblers	1-3
Royston T v Three Bridges	1-3
Aylesbury U v Faversham T	4-2
Dunstable T v Erith & Belvedere	4-1
Tooting & Mitcham U v Eastbourne T	1-2
Barton R v Peacehaven & Telscombe	0-3
Herne Bay v Merstham	0-0, 2-0
Thurrock v Corinthian Casuals	2-0
Waltham Abbey v Walton & Hersham	2-1
Uxbridge v Heybridge Swifts	1-2
Potters Bar T v Romford	2-0
Burgess Hill T v Wroxham	1-1, 2-3
Tilbury v Needham Market	3-0
AFC Sudbury v Worthing	2-0
Folkestone Invicta v Waltham Forest	6-0
Walton Casuals v Crawley Down Gatwick	1-1, 0-1
Horsham v Chipstead	4-1
Hythe T v Aveley	2-1
Barkingside v Guernsey	0-6
Hastings U v Brentwood T	3-2
Northwood v AFC Hayes	2-3
Leatherhead v Harlow T	4-0
Mangotsfield U v Thatcham T	2-1
Chalfont St Peter v Bridgwater T	1-1, 3-3*
(Bridgwater won 5-3 on penalties)	
Fleet T v Clevedon T	0-3
Didcot T v Cirencester T	1-1, 1-7
Merthyr T v Yate T	0-0, 2-1
Swindon Supermarine v Taunton T	3-0
Guildford C v Chertsey T	3-4
Tiverton T v Cinderford T	1-0
Godalming T v Slough T	1-2
Bishop's Cleeve v Paulton R	1-4
Egham T v Ashford T (Middlesex)	3-2
Wimborne T v Marlow	3-5
Shortwood U v Beaconsfield SYCOB	3-1

FIRST QUALIFYING ROUND

Trafford v Wakefield	6-1
Whitby T v Chorley	0-1
Frickley Ath v Brigg T	1-2
Cammell Laird v Curzon Ashton	0-1
AFC Fylde v Kendal T	1-1, 2-1
Ramsbottom U v Worksop T	7-2
Witton Alb v FC United of Manchester	2-2, 2-1
Ashton U v Sheffield	0-3

Mossley v Lancaster C	3-2
Northwich Vic v Radcliffe Bor	2-0
Blyth Spartans v Skelmersdale U	6-0
Droylsden v Nantwich T	0-3
Stocksbridge Park Steels v Scarborough Ath	3-4
Marine v Burscough	1-1, 1-0
Buxton v Darlington 1883	1-1, 3-3*
(Buxton won 4-3 on penalties)	
Kettering T v St Ives T	0-1
Evesham U v Leek T	0-2
Coalville T v Stafford Rangers	3-2
Halesowen T v St Neots T	1-3
Redditch U v Chasetown	2-1, 2-0
(First match abandoned after 82 mins due to	
waterlogged pitch)	
Gresley v Ilkeston	2-1
King's Lynn T v Cambridge C	1-2
Belper T v Mickleover Sports	2-3
Barwell v Rushall Olympic	0-4
Matlock T (*walkover*) v Hinckley U (*removed*)	
Stourbridge v Banbury U	3-2
Grantham T v Soham Town Rangers	2-2, 1-4*
Daventry T v Corby T	2-1
Stamford v Kidsgrove Ath	1-2
Eastbourne T v East Thurrock U	0-0, 2-6
Witham T v St Albans C	2-3
Whitstable T v Potters Bar T	2-2, 2-1
Lewes v Leatherhead	1-2
Arlesey T v Waltham Abbey	3-0
Cheshunt v Three Bridges	3-4
Thamesmead T v Metropolitan Police	1-2
AFC Sudbury v Crawley Down Gatwick	5-0
Wingate & Finchley v Hitchin T	2-2, 1-0
Hastings U v Horsham	4-2
Hampton & Richmond Bor v Bedford T	1-1, 2-0
Folkestone Invicta v Kingstonian	2-0
Leiston v Wealdstone	0-3
North Greenford U v Aylesbury	2-1
Dunstable T v Peacehaven & Telscombe	3-2
Cray W v Hendon	1-4
Chatham T v AFC Hayes	2-0
Wroxham v Margate	4-9
Biggleswade T v Chesham U	0-1
Grays Ath v Herne Bay	1-1, 2-1*
Guernsey v Billericay T	1-2
Bury T v Dereham T	2-0
Heybridge Swifts v Canvey Island	1-2
Burnham Ramblers v Carshalton Ath	0-1
Hythe T v Tilbury	3-1
Hemel Hempstead T v AFC Hornchurch	3-2
Maldon & Tiptree v Maidstone U	1-3
Dulwich Hamlet v Harrow Bor	2-1
Bognor Regis T v Thurrock	2-1
Enfield T v Lowestoft T	2-1
Aylesbury U v Ramsgate	0-1
Slough T v Merthyr T	1-2
Weymouth v Bridgwater T	1-0
AFC Totton v Clevedon T	1-2
Tiverton T v Truro C	3-2
Chippenham T v Chertsey T	3-0
Egham T v Cirencester T	3-2
Shortwood U v Mangotsfield U	0-2
Hungerford T v Bashley	4-2
Swindon Supermarine v Bideford	2-3
Frome T v Poole T	1-1, 1-3*
Marlow v North Leigh	4-1
Burnham v Paulton R	2-1

SECOND QUALIFYING ROUND

Witton Alb v Leek T	1-2
Mickleover Sports v Stourbridge	1-2
Rushall Olympic v AFC Fylde	0-1
Blyth Spartans v Ramsbottom U	0-1
Coalville T v Marine	5-0
Scarborough Ath v Cambridge C	0-0, 2-1
Redditch U v Brigg T	5-0
Kidsgrove Ath v Curzon Ashton	0-4
Northwich Vic v Mossley	2-0

Matlock T v St Neots T	2-0
Gresley v Trafford	2-0
Sheffield v Buxton	1-0
St Ives T v Nantwich T	1-4
Soham Town Rangers v Chorley	1-2
Carshalton Ath v Egham T	2-1
Chesham U v Weymouth	2-1
Folkestone Invicta v Hungerford T	1-1, 1-1*
(Hungerford won 5-4 on penalties)	
St Albans C v Billericay T	3-3, 2-2*
(St Albans C won 4-2 on penalties)	
Arlesey T v Poole T	3-2
Ramsgate v Three Bridges	4-1
Enfield T v Grays Ath	0-1
Hastings U v AFC Sudbury	0-1
Wingate & Finchley v Daventry T	1-1, 1-3
Wealdstone v Maidstone U	2-2, 0-1
Merthyr T v Dunstable T	3-2
Hampton & Richmond Bor v Metropolitan Police	2-1
Marlow v Burnham	2-0
Dulwich Hamlet v Leatherhead	3-0
Margate v Clevedon T	4-1
Bury T v Chatham T	2-1
Hemel Hempstead T v North Greenford U	9-1
Bognor Regis T v Chippenham T	4-1
Hendon v Bideford	1-0
Canvey Island v East Thurrock U	0-2
Tiverton T v Mangotsfield U	3-1
Hythe T v Whitstable T	2-2, 1-2

THIRD QUALIFYING ROUND

Barrow v Stockport Co	2-2, 3-2
Harrogate T v Bradford (Park Avenue)	1-1, 0-4
Chorley v Matlock T	2-0
Leamington v Gainsborough Trinity	2-0
Sheffield v Gresley	2-4
Stalybridge Celtic v Vauxhall Motors	3-0
Solihull Moors v Coalville T	1-2
Stourbridge v North Ferriby U	2-2, 0-4
Worcester C v Ramsbottom U	3-0
AFC Telford U v Scarborough Ath	6-0
Brackley T v Leek T	0-0, 1-2*
Hednesford T v Workington	3-0
Curzon Ashton v AFC Fylde	2-1
Northwich Vic v Nantwich T	2-0
Guiseley v Histon	3-0
Boston U v Redditch U	4-1
Colwyn Bay v Altrincham	0-2, 0-2
(First match abandoned after 81 minutes due to injury to referee)	
Basingstoke T v Hampton & Richmond Bor	3-1
Chelmsford C v St Albans C	1-2
Daventry T v Ramsgate	3-2
Sutton U v Havant & Waterlooville	1-2
Carshalton Ath v Whitstable T	1-2
Hayes & Yeading U v Bognor Regis T	2-1
Tonbridge Angels v AFC Sudbury	1-1, 1-0
East Thurrock U v Merthyr T	4-2
Boreham Wood v Gloucester C	0-1
Dover Ath v Bath C	1-0
Hungerford T v Hemel Hempstead T	5-0
Ebbsfleet U v Bromley	4-1
Hendon v Oxford C	2-1
Staines T v Farnborough	2-2, 2-0
Arlesey T v Marlow	2-0
Bury T v Grays Ath	5-1
Weston Super Mare v Tiverton T	1-1, 2-1
Whitehawk v Bishop's Stortford	2-1
Dulwich Hamlet v Concord Rangers	1-1, 3-4*
Maidstone U v Eastleigh	1-2
Eastbourne Bor v Maidenhead U	0-1
Margate v Chesham U	0-3
Gosport Bor v Dorchester T	3-0

FIRST ROUND

Leamington v Northwich Vic	0-0, 1-0
Tamworth v Macclesfield T	2-0
FC Halifax T v Guiseley	0-1
Southport v Boston U	1-2
Coalville T v Grimsby T	1-1, 0-3
Hyde v North Ferriby U	1-2
Alfreton T v Nuneaton T	0-1
Chorley v Curzon Ashton	2-1
Bradford (Park Avenue) v Kidderminster H	2-1
Worcester C v AFC Telford U	0-0, 3-0

Altrincham v Leek T	1-2
Wrexham v Gresley	2-1
Chester FC v Barrow	1-2
Gateshead v Hednesford T	4-1
Lincoln C v Stalybridge Celtic	5-1
Hereford U v Woking	0-3
Bury T v Eastleigh	0-3
Dartford v Forest Green R	1-1, 0-1
Hendon v Whitstable T	1-2
Arlesey T v Whitehawk	1-5
Tonbridge Angels v St Albans C	0-0, 0-4
Gosport Bor v Concord Rangers	1-0
Aldershot v Weston Super Mare	1-1, 5-2
Hungerford T v Chesham U	2-0
Hayes & Yeading U v Barnet	0-1
Daventry T v Maidenhead U	0-1
Staines T v Luton T	0-0, 0-2
Ebbsfleet U v Gloucester C	3-0
Braintree T v Welling U	3-0
East Thurrock U v Dover Ath	1-1, 1-3
Basingstoke T v Havant & Waterlooville	0-0, 0-1

SECOND ROUND

Luton T v Wrexham	2-0
Whitehawk v Havant & Waterlooville	1-1, 1-3
Eastleigh v Gateshead	2-0
Barnet v Grimsby T	1-2
Barrow v Maidenhead U	0-2
Gosport Bor v Nuneaton T	0-0, 0-0*
(Gosport Bor won 4-2 on penalties)	
St Albans C v Cambridge U	1-2
Guiseley v Bradford (Park Avenue)	3-0
Aldershot v Worcester C	4-1
Tamworth v Boston U	2-0
North Ferriby U v Woking	4-0
Whitstable T v Ebbsfleet U	1-2
Leek T v Hungerford T	0-1
Dover Ath v Leamington	2-0
Braintree T v Lincoln C	1-3
Chorley v Forest Green R	0-0, 0-0*
(Chorley won 3-1 on penalties)	

THIRD ROUND

Cambridge U v Luton T	2-2, 1-0
Aldershot T v Guiseley	3-0
Hungerford T v Gosport Bor	0-1
Eastleigh v Dover Ath	3-2
Tamworth v Chorley	1-1, 2-2*
(Tamworth won 6-5 on penalties)	
Lincoln C v North Ferriby U	0-4
Grimsby T v Maidenhead U	2-1
Havant & Waterlooville v Ebbsfleet U	1-0

FOURTH ROUND

Havant & Waterlooville v Aldershot T	4-1
Eastleigh v Cambridge U	0-1
North Ferriby U v Gosport Bor	1-2
Grimsby T v Tamworth	4-1

SEMI FINAL FIRST LEG

Havant & Waterlooville v Gosport Bor	1-1
Cambridge U v Grimsby T	2-1

SEMI FINAL SECOND LEG

Gosport Bor v Havant & Waterlooville	2-0
(Gosport Bor won 3-1 on aggregate)	
Grimsby T v Cambridge U	1-1
(Cambridge U won 3-2 on aggregate)	

FA CARLSBERG TROPHY FINAL 2014

Wembley, Sunday 23 March 2014

Cambridge U (1) 4 *(Bird 38, Donaldson 50, 59, Berry 78 (pen))*

Gosport Bor (0) (0)   18,120

Cambridge U: Norris; Tait, Miller, Coulson (Bonner 87), Taylor, Berry, Champion, Hughes (Arnold 73), Gillies (Pugh 61), Bird, Donaldson.
Gosport Bor: Ashmore; Molyneaux, Forbes, Pearce, Poache, Carmichael, Brown, Smith (Woodward 58), Gosney (Wooden 72), Sills (Williams 58), Bennett.
Referee: Craig Pawson.

THE FA VASE 2013–14

IN PARTNERSHIP WITH CARLSBERG

After extra time.

FIRST QUALIFYING ROUND

Birtley T v Tadcaster Alb	4-1
Penrith v Yorkshire Amateur	7-1
Marske U v Seaham Red Star	4-1
Jarrow Roofing Boldon CA v Thornaby	3-1
West Allotment Celtic v Stokesley	4-3
Billingham Synthonia v Hall Road Rangers	3-1
Whitehaven v Thackley	1-2
Chester-Le-Street T v Newcastle Benfield	1-4
Willington v Northallerton T	4-3*
Tow Law T v Durham C	0-3
Esh Winning v Liversedge	0-3
Knaresborough T v Westella Hanson	4-3*
Newton Aycliffe v Guisborough T	1-3
Whickham v Hebburn T	3-0
Alnwick T v Albion Sports	2-3
Glossop North End v Nostell MW	3-2*
Irlam v Runcorn Linnets	0-3
Wigan Robin Park v Winsford U	1-2
Cheadle T v Daisy Hill	3-1
Maltby Main v Squires Gate	0-3
Abbey Hey v Congleton T	0-2
Kinsley Boys v Appleby Frodingham	1-0
Penistone Church v Rossington Main	2-3
Worsborough Bridge Ath v Ashton T	2-1*
Armthorpe Welfare v AFC Liverpool	3-1
Stockport Sports v Atherton Collieries	5-0
Pontefract Collieries v St Helens T	2-0
Askern v Glasshoughton Welfare	2-7
Selby T v Formby	0-5
Oldham Boro v 1874 Northwich	2-1*
Hallam v Shirebrook T	1-2
Bottesford T v Ashton Ath	0-1*
Wolverhampton SC v Ellesmere Rangers	1-2
Wednesfield v Pilkington XXX	1-3
Pelsall Villa v Barnt Green Spartak	1-0
Bromyard T v Norton U	0-2
Coventry Copsewood v Nuneaton Griff	3-4
Heath Hayes v Studley	2-3
Lichfield C v Brocton	3-4*
Boldmere St Michaels v Tipton T	3-1
Malvern T v Coleshill T	2-5
Bewdley T v Stafford T	2-3*
Racing Club Warwick v Bustleholme	1-0
Dudley T v Leek CSOB	7-3
Shifnal T v Earlswood T	1-4
Black Country Rangers v Tividale	1-5
Bromsgrove Sporting v Lye T	1-0
Pegasus Juniors v Continental Star	2-3*
Pershore T v Wellington	2-1
Ellistown (removed) v Basford U (walkover)	
Blidworth Welfare v Ollerton T	1-4
Arnold T v Blaby Whetstone Ath	2-4*
Holwell Sports v Quorn	2-1*
Stewarts & Lloyds Corby v Bardon Hill Sports	4-3*
Ellistown & Ibstock U v Rothwell Corinthians	1-0*
Radcliffe Olympic v Pinxton	4-1
Harborough T v Holbrook Sports	5-3*
AFC Mansfield v Gedling MW	6-2
Mickleover Royals v Stapenhill	3-2*
Sutton T v Dunkirk	1-5
Clipstone v Belper U	4-0
Anstey Nomads v Heanor T	0-4
Radford v Desborough T	0-1
St Andrews v Lutterworth Ath	6-2
Yaxley v Peterborough Northern Star	1-2
Cambridge Regional College v Harrowby U	1-2
Boston T v Downham T	6-0
Brightlingsea Regent v Felixstowe & Walton U	1-0

Haverhill R v Stanway R	1-2*
Basildon U v Stansted	1-2
Wivenhoe T v Ipswich W	1-2
Debenham LC v Halstead T	0-2
Bowers & Pitsea v FC Clacton	2-1
Haverhill Bor v Norwich U	1-4
Hillingdon Bor v Bedford	6-0
London Colney v Codicote	2-3*
Cockfosters v Cogenhoe U	5-3*
London Tigers v Baldock T	1-2
Winslow U v Leverstock Green	6-3
Hadley v Biggleswade U	3-1
Harefield U v Wellingborough T	0-1
Berkhamsted v Hertford T	3-2*
FC Broxbourne Bor v Sporting Bengal U	0-3
Wembley v Potton U	6-0
Holmer Green v AFC Kempston R	1-0
Greenhouse London v Long Buckby	4-2*
AFC Biggleswade (removed) v	
Sileby Rangers (walkover)	
Crawley Green v London APSA	4-5
AFC Dunstable v AFC Rushden & Diamonds	1-1*, 1-3
London Lions v FC Romania	3-2
Southall v Haringey Bor	0-2
Rushden & Higham U v Northampton Spencer	0-4
Langford v Newport Pagnell T	1-5
Kings Langley v Colney Heath	1-3
Tring Ath v Eton Manor	1-0
Thame U v Carterton	8-0
Farnham T v Ardley U	2-1*
Cheltenham Saracens v Hook Norton	0-2
Kidlington v Newbury	5-2
Frimley Green v Windsor	1-3
Badshot Lea v Knaphill	0-1
Ash U v Holyport	0-1
Shrivenham v Malmesbury Vic	4-2
Brimscombe & Thrupp v Sandhurst T	3-1
Highworth T v Camberley T	1-3
Flackwell Heath v Hartley Wintney	1-3
Mile Oak v Arundel	1-1*, 0-2
Pagham v Molesey	2-1
Sevenoaks T v Canterbury C	5-0
Selsey v Littlehampton T	0-2
Saltdean U v Southwick	2-4*
Dorking W v St Francis Rangers	4-3*
Kent Football U v Lingfield	3-3*
(Lingfield won 5-4 on penalties)	
Shoreham v Horsham YMCA	2-1
Horley T v Newhaven	2-6
Chichester C v Cray Valley (PM)	3-5*
Raynes Park Vale v Holmesdale	0-2
Chessington & Hook U v Hailsham T	3-1*
Oakwood v Glebe	3-4
Steyning T v Ashford U	0-2
Croydon v Seaford T	2-0
Phoenix Sports (walkover) v Sidley U (removed)	
Colliers Wood U v Dorking	1-3*
Deal T v Epsom Ath	1-3*
East Grinstead T v AFC Uckfield	2-1
Laverstock & Ford v Cheddar	5-2
Team Solent v Horndean	1-2
Chippenham Park v Bristol Manor Farm	2-3
United Services Portsmouth v Calne T	6-1
Brockenhurst v Hayling U	5-0
Welton R v Petersfield T	0-2
Bradford T v Portishead T	5-0
Winterbourne U v Ringwood T	2-1
Warminster T v Alton T	4-3
Melksham T v Devizes T	4-1
Hythe & Dibden v Oldland Abbotonians	3-2
Fawley v Amesbury T	4-2

Keynsham T v Fleet Spurs	2-1
Hallen v Whitchurch U	2-0
Pewsey Vale v Folland Sports	0-5
Romsey T v Bournemouth	6-4
Westbury U v Ashton & Backwell U	1-3
Barnstaple T v Witheridge	3-2
Sherborne T v AFC St Austell	3-1
Bovey Tracey v Wells C	3-2*
St Blazey v Ilfracombe T	3-2*
Camelford v Torpoint Ath	2-1
Plymouth Parkway v Bridport	4-2
Elmore v Wadebridge T	2-2*, 1-4

SECOND QUALIFYING ROUND

Eccleshill U v Bishop Auckland	3-1
Newcastle Benfield v Barnoldswick T	3-1
Darlington RA v Thackley	1-5
Guisborough T v Durham C	3-1
Penrith v West Allotment Celtic	4-1
Holker OB v Ryton & Crawcrook Alb	5-1
Marske U v Knaresborough T	2-0
Jarrow Roofing Boldon CA v Willington	2-1
Albion Sports v Billingham Synthonia	2-3*
Team Northumbria v Sunderland RCA	2-4
Washington v Morpeth T	0-3
Pickering T v Crook T	2-6
Whickham v Birtley T	5-3
Consett v Nelson	3-4
South Shields v Billingham T	4-4*, 3-1
Silsden v North Shields	2-4*
Liversedge v Colne	2-1
Staveley MW v Ashton Ath	3-2
Rossington Main v West Didsbury & Chorlton	1-2
AFC Darwen v Kinsley Boys	3-4*
Glasshoughton Welfare v Armthorpe Welfare	1-4
Runcorn Linnets v Squires Gate	4-2
Winterton Rangers v AFC Blackpool	1-2
Winsford U v Pontefract Collieries	3-0
Cheadle T v Worsborough Bridge Ath	2-0
Oldham Boro v Congleton T	1-5
Parkgate v Bacup & Rossendale Bor	4-4*, 0-0*
(Parkgate won 4-2 on penalties)	
Rochdale T v Dinnington T	4-2*
Athersley Recreation v Northwich Flixton Villa	5-0
Formby v Glossop North End	0-1
Alsager T v Chadderton	0-1
Atherton LR v Shirebrook T	1-0
Worksop Parramore v Hemsworth MW	4-0
Stockport Sports v Barton Town OB	5-3*
Pilkington XXX v AFC Wulfrunians	0-3
Brocton v Wolverhampton Casuals	5-3*
Bartley Green (walkover) v	
AFC Wombourne U (removed)	
Bilston T v Stourport Swifts	0-7
Tividale v Coventry Sphinx	1-2
Shawbury U v Ellesmere Rangers	3-0
Cradley T v Southam U	2-1
Alvechurch v Eccleshall	4-1
Earlswood T v Pershore T	3-1
Norton Untied v Boldmere St Michaels	3-2*
Pelsall Villa v Sporting Khalsa	1-0
Bromsgrove Sporting v Stafford T	8-0
Bolehall Swifts v Blackwood	2-1*
Willenhall T v Racing Club Warwick	0-7
Dudley T v Studley	5-2
Causeway U v Continental Star	2-1
Dudley Sports v Atherstone T	1-3
Nuneaton Griff v Coleshill T	2-6
Desborough T v Teversal	3-0
Stewarts & Lloyds Corby v Thrapston T	1-0
Holwell Sports v Thurnby Nirvana	3-0
Grimsby Bor v AFC Mansfield	1-5
Louth T v Radcliffe Olympic	1-3
Mickleover Royals v Graham St Prims	2-4
Lincoln Moorlands Railway v Heather St Johns	3-2

Basford U v Cleethorpes T	0-2
Dunkirk v Oadby T	0-5
Ollerton T v Blaby & Whetstone Ath	0-4
Long Eaton U v Ellistown & Ibstock U	0-0*, 1-0
Shepshed Dynamo v Kirby Muxloe	0-3
St Andrews v Clipstone	3-1
Barrow T v Harborough T	0-2
Heanor T v Aylestone Park	8-2
Blackstones v Boston T	0-2
Deeping Rangers v Swaffham T	2-5
Peterborough Northern Star v Harrowby U	1-3
Eynesbury R v Fakenham T	3-1
Sleaford T v Thetford T	3-4
March Town U v Godmanchester R	0-4
Saffron Walden T v Norwich U	1-3
Walsham Le Willows v Whitton U	4-2
Mildenhall T v Stowmarket T	4-0
Brightlingsea Regent v Stanway R	3-0
Hullbridge Sports v Long Melford	4-0
Southend Manor v Bowers & Pitsea	0-1
Diss T v Stansted	3-2
Newmarket T v Woodbridge T	4-0
Cornard U v Great Yarmouth T	1-2
Halstead T v Team Bury	0-3
Ipswich W v Kirkley & Pakefield	3-1
Cockfosters v Buckingham Ath	6-2
Wembley v Hatfield T	2-1
AFC Rushden & Diamonds v Hoddesdon T	5-1
London APSA v Wellingborough Whitworths	2-0
Sporting Bengal U v Sawbridgeworth T	2-1
Berkhamsted v Buckingham T	3-2
Welwyn Garden C v Irchester U	2-1
Codicote v Sileby Rangers	1-2
Stotfold v London Lions	2-0
Winslow U v Tower Hamlets	0-4
Hadley v Holmer Green	4-3
Tring Ath v Greenhouse London	4-1
Hillingdon Bor v Newport Pagnell T	3-2
Northampton Spencer v Barking	1-5
Kentish T v Hanwell T	3-4
Wootton Blue Cross v Clapton	0-1*
Colney Heath v Broadfields U	1-0
Baldock T v Bugbrooke St Michaels	4-2
Haringey Bor v Wellingborough T	6-2
Lydney T v Highmoor Ibis	0-1
Knaphill v Tadley Calleva	5-1
Windsor v Camberley T	4-0
Milton U v Bedfont Sports	1-0
Farnham v Slimbridge	4-1
Fairford T v Kidlington	0-4
New College Swindon v Staines Lammas	0-2
Westfield v Thame U	3-0
Chinnor v Bedfont & Feltham	2-3
Bracknell T v Hartley Wintney	1-2
Brimscombe & Thrupp v Shrivenham	3-0
Abingdon T v Hook Norton	3-1
Holyport v Reading T	0-1
Pagham v East Grinstead T	1-2
Lingfield v Worthing U	2-0
Woodstock Sports v Epsom Ath	0-2
Hassocks v Ringmer	3-0
Ashford U v Cobham	4-1
Eastbourne U v Arundel	3-0
Epsom & Ewell v Whyteleafe	2-3*
Beckenham T v Haywards Heath T	3-0*
Glebe v Dorking	2-3
Littlehampton T v Shoreham	2-1
Sevenoaks T v Lancing	2-1
Croydon v Cray Valley (PM)	1-3
Fisher v AFC Croydon Ath	0-6
Crowborough Ath v Holmesdale	4-2
Chessington & Hook U v Dorking W	4-4*, 2-1
Banstead Ath v Phoenix Sports	0-2
Mole Valley SCR v Greenwich Bor	4-6
Southwick v Newhaven	2-4
Horndean v Verwood T	1-3

Bradford T v Downton	4-2
Cribbs v Hamworthy U	0-2
Odd Down v Wootton Bassett T	7-0
Hallen v Cowes Sports	2-0
Hengrove Ath v Laverstock & Ford	0-1
East Cowes VA v Lymington T	0-2
Almondsbury UWE v Radstock T	1-0
Keynsham T v Ashton & Backwell U	1-3
United Services Portsmouth v Winterbourne U	2-3
Bristol Manor Farm v Corsham T	2-1*
Folland Sports v Melksham T	4-2*
Roman Glass St George v Longwell Green Sports	2-3
Totton & Eling v Hythe & Dibden	2-3*
Fawley v Petersfield T	0-1
AFC Portchester v Romsey T	4-0
Fareham T v Bristol Academy	4-1
Brockenhurst v Warminster T	0-2
Street v Bovey Tracey	1-2
Exmouth T v Buckland Ath	0-2
Cullompton Rangers v Tavistock	0-2
Plymouth Parkway v St Blazey	6-0
Camelford v Shepton Mallet	1-3
Willand R v Sherborne T	5-3
Saltash U v Wadebridge T	5-1
Newquay v Barnstaple T	2-2*, 0-5

FIRST ROUND

Newcastle Benfield v Marske U	3-2
Jarrow Roofing Boldon CA v Nelson	2-0
Bridlington T v Sunderland RCA	2-0
Thackley v Eccleshill U	1-0
North Shields v Crook T	2-2*, 3-4*
Billingham Synthonia v Guisborough T	1-0
West Auckland T v South Shields	5-0
Penrith v Morpeth T	1-2
Whickham v Holker OB	1-0
Cheadle T v Stockport Sports	1-0
Glossop North End v Kinsley Boys	7-0
Garforth T v Winsford U	1-2*
Rochdale T v Congleton T	1-3
Bootle v Parkgate	4-5
Worksop Parramore v Runcorn Linnets	3-1
AFC Blackpool v Norton U	1-4
Liversedge v Armthorpe Welfare	3-4
Chadderton v Athersley Recreation	2-3
Maine Road v Atherton LR	3-0
Staveley MW v West Didsbury & Chorlton	2-0
Bartley Green v Alvechurch	0-6
Earlswood T v Causeway U	0-1
Westfields v Bromsgrove Sporting	3-2
Stourport Swifts v Brocton	0-2
Coleshill T v Racing Club Warwick	4-2
Pelsall Villa v Coventry Sphinx	0-2
AFC Wulfrunians v Atherstone T	5-0
Shawbury U v Bolehall Swifts	0-1
Dudley T v Cradley T	7-0
Graham St Prims v Harrowby U	3-1
Sileby Rangers v AFC Mansfield	2-5*
Harborough T v Cleethorpes T	0-5
Heanor T v Kirby Muxloe	4-2*
Woodford U v AFC Rushden & Diamonds	0-6
Stewarts & Lloyds Corby v Loughborough University	1-2
Hucknall T v Desborough T	1-3
Radcliffe Olympic v Holwell Sports	2-3*
Retford U v Oadby T	0-1
St Andrews v Lincoln Moorlands Railway	4-0
Long Eaton U v Boston T	2-0
Blaby & Whetstone Ath v Holbeach U	5-1
Norwich U v Bowers & Pitsea	2-1*
Diss T v Eynesbury R	1-3
Gorleston v Great Yarmouth T	0-1
Walsham Le Willows v Godmanchester R	5-0
Great Wakering R v Ipswich W	5-2
Newmarket T v Mildenhall T	1-1*, 2-0
Huntingdon T v Thetford T	3-0

Brightlingsea Regent v Team Bury	5-1
Swaffham T v Hullbridge Sports	2-2*, 3-4*
Tower Hamlets v Haringey Bor	0-3
Hanwell T v London APSA	4-1
Oxhey Jets v Stotfold	3-2
Hillingdon Bor v Hadley	1-2*
Ilford v Tring Ath	2-3
Baldock T v Berkhamsted	1-4
Welwyn Garden C v Bedfont & Feltham	1-0
Takeley v Sporting Bengal U	3-0
Clapton v Barking	0-1
St Margaretsbury v Colney Heath	0-3
Cockfosters v Wembley	3-0
Dorking v Knaphill	2-2*, 1-2
Farnham T v East Preston	0-1
Littlehampton T v Corinthian	2-1
Beckenham T v Westfield	4-0
Cray Valley (PM) v AFC Croydon Ath	2-0
Ashford U v Greenwich Bor	4-1
Whyteleafe v Windsor	4-2
Crowborough Ath v Epsom Ath	1-0
Staines Lammas v South Park	0-5
Chessington & Hook U v Hassocks	3-0
Newhaven v Cove	4-4*, 1-0, 0-2
(First replay abandoned after 41 mins due to *waterlogged pitch)*	
Eastbourne U v Phoenix Sports	5-4*
Erith T v Lingfield	4-3
East Grinstead T v Sevenoaks T	2-0
Winchester C v Sholing	0-1
Hamworthy U v Oxford City Nomads	1-2
Kidlington v Lymington T	5-1
Highmoor Ibis v Folland Sports	2-4
Wantage T v Abingdon T	7-0
Abingdon U v Fareham T	0-3*
Hartley Wintney v Petersfield T	4-2
Moneyfields v Christchurch	1-1*, 1-0
Bradford T v AFC Portchester	2-3
Verwood T v Laverstock & Ford	3-1
Alresford T v Hythe & Dibden	4-1
Reading T v Milton U	2-0
Binfield v Warminster T	9-1
Bishop Sutton v Odd Down	0-6
Almondsbury UWE v Barnstaple T	2-4
Cadbury Heath v Hallen	1-3
Brimscombe & Thrupp v Ashton & Backwell U	3-1
Brislington v Longwell Green Sports	1-0
Bovey Tracey v Shepton Mallet	0-2
Saltash U v Willand R	2-1
Plymouth Parkway v Gillingham T	2-0
Tavistock v Winterbourne U	3-2
Buckland Ath v Bristol Manor Farm	4-0

SECOND ROUND

Whitley Bay v Runcorn T	3-0
Cleethorpes T v Morpeth T	1-6
Maine Road v Billingham Synthonia	2-3
Norton U v Brighouse T	0-2
AFC Emley v Jarrow Roofing Boldon CA	1-3
Dunston UTS v Crook T	2-1
Staveley MW v Glossop North End	2-0
West Auckland T v Shildon	1-0
Thackley v Armthorpe Welfare	4-0
Ashington v Worksop Parramore	3-1
Winsford U v Spennymoor T	0-0*, 0-7
Whickham v Parkgate	3-0
Newcastle Benfield v Cheadle T	6-2
Athersley Recreation v Bridlington T	0-1*
Borrowash Vic v Congleton T	1-4
Causeway U v Dudley T	4-1
Walsall Wood v Spalding U	0-3
(Tie awarded to Walsall Wood 1–1 Spalding U removed)	
Bolehall Swifts v Heanor T	
(Tie awarded to Bolehall Swifts – Heanor T removed)	
Graham St Prims v Loughborough University	3-2*

Alvechurch v Oadby T	3-0
Westfields v Coventry Sphinx	6-1
Gornal Ath v Wisbech T	3-6*
Holwell Sports v Rocester	2-1*
Long Eaton U v Coleshill T	0-2*
Blaby & Whetstone Ath v Desborough T	3-0
AFC Mansfield v Huntingdon T	1-1*, 0-1
AFC Wulfrunians v AFC Rushden & Diamonds	2-4*
St Andrews v Brocton	2-1
Oxhey Jets v Hadleigh U	2-3
Tring Ath v Eynesbury R	1-0
Walsham Le Willows v Haringey Bor	1-4
Hullbridge Sports v Berkhamsted	1-0*
Great Yarmouth T v Hanwell T	1-2
Ampthill T v Barking	7-0
Great Wakering R v Cockfosters	2-0
Hadley v Brantham Ath	1-2
Takeley v Brightlingsea Regent	1-2
Ely C v Welwyn Garden C	0-0*, 0-3
Enfield 1893 v Norwich U	2-3
Colney Heath v Newmarket T	2-1
Lordswood v Whyteleafe	2-1
South Park v Cray Valley (PM)	1-1*, 3-2
Hanworth Villa v East Grinstead T	3-1
Tunbridge Wells v Crowborough Ath	1-0
Ashford U v Littlehampton T	1-0
Ascot U v Beckenham T	0-1
Chessington & Hook U v Eastbourne U	2-3
Erith T v Hartley Wintney	5-1
Knaphill v East Preston	0-4
Rye U v Cove	3-0
Buckland Ath v Saltash U	0-3
Folland Sports v Sholing	1-2
Plymouth Parkway v Wantage T	3-0
Verwood v Alresford T	1-4
Blackfield & Langley v Oxford City Nomads	1-0
Bodmin T v Bemerton Heath Harlequins	4-2
Barnstaple T v Hallen	3-4
Reading T v Brislington	1-0
Kidlington v Tavistock	3-0
Odd Down v Moneyfields	2-3
Larkhall Ath v Newport (IW)	2-0
Fareham T v Bitton	0-3
Brimscombe & Thrupp v Binfield	0-3
AFC Portchester v Shepton Mallet	3-1

THIRD ROUND

Spennymoor T v Bridlington T	2-0
West Auckland T v Billingham Synthonia	2-1
Brighouse T v Whickham	3-3*, 0-2
Staveley MW v Morpeth T	0-2
Jarrow Roofing Boldon CA v Newcastle Benfield	1-2
Ashington v Thackley	1-0
Whitley Bay v Dunston UTS	0-2
Congleton T v Huntingdon T	2-1
Blaby & Whetstone Ath v Causeway U	1-2
AFC Rushden & Diamonds v Graham St Prims	2-0
Holwell Sports v Coleshill T	1-3
Walsall Wood v Wisbech T	0-1
Alvechurch v Westfields	0-1
St Andrews v Bolehall Swifts	4-1
Great Wakering R v Hullbridge Sports	0-1
East Preston v Rye U	2-1
Hanwell T v Lordswood	5-0
Ampthill T v Beckenham T	2-1
Brightlingsea Regent v Colney Heath	2-2*, 2-0
Ashford U v Tring Ath	1-0
South Park v Eastbourne U	1-2
Hadleigh U v Welwyn Garden C	3-2*
Norwich U v Erith T	3-0
Tunbridge Wells v Hanworth Villa	0-1

Haringey Bor v Brantham Ath	2-3*
Moneyfields v Bitton	1-1
(Match abandoned after 102 mins due to player	
misconduct)	
Plymouth Parkway v Hallen	1-3
Shepton Mallet v Blackfield & Langley	1-2
Binfield v Larkhall Ath	0-1
Reading T v Sholing	1-4
Kidlington v Bodmin T	2-3*
Saltash U v Alresford T	2-7

FOURTH ROUND

Newcastle Benfield v Congleton T	3-1
Spennymoor T v Causeway U	1-0
Ashington v Wisbech T	1-2
AFC Rushden & Diamonds v St Andrews	0-2
Morpeth T v Westfields	3-0
Dunston UTS v Coleshill T	2-1*
Whickham v West Auckland T	1-3*
Larkhall Ath v Blackfield & Langley	3-0
Ampthill T v Norwich U	3-1
Hallen v Alresford T	2-0
Sholing v Hullbridge Sports	3-1
Moneyfields or Bitton v Hadleigh U	
(Tie awarded to Hadleigh U – Moneyfields & Bitton	
both removed)	
Hanworth Villa v Eastbourne U	2-7*
Hanwell T v Ashford U	2-1
Brightlingsea Regent v Bodmin T	3-1
East Preston v Brantham U	3-0

FIFTH ROUND

Eastbourne U v Morpeth T	6-1
Ampthill T v Hanwell T	3-1
Dunston UTS v Brightlingsea Regent	5-0
Sholing v Larkhall Ath	1-0
Hadleigh U v Wisbech T	1-2
Spennymoor T v Newcastle Benfield	1-2
East Preston v St Andrews	1-2
West Auckland T v Hallen	2-0

SIXTH ROUND

St Andrews v Newcastle Benfield	1-0
Eastbourne U v Ampthill T	2-1
Sholing v Wisbech T	1-0
Dunston UTS v West Auckland T	0-1

SEMI-FINALS FIRST LEG

Sholing v Eastbourne U	2-2
West Auckland T v St Andrews	0-0

SEMI-FINALS SECOND LEG

Eastbourne U v Sholing	2-4
Sholing won 6-4 on aggregate.	
St Andrews v West Auckland T	1-2
West Auckland T won 2-1 on aggregate.	

FA VASE FINAL 2014

Wembley, Saturday 10 May

Sholing (0) 1 *(McLean 71)*

West Auckland T (0) 0   5,431

Sholing: Brown; Carter, Diaper, Castle (Miller 53), Bright, Bowers (Brewster 76), Mason Barry, Fennemore (Sawyer 77), Wort, Mason Byron, McLean.
West Auckland T: Nixon; Pattinson, Green (Gibson 63), Hall, Galpin, Close, Vipond (Banks 78), Briggs, Moffat (Richardson 74), Campbell, Knight.
Referee: David Coote (West Riding FA).

THE FA YOUTH CUP 2013–14

*After extra time.

PRELIMINARY ROUND

Gateshead v Ryton & Crawcrook Alb	5-0
Formby (*withdrawn*) v Ashton T (*walkover*)	
AFC Fylde v Skelmersdale U	4-1
Northwich Vic (*withdrawn*) v Witton Alb (*walkover*)	
Buxton (*withdrawn*) v Abbey Hey (*walkover*)	
New Mills v Stalybridge Celtic	3-4
Hemsworth MW v Westella Hanson	1-3
FC Halifax T v Thackley	5-2
Hallam v Harrogate T	2-3
Worksop T v Kinsley Boys	9-0
St Andrews v Matlock T	2-0
Ilkeston v Lincoln U	8-0
Hinckley U v Spalding U	8-0
Dunkirk v Lincoln C	2-4
Pelsall Villa v Coventry Sphinx	2-5
Ellesmere Rangers v Southam U	5-0
Wednesfield v AFC Telford U	0-3
Hednesford T v Racing Club Warwick	2-1
Rugby T v Chasetown	3-2*
Stratford T v Kidderminster H	1-2
Gorleston v Dereham T	2-3
Brantham Ath v Cambridge U	1-8
Cornard U v Walsham Le Willows	2-1
Leiston (*withdrawn*) v Fakenham T (*walkover*)	
Brackley T v Barton R	1-2
AFC Kempston R (*walkover*) v Kettering T (*withdrawn*)	
Stotfold v Peterborough Northern Star	4-0
Hoddesdon T v Billericay T	2-0
Grays Ath v Tilbury	1-0
Royston T v Chelmsford C	2-4
Colney Heath v Stanway R	1-4
Clapton v AFC Hornchurch	0-2
Canvey Island v Witham T	3-2*
Hullbridge Sports v Hitchin T	0-3
Waltham Abbey v Heybridge Swifts	1-3
FC Clacton v Concord Rangers	1-2
Redbridge v Braintree T	0-2
Corinthian Casuals v Hampton & Richmond Bor	0-7
Northwood v Enfield T	2-1*
Faversham T v Chatham T	3-0
Dover Ath v Corinthian	0-1
Tonbridge Angels v Lordswood	7-2
Whitstable U v Maidstone U	2-5
Crowborough Ath v Croydon	3-2
East Grinstead T v Erith & Belvedere	1-0
Hastings U v Chipstead	6-7*
Shoreham v Pagham	7-3*
Bognor Regis T v Kingstonian	4-2
Peacehaven & Telscombe v Walton & Hersham	5-0
Lancing v Molesey	4-3
Newhaven v Dorking	0-1
Crawley Down Gatwick v Woking	2-3
Worthing v Littlehampton T	6-0
Thame U v Fleet Spurs	10-0
Thatcham T v Burnham	2-0
Banbury U v Marlow	2-4
Hartley Wintney v Flackwell Heath	3-0
Windsor v Ascot U	1-9
Cove v Sandhurst T	0-2
Kidlington v Fleet T	2-1
Salisbury C v Moneyfields	1-1*
(Moneyfields won 4-2 on penalties)	
Eastleigh v Hamworthy U	3-1
Cirencester T v Almondsbury UWE	6-0
Weston Super Mare v Wells C	6-0
Cheltenham Saracens v Hengrove Ath	4-4*
(Cheltenham Saracens won 3-1 on penalties)	
Ashton & Backwell U v Forest Green R	0-5
Taunton T v Merthyr T	1-3

FIRST QUALIFYING ROUND

Newton Aycliffe v Consett	0-4
Scarborough Ath v Gateshead	0-8
Newcastle Benfield v Chester-le-Street T	4-3
Alsager T v Ashton T	1-3
Southport v Stalybridge Celtic	0-2

Nelson v Lancaster C	7-2
Nantwich T v Abbey Hey	1-8
Runcorn T v Altrincham	4-5
AFC Fylde v Witton Alb	3-0
AFC Blackpool v Chester FC	1-6
Marine v Macclesfield T	1-1*
(Macclesfield T won 4-3 on penalties)	
Vauxhall Motors v Bootle	3-2
Wrexham v Hyde	3-0
Ashton Ath v Prescot Cables	0-3
Glossop North End v Runcorn Linnets	0-4
Warrington T v Curzon Ashton	4-1
Ossett T v Sheffield	0-4
Silsden v Westella Hanson	0-2
Grimsby T v North Ferriby U	7-0
Staveley MW v Farsley	4-0
Bottesford T v Selby T	2-6
Harrogate T v FC Halifax T	3-2
Worksop T v Ossett Alb	4-1
Guiseley v Brighouse T	2-2, 3-1
(First match abandoned after 90 mins due to serious injury to a player)	
Yorkshire Amateur (*withdrawn*) v Hall Road Rangers (*walkover*)	
Stocksbridge Park Steels v Nostell MW	2-3
Teversal v St Andrews	0-5
Deeping Rangers v Ilkeston	0-6
Holwell Sports v Boston U	0-4
Lincoln C v Basford U	7-1
Hinckley U (*walkover*) v Ellistown & Ibstock U (*withdrawn*)	
Blaby & Whetstone Ath v Mickleover Sports	1-4
Lutterworth Ath v Retford U	2-1
Gresley (*walkover*) v Oadby T (*withdrawn*)	
Stapenhill v Stamford	9-0
Rugby T v AFC Telford U	3-0
Ellesmere Rangers v Worcester C	2-4
Tipton T v Sutton Coldfield T	2-1
Boldmere St Michaels v Stourport Swifts	2-1
Leamington (*withdrawn*) v Eccleshall (*walkover*)	
Hereford U v Newcastle T	2-0
Solihull Moors v Lye T	5-0
Nuneaton T v Dudley Sports	4-0
Nuneaton Griff (*walkover*) v Malvern T (*withdrawn*)	
Kidderminster H v Romulus	5-3
Coventry Sphinx v Atherstone T	1-3
Halesowen T v Coleshill T	3-0
Walsall Wood (*withdrawn*) v Stourbridge (*walkover*)	
Pegasus Juniors v Hednesford T	5-4*
Woodbridge T v Wroxham	4-0
Stowmarket T v Newmarket T	0-4
Haverhill R v Cornard U	2-6
Needham Market v Cambridge U	2-5
Swaffham T v Dereham T	2-5*
Long Melford v Ipswich W	3-2*
Felixstowe & Walton U v Bury T	1-3
Norwich U v Fakenham T	0-2
AFC Sudbury v Whitton U	3-3*
(Whitton U won 4-2 on penalties)	
Lowestoft T v Hadleigh U	2-0
Histon v Soham Town Rangers	3-1
Stewarts & Lloyds Corby v Barton R	0-5
Corby T v AFC Kempston R	4-3*
St Neots T v Cogenhoe U	2-4
AFC Dunstable (*withdrawn*) v Rushden & Higham U (*walkover*)	
Stotfold v Yaxley	12-0
St Ives T v Leighton T	1-4
AFC Rushden & Diamonds v Bugbrooke St Michaels	4-0
Bedford T v Wellingborough T	1-3
Luton T v Rothwell Corinthians	6-0
Bishop's Stortford v Romford	3-0
Stanway R v Chelmsford C	0-1
Bowers & Pitsea v Halstead T	3-2
East Thurrock U v Braintree T	2-0
Tower Hamlets v Boreham Wood	2-6
Sawbridgeworth T v Cheshunt	3-3*
(Cheshunt won 4-2 on penalties)	

Canvey Island v Barking	1-1*
(Canvey Island won 4-3 on penalties)	
Potters Bar T v Great Wakering R	5-4
Ware v Barnet	0-4
Concord Rangers v Heybridge Swifts	2-3
Grays Ath v Hoddesdon T	3-2
St Albans C v Brentwood T	2-3
Thurrock *(walkover)* v Burnham Ramblers *(withdrawn)*	
Hitchin T v AFC Hornchurch	0-1
Staines T v Hampton & Richmond Bor	5-4
Harefield U v Northwood	2-1*
Wingate & Finchley v Wealdstone	2-2*
(Wingate & Finchley won 7-6 on penalties)	
Kings Langley v North Greenford U	2-1
Berkhamsted v Ashford T	3-1
Metropolitan Police v Oxhey Jets	3-2
Bedfont Sports v Uxbridge	4-6
Leverstock Green v Enfield 1893	0-1
Cockfosters v Hayes & Yeading U	4-3
Fisher v Dulwich Hamlet	0-6
Crowborough Ath v Tonbridge Angels	2-0
Corinthian v Eastbourne T	7-0
Thamesmead T v Erith T	5-0
Bromley v Eastbourne U	2-1
Folkestone Invicta v Colliers Wood U	1-4
Welling U v Sutton U	3-4
Sittingbourne v Holmesdale	1-0
Margate v Dartford	0-7
Ramsgate v Eastbourne Bor	1-1*
(Eastbourne Bor won 5-4 on penalties)	
East Grinstead T v Sevenoaks T	0-1
Faversham v Chipstead	0-4
Ebbsfleet U *(withdrawn)* v Cray W *(walkover)*	
Tooting & Mitcham U v VCD Ath	1-4
Carshalton Ath v Maidstone U	1-3
Godalming T v Havant & Waterlooville	3-3*
(Havant & Waterlooville won 5-4 on penalties)	
Camberley T v Redhill	3-0
Westfield v Horsham	0-6
Guildford C v Farnham T	3-1
Woking v South Park	4-1
Arundel v Horley T	0-6
Lancing v Knaphill	2-0
Peacehaven & Telscombe v Whyteleafe	3-3*
(Peacehaven & Telscombe won 4-2 on penalties)	
Three Bridges v Burgess Hill T	1-2
Leatherhead v Worthing	1-3
Dorking v Shoreham	1-2
Lewes v Bognor Regis T	3-2
Binfield v Basingstoke T	3-0
Abingdon U v Highmoor Ibis	3-0
Newport Pagnell T v Farnborough	0-1
Bracknell T v Aylesbury	2-5
Sandhurst T v Maidenhead U	1-9
Slough T v Buckingham Ath	2-3
Hartley Wintney v Chesham U	2-1
Marlow *(walkover)* v Reading T *(withdrawn)*	
Oxford C v Alton T	2-1
Didcot v Kidlington	4-0
Ascot U v Thame U	2-6
Aldershot T v Thatcham T	8-0
Eastleigh v Wimborne T	2-3
Moneyfields v Westbury U	2-0
Chippenham T v Bournemouth	0-3
AFC Totton v Gillingham T	6-0
Dorchester T v AFC Portchester	2-1
Christchurch v Poole T	2-1
Petersfield T v Chichester C	1-4
Larkhall Ath v Gloucester C	4-3
Paulton R v Cirencester T	2-3
Bitton *(removed)* v Tiverton T *(walkover)*	
Lydney T *(withdrawn)* v Bath C *(walkover)*	
Elmore v Odd Down	2-3
Cheltenham Saracens v Weston Super Mare	0-1
Forest Green R v Clevedon T	2-1
Bridgwater T v Yate T	0-3
Bishop Sutton *(withdrawn)* v Merthyr T *(walkover)*	
Mangotsfield U v Bristol Academy	1-2

SECOND QUALIFYING ROUND

Guiseley v Hall Road Rangers	1-1*
(Guiseley won 4-3 on penalties)	

Consett v Newcastle Benfield	5-1
Nelson v Gateshead	0-4
Runcorn Linnets v Stalybridge Celtic	1-2
Westella Hanson v Ashton T	3-1
Wrexham v AFC Fylde	6-0
Sheffield v Macclesfield T	0-1
Prescot Cables v Chester FC	1-3
Staveley MW v Nostell MW	1-2
Grimsby T v Harrogate T	3-1
Abbey Hey v Selby T	3-3*
(Selby T won 5-4 on penalties)	
Altrincham v Vauxhall Motors	4-1
Warrington T v Worksop T	7-2
Boston U v Lincoln C	1-0
Ilkeston v St Andrews	3-3*
(Ilkeston won 5-4 on penalties)	
Lutterworth Ath *(walkover)* v Hinckley U *(removed)*	
Gresley v Mickleover Sports	1-4
Stapenhill v Histon	0-4
Halesowen T v Eccleshall	5-0
Stourbridge v Hereford U	1-3
Solihull Moors v Rugby T	3-4*
Kidderminster H v Atherstone T	2-3
Nuneaton v Nuneaton Griff	5-0
Worcester C v Boldmere St Michaels	2-0
Tipton T v Pegasus Juniors	2-3
Cornard U v Cambridge U	1-6
Lowestoft T v Woodbridge T	0-2*
Bury T v Dereham T	1-0
Fakenham T v Long Melford	3-4
Whitton U v Newmarket T	6-1
Cogenhoe U v Rushden & Higham U	5-1
Barnet v Barton R	0-3
AFC Rushden & Diamonds v Stotfold	0-4
Wellingborough T v Leighton T	2-3*
Luton T v Corby T	5-1*
Thurrock v Boreham Wood	4-2
AFC Hornchurch v Cheshunt	1-0
Canvey Island v Bishop's Stortford	3-2
Grays Ath v Bowers & Pitsea	6-3
Potters Bar T v Concord Rangers	3-1
Chelmsford C v East Thurrock U	5-0
Brentwood T v Enfield 1893	4-2*
Wingate & Finchley v Kings Langley	4-0
Thamesmead T v Staines T	3-2
Uxbridge v Berkhamsted	3-2
Cockfosters v Harefield U	1-4
Dulwich Hamlet v Metropolitan Police	4-2
Crowborough Ath v Colliers Wood U	3-4
Sutton U v Eastbourne Bor	2-0
Maidstone U v Corinthian	2-0
Chipstead v Sevenoaks T	4-1
Sittingbourne v Dartford	0-5
Cray W v Bromley	1-0
VCD Ath v Horsham	1-0
Woking v Peacehaven & Telscombe	1-0
Lewes v Havant & Waterlooville	0-3
Worthing v Burgess Hill T	0-3
Horley T v Lancing	1-0
Shoreham v Camberley T	1-3
Didcot T v Binfield	4-3*
Wimborne T v Guildford C	0-2
Marlow v Aylesbury	2-0
Aldershot T v Buckingham Ath	2-0
Oxford C v Maidenhead U	1-3
Bournemouth v Chichester C	2-1
Moneyfields v Dorchester T	1-0
Abingdon U v AFC Totton	1-5
Farnborough v Hartley Wintney	2-1
Thame U v Christchurch	0-3
Tiverton T v Bath C	3-2
Bristol Academy v Larkhall Ath	8-0
Forest Green R v Odd Down	5-0
Yate T v Weston Super Mare	0-1
Merthyr T v Cirencester T	3-5

THIRD QUALIFYING ROUND

Warrington T v Mickleover Sports	2-1
Stalybridge Celtic v Chester FC	0-3
Altrincham v Nostell MW	10-3
Consett v Gateshead	2-6
Macclesfield T v Westella Hanson	2-1

Wrexham v Selby T	3-0
Grimsby T v Guiseley	0-2*
Histon v Cogenhoe U	5-1
Lutterworth Ath v Halesowen T	0-3
Boston U v Pegasus Juniors	3-1
Atherstone v Hereford U	2-5
Worcester C v Rugby T	1-0
Ilkeston v Nuneaton T	2-0
Luton T v Leighton T	3-0
Stotfold v Cambridge U	1-1*
(Cambridge U won 3-1 on penalties)	
Long Melford v Bury T	2-2*
(Bury T won 9-8 on penalties)	
Whitton U v Woodbridge T	0-5
Canvey Island v Dulwich Hamlet	0-1
AFC Hornchurch v Grays Ath	1-2
Barton R v Harefield U	3-1
Brentwood T v Potters Bar T	4-2
Uxbridge v Chelmsford C	2-1
Thurrock v Wingate & Finchley	0-1
Woking v Cray W	5-3
Dartford v Thamesmead T	4-2
Maidstone U v Sutton U	1-1*
(Maidstone U won 6-5 on penalties)	
Chipstead v Colliers Wood U	2-2*
(Chipstead won 4-2 on penalties)	
Farnborough v Christchurch	0-2
Horley T v Aylesbury	2-1
AFC Totton v Aldershot T	1-0
Havant & Waterlooville v Burgess Hill T	1-7
Guidford C v Camberley T	1-3
Didcot T v Bournemouth	2-1
Maidenhead U v VCD Ath	0-0*
(VCD Ath won 4-2 on penalties)	
Forest Green R v Cirencester T	3-1
Moneyfields v Weston Super Mare	0-0*
(Moneyfields won 3-1 on penalties)	
Bristol Academy v Tiverton T	4-1

FIRST ROUND

Altrincham v Wrexham	2-1
Chester FC v Chesterfield	1-1*
(Chesterfield won 5-4 on penalties)	
Tranmere R v Gateshead	4-4*
(Gateshead won 5-4 on penalties)	
Preston North End v Mansfield T	6-1
Bury v Guiseley	6-2
Accrington Stanley v Carlisle U	3-1
Macclesfield T v York C	0-3
Morecambe v Hartlepool U	3-1
Scunthorpe U v Bradford C	0-2
Warrington T v Rochdale	2-6
Oldham Ath v Sheffield U	2-2*
(Sheffield U won 4-3 on penalties)	
Rotherham U v Fleetwood T	1-1*
(Rotherham U won 7-6 on penalties)	
Notts Co v Peterborough U	1-2*
Ilkeston v Northampton T	7-4*
Hereford U v Milton Keynes Dons	3-0
Walsall v Port Vale	2-0
Boston U v Luton T	0-4
Wolverhampton W v Burton Alb	5-0
Worcester C v Halesowen T	1-0
Crewe Alexandra v Coventry C	2-0
Histon v Shrewsbury T	1-2
Barton R v Stevenage	1-0
Chipstead v Horley T	2-1
Maidstone U v Southend U	2-3
AFC Totton v Leyton Orient	0-3
Dulwich Hamlet v Brentwood T	4-1
Gillingham v Brentford	1-3
Dartford v Christchurch	6-1
Bury T v Dagenham & Redbridge	0-3
(Tie awarded to Bury T – Dagenham & Redbridge removed for fielding an ineligible player)	
Wingate & Finchley v Burgess Hill T	3-4
Crawley T v Woodbridge T	5-0
Cambridge U v Woking	2-3
AFC Wimbledon v Colchester U	1-4
Grays Ath v Uxbridge	5-2
Cheltenham T v VCD Ath	7-1

Forest Green R v Torquay U	1-2
Exeter C v Swindon T	3-4
Didcot T v Oxford U	0-3
Bristol C v Newport Co	3-0
Portsmouth v Moneyfields	12-0
Camberley T v Bristol R	1-2
Plymouth Argyle v Bristol Academy	4-1

SECOND ROUND

Sheffield U v Worcester C	9-0
Preston North End v York C	5-0
Morecambe v Bradford C	1-3
Ilkeston v Accrington Stanley	0-1
Rochdale v Crewe Alexandra	1-2
Wolverhampton W v Peterborough U	1-2
Walsall v Altrincham	4-0
Chesterfield v Hereford U	0-1
Gateshead v Luton T	1-2
Rotherham U v Bury	3-2
Grays Ath v Dartford	2-3
Shrewsbury T v Bristol R	0-1
Southend U v Oxford U	1-3
Torquay U v Chipstead	4-1
Brentford v Dulwich Hamlet	2-0
Portsmouth v Barton R	1-0
Colchester U v Plymouth Argyle	4-4*
(Plymouth Argyle won 4-2 on penalties)	
Cheltenham T v Bury T	9-0
Woking v Crawley T	1-2
Swindon T v Leyton Orient	1-4
Burgess Hill T v Bristol C	0-2

THIRD ROUND

Southampton v Portsmouth	7-0
AFC Bournemouth v Hereford U	1-1*
(Hereford U won 4-3 on penalties)	
Preston North End v Norwich C	1-6*
Bolton W v Sheffield U	1-1*
(Sheffield U won 4-3 on penalties)	
Bristol R v Crewe Alexandra	1-2*
Accrington Stanley v West Ham U	2-1*
Leeds U v Reading	1-3
Blackpool v Liverpool	3-3*
(Liverpool won 4-3 on penalties)	
Burnley v Manchester U	0-2
Hull C v Peterborough U	1-2
Sheffield Wednesday v Crystal Palace	4-4*
(Sheffield Wednesday won 4-2 on penalties)	
Nottingham Forest v Charlton Ath	2-3
Queens Park Rangers v Fulham	1-4
Crawley T v Watford	0-2
Derby Co v Wigan Ath	4-3
Leicester C v Rotherham U	3-0
Ipswich T v Sunderland	1-1*
(Sunderland won 4-2 on penalties)	
Arsenal v Torquay U	5-0
Bristol C v Brentford	1-0
Chelsea v Dartford	4-0
Cardiff C v Blackburn R	1-0
Everton v Brighton & Hove Alb	2-0
Tottenham Hotspur v Middlesbrough	2-1
Huddersfield T v Luton T	3-1*
Swansea C v Oxford U	1-3
Stoke C v Leyton Orient	2-2*
(Stoke C won 5-4 on penalties)	
West Bromwich Alb v Walsall	2-1
Bradford C v Millwall	0-3
Cheltenham T v Birmingham C	1-2
Aston Villa v Plymouth Argyle	4-3
Manchester C v Doncaster R	4-0
Barnsley v Newcastle U	1-2

FOURTH ROUND

Tottenham Hotspur v Fulham	2-3
Newcastle U v Sunderland	4-0
Reading v Crewe Alexandra	3-3*
(Reading won 4-2 on penalties)	
Leicester C v Manchester U	0-1
Oxford U v Cardiff C	2-3
Millwall v Sheffield U	2-2*
(Sheffield U won 8-7 on penalties)	

Southampton v Charlton Ath	1-3
Accrington Stanley v Bristol C	4-1
Everton v Birmingham C	4-3
West Bromwich Alb v Huddersfield T	2-4*
Chelsea v Sheffield Wednesday	4-1
Liverpool v Aston Villa	3-1
Derby Co v Stoke C	3-1
Manchester C v Hereford U	3-1*
Watford v Norwich C	3-1
Peterborough U v Arsenal	1-6

FIFTH ROUND

Cardiff C v Chelsea	0-2
Sheffield U v Everton	0-2
Charlton Ath v Arsenal	0-2
Reading v Accrington Stanley	3-0
Manchester C v Fulham	1-3
Huddersfield T v Manchester U	2-1
Watford v Liverpool	0-2
Derby Co v Newcastle U	0-1

SIXTH ROUND

Fulham v Huddersfield T	2-1
Arsenal v Everton	3-1
Reading v Liverpool	4-4*
(Reading won 5-4 on penalties).	
Newcastle U v Chelsea	2-3

SEMI-FINALS FIRST LEG

Chelsea v Arsenal	2-1
Reading v Fulham	2-2

SEMI-FINALS SECOND LEG

Arsenal v Chelsea	0-1
Chelsea won 3-1 on aggregate.	
Fulham v Reading	3-2
Fulham won 5-4 on aggregate.	

FA YOUTH CUP FINAL 2014 FIRST LEG

Monday 28 April 2014

Fulham (0) 3 *(Dembele 69, Hyndman 71, Burgess 79)*

Chelsea (0) 2 *(DaSilva 49, Musonda 83)*   4457

Fulham: Rodak; Sheckleford, Donnelly, Burgess, Evans (Baba 87), Smile (O'Halloran 63), Sambou, Hyndman, Williams, Roberts (Walker 90), Dembele.
Chelsea: Collins; Ssewankambo, Christensen, Clarke-Salter (Dabo 78), Aina, Colkett, Loftus-Cheek, Houghton (Palmer 59), Brown, DaSilva, Solanke (Musonda 73).
Referee: Jonathan Moss.

FA YOUTH CUP FINAL 2014 SECOND LEG

Monday 5 May 2014

Chelsea (2) 5 *(Colkett 22 (pen), Houghton 24, Ssewankambo 77, Solanke 82, 90)*

Fulham (3) 3 *(Dembele 5, Roberts 26, Sambou 38)* 13,125

Chelsea win 7-6 on aggregate.
Chelsea: Beeney; Dabo, Christensen, Clarke-Salter (Aina 46), DaSilva, Houghton, Colkett, Loftus-Cheek (Brown 46), Palmer (Ssewankambo 46), Solanke, Musonda.
Fulham: Rodak; Sheckleford (Smile 88), Evans, Donnelly, Burgess, Sambou, O'Halloran, Hyndman, Dembele, Roberts, Williams.
Referee: Jonathan Moss.

THE FA COUNTY YOUTH CUP 2013–14

*After extra time.

FIRST ROUND

West Riding v Westmorland	7-0
Leicestershire & Rutland v Birmingham	0-2
Northumberland v Durham	3-1
Isle of Man v Cumberland	1-6
Lancashire v East Riding	2-1
Derbyshire v Lincolnshire	1-2
Northamptonshire v Middlesex	1-2
Devon v Dorset	2-1*
Amateur Football Alliance v Gloucestershire	4-3*
Cornwall v Guernsey	4-2*
Herefordshire v Jersey	1-0*
Essex v Oxfordshire	5-1
Hertfordshire v London	2-1

SECOND ROUND

Birmingham v Cheshire	1-3
Liverpool v Manchester	0-2
Staffordshire v West Riding	0-3
Shropshire v Northumberland	1-2*
North Riding v Nottinghamshire	5-2
Sheffield & Hallamshire v Cumberland	2-1
Lancashire v Lincolnshire	4-2*
Cambridgeshire v Bedfordshire	5-3
Sussex v Essex	0-1
Middlesex v Hertfordshire	3-1*
Worcestershire v Huntingdonshire	8-1
Norfolk v Kent	2-3
Herefordshire v Somerset	4-1
Wiltshire v Devon	0-4
Suffolk v Berks & Bucks	6-1
Cornwall v Amateur Football Alliance	1-2

THIRD ROUND

Devon v Kent	1-0
Lancashire v Worcestershire	3-2
Essex v Suffolk	0-1
Cambridgeshire v Northumberland	1-2
Herefordshire v Amateur Football Alliance	1-4
West Riding v North Riding	2-1*
Sheffield & Hallamshire v Middlesex	5-2
Manchester v Cheshire	0-1

FOURTH ROUND

Suffolk v Sheffield & Hallamshire	1-1*
Suffolk won 6-5 on penalties.	
Amateur Football Alliance v West Riding	1-1*, 3-3*
Amateur Football Alliance won 4-2 on penalties.	
Cheshire v Devon	0-1*
Lancashire v Northumberland	4-3

SEMI-FINALS

Devon v Lancashire	1-2
Suffolk v Amateur Football Alliance	2-1

FA COUNTY YOUTH CUP FINAL 2014

Ipswich, Saturday 26 April 2014

Suffolk (1) 2 *(Ford 5, Thrower 58)*

Lancashire (2) 3 *(Williams 30, Khambay 38, Bent 117)*

aet.
Suffolk: Bradbrook; West (Newman 48), Mallardo, Heath, Hope, Carver, Ford (Thrower 60, Kemp 84), Crisell, Ward, Howell, Allen.
Lancashire: Lancashire: Burgess; Cooke, Higham, Vincent, Southwell, Noblet, Williams Benjamin, Smith, Williams Jack (Bent 75), Khambay (Hartley 65, Hutton 85), Linney.
Referee: Kevin Johnson (Somerset FA).

THE FA SUNDAY CUP 2013–14

*After extra time.

FIRST ROUND

Sunderland RCA Grangetown Flsts v Sportsmans	4-3
Newton Aycliffe WMC v Winlaton Commercial	1-3
Witton Park Rose & Crown v	
Stockton Rosegale N&SA	4-2
Barrington Arms v Humbledon Plains Farm	2-5
Hartlepool Rovers Quoit v	
Hartlepool Athletic Rovers	1-2
Burradon & New Fordley v Kelloe WMC	4-2
Northallerton Police v Hetton Lyons CC	1-3
HT Sports v Home & Bargain	3-1
Seacroft WMC Athletic v The Warden	1-2
Thornhill Lees v Paddock	6-2
JOB v Nicosia	2-3
Kirkdale v Netherley Woodlane Legion	1-0
West Bowling v Allerton	0-1
Campfield v The Old Bank	1-2
Alder v Hessle Rangers	2-1
Fantail v Pineapple	0-3
Seymour v Thornton United	4-1
Drum (*withdrawn*) v Canada (*walkover*)	
Garston v Larkspur	1-0
BRNESC v Lobster	0-3
Sutton Fields v Pumptec	2-1
Millhouse v Chapeltown Fforde Grene	1-3
AFC Blackburn Leisure v Queens Park	1-4
St John Fisher OB v Mariners	1-2
Birstall Stamford v Sparta Moshdock	2-4
Gedling Inn v Whitwick Compass	0-3
Star & Garter v The New Welfare	7-0
Wymeswold v T8's	2-1
Kirkby Town v Sileby Athletic	5-2
Jacksdale MW v Thurmaston PWMC	7-5*
RHP Sports & Social v FC Brimington	3-0
Bilsthorpe Celtic v Nuthall	3-1
Punchbowl v Church Hill	2-2*
(*Church Hill won 7-6 on penalties*)	
Hundred Acre v Ledbury Allstars	11-1
Halfway v Sporting Khalsa (Sunday)	1-6
Plough FC Wellington v The Royal Hotel Sutton	7-4
Burnt Oak Builders Merchants v Manor House	0-2
Upshire v Falcons	3-0
Flamstead End v New Salamis	1-7
Attero v Apoel	3-2
AC Sportsman v Bedfont Sunday	4-0
Nirankari v Two Touch	5-6*
Broadfields United v Club Lewsey	3-1
Gadeside Rangers v Rayners Lane (Sunday)	0-2
Belstone (Sunday) v NLO	3-3*
(*Belstone won 4-2 on penalties*)	
AYFCS v Dee Road Rangers	4-4*
(*AYFCS won 5-4 on penalties*)	
St Josephs (Luton) v North Wembley	2-1*
Hillbarn Athletic v AFC Kumazi Strikers	1-1, 1-3
(*First match abandoned after 33 mins due to*	
waterlogged pitch)	
Lambeth All Stars v Putney Town	4-1
Branksome Railway v Kings Tamerton CA	4-2
The Windmill v All Saints	3-1

SECOND ROUND

Lobster v Queens Park	1-0
Canada v Oyster Martyrs	0-5
Witton Park Rose & Crown v Sunderland RCA	
Grangetown Flor	0-0*
(*Witton Park Rose & Crown won 7-6 on penalties*)	
Chapeltown Fforde Grene v Garston	3-1
Seymour v Humbledon Plains Farm	3-4*
Mariners v Kirkdale	2-1
Hetton Lyons CC v Burradon & New Fordley	5-2
Buttershaw Whitestar v Nicosia	3-1
The Warden v Thornhill Lees	2-6
Allerton v Alder	4-0
Hartlepool Lion Hillcarter v Pineapple	0-3
The Old Bank v HT Sports	2-4
Sutton Fields v Winlaton Commercial	1-2

Hartlepool Athletic Rovers v Bolton Woods	6-3*
Albion v RHP Sports & Social	4-1
Wymeswold v Hundred Acre	0-1
Plough FC Wellington v Kirkby Town	5-1
Loughborough Saints v Sporting Khalsa (Sunday)	1-1*
(*Sporting Khalsa (Sunday) won 4-3 on penalties*)	
Church Hill v Star & Garter	0-3
Jacksdale MW (*withdrawn*) v Sparta Moshdock	
(*walkover*)	
Bilsthorpe Celtic v Whitwick Compass	1-2*
Lambeth All Stars v FC Houghton Centre	0-3
New Salamis v Broadfields Laurels	2-0*
Two Touch v AC Sportsman	5-1
Attero v AFC Kumazi Strikers	1-4
Rayners Lane (Sunday) v St Josephs (Luton)	1-0
Belstone (Sunday) v Manor House	7-2
Co-op Green Man v AYFCS	1-4*
Hammer v Upshire	0-5
Barnes Albion (*walkover*) v Artois United (*withdrawn*)	
Bar Sol Ona v Branksome Railway	0-4
Lebeqs Tavern Courage v The Windmill	8-0

THIRD ROUND

HT Sports v Oyster Martyrs	1-2
Allerton v Hetton Lyons CC	1-0
Mariners v Lobster	2-1
Thornhill Lees v Hartlepool Athletic Rovers	6-0
Chapeltown Fforde Grene v Buttershaw Whitestar	2-0
Pineapple v Humbledon Plains Farm	1-5
Winlaton Commercial v Witton Park Rose & Crown	3-6*
Whitwick Compass v Albion	6-1
FC Houghton Centre v Sparta Moshdock	1-0
Star & Garter v Hundred Acre	1-1*
(*Hundred Acre won 4-2 on penalties*)	
Plough FC Wellington v Sporting Khalsa (Sunday)	5-3
Two Touch v Lebeqs Tavern Courage	0-3
Upshire v Barnes Albion	1-0
New Salamis v Belstone (Sunday)	1-1*
(*New Salamis won 7-6 on penalties*)	
Branksome Railway v AFC Kumazi Strikers	4-2
AYFCS v Rayners Lane (Sunday)	4-2*

FOURTH ROUND

Witton Park Rose & Crown v Oyster Martyrs	0-4
Humbledon Plains Farm v Mariners	6-0
Allerton v Whitwick Compass	5-1
Thornhill Lees v Chapeltown Fforde Grene	2-3*
AYFCS v Plough FC Wellington	2-4
Hundred Acre v FC Houghton Centre	2-0
New Salamis v Branksome Railway	1-2*
Lebeqs Tavern Courage v Upshire	2-5

FIFTH ROUND

Chapeltown Fforde Grene v Humbledon Plains Farm	3-6
Allerton v Oyster Martyrs	1-2
Branksome Railway v Plough FC Wellington	0-5
Upshire v Hundred Acre	3-3*
(*Hundred Acre won 3-1 on penalties*)	

SEMI-FINALS

Oyster Martyrs v Plough FC Wellington	3-2*
Humbledon Plains Farm v Hundred Acre	4-2*

FA SUNDAY CUP FINAL 2014

Blackburn, Sunday 27 April 2014

Humbledon Plains Farm (2) 5 (*Davison (3), Croft, Winn*)

Oyster Martyrs (2) 2 (*Swatton, Rainford*)

Humbledon Plains Farm: Atkinson; Marshal (O'Neil 85), Wardle, Paxton, McGuiness, Croft (Johnson 39), Fairly, Coghlan, Davis (Kane 81), Winn, Davison.
Oyster Martyrs: Mano; Agger (Riley 77), Dames, Rendell, Swatton, Turner, Porter, Smith (Moore 77), Rimmer, Rainford, McGivern.
Referee: C. Boyeson.

THE FA INTER LEAGUE CUP 2013–14

After extra time.

EXTRA PRELIMINARY ROUND

Lancashire Amateur League v Wearside Football League	3-6
Lancashire & Cheshire Amateur League v Teesside League	2-3
West Cheshire League v Manchester Football League	0-1
Cheshire Football League v Northern Football Alliance	1-0
Essex Olympian Football League v Peterborough & District Football League	1-2
Suffolk & Ipswich League v West Riding County Amateur Football League	2-3*
Cambridgeshire County League v Essex & Suffolk Border League	1-2
Northants Combination League v Yorkshire Amateur League	0-1
Kent County League v Sussex County Football League (Div 3)	3-2*
Middlesex County Football League (*walkover*) v Spartan South Midlands Football League (Div 2) (*withdrew*)	
Somerset County League v Gloucestershire County League	3-1
Reading Football League v Oxfordshire Senior Football League	1-1*
(*Oxfordshire Senior League won 6-5 on penalties*)	
Northampton Town Football League v Anglian Combination	1-1*
(*Anglian Combination won 5-4 on penalties*)	

PRELIMINARY ROUND

Lincolnshire Football League v West Yorkshire Association League	2-1
Brighton Hove & District Football League v Mid Sussex Football League	3-1

FIRST ROUND

Cumberland County League v Isle of Man FA Senior League	0-5
Humber Premier League v Teesside League	4-2
Cheshire Football League v Wearside Football League	0-1
Manchester Football League v Liverpool County FA Premier League	2-1
Essex & Suffolk Border League v West Riding County Amateur Football League	1-2
Birmingham & District Amateur Football Association v Anglian Combination	
(*Anglian Combination removed for fielding an ineligible player, match awarded to Birmingham & District Amateur Football Association*)	
Bedfordshire County Football League v Yorkshire Amateur League	1-7
Peterborough & District Football League v Lincolnshire Football League	0-2
Amateur Football Combination v Surrey Elite Intermediate League	1-2
Southern Amateur League v Kent County League	5-6*
Hertfordshire Senior County League v Brighton Hove & District Football League	4-2
Worthing & District Football League (*walkover*) v Middlesex County Football League (*withdrew*)	
Oxfordshire Senior Football League v Hampshire Premier Football League	1-1*
(*Hampshire Premier League won 5-4 on penalties*)	
Jersey Football Combination v Guernsey FA League	3-1
Devon & Exeter Football League v Somerset County League	5-4*
Wiltshire Football League v Dorset Premier League	0-5

SECOND ROUND

Yorkshire Amateur League v Isle of Man FA Senior League	2-3*
Humber Premier League v Wearside Football League	2-1*
Birmingham & District Amateur Football Assoc. v Lincolnshire Football League	1-2
Manchester Football League v West Riding County Amateur Football League	1-3
Worthing & District Football League v Hampshire Premier Football League	3-2
Kent County League v Dorset Premier League	0-1
Surrey Elite Intermediate League v Hertfordshire Senior County League	
(*Surrey Elite Intermediate League removed for fielding 2 ineligible players, match awarded to Hertfordshire Senior County League*)	
Devon & Exeter Football League v Jersey Football Combination	1-2

THIRD ROUND

Lincolnshire Football League v Humber Premier League	0-2
Isle of Man FA Senior League v West Riding County Amateur Football League	3-1
Dorset Premier League v Jersey Football Combination	1-0
Hertfordshire Senior County League v Worthing & District Football League	3-0

SEMI-FINAL

Hertfordshire Senior County League v Dorset Premier League	4-2*
Humber Premier League v Isle of Man FA Senior League	1-2

FA INTER-LEAGUE CUP FINAL 2014

Douglas, Saturday 10 May 2014

Isle of Man FA Senior League (0) 3 *(Gale, Jones, Boss)*

Hertfordshire Senior County League (0) 2 *(Arthur, Ingham (pen))*

Referee: Chris Kavanagh.

FA PREMIER UNDER-21 LEAGUE 2013–14

THE FA PREMIER UNDER-21 LEAGUE TABLE

	P	W	D	L	F	A	GD	Pts
Chelsea	21	13	5	3	49	26	23	44
Liverpool	21	13	3	5	55	30	25	42
Manchester U	21	11	6	4	34	18	16	39
Manchester C	21	12	2	7	50	28	22	38
Fulham	21	11	5	5	38	30	8	38
Leicester C	21	11	4	6	37	30	7	37
Southampton	21	11	3	7	35	30	5	36
Sunderland	21	10	5	6	39	32	7	35
West Ham U	21	10	3	8	34	32	2	33
Norwich C	21	9	4	8	34	29	5	31
Everton	21	8	6	7	28	29	–1	30
Tottenham H	21	8	4	9	40	43	–3	28
Bolton W	21	8	3	10	40	47	–7	27
Arsenal	21	7	5	9	35	41	–6	26
Aston Villa	21	8	2	11	36	43	–7	26
WBA	21	8	1	12	35	43	–8	25
Reading	21	7	3	11	36	43	–7	24
Stoke C	21	6	4	11	26	34	–8	22
Middlesbrough	21	6	2	13	25	37	–12	20
Wolverhampton W	21	6	2	13	26	41	–15	20
Newcastle U	21	4	5	12	37	54	–17	17
Blackburn R	21	3	5	13	18	47	–29	14

THE FA PREMIER UNDER-21 FINAL PHASE

SEMI-FINAL

Manchester C v Chelsea	1-1*
(Chelsea won 5-4 on penalties)	
Liverpool v Manchester U	0-1

FINAL

Manchester U v Chelsea	1-2

THE FA PREMIER UNDER-21 LEAGUE CUP

After extra time.

ROUND OF 32

Middlesbrough v Everton	2-3
WBA v Nottingham F	2-1*
Blackburn R v Hull C	3-1
Bolton W v Barnsley	4-2
Leicester C v Sheffield W	4-1
Norwich C v Arsenal	0-1
Exeter C v Southampton	2-0
Notts Co v Wolverhampton W	1-2
Stoke C v Manchester C	0-2*
Aston Villa v Fulham	0-3
Birmingham C v Newcastle U†	2-1

(†Birmingham opted to withdraw from this season's U21 Premier League Cup after inadvertently fielding an ineligible player in their round-of-32 tie with Newcastle).

Burnley v Sunderland	2-1
Reading v QPR	3-1
Swansea C v Watford	0-0*
(Watford won 4-3 on penalties)	
Bristol C v West Ham U	1-2
Cardiff C v Chelsea	0-4

ROUND OF 16

Reading v Watford	6-1
Fulham v Arsenal	0-1
Exeter C v Blackburn R	2-1
Chelsea v West Ham U	2-1
Newcastle U v Leicester C	2-1
Burnley v Bolton W	3-0
Manchester C v WBA	2-0
Everton v Wolverhampton W	2-3

QUARTER-FINALS

Chelsea v Arsenal	0-1
Exeter C v Burnley	2-3*
Wolverhampton W v Reading	1-3
Newcastle U v Manchester C	2-3

SEMI-FINALS

Arsenal v Reading	1-2*
Manchester C v Burnley	3-2

FINAL FIRST LEG

Manchester C v Reading	3-2

FINAL SECOND LEG

Reading v Manchester C	2-0
Reading won 4-3 on aggregate.	

FA ACADEMY UNDER-18 LEAGUE 2013–14

THE FA PREMIER UNDER-18 LEAGUE TABLE

NORTH GROUP	P	W	D	L	F	A	GD	Pts
Manchester C	31	22	4	5	87	40	47	70
Everton	31	20	2	9	62	41	21	62
Liverpool	31	15	5	11	69	59	10	50
Manchester U	31	15	3	13	60	51	9	48
Newcastle U	31	15	2	14	49	57	–8	47
Sunderland	31	13	6	12	54	43	11	45
Wolverhampton W	31	10	7	14	47	65	–18	37
Middlesbrough	31	11	3	17	50	62	–12	36
Bolton W	31	10	3	18	49	74	–25	33
Blackburn R	31	8	5	18	61	84	–23	29
Stoke C	31	6	6	19	34	61	–27	24

SOUTH GROUP	P	W	D	L	F	A	GD	Pts
Tottenham H	31	19	6	6	82	48	34	63
West Ham U	31	17	6	8	56	36	20	57
Reading	31	16	4	11	59	57	2	52
Fulham	31	15	6	10	67	63	4	51
Chelsea	31	14	7	10	63	47	16	49
Southampton	31	12	10	9	57	50	7	46
Aston Villa	31	13	7	11	62	61	1	46
Norwich C	31	12	5	14	41	51	–10	41
Arsenal	31	8	10	13	42	48	–6	34
WBA	31	6	6	19	40	64	–24	24
Leicester C	31	6	3	22	37	66	–29	21

THE FA PREMIER UNDER-18 FINAL PHASE

SEMI-FINALS

Manchester C v West Ham U	2-1
Everton v Tottenham H	1-0

FINAL

Everton v Manchester C	1-0

FINAL THIRD DEVELOPMENT LEAGUE 2013–14

WEST DIVISION

	P	W	D	L	F	A	GD	Pts
Wigan Ath	14	9	1	4	27	12	15	28
Walsall	14	8	1	5	27	22	5	25
Port Vale	14	5	6	3	22	16	6	21
Wrexham	14	5	6	3	24	20	4	21
Morecambe	14	5	3	6	17	17	0	18
Oldham Ath	14	4	3	7	24	28	–4	15
Tranmere R	14	3	5	6	20	38	–18	14
Shrewsbury T	14	2	5	7	15	23	–8	11

EAST DIVISION

	P	W	D	L	F	A	GD	Pts
Hull C	10	7	1	2	26	10	16	22
Mansfield T	10	6	0	4	19	20	–1	18
Rotherham U	10	4	2	4	14	20	–6	14
Doncaster R	10	4	1	5	16	14	2	13
Hartlepool U	10	3	1	6	19	20	–1	10
Scunthorpe U	10	3	1	6	12	22	–10	10

FINAL THIRD DEVELOPMENT LEAGUE CUP
GROUP A

	P	W	D	L	F	A	GD	Pts
Leicester C	3	3	0	0	13	1	12	9
Port Vale	3	2	0	1	3	5	–2	6
Doncaster R	3	1	0	2	2	5	–3	3
Shrewsbury T	3	0	0	3	1	8	–7	0

GROUP B

	P	W	D	L	F	A	GD	Pts
Mansfield T	4	4	0	0	8	1	7	12
Hartlepool U	4	2	0	2	12	10	2	6
Sheffield W	4	2	0	2	11	9	2	6
Scunthorpe U	4	1	1	2	6	8	–2	4
Rotherham U	4	0	1	3	3	12	–9	1

GROUP C

	P	W	D	L	F	A	GD	Pts
Wigan Ath	4	3	0	1	5	4	1	9
Carlisle U	4	2	0	2	7	5	2	6
Fleetwood T	4	2	0	2	6	6	0	6
Tranmere R	4	2	0	2	6	6	0	6
Morecambe	4	1	0	3	4	7	–3	3

SEMI-FINALS

Leicester C v Mansfield T	2-3
Wigan Ath v Hartlepool U	2-0

FINAL THIRD DEVELOPMENT LEAGUE CUP FINAL 2014

Tuesday 6 May 2014

(at Robin Park Arena, Wigan)

Wigan Ath (1) 7 *(Jennings 16, 65, Andres 35, Redmond 59 (pen), Johnson 74, Chow 77, 90)*

Mansfield T (1) 1 *(Fletcher 19)*

Wigan Ath: Nicholls, Leigh, Lambert, Wilson, Balogun, Meadows, Jennings, Fyvie (Chow 62), Andres (Antelmi 68), Redmond (Ainscough 78), Johnson.
Mansfield T: Waldram, Koczalski, Hodget-Young, Hemshall, Brownlie, Hutchinson (Thompson R 61), Simo-Hemagou, Fitzpatrick, Fletcher, Carver, Thompson T.

FOOTBALL LEAGUE YOUTH ALLIANCE 2013–14

NORTH WEST CONFERENCE

	P	W	D	L	F	A	GD	Pts	PG
Blackpool	24	18	4	2	59	20	39	58	2.42
Oldham Ath	23	16	3	4	58	27	31	51	2.22
Rochdale	23	16	0	7	65	37	28	48	2.09
Walsall	23	14	5	4	44	17	27	47	2.04
Tranmere R	23	12	3	8	34	27	7	39	1.70
Carlisle U	24	11	3	10	48	43	5	36	1.50
Bury	24	10	6	8	44	46	–2	36	1.50
Port Vale	23	10	4	9	43	44	–1	34	1.48
Burnley	24	10	5	9	46	31	15	35	1.46
Fleetwood T	24	9	2	13	23	40	–17	29	1.21
Preston NE	24	8	4	12	39	47	–8	28	1.17
Wigan Ath	24	6	8	10	39	50	–11	26	1.08
Macclesfield T	23	7	3	13	27	41	–14	24	1.04
Accrington S	24	5	8	11	28	37	–9	23	0.96
Shrewsbury T	23	6	2	15	29	48	–19	20	0.87
Morecambe	24	5	2	17	30	75	–45	17	0.71
Wrexham	23	4	4	15	27	53	–26	16	0.70

NORTH EAST CONFERENCE

	P	W	D	L	F	A	GD	Pts
Bradford C	22	15	5	2	68	31	37	50
Doncaster R	22	14	4	4	59	29	30	46
Scunthorpe U	22	12	3	7	53	40	13	39
Notts Co	22	11	3	8	43	33	10	36
York C	22	10	4	8	33	37	–4	34
Hull C	22	10	3	9	42	29	13	33
Hartlepool U	22	9	3	10	49	60	–11	30
Burton Alb	22	8	5	9	35	46	–11	29
Rotherham U	22	5	6	11	32	49	–17	21
Grimsby T	22	4	6	12	15	43	–28	18
Chesterfield	22	4	5	13	28	44	–16	17
Lincoln C	22	4	5	13	26	42	–16	17

SOUTH WEST CONFERENCE

	P	W	D	L	F	A	GD	Pts
Exeter C	16	10	2	4	40	20	20	32
Bristol Rovers	16	9	5	2	29	15	14	32
Plymouth Arg	16	10	1	5	29	16	13	31
Oxford U	16	9	3	4	33	20	13	30
Cheltenham T	16	8	2	6	35	26	9	26
AFC Bournemouth	16	6	4	6	24	24	0	22
Swindon T	16	5	1	10	28	40	–12	16
Torquay U	16	2	2	12	17	43	–26	8
Newport Co	16	2	2	12	15	46	–31	8
Hereford U	–	–	–	–	–	–	–	–

Hereford U record expunged.

SOUTH EAST CONFERENCE

	P	W	D	L	F	A	GD	Pts	PG
Colchester U	21	14	3	4	58	31	27	45	2.14
Peterborough U	21	13	5	3	53	25	28	44	2.10
Gillingham	20	11	5	4	47	28	19	38	1.90
Watford	21	11	3	7	38	27	11	36	1.71
Luton T	21	11	3	7	33	24	9	36	1.71
Portsmouth	20	10	3	7	37	32	5	33	1.65
Southend U	20	9	4	7	37	36	1	31	1.55
Leyton Orient	20	9	1	10	39	36	3	28	1.40
AFC Wimbledon	20	8	3	9	30	31	–1	27	1.35
Northampton T	21	8	4	9	29	35	–6	28	1.33
Stevenage	21	8	3	10	43	54	–11	27	1.29
Barnet	21	7	1	13	30	39	–9	22	1.05
Milton Keynes D	21	6	3	12	45	62	–17	21	1.00
Crawley T	20	4	4	12	28	47	–19	16	0.80
Dagenham & R	20	2	1	17	22	62	–40	7	0.35

PG = points per game.

IMPORTANT ADDRESSES

The Football Association: Wembley Stadium, P.O. Box 1966, London SW1P 9EQ. *0844 980 8200*

Scotland: Hampden Park, Glasgow G42 9AY. *0141 616 6000*

Northern Ireland (Irish FA): Chief Executive, 20 Windsor Avenue, Belfast BT9 6EE. *028 9066 9458*

Wales: 11/12 Neptune Court, Vanguard Way, Cardiff CF24 5PJ. *029 2043 5830*

Republic of Ireland National Sports Campus, Abbotstown, Dublin 15. *00 353 1 8999 500*

International Federation (FIFA): Strasse 20, P.O. Box 8044, Zurich, Switzerland. *00 41 43 222 7777. Fax: 00 41 222 7878*

Union of European Football Associations: Secretary, Route de Geneve 46, P.O. Box 1260, Nyon 2, Switzerland. *Fax: 00 41 848 00 2727*

THE LEAGUES

The Premier League: Nic Coward, 30 Gloucester Place, London W1U 8PL. *0207 864 9000*

The Football League: Andy Williamson, Unit 5, Edward VII Quay, Navigation Way, Preston, Lancashire PR2 2YF. *0844 463 1888. Fax 0870 442 0 1188*

Football Conference: D. Strudwick, 3rd Floor, Wellington House, 31–34 Waterloo Street, Birmingham B2 5TJ. *0121 214 1950*

Scottish Premier League: Hampden Park, Somerville Drive, Glasgow G42 9OE. *0141 620 4140*

The Scottish League: Hampden Park, Glasgow G42 9EB. *0141 620 4160*

Football League of Ireland: D. Crowther, 80 Merrion Square, Dublin 2. *00 353 1 6765 120*

Southern League: J. Mills, Sansome Lodge, 4–6 Sansome Walk, Worcester WR1 1LH. *01905 330 444*

Northern Premier League: Ms A. Firth, 23 High Lane, Norton Tower, Halifax, W. Yorkshire HX2 0NW. *01422 410 691*

Isthmian League: Ms K. Discipline, The Base, Dartford Business Park, Victoria Park, Dartford, Kent DA1 5FS. *01322 314 999*

Eastern Counties League: N. Spurling, 16 Thanet Road, Ipswich, Suffolk IP4 5LB. *07855 279 062*

Essex Senior League: Secretary: K. Wilmot, 35 Cecil Road, Walthamstow, London E17 5DH. *07540 441 829*

Hellenic League: B. King, 7 Stoneleigh Drive, Carterton, Oxon OX18 1EE. *0845 260 6644*

Kent League: A.R. Vinter, 4 Staple Court, Chilham Castle Estate, Chilham, Canterbury CT4 8DB. *01227 730 457*

Midland Alliance: J. Shaw, 176 Springthorpe Road, Erdington, Birmingham B24 0SN. *0121 350 5869*

North West Counties League: J. Deal, 24 The Pastures, Crossens, Southport PR9 8RH. *07713 622 210*

Northern Counties East: B. Gould, 42 Thirlmere Drive, Dronfield, Derbyshire S18 2HW. *07773 653 238*

Northern League: T. Golightly, 85 Park Road North, Chester-le-Street, Co. Durham DH3 3SA. *0191 388 2056*

Spartan South Midlands League: M. Mitchell, 26 Leighton Court, Dunstable, Beds LU6 1EW. *07710 455 409*

Sussex County League: Ms K. Scott, Llandilo, Old Lane, Crowborough TN6 2AF. *07788 737 061*

United Counties League: Ms W. Newey, Riverside Pavilion, Candy Street, Peterborough PE2 9RE. *01733 566 605*

Wessex League: J. Gorman, 6 Overton House, London Road, Overton, Hants RG25 3TP. *01256 770 059*

Western League: K.A. Clarke, 32 Westmead Lane, Chippenham, Wilts SN15 3HZ. *07790 002 279*

Combined Counties League: M.J. Bidmead, 55 Grange Road, Chessington, Surrey KT9 1EZ. *0208 397 4834*

Midland Combination: N. Wood, 30 Glalsdale Road, Hall Green, Birmingham B28 8PX. *07967 440 007*

West Midlands League: N.R. Juggins, 14 Badger Way, Blackwell, Bromsgrove, Worcs B60 1EX. *07977 422 362.*

South West Peninsula League: P. Hiscox, 45a Serge Court, The Quay, Exeter, Devon EX2 4EB. *07788 897 706*

OTHER USEFUL ADDRESSES

Amateur Football Alliance: M. Brown, Unit 3, 7 Wenlock Road, London N1 7SL. *0208 733 2613*

Association of Football Badge Collectors: K. Wilkinson, 18 Hinton St, Fairfield, Liverpool L6 3AR. *0151 260 0554*

Association of Provincial Football Supporters Clubs in London: Tina A. Robertson, 45 Durham Avenue, Heston, Middlesex TW5 0HG. *0208 843 9854*

Backpass Retro Football Magazine: Greystones, Beechgrove, Kington, Herefordshire HR5 3RH. *01544 230317*

British Universities Sports Association: G. Gregory-Jones, Chief Executive: BUSA, 20–24 King's Bench Street, London SE1 0QX. *0207 633 5080*

English Schools FA: J. Read, 4 Parker Court, Staffordshire Technology Park, Stafford ST18 0WP. *01785 785 970*

Football Foundation: Whittinghton House, 19–30 Alfred Place, London WC1E 7EA. *0845 345 4555*

Football Postcard Collectors Club: PRO: Bryan Horsnell, 275 Overdown Road, Tilehurst, Reading RG31 6NX. *0118 942 4448 (and fax)*

Football Safety Officers Association: Chris Patzelt, FSOA Ltd, Suite 17, Blackburn Rovers Enterprise Centre, Ewood Park, Blackburn BB2 4JF. *01254 841 771.*

Institute of Football Management and Administration: St George's Park, Newborough, Needwood, Burton on Trent DE13 9PD. *0128 357 6350*

Institute of Groundsmanship: 19–23 Church Street, Agora, Wolverton, Milton Keynes MK12 5LG. *01908 312 511*

League Managers Association: St George's Park, Newborough, Needwood, Burton on Trent DE13 9PD. *0128 357 6350*

National Playing Fields Association: 57B, 25 Ovington Square, London SW3 1LQ. *0207 584 6445*

Professional Footballers' Association: G. Taylor, 20 Oxford Court, Bishopsgate, Off Lower Moseley Street, Manchester M2 3WQ. *0161 236 0575*

Programme Monthly & Football Collectable Magazine: 11 Tannington Terrace, London N5 1LE. *020 7359 8687*

Programme Promotions: 21 Roughwood Close, Watford WD17 3HN. *01923 861 468*
Web: www.footballprogrammes.com

Referees' Association: A.W.S. Smith, Unit 12, Ensign Business Centre, Westwood Way, Westwood Heath, Coventry CV4 8JA. *024 7642 0360*

Scottish Football Historians Association: John Lister, 46 Milton Road, Kirkcaldy, Fife KY1 1TL. *01592 268 718*

Sir Norman Chester Centre for Football Research: Department of Sociology, University of Leicester, University Road LE1 7RH. *0116 252 2741/5.*

Soccer Nostalgia: G. Wallis, Albion Chambers, 1 Albion Road, Birchington, Kent CT7 9DN. *01303 275 432.*

Sport England: 16 Upper Woburn Place, London WC1H 0QP. *0207 388 1277*

Sports Grounds Safety Authority: East Wing, 3rd Floor, Fleetbank House, 2–6 Salisbury Square, London EC4Y 8JX. *0207 930 6693*

Sports Turf Research Institute: St Ives Estate, Harden, Bingley, West Yorkshire BD16 1AU. *01274 565 131*

The Football Supporters' Federation: The Cherry Red Records Stadium, Kingsmeadow, Jack Goodchild Way, 422a Kingston Road, Kingston-upon-Thames KT1 3PB. *0330 44 000 44*

The Ninety-Two Club: Mr M. Kimberley, The Ninety-Two Club, 153 Hayes Lane, Kenley, Surrey CR8 5HP.

UK Programme Collectors Club: PM Publications, 38 Lowther Road, Norwich NR4 6QW. *01603 449 237*

Women's Football Conference: Mike Appleby, Wembley Stadium, PO Box 1966, London SW1P 9EQ. *0844 980 8200*

FOOTBALL CLUB CHAPLAINCY

Colin, the minister of a suburban parish, sat down after a tiring day. He'd made his ward rounds at the City General hospital that morning, officiated at a funeral and burial that afternoon, and conducted an interview with a young couple whom he was soon to marry. And then the phone rang.

It was Beryl, an occasional attender at Colin's church and the mother of a young footballer who played largely for the City reserve side, but who had suffered a nasty debilitating injury. It transpired the lad had become more and more depressed by his inaction, and now the psychiatric staff at the hospital thought the best place for the young man would be in a psychiatric hospital some 25 miles away. Beryl was adamant that this would only make her son's problem worse.

Colin promised an immediate visit and got on really well with the young man. Upon Colin's third visit they prayed together, with Beryl, and continued to do so subsequently whenever Colin was able to see him.

That was all a couple of years ago. Today, the young man has broken into his club's first eleven, his depression cured. Beryl and her son are regular attenders at Colin's church, and there are discussions at his football club about the possibility of appointing Colin as its honorary Chaplain.

THE REV

OFFICIAL CHAPLAINS TO FA PREMIERSHIP AND FOOTBALL LEAGUE CLUBS

Aston Villa – Rev Ken Baker
Barnsley – Rev Peter Amos
Birmingham C – Rev Kirk McAtear
Blackburn R – Rev Ken Howles
Blackpool – Rev Michael Ward
Bolton W – Mr Phil Mason
Bournemouth – Rev Andy Rimmer
Bradford C – Rev Andy Grieff
Bristol C – Rev Derek Cleave
Bristol R – Rev David Jeal
Burnley – Rev Mark Hirst
Burton A – Rev Phil Pusey
Bury – Rev David Ottley
Cardiff C – Rev Dr John Weaver
Carlisle U – Rev Alun Jones
Charlton Ath – Rev Matt Baker
Cheltenham T – Rev Malcolm Allen
Chesterfield – Rev Jim McGlade
Crawley T – Rev Gary Simmons
Crewe Alex – Rev Phil Howell
Crystal Palace – Rev Chris Roe
Dagenham & R – Rev Keiran Bush
Derby Co – Rev Tony Luke
Doncaster R – Rev Barry Miller
Everton – Co-Chaplains Rev Henry Corbett
and Rev Harry Ross
Fulham – Rev Gary Piper
Gillingham – Rev Richard Hayton
Hull C – Rev Allen Bagshawe
Ipswich T – Rev Kevan McCormack
Leeds U – Rev Paul Welch
Leicester C – Rev Andrew Hulley
Leyton Orient – Rev Alan Comfort
Liverpool – Rev Bill Bygroves
Manchester C – Rev Peter Horlock
Manchester U – Rev John Boyers
Mansfield T – Rev Ray Shaw
Millwall – Rev Canon Owen Beament

Newcastle U Academy – Rev Glyn Evans
Newport Co – Rev Keith Beardmore
Northampton T – Rev Andrew Dunlop
Norwich C – Co-Chaplains Rev Arthur
Bowles and Rev Albert Cadmore
Nottingham F – Rev Steve Silvester
Notts Co – Rev Liam O'Boyle
Oldham Ath – Rev John Simmons
Oxford U – Rev Hedley Feast
Peterborough U – Rev Richard Longfoot
Plymouth Arg – Rev Arthur Goode
Port Vale – Rev John Hibberts
Portsmouth – Co-Chaplains Mr Mick
Mellows and Rev Jonathan Jeffrey
Preston NE – Rev Chris Nelson
QPR – Co-Chaplains Rev Cameron
Collington and Rev Bob Mayo
Reading – Rev Steven Prince
Scunthorpe U – Rev Alan Wright
Sheffield U – Rev Baz Gascoyne
Sheffield W Academy – Rev Malcolm Drew
Shrewsbury T – Rev Christopher Deakin
Southampton – Rev Andy Bowerman
Southend U – Rev Stu Alleway
Sunderland – Father Marc Lyden-Smith
Swansea C – Rev Kevin Johns
Swansea C Academy – Rev Eirian Wyn
Swindon T – Rev Simon Stevenette
Torquay U – Rev Tim Smith
Walsall – Rev Peter Hart
Watford – Rev Clive Ross
West Ham U – Rev Alan Bolding
Wolverhampton W – Co-Chaplains
Rev David Wright and Mr Steve Davies
Wycombe W – Rev John Roberts
Yeovil T – Rev Jim Pearce
York C – Rev Paul Deo

The chaplains hope that those who read this page will see the value and benefit of chaplaincy work in football and will take appropriate steps to spread the word where this is possible. They would also like to thank the editors of the Football Yearbook for their continued support for this specialist and growing area of work.

For further information, please contact: Sports Chaplaincy UK, PO Box 123, Sale, Cheshire M33 4ZA. Telephone: 0161 962 6068 or email: admin@sportschaplaincy.org.uk. Website: www.sportschaplaincy.org.uk

OBITUARIES

Rex Adams (Born Oxford, 13 February 1928. Died Blackpool, 14 January 2014.) Rex Adams was a winger who signed for Blackpool in June 1948. He was mainly a reserve during his time with the Tangerines but made 18 first-team appearances before moving on to join Worcester City. He later returned to the Football League and spent a season at Oldham Athletic followed by spells with Cheshire League clubs Northwich Victoria and Mossley.

Steve Aizlewood (Born Newport, 9 October 1952. Died Newport, 6 August 2013.) Steve Aizlewood was a defender who had the distinction of making more than 100 appearances for three senior clubs: Newport County, Swindon Town and Portsmouth. He was capped for Wales U18 Schools and also for his country at U23 level.

Tony Alexander (Born Reading, 8 February 1935. Died 9 October 2013.) Tony Alexander was a versatile forward who joined the groundstaff at Reading from school and made his first-team debut as a teenager. His career at Elm Park was interrupted by National Service and he made just 11 appearances before moving on to Yeovil Town in 1956.

Frank Allen (Born Shirebrook, Derbys, 28 June 1927. Died Chesterfield, 2 February 2014.) Frank Allen was a wing half who started his career with Chesterfield when he signed for the Spireites in March 1951. He made three appearances while at Saltergate before moving to Mansfield Town where he spent a further two seasons.

Tony Allen (Born Dunkirk, Notts, 27 October 1924. Died Nottingham, 13 February 2014.) Tony Allen was a full back who made his debut for Nottingham Forest in an FA Cup tie against Watford in January 1946 before switching three years later to join neighbours Notts County. He made 30 appearances for the Magpies and later played for Corby Town and Grantham.

Wilf Allsop (Born Arbroath, 23 January 1931. Died Glenrothes, Fife, 27 December 2013.) Wilf Allsop was a creative inside forward who developed with the Hearts reserve team before joining Stirling Albion in May 1953. Although he made his senior debut at Annfield he stayed only a few months before joining Forfar. Wilf was a regular for the Loons over the next two and a half seasons, making 83 first-team appearances before concluding his career with a brief association with Arbroath.

Jim Appleby (Born Shotton Colliery, Co Durham, 15 June 1934. Died 6 January 2014.) Jim Appleby was a centre half who made his League debut for Blackpool in 1957. That was his only appearance during five years at Turf Moor and he later moved on to play for Blackburn Rovers, Southport and Chester.

Bill Atkinson (Born Sunderland, 21 December 1944. Died Nuneaton, 24 June 2013.) Winger Bill Atkinson was capped by England Schools before joining Birmingham City as an apprentice. Although he never made the first team at St Andrew's he featured regularly for Torquay United in the 1964–65 season before returning to the Midlands to play for Nuneaton Borough.

Gerry Baker (Born New Rochelle, New York State, USA, 11 April 1938. Died Wishaw, Lanarkshire, 24 August 2013.) Gerry Baker was on the groundstaff at Chelsea as a youngster then played a role in Bobby Ancell's 'Babes' at Motherwell before joining St Mirren in November 1958. A Scottish Cup winner in his first season at Love Street he netted a remarkable 65 goals in 81 games including a 10-goal haul in the record-breaking 15-0 victory over Glasgow University in January 1960. He was less successful with Manchester City but his scoring touch returned in spells with Hibernian and Ipswich Town before he ended his career at Coventry City. He was capped for the USA.

Keith Baker (Born Oxford, 15 October 1956. Died 19 December 2013.) Goalkeeper Keith Baker won two caps for England Schools before becoming an apprentice with Oxford United. He graduated to the professional ranks with the U's but his only experience of senior football came in August 1975 when he turned out for Grimsby Town during a loan spell at Blundell Park.

Eric Barnes (Born Wythenshawe, Manchester, 29 November 1937. Died Crewe, 3 January 2014.) Eric Barnes was a defender who made over 350 appearances for Crewe Alexandra after joining the club in January 1958. He captained the team for several seasons and helped Alex to two promotions during his time at Gresty Road. He also played cricket for Cheshire in the Minor Counties Championship.

Malcolm Barrass (Born Blackpool, 15 December 1924. Died Bury, 4 August 2013.) Malcolm Barrass was a versatile player who featured both at inside forward and centre half. After making three war-time appearances for Wolves he joined Bolton Wanderers for whom he made over 350 appearances, featuring in the side that won the War Cup in 1944–45 and gaining an FA Cup runners-up medal in 1953. He later had a spell with Sheffield United before joining Wigan Athletic as player-manager. He won three full caps for England and also played for the Football League representative side.

Tom Barrett (Born Salford, 16 March 1934. Died 8 March 2014.) Tom Barrett was a wing-half who spent five seasons as a professional with Manchester United without breaking into the Reds' first team. He moved on to join Plymouth Argyle in July 1957 and made 27 first-team appearances for the Pilgrims before finishing his career at Chester.

Frank Bartlett (Born Chester-le-Street, Co Durham, 8 November 1930. Died 6 December 2013.) Frank Bartlett was a versatile forward who joined Barnsley in the summer of 1950 and went on to play more than 300 first-team games during his stay at Oakwell. A regular on the left flank in 1954–55 when the Division Three North title was secured, he eventually left for Halifax at the end of the 1962–63 season before joining Goole Town.

Roger Barton (Born Jump, South Yorkshire, 25 November 1946. Died Austerfield, South Yorkshire, 4 November 2013.) Roger Barton was a slightly built winger who joined Lincoln City in the summer of 1964 after developing in the Wolverhampton Wanderers youth set-up. He was in and out of the Imps' side during two seasons at Sincil Bank, but was a near ever-present for Barnsley in 1966–67 before eventually moving on to Worcester City.

Harry Bell (Born Castletown, Sunderland, 14 October 1924. Died Newcastle upon Tyne, 22 April 2014.) Harry Bell made wartime appearances for Sunderland before signing professional forms for Middlesbrough in September 1945. After starting out as an inside forward he was converted into a tenacious right half and wenton to make over 300 appearances in 10 years at Boro before finishing his career at Darlington. He was also a talented cricketer who played for Durham in the Minor Counties Championship between 1946 and 1962.

Terry Bell (Born Nottingham, 1 August 1944. Died 15 May 2014.) Terry Bell was a forward who established himself as a first-team player with Hartlepool United after joining from non-league Nuneaton Borough in 1966. He twice topped the scoring charts with Pools and continued to find the net on a regular basis during later spells with Reading and Aldershot.

Arthur Bellamy (Born Blackhill, Co Durham, 5 April 1942. Died Burnley, 22 January 2014.) Arthur Bellamy was an inside forward who made his debut for Burnley in March 1963. He made over 200 Football League appearances for the Clarets before joining Chesterfield in July 1972. He played a further 151 senior games for the Spireites before his playing career came to an end. He later returned to Turf Moor as coach and then as assistant manager. He went on to become groundsman before retiring at the age of 65.

Bellini (Born Itapira, Brazil, 7 June 1930. Died Sao Paulo, Brazil, 20 March 2014.) Bellini was a centre half who captained the first Brazil team to win the World Cup when his country defeated Sweden to win the 1958 tournament. He made his international debut at the age of 26 and went on to win 51 caps. He played his club football for Vasco Da Gama, Sao Paulo and Atletico Paranaense.

Christian Benitez (Born Quito, Ecuador, 1 May 1986. Died Doha, Qatar, 29 July 2013.) Christian Benitez was a lively attacking player who played in Ecuador for El Nacional and then Mexico for Santos Laguna before joining Birmingham City on loan for the 2009–10 season. He made 30 Premier League appearances for Blues, scoring three goals. He subsequently spent two seasons with Club America in Mexico then signed for El Jaish of Qatar in July 2013. The day after making his debut he fell ill and died after suffering a cardiac arrest. 'Chucho', as he was known, won 28 caps for Ecuador between 2005 and 2009.

Stan Bennion (Born Blacon, Cheshire, 9 February 1938. Died Llay, Clwyd, 5 August 2013.) Stan Bennion was an inside forward or left winger who joined Wrexham after helping Saltney Juniors win the Welsh Youth Cup in 1955–56. He went on to make over 70 Football League appearances for Wrexham and Chester before joining New Brighton in 1965.

Alan Blackburn (Born Pleasley, Derbys, 4 August 1935. Died January 2014.) Alan Blackburn was a bustling centre forward who made his debut for West Ham United as an 18-year-old in December 1954. He made 17 first-team appearances for the Hammers before signing for Halifax Town in November 1957 and went on to play more than 100 games for the West Yorkshire club.

Keith Blackburn (Born Manchester, 7 July 1940. Died 4 February 2014.) Keith Blackburn was an inside forward who signed for Portsmouth in July 1959. Although mainly a reserve he gained a Division Three championship medal after featuring in the 1961–62 Pompey team and in total made 37 appearances in his five seasons with the club. He later played in South Africa before his career was cut short by injury.

Dave Blakey (Born Newburn, Newcastle upon Tyne, 22 August 1929. Died 4 April 2014.) Dave Blakey was a centre half who made his debut for Chesterfield in August 1948 and went on to complete a club record of 617 Football League appearances for the Spireites before retiring in the summer of 1967. His total included 244 consecutive League appearances between September 1952 and November 1957. Before he ended his playing career he received a Football League long service award in recognition of 20 seasons as a professional with the same club.

Kevin Blount (Born Dublin, 1930. Died Dublin, 3 July 2013.) Kevin Blount was a well-known goalkeeper in the League of Ireland in the 1950s and '60s. He won League titles with Shelbourne (1952–53) and Dundalk (1966–67) and also turned out for Transport, Cork Celtic, Limerick, Cork Hibernians and St Patrick's Athletic. He won 12 caps for the League of Ireland representative team.

Bill Boland (Born Muirkirk, Ayrshire, 30 November 1919. Died Muirkirk, Ayrshire, 24 September 2013.) Inside right Bill Boland made four appearances for Celtic in the emergency Southern League Cup competition of 1944–45, scoring twice. He later returned to Ayrshire Junior football. At the time of his death he was the oldest living Celtic player.

Ashley Booth (Born Aberdeen, circa 1937. Died Dundee, 23 March 2014.) Ashley Booth was a defender who started his career with St Johnstone, making 36 senior appearances for the Perth team after signing in September 1961. He later had a spell with East Fife before his career was cut short by injury.

Ken Booth (Born circa 1922. Died 1 July 2013.) Ken Booth rescued Rotherham United from serious financial problems early in 1987, helping the club out of administration and serving as chairman through until December 2004. A wealthy scrap metal merchant he eventually sold his interest in the club to the Millers' 05 group.

Alistair Brack (Born Aberdeen, 27 January 1940. Died Worcester, 8 May 2014.) Alistair Brack was a right back who joined Cardiff City from Scottish Junior football in September 1961. He made a single Football League appearance for the Welsh club, later moving on to play in the Southern League for Worcester City.

Peter Broadbent (Born Elvington, Kent, 15 May 1933. Died Himley, Staffs, 1 October 2013.) Peter Broadbent was introduced to senior football at Brentford but within a matter of months he was snapped up by Wolverhampton Wanderers and went on to become one of the key figures in the Molineux club's run of success during the 1950s. A member of the team that won the Football League title on three occasions, he also won an FA Cup winners' medal when Wolves beat Blackburn Rovers in the 1960 final. Peter left the club in 1964 following the dismissal of manager Stan Cullis and went on to play for Shrewsbury Town, Aston Villa and Stockport County. He won seven full caps for England and also appeared for the Football League representative side.

Sandy Brown (Born Grangemouth, Stirlingshire, 24 March 1939. Died Blackpool, 8 April 2014.) Sandy Brown was a full back who made over 150 appearances for Partick Thistle and won representative honours with the Scottish League before moving south to sign for Everton in September 1963. He spent eight years at Goodison earning a Football League championship medal in 1969–70, and later played for Shrewsbury Town and Southport.

Mick Buckley (Born Manchester, 4 November 1953. Died 7 October 2013.) Mick Buckley was a skilful midfield player who was a member of the England team that won the UEFA Youth Championship in 1972. He made over 100 appearances for both Everton and Sunderland and also won England U23 honours. Later he had injury-affected spells with Hartlepool, Carlisle United and Middlesbrough before retiring.

Allan Bushell (Born Burnley, 4 September 1932. Died Blackburn, 12 October 2013.) Allan Bushell was an amateur centre forward who made his debut for Accrington Stanley in November 1952 and made eight more first-team appearances, all in the 1952–53 season, before leaving senior football.

Dave Campbell (Born Wrexham, 18 February 1947. Died 7 December 2013.) Winger Dave Campbell was on Manchester United's books as a youngster, progressing as far as the Central League team before joining Wrexham as a 17-year-old. He went on to make 49 appearances, mostly in the 1965–66 season, but 12 months later he was released and after a brief spell at Corby Town he joined Bangor City.

Billy Carmichael (Born 1933. Died Perth, 29 December 2013.) Billy Carmichael was a wing half or inside forward who received his baptism in senior football with Clyde in March 1953 and went on to play over 30 games for the Bully Wee. He later played for Dunfermline and East Stirlingshire. Outside of football he rose to become chairman of the Scottish Stock Exchange and in 1992 he joined the Clyde board, serving as club chairman from 1995 until 2004.

Dave Carr (Born Wheatley Hill, Co Durham, 19 January 1937. Died Blackhall, Co Durham, 12 November 2013.) Dave Carr was a forward who scored 50 goals in five seasons at Darlington before following manager Ken Furphy to Workington in July 1962. He continued to find the net regularly and was a member of the Reds' team which reached the quarter-finals of the Football League Cup in successive seasons. He moved on to Watford in February 1965 but after 10 appearances for the Hornets his career was ended as a result of serious injuries he received in a road traffic accident.

Wilf Carter (Born Wednesbury, Staffs, 4 October 1933. Died Bath, 4 August 2013.) Inside forward Wilf Carter made his First Division debut for West Bromwich Albion at the age of 17. He was mostly a reserve during his stay at The Hawthorns, but proved a goalscoring revelation after joining Plymouth Argyle in March 1957. He led the club's scoring charts for five consecutive seasons and his tally of 134 Football League goals is a post-war record for the Pilgrims, whilst in December 1960 he became the first Argyle player to net five goals in a match, achieving the feat in a 6-4 win over Charlton Athletic.

George Cartmell (Born Falkirk, 4 November 1934. Died New Mexico, USA, 30 January 2014.) George Cartmell was a full back who signed for Falkirk in June 1955 from Armadale Thistle. He was mainly a reserve for the Bairns but made three Scottish League appearances before leaving the club in 1958 and later emigrating to Canada.

Ian Cashmore (Born Kilwinning, Ayrshire, 4 October 1960. Died Kilwinning, Ayrshire, 28 April 2014.) Ian Cashmore was a forward who made his senior debut for Ayr United as a teenager in March 1980. He made further first-team appearances after signing for Berwick Rangers where he scored eight goals in his first 10 games before his career ended at the age of 22 as a result of a freak training ground accident when he fractured his neck. He was later involved in coaching and in 2010 he was awarded a UEFA silver Grassroots Leaders' Award for his work.

Jack Casley (Born Torquay, 27 April 1926. Died Oxford, 31 May 2014.) Jack Casley was a utility player who became Headington United's first full-time professional when he signed for the then Southern League club in July 1949. He appeared in virtually every outfield position during his career and was also used regularly as a goalkeeper. His only Football League appearance was between the sticks for his first club Torquay United. After his playing career ended he continued to be involved as a member of the backroom staff at Oxford United, retiring as chief scout in 2002 after 53 years service to the club.

Len Chalmers (Born Corby, Northants, 4 September 1936. Died 10 February 2014.) Len Chalmers was a hard-tackling full back who made 204 senior appearances for Leicester City. He played for the Foxes in the 1961 FA Cup final but suffered an injury which forced him off early in the game. He was treated and returned to the pitch at outside left and the depleted City team went down to two late goals. He later spent two seasons at Notts County.

Bob Charles (Born Southampton, 26 November 1941. Died 7 March 2014.) Bob Charles was a goalkeeper who made his debut for Southampton as a 17-year-old in September 1959. He won a Third Division championship medal in his first season at the club but made only occasional further appearances and moved on to join Weymouth in the summer of 1961. He represented both England Schools and the England Youth team.

John Christie (Born Fraserburgh, Aberdeenshire, 26 September 1929. Died Chandler's Ford, Hants, 9 March 2014.) John Christie was a goalkeeper who began his career with Ayr United before joining Southampton in January 1951. He went on to make over 200 League and Cup appearances during eight years with the Saints. He signed for Walsall and was a member of the Saddlers' team that rose from the Fourth to the Second Division with successive promotions.

Clive Clark (Born Leeds, 19 December 1940. Died Scarborough, 2014.) Clive Clark was a winger who began his career with Queens Park Rangers before moving to West Bromwich Albion in January 1961. He went on to make over 300 appearances for the Baggies, gaining both FA Cup and Football League Cup winners' medals. He moved back to Loftus Road in the summer of 1969 and later had spells with Preston North End and Southport before playing in the USA.

Harry Clark, MBE (Born Clough Dene, Co Durham, 30 March 1913. Died 4 January 2014.) Harry Clark was a winger who played for Manchester City and Accrington Stanley during wartime. He signed for Gateshead and made 22 League and Cup appearances in 1946–47. In his later years he was an environmental activist who was still campaigning at the age of 100. He was appointed an MBE in 2001 for services to the community.

Clive Colbridge (Born Hull, 27 April 1934. Died 9 December 2013.) Clive Colbridge was a left winger who made his debut in senior football with York City in September 1955. He went on to make a total of 282 Football League appearances in a career that also took him to Workington, Crewe Alexandra, Manchester City (where he was a regular in top-flight football in 1959–60) and Wrexham. He left the full-time game in the summer of 1965, signing for Altrincham.

David Coleman, OBE (Born Alderley Edge, Cheshire, 26 April 1926. Died 21 December 2013.) David Coleman was one of the highest profile broadcasters of his generation. During a career of more than 40 years with the BBC he covered six World Cup tournaments and 11 Olympic Games and presented the Corporation's flagship sports programmes including *Grandstand*, *Sportsnight* and *Question of Sport* while also commentating on matches for *Match of the Day*.

Bobby Collins (Born Govanhill, Glasgow, 16 February 1931. Died 13 January 2014.) Bobby Collins was a diminutive midfield player who appeared 31 times for Scotland, featuring in all three games in the 1958 World Cup finals. He made his name with Celtic, making over 300 appearances and featuring in the team that won the League and Cup double in 1953–54 before moving south to sign for Everton in September 1958. Bobby made over 100 Football League appearances for the Toffees and then joined Leeds United where he was a member of the team that won the Division Two title in 1963–64 and finished runners-up in Division One the following season when they were also beaten finalists in the FA Cup. He was the 1965 Footballer of the Year before suffering a serious injury. He later played for Bury, Morton and Oldham Athletic as well as spells in Australia and Ireland before going into management at Huddersfield Town, Hull City and Barnsley.

Mario Coluna (Born Lourenco Marques, Mozambique, 6 August 1935. Died Maputo, Mozambique, 25 February 2014.) Mario Coluna was a midfield player who captained the Portugal team when they finished in third place in the 1966 World Cup. He won 54 caps for his country and captained his club Benfica to successive European Cup wins in 1961 and 1962. He had a year with Olympique Lyonnais before returning to his home country of Mozambique where he became national coach following independence and was later president of the country's football federation.

Paul Comstive (Born Southport, 25 November 1961. Died Southport, 29 December 2013.) Paul Comstive was a midfield player who developed in the youth set-up at Blackburn Rovers, making his senior debut whilst still in his teens. He went on to make over 300 League appearances in a career that saw him play for Wigan Athletic, Burnley, Wrexham, Bolton Wanderers and Chester. A highlight came when he appeared for Burnley against Wolves in the 1988 Sherpa Van Trophy final at Wembley.

Ollie Conmy (Born Mulranny, Co Mayo, 13 November 1939. Died Southport, 27 January 2014.) Ollie Conmy was a winger who won five Republic of Ireland caps after making his debut against Belgium in November 1965. He began his senior career at Huddersfield Town but was unable to break into the first team and in 1964 signed for Peterborough United. He became a regular with Posh, making over 300 appearances during the eight years he was at London Road.

Ernie Corfield (Born Wigan, 18 January 1931. Died Wigan, 26 October 2013.) Ernie Corfield was an inside forward who spent five years on the books of Bolton Wanderers from April 1948. Principally a reserve, he made just six first-team appearances then spent a season with Stockport County where he was again a second choice before switching to the non-league game with Wigan Athletic and Skelmersdale United.

Jack Crompton (Born Hulme, Manchester, 13 December 1921. Died 4 July 2013.) Goalkeeper Jack Crompton featured in wartime football for Manchester City and Stockport County before joining Manchester United in January 1945. He made over 200 appearances for United, gaining an FA Cup winners' medal in 1948 and after a brief spell as trainer at Luton he returned to Old Trafford in a similar capacity after the Munich air disaster. He was subsequently manager of Barrow from December 1971 to June 1972 and also had spells on the backroom staff at Bury and Preston North End.

Stan Crowther (Born Bilston, Staffs, 3 September 1935. Died Wolverhampton, 28 May 2014.) Stan Crowther was a wing half who was given his senior debut by Aston Villa in September 1956 and became a regular in the team playing in the club's 1957 FA Cup winning team. In the aftermath of the Munich air disaster he signed for Manchester United and although cup-tied was given permission to appear for the Reds and went on make a second successive Cup final appearance. Stan, who won three England U23 caps, later played for Chelsea and Brighton & Hove Albion.

Laurie Cunningham (Born Consett, Co Durham, 20 April 1921. Died Bournemouth, 3 October 2013.) Laurie Cunningham signed for Barnsley in November 1945 and featured regularly at right back in the first two post-war seasons before moving to Bournemouth. He enjoyed nine seasons with the Cherries, making close on 300 first-team appearances before switching to non-league football with Dorchester Town.

Andy Davidson (Born Douglas Water, Lanarkshire, 13 July 1932. Died Beverley, 6 April 2014.) Andy Davidson was a right back who joined Hull City as a teenager and went on to make a record number of appearances for the Tigers during a 16-year playing career. He made 520 Football League appearances during his time at the club and was a key figure in 1965–66 when the team won the old Division Three title and reached the quarter-finals of the FA Cup. After retiring from playing he spent a further 16 years as a member of the club's backroom staff until departing from the post of assistant manager in 1979.

Joe Davin (Born Dumbarton, 13 February 1942. Died Dumbarton, 30 September 2013.) Joe Davin was a full back who joined Hibernian from Drumchapel Amateurs after winning representative honours for Scotland Schools and Youths. He made 28 first-team appearances before signing for Ipswich Town in the summer of 1963. A fairly regular performer in his three seasons at Portman Road he later returned to Scotland where he appeared for both Morton and Dumbarton.

Ron Dellow (Born Seaforth, Lancashire, 13 July 1914. Died Almelo, Netherlands, 7 November 2013.) Ron Dellow came to prominence as a pacy outside right with Mansfield Town in the 1934–35 season and was sold to Manchester City within a matter of months of arriving at Field Mill. He later played for Tranmere Rovers (where he was a member of the team that won the Division Three North title in 1937–38) and Carlisle United. He subsequently built a career as a coach in the Netherlands, assisting a number of clubs including Volendam, Heracles Almelo and Helmond Sport.

Jackie Denver (Born Lurgan, Co Armagh, September 1926. Died Lurgan, Co Armagh, 21 July 2013.) Jackie Denver was an inside forward with the great Belfast Celtic team of the late 1940s. After the club withdrew from football in 1948 he joined Glenavon and assisted them to become the first non-Belfast team to win the Irish League in 1951–52. He won 9 caps for the Irish League representative side.

Charlie Dickson (Born Edinburgh, 7 July 1934. Died Whitburn, West Lothian, 18 October 2013.) Charlie Dickson signed for Dunfermline Athletic in January 1955 and went on to become one of the club's greatest-ever players, scoring two on his debut and creating a club record by registering 213 goals from 343 competitive games. His tally included six against St Mirren in Decmber 1951 and the Pars' decisive second goal in the replayed Scottish Cup final of 1961. He finished his career with Queen of the South.

Tommy Dixon (Born Newcastle upon Tyne, 8 June 1929. Died 2014.) Tommy Dixon was a tall forward who was strong in the air and scored regularly throughout his career. He started out at West Ham United and went on to top the Hammers' scoring chart in 1953–54, his first full season in the senior team. He moved on to Reading and later had spells at Brighton & Hove Albion, Workington and Barrow.

Henry Dodkins (Born Epping, 20 December 1929. Died 18 January 2014.) Henry Dodkins was a left half who made 26 appearances for the England Amateur team after making his debut in 1950, captaining the side on a number of occasions. He also represented Great Britain in the 1956 Olympic Games in Melbourne and was a member of the FA squad which toured Nigeria and Ghana in 1958. He played his club football for Ilford and was a member of the team which was beaten by Woking in the 1958 FA Amateur Cup final at Wembley.

Ernie Doig (Died 18 October 2013.) Ernie Doig was a wing half who played for Falkirk before signing for Kilmarnock in August 1949. He made 53 Scottish League appearances for Killie before winding up his career with brief spells at Dundee United and Leith Athletic.

Don Donovan (Born Cork, Irish Free State, 23 December 1929. Died Grimsby, 26 September 2013.) Don Donovan joined Everton in May 1949 and after waiting three years for his debut went on to play 187 first-team games for the Toffees. He signed for Grimsby Town in the 1958 close season and became a key figure for the Mariners over the next six seasons, mostly featuring at right back. He helped the club win promotion to the Second Division in 1961–61 and made 253 appearances before becoming player-manager of Boston United. He won five caps for the Republic of Ireland.

Neil Duffy (Died 17 June 2013.) Neil Duffy was an attacking player who made his name with East Stirlingshire before joining Partick Thistle in September 1960. In a four-year spell with the Jags he scored 62 times in 172 appearances before switching to St Johnstone. He eventually moved to South Africa where he played for Addington, Maritzburg and Shamrocks.

Peter Ellson (Born Audlem, Staffs, 21 August 1925. Died April 2014.) Peter Ellson was a goalkeeper who signed for Crewe Alexandra in May 1949 and went on to spend seven seasons at Gresty Road, making 234 first-team appearances for the club. He moved on to join Cheshire League club Runcorn in the summer of 1956. He was honoured in recent years by the naming of a street after him in a housing development close to the Gresty Road ground.

Eusebio da Silva Ferreira Born Maputo, Mozambique, 25 January 1942. Died 5 January 2014.) Eusebio was a key figure in the Portugal team which reached the last four of the 1966 World Cup and was leading scorer in the tournament with nine goals. He was an attacking player with power and pace as well as a ferocious shot and was widely regarded as one of the greatest footballers of the 20th century. He scored 41 goals for his country in just 64 appearances between 1961 and 1973. Eusebio was a star of the Benfica team which won the 1962 European Cup and three years later was named European Footballer of the Year. He also won the Golden Boot as the leading scorer in Europe on two occasions and played for the Rest of the World against England in 1963. He later played in the USA, Canada and Mexico.

Terry Farmer (Born Maltby, South Yorkshire, 11 May 1931. Died Rotherham, 9 May 2014.) Terry Farmer was an old fashioned centre forward who joined Rotherham United from Midland League club Gainsborough

Trinity in July 1952. He scored 24 goals in 61 Football League appearances for the Millers before joining York City in January 1958, going on to hit a further 28 League goals during his time with the Minstermen.

Ron Fenton (Born South Shields, 21 September 1940. Died Beeston, Nottingham, 25 September 2013.) Ron Fenton joined the groundstaff at Burnley on leaving school, but never managed to establish himself in the Clarets' first team. He did better at West Bromwich Albion where he scored 16 goals from 59 appearances and went on to play for Birmingham City and Brentford. On retiring as a player he joined the backroom staff at Notts County, where he was promoted to manager (September 1975 to October 1977) then worked with Brian Clough at Nottingham Forest for 16 years, latterly as assistant-manager.

Mickey Fields (Born Chester, 12 August 1935. Died Chester, 27 May 2014.) Mickey Fields was a forward who spent five seasons with his home town club of Chester after signing from local league football in 1955. He made over 20 senior appearances for the Blues before a knee injury ended his Football League career. He later played for Borough United.

Sir Tom Finney, OBE, CBE (Born Preston, 5 April 1922. Died 14 February 2014.) Sir Tom Finney was one of the all-time great internationals who was described as the most complete English footballer of any era. He won 76 caps for England and scored 30 goals for his country which was a then record, and also made 17 appearances for the Football League representative team. Sir Tom began as an inside left but switched to outside right although he played in all five forward positions during his career. He signed his first professional contract with Preston North End in January 1940 and spent 20 years at the club making a total of 433 Football League appearances and scoring 187 goals. He won a Second Division championship medal with the Lilywhites in 1951 and appeared for them in the 1954 FA Cup final when they lost to West Bromwich Albion. Sir Tom was named Footballer of the Year in 1954 and again in 1957 before retiring in the summer of 1960. He returned to his plumbing business but maintained close links with Preston and became club president.

Peter Fitzgerald (Born Waterford, 17 June 1937. Died Waterford, 29 June 2013.) Peter Fitzgerald was an attacking player who could play all across the forward-line positions when required. He began his senior career with Waterford then spent time in Belgium with Sparta Rotterdam before joining Leeds United in August 1960. However, he made little impact at Elland Road and quickly moved on to Chester where he had two seasons of regular football. In November 1963 he returned to Waterford and was a member of the team that won the League of Ireland title in 1965–66. He was capped on five occasions by the Republic of Ireland.

John Flanagan (Born Glasgow, 26 April 1942. Died 30 September 2013.) John Flanagan began his career as a winger with Albion Rovers in the early 1960s, earning a reputation as a regular goalscorer before a transfer to St Johnstone in the summer of 1963. He was less successful during his stay in Perth but at Partick, by now a deep-lying inside forward, he managed over 150 senior appearances before concluding his career with Clyde.

Bill Foulkes (Born Prescot, Lancs, 5 January 1932. Died 25 November 2013.) Centre half Bill Foulkes joined Manchester United as an 18-year-old and stayed with the club for the next 20 years. A regular in the line-up for most of that time, he amassed a total of 688 appearances for the club during which time he was a member of four Football League title-winning sides, won the FA Cup in 1963, and, most famously, the European Cup at Wembley in May 1968. A survivor of the Munich air disaster, Bill was one of two players who went on to gain a winners' medal a decade later. He won a single cap for England, appearing against Northern Ireland in October 1954.

Hughie Gallacher (Born circa 1931. Died Clydebank, 14 June 2013.) Hughie Gallacher joined Arbroath from Duntocher Hibs in December 1951 and made over 60 appearances during his stay, but he is best known for his time with Dumbarton between 1954 and 1960 and again in 1961–62. He scored a club record 205 goals from 231 appearances during the two spells and also spent time with Clyde and Queen of the South.

Eddie Garrett (Born Nethermill, Dumfriesshire, 15 February 1939. Died Rhyl, 25 February 2014.) Eddie Garrett was a hard-working forward who spent five years with Queen of the South helping the club back into top-flight football in 1962. He left the following year and joined Carlisle United before later signing for Rhyl.

Alec Gaskell (Born Leigh, Lancs, 30 July 1932. Died 8 March 2014.) Alec Gaskell was a centre forward who started out as a youngster with Manchester United before joining Southport in September 1951. His form at Haig Avenue earned him a move to Newcastle United in October 1953 but he found it difficult to break into the first team and signed for Mansfield Town at the end of the season. He later played for Tranmere Rovers.

Walter Gerrard (Born Glasgow, 1 November 1943. Died Hong Kong, 30 March 2014.) Walter Gerrard was a tall and powerful forward who scored twice on his senior debut for East Stirlingshire Clydebank in April 1965. He later appeared for East Stirlingshire, Berwick Rangers and Clydebank before becoming one of the first European professionals to play in Hong Kong after emigrating in 1970.

Brian Gibbs (Born Gillingham, Dorset, 6 October 1936. Died 27 January 2014.) Brian Gibbs was an inside left who began his career at Bournemouth before joining Gillingham in October 1962. He was leading scorer for five seasons in a row with the Gills and became the first player to score 100 Football League goals for the club. He moved to Colchester United in September 1968 and was a member of the U's team which knocked Leeds United out of the FA Cup in 1971. In total during his career he scored 154 goals in 473 Football League appearances.

Malcolm Glazer (Born Rochester, New York, USA, 1928. Died 28 May 2014.) Malcolm Glazer was a wealthy Florida-based businessman who purchased Manchester United in 2005. The club won five Premier League titles as well as the 2008 Champions League during his time as owner. He was involved in sport in the USA and owned the Tampa Bay Buccaneers NFL team from 1995.

Verdi Godwin (Born Blackburn, 11 February 1926. Died Southport, 1 December 2013.) Verdi Godwin was a powerful centre forward who played League football for nine clubs in the decade after the war ended. He moved clubs on a regular basis and his most productive spell was at Mansfield Town where he managed 31

appearances scoring 9 goals. He started out with Blackburn Rovers and his travels also took him to Manchester City, Stoke City, Grimsby Town, Brentford, Southport, Barrow and Tranmere Rovers.

Andy Graver (Born Craghead, Co Durham, 12 September 1927. Died 18 January 2014.) Andy Graver was a centre forward who was Lincoln City's all-time leading goalscorer having netted 150 goals during three spells with the club. He made his Football League debut for Newcastle United in January 1950 but was unable to break into the Magpies' first team on a regular basis and later the same year joined Lincoln. In his first full season for the Imps, in 1951–52, he was leading scorer in Division Three North with 36 goals. He was transferred to Leicester City in 1954 but soon afterwards returned to Lincoln and later spent time with Stoke City before ending his career back with Lincoln.

Jimmy Greenhalgh (Born Manchester, 27 August 1923. Died Darlington, 31 August 2013.) Jimmy Greenhalgh was a wing half who made almost 300 Football League appearances for Hull City, Bury and Gillingham in the period immediately after the war. He later had a spell as manager of Darlington (July 1966 to February 1968) and also spent time on the backroom staff of a number of clubs including Newcastle United and Middlesbrough.

Gylmar (Born Santos, Sao Paulo, Brazil, 22 August 1930. Died Sao Paulo, Brazil, 25 August 2013.) Gylmar was a goalkeeper who has the distinction of being a member of successive World Cup winning teams for Brazil in 1958 and 1962. In total he won 94 caps for his country between 1953 and 1969. At club level he spent a decade with Corinthians before switching to Santos, with whom he won two Copa Libertadores titles.

Harry Haddon (Born Cardiff, 8 April 1923. Died 10 August 2013.) Forward Harry Haddon joined Newport County from Cheshire League side Bangor City in February 1947 and went on to make 10 appearances during his time at Somerton Park. He later spent a short spell with Bristol Rovers before moving into non-league football with Trowbridge Town.

Johnny Hamilton (Born Larkhall, Lanarkshire, 22 January 1935. Died 8 August 2013.) Johnny Hamilton was a traditional-style winger with great pace and fine dribbling skills. He was on the books of Hearts between 1955 and 1967, featuring in three Scottish League Cup winning sides and making almost 400 senior appearances. He won representative honours for the Scottish League and Scotland U23s before concluding his career with spells at Watford and Berwick Rangers.

Barry Hancock (Born Hanley, Stoke-on-Trent, 30 December 1938. Died Sneyd Green, Stoke-on-Trent, 10 September 2013.) Barry Hancock was an inside forward who signed professional forms for Port Vale at the age of 19 and went on to make 22 first-team appearances. He subsequently had a brief spell with Crewe Alexandra before dropping into non-league football with Stafford Rangers.

Gordon Harris (Born Worksop, 2 June 1940. Died Langold, Notts, 10 February 2014.) Gordon Harris began his career with Burnley and appeared for the Clarets in the 1962 FA Cup final. He won an England cap four years later and was included in the initial 40-man squad for the 1966 World Cup but missed out when the final 22 were selected. He later signed for Sunderland, making over 100 Football League appearances for the Black Cats before retiring. He also made appearances for England U23s and for the Football League representative team.

Wayne Harrison (Born Stockport, 15 November 1967. Died Stockport, 25 December 2013.) Wayne Harrison was a centre forward who was something of a teenage prodigy when after just a handful of games for Oldham Athletic he joined Liverpool for a £250,000 fee in January 1985. However, he suffered a catalogue of injuries over the next few years and his only further appearances came in loan spells back at Boundary Park and with Crewe Alexandra before he was forced to leave the game.

Tony Hateley (Born Derby, 13 June 1941. Died 1 February 2014.) Tony Hateley was a centre forward who scored 211 goals in 434 Football League appearances in a career which lasted 16 seasons. He started out at Notts County where he developed into a prolific goalscorer and earned a move to Aston Villa in August 1963. He was later at Chelsea, appearing for the Blues in the 1967 FA Cup final, and then had spells at Liverpool, Coventry City and Birmingham City before returning to Notts County in November 1970. He helped the Magpies to the Fourth Division title in his first season back before finishing with Oldham Athletic.

Dave Hickson (Born Salford, 30 October 1929. Died 8 July 2013.) Dave Hickson was a bustling centre forward who is one of a select group of players to have appeared professionally for all three Merseyside clubs. He made his name as a brave and enthusiastic goalscorer for Everton, for whom he scored 95 League goals from 225 appearances in two spells. He also appeared for Aston Villa and Huddersfield Town before joining local rivals Liverpool in November 1959. He scored at a rate of a goal every other game for the Reds before ending his senior career with spells at Bury and Tranmere Rovers.

Eddie Holding (Born Wolverhampton, 15 October 1930. Died 9 February 2014.) Eddie Holding was a versatile player who signed professional forms for Walsall in January 1949. He made a number of appearances at right back for the Saddlers and then had a short spell at Derby County before returning to Walsall where he was used as a centre forward. He signed for Barrow in the summer of 1954, scoring in his first three appearances including a hat-trick on his debut, but shortly afterwards quit the full-time game to concentrate on his business interests.

Alan Hole (Born Swansea, 26 December 1930. Died Llanrhidian, Swansea, 15 April 2014.) Alan Hole was a centre half who signed for Swansea Town in July 1953 after completing his National Service. He made regular appearances in the first half of the 1953–54 campaign but then lost his place in the team and left the club at the end of the season. He later played for Kettering Town, Llanelli and Pembroke.

Ollie Hopkins (Born South Kirkby, Yorkshire, 15 November 1935. Died Chelmsford, 14 April 2014.) Ollie Hopkins was a centre half who began his career with Barnsley. He was mainly a reserve during his time with the Reds and moved on to join Peterborough United in the summer of 1961. He made over 100 first-team appearances during four seasons with Posh before joining Chelmsford City. He served the Essex club as both player and manager and at the time of his death was club president.

Harry Hughes (Born Nuneaton, 8 October 1929. Died 15 October 2013.) Harry Hughes was a powerful centre half who was given an introduction to senior football by Chelsea before joining Bournemouth, where he captained the team that defeated Wolves and Tottenham to reach the FA Cup quarter-finals in 1956–57. He later spent five seasons as a regular for Gillingham, making more than 200 appearances.

Dennis Jackson (Born Birmingham, 8 March 1932. Died March 2014.) Dennis Jackson was a full back who joined Aston Villa from local non-league club Hednesford Town in October 1954. He made eight first-team appearances for the Villa before joining Millwall and had two seasons as a regular for the Lions before returning to the Midlands to sign for Rugby Town.

Trevor Jacobs (Born Bristol, 28 November 1946. Died 18 January 2014.) Trevor Jacobs was a right back who began his career as an apprentice with Bristol City before signing professional forms in July 1965. He made over 100 first-team appearances for the club and was a member of the team which reached the Football League Cup semi-final in 1970–71. He left Ashton Gate in 1973 and crossed the city to join local rivals Bristol Rovers where he played for a further three seasons before retiring from the full-time game.

Sandy Jardine (Born Edinburgh, 31 December 1948. Died 24 April 2014.) Sandy Jardine was a defender who won 38 caps for Scotland, appearing in both the 1974 and 1978 World Cup finals and captaining the team on a number of occasions. He made his senior debut for Rangers as an 18-year-old in February 1967 and during a lengthy career with the Light Blues he completed over 650 first-team appearances. He amassed a string of honours including the European Cup Winners' Cup and was part of three Scottish League championship winning teams, captaining the club when they won the title in 1974–75, before finishing his career with six years at Hearts. He was Scottish Footballer of the Year in both 1974–75 and 1985–86, being the first player to win the award on two occasions. During his career he was mainly used at right back but also appeared as a sweeper and in midfield.

Barrie Jones (Born Barnsley, 31 October 1938. Died Sutton-in-Ashfield, Notts, 23 November 2013.) Barrie Jones was a versatile forward who spent three seasons on the books of Notts County in the early 1960s, making 50 first-team appearances before moving on to King's Lynn. In March 1962, playing only his second senior game, he scored after just six seconds at home to Torquay, one of the quickest goals in Football League history.

Dave Jones (Born Kingsley, Cheshire, 9 April 1940. Died 12 December 2013.) Forward Dave Jones won England Youth international honours and made his senior debut for Crewe Alexandra as a 16-year-old. After an injury-affected spell at Birmingham City he joined Millwall in December 1959. He was a member of the Lions' team that won the Fourth Division title in 1961–62 and scored 71 goals in 165 Football League appearances during his time at The Den.

Jimmy Jones (Born Keady, Co Armagh, 25 July 1928. Died Belfast, 13 February 2014.) Jimmy Jones was a centre forward who held the Irish League record of 332 goals during his career. He made his name with Belfast Celtic but was seriously injured after being attacked by home supporters during the club's 1948 Boxing Day derby clash at Linfield. On his return he briefly played in England before signing for Glenavon in 1951. He helped the club to three Irish League titles and was leading scorer for 10 consecutive seasons including an Irish League record of 74 goals in 1956–57. He later played for Portadown, Bangor and Newry Town. He won three caps for Northern Ireland and also appeared for the Irish League representative team.

Billy Kennedy (Born Portadown, Co Armagh, 26 May 1934. Died 23 March 2014.) Billy Kennedy was a forward who earned a Northern Ireland Amateur international cap while at Portadown before turning professional with Linfield. He won an Irish League championship medal with the Blues in 1954–55 when he was leading scorer before giving up football for religious reasons at the age of 22.

Frank Kopel (Born Falkirk, 28 March 1949. Died Kirriemuir, Angus, 16 April 2014.) Frank Kopel was a defender who made his senior debut for Manchester United as a 17-year-old and later had a spell with Blackburn Rovers before returning to his native Scotland in January 1972 when he joined Dundee United. He spent 10 years with the Arabs making over 350 first-team appearances and playing in two Scottish League Cup winning teams. He finished his career as player-coach at Arbroath.

Charlie Lemons (Born Sheffield, 1927. Died Netherthorpe, Sheffield, 18 November 2013.) Charlie Lemons was a winger who signed for Sheffield United during the war. His solitary first-team appearance came against Doncaster Rovers at Bramall Lane in February 1945.

Jim Lewis (Died Belfast, 28 September 2013.) Jim Lewis was a versatile defender who starred with Glentoran in the 1950s, featuring in the team defeated by Derry City in a second replay of the Irish Cup final in 1954. He won representative honours for Northern Ireland Amateurs and the Irish League.

John Linaker (Born Southport, 14 January 1927. Died Shipton-by-Beningbrough, York, 14 June 2013.) John Linaker was a much travelled winger who featured as a teenager for Everton and Manchester City during the war. Best known for his two spells with York City during the 1950s, he also appeared in League football for Southport, Nottingham Forest, Hull City and Crewe.

Tom Logan (Born Edinburgh, 19 September 1942. Died Edinburgh, 26 January 2014.) Tom Logan overcame polio as a child to become a professional with Hearts. He failed to break into the first team during his time at Tynecastle but went on to make 19 Scottish League appearances as a wing half for Berwick Rangers after moving on in the summer of 1967. His career was ended by injury and he later qualified as a physio working in Falkirk and Hearts. He represented Scotland at U18 level.

Billy Luke (Born Aberdeen, 19 April 1932. Died Aberdeen, 5 February 2014.) Billy Luke was an inside forward who made a handful of appearances for East Fife before moving south in October 1955 to join Crewe Alexandra. He played a single first-team game for the Alex and later played in the Southern League for Cheltenham Town and Barry Town.

John Lumsden (Born Heanor, Derbys, 1 July 1942. Died Derby, 19 February 2014.) John Lumsden was a defender who was with Aston Villa as a youngster but was unable to break into the first team and signed for Workington in February 1962. He captained the Reds' team, making almost 300 senior appearances before joining Chesterfield in March 1968. He had another three years with the Spireites before retiring from the full-time game.

Colin McAdam (Born Glasgow, 28 August 1951. Died Glasgow, 1 August 2013.) Colin McAdam was a versatile player who featured both at centre back and as a striker in a career that saw him play close on 300 Scottish League games. A big, powerful player who was effective in the air, he made his name as a defender with Dumbarton and Motherwell before joining Partick Thistle, where he was mostly used in a forward role. In the summer of 1980 he signed for Rangers, winning a Scottish League Cup winners' medal in 1983–84. He left Ibrox shortly afterwards, winding down his career with spells at Adelaide City, Hearts and, for a second time, Partick.

Albert McCann (Born Maidenhead, 1 November 1941. Died Havant, Hants, 9 January 2014.) Albert McCann was a skilful player who had spells with Luton Town and Coventry City before signing for Portsmouth in August 1962. He spent 12 years at Fratton Park scoring 98 goals in 379 senior appearances and was leading scorer for three consecutive seasons from 1965–66. He finished his career playing in South Africa.

Jimmy McColl (Born Glasgow, November 1924. Died Edinburgh, 8 August 2013.) Jimmy McColl was a full back who made 119 senior appearances in the period immediately after the war. Initially an amateur with Queen's Park, he featured for the Great Britain team at the 1948 Olympic Games. Soon afterwards he turned professional with Queen of the South and also played for Falkirk and Cowdenbeath before an ankle injury brought his career to an end.

Tommy McConville (Born Dundalk, Republic of Ireland, 19 March 1946. Died Dundalk, Republic of Ireland, 25 October 2013.) Tommy McConville was a full back best known for his three spells with Dundalk where his career spanned the period from 1964–65 to 1985–86. He made 385 League of Ireland appearances for the club and was a member of three title-winning sides. He also had spells with Waterford and Shamrock Rovers before becoming player-manager of Finn Harps. He won six full caps for the Republic of Ireland.

David MacFarlane (Born Irvine, Ayrshire, 16 January 1967. Died Kilmarnock, 30 October 2013.) David MacFarlane was a skilful midfield player who signed for Rangers straight from school, but made little impact at first-team level at Ibrox, although he won a Scottish League Cup winners' medal in 1986–87. He later had spells with Kilmarnock and Partick Thistle and also spent time in Australia before joining Glenafton Athletic, with whom he played in three consecutive Scottish Junior Cup finals.

Davie Mackie (Died Larbert, Stirlingshire, 1 November 2013.) Davie Mackie was a wing half who joined St Johnstone from Kirkintilloch Rob Roy in the summer of 1952, but he was mostly a reserve in two seasons at Muirton Park. He moved on to Stenhousemuir where he made close on 100 appearances in a three-year stay.

Andy Malcolm (Born West Ham, London, 4 May 1933. Died Port Elizabeth, South Africa, 26 December 2013.) Andy Malcolm was a hard-tackling defensive midfield player who developed with West Ham United, winning England Youth international honours. He went on to play 306 first-team games, and was an ever-present in the Division Two title winning side of 1957–58 when he also became the first recipient of the Hammer of the Year award. He went on to play for Chelsea and Queens Park Rangers before switching to play in South Africa. Andy also appeared for the Football League representative side.

Fred Martin (Born Carnoustie, 13 May 1929. Died Methven, Perthshire, 20 August 2013.) Fred Martin joined Aberdeen from Carnoustie Panmure in October 1946 as an inside forward but by the time he had worked his way into the first team he had become a goalkeeper. He was the Dons' regular 'keeper for most of the 1950s, making close on 300 appearances and was a member of the team that won the Scottish League in 1954–55 and the League Cup the following season. He won six caps for Scotland and featured in the 1954 World Cup finals.

Johnny Martin (Born Ashington, Co Durham, 4 December 1946. Died Tenerife, Spain, 16 November 2013.) Johnny Martin was a flamboyant outside left who played for Aston Villa and Colchester United before signing for Workington in July 1969. He was a fans' favourite during his five seasons with the Reds, scoring 33 goals in 226 League and Cup games and being voted the club's Player of the Year for three consecutive seasons. He later appeared for Southport.

Norrie Martin (Born Ladybank, Fife, 7 May 1939. Died Prestwick, Ayrshire, 11 October 2013.) Goalkeeper Norrie Martin spent 12 seasons on the books of Rangers from 1958, but injuries restricted him to just 110 first-team games and he never actually gained a winners' prize during his stay, although he was a member of the team that lost in extra time to Bayern Munich in the 1966–67 European Cup Winners' Cup final. Thereafter he had brief associations with East Fife, Partick, Queen of the South and Hamilton before leaving the senior game.

Cliff Mason (Born York, 27 November 1929. Died Dore, Sheffield, 22 August 2013.) Cliff Mason began his career as a left back with Darlington before joining Sheffield United in August 1955. An intelligent defender with good anticipation, he spent the best part of seven seasons at Bramall Lane, serving the Blades as captain for a while and helping them win promotion from Division Two in 1960–61. He went on to have spells with Leeds United, Scunthorpe United and Chesterfield before retiring from senior football.

Ray Mielczarek (Born Caernarvon, 10 February 1946. Died 30 October 2013.) Ray Mielczarek was a defender who joined Wrexham from Caernarvon Town as a 16-year-old. He went on to make 76 Football League appearances for the Robins before being sold to Huddersfield Town. His time at Leeds Road was affected by injuries but after moving on to Rotherham he added a further 125 games and was honoured with his only full cap for Wales against Finland in May 1971.

Peter Millar (Born 21 April 1951. Died June 2013.) Peter Millar was a tough-tackling midfield player who is best known for his time with Motherwell between 1972 and 1979 when he made a total of 238 senior

appearances and won representative honours for the Scottish League. Peter had begun his career with Arbroath and later played for Dunfermline Athletic before arriving at Fir Park. After leaving he had spells with Dundee and in the USA with Phoenix Inferno and Cleveland Force before retiring from the game.

Ernie Morgan (Born Barnsley, 13 January 1927. Died Rainham, Kent, 3 October 2013.) Centre forward Ernie Morgan spent four seasons on the books of Lincoln City from September 1949, but managed just a handful of first-team appearances. He moved on to Gillingham for the 1953–54 season and made an immediate impact, scoring 21 goals in his first season and 31 the following campaign, a new club record which remains unbeaten. In total he netted 73 times from 155 outings before injury brought his career to an end. He later managed a number of Kent non-league clubs.

Jackie Morley (Born Cork, Irish Free State, 1934. Died Cork, Republic of Ireland, 25 November 2013.) Centre half Jackie Morley was signed by West Ham United from Evergreen United in September 1955 and spent three seasons with the Hammers without making a senior appearance. He returned to Ireland where he firstly played with Cork Hibs and then, from 1967 to 1972, Waterford. During his time at Waterford the club won four out of five League of Ireland titles in what was a golden period in their history. Jackie won representative honours for the League of Ireland.

Elfed Morris (Born Colwyn Bay, 9 June 1942. Died 4 November 2013.) Elfed Morris was a tall winger who developed with Colwyn Bay, signing for Wrexham in May 1960. Two years later he moved on to Chester where his career took off in the 1964–65 season when he netted 26 goals including a hat-trick against Aldershot. In March 1968 he moved on for a brief spell at Halifax before taking on the post of player-manager at Caernarvon Town.

Tommy Newlands (Born circa 1911. Died 4 December 2013.) Tommy Newlands spent the first three post-war seasons with Berwick Rangers, who were then members of the East of Scotland League. At the time of his death he was the club's oldest living player, having reached the age of 102.

Ron Noades (Born 22 June 1937. Died Purley, Surrey, 24 December 2013.) Ron Noades was chairman of Wimbledon when they were elected to the Football League in 1977 and after moving on in 1981 he spent 17 years as chairman of Crystal Palace, guiding the Eagles to a place in the FA Cup final in 1990 and third place in the Football League the following season. He followed this with a five-year spell at Brentford, where he was also manager for the period 1998 to 2000. In his first season he took the Bees to the Division Three title, earning himself the divisional Manager of the Year award.

Dezso Novak (Born Jak, Hungary, 3 February 1939. Died 26 February 2014.) Dezso Novak was a midfield player who won Gold medals for Hungary at the 1964 and 1968 Olympic Games as well as a Bronze medal in the 1960 Games. He also appeared for Hungary in the 1964 European Championship. He played his club football for Ferencvaros for whom he scored 69 goals in 333 appearances.

Gordon Nutt (Born South Yardley, Birmingham, 8 November 1932. Died Hobart, Tasmania, 25 February 2014.) Gordon Nutt was a winger who made 82 first-team appearances for Coventry City after signing professional forms in November 1949. He moved on to Cardiff City and also saw service with Arsenal and Southend United. Later he played in the Netherlands for PSV Eindhoven before finishing his playing career in Australia. He was included in the FA team which toured the West Indies in 1955.

Parys Okai (Born Luton, 23 November 1984. Died Leicester, 30 October 2013.) A product of the Luton Town youth set-up, Parys Okai became a scholar with the club during which time he made four first-team appearances with his only start coming in an LDV Vans Trophy game in October 2003. He later moved into non-league football with Dunstable Town and a string of clubs, as well as spending time playing in Australia.

Joe O'Mahony (Born Limerick, Republic of Ireland, 8 April 1948. Died Limerick, Republic of Ireland, 7 January 2014.) Joe O'Mahoney was a centre back who made over 400 appearances for Limerick during a 20-year career with the club. He captained the team when they won the League of Ireland championship in 1980 and was also in two FAI Cup winning teams. He appeared for Ireland at youth level and also played for the League of Ireland representative team.

Bryan Orritt (Born Caernarvon, 22 February 1937. Died Johannesburg, South Africa, 24 March 2014.) Bryan Orritt was an inside forward who made over 100 appearances for Birmingham City, playing in both the 1960 and 1961 Inter Cities Fairs Cup finals. He moved on to sign for Middlesbrough where he spent a further four years and was the first substitute to be used by Boro in the Football League. He was capped three times by Wales at U23 level.

Calvin Palmer (Born Skegness, 21 October 1940. Died Brighton, 12 March 2014.) Calvin Palmer was a tough-tackling wing half who established himself at Nottingham Forest before earning a move to Stoke City in September 1963. He played over 150 games for the Potters and appeared in the 1964 Football League Cup final before moving on to Sunderland. He later had a spell in South Africa and although he returned briefly to play for Crewe Alexandra he finished his playing career back in South Africa.

Derek Panter (Born Blackpool, 22 November 1943. Died Worsley, Greater Manchester, 13 August 2013.) Centre forward Derek Panter made his debut for Manchester City in the first leg of the League Cup semi-final at Stoke City in January 1964 but managed just one other first-team appearance before moving on to Torquay at the end of the season. Here too he made little impact, scoring one from six starts and after an unproductive spell at Southport he moved into non-league with Ashton United.

Pat Parker (Born Bow, Devon, 15 July 1929. Died 28 January 2014.) Pat Parker was a defender who spent eight seasons at Southampton after signing in August 1951. He made 132 Football League appearances for the Saints and represented the Division Three South team against their northern counterparts in 1956–57. He left the club in the summer of 1959 and signed for Poole Town.

Andy Paton (Born Dreghorn, Ayrshire, 7 January 1923. Died Markinch, Fife, 8 February 2014.) Andy Paton was a centre half who was Scotland's oldest surviving internationalist at the time of his death. He joined Motherwell in 1942 and spent 16 years at the club, making over 500 senior appearances appearing in the 1950–51 Scottish League Cup winning team and in the side which won the Scottish Cup the following year. He finished his playing career at Hamilton Academical and then had a nine-year spell as manager of the Accies. He made three appearances for Scotland.

Trevor Peck (Born Llanelli, 25 May 1938. Died Kettering, 19 May 2014.) Trevor Peck was a defender who spent seven years with Cardiff City after signing from Llanelli in February 1958. He made 42 Football League appearances for the Bluebirds before leaving the club in 1965 to sign for Worcester City. He later played for Kettering Town.

Johnny Phillips (Born Portsmouth, 4 March 1937. Died 4 January 2014.) Johnny Phillips was a right half who made 81 appearances for Portsmouth during a five-year spell at Fratton Park. He moved on in the summer of 1960 to join Worcester City and later played for Salisbury.

Jimmy Pithie (Born Edinburgh, 20 January 1928. Died Edinburgh, 18 January 2014.) Jimmy Pithie was a centre half who signed professional for Hearts in April 1946. He made his senior debut as an 18-year-old and made five appearances for the club before his career was ended in the autumn of 1947 when he contracted tuberculosis.

Ken Plant (Born Nuneaton, 15 August 1925. Died Nuneaton, 22 March 2014.) Ken Plant was a forward who scored over 50 goals in a four-year spell at Bury before joining Colchester United in January 1954. He was leading scorer on three occasions during his time with the U's and netted a total of 84 goals in 197 appearances before returning to his home town to rejoin his first club Nuneaton Borough.

Ray Pointon (Born Birkenhead, 6 November 1947. Died Bebington, Merseyside, 1 July 2013.) Ray Pointon was a versatile defender who spent four seasons on the books of Tranmere Rovers after signing as a professional at the age of 18. Although mostly a reserve, he managed to make over 50 first-team appearances during his time at Prenton Park.

Johnny Poppitt (Born West Sleekburn, Northumberland, 20 January 1923. Died 12 February 2014.) Johnny Poppitt was a full back but made his Football League debut for Derby County in February 1947 as an emergency centre forward. He made 16 senior games for the Rams before joining Queens Park Rangers in 1950 where he made over 100 appearances before moving on to Chelmsford City.

Baden Powell (Born Hebburn, Northumberland, 17 June 1931. Died Sunderland, 25 January 2014.) Baden Powell was a pacy winger who joined Darlington in October 1950. He made his debut the following month on the right flank but struggled to win a regular place in the Quakers' line-up and moved on to sign for South Shields in the summer of 1954.

Charlie Purves (Born High Spen, Co Durham, 17 February 1921. Died 20 June 2013.) Charlie Purves was on the books of Newcastle United as a youngster but was unable to break into the first team. In October 1946 he joined Charlton Athletic from Spennymoor United. A creative inside forward he made 46 appearances for the Addicks and a further 30 for Southampton before moving on to Sittingbourne. At the time of his death he was Saints' oldest living player.

Vince Radcliffe (Born Manchester, 9 June 1945. Died Perth, Australia, 11 March 2014.) Vince Radcliffe was a centre half who was mainly a reserve during his time at his first club Portsmouth. He had the misfortune to suffer a broken leg which kept him out of action for 16 months and later appeared for Peterborough United and Rochdale. He concluded his playing career in Australia and then switched to coaching.

Kenny Rea (Born Liverpool, 17 February 1935. Died Liverpool, 10 April 2014.) Kenny Rea was a wing half who signed for Everton as a 16-year-old and spent eight seasons at Goodison Park. After making his first-team debut in September 1956 he went on to make a total of 51 League and Cup appearances for the Toffees before moving on to join Runcorn in the summer of 1959.

Ian Redford (Born Perth, 5 April 1960. Died Irvine, Ayrshire, 10 January 2014.) Ian Redford was a talented midfield player who started his career at Dundee before being sold at the age of 19 to Rangers in February 1980 for a then record transfer fee for a Scottish player. He made over 200 senior appearances for Rangers, gaining two Scottish League Cup winners' medals before joining Dundee United in August 1985. Later in his career he played for Ipswich Town and St Johnstone before becoming player-manager at Brechin City. He finished his career with Raith Rovers where he appeared as a substitute in their 1994–95 Scottish League Cup winning team.

Lawrie Reilly (Born Edinburgh, 26 October 1928. Died Edinburgh, 22 July 2013.) Centre forward Lawrie Reilly was one of the all-time greats for Hibernian, with whom he played from 1945 to 1958. The last surviving member of the 'Famous Five' forward line, he won Scottish League titles with Hibs in 1950–51 and 1951–52 and was top scorer seven seasons in a row. His final total of 234 competitive goals remains a record for the Easter Road club, as does his 38 caps for Scotland. He scored 22 goals for his country, the fourth highest in history, including, uniquely, in four consecutive visits to Wembley.

Geoff Richards (Born Bilston, Staffs, 24 April 1929. Died Wolverhampton, 8 May 2014.) Geoff Richards was a winger who made his Football League debut for West Bromwich Albion as a 17-year-old, marking the occasion with a goal. He made just two further Football League appearances for the club and later played for Stafford Rangers, Atherstone Town and Bilston Town before becoming player-manager of Hednesford Town.

Stan Rickaby (Born Stockton, 12 March 1924. Died Perth, Australia, 11 February 2014.) Stan Rickaby was a right back who made his senior debut for Middlesbrough in March 1948 and two years later was sold to West Bromwich Albion. He missed out on the 1954 FA Cup final through injury but was awarded a medal after

playing in all of Albion's earlier games in the competition. He won his only England cap against Northern Ireland in 1953 and also appeared for the Football League representative team.

Arthur Rowley (Born Fazakerley, Lancs, 9 May 1933. Died 12 February 2014.) Arthur Rowley was an inside left who began his career at Liverpool in May 1951. He struggled to win a regular place in the starting line-up and in November signed for Wrexham where he made 56 appearances in two seasons. He later spent time at Crewe Alexandra and Tranmere Rovers.

Harold Rudman (Born Whitworth, Lancs, 4 November 1924. Died 4 October 2013.) Harold Rudman joined Burnley as a wing half during the war, making 76 appearances in the emergency competitions. However, when peace returned he was mostly a reserve and it was not until the mid-1950s that he gained a regular place in the side, this time at right back. In July 1957 he moved on to Rochdale where he played for another season before leaving senior football.

Alex Russell (Born Kells, Co Antrim, 18 January 1923. Died 24 February 2014.) Alex Russell was a goalkeeper who made over 600 first-team appearances for Linfield during 15 years with the club after signing from Cliftonville in 1945. He won five Irish League titles while at Windsor Park and earned a single cap for Northern Ireland against England in 1946. He also appeared for the Irish League representative team.

John Ryden (Born Alexandria, Dunbartonshire, 18 February 1931. Died Keston, Kent, 16 August 2013.) Centre half John Ryden came to prominence with Alloa Athletic in the early 1950s before moving south to join the Scottish contingent at Accrington Stanley. His performances at Peel Park earned him a move to Tottenham Hotspur in November 1955. He went on to make 63 League appearances for Spurs then had a season with Watford before moving into non-league with Romford.

Djalma Santos (Born Sao Paolo, Brazil, 27 February 1929. Died Uberaba, Brazil, 23 July 2013.) Djalma Santos was one of the greatest full backs in post-war football. He won 98 caps for Brazil between 1952 and 1968 and appeared in four World Cup final tournaments, gaining winners' medals in 1958 and 1962. In 1963 he appeared for the Rest of the World against England to celebrate the FA centenary. His club football was principally played with Portuguesa and Palmeiras.

Nilton Santos (Born Governador Island, Rio de Janeiro, Brazil, 16 May 1925. Died Botafogo, Rio de Janeiro, Brazil, 27 November 2013.) Nilton Santos played at left back in the great Brazil team of the 1950s and early '60s, winning 75 caps and featuring in three World Cup final tournaments, twice (1958 and 1962) as a member of the winning team. For much of his international career he partnered his namesake Djalma Santos. Nilton spent his entire career with the Botafogo club, for whom he made over 700 appearances.

Phil Scott (Born Belfast, 24 May 1942. Died Belfast, 1 May 2014) Phil Scott was a forward who was a member of the Distillery team which won the Irish League in 1962–63 before rejoining his former club Linfield. He gained a further Irish League winners' medal with the Blues and in total made over 300 first team appearances for the club, scoring 148 goals. He was Linfield's joint all-time scorer in European competitions and represented the Irish League as well as being capped by Northern Ireland at amateur international level.

Bob Sharpe (Born Kirkcaldy, 20 December 1925. Died 21 February 2014.) Bob Sharpe was a full back who made a single appearance for Raith Rovers before crossing the border to sign for Darlington in the summer of 1952. He went on to add a further 14 appearances for the Quakers in Division Three North.

Jack Shiel (Born Seahouses, Northumberland, 13 May 1917. Died Ashington, Northumberland, 30 November 2013.) Centre forward Jack Shiel joined Newcastle United in December 1936, making his solitary first-team appearance at Barnsley in September 1937. He was then briefly attached to North Shields before joining Huddersfield Town, but here too he managed to make just a single appearance in the 1938–39 campaign before leaving senior football. At the time of his death he was Newcastle's oldest living player.

Keith Skillen (Born Cockermouth, Cumberland, 26 May 1948. Died Cockermouth, Cumbria, 1 August 2013.) Pacy forward Keith Skillen signed for Workington in December 1973 after scoring regularly with Northern Premier League club Netherfield. After scoring on his debut he went on to make 64 Football League appearances before joining Hartlepool United. He subsequently returned to Workington for another season after the club dropped out of the League.

Brian Smith (Born Bolton, 12 September 1955. Died August 2013.) Brian Smith was a versatile midfielder who came up through the ranks with Bolton Wanderers, winning England Youth international honours and graduating to a professional contract in September 1973. He made a total of 58 first-team appearances during his time at Burnden Park then had an injury-affected spell at Blackpool before concluding his career with spells at Bournemouth and Bury.

Geoff Smith (Born Cottingley, West Yorkshire, 14 March 1928. Died Keighley, West Yorkshire, 19 October 2013.) Goalkeeper Geoff Smith played in the Lancashire Combination for Nelson and Rossendale before joining Bradford City. He went on to establish a run of 200 consecutive Football League appearances for the Bantams between April 1954 and October 1958, retiring at the end of the 1958–59 season.

George Smith (Born Fleetwood, 7 February 1921. Died Bury, Greater Manchester, 14 July 2013.) George Smith joined Manchester City shortly before the outbreak of war and played a number of games in the emergency competitions that followed, also seeing active service during which he was wounded. On his return to Maine Road he scored 75 goals from 166 Football League appearances including all five against Newport County in June 1947 as City won the Division Two title in 1946–47. He was allowed to leave for Chesterfield in October 1951 and continued to be a regular scorer at Saltergate, adding a further 98 League goals. He represented Division Three North against Division Three South in 1955.

Gordon Smith (Born Glasgow, 3 July 1954. Died Glasgow, 5 April 2014.) Gordon Smith was a full back who began his career at St Johnstone where he established himself in the first team and was capped by Scotland at

U17 and U23 levels. He moved south in August 1976 signing for Aston Villa and afterwards had spells with both Tottenham Hotspur and Wolverhampton Wanderers. He later appeared in the US Indoor League for Phoenix Pride and Pittsburgh Spirit before retiring from playing.

John Smith (Born Plymouth, 12 November 1927. Died Paignton, Devon, 11 December 2013.) John Smith was a full back who joined Plymouth Argyle from local club Plymouth United in the 1950 close season. In four seasons at Home Park he was mostly a reserve but after moving on to Torquay United he experienced regular first-team football, making over 150 appearances and contributing to the club's 1959–60 promotion campaign.

Fred Stansfield (Born Cardiff, 12 December 1917. Died Cardiff, 30 March 2014.) Fred Stansfield was a stalwart centre half for Cardiff City who spent six years with the club after signing in August 1943. He captained the team to the 1946–47 Division Three South title and made over 100 appearances before finishing his career at Newport County. He won a single cap for Wales in 1948 and at the time of his death was his country's oldest surviving international.

Barry Stobart (Born Doncaster, 6 June 1938. Died 28 August 2013.) Barry Stobart was an inside forward who developed with the Wolves' nursery club Wath Wanderers before graduating to professional status in December 1955. After just four senior games he was selected to face Blackburn Rovers in the 1960 FA Cup final and returned with a winners' medal. However, he never really established himself in the line-up at Molineux. He subsequently moved on to play for Manchester City, Aston Villa and Shrewsbury Town before spending time in South Africa with Durban Spurs.

Albert Stokes (Born Darnall, Sheffield, 26 January 1933. Died Grimsby, 1 May 2014.) Albert Stokes was a bustling centre forward who signed for Grimsby Town in February 1954. He made his Football League debut later the same year but was mainly a reserve during his time with the Mariners. He later had spells with Scunthorpe United and Southport before joining Chelmsford City in 1959.

Bill Sweeney (Died 28 September 2013.) Bill Sweeney was a wing half who joined Queen of the South from Irvine Meadow in April 1952. He was mostly second-choice to Dougie McBain at Palmerston, making 40 first-team appearances during a five-year stay before moving on to Morton and then Stranraer.

Sammy Taylor (Born Gorbals, Glasgow, 23 September 1933. Died Preston, 6 November 2013.) Sammy Taylor was a pacy winger with an eye for goal who developed with Dunipace Juveniles and then Falkirk before moving south to sign for Preston North End in the summer of 1955. After settling in at Deepdale he became a regular on the left flank from where he was a regular scorer, netting 41 goals from 149 League games. In 1961 he moved on to Carlisle United, where he was a member of two promotion teams before rounding off his career with spells at Southport and Morecambe.

Jimmy Thomson (Born Edinburgh, February 1933. Died Edinburgh, 4 June 2013.) Jimmy 'Tiger' Thomson was a wing half on the books of Hibernian throughout the 1950s, making 69 competitive appearances. Although mostly a reserve he featured regularly during the 1955–56 season and was in the line-up for the historic European Cup tie away to Rot Weiss Essen in September 1955, the first occasion a British club played in the competition. He concluded his career with brief spells at Ayr United and Cowdenbeath.

Dylan Tombides (Born Perth, Australia, 8 March 1994. Died London, 18 April 2014.) Dylan Tombides was a young striker who joined West Ham United as full-time scholar in the summer of 2010 and was named Academy Player of the Year in his first season with the club. He signed a professional contract in August 2011 and after appearing in the reserves he was given his first-team debut as a substitute in a Football League Cup tie the following year. He represented Australia at U16 and U17 levels. His death came after a three-year battle with testicular cancer.

John Tomlinson (Born Bebington, Cheshire, 26 June 1934. Died Corby, Northants, 4 February 2014.) John Tomlinson was a winger who spent five seasons as a professional with Everton after signing in the summer of 1962. He made a couple of first-team appearances and later played for Chesterfield before moving on in the summer of 1959 to join Corby Town. He represented England at youth international level.

Mike Tracey (Born Blackburn, Lancs, 14 February 1935. Died 30 May 2014.) Mike Tracey was a forward who earned three England Amateur international caps. He gained an FA Amateur Cup winners' medal with Crook Town in 1959, scoring twice in the Wembley final against Barnet. He later turned professional, playing for Luton Town and Lincoln City.

Bert Trautmann, OBE (Born Bremen, Germany, 22 October 1923. Died Almenara Playara, Castellon, Spain, 19 July 2013.) Bert Trautmann came to England as a prisoner of war and after excelling in goal for St Helens Town he signed for Manchester City in November 1949. He faced hostility early in his professional career but won over fans with some brave goalkeeping displays, most memorably in the 1956 FA Cup final when he helped City defeat Newcastle 3-1 despite suffering a broken neck. In total he made 545 appearances for the Maine Road club and had a spell as manager of Stockport County (1965–66). He was Footballer of the Year in 1956 and was capped by the Football League against the Irish League in October 1960.

Rolando Ugolini (Born Lucca, Italy, 4 June 1924. Died Edinburgh, 10 April 2014.) Rolando Ugolini was a flamboyant goalkeeper who gained his first senior experience after signing for Celtic before joining Middlesbrough in May 1948. He spent eight seasons with Boro, making 335 League and Cup appearances and later had spells at Wrexham and Dundee United before finishing his career with a brief spell at Berwick Rangers.

Dave Wagstaffe (Born Manchester, 5 April 1943. Died Wolverhampton, 6 August 2013.) Dave Wagstaffe was a talented winger who developed through the Manchester City youth set-up, making his first-team debut as a 17-year-old. He made over 150 appearances during his stay at Maine Road, moving on to Wolverhampton Wanderers in December 1964, Dave became a key figure at Molineux over the next decade, playing more than 400 games. He was an ever-present in the 1966–67 promotion team and also gained a Texaco Cup winners'

medal in 1970–71 as well as appearing in a UEFA Cup final (1972) and the Football League Cup final of 1974. He concluded his career with spells at Blackburn (where he became the first English player to receive a red card) and Blackpool. He was also capped for the Football League representative side.

Nigel Walker (Born Gateshead, 7 April 1959. Died Newcastle upon Tyne, 2 February 2014.) Nigel Walker was a skilful midfield player who made his debut for Newcastle United in November 1977. He made 70 Football League appearances for the Magpies before moving on in 1982 to play for San Diego Sockers in the NASL. He later had spells with Crewe Alexandra, Sunderland, Chester and Hartlepool United.

Ottmar Walter (Born Kaiserslautern, Germany, 6 March 1924. Died Kaiserslautern, Germany, 16 June 2013.) Ottmar Walter was a centre forward who, playing alongside his brother Fritz, was a member of the West Germany team that won the 1954 World Cup in Switzerland. Ottmar, who scored 10 goals in his 21 international appearances, played most of his club football with 1.FC Kaiserslautern for whom he scored more than 300 goals in a career which ended in 1956.

Roy Warhurst (Born Sheffield, 18 September 1926. Died 7 January 2014.) Roy Warhurst began his career as an outside left with Sheffield United but later switched to become a hard-tackling wing half. He left Bramall Lane in March 1950 to join Birmingham City and went on to make over 200 League appearances for the Blues and was a key figure in their team which won the Division Two title in 1954–55. He later appeared for Manchester City, Crewe Alexandra and Oldham Athletic.

Peter Watson (Born Stapleford, Notts, 15 April 1934. Died Brighton, 17 August 2013.) Peter Watson was a centre half who was on Nottingham Forest's books for most of the 1950s, although he was generally a reserve during his stay. In the summer of 1959 he joined Southend United and he went on to make over 250 appearances for the Shrimpers before retiring through injury in 1966.

David White (Born Motherwell, 23 August 1933. Died Wishaw, Lanarkshire, 17 July 2013.) David White joined Clyde from Junior club Royal Albert in November 1957 and went on to make close on 300 first-team appearances before being appointed as manager in March 1966. He took the club to a best-ever Scottish League placing of third in 1966–67 which earned him a move to Ibrox as assistant to Scot Symon. In November 1967 he took over as manager but during his stay the team did not win any major trophies and two years later he was replaced. His final managerial post was with Dundee, where he won the Scottish League Cup in 1973–74.

Bert Williams, MBE (Born Bradley, Staffs, 31 January 1920. Died Wolverhampton, 19 January 2014.) Bert Williams was one of the great England goalkeepers who earned 24 full caps for his country between 1949 and 1955. He appeared in the 1950 World Cup finals and was a member of the England team which infamously lost 1-0 to the USA in Belo Horizonte. Bert made his first senior appearance as a 16-year-old for Walsall in October 1937 and later featured in four wartime internationals. In September 1945 he moved from Walsall to Wolverhampton Wanderers for a then record fee for a goalkeeper of £3,500. He made 420 appearances for Wolves, winning a League championship medal in 1953–54 and an FA Cup winners' medal in 1949. Bert retired in 1957 and in later years devoted his time to raising money for the Alzheimer's Society. He was appointed an MBE in 2010 for services to football and charity. At the time of his death he was the oldest England internationalist.

Stuart Williams (Born Wrexham, 9 July 1930. Died Southampton, 5 November 2013.) Stuart Williams was a full back who started out with Wrexham in the period immediately after the war before being sold to West Bromwich Albion in November 1950. A first-team regular from around 1955, he made almost 250 appearances for the Baggies, then moved on to Southampton where he added a further 150 outings and made a solid contribution to the team that won promotion to the top flight in 1965–66. He later moved into coaching. Stuart won 43 caps for Wales and was a member of the squad for the 1958 World Cup finals.

Roger Wood (Born circa 1942. Died 1 July 2013.) Roger Wood was a representative on the Birmingham County FA for more than 50 years and its chairman for 22 years. He also served as a member of the FA Council for several years.

Phil Woosnam (Born Caersws, Montgomeryshire, 22 December 1932. Died Marietta, Georgia, USA, 19 July 2013.) A skilful inside forward noted for his passing ability, Phil Woosnam spent the early years of his career as an amateur, receiving his League debut with Manchester City and becoming a regular with Leyton Orient before turning professional in January 1957. He made over 100 appearances for each of the O's, West Ham United and Aston Villa before joining Atlanta Chiefs as player-coach in January 1966. He was to stay in the United States for the remainder of his life, playing a significant role in the development of the game in that country and serving as commissioner of the North American Soccer League from 1969 to 1983. He was capped for Wales at schoolboy, youth, amateur and full international levels.

Colin Worrell (Born Great Yarmouth, 29 August 1943. Died 15 December 2013.) Full back Colin Worrell developed with Norwich City but although he broke into the first team in November 1962 he never established himself at Carrow Road and in September 1964 he moved to Leyton Orient. He had two seasons of fairly regular first-team football with the O's, making over 50 appearances but soon after joining Charlton Athletic in the summer of 1966 he was forced to retire due to a kidney problem.

John Wylie (Born Newcastle upon Tyne, 25 September 1936. Died Doncaster, 18 September 2013.) John Wylie was a wing half who began his senior career at Huddersfield, although he had to wait until he joined Preston North End before being featured in senior football. He went on to make over 300 appearances in a career that also included time with Stockport County and Doncaster Rovers. He was an ever-present in the Rovers team that won the Fourth Division title in 1965–66.

Ian Nannestad www.soccer-history.co.uk

THE FOOTBALL RECORDS

BRITISH FOOTBALL RECORDS

ALL-TIME PREMIER LEAGUE CHAMPIONSHIP SEASONS ON POINTS AVERAGE

	Team	Season	P	W	D	L	F	A	Pts	Pts Av
1	Chelsea	2004–05	38	29	8	1	72	15	95	2.50
2	Manchester U	1999–2000	38	28	7	3	97	45	91	2.39
3	Chelsea	2005–06	38	29	4	5	72	22	91	2.39
4	Arsenal	2003–04	38	26	12	0	73	26	90	2.36
	Manchester U	2008–09	38	28	6	4	68	24	90	2.36
6	Manchester C	2011–12	38	28	5	5	93	29	89	2.34
	Manchester U	2006–07	38	28	5	5	83	27	89	2.34
	Manchester U	2012–13	38	28	5	5	86	43	89	2.34
9	Arsenal	2001–02	38	26	9	3	79	36	87	2.28
	Manchester U	2007–08	38	27	6	5	80	22	87	2.28
11	Chelsea	2009–10	38	27	5	6	103	32	86	2.26
	Manchester C	2013–14	38	27	5	6	102	37	86	2.26
13	Manchester U	1993–94	42	27	11	4	80	38	92	2.19
14	Manchester U	2002–03	38	25	8	5	74	34	83	2.18
15	Manchester U	1995–96	38	25	7	6	73	35	82	2.15
16	Blackburn R	1994–95	42	27	8	7	80	39	89	2.11
17	Manchester U	2000–01	38	24	8	6	79	31	80	2.10
	Manchester U	2010–11	38	23	11	4	78	37	80	2.10
19	Manchester U	1998–99	38	22	13	3	80	37	79	2.07
20	Arsenal	1997–98	38	23	9	6	68	33	78	2.05
21	Manchester U	1992–93	42	24	12	6	67	31	84	2.00
22	Manchester U	1996–97	38	21	12	5	76	44	75	1.97

PREMIER LEAGUE EVER-PRESENT CLUBS

	P	W	D	L	F	A	Pts
Manchester U	848	547	175	126	1691	747	1816
Arsenal	848	460	221	167	1485	796	1601
Chelsea	848	448	215	185	1428	809	1559
Liverpool	848	422	213	213	1408	846	1479
Tottenham H	848	336	219	293	1193	1117	1227
Everton	848	309	242	297	1090	1058	1169
Aston Villa	848	303	259	286	1059	1053	1168

TOP TEN PREMIERSHIP APPEARANCES

1	Giggs, Ryan	632	6	Heskey, Emile	516
2	Lampard, Frank	577	7=	Carragher, Jamie	508
3	James, David	572	7=	Schwarzer, Mark	508
4	Speed, Gary	534	9	Neville, Phil	505
5	Barry, Gareth	529	10	Campbell, Sol	503

TOP TEN PREMIERSHIP GOALSCORERS

1	Shearer, Alan	260	6	Fowler, Robbie	163
2	Cole, Andy	187	7	Owen, Michael	150
3	Henry, Thierry	175	8	Ferdinand, Les	149
4	Rooney, Wayne	173	9	Sheringham, Teddy	146
5	Lampard, Frank	171	10	van Persie, Robin	134

SCOTTISH PREMIER LEAGUE SINCE 1998–99

	P	W	D	L	F	A	Pts
Celtic	604	443	88	73	1406	478	1417
Rangers	528	364	93	71	1123	418	1175
Hearts	604	239	147	218	778	735	849
Motherwell	604	217	136	251	772	899	787
Aberdeen	604	210	151	245	704	823	775
Kilmarnock	604	200	151	253	730	877	751
Dundee U	604	189	172	243	739	895	739
Hibernian	568	191	145	232	743	812	718

DOMESTIC LANDMARKS

August 2013
17   Daniel Sturridge scores the first Premier League goal of the season in the 37th minute of his side's 1-0 opener at Anfield against Stoke C.

September 2013
1   Gareth Bale signs for Real Madrid from Tottenham H in world record €100m (£83.4m) deal.
10   Frank Lampard makes his 100th appearance for England in the World Cup Qualifier in Ukraine. The match ended 0-0 with Frank inches wide with a late headed attempt.
17   Wayne Rooney scores his 200th goal for Manchester U in the 4-2 victory over Bayern Leverkusen in the Champions League at Old Trafford. He joins Sir Bobby Charlton (249), Denis Law (237) and Jack Rowley (211) as the only United players to reach 200 goals for the club.
18   Arsenal's 2-1 victory over Marseille in the Champions League means the Gunners have broken the club record by winning 10 successive away games.
23   Leyton Orient win their 8th consecutive league game in the 2-0 victory at Brentford, reinforcing the club's best ever start to a league season.

October 2013
15   England qualify for the World Cup Finals in Brazil with a 2-0 victory over Poland at Wembley. Wayne Rooney scores in the first half and a late Steven Gerrard strike settles England's nerves as they deservedly go through.
19   Liverpool captain Steven Gerrard scores his 100th Premier League goal from the penalty spot in the 2-2 draw with Newcastle U at St James' Park.

November 2013
7   Jermaine Defoe scores his 23rd European goal for Tottenham H to break Martin Chivers' record as Spurs' most prolific European marksman as Tottenham qualify for knockout stages of Europa League with a 2-1 home win over Sheriff Tiraspol.
10   Jonathan Walters makes his 100th successive Premier League appearance in Stoke's 3-3 draw at Swansea. He celebrated by scoring the opening goal in the 8th minute.

December 2013
4   Luis Suarez becomes first player to score three hat-tricks against the same opposition in Premier League history with his 4-goal haul over Norwich in the 5-1 victory at Anfield.
21   Luis Suarez scores twice for Liverpool in their 3-1 home victory over Cardiff C taking his total for December to 10, a new Premier League record by a player in a single calendar month.
20   John Terry makes his 600th appearance for Chelsea in the 2-1 victory over Liverpool at Stamford Bridge. Only Ron Harris (795), Peter Bonetti (729) and Frank Lampard (633) have made more appearances for the Blues.

January 2014
1   Luis Suarez scores his 20th Premier League goal of the season after only 15 games in Liverpool's 2-0 defeat of Hull C at Anfield, a record for the fewest number of games to achieve this feat.
11   Petr Cech keeps his 209th clean sheet for Chelsea surpassing Peter Bonnetti's record.
18   Edin Dzeko scores Manchester C's 100th goal of the season in all competitions during the 4-2 win over Cardiff C at the Etihad.
19   Wojciech Szczesny makes his 100th Premier League appearance for Arsenal in the 2-0 victory over Fulham at the Emirates.
24   Sixteen-year-old Gedion Zelalem makes Arsenal history by becoming the first player born after Arsene Wenger was appointed manager to play for the Gunners. He makes his debut as a substitute in the 4-0 defeat of Coventry C in the 4th round of the FA Cup at the Emirates.
28   Leicester C make it a club record of 8 successive league wins with a 2-1 victory over Birmingham C at St Andrew's.

February 2014
1   Craig Bellamy becomes the first player to score for seven different Premier League clubs in Cardiff C's 3-1 home victory over Norwich C.
22   Celtic goalkeeper Fraser Forster claimed a 13th consecutive clean sheet in the Scottish Premiership 2-0 win over Hearts at Tynecastle. Forster who has not conceded in 1,215 minutes of league football breaks Aberdeen's Bobby Clarke's 43-year-old record.
25   Celtic lose for the first time in the Scottish Premiership this season in a 2-1 defeat at the hands of Aberdeen at Pittodrie.

March 2014
18   Petr Cech makes his 100th Champions League appearance in Chelsea's 3-0 victory (3-1 on aggregate) over Galatasaray in the Round of 16 at Stamford Bridge. He becomes the 19th player to reach 100 appearances.
19   Ryan Giggs makes his 150th Champions League appearance as Manchester U overturn a 2-0 first leg deficit to beat Olympiacos 3-0 at Old Trafford. Robin van Persie scores his first Champions League hat-trick.
22   Arsene Wenger took charge of his 1,000th game for Arsenal against Chelsea at Stamford Bridge. Unfortunately for him his side are thrashed 6-0. Referee André Marriner sent off the wrong player in the first half, mistakingly dismissing Kieran Gibbs for handball after Alex Oxlade-Chamberlain had committed the offence.
26   Daniel Sturridge of Liverpool scores his 20th League goal of the season in Liverpool's 2-1 home victory over Sunderland. This is the first season that two Liverpool players (Luis Suarez reached the landmark earlier) have scored 20 in the same season since 1963–64.
29   Scunthorpe U manager Russ Wilcox breaks a 125-year record when his team draw 0-0 with Wycombe W to make it 24 games unbeaten from the start of his managerial reign. He surpasses the 23-match run of Preston NE's William Sudell in 1888–89.

April 2014
15   Thousands attend the 25th anniversary memorial service for the 96 victims of the Hillsborough disaster at Anfield.

May 2014
3   Ashley Westwood of Aston Villa scores the opening goal for Aston Villa against Hull C. It was the 1,000th Premier League goal scored at Villa Park.
7   Manchester C's Yaya Toure scores the club's 100th league goal of the season in a comprehensive 4-0 victory over Aston Villa at the Etihad.
11   Daniel Agger scores Liverpool's 100th league goal of the term in the season finale 2-0 victory over Newcastle U at Anfield.

EUROPEAN CUP AND CHAMPIONS LEAGUE RECORDS

MOST WINS BY CLUB

Real Madrid	10	1956, 1957, 1958, 1959, 1960, 1966, 1998, 2000, 2002, 2014.
AC Milan	7	1963, 1969, 1989, 1990, 1994, 2003, 2007.
Bayern Munich	5	1974, 1975, 1976, 2001, 2013.
Liverpool	5	1977, 1978, 1981, 1984, 2005.

MOST APPEARANCES IN FINAL
Real Madrid 13; AC Milan 11, Bayern Munich 10

MOST FINAL APPEARANCES PER COUNTRY
Italy 26 (12 wins, 14 defeats)
Spain 24 (14 wins, 10 defeats)
England 19 (12 wins, 7 defeats)
Germany 17 (7 wins, 10 defeats)

MOST CHAMPIONS LEAGUE/EUROPEAN CUP APPEARANCES
151 Ryan Giggs (Manchester U)
147 Xavi (Barcelona)
144 Raul (Real Madrid, Schalke)
142 Iker Casillas (Real Madrid)
139 Paolo Maldini (AC Milan)
130 Clarence Seedorf (Ajax, Real Madrid, Internazionale, AC Milan)
130 Paul Scholes (Manchester U)
128 Roberto Carlos (Internazionale, Real Madrid, Fenerbahce)
120 Carles Puyol (Barcelona)
116 Andriy Shevchenko (Dynamo Kyiv, AC Milan, Chelsea)

MOST WINS WITH DIFFERENT CLUBS
Clarence Seedorf (Ajax) 1995; (Real Madrid) 1998; (AC Milan) 2003, 2007.

MOST WINNERS MEDALS
6 Francisco Gento (Real Madrid) 1956, 1957, 1958, 1959, 1960, 1966.
5 Alfredo Di Stefano (Real Madrid) 1956, 1957, 1958, 1959, 1960.
5 Jose Maria Zarraga (Real Madrid) 1956, 1957, 1958, 1959, 1960.
5 Paolo Maldini (AC Milan) 1989, 1990, 1994, 2003, 2007.
4 Jose-Hector Rial (Real Madrid) 1956, 1957, 1958, 1959.
4 Marquitos (Real Madrid) 1956, 1957, 1959, 1960.
4 Phil Neal (Liverpool) 1977, 1978, 1981, 1984.
4 Clarence Seedorf (Ajax) 1995; (Real Madrid) 1998; (AC Milan) 2003, 2007.

CHAMPIONS LEAGUE BIGGEST WINS
HJK Helsinki 10, Bangor C 0 19.7.2011
Liverpool 8 Besiktas 0 6.11.2007
Juventus 7, Olympiacos 0 10.12.2003
Bayern Munich 7, FC Basel 0 13.3.2012

MOST SUCCESSIVE CHAMPIONS LEAGUE APPEARANCES
Manchester U (England) 18: 1996–97 to 2013–14.

MOST SUCCESSIVE EUROPEAN CUP APPEARANCES
Real Madrid (Spain) 15: 1955–56 to 1969–70.

MOST SUCCESSIVE WINS IN THE CHAMPIONS LEAGUE
Barcelona (Spain) 11: 2002–03.

LONGEST UNBEATEN RUN IN THE CHAMPIONS LEAGUE
Manchester U (England) 25: 2007–08 to 2009 (Final).

MOST GOALS OVERALL
71 Raul (Real Madrid, Schalke).
68 Cristiano Ronaldo (Manchester U, Real Madrid).
67 Lionel Messi (Barcelona).
60 Ruud van Nistelrooy (PSV Eindhoven, Manchester U, Real Madrid).

58 Andriy Shevchenko (Dynamo Kyiv, AC Milan, Chelsea, Dynamo Kyiv).
51 Thierry Henry (Monaco, Arsenal, Barcelona).
50 Filippo Inzaghi (Juventus, AC Milan).
49 Alfredo Di Stefano (Real Madrid).
47 Eusebio (Benfica).
44 Alessandro Del Piero (Juventus).
42 Didier Drogba (Marseille, Chelsea).
40 Zlatan Ibrahimovic (Ajax, Juventus, Inter Milan, Barcelona, AC Milan, Paris Saint-Germain).
39 Fernando Morientes (Real Madrid, Monaco, Liverpool, Valencia).

MOST GOALS IN CHAMPIONS LEAGUE MATCH
5 Lionel Messi, Barcelona v Leverkusen (25, 42, 49, 58, 84 mins) (7-1), 7.3.2012.

MOST GOALS IN ONE SEASON
17 Cristiano Ronaldo 2013–14
14 Jose Altafini 1962–63
14 Ruud van Nistelrooy 2002–03
14 Lionel Messi 2011–12

MOST GOALS SCORED IN FINALS
7 Alfredo Di Stefano (Real Madrid), 1956 (1), 1957 (1 pen), 1958 (1), 1959 (1), 1960 (3).
7 Ferenc Puskas (Real Madrid), 1960 (4), 1962 (3).

HIGHEST SCORE IN A EUROPEAN CUP MATCH
Feyenoord (Netherlands) 12, KR Reykjavik (Iceland) 2 *(First Round First Leg 1969–70)*

HIGHEST AGGREGATE IN A EUROPEAN CUP MATCH
Benfica (Portugal) 18, Dudelange (Luxembourg) 0 8-0 (h), 10-0 (a) *(Preliminary Round 1965–66)*

FASTEST GOALS SCORED IN CHAMPIONS LEAGUE

10.2 sec	Roy Makaay for Bayern Munich v Real Madrid, 7 March 2007.
20.07 sec	Gilberto Silva for Arsenal at PSV Eindhoven, 25 September 2002.
20.12 sec	Alessandro Del Piero for Juventus at Manchester U, 1 October 1997.

YOUNGEST CHAMPIONS LEAGUE GOALSCORER
Peter Ofori-Quaye for Olympiacos v Rosenborg at 17 years 195 days in 1997–98.

FASTEST HAT-TRICK SCORED IN CHAMPIONS LEAGUE
Bafetimbi Gomis, 8 mins for Lyon in Dinamo Zagreb v Lyon (1-7) 7.12.2001

HIGHEST AGGREGATE OF GOALS
11: Monaco 8, Deportivo La Coruna 3 5.11.2003

FIRST TEAM TO SCORE SEVEN GOALS
Paris St Germain 7, Rosenborg 2 24.10.2000

MOST GOALS BY A GOALKEEPER
Hans-Jorg Butt (for three different clubs)
Hamburg 13.9.2000, Leverkusen 12.5.2002, Bayern Munich 8.12.2009 – all achieved against Juventus.

LANDMARK GOALS CHAMPIONS LEAGUE
1st Daniel Amokachi, Club Brugge v CSKA Moscow 17 minutes 25.11.1992
1,000th Dmitri Khokhlov, PSV Eindhoven v Benfica 41 minutes 9.12.1998
5,000th Luisao, Benfica v Hapoel Tel Aviv 21 minutes 14.9.2010

HIGHEST SCORING DRAW
Hamburg 4, Juventus 4 13.9.2000
Chelsea 4, Liverpool 4 14.4.2009

EUROPEAN CUP AND CHAMPIONS LEAGUE RECORDS – continued

MOST CLEAN SHEETS
10: Arsenal 2005–06 (995 minutes with two goalkeepers Manuel Almunia 347 minutes and Jens Lehmann 648 minutes).

CHAMPIONS LEAGUE ATTENDANCES AND GOALS FROM GROUP STAGES ONWARDS

Season	Attendances	Average	Goals	Games
1992–93	873,251	34,930	56	25
1993–94	1,202,289	44,529	71	27
1994–95	2,328,515	38,172	140	61
1995–96	1,874,316	30,726	159	61
1996–97	2,093,228	34,315	161	61
1997–98	2,868,271	33,744	239	85
1998–99	3,608,331	42,451	238	85
1999–2000	5,490,709	34,973	442	157
2000–01	5,773,486	36,774	449	157
2001–02	5,417,716	34,508	393	157
2002–03	6,461,112	41,154	431	157
2003–04	4,611,214	36,890	309	125
2004–05	4,946,820	39,575	331	125
2005–06	5,291,187	42,330	285	125
2006–07	5,591,463	44,732	309	125
2007–08	5,454,718	43,638	330	125
2008–09	5,003,754	40,030	329	125
2009–10	5,295,708	42,366	320	125
2010–11	5,474,654	43,797	355	125
2011–12	5,225,363	41,803	345	125
2012–13	5,773,366	46,187	368	125
2013–14	5,713,049	45,704	362	125

HIGHEST AVERAGE ATTENDANCE IN ONE EUROPEAN CUP SEASON
1959–60　50,545 from a total attendance of 2,780,000.

GREATEST COMEBACKS
Werder Bremen beat Anderlecht 5-3 after being three goals down in 33 minutes on 8.12.1993. They scored five goals in 23 second-half minutes.
Deportivo La Coruna beat Paris Saint-Germain 4-3 after being three goals down in 55 minutes on 7.3.2001. They scored four goals in 27 second-half minutes.
Liverpool after being three goals down to AC Milan in the first half on 25.5.2005 in the Champions League Final. They scored three goals in five second-half minutes and won the penalty shoot-out after extra time 3-2.
Liverpool three goals down to FC Basel in 29 minutes on 12.11.2002. They scored three second half goals in 24 minutes to draw 3-3.

MOST SUCCESSFUL MANAGER
Bob Paisley 3 wins, (Liverpool) 1977, 1978, 1981; Carlo Ancelotti 3 wins, (AC Milan) 2002–03, 2006–07, (Real Madrid 2013–14).

REINSTATED WINNERS EXCLUDED FROM NEXT COMPETITION
1993 Marseille originally stripped of title. This was rescinded but they were not allowed to compete the following season.

FOREIGN LANDMARKS 2013–14

September 2013
1　Gareth Bale signs for Real Madrid from Tottenham H in world record €100m (£83.4m) deal.
　Lionel Messi scores a hat-trick for Barcelona at Valencia to become the first player to score 100 away goals in La Liga.
10　Anders Svensson makes a record 144th appearance for Sweden in the World Cup Qualifier in Kazakhstan.
18　Lionel Messi becomes the first player in Champions League to score 4 hat tricks with his treble in Barcelona's 4-0 victory over Ajax.

October 2013
23　Zlatin Ibrahimovic becomes the tenth player to score 4 goals in a Champions League game in Paris Saint-Germain's 5-0 victory at Anderlecht.

November 2013
9　Bayern Munich break a 30-year Bundesliga record by going 37 games unbeaten with a comprehensive 3-0 victory at home to Augsburg.
27　Zlatin Ibrahimovic makes his 100th Champions League appearance in the Group C home match against Olympiacos. He scored a 7th minute opener in his side's 2-1 victory. He was the 18th player to reach the landmark.
28　AC Milan score their 600th goal in European football when Mario Balotelli scored in the 60th minute of the 3-0 Champions League victory at Celtic.

December 2013
10　Cristiano Ronaldo of Real Madrid becomes the first player to score 9 goals in the group stages of the Champions League win his second-half strike at Copenhagen in his side's 2-0 win.

January 2014
13　Cristiano Ronaldo wins the Ballon d'Or for the second time. Ronaldo scored an amazing 69 goals in 59 matches during 2013 and helped Portugal secure their place in the World Cup Finals in Brazil. Lionel Messi of Barcelona came second and Frank Ribery of Bayern Munich third.

February 2014
5　David Beckham announces his MLS franchise will be based in Miami.

March 2014
16　Lionel Messi breaks all-time Barcelona goalscoring record in the 7-0 rout of Osasuna in the Nou Camp. He overtook Paulinho Alcantara's record with his second goal of the game to register his 370th Barcelona goal.
25　Bayern Munich win the Bundesliga title for the 24th time with a record 7 games still to play. They defeated Hertha Berlin 3-1 to bring home the 3rd trophy of Pep Guardiola's reign to go with the UEFA Super Cup and FIFA Club World Cup.

May 2014
4　Juventus clinch Serie A title for the third successive season (30th in total) without even playing. A 4-1 defeat for Roma at Catania meant Juve's 8-point lead became insurmountable with only 2 games to play.
　Juventus set a new Serie A League record points total of 99, beating the previous record held by Inter Milan since 2007.

June 2014
6　Miroslav Klose set new German goalscoring record. Klose broke Gerd Müller's 40-year record of 68 goals with his 69th in a 6-1 defeat of Armenia.

TOP TEN PREMIER LEAGUE AVERAGE ATTENDANCES 2013–14

1	Manchester U	75,207
2	Arsenal	60,013
3	Newcastle U	50,395
4	Manchester C	47,080
5	Liverpool	44,671
6	Chelsea	41,482
7	Sunderland	41,090
8	Everton	37,732
9	Aston Villa	36,081
10	Tottenham H	35,808

TOP TEN FOOTBALL LEAGUE AVERAGE ATTENDANCES 2013–14

1	Brighton & HA	27,283
2	Leeds U	25,088
3	Leicester C	24,995
4	Derby Co	24,933
5	Nottingham F	22,630
6	Sheffield W	21,278
7	Wolverhampton W	20,879
8	Reading	19,167
9	Sheffield U	17,507
10	Ipswich T	17,111

TOP TEN AVERAGE ATTENDANCES

1	Manchester U	2006–07	75,826
2	Manchester U	2007–08	75,691
3	Manchester U	2012–13	75,530
4	Manchester U	2011–12	75,387
5	Manchester U	2008–09	75,308
6	Manchester U	2013-14	75,207
7	Manchester U	2010–11	75,109
8	Manchester U	2009–10	74,863
9	Manchester U	2005–06	68,765
10	Manchester U	2004–05	67,871

TOP TEN AVERAGE WORLD CUP FINAL CROWDS

1	In USA	1994	68,991
2	In Brazil	2014	52,621
3	In Germany	2006	52,491
4	In Mexico	1970	50,124
5	In South Africa	2010	49,669
6	In West Germany	1974	49,098
7	In England	1966	48,847
8	In Italy	1990	48,388
9	In Brazil	1950	47,511
10	In Mexico	1986	46,039

TOP TEN ALL-TIME ENGLAND CAPS

1	Peter Shilton	125
2	David Beckham	115
3	Bobby Moore	108
4	Steven Gerrard	114
5	Ashley Cole	107
6	Bobby Charlton	106
	Frank Lampard	106
8	Billy Wright	105
9	Wayne Rooney	95
10	Bryan Robson	90

TOP TEN ALL-TIME ENGLAND GOALSCORERS

1	Bobby Charlton	49
2	Gary Lineker	48
3	Jimmy Greaves	44
4	Michael Owen	40
	Wayne Rooney	40
	Tom Finney	30
6	Nat Lofthouse	30
	Alan Shearer	30
9	Vivian Woodward	29
	Frank Lampard	29

GOALKEEPING RECORDS
(without conceding a goal)

BRITISH RECORD (all competitive games)
Chris Woods (Rangers) in 1,196 minutes from 26 November 1986 to 31 January 1987.

FA PREMIER LEAGUE
Edwin van der Sar (Manchester U) in 1,311 minutes during the 2008–09 season.

FOOTBALL LEAGUE
Steve Death (Reading) 1,103 minutes from 24 March to 18 August 1979.

MOST CLEAN SHEETS IN A SEASON
Petr Cech (Chelsea) 24 2004–05

MOST CLEAN SHEETS OVERALL IN PREMIER LEAGUE
David James (Liverpool, Aston Villa, West Ham U, Manchester C, Portsmouth and Bristol C) 173 games.

MOST GOALS FOR IN A SEASON

FA PREMIER LEAGUE		Goals	Games
2009–10	Chelsea	103	38
FOOTBALL LEAGUE **Division 4**			
1960–61	Peterborough U	134	46
SCOTTISH PREMIER LEAGUE			
2003–04	Celtic	105	38
SCOTTISH LEAGUE **Division 2**			
1937–38	Raith R	142	34

MOST GOALS AGAINST IN A SEASON

FA PREMIER LEAGUE		Goals	Games
1993–94	Swindon T	100	42
FOOTBALL LEAGUE **Division 2**			
1898–99	Darwen	141	34
SCOTTISH PREMIER LEAGUE			
1999–2000	Aberdeen	83	36
SCOTTISH LEAGUE **Division 2**			
1931–32	Edinburgh C	146	38

MOST LEAGUE GOALS IN A SEASON

FA PREMIER LEAGUE		Goals	Games
1993–94	Andy Cole (Newcastle U)	34	40
1994–95	Alan Shearer (Blackburn R)	34	42
FOOTBALL LEAGUE **Division 1**			
1927–28	Dixie Dean (Everton)	60	39
Division 2			
1926–27	George Camsell (Middlesbrough)	59	37
Division 3(S)			
1936–37	Joe Payne (Luton T)	55	39
Division 3(N)			
1936–37	Ted Harston (Mansfield T)	55	41
Division 3			
1959–60	Derek Reeves (Southampton)	39	46
Division 4			
1960–61	Terry Bly (Peterborough U)	52	46
FA CUP			
1887–88	Jimmy Ross (Preston NE)	20	8
LEAGUE CUP			
1986–87	Clive Allen (Tottenham H)	12	9
SCOTTISH PREMIER LEAGUE			
2000–01	Henrik Larsson (Celtic)	35	37
SCOTTISH LEAGUE **Division 1**			
1931–32	William McFadyen (Motherwell)	52	34
Division 2			
1927–28	Jim Smith (Ayr U)	66	38

MOST FA CUP FINAL GOALS

Ian Rush (Liverpool) 5: 1986(2), 1989(2), 1992(1)

SCORED IN EVERY PREMIERSHIP GAME

Arsenal 2001–02: 38 matches

FEWEST GOALS FOR IN A SEASON

FA PREMIER LEAGUE		Goals	Games
2007–08	Derby Co	20	38
FOOTBALL LEAGUE **Division 2**			
1899–1900	Loughborough T	18	34
SCOTTISH PREMIER LEAGUE			
2010–11	St Johnstone	23	38
SCOTTISH LEAGUE **New Division 1**			
1980–81	Stirling Alb	18	39

FEWEST GOALS AGAINST IN A SEASON

FA PREMIER LEAGUE		Goals	Games
2004–05	Chelsea	15	38
FOOTBALL LEAGUE **Division 1**			
1978–79	Liverpool	16	42
SCOTTISH PREMIER LEAGUE			
2001–02	Celtic	18	38
SCOTTISH LEAGUE **Division 1**			
1913–14	Celtic	14	38

MOST LEAGUE GOALS IN A CAREER

FOOTBALL LEAGUE			
Arthur Rowley	Goals	Games	Season
WBA	4	24	1946–48
Fulham	27	56	1948–50
Leicester C	251	303	1950–58
Shrewsbury T	152	236	1958–65
	434	619	
SCOTTISH LEAGUE			
Jimmy McGrory			
Celtic	1	3	1922–23
Clydebank	13	30	1923–24
Celtic	396	375	1924–38
	410	408	

MOST HAT-TRICKS

Career
37: Dixie Dean (Tranmere R, Everton, Notts Co, England)

Division 1 (one season post-war)
6: Jimmy Greaves (Chelsea), 1960–61

Three for one team in one match
West, Spouncer, Hooper, Nottingham F v Leicester Fosse, Division 1, 21 April 1909
Loasby, Smith, Wells, Northampton T v Walsall, Division 3S, 5 Nov 1927
Bowater, Hoyland, Readman, Mansfield T v Rotherham U, Division 3N, 27 Dec 1932
Barnes, Ambler, Davies, Wrexham v Hartlepools U, Division 4, 3 March 1962
Adcock, Stewart, White, Manchester C v Huddersfield T, Division 2, 7 Nov 1987

MOST CUP GOALS IN A CAREER

FA CUP (pre-Second World War)
Henry Cursham   48   (Notts Co)

FA CUP (post-war)
Ian Rush   43   (Chester, Liverpool)

LEAGUE CUP
Geoff Hurst   49   (West Ham U, Stoke C)
Ian Rush   49   (Chester, Liverpool, Newcastle U)

GOALS PER GAME (Football League to 1991–92)

Goals per game	Division 1		Division 2		Division 3		Division 4		Division 3(S)		Division 3(N)	
	Games	Goals	Games	Goals	Games	Goals	Games	Goals	Games	Goals	Games	Goals
0	2465	0	2665	0	1446	0	1438	0	997	0	803	0
1	5606	5606	5836	5836	3225	3225	3106	3106	2073	2073	1914	1914
2	8275	16550	8609	17218	4569	9138	4441	8882	3314	6628	2939	5878
3	7731	23193	7842	23526	3784	11352	4041	12123	2996	8988	2922	8766
4	6229	24920	5897	23588	2837	11348	2784	11136	2445	9780	2410	9640
5	3752	18755	3634	18170	1566	7830	1506	7530	1554	7770	1599	7995
6	2137	12822	2007	12042	769	4614	786	4716	870	5220	930	5580
7	1092	7644	1001	7007	357	2499	336	2352	451	3157	461	3227
8	542	4336	376	3008	135	1080	143	1144	209	1672	221	1768
9	197	1773	164	1476	64	576	35	315	76	684	102	918
10	83	830	68	680	13	130	8	80	33	330	45	450
11	37	407	19	209	2	22	7	77	15	165	15	165
12	12	144	17	204	1	12	0	0	7	84	8	96
13	4	52	4	52	0	0	0	0	2	26	4	52
14	2	28	1	14	0	0	0	0	0	0	0	0
17	0	0	0	0	0	0	0	0	0	0	1	17
	38164	117061	38140	113030	18768	51826	18631	51461	15042	46577	14374	46466

New Overall Totals (since 1992)		Totals (up to 1991–92)		Complete Overall Totals (since 1888–89)	
Games	42732	Games	143119	Games	185851
Goals	110644	Goals	426421	Goals	537065

Extensive research by statisticians has unearthed seven results from the early years of the Football League which differ from the original scores. These are 26 January 1889 Wolverhampton W 5 Everton 0 (not 4-0), 16 March 1889 Notts Co 3 Derby Co 5 (not 2-5), 4 January 1896 Arsenal 5 Loughborough 0 (not 6-0), 28 November 1896 Leicester Fosse 4 Walsall 2 (not 4-1), 21 April 1900 Burslem Port Vale 2 Lincoln City 1 (not 2-0), 25 December 1902 Glossop NE 3 Stockport Co 0 (not 3-1), 26 April 1913 Hull C 2 Leicester C 0 (not 2-1).

GOALS PER GAME (from 1992–93)

Goals per game	Premier		Championship/Div 1		League One/Div 2		League Two/Div 3	
	Games	Goals	Games	Goals	Games	Goals	Games	Goals
0	738	0	994	0	945	0	974	0
1	1576	1576	2280	2280	2274	2274	2299	2299
2	2098	4196	3083	6166	3101	6202	3028	6056
3	1801	5403	2592	7776	2643	7929	2606	7818
4	1253	5012	1679	6716	1707	6828	1594	6376
5	628	3140	914	4570	888	4440	805	4025
6	308	1848	410	2460	369	2214	356	2136
7	128	896	137	959	151	1057	141	987
8	58	464	41	328	44	352	45	360
9	12	108	7	63	18	162	18	162
10	5	50	5	50	4	40	5	50
11	1	11	2	22	0	0	3	33
	8606	22704	12144	31390	12144	31498	11874	30302

A CENTURY OF LEAGUE AND CUP GOALS IN CONSECUTIVE SEASONS

		League	Cup	Season
George Camsell				
Middlesbrough		59	5	1926–27
(101 goals)		33	4	1927–28

(Camsell's cup goals were all scored in the FA Cup.)

	League	Cup	Season
Steve Bull			
Wolverhampton W	34	18	1987–88
(102 goals)	37	13	1988–89

(Bull had 12 in the Sherpa Van Trophy, 3 Littlewoods Cup, 3 FA Cup in 1987–88; 11 Sherpa Van Trophy, 2 Littlewoods Cup in 1988–89.)

PENALTIES

Most in a Season (individual)

Division 1	Goals	Season
Francis Lee (Manchester C)	13	1971–72

Most awarded in one game

Five   Crystal Palace (4 – 1 scored, 3 missed)
v Brighton & HA (1 scored), Div 2   1988–89

Most saved in a Season

Division 1
Paul Cooper (Ipswich T)   8 (of 10)   1979–80

MOST GOALS IN A GAME

FA PREMIER LEAGUE
4 Mar 1995	Andy Cole (Manchester U) 5 goals v Ipswich T
19 Sept 1999	Alan Shearer (Newcastle U) 5 goals v Sheffield W
22 Nov 2009	Jermain Defoe (Tottenham H) 5 goals v Wigan Ath
27 Nov 2010	Dimitar Berbatov (Manchester U) 5 goals v Blackburn R

FOOTBALL LEAGUE
Division 1
14 Dec 1935	Ted Drake (Arsenal) 7 goals v Aston Villa

Division 2
5 Feb 1955	Tommy Briggs (Blackburn R) 7 goals v Bristol R
23 Feb 1957	Neville Coleman (Stoke C) 7 goals v Lincoln C

Division 3(S)
13 April 1936	Joe Payne (Luton T) 10 goals v Bristol R

Division 3(N)
26 Dec 1935	Bunny Bell (Tranmere R) 9 goals v Oldham Ath

Division 3
24 April 1965	Barrie Thomas (Scunthorpe U) 5 goals v Luton T
20 Nov 1965	Keith East (Swindon T) 5 goals v Mansfield T
16 Sept 1969	Steve Earle (Fulham) 5 goals v Halifax T
2 Oct 1971	Alf Wood (Shrewsbury T) 5 goals v Blackburn R
10 Sept 1983	Tony Caldwell (Bolton W) 5 goals v Walsall
4 May 1987	Andy Jones (Port Vale) 5 goals v Newport Co
3 April 1990	Steve Wilkinson (Mansfield T) 5 goals v Birmingham C
5 Sept 1998	Giuliano Grazioli (Peterborough U) 5 goals v Barnet
6 April 2002	Lee Jones (Wrexham) 5 goals v Cambridge U

Division 4
26 Dec 1962	Bert Lister (Oldham Ath) 6 goals v Southport

FA CUP
20 Nov 1971	Ted MacDougall (Bournemouth) 9 goals v Margate (*1st Round*)

LEAGUE CUP
25 Oct 1989	Frankie Bunn (Oldham Ath) 6 goals v Scarborough

SCOTTISH LEAGUE
Premier Division
17 Nov 1984	Paul Sturrock (Dundee U) 5 goals v Morton

Premier League
23 Aug 1996	Marco Negri (Rangers) 5 goals v Dundee U
4 Nov 2000	Kenny Miller (Rangers) 5 goals v St Mirren
25 Sept 2004	Kris Boyd (Kilmarnock) 5 goals v Dundee U
30 Dec 2009	Kris Boyd (Rangers) 5 goals v Dundee U
13 May 2012	Gary Hooper (Celtic) 5 goals v Hearts

Division 1
14 Sept 1928	Jimmy McGrory (Celtic) 8 goals v Dunfermline Ath

Division 2
1 Oct 1927	Owen McNally (Arthurlie) 8 goals v Armadale
2 Jan 1930	Jim Dyet (King's Park) 8 goals v Forfar Ath
18 April 1936	John Calder (Morton) 8 goals v Raith R
20 Aug 1937	Norman Hayward (Raith R) 8 goals v Brechin C

SCOTTISH CUP
12 Sept 1885	John Petrie (Arbroath) 13 goals v Bon Accord (*1st Round*)

LONGEST SEQUENCE OF CONSECUTIVE DEFEATS

FOOTBALL LEAGUE	Team	Games
Division 2		
1898–99	Darwen	18

LONGEST UNBEATEN SEQUENCE

FA PREMIER LEAGUE	Team	Games
May 2003–Oct 2004	Arsenal	49

FOOTBALL LEAGUE – League 1		
Jan 2011–Nov 2011	Huddersfield T	43

LONGEST UNBEATEN CUP SEQUENCE

Liverpool	25 rounds	League/Milk Cup 1980–84

LONGEST UNBEATEN SEQUENCE IN A SEASON

FA PREMIER LEAGUE	Team	Games
2003–04	Arsenal	38

FOOTBALL LEAGUE – Division 1		
1920–21	Burnley	30

SCOTTISH PREMIER LEAGUE		
2003–04	Celtic	32

LONGEST UNBEATEN START TO A SEASON

FA PREMIER LEAGUE	Team	Games
2003–04	Arsenal	38

FOOTBALL LEAGUE – Division 1		
1973–74	Leeds U	29
1987–88	Liverpool	29

LONGEST SEQUENCE WITHOUT A WIN IN A SEASON

FA PREMIER LEAGUE	Team	Games
2007–08	Derby Co	32

FOOTBALL LEAGUE	Team	Games
Division 2		
1983–84	Cambridge U	31

LONGEST SEQUENCE WITHOUT A WIN FROM SEASON'S START

FOOTBALL LEAGUE	Team	Games
Division 4		
1970–71	Newport Co	25

LONGEST SEQUENCE OF CONSECUTIVE SCORING (Individual)

FA PREMIER LEAGUE		
Ruud van Nistelrooy (Manchester U)	15 in 10 games	2003–04

FOOTBALL LEAGUE RECORD		
Tom Phillipson (Wolverhampton W)	23 in 13 games	1926–27

LONGEST WINNING SEQUENCE

FA PREMIER LEAGUE	Team	Games
2001–02 and 2002–03	Arsenal	14

FOOTBALL LEAGUE – Division 2		
1904–05	Manchester U	14
1905–06	Bristol C	14
1950–51	Preston NE	14

FROM SEASON'S START – Division 3		
1985–86	Reading	13

SCOTTISH PREMIER LEAGUE		
2003–04	Celtic	25

HIGHEST WINS

Highest win in a First-Class Match
(Scottish Cup 1st Round)
| Arbroath | 36 | Bon Accord | 0 | 12 Sept 1885 |

Highest win in an International Match
| England | 13 | Ireland | 0 | 18 Feb 1882 |

Highest win in an FA Cup Match
| Preston NE | 26 | Hyde U | 0 | 15 Oct 1887 |

(1st Round)

Highest win in a League Cup Match
| West Ham U | 10 | Bury | 0 | 25 Oct 1983 |

(2nd Round, 2nd Leg)
| Liverpool | 10 | Fulham | 0 | 23 Sept 1986 |

(2nd Round, 1st Leg)

Highest win in an FA Premier League Match
| Manchester U | 9 | Ipswich T | 0 | 4 Mar 1995 |
| Tottenham H | 9 | Wigan Ath | 1 | 22 Nov 2009 |

Highest win in a Football League Match
Division 2 – highest home win
| Newcastle U | 13 | Newport Co | 0 | 5 Oct 1946 |

Division 3(N) – highest home win
| Stockport Co | 13 | Halifax T | 0 | 6 Jan 1934 |

Division 2 – highest away win
| Burslem Port Vale | 0 | Sheffield U | 10 | 10 Dec 1892 |

Highest wins in a Scottish League Match
Scottish Premier League – highest home win
| Celtic | 9 | Aberdeen | 0 | 6 Nov 2010 |

Scottish Division 2 – highest home win
| Airdrieonians | 15 | Dundee Wanderers | 1 | 1 Dec 1894 |

Scottish Premier League – away win
| Hamilton A | 0 | Celtic | 8 | 5 Nov 1988 |

MOST HOME WINS IN A SEASON

Brentford won all 21 games in Division 3(S), 1929–30

RECORD AWAY WINS IN A SEASON

Doncaster R won 18 of 21 games in Division 3(N), 1946–47

CONSECUTIVE AWAY WINS

FA PREMIER LEAGUE
Arsenal 12 games 2012–13, 2013–14.

FOOTBALL LEAGUE
Division 1
Tottenham H 10 games (1959–60 (2), 1960–61 (8))

MOST WINS IN A SEASON

		Wins	Games
FA PREMIER LEAGUE			
2004–05	Chelsea	29	38
2005–06	Chelsea	29	38
FOOTBALL LEAGUE			
Division 3(N)			
1946–47	Doncaster R	33	42
SCOTTISH PREMIER LEAGUE			
2001–02	Celtic	33	38
SCOTTISH LEAGUE			
Division 1			
1920–21	Rangers	35	42

MOST POINTS IN A SEASON
(under old system of two points for a win)

		Points	Games
FOOTBALL LEAGUE			
Division 4			
1975–76	Lincoln C	74	46
SCOTTISH LEAGUE			
Division 1			
1920–21	Rangers	76	42

FEWEST WINS IN A SEASON

		Wins	Games
FA PREMIER LEAGUE			
2007–08	Derby Co	1	38
FOOTBALL LEAGUE			
Division 2			
1899–1900	Loughborough T	1	34
SCOTTISH PREMIER LEAGUE			
1998–99	Dunfermline Ath	4	36
SCOTTISH LEAGUE			
Division 1			
1891–92	Vale of Leven	0	22

UNDEFEATED AT HOME OVERALL

Liverpool 85 games (63 League, 9 League Cup, 7 European, 6 FA Cup), Jan 1978–Jan 1981

UNDEFEATED AT HOME LEAGUE

Chelsea 86 games, March 2004–October 2008

UNDEFEATED AWAY

Arsenal 19 games, FA Premier League 2001–02 and 2003–04 (only Preston NE with 11 in 1888–89 had previously remained unbeaten away) in the top flight.

HIGHEST AGGREGATE SCORES

FA PREMIER LEAGUE
| Portsmouth | 7 | Reading | 4 | 29 Sept 2007 |

Highest Aggregate Score England
Division 3(N)
| Tranmere R | 13 | Oldham Ath | 4 | 26 Dec 1935 |

Highest Aggregate Score Scotland
Division 2
| Airdrieonians | 15 | Dundee Wanderers | 1 | 1 Dec 1894 |

MOST POINTS IN A SEASON
(three points for a win)

		Points	Games
FA PREMIER LEAGUE			
2004–05	Chelsea	95	38
FOOTBALL LEAGUE			
Championship			
2005–06	Reading	106	46
SCOTTISH PREMIER LEAGUE			
2001–02	Celtic	103	38
SCOTTISH LEAGUE			
League One			
2013–14	Rangers	102	36

FEWEST POINTS IN A SEASON

		Points	Games
FA PREMIER LEAGUE			
2007–08	Derby Co	11	38
FOOTBALL LEAGUE			
Division 2			
1904–05	Doncaster R	8	34
1899–1900	Loughborough T	8	34
SCOTTISH PREMIER LEAGUE			
2007–08	Gretna	13	38
SCOTTISH LEAGUE			
Division 1			
1954–55	Stirling Alb	6	30

NO DEFEATS IN A SEASON

FA PREMIER LEAGUE
2003–04   Arsenal   won 26, drew 12

FOOTBALL LEAGUE
Division 1
1888–89   Preston NE   won 18, drew 4
Division 2
1893–94   Liverpool   won 22, drew 6

SCOTTISH LEAGUE DIVISION 1
1898–99   Rangers   won 18
League One
2013–14   Rangers   won 33, drew 3

ONE DEFEAT IN A SEASON

FA PREMIER LEAGUE		*Defeats*	*Games*
2004–05	Chelsea	1	38
FOOTBALL LEAGUE			
Division 1			
1990–91	Arsenal	1	38
SCOTTISH PREMIER LEAGUE			
2001–02	Celtic	1	38
2013–14	Celtic	1	38
SCOTTISH LEAGUE			
Premier Division			
Division 1			
1920–21	Rangers	1	42
Division 2			
1956–57	Clyde	1	36
1962–63	Morton	1	36
1967–68	St Mirren	1	36
New Division 1			
2011–12	Ross Co	1	36
New Division 2			
1975–76	Raith R	1	26

MOST DEFEATS IN A SEASON

FA PREMIER LEAGUE		*Defeats*	*Games*
1994–95	Ipswich T	29	42
2005–06	Sunderland	29	38
2007–08	Derby Co	29	38
FOOTBALL LEAGUE			
Division 3			
1997–98	Doncaster R	34	46
SCOTTISH PREMIER LEAGUE			
2005–06	Livingston	28	38
SCOTTISH LEAGUE			
New Division 1			
1992–93	Cowdenbeath	34	44

SENDINGS-OFF

SEASON
451 (League alone)   2003–04
(Before rescinded cards taken into account)

DAY
19 (League)   13 Dec 2003

FA CUP FINAL
Kevin Moran, Manchester U v Everton   1985
Jose Antonio Reyes, Arsenal v Manchester U   2005

QUICKEST
FA Premier League
Andreas Johansson, Wigan Ath v Arsenal 7 May 2006
and Keith Gillespie, Sheffield U v Reading 20 January
2007 both in 10 seconds
Football League
Walter Boyd, Swansea C v Darlington Div 3 as
substitute in zero seconds   23 Nov 1999

MOST IN ONE GAME
Five: Chesterfield (2) v Plymouth Arg (3) 22 Feb 1997
Five: Wigan Ath (1) v Bristol R (4)   2 Dec 1997
Five: Exeter C (3) v Cambridge U (2)   23 Nov 2002

MOST IN ONE TEAM
Wigan Ath (1) v Bristol R (4)   2 Dec 1997
Hereford U (4) v Northampton T (0)   6 Sept 1992

MOST DRAWN GAMES IN A SEASON

FA PREMIER LEAGUE		*Draws*	*Games*
1993–94	Manchester C	18	42
1993–94	Sheffield U	18	42
1994–95	Southampton	18	42
FOOTBALL LEAGUE			
Division 1			
1978–79	Norwich C	23	42
Division 3			
1997–98	Cardiff C	23	46
1997–98	Hartlepool U	23	46
Division 4			
1986–87	Exeter C	23	46
SCOTTISH PREMIER LEAGUE			
1998–99	Dunfermline Ath	16	38
SCOTTISH LEAGUE			
Premier Division			
1993–94	Aberdeen	21	44
New Division 1			
1986–87	East Fife	21	44

MOST SUCCESSFUL MANAGERS

Sir Alex Ferguson CBE
Manchester U
1986–2013, 25 major trophies:
13 Premier League, 5 FA Cup, 4 League Cup,
2 Champions League, 1 Cup-Winners' Cup.

Aberdeen
1976–86, 9 major trophies:
3 League, 4 Scottish Cup, 1 League Cup, 1 Cup-
Winners' Cup.

Bob Paisley – Liverpool
1974–83, 13 major trophies:
6 League, 3 European Cup, 3 League Cup, 1 UEFA
Cup.

Bill Struth – Rangers
1920–54, 30 major trophies:
18 League, 10 Scottish Cup, 2 League Cup

LEAGUE CHAMPIONSHIP HAT-TRICKS

Huddersfield T	1923–24 to 1925–26
Arsenal	1932–33 to 1934–35
Liverpool	1981–82 to 1983–84
Manchester U	1998–99 to 2000–01
Manchester U	2006–07 to 2008–09

MOST FA CUP MEDALS

Ashley Cole 7 (Arsenal 2002, 2003, 2005, Chelsea
2007, 2009, 2010, 2012)

MOST LEAGUE MEDALS

Ryan Giggs (Manchester U) 13: 1993, 1994, 1996, 1997,
1999, 2000, 2001, 2003, 2007, 2008, 2009, 2011 and 2013.

MOST SENIOR MATCHES

1,390 Peter Shilton (1,005 League, 86 FA Cup, 102
League Cup, 125 Internationals, 13 Under-23, 4
Football League XI, 20 European Cup, 7 Texaco Cup,
5 Simod Cup, 4 European Super Cup, 4 UEFA Cup, 3
Screen Sport Super Cup, 3 Zenith Data Systems Cup,
2 Autoglass Trophy, 2 Charity Shield, 2 Full Members
Cup, 1 Anglo-Italian Cup, 1 Football League play-offs,
1 World Club Championship)

MOST LEAGUE APPEARANCES
(750+ matches)

1,005 Peter Shilton (286 Leicester C, 110 Stoke C,
       202 Nottingham F, 188 Southampton, 175 Derby
       Co, 34 Plymouth Arg, 1 Bolton W, 9 Leyton
       Orient) 1966–97

931 Tony Ford (355 Grimsby T, 9 Sunderland (loan),
     112 Stoke C, 114 WBA, 68 Grimsby T,
     5 Bradford C (loan), 76 Scunthorpe U,
     103 Mansfield T, 89 Rochdale) 1975–2002

909 Graeme Armstrong (204 Stirling A, 83 Berwick
     R, 353 Meadowbank Th, 268 Stenhousemuir,
     1 Alloa Ath) 1975–2001

863 Tommy Hutchison (165 Blackpool, 314 Coventry
     C, 46 Manchester C, 92 Burnley, 178 Swansea C,
     68 Alloa Ath) 1965–91

833 Graham Alexander (159 Scunthorpe U,
     150 Luton T, 370 Preston NE, 154 Burnley)
     1990–2012

824 Terry Paine (713 Southampton, 111 Hereford U)
     1957–77

790 Neil Redfearn (35 Bolton W, 10 Lincoln C
     (loan), 90 Lincoln C, 46 Doncaster R, 57 Crystal
     Palace, 24 Watford, 62 Oldham Ath,
     292 Barnsley, 30 Charlton Ath, 17 Bradford C,
     22 Wigan Ath, 42 Halifax T, 54 Boston U,
     9 Rochdale) 1982–2004

788 David James (89 Watford, 214 Liverpool,
     67 Aston Villa, 91 West Ham U,
     93 Manchester C, 134 Portsmouth, 81 Bristol C,
     19 Bournemouth) 1988–2013

782 Robbie James (484 Swansea C, 48 Stoke C,
     87 QPR, 23 Leicester C, 89 Bradford C,
     51 Cardiff C) 1973–94

777 Alan Oakes (565 Manchester C, 211 Chester C,
     1 Port Vale) 1959–84

774 Dave Beasant (340 Wimbledon, 20 Newcastle U,
     133 Chelsea, 6 Grimsby T (loan),
     4 Wolverhampton W (loan), 88 Southampton,
     139 Nottingham F, 27 Portsmouth, 1 Tottenham
     H (loan), 16 Brighton & HA) 1979–2003

771 John Burridge (27 Workington, 134 Blackpool,
     65 Aston Villa, 6 Southend U (loan), 88 Crystal
     Palace, 39 QPR, 74 Wolverhampton W, 6 Derby
     Co (loan), 109 Sheffield U, 62 Southampton,
     67 Newcastle U, 65 Hibernian, 3 Scarborough,
     4 Lincoln C, 3 Aberdeen, 3 Dumbarton,
     3 Falkirk, 4 Manchester C, 3 Darlington,
     6 Queen of the S) 1968–96

770 John Trollope (all for Swindon T) 1960–80†

764 Jimmy Dickinson (all for Portsmouth) 1946–65

763 Stuart McCall (395 Bradford C, 103 Everton,
     194 Rangers, 71 Sheffield U) 1982–2004

761 Roy Sproson (all for Port Vale) 1950–72

760 Mick Tait (64 Oxford U, 106 Carlisle U, 33 Hull
     C, 240 Portsmouth, 99 Reading, 79 Darlington,
     139 Hartlepool U) 1975–97

758 Ray Clemence (48 Scunthorpe U, 470 Liverpool,
     240 Tottenham H) 1966–87

758 Billy Bonds (95 Charlton Ath, 663 West Ham U)
     1964–88

757 Pat Jennings (48 Watford, 472 Tottenham H,
     237 Arsenal) 1963–86

757 Frank Worthington (171 Huddersfield T,
     210 Leicester C, 84 Bolton W, 75 Birmingham C,
     32 Leeds U, 19 Sunderland, 34 Southampton,
     31 Brighton & HA, 59 Tranmere R, 23 Preston
     NE, 19 Stockport Co) 1966–88

752 Wayne Allison (84 Halifax T, 7 Watford,
     195 Bristol C, 101 Swindon T, 74 Huddersfield T,
     103 Tranmere R, 73 Sheffield U,
     115 Chesterfield) 1987–2008

† record for one club

CONSECUTIVE
401 Harold Bell (401 Tranmere R; 459 in all games)
     1946–55

YOUNGEST PLAYERS

FA Premier League appearance
Matthew Briggs, 16 years 65 days, Fulham v
Middlesbrough, 13.5.2007

FA Premier League scorer
James Vaughan, 16 years 271 days, Everton v Crystal
Palace 10.4.2005

Football League appearance
Reuben Noble-Lazarus 15 years 45 days, Barnsley v
Ipswich T, FL Championship 30.9.2008

Football League scorer
Ronnie Dix, 15 years 180 days, Bristol Rovers v
Norwich C, Division 3S, 3.3.1928

Division 1 appearance
Derek Forster, 15 years 185 days, Sunderland v
Leicester C, 22.8.1964

Division 1 scorer
Jason Dozzell, 16 years 57 days as substitute Ipswich T
v Coventry C, 4.2.1984

Division 1 hat-tricks
Alan Shearer, 17 years 240 days, Southampton v
Arsenal, 9.4.88
Jimmy Greaves, 17 years 10 months, Chelsea v
Portsmouth, 25.12.1957

FA Cup appearance (any round)
Andy Awford, 15 years 88 days as substitute
Worcester City v Boreham Wood, 3rd Qual. rd,
10.10.1987

FA Cup competition proper appearance
Brendon Galloway, 15 years 240 days, Milton Keynes D
v Nantwich T

FA Cup Final appearance
Curtis Weston, 17 years 119 days, Millwall v
Manchester U, 2004

FA Cup Final scorer
Norman Whiteside, 18 years 18 days, Manchester
United v Brighton & HA, 1983

FA Cup Final captain
David Nish, 21 years 212 days, Leicester C v
Manchester U, 1969

League Cup appearance
Chris Coward, 16 years 30 days, Stockport Co v
Sheffield W, 2005

League Cup Final scorer
Norman Whiteside, 17 years 324 days, Manchester U v
Liverpool, 1983

League Cup Final captain
Barry Venison, 20 years 7 months 8 days, Sunderland v
Norwich C, 1985

Scottish Premier League appearance
Scott Robinson, 16 years 45 days, Hearts v Inverness
CT, 26.4.2008

Scottish Football League appearance
Jordan Allan, 14 years 189 days, Airdrie U v
Livingston, 26.4.2013

Scottish Premier League scorer
Fraser Fyvie, 16 years 306 days, Aberdeen v Hearts,
27.1.2010

OLDEST PLAYERS

FA Premier League appearance
John Burridge, 43 years 5 months, Manchester C v
QPR, 14.5.1995

Football League appearance
Neil McBain, 52 years 4 months, New Brighton v
Hartlepools U, Div 3N, 15.3.47 (McBain was New
Brighton's manager and had to play in an emergency)

Division 1 appearance
Stanley Matthews, 50 years 5 days, Stoke C v Fulham,
6.2.65

INTERNATIONAL RECORDS

MOST GOALS IN AN INTERNATIONAL

Record/World Cup	Archie Thompson (Australia) 13 goals v American Samoa	11.4.2001
England	Howard Vaughton (Aston Villa) 5 goals v Ireland, at Belfast	18.2.1882
	Steve Bloomer (Derby Co) 5 goals v Wales, at Cardiff	16.3.1896
	Willie Hall (Tottenham H) 5 goals v Ireland, at Old Trafford	16.11.1938
	Malcolm Macdonald (Newcastle U) 5 goals v Cyprus, at Wembley	16.4.1975
Northern Ireland	Joe Bambrick (Linfield) 6 goals v Wales, at Belfast	1.2.1930
Wales	John Price (Wrexham) 4 goals v Ireland, at Wrexham	25.2.1882
	Mel Charles (Cardiff C) 4 goals v Ireland, at Cardiff	11.4.1962
	Ian Edwards (Chester) 4 goals v Malta, at Wrexham	25.10.1978
Scotland	Alexander Higgins (Kilmarnock) 4 goals v Ireland, at Hampden Park	14.3.1885
	Charles Heggie (Rangers) 4 goals v Ireland, at Belfast	20.3.1886
	William Dickson (Dundee Strathmore) 4 goals v Ireland, at Belfast	24.3.1888
	William Paul (Partick Thistle) 4 goals v Wales, at Paisley	22.3.1890
	Jake Madden (Celtic) 4 goals v Wales, at Wrexham	18.3.1893
	Duke McMahon (Celtic) 4 goals v Ireland, at Celtic Park	23.2.1901
	Bob Hamilton (Rangers) 4 goals v Ireland, at Celtic Park	23.2.1901
	Jimmy Quinn (Celtic) 4 goals v Ireland, at Dublin	14.3.1908
	Hughie Gallacher (Newcastle U) 4 goals v Ireland, at Belfast	23.2.1929
	Billy Steel (Dundee) 4 goals v N. Ireland, at Hampden Park	1.11.1950
	Denis Law (Manchester U) 4 goals v N. Ireland, at Hampden Park	7.11.1962
	Denis Law (Manchester U) 4 goals v Norway, at Hampden Park	7.11.1963
	Colin Stein (Rangers) 4 goals v Cyprus, at Hampden Park	17.5.1969

MOST GOALS IN AN INTERNATIONAL CAREER

		Goals	Games
England	Bobby Charlton (Manchester U)	49	106
Scotland	Denis Law (Huddersfield T, Manchester C, Torino, Manchester U)	30	55
	Kenny Dalglish (Celtic, Liverpool)	30	102
Northern Ireland	David Healy (Manchester U, Preston NE, Leeds U, Fulham, Sunderland, Rangers)	35	93
Wales	Ian Rush (Liverpool, Juventus)	28	73
Republic of Ireland	Robbie Keane (Wolverhampton W, Coventry C, Internazionale, Leeds U, Tottenham H, Liverpool, Tottenham H, LA Galaxy)	62	133

HIGHEST SCORES

Record/World Cup Match	Australia	31	American Samoa	0	2001
European Championship	San Marino	0	Germany	13	2006
Olympic Games	Denmark	17	France	1	1908
	Germany	16	USSR	0	1912
Other International Match	Libya	21	Oman	0	1966
European Cup	Feyenoord	12	KR Reykjavik	2	1969
European Cup-Winners' Cup	Sporting Lisbon	16	Apoel Nicosia	1	1963
Fairs & UEFA Cups	Ajax	14	Red Boys	0	1984

GOALSCORING RECORDS

World Cup Final	Geoff Hurst (England) 3 goals v West Germany	1966
World Cup Final tournament	Just Fontaine (France) 13 goals	1958
World Cup career	Miroslav Klose (Germany) 16 goals	2002, 2006, 2010, 2014
Career	Artur Friedenreich (Brazil) 1,329 goals	1910–30
	Pele (Brazil) 1,281 goals	*1956–78
	Franz 'Bimbo' Binder (Austria, Germany) 1,006 goals	1930–50
World Cup Finals fastest	Hakan Sukur (Turkey) 10.8 secs v South Korea	2002

Pele subsequently scored two goals in Testimonial matches making his total 1,283.

MOST CAPPED INTERNATIONALS IN THE BRITISH ISLES

England	Peter Shilton	125 appearances	1970–90
Northern Ireland	Pat Jennings	119 appearances	1964–86
Scotland	Kenny Dalglish	102 appearances	1971–86
Wales	Neville Southall	92 appearances	1982–97
Republic of Ireland	Robbie Keane	133 appearances	1998–2014

THE FA BARCLAYS PREMIER LEAGUE AND FOOTBALL LEAGUE FIXTURES 2014–15

*Sky Sports   All fixtures subject to change.

Friday, 8 August 2014
Sky Bet Championship
Blackburn R v Cardiff C* (7.45)

Saturday, 9 August 2014
Sky Bet Championship
Brentford v Charlton Ath
Brighton & HA v Sheffield W
Derby Co v Rotherham U
Huddersfield T v Bournemouth
Ipswich T v Fulham* (5.15)
Middlesbrough v Birmingham C
Millwall v Leeds U
Nottingham F v Blackpool
Watford v Bolton W
Wigan Ath v Reading

Sky Bet League One
Barnsley v Crawley T
Bradford C v Coventry C
Colchester U v Oldham Ath
Fleetwood T v Crewe Alex
Leyton Orient v Chesterfield
Milton Keynes D v Gillingham
Port Vale v Walsall
Preston NE v Notts Co
Rochdale v Peterborough U
Sheffield U v Bristol C* (12.15)
Swindon T v Scunthorpe U
Yeovil T v Doncaster R

Sky Bet League Two
AFC Wimbledon v Shrewsbury T
Accrington S v Southend U
Bury v Cheltenham T
Cambridge U v Plymouth Arg
Carlisle U v Luton T
Dagenham & R v Morecambe
Exeter C v Portsmouth
Newport Co v Wycombe W
Northampton T v Mansfield T
Oxford U v Burton Alb
Stevenage v Hartlepool U
Tranmere R v York C

Sunday, 10 August 2014
Sky Bet Championship
Wolverhampton W v Norwich C* (4.00)

Saturday, 16 August 2014
Barclays Premier League
Arsenal v Crystal Palace* (5.30)
Leicester C v Everton
Manchester U v Swansea C
QPR v Hull C
Stoke C v Aston Villa
WBA v Sunderland
West Ham U v Tottenham H

Sky Bet Championship
Birmingham C v Brighton & HA
Blackpool v Blackburn R
Bolton W v Nottingham F
Bournemouth v Brentford
Cardiff C v Huddersfield T
Charlton Ath v Wigan Ath
Fulham v Millwall
Leeds U v Middlesbrough* (12.15)
Norwich C v Watford
Reading v Ipswich T
Rotherham U v Wolverhampton W
Sheffield W v Derby Co

Sky Bet League One
Bristol C v Colchester U
Chesterfield v Rochdale
Coventry C v Sheffield U
Crawley T v Swindon T
Crewe Alex v Barnsley
Doncaster R v Port Vale
Gillingham v Yeovil T
Notts Co v Fleetwood T
Oldham Ath v Leyton Orient
Peterborough U v Milton Keynes D
Scunthorpe U v Preston NE
Walsall v Bradford C

Sky Bet League Two
Burton Alb v Dagenham & R
Cheltenham T v Accrington S
Hartlepool U v Bury
Luton T v AFC Wimbledon
Mansfield T v Oxford U
Morecambe v Newport Co
Plymouth Arg v Exeter C
Portsmouth v Cambridge U
Shrewsbury T v Tranmere R
Southend U v Stevenage
Wycombe W v Carlisle U
York C v Northampton T

Sunday, 17 August 2014
Barclays Premier League
Liverpool v Southampton* (1.30)
Newcastle U v Manchester C* (4.00)

Monday, 18 August 2014
Barclays Premier League
Burnley v Chelsea* (8.00)

Tuesday, 19 August 2014
Sky Bet Championship
Birmingham C v Ipswich T
Blackpool v Brentford
Bolton W v Middlesbrough
Bournemouth v Nottingham F
Cardiff C v Wigan Ath
Charlton Ath v Derby Co
Leeds U v Brighton & HA
Norwich C v Blackburn R
Reading v Huddersfield T
Rotherham U v Watford
Sheffield W v Millwall

Sky Bet League One
Bristol C v Leyton Orient
Chesterfield v Milton Keynes D
Coventry C v Barnsley
Crawley T v Bradford C
Crewe Alex v Rochdale
Doncaster R v Preston NE
Gillingham v Swindon T
Notts Co v Colchester U
Oldham Ath v Port Vale
Peterborough U v Sheffield U
Scunthorpe U v Fleetwood T
Walsall v Yeovil T

Sky Bet League Two
Burton Alb v Exeter C
Cheltenham T v Carlisle U
Hartlepool U v Dagenham & R
Luton T v Bury
Mansfield T v Newport Co
Morecambe v Oxford U
Plymouth Arg v Stevenage
Portsmouth v Northampton T
Shrewsbury T v Accrington S

Southend U v AFC Wimbledon
Wycombe W v Tranmere R
York C v Cambridge U

Wednesday, 20 August 2014
Sky Bet Championship
Fulham v Wolverhampton W

Saturday, 23 August 2014
Barclays Premier League
Aston Villa v Newcastle U
Chelsea v Leicester C
Crystal Palace v West Ham U
Everton v Arsenal* (5.30)
Southampton v WBA
Tottenham H v QPR
Swansea C v Burnley

Sky Bet Championship
Blackburn R v Bournemouth
Brentford v Birmingham C
Brighton & HA v Bolton W
Derby Co v Fulham
Huddersfield T v Charlton Ath
Ipswich T v Norwich C* (12.15)
Middlesbrough v Sheffield W
Millwall v Rotherham U
Nottingham F v Reading
Watford v Leeds U
Wigan Ath v Blackpool
Wolverhampton W v Cardiff C

Sky Bet League One
Barnsley v Gillingham
Bradford C v Peterborough U
Colchester U v Doncaster R
Fleetwood T v Chesterfield
Leyton Orient v Walsall
Milton Keynes D v Coventry C
Port Vale v Notts Co
Preston NE v Oldham Ath
Rochdale v Bristol C
Sheffield U v Crawley T
Swindon T v Crewe Alex
Yeovil T v Scunthorpe U

Sky Bet League Two
AFC Wimbledon v Hartlepool U
Accrington S v Luton T
Bury v Plymouth Arg
Cambridge U v Morecambe
Carlisle U v Southend U
Dagenham & R v Mansfield T
Exeter C v York C
Newport Co v Burton Alb
Northampton T v Shrewsbury T
Oxford U v Portsmouth
Stevenage v Wycombe W
Tranmere R v Cheltenham T

Sunday, 24 August 2014
Barclays Premier League
Hull C v Stoke C* (1.30)
Sunderland v Manchester U* (4.00)

Monday, 25 August 2014
Barclays Premier League
Manchester C v Liverpool* (8.00)

Saturday, 30 August 2014
Barclays Premier League
Aston Villa v Hull C
Burnley v Manchester U
Everton v Chelsea* (5.30)
Manchester C v Stoke C

Newcastle U v Crystal Palace
QPR v Sunderland
Swansea C v WBA
West Ham U v Southampton

Sky Bet Championship
Brighton & HA v Charlton Ath
Derby Co v Ipswich T
Fulham v Cardiff C
Leeds U v Bolton W
Middlesbrough v Reading
Millwall v Blackpool
Norwich C v Bournemouth
Rotherham U v Brentford
Sheffield W v Nottingham F* (12.15)
Watford v Huddersfield T
Wigan Ath v Birmingham C
Wolverhampton W v Blackburn R

Sky Bet League One
Colchester U v Peterborough U
Doncaster R v Oldham Ath
Fleetwood T v Leyton Orient
Gillingham v Crewe Alex
Milton Keynes D v Crawley T
Notts Co v Bristol C
Port Vale v Chesterfield
Preston NE v Sheffield U
Rochdale v Bradford C
Scunthorpe U v Walsall
Swindon T v Coventry C
Yeovil T v Barnsley

Sky Bet League Two
AFC Wimbledon v Stevenage
Bury v Accrington S
Cambridge U v Carlisle U
Cheltenham T v Hartlepool U
Mansfield T v Burton Alb
Northampton T v Exeter C
Oxford U v Dagenham & R
Plymouth Arg v Southend U
Portsmouth v Newport Co
Shrewsbury T v Luton T
Tranmere R v Morecambe
York C v Wycombe W

Sunday, 31 August 2014
Barclays Premier League
Tottenham H v Liverpool* (1.30)
Leicester C v Arsenal* (4.00)

Saturday, 6 September 2014
Sky Bet League One
Barnsley v Doncaster R
Bradford C v Yeovil T
Bristol C v Scunthorpe U
Chesterfield v Swindon T
Coventry C v Gillingham
Crawley T v Rochdale
Crewe Alex v Notts Co
Leyton Orient v Preston NE
Oldham Ath v Fleetwood T
Peterborough U v Port Vale
Sheffield U v Milton Keynes D
Walsall v Colchester U

Sky Bet League Two
Accrington S v Tranmere R
Carlisle U v AFC Wimbledon
Dagenham & R v Northampton T
Exeter C v Mansfield T
Hartlepool U v Shrewsbury T
Luton T v Plymouth Arg* (12.15)
Morecambe v Cheltenham T
Newport Co v Cambridge U
Southend U v Oxford U
Stevenage v York C
Wycombe W v Bury

Sunday, 7 September 2014
Sky Bet League Two
Burton Alb v Portsmouth* (12.15)

Saturday, 13 September 2014
Barclays Premier League
Arsenal v Manchester C
Chelsea v Swansea C
Crystal Palace v Burnley
Liverpool v Aston Villa* (5.30)
Southampton v Newcastle U
Stoke C v Leicester C
Sunderland v Tottenham H
WBA v Everton

Sky Bet Championship
Birmingham C v Leeds U* (12.15)
Blackburn R v Wigan Ath
Blackpool v Wolverhampton W
Bolton W v Sheffield W
Bournemouth v Rotherham U
Brentford v Brighton & HA
Cardiff C v Norwich C
Charlton Ath v Watford
Huddersfield T v Middlesbrough
Ipswich T v Millwall
Reading v Fulham

Sky Bet League One
Barnsley v Milton Keynes D
Bradford C v Swindon T
Bristol C v Doncaster R
Chesterfield v Scunthorpe U
Coventry C v Yeovil T
Crawley T v Fleetwood T
Crewe Alex v Port Vale
Leyton Orient v Colchester U
Oldham Ath v Gillingham
Peterborough U v Notts Co
Sheffield U v Rochdale
Walsall v Preston NE

Sky Bet League Two
Accrington S v AFC Wimbledon
Burton Alb v York C
Carlisle U v Bury
Dagenham & R v Cambridge U
Exeter C v Oxford U
Hartlepool U v Tranmere R
Luton T v Cheltenham T
Morecambe v Plymouth Arg
Newport Co v Northampton T
Southend U v Portsmouth
Stevenage v Shrewsbury T
Wycombe W v Mansfield T

Sunday, 14 September 2014
Barclays Premier League
Manchester U v QPR* (4.00)

Sky Bet Championship
Nottingham F v Derby Co* (1.15)

Sunday, 14 September 2014
Barclays Premier League
Hull C v West Ham U* (8.00)

Tuesday, 16 September 2014
Sky Bet Championship
Birmingham C v Sheffield W
Blackburn R v Derby Co
Blackpool v Watford
Bolton W v Rotherham U
Bournemouth v Leeds U
Brentford v Norwich C
Cardiff C v Middlesbrough
Charlton Ath v Wolverhampton W
Huddersfield T v Wigan Ath
Ipswich T v Brighton & HA
Reading v Millwall

Sky Bet League One
Colchester U v Sheffield U
Doncaster R v Crawley T
Fleetwood T v Barnsley
Gillingham v Peterborough U
Milton Keynes D v Bradford C
Notts Co v Leyton Orient
Port Vale v Bristol C
Preston NE v Chesterfield
Rochdale v Walsall

Scunthorpe U v Coventry C
Swindon T v Oldham Ath
Yeovil T v Crewe Alex

Sky Bet League Two
AFC Wimbledon v Burton Alb
Bury v Stevenage
Cambridge U v Exeter C
Cheltenham T v Southend U
Mansfield T v Morecambe
Northampton T v Hartlepool U
Oxford U v Accrington S
Plymouth Arg v Wycombe W
Portsmouth v Dagenham & R
Shrewsbury T v Carlisle U
Tranmere R v Newport Co
York C v Luton T

Wednesday, 17 September 2014
Sky Bet Championship
Nottingham F v Fulham

Saturday, 20 September 2014
Barclays Premier League
Aston Villa v Arsenal
Burnley v Sunderland
Everton v Crystal Palace
Newcastle U v Hull C
QPR v Stoke C
Tottenham H v WBA
Swansea C v Southampton
West Ham U v Liverpool* (5.30)

Sky Bet Championship
Brighton & HA v Blackpool
Derby Co v Cardiff C
Fulham v Blackburn R
Leeds U v Huddersfield T
Middlesbrough v Brentford
Millwall v Nottingham F
Norwich C v Birmingham C
Rotherham U v Charlton Ath
Sheffield W v Reading
Watford v Bournemouth* (12.15)
Wigan Ath v Ipswich T
Wolverhampton W v Bolton W

Sky Bet League One
Colchester U v Bradford C
Doncaster R v Chesterfield
Fleetwood T v Bristol C
Gillingham v Walsall
Milton Keynes D v Crewe Alex
Notts Co v Oldham Ath
Port Vale v Barnsley
Preston NE v Crawley T
Rochdale v Coventry C
Scunthorpe U v Leyton Orient
Swindon T v Sheffield U
Yeovil T v Peterborough U

Sky Bet League Two
AFC Wimbledon v Morecambe
Bury v Burton Alb
Cambridge U v Luton T
Cheltenham T v Dagenham & R
Mansfield T v Carlisle U
Northampton T v Accrington S
Oxford U v Stevenage
Plymouth Arg v Hartlepool U
Portsmouth v Wycombe W
Shrewsbury T v Newport Co
Tranmere R v Exeter C
York C v Southend U

Sunday, 21 September 2014
Barclays Premier League
Leicester C v Manchester U* (1.30)
Manchester C v Chelsea* (4.00)

Saturday, 27 September 2014
Barclays Premier League
Arsenal v Tottenham H* (5.30)
Chelsea v Aston Villa
Crystal Palace v Leicester C
Hull C v Manchester C
Liverpool v Everton

Manchester U v West Ham U
Southampton v QPR
Sunderland v Swansea C

Sky Bet Championship
Birmingham C v Fulham
Blackburn R v Watford
Blackpool v Norwich C
Bolton W v Derby Co
Bournemouth v Wigan Ath
Brentford v Leeds U
Cardiff C v Sheffield W
Charlton Ath v Middlesbrough
Huddersfield T v Millwall
Ipswich T v Rotherham U
Nottingham F v Brighton & HA
Reading v Wolverhampton W

Sky Bet League One
Barnsley v Swindon T
Bradford C v Port Vale
Bristol C v Milton Keynes D
Chesterfield v Notts Co
Coventry C v Preston NE
Crawley T v Yeovil T
Crewe Alex v Colchester U
Leyton Orient v Rochdale
Oldham Ath v Scunthorpe U
Peterborough U v Fleetwood T
Sheffield U v Gillingham
Walsall v Doncaster R

Sky Bet League Two
Accrington S v Plymouth Arg
Burton Alb v Cheltenham T
Carlisle U v Tranmere R
Dagenham & R v York C
Exeter C v Bury
Hartlepool U v Portsmouth
Luton T v Oxford U
Morecambe v Northampton T
Newport Co v AFC Wimbledon
Southend U v Shrewsbury T
Stevenage v Mansfield T
Wycombe W v Cambridge U

Sunday, 28 September 2014
Barclays Premier League
WBA v Burnley* (4.00)

Monday, 29 September 2014
Barclays Premier League
Stoke C v Newcastle U* (8.00)

Tuesday, 30 September 2014
Sky Bet Championship
Brighton & HA v Cardiff C
Derby Co v Bournemouth
Leeds U v Reading
Middlesbrough v Blackpool
Millwall v Birmingham C
Norwich C v Charlton Ath
Rotherham U v Blackburn R
Sheffield W v Ipswich T
Watford v Brentford
Wigan Ath v Nottingham F
Wolverhampton W v Huddersfield T

Wednesday, 1 October 2014
Sky Bet Championship
Fulham v Bolton W

Saturday, 4 October 2014
Barclays Premier League
Aston Villa v Manchester C* (5.30)
Hull C v Crystal Palace
Leicester C v Burnley
Liverpool v WBA
Manchester U v Everton
Tottenham H v Southampton
Sunderland v Stoke C
Swansea C v Newcastle U

Sky Bet Championship
Blackburn R v Huddersfield T
Blackpool v Cardiff C
Bolton W v Bournemouth
Brentford v Reading

Charlton Ath v Birmingham C
Derby Co v Millwall
Leeds U v Sheffield W
Middlesbrough v Fulham
Norwich C v Rotherham U
Nottingham F v Ipswich T
Watford v Brighton & HA
Wolverhampton W v Wigan Ath

Sky Bet League One
Bradford C v Crewe Alex
Chesterfield v Sheffield U
Coventry C v Crawley T
Fleetwood T v Port Vale
Leyton Orient v Swindon T
Notts Co v Gillingham
Peterborough U v Oldham Ath
Preston NE v Colchester U
Rochdale v Barnsley
Scunthorpe U v Doncaster R
Walsall v Bristol C
Yeovil T v Milton Keynes D

Sky Bet League Two
Burton Alb v Cambridge U
Bury v Tranmere R
Cheltenham T v AFC Wimbledon
Dagenham & R v Exeter C
Hartlepool U v Carlisle U
Mansfield T v Accrington S
Oxford U v Newport Co
Plymouth Arg v Shrewsbury T
Southend U v Morecambe
Stevenage v Luton T
Wycombe W v Northampton T
York C v Portsmouth

Sunday, 5 October 2014
Barclays Premier League
Chelsea v Arsenal* (2.05)
West Ham U v QPR* (4.15)

Saturday, 11 October 2014

Sky Bet League One
Barnsley v Bradford C
Bristol C v Chesterfield
Colchester U v Fleetwood T
Crawley T v Peterborough U
Crewe Alex v Coventry C
Doncaster R v Notts Co
Gillingham v Scunthorpe U
Milton Keynes D v Rochdale
Oldham Ath v Walsall
Port Vale v Yeovil T
Sheffield U v Leyton Orient
Swindon T v Preston NE

Sky Bet League Two
AFC Wimbledon v Bury
Accrington S v Dagenham & R
Cambridge U v Oxford U
Carlisle U v Stevenage
Exeter C v Hartlepool U
Luton T v Southend U
Morecambe v Wycombe W
Newport Co v York C
Northampton T v Burton Alb
Portsmouth v Mansfield T
Shrewsbury T v Cheltenham T
Tranmere R v Plymouth Arg

Saturday, 18 October 2014
Barclays Premier League
Arsenal v Hull C
Burnley v West Ham U
Crystal Palace v Chelsea
Everton v Aston Villa
Manchester C v Tottenham H
Newcastle U v Leicester C
Southampton v Sunderland

Sky Bet Championship
Birmingham C v Bolton W
Bournemouth v Charlton Ath
Brighton & HA v Middlesbrough
Cardiff C v Nottingham F
Fulham v Norwich C

Huddersfield T v Blackpool
Ipswich T v Blackburn R
Millwall v Wolverhampton W
Reading v Derby Co
Rotherham U v Leeds U
Sheffield W v Watford
Wigan Ath v Brentford

Sky Bet League One
Bradford C v Sheffield U
Chesterfield v Oldham Ath
Coventry C v Bristol C
Fleetwood T v Doncaster R
Leyton Orient v Milton Keynes D
Notts Co v Crawley T
Peterborough U v Barnsley
Preston NE v Port Vale
Rochdale v Gillingham
Scunthorpe U v Colchester U
Walsall v Crewe Alex
Yeovil T v Swindon T

Sky Bet League Two
Burton Alb v Morecambe
Bury v Portsmouth
Cheltenham T v Northampton T
Dagenham & R v Newport Co
Hartlepool U v Luton T
Mansfield T v Cambridge U
Oxford U v Tranmere R
Plymouth Arg v Carlisle U
Southend U v Exeter C
Stevenage v Accrington S
Wycombe W v AFC Wimbledon
York C v Shrewsbury T

Sunday, 19 October 2014
Barclays Premier League
QPR v Liverpool* (1.30)
Stoke C v Swansea C* (4.00)

Monday, 20 October 2014
Barclays Premier League
WBA v Manchester U* (8.00)

Tuesday, 21 October 2014
Sky Bet Championship
Blackburn R v Birmingham C
Blackpool v Derby Co
Bournemouth v Reading
Brentford v Sheffield W
Cardiff C v Ipswich T
Charlton Ath v Bolton W
Huddersfield T v Brighton & HA
Norwich C v Leeds U
Rotherham U v Fulham
Watford v Nottingham F
Wigan Ath v Millwall
Wolverhampton W v Middlesbrough

Sky Bet League One
Barnsley v Notts Co
Bristol C v Bradford C
Colchester U v Chesterfield
Crawley T v Walsall
Crewe Alex v Peterborough U
Doncaster R v Leyton Orient
Gillingham v Preston NE
Milton Keynes D v Fleetwood T
Oldham Ath v Coventry C
Port Vale v Scunthorpe U
Sheffield U v Yeovil T
Swindon T v Rochdale

Sky Bet League Two
AFC Wimbledon v Plymouth Arg
Accrington S v Hartlepool U
Cambridge U v Cheltenham T
Carlisle U v Burton Alb
Exeter C v Wycombe W
Luton T v Dagenham & R
Morecambe v York C
Newport Co v Southend U
Northampton T v Oxford U
Portsmouth v Stevenage
Shrewsbury T v Bury
Tranmere R v Mansfield T

Saturday, 25 October 2014
Barclays Premier League
Liverpool v Hull C
Southampton v Stoke C
Tottenham H v Newcastle U
Sunderland v Arsenal
Swansea C v Leicester C* (5.30)
WBA v Crystal Palace
West Ham U v Manchester C

Sky Bet Championship
Birmingham C v Bournemouth
Bolton W v Brentford
Brighton & HA v Rotherham U
Derby Co v Wigan Ath
Fulham v Charlton Ath
Ipswich T v Huddersfield T
Leeds U v Wolverhampton W
Middlesbrough v Watford
Millwall v Cardiff C
Nottingham F v Blackburn R
Reading v Blackpool
Sheffield W v Norwich C

Sky Bet League One
Barnsley v Bristol C
Coventry C v Peterborough U
Crewe Alex v Sheffield U
Doncaster R v Milton Keynes D
Gillingham v Crawley T
Oldham Ath v Bradford C
Port Vale v Leyton Orient
Preston NE v Fleetwood T
Scunthorpe U v Notts Co
Swindon T v Colchester U
Walsall v Chesterfield
Yeovil T v Rochdale

Sky Bet League Two
AFC Wimbledon v Tranmere R
Cambridge U v Hartlepool U
Carlisle U v Oxford U
Luton T v Northampton T
Morecambe v Exeter C
Newport Co v Accrington S
Plymouth Arg v Cheltenham T
Shrewsbury T v Portsmouth
Southend U v Bury
Stevenage v Burton Alb
Wycombe W v Dagenham & R
York C v Mansfield T

Sunday, 26 October 2014
Barclays Premier League
Burnley v Everton* (1.30)
Manchester U v Chelsea* (4.00)

Monday, 27 October 2014
Barclays Premier League
QPR v Aston Villa* (8.00)

Saturday, 1 November 2014
Barclays Premier League
Arsenal v Burnley
Chelsea v QPR
Everton v Swansea C
Hull C v Southampton
Leicester C v WBA
Newcastle U v Liverpool
Stoke C v West Ham U

Sky Bet Championship
Blackburn R v Reading
Blackpool v Ipswich T
Bournemouth v Brighton & HA
Brentford v Derby Co
Cardiff C v Leeds U
Charlton Ath v Sheffield W
Huddersfield T v Nottingham F
Norwich C v Bolton W
Rotherham U v Middlesbrough
Watford v Millwall
Wigan Ath v Fulham
Wolverhampton W v Birmingham C

Sky Bet League One
Bradford C v Doncaster R
Bristol C v Oldham Ath
Chesterfield v Yeovil T
Colchester U v Port Vale
Crawley T v Crewe Alex
Fleetwood T v Gillingham
Leyton Orient v Coventry C
Milton Keynes D v Swindon T
Notts Co v Walsall
Peterborough U v Scunthorpe U
Rochdale v Preston NE
Sheffield U v Barnsley

Sky Bet League Two
Accrington S v Morecambe
Burton Alb v Plymouth Arg
Bury v Cambridge U
Cheltenham T v York C
Dagenham & R v Shrewsbury T
Exeter C v Luton T
Hartlepool U v Newport Co
Mansfield T v Southend U
Northampton T v AFC Wimbledon
Oxford U v Wycombe W
Portsmouth v Carlisle U
Tranmere R v Stevenage

Sunday, 2 November 2014
Barclays Premier League
Manchester C v Manchester U* (1.30)
Aston Villa v Tottenham H* (4.00)

Monday, 3 November 2014
Barclays Premier League
Crystal Palace v Sunderland* (8.00)

Tuesday, 4 November 2014
Sky Bet Championship
Birmingham C v Watford
Bolton W v Cardiff C
Brighton & HA v Wigan Ath
Derby Co v Huddersfield T
Ipswich T v Wolverhampton W
Leeds U v Charlton Ath
Middlesbrough v Norwich C
Millwall v Blackburn R
Reading v Rotherham U
Sheffield W v Bournemouth

Wednesday, 5 November 2014
Sky Bet Championship
Fulham v Blackpool
Nottingham F v Brentford

Saturday, 8 November 2014
Barclays Premier League
Burnley v Hull C
Liverpool v Chelsea
Manchester U v Crystal Palace
QPR v Manchester C* (5.15)
Southampton v Leicester C
Tottenham H v Stoke C
Sunderland v Everton
West Ham U v Aston Villa

Sky Bet Championship
Birmingham C v Cardiff C
Bolton W v Wigan Ath
Brighton & HA v Blackburn R
Derby Co v Wolverhampton W
Fulham v Huddersfield T
Ipswich T v Watford
Leeds U v Blackpool
Middlesbrough v Bournemouth
Millwall v Brentford
Nottingham F v Norwich C
Reading v Charlton Ath
Sheffield W v Rotherham U

Sunday, 9 November 2014
Barclays Premier League
WBA v Newcastle U* (1.30)
Swansea C v Arsenal* (4.00)

Saturday, 15 November 2014
Sky Bet League One
Barnsley v Colchester U
Coventry C v Notts Co
Crewe Alex v Chesterfield
Doncaster R v Sheffield U
Gillingham v Leyton Orient
Oldham Ath v Crawley T
Port Vale v Rochdale
Preston NE v Bradford C
Scunthorpe U v Milton Keynes D
Swindon T v Bristol C
Walsall v Peterborough U
Yeovil T v Fleetwood T

Sky Bet League Two
AFC Wimbledon v Dagenham & R
Cambridge U v Northampton T
Carlisle U v Accrington S
Luton T v Tranmere R
Morecambe v Bury
Newport Co v Exeter C
Plymouth Arg v Portsmouth
Shrewsbury T v Mansfield T
Southend U v Hartlepool U
Stevenage v Cheltenham T
Wycombe W v Burton Alb
York C v Oxford U

Saturday, 22 November 2014
Barclays Premier League
Arsenal v Manchester U* (5.30)
Chelsea v WBA
Everton v West Ham U
Leicester C v Sunderland
Manchester C v Swansea C
Newcastle U v QPR
Stoke C v Burnley

Sky Bet Championship
Blackburn R v Leeds U
Blackpool v Bolton W
Bournemouth v Ipswich T
Brentford v Fulham
Cardiff C v Reading
Charlton Ath v Millwall
Huddersfield T v Sheffield W
Norwich C v Brighton & HA
Rotherham U v Birmingham C
Watford v Derby Co
Wigan Ath v Middlesbrough
Wolverhampton W v Nottingham F

Sky Bet League One
Bradford C v Gillingham
Bristol C v Preston NE
Chesterfield v Barnsley
Colchester U v Coventry C
Crawley T v Scunthorpe U
Fleetwood T v Walsall
Leyton Orient v Crewe Alex
Milton Keynes D v Port Vale
Notts Co v Yeovil T
Peterborough U v Swindon T
Rochdale v Doncaster R
Sheffield U v Oldham Ath

Sky Bet League Two
Accrington S v Cambridge U
Burton Alb v Luton T
Bury v Newport Co
Cheltenham T v Wycombe W
Dagenham & R v Carlisle U
Exeter C v Shrewsbury T
Hartlepool U v York C
Mansfield T v Plymouth Arg
Northampton T v Stevenage
Oxford U v AFC Wimbledon
Portsmouth v Morecambe
Tranmere R v Southend U

Sunday, 23 November 2014
Barclays Premier League
Crystal Palace v Liverpool* (1.30)
Hull C v Tottenham H* (4.00)

Monday, 24 November 2014
Barclays Premier League
Aston Villa v Southampton* (8.00)

Saturday, 29 November 2014
Barclays Premier League
Burnley v Aston Villa
Liverpool v Stoke C
Manchester U v Hull C
QPR v Leicester C
Sunderland v Chelsea* (5.30)
Swansea C v Crystal Palace
WBA v Arsenal
West Ham U v Newcastle U

Sky Bet Championship
Birmingham C v Nottingham F
Bolton W v Huddersfield T
Bournemouth v Millwall
Brentford v Wolverhampton W
Brighton & HA v Fulham
Charlton Ath v Ipswich T
Leeds U v Derby Co
Middlesbrough v Blackburn R
Norwich C v Reading
Rotherham U v Blackpool
Sheffield W v Wigan Ath
Watford v Cardiff C

Sky Bet League One
Barnsley v Scunthorpe U
Bradford C v Leyton Orient
Coventry C v Walsall
Crawley T v Chesterfield
Crewe Alex v Doncaster R
Gillingham v Port Vale
Milton Keynes D v Colchester U
Peterborough U v Bristol C
Rochdale v Oldham Ath
Sheffield U v Notts Co
Swindon T v Fleetwood T
Yeovil T v Preston NE

Sky Bet League Two
AFC Wimbledon v Cambridge U
Accrington S v Exeter C
Bury v Dagenham & R
Carlisle U v Newport Co
Cheltenham T v Oxford U
Hartlepool U v Wycombe W
Luton T v Mansfield T
Plymouth Arg v York C
Shrewsbury T v Burton Alb
Southend U v Northampton T
Stevenage v Morecambe
Tranmere R v Portsmouth

Sunday, 30 November 2014
Barclays Premier League
Southampton v Manchester C* (1.30)
Tottenham H v Everton* (4.00)

Tuesday, 2 December 2014
Barclays Premier League
Arsenal v Southampton
Burnley v Newcastle U
Crystal Palace v Aston Villa
Leicester C v Liverpool
Manchester U v Stoke C
Swansea C v QPR
WBA v West Ham U

Wednesday, 3 December 2014
Barclays Premier League
Chelsea v Tottenham H
Everton v Hull C
Sunderland v Manchester C

Saturday, 6 December 2014
Barclays Premier League
Aston Villa v Leicester C
Hull C v WBA
Liverpool v Sunderland
Manchester C v Everton
Newcastle U v Chelsea
QPR v Burnley
Southampton v Manchester U

Tottenham H v Crystal Palace
Stoke C v Arsenal
West Ham U v Swansea C

Sky Bet Championship
Blackburn R v Sheffield W
Blackpool v Birmingham C
Cardiff C v Rotherham U
Derby Co v Brighton & HA
Fulham v Watford
Huddersfield T v Brentford
Ipswich T v Leeds U
Millwall v Middlesbrough
Nottingham F v Charlton Ath
Reading v Bolton W
Wigan Ath v Norwich C
Wolverhampton W v Bournemouth

Saturday, 13 December 2014
Barclays Premier League
Arsenal v Newcastle U
Burnley v Southampton
Chelsea v Hull C
Crystal Palace v Stoke C
Everton v QPR
Leicester C v Manchester C
Manchester U v Liverpool
Sunderland v West Ham U
Swansea C v Tottenham H
WBA v Aston Villa

Sky Bet Championship
Birmingham C v Reading
Bolton W v Ipswich T
Bournemouth v Cardiff C
Brentford v Blackburn R
Brighton & HA v Millwall
Charlton Ath v Blackpool
Leeds U v Fulham
Middlesbrough v Derby Co
Norwich C v Huddersfield T
Rotherham U v Nottingham F
Sheffield W v Wolverhampton W
Watford v Wigan Ath

Sky Bet League One
Bristol C v Crawley T
Chesterfield v Bradford C
Colchester U v Rochdale
Doncaster R v Gillingham
Fleetwood T v Sheffield U
Leyton Orient v Peterborough U
Notts Co v Swindon T
Oldham Ath v Yeovil T
Port Vale v Coventry C
Preston NE v Milton Keynes D
Scunthorpe U v Crewe Alex
Walsall v Barnsley

Sky Bet League Two
Burton Alb v Hartlepool U
Cambridge U v Shrewsbury T
Dagenham & R v Tranmere R
Exeter C v Carlisle U
Mansfield T v Cheltenham T
Morecambe v Luton T
Newport Co v Stevenage
Northampton T v Plymouth Arg
Oxford U v Bury
Portsmouth v Accrington S
Wycombe W v Southend U
York C v AFC Wimbledon

Saturday, 20 December 2014
Barclays Premier League
Aston Villa v Manchester U
Hull C v Swansea C
Liverpool v Arsenal
Manchester C v Crystal Palace
Newcastle U v Sunderland
QPR v WBA
Southampton v Everton
Tottenham H v Burnley
Stoke C v Chelsea
West Ham U v Leicester C

Sky Bet Championship
Blackburn R v Charlton Ath
Blackpool v Bournemouth
Cardiff C v Brentford
Derby Co v Norwich C
Fulham v Sheffield W
Huddersfield T v Birmingham C
Ipswich T v Middlesbrough
Millwall v Bolton W
Nottingham F v Leeds U
Reading v Watford
Wigan Ath v Rotherham U
Wolverhampton W v Brighton & HA

Sky Bet League One
Barnsley v Leyton Orient
Bradford C v Scunthorpe U
Coventry C v Fleetwood T
Crawley T v Port Vale
Crewe Alex v Bristol C
Gillingham v Chesterfield
Milton Keynes D v Oldham Ath
Peterborough U v Preston NE
Rochdale v Notts Co
Sheffield U v Walsall
Swindon T v Doncaster R
Yeovil T v Colchester U

Sky Bet League Two
AFC Wimbledon v Mansfield T
Accrington S v Wycombe W
Bury v York C
Carlisle U v Northampton T
Cheltenham T v Portsmouth
Hartlepool U v Oxford U
Luton T v Newport Co
Plymouth Arg v Dagenham & R
Shrewsbury T v Morecambe
Southend U v Burton Alb
Stevenage v Exeter C
Tranmere R v Cambridge U

Friday, 26 December 2014
Barclays Premier League
Arsenal v QPR
Burnley v Liverpool
Chelsea v West Ham U
Crystal Palace v Southampton
Everton v Stoke C
Leicester C v Tottenham H
Manchester U v Newcastle U
Sunderland v Hull C
Swansea C v Aston Villa
WBA v Manchester C

Sky Bet Championship
Birmingham C v Derby Co
Bolton W v Blackburn R
Bournemouth v Fulham
Brentford v Ipswich T
Brighton & HA v Reading
Charlton Ath v Cardiff C
Leeds U v Wigan Ath
Middlesbrough v Nottingham F
Norwich C v Millwall
Rotherham U v Huddersfield T
Sheffield W v Blackpool
Watford v Wolverhampton W

Sky Bet League One
Bristol C v Yeovil T
Chesterfield v Peterborough U
Colchester U v Gillingham
Doncaster R v Coventry C
Fleetwood T v Bradford C
Leyton Orient v Crawley T
Notts Co v Milton Keynes D
Oldham Ath v Crewe Alex
Port Vale v Sheffield U
Preston NE v Barnsley
Scunthorpe U v Rochdale
Walsall v Swindon T

Sky Bet League Two
Burton Alb v Tranmere R
Cambridge U v Southend U
Dagenham & R v Stevenage

Exeter C v Cheltenham T
Mansfield T v Hartlepool U
Morecambe v Carlisle U
Newport Co v Plymouth Arg
Northampton T v Bury
Oxford U v Shrewsbury T
Portsmouth v AFC Wimbledon
Wycombe W v Luton T
York C v Accrington S

Sunday, 28 December 2014
Barclays Premier League
Aston Villa v Sunderland
Hull C v Leicester C
Liverpool v Swansea C
Manchester C v Burnley
Newcastle U v Everton
QPR v Crystal Palace
Southampton v Chelsea
Tottenham H v Manchester U
Stoke C v WBA
West Ham U v Arsenal

Sky Bet Championship
Blackburn R v Middlesbrough
Blackpool v Rotherham U
Cardiff C v Watford
Derby Co v Leeds U
Fulham v Brighton & HA
Huddersfield T v Bolton W
Ipswich T v Charlton Ath
Millwall v Bournemouth
Nottingham F v Birmingham C
Reading v Norwich C
Wigan Ath v Sheffield W
Wolverhampton W v Brentford

Sky Bet League One
Barnsley v Oldham Ath
Bradford C v Notts Co
Coventry C v Chesterfield
Crawley T v Colchester U
Crewe Alex v Preston NE
Gillingham v Bristol C
Milton Keynes D v Walsall
Peterborough U v Doncaster R
Rochdale v Fleetwood T
Sheffield U v Scunthorpe U
Swindon T v Port Vale
Yeovil T v Leyton Orient

Sky Bet League Two
AFC Wimbledon v Exeter C
Accrington S v Burton Alb
Bury v Mansfield T
Carlisle U v York C
Cheltenham T v Newport Co
Hartlepool U v Morecambe
Luton T v Portsmouth
Plymouth Arg v Oxford U
Shrewsbury T v Wycombe W
Southend U v Dagenham & R
Stevenage v Cambridge U
Tranmere R v Northampton T

Thursday, 1 January 2015
Barclays Premier League
Aston Villa v Crystal Palace
Hull C v Everton
Liverpool v Leicester C
Manchester C v Sunderland
Newcastle U v Burnley
QPR v Swansea C
Southampton v Arsenal
Tottenham H v Chelsea
Stoke C v Manchester U
West Ham U v WBA

Saturday, 3 January 2015

Sky Bet League One
Bristol C v Peterborough U
Chesterfield v Crawley T
Colchester U v Milton Keynes D
Doncaster R v Crewe Alex
Fleetwood T v Swindon T
Leyton Orient v Bradford C

Notts Co v Sheffield U
Oldham Ath v Rochdale
Port Vale v Gillingham
Preston NE v Yeovil T
Scunthorpe U v Barnsley
Walsall v Coventry C

Sky Bet League Two
Burton Alb v Shrewsbury T
Cambridge U v AFC Wimbledon
Dagenham & R v Bury
Exeter C v Accrington S
Mansfield T v Luton T
Morecambe v Stevenage
Newport Co v Carlisle U
Northampton T v Southend U
Oxford U v Cheltenham T
Portsmouth v Tranmere R
Wycombe W v Hartlepool U
York C v Plymouth Arg

Saturday, 10 January 2015
Barclays Premier League
Arsenal v Stoke C
Burnley v QPR
Chelsea v Newcastle U
Crystal Palace v Tottenham H
Everton v Manchester C
Leicester C v Aston Villa
Manchester U v Southampton
Sunderland v Liverpool
Swansea C v West Ham U
WBA v Hull C

Sky Bet Championship
Birmingham C v Wigan Ath
Blackburn R v Wolverhampton W
Blackpool v Millwall
Bolton W v Leeds U
Bournemouth v Norwich C
Brentford v Rotherham U
Cardiff C v Fulham
Charlton Ath v Brighton & HA
Huddersfield T v Watford
Ipswich T v Derby Co
Nottingham F v Sheffield W
Reading v Middlesbrough

Sky Bet League One
Barnsley v Yeovil T
Bradford C v Rochdale
Bristol C v Notts Co
Chesterfield v Port Vale
Coventry C v Swindon T
Crawley T v Milton Keynes D
Crewe Alex v Gillingham
Leyton Orient v Fleetwood T
Oldham Ath v Doncaster R
Peterborough U v Colchester U
Sheffield U v Preston NE
Walsall v Scunthorpe U

Sky Bet League Two
Accrington S v Bury
Burton Alb v Mansfield T
Carlisle U v Cambridge U
Dagenham & R v Oxford U
Exeter C v Northampton T
Hartlepool U v Cheltenham T
Luton T v Shrewsbury T
Morecambe v Tranmere R
Newport Co v Portsmouth
Southend U v Plymouth Arg
Stevenage v AFC Wimbledon
Wycombe W v York C

Saturday, 17 January 2015
Barclays Premier League
Aston Villa v Liverpool
Burnley v Crystal Palace
Everton v WBA
Leicester C v Stoke C
Manchester C v Arsenal
Newcastle U v Southampton
QPR v Manchester U
Tottenham H v Sunderland

Swansea C v Chelsea
West Ham U v Hull C

Sky Bet Championship
Brighton & HA v Brentford
Derby Co v Nottingham F
Fulham v Reading
Leeds U v Birmingham C
Middlesbrough v Huddersfield T
Millwall v Ipswich T
Norwich C v Cardiff C
Rotherham U v Bournemouth
Sheffield W v Bolton W
Watford v Charlton Ath
Wigan Ath v Blackburn R
Wolverhampton W v Blackpool

Sky Bet League One
Colchester U v Walsall
Doncaster R v Barnsley
Fleetwood T v Oldham Ath
Gillingham v Coventry C
Milton Keynes D v Sheffield U
Notts Co v Crewe Alex
Port Vale v Peterborough U
Preston NE v Leyton Orient
Rochdale v Crawley T
Scunthorpe U v Bristol C
Swindon T v Chesterfield
Yeovil T v Bradford C

Sky Bet League Two
AFC Wimbledon v Carlisle U
Bury v Wycombe W
Cambridge U v Newport Co
Cheltenham T v Morecambe
Mansfield T v Exeter C
Northampton T v Dagenham & R
Oxford U v Southend U
Plymouth Arg v Luton T
Portsmouth v Burton Alb
Shrewsbury T v Hartlepool U
Tranmere R v Accrington S
York C v Stevenage

Saturday, 24 January 2015
Sky Bet Championship
Brighton & HA v Ipswich T
Derby Co v Blackburn R
Fulham v Nottingham F
Leeds U v Bournemouth
Middlesbrough v Cardiff C
Millwall v Reading
Norwich C v Brentford
Rotherham U v Bolton W
Sheffield W v Birmingham C
Watford v Blackpool
Wigan Ath v Huddersfield T
Wolverhampton W v Charlton Ath

Sky Bet League One
Colchester U v Leyton Orient
Doncaster R v Bristol C
Fleetwood T v Crawley T
Gillingham v Oldham Ath
Milton Keynes D v Barnsley
Notts Co v Peterborough U
Port Vale v Crewe Alex
Preston NE v Walsall
Rochdale v Sheffield U
Scunthorpe U v Chesterfield
Swindon T v Bradford C
Yeovil T v Coventry C

Sky Bet League Two
AFC Wimbledon v Accrington S
Bury v Carlisle U
Cambridge U v Dagenham & R
Cheltenham T v Luton T
Mansfield T v Wycombe W
Northampton T v Newport Co
Oxford U v Exeter C
Plymouth Arg v Morecambe
Portsmouth v Southend U
Shrewsbury T v Stevenage
Tranmere R v Hartlepool U
York C v Burton Alb

Saturday, 31 January 2015
Barclays Premier League
Arsenal v Aston Villa
Chelsea v Manchester C
Crystal Palace v Everton
Hull C v Newcastle U
Liverpool v West Ham U
Manchester U v Leicester C
Southampton v Swansea C
Stoke C v QPR
Sunderland v Burnley
WBA v Tottenham H

Sky Bet Championship
Birmingham C v Norwich C
Blackburn R v Fulham
Blackpool v Brighton & HA
Bolton W v Wolverhampton W
Bournemouth v Watford
Brentford v Middlesbrough
Cardiff C v Derby Co
Charlton Ath v Rotherham U
Huddersfield T v Leeds U
Ipswich T v Wigan Ath
Nottingham F v Millwall
Reading v Sheffield W

Sky Bet League One
Barnsley v Port Vale
Bradford C v Colchester U
Bristol C v Fleetwood T
Chesterfield v Doncaster R
Coventry C v Rochdale
Crawley T v Preston NE
Crewe Alex v Milton Keynes D
Leyton Orient v Scunthorpe U
Oldham Ath v Notts Co
Peterborough U v Yeovil T
Sheffield U v Swindon T
Walsall v Gillingham

Sky Bet League Two
Accrington S v Northampton T
Burton Alb v Bury
Carlisle U v Mansfield T
Dagenham & R v Cheltenham T
Exeter C v Tranmere R
Hartlepool U v Plymouth Arg
Luton T v Cambridge U
Morecambe v AFC Wimbledon
Newport Co v Shrewsbury T
Southend U v York C
Stevenage v Oxford U
Wycombe W v Portsmouth

Saturday, 7 February 2015
Barclays Premier League
Aston Villa v Chelsea
Burnley v WBA
Everton v Liverpool
Leicester C v Crystal Palace
Manchester C v Hull C
Newcastle U v Stoke C
QPR v Southampton
Tottenham H v Arsenal
Swansea C v Sunderland
West Ham U v Manchester U

Sky Bet Championship
Brighton & HA v Nottingham F
Derby Co v Bolton W
Fulham v Birmingham C
Leeds U v Brentford
Middlesbrough v Charlton Ath
Millwall v Huddersfield T
Norwich C v Blackpool
Rotherham U v Ipswich T
Sheffield W v Cardiff C
Watford v Blackburn R
Wigan Ath v Bournemouth
Wolverhampton W v Reading

Sky Bet League One
Colchester U v Crewe Alex
Doncaster R v Walsall
Fleetwood T v Peterborough U
Gillingham v Sheffield U

Milton Keynes D v Bristol C
Notts Co v Chesterfield
Port Vale v Bradford C
Preston NE v Coventry C
Rochdale v Leyton Orient
Scunthorpe U v Oldham Ath
Swindon T v Barnsley
Yeovil T v Crawley T

Sky Bet League Two
AFC Wimbledon v Newport Co
Bury v Exeter C
Cambridge U v Wycombe W
Cheltenham T v Burton Alb
Mansfield T v Stevenage
Northampton T v Morecambe
Oxford U v Luton T
Plymouth Arg v Accrington S
Portsmouth v Hartlepool U
Shrewsbury T v Southend U
Tranmere R v Carlisle U
York C v Dagenham & R

Tuesday, 10 February 2015
Barclays Premier League
Arsenal v Leicester C
Crystal Palace v Newcastle U
Hull C v Aston Villa
Liverpool v Tottenham H
Manchester U v Burnley
Southampton v West Ham U
WBA v Swansea C

Sky Bet Championship
Birmingham C v Millwall
Blackburn R v Rotherham U
Blackpool v Middlesbrough
Bolton W v Fulham
Bournemouth v Derby Co
Brentford v Watford
Cardiff C v Brighton & HA
Charlton Ath v Norwich C
Huddersfield T v Wolverhampton W
Ipswich T v Sheffield W
Reading v Leeds U

Sky Bet League One
Barnsley v Fleetwood T
Bradford C v Milton Keynes D
Bristol C v Port Vale
Chesterfield v Preston NE
Coventry C v Scunthorpe U
Crawley T v Doncaster R
Crewe Alex v Yeovil T
Leyton Orient v Notts Co
Oldham Ath v Swindon T
Peterborough U v Gillingham
Sheffield U v Colchester U
Walsall v Rochdale

Sky Bet League Two
Accrington S v Oxford U
Burton Alb v AFC Wimbledon
Carlisle U v Shrewsbury T
Dagenham & R v Portsmouth
Exeter C v Cambridge U
Hartlepool U v Northampton T
Luton T v York C
Morecambe v Mansfield T
Newport Co v Tranmere R
Southend U v Cheltenham T
Stevenage v Bury
Wycombe W v Plymouth Arg

Wednesday, 11 February 2015
Barclays Premier League
Chelsea v Everton
Stoke C v Manchester C
Sunderland v QPR

Sky Bet Championship
Nottingham F v Wigan Ath

Saturday, 14 February 2015
Sky Bet Championship
Birmingham C v Middlesbrough
Blackpool v Nottingham F

Bolton W v Watford
Bournemouth v Huddersfield T
Cardiff C v Blackburn R
Charlton Ath v Brentford
Fulham v Ipswich T
Leeds U v Millwall
Norwich C v Wolverhampton W
Reading v Wigan Ath
Rotherham U v Derby Co
Sheffield W v Brighton & HA

Sky Bet League One
Bristol C v Sheffield U
Chesterfield v Leyton Orient
Coventry C v Bradford C
Crawley T v Barnsley
Crewe Alex v Fleetwood T
Doncaster R v Yeovil T
Gillingham v Milton Keynes D
Notts Co v Preston NE
Oldham Ath v Colchester U
Peterborough U v Rochdale
Scunthorpe U v Swindon T
Walsall v Port Vale

Sky Bet League Two
Burton Alb v Oxford U
Cheltenham T v Bury
Hartlepool U v Stevenage
Luton T v Carlisle U
Mansfield T v Northampton T
Morecambe v Dagenham & R
Plymouth Arg v Cambridge U
Portsmouth v Exeter C
Shrewsbury T v AFC Wimbledon
Southend U v Accrington S
Wycombe W v Newport Co
York C v Tranmere R

Saturday, 21 February 2015
Barclays Premier League
Aston Villa v Stoke C
Chelsea v Burnley
Crystal Palace v Arsenal
Everton v Leicester C
Hull C v QPR
Manchester C v Newcastle U
Southampton v Liverpool
Tottenham H v West Ham U
Sunderland v WBA
Swansea C v Manchester U

Sky Bet Championship
Blackburn R v Blackpool
Brentford v Bournemouth
Brighton & HA v Birmingham C
Derby Co v Sheffield W
Huddersfield T v Cardiff C
Ipswich T v Reading
Middlesbrough v Leeds U
Millwall v Fulham
Nottingham F v Bolton W
Watford v Norwich C
Wigan Ath v Charlton Ath
Wolverhampton W v Rotherham U

Sky Bet League One
Barnsley v Crewe Alex
Bradford C v Walsall
Colchester U v Bristol C
Fleetwood T v Notts Co
Leyton Orient v Oldham Ath
Milton Keynes D v Peterborough U
Port Vale v Doncaster R
Preston NE v Scunthorpe U
Rochdale v Chesterfield
Sheffield U v Coventry C
Swindon T v Crawley T
Yeovil T v Gillingham

Sky Bet League Two
AFC Wimbledon v Luton T
Accrington S v Cheltenham T
Bury v Hartlepool U
Cambridge U v Portsmouth
Carlisle U v Wycombe W
Dagenham & R v Burton Alb

Exeter C v Plymouth Arg
Newport Co v Morecambe
Northampton T v York C
Oxford U v Mansfield T
Stevenage v Southend U
Tranmere R v Shrewsbury T

Tuesday, 24 February 2015
Sky Bet Championship
Blackburn R v Norwich C
Brentford v Blackpool
Brighton & HA v Leeds U
Derby Co v Charlton Ath
Huddersfield T v Reading
Ipswich T v Birmingham C
Middlesbrough v Bolton W
Millwall v Sheffield W
Watford v Rotherham U
Wigan Ath v Cardiff C
Wolverhampton W v Fulham

Wednesday, 25 February 2015
Sky Bet Championship
Nottingham F v Bournemouth

Saturday, 28 February 2015
Barclays Premier League
Arsenal v Everton
Burnley v Swansea C
Leicester C v Chelsea
Liverpool v Manchester C
Manchester U v Sunderland
Newcastle U v Aston Villa
QPR v Tottenham H
Stoke C v Hull C
WBA v Southampton
West Ham U v Crystal Palace

Sky Bet Championship
Birmingham C v Brentford
Blackpool v Wigan Ath
Bolton W v Brighton & HA
Bournemouth v Blackburn R
Cardiff C v Wolverhampton W
Charlton Ath v Huddersfield T
Fulham v Derby Co
Leeds U v Watford
Norwich C v Ipswich T
Reading v Nottingham F
Rotherham U v Millwall
Sheffield W v Middlesbrough

Sky Bet League One
Bristol C v Rochdale
Chesterfield v Fleetwood T
Coventry C v Milton Keynes D
Crawley T v Sheffield U
Crewe Alex v Swindon T
Doncaster R v Colchester U
Gillingham v Barnsley
Notts Co v Port Vale
Oldham Ath v Preston NE
Peterborough U v Bradford C
Scunthorpe U v Yeovil T
Walsall v Leyton Orient

Sky Bet League Two
Burton Alb v Newport Co
Cheltenham T v Tranmere R
Hartlepool U v AFC Wimbledon
Luton T v Accrington S
Mansfield T v Dagenham & R
Morecambe v Cambridge U
Plymouth Arg v Bury
Portsmouth v Oxford U
Shrewsbury T v Northampton T
Southend U v Carlisle U
Wycombe W v Stevenage
York C v Exeter C

Tuesday, 3 March 2015
Barclays Premier League
Aston Villa v WBA
Hull C v Sunderland
Liverpool v Burnley
QPR v Arsenal

Southampton v Crystal Palace
West Ham U v Chelsea

Sky Bet Championship
Birmingham C v Blackpool
Bolton W v Reading
Bournemouth v Wolverhampton W
Brentford v Huddersfield T
Brighton & HA v Derby Co
Charlton Ath v Nottingham F
Leeds U v Ipswich T
Middlesbrough v Millwall
Norwich C v Wigan Ath
Rotherham U v Cardiff C
Sheffield W v Blackburn R
Watford v Fulham

Sky Bet League One
Barnsley v Coventry C
Bradford C v Crawley T
Colchester U v Notts Co
Fleetwood T v Scunthorpe U
Leyton Orient v Bristol C
Milton Keynes D v Chesterfield
Port Vale v Oldham Ath
Preston NE v Doncaster R
Rochdale v Crewe Alex
Sheffield U v Peterborough U
Swindon T v Gillingham
Yeovil T v Walsall

Sky Bet League Two
AFC Wimbledon v Southend U
Accrington S v Shrewsbury T
Bury v Luton T
Cambridge U v York C
Carlisle U v Cheltenham T
Dagenham & R v Hartlepool U
Exeter C v Burton Alb
Newport Co v Mansfield T
Northampton T v Portsmouth
Oxford U v Morecambe
Stevenage v Plymouth Arg
Tranmere R v Wycombe W

Wednesday, 4 March 2015
Barclays Premier League
Manchester C v Leicester C
Newcastle U v Manchester U
Tottenham H v Swansea C
Stoke C v Everton

Saturday, 7 March 2015
Sky Bet Championship
Blackburn R v Bolton W
Blackpool v Sheffield W
Cardiff C v Charlton Ath
Derby Co v Birmingham C
Fulham v Bournemouth
Huddersfield T v Rotherham U
Ipswich T v Brentford
Millwall v Norwich C
Nottingham F v Middlesbrough
Reading v Brighton & HA
Wigan Ath v Leeds U
Wolverhampton W v Watford

Sky Bet League One
Barnsley v Walsall
Bradford C v Chesterfield
Coventry C v Port Vale
Crawley T v Bristol C
Crewe Alex v Scunthorpe U
Gillingham v Doncaster R
Milton Keynes D v Preston NE
Peterborough U v Leyton Orient
Rochdale v Colchester U
Sheffield U v Fleetwood T
Swindon T v Notts Co
Yeovil T v Oldham Ath

Sky Bet League Two
AFC Wimbledon v York C
Accrington S v Portsmouth
Bury v Oxford U
Carlisle U v Exeter C
Cheltenham T v Mansfield T

Hartlepool U v Burton Alb
Luton T v Morecambe
Plymouth Arg v Northampton T
Shrewsbury T v Cambridge U
Southend U v Wycombe W
Stevenage v Newport Co
Tranmere R v Dagenham & R

Saturday, 14 March 2015
Barclays Premier League
Arsenal v West Ham U
Burnley v Manchester C
Chelsea v Southampton
Crystal Palace v QPR
Everton v Newcastle U
Leicester C v Hull C
Manchester U v Tottenham H
Sunderland v Aston Villa
Swansea C v Liverpool
WBA v Stoke C

Sky Bet Championship
Birmingham C v Huddersfield T
Bolton W v Millwall
Bournemouth v Blackpool
Brentford v Cardiff C
Brighton & HA v Wolverhampton W
Charlton Ath v Blackburn R
Leeds U v Nottingham F
Middlesbrough v Ipswich T
Norwich C v Derby Co
Rotherham U v Wigan Ath
Sheffield W v Fulham
Watford v Reading

Sky Bet League One
Bristol C v Gillingham
Chesterfield v Coventry C
Colchester U v Crawley T
Doncaster R v Peterborough U
Fleetwood T v Rochdale
Leyton Orient v Yeovil T
Notts Co v Bradford C
Oldham Ath v Barnsley
Port Vale v Swindon T
Preston NE v Crewe Alex
Scunthorpe U v Sheffield U
Walsall v Milton Keynes D

Sky Bet League Two
Burton Alb v Accrington S
Cambridge U v Stevenage
Dagenham & R v Southend U
Exeter C v AFC Wimbledon
Mansfield T v Bury
Morecambe v Hartlepool U
Newport Co v Cheltenham T
Northampton T v Tranmere R
Oxford U v Plymouth Arg
Portsmouth v Luton T
Wycombe W v Shrewsbury T
York C v Carlisle U

Tuesday, 17 March 2015
Sky Bet Championship
Blackburn R v Brentford
Blackpool v Charlton Ath
Cardiff C v Bournemouth
Derby Co v Middlesbrough
Huddersfield T v Norwich C
Ipswich T v Bolton W
Millwall v Brighton & HA
Reading v Birmingham C
Wigan Ath v Watford
Wolverhampton W v Sheffield W

Sky Bet League One
Bristol C v Crewe Alex
Chesterfield v Gillingham
Colchester U v Yeovil T
Doncaster R v Swindon T
Fleetwood T v Coventry C
Leyton Orient v Barnsley
Notts Co v Rochdale
Oldham Ath v Milton Keynes D
Port Vale v Crawley T
Preston NE v Peterborough U

Scunthorpe U v Bradford C
Walsall v Sheffield U

Sky Bet League Two
Burton Alb v Southend U
Cambridge U v Tranmere R
Dagenham & R v Plymouth Arg
Exeter C v Stevenage
Mansfield T v AFC Wimbledon
Morecambe v Shrewsbury T
Newport Co v Luton T
Northampton T v Carlisle U
Oxford U v Hartlepool U
Portsmouth v Cheltenham T
Wycombe W v Accrington S
York C v Bury

Wednesday, 18 March 2015
Sky Bet Championship
Fulham v Leeds U
Nottingham F v Rotherham U

Saturday, 21 March 2015
Barclays Premier League
Aston Villa v Swansea C
Hull C v Chelsea
Liverpool v Manchester U
Manchester C v WBA
Newcastle U v Arsenal
QPR v Everton
Southampton v Burnley
Tottenham H v Leicester C
Stoke C v Crystal Palace
West Ham U v Sunderland

Sky Bet Championship
Blackburn R v Brighton & HA
Blackpool v Leeds U
Bournemouth v Middlesbrough
Brentford v Millwall
Cardiff C v Birmingham C
Charlton Ath v Reading
Huddersfield T v Fulham
Norwich C v Nottingham F
Rotherham U v Sheffield W
Watford v Ipswich T
Wigan Ath v Bolton W
Wolverhampton W v Derby Co

Sky Bet League One
Barnsley v Preston NE
Bradford C v Fleetwood T
Coventry C v Doncaster R
Crawley T v Leyton Orient
Crewe Alex v Oldham Ath
Gillingham v Colchester U
Milton Keynes D v Notts Co
Peterborough U v Chesterfield
Rochdale v Scunthorpe U
Sheffield U v Port Vale
Swindon T v Walsall
Yeovil T v Bristol C

Sky Bet League Two
AFC Wimbledon v Portsmouth
Accrington S v York C
Bury v Northampton T
Carlisle U v Morecambe
Cheltenham T v Exeter C
Hartlepool U v Mansfield T
Luton T v Wycombe W
Plymouth Arg v Newport Co
Shrewsbury T v Oxford U
Southend U v Cambridge U
Stevenage v Dagenham & R
Tranmere R v Burton Alb

Saturday, 28 March 2015

Sky Bet League One
Bradford C v Oldham Ath
Bristol C v Barnsley
Chesterfield v Walsall
Colchester U v Swindon T
Crawley T v Gillingham
Fleetwood T v Preston NE
Leyton Orient v Port Vale
Milton Keynes D v Doncaster R

Notts Co v Scunthorpe U
Peterborough U v Coventry C
Rochdale v Yeovil T
Sheffield U v Crewe Alex

Sky Bet League Two
Accrington S v Newport Co
Burton Alb v Stevenage
Bury v Southend U
Cheltenham T v Plymouth Arg
Dagenham & R v Wycombe W
Exeter C v Morecambe
Hartlepool U v Cambridge U
Mansfield T v York C
Northampton T v Luton T
Oxford U v Carlisle U
Portsmouth v Shrewsbury T
Tranmere R v AFC Wimbledon

Saturday, 4 April 2015
Barclays Premier League
Arsenal v Liverpool
Burnley v Tottenham H
Chelsea v Stoke C
Crystal Palace v Manchester C
Everton v Southampton
Leicester C v West Ham U
Manchester U v Aston Villa
Sunderland v Newcastle U
Swansea C v Hull C
WBA v QPR

Sky Bet Championship
Birmingham C v Rotherham U
Bolton W v Blackpool
Brighton & HA v Norwich C
Derby Co v Watford
Fulham v Brentford
Ipswich T v Bournemouth
Leeds U v Blackburn R
Middlesbrough v Wigan Ath
Millwall v Charlton Ath
Nottingham F v Wolverhampton W
Reading v Cardiff C
Sheffield W v Huddersfield T

Sky Bet League One
Barnsley v Sheffield U
Coventry C v Leyton Orient
Crewe Alex v Crawley T
Doncaster R v Bradford C
Gillingham v Fleetwood T
Oldham Ath v Bristol C
Port Vale v Colchester U
Preston NE v Rochdale
Scunthorpe U v Peterborough U
Swindon T v Milton Keynes D
Walsall v Notts Co
Yeovil T v Chesterfield

Sky Bet League Two
AFC Wimbledon v Northampton T
Cambridge U v Bury
Carlisle U v Portsmouth
Luton T v Exeter C
Morecambe v Accrington S
Newport Co v Hartlepool U
Plymouth Arg v Burton Alb
Shrewsbury T v Dagenham & R
Southend U v Mansfield T
Stevenage v Tranmere R
Wycombe W v Oxford U
York C v Cheltenham T

Monday, 6 April 2015
Sky Bet Championship
Blackburn R v Millwall
Blackpool v Reading
Bournemouth v Birmingham C
Brentford v Nottingham F
Cardiff C v Bolton W
Charlton Ath v Fulham
Huddersfield T v Ipswich T
Norwich C v Sheffield W
Rotherham U v Brighton & HA
Watford v Middlesbrough

Wigan Ath v Derby Co
Wolverhampton W v Leeds U

Sky Bet League One
Bradford C v Preston NE
Bristol C v Swindon T
Chesterfield v Crewe Alex
Colchester U v Barnsley
Crawley T v Oldham Ath
Fleetwood T v Yeovil T
Leyton Orient v Gillingham
Milton Keynes D v Scunthorpe U
Notts Co v Coventry C
Peterborough U v Walsall
Rochdale v Port Vale
Sheffield U v Doncaster R

Sky Bet League Two
Accrington S v Carlisle U
Burton Alb v Wycombe W
Bury v Morecambe
Cheltenham T v Stevenage
Dagenham & R v AFC Wimbledon
Exeter C v Newport Co
Hartlepool U v Southend U
Mansfield T v Shrewsbury T
Northampton T v Cambridge U
Oxford U v York C
Portsmouth v Plymouth Arg
Tranmere R v Luton T

Saturday, 11 April 2015
Barclays Premier League
Burnley v Arsenal
Liverpool v Newcastle U
Manchester U v Manchester C
QPR v Chelsea
Southampton v Hull C
Tottenham H v Aston Villa
Sunderland v Crystal Palace
Swansea C v Everton
WBA v Leicester C
West Ham U v Stoke C

Sky Bet Championship
Birmingham C v Wolverhampton W
Bolton W v Norwich C
Brighton & HA v Bournemouth
Derby Co v Brentford
Fulham v Wigan Ath
Ipswich T v Blackpool
Leeds U v Cardiff C
Middlesbrough v Rotherham U
Millwall v Watford
Nottingham F v Huddersfield T
Reading v Blackburn R
Sheffield W v Charlton Ath

Sky Bet League One
Barnsley v Chesterfield
Coventry C v Colchester U
Crewe Alex v Leyton Orient
Doncaster R v Rochdale
Gillingham v Bradford C
Oldham Ath v Sheffield U
Port Vale v Milton Keynes D
Preston NE v Bristol C
Scunthorpe U v Crawley T
Swindon T v Peterborough U
Walsall v Fleetwood T
Yeovil T v Notts Co

Sky Bet League Two
AFC Wimbledon v Oxford U
Cambridge U v Accrington S
Carlisle U v Dagenham & R
Luton T v Burton Alb
Morecambe v Portsmouth
Newport Co v Bury
Plymouth Arg v Mansfield T
Shrewsbury T v Exeter C
Southend U v Tranmere R
Stevenage v Northampton T
Wycombe W v Cheltenham T
York C v Hartlepool U

Tuesday, 14 April 2015
Sky Bet Championship
Birmingham C v Blackburn R
Bolton W v Charlton Ath
Brighton & HA v Huddersfield T
Derby Co v Blackpool
Ipswich T v Cardiff C
Leeds U v Norwich C
Middlesbrough v Wolverhampton W
Millwall v Wigan Ath
Reading v Bournemouth
Sheffield W v Brentford

Sky Bet League One
Bradford C v Bristol C
Chesterfield v Colchester U
Coventry C v Oldham Ath
Fleetwood T v Milton Keynes D
Leyton Orient v Doncaster R
Notts Co v Barnsley
Peterborough U v Crewe Alex
Preston NE v Gillingham
Rochdale v Swindon T
Scunthorpe U v Port Vale
Walsall v Crawley T
Yeovil T v Sheffield U

Sky Bet League Two
Burton Alb v Carlisle U
Bury v Shrewsbury T
Cheltenham T v Cambridge U
Dagenham & R v Luton T
Hartlepool U v Accrington S
Mansfield T v Tranmere R
Oxford U v Northampton T
Plymouth Arg v AFC Wimbledon
Southend U v Newport Co
Stevenage v Portsmouth
Wycombe W v Exeter C
York C v Morecambe

Wednesday, 15 April 2015
Sky Bet Championship
Fulham v Rotherham U
Nottingham F v Watford

Saturday, 18 April 2015
Barclays Premier League
Arsenal v Sunderland
Aston Villa v QPR
Chelsea v Manchester U
Crystal Palace v WBA
Everton v Burnley
Hull C v Liverpool
Leicester C v Swansea C
Manchester C v West Ham U
Newcastle U v Tottenham H
Stoke C v Southampton

Sky Bet Championship
Blackburn R v Nottingham F
Blackpool v Fulham
Bournemouth v Sheffield W
Brentford v Bolton W
Cardiff C v Millwall
Charlton Ath v Leeds U
Huddersfield T v Derby Co
Norwich C v Middlesbrough
Rotherham U v Reading
Watford v Birmingham C
Wigan Ath v Brighton & HA
Wolverhampton W v Ipswich T

Sky Bet League One
Barnsley v Peterborough U
Bristol C v Coventry C
Colchester U v Scunthorpe U
Crawley T v Notts Co
Crewe Alex v Walsall
Doncaster R v Fleetwood T
Gillingham v Rochdale
Milton Keynes D v Leyton Orient
Oldham Ath v Chesterfield
Port Vale v Preston NE

Sheffield U v Bradford C
Swindon T v Yeovil T

Sky Bet League Two
AFC Wimbledon v Wycombe W
Accrington S v Stevenage
Cambridge U v Mansfield T
Carlisle U v Plymouth Arg
Exeter C v Southend U
Luton T v Hartlepool U
Morecambe v Burton Alb
Newport Co v Dagenham & R
Northampton T v Cheltenham T
Portsmouth v Bury
Shrewsbury T v York C
Tranmere R v Oxford U

Saturday, 25 April 2015
Barclays Premier League
Arsenal v Chelsea
Burnley v Leicester C
Crystal Palace v Hull C
Everton v Manchester U
Manchester C v Aston Villa
Newcastle U v Swansea C
QPR v West Ham U
Southampton v Tottenham H
Stoke C v Sunderland
WBA v Liverpool

Sky Bet Championship
Birmingham C v Charlton Ath
Bournemouth v Bolton W
Brighton & HA v Watford
Cardiff C v Blackpool
Fulham v Middlesbrough
Huddersfield T v Blackburn R
Ipswich T v Nottingham F
Millwall v Derby Co
Reading v Brentford
Rotherham U v Norwich C
Sheffield W v Leeds U
Wigan Ath v Wolverhampton W

Sky Bet League One
Bradford C v Barnsley
Chesterfield v Bristol C
Coventry C v Crewe Alex
Fleetwood T v Colchester U
Leyton Orient v Sheffield U
Notts Co v Doncaster R
Peterborough U v Crawley T
Preston NE v Swindon T
Rochdale v Milton Keynes D
Scunthorpe U v Gillingham
Walsall v Oldham Ath
Yeovil T v Port Vale

Sky Bet League Two
Burton Alb v Northampton T
Bury v AFC Wimbledon
Cheltenham T v Shrewsbury T
Dagenham & R v Accrington S
Hartlepool U v Exeter C
Mansfield T v Portsmouth
Oxford U v Cambridge U
Plymouth Arg v Tranmere R
Southend U v Luton T
Stevenage v Carlisle U
Wycombe W v Morecambe
York C v Newport Co

Saturday, 2 May 2015
Barclays Premier League
Aston Villa v Everton
Chelsea v Crystal Palace
Hull C v Arsenal
Leicester C v Newcastle U
Liverpool v QPR
Manchester U v WBA
Tottenham H v Manchester C
Sunderland v Southampton
Swansea C v Stoke C
West Ham U v Burnley

Sky Bet Championship
Blackburn R v Ipswich T
Blackpool v Huddersfield T
Bolton W v Birmingham C
Brentford v Wigan Ath
Charlton Ath v Bournemouth
Derby Co v Reading
Leeds U v Rotherham U
Middlesbrough v Brighton & HA
Norwich C v Fulham
Nottingham F v Cardiff C
Watford v Sheffield W
Wolverhampton W v Millwall

Sky Bet League One
Barnsley v Rochdale
Bristol C v Walsall
Colchester U v Preston NE
Crawley T v Coventry C
Crewe Alex v Bradford C
Doncaster R v Scunthorpe U
Gillingham v Notts Co
Milton Keynes D v Yeovil T
Oldham Ath v Peterborough U
Port Vale v Fleetwood T
Sheffield U v Chesterfield
Swindon T v Leyton Orient

Sky Bet League Two
AFC Wimbledon v Cheltenham T
Accrington S v Mansfield T
Cambridge U v Burton Alb
Carlisle U v Hartlepool U
Exeter C v Dagenham & R
Luton T v Stevenage
Morecambe v Southend U
Newport Co v Oxford U
Northampton T v Wycombe W
Portsmouth v York C
Shrewsbury T v Plymouth Arg
Tranmere R v Bury

Saturday, 9 May 2015
Barclays Premier League
Arsenal v Swansea C
Aston Villa v West Ham U
Chelsea v Liverpool
Crystal Palace v Manchester U
Everton v Sunderland
Hull C v Burnley
Leicester C v Southampton
Manchester C v QPR
Newcastle U v WBA
Stoke C v Tottenham H

Saturday, 16 May 2015
Barclays Premier League
Burnley v Stoke C
Liverpool v Crystal Palace
Manchester U v Arsenal
QPR v Newcastle U
Southampton v Aston Villa
Tottenham H v Hull C
Sunderland v Leicester C
Swansea C v Manchester C
WBA v Chelsea
West Ham U v Everton

Sunday, 24 May 2015
Barclays Premier League
Arsenal v WBA
Aston Villa v Burnley
Chelsea v Sunderland
Crystal Palace v Swansea C
Everton v Tottenham H
Hull C v Manchester U
Leicester C v QPR
Manchester C v Southampton
Newcastle U v West Ham U
Stoke C v Liverpool

CONFERENCE PREMIER FIXTURES 2014–15

Saturday, 9 August 2014
Aldershot T v Altrincham
Alfreton T v Woking
Bristol R v Grimsby T
Chester FC v Barnet
Dartford v Wrexham
Dover v FC Halifax T
Gateshead v Torquay U
Lincoln C v Kidderminster H
Macclesfield T v Braintree T
Nuneaton T v Eastleigh
Southport v Forest Green R
Welling U v AFC Telford U

Tuesday, 12 August 2014
AFC Telford U v Macclesfield T
Altrincham v Lincoln C
Barnet v Bristol R
Braintree T v Dover
Eastleigh v Aldershot T
FC Halifax T v Southport
Forest Green R v Chester FC
Grimsby T v Nuneaton T
Kidderminster H v Alfreton T
Torquay U v Welling U
Woking v Dartford
Wrexham v Gateshead

Saturday, 16 August 2014
AFC Telford U v Aldershot T
Altrincham v Bristol R
Barnet v Lincoln C
Braintree T v Chester FC
Eastleigh v Gateshead
FC Halifax T v Welling U
Forest Green R v Alfreton T
Grimsby T v Dover
Kidderminster H v Dartford
Torquay U v Southport
Woking v Macclesfield T
Wrexham v Nuneaton T

Saturday, 23 August 2014
Aldershot T v Forest Green R
Alfreton T v Wrexham
Bristol R v AFC Telford U
Chester FC v FC Halifax T
Dartford v Torquay U
Dover v Eastleigh
Gateshead v Grimsby T
Lincoln C v Braintree T
Macclesfield T v Kidderminster H
Nuneaton T v Barnet
Southport v Altrincham
Welling U v Woking

Monday, 25 August 2014
AFC Telford U v Southport
Altrincham v Gateshead
Barnet v Dartford
Braintree T v Nuneaton T
Eastleigh v Welling U
FC Halifax T v Lincoln C
Forest Green R v Bristol R
Grimsby T v Alfreton T
Kidderminster H v Chester FC
Torquay U v Aldershot T
Woking v Dover
Wrexham v Macclesfield T

Saturday, 30 August 2014
Aldershot T v Grimsby T
Alfreton T v Braintree T

Bristol R v FC Halifax T
Dartford v AFC Telford U
Dover v Kidderminster H
Gateshead v Chester FC
Lincoln C v Torquay U
Macclesfield T v Eastleigh
Nuneaton T v Altrincham
Southport v Barnet
Welling U v Forest Green R
Wrexham v Woking

Saturday, 6 September 2014
AFC Telford U v Dover
Altrincham v Dartford
Barnet v Alfreton T
Braintree T v Bristol R
Chester FC v Macclesfield T
Eastleigh v Southport
FC Halifax T v Aldershot T
Forest Green R v Wrexham
Grimsby T v Welling U
Kidderminster H v Gateshead
Torquay U v Nuneaton T
Woking v Lincoln C

Tuesday, 9 September 2014
Aldershot T v Woking
Alfreton T v Altrincham
Bristol R v Wrexham
Chester FC v Torquay U
Dartford v Eastleigh
Dover v Barnet
Gateshead v AFC Telford U
Lincoln C v Grimsby T
Macclesfield T v FC Halifax T
Nuneaton T v Forest Green R
Southport v Kidderminster H
Welling U v Braintree T

Saturday, 13 September 2014
AFC Telford U v Barnet
Altrincham v Eastleigh
Braintree T v Kidderminster H
Dover v Macclesfield T
Forest Green R v FC Halifax T
Gateshead v Dartford
Grimsby T v Torquay U
Lincoln C v Bristol R
Nuneaton T v Aldershot T
Southport v Alfreton T
Woking v Chester FC
Wrexham v Welling U

Tuesday, 16 September 2014
Aldershot T v Braintree T
Alfreton T v AFC Telford U
Barnet v Wrexham
Bristol R v Nuneaton T
Chester FC v Southport
Dartford v Dover
Eastleigh v Forest Green R
FC Halifax T v Grimsby T
Kidderminster H v Altrincham
Macclesfield T v Gateshead
Torquay U v Woking
Welling U v Lincoln C

Saturday, 20 September 2014
Aldershot T v Lincoln C
Alfreton T v Nuneaton T
Barnet v Altrincham
Bristol R v Woking
Chester FC v Wrexham

Dartford v Forest Green R
Eastleigh v Braintree T
FC Halifax T v AFC Telford U
Kidderminster H v Grimsby T
Macclesfield T v Southport
Torquay U v Dover
Welling U v Gateshead

Saturday, 27 September 2014
AFC Telford U v Torquay U
Altrincham v Welling U
Braintree T v FC Halifax T
Dover v Alfreton T
Forest Green R v Barnet
Gateshead v Aldershot T
Grimsby T v Chester FC
Lincoln C v Macclesfield T
Nuneaton T v Dartford
Southport v Bristol R
Woking v Kidderminster H
Wrexham v Eastleigh

Tuesday, 30 September 2014
AFC Telford U v Chester FC
Alfreton T v FC Halifax T
Altrincham v Macclesfield T
Braintree T v Barnet
Dover v Aldershot T
Eastleigh v Bristol R
Forest Green R v Torquay U
Grimsby T v Southport
Lincoln C v Gateshead
Welling U v Dartford
Woking v Nuneaton T
Wrexham v Kidderminster H

Saturday, 4 October 2014
Aldershot T v Alfreton T
Barnet v Eastleigh
Bristol R v Dover
Chester FC v Welling U
Dartford v Grimsby T
FC Halifax T v Altrincham
Gateshead v Braintree T
Kidderminster H v AFC Telford U
Macclesfield T v Forest Green R
Nuneaton T v Lincoln C
Southport v Woking
Torquay U v Wrexham

Tuesday, 7 October 2014
AFC Telford U v Forest Green R
Bristol R v Dartford
Chester FC v Aldershot T
FC Halifax T v Wrexham
Gateshead v Alfreton T
Grimsby T v Altrincham
Kidderminster H v Welling U
Macclesfield T v Barnet
Nuneaton T v Dover
Southport v Lincoln C

Saturday, 11 October 2014
Aldershot T v Bristol R
Alfreton T v Torquay U
Altrincham v Woking
Barnet v Kidderminster H
Braintree T v Southport
Dartford v Macclesfield T
Dover v Chester FC
Eastleigh v FC Halifax T
Forest Green R v Gateshead
Lincoln C v AFC Telford U

Welling U v Nuneaton T
Wrexham v Grimsby T

Saturday, 18 October 2014
Altrincham v Braintree T
Bristol R v Forest Green R
Chester FC v Alfreton T
Dartford v Aldershot T
Eastleigh v Nuneaton T
FC Halifax T v Kidderminster H
Gateshead v Barnet
Lincoln C v Wrexham
Macclesfield T v Dover
Southport v Welling U
Torquay U v Grimsby T
Woking v AFC Telford U

Tuesday, 21 October 2014
Barnet v Braintree T

Saturday, 1 November 2014
AFC Telford U v Bristol R
Aldershot T v Gateshead
Altrincham v Alfreton T
Braintree T v Woking
Eastleigh v Chester FC
Forest Green R v Lincoln C
Grimsby T v Dartford
Kidderminster H v Torquay U
Nuneaton T v Macclesfield T
Southport v Dover
Welling U v Barnet
Wrexham v FC Halifax T

Tuesday, 4 November 2014
Braintree T v Grimsby T
Lincoln C v Altrincham

Tuesday, 11 November 2014
AFC Telford U v Altrincham
Alfreton T v Bristol R
Barnet v Torquay U
Dartford v Welling U
Dover v Braintree T
Forest Green R v Eastleigh
Gateshead v Lincoln C
Grimsby T v FC Halifax T
Kidderminster H v Aldershot T
Macclesfield T v Chester FC
Woking v Wrexham

Saturday, 15 November 2014
Aldershot T v Nuneaton T
Alfreton T v Dover
Altrincham v Grimsby T
Barnet v AFC Telford U
Braintree T v Wrexham
Bristol R v Kidderminster H
Chester FC v Gateshead
Dartford v Southport
Eastleigh v Lincoln C
FC Halifax T v Woking
Torquay U v Forest Green R
Welling U v Macclesfield T

Saturday, 22 November 2014
AFC Telford U v Braintree T
Aldershot T v Eastleigh
Chester FC v Bristol R
Dover v Forest Green R
Grimsby T v Kidderminster H
Lincoln C v Dartford
Macclesfield T v Alfreton T
Nuneaton T v Southport
Torquay U v Gateshead
Welling U v FC Halifax T

Woking v Barnet
Wrexham v Altrincham

Tuesday, 25 November 2014
Braintree T v Welling U
Bristol R v Barnet
Dartford v Chester FC
Dover v Nuneaton T
Grimsby T v Woking
Kidderminster H v Wrexham
Macclesfield T v Torquay U
Southport v Aldershot T

Saturday, 29 November 2014
AFC Telford U v Grimsby T
Altrincham v Kidderminster H
Barnet v Macclesfield T
Bristol R v Welling U
FC Halifax T v Alfreton T
Forest Green R v Dartford
Gateshead v Dover
Lincoln C v Southport
Nuneaton T v Chester FC
Torquay U v Eastleigh
Woking v Braintree T
Wrexham v Aldershot T

Tuesday, 2 December 2014
Alfreton T v Gateshead
Chester FC v AFC Telford U
Dover v Torquay U
Eastleigh v Dartford
FC Halifax T v Forest Green R
Kidderminster H v Nuneaton T
Woking v Altrincham
Wrexham v Bristol R

Saturday, 6 December 2014
Aldershot T v Kidderminster H
Chester FC v Lincoln C
Dartford v FC Halifax T
Dover v Wrexham
Eastleigh v Grimsby T
Forest Green R v Altrincham
Gateshead v Woking
Macclesfield T v AFC Telford U
Nuneaton T v Alfreton T
Southport v Braintree T
Torquay U v Barnet
Welling U v Bristol R

Tuesday, 9 December 2014
AFC Telford U v Welling U
Aldershot T v Macclesfield T
Alfreton T v Eastleigh
Forest Green R v Woking
Gateshead v Southport
Lincoln C v Nuneaton T
Torquay U v FC Halifax T

Saturday, 20 December 2014
AFC Telford U v Eastleigh
Alfreton T v Macclesfield T
Altrincham v Dover
Barnet v Chester FC
Braintree T v Torquay U
Bristol R v Gateshead
FC Halifax T v Nuneaton T
Grimsby T v Forest Green R
Kidderminster H v Lincoln C
Welling U v Aldershot T
Woking v Southport
Wrexham v Dartford

Friday, 26 December 2014
Aldershot T v Barnet
Chester FC v Altrincham

Dartford v Braintree T
Dover v Welling U
Eastleigh v Woking
Forest Green R v Kidderminster H
Gateshead v FC Halifax T
Lincoln C v Alfreton T
Macclesfield T v Grimsby T
Nuneaton T v AFC Telford U
Southport v Wrexham
Torquay U v Bristol R

Sunday, 28 December 2014
AFC Telford U v Gateshead
Alfreton T v Dartford
Altrincham v Nuneaton T
Barnet v Dover
Braintree T v Eastleigh
Bristol R v Macclesfield T
FC Halifax T v Chester FC
Grimsby T v Lincoln C
Kidderminster H v Southport
Welling U v Torquay U
Woking v Aldershot T
Wrexham v Forest Green R

Thursday, 1 January 2015
AFC Telford U v Nuneaton T
Alfreton T v Lincoln C
Altrincham v Chester FC
Barnet v Aldershot T
Braintree T v Dartford
Bristol R v Torquay U
FC Halifax T v Gateshead
Grimsby T v Macclesfield T
Kidderminster H v Forest Green R
Welling U v Dover
Woking v Eastleigh
Wrexham v Southport

Sunday, 4 January 2015
Aldershot T v AFC Telford U
Chester FC v Braintree T
Dartford v Kidderminster H
Dover v Grimsby T
Eastleigh v Altrincham
Forest Green R v Welling U
Gateshead v Wrexham
Lincoln C v Barnet
Macclesfield T v Woking
Nuneaton T v Bristol R
Southport v FC Halifax T
Torquay U v Alfreton T

Saturday, 17 January 2015
Altrincham v Torquay U
Braintree T v Forest Green R
Dover v Dartford
FC Halifax T v Eastleigh
Grimsby T v Barnet
Kidderminster H v Macclesfield T
Lincoln C v Aldershot T
Nuneaton T v Gateshead
Southport v Chester FC
Welling U v Alfreton T
Woking v Bristol R
Wrexham v AFC Telford U

Saturday, 24 January 2015
AFC Telford U v FC Halifax T
Aldershot T v Dover
Alfreton T v Forest Green R
Barnet v Southport
Bristol R v Braintree T
Chester FC v Kidderminster H
Dartford v Woking
Eastleigh v Wrexham

Gateshead v Welling U
Macclesfield T v Altrincham
Nuneaton T v Grimsby T
Torquay U v Lincoln C

Saturday, 31 January 2015
Altrincham v Aldershot T
Braintree T v Macclesfield T
Dartford v Bristol R
FC Halifax T v Barnet
Forest Green R v Nuneaton T
Grimsby T v AFC Telford U
Kidderminster H v Eastleigh
Lincoln C v Dover
Southport v Gateshead
Welling U v Chester FC
Woking v Alfreton T
Wrexham v Torquay U

Saturday, 7 February 2015
Aldershot T v FC Halifax T
Alfreton T v Southport
Barnet v Woking
Bristol R v Lincoln C
Chester FC v Dartford
Dover v Altrincham
Eastleigh v AFC Telford U
Forest Green R v Grimsby T
Gateshead v Kidderminster H
Macclesfield T v Welling U
Nuneaton T v Wrexham
Torquay U v Braintree T

Tuesday, 10 February 2015
Southport v Eastleigh

Saturday, 14 February 2015
AFC Telford U v Dartford
Aldershot T v Welling U
Altrincham v Forest Green R
Braintree T v Alfreton T
Eastleigh v Torquay U
FC Halifax T v Dover
Gateshead v Nuneaton T
Grimsby T v Bristol R
Kidderminster H v Woking
Lincoln C v Chester FC
Southport v Macclesfield T
Wrexham v Barnet

Saturday, 21 February 2015
Alfreton T v Aldershot T
Barnet v Grimsby T
Bristol R v Altrincham
Chester FC v Eastleigh
Dartford v Gateshead
Dover v Southport
FC Halifax T v Braintree T
Forest Green R v AFC Telford U
Macclesfield T v Lincoln C
Nuneaton T v Kidderminster H
Welling U v Wrexham
Woking v Torquay U

Saturday, 28 February 2015
AFC Telford U v Alfreton T
Aldershot T v Dartford
Altrincham v Barnet
Eastleigh v Macclesfield T

Forest Green R v Southport
Gateshead v Bristol R
Grimsby T v Braintree T
Kidderminster H v FC Halifax T
Lincoln C v Woking
Nuneaton T v Welling U
Torquay U v Chester FC
Wrexham v Dover

Saturday, 7 March 2015
Alfreton T v Kidderminster H
Barnet v Forest Green R
Braintree T v Gateshead
Bristol R v Eastleigh
Dover v Lincoln C
FC Halifax T v Dartford
Macclesfield T v Aldershot T
Southport v Nuneaton T
Torquay U v AFC Telford U
Welling U v Altrincham
Woking v Grimsby T
Wrexham v Chester FC

Saturday, 14 March 2015
AFC Telford U v Woking
Aldershot T v Southport
Altrincham v Wrexham
Chester FC v Grimsby T
Dartford v Alfreton T
Eastleigh v Barnet
FC Halifax T v Bristol R
Forest Green R v Braintree T
Gateshead v Macclesfield T
Kidderminster H v Dover
Lincoln C v Welling U
Nuneaton T v Torquay U

Saturday, 21 March 2015
Alfreton T v Chester FC
Altrincham v FC Halifax T
Barnet v Welling U
Braintree T v AFC Telford U
Bristol R v Aldershot T
Dover v Gateshead
Grimsby T v Eastleigh
Macclesfield T v Nuneaton T
Southport v Dartford
Torquay U v Kidderminster H
Woking v Forest Green R
Wrexham v Lincoln C

Saturday, 28 March 2015
Aldershot T v Wrexham
Alfreton T v Barnet
Chester FC v Woking
Dartford v Altrincham
Dover v AFC Telford U
Gateshead v Eastleigh
Kidderminster H v Braintree T
Lincoln C v Forest Green R
Macclesfield T v Bristol R
Nuneaton T v FC Halifax T
Southport v Torquay U
Welling U v Grimsby T

Saturday, 4 April 2015
AFC Telford U v Kidderminster H
Altrincham v Southport

Barnet v Nuneaton T
Braintree T v Lincoln C
Bristol R v Chester FC
Eastleigh v Dover
FC Halifax T v Macclesfield T
Forest Green R v Aldershot T
Grimsby T v Gateshead
Torquay U v Dartford
Woking v Welling U
Wrexham v Alfreton T

Monday, 6 April 2015
Aldershot T v Torquay U
Alfreton T v Grimsby T
Chester FC v Forest Green R
Dartford v Barnet
Dover v Woking
Gateshead v Altrincham
Kidderminster H v Bristol R
Lincoln C v FC Halifax T
Macclesfield T v Wrexham
Nuneaton T v Braintree T
Southport v AFC Telford U
Welling U v Eastleigh

Saturday, 11 April 2015
AFC Telford U v Lincoln C
Barnet v FC Halifax T
Braintree T v Aldershot T
Bristol R v Southport
Chester FC v Dover
Dartford v Nuneaton T
Eastleigh v Alfreton T
Forest Green R v Macclesfield T
Grimsby T v Wrexham
Torquay U v Altrincham
Welling U v Kidderminster H
Woking v Gateshead

Saturday, 18 April 2015
Aldershot T v Chester FC
Alfreton T v Welling U
Altrincham v AFC Telford U
Dover v Bristol R
FC Halifax T v Torquay U
Gateshead v Forest Green R
Kidderminster H v Barnet
Lincoln C v Eastleigh
Macclesfield T v Dartford
Nuneaton T v Woking
Southport v Grimsby T
Wrexham v Braintree T

Saturday, 25 April 2015
AFC Telford U v Wrexham
Barnet v Gateshead
Braintree T v Altrincham
Bristol R v Alfreton T
Chester FC v Nuneaton T
Dartford v Lincoln C
Eastleigh v Kidderminster H
Forest Green R v Dover
Grimsby T v Aldershot T
Torquay U v Macclesfield T
Welling U v Southport
Woking v FC Halifax T

THE SCOTTISH PREMIER LEAGUE AND SCOTTISH LEAGUE FIXTURES 2014–15

Sky Sports   All fixtures subject to change.

Saturday, 9 August 2014
Scottish Premiership
Aberdeen v Dundee U
Celtic v Partick Thistle
Dundee v Kilmarnock
Hamilton A v Inverness CT
Motherwell v St Mirren
Ross Co v St Johnstone

Scottish Championship
Cowdenbeath v Falkirk
Hibernian v Livingston
Queen of the South v Alloa Ath
Raith R v Dumbarton

Scottish League One
Ayr U v Greenock Morton
Dunfermline Ath v Brechin C
Peterhead v Stirling Alb
Stenhousemuir v Airdrieonians
Stranraer v Forfar Ath

Scottish League Two
Albion R v Annan Ath
Berwick R v Arbroath
Elgin C v East Fife
Montrose v East Stirlingshire
Queen's Park v Clyde

Sunday, 10 August 2014
Scottish Championship
Rangers v Hearts* (1.30)

Wednesday, 13 August 2014
Scottish Premiership
Dundee U v Motherwell
Inverness CT v Dundee
Kilmarnock v Aberdeen
Partick Thistle v Ross Co
St Johnstone v Celtic* (7.45)
St Mirren v Hamilton A

Saturday, 16 August 2014
Scottish Premiership
Aberdeen v St Mirren
Celtic v Dundee U* (12.45)
Dundee v Partick Thistle
Hamilton A v St Johnstone
Motherwell v Inverness CT
Ross Co v Kilmarnock

Scottish Championship
Alloa Ath v Raith R
Dumbarton v Queen of the South
Falkirk v Rangers
Livingston v Cowdenbeath

Scottish League One
Airdrieonians v Peterhead
Brechin C v Stenhousemuir
Forfar Ath v Dunfermline Ath
Greenock Morton v Stranraer
Stirling Alb v Ayr U

Scottish League Two
Annan Ath v Queen's Park
Arbroath v Albion R
Clyde v Montrose

East Fife v Berwick R
East Stirlingshire v Elgin C

Sunday, 17 August 2014
Scottish Championship
Hearts v Hibernian* (12.30)

Saturday, 23 August 2014
Scottish Premiership
Dundee U v Ross Co
Inverness CT v Celtic
Kilmarnock v Motherwell
Partick Thistle v Hamilton A
St Johnstone v Aberdeen
St Mirren v Dundee

Scottish Championship
Cowdenbeath v Alloa Ath
Hibernian v Falkirk
Queen of the South v Livingston
Raith R v Hearts
Rangers v Dumbarton

Scottish League One
Ayr U v Forfar Ath
Dunfermline Ath v Airdrieonians
Peterhead v Greenock Morton
Stenhousemuir v Stirling Alb
Stranraer v Brechin C

Scottish League Two
Albion R v East Fife
Berwick R v East Stirlingshire
Elgin C v Clyde
Montrose v Annan Ath
Queen's Park v Arbroath

Saturday, 30 August 2014
Scottish Premiership
Aberdeen v Partick Thistle
Dundee v Celtic
Hamilton A v Ross Co
Inverness CT v Kilmarnock
Motherwell v St Johnstone
St Mirren v Dundee U

Scottish Championship
Alloa Ath v Hibernian
Cowdenbeath v Raith R
Dumbarton v Livingston
Hearts v Falkirk
Rangers v Queen of the South

Scottish League One
Airdrieonians v Stirling Alb
Brechin C v Peterhead
Forfar Ath v Greenock Morton
Stenhousemuir v Ayr U
Stranraer v Dunfermline Ath

Scottish League Two
Albion R v Queen's Park
Annan Ath v Elgin C
Arbroath v Montrose
Clyde v Berwick R
East Fife v East Stirlingshire

Saturday, 13 September 2014
Scottish Premiership
Celtic v Aberdeen
Dundee U v Hamilton A
Kilmarnock v St Mirren
Partick Thistle v Inverness CT
Ross Co v Motherwell
St Johnstone v Dundee

Scottish Championship
Dumbarton v Hearts
Falkirk v Queen of the South
Hibernian v Cowdenbeath
Livingston v Alloa Ath
Raith R v Rangers

Scottish League One
Ayr U v Stranraer
Dunfermline Ath v Stenhousemuir
Forfar Ath v Peterhead
Greenock Morton v Airdrieonians
Stirling Alb v Brechin C

Scottish League Two
Annan Ath v Berwick R
Arbroath v East Fife
East Stirlingshire v Clyde
Montrose v Albion R
Queen's Park v Elgin C

Saturday, 20 September 2014
Scottish Premiership
Aberdeen v Ross Co
Celtic v Motherwell
Dundee v Dundee U
Hamilton A v Kilmarnock
Inverness CT v St Johnstone
Partick Thistle v St Mirren

Scottish Championship
Alloa Ath v Rangers
Falkirk v Dumbarton
Hearts v Cowdenbeath
Livingston v Raith R
Queen of the South v Hibernian

Scottish League One
Airdrieonians v Stranraer
Brechin C v Ayr U
Greenock Morton v Dunfermline Ath
Peterhead v Stenhousemuir
Stirling Alb v Forfar Ath

Scottish League Two
Berwick R v Albion R
Clyde v Arbroath
East Fife v Queen's Park
East Stirlingshire v Annan Ath
Elgin C v Montrose

Saturday, 27 September 2014
Scottish Premiership
Aberdeen v Inverness CT
Dundee U v St Johnstone
Kilmarnock v Partick Thistle
Motherwell v Hamilton A

Ross Co v Dundee
St Mirren v Celtic

Scottish Championship
Cowdenbeath v Queen of the South
Dumbarton v Alloa Ath
Hearts v Livingston
Raith R v Falkirk
Rangers v Hibernian

Scottish League One
Ayr U v Airdrieonians
Dunfermline Ath v Peterhead
Forfar Ath v Brechin C
Stenhousemuir v Greenock Morton
Stranraer v Stirling Alb

Scottish League Two
Albion R v East Stirlingshire
Arbroath v Elgin C
Clyde v Annan Ath
Montrose v East Fife
Queen's Park v Berwick R

Saturday, 4 October 2014
Scottish Premiership
Celtic v Hamilton A
Dundee v Aberdeen
Inverness CT v Ross Co
Kilmarnock v Dundee U
Partick Thistle v Motherwell
St Johnstone v St Mirren

Scottish Championship
Dumbarton v Cowdenbeath
Falkirk v Alloa Ath
Hibernian v Raith R
Livingston v Rangers
Queen of the South v Hearts

Scottish League One
Airdrieonians v Forfar Ath
Brechin C v Greenock Morton
Peterhead v Ayr U
Stenhousemuir v Stranraer
Stirling Alb v Dunfermline Ath

Saturday, 11 October 2014
Scottish Championship
Alloa Ath v Hearts
Cowdenbeath v Rangers
Falkirk v Livingston
Hibernian v Dumbarton
Raith R v Queen of the South

Scottish League One
Airdrieonians v Brechin C
Ayr U v Dunfermline Ath
Forfar Ath v Stenhousemuir
Greenock Morton v Stirling Alb
Stranraer v Peterhead

Scottish League Two
Annan Ath v Arbroath
Berwick R v Montrose
East Fife v Clyde
East Stirlingshire v Queen's Park
Elgin C v Albion R

Saturday, 18 October 2014
Scottish Premiership
Dundee U v Partick Thistle
Hamilton A v Aberdeen
Motherwell v Dundee

Ross Co v Celtic
St Johnstone v Kilmarnock
St Mirren v Inverness CT

Scottish Championship
Alloa Ath v Cowdenbeath
Hearts v Dumbarton
Livingston v Hibernian
Queen of the South v Falkirk
Rangers v Raith R

Scottish League One
Brechin C v Stranraer
Dunfermline Ath v Forfar Ath
Greenock Morton v Ayr U
Peterhead v Airdrieonians
Stirling Alb v Stenhousemuir

Scottish League Two
Albion R v Clyde
Arbroath v East Stirlingshire
Berwick R v Elgin C
East Fife v Annan Ath
Queen's Park v Montrose

Saturday, 25 October 2014
Scottish Premiership
Aberdeen v Motherwell
Celtic v Kilmarnock
Dundee v Hamilton A
Inverness CT v Dundee U
Partick Thistle v St Johnstone
St Mirren v Ross Co

Scottish Championship
Dumbarton v Rangers
Falkirk v Cowdenbeath
Hibernian v Hearts
Livingston v Queen of the South
Raith R v Alloa Ath

Scottish League One
Ayr U v Brechin C
Dunfermline Ath v Greenock Morton
Forfar Ath v Stranraer
Stenhousemuir v Peterhead
Stirling Alb v Airdrieonians

Scottish League Two
Albion R v Berwick R
Annan Ath v East Stirlingshire
Clyde v Elgin C
Montrose v Arbroath
Queen's Park v East Fife

Saturday, 1 November 2014
Scottish Premiership
Celtic v Inverness CT
Dundee U v St Mirren
Hamilton A v Partick Thistle
Kilmarnock v Dundee
Ross Co v Aberdeen
St Johnstone v Motherwell

Saturday, 8 November 2014
Scottish Premiership
Aberdeen v Celtic
Dundee v St Johnstone
Inverness CT v Hamilton A
Kilmarnock v Ross Co
Motherwell v Dundee U
St Mirren v Partick Thistle

Scottish Championship
Alloa Ath v Livingston
Cowdenbeath v Hibernian
Hearts v Raith R
Queen of the South v Dumbarton
Rangers v Falkirk

Scottish League One
Airdrieonians v Stenhousemuir
Brechin C v Stirling Alb
Greenock Morton v Forfar Ath
Peterhead v Dunfermline Ath
Stranraer v Ayr U

Scottish League Two
Arbroath v Queen's Park
East Fife v Albion R
East Stirlingshire v Berwick R
Elgin C v Annan Ath
Montrose v Clyde

Saturday, 15 November 2014
Scottish Championship
Falkirk v Hearts
Hibernian v Queen of the South
Livingston v Dumbarton
Raith R v Cowdenbeath
Rangers v Alloa Ath

Scottish League One
Airdrieonians v Greenock Morton
Ayr U v Peterhead
Brechin C v Forfar Ath
Stenhousemuir v Dunfermline Ath
Stirling Alb v Stranraer

Scottish League Two
Albion R v Arbroath
Annan Ath v Montrose
Berwick R v East Fife
Clyde v East Stirlingshire
Elgin C v Queen's Park

Saturday, 22 November 2014
Scottish Premiership
Celtic v Dundee
Dundee U v Kilmarnock
Hamilton A v St Mirren
Inverness CT v Motherwell
Partick Thistle v Aberdeen
St Johnstone v Ross Co

Scottish Championship
Alloa Ath v Falkirk
Cowdenbeath v Livingston
Dumbarton v Hibernian
Hearts v Rangers
Queen of the South v Raith R

Scottish League One
Dunfermline Ath v Stirling Alb
Forfar Ath v Ayr U
Greenock Morton v Stenhousemuir
Peterhead v Brechin C
Stranraer v Airdrieonians

Scottish League Two
Arbroath v Clyde
Berwick R v Annan Ath
East Fife v Elgin C
East Stirlingshire v Montrose
Queen's Park v Albion R

Saturday, 29 November 2014
Scottish League Two
Annan Ath v Albion R
Clyde v Queen's Park
East Stirlingshire v East Fife
Elgin C v Arbroath
Montrose v Berwick R

Saturday, 6 December 2014
Scottish Premiership
Aberdeen v Hamilton A
Dundee v Inverness CT
Motherwell v Celtic
Partick Thistle v Kilmarnock
Ross Co v Dundee U
St Mirren v St Johnstone

Scottish Championship
Alloa Ath v Dumbarton
Falkirk v Hibernian
Hearts v Queen of the South
Raith R v Livingston
Rangers v Cowdenbeath

Scottish League One
Brechin C v Airdrieonians
Dunfermline Ath v Ayr U
Stenhousemuir v Forfar Ath
Stirling Alb v Peterhead
Stranraer v Greenock Morton

Scottish League Two
Albion R v Elgin C
Arbroath v Annan Ath
Berwick R v Clyde
East Fife v Montrose
Queen's Park v East Stirlingshire

Saturday, 13 December 2014
Scottish Premiership
Celtic v St Mirren
Dundee U v Aberdeen
Hamilton A v Dundee
Inverness CT v Partick Thistle
Kilmarnock v St Johnstone
Motherwell v Ross Co

Scottish Championship
Cowdenbeath v Hearts
Dumbarton v Raith R
Hibernian v Alloa Ath
Livingston v Falkirk
Queen of the South v Rangers

Scottish League One
Airdrieonians v Dunfermline Ath
Ayr U v Stenhousemuir
Forfar Ath v Stirling Alb
Greenock Morton v Brechin C
Peterhead v Stranraer

Scottish League Two
Annan Ath v East Fife
Clyde v Albion R
East Stirlingshire v Arbroath
Elgin C v Berwick R
Montrose v Queen's Park

Saturday, 20 December 2014
Scottish Premiership
Aberdeen v Kilmarnock
Dundee U v Celtic
Partick Thistle v Dundee

Ross Co v Hamilton A
St Johnstone v Inverness CT
St Mirren v Motherwell

Scottish Championship
Dumbarton v Falkirk
Hearts v Alloa Ath
Queen of the South v Cowdenbeath
Raith R v Hibernian
Rangers v Livingston

Scottish League One
Ayr U v Stirling Alb
Dunfermline Ath v Stranraer
Forfar Ath v Airdrieonians
Greenock Morton v Peterhead
Stenhousemuir v Brechin C

Scottish League Two
Albion R v Montrose
Arbroath v Berwick R
Clyde v East Fife
Elgin C v East Stirlingshire
Queen's Park v Annan Ath

Saturday, 27 December 2014
Scottish Premiership
Celtic v Ross Co
Dundee v St Mirren
Inverness CT v Aberdeen
Kilmarnock v Hamilton A
Motherwell v Partick Thistle
St Johnstone v Dundee U

Scottish Championship
Alloa Ath v Queen of the South
Cowdenbeath v Dumbarton
Falkirk v Raith R
Hibernian v Rangers
Livingston v Hearts

Scottish League One
Airdrieonians v Ayr U
Brechin C v Dunfermline Ath
Peterhead v Forfar Ath
Stirling Alb v Greenock Morton
Stranraer v Stenhousemuir

Scottish League Two
Annan Ath v Clyde
Berwick R v Queen's Park
East Fife v Arbroath
East Stirlingshire v Albion R
Montrose v Elgin C

Thursday, 1 January 2015
Scottish Premiership
Aberdeen v St Johnstone
Dundee U v Dundee
Hamilton A v Motherwell
Partick Thistle v Celtic
Ross Co v Inverness CT
St Mirren v Kilmarnock

Saturday, 3 January 2015
Scottish Championship
Cowdenbeath v Raith R
Falkirk v Alloa Ath
Hearts v Hibernian
Queen of the South v Livingston
Rangers v Dumbarton

Scottish League One
Ayr U v Stranraer

Dunfermline Ath v Peterhead
Forfar Ath v Brechin C
Greenock Morton v Airdrieonians
Stenhousemuir v Stirling Alb

Scottish League Two
Albion R v Annan Ath
Arbroath v Montrose
Berwick R v East Stirlingshire
Elgin C v East Fife
Queen's Park v Clyde

Sunday, 4 January 2015
Scottish Premiership
Dundee v Ross Co
Inverness CT v St Mirren
Kilmarnock v Celtic
Motherwell v Aberdeen
Partick Thistle v Dundee U
St Johnstone v Hamilton A

Saturday, 10 January 2015
Scottish Premiership
Celtic v St Johnstone
Dundee v Motherwell
Hamilton A v Dundee U
Kilmarnock v Inverness CT
Ross Co v Partick Thistle
St Mirren v Aberdeen

Scottish Championship
Alloa Ath v Rangers
Dumbarton v Hearts
Hibernian v Falkirk
Livingston v Cowdenbeath
Raith R v Queen of the South

Scottish League One
Airdrieonians v Peterhead
Brechin C v Ayr U
Stenhousemuir v Greenock Morton
Stirling Alb v Dunfermline Ath
Stranraer v Forfar Ath

Scottish League Two
Annan Ath v Elgin C
Arbroath v Albion R
Clyde v Berwick R
East Fife v Queen's Park
Montrose v East Stirlingshire

Saturday, 17 January 2015
Scottish Premiership
Aberdeen v Dundee
Dundee U v Inverness CT
Hamilton A v Celtic
Motherwell v Kilmarnock
Ross Co v St Mirren
St Johnstone v Partick Thistle

Scottish Championship
Falkirk v Queen of the South
Hibernian v Cowdenbeath
Livingston v Alloa Ath
Raith R v Dumbarton
Rangers v Hearts

Scottish League One
Ayr U v Greenock Morton
Dunfermline Ath v Airdrieonians
Forfar Ath v Stenhousemuir
Peterhead v Stirling Alb
Stranraer v Brechin C

Scottish League Two
Albion R v East Fife
Berwick R v Montrose
East Stirlingshire v Annan Ath
Elgin C v Clyde
Queen's Park v Arbroath

Wednesday, 21 January 2015
Scottish Premiership
Aberdeen v Ross Co
Celtic v Motherwell
Dundee v Kilmarnock
Inverness CT v St Johnstone
Partick Thistle v Hamilton A
St Mirren v Dundee U

Saturday, 24 January 2015
Scottish Premiership
Dundee U v Motherwell
Hamilton A v Inverness CT
Kilmarnock v Partick Thistle
Ross Co v Celtic
St Johnstone v Aberdeen
St Mirren v Dundee

Scottish Championship
Alloa Ath v Raith R
Cowdenbeath v Rangers
Dumbarton v Livingston
Hearts v Falkirk
Queen of the South v Hibernian

Scottish League One
Airdrieonians v Stranraer
Brechin C v Peterhead
Greenock Morton v Dunfermline Ath
Stenhousemuir v Ayr U
Stirling Alb v Forfar Ath

Scottish League Two
Annan Ath v Berwick R
Clyde v Arbroath
East Fife v East Stirlingshire
Montrose v Albion R
Queen's Park v Elgin C

Saturday, 31 January 2015
Scottish Premiership
Aberdeen v Dundee U
Celtic v Kilmarnock
Dundee v Hamilton A
Inverness CT v Ross Co
Motherwell v St Johnstone
Partick Thistle v St Mirren

Scottish Championship
Alloa Ath v Hearts
Cowdenbeath v Queen of the South
Falkirk v Dumbarton
Hibernian v Raith R
Livingston v Rangers

Scottish League One
Airdrieonians v Brechin C
Ayr U v Dunfermline Ath
Forfar Ath v Greenock Morton
Peterhead v Stenhousemuir
Stranraer v Stirling Alb

Scottish League Two
Albion R v Queen's Park
Arbroath v East Fife
Berwick R v Elgin C

East Stirlingshire v Clyde
Montrose v Annan Ath

Saturday, 7 February 2015
Scottish League One
Ayr U v Airdrieonians
Dunfermline Ath v Brechin C
Forfar Ath v Peterhead
Greenock Morton v Stirling Alb
Stenhousemuir v Stranraer

Scottish League Two
Arbroath v East Stirlingshire
Clyde v Annan Ath
East Fife v Berwick R
Elgin C v Albion R
Queen's Park v Montrose

Saturday, 14 February 2015
Scottish Premiership
Dundee v Partick Thistle
Hamilton A v Aberdeen
Kilmarnock v Dundee U
Ross Co v Motherwell
St Johnstone v Celtic
St Mirren v Inverness CT

Scottish Championship
Dumbarton v Cowdenbeath
Hearts v Livingston
Queen of the South v Alloa Ath
Raith R v Falkirk
Rangers v Hibernian

Scottish League One
Airdrieonians v Forfar Ath
Brechin C v Greenock Morton
Dunfermline Ath v Stenhousemuir
Stirling Alb v Ayr U
Stranraer v Peterhead

Scottish League Two
Albion R v Clyde
Annan Ath v Queen's Park
Berwick R v Arbroath
East Stirlingshire v Elgin C
Montrose v East Fife

Saturday, 21 February 2015
Scottish Premiership
Aberdeen v St Mirren
Celtic v Hamilton A
Dundee U v St Johnstone
Inverness CT v Kilmarnock
Motherwell v Dundee
Partick Thistle v Ross Co

Scottish Championship
Cowdenbeath v Alloa Ath
Falkirk v Livingston
Hibernian v Dumbarton
Queen of the South v Hearts
Raith R v Rangers

Scottish League One
Forfar Ath v Dunfermline Ath
Greenock Morton v Stranraer
Peterhead v Ayr U
Stenhousemuir v Airdrieonians
Stirling Alb v Brechin C

Scottish League Two
Albion R v East Stirlingshire
Annan Ath v Arbroath

East Fife v Clyde
Elgin C v Montrose
Queen's Park v Berwick R

Saturday, 28 February 2015
Scottish Premiership
Celtic v Aberdeen
Dundee U v Partick Thistle
Motherwell v Inverness CT
Ross Co v Dundee
St Johnstone v Kilmarnock
St Mirren v Hamilton A

Scottish Championship
Alloa Ath v Hibernian
Dumbarton v Queen of the South
Falkirk v Rangers
Hearts v Cowdenbeath
Livingston v Raith R

Scottish League One
Airdrieonians v Stirling Alb
Ayr U v Forfar Ath
Brechin C v Stenhousemuir
Peterhead v Greenock Morton
Stranraer v Dunfermline Ath

Scottish League Two
Arbroath v Elgin C
Berwick R v Albion R
Clyde v Montrose
East Fife v Annan Ath
East Stirlingshire v Queen's Park

Saturday, 7 March 2015
Scottish Championship
Cowdenbeath v Falkirk
Dumbarton v Alloa Ath
Hibernian v Livingston
Raith R v Hearts
Rangers v Queen of the South

Scottish League One
Brechin C v Airdrieonians
Dunfermline Ath v Ayr U
Greenock Morton v Forfar Ath
Stenhousemuir v Peterhead
Stirling Alb v Stranraer

Scottish League Two
Annan Ath v Albion R
Clyde v East Stirlingshire
Elgin C v Berwick R
Montrose v Arbroath
Queen's Park v East Fife

Saturday, 14 March 2015
Scottish Premiership
Aberdeen v Motherwell
Dundee v Celtic
Hamilton A v Ross Co
Inverness CT v Dundee U
Kilmarnock v St Mirren
Partick Thistle v St Johnstone

Scottish Championship
Alloa Ath v Falkirk
Cowdenbeath v Hibernian
Hearts v Dumbarton
Queen of the South v Raith R
Rangers v Livingston

Scottish League One
Airdrieonians v Greenock Morton

Ayr U v Stenhousemuir
Dunfermline Ath v Stirling Alb
Forfar Ath v Stranraer
Peterhead v Brechin C

Scottish League Two
Albion R v Montrose
Arbroath v Clyde
Berwick R v Annan Ath
East Stirlingshire v East Fife
Elgin C v Queen's Park

Saturday, 21 March 2015
Scottish Premiership
Celtic v Dundee U
Dundee v Aberdeen
Motherwell v Hamilton A
Partick Thistle v Inverness CT
Ross Co v Kilmarnock
St Johnstone v St Mirren

Scottish Championship
Falkirk v Hearts
Hibernian v Rangers
Livingston v Dumbarton
Queen of the South v Cowdenbeath
Raith R v Alloa Ath

Scottish League One
Brechin C v Forfar Ath
Greenock Morton v Ayr U
Stenhousemuir v Dunfermline Ath
Stirling Alb v Peterhead
Stranraer v Airdrieonians

Scottish League Two
Annan Ath v East Stirlingshire
Clyde v Elgin C
East Fife v Arbroath
Montrose v Berwick R
Queen's Park v Albion R

Saturday, 28 March 2015
Scottish Championship
Alloa Ath v Livingston
Dumbarton v Falkirk
Hearts v Queen of the South
Raith R v Hibernian
Rangers v Cowdenbeath

Scottish League One
Airdrieonians v Stenhousemuir
Ayr U v Brechin C
Dunfermline Ath v Greenock Morton
Forfar Ath v Stirling Alb
Peterhead v Stranraer

Scottish League Two
Albion R v Elgin C
Annan Ath v Clyde
Berwick R v Queen's Park
East Fife v Montrose
East Stirlingshire v Arbroath

Saturday, 4 April 2015
Scottish Premiership
Aberdeen v Partick Thistle
Dundee U v Ross Co
Hamilton A v St Johnstone
Inverness CT v Dundee
Kilmarnock v Motherwell
St Mirren v Celtic

Scottish Championship
Cowdenbeath v Dumbarton
Falkirk v Raith R
Hibernian v Queen of the South
Livingston v Hearts
Rangers v Alloa Ath

Scottish League One
Greenock Morton v Brechin C
Peterhead v Dunfermline Ath
Stenhousemuir v Forfar Ath
Stirling Alb v Airdrieonians
Stranraer v Ayr U

Scottish League Two
Albion R v Berwick R
Arbroath v Annan Ath
Clyde v East Fife
Elgin C v East Stirlingshire
Montrose v Queen's Park

Wednesday, 8 April 2015
Scottish Premiership
Aberdeen v Inverness CT
Celtic v Partick Thistle
Dundee v Dundee U
Hamilton A v Kilmarnock
Motherwell v St Mirren
Ross Co v St Johnstone

Scottish Championship
Dumbarton v Hibernian
Hearts v Alloa Ath
Livingston v Falkirk
Queen of the South v Rangers
Raith R v Cowdenbeath

Saturday, 11 April 2015
Scottish Premiership
Dundee U v Hamilton A
Inverness CT v Celtic
Kilmarnock v Aberdeen
Partick Thistle v Motherwell
St Johnstone v Dundee
St Mirren v Ross Co

Scottish Championship
Alloa Ath v Dumbarton
Cowdenbeath v Livingston
Hibernian v Hearts
Queen of the South v Falkirk
Rangers v Raith R

Scottish League One
Ayr U v Peterhead
Brechin C v Stirling Alb
Dunfermline Ath v Stranraer
Forfar Ath v Airdrieonians
Greenock Morton v Stenhousemuir

Scottish League Two
Berwick R v Clyde
East Fife v Albion R
East Stirlingshire v Montrose
Elgin C v Arbroath
Queen's Park v Annan Ath

Saturday, 18 April 2015
Scottish Championship
Alloa Ath v Queen of the South
Dumbarton v Rangers
Falkirk v Cowdenbeath

Hearts v Raith R
Livingston v Hibernian

Scottish League One
Airdrieonians v Ayr U
Brechin C v Dunfermline Ath
Peterhead v Forfar Ath
Stirling Alb v Greenock Morton
Stranraer v Stenhousemuir

Scottish League Two
Annan Ath v East Fife
Arbroath v Queen's Park
Clyde v Albion R
East Stirlingshire v Berwick R
Montrose v Elgin C

Saturday, 25 April 2015
Scottish Championship
Cowdenbeath v Hearts
Hibernian v Alloa Ath
Queen of the South v Dumbarton
Raith R v Livingston
Rangers v Falkirk

Scottish League One
Ayr U v Stirling Alb
Dunfermline Ath v Forfar Ath
Peterhead v Airdrieonians
Stenhousemuir v Brechin C
Stranraer v Greenock Morton

Scottish League Two
Albion R v Arbroath
Berwick R v East Fife
Elgin C v Annan Ath
Montrose v Clyde
Queen's Park v East Stirlingshire

Saturday, 2 May 2015
Scottish Championship
Alloa Ath v Cowdenbeath
Dumbarton v Raith R
Falkirk v Hibernian
Hearts v Rangers
Livingston v Queen of the South

Scottish League One
Airdrieonians v Dunfermline Ath
Brechin C v Stranraer
Forfar Ath v Ayr U
Greenock Morton v Peterhead
Stirling Alb v Stenhousemuir

Scottish League Two
Annan Ath v Montrose
Arbroath v Berwick R
Clyde v Queen's Park
East Fife v Elgin C
East Stirlingshire v Albion R

FOOTBALL ASSOCIATION FIXTURES 2014–15

(Not including FA Youth Cup, FA County Youth Cup, FA Sunday Cup & FA Women's Cup.)

JULY 2014

1 Tuesday	UEFA Champions League 1Q(1)
2 Wednesday	UEFA Champions League 1Q(1)
3 Thursday	UEFA Europa League 1Q(1)
8 Tuesday	UEFA Champions League 1Q(2)
9 Wednesday	UEFA Champions League 1Q(2)
10 Thursday	UEFA Europa League 1Q(2)
15 Tuesday	UEFA Champions League 2Q(1)
16 Wednesday	UEFA Champions League 2Q(1)
17 Thursday	UEFA Europa League 2Q(1)
22 Tuesday	UEFA Champions League 2Q(2)
23 Wednesday	UEFA Champions League 2Q(2)
24 Thursday	UEFA Europa League 2Q(2)
29 Tuesday	UEFA Champions League 3Q(1)
30 Wednesday	UEFA Champions League 3Q(1)
31 Thursday	UEFA Europa League 3Q(1)

AUGUST 2014

5 Tuesday	UEFA Champions League 3Q(2)
6 Wednesday	UEFA Champions League 3Q(2)
7 Thursday	UEFA Europa League 3Q(2)
9 Saturday	Football League Championship, League 1 and 2 Commences
10 Sunday	FA Community Shield
12 Tuesday	UEFA Super Cup
13 Wednesday	Football League Cup 1
16 Saturday	FA Cup Extra Preliminary Round Premier League Commences
19 Tuesday	UEFA Champions League Qualifying Play-Off(1)
20 Wednesday	UEFA Champions League Qualifying Play-Off(1)
21 Thursday	UEFA Europa League Qualifying Play-Off(1)
25 Monday	Bank Holiday
26 Tuesday	UEFA Champions League Qualifying Play-Off(2)
27 Wednesday	UEFA Champions League Qualifying Play-Off(2) Football League Cup 2
28 Thursday	UEFA Europa League Qualifying Play-Off(2)
30 Saturday	FA Cup P

SEPTEMBER 2014

3 Wednesday	Football League Trophy 1
6 Saturday	FA Vase 1Q
8 Monday	Switzerland v England – EURO 2016 Qualifier
13 Saturday	FA Cup 1Q
16 Tuesday	UEFA Champions League MD1
17 Wednesday	UEFA Champions League MD1
18 Thursday	UEFA Europa League MD1
24 Wednesday	Football League Cup 3
27 Saturday	FA Cup 2Q
30 Tuesday	UEFA Champions League MD2

OCTOBER 2014

1 Wednesday	UEFA Champions League MD2
2 Thursday	UEFA Europa League MD2
4 Saturday	FA Vase 2Q
8 Wednesday	Football League Trophy 2
9 Thursday	England v San Marino – EURO 2016 Qualifier
11 Saturday	FA Cup 3Q
12 Sunday	Estonia v England – EURO 2016 Qualifier
18 Saturday	FA Trophy P
21 Tuesday	UEFA Champions League MD3
22 Wednesday	UEFA Champions League MD3
23 Thursday	UEFA Europa League MD3
25 Saturday	FA Cup 4Q
29 Wednesday	Football League Cup 4

NOVEMBER 2014

1 Saturday	FA Trophy 1Q FA Vase 1P
4 Tuesday	UEFA Champions League MD4
5 Wednesday	UEFA Champions League MD4
6 Thursday	UEFA Europa League MD4
8 Saturday	FA Cup 1P
12 Wednesday	Football League Trophy QF
15 Saturday	FA Trophy 2Q England v Slovenia – EURO 2016 Qualifier
22 Saturday	FA Vase 2P
25 Tuesday	UEFA Champions League MD5
26 Wednesday	UEFA Champions League MD5
27 Thursday	UEFA Europa League MD5
29 Saturday	FA Trophy 3Q

DECEMBER 2014

6 Saturday	FA Cup 2P FA Vase 3P
9 Tuesday	UEFA Champions League MD6
10 Wednesday	UEFA Champions League MD6 Football League Trophy SF
11 Thursday	UEFA Europa League MD6
13 Saturday	FA Trophy 1P
17 Wednesday	Football League Cup 5
25 Thursday	Christmas Day
26 Friday	Boxing Day

JANUARY 2015

1 Thursday	New Year's Day
3 Saturday	FA Cup 3P
10 Saturday	FA Trophy 2P
14 Wednesday	Football League Trophy AF1
17 Saturday	FA Vase 4P
21 Wednesday	Football League Cup SF1
24 Saturday	FA Cup 4P FA Trophy 3P
28 Wednesday	Football League Cup SF2

FEBRUARY 2015

4 Wednesday	Football League Trophy AF2
7 Saturday	FA Trophy 4P
	FA Vase 5P
14 Saturday	FA Cup 5P
17 Tuesday	UEFA Champions League 16(1)
18 Wednesday	UEFA Champions League 16(1)
19 Thursday	UEFA Europa League 32(1)
21 Saturday	FA Trophy SF1
24 Tuesday	UEFA Champions League 16(1)
25 Wednesday	UEFA Champions League 16(1)
26 Thursday	UEFA Europa League 32(2)
28 Saturday	FA Trophy SF2
	FA Vase 6P

MARCH 2015

1 Sunday	Football League Cup Final
7 Saturday	FA Cup 6P
10 Tuesday	UEFA Champions League 16(2)
11 Wednesday	UEFA Champions League 16(2)
12 Thursday	UEFA Europa League 16(1)
17 Tuesday	UEFA Champions League 16(2)
18 Wednesday	UEFA Champions League 16(2)
19 Thursday	UEFA Europa League 16(2)
21 Saturday	FA Vase SF1
22 Sunday	Football League Trophy Final
27 Friday	England v Lithuania – EURO 2016 Qualifier
28 Saturday	FA Vase SF2
29 Sunday	FA Trophy Final

APRIL 2015

3 Friday	Good Friday
6 Monday	Easter Monday
14 Tuesday	UEFA Champions League QF(1)
15 Wednesday	UEFA Champions League QF(1)
16 Thursday	UEFA Europa League QF(1)
18 Saturday	FA Cup Semi Final
19 Sunday	FA Cup Semi Final
21 Tuesday	UEFA Champions League QF(2)
22 Wednesday	UEFA Champions League QF(2)
23 Thursday	UEFA Europa League QF (2)

MAY 2015

2 Saturday	Football League Championship, League 1 and 2 Ends
5 Tuesday	UEFA Champions League SF(1)
6 Wednesday	UEFA Champions League SF(1)
7 Thursday	UEFA Europa League SF(1)
9 Saturday	FA Vase Final
12 Tuesday	UEFA Champions League SF(2)
13 Wednesday	UEFA Champions League SF(2)
14 Thursday	UEFA Europa League SF(2)
23 Saturday	Football League 2 Play-Off Final
24 Sunday	Football League 1 Play-Off Final Premier League Ends
25 Monday	Bank Holiday Football League Championship Play-Off Final
27 Wednesday	UEFA Europa League Final
30 Saturday	FA Cup Final

JUNE 2015

6 Saturday	UEFA Champions League Final
7 Sunday	Republic of Ireland v England – International Friendly
14 Sunday	Slovenia v England – EURO 2016 Qualifier

OTHER ENGLAND INTERNATIONALS IN 2015

SEPTEMBER 2015

5 Saturday	San Marino v England – EURO 2016 Qualifier
8 Tuesday	England v Switzerland – EURO 2016 Qualifier

OCTOBER 2015

9 Friday	England v Estonia – EURO 2016 Qualifier
12 Monday	Lithuania v England – EURO 2016 Qualifier

STOP PRESS

SUMMER TRANSFER DIARY 2014

Saints sale – Lambert, Shaw, Lallana all departing for reported combined £56m ... Suarez apologizes for World Cup bite after FIFA issue 4 month ban – appeal rejected now at Court of Arbitration ... Suarez signs for Barcelona for reported £75m despite impending ban ... Arsenal go big for Sanchez at £35m ... Manchester U sign £750m shirt deal with Adidas ... Louis van Gaal arrives at Manchester U at the end of the World Cup ... Steven Gerrard retires from international football ... Leicester C smash transfer record ... Evra and Morata to Juve ... Ba to Turkey ... Iturbe, Kroos and Rodriguez in big Euro deals ... Bojan becomes a Potter ... Manchester C U21s walk off during friendly ...

Reported fees only, otherwise Free or Undisclosed.

2 June: **Colin Daniel** Mansfield T to Port Vale; **Jonathan Grounds** Oldham Ath to Birmingham C; **Jake Hyde** Barnet to York C; **Alan Judge** Blackburn R to Brentford; **Rickie Lambert** Southampton to Liverpool £4m.
3 June: **Derek Boateng** Fulham to Rayo Vallecano; **Mickey Demetriou** Kidderminster H to Shrewsbury T; **Jermaine McGlashan** Cheltenham T to Gillingham; **Liam Noble** Carlisle U to Notts Co; **Tommy Rowe** Peterborough U to Wolverhampton W; **Andrew Taylor** Cardiff C to Wigan Ath.
4 June: **James Collins** Hibernian to Shrewsbury T; **Ryan Dickson** Colchester U to Crawley T; **Paul Jones** Crawley T to Portsmouth; **Aaron Martin** Birmingham C to Yeovil T; **Kenny Miller** Vancouver Whitecaps to Rangers; **Joseph Mills** Burnley to Oldham Ath; **Jonathan Mitchell** Newcastle U to Derby Co; **Lanre Oyebanjo** York C to Crawley T; **Jon Taylor** Shrewsbury T to Peterborough U; **Aaron Taylor-Sinclair** Partick Thistle to Wigan Ath.
5 June: **Chris Basham** Blackpool to Sheffield U; **Andy Butler** Walsall to Sheffield U; **Emre Can** Bayer Leverkusen to Liverpool £10m; **Lewis Grabban** Bournemouth to Norwich C; **Mark Halstead** Blackpool to Shrewsbury T; **Shwan Jalal** Bournemouth to Bury; **Scott Loach** Ipswich T to Rotherham U; **Hayden Mullins** Birmingham C to Notts Co; **Philippe Senderos** Valencia to Aston Villa.
6 June: **Zak Ansah** Arsenal to Charlton Ath; **Jamie Jones** Leyton Orient to Preston NE; **John Mousinho** Preston NE to Burton Alb; **Ayoze Perez** Tenerife to Newcastle U; **James Wesolowski** Oldham Ath to Shrewsbury T.
7 June **Yossi Benayoun** QPR to Maccabi Haifa; **Luke Chadwick** Milton Keynes D to Cambridge U; **Simon Ferry** Portsmouth to Dundee; **Jake Jervis** Portsmouth to Ross Co.
8 June: **Gabriel Zakuani** Kalloni FC to Peterborough U.
9 June: **Kirk Broadfoot** Blackpool to Rotherham U; **Jack Colback** Sunderland to Newcastle U; **Ben Davies** Derby Co to Sheffield U; **Matt Fryatt** Hull C to Nottingham F; **Stephen Gleeson** Milton Keynes D to Birmingham C; **Gary Liddle** Notts Co to Bradford C; **Steve Sidwell** Fulham to Stoke C; **Robbie Simpson** Leyton Orient to Cambridge U; **Calum Woods** Huddersfield T to Preston NE.
10 June: **Jordan Bowery** Aston Villa to Rotherham U; **Dannie Bulman** Crawley T to AFC Wimbledon; **Alban Bunjaku** Sevilla to Derby Co; **Joe Cole** West Ham U to Aston Villa; **Damien Duff** Fulham to Melbourne C; **Mike Jones** Crawley T to Oldham Ath; **Doug Loft** Port Vale to Gillingham; **Rajiv van La Parra** Heerenveen to Wolverhampton W; **Brian Wilson** Colchester U to Oldham Ath.
11 June: **Mame Biram Diouf** Hannover 96 to Stoke C; **Jayson Leutwiler** Middlesbrough to Shrewsbury T; **Jennison Myrie-Williams** Port Vale to Scunthorpe U; **Dionatan Teixeira** Banska Bystrica to Stoke C; **Wes Thomas** Rotherham U to Birmingham C.
12 June: **Kagisho Dikgacoi** Crystal Palace to Cardiff C; **Lloyd Dyer** Leicester C to Watford; **David Edgar** Burnley to Birmingham C; **Cesc Fabregas** Barcelona to Chelsea £30m; **Gavin Gunning** Dundee U to Birmingham C; **Liam Hearn** Grimsby T to Mansfield T; **Anthony Straker** Southend U to York C; **Lars Veldwijk** Excelsior to Nottingham F.
13 June: **Adam Davies** Sheffield W to Barnsley; **Adam Legzdins** Derby Co to Leyton Orient; **David Luiz** Chelsea to Paris Saint-Germain; **Bacary Sagna** Arsenal to Manchester C; **James Wallace** Tranmere R to Sheffield U.
14 June: **Myles Weston** Gillingham to Southend U.
16 June: **Shaun Hutchinson** Motherwell to Fulham; **Carl McHugh** Bradford C to Plymouth Arg; **Costel Pantilimon** Manchester C to Sunderland.
17 June: **Sonny Bradley** Portsmouth to Crawley T; **Joe Murphy** Coventry C to Huddersfield T; **Josh Pritchard** Fulham to Gillingham; **Mat Sadler** Crawley T to Rotherham U.
18 June: **Lucas Akins** Stevenage to Burton Alb; **James Caton** Blackpool to Shrewsbury T; **Michael Ihiekwe** Wolverhampton W to Tranmere R; **Cheikhou Kouyate** Anderlecht to West Ham U; **Gavin Tomlin** Port Vale to Crawley T; **Scott Vernon** Aberdeen to Shrewsbury T.
19 June: **Neal Bishop** Blackpool to Scunthorpe U; **Ashley Chambers** Cambridge U to Dagenham & R; **Peter Hartley** Stevenage to Plymouth Arg; **Kane Hemmings** Cowdenbeath to Barnsley; **Jordan Hugill** Port Vale to Preston NE; **Chris Kettings** Blackpool to Crystal Palace; **Alan Sheehan** Notts Co to Bradford C.
20 June: **Adebayo Akinfenwa** Gillingham to AFC Wimbledon; **Danny Grainger** Dunfermline Ath to Carlisle U; **Joleon Lescott** Manchester C to WBA; **Kyle McFadzean** Crawley T to Milton Keynes D; **Peter Murphy** Accrington S to Wycombe W; **Keith Southern** Huddersfield T to Fleetwood T; **Antony Sweeney** Hartlepool U to Carlisle U; **Calvin Zola** Aberdeen to Stevenage.
21 June: **James O'Connor** Derby Co to Walsall.
23 June: **Tom Bradshaw** Shrewsbury T to Walsall; **Chris Brown** Doncaster R to Blackburn R; **Daniel Carrico** Reading to Sevilla; **Mark Cousins** Colchester U to Dagenham & R; **Conor Hourihane** Plymouth Arg to Barnsley; **Andy Little** Rangers to Preston NE; **Lee Peltier** Leeds to Huddersfield T; **Mark Phillips** Southend U to AFC Wimbledon.
24 June: **Lee Barnard** Southampton to Southend U; **Craig Cathcart** Blackpool to Watford; **David Cotterill** Doncaster R to Birmingham C; **James Dunne** Stevenage to Portsmouth; **Andy Haworth** Notts Co to Cheltenham T; **Paul McElroy** Hull C to Sheffield W; **Michael Poke** Torquay U to Portsmouth; **Jamie Proctor** Crawley T to Fleetwood T; **Kyel Reid** Bradford C to Preston NE; **Adam Taggart** Newcastle Jets to Fulham; **Byron Webster** Yeovil T to Millwall.
25 June: **Clayton Donaldson** Brentford to Birmingham C; **Wade Elliott** Birmingham C to Bristol C; **Tim Hoogland** Schalke to Fulham; **Mark Little** Peterborough U to Bristol C; **Jake Livermore** Tottenham H to Hull C £8m; **Izale McLeod** Milton Keynes D to Crawley T; **Ricky Miller** Boston to Luton T; **Marcos Tebar Ramiro** UD Almeria to Brentford; **Liam Ridgewell** WBA to Portland Timbers.
26 June: **Fernando** Porto to Manchester C £12m; **Adebayo Azeez** Charlton Ath to AFC Wimbledon; **Luke Freeman** Stevenage to Bristol C; **Ryan Hall** Milton Keynes D to Rotherham U; **Conor Henderson** Hull C to Crawley T; **Ander**

Herrera Athletic Bilbao to Manchester U – £29m; **Kelvin Mellor** Crewe Alex to Plymouth Arg; **Kayode Odejayi** Rotherham U to Tranmere R; **Stuart Parnaby** Middlesbrough to Hartlepool U; **Sascha Riether** Fulham to SC Freiburg; **Junior Stanislas** Burnley to Bournemouth; **Richard Wood** Charlton Ath to Rotherham U.

27 June: **Kris Boyd** Kilmarnock to Rangers; **Febian Brandy** Sheffield U to Rotherham U; **Billy Clarke** Crawley T to Bradford C; **Gary Dicker** Crawley T to Carlisle U; **Kelvin Etuhu** Barnsley to Bury; **Bafetimbi Gomis** Lyon to Swansea C; **Andre Gray** Luton T to Brentford; **Matt Harrold** Bristol R to Crawley T; **Alex Henshall** Manchester C to Ipswich T; **Marcus Holness** Burton Alb to Tranmere R; **Liam Kelly** Bristol C to Oldham Ath; **Michael Kightly** Stoke C to Burnley; **Kyle Lafferty** Palermo to Norwich C; **AJ Leitch-Smith** Crewe Alex to Yeovil T; **Moses Odubajo** Leyton Orient to Brentford £1m; **Billy Paynter** Doncaster R to Carlisle U; **Frazer Richardson** Middlesbrough to Rotherham U; **Luke Shaw** Southampton to Manchester U – £27m, rising to £31m; **Korey Smith** Oldham Ath to Bristol C; **Zak Whitbread** Leicester C to Derby Co.

28 June: **Alexander Buttner** Manchester U to Dynamo Moscow £4.4m; **Oriol Riera** Osasuna to Wigan Ath; **James Tavernier** Newcastle U to Wigan Ath.

30 June: **Trevor Carson** Bury to Cheltenham T; **Brennan Dickenson** Brighton & HA to Gillingham; **Andy Drury** Crawley T to Luton T £100,000; **Paul Green** Leeds U to Rotherham U; **Ronnie Henry** Luton T to Stevenage; **Stephen Kingsley** Falkirk to Swansea C; **Artur Krysiak** Exeter C to Yeovil T; **Ryan McGivern** Hibernian to Port Vale; **John-Joe O'Toole** Bristol R to Northampton T; **Robert Snodgrass** Norwich C to Hull C £6m+; **Jakub Sokolik** Liverpool to Yeovil T; **Luke Summerfield** Shrewsbury T to York C; **Lyle Taylor** Sheffield U to Scunthorpe U; **Simon Walton** Hartlepool U to Stevenage; **Chris Weale** Shrewsbury T to Yeovil T; **Chris Whelpdale** Gillingham to Stevenage; **Nicky Wroe** Preston NE to Notts Co.

1 July: **Siem de Jong** Ajax to Newcastle U; **Tom Hitchcock** QPR to Milton Keynes D; **Joe Jacobson** Shrewsbury T to Wycombe W; **Adam Lallana** Southampton to Liverpool £25m; **Chris Lewington** Dagenham & R to Colchester U; **Lindon Meikle** Mansfield T to York C; **Alefe Santos** Bristol R to Derby Co; **Cameron Stewart** Hull C to Ipswich T; **Luke Varney** Leeds U to Blackburn R.

2 July: **Jean-Louis Akpa Akpro** Tranmere R to Shrewsbury T; **Troy Archibald-Henville** Swindon T to Carlisle U; **Marvin Emnes** Middlesbrough to Swansea C; **Matt Gilks** Blackpool to Burnley; **Evan Horwood** Tranmere R to Northampton T; **Alex Lynch** Peterborough U to Wycombe W; **Mark Marshall** Coventry C to Port Vale; **Franck Moussa** Coventry C to Charlton Ath; **Dean Moxey** Crystal Palace to Bolton W; **Jordan Seabright** Dagenham & R to Torquay U; **Kay Voser** Basel to Fulham; **Aaron Wilbraham** Crystal Palace to Bristol C.

3 July: **James Berrett** Carlisle U to Yeovil T; **Emre Can** Bayer Leverkusen to Liverpool £10m; **Aaron Cresswell** Ipswich T to West Ham U; **John Egan** Sunderland to Gillingham; **Byron Moore** Crewe Alex to Port Vale; **Luke Norris** Brentford to Gillingham; **Scott Shearer** Rotherham U to Crewe Alex; **Danny Swanson** Peterborough U to Coventry C; **Stuart Taylor** Reading to Leeds U.

4 July: **Reda Johnson** Sheffield W to Coventry C; **Liam Lawrence** Barnsley to Shrewsbury T; **Tomas Mejias** Real Madrid to Middlesbrough; **Jim O'Brien** Barnsley to Coventry C; **Marvin Sordell** Bolton W to Burnley; **Matt Taylor** West Ham U to Burnley; **Callum Wilson** Coventry C to Bournemouth; **Sergei Zenjov** Karpaty Lviv to Blackpool.

5 July: **Paul Connolly** Crawley T to Luton T.

7 July: **Chris Baird** Burnley to WBA; **Ashley Cole** Chelsea to Roma; **Jordan Cook** Charlton Ath to Walsall; **Tom Ince** Blackpool to Hull C; **Jonathan Parr** Crystal Palace to Ipswich T; **Steven Reid** WBA to Burnley; **Keiren Westwood** Sunderland to Sheffield W; **Luke Wilkinson** Dagenham & R to Luton T.

8 July: **Luke Ayling** Yeovil T to Bristol C; **Gareth Barry** Manchester C to Everton; **Willy Caballero** Malaga to Manchester C £6m; **Sam Hutchinson** Chelsea to Sheffield W; **Joss Labadie** Torquay U to Dagenham & R; **Ross McCormack** Leeds U to Fulham £11m; **Brendan Moloney** Bristol C to Yeovil T; **Matt Partridge** Reading to Dagenham & R; **Diego Poyet** Charlton Ath to West Ham U; **Jack Smith** Millwall to AFC Wimbledon; **Dusan Tadic** FC Twente to Southampton £10.9m.

9 July: **Lee Angol** Wycombe W to Luton T; **Andre Bikey** Panetolikos to Charlton Ath; **Pajtim Kasami** Fulham to Olympiakos; **Mario Pasalic** Hajduk Split to Chelsea; **Marco Silvestri** Chievo to Leeds U.

10 July: **Cyrus Christie** Coventry C to Derby Co; **Don Cowie** Cardiff C to Wigan Ath; **Cameron Gayle** WBA to Shrewsbury T; **Marc Laird** Southend U to Tranmere R; **Bradley Pritchard** Charlton Ath to Leyton Orient; **Alexis Sanchez** Barcelona to Arsenal £35m.

11 July: **Fergus Bell** AC Monza to Mansfield T; **Tal Ben Haim** Standard Liege to Charlton Ath; **Gwion Edwards** Swansea C to Crawley T; **Johann Berg Gudmundsson** AZ Alkmaar to Charlton Ath; **Danny Kearns** Peterborough U to Carlisle U; **Kieran Richardson** Fulham to Aston Villa; **Marius Zaliukas** Leeds U to Rangers.

12 July: **Graziano Pelle** Feyenoord to Southampton; **Sebastien Pocognoli** Hannover 96 to WBA.

13 July: **Tommaso Bianchi** Sassuolo to Leeds U; **Remy Cabella** Montpellier to Newcastle U.

14 July: **Timothee Dieng** Stade Brestois to Oldham Ath; **Dan Hanford** Floriana FC to Carlisle U; **Aaron Hughes** QPR to Brighton & HA; **Lewis Young** Bury to Crawley T.

15 July: **Craig Alcock** Peterborough U to Sheffield U; **Bartosz Bialkowski** Notts Co to Ipswich T; **Michael Collins** Scunthorpe U to Oxford U; **Diego Costa** Atletico Madrid to Chelsea £32m; **Enrique 'Kike' Garcia** Real Murcia to Middlesbrough; **Alan Goodall** Fleetwood T to Morecambe; **Lukas Jutkiewicz** Middlesbrough to Burnley £1.5m; **Lazar Markovic** Benfica to Liverpool £20m; **Alex Marrow** Blackburn R to Carlisle U; **Roger Riera** Barcelona to Nottingham F; **Luis Suarez** Liverpool to Barcelona £75m; **George Tucudean** Standard Liege to Charlton Ath.

16 July: **Ricardo Fuller** Blackpool to Millwall; **Filipe Luis** Atletico Madrid to Chelsea; **Michael Mancienne** Hamburg to Nottingham F £1m; **Shaun Miller** Sheffield U to Coventry C; **Danny Pugh** Leeds U to Coventry C; **Emmanuel Riviere** Monaco to Newcastle U; **Laurence Wilson** Accrington S to Morecambe.

17 July: **Jordan Clark** Barnsley to Shrewsbury T; **Mathieu Debuchy** Newcastle U to Arsenal; **Rio Ferdinand** Manchester U to QPR; **Daryl Janmaat** Feyenoord to Newcastle U; **Dean Leacock** Notts Co to Crawley T; **Jaun Carlos Paredes** Granada to Watford; **Andy Robinson** Tranmere R to Shrewsbury T; **Anton Rodgers** Oldham Ath to Swindon T; **Enner Valencia** Pachuca to West Ham U £12m; **Gary Woods** Watford to Leyton Orient.

18 July: **Demba Ba** Chelsea to Besiktas £4.7m; **Ivan Calero** Atletico Madrid to Derby Co; **Brown Ideye** Dynamo Kiev to WBA £10m; **Harrison McGahey** Blackpool to Sheffield U; **Louis Rowley** Manchester U to Leicester C; **Luke Steele** Barnsley to Panathinaikos.

19 July: **Gaetano Berardi** Sampdoria to Leeds U; **Chris O'Grady** Barnsley to Brighton & HA; **George Thorne** WBA to Derby Co.

21 July: **Patrice Evra** Manchester U to Juventus £1.2m.

22 July: **Leonardo Ulloa** Brighton & HA to Leicester C £8m; **Bojan Krkic** Barcelona to Stoke C; **Steven Caulker** Cardiff C to QPR.

RIP. The football family is in mourning over the deaths of supporters John Alder and Liam Sweeney, killed in Malaysian Airways MH17 disaster over Ukraine, on their way to support their beloved Newcastle United in New Zealand.

Now you can buy any of these other bestselling sports titles from your bookshop or *direct from the publisher.*

FREE P&P AND UK DELIVERY
(Overseas and Ireland £3.50 per book)

Bend it Like Bullard	Jimmy Bullard	£16.99
Champions League Dreams	Rafa Benitez	£8.99
David Beckham	David Beckham	£20.00
Football Clichés	Adam Hurrey	£12.99
Jeffanory	Jeff Stelling	£9.99
Lions Tales	Matt Dawson	£8.99
Manchester City Ruined My Life	Colin Shindler	£8.99
Manchester United Ruined My Life	Colin Shindler	£8.99
Mr Struth: The Boss	David Mason and Ian Stewart	£9.99
My Autobiography	Luis Suarez	£20.00
My Liverpool Story	Steven Gerrard	£16.99
My Road to Wimbledon Glory	Andy Murray	£7.99
My Story	Sven-Göran Eriksson	£8.99
The Didi Man	Dietmar Hamann	£9.99
The Gaffer	Neil Warnock	£8.99
The Secret Player	Anonymous	£8.99
Tuffers' Alternative Guide to the Ashes	Phil Tufnell	£8.99
Tuffers' Cricket Tales	Phil Tufnell	£8.99
Wheelmen	Reed Albergotti and Vanessa O'Connell	£9.99

TO ORDER SIMPLY CALL THIS NUMBER

01235 400 414

or visit our website:
www.headline.co.uk

Prices and availability subject to change without notice.